*ISSN 0147-6505*

# G.K. HALL

# BIBLIOGRAPHIC GUIDE TO

# EDUCATION

## 2000

ISBN 0-7838-9209-8

# PREFACE

*G.K. Hall Bibliographic Guides* are comprehensive annual subject bibliographies. They bring together recent publications cataloged by The Research Libraries of The New York Public Library and the Library of Congress. The *G.K. Hall Bibliographic Guide to Education*, however, consists of publications cataloged by Teachers College, Columbia University, supplemented by publications cataloged by The New York Public Library.

*G.K. Hall Bibliographic Guides* provide complete LC cataloging information for each title. Access is by main entry (personal author, corporate body, name of conference, etc.), added entries (co-authors, editors, compilers, etc.), titles, series titles, and subject headings. All entries are integrated into one alphabetical sequence. Filing is on a character-by-character basis in alphanumeric sequence, with numbers preceding letters. Full bibliographic information, including tracings, is given in the main entry, with abbreviated or condensed citations for secondary entries. In certain records, the term *in process* is used to denote titles not yet assigned a call number by the Library of Congress. Subject headings appear in capital letters in boldface type. Cataloging follows the *Anglo-American Cataloging Rules*. The following is a sample entry with full bibliographic information:

(a) **Adams, Dennis M.** (b) New designs for teaching and learning: (c) promoting active learning in tomorrow's schools / Dennis Adams, Mary Hamm. 1st ed. (d) San Francisco: (e) Jossey-Bass, (f) c1994. (g) xvi, 350 p. (h) 24 cm. (i) (The Jossey-Bass education series) (j) Includes bibliographical references (p. 329-342) and indexes. (k) ISBN 0-7879-0020-6 (recycled paper) (l) DDC 371.1/09/0973 (m) 1. Education, Elementary - United States - Curricula. 2. Education, Secondary - United States - Curricula. 3. Critical thinking - Study and teaching - United States. 4. Active learning - United States. 5. Educational change - United States. (n) I. Hamm, Mary. II. Title. III. Series (o) *TC LB1570.A26 1994*

| | | | | |
|---|---|---|---|---|
| (a) | Authors name. | | (d) | Place of publication. |
| (b) | Short, or main, title. | | (e) | Publisher. |
| (c) | Subtitle and/or other title page information. | | (f) | Date of publication. |
| | | | (g) | Pagination. |

(h) Illustration statement.     (l) DDC number.
(i) Series     (m) Subject heading.
(j) Note(s).     (n) Added entry.
(k) ISBN     (o) LC Call number.

*G.K. Hall Bibliographic Guides* offer easy, multiple access to a wealth of material in each subject area. They serve as authoritative reference sources for librarians and scholars, valuable technical aids for library acquisition and cataloging, and useful research tools for students and library patrons.

*G.K. Hall Bibliographic Guides* for 2000 are available in twenty-one fields:

Anthropology and Archaeology
Art and Architecture
Black Studies
Business and Economics
Conference Publications
Dance
East Asian Studies
Education
Environment
Government Publications—Foreign
Government Publications—U.S.
Latin American Studies
Law
Maps and Atlases
Music
North American History
Psychology
Slavic, Baltic, and Eurasian Studies
Technology
Theatre Arts
Women's Studies

# INTRODUCTION

The *G.K. Hall Bibliographic Guide to Education* lists recent publications cataloged during the past year by Teachers College, Columbia University, supplemented by publications in the field of education cataloged by The Research Libraries of The New York Public Library, selected on the basis of subject headings. Non-book materials, including theses, are included in this *Guide*, with the exception of serials.

All aspects and levels of education are represented in this Guide, including such areas as: American elementary and secondary education, higher and adult education, early childhood education, history and philosophy of education, applied pedagogy, international and comparative education, educational administration, education of the culturally disadvantaged and physically handicapped, nursing education, and education of minorities and women. Also well covered are the administrative reports of departments of education for various countries and for U.S. states and large cities. The Teachers College collection covers over 200 distinct educational systems. Works in all languages are included.

The *G.K. Hall Bibliographic Guide to Education* serves in part as an annual supplement to the *Dictionary Catalog of the Teachers College Library, Columbia University* (G.K. Hall & Co., 1970) and *Supplements (First Supplement,* 1971; *Second Supplement,* 1973; *Third Supplement,* 1977).

**1 to 10 and back again :** a Getty Museum counting book. Los Angeles : J. Paul Getty Museum, c1999. [52] p. : col. ill., col. ports. ; 21 cm. SUMMARY: A counting book based on French furniture from the Getty Museum. ISBN 0-89236-525-0 DDC 513.2/11[E]
*1. Counting - Juvenile literature. 2. Furniture - France - Juvenile literature. 3. Counting. 4. Furniture. I. J. Paul Getty Museum. II. Title: One to ten and back again.*
*TC QA113 .A14 1998*

**10 best teaching practices.**
Tileston, Donna Walker. Ten best teaching practices. Thousand Oaks, Calif. : Corwin Press, c2000.
*TC LB1775.2 .T54 2000*

**10 years of research at the Institute for Research on Exceptional Children, University of Illinois, 1952-1962.**
Kirk, Samuel Alexander, 1904- [Urbana : s.n.], 1964.
*TC HQ773.7 .I4 1964*

**100 clear grammar tests.**
Folse, Keith S. Ann Arbor : University of Michigan Press, c2000.
*TC PE1128.A2 F646 2000*

**100 most popular children's authors.**
McElmeel, Sharron L. Englewood, Colo. : Libraries Unlimited, 1999.
*TC PS490 .M39 1999*

**1,000 French words.** Princeton, N.J. : Berlitz Kids, Berlitz Pub. Co., 1998. 64 p. : col. ill. ; 29 cm. Includes index. SUMMARY: Presents 1000 entries for terms in French and English with corresponding illustrations to show usage. ISBN 2-8315-6549-9 DDC 448.2/421
*1. French language - Glossaries, vocabularies, etc. - Juvenile literature. 2. English language - Glossaries, vocabularies, etc. - Juvenile literature. 3. Vocabulary. 4. French language materials - Bilingual. I. Berlitz Publishing Company. II. Title: One thousand French words*
*TC PC2680 .A15 1998 ·*

**1,000 German words.** Princeton, N.J. : Berlitz Kids, c1998. 64 p. : col. ill. ; 29 cm. Includes index. SUMMARY: Presents 1000 entries for terms in German and English with corresponding illustrations to show usage. ISBN 2-8315-6550-2 DDC 431/.2
*1. Picture dictionaries, German. 2. German language - Dictionaries - English. 3. English language - Dictionaries - German. 4. Vocabulary. 5. German language materials - Bilingual. I. Berlitz Publishing Company. II. Title: One thousand German words*
*TC PF3629 .A14 1998*

**1,000 palabras en inglés.**
1,000 Spanish words. Princeton, N.J. : Berlitz Kids, c1998.
*TC PC4680 .A13 1998*

**1,000 palabras en inglés.** Princeton : Berlitz Kids, c1998. 64 p. : col. ill. ; 29 cm. Includes index. SUMMARY: Presents 1000 entries for terms in Spanish and English with corresponding illustrations to show usage. ISBN 2-8315-6553-7 DDC 468.2/421
*1. Spanish language - Glossaries, vocabularies, etc. - Juvenile literature. 2. English language - Glossaries, vocabularies, etc. - Juvenile literature. I. Title: Mil palabras en inglés*
*TC PC4680 .A12 1998*

**1,000 Spanish words.** Princeton, N.J. : Berlitz Kids, c1998. 30 p. : col. ill. ; 28 cm. Added title page title: 1,000 palabras en inglés. SUMMARY: Presents 1000 entries for terms in Spanish and English with corresponding illustrations to show usage. ISBN 2-8315-6552-9 DDC 463/.21
*1. Spanish language - Glossaries, vocabularies, etc. - Juvenile literature. 2. English language - Glossaries, vocabularies, etc. - Juvenile literature. 3. Vocabulary. 4. Spanish language materials - Bilingual. I. Title: 1,000 palabras en inglés II. Title: One thousand Spanish words III. Title: Mil palabras en inglés*
*TC PC4680 .A13 1998*

**101 finger plays, stories, and songs to use with finger puppets.**
Briggs, Diane. 101 fingerplays, stories, and songs to use with finger puppets. Chicago : American Library Association, 1999.
*TC GV1218.F5 B74 1999*

**101 fingerplays, stories, and songs to use with finger puppets.**
Briggs, Diane. Chicago : American Library Association, 1999.
*TC GV1218.F5 B74 1999*

**101 things to do with a baby.**
Ormerod, Jan. 1st U.S. ed. New York : Lothrop, Lee & Shepard, c1984.
*TC PZ7.O634 Aad 1984*

**101 ways to integrate personal development into core curriculum.**
Conroy, Mary Ann. Lanham : University Press of America, c2000.
*TC LC311 .C65 2000*

**124 high-impact letters for busy principals.**
Grady, Marilyn L. Thousand Oaks, Calif. : Corwin Press, c2000.
*TC LB2831.9 .G72 2000*

**1776.**
The American Revolution. [videorecording]. New York, N.Y. : A&E Home Video, c1994.
*TC E208 .A447 1994*

**1900S (CENTURY).** *See* **TWENTIETH CENTURY.**

**1920S.** *See* **NINETEEN TWENTIES.**

**1st break [videorecording].**
First break [videorecording]. Boston, MA : Fanlight Productions, c1997.
*TC RC465 .F5 1997*

First break [videorecording]. Boston, MA : Fanlight Productions, c1997.
*TC RC465 .F5 1997*

**2 foolish cats.**
Uchida, Yoshiko. The two foolish cats. New York : M.K. McElderry Books, c1987.
*TC PZ8.1.U35 Tw 1987*

**2 French language teaching reformers reassessed**
Roberts, J. T. (John T.) Two French language teaching reformers reassessed. Lewiston [N.Y.] : E. Mellen Press, c1999.
*TC PB35 .R447 1999*

**20 common problems**
20 common problems in pediatrics. New York : McGraw-Hill, Health Professions Division, c2001.
*TC RJ45.T9 2001*

**20 common problems in pediatrics** / editor, Abraham B. Bergman. New York : McGraw-Hill, Health Professions Division, c2001. xii, 355 p. : 24 cm. Includes bibliographical references and index. ISBN 0-07-134901-4
*1. Pediatrics. I. Bergman, Abraham B., 1932- II. Title: Twenty common problems in pediatrics III. Series: 20 common problems*
*TC RJ45.T9 2001*

**20S (TWENTIETH CENTURY DECADE).** *See* **NINETEEN TWENTIES.**

**20TH CENTURY.** *See* **TWENTIETH CENTURY.**

**20th century day by day** / [editor in chief, Clifton Daniel]. New York, NY : DK Pub., c1999. 1542 p. : ill. (some col.) ; 30 cm. Updated ed. of: Chronicle of the 20th century. Includes index. ISBN 0-7894-4640-5
*1. History, Modern - 20th century - Chronology. I. Daniel, Clifton, 1912- II. Title: Chronicle of the 20th century. III. Title: Twentieth century day by day*
*TC D422 .C53 1999*

**20th century revolutions in technology.**
Singer, Edward. Commack, NY : Nova Science Pub., 1998.
*TC T173.8 .S568 1998*

**20th-century teen culture by the decades.**
Rollin, Lucy. Twentieth-century teen culture by the decades. Westport, Conn. : London : Greenwood Press, 1999.
*TC HQ799.U65 R65 1999*

**21 TRISOMY.** *See* **DOWN SYNDROME.**

**21ST CENTURY.** *See* **TWENTY-FIRST CENTURY.**

**25 biggest mistakes teachers make and how to avoid them.**
Orange, Carolyn. Thousand Oaks Calif. : Corwin Press, c2000.
*TC LB1033 .O73 2000*

**25 songs by Marianne Berel.**
Berel, Marianne. Musical play sessions. [S.l. : s.n.], 1994.
*TC ML3920 .B45 1994*

**26 Fairmount Avenue.**
De Paola, Tomie. New York : G.P. Putnam's Sons, c1999.
*TC PS3554.E11474 Z473 1999*

**The 329th friend.**
Sharmat, Marjorie Weinman. New York : Four Winds Press, c1979.
*TC PZ7.S5299 Tk 1979*

**The 36-hour day.**
Mace, Nancy L. 3rd ed. Baltimore : Johns Hopkins University Press, c1999.
*TC RC523 .M33 1999*

**42 up :** give me the child until he is seven, and I will show you the man / edited by Bennett Singer. New York : The New Press : Distributed by W.W. Norton, c1998. 155 p. : ill. ; 24 cm. "A book based on Michael Apted's award-winning documentary series." ISBN 1-56584-465-3 DDC 305.23/0941
*1. Children - Great Britain - Longitudinal studies. 2. Working class - Great Britain - Longitudinal studies. 3. Children in motion pictures - Great Britain. 4. Working class in motion pictures - Great Britain. 5. Documentary films - Great Britain. I. Singer, Bennett L. II. Title: Forty-two up*
*TC HQ792.G7 A18 1998*

**500 computing tips for teachers and lecturers.**
Race, Philip. 2nd ed. London : Kogan Page ; Sterling, VA : Stylus Pub., 1999.
*TC LB1028.43 .R33 1999*

**500 tips for teachers.**
Brown, Sally A. 2nd ed. London : Kogan Page ; Sterling, VA : Stylus Pub., 1998.
*TC LB3013 .B76 1998*

**500 tips on group learning.**
Race, Phil. London : Kogan Page, 2000.
*TC LB1032 .A15 2000*

**95 languages and 7 forms of intelligence.**
Hicks, D. Emily. Ninety-five languages and seven forms of intelligence. New York : P. Lang, c1999.
*TC LC196 .H53 1999*

**95 languages and seven forms of intelligence.**
Hicks, D. Emily. Ninety-five languages and seven forms of intelligence. New York : P. Lang, c1999.
*TC LC196 .H53 1999*

**A.**
Dombroski, Ann P. Administrative problem solving. 1999.
*TC 06 no. 11104*

**A child's book of art.**
Micklethwait, Lucy. 1st American ed. New York : DK Pub., c1999.
*TC N7477 .M53 1999*

**A is for aarrgh!.**
Brooke, William J. 1st ed. New York : HarperCollinsPublishers, 1999.
*TC PZ7.B78977 Ig 1999*

**A Johns Hopkins Press health book**
Sankar, Andrea. Dying at home. Rev. and updated ed. Baltimore, Md.: Johns Hopkins University Press, 1999.
*TC R726.8 .S26 1999*

**A. Lincoln and me.**
Borden, Louise. New York : Scholastic, 1999.
*TC PZ7.B64827 An 1999*

**AACRAO Task Force on Credential Fraud.**
Misrepresentation in the marketplace and beyond. Washington, DC : American Association of Collegiate Registrars and Admissions Officers, 1996.
*TC LB2331.615.U6 M57 1996*

**ABANDONED CHILDREN - CHINA.**
Evans, Karin. The lost daughters of China. New York : J.P. Tarcher/Putnam, c2000.
*TC HV1317 .E93 2000*

**Abarbanel, Albert, joint ed.**
Ellis, Albert, ed. The encyclopedia of sexual behavior, [1st ed.]. New York, Hawthorn books [1961-1964]
*TC HQ9 .E4*

**Abate, Ellen C.** Personal characteristics of nurses and their influence on professional autonomy / by Abate, Ellen C. 1998. vii, 124 leaves ; 29 cm. Issued also on microfilm. Thesis (Ed.D.)--Teachers College, Columbia University, 1998. Includes bibliographical references (leaves 105-112).
*1. Nurses - Connecticut - Attitudes. 2. Nurses - New York (State) - Attitudes. 3. Self-perception. 4. Autonomy (Psychology). 5. Nursing - Social aspects. 6. Nursing - Psychological aspects. I. Title.*
*TC 06 no. 11009*

**Abbey, Beverly, 1944-.**
Instructional and cognitive impacts of Web-based education. Hershey, PA : Idea Group Pub., c2000.
*TC LB1044.87 .I545 2000*

**Abbott, Andrew.** Department & discipline : Chicago sociology at one hundred / Andrew Abbott. Chicago, IL : University of Chicago Press, c1999. xii, 249 p. ; 24 cm. Includes bibliographical references (p. 227-243). ISBN 0-226-00098-2 (cloth : alk. paper) ISBN 0-226-00099-0

(paper) : alk. paper) DDC 301/.09
*1. Chicago school of sociology - History. 2. American journal of sociology - History. 3. University of Chicago. - Dept. of Sociology - History. 4. Sociology - United States - History. 5. Sociology - United States - Periodicals - History. 6. Sociology - Illinois - Chicago - History. I. Title. II. Title: Department and discipline*
*TC HM22.U5 A23 1999*

**Abbott, Shirley** Womenfolks, growing up down South / Shirley Abbott ; [with a new introduction by the author]. Boston : Houghton Mifflin, c1998. xiii, 210 p. ; 21 cm. "A Mariner book." Originally published: New Haven, Conn. : Ticknor & Fields, 1983. With new introd. ISBN 0-395-90144-8 (pbk.) DDC 305.4/0975
*1. Women - Southern States. 2. Rural women - Southern States. 3. Rural poor - Southern States. 4. Southern States - Social conditions. I. Title.*
*TC HQ1438.S63 A33 1998*

**ABC Multimedia.**
Sean's story [videorecording]. Princeton, N.J. : Films for the Humanities & Sciences ; [S.l. : distributed by] ABC Multimedia : Capital Cities/ABC, c1994.
*TC LC1203.M3 .S39 1994*

**ABC News.**
Heroin [videorecording]. [Princeton, N.J.] : Films for the Humanities & Sciences, c1998.
*TC HV5822.H4 H4 1998*

Sean's story [videorecording]. Princeton, N.J. : Films for the Humanities & Sciences ; [S.l. : distributed by] ABC Multimedia : Capital Cities/ABC, c1994.
*TC LC1203.M3 .S39 1994*

**ABC relaxation.**
Smith, Jonathan C. ABC relaxation theory. New York : Springer Pub., c1999.
*TC BF637.R45 S549 1999*

**ABC relaxation theory.**
Smith, Jonathan C. New York : Springer Pub., c1999.
*TC BF637.R45 S549 1999*

**The ABC's of behavior change.**
Sparzo, Frank J. Bloomington, Ind., U.S.A. : Phi Delta Kappa Educational Foundation, c1999.
*TC LB1060.2 .S62 1999*

**The ABCs of evaluation.**
Boulmetis, John. 1st ed. San Francisco, Calif. : Jossey-Bass, c2000.
*TC HD31 .B633 2000*

**ABDUCTION.** *See* KIDNAPPING.

**Abel, Chris.** Architecture and identity : responses to cultural and technological change / Chris Abel ; with a foreword by Suha Ozkan. 2nd ed. Oxford ; Boston : Architectural Press, 2000. xvii, 270 p. : ill., plans ; 28 x 28 cm. Cover title: Architecture & identity. Includes bibliographical references (p. [235]-261) and index. ISBN 0-7506-4246-7 DDC 720/.1
*1. Architecture and philosophy. 2. Architecture - Environmental aspects. 3. Regionalism in architecture. 4. Identity (Psychology) I. Title. II. Title: Architecture & identity*
*TC NA2500 .A392 2000*

**Abelsohn, David.**
Isaacs, Marla Beth. [Difficult divorce] Therapy of the difficult divorce. Northvale, N.J. ; London : J. Aronson, c2000.
*TC RC488.6 .I83 2000*

**Abelson, Herbert Irving, 1926- joint author.**
Karlins, Marvin. Persuasion; 2d ed. New York, Springer Pub. Co. [1970]
*TC BF637.P4 K27 1970*

**Abercrombie, Paul, 1968-.**
Gross, Clifford M. The new idea factory. Columbus, OH : Battelle Press, c2000.
*TC HD53 .G75 2000*

**Aberdeen, Neil.**
Italian painting before 1400 [videorecording]. [London] : The National Gallery, c1989.

Italian painting before 1400 [videorecording]. [London] : The National Gallery, c1989.
*TC ND1575 .I87 1989*

**ABILITIES.** *See* ABILITY.

**ABILITY.** *See* CREATIVE ABILITY; EDUCATIONAL ACCELERATION; EXPERTISE; INTELLECT; LEADERSHIP; MATHEMATICAL ABILITY.

**ABILITY GROUPING IN EDUCATION.** *See* EDUCATIONAL ACCELERATION; NONGRADED SCHOOLS.

**ABILITY IN CHILDREN.**
Howe, Michael J. A., 1940- The psychology of high abilities. New York : New York University Press, 1999.
*TC BF723.A25 H69 1999*

**ABILITY, INFLUENCE OF AGE ON.** *See also* MEMORY - AGE FACTORS.
The aging mind: opportunities in cognitive research. Washington, D.C. : National Academy Press, c2000.
*TC BF724.55. C63 A48 2000*

**ABILITY, SOCIAL.** *See* SOCIAL SKILLS.

**ABILITY - TESTING.** *See also* COMPETENCY BASED EDUCATION; COMPETENCY BASED EDUCATIONAL TESTS.
Prediger, D. J. Basic structure of work-relevant abilities. Iowa City, Iowa : ACT, 1998.
*TC LB3051 .A3 no. 98-9*

The psychoeducational assessment of preschool children. 3rd ed. Boston : Allyn and Bacon, c2000.
*TC LB1115 .P963 2000*

The Use of standardized ability tests in American secondary schools and their impact on students, teachers, and administrators New York] Russell Sage Foundation [1965]
*TC LB3051 .R914*

Walsh, W. Bruce, 1936- Tests and assessment. 4th ed. Upper Saddle River, N.J. : Prentice Hall, c2001.
*TC BF176 .W335 2001*

**ABILITY - UNITED STATES - TESTING - HISTORY - 20TH CENTURY.**
Lemann, Nicholas. The big test :. 1st ed. New York : Farrar, Straus and Giroux, 1999.
*TC LB3051 .L44 1999*

**Abiteboul, S. (Serge).**
ECDL '99 (3rd : 1999 : Paris, France) Research and advanced technology for digital libraries. Berlin ; New York : Springer, c1999.
*TC ZA4080 .E28 1999*

**Ableman, Paul.** The secret of consciousness : how the brain tells 'the story of me' / Paul Ableman. London ; New York : Marion Boyars, 1999. 160 p. ; 22 cm. ISBN 0-7145-3053-0 (pbk. : alk. paper) DDC 153
*1. Consciousness. 2. Memory. 3. Human information processing. 4. Psycholinguistics. I. Title.*
*TC BF311 .A195 1999*

**ABNORMAL CHILDREN.** *See* EXCEPTIONAL CHILDREN; HANDICAPPED CHILDREN.

**ABNORMAL PSYCHOLOGY.** *See* PSYCHOLOGY, PATHOLOGICAL.

**ABNORMALITIES, HUMAN.** *See* GIANTS.

**ABOLITION OF SLAVERY.** *See* SLAVERY.

**ABOLITIONISTS, AFRO-AMERICAN.** *See* AFRO-AMERICAN ABOLITIONISTS.

**ABOLITIONISTS - UNITED STATES.** *See* AFRO-AMERICAN ABOLITIONISTS.

**Aboriginal and Torres Strait Islander collection.**
Art Gallery of New South Wales. Yiribana. 2nd ed. Sydney, Australia : The Gallery, 1998.
*TC N7401 .A765 1998*

**Aboriginal art.**
Morphy, Howard. London [England] : Phaidon, 1998.
*TC N7400 .M67 1998*

**Aboriginal dot paintings of the Western Desert.**
Dreamings of the desert. Adelaide : The Gallery, c1996.
*TC ND1101 .D74 1996*

**ABORIGINES.** *See* INDIGENOUS PEOPLES.

**ABORIGINES, AMERICAN.** *See* INDIANS.

**ABORIGINES, AUSTRALIAN.** *See* AUSTRALIAN ABORIGINES.

**Aboud, Frances E.** Health psychology in global perspective / Frances E. Aboud. Thousand Oaks : Sage Publications, c1998. xiii, 329 p. : ill. ; 24 cm. (Cross-cultural psychology series ; 2) Includes bibliographical references (p. 289-310) and indexes. ISBN 0-7619-0940-0 (cloth : acid-free paper) ISBN 0-7619-0941-9 (pbk. : acid-free paper) DDC 362.1
*1. Clinical health psychology. 2. World health. 3. Clinical health psychology - Developing countries. I. Title. II. Series: Cross-cultural psychology series ; v. 2.*
*TC R726.7 .A26 1998*

**Abowitz, Kathleen Knight.** Making meaning of community in an American high school : a feminist-pragmatist critique of the liberal-communitarian debates / Kathleen Knight Abowitz. Cresskill, N.J. :

Hampton Press, c2000. ix, 206 p. ; 24 cm. (Understanding education and policy) Includes bibliographical references (p. 187-196) and indexes. ISBN 1-57273-206-7 (hbk.) ISBN 1-57273-207-5 (pbk.) DDC 370.11/4
*1. Moral education (Secondary) - United States. 2. Education, Secondary - United States - Case studies. 3. Liberalism - United States. 4. Communitarianism - United States. I. Title. II. Series.*
*TC LC311 .A36 2000*

**Abruscato, Joseph.**
Holt science. New York : Holt, Rinehart and Winston, c1986.
*TC Q161.2 .A27 1986*

Holt science. New York : Holt, Rinehart and Winston, c1986.
*TC Q161.2 .A27 1986*

Teaching children science : a discovery approach / Joseph Abruscato. 5th ed. Boston : Allyn and Bacon, c2000. xxiv, 488 p. : ill. ; 24 cm. Includes bibliographical references and index. ISBN 0-205-28410-8 (alk. paper) DDC 372.3/5
*1. Science - Study and teaching (Elementary) I. Title.*
*TC LB1585 .A29 2000*

Whizbangers and wonderments : science activities for young people / Joseph Abruscato. Boston : Allyn and Bacon, c2000. viii, 312 p. : ill. ; 28 cm. Includes index. ISBN 0-205-28409-4 (alk. paper) DDC 507/.8
*1. Science - Experiments. I. Title.*
*TC Q182.3 .A27 2000*

**ABSAHROKEE INDIANS.** *See* CROW INDIANS.

**ABSAROKA INDIANS.** *See* CROW INDIANS.

**ABSENCE FROM SCHOOL.** *See* SCHOOL ATTENDANCE.

**ABSENCE, LEAVE OF.** *See* LEAVE OF ABSENCE.

**ABSENT TREATMENT.** *See* MENTAL HEALING.

**ABSENTEEISM (LABOR).** *See* SICK LEAVE.

**ABSTRACT EXPRESSIONISM - UNITED STATES.**
Jackson Pollock [videorecording]. [Chicago, Ill.] : Home Vision ; [S.l.] : Distributed Worldwide by RM Associates, c1987.
*TC ND237.P73 J3 1987*

**ABSTRACTING AND INDEXING SERVICES.** *See* INFORMATION STORAGE AND RETRIEVAL SYSTEMS.

**Abstracting reality.**
Wolf, Mark J. P. Lanham, Md.: University Press of America, c2000.
*TC HM851 .W65 2000*

**ABSTRACTION.** *See* CATEGORIZATION (PSYCHOLOGY); MENTAL REPRESENTATION.

**Abu-Duhou, Ibtisam.** School-based management / Ibtisam Abu-Duhou. Paris : International Institute for Educational Planning (IIEP); Paris : Unesco, 1999. 134 p. ; 21 cm. (Fundamentals of educational planning ; 62) Includes bibliographical references. Other editions available: La gestion décentralisée au niveau des écoles 9280321897 fre. ISBN 92-803-1189-1 DDC 370
*1. School-based management. 2. School management and organization. 3. Educational planning. I. Title. II. Title: La gestion décentralisée au niveau des écoles fre III. Series.*
*TC LB5 .F85 1999*

**Abu-Lughod, Janet L.** New York, Chicago, Los Angeles : America's global cities / Janet L. Abu-Lughod. Minneapolis : University of Minnesota Press, c1999. x, 580 p. : ill., maps ; 26 cm. Includes bibliographical references (p. 427-553) and index. ISBN 0-8166-3335-5 (hc.) ISBN 0-8166-3336-3 (pb.) DDC 307.76/0973
*1. Cities and towns - United States - History - Case studies. 2. Metropolitan areas - United States - History - Case studies. 3. New York (N.Y.) - History. 4. Chicago (Ill.) - History. 5. Los Angeles (Calif.) - History. 6. International economic relations - History. I. Title.*
*TC HT123 .A613 1999*

**ABUSE OF CHILDREN.** *See* CHILD ABUSE.

**ABUSE OF SUBSTANCES.** *See* SUBSTANCE ABUSE.

**ABUSE, SEXUAL.** *See* SEX CRIMES.

**ABUSED CHILDREN.** *See* ADULT CHILD ABUSE VICTIMS; CHILD ABUSE; SEXUALLY ABUSED CHILDREN.

**ABUSED CHILDREN - REHABILITATION.**
Treatment of child abuse. Baltimore, Md. ; London : Johns Hopkins University Press, 2000.

*TC RJ375 .T74 2000*

ABUSED FAMILY MEMBERS. *See* VICTIMS OF FAMILY VIOLENCE.

ABUSED WIVES - SERVICES FOR - GREAT BRITAIN.
Lockley, Paul. Counselling women in violent relationships. London ; New York : Free Association Books, 1999.
*TC HV6626.23.G7 L624 1999*

ABUSED WOMEN. *See* ABUSED WIVES; BATTERED WOMAN SYNDROME.

ABUSED WOMEN - COUNSELING OF - UNITED STATES.
Gordon, Judith S., 1958- Helping survivors of domestic violence. New York : Garland Pub., 1998.
*TC HV6626.2 .G67 1998*

ABUSED WOMEN - EDUCATION.
Horsman, Jenny. Too scared to learn. Mahwah, N.J. : L. Erlbaum Associates, Publishers, 2000.
*TC LC1481 . H67 2000*

ABUSED WOMEN - SERVICES FOR - GREAT BRITAIN.
Lockley, Paul. Counselling women in violent relationships. London ; New York : Free Association Books, 1999.
*TC HV6626.23.G7 L624 1999*

ABUSED WOMEN - UNITED STATES - FAMILY RELATIONSHIPS.
Gordon, Judith S., 1958- Helping survivors of domestic violence. New York : Garland Pub., 1998.
*TC HV6626.2 .G67 1998*

ABUSED WOMEN - UNITED STATES - HEALTH ASPECTS.
Gordon, Judith S., 1958- Helping survivors of domestic violence. New York : Garland Pub., 1998.
*TC HV6626.2 .G67 1998*

ABUSED WOMEN - UNITED STATES - PSYCHOLOGY.
Gordon, Judith S., 1958- Helping survivors of domestic violence. New York : Garland Pub., 1998.
*TC HV6626.2 .G67 1998*

Aby, Stephen H., 1949-.
Academic freedom. Westport, Conn. : Greenwood Press, 2000.
*TC LC72.2 .A29 2000*

Academia in upheaval : origins, transfers, and transformations of the communist academic regime in Russia and east central Europe / edited by Michael David-Fox and György Péteri. Westport, Conn. : Bergin & Garvey, 2000. xi, 334 p. : ill. ; 24 cm. Includes bibliographical references and index. ISBN 0-89789-708-0 (alk. paper) DDC 378.47
*1. Education, Higher - Soviet Union - History - Congresses. 2. Communism and education - Soviet Union - History - Congresses. 3. Education, Higher - Europe, Eastern - History - Congresses. 4. Communism and education - Europe, Eastern - History - Congresses.*
*TC LA837 .A6 2000*

ACADEMIC ACHIEVEMENT. *See also* MOTIVATION IN EDUCATION; PREDICTION OF SCHOLASTIC SUCCESS.
Chall, Jeanne Sternlicht, 1921- The academic achievement challenge. New York ; London : Guilford Press, c2000.
*TC LB2822.8 .C49 2000*

ACADEMIC ACHIEVEMENT - CALIFORNIA - EVALUATION - HANDBOOKS, MANUALS, ETC.
Assessing literacy with the Learning Record. Portsmouth, NH : Heinemann, c1999.
*TC LB1029.P67 B37 1999b*

Barr, Mary A. (Mary Anderson) Assessing literacy with the Learning Record. Portsmouth, NH : Heinemann, c1999.
*TC LB1029.P67 B37 1999*

The academic achievement challenge.
Chall, Jeanne Sternlicht, 1921- New York ; London : Guilford Press, c2000.
*TC LB2822.8 .C49 2000*

ACADEMIC ACHIEVEMENT - CROSS-CULTURAL STUDIES.
Learning from others. Dordrecht [Netherlands] ; Boston : Kluwer Academic Publishers, c2000.
*TC LB43 .L42 2000*

ACADEMIC ACHIEVEMENT - DEVELOPING COUNTRIES - CROSS CULTURAL STUDIES.
Third World education. New York : Garland Pub., 2000.

*TC LC2607 .T55 2000*

ACADEMIC ACHIEVEMENT - EVALUATION.
Measuring student knowledge and skills. Paris : Organisation for Economic Co-operation and Development, c1999.
*TC LB3051 .M43 1999*

Organisation for Economic Co-operation and Development (Paris) Measuring student knowledge and skills. Paris : Organisation for Economic Co-operation and Development, 2000.
*TC LB3051 .M44 2000*

Tanner, David Earl, 1948- Assessing academic achievement. Boston ; London : Allyn and Bacon, c2001.
*TC LB2822.75 .T36 2001*

ACADEMIC ACHIEVEMENT - GREAT BRITAIN.
Head, John (John O.) Understanding the boys. New York : Falmer Press, 1999.
*TC LC1390 .H43 1999*

ACADEMIC ACHIEVEMENT - GREAT BRITAIN - CASE STUDIES.
Improving schools. Buckingham [England] ; Philadelphia : Open University Press, 1999.
*TC LB2822.84.G7 I68 1999*

ACADEMIC ACHIEVEMENT - MIDDLE WEST - CASE STUDIES.
MacGregor-Mendoza, Patricia, 1963- Spanish and academic achievement among Midwest Mexican youth. New York ; London : Garland Pub., 1999.
*TC LC2686.4 .M33 1999*

ACADEMIC ACHIEVEMENT - NEW ZEALAND - CASE STUDIES.
Thrupp, Martin, 1964- Schools making a difference--let's be realistic!. Buckingham [England] ; Philadelphia : Open University Press, 1999.
*TC LB2822.75 .T537 1999*

ACADEMIC ACHIEVEMENT - PAKISTAN.
Rugh, Andrea B. Teaching practices to increase student achievement. Cambridge, Mass. : B.R.I.D.G.E.S. Basic Research and Implementation in Developing Education Systems, [1991].
*TC LB1025.2 .R83 1991*

ACADEMIC ACHIEVEMENT - PSYCHOLOGICAL ASPECTS.
Purkey, William Watson. What students say to themselves. Thousand Oaks, Calif. : Corwin Press, c2000.
*TC LB1062.6 .P87 2000*

ACADEMIC ACHIEVEMENT - TESTING. *See also* COMPETENCY BASED EDUCATIONAL TESTS.
Baynes, Joyce Frisby. The development of a van Hiele-based summer geometry program and its impact on student van Hiele level and achievement in high school geometry. 1998.
*TC 06 no. 10915*

ACADEMIC ACHIEVEMENT - UNITED STATES.
Bertman, Stephen. Cultural amnesia. Westport, Conn. ; London : Praeger, 2000.
*TC HN59.2 .B474 2000*

Engaging young readers. New York : Guilford Press, c2000.
*TC LB1573 .E655 2000*

Global perspectives for local action. Washington, D.C. : National Academy Press, 1999.
*TC LB1583.3 .G56 1999*

Gregory, Sheila T. Black women in the academy. Rev. and updated ed. Lanham, Md. : University Press of America, 1999.
*TC LC2781 .G74 1999*

Meichenbaum, Donald. Nurturing independent learners. Cambridge, Mass. : Brookline Books, c1998.
*TC LB1031.4 .M45 1998*

Rathvon, Natalie. Effective school interventions. New York : Guilford Press, c1999.
*TC LC1201 .R38 1999*

ACADEMIC ACHIEVEMENT - UNITED STATES - CASE STUDIES.
Improved test scores, attitudes, and behaviors in America's schools. Westport, Conn. : Bergin & Garvey, 1999.
*TC LB2806.4 .I56 1999*

ACADEMIC ACHIEVEMENTS - PSYCHOLOGICAL ASPECTS.
Smith, Hawthorne Emery. Psychological detachment from school. 1999.

*TC 085 Sm586*

ACADEMIC ADVISING. *See* COUNSELING IN HIGHER EDUCATION.

Academic advising : a comprehensive handbook / Virginia Gordon and Wesley R. Habley, editors. 1st ed. San Francisco : Jossey-Bass, c2000. xxvi,452 p. ; 27 cm. (The Jossey-Bass higher and adult education series) Includes bibliographical references and indexes. ISBN 0-7879-5025-4 (alk. paper) DDC 378.1/94
*1. Counseling in higher education - United States - Handbooks. manuals. etc. 2. Faculty advisors - United States - Handbooks. manuals. etc. I. Gordon, Virginia N. II. Habley, Wesley R. III. Series.*
*TC LB2343 .A29 2000*

ACADEMIC ADVISORS. *See* FACULTY ADVISORS.

Academic approaches to teaching Jewish studies / edited by Zev Garber. Lanham, Md. : University Press of America, c2000. xvi, 332 p. ; 23 cm. Includes bibliographical references and indexes. ISBN 0-7618-1552-X (paperback) DDC 296/.071/1
*1. Judaism - Study and teaching (Higher) I. Garber, Zev, 1941-*
*TC BM71 .A33 2000*

The academic corporation.
Duryea, E. D. (Edwin D.) New York : Falmer Press, 2000.
*TC LB2341 .D79 2000*

ACADEMIC DEANS. *See* DEANS (EDUCATION).

ACADEMIC DECORATIONS OF HONOR. *See* DEGREES, ACADEMIC.

ACADEMIC DEGREES. *See* DEGREES, ACADEMIC.

ACADEMIC DISHONESTY. *See* CHEATING (EDUCATION).

ACADEMIC DISSERTATIONS. *See* DISSERTATIONS, ACADEMIC.

ACADEMIC FAILURE. *See* SCHOOL FAILURE.

ACADEMIC FREEDOM. *See* TEACHING, FREEDOM OF; UNIVERSITY AUTONOMY.

Academic freedom & Christian scholarship.
Diekema, Anthony J. Academic freedom and Christian scholarship. Grand Rapids, Mich. : Wm.B. Eerdmans Pub. Co., c2000.
*TC LC72.2 .D54 2000*

Academic freedom : a guide to the literature / compiled by Stephen H. Aby and James C. Kuhn, IV. Westport, Conn. : Greenwood Press, 2000. xi, 225 p. ; 23 cm. (Bibliographies and indexes in education, 0742-6917 ; no. 20) Includes bibliographical references and indexes. ISBN 0-313-30386-X (acid-free paper) DDC 378.1/21
*1. Academic freedom - United States. 2. Academic freedom - United States - History. I. Aby, Stephen H., 1949- II. Kuhn, James C., 1966- III. Series.*
*TC LC72.2 .A29 2000*

ACADEMIC FREEDOM - AFRICA.
A thousand flowers. Trenton, NJ : Africa World Press, c2000, [1999].
*TC LC67.68.A35 T56 2000*

Academic freedom and Christian scholarship.
Diekema, Anthony J. Grand Rapids, Mich. : Wm.B. Eerdmans Pub. Co., c2000.
*TC LC72.2 .D54 2000*

ACADEMIC FREEDOM - NORTH CAROLINA - HISTORY - 20TH CENTURY.
Billingsley, William J., 1953- Communists on campus. Athens, Ga. ; London : University of Georgia Press, c1999.
*TC LC72.3.N67 B55 1999*

ACADEMIC FREEDOM - UNITED STATES.
Academic freedom. Westport, Conn. : Greenwood Press, 2000.
*TC LC72.2 .A29 2000*

Brinkley, Ellen Henson, 1944- Caught off guard. Boston : Allyn and Bacon, c1999.
*TC LC72.2 .B75 1999*

Diekema, Anthony J. Academic freedom and Christian scholarship. Grand Rapids, Mich. : Wm.B. Eerdmans Pub. Co., c2000.
*TC LC72.2 .D54 2000*

Ernest, Ivan. Faculty evaluation of post-tenure review at a research university. 1999.
*TC 06 no. 11110*

Golding, Martin P. (Martin Philip), 1930- Free speech on campus. Lanham, Md. ; Oxford : Rowman & Littlefield Publishers, c2000.

*Academic freedom - United States.*

TC LC72.2 .G64 2000

**ACADEMIC FREEDOM - UNITED STATES - HISTORY.**
Academic freedom. Westport, Conn. : Greenwood Press, 2000.
*TC LC72.2 .A29 2000*

**ACADEMIC FREEDOM - UNITED STATES - HISTORY - 1945-1953.**
Foster, Stuart J., 1960- Red alert!. New York ; Canterbury [England] : P. Lang, c2000.
*TC LC72.2 .F67 2000*

**Academic intensity, attendance patterns, and bachelor's degree attainment.**
Adelman, Clifford. Answers in the tool box. Washington, DC : U.S. Dept. of Education, Office of Educational Research and Improvement, [1999]
*TC LB2390 .A34 1999*

**ACADEMIC LIBRARIANS.** *See* **COLLEGE LIBRARIANS.**

**ACADEMIC LIBRARIES - UNITED STATES.**
Librarians as learners, librarians as teachers. Chicago : Association of College and Research Libraries, 1999.
*TC Z675.U5 L415 1999*

People come first. Chicago : Association of College and Research Libraries, 1999.
*TC Z674 .A75*

**ACADEMIC MEDICAL CENTERS.** *See* **MEDICAL COLLEGES.**

**ACADEMIC MOTIVATION.** *See* **MOTIVATION IN EDUCATION.**

**ACADEMIC PROBATION.** *See* **COLLEGE ATTENDANCE.**

**Academic skills problems workbook.**
Shapiro, Edward S. (Edward Steven), 1951- New York : Guilford Press, c1996.
*TC LB1029.R4 S52 1996*

**Academic workplace.**
Austin, Ann E. Washington, D.C. : Association for the Study of Higher Education, 1983.
*TC LB2331.7 .A96 1983*

**ACADEMIC WRITING.**
Moon, Jennifer A. Learning journals. London : Kogan Page, 1999.
*TC PE1408 .M66 1999*

**ACADEMIC WRITING - ABILITY TESTING.**
Assessment of writing. New York : Modern Language Association of America, 1996.
*TC PE1404 .A88 1996*

**ACADEMIC WRITING - PROBLEMS, EXERCISES, ETC.**
Cutchin, Kay Lynch. Landscapes and language. Cambridge, UK ; New York, NY, USA : Cambridge University Press, 1999.
*TC PE1128 .C88 1999*

**ACADEMIC WRITING - SEX DIFFERENCES.**
Feminist cyberscapes. Stamford, Conn. : Ablex Pub., c1999.
*TC PE1404 .F39 1999*

**ACADEMIC WRITING - STUDY AND TEACHING.**
Flower, Linda. Learning to rival. Mahwah, New Jersey : Lawrence Erlbaum Associates, c2000.
*TC PE1404 .F59 2000*

Student writing in higher education. Philadelphia, Pa. : Open University Press, c2000.
*TC PE1404 .S84 2000*

Teaching in the 21st century. New York : Falmer Press, 1999.
*TC PE1404 .T394 1999*

Worlds apart. Mahwah, N.J. : L. Erlbaum Associates, 1999.
*TC PE1404 .W665 1999*

**ACADEMIC WRITING - STUDY AND TEACHING - DATA PROCESSING.**
Feminist cyberscapes. Stamford, Conn. : Ablex Pub., c1999.
*TC PE1404 .F39 1999*

Passions, pedagogies, and 21st century technologies. Logan : Utah State University Press ; Urbana, Ill. : National Council of Teachers of English, c1999.
*TC PE1404 .P38 1999*

**ACADEMIC WRITING - STUDY AND TEACHING - GREAT BRITAIN.**
Students writing in the university. Amsterdam ; Philadelphia : John Benjamins Pub., c1999.

TC PE1405.G7 S78 1999

**ACADEMIC WRITING - STUDY AND TEACHING (HIGHER) - POLITICAL ASPECTS - UNITED STATES.**
Parks, Stephen, 1963- Class politics. Urbana, Ill. : National Council of Teachers of English, c2000.
*TC PE1405.U6 P3 2000*

**ACADEMIC WRITING - STUDY AND TEACHING (HIGHER) - THAILAND.**
Pupipat, Apisak. Scientific writing and publishing in English in Thailand. 1998.
*TC 06 no. 10981*

**ACADEMIC WRITING - STUDY AND TEACHING - TECHNOLOGICAL INNOVATIONS.**
Passions, pedagogies, and 21st century technologies. Logan : Utah State University Press ; Urbana, Ill. : National Council of Teachers of English, c1999.
*TC PE1404 .P38 1999*

**ACADEMIES (LEARNED SOCIETIES).** *See* **SOCIETIES.**

**Academische Revue.**
Hochschul-Nachrichten. München : Academischer Verlag,

**The academy and the possibility of belief :** essays on intellectual and spiritual life / edited by Mary Louise Buley-Meissner, Mary McCaslin Thompson, Elizabeth Bachrach Tan. Cresskill, N.J. : Hampton Press, c2000. xiii, 205 p. ; 23 cm. (Critical education and ethics) Includes bibliographical references and indexes. ISBN 1-57273-220-2 ISBN 1-57273-221-0 (pbk.) DDC 378/.01
*1. Education, Higher - Aims and objectives. 2. Spirituality - Study and teaching (Higher) I. Buley-Meissner, Mary Louise. II. Thompson, Mary McCaslin. III. Tan, Elizabeth Bachrach. IV. Series.*
*TC LB2324 .A27 2000*

**ACCELERATED LEARNING.** *See* **EDUCATIONAL ACCELERATION.**

**The accelerated learning handbook.**
Meier, Dave. New York : McGraw Hill, c2000.
*TC LB1029.A22 M45 2000*

**ACCELERATION IN EDUCATION.** *See* **EDUCATIONAL ACCELERATION.**

**ACCELERATIVE LEARNING.** *See* **EDUCATIONAL ACCELERATION.**

**Accent.**
Phillips, James B. Glenview, Ill. : Scott, Foresman, 1972.
*TC PE1121 .P54 1972*

**Accessing information in a technological age.**
Whitson, Donna L. Original ed. Malabar, Fla. : Krieger Pub. Co., 1997.
*TC ZA3075 .W48 1997*

**ACCIDENTS.** *See* **DROWNING; SCHOOL ACCIDENTS.**

**ACCIDENTS - PREVENTION.** *See* **INDUSTRIAL SAFETY; SAFETY EDUCATION.**

**ACCIDENTS - PREVENTION - STUDY AND TEACHING.** *See* **SAFETY EDUCATION.**

**ACCIDENTS, SCHOOL.** *See* **SCHOOL ACCIDENTS.**

**ACCOMMODATION (PSYCHOLOGY).** *See* **ADJUSTMENT (PSYCHOLOGY).**

**Accommodations in higher education under the Americans with Disabilities Act (ADA) :** : a no-nonsense guide for clinicians, educators, administrators, and lawyers / edited by Michael Gordon, Shelby Keiser ; foreword by Alta Lapoint. DeWitt, NY : GSI Publications, 2000. xx, 236 p. : ill. ; 23 cm. Includes bibliographical references and index. CONTENTS: I. Essential concepts/administrative considerations. Underpinnings / Michael Gordon, Shelby Keiser -- Educational accommodations : a university administrator's view / Joan M. McGuire -- Test accommodations : an administrator's view / Shelby Keiser. II. Documentation of clinical conditions. Legal requirements for clinical evaluations / James G. Frierson -- Attention-deficit/ hyperactivity disorder (ADHD) / Michael Gordon, Kevin R. Murphy -- Language-based learning disabilities / Barbara J. Lorry -- Mood and anxiety disorders / Lauren Wylonis, Edward Schweizer -- Physical disabilities / Stanley F. Wainapel -- Visual disorders, dysfunctions, and disabilities / David A. Damari -- Last words / Michael Gordon, Shelby Kaiser. ISBN 1-57230-323-9
*1. Disability evaluation - United States. 2. Handicapped college students - Legal status, laws, etc. - United States. 3. Disability Evaluation - United States. 4. Handicapped -*

*Education - United States. 5. Universities and colleges - Law and legislation - United States. I. Gordon, Michael. Ph. D. II. Keiser, Shelby.*
*TC RA1055.5 A28 2000*

**ACCORDION AND PIANO MUSIC (JAZZ).** *See* **JAZZ.**

**ACCOUNTABILITY.** *See* **RESPONSIBILITY.**

**Accountability, assessment, and teacher commitment :** lessons from Kentucky's reform efforts / edited by Betty Lou Whitford and Ken Jones. Albany, N.Y. : State University of New York Press, 2000. xvi, 267 p. : ill. ; 23 cm. (SUNY series, restructuring and school change) Includes bibliographical references and indexes. ISBN 0-7914-4409-0 (alk. paper) ISBN 0-7914-4410-4 (pbk. : alk. paper) DDC 379.1/58/09769
*1. Educational accountability - Kentucky - Case studies. 2. Educational tests and measurements - Kentucky - Case studies. 3. School improvement programs - Kentucky - Case studies. 4. Teachers - Kentucky - Case studies. I. Whitford, Betty Lou. II. Jones, Ken. 1949- III. Series.*
*TC LB2806.22 .A249 2000*

**ACCOUNTABILITY IN EDUCATION.** *See* **EDUCATIONAL ACCOUNTABILITY.**

**ACCREDITATION - STANDARDS - UNITED STATES - PERIODICALS.**
Joint Commission on Accreditation of Healthcare Organizations. Hospital accreditation standards : HAS. Oakbrook Terrace, Ill. : The Commission, c1996-
*TC RA981.A2 J59a*

**ACCULTURATION.** *See also* **ASSIMILATION (SOCIOLOGY); ETHNIC RELATIONS.**
Tiago de Melo, Janine, 1969- Factors relating to Hispanic and non-Hispanic White Americans' willingness to seek psychotherapy. 1998.
*TC 085 T43*

**Accuracy or advocacy :** the politics of research in education / edited by Bruce S. Cooper, E. Vance Randall. Thousand Oaks, Calif. : Corwin Press, c1999. xii, 215 p. : ill. ; 22 cm. (Yearbook of the Politics of Education Association ; 1998) "Published simultaneously as the 1998 Yearbook of the Politics of Education Association and a special issue of Educational Policy." Includes bibliographical references and index. CONTENTS: Understanding the politics of research in education / E. Vance Randall, Bruce S. Cooper, and Steven J. Hite -- The politics of research-information use in the education policy arena / Bob L. Johnson, Jr. --Compromised positions : the ethics and politics of designing research in the postmodern age / Catherine Emihovich -- Evaluating integrated children's services : the politics of research on collaborative education and social service research / Carolyn D. Herrington and Irving Lazar -- Researching the margins : feminist critical policy analysis / Catherine Marshall -- Race, class, and gender in education research : surveying the political terrain / Michele Foster -- The politics of bilingual education / Douglas E. Mitchell ... [et al.] -- The politics of school choice research : fact, fiction, and statistics / Jeanne M. Powers and Peter W. Cookson, Jr. -- The politics of the production CONTENTS: function : the influence of political bias on the deductive process / Bruce D. Baker -- The politics of research on educational productivity / Patrick F. Galvin -- Constructing knowledge : realist and radical learning within a Canadian Royal Commission / George J. Bedard -- The extended school day in Israel : do research findings really matter? / Haim Gaziel and Nachum Blass -- Three researchers reflect : vignettes and verities / James G. Cibulka, Betty Malen, Paul E. Peterson -- Making meaning of the relationship between research and policy : an epilogue / Karen Seashore Louis. ISBN 0-8039-6778-0 (pbk. : alk. paper) ISBN 0-8039-6777-2 (cloth : alk. paper) DDC 379.072
*1. Education - Research. 2. Education - Political aspects. 3. Education and state. I. Cooper, Bruce S. II. Randall, E. Vance. III. Title: Educational policy (Los Altos, Calif.) IV. Series.*
*TC LB1028 .A312 1999*

**Accurate ways to assess student achievement.**
Ardovino, Joan. Multiple measures. Thousand Oaks, Calif. : Corwin Press, c2000.
*TC LB3051 .A745 2000*

**ACHES.** *See* **PAIN.**

**ACHIEVEMENT.**
Genius and eminence. 2nd ed. Oxford : New York : Pergamon Press, 1992.
*TC BF412 .G43 1992*

**ACHIEVEMENT, ACADEMIC.** *See* **ACADEMIC ACHIEVEMENT.**

**ACHIEVEMENT MOTIVATION - PSYCHOLOGICAL ASPECTS.**
Sosin, Adrienne. Achieving styles preferences of students in an urban graduate teacher education program. 1996.

*TC 06 no. 10701*

Sosin, Adrienne. Achieving styles preferences of students in an urban graduate teacher education program. 1996.
*TC 06 no. 10701*

**ACHIEVEMENT TESTS.** *See* **NORM-REFERENCED TESTS.**

**ACHIEVERS.** *See* **SUCCESSFUL PEOPLE.**

**Achieving educational equality.**
Grossman, Herbert, 1934- Springfield. Ill. : C.C. Thomas, c1998.
*TC LC213.2 .G76 1998*

**Achieving scientific literacy.**
Bybee, Rodger W. Portsmouth, NH : Heinemann, c1997.
*TC Q183.3.A1 B92 1997*

**Achieving styles preferences of students in an urban graduate teacher education program.**
Sosin, Adrienne. 1996.
*TC 06 no. 10701*

**Achilles, Charles M.** Let's put kids first, finally : getting class size right / Charles M. Achilles. Thousand Oaks, Calif. : Corwin Press, c1999. xii, 203 p. ; 25 cm. Includes bibliographical references (p. 178-190) and index. ISBN 0-8039-6806-X (acid-free paper) ISBN 0-8039-6807-8 (pbk. : acid-free paper) DDC 371.2/51
*1. Class size - United States. 1. Title.*
*TC LB3013.2 .A34 1999*

Problem analysis : responding to school complexity / Charles M. Achilles, John S. Reynolds, Susan H. Achilles. Larchmont, NY : Eye on Education, c1997. xiv, 165 p. : ill. ; 24 cm. (The school leadership library) Includes bibliographical references (p. 155-165). ISBN 1-88300-136-6 DDC 371.2/012
*1. School management and organization - United States - Decision making. 2. School principals - United States. 3. Problem solving. 1. Reynolds, John S., 1931- II. Achilles, Susan H. (Susan Hoover), 1950- III. Title. IV. Series.*
*TC LB2806 .A25 1997*

**Achilles, Susan H. (Susan Hoover), 1950-.**
Achilles, Charles M. Problem analysis. Larchmont, NY : Eye on Education, c1997.
*TC LB2806 .A25 1997*

**ACIDS, FATTY.** *See* **FATTY ACIDS.**

**Acker, Victor, 1940-** Célestin Freinet / Victor Acker. Westport, CT : Greenwood Press, 2000. xiii, 153 p. ; 23 cm. (Contributions to the study of education, 0196-707X ; no. 78) Includes bibliographical references and index. ISBN 0-313-30994-9 (alk. paper) DDC 370/.92
*1. Freinet, Célestin. 2. Educators - France - Biography. 3. Education - Philosophy. I. Title. II. Series.*
*TC LB775 .A255 2000*

**Ackerman, Peter.** Strategic nonviolent conflict : the dynamics of people power in the twentieth century / Peter Ackerman and Christopher Kruegler ; with forewords by Gene Sharp and Thomas C. Schelling. Westport, Conn. : Praeger, 1994. xxiv, 366 p. ; 25 cm. Includes bibliographical references (p. [351]-358) and index. ISBN 0-275-93915-4 (hc : alk. paper) ISBN 0-275-93916-2 (pb : alk. paper) DDC 303.6/1
*1. Nonviolence. 2. Protest movements. 3. Power (Social sciences) I. Kruegler, Christopher. II. Title.*
*TC JC328.3 .A28 1994*

**Acocella, Joan Ross.** Creating hysteria : women and multiple personality disorder / Joan Acocella. 1st ed. San Francisco : Jossey-Bass Publishers, c1999. ix, 214 p. ; 24 cm. Includes index. Bibliography: p. 179-195. ISBN 0-7879-4794-6 DDC 616.85/236/0082
*1. Multiple personality. 2. False memory syndrome. 1. Title.*
*TC RC569.5.M8 A28 1999*

**ACOUSTIC PHENOMENA IN NATURE.** *See* **THUNDERSTORMS.**

**ACOUSTICS.** *See* **HEARING.**

**ACQUAINTANCE RAPE.** *See* **DATING VIOLENCE.**

**ACQUAINTANCE RAPE - UNITED STATES - PREVENTION.**
d·a·t·e rape [videorecording]. [Charleston, WV] : Cambridge Educational, c1994.
*TC RC560.R36 D3 1994*

**ACQUAINTANCE RAPE - UNITED STATES - PSYCHOLOGICAL ASPECTS.**
d·a·t·e rape [videorecording]. [Charleston, WV] : Cambridge Educational, c1994.
*TC RC560.R36 D3 1994*

**ACQUIRED IMMUNE DEFICIENCY SYNDROME.** *See* **AIDS (DISEASE).**

**ACQUIRED IMMUNODEFICIENCY SYNDROME.** *See* **AIDS (DISEASE).**

**ACQUIRED IMMUNODEFICIENCY SYNDROME.**
Schoub, B. D. AIDS & HIV in perspective. 2nd ed. Cambridge ; New York, NY : Cambridge University Press, 1999.
*TC RC607.A26 S3738 1999*

**ACQUIRED IMMUNOLOGICAL DEFICIENCY SYNDROME.** *See* **AIDS (DISEASE).**

**ACQUISITION OF LANGUAGE.** *See* **LANGUAGE ACQUISITION.**

**ACRL publications in librarianship**
(no. 53) People come first. Chicago : Association of College and Research Libraries, 1999.
*TC Z674 .A75*

**ACROBATS AND ACROBATISM.** *See* **ACROBATS.**

**ACROBATS - FICTION.**
Cowley, Joy. Agapanthus Hum and the eyeglasses. New York : Philomel Books, c1999.
*TC PZ7.C8375 Ag 1999*

**Across the great divide.**
Chen, Zhe, 1964- Oxford : Blackwell, 2000.
*TC LB1103 .S6 v.65 no. 2*

**ACT (PHILOSOPHY).** *See* **INTENTIONALITY (PHILOSOPHY).**

**ACT (PHILOSOPHY) - CONGRESSES.**
International Society for Activity Theory and Cultural Research. Congress (4th : 1998 : Aarhus, Denmark) Activity theory and social practice. Aarhus : Aarhus University Press, c1999.
*TC B105.A35 I57 1998*

International Society for Activity Theory and Cultural Research. Congress (4th : 1998 : Aarhus, Denmark) Activity theory and social practice. Aarhus : Aarhus University Press, c1999.
*TC B105.A35 I57 1999*

The societal subject. Aarhus C, Denmark : Aarhus University Press, c1993.
*TC B105.A35 S68 1991*

**ACT research report series**
(98-10.) Yi, Qing. Simulating nonmodel-fitting responses in a CAT environment. Iowa City, Iowa : ACT, 1998.
*TC LB3051 .A3 no. 98-10*

(98-9.) Prediger, D. J. Basic structure of work-relevant abilities. Iowa City, Iowa : ACT, 1998.
*TC LB3051 .A3 no. 98-9*

(no. 98-3) Chang, Shun-Wen. A comparative study of item exposure control methods in computerized adaptive testing. Iowa City, IA : ACT, Inc., 1998.
*TC LB3051 .A3 no. 98-3*

**Acta Universitatis Stockholmiensis. Stockholm studies in educational psychology**
(7.) Rydberg, Sven. Bias in prediction on correction methods. Stockholm, Almqvist & Wiksell [1963]
*TC HA31.2 .R93*

**The ACTFL foreign language education series**
Foreign language standards. Lincolnwood, Ill., U.S.A. : National Textbook Company in conjunction with the American Council on the Teaching of Foreign Languages, c1999.
*TC P53 .F674 1999*

**ACTING.** *See* **DRAMA; EXPRESSION; THEATER.**

**ACTING - COMPUTER NETWORK RESOURCES.**
Theatre in cyberspace. New York : P. Lang, c1999.
*TC PN2075 .T54 1999*

**Acting out in groups** / Laurence A. Rickels, editor. Minneapolis, Minn. ; London : University of Minnesota Press, c1999. 232 p. : ill. ; 24 cm. Includes bibliographical references. ISBN 0-8166-3321-5 (pbk. : alk. paper) ISBN 0-8166-3320-7 (hbk. : alk. paper) DDC 306.4/61
*1. Acting out (Psychology) 2. Social psychology. 3. Group psychoanalysis. 4. Civilization, Modern - Psychological aspects. I. Rickels, Laurence A.*
*TC RC569.5.A25 A28 1999*

**ACTING OUT (PSYCHOLOGY).**
Acting out in groups. Minneapolis, Minn. ; London : University of Minnesota Press, c1999.
*TC RC569.5.A25 A28 1999*

**ACTING - STUDY AND TEACHING.**
Twentieth century actor training. London : New York : Routledge, 2000.
*TC PN2075 .T94 2000*

**ACTING - STUDY AND TEACHING - INTERACTIVE MULTIMEDIA.**
Theatre in cyberspace. New York : P. Lang, c1999.
*TC PN2075 .T54 1999*

**ACTING - THERAPEUTIC USE.** *See* **PSYCHODRAMA.**

**Action against child labour** / edited by Nelien Haspels and Michele Jankanish. Geneva : International Labour Office, c2000. xv, 334 p. : ill. ; 30 cm. Includes bibliographical references. ISBN 92-2-110868-6 (pbk.)
*1. Labor laws and legislation, International. 2. Child labor. 3. Children - Employment - Developing countries. I. Haspels, Nelien. II. Jankanish, M. III. International Labour Office.*
*TC HD6231 .A28 2000*

**ACTION, HUMAN.** *See* **HUMAN BEHAVIOR.**

**ACTION LEARNING.** *See* **ACTIVE LEARNING.**

**ACTION (PHILOSOPHY).** *See* **ACT (PHILOSOPHY).**

**ACTION RESEARCH IN EDUCATION.**
Michel, Patrick. Using action research for school restructuring and organizational change. 2000.
*TC 06 no. 11295*

Michel, Patrick. Using action research for school restructuring and organizational change. 2000.
*TC 06 no. 11295*

O'Neil, Judith Ann. The role of the learning advisor in action learning. 1999.
*TC 06 no. 11156*

The postmodern educator. New York : P. Lang, c1999.
*TC LB1707 .P67 1999*

Rutter, Alison Lee. Professional growth of two multidisciplinary teams within a professional development school. 1999.
*TC 06 no. 11171*

**ACTION RESEARCH IN EDUCATION - GREAT BRITAIN.**
Murray, Louis, 1944- Practitioner-based enquiry. London ; New York : Falmer Press, 2000.
*TC LB1028.24 .M87 2000*

Ozga, Jennifer. Policy research in educational settings :. Buckingham [England] ; Philadelphia : Open University Press, 2000.
*TC LB1028.25.G7 O93 2000*

**ACTION RESEARCH IN EDUCATION - IRELAND - CASE STUDIES.**
Rethinking pastoral care. London ; New York : Routledge, 1999.
*TC LB1620.53.I73 R48 1999*

**ACTION RESEARCH IN EDUCATION - UNITED STATES.**
Enhancing program quality in science and mathematics. Thousand Oaks, Calif. : Corwin Press, c1999.
*TC LB1585.3 .E55 1999*

Newman, Judith, 1943- Tensions of teaching. New York : London : Teachers College Press, c1998.
*TC LB1025.3 .N49 1998*

Research on professional development schools. Thousand Oaks, Calif. : Corwin Press, c1999.
*TC LB2154.A3 R478 1999*

**ACTION RESEARCH IN EDUCATION - UNITED STATES - CASE STUDIES.**
Fishman, Stephen M. Unplayed tapes. Urbana, Ill. : National Council of Teachers of English ; New York : Teachers College Press, c2000.
*TC LB1028.24 .F52 2000*

**ACTION THEORY - CONGRESSES.**
International Society for Activity Theory and Cultural Research. Congress (4th : 1998 : Aarhus, Denmark) Activity theory and social practice. Aarhus : Aarhus University Press, c1999.
*TC B105.A35 I57 1998*

International Society for Activity Theory and Cultural Research. Congress (4th : 1998 : Aarhus, Denmark) Activity theory and social practice. Aarhus : Aarhus University Press, c1999.
*TC B105.A35 I57 1999*

**ACTIVE LEARNING.** *See also* **EXPERIENTIAL LEARNING; PROBLEM-BASED LEARNING.**
Greene, Maxine. Active learning and aesthetic encounters. New York : NCREST, 1995.

*TC BH39 .G74 1995*

O'Neil, Judith Ann. The role of the learning advisor in action learning. 1999.
*TC 06 no. 11156*

RAE, LESLIE. Using activities in training and development. 2nd ed. London : Kogan Page ; Sterling, VA : Stylus Pub., 1999.
*TC LB1027.23 .R34 1999*

**Active learning and aesthetic encounters.**
Greene, Maxine. New York : NCREST, 1995.
*TC BH39 .G74 1995*

**Active older adults :** ideas for action / Lynn Allen, editor ; with support from the Sporting Goods Manufacturers Association (SGMA). Champaign, IL : Human Kinetics, c1999. xiv, 191 p. : ill. ; 28 cm. Includes bibliographical references (p. 184-188). ISBN 0-7360-0128-X DDC 613.7/0446
*1. Physical fitness for the aged - United States. 2. Exercise for the aged - United States. I. Allen, Lynn, 1958- II. Sporting Goods Manufacturers Association (U.S.) III. Title: Ideas for action*
*TC GV482.6 .A38 1999*

**ACTIVISM, STUDENT.** *See* **STUDENT MOVEMENTS.**

**ACTIVISTS, POLITICAL.** *See* **POLITICAL ACTIVISTS.**

**Activities, adaptation & aging.**
Caregiving--leisure and aging. New York : Haworth Press, c1999.
*TC HV1451 .C327 1999*

**Activities handbook for the teaching of psychology /** Ludy T. Benjamin, Jr., Kathleen D. Lowman, editors. Washington, D.C. : American Psychological Association, c1981-<c1999 > v. <1-4 > : ill. ; 26-28 cm. Vols. 2-3 edited by: Vivian Parker Makosky ... [et al.]. Includes bibliographical references and indexes. ISBN 0-912704-34-9 (v. 1) ISBN 1-55798-030-6 (v. 2) ISBN 1-55798-081-0 (v. 3) ISBN 1-55798-537-5 (v. 4) DDC 150/.7
*1. Psychology - Study and teaching. 2. Psychology - Problems, exercises, etc. I. Benjamin, Ludy T., 1945- II. Lowman, Kathleen D., 1948- III. Makosky, Vivian Parker.*
*TC BF78 .A28*

**ACTIVITIES, STUDENT.** *See* **STUDENT ACTIVITIES.**

**ACTIVITY LEARNING.** *See* **ACTIVE LEARNING.**

**ACTIVITY PROGRAMS IN EARLY CHILDHOOD EDUCATION.** *See* **EARLY CHILDHOOD EDUCATION - ACTIVITY PROGRAMS.**

**ACTIVITY PROGRAMS IN EDUCATION.** *See also* **CHILDREN'S LIBRARIES - ACTIVITY PROGRAMS; EARLY CHILDHOOD EDUCATION - ACTIVITY PROGRAMS; EDUCATION, ELEMENTARY - ACTIVITY PROGRAMS; EDUCATION, PRIMARY - ACTIVITY PROGRAMS; EDUCATION, SECONDARY - ACTIVITY PROGRAMS; HIGH SCHOOL LIBRARIES - ACTIVITY PROGRAMS; PROJECT METHOD IN TEACHING; SCIENCE - STUDY AND TEACHING - ACTIVITY PROGRAMS.**
Creativity in the classroom. Burbank, CA : Disney Learning Partnership, c1999.
*TC LB1062 .C7 1999*

Peterson, Carolyn Sue, 1938- Story programs. 2nd ed. Lanham, Md. : Scarecrow Press, 2000.
*TC LB1042 .P47 2000*

Ryan, Sharon Kaye. Freedom to choice. 1998.
*TC 06 no. 11034*

Toner, Patricia Rizzo, 1952- Relationships and communication activities. West Nyack, N.Y. : Center for Applied Research in Education, c1993.
*TC HM132 .T663 1993*

Toner, Patricia Rizzo, 1952- Stress-management and self-esteem activities. West Nyack, N.Y. : Center for Applied Research in Education, c1993.
*TC RA785 .T65 1993*

**ACTIVITY PROGRAMS IN EDUCATION - UNITED STATES.**
Harwayne, Shelley. Lifetime guarantees. Portsmouth, NH : Heinemann, c2000.
*TC LB1575 .H38 2000*

**ACTIVITY PROGRAMS IN ELEMENTARY EDUCATION.** *See* **EDUCATION, ELEMENTARY - ACTIVITY PROGRAMS.**

**ACTIVITY PROGRAMS IN HIGH SCHOOL LIBRARIES.** *See* **HIGH SCHOOL LIBRARIES - ACTIVITY PROGRAMS.**

**ACTIVITY PROGRAMS IN PRIMARY EDUCATION.** *See* **EDUCATION, PRIMARY - ACTIVITY PROGRAMS.**

**ACTIVITY PROGRAMS IN SECONDARY EDUCATION.** *See* **EDUCATION, SECONDARY - ACTIVITY PROGRAMS.**

**ACTIVITY PROGRAMS, THERAPEUTIC EFFECT OF.** *See* **OCCUPATIONAL THERAPY.**

**ACTIVITY SCHOOLS.** *See* **ACTIVITY PROGRAMS IN EDUCATION.**

**ACTIVITY TEACHING.** *See* **ACTIVE LEARNING.**

**Activity theory and social practice.**
International Society for Activity Theory and Cultural Research. Congress (4th : 1998 : Aarhus, Denmark) Aarhus : Aarhus University Press, c1999.
*TC B105.A35 I57 1998*

International Society for Activity Theory and Cultural Research. Congress (4th : 1998 : Aarhus, Denmark) Aarhus : Aarhus University Press, c1999.
*TC B105.A35 I57 1999*

**ACTORS.** *See* **ACTING; THEATER.**

**ACTORS AND ACTRESSES - FICTION.**
Littlesugar, Amy. Tree of hope. New York : Philomel Books, 1999.
*TC PZ7.L7362 Tr 1999*

**ACTORS - TAXATION - UNITED STATES - HANDBOOKS, MANUALS, ETC.**
Chadwick, Annie. Showbiz bookkeeper. Dorset, Vermont : Theatre Directories, 1992, c1991.
*TC HF5686.P24 C53 1991*

**ACTRESSES.** *See* **ACTING.**

**ACUI classics**
Student development in college unions and student activities. Bloomington, Ind. : Association of College Unions-International, c1996.
*TC LB2343.4 .S84 1996*

**ACULEATA.** *See* **ANTS.**

**ACUTE BRAIN SYNDROME.** *See* **DELIRIUM.**

**ACUTE CONFUSIONAL STATES.** *See* **DELIRIUM.**

**Adamopoulos, John.**
Social psychology and cultural context. Thousand Oaks, Calif. : Sage Publications, c1999.
*TC HM1033 .S64 1999*

**Adams, Annmarie.** Designing women : gender and the architectural profession / Annmarie Adams and Peta Tancred. Toronto : University of Toronto Press, c2000. xiii, 190 p. : ill. ; 24 cm. Includes bibliographical references and index. ISBN 0-8020-4417-4 (bound) ISBN 0-8020-8219-X (pbk.) DDC 720/.82
*1. Women architects - Canada. I. Tancred, Peta, 1937- II. Title.*
*TC NA1997 A32 2000*

**Adams, Anthony, 1933-.**
Teaching the mother tongue in a multilingual Europe. London : Cassell, 1998.
*TC P53.5 .T43 1998*

**Adams, Arlene.** Handbook for literacy tutors : a practical approach to effective informal instruction in reading and writing / by Arlene Adams ; with a foreword by Richard L. Allington. Springfield, Ill. : C.C. Thomas, Publisher, c1999. xii, 191 p. ; 28 cm. Includes bibliographical references (p. 185) and index. ISBN 0-398-06940-9 (spiral : pbk.) DDC 372.6
*1. Language arts - Handbooks, manuals, etc. 2. Tutors and tutoring - Handbooks, manuals, etc. 3. Language arts teachers - Handbooks, manuals, etc. I. Title.*
*TC LB1576 .A3893 1999*

**Adams, Charles Francis, 1807-1886.** Diary of Charles Francis Adams / Aida DiPace Donald and David Donald, editors. Cambridge : Belknap Press of Harvard University Press, 1964-68. 4 v. : ill. ; 26 cm. (The Adams papers ; Series I : Diaries.) Bibliography: v. 1, p. lvi-lxiv. CONTENTS: v. 1. January 1820-June 1825.--v. 2. July 1825-September 1829.--v. 3. September 1829-February 1831.--v. 4. March 1831-December 1832. Index.
*I. Donald, Aïda DiPace. ed. II. Donald, David Herbert, 1920- ed. III. Title.*
*TC KF367.A33 A3*

**Adams, David, 1950-** A handbook of diction for singers : Italian, German, French / David Adams. New York : Oxford University Press, 1999. xii, 180 p. : ill. ; 24 cm. Includes bibliographical references (p. 173-174) and index. ISBN 0-19-512567-3 ISBN 0-19-512077-9 (pbk.) DDC 783/.043
*1. Singing - Diction. 2. Italian language - Pronunciation. 3. French language - Pronunciation. 4. German language - Pronunciation. I. Title.*
*TC MT883 .A23 1999*

**Adams, Dennis M.** Media and literacy : learning in an electronic age - issues, ideas, and teaching strategies / by Dennis Adams, Mary Hamm. 2nd ed. Springfield, Ill. : C.C. Thomas, c2000. vii, 236 p. : ill. ; 27 cm. Includes bibliographical references and index. ISBN 0-398-07031-8 (cloth) ISBN 0-398-07032-6 (paper) DDC 371.33/58/0973
*1. Audio-visual education - United States. 2. Television in education - United States. 3. Visual learning - United States. 4. Computer-assisted instruction - United States. I. Hamm, Mary. II. Title.*
*TC LB1043 .A33 2000*

**Adams, Fay Greene, 1903-.**
Rogers, Lester Brown, 1875- Story of nations. New York : H.Holt, 1965.
*TC D21 .R63 1965*

**Adams, Gerald R., 1946-.**
Adolescent development. Oxford ; Malden, Mass. : Blackwell Publishers, 2000.
*TC BF724 .A275 2000*

**Adams, Jacob E.** Taking charge of curriculum : teacher networks and curriculum implementation / Jacob E. Adams, Jr. ; foreword by Ann Lieberman. New York : Teachers College Press, c2000. xi, 227 p. ; 24 cm. (The series on school reform) Includes bibliographical references (p. 203-211) and index. ISBN 0-8077-3949-9 (cloth : alk. paper) ISBN 0-8077-3948-0 (pbk. : alk. paper) DDC 375/.001/0973
*1. Curriculum planning - United States. 2. Curriculum change - United States. 3. Teachers - Social networks - United States. I. Title. II. Series.*
*TC LB2806.15 .A35 2000*

**Adams, Marilyn Jager.**
Phonics review kit [kit]. Chicago, Ill. : Open Court Pub. Co., c1995.
*TC LB1573.3 .P45 1995*

**Adams, Steven.** The Barbizon school & the origins of impressionism / Steven Adams. 1st ed. London : Phaidon, c1994. 240 p.: ill. ; 30 cm. Inlcudes bibliographical references (p. 236) and index. ISBN 0-7148-2919-6
*1. Barbizon school. 2. Painting, French. 3. Painting, Modern - 19th century - France. 4. Impressionism (Art) - France. 5. Barbizon school - Influence. I. Title. II. Title: Barbizon school and the origins of Impressionism.*
*TC N6847.5.B3 A28 1994*

**Adamski, Carol.**
Asher, James J. (James John), 1929- Learning another language through actions. 4th ed. Los Gatos, Calif. : Sky Oaks Productions, 1993.
*TC PB36 .A8 1993*

**ADAPTABILITY (PSYCHOLOGY).** *See also* **ADJUSTMENT (PSYCHOLOGY).**
Yamusah, Salifu. An investigation of the relative effectiveness of the composite approach and the phenomenological method for enhancing self-esteem in adults with mental retardation. 1998.
*TC 085 Y146*

**ADAPTABILITY (PSYCHOLOGY) IN OLD AGE.**
Hatch, Laurie Russell. Beyond gender differences. Amityville, N.Y. : Baywood Pub., c2000.
*TC HQ1061 .H375 2000*

**ADAPTATION (BIOLOGY).** *See* **STRESS (PHYSIOLOGY).**

**ADAPTATION, PHYSIOLOGICAL.**
Rowell, Loring B. Human cardiovascular control. New York : Oxford University Press, 1993.
*TC QP109 .R68 1993*

**ADAPTATION, PSYCHOLOGICAL.**
Tobin, David L. Coping strategies therapy for bulimia nervosa. Washington, DC : American Psychological Association, c2000.
*TC RC552.B84 T63 2000*

**ADAPTATION (PSYCHOLOGY).** *See* **ADAPTABILITY (PSYCHOLOGY); ADJUSTMENT (PSYCHOLOGY).**

**Adapted physical education :** regulations, recommendations, and resources. Albany, N.Y. : University of the State of New York, State Education Dept., Office of Elementary, Middle, Secondary, and Continuing Education, Office of Vocational and Educational Services for Individuals with Disabilities, 1997. vi, 46 p. : ill. ; 28 cm.
*I. University of the State of New York. Office of Vocational and Educational Services for Individuals with Disabilities. II.*

University of the State of New York. Office of Elementary,
Middle, Secondary, and Continuing Education. III. Title.
*TC GV445 .A3 1997*

**ADAPTING BEHAVIOR.** *See* **ADJUSTMENT
(PSYCHOLOGY).**

**Adapting early childhood curricula for children in
inclusive settings.**
Cook, Ruth E. 5th ed. Englewood Cliffs, N.J. :
Merrill, c2000.
*TC LC4019.2 .C66 2000*

**ADAPTIVE BEHAVIOR.** *See* **ADAPTABILITY
(PSYCHOLOGY); ADJUSTMENT
(PSYCHOLOGY).**

**ADAPTIVE COMPUTING - UNITED STATES.**
Mates, Barbara T. Adaptive technology for the
Internet. Chicago, Ill. : American Library Association,
1999.
*TC Z675.B M38 1999*

**Adaptive technology for the Internet.**
Mates, Barbara T. Chicago, Ill. : American Library
Association, 1999.
*TC Z675.B M38 1999*

**Adaptive university structures.**
Sporn, Barbara. London ; Philadelphia : Jessica
Kingsley, c1999.
*TC LB2322.2 .S667 1999*

**Adato, Perry Miller.**
Mary Cassatt [videorecording]. [Chicago, Ill.]: Home
Vision, c1977.
*TC ND237.C3 M37 1977*

**ADC (DISEASE).** *See* **AIDS DEMENTIA
COMPLEX.**

**ADC PROGRAMS.** *See* **AID TO FAMILIES WITH
DEPENDENT CHILDREN PROGRAMS.**

**ADD ADULTS.** *See* **ATTENTION-DEFICIT-
DISORDERED ADULTS.**

**ADD (CHILD BEHAVIOR DISORDER).** *See*
**ATTENTION-DEFICIT HYPERACTIVITY
DISORDER.**

**ADD CHILDREN.** *See* **ATTENTION-DEFICIT-
DISORDERED CHILDREN.**

**ADDAMS, JANE, 1860-1935.**
Jackson, Shannon, 1967- Lines of activity. Ann
Arbor : University of Michigan Press, c2000.
*TC HV4196.C4 J33 2000*

**ADDICTED PERSONS.** *See* **ADDICTS.**

**Addiction counseling.**
Miller, Geraldine A., 1955- Learning the language of
addiction counseling. Boston : Allyn and Bacon,
c1999.
*TC RC564 .M536 1999*

**Addiction is a choice.**
Schaler, Jeffrey A. Chicago, Ill. : Open Court, 2000.
*TC HV4998 .S33 2000*

**ADDICTION, SUBSTANCE.** *See* **SUBSTANCE
ABUSE.**

**ADDICTION TO ALCOHOL.** *See* **ALCOHOLISM.**

**ADDICTION TO DRUGS.** *See* **DRUG ABUSE.**

**ADDICTION TO NARCOTICS.** *See* **NARCOTIC
HABIT.**

**ADDICTION TO TOBACCO.** *See* **TOBACCO
HABIT.**

**ADDICTIVE BEHAVIOR.** *See* **COMPULSIVE
BEHAVIOR; SUBSTANCE ABUSE.**

**ADDICTIVE PERSONS.** *See* **ADDICTS.**

**ADDICTS.** *See* **ALCOHOLICS; NARCOTIC
ADDICTS; RECOVERING ADDICTS.**

**ADDICTS - PSYCHOLOGY.**
Elster, Jon, 1940- Strong feelings. Cambridge, Mass. :
MIT Press, c1999.
*TC BF531 .E475 1999*

**ADDICTS - REHABILITATION - UNITED
STATES.**
Bridges to recovery. New York ; London : Free Press,
c2000.
*TC HV5199.5 .B75 2000*

**Addison, Margaret, 1868-1940.** Diary of a European
tour, 1900 / Margaret Addison ; edited by Jean
O'Grady. Montréal : McGill-Queen's University
Press, c1999. xxxvii, 197 p. : ill., ports. ; 22 cm. Includes
bibliographical references (p. [171]-191) and index. ISBN 0-
7735-1886-X DDC 914.04/288
*1. Europe - Description and travel. 2. Addison, Margaret, -*

1868-1940 - Journeys - Europe. 3. Victoria College (Toronto,
Ont.) 4. Addison,, Margaret. - 1868-1940 - Diaries. 5. Europe -
Descriptions et voyages. 6. Addison, Margaret. - 1868-1940 -
Voyages - Europe. 7. Addison, Margaret, - 1868-1940 -
Journaux intimes. I. O'Grady, Jean, 1943- II. Title.
*TC LE3.T619 A33 1999*

**ADDISON,, MARGARET, 1868-1940 - DIARIES.**
Addison, Margaret, 1868-1940. Diary of a European
tour, 1900. Montréal : McGill-Queen's University
Press, c1999.
*TC LE3.T619 A33 1999*

**ADDISON, MARGARET, 1868-1940 - JOURNAUX
INTIMES.**
Addison, Margaret, 1868-1940. Diary of a European
tour, 1900. Montréal : McGill-Queen's University
Press, c1999.
*TC LE3.T619 A33 1999*

**ADDISON, MARGARET, 1868-1940 - JOURNEYS -
EUROPE.**
Addison, Margaret, 1868-1940. Diary of a European
tour, 1900. Montréal : McGill-Queen's University
Press, c1999.
*TC LE3.T619 A33 1999*

**ADDISON, MARGARET, 1868-1940 - VOYAGES -
EUROPE.**
Addison, Margaret, 1868-1940. Diary of a European
tour, 1900. Montréal : McGill-Queen's University
Press, c1999.
*TC LE3.T619 A33 1999*

**Addison-Wesley series on organization development.**
Chisholm, Rupert F. Developing network
organizations. Reading, Mass. : Addison-Wesley,
c1998.
*TC HD69.S8 C45 1998*

Raelin, Joseph A., 1948- Work based learning.
Reading, MA : Addison-Wesley, 1999.
*TC HD30.4 .R33 1999*

**Addressing cultural issues in organizations :** beyond
the corporate context / editor Robert T. Carter.
Thousand Oaks, Calif. : Sage Publications, 2000. xii,
297 p. : ill. ; 24 cm. (Winter roundtable series ; 1) Includes
bibliographical references (p. 247-284) and indexes. ISBN
0-7619-0548-0 (alk. paper) ISBN 0-7619-0549-9 (alk. paper)
DDC 302.3/5/08900973
*1. United States - Race relations. 2. United States - Ethnic
relations. 3. Race awareness - United States. 4. Pluralism
(Social sciences) - United States. 5. Minorities - United States -
Social conditions. 6. Diversity in the workplace - United States.
7. Organizational behavior - United States. I. Carter, Robert
T., 1948- II. Series.*
*TC E184.A1 A337 2000*

**Addressing the spiritual dimensions of adult
learning : :** what educators can do / Leona M.
English, Marie A. Gillen, editors: Susan Imel, editor-
in-chief. San Francisco : Jossey Bass, 2000. 100 p. :
ill. ; 23 cm. (New directions for adult and continuing
education, no. 85.) "Spring 2000." Includes bibliographical
references and index. CONTENTS: A spirituality epistemology:
honoring the adult learner as subject / Jane Vella -- Reckoning
with the spiritual lives of adult educators / Linda J. Vogel --
Spiritual dimensions of informal learning / Leona M. English --
The learning covenant / R.E.Y. Wickett -- Continuing
professional education: a spiritually based program / Lynda W.
Miller -- Learning from native adult education / Jeffrey A.
Orr -- Community development and adult education: locating
practice in its roots / Wilf E. Bean -- The spiritual dimensions
of lay ministry programs / Catherine P. Zeph -- Controvery,
questions, and suggestions for further reading / Marie A.
Gillen, Leona M. English. ISBN 0-7879-5364-4
*1. Spiritual life - Study and teaching. 2. Adult education. 3.
Adult learning. I. English, Leona M. 1963- II. Gillen, Marie A.
III. Imel, Susan. IV. Series: New directions for adult and
continuing education . no. 85*
*TC LC5219 .A25 2000*

**Adegboye, Akin.**
Issues on examination malpractices in Nigeria :.
Ikere-Ekiti [Nigeria] : Ondo State College of
Education, c1998.
*TC LB3058.N6 I848 1998*

**Adelman, Clifford.** Answers in the tool box : academic
intensity, attendance patterns, and bachelor's degree
attainment / Clifford Adelman. Washington, DC ; U.S.
Dept. of Education, Office of Educational Research
and Improvement, [1999] xii, 124 p. ; 28 cm. "June
1999."--T.p. verso. "PLLI-8021"--P [4] of cover. Includes
bibliographical referenes ( p. 99-108).
*1. Postsecondary education - United States. 2. Degrees,
Academic - United States. 3. United States. Office of
Educational Research and Improvement. II. Title. III. Title:
Academic intensity, attendance patterns, and bachelor's degree
attainment*

*TC LB2390 .A34 1999*

**ADELPHI UNIVERSITY - ADMINISTRATION -
CASE STUDIES.**
Lewis, Lionel S. (Lionel Stanley) When power
corrupts. New Brunswick, NJ: Transaction Publishers,
c2000.
*TC LD25.8 .L49 2000*

**ADELPHI UNIVERSITY - FACULTY - CASE
STUDIES.**
Lewis, Lionel S. (Lionel Stanley) When power
corrupts. New Brunswick, NJ: Transaction Publishers,
c2000.
*TC LD25.8 .L49 2000*

**Adetunberu, Joseph Oyekayode.**
Issues on examination malpractices in Nigeria :.
Ikere-Ekiti [Nigeria] : Ondo State College of
Education, c1998.
*TC LB3058.N6 I848 1998*

**Adger, D.**
Functional categories, argument structure and
parametric variation. Edinburgh : Centre for Cognitive
Study, University of Edinburgh, c1994.
*TC P151 .F86 1994*

**ADHD (CHILD BEHAVIOR DISORDER).** *See*
**ATTENTION-DEFICIT HYPERACTIVITY
DISORDER.**

**ADHD : :** research, practice and opinion / [edited by]
Paul Cooper and Katherine Bilton. London : Whurr,
c1999. x, 255 p. ; 24 cm. Includes bibliographical references
and index. ISBN 1-86156-108-3
*1. Attention-deficit hyperactivity disorder. I. Cooper, Paul.
1955- II. Bilton, Katherine.*
*TC RJ506.H9 A32 1999*

**ADHD** [videorecording] : what do we know? / Kevin
Dawkins, producer/writer ; New York Dawkins
Productions. New York, NY : Guilford Publications,
Inc., c1992. 1 videocassette (36 min.) : sd., col. ; 1/2 in. + 1
program manual (31 p. ; 22 cm.). VHS. Catalogued from
credits and container. Host: Dr. Russell A. Barkley. Art
director, Lee Dawkins ; program development, Dr. Russell
Barkley ; coordinating producer, Sharon Panulla. Bibliography
p. 31 in manual. "The following program is presented by
Guilford Publications."--Voice-over in opening credits. "A
Guilford Press video"--Container. For parents and educators
and all those who care for ADHD children. SUMMARY:
Describes the characteristics of Attention Deficit Hyperactivity
Disorder (ADHD), which is a biological problem involving an
underactivity in those centers of the brain responsible for
sustaining motivation and effort over time. Discusses the
differing degrees and the prevalence of this condition, as well
as problems associated with it. Parents of children with ADHD
and an adult with ADHD speak of their personal experiences of
the disorder and the three chief characteristics: inattentiveness,
impulsivity and hyperactivity. ISBN 0-89862-971-3
*1. Attention-deficit hyperactivity disorder. 2. Hyperactive
children. 3. Attention-deficit-disordered children. 4. Attention-
deficit-disordered youth. 5. Attention-deficit-disordered adults.
I. Dawkins, Kevin. II. Barkley, Russell A., 1949- III. Dawkins,
Lee. IV. Panulla. Sharon. V. Kevin Dawkins Productions. VI.
Guilford Publications. Inc. VII. Guilford Press (New York,
N.Y.) VIII. Title: ADHD : what do we know? [videorecording]
IX. Title: Attention deficit hyperactivity disorder
[videorecording] : what do we know? X. Title: What do we
know?*
*TC RJ506.H9 A3 1992*

**ADHD : what do we know? [videorecording].**
ADHD [videorecording]. New York, NY : Guilford
Publications, Inc., c1992.
*TC RJ506.H9 A3 1992*

**ADHD with comorbid disorders.**
Pliszka, Steven R. New York : Guilford Press, c1999.
*TC RJ506.H9 P55 1999*

**ADIPOSITY.** *See* **OBESITY.**

**Adjective intensification - learners versus native
speakers.**
Lorenz, Gunter R. Amsterdam ; Atlanta, GA : Rodopi,
1999.
*TC PE1074.5 .L67 1999*

**ADJUSTMENT DISORDERS.**
Newman, Stephanie. Self-silencing, depression,
gender role, and gender role conflict in women and
men. 1997.
*TC 085 N47*

**ADJUSTMENT (PSYCHOLOGY).** *See also*
**ADAPTABILITY (PSYCHOLOGY);
ADJUSTMENT (PSYCHOLOGY) IN
CHILDREN; CONFLICT (PSYCHOLOGY).**
Chrispin, Marie C. Resilient adaptation of church-
affiliated young Haitian immigrants. 1998.

*TC 06 no. 11015*

Gewirtz, Abigail Hadassah. Coping strategies and stage of change among Vietnam combat veterans diagnosed with posttraumatic stress disorder and comorbid substance use disorders. 1997.
*TC 085 G338*

Halperin, Jane Carol. The influence of causal attributions on the psychological adjustment of post-treatment adolescent cancer survivors. 1999.
*TC 085 H155*

Loss and trauma. Philadelphia, PA : Brunner-Routledge, c2000.
*TC BF575.D35 L67 2000*

Smith, Jeffery, 1961- Where the roots reach for water. New York : North Point Press, 1999.
*TC BF575.M44 S55 1999*

Stress, coping, and health in families. Thousand Oaks, Calif. : Sage Publications, c1998.
*TC RC455.4.F3 S79 1998*

**ADJUSTMENT (PSYCHOLOGY) IN CHILDREN - UNITED STATES.**
Luthar, Suniya S. Poverty and children's adjustment. Thousand Oaks, Calif. : Sage Publications, c1999.
*TC HV741 .L88 1999*

**ADJUSTMENT (PSYCHOLOGY) IN OLD AGE.**
Hatch, Laurie Russell. Beyond gender differences. Amityville, N.Y. : Baywood Pub., c2000.
*TC HQ1061 .H375 2000*

Nemeroff, Robin. Stress, social support, and psychological distress in late life. 1999.
*TC 085 N341*

**ADMINISTRATION.** *See* **MANAGEMENT; POLITICAL SCIENCE.**

**ADMINISTRATION, NURSING SERVICE.** *See* **NURSING SERVICES - ADMINISTRATION.**

**ADMINISTRATION OF CRIMINAL JUSTICE.** *See* **CRIMINAL JUSTICE, ADMINISTRATION OF.**

**ADMINISTRATION OF JUVENILE JUSTICE.** *See* **JUVENILE JUSTICE, ADMINISTRATION OF.**

**Administration of schools for young children.**
Click, Phyllis. 5th ed. Albany, NY : Delmar, 1999.
*TC LB2822.7 .C55 1999*

**ADMINISTRATION, PUBLIC.** *See* **PUBLIC ADMINISTRATION.**

**ADMINISTRATIVE AGENCIES.** *See* **EXECUTIVE DEPARTMENTS.**

**ADMINISTRATIVE AGENCIES - DATA PROCESSING - CONGRESSES.**
Digital democracy. London ; New York : Routledge, 1999.
*TC JF1525.A8 D54 1999*

**ADMINISTRATIVE AGENCIES - EVALUATION.**
Building effective evaluation capacity. New Brunswick, N.J. : Transaction Publishers, c1999.
*TC JF1351 .B83 1999*

**ADMINISTRATIVE AGENCIES - LAW AND LEGISLATION.** *See* **ADMINISTRATIVE AGENCIES.**

**ADMINISTRATIVE AGENCIES - UNITED STATES - CONGRESSES.**
Nonprofits and government. Washington, DC : Urban Institute Press, 1999.
*TC HD62.6 .N694 1999*

**ADMINISTRATIVE AGENCIES - UNITED STATES - MANAGEMENT.**
Haass, Richard. The bureaucratic entrepreneur. Washington, D.C. : Brookings Institution, c1999.
*TC JF1351 .H2 1999*

Schachter, Hindy Lauer. Reinventing government or reinventing ourselves. Albany : State University of New York Press, c1997.
*TC JK1764 .S35 1997*

**ADMINISTRATIVE AGENCIES - UNITED STATES - REORGANIZATION.**
Schachter, Hindy Lauer. Reinventing government or reinventing ourselves. Albany : State University of New York Press, c1997.
*TC JK1764 .S35 1997*

**ADMINISTRATIVE COMMUNICATION.** *See* **BUSINESS COMMUNICATION.**

**ADMINISTRATIVE LAW.** *See* **ADMINISTRATIVE AGENCIES; CONSTITUTIONAL LAW; PUBLIC ADMINISTRATION.**

**Administrative officials.**
CSG state directory. Directory III, Administrative officials. Lexington, Ky. : The Council, c1998-
*TC JK2403 .B6*

**ADMINISTRATIVE PERSONNEL.**
Simms, Lillian M. (Lillian Margaret) The professional practice of nursing administration. 3rd ed. Albany, NY : Delmar Publishers, c2000.
*TC RT89 .S58 2000*

**Administrative problem solving.**
Dombroski, Ann P. 1999.
*TC 06 no. 11104*

Dombroski, Ann P. 1999.
*TC 06 no. 11104*

**ADMINISTRATIVE TEAMS IN SCHOOLS.** *See* **SCHOOL MANAGEMENT TEAMS.**

**Administratively mandated change at Amherst College.**
Tolliver, Joseph A. 1997.
*TC 06 no. 10871*

**ADMINISTRATOR-TEACHER RELATIONSHIPS.** *See* **TEACHER-ADMINISTRATOR RELATIONSHIPS.**

**ADMINISTRATORS, NURSE.** *See* **NURSE ADMINISTRATORS.**

**Adolescence.**
Steinberg, Laurence D., 1952- 5th ed. Boston : McGraw-Hill College, c1999.
*TC BF724 .S75 1999*

**ADOLESCENCE.**
Adolescent behavior and society. 5th ed. Boston : McGraw-Hill, c1998.
*TC HQ796 .A3338 1998*

Negotiating adolescence in times of social change. Cambridge, U.K. ; New York : Cambridge University Press, 2000.
*TC HQ796 .N415 2000*

Thayer, Vivian Trow, 1886- Reorganizing secondary education; New York, Appleton-Century [c1939]
*TC LB1607 .T5*

**Adolescence, affect and health.**
Spruijt-Metz, Donna. Hove : Psychology Press, for the European Association for Research on Adolescence, 1999.
*TC RJ47.53 .S67 1999*

**Adolescence and society**
Personality development in adolescence. London ; New York : Routledge, c1998.
*TC BF724.3.P4 P47 1998*

Shucksmith, Janet, 1953- Health issues and adolescents. London ; New York : Routledge, 1998.
*TC RJ47.53 .S455 1998*

**ADOLESCENCE - JAPAN - CASE STUDIES.**
LeTendre, Gerald K. Learning to be adolescent. New Haven [Conn.] ; London : Yale University Press, c2000.
*TC LB1135 .L47 2000*

**Adolescence (New York, N.Y.)**
(4.) Adolescents and their families. New York : Garland Pub., 1999.
*TC HQ796 .A33533 1999*

**ADOLESCENCE - PSYCHOLOGY.** *See* **ADOLESCENT PSYCHOLOGY.**

**ADOLESCENCE - UNITED STATES.**
Adolescents and their families. New York : Garland Pub., 1999.
*TC HQ796 .A33533 1999*

Hurd, Paul DeHart, 1905- Transforming middle school science education. New York : Teachers College Press, c2000.
*TC LB1585.3 .H89 2000*

**ADOLESCENCE - UNITED STATES - CASE STUDIES.**
LeTendre, Gerald K. Learning to be adolescent. New Haven [Conn.] ; London : Yale University Press, c2000.
*TC LB1135 .L47 2000*

**ADOLESCENCE - UNITED STATES - HISTORY.**
Childhood in America. New York : New York University Press, c2000.

*TC HQ792.U5 C4199 1999*

Moran, Jeffrey P. Teaching sex. Cambridge, Mass. : Harvard University Press, 2000.
*TC HQ57.5.A3 M66 2000*

**ADOLESCENCE - UNITED STATES - HISTORY - SOURCES.**
Childhood in America. New York : New York University Press, c2000.
*TC HQ792.U5 C4199 1999*

**ADOLESCENT ANALYSIS.**
Sayers, Janet. Boy crazy. London ; New York : Routledge, 1998.
*TC BF724 .S325 1998*

**Adolescent behavior and society :** a book of readings / [edited by] Rolf E. Muuss, Harriet D. Porton. 5th ed. Boston : McGraw-Hill, c1998. xiii, 465 p. : ill. ; 23 cm. Rev. ed. of: Adolescent behavior and society / editor, Rolf E. Muuss. 4th ed. c1990. Includes bibliographical references and indexes. ISBN 0-07-044422-6 DDC 305.235
*1. Youth. 2. Adolescence. I. Muuss, Rolf Eduard Helmut, 1924- II. Porton, Harriet.*
*TC HQ796 .A3338 1998*

**ADOLESCENT BOYS.** *See* **TEENAGE BOYS.**

**Adolescent cultures, school & society**
(vol. 13.) Kelly, Deirdre M. Pregnant with meaning. New York : P. Lang, c2000.
*TC LC4094.2.B8 K45 2000*

(vol. 2) Peacebuilding for adolescents. New York : P. Lang, c1999.
*TC JZ5534 .P43 1999*

(vol. 9) Growing up girls. New York : P. Lang, c1999.
*TC HQ798 .G76 1999*

**Adolescent development and rapid social change :** perspectives from Eastern Europe / Judith L. Van Hoorn ... [et al.]. Albany : State University of New York Press, c2000. x, 309 p. : ill. ; 24 cm. Includes bibliographical references (p. 281-288) and index. ISBN 0-7914-4473-2 (hc. : alk. paper) ISBN 0-7914-4474-0 (pb. : alk. paper) DDC 305.235/09439
*1. Teenagers - Hungary. 2. Youth - Hungary - Social conditions. 3. Hungary - Politics and government - 1989- 4. Teenagers - Poland. 5. Youth - Poland - Social conditions. 6. Poland - Politics and government - 1989- 7. Political socialization - Europe, Eastern. 8. Adolescent psychology - Europe, Eastern. 9. Social change - Europe, Eastern. I. Van Hoorn, Judith Lieberman.*
*TC HQ799.H8 A35 2000*

**Adolescent development :** the essential readings / edited by Gerald Adams. Oxford ; Malden, Mass. : Blackwell Publishers, 2000. ix, 345 p. : ill. ; 24 cm. (Essential readings in developmental psychology) Includes bibliographical references and index. CONTENTS: Theories of adolescent development / M. Berzonsky -- Retrospective survey of parental marital relations and child reproductive development / Kenneth Kim and Peter K. Smith -- A cross-national study on the relations among prosocial moral reasoning, gender role orientation, and prosocial behaviors / Gustavo Carlo et al. -- The relations among identity development, self-consciousness, and self-focusing during middle and late adolescence / Gerald R. Adams, Kitty G. Abraham and Carol Ann Markstrom -- Classwork and homework in early adolescence / Carla M. Leone and Maryse H. Richards -- Longitudinal adjustment patterns of boys and girls experiencing early, middle, and late sexual intercourse / C. Raymond Bingham and Lisa J. Crockett -- Like father, like son? / Lor D'Angelo and Daniel A. Weinberger and S. Shirley Feldman -- Adolescent girls' relationships with mothers and best friends / Leslie A. Gavin and Wyndol Furman -- Work experience, mental health, and behavorial adjustment in adolescence / Jeylan T. Mortimer et al. -- The high school "junior theme" as an adolescent rite of passage / Reed Larson -- Social context and the subjective experience of different types of rock music / Rober L. Thompson and Reed Larson -- Alcohol use, suicidal behavior, and risky activities among adolescents / Michael Windle, Carol Miller-Tutzauer, and Donna Domenico -- Internalizing problems and their relation to the development of disruptive behaviors in adolescence / Rolf Loeber et al. -- Was Mead wrong about coming of age in Samoa? / James E. Coté. ISBN 0-631-21742-8 (hbk.) ISBN 0-631-21743-6 (pbk.) DDC 305.235/5
*1. Adolescent psychology. I. Adams, Gerald R., 1946- II. Series.*
*TC BF724 .A275 2000*

**ADOLESCENT GIRLS.** *See* **TEENAGE GIRLS.**

**ADOLESCENT GROUP PSYCHOTHERAPY.** *See* **GROUP PSYCHOTHERAPY FOR TEENAGERS.**

**ADOLESCENT HEALTH BEHAVIOR.** *See* HEALTH BEHAVIOR IN ADOLESCENCE.

**ADOLESCENT HEALTH HABITS.** *See* **HEALTH BEHAVIOR IN ADOLESCENCE.**

**The adolescent in group and family therapy** / edited by Max Sugar. 2nd ed. Northvale, NJ : Jason Aronson, 1999. xix, 28 p. ; 23 cm. Reprint. Previously published: Chicago : University of Chicago Press, 1986. Includes bibliographical references and index. ISBN 0-7657-0254-1 (pbk.) DDC 616.89/00835
*1. Adolescent psychotherapy. 2. Group psychotherapy. 3. Family psychotherapy. I. Sugar. Max. 1925-*
*TC RJ505.G7 A36 1999*

**Adolescent lives**
(1) Reiss, David, 1937- The relationship code. Cambridge, Mass. ; London : Harvard University Press, c2000.
*TC BF724 .R39 2000*

**ADOLESCENT MEDICINE.** *See* **ADOLESCENT PSYCHIATRY.**

**ADOLESCENT MOTHERS.** *See* **TEENAGE MOTHERS.**

**ADOLESCENT PREGNANCY.** *See* **TEENAGE PREGNANCY.**

**ADOLESCENT PROSTITUTION.** *See* **TEENAGE PROSTITUTION.**

**ADOLESCENT PSYCHIATRY.** *See* **INTERVIEWING IN ADOLESCENT PSYCHIATRY.**

**ADOLESCENT PSYCHIATRY - SOCIAL ASPECTS.**
Canino, Ian A. Culturally diverse children and adolescents. 2nd ed. New York : Guilford Press, c2000.
*TC RJ507.M54 C36 2000*

**ADOLESCENT PSYCHOLOGY.** *See also* EMOTIONS IN ADOLESCENCE; HEALTH BEHAVIOR IN ADOLESCENCE; IDENTITY (PSYCHOLOGY) IN ADOLESCENCE; INTERPERSONAL CONFLICT IN ADOLESCENCE; INTERPERSONAL RELATIONS IN ADOLESCENCE; PEER PRESSURE IN ADOLESCENCE; PERSONALITY IN ADOLESCENCE; SELF-ESTEEM IN ADOLESCENCE; SELF-PERCEPTION IN ADOLESCENCE; SOCIAL DESIRABILITY IN ADOLESCENCE.
Adolescent development. Oxford ; Malden, Mass. : Blackwell Publishers, 2000.
*TC BF724 .A275 2000*

Branwhite, Tony. Helping adolescents in school. Westport, Conn. ; London : Praeger, 2000.
*TC LB1027.55 .B72 2000*

Growing up girls. New York : P. Lang, c1999.
*TC HQ798 .G76 1999*

Negotiating adolescence in times of social change. Cambridge, U.K. ; New York : Cambridge University Press, 2000.
*TC HQ796 .N415 2000*

Reiss, David, 1937- The relationship code. Cambridge, Mass. ; London : Harvard University Press, c2000.
*TC BF724 .R39 2000*

Sayers, Janet. Boy crazy. London ; New York : Routledge, 1998.
*TC BF724 .S325 1998*

Scales, Peter, 1949- Developmental assets. Minneapolis : Search Institute, c1999.
*TC BF724 .S327 1999*

Smith, Mieko Kotake. Adolescents with emotional and behavioral disabilities. Lewiston, NY : E. Mellen Press, c1998.
*TC RJ503 .S63 1998*

Spruijt-Metz, Donna. Adolescence, affect and health. Hove : Psychology Press, for the European Association for Research on Adolescence, 1999.
*TC RJ47.53 .S67 1999*

Steinberg, Laurence D., 1952- Adolescence. 5th ed. Boston : McGraw-Hill College, c1999.
*TC BF724 .S75 1999*

Weisfeld, Glenn, 1943- Evolutionary principles of human adolescence. New York, NY : Basic Books, 1999.
*TC BF724 .W35 1999*

**ADOLESCENT PSYCHOLOGY - CALIFORNIA - CASE STUDIES.**
Childress, Herb, 1958- Landscapes of betrayal, landscapes of joy. Albany [N.Y.] : State University of New York Press, c2000.
*TC HQ796 .C458237 2000*

**ADOLESCENT PSYCHOLOGY - CROSS-CULTURAL STUDIES.**
LeTendre, Gerald K. Learning to be adolescent. New Haven [Conn.] ; London : Yale University Press, c2000.
*TC LB1135 .L47 2000*

**ADOLESCENT PSYCHOLOGY - EUROPE, EASTERN.**
Adolescent development and rapid social change. Albany : State University of New York Press, c2000.
*TC HQ799.H8 A35 2000*

**ADOLESCENT PSYCHOLOGY - RESEARCH.**
Research with children. New York : Falmer Press, 2000.
*TC HQ767.85 .R48 1999*

**ADOLESCENT PSYCHOPATHOLOGY.** *See* **ADOLESCENT PSYCHIATRY; ANXIETY IN ADOLESCENCE; DEPRESSION IN ADOLESCENCE; EATING DISORDERS IN ADOLESCENCE.**

**ADOLESCENT PSYCHOTHERAPY.** *See also* **GROUP PSYCHOTHERAPY FOR TEENAGERS.**
The adolescent in group and family therapy. 2nd ed. Northvale, NJ : Jason Aronson, 1999.
*TC RJ505.G7 A36 1999*

Bertolino, Bob, 1965- Therapy with troubled teenagers. New York : Wiley, c1999.
*TC RJ506.P63 B475 1999*

Bromfield, Richard. Doing child and adolescent psychotherapy. Northvale, N.J. ; London : Jason Aronson, c1999.
*TC RJ504 .B753 1999*

Child and adolescent therapy. 2nd ed. New York : Guilford Press, c2000.
*TC RJ505.C63 C45 2000*

Children's rights, therapists' responsibilities. New York : Harrington Park Press, c1997.
*TC RJ504 .C486 1997*

Gardner, Richard A. Developmental conflicts and diagnostic evaluation in adolescent psychotherapy. Northvale, N.J. : J. Aronson, c1999.
*TC RJ503 .G376 1999*

Innovative psychotherapy techniques in child and adolescent therapy. 2nd ed. New York : Wiley, c1999.
*TC RJ504 .I57 1999*

**Adolescent relationships and drug use** / Michelle A. Miller ... [et al.]. Mahwah, N.J. ; London : Lawrence Erlbaum Associates, 2000. xix, 228 p. ; 24 cm. (LEA's series on personal relationships) Includes bibliographical references (p. 193-213) and indexes. ISBN 0-8058-3435-4 (hbk. : alk. paper) ISBN 0-8058-3436-2 (pbk. : alk. paper) DDC 362.29/17/0835/0973
*1. Youth - Drug use. 2. Drug abuse - Prevention. 3. Interpersonal relations. I. Miller, Michelle A., 1960- II. Series: LEA's personal relationships series.*
*TC HV5824.Y68 A315 2000*

**ADOLESCENT SEX OFFENDERS.** *See* **TEENAGE SEX OFFENDERS.**

**Adolescent siblings in stepfamilies :** family functioning and adolescent adjustment / E. Mavis Hetherington, Sandra H. Henderson and David Reis ; in collaboration with Edward R. Anderson ... [et al.]. ; with commentary by James H. Bray. Chicago, Ill. : University of Chicago Press, 1999. vi, 222 p. : ill ; 23 cm. (Monographs of the Society for Research in Child Development, 0037-976X ; serial no. 259, vol. 64, no. 4, 1999) Includes bibliographical references.
*1. Sibling Relations. 2. Family Therapy. 3. Parent-Child Relations. I. Hetherington, E. Mavis. II. Henderson, Sandra H. III. Reis, David. IV. Anderson, Edward R. V. Bray, James H. VI. Society for Research in Child Development. VII. Series: Monographs of the Society for Research in Child Development ; 64, no. 4.*
*TC LB1103.S6 v.64 no. 4*

**ADOLESCENTS.** *See* **TEENAGERS.**

**Adolescents and their families :** structure, function, and parent-youth relationships / edited, with an introduction by Richard M. Lerner, Domini R. Castellino. New York : Garland Pub., 1999. xiii, 375 p. : ill. ; 24 cm. (Adolescence : development, diversity, and context ; 4) Includes bibliographical references. ISBN

0-8153-3293-9 (alk. paper) DDC 305.235/0973
*1. Teenagers - United States - Family relationships. 2. Teenagers - United States - Social conditions. 3. Parent and teenager - United States. 4. Minority teenagers - United States. 5. Adolescence - United States. I. Lerner, Richard M. II. Castellino, Domini R. (Domini Rose) III. Series: Adolescence (New York, N.Y.) ; 4.*
*TC HQ796 .A33533 1999*

**Adolescents' perspectives about the environmental impacts of food production practices.**
Bissonnette, Madeline Monaco. 1999.
*TC 06 no. 11084*

**Adolescents, sex, and the law.**
Levesque, Roger J. R. 1st ed. Washington, DC : American Psychological Association, c2000.
*TC KF479 .L48 2000*

**Adolescents with emotional and behavioral disabilities.**
Smith, Mieko Kotake. Lewiston, NY : E. Mellen Press, c1998.
*TC RJ503 .S63 1998*

**The Adonis complex.**
Pope, Harrison. New York : Free Press, 2000.
*TC BF697.5.B635 2000*

**ADOPTED CHILDREN - FRANCE - HISTORY.**
Gager, Kristin Elizabeth. Blood ties and fictive ties. Princeton, N.J. : Princeton University Press, c1996.
*TC HV875.58.F8 G34 1996*

**ADOPTED CHILDREN - PSYCHOLOGY.**
Groza, Victor, 1956- Clinical and practice issues in adoption. Westport, Conn. : Praeger, 1998.
*TC HV875 .G776 1998*

**ADOPTED INFANTS.** *See* **ADOPTED CHILDREN.**

**ADOPTION.** *See also* **INTERCOUNTRY ADOPTION.**
Sayles, Mary Buell, 1878- Substitute parents, New York, The Commonwealth fund; London, H. Milford, Oxford University Press, 1936.
*TC HV875 .S3*

**ADOPTION - FRANCE - HISTORY.**
Gager, Kristin Elizabeth. Blood ties and fictive ties. Princeton, N.J. : Princeton University Press, c1996.
*TC HV875.58.F8 G34 1996*

**ADOPTION - PSYCHOLOGICAL ASPECTS.**
Groza, Victor, 1956- Clinical and practice issues in adoption. Westport, Conn. : Praeger, 1998.
*TC HV875 .G776 1998*

**ADP (DATA PROCESSING).** *See* **ELECTRONIC DATA PROCESSING.**

**ADR (DISPUTE RESOLUTION).** *See* **DISPUTE RESOLUTION (LAW).**

**ADULT AND CHILD.** *See* **CHILDREN AND ADULTS.**

**ADULT CHILD ABUSE VICTIMS.** *See* **ABUSED CHILDREN; ADULT CHILD SEXUAL ABUSE VICTIMS.**

**ADULT CHILD ABUSE VICTIMS - MENTAL HEALTH.**
Shengold, Leonard. Soul murder revisited. New Haven, CT : Yale University Press, 1999.
*TC RC569.5.C55 S53 1999*

**ADULT-CHILD RELATIONSHIPS.** *See* **CHILDREN AND ADULTS.**

**ADULT CHILD SEXUAL ABUSE VICTIMS.** *See also* **SEXUALLY ABUSED CHILDREN.**
Gartner, Richard B. Betrayed as boys. New York : Guilford Press, c1999.
*TC RC569.5.A28 G37 1999*

**ADULT CHILD SEXUAL ABUSE VICTIMS - CASE STUDIES.**
With the phoenix rising. 1st ed. San Francisco : Jossey-Bass, c1999.
*TC RC569.5.A28 W57 1999*

**ADULT CHILD SEXUAL ABUSE VICTIMS - LONGITUDINAL STUDIES.**
Cameron, Catherine. Resolving childhood trauma. Thousand Oaks, Calif. : Sage Publications, c2000.
*TC RC569.5.A28 C35 2000*

**ADULT CHILD SEXUAL ABUSE VICTIMS - MENTAL HEALTH.**
Woodruff, Debra, 1967- General family functioning, parental bonding, and attachment style. 1998.
*TC 085 W858*

**ADULT CHILDREN OF DIVORCED PARENTS.** *See* **CHILDREN OF DIVORCED PARENTS.**

**ADULT EDUCATION.** *See also* **CONTINUING EDUCATION; FOLK HIGH SCHOOLS; NON-FORMAL EDUCATION; OPEN LEARNING; READING (ADULT EDUCATION).**
Addressing the spiritual dimensions of adult learning :. San Francisco : Jossey Bass, 2000.
*TC LC5219 .A25 2000*

Dominicé, Pierre. Learning from our lives. 1st ed. San Francisco : Jossey-Bass, c2000.
*TC LB1029.B55 D64 2000*

Driscoll, Margaret M. The application of adult education principles in the development of a manual for practitioners creating web-based training programs. 1999.
*TC 06 no. 11106*

Lamm, Sharon Lea. The connection between action reflection learning and transformative learning. 2000.
*TC 06 no. 11230*

Longworth, Norman. Making lifelong learning work. London : Kogan Page, 1999.
*TC LC5225.L42 L66 1999*

McKay, Heather, 1950- Teaching adult second language learners. Cambridge ; New York : Cambridge University Press, 1999.
*TC P53 .M33 1999*

Providing culturally relevant adult education. San Francisco : Jossey Bass, c1999.
*TC LC5219 .P76 1999*

Teare, Richard. The virtual university. London ; New York : Cassell, 1998.
*TC LC5215 .T42 1998*

An update on adult development theory :. San Francisco, CA : Jossey-Bass Publishers, 1999.
*TC LC5225.L42 U63 1999*

Vella, Jane Kathryn, 1931- Taking learning to task. San Francisco, Calif. : Jossey-Bass, c2000.
*TC LC5225.L42 V43 2000*

The virtual learning organization. London ; New York : Continuum, 2000.
*TC LC5215 .V574 2000*

**ADULT EDUCATION - AUSTRALIA.**
Understanding adult education and training. 2nd ed. St. Leonards, NSW, Australia : Allen & Unwin, 2000.
*TC LC5259 U53 2000*

**Adult education bulletin.**
Adult education quarterly. [s.l.] : The Dept., 1932-

[Journal of adult education (New York, N.Y.)] Journal of adult education. New York : American Association for Adult Education, 1929-[1941]

**ADULT EDUCATION - CALIFORNIA - PERIODICALS.**
California review of adult education. [Los Angeles : California State Dept. of Education, 1936.

**ADULT EDUCATION - CROSS-CULTURAL STUDIES.**
The adult university. Buckingham [England] : Philadelphia, PA : Society for Research into Higher Education & Open University Press, 1999.
*TC LC5219 .A35 1999*

**ADULT EDUCATION EDUCATORS.**
Weintraub, Robert Steven. Informal learning in the workplace through desktop technology. 1998.
*TC 06 no. 11003*

**ADULT EDUCATION - EUROPE.**
Vocational and adult education in Europe. Dordrecht ; Boston ; London : Kluwer Academic, c1999.
*TC LC1047.E8 V58 1999*

**ADULT EDUCATION - EVALUATION.**
Lamm, Sharon Lea. The connection between action reflection learning and transformative learning. 2000.
*TC 06 no. 11230*

**ADULT EDUCATION - EVALUATION - NEW YORK (STATE).**
Langer, Arthur Mark. Faculty assessment of mentoring roles at SUNY Empire State College. 1999.
*TC 06 no. 11138*

**ADULT EDUCATION - GREAT BRITAIN.**
Powell, Stuart, 1949- Returning to study. Buckingham ; Philadelphia : Open University Press, c1999.
*TC LC5256.G7 P66 1999*

Preece, Julia. Combating social exclusion in university adult education. Aldershot ; Brookfield, Vt. : Ashgate, c1999.

*TC LC5256.G7 P84 1999*

**Adult education journal.**
[Journal of adult education (New York, N.Y.)] Journal of adult education. New York : American Association for Adult Education, 1929-[1941]

**Adult education journal Jan. 1949.**
Film forum review. [New York, N.Y.] : The Institute, 1946-

**Adult education (National Education Association. Department of Adult Education).**
Adult education quarterly. [s.l.] : The Dept., 1932-

**ADULT EDUCATION OF WOMEN - GREAT BRITAIN.**
Merrill, Barbara. Gender, change and identity :. Aldershot, Hants, England ; Brookfield, Vt. : Ashgate, c1999.
*TC LC2046 .M477 1999*

**ADULT EDUCATION OF WOMEN - SOCIAL ASPECTS - GREAT BRITAIN.**
Merrill, Barbara. Gender, change and identity :. Aldershot, Hants, England ; Brookfield, Vt. : Ashgate, c1999.
*TC LC2046 .M477 1999*

**ADULT EDUCATION - PERIODICALS.**
California review of adult education. [Los Angeles : California State Dept. of Education, 1936.

Film forum review. [New York, N.Y.] : The Institute, 1946-

Fundamental and adult education. [Paris : Unesco, 1952-1960]

[Journal of adult education (New York, N.Y.)] Journal of adult education. New York : American Association for Adult Education, 1929-[1941]

Journal of the American Association for Adult Education. New York, N.Y. : The Association, [1926-1928]

**Adult education quarterly** / Official organ of the Department of Adult Education, National Education Association. [s.l.] : The Dept., 1932- v. ; 23 cm. Vol. 7, no. 3 (Jan./Feb. 1932)- . Ceased publication with vol. 8, no. 4 in Sept. 1933? Title from cover. Continues: Adult education (National Education Association. Department of Adult Education). Continued by: Adult education bulletin.
*I. National Education Association. Department of Adult Education. II. Title: Adult education (National Education Association. Department of Adult Education) III. Title: Adult education bulletin*

**ADULT EDUCATION - STUDY AND TEACHING.**
The welfare-to-work challenge for adult literacy educators. San Francisco, CA : Jossey-Bass Publishers, 1999.
*TC LC149.7 .W43 1999*

**ADULT EDUCATION - SWEDEN - PERIODICALS.**
Folk-högskolan. Stockholm : Lärarförbundet, 1979-

**ADULT EDUCATION - UNITED STATES.**
Hollenbeck, Kevin. Classrooms in the workplace. Kalamazoo, Mich. : W.E. Upjohn Institute for Employment Research, 1993.
*TC HF5549.5.T7 H598 1993*

Robbins, Carol Braswell. An examination of critical feminist pedagogy in practice. 1999.
*TC 06 no. 11067*

**ADULT EDUCATION - UNITED STATES - DIRECTORIES.**
The adult student's guide. Berkley trade pbk. ed. New York, N.Y. : Berkley Books, 1999.
*TC L901 .A494 1999*

**Adult learning.**
Food for thought. Toronto, The Canadian Association for Adult Education.

Addressing the spiritual dimensions of adult learning :. San Francisco : Jossey Bass, 2000.
*TC LC5219 .A25 2000*

Dominicé, Pierre. Learning from our lives. 1st ed. San Francisco : Jossey-Bass, c2000.
*TC LB1029.B55 D64 2000*

Hayes, Elisabeth. Women as learners. 1st ed. San Francisco : Jossey-Bass Publishers, c2000.
*TC LC5225.L42 H39 2000*

Problem-based learning in higher education. Buckingham ; Philadelphia, PA : Society for Research into Higher Education : Open University Press, 2000.

*TC LB1027.42 .S28 2000*

Providing culturally relevant adult education. San Francisco : Jossey Bass, c1999.
*TC LC5219 .P76 1999*

Taylor, Kathleen, 1943- Developing adult learners. 1st ed. San Francisco : Jossey-Bass, c2000.
*TC LC5225.L42 T39 2000*

An update on adult development theory :. San Francisco, CA : Jossey-Bass Publishers, 1999.
*TC LC5225.L42 U63 1999*

Vella, Jane Kathryn, 1931- Taking learning to task. San Francisco, Calif. : Jossey-Bass, c2000.
*TC LC5225.L42 V43 2000*

Weintraub, Robert Steven. Informal learning in the workplace through desktop technology. 1998.
*TC 06 no. 11003*

**ADULT LEARNING - EVALUATION.**
Zersen, David John. Independent learning among clergy. 1998.
*TC 06 no. 11008*

**ADULT LEARNING - PHILOSOPHY - EVALUATION.**
Eddy, Jennifer B.K. Multiple intelligences, styles, and proficiency. 1999.
*TC 085 E10*

**ADULT LITERACY.** *See* **FUNCTIONAL LITERACY.**

**The adult student's guide** / compiled by Leigh Grossman and Lesley McBain. Berkley trade pbk. ed. New York, N.Y. : Berkley Books, 1999. 560 p. ; 24 cm. "A Swordsmith production." ISBN 0-425-16919-7 DDC 374/ .973
*1. Adult education - United States - Directories. 2. Continuing education - United States - Directories. 3. Universities and colleges - United States - Directories. I. Grossman, Leigh. II. McBain, Lesley.*
*TC L901 .A494 1999*

**ADULT SURVIVORS OF CHILD ABUSE.** *See* **ADULT CHILD ABUSE VICTIMS.**

**ADULT SURVIVORS OF CHILD SEXUAL ABUSE.** *See* **ADULT CHILD SEXUAL ABUSE VICTIMS.**

**The adult university** / Etienne Bourgeois ... [et al.]. Buckingham [England] ; Philadelphia, PA : Society for Research into Higher Education & Open University Press, 1999. 194 p. : ill. ; 23 cm. Includes bibliographical references (p. [178]-185) and index. ISBN 0-335-19907-0 (pbk.) ISBN 0-335-19908-9 DDC 378
*1. Adult education - Cross-cultural studies. 2. Education, Higher - Cross-cultural studies. 3. Universities and colleges - Administration - Cross-cultural studies. 4. Educational change - Cross-cultural studies. I. Bourgeois, Etienne, 1958-*
*TC LC5219 .A35 1999*

**ADULTERATIONS.** *See* **FOOD ADULTERATION AND INSPECTION.**

**ADULTHOOD.** *See also* **AGED; MIDDLE AGE; OLD AGE; YOUNG ADULTS.**
Transcending boundaries. New York : Garland, 1999.
*TC PN1009.A1 T69 1999*

**ADULTHOOD - PSYCHOLOGICAL ASPECTS.**
Hillman, James. The force of character. 1st ed. New York : Random House, c1999.
*TC BF724.85.S45 H535 1999b*

**ADULTHOOD - PSYCHOLOGICAL ASPECTS - CONGRESSES.**
Spirituality, ethics, and relationship in adulthood. Madison, Conn. : Psychosocial Press, c2000.
*TC BF724.5 .S68 2000*

**ADULTHOOD - PSYCHOLOGICAL ASPECTS - LONGITUDINAL STUDIES.**
Smith, Mieko Kotake. Adolescents with emotional and behavioral disabilities. Lewiston, NY : E. Mellen Press, c1998.
*TC RJ503 .S63 1998*

**ADULTS.** *See* **ADULTHOOD.**

**ADULTS ABUSED AS CHILDREN.** *See* **ADULT CHILD ABUSE VICTIMS.**

**ADULTS AND CHILDREN.** *See* **CHILDREN AND ADULTS.**

**ADULTS, EDUCATION OF.** *See* **ADULT EDUCATION.**

**ADULTS SEXUALLY ABUSED AS CHILDREN.** *See* **ADULT CHILD SEXUAL ABUSE VICTIMS.**

**Advanced applications of curriculum-based measurement** / edited by Mark R. Shinn. New York : Guilford Press, c1998. x, 315 p. : ill. ; 24 cm. (The Guilford school practitioner series) Includes bibliographical references and index. ISBN 1-57230-257-7 (alk. paper) DDC 371.26/4
1. Curriculum-based assessment - United States. 1. Shinn, Mark R. II. Series.
*TC LB3060.32.C74 A38 1998*

**Advanced human nutrition.**
Wildman, Robert E. C., 1964- Boca Raton : CRC Press, c2000.
*TC QP141 .W512 2000*

**Advanced nutrition and human metabolism.**
Groff, James L. 3rd ed. Belmont, CA : West/ Wadsworth, c2000.
*TC QP141 .G76 2000*

**Advanced psychology texts**
(v. 3) Edwards, David C. Motivation & emotion. Thousand Oaks, Calif. : Sage, c1999.
*TC BF503 .E38 1999*

**The advanced theory of statistics.**
Kendall, Maurice G. (Maurice George), 1907- 4th ed. London, C. Griffin, 1948.
*TC QA276 .K4262 1948*

Kendall, Maurice George. 3d ed. New York, Hafner Pub. Co., 1951.
*TC QA276 .K38 1951*

**The advancement of learning.**
Bacon, Francis, 1561-1626. Oxford : Clarendon, 2000.
*TC B1191 .K545 2000*

**Advances in African American psychology** / Reginald L. Jones, editor. Hampton, VA : Cobb & Henry, 1999. xvii, 380 p. ; 24 cm. Includes bibliographical references and indexes. ISBN 0-943539-09-9
1. Afro-Americans - Psychology. 1. Jones, Reginald Lanier, 1931-
*TC E185.625 .A36 1999*

**Advances in applied developmental psychology (1993)**
(v. 18.) Partnerships in research, clinical, and educational settings. Stamford, Conn. : Ablex Pub., c1999.
*TC HM1106 .P37 1999*

(v. 19.) Communication. Stamford, Conn. : Ablex Pub. Corp., c2000.
*TC BF712 .A36 v.19*

**Advances in cognition and educational practice**
(v. 5) Conceptual issues in research on intelligence. Stamford, Conn. : JAI Press , 1998.
*TC BF311 .A38 v. 5 1998*

**Advances in consciousness research**
(v. 15) Stratification in cognition and consciousness. Amsterdam ; Philadelphia : J. Benjamins, c1999.
*TC BF444 .S73 1999*

(v. 19) Human cognition and social agent technology. Amsterdam ; Philadelphia : John Benjamins, c2000.
*TC BF311 .H766 2000*

**Advances in contemporary educational thought series**
(v. 17) White, Patricia, 1937- Civic virtues and public schooling. New York : Teachers College Press, c1996.
*TC LC1011 .W48 1996*

**Advances in discourse processes**
(v. 65) Hill, Clifford. Children and reading tests. Stamford, Conn. : Ablex Pub. Corp., c2000.
*TC LB1050.46 .H55 2000*

**Advances in education in diverse communities**
(1.) Edmund W. Gordon. Stamford, Conn. : Jai Press, c2000.
*TC HM1033 .E35 2000*

**Advances in exercise immunology**
Mackinnon, Laurel T., 1953- Champaign, IL : Human Kinetics, c1999.
*TC QP301 .M159 1999*

**Advances in foreign and second language pedagogy**
(v. 1) Writing across languages. Stamford, Conn. : Ablex Pub., c2000.
*TC PB36 .W77 2000*

**Advances in gender research**
(v. 4) Social change for women and children. Stamford, Conn. : JAI Press, 2000.
*TC HQ1421 .S68 2000*

**Advances in learning and instruction series**
Learning sites. 1st ed. Amsterdam ; New York : Pergamon, 1999.
*TC LB1060 .L4245 1999*

Modelling changes in understanding. Amsterdam ; New York : Pergamon, 1999.
*TC BF319 .M55 1999*

New perspectives on conceptual change. 1st ed. Amsterdam ; New York : Oxford : Pergamon, 1999.
*TC LB1062 .N49 1999*

**Advances in political science (New York, N.Y.)**
Gendering elites. Houndmills, Basingstoke, Hampshire : Macmillan Press ; New York : St. Martin's Press, 2000.
*TC HM1261 .G46 2000*

**Advances in psychology (Amsterdam, Netherlands)**
(120.) Time and behaviour. Amsterdam ; New York : Elsevier, 1997.
*TC BF468 .T538 1997*

**Advances in reading/language research**
(vol. 7) Reconceptualizing literacy in the media age. Stamford, Conn. : Jai Press, c2000.
*TC LB1050 .A38 v.7*

**Advances in social cognition**
(v. 11.) Stereotype activation and inhibition. Mahwah, N.J. : L. Erlbaum Associates, 1998.
*TC BF323.S63 S75 1998*

**Advancing the frontier, 1830-1860.**
Foreman, Grant, 1869-1953. Norman : University of Oklahoma Press, 1968 printing, c1933.
*TC E93 .F67 1968*

**Advancing the world of literacy.**
Dugan, JoAnn R. Carrollton, Ga. : College Reading Association, 1999.
*TC LB2395 .C62 1999*

**ADVENTURE AND ADVENTURERS.** *See* CONQUERORS; ENCOMENDEROS; FRONTIER AND PIONEER LIFE; SEAFARING LIFE; SHIPWRECKS.

**ADVENTURE AND ADVENTURERS - COMPUTER GAMES.** *See* COMPUTER ADVENTURE GAMES.

**ADVENTURE GAMES.** *See* COMPUTER ADVENTURE GAMES.

**ADVENTURE GAMES, COMPUTER.** *See* COMPUTER ADVENTURE GAMES.

**ADVENTURE STORIES, AMERICAN - HISTORY AND CRITICISM.**
Mensh, Elaine, 1924- Black, white, and Huckleberry Finn. Tuscaloosa : University of Alabama Press, c2000.
*TC PS1305 .M46 2000*

**ADVENTURE STORIES, AMERICAN - STUDY AND TEACHING.**
Making Mark Twain work in the classroom. Durham [N.C.] : Duke University Press, 1999.
*TC PS1338 .M23 1999*

**The adventures of Marco and Polo.**
Wiesmüller, Dieter. [Pin Kaiser und Fip Husar English] New York : Walker & Co., 2000.
*TC PZ7.W6366 Ad 2000*

**ADVERSARY SYSTEM (LAW).** *See* TRIAL PRACTICE.

**Adversity, stress, and psychopathology** / edited by Bruce P. Dohrenwend. New York : Oxford University Press, 1998. xv, 567 p. : ill. ; 26 cm. Includes bibliographical references and index. ISBN 0-19-512192-9 (acid-free paper) DDC 616.89/071
1. Mental illness - Etiology. 2. Suffering - Psychological aspects. 3. Stress (Psychology) 4. Stress (Physiology) 5. Psychology, Pathological - Etiology. I. Dohrenwend, Bruce Philip, 1927-
*TC RC455.4.S87 A39 1998*

**ADVERTISING.** *See also* COMMERCIAL ART.
Nelson, Carol, 1953- Women's market handbook. Detroit : Gale Research, c1994.
*TC HF5415 .N3495 1994*

**ADVERTISING AND CHILDREN.**
Chandler, Tomasita M. Children and adolescents in the market place. Ann Arbor, Mich. : Pierian Press, 1999.
*TC HF5822 .C43 1999*

**ADVERTISING AND CHILDREN - CHINA.**
Feeding China's little emperors. Stanford, Calif. : Stanford University Press, 2000.
*TC TX361.C5 F44 2000*

**ADVERTISING AND CHILDREN - UNITED STATES.**
Advertising to children. Thousand Oaks, Calif. : Sage Publications, c1999.
*TC HQ784.T4 A29 1999*

**ADVERTISING ART.** *See* COMMERCIAL ART.

**ADVERTISING, ART IN.** *See* COMMERCIAL ART.

**ADVERTISING, OUTDOOR.** *See* POSTERS.

**ADVERTISING, PICTORIAL.** *See* COMMERCIAL ART; POSTERS.

**Advertising to children** : concepts and controversies / M. Carole Macklin, Les Carlson, editors. Thousand Oaks, Calif. : Sage Publications, c1999. xiv, 322 p. : ill. ; 24 cm. Includes bibliographical references and index. ISBN 0-7619-1284-3 (acid-free paper) ISBN 0-7619-1285-1 (acid-free paper) DDC 302.23/45/083
1. Television advertising and children - United States. 2. Advertising and children - United States. I. Macklin, M. Carole. II. Carlson, Les.
*TC HQ784.T4 A29 1999*

**Advice for new faculty members.**
Boice, Robert. Boston ; London : Allyn and Bacon, c2000.
*TC LB1778.2 .B63 2000*

**ADVISORS.** *See* CONSULTANTS.

**ADVISORS, FACULTY.** *See* FACULTY ADVISORS.

**ADVISORY TEACHERS.** *See* MASTER TEACHERS.

**A&E Home Video (Firm).**
The American Revolution. [videorecording]. New York, N.Y. : A&E Home Video, c1994.
*TC E208 .A447 1994*

The Irish in America [videorecording]. [New York, N.Y.] : A&E Home Video ; New York, N.Y. : Distributed by the New Video Group, 1997.
*TC E184.I6 I6 1997*

**AEA.**
American education annual. Detroit : Gale, c1999-
*TC LB1028.25.U6 A44*

**Aedo-Richmond, Ruth.**
Education as a humanitarian response. London ; Herndon, VA : Cassell ; [s.l.] : UNESCO International Bureau of Education, 1998.
*TC LC3719 .E37 1998*

**AEDS journal.** Washington, Association for Educational Data Systems. 19 v. ill. 23 cm. v. 1, no. 1- Sept. 1967- . Ceased publication with v. 20, no. 1 (fall 1986). Official publication of the Association for Educational Data Systems Vols. for summer 1986-fall 1986 issued by: International Association for Computing in Education. Continued by: Journal of research on computing in education ISSN: 0888-6504. ISSN 0001-1037
1. Computer-assisted instruction - Periodicals. 2. Information storage and retrieval systems - Education - Periodicals. I. Association for Educational Data Systems. II. International Association for Computing in Education. III. Title: Journal of research on computing in education

**AEROBIC EXERCISES.** *See* SWIMMING.

**AERONAUTICS.** *See* AIRPLANES; FLIGHT; INTERPLANETARY VOYAGES; UNIDENTIFIED FLYING OBJECTS.

**AERONAUTICS - FLIGHTS.** *See* TRANSATLANTIC FLIGHTS.

**AEROPLANES.** *See* AIRPLANES.

**AES, American economic security.**
American economic security. Washington, Chamber of Commerce of the United States of America.

**Aesthetic Artist Records.**
The cello [videorecording]. Van Nuys, CA : Backstage Pass Productions ; Canoga Park, Calif. : [Distributed by] MVP, c1995.
*TC MT305 .C4 1995*

The drums [videorecording]. Van Nuys, CA : Backstage Pass Productions ; Canoga Park, Calif. : [Distributed by] MVP Home Entertainment, c1998.
*TC MT662.3 .S6 1998*

The flute [videorecording]. Van Nuys, CA : Backstage Pass Productions ; Canoga Park, Calif. : [Distributed by] MVP, c1995.

*TC MT345 .F6 1995*

The trombone [videorecording]. Van Nuys, CA :
Backstage Pass Productions : Canoga Park, Calif. :
[Distributed by] MVP, c1998.
*TC MT465 .T7 1998*

The viola [videorecording]. Van Nuys, CA :
Backstage Pass Productions : Canoga Park, Calif. :
[Distributed by] MVP Home Entertainment, c1991.
*TC MT285 .V5 1991*

The viola [videorecording]. Van Nuys, CA :
Backstage Pass Productions : Canoga Park, Calif. :
[Distributed by] MVP Home Entertainment, c1995.
*TC MT285 .V5 1995*

The violin [videorecording]. Van Nuys, CA :
Backstage Pass Productions : Canoga Park, Calif. :
[Distributed by] MVP, c1998.
*TC MT265 .V5 1998*

**AESTHETIC MOVEMENT (BRITISH ART).** *See*
**MODERNISM (ART).**

**AESTHETIC OBJECT.** *See* **OBJECT
(AESTHETICS).**

**AESTHETIC SURGERY.** *See* **SURGERY,
PLASTIC.**

**The aesthetic understanding.**
Scruton, Roger. South Bend, Ind. : St. Augustine's
Press, 1998.
*TC BH39 .S38 1998*

**AESTHETICS.** *See also* **ART; ART AND
LITERATURE; CLASSICISM; CRITICISM;
EXPRESSIONISM (ART); FEMININE
BEAUTY (AESTHETICS); IMPRESSIONISM
(ART); JUDGMENT (AESTHETICS);
MODERNISM (AESTHETICS); OBJECT
(AESTHETICS); ROMANTICISM; VALUES.**
Barone, Tom. Aesthetics, politics, and educational
inquiry. New York : P. Lang, 2000.
*TC LB1028 .B345 2000*

Beauty matters. Bloomington : Indiana University
Press, c2000.
*TC HQ1219 .B348 2000*

Development and the arts. Hillsdale, N.J. : L. Erlbaum
Associates, 1994.
*TC N71 .D495 1994*

Greene, Maxine. Active learning and aesthetic
encounters. New York : NCREST, 1995.
*TC BH39 .G74 1995*

Housen, Abigail. The eye of the beholder. 1983.
*TC BH39 .H68 1983*

Kirwan, James, 1961- Beauty. Manchester :
Manchester University Press, 1999.
*TC BH39 .K57 1999*

Léger, Fernand, 1881-1955. [Fonctions de la peinture.
English] Functions of painting. New York, Viking
Press [1973]
*TC N70 .L45213 1973*

Olson, Ivan, 1931- The arts and critical thinking in
American education. Westport, Conn. : Bergin &
Garvey, 2000.
*TC BH39 .O45 2000*

Scruton, Roger. The aesthetic understanding. South
Bend, Ind. : St. Augustine's Press, 1998.
*TC BH39 .S38 1998*

**AESTHETICS, AMERICAN.**
Torres, Louis, 1938- What art is. Chicago, Ill. : Open
Court, c2000.
*TC PS3535.A547 Z9 2000*

**AESTHETICS, BRITISH - 19TH CENTURY.**
Flint, Kate. The Victorians and the visual imagination.
Cambridge, U.K. ; New York : Cambridge University
Press, 2000.
*TC N6767 .F58 2000*

**AESTHETICS - EARLY WORKS TO 1800.**
Diderot, Denis, 1713-1784. [Selections. English.
1995] Diderot on art. New Haven : Yale University
Press, 1995.
*TC N6846 .D4613 1995*

Hogarth, William, 1697-1764. The analysis of beauty.
New Haven, Conn. : Published for the Paul Mellon
Centre for British Art by Yale University Press, c1997.
*TC BH181 .H6 1997*

**AESTHETICS, ENGLISH.** *See* **AESTHETICS,
BRITISH.**

**AESTHETICS - HISTORY.**
Wood, Robert E., 1934- Placing aesthetics. Athens,
OH : Ohio University Press, c1999.

*TC BH81 .W66 1999*

**AESTHETICS, MODERN.**
Rampley, Matthew. Nietzsche, aesthetics, and
modernity. Cambridge, U.K. ; New York : Cambridge
University Press, 2000.
*TC B3318.A4 R36 2000*

Wyss, Beat, 1947- [Trauer der Vollendung. English]
Hegel's art history and the critique of modernity.
Cambridge, U.K. ; New York : Cambridge University
Press, c1999.
*TC BH151 .W9713 1999*

**AESTHETICS, MODERN - 20TH CENTURY.**
Hagberg, Garry, 1952- Art as language. Ithaca :
Cornell University Press, c1995.
*TC B3376.W564 H25 1995*

Uncontrollable beauty. New York : Allworth Press :
School of Visual Arts, c1998.
*TC BH201 .U53 1998*

Aesthetics, politics, and educational inquiry.
Barone, Tom. New York : P. Lang, 2000.
*TC LB1028 .B345 2000*

**AESTHETICS - PSYCHOLOGICAL ASPECTS.**
Gangi, Robyn Joseph. A longitudinal case study of the
musical/aesthetic experience of adolescent choral
musicians. 1998.
*TC 06 no. 10932*

**AESTHETICS - STUDY AND TEACHING
(MIDDLE SCHOOL).**
Hafeli, Mary Claire. Drawing and painting in the
middle school. 1999.
*TC 06 no. 11055*

**AESTHETICS - STUDY AND TEACHING -
UNITED STATES.**
Detels, Claire Janice, 1953- Soft boundaries.
Westport, Conn. : Bergin & Garvey, 1999.
*TC LB1591.5.U6 D48 1999*

**AFB Deaf-Blind Project. Video Development Staff.**
Hand in hand [videorecording]. New York, N.Y. :
AFB Press, c1995.
*TC HV1597.2 .H3 1995*

**AFB Press.**
Hand in hand [videorecording]. New York, N.Y. :
AFB Press, c1995.
*TC HV1597.2 .H3 1995*

Making the most of early communication
[videorecording]. New York, NY : Distributed by
AFB Press, c1997.
*TC HV1597.2 .M3 1997*

**AFDC PROGRAMS.** *See* **AID TO FAMILIES
WITH DEPENDENT CHILDREN
PROGRAMS.**

**AFFECT (PSYCHOLOGY).** *See also* **EMOTIONS.**
Ben-Ze'ev, Aharon. The subtlety of emotions.
Cambridge, Mass. ; London : MIT Press, c2000.
*TC BF531 .B43 2000*

Berkowitz, Leonard, 1926- Causes and consequences
of feelings. Cambridge, U.K. ; New York : Cambridge
University Press ; Paris : Editions de la Maison des
sciences de l'homme, 2000.
*TC BF531 .B45 2000*

Emotion and social judgments. 1st ed. Oxford ; New
York : Pergamon Press, 1991.
*TC BF531 .E4834 1991*

Feeling and thinking. Cambridge, U.K. ; New York :
Cambridge University Press ; Paris : Editions de la
Maison des Sciences de l'Homme, 2000.
*TC BF531 .F44 2000*

Janov, Arthur. The biology of love. Amherst, N.Y. :
Prometheus Books, 2000.
*TC BF720.E45 .J36 2000*

**AFFECT (PSYCHOLOGY) - ENCYCLOPEDIAS.**
Encyclopedia of human emotions. New York :
Macmillan Reference USA, c1999.
*TC BF531 .E55 1999*

**AFFECT (PSYCHOLOGY) - STUDY AND
TEACHING.**
Bocchino, Rob. Emotional literacy. Thousand Oaks,
Calif. : Sage Publications, c1999.
*TC BF576 .B63 1999*

**AFFECTION.** *See* **FRIENDSHIP; KINDNESS;
LOVE.**

**AFFECTIVE DISORDERS.** *See also* **DEPRESSION,
MENTAL; MANIA; MANIC-DEPRESSIVE
ILLNESS; SCHIZOAFFECTIVE DISORDERS.**
Ainsworth, Patricia, M.D. Understanding depression.
Jackson : University Press of Mississippi, c2000.

*TC RC537 .A39 2000*

Clark, David A., 1954- Scientific foundations of
cognitive theory and therapy of depression. New
York : John Wiley, c1999.
*TC RC537 .C53 1999*

**AFFECTIVE DISORDERS - CHEMOTHERAPY.**
Mood disorders. Basel ; New York : Karger, c1997.
*TC RC483 .M6 1997*

**AFFECTIVE DISORDERS - DIAGNOSIS.**
Mood disorders [videorecording]. Princeton, N.J. :
Films for the Humanities & Sciences, 1998.
*TC RC537 .M6 1998*

**AFFECTIVE DISORDERS IN CHILDREN.** *See*
**DEPRESSION IN CHILDREN.**

**AFFECTIVE DISORDERS - PATIENTS.**
Mood disorders [videorecording]. Princeton, N.J. :
Films for the Humanities & Sciences, 1998.
*TC RC537 .M6 1998*

**AFFECTIVE DISORDERS, PSYCHOTIC - DRUG
THERAPY.**
Mood disorders. Basel ; New York : Karger, c1997.
*TC RC483 .M6 1997*

**AFFECTIVE DOMAIN.** *See* **AFFECTIVE
EDUCATION.**

**AFFECTIVE EDUCATION.**
Affective education. London ; New York : Cassell,
1998.
*TC LB1072 .A38 1998*

Bocchino, Rob. Emotional literacy. Thousand Oaks,
Calif. : Sage Publications, c1999.
*TC BF576 .B63 1999*

Affective education : a comparative view / edited by
Peter Lang ; with Yaacov Katz and Isabel Menezes.
London ; New York : Cassell, 1998. xii, 260 p. ; 24 cm.
(Cassell studies in pastoral care and personal and social
education) Includes bibliographical references and index. ISBN
0-304-33988-1 (pbk) ISBN 0-304-33987-3
*1. Affective education. I. Lang, Peter, 1935- II. Katz, Yaacov
Julian. III. Menezes, Isabel.*
*TC LB1072 .A38 1998*

**AFFECTIVE EDUCATION - UNITED STATES.**
Eisler, Riane Tennenhaus. Tomorrow's children.
Boulder, Colo. ; Oxford : Westview Press, 2000.
*TC LC1023 .E57 2000*

Kessler, Rachael, 1946- The soul of education.
Alexandria, Va. : Association for Supervision and
Curriculum Development, c2000.
*TC LB1072 .K48 2000*

**AFFECTIVE LEARNING.** *See* **AFFECTIVE
EDUCATION.**

**AFFECTIVE TYPE SCHIZOPHRENIFORM
PSYCHOSIS.** *See* **SCHIZOAFFECTIVE
DISORDERS.**

**AFFERENT PATHWAYS.** *See also* **AUDITORY
PATHWAYS.**
Biomechanics and neural control of posture and
movement. New York : Springer, 2000.
*TC QP303 .B5684 2000*

**AFFILIATIONS BETWEEN HEALTH
FACILITIES.** *See* **HEALTH FACILITIES -
AFFILIATIONS.**

**Affirmative action.**
Eisaguirre, Lynne, 1951- Santa Barbara, Calif. :
ABC-CLIO, c1999.
*TC HF5549.5.A34 E39 1999*

**Affirmative action and the university.**
Rai, Kul B. Lincoln : University of Nebraska Press,
2000.
*TC LC212.42 .R35 2000*

Affirmative action / Bryan J. Grapes, book editor. San
Diego, Calif. : Greenhaven Press, 2000. 74 p. ; 23 cm.
(At issue) (An Opposing viewpoints series) Includes
bibliographical references and index. ISBN 0-7377-0290-7
(lib. bdg. : alk. paper) ISBN 0-7377-0289-3 (pbk. : alk. paper)
DDC 331.13/3/0973
*1. Civil rights - United States. 2. Affirmative action programs -
United States. 3. Discrimination - United States. 4. Reverse
discrimination - United States. 5. United States - Social policy.
I. Grapes, Bryan J. II. Title: Affirmative action : At issue (San Diego, Calif.) III.
Series: Opposing viewpoints series (Unnumbered)*
*TC JC599.U5 A34685 2000*

**AFFIRMATIVE ACTION PROGRAMS -
CALIFORNIA.**
Chávez, Lydia, 1951- The color bind. Berkeley :
University of California Press, c1998.

*TC HF5549.5.A34 C484 1998*

**AFFIRMATIVE ACTION PROGRAMS - LAW AND LEGISLATION - UNITED STATES.**
Ball, Howard. The Bakke case. Lawrence, Kan. : University Press of Kansas, 2000.
*TC KF228.B34 B35 2000*

Eisaguirre, Lynne, 1951- Affirmative action. Santa Barbara, Calif. : ABC-CLIO, c1999.
*TC HF5549.5.A34 E39 1999*

**AFFIRMATIVE ACTION PROGRAMS - UNITED STATES.**
Affirmative action. San Diego, Calif. : Greenhaven Press, 2000.
*TC JC599.U5 A34685 2000*

Rai, Kul B. Affirmative action and the university. Lincoln : University of Nebraska Press, 2000.
*TC LC212.42 .R35 2000*

**AFFIRMATIVE ACTION PROGRAMS - UNITED STATES - HISTORY.**
Eisaguirre, Lynne, 1951- Affirmative action. Santa Barbara, Calif. : ABC-CLIO, c1999.
*TC HF5549.5.A34 E39 1999*

**Afflerbach, Peter.**
Hoffman, James V. Balancing principles for teaching elementary reading. Mahwah, N.J. : L. Erlbaum Associates, c2000.
*TC LB1573 . H459 2000*

**AFFLICTION.** *See* SUFFERING.

**AFFLUENCE.** *See* WEALTH.

**AFFORDABLE HOUSING.** *See* HOUSING.

**Affordable housing and urban redevelopment in the United States** / edited by Willem van Vliet--. Thousand Oaks, Calif. : Sage Publications, c1997. xv, 288 p. : ill. ; 22 cm. (Urban affairs annual reviews, 0083-4688 ; 46) Includes bibliographical references and index. CONTENTS: [1] Changes and challenges in affordable housing and urban development / Mary K. Nenno -- From BURP to BHP to Demo Dispo: lessons from affordable multifamily housing rehabilitation initiatives in Boston / Rachel G. Bratt -- The provision of affordable housing in Cleveland: patterns of organizational and financial support / Norman Krumholz -- Twenty-five years of community building in the South Bronx: Phipps Houses in West Farms / Lynda Simmons -- The revitalization of CONTENTS: [2] Boston's commonwealth public housing development / Lawrence J. Vale -- Chicago's mixed income new communities strategy: the future face of public housing? / Michael H. Schill -- Return from abandonment: the Tenant Interim Lease Program and the development of low-income cooperatives in New York City's most neglected neighborhoods / Andrew White and Susan Saegert -- Sandtown-Winchester, Baltimore: housing as community development / Edward G. Goetz -- The California Mutual Housing Association: organizational innovation for resident-controlled affordable housing / Neal Richman and Allan David Heskin -- Housing trust funds: a new approach to funding affordable housing / Mary E. Brooks -- Learning from experience: the ingredients and transferability of success / W. van Vliet--. ISBN 0-8039-7050-1 (hardcover) ISBN 0-8039-7051-X (paperback)
*1. Housing - United States. 2. Housing policy - United States. 3. Urban renewal - United States. 4. Urban policy - United States. 5. Cities and towns - United States. I. Van Vliet--, Willem, 1952- II. Series: Urban affairs annual reviews ; v. 46.*
*TC HD7293 .A55 1997*

**Affron, Matthew, 1963-.**
Exiles + emigrés. Los Angeles, Calif. : Los Angeles County Museum of Art ; New York : H.N. Abrams, c1997.
*TC N6512 .E887 1997*

**Afraid to say no! [videorecording].**
Grounded for life [videorecording]. Charleston, WV : Cambridge Research Group, Ltd., 1988.
*TC HQ759.4 .G7 1988*

**AFRICA - BIBLIOGRAPHY - PERIODICALS.**
Books for Africa. London, International Committee on Christian Literature for Africa.

**AFRICA - CIVILIZATION.** *See* AFROCENTRISM; CIVILIZATION, WESTERN - AFRICAN INFLUENCES.

**AFRICA - CIVILIZATION - ENCYCLOPEDIAS.**
Microsoft encarta Africana [computer file]. Redmond, WA : Microsoft Corp., c1999. Computer data and programs.
*TC DT14 .M527 1999*

Microsoft encarta Africana [computer file]. Redmond, WA : Microsoft Corp., c1999. Computer data and programs.

*TC DT3 .M53 1999x*

**AFRICA - CIVILIZATION - WESTERN INFLUENCES.**
Bassey, Magnus O. Western education and political domination in Africa. Westport, CT : Bergin & Garvey, 1999.
*TC LC95.A2 B37 1999*

Dove, Nah. Afrikan mothers. Albany : State University of New York Press, c1998.
*TC HQ1593 .D68 1998*

**Africa currents.** [London, Africa Publications Trust]. no. 21 cm. no. 1-  spring 1975- . Microfilm. Ann Arbor, Mich., University Microfilms International.  reels. 35mm. Africa digest ISSN: 0001-9798. ISSN 0306-8412
*1. Africa - Periodicals. I. Africa Publications Trust. II. Title: Africa digest*

**Africa digest.**
Africa currents. [London, Africa Publications Trust].

**AFRICA - PERIODICALS.**
Africa currents. [London, Africa Publications Trust].

**AFRICA - POLITICS AND GOVERNMENT - TO 1945.**
Sivonen, Seppo. White-collar or hoe handle. Helsinki : Suomen Historiallinen Seura, [1995]
*TC LA1531 .S58 1995*

**Africa Publications Trust.**
Africa currents. [London, Africa Publications Trust].

**AFRICA - SOCIAL LIFE AND CUSTOMS - ENCYCLOPEDIAS.**
Werness, Hope B. The Continuum encyclopedia of native art. New York : Continuum, 2000.
*TC E98.A7 W49 2000*

**AFRICA, SOUTHERN - SOCIAL LIFE AND CUSTOMS.**
Kuper, Adam. Among the anthropologists. London ; New Brunswick, NJ : Athlone Press ; Somerset, N.J. : Distributed in the United States by Transaction Publishers, 1999.
*TC GN325 .K89 1999*

**AFRICA - STATISTICS - HISTORY.**
Mitchell, B. R. (Brian R.) International historical statistics, Africa, Asia & Oceania, 1750-1993. 3rd ed. London : Macmillan Reference ; New York : Ggrove's Dictionaries[division of Stockton Press], 1998.
*TC HA1107 .M54 1998*

**AFRICA - STUDY AND TEACHING - UNITED STATES.**
Great ideas for teaching about Africa. Boulder : Lynne Rienner, 1999.
*TC DT19.9.U5 G74 1999*

**AFRICA, WEST - ANTQUITIES.**
Museums & archaeology in West Africa. Washington : Smithsonian Institution Press ; Oxford : J. Currey, c1997.
*TC AM91.A358 M85 1997*

**AFRICAANDERS.** *See* AFRIKANERS.

**AFRICAN AMERICAN AGED - UNITED STATES.**
Grice, Marthe Jane. Attachment, race, and gender in late life. 1999.
*TC 085 G865*

**African American authors, 1745-1945 :** bio-bibliographical critical sourcebook / edited by Emmanuel S. Nelson. Westport, Conn. : Greenwood Press, 2000. xvi, 525 p. ; 24 cm. Includes bibliographical references (p. [513]-514) and index. ISBN 0-313-30910-8 (alk. paper) DDC 810.9/896073
*1. American literature - Afro-American authors - Bio-bibliography - Dictionaries. 2. American literature - Afro-American authors - Dictionaries. 3. Afro-American authors - Biography - Dictionaries. 4. Afro-Americans in literature - Dictionaries. I. Nelson, Emmanuel S. (Emmanuel Sampath), 1954-*
*TC PS153.N5 A32 2000*

**African American children.**
Hill, Shirley A. (Shirley Ann), 1947- Thousand Oaks, Calif. : Sage Publications, c1999.
*TC E185.86 .H665 1999*

**AFRICAN AMERICAN COLLEGE PRESIDENTS - UNITED STATES.**
Tobe, Dorothy Echols. The development of cognitive leadership frames among African American female college presidents. 1999.
*TC 06 no. 11187*

**AFRICAN AMERICAN IMMERSION SCHOOLS EVALUATION PROJECT.**

African-centered schooling in theory and practice. Westport, Conn. ; London : Bergin & Garvey, 2000.
*TC LC2731 .A35 2000*

**The African-American male perspective of barriers to success** / edited by Whitney G. Harris and Gwendolyn M. Duhon. Lewiston, N.Y. : Edwin Mellen Press, c1999. 174 p. ; 25 cm. (Black studies ; v. 7) Includes bibliographical references and index. ISBN 0-7734-7884-1 (hc.) DDC 305.38/896073
*1. Afro-American men - Education. 2. Afro-American men - Education (Higher) 3. Afro-American men - Social conditions. I. Harris, Whitney G. II. Duhon, Gwendolyn M. III. Series.*
*TC LC2731 .A32 1999*

**African American quotations** / [compiled by] Richard Newman ; with a foreword by Julian Bond. Phoenix, Ariz. : Oryx Press, c1998. xvi, 504 p. ; 24 cm. Includes indexes. ISBN 1-57356-118-5 (alk. paper) DDC 081/.089/ 96073
*1. Afro-Americans - Quotations. I. Newman, Richard, 1930-*
*TC PN6081.3 .A36 1998*

**AFRICAN AMERICAN STUDENTS - EDUCATION (SECONDARY) - NEW YORK (STATE) - NEW YORK.**
Smith, Hawthorne Emery. Psychological detachment from school. 1999.
*TC 085 Sm586*

**AFRICAN AMERICAN STUDENTS - RACIAL IDENTITY.**
Smith, Hawthorne Emery. Psychological detachment from school. 1999.
*TC 085 Sm586*

**AFRICAN AMERICANS.** *See* AFRO-AMERICANS.

**AFRICAN AMERICANS - EDUCATION (HIGHER) - UNITED STATES.**
Capeheart-Meningall, Jennifer. Quality of students of color efort on a predominantly white college and the internal environmental elements that influence involvement. 1998.
*TC 06 no. 10874*

**AFRICAN AMERICANS - HEALTH AND HYGIENE - NEW YORK (STATE) - NEW YORK.**
Mendoza, Maria Adalia. A study to compare inner city Black men and women completers and non-attenders of diabetes self-care classes. 1999.
*TC 06 no. 11206*

**AFRICAN ART.** *See also* ART, AFRICAN.
World Bank. Washington, D.C. : World Bank, c1998.
*TC N7391.65 .W67 1998*

**African art in the cycle of life.**
Sieber, Roy, 1923- Washington, D.C. : Published for the National Museum of African Art by the Smithsonian Press, c1987.
*TC NB1091.65 .S54 1987*

**African-centered schooling in theory and practice** / edited by Diane S. Pollard, Cheryl S. Ajirotutu ; foreword by Edgar G. Epps. Westport, Conn. ; London : Bergin & Garvey, 2000. xii, 223 p. ; 25 cm. Includes bibliographical references and index. ISBN 0-89789-728-5 (alk. paper) DDC 371.829/96/073
*1. African American Immersion Schools Evaluation Project. 2. Afro-Americans - Education - Evaluation - Longitudinal studies. 3. Public schools - Wisconsin - Milwaukee - Longitudinal studies. 4. Afrocentrism - United States - Longitudinal studies. I. Pollard, Diane. II. Ajirotutu, Cheryl.*
*TC LC2731 .A35 2000*

**African democratization and military coups.**
Onwumechili, Chuka. Westport, Conn. : Praeger, 1998.
*TC JQ1873.5.C58 O58 1998*

**AFRICAN FOLK POETRY.** *See* FOLK POETRY, AFRICAN.

**African nomadic architecture.**
Prussin, Labelle. Washington : Smithsonian Institution Press : National Museum of African Art, c1995.
*TC NA7461.A1 P78 1995*

**AFRICAN POETRY.** *See* FOLK POETRY, AFRICAN.

**AFRICAN SCULPTURE.** *See* SCULPTURE, AFRICAN.

**African women.**
Coquery-Vidrovitch, Catherine. [Africaines. English] Boulder, Colo. : WestviewPress, 1997.
*TC HQ1787 .C6613 1997*

**AFRICANDERS.** *See* AFRIKANERS.

**AFRICANERS.** *See* **AFRIKANERS.**

**Africans in America** [videorecording] : America's journey through slavery / senior producer, Susan Bellows ; project director, Llewellyn Smith ; writer, Steve Fayer ; [a production of WGBH Boston]. [Boston, Mass.] : WGBH Educational Foundation ; South Burlington, VT : WGBH Boston Video [distributor], c1998. 4 videocassettes (ca 360 min.) : sd., col. with b&w sequences ; 1/2 in. VHS. Catalogued from credits, cassette label and container. Closed-captioned for the hearing impaired. Narrator, Angela Bassett. Music score, Bernice Johnson Reagon. Directors and producers vary for each part. Originally broadcast on PBS October 19-22, 1998. Teacher's guide for the series available at: www.pbs.org For general audiences. SUMMARY: Considers the contradictions that lay at the heart of the founding of the American nation. The infant democracy pronounced all men to be created equal while enslaving one race to benefit another. Portrays the struggles of the African people in America, from their arrival in the 1600s to the last days before the Civil War. Containers have dates at head of title for each part: 1450-1750, 1750-1805, 1791-1831, and 1831-1865, respectively. CONTENTS: [Part I]. The Terrible transformation (ca. 90 min.) -- [Part II]. Revolution (ca. 90 min.) -- [Part III]. Brotherly love (ca. 90 min.) -- [Part IV.] Judgment day (ca. 90 min.) ISBN 1-57807-144-5 (tape 1) ISBN 1-57807-146-1 (tape 2) ISBN 1-57807-145-3 (tape 3) ISBN 1-57807-147-x (tape 4) ISBN 1-57807-143-7 (set)
*1. Slavery - United States - History. 2. Afro-Americans - History. 3. Slavery - Economic aspects - United States - History. 4. Slavery - Virginia - History. 5. Slavery - Economic aspects - Virginia - History. 6. Slavery - Justification. 7. United States - History - Colonial period. ca. 1600-1775) 8. Virginia - History - Colonial period. ca. 1600-1775. 9. Historical television programs. 10. Documentary television programs. 11. Video recordings for the hearing impaired. I. Bellows, Susan. II. Smith, Llewellyn. III. Fayer, Steve, 1935- IV. Bassett, Angela. V. WGBH (Television station : Boston, Mass.) VI. WGBH Educational Foundation. VII. WGBH Video (Firm) VIII. Title: Terrible transformation [videorecording] IX. Title: Revolution [videorecording] X. Title: Brotherly love [videorecording] XI. Title: Judgment day [videorecording] XII. Title: America's journey through slavery [videorecording]*
*TC E441 .A47 1998*

**AFRICANS - UNITED STATES.** *See* **AFRO-AMERICANS.**

**AFRIKAANDERS.** *See* **AFRIKANERS.**

**AFRIKAANERS.** *See* **AFRIKANERS.**

**AFRIKAANS-SPEAKING SOUTH AFRICANS.** *See* **AFRIKANERS.**

**Afrikan mothers.**
Dove, Nah. Albany : State University of New York Press, c1998.
*TC HQ1593 .D68 1998*

**AFRIKANDERS.** *See* **AFRIKANERS.**

**AFRIKANERS - EDUCATION - HISTORY - 19TH CENTURY.**
Cross, Michael. Imagery of identity in South African education, 1880-1990. Durham, N.C. : Carolina Academic Press, c1999.
*TC LA1539 .C76 1999*

**AFRIKANERS - EDUCATION - HISTORY - 20TH CENTURY.**
Cross, Michael. Imagery of identity in South African education, 1880-1990. Durham, N.C. : Carolina Academic Press, c1999.
*TC LA1539 .C76 1999*

**AFRIKANERS - ETHNIC IDENTITY - HISTORY - 19TH CENTURY.**
Cross, Michael. Imagery of identity in South African education, 1880-1990. Durham, N.C. : Carolina Academic Press, c1999.
*TC LA1539 .C76 1999*

**AFRIKANERS - ETHNIC IDENTITY - HISTORY - 20TH CENTURY.**
Cross, Michael. Imagery of identity in South African education, 1880-1990. Durham, N.C. : Carolina Academic Press, c1999.
*TC LA1539 .C76 1999*

**AFRO-AMEICAN ARTISTS AS TEACHERS.**
Jenoure, Terry. Navigators. Albany, NY : State University of New York Press, c2000.
*TC NX396.5 .J45 2000*

**AFRO-AMERICAN ABOLITIONISTS - BIOGRAPHY - HISTORY AND CRITICISM.**
Approaches to teaching Narrative of the life of Frederick Douglass. New York : Modern Language Association of America, 1999.
*TC E449.D75 A66 1999*

**AFRO-AMERICAN ART - POLITICAL ASPECTS.**
Hooks, Bell. Art on my mind. New York : New Press : Distributed by W.W. Norton, c1995.
*TC N6537.H585 A2 1995*

**AFRO-AMERICAN ARTISTS - BIOGRAPHY.**
Marks, Carole. The power of pride. 1st ed. New York : Crown Publishers, c1999.
*TC E185.6 .M35 1999*

**AFRO-AMERICAN ARTISTS - INTERVIEWS.**
Jenoure, Terry. Navigators. Albany, NY : State University of New York Press, c2000.
*TC NX396.5 .J45 2000*

**AFRO-AMERICAN ARTS.**
Jenoure, Terry. Navigators. Albany, NY : State University of New York Press, c2000.
*TC NX396.5 .J45 2000*

**AFRO-AMERICAN ARTS - HISTORY - 20TH CENTURY - SOURCES.**
Marks, Carole. The power of pride. 1st ed. New York : Crown Publishers, c1999.
*TC E185.6 .M35 1999*

**AFRO-AMERICAN ARTS - NEW YORK STATE - NEW YORK.**
Huggins, Nathan Irvin, 1927- Harlem renaissance. London ; New York : Oxford University Press, 1973, c1971.
*TC NX511.N5 H89 1973*

**AFRO-AMERICAN ARTS - NEW YORK (STATE) - NEW YORK - HISTORY.**
Harlem on my mind : cultural capital of Black America, 1900-1968. New York : New Press : Distributed by W.W. Norton & Co., c1995.
*TC F128.68.H3 S3 1995*

**AFRO-AMERICAN AUTHORS.** *See* **AMERICAN LITERATURE - AFRO-AMERICAN AUTHORS.**

**AFRO-AMERICAN AUTHORS - BIOGRAPHY.**
Kerlin, Robert Thomas, 1866-1950. Negro poets and their poems. 3d ed., rev. and enl. Washington, D. C. : Associated Publishers, c1935.
*TC PS591.N4 K4 1935*

Marks, Carole. The power of pride. 1st ed. New York : Crown Publishers, c1999.
*TC E185.6 .M35 1999*

**AFRO-AMERICAN AUTHORS - BIOGRAPHY - DICTIONARIES.**
African American authors, 1745-1945. Westport, Conn. : Greenwood Press, 2000.
*TC PS153.N5 A32 2000*

**AFRO-AMERICAN BOYS - EDUCATION - SOCIAL ASPECTS.**
Ferguson, Ann Arnett, 1940- Bad boys. Ann Arbor : University of Michigan Press, c2000.
*TC LC2771 .F47 2000*

**AFRO-AMERICAN BOYS - PSYCHOLOGY.**
Canada, Geoffrey. Reaching up for manhood. Boston : Beacon Press, c1998.
*TC HQ775 .C35 1998*

**AFRO-AMERICAN BOYS - SOCIAL CONDITIONS.**
Canada, Geoffrey. Reaching up for manhood. Boston : Beacon Press, c1998.
*TC HQ775 .C35 1998*

**AFRO-AMERICAN CHILDREN.** *See also* **AFRO-AMERICAN BOYS.**
Hill, Shirley A. (Shirley Ann), 1947- African American children. Thousand Oaks, Calif. : Sage Publications, c1999.
*TC E185.86 .H665 1999*

**AFRO-AMERICAN CHILDREN - ATTITUDES.**
Wright, Marguerite A. I'm chocolate, you're vanilla. 1st paperback ed. San Francisco : Jossey-Bass, 2000.
*TC BF723.R3 W75 2000*

**AFRO-AMERICAN CHILDREN - EDUCATION.**
Manning, M. Lee. Multicultural education of children and adolescents. 3rd ed. Boston : Allyn and Bacon, c2000.
*TC LC1099.3 .M36 2000*

**AFRO-AMERICAN CHILDREN - EDUCATION - ALABAMA.**
Morris, Vivian Gunn, 1941- Creating caring and nurturing educational environments for African American children. Westport, Conn. ; London : Bergin & Garvey, 2000.
*TC LC2802.A2 M67 2000*

**AFRO-AMERICAN CHILDREN - EDUCATION - MASSACHUSETTS - BOSTON - HISTORY - 19TH CENTURY.**
Paul, Susan, fl. 1837. Memoir of James Jackson, the attentive and obedient scholar, who died in Boston, October 31, 1833, aged six years and eleven months. Cambridge, MA : Harvard University Press, 2000.
*TC F73.9.N4 P38 2000*

**AFRO-AMERICAN CHILDREN - ETHNIC IDENTITY.**
Wright, Marguerite A. I'm chocolate, you're vanilla. 1st paperback ed. San Francisco : Jossey-Bass, 2000.
*TC BF723.R3 W75 2000*

**AFRO-AMERICAN CHILDREN - LANGUAGE.** *See* **BLACK ENGLISH.**

**AFRO-AMERICAN CHILDREN - MASSACHUSETTS - BOSTON - BIOGRAPHY.**
Paul, Susan, fl. 1837. Memoir of James Jackson, the attentive and obedient scholar, who died in Boston, October 31, 1833, aged six years and eleven months. Cambridge, MA : Harvard University Press, 2000.
*TC F73.9.N4 P38 2000*

**AFRO-AMERICAN CHILDREN - MASSACHUSETTS - BOSTON - SOCIAL CONDITIONS - 19TH CENTURY.**
Paul, Susan, fl. 1837. Memoir of James Jackson, the attentive and obedient scholar, who died in Boston, October 31, 1833, aged six years and eleven months. Cambridge, MA : Harvard University Press, 2000.
*TC F73.9.N4 P38 2000*

**AFRO-AMERICAN CHILDREN - PSYCHOLOGY.**
Wright, Marguerite A. I'm chocolate, you're vanilla. 1st paperback ed. San Francisco : Jossey-Bass, 2000.
*TC BF723.R3 W75 2000*

**AFRO-AMERICAN CHILDREN - SOCIAL CONDITIONS.**
Edmund W. Gordon. Stamford, Conn. : Jai Press, c2000.
*TC HM1033 .E35 2000*

**AFRO-AMERICAN CHURCHES - SOUTHERN STATES - HISTORY - 19TH CENTURY.**
Cornelius, Janet Duitsman. Slave missions and the Black church in the antebellum South. Columbia : University of South Carolina Press, c1999.
*TC E449 .C82 1999*

**AFRO-AMERICAN COLLEGE ADMINISTRATORS.**
Grass roots and glass ceilings. Albany : State University of New York Press, c1999.
*TC LC212.42 .G73 1999*

**AFRO-AMERICAN COLLEGE GRADUATES.**
Dixon, Jerome C. A qualitative study of perceptions of external factors that influence the persistence of Black males at a predominantly white four-year state college. 1999.
*TC 06 no. 11050*

Gregory, Sheila T. Black women in the academy. Rev. and updated ed. Lanham, Md. : University Press of America, 1999.
*TC LC2781 .G74 1999*

**AFRO-AMERICAN COLLEGE STUDENTS.**
Gregory, Sheila T. Black women in the academy. Rev. and updated ed. Lanham, Md. : University Press of America, 1999.
*TC LC2781 .G74 1999*

**AFRO-AMERICAN COLLEGE STUDENTS - ATTITUDES.**
Dixon, Jerome C. A qualitative study of perceptions of external factors that influence the persistence of Black males at a predominantly white four-year state college. 1999.
*TC 06 no. 11050*

**AFRO-AMERICAN COLLEGE STUDENTS - BIOGRAPHY.**
Suskind, Ron. A hope in the unseen. 1st ed. New York : Broadway Books, c1998.
*TC LC2803.W3 S87 1998*

**AFRO-AMERICAN COLLEGE STUDENTS - FELLOWSHIPS.** *See* **AFRO-AMERICAN COLLEGE STUDENTS - SCHOLARSHIPS, FELLOWSHIPS, ETC.**

**AFRO-AMERICAN COLLEGE STUDENTS - SCHOLARSHIPS, FELLOWSHIPS, ETC. - UNITED STATES - DIRECTORIES.**
Financial aid for African Americans. El Dorado Hills, Calif. : Reference Service Press, c1997-
*TC LB2338 .F5643*

**AFRO-AMERICAN COLLEGE TEACHERS.** *See* **AFRO-AMERICAN WOMEN COLLEGE TEACHERS.**

**AFRO-AMERICAN COLLEGE TEACHERS - CASE STUDIES.**
Succeeding in an academic career. Westport, Conn. : Greenwood Press, 2000.
*TC LB2331.72 .S83 2000*

**AFRO-AMERICAN COLLEGE TEACHERS - SELECTION AND APPOINTMENT.**
Turner, Caroline Sotello Viernes. Faculty of color in academe. Boston : Allyn and Bacon, c2000.
*TC LB2332.72 .T87 2000*

**AFRO-AMERICAN COLLEGES.** *See* **AFRO-AMERICAN UNIVERSITIES AND COLLEGES.**

**AFRO-AMERICAN COMPOSERS - BIO-BIBLIOGRAPHY - DICTIONARIES.**
International dictionary of black composers. Chicago ; London : Fitzroy Dearborn, c1999.
*TC ML105 .I5 1999*

**AFRO-AMERICAN DIALECT.** *See* **BLACK ENGLISH.**

**AFRO-AMERICAN EDUCATION.** *See* **AFRO-AMERICANS - EDUCATION.**

**AFRO-AMERICAN EDUCATORS - BIOGRAPHY.**
Bethune, Mary McLeod, 1875-1955. [Selections. 1999] Mary McLeod Bethune. Bloomington : Indiana University Press, c1999.
*TC E185.97.B34 A25 1999*

**AFRO-AMERICAN ENGLISH.** *See* **BLACK ENGLISH.**

**AFRO-AMERICAN FAMILIES.**
Hill, Shirley A. (Shirley Ann), 1947- African American children. Thousand Oaks, Calif. : Sage Publications, c1999.
*TC E185.86 .H665 1999*

**AFRO-AMERICAN FAMILIES - HISTORY.**
Landry, Bart. Black working wives. Berkeley : University of California Press, c2000.
*TC HQ536 .L335 2000*

**AFRO-AMERICAN INTELLECTUALS.** *See* **AFRO-AMERICANS - INTELLECTUAL LIFE.**

**AFRO-AMERICAN INTELLECTUALS - BIOGRAPHY.**
Marks, Carole. The power of pride. 1st ed. New York : Crown Publishers, c1999.
*TC E185.6 .M35 1999*

**AFRO-AMERICAN LEADERSHIP.**
Gordon, Jacob U. Black leadership for social change. Westport, Conn. : Greenwood Press, 2000.
*TC E185.615 .G666 2000*

**AFRO-AMERICAN LITERATURE (ENGLISH).** *See* **AMERICAN LITERATURE - AFRO-AMERICAN AUTHORS.**

**AFRO-AMERICAN MEN - EDUCATION.**
The African-American male perspective of barriers to success. Lewiston, N.Y. : Edwin Mellen Press, c1999.
*TC LC2731 .A32 1999*

**AFRO-AMERICAN MEN - EDUCATION (HIGHER).**
The African-American male perspective of barriers to success. Lewiston, N.Y. : Edwin Mellen Press, c1999.
*TC LC2731 .A32 1999*

**AFRO-AMERICAN MEN - EDUCATION (HIGHER) - ECONOMIC ASPECTS.**
Dixon, Jerome C. A qualitative study of perceptions of external factors that influence the persistence of Black males at a predominantly white four-year state college. 1999.
*TC 06 no. 11050*

**AFRO-AMERICAN MEN - SOCIAL CONDITIONS.**
The African-American male perspective of barriers to success. Lewiston, N.Y. : Edwin Mellen Press, c1999.
*TC LC2731 .A32 1999*

**AFRO-AMERICAN MILITARY PERSONNEL.** *See* **AFRO-AMERICAN SOLDIERS.**

**AFRO-AMERICAN MUSIC.** *See* **AFRO-AMERICANS - MUSIC.**

**AFRO-AMERICAN PAINTERS - NEW YORK (STATE) - NEW YORK.**
Edward Clark. Belleville Lake, Mich. : Belleville Lake Press, c1997.

*TC ND237.C524 E393 1997*

**AFRO-AMERICAN PARENTS.** *See* **AFRO-AMERICAN SINGLE MOTHERS.**

**AFRO-AMERICAN POLITICAL ACTIVISTS - BIOGRAPHY.**
Connerly, Ward, 1939- Creating equal. San Francisco : Encounter Books, 2000.
*TC E185.97 .C74 2000*

**AFRO-AMERICAN PRESBYTERIANS - GEORGIA - DECATUR - BIOGRAPHY.**
Stroupe, Nibs. While we run this race. Maryknoll, N.Y. : Orbis Books, c1995.
*TC BX8949.D43 S77 1995*

**AFRO-AMERICAN SCHOLARSHIPS.** *See* **AFRO-AMERICANS - SCHOLARSHIPS, FELLOWSHIPS, ETC.**

**AFRO-AMERICAN SINGLE MOTHERS - INDIANA - INDIANAPOLIS - INTERVIEWS.**
Rosier, Katherine Brown. Mothering inner-city children. New Brunswick, NJ : Rutgers University Press, 2000.
*TC HV1447.I53 R67 2000*

**AFRO-AMERICAN SINGLE MOTHERS - SERVICES FOR.**
Lacy, Gary L. Head start social services. New York : Garland Pub., 1999.
*TC HV699 .L33 1999*

**AFRO-AMERICAN SLAVERY.** *See* **SLAVERY - UNITED STATES.**

**AFRO-AMERICAN SLAVES.** *See* **SLAVES - UNITED STATES.**

**AFRO-AMERICAN SOLDIERS - HISTORY - 18TH CENTURY.**
Cox, Clinton. Come all you brave soldiers. 1st ed. New York : Scholastic Press, 1999.
*TC E269.N3 C69 1999*

**AFRO-AMERICAN SOLDIERS - HISTORY - 18TH CENTURY - JUVENILE LITERATURE.**
Cox, Clinton. Come all you brave soldiers. 1st ed. New York : Scholastic Press, 1999.
*TC E269.N3 C69 1999*

**AFRO-AMERICAN SONGS.** *See* **AFRO-AMERICANS - MUSIC.**

**AFRO-AMERICAN STUDENTS.** *See also* **AFRO-AMERICAN COLLEGE STUDENTS.**
Latimer, Leah Y. Higher ground. New York : Avon Books, c1999.
*TC LC2781 .L27 1999*

**AFRO-AMERICAN STUDENTS - EDUCATION.**
Martin, Danny Bernard. Mathematics success and failure among African-American youth. Mahwah, N.J. : Lawrence Erlbaum, 2000.
*TC QA13 .M145 2000*

**AFRO-AMERICAN STUDIES.** *See* **AFRO-AMERICANS - STUDY AND TEACHING.**

**AFRO-AMERICAN TEACHERS.** *See* **AFRO-AMERICAN COLLEGE TEACHERS; AFRO-AMERICAN WOMEN TEACHERS.**

**AFRO-AMERICAN TEENAGE BOYS - EDUCATION - WASHINGTON (D.C.).**
Suskind, Ron. A hope in the unseen. 1st ed. New York : Broadway Books, c1998.
*TC LC2803.W3 S87 1998*

**AFRO-AMERICAN TEENAGE GIRLS - MASSACHUSETTS - SALEM - DIARIES - JUVENILE LITERATURE.**
Forten, Charlotte L. A free Black girl before the Civil War. Mankato, Minn. : Blue Earth Books, c2000.
*TC F74.S1 F67 2000*

**AFRO-AMERICAN TEENAGE GIRLS - SEXUAL BEHAVIOR.**
Richardson, Bonnie. Factors influencing the sexual and contraceptive behavior of sexually abused adolescents of color. 1999.
*TC 06 no. 11167*

**AFRO-AMERICAN TEENAGERS.** *See* **AFRO-AMERICAN TEENAGE GIRLS.**

**AFRO-AMERICAN UNIVERSITIES AND COLLEGES - SOCIOLOGICAL ASPECTS.**
Bracey, Earnest N. Prophetic insight. Lanham : University Press of America, c1999.
*TC LC2781 .B73 1999*

**AFRO-AMERICAN UNIVERSITY STUDENTS.** *See* **AFRO-AMERICAN COLLEGE STUDENTS.**

**AFRO-AMERICAN WOMEN COLLEGE TEACHERS.**
Gregory, Sheila T. Black women in the academy. Rev. and updated ed. Lanham, Md. : University Press of America, 1999.
*TC LC2781 .G74 1999*

**AFRO-AMERICAN WOMEN COLLEGE TEACHERS - UNITED STATES.**
Robbins, Carol Braswell. An examination of critical feminist pedagogy in practice. 1999.
*TC 06 no. 11067*

**AFRO-AMERICAN WOMEN - COUNSELING OF.**
Pack-Brown, Sherlon P. Images of me. Boston : Allyn and Bacon, c1998.
*TC HV1445 .P33 1998*

**AFRO-AMERICAN WOMEN - EDUCATION - FLORIDA - HISTORY - 20TH CENTURY - SOURCES.**
Bethune, Mary McLeod, 1875-1955. [Selections. 1999] Mary McLeod Bethune. Bloomington : Indiana University Press, c1999.
*TC E185.97.B34 A25 1999*

**AFRO-AMERICAN WOMEN - EDUCATION (HIGHER).**
Gregory, Sheila T. Black women in the academy. Rev. and updated ed. Lanham, Md. : University Press of America, 1999.
*TC LC2781 .G74 1999*

**AFRO-AMERICAN WOMEN EDUCATORS - BIOGRAPHY.**
Bethune, Mary McLeod, 1875-1955. [Selections. 1999] Mary McLeod Bethune. Bloomington : Indiana University Press, c1999.
*TC E185.97.B34 A25 1999*

**AFRO-AMERICAN WOMEN - EMPLOYMENT - HISTORY.**
Landry, Bart. Black working wives. Berkeley : University of California Press, c2000.
*TC HQ536 .L335 2000*

**AFRO-AMERICAN WOMEN - ETHNIC IDENTITY.**
Witt, Doris. Black hunger. New York : Oxford University Press, 1999.
*TC E185.86 .W58 1999*

**AFRO-AMERICAN WOMEN - RACE IDENTITY.**
Witt, Doris. Black hunger. New York : Oxford University Press, 1999.
*TC E185.86 .W58 1999*

**AFRO-AMERICAN WOMEN - SOCIAL CONDITIONS.**
Witt, Doris. Black hunger. New York : Oxford University Press, 1999.
*TC E185.86 .W58 1999*

**AFRO-AMERICAN WOMEN SOCIAL REFORMERS - BIOGRAPHY.**
Edelman, Marian Wright. Lanterns. Boston : Beacon Press, c1999.
*TC E185.97.E33 A3 1999*

**AFRO-AMERICAN WOMEN - SOUTH CAROLINA - ORANGEBURG - SOCIAL CONDITIONS.**
Mack, Kibibi Voloria C. Parlor ladies and ebony drudges. 1st ed. Knoxville : University of Tennessee Press, c1999.
*TC F279.O6 M33 1999*

**AFRO-AMERICAN WOMEN TEACHERS - NORTH CAROLINA - BIOGRAPHY.**
Wadelington, Charles Weldon. Charlotte Hawkins Brown & Palmer Memorial Institute. Chapel Hill ; London : University of North Carolina Press, c1999.
*TC LA2317.B598 W33 1999*

**AFRO-AMERICAN YOUNG MEN - EDUCATION - SOCIAL ASPECTS.**
Black sons to mothers. New York : Canterbury [England] : P. Lang, c2000.
*TC LC2731 .B53 2000*

**AFRO-AMERICAN YOUNG MEN - FAMILY RELATIONSHIPS.**
Black sons to mothers. New York ; Canterbury [England] : P. Lang, c2000.
*TC LC2731 .B53 2000*

**AFRO-AMERICAN YOUTH - BIOGRAPHY.**
Souls looking back. New York : Routledge, 1999.
*TC E185.625 .S675 1999*

**AFRO-AMERICAN YOUTH - RACE IDENTITY - CASE STUDIES.**
Souls looking back. New York : Routledge, 1999.

*TC E185.625 .S675 1999*

**AFRO-AMERICAN YOUTH - SOCIAL
CONDITIONS - CASE STUDIES.**
Souls looking back. New York : Routledge, 1999.
*TC E185.625 .S675 1999*

**AFRO-AMERICANS.**
Hooks, Bell. Yearning. Boston, MA : South End
Press, c1990.
*TC E185.86 .H742 1990*

**AFRO-AMERICANS - ALABAMA -
BIRMINGHAM - HISTORY.**
Feldman, Lynne B. A sense of place. Tuscaloosa,
Ala. ; London : University of Alabama Press, c1999.
*TC F334.B69 N437 1999*

**AFRO-AMERICANS - BIOGRAPHY.**
Forten, Charlotte L. A free Black girl before the Civil
War. Mankato, Minn. : Blue Earth Books, c2000.
*TC F74.S1 F67 2000*

Haskins, James, 1941- Bayard Rustin. 1st ed. New
York : Hyperion Books for Children, c1997.
*TC E185.97.R93 H37 1997*

**AFRO-AMERICANS - CHILDREN. *See* AFRO-
AMERICAN CHILDREN.**

**AFRO-AMERICANS - CIVIL RIGHTS.** *See also*
**CIVIL RIGHTS WORKERS - UNITED
STATES.**
Haskins, James, 1941- Bayard Rustin. 1st ed. New
York : Hyperion Books for Children, c1997.
*TC E185.97.R93 H37 1997*

**AFRO-AMERICANS - CIVIL RIGHTS -
ARKANSAS.**
Counts, I. Wilmer (Ira Wilmer), 1931- A life is more
than a moment. Bloomington, IN : Indiana University
Press, c1999.
*TC LC214.23.L56 C68 1999*

**AFRO-AMERICANS - CIVIL RIGHTS -
HISTORY.**
Howard, John R., 1933- The shifting wind. Albany :
State University of New York Press, c1999.
*TC KF4757 .H69 1999*

Klinkner, Philip A. The unsteady march. Chicago :
University of Chicago Press, c1999.
*TC E185 .K55 1999*

**AFRO-AMERICANS - CIVIL RIGHTS -
HISTORY - 19TH CENTURY.**
Lorini, Alessandra, 1949- Rituals of race.
Charlottesville : University Press of Virginia, 1999.
*TC E185.61 .L675 1999*

**AFRO-AMERICANS - CIVIL RIGHTS -
HISTORY - 20TH CENTURY.**
Cochran, David Carroll. The color of freedom.
Albany : State University of New York Press, c1999.
*TC E185.615 .C634 1999*

Lorini, Alessandra, 1949- Rituals of race.
Charlottesville : University Press of Virginia, 1999.
*TC E185.61 .L675 1999*

Without justice for all. Boulder, Colo. : Westview
Press, 1999.
*TC E185.615 .W57 1999*

**AFRO-AMERICANS - CIVIL RIGHTS -
HISTORY - 20TH CENTURY - SOURCES.**
Bethune, Mary McLeod, 1875-1955. [Selections.
1999] Mary McLeod Bethune. Bloomington : Indiana
University Press, c1999.
*TC E185.97.B34 A25 1999*

**AFRO-AMERICANS - CIVIL RIGHTS -
JUVENILE LITERATURE.**
Haskins, James, 1941- Bayard Rustin. 1st ed. New
York : Hyperion Books for Children, c1997.
*TC E185.97.R93 H37 1997*

**AFRO-AMERICANS - CIVIL RIGHTS -
MARYLAND - HISTORY - 19TH CENTURY.**
Fuke, Richard Paul, 1940- Imperfect equality. New
York : Fordham University Press, 1999.
*TC E185.93.M2 F85 1999*

**AFRO-AMERICANS - CIVIL RIGHTS -
MARYLAND - PRINCE GEORGE'S
COUNTY - HISTORY - 20TH CENTURY.**
Kohn, Howard. We had a dream. New York :
Simon & Schuster, 1998.
*TC F187.P9 K64 1998*

**AFRO-AMERICANS - CIVIL RIGHTS - TEXAS -
HOUSTON - HISTORY.**
Kellar, William Henry, 1952- Make haste slowly. 1st
ed. College Station : Texas A&M University Press,
c1999.

*TC LC214.23.H68 K45 1999*

**AFRO-AMERICANS - ECONOMIC CONDITIONS.**
Andrews, Marcellus, 1956- The political economy of
hope and fear. New York : New York University
Press, c1999.
*TC E185.8 .A77 1999*

Job creation. Washington, DC : Joint Center for
Political and Economic Studies ; Lanham, Md. ;
Oxford : University Press of America, c1998.
*TC HD8081.A65 J63 1998*

**AFRO-AMERICANS - EDUCATION.** *See also*
**AFRO-AMERICAN STUDENTS; AFRO-
AMERICAN WOMEN - EDUCATION;
AFRO-AMERICANS - SCHOLARSHIPS,
FELLOWSHIPS, ETC.; SEGREGATION IN
EDUCATION - UNITED STATES.**
Gill, Walter. A common sense guide to non-traditional
urban education. Nashville, Tenn. : James C. Winston
Publishing Co., Inc., c1998.
*TC LC5115 .G55 1998*

McWhorter, John H. Losing the race. New York :
Free Press, c2000.
*TC E185.625 .M38 2000*

**AFRO-AMERICANS - EDUCATION -
ARKANSAS - LITTLE ROCK - HISTORY -
20TH CENTURY.**
Understanding the Little Rock crisis. Fayetteville,
Ark : University of Arkansas Press, 1999.
*TC LC214.23.L56 U53 1999*

**AFRO-AMERICANS - EDUCATION (EARLY
CHILDHOOD).**
Paul, Deirdre Glenn, 1964- Raising Black children
who love reading and writing. Westport, Conn. :
Bergin & Garvey, 2000.
*TC LC2778.L34 P28 2000*

**AFRO-AMERICANS - EDUCATION
(ELEMENTARY).**
Paley, Vivian Gussin, 1929- White teacher.
Cambridge, Mass. : Harvard University Press, 2000.
*TC LC2771 .P34 2000*

Paul, Deirdre Glenn, 1964- Raising Black children
who love reading and writing. Westport, Conn. :
Bergin & Garvey, 2000.
*TC LC2778.L34 P28 2000*

**AFRO-AMERICANS - EDUCATION
(ELEMENTARY) - ALABAMA.**
Morris, Vivian Gunn, 1941- Creating caring and
nurturing educational environments for African
American children. Westport, Conn. ; London :
Bergin & Garvey, 2000.
*TC LC2802.A2 M67 2000*

**AFRO-AMERICANS - EDUCATION -
EVALUATION - LONGITUDINAL STUDIES.**
African-centered schooling in theory and practice.
Westport, Conn. ; London : Bergin & Garvey, 2000.
*TC LC2731 .A35 2000*

**AFRO-AMERICANS - EDUCATION (HIGHER).**
Latimer, Leah Y. Higher ground. New York : Avon
Books, c1999.
*TC LC2781 .L27 1999*

**AFRO-AMERICANS - EDUCATION (HIGHER) -
SOCIAL ASPECTS.**
Bracey, Earnest N. Prophetic insight. Lanham :
University Press of America, c1999.
*TC LC2781 .B73 1999*

**AFRO-AMERICANS - EDUCATION - HISTORY -
20TH CENTURY - SOURCES.**
Bethune, Mary McLeod, 1875-1955. [Selections.
1999] Mary McLeod Bethune. Bloomington : Indiana
University Press, c1999.
*TC E185.97.B34 A25 1999*

**AFRO-AMERICANS - EDUCATION -
LANGUAGE ARTS.**
Smitherman, Geneva, 1940- Talkin that talk. London ;
New York : Routledge, 2000.
*TC PE3102.N4 S63 2000*

**AFRO-AMERICANS - EDUCATION -
MARYLAND - BALTIMORE - HISTORY -
20TH CENTURY.**
Orr, Marion, 1962- Black social capital. Lawrence :
University Press of Kansas, c1999.
*TC LC2803.B35 O77 1999*

**AFRO-AMERICANS - EDUCATION - SOUTHERN
STATES - FINANCE - HISTORY.**
Anderson, Eric, 1949- Dangerous donations.
Columbia, Mo. : University of Missouri Press, c1999.
*TC LC2707 .A53 1999*

**AFRO-AMERICANS - EMPLOYMENT.**
Job creation. Washington, DC : Joint Center for
Political and Economic Studies ; Lanham, Md. :
Oxford : University Press of America, c1998.
*TC HD8081.A65 J63 1998*

**AFRO-AMERICANS - ENCYCLOPEDIAS.**
Microsoft encarta Africana [computer file]. Redmond,
WA : Microsoft Corp., c1999. Computer data and
programs.
*TC DT14 .M527 1999*

Microsoft encarta Africana [computer file]. Redmond,
WA : Microsoft Corp., c1999. Computer data and
programs.
*TC DT3 .M53 1999x*

The New York Public Library African American Desk
Reference. New york : Wiley, c1999.
*TC E185 .N487 1999*

Reference library of Black America. Detroit, MI :
Gale Group : Distributed by African American Pub.,
Proteus Enterprises, c2000.
*TC E185 .R44 2000*

**AFRO-AMERICANS - FAMILIES. *See* AFRO-
AMERICAN FAMILIES.**

**AFRO-AMERICANS - FICTION.**
Caines, Jeannette Franklin. I need a lunch box. New
York : Macmillan/McGraw-Hill, 1988.
*TC PZ7.C12 Iaan 1988*

Cummings, Pat. Clean your room, Harvey Moon!.
New York : Macmillan/McGraw-Hill School Pub.
Co., c1991.
*TC PZ8.3.C898 Cl 1991*

Curtis, Christopher Paul. Bud, not Buddy. New York :
Delacorte Press, 1999.
*TC PZ7.C94137 Bu 1999*

Draper, Sharon M. (Sharon Mills) Romiette and Julio.
1st ed. New York : Atheneum Books for Young
Readers, 1999.
*TC PZ7.D78325 Ro 1999*

Hansen, Joyce. The heart calls home. New York :
Walker & Company, 1999.
*TC PZ7.H19825 He 1999*

Hooks, Bell. Happy to be nappy. 1st ed. New York :
Hyperion Books for Children, 1999.
*TC PZ7.H7663 Hap 1999*

Jones, Joy. Tambourine moon. New York : Simon &
Schuster, 1999.
*TC PZ7.J72025 Tam 1999*

Kurtz, Jane. Faraway home. San Diego : Harcourt,
c2000.
*TC PZ7.K9626 Far 2000*

Littlesugar, Amy. Tree of hope. New York : Philomel
Books, 1999.
*TC PZ7.L7362 Tr 1999*

McGill, Alice. Molly Bannaky. Boston, Mass. :
Houghton Mifflin, 1999.
*TC PZ7.M478468 Mol 1999*

Ross, Alice. Jezebel's spooky spot. 1st ed. New
York : Dutton Children's Books, 1999.
*TC PZ7.R719694 Jf 1999*

Serfozo, Mary. What's what? a guessing game/ 1st ed.
New York, NY : Margaret K. McElderry Books,
c1996.
*TC PZ7.S482 Wg 1996*

Thomas, Joyce Carol. I have heard of a land. 1st ed.
[New York] : HarperCollins Publishers, c1998.
*TC PZ7.T36696 Iae 1998*

**AFRO-AMERICANS - FOLKLORE.**
Farmer, Nancy. Casey Jones's fireman. 1st ed. New
York : Phyllis Fogelman Books, c1998.
*TC PZ8.1.F2225 Cas 1998*

**AFRO-AMERICANS - GOVERNMENT POLICY -
HISTORY.**
Klinkner, Philip A. The unsteady march. Chicago :
University of Chicago Press, c1999.
*TC E185 .K55 1999*

**AFRO-AMERICANS - HEALTH AND HYGIENE -
UNITED STATES.**
United States. Dept. of Health and Human Services.
Task Force on Black and Minority Health. Report of
the Secretary's Task Force on Black & Minority
Health. Washington, D.C. : U.S. Dept. of Health and
Human Services, [1985-<1986 >
*TC RA448.5.N4 U55 1985*

**AFRO-AMERICANS - HEALTH AND HYGIENE - UNITED STATES - STATISTICS.**
United States. Dept. of Health and Human Services. Task Force on Black and Minority Health. Report of the Secretary's Task Force on Black & Minority Health. Washington, D.C. : U.S. Dept. of Health and Human Services, |1985-<1986 >
*TC RA448.5.N4 U55 1985*

**AFRO-AMERICANS - HISTORIOGRAPHY.**
Hall, Perry A., 1947- In the vineyard. 1st ed. Knoxville : University of Tennessee Press, c1999.
*TC E184.7 .H24 1999*

**AFRO-AMERICANS - HISTORY.**
Africans in America [videorecording]. [Boston, Mass.] : WGBH Educational Foundation ; South Burlington, VT : WGBH Boston Video [distributor], c1998.
*TC E441 .A47 1998*

Earle, Jonathan. The Routledge atlas of African American history. New York : Routledge, 2000.
*TC E185 .E125 2000*

Forten, Charlotte L. A free Black girl before the Civil War. Mankato, Minn. : Blue Earth Books, c2000.
*TC F74.S1 F67 2000*

**AFRO-AMERICANS - HISTORY - ENCYCLOPEDIAS.**
The New York Public Library African American Desk Reference. New york : Wiley, c1999.
*TC E185 .N487 1999*

**AFRO-AMERICANS - HISTORY - MAPS.**
Earle, Jonathan. The Routledge atlas of African American history. New York : Routledge, 2000.
*TC E185 .E125 2000*

**AFRO-AMERICANS - HISTORY - TO 1863.** *See* FREE AFRO-AMERICANS.

**AFRO-AMERICANS IN LITERATURE.**
MacCann, Donnarae. White supremacy in children's literature. New York : Garland Pub., 1998.
*TC PS173.N4 M33 1998*

Mensh, Elaine, 1924- Black, white, and Huckleberry Finn. Tuscaloosa : University of Alabama Press, c2000.
*TC PS1305 .M46 2000*

**AFRO-AMERICANS IN LITERATURE - BIBLIOGRAPHY.**
The Coretta Scott King awards book, 1970-1999. Chicago : American Library Association, 1999.
*TC Z1037.A2 C67 1999*

Peck, David R. American ethnic literatures. Pasadena, Calif. : Salem Press, c1992.
*TC Z1229.E87 P43 1992*

**AFRO-AMERICANS IN LITERATURE - DICTIONARIES.**
African American authors, 1745-1945. Westport, Conn. : Greenwood Press, 2000.
*TC PS153.N5 A32 2000*

**AFRO-AMERICANS - INTELLECTUAL LIFE.** *See also* AFRO-AMERICAN INTELLECTUALS.
Hooks, Bell. Yearning. Boston, MA : South End Press, c1990.
*TC E185.86 .H742 1990*

**AFRO-AMERICANS - INTELLECTUAL LIFE - 20TH CENTURY - SOURCES.**
Marks, Carole. The power of pride. 1st ed. New York : Crown Publishers, c1999.
*TC E185.6 .M35 1999*

**AFRO-AMERICANS - JUVENILE FICTION.**
Hansen, Joyce. The heart calls home. New York : Walker & Company, 1999.
*TC PZ7.H19825 He 1999*

Littlesugar, Amy. Tree of hope. New York : Philomel Books, 1999.
*TC PZ7.L7362 Tr 1999*

**AFRO-AMERICANS - LANGUAGE.**
Rickford, John R., 1949- Spoken soul. New York ; Chichester [England] : Wiley, c2000.
*TC PE3102.N42 R54 2000*

Smitherman, Geneva, 1940- Talkin that talk. London ; New York : Routledge, 2000.
*TC PE3102.N4 S63 2000*

**AFRO-AMERICANS - LANGUAGES.** *See* BLACK ENGLISH.

**AFRO-AMERICANS - LANGUAGES - DICTIONARIES.**
Smitherman, Geneva, 1940- Black talk. Rev. ed. Boston : Houghton Mifflin, 2000.

*TC PE3102.N4 S65 2000*

**AFRO-AMERICANS - LITERARY COLLECTIONS.**
The Norton anthology of African American literature. 1st ed. New York : W.W. Norton & Co., c1997.
*TC PS508.N3 N67 1996*

**AFRO-AMERICANS - MEDICAL CARE.**
Smith, David Barton. Health care divided. Ann Arbor : University of Michigan Press, 1999.
*TC RA448.5.N4 S63 1999*

**AFRO-AMERICANS - MUSIC.** *See* BLUES (MUSIC); JAZZ.

**AFRO-AMERICANS - MUSIC - HISTORY AND CRITICISM.**
Fisher, Miles Mark, 1899- Negro slave songs in the United States. Secaucus, N.J. : Citadel Press, c1953.
*TC ML3556 .F58 1953*

The jazz cadence of American culture. New York : Columbia University Press, c1998.
*TC ML3508 .J38 1998*

**AFRO-AMERICANS - NEW YORK (STATE) - NEW YORK - HISTORY.**
Harlem on my mind : cultural capital of Black America, 1900-1968. New York : New Press : Distributed by W.W. Norton & Co., c1995.
*TC F128.68.H3 S3 1995*

**AFRO-AMERICANS - NEW YORK (STATE) - NEW YORK - HISTORY - 20TH CENTURY - PICTORIAL WORKS.**
Visual journal. Washington, DC : Smithsonian Institution Press, c1996.
*TC TR820.5 .V57 1996*

**AFRO-AMERICANS - NEW YORK (STATE) - NEW YORK - RELATIONS WITH JEWS - HISTORY - 20TH CENTURY.**
Edgell, Derek. The movement for community control of New York City's schools, 1966-1970. Lewiston, N.Y. : E. Mellen Press, c1998.
*TC LB2862 .E35 1998*

**AFRO-AMERICANS - PENNSYLVANIA - PHILADELPHIA - SOCIAL CONDITIONS.**
Anderson, Elijah. Code of the street. 1st ed. New York : W.W Norton, c1999.
*TC F158.9.N4 A52 1999*

**AFRO-AMERICANS - PENNSYLVANIA - PHILADELPHIA - SOCIAL LIFE AND CUSTOMS.**
Anderson, Elijah. Code of the street. 1st ed. New York : W.W Norton, c1999.
*TC F158.9.N4 A52 1999*

**AFRO-AMERICANS - PERIODICALS.**
Black academy review. Buffalo, N.Y. : Black Academy Press, c1970-

**AFRO-AMERICANS - POLITICS AND GOVERNMENT.**
Conyers, James E., 1932- Black elected officials. New York : Russell Sage Foundation, c1976.
*TC JK1924 .C65*

Gordon, Jacob U. Black leadership for social change. Westport, Conn. : Greenwood Press, 2000.
*TC E185.615 .G666 2000*

**AFRO-AMERICANS - PORTRAITS.**
Picturing us. New York : New Press : Distributed by W.W. Norton & Co., c1994.
*TC TR680 .P53 1994*

**AFRO-AMERICANS - PSYCHOLOGY.**
Advances in African American psychology. Hampton, VA : Cobb & Henry, 1999.
*TC E185.625 .A36 1999*

Brill, Norman Q. (Norman Quintus), 1911- Being Black in America today. Springfield, Ill. : Charles C Thomas, 1999.
*TC E185.625 B754 1999*

Fullilove, Mindy Thompson. The house of Joshua. Lincoln, NE : University of Nebraska Press, c1999.
*TC BF353 .F85 1999*

Jenkins, Adelbert H. Psychology and African Americans. 2nd ed. Boston : Allyn and Bacon, 1995.
*TC E185.625 .J47 1995*

Kardiner, Abram, 1891- The mark of oppression; [1st ed.]. New York, Norton [1951]
*TC E185.625 .K3*

McWhorter, John H. Losing the race. New York : Free Press, c2000.

*TC E185.625 .M38 2000*

**AFRO-AMERICANS - QUOTATIONS.**
African American quotations. Phoenix, Ariz. : Oryx Press, c1998.
*TC PN6081.3 .A36 1998*

**AFRO-AMERICANS - RACE IDENTITY.**
Hooks, Bell. Yearning. Boston, MA : South End Press, c1990.
*TC E185.86 .H742 1990*

Jenkins, Adelbert H. Psychology and African Americans. 2nd ed. Boston : Allyn and Bacon, 1995.
*TC E185.625 .J47 1995*

**AFRO-AMERICANS - RELATIONS WITH WHITES.** *See* UNITED STATES - RACE RELATIONS.

**AFRO-AMERICANS - RELIGION.** *See also* AFRO-AMERICAN CHURCHES.
Raboteau, Albert J. A fire in the bones. Boston : Beacon Press, c1995.
*TC BR563.N4 R24 1995*

**AFRO-AMERICANS - SCHOLARSHIPS, FELLOWSHIPS, ETC.** *See* AFRO-AMERICAN COLLEGE STUDENTS - SCHOLARSHIPS, FELLOWSHIPS, ETC.

**AFRO-AMERICANS - SCHOLARSHIPS, FELLOWSHIPS, ETC. - UNITED STATES - DIRECTORIES.**
Financial aid for African Americans. El Dorado Hills, Calif. : Reference Service Press, c1997-
*TC LB2338 .F5643*

**AFRO-AMERICANS - SEGREGATION.** *See* SEGREGATION IN EDUCATION - UNITED STATES.

**AFRO-AMERICANS - SOCIAL CONDITIONS.**
Brill, Norman Q. (Norman Quintus), 1911- Being Black in America today. Springfield, Ill. : Charles C Thomas, 1999.
*TC E185.625 B754 1999*

Gordon, Jacob U. Black leadership for social change. Westport, Conn. : Greenwood Press, 2000.
*TC E185.615 .G666 2000*

Kardiner, Abram, 1891- The mark of oppression; [1st ed.]. New York, Norton [1951]
*TC E185.625 .K3*

**AFRO-AMERICANS - SOCIAL CONDITIONS - 1975-.**
McWhorter, John H. Losing the race. New York : Free Press, c2000.
*TC E185.625 .M38 2000*

**AFRO-AMERICANS - SOCIAL LIFE AND CUSTOMS.**
Smitherman, Geneva, 1940- Talkin that talk. London ; New York : Routledge, 2000.
*TC PE3102.N4 S63 2000*

**AFRO-AMERICANS - SOUTHERN STATES - RELIGION - HISTORY - 19TH CENTURY.**
Cornelius, Janet Duitsman. Slave missions and the Black church in the antebellum South. Columbia : University of South Carolina Press, c1999.
*TC E449 .C82 1999*

**AFRO-AMERICANS - STUDY AND TEACHING - HISTORY - 20TH CENTURY.**
Hall, Perry A., 1947- In the vineyard. 1st ed. Knoxville : University of Tennessee Press, c1999.
*TC E184.7 .H24 1999*

**AFRO-AMERICANS - TEXAS - DALLAS - JUVENILE POETRY.**
Livingston, Myra Cohn. No way of knowing. 1st ed. New York : Atheneum, 1980.
*TC PS3562.I945 N6 1980*

**AFRO-AMERICANS - TEXAS - DALLAS - POETRY.**
Livingston, Myra Cohn. No way of knowing. 1st ed. New York : Atheneum, 1980.
*TC PS3562.I945 N6 1980*

**AFRO-AMERICANS - UNITED STATES.** *See* AFRO-AMERICANS.

**AFRO-AMERICANS - VIRGINIA - HOLLINS - BIOGRAPHY.**
Smith, Ethel Morgan, 1952- From whence cometh my help. Columbia ; London : University of Missouri Press, c2000.
*TC F234.H65 S55 2000*

**AFRO-AMERICANS - VIRGINIA - HOLLINS - HISTORY.**
Smith, Ethel Morgan, 1952- From whence cometh my

help. Columbia : London : University of Missouri Press, c2000.
*TC F234.H65 S55 2000*

**AFRO-AMERICANS - WASHINGTON (D.C.) - HISTORY - 20TH CENTURY - PICTORIAL WORKS.**
Visual journal. Washington, DC : Smithsonian Institution Press, c1996.
*TC TR820.5 .V57 1996*

**AFRO-AMERICANS - WASHINGTON (D.C.) - SOCIAL CONDITIONS - 19TH CENTURY.**
Moore, Jacqueline M., 1965- Leading the race. Charlottesville : University Press of Virginia, 1999.
*TC E185.93.D6 M66 1999*

**AFRO-AMERICANS - WASHINGTON (D.C.) - SOCIAL CONDITIONS - 20TH CENTURY.**
Moore, Jacqueline M., 1965- Leading the race. Charlottesville : University Press of Virginia, 1999.
*TC E185.93.D6 M66 1999*

**AFRO-AMERICANS - YOUTH. See AFRO-AMERICAN YOUTH.**

**AFROCENTRICITY. See AFROCENTRISM.**

**AFROCENTRISM - PHILOSOPHY.**
Dove, Nah. Afrikan mothers. Albany : State University of New York Press, c1998.
*TC HQ1593 .D68 1998*

**AFROCENTRISM - UNITED STATES.**
Berlinerblau, Jacques. Heresy in the University. New Brunswick, N.J. : Rutgers University Press, c1999.
*TC DF78.B3983 B47 1999*

Bracey, Earnest N. Prophetic insight. Lanham : University Press of America, c1999.
*TC LC2781 .B73 1999*

**AFROCENTRISM - UNITED STATES - LONGITUDINAL STUDIES.**
African-centered schooling in theory and practice. Westport, Conn. : London : Bergin & Garvey, 2000.
*TC LC2731 .A35 2000*

**After the death of childhood.**
Buckingham, David, 1954- Malden, MA : Polity Press, 2000.
*TC HQ784.M3 B83 2000*

**After the disciplines :** the emergence of cultural studies / edited by Michael Peters. Westport, Conn. : Bergin & Garvey, 1999, xiii, 296 p. : ill ; 24 cm. (Critical studies in education and culture series, 1064-8615) Includes bibliographical references and index. ISBN 0-89789-626-2 (alk. paper) ISBN 0-89789-627-0 (pbk. : alk. paper) DDC 378.1/99
*1. Universities and colleges - New Zealand - Curricula. 2. Universities and colleges - United States - Curricula. 3. Culture - Study and teaching (Higher) - New Zealand. 4. Culture - Study and teaching (Higher) - United States. 5. Education, Humanistic. 6. Postmodernism and education. I. Peters, Michael (Michael A.), 1948- II. Series.*
*TC LB2362.N45 A48 1999*

**Agapanthus Hum and the eyeglasses.**
Cowley, Joy. New York : Philomel Books, c1999.
*TC PZ7.C8375 Ag 1999*

**Agay, Denes, ed.**
Teaching piano. New York ; London : Yorktown Music Press, Inc., c1981.
*TC MT220 .T25*

**AGE. See AGE DISTRIBUTION (DEMOGRAPHY); OLD AGE.**

**AGE AND EMPLOYMENT. See CAREER CHANGES; CHILDREN - EMPLOYMENT.**

**AGE DISTRIBUTION (DEMOGRAPHY).**
Population growth, structure and distribution. New York : United Nations, 1999.
*TC HB871.P6675 1999*

**AGE FACTORS IN DISEASE. See also AGING.**
Shephard, Roy J. Aging, physical activity, and health. Champaign, IL : Human Kinetics, c1997.
*TC QP86 .S478 1997*

**AGE FACTORS IN MEMORY. See MEMORY - AGE FACTORS.**

**AGE GROUPS. See ADULTHOOD; AGE DISTRIBUTION (DEMOGRAPHY); CHILDREN; YOUTH.**

**AGE - PHYSIOLOGICAL EFFECT. See AGING.**

**AGE (PSYCHOLOGY). See MATURATION (PSYCHOLOGY).**

**AGED. See also EXERCISE FOR THE AGED; FRAIL ELDERLY; MASS MEDIA AND THE AGED; MENTALLY HANDICAPPED AGED; OLD AGE; PHYSICAL FITNESS FOR THE AGED; POOR AGED; TELEVISION AND THE AGED.**
Caregiving systems. Hillsdale, N.J. : L. Erlbaum Associates, 1993.
*TC HV1451 .C329 1993*

**AGED AND MASS MEDIA. See MASS MEDIA AND THE AGED.**

**AGED AND TELEVISION. See TELEVISION AND THE AGED.**

**AGED, BLIND. See BLIND AGED.**

**AGED - CARE AND HYGIENE. See AGED - CARE.**

**AGED - CARE - CONGRESSES.**
Caregiving systems. Hillsdale, N.J. : L. Erlbaum Associates, 1993.
*TC HV1451 .C329 1993*

**AGED - CARE - MORAL AND ETHICAL ASPECTS.**
Handbook on ethical issues in aging. Westport, Conn. : Greenwood Press, 1999.
*TC HV1451 .H35 1999*

**AGED - CARE - UNITED STATES.**
Pearce, Benjamin W. Senior living communities. Baltimore : Johns Hopkins University Press, 1998.
*TC HD7287.92.U54 P4 1998*

**AGED - COMMUNICATION - UNITED STATES.**
Communication and aging. 2nd ed. Mahwah, NJ ; London : L. Erlbaum, 2000.
*TC HQ1064.U5 C5364 2000*

Riggs, Karen E. Mature audiences. New Brunswick, N.J. : Rutgers University Press, c1998.
*TC HQ1064.U5 R546 1998*

**AGED - COUNSELING OF.**
Nemeroff, Robin. Stress, social support, and psychological distress in late life. 1999.
*TC 085 N341*

**AGED - DISEASES - TREATMENT. See EXERCISE THERAPY FOR THE AGED.**

**AGED - DWELLINGS. See LIFE CARE COMMUNITIES.**

**AGED - EDUCATION.**
Glendenning, Frank. Teaching and learning in later life. Aldershot, Hants, Eng. ; Burlington, Vt. : Ashgate / Arena, c2000.
*TC LC5457 .G54 2000*

**AGED - EDUCATION - SOCIAL ASPECTS.**
Glendenning, Frank. Teaching and learning in later life. Aldershot, Hants, Eng. ; Burlington, Vt. : Ashgate / Arena, c2000.
*TC LC5457 .G54 2000*

**AGED - FICTION.**
Stegner, Wallace Earle, 1909- Angle of repose. New York : Modern Library, 2000.
*TC PS3537.T316 A8 2000*

**AGED, FRAIL. See FRAIL ELDERLY.**

**AGED - HEALTH AND HYGIENE.**
Ferrini, Armeda F. Health in the later years. 3rd ed. Boston : McGraw-Hill, c2000.
*TC RA777.6 .F46 2000*

Keller, Colleen, 1949- Health promotion for the elderly. Thousand Oaks, Calif. ; London : Sage Publications, c2000.
*TC RA564.8 .K438 2000*

The many dimensions of aging. New York : Springer Pub., c2000.
*TC HQ1061 .M337 2000*

**AGED - HOME CARE - CONGRESSES.**
Caregiving systems. Hillsdale, N.J. : L. Erlbaum Associates, 1993.
*TC HV1451 .C329 1993*

**AGED - HOME CARE - PSYCHOLOGICAL ASPECTS.**
Caregiving--leisure and aging. New York : Haworth Press, c1999.
*TC HV1451 .C327 1999*

**AGED - MEDICAL CARE.**
The gerontological prism. Amityville, N.Y. : Baywood Pub., c2000.
*TC HQ1061 .G416 2000*

**AGED - MEDICAL CARE - CONGRESSES.**
Caregiving systems. Hillsdale, N.J. : L. Erlbaum Associates, 1993.
*TC HV1451 .C329 1993*

**AGED MEN - NEW JERSEY.**
Smith, Irmhild Wrede. The effect of structured exercise and structured reminiscing on agitation and aggression in geriatric psychiatric patients. 1996.
*TC 06 no. 10700*

**AGED - MENTAL HEALTH. See also GERIATRIC PSYCHIATRY.**
Psychological problems of ageing. Chichester ; New York : Wiley, c1999.
*TC RC451.4.A5 P7774 1999*

**AGED - MENTAL HEALTH SERVICES.**
Assessment in geriatric psychopharmacology. New Canaan, Conn. : Mark Powley Associates, 1983.
*TC WT150 .A846 1983*

**AGED - PERSONALITY. See AGED - PSYCHOLOGY.**

**AGED, PHYSICALLY HANDICAPPED. See VISUALLY HANDICAPPED AGED.**

**AGED, POOR. See POOR AGED.**

**AGED - PSYCHIATRIC CARE. See GERIATRIC PSYCHIATRY.**

**AGED - PSYCHOLOGICAL TESTING - HANDBOOKS, MANUALS, ETC.**
Handbook of assessment in clinical gerontology. New York : Wiley, 1999.
*TC RC451.4.A5 H358 1999*

**AGED - PSYCHOLOGY. See also AGING - PSYCHOLOGICAL ASPECTS.**
Grice, Marthe Jane. Attachment, race, and gender in late life. 1999.
*TC 085 G865*

Hillman, James. The force of character. 1st ed. New York : Random House, c1999.
*TC BF724.85.S45 H535 1999b*

**AGED - PSYCHOLOGY.**
A history of geropsychology in autobiography. 1st ed. Washington, DC : London : American Psychological Association, c2000.
*TC BF724.8 .H57 2000*

**AGED - PSYCHOLOGY.**
The many dimensions of aging. New York : Springer Pub., c2000.
*TC HQ1061 .M337 2000*

Perspectives on spiritual well-being and aging. Springfield, Ill. : Charles C. Thomas, c2000.
*TC BL625.4 .P47 2000*

The self and society in aging processes. New York : Springer Pub., c1999.
*TC HQ1061 .S438 1999*

**AGED - PSYCHOLOGY - CASE STUDIES.**
Brown, Gloria M. Post-hospital care for the elderly. 1997.
*TC 06 no. 10759*

**AGED - PSYCHOLOGY - STUDY AND TEACHING - HISTORY.**
A history of geropsychology in autobiography. 1st ed. Washington, DC : London : American Psychological Association, c2000.
*TC BF724.8 .H57 2000*

**AGED - RELIGIOUS LIFE.**
Perspectives on spiritual well-being and aging. Springfield, Ill. : Charles C. Thomas, c2000.
*TC BL625.4 .P47 2000*

**AGED - SERVICES FOR - CONGRESSES.**
Caregiving systems. Hillsdale, N.J. : L. Erlbaum Associates, 1993.
*TC HV1451 .C329 1993*

**AGED - SEXUAL BEHAVIOR.**
Hillman, Jennifer L. Clinical perspectives on elderly sexuality. New York : Kluwer Academic/Plenum Publishers, c2000.
*TC HQ30 .H55 2000*

**AGED - SOCIAL CONDITIONS.**
The many dimensions of aging. New York : Springer Pub., c2000.
*TC HQ1061 .M337 2000*

The self and society in aging processes. New York : Springer Pub., c1999.
*TC HQ1061 .S438 1999*

**AGED - SUICIDAL BEHAVIOR.**
Prado, C. G. The last choice. 2nd ed. Westport,
Conn. : Greenwood Press, 1998.
*TC HV6545.2 .P7 1998*

**AGED - UNITED STATES - HOME CARE - CASE
STUDIES.**
Brown, Gloria M. Post-hospital care for the elderly.
1997.
*TC 06 no. 10759*

**AGED - UNITED STATES - PSYCHOLOGY.**
Riggs, Karen E. Mature audiences. New Brunswick,
N.J. : Rutgers University Press, c1998.
*TC HQ1064.U5 R546 1998*

**AGED, VISUALLY HANDICAPPED.** *See*
**VISUALLY HANDICAPPED AGED.**

**AGED WOMEN - NEW JERSEY - ECONOMIC
CONDITIONS - CASE STUDIES.**
Black, Helen K., 1952- Old souls. New York : A. de
Gruyter, c2000.
*TC HQ1064.U6 P424 2000*

**AGED WOMEN - NEW JERSEY - RELIGIOUS
LIFE - CASE STUDIES.**
Black, Helen K., 1952- Old souls. New York : A. de
Gruyter, c2000.
*TC HQ1064.U6 P424 2000*

**AGED WOMEN - NEW JERSEY - SOCIAL
CONDITIONS - CASE STUDIES.**
Black, Helen K., 1952- Old souls. New York : A. de
Gruyter, c2000.
*TC HQ1064.U6 P424 2000*

**AGED WOMEN - PENNSYLVANIA -
PHILADELPHIA METROPOLITAN AREA -
ECONOMIC CONDITIONS - CASE STUDIES.**
Black, Helen K., 1952- Old souls. New York : A. de
Gruyter, c2000.
*TC HQ1064.U6 P424 2000*

**AGED WOMEN - PENNSYLVANIA -
PHILADELPHIA METROPOLITAN AREA -
RELIGIOUS LIFE - CASE STUDIES.**
Black, Helen K., 1952- Old souls. New York : A. de
Gruyter, c2000.
*TC HQ1064.U6 P424 2000*

**AGED WOMEN - PENNSYLVANIA -
PHILADELPHIA METROPOLITAN AREA -
SOCIAL CONDITIONS - CASE STUDIES.**
Black, Helen K., 1952- Old souls. New York : A. de
Gruyter, c2000.
*TC HQ1064.U6 P424 2000*

**AGEING.** *See* **AGING.**

**AGENCIES, ADMINISTRATIVE.** *See*
**ADMINISTRATIVE AGENCIES.**

**AGENCIES, EMPLOYMENT.** *See*
**EMPLOYMENT AGENCIES.**

**AGENT (PHILOSOPHY).** *See* **ACT
(PHILOSOPHY).**

**Aggarwal, Anil, 1949-.**
Web-based learning and teaching technologies.
Hershey, PA ; London : Idea Group Pub., c2000.
*TC LB1044.87 .W435 2000*

**Aggarwal, J. C.**
Agrawal, S. P., 1929- Development of education in
India. New Delhi : Concept Pub. Co., 1997.
*TC LA1150 .A39 1997*

**AGGRESSION (PSYCHOLOGY).** *See*
**AGGRESSIVENESS (PSYCHOLOGY).**

**The aggressive adolescent.**
Davis, Daniel Leifeld. New York : Haworth Press,
1999.
*TC RJ506.V56 D38 1999*

**AGGRESSIVE BEHAVIOR.** *See*
**AGGRESSIVENESS (PSYCHOLOGY).**

**AGGRESSIVENESS IN CHILDREN.**
Cavell, Timothy A. Working with parents of
aggressive children. 1st ed. Washington, DC :
American Psychological Association, 2000.
*TC RJ506.A35 C38 2000*

Council of Europe. Council for Cultural Co-operation.
Bullying in schools. Strasbourg : Council of Europe
Publishing, 1999.
*TC BF637.B85 B842 1999*

**AGGRESSIVENESS (PSYCHOLOGY).** *See also*
**ASSERTIVENESS (PSYCHOLOGY);
BULLYING; VIOLENCE.**
Jack, Dana Crowley. Behind the mask. Cambridge,
Mass. ; London : Harvard University Press, 1999.

*TC HQ1206 .J26 1999*

Smith, Irmhild Wrede. The effect of structured
exercise and structured reminiscing on agitation and
aggression in geriatric psychiatric patients. 1996.
*TC 06 no. 10700*

**AGGRESSIVENESS (PSYCHOLOGY) IN
CHILDREN.** *See* **VIOLENCE IN CHILDREN.**

**AGGRESSIVENESS - UNITED STATES.**
Kosmoski, Georgia J. Managing difficult, frustrating,
and hostile conversations. Thousand Oaks, Calif. :
Sage Publications, c2000).
*TC LB3011.5 .K67 2000*

**AGING.**
Shephard, Roy J. Aging, physical activity, and health.
Champaign, IL : Human Kinetics, c1997.
*TC QP86 .S478 1997*

Weinstein, Barbara E. Geriatric audiology. New
York : Thieme, 2000.
*TC RF291.5.A35 W44 2000*

Wilson, Gail. Understanding old age :. London : Sage,
2000.
*TC HQ1061 .W54 2000*

**Aging and saging** [videorecording] / a presentation of
Films for the Humanities & Sciences. Princeton, NJ :
Films for the Humanities & Sciences : Distributed by
Canadian Broadcasting Corporation, 1998. 1
videocassette (24 min.) : sd., col. ; 1/2 in. Opening title: Man
alive... aging and saging [videorecording]. VHS. Catalogued
from credits and container. Speakers: Ram Dass and Rabbi
Zalman Schachter-Shalomi. "FFH 8491"--Container.
Videocassette release of a 1998 television production. For
adolescents through adults. SUMMARY: This program takes
place at the Omega Institute during a weekend Elder Circle
moderated by author/teachers Rabbi Zalman Schachter-
Shalomi and Ram Dass. The purpose is to help the elderly
define themselves as dignified models for graceful aging in a
society which considers them valueless.
*1. Aging - Psychological aspects. 2. Aging - Religious aspects.
3. Old age - Psychological aspects. 4. Old age - Religious
aspects. I. Ram Dass. II. Schachter-Shalomi, Zalman. 1924-
III. Canadian Broadcasting Corporation. IV. Films for the
Humanities (Firm). V. Title: Man alive (Television program).
VI. Title: Man alive... aging and saging [videorecording]*
*TC BF724.55.A35 A35 1998*

**The aging mind: opportunities in cognitive research /**
Committee on Future Directions for Cognitive
Research on Aging ; Paul C. Stern and Laura L.
Carstensen, editors. Washington, D.C. : National
Academy Press, c2000. xii, 271 p. : ill. ; 23 cm. Includes
bibliographical references and index. ISBN 0-309-06940-8
(pbk.) DDC 155.67/13
*1. Cognition - Age factors. 2. Ability. Influence of age on. I.
Stern. Paul C., 1944- II. Carstensen, Laura L. III. National
Research Council (U.S.). Committee on Future Directions for
Cognitive Research on Aging. IV. Title.*
*TC BF724.55. C63 A48 2000*

**AGING - MORAL AND ETHICAL ASPECTS.**
Handbook on ethical issues in aging. Westport,
Conn. : Greenwood Press, 1999.
*TC HV1451 .H35 1999*

**AGING PERSONS.** *See* **AGED.**

**Aging, physical activity, and health.**
Shephard, Roy J. Champaign, IL : Human Kinetics,
c1997.
*TC QP86 .S478 1997*

**AGING - PSYCHOLOGICAL ASPECTS.** *See also*
**AGED - PSYCHOLOGY.**
Aging and saging [videorecording]. Princeton, NJ :
Films for the Humanities & Sciences : Distributed by
Canadian Broadcasting Corporation, 1998.
*TC BF724.55.A35 A35 1998*

Communication and aging. 2nd ed. Mahwah, NJ ;
London : L. Erlbaum, 2000.
*TC HQ1064.U5 C5364 2000*

Hatch, Laurie Russell. Beyond gender differences.
Amityville, N.Y. : Baywood Pub., c2000.
*TC HQ1061 .H375 2000*

Models of cognitive aging. Oxford ; New York :
Oxford University Press, 2000.
*TC BF724.55.C63 M63 2000*

Psychological problems of ageing. Chichester ; New
York : Wiley, c1999.
*TC RC451.4.A5 P7774 1999*

The self and society in aging processes. New York :
Springer Pub., c1999.

*TC HQ1061 .S438 1999*

**AGING - PSYCHOLOGICAL ASPECTS - STUDY
AND TEACHING - HISTORY.**
A history of geropsychology in autobiography. 1st ed.
Washington, DC : London : American Psychological
Association, c2000).
*TC BF724.8 .H57 2000*

**AGING - RELIGIOUS ASPECTS.**
Aging and saging [videorecording]. Princeton, NJ :
Films for the Humanities & Sciences : Distributed by
Canadian Broadcasting Corporation, 1998.
*TC BF724.55.A35 A35 1998*

Perspectives on spiritual well-being and aging.
Springfield, Ill. : Charles C. Thomas, c2000.
*TC BL625.4 .P47 2000*

**AGING - RESEARCH.**
Handbook of theories of aging. New York : Springer
Pub. Co., c1999.
*TC HQ1061 .H3366 1999*

**AGING - SOCIAL ASPECTS.**
Hatch, Laurie Russell. Beyond gender differences.
Amityville, N.Y. : Baywood Pub., c2000.
*TC HQ1061 .H375 2000*

The self and society in aging processes. New York :
Springer Pub., c1999.
*TC HQ1061 .S438 1999*

**AGING - STUDY AND TEACHING
(ELEMENTARY) - UNITED STATES.**
Friedman, Barbara, 1947- Connecting generations.
Boston : Allyn and Bacon, c1999.
*TC HQ1064.U5 F755 1999*

**Agins, Alan P.** Parent & educators' drug reference : : a
guide to common medical conditions & drugs used in
school-aged children / Alan P. Agins. Cranston, R.I. :
PRN Press, c1999. ix, 265 p. : ill. ; 28 cm. Includes
bibliographical references and index. ISBN 0-9671335-0-5
(pbk.)
*1. Drugs - Handbooks, manuals, etc. 2. Drugs - Dictionaries. I.
Title.*
*TC RJ560 .A35 1999*

**Agnew, William J.**
Standards-based K-12 language arts curriculum.
Boston : Allyn and Bacon, c2000.
*TC LB1576 .S747 2000*

**AGNOSTICISM.** *See* **ATHEISM; BELIEF AND
DOUBT.**

**AGORAPHOBIA - DIAGNOSIS.**
Neurotic, stress-related, and somatoform disorders
[videorecording]. Princeton, N.J. : Films for the
Humanities & Sciences, 1998.
*TC RC530 .N4 1998*

**AGORAPHOBIA - PATIENTS.**
Neurotic, stress-related, and somatoform disorders
[videorecording]. Princeton, N.J. : Films for the
Humanities & Sciences, 1998.
*TC RC530 .N4 1998*

**AGRARIAN QUESTION.** *See* **AGRICULTURE -
ECONOMIC ASPECTS.**

**Agrawal, S. P., 1929-** Development of education in
India : select documents 1993-94 / S.P. Agrawal, J.C.
Aggarwal. New Delhi : Concept Pub. Co., 1997. 447
p. ; 22 cm. (Concepts in communication, informatics &
librarianship ; v.4) Includes index. ISBN 81-7022-661-9
*1. Education - India - History. I. Aggarwal, J. C. II. Title. III.
Series: Concepts in communication, informatics &
librarianship ; v.4*
*TC LA1150 .A39 1997*

**AGRIBUSINESS.** *See* **AGRICULTURAL
INDUSTRIES; AGRICULTURE - ECONOMIC
ASPECTS.**

**AGRICULTURAL BANKS.** *See* **BANKS AND
BANKING.**

**AGRICULTURAL ECONOMICS.** *See*
**AGRICULTURE - ECONOMIC ASPECTS.**

**AGRICULTURAL INDUSTRIES - GREAT
BRITAIN.**
Thirsk, Joan. Alternative agriculture. Oxford ; New
York : Oxford University Press, c1997.
*TC S455 .T48 1997*

**AGRICULTURAL INDUSTRIES - GREAT
BRITAIN - HISTORY.**
Thirsk, Joan. Alternative agriculture. Oxford ; New
York : Oxford University Press, c1997.
*TC S455 .T48 1997*

## AGRICULTURAL INNOVATIONS - GREAT BRITAIN.
Thirsk, Joan. Alternative agriculture. Oxford ; New York : Oxford University Press, c1997.
*TC S455 .T48 1997*

AGRICULTURAL LABORERS. *See* PEASANTRY.

AGRICULTURAL PROCESSING INDUSTRIES. *See* FOOD INDUSTRY AND TRADE.

AGRICULTURAL PRODUCTION ECONOMICS. *See* AGRICULTURE - ECONOMIC ASPECTS.

AGRICULTURE. *See* FOOD SUPPLY; GARDENING.

AGRICULTURE AND STATE. *See* RURAL DEVELOPMENT.

AGRICULTURE - ECONOMIC ASPECTS. *See* AGRICULTURAL INDUSTRIES.

AGRICULTURE - ECONOMIC ASPECTS - 1945-. *See* AGRICULTURE - ECONOMIC ASPECTS.

## AGRICULTURE - ECONOMIC ASPECTS - DEVELOPING COUNTRIES.
The paradox of plenty. Oakland, Calif. : Food First Books, c1999.
*TC HD1542 .P37 1999*

## AGRICULTURE - ECONOMIC ASPECTS - EL SALVADOR - HISTORY.
Ripton, John R. Export agriculture and social crisis. 1997.
*TC 085 R48*

## AGRICULTURE - GREAT BRITAIN.
Thirsk, Joan. Alternative agriculture. Oxford ; New York : Oxford University Press, c1997.
*TC S455 .T48 1997*

## AGRICULTURE - GREAT BRITAIN - HISTORY.
Thirsk, Joan. Alternative agriculture. Oxford ; New York : Oxford University Press, c1997.
*TC S455 .T48 1997*

AGRICULTURE - INNOVATIONS. *See* AGRICULTURAL INNOVATIONS.

## AGRICULTURE - POLITICAL ASPECTS - EL SALVADOR - HISTORY.
Ripton, John R. Export agriculture and social crisis. 1997.
*TC 085 R48*

AGRICULTURE - TECHNOLOGICAL INNOVATIONS. *See* AGRICULTURAL INNOVATIONS.

AGRICULTURE - TECHNOLOGY TRANSFER. *See* AGRICULTURAL INNOVATIONS.

## AGS algebra.
Haenisch, Siegfried Circle Pines, Minn. : AGS, American Guidance Service, c1998.
*TC QA152.2 .H33 1998*

Haenisch, Siegfried Teacher's ed. Circle Pines, Minn. : AGS, American Guidance Service, c1998.
*TC QA152.2 .H33 1998 Teacher's Ed.*

Haenisch, Siegfried Teacher's ed. Circle Pines, Minn. : AGS, American Guidance Service, c1998.
*TC QA152.2 .H33 1998 Teacher's Ed.*

Haenisch, Siegfried Teacher's ed. Circle Pines, Minn. : AGS, American Guidance Service, c1998.
*TC QA152.2 .H33 1998 Teacher's Ed.*

## AGS basic English composition.
Walker, Bonnie L. Circle Pines, Minn. : American Guidance Service, c1997.
*TC PE1408 .W34 1997*

Walker, Bonnie L. Teacher's ed. Circle Pines, Minn. : American Guidance Service, c1997.
*TC PE1408 .W34 1997 Teacher's Ed.*

Walker, Bonnie L. Teacher's ed. Circle Pines, Minn. : American Guidance Service, c1997.
*TC PE1408 .W34 1997 Teacher's Ed.*

Walker, Bonnie L. Teacher's ed. Circle Pines, Minn. : American Guidance Service, c1997.
*TC PE1408 .W34 1997 Teacher's Ed.*

## AGS basic English grammar.
Walker, Bonnie L. Circle Pines, Minn. : AGS, American Guidance Service, c1997.
*TC PE1112 .W34 1997*

Walker, Bonnie L. Teacher's ed. Circle Pines, Minn. : AGS, American Guidance Service, c1997.
*TC PE1112 .W34 1997 Teacher's Ed.*

## AGS basic math skills.
Treff, August V. Circle Pines, Minn. : AGS, American Guidance Service, c1997.
*TC QA107 .T73 1997*

Treff, August V. Teacher's ed. Circle Pines, Minn. : AGS, American Guidance Service, c1997.
*TC QA107 .T73 1997 Teacher's Ed.*

## AGS earth science.
Marshall, Robert H. Circle Pines, Minn. : AGS, American Guidance Service, c1997.
*TC QE28 .M37 1997*

Marshall, Robert H. Teacher's ed. Circle Pines, Minn. : AGS, American Guidance Service, c1997.
*TC QE28 .M37 1997 Teacher's Ed.*

## AGS English for the world of work.
Knox, Carolyn W. Circle Pines, Minn. : American Guidance Service, c1997.
*TC PE1127.W65 K66 1997*

Knox, Carolyn W. Teacher's ed. Circle Pines, Minn. : American Guidance Service, c1997.
*TC PE1127.W65 K66 1997 Teacher's Ed.*

## AGS English to use.
Trautman, Barbara A. Teacher's ed. Circle Pines, Minn. : AGS, American Guidance Service, c1998.
*TC PE1121 .T72 1998 Teacher's Ed.*

Trautman, Barbara A. Circle Pines, Minn. : AGS, American Guidance Service, c1998.
*TC PE1121 .T72 1998*

## AGS physical science.
Marshall, Robert H. Circle Pines, Minn. : AGS, American Guidance Service, c1997.
*TC QC23 .M37 1997*

Marshall, Robert H. Teacher's ed. Circle Pines, Minn. : AGS, American Guidance Service, c1997.
*TC QC23 .M37 1997 Teacher's Ed.*

## AGS pre-algebra.
Haenisch, Siegfried Circle Pines, Minn. : AGS, American Guidance Service, c1998.
*TC QA107 .H33 1998*

Haenisch, Siegfried Teacher's ed. Circle Pines, Minn. : AGS, American Guidance Service, c1998.
*TC QA107 .H33 1998 Teacher's Ed.*

Haenisch, Siegfried Teacher's ed. Circle Pines, Minn. : AGS, American Guidance Service, c1998.
*TC QA107 .H33 1998 Teacher's Ed.*

Haenisch, Siegfried Teacher's ed. Circle Pines, Minn. : AGS, American Guidance Service, c1998.
*TC QA107 .H33 1998 Teacher's Ed.*

## AGS United States government.
Smith, Jane W. (Jane Wilcox) Circle Pines, Minn. : AGS, American Guidance Service, 1997.
*TC JK40 .S639 1997*

Smith, Jane W. (Jane Wilcox) Teacher's ed. Circle Pines, Minn. : AGS, American Guidance Service, 1997.
*TC JK40 .S639 1997 Teacher's Ed.*

## AGS United States history.
King, Wayne E. Teacher's ed. Circle Pines, Minn. : AGS, American Guidance Service, c1998.
*TC E175.8 .K56 1998 Teacher's Ed.*

Napp, John L. Circle Pines, Minn. : AGS, American Guidance Service, c1998.
*TC E178.1 .N36 1998*

**Aguirre, Adalberto.** Women and minority faculty in the academic workplace : recruitment, retention, and academic culture / Adalberto Aguirre, Jr. San Francisco, Calif. : Jossey-Bass c2000. xi, 130 p. : ill. ; 23 cm. (ASHE-ERIC higher education report, 0884-0040 ; v. 27, no. 6) "Prepared ... in cooperation with ERIC Clearinghouse on Higher Education, The George Washington University, Association for the Study of Higher Education, Graduate School of Education and Human Development, The George Washington University." Includes bibliographical references (p. 91-110) and indexes. ISBN 0-7879-5574-4 (pbk.) *1. Women college teachers - United States. 2. Minority college teachers - United States. 3. Universities and colleges - United States - Faculty. I. ERIC Clearinghouse on Higher Education. II. Association for the Study of Higher Education. III. George Washington University. Graduate School of Education and Human Development. IV. Title. V. Series: ASHE-ERIC higher education report ; vol. 27, no. 6.*
*TC LB2332.3 .A35 2000*

**Aguirre, Lauren Seeley.**
In search of human origins [videorecording]. [Boston, Mass.] : WGBH Educational Foundation, c1994.
*TC GN281 .I45 1994*

**Ahmet, Kemal.**
Inspiring students :. London : Kogan Page, 1999.
*TC LB1065 .I57 1999*

AI (ARTIFICIAL INTELLIGENCE). *See* ARTIFICIAL INTELLIGENCE.

AID TO DEPENDENT CHILDREN PROGRAMS. *See* AID TO FAMILIES WITH DEPENDENT CHILDREN PROGRAMS.

## AID TO FAMILIES WITH DEPENDENT CHILDREN PROGRAMS - UNITED STATES.
Welfare, the family, and reproductive behavior. Washington, D.C. : National Academy Press, 1998.
*TC HV91 .W478 1998*

**AIDS & HIV in perspective.**
Schoub, B. D. 2nd ed. Cambridge ; New York, NY : Cambridge University Press, 1999.
*TC RC607.A26 S3738 1999*

**AIDS agenda :** emerging issues in civil rights / edited by Nan D. Hunter and William B. Rubenstein. 1st ed. New York : New Press, c1992. xv, 301 p. ; 25 cm. Includes bibliographical references. ISBN 1-56584-001-1 (cloth) ISBN 1-56584-002-X (special ed. for ACLU distribution) DDC 362.1/9697/9200973 *1. AIDS (Disease) - Law and legislation - United States. 2. AIDS (Disease) - Social aspects - United States. 3. AIDS (Disease) - Government policy - United States. I. Hunter, Nan D. II. Rubenstein, William B.*
*TC RA644.A25 A33214 1992*

**AIDS and HIV in perspective.**
Schoub, B. D. AIDS & HIV in perspective. 2nd ed. Cambridge ; New York, NY : Cambridge University Press, 1999.
*TC RC607.A26 S3738 1999*

## AIDS DEMENTIA COMPLEX - DIAGNOSIS.
Organic disorders [videorecording]. Princeton, N.J. : Films for the Humanities & Sciences, 1998.
*TC RC521 .O7 1998*

## AIDS DEMENTIA COMPLEX - PATIENTS.
Organic disorders [videorecording]. Princeton, N.J. : Films for the Humanities & Sciences, 1998.
*TC RC521 .O7 1998*

## AIDS (DISEASE).
Schoub, B. D. AIDS & HIV in perspective. 2nd ed. Cambridge ; New York, NY : Cambridge University Press, 1999.
*TC RC607.A26 S3738 1999*

AIDS (DISEASE) - COMPLICATIONS. *See also* AIDS DEMENTIA COMPLEX.
Nutritional aspects of HIV infection. London ; New York : Arnold : Co-published in the United States by Oxford University Press, 1999.
*TC RC607.A26 N895 1998*

## AIDS (DISEASE) - DIET THERAPY.
Nutritional aspects of HIV infection. London ; New York : Arnold : Co-published in the United States by Oxford University Press, 1999.
*TC RC607.A26 N895 1998*

## AIDS (DISEASE) - GOVERNMENT POLICY - UNITED STATES.
AIDS agenda. 1st ed. New York : New Press, c1992.
*TC RA644.A25 A33214 1992*

## AIDS (DISEASE) IN CHILDREN - PATIENTS - BIOGRAPHY.
Hawkins, Anne Hunsaker, 1944- A small, good thing. New York : W.W. Norton, 2000.
*TC RJ387.A25 H39 2000*

## AIDS (DISEASE) IN CHILDREN - PATIENTS - EDUCATION - UNITED STATES.
Ainsa, Patricia. Teaching children with AIDS. Lewiston, N.Y. ; Lampeter, Wales : Edwin Mellen Press, c2000.
*TC LC4561 .A55 2000*

## AIDS (DISEASE) IN CHILDREN - POPULAR WORKS.
Hawkins, Anne Hunsaker, 1944- A small, good thing. New York : W.W. Norton, 2000.
*TC RJ387.A25 H39 2000*

## AIDS (DISEASE) IN MASS MEDIA.
Treichler, Paula A. How to have theory in an epidemic. Durham : Duke University Press, 1999.
*TC RA644.A25 T78 1999*

## AIDS (DISEASE) - LAW AND LEGISLATION - UNITED STATES.
AIDS agenda. 1st ed. New York : New Press, c1992.
*TC RA644.A25 A33214 1992*

**AIDS (DISEASE) - NUTRITIONAL ASPECTS.**
Nutritional aspects of HIV infection. London : New York : Arnold : Co-published in the United States by Oxford University Press, 1999.
*TC RC607.A26 N895 1998*

**AIDS (DISEASE) - PATIENTS - ENGLAND - LONDON.**
Gatter, Philip. Identity and sexuality. New York : Cassell, 1999.
*TC HQ1075.5.G7 G37 1999*

**AIDS (DISEASE) - POLITICAL ASPECTS.**
Progress in preventing AIDS? Amityville, N.Y. : Baywood Pub. Co., 1998.
*TC RA644.A25 P7655 1998*

**AIDS (DISEASE) - POLITICAL ASPECTS - UNITED STATES.**
Boehmer, Ulrike, 1959- The personal and the political. Albany, NY : State University of New York Press, c2000.
*TC RC280.B8 B62 2000*

**AIDS (DISEASE) - PREVENTION.**
Progress in preventing AIDS? Amityville, N.Y. : Baywood Pub. Co., 1998.
*TC RA644.A25 P7655 1998*

**AIDS (DISEASE) - PREVENTION - HANDBOOKS, MANUALS, ETC.**
Handbook of HIV prevention. New York : Kluwer/ Plenum, 2000.
*TC RA644.A25 H365 2000*

**AIDS (DISEASE) - SOCIAL ASPECTS.**
Progress in preventing AIDS? Amityville, N.Y. : Baywood Pub. Co., 1998.
*TC RA644.A25 P7655 1998*

Treichler, Paula A. How to have theory in an epidemic. Durham : Duke University Press, 1999.
*TC RA644.A25 T78 1999*

**AIDS (DISEASE) - SOCIAL ASPECTS - UNITED STATES.**
AIDS agenda. 1st ed. New York : New Press, c1992.
*TC RA644.A25 A33214 1992*

Andriote, John-Manuel. Victory deferred. Chicago : The University of Chicago Press, c1999.
*TC RA644.A25 A523 1999*

Power in the blood. Mahwah, N.J. : Erlbaum, 1999.
*TC RA644.A25 P69 1999*

**AIDS (DISEASE) - UNITED STATES - HISTORY.**
Andriote, John-Manuel. Victory deferred. Chicago : The University of Chicago Press, c1999.
*TC RA644.A25 A523 1999*

**AIDS PATIENTS.** *See* **AIDS (DISEASE) - PATIENTS.**

**AIDS prevention and mental health**
Handbook of HIV prevention. New York : Kluwer/ Plenum, 2000.
*TC RA644.A25 H365 2000*

**AIDS SERODIAGNOSIS.**
HIV and AIDS. Oxford ; New York ; Oxford University Press, 1999.
*TC RA644.A25 H57855 1999*

**AIGA journal of graphic design.**
Design culture. New York : Allworth Press : American Institute of Graphic Arts, c1997.
*TC NC998.5.A1 D46 1997*

Design culture. New York : Allworth Press : American Institute of Graphic Arts, c1997.
*TC NC998.5.A1 D46 1997*

**Aiken, Lewis R., 1931-** Human differences / Lewis R. Aiken. Mahwah, N.J. : L. Erlbaum Associates, 1999. xv, 337 p. : ill. ; 23 cm. Includes bibliographical references and indexes. ISBN 0-8058-3091-X (hardcover : alk. paper) ISBN 0-8058-3092-8 (pbk. : alk. paper)
*1. Individual differences. I. Title.*
*TC BF697 .A55 1999*

Personality assessment : methods and practices / Lewis R. Aiken. 3rd rev. ed. Seattle ; Toronto : Hogrefe & Huber Publishers, 1999. x, 524 p. ; 25 cm. Includes bibliographical references and indexes. First ed. published under title: Assessment of personality. ISBN 0-88937-209-8 (bound) DDC 155.2/8
*1. Personality assessment. 2. Personnalité - Évaluation. I. Title. II. Title: Assessment of personality*
*TC BF698.4 .A54 1999*

Psychological testing and assessment / Lewis R. Aiken. 10th ed. Boston : Allyn and Bacon, c2000. ix, 501 p. : ill. ; 24 cm. Includes bibliographical references (p. 456-483) and indexes. ISBN 0-205-29567-3 DDC 150/.28/7
*1. Psychological tests. I. Title.*

*TC BF176 .A48 2000*

**Aiken, Lewis R., 1931- comp.** Readings in psychological and educational testing, edited by Lewis R. Aiken, Jr. Boston, Allyn and Bacon [1973] x, 447 p. : ill. ; 22 cm. Bibliography: p. 425-442. DDC 371.2/6/08
*1. Educational tests and measurements. 2. Psychological tests. I. Title.*
*TC LB3051 .A5625*

**AIMS AND OBJECTIVES OF EDUCATION.** *See* **EDUCATION - AIMS AND OBJECTIVES.**

**The aims of education** / edited by Roger Marples. London ; New York : Routledge, 1999. x, 213 p. ; 25 cm. Includes bibliographical references and index. ISBN 0-415-15739-0 DDC 370/.1
*1. Education - Aims and objectives. 2. Education - Philosophy. 3. Autonomy (Psychology) 4. Educational change. I. Marples, Richard.*
*TC LB41 .A36353 1999*

**Ainley, John.**
Schools and the social development of young Australians. Melbourne, Vic. : Australian Council for Educational Research, 1998.
*TC LC192.4 .S36 1998*

**Ainley, Patrick.**
Apprenticeship. London : Kogan Page, c1999.
*TC HD4885.G7 A67 1999*

Learning policy : towards the certified society / Patrick Ainley. Basingstoke, Hampshire : Macmillan Press ; New York : St. Martin's Press, 1999. vii, 236 p. ; 23 cm. Includes bibliographical references (p. 214-226) and indexes. ISBN 0-312-22230-0 (cloth) ISBN 0-333-75034-9 DDC 379.42
*1. Education and state - Great Britain. 2. Economic development - Effect of education on. 3. Occupational training - Government policy - Great Britain. 4. Vocational education - Great Britain. 5. Great Britain - Social policy. I. Title.*
*TC LC93.G7 A76 1999*

**Ainsa, Patricia.** Teaching children with AIDS / Patricia Ainsa. Lewiston, N.Y. ; Lampeter, Wales : Edwin Mellen Press, c2000. iii, 116 p. : ill. ; 24 cm. (Symposium series ; v. 60) Includes bibliographical references (p. 109-113) and index. ISBN 0-7734-7823-X DDC 371.91
*1. AIDS (Disease) in children - Patients - Education - United States. I. Title. II. Series: Symposium series (Edwin Mellen Press) ; v. 60.*
*TC LC4561 .A55 2000*

**Ainsworth, Patricia, M.D.** Understanding depression / Patricia Ainsworth. Jackson : University Press of Mississippi, c2000. xii, 174 p. : ill. ; 23 cm. (Understanding health and sickness series) Includes bibliographical references (p. 150-152) and index. ISBN 1-57806-168-7 (hbk. : alk. paper) ISBN 1-57806-169-5 (pbk. : alk. paper) DDC 616.85/27
*1. Depression, Mental. 2. Affective disorders. I. Title. II. Series.*
*TC RC537 .A39 2000*

**AIR-BORNE POLLUTANTS.** *See* **AIR - POLLUTION.**

**AIR CONTAMINANTS.** *See* **AIR - POLLUTION.**

**AIR PILOTS.**
Burleigh, Robert. Flight. New York : Philomel Books, c1991.
*TC TL540.L5 B83 1991*

**AIR POLLUTANTS.** *See* **AIR - POLLUTION.**

**AIR POLLUTION.** *See* **AIR - POLLUTION.**

**AIR - POLLUTION.** *See* **ODORS.**

**AIR POLLUTION CONTROL.** *See* **AIR - POLLUTION.**

**AIR - POLLUTION - FICTION.**
Weeks, Sarah. Little factory. 1st ed. [New York] : Laura Geringer book, c1998.
*TC PZ7.W4125 Li 1998*

**AIR - POLLUTION - MATHEMATICAL MODELS - CONGRESSES.**
Air pollution modeling and its application XII. New York : Plenum Press, c1998.
*TC TD881 .A47523 1998*

**Air pollution modeling and its application XII** / edited by Sven-Erik Gryning and Nadine Chaumerliac. New York : Plenum Press, c1998. xvi, 770 p. : ill. ; 26 cm. (NATO challenges of modern society ; v. 22.) "Published in cooperation with NATO Committee on the Challenges of Modern Society." "Proceedings of the Twenty-Second NATO/ CCMS International Technical Meeting on Air Pollution Modeling and its Application, held June 2-6, 1997, in Clermont-Ferrand, France"--T.p. verso. Includes bibliographical references and index. ISBN 0-306-45821-7 DDC 628.5/3/015118

*1. Air - Pollution - Mathematical models - Congresses. 2. Atmospheric diffusion - Mathematical models - Congresses. I. Gryning, Sven-Erik. II. Chaumerliac, Nadine. III. North Atlantic Treaty Organization. Committee on the Challenges of Modern Society. IV. NATO/CCMS International Technical Meeting on Air Pollution Modeling and its Application (22nd : 1996 : Clemont-Ferrand, France) V. Series.*
*TC TD881 .A47523 1998*

**AIR QUALITY.** *See* **AIR - POLLUTION.**

**AIR TOXICS.** *See* **AIR - POLLUTION.**

**Airasian, Peter W.**
Gay, L. R. Educational research. 6th ed. Upper Saddle River, N.J. : Merrill, c2000.
*TC LB1028 .G37 2000*

**AIRBORNE POLLUTANTS.** *See* **AIR - POLLUTION.**

**AIRCRAFT, FIXED WING.** *See* **AIRPLANES.**

**AIRCRAFT INDUSTRY.** *See* **AIRPLANES.**

**AIRPLANES - JUVENILE POETRY.**
Livingston, Myra Cohn. Up in the air. 1st ed. New York : Holiday House, c1989.
*TC PS3562.I945 U6 1989*

**AIRPLANES - POETRY.**
Livingston, Myra Cohn. Up in the air. 1st ed. New York : Holiday House, c1989.
*TC PS3562.I945 U6 1989*

**Aitchison, Jean, 1938-** Language change : progress or decay? / Jean Aitchison. 2nd ed. Cambridge [England] : New York : Cambridge University Press, 1991. xi, 258 p. : ill. ; 20 cm. (Cambridge approaches to linguistics) Includes bibliographical references (p. 237-251) and index. ISBN 0-521-41101-7 (hard) ISBN 0-521-42283-3 (pbk.) DDC 417/.7
*1. Linguistic change. I. Title. II. Series.*
*TC P142 .A37 1991*

**Ajirotutu, Cheryl.**
African-centered schooling in theory and practice. Westport, Conn. ; London : Bergin & Garvey, 2000.
*TC LC2731 .A35 2000*

**Ajmera, Maya.** Children from Australia to Zimbabwe : a photographic journey around the world / Maya Ajmera & Anna Rhesa Versola ; with a foreword by Marian Wright Edelman. Watertown, Mass. : Charlesbridge, c1997. 1 v. (unpaged) : col. ill., col. maps ; 29 cm. Originally published: Durham, N.C. : SHAKTI for Children, c1996. SUMMARY: Text and photographs depict how children live in nations across the alphabet, from Australia to Zimbawe. ISBN 0-88106-999-X (hc) DDC 305.23; E
*1. Human geography - Juvenile literature. 2. Children - Juvenile literature. 3. Human geography - Pictorial works - Juvenile literature. 4. Children - Pictorial works - Juvenile literature. 5. Human geography. 6. Alphabet. I. Versola, Anna Rhesa. II. Title.*
*TC GF48 .A45 1997*

**[Ajmo, ajde, svi u šetnju. English.]** Protest in Belgrade : winter of discontent / edited by Mladen Lazić ; [translated by Liljana Nikolić]. Budapest, Hungary ; New York, NY, USA : Central European University Press, 1999. vi, 236 p., [8] p. of plates : ill. ; 23 cm. Includes bibliographical references. ISBN 9639116726 ISBN 9639116459 (pbk.) DDC 323/.044/09497
*1. Protest movements - Yugoslavia. 2. Demonstrations - Yugoslavia - Belgrade (Serbia) 3. Student protesters - Yugoslavia - Belgrade (Serbia) - Attitudes. 4. Political activists - Yugoslavia - Belgrade (Serbia) - Attitudes. 5. Yugoslavia - Politics and government - 1992- 6. Koalicija "Zajedno." I. Lazić, Mladen. II. Title.*
*TC DR2044 .A3913 1999*

**Akhtar, Salman, 1946 July 31-.**
Brothers and sisters. Northvale, N.J. : J. Aronson, c1999.
*TC BF723.S43 B78 1999*

**Akker, J. J. H. van den, 1950-.**
Design approaches and tools in education and training. Dordrecht ; Boston : Kluwer Academic Publishers, c1999.
*TC LB1028.38 .D46 1999*

**ALA editions**
The Coretta Scott King awards book, 1970-1999. Chicago : American Library Association, 1999.
*TC Z1037.A2 C67 1999*

**Alba, Alicia de.**
Curriculum in the postmodern condition. New York : P. Lang, c2000.
*TC LB2806.15 .C694 2000*

**Albers, Peggy.** Telling pieces : art as literacy in middle school classes / Peggy Albers, Sharon Murphy. Mahwah, N.J. : L. Erlbaum Associates, 2000. xi, 163

p. : ill. ; 23 cm. Includes bibliographical references (p. 143-152) and indexes. ISBN 0-8058-3463-X (paperback : alk. paper) DDC 707/.1/273
*1. Art - Study and teaching (Middle school) - United States. 2. Art in education - United States. I. Murphy, Sharon, 1955- II. Title.*
*TC N362.5 .A43 2000*

**Albert, Robert S.**
Genius and eminence. 2nd ed. Oxford : New York : Pergamon Press, 1992.
*TC BF412 .G43 1992*

**Alberts, Joye, 1951-.**
Schwarz, Gretchen, 1952- Teacher lore and professional development for school reform. Westport, Conn : Bergin & Garvey, 1998.
*TC LB1775.2 .S38 1998*

**Albrecht, Gary L.**
Handbook of social studies in health and medicine. London ; Thousand Oaks, Calif. : Sage Publications, 2000.
*TC RA418 .H36 2000*

**Alchemies of the mind.**
Elster, Jon, 1940- Cambridge, U.K. ; New York : Cambridge University Press, 1999.
*TC BF531 .E47 1999*

**Alchemy of images.**
Livingstone, Marco. Jim Dine. New York : Monacelli Press, 1998.
*TC N6537.D5 A4 1998*

**ALCIDAE.** *See* **PUFFINS.**

**ALCOHOL.** *See* **ALCOHOLIC BEVERAGES.**

**ALCOHOL ABUSE.** *See* **ALCOHOLISM.**

**ALCOHOL AMNESIC DISORDER.** *See* **KORSAKOFF'S SYNDROME.**

**Alcohol and emerging markets :** patterns, problems, and responses / edited by Marcus Grant. Philadelphia, Penn : Brunner/Mazel, 1998. ix, 364 p. : ill. ; 24 cm. (Series on alcohol in society / International Center for Alcohol Policies) Includes bibliographical references and index. Table of contents URL: http://lcweb.loc.gov/catdir/toc/98-29521.html ISBN 0-87630-978-3 (case : alk. paper) DDC 380.1/456631
*1. Alcoholic beverage industry. 2. Alcoholic beverage industry - Government policy. 3. Drinking of alcoholic beverages - Social aspects. 4. Alcoholic beverages - Marketing. I. Grant, Marcus. II. Series: Series on alcohol in society.*
*TC HD9350.6 .A4 1998*

**Alcohol and other drugs.**
O'Brien, Robert, 1932- The encyclopedia of understanding alcohol and other drugs. New York, NY : Facts on File, c1999.
*TC HV5017 .O37 1999*

**ALCOHOL CONSUMPTION.** *See* **DRINKING OF ALCOHOLIC BEVERAGES.**

**ALCOHOL DRINKING.**
Psychological theories of drinking and alcoholism. 2nd ed. New York : Guilford Press, c1999.
*TC HV5045 .P74 1999*

**ALCOHOL DRINKING - PREVENTION & CONTROL.**
Brief Alcohol Screening and Intervention for College Students (BASICS). New York : Guilford Press, c1999.
*TC HV5135 .B74 1998*

**ALCOHOL INTOXICATION.** *See* **ALCOHOLISM.**

**ALCOHOL - PHYSIOLOGICAL EFFECT - RESEARCH.**
The hijacked brain [videorecording]. Princeton, NJ : Films for the Humanities & Sciences, c1998.
*TC RC564 .H5 1998*

**ALCOHOL USE.** *See* **DRINKING OF ALCOHOLIC BEVERAGES.**

**Alcohol use among adolescents.**
Windle, Michael T. Thousand Oaks : Sage Publications, c1999.
*TC RJ506.A4 W557 1999*

**ALCOHOL WITHDRAWAL DELIRIUM.** *See* **DELIRIUM TREMENS.**

**ALCOHOLIC BEVERAGE CONSUMPTION.** *See* **DRINKING OF ALCOHOLIC BEVERAGES.**

**ALCOHOLIC BEVERAGE INDUSTRY.**
Alcohol and emerging markets. Philadelphia, Penn : Brunner/Mazel, 1998.
*TC HD9350.6 .A4 1998*

**ALCOHOLIC BEVERAGE INDUSTRY - GOVERNMENT POLICY.**
Alcohol and emerging markets. Philadelphia, Penn : Brunner/Mazel, 1998.
*TC HD9350.6 .A4 1998*

**ALCOHOLIC BEVERAGES.** *See* **DRINKING OF ALCOHOLIC BEVERAGES.**

**ALCOHOLIC BEVERAGES - MARKETING.**
Alcohol and emerging markets. Philadelphia, Penn : Brunner/Mazel, 1998.
*TC HD9350.6 .A4 1998*

**ALCOHOLIC PSYCHOSES.** *See* **DELIRIUM TREMENS; KORSAKOFF'S SYNDROME.**

**ALCOHOLIC PSYCHOSES - DIAGNOSIS.**
Disorders due to psychoactive substance abuse [videorecording]. Princeton, N.J. : Films for the Humanities & Sciences, 1998.
*TC RC564 .D5 1998*

**ALCOHOLIC PSYCHOSES - PATIENTS.**
Disorders due to psychoactive substance abuse [videorecording]. Princeton, N.J. : Films for the Humanities & Sciences, 1998.
*TC RC564 .D5 1998*

**ALCOHOLICS.** *See* **RECOVERING ALCOHOLICS; SOCIAL WORK WITH ALCOHOLICS.**

**ALCOHOLICS ANONYMOUS.**
Raphael, Matthew J. Bill W. and Mr. Wilson. Amherst : University of Massachusetts Press, c2000.
*TC HV5032.W19 R36 2000*

**ALCOHOLICS - BIOGRAPHY.**
Raphael, Matthew J. Bill W. and Mr. Wilson. Amherst : University of Massachusetts Press, c2000.
*TC HV5032.W19 R36 2000*

**ALCOHOLICS - INTERVIEWS.**
Changing lives [videorecording]. Princeton, NJ : Films for the Humanities & Sciences, c1998.
*TC RC564 .C54 1998*

The hijacked brain [videorecording]. Princeton, NJ : Films for the Humanities & Sciences, c1998.
*TC RC564 .H5 1998*

Portrait of addiction [videorecording]. Princeton, NJ : Films for the Humanities & Sciences, c1998.
*TC HV5801 .P6 1998*

Portrait of addiction [videorecording]. Princeton, NJ : Films for the Humanities & Sciences, c1998.
*TC RC564 .P6 1998*

**ALCOHOLICS - REHABILITATION.**
Changing lives [videorecording]. Princeton, NJ : Films for the Humanities & Sciences, c1998.
*TC RC564 .C54 1998*

DuWors, George Manter, 1948- White knuckles and wishful thinking. 2nd rev. & expanded ed. Seattle : Hogrefe & Huber Publishers, c2000.
*TC RC565 .D79 2000*

Granfield, Robert, 1955- Coming clean. New York ; London : New York University Press, c1999.
*TC HV4998 .G73 1999*

The politics of addiction [videorecording]. Princeton, NJ : Films for the Humanities & Sciences, c1998.
*TC RC564 .P59 1998*

Portrait of addiction [videorecording]. Princeton, NJ : Films for the Humanities & Sciences, c1998.
*TC HV5801 .P6 1998*

Portrait of addiction [videorecording]. Princeton, NJ : Films for the Humanities & Sciences, c1998.
*TC RC564 .P6 1998*

**ALCOHOLICS - REHABILITATION - GREAT BRITAIN.**
Thom, Betsy. Dealing with drink. London ; New York : Free Association Books, 1999.
*TC HV5283.G6 T56 1999*

**ALCOHOLICS - REHABILITATION - UNITED STATES.**
Bridges to recovery. New York ; London : Free Press, c2000.
*TC HV5199.5 .B75 2000*

**ALCOHOLISM.** *See* **DRINKING OF ALCOHOLIC BEVERAGES.**

**ALCOHOLISM - COMPLICATIONS.** *See* **ALCOHOLIC PSYCHOSES.**

**ALCOHOLISM COUNSELING.**
Cohen, Monique. Counseling addicted women. Thousand Oaks, Calif. : Sage Publications, c2000.

**TC HV4999.W65 C64 2000**

**ALCOHOLISM COUNSELING - UNITED STATES.**
Bridges to recovery. New York ; London : Free Press, c2000.
*TC HV5199.5 .B75 2000*

**ALCOHOLISM - ENCYCLOPEDIAS.**
O'Brien, Robert, 1932- The encyclopedia of understanding alcohol and other drugs. New York, NY : Facts on File, c1999.
*TC HV5017 .O37 1999*

**ALCOHOLISM - PATIENTS.** *See* **ALCOHOLICS.**

**ALCOHOLISM - PHYSIOLOGICAL ASPECTS.** *See* **ALCOHOL - PHYSIOLOGICAL EFFECT.**

**ALCOHOLISM - PHYSIOLOGICAL ASPECTS - RESEARCH.**
The hijacked brain [videorecording]. Princeton, NJ : Films for the Humanities & Sciences, c1998.
*TC RC564 .H5 1998*

**ALCOHOLISM - PREVENTION.**
Brief Alcohol Screening and Intervention for College Students (BASICS). New York : Guilford Press, c1999.
*TC HV5135 .B74 1998*

Windle, Michael T. Alcohol use among adolescents. Thousand Oaks : Sage Publications, c1999.
*TC RJ506.A4 W557 1999*

**ALCOHOLISM - PREVENTION & CONTROL.**
Brief Alcohol Screening and Intervention for College Students (BASICS). New York : Guilford Press, c1999.
*TC HV5135 .B74 1998*

**ALCOHOLISM - PSYCHOLOGICAL ASPECTS.**
Kunitz, Stephen J. Drinking, conduct disorder, and social change. Oxford ; New York : Oxford University Press, 2000.
*TC E99.N3 K88 2000*

Portrait of addiction [videorecording]. Princeton, NJ : Films for the Humanities & Sciences, c1998.
*TC HV5801 .P6 1998*

Portrait of addiction [videorecording]. Princeton, NJ : Films for the Humanities & Sciences, c1998.
*TC RC564 .P6 1998*

Psychological theories of drinking and alcoholism. 2nd ed. New York : Guilford Press, c1999.
*TC HV5045 .P74 1999*

**ALCOHOLISM - PSYCHOLOGY.**
Psychological theories of drinking and alcoholism. 2nd ed. New York : Guilford Press, c1999.
*TC HV5045 .P74 1999*

**ALCOHOLISM - REHABILITATION.** *See* **ALCOHOLICS - REHABILITATION.**

**ALCOHOLISM - RELAPSE - PREVENTION.**
DuWors, George Manter, 1948- White knuckles and wishful thinking. 2nd rev. & expanded ed. Seattle : Hogrefe & Huber Publishers, c2000.
*TC RC565 .D79 2000*

**ALCOHOLISM - STUDY AND TEACHING.**
Brief Alcohol Screening and Intervention for College Students (BASICS). New York : Guilford Press, c1999.
*TC HV5135 .B74 1998*

**ALCOHOLISM - TREATMENT.**
Changing lives [videorecording]. Princeton, NJ : Films for the Humanities & Sciences, c1998.
*TC RC564 .C54 1998*

**ALCOHOLISM - TREATMENT - GREAT BRITAIN.**
Thom, Betsy. Dealing with drink. London ; New York : Free Association Books, 1999.
*TC HV5283.G6 T56 1999*

**ALCOHOLISM - TREATMENT - UNITED STATES.**
Bridges to recovery. New York ; London : Free Press, c2000.
*TC HV5199.5 .B75 2000*

**ALCOHOLISM - TREATMENT - UNITED STATES - HANDBOOKS, MANUALS, ETC.**
Kinney, Jean, 1943- Loosening the grip. 6th ed. Boston : McGraw-Hill, c2000.
*TC HV5292 .K53 2000*

**ALCOHOLISM - UNITED STATES - HANDBOOKS, MANUALS, ETC.**
Kinney, Jean, 1943- Loosening the grip. 6th ed. Boston : McGraw-Hill, c2000.

*TC HV5292 .K53 2000*

**ALCOHOLS.** *See* **ALCOHOL.**

**Alderson, Brian.**
Darton, F. J. Harvey (Frederick Joseph Harvey), 1878-1936. Children's books in England. 3rd ed. / rev. by Brian Alderson. London : British Library ; New Castle, DE : Oak Knoll Press, 1982 (1999 printing)
*TC PR990 .D3 1999*

**Aldred, Heather E.**
Sports injuries sourcebook ; 1st ed. Detroit, MI : Omnigraphics, c1999.
*TC RD97 .S736 1999*

**Alef Pictures.**
Step on a crack [videorecording]. Boston, MA : Fanlight Productions, 1996.
*TC RC533 .S7 1996*

**Alexander, Cynthia Jacqueline, 1960-.**
Digital democracy. Toronto ; New York : Oxford University Press, 1998.
*TC JC421 .D55 1998*

**Alexander, Edward P. (Edward Porter), 1907-** The museum in America : innovators and pioneers / by Edward P. Alexander. Walnut Creek : AltaMira Press, c1997. 224 p. ; 24 cm. (American Association for State and Local History book series) "Published in cooperation with the American Association for State and Local History." Includes bibliographical references and index. ISBN 0-7619-8946-3 (cloth) ISBN 0-7619-8947-1 (pbk.) DDC 069/.0973
*1. Museums - United States - History. 2. Museum curators - United States - Biography. 3. Museum directors - United States - Biography. 4. Popular culture - Museums - United States - History. 5. United States - Intellectual life - History. I. American Association for State and Local History. II. Title. III. Series.*
*TC AM11 .A55 1997*

**Alexander, George, 1949-.**
Alexander, George, 1949- Julie Rrap. [Sidney] : Piper Press, 1998.
*TC TR654 .A44 1998*

Julie Rrap / George Alexander ... [et al.]. [Sidney] : Piper Press, 1998. 128 p. : chiefly ill. ; 29 cm. Includes bibliographical references. ISBN 0-9587984-7-8
*1. Brown-Rrap, Julie. 2. Photography, Artistic - Australia. 3. Mixed media painting. 4. Women photographers - Australia. I. Alexander, George, 1949- II. Title.*
*TC TR654 .A44 1998*

**Alexander, Janet E.** Web wisdom : how to evaluate and create information quality on the Web / Janet E. Alexander, Marsha Ann Tate. Mahwah, N.J. : Lawrence Erlbaum Associates, Publishers, 1999. xv, 156 p. : ill. ; 26 cm. Includes bibliographical references (p. 141-147) and index. ISBN 0805831223c (alk. paper) ISBN 0805831231p (alk. paper) DDC 005.7/2
*1. Web sites. 2. World Wide Web (Information retrieval system) I. Tate, Marsha Ann. II. Title.*
*TC TK5105.888 .A376 1999*

**Alexander, Marthann.** Weaving on cardboard; simple looms to make & use. New York, Taplinger Pub. Co. [1972] 88 p. illus. 24 cm. SUMMARY: Instructions for making sixteen simple cardboard looms with suggestions for a variety of projects to make on them. ISBN 0-8008-8120-6 DDC 746.1/4
*1. Hand weaving. 2. Hand weaving. 3. Weaving. 4. Handicraft. I. Title.*
*TC TT848 .A67*

**Alexander, who used to be rich last Sunday.**
Viorst, Judith. 1st ed. New York : Atheneum, 1978.
*TC PZ7.V816 Am 1978*

**ALEXIA.** *See* **DYSLEXIA.**

**Alford, Brad A.**
Clark, David A., 1954- Scientific foundations of cognitive theory and therapy of depression. New York : John Wiley, c1999.
*TC RC537 .C53 1999*

**ALGEBRA.** *See also* **GROUP THEORY.**
Peters, Max, 1906- 2d ed. Princeton, N.J., Van Nostrand 1968.
*TC QA152 .P4562 1968*

**ALGEBRA.**
Haenisch, Siegfried AGS algebra. Circle Pines, Minn. : AGS, American Guidance Service, c1998.
*TC QA152.2 .H33 1998*

Haenisch, Siegfried AGS algebra. Teacher's ed. Circle Pines, Minn. : AGS, American Guidance Service, c1998.

*TC QA152.2 .H33 1998 Teacher's Ed.*
Haenisch, Siegfried AGS algebra. Teacher's ed. Circle Pines, Minn. : AGS, American Guidance Service, c1998.
*TC QA152.2 .H33 1998 Teacher's Ed.*

Haenisch, Siegfried AGS algebra. Teacher's ed. Circle Pines, Minn. : AGS, American Guidance Service, c1998.
*TC QA152.2 .H33 1998 Teacher's Ed.*

Percents [videorecording]. Princeton, N.J. : Video Tutor, 1988.

Peters, Max, 1906- Algebra. 2d ed. Princeton, N.J., Van Nostrand 1968.
*TC QA152 .P4562 1968*

Peters, Max, 1906- Algebra and trigonometry. Princeton, N.J., Van Nostrand 1965.
*TC QA152 .P4562 1965*

Pre-algebra [videorecording]. Princeton, N.J. : Video Tutor, 1988.
*TC QA152.2 .P6 1988*

**ALGEBRA, ABSTRACT.**
Chacko, Mathew Vadakkan. Public key cryptosystems. 1998.
*TC 085 C35*

**Algebra and trigonometry.**
Peters, Max, 1906- Princeton, N.J., Van Nostrand 1965.
*TC QA152 .P4562 1965*

**ALGEBRA - CONGRESSES.**
Algebra, K-theory, groups, and education. Providence, R.I. : American Mathematical Society, c1999.
*TC QA150 .A419 1999*

**Algebra, K-theory, groups, and education :** on the occasion of Hyman Bass's 65th birthday / T.Y. Lam, A.R. Magid, editors. Providence, R.I. : American Mathematical Society, c1999. ix, 238 p. ; 26 cm. (Contemporary mathematics, 0271-4132 ; 243) ISBN 0-8218-1087-1 (alk. paper) DDC 512
*1. Algebra - Congresses. 2. K-theory - Congresses. 3. Group theory - Congresses. 4. Mathematics - Study and teaching - Congresses. I. Bass, Hyman, 1932- II. Lam, T. Y. (Tsit-Yuen), 1942- III. Magid, Andy R. IV. Series: Contemporary mathematics (American Mathematical Society) ; v. 243.*
*TC QA150 .A419 1999*

**ALGEBRA - STUDY AND TEACHING (SECONDARY).**
Bumby, Douglas R. Mathematics. 2nd ed. Columbus, Ohio : C.E. Merrill, c1982-<1986.>
*TC QA154.2 .B8 1982*

Chazan, Daniel. Beyond formulas in mathematics and teaching. New York : Teachers College Press, c2000.
*TC QA159 .C48 2000*

**ALGEBRAIC TOPOLOGY.** *See* **K-THEORY.**

**ALGEBRAS, LINEAR.** *See* **TOPOLOGY.**

**Alger, Horatio, 1832-1899.** Ragged Dick, or, Street life in New York with the boot-blacks / Horatio Alger, Jr. ; introduction by Alan Trachtenberg. New York, N.Y. : Penguin Group, c1990. xx, 186 p. ; 18 cm. "A Signet classic." ISBN 0-451-52480-2
*I. Title. II. Title: Ragged Dick. III. Title: Street life in New York with the boot-blacks.*
*TC PS1029.A3 R34 1990*

**Ali, Lynda, 1946-** Moving on in your career : a guide for academic researchers and postgraduates / Lynda Ali and Barbara Graham. London ; New York : RoutledgeFalmer, 2000. xii, 188 p. ; 25 cm. Includes bibliographical references (p. [183]-186) and index. ISBN 0-415-17869-X (hard : alk. paper) ISBN 0-415-17870-3 (pbk. : alk. paper) DDC 378.1/2/02341
*1. College teaching - Vocational guidance - Great Britain. 2. College graduates - Employment - Great Britain. 3. Career changes - Great Britain. 4. Job hunting - Great Britain. I. Graham, Barbara, 1947 Aug. 3- II. Title.*
*TC LB1778.4.G7 A45 2000*

**Alice in Pastaland.**
Wright, Alexandra. Watertown, Mass. : Charlesbridge, 1997.
*TC PZ7.W9195 Al 19997*

**Alidou, Ousseina.**
A thousand flowers. Trenton, NJ : Africa World Press, c2000, [1999].
*TC LC67.68.A35 T56 2000*

**ALIEN DETENTION CENTERS.** *See* **ILLEGAL ALIENS.**

**ALIEN ENCOUNTERS WITH HUMANS.** *See* **HUMAN-ALIEN ENCOUNTERS.**

**ALIENATION, SOCIAL.** *See* **ALIENATION (SOCIAL PSYCHOLOGY).**

**ALIENATION (SOCIAL PSYCHOLOGY).** *See also* **SOCIAL ISOLATION.**
Capeheart-Meningall, Jennifer. Quality of students of color efort on a predominantly white college and the internal environmental elements that influence involvement. 1998.
*TC 06 no. 10874*

Comparative anomie research. Aldershot, Hants, England : Brookfield, Vt., USA : Ashgate, c1999.
*TC HM816 .C65 1999*

Schlanger, Dean J. An exploration of school belongingness. 1998.
*TC 06 no. 10993*

**ALIENATION (SOCIAL PSYCHOLOGY) - GREAT BRITAIN.**
Klein, Reva Defying disaffection. Staffordshire, England : Trentham Books, 1999.
*TC LC4091 .K53 1999*

**ALIENATION (SOCIAL PSYCHOLOGY) - UNITED STATES.**
Klein, Reva Defying disaffection. Staffordshire, England : Trentham Books, 1999.
*TC LC4091 .K53 1999*

**ALIENS.** *See* **ILLEGAL ALIENS; IMMIGRANTS.**

**ALIENS, ILLEGAL.** *See* **ILLEGAL ALIENS.**

**ALIENS - LEGAL STATUS, LAWS, ETC.** *See* **ILLEGAL ALIENS.**

**ALIMENTARY PASTE PRODUCTS.** *See* **PASTA PRODUCTS.**

**ALIMENTATION.** *See* **NUTRITION.**

**Alison Balter's Mastering Access 97 development.**
Balter, Alison. [Mastering Access 97 development] 2nd ed. Indianapolis, Ind. : Sams Pub., [c1997]
*TC QA76.9.D3 B32 1997*

**Alive at the core.**
Nelson, Michael, 1949- 1st ed. San Francisco : Jossey-Bass, c2000.
*TC AZ183.U5 N45 2000*

**ALL-DAY KINDERGARTEN.** *See* **FULL-DAY KINDERGARTEN.**

**ALL HALLOWS' EVE.** *See* **HALLOWEEN.**

**All India Educational and Vocational Association.**
Journal of vocational and educational guidance. [Bombay]

**All India Federation of Educational Associations.**
The Indian journal of education. Calcutta [etc] All-India Federation of Educational Associations.

**All Night Moving Pictures.**
Jazz dance class [videorecording]. W. Long Branch, NJ : Kultur, [1992?]
*TC GV1784 .J3 1992*

**All the pretty little horses :** a traditional lullaby / illustrated by Linda Saport. New York : Clarion Books, c1999. 32 p. : col. ill. ; 21 x 24 cm. SUMMARY: A traditional lullaby presented with music, a note on the origin of the song, and pastel illustrations which reflect its possible connection to slaves in the American South. ISBN 0-395-93097-9 DDC 782.4215/82/0268
*1. Lullabies - Texts. 2. Children's songs - Texts. 3. Lullabies. 4. Songs. I. Saport, Linda, ill.*
*TC PZ8.3 .A4165 1999*

**Allan, Karen Kuelthau.** Literacy and learning : strategies for middle and secondary school teachers / Karen Kuelthau Allan, Margery Staman Miller. Boston : Houghton Mifflin, c2000. xix, 522 p. : ill ; 24 cm. Includes bibliographical references (p. 499-511) and index. ISBN 0-395-74646-9 (pbk) DDC 428/.0071/2
*1. Language arts (Secondary) - United States. 2. Language arts - Correlation with content subjects - United States. 3. High school teaching - United States. I. Miller, Margary Staman. II. Title.*
*TC LB1631 .A37 2000*

**Allee, W. C. (Warder Clyde), 1885-1955.**
[Social life of animals]
Cooperation among animals : with human implications / by W.C. Allee. A rev. and amplified ed. of The social life of animals. New York : Schuman, 1951. 233 p. : ill. ; 23 cm. Bibliography: p. [215]-227. DDC 591.55
*1. Animal behavior. I. Title.*
*TC QL751 .A52 1951*

**ALLEGIANCE.** *See* **CITIZENSHIP.**

**ALLEGORY (ART).** *See* **SYMBOLISM IN ART.**

**Allen, Belinda.**
Summerhill at 70 [videorecording]. Princeton, N.J. :
Films for the Humanities, c1992.
*TC LF795.L692953 S9 1992*

**Allen, C. G. (Charles Geoffry)** A manual of European
languages for librarians / C.G. Allen. 2nd ed. New
Providence, NJ : Bowker-Saur, c1999. xiii, 994 p. ; 22
cm. ISBN 1-85739-241-8 (alk. paper) DDC 409/.4
*1. Europe - Languages - Handbooks, manuals, etc. I. Title.*
*TC P380 .A4 1999*

**Allen, Christopher, 1953-** Art in Australia : from
colonization to postmodernism / Christopher Allen.
New York, N.Y. : Thames and Hudson, 1997. 224 p. :
178 ill. (some col.) ; 21 cm. (World of art) Includes
bibliographical references (p. 218) and index. ISBN 0-500-
20301-6
*1. Art, Australian. I. Title. II. Series.*
*TC N7400 .A45 1997*

**Allen, Edith M. (Edith Marion), 1902-.**
Turk, Laurel Herbert, 1903- El español al día. Revised
ed. Lexington, Mass. : D.C. Heath, c1974.
*TC PC4111 .T87 1974*

**Allen, Edith M. (Edith Marion), 1902- joint author.**
Turk, Laurel Herbert, 1903- El español al día. 5th ed.
Lexington, Mass. : D.C. Heath, c1979.
*TC PC4111 .T87 1979*

Turk, Laurel Herbert, 1903- El español al día. 4th ed.
Lexington, Mass., Heath [1973]
*TC PC4112 .T766 1973 Teacher's Ed.*

**Allen, Kate, 1950-.**
Ingulsrud, John E. Learning to read in China.
Lewiston, N.Y. : Lampeter, Wales : Mellen, c1999.
*TC LB1577.C48 I54 1999*

**Allen, Kathleen E.** Systemic leadership : enriching the
meaning of our work / Kathleen E. Allen, Cynthia
Cherrey. Lanham, Md. : University Press of America,
c2000, xiii, 132 p. : ill. ; 23 cm. Includes bibliographical
references and index. ISBN 1-88348-519-3 (cloth : alk. paper)
ISBN 1-88348-520-7 (pbk. : alk. paper) DDC 658.4/092
*1. Leadership. 2. Organizational change. I. Cherrey, Cynthia.*
*II. Title.*
*TC HD57.7 .A42 2000*

**Allen, Lynn, 1958-.**
Active older adults. Champaign, IL : Human Kinetics,
c1999.
*TC GV482.6 .A38 1999*

**Allen-Meares, Paula, 1948-** Social work services in
schools / Paula Allen-Meares, Robert O. Washington,
Betty L. Welsh. 3rd ed. Boston : Allyn and Bacon,
c2000. xi, 354 p. : ill. ; 25 cm. Includes bibliographical
references and index. ISBN 0-205-29147-3 (hb) DDC 371.7/
0973
*1. School social work - United States. I. Washington, R. O.*
*(Robert O.) II. Welsh, Betty L., 1925- III. Title.*
*TC LB3013.4 .A45 2000*

**Allen, Sally.**
Third world peoples, a Gospel perspective. Maryknoll,
NY : Maryknoll Fathers and Brothers, c1987.
*TC F1439.T54 1987*

**ALLIANCE, THERAPEUTIC.** *See* **THERAPEUTIC
ALLIANCE.**

**ALLIANCE, WORKING (PSYCHOTHERAPY).**
*See* **THERAPEUTIC ALLIANCE.**

**ALLIED HEALTH PERSONNEL.** *See*
**OCCUPATIONAL THERAPY ASSISTANTS;
SPEECH THERAPISTS.**

**ALLIED HEALTH PERSONNEL.**
Russell, Graham, 1954- Essential psychology for
nurses and other health professionals. London ; New
York : Routledge, c1999.
*TC R726.7 .R87 1999*

**Allington, Richard L.**
Teaching struggling readers. Newark, Del. :
International Reading Association, c1998.
*TC LB1050.5 .T437 1998*

**Allison, Clinton B.**
McGarrh, Kellie, d. 1995. Kellie McGarrh's hangin'
in tough. New York : P. Lang, c2000.
*TC LA2317.D6185 M34 2000*

**Allison, David B.** Disordered mother or disordered
diagnosis? : : Munchausen by proxy syndrome / David
B. Allison, Mark S. Roberts. Hillsdale, NJ : Analytic
Press, 1998. xxxv, 297 p. ; 24 cm. Includes bibliographical
references and index. ISBN 0-88163-290-2

*1. Munchausen syndrome by proxy. I. Roberts, Mark S. II.*
*Title.*
*TC RC569.5.M83 A38 1998*

**Allison, Desmond.** Language testing and evaluation : an
introductory course / Desmond Allison. Singapore :
Singapore University Press ; Singapore ; River Edge,
N.J. : World Scientific, c1999. x, 255 p. ; 22 cm. Includes
bibliographical references (p. [239]-255) ISBN 9971-69-226-0
(pbk.)
*1. Language and languages - Ability testing. 2. Language and*
*languages - Study and teaching - Evaluation. I. Title.*
*TC P53.4 .A45 1999*

Text in education and society. Singapore : Singapore
University Press ; Singapore ; River Edge, N.J. :
World Scientific, c1998.
*TC P40.8 .T48 1998*

**Allison, Pamela C.** Constructing children's physical
education experiences : understanding the content for
teaching / Pamela C. Allison, Kate R. Barrett.
Boston : Allyn and Bacon, 2000. xiv, 332 p. : ill. ; 23 cm.
Includes bibliographical references and index. ISBN
0-205-17509-0 (alk. paper) DDC 613.7/071/073
*1. Physical education teachers - Training of. 2. Physical*
*education for children - Study and teaching. 3. Constructivism*
*(Education) I. Barrett, Kate R. II. Title.*
*TC GV363 .A512 2000*

**Allison, Sarah E.** Nursing administration in the 21st
century : a self-care theory approach / Sarah E.
Allison, Katherine E. McLaughlin-Renpenning.
Thousand Oaks : Sage Publications, c1999. xxi, 298 p. :
ill. ; 24 cm. Includes bibliographical references and index.
ISBN 0-7619-1455-2 (cloth : acid-free paper) ISBN
0-7619-1456-0 (pbk. : acid-free paper) DDC 362.1/73/068
*1. Nursing services - Administration. 2. Nursing services -*
*Forecasting. 3. Nursing - Philosophy. I. Renpenning, Kathie*
*McLaughlin. II. Title. III. Title: Nursing administration in the*
*twenty-first century*
*TC RT89. A435 1999*

**Allman, Richard M., 1955-.**
The gerontological prism. Amityville, N.Y. :
Baywood Pub., c2000.
*TC HQ1061 .G416 2000*

**ALLOCATION OF TIME.** *See* **TIME
MANAGEMENT.**

**ALLOPATHIC DOCTORS.** *See* **PHYSICIANS.**

**ALLUSIONS.** *See* **TERMS AND PHRASES.**

**Ally G. Gargano Advertising (Firm).**
The filming of a television commercial
[videorecording]. Minneapolis, Minn. : Media Loft,
c1992.
*TC HF6146.T42 F5 1992*

**The Allyn & Bacon sourcebook for college writing
teachers** / [compiled by] James C. McDonald.
Boston ; London : Allyn and Bacon, 2000. 433 p. : ill. ;
21 cm. Includes bibliographical references (p. 426-433). ISBN
0-205-31603-4 DDC 428/.0071/1
*1. English language - Rhetoric - Study and teaching. 2. Report*
*writing - Study and teaching (Higher) I. McDonald, James C.*
*II. Allyn and Bacon. III. Title: Allyn and Bacon sourcebook for*
*college writing teachers IV. Title: Sourcebook for college*
*writing teachers*
*TC PE1404 .A45 2000*

**Allyn and Bacon.**
The Allyn & Bacon sourcebook for college writing
teachers. Boston ; London : Allyn and Bacon, 2000.
*TC PE1404 .A45 2000*

**The Allyn and Bacon guide to peer tutoring.**
Gillespie, Paula. Boston : Allyn & Bacon, c2000.
*TC LB1031.5 .G55 2000*

**The Allyn and Bacon Latin program**
Jenney, Charles. Jenney's second year Latin. Newton,
Mass. : Allyn and Bacon, c1987.
*TC PA2087.5 J461 1987*

Jenney, Charles. Third year Latin. Newton, Mass. :
Allyn and Bacon, c1987.
*TC PA2087.5 J462 1987*

**Allyn and Bacon sourcebook for college writing
teachers.**
The Allyn & Bacon sourcebook for college writing
teachers. Boston ; London : Allyn and Bacon, 2000.
*TC PE1404 .A45 2000*

**ALMS AND ALMSGIVING.** *See* **CHARITIES.**

**Alper, Gerald.** Power plays : their uses and abuses in
human relations / Gerald Alper. San Francisco :
International Scholars Publications, 1998. iii, 112 p. ; 22
cm. Includes bibliographical references (p. 107-108) and index.
ISBN 1-57309-267-3 (hc : alk. paper) ISBN 1-57309-259-2

(pb : alk. paper) DDC 158.2
*1. Control (Psychology) I. Title.*
*TC BF632.5 .A465 1998*

**Alper, Sandra K.** Alternate assessment of students with
disabilities in inclusive settings / Sandra Alper, Diane
Lea Ryndak, Cynthia N. Schloss. Boston : London :
Allyn and Bacon, c2001. xv, 304 p. : ill. ; 24 cm. Includes
bibliographical references and indexes. ISBN 0-205-30615-2
(alk. paper) DDC 371.9/0973
*1. Handicapped children - Education - United States. 2.*
*Educational tests and measurements - United States. 3.*
*Inclusive education - United States. I. Ryndak, Diane Lea,*
*1952- II. Schloss, Cynthia N. III. Title.*
*TC LC4031 .A58 2001*

**ALPHABET.**
Ajmera, Maya. Children from Australia to Zimbabwe.
Watertown, Mass. : Charlesbridge, c1997.
*TC GF48 .A45 1997*

Bea, Holly, 1956- My spiritual alphabet book.
Tiburon, Calif. : H.J. Kramer, c2000.
*TC BL625.5 .B43 1999*

Edwards, Pamela Duncan. Wacky wedding. 1st ed.
New York : Hyperion Books for Children, c1999.
*TC PZ7.E26365 Wac 1999*

J. Paul Getty Museum. A is for artist. Los Angeles : J.
Paul Getty Museum, c1997.
*TC N582.M25 A513 1997*

**ALPHABET - HISTORY.**
Oauknin, Marc-Alain. [Mystères de l'alphabet.
English] The mysteries of the alphabet. 1st ed. New
York : Abbeville Press, c1999.
*TC P211 .O913 1999*

**Alphabet to email.**
Baron, Naomi S. London ; New York : Routledge,
2000.
*TC PE1075 .B28 2000*

**Alpiner, Jerome G., 1932-.**
Rehabilitative audiology. 3rd ed. Philadelphia, PA :
Lippincott Williams & Wilkins, c2000.
*TC RF297 .R44 2000*

**Alstete, Jeffrey W.** Posttenure faculty development :
building a system for faculty improvement and
appreciation / by Jeffrey W. Alstete ; prepared and
published by Jossey-Bass in cooperation with ERIC
Clearinghouse on Higher Education, Association for
the Study of Higher Education (ASHE), The George
Washington University. San Fransisco, [Calif.] :
Jossey-Bass c2000. xv, 133 p. : ill. ; 23 cm. (ASHE-ERIC
higher education report, 0884-0040 ; v. 27, no. 4) Includes
bibliographical references (p. 103-114) and index (p.115-122).
CONTENTS: Forword--Acknowledgments--Why is
development of tenured faculty a concern?--How has higher
education responded to this concern?--Posttenure faculty
development in action--Designing development programs for
tenured faculty--Conclusion--Appendix A: Resources for
faculty development--Appendix B: NUPROF program at the
University of Nebraska, Lincoln--Appendix C: Sample
guidelines for a faculty development plan--References--
Index--ASHE-ERIC Higher Education reports. ISBN 0-7879-
5572-8
*1. College teachers - Tenure - United States. 2. College*
*teachers - Promotions - United States. 3. Universities and*
*colleges - United States - Faculty. I. ERIC Clearinghouse on*
*Higher Education. II. Association for the Study of Higher*
*Education (ASHE). III. George Washington University. IV.*
*Title. V. Series: ASHE-ERIC higher education report ; vol. 27,*
*no. 4.*
*TC LB2335.7 .A47 2000*

**Alston, William P.** Illocutionary acts and sentence
meaning / William P. Alston. Ithaca : Cornell
University Press, 2000. xiii, 327 p. ; 24 cm. Includes
bibliographical references (p. 315-318) and index. ISBN
0-8014-3669-9 (cloth) DDC 306.44
*1. Speech acts (Linguistics) 2. Semantics. 3. Grammar,*
*Comparative and general - Sentences. I. Title.*
*TC P95.55 .A47 2000*

**Altbach, Philip G.**
The international academic profession. Princeton,
N.J. : Carnegie Foundation for the Advancement of
Teaching, c1996.
*TC LB1778 .I54 1996*

**Altenbaugh, Richard J.**
Historical dictionary of American education.
Westport, Conn. : Greenwood Press, 1999.
*TC LB15 .H57 1999*

**ALTERED STATES OF CONSCIOUSNESS.**
Keen, Ernest, 1937- Chemicals for the mind.
Westport, Conn. ; London : Praeger, 2000.
*TC RM315 .K44 2000*

**Alternate assessment of students with disabilities in inclusive settings.**
Alper, Sandra K. Boston : London : Allyn and Bacon, c2001.
*TC LC4031 .A58 2001*

**The alternate session.**
Buse, William Joseph. 1999.
*TC 085 B9603*

**ALTERNATING PERSONALITY.** *See* **MULTIPLE PERSONALITY.**

**Alternative agriculture.**
Thirsk, Joan. Oxford : New York : Oxford University Press, c1997.
*TC S455 .T48 1997*

**ALTERNATIVE DISPUTE RESOLUTION.** *See* **DISPUTE RESOLUTION (LAW).**

**ALTERNATIVE EDUCATION.** *See also* **ALTERNATIVE SCHOOLS.**
Chalker, Christopher S. Effective alternative education programs. Lancaster, Pa. : Technomic, c1999.
*TC LC4091 .C5 1999*

**ALTERNATIVE EDUCATION - UNITED STATES - CASE STUDIES.**
Goodman, Greg S., 1949- Alternatives in education. New York : P. Lang, c1999.
*TC LC46.4 .G66 1999*

**Alternative higher education.** [New York, Human Sciences Press] 7 v. 23 cm. Frequency: Semi annual. v. 1-7, no. 2; fall 1976-spring/summer 1983. "The journal of non-traditional studies." Indexed selectively by: Sociological abstracts 0038-0202. Indexed selectively by: Social welfare, social planning/policy & social development 0195-7988. Indexed in its entirety by: Education index 0013-1385. Indexed selectively by: Current index to journals in education 0011-3565. Continued by: Innovative higher education ISSN: 0742-5627 (DLC)  85646179 (OCoLC)10366072. ISSN 0361-6851 DDC 378.73
*1. Education, Higher - United States - Periodicals. I. Title: Innovative higher education*

**ALTERNATIVE LIFESTYLES - UNITED STATES - HISTORY.**
Smith, William L., 1956- Families and communes. Thousand Oaks, Calif. : Sage Publications, c1999.
*TC HQ971 .S55 1999*

**ALTERNATIVE MEDICINE.** *See* **MENTAL HEALING.**

**ALTERNATIVE MEDICINE.**
Hubbard, L. Ron (La Fayette Ron), 1911- Dianetics. Los Angeles, Calif. : Bridge Publications, c2000.
*TC BP605.S2 H7956 2000*

Libster, Martha. Demonstrating care. Albany, NY : Delmar Thomson Learning, 2000.
*TC RT86 .L535 2000*

**ALTERNATIVE MEDICINE - ENCYCLOPEDIAS.**
Sharma, R. (Rajendra), 1959- The family encyclopedia of health. Boston : Element Books, 1999.
*TC RC81.A2 S53 1999*

**ALTERNATIVE MEDICINE - STUDY AND TEACHING - CANADA - DIRECTORIES.**
Directory of schools for alternative and complementary health care. 2nd ed. Phoenix, AZ : Oryx Press, 1999.
*TC R733.D59 D59 1999*

**ALTERNATIVE MEDICINE - STUDY AND TEACHING - UNITED STATES - DIRECTORIES.**
Directory of schools for alternative and complementary health care. 2nd ed. Phoenix, AZ : Oryx Press, 1999.
*TC R733.D59 D59 1999*

**ALTERNATIVE PUNISHMENTS.** *See* **ALTERNATIVES TO IMPRISONMENT.**

**ALTERNATIVE SCHOOLS.** *See* **ALTERNATIVE EDUCATION; FREE SCHOOLS.**

**ALTERNATIVE SCHOOLS - NEW YORK (STATE) - NEW YORK - SOCIAL ASPECTS.**
Dreyer, Susan T. Student perceptions of their educational experiences at Satellite Academy High School and their former schools. 1999.
*TC 06 no. 11105*

**ALTERNATIVE SCHOOLS - UNITED STATES - CASE STUDIES.**
Goodman, Greg S., 1949- Alternatives in education. New York : P. Lang, c1999.

*TC LC46.4 .G66 1999*
Kennedy, Rosa L., 1938- A school for healing. New York : P. Lang, c1999.
*TC LC46.4 .K46 1999*

**Alternative teacher certification.**
Feistritzer, C. Emily. Washington, D.C. : National Center for Education Information, c2000.
*TC LB1771 .A47 2000*

**Alternatives in education.**
Goodman, Greg S., 1949- New York : P. Lang, c1999.
*TC LC46.4 .G66 1999*

**ALTERNATIVES TO IMPRISONMENT - UNITED STATES.**
Wimsatt, William Upski. No more prisons. [New York] : Soft Skull Press, [2000?]
*TC HV9276.5 .W567x 2000*

**ALTERNATIVES TO INCARCERATION.** *See* **ALTERNATIVES TO IMPRISONMENT.**

**ALTERNATIVES TO INSTITUTIONALIZATION (CORRECTIONS).** *See* **ALTERNATIVES TO IMPRISONMENT.**

**ALTERNATIVES TO PSYCHIATRIC HOSPITALIZATION.** *See* **COMMUNITY MENTAL HEALTH SERVICES.**

**Altick, Richard Daniel, 1915-** The English common reader : a social history of the mass reading public, 1800-1900 / by Richard D. Altick ; with a foreword by Jonathan Rose. 2nd ed. Columbus : Ohio State University Press, [1998], c1957. xx, 448 p. ; 24 cm. Includes bibliographical references (p. 399-427) and index. ISBN 0-8142-0793-6 (alk. paper) ISBN 0-8142-0794-4 (pbk. : alk. paper) DDC 028/.9/0941
*1. Books and reading - Great Britain - History - 19th century. I. Title.*
*TC Z1003.5.G7 A53 1998*

**Altrichter, Herbert.**
Images of educational change. Buckingham [England] ; Philadelphia : Open University Press, 2000.
*TC LB2805 .I415 2000*

**ALTRUISM.**
Integrating community service into nursing education. New York, NY : Springer Pub. Co., c1999.
*TC RT76 .I55 1999*

**ALTRUISTS.** *See* **PHILANTHROPISTS.**

**Alvermann, Donna E.** Popular culture in the classroom : teaching and researching critical media literacy / Donna E. Alvermann, Jennifer S. Moon, Margaret C. Hagood. Newark, Del. : International Reading Association ; Chicago, Ill. : National Reading Conference, c1999. xiii, 158 p. : ill. ; 23 cm. (Literacy studies series) Includes bibliographical references (p. 142-147) and indexes. ISBN 0-87207-245-2 DDC 302.23/07
*1. Media literacy - Study and teaching. 2. Popular culture - Study and teaching. I. Moon, Jennifer S. II. Hagood, Margaret C. III. Title. IV. Series.*
*TC P91.3 .A485 1999*

Reconceptualizing the literacies in adolescents' lives. Mahwah, N.J. : L. Erlbaum Associates, 1998.
*TC LB1631 .R296 1998*

**Alvesson, Mats, 1956-** Reflexive methodology : new vistas for qualitative research / Mats Alvesson and Kaj Sköldberg. London ; Thousand Oaks, Calif. : SAGE, 2000. viii, 319 p. : ill. ; 24 cm. Includes bibliographical references (p. [293]-311) and index. CONTENTS: 1. Introduction: the intellectualization of method -- 2. Data-oriented methods: empiricist techniques and procedures -- 3. Hermeneutics: interpretation and insight -- 4. Critical theory: the political and ideological dimension -- 5. Poststructuralism and postmodernism: destabilizing subject and text -- 6. Language/gender/power: discourse analysis, feminism and genealogy -- 7. On reflexive interpretation: the play of interpretive levels. ISBN 0-8039-7706-9 ISBN 0-8039-7707-7 (pbk.) DDC 001.42 DDC 001.42
*1. Social sciences - Research - Methodology. I. Sköldberg, Kaj, 1942- II. Title.*
*TC H61 .A62 2000*

**Always inventing.**
Matthews, Tom, 1949- Washington, D.C. : National Geographic Society, c1999.
*TC TK6143.B4 M37 1999*

**ALZHEIMER DISEASE.** *See* **ALZHEIMER'S DISEASE.**

**ALZHEIMER DISEASE.**
Mace, Nancy L. The 36-hour day. 3rd ed. Baltimore : Johns Hopkins University Press, c1999.
*TC RC523 .M33 1999*

**ALZHEIMER DISEASE - GENETICS.**
Concepts of Alzheimer disease. Baltimore, Md. : London : Johns Hopkins University Press, 2000.
*TC RC523 .C657 2000*

**ALZHEIMER DISEASE - HISTORY.**
Concepts of Alzheimer disease. Baltimore, Md. : London : Johns Hopkins University Press, 2000.
*TC RC523 .C657 2000*

**ALZHEIMER DISEASE - PSYCHOLOGY.**
Concepts of Alzheimer disease. Baltimore, Md. : London : Johns Hopkins University Press, 2000.
*TC RC523 .C657 2000*

**ALZHEIMER'S ASSOCIATION.**
Concepts of Alzheimer disease. Baltimore, Md. : London : Johns Hopkins University Press, 2000.
*TC RC523 .C657 2000*

**ALZHEIMER'S DEMENTIA.** *See* **ALZHEIMER'S DISEASE.**

**ALZHEIMER'S DISEASE.**
Concepts of Alzheimer disease. Baltimore, Md. : London : Johns Hopkins University Press, 2000.
*TC RC523 .C657 2000*

**ALZHEIMER'S DISEASE - GENETIC ASPECTS.**
Concepts of Alzheimer disease. Baltimore, Md. : London : Johns Hopkins University Press, 2000.
*TC RC523 .C657 2000*

**ALZHEIMER'S DISEASE - PATIENTS - HOME CARE.**
Mace, Nancy L. The 36-hour day. 3rd ed. Baltimore : Johns Hopkins University Press, c1999.
*TC RC523 .M33 1999*

**ALZHEIMER'S DISEASE - SOCIAL ASPECTS.**
Concepts of Alzheimer disease. Baltimore, Md. : London : Johns Hopkins University Press, 2000.
*TC RC523 .C657 2000*

**Amadeo, Jo-Ann.**
Civic education across countries. Amsterdam, the Netherlands : International Association for the Evaluation of Educational Achievement, c1999.
*TC JA86 .C6 1999*

**Amador, Xavier Francisco.**
Insight and psychosis. New York : Oxford University Press, 1998.
*TC RC512 .I49 1998*

**Amanat, Abbas.** Pivot of the universe : Nasir al-Din Shah Qajar and the Iranian Monarchy, 1831-1896 / Abbas Amanat. Berkeley : University of California Press, c1997. xix, 536 p. : ill. map ; 24 cm. Includes bibliographical references (p. 505-518) and index. ISBN 0-520-08321-0 (alk. paper) DDC 955/.04/092
*1. Nāsir al-Dīn Shāh, - Shah of Iran, - 1831-1896. 2. Monarchy - Iran - History - 19th century. 3. Iran - Kings and rulers - Biography. I. Title.*
*TC DS307.N38 A63 1997*

**Amatea, Ellen S., 1944-.**
Brown, Norman M., 1942- Love and intimate relationships. Philadelphia ; Hove [England] : Brunner/Mazel, c2000.
*TC BF575.L8 B75 2000*

**AMATEUR PLAYS.** *See* **CHILDREN'S PLAYS; PAGEANTS.**

**AMATEUR THEATER.** *See* **ACTING; CHILDREN'S PLAYS - PRESENTATION, ETC.**

**Amato, Adrienne.**
First break [videorecording]. Boston, MA : Fanlight Productions, c1997.
*TC RC465 .F5 1997*

First break [videorecording]. Boston, MA : Fanlight Productions, c1997.
*TC RC465 .F5 1997*

First break [videorecording]. Boston, MA : Fanlight Productions, c1997.
*TC RC465 .F5 1997*

**AMAUROSIS.** *See* **BLINDNESS.**

**Amazing mythology.**
January, Brendan, 1972- The New York Public Library amazing mythology. New York : Wiley, 2000.
*TC BL311 .J36 2000*

**The amazing potato.**
Meltzer, Milton, 1915- 1st ed. New York, NY : HarperCollins, c1992.
*TC SB211.P8 M53 1992*

**AMBASSADORS - MEXICO - BIOGRAPHY.**
Llinás Alvarez, Edgar. Vida y obra de Ramón Beteta.

1. ed. México : [s.n.], 1996 (México, D.F. : Impresora Galve)
*TC F1234.B56 L5 1996*

**The ambiguous embrace.**
Glenn, Charles Leslie, 1938- Princeton, N.J. : Princeton University Press, c2000.
*TC HV95 .G54 2000*

**Ambiguous loss.**
Boss, Pauline. Cambridge, Mass. : Harvard University Press, 1999.
*TC BF575.D35 B67 1999*

**AMBULATORY MEDICAL CARE.**
Baker, Susan Keane. Managing patient expectations. San Francisco : Jossey Bass Publishers, 1998.
*TC R727.3 .B28 1998*

**Ameis, Jerry A.** Mathematics on the Internet : a resource for K-12 teachers / Jerry A. Ameis. Upper Saddle River, N.J. : Merrill, 2000. 129 p. : ill. ; 23 cm. Includes bibliographical references. ISBN 0-13-011061-2 DDC 025.06/51
*1. Mathematics - Study and teaching - Computer network resources. 2. Internet (Computer network) I. Title.*
*TC QA41.6 .A64 2000*

**Amelia and Eleanor go for a ride.**
Ryan, Pam Muñoz. New York : Scholastic Press, 1999.
*TC PZ7.R9553 Am 1999*

**America.**
Cayton, Andrew R. L. (Andrew Robert Lee), 1954- Upper Saddle River, N.J. : Prentice Hall, c1998.
*TC E178.1 .C364 1998*

Cayton, Andrew R. L. (Andrew Robert Lee), 1954- Teacher's ed. Upper Saddle River, N.J.. : Prentice Hall, c1998.
*TC E178.1 .C364 1998 Teacher's Ed.*

Cayton, Andrew R. L. (Andrew Robert Lee), 1954- Upper Saddle River, N.J. : Prentice Hall, c1998.
*TC E178.1 .C3643 1998*

Cayton, Andrew R. L. (Andrew Robert Lee), 1954- Upper Saddle River, N.J. : Prentice Hall, c1998.
*TC E178.1 .C3643 1998*

Cayton, Andrew R. L. (Andrew Robert Lee), 1954- Teacher's ed. Upper Saddle River, N.J.. : Prentice Hall, c1998.
*TC E178.1 .C3643 1998 Teacher's Ed.*

Cayton, Andrew R. L. (Andrew Robert Lee), 1954- Upper Saddle River, N.J. : Prentice Hall, c1998.
*TC E178.1 .C3643 1998*

Cayton, Andrew R. L. (Andrew Robert Lee), 1954- Teacher's ed. Upper Saddle River, N.J.. : Prentice Hall, c1998.
*TC E178.1 .C3643 1998 Teacher's Ed.*

Cayton, Andrew R. L. (Andrew Robert Lee), 1954- Upper Saddle River, N.J. : Prentice Hall, c1998.
*TC E178.1 .C364 1998 Teacher's Ed.*

Cayton, Andrew R. L. (Andrew Robert Lee), 1954- Upper Saddle River, N.J. : Prentice Hall, c1998.
*TC E178.1 .C364 1998*

Cayton, Andrew R. L. (Andrew Robert Lee), 1954- Upper Saddle River, N.J.. : Prentice Hall, c1998.
*TC E178.1 .C3645 1998 Teacher's Ed.*

Cayton, Andrew R. L. (Andrew Robert Lee), 1954- Upper Saddle River, N.J. : Prentice Hall, c1998.
*TC E178.1 .C3645 1998*

Cayton, Andrew R. L. (Andrew Robert Lee), 1954- Upper Saddle River, N.J. : Prentice Hall, c1998.
*TC E178.1 .C3645 1998*

Cayton, Andrew R. L. (Andrew Robert Lee), 1954- Teacher's ed. Upper Saddle River, N.J.. : Prentice Hall, c1998.
*TC E178.1 .C364 1998 Teacher's Ed.*

Cayton, Andrew R. L. (Andrew Robert Lee), 1954- Upper Saddle River, N.J.. : Prentice Hall, c1998.
*TC E178.1 .C364 1998*

Cayton, Andrew R. L. (Andrew Robert Lee), 1954- Upper Saddle River, N.J. : Prentice Hall, c1998.
*TC E178.1 .C364 1998*

Cayton, Andrew R. L. (Andrew Robert Lee), 1954- Teacher's ed. Upper Saddle River, N.J.. : Prentice Hall, c1998.
*TC E178.1 .C3644 1998 Teacher's Ed.*

Cayton, Andrew R. L. (Andrew Robert Lee), 1954- Upper Saddle River, N.J. : Prentice Hall, c1998.
*TC E178.1 .C364 1998*

Cayton, Andrew R. L. (Andrew Robert Lee), 1954- Upper Saddle River, N.J. : Prentice Hall, c1998.

*TC E178.1 .C3644 1998*

Cayton, Andrew R. L. (Andrew Robert Lee), 1954- Upper Saddle River, N.J. : Prentice Hall, c1998.
*TC E178.1 .C3644 1998*

Cayton, Andrew R. L. (Andrew Robert Lee), 1954- Upper Saddle River, N.J. : Prentice Hall, c1998.
*TC E178.1 .C3644 1998*

**America in the twentieth century.**
Cayton, Andrew R. L. (Andrew Robert Lee), 1954- America. Upper Saddle River, N.J. : Prentice Hall, c1998.
*TC E178.1 .C364 1998*

Cayton, Andrew R. L. (Andrew Robert Lee), 1954- America. Teacher's ed. Upper Saddle River, N.J.. : Prentice Hall, c1998.
*TC E178.1 .C364 1998 Teacher's Ed.*

Cayton, Andrew R. L. (Andrew Robert Lee), 1954- America. Upper Saddle River, N.J. : Prentice Hall, c1998.
*TC E178.1 .C3643 1998*

Cayton, Andrew R. L. (Andrew Robert Lee), 1954- America. Upper Saddle River, N.J. : Prentice Hall, c1998.
*TC E178.1 .C3643 1998*

Cayton, Andrew R. L. (Andrew Robert Lee), 1954- America. Teacher's ed. Upper Saddle River, N.J.. : Prentice Hall, c1998.
*TC E178.1 .C3643 1998 Teacher's Ed.*

Cayton, Andrew R. L. (Andrew Robert Lee), 1954- America. Upper Saddle River, N.J. : Prentice Hall, c1998.
*TC E178.1 .C3643 1998*

**América indígena.** México. v. ill. 24-30 cm. v. 1- Oct. 1941- . Spanish (with occasional articles in English). Published by the Instituto Indigenista Interamericano. Vols. 1-2, 1941-42, with v.1.
*1. Indians - Periodicals. I. Inter-American Indian Institute.*

**AMERICA - LITERATURES - STUDY AND TEACHING.**
Teaching the literatures of early America. New York : Modern Language Association of America, 1999.
*TC PS186 .T43 1999*

**AMERICA - STATISTICS - HISTORY.**
Mitchell, B. R. (Brian R.) International historical statistics. 4th ed. London : Macmillan Reference ; New YorkGrove Dictionaries[division of : Stockton Press], 1998.
*TC HA1107 .M55 1998*

**America :** the New World in 19th-century painting / edited by Stephan Koja ; with contributions by Nicolai Cikovsky, Jr. ... [et al.]. Munich, Germany ; London ; New York : Prestel, c1999. 296 p. : col. ill. ; 31 cm. "Published on the occasion of an exhibition ... in the Österreichische Galerie Belvedere, Vienna (17 March-20 June, 1999)"--T.p. verso. Includes bibliographical references (p. 290-291) and index. ISBN 3-7913-2088-2 DDC 759.13/09/03407443613
*1. Painting, American - Exhibitions. 2. Painting, Modern - 19th century - United States - Exhibitions. 3. United States - In art - Exhibitions. I. Koja, Stephan. II. Cikovsky, Nicolai. III. Österreichische Galerie Belvedere.*
*TC ND210 .A724 1999*

**America, the West, and liberal education** / edited by Ralph C. Hancock. Lanham, Md. : Rowman & Littlefield, c1999. v, 182 p. ; 24 cm. Includes bibliographical references and index. ISBN 0-8476-9230-2 (cloth : alk. paper) ISBN 0-8476-9231-0 (paper : alk. paper) DDC 370.11/2
*1. Education, Humanistic - United States. 2. Education, Higher - United States - Philosophy. 3. Culture conflict - United States. 4. United States - Intellectual life - 20th century. 5. Civilization, Western. I. Hancock, Ralph C., 1951-*
*TC LC1023 .A44 1999*

**AMERICAN ABORIGINES.** *See* INDIANS; INDIANS OF NORTH AMERICA.

**AMERICAN ADVENTURE STORIES.** *See* ADVENTURE STORIES, AMERICAN.

**American Alliance for Health, Physical Education, Recreation, and Dance.**
Physical Best (Program) Physical Best activity guide. Champaign, IL : Human Kinetics, c1999.
*TC GV365 .P4993 1999*

Physical Best (Program) Physical education for lifelong fitness. Champaign, Ill. : Human Kinetics, c1999.

*TC GV365 .P4992 1999*

**AMERICAN ARCHITECTURE.** *See* ARCHITECTURE, AMERICAN.

**American Arithmetic.**
Upton, Clifford Brewster. 1877- 2nd ed. New York, N.Y. : American Book Company, 1963.
*TC QA103 .U67 1963*

**The American art museum.**
Einreinhofer, Nancy. London : New York : Leicester University Press, 1997.
*TC N510 .E45 1997*

**American artists in their New York studios.**
Götz, Stephan, 1960- [New Yorker Künstler in ihren Ateliers. English] Cambridge [Mass.] : Center for Conservation and Technical Studies, Harvard University Art Museums ; Stuttgart : Daco-Verlag Günter Bläse, c1992.
*TC N6535.N5 G6813 1992*

**AMERICAN ARTS.** *See* ARTS, AMERICAN.

**American Assembly.**
American Assembly (93rd : 1998 : Los Angeles, Calif.) Trust, service, and the common purpose. Indianapolis, IN : Indiana University Center on Philanthropy ; New York, NY : American Assembly, [1998]
*TC HD62.6 .A44 1998*

Health care and its costs. 1st ed. New York : Norton, c1987.
*TC RA395.A3 H392 1987*

**American Assembly (93rd : 1998 : Los Angeles, Calif.)** Trust, service, and the common purpose : philanthropy and the nonprofit sector in a changing America / the Ninety-third American Assembly, April 23-26, 1998, the Getty Center, Los Angeles, California ; [co-sponsored by] Indiana University, Center on Philanthropy [and] the American Assembly, Columbia University. Indianapolis, IN : Indiana University Center on Philanthropy ; New York, NY : American Assembly, [1998] 36 p. ; 22 cm. Cover title. "Final report of the Ninety-third American Assembly"--P. 5.
*1. Nonprofit organizations - United States. 2. Charities - United States. I. American Assembly. II. Indiana University. Center on Philanthropy. III. Title. IV. Title: Philanthropy and the nonprofit sector in a changing America.*
*TC HD62.6 .A44 1998*

**American Association for Adult Education.**
[Journal of adult education (New York, N.Y.)] Journal of adult education. New York : American Association for Adult Education, 1929-[1941]

Journal of the American Association for Adult Education. New York, N.Y. : The Association, [1926-1928]

**American Association for Adult Education. Annual report of the director.**
[Journal of adult education (New York, N.Y.)] Journal of adult education. New York : American Association for Adult Education, 1929-[1941]

**American Association for Applied Psychology.**
Journal of consulting psychology. [Lancaster, Pa., etc.] American Psychological Association.

**American Association for Comprehensive Health Planning.**
American journal of health planning. [Alexandria, Va., American Association for Comprehensive Health Planning]

**American Association for Health, Physical Education, and Recreation.**
The Journal of health and physical education. Ann Arbor, Mich., : American Physical Education Association.

**American Association for State and Local History.**
Alexander, Edward P. (Edward Porter), 1907- The museum in America. Walnut Creek : AltaMira Press, c1997.
*TC AM11 .A55 1997*

Ideas and images. Walnut Creek, CA : AltaMira Press, 1997.
*TC E172 .I34 1997*

**American Association for State and Local History book series**
Alexander, Edward P. (Edward Porter), 1907- The museum in America. Walnut Creek : AltaMira Press, c1997.
*TC AM11 .A55 1997*

Ideas and images. Walnut Creek, CA : AltaMira Press, 1997.

*TC E172 .I34 1997*

**American Association for the Study of Higher Education.**
Speck, Bruce W. Grading students' classroom writing. Washington, DC : Graduate School of Education and Human Development, The George Washington University, 2000.
*TC LB1576 .S723 2000*

**American Association for the Study of the Feeble-Minded.**
Journal of psycho-asthenics. Faribault, Minn. : Association of American Institutions for Feeble-Minded, [1896-1918]

**American Association for the Study of the Feeble-Minded. Proceedings and addresses.**
Journal of psycho-asthenics. Faribault, Minn. : Association of American Institutions for Feeble-Minded, [1896-1918]

**American Association of Colleges for Teacher Education.**
Critical knowledge for diverse teachers & learners. Washington, DC : AACTE : ERIC, c1997.
*TC LB1715 .C732 1997*

**American Association of Collegiate Registrars and Admissions Officers.**
Bulletin of the American Association of Collegiate Registrars. Philadelphia, American Association of College Registrars.

Journal of the American Association of Collegiate Registrars. Athens, Ohio [etc.] American Association of College Registrars.

Misrepresentation in the marketplace and beyond. Washington, DC : American Association of Collegiate Registrars and Admissions Officers, 1996.
*TC LB2331.615.U6 M57 1996*

**American Association of Collegiate Registrars. Bulletin of the American Association of Collegiate Registrars.**
Journal of the American Association of Collegiate Registrars. Athens, Ohio [etc.] American Association of College Registrars.

**American Association of Collegiate Registrars. Journal of the American Association of Collegiate Registrars.**
Bulletin of the American Association of Collegiate Registrars. Philadelphia, American Association of College Registrars.

**American Association of Community and Junior Colleges.**
Community and junior college journal. Washington, D.C. : American Association of Community and Junior Colleges, 1972-1985.

**American Association of Industrial Nurses.**
Industrial nursing. [Chicago : Industrial Medicine Pub. Co.,

**American Association of Junior Colleges.**
Junior college journal. Washington, D.C. [etc.]

**American Association of Museums.**
Ullberg, Alan D. Museum trusteeship. Washington : American Association of Museums, 1981.
*TC AM121 .U44*

**American Association of School Administrators.**
An educators' guide to schoolwide reform. Arlington, Va. : Educational Research Service, c1999.
*TC LB2806.35 .E38 1999*

**American Association of Suicidology.**
Life-threatening behavior. [New York, Behavioral Publications, inc.]

**AMERICAN AUTHORS.** *See* **AUTHORS, AMERICAN.**

**AMERICAN BISON - JUVENILE LITERATURE.**
Hazen-Hammond, Susan. Thunder Bear and Ko. 1st ed. New York : Dutton Children's Books, 1999.
*TC E99.T35 H36 1999*

**AMERICAN BLACK DIALECT.** *See* **BLACK ENGLISH.**

**AMERICAN BUFFALO.** *See* **AMERICAN BISON.**

**The American century.**
Haskell, Barbara. New York : Whitney Museum of American Art in association with W.W. Norton, c1999.
*TC N6512 .H355 1999*

**American Ceramic Society.**
Ceramic innovations. Westerville, Ohio : American Ceramic Society, 1999.

*TC TP807 .C473 1999*

**American Child Health Association.**
Child health bulletin. New York, American Child Health Association.

**AMERICAN CHILDREN'S LITERATURE.** *See* **CHILDREN'S LITERATURE, AMERICAN.**

**AMERICAN CHILDREN'S POETRY.** *See* **CHILDREN'S POETRY, AMERICAN.**

**AMERICAN CHILDREN'S STORIES.** *See* **CHILDREN'S STORIES, AMERICAN.**

**AMERICAN CHRISTMAS PLAYS.** *See* **CHRISTMAS PLAYS, AMERICAN.**

**An American chronology.**
Bornstein, Jerry. New York : Neal-Schuman Publishers, 2000.
*TC E169.1 .B758 2000*

**AMERICAN CIVIL WAR, 1861-1865.** *See* **UNITED STATES - HISTORY - CIVIL WAR, 1861-1865.**

**American college bulletin.**
[Christian education (Chicago, Ill.)] Christian education. Chicago : [Council of Church Boards of Education in the United States of America, -1952]

**The American college in the nineteenth century** / edited by Roger Geiger. 1st ed. Nashville : Vanderbilt University Press, 2000. ix, 363 p. : ill. ; 24 cm. (Vanderbilt issues in higher education) Includes bibliographical references (p. [277]-358) and index. CONTENTS: Introduction: New Themes in the History of Nineteenth-Century Colleges / Roger L. Geiger -- Curriculum and Enrollment: Assessing the Popularity of Antebellum Colleges / David B. Potts -- The Rights of Man and the Rites of Youth: Fraternity and Riot at Eighteenth-Century Harvard / Leon Jackson -- College As It Was in the Mid-Nineteenth Century / Roger L. Geiger and Julie Ann Bubolz -- "We Desired Our Future Rulers to Be Educated Men": South Carolina College, the Defense of Slavery, and the Development of Secessionist Politics / Michael Sugrue -- Agency, Denominations, and the Western Colleges, 1830-1860: Some Connections between Evangelicalism and American Higher Education / James Findlay -- The Era of Multipurpose Colleges in American Higher Education, 1850-1890 / Roger L. Geiger -- The Rise and Fall of Useful Knowledge: Higher Education for Science, Agriculture, and the Mechanic Arts, 1850-1875 / Roger L. Geiger -- "A Salutary Rivalry": The Growth of Higher Education for Women in Oxford, Ohio, 1855-1867 / Margaret A. Nash -- The "Superior Instruction of Women," 1836-1890 / Roger L. Geiger -- Noah Porter Writ Large? Reflections on the Modernization of American Higher Education and Its Critics, 1866-1916 / Peter Dobkin Hall -- The German Model and the Graduate School: The University of Michigan and the Origin Myth of the American University / James Turner and Paul Bernard -- CONTENTS: A "Curious Working of Cross Purposes" in the Founding of the University of Chicago / Willard J. Pugh -- The Crisis of the Old Order: The Colleges in the 1890s / Roger L. Geiger. ISBN 0-8265-1336-0 (cloth : alk. paper) ISBN 0-8265-1364-6 (paper : alk. paper) DDC 378.73 DDC 378.73
*1. Education, Higher - United States - History - 19th century. 2. Universities and colleges - United States - History - 19th century. I. Geiger, Roger L., 1943- II. Series.*
*TC LA227.1 .A64 2000*

**American College of Sports Medicine.**
Medicine and science in sports. Madison, Wisc.

**American cookery.**
The Boston Cooking School magazine of culinary science and domestic economics. Boston : Boston Cooking-School Magazine, [1896]-1914.

**American Council for the Arts.**
Nancy Hanks lecture on arts and public policy. [New York, NY] : American Council for the Arts, <1988->
*TC NX730 .N25*

**American Council on Education.**
To touch the future. Washington, D.C. : American Council on Education, c1999.
*TC LB1738 .T6 1999*

**American Council on Education/Oryx Press series on higher education**
Bogue, E. Grady (Ernest Grady), 1935- Exploring the heritage of American higher education. Phoenix, Ariz. : Oryx Press, 2000.
*TC LA227.4 .B66 2000*

Civic responsibility and higher education. Phoenix, Az. : Oryx Press, 2000.
*TC LC1091 .C5289 2000*

Lenington, Robert L. Managing higher education as a business. Phoenix, Ariz. : Oryx Press, 1996.

*TC LB2341 .L426 1996*

Postbaccalaureate futures. Phoenix, AZ : Oryx Press, 2000.
*TC LB2371.4 .P68 2000*

**American Council on the Teaching of Foreign Languages.**
Foreign language standards. Lincolnwood, Ill., U.S.A. : National Textbook Company in conjunction with the American Council on the Teaching of Foreign Languages, c1999.
*TC P53 .F674 1999*

**AMERICAN DRAMA.** *See* **CHRISTMAS PLAYS, AMERICAN; PUPPET PLAYS, AMERICAN.**

**American dream [videorecording].**
Norman Rockwell's world -- an American dream [videorecording]. [Chicago, Ill] : Home Vision, 1987, c1972.
*TC ND237.R68 N6 1987*

**American dreamtime.**
Drummond, Lee, 1944- Lanham, Md. : Littlefield Adams Books, 1996.
*TC PN1995.9.M96 D78 1996*

**American economic security.** Washington, Chamber of Commerce of the United States of America. 13 v. 23 cm. Frequency: Bimonthly. v. 1-13; Jan. 1944-Nov./Dec. 1956. Other title: AES, American economic security. "The business journal of economic security and social legislation" (varies). Includes the proceedings of the National Social Security Conference. ISSN 0098-1680 DDC 331.2544
*1. Social security - Periodicals. 2. Social security - United States - Periodicals. 3. Public welfare - Periodicals. 4. Public welfare - United States - Periodicals. 5. Economic history - Periodicals. 6. United States - Economic conditions - Periodicals. 7. United States. - Social Security Board - Periodicals. 8. United States. - Social Security Administration - Periodicals. I. Chamber of Commerce of the United States of America. II. National Social Security Conference. Proceedings. III. Title: AES, American economic security*

**American education annual.** Detroit : Gale, c1999- v. 804 p. : ill. ; 29 cm. Frequency: Annual. 1997-1998- . AEA. "Trends and issues in the educational community." Vols. for 1997/1998- called also 1st- ed. ISSN 1522-1237
*1. Education - United States - Evaluation - Periodicals. 2. Education - Research - United States - Periodicals. I. Gale Research Inc. II. Title: AEA*
*TC LB1028.25.U6 A44*

**American education fellowship. Commission on the Secondary school curriculum.**
Thayer, Vivian Trow, 1886- Reorganizing secondary education; New York, Appleton-Century [c1939]
*TC LB1607 .T5*

**American education :** Yesterday, today, and tomorrow / edited by Thomas L. Good : editor for the Society, Margaret Early. Chicago, Ill. : NSSE : Distributed by the University of Chicago Press, 2000. xiii, 346 p. ; 24 cm. (Ninety-ninth yearbook of the National Society for the Study of Education, 0077-5762 ; pt. 2) ISBN 0-226-60171-4
*1. Education - United States - History - 20th century. I. Good, Thomas L., 1943- II. Early, Margaret. III. National Society for the Study of Education. IV. Title. V. Series: Yearbook of the National Society for the Study of Education ; 99th, pt. 2.*
*TC LB5 .N25 99th pt. 2*

**American educational digest :** the school executives magazine. [Crawfordsville, Ind. : Educational Digest Co., 1923-1928] 7 v. : ill. ; 29 cm. Frequency: Monthly. [Vol. 42, no. 5] (Jan. 1923)-[v. 48, no. 4] (Dec. 1928). Title from cover. Continues: Educational digest (DLC)sf 85001136 (OCoLC)7981226. Continued by: School executives magazine (DLC)sf 85001134 (OCoLC)2496312.
*1. Education - Periodicals. 2. Education - United States - Periodicals. I. Title: Educational digest II. Title: School executives magazine*

**AMERICAN ENGLISH.** *See* **ENGLISH LANGUAGE - UNITED STATES.**

**American Enterprise Institute for Public Policy Research.**
Meeting human needs, toward a new public philosophy. Washington : American Enterprise Institute for Public Policy Research, c1982.
*TC HD60.5.U5 M427 1982*

**American ethnic literatures.**
Peck, David R. Pasadena, Calif. : Salem Press, c1992.
*TC Z1229.E87 P43 1992*

**American Eugenics Society.**
Eugenics quarterly. New York : American Eugenics Society, [1954]-c1968.

**The American family.**
Cavan, Ruth Shonle, 1896- 3d ed. New York, Crowell [1963]
*TC HQ535 .C33 1963*

**American Federation of Teachers.**
Changing education. Detroit [etc.]

An educators' guide to schoolwide reform. Arlington, Va. : Educational Research Service, c1999.
*TC LB2806.35 .E38 1999*

**American Federation of Teachers. Local 1078 (Berkeley, Calif.).**
The classroom teacher. Berkeley, Calif., Berkeley Federation of Teachers Local 1078.

**AMERICAN FICTION.** *See* **ADVENTURE STORIES, AMERICAN; CHILDREN'S STORIES, AMERICAN; SCIENCE FICTION, AMERICAN; SHORT STORIES, AMERICAN; YOUNG ADULT FICTION, AMERICAN.**

**AMERICAN FICTION - HISTORY AND CRITICISM.**
Keroes, Jo. Tales out of school. Carbondale : Southern Illinois University Press, c1999.
*TC PS374.T43 K47 1999*

**AMERICAN FICTION - STORIES, PLOTS, ETC.**
Herald, Diana Tixier. Genreflecting. 5th ed. Englewood, CO : Libraries Umlimited, 2000.
*TC PS374.P63 H47 2000*

**American Foundation for the Blind.**
Hand in hand [videorecording]. New York, N.Y. : AFB Press, c1995.
*TC HV1597.2 .H3 1995*

**American Foundation for the Blind presents ...**
Hand in hand [videorecording]. New York, N.Y. : AFB Press, c1995.
*TC HV1597.2 .H3 1995*

**American governance and public policy.**
Mintrom, Michael, 1963- Policy entrepreneurs and school choice. Washington, DC : Georgetown University Press, c2000.
*TC LB1027.9 .M57 2000*

**American Guidance Service algebra.**
Haenisch, Siegfried AGS algebra. Circle Pines, Minn. : AGS, American Guidance Service, c1998.
*TC QA152.2 .H33 1998*

Haenisch, Siegfried AGS algebra. Teacher's ed. Circle Pines, Minn. : AGS, American Guidance Service, c1998.
*TC QA152.2 .H33 1998 Teacher's Ed.*

Haenisch, Siegfried AGS algebra. Teacher's ed. Circle Pines, Minn. : AGS, American Guidance Service, c1998.
*TC QA152.2 .H33 1998 Teacher's Ed.*

Haenisch, Siegfried AGS algebra. Teacher's ed. Circle Pines, Minn. : AGS, American Guidance Service, c1998.
*TC QA152.2 .H33 1998 Teacher's Ed.*

**American Guidance Service basic English composition.**
Walker, Bonnie L. AGS basic English composition. Circle Pines, Minn. : American Guidance Service, c1997.
*TC PE1408 .W34 1997*

Walker, Bonnie L. AGS basic English composition. Teacher's ed. Circle Pines, Minn. : American Guidance Service, c1997.
*TC PE1408 .W34 1997 Teacher's Ed.*

Walker, Bonnie L. AGS basic English composition. Teacher's ed. Circle Pines, Minn. : American Guidance Service, c1997.
*TC PE1408 .W34 1997 Teacher's Ed.*

Walker, Bonnie L. AGS basic English composition. Teacher's ed. Circle Pines, Minn. : American Guidance Service, c1997.
*TC PE1408 .W34 1997 Teacher's Ed.*

**American Guidance Service basic English grammar.**
Walker, Bonnie L. AGS basic English grammar. Circle Pines, Minn. : AGS, American Guidance Service, c1997.
*TC PE1112 .W34 1997*

Walker, Bonnie L. AGS basic English grammar. Teacher's ed. Circle Pines, Minn. : AGS, American Guidance Service, c1997.
*TC PE1112 .W34 1997 Teacher's Ed.*

**American Guidance Service basic math skills.**
Treff, August V. AGS basic math skills. Circle Pines, Minn. : AGS, American Guidance Service, c1997.

*TC QA107 .T73 1997*

Treff, August V. AGS basic math skills. Teacher's ed. Circle Pines, Minn. : AGS, American Guidance Service, c1997.
*TC QA107 .T73 1997 Teacher's Ed.*

**American Guidance Service earth science.**
Marshall, Robert H. AGS earth science. Circle Pines, Minn. : AGS, American Guidance Service, c1997.
*TC QE28 .M37 1997*

Marshall, Robert H. AGS earth science. Teacher's ed. Circle Pines, Minn. : AGS, American Guidance Service, c1997.
*TC QE28 .M37 1997 Teacher's Ed.*

**American Guidance Service English for the world of work.**
Knox, Carolyn W. AGS English for the world of work. Circle Pines, Minn. : American Guidance Service, c1997.
*TC PE1127.W65 K66 1997*

Knox, Carolyn W. AGS English for the world of work. Teacher's ed. Circle Pines, Minn. : American Guidance Service, c1997.
*TC PE1127.W65 K66 1997 Teacher's Ed.*

**American Guidance Service English to use.**
Trautman, Barbara A. AGS English to use. Teacher's ed. Circle Pines, Minn. : AGS, American Guidance Service, c1998.
*TC PE1121 .T72 1998 Teacher's Ed.*

Trautman, Barbara A. AGS English to use. Circle Pines, Minn. : AGS, American Guidance Service, c1998.
*TC PE1121 .T72 1998*

**American Guidance Service physical science.**
Marshall, Robert H. AGS physical science. Circle Pines, Minn. : AGS, American Guidance Service, c1997.
*TC QC23 .M37 1997*

Marshall, Robert H. AGS physical science. Teacher's ed. Circle Pines, Minn. : AGS, American Guidance Service, c1997.
*TC QC23 .M37 1997 Teacher's Ed.*

**American Guidance Service pre-algebra.**
Haenisch, Siegfried AGS pre-algebra. Circle Pines, Minn. : AGS, American Guidance Service, c1998.
*TC QA107 .H33 1998*

Haenisch, Siegfried AGS pre-algebra. Teacher's ed. Circle Pines, Minn. : AGS, American Guidance Service, c1998.
*TC QA107 .H33 1998 Teacher's Ed.*

Haenisch, Siegfried AGS pre-algebra. Teacher's ed. Circle Pines, Minn. : AGS, American Guidance Service, c1998.
*TC QA107 .H33 1998 Teacher's Ed.*

Haenisch, Siegfried AGS pre-algebra. Teacher's ed. Circle Pines, Minn. : AGS, American Guidance Service, c1998.
*TC QA107 .H33 1998 Teacher's Ed.*

**American Guidance Service United States government.**
Smith, Jane W. (Jane Wilcox) AGS United States government. Circle Pines, Minn. : AGS, American Guidance Service, 1997.
*TC JK40 .S639 1997*

Smith, Jane W. (Jane Wilcox) AGS United States government. Teacher's ed. Circle Pines, Minn. : AGS, American Guidance Service, 1997.
*TC JK40 .S639 1997 Teacher's Ed.*

**American Guidance Service United States history.**
King, Wayne E. AGS United States history. Teacher's ed. Circle Pines, Minn. : AGS, American Guidance Service, c1998.
*TC E175.8 .K56 1998 Teacher's Ed.*

Napp, John L. AGS United States history. Circle Pines, Minn. : AGS, American Guidance Service, c1998.
*TC E178.1 .N36 1998*

**The American Heritage dictionary of the English language.** 4th ed. Boston : Houghton Mifflin, 2000. xxxv, 2074 p. : col. ; 29 cm. ISBN 0-395-82517-2 (hardcover) ISBN 0-618-08230-1 (hardcover with CD ROM) DDC 423
*1. English language - Dictionaries.*
*TC PE1628 .A623 2000*

**American Historical Association.**
Historical outlook. Philadelphia, Pa. : McKinley Pub. Co., c1918-c1933.

**AMERICAN HISTORY.** *See* **UNITED STATES - HISTORY.**

**American history, grades 7-12.**
Instructional Objectives Exchange. Los Angeles : The Exchange. [1968?]
*TC E175.8.I56*

**American Indian Historical Society.**
The Indian historian. [San Francisco, American Indian Historical Society]

**American Indian lives**
Snell, Alma Hogan. Grandmother's grandchild. Lincoln : University of Nebraska Press, c2000.
*TC E99.C92 S656 2000*

**AMERICAN INDIANS.** *See* **INDIANS; INDIANS OF NORTH AMERICA.**

**American Institute of Graphic Arts.**
Design culture. New York : Allworth Press : American Institute of Graphic Arts, c1997.
*TC NC998.5.A1 D46 1997*

Looking closer 2. New York : Allworth Press : American Institute of Graphic Arts, c1997.
*TC NC997 .L632 1997*

Looking closer. New York : Allworth Press : American Institute of Graphic Arts ; Saint Paul, MN : Distributor, Consortium Book Sales & Distribution, c1994.
*TC NC997 .L63 1994*

**American Institutes for Research.**
An educators' guide to schoolwide reform. Arlington, Va. : Educational Research Service, c1999.
*TC LB2806.35 .E38 1999*

**American Jewish desk reference** / American Jewish Historical Society. 1st ed. New York : Random House, 1999. xiv, 642 p. : ill. ; 25 cm. "Produced by the Philip Lief Group, Inc." Includes bibliographical references and index. CONTENTS: Pt. 1. History of the Jews in America -- Pt. 2. Judaism and Community in America -- Pt. 3. Rituals, Celebrations, Holidays, and Family Life -- Pt. 4. Law, Government, and Politics -- Pt. 5. American Zionism and United States Relations with Israel -- Pt. 6. Business, Labor, and Finance -- Pt. 7. Education and Intellectual Life -- Pt. 8. Sports and Games -- Pt. 9. Art, Architecture, and Photography -- Pt. 10. Music, Dance, and Theater -- Pt. 11. Radio, Television, and Film -- Pt. 12. Books, Newspapers, and Magazines -- Pt. 13. Language and Literature -- Pt. 14. Science, Medicine, and Social Science -- App. 1. Finding Out about Jews Around the World. ISBN 0-375-40243-8 DDC 973/.04924/003 DDC 973/.04924/003
*1. Jews - United States - Encyclopedias. 2. Judaism - United States - Encyclopedias. 3. United States - Civilization - Jewish influences - Encyclopedias. I. American Jewish Historical Society. II. Philip Lief Group.*
*TC E184.35 .A44 1999*

**American Jewish Historical Society.**
American Jewish desk reference. 1st ed. New York : Random House, 1999.
*TC E184.35 .A44 1999*

**American journal of care for cripples.** New York : Douglas McMurtie, 1914-1919. 8 v. : ill. ; 30 cm. Frequency: Monthly, in 2 vol. a year, 1918-June 1919. Former frequency: Quarterly, in 2 vol. a year, 1917. Former frequency: Quarterly, 1914-1916. v. 1, no. 1-v. 8, no. 6 (1914-[June 1919]). "Bibliographical notes" in v. 1-3, 7-8. Official organ of the Federation of Associations for Cripples and the Welfare Commission for Cripples.
*1. Physically handicapped - Periodicals. 2. Physically handicapped - Bibliography - Periodicals. 3. Handicapped - periodicals. I. Welfare Commission for Cripples (U.S.) II. Federation of Associations for Cripples (U.S.)*

**American journal of health planning.** [Alexandria, Va., American Association for Comprehensive Health Planning] 26 cm. v. 1- July 1976- . Official journal of the American Association for Comprehensive Health Planning. ISSN 0363-7719
*1. Health Planning - periodicals. I. American Association for Comprehensive Health Planning.*

**American journal of practical nursing v. 1-3, Mar. 1965-67.**
Bedside nurse. New York, National Federation of Licensed Practical Nurses, Inc., 1968-72.

**AMERICAN JOURNAL OF SOCIOLOGY - HISTORY.**
Abbott, Andrew. Department & discipline. Chicago, IL : University of Chicago Press, c1999.
*TC HM22.U5 A23 1999*

**AMERICAN LANGUAGE.** *See* **ENGLISH LANGUAGE - UNITED STATES.**

AMERICAN LITERATURE. *See* AMERICAN
FICTION; AMERICAN POETRY;
CHILDREN'S LITERATURE, AMERICAN;
SLAVES' WRITINGS, AMERICAN.

AMERICAN LITERATURE - 1783-1850 -
HISTORY AND CRITICISM.
Brooks, Van Wyck, 1886-1963. The world of
Washington Irving. [New York] E. P. Dutton & co.,
inc. [1944]
*TC PS208 .B7 1944*

AMERICAN LITERATURE - 1783-1850 - STUDY
AND TEACHING.
Teaching the literatures of early America. New York :
Modern Language Association of America, 1999.
*TC PS186 .T43 1999*

AMERICAN LITERATURE - 19TH CENTURY -
HISTORY AND CRITICISM.
MacCann, Donnarae. White supremacy in children's
literature. New York : Garland Pub., 1998.
*TC PS173.N4 M33 1998*

AMERICAN LITERATURE - AFRO-AMERICAN
AUTHORS. *See also* AFRO-AMERICAN
AUTHORS.
The Norton anthology of African American literature.
1st ed. New York : W.W. Norton & Co., c1997.
*TC PS508.N3 N67 1996*

AMERICAN LITERATURE - AFRO-AMERICAN
AUTHORS - BIO-BIBLIOGRAPHY -
DICTIONARIES.
African American authors, 1745-1945. Westport,
Conn. : Greenwood Press, 2000.
*TC PS153.N5 A32 2000*

AMERICAN LITERATURE - AFRO-AMERICAN
AUTHORS - DICTIONARIES.
African American authors, 1745-1945. Westport,
Conn. : Greenwood Press, 2000.
*TC PS153.N5 A32 2000*

AMERICAN LITERATURE - COLONIAL
PERIOD, CA. 1600-1775 - STUDY AND
TEACHING.
Teaching the literatures of early America. New York :
Modern Language Association of America, 1999.
*TC PS186 .T43 1999*

AMERICAN LITERATURE - CONGRESSES.
American studies in eastern Africa. Nairobi : Nairobi
University Press, 1993.
*TC E172.9 .A47 1993*

AMERICAN LITERATURE - EARLY 19TH
CENTURY - HISTORY AND CRITICISM.
Brooks, Van Wyck, 1886-1963. The world of
Washington Irving, Philadelphia, Blakiston, 1944.
*TC PS208 .B7 1944a*

AMERICAN LITERATURE - EXAMINATIONS -
STUDY GUIDES.
Cracking the GRE literature in English subject test.
New York : Random House, 1996-
*TC LB2367.4 .L58*

AMERICAN LITERATURE - HISTORY AND
CRITICISM.
Berman, Jeffrey, 1945- Surviving literary suicide.
Amherst : University of Massachusetts Press, c1999.
*TC PS169.S85 B47 1999*

Shattuck, Roger. Candor and perversion. 1st ed. New
York : W.W. Norton, c1999.
*TC PN52 .S53 1999*

True, Michael. An energy field more intense than war.
1st ed. Syracuse, N.Y. : Syracuse University Press,
1995.
*TC PS169.N65 T78 1995*

AMERICAN LITERATURE - HISTORY AND
CRITICISM - THEORY, ETC.
Caughie, Pamela L., 1953- Passing and pedagogy.
Urbana : University of Illinois Press, c1999.
*TC PN61 .C38 1999*

AMERICAN LITERATURE - ITALIAN
AMERICAN AUTHORS - HISTORY AND
CRITICISM.
The Italian American heritage. New York : Garland
Pub., 1999.
*TC E184.I8 I675 1999*

AMERICAN LITERATURE - MINORITY
AUTHORS.
Coming of age in America. New York : New Press :
Distributed by W.W. Norton, c1994.
*TC PS509.M5 C66 1994*

AMERICAN LITERATURE - MINORITY
AUTHORS - BIBLIOGRAPHY.

Peck, David R. American ethnic literatures. Pasadena,
Calif. : Salem Press, c1992.
*TC Z1229.E87 P43 1992*

AMERICAN LITERATURE - MINORITY
AUTHORS - STUDY AND TEACHING.
Teaching the literatures of early America. New York :
Modern Language Association of America, 1999.
*TC PS186 .T43 1999*

AMERICAN LITERATURE - NEGRO AUTHORS.
*See* AMERICAN LITERATURE - AFRO-
AMERICAN AUTHORS.

AMERICAN LITERATURE - PUERTO RICAN
AUTHORS.
Growing up Puerto Rican. 1st ed. New York :
Morrow, c1997.
*TC PS508.P84 G76 1997*

AMERICAN LITERATURE - REVOLUTIONARY
PERIOD, 1775-1783 - STUDY AND
TEACHING.
Teaching the literatures of early America. New York :
Modern Language Association of America, 1999.
*TC PS186 .T43 1999*

AMERICAN LITERATURE - STUDY AND
TEACHING.
Berman, Jeffrey, 1945- Surviving literary suicide.
Amherst : University of Massachusetts Press, c1999.
*TC PS169.S85 B47 1999*

AMERICAN LITERATURE - WHITE AUTHORS -
HISTORY AND CRITICISM.
MacCann, Donnarae. White supremacy in children's
literature. New York : Garland Pub., 1998.
*TC PS173.N4 M33 1998*

AMERICAN LITERATURES. *See* AMERICA -
LITERATURES.

**American Mathematical Society.**
Bulletin (new series) of the American Mathematical
Society. Providence, R.I. : The Society, 1979-

**American medical education in the 20th century.**
Ludmerer, Kenneth M. Time to heal. Oxford ; New
York : Oxford University Press, 1999.
*TC R745 .L843 1999*

**American Museum of Natural History.**
Epidemic!. New York : The New Press ; New York :
Distributed by W.W. Norton, c1999.
*TC RA651 .E596 1999*

**The American nation.**
Davidson, James West. Annotated teacher's ed. Upper
Saddle River, N.J. : Prentice Hall, c1997.
*TC E178.1 .D22 1997 Teacher's Ed.*

Davidson, James West. Upper Saddle River, N.J. :
Prentice Hall, c1997.
*TC E178.1 .D22 1997*

Davidson, James West. Annotated teacher's ed. Upper
Saddle River, N.J. : Prentice Hall, c1998.
*TC E178.1 .D22 1998 Teacher's Ed.*

**The American nation** : student study guide. Upper
Saddle River, N.J. : Prentice Hall, c1998. 271 p. : ill. ;
28 cm. Student study guide, the American nation. ISBN 0-13-
432238-X
*1. United States - History - Problems, exercises, etc. I. Title. II.
Title: Student study guide, the American nation.*
*TC E178.1 .D22 1998 Study Guide*

AMERICAN NATIONAL CHARACTERISTICS.
*See* NATIONAL CHARACTERISTICS,
AMERICAN.

**American Nurses Association. Task Force on Staff
Privileges.** Guidelines for appointment of nurses for
individual practice privileges in health care
organizations. Kansas City, MO : American Nurses
Association, Commission on Nursing Service, 1978. 4
p. ; 23 cm.
*1. Nursing. 2. Private duty nursing. 3. Health maintenance
organizations. 4. Nursing 5. Employment 6. Nurses - standards
7. Nursing Services - standards 8. Nursing Staff - standards 9.
Private Practice - standards I. Title.*
*TC RT104 .A44 1978*

**American Organization of Nurse Executives.**
Fressola, Maria C. How nurse executives learned to
become leaders. 1998.
*TC 06 no. 11115*

Fressola, Maria C. How nurse executives learned to
become leaders. 1998.
*TC 06 no. 11115*

Staffing management and methods. San Francisco :
Jossey-Bass, 2000.

*TC RT89.3 .S72 2000*

AMERICAN PAINTING. *See* PAINTING,
AMERICAN.

AMERICAN PERIODICALS.
Journal of emotional education. New York, Emotional
Education Press.

Journal of English as a second language. [New York,
American Language Institute, New York University]

AMERICAN PERIODICALS - HISTORY - 20TH
CENTURY.
Lutz, Catherine. Reading National geographic.
Chicago : University of Chicago Press, 1993.
*TC G1.N275 L88 1993*

AMERICAN PERIODICALS - INDEXES.
Schmidt, Mary. Index to nineteenth century American
art periodicals. Madison, CT : Sound View Press,
c1999.
*TC N1 Sch5*

**American Personnel and Guidance Association.**
The Humanist educator. [Washington, American
Personnel and Guidance Association]

**American photographs.**
National Museum of American Art (U.S.)
Washington, D.C. : National Museum of American
Art, Smithsonian Institution : Smithsonian Institution
Press, c1996.
*TC TR645.W18 N37 1996*

**American photojournalism comes of age.**
Carlebach, Michael L. Washington : Smithsonian
Institution Press, c1997.
*TC TR820 .C356 1997*

**American Physical Education Association.**
The Journal of health and physical education. Ann
Arbor, Mich., : American Physical Education
Association,

**American physical education review.**
The Journal of health and physical education. Ann
Arbor, Mich., : American Physical Education
Association,

**American Physical Therapy Association (1921- ).**
Journal of the American Physical Therapy
Association. [New York, N.Y.] : The Association,
[1962-1963]

AMERICAN POETRY. *See also* CHILDREN'S
POETRY, AMERICAN.
George, Kristine O'Connell. Old Elm speaks. New
York : Clarion Books, c1998.
*TC PS3557.E488 O4 1998*

Jacobs, Leland B. (Leland Blair), 1907- Just around
the corner. New York : H. Holt, 1993.
*TC PS3560.A2545 J87 1993*

Livingston, Myra Cohn. Cricket never does. New
York : Margaret K. McElderry Books, c1997.
*TC PS3562.I945 C75 1997*

Livingston, Myra Cohn. Earth songs. 1st ed. New
York : Holiday House, c1986.
*TC PS3562.I945 E3 1986*

Livingston, Myra Cohn. No way of knowing. 1st ed.
New York : Atheneum, 1980.
*TC PS3562.I945 N6 1980*

Livingston, Myra Cohn. Sea songs. 1st ed. New
York : Holiday House, c1986.
*TC PS3562.I945 S4 1986*

Livingston, Myra Cohn. Sky songs. 1st ed. New
York : Holiday House, c1984.
*TC PS3562.I945 S5 1984*

Livingston, Myra Cohn. Up in the air. 1st ed. New
York : Holiday House, c1989.
*TC PS3562.I945 U6 1989*

Livingston, Myra Cohn. The way things are, and other
poems. [1st ed.]. New York, Atheneum, 1974.
*TC PZ8.3.L75 Way*

Michelson, Richard. A book of flies. New York :
Cavendish Children's Books, 1999.
*TC PS3563.I34 B66 1999*

Sierra, Judy. Antarctic antics. 1st ed. San Diego :
Harcourt Brace & Co., c1998.
*TC PS3569.I39 A53 1998*

Swann, Brian. The house with no door. 1st ed. San
Diego : Harcourt Brace & Company., c1998.
*TC PS3569.W256 H6 1998*

Updike, John. A child's calendar. <Rev. ed.>. New
York : Holiday House, 1999.

TC PS3571.P4 C49 1999

Yolen, Jane. Ring of earth. 1st ed. San Diego : Harcourt Brace Jovanovich, c1986.
**TC PS3575.O43 R5 1986**

Zolotow, Charlotte, 1915- River winding. 1st ed. New York : Crowell, [1978]
**TC PZ8.3.Z6 Ri 1978**

**AMERICAN POETRY - 20TH CENTURY.**
When the rain sings. New York : Simon & Schuster Books for Young Readers, 1999.
**TC PS591.I55 W48 1999**

**AMERICAN POETRY - AFRO-AMERICAN AUTHORS.**
Kerlin, Robert Thomas, 1866-1950. Negro poets and their poems. 3d ed., rev. and enl. Washington, D. C. : Associated Publishers, c1935.
**TC PS591.N4 K4 1935**

**AMERICAN POETRY - COLLECTIONS.**
Heide, Florence Parry. It's about time!. New York : Clarion Books, c1999.
**TC PS3558.E427 I77 1999**

Land, sea & sky. 1st ed. Boston : Joy Street Books, c1993.
**TC PS595.N22 L36 1993**

Poems for fathers. 1st ed. New York : Holiday House, c1989.
**TC PS595.F39 P64 1989**

The sky is full of song. 1st ed. New York : Harper & Row, c1983.
**TC PS595.S42 S5 1983**

To the zoo. 1st ed. Boston : Little, Brown, c1992.
**TC PS595.Z66 T6 1992**

What's on the menu? New York : Viking, 1992.
**TC PS595.F65 W48 1992**

When the rain sings. New York : Simon & Schuster Books for Young Readers, 1999.
**TC PS591.I55 W48 1999**

Wherever home begins. New York : Orchard Books, c1995.
**TC PS595.H645 W48 1995**

**American printmakers, 1946-1996.**
Bryce, Betty Kelly, 1942- Lanham, Md. : Scarecrow Press, 1999.
**TC NE508 .B76 1999**

**AMERICAN PRINTS.** *See* **PRINTS, AMERICAN.**

**American Psychiatric Association practice guidelines**
Practice guideline for the treatment of patients with eating disorders. 2nd ed. Washington, D.C. : American Psychiatric Association, c2000.
**TC RC552.E18 P73 2000**

**American Psychiatric Association. Work Group on Eating Disorders.**
Practice guideline for the treatment of patients with eating disorders. 2nd ed. Washington, D.C. : American Psychiatric Association, c2000.
**TC RC552.E18 P73 2000**

**American Psychological Association.**
Beyond talk therapy. 1st ed. Washington, DC : American Psychological Association, c1999.
**TC RC489.A72 B49 1999**

Cumulative subject index to Psychological abstracts. Washington, D.C. : American Psychological Association, 1971-
**TC BF1 .P652**

[Graduate study in psychology (1992)] Graduate study in psychology. Washington, D.C. : American Psychological Association, c1992-
**TC BF77 .G73**

Hays, Kate F. Working it out. 1st ed. Washington, DC : American Psychological Association, c1999.
**TC RC489.E9 H39 1999**

Journal of consulting psychology. [Lancaster, Pa., etc.] American Psychological Association.

Journals in psychology. 5th ed. Washington, D.C. : American Psychological Association, c1997.
**TC BF76.8 J655 1997**

Nicol, Adelheid A. M. Presenting your findings. 1st ed. Washington, DC : American Psychological Association, c1999.
**TC HA31 .N53 1999**

The process of group psychotherapy. Washington, DC : American Psychological Association, c2000.

TC RC488 .P75 2000

Videos in psychology. 1st ed. Washington, DC : American Psychological Association, c2000.
**TC BF80.3 .V53 2000**

Work and well-being. Washington, DC : American Psychological Association, c1992.
**TC RC967.5 .W67 1992**

**American Psychological Association. Section on Clinical Child Psychology.**
Directory of internship and post-doctoral fellowships in clinical child/pediatric psychology, 1997. [Mahwah, N.J. : Lawrence Erlbaum Associates, c1997].
**TC RJ503.3 .D57 1997**

**AMERICAN PUPPET PLAYS.** *See* **PUPPET PLAYS, AMERICAN.**

**American quarterly.**
[American quarterly (Online)] American quarterly [computer file]. Baltimore, Md. : Johns Hopkins University Press, c1996-
**TC EJOURNALS**

[American quarterly (Online)] American quarterly [computer file]. Baltimore, Md. : Johns Hopkins University Press, c1996- Frequency: Quarterly. 48.1 (Mar. 1996)- . Access restricted to institutions with a site license to the Project MUSE collection. Mode of access: Internet via World Wide Web. System requirements: World Wide Web browser software. Title from title screen. HTML encoded text and graphic files (electronic journal) Also available in print version. Issued on behalf of: American Studies Association; digitized and made available by: Project Muse. URL: http:// muse.jhu.edu/journals/american%5Fquarterly/ Available in other form: American quarterly ISSN: 0003-0678 (DLC) 50004992 (OCoLC)1480637. ISSN 1080-6490 DDC 051
*1. United States - Periodicals. I. American Studies Association. II. Project Muse. III. Title: American quarterly*
**TC EJOURNALS**

**American radicals**
Buhle, Paul, 1944- William Appleman Williams. New York : Routledge, 1995.
**TC E175.5.W55 B84 1995**

**American readers**
Catching glimpses. Teacher's ed. Lexington, Mass. : D.C. Heath & Co., c1983.
**TC PE1119 .C37 1983 Teacher's Ed. Workbook**

(1) Moving on. Lexington, Mass. : D.C. Heath, c1983.
**TC PE1117 .M68 1983**

(1) Moving on. Lexington, Mass. : D.C. Heath, c1983.
**TC PE1117 .M68 1983**

(1) Moving on. Lexington, Mass. : D.C. Heath, c1983.
**TC PE1119 .M68 1983 Teacher's Ed. Workbook**

(2-1) Marching along. Teacher's ed. New York, N.Y. : American Book Company, c1980.
**TC PE1119 .M37 1980 Teacher's Ed.**

(2-1) Marching along. New York, N.Y. : American Book Company, c1980.
**TC PE1119 .M37 1980**

(2-1) Marching along. Teacher's ed. Lexington, Mass. : D.C. Heath and Company, c1983.
**TC PE1119 .M37 1983 Teacher's Ed.**

(2-1) Marching along. Lexington, Mass. : D.C. Heath and Company, c1983.
**TC PE1119 .M37 1983**

(2-1) Marching along. Teacher's ed. New York, N.Y. : D.C. Heath and Company, c1983.
**TC PE1119 .M37 1980 Teacher's Ed. Workbook**

(2-1) Marching along. Teacher's ed. Lexington, Mass. : D.C. Heath and Company, c1983.
**TC PE1119 .M37 1983 Teacher's Ed. Workbook**

(2-2) Turning corners. New York, N.Y. : American Book Company, c1980.
**TC PE1119 .T87 1980**

(2-2) Turning corners. Teacher's ed. New York, N.Y. : American Book Company, c1980.
**TC PE1119 .T87 1980 Teacher's Ed.**

(2-2) Turning corners. Lexington, Mass. : D.C. Heath and Company, c1983.
**TC PE1119 .T87 1983**

(2-2) Turning corners. Teacher's ed. New York, N.Y. : American Book Company, c1980.

**TC PE1119 .T87 1980 Teacher's Ed. Workbook**

(2-2) Turning corners. Teacher's ed. Lexington, Mass. : D.C. Heath and Company, c1983.
**TC PE1119 .T87 1983 Teacher's Ed. Workbook**

(3-1) Building dreams. New York, N.Y. : American Book Company, c1980.
**TC PE1119 .B84 1980**

(3-1) Building dreams. Teacher's ed. New York, N.Y. : American Book Company, c1980.
**TC PE1119 .B84 1980 Teacher's Ed.**

(3-1) Building dreams. Lexington, Mass. : D.C. Heath and Company, c1983.
**TC PE1119 .B84 1983**

(3-1) Building dreams. Teacher's ed. New York, N.Y. : American Book Company, c1980.
**TC PE1119 .B84 1980 Teacher's Ed. Workbook**

(3-1) Building dreams. Teacher's Ed. Lexington, Mass. : D.C. Heath and Company, c1983.
**TC PE1119 .B84 1983 Teacher's Ed. Workbook**

(4) Clearing paths. New York, N.Y. : American Book Company, c1980.
**TC PE1121 .C63 1980**

(4) Clearing paths. Teacher's ed. New York, NY : American Book Company, c1980.
**TC PE1119 .C63 1980 Teacher's Ed.**

(4) Clearing paths. Lexington, Mass. : D.C. Heath and Company, c1983.
**TC PE1121 .C63 1983**

(4) Clearing paths. Teacher's ed. New York, N.Y. : American Book Company, c1980.
**TC PE1121 .C63 1980 Teacher's Ed. Workbook**

(4) Clearing paths. Teacher's ed. Lexington, Mass. : D.C. Heath and Company, c1983.
**TC PE1121 .C63 1983 Teacher's Ed. Workbook**

(5) Crossing boundaries. Teacher's ed. Lexington, Mass. : D.C. Heath and Company, c1983.
**TC PE1121 .C76 1983 Teacher's Ed. Workbook**

(6) Making choices. Teacher's ed. New York, N.Y. : American Book Company, c1980.
**TC PE1121 .M34 1980 Teacher's Ed.**

(6) Making choices. New York, N.Y. : American Book Company, c1980.
**TC PE1121 .M34 1980**

(6) Making choices. Teacher's ed. New York, N.Y. : American Book Company, c1980.
**TC PE1121 .M34 1980 Teacher's Ed. Workbook**

(6) Workbook for making choices. Teacher's ed. Lexington, Mass. : D.C. Heath Company, c1983.
**TC PE1121 .M34 1983 Teacher's Ed. Workbook**

(7) Changing views. Teacher's ed. Lexington, Mass. : D.C. Heath and Company, c1983.
**TC PE1121 .C52 1983 Teacher's Ed.**

(7) Changing views. Teacher's ed. Lexington, Mass. : D.C. Heath and Company, c1983.
**TC PE1121 .C52 1983 Teacher's Ed. Workbook**

(8) Meeting challenges. Teacher's ed. New York, N.Y. : American Book Co., c1980.
**TC PE1121 .M43 1980 Teacher's Ed.**

(8) Meeting challenges. Teacher's ed. Lexington, Mass. : D.C. Heath and Company, c1983.
**TC PE1121 .M43 1983 Teacher's Ed.**

(8) Meeting challenges. Lexington, Mass. : D.C. Heath and Company, c1983.
**TC PE1121 .M43 1983**

(8) Meeting challenges. Teacher's ed. Lexington, Mass. : D. C. Heath and Company, c1983.
**TC PE1121 .M43 1983 Teacher's Ed. Workbook**

(K-1) Warming up. Teacher's ed. New York, N.Y. : American Book Company, c1980.
**TC PE1119 .W37 1980 Teacher's Ed.**

(K-1) Warming up. New York, N.Y. : American Book Company, c1980.
**TC PE1119 .W37 1980**

(K-1) Warming up. Teacher's ed. Lexington, Mass. : D.C. Heath and Company, c1983.
**TC PE1119 .W37 1983 Teacher's Ed.**

(K-2) Reaching out. New York, N.Y. : American Book Company, c1980.
**TC PE1119 .R42 1980**

(K-2) Reaching out. Teacher's ed. New York, N.Y. : American Book Company, c1980.

*TC PE1119 .R42 1980 Teacher's Ed.*

(K-2) Reaching out. Teacher's ed. Lexington, Mass. : D.C. Heath and Company, c1983.
*TC PE1119 .R42 1983 Teacher's Ed.*

(K-2) Reaching out. Teacher's ed. Lexington, Mass. : D.C. Heath and Company, c1986.
*TC PE1119 .R42 1986 Teacher's Ed.*

(P) Finding places. Teacher's ed. New York, N.Y. : American Book Company, c1980.
*TC PE1119 .F56 1980 Teacher's Ed.*

(P) Finding places. New York, NY : American Book Company, c1980.
*TC PE1119 .F56 1980*

(P) Finding places. Lexington, Mass. : D.C. Heath and Company, c1983.
*TC PE1119 .F56 1983*

(P) Finding places. Teacher's ed. Lexington, Mass. : D.C. Heath and Company, c1983.
*TC PE1119 .F56 1983 Teacher's Ed.*

(P) Finding places. Teacher's ed. New York, N.Y. : American Book Company, c1980.
*TC PE1119 .F56 1980 Teacher's Ed. Workbook*

(P) Finding places. Teacher's ed. Lexington, Mass. : D.C. Heath and Company, c1983.
*TC PE1119 .F56 1983 Teacher's Ed. Workbook*

(PP-2) Climbing up. New York, N.Y. : American Book Company, c1980.
*TC PE1119 .C54 1980*

(PP-3) Going far. New York, N.Y. : American Book Company, c1980.
*TC PE1119 .G64 1980*

(PP1-2-3) Looking out. Climbing up. Going far. Teacher's ed. New York, N.Y. : American Book Cpmpany, c1980.
*TC PE1119 .L66 1980 Teacher's Ed.*

(PP1-2-3) Looking out. Climbing up. Going far. Teacher's ed. New York, N.Y. : American Book Company, c1980.
*TC PE1119 .L66 1980 Teacher's Ed. Workbook*

(PP1-2-3) Looking out. Climbing up. Going far. Teacher's ed. Lexington, Mass. : D.C. Heath and Cpmpany, c1983.
*TC PE1119 .L66 1983 Teacher's Ed. Workbook*

**AMERICAN REPUBLICS.** *See* **AMERICA.**

**AMERICAN REVOLUTION.** *See* **UNITED STATES - HISTORY - REVOLUTION, 1775-1783.**

**The American Revolution.** [videorecording] / produced by Greystone Communications, Inc. in association with A&E Network ; producer, Scott Paddor ; writer, Don Cambou ; supervising producer, Don Cambou ; director, Lisa Bourgoujian. New York, N.Y. : A&E Home Video, c1994. 6 videocassettes (ca. 300 min.) : sd., col. ; 1/2 in. Title on container: History Channel presents the American Revolution. VHS. Catalogued from credits and container. Host; Bill Curtis. Executive producers, Craig Haffner and Donna E. Lusitana; photography, I-Li Chen; music, Christopher Stone; editors, Michael W. Andrews, Stephen Pomerantz. SUMMARY: This story of the American Revolution uses reenactments, commentaries by historical and military advisers and historical materials featuring the people, places and events from 1773 to the end of the war. CONTENTS: v. 1. The conflict ignites -- v. 2. 1776 -- v. 3. Washington and Arnold -- v. 4. The world at war -- v. 5. England's last chance -- v. 6. Brith of the Republic. ISBN 1-56501-437-5 (v. 1) ISBN 1-56501-438-3 (v. 2) ISBN 1-56501-439-1 (v. 3) ISBN 1-56501-440-5 (v. 4) ISBN 1-56501-441-3 (v. 5) ISBN 1-56501-442-1 (v. 6)
*1. United States - History - Revolution, 1775-1783. I. Paddor, Scott. II. Cambou, Don. III. Bourgoujian, Lisa. IV. History Channel (Firm) V. Arts and Entertainment Network. VI. A&E Home Video (Firm) VII. Greystone Communications. VIII. Title: Conflict ignites. IX. Title: 1776. X. Title: Washington and Arnold. XI. Title: World at war. XII. Title: England's last chance. XIII. Title: Birth of the Republic. XIV. Title: History Channel presents the American Revolution.*
*TC E208 .A447 1994*

**AMERICAN SCHOOLS.** *See* **SCHOOLS - UNITED STATES.**

**AMERICAN SCIENCE FICTION.** *See* **SCIENCE FICTION, AMERICAN.**

**American series in behavioral science and law**
Brill, Norman Q. (Norman Quintus), 1911- Being Black in America today. Springfield, Ill. : Charles C Thomas, 1999.
*TC E185.625 B754 1999*

**The American settlement movement.**
Barbuto, Domenica M., 1951- Westport, Conn. : Greenwood Press, 1999.
*TC Z7164.S665 B37 1999*

**American sign language.**
Baker-Shenk, Charlotte Lee. Silver Spring, Md. : T. J. Publishers, c1978, 1979 printing.
*TC HV2474 .B29*

**AMERICAN SIGN LANGUAGE.**
Baker-Shenk, Charlotte Lee. American sign language. Silver Spring, Md. : T. J. Publishers, c1978, 1979 printing.
*TC HV2474 .B29*

**AMERICAN SIGN LANGUAGE.**
Mindess, Anna. Reading between the signs. Yarmouth, Me. : Intercultural Press, c1999.
*TC HV2402 .M56 1999*

Peters, Cynthia. Deaf American literature. Washington, D.C. : Gallaudet University Press, 2000.
*TC HV2471 .P38 2000*

The signs of language revisited. Mahwah, N.J. : L.Erlbaum, 2000.
*TC HV2474 .S573 2000*

Trautman, Barbara A. AGS English to use. Teacher's ed. Circle Pines, Minn. : AGS, American Guidance Service, c1998.
*TC PE1121 .T72 1998 Teacher's Ed.*

Trautman, Barbara A. AGS English to use. Circle Pines, Minn. : AGS, American Guidance Service, c1998.
*TC PE1121 .T72 1998*

Uyechi, Linda, 1957- The geometry of visual phonology. Stanford, Calif. : CSLI Publications, 1996.
*TC HV2474 .U88 1996*

**AMERICAN SIGN LANGUAGE - GRAMMAR.**
Lillo-Martin, Diane C. (Diane Carolyn), 1959- Universal grammar and American sign language. Dordrecht ; Boston : Kluwer Academic Publishers, c1991.
*TC HV2474 .L55 1991*

**AMERICAN SIGN LANGUAGE - STUDY AND TEACHING.**
Innovative practices for teaching sign language interpreters. Washington, D.C. : Gallaudet University Press, 2000.
*TC HV2402 .I56 2000*

**AMERICAN SIGN LANGUAGE - SYNTAX.**
The syntax of American Sign Language. Cambridge, Mass. : MIT Press, c2000.
*TC HV2474 .S994 2000*

**AMERICAN SIGN LANGUAGE - UNITED STATES.** *See* **AMERICAN SIGN LANGUAGE.**

**AMERICAN SLAVES' WRITINGS.** *See* **SLAVES' WRITINGS, AMERICAN.**

**American Social Hygiene Association.**
Journal of social hygiene. New York : American Social Hygiene Association,

**American Society for Training and Development. ASTD research series**
(no. 5.) American Society for Training and Development. Issues in career and human resource development. Madison, Wisc. : American Society for Training and Development, c1980.
*TC HF5549.5.T7 A59 1980*

Issues in career and human resource development : research papers from the 1979 ASTD national conference / Judith W. Springer, editor. Madison, Wisc. : American Society for Training and Development, c1980. 164 p. : ill. ; 22 cm. (ASTD research series ; paper no. 5) Includes bibliographies. DDC 650.1/4
*1. Employees - Training of - Congresses. 2. Vocational guidance - Congresses. I. Springer, Judith W., 1938- II. Title. III. Title: Career and human resource development. IV. Series: American Society for Training and Development. ASTD research series ; no. 5.*
*TC HF5549.5.T7 A59 1980*

**AMERICAN STUDENTS - FOREIGN COUNTRIES.**
Hess, J. Daniel (John Daniel), 1937- Studying abroad/learning abroad. Yarmouth, Me., USA : Intercultural Press, c1997.
*TC LB2375 .H467 1997*

**AMERICAN STUDIES.** *See* **UNITED STATES - STUDY AND TEACHING.**

**American Studies Association.**
[American quarterly (Online)] American quarterly [computer file]. Baltimore, Md. : Johns Hopkins University Press, c1996-
*TC EJOURNALS*

**American studies in eastern Africa** / edited by Henry Indangasi, Henry Mutoro, Macharia Munene. Nairobi : Nairobi University Press, 1993. 132 p. : ill. ; 28 cm. "Based on the proceedings of the First Colloquium on American Studies in Eastern Africa, held in Nairobi, July 5th-7th, 1990." ISBN 9966-846-23-9 DDC 973/.071/0676
*1. United States - History - Congresses. 2. American literature - Congresses. 3. United States - Study and teaching - Africa, Eastern - Congresses. I. Indangasi, Henry. II. Mutoro, Henry. III. Munene, Macharia. IV. Colloquium on American Studies in Eastern Africa (1st : 1990 : Nairobi, Kenya)*
*TC E172.9 .A47 1993*

**American teacher Apr. 1971-Nov. 1972, Feb. 1975-.**
Changing education. Detroit [etc.]

**The American Thomistic revival in the philosophical papers of R.J. Henle, S.J.**
Henle, R. J. (Robert John), 1909- St. Louis, Mo. : Saint Louis University Press, c1999.
*TC B839 .H46 1999*

**American undercover.**
Teen killers [videorecording]. Princeton, NJ : Films for the Humanities and Sciences, c1998-1999.
*TC HV9067.H6 T4 1999*

**American University at Cairo. Journal of modern education.**
Majallat al-tarbiyah al-ḥadīthah. al-Qāhirah : al-Jāmiʻah al-Amrīkīyah bi-al-Qāhirah, 1928- .

Majallat al-tarbiyah al-ḥadīthah. al-Qāhirah : al-Jāmiʻah al-Amrīkīyah bi-al-Qāhirah, 1928- .

**American University at Cairo. Kullīyat al-Muʻallimīn.**
Majallat al-tarbiyah al-ḥadīthah. al-Qāhirah : al-Jāmiʻah al-Amrīkīyah bi-al-Qāhirah, 1928- .

**American University at Cairo. Kullīyat al-Tarbiyah.**
Majallat al-tarbiyah al-ḥadīthah. al-Qāhirah : al-Jāmiʻah al-Amrīkīyah bi-al-Qāhirah, 1928- .

**American university studies. Series XI, Anthropology/sociology**
(vol. 71.) Mead, George Herbert, 1863-1931. Play, school, and society. New York : Peter Lang, c1999.
*TC HQ782 .M43 1999*

**American university studies. Series XIV, Education**
(vol. 47) Teachers' pedagogical thinking. New York : P. Lang, 2000.
*TC LB1775 . T4179 2000*

**American vaudeville, its life and times.**
Gilbert, Douglas, 1889-1948. New York, Dover Publications [c1940, c1968]
*TC PN1967 .G5 1968*

**American Viewpoint Society.**
The Journal of educational sociology. [New York : American Viewpoint Society, Inc., 1927-1963]

[Journal of educational sociology (Online)] The journal of educational sociology [computer file]. New York, N.Y. : American Viewpoint Society, Inc., 1927-1963.
*TC EJOURNALS*

**AMERICAN WATERCOLOR PAINTING.** *See* **WATERCOLOR PAINTING, AMERICAN.**

**AMERICAN YOUNG ADULT FICTION.** *See* **YOUNG ADULT FICTION, AMERICAN.**

**American youth violence.**
Zimring, Franklin E. New York : Oxford University Press, 1998.
*TC HV9104 .Z57 1998*

**AMERICANISMS.** *See also* **ENGLISH LANGUAGE - UNITED STATES.**
Kovacs, George. Literal literacy II. Lewiston, NY : E. Mellen Press, c1993.
*TC PE2827 .K682 1993*

Smitherman, Geneva, 1940- Talkin that talk. London ; New York : Routledge, 2000.
*TC PE3102.N4 S63 2000*

**AMERICANISMS - DICTIONARIES.**
Smitherman, Geneva, 1940- Black talk. Rev. ed. Boston : Houghton Mifflin, 2000.
*TC PE3102.N4 S65 2000*

**AMERICAS.** *See* **AMERICA.**

**America's demographic tapestry :** baseline for the new millennium / edited by James W. Hughes and Joseph J. Seneca. New Brunswick, N.J. : Rutgers University Press, c1999. vii, 228 p. : ill. ; 24 cm. Includes bibliographical references and index. ISBN 0-8135-2646-9

*America's journey through slavery [videorecording]*

ISBN 0-8135-2647-7 (pbk.) DDC 304.6/0973
1. United States - Population. 2. United States - Population
policy. 3. Population forecasting - United States. I. Hughes,
James W. II. Seneca, Joseph J., 1943-
**TC HB3505 .A683 1999**

**America's journey through slavery [videorecording].**
Africans in America [videorecording]. [Boston,
Mass.] : WGBH Educational Foundation : South
Burlington, VT : WGBH Boston Video [distributor],
c1998.
**TC E441 .A47 1998**

**AMERINDIANS.** *See* **INDIANS.**

**AMERINDS.** *See* **INDIANS.**

**Ames, Kenneth L.**
Ideas and images. Walnut Creek, CA : AltaMira
Press, 1997.
**TC E172 .I34 1997**

**AMESLAN (SIGN LANGUAGE).** *See* **AMERICAN
SIGN LANGUAGE.**

**Amherst College.**
Tolliver, Joseph A. Administratively mandated change
at Amherst College. 1997.
**TC 06 no. 10871**

**AMHERST COLLEGE - ADMINISTRATION.**
Tolliver, Joseph A. Administratively mandated change
at Amherst College. 1997.
**TC 06 no. 10871**

**AMHERST COLLEGE - STUDENTS.**
Tolliver, Joseph A. Administratively mandated change
at Amherst College. 1997.
**TC 06 no. 10871**

**Los amigos del Hada Melina.**
Kaplan de Drimer, Alicia. Buenos Aires : Intercoop
Editora Cooperativa, [1995?]-1998.
**TC PQ7798.21.A64 A65 1995**

**Amin, Martin E. (Martin Efuetngu)** Trends in the
demand for primary education in Cameroon / Martin
E. Amin. MD : University Press of
America, 1999. xxviii, 258 p. : ill. ; 24 cm. Includes
bibliographical references and indexes. ISBN 0-7618-1397-7
(cloth : alk. paper) DDC 372.12/19/096711
1. School enrollment - Social aspects - Cameroon. 2. School
enrollment - Economic aspects - Cameroon. 3. Education
(Elementary) - Social aspects - Cameroon. 4. Education
(Elementary) - Economic aspects - Cameroon. 5. Educational
surveys - Cameroon. I. Title.
**TC LC137.C36 A55 1999**

**Amini, Fari.**
Lewis, Thomas. A general theory of love. New York :
Random House, 2000.
**TC BF575.L8 L49 2000**

**Amino acids and proteins for the athlete.**
Di Pasquale, Mauro G. Boca Raton : CRC Press,
c1997.
**TC QP551 .D46 1997**

**AMINO ACIDS IN HUMAN NUTRITION.**
Di Pasquale, Mauro G. Amino acids and proteins for
the athlete. Boca Raton : CRC Press, c1997.
**TC QP551 .D46 1997**

**Aminzade, Ronald, 1949-.**
The social worlds of higher education :. Thousand
Oaks, Calif. : Pine Forge Press, [1999].
**TC LB2331 .S573 1999 sampler**

**Amir, Yehuda.**
Enhancing education in heterogeneous schools.
Ramat-Gan : Bar-Ilan University Press, [1997]
**TC LC214 .E54 1997**

**AMISH.**
The Amish [videorecording]. Oak Forest, IL : MPI
Home Video, 1988.

The Amish [videorecording]. Oak Forest, Ill. : MPI
Home Video, c1988.
**TC BX8129.A5 A5 1988**

**AMISH - SOCIAL LIFE AND CUSTOMS.**
The Amish [videorecording]. Oak Forest, IL : MPI
Home Video, 1988.

The Amish [videorecording]. Oak Forest, Ill. : MPI
Home Video, c1988.
**TC BX8129.A5 A5 1988**

**The Amish** [videorecording] : not to be modern /
directed by Victoria Larimore ; produced by Victoria
Larimore and Michael Taylor ; cinematographer, Oren
Rudavsky. Oak Forest, IL : MPI Home Video, 1988. 1
videocassette (57 min.) : sd., col. ; 1/2 in. VHS. Catalogued
from credits and container. Editor, Ann Schaetzel; sound
editor, Barry Brown. "Made with the cooperation of Oberlin

College." For high school and adult audiences. SUMMARY:
Seldomly photographed because of the belief that graven
images are forbidden in the Bible, this video provides a rare
look at a community that separates itself from most modern
technology. Shows Amish people performing farm work,
creating elaborate quilts, and attending schools. Examines the
religious reasons for their unusual life-style and interviews one
man who broke away and became a psychoanalyst.
1. Amish. 2. Amish - Social life and customs. 3. Mennonites. 4.
Mennonites - Social life and customs. 5. Documentary
television programs. I. Larimore, Victoria. II. Taylor, Michael,
1957- III. MPI Home Video. IV. Oberlin College. V. Title: Not
to be modern [videorecording]

**The Amish** [videorecording] : not to be modern /
directed by Victoria Larimore ; produced by Victoria
Larimore and Michael Taylor ; cinematography, Oren
Rudavsky. Oak Forest, Ill. : MPI Home Video, c1988.
1 videocassette (57 min.) : sd., col. ; 1/2 in. VHS, Hi-fi, mono.
Catalogued from credits and container. Editor, Ann Schaetzel;
sound editor, Barry Brown. For high school and adult
audiences. SUMMARY: Seldomly photographed because of
the belief that graven images are forbidden in the Bible, this
video provides a rare look at a community that separates itself
from most modern technology. Shows Amish people
performing farm work, creating elaborate quilts, and attending
schools. Examines the religious reasons for their unusual lifestyle and interviews one man who broke away and became a
psychoanalyst.
1. Amish. 2. Amish - Social life and customs. 3. Documentary
films. I. Larimore, Victoria. II. Taylor, Michael, 1957- III. MPI
Home Video (Firm) IV. Oberlin College. V. Title: Not to be
modern [videorecording]
**TC BX8129.A5 A5 1988**

**Ammerman, Robert T.**
Assessment of family violence. 2nd ed. New York :
John Wiley, c1999.
**TC RC569.5.F3 A87 1999**

**AMNESTIC CONFABULATORY SYNDROME.**
*See* **KORSAKOFF'S SYNDROME.**

**AMNIOCENTESIS - SOCIAL ASPECTS - UNITED
STATES.**
Rapp, Rayna. Testing women, testing the fetus. New
York : Routledge, 1999.
**TC RG628.3.A48 R37 1999**

**AMNIOTES.** *See* **BIRDS.**

**AMNIOTIC LIQUID.** *See* **AMNIOCENTESIS.**

**Amon Carter Museum of Western Art.**
Kinsey, Joni. Plain pictures. Washington, : Published
for the University of Iowa Museum of Art by the
Smithsonian Institution Press, 1996.
**TC N8214.5.U6 K56 1996**

**Among the anthropologists.**
Kuper, Adam. London ; New Brunswick, NJ : Athlone
Press ; Somerset, N.J. : Distributed in the United
States by Transaction Publishers, 1999.
**TC GN325 .K89 1999**

**Amoral thoughts about morality.**
Kendler, Howard H., 1919- Springfield, Ill. : C.C.
Thomas, c2000.
**TC BF76.4 .K47 2000**

**Amory, Hugh.**
The colonial book in the Atlantic world. Cambridge,
U.K. ; New York : Cambridge University Press, 2000.
**TC Z473 .C686 1999**

**Amos, N. Scott.**
Anglo-Dutch Historical Conference (13th : 1997) The
education of a Christian society. Aldershot, Hants,
England ; Brookfield, Vt. : Ashgate, c1999.
**TC BR377 .E38 1999**

**AMS Planning & Research Corp.**
A planning guide to arts participation research.
Washington, DC : National Endowment for the Arts,
[1995]
**TC NX220 .P73 1995**

**Amsterdam studies in the theory and history of
linguistic science. Series IV, Current issues in
linguistic theory**
(v. 151) Discourse and perspective in cognitive
linguistics. Amsterdam ; Philadelphia : J.
Benjamins, c1997.
**TC P165 .D57 1997**

(v. 163) Lockwood, David G. Functional
approaches to language, culture, and cognition.
Amsterdam ; Philadelphia : J. Benjamins, c2000.
**TC P147 .L63 1998**

**Amstutz, Donna D.**
Whitson, Donna L. Accessing information in a
technological age. Original ed. Malabar, Fla. : Krieger
Pub. Co., 1997.

**TC ZA3075 .W48 1997**

**Amtsblatt.**
Bavaria (Germany). Staatsministerium für Unterricht,
Kultus, Wissenschaft und Kunst. Amtsblatt des
Bayerischen Staatsministeriums für Unterricht,
Kultus, Wissenschaft und Kunst. München : J. Jehle,

Bavaria (Germany). Staatsministerium für Unterricht
und Kultus. Amtsblatt des Staatsministeriums für
Unterricht und Kultus. München : Das Ministerium,
1918-

**Amtsblatt des Bayer. Staatsministeriums für
Unterricht und Kultus.**
Bavaria (Germany). Staatsministerium für Unterricht
und Kultus. Amtsblatt des Staatsministeriums für
Unterricht und Kultus. München : Das Ministerium,
1918-

**Amtsblatt des Bayerischen Staatsministeriums für
Unterricht, Kultus, Wissenschaft und Kunst.**
Bavaria (Germany). Staatsministerium für Unterricht,
Kultus, Wissenschaft und Kunst. München : J. Jehle,

**Amtsblatt des Bayerischen Staatsministeriums für
Unterricht und Kultus.**
Bavaria (Germany). Staatsministerium für Unterricht
und Kultus. Amtsblatt des Staatsministeriums für
Unterricht und Kultus. München : Das Ministerium,
1918-

**Amtsblatt des Staatsministeriums für Unterricht und
Kultus.**
Bavaria (Germany). Staatsministerium für Unterricht
und Kultus. München : Das Ministerium, 1918-

**AMUSEMENTS.** *See* **CIRCUS; DANCE;
ENTERTAINING; PLAY; RECREATION;
TOYS; VAUDEVILLE.**

**Indian Journal of Educational Administration and
Research.** New Delhi v. 1, no. 1; 1960. Edited by the
Ministry of Education Government of India.
1. Education - Research - Periodicals. 2. Education -
Research - India. I. Ministry of Education Government of
India.

**ANABAPTISTS.** *See* **MENNONITES.**

**ANALGESIA.** *See* **PAIN.**

**ANALYSIS, DREAM.** *See* **DREAM
INTERPRETATION.**

**ANALYSIS, INTERACTION (EDUCATION).** *See*
**INTERACTION ANALYSIS IN EDUCATION.**

**ANALYSIS (MATHEMATICS).** *See* **CALCULUS.**

**An analysis of 12th grade students' reasoning styles
and competencies when presented with an
environmental problem in a social and scientific
context.**
Yang, Fang-Ying. 1999.
**TC 06 no. 11076**

**The analysis of beauty.**
Hogarth, William, 1697-1764. New Haven, Conn. :
Published for the Paul Mellon Centre for British Art by
Yale University Press, c1997.
**TC BH181 .H6 1997**

**ANALYSIS OF CONVERSATION.** *See*
**CONVERSATION ANALYSIS.**

**ANALYSIS OF DIALOGUE.** *See* **DIALOGUE
ANALYSIS.**

**Analysis of discourse in an English as a second
language peer-mentoring teacher group.**
Arias, Rafael. Analysis of discourse in an ESL peer-
mentoring teacher group. 1999.
**TC 06 no. 10791**

**Analysis of discourse in an ESL peer-mentoring
teacher group.**
Arias, Rafael. 1999.
**TC 06 no. 10791**

**ANALYSIS OF FOOD.** *See* **FOOD
ADULTERATION AND INSPECTION.**

**ANALYSIS OF VARIANCE.**
Rosenthal, Robert, 1933- Contrasts and effect sizes in
behavioral research. Cambridge, U.K. ; New York :
Cambridge University Press, 2000.
**TC BF39.2.A52 R67 2000**

**ANALYSIS OF VARIANCE - DATA
PROCESSING.**
Gill, Kenneth Joseph. Social psychological artifacts in
the measurement of consumer satisfaction with health
care. 1996.
**TC 085 G396**

**ANALYSIS (PHILOSOPHY).** *See* **SEMANTICS (PHILOSOPHY).**

**ANALYSIS SITUS.** *See* **TOPOLOGY.**

**The analytic Freud** : philosophy and psychoanalysis / edited by Michael P. Levine. London ; New York : Routledge, 2000. xii, 320 p. : ill. ; 24 cm. Includes bibliographical references and indexes. ISBN 0-415-18039-2 (hb : alk. paper) ISBN 0-415-18040-6 (pbk. : alk. paper) DDC 150.19/52
*1. Freud, Sigmund. - 1856-1939. 2. Psycholanalysis and philosophy. I. Levine, Michael P. (Michael Philip)*
**TC BF109.F74 A84 2000**

**Analyzing costs in higher education** : what institutional researchers need to know / Michael F. Middaugh, editor. San Francisco, Calif. : Jossey-Bass Publishers, c2000. 107 p. : ill. ; 23 cm. (Jossey-Bass Higher and adult Education Series.) (New directions for institutional research, 0271-0560 ; no. 106) "Summer 2000." Includes bibliographical references and index. CONTENTS: The economics of higher education : focus on cost / Paul T. Brinkman -- Understanding expenditure data / Frances L. Dyke -- A guide to measuring college costs / Gordon C. Winston -- Building a consistent and reliable expenditure database / Kelli J. Armstrong -- Using comparative cost data / Michael F. Middaugh -- The importance of cost data : a view from the top / David E. Hollowell, Melvyn D. Schiavelli -- To lift the veil : new college cost studies and the quest for the perfect formula / Travis J. Reindl. ISBN 0-7879-5437-3
*1. Education, Higher - Costs. 2. Research - Finance. 3. Universities and colleges - Finance. I. Middaugh, Michael F., 1945- II. Series. III. Series: New directions institutional research ; no. 106*
**TC LB2342 .A68 2000**

**ANARCHISM.** *See* **SOCIALISM.**

**ANARCHISM AND ANARCHISTS.** *See* **ANARCHISM.**

**ANARCHISM - CUBA - HISTORY - 19TH CENTURY.**
Casanovas, Joan. Bread, or bullets!. Pittsburgh : University of Pittsburgh Press, c1998.
**TC HD8206 .C33 1998**

**ANARCHY.** *See* **ANARCHISM.**

**ANASAZI CULTURE.** *See* **PUEBLO INDIANS.**

**ANASAZI PERIOD.** *See* **PUEBLO INDIANS.**

**Anastos, Phillip.** Illegal : seeking the American dream / photographs and text by Phillip Anastos and Chris French. New York : Rizzoli, 1991. 128 p. : ill., map ; 31 cm. ISBN 0-8478-1367-3 DDC 305.9/0693
*1. Lower Rio Grande Valley (Tex.) - Emigration and immigration - Pictorial works. 2. Illegal aliens - Texas - Lower Rio Grande Valley - Pictorial works. 3. Teenage immigrants - Texas - Lower Rio Grande Valley - Pictorial works. I. French, Chris. II. Title.*
**TC F392.R5 A53 1991**

**ANATIDAE.** *See* **DUCKS; GEESE.**

**ANATINAE.** *See* **DUCKS.**

**ANATOMY.** *See* **HUMAN ANATOMY; IMMUNE SYSTEM.**

**ANATOMY, HUMAN.** *See* **HUMAN ANATOMY.**

**Anatomy of a crisis.**
Ayres, David M., 1971- Honolulu : University of Hawai'i Press, c2000.
**TC LC94.C16 A971 2000**

**The anatomy of public opinion.**
Shamir, Jacob. Ann Arbor, Mich. : University of Michigan Press, c2000.
**TC HM236 .S5 2000**

**An anatomy of thought.**
Glynn, Ian. Oxford ; New York : Oxford University Press, [1999].
**TC QP360 .G595 1999**

**ANATOMY, PRACTICAL.** *See* **HUMAN DISSECTION.**

**Chisanbop finger calculation method.**
Pai, Hang Young. New York : McCormick-Mathers Pub. Co., 1981.
**TC QA115 .P23 1981**

**ANCESTRY.** *See* **GENEALOGY.**

**ANCIENT GREEK EDUCATION.** *See* **EDUCATION, GREEK.**

**Ancient Greek psychology and the modern mind-body debate.**
Ostenfeld, Erik Nis. Aarhus, Denmark : Aarhus University Press, 1987.

**TC BF161 .O88 1987**

**ANCIENT OLYMPIC GAMES.** *See* **OLYMPIC GAMES (ANCIENT).**

**The ancient Olympic games.**
Swaddling, Judith. 2nd ed. Austin : University of Texas Press, 1999, c1980.
**TC GV23 .S9 1999**

**Ancona, George.** Charro : the Mexican cowboy / George Ancona. 1st ed. San Diego : Harcourt Brace, c1999. 1 v. (unpaged) : col. ill. ; 27 cm. SUMMARY: Text and photographs present the traditions and the annual celebration of the charro, the Mexican cowboy. ISBN 0-15-201047-5 (hardcover) ISBN 0-15-201046-7 (pbk.) DDC 972
*1. Mexico - Social life and customs - Juvenile literature. 2. Charros - Mexico - Social life and customs - Juvenile literature. 3. Charros. 4. Cowboys. 5. Mexico - Social life and customs. I. Title.*
**TC F1210 .A747 1999**

**And ebony drudges.**
Mack, Kibibi Voloria C. Parlor ladies and ebony drudges. 1st ed. Knoxville : University of Tennessee Press, c1999.
**TC F279.O6 M33 1999**

**And still we rise.**
Corwin, Miles. 1st ed. New York : Bard, 2000.
**TC LC3993.9 .C678 2000**

**And there were giants in the land.**
Beineke, John A. New York : P. Lang, c1998.
**TC LB875.K54 B44 1998**

**Andersen, Christopher Lawrence.** A microgenetic study of science reasoning in social context / Christopher Lawrence Andersen. 1998. vii, 132 leaves : ill. ; 29 cm. Issued also on microfilm. Includes tables. Thesis (Ph.D.)--Columbia University, 1998. Includes bibliographical references (leaves 105-114)
*1. Piaget, Jean - 1896-1980. 2. Science - Study and teaching (Elementary) 3. Reasoning (Psychology) - Case studies. 4. Developmental psychology. 5. Statistics. 6. Cognition. 7. Inference. I. Title.*
**TC 085 An2305**

**Andersen, Peter Bøgh.**
The Computer as medium. Cambridge [England] ; New York : Cambridge University Press, 1993.
**TC QA76.5 .C612554 1993**

**Anderson, Carl, educator.** How's it going? : a practical guide to conferring with student writers / Carl Anderson. Portsmouth, NH : Heinemann, c2000. xv, 204 p. ;c 22 cm. Includes bibliographical references and index. ISBN 0-325-00224-X (alk. paper) DDC 372.62/3044
*1. English language - Composition and exercises - Study and teaching (Elementary) 2. Creative writing (Elementary education) I. Title.*
**TC LB1576 .A6159 2000**

**Anderson, Charles M.**
Writing and healing. Urbana, Ill. : National Council of Teachers of English, c2000.
**TC RC489.W75 W756 2000**

**Anderson, Dennis S.** Mathematics and distance education on the internet : an investigation based on transactional distance education theory / Dennis S. Anderson. 1999. viii, 193 leaves : ill. ; 29 cm. Typescript; issued also on microfilm. Thesis (Ph. D.)--Columbia University, 1999. Includes bibliographical references (leaves 106-123).
*1. Moore, Michael G. 2. Distance education. 3. Mathematics - Study and teaching - Audio-visual aids. 4. Independent study. 5. Internet (Computer network) in education. 6. Teacher-student relationships. 7. Electronic mail systems in education. I. Title.*
**TC 085 An2317**

**Anderson, Edward R.**
Adolescent siblings in stepfamilies. Chicago, Ill. : University of Chicago Press, 1999.
**TC LB1103.S6 v.64 no. 4**

**Anderson, Elijah.** Code of the street : decency, violence, and the moral life of the inner city / Elijah Anderson. 1st ed. New York : W.W Norton, c1999. 352 p. ; 22 cm. Includes bibliographical references (p. [333]-342) and index. ISBN 0-393-04023-2 DDC 303.3/3/ 0896073074811
*1. Afro-Americans - Pennsylvania - Philadelphia - Social conditions. 2. Afro-Americans - Pennsylvania - Philadelphia - Social life and customs. 3. Inner cities - Pennsylvania - Philadelphia. 4. Philadelphia (Pa.) - Social conditions. 5. Philadelphia (Pa.) - Social life and customs. I. Title.*
**TC F158.9.N4 A52 1999**

**Anderson, Eric, 1949-** Dangerous donations : northern philanthropy and southern Black education, 1902-1930 / Eric Anderson and Alfred A. Moss, Jr. ; with a foreword by Louis R. Harlan. Columbia, Mo. : University of Missouri Press, c1999. xv, 245 p. : ill. ; 24 cm. Includes bibliographical references (p. 223-238) and index. ISBN 0-8262-1226-3 (cloth : alk. paper)
*1. Afro-Americans - Education - Southern States - Finance - History. 2. Endowments - Southern States - History. I. Moss, Alfred A.. 1943- II. Title.*
**TC LC2707 .A53 1999**

**Anderson, Gail (Gail O.).**
Children's rights, therapists' responsibilities. New York : Harrington Park Press, c1997.
**TC RJ504 .C486 1997**

**Anderson, Gary R., 1952-.**
The challenge of permanency planning in a multicultural society. New York : Haworth Press, c1997.
**TC HV741 .C378 1997**

**Anderson, Holly, 1949-.**
Teaching through texts. London ; New York : Routledge, 1999.
**TC LB1573 .T39 1999**

**Anderson, Holly Kathleen, 1952-.**
Perspectives in critical thinking. New York : P. Lang, c2000.
**TC LB1590.3 .P476 2000**

**Anderson, Howard R. (Howard Richmond), 1898- ed.**
Riker, Thad Weed, 1880-1952. The story of modern Europe. Boston : Houghton, Mifflin, 1942.
**TC D209 .R48**

**Anderson, John R. (John Robert), 1947-** Cognitive psychology and its implications / John R. Anderson. 5th ed. New York : Worth, 2000. xvi, 531 p. : ill. (some col.) ; 25 cm. Previous ed.: 1995. Includes bibliographical references (p. 475-510) and indexes. ISBN 0-7167-3678-0
*1. Cognition. 2. Cognitive psychology. I. Title.*
**TC BF311 .A5895 2000**

**Anderson, Lorin W.** Assessing affective characteristics in the schools / Lorin W. Anderson and Sid F. Bourke. 2nd ed. Mahwah, NJ : Lawrence Erlbaum, c2000. xix, 219 p. ; 24 cm. Includes bibliographical references (p. 205-212) and index. ISBN 0-8058-3197-5 (cloth: alk. paper) ISBN 0-8058-3198-3 (pbk. : alk. paper) DDC 371.26
*1. Educational tests and measurements. 2. Teaching. I. Bourke, S. F. II. Title.*
**TC LB3051 .A698 2000**

**Anderson, Patricia, 1950-** Contemporary jewellery in Australia and New Zealand / Patricia Anderson. North Ryde, Sydney : Craftsman House, c1998. 167, [1] p. : col. ill. ; 30 cm. Includes bibliographical references (p. [168]). ISBN 90-5703-371-2
*1. Jewelry - Australia - History - 20th century. 2. Jewelry - New Zealand - History - 20th century. 3. Jewelers - Australia - Biography. 4. Jewelers - New Zealand - Biography. I. Title. II. Title: Contemporary jewelery in Australia and New Zealand*
**TC NK7390.A1 A53 1998**

**Anderson, Paul M., 1938-.**
Professors who believe. Downers Grove, Ill. : InterVarsity Press, c1998.
**TC BR569 .P76 1998**

**Anderson, Richard E., 1943-.**
ASHE reader on finance in higher education. Needham Heights, MA : Ginn Press, c1986.
**TC LB2342 .A76 1990**

**Anderson, Rosemarie.**
Transpersonal research methods for the social sciences. Thousand Oaks, Calif. : Sage Publications, c1998.
**TC BF76.5 .T73 1998**

**Anderson, Sara Long.**
Grodner, Michele. Foundations and clinical applications of nutrition. 2nd ed. St. Louis, Mo. : Mosby, c2000.
**TC RM216 .G946 2000**

**Andorfer, Gregory.**
The blue planet [videorecording]. [New York, N.Y.?] : Unapix Entertainment, Inc. [distributor], c1996.
**TC QB631.2 .B5 1996**

The climate puzzle [videorecording]. [New York, N.Y.?] : Unapix Entertainment, Inc. [distributor], c1996.
**TC QB631.2 .C5 1996**

The living machine [videorecording]. [New York, N.Y.?] : Unapix Entertainment, Inc. [distributor], c1996.

*TC QB631.2 .L5 1996*

Fate of the earth [videorecording]. [New York, N.Y.?] : Unapix Entertainment, Inc. [distributor], c1996.

*TC QB631.2 .F3 1996*

Gifts from the earth [videorecording]. [New York, N.Y.?] : Unapix Entertainment, Inc. [distributor], c1996.

*TC QB631.2 .G5 1996*

The solar sea [videorecording]. [New York, N.Y.?] : Unapix Entertainment, Inc. [distributor], c1996.

*TC QB631.2 .S6 1996*

Tales from other worlds [videorecording]. [New York, N.Y.?] : Unapix Entertainment, Inc. [distributor], c1996.

*TC QB631.2 .T3 1996*

Tales from other worlds [videorecording]. [New York, N.Y.?] : Unapix Entertainment, Inc. [distributor], c1996.

*TC QB631.2 .T3 1996*

**ANDOVER (MASS.) - BUILDINGS, STRUCTURES, ETC.**
Montgomery, Susan J., 1947- Phillips Academy. New York : Princeton Architectural Press, 2000.
*TC LD7501.A5 M65 2000*

**ANDRAGOGICAL LEARNING.** *See* **ADULT LEARNING.**

**André, Serge.**
  [Que veut une femme? English]
  What does a woman want? / Serge André ; foreword by Frances L. Restuccia ; translated by Susan Fairfield. New York : Other Press, c1999. xxviii, 350 p. ; 21 cm. Translation of: Que veut une femme? Includes bibliographical references and index. ISBN 1-89274-628-X (pbk. : alk. paper)
  *1. Women and psychoanalysis. 2. Women - Psychology 3. Femininity. I. Title.*
  *TC BF175 .A69613 1999*

**Andress, Barbara.** Music for young children / Barbara Andress. Fort Worth, TX : Harcourt Brace College Publishers, c1998. 247 p. ; 28 cm. ISBN 0-15-503071-X
  *1. Music - Instruction and study - Juvenile. I. Title.*
  *TC MT810 .A6 1998*

**Andrews, Gavin.**
  Unmet need in psychiatry. Cambridge, U.K. : New York, NY : Cambridge University Press, 2000.
  *TC RA790.5 .U565 2000*

**Andrews, Marcellus, 1956-** The political economy of hope and fear : capitalism and the Black condition in America / Marcellus Andrews. New York : New York University Press, c1999. vii, 224 p. ; 24 cm. Includes bibliographical references (p. 215-220) and index. ISBN 0-8147-0679-7 (acid-free paper) DDC 330.973/09
  *1. Afro-Americans - Economic conditions. 2. United States - Economic conditions - 1945- 3. Capitalism - United States - History - 20th century. 4. United States - Economic policy. I. Title.*
  *TC E185.8 .A77 1999*

**Andriot, Laurie.** Internet blue pages / researched and compiled by Laurie Andriot. 1999 ed. Medford, NJ : Information Today, c1998. ix, 359 p. ; 26 cm. "The guide to Federal Government web sites"--Cover. Includes index. ISBN 0-910965-29-3 DDC 025.04
  *1. Electronic government information - United States - Directories. 2. Web sites - United States - Directories. I. Title.*
  *TC ZA5075 .A53 1998*

Uncle Sam's K-12 Web : government Internet resources for educators, students, and parents / compiled by Laurie Andriot. Medford, N.J. : CyberAge Books, 1999. xv, 244 p. ; 25 cm. Includes index. ISBN 0-910965-32-3 (pbk.) DDC 025.04 DDC 025.04
  *1. Electronic government information - United States - Directories. 2. Internet (Computer network) in education - United States - Directories. 3. Web sites - United States - Directories. I. Title.*
  *TC ZA575 .A53 1999*

**Andriote, John-Manuel.** Victory deferred : how AIDS changed gay life in America / John-Manuel Andriote. Chicago : The University of Chicago Press, c1999. xvi, 478 p. ; 24 cm. Includes bibliographical references (p. 423-459) and index. ISBN 0-226-02049-5 (cloth : alk. paper) DDC 362.1/969792/00973
  *1. AIDS (Disease) - United States - History. 2. Gay men - United States - Diseases. 3. AIDS (Disease) - Social aspects - United States. 4. Gay liberation movement - United States. I. Title.*
  *TC RA644.A25 A523 1999*

**Andrulis, Dennis P.** Managed care and the inner city : the uncertain promise for providers, plans, and communities / Dennis P. Andrulis, Betsy Carrier. San Francisco : Jossey-Bass, 1999. xxvi, 191 p. : ill. ; 24 cm. Spine title: Managed care in the inner city. Includes bibliographical references and index. ISBN 0-7879-4623-0 (hbk. : alk. paper) DDC 362.1/04258/0973
  *1. Managed care plans (Medical care) - United States. 2. Urban poor - Medical care - United States. 3. Managed Care Programs - United States. 4. Delivery of Health Care - United States. 5. Poverty - United States. I. Carrier, Betsy. II. National Public Health and Hospital Institute. III. Title. IV. Title: Managed care in the inner city*
  *TC RA413.5.U5 A57 1999*

**Andy Warhol** [videorecording] / produced and directed by Kim Evans ; edited and presented by Melvyn Bragg. [Chicago, IL] : Home Vision [distributor],cc1987. 1 videocassette (79 min.) : sd., col. with b&w sequences ; 1/2 in. (Portrait of an artist) At head of title: Home Vision... presents an RM Arts production... [videorecording]. Title on container: Warhol. VHS. Catalogued from credits and container. Graphics, Pat Gavin ; designer, Andrew Gardner ; film camera, Paul Bond ; film sound, Trevor Carless. "WAR 01"--Container. "A London Weekend Television `South Bank Show-co-production with RM Arts"--Container. For adolescents through adult. SUMMARY: A profile of Andy Warhol's life and work. This video, completed after his death in Feb. 1987, examines a career that included painting, film, television, rock music, and publishing. Includes excerpts from interviews filmed over a period of 25 years, and footage taken in London shortly before his death.
  *1. Warhol, Andy, - 1928- 2. Artists - United States - Biography. 3. Painters - United States - Biography. 4. Motion picture producers and directors - United States - Biography. 5. Documentary films. 6. Biographical films. I. Evans, Kim. II. Warhol, Andy, 1928- III. Bragg, Melvyn, 1939- IV. London Weekend Television. ltd. V. RM Arts (Firm) VI. Home Vision (Firm) VII. Title: South Bank show (Television program) VIII. Title: Home Vision... presents an RM Arts production... [videorecording] IX. Title: Warhol X. Series.*
  *TC N6537.W28 A45 1987*

**Andy Warhol** [videorecording] / produced and directed by Kim Evans ; edited and presented by Melvyn Bragg. [Chicago, IL] : Home Vision [distributor],cc1987. 1 videocassette (79 min.) : sd., col. with b&w sequences ; 1/2 in. (Portrait of an artist) At head of title: Home Vision... presents an RM Arts production... [videorecording]. Title on container: Warhol. VHS. Catalogued from credits and container. Graphics, Pat Gavin ; designer, Andrew Gardner ; film camera, Paul Bond ; film sound, Trevor Carless. "WAR 01"--Container. "A London Weekend Television `South Bank Show-co-production with RM Arts"--Container. For adolescents through adult. SUMMARY: A profile of Andy Warhol's life and work. This video, completed after his death in Feb. 1987, examines a career that included painting, film, television, rock music, and publishing. Includes excerpts from interviews filmed over a period of 25 years, and footage taken in London shortly before his death.
  *1. Warhol, Andy, - 1928- 2. Artists - United States - Biography. 3. Painters - United States - Biography. 4. Motion picture producers and directors - United States - Biography. 5. Pop art - United States. 6. Art, Modern - 20th century - United States. 7. Documentary films. 8. Biographical films. I. Evans, Kim. II. Warhol, Andy, 1928- III. Bragg, Melvyn, 1939- IV. London Weekend Television. ltd. V. RM Arts (Firm) VI. Home Vision (Firm) VII. Title: South Bank show (Television program) VIII. Title: Home Vision... presents an RM Arts production... [videorecording] IX. Title: Warhol X. Series.*
  *TC N6537.W28 A45 1987*

**Aneshensel, Carol S.**
  Handbook of the sociology of mental health. New York : Kluwer Academic/Plenum Publishers, c1999.
  *TC RC455 .H2874 1999*

**ANESTHESIOLOGY - APPARATUS AND INSTRUMENTS.** *See* **RESPIRATORS (MEDICAL EQUIPMENT).**

**Anfam, David.**
  Rothko, Mark, 1903-1970. Mark Rothko. New Haven : Yale University Press ; Washington, D.C. : National Gallery of Art, c1998.
  *TC ND237.R725 A4 1998*

**Anfinson, Olaf P.** Understanding the physical sciences. Boston, Allyn and Bacon, 1963. xv, 456 p. ill. ; 26 cm. Includes bibliography and index. DDC 500
  *1. Science. I. Title.*
  *TC Q162 .A54*

**Angel, Charlotte.**
  d·a·t·e rape [videorecording]. [Charleston, WV] : Cambridge Educational, c1994.
  *TC RC560.R36 D3 1994*

**Angel spreads her wings.**
  Delton, Judy. Boston : Houghton Mifflin, 1999.
  *TC PZ7.D388 Anf 1999*

**Angell, Carl.**
  Learning from others. Dordrecht [Netherlands] ; Boston : Kluwer Academic Publishers, c2000.
  *TC LB43 .L42 2000*

**ANGELS.**
  Sobel, Ileene Smith. Moses and the angels. New York : Delacorte Press, c1999.
  *TC BM580 .S55 1999*

**ANGEL'S FLIGHT SHELTER (LOS ANGELES, CALIF.).**
  Starting over [videorecording]. [Charleston, W.V.] : Cambridge Educational, c1994.
  *TC HV1435.C3 S7 1994*

**ANGELS (JUDAISM) - JUVENILE LITERATURE.**
  Sobel, Ileene Smith. Moses and the angels. New York : Delacorte Press, c1999.
  *TC BM580 .S55 1999*

**ANGER - FICTION.**
  Bang, Molly. When Sophie gets angry--really, really angry.... New York : Blue Sky Press, c1999.
  *TC PZ7.B2217 Wh 1999*

**Angle of repose.**
  Stegner, Wallace Earle, 1909- New York : Modern Library, 2000.
  *TC PS3537.T316 A8 2000*

**Anglin, Karin.**
  Connect with English [videorecording]. S. Burlington, Vt. : The Annenberg/CPB Collection, c1997.
  *TC PE1128 .C66 1997*

**ANGLO-AMERICAN LAW.** *See* **LAW - UNITED STATES.**

**Anglo-Dutch Historical Conference (13th : 1997)** The education of a Christian society : humanism and the Reformation in Britain and the Netherlands / edited by N. Scott Amos, Andrew Pettegree, and Henk van Nierop. Aldershot, Hants, England ; Brookfield, Vt. : Ashgate, c1999. xii, 274 p. : ill. 1 map ; 25 cm. (St. Andrews studies in Reformation history) "Papers delivered to the Thirteenth Anglo-Dutch Historical Conference, 1997." Includes bibliographical references and index. ISBN 0-7546-0001-7 (alk. paper) DDC 274.1/06
  *1. Reformation - Great Britain. 2. Humanism - Great Britain. 3. Reformation - Netherlands. 4. Humanism - Netherlands. 5. Great Britain - Church history - 16th century. 6. Netherlands - Church history - 16th century. I. Amos, N. Scott. II. Pettegree, Andrew. III. Nierop, Henk F. K. van. IV. Title. V. Series.*
  *TC BR377 .E38 1999*

**Angrosino, Michael V.** Opportunity house : ethnographic stories of mental retardation / Michael V. Angrosino. Walnut Creek, CA : AltaMira Press, c1998. 287 p. ; 23 cm. (Ethnographic alternatives book series ; v. 2) Includes bibliographical references (p. 279-285). CONTENTS: Fellow traveler -- The ghost of Dallas Lumbley -- Any port in a storm. The left stuff. Target enterprises. Midnight at the Budget Inn. Interlude -- Take pen in hand -- Where the heart is. An honest woman. Little bit of warm. The chadster steps out. Days of sunshine, days of rain. Perfect pals. Interlude. Fit to print -- The boys in the van. How sweet the sound. The lonesome trucker. By the chimney with care -- All told. ISBN 0-7619-8916-1 (cloth) ISBN 0-7619-8917-X (pbk.) DDC 362.3/0973
  *1. Mental retardation - United States. 2. Ethnology - United States. I. Title. II. Series.*
  *TC HV3006.A4 A48 1998*

**ANGST.** *See* **ANXIETY.**

**ANIMAL BABIES.** *See* **ANIMALS - INFANCY.**

**ANIMAL BEHAVIOR.** *See also* **ANIMAL MIGRATION; NOCTURNAL ANIMALS; PARENTAL BEHAVIOR IN ANIMALS; PSYCHOLOGY, COMPARATIVE; SLEEP BEHAVIOR IN ANIMALS.**
  Allee, W. C. (Warder Clyde), 1885-1955. [Social life of animals] Cooperation among animals. A rev. and amplified ed. of The social life of animals. New York : Schuman, 1951.
  *TC QL751 .A52 1951*

**ANIMAL CLINICS.** *See* **VETERINARY HOSPITALS.**

**ANIMAL COMMUNICATION.**
  Oller, D. Kimbrough. The emergence of the speech capacity. Mahwah, N.J. : Lawrence Erlbaum Associates, 2000.
  *TC P118 .O43 2000*

ANIMAL DOCTORS. *See* VETERINARIANS.

ANIMAL EVOLUTION. *See* EVOLUTION
  (BIOLOGY).

**Animal fair.**
  Stevens, Janet. New York : Holiday House, c1981.
  *TC PZ8.3.S844 An*

ANIMAL HEALTH. *See* VETERINARY
  MEDICINE.

**Animal hospital.**
  Walker-Hodge, Judith. 1st American ed. New York :
  DK Pub., 1999.
  *TC SF604.55 .H63 1999*

ANIMAL HOSPITALS. *See* VETERINARY
  HOSPITALS.

**Animal house.**
  Mathis, Melissa Bay. 1st ed. New York : Simon &
  Schuster Books for Young Readers, 1999.
  *TC PZ8.3.M4265 Ap 1999*

ANIMAL-HUMAN RELATIONSHIPS. *See*
  HUMAN-ANIMAL RELATIONSHIPS.

ANIMAL INFANCY. *See* ANIMALS - INFANCY.

ANIMAL INTELLIGENCE. *See* LEARNING,
  PSYCHOLOGY OF; PSYCHOLOGY,
  COMPARATIVE.

ANIMAL KINGDOM. *See* ZOOLOGY.

ANIMAL MAGNETISM. *See* HYPNOTISM.

ANIMAL-MAN RELATIONSHIPS. *See* HUMAN-
  ANIMAL RELATIONSHIPS.

ANIMAL MECHANICS. *See* HUMAN
  MECHANICS.

ANIMAL MIGRATION - JUVENILE
  LITERATURE.
  Sayre, April Pulley. Home at last. 1st ed. New York :
  Holt, 1998.
  *TC QL754 .S29 1998*

**Animal models of human emotion and cognition /**
  [edited by Marc Haug and Richard E. Whalen. 1st ed.
  Washington, DC : American Psychological
  Association, c1999. X, 341 p. ; 27 cm. Includes
  bibliographical references and indexes. ISBN 1-55798-583-9
  DDC 156
    *1. Psychology, Comparative. 2. Human behavior - Animal
    models. I. Haug, M. (Marc) II. Whalen, Richard E.*
  *TC BF671 .A55 1999*

**Animal music.**
  Ziefert, Harriet. Boston : Houghton Mifflin, 1999.
  *TC PZ8.3.Z47 An 1999*

ANIMAL NAMES, POPULAR. *See* ZOOLOGY -
  NOMENCLATURE (POPULAR).

ANIMAL PICTURES. *See* ANIMALS -
  PICTORIAL WORKS.

ANIMAL PSYCHOLOGY. *See* PSYCHOLOGY,
  COMPARATIVE.

ANIMAL SOUNDS. *See* BIRDSONGS.

ANIMAL SPECIALISTS. *See* VETERINARIANS.

ANIMAL SWIMMING.
  Riley, Linda Capus. Elephants swim. Boston :
  Houghton Mifflin, 1995.
  *TC QP310.S95 R55 1995*

ANIMAL YOUNG. *See* ANIMALS - INFANCY.

ANIMALS. *See also* EXTINCT ANIMALS;
  HUMAN-ANIMAL RELATIONSHIPS;
  ZOOLOGY.
  Demi. [Opposites] Demi's opposites. New York :
  Grosset & Dunlap, c1987.
  *TC PE1591 .D43 1987*

  Lesser, Carolyn. Spots. 1st ed. San Diego : Harcourt
  Brace, c1999.
  *TC QA113 .L47 1999*

  Livo, Norma J., 1929- Celebrating the earth.
  Englewood, Colo. : Teacher Ideas Press, 2000.
  *TC QL50 .L57 2000*

  Walker-Hodge, Judith. Animal hospital. 1st American
  ed. New York : DK Pub., 1999.
  *TC SF604.55 .H63 1999*

ANIMALS AND HUMANS. *See* HUMAN-ANIMAL
  RELATIONSHIPS.

ANIMALS AS PARENTS. *See* PARENTAL
  BEHAVIOR IN ANIMALS.

ANIMALS - DISEASES. *See* VETERINARY
  MEDICINE.

ANIMALS - EVOLUTION. *See* EVOLUTION
  (BIOLOGY).

ANIMALS - EXTINCTION. *See* EXTINCTION
  (BIOLOGY).

ANIMALS - FICTION.
  Cherry, Lynne. Who's sick today? 1st ed. New York :
  Dutton, c1988.
  *TC PZ8.3.C427 Wh 1988*

  Edwards, Pamela Duncan. Wacky wedding. 1st ed.
  New York : Hyperion Books for Children, c1999.
  *TC PZ7.E26365 Wac 1999*

  Ginsburg, Mirra. Mushroom in the rain. New York :
  Macmillan/McGraw-Hill, 1974.
  *TC PZ10.3 .G455Mu 1974*

  Grossman, Bill. Donna O'Neeshuck was chased by
  some cows. 1st ed. [New York] : Harper & Row,
  c1988.
  *TC PZ8.3.G914 Do 1988*

  Koide, Tan. May we sleep here tonight? New York :
  Atheneum, 1981.
  *TC PZ7.K8293 May 1981*

  Martin, Bill, 1916- Brown bear, brown bear, what do
  you see? New York : H. Holt, 1992.
  *TC PZ8.3.M418 Br 1992*

  Mathis, Melissa Bay. Animal house. 1st ed. New
  York : Simon & Schuster Books for Young Readers,
  1999.
  *TC PZ8.3.M4265 Ap 1999*

  Preston, Tim. The lonely scarecrow. 1st American ed.
  New York : Dutton Children's Books, 1999.
  *TC PZ7.P9237 Lo 1999*

  Reeves, Mona Rabun. I had a cat. 1st American ed.
  New York : Bradbury Press, c1989.
  *TC PZ8.3.R263 Iah 1989*

  Sharmat, Marjorie Weinman. The 329th friend. New
  York : Four Winds Press, c1979.
  *TC PZ7.S5299 Tk 1979*

  Stevenson, James, 1929- Don't make me laugh. 1st
  ed. New York : Farrar, Straus and Giroux, c1999.
  *TC PZ7.S84748 Do 1999*

  Taylor, Harriet Peck. Ulaq and the northern lights. 1st
  ed. New York : Farrar Straus Girous, 1998.
  *TC PZ7.T2135 Ul 1998*

  Yolen, Jane. Mouse's birthday. New York : Putnam's,
  c1993.
  *TC PZ8.3.Y76 Mo 1993*

  Ziefert, Harriet. Animal music. Boston : Houghton
  Mifflin, 1999.
  *TC PZ8.3.Z47 An 1999*

ANIMALS - FOLKLORE.
  Livo, Norma J., 1929- Celebrating the earth.
  Englewood, Colo. : Teacher Ideas Press, 2000.
  *TC QL50 .L57 2000*

ANIMALS, FOSSIL. *See* VERTEBRATES,
  FOSSIL.

ANIMALS - HABITS AND BEHAVIOR.
  Behavior monographs. Cambridge, Mass. : H. Holt &
  Company, 1911-

ANIMALS, HABITS AND BEHAVIOR OF -
  PERIODICALS.
  The Journal of animal behavior. Cambridge, Mass., H.
  Holt and Company [etc., etc., 1911-17]

ANIMALS IN ART.
  Bruegel, Jan, 1568-1625. Where's the bear? Los
  Angeles : J. Paul Getty Museum, c1997.
  *TC QL49 .B749 1997*

  Flora and fauna in Mughal art. [Bombay] : Marg
  Publications, c1999.
  *TC N7302 .F567 1999*

ANIMALS - INFANCY. *See* PARENTAL
  BEHAVIOR IN ANIMALS.

ANIMALS - INFANCY - FICTION.
  Chwast, Seymour. Traffic jam. Boston : Houghton
  Mifflin, 1999.
  *TC PZ7.C4893 Tr 1999*

ANIMALS, INFANCY OF. *See* ANIMALS -
  INFANCY.

ANIMALS - INFANCY - PERIODICALS.
  Progress in infancy research. Mahwah, NJ : Lawrence
  Erlbaum Associates, 2000-

*TC BF719 .P76*

ANIMALS - JUVENILE FICTION.
  Gannett, Ruth Stiles. My father's dragon. New York :
  Random House, 1948.
  *TC PZ7.G15 My 1948*

ANIMALS - JUVENILE LITERATURE.
  Demi. [Opposites] Demi's opposites. New York :
  Grosset & Dunlap, c1987.
  *TC PE1591 .D43 1987*

  Lesser, Carolyn. Spots. 1st ed. San Diego : Harcourt
  Brace, c1999.
  *TC QA113 .L47 1999*

ANIMALS - JUVENILE POETRY.
  Yolen, Jane. Ring of earth. 1st ed. San Diego :
  Harcourt Brace Jovanovich, c1986.
  *TC PS3575.O43 R5 1986*

ANIMALS - MIGRATION. *See also* ANIMAL
  MIGRATION.
  Sayre, April Pulley. Home at last. 1st ed. New York :
  Holt, 1998.
  *TC QL754 .S29 1998*

ANIMALS, MIGRATION OF. *See* ANIMAL
  MIGRATION.

ANIMALS, MYTHICAL. *See* DRAGONS.

ANIMALS - NAMES. *See* ZOOLOGY -
  NOMENCLATURE (POPULAR).

ANIMALS, NOCTURNAL. *See* NOCTURNAL
  ANIMALS.

ANIMALS - PICTORIAL WORKS - JUVENILE
  LITERATURE.
  Bruegel, Jan, 1568-1625. Where's the bear? Los
  Angeles : J. Paul Getty Museum, c1997.
  *TC QL49 .B749 1997*

ANIMALS - PLAY BEHAVIOR - FICTION.
  Henkes, Kevin. Oh!. New York : Greenwillow Books,
  1999.
  *TC PZ8.3.H4165 Oh 1999*

ANIMALS - POETRY.
  Dana, Katharine Floyd, 1835-1886. Over in the
  meadow. New York : Scholastic, c1992
  *TC PZ8.3.D2 Ov 1992*

  Stevens, Janet. Animal fair. New York : Holiday
  House, c1981.
  *TC PZ8.3.S844 An*

  Yolen, Jane. Ring of earth. 1st ed. San Diego :
  Harcourt Brace Jovanovich, c1986.
  *TC PS3575.O43 R5 1986*

ANIMALS - SLEEP BEHAVIOR.
  Kajikawa, Kimiko. Sweet dreams. 1st ed. New York :
  Henry Holt, c1999.
  *TC QL755.3 .K36 1999*

ANIMALS - STUDY AND TEACHING -
  ACTIVITY PROGRAMS.
  Livo, Norma J., 1929- Celebrating the earth.
  Englewood, Colo. : Teacher Ideas Press, 2000.
  *TC QL50 .L57 2000*

ANIMALS - TREATMENT - FICTION.
  Thompson, Colin (Colin Edward) Unknown. New
  York : Walker & Co., 2000.
  *TC PZ7.T371424 Un 2000*

ANIMALS, ZOO. *See* ZOO ANIMALS.

**Animating the letter.**
  Kendrick, Laura. Columbus, Ohio : Ohio State
  University Press, c1999.
  *TC NK3610 .K46 1999*

ANKARA (TURKEY).
  Seferoglu, Süleyman Sadi. Elementary school teacher
  development. 1996.
  *TC 06 no. 10693*

**Anna all year round.**
  Hahn, Mary Downing. New York : Clarion Books,
  c1999.
  *TC PZ7.H1256 An 1999*

**Anna Caroline Maxwell's contributions to nursing.**
  Smalls, Sadie Marian. 1996.
  *TC 06 no. 10698*

ANNALS. *See* HISTORY.

**Annan, Noel Gilroy Annan, Baron, 1916-** The dons :
  mentors, eccentrics and geniuses / Noel Annan.
  Chicago : University of Chicago Press ; London :
  HarperCollins Publishers, 1999. ix, 357 p., [16] p. of
  plates : ill. ; 23 cm. Includes bibliographical references and
  index. ISBN 0-226-02107-6 (cloth) DDC 378.1/2/0941

*1. Universities and colleges - Great Britain - Faculty - History. 2. College teachers - Great Britain - Biography. I. Title.*
**TC LB2331.74.G7 A55 1999**

**Annandale, Ellen.**
Gender inequalities in health. Buckingham [England] ; Philadelphia : Open University Press, 2000.
**TC RA564.85 .G4653 2000**

**Annenberg/CPB Project.**
The blue planet [videorecording]. [New York, N.Y.?] : Unapix Entertainment, Inc. [distributor], c1996.
**TC QB631.2 .B5 1996**

The climate puzzle [videorecording]. [New York, N.Y.?] : Unapix Entertainment, Inc. [distributor], c1996.
**TC QB631.2 .C5 1996**

Connect with English [videorecording]. S. Burlington, Vt. : The Annenberg/CPB Collection, c1997.
**TC PE1128 .C66 1997**

The living machine [videorecording]. [New York, N.Y.?] : Unapix Entertainment, Inc. [distributor], c1996.
**TC QB631.2 .L5 1996**

Fate of the earth [videorecording]. [New York, N.Y.?] : Unapix Entertainment, Inc. [distributor], c1996.
**TC QB631.2 .F3 1996**

Gifts from the earth [videorecording]. [New York, N.Y.?] : Unapix Entertainment, Inc. [distributor], c1996.
**TC QB631.2 .G5 1996**

The solar sea [videorecording]. [New York, N.Y.?] : Unapix Entertainment, Inc. [distributor], c1996.
**TC QB631.2 .S6 1996**

Tales from other worlds [videorecording]. [New York, N.Y.?] : Unapix Entertainment, Inc. [distributor], c1996.
**TC QB631.2 .T3 1996**

Tales from other worlds [videorecording]. [New York, N.Y.?] : Unapix Entertainment, Inc. [distributor], c1996.
**TC QB631.2 .T3 1996**

**Anning, Angela, 1944-** Promoting children's learning from birth to five : developing the new early years professional / Angela Anning and Anne Edwards. Buckingham [England] ; Philadelphia : Open University Press, 1999. viii, 184 p. : ill. ; 24 cm. Includes bibliographical references (p. [168]-177) and indexes. ISBN 0-335-20217-9 (hbk.) ISBN 0-335-20216-0 (pbk.) DDC 372.21/0941
*1. Early childhood education - Great Britain. 2. Early childhood education - Great Britain - Curricula. 3. Early childhood education - Training of - Great Britain. I. Edwards, Anne, 1946- II. Title.*
**TC LB1139.3.G7 A55 1999**

**ANNIVERSARIES.** *See* **FESTIVALS; HOLIDAYS.**

**Annuaire statistique.**
[Statistical yearbook (Unesco)] Statistical yearbook = [Paris : Unesco], 1987-
**TC AZ361 .U45**

**Annual distinguished lecture series in special education and rehabilitation.**
Annual distinguished lectures in special education and rehabilitation. Los Angeles, Dept. of Exceptional Children, University of Southern California.
**TC LC4019 .D57**

**Annual distinguished lecture series in special education and rehabilitation <1967->.**
Annual distinguished lectures in special education and rehabilitation. Los Angeles, Dept. of Exceptional Children, University of Southern California.
**TC LC4019 .D57**

**Annual distinguished lectures in special education and rehabilitation.** Los Angeles, Dept. of Exceptional Children, University of Southern California. v. 23 cm. Frequency: Annual. Began with 1962 lecture. Cover title: Annual distinguished lecture series in special education and rehabilitation <1967->. Title varies slightly. Continued by: Annual distinguished lecture series in special education and rehabilitation (DLC)sc 89037000 (OCoLC)9233262. ISSN 0070-6736 DDC 371.9/05
*1. Handicapped children - Education - Periodicals. I. University of Southern California. Dept. of Exceptional Children. II. Title: Annual distinguished lecture series in special education and rehabilitation <1967-> III. Title: Annual distinguished lecture series in special education and rehabilitation*

**TC LC4019 .D57**

**Annual editions.**
[Education (Guilford, Conn.)] Education. Guilford, Ct., Dushkin Pub. Group.
**TC LB41 .A673**

**Annual editions: Education <1980/81->.**
[Education (Guilford, Conn.)] Education. Guilford, Ct., Dushkin Pub. Group.
**TC LB41 .A673**

**Annual editions. Readings in education.**
[Education (Guilford, Conn.)] Education. Guilford, Ct., Dushkin Pub. Group.
**TC LB41 .A673**

**Annual guide to graduate nursing education.**
Annual guide to graduate nursing education programs. New York, N.Y. : National League for Nursing Press, c1995-
**TC RT75 .A5**

**Annual guide to graduate nursing education programs.** New York, N.Y. : National League for Nursing Press, c1995- v. ; 28 cm. Frequency: Annual. 1994-1995- . Issues for 1996- have new title: Annual guide to graduate nursing education. Pub. no. 19-6924 Issued by: National League for Nursing.
*1. Nursing - Study and teaching (Graduate) - United States - Directories. 2. Nursing schools - United States - Directories. 3. Education. Nursing, Graduate - United States - directories. 4. Schools, Nursing - United States - directories. I. National League for Nursing. II. Title: Annual guide to graduate nursing education*
**TC RT75 .A5**

**Annual review of The Institute for Information Studies**
(1996.) The emerging world of wireless communications. Nashville, TN : Institute for Information Studies, 1996.
**TC TK5103.2 .E44 1996**

**Annual State of American Education Address (7th : February 22, 2000 : Durham, N.C.)** The seventh annual state of American education address [videorecording / [presented by the United States Department of Education?]. [Washington, D.C. : U.S. Dept. of Education], 2000. 1 videocassette (ca. 74 min.) : sd., col. ; 1/2 in. (Satellite town meeting) VHS. Catalogued from credits and data sheet. Closed-captioned for the hearing impaired. Speaker: Secretary of education, Richard Riley. A C-span Satellite Town meeting with 250 downlinks, held at Southern High School in Durham, N.C., Tuesday, February 22, 2000, 12:00-1:00 P.M. (ET), For educators, administrators, parents and students. SUMMARY: Secretary of Education, Richard Riley discusses the challenge of the democratization of education, having new and higher expectations for all, that we might become a nation of learners, investing in our children and offering them all a first class education with better accountability and flexibility. He mentions five principles: having a healthy ties with parents and teachers; states meeting challenges and standards a step at a time; offering multiple measurement of and assessment of standards; investing in teachers and schools; offering accountability for results.
*1. Moral education - United States. 2. Civics - Study and teaching - United States. 3. Values - Study and teaching - United States. 4. Education - Parent participation - United States. 5. Respect - Study and teaching - United States. 6. Responsibility - Study and teaching - United States. 7. Work ethic - Study and teaching - United States. 8. Honesty - Study and teaching - United States. 9. Video recordings for the hearing impaired. I. Mathis, Nancy. II. Riley, Richard W. (Richard Wilson) III. United States. Dept. of Education. IV. National Alliance of Business. V. Chamber of Commerce of the United States of America. VI. Committee for Economic Development. VII. Title. VIII. Series.*

**Annual yearbook of the American Education Finance Association**
(16th) Where does the money go? Thousand Oaks, Calif. : Corwin Press, c1996.
**TC LB2825 .W415 1996**

(17th) A struggle to survive. Thousand Oaks, Calif. : Corwin Press, c1996.
**TC LB2342 .S856 1996**

(21st.) Balancing local control and state responsibility for K-12 education. Larchmont, NY : Eye on Education, 2000.
**TC LC89 .B35 2000**

**ANOMY.**
Comparative anomie research. Aldershot, Hants, England ; Brookfield, Vt., USA : Ashgate, c1999.
**TC HM816 .C65 1999**

**ANOREXIA NERVOSA.**
The management of eating disorders and obesity. Totowa, N.J. : Humana Press, c1999.

**TC RC552.E18 M364 1999**

**ANOVA (ANALYSIS OF VARIANCE).** *See* **ANALYSIS OF VARIANCE.**

**Anson's way.**
Schmidt, Gary D. New York : Clarion Books, c1999.
**TC PZ7.S3527 An 1999**

**Anspaugh, David J.** Developing health promotion programs / David J. Anspaugh, Mark B. Dignan, Susan L. Anspaugh. Boston ; London : McGraw-Hill, c2000. x, 254 p. : ill. ; 24 cm. Includes bibliographical references and index. ISBN 0-8151-4374-5 DDC 613
*1. Health promotion - Philosophy. 2. Health planning - Philosophy. I. Dignan, Mark B. II. Anspaugh, Susan L. III. Title.*
**TC RA427.8 .A57 2000**

**Anspaugh, Susan L.**
Anspaugh, David J. Developing health promotion programs. Boston ; London : McGraw-Hill, c2000.
**TC RA427.8 .A57 2000**

**Anstey, Mark.** Managing change : negotiating conflict / Mark Anstey. 2nd ed. Kenwyn : Juta, 1999. xix, 399 p. : ill. ; 25 cm. Rev. ed. of: Negotiating conflict. 1991. Includes bibliographical references (p. 373-389) and index. ISBN 0-7021-5066-5
*1. Conflict management. 2. Industrial relations. I. Anstey, Mark. Negotiating conflict. II. Title.*
**TC HD42 .A57 1999**

**Negotiating conflict.**
Anstey, Mark. Managing change. 2nd ed. Kenwyn : Juta, 1999.
**TC HD42 .A57 1999**

**Answer to everything.**
Stephen Hawking's universe [videorecording]. [Alexandria, Va.] : PBS Video; Burbank, CA : Distributed by Warner Home Video, c1997.
**TC QB982 .S7 1997**

**Answers in the tool box.**
Adelman, Clifford. Washington, DC : U.S. Dept. of Education, Office of Educational Research and Improvement, [1999]
**TC LB2390 .A34 1999**

**ANSWERS TO QUESTIONS.** *See* **QUESTIONS AND ANSWERS.**

**ANT.** *See* **ANTS.**

**Antarctic antics.**
Sierra, Judy. 1st ed. San Diego : Harcourt Brace & Co., c1998.
**TC PS3569.I39 A53 1998**

**ANTARCTIC CONTINENT.** *See* **ANTARCTICA.**

**ANTARCTIC REGIONS.** *See* **ANTARCTICA.**

**ANTARCTIC REGIONS - JUVENILE POETRY.**
Sierra, Judy. Antarctic antics. 1st ed. San Diego : Harcourt Brace & Co., c1998.
**TC PS3569.I39 A53 1998**

**ANTARCTIC REGIONS - POETRY.**
Sierra, Judy. Antarctic antics. 1st ed. San Diego : Harcourt Brace & Co., c1998.
**TC PS3569.I39 A53 1998**

**Antarctica.**
Robinson, Kim Stanley. New York : Bantam Books, c1998.
**TC PS3568.O2893 A82 1998**

**ANTARCTICA - FICTION.**
Robinson, Kim Stanley. Antarctica. New York : Bantam Books, c1998.
**TC PS3568.O2893 A82 1998**

**Antes, Richard L.**
Hopkins, Charles D. Classroom testing. 2nd ed. Itasca, Ill. : F. E. Peacock Publishers, c1989.
**TC LB3060.65 .H661 1989**

**ANTHOLOGIES.** *See* **READERS.**

**Anthology of writing from the AIGA journal of graphic design.**
Design culture. New York : Allworth Press : American Institute of Graphic Arts, c1997.
**TC NC998.5.A1 D46 1997**

**Anthony, Martin.** Neural network learning : theoretical foundations / Martin Anthony and Peter L. Bartlett. Cambridge, U.K. ; New York : Cambridge University Press, 1999. xiv, 389 p. : ill. ; 24 cm. Includes bibliographical references (p. 365-378) and indexes. ISBN 0-521-57353-X (hbk.) DDC 006.3/2
*1. Neural networks (Computer science) I. Bartlett, Peter L., 1966- II. Title.*
**TC QA76.87 .A58 1999**

**Anthony Roland Collection of Film on Art.**
Comics, the 9th art [videorecording]. [S.l.] : EPISA ; Cicero, Ill. : [Distributed by] The Roland Collection, 1990.
*TC PN6710 .C6 1990*

Etching [videorecording]. Northbrook, Ill. : Peasmarsh, East Sussex, Eng. : Roland Collection of Films on Art, c1990.
*TC NE2043 .E87 1990*

Impressionism [videorecording]. [London] : The National Gallery ; Tillingham, Peasmarsh, East Sussex, England : Ho-Ho-Kus, NJ : Distributed by The Roland Collection, c1990.
*TC ND547.5.I4 A7 1990*

Italian painting before 1400 [videorecording]. [London] : The National Gallery, c1989.

Italian painting before 1400 [videorecording]. [London] : The National Gallery, c1989.
*TC ND1575 .I87 1989*

On pictures and paintings [videorecording]. Peasmarsh, East Sussex, Eng. ; Ho-Ho-kus, NJ : Roland Collection, 1992.
*TC ND195.O45 1992*

Photomontage today, Peter Kennard [videorecording]. [London] : Art Council of Great Britain : Ho-Ho-Kus, N.J. : [distributed by] Anthony Roland Collection of Films on Art, c1982.
*TC TR685 .P45 1982*

Processing the signal [videorecording]. Cicero, Ill. : Roland Collection of Films on Art, c1989.
*TC N6494.V53 P7 1989*

Screen printing [videorecording]. [Northbrook?], Ill. ; Peasmarsh, East Sussex, Eng. : Roland Collection of Films on Art, c1992.
*TC NE2238.G7 S4 1992*

What is a good drawing? [videorecording]. Peasmarsh, East Sussex, Eng. : Ho-Ho-Kus, NJ : Roland Collection, [1980-1986?].
*TC NC703 .W45 1980*

**Anthony Roland Collection of Films on Art.**
Etching [videorecording]. Northbrook, Ill. : Peasmarsh, East Sussex, Eng. : Roland Collection of Films on Art, c1990.
*TC NE2043 .E87 1990*

Impressionism [videorecording]. [London] : The National Gallery ; Tillingham, Peasmarsh, East Sussex, England : Ho-Ho-Kus, NJ : Distributed by The Roland Collection, c1990.
*TC ND547.5.I4 A7 1990*

Italian painting before 1400 [videorecording]. [London] : The National Gallery, c1989.
*TC ND1575 .I87 1989*

Processing the signal [videorecording]. Cicero, Ill. : Roland Collection of Films on Art, c1989.
*TC N6494.V53 P7 1989*

Screen printing [videorecording]. [Northbrook?], Ill. ; Peasmarsh, East Sussex, Eng. : Roland Collection of Films on Art, c1992.
*TC NE2238.G7 S4 1992*

Tassili N'Ajjer [videorecording]. [S.l.] : Editions Cinégraphiques ; Northbrook, Ill. : [distributed by] the Roland Collection, c1968.
*TC N5310.5.A4 T3 1968*

What is a good drawing? [videorecording]. Peasmarsh, East Sussex, Eng. : Ho-Ho-Kus, NJ : Roland Collection, [1980-1986?].
*TC NC703 .W45 1980*

**Anthony Rolland Collection of Film on Art.**
Tassili N'Ajjer [videorecording]. [S.l.] : Editions Cinégraphiques ; Northbrook, Ill. : [distributed by] the Roland Collection, c1968.
*TC N5310.5.A4 T3 1968*

**ANTHROPO-GEOGRAPHY.** *See* **HUMAN GEOGRAPHY.**

**ANTHROPOGEOGRAPHY.** *See* **HUMAN GEOGRAPHY.**

**ANTHROPOLOGICAL COLLECTIONS.** *See* **ANTHROPOLOGICAL MUSEUMS AND COLLECTIONS.**

**Anthropological Institute of Great Britain and Ireland.**
[Journal of the Anthropological Institute of Great Britain and Ireland (Online)] The journal of the

Anthropological Institute of Great Britain and Ireland [computer file]. London [England] : Published for the Anthropological Institute of Great Britain and Ireland by Trübner & Co., 1872-1906.
*TC EJOURNALS*

**ANTHROPOLOGICAL MUSEUMS AND COLLECTIONS.** *See* **ARCHAEOLOGICAL MUSEUMS AND COLLECTIONS.**

**ANTHROPOLOGICAL MUSEUMS AND COLLECTIONS - WASHINGTON (D.C.) - MANAGEMENT.**
Kurin, Richard, 1950- Reflections of a culture broker. Washington, D.C. : Smithsonian Institution Press, c1997.
*TC GN36.U62 D5775 1997*

**ANTHROPOLOGISTS - ATTITUDES.**
Behar, Ruth, 1956- The vulnerable observer. Boston : Beacon Press, c1996.
*TC GN346.4 .B44 1996*

**ANTHROPOLOGISTS - PSYCHOLOGY.**
Behar, Ruth, 1956- The vulnerable observer. Boston : Beacon Press, c1996.
*TC GN346.4 .B44 1996*

**ANTHROPOLOGY.** *See* **ARCHAEOLOGY; ASSIMILATION (SOCIOLOGY); EDUCATIONAL ANTHROPOLOGY; ETHNOLOGY; HUMAN GEOGRAPHY; LANGUAGE AND LANGUAGES; SOCIAL STRUCTURE.**

**Anthropology and human movement.**
Williams, Drid, 1928- Lanham, Md. ; London : Scarecrow Press, 2000.
*TC GV1595 .W53 2000*

**ANTHROPOLOGY - BIBLIOGRAPHY - PERIODICALS.**
International bibliography of anthropology = London ; New York : Routledge, 1999-
*TC Z7161 .I593*

**ANTHROPOLOGY, CRIMINAL.** *See* **CRIMINAL ANTHROPOLOGY.**

**ANTHROPOLOGY - MUSEUMS.** *See* **ANTHROPOLOGICAL MUSEUMS AND COLLECTIONS.**

**The anthropology of child and youth care work.**
Eisikovits, Rivka Anne. New York : Haworth Press, c1997.
*TC HV713 .E47 1997*

**The anthropology of everyday life**
Rapp, Rayna. Testing women, testing the fetus. New York : Routledge, 1999.
*TC RG628.3.A48 R37 1999*

**The anthropology of friendship** / edited by Sandra Bell and Simon Coleman. Oxford ; New York : Berg, 1999. xvi, 189 p. ; 24 cm. Includes bibliographical references and index. ISBN 1-85973-310-7 ISBN 1-85973-315-8 (pbk) DDC 302.34
*1. Friendship - Cross-cultural studies. I. Bell, Sandra M. II. Coleman, Simon.*
*TC GN486.3 .A48 1999*

**ANTHROPOLOGY - PERIODICALS.**
[Journal of the Anthropological Institute of Great Britain and Ireland (Online)] The journal of the Anthropological Institute of Great Britain and Ireland [computer file]. London [England] : Published for the Anthropological Institute of Great Britain and Ireland by Trübner & Co., 1872-1906.
*TC EJOURNALS*

[Journal of the Royal Anthropological Institute of Great Britain and Ireland (Online)] The journal of the Royal Anthropological Institute of Great Britain and Ireland [computer file]. London [England] : The Institute, 1907-1965.
*TC EJOURNALS*

**ANTHROPOLOGY - STUDY AND TEACHING - UNITED STATES.**
Strategies in teaching anthropology. Upper Saddle River, N.J. : Prentice Hall, c2000.
*TC GN43 .S77 2000*

**ANTHROPOLOGY - UNITED STATES - HISTORY.**
Trencher, Susan R. Mirrored images. Westport, CT : Bergin & Garvey, 2000.
*TC GN17.3.U6 T74 2000*

**ANTHROPOLOGY - UNITED STATES - PHILOSOPHY.**
Trencher, Susan R. Mirrored images. Westport, CT : Bergin & Garvey, 2000.

*TC GN17.3.U6 T74 2000*

**ANTHROPOMETRY.** *See* **CRIMINAL ANTHROPOLOGY.**

**ANTHROPOSOPHY.**
Steiner, Rudolf, 1861-1925. [Konferenzen mit den Lehrern der Freien Waldorfschule in Stuttgart. English] Faculty meetings with Rudolf Steiner. Hudson, NY : Anthroposophic Press, c1998.
*TC LF3195.S834 S8413 1998*

**ANTI-APARTHEID MOVEMENTS.** *See* **APARTHEID.**

**ANTI-COLONIALISM.** *See* **COLONIES.**

**ANTI-COMMUNIST MOVEMENTS - NORTH CAROLINA - HISTORY - 20TH CENTURY.**
Billingsley, William J., 1953- Communists on campus. Athens, Ga. ; London : University of Georgia Press, c1999.
*TC LC72.3.N67 B55 1999*

**ANTI-COMMUNIST MOVEMENTS - UNITED STATES - HISTORY - 1945-1953.**
Foster, Stuart J., 1960- Red alert!. New York ; Canterbury [England] : P. Lang, c2000.
*TC LC72.2 .F67 2000*

**ANTI-COMMUNIST RESISTANCE.** *See* **ANTI-COMMUNIST MOVEMENTS.**

**ANTI-ENVIRONMENTALISM.** *See* **ENVIRONMENTALISM.**

**ANTI-FEMINISM.** *See* **FEMINISM.**

**ANTI-GAY BIAS.** *See* **HOMOPHOBIA.**

**ANTI-HOMOSEXUAL BIAS.** *See* **HOMOPHOBIA.**

**ANTI-IMPERIALIST MOVEMENTS.** *See* **IMPERIALISM.**

**ANTI-NUCLEAR MOVEMENT.** *See* **ANTINUCLEAR MOVEMENT.**

**ANTI-POVERTY PROGRAM (UNITED STATES).** *See* **ECONOMIC ASSISTANCE, DOMESTIC - UNITED STATES.**

**ANTI-POVERTY PROGRAMS.** *See* **ECONOMIC ASSISTANCE, DOMESTIC.**

**ANTI-SLAVERY MOVEMENTS.** *See* **ANTISLAVERY MOVEMENTS.**

**ANTICENSORSHIP ACTIVISTS.** *See* **CENSORSHIP.**

**ANTIDEPRESSANTS.**
New therapeutic indications of antidepressants. Basel ; New York : Karger, c1997.
*TC RM332 .N475 1997*

**ANTIDEPRESSANTS - EFFECTIVENESS.**
Mood disorders. Basel ; New York : Karger, c1997.
*TC RC483 .M6 1997*

**ANTIDEPRESSIVE AGENTS.** *See* **ANTIDEPRESSANTS.**

**ANTIDEPRESSIVE AGENTS - PHARMACOLOGY.**
New therapeutic indications of antidepressants. Basel ; New York : Karger, c1997.
*TC RM332 .N475 1997*

**ANTIDEPRESSIVE AGENTS - THERAPEUTIC USE.**
New therapeutic indications of antidepressants. Basel ; New York : Karger, c1997.
*TC RM332 .N475 1997*

**ANTIHEROES.** *See* **HEROES.**

**ANTILLES.** *See* **WEST INDIES.**

**ANTIMILITARISM.** *See* **MILITARISM.**

**ANTINUCLEAR MOVEMENT - SOCIAL ASPECTS.**
Gusterson, Hugh. Nuclear rites. "First paperback printing 1998". Berkeley : University of California Press, 1998.
*TC U264.4.C2 G87 1998*

**ANTINUCLEAR PROTEST MOVEMENT.** *See* **ANTINUCLEAR MOVEMENT.**

**ANTIOXIDANTS.**
Antioxidants in muscle foods. New York ; Chichester [England] : John Wiley, c2000.
*TC TX556.M4 A57 2000*

Karlsson, Jan, 1940- Antioxidants and exercise. Champaign, IL : Human Kinetics, c1997.

*TC RB170 .K37 1997*

**Antioxidants and exercise.**
Karlsson, Jan, 1940- Champaign, IL : Human Kinetics, c1997.
*TC RB170 .K37 1997*

**Antioxidants in muscle foods :** nutritional strategies to improve quality / [edited by] Eric Decker, Cameron Faustman, Clemente J. Lopez-Bote. Chichester [England] : John Wiley, c2000. xii, 499 p. : ill. ; 25 cm. "Wiley-Interscience." Includes bibliographical references and index. ISBN 0-471-31454-4 (alk. paper) DDC 664/.907
*1. Meat - Quality. 2. Antioxidants. I. Decker, Eric, 1960- II. Faustman, Cameron, 1960- III. Lopez-Bote, Clemente J.*
*TC TX556.M4 A57 2000*

**ANTIOXIDANTS - METABOLISM.**
Karlsson, Jan, 1940- Antioxidants and exercise. Champaign, IL : Human Kinetics, c1997.
*TC RB170 .K37 1997*

**Antipodean currents :** ten contemporary artists from Australia / Gordon Bennett ... [et al.] ; [contributors: Roger Benjamin ... et al.]. New York : Guggenheim Museum, c1995. 157 p. : ill. (some col.) ; 25 cm. Catalog of an exhibition held Oct. 9-16, 1994 at the John F. Kennedy Center for the Performing Arts, Washington D.C., and June 21-Aug. 6, 1995 at the Guggenheim Museum SoHo, New York. Includes bibliographical references (p. 153-155). ISBN 0-89207-145-1
*1. Art, Modern - 20th century - Australia - Exhibitions. 2. Artists - Australia - Biography. I. Bennett, Gordon. II. Benjamin, Roger, 1957- III. Guggenheim Museum Soho. IV. John F. Kennedy Center for the Performing Arts (U.S.)*
*TC N7404 .A58 1995*

**ANTIPSYCHIATRY.**
Burston, Daniel, 1954- The crucible of experience. Cambridge, Mass. : Harvard University Press, c2000.
*TC RC438.6.L34 B86 2000*

**ANTIQUARIAN BOOKSELLERS.** See OUT-OF-PRINT BOOKS.

**ANTIQUE COLLECTING.** See ANTIQUES.

**ANTIQUES - COLLECTORS AND COLLECTING.** See ANTIQUES.

**ANTIQUES - DOCUMENTATION - STANDARDS.**
Thornes, Robin. Introduction to Object ID. [Los Angeles] : Getty Information Institute, c1999.
*TC N3998 .T457 1999*

**ANTIQUITIES.** See ANTIQUES; ARCHAEOLOGY.

**ANTIQUITIES - COLLECTION AND PRESERVATION.** See ARCHAEOLOGICAL MUSEUMS AND COLLECTIONS.

**ANTIQUITIES - DOCUMENTATION - STANDARDS.**
Thornes, Robin. Introduction to Object ID. [Los Angeles] : Getty Information Institute, c1999.
*TC N3998 .T457 1999*

**ANTIQUITIES, PREHISTORIC.** See PREHISTORIC PEOPLES.

**ANTISLAVERY.** See SLAVERY.

**ANTISLAVERY MOVEMENTS.**
Forten, Charlotte L. A free Black girl before the Civil War. Mankato, Minn. : Blue Earth Books, c2000.
*TC F74.S1 F67 2000*

**ANTISLAVERY MOVEMENTS - MASSACHUSETTS - HISTORY - 19TH CENTURY - JUVENILE LITERATURE.**
Forten, Charlotte L. A free Black girl before the Civil War. Mankato, Minn. : Blue Earth Books, c2000.
*TC F74.S1 F67 2000*

**ANTISOCIAL PERSONALITY DISORDER - DIAGNOSIS.**
Personality disorders [videorecording]. Princeton, N.J. : Films for the Humanities & Sciences, 1998.
*TC RC554 .P4 1998*

**ANTISOCIAL PERSONALITY DISORDER - PATIENTS.**
Personality disorders [videorecording]. Princeton, N.J. : Films for the Humanities & Sciences, 1998.
*TC RC554 .P4 1998*

**ANTISOCIAL PERSONALITY DISORDERS.**
Kunitz, Stephen J. Drinking, conduct disorder, and social change. Oxford ; New York : Oxford University Press, 2000.
*TC E99.N3 K88 2000*

**ANTISOCIAL PERSONALITY DISORDERS - GENETIC ASPECTS - CONGRESSES.**
Genetics of criminal and antisocial behaviour. Chichester ; New York : Wiley, 1996.
*TC HV6047 .G46 1996*

**Antonides, Gerrit, 1951-** Psychology in economics and business : an introduction to economic psychology / by Gerrit Antonides ; with an introduction by W. Fred van Raaij. 2nd rev. ed. Dordrecht, Netherlands ; Boston : Kluwer Academic, c1996. xi, 430 p. ; 25 cm. Includes bibliographical references (p. 393-416) and index. ISBN 0-7923-4107-4 (hb : alk. paper) DDC 330/.01/9
*1. Economics - Psychological aspects. I. Title.*
*TC HB74.P8 A64 1996*

**ANTS - FICTION.**
Edwards, Pamela Duncan. Wacky wedding. 1st ed. New York : Hyperion Books for Children, c1999.
*TC PZ7.E26365 Wac 1999*

**Anuario estadístico 1976-.**
[Statistical yearbook (Unesco)] Statistical yearbook = [Paris : Unesco], 1987-
*TC AZ361 .U45*

**ANXIETIES.** See ANXIETY.

**ANXIETY.** *See also* FEAR; PANIC DISORDERS; POST-TRAUMATIC STRESS DISORDER; SEPARATION ANXIETY.
Brink, Andrew. The creative matrix. New York : Peter Lang, c2000.
*TC BF698.9.C74 B75 2000*

Neurotic, stress-related, and somatoform disorders [videorecording]. Princeton, N.J. : Films for the Humanities & Sciences, 1998.
*TC RC530 .N4 1998*

Wells, Adrian. Cognitive therapy of anxiety disorders. Chichester ; New York : J. Wiley & Sons, c1997.
*TC RC531 .W43 1997*

**ANXIETY (CHILD PSYCHOLOGY).** See ANXIETY IN CHILDREN.

**ANXIETY - CONGRESSES.**
Anxiety, depression, and emotion. Oxford ; New York : Oxford University Press, 2000.
*TC RC531 .A559 2000*

**Anxiety, depression, and emotion** / edited by Richard J. Davidson. Oxford ; New York : Oxford University Press, 2000. xii, 291 p., [2] p. of plates : ill. (some col.) ; 25 cm. (Series in affective science) First Wisconsin Symposium on Emotion that was held on the campus of the University of Wisconsin-Madison in April 1995. Includes bibliographical references and index. ISBN 0-19-513358-7 DDC 616.85/223
*1. Anxiety - Congresses. 2. Depression, Mental - Congresses. 3. Emotions - Congresses. I. Davidson, Richard J. II. Wisconsin Symposium on Emotion (1st : 1995 : Madison, Wis.) III. Series.*
*TC RC531 .A559 2000*

**ANXIETY IN ADOLESCENCE.**
Dacey, John S. Your anxious child. 1st ed. San Francisco : Jossey-Bass, c2000.
*TC BF723.A5 D33 2000*

**ANXIETY IN ADOLESCENCE - TREATMENT.**
Treating anxious children and adolescents. Oakland, CA : New Harbinger Publications, c2000.
*TC RJ504.A58 T74 2000*

**ANXIETY IN CHILDREN.**
Dacey, John S. Your anxious child. 1st ed. San Francisco : Jossey-Bass, c2000.
*TC BF723.A5 D33 2000*

**ANXIETY IN CHILDREN - EL SALVADOR.**
Flores, Joaquín Evelio. Psychological effects of the civil war on children from rural communities of El Salvador.
*TC 083 F67*

**ANXIETY IN CHILDREN - TREATMENT.**
Treating anxious children and adolescents. Oakland, CA : New Harbinger Publications, c2000.
*TC RJ504.A58 T74 2000*

**ANXIETY IN OLD AGE.**
Grice, Marthe Jane. Attachment, race, and gender in late life. 1999.
*TC 085 G865*

**ANXIETY IN TEENAGERS.** See ANXIETY IN ADOLESCENCE.

**ANXIOUSNESS.** See ANXIETY.

**AONE management series**
Staffing management and methods. San Francisco : Jossey-Bass, 2000.
*TC RT89.3 .S72 2000*

**Aoyama, Yuko.**
Cities in the telecommunications age. New York : Routledge, 2000.
*TC HT167 .C483 2000*

**APARTHEID - SOUTH AFRICA.**
Mahlase, Shirley Motleke. The careers of women teachers under apartheid. Harare : SAPES Books, c1997.
*TC LB2832.4.S6 M35 1997*

**APATHY.** See EMOTIONS.

**Aper, Jeffery.**
Bogue, E. Grady (Ernest Grady), 1935- Exploring the heritage of American higher education. Phoenix, Ariz. : Oryx Press, 2000.
*TC LA227.4 .B66 2000*

**APHASIA.**
Aphasia in atypical populations. Mahwah, N.J. : Lawrence Erlbaum Associates, 1998.
*TC RC425 .A637 1998*

Davis, G. Albyn (George Albyn), 1946- Aphasiology. Boston : Allyn and Bacon, 2000.
*TC RC425 .D379 2000*

Parr, Susie, 1953- Talking about aphasia. Buckingham ; Philadelphia : Open University Press, 1997.
*TC RC425 .P376 1997*

**APHASIA - CASE STUDIES.**
Parr, Susie, 1953- Talking about aphasia. Buckingham ; Philadelphia : Open University Press, 1997.
*TC RC425 .P376 1997*

**APHASIA - HISTORY.**
Jacyna, L. S. Lost words. Princeton, N.J. ; Oxford : Princeton University Press, c2000.
*TC RC425 .J33 2000*

**Aphasia in atypical populations** / edited by Patrick Coppens, Yvan Lebrun, Anna Basso. Mahwah, N.J. : Lawrence Erlbaum Associates, 1998. xiii, 336 p. : ill. ; 24 cm. Includes bibliographical references and indexes. ISBN 0-8058-1738-7 (alk. paper) DDC 616.85/52
*1. Aphasia. 2. Brain - Localization of functions. 3. Laterality. I. Coppens, Patrick, 1944- II. Lebrun, Yvan. III. Basso, Anna.*
*TC RC425 .A637 1998*

**The aphasia therapy file** / edited by Sally Byng, Kate Swinburn and Carole Pound. Hove : Psychology Press, c1999. viii, 164 p. : ill. ; 26 cm. Includes bibliographical references and index. ISBN 0-86377-566-7 DDC 616.855206
*1. Aphasia - Treatment. 2. Speech therapy. 3. Speech therapy. 4. Aphasia - Treatment. I. Pound, Carole. II. Swinburn, Kate. III. Byng, Sally, 1956-*
*TC RC425 .A665 1999*

**APHASIA - TREATMENT.**
The aphasia therapy file. Hove : Psychology Press, c1999.
*TC RC425 .A665 1999*

The aphasia therapy file. Hove : Psychology Press, c1999.
*TC RC425 .A665 1999*

**Aphasiology.**
Davis, G. Albyn (George Albyn), 1946- Boston : Allyn and Bacon, 2000.
*TC RC425 .D379 2000*

**APHRENIA.** See DEMENTIA.

**APHRONESIA.** See DEMENTIA.

**APIN (INFORMATION RETRIEVAL SYSTEM) - FORMAT.** See MARC FORMATS.

**APOCALYPTIC LITERATURE - HISTORY AND CRITICISM.**
Williams, John Tyerman. Pooh and the millennium. 1st American ed. New York : Dutton Books, 1999.
*TC PR6025.I65 Z975 1999*

**Apollo & Daphne.**
Barber, Antonia, 1932- Los Angeles : J. Paul Getty Museum, 1998.
*TC ND1420 .B37 1998*

**Apollo and Daphne.**
Barber, Antonia, 1932- Apollo & Daphne. Los Angeles : J. Paul Getty Museum, 1998.
*TC ND1420 .B37 1998*

**APOPLEXY.** See CEREBROVASCULAR DISEASE.

**APOTHEOSIS.** See HEROES.

**APPARATUS FOR THE BLIND.** *See* **BLIND, APPARATUS FOR THE.**

**APPAREL.** *See* **CLOTHING AND DRESS.**

**APPARITIONS.** *See* **GHOSTS.**

**Appeasement.**
Robbins, Keith. Oxford, UK ; New York, NY, USA : B. Blackwell, 1988.
*TC DA47.2 .R62 1988*

**APPELLATE PROCEDURE.** *See* **TRIAL PRACTICE.**

**APPERCEPTION.** *See* **ATTENTION; COMPREHENSION; CONSCIOUSNESS; KNOWLEDGE, THEORY OF; PERCEPTION.**

**APPETITE DISORDERS.** *See* **EATING DISORDERS.**

**Appiah, Anthony.**
Microsoft encarta Africana [computer file]. Redmond, WA : Microsoft Corp., c1999. Computer data and programs.
*TC DT14 .M527 1999*

Microsoft encarta Africana [computer file]. Redmond, WA : Microsoft Corp., c1999. Computer data and programs.
*TC DT3 .M53 1999x*

**Apple, Margot.** Brave Martha / written and illustrated by Margot Apple. Boston : Houghton Mifflin, 1999. 1 v. (unpaged) : col. ill. ; 23 cm. SUMMARY: One night when she has to go to bed without her cat Sophie, Martha worries about all the things she sees and hears in the dark. ISBN 0-395-59422-7 DDC [E]
*1. Cats - Fiction. 2. Fear of the dark - Fiction. 3. Bedtime - Fiction. I. Title.*
*TC PZ7.A6474 Br 1999*

**Apple, Margot, ill.**
Shaw, Nancy (Nancy E.) Sheep on a ship. Boston : Houghton Mifflin, 1989.
*TC PZ8.3.S5334 Si 1989*

**Apple, Michael W.**
Challenges of urban education. Albany : State Unviersity of New York Press, c2000.
*TC LC5131 .C38 2000*

Official knowledge : democratic education in a conservative age / Michael W. Apple. 2nd ed. New York : Routledge, 2000. xxviii, 220 p. ; 23 cm. Includes bibliographical references (p. 204-214) and index. ISBN 0-415-92614-9
*1. Education - Political aspects - United States. 2. Critical pedagogy - United States. 3. Education - United States - Philosophy. 4. Education - Social aspects - United States. I. Title.*
*TC LC89 .A815 2000*

**Appleby, R. Scott, 1956-.**
Marty, Martin E., 1928- The glory and the power. Boston : Beacon Press, c1992.
*TC BL238 .M37 1992*

**The application of adult education principles in the development of a manual for practitioners creating web-based training programs.**
Driscoll, Margaret M. 1999.
*TC 06 no. 11106*

**The application of multimedia in arts-integrated curricula.**
Carr, Richard John. 1998.
*TC 06 no. 10919*

**APPLICATION PROGRAM INTERFACES (COMPUTER SOFTWARE).**
Pfaffenberger, Bryan, 1949- Mastering GNOME. San Francisco, CA : Sybex, Inc., 1999.
*TC QA76.9.U83 P453 1999*

**APPLICATION SOFTWARE.** *See* **COMPUTER GAMES.**

**APPLICATIONS FOR POSITIONS.**
Pervola, Cindy, 1956- How to get a job if you're a teenager. Fort Atkinson, Wis. : Alleyside Press, 1998.
*TC HF5383 .P44 1998*

Pervola, Cindy, 1956- How to get a job if you're a teenager. Fort Atkinson, Wis. : Alleyside Press, 1998.
*TC HF5383 .P44 1998*

**APPLIED ARTS.** *See* **DECORATIVE ARTS.**

**Applied clinical psychology**
Haynes, Stephen N. Principles and practice of behavioral assessment. New York ; London : Kluwer Academic/Plenum, c2000.
*TC BF176.5 .H39 2000*

**APPLIED ECOLOGY.** *See* **ENVIRONMENTAL PROTECTION.**

**APPLIED LINGUISTICS.** *See also* **COMPUTATIONAL LINGUISTICS.**
Principle & practice in applied linguistics. Oxford : Oxford University Press, 1995.
*TC P129 .P75 1995*

**Applied linguistics and language study.**
From testing to assessment. London ; New York : Longman, 1994.
*TC PE1128.A2 F778 1994*

Managing evaluation and innovation in language teaching. New York : Longman, 1998.
*TC P53.63 .M36 1998*

**The applied psychologist** / edited by James Hartley and Alan Branthwaite. 2nd ed. Buckingham [England] ; Philadelphia : Open University Press, 2000. xvi, 264 p. : ill. ; 25 cm. Includes bibliographical references and index. ISBN 0-335-20285-3 (hbk.) ISBN 0-335-20284-5 (pbk.) DDC 158
*1. Psychology - Vocational guidance. 2. Psychology, Applied - Vocational guidance. I. Hartley, James, Ph. D. II. Branthwaite, Alan.*
*TC BF76 .A63 2000*

**APPLIED PSYCHOLOGY.** *See* **PSYCHOLOGY, APPLIED.**

**Applied psychology series**
Cleveland, Jeanette. Women and men in organizations. Mahwah, N.J. ; London : Lawrence Erlbaum Associates, 2000.
*TC HD6060.65.U5 C58 2000*

**Applied regression analysis and other multivariable methods.** 3rd ed. / David G. Kleinbaum ... [et al.]. Pacific Grove : Duxbury Press, c1998. xviii, 798 p. : ill. ; 25 cm. + 1 computer disk (3 1/2 in.). Rev. ed. of: Applied regression analysis and other multivariable methods / David G. Kleinbaum, Lawrence L. Kupper, Keith E. Muller. 2nd ed. c1988. "An Alexander Kugushev book." Includes bibliographical references and index. System requirements for accompanying computer disk: IBM PC or compatible; Windows. ISBN 0-534-20910-6 DDC 519.5/36
*1. Multivariate analysis. 2. Regression analysis. I. Kleinbaum, David G. II. Kleinbaum, David G. Applied regression analysis and other multivariable methods.*
*TC QA278 .A665 1998*

**APPLIED SCIENCE.** *See* **TECHNOLOGY.**

**Applied social research**
Attitudes, behavior, and social context. Mahwah, N.J. : L. Erlbaum Associates, 2000.
*TC HM132 .B48 1998*

**APPRAISAL OF BOOKS.** *See* **BOOKS AND READING; CRITICISM; LITERATURE - HISTORY AND CRITICISM.**

**The appraisal of investments in educational facilities.**
Organisation for Economic Co-operation and Development (Paris) Paris : Organisation for Economic Co-operation and Development, 2000.
*TC LB2342.3 .A7 2000*

**Appraisal procedures for counselors and helping professionals.**
Drummond, Robert J. 4th ed. Upper Saddle River, N.J. : Merrill, c2000.
*TC BF176 .D78 2000*

**APPRECIATION OF ART.** *See* **ART APPRECIATION.**

**APPREHENSION.** *See* **PERCEPTION.**

**APPRENTICES - TRAINING OF.** *See* **APPRENTICESHIP PROGRAMS.**

**APPRENTICESHIP.** *See* **APPRENTICESHIP PROGRAMS.**

**Apprenticeship in literacy.**
Dorn, Linda J. York, Me. : Stenhouse Publishers, c1998.
*TC LB1139.5.L35 D67 1998*

**APPRENTICESHIP PROGRAMS.**
Apprenticeship. London : Kogan Page, c1999.
*TC HD4885.G7 A67 1999*

**APPRENTICESHIP PROGRAMS - GREAT BRITAIN.**
Apprenticeship. London : Kogan Page, c1999.
*TC HD4885.G7 A67 1999*

**Apprenticeship :** towards a new paradigm of learning / edited by Patrick Ainley and Helen Rainbird. London : Kogan Page, c1999. xii, 211 p. ; 24 cm. (The future of education from 14+) Includes bibliographical references and index. ISBN 0-7494-2728-0

*1. Apprenticeship programs - Great Britain. 2. Apprenticeship programs. I. Ainley, Patrick. II. Rainbird, Helen. III. Series.*
*TC HD4885.G7 A67 1999*

**Approaches to semiotics**
(57) Nida, Eugène Albert, 1914- Componential analysis of meaning. The Hague : Mouton, 1975.
*TC P325 .N5*

**Approaches to teaching Narrative of the life of Frederick Douglass** / edited by James C. Hall. New York : Modern Language Association of America, 1999. xiii, 174 p. ; 24 cm. (Approaches to teaching world literature ; 63) Includes bibliographical references (p. [155]-169) and index. ISBN 0-87352-749-6 (hbk.) ISBN 0-87352-750-X (pbk.) DDC 973.8/092
*1. Douglass, Frederick, - 1817?-1895. - Narrative of the life of Frederick Douglass, an American slave. 2. Slaves' writings, American - Study and teaching. 3. Afro-American abolitionists - Biography - History and criticism. 4. Slaves - United States - Biography - History and criticism. I. Hall, James C., 1960- II. Series.*
*TC E449.D75 A66 1999*

**Approaches to teaching world literature**
(63) Approaches to teaching Narrative of the life of Frederick Douglass. New York : Modern Language Association of America, 1999.
*TC E449.D75 A66 1999*

**APPROVAL, SOCIAL.** *See* **SOCIAL DESIRABILITY.**

**APSAROKE INDIANS.** *See* **CROW INDIANS.**

**APTENODYTES.** *See* **EMPEROR PENGUIN.**

**APTENODYTES FORSTERI.** *See* **EMPEROR PENGUIN.**

**APTITUDE.** *See* **ABILITY.**

**AQUATIC ANIMALS.** *See* **FISHES.**

**AQUATIC ECOLOGY.** *See* **MARINE ECOLOGY.**

**AQUATIC SPORTS.** *See* **SWIMMING.**

**AQUATINT - TECHNIQUE.**
Etching [videorecording]. Northbrook, Ill. ; Peasmarsh, East Sussex, Eng. : Roland Collection of Films on Art, c1990.
*TC NE2043 .E87 1990*

**AQUATINTS.** *See* **AQUATINT.**

**ARACHIDES.** *See* **PEANUTS.**

**ARACHIS.** *See* **PEANUTS.**

**ARACHIS HYPOGEA.** *See* **PEANUTS.**

**Arai, Kazuhiro, 1949-**
**[Kyōiku no keizaigaku. English]**
Economics of education : an analysis of college-going behavior / Kazuhiro Arai. Tōkyō ; New York : Springer, 1998. xi, 201 p. : ill. ; 25 cm. Includes bibliographical references (p. 179-191) and index. ISBN 4-431-70224-5
*1. Education, Higher - Economic aspects - Japan 2. College attendance - Japan. I. Title.*
*TC LC67.68.J3 A72 1998*

**ARBORICULTURE.** *See* **TREES.**

**ARBOVIRUS INFECTIONS.** *See* **EPIDEMIC ENCEPHALITIS.**

**ARCADIAN ART.** *See* **PASTORAL ART.**

**ARCHAEOLOGICAL COLLECTIONS.** *See* **ARCHAEOLOGICAL MUSEUMS AND COLLECTIONS.**

**Archaeological curatorship.**
Pearce, Susan M. Washington, D.C. : Smithsonian Institution Press, 1996.
*TC AM7 .P43 1996*

**ARCHAEOLOGICAL DIGS.** *See* **EXCAVATIONS (ARCHAEOLOGY).**

**ARCHAEOLOGICAL EXCAVATIONS.** *See* **EXCAVATIONS (ARCHAEOLOGY).**

**ARCHAEOLOGICAL MUSEUMS AND COLLECTIONS - ADMINISTRATION.**
Pearce, Susan M. Archaeological curatorship. Washington, D.C. : Smithsonian Institution Press, 1996.
*TC AM7 .P43 1996*

**ARCHAEOLOGICAL MUSEUMS AND COLLECTIONS - GREAT BRITAIN - ADMINISTRATION.**
Pearce, Susan M. Archaeological curatorship. Washington, D.C. : Smithsonian Institution Press, 1996.

*TC AM7 .P43 1996*

**ARCHAEOLOGICAL SPECIMENS.** *See* ANTIQUITIES.

**ARCHAEOLOGY.** *See* ANTIQUITIES; EXCAVATIONS (ARCHAEOLOGY); HISTORIC SITES; ROCK PAINTINGS; SCULPTURE, PRIMITIVE.

**ARCHAEOLOGY AND HISTORY - NORTH CAROLINA - WINSTON-SALEM.**
South, Stanley A. Historical archaeology in Wachovia. New York : Kluwer Academic/Plenum Publishers, c1999.
*TC F264.W8 S66 1999*

**ARCHAEOLOGY - HISTORY - SOURCES - EXHIBITIONS - HANDBOOKS, MANUALS, ETC.**
Pearce, Susan M. Archaeological curatorship. Washington, D.C. : Smithsonian Institution Press, 1996.
*TC AM7 .P43 1996*

**ARCHEOLOGY.** *See* ARCHAEOLOGY.

**Archer, John, 1944-** The nature of grief : the evolution and psychology of reactions to loss / John Archer. London ; New York : Routledge, 1999. xiii, 317 p. : ill. ; 24 cm. Includes bibliographical references (p. [256]-296) and indexes. ISBN 0-415-17857-6 (hardcover) ISBN 0-415-17858-4 (pbk.) DDC 155.9/37
*1. Grief. 2. Bereavement - Psychological aspects. 3. Death - Psychological aspects. 4. Loss (Psychology) I. Title.*
*TC BF575.G7 A73 1999*

**Archer, Michael.**
Oliveira, Nicolas de. Installation art. London : Thames and Hudson, 1994.
*TC N6494.E O4 1994*

**ARCHETYPE (PSYCHOLOGY).**
Peterson, Jordan B. Maps of meaning. New York : Routledge, 1999.
*TC BF175.5.A72 P48 1999*

Stevens, Anthony. The two million-year-old self. New York : Fromm International Publishing, 1997.
*TC BF175.5.A72 S75 1997*

**Archibald, John.**
Second language acquisition and linguistic theory. Malden, Mass. : Blackwell, 2000.
*TC P118.2 .S425 2000*

**ARCHIBALD PRIZE - HISTORY.**
Ross, Peter. Let's face it. Sydney, Australia : Art Gallery of New South Wales, 1999.
*TC ND1327.A86 R67 1999*

**Archimedes.**
Stein, Sherman K. Washington, D.C. : Mathematical Association of America, c1999.
*TC QA31 .S84 1999*

Stein, Sherman K. Archimedes. Washington, D.C. : Mathematical Association of America, c1999.
*TC QA31 .S84 1999*

**Archimedes;** Anregungen und Aufgaben für Lehrer, Schuler und Freunde der Mathematik. Regensburg, Josef Habbel. 24 v. in 12. 22 cm. Jahrg. 1-24; Dez. 1948-1972. Ceased publication.
*1. Mathematics - Periodicals.*

**Archimedes' bathtub.**
Perkins, David N. 1st ed. New York : W.W. Norton, c2000.
*TC BF441 .P47 2000*

**ARCHIPELAGOES - CARIBBEAN AREA.** *See* WEST INDIES.

**ARCHITECTS.** *See* WOMEN ARCHITECTS.

**ARCHITECTS - UNITED STATES - BIOGRAPHY.**
Stein, Clarence S. The writings of Clarence S. Stein. Baltimore, Md. : Johns Hopkins University Press, 1998.
*TC NA9108 .S83 1998*

**ARCHITECTURE.** *See* ARCHITECTURE, DOMESTIC; COMMUNISM AND ARCHITECTURE; ECLECTICISM IN ARCHITECTURE; HISTORIC BUILDINGS; LIBRARY ARCHITECTURE; MONUMENTS; MUSEUM ARCHITECTURE; RESORT ARCHITECTURE.

**Architecture & identity.**
Abel, Chris. Architecture and identity. 2nd ed. Oxford : Boston : Architectural Press, 2000.
*TC NA2500 .A392 2000*

**ARCHITECTURE, AMERICAN - HISTORY - 19TH CENTURY.**
Harris, Neil, 1938- Building lives. New Haven [Conn.] : London : Yale University Press, c1999.
*TC NA2543.S6 H37 1999*

**ARCHITECTURE, AMERICAN - HISTORY - 20TH CENTURY.**
Harris, Neil, 1938- Building lives. New Haven [Conn.] : London : Yale University Press, c1999.
*TC NA2543.S6 H37 1999*

**ARCHITECTURE AND COMMUNISM.** *See* COMMUNISM AND ARCHITECTURE.

**Architecture and identity.**
Abel, Chris. 2nd ed. Oxford ; Boston : Architectural Press, 2000.
*TC NA2500 .A392 2000*

**ARCHITECTURE AND PHILOSOPHY.**
Abel, Chris. Architecture and identity. 2nd ed. Oxford : Boston : Architectural Press, 2000.
*TC NA2500 .A392 2000*

**ARCHITECTURE AND SOCIETY - UNITED STATES.**
Gelernter, Mark, 1951- A history of American architecture. Hanover, NH ; London : University Press of New England, c1999.
*TC NA705 .G35 1999*

Harris, Neil, 1938- Building lives. New Haven [Conn.] ; London : Yale University Press, c1999.
*TC NA2543.S6 H37 1999*

**ARCHITECTURE AND SOCIOLOGY.** *See* ARCHITECTURE AND SOCIETY.

**ARCHITECTURE AND YOUTH - CALIFORNIA - CASE STUDIES.**
Childress, Herb, 1958- Landscapes of betrayal, landscapes of joy. Albany [N.Y.] : State University of New York Press, c2000.
*TC HQ796 .C458237 2000*

**ARCHITECTURE, ANONYMOUS.** *See* VERNACULAR ARCHITECTURE.

**ARCHITECTURE, DOMESTIC.** *See* DWELLINGS.

**ARCHITECTURE, DOMESTIC - AFRICA, NORTHEAST.**
Prussin, Labelle. African nomadic architecture. Washington : Smithsonian Institution Press : National Museum of African Art, c1995.
*TC NA7461.A1 P78 1995*

**ARCHITECTURE, DOMESTIC - UNITED STATES.**
Ierley, Merritt. Open house. 1st ed. New York : Henry Holt and Co., 1999.
*TC NA7205 .I35 1999*

**ARCHITECTURE - ENVIRONMENTAL ASPECTS.** *See also* ORGANIC ARCHITECTURE.
Abel, Chris. Architecture and identity. 2nd ed. Oxford : Boston : Architectural Press, 2000.
*TC NA2500 .A392 2000*

**ARCHITECTURE - HUMAN FACTORS.** *See* ARCHITECTURE AND SOCIETY.

**ARCHITECTURE - INDIA.**
Cooper, Ilay. Traditional buildings of India. New York : Thames and Hudson, c1998.
*TC NA1501 .C58 1998*

**ARCHITECTURE, INDIGENOUS.** *See* VERNACULAR ARCHITECTURE.

**ARCHITECTURE, MODERN - 19TH CENTURY.** *See* ARCHITECTURE, VICTORIAN; ECLECTICISM IN ARCHITECTURE; ROMANESQUE REVIVAL (ARCHITECTURE).

**ARCHITECTURE, MODERN - 19TH CENTURY - ENGLAND.**
Vickery, Margaret Birney, 1963- Buildings for bluestockings. Newark [Del.] : University of Delaware Press ; London ; Cranbury, NJ : Associated University Presses, c1999.
*TC NA6605.G7 V53 1999*

**ARCHITECTURE, MODERN - 19TH CENTURY - NEW YORK (STATE) - NEW YORK.**
Stern, Robert A. M. New York 1880. New York, N.Y. : Monacelli Press, 1999.
*TC NA735.N5 S727 1999*

**ARCHITECTURE, MODERN - 20TH CENTURY.** *See also* ECLECTICISM IN ARCHITECTURE; ORGANIC ARCHITECTURE;

**ROMANESQUE REVIVAL (ARCHITECTURE).**
Newhouse, Victoria. Towards a new museum. New York : Monacelli Press, 1998.
*TC NA6695 .N49 1998*

**ARCHITECTURE, MODERN - 20TH CENTURY - CUBA.**
Loomis, John A., 1951- Revolution of forms. New York : Princeton Architectural Press, c1999.
*TC NA6602.A76 L66 1999*

**ARCHITECTURE, MODERN - 20TH CENTURY - UNITED STATES.**
Stein, Clarence S. The writings of Clarence S. Stein. Baltimore, Md. : Johns Hopkins University Press, 1998.
*TC NA9108 .S83 1998*

**ARCHITECTURE, ORGANIC.** *See* ORGANIC ARCHITECTURE.

**ARCHITECTURE - POLITICAL ASPECTS - CUBA - HAVANA.**
Loomis, John A., 1951- Revolution of forms. New York : Princeton Architectural Press, c1999.
*TC NA6602.A76 L66 1999*

**ARCHITECTURE, ROMANESQUE.** *See* ROMANESQUE REVIVAL (ARCHITECTURE).

**ARCHITECTURE, RURAL.** *See* ARCHITECTURE, DOMESTIC.

**ARCHITECTURE - UNITED STATES.**
Gelernter, Mark, 1951- A history of American architecture. Hanover, NH ; London : University Press of New England, c1999.
*TC NA705 .G35 1999*

**ARCHITECTURE, VERNACULAR.** *See* VERNACULAR ARCHITECTURE.

**ARCHITECTURE, VICTORIAN.**
Yanni, Carla. Nature's museums. Baltimore, Md : Johns Hopkins University Press, 2000.
*TC QH70.A1 Y25 2000*

**ARCHITECTURE, VICTORIAN - ENGLAND.**
Vickery, Margaret Birney, 1963- Buildings for bluestockings. Newark [Del.] : University of Delaware Press ; London ; Cranbury, NJ : Associated University Presses, c1999.
*TC NA6605.G7 V53 1999*

**Archiv für die gesamte Psychologie.** Leipzig : W. Englemann, 1903-1969. v : ill. ; 24 cm. Frequency: Irregular. Bd. 1 (Apr. 1903)-Bd. 121 (Dec. 1969). Imprint varies. Suspended 1944-1961. Bd. 1 (1903)-50 (1925). 1 v.; Bd. 51 (1925)-75 (1930). 1 v. Has supplement: Archiv für die gesamte Psychologie. Ergänzungsband. Continues in part: Philosophische Studien (Leipzig, Germany). Continued by: Archiv für Psychologie.
*1. Psychology - Periodicals. I. Title: Archiv für die gesamte Psychologie. Ergänzungsband II. Title: Philosophische Studien (Leipzig, Germany) III. Title: Archiv für Psychologie*

**Archiv für die gesamte Psychologie. Ergänzungsband.**
Archiv für die gesamte Psychologie. Leipzig : W. Englemann, 1903-1969.

**Archiv für Psychologie.**
Archiv für die gesamte Psychologie. Leipzig : W. Englemann, 1903-1969.

**ARCHIVAL MATERIALS - CONSERVATION AND RESTORATION - STUDY AND TEACHING.**
Ralston, Nicola L. Parchment/vellum conservation survey and bibliography. Edinburgh : Historic Scotland : Crown Copyright, c2000.
*TC Z701.4.I5 R35 2000*

**ARCHIVAL MATERIALS - DIGITIZATION.**
Kenney, Anne R., 1950- Moving theory into practice. Mountain View, CA : Research Libraries Group, 2000.
*TC Z681.3.D53 K37*

**ARCHIVES.** *See* ARCHIVAL MATERIALS; PUBLIC RECORDS.

**Archives of the History of American Psychology (University of Akron).**
Popplestone, John A. An illustrated history of American psychology. 2nd ed. Akron, Ohio : The University of Akron Press, c1999.
*TC BF108.U5 P67 1999*

**Archuleta, Margaret.**
Shared visions. 1st New Press ed. New York : New Press : Distributed by Norton, [1993], c1991.

*TC N6538.A4 A7 1993*

**ARCTIC PEOPLES.** *See* **ESKIMOS.**

**ARCTIC REGIONS - FICTION.**
George, Jean Craighead, 1919- Snow Bear. 1st ed.
New York : Hyperion Books for Children, 1999.
*TC PZ7.G2933 Sn 1999*

**ARCTIC, THE.** *See* **ARCTIC REGIONS.**

**Ardouin, Claude Daniel.**
Museums & archaeology in West Africa.
Washington : Smithsonian Institution Press ; Oxford :
J. Currey, c1997.
*TC AM91.A358 M85 1997*

**Ardovino, Joan.** Multiple measures : accurate ways to
assess student achievement / Joan Ardovino, John
Hollingsworth, Silvia Ybarra. Thousand Oaks, Calif. :
Corwin Press, c2000. vi, 114 p. : ill. ; 24 cm. Includes
bibliographical references (p. 106-108) and index. ISBN
0-7619-7679-5 (cloth : alk. paper) ISBN 0-7619-7680-9 (pbk. :
alk. paper) DDC 371.26/01/3
*1. Examinations. 2. Examinations - Design and construction. 3.
Examinations - Validity. 4. Educational tests and
measurements. I. Hollingsworth, John, 1949- II. Ybarra, Silvia.
III. Title. IV. Title: Accurate ways to assess student
achievement*
*TC LB3051 .A745 2000*

**Are we not also men?.**
Ranger, T. O. (Terence O.) Harare : Baobab ;
Portsmouth, NH : Heinemann, 1995.
*TC DT2974 .R36 1995*

**Are you sure you're the principal?.**
Villani, Susan. Thousand Oaks, Calif. : Corwin Press,
c1999.
*TC LB2831.92 .V55 1999*

**AREA LINGUISTICS.** *See* **AREAL LINGUISTICS.**

**AREA STUDIES.** *See* **GEOGRAPHY - STUDY
AND TEACHING.**

**AREAL LINGUISTICS - HANDBOOKS,
MANUALS, ETC.**
Handbook of language & ethnic identity. New York :
Oxford University Press, 1999.
*TC P35 .H34 1999*

**Arena Cultural Center (Rio de Janeiro, Brazil).**
Processing the signal [videorecording]. Cicero, Ill. :
Roland Collection of Films on Art, c1989.
*TC N6494.V53 P7 1989*

**ARENDT, HANNA - CONTRIBUTIONS IN
POLITICAL SCIENCE.**
Gorham, Eric B., 1960- The theater of politics.
Lanham, Md. : Oxford: Lexington Books, c2000.
*TC LC171 .G56 2000*

**Arendt, Hannah.** The human condition / by Hannah
Arendt. 2nd ed. / introduction by Margaret Canovan.
Chicago : University of Chicago Press, 1998. xx, 349
p. ; 24 cm. Includes bibliographical references and index.
ISBN 0-226-02599-3 (cloth : alk. paper) ISBN 0-226-02598-5
(paper : alk. paper) DDC 301
*1. Sociology. 2. Economics. 3. Technology. I. Title.*
*TC HM211 .A7 1998*

Gordon, Mordechai. Toward an integrative conception
of authority in education. 1997.
*TC 085 G656*

**ARGENTINA - PERIODICALS.**
Histonium. Buenos Aires : [s.n.], 1939-1972.

**ARGUMENTATION.** *See* **LOGIC; REASONING.**

**Arhem, Kaj.** Makuna : portrait of an Amazonian
people / Kaj Arhem ; photographs by Diego Samper.
Washington : Smithsonian Institution Press, c1998. xi,
172 p. : ill. (some col.) ; 29 cm. Includes bibliographical
references (p. 167-168) and index. ISBN 1-56098-874-6 (alk.
paper) DDC 986.1/650049843
*1. Macuna Indians - Rites and ceremonies. 2. Macuna
Indians - Religion. 3. Macuna philosophy. 4. Shamanism -
Uaupés River Valley (Colombia and Brazil) 5. Uaupés River
Valley (Colombia and Brazil) - Social life and customs. I.
Samper, Diego. II. Title.*
*TC F2270.2.M33 A68 1998*

**ARIAS.** *See* **SONGS.**

**Arias, Rafael.** Analysis of discourse in an ESL peer-
mentoring teacher group / by Rafael Arias. 1999. x,
293 leaves : ill. ; 29 cm. Includes tables. Includes
bibliographical references (leaves 282-285). Typescript; issued
also on microfilm. Thesis (Ed.D.) -- Teachers College,
Columbia University, 1997.
*1. English teachers - In-service training. 2. Interaction analysis
in education. 3. Observation (Educational method) 4.
Mentoring in education. 5. Mentoring in the professions. 6.
Peer review. 7. Video tapes in education. 8. English language -*

*Study and teaching - Foreign speakers. I. Title. II. Title:
Analysis of discourse in an English as a second language
peer-mentoring teacher group*
*TC 06 no. 10791*

**Ariasingam, David Lakshmanan, 1963-.**
Patrinos, Harry Anthony. Decentralization of
education. Washington, D.C. : World Bank, c1997.
*TC LB2826.6.D44 P38 1997*

**ARISTOTLE - CONTRIBUTIONS IN
PHILOSOPHY OF MIND.**
Ostenfeld, Erik Nis. Ancient Greek psychology and
the modern mind-body debate. Aarhus, Denmark :
Aarhus University Press, 1987.
*TC BF161 .O88 1987*

**ARITHMETICS - PROBLEMS, EXERCISES, ETC.**
McKillip, William D. Mathematics for mastery.
Teacher's ed. Morristown, N.J. : Silver Burdett, 1981.
*TC QA107 .M375 1981 Teacher's ed. K*

McKillip, William D. Mathematics for mastery.
Teacher's ed. Morristown, N.J. : Silver Burdett, 1981.
*TC QA107 .M375 1981 Teacher's ed. K*

**ARITHMETICS - STUDY AND TEACHING
(EARLY CHILDHOOD).**
McKillip, William D. Mathematics for mastery.
Teacher's ed. Morristown, N.J. : Silver Burdett, 1981.
*TC QA107 .M375 1981 Teacher's ed. K*

McKillip, William D. Mathematics for mastery.
Teacher's ed. Morristown, N.J. : Silver Burdett, 1981.
*TC QA107 .M375 1981 Teacher's ed. K*

**ARITHMETIC.** *See also* **COUNTING; DIVISION;
FRACTIONS; RATIO AND PROPORTION.**
Arithmetic for young America. Revised teachers' ed.
Yonkers-on-Hudson, N.Y. : World Book Company,
c1949
*TC QA106 .A74 1949 Teacher's Ed.*

Arithmetic for young America. Revised teachers' ed.
Yonkers-on-Hudson, N.Y. : World Book Company,
c1949
*TC QA106 .A74 1949 Teacher's Ed.*

Arithmetic for young America. Revised teachers' ed.
Yonkers-on-Hudson, N.Y. : World Book Company,
c1949
*TC QA106 .A74 1949 Teacher's Ed.*

Brueckner, Leo J. Moving ahead in arithmetic. New
York, N.Y. : Holt, Rinehart and Winston, 1963.
*TC QA107 .B78 1963*

Brueckner, Leo J. Moving ahead in arithmetic. New
York, N.Y. : Holt, Rinehart and Winston, 1963.
*TC QA107 .B78 1963*

Brueckner, Leo J. Moving ahead in arithmetic. New
York : Holt, Rinehart and Winston, 1963.
*TC QA107 .B78 1963*

Brueckner, Leo J. Moving ahead in arithmetic. New
York : Holt, Rinehart and Winston, 1963.
*TC QA107 .B78 1963*

Pai, Hang Young. Chisanbop finger calculation
method. New York : McCormick-Mathers Pub. Co.,
1981.
*TC QA115 .P23 1981*

Pai, Hang Young. Chisanbop. Teacher's annotated ed.
New York : American Book Co., 1980.
*TC QA115 .P23 1980 Teacher's Ed.*

Pai, Hang Young. Chisanbop. New York : American
Book Co., 1980.
*TC QA115 .P23 1980*

Pai, Hang Young. Chisanbop. New York : American
Book Co., 1980.
*TC QA115 .P231 1980*

Pai, Hang Young. Chisanbop. Teacher's annotated ed.
New York : American Book Co., 1980.
*TC QA115 .P231 1980 Teacher's Ed.*

Upton, Clifford Brewster. 1877- American
Arithmetic. 2nd ed. New York, N.Y. : American Book
Company, 1963.
*TC QA103 .U67 1963*

**ARITHMETIC - FICTION.**
Wright, Alexandra. Alice in Pastaland. Watertown,
Mass. : Charlesbridge, 1997.
*TC PZ7.W9195 Al 19997*

**Arithmetic for young America.** Revised teachers' ed.
Yonkers-on-Hudson, N.Y. : World Book Company,
c1949 Includes index.
*1. Arithmetic. 2. Arithmetic - Study and teaching (Elementary)
I. Title.*
*TC QA106 .A74 1949 Teacher's Ed.*

**Arithmetic for young America.** Revised teachers' ed.
Yonkers-on-Hudson, N.Y. : World Book Company,
c1949 Includes index.
*1. Arithmetic. 2. Arithmetic - Study and teaching (Elementary)
I. Title.*
*TC QA106 .A74 1949 Teacher's Ed.*

**Arithmetic for young America.** Revised teachers' ed.
Yonkers-on-Hudson, N.Y. : World Book Company,
c1949 Includes index.
*1. Arithmetic. 2. Arithmetic - Study and teaching (Elementary)
I. Title.*
*TC QA106 .A74 1949 Teacher's Ed.*

**ARITHMETIC - JUVENILE SOFTWARE.**
Carmen Sandiego [computer file]. Novato, Calif. :
Brøderbund Software, 1998. Computer data and
program.
*TC QA115 .C37 1998*

**ARITHMETIC - PROBLEMS, EXERCISES, ETC.**
McKillip, William D. Mathematics for mastery.
Teacher's ed. Morristown, N.J. : Silver Burdett, 1981.
*TC QA107 .M375 1981 Teacher's ed. K*

Number concepts [videorecording]. Princeton, N.J. :
Video Tutor, 1988.
*TC QA117 .N8 1988*

Payne, Joseph N. (Joseph Neal) Elementary
mathematics 4. Teachers' ed. New York : Harcourt,
Brace & World, 1966.
*TC QA107 .E43 1966 Teacher's Ed.*

Word problems [videorecording]. Princeton, N.J. :
Video Tutor, 1988.
*TC QA139 .W6 1988*

**ARITHMETIC - STUDY AND TEACHING
(EARLY CHILDHOOD).**
McKillip, William D. Mathematics for mastery.
Teacher's ed. Morristown, N.J. : Silver Burdett, 1981.
*TC QA107 .M375 1981 Teacher's ed. K*

**ARITHMETIC - STUDY AND TEACHING
(ELEMENTARY).**
Arithmetic for young America. Revised teachers' ed.
Yonkers-on-Hudson, N.Y. : World Book Company,
c1949
*TC QA106 .A74 1949 Teacher's Ed.*

Arithmetic for young America. Revised teachers' ed.
Yonkers-on-Hudson, N.Y. : World Book Company,
c1949
*TC QA106 .A74 1949 Teacher's Ed.*

Arithmetic for young America. Revised teachers' ed.
Yonkers-on-Hudson, N.Y. : World Book Company,
c1949
*TC QA106 .A74 1949 Teacher's Ed.*

Payne, Joseph N. (Joseph Neal) Elementary
mathematics 4. Teachers' ed. New York : Harcourt,
Brace & World, 1966.
*TC QA107 .E43 1966 Teacher's Ed.*

**ARITHMETICAL ABILITY.** *See*
**MATHEMATICAL ABILITY.**

**ARK, NOAH'S.** *See* **NOAH'S ARK.**

**Arkansas Education Association.**
The Journal of Arkansas education. [Little Rock :
Arkansas Educational Association, 1923-1975].

**Arkansas Education Association. Journal.**
The Journal of Arkansas education. [Little Rock :
Arkansas Educational Association, 1923-1975].

**Arkansas teacher.**
The Journal of Arkansas education. [Little Rock :
Arkansas Educational Association, 1923-1975].

**Arkes, Hal R., 1945-.**
Judgment and decision making. 2nd ed. Cambridge,
U.K. : New York, NY : Cambridge University Press,
2000.
*TC BF441 .J79 2000*

**ARMED FORCES.** *See* **SAILORS; SOCIOLOGY,
MILITARY; VETERANS.**

**ARMIES.** *See* **MILITARISM; SOCIOLOGY,
MILITARY.**

**Armitage, Peter B., 1939-** Political relationship and
narrative knowledge : a critical analysis of school
authoritarianism / Peter B. Armitage. Westport,
Conn. : Bergin & Garvey, 2000. xxiii, 226 p. ; 25 cm.
(Critical studies in education and culture series, 1064-8615)
Includes bibliographical references (p. 213-216) and index.
ISBN 0-89789-690-4 (alk. paper) DDC 370.11/5
*1. Politics and education - Great Britain. 2. Authoritarianism -
Great Britain. 3. Critical theory. 4. Critical pedagogy. I. Title.
II. Series.*

*TC LC93.G7 A86 2000*

**Armstrong, Alison, 1955-** The child and the machine : how computers put our children's education at risk / Alison Armstrong and Charles Casement. Beltsville, Md. : Robins Lane Press, c2000. xii, 254 p. ; 23 cm. Includes bibliographical references (p. 223-242) and index. ISBN 0-87659-210-8 DDC 372.133/4
*1. Education - Data processing. 2. Computer-assisted instruction. 3. Computers and children. 4. Child development. I. Casement, Charles. II. Title.*
*TC LB1028.43 .A76 2000*

The child and the machine : why computers may put children's education at risk / Alison Armstrong and Charles Casement. Toronto, Ont. : Key Porter Books, c1998. xiv, 257 p. ; 23 cm. Includes bibliographical references (p. [236]-249) and index. ISBN 1-55263-004-8 DDC 371.33/4
*1. Education - Data processing. 2. Computers and children. I. Casement, Charles. II. Title.*
*TC LB1028.43 .A75 1998*

**Armstrong, David G.**
Savage, Tom V. Effective teaching in elementary social studies. 4th ed. Upper Saddle River, N.J. : Merrill, c2000.
*TC LB1584 .S34 2000*

**Armstrong, Hugh, 1943-.**
Armstrong, Pat, 1945- Universal health care. New York : New Press : Distributed by W.W. Norton, c1998.
*TC RA412.5.C3 A76 1998*

**Armstrong, Michael- 1957.**
Benchmarking and threshold standards in higher education. London : Kogan Page, c1999.
*TC LB2341.8.G7 B463 1999*

**Armstrong, Pat, 1945-** Universal health care : what the United States can learn from the Canadian experience / Pat Armstrong and Hugh Armstrong, with Claudia Fegan. New York : New Press : Distributed by W.W. Norton, c1998. xv, 176 p. ; 22 cm. Includes bibliographical references and index. ISBN 1-56584-410-6 DDC 362.1/0971
*1. National health insurance - Canada. 2. Medical care - Canada. I. Armstrong, Hugh. 1943- II. Fegan, Claudia. III. Title.*
*TC RA412.5.C3 A76 1998*

**Armstrong, Peter S.** Opening gambits : the first session of psychotherapy / by Peter S. Armstrong. Northvale, N.J. : J. Aronson, 1999. xvi, 235 p. ; 24 cm. Includes index. ISBN 0-7657-0241-X DDC 616.89/14
*1. Psychoanalytic counseling. 2. Psychoanalysis. I. Title.*
*TC BF175.4.C68 .A76 1999*

**Armstrong, Rachel.**
Sci-fi aesthetics. London : Academy Group Ltd. ; Lanham, Md. : Distributed in the USA by National Book Network, c1997.
*TC N8217.F28 S34 1994*

**ARMY POSTS.** *See* **MILITARY BASES.**

**ARN journal.**
Association of Rehabilitation Nurses. [Glenview, Ill.] Association of Rehabilitation Nurses.

**Arnaud, Michèle.**
Monsieur René Magritte [videorecording]. [Chicago, Ill.] : Home Vision [distributor], c1978.
*TC ND673.M35 M6 1978*

**Arnett, Mark S.**
The cello [videorecording]. Van Nuys, CA : Backstage Pass Productions : Canoga Park, Calif. : [Distributed by] MVP, c1995.
*TC MT305 .C4 1995*

The drums [videorecording]. Van Nuys, CA : Backstage Pass Productions : Canoga Park, Calif. : [Distributed by] MVP Home Entertainment, c1998.
*TC MT662.3 .S6 1998*

The flute [videorecording]. Van Nuys, CA : Backstage Pass Productions : Canoga Park, Calif. : [Distributed by] MVP, c1995.
*TC MT345 .F6 1995*

The trombone [videorecording]. Van Nuys, CA : Backstage Pass Productions : Canoga Park, Calif. : [Distributed by] MVP, c1998.
*TC MT465 .T7 1998*

The viola [videorecording]. Van Nuys, CA : Backstage Pass Productions : Canoga Park, Calif. : [Distributed by] MVP Home Entertainment, c1991.
*TC MT285 .V5 1991*

The viola [videorecording]. Van Nuys, CA : Backstage Pass Productions : Canoga Park, Calif. : [Distributed by] MVP Home Entertainment, c1995.

*TC MT285 .V5 1995*

The violin [videorecording]. Van Nuys, CA : Backstage Pass Productions ; Canoga Park, Calif. : [Distributed by] MVP, c1998.
*TC MT265 .V5 1998*

**Arnold, Gordon B., 1954-** The politics of faculty unionization : the experience of three New England universities / Gordon B. Arnold. Westport, Conn. : London : Bergin & Garvey, 2000. x, 148 p. ; 22 cm. Includes bibliographical references (p. [139]-143) and index. ISBN 0-89789-716-1 (alk. paper) DDC 331.88/1137874
*1. College teachers' unions - New England - Case studies. 2. Collective bargaining - College teachers - New England - Case studies. 3. Universities and colleges - New England - Administration - Case studies. 4. University of Connecticut. 5. University of Rhode Island. 6. University of Massachusetts (System) I. Title.*
*TC LB2335.865.U6 A75 2000*

**Arnold, Robert M., 1957-.**
The definition of death. Baltimore : Johns Hopkins University Press, 1999.
*TC RA1063 .D44 1999*

**Arnold, Virginia A.** Macmillan predictable big books: teacher's guide / Virginia A. Arnold. New York : Macmillan Publishing Co., 1990. 7 p. : ill. ; 28 cm.
*1. Reading (Kindergarten) 2. Reading (Primary) I. Title.*
*TC LB1181.2 .A76 1990*

**Arnone, Marilyn P.**
Small, Ruth V. Turning kids on to research. Englewood, Colo. : Libraries Unlimited, 2000.
*TC LB1065 .S57 2000*

**Arnove, Robert F.**
Comparative education. Lanham : Rowman & Littlefield, c1999.
*TC LB43 .C68 1999*

**AROMAS.** *See* **ODORS.**

**Aronowitz, Stanley.** The knowledge factory : dismantling the corporate university and creating true higher learning / Stanley Aronowitz. Boston : Beacon Press, c2000. xviii, 217 p. ; 24 cm. Includes bibliographical references (p. [195]-198) and index. ISBN 0-8070-3122-4 DDC 378.73
*1. Education, Higher - Aims and objectives - United States. 2. Education, Higher - Social aspects - United States. I. Title.*
*TC LA227.4 .A76 2000*

**Arousal patterns, emotion identification, and cognitive style in depressed and nondepressed inner-city adolescent Latinas.**
Gallagher, Trish. 1997.
*TC 085 G136*

**AROUSAL (PHYSIOLOGY).** *See* **ATTENTION.**

**Arrazola, Xabier.**
Cognition, agency, and rationality. Boston : Kluwer Academic, 1999.
*TC BC177 .C45 1999*

**Ars Electronica. (1999 : Linz, Austria).**
LifeScience. Wien ; New York : Springer, 1999.
*TC T14.5 L54 1999*

**Ars Electronica 99.**
LifeScience. Wien ; New York : Springer, 1999.
*TC T14.5 L54 1999*

**ART.** *See also* **AESTHETICS; ANTIQUES; ARCHITECTURE; COMMERCIAL ART; COMMUNITY ART PROJECTS; COMPOSITION (ART); CREATION (LITERARY, ARTISTIC, ETC.); DECORATIVE ARTS; DRAWING; ETCHING; EXPRESSIONISM (ART); FEMINISM AND ART; FOLK ART; GRAPHIC ARTS; ILLUSTRATION OF BOOKS; INDIAN ART; MURAL PAINTING AND DECORATION; PASTORAL ART; PHOTOGRAPHY, ARTISTIC; PORTRAITS; POSTERS; SCULPTURE; SPACE (ART); SYMBOLISM IN ART.**
Chapman, Laura H. Discover art. Worcester, Mass. : Davis Publications, c1985.
*TC N361 .C56 1985*

Hofmann, Hans, 1880-1966. Search for the real, [Rev. ed.]. Cambridge, Mass., M.I.T. Press [c1967]
*TC N7445 .H76 1967*

Hofmann, Hans, 1880-1966. Search for the real, [Rev. ed.]. Cambridge, Mass., M.I.T. Press [c1967]
*TC N7445 .H76 1967*

**The art & craft of case writing.**
Naumes, William. Thousand Oaks, Calif. : Sage Publications, c1999.

*TC LB1029.C37 N38 1999*

**Art & design**
(v. 12, no. 9/10) Sci-fi aesthetics. London : Academy Group Ltd. ; Lanham, Md. : Distributed in the USA by National Book Network, c1997.
*TC N8217.F28 S34 1994*

**Art & design profile**
(no. 56) Sci-fi aesthetics. London : Academy Group Ltd. ; Lanham, Md. : Distributed in the USA by National Book Network, c1997.
*TC N8217.F28 S34 1994*

**Art & ideas.**
Morphy, Howard. Aboriginal art. London [England] : Phaidon, 1998.
*TC N7400 .M67 1998*

**ART - 15TH CENTURY - EUROPE.**
Art markets in Europe, 1400-1800. Aldershot ; Brookfield : Ashgate, c1998.
*TC N8600 .A737 1998*

**ART - 16TH CENTURY - EUROPE.**
Art markets in Europe, 1400-1800. Aldershot ; Brookfield : Ashgate, c1998.
*TC N8600 .A737 1998*

**ART, AFRICAN - ENCYCLOPEDIAS.**
Werness, Hope B. The Continuum encyclopedia of native art. New York : Continuum, 2000.
*TC E98.A7 W49 2000*

**ART, AFRO-AMERICAN.** *See* **AFRO-AMERICAN ART.**

**Art, alienation, and the humanities.**
Reitz, Charles. Albany : State University of New York Press, c2000.
*TC B945.M2984 R45 2000*

**ART, AMERICAN.** *See also* **INUIT ART.**
Harris, Neil. 1938- The artist in American society. Phoenix ed., with a new pref. Chicago : University of Chicago Press, 1982.
*TC N6507 .H27 1982*

**ART, AMERICAN - EXHIBITIONS.**
Haskell, Barbara. The American century. New York : Whitney Museum of American Art in association with W.W. Norton, c1999.
*TC N6512 .H355 1999*

Paris 1900. New Brunswick, N.J. : Rutgers University Press ; Montclair, N.J. : Montclair Art Museum, c1999.
*TC N6510 .P28 1999*

**ART, AMERICAN - NEW YORK (STATE) - NEW YORK.**
Götz, Stephan, 1960- [New Yorker Künstler in ihren Ateliers. English] American artists in their New York studios. Cambridge [Mass.] : Center for Conservation and Technical Studies, Harvard University Art Museums ; Stuttgart : Daco-Verlag Günter Bläse, c1992.
*TC N6535.N5 G6813 1992*

**ART - ANALYSIS, INTERPRETATION, APPRECIATION.** *See* **ART APPRECIATION; ART CRITICISM; ART - STUDY AND TEACHING.**

**Art and craft of case writing.**
Naumes, William. The art & craft of case writing. Thousand Oaks, Calif. : Sage Publications, c1999.
*TC LB1029.C37 N38 1999*

**Art and imagination.**
Scruton, Roger. South Bend, Ind. : St. Augustine's Press, 1998.
*TC BH301.J8 S37 1998*

**ART AND INDUSTRY.** *See* **ART PATRONAGE; COMMERCIAL ART.**

**ART AND LITERATURE - GREAT BRITAIN.**
Benton, Michael, 1939- Studies in the spectator role. London ; New York : Routledge, 2000.
*TC PR51.G7 B46 2000*

**ART AND LITERATURE - UNITED STATES - HISTORY - 20TH CENTURY.**
Torres, Louis, 1938- What art is. Chicago, Ill. : Open Court, c2000.
*TC PS3535.A547 Z9 2000*

**Art and logic of breakthrough thinking.**
Perkins, David N. Archimedes' bathtub. 1st ed. New York : W.W. Norton, c2000.
*TC BF441 .P47 2000*

**ART AND PHOTOGRAPHY.**
Luciana, James. The art of enhanced photography :. Gloucester, Mass. : Rockport Publishers, c1999.

TC TR654 .L83 1999

**ART AND RACE.**
Race, ethnicity and culture in the visual arts. New
York : American Council for the Arts, c1993.
*TC N70 .R32 1993*

**ART AND RELIGION.**
Schapiro, Meyer, 1904- Theory and philosophy of art.
New York : George Braziller, 1994.
*TC N66 .S345 1994*

**ART AND RELIGION - LATIN AMERICA.**
Santería aesthetics in contemporary Latin American
art. Washington : Smithsonian Institution Press,
c1996.
*TC N72.R4 S26 1996*

**Art and representation.**
Willats, John. Princeton, N.J. : Princeton University
Press, c1997.
*TC N7430.5 .W55 1997*

**ART AND REVOLUTION - MEXICO.**
Folgarait, Leonard. Mural painting and social
revolution in Mexico, 1920-1940. Cambridge ; New
York, NY : Cambridge University Press, 1998.
*TC ND2644 .F63 1998*

**ART AND SCIENCE.**
Lawrence-Lightfoot, Sara, 1944- The art and science
of portraiture. 1st ed. San Francisco : Jossey-Bass,
c1997.
*TC H62 .L33 1997*

**The art and science of digital compositing.**
Brinkman, Ronald. San Diego : Morgan Kaufmann ;
Academic Press, 1999.
*TC T385 .B75 1999*

**The art and science of portraiture.**
Lawrence-Lightfoot, Sara, 1944- 1st ed. San
Francisco : Jossey-Bass, c1997.
*TC H62 .L33 1997*

**ART AND SOCIETY.** *See also* **ART AND STATE;
STREET ART.**
Barnard, Malcolm, 1958- Art, design, and visual
culture. New York : St. Martin's Press, 1998.
*TC N71 .B32 1998*

Gombrich, E. H. (Ernst Hans), 1909- The uses of
images. London : Phaidon, 1999.
*TC N72.S6 G66 1999*

Lawrence-Lightfoot, Sara, 1944- The art and science
of portraiture. 1st ed. San Francisco : Jossey-Bass,
c1997.
*TC H62 .L33 1997*

Léger, Fernand, 1881-1955. [Fonctions de la peinture.
English] Functions of painting, New York, Viking
Press [1973]
*TC N70 .L45213 1973*

Schapiro, Meyer, 1904- Theory and philosophy of art.
New York : George Braziller, 1994.
*TC N66 .S345 1994*

Schapiro, Meyer, 1904- Worldview in painting-Art
and Society. 1st ed. New York, N.Y. : George
Braziller, 1999.
*TC N72.S6 S313 1999*

**ART AND SOCIETY - AFRICA, SUB-SAHARAN -
EXHIBITIONS.**
Sieber, Roy, 1923- African art in the cycle of life.
Washington, D.C. : Published for the National
Museum of African Art by the Smithsonian Press,
c1987.
*TC NB1091.65 .S54 1987*

**ART AND SOCIETY - ENGLAND - HISTORY -
20TH CENTURY.**
The Block reader in visual culture. London ; New
York : Routledge, 1996.
*TC N72.S6 B56 1996*

**ART AND SOCIETY - HISTORY - 19TH
CENTURY.**
Tekiner, Deniz. Modern art and the Romantic vision.
Lanham, Md. : University Press of America, c2000.
*TC N6465.R6 T43 2000*

**ART AND SOCIETY - HISTORY - 20TH
CENTURY.**
Tekiner, Deniz. Modern art and the Romantic vision.
Lanham, Md. : University Press of America, c2000.
*TC N6465.R6 T43 2000*

**ART AND SOCIETY - UNITED STATES.**
Einreinhofer, Nancy. The American art museum.
London ; New York : Leicester University Press,
1997.
*TC N510 .E45 1997*

**ART AND SOCIETY - UNITED STATES.**
Harris, Neil, 1938- The artist in American society.
Phoenix ed., with a new pref. Chicago : University of
Chicago Press, 1982.
*TC N6507 .H27 1982*

**ART AND SOCIETY - UNITED STATES -
HISTORY - 20TH CENTURY.**
Art matters. New York : New York University Press,
c1999.
*TC N72.S6 A752 1999*

Cassidy, Donna. Painting the musical city.
Washington, DC : Smithsonian Institution Press,
c1997.
*TC ML85 .C37 1997*

**ART AND SOCIOLOGY.** *See* **ART AND SOCIETY.**

**ART AND STATE.** *See* **ART COMMISSIONS.**

**ART AND STATE - PHILOSOPHY.**
Schwartz, David T. Art, education, and the democratic
commitment. Dordrecht ; Boston : Kluwer Academic
Publishers, c2000.
*TC NX720 .S33 2000*

**ART AND STATE - UNITED STATES.**
Nancy Hanks lecture on arts and public policy. [New
York, NY] : American Council for the Arts, <1988->
*TC NX730 .N25*

**Art and suburbia.**
McAuliffe, Chris. Roseville East, NSW : Craftsman
House, c1996.
*TC N7400.2 .M32 1996*

**ART AND TECHNOLOGY.**
LifeScience. Wien ; New York : Springer, 1999.
*TC T14.5 L54 1999*

**Art and the market.**
Fry, Roger Eliot, 1866-1934. Ann Arbor, Mich. :
University of Michigan Press, 1999.
*TC N8600 .F78 1999*

**ART AND WAR.** *See* **WAR MEMORIALS.**

**ART APPRECIATION.**
Belloli, Andrea P. A. Exploring world art. Los
Angeles, Calif. : J. Paul Getty Museum, 1999.
*TC N7440 .B35 1999*

Kimmelman, Michael. Portraits. 1st ed. New York :
Random House, c1998.
*TC N71 .K56 1998*

Micklethwait, Lucy. A child's book of art. 1st
American ed. New York : DK Pub., c1999.
*TC N7477 .M53 1999*

Sullivan, Missy. The Native American look book.
New York : The New Press, 1996.
*TC E98.A7 S93 1996*

What is a good drawing? [videorecording].
Peasmarsh, East Sussex, Eng. : Ho-Ho-Kus, NJ :
Roland Collection, [1980-1986?].
*TC NC703 .W45 1980*

Woolf, Felicity. Picture this century. New York :
Doubleday Book for Young Readers, c1992.
*TC N6490 .W66 1992*

**ART APPRECIATION - AUSTRALIA.**
Williams, Donald. Art now. Sydney ; New York :
McGraw-Hill Book Co., c1996.
*TC N6490 .W49 1996*

**ART APPRECIATION - JUVENILE
LITERATURE.**
Belloli, Andrea P. A. Exploring world art. Los
Angeles, Calif. : J. Paul Getty Museum, 1999.
*TC N7440 .B35 1999*

Kale, Shelly. My museum journal. Los Angeles, CA :
J. Paul Getty Museum, c2000.
*TC N7440 .K35 2000*

Kale, Shelly. My museum journal. Los Angeles, CA :
J. Paul Getty Museum, c2000.
*TC N7440 .K35 2000*

Micklethwait, Lucy. A child's book of art. 1st
American ed. New York : DK Pub., c1999.
*TC N7477 .M53 1999*

**ART APPRECIATION - PSYCHOLOGICAL
ASPECTS - SEX DIFFERENCES.**
Tuman, Donna M. Gender difference in form and
content. 1998.
*TC 06 no. 11000*

**ART APPRECIATION - STUDY AND TEACHING.**
Kárpáti, Andrea. Látni tanulunk. Budapest :
Akadémiai Kiadó, 1991.
*TC N85 .K35 1991*

**ART APPRECIATION - STUDY AND TEACHING
(MIDDLE SCHOOL) - INTERACTIVE
MULTIMEDIA.**
Tsamasiros, Katherine V. Using interactive
multimedia software to improve cognition of complex
imagery in adolescents. 1998.
*TC 06 no. 10905*

**ART APPRECIATION - STUDY AND TEACHING
(MIDDLE SCHOOL) - SOFTWARE.**
Tsamasiros, Katherine V. Using interactive
multimedia software to improve cognition of complex
imagery in adolescents. 1998.
*TC 06 no. 10905*

**Art as a basic.**
Greer, W. Dwaine. Bloomington, Ind. : Phi Delta
Kappa Education Foundation, c1997.
*TC N108 .G74 1997*

**Art as language.**
Hagberg, Garry, 1952- Ithaca : Cornell University
Press, c1995.
*TC B3376.W564 H25 1995*

**ART, ASIAN - EXHIBITIONS.**
Contemporary art in Asia. New York : Asia Society
Galleries ; Distributed by Harry N. Abrams, c1996.
*TC N7262 .C655 1996*

**ART, ASIATIC.** *See* **ART, ASIAN.**

**ART - AUSTRALIA - SYDNEY (N.S.W.) -
CATALOGS.**
Art Gallery of New South Wales. Yiribana. 2nd ed.
Sydney, Australia : The Gallery, 1998.
*TC N7401 .A765 1998*

**ART - AUSTRALIA - TORRES STRAIT ISLANDS
(QLD.) - CATALOGS.**
Art Gallery of New South Wales. Yiribana. 2nd ed.
Sydney, Australia : The Gallery, 1998.
*TC N7401 .A765 1998*

**ART, AUSTRALIAN.**
Allen, Christopher, 1953- Art in Australia. New York,
N.Y. : Thames and Hudson, 1997.
*TC N7400 .A45 1997*

Catalano, Gary, 1947- Building a picture. Sydney :
McGraw-Hill, 1997.
*TC ND1100 .C28 1997*

Drury, Nevill, 1947- Fire and shadow. Roseville East,
NWS : Craftsman House ;Australia ; United States :
G + B Arts International [distributor], c1996.
*TC N7400.2 .D78 1996*

Green, Charles. Peripheral vision. Roseville East,
N.S.W. : Craftsman House, 1995.
*TC N7400.2 .G74 1995*

McAuliffe, Chris. Art and suburbia. Roseville East,
NSW : Craftsman House, c1996.
*TC N7400.2 .M32 1996*

Voigt, Anna. New visions, new perspectives.
Roseville East, NSW : Craftsman House, 1996.
*TC N7400.2 .V65 1996*

Williams, Donald. Art now. Sydney ; New York :
McGraw-Hill Book Co., c1996.
*TC N6490 .W49 1996*

**ART, AUSTRALIAN ABORIGINAL.**
Morphy, Howard. Aboriginal art. London [England] :
Phaidon, 1998.
*TC N7400 .M67 1998*

**ART, AUSTRALIAN ABORIGINAL - CATALOGS.**
Art Gallery of New South Wales. Yiribana. 2nd ed.
Sydney, Australia : The Gallery, 1998.
*TC N7401 .A765 1998*

Morgan, Sally, 1951- The art of Sally Morgan.
Ringwood, Vic., Australia ; New York : Viking, 1996.
*TC N7405.M68 A4 1996*

**ART, AUSTRALIAN - AUSTRALIA - TORRES
STRAIT ISLANDS (QLD.) - EXHIBITIONS.**
Ilan pasin = Queensland : Cairns Regional Gallery,
[1998?].
*TC DU125.T67 I53 1998*

**ART, AUSTRALIAN - HISTORY.**
Art in diversity. 2nd. ed. Melbourne : Longman,
c1995.
*TC N5300 .A78 1995*

**ART, AUSTRALIAN - THEMES, MOTIVES.**
Sullivan, Graeme, 1951- Seeing Australia. Annandale,
NSW, Australia : Piper Press, 1994.
*TC N7400.2 .S85 1994*

**ART, BLACK - AFRICA, SUB-SAHARAN -
CATALOGS.**

World Bank. African art. Washington, D.C. : World Bank, c1998.
*TC N7391.65 .W67 1998*

**ART, CANADIAN.** *See* **INUIT ART.**

**ART CENTERS.**
Seibold, J.otto. Going to the Getty. Los Angeles : J. Paul Getty Museum, c1997.
*TC NA6813.U6 L678 1997*

**ART CENTERS - CALIFORNIA - LOS ANGELES - JUVENILE LITERATURE.**
Seibold, J.otto. Going to the Getty. Los Angeles : J. Paul Getty Museum, c1997.
*TC NA6813.U6 L678 1997*

**ART CENTERS - UNITED STATES.**
Nagy, Martin. Rural America in transition. Washington, DC : NALAA, 1996.
*TC NX798 .N3 1996*

**ART COLLECTIONS.** *See* **ART MUSEUMS.**

**ART COLLECTIONS, PRIVATE.** *See* **ART - PRIVATE COLLECTIONS.**

**ART COLLECTORS.** *See* **ART - COLLECTORS AND COLLECTING.**

**ART - COLLECTORS AND COLLECTING - EUROPE - HISTORY - 15TH CENTURY.**
Art markets in Europe, 1400-1800. Aldershot ; Brookfield : Ashgate, c1998.
*TC N8600 .A737 1998*

**ART - COLLECTORS AND COLLECTING - EUROPE - HISTORY - 16TH CENTURY.**
Art markets in Europe, 1400-1800. Aldershot ; Brookfield : Ashgate, c1998.
*TC N8600 .A737 1998*

**ART, COMMERCIAL.** *See* **COMMERCIAL ART.**

**ART COMMISSIONS - UNITED STATES.**
Building America's communities II. Washington, D.C. : Americans for the Arts (Organization) ; Institute for Community Development and the Arts, 1997.
*TC NX180.A77 B95 1997*

**ART COMMISSIONS - UNITED STATES - DIRECTORIES.**
Resource development handbook. [Washington, D.C.] : National Assembly of Local Arts Agencies, Institute for Community Development and the Arts, 1995.
*TC NX110 .R47 1995*

**ART - COMPETITIONS - AUSTRALIA - HISTORY.**
Ross, Peter. Let's face it. Sydney, Australia : Art Gallery of New South Wales, 1999.
*TC ND1327.A86 R67 1999*

**ART - COMPOSITION.** *See* **COMPOSITION (ART).**

**ART - COMPUTER NETWORK RESOURCES.**
Delivering digital images. Los Angeles, Calif. : Getty Information Institute, 1998.
*TC N59 .D45 1998*

**ART - CONSERVATION AND RESTORATION - CONGRESSES.**
Institute of Paper Conservation. Modern works, modern problems? [England] : Institute of Paper Conservation, c1994.
*TC N8560 .I59 1994*

**ART - CONSERVATION AND RESTORATION - UNITED STATES - BIBLIOGRAPHY.**
Kalfatovic, Martin R., 1961- The New Deal fine arts projects. Metuchen, N.J. : Scarecrow Press, 1994.
*TC Z5961.U5 K36 1994*

**ART CRITICISM.** *See* **ART APPRECIATION.**

**ART - CRITICISM.** *See* **ART CRITICISM.**

**ART CRITICISM.**
Uncontrollable beauty. New York : Allworth Press : School of Visual Arts, c1998.
*TC BH201 .U53 1998*

**ART CRITICISM - CANADA.**
Ryan, Allan J. The trickster shift. Vancouver, BC : UBC Press ; Seattle : University of Washington Press, c1999.
*TC E78.C2 R93 1999*

**ART CRITICISM - ENGLAND - HISTORY - 19TH CENTURY.**
Desmarais, Jane Haville. The Beardsley industry. Aldershot, Hants, England ; Brookfield, Vt. : Ashgate, c1998.
*TC NC242.B3 D475 1998*

**ART CRITICISM - ENGLAND - HISTORY - 20TH CENTURY.**
Desmarais, Jane Haville. The Beardsley industry. Aldershot, Hants, England ; Brookfield, Vt. : Ashgate, c1998.
*TC NC242.B3 D475 1998*

**ART CRITICISM - FRANCE - HISTORY - 19TH CENTURY.**
Desmarais, Jane Haville. The Beardsley industry. Aldershot, Hants, England ; Brookfield, Vt. : Ashgate, c1998.
*TC NC242.B3 D475 1998*

The New painting. San Francisco, CA : Fine Arts Museums of San Francisco, c1996.
*TC ND547.5.I4 N38 1996*

**ART CRITICISM - FRANCE - HISTORY - 20TH CENTURY.**
Desmarais, Jane Haville. The Beardsley industry. Aldershot, Hants, England ; Brookfield, Vt. : Ashgate, c1998.
*TC NC242.B3 D475 1998*

**ART DEALERS - LEGAL STATUS, LAWS, ETC. - UNITED STATES.**
DuBoff, Leonard D. The law (in plain English) for galleries. 2nd ed. New York : Allworth Press, c1999.
*TC KF2042.A76 D836 1999*

**Art, design, and visual culture.**
Barnard, Malcolm, 1958- New York : St. Martin's Press, 1998.
*TC N71 .B32 1998*

**ART - DOCUMENTATION - STANDARDS.**
Thornes, Robin. Introduction to Object ID. [Los Angeles] : Getty Information Institute, c1999.
*TC N3998 .T457 1999*

**ART - ECONOMIC ASPECTS.**
Smith, Constance, 1949- Art marketing 101. 2nd ed. Penn Valley, Calif. : ArtNetwork, c1997.
*TC N8353 .S63 1997*

**ART - EDUCATION.** *See* **ART - STUDY AND TEACHING.**

**ART EDUCATION.** *See* **ART - STUDY AND TEACHING.**

**Art, education, and the democratic commitment.**
Schwartz, David T. Dordrecht : Boston : Kluwer Academic Publishers, c2000.
*TC N720 .S33 2000*

**Art Education for the Blind.**
European modernism. New York, N.Y. : OpticalTouch Systems : Louisville, Ky. : American Printing House for the Blind, c1998-1999.
*TC N6758 .A7 1999*

**ART - EQUIPMENT AND SUPPLIES.** *See* **ARTISTS' MATERIALS.**

**ART - EUROPE - MARKETING.**
Art markets in Europe, 1400-1800. Aldershot ; Brookfield : Ashgate, c1998.
*TC N8600 .A737 1998*

**ART - EXHIBITION TECHNIQUES.**
Schlichting, Carl. Working with polyethylene foam and fluted plastic sheet. Ottawa, Ontario, Canada : Canadian Conservation Institute, Dept. of Canadian Heritage, 1994.
*TC N8554 T25 no.14*

**ART - FEDERAL AID.** *See* **FEDERAL AID TO THE ARTS.**

**ART - FINANCE.** *See* **FEDERAL AID TO THE ARTS.**

**ART, FOLK.** *See* **FOLK ART.**

**ART - FRANCE - PARIS.**
Paris [videorecording]. New York, NY : V.I.E.W. Video, c1996.
*TC DC707 .P3 1996*

**ART, FRENCH - EXHIBITIONS.**
Diderot, Denis, 1713-1784. [Selections. English. 1995] Diderot on art. New Haven : Yale University Press, 1995.
*TC N6846 .D4613 1995*

**ART GALLERIES.** *See* **ART MUSEUMS.**

**ART - GALLERIES AND MUSEUMS.** *See* **ART MUSEUMS.**

**ART GALLERIES, COMMERCIAL - LAW AND LEGISLATION - UNITED STATES.**
DuBoff, Leonard D. The law (in plain English) for galleries. New York : Allworth Press, c1999.

*TC KF2042.A76 D836 1999*

**Art Gallery of New South Wales.** Australian drawings from the gallery's collection / Hendrik Kolenberg, Prue Davidson, Anne Ryan. Sydney : Art Gallery of New South Wales, 1997. 144 p. : ill. (some col.) ; 31 cm. Cover title: Australian drawings. Catalogue of an exhibition held at the Art Gallery of New South Wales, Sydney, 13 December 1997-15 March 1998. Includes bibliographical references and index. ISBN 0-646-32833-6
*1. Drawing, Australian - Exhibitions. 2. Drawing - 20th century - Australia - Exhibitions. 3. Drawing - Australia - Sydney (N.S.W.) - Exhibitions. I. Kolenberg, Hendrik. II. Davidson, Prue. III. Ryan, Anne. IV. Title. V. Title: Australian drawings*
*TC NC369 .A78 1997*

Australian prints from the gallery's collection / Hendrik Kolenberg and Anne Ryan. Sydney : Art Gallery of New South Wales, c1998. 164 p. : ill. (some col.) ; 31 cm. Includes bibliographical references (p. 163) and index. "Published in conjunction with an exhibition at the Art Gallery of New South Wales, 6 November 1998-7 February 1999"--T.p. verso. ISBN 0-7313-8912-3 (pbk.).
*1. Art Gallery of New South Wales - Exhibitions. 2. Prints, Australian - New South Wales - Sydney - Exhibitions. I. Kolenberg, Hendrik. II. Ryan, Anne. III. Title.*
*TC NE789 .A77 1998*

Kolenberg, Hendrik. Australian watercolours from the gallery's collection. Sydney, [Australia] : Art Gallery of New South Wales, 1995.
*TC ND2089 .K64 1995*

Ross, Peter. Let's face it. Sydney, Australia : Art Gallery of New South Wales, 1999.
*TC ND1327.A86 R67 1999*

Yiribana : an introduction to the Aboriginal and Torres Strait Islander collection, the Art Gallery of New South Wales / by Margo Neale. 2nd ed. Sydney, Australia : The Gallery, 1998. 143 p. : ill. (some col.), maps ; 28 cm. Cover title: Yiribana. Spine title: Aboriginal and Torres Strait Islander collection. Includes bibliographical references (p. 140) and index. ISBN 0-7313-1565-0
*1. Art, Australian aboriginal - Catalogs. 2. Art - Australia - Torres Strait Islands (Qld.) - Catalogs. 3. Art, Modern - 20th century - Australia - Catalogs. 4. Art Gallery of New South Wales - Catalogs. 5. Art - Australia - Sydney (N.S.W.) - Catalogs. 6. Artists - Australia. I. Neale, Margo. II. Title. III. Title: Yiribana IV. Title: Aboriginal and Torres Strait Islander collection*
*TC N7401 .A765 1998*

**ART GALLERY OF NEW SOUTH WALES - CATALOGS.**
Art Gallery of New South Wales. Yiribana. 2nd ed. Sydney, Australia : The Gallery, 1998.
*TC N7401 .A765 1998*

**ART GALLERY OF NEW SOUTH WALES - EXHIBITIONS.**
Art Gallery of New South Wales. Australian drawings from the gallery's collection. Sydney : Art Gallery of New South Wales, 1997.
*TC NC369 .A78 1997*

Art Gallery of New South Wales. Australian prints from the gallery's collection. Sydney : Art Gallery of New South Wales, c1998.
*TC NE789 .A77 1998*

Kolenberg, Hendrik. Australian watercolours from the gallery's collection. Sydney, [Australia] : Art Gallery of New South Wales, 1995.
*TC ND2089 .K64 1995*

**Art Gallery of South Australia.**
Dreamings of the desert. Adelaide : The Gallery, c1996.
*TC ND1101 .D74 1996*

**ART GALLERY OF SOUTH AUSTRALIA - EXHIBITIONS.**
Dreamings of the desert. Adelaide : The Gallery, c1996.
*TC ND1101 .D74 1996*

**ART - GOVERNMENT POLICY.** *See* **ART AND STATE.**

**ART, GRAPHIC.** *See* **GRAPHIC ARTS.**

**ART, GREENLANDIC.** *See* **INUIT ART.**

**ART - HISTORY.**
Art in diversity. 2nd. ed. Melbourne : Longman, c1995.
*TC N5300 .A78 1995*

Honour, Hugh. The visual arts. 5th ed. New York : Henry N. Abrams, 1999.

*TC N5300 .H68 1999*

Stockley, Michele. Art investigator. Port Melbourne, Vic. : Heinemann, 1998.
*TC N5300 .S915 1998*

**Art history through touch & sound**
European modernism. New York, N.Y. : OpticalTouch Systems ; Louisville, Ky. : American Printing House for the Blind, c1998-1999.
*TC N6758 .A7 1999*

**ART, IBO.** *See* **ART, IGBO.**

**ART, IGBO (AFRICAN PEOPLE).** *See* **ART, IGBO.**

**ART, IGBO - INFLUENCE.**
Ottenberg, Simon. New traditions from Nigeria. Washington, DC : Smithsonian Institution Press, c1997.
*TC N7399.N52 N786 1997*

**ART IN ADVERTISING.** *See* **COMMERCIAL ART.**

**Art in America.**
Art in America. New York, Frederick Fairchild Sherman.

**Art in America.** New York, Frederick Fairchild Sherman. v. ill. 27 cm. Frequency: Bimonthly, 1914-1921. Former frequency: Quarterly, 1913. v. 1-v. 9, no. 6; 1913-Oct. 1921. Available on microfilm. Available in other form: Art in America (OCoLC)7432513. Continued by: Art in America and elsewhere (OCoLC)5844990. ISSN 0898-297X DDC 705
*1. Art - Periodicals. I. Sherman, Frederick Fairchild. II. Title: Art in America III. Title: Art in America and elsewhere*

**Art in America (1913).**
Art in America and elsewhere. Springfield, Mass., Frederick Fairchild Sherman.

**Art in America (1939).**
Art in America and elsewhere. Springfield, Mass., Frederick Fairchild Sherman.

**Art in America and elsewhere.**
Art in America. New York, Frederick Fairchild Sherman.

Art in America and elsewhere. Springfield, Mass., Frederick Fairchild Sherman.

**Art in America and elsewhere.** Springfield, Mass., Frederick Fairchild Sherman. 18 v. ill. 27 cm. Frequency: Quarterly. v. 10-v. 27, no. 2; Dec. 1921-Apr. 1939. "An illustrated quarterly magazine." Available in other form: Art in America and elsewhere (OCoLC)7432524. Continues: Art in America (1913) ISSN: 0898-297X (OCoLC)5844965. Continued by: Art in America (1939) ISSN: 0004-3214 (OCoLC)1514286.
*1. Art - Periodicals. I. Sherman, Frederick Fairchild. II. Title: Art in America and elsewhere III. Title: Art in America (1913) IV. Title: Art in America (1939)*

**Art in Australia.**
Allen, Christopher, 1953- New York, N.Y. : Thames and Hudson, 1997.
*TC N7400 .A45 1997*

**Art in diversity** / Bernard Hoffert [et al.]. 2nd. ed. Melbourne : Longman, c1995. 306 p. : ill. (some col.) ; 27 cm. Includes bibliographical references and index. CONTENTS: Part 1. Art in eighteenth and nineteenth centure Europe -- Part II. Art in the twentieth century -- Part III. Art in Australia. ISBN 0-582-80362-4
*1. Art - History. 2. Art, Australian - History. 1. Hoffert, Bernard.*
*TC N5300 .A78 1995*

**ART IN EDUCATION.**
Greene, Maxine. Active learning and aesthetic encounters. New York : NCREST, 1995.
*TC BH39 .G74 1995*

**ART IN EDUCATION - GREAT BRITAIN.**
Benton, Michael, 1939- Studies in the spectator role. London ; New York : Routledge, 2000.
*TC PR51.G7 B46 2000*

**ART IN EDUCATION - GREAT BRITAIN - CONGRESSES.**
The dynamics of now. London : Wimbledon School of Art in association with Tate, c2000.
*TC N185 .D96 2000*

**ART IN EDUCATION - UNITED STATES.**
Albers, Peggy. Telling pieces. Mahwah, N.J. : L. Erlbaum Associates, 2000.
*TC N362.5 .A43 2000*

Building America's communities II. Washington, D.C. : Americans for the Arts (Organization) ; Institute for Community Development and the Arts, 1997.

*TC NX180.A77 B95 1997*

Resource development handbook. [Washington, D.C.] : National Assembly of Local Arts Agencies, Institute for Community Development and the Arts, 1995.
*TC NX110 .R47 1995*

**ART IN LITERATURE.**
Torres, Louis, 1938- What art is. Chicago, Ill. : Open Court, c2000.
*TC PS3535.A547 Z9 2000*

**Art in the making**
Art in the making, Impressionism. London : National Gallery, in association with Yale University Press, c1991.
*TC ND547.5.I4 I4472 1991*

Impressionism [videorecording]. [London] : The National Gallery ; Tillingham, Peasmarsh, East Sussex, England : Ho-Ho-Kus, NJ : Distributed by The Roland Collection, c1990.
*TC ND547.5.I4 A7 1990*

Italian painting before 1400 [videorecording]. [London] : The National Gallery, c1989.

Italian painting before 1400 [videorecording]. [London] : The National Gallery, c1989.
*TC ND1575 .I87 1989*

**Art in the making, Impressionism** / David Bomford ... [et al.] ; with contributions by Raymond White and Louise Williams. London : National Gallery, in association with Yale University Press, c1991. 227 p. : ill. (some col.) ; 28 cm. (Art in the making) Includes bibliographical references (p. 213-227). ISBN 0-300-05035-6 DDC 759.4/09/03407442132
*1. Impressionism (Art) - France - Exhibitions. 2. Painting, French - Exhibitions. 3. Painting, Modern - 19th century - France - Exhibitions. 4. National Gallery (Great Britain) - Exhibitions. 5. Impressionism (Art) - Technique. I. Bomford, David. II. National Gallery (Great Britain) III. Title: Impressionism. IV. Series.*
*TC ND547.5.I4 I4472 1991*

**Art in the making [videorecording] : impressionisn.**
Impressionism [videorecording]. [London] : The National Gallery ; Tillingham, Peasmarsh, East Sussex, England : Ho-Ho-Kus, NJ : Distributed by The Roland Collection, c1990.
*TC ND547.5.I4 A7 1990*

**Art in the making [videorecording] : Itlian painting before 1400.**
Italian painting before 1400 [videorecording]. [London] : The National Gallery, c1989.

Italian painting before 1400 [videorecording]. [London] : The National Gallery, c1989.
*TC ND1575 .I87 1989*

**ART, INDIAN.** *See* **INDIAN ART.**

**ART, INDIAN - EXHIBITIONS.**
Shared visions. 1st New Press ed. New York : New Press ; Distributed by Norton, [1993], c1991.
*TC N6538.A4 A7 1993*

**ART INDUSTRIES AND TRADE.** *See* **DECORATIVE ARTS.**

**ART INDUSTRIES AND TRADE - STUDY AND TEACHING - PERIODICALS.**
Industrial arts magazine. Milwaukee [etc.] Bruce Publishing Co.

**Art Institute of Chicago.**
Cassatt, Mary, 1844-1926. Mary Cassatt, modern woman. 1st ed. New York : Art Institute of Chicago in association with H.N. Abrams, c1998.
*TC N6537.C35 A4 1998*

**ART, INUIT.** *See* **INUIT ART.**

**Art investigator.**
Stockley, Michele. Port Melbourne, Vic. : Heinemann, 1998.
*TC N5300 .S915 1998*

**ART - MARKETING.**
Fry, Roger Eliot, 1866-1934. Art and the market. Ann Arbor, Mich. : University of Michigan Press, 1999.
*TC N8600 .F78 1999*

Smith, Constance, 1949- Art marketing 101. 2nd ed. Penn Valley, Calif. : ArtNetwork, c1997.
*TC N8353 .S63 1997*

**Art marketing 101.**
Smith, Constance, 1949- 2nd ed. Penn Valley, Calif. : ArtNetwork, c1997.
*TC N8353 .S63 1997*

**Art marketing one hundred and one.**
Smith, Constance, 1949- Art marketing 101. 2nd ed. Penn Valley, Calif. : ArtNetwork, c1997.
*TC N8353 .S63 1997*

**Art marketing one hundred one.**
Smith, Constance, 1949- Art marketing 101. 2nd ed. Penn Valley, Calif. : ArtNetwork, c1997.
*TC N8353 .S63 1997*

**Art markets in Europe, 1400-1800** / edited by Michael North and David Ormrod. Aldershot ; Brookfield : Ashgate, c1998. ix, 250 p. : ill., map ; 25 cm. Includes bibliographical references (p. [221]-240) and index. ISBN 1-84014-630-3 (alk. paper) DDC 709/.02/4
*1. Art - Europe - Marketing. 2. Art - 15th century - Europe. 3. Art - 16th century - Europe. 4. Art - Collectors and collecting - Europe - History - 15th century. 5. Art - Collectors and collecting - Europe - History - 16th century. I. North, Michael, 1954- II. Ormrod, David.*
*TC N8600 .A737 1998*

**ART MATERIAL.** *See* **ARTISTS' MATERIALS.**

**ART MATERIALS.** *See* **ARTISTS' MATERIALS.**

**Art matters** : how the culture wars changed America / Julie Ault ... [et al.] ; edited by Brian Wallis, Marianne Weems, and Philip Yenawine. New York : New York University Press, c1999. 316 p. : ill. Includes bibliographical references. ISBN 0-8147-9351-7 (pbk. : alk. paper) ISBN 0-8147-9350-9 (cloth : alk. paper) DDC 306.4/7/097309045
*1. Art and society - United States - History - 20th century. 2. Art - Political aspects - United States - History - 20th century. 3. United States - Cultural policy - History - 20th century. I. Ault, Julie. II. Yenawine, Philip. III. Weems, Marianne. IV. Wallis, Brian, 1953-*
*TC N72.S6 A752 1999*

**ART METAL-WORKERS.** *See* **JEWELERS.**

**ART, MODERN.** *See* **NEOCLASSICISM (ART).**

**ART, MODERN - 17TH-18TH CENTURIES - FRANCE - EXHIBITIONS.**
Diderot, Denis, 1713-1784. [Selections. English. 1995] Diderot on art. New Haven : Yale University Press, 1995.
*TC N6846 .D4613 1995*

**ART, MODERN - 19H CENTURY - UNITED STATES - EXHIBITIONS.**
Paris 1900. New Brunswick, N.J. : Rutgers University Press ; Montclair, N.J. : Montclair Art Museum, c1999.
*TC N6510 .P28 1999*

**ART, MODERN - 19TH CENTURY.** *See also* **ART, VICTORIAN; IMPRESSIONISM (ART).**
Tekiner, Deniz. Modern art and the Romantic vision. Lanham, Md. : University Press of America, c2000.
*TC N6465.R6 T43 2000*

**ART, MODERN - 19TH CENTURY - EXHIBITIONS.**
Modernstarts. New York : Museum of Modern Art : Distributed by Harry N. Abrams, c1999.
*TC N620.M9 M63 1999*

**ART, MODERN - 19TH CENTURY - UNITED STATES.**
Harris, Neil, 1938- The artist in American society. Phoenix ed., with a new pref. Chicago : University of Chicago Press, 1982.
*TC N6507 .H27 1982*

**ART, MODERN - 20TH CENTURY.** *See also* **EXPRESSIONISM (ART); INSTALLATIONS (ART); MODERNISM (ART); POP ART.**
Jagodzinski, Jan, 1953- Postmodern dilemmas. Mahwah, N.J. : Lawrence Erlbaum Associates, 1997.
*TC N7445.2 .J34 1997*

Lunenfeld, Peter. Snap to grid. Cambridge, MA : MIT, 2000.
*TC QA76.9.C66 L86 2000*

Oliveira, Nicolas de. Installation art. London : Thames and Hudson, 1994.
*TC N6494.E O4 1994*

Smith, Bernard, 1916- Modernism's history. New Haven : Yale University Press, 1998.
*TC N6494.M64 S65 1998*

Tekiner, Deniz. Modern art and the Romantic vision. Lanham, Md. : University Press of America, c2000.
*TC N6465.R6 T43 2000*

Williams, Donald. Art now. Sydney ; New York : McGraw-Hill Book Co., c1996.
*TC N6490 .W49 1996*

Woolf, Felicity. Picture this century. New York : Doubleday Book for Young Readers, c1992.

*TC N6490 .W66 1992*

**ART, MODERN - 20TH CENTURY - ASIA - EXHIBITIONS.**
Contemporary art in Asia. New York : Asia Society Galleries : Distributed by Harry N. Abrams, c1996.
*TC N7262 .C655 1996*

**ART, MODERN - 20TH CENTURY - AUSTRALIA.**
Drury, Nevill, 1947- Fire and shadow. Roseville East, NWS : Craftsman House :Australia : United States : G + B Arts International [distributor], c1996.
*TC N7400.2 .D78 1996*

Green, Charles. Peripheral vision. Roseville East, N.S.W. : Craftsman House, 1995.
*TC N7400.2 .G74 1995*

Kirby, Sandy. Sight lines. Tortola, BVI : Craftsman House in association with Gordon and Breach ; New York : Distributed in the USA by STBS Ltd., 1992.
*TC N72.F45 K57 1992*

McAuliffe, Chris. Art and suburbia. Roseville East, NSW : Craftsman House, c1996.
*TC N7400.2 .M32 1996*

Voigt, Anna. New visions, new perspectives. Roseville East, NSW : Craftsman House, 1996.
*TC N7400.2 .V65 1996*

Williams, Donald. Art now. Sydney ; New York : McGraw-Hill Book Co., c1996.
*TC N6490 .W49 1996*

**ART, MODERN - 20TH CENTURY - AUSTRALIA - CATALOGS.**
Art Gallery of New South Wales. Yiribana. 2nd ed. Sydney, Australia : The Gallery, 1998.
*TC N7401 .A765 1998*

**ART, MODERN - 20TH CENTURY - AUSTRALIA - EXHIBITIONS.**
Antipodean currents. New York : Guggenheim Museum, c1995.
*TC N7404 .A58 1995*

**ART, MODERN - 20TH CENTURY - AUSTRALIA - THEMES, MOTIVES.**
Sullivan, Graeme, 1951- Seeing Australia. Annandale, NSW, Australia : Piper Press, 1994.
*TC N7400.2 .S85 1994*

**ART, MODERN - 20TH CENTURY - AUSTRALIA - TORRES STRAIT ISLANDS (QLD.) - EXHIBITIONS.**
Ilan pasin = Queensland : Cairns Regional Gallery, [1998?].
*TC DU125.T67 I53 1998*

**ART, MODERN - 20TH CENTURY - BRITISH COLUMBIA - PACIFIC COAST.**
Wyatt, Gary, 1958- Mythic beings. Vancouver : Douglas & McIntyre ; Seattle : University of Washington Press, c1999.
*TC E78.B9 W93 1999*

**ART, MODERN - 20TH CENTURY - CONSERVATION AND RESTORATION - CONGRESSES.**
Mortality immortality? Los Angeles : Getty Conservation Institute, c1999.
*TC N6485 .M67 1999*

**ART, MODERN - 20TH CENTURY - ENGLAND.**
Etching [videorecording]. Northbrook, Ill. : Peasmarsh, East Sussex, Eng. : Roland Collection of Films on Art, c1990.
*TC NE2043 .E87 1990*

**ART, MODERN - 20TH CENTURY - EUROPE.**
European modernism. New York, N.Y. : OpticalTouch Systems : Louisville, Ky. : American Printing House for the Blind, c1998-1999.
*TC N6758 .A7 1999*

**ART, MODERN - 20TH CENTURY - EUROPE - EXHIBITIONS.**
Exiles + emigrés. Los Angeles, Calif. : Los Angeles County Museum of Art ; New York : H.N. Abrams, c1997.
*TC N6512 .E887 1997*

**ART, MODERN - 20TH CENTURY - EXHIBITIONS.**
Modernstarts. New York : Museum of Modern Art : Distributed by Harry N. Abrams, c1999.
*TC N620.M9 M63 1999*

**ART, MODERN - 20TH CENTURY - GREAT BRITAIN.**
Screen printing [videorecording]. [Northbrook?], Ill. : Peasmarsh, East Sussex, Eng. : Roland Collection of Films on Art, c1992.

*TC NE2238.G7 S4 1992*

**ART, MODERN - 20TH CENTURY - JUVENILE LITERATURE.**
Woolf, Felicity. Picture this century. New York : Doubleday Book for Young Readers, c1992.
*TC N6490 .W66 1992*

**ART, MODERN - 20TH CENTURY - LATIN AMERICA.**
Santería aesthetics in contemporary Latin American art. Washington : Smithsonian Institution Press, c1996.
*TC N72.R4 S26 1996*

**ART, MODERN - 20TH CENTURY - NEW YORK (STATE) - NEW YORK.**
Götz, Stephan, 1960- [New Yorker Künstler in ihren Ateliers. English] American artists in their New York studios. Cambridge [Mass.] : Center for Conservation and Technical Studies, Harvard University Art Museums ; Stuttgart : Daco-Verlag Günter Bläse, c1992.
*TC N6535.N5 G6813 1992*

**ART, MODERN - 20TH CENTURY - NIGERIA - NSUKKA.**
Ottenberg, Simon. New traditions from Nigeria. Washington, DC : Smithsonian Institution Press, c1997.
*TC N7399.N52 N786 1997*

**ART, MODERN - 20TH CENTURY - PRIMITIVE INFLUENCES.**
Thomas, Nicholas. Possessions. New York, N.Y. : Thames and Hudson, c1999.
*TC N5313 .T46 1999*

**ART, MODERN - 20TH CENTURY - UNITED STATES.**
Andy Warhol [videorecording]. [Chicago, IL] : Home Vision [distributor].cc1987.
*TC N6537.W28 A45 1987*

Cassidy, Donna. Painting the musical city. Washington, DC : Smithsonian Institution Press, c1997.
*TC ML85 .C37 1997*

Nevelson in process [videorecording]. Chicago, IL : Public Media Inc., 1977.
*TC NB237.N43 N43 1977*

**ART, MODERN - 20TH CENTURY - UNITED STATES - EXHIBITIONS.**
Exiles + emigrés. Los Angeles, Calif. : Los Angeles County Museum of Art ; New York : H.N. Abrams, c1997.
*TC N6512 .E887 1997*

Haskell, Barbara. The American century. New York : Whitney Museum of American Art in association with W.W. Norton, c1999.
*TC N6512 .H355 1999*

Shared visions. 1st New Press ed. New York : New Press : Distributed by Norton, [1993], c1991.
*TC N6538.A4 A7 1993*

**ART, MODERN - HISTORY - STUDY AND TEACHING (MIDDLE SCHOOL) - SOFTWARE.**
Tsamasiros, Katherine V. Using interactive multimedia software to improve cognition of complex imagery in adolescents. 1998.
*TC 06 no. 10905*

**ART, MODERNIST. *See* MODERNISM (ART).**

**ART, MOGUL.**
Flora and fauna in Mughal art. [Bombay] : Marg Publications, c1999.
*TC N7302 .F567 1999*

**ART, MUNICIPAL. *See* ART COMMISSIONS; CITY PLANNING.**

**The art museum.**
Meyer, Karl Ernest. 1st ed. New York : Morrow, 1979.
*TC N510 .M47*

**ART MUSEUM ARCHITECTURE.**
Newhouse, Victoria. Towards a new museum. New York : Monacelli Press, 1998.
*TC NA6695 .N49 1998*

**ART MUSEUMS. *See* ART GALLERIES, COMMERCIAL.**

**ART - MUSEUMS. *See* ART MUSEUMS.**

**ART MUSEUMS - CALIFORNIA - SAN FRANCISCO - JUVENILE FICTION.**
Frank, Phil. The ghost of the de Young Museum. [San

Francisco : Fine Arts Museums of San Francisco, 1995]
*TC N739.5 .F72 1995*

**ART MUSEUMS - FRANCE - PARIS.**
Paris [videorecording]. New York, NY : V.I.E.W. Video, c1996.
*TC DC707 .P3 1996*

**ART MUSEUMS - UNITED STATES.**
Einreinhofer, Nancy. The American art museum. London ; New York : Leicester University Press, 1997.
*TC N510 .E45 1997*

Meyer, Karl Ernest. The art museum. 1st ed. New York : Morrow, 1979.
*TC N510 .M47*

**ART - NEW YORK (STATE) - SOUTHAMPTON - EXHIBITIONS.**
De Salvo, Donna M. Past imperfect. Southampton, N.Y. : Parrish Art Museum, in association with the New Press, New York, N.Y., c1993.
*TC N750 .D4*

**ART, NIGERIAN - NIGERIA - NSUKKA.**
Ottenberg, Simon. New traditions from Nigeria. Washington, DC : Smithsonian Institution Press, c1997.
*TC N7399.N52 N786 1997*

**Art now.**
Williams, Donald. Sydney : New York : McGraw-Hill Book Co., c1996.
*TC N6490 .W49 1996*

**ART OBJECTS. *See* ANTIQUES.**

**ART, OCCIDENTAL. *See* ART.**

**ART - OCEANIA - ENCYCLOPEDIAS.**
Werness, Hope B. The Continuum encyclopedia of native art. New York : Continuum, 2000.
*TC E98.A7 W49 2000*

**The art of classroom inquiry.**
Hubbard, Ruth, 1950- Portsmouth, N.H. : Heinemann, c1993.
*TC LB1028 .H78 1993*

**The art of classroom management.**
McEwan, Barbara, 1946- Upper Saddle River, N.J. : Merrill, c2000.
*TC LB3013 .M383 2000*

**The art of enhanced photography.**
Luciana, James. Gloucester, Mass. : Rockport Publishers, c1999.
*TC TR654 .L83 1999*

**The art of Gordon Bennett.**
McLean, Ian, Dr. Roseville East, NSW : Craftsman House, 1996.
*TC N7405.B46 M39 1996*

**The art of necessity.**
Wexler, Alice. 1999.
*TC 06 no. 11072*

**The art of performance.**
Schenker, Heinrich, 1868-1935. [Kunst des Vortrags. English] New York : Oxford University Press, 2000.
*TC MT220 .S24513 2000*

**The art of Richard Diebenkorn.**
Livingston, Jane. New York : Whitney Museum of American Art ; Berkeley : University of California Press, c1997.
*TC N6537.D447 A4 1997*

**The art of Sally Morgan.**
Morgan, Sally, 1951- Ringwood, Vic., Australia ; New York : Viking, 1996.
*TC N7405.M68 A4 1996*

**The art of spelling.**
Vos Savant, Marilyn, 1946- New York : W.W. Norton, 2000.
*TC PE1143 .V67 2000*

**The art of storytelling for teachers and pupils.**
Grugeon, Elizabeth. London : David Fulton, 2000.
*TC LB1042 .G78 2000*

**The art of teaching reading.**
Calkins, Lucy McCormick. 1st ed. New York : London : Longman, c2001.
*TC LB1573 .C185 2001*

**The art of the long view.**
Schwartz, Peter. 1st Currency pbk. ed. New York : Currency Doubleday : 1996.
*TC HD30.28 .S316 1996*

**The art of the question.**
Goldberg, Marilee C. New York : Wiley, c1998.
*TC RC489.N47 G65 1998*

**Art on my mind.**
Hooks, Bell. New York : New Press : Distributed by
W.W. Norton, c1995.
*TC N6537.H585 A2 1995*

**ART, ORIENTAL.** *See* **ART, ASIAN.**

**ART, PASTORAL.** *See* **PASTORAL ART.**

**ART PATRONAGE.**
Barnard, Malcolm, 1958- Art, design, and visual
culture. New York : St. Martin's Press, 1998.
*TC N71 .B32 1998*

**ART PATRONAGE - NEW YORK (STATE) - NEW
YORK.**
Bogart, Michele Helene, 1952- Public sculpture and
the civic ideal in New York City, 1890-1930. 1st
Smithsonian ed. Washington, D.C. : Smithsonian
Institution Press, 1997.
*TC NB235.N5 B64 1997*

**ART PATRONAGE - UNITED STATES.**
Einreinhofer, Nancy. The American art museum.
London ; New York : Leicester University Press,
1997.
*TC N510 .E45 1997*

Levy, Alan Howard. Government and the arts.
Lanham, Md. : University Press of America, c1997.
*TC NX735 .L48 1997*

**ART - PERIODICALS.**
Art in America. New York, Frederick Fairchild
Sherman.

Art in America and elsewhere. Springfield, Mass.,
Frederick Fairchild Sherman.

**ART - PERIODICALS - INDEXES.**
Schmidt, Mary. Index to nineteenth century American
art periodicals. Madison, CT : Sound View Press,
c1999.
*TC N1 Sch5*

**ART - PHILOSOPHY.**
Danto, Arthur Coleman, 1924- Philosophizing art.
Berkeley : University of California Press, c1999.
*TC N71 .D33 1999*

Housen, Abigail. The eye of the beholder. 1983.
*TC BH39 .H68 1983*

Léger, Fernand, 1881-1955. [Fonctions de la peinture.
English] Functions of painting, New York, Viking
Press [1973]
*TC N70 .L45213 1973*

Miller, Jonathan, 1934- On reflection. London :
National Gallery Publications : [New Haven, Conn.] :
Distributed by Yale University Press, c1998.
*TC N8224.M6 M54 1998*

Olson, Ivan, 1931- The arts and critical thinking in
American education. Westport, Conn. : Bergin &
Garvey, 2000.
*TC BH39 .O45 2000*

On pictures and paintings [videorecording].
Peasmarsh, East Sussex, Eng. ; Ho-Ho-kus, NJ :
Roland Collection, 1992.
*TC ND195.O45 1992*

Schapiro, Meyer, 1904- Theory and philosophy of art.
New York : George Braziller, 1994.
*TC N66 .S345 1994*

Sutton, Tiffany. The classification of visual art.
Cambridge ; New York : Cambridge University Press,
2000.
*TC N66 .S88 2000*

**ART - POLITICAL ASPECTS.**
Photomontage today, Peter Kennard [videorecording].
[London] : Art Council of Great Britain ; Ho-Ho-Kus,
N.J. : [distributed by] Anthony Roland Collection of
Films on Art, c1982.
*TC TR685 .P45 1982*

**ART - POLITICAL ASPECTS - ENGLAND.**
The Block reader in visual culture. London ; New
York : Routledge, 1996.
*TC N72.S6 B56 1996*

**ART - POLITICAL ASPECTS - UNITED STATES -
HISTORY - 20TH CENTURY.**
Art matters. New York : New York University Press,
c1999.
*TC N72.S6 A752 1999*

**ART, POP.** *See* **POP ART.**

**ART, POPULAR.** *See* **FOLK ART.**

**ART, PREHISTORIC.** *See* **ROCK PAINTINGS.**

**ART, PREHISTORIC - ALGERIA - TASSILI-N-
AJJER.**
Tassili N'Ajjer [videorecording]. [S.l.] : Editions
Cinégraphiques ; Northbrook, Ill. : [distributed by] the
Roland Collection, c1968.
*TC N5310.5.A4 T3 1968*

**ART, PRIMITIVE.** *See* **ART, PREHISTORIC;
FOLK ART; SCULPTURE, PRIMITIVE.**

**ART - PRIVATE COLLECTIONS -
WASHINGTON (D.C.) - CATALOGS.**
World Bank. African art. Washington, D.C. : World
Bank, c1998.
*TC N7391.65 .W67 1998*

**ART PROJECTS, COMMUNITY.** *See*
**COMMUNITY ART PROJECTS.**

**ART - PSYCHOLOGY.**
Gombrich, E. H. (Ernst Hans), 1909- The uses of
images. London : Phaidon, 1999.
*TC N72.S6 G66 1999*

Lowenfeld, Viktor. Creative and mental growth. Rev.
ed. New York, Macmillan [1952]
*TC N350 .L62 1952*

Wexler, Alice. The art of necessity. 1999.
*TC 06 no. 11072*

Zeki, Semir. Inner vision. Oxford ; New York :
Oxford University Press, c1999.
*TC N71 .Z45 1999*

**ART - PSYCHOLOGY - JUVENILE
LITERATURE.**
Kale, Shelly. My museum journal. Los Angeles, CA :
J. Paul Getty Museum, c2000.
*TC N7440 .K35 2000*

Kale, Shelly. My museum journal. Los Angeles, CA :
J. Paul Getty Museum, c2000.
*TC N7440 .K35 2000*

**ART - RELIGIOUS ASPECTS.** *See* **ART AND
RELIGION.**

**ART SCHOOLS.** *See* **ART - STUDY AND
TEACHING.**

**ART SCHOOLS - CUBA - HAVANA.**
Loomis, John A., 1951- Revolution of forms. New
York : Princeton Architectural Press, c1999.
*TC NA6602.A76 L66 1999*

**Art series (View Video)**
Paris [videorecording]. New York, NY : V.I.E.W.
Video, c1996.
*TC DC707 .P3 1996*

**ART SONGS.** *See* **SONGS.**

**ART, STREET.** *See* **STREET ART.**

**ART - STUDY AND TEACHING.** *See also* **ART
SCHOOLS.**
Dow, Arthur W. (Arthur Wesley), 1857-1922.
Composition. Berkeley : University of California
Press, 1997.
*TC N7430 .D68 1997*

Hofmann, Hans, 1880-1966. Search for the real, [Rev.
ed.]. Cambridge, Mass., M.I.T. Press [c1967]
*TC N7445 .H76 1967*

Hofmann, Hans, 1880-1966. Search for the real, [Rev.
ed.]. Cambridge, Mass., M.I.T. Press [c1967]
*TC N7445 .H76 1967*

Lowenfeld, Viktor. Creative and mental growth. Rev.
ed. New York, Macmillan [1952]
*TC N350 .L62 1952*

Taylor, Bruce D. The arts equation. New York, N.Y. :
Back Stage Books, c1999.
*TC N350 .T38 1999*

Walling, Donovan R., 1948- Rethinking how art is
taught. Thousand Oaks, Calif. : Corwin Press, c2000.
*TC N85 .W35 2000*

Zeki, Semir. Inner vision. Oxford ; New York :
Oxford University Press, c1999.
*TC N71 .Z45 1999*

**ART - STUDY AND TEACHING - ACTIVITY
PROGRAMS.**
Boriss-Krimsky, Carolyn. The creativity handbook.
Springfield, Ill. : C.C. Thomas, 1999.
*TC N350 .B656 1999*

**ART - STUDY AND TEACHING - CASE STUDIES.**
Curriculum, culture, and art education. Albany : State
University of New York Press, c1998.

*TC N85 .C87 1998*

**ART - STUDY AND TEACHING (ELEMENTARY).**
Chapman, Laura H. Discover art. Worcester, Mass. :
Davis Publications, c1987.
*TC N361 .C56 1987*

Wachowiak, Frank. Emphasis art. 7th ed. New York ;
London : Longman, c2001.
*TC N350 .W26 2001*

**ART - STUDY AND TEACHING
(ELEMENTARY) - PSYCHOLOGICAL
ASPECTS - SEX DIFFERENCES.**
Tuman, Donna M. Gender difference in form and
content. 1998.
*TC 06 no. 11000*

**ART - STUDY AND TEACHING
(ELEMENTARY) - UNITED STATES.**
Bates, Jane K. Becoming an art teacher. Belmont,
CA : Wadsworth/Thomson Learning, 2000.
*TC N353 .B38 2000*

Libby, Wendy M. L. Using art to make art Albany,
N.Y. : Delmar Publishers, 2000.
*TC N362 .L49 2000*

Real-world readings in art education. New York :
Falmer Press, c2000.
*TC N353 .R43 2000*

**ART - STUDY AND TEACHING - GREAT
BRITAIN.**
Benton, Michael, 1939- Studies in the spectator role.
London ; New York : Routledge, 2000.
*TC PR51.G7 B46 2000*

**ART - STUDY AND TEACHING - GREAT
BRITAIN - CONGRESSES.**
The dynamics of now. London : Wimbledon School of
Art in association with Tate, c2000.
*TC N185 .D96 2000*

**ART - STUDY AND TEACHING - HISTORY -
20TH CENTURY.**
Jagodzinski, Jan, 1953- Postmodern dilemmas.
Mahwah, N.J. : Lawrence Erlbaum Associates, 1997.
*TC N7445.2 .J34 1997*

**ART - STUDY AND TEACHING (MIDDLE
SCHOOL).**
Hafeli, Mary Claire. Drawing and painting in the
middle school. 1999.
*TC 06 no. 11055*

Wachowiak, Frank. Emphasis art. 7th ed. New York ;
London : Longman, c2001.
*TC N350 .W26 2001*

**ART - STUDY AND TEACHING (MIDDLE
SCHOOL) - UNITED STATES.**
Albers, Peggy. Telling pieces. Mahwah, N.J. : L.
Erlbaum Associates, 2000.
*TC N362.5 .A43 2000*

**ART - STUDY AND TEACHING - PHILOSOPHY.**
Readings in discipline-based art education. Reston,
Va. : National Art Education Assoc., c2000.
*TC N87 .R43 2000*

**ART - STUDY AND TEACHING (SECONDARY) -
UNITED STATES.**
Bates, Jane K. Becoming an art teacher. Belmont,
CA : Wadsworth/Thomson Learning, 2000.
*TC N353 .B38 2000*

Real-world readings in art education. New York :
Falmer Press, c2000.
*TC N353 .R43 2000*

**ART - STUDY AND TEACHING - UNITED
STATES - HISTORY - 20TH CENTURY.**
Greer, W. Dwaine. Art as a basic. Bloomington, Ind. :
Phi Delta Kappa Education Foundation, c1997.
*TC N108 .G74 1997*

**ART - SUBJECTS.** *See* **ART - THEMES,
MOTIVES.**

**ART SUPPLIES.** *See* **ARTISTS' MATERIALS.**

**Art tapes series**
(1.) Photomontage today, Peter Kennard
[videorecording]. [London] : Art Council of Great
Britain ; Ho-Ho-Kus, N.J. : [distributed by]
Anthony Roland Collection of Films on Art, c1982.
*TC TR685 .P45 1982*

**ART - THEMES, MOTIVES - JUVENILE
LITERATURE.**
Belloli, Andrea P. A. Exploring world art. Los
Angeles, Calif. : J. Paul Getty Museum, 1999.
*TC N7440 .B35 1999*

**ART THERAPY - CASE REPORT.**
Beyond talk therapy. 1st ed. Washington, DC :
American Psychological Association, c1999.
*TC RC489.A72 B49 1999*

**ART THERAPY FOR CHILDREN.**
Klorer, P. Gussie. Expressive therapy with troubled
children. Northvale, NJ : Jason Aronson, 2000.
*TC RJ505.A7 K56 2000*

**ART THERAPY FOR YOUTH.**
Wexler, Alice. The art of necessity. 1999.
*TC 06 no. 11072*

**ART, VICTORIAN - PSYCHOLOGICAL
ASPECTS.**
Flint, Kate. The Victorians and the visual imagination.
Cambridge, U.K. ; New York : Cambridge University
Press, 2000.
*TC N6767 .F58 2000*

**ART, VISUAL.** *See* **ART.**

**ART, WALL.** *See* **STREET ART.**

**ART, WEST AFRICAN.**
Frank, Barbara E. Mande potters & leatherworkers.
Washington, D.C. : Smithsonian Institution Press,
1998.
*TC DT474.6.M36 F73 1998*

**ART, WESTERN.** *See* **ART.**

**Art works! :** interdisciplinary learning powered by the
arts / edited by Dennie Palmer Wolf and Dana Balick.
Portsmouth, NH : Heinemann, c1999. xii, 169 p. : ill. ;
23 cm. (Moving middle schools) Includes bibliographical
references. ISBN 0-325-00116-2 (alk. paper) DDC 373.19
*1. Interdisciplinary approach in education - United States. 2.
Arts - Study and teaching (Middle school) - United States. 3.
Middle school education - United States - Curricula. 4. Project
method in teaching - United States. I. Wolf, Dennie. II. Balick,
Dana. III. Series: Moving middle schools*
*TC LB1628.5 .A78 1999*

**Artech House telecommunications library**
Nellist, John G. Understanding modern
telecommunications and the information
superhighway. Boston, Mass. : Artech House, 1999.
*TC TK5105.5 .N45 1999*

**ARTEFACTS (ANTIQUITIES).** *See*
**ANTIQUITIES.**

**Arthur, James, 1957-.**
Haydn, Terry, 1951- Learning to teach history in the
secondary school. London ; New York : Routledge,
1997.
*TC D16.25 .H38 1997*

Schools and community : the communitarian agenda
in education / James Arthur with Richard Bailey.
London : New York : Falmer Press, 2000. ix, 165 p. ; 23
cm. Includes bibliographical references (p. 145-156) and index.
ISBN 0-7507-0955-3 (alk. paper) ISBN 0-7507-0954-5 (pbk. :
alk. paper) DDC 371.19/0941
*1. Community and school - Great Britain. 2.
Communitarianism - Great Britain. I. Bailey, Richard, 1957-
II. Title.*
*TC LC221.4.G7 A78 2000*

**Arthur, James, 1959-.**
Issues in history teaching. London ; New York :
Routledge, 2000.
*TC D16.2 .I88 2000*

**Arthur M. Sackler Gallery (Smithsonian Institution).**
Twelve centuries of Japanese art from the Imperial
collections. Washington, DC : Freer Gallery of Art
and the Arthur M. Sackler Gallery, Smithsonian
Institution Press, c1997.
*TC ND1457.J32 W377 1997*

**Arthur Wesley Dow (1857-1922).**
Ira Spanierman Gallery. New York : Spanierman
Gallery, 1999.
*TC N44.D7442 I73 1999*

**Arthur Wesley Dow : his art and his influence.**
Ira Spanierman Gallery. Arthur Wesley Dow (1857-
1922). New York : Spanierman Gallery, 1999.
*TC N44.D7442 I73 1999*

**ARTICLES, RELIGIOUS.** *See* **RELIGIOUS
ARTICLES.**

**ARTICULATION (EDUCATION).**
General education in school and college. Cambridge :
Harvard University Press, 1952.
*TC 372G28*

**ARTICULATIONS (ANATOMY).** *See* **JOINTS.**

**ARTICULATORY PHONETICS.** *See*
**PHONETICS.**

**ARTIFACTS (ANTIQUITIES).** *See* **ANTIQUITIES.**

**ARTIFICIAL INSEMINATION, HUMAN - LAW
AND LEGISLATION - GREAT BRITAIN.**
Technologies of procreation. 2nd ed. New York :
Routledge, 1999.
*TC HQ761 .T43 1999*

**ARTIFICIAL INSEMINATION, HUMAN -
SOCIAL ASPECTS.**
Technologies of procreation. 2nd ed. New York :
Routledge, 1999.
*TC HQ761 .T43 1999*

**ARTIFICIAL INTELLIGENCE.** *See also* **EXPERT
SYSTEMS (COMPUTER SCIENCE);
MACHINE LEARNING; NEURAL
NETWORKS (COMPUTER SCIENCE).**
Clancey, William J. Conceptual coordination.
Mahwah, N.J. : L. Erlbaum Associates, 1999.
*TC BF311 .C5395 1999*

Gärdenfors, Peter. Conceptual spaces. Cambridge,
Mass. : London : MIT Press, c2000.
*TC Q335 .G358 2000*

Hayles, N. Katherine. How we became posthuman.
Chicago, Ill. : University of Chicago Press, 1999.
*TC Q335 .H394 1999*

Human cognition and social agent technology.
Amsterdam ; Philadelphia : John Benjamins, c2000.
*TC BF311 .H766 2000*

Innovative teaching and learning. Heidelberg
[Germany] ; New York : Physica-Verlag, c2000.
*TC QA76.76.E95 I54 2000*

Intelligent multimedia information retrieval. Menlo
Park, Calif. : AAAI Press ; Cambridge, Mass. : MIT
Press, c1997.
*TC QA76.575 .I577 1997*

Perspectives on cognitive science. Stamford, Conn. :
Ablex Pub. Corp., c1999.
*TC BF311 .P373 1999*

Pfeifer, Rolf, 1947- Understanding intelligence.
Cambridge, Mass. : MIT Press, c1999.
*TC Q335 .P46 1999*

Wagman, Morton. The human mind according to
artificial intelligence. Westport, Conn. : Praeger, 1999.
*TC Q335 .W342 1999*

Wagman, Morton. Scientific discovery processes in
humans and computers. Westport, CT : Praeger, 2000.
*TC Q180.55.D57 W34 2000*

**ARTIFICIAL INTELLIGENCE - QUOTATIONS,
MAXIMS, ETC.**
Historical dictionary of quotations in cognitive
science. Westport, Conn. : Greenwood Press, 2000.
*TC PN6084.C545 H57 2000*

**ARTIFICIAL LARYNX.**
The Artificial larynx handbook. New York : Grune &
Stratton, c1978.
*TC RF538 .A77*

**The Artificial larynx handbook** / editors, Shirley J.
Salmon, Lewis P. Goldstein. New York : Grune &
Stratton, c1978. xii, 157 p. : ill. ; 23 cm. & cassette (2 track
mono). Includes bibliographies and index. ISBN 0-8089-
1111-2 DDC 617/.533
*1. Artificial larynx. 2. Artificial organs. 3. Larynx. 4. Voice
production, Alaryngeal. I. Salmon, Shirley J. II. Goldstein,
Lewis P.*
*TC RF538 .A77*

**ARTIFICIAL NEURAL NETWORKS.** *See*
**NEURAL NETWORKS (COMPUTER
SCIENCE).**

**ARTIFICIAL ORGANS.**
The Artificial larynx handbook. New York : Grune &
Stratton, c1978.
*TC RF538 .A77*

**ARTIFICIAL RESPIRATION.**
Tracheostomy and ventilator dependency. New York :
Thieme, 2000.
*TC RF517 .T734 2000*

**ARTIFICIAL RESPIRATION - EQUIPMENT AND
SUPPLIES.** *See* **RESPIRATORS (MEDICAL
EQUIPMENT).**

**ARTIFICIAL SATELLITES IN
TELECOMMUNICATION.** *See* **TELEVISION.**

**ARTIFICIAL THINKING.** *See* **ARTIFICIAL
INTELLIGENCE.**

**ARTISANS.** *See* **TOYMAKERS.**

**ARTISANS - DISEASES.**
McCann, Michael, 1943- Artist beware. [2nd ed.].
New York, NY : Lyons & Burford, c1992.
*TC RC963.6.A78 M32 1992*

**ARTISANS - HEALTH AND HYGIENE -
HANDBOOKS, MANUALS, ETC.**
McCann, Michael, 1943- Health hazards manual for
artists. 4th rev. and augm. ed. New York, NY :
Lyons & Burford, c1994.
*TC RC963.6.A78 M324 1994*

**ARTIST AND ART DEALER CONTRACTS.** *See*
**ARTISTS' CONTRACTS.**

**Artist beware.**
McCann, Michael, 1943- [2nd ed.]. New York, NY :
Lyons & Burford, c1992.
*TC RC963.6.A78 M32 1992*

**The artist-gallery partnership.**
Crawford, Tad, 1946- [2nd ed.]. New York : Allworth
Press, c1998.
*TC KF947 .C7 1998*

**The artist in American society.**
Harris, Neil, 1938- Phoenix ed., with a new pref.
Chicago : University of Chicago Press, 1982.
*TC N6507 .H27 1982*

**ARTISTIC PHOTOGRAPHY.** *See*
**PHOTOGRAPHY, ARTISTIC.**

**ARTISTS.** *See* **AUTHORS; DANCERS;
ENTERTAINERS; EXPATRIATE ARTISTS;
ILLUSTRATORS; MUSICIANS; PAINTERS;
PHOTOGRAPHERS; POTTERS;
PRINTMAKERS; SCULPTORS;
TOYMAKERS; WOMEN ARTISTS.**

**ARTISTS, AFRO-AMERICAN.** *See* **AFRO-
AMERICAN ARTISTS.**

**ARTISTS AND COMMUNITY.** *See* **COMMUNITY
ART PROJECTS.**

**Artists and engravers of British and American book
plates.**
Fincham, H. W. (Henry Walter) New York : Dodd,
Mead, and Company, 1897.
*TC Z993 .F49 1897*

**Artists and issues in the theatre**
(vol. 10) Theatre in cyberspace. New York : P.
Lang, c1999.
*TC PN2075 .T54 1999*

**ARTISTS AND MUSEUMS.**
Kimmelman, Michael. Portraits. 1st ed. New York :
Random House, c1998.
*TC N71 .K56 1998*

**ARTISTS AS TEACHERS.**
Taylor, Bruce D. The arts equation. New York, N.Y. :
Back Stage Books, c1999.
*TC N350 .T38 1999*

**ARTISTS - AUSTRALIA.**
Art Gallery of New South Wales. Yiribana. 2nd ed.
Sydney, Australia : The Gallery, 1998.
*TC N7401 .A765 1998*

**ARTISTS - AUSTRALIA - BIOGRAPHY.**
Antipodean currents. New York : Guggenheim
Museum, c1995.
*TC N7404 .A58 1995*

Sullivan, Graeme, 1951- Seeing Australia. Annandale,
NSW, Australia : Piper Press, 1994.
*TC N7400.2 .S85 1994*

**ARTISTS, AUSTRALIAN - INTERVIEWS.**
Catalano, Gary, 1947- Building a picture. Sydney :
McGraw-Hill, 1997.
*TC ND1100 .C28 1997*

**ARTISTS' CONTRACTS - UNITED STATES.**
Crawford, Tad, 1946- The artist-gallery partnership.
[2nd ed.]. New York : Allworth Press, c1998.
*TC KF947 .C7 1998*

**ARTISTS' CONTRACTS - UNITED STATES -
FORMS.**
Crawford, Tad, 1946- Business and legal forms for
illustrators. Rev. ed. New York : Allworth Press,
c1998.
*TC KF390.A7 C7 1998*

**ARTISTS - DISEASES.**
McCann, Michael, 1943- Artist beware. [2nd ed.].
New York, NY : Lyons & Burford, c1992.
*TC RC963.6.A78 M32 1992*

**ARTISTS - EUROPE - EXHIBITIONS.**
Exiles + emigrés. Los Angeles, Calif. : Los Angeles
County Museum of Art ; New York : H.N. Abrams,
c1997.

*TC N6512 .E887 1997*

**ARTISTS, EXPATRIATE.** *See* **EXPATRIATE ARTISTS.**

**ARTISTS - HEALTH AND HYGIENE.**
Spandorfer, Merle, 1934- Making art safely. New York : Van Nostrand Reinhold, c1993.
*TC RC963.6.A78 S62 1993*

**ARTISTS - HEALTH AND HYGIENE - HANDBOOKS, MANUALS, ETC.**
McCann, Michael, 1943- Health hazards manual for artists. 4th rev. and augm. ed. New York, NY : Lyons & Burford, c1994.
*TC RC963.6.A78 M324 1994*

**ARTISTS - INTERVIEWS.**
Kimmelman, Michael. Portraits. 1st ed. New York : Random House, c1998.
*TC N71 .K56 1998*

**ARTISTS - LEGAL STATUS, LAWS, ETC. - UNITED STATES.**
Crawford, Tad, 1946- Legal guide for the visual artist. 3rd ed. New York : Allworth Press : Copublished with the American Council for the Arts : Cincinnati, Ohio : Distributor to the trade in the United States and Canada, North Light Books, c1995.
*TC KF390.A7 C73 1995*

**ARTISTS' MATERIALS.**
Italian painting before 1400 [videorecording]. [London] : The National Gallery, c1989.

Italian painting before 1400 [videorecording]. [London] : The National Gallery, c1989.
*TC ND1575 .I87 1989*

**ARTISTS' MATERIALS - SAFETY MEASURES.**
Spandorfer, Merle, 1934- Making art safely. New York : Van Nostrand Reinhold, c1993.
*TC RC963.6.A78 S62 1993*

**ARTISTS' MATERIALS - TOXICOLOGY.**
McCann, Michael, 1943- Artist beware. [2nd ed.]. New York, NY : Lyons & Burford, c1992.
*TC RC963.6.A78 M32 1992*

**ARTISTS - NEW YORK (STATE) - NEW YORK - INTERVIEWS.**
Götz, Stephan, 1960- [New Yorker Künstler in ihren Ateliers. English] American artists in their New York studios. Cambridge [Mass.] : Center for Conservation and Technical Studies, Harvard University Art Museums ; Stuttgart : Daco-Verlag Günter Bläse, c1992.
*TC N6535.N5 G6813 1992*

**ARTISTS - NIGERIA - NSUKKA - ATTITUDES.**
Ottenberg, Simon. New traditions from Nigeria. Washington, DC : Smithsonian Institution Press, c1997.
*TC N7399.N52 N786 1997*

**ARTISTS - PSYCHOLOGY.**
Barnard, Malcolm, 1958- Art, design, and visual culture. New York : St. Martin's Press, 1998.
*TC N71 .B32 1998*

Development and the arts. Hillsdale, N.J. : L. Erlbaum Associates, 1994.
*TC N71 .D495 1994*

Kimmelman, Michael. Portraits. 1st ed. New York : Random House, c1998.
*TC N71 .K56 1998*

Krauss, Rosalind E. The optical unconscious. 1st MIT Press pbk. ed. Cambridge, Mass. : MIT Press, 1994.
*TC N7430.5 .K73 1994*

Podro, Michael. Depiction. New Haven, CT : Yale University Press, c1998.
*TC N71 .P64 1998*

**ARTISTS' SPOUSES.** *See* **PAINTERS' SPOUSES.**

**ARTISTS - TAXATION - UNITED STATES - HANDBOOKS, MANUALS, ETC.**
Chadwick, Annie. Showbiz bookkeeper. Dorset, Vermont : Theatre Directories, 1992, c1991.
*TC HF5686.P24 C53 1991*

**ARTISTS - UNITED STATES.** *See* **AFRO-AMERICAN ARTISTS.**

**ARTISTS - UNITED STATES - BIOGRAPHY.**
Andy Warhol [videorecording]. [Chicago, IL] : Home Vision [distributor],cc1987.
*TC N6537.W28 A45 1987*

Andy Warhol [videorecording]. [Chicago, IL] : Home Vision [distributor],cc1987.

*TC N6537.W28 A45 1987*

Georgia O'Keeffe [videorecording]. [Boston?] : Home Vision : c1977.
*TC ND237.O5 G4 1977*

**ARTISTS - UNITED STATES - PSYCHOLOGY.**
Garoian, Charles R., 1943- Performing pedagogy. Albany, N.Y. : State University of New York Press, 1999.
*TC NX504 .G37 1999*

Harris, Neil, 1938- The artist in American society. Phoenix ed., with a new pref. Chicago : University of Chicago Press, 1982.
*TC N6507 .H27 1982*

**ARTISTS, WOMEN.** *See* **WOMEN ARTISTS.**

**ARTIZANS.** *See* **ARTISANS.**

**ARTS.** *See* **ART; PERFORMING ARTS.**

**The arts.**
Walters, Thomas. Lanham, MD : University Press of America, 2000.
*TC NX170 .W35 2000*

**ARTS - ADMINISTRATION.** *See* **ARTS - MANAGEMENT.**

**ARTS ADMINISTRATION.** *See* **ARTS - MANAGEMENT.**

**ARTS, AFRO-AMERICAN.** *See* **AFRO-AMERICAN ARTS.**

**ARTS, AMERICAN.** *See* **AFRO-AMERICAN ARTS.**

**ARTS, AMERICAN - EXHIBITIONS.**
Haskell, Barbara. The American century. New York : Whitney Museum of American Art in association with W.W. Norton, c1999.
*TC N6512 .H355 1999*

**Arts and crafts magazine May 1914.**
Industrial arts magazine. Milwaukee [etc.] Bruce Publishing Co.

**The arts and critical thinking in American education.**
Olson, Ivan, 1931- Westport, Conn. : Bergin & Garvey, 2000.
*TC BH39 .O45 2000*

**Arts and Entertainment Network.**
The American Revolution. [videorecording]. New York, N.Y. : A&E Home Video, c1994.
*TC E208 .A447 1994*

The Irish in America [videorecording]. [New York, N.Y.] : A&E Home Video ; New York, N.Y. : Distributed by the New Video Group, 1997.
*TC E184.I6 I6 1997*

**Arts and humanities.**
GrantFinder. Arts and humanities. New York, NY : St. Martin's Press, 2000.
*TC LB2337.2 .G72*

GrantFinder : Arts and humanities. New York, NY : St. Martin's Press, 2000.
*TC LB2337.2 .G72*

**ARTS AND SOCIETY - HISTORY - 20TH CENTURY.**
Talking visions. New York, N.Y. : New Museum of Contemporary Art ; Cambridge, Mass. : MIT Press, c1998.
*TC NX180.F4 T36 1998*

**ARTS AND SOCIETY - UNITED STATES.**
Nagy, Martin. Rural America in transition. Washington, DC : NALAA, 1996.
*TC NX798 .N3 1996*

**ARTS AND SOCIETY - UNITED STATES - HISTORY - CONGRESSES.**
Democracy & the arts. Ithaca : Cornell University Press, c1999.
*TC NX180.S6 D447 1999*

**ARTS AND SOCIOLOGY.** *See* **ARTS AND SOCIETY.**

**Arts and the Internet.**
Shiva, V. A. New York : Allworth Press, c1996.
*TC NX260 .S55 1996*

**ARTS AND YOUTH - UNITED STATES.**
Nagy, Martin. Rural America in transition. Washington, DC : NALAA, 1996.
*TC NX798 .N3 1996*

**ARTS, APPLIED.** *See* **DECORATIVE ARTS.**

**The arts as meaning makers.**
Cornett, Claudia E. Upper Saddle River, N.J. : Merrill, 1999.

*TC LB1591 .C67 1999*

**ARTS - AUDIENCES.** *See* **ARTS AUDIENCES.**

**ARTS AUDIENCES - UNITED STATES.**
A Practical guide to arts participation research. Washington, DC : National Endowment for the Arts, [1995]
*TC NX220 .P73 1995*

**ARTS - COMPARATIVE METHOD.**
Walters, Thomas. The arts. Lanham, MD : University Press of America, 2000.
*TC NX170 .W35 2000*

**ARTS - COMPUTER NETWORK RESOURCES.**
Shiva, V. A. Arts and the Internet. New York : Allworth Press, c1996.
*TC NX260 .S55 1996*

**ARTS - COMPUTER NETWORK RESOURCES - DIRECTORIES.**
Shiva, V. A. Arts and the Internet. New York : Allworth Press, c1996.
*TC NX260 .S55 1996*

**Arts Council of Great Britain.**
Photomontage today, Peter Kennard [videorecording]. [London] : Art Council of Great Britain ; Ho-Ho-Kus, N.J. : [distributed by] Anthony Roland Collection of Films on Art, c1982.
*TC TR685 .P45 1982*

**ARTS - CRITICISM.** *See* **ART CRITICISM.**

**ARTS, DECORATIVE.** *See* **DECORATIVE ARTS.**

**ARTS - ECONOMIC ASPECTS - UNITED STATES.**
Nagy, Martin. Rural America in transition. Washington, DC : NALAA, 1996.
*TC NX798 .N3 1996*

**Arts Education Partnership (U.S.).**
Champions of change. Washington, DC : Arts Education Partnership : President's Committee on the Arts and the Humanities, [1999]
*TC NX304.A1 C53 1999*

**ARTS - ENVIRONMENTAL ASPECTS - UNITED STATES.**
Nagy, Martin. Rural America in transition. Washington, DC : NALAA, 1996.
*TC NX798 .N3 1996*

**The arts equation.**
Taylor, Bruce D. New York, N.Y. : Back Stage Books, c1999.
*TC N350 .T38 1999*

**ARTS FACILITIES.** *See* **ART CENTERS; ART MUSEUMS.**

**ARTS - FEDERAL AID.** *See* **FEDERAL AID TO THE ARTS.**

**ARTS - FELLOWSHIPS.** *See* **ARTS - SCHOLARSHIPS, FELLOWSHIPS, ETC.**

**ARTS FELLOWSHIPS.** *See* **ARTS - SCHOLARSHIPS, FELLOWSHIPS, ETC.**

**ARTS - FINANCE.** *See* **FEDERAL AID TO THE ARTS.**

**ARTS, FINE.** *See* **ART; ARTS.**

**Arts funding.**
Renz, Loren. 3rd ed. [New York, N.Y.] : Foundation Center, c1998.
*TC NX711.U5 R4 1998*

**ARTS, GHANAIAN - EXHIBITIONS.**
Cole, Herbert M. The arts of Ghana. Los Angeles : Museum of Cultural History, University of California, c1977.
*TC NX589.6.G5 C64*

**ARTS - GOVERNMENT POLICY.** *See* **ART AND STATE.**

**ARTS, GRAPHIC.** *See* **GRAPHIC ARTS.**

**ARTS - GREAT BRITAIN - FINANCE.**
The Economics of the arts. Boulder, Colo. : Westview Press, 1976.
*TC NX705.5.U6 E27 1976*

**ARTS IN THE CHURCH.** *See* **ART AND RELIGION.**

**ARTS MANAGEMENT.** *See* **ARTS - MANAGEMENT.**

**ARTS - MANAGEMENT - EUROPE.**
From maestro to manager. Dublin : Oak Tree Press in association with the Graduate School of Business, University College Dublin, c1997.

*TC NX770.E85 F76 1997*

**ARTS, MINOR.** *See* **DECORATIVE ARTS.**

**ARTS, MODERN.** *See* **ART, MODERN;
LITERATURE, MODERN.**

**ARTS, MODERN - 20TH CENTURY.** *See*
**PERFORMANCE ART; POSTMODERNISM;
SURREALISM.**

**ARTS, MODERN - 20TH CENTURY - UNITED
STATES - EXHIBITIONS.**
Haskell, Barbara. The American century. New York :
Whitney Museum of American Art in association with
W.W. Norton, c1999.
*TC N6512 .H355 1999*

**ARTS, OCCIDENTAL.** *See* **ARTS.**

**The arts of Ghana.**
Cole, Herbert M. Los Angeles : Museum of Cultural
History, University of California, c1977.
*TC NX589.6.G5 C64*

**ARTS PATRONAGE.** *See* **ART PATRONAGE.**

**ARTS - POLITICAL ASPECTS - UNITED
STATES - HISTORY - CONGRESSES.**
Democracy & the arts. Ithaca : Cornell University
Press, c1999.
*TC NX180.S6 D447 1999*

**ARTS - RESEARCH GRANTS.**
GrantFinder. Arts and humanities. New York, NY :
St. Martin's Press, 2000.
*TC LB2337.2 .G72*

**ARTS - RESEARCH GRANTS - DIRECTORIES.**
GrantFinder : Arts and humanities. New York, NY :
St. Martin's Press, 2000.
*TC LB2337.2 .G72*

**ARTS SCHOLARSHIPS.** *See* **ARTS -
SCHOLARSHIPS, FELLOWSHIPS, ETC.**

**ARTS - SCHOLARSHIPS, FELLOWSHIPS, ETC. -
DIRECTORIES.**
GrantFinder : Arts and humanities. New York, NY :
St. Martin's Press, 2000.
*TC LB2337.2 .G72*

**ARTS - SOCIAL ASPECTS.** *See* **ARTS AND
SOCIETY.**

**ARTS - STUDY AND TEACHING.**
Burz, Helen L. Performance-based curriculum for
music and the visual arts. Thousand Oaks, Calif. :
Corwin Press, c1999.
*TC LB1591 .B84 1999*

Cornett, Claudia E. The arts as meaning makers.
Upper Saddle River, N.J. : Merrill, 1999.
*TC LB1591 .C67 1999*

The postmodern educator. New York : P. Lang,
c1999.
*TC LB1707 .P67 1999*

Shattuck, Roger. Candor and perversion. 1st ed. New
York : W.W. Norton, c1999.
*TC PN52 .S53 1999*

**ARTS - STUDY AND TEACHING - EUROPE,
CENTRAL - HISTORY.**
Freedman, Joseph S. Philosophy and the arts in
Central Europe, 1500-1700. Aldershot : Ashgate,
1999.
*TC B52.3.C36 F74 1999*

**ARTS - STUDY AND TEACHING (HIGHER) -
UNITED STATES.**
Caughie, Pamela L., 1953- Passing and pedagogy.
Urbana : University of Illinois Press, c1999.
*TC PN61 .C38 1999*

**ARTS - STUDY AND TEACHING -
METHODOLOGY.**
Garoian, Charles R., 1943- Performing pedagogy.
Albany, N.Y. : State University of New York Press,
1999.
*TC NX504 .G37 1999*

**ARTS - STUDY AND TEACHING (MIDDLE
SCHOOL) - UNITED STATES.**
Art works!. Portsmouth, NH : Heinemann, c1999.
*TC LB1628.5 .A78 1999*

**ARTS - STUDY AND TEACHING - UNITED
STATES.**
Champions of change. Washington, DC : Arts
Education Partnership : President's Committee on the
Arts and the Humanities, [1999]
*TC NX304.A1 C53 1999*

Detels, Claire Janice, 1953- Soft boundaries.
Westport, Conn. : Bergin & Garvey, 1999.

*TC LB1591.5.U6 D48 1999*

**ARTS SURVEYS - UNITED STATES.**
A Practical guide to arts participation research.
Washington, DC : National Endowment for the Arts,
[1995]
*TC NX220 .P73 1995*

**ARTS - THERAPEUTIC USE.**
Beyond talk therapy. 1st ed. Washington, DC :
American Psychological Association, c1999.
*TC RC489.A72 B49 1999*

**ARTS - UNITED STATES - FINANCE.**
The Economics of the arts. Boulder, Colo. : Westview
Press, 1976.
*TC NX705.5.U6 E27 1976*

Jeffri, Joan. The emerging arts. New York, N.Y. :
Praeger, 1980.
*TC NX765 .J43*

Renz, Loren. Arts funding. 3rd ed. [New York, N.Y.] :
Foundation Center, c1998.
*TC NX711.U5 R4 1998*

**ARTS - UNITED STATES - MANAGEMENT.**
Jeffri, Joan. The emerging arts. New York, N.Y. :
Praeger, 1980.
*TC NX765 .J43*

**ARTS - UNITED STATES - SOCIETIES, ETC.**
Nagy, Martin. Rural America in transition.
Washington, DC : NALAA, 1996.
*TC NX798 .N3 1996*

**ARTS, USEFUL.** *See* **INDUSTRIAL ARTS;
TECHNOLOGY.**

**ARTS, VISUAL.** *See* **ART.**

**ARTS, WESTERN.** *See* **ARTS.**

**ArtTable, Inc.**
Race, ethnicity and culture in the visual arts. New
York : American Council for the Arts, c1993.
*TC N70 .R32 1993*

**Aruego, Jose.**
Ginsburg, Mirra. Mushroom in the rain. New York :
Macmillan/McGraw-Hill, 1974.
*TC PZ10.3 .G455Mu 1974*

**Aruego, Jose, ill.**
Sierra, Judy. Antarctic antics. 1st ed. San Diego :
Harcourt Brace & Co., c1998.
*TC PS3569.I39 A53 1998*

**Arum, Richard.**
The structure of schooling. Mountain View, Calif. :
Mayfield Pub. Co., 1999.
*TC LC189 .S87 1999*

**Ascher, Carol, 1941-.**
Flaxman, Erwin. Youth mentoring: New York, N.Y. :
ERIC Clearinghouse on Urban Education, 1988.
*TC LC4065 .F53 1988*

**Ashcroft, Kate.**
Improving teaching and learning in the core
curriculum. London ; New York : Falmer Press, 2000.
*TC LB1564.G7 I475 2000*

**ASHE-ERIC higher education report**
(v. 27, no. 3) Speck, Bruce W. Grading students'
classroom writing. Washington, DC : Graduate
School of Education and Human Development, The
George Washington University, 2000.
*TC LB1576 .S723 2000*

(vol. 25, no. 1) Freed, Jann E. A culture for
academic excellence. Washington, D.C. : Graduate
School of Education and Human Development,
George Washington University, 1997.
*TC LB2341 .F688 1997*

(vol. 25, no. 2.) Dannells, Michael. From discipline
to development. Washington, DC : George
Washington University, Graduate School of
Education and Human Development, [1997]
*TC LB2344 .D36 1997*

(vol. 27, no. 2.) Stevens, Ed. Due process and
higher education. Washington, DC : Graduate
School of Education and Human Development,
George Washington University, [1999]
*TC LB2344 .S73 1999*

(vol. 27, no. 4.) Alstete, Jeffrey W. Posttenure
faculty development. San Fransisco, [Calif.] :
Jossey-Bass c2000.
*TC LB2335.7 .A47 2000*

(vol. 27, no. 5.) Van Dusen, Gerald C. Digital
dilemma. San Francisco : Jossey-Bass, c2000.

*TC LC5805 .V35 2000*

(vol. 27, no. 6.) Aguirre, Adalberto. Women and
minority faculty in the academic workplace. San
Francisco, Calif. : Jossey-Bass c2000.
*TC LB2332.3 .A35 2000*

**ASHE-ERIC/higher education research report**
(1983, no. 10.) Austin, Ann E. Academic
workplace. Washington, D.C. : Association for the
Study of Higher Education, 1983.
*TC LB2331.7 .A96 1983*

**ASHE reader on finance in higher education** / edited
by Larry L. Leslie and Richard E. Anderson.
Needham Heights, MA : Ginn Press, c1986. 419 p. :
ill. ; 28 cm. (ASHE reader series) Includes bibliographical
references. ISBN 0-536-05556-4 DDC 379.1/18/0973
*1. Education, Higher - United States - Finance. 2. Universities
and colleges - United States - Administration. 3. Higher
education and state - United States. I. Leslie, Larry L. II.
Anderson, Richard E., 1943- III. Association for the Study of
Higher Education. IV. Title: Reader on finance in higher
education. V. Series.*
*TC LB2342 .A76 1990*

**ASHE reader series**
ASHE reader on finance in higher education.
Needham Heights, MA : Ginn Press, c1986.
*TC LB2342 .A76 1990*

**Asher, James J. (James John), 1929-** Learning another
language through actions / by James J. Asher ; with
classroom-tested lessons by Carol Adamski. 4th ed.
Los Gatos, Calif. : Sky Oaks Productions, 1993. 1 v.
(various pagings) : ill. ; 22 cm. Includes bibliographical
references (section 5, p. 1-8). ISBN 1-56018-494-9
*1. Language and languages - Study and teaching. 2. Learning,
Psychology of. 3. Interactive analysis in education. I. Adamski,
Carol. II. Title.*
*TC PB36 .A8 1993*

**Asher, Mukul G.**
Ramesh, M., 1960- Welfare capitalism in southeast
Asia. New York : St. Martin's Press, c2000.
*TC HN690.8.A8 R35 2000*

**Asher, Nina.** Margins, center, and the spaces in-
between : Indian American high school students' lives
at home and school / by Nina Asher. 1999. xv, 351
leaves ; 29 cm. Typescript; issued also on microfilm. Thesis
(Ed.D.)--Teachers College, Columbia University, 1999.
Includes bibliographical references (leaves 314-323).
*1. East Indian Americans - New York (State) - New York -
Ethnic identity. 2. High school students - New York (State) -
New York. 3. East Indian Americans - Education (Secondary) -
Attitudes. 4. East Indian American teenagers - New York
(State) - New York - Cultural assimilation. 5. East Indian
American teenagers - New York (State) - New York -
Interviews. 6. East Indian American teenagers - New York
(State) - New York - Family relationships. 7. Socialization. I.
Title. II. Title: Indian American high school students' lives at
home and school*
*TC 06 no. 11080*

**Asher, R. E.**
Concise encyclopedia of educational linguistics.
Amsterdam ; New York : Elsevier, 1999.
*TC P40.8 .C66 1999*

**Ashley Entertainment.**
Headline stories of the century [videorecording].
Chicago, IL. : Distributed by Questar Video, Inc.,
c1992.
*TC D743 .H42 1992*

**Ashley, Martin.**
Improving teaching and learning in the humanities.
London : Falmer ; New York : Published in the USA
and Canada by Garland, 1999.
*TC LB1564.G7 I47 1999*

**Ashmore, Rhea A.** Teacher education in the People's
Republic of China / by Rhea A. Ashmore and Zhen
Cao. Bloomington, Ind., U.S.A. : Phi Delta Kappa
Educational Foundation, c1997. 83 p. ; 23 cm. (Phi Delta
Kappa international studies in education) Includes
bibliographical references (p. 81-82). ISBN 0-87367-494-4
*1. Teachers - Training of - China. I. Cao, Zhen. II. Title. III.
Series.*
*TC LB1727.C5 A85 1997*

**Ashton, Elizabeth, lecturer.** Religious education in the
early years / Elizabeth Ashton. London ; New York :
Routledge, 2000. xii, 203 p. : ill. ; 24 cm. (Teaching and
learning in the first three years of school) Includes
bibliographical references (p. 198-200) and index. ISBN
0-415-18386-3 (pbk. : alk. paper) DDC 268/.432
*1. Christian education of children. I. Title. II. Series.*
*TC BV1475.2 .A84 2000*

ASIA. *See* ASIA, CENTRAL.

**Asia and the Pacific Programme of Educational Innovation for Development.**
Grass roots networking for primary education :.
Bangkok : Unesco Regional Office for Education in Asia and the Pacific, 1985.
*TC LA1054 .G73 1985*

**ASIA, CENTRAL - POLITICS AND GOVERNMENT.**
Khalid, Adeeb, 1964- The politics of Muslim cultural reform. Berkeley : University of California Press, c1998.
*TC BP63.A34 K54 1998*

ASIA, EAST. *See* EAST ASIA.

ASIA, EASTERN. *See* EAST ASIA.

**Asia Society. Galleries.**
Contemporary art in Asia. New York : Asia Society Galleries : Distributed by Harry N. Abrams, c1996.
*TC N7262 .C655 1996*

**ASIA, SOUTHEASTERN - ECONOMIC CONDITIONS - CASE STUDIES.**
Ramesh, M., 1960- Welfare capitalism in southeast Asia. New York : St. Martin's Press, c2000.
*TC HN690.8.A8 R35 2000*

**ASIA, SOUTHEASTERN - SOCIAL POLICY - CASE STUDIES.**
Ramesh, M., 1960- Welfare capitalism in southeast Asia. New York : St. Martin's Press, c2000.
*TC HN690.8.A8 R35 2000*

ASIA, SOUTHWEST. *See* MIDDLE EAST.

**ASIA - STATISTICS - HISTORY.**
Mitchell, B. R. (Brian R.) International historical statistics, Africa, Asia & Oceania, 1750-1993. 3rd ed. London : Macmillan Reference ; New York : Ggrove's Dictionaries[division of Stockton Press], 1998.
*TC HA1107 .M54 1998*

ASIA, WESTERN. *See* MIDDLE EAST.

**ASIAN AMERICAN CHILDREN - EDUCATION.**
Manning, M. Lee. Multicultural education of children and adolescents. 3rd ed. Boston : Allyn and Bacon, c2000.
*TC LC1099.3 .M36 2000*

**ASIAN-AMERICAN CHILDREN - EDUCATION - NEW YORK (STATE) - CASE STUDIES.**
Schmidt, Patricia Ruggiano, 1944- Cultural conflict and struggle. New York : P. Lang, c1998.
*TC LB1181 .S36 1998*

**ASIAN AMERICAN COLLEGE STUDENTS - ATTITUDES - CASE STUDIES.**
Bhattacharya, Diya. The college experience and the construction of cultural identity among first generation Indian American undergraduates. 1999.
*TC 06 no. 11083*

**ASIAN AMERICAN COLLEGE STUDENTS - FAMILY RELATIONSHIPS.**
Bhattacharya, Diya. The college experience and the construction of cultural identity among first generation Indian American undergraduates. 1999.
*TC 06 no. 11083*

**ASIAN AMERICAN COLLEGE STUDENTS - SOCIAL IDENTITY - CASE STUDIES.**
Bhattacharya, Diya. The college experience and the construction of cultural identity among first generation Indian American undergraduates. 1999.
*TC 06 no. 11083*

**ASIAN AMERICAN COLLEGE STUDENTS - SOCIALIZATION - CASE STUDIES.**
Bhattacharya, Diya. The college experience and the construction of cultural identity among first generation Indian American undergraduates. 1999.
*TC 06 no. 11083*

**Asian-American education :** prospects and challenges / edited by Clara C. Park and Marilyn Mei-Ying Chi. Westport, Conn. : Bergin & Garvey, 1999. viii, 313 p. ; 24 cm. Includes bibliographical references and index. ISBN 0-89789-602-5 (alk. paper) ISBN 0-89789-603-3 (pbk. : alk. paper) DDC 371.82995/073
*1. Asian Americans - Education. 2. Language arts - United States. 3. Sociolinguistics - United States. I. Park, Clara C., 1944- II. Chi, Marilyn Mei-Ying, 1949-*
*TC LC2632 .A847 1999*

**ASIAN AMERICAN FAMILIES - COUNSELING OF.**
Counseling Asian families from a systems perspective. Alexandria, Va. : American Counseling Ass., c1999.

**ASIAN AMERICAN FAMILIES - MENTAL HEALTH.**
Counseling Asian families from a systems perspective. Alexandria, Va. : American Counseling Ass., c1999.
*TC RC451.5.A75 C68 1999*

**ASIAN AMERICAN FAMILIES - SOCIAL LIFE AND CUSTOMS.**
Bhattacharya, Diya. The college experience and the construction of cultural identity among first generation Indian American undergraduates. 1999.
*TC 06 no. 11083*

ASIAN AMERICAN STUDENTS. *See* ASIAN AMERICAN COLLEGE STUDENTS.

**ASIAN AMERICANS - COUNSELING OF.**
Asian and Pacific Islander Americans :. Commack, N.Y. : Nova Science Publishers, 1999.
*TC RC451.5.A75 A83 1999*

**ASIAN AMERICANS - EDUCATION.**
Asian-American education. Westport, Conn. : Bergin & Garvey, 1999.
*TC LC2632 .A847 1999*

**ASIAN AMERICANS - EDUCATION (HIGHER) - UNITED STATES.**
Capeheart-Meningall, Jennifer. Quality of students of color efort on a predominantly white college and the internal environmental elements that influence involvement. 1998.
*TC 06 no. 10874*

ASIAN AMERICANS - FAMILIES. *See* ASIAN AMERICAN FAMILIES.

**ASIAN AMERICANS IN LITERATURE - BIBLIOGRAPHY.**
Peck, David R. American ethnic literatures. Pasadena, Calif. : Salem Press, c1992.
*TC Z1229.E87 P43 1992*

**ASIAN AMERICANS - PSYCHOLOGY.**
Asian and Pacific Islander Americans :. Commack, N.Y. : Nova Science Publishers, 1999.
*TC RC451.5.A75 A83 1999*

ASIAN AMERICANS - UNITED STATES. *See* ASIAN AMERICANS.

ASIAN AND PACIFIC COUNCIL COUNTRIES. *See* ASIA.

**Asian and Pacific Islander Americans : :** issues and concerns for counseling and psychotherapy / Daya Singh Sandhu, editor. Commack, N.Y. : Nova Science Publishers, 1999. xix, 335 p. ; 26 cm. Includes bibliographical references and index. CONTENTS: Introduction to mental health issues and concerns of Asian and Pacific Islander Americans: an ecocultural analysis / Daya Singh Sandhu -- Acculturative experiences of Asian and Pacific Islander Americans: considerations for counseling and psychotherapy / Daya Singh Sandhu, Kulwinder Pal Kaur and Nita Tewari -- Multicultural counseling: an Asian American perspective / Sun-Hwan Chu -- Cultural value conflict: an examination of Asian Indian women's bicultural experience / Arpana D. Inman, Madonna G. Constantine and Nicholas Ladany -- Acculturative stress among Asians: assessment and treatment issues / Joseph A. Lippincott -- The sociocultural context of Asian Pacific American ethnic identity and self: implications for counseling / Christine J. Yeh and Mary Y. Hwang -- Political ethnic identity versus cultural ethnic identity: an understanding of research on Asian Americans / Phoebe Y. Kuo and Gargi Roysircar-Sodowsky -- A racial identity framework for understanding psychological problems and guiding treatment among Asian and Pacific Islander Americans / Karen S. Kurasaki -- Asian Americans in college: a racial identity perspective / Alvin N. Alvarez and T. Ling Yeh -- The magnitude of acculturation and its impact on Asian Americans' career development / Mei Tang and Nadya A. Fouad -- Cultural differences in self-esteem: ethnic variations in the adaptation of recent immigrant Asian adolescents / Pedro R. Portes, Madelon F. CONTENTS: Ziady and B. Phalachandra -- Counseling Asian and Pacific Islander Americans in the college/university environment / Michael J. Cuyjet and William M. Liu -- Counseling Thai Americans / Reese M. House and Methinin Pinyuchon -- A comprehensive examination of the Vietnamese refugee: culture, resettlement, assessment and treatment / Tracy Luise Leva and Kevin Wickes -- Using Confucian role approach, mean management approach in Yin-Yang theory to understand and help South-East Asian refugee families in cultural transition / Lina Y.S. Fong and Douglas K. Chung -- Asian/Pacific American "women's issues": the intersection of culture, social support, personal violence, career, and mental health / Kathleen M. Kirby and Daya Pant -- Assessment of Asian Americans in counseling: evolving issues & concerns / Kwong-Liem Karl Kwan -- Transracial children: adjustment issues and concerns /

Kevin L. Wickes and John R. Slate -- Counseling Asian Americans and Pacific Islanders with substance abuse issues / Albert L. Watson, Aiko Oda and Jennifer Williams -- From Bakla to Tongzhi: counseling and psychotherapy with gay and lesbian Asian and Pacific Islander Americans / Mark Pope and Y. Barry Chung -- Sexual abuse in Asian and Pacific-Islander populations: current research and counseling implications / Adriana G. McEachern and Maureen C. Kenny. ISBN 1-56072-663-6
*1. Asian Americans - Counseling of. 2. Pacific Islander Americans - Counseling of. 3. Asian Americans - Psychology. 4. Pacific Islander Americans - Psychology. 5. Cross-cultural counseling. I. Sandhu, Daya Singh. 1943-*
*TC RC451.5.A75 A83 1999*

ASIANS - UNITED STATES. *See* ASIAN AMERICANS.

ASIATIC ART. *See* ART, ASIAN.

**Askew, Billie J.**
Stirring the waters. Portsmouth, NH : Heinemann, c1999.
*TC LB1139.5.L35 S85 1999*

**Askins, Peggy C. (Peggy Corley).**
Misrepresentation in the marketplace and beyond. Washington, DC : American Association of Collegiate Registrars and Admissions Officers, 1996.
*TC LB2331.615.U6 M57 1996*

ASL (SIGN LANGUAGE). *See* AMERICAN SIGN LANGUAGE.

**Asmar, Christine.**
Stevens, Kate. Doing postgraduate research in Australia. Melbourne : Melbourne University Press, 1999.
*TC LB2371.6.A7 S74 1999*

**Aspen Institute.**
The emerging world of wireless communications. Nashville, TN : Institute for Information Studies, 1996.
*TC TK5103.2 .E44 1996*

ASPHYXIA. *See* DROWNING.

ASPIRATIONS, OCCUPATIONAL. *See* VOCATIONAL INTERESTS.

ASPIRATIONS, STUDENT. *See* STUDENT ASPIRATIONS.

ASPIRATIONS, VOCATIONAL. *See* VOCATIONAL INTERESTS.

ASSAULT, CRIMINAL. *See* RAPE.

ASSEMBLY, RIGHT OF. *See* FREEDOM OF SPEECH; RIOTS.

ASSEMBLY, SCHOOL. *See* SCHOOLS - EXERCISES AND RECREATIONS.

**Assertion and its social context.**
Wilson, Keithia. 1st ed. Oxford ; New York : Pergamon Press, 1993.
*TC BF575.A85 W55 1993*

ASSERTION (PSYCHOLOGY). *See* ASSERTIVENESS (PSYCHOLOGY).

ASSERTIVE BEHAVIOR. *See* ASSERTIVENESS (PSYCHOLOGY).

**ASSERTIVENESS (PSYCHOLOGY).**
Wilson, Keithia. Assertion and its social context. 1st ed. Oxford ; New York : Pergamon Press, 1993.
*TC BF575.A85 W55 1993*

**Assessing academic achievement.**
Tanner, David Earl, 1948- Boston ; London : Allyn and Bacon, c2001.
*TC LB2822.75 .T36 2001*

**Assessing adolescents in educational, counseling, and other settings.**
Hoge, Robert D. Mahwah, N.J. : Lawrence Erlbaum Associates, 1999.
*TC BF724.25 .H64 1999*

**Assessing affective characteristics in the schools.**
Anderson, Lorin W. 2nd ed. Mahwah, NJ : Lawrence Erlbaum, c2000.
*TC LB3051 .A698 2000*

**Assessing children's mathematical knowledge.**
Cooper, Barry, 1950- Buckingham ; Philadelphia : Open University Press, 2000.
*TC QA135.5 .C5955 2000*

**Assessing literacy with the Learning Record.**
Barr, Mary A. (Mary Anderson) Portsmouth, NH : Heinemann, c1999.
*TC LB1029.P67 B37 1999*

**Assessing literacy with the Learning Record :** a handbook for teachers, grades K-6 / Mary A. Barr ... [et al.] ; Anne McKittrick, editorial assistant ; [foreword by Myra Barrs]. Portsmouth, NH : Heinemann, c1999. xii, 100 p. : ill. ; 28 cm. Rev. ed. of: The Learning Record, c1998. Includes bibliographical references (p. 99-100). ISBN 0-325-00117-0 (alk. paper) DDC 372.126/4/09794
*1. Portfolios in education - California - Handbooks, manuals, etc. 2. Academic achievement - California - Evaluation - Handbooks, manuals, etc. 3. Education, Elementary - California - Evaluation - Handbooks, manuals, etc. 4. Literacy - California - Handbooks, manuals, etc. I. Barr, Mary A. (Mary Anderson) II. McKittrick, Anne. III. Barr, Mary A. (Mary Anderson). Learning Record.*
**TC LB1029.P67 B37 1999b**

**Assessing open and distance learners.**
Morgan, Chris. London : Kogan Page ; Sterling, VA : Stylus Pub., 1999.
**TC LC5800 .M67 1999**

**Assessing school improvement projects.**
Werner, Walter. Collaborative assessment of school-based projects. Vancouver : Pacific Educational Press, c1991.
**TC LB2822.8 .W47 1991**

**Assessing schools of hope.**
Heath, Douglas H. 1st ed. Bryn Mawr, PA : Conrow Pub. House, c1999.
**TC LB2822.75 .H42 1999**

**Assessing science understanding : :** a human constructivist view / edited by Joel J. Mintzes, James H. Wandersee, Joseph D. Novak. San Diego, Calif. London : Academic, 2000. xxii, 386 p. : ill. ; 24 cm. (Educational psychology series.) Includes bibliographical references and index. ISBN 0-12-498365-0
*1. Science - Study and teaching. 2. Educational tests and measurements. I. Mintzes, Joel J. II. Wandersee, James H. III. Novak, Joseph Donald. IV. Series: Educational psychology.*
**TC Q181 .A87 2000**

**Assessing students with special needs.**
Venn, John. 2nd ed. Upper Saddle River, N.J. : Merrill, c2000.
**TC LC4031 .V46 2000**

**Assessing the progress of New American Schools.**
Berends, Mark, 1962- Santa Monica, CA : RAND, 1999.
**TC LB2822.82 .B45 1999**

**Assessment as inquiry :** learning the hypothesis-test process / edited by Diane Stephens, Jennifer Story. Urbana, Ill. : National Council of Teachers of English, 1999. vi, 118 p. : ill. ; 26 cm. Includes bibliographical references. ISBN 0-8141-2785-1 (pbk. : alk. paper) DDC 371.27/2
*1. Educational tests and measurements. 2. Teacher-student relationships - Case studies. 3. Reading (Elementary) I. Stephens, Diane. II. Story, Jennifer.*
**TC LB3051 .A76665 1999**

**ASSESSMENT CENTERS (PERSONNEL MANAGEMENT PROCEDURE).** *See* **EXECUTIVES - TRAINING OF.**

**ASSESSMENT, CURRICULUM-BASED.** *See* **CURRICULUM-BASED ASSESSMENT.**

**Assessment in geriatric psychopharmacology** / edited by Thomas Crook, Steven Ferris, Raymond Bartus. New Canaan, Conn. : Mark Powley Associates, 1983. 348 p. : ill. ; 22 cm. Includes bibliographies and index. ISBN 0-943378-04-4 (pbk.)
*1. Aged - Mental health services. 2. Geriatric psychiatry. 3. Psychodiagnostics. 4. Psychological tests. 5. Psychopharmacology. 6. Mental disorders - In old age. 7. Psychiatric status rating scales. 8. Psychological tests. 9. Psychopharmacology - In old age. 10. Psychotropic drugs - Therapeutic use. I. Crook, Thomas. II. Ferris, Steven. III. Bartus, Raymond.*
**TC WT150 .A846 1983**

**Assessment in higher education.**
Heywood, John, 1930- London ; Philadelphia : Jessica Kingsley Publishers, 2000.
**TC LB2366 .H49 2000**

**Assessment in practice**
Shannon, Ann. Keeping score. Washington, D.C. : National Academy Press, 1999.
**TC QA135.5 .S45 1999x**

**Assessment in primary school science** / editor, Wynne Harlen. London : Commonwealth Secretariat, c1998. ii, 114 p. : ill. ; 30 cm. (Workshop modules for professional development.) "Unesco". Includes bibliographical references (p. 6-7). ISBN 0-85092-568-1 (pbk.)
*1. Science - Study and teaching (Elementary). 2. Science - Ability testing. I. Harlen, Wynne. II. Series.*

**TC LB1585 .A87 1998**

**Assessment in the classroom.**
Cunningham, George K. London : Falmer, 1998.
**TC LB3051 .C857 1998**

**ASSESSMENT OF BEHAVIOR.** *See* **BEHAVIORAL ASSESSMENT.**

**Assessment of exceptional students.**
Taylor, Ronald L., 1949- 5th ed. Boston : Allyn and Bacon, c2000.
**TC LC4031 .T36 2000**

**Assessment of family violence :** a clinical and legal sourcebook / edited by Robert T. Ammerman and Michel Hersen. 2nd ed. New York : John Wiley, c1999. xiv, 436 p. ; 26 cm. Includes bibliographical references and indexes. ISBN 0-471-24256-X (cloth : alk. paper) 616.85/822
*1. Family violence. 2. Family violence - Law and legislation - United States. 3. Domestic Violence - United States - legislation I. Ammerman, Robert T. II. Hersen, Michel.*
**TC RC569.5.F3 A87 1999**

**ASSESSMENT OF MEDICAL CARE NEEDS.** *See* **MEDICAL CARE - NEEDS ASSESSMENT.**

**ASSESSMENT OF PERSONALITY.** *See also* **PERSONALITY ASSESSMENT.**
Aiken, Lewis R., 1931- Personality assessment. 3rd rev. ed. Seattle ; Toronto : Hogrefe & Huber Publishers, 1999.
**TC BF698.4 .A54 1999**

**Assessment of writing :** politics, policies, practices / edited by Edward M. White, William D. Lutz, and Sandra Kamusikiri. New York : Modern Language Association of America, 1996. ix, 338 p. ; 24 cm. (Research and scholarship in composition, 1079-2554 ; 4) Includes bibliographical references (p. 305-331) and index. ISBN 0-87352-581-7 (cloth) ISBN 0-87352-582-5 (pbk.) DDC 808/.042/07
*1. English language - Rhetoric - Study and teaching. 2. English language - Ability testing. 3. Academic writing - Ability testing. 4. College prose - Evaluation. I. White, Edward M. (Edward Michael), 1933- II. Lutz, William. III. Kamusikiri, Sandra, 1949- IV. Series.*
**TC PE1404 .A88 1996**

**Assessment strategies for elementary physical education.**
Schiemer, Suzann, 1956- Champaign, IL ; Leeds, U.K. : Human Kinetics, c2000.
**TC GV436 .S27 2000**

**ASSIMILATION (SOCIOLOGY).** *See also* **EMIGRATION AND IMMIGRATION; ETHNIC RELATIONS; MARGINALITY, SOCIAL; MINORITIES.**
Chrispin, Marie C. Resilient adaptation of church-affiliated young Haitian immigrants. 1998.
**TC 06 no. 11015**

**ASSISTANT TEACHERS.** *See* **TEACHERS' ASSISTANTS.**

**ASSISTED INDEPENDENT RESIDENTIAL LIVING.** *See* **CONGREGATE HOUSING.**

**ASSISTED LIVING.** *See* **CONGREGATE HOUSING.**

**ASSISTED SUICIDE.** *See* **EUTHANASIA.**

**ASSISTED SUICIDE - LAW AND LEGISLATION - UNITED STATES - STUDY AND TEACHING (SECONDARY) - COLORADO - DENVER - PROBLEMS, EXERCISES, ETC.**
Public issues discussion [videorecording] : Diana Hess at Denver High School 1997. [Boulder, Colo.] : Social Science Education Consortium, c1997.
**TC H62.3 .P4 1997**

Socratic seminar [videorecording]. [Boulder, Colo.] : Social Science Education Consortium, c1997.

**ASSISTED SUICIDE - UNITED STATES - MORAL AND ETHICAL ASPECTS.**
Lederer, Jane. Participation in active euthanasia and assisted suicide and attitudes and interpersonal values of physicians and nurses. 1996.
**TC 06 no. 10849**

**ASSOCIATION.** *See* **SOCIAL GROUPS.**

**Association des amis de l'Université de Liège.** Bulletin trimestriel. Liège. v. ill. 25 cm. -année 39, no. 3-4 (1967). Continued by: Revue universitaire de Liège.
*1. Université de Liège - Periodicals. I. Title. II. Title: Revue universitaire de Liège*

**ASSOCIATION FOOTBALL.** *See* **SOCCER.**

**Association for Childhood Education International.**
Educators healing racism. Reston, VA : Association of Teacher Educators ; Olney, MD : Association for Childhood Education International, c1999.
**TC LC212.2 .E38 1999**

**Association for Core Texts and Courses.**
Core texts in conversation . Lanham, MD : University Press of America, 2000.
**TC LB2361.5 .C68 2000**

**Association for Educational Communications and Technology.**
Audiovisual instruction. Washington, D.C : Dept. of Audiovisual Instruction, NEA, 1956-1978.

Learning resources. [Washington, Association for Educational Communications and Technology]

**Association for Educational Data Systems.**
AEDS journal. Washington, Association for Educational Data Systems.

**Association for Humanistic Education and Development.**
The Humanist educator. [Washington, American Personnel and Guidance Association]

**Association for the Education of Teachers in Science.**
Examining pedagogical content knowledge. Dordrecht : London : Kluwer Academic, c1999.
**TC Q181 .E93 1999**

**Association for the Reform of Latin Teaching.**
Latin teaching. [Shrewsbury, Eng.? : Association for the Reform of Latin Teaching], -1986.

**Association for the Study of Higher Education.**
Aguirre, Adalberto. Women and minority faculty in the academic workplace. San Francisco, Calif. : Jossey-Bass c2000.
**TC LB2332.3 .A35 2000**

ASHE reader on finance in higher education. Needham Heights, MA : Ginn Press, c1986.
**TC LB2342 .A76 1990**

Freed, Jann E. A culture for academic excellence. Washington, D.C. : Graduate School of Education and Human Development, George Washington University, 1997.
**TC LB2341 .F688 1997**

[Review of higher education (Online)] The review of higher education [computer file]. Baltimore, Md. : Johns Hopkins University Press, c1996-
**TC EJOURNALS**

Stevens, Ed. Due process and higher education. Washington, DC : Graduate School of Education and Human Development, George Washington University, [1999]
**TC LB2344 .S73 1999**

Van Dusen, Gerald C. Digital dilemma. San Francisco : Jossey-Bass, c2000.
**TC LC5805 .V35 2000**

**Association for the Study of Higher Education (ASHE).**
Alstete, Jeffrey W. Posttenure faculty development. San Fransisco, [Calif.] : Jossey-Bass c2000.
**TC LB2335.7 .A47 2000**

**Association for Theatre in Higher Education (U.S.).**
[Theatre journal (Online)] Theatre journal [computer file]. Baltimore, Md. : Johns Hopkins University Press, c1996-
**TC EJOURNALS**

**Association of College and Research Libraries.**
ChoiceReviews.online [computer file]. Middletown, Conn. : Association of College and Reference Libraries,

**Association of College Unions-International.**
Student development in college unions and student activities. Bloomington, Ind. : Association of College Unions-International, c1996.
**TC LB2343.4 .S84 1996**

**Association of Consulting Psychologists.**
Journal of consulting psychology. [Lancaster, Pa., etc.] American Psychological Association.

**Association of Geography Teachers of India.**
The geography teacher, India. Madras : The Society for the Promotion of Education in India, 1965-

**Association of London Government.**
Richardson, Robin. Inclusive schools, inclusive society. Stoke on Trent, Staffordshire, England : Trentham Books, 1999.
**TC LC212.3.G7 R523 1999**

**Association of Medical Officers of American Institutions for Idiotic and Feeble-Minded Persons.**
Journal of psycho-asthenics. Faribault, Minn. : Association of American Institutions for Feeble-Minded, [1896-1918]

**Association of Principals of Technical Institutions (India).** Journal of Association of Principals of Technical Institutions. Delhi, The Association. v. ill. I. Title.

**Association of Rehabilitation Nurses.** ARN journal. [Glenview, Ill.] Association of Rehabilitation Nurses. 5 v. ill. 28 cm. v. 1-5; Nov./Dec. 1975-Nov./Dec. 1980. Indexed in its entirety by: Cumulative index to nursing & allied health literature 0146-5554. "Official journal of the Association of Rehabilitation Nurses." Continued by: Rehabilitation nursing ISSN: 0278-4807 (OCoLC)7154385. ISSN 0362-3505 DDC 610.73/6
*1. Rehabilitation nursing - Periodicals. 2. Nursing - periodicals 3. Rehabilitation - periodicals I. Association of Rehabilitation Nurses. Journal. II. Title. III. Title: Rehabilitation nursing*

**Journal.**
Association of Rehabilitation Nurses. ARN journal. [Glenview, Ill.] Association of Rehabilitation Nurses.

**ASSOCIATION OF RESEARCH LIBRARIES.**
Marketing and public relations activities in ARL Libraries. Washington, DC : Association of Research Libraries, Office of Leadership and Management Services, c1999.
*TC Z176.3 .M2875 1999*

**Association of Research Libraries. Office of Leadership and Management Services.**
DeCandido, GraceAnne A. Transforming libraries. Washington, D.C. : Association of Research Libraries, Office of Leadership and Management Services, c1999.
*TC Z711.92.H3 D43 1999*

Library storage facilities, management, and services. Washington, DC : Association of Research Libraries, Office of Leadership and Management Services, 1999.
*TC Z675.S75 L697 1999*

Managing the licensing of electronic products. Washington, DC : Systems and Procedures Exchange Center, Office of Leadership and Management Service, Association of Research Libraries, c1999.

Managing the licensing of electronic products. Washington, DC : Systems and Procedures Exchange Center, Office of Leadership and Management Service, Association of Research Libraries, c1999.

Managing the licensing of electronic products. Washington, DC : Systems and Procedures Exchange Center, Office of Leadership and Management Service, Association of Research Libraries, c1999.
*TC HF5429.255 .M26 1999*

Marketing and public relations activities in ARL Libraries. Washington, DC : Association of Research Libraries, Office of Leadership and Management Services, c1999.
*TC Z176.3 .M2875 1999*

**Association of Research Libraries. Systems and Procedures Exchange Center.**
Marketing and public relations activities in ARL Libraries. Washington, DC : Association of Research Libraries, Office of Leadership and Management Services, c1999.
*TC Z176.3 .M2875 1999*

**Association of Teacher Educators.**
Educators healing racism. Reston, VA : Association of Teacher Educators ; Olney, MD : Association for Childhood Education International, c1999.
*TC LC212.2 .E38 1999*

Research on professional development schools. Thousand Oaks, Calif. : Corwin Press, c1999.
*TC LB2154.A3 R478 1999*

**The Association outlook.** [Springfield, Mass. : International Young Men's Christian Association Training School,    -1900.] v ; 22 cm. -v. 9, no. 9 (July 1900). Caption title: Association outlook and Training School notes. Running title: Training School notes. Description based on: Vol. 7, no. 1 (Oct. 1897); title from cover. Continued by: Association seminar (DLC)sn 88027914 (OCoLC)8532096.
*I. International Young Men's Christian Association Training School (Springfield, Mass.) II. Title: Association seminar*

**Association seminar.**
The Association outlook. [Springfield, Mass. : International Young Men's Christian Association Training School,    -1900.]

**ASSOCIATIONS, CONTEXTUAL (PSYCHOLOGY).** *See* **CONTEXT EFFECTS (PSYCHOLOGY).**

**ASSOCIATIONS, INSTITUTIONS, ETC.** *See* **CHARITIES; COMMUNITY LIFE; NONPROFIT ORGANIZATIONS; SOCIAL GROUP WORK; SOCIETIES; VOLUNTARISM.**

**ASSOCIATIONS, INSTITUTIONS, ETC. - PERIODICALS.**
International transnational associations. [Bruxelles, Union of International Associations]

**ASSOCIATIONS, INSTITUTIONS, ETC. - UNITED STATES.**
Meeting human needs, toward a new public philosophy. Washington : American Enterprise Institute for Public Policy Research, c1982.
*TC HD60.5.U5 M427 1982*

**ASSOCIATIONS, INTERNATIONAL.** *See* **INTERNATIONAL AGENCIES.**

**Associations transnationales <1977, 1984>.**
International transnational associations. [Bruxelles, Union of International Associations]

**Associations transnationales internationales.**
International transnational associations. [Bruxelles, Union of International Associations]

**Astington, Janet W.**
Minds in the making. Oxford ; Malden, Mass. : Blackwell, 2000.
*TC BF723.C5 M56 2000*

**ASTORIA (NEW YORK, N.Y.) - SOCIAL CONDITIONS.**
Darwiche, Chirine Hijazi. The Beacons. 1997.
*TC 06 no. 10761*

**Astrolabica**
(no. 6) Learning, language, and invention. Aldershot, Hampshire, Great Britain : Variorum ; Brookfield, Vt., USA : Ashgate Pub. Co. ; Paris, France : Société internationale de l'Astrolabe, 1994.
*TC AC5 .L38 1994*

**ASTRONAUTICS.** *See* **INTERPLANETARY VOYAGES; UNIDENTIFIED FLYING OBJECTS.**

**ASTRONAUTICS - OPTICAL COMMUNICATION SYSTEMS.** *See* **TELEVISION.**

**ASTRONOMICAL GEOGRAPHY.** *See* **SEASONS.**

**ASTRONOMY.** *See* **COSMOLOGY; SEASONS; SKY.**

**ASTRONOMY - HISTORY.**
Between demonstration and imagination. Leiden, Netherlands ; Boston : Brill, 1999.
*TC QB15 .B56 1999*

**ASTRONOMY - MATHEMATICS.**
Stephen Hawking's universe [videorecording]. [Alexandria, Va.] : PBS Video; Burbank, CA : Distributed by Warner Home Video, c1997.
*TC QB982 .S7 1997*

**ASTROPHYSICS.** *See also* **NAKED SINGULARITIES (COSMOLOGY).**
Stephen Hawking's universe [videorecording]. [Alexandria, Va.] : PBS Video; Burbank, CA : Distributed by Warner Home Video, c1997.
*TC QB982 .S7 1997*

Tales from other worlds [videorecording]. [New York, N.Y.?] : Unapix Entertainment, Inc. [distributor], c1996.
*TC QB631.2 .T3 1996*

Tales from other worlds [videorecording]. [New York, N.Y.?] : Unapix Entertainment, Inc. [distributor], c1996.
*TC QB631.2 .T3 1996*

**At issue (San Diego, Calif.)**
Affirmative action. San Diego, Calif. : Greenhaven Press, 2000.
*TC JC599.U5 A34685 2000*

Interracial relationships. San Diego : Greenhaven Press, c2000.
*TC HQ1031 .I59 2000*

**At war with the word.**
Young, R. V., 1947- Wilmington, Del. : ISI Books, 1999.
*TC PN94 .Y68 1999*

**ATHABASCAN INDIANS - EDUCATION - ALASKA.**
Brown, Stephen Gilbert. Words in the wilderness. Albany : State University of New York Press, c2000.
*TC E99.A86 B76 2000*

**Athanasiadou, Angeliki.**
Speaking of emotions. Berlin ; New York : Mouton de Gruyter, 1998.
*TC BF591. S64 1998*

**ATHAPASCAN INDIANS.** *See* **NAVAJO INDIANS.**

**ATHEISM - SOVIET UNION - HISTORY.**
Husband, William. "Godless communists". DeKalb : Northern Illinois University Press, 2000.
*TC BL2765.S65 H87 2000*

**ATHEMOO.**
Theatre in cyberspace. New York : P. Lang, c1999.
*TC PN2075 .T54 1999*

**ATHENA.** *See* **ATHENA (GREEK DEITY).**

**ATHENA (GREEK DEITY).**
Woff, Richard, 1953- Bright-eyed Athena. Los Angeles, CA : J. Paul Getty Museum, 1999.
*TC BL820.M6 W64 1999*

**ATHENA (GREEK DEITY) - JUVENILE LITERATURE.**
Woff, Richard, 1953- Bright-eyed Athena. Los Angeles, CA : J. Paul Getty Museum, 1999.
*TC BL820.M6 W64 1999*

**ATHENE (GREEK DEITY).** *See* **ATHENA (GREEK DEITY).**

**Athene series**
Curry, Barbara K. Women in power. New York ; London : Teachers College Press, c2000.
*TC LB2831.62 .C87 2000*

Nidiffer, Jana, 1957- Pioneering deans of women. New York ; London : Teachers College Press, c2000.
*TC LC1620 .N53 2000*

Rosser, Sue Vilhauer. Women, science, and society. New York : Teachers College Press, c2000.
*TC QH305.5 .R67 2000*

**Athens Center for Film and Video.**
[Wide angle (Online)] Wide angle [computer file]. Baltimore, Md. : John Hopkins University Press, c1996-
*TC EJOURNALS*

**ATHLETES.** *See* **COLLEGE ATHLETES; WOMEN ATHLETES.**

**ATHLETES - DRUG USE.** *See* **DOPING IN SPORTS.**

**ATHLETES - NUTRITION.**
Benardot, Dan, 1949- Nutrition for serious athletes. Champaign, IL ; Leeds, U.K. : Human Kinetics, c2000.
*TC TX361.A8 B45 2000*

Di Pasquale, Mauro G. Amino acids and proteins for the athlete. Boca Raton : CRC Press, c1997.
*TC QP551 .D46 1997*

Energy-yielding macronutrients and energy metabolism in sports nutrition. Boca Raton, Fla. ; London : CRC Press, c2000.
*TC QP176 .E546 2000*

Nutrition in sport. Osney Mead, Oxford ; Malden, MA : Blackwell Science, 2000.
*TC QP141 .N793 2000*

**ATHLETES, WOMEN.** *See* **WOMEN ATHLETES.**

**ATHLETIC INJURIES.**
Sports injuries sourcebook ; 1st ed. Detroit, MI : Omnigraphics, c1999.
*TC RD97 .S736 1999*

**ATHLETIC MEDICINE.** *See* **SPORTS MEDICINE.**

**ATHLETIC TRAINING.** *See* **PHYSICAL EDUCATION AND TRAINING.**

**ATHLETICS.** *See* **COLLEGE SPORTS; PHYSICAL EDUCATION AND TRAINING; SPORTS; SWIMMING.**

**ATHLETICS - MEDICAL ASPECTS.** *See* **SPORTS MEDICINE.**

**ATHYMIA.** *See* **DEMENTIA.**

**Atkinson, Terry, 1948-.**
The intuitive practitioner. Buckingham [England] ; Philadelphia : Open University Press, 2000.
*TC LB1025.3 .I59 2000*

**ATLANTA (GA.) - BIOGRAPHY - JUVENILE LITERATURE.**
Berry, Carrie, b. 1854. A Confederate girl. Mankato, Minn. : Blue Earth Books, c2000.

*TC E605 .B5 2000*

**ATLANTA (GA.) - HISTORY - CIVIL WAR, 1861-1865 - PERSONAL NARRATIVES - JUVENILE LITERATURE.**
Berry, Carrie, b. 1854. A Confederate girl. Mankato, Minn. : Blue Earth Books, c2000.
*TC E605 .B5 2000*

**ATLANTA (GA.) - SOCIAL LIFE AND CUSTOMS - 19TH CENTURY - JUVENILE LITERATURE.**
Berry, Carrie, b. 1854. A Confederate girl. Mankato, Minn. : Blue Earth Books, c2000.
*TC E605 .B5 2000*

**ATLANTIC OCEAN - AERIAL CROSSINGS.** *See* **TRANSATLANTIC FLIGHTS.**

**Atlantic Provinces Special Education Authority (Canada).**
MacCuspie, P. Ann (Patricia Ann), 1950- Promoting acceptance of children with disabilities. Halifax, N.S. : Atlantic Provinces Special Education Authority, c1996.
*TC LC4301 .M33 1996*

**Atlas of African American history.**
Earle, Jonathan. The Routledge atlas of African American history. New York : Routledge, 2000.
*TC E185 .E125 2000*

**Atlas of clinical endocrinology**
(5) Human nutrition and obesity. Philadelphia : Current Medicine, 1999.
*TC RC620.5 .H846 1999*

**ATMOSPHERE.** *See* **AIR; SKY.**

**ATMOSPHERE - POLLUTION.** *See* **AIR - POLLUTION.**

**ATMOSPHERIC DEPOSITION.** *See* **AIR - POLLUTION.**

**ATMOSPHERIC DIFFUSION - MATHEMATICAL MODELS - CONGRESSES.**
Air pollution modeling and its application XII. New York : Plenum Press, c1998.
*TC TD881 .A47523 1998*

**ATMOSPHERIC PHYSICS.** *See* **ATMOSPHERIC DIFFUSION; AURORAS.**

**ATOMIC WEAPONS.** *See* **NUCLEAR WEAPONS.**

**ATOMS.** *See* **MATTER.**

**ATTACHMENT BEHAVIOR.**
Brink, Andrew. The creative matrix. New York : Peter Lang, c2000.
*TC BF698.9.C74 B75 2000*

Colin, Virginia L. Human attachment. Philadelphia : Temple University Press, c1996.
*TC BF575.A86 C65 1996*

Grice, Marthe Jane. Attachment, race, and gender in late life. 1999.
*TC 085 G865*

Nemeroff, Robin. Stress, social support, and psychological distress in late life. 1999.
*TC 085 N341*

The organization of attachment relationships. New York : Cambridge University Press, 2000.
*TC BF575.A86.O74 2000*

Woodruff, Debra, 1967- General family functioning, parental bonding, and attachment style. 1998.
*TC 085 W858*

**ATTACHMENT BEHAVIOR IN CHILDREN.**
Attachment disorganization. New York ; London : Guilford Press, c1999.
*TC RJ507.A77 A87 1999*

Colin, Virginia L. Human attachment. Philadelphia : Temple University Press, c1996.
*TC BF575.A86 C65 1996*

Levy, Terry M. Handbook of attachment interventions. San Diego, Calif. : Academic, c2000.
*TC RJ507.A77 L47 2000*

The organization of attachment relationships. New York : Cambridge University Press, 2000.
*TC BF575.A86.O74 2000*

**ATTACHMENT DISORDER IN CHILDREN.**
Attachment disorganization. New York ; London : Guilford Press, c1999.
*TC RJ507.A77 A87 1999*

**Attachment disorganization** / editors, Judith Solomon, Carol George. New York ; London : Guilford Press, c1999. xxiii, 420 p. : ill. ; 23 cm. Includes bibliographical references and index. ISBN 1-57230-480-4 DDC 618.92/89

1. Attachment disorder in children. 2. Separation anxiety in children. 3. Attachment behavior in children. 4. Child psychopathology. I. Solomon, Judith. II. George, Carol.
*TC RJ507.A77 A87 1999*

**Attachment, race, and gender in late life.**
Grice, Marthe Jane. 1999.
*TC 085 G865*

**Attainment Company.**
Break throughs [videorecording]. Boston, MA : Fanlight Productions, c1998.
*TC LC4717.5 .B7 1998*

**Attainment's breakthroughs : how to reach students with autism [videorecording].**
Break throughs [videorecording]. Boston, MA : Fanlight Productions, c1998.
*TC LC4717.5 .B7 1998*

**ATTENDANCE, COLLEGE.** *See* **COLLEGE ATTENDANCE.**

**ATTENDANCE, SCHOOL.** *See* **SCHOOL ATTENDANCE.**

**ATTENTION.** *See also* **LISTENING.**
Broadbent, Donald E. (Donald Eric) Perception and communication. New York, Pergamon Press, 1958.
*TC BF38 .B685*

Milner, Peter M. The autonomous brain. Mahwah, N.J. : L. Erlbaum Associates, 1999.
*TC BF161 .M5 1999*

**Attention and performance 11.**
International Symposium on Attention and Performance (11th : 1984 : Eugene, Or.) Attention and performance XI. Hillsdale, N.J. : L. Erlbaum Associates, 1985.
*TC BF321 .A82 1985*

**Attention and performance eleven.**
International Symposium on Attention and Performance (11th : 1984 : Eugene, Or.) Attention and performance XI. Hillsdale, N.J. : L. Erlbaum Associates, 1985.
*TC BF321 .A82 1985*

**ATTENTION - CONGRESSES.**
Attention, space, and action. Oxford ; New York : Oxford University Press, 1999.
*TC QP405 .A865 1999*

**ATTENTION - CONGRESSES.**
Attention, space, and action. Oxford ; New York : Oxford University Press, 1999.
*TC QP405 .A865 1999*

**ATTENTION - CONGRESSES.**
International Symposium on Attention and Performance (11th : 1984 : Eugene, Or.) Attention and performance XI. Hillsdale, N.J. : L. Erlbaum Associates, 1985.
*TC BF321 .A82 1985*

**ATTENTION-DEFICIT DISORDER IN ADOLESCENCE.**
Bustamante, Eduardo M. Treating the disruptive adolescent. Northvale, NJ : Jason Aronson, c2000.
*TC RJ506.O66 B87 2000*

Everett, Craig A. Family therapy for ADHD. New York : Guilford Press, 1999.
*TC RJ506.H9 E94 1999*

**ATTENTION-DEFICIT DISORDER IN ADULTS.**
Everett, Craig A. Family therapy for ADHD. New York : Guilford Press, 1999.
*TC RJ506.H9 E94 1999*

**ATTENTION-DEFICIT DISORDER IN ADULTS - PATIENTS.** *See* **ATTENTION-DEFICIT-DISORDERED ADULTS.**

**ATTENTION DEFICIT DISORDER WITH HYPERACTIVITY.** *See* **ATTENTION-DEFICIT HYPERACTIVITY DISORDER.**

**ATTENTION DEFICIT DISORDER WITH HYPERACTIVITY - DIAGNOSIS.**
Pliszka, Steven R. ADHD with comorbid disorders. New York : Guilford Press, c1999.
*TC RJ506.H9 P55 1999*

**ATTENTION DEFICIT DISORDER WITH HYPERACTIVITY - THERAPY.**
Pliszka, Steven R. ADHD with comorbid disorders. New York : Guilford Press, c1999.
*TC RJ506.H9 P55 1999*

**ATTENTION-DEFICIT-DISORDERED ADULTS.**
ADHD [videorecording]. New York, NY : Guilford Publications, Inc., c1992.
*TC RJ506.H9 A3 1992*

**ATTENTION-DEFICIT DISORDERED ADULTS - FAMILY RELATIONSHIPS.**
Everett, Craig A. Family therapy for ADHD. New York : Guilford Press, 1999.
*TC RJ506.H9 E94 1999*

**ATTENTION-DEFICIT-DISORDERED ADULTS - VOCATIONAL GUIDANCE.**
Janus, Raizi Abby. Mapping careers with LD and ADD clients. New York : Columbia University Press, c1999.
*TC HV1568.5 .J36 1999*

Janus, Raizi Abby. Mapping careers with LD and ADD clients. New York : Columbia University Press, c1999.
*TC HV1568.5 .J36 1999*

**ATTENTION-DEFICIT-DISORDERED CHILDREN.** *See also* **HYPERACTIVE CHILDREN.**
ADHD [videorecording]. New York, NY : Guilford Publications, Inc., c1992.
*TC RJ506.H9 A3 1992*

Understanding the defiant child [videorecording]. New York : Guilford Publications, c1997.
*TC HQ755.7 .U63 1997*

**ATTENTION-DEFICIT-DISORDERED CHILDREN - EDUCATION - UNITED STATES.**
Attention-Deficit/Hyperactivity disorder in the classroom. Austin, Tex. : Pro-Ed, c1998.
*TC LC4713.4 .A89 1998*

**ATTENTION-DEFICIT DISORDERED CHILDREN - FAMILY RELATIONSHIPS.**
Everett, Craig A. Family therapy for ADHD. New York : Guilford Press, 1999.
*TC RJ506.H9 E94 1999*

**ATTENTION-DEFICIT DISORDERED YOUTH.**
ADHD [videorecording]. New York, NY : Guilford Publications, Inc., c1992.
*TC RJ506.H9 A3 1992*

**ATTENTION-DEFICIT DISORDERED YOUTH - FAMILY RELATIONSHIPS.**
Everett, Craig A. Family therapy for ADHD. New York : Guilford Press, 1999.
*TC RJ506.H9 E94 1999*

**ATTENTION DEFICIT DISORDERS.** *See* **ATTENTION-DEFICIT HYPERACTIVITY DISORDER.**

**ATTENTION DEFICIT DISORDERS WITH HYPERACTIVITY - IN ADOLESCENCE.**
Everett, Craig A. Family therapy for ADHD. New York : Guilford Press, 1999.
*TC RJ506.H9 E94 1999*

**ATTENTION DEFICIT DISORDERS WITH HYPERACTIVITY - IN ADULTHOOD.**
Everett, Craig A. Family therapy for ADHD. New York : Guilford Press, 1999.
*TC RJ506.H9 E94 1999*

**ATTENTION-DEFICIT HYPERACTIVITY DISORDER.**
ADHD :. London : Whurr, c1999.
*TC RJ506.H9 A32 1999*

ADHD [videorecording]. New York, NY : Guilford Publications, Inc., c1992.
*TC RJ506.H9 A3 1992*

Everett, Craig A. Family therapy for ADHD. New York : Guilford Press, 1999.
*TC RJ506.H9 E94 1999*

Lensch, Carol R., 1949- Making sense of attention deficit/hyperactivity disorder. Westport, Conn. ; London : Bergin & Garvey, 2000.
*TC RJ506.H9 L46 2000*

Parent articles about ADHD. San Antonio, Texas : Communication Skill Builders, c1999.
*TC RJ506.H9 P37 1999*

Pliszka, Steven R. ADHD with comorbid disorders. New York : Guilford Press, c1999.
*TC RJ506.H9 P55 1999*

**ATTENTION-DEFICIT HYPERACTIVITY DISORDER - ENVIRONMENTAL ASPECTS.**
Maté, Gabor. Scattered. 1st American ed. New York, N.Y., U.S.A. : Dutton, 1999.
*TC RJ506.H9 M42326 1999*

**Attention-Deficit/Hyperactivity disorder in the classroom : a practical guide for teachers** / Carol A. Dowdy ... [et al.]. Austin, Tex. : Pro-Ed, c1998. viii, 291 p. : ill. ; 23 cm. Includes bibliographical references (p. 267-279) and index. DDC 371.93

*1. Attention-deficit-disordered children - Education - United States. 2. Attention-deficit hyperactivity disorder - United States. I. Dowdy, Carol Ammons.*
**TC LC4713.4 .A89 1998**

**ATTENTION-DEFICIT HYPERACTIVITY DISORDER - PATIENTS.** *See* **ATTENTION-DEFICIT-DISORDERED CHILDREN; HYPERACTIVE CHILDREN.**

**ATTENTION-DEFICIT HYPERACTIVITY DISORDER - PSYCHOLOGICAL ASPECTS.**
Maté, Gabor. Scattered. 1st American ed. New York, N.Y., U.S.A. : Dutton, 1999.
**TC RJ506.H9 M42326 1999**

**ATTENTION-DEFICIT HYPERACTIVITY DISORDER - UNITED STATES.**
Attention-Deficit/Hyperactivity disorder in the classroom. Austin, Tex. : Pro-Ed, c1998.
**TC LC4713.4 .A89 1998**

**Attention deficit hyperactivity disorder [videorecording] : what do we know?.**
ADHD [videorecording]. New York, NY : Guilford Publications, Inc., c1992.
**TC RJ506.H9 A3 1992**

**Attention deficit hyperactivity disorder with comorbid disorders.**
Pliszka, Steven R. ADHD with comorbid disorders. New York : Guilford Press, c1999.
**TC RJ506.H9 P55 1999**

**ATTENTION, SELECTIVE.** *See* **SELECTIVITY (PSYCHOLOGY).**

**Attention, space, and action :** studies in cognitive neuroscience / edited by Glyn W. Humphreys, John Duncan, and Anne Treisman. Oxford ; New York : Oxford University Press, 1999. x, 334 p. : ill. (some col.) ; 25 cm. "Drawn from papers reported to two linked meetings, a discussion meeting of the Royal Society ... and a meeting at the Novartis Foundation ... held in November 1997"--Pref. Includes bibliographical references and index. ISBN 0-19-852469-2 (hb : alk. paper) ISBN 0-19-852468-4 (pbk. : alk. paper) DDC 612.8/4
*1. Attention - Congresses. 2. Cognitive neuroscience - Congresses. 3. Visual perception - Congresses. 4. Visual Perception - congresses. 5. Attention - congresses. 6. Cognition - congresses. I. Humphreys, Glyn W. II. Duncan, John, Dr. III. Treisman, Anne. IV. Royal Society (Great Britain) V. Novartis Foundation for Gerontological Research.*
**TC QP405 .A865 1999**

**Atteslander, Peter M., 1926-.**
Comparative anomie research. Aldershot, Hants, England : Brookfield, Vt., USA : Ashgate, c1999.
**TC HM816 .C65 1999**

Methoden der empirischen Sozialforschung / von Peter Atteslander. Unter Mitarbeit von Klaus Baumgartner [et al.]. Berlin : De Gruyter, 1969. 313 p. : ill. ; 16 cm. (Sammlung Göschen, Bd. 1229/1229a) Bibliography: p. [302]-309. DDC 300/.1/8
*1. Social sciences - Research. 2. Social sciences - Methodology. I. Title. II. Series.*
**TC H62 .A8**

**ATTITUDE CHANGE.**
Attitudes, behavior, and social context. Mahwah, N.J. : L. Erlbaum Associates, 2000.
**TC HM132 .B48 1998**

**ATTITUDE (PSYCHOLOGY).** *See also* **ETHNIC ATTITUDES; HEALTH ATTITUDES; PREJUDICES; PUBLIC OPINION; STEREOTYPE (PSYCHOLOGY).**
Bar-Tal, Daniel. Shared beliefs in a society. Thousand Oaks, Calif. : Sage Publications, c2000.
**TC HM1041 .B37 2000**

Readings in attitude theory and measurement. New York : Wiley, 1967.
**TC BF323.C5 F5**

**ATTITUDE (PSYCHOLOGY) - TESTING.**
Foye, Stephanie Diane. Using item response theory methods to explore the effect of item wording on Likert data. 1997.
**TC 085 F82**

**Attitude theory and measurement.**
Readings in attitude theory and measurement. New York : Wiley, 1967.
**TC BF323.C5 F5**

**ATTITUDE TO DEATH - IN INFANCY & CHILDHOOD.**
Judd, Dorothy. Give sorrow words. 2nd ed. New York : Haworth Press, 1995.
**TC RJ249 .J83 1995**

**Attitudes, behavior, and social context :** the role of norms and group membership / edited by Deborah J. Terry and Michael A. Hogg. Mahwah, N.J. : L. Erlbaum Associates, 2000. viii, 347 p. : ill. ; 23 cm. (Applied social research) Includes bibliographical references (p. 293-330) and index. ISBN 0-8058-2565-7 (c : alk. paper) ISBN 0-8058-2566-5 (p : alk. paper) DDC 158.2
*1. Interpersonal relations. 2. Social groups - Psychological aspects. 3. Attitude change. 4. Social influence. 5. Persuasion (Psychology) I. Hogg, Michael A., 1954- II. Terry, Deborah J. III. Series.*
**TC HM132 .B48 1998**

**ATTITUDES (PSYCHOLOGY).** *See* **ATTITUDE (PSYCHOLOGY).**

**Atton, Tessa.**
Poorly performing staff and how to manage them. London ; New York : Routledge, 1999.
**TC LB2832.4.G7 P66 1999**

**ATTRIBUTION (SOCIAL PSYCHOLOGY).**
Halperin, Jane Carol. The influence of causal attributions on the psychological adjustment of post-treatment adolescent cancer survivors. 1999.
**TC 085 H155**

**Attwell, Graham.**
Vocational and adult education in Europe. Dordrecht ; Boston : London : Kluwer Academic, c1999.
**TC LC1047.E8 V58 1999**

**ATYPICAL CHILDREN.** *See* **EXCEPTIONAL CHILDREN.**

**Au, Kathryn Hu-Pei.**
Cooper, J. David (James David), 1942- Discover : Grade 1, level 1.5, [Themes 9 and 10]. Boston : Houghton Mifflin, 1997.
**TC LB1575.8 .C6616 1997**

**Audi, Robert, 1941-.**
The Cambridge dictionary of philosophy. 2nd ed. Cambridge ; New York : Cambridge University Press, 1999.
**TC B41 .C35 1999**

**AUDIENCES.** *See* **ARTS AUDIENCES.**

**AUDIENCES, ARTS.** *See* **ARTS AUDIENCES.**

**AUDIENCES, TELEVISION.** *See* **TELEVISION VIEWERS.**

**AUDING.** *See* **LISTENING.**

**Audio-visual communications.**
Audio-visual communications. [New York : United Business Publications, 1967-c1989.

**Audio-visual communications.** [New York : United Business Publications, 1967-c1989. 23 v. : ill. ; 29 cm. Frequency: Monthly, <Feb. 1989>-June 1989. Former frequency: Quarterly, 1967. Former frequency: Bimonthly, 1968- . Former frequency: 12 no. a year, <Feb. 1977->. [Vol. 1, no. 2] (May 1967)-v. 23, no. 6 (June 1989). Audiovisual communications. Running title: AV communications <Feb. 1989>-June 1989. Title from cover. Title varies slightly. Vols. for <Feb. 1989>-June 1989 published: Woodbury, NY : PTN Pub. Co. Indexed in its entirety by: Business periodicals index 0007-6961. Indexed in its entirety by: Trade & industry index 1981-. Indexed selectively by: Reference sources 0163-3546. Also available on microfilm. Available in other form: Audio-visual communications (OCoLC)7942202. Continues: Film and audio-visual communication (OCoLC)8044374. Continued by: AVC presentation, technology & applications (DLC) 1045-6910 (DLC) 89650722 (OCoLC)20186873. ISSN 0004-7562 DDC 621.38/044/05
*1. Audio-visual equipment - Periodicals. I. Title: Audiovisual communications II. Title: AV communications <Feb. 1989>-June 1989 III. Title: Audio-visual communications IV. Title: Film and audio-visual communication V. Title: AVC presentation, technology & applications*

**AUDIO-VISUAL EDUCATION.** *See also* **MOTION PICTURES IN EDUCATION; TELEVISION IN EDUCATION.**

**Audio-visual education.** [Delhi, Manager of Publications] no. ill. (part col.) 28 cm. Published by National Institute of Audio-Visual Education. ISSN 0571-8740
*1. Audio-visual education - Periodicals. I. Delhi. National Institute of Audio Visual Education.*

**AUDIO-VISUAL EDUCATION - EQUIPMENT AND SUPPLIES.** *See* **AUDIO-VISUAL EQUIPMENT.**

**AUDIO-VISUAL EDUCATION - PERIODICALS.**
Audio-visual education. [Delhi, Manager of Publications]

Audiovisual instruction. Washington, D.C : Dept. of Audiovisual Instruction, NEA, 1956-1978.

Instructional materials. [Washington, D.C.] : Dept. of Audio Visual Instruction, NEA, 1956.

K-eight. [Philadelphia, American Pub. Co.]

**AUDIO-VISUAL EDUCATION - UNITED STATES.**
Adams, Dennis M. Media and literacy. 2nd ed. Springfield, Ill. : C.C. Thomas, c2000.
**TC LB1043 .A33 2000**

**AUDIO-VISUAL EQUIPMENT - PERIODICALS.**
Audio-visual communications. [New York : United Business Publications, 1967-c1989.

**Audio-Visual Language Association.**
Audio-visual language journal. London.

**Audio-visual language journal.** London. 17 v. : ill. ; 24 cm. 3 no. a year. v. 1-17 ; 1962/63-1979. "The Journal of applied linguistics and language teaching technology." "Organ of the Audio-Visual Language Assiociation." Continued by: British journal of language teaching. ISSN 0004-7589
*1. Language and languages - Study and teaching - Periodicals. 2. Language and languages - Audio-visual aids - Periodicals. I. Audio-Visual Language Association. II. Title: British journal of language teaching*

**AUDIO-VISUAL LIBRARY SERVICE.** *See* **INSTRUCTIONAL MATERIALS CENTERS.**

**AUDIO-VISUAL MATERIALS.** *See* **MOTION PICTURES; VIDEO RECORDINGS.**

**AUDIO-VISUAL MATERIALS CENTERS.** *See* **INSTRUCTIONAL MATERIALS CENTERS.**

**AUDIOBOOKS.** *See* **CHILDREN'S AUDIOBOOKS.**

**AUDIOCASSETTES FOR CHILDREN - CATALOGS - PERIODICALS.**
Bowker's directory of audiocassettes for children. New Providence, N.J. : R.R. Bowker, c1998-
**TC ZA4750 .B69**

**AUDIOCASSETTES FOR CHILDREN - UNITED STATES - CATALOGS - PERIODICALS.**
Bowker's directory of audiocassettes for children. New Providence, N.J. : R.R. Bowker, c1998-
**TC ZA4750 .B69**

**Audiologie internationale.**
International audiology. Leiden, Netherlands : International Society of Audiology, 1962-1970.

**AUDIOLOGY.** *See also* **DEAFNESS; HEARING.**
Counseling for hearing aid fittings. San Diego : Singular Pub. Group, c1999.
**TC RF300 .C68 1999**

Counseling for hearing aid fittings. San Diego : Singular Pub. Group, c1999.
**TC RF300 .C68 1999**

Rehabilitative audiology. 3rd ed. Philadelphia, PA : Lippincott Williams & Wilkins, c2000.
**TC RF297 .R44 2000**

Silverman, Franklin H., 1933- Professional issues in speech-language pathology and audiology. Boston : Allyn and Bacon, c1999.
**TC RC428.5 .S55 1999**

**Audiology 1971-1995.**
International audiology. Leiden, Netherlands : International Society of Audiology, 1962-1970.

**AUDIOLOGY - DICTIONARIES.**
Martin, Michael, OBE. Dictionary of hearing. London : Whurr, 1999.
**TC QP461 .M375 1999**

Martin, Michael, OBE. Dictionary of hearing. London : Whurr, 1999.
**TC QP461 .M375 1999**

Mendel, Lisa Lucks. Singular's pocket dictionary of audiology. San Diego : Singular Pub. Group, c1999.
**TC RF290 .M4642 1999**

**AUDIOLOGY - INSTRUMENTS.** *See* **HEARING AIDS.**

**AUDIOLOGY - PRACTICE.**
Silverman, Franklin H., 1933- Professional issues in speech-language pathology and audiology. Boston : Allyn and Bacon, c1999.
**TC RC428.5 .S55 1999**

**AUDIOMETRY.**
Musiek, Frank E. Contemporary perspectives in hearing assessment. Boston : Allyn and Bacon, 1999.
**TC RF294 .M87 1999**

Vonlanthen, A. (Andy), 1961- Hearing instrument technology for the hearing healthcare professional. 2nd ed. San Diego : Singular Pub. Group, c2000.

*Audiometry.*

TC RF300 .V66 2000

**Audiovisual communications.**
Audio-visual communications. [New York : United Business Publications, 1967-c1989.

**Audiovisual instruction.**
Instructional materials. [Washington, D.C.] : Dept. of Audio Visual Instruction, NEA, 1956.

Learning resources. [Washington, Association for Educational Communications and Technology]

Learning resources. [Washington, Association for Educational Communications and Technology]

**Audiovisual instruction.** Washington, D.C : Dept. of Audiovisual Instruction, NEA, 1956-1978. 23 v. : ill. ; 28 cm. Frequency: Monthly (except July-Aug.). Vol. 1, no. 1 (Oct. 1956)-v. 23, no. 5 (May 1978). Title from cover. Indexed selectively by: Bibliography of agriculture 0006-1530. Indexed by: Biography index 0006-3053. Indexed by: Current contents. Indexed by: Current index to journals in education 0011-3565. Indexed by: Education index 0013-1385. Indexed by: Exceptional child abstracts. Indexed by: INSPEC science abstracts. Indexed by: International index to multi-media information. Indexed by: Media review digest 0363-7778. June issues, 1958-1960, lack numbering. Issue for May 1978 incorrectly called v. 23, no. 7 on cover title page, other parts of piece are called v. 23, no. 5. Issued by: Association for Educational Communications and Technology, Sept. 1970-May 1978. Some numbers for 1973-1974 include supplement: Learning resources, published separately beginning Dec. 1974. Has supplement: Learning resources ISSN: 0190-1974 (DLC)sc 78001888 (OCoLC)1149703. Continues: Instructional materials (OCoLC)5112624 (DLC) 88648800. Continued by: Audiovisual instruction with/instructional resources ISSN: 0191-3417 (OCoLC)4232254 (DLC) 79642690. ISSN 0004-7635 DDC 371
*1. Audio-visual education - Periodicals. I. National Education Association of the United States. Dept. of Audiovisual Instruction. II. Association for Educational Communications and Technology. III. Title: Learning resources IV. Title: Instructional materials V. Title: Audiovisual instruction with/instructional resources*

**Audiovisual instruction with/instructional resources.**
Audiovisual instruction. Washington, D.C : Dept. of Audiovisual Instruction, NEA, 1956-1978.

**Audit cultures :** anthropological studies in accountability, ethics and the academy / edited by Marilyn Strathern. London ; New York : Routledge, 2000. x, 310 p. ; 23 cm. (European Association of Social Anthropologists) Includes bibliographical references and index. ISBN 0-415-23326-7 (hb) ISBN 0-415-23327-5 (pb) DDC 306.43
*1. Education, Higher - Evaluation - Social aspects. 2. Educational anthropology. 3. Educational accountability - Social aspects. 4. Education, Higher - Moral and ethical aspects. I. Strathern, Marilyn. II. Series: European Association of Social Anthropologists (Series)*
TC LB2324 .A87 2000

**AUDITION (PHYSIOLOGY).** See **HEARING.**

**AUDITORY HALLUCINATIONS.**
When self-consciousness breaks. Cambridge, Mass. : MIT Press, c2000.
TC RC553.A84 S74 2000

**AUDITORY PATHWAYS.** See **HEARING.**

**AUDITORY PATHWAYS - CONGRESSES.**
The efferent auditory system. San Diego : Singular Pub. Group, c1999.
TC RF286.5 .E36 1999

**AUDITORY PATHWAYS - PHYSIOLOGY - CONGRESSES.**
The efferent auditory system. San Diego : Singular Pub. Group, c1999.
TC RF286.5 .E36 1999

**AUDITORY PERCEPTION.**
Auditory worlds. Weinheim [Germany] : Wiley-VCH, c2000.
TC QP461 .A93 2000

Bond, Zinny S. (Zinny Sans), 1940- Slips of the ear. San Diego, Calif. ; London : Academic, c1999.
TC P37.5.S67 B66 1999

**AUDITORY SYSTEM.** See **AUDITORY PATHWAYS; EAR.**

**Auditory worlds :** sensory analysis and perception in animals and man : final report of the Collaborative Research Centre 204, "Nachrichtenaufnahme und-verarbeitung im Hörsystem von Vertebraten (Munich)", 1983-1997. Weinheim [Germany] : Wiley-VCH, c2000. xix, 359 p. ; 24 cm. Includes bibliographical references. ISBN 3-527-27587-8 DDC 152.1
*1. Auditory perception I. Manley, Geoffrey A.*

TC QP461 .A93 2000

**AUFKLÄRUNG.** See **ENLIGHTENMENT.**

**Augmentative and alternative communication :** new directions in research and practice / edited by Filip T. Loncke ... [et al.]. London : Whurr, 1999. xx, 346 p. : ill. ; 24 cm. Includes bibliographical references (p. 301-338) and index. ISBN 1-86156-143-1 DDC 616.85503
*1. Handicapped - Means of communication. 2. Communication devices for the disabled. 3. Language disorders. I. Loncke, Filip.*
TC RC429 .A94 1999

**Ault, Julie.**
Art matters. New York : New York University Press, c1999.
TC N72.S6 A752 1999

**Aunt Minnie McGranahan.**
Prigger, Mary Skillings. New York : Clarion Books, c1999.
TC PZ7.P93534 Au 1999

**AUNTS - FICTION.**
Couloumbis, Audrey. Getting near to baby. New York : Putnam, 1999.
TC PZ7.C8305 Gg 1999

Prigger, Mary Skillings. Aunt Minnie McGranahan. New York : Clarion Books, c1999.
TC PZ7.P93534 Au 1999

Wiggin, Kate Douglas Smith, 1856-1923. Rebecca of Sunnybrook Farm. Boston, New York [etc.] : Houghton, Mifflin Company, [c1903] (Cambridge, Mass. : Riverside Press)
TC PZ7.W638 Re 1903

**AURORA AUSTRALIS.** See **AURORAS.**

**AURORA BOREALIS.** See **AURORAS.**

**AURORAS - FICTION.**
Taylor, Harriet Peck. Ulaq and the northern lights. 1st ed. New York : Farrar Straus Girous, 1998.
TC PZ7.T2135 Ul 1998

**Austad, Ingolv.**
Dyslexia. Dordrecht ; Boston, Mass : Kluwer Academic, 1999.
TC RC394 .D9525 1999

**Austin, Ann E.** Academic workplace : new demands, heightened tensions / by Ann E. Austin and Zelda F. Gamson ; prepared by ERIC Clearinghouse on Higher Education, the George Washington University. Washington, D.C. : Association for the Study of Higher Education, 1983. 122 p. ; 23 cm. (ASHE-ERIC higher education research report, 0737-1292 ; no. 10 (1983)) Bibliography: p. 92-109. "Index issue, 1983 series." ISBN 0-913317-09-8 (pbk.) DDC 378/.12
*1. College teachers - Psychology. 2. Universities and colleges - Administration - Psychological aspects. I. Gamson, Zelda F. II. ERIC Clearinghouse on Higher Education. III. Title. IV. Series: ASHE-ERIC/higher education research report ; 1983, no. 10.*
TC LB2331.7 .A96 1983

**Austin, Barbara J.**
Capitalizing knowledge. Toronto : University of Toronto Press, c2000.
TC HF1131 .C36 2000

**Australia. Education Research and Development Committee.**
Literacy and numeracy in Australian schools. Canberra : Australian Gov. Pub. Service, 1976-
TC LA2102 .L57 1976

**AUSTRALIAN ABORIGINAL ART.** See **ART, AUSTRALIAN ABORIGINAL.**

**AUSTRALIAN ABORIGINAL PAINTING.** See **PAINTING, AUSTRALIAN ABORIGINAL.**

**AUSTRALIAN ABORIGINES.** See **TORRES STRAIT ISLANDERS.**

**AUSTRALIAN ABORIGINES - AUSTRALIA - ARNHEM LAND (N.T.) - ART - EXHIBITIONS.**
The painters of the Wagilag sisters story 1937-1997. Canberra, ACT : The National Gallery of Australia, 1997.
TC ND1101 .P395 1997

**AUSTRALIAN ABORIGINES - ETHNIC IDENTITY.**
Thomas, Nicholas. Possessions. New York, N.Y. : Thames and Hudson, c1999.
TC N5313 .T46 1999

**AUSTRALIAN ABORIGINES - STUDY AND TEACHING (PRIMARY).**
Teaching Aboriginal studies. St Leonards, N.S.W. : Allen & Unwin, 1999.
TC GN666 .T43 1999

**AUSTRALIAN ABORIGINES - STUDY AND TEACHING (SECONDARY).**
Teaching Aboriginal studies. St Leonards, N.S.W. : Allen & Unwin, 1999.
TC GN666 .T43 1999

**AUSTRALIAN ART.** See **ART, AUSTRALIAN.**

**Australian Council for Educational Research.**
Australian education. Camberwell, Vic. : Australian Council for Educational Research, 1998.
TC LA2102.7 .A87 1998

The child's world. Camberwell, Vic. : ACER Press, 2000.
TC BF723.C5 C467 2000

Literacy and numeracy in Australian schools. Canberra : Australian Gov. Pub. Service, 1976-
TC LA2102 .L57 1976

**AUSTRALIAN DRAWING.** See **DRAWING, AUSTRALIAN.**

**Australian drawings.**
Art Gallery of New South Wales. Australian drawings from the gallery's collection. Sydney : Art Gallery of New South Wales, 1997.
TC NC369 .A78 1997

**Australian drawings from the gallery's collection.**
Art Gallery of New South Wales. Sydney : Art Gallery of New South Wales, 1997.
TC NC369 .A78 1997

**Australian education :** review of research 1965 - 1998 / edited by John Keeves and Kevin Marjoribanks. Camberwell, Vic. : Australian Council for Educational Research, 1998. viii, 364 p. 25 cm. Includes bibliographical references and index. ISBN 0-86431-295-4
*1. Education - Australia. 2. Education - Research - Australia. I. Keeves, John P. II. Marjoribanks, Kevin. III. Australian Council for Educational Research.*
TC LA2102.7 .A87 1998

**Australian journal of language and literacy. Vol. 20, no. 2.**
The changing face of whole language. Newark, Del. : International Reading Association ; Victoria, Australia : Australian Literacy Educators' Association, c1997.
TC LB1050.35 .C43 1997

**Australian Literacy Educators' Association.**
The changing face of whole language. Newark, Del. : International Reading Association ; Victoria, Australia : Australian Literacy Educators' Association, c1997.
TC LB1050.35 .C43 1997

**Australian painting, 1788-1990.**
Smith, Bernard, 1916- 3rd ed. Melbourne ; New York : Oxford University Press, 1992.
TC ND1100 .S553 1992

**AUSTRALIAN PORTRAIT PAINTING.** See **PORTRAIT PAINTING, AUSTRALIAN.**

**AUSTRALIAN POSTERS.** See **POSTERS, AUSTRALIAN.**

**Australian printmaking in the 1990s.**
Grishin, Sasha. Sydney, NSW : Craftsman House : G+B Arts International, c1997.
TC NE789.4 .G74 1997

**AUSTRALIAN PRINTS.** See **PRINTS, AUSTRALIAN.**

**Australian prints from the gallery's collection.**
Art Gallery of New South Wales. Sydney : Art Gallery of New South Wales, c1998.
TC NE789 .A77 1998

**Australian studies in school performance**
(v. 1-) Literacy and numeracy in Australian schools. Canberra : Australian Gov. Pub. Service, 1976-
TC LA2102 .L57 1976

(v. 3) Bourke, S. F. The mastery of literacy and numeracy. Canberra : Australian Govt. Pub. Service, 1977.
TC LA2102 .B68 1977

**AUSTRALIAN WATERCOLOR PAINTING.** See **WATERCOLOR PAINTING, AUSTRALIAN.**

**Australian watercolours from the gallery's collection.**
Kolenberg, Hendrik. Sydney, [Australia] : Art Gallery of New South Wales, 1995.
TC ND2089 .K64 1995

**AUSTRALIAN WIT AND HUMOR, PICTORIAL.**
Mambo. Sidney : Mambo Graphics, c1994.
*TC NC1761.M36 A4 1994*

Australian wood engravings, woodcuts and linocuts.
National Gallery of Victoria. In relief. Melbourne :
National Gallery of Victoria, c1997.
*TC NE1190.25 .G72 1997*

**AUSTRALIANS (NATIVE PEOPLE).** *See*
**AUSTRALIAN ABORIGINES.**

Authentic assessment of the young child.
Puckett, Margaret B. 2nd ed. Upper Saddle River,
N.J. : Merrill, c2000.
*TC LB3051 .P69 2000*

Authoring a life.
Daly, Brenda O., 1941- Albany, NY : State University
of New York Press, c1998.
*TC RC560.I53 D35 1998*

**AUTHORITARIANISM - GREAT BRITAIN.**
Armitage, Peter B., 1939- Political relationship and
narrative knowledge. Westport, Conn. : Bergin &
Garvey, 2000.
*TC LC93.G7 A86 2000*

Authoritative guide to evaluating information on the Internet.
Cooke, Alison. Neal-Schuman authoritative guide to
evaluating information on the Internet. New York :
Neal-Schuman Publishers, c1999.
*TC ZA4201 .C66 1999*

**AUTHORITY.** *See also* **AUTHORITARIANISM;**
**CONSENSUS (SOCIAL SCIENCES);**
**EXAMPLE.**
Gordon, Mordechai. Toward an integrative conception
of authority in education. 1997.
*TC 085 G656*

Gordon, Mordechai. Toward an integrative conception
of authority in education. 1997.
*TC 085 G656*

Obedience to authority. Mahwah, N.J. ; London :
Lawrence Erlbaum Associates, 2000.
*TC HM1251 .O24 2000*

Seligman, A. Modernity's wager. Princeton, NJ :
Princeton University Press, 2000.
*TC HM1251 .S45 2000*

Authority in language.
Milroy, James. 3rd ed. London [England] ; New
York : Routledge, 1999.
*TC P368 .M54 1999*

**AUTHORITY IN LITERATURE.**
Keroes, Jo. Tales out of school. Carbondale : Southern
Illinois University Press, c1999.
*TC PS374.T43 K47 1999*

**AUTHORS.** *See* **LITERATURE.**

**AUTHORS, AFRO-AMERICAN.** *See* **AFRO-AMERICAN AUTHORS.**

**AUTHORS, AMERICAN.** *See also* **AFRO-AMERICAN AUTHORS.**
De Paola, Tomie. 26 Fairmount Avenue. New York :
G.P. Putnam's Sons, c1999.
*TC PS3554.E11474 Z473 1999*

**AUTHORS, AMERICAN - 20TH CENTURY -**
**BIOGRAPHY.**
Gard, Robert E. (Robert Edward), 1910- Prairie
visions. Ashland, Wis. : Heartland Press, c1987.
*TC PS3513.A612 P7 1987*

**AUTHORS, AMERICAN - 20TH CENTURY -**
**BIOGRAPHY - JUVENILE LITERATURE.**
De Paola, Tomie. 26 Fairmount Avenue. New York :
G.P. Putnam's Sons, c1999.
*TC PS3554.E11474 Z473 1999*

**AUTHORS, AMERICAN - BIOGRAPHY -**
**DICTIONARIES.**
McElmeel, Sharron L. 100 most popular children's
authors. Englewood, Colo. : Libraries Unlimited,
1999.
*TC PS490 .M39 1999*

**AUTHORS, AMERICAN - STUDY AND**
**TEACHING (ELEMENTARY).**
Walmsley, Bonnie Brown. Teaching with favorite
Marc Brown books. New York : Scholastic
Professional Books, c1998.
*TC LB1576 .W258 1998*

**AUTHORS AND PUBLISHERS.** *See* **COPYRIGHT.**

**AUTHORS AND READERS.**
Kaufer, David S. Designing interactive worlds with
words. Mahwah, N.J. : Lawrence Erlbaum Associates,
2000.

*TC PE1404 .K38 2000*

Transcending boundaries. New York : Garland, 1999.
*TC PN1009.A1 T69 1999*

**AUTHORS AND READERS - GREAT BRITAIN -**
**HISTORY - 18TH CENTURY.**
Pearson, Jacqueline, 1949- Women's reading in
Britain, 1750-1835. Cambridge, UK ; New York :
Cambridge University Press, 1999.
*TC PR756.W65 P43 1999*

**AUTHORS AND READERS - GREAT BRITAIN -**
**HISTORY - 19TH CENTURY.**
Pearson, Jacqueline, 1949- Women's reading in
Britain, 1750-1835. Cambridge, UK ; New York :
Cambridge University Press, 1999.
*TC PR756.W65 P43 1999*

**AUTHORS AND READERS - UNITED STATES.**
Buzzeo, Toni. Terrific connections with authors,
illustrators, and storytellers. Englewood, Colo. :
Libraries Unlimited, 1999.
*TC LB1575.5.U5 B87 1999*

**AUTHORS, BLACK - PERIODICALS.**
Black academy review. Buffalo, N.Y. : Black
Academy Press, c1970-

**AUTHORS, ENGLISH - 20TH CENTURY -**
**BIOGRAPHY.**
Talking books. London ; New York : Routledge,
1999.
*TC PR990 .T35 1999*

**AUTHORS, ENGLISH - BIOGRAPHY -**
**CAREERS.** *See* **AUTHORS, ENGLISH -**
**BIOGRAPHY.**

**AUTHORS, ENGLISH - BIOGRAPHY -**
**DICTIONARIES.**
McElmeel, Sharron L. 100 most popular children's
authors. Englewood, Colo. : Libraries Unlimited,
1999.
*TC PS490 .M39 1999*

**AUTHORS, ENGLISH - BIOGRAPHY - EXILE.**
*See* **AUTHORS, ENGLISH - BIOGRAPHY.**

**AUTHORS, ENGLISH - BIOGRAPHY - LAST**
**YEARS AND DEATH.** *See* **AUTHORS,**
**ENGLISH - BIOGRAPHY.**

**AUTHORS, ENGLISH - BIOGRAPHY -**
**MARRIAGE.** *See* **AUTHORS, ENGLISH -**
**BIOGRAPHY.**

**AUTHORS, ENGLISH - BIOGRAPHY - YOUTH.**
*See* **AUTHORS, ENGLISH - BIOGRAPHY.**

**AUTHORS - FICTION.**
Jones, Jennifer B. Dear Mrs. Ryan, you're ruining my
life. New York : Walker & Co., 2000.
*TC PZ7.J7203 De 2000*

**AUTHORSHIP.** *See also* **ACADEMIC WRITING;**
**AUTHORS AND READERS; BUSINESS**
**WRITING; CREATIVE WRITING;**
**HISTORIOGRAPHY; LITERATURE;**
**POETRY - AUTHORSHIP; PROPOSAL**
**WRITING FOR GRANTS; PROPOSAL**
**WRITING IN EDUCATION; REPORT**
**WRITING; RHETORIC; TECHNICAL**
**WRITING.**
Haines, Dawn Denham. Writing together. 1st ed. New
York : Berkley Pub. Group, 1997.
*TC PN145 .H28 1997*

Transcending boundaries. New York : Garland, 1999.
*TC PN1009.A1 T69 1999*

**AUTHORSHIP - HANDBOOKS, MANUALS, ETC.**
Written expression. Larchmont, NY : Eye on
Education, c1997.
*TC PN145 .W78 1997*

**AUTHORSHIP - SEX DIFFERENCES.**
Haake, Katharine. What our speech disrupts. Urbana,
Ill. : National Council of Teachers of English, c2000.
*TC PE1404 .H3 2000*

**AUTHORSHIP - STYLE MANUALS.**
Gibaldi, Joseph, 1942- The MLA style manual. New
York : Modern Language Association of America,
1985.
*TC PN147 .G53 1998*

**Autism.**
Peeters, Theo. 2nd ed. London : Whurr Publishers,
1999.
*TC RJ506.A9 P44 1999*

Autism--a world apart [videorecording]. Boston, MA :
Fanlight Productions, [1989, c1988].

*TC RJ506 .A98 1988*

Gender and the interpretation of emotion
[videorecording]. Princeton, NJ : Films for the
Humanities & Sciences, c1997.
*TC BF592.F33 G4 1997*

Peeters, Theo. Autism. 2nd ed. London : Whurr
Publishers, 1999.
*TC RJ506.A9 P44 1999*

Peeters, Theo. Autism. 2nd ed. London : Whurr
Publishers, 1999.
*TC RJ506.A9 P44 1999*

**Autism--a world apart** [videorecording] / written and
produced by Karen Cunninghame ; director, Don [i.e.
Dan] Kalmanson. Boston, MA : Fanlight Productions,
[1989, c1988]. 1 videocassette (29 min.) : sd., col. ; 1/2 in.
VHS format. Cataloged from credits, container and cassette
label. Host, William Christopher. Senior high school through
college students and adults. Editors, Kiku Lani Iwata, Dan
Kalmanson ; camera, Steve Barr, I-Li Chen, James O'Keeffe ;
Original music courtesy of Sandy Owen. Broadcasting by the
University of South California School of Journalism. "...for the
Los Angeles Chapter Autism Society of America."--Container.
SUMMARY: Looks at three families with children with autism
ranging in age from six to twenty-six. Parents and siblings
discuss the heartaches, strains, and rewards of living with
autism. ISBN 1-57295-039-0 DDC 362.1
*1. Autism. 2. Autistic children - Family relationships. I.*
*Cunninghame, Karen. II. Kalmanson, Dan. III. Fanlight*
*Productions. IV. Autism Society of America. Los Angeles*
*Chapter.*
*TC RJ506 .A98 1988*

**AUTISM - CASE STUDIES.**
Break throughs [videorecording]. Boston, MA :
Fanlight Productions, c1998.
*TC LC4717.5 .B7 1998*

**Autism :** identification, education, and treatment / edited
by Dianne Berkell Zager. 2nd ed. Mahwah, N.J. :
Lawrence Erlbaum Associates, 1999. x, 380 p. ; 24 cm.
Includes bibliographical references and indexes. ISBN
0-8058-2043-4 (acid-free paper) ISBN 0-8058-2044-2 (pbk. :
acid-free paper) DDC 618.92/8982
*1. Autism in children. 2. Autism - Treatment. I. Berkell Zager,*
*Dianne, 1948-*
*TC RJ506.A9 A9223 1999*

**AUTISM IN CHILDREN.**
Autism. 2nd ed. Mahwah, N.J. : Lawrence Erlbaum
Associates, 1999.
*TC RJ506.A9 A9223 1999*

**AUTISM IN CHILDREN - CASE STUDIES.**
Break throughs [videorecording]. Boston, MA :
Fanlight Productions, c1998.
*TC LC4717.5 .B7 1998*

**AUTISM IN CHILDREN - PATIENTS.** *See*
**AUTISTIC CHILDREN.**

**Autism Society of America. Los Angeles Chapter.**
Autism--a world apart [videorecording]. Boston, MA :
Fanlight Productions, [1989, c1988].
*TC RJ506 .A98 1988*

**AUTISM - TREATMENT.**
Autism. 2nd ed. Mahwah, N.J. : Lawrence Erlbaum
Associates, 1999.
*TC RJ506.A9 A9223 1999*

**AUTISM - UNITED STATES.**
Scott, Jack, Ph. D. Students with autism. San Diego :
Singular Pub. Group, 2000.
*TC LC4718 .S36 2000*

**AUTISTIC CHILDREN - EDUCATION.**
Flowers, Toni. Reaching the child with autism through
art. Arlington, TX : Future Education, c1992.
*TC LC4717 .F56 2000*

Peeters, Theo. Autism. 2nd ed. London : Whurr
Publishers, 1999.
*TC RJ506.A9 P44 1999*

**AUTISTIC CHILDREN - EDUCATION - CASE**
**STUDIES.**
Break throughs [videorecording]. Boston, MA :
Fanlight Productions, c1998.
*TC LC4717.5 .B7 1998*

**AUTISTIC CHILDREN - EDUCATION - UNITED**
**STATES.**
Scott, Jack, Ph. D. Students with autism. San Diego :
Singular Pub. Group, 2000.
*TC LC4718 .S36 2000*

**AUTISTIC CHILDREN - FAMILY**
**RELATIONSHIPS.**
Autism--a world apart [videorecording]. Boston, MA :
Fanlight Productions, [1989, c1988].

*TC RJ506 .A98 1988*

**AUTISTIC CHILDREN - REHABILITATION.**
Flowers, Toni. Reaching the child with autism through art. Arlington, TX : Future Education, c1992.
*TC LC4717 .F56 2000*

**AUTISTIC DISORDER.** *See* **AUTISM IN CHILDREN.**

**Autoaffection.**
Clough, Patricia Ticineto, 1945- Minneapolis : University of Minnesota Press, c2000.
*TC HM846 .C56 2000*

**AUTOBIOGRAPHICAL MEMORY.**
Kuhn, Annette. Family secrets. London ; New York : Verso, 1995.
*TC CT274 .K84 1995*

**AUTOBIOGRAPHICAL MEMORY - MISCELLANEA.**
The business of memory. Saint Paul, Minn. : Graywolf Press, c1999.
*TC BF378.A87 B87 1999*

**AUTOBIOGRAPHIES.** *See* **DIARIES.**

**AUTOBIOGRAPHIES - HISTORY AND CRITICISM.** *See* **AUTOBIOGRAPHY.**

**AUTOBIOGRAPHY.**
Quigley, Jean. The grammar of autobiography. Mahwah, N.J. : Lawrence Erlbaum Associates, c2000.
*TC PE1315.M6 Q54 2000*

Rabbit in the moon [videorecording]. San Francisco, Calif. : Wabi-Sabi Productions, 1999.
*TC D753.8 .R3 1999*

**AUTOBIOGRAPHY - HISTORY AND CRITICISM.** *See* **AUTOBIOGRAPHY.**

**AUTOBIOGRAPHY - TECHNIQUE.** *See* **AUTOBIOGRAPHY.**

**AUTOBIOGRAPHY - THERAPEUTIC USE.**
Daly, Brenda O., 1941- Authoring a life. Albany, NY : State University of New York Press, c1998.
*TC RC560.I53 D35 1998*

**AUTOBIOGRAPHY - WOMEN AUTHORS.**
Bloom, Leslie Rebecca. Under the sign of hope. Albany, N.Y. : State University of New York Press, c1998.
*TC HQ1185 .B56 1998*

**AUTOMATA.** *See* **ROBOTS.**

**AUTOMATIC COMPUTERS.** *See* **COMPUTERS.**

**AUTOMATIC DATA PROCESSING.** *See* **ELECTRONIC DATA PROCESSING.**

**AUTOMATIC DATA PROCESSORS.** *See* **COMPUTERS.**

**AUTOMATIC DATA STORAGE.** *See* **INFORMATION STORAGE AND RETRIEVAL SYSTEMS.**

**AUTOMATIC INFORMATION RETRIEVAL.** *See* **INFORMATION STORAGE AND RETRIEVAL SYSTEMS.**

**AUTOMATIC LANGUAGE PROCESSING.** *See* **COMPUTATIONAL LINGUISTICS.**

**AUTOMATION IN DOCUMENTATION.** *See* **INFORMATION STORAGE AND RETRIEVAL SYSTEMS.**

**AUTOMATONS.** *See* **ROBOTS.**

**AUTOMOBILE TRUCKS.** *See* **TRUCKS.**

**The autonomous brain.**
Milner, Peter M. Mahwah, N.J. : L. Erlbaum Associates, 1999.
*TC BF161 .M5 1999*

**AUTONOMY (PSYCHOLOGY).**
Abate, Ellen C. Personal characteristics of nurses and their influence on professional autonomy. 1998.
*TC 06 no. 11009*

The aims of education. London ; New York : Routledge, 1999.
*TC LB41 .A36353 1999*

Learner autonomy in language learning. Frankfurt am Main ; New York : Peter Lang, c1999.
*TC P53 .L378 1999*

Levinson, Meira. The demands of liberal education. Oxford ; New York : Oxford University Press, 1999.
*TC LC1091 .L38 1999*

**AUTONOMY, UNIVERSITY.** *See* **UNIVERSITY AUTONOMY.**

**AUTOSUGGESTION.** *See* **HYPNOTISM.**

**AUXILIARY SCIENCES OF HISTORY.** *See* **ARCHAEOLOGY; BIOGRAPHY; CIVILIZATION; GENEALOGY; HISTORY.**

**AV communications <Feb. 1989>-June 1989.**
Audio-visual communications. [New York : United Business Publications, 1967-c1989.

**AVC presentation, technology & applications.**
Audio-visual communications. [New York : United Business Publications, 1967-c1989.

**Avellaneda Navas, José Ignacio.** The conquerors of the New Kingdom of Granada / José Ignacio Avellaneda. 1st ed. Albuquerque : University of New Mexico Press, c1995. xii, 275 p. : maps ; 24 cm. Includes bibliographical references (p. 255-264) and index. ISBN 0-8263-1612-3 DDC 986.1/02
*1. Conquerors - Colombia - History - 16th century. 2. Encomenderos - Colombia - History - 16th century. 3. Colombia - Discovery and exploration - Spanish. 4. Colombia - History - To 1810. I. Title.*
*TC F2272 .A84 1995*

**AVERSION.** *See* **HATE.**

**AVES.** *See* **BIRDS.**

**Avi, 1937-.**
Second sight. New York : Philomel Books, 1999.
*TC PZ5 .S4375 1999*

**AVOIDANCE (PSYCHOLOGY).**
Mio, Jeffrey Scott. Resistance to multiculturalism :. Philadelphia, PA : Brunner/Mazel, c2000.
*TC HM1271 .M56 2000*

**Awakuni, Gene I.**
Mio, Jeffrey Scott. Resistance to multiculturalism :. Philadelphia, PA : Brunner/Mazel, c2000.
*TC HM1271 .M56 2000*

**AWARDS - UNITED STATES - HISTORY.**
Fenn, Patricia. Rewards of merit. [Schoharie, N.Y.] : Ephemera Society of America ; Charlottesville [Va.] : Distributed by Howell Press, Inc., c1994.
*TC LA230 .F46 1994*

**AWARENESS.** *See also* **RACE AWARENESS; SELF-PERCEPTION.**
Goldsworthy, Candace L. Sourcebook of phonological awareness activities. San Diego : Singular Pub. Group, c1998.
*TC LB1050.5 .G66 1998*

Insight and psychosis. New York : Oxford University Press, 1998.
*TC RC512 .I49 1998*

**AWARENESS, RISK.** *See* **RISK PERCEPTION.**

**AXIOLOGY.** *See* **VALUES.**

**Ayeroff, Stan.**
Step on a crack [videorecording]. Boston, MA : Fanlight Productions, 1996.
*TC RC533 .S7 1996*

**Ayers, Harry.** Perspectives on behaviour : a practical guide to interventions for teachers / Harry Ayers, Don Clarke and Anne Murray. 2nd ed. London : David Fulton, 2000. xx, 108 p. : ill. ; 30 cm. Previous ed.: 1995. Includes bibliographical references and index. ISBN 1-85346-672-7 DDC 371.1024
*1. Problem children - Education. 2. Behavioral assessment of children. 3. Problem children - Behavior modification. 4. Classroom management. I. Clarke, Don. II. Murray, Anne, 1952- III. Title. IV. Series: Resource materials for teachers*
*TC LC4801 .A94 2000*

**Ayers, William, 1944-**
A simple justice. New York : Teachers College Press, 2000.
*TC LC213.2 .S56 2000*

**Ayim, Martin Ayong.** Empowerment through health education : organization, administration, and the practice of comprehensive health education in developing countries and multicultural settings / Martin Ayong Ayim. 2nd ed. Ruston, LA : Vita Press International, c1998. vii, 364 p. ; 27 cm. "Completely reorganized into parts 1, 2, and 3, and updated with new chapters." Includes bibliographical references. ISBN 0-9659474-0-8 (pbk.)
*1. Health education - Developing countries - Cross-cultural studies. 2. Health promotion - Developing countries - Cross-cultural studies. I. Title.*

*TC RA441.5 .A95 1998*

**Aylesworth, Jim.** The full belly bowl / Jim Aylesworth ; illustrated by Wendy Halperin. 1st ed. New York : Atheneum Books for Young Readers, c1998. 1 v. col. ill. 28 cm. SUMMARY: In return for the kindness he showed a wee small man, a very old man is given a magical bowl that causes problems when it is not used properly. ISBN 0-689-81033-4 (alk. paper) DDC [E]
*1. Fairy tales. I. Halperin, Wendy Anderson, ill. II. Title.*
*TC PZ8.A95 Fu 1998*

**Ayres, David M., 1971-** Anatomy of a crisis : education, development, and the state in Cambodia, 1953-1998 / David M. Ayres. Honolulu : University of Hawai'i Press, c2000. xi, 256 p. ; 24 cm. Includes bibliographical references (p. 229-249) and index. ISBN 0-8248-2238-2
*1. Education and state - Cambodia - History - 20th century. 2. Education - Social aspects - Cambodia - History - 20th century. I. Title.*
*TC LC94.C16 A971 2000*

**Ayto, Russell, ill.**
Shavick, Andrea. You'll grow soon, Alex. New York : Walker, 2000.
*TC PZ7.S5328 Yo 2000*

**AZUELA, MARIANO, 1873-1952. LOS DE ABAJO.**
Guevara-Vázquez, Fabián. El indigena en la novela de la Revolucion Mexicana. 1999.
*TC 085 G934*

**B., Beth.**
Juvenile sex offenders [videorecording]. Princeton, N.J. : Films of the Humanities & Sciences, c1998.
*TC HV9067.S48 J8 1998*

**Baade, Eric C.**
Jenney, Charles. First year Latin workbook. Newton, Mass. : Allyn and Bacon, c1987.
*TC PA2087.5 .J46 1987*

Jenney, Charles. Jenney's first year Latin. Needham, Mass. : Prentice Hall, c1990.
*TC PA2087.5 .J46 1990*

**Babbage, Keen J.** High-impact teaching : overcoming student apathy / Keen J. Babbage. Lancaster, Pa. : Technomic Pub. Co., c1998. xvii, 173 p. ; 23 cm. Includes index. ISBN 1-56676-637-0
*1. Motivation in education. 2. Effective teaching. 3. Teacher-student relationships. I. Title.*
*TC LB1065 .B23 1998*

**BABBITT, NATALIE. TUCK EVERLASTING.**
Beech, Linda Ward. Tuck everlasting by Natalie Babbitt. New York : Scholastic, c1997.
*TC LB1573 .B43 1997*

**Babe, Robert E., 1943-** Canadian communication thought : ten foundational writers / Robert E. Babe. Toronto : Buffalo : University of Toronto Press, c2000. x, 448 p. : ill. ; 24 cm. Includes bibliographical references: p. [383]-413 and index. ISBN 0-8020-4098-5 (bound) ISBN 0-8020-7949-0 (pbk.) DDC 302.23/092/271
*1. Communication. 2. Communication specialists - Canada - Biography. 3. Communicateurs - Canada - Biographies. I. Title.*
*TC P92.5.A1B32 2000*

**BABIES.** *See* **INFANTS.**

**BABIES - FICTION.**
Day, Alexandra. Carl's afternoon in the park. 1st ed. New York : Farrar, Straus & Giroux, 1991.
*TC PZ.D32915 Cars 1991*

Ormerod, Jan. 101 things to do with a baby. 1st U.S. ed. New York : Lothrop, Lee & Shepard, c1984.
*TC PZ7.O634 Aad 1984*

**Babin, Edith H.** Contemporary composition studies : a guide to theorists and terms / Edith Babin and Kimberly Harrison. Westport, Conn. : Greenwood Press, 1999. xiv, 330 p. ; 24 cm. Includes bibliographical references (p. [285]-313) and index. ISBN 0-313-30087-9 (alk. paper) DDC 808/.042/07
*1. English language - Rhetoric - Study and teaching. 2. English language - Rhetoric - Study and teaching - Terminology. 3. English language - Composition and exercises. 4. Report writing - Study and teaching. I. Harrison, Kimberly. II. Title.*
*TC PE1404 .B23 1999*

**BABY ANIMALS.** *See* **ANIMALS - INFANCY.**

**BABY SITTING.** *See* **BABYSITTING.**

**BABYSITTING - FICTION.**
Mills, Claudia. You're a brave man, Julius Zimmerman. 1st ed. New York : Farrar Straus Giroux, c1999.
*TC PZ7.M63963 Yo 1999*

**BACH, JOHANN SEBASTIAN, 1685-1750 -
FICTION.**
Ketcham, Sallie. Bach's big adventure. New York :
Orchard Books, 1999.
*TC PZ7.K488 Bac 1999*

**BACH, JOHANN SEBASTIAN, 1685-1750 -
JUVENILE FICTION.**
Ketcham, Sallie. Bach's big adventure. New York :
Orchard Books, 1999.
*TC PZ7.K488 Bac 1999*

**Bachelors.**
Krauss, Rosalind E. Cambridge, Mass. : MIT Press,
c1999.
*TC NX180.F4 K73 1999*

**Bach's big adventure.**
Ketcham, Sallie. New York : Orchard Books, 1999.
*TC PZ7.K488 Bac 1999*

**BACK.** *See* SPINE.

**BACKBONE.** *See* SPINE.

**Backstage Pass Productions.**
The cello [videorecording]. Van Nuys, CA :
Backstage Pass Productions ; Canoga Park, Calif. :
[Distributed by] MVP, c1995.
*TC MT305 .C4 1995*

The drums [videorecording]. Van Nuys, CA :
Backstage Pass Productions ; Canoga Park, Calif. :
[Distributed by] MVP Home Entertainment, c1998.
*TC MT662.3 .S6 1998*

The flute [videorecording]. Van Nuys, CA : Backstage
Pass Productions ; Canoga Park, Calif. : [Distributed
by] MVP, c1995.
*TC MT345 .F6 1995*

The trombone [videorecording]. Van Nuys, CA :
Backstage Pass Productions ; Canoga Park, Calif. :
[Distributed by] MVP, c1998.
*TC MT465 .T7 1998*

The viola [videorecording]. Van Nuys, CA :
Backstage Pass Productions ; Canoga Park, Calif. :
[Distributed by] MVP Home Entertainment, c1991.
*TC MT285 .V5 1991*

The viola [videorecording]. Van Nuys, CA :
Backstage Pass Productions ; Canoga Park, Calif. :
[Distributed by] MVP Home Entertainment, c1995.
*TC MT285 .V5 1995*

The violin [videorecording]. Van Nuys, CA :
Backstage Pass Productions ; Canoga Park, Calif. :
[Distributed by] MVP, c1998.
*TC MT265 .V5 1998*

**BACKWARD CHILDREN.** *See* MENTALLY
HANDICAPPED CHILDREN.

**BACON, FRANCIS, 1561-1626.
ADVANCEMENT OF LEARNING.**
Bacon, Francis, 1561-1626. The advancement of
learning. Oxford : Clarendon, 2000.
*TC B1191 .K545 2000*

The advancement of learning / [Francis Bacon] ;
edited with an introduction, notes and commentary by
Michael Kiernan. Oxford : Clarendon, 2000. lxxxv, 420
p. : ill. ; 23 cm. (The Oxford Francis Bacon ; 4) Includes
bibliographical references and index. ISBN 0-19-812348-5
DDC 824.3
*1. Bacon, Francis, - 1561-1626. - Advancement of learning. 2.
Bacon, Francis, - 1561-1626 - Criticism and interpretation. 3.
Logic - Early works to 1800. 4. Knowledge. Theory of - Early
works to 1800. 5. Learning - Philosophy - Early works to 1800.
6. Science - Methodology - Early works to 1800. I. Kiernan,
Michael. II. Title. III. Series: Bacon, Francis, 1561-1626.
Works. 1996; 4.*
*TC B1191 .K545 2000*

**Works. 1996;**
(4.) Bacon, Francis, 1561-1626. The advancement
of learning. Oxford : Clarendon, 2000.
*TC B1191 .K545 2000*

**BACON, FRANCIS, 1561-1626 - CRITICISM AND
INTERPRETATION.**
Bacon, Francis, 1561-1626. The advancement of
learning. Oxford : Clarendon, 2000.
*TC B1191 .K545 2000*

**Bacon, Francis, 1909-.**
Farr, Dennis, 1929- Francis Bacon. New York : Harry
N. Abrams in association with the Trust for Museum
Exhibitions, 1999.
*TC ND497.B16 A4 1999*

**BACON, FRANCIS, 1909- - EXHIBITIONS.**
Farr, Dennis, 1929- Francis Bacon. New York : Harry
N. Abrams in association with the Trust for Museum
Exhibitions, 1999.

*TC ND497.B16 A4 1999*

**BACTERIA.**
Berger, Melvin. Germs make me sick!. 1st ed. New
York : Crowell, c1985.
*TC QR57 .B47 1985*

Rowan, Kate. I know how we fight germs. Cambridge,
Mass. : Candlewick Press, 1999.
*TC QR57 .R69 1999*

**BACTERIA - JUVENILE LITERATURE.**
Berger, Melvin. Germs make me sick!. 1st ed. New
York : Crowell, c1985.
*TC QR57 .B47 1985*

Rowan, Kate. I know how we fight germs. Cambridge,
Mass. : Candlewick Press, 1999.
*TC QR57 .R69 1999*

**BACTERIAL DISEASES - JUVENILE
LITERATURE.**
Berger, Melvin. Germs make me sick!. 1st ed. New
York : Crowell, c1985.
*TC QR57 .B47 1985*

**BACTERIAL INFECTIONS.** *See* BACTERIAL
DISEASES.

**Bad boys.**
Ferguson, Ann Arnett, 1940- Ann Arbor : University
of Michigan Press, c2000.
*TC LC2771 .F47 2000*

**Bad medicine.**
O'Brien, Lawrence J. Amherst, N.Y. : Prometheus
Books, c1999.
*TC RA395.A3 O28 1999*

**Bad subjects :** political education for everyday life /
[edited by] the Bad Subjects Production Team. New
York : New York University Press, c1998. xviii, 254
p. ; 21 cm. (Cultural front) ISBN 0-8147-5792-8
(clothbound : acid-free paper) ISBN 0-8147-5793-6
(paperbound : acid-free paper) DDC 973.92
*1. United States - Civilization - 1970- 2. United States -
Politics and government - 1989- 3. Politics and culture -
United States. 4. United States - Social conditions - 1980- 1.
Bad Subjects Production Team. II. Series: Cultural front
(Series)*
*TC E169.12 .B26 1998*

**Bad Subjects Production Team.**
Bad subjects. New York : New York University Press,
c1998.
*TC E169.12 .B26 1998*

**Baddeley, Roland, 1965-.**
Information theory and the brain. Cambridge
[England] ; New York : Cambridge University Press,
2000.
*TC QP363.3 .I54 2000*

**Badders, William.**
DiscoveryWorks. Parsippany, NJ : Silver Burdett
Ginn, c1996-
*TC LB1585 .D574 1996*

**Badger, Larry.**
Teen killers [videorecording]. Princeton, NJ : Films
for the Humanities and Sciences, c1998-1999.
*TC HV9067.H6 T4 1999*

**Badran, Margot.** Feminists, Islam, and nation : gender
and the making of modern Egypt / Margot Badran.
Princeton, N.J. : Princeton University Press, c1995. xi,
352 p. ; 25 cm. Includes bibliographical references (p. [317]-
337) and index. ISBN 0-691-03706-X DDC 305.42/0962
*1. Feminism - Egypt - History. 2. Women - Egypt - History. 3.
Muslim women - Egypt - History. I. Title.*
*TC HQ1793 .B33 1995*

**Baerwald, Thomas John.** Prentice Hall world
geography : teacher's resource file / Thomas J.
Baerwald, Celeste Fraser. Englewood Cliffs, N.J. :
Prentice Hall, c1992. 15 v. : ill., maps ; 29 cm.
CONTENTS: Introduction to the teacher's resource file -- Unit
4. Western Europe -- Unit 6. The Soviet Union -- Unit 7. The
Middle East and North Africa-- Unit 8. Africa South of the
Sahara -- Unit 9. South Asia -- Unit 10. East Asia -- Unit 11.
The Pacific World and Antarctica -- Test book 1 units 1-6
(chapters 1-21) with mid-term exam -- Test book 2 units 7-11
(chapters 22-35) with final exam -- Additional test questions
and answer key - Computer test bank -- Writing process
handbook -- World data bank -- Environmentalist's handbook.
ISBN 0-13-966102-6
*1. Geography - Study and teaching. I. Fraser, Celeste. II. Title.
III. Title: World geography : teacher's resource file*
*TC G128 .B34 1992*

**BAGANDA.** *See* GANDA (AFRICAN PEOPLE).

**BAGANDA (AFRICAN PEOPLE).** *See* GANDA
(AFRICAN PEOPLE).

**Baggen, Peter.**
The university and the knowledge society. Bemmel
[Netherlands] : Concorde Publishing House, 1998.
*TC LB2322.2 .U55 1998*

**Bagin, Don, 1938-** The school and community
relations / Don Bagin, Donald R. Gallagher. 7th ed.
Boston ; London : Allyn and Bacon, c2001. x, 342 p. :
ill. ; 25 cm. Rev. ed. of : The school and community relations /
Donald R. Gallagher, Don Bagin, Leslie W. Kindred. 6th ed.
c1997. Includes bibliographical references and index. ISBN 0-
205-32200-X DDC 371.19/0973
*1. Community and school - United States. 2. Schools - Public
relations - United States. 3. Communication in education -
United States. I. Gallagher, Donald R., 1929- II. Title.*
*TC LC221 .G35 2001*

**Bagley, Mary, 1958-.**
Power, Brenda Miller. Parent power. Portsmouth,
NH : Heinemann, c1999.
*TC LC225.3 .P69 1999*

**Baguio tech journal.** [Baguio City, Philippines : Baguio
Tech., v. ; 21 cm. -v. 4, no. 1 (Jan.-June 1969). Continued by:
University of Baguio journal. ISSN 0522-0157 DDC 378
*1. Education - Philippines - Periodicals. 2. Philippines -
Periodicals. I. Title: University of Baguio journal*

**Bail me out.**
Bracey, Gerald W. (Gerald Watkins) Thousand Oaks,
Calif. : Corwin Press, c2000.
*TC LA217.2 .B72 2000*

**Bailey, C. Everett.**
Children in therapy: New York : W.W. Norton, 2000.
*TC RC488.5 .C468 2000*

**Bailey, Carolyn Sherwin, 1875-1961.**
The Kindergarten and first grade. Springfield, Mass. :
Milton Bradley Co., 1916-[1924]

**Bailey, Mildred.**
Moving on. Lexington, Mass. : D.C. Heath, c1983.
*TC PE1117 .M68 1983*

Moving on. Lexington, Mass. : D.C. Heath, c1983.
*TC PE1117 .M68 1983*

**Bailey, Patricia A. (Patricia Ann).**
Integrating community service into nursing education.
New York, NY : Springer Pub. Co., c1999.
*TC RT76 .I55 1999*

**Bailey, Richard.** Teaching physical education 5-11 /
edited by Richard Bailey and Tony Macfadyen. New
York : Continuum, 2000. 226 p. : ill. ; 24 cm. (Children,
teachers, and learning series) Includes bibliographical
references and index. ISBN 0-8264-4842-9 DDC 613.707
*1. Physical education and training - Study and teaching
(Elementary) 2. Physical education for children 3. Physical
education for teachers - Training of. I. Macfadyen, Tony. II.
Title. III. Series: Children, teachers, and learning.*
*TC GV443 .B34 2000*

**Bailey, Richard, 1957-.**
Arthur, James, 1957- Schools and community.
London ; New York : Falmer Press, 2000.
*TC LC221.4.G7 A78 2000*

**BAKED PRODUCTS.** *See* BREAD.

**Baken, R. J. (Ronald J.), 1943-** Clinical measurement
of speech and voice / R.J. Baken, Robert F. Orlikoff.
2nd ed. San Diego : Singular Thomson Learning,
c2000. xii, 610 p. : ill. ; 28 cm. Includes bibliographical
references and index. ISBN 1-56593-869-0 (soft cover : alk.
paper) DDC 616.85/5075
*1. Speech disorders - Diagnosis. 2. Voice disorders -
Diagnosis. 3. Speech - Measurement. 4. Voice - Measurement.
5. Speech Production Measurement. I. Orlikoff, Robert F. II.
Title.*
*TC RC423 .B28 2000*

**Baker, Bruce D.** A comparison of statistical and neural
network models for forecasting educational spending /
by Bruce D. Baker. 1997. xi, 149 leaves ; 29 cm. Issued
also on microfilm. Thesis (Ed.D.)--Teachers College,
Columbia University, 1997. Includes bibliographical references
(leaves 113-118).
*1. Education - United States - Statistics. 2. Education -
Finance - United States. 3. Education - United States -
Forecasting. 4. Education - Economic aspects - Econometric
models. 5. Neural networks (Computer science). I. National
Center for Education Statistics. II. Title.*
*TC 06 no. 10792*

**Baker encyclopedia of psychology.**
Baker encyclopedia of psychology & counseling. 2nd
ed. Grand Rapids, Mich. : Baker Books, c1999.
*TC BF31 .B25 1999*

**Baker encyclopedia of psychology & counseling /**
edited by David G. Benner & Peter C. Hill. 2nd ed.
Grand Rapids, Mich. : Baker Books, c1999. 1276 p. ;

*Baker encyclopedia of psychology and counseling*

26 cm. (Baker reference library) Rev. ed. of: Baker encyclopedia of psychology. Includes bibliographical references and index. ISBN 0-8010-2100-6 DDC 150/.3
*1. Psychology - Dictionaries. 2. Psychology. Pathological - Dictionaries. 3. Psychotherapy - Dictionaries. I. Benner, David G. II. Hill, Peter C., 1953- III. Title: Baker encyclopedia of psychology. IV. Title: Baker encyclopedia of psychology and counseling V. Series.*
*TC BF31 .B25 1999*

**Baker encyclopedia of psychology and counseling.**
Baker encyclopedia of psychology & counseling. 2nd ed. Grand Rapids, Mich. : Baker Books, c1999.
*TC BF31 .B25 1999*

**Baker, Justine C.** A neural network guide to teaching / by Justine C. Baker and Francis G. Martin. Bloomington, Ind. : Phi Delta Kappa Educational Foundation, c1998. 50 p. : ill. ; 18 cm. (Fastback, 431.) Includes bibliographical references (p. 45-50). ISBN 0-87367-631-9
*1. Learning - Physiological aspects. 2. Neural networks (Neurobiology). 3. Teaching. I. Martin, Francis G. II. Phi Delta Kappa. Educational Foundation. III. Title. IV. Series.*
*TC LB1057 .B35 1998*

**Baker, Leslie A.** Paris cat / Leslie Baker. 1st ed. Boston, Mass. : Little, Brown, c1999. 1 v. (unpaged) : col. ill. ; 21 x 26 cm. SUMMARY: On their first day in Paris, Annie's cat goes off to chase a mouse and wanders around the whole city before finding her way back where she belongs. ISBN 0-316-07309-1 DDC [E]
*1. Cats - Fiction. 2. Lost and found possessions - Fiction. 3. Paris (France) - Fiction. I. Title.*
*TC PZ7.B1744 Par 1999*

**Baker, Linda.**
Engaging young readers. New York : Guilford Press, c2000.
*TC LB1573 .E655 2000*

**Baker, Lynne Rudder, 1944-** Persons and bodies : a constitution view / Lynne Rudder Baker. New York : Cambridge University Press, 2000. xii, 233 p. ; 24 cm. (Cambridge studies in philosophy) Includes bibliographical references and index. ISBN 0-521-59263-1 hb ISBN 0-521-59719-6 pb DDC 128/.6
*1. Body, Human (Philosophy) 2. Personalism. I. Title. II. Series.*
*TC B105.B64 B35 2000*

**Baker, Reena.**
Chud, Gyda. Early childhood education for a multicultural society. [Vancouver] : Western Education Development Group, Faculty of Education, The University of British Columbia, c1985.
*TC LC1099 .C494 1985*

**Baker reference library**
Baker encyclopedia of psychology & counseling. 2nd ed. Grand Rapids, Mich. : Baker Books, c1999.
*TC BF31 .B25 1999*

**Baker-Shenk, Charlotte Lee.** American sign language : a look at its history, structure, and community / by Charlotte Baker, Carol Padden. Silver Spring, Md. : T. J. Publishers, c1978, 1979 printing. 22 p. : ill. ; 22 cm. Bibliography: p. 21-22. DDC 419
*1. American sign language. 2. Deaf - Education - English language. I. Padden, Carol, joint author. II. Title.*
*TC HV2474 .B29*

**Baker, Stanley B., 1935-** School counseling for the twenty-first century / Stanley B. Baker. 3rd ed. Upper Saddle River, N.J. : Merrill, c2000. xiv, 418 p. : ill. ; 25 cm. Includes bibliographical references and index. ISBN 0-13-645094-6 DDC 371.4
*1. Student counselors - Training of - United States. 2. Educational counseling - United States. I. Title. II. Title: School counseling for the 21st century*
*TC LB1731.75 .B35 2000*

**Baker, Susan Keane.** Managing patient expectations / the art of finding and keeping loyal patients / Susan Keane Baker. San Francisco : Jossey Bass Publishers, 1998. xv, 281 p. ; 24 cm. Includes bibliographical references (p. 261-269) and index. ISBN 0-7879-4158-1 (hc. : alk. paper) DDC 610.69/6
*1. Patient satisfaction. 2. Physician and patient. 3. Ambulatory medical care. 4. Consumer satisfaction. 5. Patient Satisfaction. 6. Outpatients - psychology. 7. Knowledge, Attitudes, Practice. 8. Patient Participation. 9. Physician-Patient Relations. I. Title.*
*TC R727.3 .B28 1998*

**BAKING - FICTION.**
Sathre, Vivian. Three kind mice. 1st ed. San Diego : Harcourt Brace, c1997.
*TC PZ8.3.S238 Th 1997*

**BAKKE, ALLAN PAUL - TRIALS, LITIGATION, ETC.**
Ball, Howard. The Bakke case. Lawrence, Kan. : University Press of Kansas, 2000.
*TC KF228.B34 B35 2000*

**The Bakke case.**
Ball, Howard. Lawrence, Kan. : University Press of Kansas, 2000.
*TC KF228.B34 B35 2000*

**Bakos, Zsoltné.**
Disadvantaged youth project. Budapest : Ministry of Labour, 1998.
*TC LC4096.H9 D57 1998*

**Balakian, Anna Elizabeth, 1915-** The symbolist movement : a critical appraisal / by Anna Balakian 1977 ed. New York : New York University Press, 1977 viii, 220 p. ; 22 cm. Includes index Bibliography: p. [211]-215 "Gift from Professor Maxine Greene"
*1. Symbolism in literature. 2. French literature - 19th century - History and criticism. I. Title.*
*TC PN56.S9 .B3 1977*

**BALANCE OF NATURE. See ECOLOGY.**

**Balanced reading strategies and practices.**
Reutzel, D. Ray (Douglas Ray), 1953- Upper Saddle river, N.J. : Merrill, c1999.
*TC LB1050 .R477 1999*

**Balancing acts.**
Smulyan, Lisa. Albany : State University of New York Press, c2000.
*TC LB2831.92 .S58 2000*

**Balancing local control and state responsibility for K-12 education** / edited by Neil D. Theobald and Betty Malen. Larchmont, NY : Eye on Education, 2000. xiii, 334 p. ; 24 cm. (Yearbook of the American Education Finance Association ; 21) Includes bibliographical references and index. ISBN 1-88300-196-X DDC 379.73
*1. Education and state - United States. 2. Public schools - United States - Finance. 3. Public schools - Decentralization - United States. I. Theobald. Neil D. (Neil David) II. Malen. Betty. III. Series: Annual yearbook of the American Education Finance Association ; 21st.*
*TC LC89 .B35 2000*

**Balancing principles for teaching elementary reading.**
Hoffman, James V. Mahwah, N.J. : L. Erlbaum Associates, c2000.
*TC LB1573 . H459 2000*

**Balancing the secrets of private disclosures** / edited by Sandra Petronio. Mahwah, N.J. : Lawrence Erlbaum Associates, Publishers, 2000. xvi, 355 p. ; 24 cm. (LEA's communication series) Includes bibliographical references (p. 303-335) and index. ISBN 0-8058-3114-2 (hardcover : alk. paper) DDC 302.5
*1. Self-disclosure. 2. Secrecy. 3. Privacy. 4. Interpersonal relations. I. Petronio, Sandra Sporbert. II. Series.*
*TC BF697.5.S427 B35 2000*

**Balancing the tensions of change.**
Osguthorpe, Russell T. Thousand Oaks, Calif. : Corwin Press, c1998.
*TC LB2331.53 .O74 1998*

**Baldwin, Alexinia Y.**
The many faces of giftedness. Belmont, CA : Wadsworth Pub. Co., c1999.
*TC BF723.G5 M36 1999*

**Baldwin, Harmon A. (Harmon Arthur), 1922-** Planning for disaster : a guide for school administrators / Harmon A. Baldwin. 2nd ed. Bloomington, Ind. : Phi Delta Kappa Educational Foundation, c1999. 33 p. ; 23 cm. ISBN 0-87367-818-4
*1. Schools - United States - Safety measures. 2. Disaster relief - United States - Planning. I. Phi Delta Kappa. Educational Foundation. II. Title.*
*TC LB2864.5 .B35 1999*

**Baldwin, John.** Education and welfare reform : the story of a second-chance school / by John Baldwin. Bloomington, Ind. : Phi Delta Kappa Educational Foundation, c1993. 41 p. ; 18 cm. (Fastback, 355.) Includes bibliographical references (p. 41). ISBN 0-87367-355-7 (pbk.)
*1. Handicapped - Education (Secondary) - Louisiana - Shreveport. 2. Evening and continuation schools - Louisiana - Shreveport. 3. Continuing education - Louisiana - Shreveport. 4. Public welfare - United States. 5. Public welfare - Law and legislation - United States. I. Phi Delta Kappa. Educational Foundation. II. Title. III. Title: The story of a second chance school. IV. Series.*
*TC LC4033.S61 B34 1993*

**Baldwin, Marva.**
McBride, Michael B. Meeting the national standards with handbells and handchimes. Lanham, MD : Scarecrow Press, 2000.
*TC MT711 .M35 2000*

**Balick, Dana.**
Art works!. Portsmouth, NH : Heinemann, c1999.
*TC LB1628.5 .A78 1999*

**Baliles, Gerald L.**
Educating Americans for tomorrow's world. [Washington D.C.] : NGA, [1987]
*TC LC1099 .E225 1987*

**Ball, Bill.**
Pitts, David. Red Hat Linux 6 unleashed. [Indianapolis, Ind.] : SAMS, c1999.
*TC QA76.76.O63 P56148 1999*

**BALL GAMES. See BASEBALL; CRICKET.**

**Ball, Grant T.** Civics / Grant T. Ball, Lee J. Rosch. Fifth edition. Chicago, Ill. : Follett Pub. Co., c1978. 478 p. : ill. ; 24 cm. (Follett Social Studies) Includes index. ISBN 0-695-27340-x
*1. Civics. I. Rosch. Lee J., joint author. II. Title. III. Series.*
*TC H62 .B34 1978*

**Ball, Howard.** The Bakke case : race, education, and affirmative action / Howard Ball. Lawrence, Kan. : University Press of Kansas, 2000. xv, 231 p. : ill. ; 22 cm. (Landmark law cases & American society) Includes bibliographical references and index. ISBN 0-7006-1045-6 (cloth : alk. paper) ISBN 0-7006-1046-4 (pbk. : alk. paper) DDC 344.73/0798
*1. Bakke, Allan Paul, litigation, etc. 2. University of California (System). - Regents - Trials, litigation, etc. 3. Discrimination in medical education - Law and legislation - United States. 4. Affirmative action programs - Law and legislation - United States. 5. Medical colleges - California - Admission I. Title. II. Series.*
*TC KF228.B34 B35 2000*

**Ball, Martin J. (Martin John).**
Voice quality measurement. San Diego : Singular Pub. Group, c2000.
*TC RF510 .V67 2000*

**BALL ROOM DANCING. See BALLROOM DANCING.**

**Ball, Wanda H., 1953-** Socratic seminars in the block / by Wanda H. Ball and Pam Brewer. Larchmont, N.Y. : Eye On Education, 2000. xi, 161 p. ; 28 cm. ISBN 1-88300-179-X DDC 371.3/7
*1. Questioning. 2. Lesson planning. I. Brewer. Pam. 1952- II. Title.*
*TC LB1027.44 .B35 2000*

**BALLADS. See FOLK SONGS.**

**Ballard, Danny J.**
Kolander, Cheryl A. Contemporary women's health. Boston, Mass. : WCB/McGraw-Hill, c1999.
*TC RA778 .K7245 1999*

**Ballard, Keith.**
Inclusive education. London ; Philadelphia : Falmer Press, 1999.
*TC LC1200 .I53 1999*

**Ballenger, Cynthia.** Teaching other people's children : literacy and learning in a bilingual classroom / Cynthia Ballenger ; foreword by Courtney Cazden. New York : Teachers College Press, c1999. ix, 108 p. ; 23 cm. (The practitioner inquiry series) Includes bibliographical references (p. 101-103) and index. ISBN 0-8077-3789-5 (paper : alk. paper) ISBN 0-8077-3790-9 (cloth : alk. paper) DDC 370.117/5
*1. Children of immigrants - Education (Preschool) - United States - Case studies. 2. Haitian Americans - Education (Preschool) - United States - Case studies. 3. Language arts (Preschool) - United States - Case studies. 4. Home and school - United States - Case studies. 5. Education, Bilingual - Case studies. 6. Ballenger, Cynthia. 7. Special education teachers - United States - Biography. I. Title. II. Series.*
*TC LC3746 .B336 1999*

**BALLENGER, CYNTHIA.**
Ballenger, Cynthia. Teaching other people's children. New York : Teachers College Press, c1999.
*TC LC3746 .B336 1999*

**Ballenger, Jesse F.**
Concepts of Alzheimer disease. Baltimore, Md. ; London : Johns Hopkins University Press, 2000.
*TC RC523 .C657 2000*

**BALLET. See also CHOREOGRAPHY.**
Grindley, Sally. The little ballerina. 1st American ed. New York : DK Pub., 1999.

## TC GV1787.5 .G75 1999
Wulff, Helena. Ballet across borders. Oxford ; New York : Berg, 1998.
*TC GV1787 .W85 1998*

**Ballet across borders.**
Wulff, Helena. Oxford ; New York : Berg, 1998.
*TC GV1787 .W85 1998*

**Ballet class for beginners** [videorecording] / [presented by] the Video Classroom ; with David Howard ... assisted by Frederick Wodin & Merle Hubbard ; producer and director, Lee Kraft. W. Long Branch, NJ : Kultur, c1981. 1 videocassette (35 min.) : sd., col. ; 1/2 in. (Dance instructional) VHS, Hi-fi, Mono, Stereo-Compatible, Dolby System. Catalogued from credits, container and cassette label. Instructor/host: David Howard; dancer/ demonstrator, Allison Potter; pianist, Whit Kellogg. Time listed on container, 40 minutes; actual time, 35 minutes. For the beginner ballet student and the advanced who wants a refresher course. SUMMARY: Noted ballet teacher and coach David Howard explains the basic movements of ballet as they are demonstrated by student dancer, Allison Potter. Correct posture and exercise positions are emphasized and incorporated into the basic movements of the ballet repertoire. Designed for the beginning student or as a refresher course for the more advanced student CONTENTS: Explanation of ballet posture. - Positions of feet, arms, and head. At the barre: Plié. - Tendu. - Glissé. - Ronds de jambe en terre. - Frappé. - Fondu. Petit battement. - Ronds de jambe en l'air. - Grand battement. Center floor: Explanation of 7 terms for dance movement. - Épaulement. - Port de bras. - Arabesque & attitude. - Adage. - Spotting. - Pirouettes. - Balancé & pirouettes. - Changement & soubresaut. - Glissade. - Assemblé. - Jeté derrière with temps levé. - Glissade, jeté, glissade, assemblé. - Pas de bourrée & pas de chat. - Failli & fouetté sauté. - Révérence.
*1. Ballet - Study and teaching. 2. Ballet - Terminology. I. Howard, David. II. Potter, Allison. III. Kellogg, Whit. IV. Kraft, Leland M. V. Wodin, Frederick. VI. Hubbard, Merle. VII. Kultur International Films. VIII. Video Classroom (Firm) IX. Series.*
*TC GV1589 .B3 1981*

**Ballet class : intermed/adv. [videorecording].**
Ballet class [videorecording]. W. Long Branch, NJ : Kultur, c1984.
*TC GV1589 .B33 1984*

**Ballet class** [videorecording] : intermediate-advanced / [presented by] New Age Video ; with David Howard ; [producers: Marc Chase Weinstein, Gary Jacinto ; director, Gary Donatelli]. W. Long Branch, NJ : Kultur, c1984. 1 videocassette (55 min.) : sd., color ; 1/2 in. (Dance instructional) Title on cassette label: Ballet class : intermed/adv. [videorecording]. VHS, Hi-fi, Mono, Stereo-Compatible, Dolby System. Catalogued from credits, container and cassette label. Instructor/host: David Howard. Cameras: Gary Donatelli, Dick Fisher; editors, Ira Meistrich, Gary Donatelli, Debra Zalkind; music composed & performed by Lynn Stanford ; dancers: Cynthia Harvey ... [et al.]. "A New Age Video presentation." Videotaped at the David Howard School of Ballet, New York City. For intermediate and advanced ballet students. SUMMARY: An intermediate-advanced ballet class is taught by teacher and coach David Howard in his New York City dance studio. Dancers Cynthia Harvey, Peter Fonseca, Ronnie Spiegelman, James Sewell, Natasha Beilin, Greg Larson, and Louis Navarrete demonstrate. Also includes a demonstration by Cynthia Harvey of the correct way to put on pointe shoes. CONTENTS: Plié -- Tendu -- Tendu from fifth -- Ronde de jambe -- Frappé -- Fondue -- Ronde de jambe en l'air -- Stretch -- Grand battement -- Adagio -- Relevé & développé -- Pirouette en dehors -- Pirouette en dedans -- Allégro 1 -- Allégro 2 -- Virtuoso variation -- Grand battement.
*1. Ballet - Study and teaching. 2. Ballet - Terminology. I. Howard, David. II. Harvey, Cynthia. III. Fonseca, Peter. IV. Spiegelman, Ronnie. V. Sewell, James. VI. Beilin, Natasha. VII. Larson, Greg. VIII. Navarrete, Louis. IX. Weinstein, Mark. X. Jacinto, Gary. XI. Donatelli, Gary. XII. Stanford, Lynn. XIII. New Age Video (Firm) XIV. Kultur International Films. XV. Title: Ballet class : intermed/adv. [videorecording] XVI. Series.*
*TC GV1589 .B33 1984*

**BALLET COMPANIES.**
Wulff, Helena. Ballet across borders. Oxford ; New York : Berg, 1998.
*TC GV1787 .W85 1998*

**BALLET DANCERS.**
Wulff, Helena. Ballet across borders. Oxford ; New York : Berg, 1998.
*TC GV1787 .W85 1998*

**BALLET DANCERS - RUSSIA (FEDERATION) - BIOGRAPHY.**
Solway, Diane. Nureyev, his life. 1st ed. New York : William Morrow, c1998.

## TC GV1785.N8 S66 1998
**BALLET DANCING.**
Grindley, Sally. The little ballerina. 1st American ed. New York : DK Pub., 1999.
*TC GV1787.5 .G75 1999*

**BALLET DANCING - FICTION.**
Gauch, Patricia Lee. Presenting Tanya, the Ugly Duckling. New York : Philomel Books, c1999.
*TC PZ7.G2315 Pr 1999*

Vail, Rachel. Please, please, please. New York : Scholastic, c1998.
*TC PZ7.V1916 Pl 1998*

**BALLET DANCING - JUVENILE LITERATURE.**
Grindley, Sally. The little ballerina. 1st American ed. New York : DK Pub., 1999.
*TC GV1787.5 .G75 1999*

**BALLET - ENCYCLOPEDIAS.**
International encyclopedia of dance. New York : Oxford University Press, c1998.
*TC GV1585 .I586 1998*

**BALLET - FICTION.**
Marshall, James, 1942- Swine lake. 1st ed. [New York] : Harper Collins Publishers, 1999.
*TC PZ7.M35672 Sw 1999*

**BALLET - JUVENILE LITERATURE.**
Grindley, Sally. The little ballerina. 1st American ed. New York : DK Pub., 1999.
*TC GV1787.5 .G75 1999*

**BALLET - STUDY AND TEACHING.** *See also* **BALLET DANCING.**
Ballet class for beginners [videorecording]. W. Long Branch, NJ : Kultur, c1981.
*TC GV1589 .B3 1981*

Ballet class [videorecording]. W. Long Branch, NJ : Kultur, c1984.
*TC GV1589 .B33 1984*

**BALLET TECHNIQUE.** *See* **BALLET DANCING.**

**BALLET - TERMINOLOGY.**
Ballet class for beginners [videorecording]. W. Long Branch, NJ : Kultur, c1981.
*TC GV1589 .B3 1981*

Ballet class [videorecording]. W. Long Branch, NJ : Kultur, c1984.
*TC GV1589 .B33 1984*

**Ballroom dancing for beginners** [videorecording] / producer/director, Rick Allen Lippert ; writer/ instructor, Teresa Mason. W. Long Branch, N.J. Kultur, c1993. 1 videocassette (45 min.) : sd., col. ; 1/2 in. (Dance instructional.) VHS, Hi-fi, Mono, Stereo-Compatible, Dolby System. Catalogued from credits and container and cassette label. Instructor, Teresa Mason ; demonstrating partner, Randolph Scott. Music, Richard Bugg. Running time on cassette label 57 minutes. For students of ballroom dancing. SUMMARY: Teaches the basic techniques of ballroom dancing and includes patterns for the fox trot, tango, waltz, rumba, cha cha, and swing. CONTENTS: Section one. Elements of dance -- Section two. Positions -- Section three. Music -- Section four. Patterns. ISBN 1-56127-206-X
*1. Ballroom dancing - Study and teaching. I. Mason, Teresa. II. Scott, Randolph. III. Lippert, Rick Allen. IV. Kultur International Films. V. Series.*
*TC GV1753.7 .B3 1993*

**Ballroom dancing for beginners** [videorecording] / producer/director, Rick Allen Lippert ; writer/ instructor, Teresa Mason. W. Long Branch, N.J. Kultur, c1993. 1 videocassette (45 min.) : sd., col. ; 1/2 in. (Dance instructional.) VHS, Hi-fi, Mono, Stereo-Compatible, Dolby System. Catalogued from credits and container and cassette label. Instructor, Teresa Mason ; demonstrating partner, Randolph Scott. Music, Richard Bugg. Running time on cassette label 57 minutes. For students of ballroom dancing. SUMMARY: Teaches the basic techniques of ballroom dancing and includes patterns for the fox trot, tango, waltz, rumba, cha cha, and swing. CONTENTS: Section one. Elements of dance -- Section two. Positions -- Section three. Music -- Section four. Patterns. ISBN 1-56127-206-X
*1. Ballroom dancing - Study and teaching. I. Mason, Teresa. II. Scott, Randolph. III. Lippert, Rick Allen. IV. Kultur International Films. V. Series.*
*TC GV1753.7 .B3 1993*

**BALLROOM DANCING - STUDY AND TEACHING.**
Ballroom dancing for beginners [videorecording]. W. Long Branch, N.J. Kultur, c1993.
*TC GV1753.7 .B3 1993*

Ballroom dancing for beginners [videorecording]. W. Long Branch, N.J. Kultur, c1993.
*TC GV1753.7 .B3 1993*

**BALLS (PARTIES).** *See* **DANCE.**

**BALLS (SPORTING GOODS) - FICTION.**
Willard, Nancy. The tale I told Sasha. 1st ed. Boston : Little, Brown, c1999.
*TC PZ8.3.W668 Tal 1999*

**Balog, James.**
The power of idea : [videorecording]. Minneapolis, Minn. : Media Loft, c1992.
*TC TR690 .P5 1992*

**Balter, Alison.**
**[Mastering Access 97 development]**
Alison Balter's Mastering Access 97 development / Alison Balter. 2nd ed. Indianapolis, Ind. : Sams Pub.. [c1997] xlvi, 1112 p. : ill. ; 24 cm. + 1 computer laser optical disc (4 3/4 in.). Includes index. System requirements for accompanying computer disc: Version 7 for Windows 97. ISBN 0-672-30999-8 DDC 005.75/65
*1. Microsoft Access. 2. Database management. 3. Microsoft Windows (Computer file). I. Title. II. Title: Mastering Access 97 development*
*TC QA76.9.D3 B32 1997*

**Balter, Lawrence.**
Child psychology. Philadelphia, PA : Psychology Press, c1999.
*TC BF721 .C5155 1999*

**BALTIMORE (MD.) - FICTION.**
Hahn, Mary Downing. Anna all year round. New York : Clarion Books, c1999.
*TC PZ7.H1256 An 1999*

**Bancroft, John.**
The Role of theory in sex research. Bloomington, IN : Indiana University Press, 2000.
*TC HQ60 .R65 2000*

**Bandiera, M.**
Research in science education in Europe. Dordrecht : Boston, Mass. : Kluwer Academic Publishers, c1999.
*TC Q183.4.E85 R467 1999*

**Bandman, Bertram.**
Bandman, Elsie L. Nursing ethics through the life span. 3rd ed. Norwalk, Conn. : Appleton & Lange, c1995.
*TC RT85 .B33 1995*

**Bandman, Elsie L.** Nursing ethics through the life span / Elsie L. Bandman, Bertram Bandman. 3rd ed. Norwalk, Conn. : Appleton & Lange, c1995. x, 341 p. : ill. ; 23 cm. Includes bibliographical references and index. ISBN 0-8385-6638-3 DDC 174/.2
*1. Nursing ethics. 2. Ethics, Nursing. I. Bandman, Bertram. II. Title.*
*TC RT85 .B33 1995*

**BANDS (MUSIC) - FICTION.**
Sage, James. The little band. New York : M.K. McElderry Books ; Toronto : Collier Macmillan Canada ; New York : Maxwell Macmillan International Pub. Group, c1991.
*TC PZ7.S1304 Li 1991*

Ziefert, Harriet. Animal music. Boston : Houghton Mifflin, 1999.
*TC PZ8.3.Z47 An 1999*

**Bandy, Susan J.**
Crossing boundaries. Champaign, IL : Human Kinetics, c1999.
*TC PN6071.S62 C76 1999*

**Banff Centre for the Arts.**
Juvenile sex offenders [videorecording]. Princeton, N.J. : Films of the Humanities & Sciences, c1998.
*TC HV9067.S48 J8 1998*

**Banff International Conference on Behavior Modification, 4th, 1972.** Behavior change : methodology, concepts, and practice / the Fourth Banff International Conference on Behavior Modification ; edited and introduced by Leo A. Hamerlynck, Lee C. Handy, Eric J. Mash. Champaign, Ill. : Research Press, 1974, c1973. xiv, 358 p. : graphs ; 21 cm. Conference held March 25-29 in Banff, Alberta, Canada. Includes bibliographies. ISBN 0-87822-089-5 DDC 153.8/5
*1. Behavior modification - Congresses. I. Hamerlynck, Leo A., 1929- II. Handy, Lee C. III. Mash, Eric J. IV. Title.*
*TC BF637.B4 B354 1972*

**Bang, Molly.** When Sophie gets angry--really, really angry... / by Molly Bang. New York : Blue Sky Press, c1999. 1 v. (unpaged) : col. ill. ; 26 cm. SUMMARY: A young girl is upset and doesn't know how to manage her anger but takes the time to cool off and regain her composure. ISBN

0-590-18979-4 (alk. paper) DDC [E]
*1. Anger - Fiction. I. Title.*
**TC PZ7.B2217 Wh 1999**

**Bankhead, Elizabeth.** Write it! : a guide for research /
Betty Bankhead, Janet Nichols, Dawn Vaughn. 2nd
ed./MLA version. Englewood, Colo. : Libraries
Unlimited, c1999. vii, 56 p. : ill. ; 28 cm. Rev. ed. of: Write
it / Elizabeth Bankhead ... [et al]. 1988. Includes
bibliographical references (p. 41) and index. ISBN
1-56308-689-1 (softbound) DDC 808/.02
*1. Report writing. 2. Research. I. Nichols, Janet. II. Vaughn,
Dawn. III. Title. IV. Title: Write it.*
**TC LB1047.3 .W75 1999**

**BANKING. See BANKS AND BANKING.**

**BANKING INDUSTRY. See BANKS AND
BANKING.**

**BANKS AND BANKING - UNITED STATES.**
Employee training and U.S. competitiveness.
Boulder : Westview Press, 1991.
**TC HF5549.5.T7 E46 1991**

**Banks, James A.** Cultural diversity and education :
foundations, curriculum, and teaching / James A.
Banks. 4th ed. Boston ; London : Allyn & Bacon,
c2001. xxiv, 360 p. ; 24 cm. Rev. ed. of: Multiethnic
education. 3rd ed. c1994. Includes bibliographical references
and index. ISBN 0-205-30865-1
*1. Minorities - Education - United States. 2. Multicultural
education - United States. I. Banks, James A. Multiethnic
education. II. Title.*
**TC LC3731 .B365 2001**

**Multiethnic education.**
Banks, James A. Cultural diversity and education.
4th ed. Boston : London : Allyn & Bacon, c2001.
**TC LC3731 .B365 2001**

**Banks, Nick.** White counsellors--Black clients : theory,
research and practice / Nick Banks. Aldershot, Hants,
England : Brookfield, Vt. : Ashgate, c1999. xii, 299 p. ;
23 cm. (Interdisciplinary research series in ethnic, gender, and
class relations) Includes bibliography and indexes. ISBN 1-
84014-146-8
*1. Minorities - Counseling of - Great Britain. 2. Social work
with minorities - Great Britain. 3. Cross-cultural counseling -
Great Britain. I. Title. II. Series.*
**TC HV3177.G7 B36 1999**

**BANNAKY, MOLLY, B. CA. 1666 - FICTION.**
McGill, Alice. Molly Bannaky. Boston, Mass. :
Houghton Mifflin, 1999.
**TC PZ7.M478468 Mol 1999**

**BANNAKY, MOLLY, B. CA. 1666 - JUVENILE
FICTION.**
McGill, Alice. Molly Bannaky. Boston, Mass. :
Houghton Mifflin, 1999.
**TC PZ7.M478468 Mol 1999**

**BANNEKER, BENJAMIN, 1731-1806 - FAMILY -
FICTION.**
McGill, Alice. Molly Bannaky. Boston, Mass. :
Houghton Mifflin, 1999.
**TC PZ7.M478468 Mol 1999**

**BANNEKER, BENJAMIN, 1731-1806 - FAMILY -
JUVENILE FICTION.**
McGill, Alice. Molly Bannaky. Boston, Mass. :
Houghton Mifflin, 1999.
**TC PZ7.M478468 Mol 1999**

**Banner, James M., 1935-** The elements of learning /
James M. Banner, Jr. and Harold C. Cannon. New
Haven, Conn. : Yale University Press, c1999. xii, 182
p. ; 22 cm. ISBN 0-300-07855-2 ISBN 0-300-07836-6 (alk.
paper) DDC 378.1/70281
*1. Learning. 2. Study skills. 3. Learning, Psychology of. 4.
College student orientation. I. Cannon, Harold C., 1930- II.
Title.*
**TC LB1060 .B36 1999**

**Banning, James H.**
Strange, Charles Carney. Educating by design. 1st ed.
San Francisco : Jossey-Bass, c2001.
**TC LB2324 .S77 2001**

**BANQUETS. See DINNERS AND DINING.**

**Bantoe-onderwysblad.**
Educamus. Pretoria : Govt. Printer, [1978-

**Banton, Michael P.** Racial theories / Michael Banton.
2nd ed. Cambridge : New York : Cambridge
University Press, 1998. x, 253 p. ; 24 cm. Includes
bibliographical references (p. 236-247) and index. ISBN 0-
521-62075-9 ISBN 0-521-62945-4 (pbk.) DDC 305.8
*1. Race. 2. Race relations. I. Title.*
**TC HT1521 .B345 1998**

**Bantova, M. A.**
Moro, M. I. Russian grade 1 mathematics. Chicago :
University of Chicago School of Mathematics Project,
1992.
**TC QA14.R9 R8611 1992**

Moro, M. I. Russian grade 2 mathematics. Chicago :
University of Chicago School of Mathematics Project,
1992.
**TC QA14.R9 R8711 1992**

Russian grade 3 mathematics. Chicago : University of
Chicago School of Mathematics Project, 1992.
**TC QA14.R9 R8811 1992**

**BANTU-SPEAKING PEOPLES. See GANDA
(AFRICAN PEOPLE).**

**BANTUS - SOUTH AFRICA - EDUCATION -
PERIODICALS.**
Educamus. Pretoria : Govt. Printer, [1978-

**BAPTISTS. See MENNONITES.**

**Bar-On, Reuven, 1944-.**
The handbook of emotional intelligence. 1st ed. San
Francisco, Calif. : Jossey-Bass, c2000.
**TC BF576 .H36 2000**

**Bar-Tal, Daniel.**
How children understand war and peace. 1st ed. San
Francisco : Jossey-Bass, c1999.
**TC JZ5534 .H69 1999**

Shared beliefs in a society : social psychological
analysis / Daniel Bar-Tal. Thousand Oaks, Calif. :
Sage Publications, c2000. xviii, 211 p. ; 23 cm. Includes
bibliographical references (p. 171-196) and index. ISBN
0-7619-0658-4 (cloth : alk. paper) ISBN 0-7619-0659-2 (pbk. :
alk. paper) DDC 303.3/72
*1. Social perception. 2. Social perception - Israel. 3. Social
psychology. 4. Ethnopsychology. 5. National characteristics. 6.
Social values. 7. Attitude (Psychology) I. Title.*
**TC HM1041 .B37 2000**

**Barber, Antonia, 1932-** Apollo & Daphne :
masterpieces of Greek mythology / retold by Antonia
Barber ; with paintings from great art museums of the
world. Los Angeles : J. Paul Getty Museum, 1998. 45
p. : col. ill. ; 23 x 29 cm. Includes indexes. ISBN 0-89236-
504-8 DDC 753/.7
*1. Mythology, Greek, in art. 2. Painting - Themes, motives. I.
Title. II. Title: Apollo and Daphne*
**TC ND1420 .B37 1998**

**BARBIZON SCHOOL.**
Adams, Steven. The Barbizon school & the origins of
impressionism. 1st ed. London : Phaidon, c1994.
**TC N6847.5.B3 A28 1994**

**The Barbizon school & the origins of impressionism.**
Adams, Steven. 1st ed. London : Phaidon, c1994.
**TC N6847.5.B3 A28 1994**

**Barbizon school and the origins of Impressionism.**
Adams, Steven. The Barbizon school & the origins of
impressionism. 1st ed. London : Phaidon, c1994.
**TC N6847.5.B3 A28 1994**

**BARBIZON SCHOOL - INFLUENCE.**
Adams, Steven. The Barbizon school & the origins of
impressionism. 1st ed. London : Phaidon, c1994.
**TC N6847.5.B3 A28 1994**

**Barbour, Karen, ill.**
Bunting, Eve, 1928- I have an olive tree. 1st ed. New
York : HarperCollins Publishers, c1999.
**TC PZ7.B91527 Iaar 1999**

**BARBUS (GROUP OF ARTISTS). See PAINTING,
MODERN - 19TH CENTURY - FRANCE.**

**Barbuto, Domenica M., 1951-** The American
settlement movement : a bibliography / compiled by
Domenica M. Barbuto. Westport, Conn. : Greenwood
Press, 1999. ix, 123 p. ; 24 cm. (Bibliographies and indexes
in American history, 0742-6828 ; no. 42) Includes indexes.
ISBN 0-313-30756-3 (alk. paper) DDC 016.3625/57/0973
*1. Social settlements - United States - Bibliography. I. Title. II.
Series.*
**TC Z7164.S665 B37 1999**

**Barchers, Suzanne I.** Multicultural folktales : readers
theatre for elementary students / Suzanne I. Barchers.
Englewood, Colo. : Teacher Ideas Press, 2000. xxi, 188
p. : ill. ; 28 cm. Includes bibliographical references (p. xxi).
ISBN 1-56308-760-X DDC 808.5/4
*1. Folklore and children. 2. Tales - Study and teaching
(Elementary) 3. Multicultural education. I. Title.*
**TC GR435.C4 B39 2000**

**Bard, Robert L.** Copyright duration : duration, term
extension, the European Union and the making of
copyright policy / Robert L. Bard, Lewis Kurlantzick.
San Fransisco : Austin & Winfield, 1999. 277 p. ; 24

cm. Includes bibliographical references and index. ISBN
1-57292-131-5 (cloth : alk. paper) DDC 346.7304/82
*1. Copyright - Duration - United States. I. Kurlantzick, Lewis
S. (Lewis Samuel). 1944- II. Title.*
**TC KF3010 .B37 1999**

**Bare hands.**
Moeyaert, Bart. [Blote handen. English] 1st ed.
Asheville, N.C. : Front Street, 1998.
**TC PZ7.M7227 Bar 1998**

**Barer-Stein, Thelma.** You eat what you are : people,
culture and food traditions / by Thelma Barer-Stein.
2nd ed. Toronto : Firefly Books, 1999. 544 p. : maps ; 29
cm. Includes bibliographical references (p. [469]-495) and
index. ISBN 1-55209-365-4 DDC 394.1/2
*1. Food habits. 2. Manners and customs. 3. Food -
Terminology. I. Title.*
**TC GT2850 .B37 1999**

**BARGAINING. See COLLECTIVE
BARGAINING; NEGOTIATION.**

**Bargaining for advantage.**
Shell, G. Richard, 1949- New York : Viking, 1999.
**TC BF637.N4 S44 1999**

**Barker, James R. (James Robert), 1957-** The
discipline of teamwork : participation and concertive
control / James R. Barker. Thousand Oaks, Calif. :
Sage Publications, Inc., c1999. xiv, 207 p. ; 23 cm.
Includes bibliographical references (p. 193-200) and index.
ISBN 0-7619-0369-0 (cloth : alk. paper) ISBN 0-7619-0370-4
(pbk. : alk. paper) DDC 658.4/02
*1. Teams in the workplace. I. Title.*
**TC HD66 .B364 1999**

**Barkley, Russell A., 1949-.**
ADHD [videorecording]. New York, NY : Guilford
Publications, Inc., c1992.
**TC RJ506.H9 A3 1992**

Understanding the defiant child [videorecording].
New York : Guilford Publications, c1997.
**TC HQ755.7 .U63 1997**

**Barlow, Tracie.** The COTA in the schools / Tracie
Barlow, Joanne Pinkava, Laurie L. Gombash. San
Antonio, Texas : Therapy Skill Builders, c1999. vii, 86
p. : ill. ; 23 cm. "Written to assist the certified occupational
therapy assistant (COTA) who is working in the school
system."--Preface, p. vii. Includes bibliographical references
(p. 83-86).
*1. Occupational therapy. 2. Occupational therapy assistants -
Handbooks, manuals.etc. 3. Occupational therapy - Practice. I.
Pinkava, Joanne. II. Gombash, Laurie L. III. Title. IV. Title:
Certified occupational therapy assistant in the schools.*
**TC RM735 .B37 1999**

**Barn savers.**
High, Linda Oatman. 1st ed. Honesdale, Pa. : Caroline
House/Boyds Mills Press, 1999.
**TC PZ7.H543968 Bar 1999**

**Barnard, Malcolm, 1958-** Art, design, and visual
culture : an introduction / Malcolm Barnard. New
York : St. Martin's Press, 1998. xii, 214 p. : ill. ; 23 cm.
Includes bibliographical references (p. 201-207) and index.
ISBN 0-312-21691-2 (cloth) ISBN 0-312-21692-0 (pbk.) DDC
701
*1. Artists - Psychology. 2. Creation (Literary, artistic, etc.) 3.
Visual communication. 4. Art and society. 5. Art patronage. I.
Title.*
**TC N71 .B32 1998**

**Barnes, Barbara.** Schools transformed for the 21st
century : the abc's of EFG / Barbara Barnes.
Torrance, Calif. : Griffin Pub. Group, c1999. 104 p. ; 22
cm. ISBN 1-58060-052-5 DDC 370/.973
*1. EFG Curriculum Collaborative. 2. Educational change -
United States. 3. Environmental education - United States. 4.
Multicultural education - United States. 5. Creative ability in
children. 6. Education - United States - Curricula. 7.
Instructional systems - United States. I. Title. II. Title: Schools
transformed for the twenty-first century*
**TC LA217.2 .B39 1999**

**Barnes, Colin, 1946-** Exploring disability : a
sociological introduction / Colin Barnes, Geof Mercer,
and Tom Shakespeare. Cambridge, UK : Polity Press ;
Malden, MA : Blackwell Publishers, 1999. vi, 280 p. :
ill. ; 24 cm. Includes bibliographical references (p. [228]-260)
and index. ISBN 0-7456-1477-9 (hardcover) ISBN
0-7456-1478-7 (pbk.) DDC 305.9/0816
*1. Sociology of disability. 2. Handicapped - Research. 3.
Handicapped - Government policy. I. Mercer, G. (Geoffrey) II.
Shakespeare, Tom. III. Title.*
**TC HV1568 .B35 1999**

**Barnes-Svarney, Patricia L.** The Oryx guide to natural
history : the earth and all its inhabitants / by Patricia
Barnes-Svarney and Thomas E. Svarney. Phoenix,
Ariz. : Oryx Press, 1999. xi, 252 p. : ill. ; 29 cm. Includes

bibliographical references (p. 221-222) and index. ISBN 1-57356-159-2 (alk. paper) DDC 508
*1. Natural history. I. Svarney, Thomas E. II. Title.*
***TC QH45.2 .B37 1999***

**Barnett, David W., 1946-.**
**Designing interventions for preschool learning and behavior problems.**
Barnett, David W., 1946- Designing preschool interventions. New York : Guilford Press, 1999.
***TC LC4801 .B36 1999***

Designing preschool interventions : a practitioner's guide / David W. Barnett, Susan H. Bell, Karen T. Carey. New York : Guilford Press, 1999. xvii, 380 p. ; 24 cm. (The Guilford school practitioner series) Rev. ed. of: Designing interventions for preschool learning and behavior problems. 1st ed. c1992. Includes bibliographical references (p. 315-356) and index. ISBN 1-57230-491-X DDC 649/.153
*1. Problem children - Education (Preschool) 2. Behavior disorders in children. 3. Behavior modification. 4. Socialization. I. Bell, Susan H. II. Carey, Karen T., 1952- III. Barnett, David W., 1946- Designing interventions for preschool learning and behavior problems. IV. Title. V. Series.*
***TC LC4801 .B36 1999***

**Barnett, Ronald, 1947-** Realizing the university in an age of supercomplexity / Ronald Barnett. Philadelphia, PA : Society for Research into Higher Education & Open University Press, 1999. 200 p. ; 23 cm. Includes bibliographical references and index. ISBN 0-335-20249-7 (hard) ISBN 0-335-20248-9 (pbk.) DDC 378/.01
*1. Education, Higher - Aims and objectives. 2. Universities and colleges - Philosophy. 3. Postmodernism and education. I. Title.*
***TC LB2322.2 .B37 1999***

**Barney, Richard A., 1955-** Plots of enlightenment : education and the novel in eighteenth-century England / Richard A. Barney. Stanford, Calif. : Stanford University Press, c1999. xii, 402 p. : ill. ; 23 cm. Includes bibliographical references (p. 363-383) and index. ISBN 0-8047-2978-6 (alk. paper) DDC 823/.509355
*1. English fiction - 18th century - History and criticism. 2. Education in literature. 3. Psychological fiction, English - History and criticism. 4. Didactic fiction, English - History and criticism. 5. Education - England - History - 18th century. 6. Maturation (Psychology) in literature. 7. Knowledge, Theory of, in literature. 8. Enlightenment - England. 9. Bildungsroman. I. Title.*
***TC PR858.E38 B37 1999***

**Barnhouse, Rebecca.** Recasting the past : the Middle Ages in young adult literature / Rebecca Barnhouse. Portsmouth, NH : Boynton/Cook Publishers, c2000. xvii, 103 p. ; 23 cm. (Young adult literature series) Includes bibliographical references (p. 92-99) and index. CONTENTS: Manuscripts and medicine : portrayals of books, literacy, and knowledge -- Fidelity to the infidel : religion and religious diversity -- Tales and their tellers : medieval literature in modern dress -- Saxons and Normans -- Saints and sinners : historical figures fictionalized -- Of commoners and kings : medievalism in fantasy novels -- Into the classroom. ISBN 0-86709-470-2
*1. Middle Ages in literature. 2. Medievalism in literature. 3. Young adult fiction - History and criticism. 4. Middle Ages in literature - Study and teaching. 5. Young adult fiction - Study and teaching. I. Title. II. Series: Young adult literature series (Portsmouth, N.H.).*
***TC PN3443 .B37 2000***

**Barnicle, Katherine Ann.** Evaluation of the interaction between users of screen reading technology and graphical user interface elements / Katherine Ann Barnicle. 1999. vi, 201 leaves ; 29 cm. Issued also on microfilm. Includes tables. Thesis (Ph. D.)--Columbia University, 1999. Includes bibliographical references (leaves 138-144)
*1. Microcomputers. 2. Graphical user interfaces (Computer systems) 3. Online data processing. 4. Internet (Computer network) 5. Visually handicapped. 6. Computers and the handicapped. I. Title.*
***TC 085 B265***

**BARNS - UNITED STATES - CONSERVATION AND RESTORATION - JUVENILE LITERATURE.**
High, Linda Oatman. Barn savers. 1st ed. Honesdale, Pa. : Caroline House/Boyds Mills Press, 1999.
***TC PZ7.H543968 Bar 1999***

**BARNS - UNITED STATES - HISTORY.**
High, Linda Oatman. Barn savers. 1st ed. Honesdale, Pa. : Caroline House/Boyds Mills Press, 1999.
***TC PZ7.H543968 Bar 1999***

**BARNS - UNITED STATES - HISTORY - JUVENILE FICTION.**
High, Linda Oatman. Barn savers. 1st ed. Honesdale, Pa. : Caroline House/Boyds Mills Press, 1999.
***TC PZ7.H543968 Bar 1999***

**Barnsley and Partners.**
Spon's building costs guide for educational premises. 2nd ed. London : E & FN SPON, 1999.
***TC LB3219.G7 S67 1999***

**Baroff, George S.** Mental retardation : nature, cause, and management / George S. Baroff with J. Gregory Olley. 3rd ed. Philadelphia, Pa. : Brunner/Mazel, c1999. xii, 497 p. : ill. ; 24 cm. Includes bibliographical references (p. 433-483) and index. ISBN 1-58391-000-X (case : alk. paper) ISBN 1-58391-001-8 (pbk. : alk. paper) DDC 616.85/88
*1. Mental retardation. 2. Mentally handicapped - Care. 3. Mental retardation. 4. Mental Retardation. I. Olley, J. Gregory. II. Title.*
***TC RC570 .B27 1999***

**Baron, Naomi S.** Alphabet to email : how written English evolved and where it's heading / Naomi S. Baron. London ; New York : Routledge, 2000. xiv, 316 p. : ill. ; 24 cm. Includes bibliographical references (p. 285-304) and indexes. ISBN 0-415-18685-4 DDC 421/.1
*1. English language - Written English - History. 2. Written communication - English-speaking countries - History. I. Title.*
***TC PE1075 .B28 2000***

**Barone, Diane M.** Resilient children : stories of poverty, drug exposure, and literacy development / Diane Barone. Newark, Del. : International Reading Association ; Chicago : National Reading Conference, c1999. xiii, 241 p. : ill. ; 24 cm. (Literacy studies series) Includes bibliographical references (p. 221-231) and indexes. ISBN 0-87207-199-5 DDC 371.91
*1. Children of prenatal substance abuse - Education (Primary) - Illinois - Chicago - Case studies. 2. Poor children - Education (Primary) - Illinois - Chicago - Case studies. 3. Reading (Primary) - Illinois - Chicago - Case studies. 4. Literacy - Illinois - Chicago - Case studies. I. Title. II. Series.*
***TC LC4806.4 .B37 1999***

**Barone, Tom.** Aesthetics, politics, and educational inquiry : essays and examples / Tom Barone ; foreword by William F. Pinar. New York : P. Lang, 2000. xxi, 266 p. ; 23 cm. (Counterpoints, 1058-1634 ; vol. 117) Includes bibliographical references. ISBN 0-8204-4520-7 (alk. paper) DDC 370/.7/2
*1. Education - Research - Methodology. 2. Education - Research - Social aspects. 3. Education - Philosophy. 4. Postmodernism and education. 5. Aesthetics. 6. Literature - History and criticism - Theory, etc. I. Title. II. Series: Counterpoints (New York, N.Y.) ; vol. 117.*
***TC LB1028 .B345 2000***

**Baroody, Arthur J., 1947-** Fostering children's mathematical power : an investigative approach to K-8 mathematics instruction / Arthur J. Baroody with Ronald T. Coslick. Mahwah, N.J. : Lawrence Erlbaum Associates, 1998. 1 v. (various pagings) : ill. ; 28 cm. Includes bibliographical references and indexes. ISBN 0-8058-3105-3 (pbk. : acid-free paper) DDC 372.7/044
*1. Mathematics - Study and teaching (Elementary) I. Coslick, Ronald T. II. Title.*
***TC QA135.5 .B2847 1998***

**Barr, Beryl.** Wonders, warriors, and beasts abounding. Foreword by Thomas P. F. Hoving. [1st ed.]. Garden City, N.Y., Doubleday [1967] 128 p. : ill. (part col.) ; 29 cm. DDC 704
*1. Grotesque in art - Juvenile literature. I. Title.*
***TC N8217.G8 B33***

**Barr, Catherine, 1951-.**
Reading in series. New Providence, N.J. : R.R. Bowker, c1999.
***TC Z1037 .R36 1999***

**Barr, Jeanine R.**
Communication in recovery. Cresskill, N.J. : Hampton Press, c1999.
***TC HV4998 .C64 1999***

**Barr, Margaret J.** The handbook of student affairs administration / Margaret J. Barr, Mary K. Desler, and associates. 2nd ed. San Francisco : Jossey-Bass, c2000. xxxv, 661 p. ; 24 cm. (The Jossey-Bass higher and adult education series) Includes bibliographical references and indexes. ISBN 0-7879-4720-2 (acid-free paper) DDC 378.1/94/0973
*1. Student affairs services - United States. 2. Student activities - United States - Management. I. Desler, Mary K. II. Title. III. Title: Student affairs administration IV. Series.*
***TC LB2342.92 .B37 2000***

**Barr, Mary A. (Mary Anderson)** Assessing literacy with the Learning Record : a handbook for teachers, grades 6-12 / Mary A. Barr and Margaret Syverson ; Anne McKittrick, editorial assitant. Portsmouth, NH : Heinemann, c1999. xii, 97 p. : ill. ; 28 cm. Rev. ed. of: The Learning Record, c1998. Includes bibliographical references (p. 95-97). ISBN 0-325-00118-9 (alk. paper)
*1. Portfolios in education - California - Handbooks, manuals, etc. 2. Academic achievement - California - Evaluation - Handbooks, manuals, etc. 3. Education, Secondary - California - Evaluation - Handbooks, manuals, etc. 4. Literacy - California - Evaluation - Handbooks, manuals, etc. I. Syverson, Margaret A., 1948- II. McKittrick, Anne. III. Barr, Mary A. (Mary Anderson). Learning Record. IV. Title.*
***TC LB1029.P67 B37 1999***

Assessing literacy with the Learning Record. Portsmouth, NH : Heinemann, c1999.
***TC LB1029.P67 B37 1999b***

**Learning Record.**
Assessing literacy with the Learning Record. Portsmouth, NH : Heinemann, c1999.
***TC LB1029.P67 B37 1999b***

Barr, Mary A. (Mary Anderson) Assessing literacy with the Learning Record. Portsmouth, NH : Heinemann, c1999.
***TC LB1029.P67 B37 1999***

**Barr, Rebecca.**
Handbook of reading research. New York : Longman, c1984-<2000 >
***TC LB1050 .H278 2000***

**Barr, Robert D.**
**Hope at last for at risk youth.**
Barr, Robert D. Hope fulfilled for at-risk and violent youth. 2nd ed. Boston ; London : Allyn and Bacon, c2001.
***TC LC4802 .B37 2001***

Hope fulfilled for at-risk and violent youth : K-12 programs that work / Robert D. Barr, William H. Parrett. 2nd ed. Boston ; London : Allyn and Bacon, c2001. xiv, 306 p. : ill. ; 25 cm. Rev. ed. of: Hope at last for at-risk youth. c1995. Includes bibliographical references (p. 258-284) and index. ISBN 0-205-30886-4 DDC 371.93
*1. Problem children - Education - United States. 2. Problem youth - Education - United States. 3. Socially handicapped children - Education - United States. 4. Socially handicapped youth - Education - United States. I. Parrett, William. II. Barr, Robert D. Hope at last for at-risk youth. III. Title.*
***TC LC4802 .B37 2001***

**Barrentine, Shelby J.**
Reading assessment. Newark, Del. : International Reading Association, c1999.
***TC LB1573 .R2793 1999***

**Barrett, Carolyn M., 1941-** The magic of Matsumoto : the Suzuki method of education / by Carolyn M. Barrett. Palm Springs, CA : ETC Publications, c1995. 154 p. ; 24 cm. Includes bibliographical references (p. 151-154). ISBN 0-88280-126-0 DDC 780/.7
*1. Music - Instruction and study - Juvenile. 2. Suzuki, Shin'ichi, - 1898- I. Title.*
***TC MT1 .B325 1995***

**Barrett, Kate R.**
Allison, Pamela C. Constructing children's physical education experiences. Boston : Allyn and Bacon, 2000.
***TC GV363 .A512 2000***

**Barron, Ann E.** The Internet and instruction : activities and ideas / Ann E. Barron, Karen S. Ivers. 2nd ed. Englewood, Colo. : Libraries Unlimited, 1998. xi, 244 p. : ill. ; 28 cm. Includes bibliographical references and indexes. ISBN 1-56308-613-1 DDC 371.33/4678
*1. Teaching - Computer network resources. 2. Education - Computer network resources. 3. Internet (Computer network) in education. 4. Computer managed instruction. I. Ivers, Karen S. II. Title.*
***TC LB1044.87 .B37 1998***

**Barron, James W., 1944-.**
Humor and psyche. Hillsdale, NJ : Analytic Press, c1999.
***TC BF175 .H85 1999***

**Barron, Stephanie, 1950-.**
Exiles + emigrés. Los Angeles, Calif. : Los Angeles County Museum of Art ; New York : H.N. Abrams, c1997.
***TC N6512 .E887 1997***

**Barrs, Myra.**
Dombey, Henrietta. Whole to part phonics. London : Centre for Language in Primary Education : Language Matters, c1998.
***TC LB1573.3 .D66 1998***

**Barry, Judith, 1949-.**
De Salvo, Donna M. Past imperfect. Southampton, N.Y. : Parrish Art Museum, in association with the New Press, New York, N.Y., c1993.
***TC N750 .D4***

**Barter, Judith A., 1951-.**
Cassatt, Mary, 1844-1926. Mary Cassatt, modern woman. 1st ed. New York : Art Institute of Chicago in association with H.N. Abrams, c1998.
*TC N6537.C35 A4 1998*

**BARTHOLDI, FR ED-ERIC AUGUSTE, 1834-1904.**
Maestro, Betsy. The story of the Statue of Liberty. New York : Lothrop, Lee & Shepard Books, 1986.
*TC NB553.B3 A75 1986*

**BARTHOLDI, FRÉDÉRIC AUGUSTE, 1834-1904 - JUVENILE LITERATURE.**
Maestro, Betsy. The story of the Statue of Liberty. New York : Lothrop, Lee & Shepard Books, 1986.
*TC NB553.B3 A75 1986*

**Bartlett, culture and cognition** / edited by Akiko Saito. [London] : Psychology Press ; [New York] : [Routledge], 2000. xvii, 284 p. ; 24 cm. Includes bibliographical references (p. 219-271) and indexes. ISBN 0-415-20172-1 DDC 153
*1. Cognition and culture. I. Saito, Akiko, 1964-*
*TC BF311 .B2885 2000*

**Bartlett, Peter L., 1966-.**
Anthony, Martin. Neural network learning. Cambridge, U.K. ; New York : Cambridge University Press, 1999.
*TC QA76.87 .A58 1999*

**Bartlett, Randall, 1945-** The crisis of America's cities / Randall Bartlett. Armonk, N.Y. : M.E. Sharpe, c1998. xiii, 290 p. ; 24 cm. Includes bibliographical references (p. 279-283) and index. ISBN 0-7656-0301-2 (alk. paper) ISBN 0-7656-0302-0 (pbk. : alk. paper) DDC 307.76/0973
*1. Cities and towns - United States. 2. Cities and towns - United States - History. 3. Urban policy - United States. I. Title.*
*TC HT123 .B324 1998*

**Bartolomé, Lilia I.**
Macedo, Donaldo P. (Donaldo Pereira), 1950- Dancing with bigotry. New York : St. Martin's Press, 1999.
*TC LC196.5.U6 D26 1999*

The misteaching of academic discourses : the politics of language in the classroom / Lilia I. Bartolomé. Boulder, Colo. : Westview Press, 1998. xvi, 139 p. : ill. ; 24 cm. (The edge, critical studies in educational theory) Includes bibliographical references (p. 123-133) and index. ISBN 0-8133-3144-7 (hardcover : alk. paper) DDC./1/4
*1. Communication in education - Social aspects - United States. 2. Socially handicapped children - Education - United States. 3. Language and education - Social aspects - United States. 4. Teaching - Social aspects - United States. 5. Critical pedagogy - United States. 6. Multiculturalism - United States. I. Title. II. Series.*
*TC LB1033.5 .B37 1998*

**Barton, Byron, ill.**
Weeks, Sarah. Little factory. 1st ed. [New York] : Laura Geringer book, c1998.
*TC PZ7.W4125 Li 1998*

**Barton, David, 1949-.**
Situated literacies. London ; New York : Routledge, 2000.
*TC LC149 .S52 2000*

**Barton, Harriett, ill.**
Knowlton, Jack. Maps & globes. New York : HarperCollins, c1985.
*TC GA105.6 .K58 1985*

**Bartus, Raymond.**
Assessment in geriatric psychopharmacology. New Canaan, Conn. : Mark Powley Associates, 1983.
*TC WT150 .A846 1983*

**Baruth, Leroy G.**
Manning, M. Lee. Multicultural education of children and adolescents. 3rd ed. Boston : Allyn and Bacon, c2000.
*TC LC1099.3 .M36 2000*

**Barzilai, Shuli.** Lacan and the matter of origins / Shuli Barzilai. Stanford, Calif. : Stanford University Press, 1999. x, 300 p. ; 23 cm. Includes bibliographical references (p. [271]-287) and index. ISBN 0-8047-3381-3 (alk. paper) ISBN 0-8047-3382-1 (pbk. : alk. paper) DDC 150.19/5
*1. Lacan, Jacques, - 1901- 2. Psychoanalysis. I. Title.*
*TC BF17 .B2145 1999*

**Barzun, Jacques, 1907-** From dawn to decadence : 500 years of western cultural life : 1500 to the present / Jacques Barzun. 1st ed. New York : HarperCollins, c2000. xviii, 877 p. ; 24 cm. Includes bibliographical references (p. [803]-828) and indexes. ISBN 0-06-017586-9 DDC 940.2
*1. Civilization, Western. 2. Europe - Intellectual life. 3.*

Europe - Civilization. 4. Learning and scholarship - History. I. Title.
*TC CB245 .B365 2000*

**Barzyk, Fred.**
Connect with English [videorecording]. S. Burlington, Vt. : The Annenberg/CPB Collection. c1997.
*TC PE1128 .C66 1997*

**BAS-RELIEF.** *See* SCULPTURE.

**BASAL GANGLIA - DISEASES.** *See* ALZHEIMER'S DISEASE.

**BASE-BALL.** *See* BASEBALL.

**BASEBALL - FICTION.**
Jones, Jennifer B. Dear Mrs. Ryan, you're ruining my life. New York : Walker & Co., 2000.
*TC PZ7.J7203 De 2000*

McCully, Emily Arnold. Mouse practice. 1st ed. New York : Arthur A. Levine Books/Scholastic Press, 1999.
*TC PZ7.M13913 Mo 1999*

**BASES, MILITARY.** *See* MILITARY BASES.

**Basic and clinical science of mental and addictive disorders** / volume editors, L.L. Judd, B. Saletu, V. Filip. Basel ; New York : Karger, c1997. xiii, 258 p. : ill. (some col.) ; 25 cm. (Bibliotheca psychiatrica ; no. 167) Proceedings from the Collegium Internationale Neuro-psychopharmacologicum (CINP) Regional Conference held on July 10-14, 1995 in Vienna and Prague. Includes bibliographical references and indexes. ISBN 3-8055-6385-X (hardcover : acid-free paper) DDC 616.86
*1. Psychiatry - Congresses. 2. Mental Disorders - diagnosis - congresses. 3. Mental Disorders - therapy - congresses. 4. Behavior, Addictive - diagnosis - congresses. 5. Behavior, Addictive - therapy - congresses. I. Judd, Lewis L. II. Saletu, Bernd. III. Filip, V. (Vaclav) IV. Collegium Internationale Neuro-psychopharmacologicum. Regional Conference (1995 : Vienna, Austria, and Prague, Czech Republic) V. Series.*
*TC RC327 .B37 1997*

**Basic background for test interpretation.**
Christiansen, Harley Duane. 1st ed. Tucson, Ariz. : P. Juul Press, c1981.
*TC BF176 .C472*

**Basic behavioral science**
Interpersonal psychotherapy for group. New York : Basic Books, 2000.
*TC RC489.I55 I584 2000*

Shapiro, David, 1926- Dynamics of character. New York : Basic Books, c2000.
*TC RC455.4.T45 .S46 2000*

**Basic decimals [videorecording].**
Decimals [videorecording]. Princeton, N.J. : Video Tutor, 1988.
*TC QA117 .D4 1988*

**BASIC EDUCATION.**
Shapiro, Edward S. (Edward Steven), 1951- Academic skills problems workbook. New York : Guilford Press, c1996.
*TC LB1029.R4 S52 1996*

**BASIC EDUCATION - INDIA.**
Public report on basic education in India. New Delhi ; Oxford : Oxford University Press, c1999.
*TC LA1151 .P83 1999*

**Basic English: English as a second language [videorecording].**
Basic English [videorecording]. [Roslyn Heights, N.Y.] : Video Aided Instruction, [c1995].
*TC PE1128 .B3 1995*

**Basic English** [videorecording] : ESL / [presented by] Video Aided Instruction, Inc. ; produced and directed by Peter Lanzer, Mona E. Lanzer. [Roslyn Heights, N.Y.] : Video Aided Instruction, [c1995]. 2 videocassettes (240 min.) : sd., col. ; 1/2 in. + 1 exercise booklet (62 p. ; 19 cm.). (English as a second language series) Title from container: Basic English: English as a second language [videorecording]. At head of title: Video Aided Instruction, Inc. presents Basic English [videorecording]. VHS. Catalogued from credits and container. Instructor, William W. Jex. For English-as-a-second-language students. SUMMARY: Thirty-five lesson course in basic English. Each lesson contains instruction in listening, speaking, reading, and writing. Designed for native speakers of other languages who want to learn English correctly and easily. ISBN 1-57385-001-2 (vols. 1 and 2) ISBN 1-57385-000-4 (booklet)
*1. English language - Self-instruction. 2. English language - Study and teaching - Foreign speakers - Audio-visual aids. 3. English language - Grammar. I. Lanzer, Peter. II. Lanzer, Mona E. III. Jex, William W. IV. Video Aided Instruction, Inc. V. Title: ESL [videorecording] VI. Title: Basic English: English as a second language [videorecording] VII. Title:*

Video Aided Instruction, Inc. presents Basic English [videorecording] VIII. Series: English as a second language (Roslyn Heights, N.Y.)
*TC PE1128 .B3 1995*

**Basic facts and figures (Unesco).**
[Statistical yearbook (Unesco)] Statistical yearbook = [Paris : Unesco], 1987-
*TC AZ361 .U45*

**Basic fractions [videorecording].**
Fractions [videorecording]. Princeton, N.J. : Video Tutor, 1988.
*TC QA117 .F7 1988*

**Basic geometry [videorecording].**
The high school proficiency test [videorecording]. Princeton, N.J. : Video Tutor, 1988.
*TC QA445 .H5 1988*

**BASIC NEEDS.** *See* POVERTY; QUALITY OF LIFE.

**Basic number concepts [videorecording].**
Number concepts [videorecording]. Princeton, N.J. : Video Tutor, 1988.
*TC QA117 .N8 1988*

Number concepts [videorecording]. Princeton, N.J. : Video Tutor, 1988.
*TC QA117 .N8 1988*

**Basic percents [videorecording].**
Percents [videorecording]. Princeton, N.J. : Video Tutor, 1988.
*TC QA117.P4 1988*

**Basic pre-algebra [videorecording].**
Percents [videorecording]. Princeton, N.J. : Video Tutor, 1988.

Pre-algebra [videorecording]. Princeton, N.J. : Video Tutor, 1988.
*TC QA152.2 .P6 1988*

**BASIC RIGHTS.** *See* CIVIL RIGHTS; HUMAN RIGHTS.

**BASIC SKILLS EDUCATION.** *See* BASIC EDUCATION.

**Basic structure of work-relevant abilities.**
Prediger, D. J. Iowa City, Iowa : ACT, 1998.
*TC LB3051 .A3 no. 98-9*

**Basic word problems [videorecording].**
Word problems [videorecording]. Princeton, N.J. : Video Tutor, 1988.
*TC QA139 .W6 1988*

**Basics in scope and sequence of a multi-sensory approach to language arts for specific language disability children.**
Slingerland, Beth H. A multi-sensory approach to language arts for specific language disability children. Cambridge, Mass. : Educators Pub. Service, c1976-<c1981 >
*TC LC4704.85 .S59 1976*

**Basile, Michael L., 1943-** The deployment of educational innovation through foreign aid : an inquiry into America's developmental ideology / by Michael L. Basile. 1989. xiii, 307 leaves, bound ; 29 cm. Thesis (Ed. D.)--University of Massachusetts at Amherst, 1989. Photocopy. Ann Arbor, Mich., : University Microfilms International, 1996. Bibliography: leaves [294]-307.
*1. United States. - Agency for International Development. 2. Educational innovations. 3. United States - International relations. I. Title.*
*TC LD3234.M267 B32 1989*

**BASKETS - CALIFORNIA.** *See* POMO BASKETS.

**BASKETS, POMO.** *See* POMO BASKETS.

**Baskin, Leonard, 1922- ill.**
Michelson, Richard. A book of flies. New York : Cavendish Children's Books, 1999.
*TC PS3563.I34 B66 1999*

**Baskin, Yvonne.** The work of nature : how the diversity of life sustains us / Yvonne Baskin. Washington, D.C. : Island Press, 1997. xix, 263 p. : ill. ; 24 cm. "A project of SCOPE, the Scientific Committee on Problems of the Environment." Includes bibliographical references and index. ISBN 1-55963-519-3 (cloth) DDC 333.7/2
*1. Environmentalism. 2. Biological diversity. 3. Human ecology. 4. Conservation of natural resources. I. International Council of Scientific Unions. Scientific Committee on Problems of the Environment. II. Title.*
*TC GE195 .B36 1997*

**Basmajian, Silva.**
First break [videorecording]. Boston, MA : Fanlight Productions, c1997.

*TC RC465 .F5 1997*

First break [videorecording]. Boston, MA : Fanlight Productions, c1997.
*TC RC465 .F5 1997*

First break [videorecording]. Boston, MA : Fanlight Productions, c1997.
*TC RC465 .F5 1997*

**Bass, Hyman, 1932-.**
Algebra, K-theory, groups, and education. Providence, R.I. : American Mathematical Society, c1999.
*TC QA150 .A419 1999*

**Bassett, Angela.**
Africans in America [videorecording]. [Boston, Mass.] : WGBH Educational Foundation : South Burlington, VT : WGBH Boston Video [distributor], c1998.
*TC E441 .A47 1998*

**Bassey, Magnus O.** Western education and political domination in Africa : a study in critical and dialogical pedagogy / Magnus O. Bassey. Westport, CT : Bergin & Garvey, 1999. viii, 168 p. ; 25 cm. Includes bibliographical references (p. [145]-158 and index. ISBN 0-89789-622-X (alk. paper) DDC 379.6
  *1. Politics and education - Africa - History. 2. Education - Africa - Western influences. 3. Africa - Civilization - Western influences. 4. Elite (Social sciences) - Africa. 5. Critical pedagogy - Africa. I. Title.*
*TC LC95.A2 B37 1999*

**Bassey, Michael.** Case study research in educational settings / Michael Bassey. Buckingham [England] ; Philadelphia : Open University Press, 1999. xii, 178 p. : ill. ; 23 cm. (Doing qualitative research in educational settings) Includes bibliographical references (p. [174]-176) and index. ISBN 0-335-19984-4 (pbk.) ISBN 0-335-19985-2 (hard) DDC 370/.72
  *1. Education - Research - Great Britain - Methodology. 2. Case method. I. Title. II. Series.*
*TC LB1028.25.G7 B37 1999*

**Basso, Anna.**
Aphasia in atypical populations. Mahwah, N.J. : Lawrence Erlbaum Associates, 1998.
*TC RC425 .A637 1998*

**Bastian, Misty L., 1955-.**
Great ideas for teaching about Africa. Boulder : Lynne Rienner, 1999.
*TC DT19.9.U5 G74 1999*

**Bat-Ami, Miriam.** Two suns in the sky / Miriam Bat-Ami. 1st ed. [Chicago, IL] : Front Street/Cricket Books, 1999. 223 p. ; 22 cm. ISBN 0-8126-2900-0 DDC [Fic]
  *1. Refugees. Jewish - New York (State) - Oswego - Juvenile fiction. 2. Fort Ontario Emergency Refugee Shelter - Juvenile fiction. 3. Jews - New York (State) - Oswego - Juvenile fiction. 4. Holocaust survivors - United States - Juvenile fiction. 5. World War, 1939-1945 - Jews - Rescue - Juvenile fiction. 6. Holocaust survivors - Fiction. 7. Refugees - Fiction. 8. Prejudices - Fiction. 9. Fort Ontario Emergency Refugee Shelter - Fiction. 10. Jews - United States - Fiction. I. Title.*
*TC PZ7.B2939 Tw 1999*

**Bateman, Barbara D., joint author.**
Kirk, Samuel Alexander, 1904- 10 years of research at the Institute for Research on Exceptional Children, University of Illinois, 1952-1962. [Urbana : s.n.], 1964.
*TC HQ773.7 .I4 1964*

**Bates, Ivan, ill.**
McBratney, Sam. The dark at the top of the stairs. 1st U.S. ed. Cambridge, Mass. : Candlewick Press, c1996.
*TC PZ7.M47826 DAr 1996*

**Bates, Jane K.** Becoming an art teacher / Jane K. Bates. Belmont, CA : Wadsworth/Thomson Learning, 2000. xv, 316 p. : ill. ; 28 cm. Includes bibliographical references and index. ISBN 0-534-52239-4 DDC 707/.12
  *1. Art - Study and teaching (Elementary) - United States. 2. Art - Study and teaching (Secondary) - United States. I. Title.*
*TC N353 .B38 2000*

**Bates, Robin.**
Fate of the earth [videorecording]. [New York, N.Y.?] : Unapix Entertainment, Inc. [distributor], c1996.
*TC QB631.2 .F3 1996*

Tales from other worlds [videorecording]. [New York, N.Y.?] : Unapix Entertainment, Inc. [distributor], c1996.
*TC QB631.2 .T3 1996*

Tales from other worlds [videorecording]. [New York, N.Y.?] : Unapix Entertainment, Inc. [distributor], c1996.

*TC QB631.2 .T3 1996*

**Bates, Timothy Mason.** Race, self-employment, and upward mobility : an illusive American dream / Timothy Bates. Washington, D.C. : Woodrow Wilson Center Press ; Baltimore : Johns Hopkins University Press, c1997. x, 288 p. ; 24 cm. Includes bibliographical references (p. 275-283) and index. ISBN 0-8018-5798-8 (alk. paper) DDC 331.6/3/0973
  *1. Self-employed Afro-Americans. 2. Self-employed Asian Americans. 3. Occupational mobility - United States. I. Title.*
*TC HD8037.U5 B384 1997*

**BATESON, GREGORY - PHOTOGRAPH COLLECTIONS.**
Sullivan, Gerald. Margaret Mead, Gregory Bateson, and Highland Bali. Chicago, IL : University of Chicago Press, 1999.
*TC GN635.I65 S948 1999*

**Bateson, P. P. G. (Paul Patrick Gordon), 1938-**
Design for a life : how behavior and personality develop / Patrick Bateson and Paul Martin. New York ; London : Simon & Schuster c2000. 271 p. ; 25 cm. "First published in the United Kingdom in 1999, by Jonathan Cape"--T.p. verso. Includes bibliographical references (p. [237]-254) and index. ISBN 0-684-86932-2 DDC 155.2/34
  *1. Nature and nurture. I. Martin, Paul R., 1951- II. Title.*
*TC BF341 .B37 2000*

**BATHS.** *See* **SWIMMING POOLS.**

**Batioukova, Z. I.**
Innovation in Russian schools. Bloomington, Ind. : Phi Delta Kappa Educational Foundation, c1997.
*TC LB1027 .I6575 1997*

**BATTERED CHILD SYNDROME.** *See* **ABUSED CHILDREN.**

**BATTERED CHILDREN.** *See* **ABUSED CHILDREN.**

**BATTERED WIVES.** *See* **ABUSED WIVES.**

**BATTERED WOMAN SYNDROME.** *See* **ABUSED WOMEN.**

**BATTERED WOMAN SYNDROME - UNITED STATES.**
Gordon, Judith S., 1958- Helping survivors of domestic violence. New York : Garland Pub., 1998.
*TC HV6626.2 .G67 1998*

**BATTERED WOMEN.** *See* **ABUSED WOMEN.**

**Batteries, bulbs, and wires.**
Ward, Alan, 1932- Experimenting with batteries, bulbs, and wires. New York : Chelsea Juniors, c1991.
*TC QC527.2 .W37 1991*

**Battinelli, Thomas.** Physique, fitness, and performance / Thomas Battinelli. Boca Raton : CRC Press, c2000. xix, 258 p. : ill. ; 24 cm. (CRC series in exercise physiology) Includes bibliographical references and index. ISBN 0-8493-0231-5 (alk. paper) DDC 613.7
  *1. Exercise - Physiological aspects. 2. Somatotypes. 3. Physical fitness. I. Title. II. Series.*
*TC QP301 .B364 2000*

**Bauböck, Rainer.**
The challenge of diversity. Aldershot, England : Brookfield, Vt. : Avebury, 1996.
*TC JV225 .C530 1996*

**Bauer, Anne M.** Inclusion 101 : how to teach all learners / Anne M. Bauer and Thomas M. Shea. Baltimore, Md. : P.H. Brookes Pub., c1999. xix, 324 p. : ill. ; 26 cm. Includes bibliographical references and index. ISBN 1-55766-372-6 DDC 371.102
  *1. Inclusive education - United States. 2. Classroom management - United States. 3. School management and organization - United States. I. Shea, Thomas M., 1934- II. Title. III. Title: Inclusion one hundred one IV. Title: Inclusion one hundred and one*
*TC LC1201 .B38 1999*

**Bauer, David G.** Technology funding for schools / David G. Bauer. 1st ed. San Francisco : Jossey-Bass, c2000. xv, 222 p. : ill., forms ; 28 cm. + 1 disk (3 1/2 in.). Includes bibliographical references (p. 209-222). System requirements: IBM. ISBN 0-7879-5040-8 DDC 370/.68/1
  *1. Education - Data processing - Finance. 2. Internet (Computer network) in education - United States - Finance. 3. High technology and education - United States - Finance. 4. Educational fund raising - United States. I. Title.*
*TC LB1028.43 .B38 2000*

**Bauer, Marianne, 1940-.**
Transforming universities. London ; Philadelphia : Jessica Kingsley Publishers, 1999.
*TC LA908 .T73 1999*

**Baumann, James F.**
Hoffman, James V. Balancing principles for teaching elementary reading. Mahwah, N.J. : L. Erlbaum Associates, c2000.
*TC LB1573 . H459 2000*

**Baumeister, Roy F.**
The self in social psychology. Philadelphia : Hove [England] : Psychology Press, c1999.
*TC HM1033 .S45 1999*

**Baur, Karla.**
Crooks, Robert, 1941- Our sexuality. 7th ed. Pacific Grove, CA : Brooks/Cole Pub. Co., c1999.
*TC HQ21 .C698 1999*

**Baussy, Didier.**
Matisse, voyages [videorecording]. [Chicago, Ill.] : Home Vision ; [S.l.] : Distributed worldwide by RM Associates, c1989.
*TC ND553.M37 M37 1989*

Picasso [videorecording]. Chicago, IL : Home Vision, c1986.
*TC N6853.P5 P52 1986*

**Bavaria (Germany). Königl. Staatsministerium des Innern für Kirchen- und Schulangelegenheiten. Ministerialblatt für Kirchen- und Schul-Angelegenheiten im Königreich Bayern.**
Bavaria (Germany). Staatsministerium für Unterricht und Kultus. Amtsblatt des Staatsministeriums für Unterricht und Kultus. München : Das Ministerium, 1918-

**Bavaria (Germany). Staatsministerium für Unterricht, Kultus, Wissenschaft und Kunst.**
Amtsblatt des Bayerischen Staatsministeriums für Unterricht, Kultus, Wissenschaft und Kunst. München : J. Jehle, v. ; 30 cm. Frequency: Irregular. Began in 1990. Amtsblatt. Description based on: Jahrg. 1990, T. 2, Nr. 11 (14. Nov. 1990); title from caption. Each Jahrg. consists of T. 1 and T. 2. Inhaltsverzeichnis has chronological list of articles and subject index: No. 1-20. 1988. 1 v. Continues: Bavaria (Germany). Staatsministerium für Unterricht und Kultus. Amtsblatt der Staatsministerien für Unterricht und Kultus und Wissenschaft und Kunst (DLC) 91651053 (OCoLC)24273026. DDC 379.433
  *1. Education - Germany - Bavaria - Periodicals. 2. Educational law and legislation - Germany - Bavaria - Periodicals. I. Title. II. Title: Amtsblatt III. Title: Bavaria (Germany). Staatsministerium für Unterricht und Kultus. Amtsblatt der Staatsministerien für Unterricht und Kultus und Wissenschaft und Kunst*

**Bavaria (Germany). Staatsministerium für Unterricht und Kultus.** Amtsblatt des Staatsministeriums für Unterricht und Kultus / amtlich herausgegeben vom Staatsministerium für Unterricht und Kultus. München : Das Ministerium, 1918- v. ; 22-30 cm. Frequency: Irregular. 14. Nov. 1918- . Ceased in 1986. Amtsblatt des Bayer. Amtsblatt des Bayerischen Staatsministeriums für Unterricht und Kultus. Amtsblatt. Title from caption. Issues for 1920-<1923> have title: Amtsblatt des Bayer. Staatsministeriums für Unterricht und Kultus. Issues for <1946>-1986 have title: Amtsblatt des Bayerischen Staatsministeriums für Unterricht und Kultus. Vols. for 1918-<1923> called: 54. Jahrg.-<59. Jahrg.> Suspended 1924-1925. Jahrg. 1975-Jahrg. 1986 issued in 2 parts. Supplements accompany some issues. Has supplement: Fortführungsnachweis zur bereinigten Sammlung der Verwaltungsvorschriften des Bayerischen Staatsministeriums für Unterricht und Kultus (BayBSVK) für die Zeit von 1865 bis ... (DLC) 91651062 (OCoLC)24316471. Continues: Bavaria (Germany). Königl. Staatsministerium des Innern für Kirchen- und Schulangelegenheiten. Ministerialblatt für Kirchen- und Schul-Angelegenheiten im Königreich Bayern (DLC) 91651056 (OCoLC)24272162. Continued by: Bavaria (Germany). Staatsministerium für Unterricht und Kultus. Amtsblatt der Bayerischen Staatsministerien für Unterricht und Kultus und Wissenschaft und Kunst (DLC) 91651053 (OCoLC)24273026. ISSN 0722-5105 DDC 379.433
  *1. Education - Germany - Bavaria - Periodicals. 2. Educational law and legislation - Germany - Bavaria - Periodicals. 3. Ecclesiastical law - Germany - Bavaria - Periodicals. I. Title. II. Title: Amtsblatt des Bayer. Staatsministeriums für Unterricht und Kultus III. Title: Amtsblatt des Bayerischen Staatsministeriums für Unterricht und Kultus IV. Title: Fortführungsnachweis zur bereinigten Sammlung der Verwaltungsvorschriften des Bayerischen Staatsministeriums für Unterricht und Kultus (BayBSVK) für die Zeit von 1865 bis ... VI. Title: Bavaria (Germany). Königl. Staatsministerium des Innern für Kirchen- und Schulangelegenheiten. Ministerialblatt für Kirchen- und Schul-Angelegenheiten im Königreich Bayern VII. Title: Bavaria (Germany). Staatsministerium für Unterricht und Kultus. Amtsblatt der Bayerischen Staatsministerien für Unterricht und Kultus und Wissenschaft und Kunst*

**Bavaria (Germany). Staatsministerium für Unterricht und Kultus. Amtsblatt der Bayerischen Staatsministerien für Unterricht und Kultus und Wissenschaft und Kunst.**
Bavaria (Germany). Staatsministerium für Unterricht und Kultus. Amtsblatt des Ministeriums für Unterricht und Kultus. München : Das Ministerium, 1918-

**Bavaria (Germany). Staatsministerium für Unterricht und Kultus. Amtsblatt der Bayerischen Staatsministerien für Unterricht und Kultus und Wissenschaft und Kunst.**
Bavaria (Germany). Staatsministerium für Unterricht, Kultus, Wissenschaft und Kunst. Amtsblatt des Bayerischen Staatsministeriums für Unterricht, Kultus, Wissenschaft und Kunst. München : J. Jehle.

**Baxter, Charles, 1947-.**
The business of memory. Saint Paul, Minn. : Graywolf Press, c1999.
*TC BF378.A87 B87 1999*

**Baxter Magolda, Marcia B., 1951-** Creating contexts for learning and self-authorship : constructive-developmental pedagogy / Marcia B. Baxter Magolda. 1st ed. Nashville [Tenn.] : Vanderbilt University Press, 1999. x, 345 p. ; 24 cm. (Vanderbilt issues in higher education) Includes bibliographical references (p. [328]-338) and index. ISBN 0-8265-1343-3 (hbk.) ISBN 0-8265-1346-8 (pbk.) DDC 371.102
*1. Teaching. 2. Learning. 3. Constructivism (Education) 4. Developmental psychology. I. Title. II. Series.*
*TC LB1025.3 .B39 1999*

**Baxter Magolda, Marcia B. 1951-.**
Teaching to promote intellectual and personal maturity :. San Francisco : Jossey-Bass, c2000.
*TC LB1060 .T43 2000*

**Bayard Rustin.**
Haskins, James, 1941- 1st ed. New York : Hyperion Books for Children, c1997.
*TC E185.97.R93 H37 1997*

**Bayesian methods.**
Leonard, Thomas, 1948- Cambridge, U.K. : New York : Cambridge University Press, 1999.
*TC QA279.5 .L45 1999*

**BAYESIAN STATISTICAL DECISION THEORY.**
Leonard, Thomas, 1948- Bayesian methods. Cambridge, U.K. ; New York : Cambridge University Press, 1999.
*TC QA279.5 .L45 1999*

**BAYLEY SCALES OF INFANT DEVELOPMENT.**
Black, Maureen M. Essentials of Bayley scales of infant development--II assessment. New York : Wiley, c2000.
*TC RJ151.D48 B52 2000*

**Bayne-Jardine, Colin Charles.**
Hoy, Charles, 1939- Improving quality in education. London ; New York : Falmer Press, 2000.
*TC LB2822.84.G7 H69 1999*

**Baynes, Joyce Frisby.** The development of a van Hiele-based summer geometry program and its impact on student van Hiele level and achievement in high school geometry / by Joyce Frisby Baynes. 1998. vii, 214 leaves : ill. ; 29 cm. Includes tables. Typescript; issued also on microfilm. Thesis (Ed.D.) -- Teachers College, Columbia University, 1998. Includes bibliographical references (leaves 74-79).
*1. Hiele, Pierre M. van. 2. Geometry - Study and teaching (Secondary) - Activity programs. 3. Geometry - Problems, exercises, etc. 4. Vacation schools. 5. High school students - Interviews. 6. Study skills. 7. Academic achievement - Testing. 8. Learning, Psychology of. 9. Reasoning (Psychology) I. Hiele, Pierre M. van. II. Title. III. Title: Van Hiele-based summer geometry program and its impact on student van Hiele level and achievement in high school geometryp*
*TC 06 no. 10915*

**Bayreuth contributions to glottodidactics**
(vol. 8.) Learner autonomy in language learning. Frankfurt am Main ; New York : Peter Lang, c1999.
*TC P53 .L378 1999*

**BAYUNG GEDÉ (BALI, INDONESIA) - SOCIAL LIFE AND CUSTOMS.**
Sullivan, Gerald. Margaret Mead, Gregory Bateson, and Highland Bali. Chicago, IL : University of Chicago Press, 1999.
*TC GN635.I65 S948 1999*

**Bazaar book**
(2.) Dicum, Gregory. The coffee book. New York : New Press : Distributed by W.W. Norton, c1999.
*TC HD9199.A2 D53 1999*

**Bazigos, Michael Nicholas.** The relationship of upward feedback disparities to leader performance : understanding "overestimation" / Michael Nicholas Bazigos. 1999. x, 190 leaves : 29 cm. Typescript; issued also on microfilm. Thesis (Ph.D.) -- Columbia University, 1999. Includes bibliographical references (leaves 140-153)
*1. Leaders - Rating of. 2. Self-evaluation. 3. Managers - Psychology. 4. Organizational effectiveness - Psychological aspects. 5. Social perception. 6. Corporate culture. I. Title.*
*TC 085 B33*

**BBC Worldwide Americas, Inc.**
Teen violence [videorecording]. Princeton, NJ : Films for the Humanities & Sciences, c1998.
*TC RJ506.V56 T44 1998*

**Bea, Holly, 1956-** My spiritual alphabet book / Holly Bea ; illustrated by Kim Howard. Tiburon, Calif. : H.J. Kramer, c2000. 1 v. : col. ill. ; 24 cm. SUMMARY: Rhyming verses introduce the letters of the alphabet and the concepts of God as Creator, Mother Earth, self-esteem, and joy. ISBN 0-915811-83-9 DDC 291.4/32
*1. Children - Religious life. 2. English language - Alphabet - Juvenile literature. 3. God. 4. Conduct of life. 5. Self-esteem. 6. Alphabet. I. Howard, Kim. ill. II. Title.*
*TC BL625.5 .B43 1999*

**Beabout, John L.**
Grounded for life [videorecording]. Charleston, WV : Cambridge Research Group, Ltd., 1988.
*TC HQ759.4 .G7 1988*

**Beach, Don M.** Supervisory leadership : focus on instruction / Don M. Beach, Judy Reinhartz. Boston : Allyn and Bacon, c2000. xi, 324 p. : ill. ; 25 cm. Includes bibliographical references and index. ISBN 0-205-30601-2 (alk. paper) DDC 371.2/03
*1. School supervision - United States. 2. Educational leadership - United States. I. Reinhartz, Judy. II. Title.*
*TC LB2806.4 .B433 2000*

**Beach, Richard (J. Richard).**
Introducing Canada. Washington, D.C. : National Council for the Social Studies in association with National Consortium for Teaching Canada, c1997.
*TC F1025 .I59 1997*

**BEACHES.** *See* SEASHORE.

**BEACHTOWN HIGH SCHOOL (NEW JERSEY).**
Campbell, Delois. High school students' perceptions of the impact of block scheduling on instructional effectiveness. 1999.
*TC 06 no. 11089*

**The Beacon model.**
Wright, Stanley Nathaniel. 1998.
*TC 06 no. 11007*

**The Beacons.**
Darwiche, Chirine Hijazi. 1997.
*TC 06 no. 10761*

**Beals, Ralph A. (Ralph Albert).**
[Journal of adult education (New York, N.Y.)] Journal of adult education. New York : American Association for Adult Education, 1929-[1941]

**Beamtenverein der Stadt Luzern.**
Korrespondenz-blatt. Luzern : Luzerner Staatspersonalverband, 1947-

**Bear, Donald R.**
Words their way. 2nd ed. Upper Saddle River, N.J. : Merrill, c2000.
*TC LB1050.44 .B43 2000*

**Beard, Roger.**
Reading development and the teaching of reading. Oxford, UK ; Malden, Mass. : Blackwell Publishers, 1999.
*TC LB1050.2 .R424 1999*

**BEARDSLEY, AUBREY, 1872-1898 - APPRECIATION - ENGLAND.**
Desmarais, Jane Haville. The Beardsley industry. Aldershot, Hants, England ; Brookfield, Vt. : Ashgate, c1998.
*TC NC242.B3 D475 1998*

**BEARDSLEY, AUBREY, 1872-1898 - APPRECIATION - FRANCE.**
Desmarais, Jane Haville. The Beardsley industry. Aldershot, Hants, England ; Brookfield, Vt. : Ashgate, c1998.
*TC NC242.B3 D475 1998*

**BEARDSLEY, AUBREY, 1872-1898 - CRITICISM AND INTERPRETATION.**
Desmarais, Jane Haville. The Beardsley industry. Aldershot, Hants, England ; Brookfield, Vt. : Ashgate, c1998.
*TC NC242.B3 D475 1998*

**The Beardsley industry.**
Desmarais, Jane Haville. Aldershot, Hants, England : Brookfield, Vt. : Ashgate, c1998.
*TC NC242.B3 D475 1998*

**Bearne, Eve, 1943-.**
Use of language across the primary curriculum. London ; New York : Routledge, 1998.
*TC LB1576 U74 1998*

**BEARS - FICTION.**
Day, Alexandra. Frank and Ernest on the road. New York : Scholastic Inc., c1994.
*TC PZ7.D32915 Frn 1994*

De Beer, Hans. [Kleine Eisbär und der Angsthase. English] Little Polar Bear and the brave little hare. New York : North-South Books, 1998.
*TC PZ7.D353 Liv 1998*

George, Jean Craighead, 1919- Snow Bear. 1st ed. New York : Hyperion Books for Children, 1999.
*TC PZ7.G2933 Sn 1999*

Mallat, Kathy. Brave bear. New York : Walker, 1999.
*TC PZ7.M29455 Br 1999*

Vincent, Gabrielle. [Ernest et Célestine chez le photographe. English] Smile, Ernest and Celestine. 1st American ed. New York : Greenwillow Books, c1982.
*TC PZ7.V744 Sm 1982*

**BEASTS.** *See* ZOOLOGY.

**The Beatrix Potter country cookery book.**
Lane, Margaret, 1907- London : F. Warne, 1981.
*TC TX717 .L355 1981*

**Beattie, Irenee R.**
The structure of schooling. Mountain View, Calif. : Mayfield Pub. Co., 1999.
*TC LC189 .S87 1999*

**Beauchamp, Edward R., 1933-.**
Japanese education since 1945. Armonk, N.Y. : M.E. Sharpe, c1994.
*TC LA1311.82 .J39 1994*

**BEAUTIFUL, THE.** *See* AESTHETICS.

**BEAUTY.** *See also* AESTHETICS.
Kirwan, James, 1961- Manchester : Manchester University Press, 1999.
*TC BH39 .K57 1999*

**Beauty matters** / edited by Peg Zeglin Brand. Bloomington : Indiana University Press, c2000. xv, 329 p. : ill. ; 24 cm. Includes bibliographical references and index. ISBN 0-253-33726-7 (cloth : alk. paper) ISBN 0-253-21375-4 (paper : alk. paper) DDC 305.42
*1. Aesthetics. 2. Feminine beauty (Aesthetics) I. Brand, Peggy Zeglin.*
*TC HQ1219 .B348 2000*

**BEAUTY, PERSONAL.** *See* CLOTHING AND DRESS.

**BEAUX-ARTS ARCHITECTURE.** *See* ECLECTICISM IN ARCHITECTURE.

**BEAUX-ARTS DESIGN.** *See* ECLECTICISM IN ARCHITECTURE.

**Beaux, Cecilia, 1855-1942.** Cecilia Beaux and the art of portraiture / Tara Leigh Tappert. Washington, DC : Published for the National Portrait Gallery by the Smithsonian Institution Press, 1995. x, i48 p., 31 p. of plates : ill (some col.) ; 28 cm. Exhibition held at the National Portrait Gallery, Oct. 6, 1995-Jan. 28, 1996, and at the Westmoreland Museum of Art, Greensburg, Pa., Feb. 25-May 5, 1996. ISBN 1-56098-658-1 (pbk : alk. paper) DDC 759.13
*1. Beaux, Cecilia, - 1855-1942 - Exhibitions. 2. United States - Biography - Portraits - Exhibitions. I. National Portrait Gallery (Smithsonian Institution) II. Westmoreland Museum of Art. III. Title.*
*TC ND1329.B39 A4 1995*

**BEAUX, CECILIA, 1855-1942 - EXHIBITIONS.**
Beaux, Cecilia, 1855-1942. Cecilia Beaux and the art of portraiture. Washington, DC : Published for the National Portrait Gallery by the Smithsonian Institution Press, 1995.
*TC ND1329.B39 A4 1995*

**Beck, Aaron T.**
Clark, David A., 1954- Scientific foundations of cognitive theory and therapy of depression. New York : John Wiley, c1999.
*TC RC537 .C53 1999*

**Beck, Ariadne P.**
The process of group psychotherapy. Washington, DC : American Psychological Association, c2000.
*TC RC488 .P75 2000*

**Beck, Vesna.**
Robles de Melendez, Wilma J. Teaching social studies in early education. Albany, NY : Delmar Thomson Learning, c2000.
***TC LB1139.5.S64 R62 2000***

**Becker, Evvie.** High-risk sexual behavior : interventions with vulnerable populations / Evvie Becker, Elizabeth Rankin and Annette U. Rickel. New York : Plenum Press, c1998. ix, 168 p. ; 24 cm. (Prevention in practice library) Includes bibliographical references (p. 145-162) and index. ISBN 0-306-45857-8 ISBN 0-306-45858-6 (pbk.) DDC 613.9/5
*1. Sex counseling - United States. 2. Hygiene, Sexual - United States. 3. Youth - United States - Sexual behavior. 4. Teenage pregnancy - United States. 5. Sexually transmitted diseases - United States. I. Rankin, Elizabeth Deane. II. Rickel, Annette U., 1941- III. Title. IV. Series.*
***TC HQ60.7.U6 B43 1998***

**Becker, Nancy Jane.** Implementing technology in higher education : the leadership role and perspectives of the chief information officer / by Nancy Jane Becker. 1999. xiv, 282 leaves ; 29 cm. Issued also on microfilm. Thesis (Ed.D.)--Teachers College, Columbia University, 1999. Includes bibliographical references (leaves 234-262).
*1. Universities and colleges - United States - Administration. 2. Chief information officers. 3. Educational leadership. 4. Education, Higher - United States - Effect of technological innovation on. 5. Information technology - United States. 6. Information resources management - United States. I. Title.*
***TC 06 no. 11082***

**Becker, William E.**
Teaching economics to undergraduates. Cheltenham, UK ; Northampton, MA, USA : E. Elgar, c1998.
***TC HB74.8 .T4 1998***

**Beckett, Sandra L., 1953-.**
Transcending boundaries. New York : Garland, 1999.
***TC PN1009.A1 T69 1999***

**Beckley, Bill, 1946-.**
Uncontrollable beauty. New York : Allworth Press : School of Visual Arts, c1998.
***TC BH201 .U53 1998***

**Becoming a primary school teacher.**
Duncan, Diane. Stoke on Trent, England : Trentham, 1999.
***TC LB1776.4.G7 D86 1999***

**Becoming a reader.**
O'Donnell, Michael P. 2nd ed. Boston : Allyn and Bacon, c1999.
***TC LB1050.53 .O35 1999***

**Becoming a reflective educator.**
Reagan, Timothy G. 2nd ed. Thousand Oaks Calif. : Sage Publications, c2000.
***TC LB1025.3 .R424 2000***

**Becoming adult.**
Csikszentmihalyi, Mihaly. New York : Basic Books, 2000.
***TC HQ796 .C892 2000***

**Becoming an art teacher.**
Bates, Jane K. Belmont, CA : Wadsworth/Thomson Learning, 2000.
***TC N353 .B38 2000***

**Becoming and unbecoming white :** owning and disowning a racial identity / edited by Christine Clark, James O'Donnell. Westport, Conn. : Bergin & Garvey, 1999. xiii, 283 p. ; 24 cm. (Critical studies in education and culture series, 1064-8615) Includes bibliographical references (p. [253]-268) and index. ISBN 0-89789-620-3 (alk. paper) ISBN 0-89789-621-1 (pbk. : alk. paper) DDC 305.8/00973
*1. Whites - United States - Race identity. 2. Racism - United States. 3. United States - Race relations. I. Clark, Christine, 1962- II. O'Donnell, James, 1951- III. Series.*
***TC E184.A1 B29 1999***

**Becoming good American schools :** the struggle for civic virtue in education reform / Jeannie Oakes ... [et al.]. 1st ed. San Francisco : Jossey-Bass, c2000. xxxiii, 385 p. ; 24 cm. Includes bibliographical references (p. 345-361) and index. ISBN 0-7879-4023-2 (alk. paper) DDC 371.2/00973
*1. School improvement programs - United States. 2. Educational change - United States. 3. Public schools - United States. I. Oakes, Jeannie.*
***TC LB2822.82 .B44 2000***

**Becoming multicultural.**
Ford, Terry. New York : Falmer Press, 1999.
***TC LC1099 .F674 1999***

**BEDDING (HORTICULTURE).** *See* **GARDENING.**

**Bednar, Rudy.**
Sean's story [videorecording]. Princeton, N.J. : Films for the Humanities & Sciences ; [S.l. : distributed by] ABC Multimedia : Capital Cities/ABC, c1994.
***TC LC1203.M3 .S39 1994***

**Bedside nurse.** New York, National Federation of Licensed Practical Nurses, Inc., 1968-72. 5 v. ill. Frequency: Bimonthly. v. 1-5; 1968-1972. American journal of practical nursing v. 1-3, Mar. 1965-67. Continued by: Nursing care. ISSN 0005-7665
*1. Practical nursing - Periodicals. I. National Federation of Licensed Practical Nurses, Inc. II. Title: American journal of practical nursing v. 1-3, Mar. 1965-67 III. Title: Nursing care*

**BEDTIME - FICTION.**
Apple, Margot. Brave Martha. Boston : Houghton Mifflin, 1999.
***TC PZ7.A6474 Br 1999***

Steer, Dugald. Just one more story. New York : Dutton Children's Books, 1999.
***TC PZ7.S81534 Ju 1999***

**Beech, Linda Ward.** The cay by Theodore Taylor / written by Linda Ward Beech. New York : Scholastic, c1997. 16 p. : ill. ; 28 cm. (Scholastic literature guide. Grades 4-8.) "Author biography, chapter summaries, discussion questions, vocabulary builders, assessment strategies, reproducibles, cross-curricular activities for students of all learning styles."--Cover. ISBN 0-590-36643-2
*1. Taylor, Theodore, - 1921- / - The cay. 2. Children's literature - Study and teaching. 3. Reading (Elementary) I. Title. II. Series.*
***TC LB1573 .B4312 1997***

Danny the champion of the world by Roald Dahl / written by Linda Ward Beech. New York : Scholastic, c1997. 16 p. : ill. ; 28 cm. (Scholastic literature guide. Grades 4-8.) "Author biography, chapter summaries, discussion questions, vocabulary builders, assessment strategies, reproducibles, cross-curricular activities for students of all learning styles."--Cover. ISBN 0-590-37361-7
*1. Dahl, Roald. - Danny the champion of the world. 2. Children's literature - Study and teaching. 3. Reading (Elementary) I. Title. II. Series.*
***TC LB11573 .B431 1997***

Danny the champion of the world by Roald Dahl / written by Linda Ward Beech. New York : Scholastic, c1997. 16 p. : ill. ; 28 cm. (Scholastic literature guide. Grades 4-8.) "Author biography, chapter summaries, discussion questions, vocabulary builders, assessment strategies, reproducibles, cross-curricular activities for students of all learning styles."--Cover. ISBN 0-590-37361-7
*1. Dahl, Roald. - Danny the champion of the world. 2. Children's literature - Study and teaching. 3. Reading (Elementary) I. Title. II. Series.*
***TC LB1573 .B431 1997***

The diary of a young girl by Anne Frank / written by Linda Ward Beech. New York : Scholastic, c1998. 16 p. : ill. ; 28 cm. (Scholastic literature guide. Grades 4-8.) "Author biography, chapter summaries, discussion questions, vocabulary builders, assessment strategies, reproducibles, cross-curricular activities for students of all learning styles."--Cover. ISBN 0-590-51377-x
*1. Frank, Anne, - 1929-1945. - Achterhuis. - English. 2. Children's literature - Study and teaching. 3. Reading (Elementary) I. Title. II. Series.*
***TC LB1573 .B433 1998***

The great fire by Jim Murphy / written by Linda Ward Beech. New York : Scholastic, c1996. 16 p. : ill. ; 28 cm. (Scholastic literature guide. Grades 4-8.) "Author biography, chapter summaries, discussion questions, vocabulary builders, assessment strategies, reproducibles, cross-curricular activities for students of all learning styles."--Cover. ISBN 0-590-99616-9
*1. Murphy, Jim, - 1947- / - The great fire. 2. Children's literature - Study and teaching. 3. Reading (Elementary) I. Title. II. Series.*
***TC LB11573 .B437 1996***

The great fire by Jim Murphy / written by Linda Ward Beech. New York : Scholastic, c1996. 16 p. : ill. ; 28 cm. (Scholastic literature guide. Grades 4-8.) "Author biography, chapter summaries, discussion questions, vocabulary builders, assessment strategies, reproducibles, cross-curricular activities for students of all learning styles."--Cover. ISBN 0-590-99616-9
*1. Murphy, Jim, - 1947- / - The great fire. 2. Children's literature - Study and teaching. 3. Reading (Elementary) I. Title. II. Series.*
***TC LB1573 .B437 1996***

The great Gilly Hopkins by Katherine Paterson / written by Linda Ward Beech. New York : Scholastic, c1998. 16 p. : ill. ; 28 cm. (Scholastic literature guide. Grades 4-8.) "Author biography, chapter summaries, discussion questions, vocabulary builders, assessment strategies, reproducibles, cross-curricular activities for students of all learning styles."--Cover. ISBN 0-590-04116-9
*1. Paterson, Katherine. - The great Gilly Hopkins. 2. Children's literature - Study and teaching. 3. Reading (Elementary) I. Title. II. Series.*
***TC LB1573 .B439 1998***

Guests by Michael Dorris / written by Linda Ward Beech. New York, NY : Scholastic, c1996. 16 p. : ill. ; 28 cm. (Scholastic literature guide. Grades 4-8.) "Author biography, chapter summaries, discussion questions, vocabulary builders, assessment strategies, reproducibles, cross-curricular activities for students of all learning styles."--Cover. ISBN 0-590-06570-x
*1. Dorris, Michael. - Guests. 2. Children's literature - Study and teaching. 3. Reading (Elementary) I. Title. II. Series.*
***TC LB1573 .B432 1996***

Hatchet by Gary Paulsen / written by Linda Ward Beech. New York : Scholastic, c1998. 16 p. : ill. ; 28 cm. (Scholastic literature guide. Grades 4-8.) "Author biography, chapter summaries, discussion questions, vocabulary builders, assessment strategies, reproducibles, cross-curricular activities for students of all learning styles."--Cover. ISBN 0-590-38924-6
*1. Paulsen, Gary. - Hatchet. 2. Children's literature - Study and teaching. 3. Reading (Elementary) I. Title. II. Series.*
***TC LB1573 .B4310 1998***

Island of the blue dolphins by Scott O'Dell / written by Linda Ward Beech. New York : Scholastic, c1997. 16 p. : ill. ; 28 cm. (Scholastic literature guide. Grades 4-8.) "Author biography, chapter summaries, discussion questions, vocabulary builders, assessment strategies, reproducibles, cross-curricular activities for students of all learning styles."--Cover. ISBN 0-590-37355-2
*1. O'Dell, Scott, - 1898-1989. - Island of the blue dolphins. 2. Children's literature - Study and teaching. 3. Reading (Elementary) I. Title. II. Series.*
***TC LB1573 .B438 1997***

Julie of the wolves by Jean Craighead George / written by Linda Ward Beech. New York : Scholastic, c1996. 16 p. : ill. ; 28 cm. (Scholastic literature guide. Grades 4-8.) "Author biography, chapter summaries, discussion questions, vocabulary builders, assessment strategies, reproducibles, cross-curricular activities for students of all learning styles."--Cover. ISBN 0-590-99615-0
*1. George, Jean Craighead, - 1919- / - Julie of the wolves. 2. Children's literature - Study and teaching. 3. Reading (Elementary) I. Title. II. Series.*
***TC LB1573 .B434 1996***

Maniac Magee by Jerry Spinelli / written by Linda Ward Beech. New York : Scholastic, c1997. 16 p. : ill. ; 28 cm. (Scholastic literature guide. Grades 4-8.) "Author biography, chapter summaries, discussion questions, vocabulary builders, assessment strategies, reproducibles, cross-curricular activities for students of all learning styles."--Cover. ISBN 0-590-36644-0
*1. Spinelli, Jerry, - 1940- / - Maniac Magee. 2. Children's literature - Study and teaching. 3. Reading (Elementary) I. Title. II. Series.*
***TC LB1573 .B4311 1997***

Sarah, plain and tall by Patricia MacLachlan / written by Linda Ward Beech. New York : Scholastic, c1996. 16 p. : ill. ; 28 cm. (Scholastic literature guide. Grades 4-8.) "Author biography, chapter summaries, discussion questions, vocabulary builders, assessment strategies, reproducibles, cross-curricular activities for students of all learning styles."--Cover. ISBN 0-590-06572-6
*1. MacLachlan, Patricia. - Sarah, plain and tall. 2. Children's literature - Study and teaching. 3. Reading (Elementary) I. Title. II. Series.*
***TC LB1573 .B436 1996***

Tuck everlasting by Natalie Babbitt / written by Linda Ward Beech. New York : Scholastic, c1997. 16 p. : ill. ; 28 cm. (Scholastic literature guide. Grades 4-8.) "Author biography, chapter summaries, discussion questions, vocabulary builders, assessment strategies, reproducibles, cross-curricular activities for students of all learning styles."--Cover. ISBN 0-590-37354-4
*1. Babbitt, Natalie. - Tuck everlasting. 2. Children's literature - Study and teaching. 3. Reading (Elementary) I. Title. II. Series.*
***TC LB1573 .B43 1997***

A wrinkle in time by Madeleine L'Engle / written by Linda Ward Beech. New York : Scholastic, c1997. 16 p. : ill. ; 28 cm. (Scholastic literature guide. Grades 4-8.) "Author biography, chapter summaries, discussion questions, vocabulary builders, assessment strategies, reproducibles, cross-curricular activities for students of all learning styles."--Cover. ISBN 0-590-37360-9
*1. L'Engle, Madeleine. - Wrinkle in time. 2. Children's literature - Study and teaching. 3. Reading (Elementary) I. Title. II. Series.*

*TC LB1573 .B435 1997*

**Beerens, Daniel R.** Evaluating teachers for professional growth : creating a culture of motivation and learning / Daniel R. Beerens. Thousand Oaks, Calif. : London : Corwin Press, c2000. xv, 167 p. : ill., forms ; 29 cm. Includes bibliographical references (p. 158-161) and index. ISBN 0-7619-7566-7 (cloth) ISBN 0-7619-7567-5 (paper) DDC 371.14/4/0973
*1. Teachers - Rating of - United States. 2. Teacher effectiveness - United States. I. Title.*
*TC LB2838 .B44 2000*

**Before the school bell rings.**
Hillman, Carol. Bloomington, Ind. : Phi Delta Kappa Educational Foundation, c1995.
*TC LB1140.23 .H54 1995*

**A beginner's guide to structural equation modeling.**
Schumacker, Randall E. Mahwah, N.J. : L. Erlbaum Associates, 1996.
*TC QA278 .S36 1996*

**A beginner's guide to the MMPI-2.**
Butcher, James Neal, 1933- 1st ed. Washington, DC : American Psychological Association, c1999.
*TC BF698.8.M5 B86 1999*

**Beginner's Italian and English dictionary.**
NTC's beginner's Italian and English dictionary. Lincolnwood, Ill. : NTC Pub. Group, c1995.
*TC PC1640 .N83 1995*

**BEGINNING.** See **CREATION.**

**Beginning drama 4-11.**
Winston, Joe. London : David Fulton Publishers, 1998.
*TC PN1701 .W567 1998*

**BEGINNING TEACHERS.** See **FIRST YEAR TEACHERS.**

**Begley, Paul Thomas, 1949-.**
Values and educational leadership. Albany : State University of New York Press, c1999.
*TC LB2806 .V25 1999*

The values of educational administration. London : Falmer, 1999.
*TC LB2806 .V255 1999*

**Behar-Horenstein, Linda S.**
Paradigm debates in curriculum and supervision. Westport, Conn. ; London : Bergin & Garvey, 2000.
*TC LB2806.4 .P37 2000*

**Behar, Ruth, 1956-** Translated woman : crossing the border with Esperanza's story / Ruth Behar. Boston : Beacon Press, c1993. xiv, 372 p. : ill. ; 24 cm. Includes bibliographical references (p. 345-369). ISBN 0-8070-7052-1 (cloth) DDC 305.42/0972/44
*1. Rural women - Mexico - Mexquitic - Social conditions - Case studies. 2. Hernández, Esperanza. 3. Ethnology - Mexico - Mexquitic. 4. Mexquitic (Mexico) - Rural conditions. I. Title.*
*TC HQ1465.M63 B44 1993*

The vulnerable observer : anthropology that breaks your heart / Ruth Behar. Boston : Beacon Press, c1996. xii, 195 p. ; 21 cm. Includes bibliographical references (p. 178-191) and index. ISBN 0-8070-4630-2 (cloth) DDC 301/.0723
*1. Participant observation - Psychological aspects. 2. Anthropologists - Attitudes. 3. Anthropologists - Psychology. I. Title.*
*TC GN346.4 .B44 1996*

**Behaving badly :** aversive behaviors in interpersonal relationships / edited by Robin M. Kowalski. 1st ed. Washington, D.C. : American Psychological Association, 2001. xiii, 333 p. ; 26 cm. Includes bibliographical references and indexes. ISBN 1-55798-716-5 (cloth : alk. paper) DDC 158.2
*1. Interpersonal relations. 2. Interpersonal conflict. 3. Social interaction. 4. Disorderly conduct. 5. Gossip. 6. Invective. I. Kowalski, Robin M. II. Title.*
*TC HM1106 .B45 2001*

**BEHAVIOR.**
Psychiatric and behavioural disorders in developmental disabilities and mental retardation. Cambridge, UK ; New York, NY, USA : Cambridge University Press, 1999.
*TC RC451.4.M47 P77 1999*

Rachlin, Howard, 1935- Behavior and learning. San Francisco : W. H. Freeman, c1976.
*TC BF319 .R327*

**BEHAVIOR, ADDICTIVE - DIAGNOSIS - CONGRESSES.**
Basic and clinical science of mental and addictive disorders. Basel ; New York : Karger, c1997.

*TC RC327 .B37 1997*

**BEHAVIOR, ADDICTIVE - THERAPY - CONGRESSES.**
Basic and clinical science of mental and addictive disorders. Basel : New York : Karger, c1997.
*TC RC327 .B37 1997*

**Behavior analysis.**
Leslie, Julian C. Amsterdam, Netherlands : Harwood Academic Publishers, c1999.
*TC BF199 .L47 1999*

**Behavior analysis and learning.**
Pierce, W. David. 2nd ed. Upper Saddle River, N.J. : Prentice Hall, c1999.
*TC BF199 .P54 1999*

**Behavior and learning.**
Rachlin, Howard, 1935- San Francisco : W. H. Freeman, c1976.
*TC BF319 .R327*

**BEHAVIOR ASSESSMENT.** See also **BEHAVIORAL ASSESSMENT.**
Functional analysis of problem behavior. Belmont, CA : Wadsworth Pub. Co., c1999.
*TC RC473.B43 F85 1999*

**Behavior change.**
Banff International Conference on Behavior Modification, 4th, 1972. Champaign, Ill. : Research Press, 1974, c1973.
*TC BF637.B4 B354 1972*

**BEHAVIOR, CHILD.** See **CHILD PSYCHOLOGY.**

**BEHAVIOR, COMPARATIVE.** See **PSYCHOLOGY, COMPARATIVE.**

**BEHAVIOR, COMPULSIVE.** See **COMPULSIVE BEHAVIOR.**

**BEHAVIOR DISORDERS IN CHILDREN.** See also **ANXIETY IN CHILDREN; ATTENTION-DEFICIT HYPERACTIVITY DISORDER; PROBLEM CHILDREN.**
Barnett, David W., 1946- Designing preschool interventions. New York : Guilford Press, 1999.
*TC LC4801 .B36 1999*

Developmental disability and behaviour. London, England : Mac Keith Press, 2000.
*TC RJ506.D47 D48 2000*

Understanding the defiant child [videorecording]. New York : Guilford Publications, c1997.
*TC HQ755.7 .U63 1997*

**BEHAVIOR DISORDERS IN CHILDREN - DIAGNOSIS.**
Functional analysis of problem behavior. Belmont, CA : Wadsworth Pub. Co., c1999.
*TC RC473.B43 F85 1999*

**BEHAVIOR DISORDERS IN CHILDREN - TREATMENT.**
Gardner, Richard A. Developmental conflicts and diagnostic evaluation in adolescent psychotherapy. Northvale, N.J. : J. Aronson, c1999.
*TC RJ503 .G376 1999*

**BEHAVIOR EVOLUTION.**
Cziko, Gary. The things we do. Cambridge, Mass. : MIT Press, c2000.
*TC HM1033 .C95 2000*

Dean, Alan Ph. D. Complex life. Aldershot : Ashgate, c2000.
*TC BD450 .D43 2000*

Wright, Robert, 1957- The moral animal. 1st Vintage books ed. New York : Vintage Books, 1995, c1994.
*TC GN365.9 .W75 1995*

**BEHAVIOR - FICTION.**
Stevenson, James, 1929- Don't make me laugh. 1st ed. New York : Farrar, Straus and Giroux, c1999.
*TC PZ7.S84748 Do 1999*

**BEHAVIOR GENETICS.** See also **CRIMINAL BEHAVIOR - GENETIC ASPECTS.**
Weiner, Jonathan. Time, love, memory. 1st ed. New York : Knopf, 1999.
*TC QH457 .W43 1999*

**BEHAVIOR, HEALTH.** See **HEALTH BEHAVIOR.**

**BEHAVIOR, HUMAN.** See **HUMAN BEHAVIOR.**

**BEHAVIOR IN ORGANIZATIONS.** See **ORGANIZATIONAL BEHAVIOR.**

**BEHAVIOR MODIFICATION.** See also **MENTALLY HANDICAPPED - BEHAVIOR MODIFICATION; PROBLEM CHILDREN - BEHAVIOR MODIFICATION.**

Barnett, David W., 1946- Designing preschool interventions. New York : Guilford Press, 1999.
*TC LC4801 .B36 1999*

Behavioral intervention. Baltimore, Md. : Paul H. Brookes Pub., c1999.
*TC BF637.B4 B452 1999*

Beyond behaviorism. Boston : Allyn and Bacon, c1999.
*TC LB3013 .B42 1999*

Danforth, Scot. Cases in behavior management. Upper Saddle River, N.J. : Merrill, c2000.
*TC LB3013 .D34 2000*

Hunt, Gilbert. Effective teaching. 3rd ed. Springfield, Ill. : C.C. Thomas Publisher, c1999.
*TC LB1025.3 .H86 1999*

Porter, Louise, 1958- Behaviour in schools. Buckingham [England] ; Philadelphia : Open University Press, 2000.
*TC LB3012 .P65 2000*

Rachlin, Howard, 1935- Behavior and learning. San Francisco : W. H. Freeman, c1976.
*TC BF319 .R327*

Sparzo, Frank J. The ABC's of behavior change. Bloomington, Ind., U.S.A. : Phi Delta Kappa Educational Foundation, c1999.
*TC LB1060.2 .S62 1999*

**BEHAVIOR MODIFICATION - CASE STUDIES.**
Janney, Rachel. Behavorial support. Baltimore, Md. ; London : Paul H. Brookes Pub., c2000.
*TC LB1060.2 .J26 2000*

**BEHAVIOR MODIFICATION - CONGRESSES.**
Banff International Conference on Behavior Modification, 4th, 1972. Behavior change. Champaign, Ill. : Research Press, 1974, c1973.
*TC BF637.B4 B354 1972*

**BEHAVIOR MODIFICATION - UNITED STATES.**
Behavioral management in the public schools. Westport, Conn. ; London : Praeger, 1999.
*TC LB1060.2 .B44 1999*

Kosmoski, Georgia J. Managing difficult, frustrating, and hostile conversations. Thousand Oaks, Calif. : Sage Publications, c2000.
*TC LB3011.5 .K67 2000*

McEwan, Elaine K., 1941- Managing unmanageable students. Thousand Oaks, Calif. : Corwin Press, c2000.
*TC LC4801.5 .M39 2000*

Rathvon, Natalie. Effective school interventions. New York : Guilford Press, c1999.
*TC LC1201 .R38 1999*

Tomal, Daniel R. Discipline by negotiation. 1st ed. Lancaster, Pa. : Technomic Pub. Co., c1999.
*TC LB3011.5 .T66 1999*

**Behavior monographs.** Cambridge, Mass. : H. Holt & Company, 1911- v. : ill. ; 24 cm. Frequency: Irregular. Vol. 1, no. 1- = Serial no. 1- . Ceased publication with vol. 4 in 1922/23? Each number has also a distinctive title. Continued by: Comparative psychology monographs (OCoLC)2259639.
*1. Animals - Habits and behavior. I. Title: Comparative psychology monographs*

**BEHAVIOR OF CHILDREN.** See **CHILDREN - CONDUCT OF LIFE.**

**BEHAVIOR - PERIODICALS.**
[Computers in human behavior (Online)] Computers in human behavior [computer file]. New York : Elsevier Science,
*TC EJOURNALS*

Life-threatening behavior. [New York, Behavioral Publications, inc.]

**BEHAVIOR PROBLEMS IN CHILDREN.** See **BEHAVIOR DISORDERS IN CHILDREN.**

**BEHAVIOR, SPATIAL.** See **SPATIAL BEHAVIOR.**

**BEHAVIOR THERAPY FOR CHILDREN.**
Sparzo, Frank J. The ABC's of behavior change. Bloomington, Ind., U.S.A. : Phi Delta Kappa Educational Foundation, c1999.
*TC LB1060.2 .S62 1999*

**BEHAVIOR THERAPY FOR TEENAGERS.**
Sparzo, Frank J. The ABC's of behavior change. Bloomington, Ind., U.S.A. : Phi Delta Kappa Educational Foundation, c1999.
*TC LB1060.2 .S62 1999*

**BEHAVIOR, VERBAL.** *See* **VERBAL BEHAVIOR.**

**BEHAVIORAL ANALYSIS.** *See* **BEHAVIORAL ASSESSMENT.**

**BEHAVIORAL ASSESSMENT.** *See also* **BEHAVIOR MODIFICATION.**
Golden, Valerie. Significant others' perceptions of the effects of their partners' psychotherapy. 1998.
*TC 085 G566*

Haynes, Stephen N. Principles and practice of behavioral assessment. New York ; London : Kluwer Academic/Plenum, c2000.
*TC BF176.5 .H39 2000*

**BEHAVIORAL ASSESSMENT - CHARTS, DIAGRAMS, ETC.**
McGoldrick, Monica. Genograms. 2nd ed. New York : W.W. Norton, 1999.
*TC RC488.5 .M395 1999*

**BEHAVIORAL ASSESSMENT - HANDBOOKS, MANUALS, ETC.**
Hawkins, Robert P., 1931- Measuring behavioral health outcomes. New York : Kluwer Academic/Plenum Publishers, c1999.
*TC RJ503.5 .H39 1999*

**Behavioral assessment in schools** : theory, research, and clinical foundations / edited by Edward S. Shapiro, Thomas R. Kratochwill. 2nd ed. New York : Guilford Press, c2000. xvii, 522 p. : ill. ; 25 cm. Includes bibliographical references and indexes. ISBN 1-57230-575-4 (cloth : alk. paper) DDC 370.15/3
*1. Behavioral assessment of children - United States. 2. Handicapped children - Education - United States. 3. Learning disabled children - Education - United States. I. Shapiro, Edward S. (Edward Steven), 1951- II. Kratochwill, Thomas R.*
*TC LB1124 .B435 2000*

**BEHAVIORAL ASSESSMENT OF CHILDREN.**
Ayers, Harry. Perspectives on behaviour. 2nd ed. London : David Fulton, 2000.
*TC LC4801 .A94 2000*

Council of Europe. Council for Cultural Co-operation. Bullying in schools. Strasbourg : Council of Europe Publishing, 1999.
*TC BF637.B85 B842 1999*

**BEHAVIORAL ASSESSMENT OF CHILDREN - HANDBOOKS, MANUALS, ETC.**
Conducting school-based assessments of child and adolescent behavior. New York : Guilford Press, c2000.
*TC LB1124 .C66 2000*

Hawkins, Robert P., 1931- Measuring behavioral health outcomes. New York : Kluwer Academic/Plenum Publishers, c1999.
*TC RJ503.5 .H39 1999*

**BEHAVIORAL ASSESSMENT OF CHILDREN - UNITED STATES.**
Behavioral assessment in schools. 2nd ed. New York : Guilford Press, c2000.
*TC LB1124 .B435 2000*

Venn, John. Assessing students with special needs. 2nd ed. Upper Saddle River, N.J. : Merrill, c2000.
*TC LC4031 .V46 2000*

**Behavioral disorders.**
Monograph in behavioral disorders. Severe behavior disorders of children and youth. Reston, Va. : Council for Children with Behavioral Disorders, c1978-1986.
*TC BF721 .M65*

**BEHAVIORAL DISORDERS IN CHILDREN.** *See* **BEHAVIOR DISORDERS IN CHILDREN.**

**BEHAVIORAL EVALUATION.** *See* **BEHAVIORAL ASSESSMENT.**

**BEHAVIORAL GENETICS - CONGRESSES.**
Genetics of criminal and antisocial behaviour. Chichester ; New York : Wiley, 1996.
*TC HV6047 .G46 1996*

**BEHAVIORAL HEALTH CARE.** *See* **MENTAL HEALTH SERVICES.**

**Behavioral intervention** : principles, models, and practices / edited by Joseph R. Scotti and Luanna H. Meyer. Baltimore, Md. : Paul H. Brookes Pub., c1999. xvii, 490 p. : ill. ; 26 cm. Includes bibliographical references and indexes. ISBN 1-55766-294-0 (alk. paper) DDC 153.8/5
*1. Behavior modification. I. Scotti, Joseph R. II. Meyer, Luanna H.*
*TC BF637.B4 B452 1999*

**Behavioral management in the public schools** : an urban approach / edited by Nancy R. Macciomei and Douglas H. Ruben. Westport, Conn. ; London : Praeger, 1999. x, 162 p. : ill, forms ; 25 cm. Includes

bibliographical references (p. [143]-153) and index. ISBN 0-275-96327-6 (alk. paper) DDC 371.39/3/0973
*1. Behavior modification - United States. 2. Public schools - Social aspects - United States. 3. Problem children - Behavior modification - United States. 4. Education, Urban - United States. I. Macciomei, Nancy R. II. Ruben, Douglas H.*
*TC LB1060.2 .B44 1999*

**BEHAVIORAL NEUROLOGY.** *See* **CLINICAL NEUROPSYCHOLOGY.**

**Behavioral neuroscience.**
The Journal of comparative and physiological psychology. Baltimore, 1921-82.

**BEHAVIORAL PHARMACOLOGY.** *See* **PSYCHOPHARMACOLOGY.**

**BEHAVIORAL PHYSIOLOGY.** *See* **PSYCHOPHYSIOLOGY.**

**BEHAVIORAL PROBLEMS IN CHILDREN.** *See* **BEHAVIOR DISORDERS IN CHILDREN.**

**Behavioral science of leadership.**
Misumi, Jūji, 1924- Rīdāshippu kōdō no kagaku =
*TC HM141 .M48 1978*

**BEHAVIORAL SCIENCES.** *See* **PSYCHOLOGY; SOCIAL SCIENCES.**

**BEHAVIORAL SCIENCES - PERIODICALS.**
[Computers in human behavior (Online)] Computers in human behavior [computer file]. New York : Elsevier Science,
*TC EJOURNALS*

**BEHAVIORAL SCIENTISTS.** *See* **PSYCHOLOGISTS; SOCIOLOGISTS.**

**BEHAVIORISM (PSYCHOLOGY).** *See also* **BEHAVIOR MODIFICATION.**
Kohn, Alfie. Punished by rewards. Boston : Houghton Mifflin Co., 1999, c1993.
*TC BF505.R48 K65 1999*

Leslie, Julian C. Behavior analysis. Amsterdam, Netherlands : Harwood Academic Publishers, c1999.
*TC BF199 .L47 1999*

Monograph in behavioral disorders. Severe behavior disorders of children and youth. Reston, Va. : Council for Children with Behavioral Disorders, c1978-1986.
*TC BF721 .M65*

Pierce, W. David. Behavior analysis and learning. 2nd ed. Upper Saddle River, N.J. : Prentice Hall, c1999.
*TC BF199 .P54 1999*

Uttal, William R. The war between mentalism and behaviorism. Mahwah, N.J. ; London : Lawrence Erlbaum Associates, Publishers, 2000.
*TC BF199 .U77 2000*

**BEHAVIORISTIC PSYCHOLOGY.** *See* **BEHAVIORISM (PSYCHOLOGY).**

**Behaviour and health**
Lee, Christina. Women's health. London ; Thousand Oaks, Calif. : Sage, 1998.
*TC RA564.85 .L443 1998*

**Behaviour in schools.**
Porter, Louise, 1958- Buckingham [England] ; Philadelphia : Open University Press, 2000.
*TC LB3012 .P65 2000*

**Behavorial support.**
Janney, Rachel. Baltimore, Md. ; London : Paul H. Brookes Pub., c2000.
*TC LB1060.2 .J26 2000*

**Behind closed doors [videorecording].**
d-a-t-e rape [videorecording]. [Charleston, WV] : Cambridge Educational, c1994.
*TC RC560.R36 D3 1994*

**Behind the mask.**
Jack, Dana Crowley. Cambridge, Mass. ; London : Harvard University Press, 1999.
*TC HQ1206 .J26 1999*

**Behrens, Martina.**
Evans, Karen, 1949- Learning and work in the risk society. New York : St. Martin's Press, 2000.
*TC HD6278.G4 E93 2000*

**Beier, Ellen, ill.**
Ransom, Candice F., 1952- The promise quilt. New York : Walker and Co., 1999.
*TC PZ7.R1743 Pr 1999*

**Beilin, Natasha.**
Ballet class [videorecording]. W. Long Branch, NJ : Kultur, c1984.
*TC GV1589 .B33 1984*

**Beineke, John A.** And there were giants in the land : the life of William Heard Kilpatrick / John A. Beineke. New York : P. Lang, c1998. ix, 500 p. : ill. ; 23 cm. (History of schools and schooling, 1089-0678 ; vol. 5) Includes bibliographical references (p. [433]-485) and index. ISBN 0-8204-3773-5 (pbk. : alk. paper) DDC 370/.92
*1. Kilpatrick, William Heard, - 1871-1965. 2. Educators - United States - Biography. 3. Progressive education - United States - History. I. Title. II. Title: Life of William Heard Kilpatrick III. Series: History of schools and schooling ; v. 5.*
*TC LB875.K54 B44 1998*

**Being a biracial/biethnic teen.**
Nash, Renea D. Everything you need to know about being a biracial/biethnic teen. 1st ed. New York : Rosen Pub. Group, 1995.
*TC HQ77.9 .N39 1995*

**Being and becoming.**
Combs, Arthur W. (Arthur Wright), 1912- New York : Springer Pub. Co., c1999.
*TC BF38 .C715 1999*

**Being Black in America today.**
Brill, Norman Q. (Norman Quintus), 1911- Springfield, Ill. : Charles C Thomas, 1999.
*TC E185.625 B754 1999*

**Being Catholic, being American.**
Burns, Robert E., 1927- Notre Dame, Ind. : University of Notre Dame Press, c1999.
*TC LD4113 .B87 1999*

**Being married, doing gender.**
Dryden, Caroline. London ; New York : Routledge, 1999.
*TC HQ734 .D848 1999*

**Being of two minds.**
Goldberg, Arnold, 1929- Hillsdale, NJ : Analytic Press, 1999.
*TC RC569.5.M8 G65 1999*

**Beker, Jerome.**
Residential education as an option for at-risk youth. New York : Haworth Press, c1996.
*TC HV862 .R473 1996*

**Bel canto.**
Stark, James A. (James Arthur), 1938- Toronto : University of Toronto Press, c1999.
*TC MT823 S795 1999*

**BEL CANTO.**
Stark, James A. (James Arthur), 1938- Bel canto. Toronto : University of Toronto Press, c1999.
*TC MT823 S795 1999*

Stark, James A. (James Arthur), 1938- Bel canto. Toronto : University of Toronto Press, c1999.
*TC MT823 S795 1999*

**Belanger, France, 1963-** Evaluation and implementation of distance learning : technologies, tools and techniques / France Belanger, Dianne H. Jordan. Hershey, PA ; London : Idea Group Pub., c2000. 245 p. : ill. ; 25 cm. Includes bibliographical references (p. 223-226) and index. ISBN 1-87828-963-2 (paper) DDC 371.3/5
*1. Distance education - Computer-assisted instruction. 2. Instructional systems - Design. 3. Educational technology. I. Jordan, Dianne H., 1950- II. Title.*
*TC LC5803.C65 B45 2000*

**Belcher, Michael.** Exhibitions in museums / Michael Belcher. Washington, D.C. : Smithsonian Institution Press, c1991. 230 p. : ill. ; 23 cm. "First published in 1991 in Great Britain by Leicester University Press"--T.p. verso. Bibliography: p. 215-224. Includes index. ISBN 1-56098-324-8 (paper)
*1. Museums - Exhibitions. 2. Museums - Educational aspects. I. Title.*
*TC AM7 .B3 1991*

**BELGIUM - FICTION.**
Moeyaert, Bart. [Blote handen. English] Bare hands. 1st ed. Asheville, N.C. : Front Street, 1998.
*TC PZ7.M7227 Bar 1998*

**BELIEF AND DOUBT.** *See* **RATIONALISM.**

**BELIEF AND DOUBT - CONGRESSES.**
Memory, brain, and belief. Cambridge, Mass. ; London : Harvard University Press, 2000.
*TC QP406 .M44 2000*

**BELIEFS, DELUSIONAL.** *See* **DELUSIONS.**

**BELIZE - LANGUAGES.** *See* **MAYA LANGUAGE.**

**BELL, ALEXANDER GRAHAM, 1847-1922 - JUVENILE LITERATURE.**
Matthews, Tom, 1949- Always inventing. Washington, D.C. : National Geographic Society, c1999.

*TC TK6143.B4 M37 1999*

**BELL, ALEXANDER GRAHAM, 1847-1922 -
PORTRAITS - JUVENILE LITERATURE.**
Matthews, Tom, 1949- Always inventing.
Washington, D.C. : National Geographic Society,
c1999.
*TC TK6143.B4 M37 1999*

**Bell, Cathie.**
Talking across boundaries. [New York] : [Bruner
Foundation], 1996.
*TC LB1623.5 .T35 1996*

**Bell, David.**
Psychoanalysis and culture. New York : Routledge,
1999.
*TC BF175 .P79 1999*

**Bell, David, 1965-.**
The cybercultures reader. London ; New York :
Routledge, 2000.
*TC T14.5 .C934 2000*

**Bell, Derek, 1950-** Towards effective subject leadership
in the primary school / Derek Bell and Ron Ritchie.
Buckingham [England] ; Philadelphia : Open
University Press, c1999. xiv, 190 p. ; 23 cm. Includes
bibliographical references (p. [181]-186) and index. ISBN
0-335-20183-0 (hb) ISBN 0-335-20182-2 (pbk) DDC
372.1102/0941
*1. Master teachers - Great Britain. 2. Mentoring in education -
Great Britain. 3. Teacher participation in curriculum
planning - Great Britain. 4. Elementary school teaching -
Great Britain. I. Ritchie, Ron, 1952- II. Title.*
*TC LB2832.4.G7 B45 1999*

**Bell, Inge.** This book is not required : an emotional
survival manual for students / Inge Bell and Bernard
McGrane. Rev. ed., new ed. / by Team Bell, Lynette
Albovias ... [et al.]. Thousand Oaks, Calif. : Pine
Forge Press, c1999. xvii, 316 p. ; 22 cm. Includes
bibliographical references (p. 309-312) and index.
CONTENTS: Grades : can you perform without the
pressure? -- Support your local teacher, or, The care and
feeding of professors -- An academic question -- Everybody
hates to write -- Wisdom and knowledge -- Pursuing wisdom in
the academy -- Adventures in desocialization -- Media me --
Students, media mythology, and making a difference -- The
painful avenues of upward mobility -- The career : friend or
foe? -- Love -- Trouble with parents -- Graduation, what they
forgot to mention -- Directing your own development. ISBN
0-7619-8572-7 (pbk. : acid-free paper) DDC 378.1/98
*1. College students - United States. 2. Universities and
colleges - United States. 3. College students - United States -
Psychology. 4. Universities and colleges - Social aspects -
United States. I. McGrane, Bernard. II. Title.*
*TC LA229 .B386 1999*

**Bell, Judith, 1930-** Doing your research project : a guide
for first-time researchers in education and social
science / Judith Bell. 3rd ed. Buckingham [England] ;
Philadelphia : Open University Press, 1999. xiv, 230 p. ;
ill. ; 22 cm. Includes bibliographical references (p. [216]-225)
and index. ISBN 0-335-20388-4 (pbk.) ISBN 0-335-20389-2
(hardcover) DDC 370/.7/2
*1. Education - Research. 2. Education - Research -
Methodology. 3. Social sciences - Research. 4. Social
sciences - Research - Methodology. 5. Independent study. I.
Title.*
*TC LB1028 .B394 1999*

**Bell, Julian, 1952-** What is painting? : representation
and modern art / Julian Bell. New York : Thames and
Hudson, 1999. 256 p. : ill. (some col.), ports. ; 22 cm.
Includes bibliographical references (p. 241-250) and index.
ISBN 0-500-28101-7 (pbk.) DDC 750/.1
*1. Painting - Philosophy. 2. Painting, Modern. I. Title.*
*TC ND1140 .B45 1999*

**Bell, Lisa M.** Frontal lobe dysfunction in first episode
Schizophrenia : redundancy bias in acute and
stabilized states / Lisa M. Bell. 1998. viii, 135 leaves :
ill. ; 29 cm. Issued also on microfilm. Includes tables. Thesis
(Ph.D.)--Columbia University, 1998. Includes bibliographical
references (leaves 97-122)
*1. Frontal lobes - Diseases. 2. Neuropsychological tests. 3.
Executive ability. 4. Forensic neuropsychology. 5. Intelligence
levels. 6. Schizophrenia. I. Title.*
*TC 085 B3995*

**BELL RINGING. *See* HANDBELL RINGING.**

**Bell, Sandra M.**
The anthropology of friendship. Oxford ; New York :
Berg, 1999.
*TC GN486.3 .A48 1999*

**Bell, Susan S.**
Barnett, David W., 1946- Designing preschool
interventions. New York : Guilford Press, 1999.

*TC LC4801 .B36 1999*

**Bell, Trudy E.** Engineering tomorrow : : today's
technology experts envision the next century / Janie
Fouke, editor : Trudy E. Bell and Dave Dooling,
writers. Piscataway, NJ : IEEE Press, c2000. xiv, 308
p. : col. ill., ports. (some col.) ; 29 cm. Includes index. ISBN
0-7803-5360-9 (Platinum ed.) ISBN 0-7803-5361-7 (Member
cloth ed.) ISBN 0-7803-5362-5 (Trade cloth ed.)
*1. Technological forecasting. 2. Twenty-first century -
Forecasts. 3. Engineering - Forecasting. I. Dooling, Dave. II.
Fouke, Janie. III. Title.*
*TC T174 .B451 2000*

**Bellack, Arno A., ed.**
Research into classroom processes; New York,
Teachers College Press, 1971.
*TC LB1028 .W488*

**BELLES-LETTRES. *See* LITERATURE.**

**Belloli, Andrea P. A.** Exploring world art / Andrea
Belloli. Los Angeles, Calif. : J. Paul Getty Museum,
1999. 116 p. : col. ill. ; 29 cm. Includes index. SUMMARY:
Introduces the world of art, placing Western European art in a
broad global context and discussing artistic treatment of such
themes as other worlds, daily life, history and myth, and
nature. ISBN 0-89236-510-2 DDC 709
*1. Art - Themes, motives - Juvenile literature. 2. Art
appreciation - Juvenile literature. 3. Art appreciation. I. Title.*
*TC N7440 .B35 1999*

**Bellows, Susan.**
Africans in America [videorecording]. [Boston,
Mass.] : WGBH Educational Foundation ; South
Burlington, VT : WGBH Boston Video [distributor],
c1998.
*TC E441 .A47 1998*

**BELLS. *See* HANDBELL RINGING;
HANDBELLS.**

**Bellugi, Ursula, 1931-.**
The signs of language revisited. Mahwah, N.J. :
L.Erlbaum, 2000.
*TC HV2474 .S573 2000*

**Beltyukova, G. V.**
Moro, M. I. Russian grade 1 mathematics. Chicago :
University of Chicago School of Mathematics Project,
1992.
*TC QA14.R9 R8611 1992*

Moro, M. I. Russian grade 2 mathematics. Chicago :
University of Chicago School of Mathematics Project,
1992.
*TC QA14.R9 R8711 1992*

**Bemak, Fred.** Violent and aggressive youth :
intervention and prevention strategies for changing
times / Fred Bemak, Susan Keys. Thousand Oaks,
Calif. : London : Corwin Press, c2000. xii, 106 p. ; 23
cm. (Practical skills for counselors) Includes bibliographical
references and index. ISBN 0-8039-8825-6 (cloth : alk. paper)
ISBN 0-8039-8826-4 (paper : alk. paper) DDC 371.7/8
*1. School violence - United States - Prevention. 2. Juvenile
delinquency - United States - Prevention. I. Keys, Susan. II.
Title. III. Series.*
*TC LB3013.3 .B45 2000*

**Bempechat, Janine, 1956-** Getting our kids back on
track : educating children for the future / Janine
Bempechat. 1st ed. San Francisco : Jossey-Bass,
c2000. xx, 196 p. ; 24 cm. Includes bibliographical references
(p. 185-186) and index. CONTENTS: Challenging our
assumptions -- Talking to your children about school --
Supporting achievement at home -- Dealing with homework --
Working with the teacher's values -- Balancing extra-curricular
interests with academic obligations -- Confronting negative
peer pressure -- What you say and do really matters --
Appendix: Helpful questions to ask yourself and your
children's teachers -- Notes -- Recommended reading -- The
author -- Index. ISBN 0-7879-4991-4 (acid-free paper) DDC
649/.1
*1. Education - Parent participation - United States. 2. Home
and school - United States. 3. Child rearing - United States. I.
Title.*
*TC LC225.3 .B45 2000*

**Ben-Ari, Rachel.**
Enhancing education in heterogeneous schools.
Ramat-Gan : Bar-Ilan University Press, [1997]
*TC LC214 .E54 1997*

**Ben-Peretz, Miriam.**
Routledge international companion to education.
London ; New York : Routledge, 2000.
*TC LB7 .R688 2000*

**Ben-Porath, Yossef S.**
Graham, John R. (John Robert), 1940- MMPI-2
correlates for outpatient community mental health

settings. Minneapolis : University of Minnesota Press,
c1999.
*TC RC473.M5 G733 1999*

**Ben-Ze'ev, Aharon.** The subtlety of emotions / Aaron
Ben-Ze'ev. Cambridge, Mass. : London : MIT Press,
c2000. xv, 611 p. : ill. ; 24 cm. "A Bradford book." Includes
bibliographical references (p. [567]-588) and index. ISBN
0-262-02463-2 (alk. paper) DDC 152.4
*1. Emotions. 2. Affect (Psychology) 3. Mood (Psychology) I.
Title.*
*TC BF531 .B43 2000*

**Benally, Suzanne.**
Partial recall. 1st ed. New York : New Press :
Distributed by W.W. Norton & Co., Inc., 1992.
*TC E89 .P33 1992*

**Benardot, Dan, 1949-** Nutrition for serious athletes /
Dan Benardot. Champaign, IL : Human
Kinetics, c2000. xiv, 337 p. : ill. ; 23 cm. Includes
bibliographical references (p.312-330) and index. ISBN 0-
88011-833-4 DDC 613.2/024/796
*1. Athletes - Nutrition. I. Title.*
*TC TX361.A8 B45 2000*

**Benchmarking and threshold standards in higher
education /** [edited by] Helen Smith, Michael
Armstrong and Sally Brown. London : Kogan Page,
c1999. xiii, 288 p. ; 24 cm. (Staff and educational
development series). Includes bibliographical references and
index. ISBN 0-7494-3033-8
*1. Education, Higher - Standards - Great Britain. I. Smith,
Helen, 1951- II. Armstrong, Michael- 1957 III. Brown, Sally,
1950 Feb. 1- IV. Series.*
*TC LB2341.8.G7 B463 1999*

**Bendall, A. Sarah.** A history of Emmanuel College,
Cambridge / Sarah Bendall, Christopher Brooke,
Patrick Collinson. Woodbridge, Suffolk, UK :
Rochester, NY : Boydell Press, 1999. xvii, 741 p. : ill. ;
25 cm. Includes bibliographical references and index. ISBN
0-85115-393-3 (hard : alk. paper) DDC 378.426/59
*1. Emmanuel College (University of Cambridge) - History. I.
Brooke, Christopher Nugent Lawrence. II. Collinson, Patrick.
III. Title.*
*TC LF185 .B46 1999*

**Bendall-Brunello, John, ill.**
Braun, Trudi. My goose Betsy. 1st U.S. ed.
Cambridge, MA : Candlewick Press, 1999.
*TC PZ10.3.B745 My 1998*

**Bender Gestalt screening for brain dysfunction.**
Lacks, Patricia. 2nd ed. New York : John Wiley &
Sons, c1999.
*TC RC386.6.B46 L3 1999*

**BENDER-GESTALT TEST.**
Lacks, Patricia. Bender Gestalt screening for brain
dysfunction. 2nd ed. New York : John Wiley & Sons,
c1999.
*TC RC386.6.B46 L3 1999*

Lacks, Patricia. Bender Gestalt screening for brain
dysfunction. 2nd ed. New York : John Wiley & Sons,
c1999.
*TC RC386.6.B46 L3 1999*

**Beneath thy guiding hand.**
Hoffecker, Carol E. Newark, Del. : University of
Delaware, c1994.
*TC LD1483 .H64 1994*

**BENEFACTORS. *See* PHILANTHROPISTS.**

**BENEVOLENCE. *See* KINDNESS.**

**BENEVOLENT INSTITUTIONS. *See* CHARITIES;
HOSPITALS; INSTITUTIONAL CARE;
PUBLIC WELFARE; SOCIAL SERVICE.**

**Bengtson, Vern L.**
Handbook of theories of aging. New York : Springer
Pub. Co., c1999.
*TC HQ1061 .H3366 1999*

**Benito's dream bottle.**
Nye, Naomi Shihab. 1st ed. New York : Simon &
Schuster Books for Young Readers, c1995.
*TC PZ7.N976 Be 1995*

**Benjamin, Amy, 1951-** English teacher's guide to
performance tasks and rubrics, high school / by Amy
Benjamin. Larchmont, N.Y. : Eye On Education,
2000. xiv, 189 p. ; 28 cm. Includes bibliographical references.
ISBN 1-88300-193-5 DDC 428/.0076
*1. Language arts (Secondary) - Evaluation. I. Title.*
*TC LB1631 .B383 2000*

**Benjamin, Ludy T., 1945-.**
Activities handbook for the teaching of psychology.
Washington, D.C. : American Psychological
Association, c1981-<c1999 >

*TC BF78 .A28*

**Benjamin, Roger, 1957-.**
Antipodean currents. New York : Guggenheim
Museum, c1995.
*TC N7404 .A58 1995*

**Benjamin, Roger W.**
Rediscovering the democratic purposes of education.
Lawrence : University Press of Kansas, c2000.
*TC LC89 .R43 2000*

**Benner, David G.**
Baker encyclopedia of psychology & counseling. 2nd
ed. Grand Rapids, Mich. : Baker Books, c1999.
*TC BF31 .B25 1999*

**Bennett, Gordon.**
Antipodean currents. New York : Guggenheim
Museum, c1995.
*TC N7404 .A58 1995*

**Bennett, Gordon, 1955-.**
McLean, Ian, Dr. The art of Gordon Bennett.
Roseville East, NSW : Craftsman House, 1996.
*TC N7405.B46 M39 1996*

**BENNETT, GORDON, 1955- - CRITICISM AND
INTERPRETATION.**
McLean, Ian, Dr. The art of Gordon Bennett.
Roseville East, NSW : Craftsman House, 1996.
*TC N7405.B46 M39 1996*

**Bennett, Hazel.**
Sherlock, Philip Manderson, Sir. The story of the
Jamaican people. Kingston, Jamaica : I. Randle
Publishers ; Princeton, N.J. : M. Wiener Publishers,
1998.
*TC F1881 .S5 1998*

**Bennett, James T.** From pathology to politics : public
health in America / James T. Bennett, Thomas J.
DiLorenzo. New Brunswick [N.J.] (U.S.A.) :
Transaction Publishers, c2000. 160 p. ; 24 cm. Includes
bibliographical references and index. ISBN 0-7658-0023-3
(alk. paper) DDC 362.1/0973
*1. Public health - United States - History. 2. Public health -
Social aspects - United States - History. 3. Public Health -
history - United States. 4. Social Medicine - United States. 1.
DiLorenzo, Thomas J. II. Title.*
*TC RA445 .B45 2000*

**Bennett, Joel B.** Time and intimacy : a new science of
personal relationships / Joel B. Bennett. Mahwah,
N.J. ; London : Lawrence Erlbaum Associates, 2000.
xxi, 349 p. : ill. ; 24 cm. (LEA's series on personal
relationships) Includes bibliographical references (p. 313-333)
and indexes. ISBN 0-8058-3679-9 (hbk. : alk. paper) ISBN
0-8058-3680-2 (pbk. : alk. paper) DDC 158.2
*1. Intimacy (Psychology) 2. Time. 3. Interpersonal relations. 1.
Title. II. Series.*
*TC BF575.I5 B45 2000*

**Bennett, Mark, 1956-.**
Developmental psychology. Philadelphia, PA :
Psychology Press, 1999.
*TC BF713 .D4646 1999*

**Bennett, Neville.** Skills development in higher
education and employment / Neville Bennett,
Elisabeth Dunne, Clive Carré. Buckingham
[England] ; Philadelphia : Society for Research into
Higher Education & Open University Press, 2000. x,
210 p. : ill. ; 24 cm. Includes bibliographical references (p.
[198]-205) and indexes. ISBN 0-335-20336-1 (hbk.) ISBN
0-335-20335-3 (pbk.) DDC 370.11/3/0941
*1. Training - Great Britain. 2. Occupational training - Great
Britain. 3. Education, Higher - Aims and objectives - Great
Britain. 4. Professional education - Great Britain. 5. Industry
and education - Great Britain. 1. Dunne, Elisabeth, 1952- II.
Carré, Clive. III. Society for Research into Higher Education.
IV. Title.*
*TC LB1027.47 .B46 2000*

**Bennett, Rebecca, 1969-.**
HIV and AIDS. Oxford ; New York ; Oxford
University Press, 1999.
*TC RA644.A25 H57855 1999*

**Bennett, William J. (William John), 1943-** The
educated child : a parent's guide from preschool
through eighth grade / William J. Bennett, Chester E.
Finn, Jr., John T.E. Cribb, Jr. New York : Free Press,
c1999. xxi, 666 p. ; 24 cm. Includes bibliographical
references and index. ISBN 0-684-83349-2 DDC 371.19/2
*1. Education, Elementary - Parent participation - United
States - Handbooks, manuals, etc. 2. Early childhood
education - Parent participation - United States - Handbooks,
manuals, etc. 3. Home and school - United States - Handbooks,
manuals, etc. 1. Finn, Chester E., 1944- II. Cribb, John T. E.
III. Title.*
*TC LB1048.5 .B45 1999*

**Bennington, Tammy L.**
Information technologies in evaluation. San Francisco,
Calif. : Jossey-Bass, 1999.
*TC H62 .I54 1999*

**BenShea, Noah.**
What every principal would like to say-- and what to
say next time. Thousand Oaks, Calif. : Corwin Press,
c2000.
*TC LB2831.9 .W53 2000*

**Benson, April Lane.**
I shop, therefore I am. Northvale, NJ : Jason Aronson,
c2000.
*TC RC569.5.S56 I12 2000*

**Benson, Linda.** China's last Nomads : the history and
culture of China's Kazaks / Linda Benson and Ingvar
Svanberg. Armonk, N.Y. : M.E. Sharpe, c1998. xiii,
251 p. : ill., maps ; 24 cm. (Studies on modern China) "An East
gate book." Includes bibliographical references (p. 225-240)
and index. ISBN 1-56324-781-X (cloth : alk. paper) ISBN
1-56324-782-8 (pbk. : alk. paper) ISBN 1-56324-782-8 (pbk. :
alk. paper) DDC 952/.00494345
*1. Kazakhs - China - History - 20th century. 2. Xinjiang Uygur
Zizhiqu (China) - Ethnic relations. 1. Svanberg, Ingvar, 1953-
II. Series.*
*TC DS731.K38 B46 1998*

**Benson, Richard, 1943-** A Yale album : the third
century / selection and commentary by Richard
Benson. New Haven : Yale University in association
with Yale University Press, c2000. 168 p. : ill. (some
col.) ; 32 cm. "Yale University tercentennial, 1701-2001."
ISBN 0-300-08723-3
*1. Yale University - History - 20th century - Pictorial works. 1.
Yale University. II. Title.*
*TC LD6337 .B46 2000*

**Benson, Sonja, 1968-.**
Gafner, George, 1947- Handbook of hypnotic
inductions. New York : W. W. Norton, 2000.
*TC RC495 .G27 2000*

**Benton, Lauren A.**
Employee training and U.S. competitiveness.
Boulder : Westview Press, 1991.
*TC HF5549.5.T7 E46 1991*

**Benton, Michael, 1939-** Studies in the spectator role :
literature, painting, and pedagogy / Michael Benton.
London ; New York : Routledge, 2000. xv, 220 p. : ill. ;
25 cm. Includes bibliographical references (p. [203]-211) and
index. ISBN 0-415-20827-0 (alk. paper) ISBN 0-415-20828-9
(pbk. : alk. paper) DDC 820/.71/241
*1. English literature - Study and teaching - Great Britain. 2.
Art - Study and teaching - Great Britain. 3. Art and literature -
Great Britain. 4. Art in education - Great Britain. 1. Title.*
*TC PR51.G7 B46 2000*

**Benton, Peter.**
Special needs and the beginning teacher. London ;
New York : Continuum, 2000.
*TC LC4036.G7 S684 2000*

**BENZER, SEYMOUR.**
Weiner, Jonathan. Time, love, memory. 1st ed. New
York : Knopf, 1999.
*TC QH457 .W43 1999*

**BEQUESTS. See INHERITANCE AND
SUCCESSION.**

**Berdie, Frances S., joint author.**
Finley, Carmen J. The national assessment approach
to exercise development [Ann Arbor, Mich.] National
Assessment of Educational Progress [1970]
*TC LB3051 .F53*

**BEREAVEMENT. See GRIEF.**

**BEREAVEMENT IN ADOLESCENCE.**
Christ, Grace Hyslop. Healing children's grief. New
York ; Oxford : Oxford University Press, 2000.
*TC BF723.G75 C58 2000*

**BEREAVEMENT IN CHILDREN.**
Christ, Grace Hyslop. Healing children's grief. New
York ; Oxford : Oxford University Press, 2000.
*TC BF723.G75 C58 2000*

Smith, Susan C. The forgotten mourners. 2nd ed.
London ; Philadelphia : Jessica Kingsley Publishers,
1999.
*TC BF723.G75 P46 1999*

**BEREAVEMENT - PSYCHOLOGICAL ASPECTS.**
Archer, John, 1944- The nature of grief. London ;
New York : Routledge, 1999.
*TC BF575.G7 A73 1999*

Davidman, Lynn, 1955- Motherloss. Berkeley, Calif. :
University of California Press, c2000.

*TC BF575.G7 D37 2000*

Loss and trauma. Philadelphia, PA : Brunner-
Routledge, c2000.
*TC BF575.D35 L67 2000*

Rosenblatt, Paul C. Parent grief. Philadelphia : Hove
[England] : Brunner/Mazel, c2000.
*TC BF575.G7 R673 2000*

Sanders, Catherine M. Grief. 2nd ed. New York : J.
Wiley, c1999.
*TC BF575.G7 S26 1999*

**Bereiter, Carl.**
Teacher toolbox [kit]. Chicago, Ill. : Open Court Pub.
Co., c1995.
*TC LB1573.3 .T4 1995*

**Berel, Marianne.** Musical play sessions / Marianne
Berel ; with illustrations by Peggy Lipschutz. [S.l. :
s.n.], 1994. viii, 40 p. : ill., music ; 22 x 29 cm. Subtitle on
cover: 25 songs by Marianne Berel.
*1. Music therapy. 2. Handicapped children. 3. Learning,
Psychology of. 4. Children's songs. I. Lipschutz, Peggy II.
Title. III. Title: 25 songs by Marianne Berel*
*TC ML3920 .B45 1994*

**Berends, Mark, 1962-** Assessing the progress of New
American Schools : a status report / Mark Berends
with Joanna Heilbrunn, Christopher J. McKelvey,
Thomas Sullivan. Santa Monica, CA : RAND, 1999.
xviii, 42 p. : ill. ; 23 cm. "MR-1085-EDU." Includes
bibliographical references (p. 37-42). Abstract and ordering
information for all Rand publications as well as full text
versions of selected publications available via the Internet at
the publisher's website. URL: http://www.rand.org/PUBS/
index.html ISBN 0-8330-2761-1 DDC 371.2/00973
*1. New American Schools (Organization) 2. School
improvement programs - United States - Evaluation. 3.
Educational change - United States. 1. Rand Corporation. II.
Title.*
*TC LB2822.82 .B45 1999*

Kirby, Sheila Nataraj, 1946- Staffing at-risk school
districts in Texas. Santa Monica, CA : Rand, 1999.
*TC LB2833.3.T4 K57 1999*

**Berenzy, Alix, ill.**
Sayre, April Pulley. Home at last. 1st ed. New York :
Holt, 1998.
*TC QL754 .S29 1998*

**Berg, Francie M.** Women afraid to eat : breaking free in
today's weight-obsessed world / Frances M. Berg ;
edited by Kendra Rosencrans. Hettinger, ND : Healthy
Weight Network, c2000. 376 p. : ill. ; 23 cm. Includes
bibliographical references (p. 353-368) and index. ISBN
0-918532-62-0 (pbk.) ISBN 0-918532-63-9
*1. Overweight women - Psychology. 2. Overweight women -
United States. 3. Eating disorders - United States. 4. Body
image. 5. Obesity - Social aspects - United States. 6. Obesity -
United States. 1. Rosencrans, Kendra. II. Title.*
*TC RC552.O25 B47 2000*

**Bergan, Helen, 1937-** Where the information is : a
guide to electronic research for nonprofit
organizations / by Helen Bergan. Alexandria, VA :
BioGuide Press, c1996. iv, 257 p. : ill. ; 22 cm.
"Resources": p. 233-244. Includes bibliographical references
and index. ISBN 0-9615277-2-2
*1. Nonprofit organizations - Information services. 2. Nonprofit
organizations - Computer network resources. 3. Business
information services. 4. Business enterprises - Computer
network resources. 5. Internet (Computer network) I. Title.*
*TC HD62.6 .B47 1996*

**Bergenn, Victor W.**
Beyond heredity and environment. Boulder :
Westview Press, 1995.
*TC BF341 .B48 1995*

**Berger, Elizabeth.** Raising children with character :
parents, trust, and the development of personal
integrity / Elizabeth Berger. Northvale, N.J. : J.
Aronson, c1999. xiv, 234 p. ; 23 cm. Includes
bibliographical references (p. [227]) and index. ISBN
0-7657-0214-2 (alk. paper) DDC 649/.7
*1. Personality development. 2. Child rearing. 3. Parent and
child. 1. Title.*
*TC BF723.P4 B47 1999*

**Berger, Eugenia Hepworth.** Parents as partners in
education : families and schools working together /
Eugenia Hepworth Berger. 5th ed. Upper Saddle
River, N.J. : Merrill, c2000. xii, 564 p. : ill. ; 24 cm.
Includes bibliographical references (p. 527-549) and index.
ISBN 0-13-099654-8 (pbk.) DDC 371.19/2
*1. Home and school - United States. 2. Education - Parent
participation - United States. 1. Title.*
*TC LC225.3 .B47 2000*

**Berger, Kathleen Stassen.**
The developing person through the life span. 4th
edition
Straub, Richard O. (Richard Otto) Study guide.
New York : Worth Publishers, 1998.
*TC BF713 .B463 1998 Guide*

Straub, Richard O. (Richard Otto) Study guide.
New York : Worth Publishers, 1998.
*TC BF713 .B463 1998 Guide*

Straub, Richard O. (Richard Otto) Study guide.
New York : Worth Publishers, 1998.
*TC BF713 .B463 1998 guide*

**Berger, Maurice.**
De Salvo, Donna M. Past imperfect. Southampton,
N.Y. : Parrish Art Museum, in association with the
New Press, New York, N.Y., c1993.
*TC N750 .D4*

**Berger, Melvin.** Germs make me sick! / by Melvin
Berger ; illustrated by Marylin Hafner. 1st ed. New
York : Crowell, c1985. 32 p. : col. ill. ; 19 x 23 cm. (Let's-
read-and-find-out science book) SUMMARY: Explains how
bacteria and viruses affect the human body and how the body
fights them. ISBN 0-690-04428-3 ISBN 0-690-04429-1 (lib.
bdg.) DDC 616.9/2
*1. Bacteria - Juvenile literature. 2. Viruses - Juvenile
literature. 3. Bacterial diseases - Juvenile literature. 4. Virus
diseases - Juvenile literature. 5. Bacteria. 6. Viruses. I. Hafner,
Marylin, ill. II. Title. III. Series.*
*TC QR57 .B47 1985*

**Berger, Rony.**
Preventive approaches in couples therapy.
Philadelphia : Brunner/Mazel, 1999.
*TC RC488.5 .P74 1999*

**Bergman, Abby Barry, joint author.**
Jacobson, Willard J. Science for children. Englewood
Cliffs, N.J. : Prentice-Hall, c1980.
*TC LB1585 .J32*

**Bergman, Abraham B., 1932-.**
20 common problems in pediatrics. New York :
McGraw-Hill, Health Professions Division, c2001.
*TC RJ45.T9 2001*

**Bergman, Lars R.**
Developmental science and the holistic approach.
Mahwah, N.J. : London : Lawrence Erlbaum
Associates, 2000.
*TC BF712.5 .D485 2000*

**Bergmann, Martin S., 1913-.**
The Hartmann era. New York : Other Press, 2000.
*TC BF173 .B4675 2000*

**Bergquist, William H.**
Quehl, Gary H. Fifty years of innovations in
undergraduate education. Indianapolis, Ind : USA
Group Foundation, c1999.
*TC LB1027.3 .Q43 1999*

**Bergvall, Victoria L. (Victoria Lee), 1956-.**
Rethinking language and gender research. London ;
New York : Longman, 1996.
*TC P120.S48 R48 1996*

**Berinstein, Paula.** The statistical handbook on
technology / by Paula Berinstein. Phoenix, AZ : Oryx
Press, 1999. xxiv, 277 p. : ill. ; 28 cm. Includes index. ISBN
1-57356-208-4 (alk. paper) DDC 609.73/021
*1. Technology - United States - Statistics - Handbooks,
manuals, etc. I. Title.*
*TC T21 .B47 1999*

**Berkell Zager, Dianne, 1948-.**
Autism. 2nd ed. Mahwah, N.J. : Lawrence Erlbaum
Associates, 1999.
*TC RJ506.A9 A9223 1999*

**Berkowitz, Leonard, 1926-** Causes and consequences
of feelings / Leonard Berkowitz. Cambridge, U.K. ;
New York : Cambridge University Press ; Paris :
Editions de la Maison des sciences de l'homme, 2000.
ix, 255 p. : ill. ; 23 cm. (Studies in emotion and social
interaction) Includes bibliographical references (p. 225-243)
and index. ISBN 0-521-63325-7 (hardback) ISBN 0-521-
63363-X (pbk.) DDC 152.4
*1. Emotions. 2. Affect (Psychology) I. Title. II. Series.*
*TC BF531 .B45 2000*

**Berlant, Lauren Gail, 1957-.**
Intimacy. Chicago : University of Chicago Press,
c2000.
*TC BF575.I5 I57 2000*

**Berlin, Charles I.**
The efferent auditory system. San Diego : Singular
Pub. Group, c1999.
*TC RF286.5 .E36 1999*

**Berlin, William S.**
Remy, Richard C. Government in the United States.
New York : Scribner educational publishers, 1987.
*TC JK274 .R54 1987*

**Berlinerblau, Jacques.** Heresy in the University : the
Black Athena controversy and the responsibilities of
American intellectuals / Jacques Berlinerblau. New
Brunswick, N.J. : Rutgers University Press, c1999. xii,
288 p. : map ; 25 cm. Includes bibliographical references (p.
243-273) and index. ISBN 0-8135-2587-X (alk. paper) ISBN
0-8135-2588-8 (pbk. : alk. paper) DDC 949.5
*1. Bernal, Martin. - Black Athena. 2. Greece - Civilization -
Egyptian influences. 3. Greece - Civilization - Phoenician
influences. 4. Greece - Historiography. 5. Learning and
scholarship - United States. 6. Afrocentrism - United States. 7.
United States - Intellectual life - 20th century. I. Title.*
*TC DF78.B3983 B47 1999*

**Berlitz Kids German picture dictionary.**
German picture dictionary. Princeton, NJ : Berlitz
Pub. Co., 1997.
*TC PF3629 .G47 1997*

**Berlitz kids ingles diccionario ilustrado.**
Inglés. Princeton [NJ] : Berlitz Pub. Co., 1997.
*TC PE1628.5 .I54 1997*

**Berlitz Publishing Company.**
1,000 French words. Princeton, N.J. : Berlitz Kids,
Berlitz Pub. Co., 1998.
*TC PC2680 .A15 1998*

1,000 German words. Princeton, N.J. : Berlitz Kids,
c1998.
*TC PF3629 .A14 1998*

French picture dictionary. Princeton : Berlitz Kids,
Berlitz Pub. Co., c1997.
*TC PC2629 .F74 1997*

**Berman, Jeffrey, 1945-** Surviving literary suicide /
Jeffrey Berman. Amherst : University of
Massachusetts Press, c1999. xiii, 290 p. ; 25 cm. Includes
bibliographical references (p. 277-285) and index. ISBN
1-55849-195-3 (cloth : alk. paper) ISBN 1-55849-211-9 (pbk. :
alk. paper) DDC 810.9/353
*1. American literature - History and criticism. 2. American
literature - Study and teaching. 3. Suicide in literature. I. Title.*
*TC PS169.S85 B47 1999*

**Bermuda high school student, teacher, parent, and
administrator perceptions of the causes of
misbehavior.**
Tucker, Gina Marie. Discipline. 1998.
*TC 06 no. 10999*

**Bernadac Marie-Laure.**
Picasso [videorecording]. Chicago, IL : Home Vision,
c1986.
*TC N6853.P5 P52 1986*

**BERNAL, MARTIN.**
**BLACK ATHENA.**
Berlinerblau, Jacques. Heresy in the University.
New Brunswick, N.J. : Rutgers University Press,
c1999.
*TC DF78.B3983 B47 1999*

**Bernard, Michael E. (Michael Edwin), 1950-.** Taking
the stress out of teaching / Michael E. Bernard.
Melbourne : Collins Dove, 1990. xvi, 336 p. ; 22 cm.
Includes bibliographies. ISBN 0-85924-918-2 (pbk.) DDC
371.10019
*1. Teachers - Job stress - Prevention. I. Title.*
*TC LB2840.2 .B47 1990*

**Bernardin, H. John.**
Personality assessment in organizations. New York :
Praeger, 1985.
*TC HF5548.8 .P3995 1985*

**Bernardin, James, ill.**
Farmer, Nancy. Casey Jones's fireman. 1st ed. New
York : Phyllis Fogelman Books, c1998.
*TC PZ8.1.F2225 Cas 1998*

**Berners-Lee, Tim.** Weaving the Web : the original
design and ultimate destiny of the World Wide Web
by its inventor / Tim Berners-Lee with Mark Fischetti.
1st ed. San Francisco : HarperSanFrancisco, c1999. xi,
226 p. ; 25 cm. Includes index. ISBN 0-06-251586-1 (cloth)
ISBN 0-06-251587-X (paper) DDC 025.04
*1. World Wide Web - History. 2. Berners-Lee, Tim. I. Fischetti,
Mark. II. Title.*
*TC TK5105.888 .B46 1999*

**BERNERS-LEE, TIM.**
Berners-Lee, Tim. Weaving the Web. 1st ed. San
Francisco : HarperSanFrancisco, c1999.
*TC TK5105.888 .B46 1999*

**Bernhardt, Debra E.** Ordinary people, extraordinary
lives : a pictorial history of working people in New
York City / Debra E. Bernhardt and Rachel Bernstein.
New York : New York University Press, c2000. xiv,
221 p. : ill. ; 29 cm. "A Project of the Robert F. Wagner Labor
Archives, New York University." Includes bibliographical
references and index. ISBN 0-8147-9866-7 (alk. paper) DDC
305.5/62/097471
*1. Working class - New York (State) - New York - Pictorial
works. 2. New York (N.Y.) - Pictorial works. I. Bernstein,
Rachel Amelia, 1953- II. Robert F. Wagner Labor Archives.
III. Title.*
*TC HD8085.N53 B47 2000*

**Bernhardt, Victoria L., 1952-.**
The example school portfolio. Larchmont, N.Y. : Eye
On Education, 2000.
*TC LB2822.82 .E92 2000*

**School portfolio.**
The example school portfolio. Larchmont, N.Y. :
Eye On Education, 2000.
*TC LB2822.82 .E92 2000*

**Bernstein, Barton E.** The portable lawyer for mental
health professionals : an A-Z guide to protecting your
clients, your practice, and yourself / Barton E.
Bernstein and Thomas L. Hartsell, Jr. New York : J.
Wiley, c1998. xiii, 274 p. : forms ; 24 cm. Includes
bibliographical references (p. 265) and index. ISBN 0-471-
24869-X (pbk. : alk. paper) DDC 344.73/044
*1. Mental health laws - United States - Popular works. 2.
Mental health personnel - Legal status, laws, etc. - United
States - Popular works. I. Hartsell, Thomas L. (Thomas Lee),
1955- II. Title.*
*TC KF3828.Z9 B47 1998*

**Bernstein, Basil B.** Pedagogy, symbolic control, and
identity : theory, research, critique / Basil Bernstein.
Lanham, Md. : Rowman & Littlefield, 2000. xxvi, 229
p. ; 23 cm. Originally published: London ; Washington :
Taylor & Francis. c1996, in series: Critical perspectives on
literacy and education. Includes bibliographical references (p.
215-222) and index. ISBN 0-8476-9575-1 (cloth : alk. paper)
ISBN 0-8476-9576-X (pbk. : alk. paper) DDC 306.43
*1. Educational sociology. 2. Sociolinguistics. 3. Knowledge,
Theory of. 4. Identity.*
*TC LC191 .B456 2000*

The structuring of pedagogic discourse / Basil
Bernstein. London ; New York : Routledge, 1990. x,
235 p. : ill. ; 23 cm. (Class, codes and control ; v. 4) Includes
bibliographical references (p. 219-227) and index. ISBN 0-
415-04568-1 DDC 306.4/4
*1. Sociolinguistics. 2. Educational sociology. I. Title. II. Series.*
*TC P40 .B39 1990*

**Bernstein, Rachel Amelia, 1953-.**
Bernhardt, Debra E. Ordinary people, extraordinary
lives. New York : New York University Press, c2000.
*TC HD8085.N53 B47 2000*

**Bernstein, Roberta.**
Varnedoe, Kirk, 1946- Jasper Johns. New York :
Museum of Modern Art : Distributed by Harry N.
Abrams, c1996.
*TC N6537.J6 A4 1996*

**Berntson, Gary G.**
Handbook of psychophysiology. 2nd ed. Cambridge,
UK ; New York, NY, USA : Cambridge University
Press, 2000.
*TC QP360 .P7515 2000*

**Berry, Carrie, b. 1854.** A Confederate girl : the diary of
Carrie Berry, 1864 / edited by Christy Steele with
Anne Todd ; foreword by Suzanne L. Bunkers ;
[illustrators, Linda Clavel and Kia Bielke]. Mankato,
Minn. : Blue Earth Books, c2000. 32 p. : ill. (some col.) ;
24 cm. (Diaries, letters, and memoirs) Includes bibliographical
references (p. 31) and index. SUMMARY: Excerpts from the
diary of Carrie Berry, describing her family's life in the
Confederate south in 1864. Supplemented by sidebars,
activities, and a timeline of the era. ISBN 0-7368-0343-2 DDC
973.7/82
*1. Berry, Carrie, - b. 1854 - Diaries - Juvenile literature. 2.
United States - History - Civil War, 1861-1865 - Personal
narratives, Confederate - Juvenile literature. 3. Atlanta (Ga.) -
History - Civil War, 1861-1865 - Personal narratives -
Juvenile literature. 4. Girls - Georgia - Atlanta - Diaries -
Juvenile literature. 5. Atlanta (Ga.) - Biography - Juvenile
literature. 6. Atlanta (Ga.) - Social life and customs - 19th
century - Juvenile literature. 7. United States - History - Civil
War, 1861-1865 - Social aspects - Juvenile literature. 8. Berry,
Carrie, - b. 1854. 9. United States - History - Civil War, 1861-
1865 - Personal narratives. 10. Women - Biography. 11.
Diaries. I. Steele, Christy. II. Todd, Anne. III. Clavel, Linda,
ill. IV. Bielke, Kia, ill. V. Title. VI. Series.*
*TC E605 .B5 2000*

**BERRY, CARRIE, B. 1854.**
Berry, Carrie, b. 1854. A Confederate girl. Mankato,
Minn. : Blue Earth Books, c2000.
*TC E605 .B5 2000*

**BERRY, CARRIE, B. 1854 - DIARIES - JUVENILE
LITERATURE.**
Berry, Carrie, b. 1854. A Confederate girl. Mankato,
Minn. : Blue Earth Books, c2000.
*TC E605 .B5 2000*

**Berry, John W.**
Handbook of cross-cultural psychology. 2nd ed.
Boston : Allyn and Bacon, c1997.
*TC GN502 .H36 1997*

**Berry, John W. comp.** Culture and cognition: readings
in cross-cultural psychology, edited by J. W. Berry
and P. R. Dasen. London, Methuen [1974] xiv, 487 p.
22 cm. (Methuen's manuals of modern psychology)
Bibliography: p. [429]-466. ISBN 0-416-75170-9 ISBN
0-416-75180-6 (pbk.) DDC 153.4
*1. Cognition. 2. Personality and culture - Cross-cultural
studies. I. Dasen. P. R., joint comp. II. Title.*
*TC BF311 .B48*

**Bersoff, Donald N.**
Ethical conflicts in psychology. 2nd ed. Washington,
DC : American Psychological Association, c1999.
*TC BF76.4 .E814 1999*

**Berson, Ruth.**
The New painting. San Francisco, CA : Fine Arts
Museums of San Francisco, c1996.
*TC ND547.5.I4 N38 1996*

**Bertelsen, Lars Kiel.**
Symbolic imprints. Aarhus : Aarhus University Press,
c1999.
*TC TR145 .S96 1999*

**Bertenthal, Meryl W.**
National Research Council (U.S.). Committee on
Embedding Common Test Items in State and District
Assessments. Embedding questions. Washington,
DC : National Academy Press, c1999.
*TC LB3051 .N319 1999*

**Berthoff, Ann E.** The mysterious barricades : language
and its limits / Ann E. Berthoff. Toronto ; Buffalo :
University of Toronto Press, c1999. x, 191 p. ; 24 cm.
(Toronto studies in semiotics) Includes bibliographical
references (p. [167]-188) and index. ISBN 0-8020-4706-8
(bound) DDC 401
*1. Language and languages - Philosophy. 2. Semiotics. I. Title.
II. Series.*
*TC P106 .B463 1999*

**Berthoz, Alain.**
**[Sens du Mouvement. English]**
The brain's sense of movement / Alain Berthoz ;
translated by Giselle Weiss. Cambridge, Mass. :
Harvard University Press, 2000. xi, 337 p. : ill. ; 24
cm. (Perspectives in cognitive neuroscience) Includes
bibliographical references (p. [300]-328) and index.
CONTENTS: 1. Perception Is Simulated Action. The Motor
Theory of Perception. The Concept of Acceptor of the
Results of Action. Bernstein's Comparator. Memory
Predicts the Consequences of Action. Mental Nodes. Mirror
Neurons. Simulation, Emulation, or Representation? -- 2.
The Sense of Movement: A Sixth Sense? Proprioception.
The Vestibulary System: An Inertial Center? The Functions
of the Vestibular System. Seeing Movement -- 3. Building
Coherence. How Vision Detects Movement. Visual
Movement and Vestibular Receptors. Am I in my Bed or
Hanging from the Ceiling? The Coherence between Seeing
and Hearing. The Problem of the Coherence and Unity of
Perception. Autism: The Disintegration of Coherence? -- 4.
Frames of Reference. Personal Space and Extrapersonal
Space. Egocentric and Allocentric Frames of Reference.
Natural Frames of Reference. Selecting Frames of
Reference -- 5. A Memory for Predicting. Topographic
Memory or Topokinetic Memory? The Neural Basis of
Spatial Memory: The Role of the Hippocampus.
CONTENTS: 6. Natural Movement. Pioneers. The Problem
of Number of Degrees of Freedom. The Invention of the
Eye. The Form of a Drawing Is Produced by the Law of
Maximal Smoothness -- 7. Synergies and Strategies.
Vestibular Axon Branching and Gaze Stabilization. The
Baby Fish that Wanted to Swim Flat on Its Stomach. The
Neural Bases for Encoding Movement of the Arms.
Coordination of Synergies -- 8. Capture. The Toad's
Decision. The Art of Braking. What If Newton Had Wanted
to Catch the Apple? -- 9. The Look that Investigates the
World. Gaze Orientation. "Go When I'm Looking," not
"Look Where I'm Going" Eye-to-Eye Contact. Gaze and
Emotion. The Neural Basis of Gaze-Orienting Reactions --
10. Visual Exploration. The Brain Is a Fiery Steed. A Model
of Perception-Action Relationships. Imagined Movement
and Actual Movement. Dynamic Memory and Predictive
Control of Movements. Was Piaget Right? -- 11. Balance. A

Physiology of Reaction. How to Make the University of
Edinburgh Oscillate. Toward a Projective Physiology.
CONTENTS: 12. Adaptation. Adaptation and Substitution.
The Rheumatologist and the Ophthalmologist. The Role of
Activity in Compensating for and Preventing
Disorientation -- 13. The Disoriented Brain: Illusions Are
Solutions. Illusion: The Best Possible Hypothesis. Illusions
Caused by Acceleration and Gravity. Illusions of Movement
of the Limbs. Space and Motion Sickness. A Few Other
Illusions -- 14. Architects Have Forgotten the Pleasure of
Movement -- Conclusion: Toward a Tolerant Perception.
ISBN 0-674-80109-1 (cloth : alk. paper) DDC 612.8/2
*1. Motion perception (Vision) 2. Orientation (Physiology) 3.
Proprioception. 4. Brain. 5. Neuropsychology. I. Title. II.
Series.*
*TC QP493 .B47 2000*

**Bertman, Stephen.** Cultural amnesia : America's future
and the crisis of memory / Stephen Bertman.
Westport, Conn. ; London : Praeger, 2000. 176 p. ; 25
cm. Includes bibliographical references (p. [131]-172) and
index. ISBN 0-275-96230-X (alk. paper) DDC 306/.0973
*1. Memory - Social aspects - United States. 2. Academic
achievement - United States. 3. Democracy - United States. 4.
United States - Social conditions - 1980- 5. United States -
Intellectual life - 20th century. 6. Culture. 7. Literacy - United
States. I. Title.*
*TC HN59.2 .B474 2000*

**Bertolino, Bob, 1965-** Therapy with troubled teenagers :
rewriting young lives in progress / Bob Bertolino.
New York : Wiley, c1999. xxi, 234 p. ; 23 cm. Includes
bibliographical references (p. 219-228) and index. ISBN
0-471-24996-3 (cloth : alk. paper) DDC 616.89/14/0835
*1. Problem youth - Counseling of. 2. Adolescent
psychotherapy. 3. Solution-focused therapy. I. Title.*
*TC RJ506.P63 B475 1999*

**Bertrando, Robert, 1941-.**
Eisenberger, Joanne, 1942- Self efficacy. Larchmont,
N.Y. : Eye On Education, c2000.
*TC LC4705 .C67 2000*

**Berube, Maurice R.** Eminent educators : studies in
intellectual influence / Maurice R. Berube. Westport,
Conn. : Greenwood Press, 2000. xii, 176 p. ; 24 cm.
(Contributions to the study of education, 0196-707X ; no. 76)
Includes bibliographical references and index. ISBN
0-313-31060-2 (alk. paper) DDC 370/.1
*1. Dewey, John, - 1859-1952. 2. Gardner, Howard. 3. Gilligan,
Carol, - 1936- 4. Ogbu, John U. 5. Educators - United States -
Biography. 6. Progressive education - United States. 7.
Education - Philosophy. I. Title. II. Series.*
*TC LB875.D5 B47 2000*

**Besig, Ernest.**
Rabbit in the moon [videorecording]. San Francisco,
Calif. : Wabi-Sabi Productions, 1999.
*TC D753.8 .R3 1999*

**Bess, James L.** Teaching alone, teaching together :
transforming the structure of teams for teaching /
James L. Bess and associates. 1st ed. San Francisco :
Jossey-Bass, c2000. xxxiv, 258 p. ; 23 cm. (The Jossey-
Bass higher and adult education series) Includes
bibliographical references and indexes. ISBN 0-7879-4798-9
(alk. paper) DDC 378.1/228
*1. College teaching - United States. 2. Team learning approach
in education - United States. 3. Teaching teams - United States.
4. Group work in education - United States. I. Title. II. Series.*
*TC LB2331 .B48 2000*

**BEST BOOKS.**
Littlejohn, Carol. Keep talking that book!.
Worthington, Ohio : Linworth Pub., 2000.
*TC Z716.3 .L58 2000*

Wilson, Elizabeth Laraway. Books children love.
Westchester, Ill. : Crossway Books, c1987.
*TC Z1037 .W745 1987*

**Best books for building literacy for elementary school
children.**
Gunning, Thomas G. Boston : Allyn and Bacon, 2000.
*TC LB1573 .B47 2000*

**Best books for young teen readers, grades 7 to 10 /**
John T. Gillespie, editor. New Providence, N.J. : R.R.
Bowker, 2000. xviii, 1066p. ; 27 cm. Includes index. ISBN
0-8352-4264-1 DDC 011.62/5
*1. Children's literature. English - Bibliography. 2. Young adult
literature. English - Bibliography. I. Gillespie, John Thomas,
1928-*
*TC Z1037 .B55 2000*

**Best classroom practices.**
Stone, Randi. Thousand Oaks, Calif. : Corwin Press,
c1999.
*TC LB1776.2 .S86 1999*

**Best, Ron, 1945-.**
Education for spiritual, moral, social and cultural
development. London ; New York : Continuum, 2000.
*TC LC268 .E384 2000*

**The best Web sites for teachers.**
Sharp, Richard M. 3rd ed. Eugene, OR : International
Society for Technology in Education, 2000.
*TC LB1044.87 .S52 2000*

**BETETA, RAMÓN, 1901-1965.**
Llinás Alvarez, Edgar. Vida y obra de Ramón Beteta.
1. ed. México : [s.n.], 1996 (México, D.F. : Impresora
Galve)
*TC F1234.B56 L5 1996*

**Bethune, Mary McLeod, 1875-1955.**
**[Selections. 1999]**
Mary McLeod Bethune : building a better world :
essays and selected documents / edited by Audrey
Thomas McCluskey and Elaine M. Smith.
Bloomington : Indiana University Press, c1999. xvi,
317 p. ; 25 cm. Includes bibliographical references (p.
[297]-305) and index. ISBN 0-253-33626-0 (cloth : alk.
paper) DDC 370/.92
*1. Bethune, Mary McLeod, - 1875-1955. 2. Afro-American
women educators - Biography. 3. Afro-American educators -
Biography. 4. Bethune, Mary McLeod, - 1875-1955 - Archives.
5. Afro-Americans - Education - United States - 20th century -
Sources. 6. Afro-Americans - Civil rights - History - 20th
century - Sources. 7. Afro-American women - Education -
Florida - History - 20th century - Sources. 8. United States -
Race relations - Sources. I. McCluskey, Audrey T. II. Smith,
Elaine M., 1942- III. Title.*
*TC E185.97.B34 A25 1999*

**BETHUNE, MARY MCLEOD, 1875-1955.**
Bethune, Mary McLeod, 1875-1955. [Selections.
1999] Mary McLeod Bethune. Bloomington : Indiana
University Press, c1999.
*TC E185.97.B34 A25 1999*

**BETHUNE, MARY MCLEOD, 1875-1955 -
ARCHIVES.**
Bethune, Mary McLeod, 1875-1955. [Selections.
1999] Mary McLeod Bethune. Bloomington : Indiana
University Press, c1999.
*TC E185.97.B34 A25 1999*

**Betrayed as boys.**
Gartner, Richard B. New York : Guilford Press,
c1999.
*TC RC569.5.A28 G37 1999*

**BETROTHAL.** *See* **MARRIAGE.**

**A better beginning :** supporting and mentoring new
teachers / edited by Marge Scherer. Alexandria, Va. :
Association for Supervision and Curriculum
Development, c1999. x, 244 p. : ill. ; 23 cm. Includes
bibliographical references and index. "ASCD stock no.
199236"--T.p. verso. ISBN 0-87120-355-3 (pbk. : alk. paper)
DDC 371.1
*1. First year teachers - United States. 2. Mentoring in
education - United States. I. Scherer, Marge, 1945-*
*TC LB2844.1.N4 B48 1999*

**Better books! Better readers!.**
Hart-Hewins, Linda. York, Me. : Stenhouse
Publishers ; Markham, Ont. : Pembroke Publishers,
c1999.
*TC LB1525 .H26 1999*

**Better together :** teacher's planning guide. New York :
Macmillan/McGraw-Hill, c1997. 1 v. (various pagings) :
col. ill. ; 31 cm. (Spotlight on literacy. Gr.2 l.6 u.3) (The road
to independent reading) Includes index. ISBN 0-02-181160-1
*1. Language arts (Primary) 2. Reading (Primary) I. Series. II.
Series: The road to independent reading*
*TC LB1576 .S66 1997 Gr.2 l.6 u.3*

**A better way to think about business.**
Solomon, Robert C. New York : Oxford University
Press, 1999.
*TC HF5387 .S612 1999*

**Between demonstration and imagination :** essays in
the history of science and philosophy presented to
John D. North / edited by Lodi Nauta and Arjo
Vanderjagt. Leiden, Netherlands ; Boston : Brill,
1999. xviii, 424 p. : ill., maps ; 25 cm. (Brill's studies in
intellectual history, 0920-8607 ; v. 96) Includes bibliographical
references (p. 406-417) and index. Articles in English, 1 article
each in French and German. ISBN 90-04-11468-8 (hc : acid-
free paper) DDC 520/.9
*1. Astronomy - History. 2. Philosophy. I. North, John David. II.
Nauta, Lodi. III. Vanderjagt, Arie Johan. IV. Series.*
*TC QB15 .B56 1999*

**Between politics and science.**
Guston, David H. Cambridge, U.K. ; New York, NY :
Cambridge University Press, 2000.

*TC Q127.U6 G87 2000*

**Between the lines** [videorecording] / Sophia Constantinou, director. Boston, MA : Fanlight Productions, c1997. 1 videocassette (21 min.) : sd., b&w ; 1/2 in. VHS. Catalogued from credits and container. "A film by Sophia Constantinou."--Container. Music: File Under ... [et al.]. For adolescents through adult. SUMMARY: A documentary in which women who cut themselves explain why they cross the line into self-destructive behavior and self-inflicted injury. Many come from backgrounds of sexual abuse and are full of self-hatred, intense psychic pain, emptiness and numbness, paucity of feeling or body concept-- the reasons are many although sexual abuse seems paramount. Self-mutilation is a way of getting in touch with their bodies, coping with emotional pain, seeking the spiritual or the historic-- self-preserving coping mechanisms. ISBN 1-57295-263-6
*1. Self-mutilation. 2. Self-destructive behavior. 3. Body image. 4. Body dysmorphic disorder. 5. Women - Psychology. 6. Documentary films. I. Constantinou, Sophia. II. Fanlight Productions.*
*TC RC552.S4 B4 1997*

**Betz, Nancy E.**
Walsh, W. Bruce, 1936- Tests and assessment. 4th ed. Upper Saddle River, N.J. : Prentice Hall, c2001.
*TC BF176 .W335 2001*

**BEVERAGE INDUSTRY.** *See* **ALCOHOLIC BEVERAGE INDUSTRY.**

**BEVERAGES.** *See* **ALCOHOLIC BEVERAGES.**

**BEVERAGES - GREAT BRITAIN - HISTORY.**
Burnett, John, 1925- Liquid pleasures. London ; New York : Routledge, 1999.
*TC TX815 .B87 1999*

**BEVERAGES - LAW AND LEGISLATION - UNITED STATES - HISTORY.**
Goodwin, Lorine Swainston, 1925- The pure food, drink, and crusaders, 1879-1914. Jefferson, N.C. : McFarland, 1999.
*TC HD9000.9.U5 G66 1999*

**BEVERAGES - SOCIAL ASPECTS - GREAT BRITAIN.**
Burnett, John, 1925- Liquid pleasures. London ; New York : Routledge, 1999.
*TC TX815 .B87 1999*

**Beveridge, Sally.** Special educational needs in schools / Sally Beveridge. 2nd ed. London ; New York : Routledge, 1999. 148 p. ; 21 cm. Includes bibliographical references (p. [135]-144) and index. ISBN 0-415-20293-0 hb ISBN 0-415-20294-9 pb DDC 371.9/0941
*1. Special education - Great Britain. 2. Mainstreaming in education - Great Britain. 3. Education and state - Great Britain. I. Title.*
*TC LC3986.G7 B48 1999*

**Beverley, John.** Subalternity and representation : arguments in cultural theory / John Beverley. Durham [N.C.] ; London : Duke University Press, 1999. xii, 202 p. ; 25 cm. (Post-contemporary interventions) Includes bibliographical references (p. [169]-193) and index. ISBN 0-8223-2382-6 (hbk. : alk. paper) ISBN 0-8223-2416-4 (pbk. : alk. paper) DDC 305/.6
*1. Marginality, Social. 2. Marginality, Social - Political aspects - Latin America. 3. Learning and scholarship - Political aspects. 4. Knowledge, Theory of - Political aspects. 5. Postcolonialism. 6. Culture conflict. I. Title. II. Series.*
*TC HM1136 .B48 1999*

**Bevevino, Mary M.**
Snodgrass, Dawn M., 1955- Collaborative learning in middle and secondary schools. Larchmont, N.Y. : Eye On Education, 2000.
*TC LB1032 .S62 2000*

**Beychok, Cory.**
Tap dancing for beginners [videorecording]. W. Long Branch, NJ : Kultur, c1981.
*TC GV1794 .T3 1981*

**Beyond appearance** : a new look at adolescent girls / edited by Norine G. Johnson, Michael C. Roberts, Judith Worell. 1st ed. Washington, DC : American Psychological Association, c1999. xvi, 464 p. ; 27 cm. Includes bibliographical references and indexes. ISBN 1-55798-582-0 DDC 305.235
*1. Teenage girls - United States - Social conditions. 2. Teenage girls - United States - Psychology. I. Johnson, Norine G. II. Roberts, Michael C. III. Worell, Judith, 1928-*
*TC HQ798 .B43 1999*

**Beyond behavior.**
Walters, Glenn D. Westport, Conn. ; London : Praeger, 2000.
*TC BF353 .W356 2000*

**Beyond behaviorism** : changing the classroom management paradigm / edited by H. Jerome Freiberg ; chapters by Jere Brophy ... [et al.]. Boston : Allyn and Bacon, c 1999. xiv, 178 p. : ill. ; 23 cm. Includes bibliographical references and index. ISBN 0-205-28619-4 (cloth) ISBN 0-205-28267-9 (pbk.) DDC 371.102/4
*1. Classroom management. 2. Classroom management - Case studies. 3. School discipline. 4. Behavior modification. I. Freiberg, H. Jerome. II. Brophy, Jere E.*
*TC LB3013 .B42 1999*

**Beyond fetishism and other excursions in psychopragmatics.**
Moorjani, Angela B. New York : St. Martin's Press, 2000.
*TC BF175.4.C84 M663 2000*

**Beyond formulas in high school algebra.**
Chazan, Daniel. Beyond formulas in mathematics and teaching. New York : Teachers College Press, c2000.
*TC QA159 .C48 2000*

**Beyond formulas in mathematics and teaching.**
Chazan, Daniel. New York : Teachers College Press, c2000.
*TC QA159 .C48 2000*

**Beyond fund raising.**
Grace, Kay Sprinkel. New York : Wiley, c1997.
*TC HG4027.65 .G73 1997*

**Beyond gender differences.**
Hatch, Laurie Russell. Amityville, N.Y. : Baywood Pub., c2000.
*TC HQ1061 .H375 2000*

**Beyond heredity and environment** : Myrtle McGraw and the maturation controversy / edited by Thomas C. Dalton and Victor W. Bergenn. Boulder : Westview Press, 1995. xx, 301 p. : ill. ; 24 cm. Includes bibliographical references and index. ISBN 0-8133-2153-0 (alk. paper) DDC 150/.92
*1. Nature and nurture. 2. McGraw, Myrtle B. - (Myrtle Byram), - 1899- - Contributions in child development. 3. Maturation (Psychology) 4. Child development. 5. Developmental psychobiology. I. Dalton, Thomas Carlyle. II. Bergenn, Victor W.*
*TC BF341 .B48 1995*

**Beyond room 109.**
Kent, Richard Burt. Portsmouth, NH : Heinemann, 2000.
*TC LB1049 .K45 2000*

**Beyond room one hundred nine.**
Kent, Richard Burt. Beyond room 109. Portsmouth, NH : Heinemann, 2000.
*TC LB1049 .K45 2000*

**Beyond talk therapy** : using movement and expressive techniques in clinical practice / edited by Daniel J. Wiener. 1st ed. Washington, D.C. : American Psychological Association, c1999. xix, 309 p. : ill. ; 27 cm. Includes bibliographical references and indexes. ISBN 1-55798-585-5 DDC 616.89/16
*1. Arts - Therapeutic use. 2. Mind and body therapies. 3. Psychodrama. 4. Art Therapy - Case Report. 5. Movement - Case Report. 6. Music Therapy - Case Report. 7. Psychodrama - Case Report. 8. Psychotherapy - methods - Case Report. I. Wiener, Daniel J. II. American Psychological Association.*
*TC RC489.A72 B49 1999*

**Beyond the book.**
Doggett, Sandra L. Englewood, Colo. : Libraries Unlimited, 2000.
*TC ZA4065 .D64 2000*

**Beyond the disease model of mental disorders.**
Kiesler, Donald J. Westport, Conn. : Praeger, c1999.
*TC RC454.4 .K52 1999*

**Beyond the household.**
Kierner, Cynthia A., 1958- Ithaca, NY : Cornell University Press, 1998.
*TC HQ1391.U5 K55 1998*

**Bhattacharya, Diya.** The college experience and the construction of cultural identity among first generation Indian American undergraduates / by Diya Bhattacharya. 1999. 2 v. (ix, 614 leaves) ; 29 cm. Issued also on microfilm. Thesis (Ed.D.)--Teachers College, Columbia University. 1999. Includes bibliographical references (leaves 589-597).
*1. Asian American college students - Attitudes - Case studies. 2. Asian American college students - Socialization - Case studies. 3. Asian American college students - Social identity - Case studies. 4. Asian American families - Social life and customs. 5. Asian American college students - Family relationships. 6. Intergenerational relations. I. Title.*
*TC 06 no. 11083*

**The Bi-monthly review of management research.**
[Dolton, Ill. : A. Thomas Beales 1972-1974]. 3 v. 22-28 cm. Frequency: Bimonthly. Vol. 5, nos. 1 & 2 (Jan./Feb. 1972)-v. 7 (Nov./Dec. 1974). Other title: Management research. "The monthly comprehensive research reference journal." Title from cover. Continues: Management research (Dolton, Ill. : 1971). Changed back to: Management research(Amherst, Mass.).
*I. Title: Management research II. Title: Management research (Dolton, Ill. : 1971) III. Title: Management research(Amherst, Mass.)*

**BI-RACIAL DATING.** *See* **INTERRACIAL DATING.**

**The bi-weekly school law letter.** Laramie, Wyo. : Published by R.R. Hamilton, 1951-1955. 4 v. ; 27 cm. Frequency: Biweekly (irregular). Vol. 1, no. 1 (1951)-v. 4, no. 26 (Feb. 17, 1955). Continued by: National school law reporter (OCoLC)10757681.
*1. Educational law and legislation - United States - Digests. I. Title: Biweekly school law letter II. Title: School law letter III. Title: National school law reporter*

**Biaggio, Maryka. 1950-.**
Effective brief therapies :. San Diego : Academic Press, c2000.
*TC RC480.55 .E376 2000*

**Bianco-Mathis, Virginia.**
The full-time faculty handbook. Thousand Oaks : Sage Publications, c1999.
*TC LB1778.2 .F85 1999*

**BIAS.** *See* **DISCRIMINATION.**

**Bias in prediction on correction methods.**
Rydberg, Sven. Stockholm, Almqvist & Wiksell [1963]
*TC HA31.2 .R93*

**BIAS IN TESTS.** *See* **TEST BIAS.**

**BIAS, JOB.** *See* **DISCRIMINATION IN EMPLOYMENT.**

**BIAS (PSYCHOLOGY).** *See* **PREJUDICES.**

**BIAS, RACIAL.** *See* **RACE DISCRIMINATION; RACISM.**

**Bibace, Roger.**
Partnerships in research, clinical, and educational settings. Stamford, Conn. : Ablex Pub., c1999.
*TC HM1106 .P37 1999*

**BIBLE IN THE SCHOOLS.** *See* **RELIGION IN THE PUBLIC SCHOOLS.**

**BIBLE. N.T. GOSPELS - HISTORY OF CONTEMPORARY EVENTS.**
Millard, A. R. (Alan Ralph) Reading and writing in the time of Jesus. New York : New York University Press, 2000.
*TC BS2555.5 .M55 2000*

**BIBLE. O.T. - BIOGRAPHY - JUVENILE LITERATURE.**
Sobel, Ileene Smith. Moses and the angels. New York : Delacorte Press, c1999.
*TC BM580 .S55 1999*

**BIBLE STORIES, ENGLISH - O.T. - GENESIS.**
Gerstein, Mordicai. Noah and the great flood. 1st ed. New York : Simon & Schuster for Young Readers, c1999.
*TC BS580.N6 G47 1999*

**BIBLE STORIES - O.T.**
Gerstein, Mordicai. Noah and the great flood. 1st ed. New York : Simon & Schuster for Young Readers, c1999.
*TC BS580.N6 G47 1999*

**BIBLICAL COSMOGONY.** *See* **CREATION.**

**BIBLICAL COSMOLOGY.** *See* **CREATION.**

**BIBLIOGRAPHIC INSTRUCTION.** *See* **LIBRARY ORIENTATION.**

**Bibliographie internationale d'anthropologie.**
International bibliography of anthropology = London ; New York : Routledge, 1999-
*TC Z7161 .I593*

**Bibliographies and indexes in American history**
(no. 42) Barbuto, Domenica M., 1951- The American settlement movement. Westport, Conn. : Greenwood Press, 1999.
*TC Z7164.S665 B37 1999*

**Bibliographies and indexes in education**
(no. 20) Academic freedom. Westport, Conn. : Greenwood Press, 2000.
*TC LC72.2 .A29 2000*

**BIBLIOGRAPHY.** *See* **BOOKS; ELECTRONIC PUBLICATIONS; PERIODICALS - INDEXES.**

**BIBLIOGRAPHY - CHILDREN'S BOOKS ISSUED IN SERIES.** *See* **CHILDREN'S LITERATURE IN SERIES.**

**BIBLIOGRAPHY - METHODOLOGY.** *See* **CATALOGING.**

**Bibliography of composition and rhetoric.**
CCCC bibliography of composition and rhetoric. Carbondale : Southern Illinois University Press, c1990-
*TC Z5818.E5 L66*

**BIBLIOGRAPHY - OUT-OF-PRINT BOOKS.** *See* **OUT-OF-PRINT BOOKS.**

**BIBLIOGRAPHY - PERIODICALS.**
Books abroad; Norman, Okla., The University of Oklahoma Press.

Books for Africa. London, International Committee on Christian Literature for Africa.

**BIBLIOGRAPHY - REPRINT EDITIONS.** *See* **REPRINTS (PUBLICATIONS).**

**BIBLIOGRAPHY - VELLUM PRINTED BOOKS.** *See* **VELLUM PRINTED BOOKS.**

**Bibliotheca historica (Helsinki, Finland)**
(4.) Sivonen, Seppo. White-collar or hoe handle. Helsinki : Suomen Historiallinen Seura, [1995]
*TC LA1531 .S58 1995*

**Bibliotheca psychiatrica**
(no. 167) Basic and clinical science of mental and addictive disorders. Basel ; New York : Karger, c1997.
*TC RC327 .B37 1997*

**BIBLIOTHERAPY.** *See also* **PSYCHODRAMA.**
Daly, Brenda O., 1941- Authoring a life. Albany, NY : State University of New York Press, c1998.
*TC RC560.153 D35 1998*

**BICAMERALISM.** *See* **LEGISLATIVE BODIES.**

**Bickart, Toni S.** Building the primary classroom : a complete guide to teaching and learning / Toni S. Bickart, Judy R. Jablon, Diane Trister Dodge. Washington, DC : Teaching Strategies ; Portsmouth, NH : Heinemann, 1999. v, 462 p. : ill. ; 28 cm. Includes bibliographical references and index. ISBN 1-87953-738-9 DDC 372.24'1
*1. Education, Primary. 2. Education, Primary - Curricula. 3. Teaching. I. Jablon, Judy R. II. Dodge, Diane Triste. III. Title. IV. Title: Complete guide to teaching and learning*
*TC LB1507 .B53 1999*

**Bickel, Warren K.**
Reframing health behavior change with behavioral economics. Mahwah, N.J. ; London : Lawrence Erlbaum, 2000.
*TC RA776.9 .R433 2000*

**Bickerton, Derek.**
Calvin, William H., 1939- Lingua ex machina. Cambridge, Mass. ; London : MIT Press, c2000.
*TC QP399 .C35 2000*

**Bickford, Beth.**
The nutty, nougat-filled world of human nutrition [videorecording]. [Arlington, Va.] : Cerebellum Corp., c1998.
*TC QP141 .N8 1998*

**Biddle, Arthur W.**
Teaching critical thinking. Englewood Cliffs, N.J. : Prentice Hall, c1993.
*TC LB1590.3 .T4 1993*

**Biehle, James T.** NSTA guide to school science facilities / James T. Biehle, LaMoine L. Motz, Sandra S. West. Arlington, VA : National Science Teachers Association, c1999. vi, 100 p. : ill. ; 22 x 28 cm. Includes bibliographical references (p. 98-100). ISBN 0-87355-174-5
*1. Laboratories. 2. Science - Study and teaching (Elementary) 3. Science - Study and teaching (Secondary) I. Motz, LaMoine L. II. West, Sandra S. III. National Science Teachers Association. IV. Title. V. Title: School science facilities*
*TC Q183.3.A1 B54 1999*

**Bielke, Kia, ill.**
Berry, Carrie, b. 1854. A Confederate girl. Mankato, Minn. : Blue Earth Books, c2000.
*TC E605 .B5 2000*

**Biemiller, Andrew, 1939-** Language and reading success / by Andrew Biemiller. Cambridge, Mass. : Brookline Books, c1999. 75 p. : ill. ; 23 cm. (From reading research to practice ; v. 5) Includes bibliographical references (p. [71]-75). ISBN 1-57129-068-0 DDC 372.62/2

*1. Children - Language. 2. Reading comprehension. 3. Reading (Elementary) I. Title. II. Series.*
*TC LB1139.L3 B48 1999*

Meichenbaum, Donald. Nurturing independent learners. Cambridge, Mass. : Brookline Books, c1998.
*TC LB1031.4 .M45 1998*

**Bierhorst, John.** The people with five fingers : a native Californian creation tale / retold by John Bierhorst ; illustrated by Robert Andrew Parker. New York : Marshall Cavendish, 2000. 1v. (unpaged) : col. ill. ; 24 cm. SUMMARY: A tale shared by the different native peoples of California tells how Coyote and other animals created the world and the people who came to live in it. ISBN 0-7614-5058-0 DDC 398.2/08997
*1. Indians of North America - California - Folklore. 2. Creation - Mythology. 3. Tales - California. 4. Creation - Folklore. 5. Indians of North America - California - Folklore. 6. Folklore - California. I. Parker, Robert Andrew, ill. II. Title.*
*TC E78.C15 B523 2000*

**Bierut, Michael.**
Looking closer 2. New York : Allworth Press : American Institute of Graphic Arts, c1997.
*TC NC997 .L632 1997*

Looking closer. New York : Allworth Press : American Institute of Graphic Arts ; Saint Paul, MN : Distributor, Consortium Book Sales & Distribution, c1994.
*TC NC997 .L63 1994*

**Biesanz, Karen Zubris.**
Biesanz, Mavis Hiltunen. The Ticos. Boulder, Colo. : Lynne Rienner Publishers, 1999.
*TC F1543 .B563 1999*

**Biesanz, Mavis Hiltunen.** The Ticos : culture and social change in Costa Rica / Mavis Hiltunen Biesanz, Richard Biesanz, Karen Zubris Biesanz. Boulder, Colo. : Lynne Rienner Publishers, 1999. x, 307 p. : ill., maps ; 24 cm. Includes bibliographical references (p. 291-292) and index. ISBN 1-55587-724-9 (alk. paper) ISBN 1-55587-737-0 (pbk. : alk. paper) DDC 972.8605
*1. Costa Rica. I. Biesanz, Richard. II. Biesanz, Karen Zubris. III. Title.*
*TC F1543 .B563 1999*

**Biesanz, Richard.**
Biesanz, Mavis Hiltunen. The Ticos. Boulder, Colo. : Lynne Rienner Publishers, 1999.
*TC F1543 .B563 1999*

**Bieschke, Kathleen J.**
Handbook of counseling and psychotherapy with lesbian, gay, and bisexual clients. 1st ed. Washington, DC ; London : American Psychological Association, c2000.
*TC BF637.C6 H3125 2000*

**Biever, John.**
Sport photography today! [videorecording]. Minneapolis, Minn. : Media Loft, c1992.
*TC TR821 .S64 1992*

**Big bang.**
Stephen Hawking's universe [videorecording]. [Alexandria, Va.] : PBS Video; Burbank, CA : Distributed by Warner Home Video, c1997.
*TC QB982 .S7 1997*

**BIG BANG THEORY.**
Stephen Hawking's universe [videorecording]. [Alexandria, Va.] : PBS Video; Burbank, CA : Distributed by Warner Home Video, c1997.
*TC QB982 .S7 1997*

**BIG BUSINESS.**
Shiva, Vandana. Stolen harvest. Cambridge, MA : South End Press, c2000.
*TC HD9000.5 .S454 2000*

**Big cities in the welfare transition.**
Kahn, Alfred J., 1919- New York City : Cross-National Studies Research Program, Columbia University School of Social Work, 1998.
*TC HV91 .K27 1998*

**The big test.**
Lemann, Nicholas. 1st ed. New York : Farrar, Straus and Giroux, 1999.
*TC LB3051 .L44 1999*

**Bigge, June L.** Curriculum, assessment, and instruction for students with disabilities / June Lee Bigge, Colleen Shea Stump with Michael Edward Spagna, Rosanne K. Silberman. Belmont, CA : Wadsworth Pub., c1999. xix, 492 p. : ill. ; 28 cm. (The Wadsworth special educator series) Includes bibliographical references (p. 466-480) and index. ISBN 0-534-16770-5 (alk. paper) DDC 371.9/0973
*1. Handicapped children - Education - United States - Curricula. 2. Educational tests and measurements - United*

States. 3. Special education - United States. I. Stump, Colleen Shea. II. Title. III. Series.
*TC LC4031 .B46 1999*

**Biggs, John B. (John Burville).** Teaching for quality learning at university : : what the student does / John Biggs. Buckingham, UK ; Philadelphia : Society for Research into Higher Education : Open University Press, 1999. xiv, 250 p. : ill. ; 23 cm. Includes bibliographical references and index. ISBN 0-335-20172-5 ISBN 0-335-20171-7 (pbk.)
*1. College teaching. 2. Learning. 3. College students - Rating of. 4. Effective teaching. I. Title.*
*TC LB2331 .B526 1999*

**Bigham, George.**
Bigham, Vicki Smith. The Prentice Hall directory of online education resources. Paramus, N.J. : Prentice Hall, c1998.
*TC LB1044.87 .B54 1998*

**Bigham, Vicki Smith.** The Prentice Hall directory of online education resources / Vicki Smith Bigham, George Bigham. Paramus, N.J. : Prentice Hall, c1998. x, 390 p. : ill. ; 28 cm. Includes index. ISBN 0-13-618588-6 DDC 025.06/37
*1. Education - Computer network resources - Directories. 2. Internet (Computer network) in education - Directories. 3. World Wide Web - Directories. I. Bigham, George. II. Title. III. Title: Directory of online education resources IV. Title: Online education resources*
*TC LB1044.87 .B54 1998*

**BILDUNGSROMAN.**
Barney, Richard A., 1955- Plots of enlightenment. Stanford, Calif. : Stanford University Press, c1999.
*TC PR858.E38 B37 1999*

**Bilingual acquisition.**
Deuchar, M. (Margaret) Oxford ; New York : Oxford University Press, 2000.
*TC P118 .D439 2000*

**BILINGUAL EDUCATION.** *See* **EDUCATION, BILINGUAL.**

**Bilingual education and bilingualism**
(14) Freeman, Rebecca D. (Rebecca Diane), 1960- Bilingual education and social change. Clevedon [England] ; Philadelphia : Multilingual Matters, c1998.
*TC LC3731 .F72 1998*

(16) Woods, Peter, 1934- Multicultural children in the early years. Clevedon ; Philadelphia : Multilingual Matters Ltd, c1999.
*TC LC3736.G6 W66 1999*

(18) Thompson, Linda, 1949- Young bilingual children in nursery school. Clevedon, UK ; Buffalo, NY : Multilingual Matters, c2000.
*TC LC3723 .T47 2000*

(20) Toohey, Kelleen, 1950- Learning English at school. Clevedon, [England] ; Buffalo : Multilingual Matters, 2000.
*TC PE1128.A2 T63 2000*

(21) The sociopolitics of English language teaching. Clevedon ; Buffalo [N.Y.] : Multilingual Matters, c2000.
*TC PE1128.A2 S5994 2000*

(23) Cummins, Jim, 1949- Language, power, and pedagogy. Clevedon [England] ; Buffalo [N.Y.] : Multilingual Matters, c2000.
*TC LC3719 .C86 2000*

**Bilingual education and social change.**
Freeman, Rebecca D. (Rebecca Diane), 1960- Clevedon [England] : Philadelphia : Multilingual Matters, c1998.
*TC LC3731 .F72 1998*

**BILINGUALISM.** *See also* **EDUCATION, BILINGUAL; INTERFERENCE (LINGUISTICS).**
Hamers, Josiane F. Bilinguality and bilingualism. 2nd ed. Cambridge, England ; New York, NY : Cambridge University Press, 2000.
*TC P115 .H3613 2000*

**BILINGUALISM - ASIA - CONGRESSES.**
Bilingualism Through the Classroom : Strategies and Practices (1995 : Universiti Brunei Darussalam) Bilingualism through the classroom : strategies and practices. [Bandar Seri Begawan : Universiti Brunei Darussalam, 1995]
*TC P115 .B57 1995*

**BILINGUALISM - CONGRESSES.**
Bilingualism Through the Classroom : Strategies and Practices (1995 : Universiti Brunei Darussalam) Bilingualism through the classroom : strategies and

practices. [Bandar Seri Begawan : Universiti Brunei Darussalam, 1995]
*TC P115 .B57 1995*

## BILINGUALISM IN CHILDREN - CASE STUDIES.
Deuchar, M. (Margaret) Bilingual acquisition. Oxford : New York : Oxford University Press, 2000.
*TC P118 .D439 2000*

**Bilingualism through the classroom : strategies and practices.**
Bilingualism Through the Classroom : Strategies and Practices (1995 : Universiti Brunei Darussalam) [Bandar Seri Begawan : Universiti Brunei Darussalam, 1995]
*TC P115 .B57 1995*

**Bilingualism Through the Classroom : Strategies and Practices (1995 : Universiti Brunei Darussalam)**
Bilingualism through the classroom : strategies and practices : papers and discussants' comments for a colloquium held at Universiti Brunei Darussalam, 5-9 June 1995. [Bandar Seri Begawan : Universiti Brunei Darussalam, 1995] 1 v. (various pagings) : ill., map ; 30 cm. Includes bibliographical references.
*1. Bilingualism - Congresses. 2. Bilingualism - Asia - Congresses. 3. Education, Bilingual - Congresses. 4. Education, Bilingual - Asia - Congresses. 5. Language policy - Congresses. 6. Language policy - Asia - Congresses. 7. English language - Study and teaching - Congresses. 8. English language - Study and teaching - Asia - Congresses. I. Title. II. Title: Papers and discussants' comments*
*TC P115 .B57 1995*

## BILINGUALISM - UNITED STATES.
So much to say. New York : Teachers College Press, c1999.
*TC PE1128.A2 S599 1999*

**Bilinguality and bilingualism.**
Hamers, Josiane F. 2nd ed. Cambridge, England : New York, NY : Cambridge University Press, 2000.
*TC P115 .H3613 2000*

## BILL-POSTING. *See* POSTERS.

**Bill W. and Mister Wilson.**
Raphael, Matthew J. Bill W. and Mr. Wilson. Amherst : University of Massachusetts Press, c2000.
*TC HV5032.W19 R36 2000*

**Bill W. and Mr. Wilson.**
Raphael, Matthew J. Amherst : University of Massachusetts Press, c2000.
*TC HV5032.W19 R36 2000*

**Biller, Peter.**
The medieval church. Woodbridge, Suffolk ; Rochester, NY : Published for the Ecclesiastical History Society by the Boydell Press, 1999.
*TC BR270 .M43 1999*

**Billig, Michael.** Freudian repression : conversation creating the unconscious / Michael Billig. New York : Cambridge University Press, 1999. vii, 290 p. ; 23 cm. Includes bibliographical references and indexes. ISBN 0-521-65052-6 (hardcover) ISBN 0-521-65956-6 (pbk.) DDC 154.2/4
*1. Repression (Psychology) 2. Psychoanalysis. 3. Freud, Sigmund, - 1856-1939. I. Title.*
*TC BF175.5.R44 B55 1999*

**Billingsley, William J., 1953-** Communists on campus : race, politics, and the public university in sixties North Carolina / William J. Billingsley. Athens, Ga. ; London : University of Georgia Press, c1999. xvi, 308 p., [6] p. of plates ; 24 cm. Includes bibliographical references (p. 245-299) and index. ISBN 0-8203-2109-5 (alk. paper) DDC 378.1/21
*1. Academic freedom - North Carolina - History - 20th century. 2. Universities and colleges - Law and legislation - North Carolina. 3. Politics and education - North Carolina - History - 20th century. 4. Anti-communist movements - North Carolina - History - 20th century. I. Title.*
*TC LC72.3.N67 B55 1999*

**Billstein, Rick.**
  **Problem solving approach to mathematics. 5th ed.**
  Billstein, Rick. A problem solving approach to mathematics for elementary school teachers. 5th ed. Reading, Mass. : Addison-Wesley, c1993.
*TC QA135.5 .B49 1993*

A problem solving approach to mathematics for elementary school teachers / Rick Billstein, Shlomo Libeskind, Johnny W. Lott. 5th ed. Reading, Mass. : Addison-Wesley, c1993. xxii, 905 p. : ill. (some col.) ; 27 cm. Fifth ed. also published under title: A problem solving approach to mathematics. Includes bibliographical references and index. ISBN 0-201-52565-8 DDC 372.7
*1. Mathematics - Study and teaching (Elementary) 2. Problem solving. I. Libeskind, Shlomo. II. Lott, Johnny W., 1944- III.*

*Billstein, Rick. Problem solving approach to mathematics. 5th ed. IV. Title. V. Title: Mathematics for elementary school teachers.*
*TC QA135.5 .B49 1993*

**Bilodeau, Martin, 1961-** Theory of multivariate statistics / Martin Bilodeau, David Brenner. New York : Springer, c1999. xiv, 288 p. : ill. ; 25 cm. (Springer texts in statistics) Includes bibliographical references (p. [263]-276) and indexes. ISBN 0-387-98739-8 (hardcover : alk. paper) DDC 519.5/35
*1. Multivariate analysis. I. Brenner, David, 1946- II. Title. III. Series.*
*TC QA278 .B55 1999*

**Bilton, Katherine.**
ADHD :. London : Whurr, c1999.
*TC RJ506.H9 A32 1999*

**Binder, Marc D.**
Peripheral and spinal mechanisms in the neural control of movement. Amsterdam ; Oxford : Elsevier, 1999.
*TC QP376.A1 P7 1999*

## BINDING OF BOOKS. *See* BOOKBINDING.

## BINDING THEORY (LINGUISTICS). *See* GOVERNMENT-BINDING THEORY (LINGUISTICS).

**Bing, Janet Mueller, 1937-.**
Rethinking language and gender research. London ; New York : Longman, 1996.
*TC P120.S48 R48 1996*

## BINGE-PURGE BEHAVIOR. *See* BULIMIA.

**Binnie, Alison.** Freedom to practise : the development of patient-centred nursing / Alison Binnie and Angie Tichen ; edited by Judith Lathlean ; with a foreword by Marie Manthey. Oxford ; Boston : Butterworth-Heinemann, 1999. xiv, 251 p. : ill. ; 24 cm. Includes bibliographical references (p. [236]-246) and index. ISBN 0-7506-4075-8 DDC 610.73
*1. Nursing. 2. Nurse and patient. 3. Nursing. 4. Patient-Centered Care. I. Tichen, Angie. II. Lathlean, Judith. III. Title.*
*TC RT41 .B56 1999*

**Bins, Susan K.**
Kraus, Anne Marie. Folktale themes and activities for children. Englewood, Colo. : Teacher Ideas Press, c1998-1999.
*TC GR45 .K73 1998*

## BIO-BIBLIOGRAPHY. *See* AUTHORS.

## BIOACOUSTICS. *See* HEARING.

## BIOACTIVE COMPOUNDS. *See* DRUGS.

**Biochemical and physiological aspects of human nutrition** / Martha H. Stipanuk. Philadelphia : W.B. Saunders, c1999. xxx, 100 p. : ill. ; 25 cm. Includes bibliographical references and index. ISBN 0-7216-4452-X DDC 612.3/9
*1. Nutrition. 2. Metabolism. 3. Biochemistry. I. Stipanuk, Martha H.*
*TC QP141 .B57 1999*

## BIOCHEMISTRY.
Biochemical and physiological aspects of human nutrition. Philadelphia : W.B. Saunders, c1999.
*TC QP141 .B57 1999*

Houston, Michael E., 1941- Biochemistry primer for exercise science. Champaign, IL : Human Kinetics, c1995.
*TC QP514.2 .H68 1995*

**Biochemistry primer for exercise science.**
Houston, Michael E., 1941- Champaign, IL : Human Kinetics, c1995.
*TC QP514.2 .H68 1995*

**Biocultural approaches to the emotions** / edited by Alexander Laban Hinton. Cambridge, U.K. ; New York : Cambridge University Press, 1999. xiii, 369 p. : ill. ; 23 cm. (Publications of the Society for Psychological Anthropology ; [10]) Includes bibliographical references and index. ISBN 0-521-65211-1 (hardcover) ISBN 0-521-65569-2 (pbk.)
*1. Ethnopsychology. 2. Emotions - Physiology. 3. Emotions - Social aspects. I. Hinton, Alexander Laban. II. Series.*
*TC GN502 .B53 1999*

## BIODIVERSITY. *See* BIOLOGICAL DIVERSITY.

## BIOENERGETICS.
Exercise physiology. 3rd ed. Mountain View, Calif. : Mayfield Pub., c2000.
*TC QP301 .B885 2000*

## BIOETHICS. *See also* MEDICAL ETHICS.
Embodying bioethics. Lanham : Rowman & Littlefield Publishers, c1999.

*TC QH332 .E43 1999*

## BIOGENIC AMINES. *See* DOPAMINE.

**Biographical encyclopedia of famous American women [computer file].**
Her heritage [computer file]. Cambridge, MA : Pilgrim New Media, c1994. Interactive multimedia.
*TC HQ1412 .A43 1994*

## BIOGRAPHICAL FILMS.
Andy Warhol [videorecording]. [Chicago, IL] : Home Vision [distributor],cc1987.
*TC N6537.W28 A45 1987*

Andy Warhol [videorecording]. [Chicago, IL] : Home Vision [distributor],cc1987.
*TC N6537.W28 A45 1987*

Georgia O'Keeffe [videorecording]. [Boston?] : Home Vision : c1977.
*TC ND237.O5 G4 1977*

Mary Cassatt [videorecording]. [Chicago, Ill.]: Home Vision, c1977.
*TC ND237.C3 M37 1977*

Nevelson in process [videorecording]. Chicago, IL : Public Media Inc., 1977.
*TC NB237.N43 N43 1977*

Norman Rockwell's world -- an American dream [videorecording]. [Chicago, Ill] : Home Vision, 1987, c1972.
*TC ND237.R68 N6 1987*

Picasso [videorecording]. Chicago, IL : Home Vision, c1986.
*TC N6853.P5 P52 1986*

Roy Lichtenstein [videorecording]. [Chicago, IL] : Home Vision : [S.l.] : distributed worldwide by RM Asssociates, c1991.
*TC ND237.L627 R6 1991*

## BIOGRAPHY. *See also* CHRISTIAN BIOGRAPHY; GENEALOGY; LETTERS; PORTRAITS; RELIGIOUS BIOGRAPHY.
Jung on film [videorecording]. [Chicago, Ill.?] : Public Media Video, c1990.
*TC BF109.J8 J4 1990*

Jung on film [videorecording]. [Chicago, Ill.?] : Public Media Video, c1990.
*TC BF109.J8 J4 1990*

## BIOGRAPHY AS A LITERARY FORM. *See* AUTOBIOGRAPHY.

**Biography (Public Media Video)**
Jung on film [videorecording]. [Chicago, Ill.?] : Public Media Video, c1990.
*TC BF109.J8 J4 1990*

Jung on film [videorecording]. [Chicago, Ill.?] : Public Media Video, c1990.
*TC BF109.J8 J4 1990*

## BIOGRAPHY - STUDY AND TEACHING.
Druce, Arden. Paper bag puppets. Lanham, MD : Scarecrow Press, 1999.
*TC Z718.3 .D78 1999*

Marsh, Valerie. True tales of heroes & heroines. Fort Atkinson, Wis. : Alleyside Press, c1999.
*TC CT85 .M37 1999*

## BIOLINGUISTICS.
Loritz, Donald, 1947- How the brain evolved language. New York : Oxford University Press, 1999.
*TC P116 .L67 1999*

**A biological brain in a cultural classroom.**
Sylwester, Robert. Thousand Oaks, Calif. : Corwin Press, c2000.
*TC LB3011.5 .S95 2000*

## BIOLOGICAL DIVERSIFICATION. *See* BIOLOGICAL DIVERSITY.

## BIOLOGICAL DIVERSITY.
Baskin, Yvonne. The work of nature. Washington, D.C. : Island Press, 1997.
*TC GE195 .B36 1997*

## BIOLOGICAL DIVERSITY - CONGRESSES.
Forum on Biodiversity (1997 : National Academy of Sciences) Nature and human society. Washington, D.C. : National Academy Press, 2000.
*TC QH541.15.B56 F685 1997*

## BIOLOGICAL EVOLUTION. *See* EVOLUTION (BIOLOGY).

## BIOLOGICAL NEURAL NETWORKS. *See* NEURAL NETWORKS (NEUROBIOLOGY).

**BIOLOGICAL OCEANOGRAPHY.** *See* **MARINE ECOLOGY.**

**Biological Sciences Curriculum Study.** The BSCS journal. Boulder, Colo., Biological Sciences Curriculum Study. v. ill. 28 cm. v. 2, no. 4-   Nov. 1979- . Continues: Biological Sciences Curriculum Study. The Biological Sciences Curriculum Study journal.
*I. Biological Sciences Curriculum Study. Journal. II. Title. III. Title: Biological Sciences Curriculum Study journal*

**Journal.**
Biological Sciences Curriculum Study. The BSCS journal. Boulder, Colo., Biological Sciences Curriculum Study.

**Biological Sciences Curriculum Study journal.**
Biological Sciences Curriculum Study. The BSCS journal. Boulder, Colo., Biological Sciences Curriculum Study.

**BIOLOGISTS.** *See also* **WOMEN BIOLOGISTS.**
Ruse, Michael. Mystery of mysteries. Cambridge, Mass. : Harvard University Press, 1999.
*TC QH360.5 .R874 1999*

**BIOLOGY.** *See also* **BIOLOGICAL DIVERSITY; DEVELOPMENTAL BIOLOGY; ECOLOGY; EVOLUTION (BIOLOGY); EXTINCTION (BIOLOGY); NATURAL HISTORY; ZOOLOGY.**
Children's understanding of biology and health. 1st ed. Cambridge, U.K. ; New York : Cambridge University Press, 1999.
*TC BF723.C5 C514 1999*

**Biology and behavior**
Environmental influences: New York, Rockefeller University Press ; Russell Sage Foundation, 1968.
*TC BF353 .E5*

**BIOLOGY - ECOLOGY.** *See* **ECOLOGY.**

**BIOLOGY - FIELD WORK.** *See* **NATURE STUDY.**

**The biology of love.**
Janov, Arthur. Amherst, N.Y. : Prometheus Books, 2000.
*TC BF720.E45 .J36 2000*

**Biology of music making.**
Music and child development. St. Louis, Mo. : MMB Music, c1990.
*TC ML3820 .M87 1990*

**Biology of Music Making Conference (2nd : 1987 : Denver, Colo.).**
Music and child development. St. Louis, Mo. : MMB Music, c1990.
*TC ML3820 .M87 1990*

**BIOLOGY - STUDY AND TEACHING (HIGHER) - PERIODICALS.**
Commission on Undergraduate Education in the Biological Sciences. CUEBS news. [Washington, D.C.] Commission on Undergradute Education in the Biological Sciences.

**BIOMASS.** *See* **BIOLOGY.**

**Biomechanics and neural control of posture and movement** / edited by Jack M. Winters, Patrick E. Crago. New York : Springer, 2000. xxii, 683 p. : ill. ; 25 cm. Includes bibliographical references and index. ISBN 0-387-94974-7 (alk. paper) DDC 612.7/6
*1. Human locomotion - Mathematical models. 2. Posture - Mathematical models. 3. Human mechanics - Mathematical models. 4. Afferent pathways. I. Winters, Jack M., 1957- II. Crago, Patrick E.*
*TC QP303 .B5684 2000*

**BIOMEDICAL ETHICS.** *See* **MEDICAL ETHICS.**

**BIOMEDICAL RESEARCH.** *See* **MEDICINE - RESEARCH.**

**BIOMETRY.**
Katz, Mitchell H. Multivariable analysis. Cambridge, UK ; New York : Cambridge University Press, 1999.
*TC R853.S7 K38 1999*

**BIOMOLECULES.** *See* **LIPIDS; PROTEINS.**

**BIONICS.** *See* **ARTIFICIAL INTELLIGENCE.**

**BIONOMICS.** *See* **ECOLOGY.**

**BIOSCIENCES.** *See* **LIFE SCIENCES.**

**BIOTECHNOLOGY.** *See* **GENETIC ENGINEERING.**

**BIOTIC COMMUNITIES.** *See* **NICHE (ECOLOGY).**

**BIOTIC DIVERSITY.** *See* **BIOLOGICAL DIVERSITY.**

**BIPOLAR DEPRESSION.** *See* **MANIC-DEPRESSIVE ILLNESS.**

**BIPOLAR DISORDER.** *See* **MANIC-DEPRESSIVE ILLNESS.**

**BIRACIAL DATING.** *See* **INTERRACIAL DATING.**

**Bircher, William, 1845-1917.** A Civil War drummer boy : the diary of William Bircher, 1861-1865 / edited by Shelley Swanson Sateren ; foreword by Suzanne L. Bunkers. Mankato, Minn. : Blue Earth Books, c2000. 32 p. : ill. (some col.) ; 24 cm. (Diaries, letters, and memoirs) Includes bibliographical references (p. 31) and index. SUMMARY: Excerpts from the diary of William Bircher, a fifteen-year-old Minnesotan who was a drummer during the Civil War. Supplemented by sidebars, activities, and a timeline of the era. ISBN 0-7368-0348-3 DDC 973.7/81
*1. Bircher, William, - 1845-1917 - Diaries - Juvenile literature. 2. United States. - Army. - Minnesota Infantry Regiment, 2nd (1861-1865) - Biography - Juvenile literature. 3. United States - History - Civil War, 1861-1865 - Personal narratives - Juvenile literature. 4. Minnesota - History - Civil War, 1861-1865 - Personal narratives - Juvenile literature. 5. United States - History - Civil War, 1861-1865 - Participation, Juvenile - Juvenile literature. 6. Boys - Minnesota - Saint Paul Region - Diaries - Juvenile literature. 7. Bircher, William, - 1845-1917. 8. United States - History - Civil War, 1861-1865 - Personal narratives. 9. Diaries. I. Sateren, Shelley Swanson. II. Title. III. Series.*
*TC E601 .B605 2000*

**BIRCHER, WILLIAM, 1845-1917.**
Bircher, William, 1845-1917. A Civil War drummer boy. Mankato, Minn. : Blue Earth Books, c2000.
*TC E601 .B605 2000*

**BIRCHER, WILLIAM, 1845-1917 - DIARIES - JUVENILE LITERATURE.**
Bircher, William, 1845-1917. A Civil War drummer boy. Mankato, Minn. : Blue Earth Books, c2000.
*TC E601 .B605 2000*

**BIRD CALLS.** *See* **BIRDSONGS.**

**Bird, Lois Bridges.**
Coughlin, Debbie. The mainstreaming handbook. Portsmouth, NH : Heinemann, c2000.
*TC LC1201 .C68 2000*

Frank, Carolyn. Ethnographic eyes. Portsmouth, NH : Heinemann, c1999.
*TC LB1027.28 .F73 1999*

**BIRD-SONG.** *See* **BIRDSONGS.**

**BIRD SONGS.** *See* **BIRDSONGS.**

**BIRDS.** *See* **GREBES; OWLS; PENGUINS.**

**BIRDS - FICTION.**
Fleming, Candace. When Agnes caws. 1st ed. New York : Atheneum Books for Young Readers, 1999.
*TC PZ7.F59936 Wh 1999*

Jennings, Patrick. Putnam and Pennyroyal. 1st ed. New York : Scholastic Press, 1999.
*TC PZ7.J4298715 Co 1999*

Mallat, Kathy. Brave bear. New York : Walker, 1999.
*TC PZ7.M29455 Br 1999*

**BIRDS - PICTORIAL WORKS.**
[Nature study class, P.S. 165] [picture] 1935.
*TC BE5564*

[Nature study class, P.S. 165] [picture] 1935.
*TC BE5564*

[Nature study class, P.S. 165] [picture] 1935.
*TC BE5564*

**BIRDSONGS - FICTION.**
Fleming, Candace. When Agnes caws. 1st ed. New York : Atheneum Books for Young Readers, 1999.
*TC PZ7.F59936 Wh 1999*

**Birke, Lynda I. A.** Feminism and the biological body / Lynda Birke. New Brunswick, N.J. : Rutgers University Press, 2000. viii, 204 p. : ill. ; 25 cm. First published: Edinburgh : Edinburgh University Press, 1999. Includes bibliographical references (p. 188-200) and index. ISBN 0-8135-2822-4 (cloth : alk.) ISBN 0-8135-2823-2 (paper : alk.) DDC 305.42/01
*1. Feminist theory. 2. Women - Physiology. 3. Body, Human - Social aspects. 4. Body, Human - Symbolic aspects. I. Title.*
*TC HQ1190 .B56 2000*

**BIRMINGHAM (ALA.) - HISTORY.**
Feldman, Lynne B. A sense of place. Tuscaloosa, Ala. ; London : University of Alabama Press, c1999.
*TC F334.B69 N437 1999*

**Birnbaum, Barry W.** Connecting special education and technology for the 21st century / Barry W. Birnbaum. Lewiston, N.Y. ; Lampeter, Wales : E. Mellen Press,

c1999. i, 117 p. : ill. ; 24 cm. (Mellen studies in education : v. 45) Includes bibliographical references (p. 109-113) and index. ISBN 0-7734-7991-0 DDC 371.9/0285
*1. Special education - United States - Computer-assisted instruction. 2. Educational technology - United States. I. Title. II. Series.*
*TC LC3969.5 .B57 1999*

**Birnbaum, Michael H.**
Psychological experiments on the Internet. San Diego : Academic Press, c2000.
*TC BF198.7 .P79 2000*

**Birnbaum, Robert.** Management fads in higher education : where they come from, what they do, why they fail / Robert Birnbaum. San Francisco : Jossey-Bass, 2000. xxii, 287 p. ; 24 cm. Includes bibliographical references (p. 243-266) and indexes. ISBN 0-7879-4456-4 DDC 378.1/01
*1. Education, Higher - United States - Management. 2. Fads - United States. 3. Organizational effectiveness. I. Title.*
*TC LB2341 .B49 2000*

**Birren, James E.**
A history of geropsychology in autobiography. 1st ed. Washington, DC ; London : American Psychological Association, c2000.
*TC BF724.8 .H57 2000*

**BIRTH CONTROL.** *See* **CONTRACEPTION.**

**BIRTH CONTROL - GOVERNMENT POLICY - UNITED STATES.**
Welfare, the family, and reproductive behavior. Washington, D.C. : National Academy Press, 1998.
*TC HV91 .W478 1998*

**BIRTH CONTROL - PERIODICALS.**
Eugenics quarterly. New York : American Eugenics Society, [1954]-c1968.

**Birth of the Republic.**
The American Revolution. [videorecording]. New York, N.Y. : A&E Home Video, c1994.
*TC E208 .A447 1994*

**BIRTHDAYS - FICTION.**
Gould, Deborah Lee. Brendan's best-timed birthday. New York : Bradbury Press, 1988.
*TC PZ7.G723 Br 1988*

Sathre, Vivian. Three kind mice. 1st ed. San Diego : Harcourt Brace, c1997.
*TC PZ8.3.S238 Th 1997*

Uff, Caroline. Happy birthday, Lulu!. New York : Walker & Company, 2000.
*TC PZ7.U285 Hap 2000*

Yolen, Jane. Mouse's birthday. New York : Putnam's, c1993.
*TC PZ8.3.Y76 Mo 1993*

**BIRTHFLOWERS.** *See* **BIRTHDAYS.**

**BIRTHSTONES.** *See* **BIRTHDAYS.**

**BISEXUAL COLLEGE STUDENTS - UNITED STATES - BIOGRAPHY.**
Out & about campus. 1st ed. Los Angeles : Alyson Books, 2000.
*TC LC2574.6 .O87 2000*

**BISEXUAL COLLEGE STUDENTS - UNITED STATES - SOCIAL CONDITIONS.**
Toward acceptance. Lanham, Md. : University Press of America, 1999.
*TC LC192.6 .T69 1999*

**BISEXUAL PERSONS.** *See* **BISEXUALS.**

**BISEXUALITY.** *See* **HOMOSEXUALITY.**

**BISEXUALS - COUNSELING OF.**
Handbook of counseling and psychotherapy with lesbian, gay, and bisexual clients. 1st ed. Washington, DC ; London : American Psychological Association, c2000.
*TC BF637.C6 H3125 2000*

Therapeutic perspectives on working with lesbian, gay and bisexual clients. Buckingham [England] ; Philadelphia : Open University Press, 2000.
*TC RC451.4.G39 T476 2000*

**Bishop, Anne H., 1935-** Nursing ethics : holistic caring practice / Anne H. Bishop, John R. Scudder, Jr. 2nd ed. Sudbury, Mass. : Jones and Bartlett, c2001. xv, 136 p. ; 23 cm. Includes bibliographical references and index. ISBN 0-7637-1426-7
*1. Ethics, Nursing. 2. Holistic Nursing. 3. Philosophy, Nursing. I. Scudder, John R., 1926- II. Title.*
*TC RT85 .B57 2001*

**Bishop, Wendy.**
The subject is reading. Portsmouth, NH : Heinemann c2000.

TC LB2395.3 .S82 2000

**BISON.** *See also* **AMERICAN BISON.**
Hazen-Hammond, Susan. Thunder Bear and Ko. 1st ed. New York : Dutton Children's Books, 1999.
*TC E99.T35 H36 1999*

**BISON, AMERICAN.** *See* **AMERICAN BISON.**

**BISON BISON.** *See* **AMERICAN BISON.**

**Bissonnette, Madeline Monaco.** Adolescents' perspectives about the environmental impacts of food production practices / by Madeline Monaco Bissonnette. 1999. xi, 248 leaves ; 29 cm. Typescript; issued also on microfilm. Thesis (Ed.D.)--Teachers College, Columbia University, 1999. Includes bibliographical references (leaves 186-193).
*1. High school seniors - New York (State) - Nutrition. 2. Food habits. 3. Food preferences - Social aspects. 4. Food industry and trade - Environmental aspects. 5. Social influence. I. Title. II. Title: Environmental impacts of food production practices*
*TC 06 no. 11084*

**Bitters in the honey.**
Roy, Beth. Fayetteville : University of Arkansas Press, 1999.
*TC LC214.23.L56 R69 1999*

**Bitz, Michael Eric.** A description and investigation of strategies for teaching classroom music improvisation / by Michael Bitz. 1998. vi, 117 leaves : music ; 29 cm. Issued also on microfilm. Thesis (Ed.D.)--Teachers College, Columbia University, 1998. Includes bibliographical references (leaves 87-95).
*1. School music - Instruction and study - New York (State) - New York. 2. School music - Instruction and study - Activity programs. 3. Improvisation (Music). 4. Imitation. I. Title.*
*TC 06 no. 11012*

**Biweekly school law letter.**
The bi-weekly school law letter. Laramie, Wyo. : Published by R.R. Hamilton, 1951-1955.

**Bizar, Marilyn.**
Daniels, Harvey, 1947- Methods that matter. York, Me. : Stenhouse Publishers, c1998.
*TC LB1027 .D24 1998*

**Bjorklund, David F., 1949-.**
False-memory creation in children and adults. Mahwah, N.J. : London : L. Erlbaum, 2000.
*TC RC455.2.F35 F34 2000*

**Blachman, Benita A.** Road to the code : a phonological awareness program for young children / by Benita A. Blachman ... [et al.]. Baltimore : Paul H. Brookes, c2000. xxiii, 391 p. : ill. ; 28 cm. Includes bibliographical references (p. 387-391). ISBN 1-55766-438-2 DDC 372.46/5
*1. Children - Language. 2. English language - Phonetics - Study and teaching (Early childhood) 3. Reading - Phonetic method. 4. Language awareness in children.*
*TC LB1139.L3 B53 2000*

**Black academy review.** Buffalo, N.Y. : Black Academy Press, c1970- v. ; 22 cm. Frequency: Quarterly. Vol. 1, no. 1 (spring 1970)- . Title from cover. Vol. 4, no. 1-2 never published? Cf. University Microfilms International. Suspended 1975-1994. SUMMARY: "Quarterly of the black world." Separately paged supplement at end of v. 1, also includes index. ISSN 0006-4084 DDC 301
*1. Afro-Americans - Periodicals. 2. Authors, Black - Periodicals.*

**Black America.**
Reference library of Black America. Detroit, MI : Gale Group : Distributed by African American Pub., Proteus Enterprises, c2000.
*TC E185 .R44 2000*

**BLACK AMERICANS.** *See* **AFRO-AMERICANS.**

**BLACK ART.** *See* **ART, BLACK.**

**BLACK ART (WITCHCRAFT).** *See* **WITCHCRAFT.**

**BLACK AUTHORS.** *See* **AUTHORS, BLACK.**

**Black, Barbara J., 1962-** On exhibit : Victorians and their museums / Barbara J. Black. Charlottesville ; London : University Press of Virginia, 2000. viii, 242 p. : ill. ; 24 cm. (Victorian literature and culture series) Includes bibliographical references (p. [195]-233) and index. ISBN 0-8139-1897-9 (cloth : alk. paper) DDC 069/.09421
*1. Museums - England - London - History - 19th century. 2. London (England) - Intellectual life - 19th century. 3. London (England) - Civilization - 19th century. 4. Literature and society - England - London - History - 19th century. 5. Popular culture - Great Britain - History - 19th century. 6. Great Britain - History - Victoria, 1837-1901. I. Title. II. Series.*
*TC AM43.L6 B53 2000*

**BLACK CARIB WOMEN - CANADA - SOCIAL CONDITIONS - CASE STUDIES.**
Henry, Annette, 1955- Taking back control. Albany : State University of New York Press, c1998.
*TC LB1775.4.C2 H45 1998*

**BLACK CHILDREN.** *See* **CHILDREN, BLACK.**

**BLACK COMPOSERS.** *See* **COMPOSERS, BLACK.**

**Black, Dora.**
Hendriks, Jean Harris. When father kills mother. 2nd ed. London : Philadelphia : Routledge, 2000.
*TC RJ506.U96 .B53 2000*

**Black elected officials.**
Conyers, James E., 1932- New York : Russell Sage Foundation, c1976.
*TC JK1924 .C65*

**BLACK ENGLISH.**
Smitherman, Geneva, 1940- Talkin that talk. London ; New York : Routledge, 2000.
*TC PE3102.N4 S63 2000*

**BLACK ENGLISH - UNITED STATES.**
Rickford, John R., 1949- Spoken soul. New York : Chichester [England] : Wiley, c2000.
*TC PE3102.N42 R54 2000*

**BLACK ENGLISH - UNITED STATES - DICTIONARIES.**
Smitherman, Geneva, 1940- Black talk. Rev. ed. Boston : Houghton Mifflin, 2000.
*TC PE3102.N4 S65 2000*

**Black, Helen K., 1952-** Old souls : aged women, poverty, and the experience of God / Helen K. Black, Robert L. Rubinstein. New York : A. de Gruyter, c2000. x, 243 p. ; 24 cm. Includes bibliographical references (p. 237-240) and index. ISBN 0-202-30633-X (cloth : acid-free paper) ISBN 0-202-30634-8 (paper : acid-free paper) DDC 305.26/09748/11
*1. Aged women - Pennsylvania - Philadelphia Metropolitan Area - Economic conditions - Case studies. 2. Aged women - New Jersey - Economic conditions - Case studies. 3. Aged women - Pennsylvania - Philadelphia Metropolitan Area - Social conditions - Case studies. 4. Aged women - New Jersey - Social conditions - Case studies. 5. Poor aged - Pennsylvania - Philadelphia Metropolitan Area - Case studies. 6. Poor aged - New Jersey - Case studies. 7. Aged women - Pennsylvania - Philadelphia Metropolitan Area - Religious life - Case studies. 8. Aged women - New Jersey - Religious life - Case studies. I. Rubinstein, Robert L. II. Title.*
*TC HQ1064.U6 P424 2000*

**Black, Henry Campbell, 1860-1927.** Black's law dictionary. 7th ed. / Bryan A. Garner, editor in chief. St. Paul, MN : West Group, 1999. xxiii, 1738 p. : map ; 27 cm. Includes bibliographical references. ISBN 0-314-22864-0
*1. Law - United States - Dictionaries. 2. Law - Dictionaries. I. Garner, Bryan A. II. Title. III. Title: Law dictionary*
*TC KF156 .B53 1999*

**BLACK HISTORY.** *See* **AFRO-AMERICANS - HISTORY.**

**Black holes and beyond.**
Stephen Hawking's universe [videorecording]. [Alexandria, Va.] : PBS Video; Burbank, CA : Distributed by Warner Home Video, c1997.
*TC QB982 .S7 1997*

**BLACK HOLES (ASTRONOMY).**
Stephen Hawking's universe [videorecording]. [Alexandria, Va.] : PBS Video; Burbank, CA : Distributed by Warner Home Video, c1997.
*TC QB982 .S7 1997*

**Black hunger.**
Witt, Doris. New York : Oxford University Press, 1999.
*TC E185.86 .W58 1999*

**Black, Janet K.**
Puckett, Margaret B. Authentic assessment of the young child. 2nd ed. Upper Saddle River, N.J. : Merrill, c2000.
*TC LB3051 .P69 2000*

**Black leadership for social change.**
Gordon, Jacob U. Westport, Conn. : Greenwood Press, 2000.
*TC E185.615 .G666 2000*

**Black lines.** [Pittsburgh, Dept. of Black Studies, University of Pittsburgh. 3 v. ill. 28 cm. Frequency: Quarterly. v. 1-3, no. 2; fall 1970-winter 1972. "A journal of Black studies." Vols. for 19 -winter 1972 issued by the Dept. of Black Studies, University of Pittsburgh. DDC 917.3/06/96073
*1. University of Pittsburgh. Dept. of Black Studies.*

**BLACK LITERATURE (AMERICAN).** *See* **AMERICAN LITERATURE - AFRO-AMERICAN AUTHORS.**

**Black, Maureen M.** Essentials of Bayley scales of infant development--II assessment / Maureen M. Black and Kathleen Matula. New York : Wiley, c2000. xii, 162 p. ; 22 cm. (Essentials of psychological assessment series) Includes bibliographical references and index. ISBN 0-471-32651-8 (pbk. : alk. paper) DDC 618.92/89075
*1. Bayley Scales of Infant Development. I. Matula, Kathleen. II. Title. III. Series.*
*TC RJ151.D48 B52 2000*

**Black, P. J. (Paul Joseph), 1930-** Testing, friend or foe? : the theory and practice of assessment and testing / Paul J. Black. London : Washington : Falmer Press, 1998. x, 173 p. : ill. ; 25 cm. (Master classes in education series) Includes bibl. references and index. ISBN 0-7507-0614-7 (pbk.) ISBN 0-7507-0729-1 DDC 371.26
*1. Educational tests and measurements - England. 2. Educational tests and measurements - United States. 3. Education - Aims and objectives - England. 4. Education - Aims and objectives - United States. 5. Education - England - Evaluation. 6. Education - United States - Evaluation. I. Title. II. Series.*
*TC LB3056.E54 B53 1998*

**BLACK SCULPTURE.** *See* **SCULPTURE, BLACK.**

**Black social capital.**
Orr, Marion, 1962- Lawrence : University Press of Kansas, c1999.
*TC LC2803.B35 O77 1999*

**Black sons to mothers** : compliments, critiques, and challenges for cultural workers in education / edited by M. Christopher Brown II and James Earl Davis. New York : Canterbury [England] : P. Lang, c2000. x, 237 p. ; 23 cm. (Counterpoints ; v. 107) Includes bibliographical references (p. 233-234). ISBN 0-8204-4292-5 DDC 371.829/6073
*1. Afro-American young men - Education - Social aspects. 2. Afro-American young men - Family relationships. 3. Mothers and sons - United States. 4. Home and school - United States. I. Brown, M. Christopher. II. Davis, James Earl, 1960- III. Series: Counterpoints (New York, N.Y.) ; vol. 107.*
*TC LC2731 .B53 2000*

**BLACK STUDENTS.** *See* **STUDENTS, BLACK.**

**Black studies**
(v. 7) The African-American male perspective of barriers to success. Lewiston, N.Y. : Edwin Mellen Press, c1999.
*TC LC2731 .A32 1999*

**Black talk.**
Smitherman, Geneva, 1940- Rev. ed. Boston : Houghton Mifflin, 2000.
*TC PE3102.N4 S65 2000*

**Black, white, and Huckleberry Finn.**
Mensh, Elaine, 1924- Tuscaloosa : University of Alabama Press, c2000.
*TC PS1305 .M46 2000*

**BLACK WOMEN.** *See* **WOMEN, BLACK.**

**BLACK WOMEN COLLEGE TEACHERS.** *See* **WOMEN COLLEGE TEACHERS, BLACK.**

**Black women in South African universities.**
Makosana, I. Nokuzola Zola. Social factors in the positioning of black women in South African universities. 1997.
*TC 06 no. 10825*

**Black women in the academy.**
Gregory, Sheila T. Rev. and updated ed. Lanham, Md. : University Press of America, 1999.
*TC LC2781 .G74 1999*

**BLACK WOMEN TEACHERS.** *See* **WOMEN TEACHERS, BLACK.**

**Black worker in the 21st century.**
Job creation. Washington, DC : Joint Center for Political and Economic Studies : Lanham, Md. : Oxford : University Press of America, c1998.
*TC HD8081.A65 J63 1998*

**Black working wives.**
Landry, Bart. Berkeley : University of California Press, c2000.
*TC HQ536 .L335 2000*

**Blackburn, Lois.** Whole music : a whole language approach to teaching music / Lois Blackburn. Portsmouth, N.H. : Heinemann, c1998. vi, 212 p. : ill. ; 23 cm. Includes bibliographical references (167-177) and index. ISBN 0-435-07043-6 DDC 780/.71
*1. Music - Instruction and study. 2. School music - Instruction and study. I. Title.*

*TC MT1 .B643 1998*

**Blacking, John.** Music, culture, & experience : selected papers of John Blacking / edited and with an introduction by Reginald Byron ; with a forward by Bruno Nettl. Chicago : University of Chicago Press, c1995. xii, 269 p. : ill. ; 24 cm. (Chicago studies in ethnomusicology) Works by John Blacking (p. 247-252). Includes bibliographical references (p. 253-259) and index. ISBN 0-226-08829-4 (cloth) ISBN 0-226-08830-8 (paper) DDC 780/.89
*1. Ethnomusicology. 2. Music - Social aspects. 3. Folk music - History and criticism. I. Byron, Reginald. II. Nettl, Bruno, 1930- III. Title. IV. Title: Music, culture, and experience V. Series.*
*TC ML60 .B63 1995*

**BLACKLEDGE, ADRIAN.** Literacy, power and social justice. Stoke on Trent, Staffordshire, England : Trentham Books, 2000. v, 159 p. ; 23 cm. Includes bibliographical references and index. ISBN 1-85856-157-4 (cloth) ISBN 1-85856-158-2 (paper) DDC 302.2
*1. Education, Bilingual - Cross-cultural studies.*
*TC LC149 .B53 2000*

**BLACKS - BRAZIL - SOCIAL CONDITIONS.**
Race in contemporary Brazil. University Park, Pa. : Pennsylvania State University Press, 1999.
*TC F2659.N4 R245 1999*

**BLACKS - CHILDREN.** *See* CHILDREN, BLACK.

**BLACKS - EDUCATION.** *See* STUDENTS, BLACK.

**BLACKS - EDUCATION - SOUTH AFRICA - HISTORY - 19TH CENTURY.**
Cross, Michael. Imagery of identity in South African education, 1880-1990. Durham, N.C. : Carolina Academic Press, c1999.
*TC LA1539 .C76 1999*

**BLACKS - EDUCATION - SOUTH AFRICA - HISTORY - 20TH CENTURY.**
Cross, Michael. Imagery of identity in South African education, 1880-1990. Durham, N.C. : Carolina Academic Press, c1999.
*TC LA1539 .C76 1999*

**BLACKS - EDUCATION - SOUTH AFRICA - PERIODICALS.**
Educamus. Pretoria : Govt. Printer, [1978-

**BLACKS - EDUCATION - UNITED STATES - DIRECTORIES.**
Financial aid for African Americans. El Dorado Hills, Calif. : Reference Service Press, c1997-
*TC LB2338 .F5643*

**Black's law dictionary.**
Black, Henry Campbell, 1860-1927. 7th ed. / Bryan A. Garner, editor in chief. St. Paul, MN : West Group, 1999.
*TC KF156 .B53 1999*

**BLACKS - PUERTO RICO - SOCIAL CONDITIONS.**
Kinsbruner, Jay. Not of pure blood. Durham : Duke University Press, 1996.
*TC F1983.B55 K56 1996*

**BLACKS - RACE IDENTITY - SOUTH AFRICA - HISTORY - 19TH CENTURY.**
Cross, Michael. Imagery of identity in South African education, 1880-1990. Durham, N.C. : Carolina Academic Press, c1999.
*TC LA1539 .C76 1999*

**BLACKS - RACE IDENTITY - SOUTH AFRICA - HISTORY - 20TH CENTURY.**
Cross, Michael. Imagery of identity in South African education, 1880-1990. Durham, N.C. : Carolina Academic Press, c1999.
*TC LA1539 .C76 1999*

**BLACKS - UNITED STATES.** *See* AFRO-AMERICANS.

**Blackwater.**
Bunting, Eve, 1928- 1st ed. New York : Joanna Cotler Books, 1999.
*TC PZ7.B91527 Bne 1999*

**Blackwell, James M.**
Grounded for life [videorecording]. Charleston, WV : Cambridge Research Group, Ltd., 1988.
*TC HQ759.4 .G7 1988*

**Blackwell philosophy anthologies**
(8) Mind and cognition. 2nd ed. Malden, Mass. : Blackwell Publishers, 1999.
*TC BF171 .M55 1999*

**Blades, Ann, 1947-** Wolf and the seven little kids / Ann Blades. Toronto : Douglas & McIntyre, c1999. [32] p. : col. ill. ; 24 cm. A Groundwood book. Based on the tale from the Brothers Grimm. ISBN 0-88899-364-1 DDC j398.20943/04529648
*I. Title.*
*TC PS8553.L33 W64 1999*

**Blades, Mark.**
Children's source monitoring. Mahwah, N.J. : London : Lawrence Erlbaum Associates, 2000.
*TC BF723.M4 C45 2000*

**Blaine, Nell, 1922-.**
Sawin, Martica. Nell Blaine. 1st ed. New York : Hudson Hills Press ; [Lanham, MD] : Distributed in the USA, its territories and possessions, and Canada by National Book Network, c1998.
*TC ND237.B597 S28 1998*

**BLAINE, NELL, 1922-.**
Sawin, Martica. Nell Blaine. 1st ed. New York : Hudson Hills Press ; [Lanham, MD] : Distributed in the USA, its territories and possessions, and Canada by National Book Network, c1998.
*TC ND237.B597 S28 1998*

**Blair, Kristine.**
Feminist cyberscapes. Stamford, Conn. : Ablex Pub., c1999.
*TC PE1404 .F39 1999*

**Blair, Margot.** The red string / conceived by Margot Blair ; drawings by Greg Colson. Malibu, Calif. : J. Paul Getty Museum and Childrens Library Press, c1996. 1 v. (unpaged) : col. ill. ; 27 cm. SUMMARY: The adventures of a piece of red string as it winds its way from an open drawer across the world. ISBN 0-89236-340-1 DDC [E]
*1. String - Fiction. 2. Stories without words. I. Colson, Greg, ill. II. Title.*
*TC PZ7.B537865 Re 1996*

**Blake, Quentin.** Clown / Quentin Blake. 1st American ed. New York : H. Holt, 1996. 1 v. (unpaged) : col. ill. ; 33 cm. SUMMARY: After being discarded, Clown makes his way through town having a series of adventures as he tries to find a home for himself and his other toy friends. ISBN 0-8050-4399-3 DDC [E]
*1. Toys - Fiction. 2. Home - Fiction. 3. Stories without words. I. Title.*
*TC PZ7.B56 Cl 1996*

**Blake, Robert J.** Yudonsi : a tale from the canyons / Robert J. Blake. New York : Philomel Books, 1999. 1 v. (unpaged) : col. ill. ; 29 cm. SUMMARY: Yusi wants people to notice that he is different, so he puts his "tag" on desks, walls, and even trees, alienating everyone in his village. ISBN 0-399-23320-2 DDC [E]
*1. Indians of North America - Southwest. New - Fiction. I. Title.*
*TC PZ7.B564 Yu 1999*

**Blakely, Edward James, 1938-** Fortress America : gated communities in the United States / Edward J. Blakely and Mary Gail Snyder. Washington, D.C. : Brookings Institution Press ; c1997. xi, 209 p. : ill., maps ; 23 cm. Includes bibliographical references (p. 194-201) and index. CONTENTS: Forting up -- The search for community -- Gates to paradise : lifestyle communities -- I have a dream : the prestige communities -- Enclaves of fear : security zone communities -- You can run, but you can't hide -- Not-so-brave world -- Building better communities. ISBN 0-8157-1002-X (cloth) DDC 307.76
*1. Gated communities - United States. 2. Community life - United States. I. Snyder, Mary Gail. II. Title.*
*TC HT169.59.U6 B53 1997*

**Blakemore, Colin.**
Gender and society. Oxford ; New York : Oxford University Press, 2000.
*TC HQ1075 .G4619 2000*

**Blakeslee, Sandra.**
Ramachandran, V. S. Phantoms in the brain. 1st ed. New York : William Morrow, c1998.
*TC RC351 .R24 1998*

**Blanc, Michel, sociolinguiste.**
Hamers, Josiane F. Bilinguality and bilingualism. 2nd ed. Cambridge, England ; New York, NY : Cambridge University Press, 2000.
*TC P115 .H3613 2000*

**Blanchard, Jay S.**
Educational computing in the schools. New York : Haworth Press, 1999.
*TC LB1028.3 .E332 1999*

**Blandford, Sonia.** Managing professional development in schools / Sonia Blandford ; foreword by John Welton. London ; New York : Routledge, 2000. xviii, 226 p. : ill. ; 24 cm. (Educational management series) Includes bibliographical references (p. 207-218) and index. ISBN

0-415-19759-7 (pbk. : alk. paper) DDC 370/.71/55
*1. Teachers - In-service training - Great Britain - Administration. I. Title. II. Series.*
*TC LB1731 .B57 2000*

**Blane, Howard T., 1926-.**
Psychological theories of drinking and alcoholism. 2nd ed. New York : Guilford Press, c1999.
*TC HV5045 .P74 1999*

**Blank, Leonard.** Confrontation: encounters in self and interpersonal awareness. Edited by Leonard Blank, Gloria B. Gottsegen [and] Monroe G. Gottsegen. New York, Macmillan [1971] xi, 516 p. illus. 24 cm. Includes bibliographies. DDC 301.18
*1. Group relations training. 2. Interpersonal confrontation. I. Gottsegen, Gloria B., joint author. II. Gottsegen, Monroe G., joint author. III. Title.*
*TC HM132 .B55*

**Blase, Joseph.** Bringing out the best in teachers : what effective principals do / Joseph Blase, Peggy C. Kirby. 2nd ed. Thousand Oaks, Calif. : Corwin Press, c2000. xvi, 144 p. : ill. ; 24 cm. Includes bibliographical references and index. CONTENTS: Effective school principals -- The power of praise -- Influencing by expecting -- Influencing by involving -- Granting professional autonomy -- Leading by standing behind -- Gentle nudges : suggesting versus directing -- Positive use of formal authority -- Mirrors to the possible -- Conclusions, caveats, and challenges. ISBN 0-8039-6861-2 (cloth: acid-free paper) ISBN 0-8039-6862-0 (pbk.: acid-free paper) DDC 371.1/06
*1. Teacher-principal relationships. I. Kirby, Peggy C. II. Title.*
*TC LB2840 .B57 2000*

**Blass, Thomas.**
Obedience to authority. Mahwah, N.J. ; London : Lawrence Erlbaum Associates, 2000.
*TC HM1251 .O24 2000*

**Blatner, Adam.** Foundations of psychodrama : history, theory, and practice / Adam Blatner. 4th ed. New York : Springer Pub. Co., c2000. xxi, 285 p. : ill. ; 23 cm. Includes bibliographical references and index. ISBN 0-8261-6041-7 DDC 616.89/1523
*1. Psychodrama. I. Title.*
*TC RC489.P7 B475 2000*

**Blatt.**
Korrespondenz-blatt. Luzern : Luzerner Staatspersonalverband, 1947-

**Blaug, Mark.**
The Economics of the arts. Boulder, Colo. : Westview Press, 1976.
*TC NX705.5.U6 E27 1976*

**Blaz, Deborah.** Teaching foreign languages in the block / Deborah Blaz. Larchmont, NY : Eye on Education, c1998. xiv, 200 p. : ill. ; 28 cm. Includes bibliographical references (p. 197-200). ISBN 1-88300-152-8 DDC 407
*1. Language and languages - Study and teaching. I. Title.*
*TC P51 .B545 1998*

**Blazer, Dan G. (Dan German), 1944-.**
Depression in older adults [videorecording]. Boston, MA : Fanlight Productions ; [Chicago, Ill.] : Distributed by Terra Nova Films, Inc., 1997.
*TC RC537.5 .D4 1997*

**Bleach, Kevan.** The induction and mentoring of newly qualified teachers : : a new deal for teachers / Kevan Bleach. London : David Fulton, 1999. vii, 134 p. ; 25 cm. Includes bibliographical references and index. ISBN 1-85346-635-2
*1. Teacher orientation - Great Britain. 2. Mentoring in education - Great Britain. 3. First year teachers - Supervision of - Great Britain. I. Title.*
*TC LB1729 .B584 1999*

**BLEACHING.** *See* DYES AND DYEING.

**Blechman, Rachel S., 1938-.**
Goonen, Norma M. Higher education administration. Westport, Conn. ; London : Greenwood Press, 1999.
*TC LB2341 .G573 1999*

**Bledsoe, Caroline H.**
Critical perspectives on schooling and fertility in the developing world. Washington, D.C. : National Academy Press, 1999.
*TC LC2572 .C75 1998*

**Bleiklie, Ivar, 1948-** Policy and practice in higher education : reforming Norwegian Universities / Ivar Bleiklie, Roar Høstaker and Agnete Vabø. London ; Philadelphia : J. Kingsley Publishers, 2000. 350 p. ; 24 cm. (International study of higher education reforms) (Higher education policy series ; 49) Includes bibliographical references (p. 315-336) and indexes. ISBN 1-85302-705-7 (alk. paper) DDC 378.481
*1. Higher education and state - Norway. 2. Educational*

change - Norway. 3. Education. Higher - Social aspects - Norway. I. Høstaker, Roar. II. Vabø. Agnete. III. Title. IV. Series.
*TC LC178.N8 B44 2000*

**Blending genre, altering style.**
Romano, Tom. Portsmouth, NH : Boynton/Cook ; Heinemann, c2000.
*TC PE1404 .R635 2000*

**Bless, Herbert.**
The message within. Philadelphia, Pa. : Psychology Press, 2000.
*TC BF697 .M457 2000*

**Bligh, Donald, 1936-** Understanding higher education : an introduction for parents, staff, employers and students / Donald Bligh, Harold Thomas & Ian McNay. Oxford : Intellect, 1999. x, 150 p. : ill. ; 23 cm. Includes bibliographical references and index. ISBN 1-87151-674-9 DDC 378.41
*1. Education, Higher - Great Britain. 2. Education, Higher - Great Britain - History. 3. Higher education and state - Great Britain. I. McNay, Ian. II. Thomas. H. G. (Harold G) III. Title.*
*TC LA637 .B55 1999*

**Bligh, Donald A.** What's the point in discussion? / by Donald Bligh. Exeter, Eng. ; Portland, OR : Intellect, 2000. viii, 312 p. : ill. ; 24 cm. Includes bibliographical references (p. 277-306) and index. ISBN 1-87151-669-2 (pbk)
*1. Discussion. 2. Group work in education. 3. Learning - Study and teaching. 4. Forums (Discussion and debate) I. Title.*
*TC LC6519 .B555 2000*

**BLIND.** *See* **BLIND AGED; CHILDREN, BLIND; LIBRARIES AND THE BLIND.**

**BLIND AGED - SERVICES FOR.**
Brighter visions [videorecording. Burbank, CA : RCA/Columbia Pictures Home Video ; Toluca Lake, CA : [Distributed by] Corporate Productions, c1991.
*TC HV1597.5 .B67 1991*

**BLIND AND LIBRARIES.** *See* **LIBRARIES AND THE BLIND.**

**BLIND, APPARATUS FOR THE - UNITED STATES.**
Mates, Barbara T. Adaptive technology for the Internet. Chicago, Ill. : American Library Association, 1999.
*TC Z675.B M38 1999*

**BLIND - BOOKS AND READING.**
European modernism. New York, N.Y. : OpticalTouch Systems : Louisville, Ky. : American Printing House for the Blind, c1998-1999.
*TC N6758 .A7 1999*

**BLIND CHILDREN.** *See* **CHILDREN, BLIND.**

**BLIND-DEAF CHILDREN - EDUCATION.**
Hand in hand [videorecording]. New York, N.Y. : AFB Press, c1995.
*TC HV1597.2 .H3 1995*

**BLIND-DEAF CHILDREN - EDUCATION (EARLY CHILDHOOD).**
Making the most of early communication [videorecording]. New York, NY : Distributed by AFB Press, c1997.
*TC HV1597.2 .M3 1997*

**BLIND-DEAF CHILDREN - LANGUAGE.**
Hand in hand [videorecording]. New York, N.Y. : AFB Press, c1995.
*TC HV1597.2 .H3 1995*

Making the most of early communication [videorecording]. New York, NY : Distributed by AFB Press, c1997.
*TC HV1597.2 .M3 1997*

**BLIND-DEAF CHILDREN - MEANS OF COMMUNICATION.**
Hand in hand. New York : AFB Press, c1995.
*TC HV1597.2 .H342 1995*

Hand in hand. New York : AFB Press, c1995.
*TC HV1597.2 .H34 1995*

Making the most of early communication [videorecording]. New York, NY : Distributed by AFB Press, c1997.
*TC HV1597.2 .M3 1997*

**BLIND-DEAF CHILDREN - ORIENTATION AND MOBILITY.**
Hand in hand. New York : AFB Press, c1995.
*TC HV1597.2 .H342 1995*

Hand in hand. New York : AFB Press, c1995.
*TC HV1597.2 .H34 1995*

**BLIND-DEAF CHILDREN - PSYCHOLOGY.**
Hand in hand [videorecording]. New York, N.Y. : AFB Press, c1995.
*TC HV1597.2 .H3 1995*

Making the most of early communication [videorecording]. New York, NY : Distributed by AFB Press, c1997.
*TC HV1597.2 .M3 1997*

**BLIND-DEAF CHILDREN - REHABILITATION.**
Hand in hand [videorecording]. New York, N.Y. : AFB Press, c1995.
*TC HV1597.2 .H3 1995*

Making the most of early communication [videorecording]. New York, NY : Distributed by AFB Press, c1997.
*TC HV1597.2 .M3 1997*

**BLIND-DEAF CHILDREN - STUDY AND TEACHING.**
Hand in hand. New York : AFB Press, c1995.
*TC HV1597.2 .H342 1995*

Hand in hand. New York : AFB Press, c1995.
*TC HV1597.2 .H34 1995*

**BLIND-DEAF - EDUCATION.** *See* **TEACHERS OF THE BLIND-DEAF.**

**BLIND-DEAF, TEACHERS OF THE.** *See* **TEACHERS OF THE BLIND-DEAF.**

**BLIND - EDUCATION.**
Bridges to independence [videorecording. Burbank, CA : RCA/Columbia Pictures Home Video ; [S.l. : Distributed by] Rank Video Services Production, c1991.
*TC HV1646 .B7 1991*

**BLIND - EMPLOYMENT.**
Work sight [videorecording]. Burbank, Ca. : RCA/Columbia Pictures Home Video, c1991.
*TC HV1652 .W6 1991*

**BLIND, LIBRARIES FOR THE.** *See* **LIBRARIES AND THE BLIND.**

**BLIND - ORIENTATION AND MOBILITY.**
Touch 'n' go [videorecording. Burbank, Calif. : Columbia Tristar Home Video ; [S.l. : Distributed by] Rank Video Services Production, c1991.
*TC HV1626 .T6 1991*

**BLIND - REHABILITATION.**
Touch 'n' go [videorecording. Burbank, Calif. : Columbia Tristar Home Video ; [S.l. : Distributed by] Rank Video Services Production, c1991.
*TC HV1626 .T6 1991*

**BLIND - SERVICES FOR.**
Bright beginnings [videorecording. Burbank, CA : RCA/Columbia Pictures Home Video ; Toluca Lake, CA : [Distributed by] Corporate Productions, c1991.
*TC HV1642 .B67 1991*

Bright beginnings [videorecording. Burbank, CA : RCA/Columbia Pictures Home Video ; [S.l. : Distributed by] Rank Video Services America, c1991.
*TC HV1642 .B67 1991*

Brighter visions [videorecording. Burbank, CA : RCA/Columbia Pictures Home Video ; Toluca Lake, CA : [Distributed by] Corporate Productions, c1991.
*TC HV1597.5 .B67 1991*

Touch 'n' go [videorecording. Burbank, Calif. : Columbia Tristar Home Video ; [S.l. : Distributed by] Rank Video Services Production, c1991.
*TC HV1626 .T6 1991*

Work sight [videorecording]. Burbank, Ca. : RCA/Columbia Pictures Home Video, c1991.
*TC HV1652 .W6 1991*

**BLIND - UNITED STATES - BOOKS AND READING.**
Leibs, Andrew. A field guide for the sight-impaired reader. Westport, Conn. ; London : Greenwood Press, 1999.
*TC HV1731 .L45 1999*

**BLINDNESS IN CHILDREN.** *See* **CHILDREN, BLIND.**

**BLINDNESS - PATIENTS.** *See* **BLIND.**

**BLINDNESS - PSYCHOLOGICAL ASPECTS.**
Touch, representation, and blindness. Oxford ; New York : Oxford University Press, 2000.
*TC BF275 .T68 2000*

**Bliss, Joan.**
Learning sites. 1st ed. Amsterdam ; New York : Pergamon, 1999.

*TC LB1060 .L4245 1999*

**Blixrud, Julia C., 1954-.**
DeCandido, GraceAnne A. Transforming libraries. Washington, D.C. : Association of Research Libraries, Office of Leadership and Management Services, c1999.
*TC Z711.92.H3 D43 1999*

**Blobaum, Robert.** Rewolucja : Russian Poland, 1904-1907 / Robert E. Blobaum. Ithaca : Cornell University Press, 1995. xx, 300 p. : ill. ; 24 cm. Includes bibliographical references and index. ISBN 0-8014-3054-2 (alk. paper) DDC 943.8/033
*1. Poland - History - Revolution, 1905-1907. I. Title.*
*TC DK4385 .B57 1995*

**Blocher, Donald H.** Counseling : a developmental approach / Donald H. Blocher. 4th ed. New York : Wiley, c2000. xiii, 418 p. : ill. ; 25 cm. Rev. ed. of: The professional counselor. 1987. Includes bibliographical references (p. 386-406) and indexes. ISBN 0-471-25462-2 (cloth : alk. paper) DDC 158/.3
*1. Counseling. 2. Counselors. I. Blocher, Donald H. Professional counselor. II. Title.*
*TC BF637.C6 B48 2000*

The evolution of counseling psychology / Donald H. Blocher. New York : Springer, c2000. xiii, 343 p. : ports. ; 23 cm. Includes bibliographical references and indexes. ISBN 0-8261-1348-6 DDC 158/.3
*1. Counseling - United States - History. I. Title.*
*TC BF637.C6 .B473 2000*

**Professional counselor.**
Blocher, Donald H. Counseling. 4th ed. New York : Wiley, c2000.
*TC BF637.C6 B48 2000*

**Block (East Barnet, England).**
The Block reader in visual culture. London ; New York : Routledge. 1996.
*TC N72.S6 B56 1996*

**Block, Martin E., 1958-** A teacher's guide to including students with disabilities in general physical education / by Martin E. Block. 2nd ed. Baltimore, Md. : Paul H. Brookes Pub. Co., c2000. xii, 397 p. : ill. ; 26 cm. Includes bibliographical references (p. [355]-365) and index. ISBN 1-55766-463-3 DDC 371.9/04486
*1. Physical education for handicapped persons. 2. Mainstreaming in education. I. Title.*
*TC GV445 .B56 2000*

**The Block reader in visual culture.** London ; New York : Routledge, 1996. xiv, 342 p. : ill. ; 24 cm. Includes bibliographical references and index. ISBN 0-415-13988-0 (hbk) ISBN 0-415-13989-9 (pbk). DDC 701/.03/0942
*1. Art and society - England - History - 20th century. 2. Popular culture - Psychological aspects - England. 3. Art - Political aspects - England. I. Title: Block (East Barnet, England)*
*TC N72.S6 B56 1996*

**BLOCK SCHEDULING (EDUCATION).**
Robbins, Pamela. Thinking inside the block schedule. Thousand Oaks, Calif. : Corwin Press, c2000.
*TC LB3032.2 .R63 2000*

**BLOCK SCHEDULING (EDUCATION) - NEW JERSEY.**
Campbell, Delois. High school students' perceptions of the impact of block scheduling on instructional effectiveness. 1999.
*TC 06 no. 11089*

**BLOCK SCHEDULING (EDUCATION) - PLANNING.**
Zepeda, Sally J., 1956- Supervision and staff development in the block. Larchmont, N.Y. : Eye On Education, c2000.
*TC LB3032.2 .Z46 2000*

**BLOCK SCHEDULING (EDUCATION) - UNITED STATES.**
Block scheduling. Bloomington, IN : Phi Delta Phi International, c1999.
*TC LB3032.2 .B47 1999*

Rettig, Michael D., 1950- Scheduling strategies for middle schools. Larchmont, NY : Eye On Education, 2000.
*TC LB3032.2 .R48 2000*

**Block scheduling :** restructuring the school day / David J. Flinders, editor. Bloomington, IN : Phi Delta Phi International, c1999. 288 p. ; ill. ; 28 cm. (Hot topics series) "January 2000." Includes bibliographical references (p. 277-288). DDC 373.12/4
*1. Block scheduling (Education) - United States. 2. Schedules, School - United States. I. Flinders, David J., 1955- II. Series.*
*TC LB3032.2 .B47 1999*

**BLOCKS (TOYS) - FICTION.**
Wynne-Jones, Tim. Builder of the moon. New York
M.K. McElderry Books, c1988.
*TC PZ7.W993 Bu 1988*

**Blocksidge, Martin.**
Teaching literature 11-18. London & New York :
Continuum, 2000.
*TC PR51.G7 T43 2000*

**Blood, Charles L., 1929-** The goat in the rug / by
Geraldine, as told to Charles L. Blood & Martin Link ;
illustrated by Nancy Winslow Parker. New York :
Four Winds Press, 1976. [32] p. : col. ill. ; 46 x 34 cm.
Originally published by Parents' Magazine Press, New York.
SUMMARY: Geraldine, a goat, describes each step as she and
her Navajo friend make a rug, from the hair clipping and
carding to the dyeing and actual weaving. ISBN 0-02-109114-5
*1. Navajo textile fabrics - Juvenile fiction. 2. Navajo textile
fabrics - Fiction. 3. Rugs - Fiction. 4. Hand weaving - Fiction.
5. Indian textile fabrics - Southwest. New - Fiction. I. Link,
Martin A., joint author. II. Parker, Nancy Winslow, ill. III.
Title.*
*TC PZ7.B6227 Go 1976*

**BLOOD - CIRCULATION.** *See also*
**CARDIOVASCULAR SYSTEM.**
Exercise and circulation in health and disease.
Champaign, IL ; Leeds, U.K. : Human Kinetics,
c2000.
*TC QP301 .E9346 2000*

**BLOOD - CIRCULATION - REGULATION.**
Rowell, Loring B. Human cardiovascular control.
New York : Oxford University Press, 1993.
*TC QP109 .R68 1993*

**BLOOD - PRESSURE.** *See* **BLOOD PRESSURE.**

**BLOOD PRESSURE - REGULATION.**
Rowell, Loring B. Human cardiovascular control.
New York : Oxford University Press, 1993.
*TC QP109 .R68 1993*

**Blood ties and fictive ties.**
Gager, Kristin Elizabeth. Princeton, N.J. : Princeton
University Press, c1996.
*TC HV875.58.F8 G34 1996*

**Bloom, Harold.** How to read and why / Harold Bloom.
New York : Scribner, c2000. 283 p. : 23 cm. ISBN 0-
684-85906-8
*1. Reading. I. Title.*
*TC LB1050 .B56 2000*

**Bloom, Leslie Rebecca.** Under the sign of hope :
feminist methodology and narrative interpretation /
Leslie Rebecca Bloom. Albany, N.Y. : State
University of New York Press, c1998. xv, 188 p. ; 24
cm. (SUNY series, identities in the classroom) Includes
bibliographical references (p. 167-179) and index. ISBN
0-7914-3917-8 (hbk. : alk. paper) ISBN 0-7914-3918-6 (pbk. :
alk. paper) DDC 305.4/07
*1. Women's studies - Biographical methods. 2. Women -
Research - Methodology. 3. Feminism - Research -
Methodology. 4. Autobiography - Women authors. I. Title. II.
Series.*
*TC HQ1185 .B56 1998*

**Bloom, Lloyd, ill.**
Gray, Libba Moore. When Uncle took the fiddle. New
York : Orchard Books, 1999.
*TC PZ7.G7793 Wh 1999*

Recorvits, Helen. Goodbye, Walter Malinski. 1st ed.
New York : Farrar, Straus and Giroux, c1999.
*TC PZ7.R24435 Go 1999*

**Bloom, Paul, 1963-** How children learn the meanings of
words / Paul Bloom. Cambridge, MA : MIT Press,
c2000. xii, 300 p. ; 24 cm. Includes bibliographical references
(p. [267]-290) and indexes. ISBN 0-262-02469-1 (alk. paper)
DDC 401/.93
*1. Language acquisition. 2. Semantics. I. Title.*
*TC P118 .B623 2000*

**BLOOMSBURY GROUP.**
Women in the milieu of Leonard and Virginia Woolf.
New York : Pace University Press, 1998.
*TC PR6045.O72 Z925 1998*

**BLPES.**
International bibliography of anthropology = London ;
New York : Routledge, 1999-
*TC Z7161 .I593*

**The blue planet** [videorecording] / a production of
WQED Pittsburgh in association with the National
Academy of Sciences ; series producer, Gregory
Andorfer ; producer, Theodore Thomas ; written by
Theodore Thomas. [New York, N.Y.?] : Unapix
Entertainment, Inc. [distributor]. 1 videocassette
(57 min.) : sd., col. ; 1/2 in. (Planet Earth ; 2) At head of title:
Unapix Consumer Products feature presentation

[videorecording]. VHS. Catalogued from credits and container.
Narrator, Richard Kiley. Sound, Mike de Gruy, Ken King,
Albee Gordon; photographers, Christopher Woods, Paul
Atkins, Eric Camiel; music, Jack Tillar and William Loose.
"Major funding by the Annenberg/CPB Project"--Container.
Originally produced in 1986. For adolescent through adult.
SUMMARY: The oceans may still be the last great unexplored
frontier on earth. Major revelations about the sea include a
scientist aboard the space shuttle exploring a new chapter in
oceanography and startling findings about the El Niño current
that has caused worldwide devastation. A dive takes the viewer
to the site of sea floor spreading and visits the depths of the
"middle ocean" to see new species for the first time.
*1. Earth sciences. 2. Earth. 3. Geology. 4. Oceanography. 5. El
Niño Current. 6. Documentary television programs. I.
Andorfer, Gregory. II. Thomas, Theodore, 1951- III. Kiley,
Richard. IV. WQED (Television station : Pittsburgh, Pa.) V.
National Academy of Sciences (U.S.) VI. Annenberg/CPB
Project. VII. Unapix Entertainment, Inc. VIII. Unapix
Consumer Products. IX. Title: Unapix Consumer Products
feature presentation [videorecording] X. Series.*
*TC QB631.2 .B5 1996*

**Blue willow.**
Conrad, Pam. New York : Philomel Books, c1999.
*TC PZ7.C76476 Bl 1999*

**BLUES (MUSIC) - HISTORY AND CRITICISM.**
The jazz cadence of American culture. New York :
Columbia University Press, c1998.
*TC ML3508 .J38 1998*

**BLUES (MUSIC) - UNITED STATES.** *See* **BLUES
(MUSIC).**

**BLUES (SONGS, ETC.).** *See* **BLUES (MUSIC).**

**Blumenfeld, Yorick.**
Scanning the future. New York : Thames & Hudson,
c1999.
*TC CB161 .S44 1999*

**Blumenthal, Nancy.** Count-a-saurus / by Nancy
Blumenthal ; illustrated by Robert Jay Kaufman. New
York : Four Winds Press, c1989. [24] p. : col. ill. ; 38 x
38 cm. SUMMARY: Depicts numbered groups of dinosaurs
and other prehistoric creatures, from one Stegosaurus standing
in the sun to ten Hadrosaurids sporting funny hats. Additional
text in the back provides more information about each species.
ISBN 0-02-109105-6
*1. Counting - Juvenile literature. 2. Dinosaurs - Juvenile
literature. 3. Dinosaurs. 4. Counting. I. Kaufman, Robert Jay,
ill. II. Title.*
*TC QA113 .B57 1989*

**BLUNDELL, MICHAEL, SIR, 1907-.**
Mungazi, Dickson A. The last British liberals in
Africa. Westport, Conn. : Praeger, 1999.
*TC DT2979.T63 M86 1999*

**Blurring the edges.**
Chatton, Barbara. Portsmouth, NH : Heinemann,
c1999.
*TC LB1576 .C46 1999*

**B'nai B'rith. Anti-defamation League.** Human
relations materials for the school, church &
community / Anti-defamation League of B'nai b'rith.
[New York : Anti-defamation League of B'nai B'rith,
1981?] [69] p. : ill. ; 29 cm. Includes index.
*1. Interpersonal relations - Bibliography - Catalogs. 2.
Interpersonal relations - Audiovisual aids - Catalogs. I. Title.*
*TC Z7204.S67 A5 1981*

**BNA's health law & business series**
Demetriou, Andrew J. Health care integration.
Washington, D.C. : Bureau of National Affairs, Inc.,
c1996.
*TC KF3825 .D394 1996*

**Boahen, A. Adu.** Mfantsipim and the making of Ghana :
a centenary history, 1876-1976 / by A. Adu Boahen.
Accra, Ghana : Sankofa Educational Publishers,
c1996. x, 541 p. : ill. ; 24 cm. Includes bibliographical
references (p. 540-541). ISBN 9988763115
*1. Mfantsipim School - History. 2. Ghana - History. I. Title.*
*TC LG497.M42 B62 1996*

**Board on Children, Youth, and Families (U.S.).
Committee on the Assessment of Family Violence
Interventions.**
Violence in families. Washington, D.C. : National
Academy Press, 1998.
*TC HV6626.2 .V56 1998*

**BOARDING SCHOOLS - ENGLAND - LONDON -
HISTORY - 19TH CENTURY.**
Elledge, Paul. Lord Byron at Harrow School.
Baltimore : Johns Hopkins University Press, c2000.
*TC PR4382 .E36 2000*

**BOARDING SCHOOLS - FICTION.**
Gordon, Amy, 1949- When JFK was my father.
Boston : Houghton Mifflin, 1999.
*TC PZ7.G65 Wh 1999*

**BOARDING SCHOOLS - FRANCE - HISTORY -
19TH CENTURY.**
Knottnerus, J. David. The social worlds of male and
female children in the nineteenth century French
educational system. Lewiston, N.Y. ; Lampeter,
Wales : Edwin Mellen Press, c1999.
*TC LC191.8.F8 K66 1999*

**BOARDINGHOUSES.** *See* **HOTELS.**

**BOARDS OF EDUCATION.** *See* **SCHOOL
BOARDS.**

**BOATS AND BOATING.** *See* **SHIPS.**

**Bocchino, Rob.** Emotional literacy : to be a different
kind of smart / Rob Bocchino. Thousand Oaks, Calif. :
Sage Publications, c1999. xiv, 160 p. : ill. ; 27 cm.
Includes bibliographical references (p. 150-152) and index.
ISBN 0-8039-6823-X (cloth: alk. paper) ISBN 0-8039-6824-8
(paperback: alk. paper) DDC 152.4
*1. Emotional intelligence. 2. Affect (Psychology) - Study and
teaching. 3. Affective education. 4. Emotions in children. 5.
Emotions and cognition. I. Title.*
*TC BF576 .B63 1999*

**Bock, Gregory.**
Genetics of criminal and antisocial behaviour.
Chichester ; New York : Wiley, 1996.
*TC HV6047 .G46 1996*

**Bode, Peer.**
Processing the signal [videorecording]. Cicero, Ill. :
Roland Collection of Films on Art, c1989.
*TC N6494.V53 P7 1989*

**Bodenhausen, Galen Von. 1961-.**
Stereotype activation and inhibition. Mahwah, N.J. :
L. Erlbaum Associates, 1998.
*TC BF323.S63 S75 1998*

**Bodine, Richard J.** Developing emotional intelligence :
a guide to behavior management and conflict
resolution in schools / Richard J. Bodine ; Donna K.
Crawford. Champaign, Ill : Research Press, c1999.
xiii, 216 p. ; 23 cm. Includes bibliographical references. ISBN
0-87822-421-1
*1. Classroom management. 2. Emotional intelligence. 3.
Conflict management. I. Crawford, Donna K. II. Title.*
*TC BF561 .B6 1999*

**Bodkin, Odds.** Ghost of the Southern Belle : a sea tale /
by Odds Bodkin ; paintings by Bernie Fuchs. 1st ed.
Boston : Little, Brown, 1999. 1v. (unpaged) :bcol. ill. ;c29
cm. SUMMARY: The young son of a ship's captain finds a
way to end the curse of a ghost ship whose daring Confederate
captain had once given him a lucky ball. ISBN 0-316-02608-5
DDC [Fic]
*1. Shipwrecks - Fiction. 2. Ghosts - Fiction. I. Fuchs, Bernie,
ill. II. Title.*
*TC PZ7.B6355 Gh 1999*

**BODY AND MIND.** *See* **MIND AND BODY.**

**BODY AND SOUL (PHILOSOPHY).** *See* **MIND
AND BODY.**

**The body/body problem.**
Danto, Arthur Coleman, 1924- Berkeley : University
of California Press, c1999.
*TC B105.R4 D36 1999*

**BODY CARE.** *See* **HYGIENE.**

**BODY COVERING (ANATOMY).** *See* **HAIR.**

**Body decoration.**
Gröning, Karl. New York : Vendome Press :
Distributed in the USA by Rizzoli, 1998.
*TC GT2343 .G76 1998*

**BODY DYSMORPHIC DISORDER.** *See also* **BODY
IMAGE.**
Between the lines [videorecording]. Boston, MA :
Fanlight Productions, c1997.
*TC RC552.S4 B4 1997*

**BODY FLUIDS.** *See* **BLOOD.**

**BODY FLUIDS - PRESSURE.** *See* **BLOOD
PRESSURE.**

**BODY, HUMAN.** *See also* **BODY IMAGE; HUMAN
ANATOMY; MIND AND BODY.**
Vital signs. Edinburgh : Edinburgh University Press,
c1998.
*TC HQ1190 .V56 1998*

**BODY, HUMAN - CARE AND HYGIENE.** *See*
**HYGIENE.**

**BODY, HUMAN (PHILOSOPHY).**
Baker, Lynne Rudder, 1944- Persons and bodies. New York : Cambridge University Press, 2000.
*TC B105.B64 B35 2000*

Taught bodies. New York : P. Lang, c2000.
*TC LB14.7 .T38 2000*

**BODY, HUMAN - POLITICAL ASPECTS.**
Brook, Barbara, 1949- Feminist perspective on the body. New York : Longman, 1999.
*TC GT495 .B76 1999*

**BODY, HUMAN - PSYCHOLOGICAL ASPECTS.**
*See* MIND AND BODY.

**BODY, HUMAN - SOCIAL ASPECTS.**
Birke, Lynda I. A. Feminism and the biological body. New Brunswick, N.J. : Rutgers University Press, 2000.
*TC HQ1190 .B56 2000*

Brook, Barbara, 1949- Feminist perspective on the body. New York : Longman, 1999.
*TC GT495 .B76 1999*

Vital signs. Edinburgh : Edinburgh University Press, c1998.
*TC HQ1190 .V56 1998*

**BODY, HUMAN - SYMBOLIC ASPECTS.**
Birke, Lynda I. A. Feminism and the biological body. New Brunswick, N.J. : Rutgers University Press, 2000.
*TC HQ1190 .B56 2000*

Vital signs. Edinburgh : Edinburgh University Press, c1998.
*TC HQ1190 .V56 1998*

**Body image.**
Grogan, Sarah, 1959- London ; New York : Routledge, 1999.
*TC BF697.5.B63 G76 1999*

Berg, Francie M. Women afraid to eat. Hettinger, ND : Healthy Weight Network, c2000.
*TC RC552.O25 B47 2000*

Between the lines [videorecording]. Boston, MA : Fanlight Productions, c1997.
*TC RC552.S4 B4 1997*

Druss, Richard G., 1933- Listening to patients :. Oxford ; New York : Oxford University Press, 2000.
*TC RC480.8 .D78 2000*

Goldfein, Juli Ann. The importance of shape and weight in normal-weight women with bulimia nervosa, restrained eaters (dieters), and normal controls (Non-dieters). 1997.
*TC 085 G5675*

Solovay, Sondra, 1970- Tipping the scales of justice. Amherst, N.Y. : Prometheus Books, 2000.
*TC BF697.5.B63 S65 2000*

Weiss, Gail, 1959- Body images. New York : Routledge, 1999.
*TC BF697.5.B63 W45 1999*

Working with groups to explore food & body connections. Duluth, Minn. : Whole Person Associates, c1996.
*TC RC552.E18 W67 1996*

**BODY IMAGE IN ADOLESCENCE.**
Nichter, Mimi. Fat talk. Cambridge, Mass. : Harvard University Press, 2000.
*TC RJ399.C6 N53 2000*

**BODY IMAGE IN MEN.**
Pope, Harrison. The Adonis complex. New York : Free Press, 2000.
*TC BF697.5.B635 2000*

**BODY IMAGE IN WOMEN.**
Brook, Barbara, 1949- Feminist perspective on the body. New York : Longman, 1999.
*TC GT495 .B76 1999*

**BODY IMAGE - SOCIAL ASPECTS.**
Lippert, Robin Alissa. Conflating the self with the body. 1999.
*TC 085 L655*

Solovay, Sondra, 1970- Tipping the scales of justice. Amherst, N.Y. : Prometheus Books, 2000.
*TC BF697.5.B63 S65 2000*

**BODY IMAGE - SOCIAL ASPECTS - GREAT BRITAIN.**
Grogan, Sarah, 1959- Body image. London ; New York : Routledge, 1999.
*TC BF697.5.B63 G76 1999*

**BODY IMAGE - SOCIAL ASPECTS - UNITED STATES.**
Grogan, Sarah, 1959- Body image. London ; New York : Routledge, 1999.
*TC BF697.5.B63 G76 1999*

**Body images.**
Weiss, Gail, 1959- New York : Routledge, 1999.
*TC BF697.5.B63 W45 1999*

**The body in mind.**
Rowlands, Mark. Cambridge, U.K. ; New York : Cambridge University Press, 1999.
*TC BD418.3 .R78 1999*

**The body, in theory**
Too, Yun Lee. The pedagogical contract. Ann Arbor: University of Michigan Press, c2000.
*TC LB1033 .T66 2000*

**BODY LANGUAGE.** *See also* **FACIAL EXPRESSION.**
The social context of nonverbal behavior. Cambridge, U.K. ; New York : Cambridge University Press ; Paris : Editions de la Maison des Sciences de l'Homme, 1999.
*TC BF637.N66 S63 1999*

**BODY MARKING.**
Gröning, Karl. Body decoration. New York : Vendome Press : Distributed in the USA by Rizzoli, 1998.
*TC GT2343 .G76 1998*

**BODY MECHANICS, HUMAN.** *See* **HUMAN MECHANICS.**

**BODY PAINTING.**
Gröning, Karl. Body decoration. New York : Vendome Press : Distributed in the USA by Rizzoli, 1998.
*TC GT2343 .G76 1998*

**BODY POSITION.** *See* **POSTURE.**

**BODY SCHEMA.**
Weiss, Gail, 1959- Body images. New York : Routledge, 1999.
*TC BF697.5.B63 W45 1999*

**BODY WEIGHT.** *See* **OBESITY; WEIGHT LOSS.**

**Boehm, Beth.**
History, reflection, and narrative. Stamford, Conn. : Ablex Pub., c1999.
*TC PE1405.U6 H56 1999*

**Boehmer, Ulrike, 1959-** The personal and the political : women's activism in response to the breast cancer and AIDS epidemics / Ulrike Boehmer. Albany, NY : State University of New York Press, c2000. x, 208 p. ; 24 cm. Includes bibliographical references (p. 193-203) and index. ISBN 0-7914-4549-6 (hardcover : alk. paper) ISBN 0-7914-4550-X (pbk. : alk. paper) DDC 362.1/969792/0082
*1. Breast - Cancer - Political aspects - United States. 2. AIDS (Disease) - Political aspects - United States. 3. Women political activists - United States. I. Title.*
*TC RC280.B8 B62 2000*

**Boehnlein, James K.**
Psychiatry and religion. 1st ed. Washington, DC : American Psychiatric Press, c2000.
*TC RC455.4.R4 P755 2000*

**Boekaerts, Monique.**
Handbook of self-regulation. San Diego : Academic, 2000.
*TC BF632 .H254 2000*

**Boer, Theodoor Adriaan, 1960-.**
Meaningful care. Dordrecht ; Boston ; London : Kluwer Academic Publishers, c2000.
*TC HV3004 .M34 2000*

**BOERS.** *See* **AFRIKANERS.**

**Bogart, Michele Helene, 1952-** Public sculpture and the civic ideal in New York City, 1890-1930 / Michele H. Bogart. 1st Smithsonian ed. Washington, D.C. : Smithsonian Institution Press, 1997. xvi, 390 p. : ill., map ; 21 cm. Originally published: Chicago : University of Chicago Press, 1989. Includes bibliographical references (p. 321-380) and index. ISBN 1-56098-766-9 (paper : alk. paper) DDC 731,76/09747109041
*1. Public sculpture - New York (State) - New York - Themes, motives. 2. Art patronage - New York (State) - New York. I. Title.*
*TC NB235.N5 B64 1997*

**Bogle, Michael.** Design in Australia, 1880-1970 / Michael Bogle. Sydney : Craftsman House : G+B Arts International, c1998. 156 p. : ill. (some col.) ; 31 cm. Includes bibliographical references (p. 147-151) and index. ISBN 90-5703-461-1

*1. Design - Australia - History - 19th century. 2. Design - Australia - Hitory - 20th century. I. Title.*
*TC NK1490.A1 B64 1998*

**Bogue, E. Grady (Ernest Grady), 1935-** Exploring the heritage of American higher education : the evolution of philosophy and policy / by E. Grady Bogue and Jeffery Aper. Phoenix, Ariz. : Oryx Press, 2000. xiii, 258 p. : ill. ; 24 cm. (American Council on Education/Oryx Press series on higher education) Includes bibliographical references (p. 219-236) and index. ISBN 1-57356-310-2 (alk. paper) DDC 378.73
*1. Education, Higher - United States. 2. Education, Higher - Aims and objectives - United States. 3. Higher education and state - United States. I. Aper, Jeffery. II. Title. III. Series.*
*TC LA227.4 .B66 2000*

**Bogue, Nila.**
The Choice of a lifetime [videorecording]. Hohokus, NJ : New Day Films, c1996.
*TC RC569 .C45 1996*

**Bohannan, April.**
Saye, Jerry D. Manheimer's cataloging and classification. 4th ed., rev. and expanded. New York : Marcel Dekker, c2000.
*TC Z693 .S28 2000*

**Bohart, Arthur C.** How clients make therapy work : the process of active self-healing / Arthur C. Bohart and Karen Tallman. 1st ed. Washington, DC : American Psychological Association, c1999. xvi, 347 p. ; 26 cm. Includes bibliographical references (p. 305-328) and indexes. ISBN 1-55798-571-5 (case : alk. paper) DDC 616.89/14
*1. Psychotherapy. 2. Patient participation. I. Tallman, Karen. II. Title.*
*TC RC480.5 .B64 1999*

**BOHM, DAVID.**
Peat, F. David, 1938- Infinite potential. Reading, Mass. : Addison Wesley, c1997.
*TC QC16.B627 P43 1997*

**Bohmer, Carol.** The wages of seeking help : sexual exploitation by professionals / Carol Bohmer. Westport, Conn. ; London : Praeger, 2000. ix, 209 p. ; 25 cm. Includes bibliographical references (p. [189]-204) and index. ISBN 0-275-96793-X (alk. paper) DDC 616.85/83
*1. Sexually abused patients. 2. Medical personnel and patient. 3. Medical personnel - Sexual behavior. 4. Sexual abuse victims. I. Title.*
*TC RC560.S44 B67 2000*

**Boice, Robert.** Advice for new faculty members : nihil nimus / Robert Boice. Boston ; London : Allyn and Bacon, c2000. xiv, 319 p. : ill. ; 23 cm. Includes bibliographical references (p. 299-309) and indexes. ISBN 0-205-28159-1 DDC 378.1/2
*1. College teachers - United States. 2. College personnel management - United States. 3. Professional socialization - United States. I. Title.*
*TC LB1778.2 .B63 2000*

**Bois, Yve Alain.**
Piet Mondrian, 1872-1944. Milan : Leonardo Arte, 1994.
*TC N6953.M64 A4 1994*

**Bold, Christine.** Progression in primary design and technology / Christine Bold. London : David Fulton, 1999. 104 p. : ill., forms ; 30 cm. Includes bibliographical references (p. [99]-101) and index. ISBN 1-85346-605-0
*1. Design - Study and teaching (Elementary) - Great Britain. 2. Technology - Study and teaching (Elementary) - Great Britain. 3. Child development. I. Title.*
*TC LB1541 .B65 1999*

**Bolles, Augusta Lynn.** We paid our dues : women trade union leaders of the Caribbean / A. Lynn Bolles. Washington, D.C. : Howard University Press, 1996. xxxviii, 250 p. : ill. ; 23 cm. Includes bibliographical references (p. 231-239) and index. ISBN 0-88258-086-8 (cloth : alk. paper) ISBN 0-88258-087-6 (pbk. : alk. paper) DDC 331.4/7/09729
*1. Women labor union members - Caribbean. English-speaking. 2. Women labor leaders - Caribbean. English-speaking. I. Title.*
*TC HD6079.2.C27 B64 1996*

**Bolles, Richard Nelson.**
Figler, Howard E. The career counselor's handbook. Berkeley, Calif. : Ten Speed Press, c1999.
*TC HF5549.5.C35 F54 1999*

**Parachute library.**
Figler, Howard E. The career counselor's handbook. Berkeley, Calif. : Ten Speed Press, c1999.
*TC HF5549.5.C35 F54 1999*

**Bolt, David B., 1954-** Digital divide : computers and our children's future / David B. Bolt, Ray A.K. Crawford. New York : TV Books, c2000. 207 p. : ill. ; 24 cm. ISBN

1-57500-086-5 DDC 371.33/4
*1. Education - United States - Data processing. 2. Computer-assisted instruction - Social aspects - United States. 3. Educational equalization - United States. 4. Computers and children. I. Crawford, Ray A. K., 1954- II. Title.*
**TC LB1028.43 .B64 2000**

**Bolter, J. David, 1951-** Remediation : understanding new media / Jay David Bolter and Richard Grusin. Cambridge, Mass. : MIT Press, c1999. xi, 295 p. : ill. (some col.) ; 24 cm. Includes bibliographical references (p. [276]-284) and index. ISBN 0-262-02452-7 (hardcover : alk. paper) DDC 302.2223
*1. Mass media - Technological innovations. I. Grusin, Richard. II. Title.*
**TC P96.T42 B59 1998**

**Bolton, Allan.** Managing the academic unit / Allan Bolton. Buckingham [England] ; Philadelphia : Open University Press, c2000. xi, 152 p. ; 22 cm. (Managing universities and colleges) Includes bibliographical references (p. [146]-149) and index. ISBN 0-335-20404-X ISBN 0-335-20403-1 (pbk.) DDC 378.1/11
*1. Departmental chairmen (Universities) - Great Britain. 2. Deans (Education) - Great Britain. 3. College administrators - Great Britain. 4. Universities and colleges - Great Britain - Administration. I. Title. II. Series.*
**TC LB2341 .B583 2000**

**Bomford, David.**
Art in the making, Impressionism. London : National Gallery, in association with Yale University Press, c1991.
**TC ND547.5.I4 I4472 1991**

Colour / David Bomford and Ashok Roy. London : National Gallery Company ; [New Haven, Conn.] : Distributed by Yale University Press, 2000. 80 p. : col. ill. ; 23 cm. (Pocket guides) Includes bibliographical references (p. 80). ISBN 1-85709-248-1
*1. Color in art. 2. National Gallery (Great Britain) - Guidebooks. 3. Pigments. I. Roy, Ashok. II. Title. III. Series: Pocket guides (National Gallery (Great Britain))*
**TC ND1489 B66 2000**

**Bommarito, James W., 1922- joint author.**
Johnson, Orval G., 1917- Tests and measurements in child development: [1st ed.]. San Francisco, Jossey-Bass, 1971.
**TC BF722 .J64**

**Bonacci, Mark A.**
Staines, Gail M., 1961- Social sciences research. Lanham, Md. ; London : Scarecrow Press, 2000.
**TC H62 .S736 2000**

**Bonar, Eulalie H.**
Woven by the grandmothers. Washington : Smithsonian Institution Press in association with the National Museum of the American Indian, Smithsonian Institution, c1996.
**TC E99.N3 W79 1996**

**Bond, Sheryl.**
A new world of knowledge. Ottawa : International Development Research Centre, c1999.
**TC LC1090 N38 1999**

**Bond, Zinny S. (Zinny Sans), 1940-** Slips of the ear : errors in the perception of casual conversation / Zinny S. Bond. San Diego, Calif. ; London : Academic, c1999. xvii, 212 p. ; 24 cm. Includes bibliographical references (p. 205-208) and index. CONTENTS: Foreword -- Preface -- ch. 1. Introduction -- ch. 2. Vowel misperceptions -- ch. 3. Consonant misperceptions -- ch. 4. Misperceptions of the shape of words -- ch. 5. Children's misperceptions -- ch. 6. The lexicon -- ch. 7. Syntax -- ch. 8. Summary and conclusions -- Appendix A: Experimental errors -- Appendix B. Data set -- References -- Subject index. ISBN 0-12-113340-0 DDC 302.346
*1. Conversation analysis. 2. Speech perception. 3. Auditory perception. 4. Conversation analysis. I. Title.*
**TC P37.5.S67 B66 1999**

**Bondi, Joseph.**
Wiles, Jon. Supervision. 5th ed. Upper Saddle River, N.J. : Merrill, c2000.
**TC LB2806.4 .W55 2000**

**BONDS, SCHOOL.** *See* **SCHOOL BONDS.**

**BONES.** *See* **SPINE.**

**Boney, F. N.** A pictorial history of the University of Georgia / F.N. Boney. 2nd ed. Athens : University of Georgia Press, c2000. ix, 302 p. : ill. ; 29 cm. Includes bibliographical references (p. 295) and index. ISBN 0-8203-2198-2 (alk. paper) DDC 378.758/18
*1. University of Georgia - History. 2. University of Georgia - History - Pictorial works. I. Title. II. Title: University of Georgia*
**TC LD1983 .B6 2000**

**BONIFACIO SÁNCHEZ HIGH SCHOOL (AIBONITO, P.R.).**
Laborde, Ilia M. Rediscovering San Cristóbal Canyon. 1996.
**TC 06 no. 10660**

Laborde, Ilia M. Rediscovering San Cristóbal Canyon. 1996.
**TC 06 no. 10660**

**Bonnard.**
Whitfield, Sarah, 1942- New York, N.Y. : Harry N. Abrams, 1998.
**TC ND553.B65 W45 1998**

**BONNARD, PIERRE, 1867-1947 - CRITICISM AND INTERPRETATION.**
Whitfield, Sarah, 1942- Bonnard. New York, N.Y. : Harry N. Abrams, 1998.
**TC ND553.B65 W45 1998**

**Bonnell, Victoria E.** Iconography of power : Soviet political posters under Lenin and Stalin / Victoria E. Bonnell. Berkeley : University of California Press, c1997. xxii, 363 p. : ill. (some col.) ; 25 cm. (Studies on the history of society and culture ; 27) Includes bibliographical references (p. 333-344) and index. ISBN 0-520-08712-7 (alk. paper) DDC 947.084
*1. Soviet Union - Politics and government - 1917-1936 - Posters. 2. Soviet Union - Politics and government - 1936-1953 - Posters. 3. Political posters. Russian. I. Title. II. Series.*
**TC DK266.3 .B58 1997**

**BONS MOTS.** *See* **WIT AND HUMOR.**

**Boo!.**
Hubbell, Patricia. 1st ed. New York : Marshall Cavendish, 1998.
**TC PS3558.U22 B66 1998**

**BOOK.**
Hays, Kate F. Working it out. 1st ed. Washington, DC : American Psychological Association, c1999.
**TC RC489.E9 H39 1999**

Smith, Richard Mason, 1881- From infancy to childhood. Boston : Atlantic monthly press, [c1925]
**TC RJ61 .S675**

**BOOK CENSORSHIP.** *See* **CENSORSHIP.**

**BOOK CLUBS.** *See* **GROUP READING.**

**BOOK ILLUSTRATION.** *See* **ILLUSTRATION OF BOOKS.**

**BOOK INDUSTRIES AND TRADE.** *See* **PUBLISHERS AND PUBLISHING.**

**BOOK INDUSTRIES AND TRADE - UNITED STATES - HISTORY - 17TH CENTURY.**
The colonial book in the Atlantic world. Cambridge, U.K. : New York : Cambridge University Press, 2000.
**TC Z473 .C686 1999**

**BOOK INDUSTRIES AND TRADE - UNITED STATES - HISTORY - 18TH CENTURY.**
The colonial book in the Atlantic world. Cambridge, U.K. : New York : Cambridge University Press, 2000.
**TC Z473 .C686 1999**

**A book of flies.**
Michelson, Richard. New York : Cavendish Children's Books, 1999.
**TC PS3563.I34 B66 1999**

**The book of leadership wisdom :** classic writings by legendary business leaders / edited by Peter Krass. New York : Wiley, c1998. xiv, 493 p. ; 24 cm. Includes bibliographical references (p. 478-487) and indexes. ISBN 0-471-29455-1 (alk. paper) DDC 658.4/092
*1. Leadership. I. Krass, Peter.*
**TC HD57.7 .B66 1998**

**Book of lists.**
Fry, Edward Bernard, 1925- The reading teacher's book of lists. 3rd ed. Englewood Cliffs, NJ : Prentice Hall, c1993.
**TC LB1050.2 .F79 1993**

Fry, Edward Bernard, 1925- The reading teacher's book of lists. 4th ed. Paramus, N.J. : Prentice Hall, c2000.
**TC LB1050.2 .F79 2000**

**Book of trucks.**
Simon, Seymour. Seymour Simon's book of trucks. New York : HarperCollins Publishers, 2000.
**TC TL230.15 .S56 2000**

**BOOK PUBLISHING.** *See* **PUBLISHERS AND PUBLISHING.**

**BOOK REGISTRATION, NATIONAL.** *See* **COPYRIGHT.**

**BOOK REPAIRING.** *See* **BOOKS - CONSERVATION AND RESTORATION.**

**BOOK REVIEWS.** *See* **BOOKS - REVIEWS.**

**BOOK SELECTION.** *See also* **INSTRUCTIONAL MATERIALS CENTERS - BOOK SELECTION.**
Hart-Hewins, Linda. Better books! Better readers!. York, Me. : Stenhouse Publishers ; Markham, Ont. : Pembroke Publishers, c1999.
**TC LB1525 .H26 1999**

**BOOK-STUDY GROUPS.** *See* **GROUP READING.**

**BOOK TALKS.**
Littlejohn, Carol. Keep talking that book!. Worthington, Ohio : Linworth Pub., 2000.
**TC Z716.3 .L58 2000**

Littlejohn, Carol. Talk that book! booktalks to promote reading. Worthington, Ohio : Linworth Publishing, 1999.
**TC Z1037.A2 L58 1999**

**BOOK TRADE.** *See* **BOOK INDUSTRIES AND TRADE.**

**BOOK-WORMS.** *See* **BOOKS - CONSERVATION AND RESTORATION.**

**BOOKBINDERS - GREAT BRITAIN - BIOGRAPHY.**
Middleton, Bernard C., 1924- Recollections. New Castle, Del. : Oak Knoll Press, 2000.
**TC Z269.2.M53 A3 2000**

**BOOKBINDING - GREAT BRITAIN - HISTORY - 19TH CENTURY.**
Darling, Harold. From Mother Goose to Dr. Seuss. San Francisco : Chronicle Books, c1999.
**TC Z270.G7 D37 1999**

**BOOKBINDING - GREAT BRITAIN - HISTORY - 20TH CENTURY.**
Darling, Harold. From Mother Goose to Dr. Seuss. San Francisco : Chronicle Books, c1999.
**TC Z270.G7 D37 1999**

**BOOKBINDING - UNITED STATES - HISTORY - 19TH CENTURY.**
Darling, Harold. From Mother Goose to Dr. Seuss. San Francisco : Chronicle Books, c1999.
**TC Z270.G7 D37 1999**

**BOOKBINDING - UNITED STATES - HISTORY - 20TH CENTURY.**
Darling, Harold. From Mother Goose to Dr. Seuss. San Francisco : Chronicle Books, c1999.
**TC Z270.G7 D37 1999**

**BOOKER T. WASHINGTON NATIONAL MONUMENT (VA.).**
West, Patricia, 1958- Domesticating history. Washington [D.C.] : Smithsonian Institution Press, c1999.
**TC E159 .W445 1999**

**Bookmarks.**
Ruszkiewicz, John J., 1950- New York : Harlow, England : Longman, c2000.
**TC LB2369 .R88 2000**

**BOOKPLATES, AMERICAN.**
Fincham, H. W. (Henry Walter) Artists and engravers of British and American book plates. New York : Dodd, Mead, and Company, 1897.
**TC Z993 .F49 1897**

**BOOKPLATES, ENGLISH.**
Fincham, H. W. (Henry Walter) Artists and engravers of British and American book plates. New York : Dodd, Mead, and Company, 1897.
**TC Z993 .F49 1897**

**BOOKS.** *See* **CATALOGING; CHILDREN'S BOOKS; ILLUSTRATION OF BOOKS; PICTURE BOOKS.**

**Books abroad;** an international literary quarterly. Norman, Okla., The University of Oklahoma Press. 50 v. ill., ports. 23-26 cm. v. 1-50; Jan. 1927-autumn 1976. Subtitle varies. Indexed by: International index. Indexed by: Social science and humanities index. Continued by World literature today ISSN: 0196-3570. ISSN 0006-7431
*1. Books - Reviews. 2. Bibliography - Periodicals. I. Title: World literature today*

**BOOKS AND READING.** *See also* **BOOKS - REVIEWS; POPULAR LITERATURE.**
Transcending boundaries. New York : Garland, 1999.
**TC PN1009.A1 T69 1999**

**BOOKS AND READING - FICTION.**
Steer, Dugald. Just one more story. New York : Dutton Children's Books, 1999.

TC PZ7.S81534 Ju 1999

**BOOKS AND READING FOR CHILDREN.** See **CHILDREN - BOOKS AND READING.**

**BOOKS AND READING - GREAT BRITAIN - HISTORY - 19TH CENTURY.**
Altick, Richard Daniel, 1915- The English common reader. 2nd ed. Columbus : Ohio State University Press, [1998], c1957.
*TC Z1003.5.G7 A53 1998*

**BOOKS AND READING IN LITERATURE.**
Pearson, Jacqueline, 1949- Women's reading in Britain, 1750-1835. Cambridge, UK ; New York : Cambridge University Press, 1999.
*TC PR756.W65 P43 1999*

**BOOKS AND READING - MEDITERRANEAN REGION - HISTORY.**
Millard, A. R. (Alan Ralph) Reading and writing in the time of Jesus. New York : New York University Press, 2000.
*TC BS2555.5 .M55 2000*

**BOOKS AND READING - UNITED STATES.**
I hear America reading. Portsmouth, NH : Heinemann, c1999.
*TC Z1003.2 .I34 1999*

**BOOKS AND READING - UNITED STATES - HISTORY - 20TH CENTURY.**
Lutz, Catherine. Reading National geographic. Chicago : University of Chicago Press, 1993.
*TC G1.N275 L88 1993*

**BOOKS - APPRAISAL.** See **BOOKS AND READING; CRITICISM; LITERATURE - HISTORY AND CRITICISM.**

**BOOKS - CARE.** See **BOOKS - CONSERVATION AND RESTORATION.**

**BOOKS - CENSORSHIP.** See **CENSORSHIP.**

**Books children love.**
Wilson, Elizabeth Laraway. Westchester, Ill. : Crossway Books, c1987.
*TC Z1037 .W745 1987*

**BOOKS - CONSERVATION AND RESTORATION - GREAT BRITAIN - HISTORY - 20TH CENTURY.**
Middleton, Bernard C., 1924- Recollections. New Castle, Del. : Oak Knoll Press, 2000.
*TC Z269.2.M53 A3 2000*

**Books for Africa.** London, International Committee on Christian Literature for Africa. 33 v. 22 cm. v. 1-33, no. 3; Jan. 1931-July 1963. The bulletin of the International Committee on Christian Literature for Africa. Vols. 30-33 published by the Christian Literature Council. ISSN 0567-3348
*1. Bibliography - Periodicals. 2. Africa - Bibliography - Periodicals. I. International Committee on Christian Literature for Africa.*

**BOOKS FOR TEENAGERS.** See **YOUNG ADULT LITERATURE.**

**BOOKS - HISTORY - EXHIBITIONS.** See **LIBRARY EXHIBITS.**

**BOOKS, ILLUSTRATION OF.** See **ILLUSTRATION OF BOOKS.**

**Books in library and information science**
(v. 59) Saye, Jerry D. Manheimer's cataloging and classification. 4th ed., rev. and expanded. New York : Marcel Dekker, c2000.
*TC Z693 .S28 2000*

**BOOKS - MUTILATION, DEFACEMENT, ETC.** See **BOOKS - CONSERVATION AND RESTORATION.**

**BOOKS OF KNOWLEDGE.** See **ENCYCLOPEDIAS AND DICTIONARIES.**

**Books of the body.**
Carlino, Andrea, 1960- [Fabbrica del corpo. English] Chicago : University of Chicago Press, c1999.
*TC QM33.4 .C3613 1999*

**BOOKS, OUT-OF-PRINT.** See **OUT-OF-PRINT BOOKS.**

**BOOKS PALS (PROGRAM).**
Glass, Laurie. Read! read! read!. Thousand Oaks, Calif. : Corwin Press, c2000.
*TC LB1050.2 .G54 2000*

**BOOKS - PRESERVATION.** See **BOOKS - CONSERVATION AND RESTORATION.**

**BOOKS - PUBLISHING.** See **PUBLISHERS AND PUBLISHING.**

**BOOKS - REPAIRING.** See **BOOKS - CONSERVATION AND RESTORATION.**

**BOOKS - RESTORATION.** See **BOOKS - CONSERVATION AND RESTORATION.**

**BOOKS - REVIEWS.**
Books abroad; Norman, Okla., The University of Oklahoma Press.

**BOOKS - REVIEWS - PERIODICALS.**
CAS. Chicago : Curriculum Advisory Service, 1969-1974.

**Books to build on.**
Hirsch, E. D. (Eric Donald), 1928- New York : Delta, 1996.
*TC Z1037 .H646 1996*

**BOOKS, VELLUM PRINTED.** See **VELLUM PRINTED BOOKS.**

**BOOKS - WANT LISTS.** See **OUT-OF-PRINT BOOKS.**

**BOOKSELLERS AND BOOKSELLING.** See **PUBLISHERS AND PUBLISHING.**

**Booktalks to promotion reading.**
Littlejohn, Carol. Talk that book! booktalks to promote reading. Worthington, Ohio : Linworth Publishing, 1999.
*TC Z1037.A2 L58 1999*

**Boone, Daniel R.** The voice and voice therapy / Daniel R. Boone, Stephen C. McFarlane. 6th ed. Boston ; London : Allyn & Bacon, c2000. xi, 308 p., [2] p. of plates : ill. (some col.) ; 25 cm. + 1 sound disc (4 3/4 in.). Includes bibliographical references (p. 293-303) and index. ISBN 0-205-30843-0 (alk. paper) DDC 616.85/5
*1. Voice disorders. 2. Larynx - Diseases. 3. Voice Disorders - diagnosis. 4. Speech, Alaryngeal. 5. Voice - physiology. 6. Voice Disorders - etiology. 7. Voice Disorders - therapy. 8. Voice Training. I. McFarlane, Stephen C. II. Title.*
*TC RF540 .B66 2000*

**BOOTBLACKS.** See **SHOE SHINERS.**

**Booth, Alan, 1935-.**
Transitions to adulthood in a changing economy. Westport, Conn. : Praeger, c1999.
*TC HQ799.7 .T73 1999*

**Booth, Wayne C.** For the love of it : amateuring and its rivals / Wayne Booth. Chicago : University of Chicago Press, c1999. x, 237 p. : ill. ; 24 cm. Includes bibliographical references (p. [215]-226) and index. ISBN 0-226-06585-5 (cloth : alk. paper) DDC 787.4/092
*1. Booth, Wayne C. 2. Violoncellists - United States - Biography. I. Title.*
*TC ML418.B49 A3 1999*

**BOOTH, WAYNE C.**
Booth, Wayne C. For the love of it. Chicago : University of Chicago Press, c1999.
*TC ML418.B49 A3 1999*

**BOOTS AND SHOES.** See **FOOTWEAR.**

**Bootzin, Richard R., 1940-.**
Psychology today. 7th ed. New York : McGraw-Hill, c1991.
*TC BF121 .P85 1991*

**Bor, Robert.**
The practice of counselling in primary care. London ; Thousand Oaks, Calif. : SAGE Publications, 1999.
*TC R727.4 .P733 1999*

**Borasi, Raffaella.** Reading counts : expanding the role of reading in mathematics classrooms / Raffaella Borasi & Marjorie Siegel ; foreword by David Pimm. New York ; London : Teachers College Press, c2000. xii, 227 p. : ill. ; 24 cm. (Ways of knowing in science series) Includes bibliographical references (p. 213-221) and index. ISBN 0-8077-3921-9 (hbk.) ISBN 0-8077-3920-0 (pbk.) DDC 510/.71
*1. Mathematics - Study and teaching. 2. Literature in mathematics education. I. Siegel, Marjorie Gail, 1952- II. Title. III. Series.*
*TC QA11 .B6384 2000*

**Borden, Louise.** A. Lincoln and me / story by Louise Borden and pictures by Ted Lewin. New York : Scholastic, 1999. 1v. (unpaged) : col. ill. ; 30 cm. SUMMARY: With the help of his teacher, a young boy realizes that he not only shares his birthday and similar physical appearance with Abraham Lincoln, but that he is like him in other ways as well. ISBN 0-590-45714-4 (hc.) DDC [E]
*1. Lincoln, Abraham, - 1809-1865 - Juvenile fiction. 2. Lincoln, Abraham, - 1809-1865 - Fiction. 3. Self-perception - Fiction. I. Lewin, Ted, ill. II. Title.*
*TC PZ7.B64827 An 1999*

**Borden, William.**
Comparative approaches in brief dynamic psychotherapy. New York : Haworth Press, c1999.
*TC RC480.55 .C658 1999*

**BORDER LIFE.** See **FRONTIER AND PIONEER LIFE.**

**Borderline patients : :** extending the limits of treatability / Harold W. Koenigsberg ... [et al.]. 1st ed. New York : BasicBooks, c2000. ix, 293 p. : ill. ; 25 cm. ISBN 0-465-09560-7
*1. Borderline personality disorder - Treatment. 2. Transference (Psychology).*
*TC RC569.5.B67 B685 2000*

**BORDERLINE PERSONALITY DISORDER.**
Gutin, Nina J. Differential object representations in inpatients with narcissistic and borderline personality disorders and normal controls. 1997.
*TC 085 G975*

McCormack, Charles C. Treating borderline states in marriage. Northvale, NJ : Jason Aronson, 2000.
*TC RC488.5 .M392 2000*

**BORDERLINE PERSONALITY DISORDER - TREATMENT.**
Borderline patients :. 1st ed. New York : BasicBooks, c2000.
*TC RC569.5.B67 B685 2000*

**Bordin, Ruth Birgitta Anderson, 1917-** Women at Michigan : the "dangerous experiment," 1870s to the present / by Ruth Bordin ; foreword by Martha Vicinus ; introduction by Kathryn Kish Sklar and Lynn Y. Weiner. Ann Arbor : University of Michigan Press, c1999. xxxii, 138 p. : ill. ; 24 cm. Includes bibliographical references (p. 123-126) and index. CONTENTS: Pursuing the cause -- A most hopeful experiment -- Change and redefinition -- Women, war, and crisis -- From the age of conformity to the stirrings of dissent -- Change and resistance -- Victory or accommodation. ISBN 0-472-10871-9 (cloth : acid-free paper) DDC 378.774/35
*1. University of Michigan - History. 2. Women - Education (Higher) - Michigan - Ann Arbor - History. 3. Women college teachers - Michigan - Ann Arbor - History. 4. McGuigan, Dorothy Gies. - Dangerous experiment. I. Title.*
*TC LD3280 .B67 1999*

**Borgman, Christine L., 1951-** From Gutenberg to the global information infrastructure : access to information in the networked world / Christine L. Borgman. Cambridge, Mass. : MIT Press, 2000. xviii, 324 p. ; 24 cm. (Digital libraries and electronic publishing.) Includes bibliographical references (p. [271]-310) and index. ISBN 0-262-02473-X (alk. paper)
*1. Information superhighway. 2. Digital libraries. 3. Libraries - Special collections - Electronic information resources. 4. Information superhighway - United States. 5. Digital libraries - United States. 6. Libraries - United States - Special collections - Electronic information resources. I. Title. II. Series.*
*TC ZA3225 .B67 2000*

**Borich, Gary D.** Effective teaching methods / Gary D. Borich. 4th ed. Upper Saddle River, N.J. : Merrill, c2000. xx, 515 p. : ill. (some col.), forms ; 24 cm. + 1 booklet. Includes booklet: Bridge: activity guide and assessment options to accompany Effective teaching methods, prepared by Debra Bayles Martin, c2000. Booklet measures 22 x 28.5 cm. Includes bibliographical references (p. 495-508) and indexes. ISBN 0-13-936130-8 (text) ISBN 0-13-007813-1 (booklet) DDC 371.102
*1. Effective teaching. 2. Lesson planning - United States. I. Martin, Debra Bayles. Bridge. II. Title.*
*TC LB1025.3 .B67 2000*

Kubiszyn, Tom. Educational testing and measurement. 6th ed. New York : J. Wiley & Sons, c2000.
*TC LB3051 .K8 2000*

**Boris, Elizabeth T.**
Nonprofits and government. Washington, DC : Urban Institute Press, 1999.
*TC HD62.6 .N694 1999*

**Boriss-Krimsky, Carolyn.** The creativity handbook : a visual arts guide for parents and teachers / Carolyn Boriss-Krimsky. Springfield, Ill. : C.C. Thomas, 1999. xiii, 171 p. : ill. ; 26 cm. Includes bibliographical references (p. 163-164) and index. ISBN 0-398-06962-X (paper) DDC 707/.1
*1. Art - Study and teaching - Activity programs. 2. Creative ability in children. 3. Creative ability in adolescence. I. Title.*
*TC N350 .B656 1999*

**Bornet, Vaughn Davis, 1917-** An independent scholar in twentieth century America : the autobiography of Vaughn Davis Bornet. Talent, Or. : Bornet Books, 1995. xl, 383 p. : ill. ; 23 cm. Includes bibliographical references (p. 369-382) and index.

*1. Bornet, Vaughn Davis. - 1917- 2. Social scientists - United States - Biography. I. Title. II. Title: Independent scholar in 20th century America*
**TC H59.B63 A3 1995**

**BORNET, VAUGHN DAVIS, 1917-.**
Bornet, Vaughn Davis, 1917- An independent scholar in twentieth century America. Talent, Or. : Bornet Books, 1995.
**TC H59.B63 A3 1995**

**Bornstein, Jerry.** An American chronology / Jerry Bornstein. New York : Neal-Schuman Publishers, 2000. xi, 303 p. ; 28 cm. ISBN 1-55570-369-0 DDC 973
*1. United States - Civilization - 19th century - Chronology. 2. United States - Civilization - 20th century - Chronology. I. Title.*
**TC E169.1 .B758 2000**

**Bornstein, Robert F.**
Empirical perspectives on object relations theory. 1st ed. Washington, DC : American Psychological Association, c1994.
**TC BF175.5.O24 E85 1994**

**Borofsky, Jonathan, 1942-** Jonathan Borofsky. New York : Whitney Museum of American Art, c1984. [13] p. : ill. ; 23 cm. Exhibition itinerary: Philadelphia Museum of Art, Oct. 7-Dec. 2, 1984; Whitney Museum of American Art, New York, Dec. 22, 1984-March 10, 1985; University Art Museum, Berkeley, Apr. 17-June 16, 1985; Walker Art Center, Minneapolis, Sept. 13-Nov. 3, 1985; The Corcoran Gallery of Art, Wash., D.C., Dec. 14, 1985-Feb. 9, 1986. Catalog essay by Richard Marshall. "Gift from Professor Maxine Greene"
*1. Borofsky, Jonathan. - 1942- - Exhibitions. I. Whitney Museum of American Art.*
**TC N6537.B68 W5 1984**

**BOROFSKY, JONATHAN, 1942 - -EXHIBITIONS.**
Borofsky, Jonathan, 1942- Jonathan Borofsky. New York : Whitney Museum of American Art, c1984.
**TC N6537.B68 W5 1984**

**Bos, Candace S., 1950-.**
Helping individuals with disabilities and their families. Tempe, Ariz. : Bilingual Review/Press, c1999.
**TC LC4035.M6 H45 1999**

Vaughn, Sharon, 1952- Teaching exceptional, diverse, and at-risk students in the general education classroom. 2nd ed. Boston : Allyn and Bacon, 2000.
**TC LC3981 .V28 2000**

**Boscardin, Mary Lynn.**
Learning disabilities and life stories. Boston : Allyn and Bacon, c2001.
**TC LC4818.38 .L42 2001**

**Boschee, Floyd.** School bond success : a strategy for building America's schools / Floyd Boschee, Carleton R. Holt with contributions from Patricia M. Peterson ; foreword by Paul D. Houston ; afterword by Senator Tom Daschle. 1st ed. Lancaster, Pa. : Technomic Publishing Co., c1999. xvi, 171 p. : ill. ; 23 cm. Includes bibliographical references and index. ISBN 1-56676-705-9 (pbk. : acid-free paper)
*1. School bonds - United States. 2. Education - United States - Finance. I. Holt, Carleton R. II. Peterson, Patricia M. III. Title.*
**TC LB2825 .B63 1999**

**Boshyk, Yuri.**
Business-driven action learning. New York : St. Martin's Press, 2000.
**TC HD58.82 .B87 2000**

**Bosker, R. J. (Roel J.).**
Enhancing educational excellence, equity, and efficiency. Dordrecht ; Boston : Kluwer Academic Publishers, c1999.
**TC LB2921 .E54 1999**

Snijders, Tom A. B. Multilevel analysis. Thousand Oaks, Calif. ; London : SAGE, 1999.
**TC QA278 .S645 1999**

**Bosman, Paul.**
Hall-Martin, Anthony. Cats of Africa. Washington, D.C. : Smithsonian Institution Press, 1998.
**TC QL737.C23 H335 1997**

**Boss, Pauline.** Ambiguous loss : learning to live with unresolved grief / Pauline Boss. Cambridge, Mass. : Harvard University Press, 1999. 155 p. ; 22 cm. Includes bibliographical references (p. 143-151). ISBN 0-674-01738-2 (alk. paper) DDC 155.9/3
*1. Loss (Psychology) 2. Grief. 3. Family - Psychological aspects. 4. Interpersonal relations. I. Title.*
**TC BF575.D35 B67 1999**

**Boston Cooking School (Boston, Mass.).**
The Boston Cooking School magazine of culinary

science and domestic economics. Boston : Boston Cooking-School Magazine, [1896]-1914.

**Boston Cooking-School magazine.**
The Boston Cooking School magazine of culinary science and domestic economics. Boston : Boston Cooking-School Magazine, [1896]-1914.

**Boston Cooking-School magazine of culinary science and domestic economics.**
The Boston Cooking School magazine of culinary science and domestic economics. Boston : Boston Cooking-School Magazine, [1896]-1914.

**The Boston Cooking School magazine of culinary science and domestic economics.** Boston : Boston Cooking-School Magazine, [1896]-1914. 18 v. : ill. ; 25 cm. Frequency: Ten times a year, June 1901-May 1914. Former frequency: Bimonthly, June 1897-May 1901. Former frequency: Quarterly, June 1896-May 1897. Vol. 1 (June 1896)-v. 18, no. [10] (May 1914). Title from cover. Official journal of the Boston Cooking-School Corporation, June 1896-Nov. 1905. Founded and for many years edited by Janet M. Hill. Continued by: American cookery ISSN: 0191-2658 (DLC)sc 79002656 (OCoLC)1479708.
*1. Home economics - Periodicals. 2. Cookery - Periodicals. I. Boston Cooking School (Boston, Mass.) II. Title: Boston Cooking-School magazine of culinary science and domestic economics III. Title: Boston Cooking-School magazine IV. Title: American cookery*

**BOSTON (MASS.) - BIOGRAPHY.**
Paul, Susan, fl. 1837. Memoir of James Jackson, the attentive and obedient scholar, who died in Boston, October 31, 1833, aged six years and eleven months. Cambridge, MA : Harvard University Press, 2000.
**TC F73.9.N4 P38 2000**

**Boston review (Cambridge, Mass. : 1982).**
Will standards save public education? Boston : Beacon Press, c2000.
**TC LB3060.83 .W55 2000**

**Bosworth, Kris.**
Preventing student violence. Bloomington, IN (P.O. Box 789, Bloomington 47402-0789) : Phi Delta Kappa International, c1999.
**TC LB3013.3 .P755 1999**

**BOTANY. See TREES.**

**Botel, Morton.** Communicating : book A/ Morton Botel, John Dawkins. Lexington, Mass. : D. C. Heath, c1973. 53 p. : ill. (some col.) ; 23 x 30 cm. (Heath English series) ISBN 0-669-58214-x
*1. Readers (Elementary) 2. English language - Problems, exercises, etc. I. Dawkins, John. II. Title. III. Series.*
**TC PE1121 .B67 1973 Bk A**

Communicating / Morton Botel, John Dawkins. Lexington, Mass. : D. C. Heath, c1973. v. : ill. (some col.) ; 24 cm. (Heath English series) Includes index. ISBN 0-669-58230-1 (level 2) ISBN 0-669-58255-7 (level 3) ISBN 0-669-58271-9 (level 4) ISBN 0-669-58297-2 (level 5) ISBN 0-669-58313-8 (level 6)
*1. Readers (Elementary) 2. English language - Composition and exercises. I. Dawkins, John. II. Title. III. Series.*
**TC PE1121 .B67 1973**

**Bottenberg, Robert Alan.** Applied multiple linear regression, by Robert A. Bottenberg [and] Joe. H. Ward. Lackland Air Force Base, Texas, 6570th Personnel Research Laboratory Aerospace Medical Division, Air Force Systems Command, 1963 viii, 139 p. : ill. ; 28 cm. "Technical documentary report PRL-TDR-63-6." Includes bibliographical references and index.
*1. Mathematical statistics. I. Ward, Joe H., joint author.*
**TC QA276 .B67 1963**

**Bottery, Mike.** Teachers and the state : towards a directed profession / Mike Bottery and Nigel Wright. London ; New York : Routledge, c2000. viii, 176 p. ; 25 cm. (Routledge research in education ; 3) Includes bibliographical references (p. 164-171) and index. ISBN 0-415-21347-9 DDC 371.1/00941
*1. Teachers - Great Britain. 2. Education and state - Great Britain. 3. Teachers - Training of - Great Britain. 4. Teachers - Cross-cultural studies. I. Wright, Nigel. II. Title. III. Series.*
**TC LB1775.4.G7 B68 2000**

**Boucher, Douglas H.**
The paradox of plenty. Oakland, Calif. : Food First Books, c1999.
**TC HD1542 .P37 1999**

**Boufis, Christina.**
On the market. 1st Riverhead ed. New York : Riverhead Books, 1997.
**TC LB2331.72 .O5 1997**

**Boulmetis, John.** The ABCs of evaluation : timeless techniques for program and project managers / John Boulmetis, Phyllis Dutwin. 1st ed. San Francisco,

Calif. : Jossey-Bass, c2000. xvi, 207 p. : ill. ; 24 cm. Includes bibliographical references (p. 201-202) and index. CONTENTS: What is evaluation? -- Why evaluate? -- Decision making : whom to involve, how, and why? -- Starting point : the evaluator's program description -- Choosing an evaluation model -- Data sources -- Data analysis -- Is it evaluation or is it research -- Writing the evaluation report. ISBN 0-7879-4432-7 (hard : perm. paper) DDC 658.4/032
*1. Management - Evaluation. I. Dutwin, Phyllis. II. Title.*
**TC HD31 .B633 2000**

**Bouras, Nick.**
Psychiatric and behavioural disorders in developmental disabilities and mental retardation. Cambridge, UK ; New York, NY, USA : Cambridge University Press, 1999.
**TC RC451.4.M47 P77 1999**

**BOURDIEU, PIERRE.**
Pierre Bourdieu. Bern ; New York : P. Lang, c1999.
**TC HM621 .P54 1999**

Swartz, David, 1945- Culture & power. Chicago : University of Chicago Press, 1997.
**TC HM22.F8 S93 1997**

**Bourgeois, Etienne, 1958-.**
The adult university. Buckingham [England] ; Philadelphia, PA : Society for Research into Higher Education & Open University Press, 1999.
**TC LC5219 .A35 1999**

**BOURGEOISIE. See MIDDLE CLASS.**

**Bourgoujian, Lisa.**
The American Revolution. [videorecording]. New York, N.Y. : A&E Home Video, c1994.
**TC E208 .A447 1994**

**Bourisaw, Diana, 1956-.**
Sweeney, Jim, 1937- Judgment. Larchmont, NY : Eye on Education, c1997.
**TC LB2806 .S88 1997**

**Bourke, Joanna.** An intimate history of killing : face-to-face killing in twentieth-century warfare / Joanna Bourke. [New York, NY] : Basic Books, c1999. xxiii, 509 p., [8] p. of plates : ill., ports. ; 25 cm. Includes bibliographical references (p. [365]-499) and index. ISBN 0-465-00737-6
*1. Psychology, Military. 2. Combat - Psychological aspects. 3. Homicide - Psychological aspects. 4. War - History - 20th century. 5. World War, 1914-1918. 6. World War, 1939-1945. 7. Vietnamese Conflict, 1961-1975. I. Title.*
**TC U22.3 .B68 1999**

**Bourke, S. F.**
Anderson, Lorin W. Assessing affective characteristics in the schools. 2nd ed. Mahwah, NJ : Lawrence Erlbaum, c2000.
**TC LB3051 .A698 2000**

The mastery of literacy and numeracy : final report / S. R. Bourke and J. P. Keeves. Canberra : Australian Govt. Pub. Service, 1977. 334 p. : diagrs ; 26 cm. (Australian studies in school performance ; v. 3) (ERDC report ; no. 13) ISBN 0-642-03071-5 DDC 370/.94
*1. Education - Australia - Addresses, essays, lectures. 2. Minorities - Education - Australia - Addresses, essays, lectures. 3. Numeracy - Australia - Addresses, essays, lectures. I. Keeves, John P., joint author. II. Title. III. Series. IV. Series: E.R.D.C. report ; no. 13.*
**TC LA2102 .B68 1977**

**Bourne, Barbara.**
Taking inquiry outdoors. York, Me. : Stenhouse Publishers, c2000.
**TC QH51 .T35 2000**

**Boutwell, Clinton E.** Shell game : corporate America's agenda for schools / Clinton E. Boutwell. Bloomington, Ind. : Phi Delta Kappa Educational Foundation, c1997. 361 p. ; 24 cm. Includes bibliographical references. ISBN 0-87367-499-5 DDC 371.19/5/0973
*1. Industry and education - United States. 2. Education - Economic aspects - United States. 3. Education - Aims and objectives - United States. I. Title.*
**TC LC1085.2 .B68 1997**

**Bowden, William W.**
Humphrey, James Harry, 1911- Stress in college athletics. New York : Haworth Press, c2000.
**TC GV347 .H86 2000**

**Bowe, Frank.** Universal design in education : teaching nontraditional students / Frank G. Bowe. Westport, Conn. : London : Bergin & Garvey, 2000. x, 133 p. ; 24 cm. Includes bibliographical references (p. [125]-129) and index. ISBN 0-89789-688-2 (alk. paper) DDC 371.9/045
*1. Instructional systems - Design. 2. Educational technology. 3. Handicapped - Education. 4. Minorities - Education. I. Title.*
**TC LB1028.38 .B69 2000**

**Bowen, Craigen W.-**
Götz, Stephan, 1960- [New Yorker Künstler in ihren Ateliers. English] American artists in their New York studios. Cambridge [Mass.] : Center for Conservation and Technical Studies, Harvard University Art Museums ; Stuttgart : Daco-Verlag Günter Bläse, c1992.
*TC N6535.N5 G6813 1992*

**Bowen, Don R., joint author.**
Masotti, Louis H. Riots and rebellion: Beverly Hills, Calif., Sage Publications [1968]
*TC HV6477 .M37*

**Bowen, Raymond C.**
Gateways to democracy. San Francisco : Jossey-Bass, 1999.
*TC LB2328.N53 1999*

**Bowers, Patricia joint editor.**
Rhoton, Jack Issues in science education. Arlington, Va. National Science Teachers Association: National Science Education Leadership Association, c1997.
*TC Q181 .R56 1996*

**Bowker's directory.**
Bowker's directory of videocassettes for children. New Providence, N.J. : R.R. Bowker, c1998-
*TC PN1992.945 .B66*

**Bowker's directory of audiocassettes for children.**
New Providence, N.J. : R.R. Bowker, c1998- v. ; 28 cm. Frequency: Annual. 1998- . Directory of audiocassettes for children. ISSN 0000-1740 DDC 011/.37
*1. Audiocassettes for children - United States - Catalogs - Periodicals. 2. Children's audiobooks - United States - Audiotape catalogs - Periodicals. 3. Audiocassettes for children - Catalogs - Periodicals. I. R.R. Bowker Company. II. Title: Directory of audiocassettes for children*
*TC ZA4750 .B69*

**Bowker's directory of videocassettes for children.**
New Providence, N.J. : R.R. Bowker, c1998- v. ; 28 cm. Frequency: Annual. 1998- . Directory of videocassettes for children. Running title: Videocassettes for children. Running title: Bowker's directory. DDC 011/.37
*1. Video recordings for children - Catalogs - Periodicals. 2. Children's films - Catalogs - Periodicals. I. Title: Directory of videocassettes for children II. Title: Videocassettes for children III. Title: Bowker's directory*
*TC PN1992.945 .B66*

**Bownas, David A.**
Personality assessment in organizations. New York : Praeger, 1985.
*TC HF5548.8 .P3995 1985*

**BOY COUTS OF AMERICA.**
Boy Scouts of America. Annual report of the Boy Scouts of America. Washington, D.C., Govt. Print. Off.
*TC HS3313.B7 A15*

**Boy crazy.**
Sayers, Janet. London ; New York : Routledge, 1998.
*TC BF724 .S325 1998*

**Boy Scouts of America.** Annual report of the Boy Scouts of America. Letter from the chief scout executive transmitting the annual report of the Boy Scouts of America ... as required by federal charter. Washington, D.C., Govt. Print. Off. v. 23 cm. Vols. for 1917- published in the United States. Congress. House. Documents. Vols. for 1956- issued with the Report of the Girl Scouts of America. Subseries of: United States. Congress. House. Documents. Issued with: Girl Scouts of America. Report.
*1. Boy Couts of America I. Title: United States. Congress. House. Documents II. Title: Girl Scouts of America. Report*
*TC HS3313.B7 A15*

**Boyd-Franklin, Nancy.** Reaching out in family therapy : home-based, school, and community interventions / Nancy Boyd-Franklin, Brenna Hafer Bry. New York : Guilford Press, 2000. xii, 244 p. : ill. ; 24 cm. Includes bibliographical references and index. ISBN 1-57230-519-3 (acid-free paper) DDC 616.89/156
*1. Family psychotherapy. I. Bry, Brenna Hafer. II. Title.*
*TC RC488.5 .B678 2000*

**Boyd Lee Spahr lectures in Americana**
(1962-1969.) Dickinson College. The Spahr lectures, Dickinson College, Carlisle, Pa., : Dickinson College 1970.
*TC LD1663 .A5 1970*

**Boyd, Susan C.,** 1953- Mothers and illicit drugs : transcending the myths / Susan C. Boyd. Toronto ; Buffalo, NY : University of Toronto Press, 1999. viii, 243 p. ; 24 cm. Includes bibliographical references (p. <219>-238) and index. ISBN 0-8020-4331-3 (bound) ISBN 0-8020-8151-7 (pbk.) DDC 362.29/085/2

*1. Mothers - Drug use - Canada. 2. Mothers - Drug use - United States. I. Title.*
*TC HV5824.W6 B69 1999*

**Boyer-Alexander, René.**
Rozmajzl, Michon. Music fundamentals, methods, and materials for the elementary classroom teacher. 3rd ed. New York : Harlow, England : Longman, c2000.
*TC MT1 .R85 2000*

**Boyle, Joseph R.**
Danforth, Scot. Cases in behavior management. Upper Saddle River, N.J. : Merrill, c2000.
*TC LB3013 .D34 2000*

**Boyle, Mari.**
Woods, Peter, 1934- Multicultural children in the early years. Clevedon ; Philadelphia : Multilingual Matters Ltd, c1999.
*TC LC3736.G6 W66 1999*

**Boyle, Richard,** 1955-.
Building effective evaluation capacity. New Brunswick, N.J. : Transaction Publishers, c1999.
*TC JF1351 .B83 1999*

**BOYS.** *See* TEENAGE BOYS.

**BOYS AS SOLDIERS - POSTERS.**
Civil war [picture]. Amawalk, NY : Jackdaw Publications, c1999.
*TC TR820.5 .C56 1999*

**BOYS - BOOKS AND READING.**
Girls, boys, books, toys. Baltimore : Johns Hopkins University Press, 1999.
*TC PN1009.5.S48 G57 1999*

**BOYS - EDUCATION - SOCIAL ASPECTS.**
Masculinities at school. Thousand Oaks, Calif. : SAGE, c2000.
*TC LC1390 .M37 2000*

**BOYS - EMPLOYMENT.** *See* CHILDREN - EMPLOYMENT.

**BOYS - MINNESOTA - SAINT PAUL REGION - DIARIES - JUVENILE LITERATURE.**
Bircher, William, 1845-1917. A Civil War drummer boy. Mankato, Minn. : Blue Earth Books, c2000.
*TC E601 .B605 2000*

**BOYS - UNITED STATES.** *See* AFRO-AMERICAN BOYS.

**BOYS - UNITED STATES - PSYCHOLOGY.**
Canada, Geoffrey. Reaching up for manhood. Boston : Beacon Press, c1998.
*TC HQ775 .C35 1998*

**BOYS - UNITED STATES - SOCIAL CONDITIONS.**
Canada, Geoffrey. Reaching up for manhood. Boston : Beacon Press, c1998.
*TC HQ775 .C35 1998*

**Brabeck, Mary M.**
Practicing feminist ethics in psychology. 1st ed. Washington, DC : American Psychological Association, c2000.
*TC BF201.4 .P73 2000*

**Bracey, Earnest N.** Prophetic insight : the higher education and pedagogy of African Americans / Earnest N. Bracey. Lanham : University Press of America, c1999. vii, 143 p. ; 23 cm. Includes bibliographical references (p. [125]-134) and index. ISBN 0-7618-1383-7 (cloth : alk. paper) ISBN 0-7618-1384-5 (pbk. : alk. paper) DDC 378/.0089/96073
*1. Afro-Americans - Education (Higher) - Social aspects. 2. Afro-American universities and colleges - Sociological aspects. 3. Afrocentrism - United States. 4. Education, Higher - Aims and objectives - United States. I. Title.*
*TC LC2781 .B73 1999*

**Bracey, Gerald W. (Gerald Watkins)** Bail me out : an educator's guide to handling tough questions about public schools / by Gerald W. Bracey. Thousand Oaks, Calif. : Corwin Press, c2000. ix, 213 p. : ill. ; 27 cm. Includes bibliographical references. ISBN 0-7619-7602-7 (cloth : alk. paper) ISBN 0-7619-7603-5 (pbk. : acid-free paper) DDC 371.01/0973
*1. Public schools - United States. 2. Teachers - United States. I. Title.*
*TC LA217.2 .B72 2000*

The truth about America's schools : the Bracey reports, 1991-97 / Gerald W. Bracey. Bloomington, Ind. : Phi Delta Kappa Educational Foundation, c1997. 264 p. ; 23 cm. Includes bibliographical references. ISBN 0-87367-395-6 DDC 371.01/0973
*1. Public schools - United States. 2. Education - United States. I. Title.*

*TC LA217.2 .B75 1997*

**Bracken, Bruce A.**
The psychoeducational assessment of preschool children. 3rd ed. Boston : Allyn and Bacon, c2000.
*TC LB1115 .P963 2000*

**Braden, Jennifer S.**
Good, Thomas L., 1943- The great school debate. Mahwah, N.J. : L. Erlbaum Associates, 2000.
*TC LB2806.36 .G66 2000*

**Bradley, Elizabeth H.,** 1962-.
Public and private responsibilities in long-term care. Baltimore : Johns Hopkins University Press, 1998.
*TC RA644.6 .P8 1998*

**Bradley, Phil,** 1959- Internet power searching : the advanced manual / Phil Bradley. New York : Neal-Schuman Publishers, 1999. xv, 232 p. : ill. ; 25 cm. Includes index. ISBN 1-55570-350-X DDC 025.04
*1. Internet searching. I. Title.*
*TC ZA4201 .B69 1999*

**Bradshaw, C. M. (Christopher M.).**
Time and behaviour. Amsterdam ; New York : Elsevier, 1997.
*TC BF468 .T538 1997*

**BRADY, MATHEW B., 1823 (CA.)-1896 - EXHIBITIONS.**
Panzer, Mary. Mathew Brady and the image of history. Washington, D.C. : Smithsonian Institution Press for the National Portrait Gallery, c1997.
*TC TR140.B7 P36 1997*

**Brady, Michael P.**
Scott, Jack, Ph. D. Students with autism. San Diego : Singular Pub. Group, 2000.
*TC LC4718 .S36 2000*

**Bragg, Melvyn.**
Jackson Pollock [videorecording]. [Chicago, Ill.] : Home Vision : [S.l.] : Distributed Worldwide by RM Associates, c1987.
*TC ND237.P73 J3 1987*

**Bragg, Melvyn,** 1931-.
Roy Lichtenstein [videorecording]. [Chicago, IL] : Home Vision : [S.l.] : distributed worldwide by RM Asssociates, c1991.
*TC ND237.L627 R6 1991*

**Bragg, Melvyn,** 1939-.
Andy Warhol [videorecording]. [Chicago, IL] : Home Vision [distributor],cc1987.
*TC N6537.W28 A45 1987*

Andy Warhol [videorecording]. [Chicago, IL] : Home Vision [distributor],cc1987.
*TC N6537.W28 A45 1987*

Marc Chagall [videorecording]. [Chicago, Ill.] : Home Vision [distributor], c1985.
*TC ND699.C5 C5 1985*

**Brahier, Daniel J.** Teaching secondary and middle school mathematics / Daniel J. Brahier. Boston : Allyn and Bacon, 2000. xviii, 405 p. : ill. ; 24 cm. Includes bibliographical references and index. ISBN 0-205-28614-3 DDC 510/.71/2
*1. Mathematics - Study and teaching (Middle school) 2. Mathematics - Study and teaching (Secondary) I. Title.*
*TC QA11 .B6999 2000*

**BRAHMANISM.** *See* HINDUISM.

**BRAIDISM.** *See* HYPNOTISM.

**Braille Institute insight series**
Bridges to independence [videorecording. Burbank, CA : RCA/Columbia Pictures Home Video : [S.l. : Distributed by] Rank Video Services Production, c1991.
*TC HV1646 .B7 1991*

Bright beginnings [videorecording. Burbank, CA : RCA/Columbia Pictures Home Video : Toluca Lake, CA : [Distributed by] Corporate Productions, c1991.
*TC HV1642 .B67 1991*

Bright beginnings [videorecording. Burbank, CA : RCA/Columbia Pictures Home Video : [S.l.] : Distributed by] Rank Video Services America, c1991.
*TC HV1642 .B67 1991*

Brighter visions [videorecording. Burbank, CA : RCA/Columbia Pictures Home Video : Toluca Lake, CA : [Distributed by] Corporate Productions, c1991.
*TC HV1597.5 .B67 1991*

Touch 'n' go [videorecording. Burbank, Calif. : Columbia Tristar Home Video ; [S.l. : Distributed by] Rank Video Services Production, c1991.

*TC HV1626 .T6 1991*

Work sight [videorecording]. Burbank, Ca. : RCA/
Columbia Pictures Home Video, c1991.
*TC HV1652 .W6 1991*

**Braille Institute of America.**
Bridges to independence [videorecording. Burbank,
CA : RCA/Columbia Pictures Home Video : [S.l. :
Distributed by] Rank Video Services Production,
c1991.
*TC HV1646 .B7 1991*

Bright beginnings [videorecording. Burbank, CA :
RCA/Columbia Pictures Home Video : Toluca Lake,
CA : [Distributed by] Corporate Productions, c1991.
*TC HV1642 .B67 1991*

Bright beginnings [videorecording. Burbank, CA :
RCA/Columbia Pictures Home Video : [S.l. :
Distributed by] Rank Video Services America, c1991.
*TC HV1642 .B67 1991*

Brighter visions [videorecording. Burbank, CA :
RCA/Columbia Pictures Home Video : Toluca Lake,
CA : [Distributed by] Corporate Productions, c1991.
*TC HV1597.5 .B67 1991*

Touch 'n' go [videorecording. Burbank, Calif. :
Columbia Tristar Home Video ; [S.l. : Distributed by]
Rank Video Services Production, c1991.
*TC HV1626 .T6 1991*

Work sight [videorecording]. Burbank, Ca. : RCA/
Columbia Pictures Home Video, c1991.
*TC HV1652 .W6 1991*

**BRAIN.** *See also* **MIND AND BODY.**
Berthoz, A. [Sens du Mouvement. English] The
brain's sense of movement. Cambridge, Mass. :
Harvard University Press, 2000.
*TC QP493 .B47 2000*

Dowling, John E. Creating mind. 1st ed. New York :
W.W. Norton, c1998.
*TC QP376 .D695 1998*

Gillett, Grant, 1950- The mind and its discontents.
Oxford ; New York : Oxford University Press, c1999.
*TC BD418.3 .G555 1999*

Glynn, Ian. An anatomy of thought. Oxford ; New
York : Oxford University Press, [1999].
*TC QP360 .G595 1999*

Mind myths. Chichester, England ; New York : J.
Wiley & Sons, c1999.
*TC BF161 .M556 1999*

Mind myths. Chichester, England ; New York : J.
Wiley & Sons, c1999.
*TC BF161 .M556 1999*

Morgan, Brian L. G. Brainfood. Tucson, Ariz. : Body
Press, c1987.
*TC QP376 .M62 1987*

Shore, Rima. Rethinking the brain. New York :
Families and Work Institute, c1997.
*TC RJ486.5 .S475 1997*

Sylwester, Robert. A biological brain in a cultural
classroom. Thousand Oaks, Calif. : Corwin Press,
c2000.
*TC LB3011.5 .S95 2000*

Wagman, Morton. The human mind according to
artificial intelligence. Westport, Conn. : Praeger, 1999.
*TC Q335 .W342 1999*

**BRAIN - BLOOD-VESSELS - DISEASES.** *See*
**CEREBROVASCULAR DISEASE.**

**BRAIN - CONGRESSES.**
Memory, brain, and belief. Cambridge, Mass. ;
London : Harvard University Press, 2000.
*TC QP406 .M44 2000*

**BRAIN DAMAGE.** *See also* **CEREBRAL PALSY.**
Myers, Penelope S. Right hemisphere damage. San
Diego : Singular Pub., c1999.
*TC RC423 .M83 1999*

When the brain goes wrong [videorecording]. Short
version. Boston, MA : Fanlight Productions [dist.],
c1992.
*TC RC386 .W54 1992*

**Brain damage, behaviour, and cognition.**
Communication disorders following traumatic brain
injury. Hove, East Sussex, UK : Psychology Press,
c1999.
*TC RD594 .C648 1999*

**Brain damage, behaviour and cognition.**
Temple, Christine. Developmental cognitive
neuropsychology. Hove, East Sussex, UK :
Psychology Press, c1997.

*TC RC553.C64 T46 1997*

**BRAIN DAMAGE, CHRONIC -
   COMPLICATIONS.**
Myers, Penelope S. Right hemisphere damage. San
Diego : Singular Pub., c1999.
*TC RC423 .M83 1999*

**BRAIN DAMAGE - PATIENTS -
   REHABILITATION.**
Cognitive neurorehabilitation. Cambridge, UK ; New
York : Cambridge University Press, c1999.
*TC RC553.C64 C654 1999*

**BRAIN DAMAGE - PATIENTS -
   REHABILITATION - HANDBOOKS,
   MANUALS, ETC.**
International handbook of neuropsychological
rehabilitation. New York : Kluwer Academic/Plenum
Publishers, c2000.
*TC RC387.5 .I478 2000*

**BRAIN-DAMAGED CHILDREN.**
Childhood epilepsies and brain development.
London : John Libbey, c1999.
*TC RJ496.E6 C45 1999*

**BRAIN DEATH.**
The definition of death. Baltimore : Johns Hopkins
University Press, 1999.
*TC RA1063 .D44 1999*

**BRAIN - DISEASES.** *See* **APHASIA; BRAIN
DAMAGE.**

**BRAIN DISEASES.** *See* **BRAIN - DISEASES.**

**BRAIN - DISEASES.** *See* **CEREBROVASCULAR
DISEASE; DEMENTIA; EPILEPSY;
KORSAKOFF'S SYNDROME;
PSYCHOLOGY, PATHOLOGICAL.**

**BRAIN - DISEASES - DIAGNOSIS.**
Lacks, Patricia. Bender Gestalt screening for brain
dysfunction. 2nd ed. New York : John Wiley & Sons,
c1999.
*TC RC386.6.B46 L3 1999*

**BRAIN DISEASES - IN INFANCY &
   CHILDHOOD - PERIODICALS.**
Child's brain. Basel, New York, Karger.

**BRAIN - EVOLUTION.**
Calvin, William H., 1939- Lingua ex machina.
Cambridge, Mass. ; London : MIT Press, c2000.
*TC QP399 .C35 2000*

McNamara, Patrick, 1956- Mind and variability.
Westport, Conn. : Praeger, 1999.
*TC BF371 .M385 1999*

**Brain food.**
Fleisher, Paul, 1951- Tucson, AZ : Zephyr Press,
c1997.
*TC GV1480 .F54 1997*

**BRAIN - GROWTH.**
Shore, Rima. Rethinking the brain. New York :
Families and Work Institute, c1997.
*TC RJ486.5 .S475 1997*

**BRAIN - GROWTH & DEVELOPMENT.**
Shore, Rima. Rethinking the brain. New York :
Families and Work Institute, c1997.
*TC RJ486.5 .S475 1997*

**BRAIN INJURIES - COMPLICATIONS.**
Communication disorders following traumatic brain
injury. Hove, East Sussex, UK : Psychology Press,
c1999.
*TC RD594 .C648 1999*

**BRAIN INJURIES - REHABILITATION.**
International handbook of neuropsychological
rehabilitation. New York : Kluwer Academic/Plenum
Publishers, c2000.
*TC RC387.5 .I478 2000*

**BRAIN - LOCALIZATION OF FUNCTIONS.** *See
also* **BRAIN MAPPING.**
Aphasia in atypical populations. Mahwah, N.J. :
Lawrence Erlbaum Associates, 1998.
*TC RC425 .A637 1998*

**BRAIN MAPPING - RESEARCH.**
The hijacked brain [videorecording]. Princeton, NJ :
Films for the Humanities & Sciences, c1998.
*TC RC564 .H5 1998*

**BRAIN - PHYSIOLOGY.**
Grigsby, Jim. Neurodynamics of personality. New
York : Guilford Press, 2000.
*TC BF698.9.B5 G741 2000*

**BRAIN - PHYSIOLOGY.**
Grigsby, Jim. Neurodynamics of personality. New
York : Guilford Press, 2000.

*TC BF698.9.B5 G741 2000*

**BRAIN - PHYSIOLOGY.**
Zeki, Semir. Inner vision. Oxford : New York :
Oxford University Press, c1999.
*TC N71 .Z45 1999*

**BRAIN - PHYSIOLOGY - CONGRESSES.**
International School of Biocybernetics (1997 : Naples,
Italy) Neuronal bases and psychological aspects of
consciousness. Singapore ; River Edge, N.J : World
Scientific, c1999.
*TC QP411 .I56 1997*

**BRAIN - POPULAR WORKS.**
Ramachandran, V. S. Phantoms in the brain. 1st ed.
New York : William Morrow, c1998.
*TC RC351 .R24 1998*

**BRAIN - PSYCHOPHYSIOLOGY.**
Milner, Peter M. The autonomous brain. Mahwah,
N.J. : L. Erlbaum Associates, 1999.
*TC BF161 .M5 1999*

**BRAIN RESEARCH.** *See* **BRAIN - RESEARCH.**

**BRAIN - RESEARCH - HISTORY.**
Finger, Stanley. Minds behind the brain. Oxford ;
New York : Oxford University Press, 2000.
*TC QP353 .F549 2000*

**Brain series**
When the brain goes wrong [videorecording]. Short
version. Boston, MA : Fanlight Productions [dist.],
c1992.
*TC RC386 .W54 1992*

**BRAIN SYNDROME, ACUTE.** *See* **DELIRIUM.**

**BRAIN - WOUNDS AND INJURIES.** *See also*
**BRAIN DAMAGE.**
Communication disorders following traumatic brain
injury. Hove, East Sussex, UK : Psychology Press,
c1999.
*TC RD594 .C648 1999*

When the brain goes wrong [videorecording]. Short
version. Boston, MA : Fanlight Productions [dist.],
c1992.
*TC RC386 .W54 1992*

**BRAIN - WOUNDS AND INJURIES -
   COMPLICATIONS.**
Communication disorders following traumatic brain
injury. Hove, East Sussex, UK : Psychology Press,
c1999.
*TC RD594 .C648 1999*

**Brainfood.**
Morgan, Brian L. G. Tucson, Ariz. : Body Press,
c1987.
*TC QP376 .M62 1987*

**The brain's sense of movement.**
Berthoz, A. [Sens du Mouvement. English]
Cambridge, Mass. : Harvard University Press, 2000.
*TC QP493 .B47 2000*

**Bramadat, Paul A.** The church on the world's turf : an
evangelical Christian group at a secular university /
Paul A. Bramadat. Oxford ; New York : Oxford
University Press, 2000. viii, 205 p. ; 25 cm. (Religion in
America series) Includes bibliographical references (p. 183-
199) and index. ISBN 0-19-513499-0 (alk. paper) DDC 306.6/
6761/0971352
   *1. Inter-Varsity Christian Fellowship. 2. Christian college
students - Religious life - Ontario - Hamilton. 3. Christianity
and culture - Ontario - Hamilton. 4. McMaster University -
Students - Religious life. I. Title. II. Series: Religion in America
series (Oxford University Press)*
*TC BV970.16 B73 2000*

**Bramlett-Jackson, E. (Elizabeth).**
Deuschle, C. (Constance) Stop the bus. Lanham, Md. :
University Press of America, c2000.
*TC LB1027.5 .D4567 2000*

**Brand, Peggy Zeglin.**
Beauty matters. Bloomington : Indiana University
Press, c2000.
*TC HQ1219 .B348 2000*

**Brandom, Ann-Marie.**
Wright, Andrew, 1958- Learning to teach religious
education in the secondary school. London ; New
York : Routledge, 2000.
*TC LC410.G7 W75 2000*

**Brandsma, T. F.**
Bridging the skills gap between work and education.
Dordrecht ; Boston : Kluwer Academic Publishers,
c1999.
*TC LC5056.A2 B75 1999*

**Brandwein, Paul F. (Paul Franz), 1912-** Matter : an earth science / Paul F. Brandwein, Warren E. Yasso, Daniel J. Brovey. Curie ed. New York : Harcourt Brace Jovanovich, 1980. xiii, 446 p. : ill. ; 24 cm. (Concepts in science) Includes index. ISBN 0-15-365739-1
*1. Earth sciences. I. Yasso, Warren E. II. Brovey, Daniel J. III. Title. IV. Series.*
*TC Q161.2 .C66 1980*

**Brandy, Tim.** So what? : teaching children what matters in math / Tim Brandy ; [foreword by Susan Ohanian]. Portsmouth, NH : Heinemann, c1999. viii, 120 p. : ill. ; 23 cm. ISBN 0-325-00176-6 (acid-free paper) DDC 372.7
*1. Mathematics - Study and teaching (Elementary) I. Title. II. Title: Teaching children what matters in math*
*TC QA135.5 .B6785 1999*

**Bransford, John.**
How people learn. Expanded ed. Washington, D.C. : National Academy Press, c2000.
*TC LB1060 .H672 2000*

**Branthwaite, Alan.**
The applied psychologist. 2nd ed. Buckingham [England] ; Philadelphia : Open University Press, 2000.
*TC BF76 .A63 2000*

**Branwhite, Tony.** Helping adolescents in school / Tony Branwhite. Westport, Conn. ; London : Praeger, 2000. 188 p. : ill. ; 25 cm. Includes bibliographical references (p. [135]-178) and indexes. ISBN 0-275-96898-7 (alk. paper) DDC 155.5
*1. School psychology. 2. Adolescent psychology. I. Title.*
*TC LB1027.55 .B72 2000*

**Braskamp, Larry A.**
Utilization of evaluative information. San Francisco : Jossey-Bass, 1980.
*TC H62.5.U5 U86*

**BRASS INSTRUMENTS.**
Whitener, Scott. A complete guide to brass. 2nd ed. New York : Schirmer Books, c1997.
*TC ML933 .W52 1997*

**BRASS INSTRUMENTS - INSTRUCTION AND STUDY.**
Whitener, Scott. A complete guide to brass. 2nd ed. New York : Schirmer Books, c1997.
*TC ML933 .W52 1997*

**BRASSES (MUSICAL INSTRUMENTS).** *See* **BRASS INSTRUMENTS.**

**Braud, William.**
Transpersonal research methods for the social sciences. Thousand Oaks, Calif. : Sage Publications, c1998.
*TC BF76.5 .T73 1998*

**Bräuer, Gerd.**
Writing across languages. Stamford, Conn. : Ablex Pub., c2000.
*TC PB36 .W77 2000*

**Braun, Dietmar.**
Towards a new model of governance for universities? London ; Philadelphia : Jessica Kingsley, c1999.
*TC LC171 .T683 1999*

**Braun, Joseph A., 1947-.**
Surfing social studies. Washington, DC : National Council for the Social Studies, c1999.
*TC LB1044.87 .S97 1999*

**Braun, Trudi.** My goose Betsy / Trudi Braun ; illustrated by John Bendall-Brunello. 1st U.S. ed. Cambridge, MA : Candlewick Press, 1999. 29 p. : col. ill. ; 28 cm. Includes index. SUMMARY: Betsy the goose makes a cozy nest, lays her eggs, and tends to them until her little goslings are hatched. Includes a section with facts about geese. ISBN 0-7636-0449-6 DDC [E]
*1. Geese - Juvenile fiction. 2. Geese - Fiction. I. Bendall-Brunello, John, ill. II. Title.*
*TC PZ10.3.B745 My 1998*

**Brave bear.**
Mallat, Kathy. New York : Walker, 1999.
*TC PZ7.M29455 Br 1999*

**Brave Martha.**
Apple, Margot. Boston : Houghton Mifflin, 1999.
*TC PZ7.A6474 Br 1999*

**Brave new mind.**
Dodwell, P. C. New York : Oxford University Press, 2000.
*TC BF311 .D568 2000*

**BRAVERY.** *See* **COURAGE.**

**Braxton, Beverly.**
Math around the world. Berkeley, CA : Lawrence Hall

of Science, University of California at Berkeley, c1995.
*TC QA20.G35 M384 1995*

**Braxton, John M.**
Perspectives on scholarly misconduct in the sciences. Columbus : Ohio State University Press, c1999.
*TC Q147 .P47 1999*

**Bray, James H.**
Adolescent siblings in stepfamilies. Chicago, Ill. : University of Chicago Press, 1999.
*TC LB1103.S6 v.64 no. 4*

**Bray, John N.**
Collaborative inquiry in practice. Thousand Oaks [Calif.] : Sage Publications, c2000.
*TC H62 .C5657 2000*

**Bray, Mark.** The shadow education system : : private tutoring and its implications for planners / Mark Bray. Paris : Unesco, International Institute for Educational Planning, 1999. 97 p. : ill. ; 21 cm. (Fundamentals of educational planning, 61.) Includes bibliographical references (p. 88-97). ISBN 92-803-1187-5
*1. Tutors and tutoring. I. Title. II. Series.*
*TC LC41 .B73 1999*

**BRAZIL - RACE QUESTION.**
Ford, Richard B., 1935- Tradition and change in four societies; New York, Holt, Rinehart and Winston, 1968.
*TC HT1521 .F6 1968*

**BRAZIL - RACE RELATIONS.**
Race in contemporary Brazil. University Park, Pa. : Pennsylvania State University Press, 1999.
*TC F2659.N4 R245 1999*

**BREACH OF THE PEACE.** *See* **RIOTS.**

**BREAD.**
Robbins, Ken. Make me a peanut butter sandwich and a glass of milk. New York : Scholastic, c1992.
*TC TX814.5.P38 R63 1992*

**BREAD - JUVENILE LITERATURE.**
Robbins, Ken. Make me a peanut butter sandwich and a glass of milk. New York : Scholastic, c1992.
*TC TX814.5.P38 R63 1992*

**Bread, or bullets!.**
Casanovas, Joan. Pittsburgh : University of Pittsburgh Press, c1998.
*TC HD8206 .C33 1998*

**BREADSTUFFS.** *See* **WHEAT.**

**Break throughs** [videorecording] : how to reach students with autism / written, produced and directed by Jeff Schultz. Boston, MA : Fanlight Productions, c1998. 1 videocassette (25 min.) : sd., col. ; 1/2 in. Title on videocassette label: Breakthroughs : how to reach students with autism [videorecording]. Title on container: Attainment's breakthroughs : how to reach students with autism [videorecording]. VHS. Catalogued from credits, container and cassette label. Closed captioned. Presenter: Karen Sewell. Camera, Dan Ryan, Melissa Ryan, Rich Reilly; editor, Jeff Schultz; music, Rich Reilly. Previously published by Attainment Co., Verona, WI. Publisher from label mounted on container over previous publisher. For special education teachers, parents of autistic children and all those who work with autistic children. SUMMARY: Karen Sewell, a special education teacher for 20 years, displays her experience in dealing with autistic children by working successfully with a 3-year-old girl. Sewell uses perseverance, patience, tough love and comprehensive planning to work with austistic children. She demonstrates how the child learns to imitate and unlearns "learned helplessness", among many other lessons.
*1. Autism - Case studies. 2. Autism in children - Case studies. 3. Autistic children - Education - Case studies. 4. Video recordings for the hearing impaired. I. Sewell, Karen. II. Schultz, Jeffrey Alan. 1946- III. Attainment Company. IV. Fanlight Productions. V. Title: How to reach students with autism [videorecording] VI. Title: Breakthroughs : how to reach students with autism [videorecording] VII. Title: Attainment's breakthroughs : how to reach students with autism [videorecording]*
*TC LC4717.5 .B7 1998*

**Breakfast at the Liberty Diner.**
Kirk, Daniel. 1st ed. New York : Hyperion Books for Children, c1997.
*TC PZ7.K6339 Br 1997*

**Breaking out.**
Brodie, Laura Fairchild. 1st ed. New York : Pantheon Books, c2000.
*TC LC212.862 .B75 2000*

**Breaking up (at) totality.**
Davis, D. Diane (Debra Diane), 1963- Carbondale : Southern Illinois University Press, c2000.

*TC PE1404 .D385 2000*

**Breakthroughs : how to reach students with autism** [videorecording].
Break throughs [videorecording]. Boston, MA : Fanlight Productions, c1998.
*TC LC4717.5 .B7 1998*

**BREAKTHROUGHS, TECHNOLOGICAL.** *See* **TECHNOLOGICAL INNOVATIONS.**

**BREARLEY SCHOOL - ALUMNI AND ALUMNAE - BIOGRAPHY.**
Fishel, Elizabeth. Reunion. 1st ed. New York : Random House, c2000.
*TC LD7501.N494 F575 2000*

**BREARLEY SCHOOL. CLASS OF 1968.**
Fishel, Elizabeth. Reunion. 1st ed. New York : Random House, c2000.
*TC LD7501.N494 F575 2000*

**BREAST - CANCER - POLITICAL ASPECTS - UNITED STATES.**
Boehmer, Ulrike, 1959- The personal and the political. Albany, NY : State University of New York Press, c2000.
*TC RC280.B8 B62 2000*

**Brecher, Jeremy.**
Global visions. 1st ed. Boston : South End Press, c1993.
*TC HF1359 .G58 1993*

**Bredekamp, Sue.**
Developmentally appropriate practice in early childhood programs. Rev. ed. Washington, D.C. : National Association for the Education of Young Children, 1997.
*TC LB1139.25 .D48 1997*

Reaching potentials. Washington, DC : National Association for the Education of Young Children, c1992-<1995>
*TC LB1140.23 .R36 1992*

**BREGLER, CHARLES - PHOTOGRAPH COLLECTIONS - CATALOGS.**
Pennsylvania Academy of the Fine Arts. Eakins and the photograph. Washington : Published for the Pennsylvania Academy of the Fine Arts by the Smithsonian Institution Press, c1994.
*TC TR652 .P46 1994*

**Breisch, Kenneth A.** Henry Hobson Richardson and the small public library in America : a study in typology / Kenneth A. Breisch. Cambridge, Mass. : MIT Press, c1997. xii, 354 p. : ill. ; 26 cm. Includes bibliographical references (p. 314-334) and index. ISBN 0-262-02416-0 (hc : alk. paper) DDC 727/.82473
*1. Library architecture - United States - History - 19th century. 2. Richardson. H. H. - (Henry Hobson). - 1838-1886. 3. Public libraries - United States - History - 19th century. 4. Small libraries - United States - History - 19th century. 5. Romanesque revival (Architecture) - United States. I. Title.*
*TC Z679.2.U54 B74 1997*

**Brems, Christiane.** Dealing with challenges in psychotherapy and counseling / Christiane Brems. Belmont, Calif. : Wadsworth Pub., Brooks/Cole, c2000. xiv, 321 p. ; 24 cm. Includes bibliographical references (p. 297-311) and indexes. ISBN 0-534-36471-3 (pbk. : alk. paper) DDC 616.89/14
*1. Counseling. 2. Psychotherapy. I. Title.*
*TC BF637.C6 B723 2000*

**Brencick, Janice M.** Philosophy of nursing : a new vision for health care / Janice M. Brencick, Glenn A. Webster. Albany : State University of New York Press, c2000. ix, 247 p. ; 23 cm. Includes bibliographical references and index. ISBN 0-7914-4379-5 (hc : alk. paper) ISBN 0-7914-4380-9 (pb : alk. paper) DDC 610.73/01
*1. Nursing - Philosophy. I. Webster, Glenn A. II. Title.*
*TC RT84.5 .B74 2000*

**Brendan's best-timed birthday.**
Gould, Deborah Lee. New York : Bradbury Press, 1988.
*TC PZ7.G723 Br 1988*

**Brennan, J. L. (John Leslie), 1947-.**
What kind of university? 1st ed. Buckingham ; Philadelphia, PA : Society for Research into Higher Education : Open University Press, 1999.
*TC LB2322.2 .W43 1999*

**Brenner, David, 1946-.**
Bilodeau, Martin, 1961- Theory of multivariate statistics. New York : Springer, c1999.
*TC QA278 .B55 1999*

**Brenson, Michael.**
Catlett, Elizabeth, 1915- Elizabeth Catlett sculpture. [Purchase, N.Y.] : Neuberger Museum of Art,

Purchase College, State University of New York : Seattle : Distributed by University of Washington Press, c1998.
*TC NB259.C384 A4 1998*

**BRETHREN, UNITED.** *See* **MORAVIANS.**

**Brewer, Charles L.**
Handbook for teaching statistics and research methods. 2nd ed. Mahwah, N.J. : Lawrence Erlbaum Associates, c1999.
*TC QA276.18 .H36 1999*

**Brewer, Pam, 1952-.**
Ball, Wanda H., 1953- Socratic seminars in the block. Larchmont, N.Y. : Eye On Education, 2000.
*TC LB1027.44 .B35 2000*

**BRIDGES - NEW YORK (STATE).** *See* **BROOKLYN BRIDGE (NEW YORK, N.Y.).**

**Bridges not walls :** a book about interpersonal communication / edited by John Stewart. 7th ed. Boston : McGraw Hill College, c1999. xvi, 603 p. : ill. ; 24 cm. Includes bibliographical references and index. ISBN 0-07-290435-6 (alk. paper) DDC 158.2
*1. Interpersonal communication. I. Stewart, John Robert, 1941-*
*TC BF637.C45 B74 1999*

**BRIDGES research report series**
(no. 8.) Rugh, Andrea B. Teaching practices to increase student achievement. Cambridge, Mass. : B.R.I.D.G.E.S. Basic Research and Implementation in Developing Education Systems, [1991].
*TC LB1025.2 .R83 1991*

(no. 9.) Nielsen, H. Dean. The cost-effectiveness of distance education for teacher training. Cambridge, Mass. : B.R.I.D.G.E.S. Basic Research and Implementation in Developing Education Systems, [1991].
*TC LB1731 .N43 1991*

**Bridges to independence** [videorecording / Braille Institute of America]. Burbank, CA : RCA/Columbia Pictures Home Video ; [S.l. : Distributed by] Rank Video Services Production, c1991. 1 videocassette (27 min.) : sd., col. ; 1/2 in. (Braille Institute insight series) VHS. Catalogued from credits and container. Introduction by Sidney Poitier. Photography: Brad Fowler. Originally produced by the Braille Institute of America by Corporate Productions, Toluca Lake, CA. For teachers, families and professionals working with blind and visually impaired adolescents. SUMMARY: Provides information to visually impaired teens, their parents and the professionals who serve them, including ways of developing teens' social skills and communication techniques. ISBN 0-8001-0873-6
*1. Visually handicapped children - Education. 2. Children, Blind - Education. 3. Physically handicapped teenagers - Education. 4. Social skills - Study and teaching. 5. Blind - Education. 6. Visually handicapped - Education. I. Poitier, Sidney. II. Braille Institute of America. III. RCA/Columbia Pictures of America. IV. Corporate Productions. V. Rank Video Services America. VI. Series.*
*TC HV1646 .B7 1991*

**Bridges to recovery :** addiction, family therapy, and multicultural treatment / edited by Jo-Ann Krestan. New York ; London : Free Press, c2000. xii, 323 p. ; 25 cm. Includes bibliographical references and index. ISBN 0-684-84649-7 DDC 362.29/089/00973
*1. Minorities - Alcohol use - United States - Prevention. 2. Minorities - Substance use - United States - Prevention. 3. Alcoholics - Rehabilitation - United States. 4. Addicts - Rehabilitation - United States. 5. Alcoholism - Treatment - United States. 6. Substance abuse - Treatment - United States. 7. Alcoholism counseling - United States. 8. Drug abuse counseling - United States. 9. Cross-cultural counseling - United States. 10. Family psychotherapy - United States. I. Krestan, Jo Ann.*
*TC HV5199.5 .B75 2000*

**Bridging the family-professional gap :** facilitating interdisciplinary services for children with disabilities / edited by Billy T. Ogletree, Martin A. Fischer, Jane B. Schulz. Springfield, Ill. : Charles C. Thomas, c1999. xvi, 284 p. ; 27 cm. Includes bibliographical references and indexes. ISBN 0-398-06988-3 (cloth) ISBN 0-398-06989-1 (paper) DDC 362.4/048/0830973
*1. Handicapped children - Services for - United States. 2. Parents of handicapped children - Services for - United States. I. Ogletree, Billy T. II. Fischer, Martin A. (Martin Alan), 1950- III. Schulz, Jane B., 1924-*
*TC HV888.5 .B74 1999*

**Bridging the skills gap between work and education /** edited by Wim J. Nijhof & Jittie Brandsma. Dordrecht ; Boston : Kluwer Academic Publishers, c1999. xvii, 225 p. : ill. ; 25 cm. Includes bibliographical references and index. ISBN 0-7923-5653-5 (alk. paper) DDC 370.113/094
*1. Vocational education - Europe. 2. Career education - Europe. 3. School-to-work transition - Europe. I. Nijhof, Wim J., 1941- II. Brandsma, T. F.*
*TC LC5056.A2 B75 1999*

**Brief Alcohol Screening and Intervention for College Students (BASICS) :** a harm reduction approach / Linda A. Dimeff ... [et al.]. New York : Guilford Press, c1999. xii, 200 p. ; 27 cm. Includes bibliographical references (p. 185-196) and index. ISBN 1-57230-392-1 DDC 362.292/7/0842
*1. College students - Alcohol use. 2. Alcoholism - Prevention. 3. Alcoholism - Study and teaching. 4. College students - Counseling of. 5. Alcohol Drinking - prevention & control. 6. Student Health Services - methods. 7. Alcoholism - prevention & control. 8. Students - psychology. 9. Counseling - methods. 10. Cognitive Therapy - methods. I. Dimeff, Linda A.*
*TC HV5135 .B74 1998*

**Brief counseling in action.**
Littrell, John M., 1944- 1st ed. New York : W. W. Norton, c1998.
*TC RC480.55 .L58 1998*

**Brief intervention for school problems.**
Murphy, John J. (John Joseph), 1955- New York : Guilford Press, c1997.
*TC LC4802 .M87 1997*

**BRIEF PSYCHOTHERAPY.**
Bromfield, Richard. Doing child and adolescent psychotherapy. Northvale, N.J. ; London : Jason Aronson, c1999.
*TC RJ504 .B753 1999*

Comparative approaches in brief dynamic psychotherapy. New York : Haworth Press, c1999.
*TC RC480.55 .C658 1999*

Effective brief therapies :. San Diego : Academic Press, c2000.
*TC RC480.55 .E376 2000*

Johnson, Lynn D. Psychotherapy in the age of accountability. 1st ed. New York : W.W. Norton & Co., c1995.
*TC RC480.55 .J64 1995*

Littrell, John M., 1944- Brief counseling in action. 1st ed. New York : W. W. Norton, c1998.
*TC RC480.55 .L58 1998*

Magnavita, Jeffrey J. Relational therapy for personality disorders. New York : Wiley, c2000.
*TC RC554 .M228 2000*

McNeilly, Robert B. Healing the whole person. New York ; Chichester [England] : John Wiley & Sons, c2000.
*TC RC489.S65 M38 2000*

**Brief therapies series**
O'Connell, Bill. Solution-focused therapy. London ; Thousand Oaks, Calif. : Sage Publications, 1998.
*TC RC489.S65 O26 1998*

**BRIEF THERAPY.**
Walter, John L., 1945- Recreating brief therapy. New York : W.W. Norton & Co., 2000.
*TC RC480.5 .W276 2000*

**Briggs, Diane.** 101 fingerplays, stories, and songs to use with finger puppets / Diane Briggs. Chicago : American Library Association, 1999. x, 129 p. : ill. ; 26 cm. Includes bibliographical references (p. 117-227) and discography (p. 129. ISBN 0-8389-0749-0 DDC 791.5/3
*1. Finger play. 2. Finger puppets. I. Title. II. Title: One hundred one fingerplays, stories, and songs to use with finger puppets III. Title: One hundred and one fingerplays, stories, and songs to use with finger puppets IV. Title: 101 finger plays, stories, and songs to use with finger puppets*
*TC GV1218.F5 B74 1999*

**Briggs, Lynn Craigue, 1960-.**
Stories from the center. Urbana, Ill. National Council of Teachers of English, c2000.
*TC PE1404 .S834 2000*

**Brigham, Janet.** Dying to quit : why we smoke and how we stop / Janet Brigham. Washington, D.C. : Joseph Henry Press, 1998. xv, 289 p. : ill. ; 24 cm. Includes bibliographical references (p. 251-267) and index. ISBN 0-309-06409-0 (alk. paper) DDC 613.85
*1. Cigarette habit - Psychological aspects. 2. Cigarette habit - Prevention. 3. Tobacco - Physiological effect. I. Title.*
*TC HV5740 .B75 1998*

**Brighouse, Harry.** School choice and social justice / Harry Brighouse. Oxford ; New York : Oxford University Press, 2000. viii, 222 p. ; 25 cm. Includes bibliographical references and index. ISBN 0-19-829586-3 DDC 379.1/11
*1. School choice - Social aspects. 2. Educational equalization. 3. Education and state. I. Title.*
*TC LB1027.9 .B75 2000*

**Brighouse, Tim.** How to improve your school / Tim Brighouse and David Woods. London ; New York : Routledge, 1999. viii, 176 p. : ill. ; 24 cm. Includes bibliographical references (p. 169-170) and index. ISBN 0-415-19444-X (alk. paper) DDC 371.2/00941
*1. School improvement programs - Great Britain. 2. Educational leadership - Great Britain. I. Woods, David, 1942- II. Title.*
*TC LB2822.84.G7 B75 1999*

**Bright beginnings** [videorecording / Braille Institute of America]. Burbank, CA : RCA/Columbia Pictures Home Video ; Toluca Lake, CA : [Distributed by] Corporate Productions, c1991. 1 videocassette (27 min.) : sd., col. ; 1/2 in. (Braille Institute insight series) VHS. Catalogued from credits and container. Introduced by Robert Stack. Photography: Brad Fowler. Originally produced by the Braille Institute of America. For teachers, parents and professionals working with the blind. SUMMARY: This documentary helps parents and teachers to enrich the lives of blind and visually impaired children. It offers a team approach involving parents, teachers and other professionals. ISBN 0-8001-0869-8
*1. Children, Blind - Education (Early childhood) 2. Visually handicapped children - Education (Early childhood) 3. Early childhood education - Parent participation. 4. Special education - Parent participation. 5. Teaching teams. 6. Blind - Services for. 7. Documentary television programs. I. Stack, Robert. II. Braille Institute of America. III. RCA/Columbia Pictures Home Video. IV. Corporate Productions. V. Series.*
*TC HV1642 .B67 1991*

**Bright beginnings** [videorecording / Braille Institute of America]. Burbank, CA : RCA/Columbia Pictures Home Video ; [S.l. : Distributed by] Rank Video Services America, c1991. 1 videocassette (27 min.) : sd., col. ; 1/2 in. (Braille Institute insight series) VHS. Catalogued from credits and container. Introduced by Robert Stack. Photography: Brad Fowler. Originally produced by the Braille Institute of America by Corporate Productions, Toluca Lake, CA. For teachers, parents and professionals working with the blind. SUMMARY: This documentary helps parents and teachers to enrich the lives of blind and visually impaired children. It offers a team approach involving parents, teachers and other professionals. ISBN 0-8001-0869-8
*1. Children, Blind - Education (Early childhood) 2. Visually handicapped children - Education (Early childhood) 3. Early childhood education - Parent participation. 4. Special education - Parent participation. 5. Teaching teams. 6. Blind - Services for. 7. Documentary television programs. I. Stack, Robert. II. Braille Institute of America. III. RCA/Columbia Pictures Home Video. IV. Corporate Productions. V. Rank Video Services America. VI. Series.*
*TC HV1642 .B67 1991*

**The bright boys.**
Lebow, Eileen F. Westport, Conn. : Greenwood Press, c2000.
*TC LD7501.N5 T692 2000*

**BRIGHT CHILDREN.** *See* **GIFTED CHILDREN.**

**Bright-eyed Athena.**
Woff, Richard, 1953- Los Angeles, CA : J. Paul Getty Museum, 1999.
*TC BL820.M6 W64 1999*

**Brighter visions** [videorecording / Braille Institute of America]. Burbank, CA : RCA/Columbia Pictures Home Video ; Toluca Lake, CA : [Distributed by] Corporate Productions, c1991. 1 videocassette (27 min.) : sd., col. ; 1/2 in. (Braille Institute insight series) VHS. Catalogued from credits and container. Introduced by Charlton Heston. Photography: Brad Fowler. Originally produced by the Braille Institute of America. For families and professionals working with the aged blind. SUMMARY: This video demonstrates how visually impaired senior citizens, with newly acquired skills, a little help from others, and the support of family, friends and professionals, can enjoy greater independence. ISBN 0-8001-0870-1
*1. Blind aged - Services for. 2. Visually handicapped aged - Services for. 3. Blind - Services for. 4. Documentary television programs. I. Heston, Charlton. II. Braille Institute of America. III. RCA/Columbia Pictures Home Video. IV. Corporate Productions. V. Series.*
*TC HV1597.5 .B67 1991*

**Brighton Polytechnic. Media Services.**
Etching [videorecording]. Northbrook, Ill. : Peasmarsh, East Sussex, Eng. : Roland Collection of Films on Art, c1990.
*TC NE2043 .E87 1990*

Screen printing [videorecording]. [Northbrook?], Ill. ; Peasmarsh, East Sussex, Eng. : Roland Collection of Films on Art, c1992.

*Brighton Polytechnic. Media Services.*

*TC NE2238.G7 S4 1992*

What is a good drawing? [videorecording].
Peasmarsh, East Sussex, Eng. : Ho-Ho-Kus, NJ :
Roland Collection, [1980-1986?].
*TC NC703 .W45 1980*

**Brill, Norman Q. (Norman Quintus), 1911-** Being
Black in America today : a multiperspective review of
the problem / by Norman Q. Brill. Springfield, Ill. :
Charles C Thomas, 1999. xiii, 179 p. ; 27 cm. (American
series in behavioral science and law) Includes bibliographical
references and index. ISBN 0-398-06917-4 (cloth) ISBN
0-398-06918-2 (pbk.) DDC 305.896/073
*1. Afro-Americans - Psychology. 2. Afro-Americans - Social
conditions. I. Title. II. Series.*
*TC E185.625 B754 1999*

**Brill's studies in intellectual history**
(v. 96) Between demonstration and imagination.
Leiden, Netherlands ; Boston : Brill, 1999.
*TC QB15 .B56 1999*

**Brim, Orville Gilbert, 1923-.**
The Use of standardized ability tests in American
secondary schools and their impact on students,
teachers, and administrators New York] Russell Sage
Foundation [1965]
*TC LB3051 .R914*

**Brinckloe, Julie, ill.**
Sachar, Louis, 1954- Sideways stories from Wayside
School. New York : Morrow Junior Books, 1998.
*TC PZ7.S1185 Si 1998*

**Brinegar, Todd.**
The cello [videorecording]. Van Nuys, CA :
Backstage Pass Productions ; Canoga Park, Calif. :
[Distributed by] MVP, c1995.
*TC MT305 .C4 1995*

The drums [videorecording]. Van Nuys, CA :
Backstage Pass Productions ; Canoga Park, Calif. :
[Distributed by] MVP Home Entertainment, c1998.
*TC MT662.3 .S6 1998*

The flute [videorecording]. Van Nuys, CA : Backstage
Pass Productions ; Canoga Park, Calif. : [Distributed
by] MVP, c1995.
*TC MT345 .F6 1995*

The trombone [videorecording]. Van Nuys, CA :
Backstage Pass Productions ; Canoga Park, Calif. :
[Distributed by] MVP, c1998.
*TC MT465 .T7 1998*

The viola [videorecording]. Van Nuys, CA :
Backstage Pass Productions ; Canoga Park, Calif. :
[Distributed by] MVP Home Entertainment, c1991.
*TC MT285 .V5 1991*

The viola [videorecording]. Van Nuys, CA :
Backstage Pass Productions ; Canoga Park, Calif. :
[Distributed by] MVP Home Entertainment, c1995.
*TC MT285 .V5 1995*

The violin [videorecording]. Van Nuys, CA :
Backstage Pass Productions ; Canoga Park, Calif. :
[Distributed by] MVP, c1998.
*TC MT265 .V5 1998*

**Brinegar Video/Film Productions, Inc.**
The cello [videorecording]. Van Nuys, CA :
Backstage Pass Productions ; Canoga Park, Calif. :
[Distributed by] MVP, c1995.
*TC MT305 .C4 1995*

The drums [videorecording]. Van Nuys, CA :
Backstage Pass Productions ; Canoga Park, Calif. :
[Distributed by] MVP Home Entertainment, c1998.
*TC MT662.3 .S6 1998*

The flute [videorecording]. Van Nuys, CA : Backstage
Pass Productions ; Canoga Park, Calif. : [Distributed
by] MVP, c1995.
*TC MT345 .F6 1995*

The trombone [videorecording]. Van Nuys, CA :
Backstage Pass Productions ; Canoga Park, Calif. :
[Distributed by] MVP, c1998.
*TC MT465 .T7 1998*

The viola [videorecording]. Van Nuys, CA :
Backstage Pass Productions ; Canoga Park, Calif. :
[Distributed by] MVP Home Entertainment, c1991.
*TC MT285 .V5 1991*

The viola [videorecording]. Van Nuys, CA :
Backstage Pass Productions ; Canoga Park, Calif. :
[Distributed by] MVP Home Entertainment, c1995.
*TC MT285 .V5 1995*

The violin [videorecording]. Van Nuys, CA :
Backstage Pass Productions ; Canoga Park, Calif. :
[Distributed by] MVP, c1998.

*TC MT265 .V5 1998*

**Bringing out the best in students.**
Scheidecker, David, 1950- Thousand Oaks, Calif. :
Corwin Press, c1999.
*TC LB1065 .S344 1999*

**Bringing out the best in teachers.**
Blase, Joseph. 2nd ed. Thousand Oaks, Calif. :
Corwin Press, c2000.
*TC LB2840 .B57 2000*

**Bringing the story home.**
Lipkin, Lisa. New York : W.W. Norton & Co., c2000.
*TC LB1042 .L515 2000*

**Bringing up a challenging child at home.**
Gregory, Jane, 1960- London ; Philadelphia : Jessica
Kingsley Publishers, 2000.
*TC HQ759.913 .G74 2000*

**Bringle, Robert G.**
Colleges and universities as citizens. Boston : Allyn
and Bacon, c1999.
*TC LC220.5 .C644 1999*

**Brink, Andrew.** The creative matrix : anxiety and the
origin of creativity / Andrew Brink. New York : Peter
Lang, c2000. 221 p. : ill. ; 24 cm. (The reshaping of
psychoanalysis, 1059-3551 ; vol. 10) Includes bibliographical
references (p. [203]-216) and index. ISBN 0-8204-4480-4
DDC 153.3/5
*1. Personality and creative ability. 2. Creation (Literary,
artistic, etc.) - Psychological aspects. 3. Anxiety. 4. Attachment
behavior. 5. Psychoanalysis. I. Title. II. Series.*
*TC BF698.9.C74 B75 2000*

**BRINK, CAROL RYRIE, 1895- /.
CADDIE WOODLAWN.**
Gutner, Howard. Caddie Woodlawn by Carol Ryrie
Brink. New York : Scholastic, c1997.
*TC LB1573 .G87 1997*

**Brinkley, Alan.**
The Chicago handbook for teachers. Chicago :
University of Chicago Press, 1999.
*TC LB2331 .C52332 1999*

**Brinkley, Ellen Henson, 1944-** Caught off guard :
teachers rethinking censorship and controversy / Ellen
Henson Brinkley. Boston : Allyn and Bacon, c1999.
xvii, 283 p. : ill. ; 24 cm. Includes bibliographical references
and index. ISBN 0-205-18529-0 DDC 379.1/56/0973
*1. Teaching, Freedom of - United States. 2. Public schools -
United States - Curricula - Censorship. 3. Textbooks -
Censorship - United States. 4. Academic freedom - United
States. I. Title.*
*TC LC72.2 .B75 1999*

**Brinkman, Ronald.** The art and science of digital
compositing / Ron Brinkman. San Diego : Morgan
Kaufmann : Academic Press, 1999. xviii, 364 p., [40] p.
of plates : ill. (some col.) ; 25 cm. + 1 computer optical disc.
Includes bibliographical references and index. Computer
optical disc in pocket attached to inside back cover. ISBN 0-
12-133960-2 ISBN 0-12-133961-0 (disc)
*1. CD-ROMs. 2. Computer graphics. 3. Image processing -
Digital techniques. I. Title.*
*TC T385 .B75 1999*

**Brinson, Kenneth, 1961-.**
Short, Paula M. Information collection. Larchmont,
NY : Eye on Education, c1998.
*TC LB1028.27.U6 S46 1998*

**Brint, Steven G.** Schools and societies / Steven Brint.
Thousand Oaks : Pine Forge Press, c1998. xviii, 349 p. :
ill., maps ; 24 cm. (Sociology for a new century) Includes
bibliographical references (p. [305]-332) and index.
CONTENTS: Schools as social institutions -- Schooling in the
industrialized world -- Schooling in the developing world --
Schools and the transmission of knowledge -- Schools and
socialization -- Schools and social selection, 1 : Opportunity --
Schools and social selection, 2 : Inequality -- Teaching and
learning in comparative perspective -- School reform and the
possibilities of schooling. ISBN 0-8039-9059-6 (pbk. : acid-
free paper) DDC 306.43
*1. Educational sociology - United States. 2. Schools - United
States - Sociological aspects. I. Title. II. Series.*
*TC LC191.4 .B75 1998*

**Brisk, Maria.** Literacy and bilingualism : a handbook
for all teachers / Maria Estela Brisk and Margaret M.
Harrington. Mahwah, N.J. : L. Erlbaum Associates,
c2000. xiii, 168 p. ; 23 cm. Includes bibliographical
references and indexes. ISBN 0-8058-3165-7 (pbk. : alk.
paper) DDC 370.117/5/0973
*1. Education, Bilingual - United States. 2. Literacy - United
States. 3. English language - Study and teaching - United
States - Foreign speakers. 4. Second language acquisition. I.
Harrington, Margaret M. II. Title.*
*TC LC3731 .B684 2000*

**Britain, Mat.**
The drums [videorecording]. Van Nuys, CA :
Backstage Pass Productions ; Canoga Park, Calif. :
[Distributed by] MVP Home Entertainment, c1998.
*TC MT662.3 .S6 1998*

**BRITISH AESTHETICS. See AESTHETICS,
BRITISH.**

**British Broadcasting Corporation.**
Gender and the interpretation of emotion
[videorecording]. Princeton, NJ : Films for the
Humanities & Sciences, c1997.
*TC BF592.F33 G4 1997*

On pictures and paintings [videorecording].
Peasmarsh, East Sussex, Eng. ; Ho-Ho-kus, NJ :
Roland Collection, 1992.
*TC ND195.O45 1992*

Teen violence [videorecording]. Princeton, NJ : Films
for the Humanities & Sciences, c1998.
*TC RJ506.V56 T44 1998*

**British Broadcasting Corporation. Television
Service.**
Stephen Hawking's universe [videorecording].
[Alexandria, Va.] : PBS Video; Burbank, CA :
Distributed by Warner Home Video, c1997.
*TC QB982 .S7 1997*

**British Columbia Centre for International
Education.**
McKellin, Karen, 1950- Maintaining the momentum.
Victoria, B.C. : British Columbia Centre for
International Education, c1998.
*TC LC1090 .M24 1998*

**BRITISH COMMONWEALTH COUNTRIES. See
COMMONWEALTH COUNTRIES.**

**BRITISH COMMONWEALTH NATIONS. See
COMMONWEALTH COUNTRIES.**

**BRITISH DOMINIONS. See COMMONWEALTH
COUNTRIES.**

**BRITISH EMPIRE. See GREAT BRITAIN -
COLONIES.**

**BRITISH - INDIA - SOCIAL LIFE AND
CUSTOMS.**
Burton, David, 1952- The Raj at table. London ;
Boston : Faber, 1994.
*TC TX724.5.I4 B87 1993*

**British Journal of educational psychology.**
Forum of education. London, Longmans Green.

**British journal of educational technology.** London,
Councils and Education Press. v. 1- Jan. 1970- . Title
varies: Journal of educational technology 1970. "Journal of the
National Council for Educational Technology."
*1. Teaching - Aids and devices - Periodicals. I. National
Council for Educational Technology. II. Title: Journal of
educational technology 1970*

**British journal of language teaching.**
Audio-visual language journal. London.

**British Library of Political and Economic Science.**
International bibliography of anthropology = London ;
New York : Routledge, 1999-
*TC Z7161 .I593*

**BRITISH LIBRARY - PLANNING.**
Towards the digital library. London : The British
Library, 1998.
*TC Z664.B75 T683 1998*

**British Library. Science Technology and Business.**
Grimshaw, Jennie. Employment and health. London :
British Library, 1999.
*TC HF5548.85 .G75 1999*

**British Library's Initiatives for Access programme.**
Towards the digital library. London : The British
Library, 1998.
*TC Z664.B75 T683 1998*

**BRITISH LITERATURE. See ENGLISH
LITERATURE.**

**British Psychological Society.**
Noon, J. Mitchell. Counselling and helping carers.
Leicester : BPS Books, 1999.
*TC R727.4 .N66 1999*

**BRITISHERS. See BRITISH.**

**BRITTLE DIABETES. See DIABETES.**

**Britton, Edward.**
Connecting mathematics and science to workplace
contexts. Thousand Oaks, Calif. : Corwin Press,
c1999.
*TC QA11 .C655 1999*

**Britzman, Deborah P., 1952-** Lost subjects, contested objects : toward a psychoanalytic inquiry of learning / Deborah P. Britzman. Albany : State University of New York Press, c1998. viii, 199 p. ; 24 cm. Includes bibliographical references (p. 169-187) and index. ISBN 0-7914-3807-4 (hc : alk. paper) ISBN 0-7914-3808-2 (pb : alk. paper) DDC 370.15/23
*1. Learning. 2. Psychoanalysis. 3. Ethics. 4. Critical pedagogy. I. Title.*
**TC LB1060 .B765 1998**

**Broad, Kenneth.** Climate, culture, and values : the 1997-98 El Niño and Peruvian fisheries / Kenneth Broad. 1999. viii, 311 leaves : charts (some col.) ; 29 cm. Issued also on microfilm. Includes tables. Thesis (Ph. D.)-- Columbia University, 1999. Includes bibliographical references (leaves 283-299)
*1. Fisheries - Peru - Climatic factors. 2. Fisheries - Chile - Climatic factors. 3. Weather forecasting. 4. Global environmental change. 5. Climatic changes. 6. El Niño Current. 7. Southern Oscillation. I. Title.*
**TC 085 B7775**

**Broadbent, Donald E. (Donald Eric)** Perception and communication. New York, Pergamon Press, 1958. 338 p. : ill. ; 22 cm. Includes bibliography. DDC 150.151
*1. Information theory in psychology. 2. Attention. 3. Hearing. I. Title.*
**TC BF38 .B685**

**BROADCASTING. See RADIO BROADCASTING; TELEVISION BROADCASTING.**

**Broadfoot, Patricia.**
Promoting quality in learning. London ; New York : Cassell, 2000.
**TC LA632.b.P76 2000**

**Brock, Avril.**
Into the enchanted forest. Stoke on Trent, Staffordshire : Trentham Books, 1999.
**TC LB1528 .I68 1999**

**Brock, Barbara L.** Rekindling the flame : principals combating teacher burnout / Barbara L. Brock, Marilyn L. Grady. Thousand Oaks, Calif. : Corwin Press, c2000. xii, 139 p. : ill. ; 25 cm. Includes bibliographical references (p. 125-131) and index. ISBN 0-8039-6792-6 (cloth : alk. paper) ISBN 0-8039-6793-4 (pbk. : alk. paper) DDC 371.1/001/9
*1. Teachers - Job stress. 2. Burn out (Psychology) - Prevention. 3. Teacher-principal relationships. I. Grady, Marilyn L. II. Title.*
**TC LB2840.2 .B76 2000**

**Brock-Utne, Birgit, 1938-** Whose education for all? : the recolonization of the African mind / Birgit Brock-Utne. New York ; London : Falmer Press, 2000. xxx, 340 p. ; 23 cm. (Garland reference library of social science ; v. 1445. Studies in education/politics ; v. 6) Includes bibliographical references (p. 291-325) and index. ISBN 0-8153-3478-8 (alk. paper) DDC 379.1/296
*1. Education - Economic aspects - Africa, Sub-Saharan. 2. Education - Aims and objectives - Africa, Sub-Saharan. 3. Educational assistance - Africa, Sub-Saharan. I. Title. II. Series: Garland reference library of social science ; v. 1445. III. Series: Garland reference library of social science. Studies in education/politics ; vol. 6.*
**TC LC67.A435 B76 2000**

**Brock, W. H. (William Hodson)** Science for all : studies in the history of Victorian science and education / William H. Brock. Brookfield, VT : Variorum, 1996. 1 v. (various pagings) : ill. ; 23 cm. (Collected studies series ; CS518) Includes bibliographical references and index. ISBN 0-86078-542-4 (hc : alk. paper) DDC 509.41/09/034
*1. Science - Great Britain - History - 19th century. 2. Science - Social aspects - Great Britain - History - 19th century. 3. Science - Study and teaching - Great Britain - History - 19th century. 4. Great Britain - History - Victoria, 1837-1901. I. Title. II. Series: Collected studies ; CS518.*
**TC Q127.G5 B76 1996**

**Brøderbund.**
Carmen Sandiego [computer file]. Novato, Calif. : Brøderbund Software, 1998. Computer data and program.
**TC QA115 .C37 1998**

Dr. Seuss kindergarten [computer file] Windows / Macintosh CD-ROM ; v. 1.0. Novato, CA : Brøderbund, c1998.
**TC LB1195 .D77 1998**

**Brodie, Laura Fairchild.** Breaking out : VMI and the coming of women / Laura Fairchild Brodie. 1st ed. New York : Pantheon Books, c2000. xv, 350 p. : ill. ; 25 cm. CONTENTS: 1. What Is/Was VMI? -- 2. Coeducation: The Initial Blueprints -- 3. The Case of the "Privateers" -- 4. The Language of Assimilation -- 5. Recruiting for a New Era -- 6. Sweating the Details: Modifications to Facilities -- 7.

Femininity and Fraternization -- 8. The VFT and the Varsity -- 9. Preparing the Corps -- Interlude: Farewell to the All-Male Corps -- 10. The Dress Rehearsal: VMI'S Summer Transition Program -- 11. Memories from Hell -- 12. Problems and Procedures -- 13. Rat/Woman -- 14. Breakout -- 15. Looking Back at the Year -- Epilogue: Third Class Year. ISBN 0-375-40614-X (alk. paper) DDC 379.2/6 DDC 379.2/6
*1. Sexism in higher education - United States - Case studies. 2. Feminism and education - United States - Case studies. 3. Educational equalization - United States - Case studies. 4. Virginia Military Institute - History - 20th century. I. Title.*
**TC LC212.862 .B75 2000**

**Broek, Paul van den.**
Reading for meaning. New York : London : Teachers College Press, c2000.
**TC LB1050.45 .R443 2000**

**Bromberg, Walter, 1900-** The mind of man : a history of psychotherapy and psychoanalysis / Walter Bromberg. Harper colophon ed. New York : Harper & Row, 1963. xxi, 344 p., [16] p. of plates : ill., ports. ; 21 cm. (Harper colophon books ; CN/34) "Originally entitled Man above humanity: a history of psychotherapy, published in 1954." Includes bibliographical references and index.
*1. Psychotherapy - History. 2. Mentally ill - Care. I. Title. II. Title: History of psychotherapy and psychoanalysis*
**TC RC480 .B7 1963**

The mind of man : the story of man's conquest of mental illness / by Walter Bromberg. 4th ed. New York : Harper & Brothers, 1937. xiv, 323 p., [16] leaves of plates ; 23 cm. Includes bibliographical references and index.
*1. Psychiatry - History. 2. Mental healing - History. 3. Mentally ill - Care. I. Title. II. Title: Story of man's conquest of mental illness*
**TC RC480 .B7**

**Bromfield, Richard.** Doing child and adolescent psychotherapy : the ways and whys / Richard Bromfield. Northvale, N.J. ; London : Jason Aronson, c1999. ix, 297 p. : ill. ; 24 cm. Includes bibliographical references (p. 287) and index. CONTENTS: 1. Easy Does It: Beginning Therapy -- 2. Can I Help You?: Evaluating the Child and Offering Treatment -- 3. The Not-So-Magic of Therapy: How Therapy Works -- 4. Do Fence Me In: The Bounds and Limits -- 5. Tell Me Where It Hurts: On Talking and Querying -- 6. The Lowdown on High Drama: Playing with Puppets and Action Figures -- 7. Shoot, Topple, and Roll: Using Games, Building Toys, and Guns -- 8. Drawing Out the Child: Artwork in Therapy -- 9. All Together Now: Balancing Play and Talk -- 10. Pushing the Envelope: On Giving, Telling, and Other Exceptions -- 11. Handle with Care: Working with Parents -- 12. Hard Times: Unwilling Patients and Therapeutic Crises -- 13. When Therapy Is Not Enough: Medication -- 14. All's Well That Ends Well: Closing Therapy. ISBN 0-7657-0220-7 DDC 618.92/8914 DDC 618.92/8914
*1. Child psychotherapy. 2. Adolescent psychotherapy. 3. Brief psychotherapy. I. Title.*
**TC RJ504 .B753 1999**

**BROMOCRIPTINE. See DOPAMINE.**

**Bronson, Martha.** Self-regulation in early childhood : nature and nurture / Martha B. Bronson. New York ; London : Guilford Press, c2000. viii, 296 p. ; 24 cm. Includes bibliographical references (p. 247-285) and index. ISBN 1-57230-532-0 (hardcover) DDC 155.4/1825
*1. Self-control in children. 2. Child rearing. I. Title.*
**TC BF723.S25 B76 2000**

**BRONX (NEW YORK, N.Y.).**
Mendoza, Maria Adalia. A study to compare inner city Black men and women completers and non-attenders of diabetes self-care classes. 1999.
**TC 06 no. 11206**

**BRONX VETERANS AFFAIRS MEDICAL CENTER (BRONX, N.Y.).**
Fenichel, Ann. The relationship between health care clinicians' relational abilities and psychosocial orientation to patient care, and patient adherence with medical treatment. 1998.
**TC 085 F352**

**BRONZE SCULPTORS. See SCULPTORS.**

**Brook, Barbara, 1949-** Feminist perspective on the body / Barbara Brook. New York : Longman, 1999. xiv, 183 p. ; 22 cm. (Feminist perspectives series) Includes bibliographical references and index. ISBN 0-582-35639-3 DDC 391.6/082
*1. Body, Human - Social aspects. 2. Body, Human - Political aspects. 3. Women - Physiology. 4. Human reproduction. 5. Body image in women. 6. Surgery, Plastic - Psychological aspects. 7. Feminist theory. I. Title. II. Series.*
**TC GT495 .B76 1999**

**Brooke, Christopher Nugent Lawrence.**
Bendall, A. Sarah. A history of Emmanuel College,

Cambridge. Woodbridge, Suffolk, UK : Rochester, NY : Boydell Press, 1999.
**TC LF185 .B46 1999**

**Brooke, Roger, 1953-.**
Pathways into the Jungian world. London ; New York : Routledge, 2000.
**TC BF175 .P29 2000**

**Brooke, William J.** A is for aarrgh! / William J. Brooke. 1st ed. New York : HarperCollinsPublishers, 1999. 249 p. ; 22 cm. "Joanna Cotler books." SUMMARY: Mog, a young boy living during the Stone Age, discovers words and language and teaches his fellow cave dwellers how to talk, thus altering the course of history. ISBN 0-06-023393-1 ISBN 0-06-023394-X (lib. bdg.) DDC [Fic]
*1. Language and languages - Fiction. 2. Communication - Fiction. 3. Prehistoric peoples - Fiction. I. Title.*
**TC PZ7.B78977 Ig 1999**

**Brookings Institution. Brown Center on Education Policy.**
Brookings papers on education policy, 2000. Washington, D.C. : Brookings Institution Press, c2000.
**TC LC89 .B7472 2000**

**Brookings papers on education policy, 2000** / Diane Ravitch, editor ; sponsored by the Brown Center for Education Policy. Washington, D.C. : Brookings Institution Press, c2000. 396 p. : ill. ; 23 cm. Contains edited versions of the papers and comments presented at the annual conference of the Brown Center on Education Policy of the Brookings Institution, held May 1999. Includes bibliographical references. ISBN 0-8157-7357-9
*1. Education and state - United States - Congresses. 2. Education - Standards - United States - Congresses. 3. Educational change - United States - Congresses. I. Ravitch, Diane. II. Brookings Institution. Brown Center on Education Policy.*
**TC LC89 .B7472 2000**

**Brooklyn Bridge.**
Trachtenberg, Alan. Phoenix ed. Chicago : University of Chicago Press, 1979.
**TC TG25.N53 T7 1979**

**BROOKLYN BRIDGE (NEW YORK, N.Y.).**
Trachtenberg, Alan. Brooklyn Bridge. Phoenix ed. Chicago : University of Chicago Press, 1979.
**TC TG25.N53 T7 1979**

**Brooklyn Museum.**
Sullivan, Missy. The Native American look book. New York : The New Press, 1996.
**TC E98.A7 S93 1996**

**Brooklyn Museum of Art.**
Carbone, Teresa A. Eastman Johnson. New York : Brooklyn Museum of Art in association with Rizzoli International Publications, 1999.
**TC ND237.J7 A4 1999**

Ferber, Linda S. Masters of color and light. Washington : Brooklyn Museum of Art in Association with Smithsonian Institution Press, c1998.
**TC ND1807 .F47 1998**

Microsoft encarta Africana [computer file]. Redmond, WA : Microsoft Corp., c1999. Computer data and programs.
**TC DT14 .M527 1999**

Microsoft encarta Africana [computer file]. Redmond, WA : Microsoft Corp., c1999. Computer data and programs.
**TC DT3 .M53 1999x**

**BROOKLYN MUSEUM OF ART - EXHIBITIONS.**
Ferber, Linda S. Masters of color and light. Washington : Brooklyn Museum of Art in Association with Smithsonian Institution Press, c1998.
**TC ND1807 .F47 1998**

**BROOKLYN (NEW YORK, N.Y.).**
Tsamasiros, Katherine V. Using interactive multimedia software to improve cognition of complex imagery in adolescents. 1998.
**TC 06 no. 10905**

**BROOKS. See RIVERS.**

**Brooks, George A. (George Austin), 1944-.**
Exercise physiology. 3rd ed. Mountain View, Calif. : Mayfield Pub., c2000.
**TC QP301 .B885 2000**

**Brooks, Nigel.** Town mouse house : how we lived one hundred years ago / Nigel Brooks & Abigail Horner. New York : Walker & Co., 2000. 1v. (unpaged) :bcol. ill. ; 25 cm. SUMMARY: A wealthy young mouse describes his home and family and the comfortable life that they lead in their large city house in 1900. ISBN 0-8027-8732-0 DDC [E]

*1. Mice - Fiction. 2. City and town life - Fiction. I. Horner, Abigail. II. Title.*
**TC PZ7.B7977 To 2000**

**Brooks, Philip, 1955-** Invaders from outer space : real-life stories of UFOs / written by Philip Brooks. 1st American ed. New York : DK, 1999. 48 p. : col. ill., col. maps ; 24 cm. (Eyewitness readers. Level 3) "Grades 2 and 3." SUMMARY: Examines the phenomena of unidentified flying objects and encounters with alien beings. ISBN 0-7894-3999-9 (hc) ISBN 0-7894-3998-0 (pb) DDC 001.942
*1. Unidentified flying objects - Sightings and encounters - Juvenile literature. 2. Human-alien encounters - Juvenile literature. 3. Unidentified flying objects. 4. Extraterrestrial beings. I. Title. II. Series.*
**TC TL789.2 .B76 1999**

**Brooks, Van Wyck, 1886-1963.**
**Makers and finders: a history of the writer in America, 1800-1915**
(1.) Brooks, Van Wyck, 1886-1963. The world of Washington Irving, Philadelphia, Blakiston, 1944.
**TC PS208 .B7 1944a**

The world of Washington Irving, by Van Wyck Brooks. Philadelphia, Blakiston, 1944. 495 p. ; 22 cm. (His Makers and finders: a history of the writer in America, 1800-1915, 1) Includes bliographical footnotes and index.
*1. American literature - Early 19th century - History and criticism. I. Title. II. Series: Brooks, Van Wyck, 1886-1963. Makers and finders: a history of the writer in America, 1800-1915, 1.*
**TC PS208 .B7 1944a**

The world of Washington Irving, by Van Wyck Brooks. [New York] E. P. Dutton & co., inc. [1944] 5 p. 1., 495 p. 22 cm. ([His Makers and finders: a history of the writer in America, 1800-1915, 1]) "First edition." Bibliographical foot-notes. Sequel to New England: Indian Summer. DDC 810.903
*1. American literature - 1783-1850 - History and criticism. 2. United States - Intellectual life - 1783-1865. I. Title.*
**TC PS208 .B7 1944**

**Brophy, Jere E.**
Beyond behaviorism. Boston : Allyn and Bacon, c 1999.
**TC LB3013 .B42 1999**

**Brotherly love [videorecording].**
Africans in America [videorecording]. [Boston, Mass.] : WGBH Educational Foundation : South Burlington, VT : WGBH Boston Video [distributor], c1998.
**TC E441 .A47 1998**

**BROTHERS AND SISTERS.** *See also* **BROTHERS; SISTERS; TRIPLETS; TWINS.**
Brothers and sisters. Northvale, N.J. : J. Aronson, c1999.
**TC BF723.S43 B78 1999**

**Brothers and sisters :** developmental, dynamic, and technical aspects of the sibling relationship / edited by Salman Akhtar and Selma Kramer. Northvale, N.J. : J. Aronson, c1999. xii, 187 p. ; 23 cm. "The chapters in this book ... were originally presented as papers at the 29th Annual Margaret S. Mahler Symposium on Child Development held on May 2, 1998, in Philadelphia"--P. ix. Includes bibliographical references and index. ISBN 0-7657-0203-7 (alk. paper) DDC 306.875
*1. Brothers and sisters. 2. Sibling rivalry. I. Akhtar, Salman, 1946 July 31- II. Kramer, Selma. III. Margaret S. Mahler Symposium on Child Development (29th : 1998 : Philadelphia, Pa.)*
**TC BF723.S43 B78 1999**

**BROTHERS AND SISTERS - FICTION.**
Graham, Bob, 1942- Crusher is coming!. New York, N.Y., U.S.A. : Puffin Books, 1990.
**TC PZ7.G751667 Cr 1990**

Holm, Jennifer L. Our only May Amelia. 1st ed. New York : HarperCollinsPublishers, c1999.
**TC PZ7.H732226 Ou 1999**

Ormerod, Jan. 101 things to do with a baby. 1st U.S. ed. New York : Lothrop, Lee & Shepard, c1984.
**TC PZ7.O634 Aad 1984**

Recorvits, Helen. Goodbye, Walter Malinski. 1st ed. New York : Farrar, Straus and Giroux, c1999.
**TC PZ7.R24435 Go 1999**

**Brothers, Barbara Jo, 1940-.**
Couples therapy in managed care. New York : Haworth Press, c1999.
**TC RC488.5 .C64385 1999**

**BROTHERS - FICTION.**
Naylor, Phyllis Reynolds. A traitor among the boys. New York : Delacorte Press, 1999.

**TC PZ7.N24 Tpr 1999**
Naylor, Phyllis Reynolds. Walker's Crossing. New York : Atheneum Books for Young Readers, c1999.
**TC PZ7.N24 Wai 1999**

**Brovey, Daniel J.**
Brandwein, Paul F. (Paul Franz), 1912- Matter. Curie ed. New York : Harcourt Brace Jovanovich, 1980.
**TC Q161.2 .C66 1980**

**Brown, B. Bradford (Benson Bradford), 1949-.**
The development of romantic relationships in adolescence. Cambridge, U.K. ; New York : Cambridge University Press, 1999.
**TC BF724.3.L68 D48 1999**

**Brown bear, brown bear, what do you see?.**
Martin, Bill, 1916- New York : H. Holt, 1992.
**TC PZ8.3.M418 Br 1992**

**BROWN, CHARLOTTE HAWKINS, 1883-1961.**
Wadelington, Charles Weldon. Charlotte Hawkins Brown & Palmer Memorial Institute. Chapel Hill ; London : University of North Carolina Press, c1999.
**TC LA2317.B598 W33 1999**

**Brown, Cheryl.**
Grounded for life [videorecording]. Charleston, WV : Cambridge Research Group, Ltd., 1988.
**TC HQ759.4 .G7 1988**

**Brown, Colin M.**
The neurocognition of language. Oxford ; New York : Oxford University Press, 1999.
**TC QP399 .N483 1999**

**Brown, Deborah Edler.**
De Toledo, Sylvie. Grandparents as parents. New York : Guilford Press, c1995.
**TC HQ759.9 .D423 1995**

**Brown, Fredda.**
Instruction of students with severe disabilities. 5th ed. Upper Saddle River, N.J. : Merrill, c2000.
**TC LC4031 .I572 2000**

**Brown, Gloria M.** Post-hospital care for the elderly : a gap to be filled / Gloria Margarita Brown. 1997. iv, 108 leaves ; 29 cm. Issued also on microfilm. Thesis (Ed.D.)--Teachers College, Columbia University, 1997. Includes bibliographical references (leaves 107-108).
*1. Aged - United States - Home care - Case studies. 2. Aged - Psychology - Case studies. 3. Home care services - United States. 4. Caregivers - United States - Attitudes - Case studies. 5. Interpersonal relations - Psychological aspects - Case studies. 6. Hospitals - United States - Home care programs. I. Title. II. Title: Posthospital care for the elderly*
**TC 06 no. 10759**

**Brown, H. Douglas, 1941-** Principles of language learning and teaching / H. Douglas Brown. 2nd ed. Englewood Cliffs, N.J. : Prentice-Hall, c1987. xvi, 285 ; 23 cm. Bibliography: p. 252-277. Includes index. ISBN 0-13-701491-0 DDC 418/.007
*1. Language and languages - Study and teaching. 2. Language acquisition. I. Title.*
**TC P51 .B775 1987**

**Brown, John Seely.** The social life of information / John Seely Brown and Paul Duguid. Boston : Harvard Business School Press, c2000. x, 320 p. ; 22 cm. Includes bibliographical references (p. 289-305) and index. ISBN 0-87584-762-5 (alk. paper) DDC 303.48/33
*1. Information society. 2. Information technology - Social aspects. I. Duguid, Paul, 1954- II. Title.*
**TC HM851 .B76 2000**

**Brown, Kimila S.**
Chalker, Christopher S. Effective alternative education programs. Lancaster, Pa. : Technomic, c1999.
**TC LC4091 .C5 1999**

**Brown, Lee E., 1956-.**
Isokinetics in human performance. Champaign, Ill. : Human Kinetics, 2000.
**TC QP303 .I82 2000**

**Brown, Lester Russell, 1934-** Vital signs 2000 : : the environmental trends that are shaping our future / Lester R. Brown, Michael Renner, Brian Halweil ; editor, Linda Starke. New York : Norton, c2000. 192 p. : ill. ; 24 cm. Includes bibliographical references. CONTENTS: Food trends -- Agricultural resource trends -- Energy trends -- Atmospheric trends -- Economic trends -- Transportation trends -- Communication trends -- Social trends -- Military trends -- Environmental features -- Economic features -- Social features -- Military features. ISBN 0-393-32022-7
*1. Environmental impact analysis. 2. Nature - Effect of human beings on - Forecasting. 3. Consumption (Economics) - Forecasting. I. Renner, Michael. 1957- II. Starke, Linda. III. Halwell, Brian. IV. Title.*

**TC HD75.6 .B768 2000**

**Brown, Lois, 1966-.**
Paul, Susan, fl. 1837. Memoir of James Jackson, the attentive and obedient scholar, who died in Boston, October 31, 1833, aged six years and eleven months. Cambridge, MA : Harvard University Press, 2000.
**TC F73.9.N4 P38 2000**

**Brown, M. Christopher.**
Black sons to mothers. New York : Canterbury [England] : P. Lang, c2000.
**TC LC2731 .B53 2000**

**BROWN, MARC TOLON - STUDY AND TEACHING (ELEMENTARY).**
Walmsley, Bonnie Brown. Teaching with favorite Marc Brown books. New York : Scholastic Professional Books, c1998.
**TC LB1576 .W258 1998**

**Brown, Nina W.**
Wetzel, Roberta, 1946- Student-generated sexual harassment in secondary schools. Westport, Conn. ; London : Bergin & Garvey, 2000.
**TC LC212.82 .W47 2000**

**Brown, Norman M., 1942-** Love and intimate relationships : journeys of the heart / Norman M. Brown, Ellen S. Amatea. Philadelphia ; Hove [England] : Brunner/Mazel, c2000. xxii, 618 p. : ill. ; 24 cm. Includes bibliographical references (p. 529-588) and index. ISBN 0-87630-979-1 (alk. paper) DDC 306.7
*1. Love. 2. Intimacy (Psychology) I. Amatea, Ellen S., 1944- II. Title.*
**TC BF575.L8 B75 2000**

**Brown, Richard Harvey.**
Knowledge and power in higher education. New York ; London : Teachers College Press, c2000.
**TC LC171 .K62 2000**

**Brown, Robert Donald, 1931-.**
Utilization of evaluative information. San Francisco : Jossey-Bass, 1980.
**TC H62.5.U5 U86**

**Brown, Ronald T.** Medications for school-age children : effects on learning and behavior / Ronald T. Brown, Michael G. Sawyer ; foreword by Martin T. Stein. New York : Guilford Press, c1998. xii, 228 p. : ill. ; 24 cm. (The Guilford school practitioner series) Includes bibliographical references (p. 187-221) and index. ISBN 1-57230-316-6 (alk. paper) DDC 615/.1/083
*1. Pediatric pharmacology. 2. School nursing. 3. Drugs - Administration. I. Sawyer, Michael G. II. Title. III. Series.*
**TC RJ560 .B76 1998**

**BROWN-RRAP, JULIE.**
Alexander, George, 1949- Julie Rrap. [Sidney] : Piper Press, 1998.
**TC TR654 .A44 1998**

**Brown, Rupert, 1950-** Group processes : dynamics within and between groups / Rupert Brown. 2nd ed. Oxford : Malden, Mass. : Blackwell Publishers, 2000. xxiii, 417 p. : ill. ; 24 cm. Includes bibliographical references (p. 361-409) and indexes. ISBN 0-631-21852-1 (hbk. : alk. paper) ISBN 0-631-18496-1 (pbk. : alk. paper) DDC 302.3
*1. Social groups. 2. Interpersonal relations. 3. Intergroup relations. I. Title.*
**TC HM131 .B726 2000**

**Brown, Ruth.** Mad summer night's dream / by Ruth Brown. 1st American ed. New York : Dutton Children's Books, 1999. 1 v. (unpaged) : col. ill. ; 28 cm. SUMMARY: A strange dream on a midsummer night in winter produces many contradictions and unusual sights, from singing flowers and blooming trees to dancing stone monkeys. ISBN 0-525-46010-1 hc DDC [E]
*1. Dreams - Fiction. 2. Stories in rhyme. I. Title.*
**TC PZ8.3.B8155 Mad 1999**

**Brown, Sally.**
Routledge international companion to education. London ; New York : Routledge, 2000.
**TC LB7 .R688 2000**

**Brown, Sally. 1950 Feb. 1-.**
Benchmarking and threshold standards in higher education. London : Kogan Page, c1999.
**TC LB2341.8.G7 B463 1999**

**Brown, Sally A.** 500 tips for teachers / Sally Brown, Carolyn Earlam and Phil Race. 2nd ed. London : Kogan Page ; Sterling, VA : Stylus Pub., 1998. vi, 154 p. ; 24 cm. Includes bibliographical references (p. 151) and index. ISBN 0-7494-2835-X
*1. Classroom management - Handbooks, manuals, etc. 2. Teaching - Handbooks, manuals, etc. I. Earlam, Carolyn. II. Race, Philip. III. Title. IV. Title: Five hundred tips for teachers.*

**TC LB3013 .B76 1998**
Computer-assisted assessment in higher education.
London : Kogan Page, 1999.
**TC LB2366 .C65 1999**

**Brown, Stephen Gilbert.** Words in the wilderness :
critical literacy in the borderlands / Stephen Gilbert
Brown ; foreword by Gary A. Olson. Albany : State
University of New York Press, c2000. xi, 229 p. ; 24 cm.
(SUNY series, interruptions -- border testimony(ies) and
critical discourse/s) Includes bibliographical references (p.
217-224) and index. ISBN 0-7914-4405-8 (alk. paper) ISBN
0-7914-4406-6 (pbk. : alk. paper) DDC 371.829/972
*1. Athabascan Indians - Education - Alaska. 2. Brown, Stephen
Gilbert. - 1949- 3. Critical pedagogy. 4. Literacy. 5. Teachers -
Alaska - Biography. I. Title. II. Series.*
**TC E99.A86 B76 2000**

**BROWN, STEPHEN GILBERT, 1949-.**
Brown, Stephen Gilbert. Words in the wilderness.
Albany : State University of New York Press, c2000.
**TC E99.A86 B76 2000**

**Brown, Steven D. (Steven Douglas), 1947-.**
Handbook of counseling psychology. 3rd ed. New
York : J. Wiley, c2000.
**TC BF637.C6 H315 2000**

**Brown, Trisha.**
Hopps, Walter. Robert Rauschenberg. New York :
Guggenheim Museum, c1997.
**TC N6537.R27 H66 1997**

**BROWN UNIVERSITY - STUDENTS -
    BIOGRAPHY.**
Suskind, Ron. A hope in the unseen. 1st ed. New
York : Broadway Books, c1998.
**TC LC2803.W3 S87 1998**

**Brown, Victoria (Victoria L.)** The dramatic difference :
drama in the preschool and kindergarten classroom /
Victoria Brown and Sarah Pleydell ; foreword by
Gavin Bolton. Portsmouth, NH : Heinemann, c1999.
xiv, 177 p. ; 23 cm. Includes bibliographical references (p.
173-177). ISBN 0-325-00121-9 (alk. paper) DDC 372.13/32
*1. Drama in education. 2. Play. 3. Early childhood education -
Activity programs. I. Pleydell, Sarah. II. Title.*
**TC PN3171 .B76 1999**

**Brown, Walker, 1894-.**
Rogers, Lester Brown, 1875- Story of nations. New
York : H.Holt, 1965.
**TC D21 .R63 1965**

**Browndeer Press**
Swann, Brian. The house with no door. 1st ed. San
Diego : Harcourt Brace & Company., c1998.
**TC PS3569.W256 H6 1998**

**Browne, Ray Broadus.**
Pioneers in popular culture studies. Bowling Green,
OH : Bowling Green State University Popular Press,
c1999.
**TC E169.04 .P563 1999**

**Brownell, Gregg.** A PC for the teacher : Microsoft
Office 97, HyperStudio 3.1, Internet Explorer / Gregg
Brownell, Carol Youngs, Jan Metzger. Belmont, CA :
Wadsworth Pub. Co., c1999. xviii, 445 p. : ill. ; 25 cm. + 1
computer optical disc (4 3/4 in.). Includes index. ISBN
0-534-53862-2 (alk. paper) DDC 371.33/4
*1. Education - Data processing. 2. Computer-assisted
instruction. 3. Computer managed instruction. 4. Education -
Computer programs. 5. Microcomputers. I. Youngs, Carol. II.
Metzger, Jan. III. Title. IV. Title: Personal computer for the
teacher*
**TC LB1028.43 .B755 1999**

**Brownlee, David Bruce.**
Thomas, George E. Building America's first
university. Philadelphia : University of Pennsylvania
Press, c2000.
**TC LD4531 .T56 1999**

**Brozo, William G.** Readers, teachers, learners :
expanding literacy across the content areas / William
G. Brozo, Michele L. Simpson. 3rd ed. Upper Saddle
River, N.J. : Merrill, c1999. xx, 484 p. : ill. ; 26 cm.
Includes bibliographical references and indexes. ISBN 0-13-
647272-9 DDC 428.4/071/273
*1. Reading (Secondary) - United States. 2. Language arts
(Secondary) - United States. I. Simpson, Michele L. II. Title.*
**TC LB1632 .B7 1999**

**Brubacher, John W.**
Reagan, Timothy G. Becoming a reflective educator.
2nd ed. Thousand Oaks Calif. : Sage Publications,
c2000.
**TC LB1025.3 .R424 2000**

**Brubaker, Dale L.**
Thomas, R. Murray (Robert Murray), 1921- Theses

and dissertations. Westport, Conn. : Bergin & Garvey,
2000.
**TC LB2369 .T458 2000**

**Brueckner, Leo J.** Moving ahead in arithmetic / by Leo
J. Brueckner, Elda L. Merton, Foster E. Grossnickle.
New York, N.Y. : Holt, Rinehart and Winston, 1963.
v. : ill. (some col.) ; 24 cm.
*1. Arithmetic. I. Merton. Elda L. II. Grossnickle. Foster E. III.
Title.*
**TC QA107 .B78 1963**

Moving ahead in arithmetic / by Leo J. Brueckner,
Elda L. Merton, Foster E. Grossnickle. New York,
N.Y. : Holt, Rinehart and Winston, 1963. v. : ill. (some
col.) ; 24 cm.
*1. Arithmetic. I. Merton. Elda L. II. Grossnickle. Foster E. III.
Title.*
**TC QA107 .B78 1963**

Moving ahead in arithmetic / by Leo J. Brueckner,
Elda L. Merton, Foster E. Grossnickle. New York :
Holt, Rinehart and Winston, 1963. 6 v. : ill. (some col.) ;
24 cm.
*1. Arithmetic. I. Merton. Elda L. II. Grossnickle. Foster E. III.
Title.*
**TC QA107 .B78 1963**

Moving ahead in arithmetic / by Leo J. Brueckner,
Elda L. Merton, Foster E. Grossnickle. New York :
Holt, Rinehart and Winston, 1963. 6 v. : ill. (some col.) ;
24 cm.
*1. Arithmetic. I. Merton. Elda L. II. Grossnickle. Foster E. III.
Title.*
**TC QA107 .B78 1963**

**Bruegel, Jan, 1568-1625.** Where's the bear? : a look-
and-find book. Los Angeles : J. Paul Getty Museum,
c1997. 1 v. (unpaged) : col. ill. ; 21 cm. SUMMARY: Details
from the painting "The Entry of the Animals into Noah's Ark,"
by Jan Bruegel, present twenty-two different animals with their
names in English, French, German, Italian, and Japanese. ISBN
0-89236-378-9 DDC 590
*1. Animals - Pictorial works - Juvenile literature. 2. Zoology -
Nomenclature (Popular) - Polyglot - Juvenile literature. 3.
Animals in art. 4. Polyglot materials. I. J. Paul Getty Museum.
II. Title.*
**TC QL49 .B749 1997**

**Bruer, John T., 1949-** The myth of the first three years :
a new understanding of early brain development and
lifelong learning / John T. Bruer. New York : Free
Press, c1999. x, 244 p. : ill. ; 24 cm. Includes bibliographical
references (p. 211-235) and index. ISBN 0-684-85184-9 DDC
155.4/13
*1. Learning, Psychology of. 2. Educational psychology. 3.
Pediatric neuropsychology. I. Title.*
**TC BF318 .B79 1999**

**Bruestle, Doug.**
The cello [videorecording]. Van Nuys, CA :
Backstage Pass Productions ; Canoga Park, Calif. :
[Distributed by] MVP, c1995.
**TC MT305 .C4 1995**

**Brumbaugh, Douglas K., 1939-.**
Teaching secondary mathematics. Mahwah, N.J. : L.
Erlbaum Associates, 1997.
**TC QA11 .T357 1997**

**Brumfitt, Shelagh.** The social psychology of
communication impairment / Shelagh Brumfitt.
London : Whurr, 1999. ix, 126 p. ; 24 cm. Includes
bibliographical references (p. 111-119) and index. ISBN 1-
86156-095-8
*1. Social psychology. 2. Communicative disorders. I. Title.*
**TC HM251 .B758 1999**

**BRUNDAGE, AVERY.**
Senn, Alfred Erich. Power, politics, and the Olympic
Games. Champaign, IL : Human Kinetics, c1999.
**TC GV721.5 .S443 1999**

**Brunello, Nicoletta.**
New therapeutic indications of antidepressants.
Basel ; New York : Karger, c1997.
**TC RM332 .N475 1997**

**Bruner Foundation.**
Talking across boundaries. [New York] : [Bruner
Foundation], 1996.
**TC LB1623.5 .T35 1996**

**Bruner, Jerome Seymour.** On knowing; essays for the
left hand. Cambridge, Belknap Press of Harvard
University Press, 1962. 165 p. illus. 21 cm. DDC 121
*1. Learning. 2. Knowledge. Theory of. I. Title.*
**TC LB885 .B778**

**Bruning, Roger H.** Cognitive psychology and
instruction / Roger H. Bruning, Gregory J. Schraw,
Royce R. Ronning. 3rd ed. Upper Saddle River, N.J. :
Merrill, c1999. xiv, 433 p. : ill. ; 23 cm. Includes

bibliographical references (p. 373-409) and indexes. ISBN
0-13-716606-0 (pbk.) DDC 370.15/23
*1. Learning. 2. Cognitive psychology. 3. Cognitive learning. 4.
Instructional systems - Design. I. Schraw. Gregory J. II.
Ronning. Royce R. III. Title.*
**TC LB1060 .B786 1999**

**Brunk, Terence.**
Literacies. 2nd ed. New York : W.W. Norton, c2000.
**TC PE1417 .L62 2000**

**Brunner, C. Cryss.** Principles of power : women
superintendents and the riddle of the heart / C. Cryss
Brunner. Albany, NY : State University of New York
Press, c2000. xix, 200 p. ; 23 cm. Includes bibliographical
references and index. ISBN 0-7914-4569-0 (hc : alk. paper)
ISBN 0-7914-4570-4 (pbk. : alk. paper) DDC 025.06/37
*1. Women school superintendents - United States. 2.
Castaneda, Carlos, - 1931- I. Title.*
**TC LB2831.72 .B78 2000**

Sacred dreams. Albany : State University of New
York Press, c1999.
**TC LB2831.72 .S23 1999**

**Brunner, Cornelia, Dr.** The new media literacy
handbook : an educator's guide to bringing new media
into the classroom / Cornelia Brunner and William
Tally. New York : Anchor Books, 1999. 228 p. : ill. ; 24
cm. Includes bibliographical references and index. ISBN
0-385-49614-1 (paperback) DDC 371.33/4
*1. Educational technology - Handbooks, manuals. etc. 2.
Media literacy - Handbooks, manuals. etc. 3. Interactive
multimedia - Handbooks, manuals. etc. 4. Computer-assisted
instruction - Handbooks, manuals. etc. I. Tally, William. II.
Title.*
**TC LB1028.3 .B77 1999**

**Brusko, Mike.** Writing rules! : teaching kids to write for
life, grades 4-8 / Mike Brusko. Portsmouth, NH :
Heinemann, c1999. xviii, 93 p. ; 24 cm. Includes
bibliographical references (p. 92-93). ISBN 0-325-00157-X
DDC 372.62/3/044
*1. English language - Composition and exercises - Study and
teaching (Elementary) - United States. I. Title.*
**TC LB1576 .B876 1999**

**Bry, Brenna Hafer.**
Boyd-Franklin, Nancy. Reaching out in family
therapy. New York : Guilford Press, 2000.
**TC RC488.5 .B678 2000**

**Bryan, Ashley, ill.**
Swann, Brian. The house with no door. 1st ed. San
Diego : Harcourt Brace & Company., c1998.
**TC PS3569.W256 H6 1998**

**Bryce, Betty Kelly, 1942-** American printmakers,
1946-1996 : an index to reproductions and biocritical
information / Betty Kelly Bryce. Lanham, Md. :
Scarecrow Press, 1999. xxxiv, 570 p. ; 23 cm. Includes
bibliographical references and indexes. ISBN 0-8108-3586-X
(alk. paper) DDC 016.76992/273
*1. Prints, American - Indexes. 2. Prints - 20th century - United
States - Indexes. 3. Printmakers - United States - Indexes. I.
Title.*
**TC NE508 .B76 1999**

**Bryce, T. G. K.**
Scottish education. Edinburgh : Edinburgh University
Press, c1999.
**TC LA652 .S34 1999**

**The BSCS journal.**
Biological Sciences Curriculum Study. Boulder,
Colo., Biological Sciences Curriculum Study.

**BT FACTOR. See CARNITINE.**

**Buchan, P. Bruce (Peter Bruce), 1932-.**
Daub, Mervin, 1943- Getting down to business.
Montreal ; Ithaca : McGill-Queen's University Press,
c1999.
**TC HF1134.Q442 D38 1999**

**Buchanan, David Ross.** An ethic for health promotion :
rethinking the sources of human well-being / David R.
Buchanan. New York : Oxford : Oxford University
Press, 2000. xii, 214 p. : ill. ; 24 cm. Includes bibliographical
references (p. 171-207) and index. ISBN 0-19-513057-X DDC
613/.01
*1. Health promotion - Moral and ethical aspects. 2. Health
promotion - Philosophy. I. Title.*
**TC RA427.8 .B83 2000**

Progress in preventing AIDS? Amityville, N.Y. :
Baywood Pub. Co., 1998.
**TC RA644.A25 P7655 1998**

**Buchanan, Robert (Robert M.)** Illusions of equality :
deaf Americans in school and factory, 1850-1950 /
Robert M. Buchanan. Washington, D.C. : Gallaudet
University Press, 1999. xvii, 214 p. : ill. ; 24 cm. Includes
bibliographical references (p. 129-204) and index. ISBN 1-

56368-084-X (hardcover : alk. paper) DDC 305.9/08162
1. *Deaf - Education - United States - History.* 2. *Deaf - Employment - United States - History.* I. *Title.*
*TC HV2530 .B83 1999*

**Bucher, Katherine Toth, 1947-** Information technology for schools / Katherine Toth Bucher. 2nd ed. Worthington, Ohio : Linworth Pub., c1998. xvi, 400 p. : ill. ; 28 cm. (Professional growth series) Includes bibliographical references and index. ISBN 0-938865-65-X DDC 027.8/0285 ·
1. *School libraries - United States - Data processing.* 2. *Instructional materials centers - United States - Data processing.* 3. *Computer-assisted instruction - United States.* 4. *Media programs (Education) - United States.* I. *Title.* II. *Series.*
*TC Z675.S3 B773 1998*

**Buchert, Lene.**
Changing international aid to education. Paris : Unesco Pub./NORRAG, 1999.
*TC LC2607 .C42 1999*

Learning from experience. The Hague : Centre for the Study of Education in Developing Countries, c1995.
*TC LC2610 .L43 1995*

**Büchner, Louise, 1821-1877.**
[Frauen und ihr Beruf. English]
Women and their vocation : a nineteenth-century view / by Luise Büchner ; translated and with an introduction by Susan L. Piepke. New York : P. Lang, c1999. 127 p. : ill. ; 25 cm. (Women in German literature ; vol. 5) Includes bibliographical references (p. [125]-127). ISBN 0-8204-4142-2 (alk. paper) DDC 305.42
1. *Women - Germany - Conduct of life.* I. *Title.* II. *Series.*
*TC BJ1610 .B8313 1998*

**Buckingham, David, 1954-** After the death of childhood : growing up in the age of electronic media / David Buckingham. Malden, MA : Polity Press, 2000. vii, 245 p. ; 23 cm. Includes bibliographical references and index. DDC 302.23
1. *Mass media and children.* 2. *Digital media - Social aspects.* 3. *Children - Social conditions.* 4. *Children's rights.* I. *Title.*
*TC HQ784.M3 B83 2000*

The making of citizens : young people, news, and politics / David Buckingham. London : New York : Routledge, 2000. x, 235 p. : ill. ; 24 cm. (Media, education and culture) Includes bibliographical references (p. 225-232) and index. DDC 302.23/45/083
1. *Television and children.* 2. *Television broadcasting of news.* 3. *Children - Political activity.* I. *Title.* II. *Series.*
*TC HQ784.T4 .B847 2000*

**Buckley, Francis J.** Team teaching : what, why, and how? / Francis J. Buckley. Thousand Oaks, Calif. : Sage Publications, c2000. xiii, 127 p. ; 23 cm. Includes bibliographical references (p. 103-121) and index. ISBN 0-7619-0744-0 (pbk. : acid-free paper) DDC 371.14/8
1. *Teaching teams.* 2. *Teaching teams - Planning.* 3. *Teaching.* 4. *Teaching - Planning.* I. *Title.*
*TC LB1029.T4 B83 2000*

**Buckley, Keith.**
Pauwels, Colleen Kristl, 1946- Legal research. Bloomington, Ind. : Phi Delta Kappa Educational Foundation, c1999.
*TC KF240 .P38 1999*

**BUCOLIC ART.** *See* **PASTORAL ART.**

**Bud.**
O'Malley, Kevin, 1961- New York : Walker, 2000.
*TC PZ7.O526 Bu 2000*

**Bud, not Buddy.**
Curtis, Christopher Paul. New York : Delacorte Press, 1999.
*TC PZ7.C94137 Bu 1999*

**Buddy reading.**
Samway, Katharine Davies. Portsmouth, NH : Heinemann, c1995.
*TC LB1031.5 .S36 1995*

**BUDGETS, TIME.** *See* **TIME MANAGEMENT.**

**Budwig, Nancy.**
Communication. Stamford, Conn. : Ablex Pub. Corp., c2000.
*TC BF712 .A36 v.19*

**Buechner, Thomas S.** How I paint / Thomas S. Buechner. New York : Harry N. Abrams, 2000. 127 p. : col. ; 27 cm. Includes bibliographical references and index. ISBN 0-8109-4153-8 (hardcover) DDC 751.4
1. *Buechner, Thomas S. - Contributions in painting technique.* 2. *Painting - Technique.* I. *Title.*
*TC ND237.B8827 A4 2000*

**BUECHNER, THOMAS S. - CONTRIBUTIONS IN PAINTING TECHNIQUE.**

Buechner, Thomas S. How I paint. New York : Harry N. Abrams, 2000.
*TC ND237.B8827 A4 2000*

**Buell, John.**
Kralovec, Etta. The end of homework. Boston, Mass. : Beacon Press, c2000.
*TC LB1048 .K73 2000*

**BUFFALO, AMERICAN.** *See* **AMERICAN BISON.**

**BUFFALO BILL, 1846-1917 - EXHIBITIONS.**
White, Richard, 1947- The frontier in American culture. Chicago : The Library ; Berkeley : University of California Press, c1994.
*TC F596 .W562 1994*

**BUFFALO MEAT.** *See* **AMERICAN BISON.**

**BUHÁGANA INDIANS.** *See* **MACUNA INDIANS.**

**Buhle, Paul, 1944-** William Appleman Williams : the tragedy of empire / Paul M. Buhle and Edward Rice-Maximin. New York : Routledge, 1995. xv, 318 p. ; 24 cm. (American radicals) Includes bibliographical references (p. [297]-306) and index. ISBN 0-415-91130-3 (acid-free paper) ISBN 0-415-91131-1 (corrected : pbk. : acid-free paper) DDC 973.92/092
1. *Williams, William Appleman.* 2. *Historians - United States - Biography.* I. *Rice-Maximin, Edward Francis, 1941-* II. *Title.* III. *Series.*
*TC E175.5.W55 B84 1995*

**BUIGANA INDIANS.** *See* **MACUNA INDIANS.**

**Build it! festival.**
Gonsalves, Philip. Berkeley, CA : Great Explorations in Math and Science (GEMS), Lawrence Hall of Science, University of California at Berkeley, c1995.
*TC QA462 .G66 1995*

**Builder of the moon.**
Wynne-Jones, Tim. New York M.K. McElderry Books, c1988.
*TC PZ7.W993 Bu 1988*

**Builders and deserters.**
Konecny, Peter, 1963- Montreal : McGill-Queen's University Press, 1999.
*TC LA839.5.L45 K65 1999*

**BUILDING.** *See* **ARCHITECTURE.**

**Building a picture.**
Catalano, Gary, 1947- Sydney : McGraw-Hill, 1997.
*TC ND1100 .C28 1997*

**Building a successful school.**
Walsh, Mike. London : Kogan Page, 1999.
*TC LB2900.5 .W37 1999*

**Building America.** [New York : Published for the Dept. of Supervision and Curriculum Development by the Society for Curriculum Study, Inc. ; distributed by Americana Corporation, 1935- 13 v. : ill. ; 31 cm. Frequency: Monthly (Oct.-May). Vol. 1, no. 1 (Oct. 1935)- . Ceased publication with v. 13, 1948. Cf. Union list of serials. "Illustrated studies on modern problems" (varies). Title from cover. Individual numbers have title: Building America ; a photographic magazine of modern problems. Vol. 1 includes special edition "Housing" (undated). Published with the assistance of the Lincoln School of Teachers College, Columbia University, and the U. S. Works Progress Administration, New York. Includes bibliographies. Some nos. issued in revised editions. Vol. 1, no. 1 preceded by v. 1, special issue. DDC 051
1. *Education - Curricula - Periodicals.* 2. *Project method in teaching - Periodicals.* 3. *Social history - Periodicals.* 4. *Social problems - Periodicals.* 5. *United States - Social life and customs - Periodicals.* 6. *United States - Economic conditions - 1918-1945 - Periodicals.* 7. *United States - Social conditions - Periodicals.* 8. *United States - Social conditions - Bibliography - Periodicals.* I. *Society for Curriculum Study.* II. *National Education Association of the United States. Dept. of Supervision and Curriculum Development.*

**Building America's communities II :** a compendium of arts and community development programs / Dian Magie, contributing writer ; edited by Julie Nadezna. Washington, D.C. : Americans for the Arts (Organization) ; Institute for Community Development and the Arts, 1997. 44 p. : ill. ; 28 cm.
1. *Community art projects - United States.* 2. *Art in education - United States.* 3. *Art commissions - United States.* 4. *Community development - United States.* I. *Magie, Dian.* II. *Nadezna, Julie.* III. *Title: Compendium of arts and community development programs*
*TC NX180.A77 B95 1997*

**Building America's first university.**
Thomas, George E. Philadelphia : University of Pennsylvania Press, c2000.
*TC LD4531 .T56 1999*

**Building an emergency plan :** a guide for museums and other cultural institutions / compiled by Valerie Dorge and Sharon L. Jones. Los Angeles, Calif. : Getty Conservation Institute, c1999. viii, 272 p. : ill. ; 28 cm. Includes bibliographical references and index. ISBN 0-89236-551-X DDC 069/.2
1. *Museums - Management - Planning - Handbooks, manuals, etc.* 2. *Emergency management - Handbooks, manuals, etc.* 3. *Cultural property - Protection - Handbooks, manuals, etc.* I. *Dorge, Valerie, 1946-* II. *Jones, Sharon L., 1961-* III. *Getty Conservation Institute.*
*TC AM121 .B85 1999*

**BUILDING BLOCKS (TOYS).** *See* **BLOCKS (TOYS).**

**Building bridges :** connecting classroom and community through service-learning in social studies / edited by Rahima C. Wade. Washington, DC : National Council for the Social Studies, 2000. 116 p. ; 23 cm. (NCSS bulletin ; 97) Includes bibliographical references and index.
1. *Student service - United States.* I. *Wade, Rahima Carol.* II. *Series: Bulletin (National Council for the Social Studies) ; 97.*

**Building character and culture.**
Hutcheon, Pat Duffy. Westport, Conn. : Praeger, 1999.
*TC HQ783 .H88 1999*

**Building costs guide for educational premises.**
Spon's building costs guide for educational premises. 2nd ed. London : E & FN SPON, 1999.
*TC LB3219.G7 S67 1999*

**Building cultural reciprocity with families.**
Harry, Beth. Baltimore, Md. : P.H. Brookes Pub. Co., c1999.
*TC LC3969 .H377 1999*

**BUILDING DESIGN.** *See* **ARCHITECTURE.**

**Building dreams.** New York, N.Y. : American Book Company, c1980. 320 p. : col. ill. ; 24 cm. (American readers ; 3-1) ISBN 0-278-45821-1
1. *Readers (Primary)* I. *Series.*
*TC PE1119 .B84 1980*

**Building dreams.** Teacher's ed. New York, N.Y. : American Book Company, c1980. xvi, 519 p. : ill. (some col.) ; 28 cm. (American readers ; 3-1) Includes index. ISBN 0-278-45852-1
1. *Readers (Primary)* 2. *Reading (Primary)* I. *Series.*
*TC PE1119 .B84 1980 Teacher's Ed.*

**Building dreams.** Lexington, Mass. : D.C. Heath and Company, c1983. 352 p. : ill. (some col.) ; 24 cm. (American readers ; 3-1) ISBN 0-669-05012-1
1. *Readers (Primary)* I. *Series.*
*TC PE1119 .B84 1983*

**Building dreams.** Teacher's ed. Lexington, Mass. : D.C. Heath and Company, c1986. T32, 575 p. : ill. (some col.) ; 28 cm. (American readers ; 3-1) Includes index. ISBN 0-669-08051-9
1. *Readers (Primary)* 2. *Reading (Primary)* I. *Series.*
*TC PE1119 .B84 1986 Teacher's Ed.*

**Building dreams :** workbook. Teacher's ed. New York, N.Y. : American Book Company, c1980. 128 p. : col. ill. ; 24 cm. (American readers ; 3-1) Includes index. ISBN 0-278-45932-3
1. *Readers (Primary)* 2. *Reading (Primary)* I. *Series.*
*TC PE1119 .B84 1980 Teacher's Ed. Workbook*

**Building dreams :** workbook. Teacher's ed. Lexington, Mass. : D.C. Heath and Company, c1983. 128 p. : col. ill. ; 28 cm. (American readers ; 3-1) Includes index. ISBN 0-669-05019-9
1. *Readers (Primary)* 2. *Reading (Primary)* I. *Series.*
*TC PE1119 .B84 1983 Teacher's Ed. Workbook*

**Building effective evaluation capacity :** lessons from practice / Richard Boyle, Donald Lemaire, editors. New Brunswick, N.J. : Transaction Publishers, c1999. 202 p. ; 24 cm. (Comparative policy analysis series) Includes bibliographical references and index. ISBN 1-56000-396-0 (alk. paper) DDC 352.3/0973
1. *Administrative agencies - Evaluation.* 2. *Executive departments - Evaluation.* 3. *Bureaucracy - Evaluation.* I. *Boyle, Richard, 1955-* II. *Lemaire, Donald.* III. *Series.*
*TC JF1351 .B83 1999*

**Building family literacy in an urban community.**
Handel, Ruth D. New York : Teachers College Press, c1999.
*TC LC152.N58 H36 1999*

**Building healthy minds.**
Greenspan, Stanley I. Cambridge, MA : Perseus, 1999.
*TC HQ772 .G672 1999*

**Building lives.**
Harris, Neil, 1938- New Haven [Conn.] ; London : Yale University Press, c1999.
*TC NA2543.S6 H37 1999*

**BUILDING MATERIALS. See CERAMICS.**

**Building the best faculty.**
Clement, Mary C. Lanham, Md. : Scarecrow Press, 2000.
*TC LB2833 .C53 2000*

**Building the invisible orphanage.**
Crenson, Matthew A., 1943- Cambridge, Mass. : Harvard University Press, 1998.
*TC HV91 .C74 1998*

**Building the primary classroom.**
Bickart, Toni S. Washington, DC : Teaching Strategies ; Portsmouth, NH : Heinemann, 1999.
*TC LB1507 .B53 1999*

**Building the responsive campus.**
Tierney, William G. Thousand Oaks, Calif. : Sage, c1999.
*TC LB2341 .T584 1999*

**Building university electronic educational environments.**
IFIP TC3 WG3.2/3.6 International Working Conference on Building University Electronic Educational Environments (1999 : Irvine, Calif.) Boston : Kluwer Academic Publishers, c2000.
*TC LC5803.C65 .I352 2000*

**Building words.**
Gunning, Thomas G. Boston : London : Allyn and Bacon, c2001.
*TC LB1573.3 .G83 2001*

**BUILDINGS. See ARCHITECTURE; CHURCH BUILDINGS; DWELLINGS; HISTORIC BUILDINGS.**

**BUILDINGS - DESIGN AND CONSTRUCTION. See ARCHITECTURE.**

**Buildings for bluestockings.**
Vickery, Margaret Birney, 1963- Newark [Del.] : University of Delaware Press ; London ; Cranbury, NJ : Associated University Presses, c1999.
*TC NA6605.G7 V53 1999*

**BUILDINGS, SCHOOL. See SCHOOL BUILDINGS.**

**Bukowski, William M.**
Recent advances in the measurement of acceptance and rejection in the peer system. San Francisco : Jossey-Bass Publishers, c2000.
*TC BF723.I65 R4 2000*

**Bukowski, Wolf.**
Step on a crack [videorecording]. Boston, MA : Fanlight Productions, 1996.
*TC RC533 .S7 1996*

**Buley-Meissner, Mary Louise.**
The academy and the possibility of belief. Cresskill, N.J. : Hampton Press, c2000.
*TC LB2324 .A27 2000*

**BULIMAREXIA. See BULIMIA.**

**BULIMIA.**
Goldfein, Juli Ann. The importance of shape and weight in normal-weight women with bulimia nervosa, restrained eaters (dieters), and normal controls (Non-dieters). 1997.
*TC 085 G5675*

The management of eating disorders and obesity. Totowa, N.J. : Humana Press, c1999.
*TC RC552.E18 M364 1999*

Tobin, David L. Coping strategies therapy for bulimia nervosa. Washington, DC : American Psychological Association, c2000.
*TC RC552.B84 T63 2000*

**BULIMIA NERVOSA. See BULIMIA.**

**BULIMIA - THERAPY.**
Tobin, David L. Coping strategies therapy for bulimia nervosa. Washington, DC : American Psychological Association, c2000.
*TC RC552.B84 T63 2000*

**Bulkeley, Kelly, 1962-** Visions of the night : dreams, religion, and psychology / Kelly Bulkeley. Albany, NY : State University of New York Press, c1999. ix, 217 p. ; 24 cm. (SUNY series in dream studies) Includes bibliographical references (p. 177-211) and index. ISBN 0-7914-4283-7 (alk. paper) ISBN 0-7914-4284-5 (pbk. : alk. paper) DDC 154.6/3
*1. Dreams. 2. Dreams - Religious aspects. 3. Dream interpretation. I. Title. II. Series.*

*TC BF1091 .B94 1999*

**Bull, Joanna.**
Computer-assisted assessment in higher education. London : Kogan Page, 1999.
*TC LB2366 .C65 1999*

**Bulletin.**
University of Illinois (Urbana-Champaign campus). Bureau of Educational Research. Urbana, 1918-47.

The University of Michigan School of Education bulletin. [Ann Arbor] : The School, 1929-1964.

**Bulletin de la coopération intellectuelle.**
League of Nations. Paris : Institut international de coopération intellectuelle, [1931?-1932?]

**Bulletin (Federation for Child Study (U.S.).**
[Child study (New York, N.Y.)] Child study. [New York City] : Federation for Child Study, 1925-1960.

**Bulletin - National Catholic Educational Association.**
National Catholic Educational Association. [Washington] National Catholic Educational Association.

**Bulletin (National Council for the Social Studies)**
(94.) Introducing Canada. Washington, D.C. : National Council for the Social Studies in association with National Consortium for Teaching Canada, c1997.
*TC F1025 .I59 1997*

(96.) Surfing social studies. Washington, DC : National Council for the Social Studies, c1999.
*TC LB1044.87 .S97 1999*

(97.) Building bridges. Washington, DC : National Council for the Social Studies, 2000.

**Bulletin (new series) of the American Mathematical Society.** Providence, R.I. : The Society, 1979- v. : ill. ; 25 cm. Frequency: Quarterly, <1984->. Former frequency: Bimonthly, 1979- . Vol. 1, no. 1 (Jan. 1979)- . Bulletin of the American Mathematical Society. Title from cover. Indexed in its entirety by: General science index 0162-1963 1992-. Indexed in its entirety by: Mathematical reviews 0025-5629. Issued also online via the World Wide Web; available to subscribers with a subscription to the print version and/or with a site license, <1992-> ; files in DVI, TeX, PostScript, and PDF formats. Selected articles are reprinted in: Reprints from the Bulletin of the American Mathematical Society. URL: http://www.ams.org/journals/bull/ Available in other form: Bulletin (new series) of the American Mathematical Society (Online) ISSN: 1088-9485 (DLC)sn 96003965 (OCoLC)34778342. Continues: Bulletin of the American Mathematical Society ISSN: 0002-9904 (DLC) 15001248 (OCoLC)5797393. Reprints from the Bulletin of the American Mathematical Society ISSN: 1064-9662 (DLC)sn 92000284. ISSN 0273-0979 DDC 510/.5
*1. Mathematics - Periodicals. I. American Mathematical Society. II. Title: Bulletin of the American Mathematical Society III. Title: Bulletin (new series) of the American Mathematical Society (Online) IV. Title: Bulletin of the American Mathematical Society (Online) V. Title: Reprints from the Bulletin of the American Mathematical Society*

**Bulletin (new series) of the American Mathematical Society (Online).**
Bulletin (new series) of the American Mathematical Society. Providence, R.I. : The Society, 1979-

**Bulletin (New York State School of Industrial and Labor Relations)**
(no. 44.) Doherty, Robert Emmett, 1923- Industrial and labor relations terms. 5th ed., rev. Ithaca, NY : ILR Press, c1989.
*TC HD4839 .D6 1989*

(no. 66.) Gold, Michael Evan. An introduction to labor law. 2nd ed. Ithaca : ILR Press, c1998.
*TC KF3319 .G62 1998*

**Bulletin of Adult Education Department.**
[Journal of adult education (New York, N.Y.)] Journal of adult education. New York : American Association for Adult Education, 1929-[1941]

**Bulletin of education** / University of Kansas. Lawrence, Kan. : Bureau of School Service and Research, University of Kansas, 1926-1969. 23 v. ; 23 cm. Frequency: Three no. a year, 1932- . Former frequency: Bimonthly, 1927-1931. Vol. 1, no. 1 (Dec. 1926)-v. 23, no. 1 (Feb. 1969). Other title: University of Kansas bulletin of education. Title from cover. Suspended 1932-1949? Issued by: the Bureau of School Service and Research, 1927-193 ; by the School of Education, 193 -1969.
*1. Education - Kansas - Periodicals. 2. Education - Periodicals. I. University of Kansas. Bureau of School Service and Research. II. University of Kansas. School of Education. III. Title: University of Kansas bulletin of education*

**Bulletin of high points in the work of the high schools of New York City.**
High points in the work of the high schools of New York City. New York City : Board of Education, 1931-1966.

**Bulletin of the American Association of Collegiate Registrars.** Philadelphia, American Association of College Registrars. 12 v. ill. 23 cm. Frequency: Quarterly. v. 1-12; July 1925-July 1937. FOR HOLDINGS AND LOCATIONS SEE SERIALS SHELFLIST FOR HOLDINGS IN MICROFORM HOLDINGS SEE: Microfilm 2104 Vol. 6, no. 1 erroneously numbered v. 5, no.1. Continued by: American Association of Collegiate Registrars. Journal of the American Association of Collegiate Registrars (OCoLC)4107237.
*1. Education - Periodicals. 2. Universities and colleges - United States - Periodicals. I. American Association of Collegiate Registrars and Admissions Officers. II. Title. III. Title: American Association of Collegiate Registrars. Journal of the American Association of Collegiate Registrars*

**Bulletin of the American Mathematical Society.**
Bulletin (new series) of the American Mathematical Society. Providence, R.I. : The Society, 1979-

Bulletin (new series) of the American Mathematical Society. Providence, R.I. : The Society, 1979-

**The Bulletin of the New Hampshire State Teachers' Association.** [Manchester, N.H.] : The Association, [1946] 1 v. : ill. ; 24 cm. Frequency: Quarterly. Vol. 26, no. 1 (Jan. 1946)-v. 26, no. 4 (Oct. 1946). Title from cover. Continues: N.H.S.T.A. bulletin (OCoLC)7559661 (DLC)sc 84007494. Continued by: New Hampshire educator (DLC) 60035528 (OCoLC)7559657.
*I. New Hampshire State Teachers' Association. II. Title: N.H.S.T.A. bulletin III. Title: New Hampshire educator*

**Bulletin of the New York Society for the Experimental Study of Education.** [New York : The Society, v. : ill. ; 23-28 cm. Frequency: Monthly (Oct.-May). Ceased publication with May 1936 issue? Description based on: Vol. 3, no. 1 (Oct. 1921); title from caption. Continued in part by: Yearbook of the New York Society for the Experimental Study of Education.
*1. Education - Experimental methods - Periodicals. I. New York Society for the Experimental Study of Education. II. Title: Yearbook of the New York Society for the Experimental Study of Education*

**Bulletin to the schools ...**
University of the State of New York Albany, The University of the State of New York Press [1928-

**Bulletin trimestriel.**
Association des amis de l'Université de Liège. Liège.

**BULLYING - GREAT BRITAIN - CASE STUDIES.**
Duncan, Neil, 1956- Sexual bullying. London ; New York : Routledge, 1999.
*TC LC212.83.G7 D85 1999*

**Bullying in schools.**
Council of Europe. Council for Cultural Co-operation. Strasbourg : Council of Europe Publishing, 1999.
*TC BF637.B85 B842 1999*

**BULLYISM. See BULLYING.**

**Bulman, Chris.**
Reflective practice in nursing. 2nd ed. Oxford : Malden, MA : Blackwell Scientific, 2000.
*TC RT73 .R3461 2000*

**Bumby, Douglas R.** Mathematics : a topical approach / Douglas Bumby, Richard Klutch. 2nd ed. Columbus, Ohio : C.E. Merrill, c1982-<1986.> <v.2> : col. ill., ports., photos. ; 25 cm. High school text, integrating algebra and geometry. Includes indexes. ISBN 0-675-05754-X (course 1, teacher's ed.) ISBN 0-675-05757-4 (course 2, teacher's ed.) ISBN 0-675-05756-6 (course 2) ISBN 0-675-05424-9 (course 3, teacher's ed.)
*1. Algebra - Study and teaching (Secondary) 2. Geometry - Study and teaching (Secondary) 3. Mathematics - Study and teaching (Secondary) I. Klutch. Richard J. II. Charles E. Merrill Publishing Company. III. Title.*

*TC QA154.2 .B8 1982*

Mathematics : a topical approach / Douglas R. Bumby, Richard J. Klutch. Columbus, Ohio : C.E. Merrill, c1978-1979. 3 v. : ill. ; 24 cm. Includes indexes. ISBN 0-675-05410-9 (v. 1) ISBN 0-675-05416-8 (v. 3)
*1. Mathematics. I. Klutch, Richard J., joint author. II. Title.*

*TC QA39.2 .B85 1980*

**Bunkers, Suzanne L.**
Gillespie, Sarah (Sarah L.) A pioneer farm girl. Mankato, Minn. : Blue Earth Books, c2000.
*TC F629.M28 G55 2000*

**Bunting, Eve, 1928-** Blackwater / Eve Bunting. 1st ed. New York : Joanna Cotler Books, 1999. 146 p. ; 22 cm. SUMMARY: When a boy and girl are drowned in the

Blackwater River, thirteen-year-old Brodie must decide whether to confess that he may have caused the accident. ISBN 0-06-027838-2 ISBN 0-06-027843-9 (lib. bdg.) DDC [Fic]
*1. Drowning - Fiction. 2. Death - Fiction. 3. Guilt - Fiction. I. Title.*
*TC PZ7.B91527 Bne 1999*

I have an olive tree / by Eve Bunting ; illustrated by Karen Barbour. 1st ed. New York : HarperCollins Publishers, c1999. 1 v. (unpaged) : col. ill. ; 23 x 26 cm. "Joanna Cotler books." SUMMARY: After her grandfather's death, eight-year-old Sophia fulfills his last request and journeys to Greece with her mother to see the land where her roots are. ISBN 0-06-027573-1 ISBN 0-06-027574-X (lib. bdg.) DDC [E]
*1. Greek Americans - Juvenile fiction. 2. Greek Americans - Fiction. 3. Greece - Fiction. I. Barbour, Karen, ill. II. Title.*
*TC PZ7.B91527 Iaar 1999*

**Bunwaree, Sheila S.**
Gender, education, and development. London : New York : Zed Books ; New York : Distributed in USA exclusively by St. Martin's Press, c1999.
*TC LC2607 .G46 1998*

**Buqtur, Amīr, 1896-1966.**
Majallat al-tarbiyah al-ḥadīthah. al-Qāhirah : al-Jāmi'ah al-Amrīkīyah bi-al-Qāhirah, 1928- .

**Buranen, Lise, 1954-.**
Perspectives on plagiarism and intellectual property in a postmodern world. Albany : State University of New York Press, c1999.
*TC PN167 .P47 1999*

**Burbules, Nicholas C.**
Globalization and education. New York : Routledge, 1999.
*TC LC191 .G545 1999*

Watch IT : the risks and promises of information technologies for education / Nicholas C. Burbules, Thomas A. Callister, Jr. Boulder, Colo. : Westview Press, 2000. xiii, 188 p. ; 23 cm. Includes bibliographical references and index. ISBN 0-8133-9083-4 (alk. paper) ISBN 0-8133-9082-6 (pbk. : alk. paper) DDC 370.11/5
*1. Educational technology - United States. 2. Education - Technological innovations - United States. 3. Educational anthropology - United States. 4. Information technology - United States. I. Callister, Thomas A. II. Title.*
*TC LB1028.43 .B87 2000*

**Burch, Kerry T., 1957-** Eros as the educational principle of democracy / Kerry T. Burch. New York : P. Lang, c2000. xiv, 223 p. ; 23 cm. (Counterpoints ; vol. 114) Includes bibliographical references (p. [205]-216) and index. ISBN 0-8204-4481-2 (pbk. : alk. paper) DDC 370.11/5
*1. Critical pedagogy. 2. Democracy - Study and teaching. 3. Love. 4. Feminism and education. I. Title. II. Series: Counterpoints (New York, N.Y.) ; vol. 114.*
*TC LC196 .B75 2000*

**Burdick, Eugene.** Fail-safe / Eugene Burdick & Harvey Wheeler. 1st Ecco ed. Hopewell, N.J. : Ecco Press ; New York, NY : Distributed by W.W. Norton, 1999. 286 p. ; 21 cm. ISBN 0-88001-654-X (pbk.) DDC 813/.54
*1. Political fiction. 2. United States - Foreign relations - Soviet Union - Fiction. 3. Soviet Union - Foreign relations - United States - Fiction. 4. Nuclear weapons - Accidents - Fiction. 5. Cold war - Fiction. I. Wheeler, Harvey, 1918- II. Title.*
*TC PS3552.U7116 F35 1999*

Lederer, William J., 1912- The ugly American. 1st ed. New York : Norton, 1958.
*TC PS3523 .E27U35 1958*

**BUREAU OF MUNICIPAL RESEARCH (NEW YORK, N.Y.) - HISTORY.**
Schachter, Hindy Lauer. Reinventing government or reinventing ourselves. Albany : State University of New York Press, c1997.
*TC JK1764 .S35 1997*

**Bureau of National Affairs (Washington, D.C.).**
Demetriou, Andrew J. Health care integration. Washington, D.C. : Bureau of National Affairs, Inc., c1996.
*TC KF3825 .D394 1996*

**BUREAUCRACY.**
Haass, Richard. The bureaucratic entrepreneur. Washington, D.C. : Brookings Institution, c1999.
*TC JF1351 .H2 1999*

**BUREAUCRACY - EVALUATION.**
Building effective evaluation capacity. New Brunswick, N.J. : Transaction Publishers, c1999.
*TC JF1351 .B83 1999*

**The bureaucratic entrepreneur.**
Haass, Richard. Washington, D.C. : Brookings Institution, c1999.

*TC JF1351 .H2 1999*

**Burgess, Thomas K.**
Jenney, Charles. Jenney's first year Latin. Needham, Mass. : Prentice Hall, c1990.
*TC PA2087.5 .J46 1990*

**Burke, Jim, 1961-** The English teachers' companion : a complete guide to classroom, curriculum, and the profession / Jim Burke ; [foreword by Fran Claggett]. Portsmouth, NH : Boynton/Cook, c1999. xviii, 366 p. : ill. ; 24 cm. Includes bibliographical references (p. 349-354) and index. ISBN 0-86709-475-3 (acid-free paper) DDC 428/.0071/2
*1. English philology - Study and teaching - Handbooks, manuals, etc. I. Claggett, Mary Frances. II. Title.*
*TC PE65 .B87 1999*

I hear America reading. Portsmouth, NH : Heinemann, c1999.
*TC Z1003.2 .I34 1999*

**Burleigh, Robert.** Flight : the journey of Charles Lindbergh / Robert Burleigh ; illustrated by Mike Wimmer ; introduction by Jean Fritz. New York : Philomel Books, c1991. 1 v. (unpaged) : col. ill. ; 29 cm. SUMMARY: Describes how Charles Lindbergh achieved the remarkable feat of flying nonstop and solo from New York to Paris in 1927. ISBN 0-399-22272-3 DDC 629.13/09111; 92
*1. Lindbergh, Charles A. - (Charles Augustus), - 1902-1974 - Juvenile literature. 2. Transatlantic flights - Juvenile literature. 3. Lindbergh, Charles A. - (Charles Augustus), - 1902-1974. 4. Air pilots. 5. Transatlantic flights. I. Wimmer, Mike. II. Title.*
*TC TL540.L5 B83 1991*

**BURN OUT (PSYCHOLOGY).**
Jevne, Ronna Fay. When dreams don't work. Amityville, N.Y. : Baywood Pub., c1998.
*TC BF481 .J48 1998*

Professional burnout. Washington, DC : Taylor & Francis, c1993.
*TC BF481 .P77 1993*

**BURN OUT (PSYCHOLOGY) - PREVENTION.**
Brock, Barbara L. Rekindling the flame. Thousand Oaks, Calif. : Corwin Press, c2000.
*TC LB2840.2 .B76 2000*

**Burnard, Philip.** Counselling skills for health professionals / Philip Burnard. 3rd ed. Cheltenham, U.K. : Stanley Thornes, 1999. ix, 256 p. : ill. ; 24 cm. Includes bibliographical references (p. 242-250) and index. ISBN 0-7487-3976-9 DDC 158/.3
*1. Counseling. 2. Medical personnel - Psychology. I. Title.*
*TC BF637.C6 B82 1999*

**Burnett, Frances Hodgson, 1849-1924.**
**Secret garden.**
Cotler, Amy. The secret garden cookbook. 1st ed. New York : HarperCollins Publishers, c1999.
*TC TX717 .C588 1999*

**Burnett, Joanne, 1961-.**
Foreign language standards. Lincolnwood, Ill., U.S.A. : National Textbook Company in conjunction with the American Council on the Teaching of Foreign Languages, c1999.
*TC P53 .F674 1999*

**Burnett, John, 1925-** Liquid pleasures : a social history of drinks in modern Britain / John Burnett. London ; New York : Routledge, 1999. viii, 254 p. : ill. ; 24 cm. Includes bibliographical references (p. [191]-244) and index. ISBN 0-415-13181-2 (hbk.) ISBN 0-415-13182-0 (pbk.) DDC 641.2/0941
*1. Beverages - Great Britain - History. 2. Beverages - Social aspects - Great Britain. I. Title.*
*TC TX815 .B87 1999*

**Burning up.**
Cooney, Caroline B. New York : Delacorte Press, c1999.
*TC PZ7.C7834 Bu 1999*

**Burningham, John.** Whaddayamean / John Burningham. 1st American ed. New York : Crown Publishers, 1999. 1 v. (unpaged) : col. ill. ; 24 x 30 cm. SUMMARY: When God sees what a mess has been made of the world, God gets two children to convince everyone to help make it the lovely place it was meant to be. ISBN 0-375-80177-4 (tr.) ISBN 0-375-90177-9 (GLB) ISBN 0-517-80066-7 (trade) ISBN 0-517-80067-5 (lib. bdg.)
*1. God - Fiction. <Juvenile subject heading>. 2. Environmental protection - Fiction. <Juvenile subject heading>. I. Title.*
*TC PZ7.B936 We 1999*

**BURNOUT, PROFESSIONAL - CONGRESSES.**
Professional burnout. Washington, DC : Taylor & Francis, c1993.
*TC BF481 .P77 1993*

**BURNOUT (PSYCHOLOGY).** *See* **BURN OUT (PSYCHOLOGY).**

**Burns, Catherine E.**
Pocket reference for Pediatric primary care. Philadelphia ; London : Saunders, c2001.
*TC RJ45 .P525 2001*

**Burns, Robert E., 1927-** Being Catholic, being American : the Notre Dame story, 1842-1934 / Robert E. Burns. Notre Dame, Ind. : University of Notre Dame Press, c1999. xii, 595 p. : ill. ; 24 cm. (The Mary and Tim Gray series for the study of Catholic higher education) Includes bibliographical references (p. 579-583) and index. ISBN 0-268-02156-2 (hc. : acid-free paper) DDC 378.772/89
*1. University of Notre Dame - History. I. Title. II. Title: Notre Dame story, 1842-1934 III. Series.*
*TC LD4113 .B87 1999*

**Burns, Sarah, DN.**
Reflective practice in nursing. 2nd ed. Oxford ; Malden, MA : Blackwell Scientific, 2000.
*TC RT73 .R3461 2000*

**Burreson, C. (Cynthia).**
Deuschle, C. (Constance) Stop the bus. Lanham, Md. : University Press of America, c2000.
*TC LB1027.5 .D4567 2000*

**Burridge, Keith R.**
Landy, Joanne M. Ready-to-use fundamental motor skills & movement activities for young children. West Nyack, NY : Center for Applied Research in Education, c1999.
*TC GV452 .L355 1999*

**Bursak, George J., 1913-** If I can do it, so can you : triumph over dyslexia / by George J. Bursak. [S.l.] : G.J. Bursak, c1999. xiii, 47 p. : ill. ; 24 cm. DDC 362.1/968553/0092
*1. Bursak, George J. - 1913- 2. Dyslexics - United States - Biography. 3. Industrial designers - United States - Biography. I. Title.*
*TC RC394.W6 B87 1999*

**BURSAK, GEORGE J., 1913-.**
Bursak, George J., 1913- If I can do it, so can you. [S.l.] : G.J. Bursak, c1999.
*TC RC394.W6 B87 1999*

**BURSARIES.** *See* **SCHOLARSHIPS.**

**Burston, Daniel, 1954-** The crucible of experience : R.D. Laing and the crisis of psychotherapy / Daniel Burston. Cambridge, Mass. : Harvard University Press, c2000. viii, 168 p. ; 24 cm. Includes bibliographical references (p. [157]-164) and index. ISBN 0-674-00217-2 (alk. paper) DDC 616.89/14/01
*1. Laing, R. D. - (Ronald David), - 1927- 2. Psychotherapy - Philosophy. 3. Existential psychotherapy. 4. Antipsychiatry. I. Title.*
*TC RC438.6.L34 B86 2000*

**Burstyn, Varda.** The rites of men : manhood, politics, and the culture of sport / Varda Burstyn. Toronto ; Buffalo : University of Toronto Press, 1999. xvi, 388 p. ; 24 cm. Includes bibliographical references and index. ISBN 0-8020-2844-6 (bound) ISBN 0-8020-7725-0 (pbk.) DDC 306.4/83
*1. Sports - Social aspects. 2. Masculinity (Psychology) I. Title.*
*TC GV706.5 .B87 1999*

**Burton, David, 1952-** The Raj at table : a culinary history of the British in India / David Burton. London ; Boston : Faber, 1994. xii, 240 p. : ill., map ; 24 cm. ISBN 0-571-14389-X DDC 641.5954
*1. Cookery, Indic. 2. Cookery, British. 3. British - India - Social life and customs. I. Title.*
*TC TX724.5.I4 B87 1993*

**Burton, John W. (John Wear), 1915-** Conflict resolution : its language and processes / John W. Burton. Lanham, Md. : Scarecrow Press, 1996. 86 p. ; 22 cm. Includes bibliographical references and index. ISBN 0-8108-3265-8 ISBN 0-8108-3214-5 (pbk.: alk. paper) DDC 303.6/9
*1. Conflict management. 2. Conflict management - Terminology. I. Title.*
*TC HM136 .B786 1996*

**Burwell, Helen P.** Online competitive intelligence : Increase your profits using cyber-intelligence / Helen P. Burwell. Tempe, AZ : Facts on Demand Press, c1999. [x], 464 p. : ill. ; 25 cm. Includes bibliographical references and index. ISBN 1-88915-008-8 (pbk.)
*1. Business intelligence. 2. Business intelligence - Computer network resources. 3. Internet. 4. Web sites. I. Title.*
*TC HD38.7 .B974 1999*

**Burwood, Sarah.**
Phillips, Diane. Projects with young learners. Oxford ; New York : Oxford University Press, c1999.

*TC LB1576 .P577 1999*

**Burz, Helen L.**
**From knowing to showing.**
Burz, Helen L. Performance-based curriculum for music and the visual arts. Thousand Oaks, Calif. : Corwin Press, c1999.
*TC LB1591 .B84 1999*

Performance-based curriculum for music and the visual arts : from knowing to showing / Helen L. Burz, Kit Marshall. Thousand Oaks, Calif. : Corwin Press, c1999. viii, 127 p. : ill. ; 30 cm. (From knowing to showing) Includes bibliographical references (p. 125-127).
ISBN 0-7619-7535-7 (cloth : acid-free paper) ISBN 0-7619-7536-5 (pbk. : acid-free paper) DDC 700/.71
*1. Arts - Study and teaching. 2. Music - Instruction and study. 3. Competency based education. I. Marshall, Kit. II. Title. III. Series: Burz, Helen L. From knowing to showing.*
*TC LB1591 .B84 1999*

**Buschman, Isabel, 1927-** Handweaving : an annotated bibliography / by Isabel Buschman. Metuchen, N.J. : Scarecrow Press, 1991. vii, 250 p. ; 23 cm. Includes indexes. ISBN 0-8108-2403-5 (acid-free paper) DDC 016.7461/4
*1. Hand weaving - Bibliography. I. Title.*
*TC Z6153.T4 B87 1991*

**Buse, William Joseph.** The alternate session : memory and membership in a psychoanalytic society / by William Joseph Buse. 1999. ix, 282 leaves : ill. ; 29 cm. Typescript; issued also on microfilm. Thesis (Ph.D.)-- Columbia University, 1999. Includes bibliographical references (leaves 270-278).
*1. Nietzsche, Friedrich Wilhelm, - 1844-1900. 2. Freud, Sigmund, - 1856-1939. 3. Psychoanalysis - United States. 4. Psychoanalysts - Training of - United States. 5. Psychoanalytic interpretation - United States. 6. Memory - Research - United States. 7. Societies - United States. I. Title.*
*TC 085 B9603*

**Bush, Julia.** Edwardian ladies and imperial power / Julia Bush. London ; New York : Leicester University Press, 2000. xi, 242 p., 8 p. of plates : ill. ; 25 cm. (Women, power, and politics) Includes bibliographical references (p. [223]-231) and index. ISBN 0-7185-0061-X (hardcover) DDC 325/.32/0820941
*1. Women in politics - Great Britain - History - 20th century. 2. Imperialism - Social aspects - Great Britain - History - 20th century. 3. Power (Social sciences) - Great Britain - History - 20th century. 4. Great Britain - Colonies - Politics and government. 5. Great Britain - Politics and government - 1901-1910. I. Title. II. Series.*
*TC DA16 .B87 2000*

**Bush, Timothy, ill.**
Ketcham, Sallie. Bach's big adventure. New York : Orchard Books, 1999.
*TC PZ7.K488 Bac 1999*

**BUSINESS.** *See also* **BUSINESS ENTERPRISES; INDUSTRIAL MANAGEMENT; SMALL BUSINESS; SOCIAL RESPONSIBILITY OF BUSINESS; WEALTH.**
Viney, John. Drive. 1st U.S. ed. New York, N.Y. : Bloomsbury, 1999.
*TC HD57.7 .V564 1999*

**Business @ the speed of thought.**
Gates, Bill, 1955- New York, NY : Warner Books, c1999.
*TC HD30.37 .G38 1999*

**BUSINESS ADMINISTRATION.** *See* **INDUSTRIAL MANAGEMENT.**

**BUSINESS AND EDUCATION.** *See* **INDUSTRY AND EDUCATION.**

**Business and legal forms for illustrators.**
Crawford, Tad, 1946- Rev. ed. New York : Allworth Press, c1998.
*TC KF390.A7 C7 1998*

**BUSINESS AND SOCIAL PROBLEMS.** *See* **INDUSTRIES - SOCIAL ASPECTS.**

**BUSINESS - AUTHORSHIP.** *See* **BUSINESS WRITING.**

**BUSINESS, CHOICE OF.** *See* **VOCATIONAL GUIDANCE.**

**BUSINESS COMMUNICATION.** *See* **BUSINESS WRITING.**

**BUSINESS COMMUNICATION - INTERACTIVE MULTIMEDIA.**
Weintraub, Robert Steven. Informal learning in the workplace through desktop technology. 1998.
*TC 06 no. 11003*

**BUSINESS CORPORATIONS.** *See* **CORPORATIONS.**

**BUSINESS CYCLES.** *See* **DEPRESSIONS.**

**Business-driven action learning :** global best practices / edited by Yury Boshyk. New York : St. Martin's Press, 2000. xvii, 264 p. : ill. ; 25 cm. Includes bibliographical references and index. ISBN 0-312-23094-X (cloth) DDC 658.3/124
*1. Organizational learning - Case studies. 2. International business enterprises - Management - Study and teaching - Case studies. 3. Executives - Training of - Case studies. I. Boshyk, Yuri.*
*TC HD58.82 .B87 2000*

**BUSINESS EDUCATION.**
Business education and training. Lanham, Md. : University Press of America, c1997-<c2000 >
*TC LC1059 .B87*

**Business education and training :** a value-laden process / editor, Samuel M. Natale, assistant editor, Mark B. Fenton. Lanham, Md. : University Press of America, c1997-<c2000 > v. 6-7 > : ill. ; 24 cm. Includes bibliographical references and indexes. CONTENTS: v. 1. Education and value conflict -- v. 3. Instilling values in the educational process -- v. 4. Corporate structures, business, and the management of values -- v. 5. The management of values : organizational and educational issues -- v. 6. On the threshold of the millennium -- v.7. New wine in old bottles ISBN 0-7618-0568-0 (v. 1 : cloth : alk. paper) ISBN 0-7618-0569-9 (v. 1 : paper : alk. paper) DDC 378/.013
*1. Professional education. 2. Professional employees - Training of. 3. Business education. 4. Values. I. Natale, Samuel M. II. Fenton, Mark B.*
*TC LC1059 .B87*

**BUSINESS EDUCATION - CANADA - HISTORY.**
Capitalizing knowledge. Toronto : University of Toronto Press, c2000.
*TC HF1131 .C36 2000*

**BUSINESS EDUCATION - CONGRESSES.**
Educating entrepreneurs for wealth creation. Aldershot, Hants, England ; Brookfield, USA : Ashgate, 1998.
*TC HF1106 .E378 1998*

Education, leadership, and business ethics. Boston, MA : Kluwer Academic Publishers, c1998.
*TC HF5387 .E346 1998*

Educational innovation in economics and business. IV, Learning in a changing environment. Boston, MA : Kluwer Academic Publishers, c1999.
*TC HB74.5 .E3333 1999*

**Business education forum.**
Business education forum. Reston, Va., National Business Education Association.

**Business education forum.** Reston, Va., National Business Education Association. v. ill. 29 cm. Frequency: Eight nos. a year (Oct. to May). "Official journal of the National Business Education Association." Indexed by: Business education index. Indexed in its entirety by: Education index 0013-1385. Indexed selectively by: Current index to journals in education 0011-3565. Available on microfilm. Available in other form: Business education forum ISSN: 0007-6678. Continues: UBEA forum. Absorbed: National business education quarterly v.25, no. 1, Oct. 1970. ISSN 0007-6678
*I. National Business Education Association. II. Title: Business education forum III. Title: UBEA forum IV. Title: National business education quarterly v.25, no. 1, Oct. 1970*

**BUSINESS EDUCATION - PERIODICALS.**
The Journal of business education New York City, The Haire Publishing Company.

Management learning. London ; Thousand Oaks, CA : Sage Publications, c1994-

**BUSINESS ENGLISH.** *See* **ENGLISH LANGUAGE - BUSINESS ENGLISH.**

**BUSINESS ENTERPRISES.** *See* **CORPORATIONS; INTERNATIONAL BUSINESS ENTERPRISES; WOMEN-OWNED BUSINESS ENTERPRISES.**

**BUSINESS ENTERPRISES - COMMUNICATION SYSTEMS.**
Gates, Bill, 1955- Business @ the speed of thought. New York, NY : Warner Books, c1999.
*TC HD30.37 .G38 1999*

**BUSINESS ENTERPRISES - COMPUTER NETWORK RESOURCES.**
Bergan, Helen, 1937- Where the information is. Alexandria, VA : BioGuide Press, c1996.

*TC HD62.6 .B47 1996*

**BUSINESS ENTERPRISES - COMPUTER NETWORKS.**
Gates, Bill, 1955- Business @ the speed of thought. New York, NY : Warner Books, c1999.
*TC HD30.37 .G38 1999*

**BUSINESS ENTERPRISES, INTERNATIONAL.** *See* **INTERNATIONAL BUSINESS ENTERPRISES.**

**BUSINESS ENTERPRISES - MANAGEMENT.** *See* **INDUSTRIAL MANAGEMENT.**

**BUSINESS ENTERPRISES - SOCIAL ASPECTS.** *See* **INDUSTRIES - SOCIAL ASPECTS.**

**BUSINESS ESPIONAGE.** *See* **BUSINESS INTELLIGENCE.**

**BUSINESS ETHICS.** *See also* **BUSINESS INTELLIGENCE; SOCIAL RESPONSIBILITY OF BUSINESS.**
Managerial ethics. Mahwah, N.J. : Lawrence Erlbaum Assocs., 1998.
*TC HF5387 .M3345 1998*

Solomon, Robert C. A better way to think about business. New York : Oxford University Press, 1999.
*TC HF5387 .S612 1999*

**BUSINESS ETHICS - CONGRESSES.**
Education, leadership, and business ethics. Boston, MA : Kluwer Academic Publishers, c1998.
*TC HF5387 .E346 1998*

**BUSINESS ETHICS - STUDY AND TEACHING - CONGRESSES.**
Education, leadership, and business ethics. Boston, MA : Kluwer Academic Publishers, c1998.
*TC HF5387 .E346 1998*

**BUSINESS ETIQUETTE.**
Pervola, Cindy, 1956- How to get a job if you're a teenager. Fort Atkinson, Wis. : Alleyside Press, 1998.
*TC HF5383 .P44 1998*

**BUSINESS EXECUTIVES.** *See* **EXECUTIVES.**

**BUSINESS FORECASTING.**
Schwartz, Peter. The art of the long view. 1st Currency pbk. ed. New York : Currency Doubleday ; 1996.
*TC HD30.28 .S316 1996*

**BUSINESS INCUBATORS.** *See* **ENTREPRENEURSHIP.**

**BUSINESS INFORMATION SERVICES.**
Bergan, Helen, 1937- Where the information is. Alexandria, VA : BioGuide Press, c1996.
*TC HD62.6 .B47 1996*

**BUSINESS INTELLIGENCE.**
Burwell, Helen P. Online competitive intelligence. Tempe, AZ : Facts on Demand Press, c1999.
*TC HD38.7 .B974 1999*

**BUSINESS INTELLIGENCE - COMPUTER NETWORK RESOURCES.**
Burwell, Helen P. Online competitive intelligence. Tempe, AZ : Facts on Demand Press, c1999.
*TC HD38.7 .B974 1999*

**BUSINESS MANAGEMENT.** *See* **INDUSTRIAL MANAGEMENT.**

**BUSINESS MEN.** *See* **BUSINESSMEN.**

**BUSINESS NETWORKING.** *See* **BUSINESS NETWORKS.**

**BUSINESS NETWORKS.**
Chisholm, Rupert F. Developing network organizations. Reading, Mass. : Addison-Wesley, c1998.
*TC HD69.S8 C45 1998*

**BUSINESS NETWORKS - CASE STUDIES.**
Chisholm, Rupert F. Developing network organizations. Reading, Mass. : Addison-Wesley, c1998.
*TC HD69.S8 C45 1998*

**The business of memory :** the art of remembering in an age of forgetting / edited by Charles Baxter. Saint Paul, Minn. : Graywolf Press, c1999. x, 174 p. ; 23 cm. (Graywolf forum, 1088-3347 ; 3) ISBN 1-55597-287-X DDC 153.1/2
*1. Autobiographical memory - Miscellanea. I. Baxter, Charles, 1947- II. Series.*
*TC BF378.A87 B87 1999*

**BUSINESS ORGANIZATIONS.** *See* **BUSINESS ENTERPRISES.**

**BUSINESS PATRONAGE OF THE ARTS.** *See* ART PATRONAGE.

**BUSINESS PEOPLE.** *See* BUSINESSPEOPLE.

**BUSINESS PERSONS.** *See* BUSINESSPEOPLE.

**BUSINESS PLANNING.** *See* STRATEGIC PLANNING.

**BUSINESS PSYCHOLOGY.** *See* PSYCHOLOGY, INDUSTRIAL.

**Business school journal.**
The Journal of business education New York City, The Haire Publishing Company.

**BUSINESS SCHOOLS.**
Crainer, Stuart. Gravy training. 1st ed. San Francisco : Jossey-Bass Publishers, c1999.
*TC HF1111 .C7 1999*

**BUSINESS - SOCIAL ASPECTS.** *See* INDUSTRIES - SOCIAL ASPECTS.

**BUSINESS - SOCIAL RESPONSIBILITY.** *See* SOCIAL RESPONSIBILITY OF BUSINESS.

**BUSINESS - STUDY AND TEACHING.** *See* BUSINESS EDUCATION.

**BUSINESS TELEVISION.** *See* INDUSTRIAL TELEVISION.

**BUSINESS WRITING.**
Stockard, Olivia. The write approach. San Diego, Calif. : Academic Press, c1999.
*TC HF5718.3 .S764 1999*

**BUSINESS WRITING - STUDY AND TEACHING.**
Worlds apart. Mahwah, N.J. : L. Erlbaum Associates, 1999.
*TC PE1404 .W665 1999*

**BUSINESSMEN - UNITED STATES - BIOGRAPHY.**
Sanger, Martha Frick Symington. Henry Clay Frick. 1st ed. New York : Abbeville Press Publishers, c1998.
*TC HC102.5.F75 S32 1998*

**BUSINESSPEOPLE.** *See* BUSINESSMEN; BUSINESSWOMEN; CAPITALISTS AND FINANCIERS.

**BUSINESSPEOPLE - PROFESSIONAL ETHICS.** *See* BUSINESS ETHICS.

**BUSINESSPEOPLE - TRAINING OF - CONGRESSES.**
Educating entrepreneurs for wealth creation. Aldershot, Hants, England ; Brookfield, USA : Ashgate, 1998.
*TC HF1106 .E378 1998*

**BUSINESSPERSONS.** *See* BUSINESSPEOPLE.

**BUSINESSWOMEN.** *See* WOMEN-OWNED BUSINESS ENTERPRISES.

**BUSINESSWOMEN - UNITED STATES - CONGRESSES.**
A look backward and forward at American professional women and their families. Lanham : University Press of America, 1999.
*TC HQ759.48 .L66 1999*

**BUSINESSWOMEN - UNITED STATES - HISTORY.**
Kwolek-Folland, Angel. Incorporating women. New York : Twayne Publishers, 1998.
*TC HD6095 .K85 1998*

**Buss, David M.** The dangerous passion : why jealousy is as necessary as love and sex / David M. Buss. New York : Free Press, 2000. xi, 258 p. ; 25 cm. Includes bibliographical references and index. ISBN 0-684-85081-8 DDC 152.4/8
*1. Jealousy. I. Title.*
*TC BF575.J4 B87 2000*

**Bustamante, Eduardo M.** Treating the disruptive adolescent : finding the real child behind oppositional defiant disorders / Eduardo M. Bustamante. Northvale, NJ : Jason Aronson, c2000. xxv, 468 p. ; 24 cm. Includes bibliographical references and index. ISBN 0-7657-0235-5 DDC 616.89/00835
*1. Oppositional defiant disorder in adolescence. 2. Attention-deficit disorder in adolescence. I. Title.*
*TC RJ506.O66 B87 2000*

**Butcher, James Neal, 1933-** A beginner's guide to the MMPI-2 / James N. Butcher. 1st ed. Washington, DC : American Psychological Association, c1999. xiii, 225 p. : ill. ; 27 cm. Includes bibliographical references (p. 207-212) and index. ISBN 1-55798-564-2 (hardcover : alk. paper) DDC 155.2/83
*1. Minnesota Multiphasic Personality Inventory. I. Title.*

*TC BF698.8.M5 B86 1999*

**Butler, Brian S.**
Kaufer, David S. Designing interactive worlds with words. Mahwah, N.J. : Lawrence Erlbaum Associates, 2000.
*TC PE1404 .K38 2000*

**Butler, John M.** Quantitative naturalistic research; an introduction to naturalistic observation and investigation [by] John M. Butler, Laura N. Rice [and] Alice K. Wagstaff in collaboration with Sarah Counts Knapp. Englewood Cliffs, N.J., Prentice-Hall [1963] 122 p. illus. 24 cm. DDC 151.26
*1. Factor analysis. I. Title.*
*TC BF39 .B83*

**Butler, Roger.** Poster art in Australia : the streets as art galleries : walls sometimes speak / Roger Butler. Canberra : National Gallery of Australia, 1993. 104 p. : col. ill. ; 30 cm. "Published ... in conjunction with the exhibition The streets as art galleries-- walls sometimes speak: poster art in Australia, National Gallery of Australia, Canberra, 5 November 1993-6 February 1994"--T.p. verso. Includes bibliographical references (p. 103-104). ISBN 0-642-13020-5 DDC 741.6/74/09940749471
*1. Posters, Australian - Exhibitions. 2. Posters - 19th century - Australia - Exhibitions. 3. Posters - 20th century - Australia - Exhibitions. 4. Posters - Australia - Canberra (A.C.T.) - Exhibitions. 5. National Gallery of Australia - Exhibitions. I. National Gallery of Australia. II. Title. III. Title: Streets as art galleries IV. Title: Walls sometimes speak*
*TC NC1807.A78 B88 1993*

**Butler, Tim, 1949-.**
Eastern promise. London : Lawrence and Wishart, 2000.
*TC LC238.4.G73 L66 2000*

**Butler, William T.**
Institute of Medicine (U.S.). Committee on Prevention and Control of Sexually Transmitted Diseases. The hidden epidemic. Washington, D.C. : National Academy Press, 1997.
*TC RA644.V4 I495 1997*

**Butor, Michael.**
Photomontage today, Peter Kennard [videorecording]. [London] : Art Council of Great Britain ; Ho-Ho-Kus, N.J. : [distributed by] Anthony Roland Collection of Films on Art, c1982.
*TC TR685 .P45 1982*

**Buttlar, Lois, 1934-.**
Education, a guide to reference and information sources.
O'Brien, Nancy P. Education, a guide to reference and information sources. 2nd ed. Englewood, Colo. : Libraries Unlimited, 2000.
*TC Z5811 .B89 2000*

**Buttons.**
Cole, Brock. 1st ed. New York : Farrar Straus Giroux, 2000.
*TC PZ7.C67342 Bu 2000*

**BUYERS' GUIDES.** *See* CONSUMER EDUCATION.

**Buzzeo, Toni.** Terrific connections with authors, illustrators, and storytellers : real space and virtual links / Toni Buzzeo, Jane Kurtz. Englewood, Colo. : Libraries Unlimited, 1999. xii, 185 p. ; 28 cm. Includes bibliographical references (p. 161-171) and indexes. ISBN 1-56308-744-8 (paper) DDC 372.64/044
*1. Children's literature - Study and teaching (Elementary) - United States. 2. Authors and readers - United States. 3. Internet (Computer network) in education - United States. I. Kurtz, Jane. II. Title. III. Title: Terrific connections*
*TC LB1575.5.U5 B87 1999*

**BWS (BATTERED WOMAN SYNDROME).** *See* BATTERED WOMAN SYNDROME.

**By a blazing blue sea.**
Garne, S. T. San Diego : Harcourt Brace & Co., 1999.
*TC PZ8.3.G1866 By 1999*

**Bybee, Rodger W.** Achieving scientific literacy : from purposes to practices / Rodger W. Bybee. Portsmouth, NH : Heinemann, c1997. xvi, 265 p. ; 24 cm. Includes bibliographical references (p. 233-254) and index. ISBN 0-435-07134-3 DDC 507.1/073
*1. Science - Study and teaching - United States. 2. Literacy - United States. I. Title.*
*TC Q183.3.A1 B92 1997*

**Byng, Sally, 1956-.**
The aphasia therapy file. Hove : Psychology Press, c1999.
*TC RC425 .A665 1999*

Parr, Susie, 1953- Talking about aphasia. Buckingham ; Philadelphia : Open University Press, 1997.
*TC RC425 .P376 1997*

**Byrd, David M.**
Research on effective models for teacher education. Thousand Oaks, Calif. : Corwin Press, Inc., c2000.
*TC LB1715 .R42 2000*

Research on professional development schools. Thousand Oaks, Calif. : Corwin Press, c1999.
*TC LB2154.A3 R478 1999*

**Byrne, Barbara M.** Structural equation modeling with LISREL, PRELIS, and SIMPLIS : basic concepts, applications, and programming / Barbara M. Byrne. Mahwah, N.J. : L. Erlbaum Associates, 1998. xiii, 412 p. : ill. ; 24 cm. (Multivariate applications book series) Includes bibliographical references and indexes. ISBN 0-8058-2924-5 (acid-free paper) DDC 519.5/35
*1. Multivariate analysis. 2. Social sciences - Statistical methods. I. Title. II. Series.*
*TC QA278 .B97 1998*

**Byrne, F. J. (Francis John), 1934-.**
A new history of Ireland. Oxford [England] : Clarendon Press ; New York : Oxford University Press, <1976-1986 >
*TC DA912 .N48*

**Byrne, Peter, 1950-** Philosophical and ethical problems in mental handicap / Peter Byrne. New York : St. Martin's Press , 2000. xiii, 175 p. ; 23 cm. Includes bibliographical references and index. ISBN 0-312-23460-0 DDC 362.3
*1. Mentally handicapped. 2. Mental retardation - Moral and ethical aspects. I. Title.*
*TC HV3004 .B95 2000*

**BYRON, GEORGE GORDON BYRON, BARON, 1788-1824 - CHILDHOOD AND YOUTH.**
Elledge, Paul. Lord Byron at Harrow School. Baltimore : Johns Hopkins University Press, c2000.
*TC PR4382 .E36 2000*

**BYRON, GEORGE GORDON BYRON, BARON, 1788-1824 - HOMES AND HAUNTS - ENGLAND - LONDON.**
Elledge, Paul. Lord Byron at Harrow School. Baltimore : Johns Hopkins University Press, c2000.
*TC PR4382 .E36 2000*

**BYRON, GEORGE GORDON BYRON, BARON, 1788-1824 - KNOWLEDGE AND LEARNING.**
Elledge, Paul. Lord Byron at Harrow School. Baltimore : Johns Hopkins University Press, c2000.
*TC PR4382 .E36 2000*

**Byron, Reginald.**
Blacking, John. Music, culture, & experience. Chicago : University of Chicago Press, c1995.
*TC ML60 .B63 1995*

**C CORPORATIONS.** *See* CORPORATIONS.

**CA (INTERPERSONAL COMMUNICATION).** *See* CONVERSATION ANALYSIS.

**CABINETWORK.** *See* FURNITURE.

**Cacioppo, John T.**
Handbook of psychophysiology. 2nd ed. Cambridge, UK ; New York, NY, USA : Cambridge University Press, 2000.
*TC QP360 .P7515 2000*

**Caddie Woodlawn by Carol Ryrie Brink.**
Gutner, Howard. New York : Scholastic, c1997.
*TC LB1573 .G87 1997*

**Cadnum, Michael.** In a dark wood / Michael Cadnum. New York : Orchard Books, c1998. 246 p. ; 22 cm. SUMMARY: On orders from the King, the Sheriff of Nottingham seeks to capture the outlaw Robin Hood, but he finds him to be a tricky and elusive foe. ISBN 0-531-30071-4 (trade) ISBN 0-531-33071-0 (lib. bdg.) DDC [Fic]
*1. Sheriff of Nottingham (Legendary character) - Juvenile fiction. 2. Robin Hood (Legendary character) - Juvenile fiction. 3. Great Britain - History - Richard I, 1189-1199 - Juvenile fiction. 4. Sheriff of Nottingham (Legendary character) - Fiction. 5. Robin Hood (Legendary character) - Fiction. 6. Great Britain - History - Richard I, 1189-1199 - Fiction. 7. Robbers and outlaws - Fiction. I. Title.*
*TC PZ7.C11724 In 1998*

Rundown / by Michael Cadnum. New York : Viking, c1999. 168 p. ; 22 cm. SUMMARY: As a game, sixteen-year-old Jennifer pretends that she has been attacked by a serial rapist, but then she finds herself getting more attention than she wanted, from the police and her parents. ISBN 0-670-88377-8 DDC [Fic]
*1. Honesty - Fiction. 2. Rape - Fiction. 3. Criminal investigation - Fiction. 4. Parent and child - Fiction. I. Title.*

*TC PZ7.C11724 Ru 1999*

CAESARISM. *See* IMPERIALISM.

**Caffarella, Rosemary S. (Rosemary Shelley), dd 1946-).**
An update on adult development theory :. San Francisco, CA : Jossey-Bass Publishers, 1999.
*TC LC5225.L42 U63 1999*

**Caffentzis, Constantine George, 1945-.**
A thousand flowers. Trenton, NJ : Africa World Press, c2000, [1999].
*TC LC67.68.A35 T56 2000*

**Cahill, George F., 1927-.**
The Horizons of health. Cambridge, Mass. : Harvard University Press, 1977.
*TC R850 .H67*

**Cahn, Dudley D.**
Lulofs, Roxane Salyer. Conflict. 2nd ed. Boston : Allyn and Bacon, c2000.
*TC BF637.I48 L85 2000*

CAI. *See* COMPUTER-ASSISTED INSTRUCTION.

**Cain, Michael Scott.** The community college in the twenty-first century : a systems approach / Michael Scott Cain. Lanham, MD : University Press of America, c1999. 139, [8] p. ; 23 cm. Includes bibliographical references (p. [141]-[147]) and index. ISBN 0-7618-1357-8 (cloth) DDC 378.1/543
*1. Community colleges - United States. 2. Community colleges - United States - Administration. 3. System theory. I. Title.*
*TC LB2328.15.U6 C33 1999*

**Caines, Jeannette Franklin.** I need a lunch box / by Jeannette Caines ; pictures by Pat Cummings. New York : Macmillan/McGraw-Hill, 1988. [32] p. : col. ill. ; 39 x 38 cm. ISBN 0-02-109103-x
*1. Wishes - Fiction. 2. Afro-Americans - Fiction. I. Cummings, Pat, ill. II. Title.*
*TC PZ7.C12 Iaan 1988*

**Cairns, Jo.**
Education for values. London ; Sterling, VA : Kogan Page, 2000.
*TC LC268 .E38 2000*

**Cairns Regional Gallery.**
Ilan pasin = Queensland : Cairns Regional Gallery, [1998?].
*TC DU125.T67 I53 1998*

CAISSE CLAIRE. *See* SNARE DRUM.

CALCULATORS. *See* ARITHMETIC; COMPUTERS.

**Calculus renewal** : issues for undergraduate mathematics education in the next decade / edited by Susan L. Ganter. New York : Kluwer Academic/ Plenum Publishers, c2000. xii, 167 p. : ill. ; 24 cm. Includes bibliographical references and index. ISBN 0-306-46322-9 DDC 515/.071/1
*1. Calculus - Study and teaching (Higher) - United States. I. Ganter, Susan L.*
*TC QA303.3 .C34 2000*

CALCULUS - STUDY AND TEACHING (HIGHER) - UNITED STATES.
Calculus renewal. New York : Kluwer Academic/ Plenum Publishers, c2000.
*TC QA303.3 .C34 2000*

**Calderwood, Patricia E., 1954-** Learning community : finding common ground in difference / Patricia E. Calderwood. New York : Teachers College Press, c2000. viii, 168 p. : ill. ; 23 cm. Includes bibliographical references (p. 155-161) and index. ISBN 0-8077-3953-7 (cloth : acid-free paper) ISBN 0-8077-3952-9 (pbk. : acid-free paper) DDC 370.11
*1. Group work in education - United States. 2. Group identity - United States. 3. Interpersonal relations - United States. I. Title.*
*TC LB1032 .C34 2000*

**Caldwell, Michael D.**
Clinical nutrition. 2nd ed. Philadelphia : Saunders, 1993.
*TC RM224 .P24 1993*

CALENDAR. *See* MONTHS.

**Calfee, Robert C.** Teach your children well : bringing K-12 education into the 21st century / by Robert C. Calfee and Cynthia L. Patrick. Stanford, CA : Stanford Alumni Association, c1995. 234 p. : ill. ; 23 cm. (Portable Stanford Book Series) Cover title : Teach our Children well : bringing K-12 education into the 21st century. Includes bibliographical references. ISBN 0-916318-55-9
*1. Education - United States. 2. Education - Aims and objectives. I. Patrick, Cynthia L. II. Title. III. Title: Teach our*

children well : bringing K-12 education into the 21st century IV. Series.
*TC LB2822.82 .C32 1995*

**Calhoun, Emily.**
Joyce, Bruce R. The new structure of school improvement. Buckingham [England] ; Philadelphia : Open University Press, 1999.
*TC LB2822.84.G7 J69 1999*

**Caliendo, Stephen M., 1971-** Teachers matter : the trouble with leaving political education to the coaches / Stephen M. Caliendo. Westport, Conn. : Praeger, 2000. xvii, 131 p. : ill. ; 24 cm. Includes bibliographical references (p. [123]-127) and index. ISBN 0-275-96907-X (alk. paper) DDC 320/.071/273
*1. Political science - Study and teaching (Secondary) - United States. 2. United States - Politics and government - Study and teaching (Secondary) 3. Political socialization - United States. 4. United States. - Supreme Court - Public opinion. 5. Public opinion - United States. I. Title.*
*TC JA88.U6 C24 2000*

**California Association for Adult Education.**
California review of adult education. [Los Angeles : California State Dept. of Education, 1936.

**California Association of Secondary School Administrators.**
Journal of secondary education. [Burlingame, Calif. : California Association of Secondary School Administrators, 1961-1971]

**California. Bureau of Juvenile Research. Dept. of Research.**
The Journal of delinquency. Whittier, Calif. : Whittier State School, Dept. of Research, 1916-c1928.

**California. Dept. of Education.**
California journal of elementary education. Sacramento, California, State Department of Education.
*TC L11 .C27*

**California. Education Department. California education.**
California journal of elementary education. Sacramento, California, State Department of Education.
*TC L11 .C27*

**California education** / official publication of the California State Department of Education. [Sacramento : California State Dept. of Education, 1963-1966] 3 v. : ill., tables ; 27 cm. Frequency: Monthly (Sept.-June). Vol. 1, no. 1 (Sept. 1963)-v. 3, no. 10 (June 1966). Title from cover. Continues in part: Education in depth; and formed by the union of California schools and California journal of elementary education. DDC 370.9794 DDC qC153e
*1. Education - California - Periodicals. I. California. State Dept. of Education. II. Title: Education in depth III. Title: California schools IV. Title: California journal of elementary education*

**California education** / official publication of the California State Department of Education. [Sacramento : California State Dept. of Education, 1963-1966] 3 v. : ill., tables ; 27 cm. Frequency: Monthly (Sept.-June). Vol. 1, no. 1 (Sept. 1963)-v. 3, no. 10 (June 1966). Title from cover. Continues in part: Education in depth; and formed by the union of California schools and California journal of elementary education. DDC 370.9794 DDC qC153e
*1. Education - California - Periodicals. I. California. State Dept. of Education. II. Title: Education in depth III. Title: California schools IV. Title: California journal of elementary education*

**California education** / official publication of the California State Department of Education. [Sacramento : California State Dept. of Education, 1963-1966] 3 v. : ill., tables ; 27 cm. Frequency: Monthly (Sept.-June). Vol. 1, no. 1 (Sept. 1963)-v. 3, no. 10 (June 1966). Title from cover. Continues in part: Education in depth; and formed by the union of California schools and California journal of elementary education. DDC 370.9794 DDC qC153e
*1. Education - California - Periodicals. I. California. State Dept. of Education. II. Title: Education in depth III. Title: California schools IV. Title: California journal of elementary education*

**California elementary school principals' association.**
California journal of elementary education. Sacramento, California, State Department of Education.
*TC L11 .C27*

CALIFORNIA - FICTION.
Stegner, Wallace Earle, 1909- Angle of repose. New York : Modern Library, 2000.
*TC PS3537.T316 A8 2000*

CALIFORNIA INSTITUTE OF TECHNOLOGY - BUILDINGS.
Wyllie, Romy. Caltech's architectural heritage. Los Angeles : Balcony Press, c2000.
*TC NA6603 .W95 2000*

CALIFORNIA INSTITUTE OF TECHNOLOGY - HISTORY.
Wyllie, Romy. Caltech's architectural heritage. Los Angeles : Balcony Press, c2000.
*TC NA6603 .W95 2000*

**California Institute of Technology's architectural heritage.**
Wyllie, Romy. Caltech's architectural heritage. Los Angeles : Balcony Press, c2000.
*TC NA6603 .W95 2000*

**California journal of elementary education.**
California education. [Sacramento : California State Dept. of Education, 1963-1966]

California education. [Sacramento : California State Dept. of Education, 1963-1966]

California education. [Sacramento : California State Dept. of Education, 1963-1966]

**California journal of elementary education.**
Sacramento, California, State Department of Education. 31 v. in 16. v. 1-31; August 1932-May 1963. Ceased publication with v. 31, no. 4, 1963. "The California elementary principals' association is cooperating with the State Department of Education in the preparation of materials to be presented in this journal". Volume 1, no. 1. Includes bibliographies. Superseded by: California. Education Department. California education.
*1. Education - Periodicals. I. California. Dept. of Education. II. California elementary school principals' association. III. Title: California. Education Department. California education*
*TC L11 .C27*

**California journal of secondary education.**
California quarterly of secondary education. Berkeley, Cal. : The Society, 1925-

Journal of secondary education. [Burlingame, Calif. : California Association of Secondary School Administrators, 1961-1971]

CALIFORNIA - POLITICS AND GOVERNMENT - 1951-.
Connerly, Ward, 1939- Creating equal. San Francisco : Encounter Books, 2000.
*TC E185.97 .C74 2000*

**California quarterly of secondary education** / California Society for the Study of Secondary Education. Berkeley, Cal. : The Society, 1925- v. ; 24 cm. Vol. 1, no. 1 (Oct. 1925)-v. 9, no. 4 (June 1934). Continued by: California journal of secondary education (OCoLC)1552561.
*1. Education. Secondary - Periodicals. I. California Society for the Study of Secondary Education. II. Title: California journal of secondary education*

CALIFORNIA - RACE RELATIONS.
Connerly, Ward, 1939- Creating equal. San Francisco : Encounter Books, 2000.
*TC E185.97 .C74 2000*

**California review of adult education.** [Los Angeles : California State Dept. of Education, 1936. 1 v. ; 25 cm. Frequency: Quarterly. Vol. 1, no. 1 (Apr. 1936)-v. 1, no. 4 (Dec. 1936). Title from cover. Published in cooperation with: the California Association for Adult Education.
*1. Education - Periodicals. 2. Adult education - Periodicals. 3. Education - California - Periodicals. 4. Adult education - California - Periodicals. I. California. State Dept. of Education. II. California Association for Adult Education.*

**California schools.**
California education. [Sacramento : California State Dept. of Education, 1963-1966]

California education. [Sacramento : California State Dept. of Education, 1963-1966]

California education. [Sacramento : California State Dept. of Education, 1963-1966]

**California Society for the Study of Secondary Education.**
California quarterly of secondary education. Berkeley, Cal. : The Society, 1925-

**California. State Dept. of Education.**
California education. [Sacramento : California State Dept. of Education, 1963-1966]

California education. [Sacramento : California State Dept. of Education, 1963-1966]

California education. [Sacramento : California State Dept. of Education, 1963-1966]

California review of adult education. [Los Angeles : California State Dept. of Education, 1936.

**California State University, Northridge.**
Making the most of early communication [videorecording]. New York, NY : Distributed by AFB Press, c1997.
*TC HV1597.2 .M3 1997*

**Calkins, Lucy McCormick.** The art of teaching reading / Lucy McCormick Calkins ; photography by Peter Cunningham. 1st ed. New York ; London : Longman, c2001. xii, 580 p. : ill. ; 24 cm. Includes bibliographical references (p. 565-574) and index. ISBN 0-321-08059-9 DDC 372.41/6
*1. Reading (Elementary) - United States. 2. Group reading - United States. I. Title.*
*TC LB1573 .C185 2001*

**Call it courage :** teacher's planning guide. New York : Macmillan/McGraw-Hill, c1997. 1 v. (various pagings) : col. ill. ; 31 cm. (Spotlight on literacy ; Gr.6 l.12 u.6) (The road to independent reading) Includes index. ISBN 0-02-183199-8
*1. Language arts (Elementary) 2. Reading (Elementary) I. Series. II. Series: The road to independent reading*
*TC LB1576 .S66 1997 Gr.6 l.12 u.6*

**Callahan, Daniel, 1930-.**
Promoting healthy behavior. Washington, D.C. : Georgetown University Press, c2000.
*TC RA427.8 .P766 2000*

**Callaway, Alison.** Deaf children in China / Alison Callaway. Washington, D.C. : Gallaudet University Press, 2000. x, 320 p. : ill. ; 24 cm. Originally presented as the author's thesis (Ph.D.--Bristol University). Includes bibliographical references (p. 277-305) and index. ISBN 1-56368-085-8 DDC 362.4/2/0830951
*1. Deaf children - China. 2. Deaf children - China - Family relationships. 3. Hearing impaired children - China - Family relationships. I. Title.*
*TC HV2888 .C35 2000*

**CALLIGRAPHY, JAPANESE - EXHIBITIONS.**
Twelve centuries of Japanese art from the Imperial collections. Washington, DC : Freer Gallery of Art and the Arthur M. Sackler Gallery, Smithsonian Institution Press, c1997.
*TC ND1457.J32 W377 1997*

**Calling all toddlers.**
Simon, Francesca. 1st American ed. New York : Orchard Books, 1999.
*TC PZ8.3.S5875 Cal 1999*

**The calling of Katie Makanya.**
McCord, Margaret (McCord Nixon) New York : J. Wiley, 1995.
*TC CT1929.M34 M38 1995*

**Callison, William.** Elementary school principal's handbook / William Callison, Carol H. McAllister. Lancaster, Pa. : Technomic, c1999. xv, 267 p. : ill. ; 30 cm. Includes bibliographical references and index. CONTENTS: School leadership -- Introducing change -- Helping individuals change within the school organization -- Establishing a plan to promote change and agreement within the school organization -- Steps in the decision process -- A positive work climate through effective human resource management -- Selection of staff -- Supervision of staff -- Collective bargaining -- Fiscal management -- The budgeting process at a school site -- Fundraising -- Managing a school site -- Parent involvement -- Self-evaluation -- Improvement of the instructional program -- Identifying special needs students : elementary risk assessment -- Planning and supervision of curriculum -- Planning and supervision of instruction and the learning environment -- Planning and supervising the use of technology -- Establishing a climate for staff acceptance of assessment and evaluation -- Assessing student progress -- Many kinds of minds : a neurodevelopmental perspective for understanding why some students fail in school -- Clinical supervision and evaluation -- Evaluation of program effectiveness -- Legal responsibilities of the principal -- Public relations and media relations -- Understanding different political positions in schools -- Utilizing federal, state, and community resources -- Using CONTENTS: the internet and CD ROM -- Strategies for teaching or reaching many kinds of minds -- A tutoring program for at-risk students that works -- An evaluation case study at Los Naranjos Elementary School.
*1. Elementary school principals - Handbooks, manuals, etc. 2. School management and organization - United States - Handbooks, manuals, etc. 3. School management and organization - Handbooks, manuals, etc. 4. Elementary school administration - United States - Handbooks, manuals, etc. I. McAllister, Carol H. II. Title.*
*TC LB2822.5 .C34 1999*

**Callister, Thomas A.**
Burbules, Nicholas C. Watch IT. Boulder, Colo. : Westview Press, 2000.

*TC LB1028.43 .B87 2000*

**CALLISTHENICS.** *See* **PHYSICAL EDUCATION AND TRAINING.**

**Caltech's architectural heritage.**
Wyllie, Romy. Los Angeles : Balcony Press, c2000.
*TC NA6603 .W95 2000*

**Calvert, Sandra L.** Children's journeys through the information age / Sandra L. Calvert. 1st ed. Boston : McGraw-Hill College, c1999. xxii, 298 p. : ill. ; 24 cm. (McGraw-Hill series in developmental psychology) Includes bibliographical references (p. 258-282) and indexes. ISBN 0-07-011664-4 DDC 303.48/33/083
*1. Television and children - United States. 2. Computers and children - United States. 3. Internet (Computer network) and children - United States. 4. Mass media and children - United States. 5. Sex role in mass media - United States. 6. Violence in mass media - United States. I. Title. II. Series.*
*TC HQ784.T4 C24 1999*

**CALVIN COLLEGE - HISTORY.**
DeBoer, Peter P. Origins of teacher education at Calvin College, 1900-1930. Lewiston : E. Mellen Press, c1991.
*TC LD785 .D43 1991*

**Calvin, William H., 1939-** Lingua ex machina : reconciling Darwin and Chomsky with the human brain / William H. Calvin, Derek Bickerton. Cambridge, Mass. ; London : MIT Press, c2000. 298 p. : ill. ; 24 cm. "A Bradford book." Includes bibliographical references (p. [261]-280) and index. ISBN 0-262-03273-2 (hc. : alk. paper) DDC 612.8/2
*1. Neurolinguistics. 2. Brain - Evolution. 3. Chomsky, Noam. 4. Darwin, Charles, - 1809-1882. I. Bickerton, Derek. II. Title.*
*TC QP399 .C35 2000*

**Camara, Evandro de Morais, 1946-** The cultural one or the racial many : religion, culture and the interethnic experience / Evandro Camara. Aldershot, Hants, England : Brookfield, Vt., USA : Ashgate, c1997. ix, 294 p. ; 23 cm. (Research in ethnic relations series) Includes bibliographical references (p. 276-291) and index. CONTENTS: Cultural explanation and the question of intergroup life--Culture and ethnicity: a crossnational contrast--The meeting of dominant and minority cultures: Integration vs. separatism--Miscegenation and intermarriage in the formation of society--The psychosocial aspect: Group consciousness and cultural identity--Revisiting secularization: Religion as implicit normative system--The Church in Brazil: Folk Catholicism and ethnic assimilation--The Church in the United States: Calvinistic Protestantism and ethnic assimilation. ISBN 1-84014-119-0 DDC 305.8
*1. Race relations. 2. Ethnic relations. I. Title. II. Series.*
*TC HT1521 .C343 1997*

**CAMBODIA - SOCIAL LIFE AND CUSTOMS.**
Phim, Toni Samantha, 1957- Dance in Cambodia. [Kuala Lumpur] Malaysia ; Oxford ; New York : Oxford University Press, 1999.
*TC GV1703.C3 P55 1999*

**Cambou, Don.**
The American Revolution. [videorecording]. New York, N.Y. : A&E Home Video, c1994.
*TC E208 .A447 1994*

**Cambourne, Brian.**
Geekie, Peter. Understanding literacy development. Stoke on Trent, England : Trentham Books, 1999.
*TC LC149 .G44 1999*

**Cambourne, Brian, edt.**
The changing face of whole language. Newark, Del. : International Reading Association ; Victoria, Australia : Australian Literacy Educators' Association, c1997.
*TC LB1050.35 .C43 1997*

**Cambridge applied linguistics series**
Culture in second language teaching and learning. Cambridge, U.K. ; New York : Cambridge University Press, 1999.
*TC P53 .C77 1999*

Network-based language teaching. Cambridge, U.K. : New York : Cambridge University Press, 2000.
*TC P53.285 .N48 2000*

**Cambridge approaches to linguistics**
Aitchison, Jean, 1938- Language change. 2nd ed. Cambridge [England] ; New York : Cambridge University Press, 1991.
*TC P142 .A37 1991*

Chiat, Shula. Understanding children with language problems. Oxford [England] ; New York : Cambridge University Press, 2000.
*TC RJ496.L35 C46 2000*

**Cambridge Career Products.**
Grounded for life [videorecording]. Charleston, WV : Cambridge Research Group, Ltd., 1988.
*TC HQ759.4 .G7 1988*

**Cambridge Career Products (Firm).**
Grounded for life [videorecording]. Charleston, WV : Cambridge Research Group, Ltd., 1988.
*TC HQ759.4 .G7 1988*

**Cambridge criminology series**
Violence and childhood in the inner city. Cambridge, UK : New York : Cambridge University Press, 1997.
*TC HN90.V5 V532 1997*

**The Cambridge dictionary of philosophy** / edited by Robert Audi. 2nd ed. Cambridge ; New York : Cambridge University Press, 1999. xxxv, 1001 p. : ill. ; 26 cm. Includes index. ISBN 0-521-63136-X ISBN 0-521-63722-8 (pbk.) DDC 103
*1. Philosophy - Dictionaries. I. Audi, Robert, 1941- II. Title: Dictionary of philosophy*
*TC B41 .C35 1999*

**Cambridge Educational.**
Children of the night [videorecording]. [Charleston, W.V.] : Cambridge Educational, c1994.
*TC HV1435.C3 C45 1994*

Children of the night [videorecording]. [Charleston, W.V.] : Cambridge Educational, c1994.
*TC HV1435.C3 C45 1994*

Starting over [videorecording]. [Charleston, W.V.] : Cambridge Educational, c1994.
*TC HV1435.C3 S7 1994*

**Cambridge Educational (Firm).**
Children of the night [videorecording]. [Charleston, W.V.] : Cambridge Educational, c1994.
*TC HV1435.C3 C45 1994*

Children of the night [videorecording]. [Charleston, W.V.] : Cambridge Educational, c1994.
*TC HV1435.C3 C45 1994*

Children of the night [videorecording]. [Charleston, W.V.] : Cambridge Educational, c1994.
*TC HV1435.C3 C45 1994*

d·a·t·e rape [videorecording]. [Charleston, WV] : Cambridge Educational, c1994.
*TC RC560.R36 D3 1994*

Grounded for life [videorecording]. Charleston, WV : Cambridge Research Group, Ltd., 1988.
*TC HQ759.4 .G7 1988*

Starting over [videorecording]. [Charleston, W.V.] : Cambridge Educational, c1994.
*TC HV1435.C3 S7 1994*

**Cambridge handbooks for language teachers**
McKay, Heather, 1950- Teaching adult second language learners. Cambridge ; New York : Cambridge University Press, 1999.
*TC P53 .M33 1999*

**The Cambridge history of American music** / edited by David Nicholls. Cambridge, UK ; New York, NY : Cambridge University Press, 1998. xv, 637 p. : ill. ; 24 cm. (The Cambridge history of music) Includes bibliographical references (p. 567-609) and index. ISBN 0-521-45429-8 (hardback) DDC 780/.973
*1. Music - United States - History and criticism. I. Nicholls, David, 1955- II. Series.*
*TC ML200 .C36 1998*

**The Cambridge history of music**
The Cambridge history of American music. Cambridge, UK ; New York, NY : Cambridge University Press, 1998.
*TC ML200 .C36 1998*

**Cambridge language teaching library**
New immigrants in the United States. Cambridge, U.K. ; New York : Cambridge University Press, 2000.
*TC PE1128 .N384 1999*

Richards, Jack C. The language teaching matrix. Cambridge [England] ; New York : Cambridge University Press, 1990.
*TC P51 .R48 1990*

**Cambridge music handbooks**
Hefling, Stephen E. Mahler, Das Lied von der Erde = Cambridge, UK ; New York : Cambridge University Press, c2000.
*TC MT121.M34 H44 2000*

**Cambridge Research Group, Ltd.**
Children of the night [videorecording]. [Charleston, W.V.] : Cambridge Educational, c1994.
*TC HV1435.C3 C45 1994*

Children of the night [videorecording]. [Charleston, W.V.] : Cambridge Educational, c1994.
*TC HV1435.C3 C45 1994*

Children of the night [videorecording]. [Charleston, W.V.] : Cambridge Educational, c1994.
*TC HV1435.C3 C45 1994*

Grounded for life [videorecording]. Charleston, WV : Cambridge Research Group, Ltd., 1988.
*TC HQ759.4 .G7 1988*

Starting over [videorecording]. [Charleston, W.V.] : Cambridge Educational, c1994.
*TC HV1435.C3 S7 1994*

**Cambridge series on judgment and decision making**
Chapman, Gretchen B., 1965- Decision making in health care. New York : Cambridge University Press, 2000.
*TC R723.5 .C48 2000*

Judgment and decision making. 2nd ed. Cambridge, U.K. ; New York, NY : Cambridge University Press, 2000.
*TC BF441 .J79 2000*

**Cambridge series on statistical and probabilistic mathematics.**
Leonard, Thomas, 1948- Bayesian methods. Cambridge, U.K. ; New York : Cambridge University Press, 1999.
*TC QA279.5 .L45 1999*

**Cambridge studies in American visual culture**
Dabakis, Melissa. Visualizing labor in American sculpture. New York : Cambridge University Press, 1999.
*TC NB1952.L33 D24 1999*

**Cambridge studies in cognitive and perceptual development**
Light, Paul. Social processes in children's learning. Cambridge, U.K. ; New York : Cambridge University Press, 1999.
*TC LB1060 .L533 1999*

**Cambridge studies in cognitive perceptual development**
Children's understanding of biology and health. 1st ed. Cambridge, U.K. ; New York : Cambridge University Press, 1999.
*TC BF723.C5 C514 1999*

**Cambridge studies in French**
Forrester, John. The seductions of psychoanalysis. 1st pbk. ed. Cambridge : New York : Cambridge University Press, 1991 (1992 printing)
*TC RC504 .F63 1991*

**Cambridge studies in medieval life and thought**
(4th ser.) Courtenay, William J. Parisian scholars in the early fourteenth century. Cambridge, U.K. ; New York, NY : Cambridge University Press, 1999.
*TC LF2165 .C68 1999*

**Cambridge studies in philosophy**
Baker, Lynne Rudder, 1944- Persons and bodies. New York : Cambridge University Press, 2000.
*TC B105.B64 B35 2000*

Rowlands, Mark. The body in mind. Cambridge, U.K. ; New York : Cambridge University Press, 1999.
*TC BD418.3 .R78 1999*

**Cambridge studies in social and emotional development**
The development of romantic relationships in adolescence. Cambridge, U.K. ; New York : Cambridge University Press, 1999.
*TC BF724.3.L68 D48 1999*

Hoffman, Lois Norma Wladis, 1929- Mothers at work. Cambridge ; New York : Cambridge University Press, 1999.
*TC HQ759.48 .H63 1999*

**CAMERA JOURNALISM.** *See* **PHOTOJOURNALISM.**

**Camerini, Michael.**
The frescoes of Diego Rivera [videorecording]. [Detroit, Mich.] : Founders Society, Detroit Institute of Arts ; [Chicago, Ill.?] : Home Vision [distributor], c1986.
*TC ND259.R5 F6 1986*

**Cameron, Catherine.** Resolving childhood trauma : a long-term study of abuse survivors / by Catherine Cameron. Thousand Oaks, Calif. : Sage Publications, c2000. xi, 338 p. ; 24 cm. Includes bibliographical references (p. 327-332) and indexes. CONTENTS: Background -- A study of sexual abuse survivors -- The women and their families -- Childhood trauma -- Cumulative developmental damage --

Amnesia and posttraumatic stress -- Long silent years -- Triggering of memories -- Flashbacks and the crisis of recall -- Personal response to remembering -- Reactions of others -- Confronting the abuser -- Changed lives -- Epilogue : gaining closure. ISBN 0-7619-2128-1 ISBN 0-7619-2129-X DDC 616.85/8369
*1. Adult child sexual abuse victims - Longitudinal studies. 2. Recovered memory. I. Title.*
*TC RC569.5.A28 C35 2000*

**Cameron, Keith.**
Computer assisted language learning (CALL). Lisse [Netherlands] ; Exton, PA : Swets & Zeitlinger, 1999.
*TC P53.28 .C6634 1999*

**Camilleri, George.**
Introducing learner autonomy in teacher education. Strasbourg : Council of Europe Pub., c1999.
*TC PB38.E8 I567 1999*

Learner autonomy. Strasbourg : Council of Europe Pub., c1999.
*TC PB38.E8 L424 1999*

**Camp, Lindsay.** Why? / written by Lindsay Camp ; illustrated by Tony Ross. New York : Putnam, c1998. 1 v. (unpaged) : col. ill. ; 29 cm. SUMMARY: Lily's continual questioning sometimes annoys her father, but one day it proves very useful. ISBN 0-399-23396-2 DDC [E]
*1. Questions and answers - Fiction. 2. Fathers and daughters - Fiction. 3. Extraterrestrial beings - Fiction. I. Ross, Tony, ill. II. Title.*
*TC PZ7.C1475 Wf 1998*

**Campbell, Cherry.** Teaching second-language writing : interacting with text / Cherry Campbell. Pacific Grove : Heinle & Heinle, c1998. xi, 95 p. : ill. ; 24 cm. (TeacherSource book) (Newbury House teacher development) Includes bibliographical references (p. 91-94). ISBN 0-8384-7892-1 DDC 428/.007
*1. English language - Study and teaching - Foreign speakers. 2. English language - Composition and exercises. I. Title. II. Series. III. Series: TeacherSource*
*TC PE1128.A2 C325 1998*

**Campbell, Christine.**
Hill, Paul Thomas, 1943- It takes a city. Washington, D.C. : Brookings Institution Press, c2000.
*TC LC5131 .H48 2000*

**Campbell, Delois.** High school students' perceptions of the impact of block scheduling on instructional effectiveness / by Delois Campbell. 1999. x, 193 leaves : ill. ; 29 cm. Typescript; issued also on microfilm. Thesis (Ed.D.)--Teachers College, Columbia University, 1999. Includes bibliographical references (leaves 178-184).
*1. Block scheduling (Education) - New Jersey. 2. Schedules. School - New Jersey. 3. High school students - Education - New Jersey - Attitudes. 4. High school teaching - New Jersey - Evaluation. 5. Education. Secondary - New Jersey. 6. Education - New Jersey - Curricula. 7. School management and organization - New Jersey. 8. Beachtown High School (New Jersey) I. Title. II. Title: Impact of block scheduling on instructional effectiveness*
*TC 06 no. 11089*

**Campbell, Dorothy M.**
Portfolio and performance assessment in teacher education. Boston : Allyn and Bacon, c2000.
*TC LB1728 .P667 2000*

**Campbell, Duane E.** Choosing democracy : a practical guide to multicultural education / Duane E. Campbell ; with contributions by Delores Delgado-Campbell ... [et al.]. 2nd ed. Upper Saddle River, N.J. : Merrill, c2000. xxii, 410 p. ; 23 cm. Includes bibliographical references and index. ISBN 0-13-096102-7 DDC 370.117
*1. Multicultural education - United States. 2. Education - Social aspects - United States. 3. Pluralism (Social sciences) - United States. 4. Racism - United States. 5. United States - Race relations. 6. Social classes - United States. 7. Sex differences in education - United States. I. Delgado-Campbell, Delores. II. Title.*
*TC LC1099.3 .C36 2000*

**Campbell, Hope.** Managing technology in the early childhood classroom / author, Hope Campbell. Westminster, CA : Teacher Created Materials, c1999. 256 p. : ill. ; 28 cm. At head of title on cover: Techknowledgey. "TCM 2434"--Cover. "References and web sites": p. 249-256. ISBN 1-57690-434-2 DDC 372.133
*1. Early childhood education - Computer-assisted instruction. 2. Computers and children. 3. Educational technology. I. Title. II. Title: Techknowledgey*
*TC LB1139.35.C64 C36 1999*

**Campbell, Jack, Ed. D.** Student discipline and classroom management : preventing and managing discipline problems in the classroom / by Jack Campbell. Springfield, Ill. : C.C. Thomas, c1999. xiii, 112 p. : ill. ; 24 cm. Includes bibliographical references and

index. ISBN 0-398-07003-2 (cloth) ISBN 0-398-07004-0 (paper) DDC 371.102/4
*1. School discipline. 2. Classroom management. 3. Motivation in education. I. Title.*
*TC LB3012 .C34 1999*

**Campbell, Robin, 1937-** Literacy from home to school : : reading with Alice / Robin Campbell. Stoke on Trent, Staffordshire, Eng. : Trentham Books, 1999. v, 168 p. : ill., ports. ; 21 cm. Includes bibliographical references (p. 163-168). ISBN 1-85856-166-3
*1. Education. Preschool. 2. Literacy - Study and teaching (Early childhood). I. Title. II. Title: Reading with Alice.*
*TC LB1140.2 .C35 1999*

**Campbell, Ruth, 1944-.**
Gesture, speech, and sign. Oxford [England] ; New York : Oxford University Press, c1999.
*TC P117 .G469 1999*

**Campbell, Vicki Lynn.**
Testing and assessment in counseling practice. 2nd ed. Mahwah, N.J. : L. Erlbaum Associates, 2000.
*TC BF176 .T423 2000*

**Campbell, Will D.**
Counts, I. Wilmer (Ira Wilmer), 1931- A life is more than a moment. Bloomington, IN : Indiana University Press, c1999.
*TC LC214.23.L56 C68 1999*

**CAMPING - EQUIPMENT AND SUPPLIES.** *See* **TENTS.**

**Campoy, Renee W.** A professional development school partnership : conflict and collaboration / Renee W. Campoy. Westport, Conn. : Bergin & Garvey, 2000. viii, 149 p. ; 25 cm. Includes bibliographical references (p. [141]-146) and index. ISBN 0-89789-705-6 (alk. paper) DDC 370.19
*1. Laboratory schools - United States - Case studies. 2. College-school cooperation - United States - Case studies. I. Title.*
*TC LB2154.A3 C36 2000*

**CAMPS, ANNA.**
Metalinguistic activity in learning to write. Amsterdam : Amsterdam University Press, c2000.
*TC PN181 .M48 2000*

**CAMPUS CULTURES.** *See* **EDUCATIONAL ANTHROPOLOGY.**

**CAMPUS DISORDERS.** *See* **STUDENT MOVEMENTS.**

**Campus guide (New York, N.Y.)**
Joncas, Richard, 1953- Stanford University. 1st ed. New York : Princeton Architectural Press, 1999.
*TC LD3031 .J65 1999*

Montgomery, Susan J., 1947- Phillips Academy. New York : Princeton Architectural Press, 2000.
*TC LD7501.A5 M65 2000*

**CAMPUS PLANNING - UNITED STATES.**
Dober, Richard P. Campus landscape. New York : Wiley, c2000.
*TC LB3223.3 .D65 2000*

Strange, Charles Carney. Educating by design. 1st ed. San Francisco : Jossey-Bass, c2001.
*TC LB2324 .S77 2001*

**CAMPUS SCHOOLS.** *See* **LABORATORY SCHOOLS.**

**Can we wear our pearls and still be feminists?.**
Mandle, Joan D. Columbia : University of Missouri Press, c2000.
*TC HQ1181.U5 M37 2000*

**Can you count ten toes?.**
Evans, Lezlie. Boston, Mass. : Houghton Mifflin, 1999.
*TC QA113 .E84 1999*

**CANADA - CIVILIZATION - COMPUTER NETWORK RESOURCES - DIRECTORIES.**
Gregory, Vicki L., 1950- Multicultural resources on the Internet. The United States and Canada. Englewood, Colo. : Libraries Unlimited, 1999.
*TC E184.A1 G874 1999*

**Canada, Geoffrey.** Reaching up for manhood : transforming the lives of boys in America / Geoffrey Canada. Boston : Beacon Press, c1998. xiv, 160 p. ; 24 cm. ISBN 0-8070-2316-7 (cloth) DDC 305.23
*1. Boys - United States - Psychology. 2. Boys - United States - Social conditions. 3. Afro-American boys - Psychology. 4. Afro-American boys - Social conditions. 5. Masculinity - United States. I. Title.*
*TC HQ775 .C35 1998*

**CANADA - LANGUAGES.** *See* **AMERICAN SIGN LANGUAGE.**

**CANADA - RACE RELATIONS - CASE STUDIES.**
Souls looking back. New York : Routledge, 1999.
*TC E185.625 .S675 1999*

**CANADA - RACE RELATIONS - HANDBOOKS, MANUALS, ETC.**
Kehoe, John W. A handbook for enhancing the multicultural climate of the school. [Vancouver, B.C.] : Western Education Development Group, Faculty of Education, University of British Colombia, c1984.
*TC LC1099 .K438 1984*

**CANADA - STUDY AND TEACHING.**
Introducing Canada. Washington, D.C. : National Council for the Social Studies in association with National Consortium for Teaching Canada, c1997.
*TC F1025 .I59 1997*

**The Canadian anthology of social studies** : issues and strategies for teachers / Roland Case, Penney Clark, editors. Vancouver : Pacific Educational Press, c1999. vii, 424 p. : ill. ; 28 cm. Includes bibliographical references. Previous ed. published by: Simon Fraser University, Faculty of Education, Field Relations and Teacher In-Service Education. ISBN 1-89576-639-7 DDC 300/.71/071
*1. Social sciences - Study and teaching. 2. Sciences sociales - Étude et enseignement. I. Case, Roland. 1951- II. Clark, Penney, 1950-*
*TC H62.5.C3 C32 1999*

**Canadian Association for Adult Education.**
Food for thought. Toronto, The Canadian Association for Adult Education.

Learning for living series. [Toronto]

**Canadian Association of Sports Sciences.**
Canadian journal of applied sport sciences = Windsor, Ont. : Canadian Association of Sports Sciences,

**Canadian Broadcasting Corporation.**
Aging and saging [videorecording]. Princeton, NJ : Films for the Humanities & Sciences : Distributed by Canadian Broadcasting Corporation, 1998.
*TC BF724.55.A35 A35 1998*

**Canadian communication thought.**
Babe, Robert E., 1943- Toronto ; Buffalo : University of Toronto Press, c2000.
*TC P92.5.A1B32 2000*

**Canadian Conservation Institute.**
Strang, Thomas J. K. Controlling museum fungal problems. Ottawa : Canadian Conservation Institute, Department of Communications, [1991]
*TC TH9031 .S75 1991*

**CANADIAN HANDICRAFTS GUILD - HISTORY.**
McLeod, Ellen Mary Easton, 1945- In good hands. Montreal ; Ithaca : Published for Carleton University by McGill-Queen's University Press, c1999.
*TC NK841 .M38 1999*

**Canadian journal of applied sport sciences** = Journal canadien des sciences appliquées au sport. Windsor, Ont. : Canadian Association of Sports Sciences, v. : ill. ;c 28 cm. Began publication 1976; ceased with v. 11, no. 4 (Dec. 1986). Journal canadien des sciences appliquées au sport. Description based on: Vol. 11, no. 1 (Mar. 86); title from cover. Includes some text in French. Continued by: Canadian journal of sport sciences. ISSN 0700-3978 DDC 796/.05
*1. Sports - Periodicals. 2. Sports medicine - Periodicals. I. Canadian Association of Sports Sciences. II. Title: Journal canadien des sciences appliquées au sport III. Title: Canadian journal of sport sciences*

**Canadian journal of sport sciences.**
Canadian journal of applied sport sciences = Windsor, Ont. : Canadian Association of Sports Sciences,

**Canadian Teachers' Federation.**
Racism and education. Ottawa : Canadian Teachers' Federation, 1992.
*TC LC212.3.C3 R32 1992*

**Canadian universities and globalization.**
A new world of knowledge. Ottawa : International Development Research Centre, c1999.
*TC LC1090 N38 1999*

**Canady, Robert Lynn.**
Rettig, Michael D., 1950- Scheduling strategies for middle schools. Larchmont, NY : Eye On Education, 2000.
*TC LB3032.2 .R48 2000*

**Canagarajah, A. Suresh.** Resisting linguistic imperialism in English teaching / A. Suresh Canagarajah. Oxford : Oxford University Press, 1999. viii, 216 p. ; 24 cm. (Oxford applied linguistics.) Includes bibliographical references and index. ISBN 0-19-442154-6

*1. English language - Study and teaching - Sri Lanka. 2. English language - Study and teaching - Social aspects - Sri Lanka. 3. English language - Study and teaching - Political aspects - Sri Lanka. 4. English language - Study and teaching - Foreign speakers. I. Title.*
*TC PE1068.S7 C36 1999*

**CANANDAIGUA (N.Y.) - BIOGRAPHY - JUVENILE LITERATURE.**
Richards, Caroline Cowles, 1842-1913. A nineteenth-century schoolgirl. Mankato, Minn. : Blue Earth Books, c2000.
*TC F129.C2 R53 2000*

**CANANDAIGUA (N.Y.) - SOCIAL LIFE AND CUSTOMS - 19TH CENTURY - JUVENILE LITERATURE.**
Richards, Caroline Cowles, 1842-1913. A nineteenth-century schoolgirl. Mankato, Minn. : Blue Earth Books, c2000.
*TC F129.C2 R53 2000*

**CANCER - NURSING.**
Quality of life from nursing and patient perspectives. Sudbury, Mass. ; London : Jones and Bartlett, c1998.
*TC RC262 .Q34 1998*

**CANCER PATIENTS.** *See* **CANCER - PATIENTS.**

**CANCER - PATIENTS - REHABILITATION.**
Halperin, Jane Carol. The influence of causal attributions on the psychological adjustment of post-treatment adolescent cancer survivors. 1999.
*TC 085 H155*

**CANCER - PSYCHOLOGICAL ASPECTS.**
Quality of life from nursing and patient perspectives. Sudbury, Mass. ; London : Jones and Bartlett, c1998.
*TC RC262 .Q34 1998*

**CANCER - SOCIAL ASPECTS.**
Quality of life from nursing and patient perspectives. Sudbury, Mass. ; London : Jones and Bartlett, c1998.
*TC RC262 .Q34 1998*

**CANCERS.** *See* **CANCER.**

**Candor and perversion.**
Shattuck, Roger. 1st ed. New York : W.W. Norton, c1999.
*TC PN52 .S53 1999*

**Cangelosi, James S.** Classroom management strategies : gaining and maintaining students' cooperation / James S. Cangelosi. 3rd ed. White Plains, N.Y. : Longman, c1997. xv, 383 p. : ill. ; 24 cm. Includes bibliographical references (p. 365-375) and index. ISBN 0-8013-1623-5 ISBN 0-8013-7624-6 DDC 371.1/024
*1. Classroom management - United States. 2. Teacher-student relationships - United States. 3. Rewards and punishments in education - United States. I. Title.*
*TC LB3013 .C3259 1997*

Classroom management strategies : gaining and maintaining students' cooperation / James S. Cangelosi. 4th ed. New York : J. Wiley, c2000. xvi, 432 p. : ill. ; 24 cm. Includes bibliographical references (p. 411-424) and index. ISBN 0-8013-3059-9 DDC 371.102/4
*1. Classroom management - United States. 2. Teacher-student relationships - United States. 3. Rewards and punishments in education - United States. I. Title.*
*TC LB3013 .C3259 2000*

**CANIDAE.** *See* **FOXES.**

**Canino, Ian A.** Culturally diverse children and adolescents : assessment, diagnosis, and treatment / Ian A. Canino, Jeanne Spurlock ; foreword by Clarice J. Kestenbaum. 2nd ed. New York : Guilford Press, c2000. xii, 228 p. ; 23 cm. Includes bibliographical references (p. 195-221) and index. ISBN 1-57230-583-5 (acid-free paper) DDC 618.92/89/0089
*1. Children of minorities - Mental health. 2. Child psychiatry - Social aspects. 3. Minority teenagers - Mental health. 4. Adolescent psychiatry - Social aspects. 5. Mental Disorders - Adolescence. 6. Mental Disorders - Child. 7. Cultural Characteristics. 8. Ethnic Groups - psychology. 9. Psychotherapy. I. Spurlock, Jeanne. II. Title.*
*TC RJ507.M54 C36 2000*

**CANIS.** *See* **COYOTES; WOLVES.**

**CANIS LATRANS.** *See* **COYOTES.**

**CANIS LUPUS.** *See* **WOLVES.**

**Cann, Helen.**
Evetts-Secker, Josephine. Father and son tales. Richmond Hill, Ont. : Scholastic Canada, 1998.
*TC GR469 E93 1998*

**Cann, Helen, ill.**
Gilchrist, Cherry. Calendar of festivals. Kingswood, Bristol, U.K. : Barefoot Books, c1998.

*TC GT3932 .G54 1998*

**Cannon, Harold C., 1930-.**
Banner, James M., 1935- The elements of learning. New Haven, Conn. : Yale University Press, c1999.
*TC LB1060 .B36 1999*

**CANON LAW.** *See* **ECCLESIASTICAL LAW.**

**CANONIZATION.** *See* **CHRISTIAN SAINTS.**

**Cantrill, James G. (James Gerard),-.**
Honeycutt, James M. Cognition, communication, and romantic relationships. Mahwah, N.J. ; London : L. Erlbaum Associates, 2001.
*TC BF575.I5 H66 2001*

**CANVASSING.** *See* **PEDDLERS AND PEDDLING.**

**Cao, Zhen.**
Ashmore, Rhea A. Teacher education in the People's Republic of China. Bloomington, Ind., U.S.A. : Phi Delta Kappa Educational Foundation, c1997.
*TC LB1727.C5 A85 1997*

**CAPACITY AND DISABILITY.** *See* **GUARDIAN AND WARD.**

**Capaldi, E. John.** Contextualism in psychological research? : a critical review / E.J. Capaldi, Robert W. Proctor. Thousand Oaks, Calif. : Sage, c1999. xiii, 193 p. ; 24 cm. Includes bibliographical references (p. 175-184) and indexes. ISBN 0-7619-0997-4 (hardcover : alk. paper) ISBN 0-7619-0998-2 (pbk. : alk. paper) DDC 150.19/8
*1. Context effects (Psychology) 2. Relativity. I. Proctor, Robert W. II. Title.*
*TC BF315.2 .C37 1999*

**CAPE COLOURED PEOPLE.** *See* **COLORED PEOPLE (SOUTH AFRICA).**

**Capeheart-Meningall, Jennifer.** Quality of students of color efort on a predominantly white college and the internal environmental elements that influence involvement / by Jennifer Capeheart- Meningall. 1998. ix, 184 leaves ; 29 cm. Typescript; issued also on microfilm. Thesis (Ed.D.)--Teachers College, Columbia University, 1998. Includes bibliographical references (leaves 154-165).
*1. Minorities - Education (Higher) - United States. 2. African Americans - Education (Higher) - United States. 3. Asian Americans - Education (Higher) - United States. 4. Hispanic Americans - Education (Higher) - United States. 5. Indians of North America - Education (Higher) - United States. 6. College students - Attitudes. 7. College environment - United States - Evaluation. 8. Race awareness - United States. 9. Alienation (Social psychology) I. Title.*
*TC 06 no. 10874*

**Capel, Susan Anne, 1953-.**
Learning to teach in the secondary school. 2nd ed. London ; New York : Routledge, 1999.
*TC LB1737.A3 L43 1999*

**Caper, Robert.** Immaterial facts : Freud's discovery of psychic reality and Klein's development of his work / Robert Caper. London ; New York : Routledge, 2000. xiv, 161 p. ; 24 cm. Includes bibliographical references (p. [153]-156) and index. ISBN 0-415-22083-1 ISBN 0-415-22084-X (pbk.) DDC 150.19/52
*1. Psychoanalysis. 2. Freud, Sigmund, - 1856-1939 - Influence. 3. Klein, Melanie. I. Title.*
*TC BF173 .C35 2000*

**CAPITAL.** *See* **CAPITALISM; HUMAN CAPITAL; WEALTH.**

**CAPITAL AND LABOR.** *See* **INDUSTRIAL RELATIONS.**

**Capital Cities/ABC, Inc.**
Sean's story [videorecording]. Princeton, N.J. : Films for the Humanities & Sciences ; [S.l. : distributed by] ABC Multimedia : Capital Cities/ABC, c1994.
*TC LC1203.M3 .S39 1994*

**CAPITAL, INTELLECTUAL.** *See* **INTELLECTUAL CAPITAL.**

**CAPITAL INVESTMENTS.**
Organisation for Economic Co-operation and Development (Paris) The appraisal of investments in educational facilities. Paris : Organisation for Economic Co-operation and Development, 2000.
*TC LB2342.3 .A7 2000*

**CAPITALISM.** *See* **ENTREPRENEURSHIP; MIXED ECONOMY.**

**CAPITALISM - UNITED STATES - HISTORY - 20TH CENTURY.**
Andrews, Marcellus, 1956- The political economy of hope and fear. New York : New York University Press, c1999.
*TC E185.8 .A77 1999*

**CAPITALISTS AND FINANCIERS - UNITED STATES - BIOGRAPHY.**
Sanger, Martha Frick Symington. Henry Clay Frick. 1st ed. New York : Abbeville Press Publishers, c1998.
*TC HC102.5.F75 S32 1998*

**Capitalizing knowledge :** essays on the history of business education in Canada / edited by Barbara Austin. Toronto : University of Toronto Press, c2000. viii, 371 p. : ill. ; 24 cm. ISBN 0-8020-4234-1 DDC 650/.071/171
*1. Business education - Canada - History. 2. Enseignement commercial - Canada - Histoire. I. Austin, Barbara J.*
*TC HF1131 .C36 2000*

**CAPITULATIONS, MILITARY. See PRISONERS OF WAR.**

**Capozzoli, Thomas.** Kids killing kids : managing violence and gangs in schools / Thomas K. Capozzoli and R. Steve McVey. Boca Raton, Fla. ; London : St. Lucie Press, c2000. x, 156 p. : ill., maps ; 24 cm. Includes bibliographical references (p. 147-149) and index. ISBN 1-57444-283-X (alk. paper) DDC 371.7/82/0973
*1. School violence - United States - Prevention. 2. Schools - United States - Safety measures. I. McVey, R. Steve. II. Title.*
*TC LB3013.3 .C37 2000*

**Cappella, David.**
Wormser, Baron. Teaching the art of poetry. Mahwah, N.J. : Lawrence Erlbaum Assoc., 2000.
*TC PN1101 .W67 2000*

**Capper, Colleen A., 1960-** Meeting the needs of students of all abilities : how leaders go beyond inclusion / Colleen A. Capper, Elise Frattura, Maureen W. Keyes. Thousand Oaks, Calif. : Corwin Press, c2000. xx, 201 p. : ill. ; 29 cm. Includes bibliographical references (p. 191-194) and index. ISBN 0-7619-7500-4 (alk. paper) ISBN 0-7619-7501-2 (pbk. : alk. paper) DDC 371.9/046
*1. Inclusive education - United States. 2. School districts - United States. 3. School management and organization - United States. I. Frattura, Elise. II. Keyes, Maureen W. III. Title.*
*TC LC1201 .C36 2000*

**Captain Underpants and the invasion of the incredibly naughty cafeteria ladies from outer space ...**
Pilkey, Dav, 1966- New York : Blue Sky Press, c1999.
*TC PZ7.P63123 Cat 1999*

**CAPTIVE WILD ANIMALS. See ZOO ANIMALS.**

**Carabins ou activistes?.**
Neatby, Nicole, 1962- Montréal ; Ithaca : McGill-Queen's University Press, [1999?], c1997.
*TC LA418.Q8 N42 1999*

**CARBOHYDRATE INTOLERANCE. See DIABETES.**

**Carbone, Elisa Lynn.** Teaching large classes : tools and strategies / Elisa Carbone. Thousand Oaks, Calif. : Sage Publications, c1998. xviii, 97 p. ; 23 cm. (Survival skills for scholars ; v. 19) Includes bibliographical references and index. CONTENTS: Starting the semester : the first class -- Personalizing the large class -- Lecturing 101 : getting your students to listen -- Lecturing 102 : using stories and examples -- Using demonstrations, visual aids and technology -- Active learning in a large class -- Are there any questions? -- Assessment and feedback in large classes -- Managing student behavior -- Working effectively with teaching assistants (TAs). ISBN 0-7619-0974-5 (cloth : acid-free paper) ISBN 0-7619-0975-3 (pbk. : acid-free paper) DDC 378.12
*1. College teaching - United States. 2. Class size - United States. 3. Lecture method in teaching. I. Title. II. Series.*
*TC LB2331 .C336 1998*

**Carbone, Teresa A.** Eastman Johnson : painting America / Teresa A. Carbone, Patricia Hills ; with contributions by Jane Weiss, Sarah Burns, Anne C. Rose ; edited by Teresa A. Carbone. New York : Brooklyn Museum of Art in association with Rizzoli International Publications, 1999. 272 p. : col. ill. ; 32 cm. Catalog of the exhibition held at the Brooklyn Museum of Art, Oct. 29, 1999 to Feb. 6, 2000; San Diego Museum of Art, Feb. 26 to May 21, 2000; and Seattle Art Museum, June 8 to Sept. 10, 2000. Includes bibliographical references (p. [267]) and index. ISBN 0-8478-2214-1 (Rizzoli : pbk.) ISBN 0-87273-138-3 (Brooklyn Museum : pbk.) DDC 759.13
*1. Johnson, Eastman, - 1824-1906 - Exhibitions. I. Johnson, Eastman, 1824-1906. II. Hills, Patricia. III. Brooklyn Museum of Art. IV. San Diego Museum of Art. V. Seattle Art Museum. VI. Title.*
*TC ND237.J7 A4 1999*

**CARBOXYLIC ACIDS. See FATTY ACIDS.**

**CARCINOMA. See CANCER.**

**Cardiff papers in qualitative research**
Gender and qualitative research. Aldershot, Hants, England : Brookfield, Vt., USA : Avebury, c1996.
*TC HQ1075 .G4617 1996*

Qualitative research. Aldershot, Hants, England : Brookfield, Vt. : Avebury, c1996.
*TC H62 .Q355 1996*

**CARDIOVASCULAR SYSTEM. See BLOOD - CIRCULATION.**

**CARDIOVASCULAR SYSTEM - PHYSIOLOGY.**
Exercise and circulation in health and disease. Champaign, IL ; Leeds, U.K. : Human Kinetics, c2000.
*TC QP301 .E9346 2000*

**CARDIOVASCULAR SYSTEM - PHYSIOLOGY.**
Rowell, Loring B. Human cardiovascular control. New York : Oxford University Press, 1993.
*TC QP109 .R68 1993*

**CARDS, POSTAL. See POSTCARDS.**

**Cardwell, Mike.**
**Complete A Z psychology handbook.**
Cardwell, Mike. The dictionary of psychology. London ; Chicago : Fitzroy Dearborn Publishers, 1999, c1996.
*TC BF31 .C33 1999*

The dictionary of psychology / Mike Cardwell ; series editor, Ian Marcousé. London ; Chicago : Fitzroy Dearborn Publishers, 1999, c1996. vi, 249 p. ; 24 cm. "First published 1996 in the United Kingdom by Hodder and Stoughton Educational as 'The complete A-Z psychology handbook'"--T.p. verso. ISBN 1-57958-064-5
*1. Psychology - Dictionaries. 2. Psychiatry - Dictionaries. 3. Psychology - dictionary. 4. Psychiatry - dictionary. I. Cardwell, Mike. Complete A-Z psychology handbook. II. Title.*
*TC BF31 .C33 1999*

**Care about education.**
Morgan, Sally, 1951- London : DfEE, 1999.
*TC HV59 .M67 1999*

**The care and education of a deaf child.**
Knight, Pamela, 1940- Clevedon [England] ; Buffalo [N.Y.] : Multilingual Matters, c1999.
*TC HV2716 .K65 1999*

**CARE GIVERS. See CAREGIVERS.**

**CARE, INSTITUTIONAL. See INSTITUTIONAL CARE.**

**CARE OF CHILDREN. See CHILD CARE.**

**CARE OF SOULS. See PASTORAL COUNSELING.**

**CARE OF THE SICK. See LONG-TERM CARE OF THE SICK; NURSING; TERMINAL CARE.**

**CARE OF THE YOUNG (ANIMALS). See PARENTAL BEHAVIOR IN ANIMALS.**

**CAREER ADVANCEMENT. See CAREER DEVELOPMENT.**

**Career and human resource development.**
American Society for Training and Development. Issues in career and human resource development. Madison, Wisc. : American Society for Training and Development, c1980.
*TC HF5549.5.T7 A59 1980*

**CAREER CHANGES - GREAT BRITAIN.**
Ali, Lynda, 1946- Moving on in your career. London ; New York : RoutledgeFalmer, 2000.
*TC LB1778.4.G7 A45 2000*

**CAREER CHOICE. See VOCATIONAL GUIDANCE.**

**CAREER COUNSELING. See VOCATIONAL GUIDANCE.**

**Career counseling of college students :** an empirical guide to strategies that work / edited by Darrell Anthony Luzzo. Washington, DC : American Psychological Association, c2000. xx, 353 p. : ill. ; 27 cm. Includes bibliographical references and indexes. ISBN 1-55797-708-4 (casebound : alk. paper) DDC 378.1/9425/0973
*1. Counseling in higher education - United States. 2. Vocational guidance - United States. 3. College students - United States. I. Luzzo, Darrell Anthony.*
*TC LB2343 .C3273 2000*

**The career counselor's handbook.**
Figler, Howard E. Berkeley, Calif. : Ten Speed Press, c1999.
*TC HF5549.5.C35 F54 1999*

**CAREER COUPLES. See DUAL-CAREER FAMILIES.**

**Career development.**
Peatling, John H. Muncie, Ind. : Accelerated Development, c1977.
*TC BF697 .P384*

**CAREER DEVELOPMENT.**
Career development and planning. Belmont, CA ; London : Brooks/Cole/Thomson Learning, c2000.
*TC HF5381 .C265275 2000*

Career frontiers. New York : Oxford University Press 2000.
*TC HF5549.5.C35 C367 2000*

McCabe, Linda. How to succeed in academics. San Diego, Calif. : Academic, c2000.
*TC LB2331.7 .M34 2000*

**Career development and planning :** a comprehensive approach / Robert C. Reardon ... [et al.]. Belmont, CA ; London : Brooks/Cole/Thomson Learning, c2000. xxvii, 379 p. : ill. ; 25 cm. Includes bibliographical references (p. 357-366) and indexes. ISBN 0-534-36472-1 (alk. paper) DDC 650.14
*1. Career development. I. Reardon, Robert C.*
*TC HF5381 .C265275 2000*

**CAREER DEVELOPMENT - CASE STUDIES.**
Swanson, Jane Laurel. Career theory and practice. Thousand Oaks, Calif. : Sage Publications, c1999.
*TC HF5381 .S937 1999*

**Career discovery encyclopedia.** 4th ed. Chicago : Ferguson Pub. Co., 2000. 8 v. : ill. ; 24 cm. Includes index. SUMMARY: Six volumes with over 500 articles on all categories of occupations present such information as job descriptions, salaries, educational and training requirements, sources of further information, and other pertinent facts. ISBN 0-89434-275-4 DDC 331.7/02
*1. Vocational guidance - Dictionaries - Juvenile literature. 2. Vocational guidance - Dictionaries. 3. Occupations. I. J.G. Ferguson Publishing Company.*
*TC HF5381.2 .C37 2000*

**CAREER EDUCATION. See also PROFESSIONAL EDUCATION; SCHOOL-TO-WORK TRANSITION.**
Organisation for Economic Co-operation and Development (Paris) From initial education to working life. Paris : Organisation for Economic Co-operation and Development, 2000.
*TC LC1037 .O74 2000*

Weintraub, Robert Steven. Informal learning in the workplace through desktop technology. 1998.
*TC 06 no. 11003*

**CAREER EDUCATION - EUROPE.**
Bridging the skills gap between work and education. Dordrecht ; Boston : Kluwer Academic Publishers, c1999.
*TC LC5056.A2 B75 1999*

**CAREER EDUCATION - UNITED STATES.**
Steinberg, Adria. Schooling for the real world. 1st ed. San Francisco : Jossey-Bass, c1999.
*TC LC1037.5 .S843 1999*

**Career frontiers :** new conceptions of working lives / edited by Maury Peiperl ... [et al.]. New York : Oxford University Press 2000. xvii, 290 p. : ill. ; 25 cm. Includes bibliographical references and index. DDC 331.7
*1. Career development. I. Peiperl, Maury.*
*TC HF5549.5.C35 C367 2000*

**Career Guidance Foundation (La Jolla, San Diego, Calif.).**
[CollegeSource (Online)] CollegeSource [computer file]. San Diego, Calif. : The Foundation, [1997-

CollegeSource online [computer file]. San Diego, CA : The Foundation, c1999-
*TC NETWORKED RESOURCE*

**CAREER LADDER. See CAREER DEVELOPMENT.**

**CAREER MANAGEMENT. See CAREER DEVELOPMENT.**

**CAREER PATTERNS. See OCCUPATIONS; PROFESSIONS; VOCATIONAL GUIDANCE.**

**CAREER PLANNING. See CAREER DEVELOPMENT; VOCATIONAL GUIDANCE.**

**Career theory and practice.**
Swanson, Jane Laurel. Thousand Oaks, Calif. : Sage Publications, c1999.
*TC HF5381 .S937 1999*

**CAREERS.** *See* OCCUPATIONS; PROFESSIONS; VOCATIONAL GUIDANCE.

**Careers by design.**
Goldfarb, Roz. Rev. ed. New York, NY : Allworth Press Council, c1997.
*TC NC1001 .G65 1997*

**The careers of women teachers under apartheid.**
Mahlase, Shirley Motleke. Harare : SAPES Books, c1997.
*TC LB2832.4.S6 M35 1997*

**CAREGIVERS.**
Mace, Nancy L. The 36-hour day. 3rd ed. Baltimore : Johns Hopkins University Press, c1999.
*TC RC523 .M33 1999*

Noon, J. Mitchell. Counselling and helping carers. Leicester : BPS Books, 1999.
*TC R727.4 .N66 1999*

**CAREGIVERS - CONGRESSES.**
Caregiving systems. Hillsdale, N.J. : L. Erlbaum Associates, 1993.
*TC HV1451 .C329 1993*

**CAREGIVERS - CONGRESSES.**
Caregiving systems. Hillsdale, N.J. : L. Erlbaum Associates, 1993.
*TC HV1451 .C329 1993*

**CAREGIVERS - RECREATION.**
Caregiving--leisure and aging. New York : Haworth Press, c1999.
*TC HV1451 .C327 1999*

**CAREGIVERS - UNITED STATES - ATTITUDES - CASE STUDIES.**
Brown, Gloria M. Post-hospital care for the elderly. 1997.
*TC 06 no. 10759*

**Caregiving--leisure and aging** / M. Jean Keller, editor. New York : Haworth Press, c1999. xiv, 103 p. ; 22 cm. "Caregiving--leisure and aging has been co-published simultaneously as Activities, adaptation & aging, Volume 24, Number 2 1999." Includes bibliographical references and index. ISBN 0-7890-0799-1 (alk. paper) DDC 362.6
*1. Aged - Home care - Psychological aspects. 2. Caregivers - Recreation. 3. Leisure. I. Keller, M. Jean. II. Title: Activities, adaptation & aging.*
*TC HV1451 .C327 1999*

**Caregiving systems** : informal and formal helpers / edited by Steven H. Zarit, Leonard I. Pearlin, K. Warner Schaie. Hillsdale, N.J. : L. Erlbaum Associates, 1993. x, 332 p. : ill. ; 24 cm. (Social structure and aging) "Edited proceedings of a conference held at the Pennsylvania State University, October 13-14, 1989"--Pref. Includes bibliographical references and indexes. ISBN 0-8058-1094-3 (acid-free paper) DDC 362.6
*1. Aged - Care - Congresses. 2. Caregivers - Congresses. 3. Aged - Services for - Congresses. 4. Aged - Medical care - Congresses. 5. Aged - Home care - Congresses. 6. Aged. 7. Caregivers - congresses. 8. Home Care Services. 9. Home Nursing. I. Zarit, Steven H. II. Pearlin, Leonard I. (Leonard Irving), 1924- III. Schaie, K. Warner (Klaus Warner), 1928- IV. Series.*
*TC HV1451 .C329 1993*

**CARERS.** *See* CAREGIVERS.

**The CARES directory in electronic form** [computer file] Maywood, NJ : ACIT, computer optical discs ; 4 3/4 in. + user manual (20 p. ; 22 cm.). Frequency: Annual. 1994-1999- . "Contains social and health services in the greater New York City area." Also available in print version and online via World Wide Web. Derived from the CARES database maintained by United Way of New York City in partnership with the New York City Human Resources Administration. URL: http://www.uwnyc.org/ Continues: Source book ISSN: 0740-4549 (IaU)ADV6653.
*1. Social service - New York Metropolitan Area - Directories. 2. Public health - New York Metropolitan Area - Directories. 3. Health facilities - New York Metropolitan Area - Directories. 4. Social service - New York (City) - directories. 5. Health Services - New York (City) - directories. 6. Health Facilities - New York (City) - directories. 7. Health (N.Y.) - Directories. 8. Social service - New York (N.Y.) - Directories. I. United Way of New York City. II. New York (N.Y.). Human Resources Administration. III. Title: Community access to resources directory IV. Title: Source book*
*TC HV99.N59 S58*

**Carey, Karen T., 1952-**
Barnett, David W., 1946- Designing preschool interventions. New York : Guilford Press, 1999.
*TC LC4801 .B36 1999*

**Carey, Lou.** Measuring and evaluating school learning / Lou M. Carey. 2nd ed. Boston : Allyn and Bacon, c1994. xxiii, 534 p. ; 24 cm. + 1 computer disk. Includes bibliographical references and index. ISBN 0-205-12865-3

DDC 371.2/6/0973
*1. Educational tests and measurements - United States. I. Title.*
*TC LB3051 .C36 1994*

Measuring and evaluating school learning / Lou M. Carey. 3rd ed. Boston : London : Allyn and Bacon, c2001. xxiii, 550 p. : ill. ; 25 cm. Includes bibliographical references and index. ISBN 0-205-32388-X (alk. paper) DDC 371.2/6/0973
*1. Educational tests and measurements - United States. I. Title.*
*TC LB3051 .C36 2001*

**CARIBBEAN AREA - FICTION.**
Garne, S. T. By a blazing blue sea. San Diego : Harcourt Brace & Co., 1999.
*TC PZ8.3.G1866 By 1999*

**CARIBBEAN AREA - JUVENILE FICTION.**
Garne, S. T. By a blazing blue sea. San Diego : Harcourt Brace & Co., 1999.
*TC PZ8.3.G1866 By 1999*

**CARIBBEAN FREE TRADE ASSOCIATION COUNTRIES.** *See* CARIBBEAN AREA.

**CARIBBEAN ISLANDS.** *See* WEST INDIES.

**CARIBBEAN REGION.** *See* CARIBBEAN AREA.

**CARIBBEAN SEA REGION.** *See* CARIBBEAN AREA.

**CARICATURE.** *See* CARTOONING; WIT AND HUMOR.

**CARICATURES AND CARTOONS.** *See also* CARTOONING; COMIC BOOKS, STRIPS, ETC.
Comics, the 9th art [videorecording]. [S.l.] : EPISA : Cicero, Ill. : [Distributed by] The Roland Collection, 1990.
*TC PN6710 .C6 1990*

**CARILLONS.** *See* HANDBELL RINGING.

**CARING.**
Lyman, Linda L. How do they know you care? New York : Teachers College Press, c2000.
*TC LB2831.924.13 L96 2000*

**Caring as tenacity** : stories of urban school survival / edited by Mary Anne Pitman, Debbie Zorn. Cresskill, N.J. : Hampton Press, c2000. viii, 141 p. ; 24 cm. (Understanding education and policy) Includes bibliographical references (p. 131-135) and indexes. ISBN 1-57273-210-5 (hbk.) 1-57273-211-3 (pbk.) DDC 370/.9173/2
*1. Education. Urban - United States. 2. Socially handicapped children - Services for - United States. 3. Mentoring in education - United States. I. Pitman, Mary Anne. II. Zorn, Debbie. III. Series.*
*TC LC5131 .C35 2000*

**Caring enough to lead.**
Pellicer, Leonard O. Thousand Oaks, Calif. : Corwin Press, c1999.
*TC LB2805 .P375 1999*

**Caring for children**
(no.7.) Murphy, Lois Barclay, 1902- The individual child. Washington : Department of Health Education, and Welfare : for sale by the Supt. of Docs., U. S. Govt. Print. Off., 1973.

**A caring world** : the new social policy agenda / Organisation for Economic Co-operation and Development. Paris : The Organisation, c1999. 156 p. : ill. (some col.) ; 27 cm. Includes bibliographical references (p. 149-156). Other editions available: Pour un monde solidaire : le nouvel agenda social 9264270078. ISBN 92-64-17007-3 DDC 361.6/1
*1. OECD countries - Social policy. I. Organisation for Economic Co-operation and Development. II. Title: Pour un monde solidaire : le nouvel agenda social*
*TC HN17.5 .C323 1999*

**Carini, Patricia F.**
From another angle. New York : Teachers College Press, c2000.
*TC LB1117 .F735 2000*

**Carl Gustav Jung interviewed in Zurich, Switzerland on August 5-8, 1957 [videorecording].**
Jung on film [videorecording]. [Chicago, Ill.?] : Public Media Video, c1990.
*TC BF109.J8 J4 1990*

Jung on film [videorecording]. [Chicago, Ill.?] : Public Media Video, c1990.
*TC BF109.J8 J4 1990*

**Carle, Eric, ill.**
Martin, Bill, 1916- Brown bear, brown bear, what do you see? New York : H. Holt, 1992.
*TC PZ8.3.M418 Br 1992*

**Carlebach, Michael L.** American photojournalism comes of age / Michael L. Carlebach. Washington : Smithsonian Institution Press, c1997. ix, 217 p. : ill. ; 28 cm. Includes bibliographical references (p. 209-212) and index. ISBN 1-56098-786-3 (alk. paper) DDC 070.4/9/0973
*1. Photojournalism - United States - History. I. Title.*
*TC TR820 .C356 1997*

The origins of photojournalism in America / Michael L. Carlebach. Washington : Smithsonian Institution Press, c1992. x, 194 p. : ill. ; 28 cm. Includes bibliographical references (p. 184-189) and index. ISBN 1-56098-159-8 DDC 070.4/9/097309034
*1. Photojournalism - United States - History. I. Title.*
*TC TR820 .C357 1992*

**Carling, M.** Linux system administration / M. Carling, Stephen Degler, James Dennis. Indianapolis, IN : New Riders, c2000. xx, 337 p. : ill. ; 23 cm. Includes bibliographical references (p. [295]-296) and index. ISBN 1-56205-934-3
*1. Linux. 2. Operating systems (Computers) I. Degler, Stephen. II. Dennis, James. III. Title.*
*TC QA76.76.O63 C3755 2000*

**Carlino, Andrea, 1960-**
**[Fabbrica del corpo. English]**
Books of the body : anatomical ritual and renaissance learning / Andrea Carlino ; translated by John Tedeschi and Anne C. Tedeschi. Chicago : University of Chicago Press, c1999. xiv, 266 p. : ill. ; 24 cm. Includes bibliographical references (p. 233-250) and index. Table of Contents URL: http://lcweb.loc.gov/catdir/toc/99025338.html ISBN 0-226-09287-9 (cloth : alk. paper) DDC 611/.009/031
*1. Human dissection - History - 16th century. 2. Human anatomy - History - 16th century. 3. Renaissance. I. Title.*
*TC QM33.4 .C3613 1999*

**Carl's afternoon in the park.**
Day, Alexandra. 1st ed. New York : Farrar, Straus & Giroux, 1991.
*TC PZ7.D32915 Cars 1991*

**Carlson, Caryn L.**
Pliszka, Steven R. ADHD with comorbid disorders. New York : Guilford Press, c1999.
*TC RJ506.H9 P55 1999*

**Carlson, Laurie M., 1952-** A fever in Salem : a new interpretation of the New England witch trials / Laurie Winn Carlson. Chicago : I.R. Dee, 1999. xvi, 197 p. ; 22 cm. Includes bibliographical references and index. ISBN 1-56663-253-6 (alk. paper) DDC 133.4/3/097445
*1. Witchcraft - Massachusetts - Salem - History - 17th century. 2. Epidemic encephalitis - Massachusetts - Salem - History - 17th century. I. Title.*
*TC BF1576 .C37 1999*

**Carlson, Les.**
Advertising to children. Thousand Oaks, Calif. : Sage Publications, c1999.
*TC HQ784.T4 A29 1999*

**Carly.**
Fuchshuber, Annegert. [Karlinchen. English] 1st ed. New York : The Feminist Press, c1997.
*TC PZ7.F94 Car 1997*

**Carmen Sandiego** [computer file] : math detective. Novato, Calif. : Brøderbund Software, 1998. Computer data and program. 1 computer optical disc : sd., col. ; 4 3/4 in. + 1 Acme agent handbook (28 p. : ill. ; 23 cm.) + 1 troubleshooting guide. System requirements for Macintosh: System 7.5.1 or higher ; 100MHz PowerPC (603e) or faster ; 16MB RAM ; minimum 20MB hard disk space; 4X CD-ROM drive or faster ; 640x480 display, 256 colors. System requirements for Windows: Windows 95 or Windows 98, 66Mhz 486 or faster, Pentium recommended ; 16MB RAM ; 20MB hard disk space ; 4X CD-ROM drive or faster ; 640x480 display, 256 colors ; Windows compatible sound device. Title from disc label. "Thrilling missions for math success."--Promotional container. SUMMARY: The villain Carmen Sandiego is shrinking famous landmarks. The user is invited to apply 4th-, 5th, and 6th-grade mathematics and geometry skills to thwart her. Includes three levels of difficulty. "Ages 8 to 14"--Container. ISBN 1-57382-151-9
*1. Arithmetic - Juvenile software. 2. Educational games - Software. 3. Computer adventure games - Juvenile software. 4. Sandiego, Carmen (Fictitious character). I. Brøderbund. II. Title: Math detective [computer file]*
*TC QA115 .C37 1998*

**CARNEGIE CORPORATION OF NEW YORK.**
Lagemann, Ellen Condliffe, 1945- The politics of knowledge. 1st ed. Middletown, Conn. : Wesleyan University Press, c1989.
*TC HV97.C3 L34 1989*

**Carnegie Foundation for the Advancement of Teaching.**
The international academic profession. Princeton,

N.J. : Carnegie Foundation for the Advancement of
Teaching, c1996.
*TC LB1778 .I54 1996*

**The carnitine defense.**
DeFelice, Stephen L., 1936- [Emmaus, Pa.] : Rodale
Press ; [New York] : Distributed to the book trade by
St. Martin's Press, c1999.
*TC RC685.C6 D4235 1999*

**CARNITINE - THERAPEUTIC USE.**
DeFelice, Stephen L., 1936- The carnitine defense.
[Emmaus, Pa.] : Rodale Press ; [New York] :
Distributed to the book trade by St. Martin's Press,
c1999.
*TC RC685.C6 D4235 1999*

**CARNITINE - THERAPEUTIC USE.**
DeFelice, Stephen L., 1936- The carnitine defense.
[Emmaus, Pa.] : Rodale Press ; [New York] :
Distributed to the book trade by St. Martin's Press,
c1999.
*TC RC685.C6 D4235 1999*

**CARNIVORA.** *See* BEARS; FELIDAE.

**Carnoy, Martin.** Globalization and educational reform :
What planners need to know / Martin Carnoy. Paris :
International Institute for Educational Planning (IIEP),
1999. 96 p. ; 21 cm. (Fundamentals of educational planning ;
63) Includes bibliographical references. ISBN 92-803-1192-1
DDC 370
*1. Educational planning. 2. Educational change. I. Title. II.
Series.*
*TC LB5 .F85 v.63*

**Carolyn and Ernest Fay series in analytical
psychology**
(no. 3) Stevens, Anthony. The two million-year-old
self. New York : Fromm International Publishing,
1997.
*TC BF175.5.A72 S75 1997*

**Carothers, Jacqueline.**
Dyer, Karen M. The intuitive principal. Thousand
Oaks, Calif. : Corwin Press, c2000.
*TC LB2831.92 .D94 2000*

**Carpenter, Charles H.**
Portraits of native Americans. New York : New
Press : Distributed by W.W. Norton, c1994.
*TC TR140.C388 C48*

**CARPENTER, CHARLES H.**
Portraits of native Americans. New York : New
Press : Distributed by W.W. Norton, c1994.
*TC TR140.C388 C48*

**Carpenter, Dona Rinaldi.**
Integrating community service into nursing education.
New York, NY : Springer Pub. Co., c1999.
*TC RT76 .I55 1999*

Streubert, Helen J. Qualitative research in nursing.
2nd ed. Philadelphia : Lippincott, c1999.
*TC RT81.5 .S78 1999*

**Carpenter, Hattie H., ed.**
Florida school exponent Miami, Fla.,

**Carpenter, Leona.**
Towards the digital library. London : The British
Library, 1998.
*TC Z664.B75 T683 1998*

**CARPETBAG RULE.** *See* RECONSTRUCTION.

**CARPETS.** *See* RUGS.

**Carr, Alan, Dr.**
Clinical psychology in Ireland. Lewiston, N.Y. : E.
Mellen, 2000.
*TC RC466.83.I73 C56 2000*

**Carr, David, 1944-** Professionalism and ethics in
teaching / David Carr. London ; New York :
Routledge, 2000. xvi, 275 p. ; 23 cm. (Professional ethics)
Includes bibliographical references (p. 263-270) and index.
ISBN 0-415-18459-2 (hard) ISBN 0-415-18460-6 (pbk.) DDC
174/.937
*1. Teachers - Professional ethics. 2. Moral education. 3. Moral
education. 4. Teachers - Professional ethics. I. Title. II. Series.*
*TC LB1779 .C37 2000*

**Carr, Janine Chappell.** A child went forth : reflective
teaching with young readers and writers / Janine
Chappell Carr. Portsmouth, NH : Heinemann, 1999.
xxvi, 390 p. : ill. ; 25 cm. Includes bibliographical references
(p. 377-379) and index. ISBN 0-325-00171-5 DDC 372.6/044
*1. Language arts (Elementary) - United States. 2. Reading
(Elementary) - United States. 3. English language -
Composition and exercises - Study and teaching (Elementary) -
United States. 4. Carr, Janine Chappell. 5. Elementary school
teachers - United States - Biography. I. Title.*

*TC LB1576 .C31714 1999*

**CARR, JANINE CHAPPELL.**
Carr, Janine Chappell. A child went forth. Portsmouth,
NH : Heinemann, 1999.
*TC LB1576 .C31714 1999*

**Carr, Richard John.** The application of multimedia in
arts-integrated curricula / by Richard John Carr. 1998.
294 leaves : ill. ; 29 cm. Typescript; issued also on microfilm.
Thesis (Ed.D.)--Teachers College, Columbia University, 1998.
Includes bibliographical references (leaves 289-294).
*1. Middle schools - New York (State) - Curricula - Case
studies. 2. Interaction analysis in education - Audio-visual
aids. 3. Interdisciplinary approach in education - Case studies.
4. Problem solving - Study and teaching (Middle school) - New
York (State) - Case studies. 5. Creative thinking - Study and
teaching (Middle school) - New York (State) - Case studies. 6.
Creation (Literary, artistic, etc.) I. Title.*
*TC 06 no. 10919*

**Carrasquillo, Angela.**
The teaching of reading in Spanish to the bilingual
student = 2nd ed. Mahwah, N.J. : L. Erlbaum
Associates, 1998.
*TC LB1573 .T365 1998*

**Carré, Clive.**
Bennett, Neville. Skills development in higher
education and employment. Buckingham [England] ;
Philadelphia : Society for Research into Higher
Education & Open University Press, 2000.
*TC LB1027.47 .B46 2000*

**Carrell, Susan.** Group exercises for adolescents : a
manual for therapists / Susan Carrell. 2nd ed.
Thousand Oaks : Sage Publications, c2000. xii, 188 p. :
ill. ; 28 cm. Includes bibliographical references (p. 186). ISBN
0-7619-1953-8 (pbk.) DDC 616.89/152/0835
*1. Group psychotherapy for teenagers - Problems, exercises,
etc. I. Title.*
*TC RJ505.G7 C37 2000*

**Carretero, Mario.**
New perspectives on conceptual change. 1st ed.
Amsterdam ; New York ; Oxford : Pergamon, 1999.
*TC LB1062 .N49 1999*

**Carrick, Carol.** Patrick's dinosaurs on the Internet /
Carol Carrick ; illustrated by David Milgrim. New
York : Clarion Books, 1999. 1 v. (unpaged) : col. ill. ; 26
cm. SUMMARY: After looking up information about
dinosaurs on his computer, Patrick is awakened by a dinosaur
who arrives in a spaceship to take Patrick to his planet for
show and tell. ISBN 0-395-50949-1 DDC [E]
*1. Dinosaurs - Fiction. 2. Interplanetary voyages - Fiction. 3.
Computers - Fiction. 4. Show-and-tell presentations - Fiction.
5. Schools - Fiction. I. Milgrim, David, ill. II. Title.*
*TC PZ7.C2344 Patf 1999*

**Carrier, Betsy.**
Andrulis, Dennis P. Managed care and the inner city.
San Francisco : Jossey-Bass, 1999.
*TC RA413.5.U5 A57 1999*

**Carrier, Martin.**
Science at century's end. Pittsburgh, Pa. : University
of Pittsburgh Press, c2000.
*TC Q175 .S4193 2000*

**Carroll, Noël (Noël E.)** A philosophy of mass art / Noël
Carroll. Oxford : Clarendon Press ; New York :
Oxford University Press, 1998. xii, 425 p. ; 24 cm.
Includes bibliographical references and index. ISBN
0-19-871129-8 (hard : alk. paper) ISBN 0-19-874237-1 (pbk. :
alk. paper) DDC 700/.1/03
*1. Mass media and the arts. 2. Popular culture. I. Title.*
*TC NX180.M3 C37 1998*

**Carstensen, Laura L.**
The aging mind: opportunities in cognitive research.
Washington, D.C. : National Academy Press, c2000.
*TC BF724.55 .C63 A48 2000*

**Cart, Michael.**
Tomorrowland. New York : Scholastic Press, 1999.
*TC PZ5 .T6235 1999*

**Carter, Carol.** Majoring in the rest of your life : college
and career secrets for students / Carol Carter, Lynn
Quitman Troyka. Upper Saddle River, NJ : Prentice
Hall, c2000. xix, 332 p. : ill. ; 28 cm. Includes
bibliographical references (p. 313-315) and index. ISBN 0-13-
013154-7 DDC 650.14
*1. Vocational guidance - United States. 2. College students -
Employment - United States. I. Troyka, Lynn Quitman, 1938-
II. Title.*
*TC HF5382.5.U5 C373 2000*

**Carter, David A., ill.**
Dana, Katharine Floyd, 1835-1886. Over in the
meadow. New York : Scholastic, c1992

*TC PZ8.3.D2 Ov 1992*

**Carter, Dennis.** Teaching poetry in the primary school :
perspectives for a new generation / Dennis Carter.
London : David Fulton, 1998. 148 p. ; 25 cm. Includes
bibliographical references and index. ISBN 1-85346-567-4
DDC 372.64
*1. Poetry - Study and teaching (Elementary) - Great Britain. I.
Title.*
*TC LB1575 .C27 1998*

**Carter, Erik W.**
Hughes, Carolyn, 1946- The transition handbook.
Baltimore : P.H. Brookes Pub., c2000.
*TC LC4019 .H84 2000*

**Carter G. Woodson Institute series in Black studies**
Lorini, Alessandra, 1949- Rituals of race.
Charlottesville : University Press of Virginia, 1999.
*TC E185.61 .L675 1999*

**Carter, James, 1959-.**
Talking books. London ; New York ; Routledge,
1999.
*TC PR990 .T35 1999*

**Carter, Keith.**
Qualitative research. Aldershot, Hants, England ;
Brookfield, Vt. : Avebury, c1996.
*TC H62 .Q355 1996*

**Carter, Robert T., 1948-.**
Addressing cultural issues in organizations. Thousand
Oaks, Calif. : Sage Publications, 2000.
*TC E184.A1 A337 2000*

**Carthage reprint**
Scruton, Roger. The aesthetic understanding. South
Bend, Ind. : St. Augustine's Press, 1998.
*TC BH39 .S38 1998*

**CARTOONING - HISTORY.**
Comics, the 9th art [videorecording]. [S.l.] : EPISA ;
Cicero, Ill. : [Distributed by] The Roland Collection,
1990.
*TC PN6710 .C6 1990*

**CARTOONS AND COMICS - FICTION.**
Pilkey, Dav, 1966- Captain Underpants and the
invasion of the incredibly naughty cafeteria ladies
from outer space .... New York : Blue Sky Press,
c1999.
*TC PZ7.P63123 Cat 1999*

**Cartwright, Morse A. (Morse Adams), 1890-.**
[Journal of adult education (New York, N.Y.)] Journal
of adult education. New York : American Association
for Adult Education, 1929-[1941]

**Caruana, Wally.**
The painters of the Wagilag sisters story 1937-1997.
Canberra, ACT : The National Gallery of Australia,
1997.
*TC ND1101 .P395 1997*

**Carver, Charles S.**
Perspectives on behavioral self-regulation. Mahwah,
N.J. : Lawrence Erlbaum Associates, 1999.
*TC HM291 A345 1999*

**Carver, Ronald P.** The causes of high and low reading
achievement / by Ronald P. Carver. Mahway, N.J. :
Lawrence Erlbaum Associates, 2000. xii, 443 p. : ill ; 24
cm. Includes bibliographical references (p.411-429) and index.
ISBN 0-8058-3529-6 (cloth : alk. paper) DDC 428/.4
*1. Reading. 2. Reading comprehension. 3. Reading disability. I.
Title.*
*TC LB1050.2 .C27 2000*

**CARVING (DECORATIVE ARTS).** *See* WOOD-
CARVING.

**Cary, Stephen.** Working with second language
learners : answers to teachers' top ten questions /
Stephen Cary. Portsmouth, NH : Heinemann, c2000.
xv, 142 p. ; 24 cm. Includes bibliographical references (p.
129-139) and index. ISBN 0-325-00250-9 DDC 418/.0071
*1. Language and languages - Study and teaching. 2. Second
language acquisition. I. Title.*
*TC P53 .C286 2000*

**CAS.** Chicago : Curriculum Advisory Service, 1969-
1974. 6 v. ; 28 cm. Frequency: Quarterly. Vol. 8, no. 1 (winter
1969)-v. 13, no. 5 (Nov. 1974). Curriculum Advisory Service
quarterly. Vol. 8, no. 3-v. 13, no. 5 have subtitle: Curriculum
Advisory Service quarterly. CAS bulletin. CAS review 1975.
*1. Text-books - Bibliography - Periodicals. 2. Books -
Reviews - Periodicals. 3. Education - Curricula - Periodicals.
I. Curriculum Advisory Service. II. Title: Curriculum Advisory
Service quarterly III. Title: CAS bulletin IV. Title: CAS review
1975*

**CAS bulletin.**
CAS. Chicago : Curriculum Advisory Service, 1969-
1974.

**CAS review 1975.**
CAS. Chicago : Curriculum Advisory Service, 1969-1974.

**Casanave, Christine Pearson, 1944-.**
On becoming a language educator. Mahwah, NJ : Lawrence Erlbaum, 1997.
*TC P53.85 .O5 1997*

**Casanovas, Joan.** Bread, or bullets! : urban labor and Spanish colonialism in Cuba, 1850-1898 / Joan Casanovas. Pittsburgh : University of Pittsburgh Press, c1998. xiii, 320 p. : ill., maps ; 25 cm. (Pitt Latin American series) Includes bibliographical references (p. 284-312) and index. CONTENTS: Maps, figures, and tables -- Acknowledgments -- Introduction -- Urban space and labor -- The heyday of colonialism and the first artisans' associations -- The labor movement of the 1860s and Spain's search for a new colonial policy -- The ten years' war -- The rebuilding of the Cuban labor movement -- From reformism to anarchism -- Postemancipation party politics -- The turning point of the labor movement -- Conclusion and epilogue -- Notes -- Glossary -- References -- Index. ISBN 0-8229-4070-1 (acid-free paper) ISBN 0-8229-5675-6 (pbk. : acid-free paper) DDC 331.8/097291
*1. Labor movement - Cuba - History - 19th century. 2. Slavery - Cuba - History - 19th century. 3. Social classes - Cuba - History - 19th century. 4. Spain - Colonies - America - Administration. 5. Working class - Cuba - History - 19th century. 6. Anarchism - Cuba - History - 19th century. I. Title. II. Series.*
*TC HD8206 .C33 1998*

**Casciato, Tom.**
The next generation [videorecording]. Princeton, NJ : Films for the Humanities & Sciences, c1998.
*TC RC564 .N4 1998*

**Case, Charles W.**
Reagan, Timothy G. Becoming a reflective educator. 2nd ed. Thousand Oaks Calif. : Sage Publications, c2000.
*TC LB1025.3 .R424 2000*

**CASE currents.**
Council for Advancement and Support of Education. [Washington] Council for Advancement and Support of Education.

**CASE HISTORY METHOD.** *See* **CASE METHOD.**

**CASE METHOD.**
Bassey, Michael. Case study research in educational settings. Buckingham [England] ; Philadelphia : Open University Press, 1999.
*TC LB1028.25.G7 B37 1999*

Case study applications for teacher education. Boston : Allyn and Bacon, c1999.
*TC LB1715 .S796 1999*

Hinely, Reg. Education in Edge City. 2nd ed. Mahwah, N.J. : L. Erlbaum Associates, 2000.
*TC LB1029.C37 H45 2000*

Merriam, Sharan B. Qualitative research and case study applications in education. 2nd ed. San Francisco : Jossey-Bass Publishers, c1998.
*TC LB1028 .M396 1998*

Naumes, William. The art & craft of case writing. Thousand Oaks, Calif. : Sage Publications, c1999.
*TC LB1029.C37 N38 1999*

**CASE METHOD - STUDY AND TEACHING - UNITED STATES.**
Who learns what from cases and how? Mahwah, N.J. : L. Erlbaum Associates, 1999.
*TC LB1029.C37 W56 1999*

**The case of the firecrackers.**
Yep, Laurence. 1st ed. New York : HarperCollins, c1999.
*TC PZ7.Y44 Cag 1999*

**Case, Roland, 1951-.**
The Canadian anthology of social studies. Vancouver : Pacific Educational Press, c1999.
*TC H62.5.C3 C32 1999*

Critical challenges in social studies for junior high students. Burnaby, B.C. : Field Relations and Teacher In-Service Education, Faculty of Education, Simon Fraser University, 1996.
*TC D16.2 .C75 1996*

Werner, Walter. Collaborative assessment of school-based projects. Vancouver : Pacific Educational Press, c1991.
*TC LB2822.8 .W47 1991*

**Case stories in early intervention.**
McWilliam, P. J. Lives in progress. Baltimore : P.H. Brookes, c2000.

*TC HV741 .M3128 2000*

**Case studies for school administrators** : managing change in education / [edited by] Maenette K. P. Ah Nee-Benham. 1st ed. Lancaster, PA : Technomic Pub. Co., c1999. xvii, 298 p. ; 24 cm. Includes bibliographical references. ISBN 1-56676-689-3 (acid-free paper)
*1. School management and organization - United States - Case studies. 2. Educational change - United States - Case studies. 3. School administrators - United States - Case studies. I. Nee-Benham, Maenette K. P.*
*TC LB2806 .C316 1999*

**Case studies in the neuropsychology of reading** / edited by Elaine Funnell. Hove, East Sussex : Psychology Press, c2000. v, 154 p. : ill. ; 25 cm. Includes bibliographical references and indexes. ISBN 0-86377-558-6 DDC 371.9144
*1. Dyslexia - Case studies. 2. Neuropsychology. 3. Reading, Psychology of I. Funnell, Elaine.*
*TC RC394.W6 .C37 2000*

**Case studies of the superintendency** / edited by Paula M. Short and Jay Paredes Scribner. Lanham, Md. : Scarecrow Press, c2000. vi, 186 p. ; 24 cm. Includes bibliographical references and index. ISBN 0-8108-3752-8 (alk. paper) DDC 371.2/011
*1. School superintendents - United States - Case studies. 2. School management and organization - United States - Case studies. I. Short, Paula M. II. Scribner, Jay Paredes, 1963-*
*TC LB2831.72 .C38 2000*

**Case study applications for teacher education** : cases of teaching and learning in the content areas / edited by Mary R. Sudzina. Boston : Allyn and Bacon, c1999. xiv, 240 p. : ill. ; 23 cm. Includes bibliographical references and index. ISBN 0-205-28762-X (pb) DDC 370/.71
*1. Teachers - Training of - United States. 2. Case method. I. Sudzina, Mary R.*
*TC LB1715 .S796 1999*

**A case study in teaching to civic standards using a portfolio approach 1996 : "Office of Citizen"** / produced by the Social Science Education Consortium. [Boulder, Colo.] : Social Science Education Consortium, c1997. 1 videocassette (17 min.) : sd., col. ; 1/2 in. VHS. Catalogued from credits and cassette label. Title from cassette label. Video production by Vicki Murray-Kurzban. For educators, especially civics middle school teachers and students. SUMMARY: Jackie Johnson, Social Science teacher at Campus Middle School, outlines the portfolio approach she uses to teach civics to middle school students. The students, Matt Walker, Jeff Bloom, Pavar Sekhar and others discuss what they learned from the approach. The portfolio contains the student's resume based on the experiences and projects from the civics class, which include: a "Socratic Seminar", a mock trial, and a simulated congressional hearing. CONTENTS: A case study in teaching to civic standards using a portfolio approach : "Office of citizen" -- Student reflections on a portfolio approach -- Contents of the portfolio : experiences, performances, projects, knowledge and skills -- Teaching reflection.
*1. Civics - Study and teaching (Middle school) - United States. 2. Citizenship - Study and teaching (Middle school) - United States. 3. Education - Standards - United States. I. Social Science Education Consortium. II. Title: "Office of Citizen" [videorecording]*
*TC LC1091 .C37 1997*

**CASE STUDY METHOD.** *See* **CASE METHOD.**

**A case study of Japanese middle schools, 1983-1998.**
Whitman, Nancy C. Lanham, Md. ; Oxford : University Press of America, c2000.
*TC LA1316 .W45 2000*

**Case study research in educational settings.**
Bassey, Michael. Buckingham [England] ; Philadelphia : Open University Press, 1999.
*TC LB1028.25.G7 B37 1999*

**CASE WORK, SOCIAL.** *See* **SOCIAL CASE WORK.**

**Casebook in family therapy** / edited by David M. Lawson, Frances F. Prevatt. Belmont : Brooks/Cole, c1999. xviii, 358 p. : ill. ; 24 cm. Includes bibliographical references and indexes. ISBN 0-534-34415-1 (pbk.) DDC 616.89/156
*1. Family psychotherapy - Case studies. I. Lawson, David M. II. Prevatt, Frances F., 1955-*
*TC RC488.5 .C369 1999*

**Caseley, Judith.** Losing Louisa / Judith Caseley. 1st ed. New York : Farrar, Straus and Giroux, c1999. 235 p. ; 22 cm. "Frances Foster books" SUMMARY: Sixteen-year-old Lacey worries about the effect of her parents' divorce on her family, especially her mother, and about her older sister's sexual activity, which may have made her pregnant. ISBN 0-374-34665-8 DDC [Fic]
*1. Divorce - Fiction. 2. Sexual ethics - Fiction. 3. Pregnancy - Fiction. I. Title.*

*TC PZ7.C2677 Lo 1999*

**Casement, Charles.**
Armstrong, Alison, 1955- The child and the machine. Beltsville, Md. : Robins Lane Press, c2000.
*TC LB1028.43 .A76 2000*

Armstrong, Alison, 1955- The child and the machine. Toronto, Ont. : Key Porter Books, c1998.
*TC LB1028.43 .A75 1998*

**Cases for middle school educators.**
Siskind, Theresa Gayle, 1951- Lanham, Md. ; London : Scarecrow Press, 2000.
*TC LB1623.5 .S57 2000*

**Cases in behavior management.**
Danforth, Scot. Upper Saddle River, N.J. : Merrill, c2000.
*TC LB3013 .D34 2000*

**Cases in middle and secondary science education** : the promise and dilemmas / [edited by] Thomas R. Koballa, Jr., Deborah J. Tippins. Upper Saddle River, N.J. : Merrill, c2000. xvi, 281 p. : ill. ; 24 cm. Includes bibliographical references and index. ISBN 0-13-082468-2 DDC 507/.1/2
*1. Science - Study and teaching (Middle school) - Case studies. 2. Science - Study and teaching (Secondary) - Case studies. I. Koballa, Thomas R. II. Tippins, Deborah J.*
*TC Q181 .C348 2000*

**Cases studies on information technology in higher education** : implications for policy and practice / [edited by] Lisa Ann Petrides. Hershey, PA : Idea Group Pub., c2000. iv, 257 p. ; 24 cm. Includes bibliographical references and index. ISBN 1-87828-974-8 DDC 378/.00285
*1. Education, Higher - Data processing - Case studies. 2. Educational technology - Case studies. 3. Information technology - Case studies. I. Petrides, Lisa Ann, 1961-*
*TC LB2395.7 .C39 2000*

**Casey, Jean Marie.** Creating the early literacy classroom : activities for using technology to empower elementary students / Jean M. Casey. Englewood, Colo. : Libraries Unlimited, c2000. xi, 111 p. : ill. ; 26 cm. Includes bibliographical references (p. 103-105) and index. ISBN 1-56308-712-X (pbk.) DDC 372.133/4
*1. Language arts (Elementary) - Computer-assisted instruction. 2. Computers and literacy. 3. English language - Computer-assisted instruction. I. Title.*
*TC LB1576.7 .C38 2000*

Early literacy : the empowerment of technology / Jean M. Casey. Rev. ed. Englewood, Colo. : Libraries Unlimited, 2000. xiv, 198 p. : ill. ; 26 cm. Includes bibliographical references (p. 175-184) and index. ISBN 1-56308-865-7 DDC 372.133/4
*1. Language arts (Early childhood) - Computer-assisted instruction. 2. Reading (Early childhood) - Computer-assisted instruction. 3. Computers and literacy. 4. Educational technology. I. Title.*
*TC LB1139.5.L35 C37 2000*

**Casey Jones's fireman.**
Farmer, Nancy. 1st ed. New York : Phyllis Fogelman Books, c1998.
*TC PZ8.1.F2225 Cas 1998*

**Casey, Mary Anne.**
Krueger, Richard A. Focus groups. 3rd ed. Thousand Oaks, Calif. : Sage Publications, c2000.
*TC H61.28 .K78 2000*

**Casey, Patricia.** My cat Jack / Patricia Casey. 1st U.S. ed. Cambridge, Mass. : Candlewick Press, c1994. 1 v. (unpaged) : col. ill. ; 26 cm. (Read and wonder) "Published in Great Britain in 1994"--page facing t.p. SUMMARY: A close-up look at the day-to-day doings of a pet cat. ISBN 1-56402-410-5 DDC [E]
*1. Cats - Fiction. I. Title. II. Series.*
*TC PZ7.C2679 My 1994*

**Casey, Ron.**
Mathematics for primary teachers. London ; New York : Routledge, 2000.
*TC QA135.5 .K67 2000*

**Cashdan, Asher.**
Teaching in primary schools. London : Cassell, 1998.
*TC LB1776.T43 1998*

**Cashdan, Sheldon.** The witch must die : how fairy tales shape our lives / Sheldon Cashdan. New York : Basic Books, 1999. x, 283 p. : ill. ; 24 cm. ISBN 0-465-09148-2 (cloth) DDC 398/.45
*1. Fairy tales - History and criticism. 2. Fairy tales - Social aspects. I. Title.*
*TC GR550 .C39 1999*

**Casilla, Robert, ill.**
Poems for fathers. 1st ed. New York : Holiday House, c1989.

[Washington] National Catholic Educational Association.

**Catholic foreign mission society of America.**
Third world peoples, a Gospel perspective. Maryknoll, NY : Maryknoll Fathers and Brothers, c1987.
*TC F1439.T54 1987*

**Catholic Health Association of the United States.**
Hospital progress. St. Louis [etc.] Catholic Health Association of the United States [etc.]

**CATHOLIC HIGH SCHOOLS - IRELAND - CURRICULA - HISTORY - 20TH CENTURY.**
O'Donoghue, T. A. (Tom A.), 1953- The Catholic Church and the secondary school curriculum in Ireland, 1922-1962. New York : P. Lang, c1999.
*TC LC506.G72 1745 1999*

**Catholic Hospital Association.**
Hospital progress. St. Louis [etc.] Catholic Health Association of the United States [etc.]

**Catholic Hospital Association of the United States and Canada.**
Hospital progress. St. Louis [etc.] Catholic Health Association of the United States [etc.]

**Catholic school leadership :** an invitation to lead / edited by Thomas C. Hunt, Thomas E. Oldenski, and Theodore J. Wallace. London ; New York : Falmer Press, 2000. xv, 284 p. : ill. ; 25 cm. Includes bibliographical references and index. ISBN 0-7507-0854-9 (hbk. : alk. paper) ISBN 0-7507-0853-0 (pbk. : alk. paper) DDC 371.071/2/73
*1. Catholic schools - United States - Administration. 2. School management and organization - United States. 3. Educational leadership - United States. I. Hunt, Thomas C., 1930- II. Oldenski, Thomas. III. Wallace, Theodore J. (Theodore Joseph), 1954-*
*TC LC501 .C3484 2000*

**CATHOLIC SCHOOLS - FRANCE - HISTORY - 19TH CENTURY.**
Curtis, Sarah Ann. Educating the faithful. DeKalb : Northern Illinois University Press, 2000.
*TC LC506.F7 C87 2000*

**CATHOLIC SCHOOLS - ONTARIO - TORONTO - CASE STUDIES.**
McLaren, Peter, 1948- Schooling as a ritual performance. 3rd ed. Lanham, Md. : Rowman & Littlefield, c1999.
*TC LC504.3.T67 M35 1999*

**CATHOLIC SCHOOLS - PERIODICALS.**
National Catholic Educational Association. Bulletin - National Catholic Educational Association. [Washington] National Catholic Educational Association.

**CATHOLIC SCHOOLS - UNITED STATES - ADMINISTRATION.**
Catholic school leadership. London ; New York : Falmer Press, 2000.
*TC LC501 .C3484 2000*

**CATHOLIC UNIVERSITIES AND COLLEGES - UNITED STATES - HISTORY - 20TH CENTURY.**
Gallin, Alice. Negotiating identity. Notre Dame, Ind. : University of Notre Dame Press, c2000.
*TC LC501 .G36 2000*

**Catlett, Elizabeth, 1915-** Elizabeth Catlett sculpture : a fifty-year retrospective / organized by Lucinda H. Gedeon ; essays by Michael Brenson and Lowery Stokes Sims. [Purchase, N.Y.] : Neuberger Museum of Art, Purchase College, State University of New York : Distributed by University of Washington Press, c1998. 119 p. : ill. (some col.) ; 24 x 26 cm. Published to accompany an exhibition appearing initially at the Neuberger Museum of Art, Purchase, N.Y., 8 February-7 June, 1998. Includes bibliographical references (p. 115-118). CONTENTS: Elizabeth Catlett : a life in art and politics / Lowery Stokes Sims -- Elizabeth Catlett's sculptural aesthetics / Michael Brenson. ISBN 0-295-97722-1
*1. Catlett, Elizabeth. - 1915- - Exhibitions. 2. Sculpture, Black - Mexico - Exhibitions. I. Gedeon, Lucinda H. II. Brenson, Michael. III. Sims, Lowery Stokes. IV. Neuberger Museum of Art. V. Title.*
*TC NB259.C384 A4 1998*

**CATLETT, ELIZABETH, 1915- - EXHIBITIONS.**
Catlett, Elizabeth, 1915- Elizabeth Catlett sculpture. [Purchase, N.Y.] : Neuberger Museum of Art, Purchase College, State University of New York : Seattle : Distributed by University of Washington Press, c1998.
*TC NB259.C384 A4 1998*

**Catlett, Joyce.**
Firestone, Robert. Fear of intimacy. 1st ed.

Washington, DC : American Psychological Association, c1999.
*TC BF575.I5 F57 1999*

**Catlin, Stanton L. (Stanton Loomis).**
The frescoes of Diego Rivera [videorecording]. [Detroit, Mich.] : Founders Society, Detroit Institute of Arts : [Chicago, Ill.?] : Home Vision [distributor], c1986.
*TC ND259.R5 F6 1986*

**CATS. See FELIDAE.**

**CATS - FICTION.**
Apple, Margot. Brave Martha. Boston : Houghton Mifflin, 1999.
*TC PZ7.A6474 Br 1999*

Baker, Leslie A. Paris cat. 1st ed. Boston, Mass. : Little, Brown, c1999.
*TC PZ7.B1744 Par 1999*

Casey, Patricia. My cat Jack. 1st U.S. ed. Cambridge, Mass. : Candlewick Press, c1994.
*TC PZ7.C2679 My 1994*

Chwast, Seymour. Traffic jam. Boston : Houghton Mifflin, c1999.
*TC PZ7.C4893 Tr 1999*

Purdy, Carol. Mrs. Merriwether's musical cat. New York : Putnam, c1994.
*TC PZ7.P9745 Mr 1994*

Schachner, Judith Byron. The Grannyman. 1st ed. New York : Dutton Children's Books, c1999.
*TC PZ7.S3286 Gr 1999*

**CATS - FOLKLORE.**
Uchida, Yoshiko. The two foolish cats. New York : M.K. McElderry Books, c1987.
*TC PZ8.1.U35 Tw 1987*

**Cats of Africa.**
Hall-Martin, Anthony. Washington, D.C. : Smithsonian Institution Press, 1998.
*TC QL737.C23 H335 1997*

**CATS SYSTEM - FORMAT. See MARC FORMATS.**

**CAUCASIAN RACE. See WHITES.**

**Caughie, Pamela L., 1953-** Passing and pedagogy : the dynamics of responsibility / Pamela L. Caughie. Urbana : University of Illinois Press, c1999. xii, 286 p. : ill. ; 24 cm. Includes bibliographical references (p. 261-275) and index. ISBN 0-252-02466-4 (cloth : alk. paper) ISBN 0-252-06770-3 (pbk. : alk. paper) DDC 807/.1/173
*1. Literature - Study and teaching (Higher) - United States. 2. American literature - History and criticism - Theory, etc. 3. English literature - History and criticism - Theory, etc. 4. Arts - Study and teaching (Higher) - United States. 5. Passing (Identity) in literature. 6. Passing (Identity) I. Title.*
*TC PN61 .C38 1999*

**Caught off guard.**
Brinkley, Ellen Henson, 1944- Boston : Allyn and Bacon, c1999.
*TC LC72.2 .B75 1999*

**Cauley, Lorinda Bryan, ill.**
Ivimey, John W. (John William), b. 1868. [Complete version of ye Three blind mice] Three blind mice. New York : G.P. Putnam's Sons, c1991.
*TC PZ8.3.I83 Th 1991*

**Causality.**
Pearl, Judea. Cambridge ; New York : Cambridge University Press, 2000.
*TC BD541 .P43 2000*

**CAUSATION.**
Halperin, Jane Carol. The influence of causal attributions on the psychological adjustment of post-treatment adolescent cancer survivors. 1999.
*TC O85 H155*

Pearl, Judea. Causality. Cambridge ; New York : Cambridge University Press, 2000.
*TC BD541 .P43 2000*

**Causes and consequences of feelings.**
Berkowitz, Leonard, 1926- Cambridge, U.K. : New York : Cambridge University Press ; Paris : Editions de la Maison des sciences de l'homme, 2000.
*TC BF531 .B45 2000*

**The causes of exclusion.**
Cullingford, Cedric. London : Kogan Page ; Sterling, VA : Stylus, 1999.
*TC HV6166 .C85 1999*

**The causes of high and low reading achievement.**
Carver, Ronald P. Mahway, N.J. : Lawrence Erlbaum Associates, 2000.

*TC LB1050.2 .C27 2000*

**Cava, Margaret T.** Second language learner strategies and the unsuccessful second language writer / by Margaret T. Cava. 1999. v, 175 leaves ; 29 cm. Typescript; issued also on microfilm. Includes tables. Thesis (Ph.D.)-- Columbia University, 1999. Includes bibliographical references (leaves 105-129).
*1. Language and languages - Study and teaching. 2. English language - Composition and exercises - Study and teaching. 3. Second language aquisition. 4. English language - Study and teaching - Foreign speakers. 5. Cognitive learning. 6. Metacognition. I. Title.*
*TC O85 C295*

**Cavalier, Robert P., 1933-** Personal motivation : a model for decision making / Robert P. Cavalier. Westport, Conn. : London : Praeger, 2000. xv, 160 p. : ill. ; 25 cm. Includes bibliographical references (p. [144]-149) and index. CONTENTS: 1. Thank You, Dr. Allport -- 2. Self and Will -- 3. Nature and Freedom -- 4. Personal Motivation -- 5. Three Ways to Go -- 6. Setting a Course -- 7. Territories Within -- 8. Deciding -- 9. Work and Leaders -- Epilogue: White Coats and Robots. ISBN 0-275-96168-0 (alk. paper) DDC 153.8 DDC 153.8
*1. Motivation (Psychology) 2. Decision making. I. Title.*
*TC BF503 .C39 2000*

**Cavaliere, Barbara.**
Edward Clark. Belleville Lake, Mich. : Belleville Lake Press, c1997.
*TC ND237.C524 E393 1997*

**Cavan, Ruth Shonle, 1896-** The American family. 3d ed. New York, Crowell [1963] 548 p. illus. 24 cm. Includes bibliography. DDC 392
*1. Family - U.S. 2. United States - Social conditions. I. Title.*
*TC HQ535 .C33 1963*

**Cavan, Ruth (Shonle) 1896- ed.** Marriage and family in the modern world, a book of readings. 2d ed. New York, Crowell [1965] xiii, 609 p. : illus. ; 23 cm. Includes index. Bibliographical footnotes. DDC 301.42082
*1. Family. 2. Marriage. I. Title.*
*TC HQ734 .C382 1965*

**CAVE-DRAWINGS. See CAVE PAINTINGS.**

**CAVE PAINTINGS - ALGERIA - TASSILI-N-AJJER.**
Tassili N'Ajjer [videorecording]. [S.l.] : Editions Cinégraphiques : Northbrook, Ill. : [distributed by] the Roland Collection, c1968.
*TC N5310.5.A4 T3 1968*

**Cave, Sue, 1949-** Therapeutic approaches in psychology / Sue Cave. London ; New York : Routledge, 1999. xix, 178 p. ; 21 cm. (Routledge modular psychology) Includes bibliographical references (p. [161]-174) and index. ISBN 0-415-18870-9 (hardcover) ISBN 0-415-18871-7 (pbk.) DDC 616.89/14
*1. Psychotherapy. I. Title. II. Series.*
*TC RC480 .C37 1999*

**Caveat homo sapiens.**
Friedberg, Felix. Lanham, Md. : Oxford : University Press of America, c2000.
*TC BF41 .F75 2000*

**Cavell, Timothy A.** Working with parents of aggressive children : a practitioner's guide / Timothy A. Cavell. 1st ed. Washington, DC : American Psychological Association, 2000. xiii, 267 p. ; 26 cm. Includes bibliographical references and index. ISBN 1-55798-637-1 (cloth : acid-free paper) DDC 155.4/8232
*1. Aggressiveness in children. 2. Violence in children. 3. Parent and child. 4. Parent-child interaction therapy. I. Title.*
*TC RJ506.A35 C38 2000*

**Caverly, David C.**
Handbook of college reading and study strategy research. Mahwah, N.J. : Lawrence Erlbaum Associates, c2000.
*TC LB2395.3 .H36 2000*

**The cay by Theodore Taylor.**
Beech, Linda Ward. New York : Scholastic, c1997.
*TC LB1573 .B4312 1997*

**Cayton, Andrew R. L. (Andrew Robert Lee), 1954-**
America : pathways to the present : America in the twentieth century / Andrew Cayton, Elisabeth Israels Perry, Allan M. Winkler. Upper Saddle River, N.J. : Prentice Hall, c1998. xxii, 1018 p. : ill. (some col.), maps (some col.) ; 27 cm. Includes index. ISBN 0-13-432386-6
*1. United States - History. I. Perry, Elisabeth Israels. II. Winkler, Allan M., 1945- III. Title. IV. Title: America in the twentieth century*
*TC E178.1 .C364 1998*

America : pathways to the present : America in the twentieth century / Andrew Cayton, Elisabeth Israels Perry, Allan M. Winkler. Teacher's ed. Upper Saddle

River, N.J.. : Prentice Hall, c1998. T28, xxii, 1032 p. : ill. (some col.), maps (some col.) ; 29 cm. Includes index. ISBN 0-13-432444-7
*1. United States - History. I. Perry, Elisabeth Israels. II. Winkler, Allan M., 1945- III. Title. IV. Title: America in the twentieth century*
**TC E178.1 .C364 1998 Teacher's Ed.**

America : pathways to the present : America in the twentieth century / Andrew Cayton, Elisabeth Israels Perry, Allan M. Winkler. Upper Saddle River, N.J. : Prentice Hall, c1998. xxii, 1018 p. : ill. (some col.), maps (some col.) ; 27 cm. Includes index. ISBN 0-13-432386-6
*1. United States - History. I. Perry, Elisabeth Israels. II. Winkler, Allan M., 1945- III. Title. IV. Title: America in the twentieth century*
**TC E178.1 .C3643 1998**

America : pathways to the present : America in the twentieth century / Andrew Cayton, Elisabeth Israels Perry, Allan M. Winkler. Upper Saddle River, N.J. : Prentice Hall, c1998. xxii, 1018 p. : ill. (some col.), maps (some col.) ; 27 cm. Includes index. ISBN 0-13-432386-6
*1. United States - History. I. Perry, Elisabeth Israels. II. Winkler, Allan M., 1945- III. Title. IV. Title: America in the twentieth century*
**TC E178.1 .C3643 1998**

America : pathways to the present : America in the twentieth century / Andrew Cayton, Elisabeth Israels Perry, Allan M. Winkler. Teacher's ed. Upper Saddle River, N.J.. : Prentice Hall, c1998. T28, xxii, 1032 p. : ill. (some col.), maps (some col.) ; 29 cm. Includes index. ISBN 0-13-432444-7
*1. United States - History. I. Perry, Elisabeth Israels. II. Winkler, Allan M., 1945- III. Title. IV. Title: America in the twentieth century*
**TC E178.1 .C3643 1998 Teacher's Ed.**

America : pathways to the present : America in the twentieth century / Andrew Cayton, Elisabeth Israels Perry, Allan M. Winkler. Upper Saddle River, N.J. : Prentice Hall, c1998. xxii, 1018 p. : ill. (some col.), maps (some col.) ; 27 cm. Includes index. ISBN 0-13-432386-6
*1. United States - History. I. Perry, Elisabeth Israels. II. Winkler, Allan M., 1945- III. Title. IV. Title: America in the twentieth century*
**TC E178.1 .C3643 1998**

America : pathways to the present / Andrew Cayton, Elisabeth Israels Perry, Allan M. Winkler. Teacher's ed. Upper Saddle River, N.J.. : Prentice Hall, c1998. T34, xxii, 1184 p. : ill. (some col.), maps (some col.) ; 29 cm. Includes index. ISBN 0-13-432402-1
*1. United States - History. I. Perry, Elisabeth Israels. II. Winkler, Allan M., 1945- III. Title.*
**TC E178.1 .C364 1998 Teacher's Ed.**

America : pathways to the present / Andrew Cayton, Elisabeth Israels Perry, Allan M. Winkler. Upper Saddle River, N.J. : Prentice Hall, c1998. xxii, 1178 p. : ill. (some col.), maps (some col.) ; 27 cm. Includes index. ISBN 0-13-432345-9
*1. United States - History. I. Perry, Elisabeth Israels. II. Winkler, Allan M., 1945- III. Title.*
**TC E178.1 .C364 1998**

America : pathways to the present / Andrew Cayton, Elisabeth Israels Perry, Allan M. Winkler. Teacher's ed. Upper Saddle River, N.J.. : Prentice Hall, c1998. T34, xxii, 1184 p. : ill. (some col.), maps (some col.) ; 29 cm. Includes index. ISBN 0-13-432402-1
*1. United States - History. I. Perry, Elisabeth Israels. II. Winkler, Allan M., 1945- III. Title.*
**TC E178.1 .C3645 1998 Teacher's Ed.**

America : pathways to the present / Andrew Cayton, Elisabeth Israels Perry, Allan M. Winkler. Upper Saddle River, N.J. : Prentice Hall, c1998. xxii, 1178 p. : ill. (some col.), maps (some col.) ; 27 cm. Includes index. ISBN 0-13-432345-9
*1. United States - History. I. Perry, Elisabeth Israels. II. Winkler, Allan M., 1945- III. Title.*
**TC E178.1 .C3645 1998**

America : pathways to the present / Andrew Cayton, Elisabeth Israels Perry, Allan M. Winkler. Upper Saddle River, N.J. : Prentice Hall, c1998. xxii, 1178 p. : ill. (some col.), maps (some col.) ; 27 cm. Includes index. ISBN 0-13-432345-9
*1. United States - History. I. Perry, Elisabeth Israels. II. Winkler, Allan M., 1945- III. Title.*
**TC E178.1 .C3645 1998**

America : pathways to the present : Civil War to the present / Andrew Cayton, Elisabeth Israels Perry, Allan M. Winkler. Teacher's ed. Upper Saddle River, N.J.. : Prentice Hall, c1998. T33, xxii, 1036 p. : ill. (some col.), maps (some col.) ; 29 cm. Includes index. ISBN 0-13-432436-6
*1. United States - History. I. Perry, Elisabeth Israels. II.*

---

*Winkler, Allan M., 1945- III. Title. IV. Title: Civil War to the present*
**TC E178.1 .C364 1998 Teacher's Ed.**

America : pathways to the present : Civil War to the present / Andrew Cayton, Elisabeth Israels Perry, Allan M. Winkler. Upper Saddle River, N.J.. : Prentice Hall, c1998. xxii, 1034 p. : ill. (some col.), maps (some col.) ; 27 cm. Includes index. ISBN 0-13-432378-5
*1. United States - History. I. Perry, Elisabeth Israels. II. Winkler, Allan M., 1945- III. Title. IV. Title: Civil War to the present*
**TC E178.1 .C364 1998**

America : pathways to the present : Civil War to the present / Andrew Cayton, Elisabeth Israels Perry, Allan M. Winkler. Upper Saddle River, N.J. : Prentice Hall, c1998. xxii, 1034 p. : ill. (some col.), maps (some col.) ; 27 cm. Includes index. ISBN 0-13-432378-5
*1. United States - History. I. Perry, Elisabeth Israels. II. Winkler, Allan M., 1945- III. Title. IV. Title: Civil War to the present*
**TC E178.1 .C364 1998**

America : pathways to the present : Civil War to the present / Andrew Cayton, Elisabeth Israels Perry, Allan M. Winkler. Teacher's ed. Upper Saddle River, N.J.. : Prentice Hall, c1998. T33, xxii, 1036 p. : ill. (some col.), maps (some col.) ; 29 cm. Includes index. ISBN 0-13-432436-6
*1. United States - History. I. Perry, Elisabeth Israels. II. Winkler, Allan M., 1945- III. Title. IV. Title: Civil War to the present*
**TC E178.1 .C3644 1998 Teacher's Ed.**

America : pathways to the present : Civil War to the present / Andrew Cayton, Elisabeth Israels Perry, Allan M. Winkler. Upper Saddle River, N.J. : Prentice Hall, c1998. xxii, 1034 p. : ill. (some col.), maps (some col.) ; 27 cm. Includes index. ISBN 0-13-432378-5
*1. United States - History. I. Perry, Elisabeth Israels. II. Winkler, Allan M., 1945- III. Title. IV. Title: Civil War to the present*
**TC E178.1 .C364 1998**

America : pathways to the present : Civil War to the present / Andrew Cayton, Elisabeth Israels Perry, Allan M. Winkler. Upper Saddle River, N.J. : Prentice Hall, c1998. xxii, 1034 p. : ill. (some col.), maps (some col.) ; 27 cm. Includes index. ISBN 0-13-432378-5
*1. United States - History. I. Perry, Elisabeth Israels. II. Winkler, Allan M., 1945- III. Title. IV. Title: Civil War to the present*
**TC E178.1 .C3644 1998**

America : pathways to the present : Civil War to the present / Andrew Cayton, Elisabeth Israels Perry, Allan M. Winkler. Upper Saddle River, N.J. : Prentice Hall, c1998. xxii, 1034 p. : ill. (some col.), maps (some col.) ; 27 cm. Includes index. ISBN 0-13-432378-5
*1. United States - History. I. Perry, Elisabeth Israels. II. Winkler, Allan M., 1945- III. Title. IV. Title: Civil War to the present*
**TC E178.1 .C3644 1998**

America : pathways to the present : Civil War to the present / Andrew Cayton, Elisabeth Israels Perry, Allan M. Winkler. Upper Saddle River, N.J. : Prentice Hall, c1998. xxii, 1034 p. : ill. (some col.), maps (some col.) ; 27 cm. Includes index. ISBN 0-13-432378-5
*1. United States - History. I. Perry, Elisabeth Israels. II. Winkler, Allan M., 1945- III. Title. IV. Title: Civil War to the present*
**TC E178.1 .C3644 1998**

**CB RADIO.** *See* **CITIZENS BAND RADIO.**

**CBA (EDUCATIONAL TEST).** *See* **CURRICULUM-BASED ASSESSMENT.**

**CBS Fox Video.**
Vietnam [videorecording]. [Beverly Hills, Calif.?] : CBS Fox Video : Distributed by Fox Video, c1993.
**TC DS557.7 .V53 1993**

**CBS News.**
Vietnam [videorecording]. [Beverly Hills, Calif.?] : CBS Fox Video : Distributed by Fox Video, c1993.
**TC DS557.7 .V53 1993**

**CBS News Archives.**
Vietnam [videorecording]. [Beverly Hills, Calif.?] : CBS Fox Video : Distributed by Fox Video, c1993.
**TC DS557.7 .V53 1993**

**CBS News collectors series.**
Vietnam [videorecording]. [Beverly Hills, Calif.?] : CBS Fox Video : Distributed by Fox Video, c1993.
**TC DS557.7 .V53 1993**

**CBS Television Network.**
Vietnam [videorecording]. Beverly Hills, CA : CBS/Fox Video, c1981.

---

**CBS Video (Firm).**
Vietnam [videorecording]. [Beverly Hills, Calif.?] : CBS Fox Video : Distributed by Fox Video, c1993.
**TC DS557.7 .V53 1993**

**CCCC bibliography of composition and rhetoric.**
Carbondale : Southern Illinois University Press, c1990- v. ; 26 cm. Frequency: Annual. 1987- . Bibliography of composition and rhetoric. Continues: Longman bibliography of composition and rhetoric ISSN: 0897-3385 (DLC) 87642756 (OCoLC)16185914. ISSN 1046-0675 DDC 808
*1. English language - Rhetoric - Study and teaching - Bibliography - Periodicals. 2. English language - Composition and exercises - Study and teaching - Bibliography - Periodicals. I. Conference on College Composition and Communication (U.S.) II. Title: Bibliography of composition and rhetoric III. Title: Longman bibliography of composition and rhetoric*
**TC Z5818.E5 L66**

**CD-ROM.** *See* **CD-ROMS.**

**CD-ROMS.**
Brinkman, Ronald. The art and science of digital compositing. San Diego : Morgan Kaufmann ; Academic Press, 1999.
**TC T385 .B75 1999**

**CD-ROMS - CATALOGS.**
Culturally diverse videos, audios, and CD-ROMS for children and young adults. New York : Neal-Schuman Publishers, 1999.
**TC PN1998 .M85 1999**

**CD-ROMS for kids : :** Booklist's best bets / edited by Irene Wood. [Chicago, Ill.] : American Library Association, Booklist Publications, 1997. 47 p. ; 23 cm. Includes index. ISBN 0-8389-7887-8 (pbk.).
*1. CD-ROMs - United States - Catalogs - Juvenile software. 2. Children's software - United States - Catalogs. I. Wood, Irene. II. Title.*
**TC QA76.76.C54 C47 1997**

**CD-ROMS - UNITED STATES - CATALOGS - JUVENILE SOFTWARE.**
CD-ROMS for kids :. [Chicago, Ill.] : American Library Association, Booklist Publications, 1997.
**TC QA76.76.C54 C47 1997**

**CDROMS.** *See* **CD-ROMS.**

**Ceci, Stephen J.**
The nature-nurture debate. Oxford ; Malden, Mass. : Blackwell, 1999.
**TC BF341 .N39 1999**

**Cecilia Beaux and the art of portraiture.**
Beaux, Cecilia, 1855-1942. Washington, DC : Published for the National Portrait Gallery by the Smithsonian Institution Press, 1995.
**TC ND1329.B39 A4 1995**

**CEILINGS, PAINTED.** *See* **MURAL PAINTING AND DECORATION.**

**Celebrating the earth.**
Livo, Norma J., 1929- Englewood, Colo. : Teacher Ideas Press, 2000.
**TC QL50 .L57 2000**

**Celebrating the fourth.**
Servis, Joan. Portsmouth, NH : Heinemann, c1999.
**TC LB1571 4th .S47 1999**

**A celebration of literature and response.**
Hancock, Marjorie R. Upper Saddle River, N.J. : Merrill, c2000.
**TC LB1575 .H36 2000**

**Celebration of reading, writing, and reflective practice at the middle level.**
A middle mosaic. Urbana, Ill. : National Council of Teachers of English, c2000.
**TC LB1631 .A2 2000**

**Celebrations.**
Livingston, Myra Cohn. 1st ed. New York : Holiday House, c1985.
**TC PS3562.I945 C4 1985**

**CELEBRITIES - INTERVIEWS.**
Dreifus, Claudia. Interview. New York : Seven Stories : London : Turnaround, 1999.
**TC PN4874.D74158 1999**

**CELEBRITIES - PSYCHOLOGY.**
Giles, David, 1964- Illusions of immortality. Houndmills [England] : Macmillan Press ; New York : St. Martin's Press, 2000.
**TC BJ1470.5 .G55 2000**

**CELEBRITY.** *See* **FAME.**

**CELESTIAL MECHANICS.**
Stephen Hawking's universe [videorecording].
[Alexandria, Va.] : [PBS Video; Burbank, CA :
Distributed by Warner Home Video, c1997.
*TC QB982 .S7 1997*

**Célestin Freinet.**
Acker, Victor, 1940- Westport, CT : Greenwood
Press, 2000.
*TC LB775 .A255 2000*

**CELLISTS.** *See* **VIOLONCELLISTS.**

**CELLO.** *See* **VIOLONCELLO.**

**Cello for beginners.**
The cello [videorecording]. Van Nuys, CA :
Backstage Pass Productions ; Canoga Park, Calif. :
[Distributed by] MVP, c1995.
*TC MT305 .C4 1995*

**CELLO PLAYERS.** *See* **VIOLONCELLISTS.**

**The cello** [videorecording] / director, Todd Brinegar :
producer, Mark S. Arnett ; a production of Aesthetic
Artist Records and Brinegar Video/Film Productions,
Inc. in association with Backstage Pass Instructional
Video. Van Nuys, CA : Backstage Pass Productions ;
Canoga Park, Calif. : [Distributed by] MVP, c1995. 1
videocassette (59 min.) : sd., col. ; 1/2 in. + 1 instruction
booklet (12 p. : music ; 18 cm.). (Maestro music instrument
instructional video ... for) Title on container: Cello for
beginners. VHS, Hi-Fi, Stereo. Cataloged from credits, cassette
label and container. Instructor: Doug Bruestle. Audio, Mark S.
Arnett. For beginners. SUMMARY: Doug Bruestle teaches the
basics of learning to play the cello, from handling to
rudimentary playing, and demonstrates the technique along
with two of his pupils. CONTENTS: The parts -- Holding your
cello -- The bow -- Using the bow -- Your left hand -- Putting
it together -- Advanced topics -- Wrapping it up.
*1. Violoncello - Instruction and study. 2. Violoncello - Studies
and exercises. I. Bruestle, Doug. II. Brinegar, Todd. III. Arnett,
Mark S. IV. Backstage Pass Productions. V. Aesthetic Artist
Records. VI. Brinegar Video/Film Productions, Inc. VII. MVP
Home Entertainment (Firm) VIII. Title: Cello for beginners IX.
Series.*
*TC MT305 .C4 1995*

**Censorship in America.**
Hull, Mary. Santa Barbara, Calif. : ABC-CLIO,
c1999.
*TC Z658.U5 H84 1999*

**CENSORSHIP - UNITED STATES.**
Hull, Mary. Censorship in America. Santa Barbara,
Calif. : ABC-CLIO, c1999.
*TC Z658.U5 H84 1999*

**The centennial series of the Association of Former
Students, Texas A&M University**
(no. 80) Kellar, William Henry, 1952- Make haste
slowly. 1st ed. College Station : Texas A&M
University Press, c1999.
*TC LC214.23.H68 K45 1999*

**Center for Applied Linguistics.**
Language and automation. Washington, Center for
Applied Linguistics.

**Center for Applied Research in Education.**
Toner, Patricia Rizzo, 1952- Sex education activities.
West Nyack, N.Y. : Center for Applied Research in
Education, c1993.
*TC HQ35 .T65 1993*

**Center for Dewey Studies.**
Dewey, John, 1859-1952. The correspondence of John
Dewey. [computer file]. Windows version.
Charlottesville, VA : InteLex Corp., 1999- Computer
data and program.
*TC B945.D44 A4 1999*

**Center for Migration Studies (U.S.).**
National Legal Conference on Immigration and
Refugee Policy (6th : 1983 : Washington, D.C.)
Immigration and refugee policy. 1st ed. New York :
Center for Migration Studies, 1984.
*TC KF4819.A2 N375 1983*

**Center for Science, Mathematics, and Engineering
Education. Committee on Developing the Capacity
to Select Effective Instructional Materials.**
Selecting instructional materials : a guide for K-12
science / Committee on Developing the Capacity to
Select Effective Instructional Materials, Center for
Science, Mathematics, and Engineering Education,
National Research Council ; Maxine Singer and Jan
Tuomi, editors. Washington, D.C. : National Academy
Press, c1999. xi, 121 p. : ill. ; 28 cm. Includes
bibliographical references (p. 113-116) and index. ISBN 0-
309-06533-X DDC 507.8
*1. Science - Study and teaching - United States - Aids and
devices. 2. Science - Study and teaching - Aids and devices -*

*Pruchasing - United States. I. Singer, Maxine. II. Tuomi, Jan.
III. Title.*
*TC LB1585.3 .C45 1999*

**Center for Science, Mathematics, and Engineering
Education. Committee on Development of an
Addendum to the National Science Education
Standards on Scientific Inquiry.**
Inquiry and the National Science Education Standards.
Washington, D.C. : National Academy Press, c2000.
*TC LB1585.3 .I57 2000*

**Center for Science, Mathematics, and Engineering
Education. Committee on Undergraduate Science
Education.**
Transforming undergraduate education in science,
mathematics, engineering, and technology.
Washington, DC : National Academy Press, 1999.
*TC Q183.3.A1 T73 1999*

**Center for Urban Education.**
The Center forum. New York, Center for Urban
Education.

**The Center forum.** New York, Center for Urban
Education. v. 31 cm. -v. 4, no. 1;  -Sept. 1969.
*1. Education, Urban - Periodicals I. Center for Urban
Education.*

**Center on Nonprofits and Philanthropy (Urban
Institute).**
Nonprofits and government. Washington, DC : Urban
Institute Press, 1999.
*TC HD62.6 .N694 1999*

**CENTRAL AMERICA - HISTORY - 1979 - -
OUTLINES, SYLLABI, ETC.**
Third world peoples, a Gospel perspective. Maryknoll,
NY : Maryknoll Fathers and Brothers, c1987.
*TC F1439.T54 1987*

**CENTRAL AMERICA - SOCIAL CONDITIONS -
1979 - -OUTLINES, SYLLABI, ETC.**
Third world peoples, a Gospel perspective. Maryknoll,
NY : Maryknoll Fathers and Brothers, c1987.
*TC F1439.T54 1987*

**CENTRAL ASIA.** *See* **ASIA, CENTRAL.**

**CENTRAL CITIES.** *See* **INNER CITIES.**

**CENTRAL HIGH SCHOOL (LITTLE ROCK,
ARK.) - HISTORY.**
Counts, I. Wilmer (Ira Wilmer), 1931- A life is more
than a moment. Bloomington, IN : Indiana University
Press, c1999.
*TC LC214.23.L56 C68 1999*

Understanding the Little Rock crisis. Fayetteville,
Ark : University of Arkansas Press, 1999.
*TC LC214.23.L56 U53 1999*

**CENTRAL HIGH SCHOOL (LITTLE ROCK,
ARK.) - HISTORY - 20TH CENTURY.**
Roy, Beth. Bitters in the honey. Fayetteville :
University of Arkansas Press, 1999.
*TC LC214.23.L56 R69 1999*

**CENTRAL NERVOUS SYSTEM.** *See* **BRAIN;
EFFERENT PATHWAYS.**

**CENTRALIZATION OF SCHOOLS.** *See*
**SCHOOLS - CENTRALIZATION.**

**Centre du cinéma et de l'audio-visuel de la
communauté Française de Belgique.**
Ecole 27 [videorecording]. Bruxelles : Paradise
Films ; New York, N.Y. : [distributed by] First Run/
Icarus Films, 1997, c1996.
*TC LC746.P7 E2 1997*

**Centre for Advanced Studies in Music Education.
Faculty of Education.**
Singing development. London : Roehampton Institute,
Centre for Advanced Studies in Music Education,
Faculty of Education, [1997?]
*TC MT898 .S55 1997*

**Centre for Educational Research and Innovation.**
Human capital investment. Paris : Organisation for
Economic Co-operation and Development, c1998.
*TC HD4904.7 .H843 1998*

Inclusive education at work. Paris : Organisation for
Economic Co-operation and Development, 1999.
*TC LC4015 .I525 1999*

Knowledge management in the learning society /
Centre for Educational Research and Innovation.
Paris : Organisation for Economic Co-operation and
Development, 2000. 257 p. ; 27 cm. (Education and Skills)
Includes bibliographical references (p. 255-257). Other editions
available: Société du savoir et gestion des connaissances
9264271821 fre. ISBN 92-64-17182-7 DDC 370
*1. Knowledge management. I. Title. II. Title: Société du savoir
et gestion des connaissances fre III. Series.*

**TC HD30.2 .C462 2000**
Motivating students for lifelong learning. Paris :
Organisation for Economic Co-operation and
Development, c2000.
*TC LB1065 .M669 2000*

**Centre for Language in Primary Education (London,
England).**
Dombey, Henrietta. Whole to part phonics. London :
Centre for Language in Primary Education : Language
Matters, c1998.
*TC LB1573.3 .D66 1998*

**Centre for Social Development and Humanitarian
Affairs (United Nations).**
[Family (New York, N.Y. : 1984)] The family. New
York : United Nations, 1984-

[Family (New York, N.Y. : 1984)] The Family. New
York : United Nations, 1984-

**Centre Georges Pompidou.**
Matisse, voyages [videorecording]. [Chicago, Ill.] :
Home Vision ; [S.l.] : Distributed worldwide by RM
Associates, c1989.
*TC ND553.M37 M37 1989*

**Centre on Transnational Corporations (United
Nations).**
University curriculum on transnational corporations.
New York : United Nations, 1991.
*TC HD2755.5 .U55 1991*

**Centro de Estudios Educativos.**
[Folleto de divulgación (Centro de Estudios
Educativos).] Folleto de divulgación. México : Centro
de Estudios Educativos,

**Centro di Educazione Professionale per Assistenti
Sociali.**
Centro sociale. Roma.

**Centro sociale.** Roma. v. ill. anno 1- luglio/sett. 1954- .
"Inchieste sociale, servizio sociale di Gruppo, educazione degli
adulti." Beginning 1965 each volume includes an international
issue: International review of community development.
Indexed selectively by: Social welfare, social planning/
policy & social development 0195-7988. Indexed selectively
by: Sociological abstracts 0038-0202. Anno 2-  1955- also
numbered consecutively n. 1- Anno numbering irregular. Anno
2-25 also numbered 1-142/144. Ceased with v. 25. Issued
1954-  by the Centro di Educazione Professionale per
Assistenti Sociali (CEPAS). Vols. for 1972-73, 1974-75. ISSN
0528-5852 DDC 362
*1. Community development - Periodicals. 2. Social sciences -
Periodicals. I. Centro di Educazione Professionale per
Assistenti Sociali. II. Title: International review of community
development.*

**Centrum voor Studies van het Hoger
Onderwijsbeleid (Enschede, Netherlands).**
From the eye of the storm. Dordrecht ; Boston ;
London : Kluwer Academic Publishers, c1999.
*TC LB2341.8.E85 F76 1999*

**Century May 1940.**
Current history and Forum. New York [C-H
Publishing Corporation; etc., etc., 1914-41]

**Cepeda, Claudio, 1942-** Concise guide to the
psychiatric interview of children and adolescents /
Claudio Cepeda. Washington, DC : American
Psychiatric Press, c2000. xxxiii, 382 p. : ill. ; 17 cm.
(Concise guides / American Psychiatric Press) Spine title:
Psychiatric interview of children and adolescents. Includes
bibliographical references and index. ISBN 0-88048-330-X
DDC 618.92/89
*1. Interviewing in child psychiatry - Handbooks, manuals, etc.
2. Interviewing in adolescent psychiatry - Handbooks,
manuals, etc. 3. Interview, Psychological -
Adolescence - Handbooks. 4. Interview, Psychological -
methods - Child - Handbooks. 5. Interview, Psychological -
methods - Child, Preschool - Handbooks. 6. Psychiatry -
methods - Adolescence - Handbooks. 7. Psychiatry - methods -
Child - Handbooks. 8. Psychiatry - methods - Child,
Preschool - Handbooks. I. Title. II. Title: Psychiatric interview
of children and adolescents III. Series: Concise guides
(American Psychiatric Press).*
*TC RJ503.6 .C46 2000*

**CERAMIC ART.** *See* **POTTERY.**

**CERAMIC ARTISTS.** *See* **POTTERS.**

**Ceramic innovations** : in the 20th century / edited by
John B. Wachtman. Westerville, Ohio : American
Ceramic Society, 1999. xiii, 307 p. : ill. ; 24 cm. Includes
bibliographical references (p. 295-296) and index. "Gift from
professor Maxine Greene" ISBN 1-57498-093-9
*1. Ceramics - History. I. Wachtman, J. B. 1928- II. American
Ceramic Society.*
*TC TP807 .C473 1999*

CERAMIC TECHNOLOGY. *See* CERAMICS.

CERAMICS. *See also* POTTERY.
Minogue, Coll. Wood-fired ceramics. London : A & C Black : Philadelphia : University of Pennsylvania Press, 2000.
*TC TP841 .M57 2000*

CERAMICS (ART). *See* POTTERY.

CERAMICS - HISTORY.
Ceramic innovations. Westerville, Ohio : American Ceramic Society, 1999.
*TC TP807 .C473 1999*

Cereb palsy j.
Cerebral palsy journal. Wichita, Kan., Institute of Logopedics, inc.

Cerebellum Corporation.
The nutty, nougat-filled world of human nutrition [videorecording]. [Arlington, Va.] : Cerebellum Corp., c1998.
*TC QP141 .N8 1998*

The salsa-riffic world of Spanish [videorecording]. [Arlington, Va.] : Cerebellum Corp., c1998.
*TC PC4112.7 .S25 1998*

CEREBRAL CIRCULATION DISORDERS. *See* CEREBROVASCULAR DISEASE.

CEREBRAL CORTEX. *See* FRONTAL LOBES.

CEREBRAL HEMISPHERES.
Myers, Penelope S. Right hemisphere damage. San Diego : Singular Pub., c1999.
*TC RC423 .M83 1999*

CEREBRAL PALSIED CHILDREN.
Love, Russell J. Childhood motor speech disability. 2nd ed. Boston : London : Allyn and Bacon, c2000.
*TC RJ496.S7 L68 2000*

Cerebral palsy journal. Wichita, Kan., Institute of Logopedics, inc. 29 v. ill. 28 cm. Frequency: Bimonthly (1940- monthly). v.1-28, no.4; Apr.1940-July/Aug.1968. Cover title: C.P. review -Mar./Apr. 1965. Other title: Cereb palsy j.
*1. Cerebral palsy - Periodicals. 2. Rehabilitation - Periodicals. I. Institute of Logopedics. II. Title: C.P. review -Mar./Apr. 1965 III. Title: Cereb palsy j IV. Title: Spastic review v.1-10, 1940-1949 V. Title: Cerebral palsy review v.11-26, no.2, 1950-Mar./Apr. 1965*

Cerebral palsy journal May/June 1965-.
Cerebral palsy review. Wichita, Kan., Institute of Logopedics.

CEREBRAL PALSY - PERIODICALS.
Cerebral palsy journal. Wichita, Kan., Institute of Logopedics, inc.

Cerebral palsy review. Wichita, Kan., Institute of Logopedics.

CEREBRAL PALSY - REHABILITATION - PERIODICALS.
Cerebral palsy review. Wichita, Kan., Institute of Logopedics.

Cerebral palsy review. Wichita, Kan., Institute of Logopedics. v. : ill. Frequency: Bimonthly. v. 11-26, no. 2; Jan. 1950-Mar./Apr. 1965. Caption title: CP review. Continues: Spastic review 1940-49. Continued by: Cerebral palsy journal May/June 1965-.
*1. Cerebral palsy - Periodicals. 2. Rehabilitation - Periodicals. 3. Cerebral palsy - Rehabilitation - Periodicals. 4. Paralysis, Cerebral - periodicals. I. Institute of Logopedics. II. Title: CP review III. Title: Spastic review 1940-49 IV. Title: Cerebral palsy journal May/June 1965-*

Cerebral palsy review v.11-26, no.2, 1950-Mar./Apr. 1965.
Cerebral palsy journal. Wichita, Kan., Institute of Logopedics, inc.

CEREBRAL PARALYSIS. *See* CEREBRAL PALSY.

CEREBROPATHIA PSYCHICA TOXAEMICA. *See* KORSAKOFF'S SYNDROME.

CEREBROVASCULAR ACCIDENT. *See* CEREBROVASCULAR DISEASE.

CEREBROVASCULAR DISEASE.
When the brain goes wrong [videorecording]. Short version. Boston, MA : Fanlight Productions [dist.], c1992.
*TC RC386 .W54 1992*

CEREBROVASCULAR DISEASE - COMPLICATIONS.
Parr, Susie, 1953- Talking about aphasia. Buckingham ; Philadelphia : Open University Press, 1997.

*TC RC425 .P376 1997*

CEREBROVASCULAR DISORDERS. *See* CEREBROVASCULAR DISEASE.

CEREBROVASCULAR SYNDROME. *See* CEREBROVASCULAR DISEASE.

CEREBRUM. *See* BRAIN.

CEREMONIES. *See* RITES AND CEREMONIES.

Cernada, George Peter.
Progress in preventing AIDS? Amityville, N.Y. : Baywood Pub. Co., 1998.
*TC RA644.A25 P7655 1998*

Cerruto, Audra. The effects of training on theory of mind tasks with children who are deaf / by Audra Cerruto. 1999. viii, 144 leaves ; 29 cm. Typescript; issued also on microfilm. Includes tables. Thesis (Ph.D.)--Columbia University, 1999. Includes bibliographical references (leaves 117-128).
*1. Children, deaf - Education. 2. Performance in children. 3. Child rearing. 4. Child development. 5. Philosophy of mind. 6. Parent and child. I. Title.*
*TC 085 C34*

CERTAINTY.
Sorrentino, Richard M. The uncertain mind. Philadelphia : Psychology Press, c2000.
*TC BF697 .S674 2000*

CERTIFICATION, FALSE. *See* FALSE CERTIFICATION.

CERTIFICATION OF LIBRARIANS. *See* LIBRARIANS - CERTIFICATION.

Certified occupational therapy assistant in the schools.
Barlow, Tracie. The COTA in the schools. San Antonio, Texas : Therapy Skill Builders, c1999.
*TC RM735 .B37 1999*

CESO paperback
(no. 24) Learning from experience. The Hague : Centre for the Study of Education in Developing Countries, c1995.
*TC LC2610 .L43 1995*

Chacko, Mathew Vadakkan. Public key cryptosystems : history and development / Mathew Vadakkan Chacko. 1998. iv, 266 leaves : ill. ; 29 cm. Typescript; issued also on microfilm. Thesis (Ph.D.)--Columbia University, 1998. Includes bibliographical references (leaves 124-131).
*1. Computers - Access control. 2. Cryptography. 3. Computer security. 4. Data encryption (Computer science) 5. Data protection. 6. Algebra, Abstract. I. Title.*
*TC 085 C35*

Chadwick, Annie. Showbiz bookkeeper : the tax record-keeping system for professionals working in the arts, 1992 & 1993 / by Annie Chadwick with Wallace Norman. Dorset, Vermont : Theatre Directories, 1992, c1991. 1 v. (unpaged) ; 28 cm. Chiefly tables. Label mounted on title page: "This edition was revised and reprinted in Dec. 1994 and is accurate for 1995." ISBN 0-933919-22-0
*1. Artists - Taxation - United States - Handbooks, manuals, etc. 2. Actors - Taxation - United States - Handbooks, manuals, etc. 3. Entertainers - Taxation - United States - Handbooks, manuals, etc. I. Norman, Wallace. II. Title.*
*TC HF5686.P24 C53 1991*

Chadwick, Bruce A.
Heaton, Tim B. Statistical handbook on racial groups in the United States. Phoenix, AZ : Oryx Press, 2000.
*TC E184.A1 H417 2000*

Chafetz, Morris E.
O'Brien, Robert, 1932- The encyclopedia of understanding alcohol and other drugs. New York, NY : Facts on File, c1999.
*TC HV5017 .O37 1999*

CHAGA (AFRICAN PEOPLE) - EDUCATION.
Mosha, R. Sambuli. The heartbeat of indigenous Africa. New York : London : Garland Publishing : [Falmer Press], 2000.
*TC LC191.8.T29 M67 2000*

Chagall.
Marc Chagall [videorecording]. [Chicago, Ill.] : Home Vision [distributor], c1985.
*TC ND699.C5 C5 1985*

Chagall, Marc, 1887-.
La Fontaine, Jean de, 1621-1695. [Fables. English. Selections] Marc Chagall. New York : New Press : Distributed by W.W. Norton, [1997]
*TC PQ1811.E3 W6 1997*

Marc Chagall [videorecording]. [Chicago, Ill.] : Home Vision [distributor], c1985.

*TC ND699.C5 C5 1985*

CHAGALL, MARC, 1887-.
Marc Chagall [videorecording]. [Chicago, Ill.] : Home Vision [distributor], c1985.
*TC ND699.C5 C5 1985*

CHAGALL, MARC, 1887 - -EXHIBITIONS.
La Fontaine, Jean de, 1621-1695. [Fables. English. Selections] Marc Chagall. New York : New Press : Distributed by W.W. Norton, [1997]
*TC PQ1811.E3 W6 1997*

CHAGGA (AFRICAN PEOPLE). *See* CHAGA (AFRICAN PEOPLE).

Chaiklin, Seth.
International Society for Activity Theory and Cultural Research. Congress (4th : 1998 : Aarhus, Denmark) Activity theory and social practice. Aarhus : Aarhus University Press, c1999.
*TC B105.A35 I57 1998*

International Society for Activity Theory and Cultural Research. Congress (4th : 1998 : Aarhus, Denmark) Activity theory and social practice. Aarhus : Aarhus University Press, c1999.
*TC B105.A35 I57 1999*

Chaim Soutine.
Kleeblatt, Norman L. An expressionist in Paris. Munich ; New York : Jewish Museum, c1998.
*TC ND553.S7 A4 1998*

Chaisson, Eric.
The thirteenth labor. Amsterdam : Gordon and Breach Publishers, c1999.
*TC Q181.3 .T45 1999*

Chalifoux, Debbie.
Jazz dance class [videorecording]. W. Long Branch, NJ : Kultur, [1992?]
*TC GV1784 .J3 1992*

The chalk doll.
Pomerantz, Charlotte. New York : Lippincott, c1989.
*TC PZ7.P77 Ch 1989*

Chalk, Rosemary A.
Violence in families. Washington, D.C. : National Academy Press, 1998.
*TC HV6626.2 .V56 1998*

Chalker, Christopher S. Effective alternative education programs : solutions for K-8 students at risk / Christopher S. Chalker, Kimila S. Brown. Lancaster, Pa. : Technomic, c1999. xvi, 239 p. : ill. ; 23 cm. ISBN 1-56676-732-6
*1. High risk students. 2. Socially handicapped children - Education - United States. 3. Alternative education. I. Brown, Kimila S. II. Title.*
*TC LC4091 .C5 1999*

Chall, Jeanne Sternlicht, 1921- The academic achievement challenge : what really works in the classroom? / Jeanne S. Chall. New York ; London : Guilford Press, c2000. xii, 210 p. ; 24 cm. Includes bibliographical references (p. 193-202) and index. ISBN 1-57230-500-2 DDC 371.3
*1. School improvement programs. 2. Academic achievement. 3. Teaching. I. Title.*
*TC LB2822.8 .C49 2000*

Challenge cases for differential diagnosis.
Challenge cases [videorecording]. Princeton, N.J. : Films for the Humanities & Sciences, 1998.
*TC RC455.2.C4 C4 1998*

Challenge cases [videorecording] / a presentation of Films for the Humanities & Sciences : University of Sheffield ; produced and directed by Steve Collier ; written by Dr. Steve Peters : Sheffield University Television. Princeton, N.J. : Films for the Humanities & Sciences, 1998. 1 videocassette (35 min.) : sd., col. ; 1/2 in. (Differential diagnosis in psychiatry) Series subtitle: Visual aided on ICD 10. Title on container: Challenge cases for differential diagnosis. VHS. Catalogued from credits and container. Commentary: John Graham Davies. Sound: Ken Hardy; cameras: Jackie Jones, Mark Parkin, Gary Wraith; graphics: Sean Purcell. Originally produced 1995-1997 at the University of Sheffield. "Clinical features of myotonic dystrophy and Huntington's disease" included in list of complete series on container no longer part of series. For students of psychiatry, clinical psychology and social work, and counselling. SUMMARY: "This program offers viewers a chance to watch interviews with four patients and then, based on their symptoms, come up with their own differential diagnoses. The cases include a 22-year old man who continually complains about body odor, when he does not have body odor; a 26-year old man in a seemingly confused metnal state; a 30-year old woman with anxiety symptoms; and a seemingly normal young man who throws bricks through his neighbor's window."--Container.

*1. Mental illness - Diagnosis. 2. Delusions - Case studies. 3. Panic disorders - Patients. 4. Dissociative disorders - Patients. 5. Paranoia - Patients. 6. Diagnosis. Differential. I. Peters, Steve. Dr. II. Collier. Steve. III. Davies. John Graham. IV. University of Sheffield. V. Sheffield University Television. VI. Films for the Humanities (Firm) VII. Title: Visual aid based on ICD 10 VIII. Title: Challenge cases for differential diagnosis IX. Series.*
***TC RC455.2.C4 C4 1998***

**The challenge of change in physical education.** Webb, Ida M. London : Falmer Press, 1999.
***TC GV246.E3 B79 1999***

**The challenge of diversity :** integration and pluralism in societies of immigration / Rainer Bauböck, Agnes Heller, Aristide R. Zolberg (eds.). Aldershot, England ; Brookfield, Vt. : Avebury, 1996. 278 p. : ill. ; 24 cm. (Public policy and social welfare ; v. 21) Includes bibliographical references. "European Centre Vienna."--T.p. verso. ISBN 1-85972-401-9
*1. Emigration and immigration - Social aspects. 2. Immigrants - Social conditions. 3. Multiculturalism. 4. Social integration. I. Bauböck, Rainer. II. Heller, Agnes. III. Zolberg, Aristide R. IV. European Centre for Social Welfare Policy and Research. V. Series.*
***TC JV225 .C530 1996***

**The challenge of permanency planning in a multicultural society** / Gary R. Anderson, Angela Shen Ryan, Bogart R. Leashore, editors. New York : Haworth Press, c1997. xiii, 215 p. : ill. ; 22 cm. "Has also been published as Journal of multicultural social work, volume 5, numbers 1/2 and 3/4 1997"--T.p. verso. Includes bibliographical references and index. ISBN 0-7890-0034-2 (acid-free paper) ISBN 0-7890-0302-3 (acid-free paper) DDC 362.7/0973
*1. Social work with children - United States. 2. Social work with minorities - United States. 3. Family social work - United States. 4. Foster children - United States. 5. Child welfare - United States. 6. Pluralism (Social sciences) - United States. I. Anderson, Gary R., 1952- II. Ryan, Angela Shen. III. Leashore, Bogart R.*
***TC HV741 .C378 1997***

**A challenge to change :** the language learning continuum : strategies for more effective language instruction & lessons learned from the articulation and achievement project / Claire W. Jackson, executive editor. New York : College Entrance Examination Board, 1999. xii, 208 p. : ill. ; 23 cm. "A project in foreign language education"--Cover. Includes bibliographical references. DDC 418/.007
*1. Language and languages - Study and teaching. I. Jackson, Claire W. II. College Entrance Examination Board.*
***TC P51 .C427 1999***

**CHALLENGED BOOKS.** *See* **CENSORSHIP.**

**Challenges and opportunities for education in the 21st century** / edited by James J. Van Patten. Lewiston, NY : Edwin Mellen Press, c1999. xii, 203 p. ; 24 cm. (Mellen studies in education ; v. 44) Includes bibliographical references and index. ISBN 0-7734-8045-5 DDC 370/.1
*1. Education - United States. 2. Educational planning - United States. 3. School management and organization - United States. 4. Educational change - United States. 5. Education - Philosophy. I. Van Patten, James J. II. Series.*
***TC LA209.2 .C45 1999***

**The challenges of science education :** Education Committee forum, 30 March 1999, Strasbourg, France / Council for Cultural Co-operation. Strasbourg : Council of Europe Pub., c1999. 75 p. : ill. ; 21 cm. Includes bibliographical references. ISBN 92-871-4095-2
*1. Science - Study and teaching - Europe - Congresses. I. Council of Europe. Council for Cultural Co-operation. Education Committee.*
***TC Q183.4.E85 C475 1999***

**The challenges of the information and communication technologies facing history teaching :** symposium, 25-27 March 1999, Andorra la Vella (Andorra) : general report / by Jacques Tardif. Strasbourg : Council of Europe Pub., c1999. 55 p. ; 21 cm. (Education) "Council for Cultural Co-operation." ISBN 92-871-3998-9
*1. History - Study and teaching - Europe. 2. Information technology - Europe - Congresses. 3. Communication and technology - Europe - Congresses. 4. Europe - History - 20th century - Study and teaching - Europe - Congresses. I. Tardif, Jacques, 1947- II. Council of Europe. III. Council of Europe. Council for Cultural Co-operation. IV. Title: Learning and teaching about the history of Europe in the 20th century V. Series: Collection Education (Strasbourg, France)*
***TC D424 .C425 1999***

**Challenges of urban education :** sociological perspectives for the next century / edited by Karen A. McClafferty, Carlos Alberto Torres, Theodore R. Mitchell ; [Michael W. Apple, et al.]. Albany : State Unviersity of New York Press, c2000. ix, 357 p. ; 23 cm. Includes bibliographical references and index. ISBN 0-7914-4433-3 (alk. paper) ISBN 0-7914-4434-1 (pbk. : alk. paper) DDC 370/.9173/2
*1. Education, Urban - Social aspects - United States. 2. Children of minorities - Education - United States. 3. Educational change - United States. I. McClafferty, Karen A. II. Torres, Carlos Alberto. III. Mitchell, Theodore R. IV. Apple, Michael W.*
***TC LC5131 .C38 2000***

**The challenges to sustaining Unification faith and the spiritual quest after seminary.**
Stewart, Therese Marie Klein. 1996.
***TC 06 no. 10751***

**Challenging behaviour :** principles and practices / edited by Dave Hewett. London : D. Fulton, 1998. viii, 232 p. : ill. ; 24 cm. Includes bibliographical references and indexes. ISBN 1-85346-451-1 DDC 616.85/889
*1. Mentally handicapped - Behavior modification. 2. Mentally handicapped - Behavior modification - Great Britain - Case studies. I. Hewett, Dave.*
***TC RC451.4.M47 C492 1998***

**Challenging women.**
Maddock, Su. London ; Thousand Oaks, Calif. : Sage, 1999.
***TC HQ1236 .M342 1999***

**Challis, Bradford H.**
Stratification in cognition and consciousness. Amsterdam ; Philadelphia : J. Benjamins, c1999.
***TC BF444 .S73 1999***

**Chalmers, David John, 1966-.**
Toward a science of consciousness III. Cambridge, Mass. : MIT Press, c1999.
***TC BF311 .T67 1999***

**Chalofsky, Neal, 1945-.**
The full-time faculty handbook. Thousand Oaks : Sage Publications, c1999.
***TC LB1778.2 .F85 1999***

**Chaloupka, Frank J.**
The economic analysis of substance use and abuse. Chicago : University of Chicago Press, 1999.
***TC HV4999.2 .E25 1999***

**Chamber of Commerce of the United States of America.**
American economic security. Washington, Chamber of Commerce of the United States of America.

Annual State of American Education Address (7th : February 22, 2000 : Durham, N.C.) The seventh annual state of American education address [videorecording. [Washington, D.C. : U.S. Dept. of Education], 2000.

Modernizing schools : technology and buildings for a new century (September 19, 2000 : Washington, D.C.) Modernizing schools [videorecording]. [Washington, D.C.] : U.S. Dept. of Education, [2000].
***TC LB3205 .M64 2000***

Modernizing schools : technology and buildings for a new century (September 19, 2000 : Washington, D.C.) Modernizing schools [videorecording]. [Washington, D.C.] : U.S. Dept. of Education, [2000].
***TC LB3205 .M64 2000***

**Chamber of the United States of America.**
Powerful middle schools : teaching and learning for young adolescents (2000) Powerful middle schools [videorecording]. [Washington, D.C.?] : U.S. Dept. of Education, [2000].
***TC LB1623 .P6 2000***

**Chamberlain, Kathryn A.** The JCAHO mock survey made simple / Kathryn Chamberlain, Candace Hamner. 1998 ed. Marblehead, MA : Opus Communications, c1998. 1 v. (various pagings) ; 28 cm. ISBN 1-57839-023-0 DDC 362.1/1/021873
*1. Hospitals - Accreditation - United States - Problems, exercises, etc. 2. Hospitals - Standards - United States - Problems, exercises, etc. I. Hamner, Candace J. II. Title.*
***TC RA981.A2 C45 1999***

**Chamberlain, Margaret, ill.**
Hendry, Diana, 1941- Dog Donovan. 1st U.S. ed. Cambridge, Mass. : Candlewick Press, 1995.
***TC PZ7.H38586 Dm 1995***

**Chamberlain, Marisha.**
The power of idea : [videorecording]. Minneapolis, Minn. : Media Loft, c1992.
***TC TR690 .P5 1992***

**Chamberlin, J. Gordon (John Gordon)** Upon whom we depend : the American poverty system / J. Gordon Chamberlin. New York : Peter Lang, c1999. 190 p. : ill. ; 23 cm. (Counterpoints, 1058-1634 ; vol. 98) Includes bibliographical references (p. [177]-179) and index. ISBN 0-8204-4151-1 (pbk. : alk. paper) DDC 339.4/6/0973
*1. Poverty - United States. 2. Poor - United States. 3. Social classes - United States. I. Title. II. Series: Counterpoints (New York, N.Y.) ; vol. 98.*
***TC HC110.P6 C326 1999***

**Chambers, Gary N., 1956-** Motivating language learners / Gary N. Chambers. Clevedon [U.K.] ; Buffalo : Multilingual Matters, c1999. xi, 242 p. ; 21 cm. (Modern languages in practice ; 12) Includes bibliographical references (p. 231-240) and index. ISBN 1-85359-449-0 (alk. paper) ISBN 1-85359-448-2 (pbk. : alk. paper) DDC 418/.007
*1. Languages, Modern - Study and teaching. I. Title. II. Series.*
***TC PB35 .C517 1999***

**Chambers, J. K.** Sociolinguistic theory : linguistic variation and its social significance / J.K. Chambers. Oxford, UK ; Cambridge, Mass., USA : Blackwell, 1995. xxi, 284 p. ; 24 cm. (Language in society) Includes bibliographical references (p. [260]-276) and index. ISBN 0-631-18325-6 ISBN 0-631-18326-4 (pbk.) DDC 306.4/4
*1. Sociolinguistics. I. Title. II. Series: Language in society (Oxford, England)*
***TC P40 .C455 1995***

**Chambliss, William J.** Power, politics, and crime / William J. Chambliss. Boulder, CO : Westview Press, c1999. xiv, 173 p. : ill. ; 24 cm. (Crime & society) Includes bibliographical references and index. ISBN 0-8133-3486-1 (alk. paper) DDC 364.973
*1. Crime - Political aspects - United States. 2. Criminal justice, Administration of - Political aspects - United States. I. Title. II. Series: Crime & society (Boulder, Colo.)*
***TC HV6789 .C395 1999***

**Chamot, Anna Uhl.**
The learning strategies handbook. White Plains, NY : Longman, c1999.
***TC P51 .L43 1999***

**CHAMPIGNONS.** *See* **MUSHROOMS.**

**Champions of change :** the impact of the arts on learning / edited by Edward B. Fiske. Washington, DC : Arts Education Partnership : President's Committee on the Arts and the Humanities, [1999] xii, 98 p. : ill. ; 28 cm. Includes bibliographical references.
*1. Arts - Study and teaching - United States. 2. Learning. I. Fiske, Edward B. II. Arts Education Partnership (U.S.) III. United States. President's Committee on the Arts and the Humanities.*
***TC NX304.A1 C53 1999***

**Chan, Mary, 1965-.**
Modernstarts. New York : Museum of Modern Art : Distributed by Harry N. Abrams, c1999.
***TC N620.M9 M63 1999***

**CHANCE.** *See also* **PROBABILITIES.**
Everitt, Brian. Chance rules. New York : Copernicus, c1999.
***TC QA273 .E84 1999***

**Chance rules.**
Everitt, Brian. New York : Copernicus, c1999.
***TC QA273 .E84 1999***

**Chandler, Cynthia K.**
Kolander, Cheryl A. Contemporary women's health. Boston, Mass. : WCB/McGraw-Hill, c1999.
***TC RA778 .K7245 1999***

**Chandler, Tomasita M.** Children and adolescents in the market place : twenty-five years of academic research / Tomasita M. Chandler and Barbara M. Heinzerling. Ann Arbor, Mich. : Pierian Press, 1999. x, 669 p. ; 29 cm. Includes indexes. ISBN 0-87650-383-0
*1. Marketing research. 2. Advertising and children. 3. Child consumers - United States - Bibliography. I. Heinzerling, Barbara M. II. Title.*
***TC HF5822 .C43 1999***

**Chang, Edward C. (Edward Chin-Ho).**
Optimism & pessimism. 1st ed. Washington, DC : American Psychological Association, c2001.
***TC BF698.35.O57 O68 2001***

**Chang, Shun-Wen.** A comparative study of item exposure control methods in computerized adaptive testing / Shun-Wen Chang, Bor-Yaun Twu. Iowa City, IA : ACT, Inc., 1998. v, 46 p. : ill. ; 28 cm. (ACT research report series ; no. 98-3) Includes bibliographical references (p. 33-34).
*1. Educational tests and measurements - United States - Data Processing. 2. Computer adaptive testing. 3. Examinations - Evaluation. I. Twu, Bor-Yaun II. Title. III. Series.*
***TC LB3051 .A3 no. 98-3***

**Change.**
Change in higher education. [New York, Science and University Affairs for Educational Change, Inc.]

**CHANGE, EDUCATIONAL.** *See* **EDUCATIONAL CHANGE.**

**Change in higher education.**
Change in higher education. [New York, Science and University Affairs for Educational Change, Inc.]

**Change in higher education.** [New York, Science and University Affairs for Educational Change, Inc.] 2 v. ill. 26 cm. Frequency: Bimonthly. v. 1-2, no. 3; Jan./Feb. 1969-May/June 1970. Running title: Change. "Conceived under the auspices of the Union for Research and Experimentation in Higher Education and funded by a grant from the Esso Educational Foundation." Available on microfilm. Available in other form: Change in higher education ISSN: 0363-6291 (OCoLC)4320411. Continued by: Change (New Rochelle, N.Y.) ISSN: 0009-1383 (DLC) 80643795 (OCoLC)1553876. ISSN 0363-6291 DDC 378.1/005
*1. Education, Higher - Periodicals. I. Educational Change, inc. II. Title: Change III. Title: Change in higher education IV. Title: Change (New Rochelle, N.Y.)*

**CHANGE, LINGUISTIC.** *See* **LINGUISTIC CHANGE.**

**Change (New Rochelle, N.Y.).**
Change in higher education. [New York, Science and University Affairs for Educational Change, Inc.]

**CHANGE, ORGANIZATIONAL.** *See* **ORGANIZATIONAL CHANGE.**

**CHANGE (PSYCHOLOGY).**
Fosha, Diana. The transforming power of affect. 1st ed. New York : BasicBooks, 2000.
*TC BF637.C4 F67 2000*

Modelling changes in understanding. Amsterdam ; New York : Pergamon, 1999.
*TC BF319 .M55 1999*

Walters, Glenn D. The self-altering process. Westport, Conn. : Praeger, 2000.
*TC BF637.C4 W35 2000*

Weber, Robert J. (Robert John), 1936- The created self. 1st ed. New York ; London : W.W. Norton, c2000.
*TC BF697.5.S44 W43 2000*

**CHANGE, SOCIAL.** *See* **SOCIAL CHANGE.**

**CHANGES, CAREER.** *See* **CAREER CHANGES.**

**Changes, changes.**
Hutchins, Pat, 1942- New York, Macmillan c1971.
*TC PZ8.9 .H95 1971*

Hutchins, Pat, 1942- New York, Macmillan c1971.
*TC PZ8.9.H95 Ch 1971*

**Changing academic work.**
Martin, Elaine, 1948- Buckingham ; Philadelphia : Society for Research into Higher Education : Open University Press, 1999.
*TC LA184 .M37 1999*

**CHANGING CAREERS.** *See* **CAREER CHANGES.**

**Changing education**
Helsby, Gill. Changing teachers' work. Buckingham [England] ; Philadelphia : Open University Press, 1999.
*TC LA635 .H375 1999*

Leithwood, Kenneth A. Changing leadership for changing times. Buckingham ; Philadelphia : Open University Press, 1999.
*TC LB2805 .L358 1999*

**Changing education.** Detroit [etc.] 6 v. ill. 26 cm. v. 1-6, no. 1; spring 1966-summer 1974. "A journal of the American Federation of Teachers." Issues for winter/spring 1968 and summer/fall 1968 are unnumbered but constitute v. 2, no. 4-v. 3, no. 3; issues for spring and summer 1973 are unnumbered but constitute v. 5, no. 1-2. Absorbed by: American teacher Apr. 1971-Nov. 1972, Feb. 1975-. ISSN 0009-1413 DDC 370 DDC 370
*1. Education - Periodicals. 2. Teachers - Periodicals. I. American Federation of Teachers. II. Title: American teacher Apr. 1971-Nov. 1972, Feb. 1975-*

**The changing face of whole language** / Jan Turbill, Brian Cambourne, guest editors. Newark, Del. : International Reading Association ; Victoria, Australia : Australian Literacy Educators' Association, c1997. v, 83 p. ; ill. ; 23 cm. "Reprinted from the May 1997 themed issue of The Australian journal of language and literacy, vol. 20, no. 2." Includes bibliographical references. CONTENTS: Guest editors' introduction / Jan Turbill and Brian Cambourne -- Whole language: are we critical enough? / Beth Berghoff, Jerry Harste, and Chris

Leland -- This is literacy: three challenges for teachers of reading and writing / David Bloome -- Defining whole language in a postmodern age / Lorraine Wilson -- Towards a personal theory of whole language: a teacher-researcher-writer reflects / Mem Fox -- Teaching factual writing: purpose and structure / David Wray and Maureen Lewis -- They don't teach spelling anymore--or do they? / Chrystine Bouffler -- Real(ly) writing in school: generic practice? / Jo-Anne Reid -- Whole language and its critics: a New Zealand perspective / John Smith.
*1. Language experience approach in education. 2. Reading - Language experience approach. 3. Language arts. I. Turbill, Jan. edt. II. Cambourne, Brian. edt. III. International Reading Association. IV. Australian Literacy Educators' Association. V. Title: Australian journal of language and literacy. Vol. 20, no. 2.*
*TC LB1050.35 .C43 1997*

**Changing families, changing responsibilities.**
Ganong, Lawrence H. Mahwah, N.J. : Lawrence Erlbaum Associates, 1999.
*TC HQ834 .G375 1999*

**The changing family and child development** / edited by Claudio Violato, Elizabeth Oddone-Paolucci, Mark Genuis. Aldershot : Ashgate, c2000. xxiv, 301 p. ; 23 cm. Papers from the First International Congress on the Changing Family and Child Development held at the University of Calgary, July 1997. Includes bibliographical references. ISBN 0-7546-1025-X DDC 306.85
*1. Family - Congresses. 2. Child development - Congresses. I. Genuis, Mark. II. Violato, Claudio. III. Oddone-Paolucci, Elizabeth. IV. International Congress on the Changing Family and Child Development (1st : 1997 : University of Calgary)*
*TC HQ518 .C478 2000*

**Changing images of pictorial space.**
Dunning, William V., 1933- 1st ed. Syracuse : Syracuse University Press, 1991.
*TC ND1475 .D86 1991*

**Changing international aid to education :** global patterns and national contexts / edited by Kenneth King and Lene Buchert. Paris : Unesco Pub./ NORRAG, 1999. 326 p. ; 24 cm. (Education on the move) Includes bibliographical references. ISBN 92-3-103514-2 (pbk.)
*1. Educational assistance - Developing countries. 2. Educational assistance - Africa. 3. Education - International cooperation. I. King, Kenneth, 1940- II. Buchert, Lene. III. Unesco. IV. Northern Policy, Review, Research Advisory Network on Education and Training V. Series.*
*TC LC2607 .C42 1999*

**Changing leadership for changing times.**
Leithwood, Kenneth A. Buckingham ; Philadelphia : Open University Press, 1999.
*TC LB2805 .L358 1999*

**Changing lives** [videorecording] / a presentation of Films for the Humanities & Sciences ; a production of Public Affairs Television, Inc. ; a presentation of Thirteen/WNET New York ; produced and directed by Pamela Mason Wagner. Princeton, NJ : Films for the Humanities & Sciences, c1998. 1 videocassette (81 min.) : sd., col. ; 1/2 in. (The Moyers collection) (Close to home. Moyers on addiction) Title on cassette label: Close to home, changing lives [videorecording]. VHS. Catalogued from credits and cassette label and container. Host, Bill Moyers. Editor, Susan Fanshel ; photography, Bob Ellfstrom ; music, Thomas Wagner; sound, Greg Linton, Alfred Livecchi. "FFH 7861"--Cassette label. For adolescents through adult. SUMMARY: Bill Moyers focuses on the point that no single treatment program will work for all addicts. He visits the Ridgeview Institute to interview recovering addicts and sit in on a group therapy session. The program also visits Project Safe, a treatment program that reaches out to disadvantaged mothers who are addicts and to their children who are at serious risk of becoming addicts.
*1. Ridgeview Institute. 2. Project Safe. 3. Drug abuse - Treatment. 4. Narcotic addicts - Rehabilitation. 5. Narcotic addicts - Interviews. 6. Alcoholism - Treatment. 7. Alcoholics - Interviews. 8. Alcoholics - Rehabilitation. 9. Recovering addicts - Interviews. 10. Recovering alcoholics - Interviews. 11. Group psychotherapy. 12. Substance abuse. 13. Documentary television programs. I. Moyers, Bill D. II. Wagner, Pamela Mason. III. Public Affairs Television (Firm) IV. WNET (Television station : New York, N.Y.) V. Films for the Humanities (Firm) VI. Title: Close to home, changing lives [videorecording] VII. Series. VIII. Series: Close to home (Series)*
*TC RC564 .C54 1998*

**Changing minds.**
DiSessa, Andrea A. Cambridge, MA : MIT Press, c2000.
*TC LB1028.43 .D57 2000*

**Changing teachers' work.**
Helsby, Gill. Buckingham [England] ; Philadelphia : Open University Press, 1999.
*TC LA635 .H375 1999*

**Changing traditions in Germany's public schools.**
Dichanz, Horst, 1937- Bloomington, Ind. : Phi Delta Kappa Educational Foundation, c1998.
*TC LA723 .D53 1998*

**Changing university teaching : :** reflections on creating educational technologies / [edited by] Terry Evans and Daryl Nation. London : Kogan Page ; Sterling, VA : Stylus Pub., 2000. xiii, 194 p. ; 25 cm. (Open and distance learning series.) Includes bibliographical references (p. 176-187) and index. ISBN 0-7494-3034-6 ISBN 0-7494-3064-8 (pbk.)
*1. College teaching. 2. Educational technology. I. Nation, Daryl. II. Evans, Terry D. (Terry Denis) III. Series.*
*TC LB2331 .C53 2000*

**Changing views.** Teacher's ed. Lexington, Mass. : D.C. Heath and Company, c1983. xxxiv, 365 p. : ill. (some col.) ; 28 cm. (American readers ; 7) Includes index. ISBN 0-669-05085-7
*1. Readers (Elementary) 2. Reading (Elementary) I. Series.*
*TC PE1121 .C52 1983 Teacher's Ed.*

**Changing views :** workbook. Teacher's ed. Lexington, Mass. : D.C. Heath and Company, c1983. 96 p. : ill. ; 28 cm. (American readers ; 7) Includes index. ISBN 0-669-05088-1
*1. Readers (Elementary) 2. Reading (Elementary) I. Series.*
*TC PE1121 .C52 1983 Teacher's Ed. Workbook*

**Channel Four (Great Britain).**
Picasso [videorecording]. Chicago, IL : Home Vision, c1986.
*TC N6853.P5 P52 1986*

Summerhill at 70 [videorecording]. Princeton, N.J. : Films for the Humanities, c1992.
*TC LF795.L692953 S9 1992*

**Channel surfing.**
Giroux, Henry A. 1st ed. New York : St. Martin's Press, 1997.
*TC HQ799.7 .G57 1997*

**CHANT - HISTOIRE.**
Stark, James A. (James Arthur), 1938- Bel canto. Toronto : University of Toronto Press, c1999.
*TC MT823 S795 1999*

**CHAOS IN SYSTEMS.** *See* **CHAOTIC BEHAVIOR IN SYSTEMS.**

**CHAOTIC BEHAVIOR IN SYSTEMS.**
Wheatley, Margaret J. Leadership and the new science. 2nd ed. San Francisco : Berrett-Koehler Publishers, c1999.
*TC HD57.7 .W47 1999*

**CHAOTIC BEHAVIOR IN SYSTEMS - MISCELLANEA.**
The Psychological meaning of chaos. 1st ed. Washington, D.C. : American Psychological Association, c1997.
*TC RC437.5 .P762 1997*

**CHAOTIC MOTION IN SYSTEMS.** *See* **CHAOTIC BEHAVIOR IN SYSTEMS.**

**Chaplin, Jocelyn.** Feminist counselling in action / Jocelyn Chaplin. 2nd ed. Thousand Oaks, Calif. : SAGE, 1999. x, 144 p. : ill. ; 23 cm. (Counselling in action.) Previous ed.: 1988. Includes bibliographical references and index. ISBN 0-7619-6311-1 ISBN 0-7619-6310-3 (hbk.)
*1. Counseling. 2. Feminist psychology. I. Title. II. Title: Feminist counseling in action. III. Series. IV. Series: Counselling in action.*
*TC HQ1206 .C447 1999*

**Chapman, Gretchen B., 1965-** Decision making in health care : theory, psychology, and applications / Gretchen B. Chapman, Frank A. Sonnenberg. New York : Cambridge University Press, 2000. xiii, 438 p. ; 24 cm. (Cambridge series on judgment and decision making) Includes bibliographical references and index. ISBN 0-521-64159-4 (hc.) DDC 362.1
*1. Medical care - Decision making - Philosophy. 2. Medical care - Decision making - Psychological aspects. I. Sonnenberg, Frank A. II. Title. III. Series.*
*TC R723.5 .C48 2000*

**Chapman, Jane, 1970- ill.**
Jenkins, Martin. The emperor's egg. 1st U.S. ed. Cambridge, Mass. : Candlewick Press, 1999.
*TC QL696.S473 J45 1999*

**Chapman, Laura H.** Discover art : art print guide 1-3 / Laura H. Chapman. Worcester, Mass. : Davis Publications, c1987. xii, 36 p. : ill. ; 28 cm. "This set of fine art prints and teacher's guide for grades 1 to 3 is designed to

help elementary teachers offer an art program that meets contemporary expectations for art education"--Introduction.
*1. Art - Study and teaching (Elementary) I. Title.*
*TC N361 .C56 1987*

Discover art / Laura H. Chapman. Worcester, Mass. : Davis Publications, c1985. 6 v. : ill. (some col.) ; 28 cm. A sequential art curriculum for grades 1 through 6. ISBN 0-87192-153-7 (grade 1) ISBN 0-87192-154-5 (grade 2) ISBN 0-87192-155-3 (grade 3) ISBN 0-87192-156-1 (grade 4) ISBN 0-87192-157-X (grade 5) ISBN 0-87192-158-8 (grade 6)
*1. Art. I. Davis Publications. II. Title.*
*TC N361 .C56 1985*

**Chapman, Wayne K.**
Women in the milieu of Leonard and Virginia Woolf. New York : Pace University Press, 1998.
*TC PR6045.O72 Z925 1998*

**Chapnick, Howard.**
The power of idea : [videorecording]. Minneapolis, Minn. : Media Loft, c1992.
*TC TR690 .P5 1992*

**CHAPNICK, HOWARD.**
The power of idea : [videorecording]. Minneapolis, Minn. : Media Loft, c1992.
*TC TR690 .P5 1992*

**Chappell, Peter, 1948-.**
Our friends at the bank [videorecording]. New York, NY : First Run/Icarus Films, 1997.
*TC HG3881.5.W57 O87 1997*

**CHARACTER.**
Hillman, James. The force of character. 1st ed. New York : Random House, c1999.
*TC BF724.85.S45 H535 1999b*

Hutcheon, Pat Duffy. Building character and culture. Westport, Conn. : Praeger, 1999.
*TC HQ783 .H88 1999*

Sabini, John, 1947- Emotion, character, and responsibility. New York : Oxford University Press, 1998.
*TC BF531 .S23 1998*

Shapiro, David, 1926- Dynamics of character. New York : Basic Books, c2000.
*TC RC455.5.T45 .S46 2000*

**Character and personality.** Durham, N.C. : Duke Univ. Press, 1932-1945. v. : ill. ; 24 cm. Vol. 1, no. 1 (Sept. 1932)- . Ceased with v. 13 in 1945. Continued by: Journal of personality ISSN : 0022-3506. ISSN 0730-6407 DDC 137.05
*1. Psychology - Periodicals. 2. Character - Periodicals. 3. Personality - Periodicals. I. Title: Journal of personality*

**CHARACTER EDUCATION.** *See* **MORAL EDUCATION.**

**CHARACTER - PERIODICALS.**
Character and personality. Durham, N.C. : Duke Univ. Press, 1932-1945.

**CHARACTER TESTS.** *See also* **PERSONALITY TESTS.**
Katz, Tal Y. Self-construal as a moderator of the effects of task and reward interdependence of group performance. 1999.
*TC 085 K1524*

**CHARACTERS AND CHARACTERISTICS.** *See* **TYPOLOGY (PSYCHOLOGY).**

**CHARACTERS AND CHARACTERISTICS IN LITERATURE.**
Gillespie, John Thomas, 1928- Characters in young adult literature. Detroit : Gale Research, c1997.
*TC Z1037.A1 G47 1997*

Guevara-Vázquez, Fabián. El indigena en la novela de la Revolucion Mexicana. 1999.
*TC 085 G934*

MacCann, Donnarae. White supremacy in children's literature. New York : Garland Pub., 1998.
*TC PS173.N4 M33 1998*

**CHARACTERS IN LITERATURE - FICTION.**
Wright, Alexandra. Alice in Pastaland. Watertown, Mass. : Charlesbridge, 1997.
*TC PZ7.W9195 Al 1999?*

**Characters in young adult literature.**
Gillespie, John Thomas, 1928- Detroit : Gale Research, c1997.
*TC Z1037.A1 G47 1997*

**CHARITABLE INSTITUTIONS.** *See* **CHARITIES; INSTITUTIONAL CARE.**

**CHARITABLE USES, TRUSTS, AND FOUNDATIONS.** *See* **ENDOWMENTS.**

**CHARITIES.** *See* **CHURCH CHARITIES; COMMUNITY ORGANIZATION; ENDOWMENTS; INSTITUTIONAL CARE; SOCIAL SETTLEMENTS.**

**CHARITIES, MEDICAL.** *See* **AGED - MEDICAL CARE; HOSPITALS; POOR - MEDICAL CARE.**

**CHARITIES - NEW YORK (STATE) - NEW YORK.**
Ostrower, Francie. Why the wealthy give. Princeton, N.J. : Princeton University Press, c1995.
*TC HV99.N59 O85 1995*

**CHARITIES - SOCIETIES, ETC.** *See* **CHARITIES.**

**CHARITIES - UNITED STATES.**
American Assembly (93rd : 1998 : Los Angeles, Calif.) Trust, service, and the common purpose. Indianapolis, IN : Indiana University Center on Philanthropy ; New York, NY : American Assembly, [1998]
*TC HD62.6 .A44 1998*

Sagawa, Shirley, 1961- Common interest, common good. Boston : Harvard Business School Press, c2000.
*TC HD60.5.U5 S24 2000*

**CHARITY.** *See* **KINDNESS.**

**CHARITY ORGANIZATION - UNITED STATES.**
Wimsatt, William Upski. No more prisons. [New York] : Soft Skull Press, [2000?]
*TC HV9276.5 .W567x 2000*

Charles, C. M. Elementary classroom management / C.M. Charles, Gail W. Senter. 2nd ed. White Plains, N.Y. : Longman, c1995. xv, 299 p. : ill. ; 24 cm. Includes bibliographical references and index. ISBN 0-8013-1474-7 DDC 372.11/024
*1. Classroom management. 2. Education, Elementary. I. Senter, Gail W. II. Title.*
*TC LB3013 .C465 1995*

The synergetic classroom : joyful teaching and gentle discipline / C.M. Charles. New York : Longman, c2000. viii, 184 p. ; 24 cm. Includes bibliographical references and index. ISBN 0-321-04912-8 DDC 371.102/4
*1. Classroom management. 2. School discipline. I. Title.*
*TC LB3013 .C4653 2000*

**Charles E. Merrill Publishing Company.**
Bumby, Douglas R. Mathematics. 2nd ed. Columbus, Ohio : C.E. Merrill, c1982-<1986.>
*TC QA154.2 .B8 1982*

**Charlesworth, Rosalind.** Math and science for young children / Rosalind Charlesworth, Karen K. Lind. 3rd ed. Albany, NY : Delmar Publishers, c1999. viii, 581 p. : ill. (some col) ; 24 cm. Includes bibliographical references (p. 547-560) and index. ISBN 0-8273-8635-4 DDC 372.7/044
*1. Mathematics - Study and teaching (Primary) 2. Science - Study and teaching (Primary) I. Lind, Karen. II. Title.*
*TC QA135.5 .C463 1999*

**Charlotte Hawkins Brown & Palmer Memorial Institute.**
Wadelington, Charles Weldon. Chapel Hill ; London : University of North Carolina Press, c1999.
*TC LA2317.B598 W33 1999*

**Charlotte Hawkins Brown and Palmer Memorial Institute.**
Wadelington, Charles Weldon. Charlotte Hawkins Brown & Palmer Memorial Institute. Chapel Hill ; London : University of North Carolina Press, c1999.
*TC LA2317.B598 W33 1999*

**Charro.**
Ancona, George. 1st ed. San Diego : Harcourt Brace, c1999.
*TC F1210 .A747 1999*

**CHARROS.**
Ancona, George. Charro. 1st ed. San Diego : Harcourt Brace, c1999.
*TC F1210 .A747 1999*

**CHARROS - MEXICO - SOCIAL LIFE AND CUSTOMS - JUVENILE LITERATURE.**
Ancona, George. Charro. 1st ed. San Diego : Harcourt Brace, c1999.
*TC F1210 .A747 1999*

**CHARTER SCHOOLS.** *See* **PRIVATIZATION IN EDUCATION.**

**Charter schools in action.**
Finn, Chester E., 1944- Princeton, N.J. : Princeton University Press, c2000.
*TC LB2806.36 .F527 2000*

**CHARTER SCHOOLS - UNITED STATES.**
Education's big gamble [videorecording]. New York, NY : Merrow Report, c1997.

*TC LB2806.36 .E3 1997*

Engel, Michael, 1944- The struggle for control of public education. Philadelphia, Pa. : Temple University Press, c2000.
*TC LA217.2 .E533 2000*

Finn, Chester E., 1944- Charter schools in action. Princeton, N.J. : Princeton University Press, c2000.
*TC LB2806.36 .F527 2000*

Good, Thomas L., 1943- The great school debate. Mahwah, N.J. : L. Erlbaum Associates, 2000.
*TC LB2806.36 .G66 2000*

Public charter schools : new choices in public education (May 3, 2000 : Washington, D.C.) Public charter schools [videorecording]. [Washington, D.C.] : U.S. Dept. of Education, [2000].
*TC LB2806.36 .P9 2000*

Rufo-Lignos, Patricia Marie. Towards a new topology of public and private schools. 1999.
*TC 06 no. 11170*

Rufo-Lignos, Patricia Marie. Towards a new typology of public and private schools. 1999.
*TC 06 no. 11170*

**Charter schools [videorecording].**
Education's big gamble [videorecording]. New York, NY : Merrow Report, c1997.
*TC LB2806.36 .E3 1997*

**CHARTERED SCHOOLS.** *See* **CHARTER SCHOOLS.**

**Charting a course for continuing professional education : :** reframing professional practice / Vivian W. Mott, Barbara J. Daley, editors. San Francisco : Jossey-Bass, c2000. 90 p. : ill. ; 23 cm. (New directions for adult and continuing education, no. 86.) "Summer 2000." Includes bibliographical references and index. CONTENTS: Trends and issues in continuing professional education / Ronald M. Cervero -- The continuum of professional education and practice / Alan B. Knox -- The development of professional expertise in the workplace / Vivian W. Mott -- Learning in professional practice / Barbara J. Daley -- Evaluation of continuing professional education : toward a theory of our own / Judith M. Ottoson -- Marketing realities in continuing professional education / Ruth F. Craven, Martha B. DuHamel -- Ethical issues in continuing professional education / Patricia Ann Lawler -- Professional practice in the modern world / Arthur L. Wilson -- Continuing professional education : from vision to reality / Barbara J. Daley, Vivian W. Mott. ISBN 0-7879-5424-1
*1. Professional education. 2. Continuing education. I. Mott, Vivian W. II. Daley, Barbara J. III. Series: New directions for adult and continuing education : no.86*
*TC LC1072.C56 C55 2000*

**Charting terrains of Chicana/Latina education.**
Charting terrains of Chicana(o)/Latina(o) education. Cresskill, N.J. : Hampton Press, c2000.
*TC LC2669 .C42 2000*

**Charting terrains of Chicana(o)/Latina(o) education /** edited by Corinne Martínez, Zeus Leonardo, Carlos Tejeda. Cresskill, N.J. : Hampton Press, c2000. xiii, 248 p. ; 25 cm. (Themes of urban and inner city education) Includes bibliographical references and indexes. ISBN 1-57273-291-1 ISBN 1-57273-292-x (pbk.) DDC 371.829/68/72073
*1. Hispanic Americans - Education - Social aspects. 2. Discrimination in education - United States. 3. Educational equalization - United States. I. Martínez, Corinne, 1965- II. Leonardo, Zeus, 1968- III. Tejeda, Carlos, 1968- IV. Title: Charting terrains of Chicana/Latina education V. Title: Charting terrains of Chicano/Latino education VI. Series*
*TC LC2669 .C42 2000*

**Charting terrains of Chicano/Latino education.**
Charting terrains of Chicana(o)/Latina(o) education. Cresskill, N.J. : Hampton Press, c2000.
*TC LC2669 .C42 2000*

**Chartock, Roselle.**
Educational foundations. Upper Saddle River, N.J. : Merrill, c2000.
*TC LB17 .E393 2000*

**Chastain, Garvin D.**
Protecting human subjects. 1st ed. Washington, DC : American Psychological Association, c1999.
*TC BF181 .P65 1999*

**Chastain, Kenneth.** Spanish grammar in review / Kenneth Chastain. Lincolnwood, Ill., USA : National Textbook Co., c1994. x, 398 p. ; 28 cm. "Second edition"-- P. x. Includes index. ISBN 0-8442-7670-7 DDC 468.2/421
*1. Spanish language - Grammar. I. Title.*
*TC PC4112 .C4 1994*

**CHATINO INDIANS.** *See* **ZAPOTEC INDIANS.**

**Chatton, Barbara.** Blurring the edges : integrated curriculum through writing and children's literature / Barbara Chatton and N. Lynne Decker Collins. Portsmouth, NH : Heinemann, c1999. xv, 144 p. ; 24 cm. Includes bibliographical references (p. 131-137) and index. ISBN 0-325-00144-8 (alk. paper) DDC 372.6/043
*1. Language arts - Correlation with content subjects. 2. Children's literature - Study and teaching (Elementary) 3. Interdisciplinary approach in education. 4. Children - Books and reading. I. Collins, Lynne Decker. II. Title.*
*TC LB1576 .C46 1999*

**Chaumerliac, Nadine.**
Air pollution modeling and its application XII. New York : Plenum Press, c1998.
*TC TD881 .A47523 1998*

**CHAUNCEY, HENRY, 1905-.**
Lemann, Nicholas. The big test :. 1st ed. New York : Farrar, Straus and Giroux, 1999.
*TC LB3051 .L44 1999*

**CHAUVINISM AND JINGOISM.** *See* **IMPERIALISM; MILITARISM.**

**Chávez, Lydia, 1951-** The color bind : California's battle to end affirmative action / Lydia Chávez. Berkeley : University of California Press, c1998. xiv, 305 p. ; 23 cm. Includes bibliographical references (p. [293]-298) and index. ISBN 0-520-20687-8 (cloth : alk. paper) ISBN 0-520-21344-0 (pbk. : alk. paper) DDC 331.13/3/09794
*1. Affirmative action programs - California. I. Title.*
*TC HF5549.5.A34 C484 1998*

**Chazan, Daniel.** Beyond formulas in mathematics and teaching : dynamics of the high school algebra classroom / Daniel Chazan ; foreword by Penelope Peterson. New York : Teachers College Press, c2000. xvi, 200 p. : ill. ; 24 cm. (The series on school reform) Title on CIP record: Beyond formulas in high school algebra. Includes bibliographical references (p. 179-191) and index. ISBN 0-8077-3918-9 (pbk. : alk. paper) ISBN 0-8077-3919-7 (cloth : alk. paper) DDC 512/.071/2
*1. Algebra - Study and teaching (Secondary) I. Title. II. Title: Dynamics of the high school algebra classroom III. Title: Beyond formulas in high school algebra IV. Series.*
*TC QA159 .C48 2000*

Designing learning environments for developing understanding of geometry and space. Mahwah, N.J. : Lawrence Erlbaum, c1998.
*TC QA461 .L45 1998*

**Che Guevara, Paulo Freire, and the pedagogy of revolution.**
McLaren, Peter, 1948- Lanham [Md.] : Rowman & Littlefield Publishers, c2000.
*TC LC196 .M29 2000*

**CHEATING (EDUCATION).**
Cizek, Gregory J. Cheating on tests. Mahwah, N.J. ; London : L. Erlbaum Associates, 1999.
*TC LB3609 .C47 1999*

Lathrop, Ann. Student cheating and plagiarism in the Internet era. Englewood, Colo. : Libraries Unlimited, 2000.
*TC LB3609 .L28 2000*

**Cheating on tests.**
Cizek, Gregory J. Mahwah, N.J. ; London : L. Erlbaum Associates, 1999.
*TC LB3609 .C47 1999*

**CHELSEA COLLEGE OF PHYSICAL EDUCATION.**
Webb, Ida M. The challenge of change in physical education :. London : Falmer Press, 1999.
*TC GV246.E3 B79 1999*

**CHEMICAL DEPENDENCY.** *See* **SUBSTANCE ABUSE.**

**CHEMICAL ELEMENTS.**
Stephen Hawking's universe [videorecording]. [Alexandria, Va.] : PBS Video; Burbank, CA : Distributed by Warner Home Video, c1997.
*TC QB982 .S7 1997*

**CHEMICAL ENGINEERING.** *See* **CHEMISTRY, TECHNICAL.**

**CHEMICAL INHIBITORS.** *See* **ANTIOXIDANTS.**

**CHEMICAL TECHNOLOGY.** *See* **CHEMISTRY, TECHNICAL.**

**Chemicals for the mind.**
Keen, Ernest, 1937- Westport, Conn. : London : Praeger, 2000.
*TC RM315 .K44 2000*

**CHEMISTRY.** *See* **CHEMISTRY, TECHNICAL; COLOR.**

**CHEMISTRY, TECHNICAL.** *See* **CERAMICS.**

**CHEMISTRY, TECHNICAL - PERIODICALS.**
Ciba review. Basle, Switzerland Ciba Limited.

**CHEMOTHERAPY.** *See* **DRUGS; PSYCHOPHARMACOLOGY.**

**Chen, Deborah.**
Making the most of early communication [videorecording]. New York, NY : Distributed by AFB Press, c1997.
*TC HV1597.2 .M3 1997*

**Chen, Sheying.** Mastering research : a guide to the methods of social and behavioral sciences / Sheying Chen. Chicago : Nelson-Hall, c1998. ix, 229 p. ; 26 cm. Includes bibliographical references (p. 214-219) and index. ISBN 0-8304-1531-9 (pbk. : alk. paper) DDC 300/.7/2
*1. Psychology - Research - Methodology. 2. Social sciences - Research - Methodology. I. Title.*
*TC BF76.5 .C44 1998*

Measurement and analysis in psychosocial research : the failing and saving of theory / Sheying Chen. Aldershot, Hants, UK ; Brookfield USA : Avebury, c1997. xv, 317 p. ; 23 cm. Includes bibliographical references (p. 303-317). ISBN 1-85972-571-6 DDC 150/.1/05195
*1. Psychometrics. 2. Psychiatry - Research - Methodology. 3. Mental health - Research - Methodology. 4. Scaling (Social sciences) I. Title.*
*TC RC473.P79 C46 1997*

Remedial education and grading : a case study approach to two critical issues in American higher education / Sheying Chen, David X. Cheng. New York : the City University of New York, 1999. viii, 51 p. : ill. ; 28 cm. "A research report submitted to the Research Foundation of the City University of New York." "June 1999." "PSC-CUNY Research Grant no. 669282." Includes bibliographical references. Cover title.
*1. Education, Higher - United States - Case studies. 2. Remedial teaching - United States - Case studies. 3. Grading and marking (Students) - United States - Case studies. 4. Educational tests and measurements - United States. I. City University of New York. Research Foundation. II. Title.*
*TC LB1029.R4 C54 1999*

**Chen, Zhe, 1964-** Across the great divide : bridging the gap between understanding of toddlers' and older children's thinking / Zhe Chen, Robert S. Siegler; with commentary by Marvin W. Daehler. Oxford : Blackwell, 2000. vii, 108 p. : ill. ; 23 cm. (Monographs of the Society for Research in Child Development ; serial no. 261, vol. 65, no. 2) Includes bibliographical references. ISBN 0-631-22153-0 (pbk.)
*1. Cognition in children. 2. Child development. 3. Human information processing in children. 4. Communicative competence. 5. Social perception. I. Dachler, Marvin W., 1942- II. Siegler, Robert S. III. Society for Research in Child Development. IV. Title. V. Series: Monographs of the Society for Research in Child Development ; v. 65, no. 2.*
*TC LB1103 .S6 v.65 no. 2*

**Chepaitis, Barbara.**
North, Stephen M. Refiguring the Ph.D. in English studies. Urbana, Ill. : National Council of Teachers of English, c2000.
*TC PE69.A47 N67 2000*

**Cherrey, Cynthia.**
Allen, Kathleen E. Systemic leadership. Lanham, Md. : University Press of America, c2000.
*TC HD57.7 .A42 2000*

**Cherry, Lynne.** Who's sick today? / by Lynne Cherry. 1st ed. New York : Dutton, c1988. [24] p. : col. ill. ; 27 cm. SUMMARY: Rhyming text and illustrations introduce a variety of animals with different ailments. ISBN 0-525-44380-0 (lib. bdg.) DDC [E]
*1. Sick - Fiction. 2. Animals - Fiction. 3. Stories in rhyme. I. Title.*
*TC PZ8.3.C427 Wh 1988*

**Cherry, Roger Dennis.**
A Rhetoric of doing. Carbondale : Southern Illinois University Press, c1992.
*TC PE1404 .R496 1992*

**Chester, David.**
Feistritzer, C. Emily. Alternative teacher certification. Washington, D.C. : National Center for Education Information, c2000.
*TC LB1771 .A47 2000*

**Chevalier, Gérard.**
Monsieur René Magritte [videorecording]. [Chicago, Ill.] : Home Vision [distributor], c1978.
*TC ND673.M35 M6 1978*

**Chi, Marilyn Mei-Ying, 1949-.**
Asian-American education. Westport, Conn. : Bergin & Garvey, 1999.
*TC LC2632 .A847 1999*

**CHIANG-HSI KUNG CH'AN CHU I LAO TUNG TA HSÜEH - HISTORY.**
Cleverley, John F. In the lap of tigers. Lanham, Md. : Oxford : Rowman & Littlefield, c2000.
*TC S539.C6 C64 2000*

**Chiat, Shula.** Understanding children with language problems / Shula Chiat. Oxford [England] : New York : Cambridge University Press, 2000. xii, 286 p. : ill. ; 20 cm. (Cambridge approaches to linguistics) Includes bibliographical references and index. ISBN 0-521-57386-6 ISBN 0-521-57474-9 (pbk.) DDC 618.92/855
*1. Language disorders in children - Case studies. 2. Speech disorders in children - Case studies. 3. Children - Language. I. Title. II. Series.*
*TC RJ496.L35 C46 2000*

**The Chicago handbook for teachers :** a practical guide to the college classroom / Alan Brinkley ... [et al.]. Chicago : University of Chicago Press, 1999. x, 185 p. ; 21 cm. Includes bibliographical references (p. 171-176) and index. ISBN 0-226-07511-7 (cloth : alk. paper) ISBN 0-226-07512-5 (pbk. : alk. paper) DDC 378.1/25
*1. College teaching - Handbooks, manuals, etc. 2. College teachers - Handbooks, manuals, etc. I. Brinkley, Alan.*
*TC LB2331 .C52332 1999*

**Chicago (Ill.). Board of Education.**
Chicago schools journal. Chicago, Board of Education.

**CHICAGO (ILL.) - HISTORY.**
Abu-Lughod, Janet L. New York, Chicago, Los Angeles. Minneapolis : University of Minnesota Press, c1999.
*TC HT123 .A613 1999*

**CHICAGO SCHOOL OF SOCIOLOGY - HISTORY.**
Abbott, Andrew. Department & discipline. Chicago, IL : University of Chicago Press, c1999.
*TC HM22.U5 A23 1999*

**Chicago schools journal.**
Illinois schools journal. Chicago, Ill. : Illinois State Teachers College Chicago-South, 1967-

**Chicago schools journal.** Chicago, Board of Education. 46 V. ill.(incl.ports.)diagrs. 28 cm. Frequency: Monthly, Sept.-June. Vol. [1] (Sept. 1918)-v. 46 (May 1965). Publication suspended Sept. 1933-June 1934. Continues: Educational bimonthly. Continued by: Illinois school journal ISSN: 0019-2236.
*1. Education - Periodicals. 2. Education - Illinois - Chicago - Periodicals. I. Chicago (Ill.). Board of Education. II. Title: Educational bimonthly III. Title: Illinois school journal*

**CHICAGO SOCIOLOGISTS.** *See* **CHICAGO SCHOOL OF SOCIOLOGY.**

**Chicago State College.**
Illinois schools journal. Chicago, Ill. : Illinois State Teachers College Chicago-South, 1967-

**Chicago State University.**
Illinois schools journal. Chicago, Ill. : Illinois State Teachers College Chicago-South, 1967-

**Chicago studies in ethnomusicology**
Blacking, John. Music, culture, & experience. Chicago : University of Chicago Press, c1995.
*TC ML60 .B63 1995*

Wade, Bonnie C. Imaging sound. Chicago : University of Chicago Press, c1998.
*TC ML338 .W318 1998*

**Chicano empowerment and bilingual education.**
Trujillo, Armando L. New York : Garland Pub., c1998.
*TC LC2688.C79 T78 1998*

**CHICANOS.** *See* **MEXICAN AMERICANS.**

**Chichester Clark, Emma.** More! / Emma Chichester Clark. 1st American ed. New York : Doubleday Books for Young Readers/Bantam Doubleday Dell Pub., 1999. 1 v. (unpaged) : col. ill. ; 28 cm. SUMMARY: Billy, a boy who always wants more of everything, travels to an imaginary land where he finally has enough but finds that he misses his mother. ISBN 0-385-32630-0 DDC [E]
*1. Play - Fiction. 2. Mothers and sons - Fiction. I. Title.*
*TC PZ7.C4335 Mo 1999*

**CHIEF EDUCATION OFFICERS.** *See* **SCHOOL SUPERINTENDENTS.**

**CHIEF EXECUTIVE OFFICERS.**
Judge, William Q. The leader's shadow. Thousand Oaks, Calif. : Sage Publications, c1999.

*Chief information officers.*

*TC HD57.7 .J83 1999*

**CHIEF INFORMATION OFFICERS.**
Becker, Nancy Jane. Implementing technology in higher education. 1999.
*TC 06 no. 11082*

**Child & youth services series**
Eisikovits, Rivka Anne. The anthropology of child and youth care work. New York : Haworth Press, c1997.
*TC HV713 .E47 1997*

**CHILD ABUSE.** *See also* **ABUSED CHILDREN; CHILD SEXUAL ABUSE.**
Wolfe, David A. 2nd ed. Thousands Oaks, Calif. : Sage Publications, 1999.
*TC HV6626.5 .W58 1999*

**CHILD ABUSE.**
Wolfe, David A. Child abuse. 2nd ed. Thousands Oaks, Calif. : Sage Publications, 1999.
*TC HV6626.5 .W58 1999*

**CHILD ABUSE - CONGRESSES.**
Developmental perspectives on trauma. Rochester, N.Y., USA : University of Rochester Press, 1997.
*TC RJ499 .D4825 1997*

**CHILD ABUSE - CONGRESSES.**
Developmental perspectives on trauma. Rochester, N.Y., USA : University of Rochester Press, 1997.
*TC RJ499 .D4825 1997*

**CHILD ABUSE IN LITERATURE.**
Shengold, Leonard. Soul murder revisited. New Haven, CT : Yale University Press, 1999.
*TC RC569.5.C55 S53 1999*

**CHILD ABUSE - PREVENTION - PROBLEMS, EXERCISES, ETC.**
Johnson, Toni Cavanagh. Sexual, physical, and emotional abuse in out-of-home care. New York : The Haworth Maltreatment and Trauma Press, c1997.
*TC RJ507.A29 J64 1997*

**CHILD ABUSE, SEXUAL - PSYCHOLOGY.**
Sexual aggression. 1st ed. Washington, DC : American Psychiatric Press, c1999.
*TC RC560.S47 S488 1999*

**CHILD ABUSE, SEXUAL - THERAPY.**
Gartner, Richard B. Betrayed as boys. New York : Guilford Press, c1999.
*TC RC569.5.A28 G37 1999*

**CHILD ABUSE SURVIVORS.** *See* **ADULT CHILD ABUSE VICTIMS.**

**CHILD ABUSE - TREATMENT.**
Treatment of child abuse. Baltimore, Md. ; London : Johns Hopkins University Press, 2000.
*TC RJ375 .T74 2000*

**CHILD ABUSE - UNITED STATES.**
Hyman, Irwin A. Dangerous schools. 1st ed. San Francisco : Jossey-Bass Publishers, c1999.
*TC LB3013 .H897 1999*

**CHILD ABUSE - UNITED STATES - HISTORY - 19TH CENTURY - PICTORIAL WORKS.**
Child labor [picture]. Amawalk, NY : Jackdaw Publications, c1997.
*TC HD6250.U5 C4 1997*

**CHILD ABUSE - UNITED STATES - HISTORY - 20TH CENTURY - PICTORIAL WORKS.**
Child labor [picture]. Amawalk, NY : Jackdaw Publications, c1997.
*TC HD6250.U5 C4 1997*

**CHILD ABUSE VICTIMS.** *See* **ABUSED CHILDREN.**

**CHILD ABUSE VICTIMS, ADULT.** *See* **ADULT CHILD ABUSE VICTIMS.**

**CHILD-ADULT RELATIONSHIPS.** *See* **CHILDREN AND ADULTS.**

**CHILD ANALYSIS - CASE STUDIES.**
Mathelin, Catherine. [Raisins verts et dents agacées. English] Lacanian psychotherapy with children. New York : The Other Press, 1999.
*TC RJ504.2 .M3913 1999*

**Child and adolescent therapy** : cognitive-behavioral procedures / edited by Philip C. Kendall. 2nd ed. New York : Guilford Press, c2000. xvi, 432 p. : ill. ; 24 cm. Includes bibliographical references and index. ISBN 1-57230-556-8 (acid-free paper) DDC 618.92/92/89142
*1. Cognitive therapy for children. 2. Cognitive therapy for teenagers. 3. Child psychotherapy. 4. Adolescent psychotherapy. 5. Clinical child psychology. I. Kendall, Philip C.*

*TC RJ505.C63 C45 2000*

**CHILD AND ADULT.** *See* **CHILDREN AND ADULTS.**

**CHILD AND FATHER.** *See* **FATHER AND CHILD.**

**CHILD AND MOTHER.** *See* **MOTHER AND CHILD.**

**CHILD AND PARENT.** *See* **PARENT AND CHILD.**

**The child and the machine.**
Armstrong, Alison, 1955- Beltsville, Md. : Robins Lane Press, c2000.
*TC LB1028.43 .A76 2000*

Armstrong, Alison, 1955- Toronto, Ont. : Key Porter Books, c1998.
*TC LB1028.43 .A75 1998*

**CHILD ARTISTS.**
Khatena, Joe. Developing creative talent in art. Stamford, Conn. : Ablex Publ., c1999.
*TC NX164.C47 K53 1999*

**CHILD BEHAVIOR.** *See* **CHILD PSYCHOLOGY; CHILDREN - CONDUCT OF LIFE.**

**CHILD BEHAVIOR DISORDERS.** *See* **BEHAVIOR DISORDERS IN CHILDREN.**

**Child, Brenda.**
Portraits of native Americans. New York : New Press : Distributed by W.W. Norton, c1994.
*TC TR140.C388 C48*

**CHILD CARE.** *See* **CHILD REARING.**

**CHILD CARE - BIBLIOGRAPHY.**
Infants & toddlers. 2nd ed. Seattle, Wash. : Resourse Pathways, 1999.
*TC HQ755.8 .I54 1999*

**CHILD CARE CENTERS.** *See* **DAY CARE CENTERS.**

**CHILD CARE - GOVERNMENT POLICY - UNITED STATES.**
Gormley, William T., 1950- Everybody's children. Washington, D.C. : Brookings Institution, c1995.
*TC HQ778.63 .G674 1995*

**CHILD CARE - GOVERNMENT POLICY - UNITED STATES - HISTORY.**
Michel, Sonya, 1942- Children's interests/mothers' rights. New Haven, CT : Yale University Press, c1999.
*TC HQ778.63 .M52 1999*

**CHILD CARE - GREAT BRITAIN.**
Morgan, Sally, 1951- Care about education. London : DfEE, 1999.
*TC HV59 .M67 1999*

Siraj-Blatchford, Iram. Supporting identity, diversity and language in the early years. Buckingham [England] ; Philadelphia : Open University Press, 2000.
*TC LB1139.3.G7 S57 2000*

**CHILD CARE - JAPAN - HISTORY - 20TH CENTURY.**
Uno, Kathleen S., 1951- Passages to modernity. Honolulu : University of Hawai'i Press, c1999.
*TC HQ778.7.J3 U56 1999*

**CHILD CARE - PERIODICALS.**
Parents' magazine. New York.

**CHILD CARE SERVICES.** *See* **BABYSITTING; CHILD GUIDANCE CLINICS; DAY CARE CENTERS; FOSTER HOME CARE.**

**CHILD CARE SERVICES - CROSS-CULTURAL STUDIES.**
Families speak. Ypsilanti, Mich. : High/Scope Press, c1994.
*TC LB1139.23 .F36 1994*

How nations serve young children. Ypsilanti, Mich. : High/Scope Press, c1989.
*TC HQ778.5 .H69 1989*

**CHILD CARE SERVICES - EUROPE.**
Early childhood services. Buckingham [England] ; Philadelphia, PA : Open University Press, 2000.
*TC LB1139.3.E85 E35 2000*

**CHILD CARE SERVICES - GOVERNMENT POLICY - UNITED STATES.**
Gormley, William T., 1950- Everybody's children. Washington, D.C. : Brookings Institution, c1995.
*TC HQ778.63 .G674 1995*

**CHILD CARE SERVICES - GREAT BRITAIN.**
Early childhood services. Buckingham [England] ; Philadelphia, PA : Open University Press, 2000.

*TC LB1139.3.E85 E35 2000*

**CHILD CARE SERVICES - UNITED STATES - HISTORY.**
Michel, Sonya, 1942- Children's interests/mothers' rights. New Haven, CT : Yale University Press, c1999.
*TC HQ778.63 .M52 1999*

**CHILD CARE - SOCIAL ASPECTS.**
Johnson, Richard T., 1956- Hands off!. New York ; Canterbury [England] : P. Lang, c2000.
*TC LB1033 .J63 2000*

**CHILD CARE - UNITED STATES.**
Cromwell, Ellen, 1937- Nurturing readiness in early childhood education. 2nd ed. Boston : Allyn & Bacon, c2000.
*TC LB1140.4 .C76 2000*

Gormley, William T., 1950- Everybody's children. Washington, D.C. : Brookings Institution, c1995.
*TC HQ778.63 .G674 1995*

Hillman, Carol. Before the school bell rings. Bloomington, Ind. : Phi Delta Kappa Educational Foundation, c1995.
*TC LB1140.23 .H54 1995*

Quality in child care. Washington, D.C. : National Association for the Education of Young Children, c1987.
*TC HQ778.7.U6 Q35 1987*

**CHILD CARE - UNITED STATES - EVALUATION.**
Quality in child care. Washington, D.C. : National Association for the Education of Young Children, c1987.
*TC HQ778.7.U6 Q35 1987*

**Child clinician's handbook.**
Kronenberger, William G. 2nd ed. Boston : Allyn and Bacon, c2001.
*TC RJ499.3 .K76 2001*

**CHILD CONSUMERS - UNITED STATES.**
Kids' media culture. Durham [N.C.] ; London : Duke University Press, 1999.
*TC HQ784.M3 K54 1999*

**CHILD CONSUMERS - UNITED STATES - BIBLIOGRAPHY.**
Chandler, Tomasita M. Children and adolescents in the market place. Ann Arbor, Mich. : Pierian Press, 1999.
*TC HF5822 .C43 1999*

**CHILD DEATH.** *See* **CHILDREN - DEATH.**

**CHILD DEVELOPMENT.** *See also* **CHILD PSYCHOLOGY; CHILD REARING.**
Armstrong, Alison, 1955- The child and the machine. Beltsville, Md. : Robins Lane Press, c2000.
*TC LB1028.43 .A76 2000*

Beyond heredity and environment. Boulder : Westview Press, 1995.
*TC BF341 .B48 1995*

Bold, Christine. Progression in primary design and technology. London : David Fulton, 1999.
*TC LB1541 .B65 1999*

Cerruto, Audra. The effects of training on theory of mind tasks with children who are deaf. 1999.
*TC 085 C34*

Chen, Zhe, 1964- Across the great divide. Oxford : Blackwell, 2000.
*TC LB1103 .S6 v.65 no. 2*

Child Study Association of America. Guidance of childhood and youth; New York, Macmillan, 1926.
*TC HQ772 .C45*

Childhood social development. Malden, Mass. ; Oxford : Blackwell Publishers, 2000.
*TC BF721 .C6675 2000*

Children achieving. Newark, Del. : International Reading Association, c1998.
*TC LB1139.5.R43 C55 1998*

Cullingford, Cedric. The human experience. Aldershot : Brookfield, Vt. : Ashgate, c1999.
*TC BF723.E95 C84 1999*

Current issues in developmental psychology. Dordrecht ; Boston : London : Kluwer Academic Publishers, c1999.
*TC RJ134 .C868 1999*

The deaf child in the family and at school. Mahwah, N.J. : Lawrence Erlbaum Associates, 2000.

*TC HV2392.2 .D43 2000*

Developmental psychopathology. Australia : Harwood Academic Publishers, c1997.
*TC RJ499 .D48 1997*

Diversity [videorecording]. Barrington, IL : Magna Systems, Inc., 1996.
*TC LB1139.25 .D5 1996*

Greenspan, Stanley I. Building healthy minds. Cambridge, MA : Perseus, 1999.
*TC HQ772 .G672 1999*

## CHILD DEVELOPMENT.
Handbook of infant mental health. New York : Wiley, c2000.
*TC RJ502.5 .H362 2000*

## CHILD DEVELOPMENT.
Hashway, Robert M. Developmental cognitive styles. San Francisco : Austin & Winfield Publishers, 1998.
*TC LB1060 .H373 1998*

Kim, Jinyoung. Effects of word type, context, and vocal assistance on children's pitch-matching abilities. 1998.
*TC 06 no. 10954*

Lavatelli, Celia Stendler, 1911- Piaget's theory applied to an early childhood curriculum. [1st ed.]. Boston : American Science and Engineering. [c1970].
*TC LB1140.2 .L3*

Leventhal, Tama. Poverty and turbulence. 1999.
*TC 085 L5515*

Making sense of social development. London ; New York : Routledge in association with the Open University, 1999.
*TC HQ783 .L57 1999*

Page, Nick. Music as a way of knowing. York, Me. : Stenhouse Publishers ; Los Angeles, Calif. : Galef Institute, c1995.
*TC MT1 .P234 1995*

Piaget, Jean, 1896-1980. [Représentation du monde chez l'enfant. English] The child's conception of the world. Translated by Joan and Andrew Tomlinson. Paterson, N.J., Littlefield, Adams, 1960.
*TC BF721 .P513 1960*

Pringle, Sheila M. Promoting the health of children. St. Louis : Mosby, 1982.
*TC RJ101 .P66 1982*

Reutzel, D. Ray (Douglas Ray), 1953- Balanced reading strategies and practices. Upper Saddle river, N.J. : Merrill, c1999.
*TC LB1050 .R477 1999*

Revisiting a progressive pedagogy. Albany : State University of New York Press, c2000.
*TC LB1117 .R44 2000*

Rights and wrongs. San Francisco, [CA] : Jossey-Bass, c2000.
*TC BF723.M54 L38 2000*

Shore, Rima. Rethinking the brain. New York : Families and Work Institute, c1997.
*TC RJ486.5 .S475 1997*

## CHILD DEVELOPMENT.
Shore, Rima. Rethinking the brain. New York : Families and Work Institute, c1997.
*TC RJ486.5 .S475 1997*

## CHILD DEVELOPMENT.
Shore, Rima. Rethinking the brain. New York : Families and Work Institute, c1997.
*TC RJ486.5 .S475 1997*

Thomas, R. Murray (Robert Murray), 1921- Human development theories. Thousand Oaks : Sage Publications, c1999.
*TC HQ783 .T57 1999*

Trawick-Smith, Jeffrey W. Early childhood development. 2nd ed. Upper Saddle River, N.J. : Merrill, c2000.
*TC LB1115 .T73 2000*

Washburn, Ruth Wendell, 1890- Children have their reasons. New York, D. Appleton-Century, 1942.
*TC HQ772 .W24*

Wolfe, David A. Child abuse. 2nd ed. Thousands Oaks, Calif. : Sage Publications, 1999.
*TC HV6626.5 .W58 1999*

Wyness, Michael G. Contesting childhood. London ; New York : Falmer Press, 2000.
*TC HQ767.9 .W96 2000*

## CHILD DEVELOPMENT - CONGRESSES.
The changing family and child development. Aldershot : Ashgate, c2000.
*TC HQ518 .C478 2000*

Developmental perspectives on trauma. Rochester, N.Y., USA : University of Rochester Press, 1997.
*TC RJ499 .D4825 1997*

## CHILD DEVELOPMENT - CONGRESSES.
Developmental perspectives on trauma. Rochester, N.Y., USA : University of Rochester Press, 1997.
*TC RJ499 .D4825 1997*

## CHILD DEVELOPMENT - CROSS-CULTURAL STUDIES.
Infancy and culture. New York : Falmer Press, 1999.
*TC GN482 .I53 1999*

Valsiner, Jaan. Culture and human development. London ; Thousand Oaks, Calif. : Sage, 2000.
*TC BF713 .V35 2000*

## CHILD DEVELOPMENT - DEVELOPING COUNTRIES.
Strengthening the family. Tokyo ; New York : United Nations University Press, c1995.
*TC HQ727.9 .S77 1995*

## CHILD DEVELOPMENT DEVIATIONS. *See* AUTISM IN CHILDREN; DEVELOPMENTALLY DISABLED CHILDREN.

## CHILD DEVELOPMENT - EVALUATION.
The psychoeducational assessment of preschool children. 3rd ed. Boston : Allyn and Bacon, c2000.
*TC LB1115 .P963 2000*

Puckett, Margaret B. Authentic assessment of the young child. 2nd ed. Upper Saddle River, N.J. : Merrill, c2000.
*TC LB3051 .P69 2000*

## CHILD DEVELOPMENT - HANDBOOKS, MANUALS, ETC.
Ramey, Sharon L. Going to school. New York : Goddard Press ; Lanham, MD : Distributed to the trade by National Book Network, c1999.
*TC LB1139.35.P37 R26 1999*

## CHILD DEVELOPMENT - INDIA.
Culture, socialization and human development. New Delhi : Thousand Oaks, CA : Sage Publications, c1999.
*TC HQ783 .C85 1999*

## CHILD DEVELOPMENT - PERIODICALS.
[Child study (New York, N.Y.)] Child study. [New York City] : Federation for Child Study, 1925-1960.

Parents' magazine. New York.

Progress in infancy research. Mahwah, NJ : Lawrence Erlbaum Associates, 2000-
*TC BF719 .P76*

## CHILD DEVELOPMENT - RESEARCH.
Childhood studies. London ; New York : Routledge, 2000.
*TC HQ767.85 .C483 2000*

Research with children. New York : Falmer Press, 2000.
*TC HQ767.85 .R48 1999*

## CHILD DEVELOPMENT - SCANDINAVIA - BIBLIOGRAPHY.
Research on socialization of young children in the Nordic countries. Aarhus : Aarhus University Press, c1989.
*TC Z7164.S678 R47 1989*

## CHILD DEVELOPMENT - UNITED STATES.
Cromwell, Ellen, 1937- Nurturing readiness in early childhood education. 2nd ed. Boston : Allyn & Bacon, c2000.
*TC LB1140.4 .C76 2000*

Curriculum planning. 7th ed. Boston : Allyn and Bacon, c2000.
*TC LB2806.15 .C868 2000*

Developmentally appropriate practice in early childhood programs. Rev. ed. Washington, D.C. : National Association for the Education of Young Children, 1997.
*TC LB1139.25 .D48 1997*

Hillman, Carol. Before the school bell rings. Bloomington, Ind. : Phi Delta Kappa Educational Foundation, c1995.
*TC LB1140.23 .H54 1995*

Umansky, Warren. Young children with special needs. 3rd ed. Upper Saddle River, N.J. : Merrill, c1998.

*TC LC4031 .U425 1998*

## CHILD DEVELOPMENT - VERMONT - BENNINGTON.
From another angle. New York : Teachers College Press, c2000.
*TC LB1117 .F735 2000*

## CHILD GUIDANCE CENTERS. *See* CHILD GUIDANCE CLINICS.

## CHILD GUIDANCE CLINICS - UNITED STATES - HISTORY - 20TH CENTURY.
Jones, Kathleen W. Taming the troublesome child. Cambridge, Mass : Harvard University Press, 1999.
*TC RJ501.A2 J64 1999*

## CHILD HEALTH. *See* CHILDREN - HEALTH AND HYGIENE.

**Child health bulletin.** New York, American Child Health Association. 11 v. ill., diagrs. 23 cm. v. 1-11; Mar. 1925-Sept./Nov. 1935. Caption title. Irregular. SUMMARY: Includes section "Child health literature". With supplements. Child health magazine.
*1. Children - Health and hygiene - Periodicals. I. American Child Health Association. II. Title: Child health magazine*

**Child health magazine.**
Child health bulletin. New York, American Child Health Association.

## CHILD HEALTH SERVICES. *See* CHILD MENTAL HEALTH SERVICES.

## CHILD HEALTH SERVICES - PERIODICALS.
Family and child mental health journal. New York, NY : Human Sciences Press, [c1980-c1982]

Issues in child mental health. [New York, Human Sciences Press]

**The child in focus.**
Clark, Alison. London : National Children's Bureau Enterprise, c1999.
*TC KD785 .C43 1999*

## CHILD LABOR. *See also* CHILDREN - EMPLOYMENT.
Hobbs, Sandy. Santa Barbara, Calif. : ABC-CLIO, 1999.
*TC HD6231 .H63 1999*

## CHILD LABOR.
Action against child labour. Geneva : International Labour Office, c2000.
*TC HD6231 .A28 2000*

## CHILD LABOR - HISTORY.
Hobbs, Sandy. Child labor. Santa Barbara, Calif. : ABC-CLIO, 1999.
*TC HD6231 .H63 1999*

**Child labor [picture] : the shame of the nation.** Amawalk, NY : Jackdaw Publications, c1997. 12 posters : b&w ; 43 x 56 cm. + 1 leaflet ([6] p. : ill. ; 28 cm.). (Jackdaw photo collections ; PC 100) Compiled by Enid Goldberg & Norman Itzkowitz. SUMMARY: 12 historical photo-posters depicting chidren at work in factories, coal mines, canneries, farms as newsboys, farmers, factory workers, miners and, finally, in night school. CONTENTS: 1. The littlest laborers: the cranberry picker -- 2. Working in canneries: preparing beans -- 3. At work in the fields: a toddler picking cotton -- 4. Safety is not a concern: boy at work in a glass factory -- 5. Slaving in the coal mines: breaker boys in a coal chute -- 6. Factory labor: boys in front of a manufacturing plant -- 7. Home is no haven: doing piece work at home -- 8. Entertaining adults: setting pins in a bowling alley -- 9. Dignity in poverty: barefoot girl in cotton mill -- 10. A life of misery: a young boy in the coal mines -- 11. No time for rest: a newsboy asleep on the job -- 12. Trying to better themselves: night school. ISBN 1-56696-156-4
*1. Children - Employment - United States - History - 19th century - Pictorial works. 2. Children - Employment - United States - History - 20th century - Pictorial works. 3. Child abuse - United States - History - 19th century - Pictorial works. 4. Child abuse - United States - History - 20th century - Pictorial works. 5. Documentary photography - United States. I. Goldberg, Enid. II. Itzkowitz, Norman. III. Jackdaw Publications. IV. Title: Shame of the nation [picture] V. Series.*
*TC HD6250.U5 C4 1997*

**Child language.**
Peccei, Jean Stilwell. 2nd ed. London ; New York : Routledge, 1999.
*TC P118 .P38 1999*

**Child Language Data Exchange System project.**
MacWhinney, Brian. The CHILDES project. 3rd ed. Mahwah, N.J. : Lawrence Erlbaum, 2000.
*TC LB1139.L3 M24 2000*

**Child language research forum.**
Child Language Research Forum (29th : 1997 : Stanford University) The proceedings of the twenty-

ninth Annual Child Language Research Forum. [Stanford] : Published for the Stanford Linguistics Association by the Center for the Study of Language and Information, c1998.
*TC P118 .C4558 1997*

**Child Language Research Forum (29th : 1997 : Stanford University)** The proceedings of the twenty-ninth Annual Child Language Research Forum / edited by Eve V. Clark. [Stanford] : Published for the Stanford Linguistics Association by the Center for the Study of Language and Information, c1998. vii, 240 p. : ill. ; 24 cm. Held April 25-27, 1997, at Stanford University. Includes bibliographical references. CONTENTS: "ISSN: 1042-1080"--t.p. verso ISBN 1-57586-119-4 (cloth) ISBN 1-57586-118-6 (paper)
*1. Language acquisition - Congresses 2. Children - Language - Congresses. I. Clark, Eve V. II. Title. III. Title: Child language research forum*
*TC P118 .C4558 1997*

**Child Language Seminar (1998 : University of Sheffield).**
New directions in language development and disorders. New York : Kluwer Academic/Plenum Publishers, c2000.
*TC P118 .N49 2000*

**Child life.** London, G. Philip & Son. Frequency: MOnthly. v. 1- 1891- ;n.s., v.1- 1899- . "A magazine for kindergarten teachers, parents, and all interested in the education and development of young children." Ceased publication?
*1. Education - Periodicals. 2. Kindergarten - Periodicals.*

**Child, Lydia Maria Francis, 1802-1880.**
Jacobs, Harriet A. (Harriet Ann), 1813-1897. Incidents in the life of a slave girl : written by herself. Cambridge, Mass. : Harvard University Press, 2000.
*TC E444.J17 A3 2000c*

**CHILD MALTREATMENT.** See **CHILD ABUSE.**

**CHILD MENTAL HEALTH.** See **CHILD PSYCHIATRY; CHILD PSYCHOPATHOLOGY.**

**CHILD MENTAL HEALTH - PERIODICALS.**
Family and child mental health journal. New York, NY : Human Sciences Press, [c1980-c1982]

**CHILD MENTAL HEALTH SERVICES.** See also **CHILD GUIDANCE CLINICS; CHILD PSYCHIATRY; CHILD PSYCHOTHERAPY.**
Donahue, Paul J. Mental health consultation in early childhood. Baltimore, MD : Paul H. Brookes Publishing, 2000.
*TC RJ499 .D595 2000*

**CHILD MENTAL HEALTH SERVICES - UNITED STATES - HISTORY - 20TH CENTURY.**
Jones, Kathleen W. Taming the troublesome child. Cambridge, Mass : Harvard University Press, 1999.
*TC RJ501.A2 J64 1999*

**CHILD MOLESTING.** See **CHILD SEXUAL ABUSE.**

**CHILD MUSICIANS - CONGRESSES.**
Music and child development. St. Louis, Mo. : MMB Music, c1990.
*TC ML3820 .M87 1990*

**CHILD NEGLECT.** See **CHILD ABUSE.**

**CHILD NUTRITION.** See **CHILDREN - NUTRITION.**

**CHILD-PARENT CENTER PROGRAM (CHICAGO, ILL.).**
Reynolds, Arthur J. Success in early intervention. Lincoln, Neb. : University of Nebraska Press, c2000.
*TC HV743.C5 R48 2000*

**CHILD PIONEERS.** See **PIONEER CHILDREN.**

**CHILD PLACING.** See **ADOPTION; FOSTER HOME CARE.**

**CHILD PRODIGIES.** See **GIFTED CHILDREN.**

**CHILD PROTECTIVE SERVICES.** See **CHILD WELFARE.**

**CHILD PROTECTIVE SERVICES PERSONNEL.** See **CHILD WELFARE.**

**CHILD PSYCHIATRIC INTERVIEWING.** See **INTERVIEWING IN CHILD PSYCHIATRY.**

**CHILD PSYCHIATRY.** See also **ADOLESCENT PSYCHIATRY; CHILD MENTAL HEALTH; CHILD PSYCHOPATHOLOGY; CHILD PSYCHOTHERAPY; INFANT PSYCHIATRY; INTERVIEWING IN CHILD PSYCHIATRY; MENTALLY ILL CHILDREN.**
Donahue, Paul J. Mental health consultation in early

childhood. Baltimore, MD : Paul H. Brookes Publishing, 2000.
*TC RJ499 .D595 2000*

Gerard, Margaret Elizabeth Wilson, 1894-1954. The emotionally disturbed child; New York, Child Welfare League of America [1956?]
*TC RJ499 .G4*

Group for the Advancement of Psychiatry. Committee on Child Psychiatry. Psychopathological disorders in childhood; [New York, 1966]
*TC RJ499 .G76*

The Journal of child psychiatry. New York : Child Care Publications, 1947-1956.

Siskind, Diana. A primer for child psychotherapists. Northvale, NJ : Jason Aronson, c1999.
*TC RJ504 .S543 1999*

**CHILD PSYCHIATRY - PERIODICALS.**
Family and child mental health journal. New York, NY : Human Sciences Press, [c1980-c1982]

Issues in child mental health. [New York, Human Sciences Press]

**CHILD PSYCHIATRY - PERIODICALS.**
The Journal of child psychiatry. New York : Child Care Publications, 1947-1956.

**CHILD PSYCHIATRY - SOCIAL ASPECTS.**
Canino, Ian A. Culturally diverse children and adolescents. 2nd ed. New York : Guilford Press, c2000.
*TC RJ507.M54 C36 2000*

**CHILD PSYCHOANALYSIS.** See **CHILD ANALYSIS.**

**CHILD PSYCHOLOGY.** See also **ADJUSTMENT (PSYCHOLOGY) IN CHILDREN; ANXIETY IN CHILDREN; CHILD MENTAL HEALTH; CHILD PSYCHIATRY; CHILD REARING; CHILDREN AND ADULTS; CLINICAL CHILD PSYCHOLOGY; COGNITIVE STYLES IN CHILDREN; CREATIVE ABILITY IN CHILDREN; EDUCATIONAL PSYCHOLOGY; IMAGERY (PSYCHOLOGY) IN CHILDREN; INFANT PSYCHOLOGY; INTERPERSONAL RELATIONS IN CHILDREN; LEARNING, PSYCHOLOGY OF; MEMORY IN CHILDREN; PSYCHOHISTORY; RACE AWARENESS IN CHILDREN; REWARD (PSYCHOLOGY) IN CHILDREN; SOCIAL DESIRABILITY IN CHILDREN; SOCIAL INTERACTION IN CHILDREN; SOCIAL SKILLS IN CHILDREN.**
Hetherington, E. Mavis (Eileen Mavis), 1926- 5th ed. Boston : McGraw-Hill College, c1999.
*TC BF721 .H418 1999*

**CHILD PSYCHOLOGY.**
Child psychology. Philadelphia, PA : Psychology Press, c1999.
*TC BF721 .C5155 1999*

Childhood social development. Malden, Mass. ; Oxford : Blackwell Publishers, 2000.
*TC BF721 .C6675 2000*

Clarke, Ann M. (Ann Margaret) Early experience and the life path. London ; Philadelphia : Jessica Kingsley, 2000.
*TC BF721 .C5457 2000*

Cullingford, Cedric. The human experience. Aldershot ; Brookfield, Vt. : Ashgate, c1999.
*TC BF723.E95 C84 1999*

Current issues in developmental psychology. Dordrecht ; Boston ; London : Kluwer Academic Publishers, c1999.
*TC RJ134 .C868 1999*

Golombok, Susan. Parenting. London ; Philadelphia : Routledge, 2000.
*TC HQ755.8 .G655 2000*

**CHILD PSYCHOLOGY.**
Handbook of infant mental health. New York : Wiley, c2000.
*TC RJ502.5 .H362 2000*

Handbook of research in pediatric and clinical child psychology. New York : Kluwer Academic/Plenum Publishers, c 2000.
*TC RJ499.3 .H367 2000*

**CHILD PSYCHOLOGY.**
Hetherington, E. Mavis (Eileen Mavis), 1926- Child psychology. 5th ed. Boston : McGraw-Hill College, c1999.

*TC BF721 .H418 1999*

[Kindheit und Trauma. English.] Childhood and trauma. Aldershot, Hants, UK ; Brookfield, Vt., USA : Ashgate, c1999.
*TC RJ506.P66 K613 1999*

Play diagnosis and assessment. 2nd ed. New York : John Wiley & Sons, c2000.
*TC RJ505.P6 P524 1999*

Rights and wrongs. San Francisco, [CA] : Jossey-Bass, c2000.
*TC BF723.M54 L38 2000*

Variability in the social construction of the child. San Francisco : Jossey-Bass, 2000.
*TC BF723.S62 .V37 2000*

**Child psychology :** a handbook of contemporary issues / edited by Lawrence Balter, Catherine S. Tamis-LeMonda. Philadelphia, PA : Psychology Press, c1999. xviii, 542 p. : ill. ; 26 cm. Includes bibliographical references and index. ISBN 1-84169-000-7 (alk. paper) DDC 155.4
*1. Child psychology. I. Balter, Lawrence. II. Tamis-LeMonda, Catherine S. (Catherine Susan), 1958-*
*TC BF721 .C5155 1999*

**CHILD PSYCHOLOGY - CROSS-CULTURAL STUDIES.**
Infancy and culture. New York : Falmer Press, 1999.
*TC GN482 .I53 1999*

**CHILD PSYCHOLOGY - METHODOLOGY.** See **BEHAVIORAL ASSESSMENT OF CHILDREN.**

**CHILD PSYCHOLOGY - METHODOLOGY - HANDBOOKS, MANUALS, ETC.**
Hawkins, Robert P., 1931- Measuring behavioral health outcomes. New York : Kluwer Academic/Plenum Publishers, c1999.
*TC RJ503.5 .H39 1999*

**CHILD PSYCHOLOGY - PERIODICALS.**
Issues in child mental health. [New York, Human Sciences Press]

**CHILD PSYCHOPATHOLOGY.** See also **BEHAVIOR DISORDERS IN CHILDREN; CHILD PSYCHIATRY; EATING DISORDERS IN CHILDREN; MENTALLY ILL CHILDREN; POST-TRAUMATIC STRESS DISORDER IN CHILDREN; VIOLENCE IN CHILDREN.**
Attachment disorganization. New York ; London : Guilford Press, c1999.
*TC RJ507.A77 A87 1999*

Developmental psychopathology. Australia : Harwood Academic Publishers, c1997.
*TC RJ499 .D48 1997*

House, Alvin E. DSM-IV diagnosis in the schools. New York : Guilford Press, c1999
*TC RJ503.5 .H68 1999*

Wolfe, David A. Child abuse. 2nd ed. Thousand Oaks, Calif. : Sage Publications, 1999.
*TC HV6626.5 .W58 1999*

**CHILD PSYCHOPATHOLOGY - CONGRESSES.**
Developmental perspectives on trauma. Rochester, N.Y., USA : University of Rochester Press, 1997.
*TC RJ499 .D4825 1997*

**CHILD PSYCHOPATHOLOGY - ETIOLOGY.**
The effects of early adversity on neurobehavioral development. Mahwah, N.J. : L. Erlbaum Associates, 2000.
*TC RJ499 .E34 2000*

**CHILD PSYCHOPATHOLOGY - LONGITUDINAL STUDIES.**
In the long run--longitudinal studies of psychopathology in children. Washington, DC : American Psychiatric Press, c1999.
*TC RC321 .G7 no. 143*

**CHILD PSYCHOPATHOLOGY - PREVENTION - HANBOOKS, MANUALS, ETC.**
Handbook of infant mental health. New York : Wiley, c2000.
*TC RJ502.5 .H362 2000*

**CHILD PSYCHOPATHOLOGY - UNITED STATES.**
Luthar, Suniya S. Poverty and children's adjustment. Thousand Oaks, Calif. : Sage Publications, c1999.
*TC HV741 .L88 1999*

**CHILD PSYCHOTHERAPY.** See also **CHILD ANALYSIS.**
Bromfield, Richard. Doing child and adolescent

psychotherapy. Northvale, N.J. ; London : Jason Aronson, c1999.
*TC RJ504 .B753 1999*

Child and adolescent therapy. 2nd ed. New York : Guilford Press, c2000.
*TC RJ505.C63 C45 2000*

Children in therapy: New York : W.W. Norton, 2000.
*TC RC488.5 .C468 2000*

Children's rights, therapists' responsibilities. New York : Harrington Park Press, c1997.
*TC RJ504 .C486 1997*

Daniels, Debbie. Therapy with children :. London ; Thousand Oaks, Calif. : SAGE, 2000.
*TC RJ504 .D36 2000*

Handbook of psychotherapies with children and families. New York ; London : Kluwer Academic/ Plenum Publishers, c1999.
*TC RJ504 .H3619 1999*

Innovative psychotherapy techniques in child and adolescent therapy. 2nd ed. New York : Wiley, c1999.
*TC RJ504 .I57 1999*

Nevas, Debra Baron. Factors affecting parental attitudes toward a child's therapist and therapy. 1997.
*TC 085 N401*

Siskind, Diana. A primer for child psychotherapists. Northvale, NJ : Jason Aronson, c1999.
*TC RJ504 .S543 1999*

**CHILD PSYCHOTHERAPY - CASE STUDIES.**
Roemmelt, Arthur F., 1944- Haunted children. Albany : State University of New York Press, c1998.
*TC RJ504 .R64 1998*

**CHILD PSYCHOTHERAPY - PARENT PARTICIPATION.**
Nevas, Debra Baron. Factors affecting parental attitudes toward a child's therapist and therapy. 1997.
*TC 085 N401*

**CHILD PSYCHOTHERAPY - PHILOSOPHY.**
Roemmelt, Arthur F., 1944- Haunted children. Albany : State University of New York Press, c1998.
*TC RJ504 .R64 1998*

**CHILD PSYCHOTHERAPY - RESIDENTIAL TREATMENT.**
Outcome assessment in residential treatment. New York : Haworth Press, c1996.
*TC RJ504.5 .O98 1996*

**CHILD RAISING.** *See* **CHILD REARING.**

**CHILD REARING.** *See also* **CHILD DEVELOPMENT; CHILD PSYCHOLOGY; MORAL EDUCATION; PARENTING.**
Berger, Elizabeth. Raising children with character. Northvale, N.J. : J. Aronson, c1999.
*TC BF723.P4 B47 1999*

Bronson, Martha. Self-regulation in early childhood. New York ; London : Guilford Press, c2000.
*TC BF723.S25 B76 2000*

Cerruto, Audra. The effects of training on theory of mind tasks with children who are deaf. 1999.
*TC 085 C34*

De Toledo, Sylvie. Grandparents as parents. New York : Guilford Press, c1995.
*TC HQ759.9 .D423 1995*

Family and peers. Westport, Conn. : Praeger, 2000.
*TC HQ755.85 .F365 2000*

Groves, Ernest Rutherford, 1878-1946. Wholesome childhood, Boston, Houghton Mifflin Company, 1924.
*TC HQ772 .G75*

Understanding the defiant child [videorecording]. New York : Guilford Publications, c1997.
*TC HQ755.7 .U63 1997*

**CHILD REARING - HISTORY - PERIODICALS.**
History of childhood quarterly. [Broadway, N.Y., Atcom]

**CHILD REARING - INDIANA - INDIANAPOLIS - CASE STUDIES.**
Rosier, Katherine Brown. Mothering inner-city children. New Brunswick, NJ : Rutgers University Press, 2000.
*TC HV1447.I53 R67 2000*

**CHILD REARING - PERIODICALS.**
[Child study (New York, N.Y.)] Child study. [New York City] : Federation for Child Study, 1925-1960.

**CHILD REARING - UNITED STATES.**
Bempechat, Janine, 1956- Getting our kids back on track. 1st ed. San Francisco : Jossey-Bass, c2000.

*TC LC225.3 .B45 2000*
Variability in the social construction of the child. San Francisco : Jossey-Bass, 2000.
*TC BF723.S62 .V37 2000*

**CHILD RESEARCH.** *See* **CHILDREN - RESEARCH.**

**CHILD SEXUAL ABUSE.**
Sexual aggression. 1st ed. Washington, DC : American Psychiatric Press, c1999.
*TC RC560.S47 S488 1999*

**CHILD SEXUAL ABUSE - LAW AND LEGISLATION.** *See* **CHILD SEXUAL ABUSE.**

**CHILD SEXUAL ABUSE - PREVENTION.**
Johnson, Richard T., 1956- Hands off!. New York ; Canterbury [England] : P. Lang, c2000.
*TC LB1033 .J63 2000*

**CHILD SEXUAL ABUSE VICTIMS.** *See* **SEXUALLY ABUSED CHILDREN.**

**CHILD SEXUAL ABUSE VICTIMS, ADULT.** *See* **ADULT CHILD SEXUAL ABUSE VICTIMS.**

**CHILD SOCIALIZATION.** *See* **SOCIALIZATION.**

**CHILD STUDY.** *See also* **CHILD DEVELOPMENT; CHILD PSYCHOLOGY.**
[Child study (New York, N.Y.)] Child study. [New York City] : Federation for Child Study, 1925-1960.

**Child Study Association of America.**
[Child study (New York, N.Y.)] Child study. [New York City] : Federation for Child Study, 1925-1960.

Guidance of childhood and youth; readings in child study; compiled by Child Study Association of America, edited by Benjamin C. Gruenberg. New York, Macmillan, 1926. xxi, 324 p. 24 cm. Includes index.
*1. Child development. I. Gruenberg, Benjamin Charles, 1875- ed. II. Title.*
*TC HQ772 .C45*

[Child study (New York, N.Y.)] Child study. [New York City] : Federation for Child Study, 1925-1960.
36 v. ; 26-28 cm. Frequency: Quarterly, fall 1939-summer 1960. Former frequency: Monthly (Oct.-May), Feb. 1925-May 1939. Vol. 2, no. 3 (Feb. 1925)- v. 37, no. 3 (summer 1960). Separately paged supplements accompany some numbers. Available on microfilm. Issued by the Child Study Association of America, Oct. 1925-summer 1960. Available in other form: Child study (OCoLC)7490655. Continues: Bulletin (Federation for Child Study (U.S.) (OCoLC)5984039.
*1. Parenting - Study and teaching - Periodicals. 2. Child development - Periodicals. 3. Child rearing - Periodicals. I. Federation for Child Study (U.S.) II. Child Study Association of America. III. Title: Child study IV. Title: Bulletin (Federation for Child Study (U.S.)*

**CHILD STUDY - PERIODICALS.**
The Journal of childhood and adolescence. Seattle.

**CHILD SUICIDE.** *See* **CHILDREN - SUICIDAL BEHAVIOR.**

**CHILD WELFARE.** *See also* **CHILD ABUSE; FOSTER HOME CARE.**
United States. General Accounting Office. Washington, D.C. (P.O. Box 37050, Washington, D.C. 20013) : The Office, [1998]
*TC HV741 .U525 1998a*

**CHILD WELFARE.**
Sayles, Mary Buell, 1878- Substitute parents, New York, The Commonwealth fund; London, H. Milford, Oxford University Press, 1936.
*TC HV875 .S3*

**CHILD WELFARE - GOVERNMENT POLICY - UNITED STATES.**
Welfare, the family, and reproductive behavior. Washington, D.C. : National Academy Press, 1998.
*TC HV91 .W478 1998*

**CHILD WELFARE - ILLINOIS - CHICAGO.**
McMahon, Anthony. Damned if you do, damned if you don't. Aldershot, England ; Brookfield, USA : Ashgate, 1998.
*TC HV743.C5 M35 1998*

**CHILD WELFARE - LAW AND LEGISLATION.** *See* **CHILDREN - LEGAL STATUS, LAWS, ETC.**

**CHILD WELFARE - MICHIGAN.**
Schwartz, Ira M. Kids raised by the government. Westport, Conn. : Praeger, 1999.
*TC HV741 .S367 1999*

**CHILD WELFARE - UNITED STATES.**
The challenge of permanency planning in a multicultural society. New York : Haworth Press, c1997.

*TC HV741 .C378 1997*
Schwartz, Ira M. Kids raised by the government. Westport, Conn. : Praeger, 1999.
*TC HV741 .S367 1999*

Securing the future. New York : Russell Sage Foundation, c2000.
*TC HV741 .S385 2000*

United States. General Accounting Office. Child welfare. Washington, D.C. (P.O. Box 37050, Washington, D.C. 20013) : The Office, [1998]
*TC HV741 .U525 1998a*

**CHILD WELFARE - UNITED STATES - HISTORY.**
Crenson, Matthew A., 1943- Building the invisible orphanage. Cambridge, Mass. : Harvard University Press, 1998.
*TC HV91 .C74 1998*

**A child went forth.**
Carr, Janine Chappell. Portsmouth, NH : Heinemann, 1999.
*TC LB1576 .C31714 1999*

**Child, youth, and family sevices.**
Reynolds, Arthur J. Success in early intervention. Lincoln, Neb. : University of Nebraska Press, c2000.
*TC HV743.C5 R48 2000*

**CHILDCARE.** *See* **CHILD CARE.**

**The CHILDES project.**
MacWhinney, Brian. 3rd ed. Mahwah, N.J. : Lawrence Erlbaum, 2000.
*TC LB1139.L3 M24 2000*

**CHILDHOOD.** *See* **CHILDREN.**

**Childhood and trauma.**
[Kindheit und Trauma. English.] Aldershot, Hants, UK : Brookfield, Vt., USA : Ashgate, c1999.
*TC RJ506.P66 K613 1999*

**CHILDHOOD AUTISM.** *See* **AUTISM IN CHILDREN.**

**Childhood cognitive development :** the essential readings / edited by Kang Lee. Malden, Mass. : Blackwell, 2000. xii, 340 p. : ill. ; 23 cm. (Essential readings in developmental psychology) Includes bibliographical references and index. ISBN 0-631-21655-3 (alk. paper) ISBN 0-631-21656-1 (pbk. : alk. paper) DDC 155.4/13
*1. Cognition in children. I. Lee, Kang. II. Series.*
*TC BF723.C5 C487 2000*

**CHILDHOOD DISEASES.** *See* **CHILDREN - DISEASES.**

**Childhood epilepsies and brain development** / editors, Astrid Nehlig ... [et al.]. London : John Libbey, c1999. vii, 311 p. : ill. (some col.) ; 25 cm. (Current problems in epilepsy, 0950-4591 ; 14) Includes bibliographical references and author index. ISBN 0-86196-578-7
*1. Epilepsy in children. 2. Brain-damaged children. I. Nehlig, Astrid. II. Series.*
*TC RJ496.E6 C45 1999*

**Childhood in America** / edited by Paula S. Fass and Mary Ann Mason. New York : New York University Press, c2000. xxii, 725 p. ; 25 cm. Includes bibliographical references and index. ISBN 0-8147-2692-5 (alk. paper) ISBN 0-8147-2693-3 (pbk. : alk. paper)
*1. Children - United States - History. 2. Children - United States - History - Sources. 3. Youth - United States - History. 4. Youth - United States - History - Sources. 5. Adolescence - United States - History. 6. Adolescence - United States - History - Sources. I. Fass, Paula S. II. Mason, Mary Ann.*
*TC HQ792.U5 C4199 1999*

**Childhood language disorders in context.**
Nelson, Nickola. 2nd ed. Boston : Allyn & Bacon, c1998.
*TC RJ496.L35 N46 1998*

**Childhood motor speech disability.**
Love, Russell J. 2nd ed. Boston ; London : Allyn and Bacon, c2000.
*TC RJ496.S7 L68 2000*

**Childhood social development :** the essential readings / edited by Wendy Craig. Malden, Mass. ; Oxford : Blackwell Publishers, 2000. xi, 375 p. ; 24 cm. (Essential readings in developmental psychology) Includes bibliographical references and index. CONTENTS: Attachments / M.D.S. Ainsworth -- Parenting / G.S. Pettit, J.E. Bates, and K.A. Dodge. -- Friendships /W.W. Hartup -- Peer relations / C.L. Bagwell, A.F. Newcomb, and W.M. Bukowski. -- Bullying and victimization / W.M. Craig and D.J. Pepler -- Friendship and school adjustment / G.W. Ladd, B.J. Kochenderfer, and C.C. Coleman -- Extracurricular activities / J.L. Mahoney and R.B. Cairns -- Gender differences / E.E. Maccoby -- Self-concept / H.W. Marsh, R. Craven, and R.

Debus -- Moral reasoning / J.G. Smetana, M. Killen, and E. Turiel -- Forms of aggression / N.R. Crick -- Development of antisocial behavior / G.R. Patterson, B.D. DeBaryshe, and E. Ramsey -- Prevention of conduct disorders / J.D. Coie and M.R. Jacobs. ISBN 0-631-21740-1 (hbk. : alk. paper) ISBN 0-631-21741-X (pbk. : alk. paper) DDC 305.231
*1. Child psychology. 2. Child development. I. Craig, Wendy (Wendy M.). II. Series.*
**TC BF721 .C6675 2000**

**Childhood studies :** a reader in perspectives of childhood / edited by Jean Mills and Richard Mills. London ; New York : Routledge, 2000. xiii, 204 p. ; 24 cm. Includes bibliographical references and index. ISBN 0-415-21414-9 (hard : alk. paper) ISBN 0-415-21415-7 (pbk. : alk. paper) DDC 305.23/07/2
*1. Children - Research. 2. Child development - Research. 3. Children - Attitudes. I. Mills, Jean, 1947- II. Mills, Richard W.*
**TC HQ767.85 .C483 2000**

**Childhood's deadly scourge.**
Hammonds, Evelynn Maxine. Baltimore, Md. : Johns Hopkins University Press, c1999.
**TC RA644.D6 H36 1999**

**CHILDREN.** *See also* **ABUSED CHILDREN; ADOPTED CHILDREN; ADVERTISING AND CHILDREN; BILINGUALISM IN CHILDREN; BOYS; CHILD DEVELOPMENT; CITY CHILDREN; COMPUTERS AND CHILDREN; EXCEPTIONAL CHILDREN; FOSTER CHILDREN; GIRLS; HOMELESS CHILDREN; INFANTS; INTERNET (COMPUTER NETWORK) AND CHILDREN; MASS MEDIA AND CHILDREN; MOTION PICTURES FOR CHILDREN; ORPHANS; OVERWEIGHT CHILDREN; PIONEER CHILDREN; POOR CHILDREN; PRESCHOOL CHILDREN; PROBLEM CHILDREN; SCHOOL CHILDREN; SICK CHILDREN; SOCIAL WORK WITH CHILDREN; STEPCHILDREN; STREET CHILDREN; TELEVISION ADVERTISING AND CHILDREN; TELEVISION AND CHILDREN; TODDLERS; VIDEO RECORDINGS FOR CHILDREN.**
Children's geographies. London ; New York : Routledge, 2000.
**TC HQ767.9 .C4559 2000**

Wyness, Michael G. Contesting childhood. London : New York : Falmer Press, 2000.
**TC HQ767.9 .W96 2000**

**CHILDREN, ABANDONED.** *See* **ABANDONED CHILDREN.**

**CHILDREN, ABNORMAL AND BACKWARD.** *See* **EXCEPTIONAL CHILDREN; HANDICAPPED CHILDREN.**

**CHILDREN - ABUSE OF.** *See* **CHILD ABUSE.**

**Children achieving :** best practices in early literacy / Susan B. Neuman, Kathleen A. Roskos, editors. Newark, Del. : International Reading Association, c1998. xii, 323 p. : ill. ; 23 cm. Includes bibliographical references and indexes. ISBN 0-87207-193-6 DDC 372.6
*1. Reading (Early childhood) 2. English language - Composition and exercises - Study and teaching (Early childhood) 3. Literacy. 4. Language arts (Early childhood) 5. Child development. I. Neuman, Susan B. II. Roskos, Kathy. III. International Reading Association.*
**TC LB1139.5.R43 C55 1998**

**CHILDREN, ADOPTED.** *See* **ADOPTED CHILDREN.**

**CHILDREN, AFRO-AMERICAN.** *See* **AFRO-AMERICAN CHILDREN.**

**Children and adolescents in the market place.**
Chandler, Tomasita M. Ann Arbor, Mich. : Pierian Press, 1999.
**TC HF5822 .C43 1999**

**CHILDREN AND ADULTS.** *See also* **PARENT AND CHILD; TEACHER-STUDENT RELATIONSHIPS.**
Giroux, Henry A. Stealing innocence. 1st ed. New York : St. Martin's Press, 2000.
**TC HM621 .G57 2000**

Peterson, Susan Louise, 1960- Why children make up stories. San Francisco ; London : International Scholars Publications, 1999.
**TC BF723.C57 P47 1999**

**CHILDREN AND ADULTS - STUDY AND TEACHING (ELEMENTARY) - UNITED STATES.**

Friedman, Barbara, 1947- Connecting generations. Boston : Allyn and Bacon, c1999.
**TC HQ1064.U5 F755 1999**

**CHILDREN AND COMPUTERS.** *See* **COMPUTERS AND CHILDREN.**

**CHILDREN AND DEATH.**
Christ, Grace Hyslop. Healing children's grief. New York : Oxford University Press, 2000.
**TC BF723.G75 C58 2000**

Judd, Dorothy. Give sorrow words. 2nd ed. New York : Haworth Press, 1995.
**TC RJ249 .J83 1995**

Silverman, Phyllis R. Never too young to know. New York : Oxford University Press, 2000.
**TC BF723.D3 S58 2000**

Smith, Susan C. The forgotten mourners. 2nd ed. London ; Philadelphia : Jessica Kingsley Publishers, 1999.
**TC BF723.G75 P46 1999**

**CHILDREN AND INTERNET.** *See* **INTERNET (COMPUTER NETWORK) AND CHILDREN.**

**Children and interparental violence.**
Rossman, B. B. Robbie. Philadelphia, Pa. ; London : Brunner/Mazel, c2000.
**TC HQ784.V55 R675 2000**

**CHILDREN AND MASS MEDIA.** *See* **MASS MEDIA AND CHILDREN.**

**CHILDREN AND PARENTS.** *See* **PARENT AND CHILD.**

**CHILDREN AND PEACE.**
How children understand war and peace. 1st ed. San Francisco : Jossey-Bass, c1999.
**TC JZ5534 .H69 1999**

**Children and reading tests.**
Hill, Clifford. Stamford, Conn. : Ablex Pub. Corp., c2000.
**TC LB1050.46 .H55 2000**

**CHILDREN AND TELEVISION.** *See* **TELEVISION AND CHILDREN.**

**CHILDREN AND THE INTERNET.** *See* **INTERNET (COMPUTER NETWORK) AND CHILDREN.**

**CHILDREN AND VIOLENCE.** *See also* **VIOLENCE IN CHILDREN.**
Rossman, B. B. Robbie. Children and interparental violence. Philadelphia, Pa. ; London : Brunner/Mazel, c2000.
**TC HQ784.V55 R675 2000**

**CHILDREN AND VIOLENCE - UNITED STATES.**
Violence and childhood in the inner city. Cambridge, UK ; New York : Cambridge University Press, 1997.
**TC HN90.V5 V532 1997**

**CHILDREN AND WAR.**
[Kindheit und Trauma. English.] Childhood and trauma. Aldershot, Hants, UK ; Brookfield, Vt., USA : Ashgate, c1999.
**TC RJ506.P66 K613 1999**

**The children are watching.**
Cortés, Carlos E. New York : Teachers College Press, c2000.
**TC P96.M83 C67 2000**

**CHILDREN AS ARTISTS.**
Lowenfeld, Viktor. Creative and mental growth. Rev. ed. New York, Macmillan [1952]
**TC N350 .L62 1952**

**CHILDREN AS CONSUMERS.** *See* **CHILD CONSUMERS.**

**CHILDREN AS MUSICIANS.** *See* **CHILD MUSICIANS.**

**Children as partners for health.**
Pridmore, Pat, 1947- London ; New York : Zed Books ; New York : Distributed exclusively in the USA by St. Martin's Press, 2000.
**TC LB1587.A3 P75 2000**

**CHILDREN, ASIAN AMERICAN.** *See* **ASIAN AMERICAN CHILDREN.**

**Children at the center.**
Taylor, Kathe. Portsmouth, NH : Heinemann, c1998.
**TC LB3060.57 .T39 1998**

**CHILDREN - ATTITUDES.**
Childhood studies. London ; New York : Routledge, 2000.
**TC HQ767.85 .C483 2000**

Lewis, Ann, 1950- Researching children's perspectives. Buckingham ; Philadelphia : Open University Press, 2000.
**TC HQ767.85 .L49 2000**

Tobin, Joseph Jay. "Good guys don't wear hats". New York : Teachers College Press, c2000.
**TC HQ784.M3 T63 2000**

**CHILDREN, AUTISTIC.** *See* **AUTISTIC CHILDREN.**

**CHILDREN, BACKWARD.** *See* **MENTALLY HANDICAPPED CHILDREN.**

**CHILDREN, BLACK - EDUCATION (ELEMENTARY) - SOCIAL ASPECTS - CANADA - CASE STUDIES.**
Henry, Annette, 1955- Taking back control. Albany : State University of New York Press, c1998.
**TC LB1775.4.C2 H45 1998**

**CHILDREN, BLIND.** *See* **VISUALLY HANDICAPPED CHILDREN.**

**CHILDREN, BLIND - EDUCATION.**
Bridges to independence [videorecording. Burbank, CA : RCA/Columbia Pictures Home Video ; [S.l. : Distributed by] Rank Video Services Production, c1991.
**TC HV1646 .B7 1991**

Hand in hand [videorecording]. New York, N.Y. : AFB Press, c1995.
**TC HV1597.2 .H3 1995**

**CHILDREN, BLIND - EDUCATION (EARLY CHILDHOOD).**
Bright beginnings [videorecording. Burbank, CA : RCA/Columbia Pictures Home Video ; Toluca Lake, CA : [Distributed by] Corporate Productions, c1991.
**TC HV1642 .B67 1991**

Bright beginnings [videorecording. Burbank, CA : RCA/Columbia Pictures Home Video ; [S.l. : Distributed by] Rank Video Services America, c1991.
**TC HV1642 .B67 1991**

Making the most of early communication [videorecording]. New York, NY : Distributed by AFB Press, c1997.
**TC HV1597.2 .M3 1997**

**CHILDREN, BLIND - LANGUAGE.**
Hand in hand [videorecording]. New York, N.Y. : AFB Press, c1995.
**TC HV1597.2 .H3 1995**

Making the most of early communication [videorecording]. New York, NY : Distributed by AFB Press, c1997.
**TC HV1597.2 .M3 1997**

Pérez Pereira, Miguel. Language development and social interaction in blind children. Hove, UK : Psychology Press, c1999.
**TC P118 .P37 1999**

**CHILDREN, BLIND - PSYCHOLOGY.**
Hand in hand [videorecording]. New York, N.Y. : AFB Press, c1995.
**TC HV1597.2 .H3 1995**

Making the most of early communication [videorecording]. New York, NY : Distributed by AFB Press, c1997.
**TC HV1597.2 .M3 1997**

**CHILDREN, BLIND - REHABILITATION.**
Hand in hand [videorecording]. New York, N.Y. : AFB Press, c1995.
**TC HV1597.2 .H3 1995**

Making the most of early communication [videorecording]. New York, NY : Distributed by AFB Press, c1997.
**TC HV1597.2 .M3 1997**

**CHILDREN - BOOKS AND READING.**
Chatton, Barbara. Blurring the edges. Portsmouth, NH : Heinemann, c1999.
**TC LB1576 .C46 1999**

Hancock, Marjorie R. A celebration of literature and response. Upper Saddle River, N.J. : Merrill, c2000.
**TC LB1575 .H36 2000**

Hart-Hewins, Linda. Better books! Better readers!. York, Me. : Stenhouse Publishers ; Markham, Ont. : Pembroke Publishers, c1999.
**TC LB1525 .H26 1999**

Hill, Clifford. Children and reading tests. Stamford, Conn. : Ablex Pub. Corp., c2000.

*TC LB1050.46 .H55 2000*

Hunt, Gladys M. Honey for a child's heart. 3rd ed. Grand Rapids, Mich. : Zondervan Books, c1989.
*TC Z1037 .H945 1989*

Jobe, Ron. Reluctant readers. Markham, Ont. : Pembroke Pub., 1999.
*TC LB1573 .J58 1999*

Literature and the child. Iowa City : University of Iowa Press, c1999.
*TC PR990 .L58 1999*

Mikkelsen, Nina. Words and pictures. Boston : McGraw-Hill, c2000.
*TC LB1575 .M55 2000*

Morris, Timothy, 1959- You're only young twice. Urbana : University of Illinois Press, c2000.
*TC PR990 .M67 2000*

Savage, John F., 1938- For the love of literature. Boston : McGraw-Hill, c2000.
*TC LB1575 .S28 2000*

Sawyer, Walter. Growing up with literature. 3rd ed. Albany, N.Y. : Delmar, c2000.
*TC LB1140.5.L3 S28 2000*

Schon, Isabel. Recommended books in Spanish for children and young adults, 1996 through 1999. Lanham, Md. : Scarecrow Press, 2000.
*TC Z1037.7 .S387 2000*

Stewig, John W. Language arts in the early childhood classroom. Belmont [Calif.] : Wadsworth Pub. Co., c1995.
*TC LB1140.5.L3 S72 1995*

Transcending boundaries. New York : Garland, 1999.
*TC PN1009.A1 T69 1999*

**CHILDREN - BOOKS AND READING - PSYCHOLOGICAL ASPECTS.**
Spitz, Ellen Handler, 1939- Inside picture books. New Haven : Yale University Press, c1999.
*TC BF456.R2 S685 1999*

**CHILDREN - BOOKS AND READING - UNITED STATES.**
Glazer, Joan I. Literature for young children. 4th ed. Upper Saddle River, N.J. : Merrill, 2000.
*TC Z1037.A1 G573 2000*

Gunning, Thomas G. Best books for building literacy for elementary school children. Boston : Allyn and Bacon, 2000.
*TC LB1573 .B47 2000*

Littlejohn, Carol. Talk that book! booktalks to promote reading. Worthington, Ohio : Linworth Publishing, 1999.
*TC Z1037.A2 L58 1999*

Nelsen, Marjorie R. Peak with books. 3rd ed. Thousand Oaks, Calif. : Corwin Press, c1999.
*TC Z1037.A1 N347 1999*

**CHILDREN - CARE.** *See* **CHILD CARE.**

**CHILDREN - CARE AND HYGIENE.** *See also* **CHILD CARE; CHILDREN - HEALTH AND HYGIENE.**
Smith, Richard Mason, 1881- From infancy to childhood. Boston : Atlantic monthly press, [c1925]
*TC RJ61 .S675*

**CHILDREN - CHARITIES.** *See* **CHILD WELFARE.**

**CHILDREN - CHARITIES, PROTECTION, ETC.** *See* **CHILD WELFARE.**

**CHILDREN - CHINA - NUTRITION.**
Feeding China's little emperors. Stanford, Calif. : Stanford University Press, 2000.
*TC TX361.C5 F44 2000*

**CHILDREN, CHINESE AMERICAN.** *See* **CHINESE AMERICAN CHILDREN.**

**CHILDREN - CONDUCT OF LIFE - EARLY WORKS TO 1800.**
Jocelin, Elizabeth, 1596-1622. The mothers legacy to her vnborn [i.e. unborn] childe [i.e. child]. Toronto : University of Toronto Press, 2000.
*TC BV4570 .J62 2000*

**CHILDREN - COUNSELING OF.**
Epps, Susan. Empowered families, successful children. 1st ed. Washington, DC : American Psychological Association, c2000.
*TC BF637.C6 E66 2000*

Goldman, Linda, 1946- Life & loss. 2nd ed. Philadelphia : Accelerated Development, c2000.

*TC BF723.G75 G65 2000*

Smith, Susan C. The forgotten mourners. 2nd ed. London : Philadelphia : Jessica Kingsley Publishers, 1999.
*TC BF723.G75 P46 1999*

**CHILDREN - CRIMES AGAINST.** *See* **CHILD ABUSE.**

**CHILDREN - CROSS-CULTURAL STUDIES.**
Infancy and culture. New York : Falmer Press, 1999.
*TC GN482 .I53 1999*

Variability in the social construction of the child. San Francisco : Jossey-Bass, 2000.
*TC BF723.S62 .V37 2000*

**CHILDREN, DEAF.** *See* **HEARING IMPAIRED CHILDREN.**

**CHILDREN, DEAF - EDUCATION.**
Cerruto, Audra. The effects of training on theory of mind tasks with children who are deaf. 1999.
*TC 085 C34*

**CHILDREN, DEAF - EDUCATION.**
Hand in hand [videorecording]. New York, N.Y. : AFB Press, c1995.
*TC HV1597.2 .H3 1995*

**CHILDREN, DEAF - EDUCATION (EARLY CHILDHOOD).**
Making the most of early communication [videorecording]. New York, NY : Distributed by AFB Press, c1997.
*TC HV1597.2 .M3 1997*

**CHILDREN, DEAF - LANGUAGE.**
Hand in hand [videorecording]. New York, N.Y. : AFB Press, c1995.
*TC HV1597.2 .H3 1995*

Making the most of early communication [videorecording]. New York, NY : Distributed by AFB Press, c1997.
*TC HV1597.2 .M3 1997*

**CHILDREN, DEAF - PSYCHOLOGY.**
Hand in hand [videorecording]. New York, N.Y. : AFB Press, c1995.
*TC HV1597.2 .H3 1995*

Making the most of early communication [videorecording]. New York, NY : Distributed by AFB Press, c1997.
*TC HV1597.2 .M3 1997*

**CHILDREN, DEAF - REHABILITATION.**
Hand in hand [videorecording]. New York, N.Y. : AFB Press, c1995.
*TC HV1597.2 .H3 1995*

Making the most of early communication [videorecording]. New York, NY : Distributed by AFB Press, c1997.
*TC HV1597.2 .M3 1997*

**CHILDREN - DEATH AND FUTURE STATE.** *See* **CHILDREN - DEATH.**

**CHILDREN - DEATH - PSYCHOLOGICAL ASPECTS.**
Rosenblatt, Paul C. Parent grief. Philadelphia ; Hove [England] : Brunner/Mazel, c2000.
*TC BF575.G7 R673 2000*

**CHILDREN - DEATH - PSYCHOLOGICAL ASPECTS - CASE STUDIES.**
Rosenblatt, Paul C. Parent grief. Philadelphia ; Hove [England] : Brunner/Mazel, c2000.
*TC BF575.G7 R673 2000*

**CHILDREN - DEVELOPMENT.** *See* **CHILD DEVELOPMENT.**

**CHILDREN - DEVELOPMENT AND GUIDANCE.** *See* **CHILD REARING.**

**CHILDREN - DISEASES.** *See also* **PEDIATRICS.**
The Crippled child. Chicago [etc.] National Society for Crippled Children and Adults [etc.]

Pringle, Sheila M. Promoting the health of children. St. Louis : Mosby, 1982.
*TC RJ101 .P66 1982*

**CHILDREN - DISEASES - NURSING.** *See* **PEDIATRIC NURSING.**

**CHILDREN - DISEASES - TREATMENT.** *See also* **CHILD PSYCHOTHERAPY; SPEECH THERAPY FOR CHILDREN.**
Siskind, Diana. A primer for child psychotherapists. Northvale, NJ : Jason Aronson, c1999.

*TC RJ504 .S543 1999*

**CHILDREN - EDUCATION.** *See* **EDUCATION.**

**CHILDREN - EDUCATION (ELEMENTARY).** *See* **EDUCATION, ELEMENTARY.**

**CHILDREN - EDUCATION (PRESCHOOL).** *See* **EDUCATION, PRESCHOOL.**

**CHILDREN - EDUCATION (PRIMARY).** *See* **EDUCATION, PRIMARY.**

**CHILDREN - EDUCATION (SECONDARY).** *See* **EDUCATION, SECONDARY.**

**CHILDREN - EL SALVADOR - SOCIAL CONDITIONS.**
Flores, Joaquín Evelio. Psychological effects of the civil war on children from rural communities of El Salvador.
*TC 083 F67*

**CHILDREN - EMPLOYMENT - DEVELOPING COUNTRIES.**
Action against child labour. Geneva : International Labour Office, c2000.
*TC HD6231 .A28 2000*

**CHILDREN - EMPLOYMENT - UNITED STATES - HISTORY - 19TH CENTURY - PICTORIAL WORKS.**
Child labor [picture]. Amawalk, NY : Jackdaw Publications, c1997.
*TC HD6250.U5 C4 1997*

**CHILDREN - EMPLOYMENT - UNITED STATES - HISTORY - 20TH CENTURY - PICTORIAL WORKS.**
Child labor [picture]. Amawalk, NY : Jackdaw Publications, c1997.
*TC HD6250.U5 C4 1997*

**CHILDREN - ENGLAND - BOOKS AND READING.**
Darton, F. J. Harvey (Frederick Joseph Harvey), 1878-1936. Children's books in England. 3rd ed. / rev. by Brian Alderson. London : British Library ; New Castle, DE : Oak Knoll Press, 1982 (1999 printing)
*TC PR990 .D3 1999*

**CHILDREN, EXCEPTIONAL.** *See* **EXCEPTIONAL CHILDREN.**

**CHILDREN EXPOSED PRENATALLY TO SUBSTANCES.** *See* **CHILDREN OF PRENATAL SUBSTANCE ABUSE.**

**CHILDREN EXPOSED TO PRENATAL SUBSTANCE ABUSE.** *See* **CHILDREN OF PRENATAL SUBSTANCE ABUSE.**

**CHILDREN - FOOD.** *See* **CHILDREN - NUTRITION.**

**CHILDREN - FOREIGN COUNTRIES - ATTITUDES.**
Pollock, David C. The third culture kid experience. Yarmouth, Me. : Intercultural Press, c1999.
*TC HQ784.S56 P65 1999*

**Children from Australia to Zimbabwe.**
Ajmera, Maya. Watertown, Mass. : Charlesbridge, c1997.
*TC GF48 .A45 1997*

**CHILDREN, GIFTED.** *See* **GIFTED CHILDREN.**

**CHILDREN - GOVERNMENT POLICY.**
Governing childhood. Aldershot, England ; Brookfield, Vt. : Dartmouth, c1997.
*TC HQ789 .G68 1997*

**CHILDREN - GOVERNMENT POLICY - UNITED STATES.**
Securing the future. New York : Russell Sage Foundation, c2000.
*TC HV741 .S385 2000*

United States. General Accounting Office. Child welfare. Washington, D.C. (P.O. Box 37050, Washington, D.C. 20013) : The Office, [1998]
*TC HV741 .U525 1998a*

**CHILDREN - GREAT BRITAIN - BOOKS AND READING.**
Coles, Martin, 1952- Children's reading choices. London ; New York : Routledge, 1999.
*TC Z1037.A1 C59 1999*

**CHILDREN - GREAT BRITAIN - LONGITUDINAL STUDIES.**
42 up. New York : The New Press : Distributed by W.W. Norton, c1998.
*TC HQ792.G7 A18 1998*

**CHILDREN - GROWTH.**
Symposium on Issues in Human Development (1967 : Philadelphia) Issues in human development; Washington, For sale by the Supt. of Docs., U. S. Govt. Print. Off. [1970?]
*TC RJ131.A1 S93 1967*

**CHILDREN, HANDICAPPED.** *See* **HANDICAPPED CHILDREN.**

**Children have their reasons.**
Washburn, Ruth Wendell, 1890- New York, D. Appleton-Century, 1942.
*TC HQ772 .W24*

**CHILDREN - HEALTH.** *See* **CHILDREN - HEALTH AND HYGIENE.**

**CHILDREN - HEALTH AND HYGIENE.** *See also* **PEDIATRICS; PHYSICAL EDUCATION FOR CHILDREN.**
Groves, Ernest Rutherford, 1878-1946. Wholesome childhood, Boston, Houghton Mifflin Company, 1924.
*TC HQ772 .G75*

Pringle, Sheila M. Promoting the health of children. St. Louis : Mosby, 1982.
*TC RJ101 .P66 1982*

**CHILDREN - HEALTH AND HYGIENE - NEW YORK (STATE) - STATISTICS.**
Maternal, child and adolescent health profile. Albany, N.Y. : New York State Dept. of Health, 1996.
*TC HV742.N7 B83 1996*

**CHILDREN - HEALTH AND HYGIENE - PERIODICALS.**
Child health bulletin. New York, American Child Health Association.

**CHILDREN - HEALTH AND HYGIENE - STATISTICS - PERIODICALS.**
The progress of nations. New York, NY : UNICEF, 1993-
*TC RA407.A1 P76*

**CHILDREN, HEARING IMPAIRED.** *See* **HEARING IMPAIRED CHILDREN.**

**CHILDREN, HISPANIC AMERICAN.** *See* **HISPANIC AMERICAN CHILDREN.**

**CHILDREN - HISTORY - 20TH CENTURY.**
Werner, Emmy E. Through the eyes of innocents. Boulder, CO : Westview Press, 2000.
*TC D810.C4 W45 1999*

**CHILDREN - HISTORY - PERIODICALS.**
History of childhood quarterly. [Broadway, N.Y., Atcom]

**CHILDREN, HOMELESS.** *See* **HOMELESS CHILDREN.**

**CHILDREN - HYGIENE.** *See* **CHILDREN - HEALTH AND HYGIENE.**

**CHILDREN IN CITIES.** *See* **CITY CHILDREN.**

**CHILDREN IN FOREIGN COUNTRIES.** *See* **CHILDREN - FOREIGN COUNTRIES.**

**CHILDREN IN MOTION PICTURES - GREAT BRITAIN.**
42 up. New York : The New Press : Distributed by W.W. Norton, c1998.
*TC HQ792.G7 A18 1998*

**CHILDREN IN THE UNITED STATES.** *See* **CHILDREN - UNITED STATES.**

**Children in therapy:** using the family as a resource. / C. Everett Bailey, editor. New York : W.W. Norton, 2000. xxvi, 529 p. ; 25 cm. "A Norton professional book." Includes bibliographical references and index. ISBN 0-393-70289-8 DDC 616.89/156
1. Family psychotherapy. 2. Child psychotherapy. I. Bailey, C. Everett.
*TC RC488.5 .C468 2000*

**CHILDREN - INSTITUTIONAL CARE.** *See also* **DAY CARE CENTERS; FOSTER HOME CARE; ORPHANAGES; REFORMATORIES.**
Johnson, Toni Cavanagh. Sexual, physical, and emotional abuse in out-of-home care. New York : The Haworth Maltreatment and Trauma Press, c1997.
*TC RJ507.A29 J64 1997*

**CHILDREN - JUVENILE LITERATURE.**
Ajmera, Maya. Children from Australia to Zimbabwe. Watertown, Mass. : Charlesbridge, c1997.
*TC GF48 .A45 1997*

**CHILDREN - LANGUAGE.**
Biemiller, Andrew, 1939- Language and reading success. Cambridge, Mass. : Brookline Books, c1999.

*TC LB1139.L3 B48 1999*

Blachman, Benita A. Road to the code. Baltimore : Paul H. Brookes, c2000.
*TC LB1139.L3 B53 2000*

Chiat, Shula. Understanding children with language problems. Oxford [England] ; New York : Cambridge University Press, 2000.
*TC RJ496.L35 C46 2000*

Cramer, Ronald L. Creative power. New York ; London : Longman, c2001.
*TC LB1576 .C758 2001*

Fahey, Kathleen R. Language development, differences, and disorders. Austin, Tex. : PRO-ED, c2000.
*TC LB1139.L3 F35 2000*

Kress, Gunther R. Early spelling. London ; New York : Routledge, 2000.
*TC P240.2 .K74 2000*

Minds in the making. Oxford ; Malden, Mass. : Blackwell, 2000.
*TC BF723.C5 M56 2000*

Quigley, Jean. The grammar of autobiography. Mahwah, N.J. : Lawrence Erlbaum Associates, c2000.
*TC PE1315.M6 Q54 2000*

Stirring the waters. Portsmouth, NH : Heinemann, c1999.
*TC LB1139.5.L35 S85 1999*

Tobin, Joseph Jay. "Good guys don't wear hats". New York : Teachers College Press, c2000.
*TC HQ784.M3 T63 2000*

Whitehead, Marian R. Supporting language and literacy development in the early years. Buckingham [England] ; Philadelphia : Open University Press, 1999.
*TC LB1139.5.L35 W53 1999*

**CHILDREN - LANGUAGE - CONGRESSES.**
Child Language Research Forum (29th : 1997 : Stanford University) The proceedings of the twenty-ninth Annual Child Language Research Forum. [Stanford] : Published for the Stanford Linguistics Association by the Center for the Study of Language and Information, c1998.
*TC P118 .C4558 1997*

**CHILDREN - LANGUAGE - DATA PROCESSING.**
MacWhinney, Brian. The CHILDES project. 3rd ed. Mahwah, N.J. : Lawrence Erlbaum, 2000.
*TC LB1139.L3 M24 2000*

**CHILDREN - LANGUAGE - EVALUATION.**
Retherford, Kristine S., 1950- Guide to analysis of language transcripts. 2nd ed. Eau Claire, WI : Thinking Publications, 1993.
*TC RJ496.L35 S84 1993*

**CHILDREN - LAW.** *See* **CHILDREN - LEGAL STATUS, LAWS, ETC.**

**CHILDREN - LEGAL STATUS, LAWS, ETC.**
Governing childhood. Aldershot, England ; Brookfield, Vt. : Dartmouth, c1997.
*TC HQ789 .G68 1997*

[Kindheit und Trauma. English.] Childhood and trauma. Aldershot, Hants, UK ; Brookfield, Vt., USA : Ashgate, c1999.
*TC RJ506.P66 K613 1999*

Parker-Jenkins, Marie. Sparing the rod. Stoke-on-Trent : Trentham, 1999.
*TC LB3012 .P37 1999*

**CHILDREN - LEGAL STATUS, LAWS, ETC. - CONGRESSES.**
Children's rights and traditional values. Aldershot ; Brookfield, USA : Ashgate/Dartmouth, c1998.
*TC K639 .A55 1998*

**CHILDREN - LEGAL STATUS, LAWS, ETC. - GREAT BRITAIN.**
Clark, Alison. The child in focus. London : National Children's Bureau Enterprise, c1999.
*TC KD785 .C43 1999*

**CHILDREN - LEGAL STATUS, LAWS, ETC. - ISRAEL - CONGRESSES.**
Children's rights and traditional values. Aldershot ; Brookfield, USA : Ashgate/Dartmouth, c1998.
*TC K639 .A55 1998*

**CHILDREN - MANAGEMENT.** *See* **CHILD REARING.**

**CHILDREN - MENTAL DISORDERS.** *See* **CHILD PSYCHIATRY; CHILD PSYCHOPATHOLOGY.**

**CHILDREN - MENTAL HEALTH.** *See* **CHILD MENTAL HEALTH.**

**CHILDREN - MENTAL HEALTH SERVICES.** *See* **CHILD MENTAL HEALTH SERVICES.**

**CHILDREN - NEW YORK (STATE) - LANGUAGE - CASE STUDIES.**
Schmidt, Patricia Ruggiano, 1944- Cultural conflict and struggle. New York : P. Lang, c1998.
*TC LB1181 .S36 1998*

**CHILDREN - NEW YORK (STATE) - NEW YORK - SOCIAL CONDITIONS.**
Kozol, Jonathan. Ordinary resurrections. 1st ed. New York : Crown Publishers, c2000.
*TC HQ792.U5 K69 2000*

**CHILDREN - NUTRITION - STATISTICS - PERIODICALS.**
The progress of nations. New York, NY : UNICEF, 1993-
*TC RA407.A1 P76*

**CHILDREN OF DEAF PARENTS - UNITED STATES - BIOGRAPHY.**
Davis, Lennard J., 1949- My sense of silence. Urbana : University of Illinois Press, c2000.
*TC HQ759.912 .D38 2000*

**CHILDREN OF DIVORCED PARENTS - MENTAL HEALTH.**
Ellis, Elizabeth M. Divorce wars. 1st ed. Washington, D.C. : American Psychological Association, c2000.
*TC RC488.6 .E45 2000*

**CHILDREN OF DIVORCED PARENTS - UNITED STATES.**
Ganong, Lawrence H. Changing families, changing responsibilities. Mahwah, N.J. : Lawrence Erlbaum Associates, 1999.
*TC HQ834 .G375 1999*

**CHILDREN OF GAY MEN.** *See* **CHILDREN OF GAY PARENTS.**

**CHILDREN OF GAY PARENTS - UNITED STATES.**
Ryan, Daniel Prentice. Gay/lesbian parents and school personnel. 1998.
*TC 06 no. 10988*

**CHILDREN OF HOMOSEXUAL PARENTS.** *See* **CHILDREN OF GAY PARENTS.**

**CHILDREN OF IMMIGRANTS - EDUCATION (ELEMENTARY) - UNITED STATES - CASE STUDIES.**
Paratore, Jeanne R. What should we expect of family literacy? Newark, Del. : International Reading Association ; Chicago , Ill. : National Reading Conference, c1999.
*TC LC151 .P37 1999*

**CHILDREN OF IMMIGRANTS - EDUCATION (PRESCHOOL) - GREAT BRITAIN.**
Thompson, Linda, 1949- Young bilingual children in nursery school. Clevedon, UK ; Buffalo, NY : Multilingual Matters, c2000.
*TC LC3723 .T47 2000*

**CHILDREN OF IMMIGRANTS - EDUCATION (PRESCHOOL) - UNITED STATES - CASE STUDIES.**
Ballenger, Cynthia. Teaching other people's children. New York : Teachers College Press, c1999.
*TC LC3746 .B336 1999*

**CHILDREN OF IMMIGRANTS - EDUCATION (SECONDARY) - TEXAS - CASE STUDIES.**
Valenzuela, Angela. Subtractive schooling. Albany : State University of New York Press, c1999.
*TC LC2683.4 .V35 1999*

**Children of immigrants :** health, adjustment, and public assistance / Donald J. Hernandez, editor ; Committee on the Health and Adjustment of Immigrant Children and Families, Board on Children, Youth, and Families, National Research Council and Institute of Medicine. Washington, D.C. : National Academy Press, c1999. x, 660 p : ill. ; 23 cm. Includes bibliographical references. CONTENTS: Children of immigrants : health, adjustment, and public assistance / Donald J. Hernandez -- Socioeconomic and demographic risk factors and resources among children in immigrant and native-born families : 1910, 1960, and 1990 / Donald J. Hernandez and Katherine Darke -- Access to health insurance and health care for children in immigrant families / E. Richard Brown, Roberta Wyn, Hongjian Yu, Abel Valenzuela, and Liane Dong -- The health and nutritional status of immigrant Hispanic children : analyses of the Hispanic health and nutrition examination survey / Fernando S. Mendoza and Lori Beth Dixon -- Immigration and infant health : birth outcomes of immigrant and native-born women / Nancy S. Landale, R.S. Oropesa, and

Bridget K. Gorman -- The health status and risk behaviors of adolescents in immigrant families / Kathleen Mullan Harris -- Educational profile of 3- to 8-year-old children of immigrants / Christine Winquist Nord and James A. Griffin -- Psychological well-being and educational achievement among immigrant youth / Grace Kao -- Passages to adulthood : the adaptation of children of immigrants in Southern California / Rubén G. Rumbaut -- Receipt of public assistance by Mexican American and Cuban American children in native and immigrant families / Sandra L. Hofferth -- Receipt of public assistance by immigrant children and their families : evidence from the survey of income and program participation / Peter David CONTENTS: Brandon -- Children in immigrant and nonimmigrant farmworker families : findings from the National Agricultural Workers survey / Richard Mines. ISBN 0-309-06545-3 (pbk. : alk. paper) DDC 362.7/086/91
*1. Children of immigrants - United States - Social conditions. 2. Children of immigrants - United States - Economic conditions. 3. Children of immigrants - Health and hygiene - United States. I. Hernandez, Donald J. II. Committee on the Health and Adjustment of Immigrant Children and Families (U.S.)*
***TC HV741 .C536157 1999***

**CHILDREN OF IMMIGRANTS - HEALTH AND HYGIENE - UNITED STATES.**
Children of immigrants. Washington, D.C. : National Academy Press, c1999.
***TC HV741 .C536157 1999***

**CHILDREN OF IMMIGRANTS - UNITED STATES - ECONOMIC CONDITIONS.**
Children of immigrants. Washington, D.C. : National Academy Press, c1999.
***TC HV741 .C536157 1999***

**CHILDREN OF IMMIGRANTS - UNITED STATES - SOCIAL CONDITIONS.**
Children of immigrants. Washington, D.C. : National Academy Press, c1999.
***TC HV741 .C536157 1999***

**CHILDREN OF LESBIANS.** *See* **CHILDREN OF GAY PARENTS.**

**CHILDREN OF MIGRANT LABORERS - EDUCATION - UNITED STATES.**
Lopez, Marianne Exum, 1960- When discourses collide. New York : P. Lang, c1999.
***TC HQ792.U5 L665 1999***

**CHILDREN OF MIGRANT LABORERS - SERVICES FOR - UNITED STATES.**
Lopez, Marianne Exum, 1960- When discourses collide. New York : P. Lang, c1999.
***TC HQ792.U5 L665 1999***

**CHILDREN OF MIGRANT LABORERS - UNITED STATES.**
Lopez, Marianne Exum, 1960- When discourses collide. New York : P. Lang, c1999.
***TC HQ792.U5 L665 1999***

**CHILDREN OF MINORITIES - EDUCATION (EARLY CHILDHOOD) - GREAT BRITAIN - CASE STUDIES.**
Woods, Peter, 1934- Multicultural children in the early years. Clevedon ; Philadelphia : Multilingual Matters Ltd, c1999.
***TC LC3736.G6 W66 1999***

**CHILDREN OF MINORITIES - EDUCATION (MIDDLE SCHOOL) - NEW YORK (STATE) - NEW YORK.**
Graham, Sheila L. Urban minority gifted students. 1999.
***TC 06 no. 11119***

**CHILDREN OF MINORITIES - EDUCATION (PRESCHOOL) - GREAT BRITAIN.**
Thompson, Linda, 1949- Young bilingual children in nursery school. Clevedon, UK ; Buffalo, NY : Multilingual Matters, c2000.
***TC LC3723 .T47 2000***

**CHILDREN OF MINORITIES - EDUCATION - TEXAS - LONGITUDINAL STUDIES.**
Kirby, Sheila Nataraj, 1946- Staffing at-risk school districts in Texas. Santa Monica, CA : Rand, 1999.
***TC LB2833.3.T4 K57 1999***

**CHILDREN OF MINORITIES - EDUCATION - UNITED STATES.**
Challenges of urban education. Albany : State Unviersity of New York Press, c2000.
***TC LC5131 .C38 2000***

Creativity and giftedness in culturally diverse students. Cresskill, N.J. : Hampton Press, c2000.
***TC LC3993.2 .C74 2000***

Grossman, Herbert, 1934- Achieving educational equality. Springfield, Ill. : C.C. Thomas, c1998.
***TC LC213.2 .G76 1998***

Kozol, Jonathan. Savage inequalities. 1st Harper Perennial ed. New York : HarperPerennial, 1992.
***TC LC4091 .K69 1992***

Literacy instruction for culturally and linguistically diverse students. Newark, Del. : International Reading Association, c1998.
***TC LC3731 .L566 1998***

**CHILDREN OF MINORITIES - MENTAL HEALTH.**
Canino, Ian A. Culturally diverse children and adolescents. 2nd ed. New York : Guilford Press, c2000.
***TC RJ507.M54 C36 2000***

**CHILDREN OF MINORITIES - UNITED STATES - LITERARY COLLECTIONS.**
Coming of age in America. New York : New Press : Distributed by W.W. Norton, c1994.
***TC PS509.M5 C66 1994***

**Children of poverty**
Dunlap, Katherine M. Family empowerment. New York : London : Garland Pub., 2000.
***TC LB1140.35.P37 D86 2000***

Lacy, Gary L. Head start social services. New York : Garland Pub., 1999.
***TC HV699 .L33 1999***

Newman, Rebecca. Educating homeless children. New York : London : Garland, 1999.
***TC LC5144.22.C2 N49 1999***

**CHILDREN OF PRENATAL SUBSTANCE ABUSE - EDUCATION (PRIMARY) - ILLINOIS - CHICAGO - CASE STUDIES.**
Barone, Diane M. Resilient children. Newark, Del. : International Reading Association ; Chicago : National Reading Conference, c1999.
***TC LC4806.4 .B37 1999***

**CHILDREN OF SINGLE PARENTS.** *See* **CHILDREN OF DIVORCED PARENTS.**

**The children of Telstar.**
Moody, Kate. 1st ed. New York : Center for Understanding Media : Vantage Press, c1999.
***TC LB1044.7 .M616 1999***

**Children of the land.**
Elder, Glen H. Chicago : University of Chicago Press, 2000.
***TC HQ796 .E525 2000***

**CHILDREN OF THE NIGHT.**
Children of the night [videorecording]. [Charleston, W.V.] : Cambridge Educational, c1994.
***TC HV1435.C3 C45 1994***

**CHILDREN OF THE NIGHT (VAN NUYS, CALIF.).**
Children of the night [videorecording]. [Charleston, W.V.] : Cambridge Educational, c1994.
***TC HV1435.C3 C45 1994***

Children of the night [videorecording]. [Charleston, W.V.] : Cambridge Educational, c1994.
***TC HV1435.C3 C45 1994***

Starting over [videorecording]. [Charleston, W.V.] : Cambridge Educational, c1994.
***TC HV1435.C3 S7 1994***

**Children of the night** [videorecording] / producer & director, Janet Gardner ; screenwriter, Janet Gardner ; Cambridge Educational. [Charleston, W.V.] : Cambridge Educational, c1994. 1 videorecording (35 min.) : sd., col. ; 1/2 in. (Running away, dropping out series) VHS. Catalogued from credits, cassette label and container. Narrator, Eric Conger. Music and lyrics by Richard Marx, published by Chi-Boy Music; director of photography, Len McClure; audio, Isak Ben Meir; editor, Jessie Weiner, Marlo Paoll. Copyright holder on cassette label: Cambridge Research Group, Ltd. For pre-adolescents through adult. SUMMARY: Runaways discuss their reasons for turning away from their lives and families and moving to the streets. 95% of the kids have been sexually abused by families or some other trusted adult. 100% of the kids have suffered abuse of any kind. Viewers learn how homeless kids survive-- by turning to drug-dealing, prostitution and panhandling. The addictiveness of street life, despite its hardships, is described and other methods of handling the runaways' problems are addressed. The viewer also goes along with an employee of the shelter, Children of the Night, as she makes her rounds and attempts to help these children.
*1. Runaway teenagers - California - Los Angeles. 2. Runaway teenagers - New York (State) - New York. 3. Youth - Crimes against - California - Los Angeles. 4. Youth - Crimes against - New York (State) - New York. 5. Homeless youth - California - Los Angeles. 6. Homeless youth - New York (State) - New York. 7. Teenage prostitution - United States. 8. Teenagers - Drug use - United States. 9. Runaway teenagers - United States - Family relationships. 10. Runaway teenagers - United States - Social conditions. 11. Children of the Night. 12. Documentary films. I. Gardner, Janet. II. Conger, Eric. III. Cambridge Educational (Firm) IV. Cambridge Research Group, Ltd. V. Series.*
***TC HV1435.C3 C45 1994***

**Children of the night** [videorecording] / producer & director, Janet Gardner ; screenwriter, Janet Gardner ; Cambridge Educational. [Charleston, W.V.] : Cambridge Educational, c1994. 1 videorecording (35 min.) : sd., col. ; 1/2 in. (Running away, dropping out) At head of title: Cambridge Educational. VHS. Catalogued from credits, cassette label and container. Narrator, Eric Conger. Music and lyrics by Richard Marx, published by Chi-Boy Music; director of photography, Len McClure; audio, Isak Ben Meir; editor, Jessie Weiner, Marlo Paoll. Copyright holder on cassette label: Cambridge Research Group, Ltd. For pre-adolescents through adult. SUMMARY: Runaways discuss their reasons for turning away from their lives and families and moving to the streets. 95% of the kids have been sexually abused by their families or some other trusted adult. 100% of the kids have suffered abuse of some kind. Viewers learn how homeless kids survive-- by turning to drug-dealing, prostitution and panhandling. The addictiveness of street life, despite its hardships, is described and other methods of handling the runaways' problems are addressed. The viewer also goes along with an employee of the shelter, Children of the Night, as she makes her rounds and attempts to help these children.
*1. Runaway teenagers - California - Los Angeles. 2. Runaway teenagers - New York (State) - New York. 3. Youth - Crimes against - California - Los Angeles. 4. Youth - Crimes against - New York (State) - New York. 5. Homeless youth - California - Los Angeles. 6. Homeless youth - New York (State) - New York. 7. Teenage prostitution - United States. 8. Teenagers - Drug use - United States. 9. Runaway teenagers - United States - Family relationships. 10. Runaway teenagers - United States - Social conditions. 11. Children of the Night (Van Nuys, Calif.) 12. Documentary films. I. Gardner, Janet. II. Conger, Eric. III. Cambridge Educational (Firm) IV. Cambridge Research Group, Ltd. V. Title: Cambridge Educational VI. Series.*
***TC HV1435.C3 C45 1994***

**Children of the night** [videorecording] / producer & director, Janet Gardner ; screenwriter, Janet Gardner ; Cambridge Educational. [Charleston, W.V.] : Cambridge Educational, c1994. 1 videorecording (35 min.) : sd., col. ; 1/2 in. (Running away, dropping out) At head of title: Cambridge Educational. VHS. Catalogued from credits, cassette label and container. Narrator, Eric Conger. Music and lyrics by Richard Marx, published by Chi-Boy Music; director of photography, Len McClure; audio, Isak Ben Meir; editor, Jessie Weiner, Marlo Paoll. Copyright holder: Cambridge Research Group, Ltd. For pre-adolescents through adult. SUMMARY: Runaways discuss their reasons for turning away from their lives and families and moving to the streets. 95% of the kids have been sexually abused by their families or some other trusted adult. 100% of the kids have suffered abuse of some kind. Viewers learn how homeless kids survive-- by turning to drug-dealing, prositution and panhandling. The addictiveness of street life, despite its hardships, is described and other methods of handling the runaways' problems are addressed. The viewer also goes along with an employee of the shelter, Children of the Night, as she makes her rounds and attempts to help these children.
*1. Runaway teenagers - California - Los Angeles. 2. Runaway teenagers - New York (State) - New York. 3. Youth - Crimes against - California - Los Angeles. 4. Youth - Crimes against - New York (State) - New York. 5. Homeless youth - California - Los Angeles. 6. Homeless youth - New York (State) - New York. 7. Homeless youth - Drug use - United States. 8. Teenage prostitution - United States. 9. Runaway teenagers - United States - Family relationships. 10. Runaway teenagers - United States - Social conditions. 11. Runaway teenagers - Drug use - United States. 12. Children of the Night (Van Nuys, Calif.) 13. Documentary films. I. Gardner, Janet. II. Conger, Eric. III. Cambridge Educational (Firm) IV. Cambridge Research Group, Ltd. V. Title: Cambridge Educational VI. Series.*
***TC HV1435.C3 C45 1994***

**CHILDREN OF THE POOR.** *See* **POOR CHILDREN.**

**CHILDREN OF THE STREETS.** *See* **STREET CHILDREN.**

**CHILDREN OF UXORICIDES - MENTAL HEALTH.**
Hendriks, Jean Harris. When father kills mother. 2nd ed. London ; Philadelphia : Routledge, 2000.
***TC RJ506.U96 .B53 2000***

**CHILDREN OF UXORICIDES - REHABILITATION.**
Hendriks, Jean Harris. When father kills mother. 2nd ed. London ; Philadelphia : Routledge, 2000.

*TC RJ506.U96 .B53 2000*

**CHILDREN OF WORKING MOTHERS - UNITED STATES.**
Hoffman, Lois Norma Wladis, 1929- Mothers at work. Cambridge ; New York : Cambridge University Press, 1999.
*TC HQ759.48 .H63 1999*

**Children on the streets of the Americas :**
homelessness, education and globalization in the United States, Brazil and Cuba / edited by Roslyn Arlin Mickelson. London ; New York : Routledge, 2000. 300 p. : ill., maps ; 24 cm. Includes bibliographical references and index. ISBN 0-415-92321-2 (hb) ISBN 0-415-92322-0 (pb) DDC 362.74
*1. Street children - Brazil - Social conditions. 2. Street children - Cuba - Social conditions. 3. Street children - United States - Social conditions. 4. Street children - Education - Brazil. 5. Street children - Education - Cuba. 6. Street children - Education - United States. 7. Street children - Services for - Brazil - Case studies. 8. Street children - Services for - Cuba - Case studies. 9. Street children - Services for - United States - Case studies. I. Mickelson, Roslyn Arlin. 1948-*
*TC HV887.B8 C475 2000*

**CHILDREN - PICTORIAL WORKS - JUVENILE LITERATURE.**
Ajmera, Maya. Children from Australia to Zimbabwe. Watertown, Mass. : Charlesbridge, c1997.
*TC GF48 .A45 1997*

**CHILDREN - POLITICAL ACTIVITY.**
Buckingham, David, 1954- The making of citizens. London ; New York : Routledge, 2000.
*TC HQ784.T4 .B847 2000*

**CHILDREN, POOR.** *See* **POOR CHILDREN.**

**CHILDREN, PRESCHOOL.** *See* **PRESCHOOL CHILDREN.**

**CHILDREN - PROTECTION.** *See* **CHILD WELFARE.**

**CHILDREN - PSYCHOLOGY.** *See* **CHILD PSYCHOLOGY.**

**CHILDREN, PUERTO RICAN.** *See* **PUERTO RICAN CHILDREN.**

**CHILDREN - RELATIONSHIP WITH ADULTS.** *See* **CHILDREN AND ADULTS.**

**CHILDREN - RELIGIOUS LIFE.**
Bea, Holly, 1956- My spiritual alphabet book. Tiburon, Calif. : H.J. Kramer, c2000.
*TC BL625.5 .B43 1999*

Hunt, Gladys M. Honey for a child's heart. 3rd ed. Grand Rapids, Mich. : Zondervan Books, c1989.
*TC Z1037 .H945 1989*

**CHILDREN - RELIGIOUS LIFE - EARLY WORKS TO 1800.**
Jocelin, Elizabeth, 1596-1622. The mothers legacy to her vnborn [i.e. unborn] childe [i.e. child]. Toronto : University of Toronto Press, 2000.
*TC BV4570 .J62 2000*

**CHILDREN - RELIGIOUS LIFE - PERSONAL NARRATIVES.** *See* **CHILDREN - RELIGIOUS LIFE.**

**CHILDREN - RESEARCH.**
Childhood studies. London ; New York : Routledge, 2000.
*TC HQ767.85 .C483 2000*

**CHILDREN - RESEARCH - METHODOLOGY.**
Lewis, Ann, 1950- Researching children's perspectives. Buckingham ; Philadelphia : Open University Press, 2000.
*TC HQ767.85 .L49 2000*

Research with children. New York : Falmer Press, 2000.
*TC HQ767.85 .R48 1999*

**CHILDREN, RETARDED.** *See* **MENTALLY HANDICAPPED CHILDREN.**

**CHILDREN - SCANDINAVIA - SOCIAL CONDITIONS - BIBLIOGRAPHY.**
Research on socialization of young children in the Nordic countries. Aarhus : Aarhus University Press, c1989.
*TC Z7164.S678 R47 1989*

**CHILDREN - SERVICES FOR.** *See* **CHILD CARE SERVICES.**

**CHILDREN - SERVICES FOR - UNITED STATES.**
Collaborative practice. Westport, Conn. ; London : Praeger, 1999.
*TC HV741 .C5424 1999*

**CHILDREN - SERVICES FOR - UNITED STATES - COST CONTROL.**
United States. General Accounting Office. Child welfare. Washington, D.C. (P.O. Box 37050, Washington, D.C. 20013) : The Office, [1998]
*TC HV741 .U525 1998a*

**CHILDREN, SICK.** *See* **SICK CHILDREN.**

**CHILDREN - SOCIAL CONDITIONS.** *See also* **ETHNICITY IN CHILDREN.**
Buckingham, David, 1954- After the death of childhood. Malden, MA : Polity Press, 2000.
*TC HQ784.M3 B83 2000*

Social change for women and children. Stamford, Conn. : JAI Press, 2000.
*TC HQ1421 .S68 2000*

Wyness, Michael G. Contesting childhood. London ; New York : Falmer Press, 2000.
*TC HQ767.9 .W96 2000*

**CHILDREN - SOCIALIZATION.** *See* **SOCIALIZATION.**

**CHILDREN - SUICIDAL BEHAVIOR - UNITED STATES.**
Jamison, Kay R. Night falls fast. 1st ed. New York : Knopf : Distributed by Random House, 1999.
*TC RC569 .J36 1999*

**Children, teachers, and learning.**
Bailey, Richard. Teaching physical education 5-11. New York : Continuum, 2000.
*TC GV443 .B34 2000*

**Children: the magazine for parents. Oct. 1926-July 1929.**
Parents' magazine. New York.

**CHILDREN - TRAINING.** *See* **CHILD REARING.**

**CHILDREN - TRAVEL - FOREIGN COUNTRIES.**
Pollock, David C. The third culture kid experience. Yarmouth, Me. : Intercultural Press, c1999.
*TC HQ784.S56 P65 1999*

**CHILDREN - UNITED STATES.** *See* **AFRO-AMERICAN CHILDREN; ASIAN AMERICAN CHILDREN; CHINESE AMERICAN CHILDREN; HISPANIC AMERICAN CHILDREN; PUERTO RICAN CHILDREN; UNITED STATES - HISTORY - CIVIL WAR, 1861-1865 - PARTICIPATION, JUVENILE.**

**CHILDREN - UNITED STATES - BOOKS AND READING.**
Hirsch, E. D. (Eric Donald), 1928- Books to build on. New York : Delta, 1996.
*TC Z1037 .H646 1996*

Jody, Marilyn, 1932- Using computers to teach literature. 2nd ed. Urbana, Ill. : National Council of Teachers of English, c1998.
*TC LB1050.37 .J63 1998*

**CHILDREN - UNITED STATES - CONDUCT OF LIFE.**
Edelman, Marian Wright. Lanterns. Boston : Beacon Press, c1999.
*TC E185.97.E33 A3 1999*

**CHILDREN - UNITED STATES - DIARIES.**
Madigan, Dan. The writing lives of children. York, ME : Stenhouse Publishers, 1997.
*TC LB1042 .M24 1997*

**CHILDREN - UNITED STATES - HISTORY.**
Childhood in America. New York : New York University Press, c2000.
*TC HQ792.U5 C4199 1999*

**CHILDREN - UNITED STATES - HISTORY - SOURCES.**
Childhood in America. New York : New York University Press, c2000.
*TC HQ792.U5 C4199 1999*

**CHILDREN - UNITED STATES - INTELLIGENCE TESTING - LONGITUDINAL STUDIES.**
Leventhal, Tama. Poverty and turbulence. 1999.
*TC 085 L5515*

**CHILDREN - UNITED STATES - SOCIAL CONDITIONS.**
Securing the future. New York : Russell Sage Foundation, c2000.
*TC HV741 .S385 2000*

**CHILDREN - VOCABULARY.** *See* **CHILDREN - LANGUAGE.**

**CHILDREN'S ART.** *See* **CHILDREN'S DRAWINGS.**

**CHILDREN'S AUDIOBOOKS - UNITED STATES - AUDIOTAPE CATALOGS - PERIODICALS.**
Bowker's directory of audiocassettes for children. New Providence, N.J. : R.R. Bowker, c1998-
*TC ZA4750 .B69*

**CHILDREN'S BOOKS.** *See* **ILLUSTRATED CHILDREN'S BOOKS.**

**CHILDREN'S BOOKS - GREAT BRITAIN - HISTORY - 19TH CENTURY.**
Darling, Harold. From Mother Goose to Dr. Seuss. San Francisco : Chronicle Books, c1999.
*TC Z270.G7 D37 1999*

**CHILDREN'S BOOKS - GREAT BRITAIN - HISTORY - 20TH CENTURY.**
Darling, Harold. From Mother Goose to Dr. Seuss. San Francisco : Chronicle Books, c1999.
*TC Z270.G7 D37 1999*

**Children's books in England.**
Darton, F. J. Harvey (Frederick Joseph Harvey), 1878-1936. 3rd ed. / rev. by Brian Alderson. London : British Library ; New Castle, DE : Oak Knoll Press, 1982 (1999 printing)
*TC PR990 .D3 1999*

**CHILDREN'S BOOKS - UNITED STATES - HISTORY - 19TH CENTURY.**
Darling, Harold. From Mother Goose to Dr. Seuss. San Francisco : Chronicle Books, c1999.
*TC Z270.G7 D37 1999*

**CHILDREN'S BOOKS - UNITED STATES - HISTORY - 20TH CENTURY.**
Darling, Harold. From Mother Goose to Dr. Seuss. San Francisco : Chronicle Books, c1999.
*TC Z270.G7 D37 1999*

**Children's classic literature.**
Goldsworthy, Candace L. Sourcebook of phonological awareness activities. San Diego : Singular Pub. Group, c1998.
*TC LB1050.5 .G66 1998*

**Children's construction of personal meanings of mathematical symbolism in a reform-oriented classroom.**
Seo, Kyoung-Hye. 2000.
*TC 06 no. 11310*

**CHILDREN'S DAY CARE CENTERS.** *See* **DAY CARE CENTERS.**

**CHILDREN'S DISEASES.** *See* **CHILDREN - DISEASES.**

**CHILDREN'S DRAMA.** *See* **CHILDREN'S PLAYS.**

**CHILDREN'S DRAWINGS - PSYCHOLOGICAL ASPECTS.**
Hafeli, Mary Claire. Drawing and painting in the middle school. 1999.
*TC 06 no. 11055*

**CHILDREN'S DRAWINGS - PSYCHOLOGICAL ASPECTS - SEX DIFFERENCES.**
Tuman, Donna M. Gender difference in form and content. 1998.
*TC 06 no. 11000*

**CHILDREN'S DRAWINGS - THEMES, MOTIVES - SEX DIFFERENCES.**
Tuman, Donna M. Gender difference in form and content. 1998.
*TC 06 no. 11000*

**Children's dreaming and the development of consciousness.**
Foulkes, David, 1935- Cambridge, Mass. : Harvard University Press, 1999.
*TC BF1099.C55 F67 1999*

**CHILDREN'S DREAMS.**
Foulkes, David, 1935- Children's dreaming and the development of consciousness. Cambridge, Mass. : Harvard University Press, 1999.
*TC BF1099.C55 F67 1999*

**CHILDREN'S ENCYCLOPEDIAS AND DICTIONARIES.**
Children's illustrated encyclopedia. [2nd] rev. ed. New York : DK Pub., 1998.
*TC AG5 .C535 1998*

**Children's films.**
Wojcik-Andrews, Ian, 1952- New York : Garland Pub., 2000.
*TC PN1995.9.C45 W59 2000*

**CHILDREN'S FILMS - CATALOGS - PERIODICALS.**
Bowker's directory of videocassettes for children. New Providence, N.J. : R.R. Bowker, c1998-

**TC** *PN1992.945 .B66*

**CHILDREN'S FILMS - HISTORY AND CRITICISM.**
Wojcik-Andrews, Ian, 1952- Children's films. New York : Garland Pub., 2000.
**TC** *PN1995.9.C45 W59 2000*

**Children's games from around the world.**
Kirchner, Glenn. 2nd ed. Boston : Allyn and Bacon, c2000.
**TC** *GV1203 .K65 2000*

**Children's geographies :** playing, living, learning / edited by Sarah L. Holloway and Gill Valentine. London ; New York : Routledge, 2000. xvii, 275 p. : ill., maps ; 24 cm. (Critical geographies ; 8) Includes bibliographical references and index. ISBN 0-415-20729-0 (hbk. : acid-free paper) ISBN 0-415-20730-4 (pbk. : acid-free paper) DDC 305.23
*1. Children. 2. Human geography. I. Holloway, Sarah, 1970- II. Valentine, Gill, 1965- III. Series.*
**TC** *HQ767.9 .C4559 2000*

**CHILDREN'S ILLUSTRATED BOOKS.** *See* **ILLUSTRATED CHILDREN'S BOOKS.**

**Children's illustrated encyclopedia.** [2nd] rev. ed. New York : DK Pub., 1998. 644 p. : col. ill. ; 29 cm. Rev. ed. of: The Random House children's encyclopedia. Rev. ed. 1993. Includes index. SUMMARY: A highly illustrated one-volume encyclopedia containing 450 main entries ranging from Aboriginal Australians to Zoos. ISBN 0-7894-2787-7
*1. Children's encyclopedias and dictionaries. 2. Encyclopedias and dictionaries. <Juvenile subject heading>. I. DK Publishing, Inc. II. Title: Random House children's encyclopedia.*
**TC** *AG5 .C535 1998*

**Children's interests/mothers' rights.**
Michel, Sonya, 1942- New Haven, CT : Yale University Press, c1999.
**TC** *HQ778.63 .M52 1999*

**Children's journeys through the information age.**
Calvert, Sandra L. 1st ed. Boston : McGraw-Hill College, c1999.
**TC** *HQ784.T4 C24 1999*

**CHILDREN'S LIBRARIES.** *See* **LIBRARIES AND HANDICAPPED CHILDREN; LIBRARIES - SERVICES TO PRESCHOOL CHILDREN.**

**CHILDREN'S LIBRARIES - ACTIVITY PROGRAMS - UNITED STATES.**
Cullum, Carolyn N. The storytime sourcebook. 2nd ed. New York ; London : Neal-Schuman Publishers, c1999.
**TC** *Z718.3 .C85 1999*

Druce, Arden. Paper bag puppets. Lanham, MD : Scarecrow Press, 1999.
**TC** *Z718.3 .D78 1999*

**CHILDREN'S LIBRARIES - BOOK LISTS.**
Schon, Isabel. Recommended books in Spanish for children and young adults, 1996 through 1999. Lanham, Md. : Scarecrow Press, 2000.
**TC** *Z1037.7 .S387 2000*

**CHILDREN'S LIBRARIES - BOOK SELECTION.**
Reading in series. New Providence, N.J. : R.R. Bowker, c1999.
**TC** *Z1037 .R36 1999*

**CHILDREN'S LITERATURE.** *See* **CHILDREN'S LITERATURE IN SERIES; CHILDREN'S PLAYS; CHILDREN'S STORIES.**

**CHILDREN'S LITERATURE, AMERICAN - AFRO-AMERICAN AUTHORS - AWARDS.**
The Coretta Scott King awards book, 1970-1999. Chicago : American Library Association, 1999.
**TC** *Z1037.A2 C67 1999*

**CHILDREN'S LITERATURE, AMERICAN - AFRO-AMERICAN AUTHORS - BIBLIOGRAPHY.**
The Coretta Scott King awards book, 1970-1999. Chicago : American Library Association, 1999.
**TC** *Z1037.A2 C67 1999*

**CHILDREN'S LITERATURE, AMERICAN - BIBLIOGRAPHY.**
Gunning, Thomas G. Best books for building literacy for elementary school children. Boston : Allyn and Bacon, 2000.
**TC** *LB1573 .B47 2000*

**CHILDREN'S LITERATURE, AMERICAN - BIO-BIBLIOGRAPHY - DICTIONARIES.**
McElmeel, Sharron L. 100 most popular children's authors. Englewood, Colo. : Libraries Unlimited, 1999.

**TC** *PS490 .M39 1999*

**CHILDREN'S LITERATURE, AMERICAN - HISTORY AND CRITICISM.**
Literature and the child. Iowa City : University of Iowa Press, c1999.
**TC** *PR990 .L58 1999*

MacCann, Donnarae. White supremacy in children's literature. New York : Garland Pub., 1998.
**TC** *PS173.N4 M33 1998*

Morris, Timothy, 1959- You're only young twice. Urbana : University of Illinois Press, c2000.
**TC** *PR990 .M67 2000*

Rollin, Lucy. Psychoanalytic responses to children's literature. Jefferson, N.C. : McFarland, c1999.
**TC** *PR990 .R65 1999*

**CHILDREN'S LITERATURE, AMERICAN - ILLUSTRATIONS - EXHIBITIONS.**
Myth, magic and mystery. Boulder, Colo. : Roberts Rinehart Publishers ; [Norfolk, Va.] : in cooperation with the Chrysler Museum of Art, c1996.
**TC** *NC975 .M98 1996*

**Children's literature and culture**
(v. 10) McGillis, Roderick. Voices of the other. New York : Garland Publishing., Inc., c2000.
**TC** *PN344 .M35 2000*

**CHILDREN'S LITERATURE - AUTHORSHIP.**
Talking books. London ; New York : Routledge, 1999.
**TC** *PR990 .T35 1999*

Transcending boundaries. New York : Garland, 1999.
**TC** *PN1009.A1 T69 1999*

**CHILDREN'S LITERATURE - BIBLIOGRAPHY.**
Littlejohn, Carol. Talk that book! booktalks to promote reading. Worthington, Ohio : Linworth Publishing, 1999.
**TC** *Z1037.A2 L58 1999*

Savage, John F., 1938- For the love of literature. Boston : McGraw-Hill, c2000.
**TC** *LB1575 .S28 2000*

Wilson, Elizabeth Laraway. Books children love. Westchester, Ill. : Crossway Books, c1987.
**TC** *Z1037 .W745 1987*

**Children's literature, briefly.**
Tunnell, Michael O. 2nd ed. Upper Saddle River, N.J. : Merrill, c2000.
**TC** *PN1008.8 .J33 2000*

**CHILDREN'S LITERATURE, CANADIAN (ENGLISH) - STUDY AND TEACHING (ELEMENTARY).**
Young adolescents meet literature. Vancouver : Pacific Education Press, 2000.
**TC** *LB1575.5.C3 Y68 2000*

**CHILDREN'S LITERATURE, ENGLISH - BIBLIOGRAPHY.**
Best books for young teen readers, grades 7 to 10. New Providence, N.J. : R.R. Bowker, 2000.
**TC** *Z1037 .B55 2000*

Darton, F.J. Harvey (Frederick Joseph Harvey), 1878-1936. Children's books in England. 3rd ed. / rev. by Brian Alderson. London : British Library ; New Castle, DE : Oak Knoll Press, 1982 (1999 printing)
**TC** *PR990 .D3 1999*

**CHILDREN'S LITERATURE, ENGLISH - BIO-BIBLIOGRAPHY - DICTIONARIES.**
McElmeel, Sharron L. 100 most popular children's authors. Englewood, Colo. : Libraries Unlimited, 1999.
**TC** *PS490 .M39 1999*

**CHILDREN'S LITERATURE, ENGLISH - BOOK REVIEWS.**
Cianciolo, Patricia J. Informational picture books for children. Chicago : American Library Association, 2000.
**TC** *Z1037.A1 C54 1999*

**CHILDREN'S LITERATURE, ENGLISH - HISTORY AND CRITICISM.**
Darton, F. J. Harvey (Frederick Joseph Harvey), 1878-1936. Children's books in England. 3rd ed. / rev. by Brian Alderson. London : British Library ; New Castle, DE : Oak Knoll Press, 1982 (1999 printing)
**TC** *PR990 .D3 1999*

Literature and the child. Iowa City : University of Iowa Press, c1999.
**TC** *PR990 .L58 1999*

Morris, Timothy, 1959- You're only young twice. Urbana : University of Illinois Press, c2000.

**TC** *PR990 .M67 2000*

Rollin, Lucy. Psychoanalytic responses to children's literature. Jefferson, N.C. : McFarland, c1999.
**TC** *PR990 .R65 1999*

**CHILDREN'S LITERATURE, ENGLISH - HISTORY AND CRITICISM - THEORY, ETC.**
Talking books. London ; New York ; Routledge, 1999.
**TC** *PR990 .T35 1999*

**CHILDREN'S LITERATURE - FILM AND VIDEO ADAPTATIONS.**
Morris, Timothy, 1959- You're only young twice. Urbana : University of Illinois Press, c2000.
**TC** *PR990 .M67 2000*

**Children's literature for the primary inclusive classroom.**
Turner, Nancy D'Isa. Albany, N.Y. : Delmar Publishers, c2000.
**TC** *LC4028 .T87 2000*

**CHILDREN'S LITERATURE - HISTORY AND CRITICISM.**
Girls, boys, books, toys. Baltimore : Johns Hopkins University Press, 1999.
**TC** *PN1009.5.S48 G57 1999*

McGillis, Roderick. Voices of the other. New York : Garland Publishing., Inc., c2000.
**TC** *PN344 .M35 2000*

Nikolajeva, Maria. From mythic to linear. Lanham, Md. : Children's Literature Association : Scarecrow Press, 2000.
**TC** *PN1009.5.T55 N55 2000*

Savage, John F., 1938- For the love of literature. Boston : McGraw-Hill, c2000.
**TC** *LB1575 .S28 2000*

Stephens, John, 1944- Retelling stories, framing culture. New York : Garland Pub., 1998.
**TC** *PN1009.A1 S83 1998*

Transcending boundaries. New York : Garland, 1999.
**TC** *PN1009.A1 T69 1999*

Tunnell, Michael O. Children's literature, briefly. 2nd ed. Upper Saddle River, N.J. : Merrill, c2000.
**TC** *PN1008.8 .J33 2000*

Understanding children's literature. London ; New York : Routledge, 1999.
**TC** *PN1009.A1 U44 1999*

**CHILDREN'S LITERATURE - HISTORY AND CRITICISM - PERIODICALS.**
[Lion and the unicorn (Baltimore, Md. : Online)] The lion and the unicorn [computer file]. Baltimore, MD : Johns Hopkins University Press, c1995-
**TC** *EJOURNALS*

**CHILDREN'S LITERATURE - ILLUSTRATIONS - PSYCHOLOGICAL ASPECTS.**
Rollin, Lucy. Psychoanalytic responses to children's literature. Jefferson, N.C. : McFarland, c1999.
**TC** *PR990 .R65 1999*

**CHILDREN'S LITERATURE IN MATHEMATICS EDUCATION.**
Whitin, David Jackman, 1947- It's the story that counts. Portsmouth, NH : Heinemann, c1995.
**TC** *QA135.5 .W465 1995*

**CHILDREN'S LITERATURE IN SERIES - BIBLIOGRAPHY.**
Reading in series. New Providence, N.J. : R.R. Bowker, c1999.
**TC** *Z1037 .R36 1999*

**Children's literature in the elementary school /** Charlotte S. Huck ... [et al.]. 7th ed. Dubuque, IA : McGraw-Hill, c2001. xx, 682 p. : ill. (some col.) ; 29 cm. + computer optical disk (4 3/4 in.). Includes bibliographical references and indexes. ISBN 0-07-232228-4 (acid-free paper) DDC 372.64
*1. Literature - Study and teaching (Elementary) - United States. 2. Children's literature - Study and teaching (Elementary) - United States. I. Huck, Charlotte S.*
**TC** *LB1575.5.U5 H79 2001*

**CHILDREN'S LITERATURE - PSYCHOLOGICAL ASPECTS.**
Rollin, Lucy. Psychoanalytic responses to children's literature. Jefferson, N.C. : McFarland, c1999.
**TC** *PR990 .R65 1999*

**CHILDREN'S LITERATURE - PUBLISHING - ENGLAND - HISTORY.**
Darton, F. J. Harvey (Frederick Joseph Harvey), 1878-1936. Children's books in England. 3rd ed. / rev. by Brian Alderson. London : British Library ; New Castle, DE : Oak Knoll Press, 1982 (1999 printing)

*TC PR990 .D3 1999*

## CHILDREN'S LITERATURE, SPANISH AMERICAN - BIBLIOGRAPHY.
Schon, Isabel. Recommended books in Spanish for children and young adults, 1996 through 1999. Lanham, Md. : Scarecrow Press, 2000.
*TC Z1037.7 .S387 2000*

## CHILDREN'S LITERATURE, SPANISH - BIBLIOGRAPHY.
Schon, Isabel. Recommended books in Spanish for children and young adults, 1996 through 1999. Lanham, Md. : Scarecrow Press, 2000.
*TC Z1037.7 .S387 2000*

## CHILDREN'S LITERATURE - STUDY AND TEACHING.
Beech, Linda Ward. The cay by Theodore Taylor. New York : Scholastic, c1997.
*TC LB1573 .B4312 1997*

Beech, Linda Ward. Danny the champion of the world by Roald Dahl. New York : Scholastic, c1997.
*TC LB11573 .B431 1997*

Beech, Linda Ward. Danny the champion of the world by Roald Dahl. New York : Scholastic, c1997.
*TC LB1573 .B431 1997*

Beech, Linda Ward. The diary of a young girl by Anne Frank. New York : Scholastic, c1998.
*TC LB1573 .B433 1998*

Beech, Linda Ward. The great fire by Jim Murphy. New York : Scholastic, c1996.
*TC LB11573 .B437 1996*

Beech, Linda Ward. The great fire by Jim Murphy. New York : Scholastic, c1996.
*TC LB1573 .B437 1996*

Beech, Linda Ward. The great Gilly Hopkins by Katherine Paterson. New York : Scholastic, c1998.
*TC LB1573 .B439 1998*

Beech, Linda Ward. Guests by Michael Dorris. New York, NY : Scholastic, c1996.
*TC LB1573 .B432 1996*

Beech, Linda Ward. Hatchet by Gary Paulsen. New York : Scholastic, c1998.
*TC LB1573 .B4310 1998*

Beech, Linda Ward. Island of the blue dolphins by Scott O'Dell. New York : Scholastic, c1997.
*TC LB1573 .B438 1997*

Beech, Linda Ward. Julie of the wolves by Jean Craighead George. New York : Scholastic, c1996.
*TC LB1573 .B434 1996*

Beech, Linda Ward. Maniac Magee by Jerry Spinelli. New York : Scholastic, c1997.
*TC LB1573 .B4311 1997*

Beech, Linda Ward. Sarah, plain and tall by Patricia MacLachlan. New York : Scholastic, c1996.
*TC LB1573 .B436 1996*

Beech, Linda Ward. Tuck everlasting by Natalie Babbitt. New York : Scholastic, c1997.
*TC LB1573 .B43 1997*

Beech, Linda Ward. A wrinkle in time by Madeleine L'Engle. New York : Scholastic, c1997.
*TC LB1573 .B435 1997*

Gutner, Howard. Caddie Woodlawn by Carol Ryrie Brink. New York : Scholastic, c1997.
*TC LB1573 .G87 1997*

McCarthy, Tara. My brother Sam is dead by James Lincoln Collier and Christopher Collier. New York : Scholastic, c1997.
*TC LB1573 .M32 1997*

Rawlings, Carol Miller. The lion, the witch and the wardrobe by C. S. Lewis. New York : Scholastic, c1997.
*TC LB1573 .R38 1997*

Tunnell, Michael O. Children's literature, briefly. 2nd ed. Upper Saddle River, N.J. : Merrill, c2000.
*TC PN1008.8 .J33 2000*

## CHILDREN'S LITERATURE - STUDY AND TEACHING (EARLY CHILDHOOD) - UNITED STATES.
Glazer, Joan I. Literature for young children. 4th ed. Upper Saddle River, N.J. : Merrill, 2000.
*TC Z1037.A1 G573 2000*

## CHILDREN'S LITERATURE - STUDY AND TEACHING (ELEMENTARY).
Chatton, Barbara. Blurring the edges. Portsmouth, NH : Heinemann, c1999.

*TC LB1576 .C46 1999*

Hancock, Marjorie R. A celebration of literature and response. Upper Saddle River, N.J. : Merrill, c2000.
*TC LB1575 .H36 2000*

Mikkelsen, Nina. Words and pictures. Boston : McGraw-Hill, c2000.
*TC LB1575 .M55 2000*

PHINN, GERVASE. Young readers and their books. London : David Fulton, 2000.
*TC LB1575 .P45 2000*

Savage, John F., 1938- For the love of literature. Boston : McGraw-Hill, c2000.
*TC LB1575 .S28 2000*

## CHILDREN'S LITERATURE - STUDY AND TEACHING (ELEMENTARY) - UNITED STATES.
Buzzeo, Toni. Terrific connections with authors, illustrators, and storytellers. Englewood, Colo. : Libraries Unlimited, 1999.
*TC LB1575.5.U5 B87 1999*

Children's literature in the elementary school. 7th ed. Dubuque, IA : McGraw-Hill, c2001.
*TC LB1575.5.U5 H79 2001*

Fredericks, Anthony D. More social studies through children's literature. Englewood, Colo. : Teacher Ideas Press, 2000.
*TC LB1584 .F659 2000*

Singleton, Laurel R., 1950- H is for history. Boulder, Colo. : Social Science Education Consortium, 1995.
*TC LB1582.U6 S56 1995*

## CHILDREN'S LITERATURE - STUDY AND TEACHING (PRESCHOOL) - UNITED STATES.
Sawyer, Walter. Growing up with literature. 3rd ed. Albany, N.Y. : Delmar, c2000.
*TC LB1140.5.L3 S28 2000*

## CHILDREN'S LITERATURE - STUDY AND TEACHING (PRIMARY).
Opitz, Michael F. Rhymes & reasons. Portsmouth, NH : Heinemann, c2000.
*TC LB1528 .O65 2000*

## CHILDREN'S LITERATURE - STUDY AND TEACHING (PRIMARY) - GREAT BRITAIN.
Teaching through texts. London ; New York : Routledge, 1999.
*TC LB1573 .T39 1999*

## CHILDREN'S LITERATURE - STUDY AND TEACHING (PRIMARY) - UNITED STATES.
Turner, Nancy D'Isa. Children's literature for the primary inclusive classroom. Albany, N.Y. : Delmar Publishers, c2000.
*TC LC4028 .T87 2000*

## CHILDREN'S LITERATURE - TRANSLATIONS INTO SPANISH - BIBLIOGRAPHY.
Schon, Isabel. Recommended books in Spanish for children and young adults, 1996 through 1999. Lanham, Md. : Scarecrow Press, 2000.
*TC Z1037.7 .S387 2000*

## CHILDREN'S MASS MEDIA. *See* AUDIOCASSETTES FOR CHILDREN.

**Children's music for children.**
James, Phoebe L. Accompaniments for rhythmic expressions. [Los Angeles? : s.n.], c1946.
*TC M1993.J18 A3*

## CHILDREN'S PARAPHERNALIA. *See* CHILDREN'S BOOKS; TOYS.

**Children's peer relations** / edited by Phillip T. Slee and Ken Rigby. London ; New York : Routledge, 1998. xv, 340 p. : ill. ; 24 cm. (International library of psychology) Includes bibliographical references (p. [288]-331) and indexes. ISBN 0-415-15392-1 (hardcover) DDC 155.4/18
*1. Interpersonal relations in children. I. Slee, Phillip T. II. Rigby, Ken. III. Series.*
*TC BF723.I646 C47 1998*

## CHILDREN'S PICTURE BOOKS. *See* PICTURE BOOKS FOR CHILDREN.

## CHILDREN'S PLAYHOUSES. *See* TREE HOUSES.

## CHILDREN'S PLAYS - PRESENTATION, ETC.
Croteau, Jan Helling. Perform it!. Portsmouth, NH : Heinemann, c2000.
*TC PN3157 .C76 2000*

## CHILDREN'S POETRY. *See also* LULLABIES.
Dana, Katharine Floyd, 1835-1886. Over in the meadow. New York : Scholastic, c1992

*TC PZ8.3.D2 Ov 1992*

Ivimey, John W. (John William), b. 1868. [Complete version of ye Three blind mice] Three blind mice. New York : G.P. Putnam's Sons, c1991.
*TC PZ8.3.I83 Th 1991*

Johnson, Eleanor M. (Eleanor Murdoch), 1892-1987. Treat shop. Columbus, Ohio : Charles E. Merrill, c1954.
*TC PE1119 .J63 1954*

A journey through time in verse and rhyme. Rev. ed. Edinburgh : Floris Books, 1998.
*TC PN6109.97 .J68 1998*

My mane catches the wind. 1st ed. New York : Harcourt Brace Jovanovich, c1979.
*TC PN6110.H7 M9*

Time is the longest distance. 1st ed. New York, NY : HarperCollins, c1991.
*TC PN6109.97 .T56 1991*

## CHILDREN'S POETRY, AMERICAN.
George, Kristine O'Connell. Old Elm speaks. New York : Clarion Books, c1998.
*TC PS3557.E488 O4 1998*

Heide, Florence Parry. It's about time!. New York : Clarion Books, c1999.
*TC PS3558.E427 I77 1999*

Hubbell, Patricia. Boo!. 1st ed. New York : Marshall Cavendish, 1998.
*TC PS3558.U22 B66 1998*

Jacobs, Leland B. (Leland Blair), 1907- Just around the corner. New York : H. Holt, 1993.
*TC PS3560.A2545 J87 1993*

Land, sea & sky. 1st ed. Boston : Joy Street Books, c1993.
*TC PS595.N22 L36 1993*

Livingston, Myra Cohn. Celebrations. 1st ed. New York : Holiday House, c1985.
*TC PS3562.I945 C4 1985*

Livingston, Myra Cohn. Cricket never does. New York : Margaret K. McElderry Books, c1997.
*TC PS3562.I945 C75 1997*

Livingston, Myra Cohn. Earth songs. 1st ed. New York : Holiday House, c1986.
*TC PS3562.I945 E3 1986*

Livingston, Myra Cohn. Flights of fancy and other poems. 1st ed. New York : M.K. McElderry Books ; Toronto : Maxwell Macmillan Canada ; New York : Maxwell Macmillan International, c1994.
*TC PS3562.I945 F58 1994*

Livingston, Myra Cohn. No way of knowing. 1st ed. New York : Atheneum, 1980.
*TC PS3562.I945 N6 1980*

Livingston, Myra Cohn. Sea songs. 1st ed. New York : Holiday House, c1986.
*TC PS3562.I945 S4 1986*

Livingston, Myra Cohn. Sky songs. 1st ed. New York : Holiday House, c1984.
*TC PS3562.I945 S5 1984*

Livingston, Myra Cohn. Up in the air. 1st ed. New York : Holiday House, c1989.
*TC PS3562.I945 U6 1989*

Michelson, Richard. A book of flies. New York : Cavendish Children's Books, 1999.
*TC PS3563.I34 B66 1999*

Poems for fathers. 1st ed. New York : Holiday House, c1989.
*TC PS595.F39 P64 1989*

Sierra, Judy. Antarctic antics. 1st ed. San Diego : Harcourt Brace & Co., c1998.
*TC PS3569.I39 A53 1998*

The sky is full of song. 1st ed. New York : Harper & Row, c1983.
*TC PS595.S42 S5 1983*

Swann, Brian. The house with no door. 1st ed. San Diego : Harcourt Brace & Company., c1998.
*TC PS3569.W256 H6 1998*

To the zoo. 1st ed. Boston : Little, Brown, c1992.
*TC PS595.Z66 T6 1992*

Updike, John. A child's calendar. <Rev. ed.>. New York : Holiday House, 1999.
*TC PS3571.P4 C49 1999*

What's on the menu? New York : Viking, 1992.

TC PS595.F65 W48 1992
Wherever home begins. New York : Orchard Books,
c1995.
*TC PS595.H645 W48 1995*

Yolen, Jane. Ring of earth. 1st ed. San Diego :
Harcourt Brace Jovanovich, c1986.
*TC PS3575.O43 R5 1986*

**CHILDREN'S POETRY, AMERICAN - INDIAN
AUTHORS.**
When the rain sings. New York : Simon & Schuster
Books for Young Readers, 1999.
*TC PS591.I55 W48 1999*

**CHILDREN'S POETRY, ENGLISH.**
Poems for fathers. 1st ed. New York : Holiday House,
c1989.
*TC PS595.F39 P64 1989*

Simon, Francesca. Calling all toddlers. 1st American
ed. New York : Orchard Books, 1999.
*TC PZ8.3.S5875 Cal 1999*

**CHILDREN'S POETRY, RUSSIAN - 20TH
CENTURY.**
Mayakovsky, Vladimir, 1893-1930. Kem byt'?
[Moskva] : Gosudarstvennoe izdatel'stvo, 1929.
*TC PN6110.O32 M39 1929 Rus*

**Children's reading choices.**
Coles, Martin, 1952- London ; New York : Routledge,
1999.
*TC Z1037.A1 C59 1999*

**Children's reasoning and the mind** / edited by Pete
Mitchell, Kevin John Riggs. Hove : Psychology,
c2000. xiv, 415 p. : ill. ; 25 cm. Includes bibliographical
references and indexes. ISBN 0-86377-854-2 DDC 155.41343
*1. Reasoning in children. 2. Philosophy of mind in children. I.
Riggs, Kevin John. II. Mitchell, Peter, 1959-*
*TC BF723.R4 C555 2000*

**CHILDREN'S RIGHTS.**
Buckingham, David, 1954- After the death of
childhood. Malden, MA : Polity Press, 2000.
*TC HQ784.M3 B83 2000*

**Children's rights and traditional values** / edited by
Gillian Douglas, Leslie Sebba. Aldershot ; Brookfield,
USA : Ashgate/Dartmouth, c1998. xv, 335 p. ; 23 cm.
(Programme on International Rights of the Child) Papers
originally presented at a symposium held at the Faculty of Law
of the Hebrew University of Jerusalem in March 1996.
Includes bibliographical references. ISBN 1-85521-956-5 (hb)
DDC 346.01/35
*1. Children - Legal status, laws, etc. - Congresses. 2.
Children - Legal status, laws, etc. - Israel - Congresses. I.
Douglas, Gillian. II. Sebba, Leslie. III. Series: Programme on
the International Rights of the Child (Series)*
*TC K639 .A55 1998*

**Children's rights, therapists' responsibilities :**
feminist commentaries / Gail Anderson, Marcia Hill,
editors. New York : Harrington Park Press, c1997. 141
p. ; 22 cm. "Simultaneously issued by the Haworth Press, Inc.,
under the same title, as a special issue of the journal Women &
therapy, volume 20, number 2, 1997." Includes bibliographical
references and index. ISBN 0-7890-0326-0 (alk. paper) ISBN
1-56023-100-9 (alk. paper) DDC 618.92/8914
*1. Child psychotherapy. 2. Feminist therapy. 3. Adolescent
psychotherapy. I. Anderson, Gail (Gail O.) II. Hill, Marcia.*
*TC RJ504 .C486 1997*

**CHILDREN'S SOFTWARE - UNITED STATES -
CATALOGS.**
CD-ROMS for kids :. [Chicago, Ill.] : American
Library Association, Booklist Publications, 1997.
*TC QA76.76.C54 C47 1997*

**CHILDREN'S SONGS.** *See also* **LULLABIES.**
Berel, Marianne. Musical play sessions. [S.l. : s.n.],
1994.
*TC ML3920 .B45 1994*

James, Phoebe L. Accompaniments for rhythmic
expressions. [Los Angeles? : s.n.], c1946.
*TC M1993.J18 A3*

**CHILDREN'S SONGS - STUDY AND TEACHING
(PRIMARY).**
Teacher toolbox [kit]. Chicago, Ill. : Open Court Pub.
Co., c1995.
*TC LB1573.3 .T4 1995*

**CHILDREN'S SONGS - TEXTS.**
All the pretty little horses. New York : Clarion Books,
c1999.
*TC PZ8.3 .A4165 1999*

**Children's source monitoring** / [edited by] Kim P.
Roberts, Mark Blades. Mahwah, N.J. ; London :
Lawrence Erlbaum Associates, 2000. ix, 359 p. : ill. ; 24
cm. Includes bibliographical references and indexes. ISBN

0-8058-3326-9 (alk. paper) DDC 155.4/1312
*1. Memory in children. 2. Cognition in children. I. Roberts,
Kim P. II. Blades, Mark.*
*TC BF723.M4 C45 2000*

**CHILDREN'S STORIES.** *See also* **FAIRY TALES;
STORYTELLING.**
Johnson, Eleanor M. (Eleanor Murdoch), 1892-1987.
Treat shop. Columbus, Ohio : Charles E. Merrill,
c1954.
*TC PE1119 .J63 1954*

**CHILDREN'S STORIES, AMERICAN.**
Second sight. New York : Philomel Books, 1999.
*TC PZ5 .S4375 1999*

Tomorrowland. New York : Scholastic Press, 1999.
*TC PZ5 .T6235 1999*

**CHILDREN'S STORIES, AMERICAN -
BIBLIOGRAPHY.**
Reading in series. New Providence, N.J. : R.R.
Bowker, c1999.
*TC Z1037 .R36 1999*

**CHILDREN'S STORIES, AMERICAN - HISTORY
AND CRITICISM.**
O'Keefe, Deborah. Good girl messages. New York :
Continuum, 2000.
*TC PS374.G55 O44 2000*

**CHILDREN'S STORIES, ENGLISH - HISTORY
AND CRITICISM.**
Kutzer, M. Daphne. Empire's children. New York :
Garland Pub., 2000.
*TC PR830.I54 K88 2000*

O'Keefe, Deborah. Good girl messages. New York :
Continuum, 2000.
*TC PS374.G55 O44 2000*

Williams, John Tyerman. Pooh and the millennium.
1st American ed. New York : Dutton Books, 1999.
*TC PR6025.I65 Z975 1999*

**CHILDREN'S STORIES - HISTORY AND
CRITICISM.**
McCallum, Robyn. Ideologies of identity in
adolescent fiction. New York : Garland Pub., 1999.
*TC PN3443 .M38 1999*

**CHILDREN'S STORIES - STUDY AND
TEACHING - UNITED STATES.**
Nelsen, Marjorie R. Peak with books. 3rd ed.
Thousand Oaks, Calif. : Corwin Press, c1999.
*TC Z1037.A1 N347 1999*

**CHILDREN'S THEATER.** *See* **CHILDREN'S
PLAYS - PRESENTATION, ETC.**

**Children's understanding of biology and health** /
edited by Michael Siegal and Candida C. Peterson. 1st
ed. Cambridge, U.K. ; New York : Cambridge
University Press, 1999. xiii, 291 p. : ill. ; 24 cm.
(Cambridge studies in cognitive perceptual development)
Includes bibliographical references and indexes. ISBN
0-521-62098-8 (hbk.) DDC 370.15/2
*1. Cognition in children. 2. Biology. 3. Health. I. Siegal,
Michael. II. Peterson, Candida D. (Candida Clifford) III.
Series.*
*TC BF723.C5 C514 1999*

**CHILDREN'S WEB SITES - DIRECTORIES.**
Polly, Jean Armour. The Internet kids & family
yellow pages. Millenium ed. Berkeley, Calif. :
Osborne McGraw-Hill, c2000.
*TC ZA4226 .P6 2000*

**CHILDREN'S WRITINGS.**
When the rain sings. New York : Simon & Schuster
Books for Young Readers, 1999.
*TC PS591.I55 W48 1999*

**CHILDREN'S WRITINGS, AMERICAN.**
When the rain sings. New York : Simon & Schuster
Books for Young Readers, 1999.
*TC PS591.I55 W48 1999*

**Childress, Herb, 1958-** Landscapes of betrayal,
landscapes of joy : Curtisville in the lives of its
teenagers / Herb Childress. Albany [N.Y.] : State
University of New York Press, c2000. xx, 351 p. : ill.,
plans ; 24 cm. (SUNY series in environmental and architectural
phenomenology) Includes bibliographical references (p. 317-
344) and index. ISBN 0-7914-4577-1 (hbk : alk. paper) ISBN
0-7914-4578-X (pbk : alk. paper) DDC 305.235/09794
*1. Teenagers - California - Social conditions - Case studies. 2.
Adolescent psychology - California - Case studies. 3. Spatial
behavior - California - Case studies. 4. Environment and
teenagers - California - Case studies. 5. Architecture and
youth - California - Case studies. I. Title. II. Series.*
*TC HQ796 .C458237 2000*

**Child's brain.** Basel, New York, Karger. 11 v. ill. 25 cm.
Frequency: Bimonthly. Former frequency: Bimonthly. Former
frequency: Monthly. v. 1-11; 1975-1984. Official journal of the
International Society for Paediatric Neurosurgery. Indexed in
its entirety by: Excerpta medica. Indexed selectively by:
Biological abstracts 0006-3169. Indexed selectively by: Index
medicus 0019-3879. Indexed selectively by: Life sciences
collection. Indexed by: Current contents. Continued by:
Pediatric neuroscience ISSN: 0255-7975 (OCoLC)13028013.
ISSN 0302-2803
*1. Brain Diseases - in infancy & childhood - periodicals. 2.
Neuroscience - in infancy & childhood - periodicals. I.
International Society for Paediatric Neurosurgery. II. Title:
Pediatric neuroscience*

**A child's calendar.**
Updike, John. <Rev. ed.> New York : Holiday
House, 1999.
*TC PS3571.P4 C49 1999*

**The child's conception of the world. Translated by
Joan and Andrew Tomlinson.**
Piaget, Jean, 1896-1980. [Représentation du monde
chez l'enfant. English] Paterson, N.J., Littlefield,
Adams, 1960.
*TC BF721 .P513 1960*

**Childs, John Brown.**
Global visions. 1st ed. Boston : South End Press,
c1993.
*TC HF1359 .G58 1993*

**The child's world :** triggers for learning / edited by
Margaret Robertson, Rod Gerber. Camberwell, Vic. :
ACER Press, 2000. xvii, 378 p. : ill. ; 27 cm. Includes
bibliographical references and indexes. ISBN 0-86431-301-2
(pbk.)
*1. Cognition in children. 2. Reasoning in children. 3.
Experience in children. I. Robertson, Margaret. II. Gerber,
Rodney. III. Australian Council for Educational Research.*
*TC BF723.C5 C467 2000*

**CHIMES.** *See* **HANDCHIMES.**

**Chin, Tiffani.**
Rabow, Jerome. Tutoring matters. Philadelphia :
Temple University Press, 1999.
*TC LC41 .R33 1999*

**CHINA - FOREIGN PUBLIC OPINION,
AMERICAN - HISTORY - 18TH CENTURY.**
Tchen, John Kuo Wei. New York before Chinatown.
Baltimore : Johns Hopkins University Press, 1999.
*TC DS706 .T4 1999*

**CHINA - FOREIGN PUBLIC OPINION,
AMERICAN - HISTORY - 19TH CENTURY.**
Tchen, John Kuo Wei. New York before Chinatown.
Baltimore : Johns Hopkins University Press, 1999.
*TC DS706 .T4 1999*

**CHINA - POLITICS AND GOVERNMENT.**
Ford, Richard B., 1935- Tradition and change in four
societies; New York, Holt, Rinehart and Winston,
1968.
*TC HT521 .F6 1968*

**CHINA (PORCELAIN).** *See* **PORCELAIN.**

**China (Republic : 1949- ). Chu chi ch'u.**
Statistical yearbook of the Republic of China. [Taipei]
Directorate-General of Budget, Accounting &
Statistics, Executive Yuan, Republic of China.

**CHINA - SOCIAL CONDITIONS - 1949-1976.**
Diamant, Neil Jeffrey, 1964- Revolutionizing the
family. Berkeley : University of California Press,
c2000.
*TC HQ684 .D53 2000*

**CHINATOWN (SAN FRANCISCO, CALIF.) -
FICTION.**
Yep, Laurence. The case of the firecrackers. 1st ed.
New York : HarperCollins, c1999.
*TC PZ7.Y44 Cag 1999*

**CHINAWARE.** *See* **PORCELAIN; POTTERY.**

**Chinese adolescents in Britain and Hong Kong :**
identity and aspirations / Gajendra Verma ... [et al.].
Aldershot ; Brookfield, USA : Ashgate, c2000. xii, 204
p. ; 22 cm. Includes bibliographical references (p. 190-201).
ISBN 1-84014-986-8 DDC 305.235089951045
*1. Chinese - Great Britain. 2. Chinese - China - Hong Kong. 3.
Minority teenagers - Great Britain. 4. Minority teenagers -
China - Hong Kong. 5. Chinese - Great Britain - Ethnic
identity. 6. Chinese - China - Hong Kong - Ethnic identity. I.
Verma, Gajendra K.*
*TC DA125.C5 C47 1999*

**CHINESE AMERICAN CHILDREN -
EDUCATION (SECONDARY) - NEW YORK
(STATE) - NEW YORK - SOCIAL
CONDITIONS - CASE STUDIES.**

Woo, Kimberley Ann. "Double happiness," double
jeopardy. 1999.
*TC 06 no. 11075*

**CHINESE AMERICAN WOMEN - LANGUAGE.**
Li, Duan-Duan. Expressing needs and wants in a
second language. 1998.
*TC 06 no. 10958*

**CHINESE AMERICANS - FAMILY
RELATIONSHIP.**
Woo, Kimberley Ann. "Double happiness," double
jeopardy. 1999.
*TC 06 no. 11075*

**CHINESE AMERICANS - FICTION.**
Yep, Laurence. The case of the firecrackers. 1st ed.
New York : HarperCollins, c1999.
*TC PZ7.Y44 Cag 1999*

**CHINESE AMERICANS - UNITED STATES.** *See*
**CHINESE AMERICANS.**

**CHINESE CHARACTERS - STUDY AND
TEACHING (ELEMENTARY) - CHINA.**
Ingulsrud, John E. Learning to read in China.
Lewiston, N.Y. ; Lampeter, Wales : Mellen, c1999.
*TC LB1577.C48 I54 1999*

**CHINESE - CHINA - HONG KONG.**
Chinese adolescents in Britain and Hong Kong.
Aldershot ; Brookfield, USA : Ashgate, c1999.
*TC DA125.C5 C47 1999*

**CHINESE - CHINA - HONG KONG - ETHNIC
IDENTITY.**
Chinese adolescents in Britain and Hong Kong.
Aldershot ; Brookfield, USA : Ashgate, c1999.
*TC DA125.C5 C47 1999*

**Chinese glazes.**
Wood, Nigel. Philadelphia, Pa. : University of
Pennylvania Press, 1999.
*TC TP812 .W65 1999*

**CHINESE - GREAT BRITAIN.**
Chinese adolescents in Britain and Hong Kong.
Aldershot ; Brookfield, USA : Ashgate, c1999.
*TC DA125.C5 C47 1999*

**CHINESE - GREAT BRITAIN - ETHNIC
IDENTITY.**
Chinese adolescents in Britain and Hong Kong.
Aldershot ; Brookfield, USA : Ashgate, c1999.
*TC DA125.C5 C47 1999*

**CHINESE LANGUAGE - ALPHABET.** *See*
**CHINESE CHARACTERS.**

**CHINESE LANGUAGE - STUDY AND
TEACHING (ELEMENTARY) - CHINA.**
Ingulsrud, John E. Learning to read in China.
Lewiston, N.Y. ; Lampeter, Wales : Mellen, c1999.
*TC LB1577.C48 I54 1999*

**CHINESE LANGUAGE - WRITING.** *See*
**CHINESE CHARACTERS.**

**CHINESE LOGOGRAPHS.** *See* **CHINESE
CHARACTERS.**

**CHINESE - UNITED STATES.** *See also* **CHINESE
AMERICANS.**
Evans, Karin. The lost daughters of China. New
York : J.P. Tarcher/Putnam, c2000.
*TC HV1317 .E93 2000*

**Chinn, Peggy L.** Peace and power : building
communities for the future / Peggy L. Chinn. 5th ed.
Boston : Jones and Bartlett Publishers, c2001. ix, 106
p. ; 23 cm. Includes bibliographical references. ISBN 0-7637-
1418-6 DDC 305.42/0973
*1. Feminism - United States. 2. Women and peace. I. Title.*
*TC HQ1426 .W454 2001*

**Chiozza, Luis A.** Why do we fall ill? : the story hiding
in the body / Luis A. Chiozza. Madison, Conn. :
Psychosocial Press, c1999. vii, 125 p. ; 24 cm. Includes
bibliographical references (p. 121-125). ISBN 1-88784-118-0
DDC 616/.001/9
*1. Sick - Psychology. 2. Personality - Health aspects. 3.
Diseases - Causes and theories of causation. 4. Medicine and
psychology. 5. Mind and body. I. Title.*
*TC R726.7 .C48 1999*

**Chipman, Susan F.**
Cognitive task analysis. Mahwah, N.J. : L. Erlbaum
Associates, 2000.
*TC BF311 .C55345 2000*

**CHIROGRAPHY.** *See* **WRITING.**

**Chisanbop.**
Pai, Hang Young. Teacher's annotated ed. New York :
American Book Co., 1980.

*TC QA115 .P23 1980 Teacher's Ed.*

Pai, Hang Young. New York : American Book Co.,
1980.
*TC QA115 .P23 1980*

Pai, Hang Young. New York : American Book Co.,
1980.
*TC QA115 .P231 1980*

Pai, Hang Young. Teacher's annotated ed. New York :
American Book Co., 1980.
*TC QA115 .P231 1980 Teacher's Ed.*

**Chisholm, Margaret E.**
Lane, Nancy D. Techniques for student research. New
York : Neal-Schuman Publishers, 2000.
*TC Z710 .L36 2000*

**Chisholm, Rupert F.** Developing network
organizations : learning from practice and theory /
Rupert F. Chisholm. Reading, Mass. : Addison-
Wesley, c1998. xxxiii, 239 p. : ill. ; 21 cm. (Addison-
Wesley series on organizational development) Includes
bibliographical references (p. 231-233) and indexes. ISBN 0-
201-87444-X DDC 302.3/5
*1. Business networks. 2. Business networks - Case studies. I.
Title. II. Series: Addison-Wesley series on organization
development.*
*TC HD69.S8 C45 1998*

**Chitty, Clyde.**
State schools. London ; Portland, OR : Woburn Press,
1999.
*TC LC93.G7 S73 1999*

**CHIVALRY.** *See* **CIVILIZATION, MEDIEVAL.**

**Chmiel, Nik.**
Introduction to work and organizational psychology.
Malden, Mass. : Blackwell, 1999.
*TC HF5548.8 .I576 1999*

**Choate, Joyce S.**
Successful inclusive teaching. 3rd ed. Boston : Allyn
and Bacon, c2000.
*TC LC1201 .S93 2000*

**Choice (Chicago, Ill.).**
ChoiceReviews.online [computer file]. Middletown,
Conn. : Association of College and Reference
Libraries,

**The Choice of a lifetime** [videorecording] : returning
from the brink of suicide / produced and directed by
Nila Bogue. Hohokus, NJ : New Day Films, c1996. 1
videocassette (53 min.) : sd., col. ; 1/2 in. VHS. Catalogued
from credits and container. Narrator and interviewer: Nila
Bogue. Editor, Heidi Jane Rahlmann ; cinematographers,
Frances Reid... [et al.] ; music composed by Stephen
O'Connor ; sound, Molly McBride, Patricia Sielski, Laura
Scheerer Whitney. For adolescent through adult. SUMMARY:
Six diverse people-- including an elderly widower, a Native
American son of an alcoholic and victim of sexual abuse, a
lesbian who had problems coming out, a Mexican immigrant
who got involved in dangerous crimes, an unloved and abused
black woman, and a woman depressed and filled with self-
hatred ever since childhood-- all speak openly and honestly
about the roots of their despair and their eventual way back to
life. They found their healing in different ways-- support
groups, therapy, spirituality, religious ecstasy, and artistic
expression. The author of this video herself attempted suicide
and made this video part of her own recovery, after
interviewing recovered potential suicide victims across the
country to find out why others "came back", and found a will to
live.
*1. Suicide - Personal narratives. 2. Depression, Mental -
Personal narratives. 3. Depression in children - Personal
narratives. 4. Depression in adolescence - Personal narratives.
5. Depression in old age - Personal narratives. I. Bogue, Nila.
II. New Day Films. III. Title: Returning from the brink of
suicide [videorecording]*
*TC RC569 .C45 1996*

**CHOICE OF BOOKS.** *See* **BOOKS AND
READING.**

**CHOICE OF PROFESSION.** *See* **VOCATIONAL
GUIDANCE.**

**CHOICE OF SCHOOL.** *See* **SCHOOL CHOICE.**

**Choice online.**
ChoiceReviews.online [computer file]. Middletown,
Conn. : Association of College and Reference
Libraries.

**CHOICE (PSYCHOLOGY).**
Elster, Jon, 1940- Strong feelings. Cambridge, Mass. :
MIT Press, c1999.
*TC BF531 .E475 1999*

Schaler, Jeffrey A. Addiction is a choice. Chicago,
Ill. : Open Court, 2000.

*TC HV4998 .S33 2000*

**ChoiceReviews.online** [computer file]. Middletown,
Conn. : Association of College and Reference
Libraries, Frequency: Monthly. Other title: Choice online.
HTML Mode of access: World Wide Web. URL: http://
www.choicereviews.org Available in other form: Choice
(Chicago, Ill.) ISSN: 0009-4978 (DLC)   64009413. ISSN
1523-8253
*I. Association of College and Research Libraries. II. Title:
Choice online III. Title: Choice (Chicago, Ill.)*

**CHOIRS (MUSIC).** *See* **CHORAL MUSIC;
CHORAL SINGING.**

**Chomsky, Noam.** Chomsky on miseducation / Noam
Chomsky ; edited and introduced by Donaldo
Macedo. Lanham, Md. ; Oxford : Rowman &
Littlefield Publishers, c2000. 199 p. ; 23 cm. (Critical
perspective series) Includes bibliographical references and
index. ISBN 0-7425-0129-9 (alk. paper) DDC 370.1
*1. Chomsky, Noam - Contributions in education. 2. Education -
Philosophy. 3. Critical pedagogy. I. Macedo, Donaldo P.
(Donaldo Pereira), 1950- II. Title. III. Series: Critical
perspectives series.*
*TC LB885.C522 A3 2000*

Language and mind / Noam Chomsky. Enl. ed. New
York : Harcourt Brace Jovanovich, [1972]. xii, 194 p. ;
24 cm. Includes bibliographical references. ISBN 0-15-
147810-4 ISBN 0-15-549257-8 (pbk) DDC 401/.9
*1. Psycholinguistics. 2. Thought and thinking. I. Title.*
*TC P106 .C52 1972*

**CHOMSKY, NOAM.**
Calvin, William H., 1939- Lingua ex machina.
Cambridge, Mass. : London : MIT Press, c2000.
*TC QP399 .C35 2000*

Cook, V. J. (Vivian James), 1940- Chomsky's
universal grammar. 2nd [updated] ed. Oxford, OX,
UK ; Cambridge, Mass., USA : Blackwell Publishers,
1996.
*TC P85.C47 C66 1996*

**CHOMSKY, NOAM - CONTRIBUTIONS IN
EDUCATION.**
Chomsky, Noam. Chomsky on miseducation.
Lanham, Md. ; Oxford : Rowman & Littlefield
Publishers, c2000.
*TC LB885.C522 A3 2000*

**Chomsky on miseducation.**
Chomsky, Noam. Lanham, Md. ; Oxford : Rowman &
Littlefield Publishers, c2000.
*TC LB885.C522 A3 2000*

**Chomsky's universal grammar.**
Cook, V. J. (Vivian James), 1940- 2nd [updated] ed.
Oxford, OX, UK ; Cambridge, Mass., USA :
Blackwell Publishers, 1996.
*TC P85.C47 C66 1996*

**Choosing a counselling or psychotherapy training.**
Schapira, Sylvie K., 1940- London ; New York :
Routledge, 2000.
*TC BF637.C6 S355 2000*

**Choosing democracy.**
Campbell, Duane E. 2nd ed. Upper Saddle River,
N.J. : Merrill, c2000.
*TC LC1099.3 .C36 2000*

**Choosing equality.**
Viteritti, Joseph P., 1946- Washington, D.C. :
Brookings Institution Press, c1999.
*TC LB1027.9 .V58 1999*

**Choosing schools.**
Schneider, Mark, 1946- Princeton, N.J. ; Oxford :
Princeton University Press, c2000.
*TC LB1027.9 .S32 2000*

**CHORAL MUSIC - ANALYSIS, APPRECIATION -
LONGITUDINAL STUDIES.**
Gangi, Robyn Joseph. A longitudinal case study of the
musical/aesthetic experience of adolescent choral
musicians. 1998.
*TC 06 no. 10932*

**CHORAL SINGING - PSYCHOLOGICAL
ASPECTS - CASE STUDIES.**
Gangi, Robyn Joseph. A longitudinal case study of the
musical/aesthetic experience of adolescent choral
musicians. 1998.
*TC 06 no. 10932*

**CHORAL SOCIETIES.** *See* **CHORAL MUSIC.**

**CHOREOGRAPHERS - BIOGRAPHY.**
Mazo, Joseph H. Prime movers. 2nd revised edition.
Princeton, NJ. : Princeton Book Co. Pub., c2000.
*TC GV1783 .M347 2000*

**CHOREOGRAPHERS - UNITED STATES - BIOGRAPHY.**
Limón, José. José Limón. Hanover, NH : University Press of New England, [1998?]
*TC GV1785.L515 A3 1998*

Vaughan, David, 1924- Merce Cunningham. 1st ed. New York, NY : Aperture, c1997.
*TC GV1785.C85 V38 1997*

**CHOREOGRAPHY.** *See* **BALLET; CHOREOGRAPHERS.**

**CHOREOGRAPHY - PICTORIAL WORKS.**
Vaughan, David, 1924- Merce Cunningham. 1st ed. New York, NY : Aperture, c1997.
*TC GV1785.C85 V38 1997*

**Chow, Ching Kuang, 1940-.**
Fatty acids in foods and their health implications. 2nd ed., rev. and expanded. New York : M. Dekker, c2000.
*TC QP752.F35 F38 2000*

**CHOWDERS.** *See* **SOUPS.**

**CHRESTOMATHIES.** *See* **READERS.**

**Chrispin, Marie C.** Resilient adaptation of church-affiliated young Haitian immigrants : a seach for protective resources / by Marie C. Chrispin. 1998. xi, 225 leaves ; 29 cm. Typescript; issued also on microfilm. Thesis (Ed.D.)--Teachers College, Columbia University, 1998. Includes bibliographical references (leaves 163-195).
*1. Haitian American teenagers - New York (State) - New York - Ethnic identity. 2. Haitian American teenagers - New York (State) - New York - Religious life. 3. Haitian American teenagers - New York (State) - New York - Education. 4. Haitian Americans - New York (State) - New York - Cultural assimilation. 5. Social interaction. 6. Psychological adaptation. 7. Stress (Psychology) 8. Assimilation (Sociology) 9. Adjustment (Psychology) I. Title.*
*TC 06 no. 11015*

**Chriss, James J., 1955-.**
Counseling and the therapeutic state. New York : Aldine de Gruyter, c1999.
*TC HV95.C675 1999*

**Christ, Grace Hyslop.** Healing children's grief : surviving a parent's death from cancer / Grace Hyslop Christ. New York ; Oxford : Oxford University Press, 2000. xxi, 264 p. : ill. ; 25 cm. Includes bibliographical references (p. 245-252) and indexes. ISBN 0-19-510590-7 (hbk. : alk. paper) ISBN 0-19-510591-5 (pbk. : alk. paper) DDC 155.9/37/083
*1. Grief in children. 2. Grief in adolescence. 3. Bereavement in children. 4. Bereavement in adolescence. 5. Parents - Death - Psychological aspects. 6. Children and death. 7. Teenagers and death. I. Title.*
*TC BF723.G75 C58 2000*

**Christ, Henry I. (Henry Irving), 1915-** Modern English in action / [by] Henry I. Christ. Lexington, Mass. : D. C. Heath, 1978 v. : ill. ; 24 cm. ISBN 0-669-00769-2 (level 12)
*1. English language - Grammar - Problems, exercises, etc. 2. English language - Composition and exercises. I. Title.*
*TC PE1112.C47 1978*

Modern English in action / by Henry I. Christ, Margaret M. Starkey, contributing author. Lexington, Mass. : D. C. Heath, 1975 v. : ill. ; 24 cm. ISBN 0-669-97097-2 (level 12)
*1. English language - Grammar - Problems, exercises, etc. 2. English language - Composition and exercises. I. Starkey, Margaret M. II. Title.*
*TC PE1112.C47 1975*

Modern English in action : manual and answer book / by Henry I. Christ. Teacher's ed. Lexington, Mass. : D. C. Heath, 1975 v. : ill. ; 24 cm. ISBN 0-669-99192-9 (level 7) ISBN 0-669-99218-6 (level 8) ISBN 0-669-96982-6 (level 9) ISBN 0-669-97063-8 (level 11)
*1. English language - Study and teaching (Elementary) 2. English language - Grammar - Problems, exercises, etc. 3. English language - Composition and exercises. I. Title.*
*TC PE1112.C47 1975 Teacher's Ed.*

Modern English in action : manual and answer book / by Henry I. Christ. Teacher's ed. Lexington, Mass. : D. C. Heath, 1978 v. : ill. ; 24 cm. ISBN 0-669-00762-5 (level 10) ISBN 0-669-00766-8 (level 11)
*1. English language - Study and teaching (Elementary) 2. English language - Grammar - Problems, exercises, etc. 3. English language - Composition and exercises. I. Title.*
*TC PE1112.C47 1978 Teacher's ed.*

Modern English in action : manual and answer book / by Henry I. Christ. Teacher's ed. Lexington, Mass. : D. C. Heath, 1978 v. : ill. ; 24 cm. ISBN 0-669-00762-5 (level 10) ISBN 0-669-00766-8 (level 11)
*1. English language - Study and teaching (Elementary) 2.*

*English language - Grammar - Problems, exercises, etc. 3. English language - Composition and exercises. I. Title.*
*TC PE1112.C47 1978 Teacher's Ed.*

Modern English in action : manual and answer book / by Henry I. Christ. Teacher's ed. Lexington, Mass. : D. C. Heath, 1978 v. : ill. ; 24 cm. ISBN 0-669-00762-5 (level 10) ISBN 0-669-00766-8 (level 11)
*1. English language - Study and teaching (Elementary) 2. English language - Grammar - Problems, exercises, etc. 3. English language - Composition and exercises. I. Title.*
*TC PE1112.C47 1978 Teacher's Ed.*

**Christenbury, Leila.** Making the journey : being and becoming a teacher of English language arts / Leila Christenbury. 2nd ed. Portsmouth, NH : Boynton/ Cook Publishers, c2000. xiv, 322 p. ; 26 cm. Includes bibliographical references and index. ISBN 0-86709-476-1 (alk. paper) DDC 428/.0071/2
*1. Language arts (Secondary) - United States. 2. Teaching. 3. English philology - Study and teaching - United States - Vocational guidance. 4. English language - Study and teaching - United States. 5. Classroom management - United States. 6. English teachers - Training of. I. Title.*
*TC LB1631.C4486 2000*

**Christensen, Anne-Lise.**
International handbook of neuropsychological rehabilitation. New York : Kluwer Academic/Plenum Publishers, c2000.
*TC RC387.5.I478 2000*

**Christensen, Larry B., 1941-.**
Johnson, Burke. Educational research. Boston : Allyn and Bacon, c2000.
*TC LB1028.J59 2000*

**Christensen, Pia Monrad.**
Research with children. New York : Falmer Press, 2000.
*TC HQ767.85.R48 1999*

**CHRISTIAN BIOGRAPHY - UNITED STATES.**
Professors who believe. Downers Grove, Ill. : InterVarsity Press, c1998.
*TC BR569.P76 1998*

**CHRISTIAN COLLEGE STUDENTS - RELIGIOUS LIFE - ONTARIO - HAMILTON.**
Bramadat, Paul A. The church on the world's turf. Oxford ; New York : Oxford University Press, 2000.
*TC BV970.16 B73 2000*

**CHRISTIAN COLLEGE TEACHERS - UNITED STATES - BIOGRAPHY.**
Professors who believe. Downers Grove, Ill. : InterVarsity Press, c1998.
*TC BR569.P76 1998*

**CHRISTIAN COLLEGES.** *See* **CHURCH COLLEGES.**

**CHRISTIAN EDUCATION.** *See also* **SUNDAY SCHOOLS.**
[Christian education (Chicago, Ill.)] Christian education. Chicago : [Council of Church Boards of Education in the United States of America, -1952]

**CHRISTIAN EDUCATION.**
Groome, Thomas H. Educating for life. Allen, Tex. : T. More, c1998.
*TC BV1471.2.G6874 1998*

[Christian education (Chicago, Ill.)] Christian education. Chicago : [Council of Church Boards of Education in the United States of America, -1952] 34 v. : ill. ; 23-26 cm. Frequency: Quarterly, 1942-1952. Former frequency: Monthly (omitting Aug. and Sept.), Mar. 1919-Mar. 1924. Former frequency: Monthly (omitting July, Aug., and Sept.), Apr. 1924-June 1932. Former frequency: 5 no. a year, Oct. 1932-1941. Began in 1919 with v. 2, no. 11. -v. 35, 4 (Dec. 1952). Description based on: Vol. 4, no. 10 (Oct. 1920); title from cover. Has supplements. Issued also on microfilm from University Microfilms International. Issued by: Council of Church Boards of Education in the United States of America, <1920>-1946; National Protestant Council on Higher Education, 1947-1950; Commission on Christian Higher Education of the National Council of the Churches of Christ in the United States of America, 1951-1952. Issues for May 1928, Jan. 1931 and Apr./June 1934 called Handbook, 1928-1934 (1928 lacks title). Beginning in 1940 the Handbook was issued separately under title: Christian higher education. A handbook. Available in other form: Christian education (OCoLC)6502764. Continues: American college bulletin (OCoLC)1776361. Continued by: Christian scholar ISSN: 0361-8234 (DLC) 54038490 (OCoLC)1554485. Continued in part by: National Association of Biblical Instructors. Journal of the National Association of Biblical Instructors (OCoLC)1964178.
*1. Religious education - Periodicals. I. Council of Church Boards of Education in the United States of America. II. National Protestant Council on Higher Education (U.S.) III.*

*National Council of the Churches of Christ in the United States of America. Commission on Christian Higher Education. IV. Title: Christian education V. Title: American college bulletin VI. Title: Christian scholar VII. Title: National Association of Biblical Instructors. Journal of the National Association of Biblical Instructors*

**CHRISTIAN EDUCATION - ENGLAND.**
Levitt, Mairi. Nice when they are young. Aldershot, Hants, England ; Brookfield, Vt. : Avebury, c1996.
*TC BV1475.2.L45 1996*

**CHRISTIAN EDUCATION - ENGLAND - CORNWALL (COUNTY) - CASE STUDIES.**
Levitt, Mairi. Nice when they are young. Aldershot, Hants, England ; Brookfield, Vt. : Avebury, c1996.
*TC BV1475.2.L45 1996*

**CHRISTIAN EDUCATION - MICHIGAN - HISTORY.**
DeBoer, Peter P. Origins of teacher education at Calvin College, 1900-1930. Lewiston : E. Mellen Press, c1991.
*TC LD785.D43 1991*

**CHRISTIAN EDUCATION OF CHILDREN.**
Ashton, Elizabeth, lecturer. Religious education in the early years. London ; New York : Routledge, 2000.
*TC BV1475.2.A84 2000*

**CHRISTIAN EDUCATION OF THE MENTALLY HANDICAPPED.**
Clark, Doris C., 1938- Feed all my sheep. 1st ed. Louisville, Ky. : Geneva Press, c2000.
*TC BV1615.M37 C53 2000*

**CHRISTIAN EDUCATION - PHILOSOPHY.**
Martin, Robert K., 1959- The incarnate ground of Christian faith. Lanham, Md. : University Press of America, c1998.
*TC BV1464.M37 1998*

**CHRISTIAN ETHICS.** *See* **GUILT; SOCIAL ETHICS.**

**CHRISTIAN HERESIES.** *See* **HERESIES, CHRISTIAN.**

**Christian liberal arts.**
Mannoia, V. James. Lanham, Md. : Rowman & Littlefield, c2000.
*TC LC427.M26 2000*

**CHRISTIAN LIFE - BIOGRAPHY.** *See* **CHRISTIAN BIOGRAPHY.**

**CHRISTIAN MISSIONS.** *See* **MISSIONS.**

**CHRISTIAN SAINTS - FRANCE - BIOGRAPHY - JUVENILE LITERATURE.**
Hodges, Margaret, 1911- Joan of Arc. 1st ed. New York : Holiday House, c1999.
*TC DC103.5.H64 1999*

**Christian, Sandy Stewart.**
Working with groups to explore food & body connections. Duluth, Minn. : Whole Person Associates, c1996.
*TC RC552.E18 W67 1996*

**Christian scholar.**
[Christian education (Chicago, Ill.)] Christian education. Chicago : [Council of Church Boards of Education in the United States of America, -1952]

**The christian scholar.** [Somerville, N.J., etc.] ill., diagrs. 23-26 cm. Frequency: Frequency varies. Title varies: Christian education Oct. 1917-Dec. 1952. Issues for May, 1928, Jan. 1931, and April-June 1934 called handbook, 1928-34 (1928 lacks title) beginning in 1940 the handbook is issued separately under title:'christian higher education. a handbook.' Ceased publication with v.50, no.4. Suppl. to v.37 (autumn 1954- ) Continued by: Soundings.
*1. Religious education - Periodicals. I. National Protestant Council on Higher Education. II. National Council of the Churches of Chirst in the United States of America. III. Title: Soundings*

**CHRISTIAN SCHOOLS.** *See* **CHURCH SCHOOLS.**

**CHRISTIAN SCIENCE - UNITED STATES - HISTORY.**
Satter, Beryl, 1959- Each mind a kingdom. Berkeley : University of California Press, c1999.
*TC BF639.S124 1999*

**CHRISTIAN SECTS.** *See* **CHRISTIAN SCIENCE; HERESIES, CHRISTIAN; LUTHERAN CHURCH; MENNONITES; METHODIST CHURCH.**

**CHRISTIAN SECTS - UNITED STATES.** *See* **AFRO-AMERICAN CHURCHES.**

**Christiana, David, ill.**
Gauch, Patricia Lee. Poppy's puppet. 1st ed. New York : Holt, 1999.
*TC PZ7.G2315 Po 1999*

Willard, Nancy. The tale I told Sasha. 1st ed. Boston : Little, Brown, c1999.
*TC PZ8.3.W668 Tal 1999*

**CHRISTIANITY.** *See* **CHURCH HISTORY.**

**CHRISTIANITY AND CULTURE - ONTARIO - HAMILTON.**
Bramadat, Paul A. The church on the world's turf. Oxford ; New York : Oxford University Press, 2000.
*TC BV970.16 B73 2000*

**CHRISTIANITY AND OTHER RELIGIONS.**
Eck, Diana L. Encountering God. Boston : Beacon Press, c1993.
*TC BR127 .E25 1993*

**CHRISTIANITY AND OTHER RELIGIONS - HINDUISM.**
Eck, Diana L. Encountering God. Boston : Beacon Press, c1993.
*TC BR127 .E25 1993*

**CHRISTIANITY AND OTHER RELIGIONS - HISTORY.** *See* **CHRISTIANITY AND OTHER RELIGIONS.**

**CHRISTIANITY AND POLITICS - UNITED STATES.**
New school order [videorecording]. New York : First Run/Icarus Films, 1996.
*TC LB2831.583.P4 N4 1996*

**CHRISTIANITY - BIOGRAPHY.** *See* **CHRISTIAN BIOGRAPHY.**

**CHRISTIANITY - CONTROVERSIAL LITERATURE.** *See* **SECULARISM.**

**CHRISTIANITY - HISTORY.** *See* **CHURCH HISTORY.**

**CHRISTIANITY - MISSIONS.** *See* **MISSIONS.**

**CHRISTIANITY - POLITICAL ASPECTS.** *See* **CHRISTIANITY AND POLITICS.**

**CHRISTIANS - BIOGRAPHY.** *See* **CHRISTIAN BIOGRAPHY.**

**Christiansen, Harley Duane.** Basic background for test interpretation / Harley D. Christiansen. 1st ed. Tucson, Ariz. : P. Juul Press, c1981. 96 p. : ill. ; 28 cm. Includes bibliographical references (p.90-92) and index. ISBN 0-915456-04-4 DDC 371.2/6/013
*1. Psychological tests - Evaluation. 2. Psychometrics. I. Title. II. Title: Test interpretation.*
*TC BF176 .C472*

Key readings in testing. 1st ed. Tucson, Ariz. : P. Juul Press, c1985.
*TC BF176 .K48 1985*

**Christie, Frances.**
Genre and institutions. London : Washington : Cassell, 1997.
*TC P302.84 .G46 1997*

**Christie, James F.**
Play and literacy in early childhood. Mahwah, N.J. : Lawrence Erlbaum Associates, Publishers, 2000.
*TC LB1140.35.P55 P557 2000*

**CHRISTMAS.** *See* **SANTA CLAUS.**

**CHRISTMAS BOOKS.** *See* **CHRISTMAS.**

**CHRISTMAS - CENTRAL AMERICA.** *See* **POSADAS (SOCIAL CUSTOM).**

**CHRISTMAS - FICTION.**
Polacco, Patricia. Welcome Comfort. New York : Philomel Books, 1999.
*TC PZ7.P75186 Wg 1999*

**CHRISTMAS - MEXICO.** *See* **POSADAS (SOCIAL CUSTOM).**

**CHRISTMAS PLAYS, AMERICAN - NEW YORK (STATE) - NEW YORK.**
Milbank Memorial Library story hour [videorecording]. [New York : Milbank Memorial Library, 1999].
*TC Z718.3 .M5 1999 Series 3 Prog. 11*

**CHRISTMAS - SOUTHWEST, NEW.** *See* **POSADAS (SOCIAL CUSTOM).**

**Christopher, Elphis, 1936-.**
Jungian thought in the modern world. London ; New York : Free Association, 2000.
*TC BF173.J85 J85 2000*

**Christy, Teresa E.** Cornerstone for nursing education : a history of the Division of Nursing Education of Teachers College, Columbia University, 1899-1947: [by] Teresa E. Christy. New York : Teachers College Press, Columbia University, [1969] xii, 123 p. 24 cm. (Nursing education monographs) Bibliography: p. 113-117. Library has a copy in the Adelaide Nutting Collection. DDC 610.73/071/107471
*1. Columbia University. - Teachers College. - Dept. of Nursing Education. I. Title. II. Series.*
*TC RT81.N3 C45*

**CHROMATICS.** *See* **COLOR.**

**CHRONIC ALCOHOLIC DELIRIUM.** *See* **KORSAKOFF'S SYNDROME.**

**CHRONIC DISEASES.**
Evolutionary aspects of nutrition and health. Basel : New York : Karger, c1999.
*TC QP141 .E95 1999*

**CHRONICALLY ILL.** *See* **DIABETICS; NURSING HOME PATIENTS.**

**CHRONICALLY ILL CHILDREN - EDUCATION - GREAT BRITAIN.**
The education of children with medical conditions. London : D. Fulton Publishers, 2000.
*TC LC4564.G7 E38 2000*

**CHRONICALLY ILL CHILDREN - EDUCATION - UNITED STATES.**
Wishnietsky, Dorothy Botsch. Managing chronic illness in the classroom. Bloomington, Ind. : Phi Delta Kappa Educational Foundation, c1996.
*TC LC4561 .W57 1996*

**CHRONICALLY ILL CHILDREN - SERVICES FOR - UNITED STATES.**
Social work in pediatrics. New York : Haworth Press, c1995.
*TC HV688.U5 S63 1995*

**Chronicle of a war [videorecording].**
Vietnam [videorecording]. [Beverly Hills, Calif.?] : CBS Fox Video : Distributed by Fox Video, c1993.
*TC DS557.7 .V53 1993*

**Chronicle of the 20th century.**
20th century day by day. New York, NY : DK Pub., c1999.
*TC D422 .C53 1999*

**Chronicle of the Olympics, 1896-2000.** 1st American ed. New York : DK Pub., c1998. 330 p. : ill. ; 30 cm. Includes index. ISBN 0-7894-2312-X DDC 796.48
*1. Olympics - History. 2. Olympics - Pictorial works. 3. Olympics - Records. I. DK Publishing, Inc.*
*TC GV721.5 .C474 1998*

**CHRONOLOGY.** *See* **CLOCKS AND WATCHES; DAY; MONTHS; NIGHT.**

**CHRONOPHOTOGRAPHY.** *See* **CINEMATOGRAPHY.**

**Chrysler Museum.**
Myth, magic and mystery. Boulder, Colo. : Roberts Rinehart Publishers ; [Norfolk, Va.] : in cooperation with the Chrysler Museum of Art, c1996.
*TC NC975 .M98 1996*

**Chubin, Daryl E.**
Science, technology, and society. New York : Kluwer Academic/Plenum, c2000.
*TC Q181 .S38225 1999*

**Chud, Gyda.** Early childhood education for a multicultural society / Gyda Chud, Ruth Fahlman ; with Reena Baker ... [et al.]. [Vancouver] : Western Education Development Group, Faculty of Education, The University of British Columbia, c1985. 138 p. : ill. ; 22 x 28 cm. Includes bibliographies. ISBN 0-88865-047-7 (pbk.)
*1. Intercultural education - Canada. 2. Pluralism (Social sciences) - Study and teaching (Preschool) - Canada. 3. Minorities - Education (Preschool) - Canada. I. Baker, Reena. II. Fahlman, Ruth. III. Title.*
*TC LC1099 .C494 1985*

**Chung-kuo chiao hui ta hsüeh li shih wen hsien yen t'ao hui lun wen chi.**
International Symposium on Historical Archives of Pre-1949 Christian Higher Education in China (1993 : Hong Kong) Hsiang-kang : Chung wen ta hsüeh ch'u pan she, 1995.
*TC LC432.C5 158 1995*

**CHURCH.** *See* **SLAVERY AND THE CHURCH.**

**CHURCH AND EDUCATION.** *See* **CHURCH SCHOOLS; RELIGION IN THE PUBLIC SCHOOLS.**

**CHURCH AND EDUCATION - ENGLAND - HISTORY - 19TH CENTURY.**
Phillips, Francis R. Creating an education system for England and Wales. Lewiston, N.Y. : E. Mellen Press, 1992.
*TC LA633 .P48 1992*

**CHURCH AND EDUCATION - UNITED STATES.**
Diekema, Anthony J. Academic freedom and Christian scholarship. Grand Rapids, Mich. : Wm.B. Eerdmans Pub. Co., c2000.
*TC LC72.2 .D54 2000*

New school order [videorecording]. New York : First Run/Icarus Films, 1996.
*TC LB2831.583.P4 N4 1996*

**CHURCH AND SLAVERY.** *See* **SLAVERY AND THE CHURCH.**

**CHURCH AND SOCIAL PROBLEMS.** *See* **CHURCH CHARITIES.**

**CHURCH AND SOCIAL PROBLEMS - CENTRAL AMERICA - OUTLINES, SYLLABI, ETC.**
Third world peoples, a Gospel perspective. Maryknoll, NY : Maryknoll Fathers and Brothers, c1987.
*TC F1439.T54 1987*

**CHURCH AND STATE.** *See* **ECCLESIASTICAL LAW; RELIGION IN THE PUBLIC SCHOOLS.**

**CHURCH AND STATE - EUROPE.**
Glenn, Charles Leslie, 1938- The ambiguous embrace. Princeton, N.J. : Princeton University Press, c2000.
*TC HV95 .G54 2000*

**CHURCH AND STATE - UNITED STATES.**
Glenn, Charles Leslie, 1938- The ambiguous embrace. Princeton, N.J. : Princeton University Press, c2000.
*TC HV95 .G54 2000*

**CHURCH ARCHITECTURE.** *See* **CHURCH BUILDINGS.**

**CHURCH BIOGRAPHY.** *See* **CHRISTIAN BIOGRAPHY.**

**CHURCH BUILDINGS - FICTION.**
Otto, Carolyn. Pioneer church. 1st ed. New York : Henry Holt, 1999
*TC PZ7.O8794 Pi 1999*

**CHURCH CHARITIES - EUROPE.**
Glenn, Charles Leslie, 1938- The ambiguous embrace. Princeton, N.J. : Princeton University Press, c2000.
*TC HV95 .G54 2000*

**CHURCH CHARITIES - UNITED STATES.**
Glenn, Charles Leslie, 1938- The ambiguous embrace. Princeton, N.J. : Princeton University Press, c2000.
*TC HV95 .G54 2000*

**CHURCH COLLEGES - CHINA - ARCHIVAL RESOURCES - CONGRESSES.**
International Symposium on Historical Archives of Pre-1949 Christian Higher Education in China (1993 : Hong Kong) Chung-kuo chiao hui ta hsüeh li shih wen hsien yen t'ao hui lun wen chi. Hsiang-kang : Chung wen ta hsüeh ch'u pan she, 1995.
*TC LC432.C5 158 1995*

**CHURCH COLLEGES - UNITED STATES.**
Mannoia, V. James. Christian liberal arts. Lanham, Md. : Rowman & Littlefield, c2000.
*TC LC427 .M26 2000*

**CHURCH COLLEGES - UNITED STATES - CURRICULA.**
Diekema, Anthony J. Academic freedom and Christian scholarship. Grand Rapids, Mich. : Wm.B. Eerdmans Pub. Co., c2000.
*TC LC72.2 .D54 2000*

**CHURCH FACILITIES.** *See* **CHURCH BUILDINGS.**

**CHURCH FINANCE.** *See* **CHURCH CHARITIES.**

**CHURCH HISTORY - 16TH CENTURY.** *See* **REFORMATION.**

**CHURCH HISTORY - MIDDLE AGES, 600-1500.**
The medieval church. Woodbridge, Suffolk ; Rochester, NY : Published for the Ecclesiastical History Society by the Boydell Press, 1999.
*TC BR270 .M43 1999*

**CHURCH LAW.** *See* **ECCLESIASTICAL LAW.**

**CHURCH MUSIC.** *See* **CHORAL MUSIC.**

**CHURCH OF CHRIST, SCIENTIST.** *See* **CHRISTIAN SCIENCE.**

**The church on the world's turf.**
Bramadat, Paul A. Oxford ; New York : Oxford University Press, 2000.
*TC BV970.16 B73 2000*

**CHURCH POLITY.** *See* ECCLESIASTICAL LAW.

**CHURCH-RELATED COLLEGES.** *See* CHURCH COLLEGES.

**CHURCH SCHOOLS - EUROPE.**
Glenn, Charles Leslie, 1938- The ambiguous embrace. Princeton, N.J. : Princeton University Press, c2000.
*TC HV95 .G54 2000*

**CHURCH SCHOOLS - LAW AND LEGISLATION - UNITED STATES.**
Mawdsley, Ralph D. Legal problems of religious and private schools. 4th ed. Dayton, OH : Education Law Association, c2000.
*TC KF4124.5 .M38 2000*

**CHURCH SCHOOLS - UNITED STATES.**
Glenn, Charles Leslie, 1938- The ambiguous embrace. Princeton, N.J. : Princeton University Press, c2000.
*TC HV95 .G54 2000*

**CHURCH SETTLEMENTS.** *See* SOCIAL SETTLEMENTS.

**CHURCH YEAR.** *See* CHRISTMAS.

**CHURCHES.** *See* CHURCH BUILDINGS.

**CHURCHES, AFRO-AMERICAN.** *See* AFRO-AMERICAN CHURCHES.

**Churukian, George Allen, 1932-.**
International narratives on becoming a teacher educator. Lewiston, N.Y. ; Lampeter,Wales : E. Mellen Press, c2000.
*TC LB1737.5 .I58 2000*

**Chuska, Kenneth R.** Improving classroom questions / by Kenneth R. Chuska. Bloomington, Ind. : Phi Delta Kappa Educational Foundation, 1995. 87 p. ; 23 cm. Includes bibliographical references (p. 85-86). ISBN 0-87367-474-X DDC 371.3/7
*1. Questioning. 2. Teaching. 3. Learning. 4. Motivation in education. 5. Teacher-student relationships. 6. Classroom environment. I. Title.*
*TC LB1027.44 .C58 1995*

**Chwast, Seymour.** Traffic jam / Seymour Chwast. Boston : Houghton Mifflin, 1999. 1 v. (unpaged) : col. ill. ; 21 x 26 cm. "Walter Lorraine books." One page folds out to show the traffic jam. SUMMARY: When Babs the cat decides to take her kitten home to keep her out of trouble, she creates a traffic jam at the corner where Officer Grumm stops the traffic to let them cross. ISBN 0-395-97495-X DDC [E]
*1. Cats - Fiction. 2. Animals - Infancy - Fiction. 3. Mother and child - Fiction. 4. Traffic congestion - Fiction. I. Title.*
*TC PZ7.C4893 Tr 1999*

**Cianciolo, Patricia J.** Informational picture books for children / Patricia J. Cianciolo. Chicago : American Library Association, 2000. x, 205 p. : ill. ; 26 cm. Includes bibliographical references and index. ISBN 0-8389-0774-1 DDC 028.1/62
*1. Children's literature, English - Book reviews. 2. Picture books for children - United States - Book reviews. I. Title.*
*TC Z1037.A1 C54 1999*

**Ciba foundation symposium**
(194) Genetics of criminal and antisocial behaviour. Chichester ; New York : Wiley, 1996.
*TC HV6047 .G46 1996*

**Ciba-Geigy review.**
Ciba review. Basle, Switzerland Ciba Limited.

**CIBA Limited.**
Ciba review. Basle, Switzerland Ciba Limited.

**Ciba review.** Basle, Switzerland Ciba Limited. v. ill., ports. 25 cm. Frequency: 4 no. a year, 1961-1970. Former frequency: Frequency varies, 1937-1960. no. 1-141, Sept. 1937-Dec. 1960; 1961/1-1970/4. Issues no. 1-141 constitute v. 1-12. With supplements. Issued by Ciba Ltd. (called, Sept. 1937-Apr. 1954, Society of Chemical Industry in Basel). No. 1-24, Sept. 1937-Aug. 1939, with no. 24; no. 25-72, Sept. 1939-Feb. 1949. 1 v.; no. 73-120, Apr. 1949-June 1957. 1 v. Continued by: Ciba-Geigy review (DLC)sn 88015440 (OCoLC)1554687. DDC 660.5
*1. Chemistry, Technical - Periodicals. 2. Dyes and dyeing - Periodicals. I. CIBA Limited. II. Title: Ciba-Geigy review*

**Cicchetti, Dante.**
Developmental perspectives on trauma. Rochester, N.Y., USA : University of Rochester Press, 1997.
*TC RJ499 .D4825 1997*

**CIGARETTE HABIT - PREVENTION.**
Brigham, Janet. Dying to quit. Washington, D.C. : Joseph Henry Press, 1998.

---

*TC HV5740 .B75 1998*

**CIGARETTE HABIT - PSYCHOLOGICAL ASPECTS.**
Brigham, Janet. Dying to quit. Washington, D.C. : Joseph Henry Press, 1998.
*TC HV5740 .B75 1998*

**Cikovsky, Nicolai.**
America. Munich, Germany ; London ; New York : Prestel, c1999.
*TC ND210 .A724 1999*

Winslow Homer / Nicolai Cikovsky, Jr., Franklin Kelly with contributions by Judith Walsh and Charles Brock. Washington, D.C. : National Gallery of Art, 1995. 420 p. : ill. (some col.), ports. ; 32 cm. "Exhibition dates, National Gallery of Art, Washington 15 October 1995-28 January 1996, Boston Museum of Fine Arts 21 February-26 May 1996, Metropolitan Museum of Art, New York 20 June-22 September 1996"--T.p. verso. Includes bibliographical references (p. 414-418) and index. CONTENTS: The School of War / Nicolai Cikovsky, Jr. -- Modern and National / Nicolai Cikovsky, Jr. -- Reconstruction / Nicolai Cikovsky, Jr. -- A Process of Change / Franklin Kelly -- Something More than Meets the Eye / Nicolai Cikovsky, Jr. -- Innovation in Homer's Late Watercolors / Judith Walsh -- Time and Narrative Erased / Franklin Kelly -- Good Pictures / Nicolai Cikovsky, Jr. -- Chronology / Charles Brock -- Exhibitions in Homer's Lifetime / Charles Brock. ISBN 0-89468-217-2 DDC 759.13
*1. Homer, Winslow, - 1836-1910 - Exhibitions. 2. Nationalism in art - Exhibitions. I. Kelly, Franklin. II. National Gallery of Art (U.S.) III. Museum of Fine Arts, Boston. IV. Metropolitan Museum of Art (New York, N.Y.) V. Homer, Winslow, 1836-1910. VI. Title.*
*TC N6537.H58 A4 1995*

**Cillessen, Antonius H.**
Recent advances in the measurement of acceptance and rejection in the peer system. San Francisco : Jossey-Bass Publishers, c2000.
*TC BF723.I65 R4 2000*

**Cincinnati Art Museum.**
Kleeblatt, Norman L. An expressionist in Paris. Munich ; New York : Jewish Museum, c1998.
*TC ND553.S7 A4 1998*

**CINEMA.** *See* MOTION PICTURES.

**Cinéma.**
Intercine. Rome.

**CINEMATOGRAPHY - PERIODICALS.**
Journal of the SMPTE. New York, N.Y. : SMPTE, 1956-1975.

**Cioffari, Angelina Grimaldi, 1913-.**
Cioffari, Vincenzo, 1905- Graded Italian reader. 3rd ed. Lexington, Mass. : D.C. Heath, c1991.
*TC PC1113 .C5 1991*

Graded Italian reader : seconda tappa / Angelina Grimaldi Cioffari, Vincenzo Cioffari. 2nd ed. Lexington, Mass. : D.C. Heath, c1984. v, 218 p. ; 21 cm. English and Italian. ISBN 0-669-06325-8 (pbk.) DDC 458.6/421
*1. Italian language - Readers. I. Cioffari, Vincenzo, 1905- II. Title.*
*TC PC1113 .C48 1984*

**Cioffari, Vincenzo, 1905-.**
Cioffari, Angelina Grimaldi, 1913- Graded Italian reader. 2nd ed. Lexington, Mass. : D.C. Heath, c1984.
*TC PC1113 .C48 1984*

Graded Italian reader : prima tappa / Vincenzo Cioffari, Angelina Grimaldi Cioffari. 3rd ed. Lexington, Mass. : D.C. Heath, c1991. ix, 246 p. ; 21 cm. English and Italian. ISBN 0-669-20296-7 DDC 458/.6/421
*1. Italian language - Readers. I. Cioffari, Angelina Grimaldi, 1913- II. Title.*
*TC PC1113 .C5 1991*

**Cioffi, Frank.** Freud and the question of pseudoscience / Frank Cioffi. Chicago : Open Court, c1998. ix, 313 p. ; 23 cm. Includes bibliographical references and index. ISBN 0-8126-9385-X (alk. paper) DDC 150.19/52/092
*1. Psychoanalysis. 2. Freud, Sigmund, - 1856-1939. I. Title.*
*TC BF173 .C495 1998*

**CIPHERS.** *See* WRITING.

**CIRCLE - FICTION.**
Joyce, William. Rolie Polie Olie. 1st ed. New York : Laura Geringer Book, c1999.
*TC PZ8.3.J835 Ro 1999*

**CIRCULATION OF THE BLOOD.** *See* BLOOD - CIRCULATION.

**CIRCULATORY SYSTEM.** *See* CARDIOVASCULAR SYSTEM.

---

**CIRCUMSTELLAR MATTER.** *See* STARS.

**Circus!.**
Spier, Peter. [Circus!] Peter Spier's circus!. 1st ed. New York : Doubleday, c1992.
*TC PZ7.S7544 Cj 1992*

**CIRCUS - FICTION.**
Spier, Peter. [Circus!] Peter Spier's circus!. 1st ed. New York : Doubleday, c1992.
*TC PZ7.S7544 Cj 1992*

**CIRCUSES.** *See* CIRCUS.

**CITADEL, THE MILITARY COLLEGE OF SOUTH CAROLINA - TRIALS, LITIGATION, ETC.**
Manegold, Catherine S. In glory's shadow. 1st ed. New York : Alfred A. Knopf, 1999.
*TC KF228.C53 M36 1999*

**Cities & planning series**
Rebuilding urban neighborhoods. Thousand Oaks, Calif. : Sage Publications, c1999.
*TC HT175 .R425 1999*

**CITIES AND STATE.** *See* URBAN POLICY.

**CITIES AND TOWNS.** *See also* COMMUNITY; EDUCATION, URBAN; INNER CITIES; PUBLIC SPACES.
Mental health in our future cities. Hove, England : Psychology Press, c1998.
*TC RA790.5 .M4196 1998*

Mitchell, William J. (William John), 1944- E-topia. Cambridge, Mass. : MIT Press, 1999.
*TC HE7631 .M58 1999*

**CITIES AND TOWNS - EFFECT OF TECHNOLOGICAL INNOVATIONS ON - UNITED STATES.**
Cities in the telecommunications age. New York : Routledge, 2000.
*TC HT167 .C483 2000*

**CITIES AND TOWNS - GROWTH.** *See* METROPOLITAN AREAS; SUBURBS.

**CITIES AND TOWNS - PLANNING.** *See* CITY PLANNING.

**CITIES AND TOWNS - UNITED STATES.**
Affordable housing and urban redevelopment in the United States. Thousand Oaks, Calif. : Sage Publications, c1997.
*TC HD7293 .A55 1997*

Bartlett, Randall, 1945- The crisis of America's cities. Armonk, N.Y. : M.E. Sharpe, c1998.
*TC HT123 .B324 1998*

Kahn, Alfred J., 1919- Big cities in the welfare transition. New York City : Cross-National Studies Research Program, Columbia University School of Social Work, 1998.
*TC HV91 .K27 1998*

Withers, Carl. Plainville, U.S.A.. New York : Columbia University Press, [c1945]
*TC HN57 .W58 1945*

**CITIES AND TOWNS - UNITED STATES - HISTORY.**
Bartlett, Randall, 1945- The crisis of America's cities. Armonk, N.Y. : M.E. Sharpe, c1998.
*TC HT123 .B324 1998*

**CITIES AND TOWNS - UNITED STATES - HISTORY - CASE STUDIES.**
Abu-Lughod, Janet L. New York, Chicago, Los Angeles. Minneapolis : University of Minnesota Press, c1999.
*TC HT123 .A613 1999*

**Cities in the telecommunications age** : the fracturing of geographies / James O. Wheeler, Yuko Aoyama, and Barney Warf, editors. New York : Routledge, 2000. 350 p. : ill., maps ; 23 cm. Includes bibliographical references and index. ISBN 0-415-92441-3 (hb.) ISBN 0-415-92442-1 (pb.) DDC 384/.0973
*1. Cities and towns - Effect of technological innovations on - United States. 2. Telecommunication - Social aspects - United States. I. Wheeler, James O. II. Aoyama, Yuko. III. Warf, Barney, 1956-*
*TC HT167 .C483 2000*

**Cities in transition.**
Stanback, Thomas M. Totowa, N.J. : Allanheld, Osmun, 1982.
*TC HD5724 .S649 1982*

**CITIZEN 2000 (PHOENIX, ARIZ.).**
Education's big gamble [videorecording]. New York, NY : Merrow Report, c1997.

*Citizen participation*

*TC LB2806.36 .E3 1997*

**CITIZEN PARTICIPATION.** *See* **POLITICAL PARTICIPATION.**

**CITIZENS BAND RADIO - SLANG - FICTION.**
Day, Alexandra. Frank and Ernest on the road. New York : Scholastic Inc., c1994.
*TC PZ7.D32915 Frn 1994*

**CITIZENS RADIO SERVICE.** *See* **CITIZENS BAND RADIO.**

**CITIZENS RADIO SERVICE (CLASS D).** *See* **CITIZENS BAND RADIO.**

**CITIZENSHIP.** *See also* **CIVICS.**
Crick, Bernard R. Essays on citizenship. London : New York : Continuum, 2000.
*TC JF801 .C75 2000*

**Citizenship for the 21st century :** an international perspective on education / edited by John J. Cogan and Ray Derricott. [Rev. ed.]. London : Kogan Page, 2000. xviii, 197 p. : ill. ; 25 cm. Other title: Citizenship for the twenty-first century. Includes bibliographical references and indexes. CONTENTS: Ch. 1. Citizenship education for the 21st century: Setting the context / John J. Cogan -- Ch. 2. National case studies of citizenship education / Ray Derricott, Athan Gotovos and Zsuzsa Matrai [et al.] -- Ch. 3. Using the Delphi cross-culturally: Towards the development of policy / Ruthanne Kurth-Schai, Chumpol Poolpatarachewin and Somwung Pitiyanuwat -- Ch. 4. Challenges facing the 21st century citizen: Views of policy makers / Sjoerd Karsten, Patricia Kubow and Zsuzsa Matrai / [et al.] -- Ch. 5. Multidimensional citizenship: Educational policy for the 21st century / Patricia Kubow, David Grossman and Akira Ninomiya -- Ch. 6. Making it work: Implementing multidimensional citizenship / Walter Parker, David Grossman and Patricia Kubow / [et al.] -- Ch. 7. The challenge of multidimensional citizenship for the 21st century / John J. Cogan. ISBN 0-7494-3201-2
*1. Citizenship - Study and teaching - Cross-cultural studies. I. Cogan, John J. II. Derricott, R. III. Title: Citizenship for the twenty-first century*
*TC LC1091 .C575 2000*

**Citizenship for the twenty-first century.**
Citizenship for the 21st century. [Rev. ed.]. London : Kogan Page, 2000.
*TC LC1091 .C575 2000*

**CITIZENSHIP - STUDY AND TEACHING.**
Civic education across countries. Amsterdam, the Netherlands : International Association for the Evaluation of Educational Achievement, c1999.
*TC JA86 .C6 1999*

Levinson, Meira. The demands of liberal education. Oxford ; New York : Oxford University Press, 1999.
*TC LC1091 .L38 1999*

Politics, education and citizenship. London ; New York : Falmer Press, 2000.
*TC LC1091 .P54 2000*

**CITIZENSHIP - STUDY AND TEACHING - CROSS-CULTURAL STUDIES.**
Citizenship for the 21st century. [Rev. ed.]. London : Kogan Page, 2000.
*TC LC1091 .C575 2000*

**CITIZENSHIP - STUDY AND TEACHING - GREAT BRITAIN.**
Davies, Ian, 1957- Good citizenship and educational provision. London ; New York : Falmer Press, c1999.
*TC LC1091 .D28 1999*

**CITIZENSHIP - STUDY AND TEACHING (HIGHER) - UNITED STATES.**
Civic responsibility and higher education. Phoenix, Az. : Oryx Press, 2000.
*TC LC1091 .C5289 2000*

Colleges and universities as citizens. Boston : Allyn and Bacon, c1999.
*TC LC220.5 .C644 1999*

**CITIZENSHIP - STUDY AND TEACHING (MIDDLE SCHOOL) - UNITED STATES.**
A case study in teaching to civic standards using a portfolio approach 1996 : "Office of Citizen". [Boulder, Colo.] : Social Science Education Consortium, c1997.
*TC LC1091 .C37 1997*

Democratic dialogue with special needs students. [Boulder, Colo.] : Social Science Education Consortium, c1997.

**CITIZENSHIP - STUDY AND TEACHING - UNITED STATES.**
Macedo, Stephen, 1957- Diversity and distrust. Cambridge, Mass. ; London : Harvard University Press, 2000.

*TC LA217.2 .M33 2000*

**CITIZENSHIP - STUDY AND TEACHING - UNITED STATES - CONGRESSES.**
Thomas Jefferson and the education of a citizen. Washington, DC : Library of Congress, 1999.
*TC Z663 .T425 1999*

**CITY AND TOWN LIFE.** *See* **URBAN POLICY.**

**CITY AND TOWN LIFE - FICTION.**
Brooks, Nigel. Town mouse house. New York : Walker & Co., 2000.
*TC PZ7.B7977 To 2000*

**CITY AND TOWN LIFE - NEW ENGLAND - FICTION.**
Wiggin, Kate Douglas Smith, 1856-1923. Rebecca of Sunnybrook Farm. Boston, New York [etc.] : Houghton, Mifflin Company, [c1903] (Cambridge, Mass. : Riverside Press)
*TC PZ7.W638 Re 1903*

**CITY AND TOWN LIFE - PUERTO RICO - SAN JUAN - HISTORY.**
Matos Rodríguez, Félix V., 1962- Women and urban change in San Juan, Puerto Rico, 1820-1868. Gainesville, Fla. : University Press of Florida, c1999.
*TC HQ1522 .M38 1999*

**CITY CHILDREN.** *See* **URBAN YOUTH.**

**CITY CHILDREN - EDUCATION (PRESCHOOL) - UNITED STATES - CASE STUDIES.**
Meier, Daniel R. Scribble scrabble--teaching children to become successful readers and writers. New York : Teachers College Press, c2000.
*TC LB1140.5.L3 M45 2000*

**CITY CHILDREN - UNITED STATES.**
Violence and childhood in the inner city. Cambridge, UK ; New York : Cambridge University Press, 1997.
*TC HN90.V5 V532 1997*

**CITY CRIME.** *See* **CRIME.**

**CITY DWELLERS.** *See* **CITY CHILDREN; URBAN WOMEN; URBAN YOUTH.**

**CITY LIFE.** *See* **CITY AND TOWN LIFE.**

**City of light [videorecording].**
Paris [videorecording]. New York, NY : V.I.E.W. Video, c1996.
*TC DC707 .P3 1996*

**CITY PLANNING.** *See* **HOUSING; SUBURBS; URBAN POLICY; URBAN RENEWAL.**

**CITY PLANNING - GOVERNMENT POLICY.** *See* **CITY PLANNING.**

**CITY PLANNING - NEW YORK (STATE) - NEW YORK - HISTORY - 19TH CENTURY.**
Stern, Robert A. M. New York 1880. New York, N.Y. : Monacelli Press, 1999.
*TC NA735.N5 S727 1999*

**CITY PLANNING - UNITED STATES - HISTORY - 20TH CENTURY.**
Stein, Clarence S. The writings of Clarence S. Stein. Baltimore, Md. : Johns Hopkins University Press, 1998.
*TC NA9108 .S83 1998*

**City schools and city politics.**
Portz, John, 1953- Lawrence : University Press of Kansas, c1999.
*TC LC5131 .P67 1999*

**City schools :** lessons from New York / edited by Diane Ravitch and Joseph P. Viteritti. Baltimore : Johns Hopkins University Press, c2000. ix, 405 p. ; 23 cm. Includes bibliographical references and index. ISBN 0-8018-6341-4 (alk. paper) ISBN 0-8018-6342-2 (pbk. : alk. paper) DDC 370/.9747/1
*1. Education, Urban - New York (State) - New York. I. Ravitch, Diane. II. Viteritti, Joseph P., 1946-*
*TC LC5133.N4 C57 2000*

**CITY UNIVERSITY OF NEW YORK - HISTORY.**
Roff, Sandra Shoiock. From the Free Academy to CUNY. New York : Fordham University Press, c2000.
*TC LD3835 .R64 2000*

**City University of New York. Research Foundation.**
Chen, Sheying. Remedial education and grading. New York : the City University of New York, 1999.
*TC LB1029.R4 C54 1999*

**City works : exploring your community.**
Steinberg, Adria. CityWorks. New York : New Press, c1999.
*TC LC1036 .S74 1999*

**CityWorks.**
Steinberg, Adria. New York : New Press, c1999.
*TC LC1036 .S74 1999*

**Civic education across countries :** twenty-four national case studies from the IEA civic education project / edited by Judith Torney-Purta, John Schwille and Jo-Ann Amadeo. Amsterdam, the Netherlands : International Association for the Evaluation of Educational Achievement, c1999. 624 p. : ill. ; 24 cm. Includes bibliographical references. ISBN 90-5166-671-3 (pbk.)
*1. Civics - Study and teaching 2. Citizenship - Study and teaching. 3. Political socialization I. Schwille, John. II. Amadeo, Jo-Ann. III. International Association for the Evaluation of Educational Achievement.*
*TC JA86 .C6 1999*

**CIVIC IMPROVEMENT.** *See* **CITY PLANNING.**

**CIVIC LEADERS.** *See* **WOMEN CIVIC LEADERS.**

**CIVIC LEADERS - TRAINING OF.**
Robinson, Anna Bess. Leadership development in women's civic organizations. 1999.
*TC 06 no. 11168*

**CIVIC PLANNING.** *See* **CITY PLANNING.**

**Civic responsibility and higher education** / edited by Thomas Ehrlich. Phoenix, Az. : Oryx Press, 2000. xliii, 403 p. ; 23 cm. (American Council on Education/Oryx Press series on higher education) Includes bibliographical references and index. ISBN 1-57356-289-0 (alk.) DDC 378/.015 DDC 378/.01/5
*1. Citizenship - Study and teaching (Higher) - United States. 2. Education, Higher - Aims and objectives - United States. I. Ehrlich, Thomas, 1934- II. Series.*
*TC LC1091 .C5289 2000*

**Civic virtues and public schooling.**
White, Patricia, 1937- New York : Teachers College Press, c1996.
*TC LC1011 .W48 1996*

**CIVICS.** *See also* **CITIZENSHIP.**
Ball, Grant T. Fifth edition. Chicago, Ill. : Follett Pub. Co., c1978.
*TC H62 .B34 1978*

**CIVICS.**
Ball, Grant T. Civics. Fifth edition. Chicago, Ill. : Follett Pub. Co., c1978.
*TC H62 .B34 1978*

**CIVICS, AMERICAN.** *See* **CIVICS.**

**CIVICS - STUDY AND TEACHING.**
Civic education across countries. Amsterdam, the Netherlands : International Association for the Evaluation of Educational Achievement, c1999.
*TC JA86 .C6 1999*

**CIVICS - STUDY AND TEACHING (MIDDLE SCHOOL) - UNITED STATES.**
A case study in teaching to civic standards using a portfolio approach 1996 : "Office of Citizen". [Boulder, Colo.] : Social Science Education Consortium, c1997.
*TC LC1091 .C37 1997*

Democratic dialogue with special needs students. [Boulder, Colo.] : Social Science Education Consortium, c1997.

**CIVICS - STUDY AND TEACHING (SECONDARY) - UNITED STATES.**
Socratic seminar [videorecording]. [Boulder, Colo.] : Social Science Education Consortium, c1997.
*TC LB1027.44 .S6 1997*

**CIVICS - STUDY AND TEACHING - UNITED STATES.**
Annual State of American Education Address (7th : February 22, 2000 : Durham, N.C.) The seventh annual state of American education address [videorecording]. [Washington, D.C. : U.S. Dept. of Education], 2000.

**CIVIL DEFENSE.** *See* **EMERGENCY MANAGEMENT.**

**CIVIL DISORDERS.** *See* **RIOTS.**

**CIVIL GOVERNMENT.** *See* **POLITICAL SCIENCE.**

**CIVIL LAW (ISLAMIC LAW).** *See* **ISLAMIC LAW.**

**CIVIL LIBERATION MOVEMENTS.** *See* **CIVIL RIGHTS MOVEMENTS.**

**CIVIL LIBERTIES.** *See* **CIVIL RIGHTS.**

**CIVIL LIBERTY.** *See* **LIBERTY.**

**CIVIL-MILITARY RELATIONS - AFRICA.**
Onwumechili, Chuka. African democratization and military coups. Westport, Conn. : Praeger, 1998.
*TC JQ1873.5.C58 O58 1998*

**CIVIL PROCEDURE.** *See* **INTERVENTION (CIVIL PROCEDURE); TRIAL PRACTICE.**

**CIVIL RIGHTS.** *See* **FREEDOM OF INFORMATION; FREEDOM OF SPEECH; PRIVACY, RIGHT OF.**

**CIVIL RIGHTS (INTERNATIONAL LAW).** *See* **HUMAN RIGHTS.**

**CIVIL RIGHTS (JEWISH LAW).**
Novak, David, 1941- Covenantal rights. Princeton, N.J. : Princeton University Press, 2000.
*TC KC3 .N68 2000*

**CIVIL RIGHTS MOVEMENTS - UNITED STATES - HISTORY - 20TH CENTURY - JUVENILE LITERATURE.**
Haskins, James, 1941- Bayard Rustin. 1st ed. New York : Hyperion Books for Children, c1997.
*TC E185.97.R93 H37 1997*

**CIVIL RIGHTS - UNITED STATES.** *See also* **AFRO-AMERICANS - CIVIL RIGHTS.**
Affirmative action. San Diego, Calif. : Greenhaven Press, 2000.
*TC JC599.U5 A34685 2000*

**CIVIL RIGHTS - UNITED STATES - HISTORY.**
Howard, John R., 1933- The shifting wind. Albany : State University of New York Press, c1999.
*TC KF4757 .H69 1999*

**CIVIL RIGHTS WORKERS.**
Haskins, James, 1941- Bayard Rustin. 1st ed. New York : Hyperion Books for Children, c1997.
*TC E185.97.R93 H37 1997*

**CIVIL RIGHTS WORKERS - UNITED STATES - BIOGRAPHY - JUVENILE LITERATURE.**
Haskins, James, 1941- Bayard Rustin. 1st ed. New York : Hyperion Books for Children, c1997.
*TC E185.97.R93 H37 1997*

**CIVIL SERVICE.** *See* **LOCAL OFFICIALS AND EMPLOYEES.**

**CIVIL SOCIETY.**
Giroux, Henry A. Stealing innocence. 1st ed. New York : St. Martin's Press, 2000.
*TC HM621 .G57 2000*

**CIVIL SOCIETY - EUROPE.**
Glenn, Charles Leslie, 1938- The ambiguous embrace. Princeton, N.J. : Princeton University Press, c2000.
*TC HV95 .G54 2000*

**CIVIL SOCIETY - UNITED STATES.**
Glenn, Charles Leslie, 1938- The ambiguous embrace. Princeton, N.J. : Princeton University Press, c2000.
*TC HV95 .G54 2000*

**CIVIL SOCIETY - UNITED STATES - HISTORY - 20TH CENTURY.**
Cochran, David Carroll. The color of freedom. Albany : State University of New York Press, c1999.
*TC E185.615 .C634 1999*

**CIVIL WAR.** *See* **INSURGENCY.**

**Civil War artist.**
Morrison, Taylor. Boston : Houghton Mifflin, 1999.
*TC E468.9 .M86 1999*

**A Civil War drummer boy.**
Bircher, William, 1845-1917. Mankato, Minn. : Blue Earth Books, c2000.
*TC E601 .B605 2000*

**Civil war** [picture] : young soldiers. Amawalk, NY : Jackdaw Publications, c1999. 12 posters : b&w ; 43 x 56 cm. + 1 leaflet ([6] p. : ill. ; 28 cm.). (Jackdaw photo collections ; PC 104) Compiled by Bill Eames. SUMMARY: 12 historical photo-posters depicting the young, in some case, child, soldiers of the Civil War. CONTENTS: 1. Union drummer boy -- 2. Teen-age Private, Georgia Infantry -- 3. 93rd New York Infantry Drum Corps -- 4. Youngest wounded soldier of the Civil War -- 5. Twelve-year-old Shiloh veteran -- 6. Union Colored Infantry drummer boy -- 7. "Powder Monkey" -- 8. Youthful Confederate Calvaryman -- 9. Federal soldier -- 10. Pvt. William S. Askew, 1st Georgia Regiment -- 11. Pvt. George Graffman, Maine Infantry -- 12. Private of Fourth Michigan Infantry. ISBN 1-56696-161-0
*1. Jewish children in the Holocaust - Posters. 2. Holocaust, Jewish - Posters. 3. Holocaust survivors - Posters. 4. Documentary photography - United States - Posters. I. Eames, Bill. II. Jackdaw Publications. III. Title: Young soldiers [picture] IV. Series.*

**Civil war** [picture] : young soldiers. Amawalk, NY : Jackdaw Publications, c1999. 12 posters : b&w ; 43 x 56 cm. + 1 leaflet ([6] p. : ill. ; 28 cm.). (Jackdaw photo collections ; PC 104) Compiled by Bill Eames. SUMMARY: 12 historical photo-posters depicting the young, in some case, child, soldiers of the Civil War. CONTENTS: 1. Union drummer boy -- 2. Teen-age Private, Georgia Infantry -- 3. 93rd New York Infantry Drum Corps -- 4. Youngest wounded soldier of the Civil War -- 5. Twelve-year-old Shiloh veteran -- 6. Union Colored Infantry drummer boy -- 7. "Powder Monkey" -- 8. Youthful Confederate Calvaryman -- 9. Federal soldier -- 10. Pvt. William S. Askew, 1st Georgia Regiment -- 11. Pvt. George Graffman, Maine Infantry -- 12. Private of Fourth Michigan Infantry. ISBN 1-56696-161-0
*1. United States - History - Civil War, 1861-1865 - Posters. 2. United States - History - Civil War, 1861-1865 - Participation, Juvenile - Posters. 3. Boys as soldiers - Posters. 4. Documentary photography - United States - Posters. I. Eames, Bill. II. Jackdaw Publications. III. Title: Young soldiers [picture] IV. Series.*
*TC TR820.5 .C56 1999*

**Civil War to the present.**
Cayton, Andrew R. L. (Andrew Robert Lee), 1954- America. Teacher's ed. Upper Saddle River, N.J.. : Prentice Hall, c1998.
*TC E178.1 .C364 1998 Teacher's Ed.*

Cayton, Andrew R. L. (Andrew Robert Lee), 1954- America. Upper Saddle River, N.J.. : Prentice Hall, c1998.
*TC E178.1 .C364 1998*

Cayton, Andrew R. L. (Andrew Robert Lee), 1954- America. Upper Saddle River, N.J. : Prentice Hall, c1998.
*TC E178.1 .C364 1998*

Cayton, Andrew R. L. (Andrew Robert Lee), 1954- America. Teacher's ed. Upper Saddle River, N.J.. : Prentice Hall, c1998.
*TC E178.1 .C3644 1998 Teacher's Ed.*

Cayton, Andrew R. L. (Andrew Robert Lee), 1954- America. Upper Saddle River, N.J. : Prentice Hall, c1998.
*TC E178.1 .C364 1998*

Cayton, Andrew R. L. (Andrew Robert Lee), 1954- America. Upper Saddle River, N.J. : Prentice Hall, c1998.
*TC E178.1 .C3644 1998*

Cayton, Andrew R. L. (Andrew Robert Lee), 1954- America. Upper Saddle River, N.J. : Prentice Hall, c1998.
*TC E178.1 .C3644 1998*

**CIVIL WAR, U. S., 1861-1865.** *See* **UNITED STATES - HISTORY - CIVIL WAR, 1861-1865.**

**Civilisations.** Bruxelles, Institut International des Civilisations Différentes. v. 24 cm. Frequency: 4 no. a year. v. 1- Jan. 1951- . Indexed selectively by: ABC pol sci 0001-0456. Indexed selectively by: America, history and life 0002-7065 1955-. Indexed selectively by: Historical abstracts. Part A. Modern history abstracts 0363-2717 1955-. Indexed selectively by: Historical abstracts. Part B. Twentieth century abstracts 0363-2725 1955-. Indexed selectively by: Foreign language index 0048-5810 -1984. Indexed selectively by: PAIS bulletin 0898-2201 1986-. Indexed selectively by: PAIS foreign language index 0896-792X 1985-. Indexed selectively by: Public Affairs Information Service bulletin 0033-3409 - 1985. English or French. 1951-52, issued by the Institute under its former name: International Institute of Political and Social Sciences Concerning Countries of Differing Civilizations. ISSN 0009-8140 DDC 054
*1. Social sciences - Periodicals. 2. Colonies - Periodicals. I. International Institute of Differing Civilizations.*

**CIVILIZATION.** *See also* **CULTURE; EDUCATION; LEARNING AND SCHOLARSHIP; PERSONALITY AND CULTURE; RELIGIONS; SOCIAL SCIENCES.**
Hogben, Lancelot Thomas,d1895- Science for the citizen; [2d ed.]. New York, W. W. Norton & Co. c1938.
*TC Q162 .H7 1938*

**CIVILIZATION, AMERICAN.** *See* **UNITED STATES - CIVILIZATION.**

**CIVILIZATION, ANCIENT.** *See* **CIVILIZATION, CLASSICAL.**

**CIVILIZATION AND PERSONALITY.** *See* **PERSONALITY AND CULTURE.**

**CIVILIZATION, CLASSICAL.** *See also* **CLASSICISM; ROME - CIVILIZATION.**
Garnsey, Peter. Food and society in classical antiquity. Cambridge, U.K. : New York : Cambridge University Press, 1999.
*TC GT2853.G8 G37 1999*

**CIVILIZATION, CLASSICAL - STUDY AND TEACHING - UNITED STATES.**
Kopff, E. Christian. The devil knows Latin. Wilmington, Del. : ISI Books, 1999.
*TC PA78.U6 K67 1999*

**CIVILIZATION, GREEK.** *See* **GREECE - CIVILIZATION.**

**CIVILIZATION - HISTORY.** *See* **CIVILIZATION, MEDIEVAL; CIVILIZATION, MODERN.**

**CIVILIZATION, LATIN.** *See* **ROME - CIVILIZATION.**

**CIVILIZATION, MEDIEVAL.** *See* **EDUCATION, MEDIEVAL; MIDDLE AGES.**

**CIVILIZATION, MEDIEVAL - HISTORY.** *See* **CIVILIZATION, MEDIEVAL.**

**CIVILIZATION, MEDIEVAL - JUVENILE LITERATURE.**
Honan, Linda. Picture the Middle Ages. Amawalk, N.Y. : Golden Owl Pub. Co. : Higgins Armory Museum, c1994.
*TC CB351 .H58 1994*

**CIVILIZATION, MEDIEVAL - STUDY AND TEACHING (ELEMENTARY).**
Honan, Linda. Picture the Middle Ages. Amawalk, N.Y. : Golden Owl Pub. Co. : Higgins Armory Museum, c1994.
*TC CB351 .H58 1994*

**CIVILIZATION, MODERN.**
Scanning the future. New York : Thames & Hudson, c1999.
*TC CB161 .S44 1999*

**CIVILIZATION, MODERN - 20TH CENTURY.**
Langan, Thomas. Surviving the age of virtual reality. Columbia, Mo. : London : University of Missouri Press, c2000.
*TC B105.M4 L355 2000*

**CIVILIZATION, MODERN - 20TH CENTURY - PSYCHOLOGICAL ASPECTS.**
Stevens, Anthony. The two million-year-old self. New York : Fromm International Publishing, 1997.
*TC BF175.5.A72 S75 1997*

**CIVILIZATION, MODERN - PSYCHOLOGICAL ASPECTS.**
Acting out in groups. Minneapolis, Minn. : London : University of Minnesota Press, c1999.
*TC RC569.5.A25 A28 1999*

**CIVILIZATION, OCCIDENTAL.** *See* **CIVILIZATION, WESTERN.**

**Civilization of the American Indian series**
(v. 4.) Foreman, Grant, 1869-1953. Advancing the frontier, 1830-1860. Norman : University of Oklahoma Press, 1968 printing, c1933.
*TC E93 .F67 1968*

**CIVILIZATION, ORIENTAL.** *See* **EAST ASIA - CIVILIZATION.**

**CIVILIZATION, WESTERN.**
America, the West, and liberal education. Lanham, Md. : Rowman & Littlefield, c1999.
*TC LC1023 .A44 1999*

Barzun, Jacques, 1907- From dawn to decadence. 1st ed. New York : HarperCollins, c2000.
*TC CB245 .B365 2000*

**CIVILIZATION, WESTERN - AFRICAN INFLUENCES.** *See* **AFROCENTRISM.**

**CIVILIZATION, WESTERN - AFRICAN INFLUENCES - ENCYCLOPEDIAS.**
Microsoft encarta Africana [computer file]. Redmond, WA : Microsoft Corp., c1999. Computer data and programs.
*TC DT14 .M527 1999*

Microsoft encarta Africana [computer file]. Redmond, WA : Microsoft Corp., c1999. Computer data and programs.
*TC DT3 .M53 1999x*

**CIVILIZATION, WESTERN - CLASSICAL INFLUENCES.**

**Cizek, Gregory J.**

The eye expanded. Berkeley : University of California Press, c1999.
*TC DE59 .E93 1999*

**Cizek, Gregory J.** Cheating on tests : how to do it, detect it, and prevent it / Gregory J. Cizek. Mahwah, N.J. ; London : L. Erlbaum Associates, 1999. xi, 268 p. : ill. ; 27 cm. Includes bibliographical references (p. 233-248) and indexes. ISBN 0-8058-3144-4 (hbk. : alk. paper) ISBN 0-8058-3145-2 (pbk. : alk. paper) DDC 371.26
*1. Cheating (Education) 2. Educational tests and measurements. I. Title.*
*TC LB3609 .C47 1999*

**Claggett, Mary Frances.**
Burke, Jim, 1961- The English teachers' companion. Portsmouth, NH : Boynton/Cook, c1999.
*TC PE65 .B87 1999*

**Clair, Jeffrey M., 1958-.**
The gerontological prism. Amityville, N.Y. : Baywood Pub., c2000.
*TC HQ1061 .G416 2000*

**Clamp, Cynthia G. L.** Resources for nursing research : an annotated bibliography / Cynthia G.L. Clamp and Stephen Gough. 3rd ed. London ; Thousand Oaks, Calif. : Sage, 1999. xiv, 402 p. ; 25 cm. Includes bibliographical references and index. ISBN 0-7619-6065-1 ISBN 0-7619-6066-X (pbk) DDC 016.61073
*1. Nursing - Research - Bibliography. 2. Nursing - Bibliography of bibliographies. 3. Nursing research - Bibliography. 4. Nursing - Bibliography. I. Gough, Stephen. II. Title.*
*TC Z6675.N7 C53 1999*

**Clancey, William J.** Conceptual coordination : how the mind orders experience in time / William J. Clancey. Mahwah, N.J. : L. Erlbaum Associates, 1999. xix, 395 p. : ill. ; 23 cm. Includes bibliographical references (p. 363-382) and indexes. ISBN 0-8058-3143-6 (alk. paper) DDC 153
*1. Cognitive science. 2. Cognition. 3. Knowledge, Theory of. 4. Artificial intelligence. I. Title.*
*TC BF311 .C5395 1999*

**Clandinin, D. Jean.** Narrative inquiry : experience and story in qualitative research / D. Jean Clandinin, F. Michael Connelly. 1st ed. San Francisco : Jossey-Bass Inc., c2000. xxvi, 211 p. ; 24 cm. Includes bibliographical references (p 191-197) and index. ISBN 0-7879-4343-6 (alk. paper) DDC 370/.7/2
*1. Education - Research - Methodology. 2. Narration (Rhetoric) 3. Storytelling. I. Connelly, F. Michael. II. Title.*
*TC LB1028 .C55 2000*

**Claremont College Reading Conference. Yearbook - Claremont College Reading Conference.**
Claremont Reading Conference. Yearbook. Claremont, Calif. : Claremont Graduate School Curriculum Laboratory, c1961-
*TC BF456.R2 A24*

**Claremont Graduate School.**
Claremont Reading Conference. Yearbook. Claremont, Calif. : Claremont Graduate School Curriculum Laboratory, c1961-
*TC BF456.R2 A24*

**Claremont Reading Conference.** Yearbook / Claremont Reading Conference. Claremont, Calif. : Claremont Graduate School Curriculum Laboratory, c1961- v. : ill. ; 17-22 cm. Frequency: Annual. 25th (1961)- Yearbook of the Claremont Reading Conference. Vols. for <1963- > have title: Yearbook of the Claremont Reading Conference. Publisher varies. Indexed in its entirety by: Education index 0013-1385. Sponsored by Claremont Graduate School. 1st (1936)-51st (1987) with 52nd (1988). (Includes index to earlier title) Continues: Claremont College Reading Conference. Yearbook - Claremont College Reading Conference. (OCoLC)2259436. ISSN 0886-6880 DDC 372.4
*1. Reading - Congresses. I. Claremont Graduate School. II. Title. III. Title: Yearbook of the Claremont Reading Conference IV. Title: Claremont College Reading Conference. Yearbook - Claremont College Reading Conference.*
*TC BF456.R2 A24*

**Clarence S. Stein.**
Stein, Clarence S. The writings of Clarence S. Stein. Baltimore, Md. : Johns Hopkins University Press, 1998.
*TC NA9108 .S83 1998*

**CLARINET AND PIANO MUSIC (JAZZ).** *See* JAZZ.

**Clark, Alison.** The child in focus : the evolving role of the guardian ad litem / Alison Clark and Ruth Sinclair. London : National Children's Bureau Enterprise, c1999. vi, 125 p. : ill. ; 30 cm. Includes bibliographical references (p. 122-125). ISBN 1-900990-50-4
*1. Guardian and ward - Great Britain. 2. Children - Legal status, laws, etc. - Great Britain. I. Sinclair, Ruth. II. Title. III. Title: Evolving role of the guardian ad litem*
*TC KD785 .C43 1999*

**Clark, Ann, 1961-.**
Gender in the secondary curriculum. London ; New York : Routledge, 1998.
*TC LC212.93.G7 G46 1998*

**Clark, Beverly Lyon.**
Girls, boys, books, toys. Baltimore : Johns Hopkins University Press, 1999.
*TC PN1009.5.S48 G57 1999*

**Clark, Catherine, 1944-.**
Theorising special education. London ; New York : Routledge, 1998.
*TC LC3986.G7 T54 1998*

**Clark, Charles E., 1960-.**
**Doloi negramotnost.**
Clark, Charles E., 1960- Uprooting otherness. Selinsgrove [Pa.] : Susquehanna University Press ; London : Associated University Presses, c2000.
*TC LC156.S65 C56 2000*

Uprooting otherness : the literacy campaign in NEP-Era Russia / Charles E. Clark. Selinsgrove [Pa.] : Susquehanna University Press ; London : Associated University Presses, c2000. 235 p. ; 25 cm. Originally presented as the author's thesis (Ph.D.--University of Illinois at Urbana-Champaign, 1993) under the title: Doloi negramotnost'. Includes bibliographical references (p. 181-229) and index. ISBN 1-57591-030-6 (alk. paper) DDC 302.2/244/0947
*1. Literacy - Soviet Union - History - 20th century. 2. Literacy programs - Soviet Union - History - 20th century. 3. Soviet Union - Economic policy - 1917-1928. I. Clark, Charles E., 1960- Doloi negramotnost' . II. Title. III. Title: Literacy campaign in NEP-Era Russia*
*TC LC156.S65 C56 2000*

**Clark, Christine, 1962-.**
Becoming and unbecoming white. Westport, Conn. : Bergin & Garvey, 1999.
*TC E184.A1 B29 1999*

**Clark, Claiborne M.**
Depression in older adults [videorecording]. Boston, MA : Fanlight Productions ; [Chicago, Ill.] : Distributed by Terra Nova Films, Inc., 1997.
*TC RC537.5 .D4 1997*

**Clark, Claudia, 1950-.**
Scott, Jack, Ph. D. Students with autism. San Diego : Singular Pub. Group, 2000.
*TC LC4718 .S36 2000*

**Clark, David A., 1954-** Scientific foundations of cognitive theory and therapy of depression / David A. Clark and Aaron T. Beck, with Brad A. Alford. New York : John Wiley, c1999. ix, 494 p. ; 24 cm. Includes bibliographical references (p. 421-475) and indexes. ISBN 0-471-18970-7 (cloth : alk. paper) DDC 616.85/270651
*1. Depression, Mental. 2. Cognitive therapy. 3. Affective disorders. I. Beck, Aaron T. II. Alford, Brad A. III. Title.*
*TC RC537 .C53 1999*

**Clark, Doris C., 1938-** Feed all my sheep : a guide and curriculum for adults with developmental disabilities / Doris C. Clark ; with music by Kinley Lange. 1st ed. Louisville, Ky. : Geneva Press, c2000. ix, 109 p. : ill., music ; 28 cm. Includes bibliographical references (p. 107-109). ISBN 0-664-50113-3 (alk. paper) DDC 268/.434/0875
*1. Christian education of the mentally handicapped. I. Title.*
*TC BV1615.M37 C53 2000*

**CLARK, EDWARD, 1926- - EXHIBITIONS.**
Edward Clark. Belleville Lake, Mich. : Belleville Lake Press, c1997.
*TC ND237.C524 E393 1997*

**Clark, Eve V.**
Child Language Research Forum (29th : 1997 : Stanford University) The proceedings of the twenty-ninth Annual Child Language Research Forum. [Stanford] : Published for the Stanford Linguistics Association by the Center for the Study of Language and Information, c1998.
*TC P118 .C4558 1997*

**Clark, Henry Nichols Blake.**
Myth, magic and mystery. Boulder, Colo. : Roberts Rinehart Publishers ; [Norfolk, Va.] : in cooperation with the Chrysler Museum of Art, c1996.
*TC NC975 .M98 1996*

**Clark, Leonard H.** Secondary and middle school teaching methods / Leonard H. Clark, Irving S. Starr. 7th ed. Englewood Cliffs, N.J. : Merrill, c1996. xii, 477 p. : ill. ; 28 cm. Includes bibliographical references and index. ISBN 0-02-322871-7 DDC 373.11/02
*1. High school teaching. 2. Middle school teaching. I. Starr, Irving S. II. Title.*
*TC LB1737.A3 C53 1996*

**Clark, M. Carolyn.**
An update on adult development theory :. San Francisco, CA : Jossey-Bass Publishers, 1999.
*TC LC5225.L42 U63 1999*

**Clark, Matt.**
d·a·t·e rape [videorecording]. [Charleston, WV] : Cambridge Educational, c1994.
*TC RC560.R36 D3 1994*

**Clark, Penney, 1950-.**
The Canadian anthology of social studies. Vancouver : Pacific Educational Press, c1999.
*TC H62.5.C3 C32 1999*

**Clark, Trinkett.**
Myth, magic and mystery. Boulder, Colo. : Roberts Rinehart Publishers ; [Norfolk, Va.] : in cooperation with the Chrysler Museum of Art, c1996.
*TC NC975 .M98 1996*

**Clarke, A. D. B. (Alan Douglas Benson).**
Clarke, Ann M. (Ann Margaret) Early experience and the life path. London ; Philadelphia : Jessica Kingsley, 2000.
*TC BF721 .C5457 2000*

**Clarke, Ann M. (Ann Margaret)** Early experience and the life path / Ann M. Clarke and Alan D.B. Clarke. London ; Philadelphia : Jessica Kingsley, 2000. 127 p. ; 22 cm. Includes bibliographical references (p. 109-122) and indexes. ISBN 1-85302-858-4 (pbk.) DDC 155.2/5
*1. Child psychology. 2. Parental deprivation. I. Clarke, A. D. B. (Alan Douglas Benson) II. Title.*
*TC BF721 .C5457 2000*

**Clarke, Don.**
Ayers, Harry. Perspectives on behaviour. 2nd ed. London : David Fulton, 2000.
*TC LC4801 .A94 2000*

**Clarke, John H., 1943-.**
Teaching critical thinking. Englewood Cliffs, N.J. : Prentice Hall, c1993.
*TC LB1590.3 .T4 1993*

**Clarke, Paul, 1961-** Learning schools, learning systems / Paul Clarke. London ; New York : Continuum, 2000. xvi, 160 p. : ill. ; 25 cm. (School development series) Includes bibliographical references (p. 150-156) and index. ISBN 0-8264-4804-6 ISBN 0-8264-4800-3 (pbk.)
*1. Educational change. 2. Educational innovations. I. Title. II. Series.*
*TC LB1027 .C468 2000*

**Clarke, Priscilla, 1943-.**
Siraj-Blatchford, Iram. Supporting identity, diversity and language in the early years. Buckingham [England] ; Philadelphia : Open University Press, 2000.
*TC LB1139.3.G7 S57 2000*

**Clarkson, Rich.**
The power of idea : [videorecording]. Minneapolis, Minn. : Media Loft, c1992.
*TC TR690 .P5 1992*

Sport photography today! [videorecording]. Minneapolis, Minn. : Media Loft, c1992.
*TC TR821 .S64 1992*

**Class, codes and control**
(v. 4) Bernstein, Basil B. The structuring of pedagogic discourse. London ; New York : Routledge, 1990.
*TC P40 .B39 1990*

**CLASS CONFLICT.** *See* **SOCIAL CONFLICT.**

**CLASS DISTINCTION.** *See* **SOCIAL CLASSES.**

**Class politics.**
Parks, Stephen, 1963- Urbana, Ill. : National Council of Teachers of English, c2000.
*TC PE1405.U6 P3 2000*

**CLASS REUNIONS - UNITED STATES.**
Ikeda, Keiko. A room full of mirrors. Stanford, Calif. : Stanford University Press; 1998.
*TC LB3618 .I54 1998*

**CLASS ROOMS.** *See* **CLASSROOMS.**

**CLASS SCHEDULES.** *See* **SCHEDULES, SCHOOL.**

**CLASS SIZE - UNITED STATES.**
Achilles, Charles M. Let's put kids first, finally. Thousand Oaks, Calif. : Corwin Press, c1999.
*TC LB3013.2 .A34 1999*

Carbone, Elisa Lynn. Teaching large classes.
Thousand Oaks, Calif. : Sage Publications, c1998.
*TC LB2331 .C336 1998*

CLASS STRUGGLE. *See* SOCIAL CONFLICT.

CLASSES, SOCIAL. *See* SOCIAL CLASSES.

CLASSICAL ANTIQUITIES. *See* CLASSICAL
PHILOLOGY.

CLASSICAL CIVILIZATION. *See*
CIVILIZATION, CLASSICAL.

CLASSICAL EDUCATION. *See* EDUCATION,
HUMANISTIC; HUMANISM; HUMANITIES.

CLASSICAL EDUCATION - ENGLAND -
HISTORY - 19TH CENTURY.
Stray, Christopher. Classics transformed. Oxford :
Clarendon Press ; New York : Oxford University
Press, 1998.
*TC PA78.E53 S87 1998*

CLASSICAL EDUCATION - ENGLAND -
HISTORY - 20TH CENTURY.
Stray, Christopher. Classics transformed. Oxford :
Clarendon Press ; New York : Oxford University
Press, 1998.
*TC PA78.E53 S87 1998*

CLASSICAL EDUCATION - UNITED STATES.
Kopff, E. Christian. The devil knows Latin.
Wilmington, Del. : ISI Books, 1999.
*TC PA78.U6 K67 1999*

CLASSICAL EDUCATION - UNITED STATES -
HISTORY.
Rabil, Alison. Content, context, and continuity. 1998.
*TC 06 no. 10901*

CLASSICAL LANGUAGES. *See* LATIN
LANGUAGE.

CLASSICAL MUSIC. *See* MUSIC.

CLASSICAL PHILOLOGY. *See* HUMANISM;
LATIN LANGUAGE.

CLASSICAL PHILOLOGY - STUDY AND
TEACHING - ENGLAND - HISTORY.
Stray, Christopher. Classics transformed. Oxford :
Clarendon Press ; New York : Oxford University
Press, 1998.
*TC PA78.E53 S87 1998*

CLASSICAL PHILOLOGY - STUDY AND
TEACHING - HISTORY - 19TH CENTURY.
Stray, Christopher. Classics transformed. Oxford :
Clarendon Press ; New York : Oxford University
Press, 1998.
*TC PA78.E53 S87 1998*

CLASSICAL PHILOLOGY - STUDY AND
TEACHING - HISTORY - 20TH CENTURY.
Stray, Christopher. Classics transformed. Oxford :
Clarendon Press ; New York : Oxford University
Press, 1998.
*TC PA78.E53 S87 1998*

CLASSICAL PHILOLOGY - STUDY AND
TEACHING - UNITED STATES.
Kopff, E. Christian. The devil knows Latin.
Wilmington, Del. : ISI Books, 1999.
*TC PA78.U6 K67 1999*

CLASSICISM. *See* CIVILIZATION, CLASSICAL.

CLASSICISM - ENGLAND.
Stray, Christopher. Classics transformed. Oxford :
Clarendon Press ; New York : Oxford University
Press, 1998.
*TC PA78.E53 S87 1998*

CLASSICISM IN ART. *See* NEOCLASSICISM
(ART).

CLASSICISM - UNITED STATES.
Kopff, E. Christian. The devil knows Latin.
Wilmington, Del. : ISI Books, 1999.
*TC PA78.U6 K67 1999*

Classics transformed.
Stray, Christopher. Oxford : Clarendon Press ; New
York : Oxford University Press, 1998.
*TC PA78.E53 S87 1998*

CLASSIFICATION - BOOKS - PROBLEMS,
EXERCISES, ETC.
Saye, Jerry D. Manheimer's cataloging and
classification. 4th ed., rev. and expanded. New York :
Marcel Dekker, c2000.
*TC Z693 .S28 2000*

CLASSIFICATION - CONGRESSES.
International Federation of Classification Societies.
Conference. 5th, 1996, Kobe, Japan. Data science,

classification, and related methods :. Tokyo ; New
York : Springer, c1998.
*TC QA278 I53 1996*

The classification of visual art.
Sutton, Tiffany. Cambridge ; New York : Cambridge
University Press, 2000.
*TC N66 .S88 2000*

CLASSIFICATION (PSYCHOLOGY). *See*
CATEGORIZATION (PSYCHOLOGY).

CLASSROOM CLIMATE. *See* CLASSROOM
ENVIRONMENT.

Classroom Connect.
McLain, Tim, 1970- How to create successful Internet
projects. El Segundo, Calif. : Classroom Connect,
c1999.
*TC LB1044.87 .M35 1999*

CLASSROOM ENVIRONMENT.
Chuska, Kenneth R. Improving classroom questions.
Bloomington, Ind. : Phi Delta Kappa Educational
Foundation, 1995.
*TC LB1027.44 .C58 1995*

Gore, M. C. Taming the time stealers. Thousand
Oaks, Calif. : Corwin Press, c1999.
*TC LB2838.8 .G67 1999*

Page, Randy M. Fostering emotional well-being in the
classroom. 2nd ed. Sudbury, Mass. ; London : Jones
and Bartlett Publishers, c2000.
*TC LB3430 .P34 2000*

Reflections of first-year teachers on school culture.
San Francisco : Jossey-Bass Inc., 1999.
*TC LB2844.1.N4 R44 1999*

Ryan, Sharon Kaye. Freedom to choice. 1998.
*TC 06 no. 11034*

Stories out of school. Stamford, Conn. : Ablex Pub.,
c2000.
*TC LC196 .S6994 2000*

CLASSROOM ENVIRONMENT - EVALUATION.
School climate. London ; Philadelphia : Falmer Press,
1999.
*TC LC210 .S35 1999*

Classroom interviews.
Rogovin, Paula. Portsmouth, NH : Heinemann, c1998.
*TC LB1537 .R58 1998*

Classroom issues : practice, pedagogy and curriculum /
edited by Mal Leicester, Celia Modgil and Sohan
Modgil. London ; New York : Falmer Press, 2000. 259
p. : ill. ; 29 cm. (Education, culture, and values ; v. 3) Includes
bibliographical references and index. ISBN 0-7507-1004-7
DDC 370.11/4
*1. Moral education. 2. Teaching. 3. Learning. 4. Curriculum
planning. 5. Multicultural education. I. Leicester, Mal. II.
Modgil. Celia. III. Modgil. Sohan. IV. Series.*
*TC LC268 .C52 2000*

Classroom killers? hallway hostages?.
Trump, Kenneth S. Thousand Oaks, Calif. : Corwin
Press, c2000.
*TC LB2866.5 .T78 2000*

CLASSROOM LEARNING CENTERS.
Strategies for energizing large classes : from small
groups to learning communities. San Francisco,
Calif. : Jossey-Bass, 2000.
*TC LB2361.5 .S77 2000*

CLASSROOM MANAGEMENT. *See also*
CLASSROOM ENVIRONMENT.
Tauber, Robert T. 3rd ed. Westport, Conn. : Bergin &
Garvey, 1999.
*TC LB3011 .T38 1999*

CLASSROOM MANAGEMENT.
Ayers, Harry. Perspectives on behaviour. 2nd ed.
London : David Fulton, 2000.
*TC LC4801 .A94 2000*

Beyond behaviorism. Boston : Allyn and Bacon, c
1999.
*TC LB3013 .B42 1999*

Bodine, Richard J. Developing emotional intelligence.
Champaign, Ill : Research Press, c1999.
*TC BF561 .B6 1999*

Campbell, Jack, Ed. D. Student discipline and
classroom management. Springfield, Ill. : C.C.
Thomas, c1999.
*TC LB3012 .C34 1999*

Charles, C. M. Elementary classroom management.
2nd ed. White Plains, N.Y. : Longman, c1995.

*TC LB3013 .C465 1995*

Charles, C. M. The synergetic classroom. New York :
Longman, c2000.
*TC LB3013 .C4653 2000*

Danforth, Scot. Cases in behavior management. Upper
Saddle River, N.J. : Merrill, c2000.
*TC LB3013 .D34 2000*

Dreyer, Susan T. Student perceptions of their
educational experiences at Satellite Academy High
School and their former schools. 1999.
*TC 06 no. 11105*

Emmer, Edmund T. Classroom management for
secondary teachers. 5th ed. Boston : Allyn and Bacon,
c2000.
*TC LB3013 .C53 2000*

Evertson, Carolyn M., 1935- Classroom management
for elementary teachers. 5th ed. Boston : Allyn and
Bacon, c2000.
*TC LB3013 .C528 2000*

Freiberg, H. Jerome. Universal teaching strategies. 3rd
ed. Boston : Allyn and Bacon, c2000.
*TC LB1025.3 .F74 2000*

Froyen, Len A. Schoolwide and classroom
management. 3rd ed. Upper Saddle River, N.J. :
Merrill, c1999.
*TC LB3013 .F783 1999*

Jones, Vernon F., 1945- Comprehensive classroom
management. 6th ed. Boston : Allyn and Bacon,
c2001.
*TC LB3013 .J66 2001*

Kohn, Alfie. What to look for in a classroom. 1st ed.
San Francisco : Jossey-Bass, c1998.
*TC LB1775 .K643 1998*

Koshewa, Allen. Discipline and democracy.
Portsmouth, NH : Heinemann, c1999.
*TC LB3011 .K66 1999*

Olson, Judy L. Teaching children and adolescents
with special needs. 3rd ed. Upper Saddle River, N.J. :
Merrill, c2000.
*TC LC3969 .O47 2000*

Peters, Dorothy. Taking cues from kids. Portsmouth,
NH : Heinemann, c2000.
*TC LB3013 .P43 2000*

Porter, Louise, 1958- Behaviour in schools.
Buckingham [England] ; Philadelphia : Open
University Press, 2000.
*TC LB3012 .P65 2000*

Robbins, Pamela. Thinking inside the block schedule.
Thousand Oaks, Calif. : Corwin Press, c2000.
*TC LB3032.2 .R63 2000*

Seeman, Howard. Preventing classroom discipline
problems. 3rd ed. Lanham, Md. : Scarecrow Press,
2000.
*TC LB3013 .S44 2000*

CLASSROOM MANAGEMENT - BERMUDA
ISLANDS.
Tucker, Gina Marie. Discipline. 1998.
*TC 06 no. 10999*

CLASSROOM MANAGEMENT - CASE STUDIES.
Beyond behaviorism. Boston : Allyn and Bacon, c
1999.
*TC LB3013 .B42 1999*

Classroom management for elementary teachers.
Evertson, Carolyn M., 1935- 5th ed. Boston : Allyn
and Bacon, c2000.
*TC LB3013 .C528 2000*

Classroom management for secondary teachers.
Emmer, Edmund T. 5th ed. Boston : Allyn and Bacon,
c2000.
*TC LB3013 .C53 2000*

CLASSROOM MANAGEMENT - GREAT
BRITAIN.
Harris, Alma, 1958- Teaching and learning in the
effective school. Aldershot, England ; Brookfield,
Vt. : Ashgate, c1999.
*TC LB2822.84.G7 H37 1999*

McNamara, Eddie. Positive pupil management and
motivation :. London : David Fulton, 1999.
*TC LB3013 .M336 1999*

CLASSROOM MANAGEMENT - HANDBOOKS,
MANUALS, ETC.
Brown, Sally A. 500 tips for teachers. 2nd ed.
London : Kogan Page ; Sterling, VA : Stylus Pub.,
1998.

**TC LB3013 .B76 1998**

Learning to teach in the secondary school. 2nd ed.
London ; New York : Routledge, 1999.
**TC LB1737.A3 L43 1999**

**CLASSROOM MANAGEMENT -
PSYCHOLOGICAL ASPECTS.**
Sylwester, Robert. A biological brain in a cultural
classroom. Thousand Oaks, Calif. : Corwin Press,
c2000.
**TC LB3011.5 .S95 2000**

**CLASSROOM MANAGEMENT - SOCIAL
ASPECTS - UNITED STATES.**
McEwan, Barbara, 1946- The art of classroom
management. Upper Saddle River, N.J. : Merrill,
c2000.
**TC LB3013 .M383 2000**

**Classroom management strategies.**
Cangelosi, James S. 3rd ed. White Plains, N.Y. :
Longman, c1997.
**TC LB3013 .C3259 1997**

Cangelosi, James S. 4th ed. New York : J. Wiley,
c2000.
**TC LB3013 .C3259 2000**

**CLASSROOM MANAGEMENT - UNITED
STATES.**
Bauer, Anne M. Inclusion 101. Baltimore, Md. : P.H.
Brookes Pub., c1999.
**TC LC1201 .B38 1999**

Cangelosi, James S. Classroom management
strategies. 3rd ed. White Plains, N.Y. : Longman,
c1997.
**TC LB3013 .C3259 1997**

Cangelosi, James S. Classroom management
strategies. 4th ed. New York : J. Wiley, c2000.
**TC LB3013 .C3259 2000**

Christenbury, Leila. Making the journey. 2nd ed.
Portsmouth, NH : Boynton/Cook Publishers, c2000.
**TC LB1631 .C4486 2000**

DiGiulio, Robert C., 1949- Positive classroom
management. 2nd ed. Thousand Oaks, CA. : Corwin
Press, c2000.
**TC LB3013 .D54 2000**

Dynamics of effective teaching. 4th ed. New York ;
Harlow, England : Longman, c2000.
**TC LB1737.U6 K56 2000**

Frank, Carolyn. Ethnographic eyes. Portsmouth, NH :
Heinemann, c1999.
**TC LB1027.28 .F73 1999**

Janney, Rachel. Modifying schoolwork. Baltimore,
Md. : Paul H. Brookes Pub., c2000.
**TC LC1201 .J26 2000**

Paley, Vivian Gussin, 1929- White teacher.
Cambridge, Mass. : Harvard University Press, 2000.
**TC LC2771 .P34 2000**

Rathvon, Natalie. Effective school interventions. New
York : Guilford Press, c1999.
**TC LC1201 .R38 1999**

Savage, Tom V. Teaching self-control through
management and discipline. 2nd ed. Boston : London :
Allyn and Bacon, c1999.
**TC LB3012.2 .S38 1999**

Tauber, Robert T. Classroom management. 3rd ed.
Westport, Conn. : Bergin & Garvey, 1999.
**TC LB3011 .T38 1999**

Tomal, Daniel R. Discipline by negotiation. 1st ed.
Lancaster, Pa. : Technomic Pub. Co., c1999.
**TC LB3011.5 .T66 1999**

**CLASSROOM MANAGEMENT - UNITED
STATES - HANDBOOKS, MANUALS, ETC.**
Niebrand, Chris. The pocket mentor. Boston, Mass. :
Allyn and Bacon, 2000.
**TC LB1775.2 .N54 2000**

**CLASSROOM MANAGEMENT - UNITED
STATES - PROBLEMS, EXERCISES, ETC.**
Levin, James, 1946- Principles of classroom
management. 3rd ed. Boston : Allyn and Bacon,
c2000.
**TC LB3013 .L475 2000**

**CLASSROOM OBSERVATION.** *See*
**OBSERVATION (EDUCATIONAL
METHOD).**

**Classroom resource materials**
Stein, Sherman K. Archimedes. Washington, D.C. :
Mathematical Association of America, c1999.

**TC QA31 .S84 1999**

**The classroom teacher.** Berkeley, Calif., Berkeley
Federation of Teachers Local 1078. v. 28 cm. Title
varies: News bulletin <Feb. 1952>-Mar. 1953, June 1953-Dec.
1953. Title varies: Salary bulletin May 1953-June 1953. Title
varies: Gadfly <Oct. 1964-Apr. 1968>. Vol. 11 never
published. <Nov. 1952-Mar. 1953> called no. <3-7>; <Nov.
18, 1954>-June 16, 1955, Bulletin no. <3>-10; Sept. 15, 1955-
<Apr. 26, 1956>, no. 1-<14>; <Oct. 1964-Apr. 1968>, <v. 12,
no. 1-v. 16, no. 2>
*1. Teachers - California - Periodicals. I. American Federation
of Teachers. Local 1078 (Berkeley, Calif.) II. Title: Labor
union collection. III. Title: News bulletin <Feb. 1952>-Mar.
1953, June 1953-Dec. 1953 IV. Title: Salary bulletin May
1953-June 1953 V. Title: Gadfly <Oct. 1964-Apr. 1968>*

**Classroom testing.**
Hopkins, Charles D. 2nd ed. Itasca, Ill. : F. E. Peacock
Publishers, c1989.
**TC LB3060.65 .H661 1989**

**Classroom volunteers.**
Wachter, Joanne C. Thousand Oaks, Calif. : Corwin
Press, c1999.
**TC LB2844.1.V6 W33 1999**

**CLASSROOMS - HISTORY - CONGRESSES.**
Silences & images. New York : P. Lang, c1999.
**TC LA128 .S55 1999**

**Classrooms in the work place.**
Hollenbeck, Kevin. Classrooms in the workplace.
Kalamazoo, Mich. : W.E. Upjohn Institute for
Employment Research, 1993.
**TC HF5549.5.T7 H598 1993**

**Classrooms in the workplace.**
Hollenbeck, Kevin. Kalamazoo, Mich. : W.E. Upjohn
Institute for Employment Research, 1993.
**TC HF5549.5.T7 H598 1993**

**CLASSROOMS - PICTORIAL WORKS.**
[Nature study class, P.S. 165] [picture] 1935.
**TC BE5564**

[Nature study class, P.S. 165] [picture] 1935.
**TC BE5564**

[Nature study class, P.S. 165] [picture] 1935.
**TC BE5564**

**Classrooms under the influence.**
Powell, Richard R., 1951- Newbury Park, Calif. :
Corwin Press, c1995.
**TC HV5824.Y68 P69 1995**

**CLASSROOMS - UNITED STATES - HISTORY -
CONGRESSES.**
Silences & images. New York : P. Lang, c1999.
**TC LA128 .S55 1999**

**Clauss, Caroline Seay.** Degrees of distance : the
relationship between white racial identity and social
distance phenomena in American society / by
Caroline Seay Clauss. 1999. ix, 171 leaves ; 29 cm.
Includes tables. Typescript; issued also on microfilm. Thesis
(Ph.D.)--Columbia University, 1999. Includes bibliographical
references (leaves 131-144).
*1. Whites - United States - Race identity. 2. Ethnicity - United
States. 3. Social distance. 4. Social change - United States -
Cross-cultural studies. 5. Intercultural communication - United
States. 6. United States - Social conditions. 7. United States -
Race relations - Psychological aspects. I. Title.*
**TC 085 C58**

**Claussen, Angelika Hartl.**
The organization of attachment relationships. New
York : Cambridge University Press, 2000.
**TC BF575.A86.O74 2000**

**Clavel, Linda, ill.**
Berry, Carrie, b. 1854. A Confederate girl. Mankato,
Minn. : Blue Earth Books, c2000.
**TC E605 .B5 2000**

Forten, Charlotte L. A free Black girl before the Civil
War. Mankato, Minn. : Blue Earth Books, c2000.
**TC F74.SI F67 2000**

**Claverie, Jean, 1946- ill.**
Nikly, Michelle. [Royaume des parfums. English] The
perfume of memory. 1st American ed. New York :
A.A. Levine Books, 1998.
**TC PZ7.N585 Pe 1998**

**Claxton, Guy.**
The intuitive practitioner. Buckingham [England] ;
Philadelphia : Open University Press, 2000.
**TC LB1025.3 .I59 2000**

Wise up : the challenge of lifelong learning / Guy
Claxton. 1st U.S. ed. New York, N.Y. : Bloomsbury :
Distributed to the trade by St. Martin's Press, 1999. x,
374 p. : ill. ; 25 cm. Includes bibliographical references (p.

[344]-366) and index. ISBN 1-58234-039-0
*1. Learning, Psychology of. 2. Continuing education. 3.
Thought and thinking. 4. Cognition. I. Title.*
**TC BF318 .C55 1999**

**CLAY.** *See* **CERAMICS.**

**Clay, Cheryl D., 1947-** Schooling at-risk Native
American children : a journey from reservation Head
Start to public school kindergarten / Cheryl D. Clay.
New York : Garland Pub., 1998. xvi, 185 p. : ill. ; 22 cm.
(Native Americans) Includes bibliographical references (p.
171-182) and index. ISBN 0-8153-3137-1 (alk. paper) DDC
372.1829/9745
*1. Ute children - Education (Early childhood) - Colorado. 2.
Ute children - Socialization. 3. Ute children - Social
conditions. 4. Social handicapped children - Education (Early
childhood) - Colorado. 5. Head Start programs - Colorado. 6.
Kindergarten - Colorado. 7. Mainstreaming in education -
Colorado. 8. Social skills in children - Colorado. 9. Education
and state - Colorado. I. Title. II. Series: Native Americans
(Garland Publishing, Inc.)*
**TC E99.U8 C53 1998**

**CLAY, MARIE M.**
Stirring the waters. Portsmouth, NH : Heinemann,
c1999.
**TC LB1139.5.L35 S85 1999**

**Clean living movements.**
Engs, Ruth C. Westport, Conn. ; London : Praeger,
2000.
**TC RA427.8 .E54 2000**

**Clean your room, Harvey Moon!.**
Cummings, Pat. New York : Macmillan/McGraw-Hill
School Pub. Co., c1991.
**TC PZ8.3.C898 Cl 1991**

**CLEANING AND DYEING INDUSTRY.** *See* **DYES
AND DYEING.**

**CLEANLINESS.** *See* **HYGIENE; SANITATION.**

**Clearing paths.** New York, N.Y. : American Book
Company, c1980 448 p. : ill. (some col.) ; 24 cm. (American
readers ; 4) ISBN 0-278-45826-2
*1. Readers (Elementary) I. Series.*
**TC PE1121 .C63 1980**

**Clearing paths.** Teacher's ed. New York, NY :
American Book Company, c1980 xiv, 528 p. : ill. (some
col.) ; 28 cm. (American readers ; 4) Includes index. ISBN 0-
278-45857-2
*1. Readers (Primary) 2. Reading (Primary) I. Series.*
**TC PE1119 .C63 1980 Teacher's Ed.**

**Clearing paths.** Lexington, Mass. : D.C. Heath and
Company, c1983. 592 p. : ill. (some col.) ; 24 cm.
(American readers ; 4) ISBN 0-669-05040-7
*1. Readers (Elementary) I. Series.*
**TC PE1121 .C63 1983**

**Clearing paths : workbook.** Teacher's ed. New York,
N.Y. : American Book Company, c1980 126 p. : ill.
(some col.) ; 28 cm. (American readers ; 4) Includes index.
ISBN 0-278-45938-2
*1. Readers (Elementary) 2. Reading (Elementary) I. Series.*
**TC PE1121 .C63 1980 Teacher's Ed. Workbook**

**Clearing paths : Workbook.** Teacher's ed. Lexington,
Mass. : D.C. Heath and Company, c1983, 142 p. : ill.
(some col.) ; 28 cm. (American readers ; 4) Includes index.
ISBN 0-669-05049-0
*1. Readers (Elementary) 2. Reading (Elementary) I. Series.*
**TC PE1121 .C63 1983 Teacher's Ed. Workbook**

**Clement, Mary C.** Building the best faculty : strategies
for hiring and supporting new teachers / Mary C.
Clement. Lanham, Md. : Scarecrow Press, 2000. xv,
153 p. ; 24 cm. Includes bibliographical references (p. 147-
149) and index. ISBN 1-56676-735-0
*1. Teachers - Recruiting 2. Teachers - In-service training. 3.
Teachers - Selection and appointment. I. Title.*
**TC LB2833 .C53 2000**

**Clement, Rod.** Frank's great museum adventure /
Rod Clement. 1st American ed. [New York] :
HarperCollinsPublishers, 1999. 1 v. (unpaged) : col. ill. ;
26 cm. "Ages 4-8"--Bk. jacket. SUMMARY: Frank the dog
and his owner travel through history when they visit the
museum. ISBN 0-06-027673-8 ISBN 0-06-027674-6 (lib. bdg.)
DDC [E]
*1. Museums - Fiction. 2. Dogs - Fiction. I. Title.*
**TC PZ7.C59114 Fr 1999**

**Clements, Robert D.**
Wachowiak, Frank. Emphasis art. 7th ed. New York ;
London : Longman, c2001.
**TC N350 .W26 2001**

**Cleveland Board of Education (Ohio).** Cleveland's
plan for gifted children : a handbook for
administrators, parents, and the lay public, showing

the need for education of gifted children. [Cleveland] : Cleveland Board of Education, c1956. 32 p. : ill. : 23 cm. "A handbook for administrators, parents and the lay public showing the need for education of gifted children."
*1. Gifted children - Education. I. Title.*
**TC LC3983.C5 A3**

**Cleveland, Jeanette.** Women and men in organizations : sex and gender issues at work / Jeanette N. Cleveland, Margaret Stockdale, Kevin R. Murphy. Mahwah, N.J. ; London : Lawrence Erlbaum Associates, 2000. xiv, 463 p. : ill. ; 24 cm. (Applied psychology series) Includes bibliographical references (p. 384-443) and indexes. ISBN 0-8058-1267-9 (hbk. : alk. paper) ISBN 0-8058-1268-7 (pbk. : alk. paper) DDC 331.11/43
*1. Sex role in the work environment - United States. I. Stockdale, Margaret S. II. Murphy, Kevin R., 1952- III. Title. IV. Series.*
**TC HD6060.65.U5 C58 2000**

**Cleveland's plan for gifted children.**
Cleveland Board of Education (Ohio). [Cleveland] : Cleveland Board of Education, c1956.
**TC LC3983.C5 A3**

**Cleverley, John F.** In the lap of tigers : the Communist Labor University of Jiangxi Province / John Cleverley. Lanham, Md. ; Oxford : Rowman & Littlefield, c2000. xxiv, 249 p. , [20] p. of plates : ill., maps ; 24 cm. Includes bibliographical references (p. 215-235) and index. ISBN 0-8476-9936-6 (cloth : alk. paper) ISBN 0-8476-9937-4 (paper : alk. paper) DDC 630/.71/151222
*1. Chiang-hsi kung ch'an chu i lao tung ta hsüeh - History. I. Title. II. Title: Communist Labor University of Jiangxi Province*
**TC S539.C6 C64 2000**

**Click, Phyllis.** Administration of schools for young children / Phyllis M. Click. 5th ed. Albany, NY : Delmar, 1999. xi, 468 p. : ill. ; 24 cm. Includes bibliographical references (p.455-459 ) and index. ISBN 0-7668-0354-6 DDC 372.21/6/0973
*1. Nursery schools - United States - Administration. 2. Day care centers - United States - Administration. 3. Early childhood education - United States. I. Title.*
**TC LB2822.7 .C55 1999**

**Clifford, Geraldine Jonçich.**
Thorndike, Edward L. (Edward Lee), 1874-1949. Human nature and the social order Cambridge, Mass., M.I.T. Press [1969]
**TC BF121 .T442]**

**CLIFTON (ARIZ.) - RACE RELATIONS.**
Gordon, Linda. The great Arizona orphan abduction. Cambridge, Mass. : Harvard University Press, 1999.
**TC F819.C55 G67 1999**

**CLIMATE, CLASSROOM.** *See* **CLASSROOM ENVIRONMENT.**

**Climate, culture, and values.**
Broad, Kenneth. 1999.
**TC 085 B7775**

**The climate puzzle** [videorecording] / a production of WQED Pittsburgh in association with the National Academy of Sciences ; series producer, Gregory Andorfer ; producer, Gregory Andorfer ; written by Gregory Andorfer, Georgann Kane, Deane Rink. [New York, N.Y.?] : Unapix Entertainment, Inc. [distributor], c1996. 1 videocassette (60 min.) : sd., col. ; 1/2 in. (Planet Earth ; 3) At head of title: Unapix Consumer Products feature presentation [videorecording]. VHS. Catalogued from credits and container. Narrator, Richard Kiley. Sound, Mike deGruy... [et al.]; photography by Paul Atkins, Norris Brock, Chris Woods. "Major funding by the Annenberg/CPB Project"--Container. Originally produced in 1986. For adolescent through adult. SUMMARY: This video explains why no human being has ever experienced the earth's normal climate and questions whether the climate will change again and why, and is the earth entering a new ice age, or will the current global warming trend hold off the inevitable?
*1. Climatic changes. 2. Earth. 3. Global warming. 4. Termites - Environmental aspects. 5. Documentary television programs. I. Andorfer, Gregory. II. Kane, Georgann. III. Rink, Deane. IV. Kiley, Richard. V. WQED (Television station : Pittsburgh, Pa.) VI. National Academy of Sciences (U.S.) VII. Annenberg/CPB Project. VIII. Unapix Entertainment, Inc. IX. Unapix Consumer Products. X. Title: Unapix Consumer Products feature presentation [videorecording] XI. Series.*
**TC QB631.2 .C5 1996**

**Climates and constitutions.**
Harrison, Mark, lecturer. Climates & constitutions :. New Delhi ; New York : Oxford University Press, c1999.
**TC RA395.15 H37 1999**

**CLIMATIC CHANGES.**
Broad, Kenneth. Climate, culture, and values. 1999.

---

**TC 085 B7775**
The climate puzzle [videorecording]. [New York, N.Y.?] : Unapix Entertainment, Inc. [distributor], c1996.
**TC QB631.2 .C5 1996**

**CLIMATOLOGY.** *See* **SEASONS.**

**Climbing up.** New York, N.Y. : American Book Company, c1980. 72 p. : col. ill. : 23x22 cm. (American readers ; PP-2) ISBN 0-278-45807-6
*1. Readers (Primary) I. Series.*
**TC PE1119 .C54 1980**

**Clinchy, Evans.**
Creating new schools. New York : London : Teachers College Press, c2000.
**TC LB2822.82 .C76 2000**

Reforming American education from the bottom to the top. Portsmouth, NH : Heinemann, c1999.
**TC LA210 .R44 1999**

**Clinical and practice issues in adoption.**
Groza, Victor, 1956- Westport, Conn. : Praeger, 1998.
**TC HV875 .G776 1998**

**CLINICAL CHILD PSYCHOLOGY.**
Child and adolescent therapy. 2nd ed. New York : Guilford Press, c2000.
**TC RJ505.C63 C45 2000**

**Clinical child psychology library**
Hawkins, Robert P., 1931- Measuring behavioral health outcomes. New York : Kluwer Academic/ Plenum Publishers, c1999.
**TC RJ503.5 .H39 1999**

**CLINICAL CHILD PSYCHOLOGY - SCHOLARSHIPS, FELLOWSHIPS, ETC. - DIRECTORIES.**
Directory of internship and post-doctoral fellowships in clinical child/pediatric psychology, 1997. [Mahwah, N.J. : Lawrence Erlbaum Associates, c1997].
**TC RJ503.3 .D57 1997**

**CLINICAL CHILD PSYCHOLOGY - STUDY AND TEACHING (INTERNSHIP) - DIRECTORIES.**
Directory of internship and post-doctoral fellowships in clinical child/pediatric psychology, 1997. [Mahwah, N.J. : Lawrence Erlbaum Associates, c1997].
**TC RJ503.3 .D57 1997**

**Clinical competence series**
Golper, Lee Ann C., 1948- Sourcebook for medical speech pathology. 2nd ed. San Diego, Calif. : Singular Pub. Group, c1998.
**TC RC423 .G64 1998**

**Clinical counselling in context** : an introduction / edited by John Lees. London ; New York : Routledge, 1999. xi, 153 p. ; 23 cm. (Clinical counselling in context) Includes bibliographical references and index. ISBN 0-415-17955-6 (hardbound) ISBN 0-415-17956-4 (pbk.) DDC 362.2/04256
*1. Mental health counseling. 2. Clinical psychology. 3. Counseling. 4. Psychotherapy - methods. 5. Psychology, Clinical. I. Lees, John, 1951- II. Series: Clinical counselling in context series.*
**TC RC466 .C55 1999**

**Clinical counselling in context series.**
Clinical counselling in context. London ; New York : Routledge, 1999.
**TC RC466 .C55 1999**

**Clinical genetics in nursing practice.**
Lashley, Felissa R., 1941- 2nd ed. New York : Springer, c1998.
**TC RB155 .L37 1998**

**Clinical handbook of weight management.**
Lean, Michael E. J. London : Martin Dunitz, Ltd. ; Malden, MA : distributed in the USA, Canada and Brazil by Blackwell Science, Ltd., c1998.
**TC RC628 .L436 1998**

**CLINICAL HEALTH PSYCHOLOGY.**
Aboud, Frances E. Health psychology in global perspective. Thousand Oaks : Sage Publications, c1998.
**TC R726.7 .A26 1998**

Hormones, health, and behavior. Cambridge ; New York : Cambridge University Press, 1999.
**TC QP356.45 .H67 1999**

Jonas, Steven. Talking about health and wellness with patients. New York : Springer, c2000.
**TC RA427.8 .J66 2000**

Russell, Graham, 1954- Essential psychology for nurses and other health professionals. London ; New York : Routledge, c1999.

---

**TC R726.7 .R87 1999**

**CLINICAL HEALTH PSYCHOLOGY - DEVELOPING COUNTRIES.**
Aboud, Frances E. Health psychology in global perspective. Thousand Oaks : Sage Publications, c1998.
**TC R726.7 .A26 1998**

**CLINICAL HEALTH PSYCHOLOGY - HANDBOOKS, MANUALS, ETC.**
Handbook of rehabilitation psychology. 1st ed. Washington, DC : American Psychological Association c2000.
**TC R726.7 .H366 2000**

**Clinical interviewing.**
Sommers-Flanagan, Rita, 1953- 2nd ed. New York : Wiley, c1999.
**TC RC480.7 .S66 1999**

**Clinical management of communication disorders in culturally diverse children** / [edited by] Thalia J. Coleman. Boston : Allyn & Bacon, c2000. xxiv, 344 p. ; 23 cm. Includes bibliographical references and index. ISBN 0-205-26724-6 DDC 618.92/855
*1. Communicative disorders in children. 2. Communicative disorders in children - Miscellanea. 3. Communication Disorders - therapy - Child - United States. 4. Cultural Diversity - United States. 5. Early Intervention (Education) - United States. I. Coleman, Thalia J., 1948-*
**TC RJ496.C67 C556 2000**

**Clinical measurement of speech and voice.**
Baken, R. J. (Ronald J.), 1943- 2nd ed. San Diego : Singular Thomson Learning, c2000.
**TC RC423 .B28 2000**

**CLINICAL MEDICINE.**
Nurse practitioner's clinical companion. Springhouse, Pa. : Springhouse Corp., c2000.
**TC RT82.8 .N8638 2000**

**CLINICAL MEDICINE - HANDBOOKS.**
Golper, Lee Ann C., 1948- Sourcebook for medical speech pathology. 2nd ed. San Diego, Calif. : Singular Pub. Group, c1998.
**TC RC423 .G64 1998**

**CLINICAL MEDICINE - HANDBOOKS, MANUALS, ETC.**
Nurse practitioner's clinical companion. Springhouse, Pa. : Springhouse Corp., c2000.
**TC RT82.8 .N8638 2000**

**CLINICAL NEUROPSYCHOLOGY.**
Clinician's guide to neuropsychological assessment. 2nd ed. Mahwah, N.J. : Lawrence Erlbaum Associates, c2000.
**TC RC386.6.N48 G85 2000**

**CLINICAL NEUROPSYCHOLOGY - HANDBOOKS, MANUALS, ETC.**
International handbook of neuropsychological rehabilitation. New York : Kluwer Academic/Plenum Publishers, c2000.
**TC RC387.5 .I478 2000**

**CLINICAL NURSE SPECIALISTS.** *See* **NURSE PRACTITIONERS.**

**CLINICAL NURSING.** *See* **NURSING.**

**Clinical nutrition** : parenteral nutrition / [edited by] John L. Rombeau, Michael D. Caldwell ; illustrations by David W. Low. 2nd ed. Philadelphia : Saunders, 1993. xxix, 889 p. : ill., ports. ; 27 cm. (Clinical nutrition ; [2]) Includes bibliographies and index. ISBN 0-7216-3600-4
*1. Nutrition. 2. Parenteral Nutrition. 3. Parenteral feeding. I. Rombeau, John L. II. Caldwell, Michael D. III. Title: Parenteral nutrition*
**TC RM224 .P24 1993**

**Clinical obstetrics and gynecology.** [New York] Hoeber Medical Division, Harper & Row. v. ill. 24 cm. Began publication Mar. 1958. ISSN 0009-9201
*1. Obstetrics - Periodicals. 2. Gynecology - Periodicals.*

**Clinical perspectives on elderly sexuality.**
Hillman, Jennifer L. New York : Kluwer Academic/Plenum Publishers, c2000.
**TC HQ30 .H55 2000**

**The clinical pharmacology of sport and exercise.**
Fundacion Dr. Antonio Esteve. Symposium (7th : 1996 : Sitges, Spain) Amsterdam ; New York : Elsevier Science B.V., Excerpta Medica, 1997.
**TC RC1230 .F86 1996**

**Clinical practice**
(no. 38) Sexual harassment in the workplace and academia. 1st ed. Washington, DC : American Psychiatric Press, c1996.
**TC RC560.S47 S495 1996**

CLINICAL PSYCHOLOGY. *See also* CLINICAL CHILD PSYCHOLOGY; CLINICAL HEALTH PSYCHOLOGY; CLINICAL NEUROPSYCHOLOGY; PSYCHODIAGNOSTICS; PSYCHOLOGICAL TESTS.
Clinical counselling in context. London ; New York : Routledge, 1999.
*TC RC466 .C55 1999*

CLINICAL PSYCHOLOGY - HANDBOOKS, MANUALS, ETC.
Psychologists' desk reference. New York : Oxford University Press, 1998.
*TC RC467.2 .P78 1998*

Clinical psychology in Ireland : empirical studies of professional practice / edited by Alan Carr. Lewiston, N.Y. : E. Mellen, 2000. xii, 246 p. ; 24 cm. (Studies in health and human services ; v. 36) Includes bibliographical references and index. ISBN 0-7734-7831-0 DDC 616.89/009415
*1. Clinical psychology - Ireland - History. I. Carr, Alan, Dr. II. Series.*
*TC RC466.83.I73 C56 2000*

CLINICAL PSYCHOLOGY - IRELAND - HISTORY.
Clinical psychology in Ireland. Lewiston, N.Y. : E. Mellen, 2000.
*TC RC466.83.I73 C56 2000*

CLINICAL PSYCHOLOGY - PERIODICALS.
Journal of consulting psychology. [Lancaster, Pa., etc.] American Psychological Association.

CLINICAL SCIENCES. *See* MEDICINE.

CLINICAL SOCIOLOGY. *See also* COUNSELING; PSYCHOTHERAPY; SOCIAL PSYCHIATRY.
Darling, Rosalyn Benjamin. The partnership model in human services. New York : Kluwer Academic/Plenum Publishers, c2000.
*TC HV43 .D2 2000*

CLINICAL SOCIOLOGY.
Darling, Rosalyn Benjamin. The partnership model in human services. New York : Kluwer Academic/Plenum Publishers, c2000.
*TC HV43 .D2 2000*

Hall, C. Margaret (Constance Margaret) Heroic self. Springfield, Ill. : C.C. Thomas, c1998.
*TC RC489.S62 H35 1998*

CLINICAL SUPERVISION OF NURSES. *See* NURSES - SUPERVISION OF.

Clinical teaching strategies in nursing.
Gaberson, Kathleen B. New York : Springer, c1999.
*TC RT73 .G26 1999*

Clinical voice pathology.
Stemple, Joseph C. 3rd ed. San Diego : Singular Pub. Group, c2000.
*TC RF510 .S74 2000*

Clinician's guide to neuropsychological assessment / edited by Rodney D. Vanderploeg. 2nd ed. Mahwah, N.J. : Lawrence Erlbaum Associates, c2000. x, 551 p. : ill. ; 23 cm. Includes bibliographical references and indexes. ISBN 0-8058-2834-6 (alk. paper) DDC 616.8/0475
*1. Neuropsychological tests. 2. Clinical neuropsychology. 3. Neuropsychology - methods. 4. Cognition Disorders - diagnosis. 5. Interview, Psychological. 6. Neuropsychological Tests. 7. Personality Assessment. I. Vanderploeg, Rodney D.*
*TC RC386.6.N48 G85 2000*

Clinics in developmental medicine
(no. 149) Developmental disability and behaviour. London, England : Mac Keith Press, 2000.
*TC RJ506.D47 D48 2000*

(no.148) Dubowitz, Lilly M. S. The neurological assessment of the preterm and full-term newborn infant. 2nd ed. London : Mac Keith, 1999.
*TC RJ486 .D85 1999*

Clinton, Catherine, 1952- Scholastic encyclopedia of the Civil War / by Catherine Clinton. New York : Scholastic Reference, 1999. 112 p. : ill. 28 cm. Includes index. SUMMARY: Traces the course of the Civil War, year by year, using profiles of important people, eyewitness accounts, and period art. ISBN 0-590-37227-0 DDC 973.7/03
*1. United States - History - Civil War, 1861-1865 - Encyclopedias, Juvenile. 2. United States - History - Civil War, 1861-1865. I. Title.*
*TC E468 .C67 1999*

Clinton, Helen G.
Social work in pediatrics. New York : Haworth Press, c1995.
*TC HV688.U5 S63 1995*

Clipson-Boyles, Suzi. Drama in primary English teaching / Suzi Clipson-Boyles. London : David Fulton, 1998. iv, 123 p. : ill. ; 30 cm. Includes bibliographical references (p. 121-122) and index. ISBN 1-85346-540-2 (pbk)
*1. Drama - Study and teaching (Elementary) 2. Drama in education. I. Title.*
*TC PN1701 .C556 1998*

CLOCK AND WATCH MAKING. *See* CLOCKS AND WATCHES.

CLOCKS AND WATCHES - FICTION.
Gould, Deborah Lee. Brendan's best-timed birthday. New York : Bradbury Press, 1988.
*TC PZ7.G723 Br 1988*

CLONING - FICTION.
Lasky, Kathryn. Star split. 1st ed. New York : Hyperion Books for Children, 1999.
*TC PZ7.L3274 St 1999*

Close, Elizabeth, 1941-.
A middle mosaic. Urbana, Ill. : National Council of Teachers of English, c2000.
*TC LB1631 .A2 2000*

CLOSE ENCOUNTERS OF THE FIRST KIND. *See* UNIDENTIFIED FLYING OBJECTS - SIGHTINGS AND ENCOUNTERS.

CLOSE ENCOUNTERS OF THE SECOND KIND. *See* UNIDENTIFIED FLYING OBJECTS - SIGHTINGS AND ENCOUNTERS.

CLOSE ENCOUNTERS OF THE THIRD KIND. *See* HUMAN-ALIEN ENCOUNTERS.

Close relationships : a sourcebook / Clyde Hendrick, Susan S. Hendrick, editors. Thousand Oaks, Calif. : Sage Publications, c2000. xxiii, 476 p. ; 25 cm. Includes bibliographical references (p. 371-436) and indexes. ISBN 0-7619-1605-9 (alk. paper) DDC 302
*1. Interpersonal relations. 2. Friendship. 3. Love. 4. Interpersonal conflict. I. Hendrick, Clyde. II. Hendrick, Susan, 1944- III. Title.*
*TC HM1106 .C55 2000*

Close to home, changing lives [videorecording].
Changing lives [videorecording]. Princeton, NJ : Films for the Humanities & Sciences, c1998.
*TC RC564 .C54 1998*

Close to home, portrait of addiction [videorecording].
Portrait of addiction [videorecording]. Princeton, NJ : Films for the Humanities & Sciences, c1998.
*TC HV5801 .P6 1998*

Portrait of addiction [videorecording]. Princeton, NJ : Films for the Humanities & Sciences, c1998.
*TC RC564 .P6 1998*

Close to home (Series)
Changing lives [videorecording]. Princeton, NJ : Films for the Humanities & Sciences, c1998.
*TC RC564 .C54 1998*

The hijacked brain [videorecording]. Princeton, NJ : Films for the Humanities & Sciences, c1998.
*TC RC564 .H5 1998*

The next generation [videorecording]. Princeton, NJ : Films for the Humanities & Sciences, c1998.
*TC RC564 .N4 1998*

The politics of addiction [videorecording]. Princeton, NJ : Films for the Humanities & Sciences, c1998.
*TC RC564 .P59 1998*

Portrait of addiction [videorecording]. Princeton, NJ : Films for the Humanities & Sciences, c1998.
*TC HV5801 .P6 1998*

Portrait of addiction [videorecording]. Princeton, NJ : Films for the Humanities & Sciences, c1998.
*TC RC564 .P6 1998*

Close to home, the hijacked brain [videorecording].
The hijacked brain [videorecording]. Princeton, NJ : Films for the Humanities & Sciences, c1998.
*TC RC564 .H5 1998*

Close to home, the next generation [videorecording].
The next generation [videorecording]. Princeton, NJ : Films for the Humanities & Sciences, c1998.
*TC RC564 .N4 1998*

Close to home, the politics of addiction [videorecording].
The politics of addiction [videorecording]. Princeton, NJ : Films for the Humanities & Sciences, c1998.
*TC RC564 .P59 1998*

CLOSED-CIRCUIT TELEVISION. *See* INDUSTRIAL TELEVISION; TELEVISION IN EDUCATION.

Closing the education gap.
Vernez, Georges. Santa Monica, CA : RAND, 1999.
*TC LC213.2 .V47 1999*

Closs, Alison.
The education of children with medical conditions. London : D. Fulton Publishers, 2000.
*TC LC4564.G7 E38 2000*

CLOTH. *See* TEXTILE FABRICS.

Cloth and human experience / edited by Annette B. Weiner & Jane Schneider. Washington : Smithsonian Institution Press, c1989. xv, 431 p. : ill. ; 24 cm. (Smithsonian series in ethnographic inquiry) Includes bibliographical references and index. ISBN 0-87474-986-7 (alk. paper) DDC 391
*1. Costume - Social aspects. 2. Textile fabrics - Social aspects. I. Weiner, Annette B., 1933- II. Schneider, Jane, 1938- III. Series.*
*TC GT525 .C57 1989*

CLOTHES. *See* CLOTHING AND DRESS.

CLOTHING. *See* CLOTHING AND DRESS.

CLOTHING AND DRESS. *See* COATS; COSTUME; FOOTWEAR.

CLOTHING AND DRESS - FICTION.
Taback, Simms. Joseph had a little overcoat. New York : Viking, 1999.
*TC PZ7.T1115 Jo 1999*

CLOTHING AND DRESS, PRIMITIVE. *See* COSTUME.

CLOTHING AND DRESS - STUDY AND TEACHING (SECONDARY) - CANADA, WESTERN.
Peterat, Linda, 1946- Making textile studies matter. Vancouver : Pacific Educational Press, 1999.
*TC TX340 .P47 1999*

CLOUD FORESTS. *See* RAIN FORESTS.

Cloud, William, 1947-.
Granfield, Robert, 1955- Coming clean. New York ; London : New York University Press, c1999.
*TC HV4998 .G73 1999*

CLOUDS - FICTION.
Wiesner, David. Sector 7. New York : Clarion Books, c1999.
*TC PZ7.W6367 Se 1999*

Clough, Patricia Ticineto, 1945- Autoaffection : unconscious thought in the age of teletechnology / Patricia Ticineto Clough. Minneapolis : University of Minnesota Press, c2000. x, 213 p. ; 23 cm. Includes bibliographical references and index. ISBN 0-8166-2888-2 (alk. paper) ISBN 0-8166-2889-0 (pbk. : alk. paper) DDC 303.48/33
*1. Technology - Social aspects. 2. Telecommunication - Social aspects. 3. Thought and thinking. 4. Subconsciousness. 5. Cognition and culture. 6. Psychoanalysis and culture. 7. Poststructuralism. 8. Postmodernism. I. Title.*
*TC HM846 .C56 2000*

Clown.
Blake, Quentin. 1st American ed. New York : H. Holt, 1996.
*TC PZ7.B56 Cl 1996*

CLUBS. *See* SOCIAL GROUP WORK; SOCIETIES.

CLUSTER ANALYSIS - CONGRESSES.
International Federation of Classification Societies. Conference. 5th, 1996, Kobe, Japan. Data science, classification, and related methods :. Tokyo ; New York : Springer, c1998.
*TC QA278 I53 1996*

CMC SYSTEMS. *See* TELEMATICS.

CO-EDS. *See* WOMEN COLLEGE STUDENTS.

Coaching & mentoring first-year and student teachers.
Podsen, India, 1945- Larchmont, NY : Eye On Education, c2000.
*TC LB1731.4 .P63 2000*

Coaching and mentoring first-year and student teachers.
Podsen, India, 1945- Coaching & mentoring first-year and student teachers. Larchmont, NY : Eye On Education, c2000.
*TC LB1731.4 .P63 2000*

COAL-TAR COLORS. *See* DYES AND DYEING.

Coarticulation : theory, data and techniques / edited by William J. Hardcastle and Nigel Hewlett. Cambridge, U.K. ; New York : Cambridge University Press, 1999. xiii, 386 p. : ill. ; 24 cm. Includes bibliographical references (p.

337-382) and index. ISBN 0-521-44027-0 (hbk.) DDC 612.7/8
1. Speech - Physiological aspects. 2. Phonetics. I. Hardcastle,
William J., 1943- II. Hewlett, Nigel.
*TC QP306 .C68 1999*

**COASTS. See SEASHORE.**

**Coates, Jennifer.** Women talk : conversation between
women friends / Jennifer Coates. Oxford, U.K. ;
Cambridge, Mass. : Blackwell Publishers, 1996. xiv,
324 p. : ill. ; 24 cm. Includes bibliographical references (p.
[311]-319) and index. ISBN 0-631-18252-7 (hbk. : alk. paper)
ISBN 0-631-18253-5 (pbk. : alk. paper) DDC 302.3/46/082
1. Conversation analysis. 2. Women - Language. I. Title.
*TC P120.W66 C6 1996*

**Coats, Erik J., 1968-.**
The social context of nonverbal behavior. Cambridge,
U.K. ; New York : Cambridge University Press ;
Paris : Editions de la Maison des Sciences de
l'Homme, 1999.
*TC BF637.N66 S63 1999*

**COATS - FICTION.**
Taback, Simms. Joseph had a little overcoat. New
York : Viking, 1999.
*TC PZ7.T1115 Jo 1999*

**Cobb, Paul.**
Symbolizing and communicating in mathematics
classrooms. Mahwah, N.J. : Lawrence Erlbaum
Associates, 2000.
*TC QA11 .S873 2000*

**Cobb, William H.** Radical education in the rural South :
Commonwealth College, 1922-1940 / William H.
Cobb. Detroit : Wayne State University Press, 2000.
263 p. : ill. ; 24 cm. Includes bibliographical references (p.
217-255) and index. ISBN 0-8143-2773-7 (alk. paper) DDC
378.767/45
1. Commonwealth College (Mena, Ark.) - History. 2. Working
class - Education (Higher) - Arkansas - History. 3. Labor
movement - United States - History. I. Title.
*TC LD1276 .C63 2000*

**COCAINE HABIT - PHYSIOLOGICAL
ASPECTS - RESEARCH.**
The hijacked brain [videorecording]. Princeton, NJ :
Films for the Humanities & Sciences, c1998.
*TC RC564 .H5 1998*

**COCAINE HABIT - PHYSIOLOGICAL EFFECT -
RESEARCH.**
The hijacked brain [videorecording]. Princeton, NJ :
Films for the Humanities & Sciences, c1998.
*TC RC564 .H5 1998*

**COCAINE HABIT - PSYCHOLOGICAL
ASPECTS.**
Portrait of addiction [videorecording]. Princeton, NJ :
Films for the Humanities & Sciences, c1998.
*TC HV5801 .P6 1998*

Portrait of addiction [videorecording]. Princeton, NJ :
Films for the Humanities & Sciences, c1998.
*TC RC564 .P6 1998*

**COCHLEA - PHYSIOLOGY.**
Venema, Ted. Compression for clinicians. San Diego,
Calif. : Singular Pub. Group, c1998.
*TC RF300 .V46 1999*

**COCHLEAR IMPLANTATION.**
Cochlear implants. Philadelphia : Lippincott
Williams & Wilkins, c2000.
*TC RF305 .C6295 2000*

**COCHLEAR IMPLANTS.**
Cochlear implants. Philadelphia : Lippincott
Williams & Wilkins, c2000.
*TC RF305 .C6295 2000*

**COCHLEAR IMPLANTS.**
Cochlear implants. Philadelphia : Lippincott
Williams & Wilkins, c2000.
*TC RF305 .C6295 2000*

**Cochlear implants** : principles & practices / editors,
John K. Niparko ... [et al.]. Philadelphia : Lippincott
Williams & Wilkins, c2000. xiii, 396 p. : ill. ; 26 cm.
Includes bibliographical references and index. ISBN 0-7817-
1782-5 DDC 617.89
1. Cochlear implants. 2. Cochlear Implantation. 3. Cochlear
Implants. 4. Deafness - rehabilitation. I. Niparko, John K.
*TC RF305 .C6295 2000*

**Cochran, David Carroll.** The color of freedom : race
and contemporary American liberalism / David
Carroll Cochran. Albany : State University of New
York Press, c1999. ix, 207 p. ; 24 cm. (SUNY series in
Afro-American studies) Includes bibliographical references (p.
179-197) and index. ISBN 0-7914-4185-7 (hardcover : alk.
paper) ISBN 0-7914-4186-5 (pbk. : alk. paper) DDC 305.8/
00973

1. United States - Race relations - Political aspects - History -
20th century. 2. Racism - Political aspects - United States -
History - 20th century. 3. Race discrimination - Political
aspects - United States - History - 20th century. 4. Liberalism -
United States - History - 20th century. 5. Afro-Americans -
Civil rights - History - 20th century. 6. Civil society - United
States - History - 20th century. I. Title. II. Series.
*TC E185.615 .C634 1999*

**Cocklin, Barry, 1946-.**
Learning communities in education. London : New
York : Routledge, 1999.
*TC LB14.7 .L43 1999*

**Codding, Judy B., 1944-.**
The new American high school. Thousand Oaks,
Calif. : Corwin Press, c1999.
*TC LA222 .N49 1999*

**Code, Christopher, 1942-.**
Communication disorders following traumatic brain
injury. Hove, East Sussex, UK : Psychology Press,
c1999.
*TC RD594 .C648 1999*

**Code of the street.**
Anderson, Elijah. 1st ed. New York : W.W Norton,
c1999.
*TC F158.9.N4 A52 1999*

**Codes and contradictions.**
Weiler, Jeanne. Albany : State University of New
York Press, c2000.
*TC LC1755 .W45 2000*

**COEDUCATION. See EDUCATION; WOMEN -
EDUCATION.**

**COEDUCATION - UNITED STATES -
LONGITUDINAL STUDIES.**
Miller-Bernal, Leslie, 1946- Separate by degree. New
York : P. Lang, c2000.
*TC LC1601 .M55 2000*

**COEXISTENCE. See INTERNATIONAL
RELATIONS; PEACE; WORLD POLITICS -
1945-.**

**COFFEE.**
Dicum, Gregory. The coffee book. New York : New
Press : Distributed by W.W. Norton, c1999.
*TC HD9199.A2 D53 1999*

**The coffee book.**
Dicum, Gregory. New York : New Press : Distributed
by W.W. Norton, c1999.
*TC HD9199.A2 D53 1999*

**COFFEE INDUSTRY.**
Dicum, Gregory. The coffee book. New York : New
Press : Distributed by W.W. Norton, c1999.
*TC HD9199.A2 D53 1999*

**COFFEE SHOPS - IOWA - EMPLOYEES -
BIOGRAPHY.**
Walz, Thomas, 1933- The unlikely celebrity.
Carbondale : Southern Illinois University Press,
c1998.
*TC HV3006.S33 W35 1998*

**Coffey, Amanda, 1967-.**
Gender and qualitative research. Aldershot, Hants,
England ; Brookfield, Vt., USA : Avebury, c1996.
*TC HQ1075 .G4617 1996*

**Coffin, David D.**
Jenney, Charles. Fourth year Latin. Needham, Mass. :
Prentice Hall, c1990.
*TC PA2087.5 .J463 1990*

Jenney, Charles. Third year Latin. Newton, Mass. :
Allyn and Bacon, c1987.
*TC PA2087.5 .J462 1987*

**Cogan, John J.**
Citizenship for the 21st century. [Rev. ed.]. London :
Kogan Page, 2000.
*TC LC1091 .C575 2000*

**COGNITION. See also ATTRIBUTION (SOCIAL
PSYCHOLOGY); COGNITION AND
CULTURE; COGNITIVE STYLES;
DIFFERENTIATION (COGNITION);
SELECTIVITY (PSYCHOLOGY).**
Andersen, Christopher Lawrence. A microgenetic
study of science reasoning in social context. 1998.
*TC 085 An2305*

Anderson, John R. (John Robert), 1947- Cognitive
psychology and its implications. 5th ed. New York :
Worth, 2000.
*TC BF311 .A5895 2000*

Berry, John W. comp. Culture and cognition: readings
in cross-cultural psychology. London, Methuen [1974]

*TC BF311 .B48*
Clancey, William J. Conceptual coordination.
Mahwah, N.J. : L. Erlbaum Associates, 1999.
*TC BF311 .C5395 1999*

Claxton, Guy. Wise up. 1st U.S. ed. New York, N.Y. :
Bloomsbury : Distributed to the trade by St. Martin's
Press, 1999.
*TC BF311 .C55 1999*

Cognitive task analysis. Mahwah, N.J. : L. Erlbaum
Associates, 2000.
*TC BF311 .C55345 2000*

Explanation and cognition. Cambridge, Mass. : MIT
Press, c2000.
*TC BF311 .E886 2000*

Glynn, Ian. An anatomy of thought. Oxford ; New
York : Oxford University Press, [1999].
*TC QP360 .G595 1999*

Gopnik, Alison. The scientist in the crib. New York :
William Morrow & Co., 1999.
*TC BF311 .G627 1999*

Halpern, Diane F. Sex differences in cognitive
abilities. 3rd ed. Mahwah, N.J. : L. Erlbaum
Associates, 2000.
*TC BF311 .H295 2000*

Handbook of contemporary learning theories.
Mahwah, N.J. ; London : Lawrence Erlbaum
Associates, 2001.
*TC LB1060 .H3457 2001*

Honeycutt, James M. Cognition, communication, and
romantic relationships. Mahwah, N.J. ; London : L.
Erlbaum Associates, 2001.
*TC BF575.I5 H66 2001*

Human cognition and social agent technology.
Amsterdam ; Philadelphia : John Benjamins, c2000.
*TC BF311 .H766 2000*

Language and conceptualization. 1st paperback ed.
Cambridge [England] ; New York : Cambridge
University Press, 1999.
*TC P37 .L354 1999*

Perception, cognition, and language. Cambridge,
Mass. : MIT, c2000.
*TC BF455 .P389 2000*

Perspectives on cognitive science. Stamford, Conn. :
Ablex Pub. Corp., c1999.
*TC BF311 .P373 1999*

Rowlands, Mark. The body in mind. Cambridge,
U.K. ; New York : Cambridge University Press, 1999.
*TC BD418.3 .R78 1999*

Schunk, Dale H. Learning theories. 3rd ed. Upper
Saddle River, N.J. : Merrill, c2000.
*TC LB1060 .S37 2000*

Skehan, Peter. A cognitive approach to language
learning. Oxford ; New York : Oxford University
Press, 1998.
*TC P118.2 .S567 1998*

Valencia, Richard R. Intelligence testing and minority
students. Thousand Oaks, Calif. : Sage Publications,
[2000]
*TC BF431.5.U6 V35 2000*

What is cognitive science? Malden, Mass. :
Blackwell, 1999.
*TC BF311 .W48 1999*

**COGNITION - AGE FACTORS.**
The aging mind: opportunities in cognitive research.
Washington, D.C. : National Academy Press, c2000.
*TC BF724.55. C63 A48 2000*

Cognitive aging. Philadelphia, PA : Psychology Press,
c2000.
*TC BF724.85.C64 A35 2000*

Kinnamon, James C. A comparison of structural
knowledge in eighth graders and college students.
1999.
*TC 085 K6194*

Models of cognitive aging. Oxford ; New York :
Oxford University Press, 2000.
*TC BF724.55.C63 M63 2000*

**Cognition, agency, and rationality** / edited by Kepa
Korta, Ernest Sosa, and Xabier Arrazola. Boston :
Kluwer Academic, 1999. xi, 198 p. ; 25 cm. "Fifth
International Colloquium on Cognitive Science"--Introd.
Includes indexes. ISBN 0-7923-5973-9 (alk. paper) DDC
153.4/3
1. Reasoning - Congresses. 2. Cognitive science - Congresses.
I. Korta, Kepa. II. Sosa, Ernest. III. Arrazola, Xabier. IV.

*Cognition and culture.*

Brunswick, New Jersey, at the Rutgers Graduate School of Education"--Series fwd. Includes bibliographical references (p. 319-344) and indexes. ISBN 0-8058-2447-2 (cloth : alk. paper) ISBN 0-8058-2448-0 (pbk.) DDC 370.15/23
*1. Peer-group tutoring of students - Congresses. 2. Cognitive learning - Congresses. 3. Learning, Psychology of - Congresses. I. O'Donnell. Angela M. II. King. Alison. III. Series: Rutgers invitational symposium on education series*
*TC LB1031.5 .C65 1999*

## COGNITIVE PSYCHOLOGY.
Anderson, John R. (John Robert), 1947- Cognitive psychology and its implications. 5th ed. New York : Worth, 2000.
*TC BF311 .A5895 2000*

Bruning, Roger H. Cognitive psychology and instruction. 3rd ed. Upper Saddle River, N.J. : Merrill, c1999.
*TC LB1060 .B786 1999*

Dombroski, Ann P. Administrative problem solving. 1999.
*TC 06 no. 11104*

Dombroski, Ann P. Administrative problem solving. 1999.
*TC 06 no. 11104*

The neurocognition of language. Oxford ; New York : Oxford University Press, 1999.
*TC QP399 .N483 1999*

Perspectives on cognitive science. Stamford, Conn. : Ablex Pub. Corp., c1999.
*TC BF311 .P373 1999*

Uttal, William R. The war between mentalism and behaviorism. Mahwah, N.J. ; London : Lawrence Erlbaum Associates, Publishers, 2000.
*TC BF199 .U77 2000*

**Cognitive psychology and instruction.**
Bruning, Roger H. 3rd ed. Upper Saddle River, N.J. : Merrill, c1999.
*TC LB1060 .B786 1999*

**Cognitive psychology and its implications.**
Anderson, John R. (John Robert), 1947- 5th ed. New York : Worth, 2000.
*TC BF311 .A5895 2000*

## COGNITIVE SCIENCE. *See also* ARTIFICIAL INTELLIGENCE; COGNITIVE NEUROSCIENCE; PHILOSOPHY OF MIND.
Clancey, William J. Conceptual coordination. Mahwah, N.J. : L. Erlbaum Associates, 1999.
*TC BF311 .C5395 1999*

Cognitive dynamics. Mahwah, N.J. ; London : L. Erlbaum, 2000.
*TC BF316.6 .C64 2000*

Dodwell, P. C. Brave new mind. New York : Oxford University Press, 2000.
*TC BF311 .D568 2000*

Gärdenfors, Peter. Conceptual spaces. Cambridge, Mass. ; London : MIT Press, c2000.
*TC Q335 .G358 2000*

Mind and cognition. 2nd ed. Malden, Mass. : Blackwell Publishers, 1999.
*TC BF171 .M55 1999*

Naturalizing phenomenology. Stanford, Calif. : Stanford University Press, c1999.
*TC B829.5 .N38 1999*

Perspectives on cognitive science. Stamford, Conn. : Ablex Pub. Corp., c1999.
*TC BF311 .P373 1999*

Pfeifer, Rolf, 1947- Understanding intelligence. Cambridge, Mass. : MIT Press, c1999.
*TC Q335 .P46 1999*

Wagman, Morton. Scientific discovery processes in humans and computers. Westport, CT : Praeger, 2000.
*TC Q180.55.D57 W34 2000*

What is cognitive science? Malden, Mass. : Blackwell, 1999.
*TC BF311 .W48 1999*

## COGNITIVE SCIENCE - CONGRESSES.
Cognition, agency, and rationality. Boston : Kluwer Academic, 1999.
*TC BC177 .C45 1999*

Metarepresentations. Oxford ; New York : Oxford University Press, c2000.
*TC BF316.6 .M48 2000*

## COGNITIVE SCIENCE - QUOTATIONS, MAXIMS, ETC.

Historical dictionary of quotations in cognitive science. Westport, Conn. : Greenwood Press, 2000.
*TC PN6084.C545 H57 2000*

## COGNITIVE STYLES.
Lazear, David G. Eight ways of knowing. 3rd ed. Arlington Heights, Ill. : SkyLight Training and Pub., c1999.
*TC LB1060 .L39 1999*

Zersen, David John. Independent learning among clergy. 1998.
*TC 06 no. 11008*

## COGNITIVE STYLES IN CHILDREN.
Hashway, Robert M. Developmental cognitive styles. San Francisco : Austin & Winfield Publishers, 1998.
*TC LB1060 .H373 1998*

## COGNITIVE STYLES IN CHILDREN - SEX DIFFERENCES.
Tuman, Donna M. Gender difference in form and content. 1998.
*TC 06 no. 11000*

## COGNITIVE STYLES - PSYCHOLOGICAL ASPECTS.
Eddy, Jennifer B.K. Multiple intelligences, styles, and proficiency. 1999.
*TC 085 E10*

## COGNITIVE STYLES - UNITED STATES.
Durocher, Elizabeth Antoinette. Leadership orientations of school administrators. 1995.
*TC 06 no. 10583a*

Gallagher, Trish. Arousal patterns, emotion identification, and cognitive style in depressed and nondepressed inner-city adolescent Latinas. 1997.
*TC 085 G136*

**Cognitive task analysis** / edited by Jan Maarten Schraagen, Susan F. Chipman, Valerie L. Shalin. Mahwah, N.J. : L. Erlbaum Associates, 2000. xiv, 531 p. : ill. ; 24 cm. (Expertise, research and applications) Includes bibliographical references and indexes. ISBN 0-8058-3383-8 (alk. paper) DDC 153.4
*1. Cognition. 2. Task analysis. I. Schraagen, Jan Maarten. II. Chipman, Susan F. III. Shalin, Valerie L. IV. Series.*
*TC BF311 .C55345 2000*

## COGNITIVE THERAPY.
Clark, David A., 1954- Scientific foundations of cognitive theory and therapy of depression. New York : John Wiley, c1999.
*TC RC537 .C53 1999*

Davidson, Kate M. Cognitive therapy for personality disorders :. Oxford ; Boston : Butterworth-Heinemann, 2000.
*TC RC554 .D38 2000*

Maass, Vera Sonja. Counseling single parents. New York : Springer Pub. Co., c2000.
*TC HQ759.915 .M23 2000*

Wells, Adrian. Cognitive therapy of anxiety disorders. Chichester ; New York : J. Wiley & Sons, c1997.
*TC RC531 .W43 1997*

## COGNITIVE THERAPY FOR CHILDREN.
Child and adolescent therapy. 2nd ed. New York : Guilford Press, c2000.
*TC RJ505.C63 C45 2000*

**Cognitive therapy for personality disorders.**
Davidson, Kate M. Oxford ; Boston : Butterworth-Heinemann, 2000.
*TC RC554 .D38 2000*

## COGNITIVE THERAPY FOR TEENAGERS.
Child and adolescent therapy. 2nd ed. New York : Guilford Press, c2000.
*TC RJ505.C63 C45 2000*

## COGNITIVE THERAPY - METHODS.
Brief Alcohol Screening and Intervention for College Students (BASICS). New York : Guilford Press, c1999.
*TC HV5135 .B74 1998*

**Cognitive therapy of anxiety disorders.**
Wells, Adrian. Chichester ; New York : J. Wiley & Sons, c1997.
*TC RC531 .W43 1997*

## COHABITATION. *See* UNMARRIED COUPLES.

**Cohen, Elliot D.** The virtuous therapist : ethical practice of counseling & psychotherapy / Elliot D. Cohen, Gale Spieler Cohen. Belmont, CA : Brooks/Cole Wadworth, 1999. xiv, 349 p. ; 24 cm. Includes bibliographical references (p. 259-267) and index. ISBN 0-534-34408-9 (pbk.) DDC 174/.915
*1. Counselors - Professional ethics. 2. Psychotherapists - Professional ethics. 3. Counseling - Moral and ethical aspects.*

*4. Counseling - Moral and ethical aspects - Case studies. 5. Psychotherapy - Moral and ethical aspects. 6. Psychotherapy - Moral and ethical aspects - Case studies. I. Cohen. Gale Spieler. 1952- II. Title.*
*TC BF637.C6 C46 1999*

**Cohen, Gale Spieler, 1952-.**
Cohen, Elliot D. The virtuous therapist. Belmont, CA : Brooks/Cole Wadworth, 1999.
*TC BF637.C6 C46 1999*

**Cohen, Joseph W., ed.** The superior student in American higher education / edited by Joseph W. Cohen. New York : McGraw-Hill, [c1966] xxiv, 299 p. ; 22 cm. (The Carnegie series in American education) Bibliographical footnotes. DDC 378.179420973
*1. Gifted students. I. Title. II. Series.*
*TC 371.95C66*

**Cohen, Joshua, 1951-.**
Will standards save public education? Boston : Beacon Press, c2000.
*TC LB3060.83 .W55 2000*

**Cohen, Monique.** Counseling addicted women : a practical guide / Monique Cohen. Thousand Oaks, Calif. : Sage Publications, c2000. ix, 251 p. ; 28 cm. Includes bibliographical references and index. CONTENTS: pt. 1. Putting women's substance abuse in social and cultural context -- Perspectives on the socialization of women -- Substance abusing women in relationships -- Types of drug abuse and counseling strategies -- pt. 2. Special issues in enhancing women's treatment -- Guidelines for counseling -- Designing treatment programs -- Pregnancy and paarenting issues -- HIV, AIDS, and women -- Dual diagnose issues among women -- Pt. 3. Trends and considerations for special populations -- Young women -- Women of color and multicultural counseling -- Lesbians and bisexual women -- Disabled women and substance abuse -- Homeless women -- Elderly women -- Substance-abusing women in the workplace -- Wellness for women in recovery. ISBN 0-7619-0910-9 (alk. paper) DDC 362.29/18/082
*1. Women - Substance use - Prevention. 2. Alcoholism counseling. 3. Drug abuse counseling. I. Title.*
*TC HV4999.W65 C64 2000*

**Cohen, Ronald Jay.** Sixty-five exercises in psychological testing and assessment / Ronald Jay Cohen. 2nd ed. Mountain View, CA : Mayfield, c1992. 240 p. : ill., map ; 27 cm. Includes bibliographical references. ISBN 0-87484-980-2 (pbk.) DDC 150/.28/7
*1. Psychological tests - Problems. exercises, etc. 2. Psychometrics - Problems. exercises. etc. I. Title.*
*TC BF176 .C64 1992*

**Cohen, Selma Jeanne, 1920-.**
International encyclopedia of dance. New York : Oxford University Press, c1998.
*TC GV1585 .I586 1998*

**Cohen, Sidney, 1910-.**
O'Brien, Robert, 1932- The encyclopedia of understanding alcohol and other drugs. New York, NY : Facts on File, c1999.
*TC HV5017 .O37 1999*

**Cohen, Steven Martin.**
National variations in Jewish identity. Albany, N.Y. : State University of New York Press, 1999.
*TC DS143 .N27 1999*

**Cohn, Amy L.**
Morton, Jessica G. Kids on the 'Net. Portsmouth, NH : Heinemann, c1998.
*TC LB1044.87 .M67 1998*

**Cohn, John M.** Writing and updating technology plans : a guidebook with sample policies on CD-ROM / John M. Cohn, Ann L. Kelsey, Keith Michael Fiels. New York : Neal-Schuman Publishers, 2000. 101 p. ; 28 cm. 1 computer optical disc. Includes bibliographical references and index. ISBN 1-55570-365-8 DDC 025/.00285
*1. Libraries - United States - Data processing - Planning. I. Kelsey, Ann L. II. Fiels, Keith Michael. III. Title.*
*TC Z678.9.A4 U623 2000*

**Coit, Stanton, 1857-1944 tr.**
Hartmann, Nicolai, 1882-1950. Ethics. London, G. Allen & Unwin ltd,; New York, The Macmillan company [1932]
*TC BJ1114 .H3C6 1932*

## COLD WAR - FICTION.
Burdick, Eugene. Fail-safe. 1st Ecco ed. Hopewell, N.J. : Ecco Press ; New York, NY : Distributed by W.W. Norton, 1999.
*TC PS3552.U7116 F35 1999*

**Cole, Brock.** Buttons / Brock Cole. 1st ed. New York : Farrar Straus Giroux, 2000. [32] p. : col. ill. ; 25 x 27 cm. SUMMARY: When their father eats so much that he pops the buttons off his britches, each of his three daughters tries a different plan to find replacements. ISBN 0-374-31001-7 DDC

*Cole, David.*

[Fic]
*1. Fathers and daughters - Fiction. 2. Humorous stories. I. Title.*
**TC PZ7.C67342 Bu 2000**

**Cole, David.** No equal justice : race and class in the American criminal justice system / David Cole. New York : The New Press : Distributed by W. W. Norton, c1999. 2128 p. ; 24 cm. Includes bibliographical references and index. ISBN 1-56584-473-4 DDC 362 DDC 362
*1. Discrimination in criminal justice administration - United States. 2. Criminal justice. Administration of - United States. 3. Race discrimination - United States. I. Title. II. Title: Race and class in the American criminal justice system*
**TC HV9950 .C65 1999**

**Cole, Donna J.**
Portfolios across the curriculum and beyond. 2nd ed. Thousand Oaks, Calif. : Corwin Press, 2000.
**TC LB1029.P67 C65 2000**

**Cole, Henry, 1955- ill.**
Edwards, Pamela Duncan. Wacky wedding. 1st ed. New York : Hyperion Books for Children, c1999.
**TC PZ7.E26365 Wac 1999**

**Cole, Herbert M.** The arts of Ghana : exhibition dates : Frederick S. Wight Gallery, University of California, Los Angeles, California, October 11 to December 11, 1977 : Walker Art Center, Minneapolis, Minnesota, February 11 to March 26, 1978 : Dallas Museum of Fine Arts, Dallas, Texas, May 3 to July 2, 1978 / by Herbert M. Cole and Doran H. Ross. Los Angeles : Museum of Cultural History, University of California, c1977. xv, 230 p. : ill. (some col.) ; 28 cm. Bibliography: p. 222-227. DDC 700/.9667/074013
*1. Arts, Ghanaian - Exhibitions. I. Ross, Doran H., joint author. II. Frederick S. Wight Art Gallery. III. Walker Art Center. IV. Dallas Museum of Fine Arts. V. University of California, Los Angeles. Museum of Cultural History. VI. Title.*
**TC NX589.6.G5 C64**

**Cole, Mike, 1946-.**
Professional issues for teachers and student teachers. London : David Fulton, 1999.
**TC LB1775.4.G7 P73 1999**

Promoting equality in secondary schools. London ; New York : Cassell, 1999.
**TC LC212.3.G7 P77 1999**

**Cole, Robert A., 1958-.**
Issues in Web-based pedagogy. Westport, Conn. : Greenwood Press, 2000.
**TC LB1044.87 .I88 2000**

**Cole, Robert E.** Managing quality fads : how American business learned to play the quality game / Robert E. Cole. New York : Oxford University Press, 1999. viii, 284 p. ; 24 cm. Includes bibliographical references (p. 259-272) and index. ISBN 0-19-512260-7 (alk. paper) DDC 658.5/62
*1. Quality circles. 2. Quality circles - United States - History. 3. Industrial management - United States - History. 4. Industrial management - Japan - History. I. Title.*
**TC HD66 .C539 1999**

**Coleman, Marilyn.**
Ganong, Lawrence H. Changing families, changing responsibilities. Mahwah, N.J. : Lawrence Erlbaum Associates, 1999.
**TC HQ834 .G375 1999**

**Coleman, Satis N. (Satis Narrona), 1878-1961.**
Volcanoes, new and old, with 97 illustrations and two maps. New York, The John Day Company [1946] vii, [2], 222 p. col. front., illus. (incl. maps) 24 cm. At head of title: Satis N. Coleman. "References for further reading": p. 215-216. DDC 551.21
*1. Volcanoes. I. Title.*
**TC QE522 .C56**

**Coleman, Simon.**
The anthropology of friendship. Oxford : New York : Berg, 1999.
**TC GN486.3 .A48 1999**

**Coleman, Thalia J., 1948-.**
Clinical management of communication disorders in culturally diverse children. Boston : Allyn & Bacon, c2000.
**TC RJ496.C67 C556 2000**

**Coleman, Tracey.**
Get a grip [videorecording]. Racine, WI : S.C. Johnson and Son, Inc., 1999, c1998.
**TC TD170 .G4 1999**

**Coles, Gerald.** Misreading reading : the bad science that hurts children / Gerald Coles. Portsmouth, NH : Heinemann, c2000. xix, 138 p. : ill. ; 24 cm. Includes bibliographical references (p. 110-126) and index. ISBN 0-325-00060-3 DDC 428/.4/072

*1. Reading - Research. 2. Reading - Phonetic method - Research. 3. Reading - Language experience approach - Research. I. Title.*
**TC LB1050.6 .C65 2000**

**Coles, Honi, 1911-.**
Tap dancing for beginners [videorecording]. W. Long Branch, NJ : Kultur, c1981.
**TC GV1794 .T3 1981**

**Coles, Martin, 1952-** Children's reading choices / Martin Coles and Christine Hall. London : New York : Routledge, 1999. xv, 185 p. : ill. ; 23 cm. Includes index. ISBN 0-415-18387-1 DDC 028.5/0941
*1. Children - Great Britain - Books and reading. I. Hall, Christine, 1951- II. Title.*
**TC Z1037.A1 C59 1999**

**Coles, Robert.** Lives of moral leadership / Robert Coles. 1st ed. New York : Random House, c2000. xvii, 247 p. ; 25 cm. ISBN 0-375-50108-8 DDC 170/.92/2
*1. Conduct of life - Case studies. 2. Leadership - Moral and ethical aspects - Case studies. I. Title.*
**TC BJ1547.4 .C64 2000**

The secular mind / Robert Coles. Princeton, N.J. : Princeton University Press, c1999. 189 p. ; 23 cm. ISBN 0-691-05805-9 (alk. paper) DDC 291.1/7
*1. Secularism - United States. I. Title.*
**TC BL2760 .C65 1999**

**COLGATE UNIVERSITY.**
Mandle, Joan D. Can we wear our pearls and still be feminists? Columbia : University of Missouri Press, c2000.
**TC HQ1181.U5 M37 2000**

**Colin, Virginia L.** Human attachment / Virginia L. Colin. Philadelphia : Temple University Press, c1996. xxi, 391 p. : ill. ; 25 cm. Includes bibliographical references (p. 347-372) and indexes. ISBN 1-56639-459-7 (cl. : acid-free paper) DDC 155.4/18
*1. Attachment behavior. 2. Attachment behavior in children. 3. Parent and child. I. Title.*
**TC BF575.A86 C65 1996**

**Collaborating to improve community health :** workbook and guide to best practices in creating healthier communities and populations / Kathryn Johnson, Wynne Grossman, Anne Cassidy, editors ; foreword by Tyler Norris. San Francisco : Jossey-Bass Publishers, c1996. xxvi, 227 p. : ill. ; 28 cm. Includes bibliographical references (p. [205]-227). ISBN 0-7879-1079-1 (pbk) DDC 362.1/2
*1. Community health services. 2. Health planning. I. Johnson, Kathryn, 1947- II. Grossman, Wynne, 1950- III. Cassidy, Anne, 1965-*
**TC RA427 .C59 1996**

**Collaboration for inclusive education :** developing successful programs / Chriss Walther-Thomas ... [et al.]. Boston ; London : Allyn and Bacon, c2000. xvii, 332 p. : ill. ; 24 cm. Includes bibliographical references (p. 291-319) and index. ISBN 0-205-27368-8 (pbk) DDC 371.9/046
*1. Inclusive education - United States. 2. Teaching teams - United States. I. Walther-Thomas, Chriss.*
**TC LC1201 .C63 1999**

**Collaborative approaches to resolving conflict.**
Isenhart, Myra Warren. Thousand Oaks, Calif. : Sage Publications, c2000.
**TC HM1126 .I74 2000**

**Collaborative assessment of school-based projects.**
Werner, Walter. Vancouver : Pacific Educational Press, c1991.
**TC LB2822.8 .W47 1991**

**Collaborative consultation.**
Idol, Lorna. 3rd ed. Austin, Tex. : PRO-ED, c2000.
**TC LC4019 .I35 2000**

**Collaborative consultation in the schools.**
Kampwirth, Thomas J. Upper Saddle River, N.J. : Merrill, c1999.
**TC LB1027.5 .K285 1999**

**Collaborative inquiry in practice :** action, reflection, and meaning making [sic] / John N. Bray ... [et al.] ; foreward by Elizabeth Kasl. Thousand Oaks [Calif.] : Sage Publications, c2000. xviii, 162 p. : ill. ; 23 cm. Includes bibliographical references (p. 141-149) and index. ISBN 0-7619-0646-0 (acid-free paper) ISBN 0-7619-0647-9 (pbk. : acid-free paper) DDC 300/.7/2
*1. Social sciences - Research. 2. Group work in research. I. Bray, John N. II. Title.*
**TC H62 .C5657 2000**

**Collaborative learning in middle and secondary schools.**
Snodgrass, Dawn M., 1955- Larchmont, N.Y. : Eye On Education, 2000.

**TC LB1032 .S62 2000**

**Collaborative negotiation of meaning.**
Jauregi Ondarra, Kristi. Amsterdam : Atlanta, GA : Rodopi, 1997.
**TC P118.2 .J38 1997**

**Collaborative practice :** school and human service partnerships / edited by Robbie W.C. Tourse and Jean F. Mooney ; foreword by Mary Ann Quaranta. Westport, Conn. ; London : Praeger, 1999. xx, 318 p. : ill. ; 25 cm. Includes bibliographical references (p. [303]-305) and index. CONTENTS: Foreword / Mary Ann Quaranta -- Pt. I. Interprofessional Collaboration: A Rationale. 1. Socioeducational Realities of the Twenty-First Century: A Need for Change / Kathleen McInnis-Dittrich, Otherine J. Neisler and Robbie W. C. Tourse. 2. Socioeconomic Forces and Educational Reform / Sandra A. Waddock -- Pt. II. An Approach to Collaborative Practice: Social Work and Education Partnerships. 3. The Collaborative Alliance: Supporting Vulnerable Children in School / Robbie W. C. Tourse and Jane Sulick. 4. Interprofessional Collaboration in the Process of Assessment / Otherine J. Neisler, Kathleen McInnis-Dittrich and Jean F. Mooney. 5. Collaborative Interventions: Promoting Psychosocial Competence and Academic Achievement / Jean F. Mooney, Paul M. Kline and Jeanne C. Davoren. 6. Resolution-Focused Evaluation: Monitoring Progress / Pauline M. Collins -- Pt. III. Other Disciplines in the Interprofessional Mix. 7. Issues in School Health and Expanding Partnerships / Kathleen M. Theis, Rosemary M. Krawczyk and Nancy Gaspard. 8. Pastoral Counseling: An Emerging Partner in the Field of Social Service / Hugo A. Kamya and Claire Lowery. 9. Law in the School-Linked Services Model: Problems and Possibilities / Francine T. Sherman. 10. The Role of Counseling Psychology in Full-Service Schools / Elizabeth Sparks -- Pt. IV. The Realities and Ethical Dilemmas of Full-Service Schools. 11. Organizational Change to Promote Psychosocial and Academic Development / C. Warren Moses and Philip Coltoff. 12. Evaluating Extended-Service Schools: Lessons from the Battlefront / Ellen Brickman. 13. Ethics and Collaborative Practice in Public Schools / Paul M. Kline and Mary M. Brabeck -- App. A. Observable Behavior Patterns for Classroom Teacher Preassessment Data Collection -- App. B. Healthy People 2000 Objectives Related to School Health Education. ISBN 0-275-96307-1 (alk. paper) DDC 362.71/0973 DDC 362.71/0973
*1. Children - Services for - United States. 2. Students - Services for - United States. 3. School social work - United States. 4. Community and school - United States. 5. Interprofessional relations - United States. I. Tourse, Robbie W. C. (Robbie Welch Christler) II. Mooney, Jean F.*
**TC HV741 .C5424 1999**

**Collaborative reform and other improbable dreams :** the challenges of professional development schools / edited by Marilyn Johnston ... [et al.]. Albany, N.Y. : State University of New York Press, 2000. xiii, 297 p. ; 23 cm. (SUNY series, teacher preparation and development) Includes bibliographical references and index. ISBN 0-7914-4465-1 (hard : alk. paper) ISBN 0-7914-4466-X (pbk. : alk. paper) DDC 370/.71/1
*1. Laboratory schools - United States. 2. Educational change - United States. I. Johnston, Marilyn, 1942- II. Series: SUNY series in teacher preparation and development.*
**TC LB2154.A3 C65 2000**

**Collaborative teaming.**
Snell, Martha E. Baltimore : Paul H. Brookes Pub., c2000.
**TC LC1201 .S64 2000**

**The collapse of the self and its therapeutic restoration.**
Kainer, Rochelle G. K., 1936- Hillsdale, NJ ; London : Analytic Press, 1999.
**TC RC489.S43 K35 1999**

**Collay, Michelle.**
Learning circles. Thousand Oaks, Calif. : Corwin Press, c1998.
**TC LB1032 .L355 1998**

**Collected papers.**
Freud, Sigmund, 1856-1939. [Sammlung kleiner schriften zur neurosenlehre. eng] 1st American ed. New York : Basic Books, 1959.
**TC BF173 .F672 1959**

**Collected studies**
(CS518.) Brock, W. H. (William Hodson) Science for all. Brookfield, VT : Variorum, 1996.
**TC Q127.G5 B76 1996**

(CS626.) Freedman, Joseph S. Philosophy and the arts in Central Europe, 1500-1700. Aldershot : Ashgate, 1999.
**TC B52.3.C36 F74 1999**

(CS636.) Gascoigne, John, Ph. D. Science, politics, and universities in Europe, 1600-1800. Aldershot [England] ; Brookfield, Vt. : Ashgate, c1998.
*TC LA621.5 .G37 1998*

**The collected works of John Dewey, 1882-1953. [computer file].**
Dewey, John, 1859-1952. [Works.] Windows version. Charlottesville, VA : InteLex Corp, 1997, c1992. Computer program.
*TC LB875 .D363 1997*

**COLLECTIBLES.** *See* ANTIQUES.

**Collection Education (Strasbourg, France)**
The challenges of the information and communication technologies facing history teaching. Strasbourg : Council of Europe Pub., c1999.
*TC D424 .C425 1999*

Council of Europe. Council for Cultural Co-operation. Bullying in schools. Strasbourg : Council of Europe Publishing, 1999.
*TC BF637.B85 B842 1999*

Towards a pluralist and tolerant approach to teaching history. Strasbourg : Council of Europe Pub., c1999.
*TC D424 .T665 1999*

**A collection of performance tasks and rubrics.**
Danielson, Charlotte. Larchnmont, NY : Eye On Education, c1999.
*TC QA135.5 .D244 1999*

**Collections for Young Scholars**
Phonics review kit [kit]. Chicago, Ill. : Open Court Pub. Co., c1995.
*TC LB1573.3 .P45 1995*

Pocket chart kit [kit]. Chicago, Ill. : Open Court Publishing Company, c1995.
*TC LB1573.3 .P6 1995*

Teacher toolbox [kit]. Chicago, Ill. : Open Court Pub. Co., c1995.
*TC LB1573.3 .T4 1995*

**COLLECTIONS OF PHOTOGRAPHS.** *See* PHOTOGRAPH COLLECTIONS.

**COLLECTIVE BARGAINING - COLLEGE TEACHERS - NEW ENGLAND - CASE STUDIES.**
Arnold, Gordon B., 1954- The politics of faculty unionization. Westport, Conn. ; London : Bergin & Garvey, 2000.
*TC LB2335.865.U6 A75 2000*

**COLLECTIVE BARGAINING - COLLEGE TEACHERS - UNITED STATES.**
Rhoades, Gary. Managed professionals. Albany : State University of New York Press, c1998.
*TC LB2331.72 .R56 1998*

**COLLECTIVE BARGAINING - TEACHERS.** *See* TEACHERS' CONTRACTS.

**COLLECTIVE BEHAVIOR.** *See* DEMONSTRATIONS.

**COLLECTIVE EDUCATION - ISRAEL.**
The transformation of collective education in the kibbutz. Frankfurt am Main ; New York : P. Lang, 1999.
*TC LC1027.I75 T73 1999*

**COLLECTIVE FARMS.** *See* COLLECTIVE SETTLEMENTS.

**COLLECTIVE IDENTITY.** *See* GROUP IDENTITY.

**COLLECTIVE PSYCHOTHERAPY.** *See* GROUP PSYCHOTHERAPY.

**COLLECTIVE SETTLEMENTS.** *See* COMMUNAL LIVING; COMMUNITARIANISM.

**COLLECTIVE SETTLEMENTS - EDUCATION.** *See* COLLECTIVE EDUCATION.

**COLLECTIVE SETTLEMENTS - UNITED STATES - HISTORY.**
Smith, William L., 1956- Families and communes. Thousand Oaks, Calif. : Sage Publications, c1999.
*TC HQ971 .S55 1999*

**COLLECTIVISM.** *See* SOCIALISM.

**COLLECTORS AND COLLECTING.** *See* ANTIQUES.

**COLLEGE ADMINISTRATORS.** *See* COLLEGE PRESIDENTS; COLLEGE STUDENT PERSONNEL ADMINISTRATORS; DEPARTMENTAL CHAIRMEN

(UNIVERSITIES); MINORITY COLLEGE ADMINISTRATORS.

**COLLEGE ADMINISTRATORS - GREAT BRITAIN.**
Bolton, Allan. Managing the academic unit. Buckingham [England] : Philadelphia : Open University Press, c2000.
*TC LB2341 .B583 2000*

**COLLEGE ADMINISTRATORS - PROFESSIONAL RELATIONSHIPS.**
Understanding the work and career paths of midlevel administrators. San Francisco : Jossey-Bass, 2000.
*TC LB2341 .N5111 2000*

**COLLEGE ADMINISTRATORS - UNITED STATES - BIOGRAPHY.**
Odegaard, Charles E. A pilgrimage through universities. Seattle : University of Washington Press, c1999.
*TC LD5752.1 .O34 1999*

**COLLEGE AND COMMUNITY.** *See* COMMUNITY AND COLLEGE.

**COLLEGE AND SCHOOL DRAMA.** *See* CHILDREN'S PLAYS.

**College and university.**
Journal of the American Association of Collegiate Registrars. Athens, Ohio [etc.] American Association of College Registrars.

**COLLEGE ATHLETES - PSYCHOLOGY.**
Humphrey, James Harry, 1911- Stress in college athletics. New York : Haworth Press, c2000.
*TC GV347 .H86 2000*

**COLLEGE ATHLETICS.** *See* COLLEGE SPORTS.

**COLLEGE ATTENDANCE - JAPAN.**
Arai, Kazuhiro, 1949- [Kyōiku no keizaigaku. English] Economics of education. Tōkyō ; New York : Springer, 1998.
*TC LC67.68.J3 A72 1998*

**COLLEGE AUTONOMY.** *See* UNIVERSITY AUTONOMY.

**COLLEGE BUILDINGS - CALIFORNIA - PASADENA.**
Wyllie, Romy. Caltech's architectural heritage. Los Angeles : Balcony Press, c2000.
*TC NA6603 .W95 2000*

**COLLEGE BUILDINGS - MASSACHUSETTS - ANDOVER.**
Montgomery, Susan J., 1947- Phillips Academy. New York : Princeton Architectural Press, 2000.
*TC LD7501.A5 M65 2000*

**College catalog collection (San Diego, Calif. : 1987).**
[CollegeSource (Online)] CollegeSource [computer file]. San Diego, Calif. : The Foundation, [1997-

[CollegeSource (Online)] CollegeSource [computer file]. San Diego, Calif. : The Foundation, [1997-

CollegeSource online [computer file]. San Diego, CA : The Foundation, c1999-
*TC NETWORKED RESOURCE*

CollegeSource online [computer file]. San Diego, CA : The Foundation, c1999-
*TC NETWORKED RESOURCE*

**COLLEGE CATALOGS.** *See* CATALOGS, COLLEGE.

**COLLEGE CHAPLAINS.**
Winings, Kathy. What has the church/synagogue to do with the academy. 1996.
*TC 06 no. 10718*

**COLLEGE COMMUNITY CENTERS.** *See* STUDENT UNIONS.

**COLLEGE COSTS - UNITED STATES.**
Kane, Thomas J. The price of admission. Washington, D.C. : Brookings Institution Press ; New York : Russell Sage Foundation, c1999.
*TC LB2342 .K35 1999*

Smith, Charles W., 1938- Market values in American higher education. Lanham, Md. : Oxford : Rowman & Littlefield, 2000.
*TC LB2342 .S55 2000*

**COLLEGE COUNSELING.** *See* COUNSELING IN HIGHER EDUCATION.

**COLLEGE DEGREES.** *See* DEGREES, ACADEMIC.

**COLLEGE DISCIPLINE - UNITED STATES.**
Dannells, Michael. From discipline to development. Washington, DC : George Washington University,

Graduate School of Education and Human Development, [1997]
*TC LB2344 .D36 1997*

**COLLEGE EDUCATION COSTS.** *See* COLLEGE COSTS.

**COLLEGE EMPLOYEES.** *See* UNIVERSITIES AND COLLEGES - EMPLOYEES.

**COLLEGE ENROLLMENT.** *See* COLLEGE ATTENDANCE.

**College Entrance Examination Board.**
A challenge to change. New York : College Entrance Examination Board, 1999.
*TC P51 .C427 1999*

**COLLEGE ENVIRONMENT - EVALUATION.**
Dixon, Jerome C. A qualitative study of perceptions of external factors that influence the persistence of Black males at a predominantly white four-year state college. 1999.
*TC 06 no. 11050*

**COLLEGE ENVIRONMENT - UNITED STATES.**
Strange, Charles Carney. Educating by design. 1st ed. San Francisco : Jossey-Bass, c2001.
*TC LB2324 .S77 2001*

**COLLEGE ENVIRONMENT - UNITED STATES - EVALUATION.**
Capeheart-Meningall, Jennifer. Quality of students of color efort on a predominantly white college and the internal environmental elements that influence involvement. 1998.
*TC 06 no. 10874*

**The college experience and the construction of cultural identity among first generation Indian American undergraduates.**
Bhattacharya, Diya. 1999.
*TC 06 no. 11083*

**COLLEGE FACILITIES.** *See* COLLEGE BUILDINGS; COLLEGE RADIO STATIONS.

**COLLEGE FACILITIES - GREAT BRITAIN.**
Ruddiman, Ken. Strategic management of college premises. London : Falmer, 1999.
*TC LB3223.5.G7 R84 1999*

**COLLEGE FACILITIES - MANAGEMENT - CONGRESSES.**
Programme on Educational Building. Strategic asset management for tertiary institutions. Paris : Organisation for Economic Co-operation and Development, c1999.
*TC LB3223 .P76 1999*

**COLLEGE FACULTY.** *See* COLLEGE TEACHERS; UNIVERSITIES AND COLLEGES - FACULTY.

**COLLEGE GRADUATES - EMPLOYMENT - GERMANY (EAST).**
Evans, Karen, 1949- Learning and work in the risk society. New York : St. Martin's Press, 2000.
*TC HD6278.G4 E93 2000*

**COLLEGE GRADUATES - EMPLOYMENT - GREAT BRITAIN.**
Ali, Lynda, 1946- Moving on in your career. London ; New York : RoutledgeFalmer, 2000.
*TC LB1778.4.G7 A45 2000*

**COLLEGE GUIDANCE.** *See* COUNSELING IN HIGHER EDUCATION.

**COLLEGE-HIGH SCHOOL COOPERATION.** *See* COLLEGE-SCHOOL COOPERATION.

**COLLEGE LEADERSHIP.** *See* EDUCATIONAL LEADERSHIP.

**COLLEGE LIBRARIANS - UNITED STATES.**
Librarians as learners, librarians as teachers. Chicago : Association of College and Research Libraries, 1999.
*TC Z675.U5 L415 1999*

**COLLEGE LIBRARIES.** *See* ACADEMIC LIBRARIES.

**COLLEGE LIFE.** *See* COLLEGE STUDENTS.

**College of Hawaii. Extension Dept.**
Hawaii educational review. [Honolulu : Dept. of Public Instruction and the Extension Dept. of the College of Hawaii], 1913-1954.

**COLLEGE OFFICIALS.** *See* COLLEGE ADMINISTRATORS.

**COLLEGE PERSONNEL MANAGEMENT - UNITED STATES.**
Boice, Robert. Advice for new faculty members. Boston ; London : Allyn and Bacon, c2000.

*College Placement Council.*

TC LB1778.2 .B63 2000

**College Placement Council.**
Journal of college placement. [Philadelphia, Pa. etc.],
The College Placement Council, inc. [etc.]

**COLLEGE PREPARATORY SCHOOLS.** *See*
**PREPARATORY SCHOOLS.**

**COLLEGE PRESIDENTS.** *See* **WOMEN
COLLEGE PRESIDENTS.**

**COLLEGE PRESIDENTS - PROFESSIONAL
ETHICS - UNITED STATES.**
Nelson, Stephen James, 1947- Leaders in the crucible.
Westport, Conn. : Bergin & Garvey, 2000.
TC LB2341 .N386 2000

**COLLEGE PROSE - EVALUATION.**
Assessment of writing. New York : Modern Language
Association of America, 1996.
TC PE1404 .A88 1996

A sourcebook for responding to student writing.
Cresskill, N.J. : Hampton Press, c1999.
TC PE1404 .S683 1999

**COLLEGE PUBLICATIONS.** *See* **CATALOGS,
COLLEGE.**

**COLLEGE RADIO STATIONS - UNITED
STATES.**
Sauls, Samuel J. The culture of American college
radio. 1st ed. Ames : Iowa State University Press,
2000.
TC PN1991.67.C64 S38 2000

**COLLEGE READERS.**
Cutchin, Kay Lynch. Landscapes and language.
Cambridge, UK ; New York, NY, USA : Cambridge
University Press, 1999.
TC PE1128 .C88 1999

Hutchinson, Helene D. Mixed bag ; [Glenview, Ill.]
Scott, Foresman [1970]
TC PE1122 .H85

Literacies. 2nd ed. New York : W.W. Norton, c2000.
TC PE1417 .L62 2000

**College Reading Association.**
The Journal of the reading specialist. Bethlehem, Pa. :
The Association, c1962-

**The College Reading Association monograph series**
College reading. Carrollton, GA : The College
Reading Association, 1999.
TC LB2395 .C64 1999

**College reading :** perspectives and practices / Barbara
Martin Palmer, editor. Carrollton, GA : The College
Reading Association, 1999. 93 p. ; 23 cm. (The College
Reading Association monograph series) Includes
bibliographical references. ISBN 1-88360-427-3 (pbk)
*1. Reading (Higher education) I. Palmer, Barbara Martin, ed.
II. Series.*
TC LB2395 .C64 1999

**COLLEGE-SCHOOL COLLABORATION.** *See*
**COLLEGE-SCHOOL COOPERATION.**

**COLLEGE-SCHOOL COOPERATION.**
Lawrence, Alexandria Teresa. Cooperating teachers'
perceptions of the nature and quality of professional
development in a professional development school
collaboration. 1999.
TC 06 no. 11141

Lawrence, Alexandria Teresa. Cooperating teachers'
perceptions of the nature and quality of professional
development in a professional development school
collaboration. 1999.
TC 06 no. 11141

Lawrence, Alexandria Teresa. Cooperating teachers'
perceptions of the nature and quality of professional
development in a professional development school
collaboration. 1999.
TC 06 no. 11141

Osguthorpe, Russell T. Balancing the tensions of
change. Thousand Oaks, Calif. : Corwin Press, c1998.
TC LB2331.53 .O74 1998

**COLLEGE-SCHOOL COOPERATION - UNITED
STATES.**
Research on professional development schools.
Thousand Oaks, Calif. : Corwin Press, c1999.
TC LB2154.A3 R478 1999

**COLLEGE-SCHOOL COOPERATION - UNITED
STATES - CASE STUDIES.**
Campoy, Renee W. A professional development
school partnership. Westport, Conn. : Bergin &
Garvey, 2000.
TC LB2154.A3 C36 2000

**COLLEGE-SCHOOL COOPERATION - UNITED
STATES - DIRECTORIES.**
Linking America's schools and colleges. Washington,
D.C. : American Association for Higher Education,
1991.
TC LB2331.53 .L56 1991

**COLLEGE-SCHOOL COOPERATION - UNITED
STATES - LONGITUDINAL STUDIES.**
Teaching to teach. Washington, DC : National
Education Association, 1999.
TC LB1715 .T436 1999

**COLLEGE-SCHOOL PARTNERSHIPS.** *See*
**COLLEGE-SCHOOL COOPERATION.**

**COLLEGE SETTLEMENTS.** *See* **SOCIAL
SETTLEMENTS.**

**College source.**
[CollegeSource (Online)] CollegeSource [computer
file]. San Diego, Calif. : The Foundation, [1997-

**College Source.**
CollegeSource online [computer file]. San Diego,
CA : The Foundation, c1999-
*TC NETWORKED RESOURCE*

**College source online.**
[CollegeSource (Online)] CollegeSource [computer
file]. San Diego, Calif. : The Foundation, [1997-

**College Source online.**
CollegeSource online [computer file]. San Diego,
CA : The Foundation, c1999-
*TC NETWORKED RESOURCE*

**COLLEGE SPORTS - CORRUPT PRACTICES -
UNITED STATES.**
Duderstadt, James J., 1942- Intercollegiate athletics
and the American university. Ann Arbor [Mich.] :
University of Michigan Press, c2000.
TC GV351 .D83 2000

**COLLEGE SPORTS - MORAL AND ETHICAL
ASPECTS - UNITED STATES.**
Duderstadt, James J., 1942- Intercollegiate athletics
and the American university. Ann Arbor [Mich.] :
University of Michigan Press, c2000.
TC GV351 .D83 2000

**COLLEGE SPORTS - SOCIAL ASPECTS -
UNITED STATES.**
Duderstadt, James J., 1942- Intercollegiate athletics
and the American university. Ann Arbor [Mich.] :
University of Michigan Press, c2000.
TC GV351 .D83 2000

**COLLEGE SPORTS - UNITED STATES -
MANAGEMENT.**
Duderstadt, James J., 1942- Intercollegiate athletics
and the American university. Ann Arbor [Mich.] :
University of Michigan Press, c2000.
TC GV351 .D83 2000

**COLLEGE STUDENT DEVELOPMENT
PROGRAMS.**
Love, Patrick G. Understanding and applying
cognitive development theory. San Francisco :
Jossey-Bass, c1999.
TC LB2343 .L65 1999

**COLLEGE STUDENT DEVELOPMENT
PROGRAMS - UNITED STATES.**
Dannells, Michael. From discipline to development.
Washington, DC : George Washington University,
Graduate School of Education and Human
Development, [1997]
TC LB2344 .D36 1997

Student development in college unions and student
activities. Bloomington, Ind. : Association of College
Unions-International, c1996.
TC LB2343.4 .S84 1996

**COLLEGE STUDENT ORIENTATION.**
Banner, James M., 1935- The elements of learning.
New Haven, Conn. : Yale University Press, c1999.
TC LB1060 .B36 1999

**COLLEGE STUDENT PERSONNEL
ADMINISTRATORS, TRAINING OF.** *See*
**COLLEGE STUDENT PERSONNEL
ADMINISTRATORS - TRAINING OF.**

**COLLEGE STUDENT PERSONNEL
ADMINISTRATORS - TRAINING OF -
UNITED STATES.**
Linking theory to practice. 2nd ed. Philadelphia, Pa. :
Taylor and Francis, 2000.
TC LB2342.9 .L56 2000

**COLLEGE STUDENT PERSONNEL
ADMINISTRATORS - UNITED STATES.**
Creating successful partnerships between academic

and student affairs. San Francisco : Jossey-Bass
Publishers, 1999.
TC LB2342.9 .C75 1999

Deegan, William L. Translating theory into practice.
1st ed. [Columbus, Ohio] : National Association of
Student Personnel Administrators, c1985.
TC LB2343 .D356 1985

**COLLEGE STUDENTS.** *See also* **BISEXUAL
COLLEGE STUDENTS; GAY COLLEGE
STUDENTS; GRADUATE STUDENTS;
HANDICAPPED COLLEGE STUDENTS;
TEACHERS COLLEGE STUDENTS;
WOMEN COLLEGE STUDENTS.**
Kinnamon, James C. A comparison of structural
knowledge in eighth graders and college students.
1999.
TC 085 K6194

Teaching to promote intellectual and personal
maturity :. San Francisco : Jossey-Bass, c2000.
TC LB1060 .T43 2000

What kind of university? 1st ed. Buckingham :
Philadelphia, PA : Society for Research into Higher
Education : Open University Press, 1999.
TC LB2322.2 .W43 1999

**COLLEGE STUDENTS, AFRO-AMERICAN.** *See*
**AFRO-AMERICAN COLLEGE STUDENTS.**

**COLLEGE STUDENTS - ALCOHOL USE.**
Brief Alcohol Screening and Intervention for College
Students (BASICS). New York : Guilford Press,
c1999.
TC HV5135 .B74 1998

**COLLEGE STUDENTS, ASIAN AMERICAN.** *See*
**ASIAN AMERICAN COLLEGE STUDENTS.**

**COLLEGE STUDENTS - ATTITUDES.**
Capeheart-Meningall, Jennifer. Quality of students of
color efort on a predominantly white college and the
internal environmental elements that influence
involvement. 1998.
TC 06 no. 10874

Tolliver, Joseph A. Administratively mandated change
at Amherst College. 1997.
TC 06 no. 10871

**COLLEGE STUDENTS - CIVIL RIGHTS -
UNITED STATES.**
Golding, Martin P. (Martin Philip), 1930- Free speech
on campus. Lanham, Md. : Oxford : Rowman &
Littlefield Publishers, c2000.
TC LC72.2 .G64 2000

**COLLEGE STUDENTS - COUNSELING OF.** *See
also* **COUNSELING IN HIGHER
EDUCATION.**
Brief Alcohol Screening and Intervention for College
Students (BASICS). New York : Guilford Press,
c1999.
TC HV5135 .B74 1998

**COLLEGE STUDENTS - EMPLOYMENT -
UNITED STATES.**
Carter, Carol. Majoring in the rest of your life. Upper
Saddle River, NJ : Prentice Hall, c2000.
TC HF5382.5.U5 C373 2000

**COLLEGE STUDENTS - GREAT BRITAIN -
LANGUAGE.**
Students writing in the university. Amsterdam ;
Philadelphia : John Benjamins Pub., c1999.
TC PE1405.G7 S78 1999

**COLLEGE STUDENTS - GREAT BRITAIN -
SOCIAL CONDITIONS.**
Students writing in the university. Amsterdam ;
Philadelphia : John Benjamins Pub., c1999.
TC PE1405.G7 S78 1999

**COLLEGE STUDENTS - LEGAL STATUS, LAWS,
ETC. - UNITED STATES.**
Hawke, Constance S., 1952- Computer and Internet
use on campus. 1st ed. San Francisco : Jossey-Bass,
c2001.
TC KF390.5.C6 H39 2001

**COLLEGE STUDENTS, NEGRO.** *See* **AFRO-
AMERICAN COLLEGE STUDENTS.**

**COLLEGE STUDENTS, RATING OF.** *See*
**COLLEGE STUDENTS - RATING OF.**

**COLLEGE STUDENTS - RATING OF.**
Biggs, John B. (John Burville). Teaching for quality
learning at university :. Buckingham, UK ;
Philadelphia : Society for Research into Higher
Education : Open University Press, 1999.
TC LB2331 .B526 1999

Huba, Mary E. Learner-centered assessment on college campuses. Boston ; London : Allyn and Bacon, c2000.
*TC LB2331 .H83 2000*

**COLLEGE STUDENTS - RATING OF - DATA PROCESSING.**
Computer-assisted assessment in higher education. London : Kogan Page, 1999.
*TC LB2366 .C65 1999*

**COLLEGE STUDENTS - RATING OF - HANDBOOKS, MANUALS, ETC.**
George, Judith W. A handbook of techniques for formative evaluation :. London : Kogan Page, 1999.
*TC LB2333 .G46 1999*

**COLLEGE STUDENTS - RECRUITING - GREAT BRITAIN.**
Humfrey, Christine, 1947- Managing international students. Philadelphia, Penn : Society for Research into Higher Education & Open University Press, 1999.
*TC LB2376.6.G7 H86 1999*

**COLLEGE STUDENTS - RELIGIOUS LIFE - HISTORY.**
Winings, Kathy. What has the church/synagogue to do with the academy. 1996.
*TC 06 no. 10718*

**COLLEGE STUDENTS - SEXUAL BEHAVIOR.**
Gordon, Sol, 1923- Personal issues in human sexuality. Boston : Allyn and Bacon, 1986.
*TC HQ35.2 .G67 1986*

**COLLEGE STUDENTS - SOCIAL LIFE AND CUSTOMS.**
Tolliver, Joseph A. Administratively mandated change at Amherst College. 1997.
*TC 06 no. 10871*

**COLLEGE STUDENTS - UNITED STATES.** *See also* **AFRO-AMERICAN COLLEGE STUDENTS; ASIAN AMERICAN COLLEGE STUDENTS.**
Bell, Inge. This book is not required. Rev. ed., new ed. / by Team Bell, Lynette Albovias ... [et al.]. Thousand Oaks, Calif. : Pine Forge Press, c1999.
*TC LA229 .B386 1999*

Career counseling of college students. Washington, DC : American Psychological Association, c2000.
*TC LB2343 .C3273 2000*

Powerful programming for student learning. San Francisco : Jossey-Bass, c2000.
*TC LB2343 .P643 2000*

**COLLEGE STUDENTS - UNITED STATES - ATTITUDES.**
Dannells, Michael. From discipline to development. Washington, DC : George Washington University, Graduate School of Education and Human Development, [1997].
*TC LB2344 .D36 1997*

Strange, Charles Carney. Educating by design. 1st ed. San Francisco : Jossey-Bass, c2001.
*TC LB2324 .S77 2001*

**COLLEGE STUDENTS - UNITED STATES - LANGUAGE.**
Parks, Stephen, 1963- Class politics. Urbana, Ill. : National Council of Teachers of English, c2000.
*TC PE1405.U6 P3 2000*

**COLLEGE STUDENTS - UNITED STATES - POLITICAL ACTIVITY.**
Parks, Stephen, 1963- Class politics. Urbana, Ill. : National Council of Teachers of English, c2000.
*TC PE1405.U6 P3 2000*

**COLLEGE STUDENTS - UNITED STATES - PSYCHOLOGY.**
Bell, Inge. This book is not required. Rev. ed., new ed. / by Team Bell, Lynette Albovias ... [et al.]. Thousand Oaks, Calif. : Pine Forge Press, c1999.
*TC LA229 .B386 1999*

**COLLEGE STUDENTS' WRITINGS.** *See* **COLLEGE PROSE.**

**COLLEGE TEACHER AIDES.** *See* **GRADUATE TEACHING ASSISTANTS.**

**COLLEGE TEACHER ASSISTANTS.** *See* **GRADUATE TEACHING ASSISTANTS.**

**COLLEGE TEACHERS.** *See also* **COMMUNITY COLLEGE TEACHERS; GRADUATE TEACHING ASSISTANTS; MINORITY COLLEGE TEACHERS; TEACHER EDUCATORS; UNIVERSITIES AND COLLEGES - FACULTY; WOMEN COLLEGE TEACHERS.**

A handbook for teaching and learning in higher education. London : Kogan Page, 1999.
*TC LB2331 .H29 1999*

Taylor, Peter G., 1951- Making sense of academic life. Philadelphia, PA : Open University Press, 1999.
*TC LB1778 .T39 1999*

**COLLEGE TEACHERS, AFRO-AMERICAN.** *See* **AFRO-AMERICAN COLLEGE TEACHERS.**

**COLLEGE TEACHERS - ATTITUDES - CROSS-CULTURAL STUDIES.**
The international academic profession. Princeton, N.J. : Carnegie Foundation for the Advancement of Teaching, c1996.
*TC LB1778 .I54 1996*

**COLLEGE TEACHERS - COLLECTIVE BARGAINING.** *See* **COLLECTIVE BARGAINING - COLLEGE TEACHERS.**

**COLLEGE TEACHERS - EMPLOYMENT.**
Sadler, D. Royce (David Royce) Managing your academic career. St Leonards, N.S.W., Australia : Allen & Unwin, 1999.
*TC LB1778 .S23 1999*

**COLLEGE TEACHERS - EMPLOYMENT - UNITED STATES.**
On the market. 1st Riverhead ed. New York : Riverhead Books, 1997.
*TC LB2331.72 .O5 1997*

**COLLEGE TEACHERS - EMPLOYMENT - UNITED STATES - HANDBOOKS, MANUALS, ETC.**
Vesilind, P. Aarne. So you want to be a professor? Thousand Oaks, Calif. : Sage Publications, c2000.
*TC LB1778.2 .V47 2000*

**COLLEGE TEACHERS - GREAT BRITAIN - BIOGRAPHY.**
Annan, Noel Gilroy Annan, Baron, 1916- The dons. Chicago : University of Chicago Press ; London : HarperCollins Publishers, 1999.
*TC LB2331.74.G7 A55 1999*

**COLLEGE TEACHERS - HANDBOOKS, MANUALS, ETC.**
The Chicago handbook for teachers. Chicago : University of Chicago Press, 1999.
*TC LB2331 .C52332 1999*

**COLLEGE TEACHERS, HISPANIC AMERICAN.** *See* **HISPANIC AMERICAN COLLEGE TEACHERS.**

**COLLEGE TEACHERS - IN-SERVICE TRAINING.**
Staff development in open and flexible learning. London ; New York : Routledge, 1998.
*TC LC5800 .S83 1998*

**COLLEGE TEACHERS - IN-SERVICE TRAINING - INDIA.**
Staff development in higher and distance education. New Delhi : Aravali Books International, 1997.
*TC LB2331 .S692 1997*

**COLLEGE TEACHERS - IN-SERVICE TRAINING - UNITED STATES - CASE STUDIES.**
Themes and issues in faculty development. Lanham, MD : University Press of America, 1999.
*TC LB1738 .T54 1999*

**COLLEGE TEACHERS - JOB SATISFACTION - UNITED STATES.**
What contributes to job satisfaction among faculty and staff. San Francisco, Calif. : Jossey-Bass Publishers, c2000.
*TC LB2331.7 .W45 2000*

**COLLEGE TEACHERS - JOB STRESS.**
Martin, Elaine, 1948- Changing academic work. Buckingham ; Philadelphia : Society for Research into Higher Education : Open University Press, 1999.
*TC LA184 .M37 1999*

**COLLEGE TEACHERS - JOB STRESS - GREAT BRITAIN.**
Edworthy, Ann, 1952- Managing stress. Buckingham [England] ; Philadelphia : Open University Press, 2000.
*TC LB2333.3 .E39 2000*

**COLLEGE TEACHERS - NEW JERSEY - TENURE.**
Ernest, Ivan. Faculty evaluation of post-tenure review at a research university. 1999.
*TC 06 no. 11110*

**COLLEGE TEACHERS, PART-TIME - SALARIES, ETC. - UNITED STATES.**
Rhoades, Gary. Managed professionals. Albany : State University of New York Press, c1998.
*TC LB2331.72 .R56 1998*

**COLLEGE TEACHERS - PROMOTIONS - UNITED STATES.**
Alstete, Jeffrey W. Posttenure faculty development. San Fransisco, [Calif.] : Jossey-Bass c2000.
*TC LB2335.7 .A47 2000*

**COLLEGE TEACHERS - PSYCHOLOGY.**
Austin, Ann E. Academic workplace. Washington, D.C. : Association for the Study of Higher Education, 1983.
*TC LB2331.7 .A96 1983*

**COLLEGE TEACHERS - SALARIES, ETC. - UNITED STATES.**
Rhoades, Gary. Managed professionals. Albany : State University of New York Press, c1998.
*TC LB2331.72 .R56 1998*

**COLLEGE TEACHERS - SALARIES, PENSIONS, ETC.** *See* **COLLEGE TEACHERS - SALARIES, ETC.**

**COLLEGE TEACHERS - SASKATCHEWAN - SASKATOON.**
Spafford, Shirley. No ordinary academics. Toronto : University of Toronto Press, 1999.
*TC HB74.9.C3 S62 1999*

**COLLEGE TEACHERS - SELECTION AND APPOINTMENT - UNITED STATES.**
On the market. 1st Riverhead ed. New York : Riverhead Books, 1997.
*TC LB2331.72 .O5 1997*

**COLLEGE TEACHERS - TENURE - EVALUATION.**
Ernest, Ivan. Faculty evaluation of post-tenure review at a research university. 1999.
*TC 06 no. 11110*

**COLLEGE TEACHERS - TENURE - UNITED STATES.**
Alstete, Jeffrey W. Posttenure faculty development. San Fransisco, [Calif.] : Jossey-Bass c2000.
*TC LB2335.7 .A47 2000*

Woodring, Carl, 1919- Literature. New York : Columbia University Press, 1999.
*TC PN70 .W66 1999*

**COLLEGE TEACHERS - TRAINING OF - UNITED STATES.**
To touch the future. Washington, D.C. : American Council on Education, c1999.
*TC LB1738 .T6 1999*

**COLLEGE TEACHERS' UNIONS - NEW ENGLAND - CASE STUDIES.**
Arnold, Gordon B., 1954- The politics of faculty unionization. Westport, Conn. : London : Bergin & Garvey, 2000.
*TC LB2335.865.U6 A75 2000*

**COLLEGE TEACHERS' UNIONS - UNITED STATES.**
Rhoades, Gary. Managed professionals. Albany : State University of New York Press, c1998.
*TC LB2331.72 .R56 1998*

**COLLEGE TEACHERS - UNITED STATES.** *See also* **AFRO-AMERICAN COLLEGE TEACHERS; HISPANIC AMERICAN COLLEGE TEACHERS.**
Boice, Robert. Advice for new faculty members. Boston ; London : Allyn and Bacon, c2000.
*TC LB1778.2 .B63 2000*

Rhoades, Gary. Managed professionals. Albany : State University of New York Press, c1998.
*TC LB2331.72 .R56 1998*

**COLLEGE TEACHERS - UNITED STATES - BIOGRAPHY.**
Comp tales. New York : Longman, c2000.
*TC PE1404 .C617 2000*

**COLLEGE TEACHERS - UNITED STATES - SOCIAL CONDITIONS.**
The full-time faculty handbook. Thousand Oaks : Sage Publications, c1999.
*TC LB1778.2 .F85 1999*

The social worlds of higher education :. Thousand Oaks, Calif. : Pine Forge Press, [1999].
*TC LB2331 .S573 1999 sampler*

**COLLEGE TEACHERS - UNITED STATES - WORKLOAD.**

*College teaching*

Faculty productivity :. New York : Falmer Press, 1999.
*TC LB2331.7 .F33 1999*

**COLLEGE TEACHING.** *See also* **SEMINARS.**
Improving college and university teaching.
[Corvallis : Graduate School, Oregon State College,

**COLLEGE TEACHING.**
Biggs, John B. (John Burville). Teaching for quality learning at university :. Buckingham, UK : Philadelphia : Society for Research into Higher Education : Open University Press, 1999.
*TC LB2331 .B526 1999*

Changing university teaching :. London : Kogan Page ; Sterling, VA : Stylus Pub., 2000.
*TC LB2331 .C53 2000*

Huba, Mary E. Learner-centered assessment on college campuses. Boston ; London : Allyn and Bacon, c2000.
*TC LB2331 .H83 2000*

Martin, Elaine, 1948- Changing academic work. Buckingham ; Philadelphia : Society for Research into Higher Education : Open University Press, 1999.
*TC LA184 .M37 1999*

Taylor, Peter G., 1951- Making sense of academic life. Philadelphia, PA : Open University Press, 1999.
*TC LB1778 .T39 1999*

Teaching and learning on the edge of the millennium :. San Francisco : Jossey-Bass, c1999.
*TC LB2331 .T35 1999*

Teaching to promote intellectual and personal maturity :. San Francisco : Jossey-Bass, c2000.
*TC LB1060 .T43 2000*

**COLLEGE TEACHING - COMPUTER NETWORK RESOURCES.**
The online teaching guide :. Boston, Mass. : Allyn and Bacon, c2000.
*TC LB1044.87 .O45 1999*

Salmon, Gilly. E-moderating. London : Kogan Page ; Sterling, VA : Stylus, 2000.
*TC LB1044.87 .S25 2000*

**COLLEGE TEACHING - CROSS-CULTURAL STUDIES.**
The international academic profession. Princeton, N.J. : Carnegie Foundation for the Advancement of Teaching, c1996.
*TC LB1778 .I54 1996*

**COLLEGE TEACHING - EUROPE - CONGRESSES.**
Learning institutionalized. Notre Dame, Ind. : University of Notre Dame Press, c2000.
*TC LA177 .L43 2000*

**COLLEGE TEACHING - EVALUATION.**
Heywood, John, 1930- Assessment in higher education. London ; Philadelphia : Jessica Kingsley Publishers, 2000.
*TC LB2366 .H49 2000*

**COLLEGE TEACHING - EVALUATION - HANDBOOKS, MANUALS, ETC.**
George, Judith W. A handbook of techniques for formative assessment :. London : Kogan Page, 1999.
*TC LB2333 .G46 1999*

**COLLEGE TEACHING - HANDBOOKS, MANUALS, ETC.**
The Chicago handbook for teachers. Chicago : University of Chicago Press, 1999.
*TC LB2331 .C52332 1999*

A handbook for teaching and learning in higher education. London : Kogan Page, 1999.
*TC LB2331 .H29 1999*

**COLLEGE TEACHING - INDIA.**
Staff development in higher and distance education. New Delhi : Aravali Books International, 1997.
*TC LB2331 .S692 1997*

**COLLEGE TEACHING - MORAL AND ETHICAL ASPECTS.**
Ethical issues in college writing. New York ; Canterbury [England] : Peter Lang, c1999.
*TC PE1404 .E84 1999*

**COLLEGE TEACHING - NETHERLANDS - DELFT.**
Klaassen, R. G. Effective lecturing behaviour in English-medium instruction. Delft, Netherlands : Delft University Press, 1999.
*TC LB2393 .K53 1999*

**COLLEGE TEACHING - PERIODICALS.**
Improving college and university teaching.
[Corvallis : Graduate School, Oregon State College.

**COLLEGE TEACHING - SOCIAL ASPECTS - UNITED STATES.**
The social worlds of higher education :. Thousand Oaks, Calif. : Pine Forge Press, [1999].
*TC LB2331 .S573 1999 sampler*

**COLLEGE TEACHING - UNITED STATES.**
Bess, James L. Teaching alone, teaching together. 1st ed. San Francisco : Jossey-Bass, c2000.
*TC LB2331 .B48 2000*

Carbone, Elisa Lynn. Teaching large classes. Thousand Oaks, Calif. : Sage Publications, c1998.
*TC LB2331 .C336 1998*

Curzan, Anne. First day to final grade. Ann Arbor [Mich.] : University of Michigan Press, c2000.
*TC LB2335.4 .C87 2000*

Mentkowski, Marcia. Learning that lasts. 1st ed. San Francisco : Jossey-Bass, c2000.
*TC LB1060 .M464 2000*

Rojstaczer, Stuart. Gone for good. Oxford : Oxford University Press, 1999.
*TC LA227.4 .R65 1999*

Sarkisian, Ellen. Teaching American students. Rev. ed. Cambridge, Mass. : The President and Fellows of Harvard University, Derek Bok Center for Teaching and Learning, 1997, c1990.
*TC LB1738 .S371 1997*

To touch the future. Washington, D.C. : American Council on Education, c1999.
*TC LB1738 .T6 1999*

**COLLEGE TEACHING - UNITED STATES - EVALUATION.**
Faculty productivity :. New York : Falmer Press, 1999.
*TC LB2331.7 .F33 1999*

**COLLEGE TEACHING - VOCATIONAL GUIDANCE.**
Sadler, D. Royce (David Royce) Managing your academic career. St Leonards, N.S.W., Australia : Allen & Unwin, 1999.
*TC LB1778 .S23 1999*

**COLLEGE TEACHING - VOCATIONAL GUIDANCE - GREAT BRITAIN.**
Ali, Lynda, 1946- Moving on in your career. London ; New York : RoutledgeFalmer, 2000.
*TC LB1778.4.G7 A45 2000*

**COLLEGE TEACHING - VOCATIONAL GUIDANCE - UNITED STATES.**
The full-time faculty handbook. Thousand Oaks : Sage Publications, c1999.
*TC LB1778.2 .F85 1999*

**COLLEGE TEACHING - VOCATIONAL GUIDANCE - UNITED STATES - HANDBOOKS, MANUALS, ETC.**
Vesilind, P. Aarne. So you want to be a professor? Thousand Oaks, Calif. : Sage Publications, c2000.
*TC LB1778.2 .V47 2000*

**COLLEGE TEACHING - YEARBOOKS.**
Improving college and university teaching yearbook. Corvallis, Ore., Oregon State University Press.

**COLLEGE UNIONS.** *See* **STUDENT UNIONS.**

**COLLEGES.** *See* **UNIVERSITIES AND COLLEGES.**

**COLLEGES, AFRO-AMERICAN.** *See* **AFRO-AMERICAN UNIVERSITIES AND COLLEGES.**

**Colleges and universities as citizens** / edited by Robert G. Bringle, Richard Games, Edward A. Malloy. Boston : Allyn and Bacon, c1999. xiv, 210 p. : ill. ; 24 cm. Includes bibliographical references and indexes. ISBN 0-205-28696-8 (alk. paper) DDC 378/.015
*1. Student service - United States. 2. Citizenship - Study and teaching (Higher) - United States. 3. Education, Higher - Aims and objectives - United States. I. Bringle, Robert G. II. Games, Richard. III. Malloy, Edward A.*
*TC LC220.5 .C644 1999*

**COLLEGES FOR WOMEN.** *See* **WOMEN'S COLLEGES.**

**COLLEGES, SMALL.** *See* **SMALL COLLEGES.**

**COLLEGES, STATE.** *See* **STATE UNIVERSITIES AND COLLEGES.**

**CollegeSource.**
[CollegeSource (Online)] CollegeSource [computer file]. San Diego, Calif. : The Foundation, [1997-

CollegeSource online [computer file]. San Diego, CA : The Foundation, c1999-
*TC NETWORKED RESOURCE*

**CollegeSource on line.**
[CollegeSource (Online)] CollegeSource [computer file]. San Diego, Calif. : The Foundation, [1997-

**[CollegeSource (Online)]** CollegeSource [computer file] / Career Guidance Foundation. San Diego, Calif. : The Foundation, [1997- Frequency: Biweekly, with annual cumulations. Title from home page. Account required to access full catalog information. SUMMARY: Consists of college profiles and full-text college catalogs. Also available on CD-ROM. Mode of access: Internet via World Wide Web. System requirements: PC; internet browser (Netscape Navigator 3.0 or Microsoft Internet Explorer 3.0 recommended); Adobe Acrobat 3.0 reader; modem. Online version of microfiche: College catalog collection (San Diego, Calif. : 1987). URL: http://www.cgf.org Other editions available: CollegeSource (DLC)sn 96047057 (OCoLC)31383845. Available in other form: College catalog collection (San Diego, Calif. : 1987) (DLC) 90640043 (OCoLC)18267299.
*1. Catalogs, College - United States. 2. Catalogs, College I. Career Guidance Foundation (La Jolla, San Diego, Calif.) II. Title: College catalog collection (San Diego, Calif. : 1987) III. Title: CollegeSource on line IV. Title: College source online V. Title: College source VI. Title: CollegeSource VII. Title: College catalog collection (San Diego, Calif. : 1987)*

**CollegeSource online** [computer file] / Career Guidance Foundation. San Diego, CA : The Foundation, c1999- Frequency: Weekly. Title from home page. Access restricted to institutions with a subscription. SUMMARY: Contains over 11,400 college catalogs in complete cover-to-cover original page format including 2-year, 4-year, graduate and professional schools; extensive files beginning 1994, but some catalogs archived as far back as 1991. Online version of microfiche: College catalog collection (San Diego, Calif. : 1987); also available on CD-ROM. Mode of access: Internet via World Wide Web. System requirements: PC; internet browser (Netscape Navigator 3.0 or Microsoft Internet Explorer 3.0 recommended); Adobe Acrobat 3.0 reader; modem. URL: http://www.cgf.org Other editions available: CollegeSource. Available in other form: College catalog collection (San Diego, Calif. : 1987).
*1. Catalogs, College. I. Career Guidance Foundation (La Jolla, San Diego, Calif.) II. Title: College catalog collection (San Diego, Calif. : 1987) III. Title: College Source online IV. Title: College Source V. Title: CollegeSource VI. Title: College catalog collection (San Diego, Calif. : 1987)*
*TC NETWORKED RESOURCE*

**COLLEGIATE SPORTS.** *See* **COLLEGE SPORTS.**

**Collegium Internationale Neuro-psychopharmacologicum. Regional Conference (1995 : Vienna, Austria, and Prague, Czech Republic).**
Basic and clinical science of mental and addictive disorders. Basel ; New York : Karger, c1997.
*TC RC327 .B37 1997*

**Collett, Anne.**
Teaching post-colonialism and post-colonial literatures. Aarhus, Denmark ; Oakville, Conn. : Aarhus University Press, c1997.
*TC PR9080.A53 T43 1997*

**Colley, Kenna M.**
Snell, Martha E. Social relationships and peer support. Baltimore, Md. ; London : Paul H. Brookes Pub. Co., c2000.
*TC LC4069 .S54 2000*

**COLLIER, CHRISTOPHER, 1930- /.**
**MY BROTHER SAM IS DEAD.**
McCarthy, Tara. My brother Sam is dead by James Lincoln Collier and Christopher Collier. New York : Scholastic, c1997.
*TC LB1573 .M32 1997*

**COLLIER, JAMES LINCOLN, 1928- /.**
**MY BROTHER SAM IS DEAD.**
McCarthy, Tara. My brother Sam is dead by James Lincoln Collier and Christopher Collier. New York : Scholastic, c1997.
*TC LB1573 .M32 1997*

**Collier, Steve.**
Challenge cases [videorecording]. Princeton, N.J. : Films for the Humanities & Sciences, 1998.
*TC RC455.2.C4 C4 1998*

Disorders due to psychoactive substance abuse [videorecording]. Princeton, N.J. : Films for the Humanities & Sciences, 1998.

*TC RC564 .D5 1998*

Mood disorders [videorecording]. Princeton, N.J. : Films for the Humanities & Sciences, 1998.
*TC RC537 .M6 1998*

Neurotic, stress-related, and somatoform disorders [videorecording]. Princeton, N.J. : Films for the Humanities & Sciences, 1998.
*TC RC530 .N4 1998*

Organic disorders [videorecording]. Princeton, N.J. : Films for the Humanities & Sciences, 1998.
*TC RC521 .O7 1998*

Personality disorders [videorecording]. Princeton, N.J. : Films for the Humanities & Sciences, 1998.
*TC RC554 .P4 1998*

Schizophrenia and delusional disorders [videorecording]. Princeton, N.J. : Films for the Humanities & Sciences, c1998.
*TC RC514 .S3 1998*

**Collington, Peter.** The tooth fairy / Peter Collington. 1st U.S. ed. New York : Knopf ; Distributed by Random House, 1995. 1 v. (unpaged) : col. ill. ; 29 cm. SUMMARY: A resourceful tooth fairy goes to great lengths when a little girl loses a tooth. ISBN 0-679-87168-3 (trade) ISBN 0-679-97168-8 (GLB) DDC [E]
*1. Tooth Fairy - Fiction. 2. Teeth - Fiction. 3. Stories without words. I. Title.*
*TC PZ7.C686 To 1995*

**Collingwood, R. G. (Robin George), 1889-1943.** Outlines of a philosophy of art / R. G. Collingwood. Bristol : Thoemmes, 1994, c1925. 104 p. ; 22 c mm. (Key texts : classic studies in the history of ideas) Originally published: London: Oxford University Press, 1925. Includes index. ISBN 1-85506-316-6 (pbk) DDC 700.1
*1. Title. II. Series: Key texts (Bristol, England)*
*TC N70 .C6 1994*

**Collins, Christopher G.** Teaching the emotionally handicapped child : a practical guide for teachers / Christopher G. Collins. Danville, Ill. : Interstate Printers & Publishers, c1983. xiii, 185 p. : ill. ; 25 cm. Includes the text of the Education for All Handicapped Children Act of 1975. Bibliography: p. 181-185. ISBN 0-8134-2257-4 (pbk.) DDC 371.94
*1. Mentally ill children - Education. I. United States. Education for All Handicapped Children Act. 1983. II. Title.*
*TC LC4165 .C62 1983*

**Collins, David, 1966-** Organizational change : sociological perspectives / David Collins. New York : Routledge, 1998. xiv, 214 p. ; 24 cm. Includes bibliographical references (p. 199-206) and index. ISBN 0-415-17155-5 ISBN 0-415-17156-3 (pbk.) DDC 302.3/5
*1. Organizational change - Social aspects. 2. Corporate culture. 3. Organizational behavior. 4. Organizational sociology. I. Title.*
*TC HD58.8 .C642 1998*

**Collins, Harold W.** Educational measurement and evaluation, a worktext / [by] Harold W. Collins, John H. Johansen [and] James A. Johnson. [Glenview, Ill.], Scott, Foresman, [c1969]. [xi], 196 p. : ill., forms. ; 26 cm. Includes bibliographical references.
*1. Educational tests and measurements I. Johansen. John H. II. Johnson, James A. III. Title.*
*TC LB3051 .C645*

**Collins, Jane Lou, 1954-.** Lutz, Catherine. Reading National geographic. Chicago : University of Chicago Press, 1993.
*TC G1.N275 L88 1993*

**Collins, Karen Scott.** Minority health in America. Baltimore, Md. : Johns Hopkins University Press, 2000.
*TC RA448.4 .M566 2000*

**Collins, Lynne Decker.** Chatton, Barbara. Blurring the edges. Portsmouth, NH : Heinemann, c1999.
*TC LB1576 .C46 1999*

**Collins, Michael, 1939-** Critical crosscurrents in education / Michael Collins. Original ed. Malabar, Fla. : Krieger Pub. Co., 1998. xi, 201 p. ; 24 cm. Includes bibliographical references (p. 187-192) and index. ISBN 0-89464-755-5 (hardcover : alk. paper) DDC 370.11/5
*1. Critical pedagogy. 2. Critical theory. 3. Continuing education. I. Title.*
*TC LC196 .C65 1998*

**Collins, Pat Lowery.** Signs and wonders / Pat Lowery Collins. Boston : Houghton Mifflin, 1999. 176 p. ; 22 cm. SUMMARY: In a series of letters, a fourteen-year-old convent school student who never knew her mother and resents her father, grapples with her belief that God has chosen her to give birth to a prophet. ISBN 0-395-97119-5 DDC [Fic]
*1. Parent and child - Fiction. 2. Letters - Fiction. I. Title.*

*TC PZ7.C69675 Si 1999*

**Collins, Úna M.** Rethinking pastoral care. London : New York : Routledge, 1999.
*TC LB1620.53.I73 R48 1999*

**Collinson, Patrick.** Bendall, A. Sarah. A history of Emmanuel College, Cambridge. Woodbridge, Suffolk, UK ; Rochester, NY : Boydell Press, 1999.
*TC LF185 .B46 1999*

**COLLISIONS AT SEA.** *See* **SHIPWRECKS.**

**COLLOQUIAL ENGLISH.** *See* **ENGLISH LANGUAGE - SPOKEN ENGLISH.**

**COLLOQUIAL LANGUAGE.** Connect with English [videorecording]. S. Burlington, Vt. : The Annenberg/CPB Collection, c1997.
*TC PE1128 .C66 1997*

**Colloquium on American Studies in Eastern Africa** (1st : 1990 : Nairobi, Kenya). American studies in eastern Africa. Nairobi : Nairobi University Press, 1993.
*TC E172.9 .A47 1993*

**Colloquium publications (American Mathematical Society)** (v.30) Radó, Tibor, 1895-1965. Length and area. New York, American Mathematical Society, 1948.
*TC QA611 .R3*

**Colmer, David, 1964-.** Moeyaert, Bart. [Blote handen. English] Bare hands. 1st ed. Asheville, N.C. : Front Street, 1998.
*TC PZ7.M7227 Bar 1998*

**COLOMBIA - DISCOVERY AND EXPLORATION - SPANISH.** Avellaneda Navas, José Ignacio. The conquerors of the New Kingdom of Granada. 1st ed. Albuquerque : University of New Mexico Press, c1995.
*TC F2272 .A84 1995*

**COLOMBIA - HISTORY - TO 1810.** Avellaneda Navas, José Ignacio. The conquerors of the New Kingdom of Granada. 1st ed. Albuquerque : University of New Mexico Press, c1995.
*TC F2272 .A84 1995*

**COLONIAL AFFAIRS.** *See* **COLONIES.**

**The colonial book in the Atlantic world** / edited by Hugh Amory & David D. Hall. Cambridge, U.K. ; New York : Cambridge University Press, 2000. xxiv, 638 p. : ill., maps ; 24 cm. (A history of the book in America ; v. 1) On t.p.: American Antiquarian Society. Includes bibliographical references and index. "A select bibliography" by Hugh Amory: P. 486-503. ISBN 0-521-48256-9
*1. Book industries and trade - United States - History - 17th century. 2. Book industries and trade - United States - History - 18th century. I. Amory, Hugh. II. Hall, David D. III. Series: History of the book in America ; v. 1.*
*TC Z473 .C686 1999*

**COLONIAL POTTERY.** *See* **POTTERY, COLONIAL.**

**A colonial Quaker girl.** Wister, Sarah, 1761-1804. Mankato, Minn. : Blue Earth Books, c2000.
*TC F158.44 .W75 2000*

**Colonial Williamsburg Foundation.** Waters, Kate. Mary Geddy's day :. 1st ed. New York : Scholastic Press, 1999.
*TC PZ7.W26434 Mar 1999*

**COLONIALISM.** *See* **COLONIES; IMPERIALISM; WORLD POLITICS.**

**COLONIALISM - HISTORY - UNITED STATES.** Reiss, Oscar, 1925- Medicine in colonial America. Lanham : University Press of America, 2000.
*TC RC151 .R44 2000*

**COLONIES.** *See* **DECOLONIZATION.**

**COLONIES IN LITERATURE.** Kutzer, M. Daphne. Empire's children. New York : Garland Pub., 2000.
*TC PR830.154 K88 2000*

**COLONIES - PERIODICALS.** Civilisations. Bruxelles, Institut International des Civilisations Différentes.

**COLONIZATION.** *See* **COLONIES; DECOLONIZATION; EMIGRATION AND IMMIGRATION.**

**Colonization of Islam.** Malik, Jamal. New Delhi : Manohar, 1996.

*TC BP173.25 .M34 1996*

**COLOR.** *See also* **DYES AND DYEING.** Hoban, Tana. Of colors and things. 1st Tupelo Board Book ed. New York : Tupelo Books, 1998.
*TC QC495.5 .H62 1998*

**Color and shape books for all ages.** Cooper, Cathie Hilterbran, 1953- Lanham, Md. ; London : Scarecrow Press, 2000.
*TC QC496 .C66 2000*

**The color bind.** Chávez, Lydia, 1951- Berkeley : University of California Press, c1998.
*TC HF5549.5.A34 C484 1998*

**COLOR - FICTION.** Garne, S. T. By a blazing blue sea. San Diego : Harcourt Brace & Co., 1999.
*TC PZ8.3.G1866 By 1999*

Martin, Bill, 1916- Brown bear, brown bear, what do you see? New York : H. Holt, 1992.
*TC PZ8.3.M418 Br 1992*

**COLOR-HEARING.** *See* **PERCEPTION.**

**COLOR IN ART.** Bomford, David. Colour. London : National Gallery Company ; [New Haven, Conn.] : Distributed by Yale Universtiy Press, 2000.
*TC ND1489 B66 2000*

**COLOR IN THE TEXTILE INDUSTRIES.** *See* **DYES AND DYEING.**

**COLOR - JUVENILE LITERATURE - BIBLIOGRAPHY.** Cooper, Cathie Hilterbran, 1953- Color and shape books for all ages. Lanham, Md. ; London : Scarecrow Press, 2000.
*TC QC496 .C66 2000*

**The color of excellence.** Orsini, Alfonso J. 1999.
*TC 06 no. 11209*

**The color of freedom.** Cochran, David Carroll. Albany : State University of New York Press, c1999.
*TC E185.615 .C634 1999*

**The color of teaching.** Gordon, June A., 1950- London ; New York : RoutledgeFalmer, c2000.
*TC LB2835.25 .G67 2000*

**The color of words.** Herbst, Philip. Yarmouth, Me., USA : Intercultural Press, [1997]
*TC E184.A1 H466 1997*

**COLOR - PICTORIAL WORKS - JUVENILE LITERATURE.** Hoban, Tana. Of colors and things. 1st Tupelo Board Book ed. New York : Tupelo Books, 1998.
*TC QC495.5 .H62 1998*

**COLOR PRINTING.** *See* **SERIGRAPHY.**

**COLOR - STUDY AND TEACHING (ELEMENTARY) - ACTIVITY PROGRAMS - UNITED STATES.** Cooper, Cathie Hilterbran, 1953- Color and shape books for all ages. Lanham, Md. ; London : Scarecrow Press, 2000.
*TC QC496 .C66 2000*

**COLORED PEOPLE (SOUTH AFRICA) - EDUCATION - HISTORY - 19TH CENTURY.** Cross, Michael. Imagery of identity in South African education, 1880-1990. Durham, N.C. : Carolina Academic Press, c1999.
*TC LA1539 .C76 1999*

**COLORED PEOPLE (SOUTH AFRICA) - EDUCATION - HISTORY - 20TH CENTURY.** Cross, Michael. Imagery of identity in South African education, 1880-1990. Durham, N.C. : Carolina Academic Press, c1999.
*TC LA1539 .C76 1999*

**COLORED PEOPLE (SOUTH AFRICA) - RACE IDENTITY - HISTORY - 19TH CENTURY.** Cross, Michael. Imagery of identity in South African education, 1880-1990. Durham, N.C. : Carolina Academic Press, c1999.
*TC LA1539 .C76 1999*

**COLORED PEOPLE (SOUTH AFRICA) - RACE IDENTITY - HISTORY - 20TH CENTURY.** Cross, Michael. Imagery of identity in South African education, 1880-1990. Durham, N.C. : Carolina Academic Press, c1999.

*Colored people (United States)*

TC LA1539 .C76 1999

**COLORED PEOPLE (UNITED STATES).** *See* AFRO-AMERICANS.

**COLORING MATTER.** *See* DYES AND DYEING.

**Coloring outside the lines.**
Gardiner, Mary E., 1953- Albany : State University of New York Press, c2000.
*TC LB2831.82 .G37 2000*

**COLORS.** *See* COLOR.

**The colors of us.**
Katz, Karen. 1st ed. New York : Holt, 1999.
*TC PZ7.K15745 Co 1999*

**Colour.**
Bomford, David. London : National Gallery Company ; [New Haven, Conn.] : Distributed by Yale Universtiy Press, 2000.
*TC ND1489 B66 2000*

**COLOURED PERSONS (SOUTH AFRICA).** *See* COLORED PEOPLE (SOUTH AFRICA).

**Colson, Greg, ill.**
Blair, Margot. The red string. Malibu, Calif. : J. Paul Getty Museum and Childrens Library Press, c1996.
*TC PZ7.B537865 Re 1996*

**Colson, Jeff, ill.**
Hill, T. L. Morris and the kingdom of Knoll. Malibu, Calif. : J. Paul Getty Museum and Children's Library Press, c1996.
*TC PZ7.H55744 Mo 1996*

**Columbia College (Chicago, Ill.). Center for Black Music Research.**
International dictionary of black composers. Chicago ; London : Fitzroy Dearborn, c1999.
*TC ML105 .I5 1999*

**Columbia Tristar Home Video (Firm).**
Touch 'n' go [videorecording]. Burbank, Calif. : Columbia Tristar Home Video ; [S.l. : Distributed by] Rank Video Services Production, c1991.
*TC HV1626 .T6 1991*

**Columbia University. School of Social Work. Cross-National Studies Research Program.**
Kahn, Alfred J., 1919- Big cities in the welfare transition. New York City : Cross-National Studies Research Program, Columbia University School of Social Work, 1998.
*TC HV91 .K27 1998*

**COLUMBIA UNIVERSITY. TEACHERS COLLEGE. DEPT. OF NURSING EDUCATION.**
Christy, Teresa E. Cornerstone for nursing education. New York : Teachers College Press, Columbia University, [1969]
*TC RT81.N3 C45*

**Columbia University. Teachers College. Institute of Adult Education.**
Film forum review. [New York, N.Y.] : The Institute, 1946-

**Columbus (Ohio). Board of Education.** Rules, 1905, 1910, 1922. Columbus : [s.n.], 1905-1922. 3 v.
*1. School management and organization - Ohio - Columbus.*
*TC 379.7830C722*

**COLUMNA VERTEBRALIS.** *See* SPINE.

**Colvin, A. Vonnie, 1951-** Teaching the nuts and bolts of physical education : building basic movement skills / A. Vonnie Colvin, Nancy J. Egner Markos, Pam Walker. Champaign, IL : Human Kinetics, c2000. vii, 279 p. : ill. ; 28 cm. Includes bibliographical references. ISBN 0-88011-883-0 DDC 372.86
*1. Physical education for children. 2. Movement education. I. Markos, Nancy J. Egner. 1949- II. Walker, Pam, 1953- III. Title.*
*TC GV443 .C59 2000*

**COMBAT - PSYCHOLOGICAL ASPECTS.**
Bourke, Joanna. An intimate history of killing. [New York, NY] : Basic Books, c1999.
*TC U22.3 .B68 1999*

**Combating educational disadvantage :** meeting the needs of vulnerable children / edited by Theo Cox. London ; New York : Falmer Press, 2000. xii, 288 p. : ill. ; 25 cm. Includes bibliographical references and indexes. ISBN 0-7507-0901-4 (hb : alk. paper) ISBN 0-7507-0900-6 (pb : alk. paper) DDC 371.9
*1. Socially handicapped children - Education. 2. School improvement programs. 3. Educational change. 4. Education and state. I. Cox, T. (Theodore)*
*TC LC4065 .C66 1999*

**Combating social exclusion in university adult education.**
Preece, Julia. Aldershot ; Brookfield, Vt. : Ashgate, c1999.
*TC LC5256.G7 P84 1999*

**Combatting racism in the workplace.**
Thomas, Barb, 1946- Toronto : Cross Cultural Communication Centre, c1983.
*TC HD4903.5.C3 T56 1983*

**COMBINATIONS.** *See* PROBABILITIES.

**Combining service and learning in higher education :** evaluation of the Learn and Serve America Higher Education program / Maryann J. Gray ... [et al.]. Santa Monica, CA : RAND Education, 1999. xxiii, 108 p. : ill. ; 28 cm. Includes bibliographical references (p. 107-108). ISBN 0-8330-2725-5 DDC 378/.015/0973
*1. Student service - United States. 2. Community and college - United States. 3. Learn and Serve America Higher Education (Program) - Evaluation. I. Gray, Maryann Jacobi.*
*TC LC220.5 .C646 1999*

**Combs, Arthur W. (Arthur Wright), 1912-** Being and becoming : a field approach to psychology / Arthur W. Combs. New York : Springer Pub. Co., c1999. ix, 277 p. : ill. ; 24 cm. Includes bibliographical references (p. 257-265) and index. ISBN 0-8261-1257-9 (hardcover) DDC 150.19/84
*1. Psychology - Philosophy. 2. Unified field theories. I. Title.*
*TC BF38 .C715 1999*

**Come all you brave soldiers.**
Cox, Clinton. 1st ed. New York : Scholastic Press, 1999.
*TC E269.N3 C69 1999*

**Comedia**
Robins, Kevin. Times of the technoculture. London ; New York : Routledge, 1999.
*TC T58.5 .R65 1999*

**COMEDY FILMS.**
Jones, Carl Mounsey. The film-audience relationship. 1997.
*TC 06 no. 10769*

Jones, Carl Mounsey. The film-audience relationship. 1997.
*TC 06 no. 10769*

**COMIC BOOKS, STRIPS, ETC.**
Comics, the 9th art [videorecording]. [S.l.] : EPISA ; Cicero, Ill. : [Distributed by] The Roland Collection, 1990.
*TC PN6710 .C6 1990*

**COMIC BOOKS, STRIPS, ETC. - HISTORY.**
Comics, the 9th art [videorecording]. [S.l.] : EPISA ; Cicero, Ill. : [Distributed by] The Roland Collection, 1990.
*TC PN6710 .C6 1990*

**COMIC BOOKS, STRIPS, ETC., IN ART.**
Roy Lichtenstein [videorecording]. [Chicago, IL] : Home Vision ; [S.l.] : distributed worldwide by RM Asssociates, c1991.
*TC ND237.L627 R6 1991*

**COMIC BOOKS, STRIPS, ETC. - SOCIAL ASPECTS.**
Comics, the 9th art [videorecording]. [S.l.] : EPISA ; Cicero, Ill. : [Distributed by] The Roland Collection, 1990.
*TC PN6710 .C6 1990*

**COMIC BOOKS, STRIPS, ETC. - THEMES, MOTIVES.**
Comics, the 9th art [videorecording]. [S.l.] : EPISA ; Cicero, Ill. : [Distributed by] The Roland Collection, 1990.
*TC PN6710 .C6 1990*

**COMIC STRIP CHARACTERS IN MOTION PICTURES.**
Comics, the 9th art [videorecording]. [S.l.] : EPISA ; Cicero, Ill. : [Distributed by] The Roland Collection, 1990.
*TC PN6710 .C6 1990*

**COMIC STRIPS.** *See* COMIC BOOKS, STRIPS, ETC.

**COMICS.** *See* COMIC BOOKS, STRIPS, ETC.

**Comics, the 9th art** [videorecording] / EPISA (Euskal Pictures International, S.A.) ; [director, Alejandro Vallejo ; producer], Inigo Silva. [S.l.] : EPISA ; Cicero, Ill. : [Distributed by] The Roland Collection, 1990. 1 videocassette (28 min.) : sd., col. with b&w sequences ; 1/2 in. (28 min.) in the ninth art ; [1]) VHS, NTSC. Catalogued from credits, cassette label and container. Credits from container; more extensive credits given at the end of the film in Basque. Script, Carmen Dominguez, Maite Ruiz de Austri, Alejandro Vallejo. Place of distribution from cassette label; addresses for the Roland Collection on container: Peasmarsh, East Sussex, England and Ho-Ho-Kus, NJ. On spine of container and cassette case: "781." Age 9 and up. SUMMARY: This is the opening film in a series which explores the history and development of the comic-book as an artistic entity in its own right. In a moving collage of images, part still photographs, part animation and part documentary film clips, the subject matter, various types of characters, and various types of artistic dipiction are presented in samples from a vast selection of work by an international group of comic book artists. The film thus relates the relatively short history of the form which, despite the criticism routinely leveled against it, has becom one of the pillars of twentieth-century mass culture.
*1. Comic books, strips, etc. 2. Comic books, strips, etc. - History. 3. Comic books, strips, etc. - Themes, motives. 4. Comic books, strips, etc. - Social aspects. 5. Comic strip characters in motion pictures. 6. Wit and humor, Pictorial. 7. Caricatures and cartoons. 8. Cartooning - History. 9. Documentary films. I. Vallejo, Alejandro. II. Dominguez, Carmen. III. Ruiz de Austri, Maite. IV. Silva, Inigo. V. Anthony Roland Collection of Film on Art. VI. EPISA (Firm) VII. Title: Comics, the ninth art [videorecording] VIII. Series.*
*TC PN6710 .C6 1990*

**Comics, the ninth art**
([1]) Comics, the 9th art [videorecording]. [S.l.] : EPISA ; Cicero, Ill. : [Distributed by] The Roland Collection, 1990.
*TC PN6710 .C6 1990*

**Comics, the ninth art [videorecording].**
Comics, the 9th art [videorecording]. [S.l.] : EPISA ; Cicero, Ill. : [Distributed by] The Roland Collection, 1990.
*TC PN6710 .C6 1990*

**Coming clean.**
Granfield, Robert, 1955- New York ; London : New York University Press, c1999.
*TC HV4998 .G73 1999*

**Coming home :** teacher's planning guide. New York : Macmillan/McGraw-Hill, c1997. 1 v. (various pagings) : col. ill. ; 31 cm. (Spotlight on literacy ; Gr.6 l.12 u.5) (The road to independent reading) Includes index. ISBN 0-02-183198-x
*1. Language arts (Elementary) 2. Reading (Elementary) I. Series. II. Series: The road to independent reading*
*TC LB1576 .S66 1997 Gr.6 L.12 u.5*

**Coming into her own :** educational success in girls and women / Sara N. Davis, Mary Crawford, and Jadwiga Sebrechts, Editors. San Francisco, Calif. : Jossey-Bass, c1999. xix, 361 p. ; 24 cm. Includes bibliographical references and index. CONTENTS: Charting the history of women's studies programs / Judith Giblin James -- The women's college difference / Jadwiga Sebrechts -- Principles and strategies of feminist teaching / Ellen Kimmel -- Teaching through narratives of women's lives / Debbie Cottrell -- Studying women's lives in an interdisciplinary context / Sara N. Davis and Virginia Kaib Ratigan -- The influence of the personal on classroom interaction / Helene Elting -- Creating collaborative classroom / Sara N. Davis -- Encouraging participation in the classroom / Estelle Disch -- Overcoming resistance to feminism in the classroom / Mary Crawford and Jessica A. Suckle -- Creating expectations in adolescent girls / Rebecca L. Pierce and Mary E. Kite -- Successful strategies for teaching statistics / Mary B. Harris and Candace Schau -- Mentoring the whole life of emerging scientists / Neal B. Abraham -- Mentoring diverse population / Roxana Moayedi -- Advising young women of color / Susan E. Murphy, Sharon G. Goto, and Ellen A. Ensher -- Lessons from self-defense training / Glenda M. Russell and Kari L. Fraser -- Including lesbian, gay, and bisexual students in student life / Janis S. Bohan and Glenda M. Russell -- College women and alcohol use / Mary Crawford, George Dowdall, and Henry Wechsler -- Preventing dating violence / Deborah Mahlstedt and Carole Baroody Corcoran -- Defining supportive educational environment for low-income women / Erika Kates. ISBN 0-7879-4490-4 (acid-free paper) DDC 371.822/0973
*1. Women - Education - United States. 2. Women - Education (Higher) - United States. 3. Feminism and education - United States. 4. Women's studies - United States. I. Davis, Sara N., 1946- II. Crawford, Mary (Mary E.) III. Sebrechts, Jadwiga, 1953-*
*TC LC1503 .C65 1999*

**Coming of age in academe.**
Martin, Jane Roland, 1929- New York ; London : Routledge, 2000.
*TC LC197 .M37 2000*

**Coming of age in America :** a multicultural anthology / edited by Mary Frosch ; foreword by Gary Soto. New York : New Press : Distributed by W.W. Norton, c1994. xiv, 274 p. ; 21 cm. Includes bibliographical references (p. 265-266). ISBN 1-56584-146-8 DDC 813.008/ 0920693
*1. Children of minorities - United States - Literary collections.*

2. Ethnic groups - United States - Literary collections. 3.
American literature - Minority authors. I. Frosch, Mary.
*TC PS509.M5 C66 1994*

**COMING OUT (SEXUAL ORIENTATION).**
Rogers, Richard Randall. The impact of gay identity
and perceived milieu toward gay employees on job
involvement and organizational commitment of gay
men. 1998.
*TC 085 R635*

**COMMAND OF TROOPS.** *See* **LEADERSHIP.**

**COMMERCE.** *See* **COMPETITION;
INTERNATIONAL TRADE; RETAIL TRADE.**

**COMMERCIAL ART.**
Looking closer 2. New York : Allworth Press :
American Institute of Graphic Arts, c1997.
*TC NC997 .L632 1997*

Looking closer. New York : Allworth Press :
American Institute of Graphic Arts ; Saint Paul, MN :
Distributor, Consortium Book Sales & Distribution,
c1994.
*TC NC997 .L63 1994*

**COMMERCIAL ART GALLERIES.** *See* **ART
GALLERIES, COMMERCIAL.**

**COMMERCIAL ART - HISTORY.**
Heller, Steven. Design literacy. New York : Allworth
Press, c1997.
*TC NC998 .H45 1997*

**COMMERCIAL ART - INDIA - PICTORIAL
WORKS.**
Dawson, Barry. Street graphics India. London :
Thames & Hudson, 1999.
*TC NC998.6.I6 D38 1999*

Dawson, Barry. Street graphics India. London :
Thames & Hudson, 1999.
*TC NC998.6.I6 D38 1999*

**COMMERCIAL ART - STUDY AND TEACHING.**
The education of a graphic designer. New York :
Allworth Press [in association with the] School of
Visual Arts, c1998
*TC NC590 .E38 1998*

**COMMERCIAL ART - VOCATIONAL
GUIDANCE - UNITED STATES.**
Goldfarb, Roz. Careers by design. Rev. ed. New York,
NY : Allworth Press Council, c1997.
*TC NC1001 .G65 1997*

**COMMERCIAL BANKS.** *See* **BANKS AND
BANKING.**

**COMMERCIAL BUILDINGS.** *See* **STORES,
RETAIL.**

**COMMERCIAL CORRESPONDENCE.** *See* **FORM
LETTERS.**

**COMMERCIAL CRISES.** *See* **DEPRESSIONS.**

**COMMERCIAL DESIGN.** *See* **COMMERCIAL
ART.**

**COMMERCIAL EDUCATION.** *See* **BUSINESS
EDUCATION.**

**COMMERCIAL ETHICS.** *See* **BUSINESS ETHICS.**

**COMMERCIAL FISHING.** *See* **FISHERIES.**

**COMMERCIAL LAW.** *See* **FOOD LAW AND
LEGISLATION.**

**COMMERCIAL PHOTOGRAPHY.** *See also*
**PHOTOJOURNALISM.**
The power of idea : [videorecording]. Minneapolis,
Minn. : Media Loft, c1992.
*TC TR690 .P5 1992*

Sport photography today! [videorecording].
Minneapolis, Minn. : Media Loft, c1992.
*TC TR821 .S64 1992*

**COMMERCIAL POLICY.** *See* **CONSUMER
PROTECTION.**

**COMMERCIAL VEHICLES.** *See* **TRUCKS.**

**COMMISSION MERCHANTS.** *See*
**CONSIGNMENT SALES.**

**Commission on Family and Medical Leave (U.S.)** A
Workable balance : report to Congress on family and
medical leave policies. Washington, DC :
Commission on Leave ; Women's Bureau, U.S. Dept.
of Labor, [1996] 2, 2, xxiii, 314 p. : ill. ; 28 cm. "April 30,
1996"--P. 2 (1st. group). Shipping list no.: 96-0227-P. Includes
bibliographical references (p. 307-314).
*1. Sick leave - United States. 2. Maternity leave - United states.
3. Parental leave - United States. 4. Leave of absence - United
states. 5. Sick leave - Law and legislation - United states. 6.*

*Maternity leave - Law and legislation - United states. 7.
Parental leave - Law and legislation - United states. 8. Leave
of absence - Law and legislation - United States. I. United
States. Women's Bureau. II. Title. III. Title: Report to
Congress on family and medical leave policies*
*TC HD5115.6.U5 C66 1996*

**Commission on Undergraduate Education in the
Biological Sciences.** CUEBS news. [Washington,
D.C.] Commission on Undergradute Education in the
Biological Sciences. v. ports. 28 cm. v. 1-  Feb. 1965-Jan.
1972. ISSN 0574-9816 DDC 507/.1/173
*1. Biology - Study and teaching (Higher) - Periodicals. I.
Commission on Undergraduate Education in the Biological
Sciences. News. II. Title.*

**News.**
Commission on Undergraduate Education in the
Biological Sciences. CUEBS news. [Washington,
D.C.] Commission on Undergradute Education in
the Biological Sciences.

**COMMISSIONS, ART.** *See* **ART COMMISSIONS.**

**COMMITMENT (PSYCHOLOGY).**
Rogers, Richard Randall. The impact of gay identity
and perceived milieu toward gay employees on job
involvement and organizational commitment of gay
men. 1998.
*TC 085 R635*

**Committee for Economic Development.**
Annual State of American Education Address (7th :
February 22, 2000 : Durham, N.C.) The seventh
annual state of American education address
[videorecording. [Washington, D.C. : U.S. Dept. of
Education], 2000.

Modernizing schools : technology and buildings for a
new century (September 19, 2000 : Washington, D.C.)
Modernizing schools [videorecording]. [Washington,
D.C.] : U.S. Dept. of Education, [2000].
*TC LB3205 .M64 2000*

Modernizing schools : technology and buildings for a
new century (September 19, 2000 : Washington, D.C.)
Modernizing schools [videorecording]. [Washington,
D.C.] : U.S. Dept. of Education, [2000].
*TC LB3205 .M64 2000*

Powerful middle schools : teaching and learning for
young adolescents (2000) Powerful middle schools
[videorecording]. [Washington, D.C.?] : U.S. Dept. of
Education, [2000].
*TC LB1623 .P6 2000*

**Committee on Science, Engineering, and Public
Policy (U.S.).**
Enhancing the postdoctoral experience for scientists
and engineers. Washington, DC : National Academy
Press, 2000.
*TC Q147 .E53 2000*

**Committee on the Health and Adjustment of
Immigrant Children and Families (U.S.).**
Children of immigrants. Washington, D.C. : National
Academy Press, c1999.
*TC HV741 .C536157 1999*

**Common, delinquent, and special.**
Richardson, John G. New York : Falmer Press, 1999.
*TC LC3981 .R525 1999*

**COMMON GOOD.** *See also* **CONSENSUS
(SOCIAL SCIENCES).**
Kane, Francis, 1944- Neither beasts nor gods. Dallas :
Southern Methodist University Press, 1998.
*TC JC330.15 .K36 1998*

**Common interest, common good.**
Sagawa, Shirley, 1961- Boston : Harvard Business
School Press, c2000.
*TC HD60.5.U5 S24 2000*

**COMMON LAW MARRIAGE.** *See* **UNMARRIED
COUPLES.**

**COMMON NAMES OF ANIMALS.** *See*
**ZOOLOGY - NOMENCLATURE (POPULAR).**

**COMMON SCHOOLS.** *See* **PUBLIC SCHOOLS.**

**A common sense guide to non-traditional urban
education.**
Gill, Walter. Nashville, Tenn. : James C. Winston
Publishing Co., Inc., c1998.
*TC LC5115 .G55 1998*

**COMMONPLACE-BOOKS.** *See* **HANDBOOKS,
VADE-MECUMS, ETC.**

**COMMONS.** *See* **PARKS.**

**COMMONS (SOCIAL ORDER).** *See* **MIDDLE
CLASS; WORKING CLASS.**

**COMMONS, STUDENT.** *See* **STUDENT UNIONS.**

**Commonsense copyright.**
Talab, R. S., 1948- 2nd ed. Jefferson, N.C. :
McFarland & Co., 1999.
*TC KF2994 .T36 1999*

**COMMONWEALTH COLLEGE (MENA, ARK.) -
HISTORY.**
Cobb, William H. Radical education in the rural
South. Detroit : Wayne State University Press, 2000.
*TC LD1276 .C63 2000*

**COMMONWEALTH COUNTRIES - IN
LITERATURE - STUDY AND TEACHING.**
Teaching post-colonialism and post-colonial
literatures. Aarhus, Denmark ; Oakville, Conn. :
Aarhus University Press, c1997.
*TC PR9080.A53 T43 1997*

**Commonwealth Fund.**
Minority health in America. Baltimore, Md. : Johns
Hopkins University Press, 2000.
*TC RA448.4 .M566 2000*

**COMMONWEALTH LITERATURE (ENGLISH) -
STUDY AND TEACHING.**
Teaching post-colonialism and post-colonial
literatures. Aarhus, Denmark ; Oakville, Conn. :
Aarhus University Press, c1997.
*TC PR9080.A53 T43 1997*

**COMMONWEALTH NATIONS.** *See*
**COMMONWEALTH COUNTRIES.**

**COMMONWEALTH OF NATIONS LITERATURE
(ENGLISH).** *See* **COMMONWEALTH
LITERATURE (ENGLISH).**

**COMMONWEALTH (ORGANIZATION)
COUNTRIES.** *See* **COMMONWEALTH
COUNTRIES.**

**Commonwealth Secretariat.**
Leo-Rhynie, Elsa. Gender mainstreaming in
education. London : Commonwealth Secretariat,
c1999.
*TC LC2572 .L46 1999*

**COMMONWEALTH, THE.** *See* **POLITICAL
SCIENCE.**

**COMMUNAL LIVING.** *See* **COLLECTIVE
SETTLEMENTS.**

**COMMUNAL LIVING - UNITED STATES -
HISTORY.**
Smith, William L., 1956- Families and communes.
Thousand Oaks, Calif. : Sage Publications, c1999.
*TC HQ971 .S55 1999*

**COMMUNAL SETTLEMENTS.** *See*
**COLLECTIVE SETTLEMENTS;
COMMUNAL LIVING.**

**COMMUNES.** *See* **COMMUNAL LIVING.**

**COMMUNICABLE DISEASES.** *See also*
**BACTERIAL DISEASES; SEXUALLY
TRANSMITTED DISEASES; VIRUS
DISEASES.**
Epidemic!. New York : The New Press ; New York :
Distributed by W.W. Norton, c1999.
*TC RA651 .E596 1999*

**COMMUNICABLE DISEASES - LAW AND
LEGISLATION.** *See* **PUBLIC HEALTH
LAWS.**

**COMMUNICATEURS - CANADA -
BIOGRAPHIES.**
Babe, Robert E., 1943- Canadian communication
thought. Toronto ; Buffalo : University of Toronto
Press, c2000.
*TC P92.5.A1B32 2000*

**Communicating.**
Botel, Morton. Lexington, Mass. : D. C. Heath, c1973.
*TC PE1121 .B67 1973 Bk A*

Botel, Morton. Lexington, Mass. : D. C. Heath, c1973.
*TC PE1121 .B67 1973*

**Communicating emotion.**
Planalp, Sally, 1950- Cambridge ; New York :
Cambridge University Press ; Paris ; Editions de la
Maison des sciences de l'homme, 1999.
*TC BF591. .P57 1999*

**Communicating science.** London ; New York :
Routledge in association with The Open University,
1999. 2 v. : ill. ; 24 cm. Includes bibliographical references
and index. Library lacks v. 1 CONTENTS: Reader 1.
Professional contexts / edited by Eileen Scanlon, Roger Hill,
and Kirk Junker -- Reader 2. Contexts and channels / edited by
Eileen Scanlon, Elizabeth Whitelegg and Simeon Yates. ISBN
0-415-19750-3 (hbk) ISBN 0-415-19751-1 (pbk). DDC 501/.4

*Communication*

*1. Communication in science. 2. Science news. I. Scanlon. Eileen.*
*TC Q223 .C6542 1999*

**COMMUNICATION.** *See also* AGED - COMMUNICATION; BUSINESS COMMUNICATION; DEAF - MEANS OF COMMUNICATION; INTERCULTURAL COMMUNICATION; LANGUAGE AND LANGUAGES; LANGUAGE ARTS; ORAL COMMUNICATION; PERSUASION (PSYCHOLOGY); POPULAR CULTURE; TELECOMMUNICATION; WRITTEN COMMUNICATION.
Babe, Robert E., 1943- Canadian communication thought. Toronto ; Buffalo : University of Toronto Press, c2000.
*TC P92.5.A1B32 2000*

Communication in recovery. Cresskill, N.J. : Hampton Press, c1999.
*TC HV4998 .C64 1999*

The emerging world of wireless communications. Nashville, TN : Institute for Information Studies, 1996.
*TC TK5103.2 .E44 1996*

Jones, Carl Mounsey. The film-audience relationship. 1997.
*TC 06 no. 10769*

Jones, Carl Mounsey. The film-audience relationship. 1997.
*TC 06 no. 10769*

Nursing documentation. Thousand Oaks, Calif. : Sage Publications, c1999.
*TC RT50 .N87 1999*

Webster, Douglas B., 1934- Neuroscience of communication. 2nd ed. San Diego : Singular Publishing Group, c1999.
*TC QP355.2 .W43 1999*

**COMMUNICATION, ADMINISTRATIVE.** *See* BUSINESS COMMUNICATION.

**Communication :** an arena of development / edited by Nancy Budwig, Ina Č. Užgiris, James V. Wertsch. Stamford, Conn. : Ablex Pub. Corp., c2000. xv, 242 p. : ill. ; 24 cm. (Advances in applied developmental psychology ; vol. 19) Includes bibliographical references and indexes. ISBN 1-56750-456-6 (hbk.) ISBN 1-56750-457-4 (pbk.) DDC 153.6
*1. Interpersonal communication in infants. 2. Interpersonal communication in children. 3. Communication and culture. I. Budwig, Nancy. II. Užgiris, Ina Č. III. Wertsch, James V. IV. Series: Advances in applied developmental psychology (1993) ; v. 19.*
*TC BF712 .A36 v.19*

**Communication and aging** / Jon F. Nussbaum ... [et al.]. 2nd ed. Mahwah, NJ ; London : L. Erlbaum, 2000. xxi, 368 p. ; 24 cm. (LEA's communication series) Includes bibliographical references and index. ISBN 0-8058-3331-5 (alk. paper) ISBN 0-8058-3332-3 (pbk. : alk. paper) DDC 305.26
*1. Aged - Communication - United States. 2. Interpersonal communication. 3. Aging - Psychological aspects. 4. Old age - Social aspects - United States. I. Nussbaum, Jon F. II. Series.*
*TC HQ1064.U5 C5364 2000*

**Communication and counselling in health care.** Noon, J. Mitchell. Counselling and helping carers. Leicester : BPS Books, 1999.
*TC R727.4 .N66 1999*

**COMMUNICATION AND CULTURE.**
Communication. Stamford, Conn. : Ablex Pub. Corp., c2000.
*TC BF712 .A36 v.19*

Global literacies and the World-Wide Web. London ; New York : Routledge, 2000.
*TC P94.6 .G58 2000*

Kavanagh, Gaynor. Dream spaces. New York : Leicester University Press, 2000.
*TC AM7 .K37 2000*

Li, Duan-Duan. Expressing needs and wants in a second language. 1998.
*TC 06 no. 10958*

Robins, Kevin. Times of the technoculture. London ; New York : Routledge, 1999.
*TC T58.5 .R65 1999*

Wierzbicka, Anna. Emotions across languages and cultures. Cambridge : Cambridge University Press, 1999.
*TC BF531 .W54 1999*

**COMMUNICATION AND CULTURE - UNITED STATES.**
Mindess, Anna. Reading between the signs. Yarmouth, Me. : Intercultural Press, c1999.
*TC HV2402 .M56 1999*

**Communication and personal relationships :** edited by Steve Duck and Kathryn Dindia. New York : Wiley, 2000. xiv, 217 p. ; 25 cm. Includes bibliographical references and indexes. ISBN 0-471-49133-0 DDC 302.3/4
*1. Interpersonal communication. 2. Interpersonal relations. I. Duck, Steve. II. Dindia, Kathryn.*
*TC HM1116 .C65 2000*

**COMMUNICATION AND TECHNOLOGY.**
Global literacies and the World-Wide Web. London ; New York : Routledge, 2000.
*TC P94.6 .G58 2000*

Wolf, Mark J. P. Abstracting reality. Lanham, Md.: University Press of America, c2000.
*TC HM851 .W65 2000*

**COMMUNICATION AND TECHNOLOGY - EUROPE - CONGRESSES.**
The challenges of the information and communication technologies facing history teaching. Strasbourg : Council of Europe Pub., c1999.
*TC D424 .C425 1999*

**COMMUNICATION AND TECHNOLOGY - UNITED STATES - HISTORY.**
Gitelman, Lisa. Scripts, grooves, and writing machines. Stanford, Calif. : Stanford University Press, c1999.
*TC P96.T422 U6343*

**COMMUNICATION AND TRAFFIC.** *See* RAILROADS.

**COMMUNICATION ARTS.** *See* LANGUAGE ARTS.

**COMMUNICATION - ASPECT POLITIQUE.**
Digital democracy. Toronto ; New York : Oxford University Press, 1998.
*TC JC421 .D55 1998*

**COMMUNICATION, BUSINESS.** *See* BUSINESS COMMUNICATION.

**COMMUNICATION DEVICES FOR THE DISABLED.** *See also* BLIND, APPARATUS FOR THE.
Augmentative and alternative communication. London : Whurr, 1999.
*TC RC429 .A94 1999*

**COMMUNICATION DISORDERS - COMPLICATIONS.**
Myers, Penelope S. Right hemisphere damage. San Diego : Singular Pub., c1999.
*TC RC423 .M83 1999*

**COMMUNICATION DISORDERS - DIAGNOSIS.**
Communication disorders following traumatic brain injury. Hove, East Sussex, UK : Psychology Press, c1999.
*TC RD594 .C648 1999*

**COMMUNICATION DISORDERS - ETIOLOGY.**
Gerber, Sanford E. Etiology and prevention of communicative disorders. 2nd ed. San Diego : Singular Pub. Group, c1998.
*TC RJ496.C67 G47 1998*

**Communication disorders following traumatic brain injury** / edited by Skye McDonald, Leanne Togher, Chris Code. Hove, East Sussex, UK : Psychology Press, c1999. xiv, 338 p. : ill. ; 24 cm. (Brain damage, behaviour, and cognition series, 0967-9944) Includes bibliographical references and indexes. ISBN 0-86377-724-4 DDC 616.8552
*1. Communication Disorders - diagnosis 2. Communication Disorders - rehabilitation 3. Brain Injuries - complications 4. Communicative disorders. 5. Brain - Wounds and injuries. 6. Brain - Wounds and injuries - Complications. 7. Communicative disorders. I. McDonald, Skye. II. Togher, Leanne. III. Code, Christopher, 1942- IV. Series: Brain damage, behaviour, and cognition.*
*TC RD594 .C648 1999*

**COMMUNICATION DISORDERS - IN INFANCY & CHILDHOOD.**
Gerber, Sanford E. Etiology and prevention of communicative disorders. 2nd ed. San Diego : Singular Pub. Group, c1998.
*TC RJ496.C67 G47 1998*

**COMMUNICATION DISORDERS (MEDICINE).** *See* COMMUNICATIVE DISORDERS.

**COMMUNICATION DISORDERS - PREVENTION & CONTROL.**
Gerber, Sanford E. Etiology and prevention of

communicative disorders. 2nd ed. San Diego : Singular Pub. Group, c1998.
*TC RJ496.C67 G47 1998*

**COMMUNICATION DISORDERS - REHABILITATION.**
Communication disorders following traumatic brain injury. Hove, East Sussex, UK : Psychology Press, c1999.
*TC RD594 .C648 1999*

Neurogenic communication disorders. New York : Thieme, 2000.
*TC RC423 .N48 2000*

**COMMUNICATION DISORDERS - THERAPY - CHILD - UNITED STATES.**
Clinical management of communication disorders in culturally diverse children. Boston : Allyn & Bacon, c2000.
*TC RJ496.C67 C556 2000*

**COMMUNICATION - FICTION.**
Brooke, William J. A is for aarrgh!. 1st ed. New York : HarperCollinsPublishers, 1999.
*TC PZ7.B78977 Ig 1999*

**COMMUNICATION IN COMMUNITY DEVELOPMENT.**
Moemeka, Andrew A. (Andrew Azukaego) Development communication in action. Lanham, Md. : University Press of America, c2000.
*TC HD76 .M644 2000*

**COMMUNICATION IN ECONOMIC DEVELOPMENT.**
Moemeka, Andrew A. (Andrew Azukaego) Development communication in action. Lanham, Md. : University Press of America, c2000.
*TC HD76 .M644 2000*

**COMMUNICATION IN EDUCATION.**
Fennimore, Beatrice Schneller. Talk matters. New York : London : Teachers College Press, c2000.
*TC LB1033.5 F46 2000*

Flecha, Ramón. [Compartiendo palabras. English] Sharing words. Lanham, Md. : Oxford : Rowman & Littlefield Publishers, c2000.
*TC LB1060 .F5913 2000*

Friend, Marilyn Penovich, 1953- Interactions. 3rd ed. New York : Longman, 1999.
*TC LC3969.45 .F75 1999*

McCaslin, Mary M. Listening in classrooms. 1st ed. New York : HarperCollins College Publishers, c1996.
*TC LB1033 .M34 1996*

Muse, Ivan. Oral and nonverbal expression. Princeton, NJ : Eye On Education, c1996.
*TC P95 .M86 1996*

Seo, Kyoung-Hye. Children's construction of personal meanings of mathematical symbolism in a reform-oriented classroom. 2000.
*TC 06 no. 11310*

Strategies for energizing large classes : from small groups to learning communities. San Francisco, Calif. : Jossey-Bass, 2000.
*TC LB2361.5 .S77 2000*

**COMMUNICATION IN EDUCATION - SOCIAL ASPECTS - UNITED STATES.**
Bartolomé, Lilia I. The misteaching of academic discourses. Boulder, Colo. : Westview Press, 1998.
*TC LB1033.5 .B37 1998*

**COMMUNICATION IN EDUCATION - TAIWAN - CASE STUDIES.**
Tian, Shiau-ping. TOEFL reading comprehension. 2000.
*TC 06 no. 11316*

**COMMUNICATION IN EDUCATION - UNITED STATES.**
Bagin, Don, 1938- The school and community relations. 7th ed. Boston ; London : Allyn and Bacon, c2001.
*TC LC221 .G35 2001*

Garoian, Charles R., 1943- Performing pedagogy. Albany, N.Y. : State University of New York Press, 1999.
*TC NX504 .G37 1999*

**COMMUNICATION IN MARRIAGE - UNITED STATES.**
Gottman, John Mordechai. Why marriages succeed or fail :. 1st Fireside ed. New York : Fireside, 1995.
*TC HQ536 .G68 1994*

**COMMUNICATION IN MEDICINE.** *See* HEALTH EDUCATION.

**COMMUNICATION IN NURSING.** *See* **NURSING RECORDS.**

**COMMUNICATION IN NURSING - MISCELLANEA - HANDBOOKS, MANUALS, ETC.**
Nursing documentation. Thousand Oaks, Calif. : Sage Publications, c1999.
*TC RT50 .N87 1999*

**COMMUNICATION IN ORGANIZATIONS.**
Organizational communication and change. Cresskill, N.J. : Hampton Press, 1999.
*TC HD30.3 .O722 1999*

Talk, work, and institutional order. Berlin ; New York : Mouton de Gruyter, 1999.
*TC P95 .T286 1999*

**COMMUNICATION IN ORGANIZATIONS - SPAIN.**
Sauquet, Alfonso. Conflict and team learning:. 2000.
*TC 06 no. 11308*

**COMMUNICATION IN PUBLIC ADMINISTRATION.** *See* **GOVERNMENT PUBLICITY.**

**Communication in recovery :** perspectives on twelve-step groups / edited by Lynette S. Eastland, Sandra L. Herndon, Jeanine R. Barr. Cresskill, N.J. : Hampton Press, c1999. viii, 388 p. : ill. ; 24 cm. (Health communication) Includes bibliographical references and indexes. ISBN 1-57273-187-7 ISBN 1-57273-188-5 (pbk.) DDC 616.86/03
*1. Twelve-step programs. 2. Recovery movement. 3. Communication. I. Eastland, Lynette S. II. Herndon, Sandra L. III. Barr, Jeanine R. IV. Series: Health communication (Cresskill, N.J.)*
*TC HV4998 .C64 1999*

**COMMUNICATION IN SCIENCE.**
Communicating science. London ; New York : Routledge in association with The Open University, 1999.
*TC Q223 .C6542 1999*

**COMMUNICATION IN THE FAMILY.**
Woodruff, Debra, 1967- General family functioning, parental bonding, and attachment style. 1998.
*TC 085 W858*

**COMMUNICATION, INDUSTRIAL.** *See* **BUSINESS COMMUNICATION.**

**COMMUNICATION, INTERCULTURAL.** *See also* **INTERCULTURAL COMMUNICATION.**
Flower, Linda. Learning to rival. Mahwah, New Jersey : Lawrence Erlbaum Associates, c2000.
*TC PE1404 .F59 2000*

**COMMUNICATION, INTERNATIONAL.**
From testing to assessment. London ; New York : Longman, 1994.
*TC PE1128.A2 F778 1994*

Pelton, Joseph N. e-Sphere. Westport, Conn. ; London : Quorum Books, 2000.
*TC P96.I5 P33 2000*

Tehranian, Majid. Global communication and world politics. Boulder, Colo. : Lynne Rienner Publishers, 1999.
*TC P95.8 .T44 1999*

**COMMUNICATION OF TECHNICAL INFORMATION.** *See* **TECHNICAL WRITING.**

**COMMUNICATION - PHILOSOPHY - HISTORY.**
Peters, John Durham. Speaking into the air. Chicago : University of Chicago Press, 1999.
*TC P90 .P388 1999*

**COMMUNICATION POLICY.** *See* **LANGUAGE POLICY.**

**COMMUNICATION - POLITICAL ASPECTS.**
Digital democracy. Toronto ; New York : Oxford University Press, 1998.
*TC JC421 .D55 1998*

Tehranian, Majid. Global communication and world politics. Boulder, Colo. : Lynne Rienner Publishers, 1999.
*TC P95.8 .T44 1999*

**COMMUNICATION, PRIMITIVE.** *See* **COMMUNICATION.**

**COMMUNICATION - PSYCHOLOGICAL ASPECTS.** *See also* **INTERPERSONAL COMMUNICATION.**
Wallace, Patricia M. The psychology of the Internet. Cambridge ; New York : Cambridge University Press, 1999.

*TC BF637.C45 W26 1999*

**Communication research.**
Rubin, Rebecca B. 5th ed. Belmont, CA : Wadsworth Thomson Learning, 1999.
*TC P91.3 .R83 1999*

**COMMUNICATION - RESEARCH - METHODOLOGY.**
Rubin, Rebecca B. Communication research. 5th ed. Belmont, CA : Wadsworth Thomson Learning, 1999.
*TC P91.3 .R83 1999*

**Communication sciences and disorders :** from science to clinical practice / [edited by] Ronald B. Gillam, Thomas P. Marquardt, Frederick N. Martin. San Diego : Singular Pub. Group/Thomson Learning, c2000. xxii, 503 p. : ill. ; 26 cm. + 2 computer optical discs (4 3/4 in.). Includes bibliographical references and index. System requirements for computer discs (IBM): IBM-PC or compatible (Pentium I processor or faster); 32MB RAM (64MB recommended); Windows 95, 98 or NT 4.0 with Service Pack 3 or later; SoundBlaster or compatible sound card; speakers or headphones; 8x CD-ROM drive. System requirements for computer discs (Mac): PowerPC running 166 MHz or higher; 32MB RAM (64MB recommended); Mac OS 7.1.2 or later; speakers or headphones; 8x CD-ROM drive. ISBN 0-7693-0040-5 DDC 616.85/5
*1. Communicative disorders. I. Gillam, Ronald B. (Ronald Bradley), 1955- II. Marquardt, Thomas P. III. Martin, Frederick N.*
*TC RC423 .C647 2000*

**COMMUNICATION SKILLS (ELEMENTARY EDUCATION).** *See* **ENGLISH LANGUAGE - STUDY AND TEACHING (ELEMENTARY).**

**COMMUNICATION - SOCIAL ASPECTS.**
Li, Duan-Duan. Expressing needs and wants in a second language. 1998.
*TC 06 no. 10958*

**COMMUNICATION SPECIALISTS - CANADA - BIOGRAPHY.**
Babe, Robert E., 1943- Canadian communication thought. Toronto ; Buffalo : University of Toronto Press, c2000.
*TC P92.5.A1B32 2000*

**COMMUNICATION - STUDY AND TEACHING.**
Penman, Robyn. Reconstructing communicating. Mahwah, N.J. ; London : Lawrence Erlbaum Associates, 2000.
*TC BF637.C45 P435 2000*

**COMMUNICATION SYSTEMS, COMPUTER.** *See* **COMPUTER NETWORKS.**

**COMMUNICATION - TECHNOLOGICAL INNOVATIONS.**
Pelton, Joseph N. e-Sphere. Westport, Conn. ; London : Quorum Books, 2000.
*TC P96.I5 P33 2000*

**COMMUNICATION - UNITED STATES - SEX DIFFERENCES.**
Newman, Stephanie. Self-silencing, depression, gender role, and gender role conflict in women and men. 1997.
*TC 085 N47*

**Communications and networking in education.**
IFIP TC3 WG3.1/3.5 Open Conference on Communications and Networking in Education (1999 : Aulanko, Finland) Boston : Kluwer Academic Publishers, 2000.
*TC LB1044.87 .I45 2000*

**Communications and Society Program (Aspen Institute).**
Investing in diversity. Washington, D.C. : Aspen Institute, Communications and Society Program, c1998.
*TC P94.5.M552 U647 1997*

**COMMUNICATIONS, CONFIDENTIAL.** *See* **CONFIDENTIAL COMMUNICATIONS.**

**Communications, media and culture**
Riggs, Karen E. Mature audiences. New Brunswick, N.J. : Rutgers University Press, c1998.
*TC HQ1064.U5 R546 1998*

**COMMUNICATIONS RESEARCH.** *See* **COMMUNICATION - RESEARCH.**

**COMMUNICATIVE COMPETENCE.**
Chen, Zhe, 1964- Across the great divide. Oxford : Blackwell, 2000.
*TC LB1103 .S6 v.65 no. 2*

North, Brian, 1950- The development of a common framework scale of language proficiency. New York : P. Lang, c2000.

*TC P53.4 .N67 2000*

**COMMUNICATIVE DISORDERS.** *See also* **LANGUAGE DISORDERS; SPEECH DISORDERS.**
Brumfitt, Shelagh. The social psychology of communication impairment. London : Whurr, 1999.
*TC HM251 .B758 1999*

Communication disorders following traumatic brain injury. Hove, East Sussex, UK : Psychology Press, c1999.
*TC RD594 .C648 1999*

Communication disorders following traumatic brain injury. Hove, East Sussex, UK : Psychology Press, c1999.
*TC RD594 .C648 1999*

Communication sciences and disorders. San Diego : Singular Pub. Group/Thomson Learning, c2000.
*TC RC423 .C647 2000*

Gerber, Sanford E. Etiology and prevention of communicative disorders. 2nd ed. San Diego : Singular Pub. Group, c1998.
*TC RJ496.C67 G47 1998*

Myers, Penelope S. Right hemisphere damage. San Diego : Singular Pub., c1999.
*TC RC423 .M83 1999*

**COMMUNICATIVE DISORDERS IN CHILDREN.** *See also* **LANGUAGE DISORDERS IN CHILDREN; SPEECH DISORDERS IN CHILDREN.**
Clinical management of communication disorders in culturally diverse children. Boston : Allyn & Bacon, c2000.
*TC RJ496.C67 C556 2000*

**COMMUNICATIVE DISORDERS IN CHILDREN - ETIOLOGY.**
Gerber, Sanford E. Etiology and prevention of communicative disorders. 2nd ed. San Diego : Singular Pub. Group, c1998.
*TC RJ496.C67 G47 1998*

**COMMUNICATIVE DISORDERS IN CHILDREN - MISCELLANEA.**
Clinical management of communication disorders in culturally diverse children. Boston : Allyn & Bacon, c2000.
*TC RJ496.C67 C556 2000*

**COMMUNICATIVE DISORDERS IN CHILDREN - PREVENTION.**
Gerber, Sanford E. Etiology and prevention of communicative disorders. 2nd ed. San Diego : Singular Pub. Group, c1998.
*TC RJ496.C67 G47 1998*

**COMMUNICATIVE DISORDERS - PATIENTS - COUNSELING OF.**
Shames, George H., 1926- Counseling the communicatively disabled and their families. Boston ; London : Allyn and Bacon, c2000.
*TC RC428.8 .S53 2000*

**COMMUNICATIVE DISORDERS - PATIENTS - COUNSELING OF - CASE STUDIES.**
Wanting to talk. London : Whurr, c1998.
*TC RC423 .W26 1998*

**COMMUNICATIVE DISORDERS - PATIENTS - REHABILITATION.**
Klein, Harriet B. Intervention planning for adults with communication problems : Volume 2. Boston : Allyn and Bacon, c1999.
*TC RC423 .K57 1999*

**COMMUNICATIVE DISORDERS - PHYSIOLOGICAL ASPECTS.**
Webster, Douglas B., 1934- Neuroscience of communication. 2nd ed. San Diego : Singular Publishing Group, c1999.
*TC QP355.2 .W43 1999*

**COMMUNICATIVE DISORDERS - REHABILITATION.**
Neurogenic communication disorders. New York : Thieme, 2000.
*TC RC423 .N48 2000*

**COMMUNICATIVE DISORDERS - TREATMENT.**
Klein, Harriet B. Intervention planning for adults with communication problems : Volume 2. Boston : Allyn and Bacon, c1999.
*TC RC423 .K57 1999*

**COMMUNISM.** *See also* **ANTI-COMMUNIST MOVEMENTS; COLLECTIVE SETTLEMENTS; SOCIALISM.**
James, C. L. R. (Cyril Lionel Robert), 1901- Marxism

for our times. Jackson, Miss: University Press of Mississippi, c1999.
*TC HX44 .J25 1999*

**COMMUNISM AND ARCHITECTURE - CUBA - HAVANA.**
Loomis, John A., 1951- Revolution of forms. New York : Princeton Architectural Press, c1999.
*TC NA6602.A76 L66 1999*

**COMMUNISM AND CULTURE - SOVIET UNION - HISTORY.**
Holmes, Larry E. (Larry Eugene), 1942- Stalin's school. Pittsburgh, Pa. : University of Pittsburgh Press, c1999.
*TC LF4435.M657 H65 1999*

**COMMUNISM AND EDUCATION - EUROPE, EASTERN - HISTORY - CONGRESSES.**
Academia in upheaval. Westport, Conn. : Bergin & Garvey, 2000.
*TC LA837 .A6 2000*

**COMMUNISM AND EDUCATION - SOVIET UNION - HISTORY.**
Holmes, Larry E. (Larry Eugene), 1942- Stalin's school. Pittsburgh, Pa. : University of Pittsburgh Press, c1999.
*TC LF4435.M657 H65 1999*

**COMMUNISM AND EDUCATION - SOVIET UNION - HISTORY - CONGRESSES.**
Academia in upheaval. Westport, Conn. : Bergin & Garvey, 2000.
*TC LA837 .A6 2000*

**Communist Labor University of Jiangxi Province.**
Cleverley, John F. In the lap of tigers. Lanham, Md. ; Oxford : Rowman & Littlefield, c2000.
*TC S539.C6 C64 2000*

**COMMUNISTIC SETTLEMENTS.** *See* **COLLECTIVE SETTLEMENTS.**

**Communists on campus.**
Billingsley, William J., 1953- Athens, Ga. ; London : University of Georgia Press, c1999.
*TC LC72.3.N67 B55 1999*

**COMMUNITARIANISM - GREAT BRITAIN.**
Arthur, James, 1957- Schools and community. London : New York : Falmer Press, 2000.
*TC LC221.4.G7 A78 2000*

**COMMUNITARIANISM - HEALTH ASPECTS.**
Ethics and community in the health care professions. London ; New York : Routledge, 1999.
*TC R725.5 .E87 1999*

**COMMUNITARIANISM - UNITED STATES.**
Abowitz, Kathleen Knight. Making meaning of community in an American high school. Cresskill, N.J. : Hampton Press, c2000.
*TC LC311 .A36 2000*

**COMMUNITIES, GATED.** *See* **GATED COMMUNITIES.**

**COMMUNITY.** *See* **COMMUNITARIANISM; COMMUNITY LIFE; COMMUNITY ORGANIZATION; GATED COMMUNITIES.**

**Community access to resources directory.**
The CARES directory in electronic form [computer file] Maywood, NJ : ACIT,
*TC HV99.N59 S58*

**COMMUNITY ACTION.** *See* **POLITICAL PARTICIPATION.**

**COMMUNITY AND COLLEGE - CASE STUDIES.**
The response of higher education institutions to regional needs. Paris : Organisation for Economic Co-operation and Development, 1999.
*TC LC237 .R47 1999*

**COMMUNITY AND COLLEGE - EUROPE.**
Groof, Jan de. Democracy and governance in higher education. The Hague : Boston : Kluwer Law International, 1998.
*TC LB2341.8.E85 G76 1998*

**COMMUNITY AND COLLEGE - UNITED STATES.**
Combining service and learning in higher education. Santa Monica, CA : RAND Education, 1999.
*TC LC220.5 .C646 1999*

Transforming social inquiry, transforming social action. Boston ; London : Kluwer Academic, c2000.
*TC LC238 .T73 2000*

**Community and junior college journal.**
Junior college journal. Washington, D.C. [etc.]

**Community and junior college journal.** Washington, D.C. : American Association of Community and

Junior Colleges, 1972-1985. 13 v. : ill. ; 28 cm. Frequency: 8 no. a year. Former frequency: Monthly. Vol. 43, no. 1 (Aug./Sept. 1972)-v. 55, no. 8 (May/June 1985). Title from cover. Indexed in its entirety by: Current index to journals in education 0011-3565. Indexed in its entirety by: Education index 0013-1385. Indexed selectively by: Energy research abstracts 0160-3604 1982-1985. Available on microfilm. Continued in Aug./Sept. 1985 by: Community, technical, and junior college journal. Continues: Junior college journal (DLC) a33000196 (OCoLC)1800231. ISSN 0190-3160 DDC 378.15/43/05
*1. Junior colleges - Periodicals. I. American Association of Community and Junior Colleges. II. Title: Junior college journal III. Title: Community, technical, and junior college journal*

**COMMUNITY AND SCHOOL.** *See also* **COMMUNITY AND COLLEGE; TEACHERS AND COMMUNITY.**
Public relations in schools. 2nd ed. Upper Saddle River, N.J. : Merrill, c2000.
*TC LB2847 .P82 2000*

Speck, Marsha. The principalship. Upper Saddle River, N.J. : Merrill, c1999.
*TC LB1738.5 .S64 1999*

**COMMUNITY AND SCHOOL - CASE STUDIES.**
Public relations in schools. 2nd ed. Upper Saddle River, N.J. : Merrill, c2000.
*TC LB2847 .P82 2000*

**COMMUNITY AND SCHOOL - GREAT BRITAIN.**
Arthur, James, 1957- Schools and community. London : New York : Falmer Press, 2000.
*TC LC221.4.G7 A78 2000*

**COMMUNITY AND SCHOOL - NEW YORK (STATE) - HERKIMER COUNTY - CASE STUDIES.**
O'Connor-Pirkle, Marilyn. Tracking systemic change in an interagency partnership. 1996.
*TC 06 no. 10677*

O'Connor-Pirkle, Marilyn. Tracking systemic change in an interagency partnership. 1996.
*TC 06 no. 10677*

**COMMUNITY AND SCHOOL - NEW YORK (STATE) - NEW YORK.**
Wright, Stanley Nathaniel. The Beacon model. 1998.
*TC 06 no. 11007*

**COMMUNITY AND SCHOOL - NEW YORK (STATE) - NEW YORK - EVALUATION.**
Darwiche, Chirine Hijazi. The Beacons. 1997.
*TC 06 no. 10761*

**COMMUNITY AND SCHOOL - NEW YORK (STATE) - NEW YORK - HISTORY - 20TH CENTURY.**
Edgell, Derek. The movement for community control of New York City's schools, 1966-1970. Lewiston, N.Y. : E. Mellen Press, c1998.
*TC LB2862 .E35 1998*

**COMMUNITY AND SCHOOL - NIGERIA.**
Francis, Paul A. Hard lessons. Washington, D.C. : World Bank, c1998.
*TC LA1632 .F73 1998*

**COMMUNITY AND SCHOOL - UNITED STATES.**
Bagin, Don, 1938- The school and community relations. 7th ed. Boston ; London : Allyn and Bacon, c2001.
*TC LC221 .G35 2001*

Collaborative practice. Westport, Conn. ; London : Praeger, 1999.
*TC HV741 .C5424 1999*

Conners, Gail A. Good news!. Thousand Oaks, Calif. : Corwin Press, c2000.
*TC LB2847 .C65 2000*

Hughes, Carolyn, 1946- The transition handbook. Baltimore : P.H. Brookes Pub., c2000.
*TC LC4019 .H84 2000*

Otterbourg, Susan D. Using technology to strengthen employee and family involvement in education. [New York] : Conference Board, c1998.
*TC LB1028.3 .O88 1998*

Powerful middle schools : teaching and learning for young adolescents (2000) Powerful middle schools [videorecording]. [Washington, D.C.?] : U.S. Dept. of Education, [2000].
*TC LB1623 .P6 2000*

**COMMUNITY AND SCHOOL - UNITED STATES - CASE STUDIES.**
Doyle, Denis P. Raising the standard. 2nd ed. Thousand Oaks, Calif. : Corwin Press, c1999.

*TC LB2822.82 .D69 1999*
Hughes, Larry W., 1931- Public relations for school leaders. Boston : London : Allyn and Bacon, c2000.
*TC LB2847 .H84 2000*

**COMMUNITY AND TEACHERS.** *See* **TEACHERS AND COMMUNITY.**

**COMMUNITY ART CENTERS.** *See* **ART CENTERS.**

**COMMUNITY ART PROJECTS - UNITED STATES.**
Building America's communities II. Washington, D.C. : Americans for the Arts (Organization) ; Institute for Community Development and the Arts, 1997.
*TC NX180.A77 B95 1997*

**COMMUNITY ART PROJECTS - UNITED STATES - DIRECTORIES.**
Resource development handbook. [Washington, D.C.] : National Assembly of Local Arts Agencies, Institute for Community Development and the Arts, 1995.
*TC NX110 .R47 1995*

**COMMUNITY CENTERS.** *See* **ART CENTERS; RECREATION; STUDENT UNIONS.**

**Community college curriculum.**
Trends in community college curriculum. San Francisco : Jossey-Bass, c1999.
*TC LB2328.15.U6 T75 1999*

**The community college in the twenty-first century.**
Cain, Michael Scott. Lanham, MD : University Press of America, c1999.
*TC LB2328.15.U6 C33 1999*

**COMMUNITY COLLEGE STUDENTS.**
Miller, Estelle L. Fears expressed by female reentry students at an urban community college : qualitative study. 1997.
*TC 06 no. 10864*

**COMMUNITY COLLEGE TEACHERS - IN-SERVICE TRAINING - UNITED STATES.**
Miller, Richard I. Evaluating, improving, and judging faculty performance in two-year colleges. Westport, Conn. ; London : Bergin & Garvey, 2000.
*TC LB2333 .M49 2000*

**COMMUNITY COLLEGE TEACHERS - RATING OF - UNITED STATES.**
Miller, Richard I. Evaluating, improving, and judging faculty performance in two-year colleges. Westport, Conn. ; London : Bergin & Garvey, 2000.
*TC LB2333 .M49 2000*

**COMMUNITY COLLEGES.**
Gateways to democracy. San Francisco : Jossey-Bass, 1999.
*TC LB2328.N53 1999*

**COMMUNITY COLLEGES - ADMINISTRATION.**
Dimensions of managing academic affairs in the community college. San Francisco : Jossey-Bass, 2000.
*TC LB2341 .D56 2000*

**COMMUNITY COLLEGES - CURRICULA.**
Trends in community college curriculum. San Francisco : Jossey-Bass, c1999.
*TC LB2328.15.U6 T75 1999*

**COMMUNITY COLLEGES - FACULTY.** *See also* **COMMUNITY COLLEGE TEACHERS.**
Dimensions of managing academic affairs in the community college. San Francisco : Jossey-Bass, 2000.
*TC LB2341 .D56 2000*

**COMMUNITY COLLEGES - UNITED STATES.**
Cain, Michael Scott. The community college in the twenty-first century. Lanham, MD : University Press of America, c1999.
*TC LB2328.15.U6 C33 1999*

**COMMUNITY COLLEGES - UNITED STATES - ADMINISTRATION.**
Cain, Michael Scott. The community college in the twenty-first century. Lanham, MD : University Press of America, c1999.
*TC LB2328.15.U6 C33 1999*

Dimensions of managing academic affairs in the community college. San Francisco : Jossey-Bass, 2000.
*TC LB2341 .D56 2000*

**COMMUNITY COLLEGES - UNITED STATES - CASE STUDIES.**
Two-year colleges for women and minorities. New York : Falmer Press, 1999.

TC LB2328.15.U6 T96 1999

**COMMUNITY COLLEGES - UNITED STATES - CURRICULA.**
Trends in community college curriculum. San Francisco : Jossey-Bass, c1999.
*TC LB2328.15.U6 T75 1999*

**COMMUNITY COLLEGES - UNITED STATES - SOCIOLOGICAL ASPECTS.**
Herideen, Penelope E., 1960- Policy, pedagogy, and social inequality. Westport, Conn. : Bergin & Garvey, 1998.
*TC LB2328.15.U6 H47 1998*

**COMMUNITY COUNCILS.** *See* **COMMUNITY ORGANIZATION.**

**COMMUNITY DEVELOPMENT.** *See* **FUNDAMENTAL EDUCATION; RURAL DEVELOPMENT.**

**COMMUNITY DEVELOPMENT - CASE STUDIES.**
The response of higher education institutions to regional needs. Paris : Organisation for Economic Co-operation and Development, 1999.
*TC LC237 .R47 1999*

**COMMUNITY DEVELOPMENT - CITIZEN PARTICIPATION.** *See* **COMMUNITY DEVELOPMENT.**

**COMMUNITY DEVELOPMENT - GOVERNMENT POLICY.** *See* **COMMUNITY DEVELOPMENT.**

**COMMUNITY DEVELOPMENT - PERIODICALS.**
Centro sociale. Roma.

**COMMUNITY DEVELOPMENT, RURAL.** *See* **RURAL DEVELOPMENT.**

**COMMUNITY DEVELOPMENT - UNITED STATES.**
Building America's communities II. Washington, D.C. : Americans for the Arts (Organization) ; Institute for Community Development and the Arts, 1997.
*TC NX180.A77 B95 1997*

De Pree, Max. Leading without power. 1st ed. San Francisco, Calif. : Jossey-Bass, c1997.
*TC HN90.V64 D4 1997*

**COMMUNITY EDUCATION.** *See also* **POPULAR EDUCATION.**
Indigenous community-based education. Clevedon [England] ; Philadelphia : Multilingual Matters, c1999.
*TC LC1036 .I43 1999*

**COMMUNITY HEALTH.** *See* **PUBLIC HEALTH.**

**COMMUNITY HEALTH NURSING.**
Poirrier, Gail P. Service learning. Boston : Jones and Bartlett Publishers, 2001.
*TC RT73 .P64 2001*

**COMMUNITY HEALTH NURSING.**
Poirrier, Gail P. Service learning. Boston : Jones and Bartlett Publishers, 2001.
*TC RT73 .P64 2001*

**COMMUNITY HEALTH SERVICES.** *See also* **ABUSED WIVES - SERVICES FOR; COMMUNITY MENTAL HEALTH SERVICES; HOME CARE SERVICES.**
Collaborating to improve community health. San Francisco : Jossey-Bass Publishers, c1996.
*TC RA427 .C59 1996*

**COMMUNITY HEALTH SERVICES - GREAT BRITAIN.**
Thom, Betsy. Dealing with drink. London ; New York : Free Association Books, 1999.
*TC HV5283.G6 T56 1999*

**COMMUNITY IDENTITY.** *See* **GROUP IDENTITY.**

**COMMUNITY-INSTITUTIONAL RELATIONS.**
Integrating community service into nursing education. New York, NY : Springer Pub. Co., c1999.
*TC RT76 .I55 1999*

**COMMUNITY JUNIOR COLLEGES.** *See* **COMMUNITY COLLEGES.**

**COMMUNITY LEADERS.** *See* **CIVIC LEADERS.**

**COMMUNITY LIFE.** *See* **COMMUNITY AND SCHOOL; COMMUNITY ORGANIZATION; NEIGHBORHOOD; SOCIAL PARTICIPATION.**

**COMMUNITY LIFE - ENGLAND - LONDON.**
Gatter, Philip. Identity and sexuality. New York : Cassell, 1999.
*TC HQ1075.5.G7 G37 1999*

**COMMUNITY LIFE - UNITED STATES.**
Blakely, Edward James, 1938- Fortress America. Washington, D.C. : Brookings Institution Press, c1997.
*TC HT169.59.U6 B53 1997*

**COMMUNITY MENTAL HEALTH SERVICES.**
Graham, John R. (John Robert), 1940- MMPI-2 correlates for outpatient community mental health settings. Minneapolis : University of Minnesota Press, c1999.
*TC RC473.M5 G733 1999*

**COMMUNITY MENTAL HEALTH SERVICES.**
Mental health in our future cities. Hove, England : Psychology Press, c1998.
*TC RA790.5 .M4196 1998*

**COMMUNITY MENTAL HEALTH SERVICES - CONGRESSES.**
Unmet need in psychiatry. Cambridge, U.K. ; New York, NY : Cambridge University Press, 2000.
*TC RA790.5 .U565 2000*

**COMMUNITY MENTAL HEALTH SERVICES - ECONOMIC ASPECTS - UNITED STATES.**
Kenig, Sylvia. Who plays? who pays? who cares? Amityville, N.Y. : Baywood Pub. Co., c1992.
*TC RA790.6 .K46 1992*

**COMMUNITY MENTAL HEALTH SERVICES FOR TEENAGERS - UNITED STATES.**
Juvenile sex offenders [videorecording]. Princeton, N.J. : Films of the Humanities & Sciences, c1998.
*TC HV9067.S48 J8 1998*

**COMMUNITY MENTAL HEALTH SERVICES - HANDBOOKS, MANUALS, ETC.**
Crisis intervention handbook. 2nd ed. Oxford ; New York : Oxford University Press, 2000.
*TC RC480.6 .C744 2000*

**COMMUNITY MENTAL HEALTH SERVICES - POLITICAL ASPECTS - UNITED STATES.**
Kenig, Sylvia. Who plays? who pays? who cares? Amityville, N.Y. : Baywood Pub. Co., c1992.
*TC RA790.6 .K46 1992*

**COMMUNITY ORGANIZATION.** *See* **URBAN RENEWAL.**

**COMMUNITY ORGANIZATION - UNITED STATES.**
Loeb, Paul Rogat, 1952- Soul of a citizen. 1st St. Martin's Griffin ed. New York : St. Martin's Griffin, 1999.
*TC HN65 .L58 1999*

Wimsatt, William Upski. No more prisons. [New York] : Soft Skull Press, [2000?]
*TC HV9276.5 .W567x 2000*

**COMMUNITY PSYCHIATRY.** *See* **COMMUNITY MENTAL HEALTH SERVICES.**

**COMMUNITY PSYCHOLOGY - HANDBOOKS, MANUALS, ETC.**
Handbook of community psychology. New York ; London : Kluwer Academic/Plenum, c2000.
*TC RA790.55 .H36 2000*

**COMMUNITY SERVICE (EDUCATION).** *See* **STUDENT SERVICE.**

**Community spirit :** teacher's planning guide. New York : Macmillan/McGraw-Hill, c1997. 1 v. (various pagings) : col. ill. ; 31 cm. (Spotlight on literacy ; Gr.3 L.9 u.1) (The road to independent reading) Includes index. ISBN 0-02-181168-7
*1. Language arts (Primary) 2. Reading (Primary) I. Series. II. Series: The road to independent reading*
*TC LB1576 .S66 1997 Gr.3 L.9 u.1*

**COMMUNITY - STUDY AND TEACHING (PRIMARY) - UNITED STATES.**
Rogovin, Paula. Classroom interviews. Portsmouth, NH : Heinemann, c1998.
*TC LB1537 .R58 1998*

**COMMUNITY - STUDY AND TEACHING (SECONDARY).**
Steinberg, Adria. CityWorks. New York : New Press, c1999.
*TC LC1036 .S74 1999*

**Community, technical, and junior college journal.**
Community and junior college journal. Washington, D.C. : American Association of Community and Junior Colleges, 1972-1985.

**Community treatment of drug misuse.**
Seivewright, Nicholas. Cambridge, UK ; New York : Cambridge University Press, 2000.
*TC RC564 .S45 2000*

**COMMUTING COLLEGE STUDENTS.**
Involving commuter students in learning. San Francisco, Calif. : Jossey-Bass, 2000.
*TC LB2343.6 .I68 2000*

**COMORBIDITY.**
Pliszka, Steven R. ADHD with comorbid disorders. New York : Guilford Press, c1999.
*TC RJ506.H9 P55 1999*

Pliszka, Steven R. ADHD with comorbid disorders. New York : Guilford Press, c1999.
*TC RJ506.H9 P55 1999*

**Comp tales :** an introduction to college composition through its stories / Richard H. Haswell, Min-Zhan Lu, and contributors. New York : Longman, c2000. xii, 244 p. ; 21 cm. Includes bibliographical references (p. 237-244) and index. ISBN 0-321-05088-6 (pbk.)
*1. English language - Rhetoric - Study and teaching. 2. Report writing - Study and teaching. 3. English language - Rhetoric - Study and teaching (Higher) - United States. 4. Report writing - Study and teaching (Higher) - United States. 5. English teachers - United States - Biography. 6. College teachers - United States - Biography. I. Haswell, Richard H. II. Lu, Min-Zhan, 1946-*
*TC PE1404 .C617 2000*

**COMPACT DISC READ-ONLY MEMORY.** *See* **CD-ROMS.**

**COMPACT DISCS.** *See* **CD-ROMS.**

**COMPACT DISK READ-ONLY MEMORY.** *See* **CD-ROMS.**

**COMPANIES.** *See* **BUSINESS ENTERPRISES.**

**COMPANY OFFICERS.** *See* **EXECUTIVES.**

**Comparative anomie research :** hidden barriers, hidden potential for social development / edited by Peter Atteslander, Bettina Gransow, John Western. Aldershot, Hants, England ; Brookfield, Vt., USA : Ashgate, c1999. xvi, 256 p. : ill. ; 23 cm. Includes bibliographical references and index. ISBN 1-84014-887-X (hbk.) ISBN 0-7546-1121-3 (pbk.)
*1. Anomy. 2. Marginality, Social. 3. Alienation (Social psychology) 4. Economic development - Sociological aspects. I. Western, John. II. Gransow, Bettina. III. Atteslander, Peter M., 1926-*
*TC HM816 .C65 1999*

**Comparative approaches in brief dynamic psychotherapy** / William Borden, editor. New York : Haworth Press, c1999. 245 p. ; 22 cm. "Has been co-published simultaneously as Psychoanalytic social work, volume 6, numbers 3/4 1999." Includes bibliographical references and index. ISBN 0-7890-0833-5 (alk. paper) ISBN 0-7890-0844-0 (pbk. : alk. paper) DDC 616.89/14
*1. Brief psychotherapy. 2. Psychodynamic psychotherapy. I. Borden, William.*
*TC RC480.55 .C658 1999*

**COMPARATIVE BEHAVIOR.** *See* **PSYCHOLOGY, COMPARATIVE.**

**COMPARATIVE EDUCATION.**
Competitor or ally? New York : Falmer Press, 1999.
*TC LA1312 .C667 1999*

Education in a global society. Boston : Allyn and Bacon, c2000.
*TC LB43 .E385 2000*

The future of literacy in a changing world. Rev. ed. Cresskill, N.J. : Hampton Press, c1998.
*TC LC149 .F87 1998*

Learning from others. Dordrecht [Netherlands] ; Boston : Kluwer Academic Publishers, c2000.
*TC LB43 .L42 2000*

Ma, Liping. Knowing and teaching elementary mathematics. Mahwah, N.J. : Lawrence Erlbaum Associates, 1999.
*TC QA135.5 .M22 1999*

Promoting quality in learning. London ; New York : Cassell, 2000.
*TC LA632.b.P76 2000*

**COMPARATIVE EDUCATION - PHILOSOPHY.**
Comparative education. Lanham : Rowman & Littlefield, c1999.
*TC LB43 .C68 1999*

**Comparative education :** the dialectic of the global and the local / edited by Robert F. Arnove and Carlos Alberto Torres. Lanham : Rowman & Littlefield, c1999. vi, 434 p. ; 25 cm. Includes bibliographical references

(p. 428-431) and index. ISBN 0-8476-8460-1 (cloth : alk. paper) ISBN 0-8476-8461-X (pbk. : alk. paper) DDC 370.9
1. Comparative education - Philosophy. I. Arnove, Robert F. II. Torres, Carlos Alberto.
*TC LB43 .C68 1999*

**COMPARATIVE GRAMMAR.** See **GRAMMAR, COMPARATIVE AND GENERAL.**

**COMPARATIVE LINGUISTICS.** See **SEMANTICS.**

**Comparative perspectives on racism** / edited by Jessika Ter Wal & Maykel Verkuyten. Aldershot, Hants, UK ; Burlington, VT, USA : Ashgate, c2000. xiv, 290 p. ; 22 cm. (Research in migration and ethnic relations series) Includes bibliographical references and indexes. ISBN 0-7546-1123-X DDC 305.8
1. Racism - Cross-cultural studies. I. Ter Wal, Jessika. II. Verkuyten, M. III. Series.
*TC GN269 .C646 2000*

**COMPARATIVE PHYSIOLOGY.** See **PHYSIOLOGY, COMPARATIVE.**

**Comparative policy analysis series.** Building effective evaluation capacity. New Brunswick, N.J. : Transaction Publishers, c1999.
*TC JF1351 .B83 1999*

**Comparative political systems.** Schultz, Mindella. New York, Holt, Rinehart and Winston [1967]
*TC JF51 .S34 1967*

**COMPARATIVE PSYCHOLOGY.** See **PSYCHOLOGY, COMPARATIVE.**

**Comparative psychology monographs.** Behavior monographs. Cambridge, Mass. : H. Holt & Company, 1911-

**COMPARATIVE RELIGION.** See **RELIGIONS.**

**Comparative studies on Muslim societies.** (27) Khalid, Adeeb, 1964- The politics of Muslim cultural reform. Berkeley : University of California Press, c1998.
*TC BP63 .A34 K54 1998*

**A comparative study of item exposure control methods in computerized adaptive testing.** Chang, Shun-Wen. Iowa City, IA : ACT, Inc., 1998.
*TC LB3051 .A3 no. 98-3*

**The comparative understanding of intergroup realtions [i.e. relations].** Kinloch, Graham Charles. Boulder, CO : Westview Press, 1999.
*TC HM131 .K495 1999*

**Comparing standards internationally** : research and practice in mathematics and beyond / edited by Barbara Jaworski & David Phillips. Wallingford : Symposium, 1999. 207 p. : ill. ; 24 cm. (Oxford studies in comparative education, 0961-2149 ; v.9, no.1) Includes bibliographical references. ISBN 1-87392-768-1 DDC 510.71
I. Jaworski, Barbara. II. Phillips, David, 1944 Dec. 15- III. Series: Oxford studies in comparative education ; v.9, no.1
*TC QA11 .C64 1999*

**COMPARISON OF CULTURES.** See **CROSS-CULTURAL STUDIES.**

**A comparison of different types of mathematical problem-solving hints selected by concrete and formal operational subjects in a hypercard environment.** Feldberg, Suzanne. 1998.
*TC 085 F316*

**Comparison of Hannah Arendt's and John Dewey's views on authority.** Gordon, Mordechai. Toward an integrative conception of authority in education. 1997.
*TC 085 G656*

**A comparison of statistical and neural network models for forecasting educational spending.** Baker, Bruce D. 1997.
*TC 06 no. 10792*

**A comparison of structural knowledge in eighth graders and college students.** Kinnamon, James C. 1999.
*TC 085 K6194*

**COMPARISON (PSYCHOLOGY).** See **IDENTITY.**

**Compendium of arts and community development programs.** Building America's communities II. Washington, D.C. : Americans for the Arts (Organization) ; Institute for Community Development and the Arts, 1997.

*TC NX180 .A77 B95 1997*

**COMPENSATORY EDUCATION - GOVERNMENT POLICY - UNITED STATES.** Testing, teaching, and learning. Washington, D.C. : National Academy Press, c1999.
*TC LC3981 .T4 1999*

**COMPENSATORY EDUCATION - STANDARDS - UNITED STATES.** Testing, teaching, and learning. Washington, D.C. : National Academy Press, c1999.
*TC LC3981 .T4 1999*

**COMPETENCE.** See **PERFORMANCE.**

**COMPETENCE AND PERFORMANCE (LINGUISTICS).** See **CREATIVITY (LINGUISTICS).**

**COMPETENCE, INTERPERSONAL.** See **SOCIAL SKILLS.**

**COMPETENCE, SOCIAL.** See **SOCIAL SKILLS.**

**COMPETENCY BASED EDUCATION.** See also **COMPETENCY BASED EDUCATIONAL TESTS.** Burz, Helen L. Performance-based curriculum for music and the visual arts. Thousand Oaks, Calif. : Corwin Press, c1999.
*TC LB1591 .B84 1999*

**COMPETENCY-BASED EDUCATION.** Educational competencies for graduates of associate degree nursing programs. [Rev.]. Sudbury, Mass. : Jones and Bartlett, 2000.
*TC RT74.5 .E38 2000*

**COMPETENCY BASED EDUCATION - OECD COUNTRIES.** Measuring student knowledge and skills. Paris : Organisation for Economic Co-operation and Development, c1999.
*TC LB3051 .M43 1999*

Organisation for Economic Co-operation and Development (Paris) Measuring student knowledge and skills. Paris : Organisation for Economic Co-operation and Development, 2000.
*TC LB3051 .M44 2000*

**COMPETENCY BASED EDUCATION - UNITED STATES.** Hibbard, K. Michael. Performance-based learning and assessment in middle school science. Larchmont, NY : Eye On Education, 2000.
*TC Q181 .H52 2000*

**COMPETENCY BASED EDUCATIONAL TESTS - NEW YORK (STATE).** Southworth, Robert A. Evidence of student learning and implications for alternative policies that support instructional use of assessment. 1999.
*TC 06 no. 11218*

**COMPETENCY TESTS (EDUCATION).** See **COMPETENCY BASED EDUCATIONAL TESTS.**

**COMPETENCY TRAINING.** See **COMPETENCY BASED EDUCATION.**

**COMPETITION (BIOLOGY).** See **NICHE (ECOLOGY).**

**COMPETITION, INTERNATIONAL.** Critical technologies and competitiveness. Huntington, New York : Nova Science Publishers, c2000.
*TC HC110.T4 C74 2000*

Employee training and U.S. competitiveness. Boulder : Westview Press, 1991.
*TC HF5549.5.T7 E46 1991*

**COMPETITION - PSYCHOLOGY.** Katz, Tal Y. Self-construal as a moderator of the effects of task and reward interdependence of group performance. 1999.
*TC 085 K1524*

**COMPETITION, UNFAIR.** See **BUSINESS INTELLIGENCE.**

**COMPETITIVE EXAMINATIONS.** See **EXAMINATIONS.**

**COMPETITIVENESS (ECONOMICS).** See **COMPETITION.**

**Competitor or ally?** : Japan's role in American educational debates / edited by Gerald K. LeTendre. New York : Falmer Press, 1999. xxii, 171 p. : ill. ; 23 cm. (Garland reference library of social science ; v. 1407. Reference books in international education ; v. 45.) Includes bibliographical references (p. 151-163) and index. ISBN 0-

8153-3273-4
1. Education - Japan. 2. Education - United States. 3. Comparative education. I. LeTendre, Gerald K. II. Series: Garland reference library of social science ; v. 1407 III. Series: Garland reference library of social science. Reference books in international education ; v. 45.
*TC LA1312 .C667 1999*

**COMPLEMENTARY MEDICINE.** See **ALTERNATIVE MEDICINE.**

**Complete encyclopedia [computer file].** Education [computer file]: Version 1.1. [Oxford, Eng.] : Pergamon, c1998. Computer program.
*TC LB15 .E3 1998*

**Complete family reference guide to alternative & orthodoxe medical diagnosis, treatment & preventive healthcare.** Sharma, R. (Rajendra), 1959- The family encyclopedia of health. Boston : Element Books, 1999.
*TC RC81.A2 S53 1999*

**Complete family reference guide to alternative and orthodoxe medical diagnosis, treatment and preventive healthcare.** Sharma, R. (Rajendra), 1959- The family encyclopedia of health. Boston : Element Books, 1999.
*TC RC81.A2 S53 1999*

**A complete guide to brass.** Whitener, Scott. 2nd ed. New York : Schirmer Books, c1997.
*TC ML933 .W52 1997*

**The complete guide to graduate school admission.** Keith-Spiegel, Patricia. 2nd ed. Mahwah, N.J. ; London : L. Erlbaum Associates, 2000.
*TC BF77 .K35 2000*

**Complete guide to postgraduate funding worldwide.** GrantFinder : Arts and humanities. New York, NY : St. Martin's Press, 2000.
*TC LB2337.2 .G72*

GrantFinder : Medicine. New York, NY : St. Martin's Press,
*TC LB2337.2 .G73*

GrantFinder : Social sciences. New York, NY : St. Martin's Press,
*TC LB2337.2 .G7 2000*

**The complete guide to rubber stamping.** Taormina, Grace. New York : Watson-Guptill Publications, c1996.
*TC TT867 .T36 1996*

**Complete guide to special education transition services.** Pierangelo, Roger. West Nyack, NY : Center for Applied Research in Education, c1997.
*TC HV1569.3.Y68 P55 1997*

**Complete guide to storytelling for parents.** Lipkin, Lisa. Bringing the story home. New York : W.W. Norton & Co., c2000.
*TC LB1042 .L515 2000*

**A complete guide to student grading.** Haladyna, Thomas M. Boston : Allyn and Bacon, c1999.
*TC LB3051 .H296 1999*

**The complete guide to teaching a course.** Forsyth, Ian. 2nd ed. London : Kogan Page ; Sterling, VA : Stylus Publishing, 1999.
*TC LB1025.3 .F67 1999*

**Complete guide to teaching and learning.** Bickart, Toni S. Building the primary classroom. Washington, DC : Teaching Strategies ; Portsmouth, NH : Heinemann, 1999.
*TC LB1507 .B53 1999*

**Complex adaptive systems.** Thornton, Christopher James. Truth from trash. Cambridge, Mass. ; London : MIT Press, c2000.
*TC Q325.4 .T47 2000*

Toward a science of consciousness III. Cambridge, Mass. : MIT Press, c1999.
*TC BF311 .T67 1999*

**Complex life.** Dean, Alan Ph. D. Aldershot : Ashgate, c2000.
*TC BD450 .D43 2000*

**COMPLEX ORGANIZATIONS.** See also **INTERORGANIZATIONAL RELATIONS.** Multilevel theory, research, and methods in organizations. 1st ed. San Francisco : Jossey-Bass, c2000.

**TC HF5548.8 .M815 2000**
Parker, Glenn M., 1938- Cross-functional teams. 1st ed. San Francisco, Calif. : Jossey-Bass, c1994.
**TC HD66 .P345 1994**

**Compliance and the law;** a multi-disciplinary approach. Edited by Samuel Krislov [and others] Beverly Hills, Sage Publications [1972] 391 p. ; 25 cm. "Portions of this volume have previously appeared in issues of the Law and society review." Includes index. Bibliography: p. 354-382. ISBN 0-8039-0119-4 DDC 301.15/7
1. Sociological jurisprudence. 2. Obedience. I. Krislov. Samuel. ed.
**TC K376 .C66**

**COMPONENTIAL ANALYSIS (LINGUISTICS).**
Nida, Eugène Albert, 1914- Componential analysis of meaning. The Hague : Mouton, 1975.
**TC P325 .N5**

**Componential analysis of meaning.**
Nida, Eugène Albert, 1914- The Hague : Mouton, 1975.
**TC P325 .N5**

**COMPOSERS, AFRO-AMERICAN.** See **AFRO-AMERICAN COMPOSERS.**

**COMPOSERS, BLACK - BIO-BIBLIOGRAPHY - DICTIONARIES.**
International dictionary of black composers. Chicago ; London : Fitzroy Dearborn, c1999.
**TC ML105 .I5 1999**

**COMPOSERS - GERMANY - BIOGRAPHY.**
Kennedy, Michael, 1926- Richard Strauss. Cambridge, UK ; New York, NY, USA : Cambridge University Press, 1999.
**TC ML410.S93 K46 1999**

**COMPOSERS - UNITED STATES.** See **AFRO-AMERICAN COMPOSERS.**

**COMPOSITE PHOTOGRAPHY.** See **PHOTOMONTAGE.**

**Composition.**
Dow, Arthur W. (Arthur Wesley), 1857-1922. Berkeley : University of California Press, 1997.
**TC N7430 .D68 1997**

**COMPOSITION (ART).**
Dow, Arthur W. (Arthur Wesley), 1857-1922. Composition. Berkeley : University of California Press, 1997.
**TC N7430 .D68 1997**

Dunning, William V., 1933- Changing images of pictorial space. 1st ed. Syracuse : Syracuse University Press, 1991.
**TC ND1475 .D86 1991**

**COMPOSITION (LANGUAGE ARTS).**
Hoffman, Eric. An introduction to teaching composition in an electronic environment. Needham Heights, Mass. : Allyn & Bacon, c2000.
**TC LB1028.3 .H63 2000**

**COMPOSITION (LANGUAGE ARTS) - STUDY AND TEACHING.**
Metalinguistic activity in learning to write. Amsterdam : Amsterdam University Press, c2000.
**TC PN181 .M48 2000**

**COMPOSITION (RHETORIC).** See **COMPOSITION (LANGUAGE ARTS).**

**COMPREHENSION.** See **LEARNING; LEARNING, PSYCHOLOGY OF; LISTENING; MEMORY; READING COMPREHENSION.**

**COMPREHENSION - PROBLEMS, EXERCISES, ETC.**
Whimbey, Arthur. Problem solving and comprehension. 6th ed. Mahwah, N.J. : Lawrence Erlbaum Associates, 1999.
**TC BF449 .W45 1999**

**Comprehensive accreditation manual for hospitals.**
Joint Commission on Accreditation of Healthcare Organizations. Hospital accreditation standards : HAS. Oakbrook Terrace, Ill. : The Commission, c1996-
**TC RA981.A2 J59a**

**Comprehensive catalogue of vocal chamber duets.**
Newman, Marilyn Stephanie Mercedes, 1954- Duet literature for female voices with piano, organ or unaccompanied. 1998.
**TC 06 no. 10897**

**Comprehensive classroom management.**
Jones, Vernon F., 1945- 6th ed. Boston : Allyn and Bacon, c2001.

**TC LB3013 .J66 2001**

**Comprehensive guide to interpersonal psychotherapy.**
Weissman, Myrna M. New York: Basic Books, c2000.
**TC RC480.8 .W445 2000**

**COMPREHENSIVE HEALTH PLANNING.** See **HEALTH PLANNING.**

**Comprehensive school health education.**
Meeks, Linda Brower. 2nd edition. Blacklick, OH : Meeks Heit Pub. Co., c1996.
**TC RA440.3.U5 M445 1996**

**COMPRESSION (AUDIOLOGY).**
Venema, Ted. Compression for clinicians. San Diego, Calif. : Singular Pub. Group, c1998.
**TC RF300 .V46 1998**

**Compression for clinicians.**
Venema, Ted. San Diego, Calif. : Singular Pub. Group, c1998.
**TC RF300 .V46 1998**

**COMPULSION (PSYCHOLOGY).** See **COMPULSIVE BEHAVIOR.**

**COMPULSIVE BEHAVIOR.** See also **OBSESSIVE-COMPULSIVE DISORDER.**
Schaler, Jeffrey A. Addiction is a choice. Chicago, Ill. : Open Court, 2000.
**TC HV4998 .S33 2000**

**COMPULSIVE BEHAVIOR - ETIOLOGY.**
Elster, Jon, 1940- Strong feelings. Cambridge, Mass. : MIT Press, c1999.
**TC BF531 .E475 1999**

**COMPULSIVE BEHAVIOR - SOCIAL ASPECTS.**
Powell, Richard R., 1951- Classrooms under the influence. Newbury Park, Calif. : Corwin Press, c1995.
**TC HV5824.Y68 P69 1995**

**COMPULSIVE DISORDER.** See **OBSESSIVE-COMPULSIVE DISORDER.**

**COMPULSIVE GAMBLING.**
Castellani, Brian, 1966- Pathological gambling. Albany : State University of New York Press, c2000.
**TC RC569.5.G35 C37 2000**

**COMPULSIVE SHOPPING.**
I shop, therefore I am. Northvale, NJ : Jason Aronson, c2000.
**TC RC569.5.S56 I12 2000**

**COMPULSORY SCHOOL ATTENDANCE.** See **EDUCATIONAL LAW AND LEGISLATION.**

**COMPULSORY STERILIZATION.** See **STERILIZATION, EUGENIC.**

**COMPUTATIONAL LINGUISTICS.**
Lorenz, Gunter R. Adjective intensification--learners versus native speakers. Amsterdam : Atlanta, GA : Rodopi, 1999.
**TC PE1074.5 .L67 1999**

Partington, Alan. Patterns and meanings. Amsterdam ; Philadelphia : J. Benjamins Pub., c1998.
**TC PE1074.5 .P37 1998**

**COMPUTATIONAL LINGUISTICS - BIBLIOGRAPHY - PERIODICALS.**
Language and automation. Washington, Center for Applied Linguistics.

**COMPUTER ADAPTIVE TESTING.**
Chang, Shun-Wen. A comparative study of item exposure control methods in computerized adaptive testing. Iowa City, IA : ACT, Inc., 1998.
**TC LB3051 .A3 no. 98-3**

Computerized adaptive testing. Dordrecht ; Boston : Kluwer Academic, c2000.
**TC LB3060.32.C65 C66 2000**

Wainer, Howard. Computerized adaptive testing. 2nd ed. Mahwah, N.J. : Lawrence Erlbaum Associates, 2000.
**TC LB3060.32.C65 W25 2000**

Yi, Qing. Simulating nonmodel-fitting responses in a CAT environment. Iowa City, Iowa : ACT, 1998.
**TC LB3051 .A3 no. 98-10**

**COMPUTER ADVENTURE GAMES - JUVENILE SOFTWARE.**
Carmen Sandiego [computer file]. Novato, Calif. : Brøderbund Software, 1998. Computer data and program.
**TC QA115 .C37 1998**

**COMPUTER-AIDED INSTRUCTION.** See also **COMPUTER-ASSISTED INSTRUCTION.**
Innovative teaching and learning. Heidelberg [Germany] ; New York : Physica-Verlag, c2000.
**TC QA76.76.E95 I54 2000**

**Computer and Internet use on campus.**
Hawke, Constance S., 1952- 1st ed. San Francisco : Jossey-Bass, c2001.
**TC KF390.5.C6 H39 2001**

**COMPUTER ART.**
LifeScience. Wien ; New York : Springer, 1999.
**TC T14.5 L54 1999**

**The computer as an educational tool.**
Forcier, Richard C. 2nd ed. Upper Saddle River, N.J. : Merrill, c1999.
**TC LB1028.43 .F67 1999**

**The Computer as medium** / [edited by] Peter Bøgh Andersen, Berit Holmqvist, Jens F. Jensen. Cambridge [England] ; New York : Cambridge University Press, 1993. vii, 495 p. : ill. ; 24 cm. (Learning in doing) Includes bibliographical references and index. ISBN 0-521-41995-6 (hardback) DDC 302.23
1. Computers. 2. Mass media. 3. Interactive multimedia. I. Andersen, Peter Bøgh. II. Holmqvist, Berit. III. Jensen, Jens F. IV. Series.
**TC QA76.5 .C612554 1993**

**Computer-assisted assessment in higher education** / [edited by] Sally Brown, Phil Race and Joanna Bull. London : Kogan Page, 1999. xi, 205 p. : ill. ; 24 cm. (Staff and educational development series.) Includes bibliographical references and index. ISBN 0-7494-3035-4
1. Universities and colleges - Examinations - Data processing. 2. Educational tests and measurements - Data processing. 3. College students - Rating of - Data processing. 4. Computer-assisted instruction. I. Brown, Sally A. II. Race, Philip. III. Bull. Joanna. IV. Series.
**TC LB2366 .C65 1999**

**COMPUTER-ASSISTED INSTRUCTION.**
Armstrong, Alison, 1955- The child and the machine. Beltsville, Md. : Robins Lane Press, c2000.
**TC LB1028.43 .A76 2000**

Brownell, Gregg. A PC for the teacher. Belmont, CA : Wadsworth Pub. Co., c1999.
**TC LB1028.43 .B755 1999**

Computer-assisted assessment in higher education. London : Kogan Page, 1999.
**TC LB2366 .C65 1999**

Cook, Deirdre, 1943- Interactive children, communicative teaching. Buckingham [England] : Philadelphia : Open University Press, 1999.
**TC LB1028.46 .C686 1999**

Design approaches and tools in education and training. Dordrecht ; Boston : Kluwer Academic Publishers, c1999.
**TC LB1028.38 .D46 1999**

Forcier, Richard C. The computer as an educational tool. 2nd ed. Upper Saddle River, N.J. : Merrill, c1999.
**TC LB1028.43 .F67 1999**

Geisert, Paul. Teachers, computers, and curriculum. 3rd ed. Boston : Allyn and Bacon, c2000.
**TC LB1028.43 .G42 2000**

Gibbons, Andrew S. Computer-based instruction. Englewood Cliffs, N.J. : Educational Technology Publications, c1998.
**TC LB1028.5 .G487 1998**

Instructional technology for teaching and learning. 2nd ed. Upper Saddle River, N.J. : Merrill, c2000.
**TC LB1028.38 .I587 2000**

Kahn, Jessica L. Ideas and strategies for the one-computer classroom. Eugene, OR : International Society for Technology in Education, c1998.
**TC LB1028.5 .K25 1998**

Keates, Anita. Dyslexia and information and communications technology. London : D. Fulton Publishers, 2000.
**TC LC4708.5K43 2000**

Modeling and simulation in science and mathematics education. New York : Springer, c1999.
**TC Q181 .M62 1999**

Morrison, Gary R. Integrating computer technology into the classroom. Upper Saddle River, N.J. : Merrill, c1999.
**TC LB1028.5 .M6373 1999**

Net-working. Dunedin, N.Z. : University of Otago Press, 1999.

TC LB1044.87 .N47 1999

Race, Philip. 500 computing tips for teachers and lecturers. 2nd ed. London : Kogan Page : Sterling, VA : Stylus Pub., 1999.
TC LB1028.43 .R33 1999

Sharp, Vicki F. Computer education for teachers. 3rd ed. Boston, Mass. : McGraw-Hill College, c1999.
TC LB1028.43 .S55 1999

Stoll, Clifford. High tech heretic. 1st ed. New York : Doubleday, c1999.
TC LB1028.5 .S77 1999

Weintraub, Robert Steven. Informal learning in the workplace through desktop technology. 1998.
TC 06 no. 11003

**COMPUTER-ASSISTED INSTRUCTION - AUTHORSHIP.**
Keegan, Mark. Scenario educational software. Englewood Cliffs, N.J. : Educational Technology Publications, c1995.
TC LB1028.6 .K44 1995

**COMPUTER-ASSISTED INSTRUCTION - CATALOGS.**
The ... Educational software preview guide. Redwood City, CA : California TECC Software Library & Clearinghouse.
TC LB1028.7 .E35

**COMPUTER-ASSISTED INSTRUCTION - CONGRESSES.**
IFIP TC3 WG3.1/3.5 Open Conference on Communications and Networking in Education (1999 : Aulanko, Finland) Communications and networking in education. Boston : Kluwer Academic Publishers, 2000.
TC LB1044.87 .I45 2000

**COMPUTER-ASSISTED INSTRUCTION - GREAT BRITAIN - CASE STUDIES.**
Learning to teach using ICT in the secondary school. London ; New York : Routledge, 1999.
TC LB1028.5 .L3884 1999

**COMPUTER-ASSISTED INSTRUCTION - HANDBOOKS, MANUALS, ETC.**
Brunner, Cornelia, Dr. The new media literacy handbook. New York : Anchor Books, 1999.
TC LB1028.3 .B77 1999

Gardner, Paul (Paul Henry) Managing technology in the middle school classroom. Huntington Beach, CA : Teacher Created Materials, c1996.
TC LB1028.5 .C353 1996

**COMPUTER-ASSISTED INSTRUCTION - JUVENILE LITERATURE.**
Drake, Jim, 1955- Computers and schools. Des Plaines, Ill. : Heinemann Library, c1999.
TC LB1028.5 .D69 1999

**COMPUTER-ASSISTED INSTRUCTION - PERIODICALS.**
AEDS journal. Washington, Association for Educational Data Systems.

**COMPUTER-ASSISTED INSTRUCTION - SOCIAL ASPECTS.**
International perspectives on tele-education and virtual learning environments. Aldershot : Ashgate, 2000.
TC LB1044.87 .I55 2000

**COMPUTER-ASSISTED INSTRUCTION - SOCIAL ASPECTS - UNITED STATES.**
Bolt, David B., 1954- Digital divide. New York : TV Books, c2000.
TC LB1028.43 .B64 2000

**COMPUTER-ASSISTED INSTRUCTION - SOFTWARE.**
Keegan, Mark. Scenario educational software. Englewood Cliffs, N.J. : Educational Technology Publications, c1995.
TC LB1028.6 .K44 1995

**COMPUTER-ASSISTED INSTRUCTION - UNITED STATES.**
Adams, Dennis M. Media and literacy. 2nd ed. Springfield, Ill. : C.C. Thomas, c2000.
TC LB1043 .A33 2000

Bucher, Katherine Toth, 1947- Information technology for schools. 2nd ed. Worthington, Ohio : Linworth Pub., c1998.
TC Z675.S3 B773 1998

Doggett, Sandra L. Beyond the book. Englewood, Colo. : Libraries Unlimited, 2000.

TC ZA4065 .D64 2000

The Jossey-Bass reader on technology and learning. 1st ed. San Francisco, Calif. : Jossey-Bass, c2000.
TC LB1028.3 .J66 2000

Teaching with technology. Washington, D.C. : National Education Association of the United States, 1999.
TC LB1044.88 .T44 1999

**COMPUTER-ASSISTED INSTRUCTION - UNITED STATES - CASE STUDIES.**
Linn, Marcia C. Computers, teachers, peers. Mahwah, N.J. : L. Erlbaum Associates, 2000.
TC LB1585.3 .L56 2000

**Computer assisted language learning (CALL) :** media, design, and applications / introduced and edited by Keith Cameron,. Lisse [Netherlands] ; Exton, PA : Swets & Zeitlinger, 1999. 321 p. : ill. : 25 cm. (Contexts of learning) Includes bibliographical references and index. ISBN 90-265-1543-X (hard) DDC 418/.00285
*1. Language and languages - Computer-assisted instruction. I. Cameron, Keith. II. Series.*
TC P53.28 .C6634 1999

**COMPUTER-ASSISTED LEARNING.** *See* **COMPUTER-ASSISTED INSTRUCTION.**

**Computer-assisted text analysis.**
Popping, Roel. Thousand Oaks, Calif. ; London : SAGE, c2000.
TC P302 .P636 2000

**COMPUTER-BASED INFORMATION SYSTEMS.** *See* **INFORMATION STORAGE AND RETRIEVAL SYSTEMS.**

**COMPUTER BASED INSTRUCTION.** *See* **COMPUTER-ASSISTED INSTRUCTION.**

**Computer-based instruction.**
Gibbons, Andrew S. Englewood Cliffs, N.J. : Educational Technology Publications, c1998.
TC LB1028.5 .G487 1998

**COMPUTER-BASED MULTIMEDIA INFORMATION SYSTEMS.** *See* **MULTIMEDIA SYSTEMS.**

**COMPUTER COMMUNICATION SYSTEMS.** *See* **COMPUTER NETWORKS.**

**COMPUTER CONFERENCING IN EDUCATION.**
McConnell, David, 1951- Implementing computer supported cooperative learning.. 2nd ed. London : Kogan Page, 2000.
TC LB1032 .M38 2000

**COMPUTER CRIMES.** *See* **PRIVACY, RIGHT OF.**

**Computer education for teachers.**
Sharp, Vicki F. 3rd ed. Boston, Mass. : McGraw-Hill College, c1999.
TC LB1028.43 .S55 1999

**COMPUTER GAMES.** *See* **COMPUTER ADVENTURE GAMES.**

**COMPUTER GAMES - SOCIAL ASPECTS.**
Digital diversions. London : UCL Press, 1998.
TC QA76.575 .D536 1998

**COMPUTER GRAPHICS.**
Brinkman, Ronald. The art and science of digital compositing. San Diego : Morgan Kaufmann ; Academic Press, 1999.
TC T385 .B75 1999

**COMPUTER HARDWARE.** *See* **COMPUTERS.**

**COMPUTER INDUSTRY.** *See also* **COMPUTERS.**
Weil, Ulric. Information systems in the 80's. Englewood Cliffs, N.J. : Prentice-Hall, c1982.
TC HD9696.C63 U5954 1982

**COMPUTER INDUSTRY - UNITED STATES.**
Weil, Ulric. Information systems in the 80's. Englewood Cliffs, N.J. : Prentice-Hall, c1982.
TC HD9696.C63 U5954 1982

**COMPUTER LITERACY - STANDARDS - UNITED STATES.**
International Society for Technology in Education. National educational technology standards for students. Eugene, OR : The Society, c1998.
TC LB1028.3 .I569 1998

**COMPUTER LITERACY - UNITED STATES.**
Librarians as learners, librarians as teachers. Chicago : Association of College and Research Libraries, 1999.
TC Z675.U5 L415 1999

**COMPUTER MANAGED INSTRUCTION.**
Barron, Ann E. The Internet and instruction. 2nd ed. Englewood, Colo. : Libraries Unlimited, 1998.

TC LB1044.87 .B37 1998

Brownell, Gregg. A PC for the teacher. Belmont, CA : Wadsworth Pub. Co., c1999.
TC LB1028.43 .B755 1999

Forcier, Richard C. The computer as an educational tool. 2nd ed. Upper Saddle River, N.J. : Merrill, c1999.
TC LB1028.43 .F67 1999

Geisert, Paul. Teachers, computers, and curriculum. 3rd ed. Boston : Allyn and Bacon, c2000.
TC LB1028.5 .G42 2000

Morrison, Gary R. Integrating computer technology into the classroom. Upper Saddle River, N.J. : Merrill, c1999.
TC LB1028.5 .M6373 1999

Williams, Bard. The Internet for teachers. 3rd ed. Foster City, CA : IDG Books Worldwide, c1999.
TC LB1044.87 .W55 1999

**COMPUTER-MEDIATED COMMUNICATION.** *See* **TELEMATICS.**

**COMPUTER NETWORK RESOURCES.**
Henninger, Maureen, 1940- Don't just surf. 2nd ed. Sydney : UNSW Press, 1999.
TC ZA4201 .H46 1999

**COMPUTER NETWORK RESOURCES - EVALUATION.**
Cooke, Alison. Neal-Schuman authoritative guide to evaluating information on the Internet. New York : Neal-Schuman Publishers, c1999.
TC ZA4201 .C66 1999

**COMPUTER NETWORK RESOURCES - STUDY AND TEACHING.**
McLain, Tim, 1970- How to create successful Internet projects. El Segundo, Calif. : Classroom Connect, c1999.
TC LB1044.87 .M35 1999

**COMPUTER NETWORK RESOURCES - STUDY AND TEACHING (CONTINUING EDUCATION) - UNITED STATES.**
Hollands, William D. Teaching the Internet to library staff and users. New York : Neal-Schuman, c1999.
TC ZA4201 .H65 1999

**COMPUTER NETWORK RESOURCES - UNITED STATES - EVALUATION.**
Cooke, Alison. Neal-Schuman authoritative guide to evaluating information on the Internet. New York : Neal-Schuman Publishers, c1999.
TC ZA4201 .C66 1999

**COMPUTER NETWORKS.**
Nellist, John G. Understanding modern telecommunications and the information superhighway. Boston, Mass. : Artech House, 1999.
TC TK5105.5 .N45 1999

**COMPUTER NETWORKS - DICTIONARIES.**
Saigh, Robert A. The international dictionary of data communications. Chicago : Glenlake Pub. Co. : New York : American Management Association, c1998.
TC TK5102 .S25 1998

**COMPUTER NETWORKS - LAW AND LEGISLATION - UNITED STATES.**
Hawke, Constance S., 1952- Computer and Internet use on campus. 1st ed. San Francisco : Jossey-Bass, c2001.
TC KF390.5.C6 H39 2001

**COMPUTER NETWORKS - MANAGEMENT.**
Maxwell, Steven. Red hat linux network management tools. New York : McGraw Hill, c2000.
TC QA76.76.O63 M373339 2000

**COMPUTER NETWORKS - PSYCHOLOGICAL ASPECTS.**
Wallace, Patricia M. The psychology of the Internet. Cambridge ; New York : Cambridge University Press, 1999.
TC BF637.C45 W26 1999

**COMPUTER NETWORKS - SOCIAL ASPECTS.**
Mitchell, William J. (William John), 1944- E-topia. Cambridge, Mass. : MIT Press, 1999.
TC HE7631 .M58 1999

Race in cyberspace. New York : London : Routledge, 2000.
TC HT1523 .R252 2000

**COMPUTER OPERATING SYSTEMS.** *See* **OPERATING SYSTEMS (COMPUTERS).**

**COMPUTER PRIVACY.** *See* **COMPUTER SECURITY.**

**COMPUTER SCIENCE.**
Hayles, N. Katherine. How we became posthuman. Chicago, Ill. : University of Chicago Press, 1999.
*TC Q335 .H394 1999*

**COMPUTER SCIENCE - PHILOSOPHY.**
Floridi, Luciano, 1964- Philosophy and computing. London : New York: Routledge, 1999.
*TC QA76.167 .F56 1999*

**COMPUTER SECURITY.** *See also* **DATA ENCRYPTION (COMPUTER SCIENCE).**
Chacko, Mathew Vadakkan. Public key cryptosystems. 1998.
*TC 085 C35*

Maximum Linux security. Indianapolis, Ind. : Sams, c2000.
*TC QA76.9.A25 M385 2000*

**COMPUTER SECURITY - UNITED STATES.**
Garfinkel, Simson. Database nation. 1st ed. Beijing ; Cambridge : O'Reilly, c2000.
*TC JC596.2.U5 G37 2000*

**COMPUTER SOFTWARE.** *See* **CHILDREN'S SOFTWARE; COMPUTERS; INTERACTIVE MULTIMEDIA.**

**COMPUTER SOFTWARE - CATALOGS.**
The ... Educational software preview guide. Redwood City, CA : California TECC Software Library & Clearinghouse,
*TC LB1028.7 .E35*

**COMPUTER SOFTWARE - DEVELOPMENT.**
Keegan, Mark. Scenario educational software. Englewood Cliffs, N.J. : Educational Technology Publications, c1995.
*TC LB1028.6 .K44 1995*

**COMPUTER SYSTEM SECURITY.** *See* **COMPUTER SECURITY.**

**COMPUTER USES IN EDUCATION.** *See* **EDUCATION - DATA PROCESSING.**

**Computerized adaptive testing.**
Wainer, Howard. 2nd ed. Mahwah, N.J. : Lawrence Erlbaum Associates, 2000.
*TC LB3060.32.C65 W25 2000*

**Computerized adaptive testing : theory and practice /** edited by Wim J. van der Linden and Cees A. W. Glas. Dordrecht ; Boston : Kluwer Academic, c2000. xii, 323 p. : ill. ; 24 cm. Includes bibliographical references and indexes. ISBN 0-7923-6425-2 (hardcover : alk. paper) DDC 371.26/0285
*1. Computer adaptive testing. I. Linden. Wim J. van der. II. Glas. Cees A. W.*
*TC LB3060.32.C65 C66 2000*

**COMPUTERS.** *See also* **COMPUTER SOFTWARE; CYBERSPACE; ELECTRONIC DATA PROCESSING; INFORMATION STORAGE AND RETRIEVAL SYSTEMS.**
The Computer as medium. Cambridge [England] ; New York : Cambridge University Press, 1993.
*TC QA76.5 .C612554 1993*

Drake, Jim, 1955- Computers and schools. Des Plaines, Ill. : Heinemann Library, c1999.
*TC LB1028.5 .D69 1999*

**COMPUTERS - ACCESS CONTROL.**
Chacko, Mathew Vadakkan. Public key cryptosystems. 1998.
*TC 085 C35*

**COMPUTERS AND CHILDREN.**
Armstrong, Alison, 1955- The child and the machine. Beltsville, Md. : Robins Lane Press, c2000.
*TC LB1028.43 .A76 2000*

Armstrong, Alison, 1955- The child and the machine. Toronto, Ont. : Key Porter Books, c1998.
*TC LB1028.43 .A75 1998*

Bolt, David B., 1954- Digital divide. New York : TV Books, c2000.
*TC LB1028.43 .B64 2000*

Campbell, Hope. Managing technology in the early childhood classroom. Westminster, CA : Teacher Created Materials, c1999.
*TC LB1139.35.C64 C36 1999*

Digital diversions. London : UCL Press, 1998.
*TC QA76.575 .D536 1998*

**COMPUTERS AND CHILDREN - UNITED STATES.**
Calvert, Sandra L. Children's journeys through the information age. 1st ed. Boston : McGraw-Hill College, c1999.

**COMPUTERS AND CIVILIZATION.**
*TC HQ784.T4 C24 1999*
The cybercultures reader. London : New York : Routledge, 2000.
*TC T14.5 .C934 2000*

Hakken, David. Cyborgs@cyberspace? New York : Routledge, 1999.
*TC QA76.9.C66 H34 1999*

Lunenfeld, Peter. Snap to grid. Cambridge, MA : MIT, 2000.
*TC QA76.9.C66 L86 2000*

Robertson, Douglas S. The new renaissance. New York : Oxford University Press, 1998.
*TC QA76.9.C66 R618 1998*

Slevin, James. The internet and society. Malden, MA : Polity Press, 2000.
*TC HM851 .S58 2000*

Social dimensions of information technology. Hershey, Pa. : Ideas Group Pub., 2000.
*TC HM851 .S63 2000*

Stefik, Mark. The Internet edge. Cambridge, Mass. : MIT Press, c1999.
*TC HM851 .S74 1999*

Stoll, Clifford. High tech heretic. 1st ed. New York : Doubleday, c1999.
*TC LB1028.5 .S77 1999*

Wertheim, Margaret. The pearly gates of cyberspace. 1st ed. New York : W.W. Norton, c1999.
*TC QA76.9.C66 W48 1999*

**COMPUTERS AND LITERACY.**
Casey, Jean Marie. Creating the early literacy classroom. Englewood, Colo. : Libraries Unlimited, c2000.
*TC LB1576.7 .C38 2000*

Casey, Jean Marie. Early literacy. Rev. ed. Englewood, Colo. : Libraries Unlimited, 2000.
*TC LB1139.5.L35 C37 2000*

Linking literacy and technology. Newark, Del. : International Reading Association, c2000.
*TC LB1576.7 .L56 2000*

Page to screen. London ; New York : Routledge, 1998.
*TC LC149.5 .P35 1998*

Welch, Kathleen E. Electric rhetoric. Cambridge, Mass. : MIT Press, c1999.
*TC P301.5.D37 W45 1999*

**COMPUTERS AND LITERACY - UNITED STATES.**
Selfe, Cynthia L., 1951- Technology and literacy in the twenty-first century. Carbondale : Southern Illinois University Press, c1999.
*TC LC149.5 .S45 1999*

**Computers and school.**
Drake, Jim, 1955- Computers and schools. Des Plaines, Ill. : Heinemann Library, c1999.
*TC LB1028.5 .D69 1999*

**Computers and schools.**
Drake, Jim, 1955- Des Plaines, Ill. : Heinemann Library, c1999.
*TC LB1028.5 .D69 1999*

**COMPUTERS AND THE HANDICAPPED.** *See also* **ADAPTIVE COMPUTING.**
Barnicle, Katherine Ann. Evaluation of the interaction between users of screen reading technology and graphical user interface elements. 1999.
*TC 085 B265*

**COMPUTERS, ELECTRONIC.** *See* **COMPUTERS.**

**COMPUTERS - FICTION.**
Carrick, Carol. Patrick's dinosaurs on the Internet. New York : Clarion Books, 1999.
*TC PZ7.C2344 Patf 1999*

**COMPUTERS IN EDUCATION.** *See* **EDUCATION - DATA PROCESSING.**

**Computers in human behavior.**
[Computers in human behavior (Online)] Computers in human behavior [computer file]. New York : Elsevier Science,
*TC EJOURNALS*

**[Computers in human behavior (Online)]** Computers in human behavior [computer file]. New York : Elsevier Science, Coverage as of Mar. 17, 1998: Vol. 13, issue 1 (Jan. 1997)- . Mode of access: Internet via the World Wide Web. Electronic journal Abstracts, tables of contents, and citation information are HTML encoded; articles are available in portable document format (PDF) and as Postscript Level 2

files. Subscription and registration required for access. Online version of the print title: Computers in human behavior. System requirements: Internet connectivity, World Wide Web browser, and Adobe Acrobat reader. Description based on: Vol. 13, issue 1 (Jan. 1997); title from general information screen (viewed Mar. 17, 1998). URL: http:// www.sciencedirect.com/science/journal/07475632 URL: http://www.columbia.edu/cu/libraries/indexes/science-direct.html URL: http://www.sciencedirect.com/ Available in other form: Computers in human behavior ISSN: 0747-5632 (DLC) 85643678 (OCoLC)10746756. ISSN 0747-5632
*1. Psychology - Data processing - Periodicals. 2. Computers - Psychological aspects - Periodicals. 3. Behavior - periodicals. 4. Behavioral Sciences - periodicals. 5. Computers - periodicals. I. Title: ScienceDirect. II. Title: Computers in human behavior*
*TC EJOURNALS*

**Computers in the schools.**
Educational computing in the schools. New York : Haworth Press, 1999.
*TC LB1028.3 .E332 1999*

Information technology in educational research and statistics. New York : Haworth Press, 1999.
*TC LB1028.3 .I51945 1999*

**COMPUTERS - JUVENILE LITERATURE.**
Drake, Jim, 1955- Computers and schools. Des Plaines, Ill. : Heinemann Library, c1999.
*TC LB1028.5 .D69 1999*

**COMPUTERS - LAW AND LEGISLATION - UNITED STATES.**
Hawke, Constance S., 1952- Computer and Internet use on campus. 1st ed. San Francisco : Jossey-Bass, c2001.
*TC KF390.5.C6 H39 2001*

**COMPUTERS - OPERATING SYSTEMS.** *See* **OPERATING SYSTEMS (COMPUTERS).**

**COMPUTERS - PERIODICALS.**
[Computers in human behavior (Online)] Computers in human behavior [computer file]. New York : Elsevier Science,
*TC EJOURNALS*

**COMPUTERS - PSYCHOLOGICAL ASPECTS.**
Fink, Jeri. Cyberseduction. Amherst, N.Y. : Prometheus Books, 1999.
*TC QA76.9.P75 F53 1999*

**COMPUTERS - PSYCHOLOGICAL ASPECTS - PERIODICALS.**
[Computers in human behavior (Online)] Computers in human behavior [computer file]. New York : Elsevier Science,
*TC EJOURNALS*

**COMPUTERS - SECURITY MEASURES.** *See* **COMPUTER SECURITY.**

**COMPUTERS - SOCIAL ASPECTS.**
Hakken, David. Cyborgs@cyberspace? New York : Routledge, 1999.
*TC QA76.9.C66 H34 1999*

**COMPUTERS - STUDY AND TEACHING.**
Morrison, Gary R. Integrating computer technology into the classroom. Upper Saddle River, N.J. : Merrill, c1999.
*TC LB1028.5 .M6373 1999*

Sharp, Vicki F. Computer education for teachers. 3rd ed. Boston, Mass. : McGraw-Hill College, c1999.
*TC LB1028.43 .S55 1999*

**COMPUTERS - STUDY AND TEACHING (ELEMENTARY).**
Saltveit, Elin Kordahl, 1964- Hit enter. Portsmouth, NH : Heinemann, c1999.
*TC LB1028.5 .S233 1999*

**COMPUTERS - STUDY AND TEACHING (HIGHER).**
Forcier, Richard C. The computer as an educational tool. 2nd ed. Upper Saddle River, N.J. : Merrill, c1999.
*TC LB1028.43 .F67 1999*

**Computers, teachers, peers.**
Linn, Marcia C. Mahwah, N.J. : L. Erlbaum Associates, 2000.
*TC LB1585.3 .L56 2000*

**COMPUTING MACHINES (COMPUTERS).** *See* **COMPUTERS.**

**Comstock, George A.** Television : what's on, who's watching, and what it means / George Comstock, Erica Scharrer. San Diego : Academic Press, c1999. xi, 388 p. : ill. ; 24 cm. Includes bibliographical references (p. 311-369) and index. DDC 302.23/45

*1. Television broadcasting - Social aspects. 2. Television broadcasting - Influence. I. Scharrer, Erica. II. Title.*
**TC PN1992.6 .C645 1999**

**Comstock, Kenneth.**
Jazz dance class [videorecording]. W. Long Branch, NJ : Kultur, [1992?]
**TC GV1784 .J3 1992**

**CONCENTRATION CAMPS - ARIZONA.**
Rabbit in the moon [videorecording]. San Francisco, Calif. : Wabi-Sabi Productions, 1999.
**TC D753.8 .R3 1999**

**CONCENTRATION CAMPS - CALIFORNIA.**
Rabbit in the moon [videorecording]. San Francisco, Calif. : Wabi-Sabi Productions, 1999.
**TC D753.8 .R3 1999**

**CONCENTRATION CAMPS - PSYCHOLOGICAL ASPECTS.**
Madsen, Benedicte, 1943- Survival in the organization. Aarhus [Denmark] ; Oakville, Conn. : Aarhus University Press, c1996.
**TC D805.G3 M24 1996**

**CONCENTRATION CAMPS - UNITED STATES.**
*See also* **JAPANESE AMERICANS - EVACUATION AND RELOCATION, 1942-1945.**
Rabbit in the moon [videorecording]. San Francisco, Calif. : Wabi-Sabi Productions, 1999.
**TC D753.8 .R3 1999**

**CONCENTRATION CAMPS - UNITED STATES - POSTERS.**
[Japanese-American internment picture. Amawalk, NY : Jackdaw Publications, c1999.
**TC TR820.5 .J3 1999**

**CONCENTRATION CAMPS - WYOMING.**
Rabbit in the moon [videorecording]. San Francisco, Calif. : Wabi-Sabi Productions, 1999.
**TC D753.8 .R3 1999**

**CONCENTRATION OF SCHOOLS.** *See* **SCHOOLS - CENTRALIZATION.**

**CONCENTRATION (PSYCHOLOGY).** *See* **ATTENTION.**

**Concept development in nursing :** foundations, technqiues, and applications / [edited by] Beth L. Rodgers, Kathleen A. Knafl. 2nd ed. Philadelphia : Saunders, c2000. xiv, 458 p. ; 23 cm. Includes bibliographical references and index. ISBN 0-7216-8243-X DDC 610.73/01
*1. Nursing - Philosophy. 2. Concepts. 3. Nursing. 4. Concept Formation. I. Rodgers, Beth L. II. Knafl, Kathleen Astin.*
**TC RT84.5 .C6624 2000**

**CONCEPT FORMATION.**
Concept development in nursing. 2nd ed. Philadelphia : Saunders, c2000.
**TC RT84.5 .C6624 2000**

**CONCEPT LEARNING.**
New perspectives on conceptual change. 1st ed. Amsterdam ; New York ; Oxford : Pergamon, 1999.
**TC LB1062 .N49 1999**

**CONCEPTION.** *See* **PREGNANCY.**

**CONCEPTION - PREVENTION.** *See* **CONTRACEPTION.**

**CONCEPTS.** *See also* **EXAMPLE.**
Concept development in nursing. 2nd ed. Philadelphia : Saunders, c2000.
**TC RT84.5 .C6624 2000**

Language and conceptualization. 1st paperback ed. Cambridge [England] ; New York : Cambridge University Press, 1999.
**TC P37 .L354 1999**

Modelling changes in understanding. Amsterdam ; New York : Pergamon, 1999.
**TC BF319 .M55 1999**

**CONCEPTS IN CHILDREN.**
Embiricos, Anne-Marie T. The effects of content knowledge and strategies on memory development among 4- and 6-year-old children. 1998.
**TC 085 Em22**

Embiricos, Anne-Marie T. The effects of content knowledge and strategies on memory development among 4- and 6-year-old children. 1998.
**TC 085 Em22**

**Concepts in communication, informatics & librarianship**
(4) Agrawal, S. P., 1929- Development of education in India. New Delhi : Concept Pub. Co., 1997.

**TC LA1150 .A39 1997**

**Concepts in fitness programming.**
McMurray, Robert G. Boca Raton : CRC Press, c1999.
**TC QP301 .M3754 1999**

**Concepts in science**
Brandwein, Paul F. (Paul Franz), 1912- Matter. Curie ed. New York : Harcourt Brace Jovanovich, 1980.
**TC Q161.2 .C66 1980**

**Concepts of Alzheimer disease :** biological, clinical, and cultural perspectives / edited by Peter J. Whitehouse, Konrad Maurer, and Jesse F. Ballenger. Baltimore, Md. ; London : Johns Hopkins University Press, 2000. xx, 321 p. : ill., facsims. ; 24 cm. Includes bibliographical references and index. ISBN 0-8018-6233-7 (alk. paper) DDC 616.8/31
*1. Alzheimer's Association. 2. Alzheimer's disease. 3. Alzheimer's disease - Genetic aspects. 4. Alzheimer's disease - Social aspects. 5. Alzheimer Disease - genetics. 6. Alzheimer Disease - history. 7. Alzheimer Disease - psychology. 8. Neuroscience - history. I. Whitehouse, Peter J. II. Maurer, Konrad, 1943- III. Ballenger, Jesse F.*
**TC RC523 .C657 2000**

**Concepts Unlimited.**
Norman Rockwell's world -- an American dream [videorecording]. [Chicago, Ill] : Home Vision, 1987, c1972.
**TC ND237.R68 N6 1987**

**Conceptual coordination.**
Clancey, William J. Mahwah, N.J. : L. Erlbaum Associates, 1999.
**TC BF311 .C5395 1999**

**Conceptual issues in research on intelligence** / Welko Tomic and Johannes Kingma, editors. Stamford, Conn. : JAI Press , 1998. x, 320 p. : ill. ; 23 cm. (Advances in cognition and educational practice, v. 5) Includes bibliographical references.
*1. Intelligence levels - Research. 2. Educational psychology - Research. I. Kingma, Johannes. II. Tomic, W. (Welko), 1946- III. Title. IV. Series.*
**TC BF311 .A38 v. 5 1998**

**Conceptual spaces.**
Gärdenfors, Peter. Cambridge, Mass. ; London : MIT Press, c2000.
**TC Q335 .G358 2000**

**CONCESSIONS.** *See* **RAILROADS.**

**Concise encyclopedia of educational linguistics** / edited by Bernard Spolsky ; consulting editor, R.E. Asher. Amsterdam ; New York : Elsevier, 1999. xxiv, 877 p. ; 26 cm. Includes bibliographical references and indexes. ISBN 0-08-043163-1 DDC 306.44/03
*1. Language and education - Encyclopedias. I. Spolsky, Bernard. II. Asher, R. E.*
**TC P40.8 .C66 1999**

**Concise guide to the psychiatric interview of children and adolescents.**
Cepeda, Claudio, 1942- Washington, DC : American Psychiatric Press, c2000.
**TC RJ503.6 .C46 2000**

**Concise guides (American Psychiatric Press).**
Cepeda, Claudio, 1942- Concise guide to the psychiatric interview of children and adolescents. Washington, DC : American Psychiatric Press, c2000.
**TC RJ503.6 .C46 2000**

**The condition of madness.**
Grant, Brian W., 1939- Lanham, Md : University Press of America, 1999.
**TC RC437.5 .G73 1999**

**CONDITIONED RESPONSE.** *See also* **BEHAVIOR MODIFICATION; VERBAL BEHAVIOR.**
Leslie, Julian C. Behavior analysis. Amsterdam, Netherlands : Harwood Academic Publishers, c1999.
**TC BF199 .L47 1999**

Rachlin, Howard, 1935- Behavior and learning. San Francisco : W. H. Freeman, c1976.
**TC BF319 .R327**

Wyrwicka, Wanda. Conditioning. New Brunswick, N.J. : Transaction Publishers, c2000.
**TC BF319 .W94 2000**

**Conditioning.**
Wyrwicka, Wanda. New Brunswick, N.J. : Transaction Publishers, c2000.
**TC BF319 .W94 2000**

**CONDUCT DISORDERS IN CHILDREN.** *See* **JUVENILE DELINQUENCY; JUVENILE HOMICIDE.**

**CONDUCT OF LIFE.** *See also* **COURAGE; FRIENDSHIP; KINDNESS; RESPECT; SHARING; SUCCESS.**
Bea, Holly, 1956- My spiritual alphabet book. Tiburon, Calif. : H.J. Kramer, c2000.
**TC BL625.5 .B43 1999**

Edelman, Marian Wright. Lanterns. Boston : Beacon Press, c1999.
**TC E185.97.E33 A3 1999**

**CONDUCT OF LIFE - CASE STUDIES.**
Coles, Robert. Lives of moral leadership. 1st ed. New York : Random House, c2000.
**TC BJ1547.4 .C64 2000**

**CONDUCT OF LIFE IN LITERATURE.**
O'Keefe, Deborah. Good girl messages. New York : Continuum, 2000.
**TC PS374.G55 O44 2000**

**Conducting drug abuse research with minority populations :** advances and issues / Mario R. De La Rosa, Bernard Segal, Richard Lopez, editors. New York : Haworth Press, c1999. xxiii, 297 p. : ill. ; 23 cm. "Co-published simultaneously as Drugs & society, volume 14, numbers 1/2 1999." Includes bibliographical references and index. ISBN 0-7890-0530-1 (alk. paper) DDC 362.29/12/08900973
*1. Minorities - United States - Drug use - Research. 2. Drug abuse - Research - United States. I. De la Rosa, Mario. II. Segal, Bernard, 1936- III. Lopez, Richard. IV. Title: Drugs & society (New York, N.Y.)*
**TC HV5824.E85 C66 1999**

**Conducting effective conferences with parents of children with disabilities.**
Seligman, Milton, 1937- New York : Guilford Press, c2000.
**TC LC4019 .S385 2000**

**Conducting school-based assessments of child and adolescent behavior** / edited by Edward S. Shapiro, Thomas R. Kratochwill. New York : Guilford Press, c2000. xvi, 318 p. : ill. ; 24 cm. (The Guilford school practitioner series) Includes bibliographical references and index. DDC 370.15/3
*1. Behavioral assessment of children - Handbooks, manuals, etc. 2. School psychology - Handbooks, manuals, etc. I. Shapiro, Edward S. (Edward Steven), 1951- II. Kratochwill, Thomas R. III. Series.*
**TC LB1124 .C66 2000**

**A Confederate girl.**
Berry, Carrie, b. 1854. Mankato, Minn. : Blue Earth Books, c2000.
**TC E605 .B5 2000**

**CONFEDERATE STATES OF AMERICA.** *See* **UNITED STATES - HISTORY - CIVIL WAR, 1861-1865.**

**Conference Board.**
Otterbourg, Susan D. Using technology to strengthen employee and family involvement in education. [New York] : Conference Board, c1998.
**TC LB1028.3 .O88 1998**

**Conference Board report**
(no. 1223-98-RR.) Otterbourg, Susan D. Using technology to strengthen employee and family involvement in education. [New York] : Conference Board, c1998.
**TC LB1028.3 .O88 1998**

**Conference on College Composition and Communication (U.S.).**
CCCC bibliography of composition and rhetoric. Carbondale : Southern Illinois University Press, c1990-
**TC Z5818.E5 L66**

**Conference on Population and Economic Change in Less Developed Countries (1976 : Philadelphia, Pa.)** Population and economic change in developing countries / edited by Richard A. Easterlin. Chicago : University of Chicago Press, 1980. x, 581 p. ; 24 cm. (A Conference report, Universities-National Bureau Committee for Economic Research ; no. 30) Sponsored by the Universities-National Bureau Committee for Economic Research. Includes bibliographies and indexes. ISBN 0-226-18026-3 DDC 301.32/9/1724
*1. Developing countries - Population - Congresses. 2. Population - Economic aspects - Congresses. I. Easterlin, Richard A., 1926- II. Universities-National Bureau Committee for Economic Research. III. Title. IV. Series: Conference report (Universities--National Bureau Committee for Economic Research) ; no. 30.*
**TC HB849 .C59 1976**

**Conference report (National Bureau of Economic Research)**

The economic analysis of substance use and abuse. Chicago : University of Chicago Press, 1999.
*TC HV4999.2 .E25 1999*

**Conference report (Universities--National Bureau Committee for Economic Research)** (no. 30.) Conference on Population and Economic Change in Less Developed Countries (1976 : Philadelphia, Pa.) Population and economic change in developing countries. Chicago : University of Chicago Press, 1980.
*TC HB849 .C59 1976*

**CONFERENCES.** *See* **CONGRESSES AND CONVENTIONS; FORUMS (DISCUSSION AND DEBATE).**

**CONFESSION.** *See* **CONFIDENTIAL COMMUNICATIONS.**

**Confessions of a teenage drama queen.** Sheldon, Dyan. 1st ed. Cambridge, Mass. : Candlewick Press, 1999.
*TC PZ7.S54144 Co 1999*

**CONFIDENTIAL COMMUNICATIONS.** *See* **PRIVACY, RIGHT OF.**

**CONFIDENTIAL COMMUNICATIONS - PHYSICIANS.** HIV and AIDS. Oxford ; New York : Oxford University Press, 1999.
*TC RA644.A25 H57855 1999*

**CONFIDENTIAL RELATIONSHIPS.** *See* **CONFIDENTIAL COMMUNICATIONS.**

**CONFIDENTIALITY.** *See also* **CONFIDENTIAL COMMUNICATIONS.** HIV and AIDS. Oxford ; New York : Oxford University Press, 1999.
*TC RA644.A25 H57855 1999*

**Conflating the self with the body.** Lippert, Robin Alissa. 1999.
*TC 085 L655*

**Conflict.** Lulofs, Roxane Salyer. 2nd ed. Boston : Allyn and Bacon, c2000.
*TC BF637.I48 L85 2000*

**Conflict and team learning.** Sauquet, Alfonso. 2000.
*TC 06 no. 11308*

**CONFLICT CONTROL.** *See* **CONFLICT MANAGEMENT.**

**CONFLICT, ETHNIC.** *See* **ETHNIC RELATIONS.**

**Conflict ignites.** The American Revolution. [videorecording]. New York, N.Y. : A&E Home Video, c1994.
*TC E208 .A447 1994*

**CONFLICT, INTERGROUP.** *See* **INTERGROUP RELATIONS.**

**CONFLICT MANAGEMENT.** *See also* **MEDIATION.** Anstey, Mark. Managing change. 2nd ed. Kenwyn : Juta, 1999.
*TC HD42 .A57 1999*

Bodine, Richard J. Developing emotional intelligence. Champaign, Ill : Research Press, c1999.
*TC BF561 .B6 1999*

Burton, John W. (John Wear), 1915- Conflict resolution. Lanham, Md. : Scarecrow Press, 1996.
*TC HM136 .B786 1996*

Isenhart, Myra Warren. Collaborative approaches to resolving conflict. Thousand Oaks, Calif. : Sage Publications, c2000.
*TC HM1126 .I74 2000*

Lulofs, Roxane Salyer. Conflict. 2nd ed. Boston : Allyn and Bacon, c2000.
*TC BF637.I48 L85 2000*

Mayer, Bernard S., 1946- The dynamics of conflict resolution. 1st ed. San Francisco : Jossey-Bass Publishers, c2000.
*TC BF637.I48 M39 2000*

Miall, Hugh. Contemporary conflict resolution. Cambridge, UK : Polity Press ; Malden, MA : Blackwell, 1999.
*TC JZ6010 .M53 1999*

Tillett, Gregory, Ph. D. Resolving conflict :. 2nd ed. Oxford ; New York : Oxford University Press, 1999.
*TC HM132 .T55 1999*

Tolliver, Joseph A. Administratively mandated change at Amherst College. 1997.

**TC 06 no. 10871**
Wagner Pacifici, Robin Erica. Theorizing the standoff. Cambridge : Cambridge University Press, 2000.
*TC HM1121 .W34 2000*

Wilde, Jerry, 1962- An educators guide to difficult parents. Huntington, N.Y. : Kroshka Books, c2000.
*TC LC225.3 .W54 2000*

Working with conflict. New York : Zed Books ; Birmingham, UK : In association with Responding to Conflict ; New York : Distributed in the USA exclusively by St. Martin's Press, 2000.
*TC HM1126 .W67 2000*

**CONFLICT MANAGEMENT - GREAT BRITAIN.** Traynor, Michael, 1956- Managerialism and nursing. London ; New York : Routledge, 1999.
*TC RT86.45 .T73 1999*

**CONFLICT MANAGEMENT - HANDBOOKS, MANUALS, ETC.** The consensus building handbook. Thousand Oaks, Calif. : Sage Publications, c1999.
*TC HM746 .C66 1999*

**CONFLICT MANAGEMENT - SPAIN - CASE STUDIES.** Sauquet, Alfonso. Conflict and team learning:. 2000.
*TC 06 no. 11308*

**CONFLICT MANAGEMENT - STUDY AND TEACHING.** Gilhooley, James. Using peer mediation in classrooms and schools. Thousand Oaks, Calif. : Corwin Press, c2000.
*TC LB1027.5 .G48 2000*

**CONFLICT MANAGEMENT - STUDY AND TEACHING (MIDDLE SCHOOL) - UNITED STATES.** Promoting nonviolence in early adolescence. New York : Kluwer Academic/Plenum Publishers, c2000.
*TC HM1126 .P76 2000*

**CONFLICT MANAGEMENT - TERMINOLOGY.** Burton, John W. (John Wear), 1915- Conflict resolution. Lanham, Md. : Scarecrow Press, 1996.
*TC HM136 .B786 1996*

**CONFLICT MANAGEMENT - UNITED STATES.** Kosmoski, Georgia J. Managing difficult, frustrating, and hostile conversations. Thousand Oaks, Calif. : Sage Publications, c2000.
*TC LB3011.5 .K67 2000*

**CONFLICT (PSYCHOLOGY).** Lulofs, Roxane Salyer. Conflict. 2nd ed. Boston : Allyn and Bacon, c2000.
*TC BF637.I48 L85 2000*

Mayer, Bernard S., 1946- The dynamics of conflict resolution. 1st ed. San Francisco : Jossey-Bass Publishers, c2000.
*TC BF637.I48 M39 2000*

Smith, Clagett G., 1930- comp. Conflict resolution: contributions of the behavioral sciences. Notre Dame [Ind.] University of Notre Dame Press [1971]
*TC JX1291 .S45*

**CONFLICT RESOLUTION.** *See also* **CONFLICT MANAGEMENT; DISPUTE RESOLUTION (LAW).** Burton, John W. (John Wear), 1915- Lanham, Md. : Scarecrow Press, 1996.
*TC HM136 .B786 1996*

**Conflict resolution: contributions of the behavioral sciences.** Smith, Clagett G., 1930- comp. Notre Dame [Ind.] University of Notre Dame Press [1971]
*TC JX1291 .S45*

**CONFLICT, SOCIAL.** *See* **SOCIAL CONFLICT.**

**Conflicting missions? :** teachers unions and educational reform / Tom Loveless, editor. Washington, D.C. : Brookings Institution Press, c2000. vi, 328 p. ; 25 cm. Includes bibliographical references and index. CONTENTS: Reform bargaining and its promise for school improvement / Susan Moore Johnson and Susan M. Kardos -- Collective bargaining and public schools / Joe A. Stone -- Gaining control of professional licensing and advancement / Dale Ballou and Michael Podgursky -- Collective bargaining in Milwaukee Public Schools / Howard L. Fuller, George A. Mitchell, and Michael E. Hartmann -- The NEA and school choice / James G. Cibulka -- Teachers unions in hard times / William Lowe Boyd, David N. Plank, and Gary Sykes -- Teachers unions and educational research and development / Maris A. Vinovskis -- An international perspective on teachers unions / Bruce S. Cooper -- Organizing around quality : the frontiers of teacher unionism / Charles Taylor Kerchner and Julia E. Koppich. ISBN 0-8157-5304-7 ISBN 0-8157-5303-9 (pbk.) DDC

331.88/113711/00973
*1. Teachers' unions - United States. 2. Educational change - United States. I. Loveless, Tom, 1954- II. Title: Teachers unions and educational reform*
*TC LB2844.53.U62 C66 2000*

**CONFORMITY.** *See also* **INFLUENCE (PSYCHOLOGY); PERSUASION (PSYCHOLOGY).** Hollander, Edwin Paul, 1927- Leaders, groups, and influence New York, Oxford University Press, 1964.
*TC HM141 .H58*

**Confrontation.** Blank, Leonard. New York, Macmillan [1971]
*TC HM132 .B55*

**Confronting the drug control establishment.** Keys, David Patrick, 1955- Albany, N.Y. : State University of New York Press, c2000.
*TC HM1031.L56 K49 2000*

**Confusable words.** Dictionary of confusable words. Chicago, IL : Fitzroy Dearborn Publ., 2000.
*TC PE1591 .D53 2000*

**CONFUSIONAL STATES, ACUTE.** *See* **DELIRIUM.**

**Conger, Eric.** Children of the night [videorecording]. [Charleston, W.V.] : Cambridge Educational, c1994.
*TC HV1435.C3 C45 1994*

Children of the night [videorecording]. [Charleston, W.V.] : Cambridge Educational, c1994.
*TC HV1435.C3 C45 1994*

Children of the night [videorecording]. [Charleston, W.V.] : Cambridge Educational, c1994.
*TC HV1435.C3 C45 1994*

Starting over [videorecording]. [Charleston, W.V.] : Cambridge Educational, c1994.
*TC HV1435.C3 S7 1994*

**Conger, Rand.** Elder, Glen H. Children of the land. Chicago : University of Chicago Press, 2000.
*TC HQ796 .E525 2000*

**CONGESTION, TRAFFIC.** *See* **TRAFFIC CONGESTION.**

**CONGLOMERATE CORPORATIONS.** *See* **COMPETITION.**

**CONGREGATE HOUSING - UNITED STATES - MANAGEMENT.** Pearce, Benjamin W. Senior living communities. Baltimore : Johns Hopkins University Press, 1998.
*TC HD7287.92.U54 P4 1998*

**CONGRESSES AND CONVENTIONS.** *See* **POLITICAL CONVENTIONS.**

**CONGRESSES AND CONVENTIONS - PERIODICALS.** International transnational associations. [Bruxelles, Union of International Associations]

**CONGRESSIONAL HEARINGS.** *See* **LEGISLATIVE HEARINGS - UNITED STATES.**

**CONGRESSMEN.** *See* **LEGISLATORS - UNITED STATES.**

**Conisbee, Philip.** Ingres, Jean-Auguste-Dominique, 1780-1867. Portraits by Ingres. New York : Metropolitan Museum of Art : Distributed by Harry N. Abrams, c1999.
*TC ND1329.I53 A4 1999*

**Conlin, Joseph Robert.** Our land, our time : a history of the United States / Joseph R. Conlin. Annotated teacher's ed. San Diego : Coronado Publishers, c1987. T159, xiii, 872 p. : ill. (some col.), col. maps ; 27 cm. Other title: History of the United States. Includes tables. Includes bibliographical references (p. T155-T159) and index. SUMMARY: Traces the history of the United States from the arrival of the first Indians to the present day. ISBN 0-15-772001-2
*1. United States - History. 2. United States - History - Study and teaching (Secondary) I. Title. II. Title: History of the United States.*
*TC E178.1 .C762 1987*

**Connect with English** [videorecording] / Annenberg/ CPB Collection ; associate producer, Julia Haslett ; co-producers, Roberto Rodriguez, Olivia Tappan. S. Burlington, Vt. : The Annenberg/CPB Collection, c1997. 8 videocassettes (12 hrs.) : sd., col. ; 1/2 in. VHS. Catalogued from credits and container for tape 1 (ie., unit 1, episodes 1-6). Closed-captioned. Rebecca: Karin Anglin.

Music: Misha Segal. "Producer: WGBH/Boston with McGraw-Hill"--Container. Based on the Connections novella series. For speakers of other languages who want to learn colloquial English. SUMMARY: "Connect with English is a dramatic new way for speakers of other languages to learn English. Through the story of Rebecca, an aspiring singer on a journey across America, the series touches on life's important issues: leaving home, parenting, education, work, love, success, and loss."--Container. CONTENTS: [Tape 1]. Introduction, 1. Rebecca's dream, 2. Differences, 3. A visit to the doctor, 4. Celebrations, 5. Breaking the news, 6. Saying goodbye -- [Tape 2]. 7. Leaving home, 8. The stranger, 9. The motel, 10. Negotiations, 11. Photos and farewells, 12. A new home -- [Tape 3]. 13. Job hunting, 14. A bad day, 15. A night out, 16. First day of class, 17. Casey at the bat -- 18. The art gallery -- [Tape 4]. 19. The picnic, 20. Prejudice, 21. A difficult decision, 22. Guitar lessons, 23. Retirement party, 24. The phone call -- [Tape 5]. 25. Review, 26. The emergency, 27. Bad news, 28. Brothers, 29. Grief, 30. Life goes on -- [Tape 6] 31. A box of memories, 32. The missing car, 33. A breakdown, 34. A call for help, 35. Changes, 36. The farm -- [Tape 7]. 37. Thanksgiving, 38. Starting over, 39. The pressure's on, 40. Sharing feelings, 41. Unexpected offers, 42. The audition -- [Tape 8]. 43. Dreamcatcher, 44. Gifts, 45. True love, 46. Friendship, 47. The lost boys, 48. A very good year. ISBN 1-57680-002-4
*1. English language - Study and teaching - Audio-visual aids. 2. English language - Study and teaching - Foreign speakers. 3. Colloquial language. 4. English language - Films for foreign speakers. 5. English language - Self-instruction. I. Anglin, Karin. II. Barzyk, Fred. III. Haslett, Julia. IV. Rodriguez, Roberto. V. Tappan, Olivia. VI. WGBH Educational Foundation. VII. McGraw-Hill, inc. VIII. Annenberg/CPB Project. IX. Title: Connections novella series.*
**TC PE1128 .C66 1997**

**Connecticut. Board of Education.** Connecticut schools ... [Hartford.], Connecticut Board of Education. v. pl., diagrs. 22 cm. v. 1- 1920-May 1938. "Successor to the Connecticut common school journal founded in 1838 by Henry Barnard." Some months issued in combined numbers.
*1. Education - Connecticut. I. Title. II. Title: Connecticut common school journal*

**Connecticut common school journal.**
Connecticut. Board of Education. Connecticut schools ... [Hartford.], Connecticut Board of Education.

**Connecticut school directory.**
MDR's school directory. Connecticut. Shelton, CT : Market Data Retrieval, c1995-
**TC L903.C8 M37**

**Connecticut schools ...**
Connecticut. Board of Education. [Hartford.], Connecticut Board of Education.

**Connecticut State Teacher's Association.**
Connecticut teacher. Hartford, Conn. : The Association, [1933-

**Connecticut teacher :** official publication of the Connecticut State Teacher's Association. Hartford, Conn. : The Association, [1933- v. : ill., ports. ; 28-29 cm. Frequency: Monthly (during the school year). Vol. 1, no. 1 (Oct. 1933)- . Title from cover.
*1. Education - Societies. 2. Education - Periodicals. 3. Education - Connecticut. 4. Education - Connecticut - Periodicals. I. Connecticut State Teacher's Association.*

**Connecting generations.**
Friedman, Barbara, 1947- Boston : Allyn and Bacon, c1999.
**TC HQ1064.U5 F755 1999**

**Connecting mathematics and science to workplace contexts :** a guide to curriculum materials / Edward Britton ... [et al.]. Thousand Oaks, Calif. : Corwin Press, c1999. xviii, 254 p. : ill. ; 27 cm. Includes bibliographical references (p. 239-242). ISBN 0-8039-6866-3 (acid-free paper) ISBN 0803968671(pbk. : (acid-free paper) DDC 507.1/2
*1. Mathematics - Study and teaching (Secondary) 2. Science - Study and teaching (Secondary) 3. School-to-work transition. I. Britton, Edward.*
**TC QA11 .C655 1999**

**Connecting special education and technology for the 21st century.**
Birnbaum, Barry W. Lewiston, N.Y. : Lampeter, Wales : E. Mellen Press, c1999.
**TC LC3969.5 .B57 1999**

**The connection between action reflection learning and transformative learning.**
Lamm, Sharon Lea. 2000.
**TC 06 no. 11230**

**CONNECTIONISM.**
Development of mental representation. Mahwah, NJ : L. Erlbaum Associates, c1999.
**TC BF723.M43 T47 1999**

**Connections novella series.**
Connect with English [videorecording]. S. Burlington, Vt. : The Annenberg/CPB Collection, c1997.
**TC PE1128 .C66 1997**

**Connelly, F. Michael.**
Clandinin, D. Jean. Narrative inquiry. 1st ed. San Francisco : Jossey-Bass Inc., c2000.
**TC LB1028 .C55 2000**

**Connerly, Ward, 1939-** Creating equal : my fight against race preferences / Ward Connerly. San Francisco : Encounter Books, 2000. 286 p., [8] p. of plates : ill. ; 24 cm. Includes index. ISBN 1-89355-404-X DDC 305.896073/0092
*1. Connerly, Ward. - 1939- 2. Afro-American political activists - Biography. 3. Political activists - United States - Biography. 4. University of California (System). - Regents - Biography. 5. California - Race relations. 6. Race discrimination - California. 7. California - Politics and government - 1951- 8. United States - Race relations. 9. Race discrimination - United States. 10. United States - Politics and government - 1989- I. Title.*
**TC E185.97 .C74 2000**

**CONNERLY, WARD, 1939-.**
Connerly, Ward, 1939- Creating equal. San Francisco : Encounter Books, 2000.
**TC E185.97 .C74 2000**

**Conners, Gail A.** Good news! : how to get the best possible media coverage for your school / Gail A. Conners. Thousand Oaks, Calif. : Corwin Press, c2000. xii, 116 p. : ill. ; 28 cm. Includes bibliographical references. CONTENTS: Using "the Bleiker lifepreserver" for positive school-community relations : putting Bleiker to work -- Building credibility and accountability with the community -- Developing a communications plan -- Creating a positive relationship with the media -- Crisis communications : schools in turmoil -- Forming partnerships in communications -- Designing newsletters and Web sites. ISBN 0-7619-7506-3 (alk. paper) ISBN 0-7619-7507-1 (pbk. : alk. paper) DDC 659.2/9371
*1. Schools - Public relations - United States. 2. Community and school - United States. 3. Education in mass media. I. Title.*
**TC LB2847 .C65 2000**

**Connerton, Paul.**
Critical sociology. Harmondsworth ; New York [etc.] : Penguin, 1976.
**TC HM24 .C74**

**Connolly, Terry.**
Judgment and decision making. 2nd ed. Cambridge, U.K. : New York, NY : Cambridge University Press, 2000.
**TC BF441 .J79 2000**

**Conolly, L. W. (Leonard W.).**
Theatrical touring and founding in North America. Westport, Conn. : Greenwood Press, 1982.
**TC PN2219.5 .T5 1982**

**Conquering the beast within.**
Irwin, Cait. New York : Times Books, 1999.
**TC RC537 .I77 1999**

**CONQUERORS - COLOMBIA - HISTORY - 16TH CENTURY.**
Avellaneda Navas, José Ignacio. The conquerors of the New Kingdom of Granada. 1st ed. Albuquerque : University of New Mexico Press, c1995.
**TC F2272 .A84 1995**

**The conquerors of the New Kingdom of Granada.**
Avellaneda Navas, José Ignacio. 1st ed. Albuquerque : University of New Mexico Press, c1995.
**TC F2272 .A84 1995**

**CONQUISTADORS.** *See* CONQUERORS.

**Conrad, Pam.** Blue willow / Pam Conrad ; illustrated by S. Saelig Gallagher. New York : Philomel Books, c1999. 1 v. (unpaged) : col. ill. ; 23 x 28 cm. SUMMARY: Kung Shi Fair's wealthy father gives her everything she asks of him; but when she requests permission to marry, he learns too late the value of listening. ISBN 0-399-22904-3 (hc) DDC [Fic]
*1. Fathers and daughters - Fiction. 2. Listening - Fiction. I. Gallagher, S. Saelig, ill. II. Title.*
**TC PZ7.C76476 Bl 1999**

**Conroy, Mary Ann.** 101 ways to integrate personal development into core curriculum : lessons in character education for grades K-12 / Mary Ann Conroy. Lanham : University Press of America, c2000. xvii, 301 p. ; 22 cm. Includes bibliographical references (p. 293) and index. ISBN 0-7618-1642-9 (pbk. : alk.

paper) DDC 370.11/4
*1. Moral education - United States - Curricula. 2. Moral education - United States - Handbooks, manuals, etc. 3. Lesson planning - United States - Handbooks, manuals, etc. I. Title. II. Title: One hundred one ways to integrate personal development into core curriculum III. Title: One hundred and one ways to integrate personal development into core curriculum*
**TC LC311 .C65 2000**

**CONSANGUINITY.** *See* INCEST.

**CONSCIENCE.** *See also* GUILT.
Stilwell, Barbara M. Right vs. wrong--. Bloomington : Indiana University Press, c2000.
**TC BJ1471 .S69 2000**

**CONSCIOUSNESS.** *See also* BELIEF AND DOUBT; INTUITION; KNOWLEDGE, THEORY OF; PERSONALITY; SELF.
Ableman, Paul. The secret of consciousness. London : New York : Marion Boyars, 1999.
**TC BF311 .A195 1999**

Dodwell, P. C. Brave new mind. New York : Oxford University Press, 2000.
**TC BF311 .D568 2000**

Foulkes, David, 1935- Children's dreaming and the development of consciousness. Cambridge, Mass. : Harvard University Press, 1999.
**TC BF1099.C55 F67 1999**

Hobson, J. Allan, 1933- [Chemistry of conscious states] Dreaming as delirium. 1st MIT Press ed. Cambridge, Mass. : MIT Press, 1999.
**TC QP426 .H629 1999**

Keen, Ernest, 1937- Chemicals for the mind. Westport, Conn. : London : Praeger, 2000.
**TC RM315 .K44 2000**

O'Shaughnessy, Brian. Consciousness and the world. Oxford : Clarendon Press ; New York : Oxford University Press, 2000.
**TC B808.9 .O74 2000**

Wilton, Richard. Consciousness, free will, and the explanation of human behavior. Lewiston, N.Y. : E. Mellen Press, c2000.
**TC BF161 .W495 2000**

**Consciousness and the world.**
O'Shaughnessy, Brian. Oxford : Clarendon Press ; New York : Oxford University Press, 2000.
**TC B808.9 .O74 2000**

**CONSCIOUSNESS - CONGRESSES.**
International School of Biocybernetics (1997 : Naples, Italy) Neuronal bases and psychological aspects of consiousness. Singapore : River Edge, N.J : World Scientific, c1999.
**TC QP411 .I56 1997**

Memory, consciousness, and the brain. Philadelphia ; London : Psychology Press, c2000.
**TC BF371 .M4483 2000**

Toward a science of consciousness III. Cambridge, Mass. : MIT Press, c1999.
**TC BF311 .T67 1999**

**Consciousness, free will, and the explanation of human behavior.**
Wilton, Richard. Lewiston, N.Y. : E. Mellen Press, c2000.
**TC BF161 .W495 2000**

**CONSCIOUSNESS, MULTIPLE.** *See* MULTIPLE PERSONALITY.

**CONSCIOUSNESS, NATIONAL.** *See* NATIONALISM.

**CONSCIOUSNESS - PHYSIOLOGY - CONGRESSES.**
International School of Biocybernetics (1997 : Naples, Italy) Neuronal bases and psychological aspects of consiousness. Singapore : River Edge, N.J : World Scientific, c1999.
**TC QP411 .I56 1997**

**CONSCIOUSNESS-RAISING GROUPS.** *See* GROUP RELATIONS TRAINING.

**The consensus building handbook :** a comprehensive guide to reaching agreement / editors, Lawrence Susskind, Sarah McKearnan, Jennifer Thomas-Larmer. Thousand Oaks, Calif. : Sage Publications, c1999. xxiv, 1147 p. ; 26 cm. Includes bibliographical references and index. ISBN 0-7619-0844-7 (acid-free paper) DDC 302.3
*1. Group decision-making - Handbooks, manuals, etc. 2. Consensus (Social sciences) - Handbooks, manuals, etc. Consensus (Social sciences) - Case studies. 4. Conflict management - Handbooks, manuals, etc. I. Susskind,*

Lawrence. II. McKearnan. Sarah. III. Thomas-Larmer.
Jennifer.
*TC HM746 .C66 1999*

**CONSENSUS (SOCIAL SCIENCES).** *See* **POWER
(SOCIAL SCIENCES).**

**CONSENSUS (SOCIAL SCIENCES) - CASE
STUDIES.**
The consensus building handbook. Thousand Oaks,
Calif. : Sage Publications, c1999.
*TC HM746 .C66 1999*

**CONSENSUS (SOCIAL SCIENCES) -
HANDBOOKS, MANUALS, ETC.**
The consensus building handbook. Thousand Oaks,
Calif. : Sage Publications, c1999.
*TC HM746 .C66 1999*

**CONSENT, INFORMED.** *See* **INFORMED
CONSENT (MEDICAL LAW).**

**CONSENT (LAW).** *See* **INFORMED CONSENT
(MEDICAL LAW).**

**CONSENT TO TREATMENT.** *See* **INFORMED
CONSENT (MEDICAL LAW).**

**CONSERVATION OF BOOKS.** *See* **BOOKS -
CONSERVATION AND RESTORATION.**

**Conservation of human resources series**
(15) Stanback, Thomas M. Cities in transition.
Totowa, N.J. : Allanheld, Osmun, 1982.
*TC HD5724 .S649 1982*

**The conservation of leather artefacts.**
Sturge, Theodore. London : The Leather Conservation
Centre, 2000.
*TC N8555 .S8 2000*

**CONSERVATION OF MINERAL RESOURCES.**
*See* **MINERAL RESOURCES
CONSERVATION.**

**CONSERVATION OF NATURAL RESOURCES.**
*See also* **MINERAL RESOURCES
CONSERVATION.**
Baskin, Yvonne. The work of nature. Washington,
D.C. : Island Press, 1997.
*TC GE195 .B36 1997*

**CONSERVATISM AND LITERATURE.** *See*
**POLITICS AND LITERATURE.**

**CONSERVATISM - RELIGIOUS ASPECTS.**
Spinner-Halev, Jeff. Surviving diversity. Baltimore :
Johns Hopkins University Press, 2000.
*TC BL2525 .S588 2000*

**CONSERVATIVE JUDAISM - UNITED STATES -
HISTORY.**
Tradition renewed. 1st ed. New York, N.Y. : The
Seminary, 1997.
*TC BM90.J56 T83 1997*

**CONSERVATORIES OF MUSIC - NEW YORK
(STATE) - NEW YORK.**
Olmstead, Andrea. Juilliard. Urbana : University of
Illinois Press, c1999.
*TC MT4.N5 J846 1999*

**CONSERVATORSHIPS.** *See* **GUARDIAN AND
WARD.**

**CONSIGNMENT BUYING.** *See* **CONSIGNMENT
SALES.**

**CONSIGNMENT SALES - UNITED STATES.**
Crawford, Tad, 1946- The artist-gallery partnership.
[2nd ed.]. New York : Allworth Press, c1998.
*TC KF947 .C7 1998*

DuBoff, Leonard D. The law (in plain English) for
galleries. 2nd ed. New York : Allworth Press, c1999.
*TC KF2042.A76 D836 1999*

**CONSOLATION.** *See* **BEREAVEMENT.**

**Console-ing passions**
Kids' media culture. Durham [N.C.] ; London : Duke
University Press, 1999.
*TC HQ784.M3 K54 1999*

**CONSOLIDATION OF SCHOOLS.** *See*
**SCHOOLS - CENTRALIZATION.**

**The conspiracy of ignorance.**
Gross, Martin L. (Martin Louis), 1925- New York :
HarperCollins, c1999.
*TC LA217.2 .G76 1999*

**Constant Communications Productions.**
New school order [videorecording]. New York : First
Run/Icarus Films, 1996.
*TC LB2831.583.P4 N4 1996*

**Constantinou, Sophia.**
Between the lines [videorecording]. Boston, MA :
Fanlight Productions, c1997.
*TC RC552.S4 B4 1997*

**CONSTITUTIONAL LAW.** *See* **CIVIL RIGHTS;
LEGISLATIVE BODIES.**

**CONSTITUTIONAL LAW - INTERPRETATION
AND CONSTRUCTION.** *See*
**CONSTITUTIONAL LAW.**

**CONSTITUTIONAL LAW - UNITED STATES.**
Renstrom, Peter G., 1943- Constitutional rights
sourcebook. Santa Barbara, Calif. : ABC-CLIO, 1999.
*TC KF4550.Z9 R463 1999*

**CONSTITUTIONAL LAW - UNITED STATES -
COMPETITIONS - COLORADO.**
We the people simulated congressional hearing
[videorecording]. [Boulder, Colo.] : Social Science
Education Consortium, c1997.
*TC KF4208.5.L3 W4 1997*

**CONSTITUTIONAL LAW - UNITED STATES -
STUDY AND TEACHING (SECONDARY) -
COLORADO - DENVER - PROBLEMS,
EXERCISES, ETC.**
Public issues discussion [videorecording] : Diana
Hess at Denver High School 1997. [Boulder, Colo.] :
Social Science Education Consortium, c1997.
*TC H62.3 .P4 1997*

Socratic seminar [videorecording]. [Boulder, Colo.] :
Social Science Education Consortium, c1997.

**CONSTITUTIONAL LAW - UNITED STATES -
STUDY AND TEACHING (SECONDARY) -
COLORADO - EVALUATION.**
We the people simulated congressional hearing
[videorecording]. [Boulder, Colo.] : Social Science
Education Consortium, c1997.
*TC KF4208.5.L3 W4 1997*

**CONSTITUTIONAL LAW - UNITED STATES -
STUDY AND TEACHING (SECONDARY) -
SIMULATION METHODS - COLORADO.**
We the people simulated congressional hearing
[videorecording]. [Boulder, Colo.] : Social Science
Education Consortium, c1997.
*TC KF4208.5.L3 W4 1997*

**CONSTITUTIONAL LIMITATIONS.** *See*
**CONSTITUTIONAL LAW.**

**CONSTITUTIONAL RIGHTS.** *See* **CIVIL
RIGHTS.**

**Constitutional rights sourcebook.**
Renstrom, Peter G., 1943- Santa Barbara, Calif. :
ABC-CLIO, 1999.
*TC KF4550.Z9 R463 1999*

**CONSTITUTIONS.** *See* **CONSTITUTIONAL LAW.**

**CONSTITUTIONS - INTERPRETATION AND
CONSTRUCTION.** *See* **CONSTITUTIONAL
LAW.**

**Constructing children's physical education
experiences.**
Allison, Pamela C. Boston : Allyn and Bacon, 2000.
*TC GV363 .A512 2000*

**Constructing female identities.**
Proweller, Amira. Albany : State University of New
York Press, c1998.
*TC LC1755 .P76 1998*

**Constructing gender and difference :** critical research
perspectives on early childhood / edited by Barbara
Kamler. Cresskill, N.J. : Hampton Press, c1999. x, 228
p. : ill. ; 23 cm. (Language & social processes) Includes
bibliographical references and indexes. ISBN 1-57273-222-9
(hardcover) ISBN 1-57273-223-7 (pbk.) DDC 155.4/1
*1. Sex role in children. 2. Sex differences (Psychology) in
children. 3. Psychosexual development. I. Kamler, Barbara. II.
Series: Language & social processes*
*TC BF723.S42 C66 1999*

**CONSTRUCTION.** *See* **ARCHITECTURE;
ENGINEERING.**

**The construction and analysis of educational and
psychological tests.**
Sax, Gilbert. Madison, Wisconsin : College Printing
and Typing Co., 1962.
*TC BF39 .S27*

**CONSTRUCTION INDUSTRY - EMPLOYEES.**
*See* **CONSTRUCTION WORKERS.**

**CONSTRUCTION WORKERS - PICTORIAL
WORKS.**
Hine, Lewis Wickes, 1874-1940. The Empire State
Building. Munich ; New York : Prestel, c1998.

*TC TR820.5 .H5634 1998*

**Constructions of disorder :** meaning-making
frameworks for psychotherapy / edited by Robert A.
Neimeyer and Jonathan D. Raskin. 1st ed.
Washington, DC : American Psychological
Association, c2000. xiii, 373 p. ; 26 cm. Includes
bibliographical references and indexes. ISBN 1-55798-629-0
(alk. paper)
*1. Psychotherapy - Philosophy. 2. Postmodernism -
Psychological aspects. 3. Constructivism (Psychology) 4.
Personal construct therapy. 5. Storytelling - Therapeutic use. I.
Niemeyer. Robert A., 1954- II. Raskin, Jonathan D. III. Title:
Meaning-making frameworks for psychotherapy*
*TC RC437.5 .C647 2000*

**CONSTRUCTIVISM (EDUCATION).**
Allison, Pamela C. Constructing children's physical
education experiences. Boston : Allyn and Bacon,
2000.
*TC GV363 .A512 2000*

Baxter Magolda, Marcia B., 1951- Creating contexts
for learning and self-authorship. 1st ed. Nashville
[Tenn.] : Vanderbilt University Press, 1999.
*TC LB1025.3 .B39 1999*

Constructivism in education. Chicago, Ill. : NSSE :
Distributed by the University of Chicago Press,
2000.
*TC LB5 .N25 99th pt. 1*

Dhingra, Koshi. An ethnographic study of the
construction of science on television. 1999.
*TC 06 no. 11101*

Nord, Michael B. Music in the classroom (MITC).
1998.
*TC 06 no. 10974*

Oldfather, Penny. Learning through children's eyes.
1st ed. Washington, DC : American Psychological
Association, c1999.
*TC LB1060 .O43 1999*

Tsai, Chin-Chung. The interrelationships between
junior high school students' scientific epistemologicl
beliefs, learning environment preferences and their
cognitive structure outcomes. 1996.
*TC 06 no. 10713*

**CONSTRUCTIVISM (EDUCATION) -
LONGITUDINAL STUDIES.**
Painter, Clare, 1947- Learning through language in
early childhood. London ; New York : Cassell, 1999.
*TC LB1139.5.L35 P35 1999*

**CONSTRUCTIVISM (EDUCATION) - UNITED
STATES.**
Martin, David Jerner. Elementary science methods.
2nd ed. Belmont, CA : Wadsworth, c2000.
*TC LB1585.3 .M37 2000*

**Constructivism in education :** Opinions and second
opinions on controversial issues / edited by D. C.
Phillips ; editor for the Society, Margaret Early.
Chicago, Ill. : NSSE : Distributed by the University
of Chicago Press, 2000. xii, 340 p. ; 24 cm. (Ninety-
ninth yearbook of the National Society for the Study of
Education, 0077-5762 ; pt. 1) ISBN 0-226-60171-4
*1. Constructivism (Education). I. Phillips, D. C. (Denis
Charles), 1938- II. Early, Margaret. III. National Society for
the Study of Education. IV. Title. V. Series: Yearbook of the
National Society for the Study of Education ; 99th, pt. 1.*
*TC LB5 .N25 99th pt. 1*

**Constructivism in science education :** a philosophical
examination / edited by Michael R. Matthews.
Dordrecht ; Boston : Kluwer Academic, c1998. xii, 234
p. ; 25 cm. Includes bibliographical references and indexes.
ISBN 0-7923-5033-2 (alk. paper) DDC 507/.1
*1. Science - Study and teaching - Philosophy. 2. Constructivism
(Philosophy) I. Matthews, Michael R.*
*TC Q181 .C612 1998*

**CONSTRUCTIVISM (PHILOSOPHY).**
Constructivism in science education. Dordrecht ;
Boston : Kluwer Academic, c1998.
*TC Q181 .C612 1998*

**CONSTRUCTIVISM (PSYCHOLOGY).**
Constructions of disorder. 1st ed. Washington, DC :
American Psychological Association, c2000.
*TC RC437.5 .C647 2000*

**CONSTRUCTIVIST EDUCATION.** *See*
**CONSTRUCTIVISM (EDUCATION).**

**CONSULTANTS.** *See also* **EDUCATIONAL
CONSULTANTS.**
Salacuse, Jeswald W. The wise advisor. Westport,
Conn. : Praeger, 2000.

*TC BF637.C56 .S26 2000*

**CONSULTANTS - IN-SERVICE TRAINING.**
O'Neil, Judith Ann. The role of the learning advisor in
action learning. 1999.
*TC 06 no. 11156*

**CONSUMER AFFAIRS DEPARTMENTS.** *See*
**CONSUMER EDUCATION; CONSUMER
PROTECTION.**

**CONSUMER DEMAND.** *See* **CONSUMPTION
(ECONOMICS).**

**CONSUMER EDUCATION.** *See also* **HOME
ECONOMICS.**
Nathan, Peter E. Treating mental disorders. New
York : Oxford University Press, 1999.
*TC RC480.515 .N38 1999*

**CONSUMER EDUCATION - UNITED STATES -
PROBLEMS, EXERCISES, ETC.**
Toner, Patricia Rizzo, 1952- Consumer health and
safety activities. West Nyack, N.Y. : Center for
Applied Research in Education, c1993.
*TC RA440.3.U5 T66 1993*

**Consumer health and safety activities.**
Toner, Patricia Rizzo, 1952- West Nyack, N.Y. :
Center for Applied Research in Education, c1993.
*TC RA440.3.U5 T66 1993*

**CONSUMER PROTECTION.** *See* **FOOD
ADULTERATION AND INSPECTION.**

**CONSUMER PROTECTION - LAW AND
LEGISLATION.** *See* **FOOD LAW AND
LEGISLATION.**

**CONSUMER PROTECTION - UNITED STATES -
HISTORY.**
Goodwin, Lorine Swainston, 1925- The pure food,
drink, and drug crusaders, 1879-1914. Jefferson,
N.C. : McFarland, 1999.
*TC HD9000.9.U5 G66 1999*

**CONSUMER SATISFACTION.**
Baker, Susan Keane. Managing patient expectations.
San Francisco : Jossey Bass Publishers, 1998.
*TC R727.3 .B28 1998*

Gill, Kenneth Joseph. Social psychological artifacts in
the measurement of consumer satisfaction with health
care. 1996.
*TC 085 G396*

**CONSUMER SPENDING.** *See* **CONSUMPTION
(ECONOMICS).**

**CONSUMERS.** *See* **CHILD CONSUMERS;
YOUNG CONSUMERS.**

**CONSUMERS' LEAGUES.** *See* **CONSUMER
EDUCATION.**

**CONSUMPTION (ECONOMICS) -
FORECASTING.**
Brown, Lester Russell, 1934- Vital signs 2000 :. New
York : Norton, c2000.
*TC HD75.6 .B768 2000*

**CONSUMPTION (ECONOMICS) - UNITED
STATES - STATISTICS.**
Statistical handbook on consumption and wealth in the
United States. Phoenix, Ariz. : Oryx Press, 1999.
*TC HC110.C6 S73 1999*

**CONSUMPTION OF ALCOHOLIC BEVERAGES.**
*See* **DRINKING OF ALCOHOLIC
BEVERAGES.**

**CONTACTS OF HUMANS WITH ALIENS.** *See*
**HUMAN-ALIEN ENCOUNTERS.**

**CONTAMINANTS, AIR.** *See* **AIR - POLLUTION.**

**Contemporary aboriginal painting** / [introduction by
Nevill Drury]. East Roseville, Australia : Craftsmen
House, c1993. 30 p. : chiefly col. ill. ; 40 cm. (Poster book)
Includes bibliographical references (p. 6) ISBN 976-8097-49-3
*1. Painting, Australian aboriginal. 2. Painting, Modern - 20th
century - Australia. I. Drury, Nevill, 1947- II. Series.*
*TC ND1101 .C66 1993*

**CONTEMPORARY ART.** *See* **ART, MODERN -
20TH CENTURY.**

**Contemporary art in Asia** : traditions, tensions / guest
curator Apinan Poshyananda ; essays by Apinan
Poshyananda ... [et al.]. New York : Asia Society
Galleries ; Distributed by Harry N. Abrams, c1996.
239 p. : ill. (some col.) ; 29 cm. "Published in conjunction with
the exhibition Contemporary art in Asia: traditions/tensions
organized by the Asia Society Galleries, New York"--T.p.
verso. Errata slip inserted at end. Includes bibliographical
references and index. ISBN 0-87848-083-8 (Asia Society
Galleries : pbk.) ISBN 0-8109-6331-0 (Abrams) ISBN

90-5704-091-3 (G+B)
*1. Art, Asian - Exhibitions. 2. Art, Modern - 20th century -
Asia - Exhibitions. I. Poshyananda, Apinan, 1956- II. Asia
Society. Galleries III. Title: Traditions, tensions*
*TC N7262 .C655 1996*

**Contemporary ceramic art in Australia and New
Zealand.**
Mansfield, Janet. Roseville East, NSW : Craftsman
House, 1995.
*TC NK4179 .M36 1995*

**Contemporary composition studies.**
Babin, Edith H. Westport, Conn. : Greenwood Press,
1999.
*TC PE1404 .B23 1999*

**Contemporary conflict resolution.**
Miall, Hugh. Cambridge, UK : Polity Press ; Malden,
MA : Blackwell, 1999.
*TC JZ6010 .M53 1999*

**Contemporary curriculum discourses** : twenty years
of JCT / edited by William F. Pinar. New York : P.
Lang, c1999. xxx, 578 p. ; 23 cm. (Counterpoints ; vol. 70)
Includes bibliographical references and indexes. DDC 375/
.001/0973
*1. Curriculum planning - United States - Philosophy. 2.
Curriculum change - United States - Philosophy. I. Pinar,
William. II. Title: JCT. III. Series: Counterpoints (New York,
N.Y.) ; vol. 70.*
*TC LB2806.15 .C6753 1999*

**Contemporary issues in museum culture**
Einreinhofer, Nancy. The American art museum.
London ; New York : Leicester University Press,
1997.
*TC N510 .E45 1997*

Moore, Kevin, 1960- Museums and popular culture.
London ; New York : Leicester University Press,
1997.
*TC AM41 .M66 1997*

**Contemporary jewelery in Australia and New
Zealand.**
Anderson, Patricia, 1950- Contemporary jewellery in
Australia and New Zealand. North Ryde, Sydney :
Craftsman House, c1998.
*TC NK7390.A1 A53 1998*

**Contemporary jewellery in Australia and New
Zealand.**
Anderson, Patricia, 1950- North Ryde, Sydney :
Craftsman House, c1998.
*TC NK7390.A1 A53 1998*

**Contemporary learning theories.**
Handbook of contemporary learning theories.
Mahwah, N.J. ; London : Lawrence Erlbaum
Associates, 2001.
*TC LB1060 .H3457 2001*

**Contemporary mathematics (American
Mathematical Society)**
(v. 243). Algebra, K-theory, groups, and education.
Providence, R.I. : American Mathematical Society,
c1999.
*TC QA150 .A419 1999*

**CONTEMPORARY PAINTING.** *See* **PAINTING,
MODERN - 20TH CENTURY.**

**Contemporary perspectives in hearing assessment.**
Musiek, Frank E. Boston : Allyn and Bacon, 1999.
*TC RF294 .M87 1999*

**CONTEMPORARY SCULPTURE.** *See*
**SCULPTURE, MODERN - 20TH CENTURY.**

**Contemporary special education research** : syntheses
of the knowledge base on critical instructional issues /
edited by Russell Gersten, Ellen P. Schiller and
Sharon Vaughn. Mahwah, N.J. : Lawrence Erlbaum,
c2000. xi, 341 p. : ill. ; 23 cm. (The LEA series on special
education and disability) Includes bibliographical references
and indexes. ISBN 0-8058-2879-6 (cloth : alk. paper) ISBN 0-
8058-2880-X (pbk. : alk. paper) DDC 371.9/07/2
*1. Handicapped - Education - Research - United States -
Methodology. 2. Special education - Research - United States -
Methodology. 3. Meta-analysis. I. Gersten, Russell Monroe,
1947- II. Schiller, Ellen P. III. Vaughn, Sharon, 1952- IV.
Series.*
*TC LC4019 .C575 2000*

**Contemporary studies in social and policy issues in
education**
Stories out of school. Stamford, Conn. : Ablex Pub.,
c2000.
*TC LC196 .S6994 2000*

**The contemporary thesaurus of search terms and
synonyms.**

Knapp, Sara D. 2nd ed. Phoenix, Ariz. : Oryx Press,
2000.
*TC ZA4060 .K58 2000*

**Contemporary women's health.**
Kolander, Cheryl A. Boston, Mass. : WCB/McGraw-
Hill, c1999.
*TC RA778 .K7245 1999*

**Contemporary world issues**
Eisaguirre, Lynne, 1951- Affirmative action. Santa
Barbara, Calif. : ABC-CLIO, c1999.
*TC HF5549.5.A34 E39 1999*

Hull, Mary. Censorship in America. Santa Barbara,
Calif. : ABC-CLIO, c1999.
*TC Z658.U5 H84 1999*

Kinnear, Karen L. Single parents. Santa Barbara,
Calif. : ABC-CLIO, c1999.
*TC HQ759.915 .K56 1999*

**CONTENT AREA LANGUAGE ARTS
INSTRUCTION.** *See* **LANGUAGE ARTS -
CORRELATION WITH CONTENT
SUBJECTS.**

**CONTENT AREA READING.**
Ubbes, Valerie A. Literature links for nutrition and
health. Boston : Allyn and Bacon, c2000.
*TC TX364 .U253 2000*

**CONTENT AREA READING - UNITED STATES.**
Miller, Wilma H. Ready-to-use activities & materials
for improving content reading skills. West Nyack,
NY : Center For Applied Research in Education,
c1999.
*TC LB1576 .M52 1999*

**Content-based college ESL instruction.**
Kasper, Loretta F. (Loretta Frances), 1951- Mahwah,
N.J. : Lawrence Erlbaum Associates, 2000.
*TC PE1128.A2 K376 2000*

**Content, context, and continuity.**
Rabil, Alison. 1998.
*TC 06 no. 10901*

**CONTENTMENT - FICTION.**
McDonald, Megan. The night Iguana left home. 1st
ed. New York : DK Ink. 1999.
*TC PZ7.M478419 Ni 1999*

**Contested childhood.**
Holloway, Susan D. New York : Routledge, 2000.
*TC LB1140.25.J3 H69 2000*

**Contesting childhood.**
Wyness, Michael G. London ; New York : Falmer
Press, 2000.
*TC HQ767.9 .W96 2000*

**CONTEXT EFFECTS (PSYCHOLOGY).**
Capaldi, E. John. Contextualism in psychological
research? Thousand Oaks, Calif. : Sage, c1999.
*TC BF315.2 .C37 1999*

Learning sites. 1st ed. Amsterdam ; New York :
Pergamon, 1999.
*TC LB1060 .L4245 1999*

Social identity. Malden, MA : Blackwell Publishers,
1999.
*TC HM131 .S58433 1999*

Social psychology and cultural context. Thousand
Oaks, Calif. : Sage Publications, c1999.
*TC HM1033 .S64 1999*

**CONTEXT (PSYCHOLOGY).** *See* **CONTEXT
EFFECTS (PSYCHOLOGY).**

**Contexts and connections.**
Shaddock, David. New York : Basic Books, 2000.
*TC RC488.5 .S483 2000*

**Contexts of learning**
Computer assisted language learning (CALL). Lisse
[Netherlands] : Exton, PA : Swets & Zeitlinger, 1999.
*TC P53.28 .C6634 1999*

Sammons, Pam. School effectiveness. Lisse,
Netherlands ; Abingdon [England] : Exton, PA :
Swets & Zeitlinger Publishers, c1999.
*TC LB2822.75 .S24 1999*

Teaching and learning thinking skills. Lisse
[Netherlands] ; Exton, PA : Swets & Zeitlinger,
c1999.
*TC LB1590.3 .T36 1999*

**CONTEXTS (PSYCHOLOGY).** *See* **CONTEXT
EFFECTS (PSYCHOLOGY).**

**CONTEXTUAL ASSOCIATIONS
(PSYCHOLOGY).** *See* **CONTEXT EFFECTS
(PSYCHOLOGY).**

**Contextualism in psychological research?.**
Capaldi, E. John. Thousand Oaks, Calif. : Sage, c1999.
*TC BF315.2 .C37 1999*

**CONTEXTUALISM (PSYCHOLOGY).** *See*
**CONTEXT EFFECTS (PSYCHOLOGY).**

**CONTEXTUALIZATION (CHRISTIAN THEOLOGY).** *See* **CHRISTIANITY AND CULTURE.**

**Conti-D'Antonio, Marcia, 1953-.**
Eisenberger, Joanne, 1942- Self efficacy. Larchmont, N.Y. : Eye On Education, c2000.
*TC LC4705 .C67 2000*

**Conti-Ramsden, Gina.**
Pérez Pereira, Miguel. Language development and social interaction in blind children. Hove, UK : Psychology Press, c1999.
*TC P118 .P37 1999*

**CONTINUATION SCHOOLS.** *See* **EVENING AND CONTINUATION SCHOOLS.**

**CONTINUING CARE COMMUNITIES.** *See* **LIFE CARE COMMUNITIES.**

**CONTINUING CARE RETIREMENT COMMUNITIES.** *See* **LIFE CARE COMMUNITIES.**

**CONTINUING EDUCATION.** *See also* **ADULT EDUCATION; EVENING AND CONTINUATION SCHOOLS.**
Charting a course for continuing professional education :. San Francisco : Jossey-Bass, c2000.
*TC LC1072.C56 C55 2000*

Claxton, Guy. Wise up. 1st U.S. ed. New York, N.Y. : Bloomsbury : Distributed to the trade by St. Martin's Press, 1999.
*TC BF318 .C55 1999* ·

Collins, Michael, 1939- Critical crosscurrents in education. Original ed. Malabar, Fla. : Krieger Pub. Co., 1998.
*TC LC196 .C65 1998*

Knapper, Christopher. Lifelong learning in higher education. 3rd ed. London : Kogan Page, 2000.
*TC LC5215 .K593 2000*

Lifelong and continuing education :. Aldershot, Hants, England ; Brookfield, Vt. : Ashgate, c1999.
*TC LC5215 L464 1999*

Longworth, Norman. Making lifelong learning work. London : Kogan Page, 1999.
*TC LC5225.L42 L66 1999*

Miller, Estelle L. Fears expressed by female reentry students at an urban community college : qualitative study. 1997.
*TC 06 no. 10864*

Teare, Richard. The virtual university. London ; New York : Cassell, 1998.
*TC LC5215 .T42 1998*

The virtual learning organization. London ; New York : Continuum, 2000.
*TC LC5215 .V574 2000*

**CONTINUING EDUCATION - AUSTRALIA.**
Understanding adult education and training. 2nd ed. St. Leonards, NSW, Australia : Allen & Unwin, 2000.
*TC LC5259 U53 2000*

**CONTINUING EDUCATION - CASE STUDIES.**
Zersen, David John. Independent learning among clergy. 1998.
*TC 06 no. 11008*

**CONTINUING EDUCATION - ECONOMIC ASPECTS.**
Tuijnman, Albert. Recurrent education and socioeconomic success. [Stockholm] : Institute of International Education, University of Stockholm, c1986.
*TC LC5215 .T84 1986*

**CONTINUING EDUCATION - GREAT BRITAIN.**
Powell, Stuart, 1949- Returning to study. Buckingham ; Philadelphia : Open University Press, c1999.
*TC LC5256.G7 P66 1999*

**CONTINUING EDUCATION - INDIA.**
Staff development in higher and distance education. New Delhi : Aravali Books International, 1997.
*TC LB2331 .S692 1997*

**CONTINUING EDUCATION - LOUISIANA - SHREVEPORT.**
Baldwin, John. Education and welfare reform.

Bloomington, Ind. : Phi Delta Kappa Educational Foundation, c1993.
*TC LC4033.S61 B34 1993*

**CONTINUING EDUCATION - OECD COUNTRIES - CASE STUDIES.**
Motivating students for lifelong learning. Paris : Organisation for Economic Co-operation and Development, c2000.
*TC LB1065 .M669 2000*

**CONTINUING EDUCATION - PERIODICALS.**
Journal of continuing education and training. [Farmingdale, N.Y.] Baywood Pub. Co.

**CONTINUING EDUCATION - PHILOSOPHY.**
Lifelong and continuing education :. Aldershot, Hants, England ; Brookfield, Vt. : Ashgate, c1999.
*TC LC5215 L464 1999*

**CONTINUING EDUCATION - SOCIAL ASPECTS.**
Tuijnman, Albert. Recurrent education and socioeconomic success. [Stockholm] : Institute of International Education, University of Stockholm, c1986.
*TC LC5215 .T84 1986*

**CONTINUING EDUCATION - UNITED STATES - CONGRESSES.**
Postbaccalaureate futures. Phoenix, AZ : Oryx Press, 2000.
*TC LB2371.4 .P68 2000*

**CONTINUING EDUCATION - UNITED STATES - DIRECTORIES.**
The adult student's guide. Berkley trade pbk. ed. New York, N.Y. : Berkley Books, 1999.
*TC L901 .A494 1999*

**Continuous learning.**
Food for thought. Toronto, The Canadian Association for Adult Education.

**The Continuum encyclopedia of native art.**
Werness, Hope B. New York : Continuum, 2000.
*TC E98.A7 W49 2000*

**Continuum studies in pastoral care and personal and social education**
Education for spiritual, moral, social and cultural development. London : Continuum, 2000.
*TC LC268 .E384 2000*

**CONTRACEPTION.** *See also* **BIRTH CONTROL.**
Richardson, Bonnie. Factors influencing the sexual and contraceptive behavior of sexually abused adolescents of color. 1999.
*TC 06 no. 11167*

**Contraception across cultures :** : technologies, choices, constraints / edited by Andrew Russell, Elisa J. Sobo and Mary S. Thompson. Oxford ; New York : Berg, 2000. 224 p. : ill. ; 22 cm. (Cross-cultural perspectives on women, [v. 22].) Includes bibliographical references and index. ISBN 1-85973-381-6 ISBN 1-85973-386-7 (pbk.)
*1. Contraception - Social aspects. I. Thompson, Mary. II. Russell, Andrew. 1958- III. Sobo, Elisa Janine. 1963- IV. Series.*
*TC RG136 .C574 2000*

**CONTRACEPTION - SOCIAL ASPECTS.**
Contraception across cultures :. Oxford ; New York : Berg, 2000.
*TC RG136 .C574 2000*

**CONTRACT LABOR.** *See* **INDENTURED SERVANTS.**

**CONTRACTING OUT.** *See* **HUMAN SERVICES - CONTRACTING OUT; PRIVATIZATION; SOCIAL SERVICE - CONTRACTING OUT.**

**CONTRACTS.** *See* **ARTISTS' CONTRACTS; TEACHERS' CONTRACTS.**

**Contradictions of reform.**
McNeil, Linda M. Contradictions of school reform. New York : Routledge, 2000.
*TC LB3060.83 .M38 2000*

**Contradictions of school reform.**
McNeil, Linda M. New York : Routledge, 2000.
*TC LB3060.83 .M38 2000*

**Contrasts and effect sizes in behavioral research.**
Rosenthal, Robert, 1933- Cambridge, U.K. ; New York : Cambridge University Press, 2000.
*TC BF39.2.A52 R67 2000*

**Contreras, Josefina M., 1960-.**
Family and peers. Westport, Conn. : Praeger, 2000.
*TC HQ755.85 .F365 2000*

**The contribution of parents to school effectiveness.**
London : David Fulton Publishers, c2000. viii, 168 p. ; 24 cm. (Home and school -- a working alliance) Includes

bibliographical references and index. ISBN 1-85346-633-6 DDC 371.1
*1. Education - Parent participation - Great Britain. I. Wolfendale, Sheila.*
*TC LC225.33.G7 C66 2000*

**Contributions in Afro-American and African studies**
(no. 196) Hlatshwayo, Simphiwe A. (Simphiwe Abner) Education and independence. Westport, Conn : Greenwood Press, 2000.
*TC LA1536 .H53 2000*

(no. 200) Gordon, Jacob U. Black leadership for social change. Westport, Conn. : Greenwood Press, 2000.
*TC E185.615 .G666 2000*

**Contributions in drama and theatre studies**
(no. 5) Theatrical touring and founding in North America. Westport, Conn. : Greenwood Press, 1982.
*TC PN2219.5 .T5 1982*

**Contributions in philosophy**
(no. 63) Prado, C. G. The last choice. 2nd ed. Westport, Conn. : Greenwood Press, 1998.
*TC HV6545.2 .P7 1998*

**Contributions to the sociology of language**
(77) The multilingual Apple. Berlin ; New York : Mouton de Gruyter, 1997.
*TC P40.5.L56 M8 1997*

**Contributions to the study of education**
(no. 76) Berube, Maurice R. Eminent educators. Westport, Conn. : Greenwood Press, 2000.
*TC LB875.D5 B47 2000*

(no. 78) Acker, Victor, 1940- Célestin Freinet. Westport, CT : Greenwood Press, 2000.
*TC LB775 .A255 2000*

(no. 79) Reforming college composition. Westport, Conn. : Greenwood Press, 2000.
*TC PE1404 .R383 2000*

(no. 80) Lebow, Eileen F. The bright boys. Westport, Conn. : Greenwood Press, c2000.
*TC LD7501.N5 T692 2000*

**Contributions to the study of science fiction and fantasy**
(no. 79) Young adult science fiction. Westport, Conn. : Greenwood Press, 1999.
*TC PS374.S35 Y63 1999*

**CONTROL OF GUNS.** *See* **GUN CONTROL.**

**Control of human behavior, mental processes, and consciousness :** essays in honor of the 60th birthday of August Flammer / edited by Walter J. Perrig, Alexander Grob. Mahwah, N.J. : Lawrence Erlbaum Associates, c2000. xi, 603 p. : ill. ; 24 cm. Includes bibliographical references and indexes. ISBN 0-8058-2915-6 (hardcover : alk. paper) DDC 153
*1. Control (Psychology) 2. Self-control. 3. Perceptual control theory. 4. Human information processing. I. Flammer, August. II. Perrig, Walter J. III. Grob, Alexander, 1958-*
*TC BF611 .C67 2000*

**CONTROL (PSYCHOLOGY).** *See also* **SELF-CONTROL.**
Alper, Gerald. Power plays. San Francisco : International Scholars Publications, 1998.
*TC BF632.5 .A465 1998*

Control of human behavior, mental processes, and consciousness. Mahwah, N.J. : Lawrence Erlbaum Associates, c2000.
*TC BF611 .C67 2000*

Fisher, S. (Shirley) Stress and strategy. London ; Hillsdale, N.J. : Lawrence Erlbaum Associates, c1986.
*TC BF575.S75 F52 1986*

Halperin, Jane Carol. The influence of causal attributions on the psychological adjustment of post-treatment adolescent cancer survivors. 1999.
*TC 085 H155*

**Le controle des moisissures dans les museés.**
Strang, Thomas J. K. Controlling museum fungal problems. Ottawa : Canadian Conservation Institute, Department of Communications. [1991]
*TC TH9031 .S75 1991*

**CONTROLLED DRINKING.** *See* **ALCOHOLISM.**

**Controlling museum fungal problems.**
Strang, Thomas J. K. Ottawa : Canadian Conservation Institute, Department of Communications, [1991]
*TC TH9031 .S75 1991*

**Controlling public education.**
McDermott, Kathryn A., 1969- Lawrence : University Press of Kansas, c1999.

**Controversial issues in education**
Lockwood, Anne Turnbaugh. Standards. Thousand Oaks, Calif. : Corwin Press, c1998.
*TC LB3060.83 .L63 1998*

**CONURBATIONS.** See **METROPOLITAN AREAS.**

**CONVENTION FACILITIES.** See **CONGRESSES AND CONVENTIONS.**

**CONVENTIONS (CONGRESSES).** See **CONGRESSES AND CONVENTIONS.**

**CONVENTIONS, POLITICAL.** See **POLITICAL CONVENTIONS.**

**The convergence of race, ethnicity, and gender.**
Robinson, Tracy L. Upper Saddle River, N.J. : Merrill, c2000.
*TC BF637.C6 R583 2000*

**Converging methods for understanding reading and dyslexia** / edited by Raymond M. Klein and Patricia McMullen. Cambridge, Mass. ; London : MIT Press, c1999. xi, 524 p. : ill. ; 24 cm. ([Language, speech, and communication series]) Series statement on jacket. Includes bibliographical references and indexes. CONTENTS: Introduction: The Reading Brain / Raymond M. Klein and Patricia McMullen — Normal Adult Reading and Its Development. 1. What Have We Learned about Eye Movements during Reading? / Keith Rayner. 2. Integrating Orthographic and Phonological Knowledge as Reading Develops: Onsets, Rimes, and Analogies in Children's Reading / Usha Goswami. 3. Whole Words, Segments, and Meaning: Approaches to Reading Education / Betty Ann Levy -- Developmental Dyslexia. 4. Defining and Remediating the Core Deficits of Developmental Dyslexia: Lessons from Remedial Outcome Research with Reading Disabled Children / Maureen W. Lovett. 5. A Behavioral-Genetic Analysis of Reading Disabilities and Component Processes / Richard K. Olson, Helen Datta and Javier Gayan / [et al.] -- Acquired Dyslexia. 6. Pure Alexia: Underlying Mechanisms and Remediation / Marlene Behrmann. 7. Phonological Processing in Acquired Deep Dyslexia Reexamined / Lori Buchanan, Nancy Hildebrandt and G. E. MacKinnon. 8. Are there Orthography Specific Brain Regions? Neuropsychological and Computational Investigations / Martha J. Farah -- Brain Imaging of Reading Subprocesses. 9. Functional Neuroimaging of Word Processing in Normal and Dyslexic Readers / Jonthan B. Demb, Russell A. Poldrack and John D. E. Gabrieli. 10. Brain Circuitry during Reading / Michael I. Posner and Bruce D. McCandliss -- CONTENTS: Computational Modeling of Reading, Dyslexia, and Remediation. 11. Computation Modeling of Word Reading, Acquired Dyslexia, and Remediation / David C. Plaut. 12. Interactive Processes in Word Identification: Modeling Context Effects in a Distributed Memory System / Michael E. J. Masson. 13. Basic Processes in Reading: Multiple Routines in Localist and Connectionist Models / Derek Besner -- Integrating Themes in Reading Research. 14. Trying to Understand Reading and Dyslexia: Mental Chronometry, Individual Differences, Cognitive Neuroscience and the Impact of Instruction as Converging Sources of Evidence / Thomas H. Carr. ISBN 0-262-11247-7 (alk. paper) DDC 371.91/44 DDC 371.91/44
*1. Dyslexia. 2. Reading - Remedial teaching. I. Klein, Raymond M. II. McMullen, Patricia A. III. Series: Language, speech, and communication.*
*TC LB1050.5 .C662 1999*

**CONVERSATION.** See **INTERVIEWS.**

**Conversation analysis.**
Markee, Numa. Mahwah, N.J. : L. Erlbaum Associates, c2000.
*TC P95.45 .M35 2000*

**CONVERSATION ANALYSIS.**
Bond, Zinny S. (Zinny Sans), 1940- Slips of the ear. San Diego, Calif. ; London : Academic, c1999.
*TC P37.5.S67 B66 1999*

Bond, Zinny S. (Zinny Sans), 1940- Slips of the ear. San Diego, Calif. ; London : Academic, c1999.
*TC P37.5.S67 B66 1999*

Coates, Jennifer. Women talk. Oxford, U.K. ; Cambridge, Mass. : Blackwell Publishers, 1996.
*TC P120.W66 C6 1996*

Jones, Carl Mounsey. The film-audience relationship. 1997.
*TC 06 no. 10769*

Jones, Carl Mounsey. The film-audience relationship. 1997.
*TC 06 no. 10769*

Markee, Numa. Conversation analysis. Mahwah, N.J. : L. Erlbaum Associates, c2000.

*TC P95.45 .M35 2000*
Svennevig, Jan. Getting acquainted in conversation. Amsterdam : Philadelphia : J. Benjamins Pub. Co., c1999.
*TC P95.45 .S89 1999*

**CONVERSATION ANALYSIS - JAPAN.**
Tanaka, Hiroko. Turn-taking in Japanese conversation. Amsterdam : Philadelphia, PA : John Benjamins Pub. Co., c1999.
*TC PL640.5 .T36 1999*

**Conversations.**
Routman, Regie. Portsmouth, NH : Heinemann, c2000.
*TC LB1576 .R757 1999*

**CONVICTION.** See **BELIEF AND DOUBT.**

**CONVULSIONS.** See **EPILEPSY.**

**CONWAY, MONCURE DANIEL, 1832-1907.**
Dickinson College. The Spahr lectures, Dickinson College, Carlisle, Pa., : Dickinson College 1970.
*TC LD1663 .A5 1970*

**Conwill, Kinshasha Holman.**
Race, ethnicity and culture in the visual arts. New York : American Council for the Arts, c1993.
*TC N70 .R32 1993*

**Conyers, James E., 1932-** Black elected officials : a study of Black Americans holding governmental office / James E. Conyers, Walter L. Wallace. New York : Russell Sage Foundation, c1976. xii, 190 p. ; 24 cm. Bibliography: p. 161-162. Includes index. ISBN 0-87154-206-4 DDC 320.9/73/092
*1. Afro-Americans - Politics and government. 2. United States - Politics and government - 1945-1989. 3. Local officials and employees - United States. I. Wallace, Walter L., joint author. II. Title.*
*TC JK1924 .C65*

**Coogan, David.** Electronic writing centers : computing the field of composition / by David Coogan. Stamford, Conn. : Ablex Pub. Corp., c1999. xxi, 146 p. ; 24 cm. (New directions in computers and composition studies) Includes bibliographical references (p. 133-140) and indexes. ISBN 1-56750-428-0 (cloth) ISBN 1-56750-429-9 (pbk.) DDC 808/.042/0785
*1. English language - Rhetoric - Study and teaching - Data processing. 2. English language - Composition and exercises - Data processing. 3. Report writing - Study and teaching - Data processing. 4. English language - Computer-assisted instruction. 5. Report writing - Computer-assisted instruction. 6. Writing centers - Automation. I. Title. II. Series.*
*TC PE1404 .C6347 1999*

**COOK-BOOKS.** See **COOKERY.**

**Cook, Deirdre, 1943-** Interactive children, communicative teaching : ICT and classroom teaching / Deirdre Cook and Helen Finlayson. Buckingham [England] ; Philadelphia : Open University Press, 1999. xv, 142 p. : ill. ; 23 cm. (Enriching the primary curriculum--child, teacher, context) Includes bibliographical references (p. [132]-137) and index. ISBN 0-335-20021-4 (hbk.) ISBN 0-335-20020-6 (pbk.) DDC 371.33/4
*1. Computer-assisted instruction. 2. Information technology. 3. Telecommunication in education. I. Finlayson, Helen, 1945- II. Title. III. Series.*
*TC LB1028.46 .C686 1999*

**Cook, Gary, 1951-** Teaching percussion / Gary Cook. 2nd ed. New York : Schirmer Books : London : Prentice Hall International, c1997. xxiv, 499 p. : ill. ; 28 cm. Discography: p. 439-444. Includes bibliographical references (p. 491-493) and index. ISBN 0-02-870191-7 (alk. paper) DDC 786.8/07
*1. Percussion instruments - Instruction and study. I. Title.*
*TC MT655 .C67 1997*

**Cook, Gillian Elizabeth, 1934-.**
Martinello, Marian L. Interdisciplinary inquiry in teaching and learning. 2nd. ed. Upper Saddle River, N.J. : Merrill, c2000.
*TC LB1570 .M3675 2000*

**Cook-Greuter, Susanne R.**
Creativity, spirituality, and transcendence. Stamford, Conn. : Ablex, c2000.
*TC BF411 .C76 2000*

**Cook, Guy.**
Principle & practice in applied linguistics. Oxford : Oxford University Press, 1995.
*TC P129 .P75 1995*

**Cook, Haruko M.**
New trends & issues in teaching Japanese language & culture. Honolulu ; Second Language Teaching and Curriculum, University of Hawai'i at Manoa, 1997.

*TC PL519 .N45 1997*

**Cook, Lynne.**
Friend, Marilyn Penovich, 1953- Interactions. 3rd ed. New York : Longman, 1999.
*TC LC3969.45 .F75 1999*

**Cook, Ruth E.** Adapting early childhood curricula for children in inclusive settings / Ruth E. Cook, Annette Tessier, M. Diane Klein. 5th ed. Englewood Cliffs, N.J. : Merrill, c2000. xvi, 477 p. : ill. ; 24 cm. Includes bibliographical references and indexes. ISBN 0-13-083201-4 DDC 371.9/0472
*1. Handicapped children - Education (Preschool) 2. Handicapped children - Education (Preschool) - Curricula. 3. Mainstreaming in education. I. Tessier, Annette. II. Klein, M. Diane. III. Title.*
*TC LC4019.2 .C66 2000*

**Cook, V. J. (Vivian James), 1940-** Chomsky's universal grammar : an introduction / Vivian Cook and Mark Newson. 2nd [updated] ed. Oxford, OX, UK ; Cambridge, Mass., USA : Blackwell Publishers, 1996. vii, 369 p. : ill. ; 23 cm. Includes bibliographical references (p. [351]-362) and index. ISBN 0-631-19796-6 (acid-free paper) ISBN 0-631-19556-4 (pbk. : acid-free paper) DDC 415
*1. Chomsky, Noam. 2. Grammar, Comparative and general. 3. Generative grammar. 4. Principles and parameters (Linguistics) 5. Government-binding theory (Linguistics) 6. Language acquisition. 7. Minimalist theory (Linguistics) I. Newson, Mark. II. Title.*
*TC P85.C47 C66 1996*

**COOKBOOKS.** See **COOKERY.**

**Cooke, Alison.** Neal-Schuman authoritative guide to evaluating information on the Internet / Alison Cooke. New York : Neal-Schuman Publishers, c1999. ix, 169 p. : ill. ; 28 cm. (Neal-Schuman netguide series) Spine title: Authoritative guide to evaluating information on the Internet. Includes bibliographical references (p. [135]-152) and index. ISBN 1-55570-356-9 DDC 025.04
*1. Computer network resources - Evaluation. 2. Computer network resources - United States - Evaluation. I. Title. II. Title: Authoritative guide to evaluating information on the Internet III. Series: Neal-Schuman net-guide series.*
*TC ZA4201 .C66 1999*

**COOKERY.** See **BAKING; DINNERS AND DINING; FOOD; SOUPS.**

**COOKERY (BEAR MEAT).** See **BEARS.**

**COOKERY (BREAD).** See **BREAD.**

**COOKERY, BRITISH.** See also **COOKERY, ENGLISH.**
Burton, David, 1952- The Raj at table. London ; Boston : Faber, 1994.
*TC TX724.5.14 B87 1993*

Lane, Margaret, 1907- The Beatrix Potter country cookery book. London : F. Warne, 1981.
*TC TX717 .L355 1981*

**COOKERY (DUCK).** See **DUCKS.**

**COOKERY - ENCYCLOPEDIAS.**
Davidson, Alan, 1924- The Oxford companion to food. Oxford : Oxford University Press, 1999.
*TC TX349 .D38 1999*

Davidson, Alan, 1924- The Oxford companion to food. Oxford : Oxford University Press, 1999.
*TC TX349 .D38 1999*

**COOKERY, ENGLISH.**
Cotler, Amy. The secret garden cookbook. 1st ed. New York : HarperCollins Publishers, c1999.
*TC TX717 .C588 1999*

**COOKERY, ENGLISH - JUVENILE LITERATURE.**
Cotler, Amy. The secret garden cookbook. 1st ed. New York : HarperCollins Publishers, c1999.
*TC TX717 .C588 1999*

**COOKERY (FLOWERS).** See **FLOWERS.**

**COOKERY (HARES).** See **HARES.**

**COOKERY, INDIC.**
Burton, David, 1952- The Raj at table. London ; Boston : Faber, 1994.
*TC TX724.5.14 B87 1993*

**COOKERY, INTERNATIONAL.**
Webb, Lois Sinaiko. Multicultural cookbook of life-cycle celebrations. Phoenix, AZ : Oryx Press, 2000.
*TC TX725.A1 W43 2000*

**COOKERY (MEAT).** See **MEAT.**

**COOKERY, MEDIEVAL - JUVENILE LITERATURE.**

Martell, Hazel. Food & feasts with the Vikings. Parsippany, N.J. : New Discovery Books, c1995.
*TC DL65 .M359 1995*

**COOKERY (MILK).** *See* **MILK.**

**COOKERY (PASTA).** *See* **PASTA PRODUCTS.**

**COOKERY (PEANUT BUTTER).** *See* **PEANUT BUTTER.**

**COOKERY (PEANUTS).** *See* **PEANUTS.**

**COOKERY - PERIODICALS.**
The Boston Cooking School magazine of culinary science and domestic economics. Boston : Boston Cooking-School Magazine, [1896]-1914.

**COOKERY (POTATOES).** *See* **POTATOES.**

**COOKERY (RABBITS).** *See* **RABBITS.**

**COOKERY, SCANDINAVIAN.**
Martell, Hazel. Food & feasts with the Vikings. Parsippany, N.J. : New Discovery Books, c1995.
*TC DL65 .M359 1995*

**COOKERY (VEGETABLES).** *See* **VEGETABLES.**

**COOKERY, VIKING - JUVENILE LITERATURE.**
Martell, Hazel. Food & feasts with the Vikings. Parsippany, N.J. : New Discovery Books, c1995.
*TC DL65 .M359 1995*

**COOKERY (WHEAT).** *See* **WHEAT.**

**COOKING.** *See* **COOKERY.**

**Cooks, Roberta.**
When the brain goes wrong [videorecording]. Short version. Boston, MA : Fanlight Productions [dist.], c1992.
*TC RC386 .W54 1992*

**Cookson, Peter W.**
Sadovnik, Alan R. Exploring education. Boston : Allyn and Bacon, c1994.
*TC LB17 .S113 1994*

Sadovnik, Alan R. Exploring education. 2nd ed. Boston : Allyn and Bacon, 2000.
*TC LA217.2 . S23 2000*

**Cooley, Sandra M.**
The developmental process of positive attitudes and mutual respect. Lewiston, N.Y. : E. Mellen Press, c1999.
*TC LB2822.82 .D49 1999*

**Coombe, Kennece, 1954-.**
Learning communities in education. London ; New York : Routledge, 1999.
*TC LB14.7 .L43 1999*

**Coombes, Yolande.**
Evaluating health promotion. Oxford ; New York : Oxford University Press, 2000.
*TC RA427.8 .E95 2000*

**Coomes, Michael D., 1951-.**
The role student aid plays in enrollment management. San Francisco : Jossey-Bass Publishers, 2000.
*TC LB2337.4 .R655 2000*

**Cooney, Caroline B.** Burning up : a novel/ by Caroline B. Cooney. New York : Delacorte Press, c1999. 230 p. ; 22 cm. SUMMARY: When a girl she had met at an innercity church is murdered, fifteen-year-old Macey channels her grief into a school project that leads her to uncover prejudice she had not imagined in her grandparents and their wealthy Connecticut community. ISBN 0-385-32318-2 DDC [Fic]
*1. Racism - Fiction. I. Title.*
*TC PZ7.C7834 Bu 1999*

Tune in anytime / Caroline B. Cooney. New York : Delacorte Press, 1999. 186 p. ; 18 cm. SUMMARY: When Sophie's father suddenly decides to divorce Sophie's mother and marry her sister Marley's college roommate, Sophie feels like she is trapped in an endless soap opera. ISBN 0-385-32649-1 DDC [Fic]
*1. Divorce - Fiction. 2. Family problems - Fiction. 3. Parent and child - Fiction. I. Title.*
*TC PZ7.C7834 Tu 1999*

**Coontz, Stephanie.** The way we never were : American families and the nostalgia trap / Stephanie Coontz. New York, NY : BasicBooks, c1992. viii, 391 p. ; 24 cm. Includes bibliographical references (p. [377]-379) and index. ISBN 0-465-00135-1 DDC 306.85/0973
*1. Family - United States - History - 20th century. 2. United States - Social conditions. 3. Nostalgia. I. Title.*
*TC HQ535 .C643 1992*

**Cooper, Barry, 1950-** Assessing children's mathematical knowledge : social class, sex, and problem-solving / Barry Cooper and Mairead Dunne. Buckingham ; Philadelphia : Open University Press,

2000. xv, 215 p. : ill. ; 23 cm. Includes bibliographical references (p. [206]-212) and index. ISBN 0-335-20317-5 (HB) ISBN 0-335-20316-7 (PB) DDC 372.7/0942
*1. Mathematics - Study and teaching (Elementary) - England - Evaluation. 2. Mathematics - Study and teaching (Elementary) - England - Social aspects. 3. Mathematical ability - Sex differences. I. Dunne, Mairéad. II. Title.*
*TC QA135.5 .C5955 2000*

**Cooper, Bruce S.**
Accuracy or advocacy. Thousand Oaks, Calif. : Corwin Press, c1999.
*TC LB1028 .A312 1999*

**Cooper, Cary L.**
Industrial and organizational psychology. Oxford, UK ; Malden, Mass. : Blackwell Business, 2000.
*TC HF5548.8 .I5233 2000*

**Cooper, Cathie Hilterbran, 1953-** Color and shape books for all ages / by Cathie Hilterbran Cooper. Lanham, Md. ; London : Scarecrow Press, 2000. 129 p. : ill., forms ; 28 cm. (School library media series ; no. 18) Includes bibliographical references (p. 117-118) and index. ISBN 0-8108-3542-8 (alk. paper) DDC 535.6/071/073
*1. Color - Study and teaching (Elementary) - Activity programs - United States. 2. Geometry - Study and teaching (Elementary) - Activity programs - United States. 3. Color - Juvenile literature - Bibliography. 4. Geometry - Juvenile literature - Bibliography. I. Title. II. Series.*
*TC QC496 .C66 2000*

**Cooper, Emmanuel.** Fully exposed : the male nude in photography / Emmanuel Cooper. 2nd ed. London ; New York : Routledge, c1995. 296 p. : ill. ; 26 cm. Male nude in photography. Includes bibliographical references and index. ISBN 0-415-03279-2 (hc) ISBN 0-415-03280-6 (pbk.) DDC 778.9/23
*1. Photography of the nude - History. 2. Photography of men - History. 3. Male nude in art. I. Title. II. Title: Male nude in photography*
*TC TR674 .C66 1995*

**Cooper, Floyd, ill.**
Littlesugar, Amy. Tree of hope. New York : Philomel Books, 1999.
*TC PZ7.L7362 Tr 1999*

Thomas, Joyce Carol. I have heard of a land. 1st ed. [New York] : HarperCollins Publishers, c1998.
*TC PZ7.T36696 Iae 1998*

**Cooper, Ilay.** Traditional buildings of India / Ilay Cooper, Barry Dawson. New York : Thames and Hudson, c1998. 192 p. : ill. (some col.) ; 26 cm. Includes bibliographical references (p. 186-188) and index. ISBN 0-500-34161-3 DDC 720/.954
*1. Architecture - India. 2. Vernacular architecture - India. I. Dawson, Barry. II. Title.*
*TC NA1501 .C58 1998*

**Cooper, J. David (James David), 1942-** Discover : teacher's book : a resource for planning and teaching. Grade 1, level 1.5, [Themes 9 and 10] / senior authors J. David Cooper, John J. Pikulski ; authors Kathryn H. Au ... [et al.]. Boston : Houghton Mifflin, 1997. T428, H29 p. : col. ill. ; 31 cm. + 4 cassettes, 6 booklets, 1 anthology. (Invitations to literacy) Cover title: Houghton Mifflin teacher's book: a resource for planning and teaching. Includes bibliographical references and index. CONTENTS: Theme 9. Family treasures: [bk. 1]. On mother's lap -- [bk. 1a]. On mother's lap: teacher's resource -- [bk. 2]. A mother for Choco. CONTENTS: Theme 10. Something fishy: [bk. 3]. Fishy facts -- [bk. 4]. Is this a house for hermit crab? -- [bk. 4a]. Is this a house for hermit crab: teacher's resource. ISBN 0-395-79555-9
*1. Language arts (Elementary) 2. Reading (Elementary) 3. Literature - Study and teaching (Elementary) I. Pikulski. John J. II. Au, Kathryn Hu-Pei. III. Title. IV. Title: Teacher's book : a resource for planning and teaching. level 1.5 V. Title: Houghton Mifflin teacher's book: a resource for planning and teaching VI. Series.*
*TC LB1575.8 .C6616 1997*

Literacy : helping children construct meaning / J. David Cooper ; with an introduction by Kathryn H. Au. 4th ed. Boston : Houghton Mifflin Co., c2000. xxii, 617 p. : ill. (some col.) ; 24 cm. Includes bibliographical references (p. 585-601) and indexes. ISBN 0-395-96132-7 (pbk.) DDC 372.4
*1. Reading comprehension. 2. Reading. 3. Literacy. I. Title.*
*TC LB1050.45 .C76 2000*

**Cooper, Jeremy.**
On pictures and paintings [videorecording]. Peasmarsh, East Sussex, Eng. ; Ho-Ho-kus, NJ : Roland Collection, 1992.
*TC ND195.O45 1992*

**Cooper, Joanne E.**
Indigenous educational models for contemporary practice. Mahwah, N.J. : L. Erlbaum Associates, 2000.

*TC LC3719 .I53 2000*

**Cooper, Paul. 1955-.**
ADHD :. London : Whurr, c1999.
*TC RJ506.H9 A32 1999*

**Cooperating teachers' perceptions of the nature and quality of professional development in a professional development school collaboration.**
Lawrence, Alexandria Teresa. 1999.
*TC 06 no. 11141*

Lawrence, Alexandria Teresa. 1999.
*TC 06 no. 11141*

Lawrence, Alexandria Teresa. 1999.
*TC 06 no. 11141*

**COOPERATION.** *See* **COLLECTIVE SETTLEMENTS; INTERNATIONAL COOPERATION; INTERPROFESSIONAL RELATIONS; PUBLIC-PRIVATE SECTOR COOPERATION.**

**Cooperation among animals.**
Allee, W. C. (Warder Clyde), 1885-1955. [Social life of animals] A rev. and amplified ed. of The social life of animals. New York : Schuman, 1951.
*TC QL751 .A52 1951*

**COOPERATION BETWEEN HEALTH FACILITIES.** *See* **HEALTH FACILITIES - AFFILIATIONS.**

**COOPERATION, COLLEGE-SCHOOL.** *See* **COLLEGE-SCHOOL COOPERATION.**

**COOPERATION, INTELLECTUAL.** *See* **INTELLECTUAL COOPERATION.**

**Coopération intellectuelle (Paris, France : 1929).**
League of Nations. Bulletin de la coopération intellectuelle. Paris : Institut international de coopération intellectuelle, [1931?-1932?]

**COOPERATION, INTERNATIONAL.** *See* **INTERNATIONAL COOPERATION.**

**COOPERATION (PSYCHOLOGY).** *See* **COOPERATIVENESS.**

**COOPERATIVE LEARNING.** *See* **GROUP WORK IN EDUCATION.**

**COOPERATIVE LIVING.** *See* **COMMUNAL LIVING.**

**COOPERATIVENESS - UNITED STATES.**
Learning circles. Thousand Oaks, Calif. : Corwin Press, c1998.
*TC LB1032 .L355 1998*

**Coordinating assessment practice across the primary school.**
Wintle, Mike. London ; Philadelphia, PA : Falmer Press, 1999.
*TC LB3060.37 .W56 1999*

**Coordinator.**
The Family life coordinator. Eugene, Ore. : E. C. Brown Trust Foundation.

**Cooter, Robert B.**
Reutzel, D. Ray (Douglas Ray), 1953- Balanced reading strategies and practices. Upper Saddle river, N.J. : Merrill, c1999.
*TC LB1050 .R477 1999*

**Cope, Bill.**
Multiliteracies. London ; New York : Routledge, 2000.
*TC LC149 .M85 2000*

**Copeland, James E.**
Lockwood, David G. Functional approaches to language, culture, and cognition. Amsterdam ; Philadelphia : J. Benjamins, c2000.
*TC P147 .L63 1998*

**COPING BEHAVIOR.** *See* **ADJUSTMENT (PSYCHOLOGY).**

**Coping strategies and stage of change among Vietnam combat veterans diagnosed with posttraumatic stress disorder and comorbid substance use disorders.**
Gewirtz, Abigail Hadassah. 1997.
*TC 085 G338*

**Coping strategies and stage of change among Vietnam combat veterans diagnosed with posttraumatic stress disorder and comorbid substance use disorders [microform].**
Gewirtz, Abigail Hadassah. 1997.

**Coping strategies therapy for bulimia nervosa.**
Tobin, David L. Washington, DC : American Psychological Association, c2000.

*TC RC552.B84 T63 2000*

**Coppens, Patrick, 1944-.**
Aphasia in atypical populations. Mahwah, N.J. : Lawrence Erlbaum Associates, 1998.
*TC RC425 .A637 1998*

**Copple, Carol.**
Developmentally appropriate practice in early childhood programs. Rev. ed. Washington, D.C. : National Association for the Education of Young Children, 1997.
*TC LB1139.25 .D48 1997*

**COPYRIGHT AND ELECTRONIC DATA PROCESSING - UNITED STATES.**
The digital dilemma. Washington, D.C. : National Academy Press, c2000.
*TC KF2979 .D53 2000*

**Copyright duration.**
Bard, Robert L. San Fransisco : Austin & Winfield, 1999.
*TC KF3010 .B37 1999*

**COPYRIGHT - DURATION - UNITED STATES.**
Bard, Robert L. Copyright duration. San Fransisco : Austin & Winfield, 1999.
*TC KF3010 .B37 1999*

**COPYRIGHT - FAIR USE.** *See* **FAIR USE (COPYRIGHT).**

**COPYRIGHT INFRINGEMENT.** *See* **COPYRIGHT AND ELECTRONIC DATA PROCESSING; FAIR USE (COPYRIGHT).**

**COPYRIGHT - LAW AND LEGISLATION.** *See* **COPYRIGHT.**

**COPYRIGHT - RENEWAL.** *See* **COPYRIGHT - DURATION.**

**COPYRIGHT - UNITED STATES - POPULAR WORKS.**
Talab, R. S., 1948- Commonsense copyright. 2nd ed. Jefferson, N.C. : McFarland & Co., 1999.
*TC KF2994 .T36 1999*

**Coquery-Vidrovitch, Catherine.**
[Africaines. English]
African women : a modern history / Catherine Coquery-Vidrovitch ; translated by Beth Gillian Raps. Boulder, Colo. : WestviewPress, 1997. xviii, 308 p. : ill. ; map ; 24 cm. (Social change in global perspective) Includes bibliographical references (p. 265-285) and index. ISBN 0-8133-2360-6 (hardcover) ISBN 0-8133-2361-4 DDC 305.4/0967
*1. Women - Africa, Sub-Saharan - History - 19th century. 2. Women - Africa, Sub-Saharan - History - 20th century. I. Title. II. Series.*
*TC HQ1787 .C6613 1997*

**Corbett, Edward P. J.**
The writing teacher's sourcebook. 4th ed. New York : Oxford University Press, 2000.
*TC PE1404 .W74 2000*

**Corboz-Warnery, Antoinette.**
Fivaz-Depeursinge, Elisabeth. The primary triangle :. New York : Basic Books, c1999.
*TC HQ755.85 .F583 1999*

**Corcoran, Kevin (Kevin J.)** Measures for clinical practice : a sourcebook / Kevin Corcoran, Joel Fischer. 3rd ed. New York : London : Free Press, c2000. 2 v. : forms ; 25 cm. CONTENTS: v. 1. Couples, families, and children -- v. 2. Adults. ISBN 0-684-84830-9 (v. 1) ISBN 0-684-84831-7 (v. 2) DDC 150/.28/7
*1. Psychological tests. I. Fischer, Joel. II. Title.*
*TC BF176 .C66 2000*

**CORDAGE.** *See* **STRING.**

**Cordeiro, Paula A.**
Cunningham, William G. Educational administration. Boston : London : Allyn & Bacon, c2000.
*TC LB1738.5 .C86 2000*

**Cordes, Anne K.**
Treatment efficacy for stuttering. San Diego, Calif. : Singular Pub. Group, c1998.
*TC RC424 .T698 1998*

**Corduroy.**
Freeman, Don. Harmondsworth, Middlesex : New York : Puffin Books, 1976.
*TC PZ8.9.F85 C5 1976*

**CORE CURRICULUM.** *See* **EDUCATION - CURRICULA.**

**The core knowledge series**
Hirsch, E. D. (Eric Donald), 1928- Books to build on. New York : Delta, 1996.

*TC Z1037 .H646 1996*

**The Core knowledge series**
(bk. 5) What your fifth grader needs to know. New York : Doubleday, c1993.
*TC LB1571 5th .W43 1993*

**Core knowledge series**
(bk. 6) What your sixth grader needs to know. New York : Doubleday, c1993.
*TC LB1571 6th .W43 1993*

**Core texts in conversation** / edited by Jane Kelley Rodeheffer, David Sokolowski, J. Scott Lee ; Association for Core Texts and Courses. Lanham, MD : University Press of America, 2000. xviii, 203 p. ; 24 cm. Includes bibliographical references. ISBN 0-7618-1679-8 (pbk. : alk. paper) DDC 378.1/99/0973
*1. Universities and colleges - United States - Curricula. 2. Education, Higher - United States - Curricula. 3. Postmodernism and education. I. Rodeheffer, Jane Kelley. II. Sokolowski, David. III. Lee, J. Scott, 1948- IV. Association for Core Texts and Courses.*
*TC LB2361.5 .C68 2000*

**CORETTA SCOTT KING AWARD.**
The Coretta Scott King awards book, 1970-1999. Chicago : American Library Association, 1999.
*TC Z1037.A2 C67 1999*

**The Coretta Scott King awards book, 1970-1999** / edited by Henrietta M. Smith. Chicago : American Library Association, 1999. xii, 135 p., [16] p. of plates : ill. (some col.) ; 28 cm. (ALA editions) Includes index. ISBN 0-8389-3496-X (alk. paper) DDC 016.8108/09282/08996073
*1. Coretta Scott King Award. 2. Children's literature, American - Afro-American authors - Bibliography. 3. Children's literature, American - Afro-American authors - Awards. 4. Afro-Americans in literature - Bibliography. I. Smith, Henrietta M. II. Series.*
*TC Z1037.A2 C67 1999*

**Corey, Gerald.** Theory and practice of counseling and psychotherapy / Gerald Corey. 6th ed. Stamford, Conn : Brooks/Cole, 2000. xvii, 556 p. : ill. ; 25 cm. Includes bibliographical references and index. ISBN 0-534-34823-8 (alk. paper) DDC 158/.3
*1. Counseling. 2. Psychotherapy. I. Title.*
*TC BF637.C6 C574 2000*

**Cornbleth, Catherine.**
Curriculum politics, policy, practice. Albany : State University of New York Press, c2000.
*TC LC71.3 .C87 2000*

**Cornelius, Janet Duitsman.** Slave missions and the Black church in the antebellum South / Janet Duitsman Cornelius. Columbia : University of South Carolina Press, c1999. x, 305 p. : ill. ; 24 cm. Includes bibliographical references (p. 253-284) and index. ISBN 1-57003-247-5 DDC 277.5/081/08996073
*1. Slavery and the church - Southern States - History - 19th century. 2. Slaves - Religious life - Southern States - History - 19th century. 3. Afro-Americans - Southern States - Religion - History - 19th century. 4. Afro-American churches - Southern States - History - 19th century. 5. Southern States - Church history - 19th century. 6. Southern States - History - 1775-1865. I. Title.*
*TC E449 .C82 1999*

**Cornell studies in the history of psychiatry**
Dreams 1900-2000. Binghamton : Cornell University Press : Binghamton University Art Museum, State University of New York, 2000.
*TC BF1078 .D729 2000*

**Cornerstone for nursing education.**
Christy, Teresa E. New York : Teachers College Press, Columbia University, [1969]
*TC RT81.N3 C45*

**CORNET AND PIANO MUSIC (JAZZ).** *See* **JAZZ.**

**Cornett, Claudia E.** The arts as meaning makers : integrating literature and the arts throughout the curriculum / Claudia E. Cornett. Upper Saddle River, N.J. : Merrill, 1999. viii, 456 p. : ill. ; 26 cm. Includes bibliographical references and index. ISBN 0-13-792920-X DDC 372.64
*1. Arts - Study and teaching. 2. Literature - Study and teaching. 3. Interdisciplinary approach in education. I. Title. II. Title: Integrating literature and the arts throughout the curriculum*
*TC LB1591 .C67 1999*

**Cornfield, Robert.**
Denby, Edwin, 1903- Dance writings & poetry. New Haven [CT] : Yale University Press, c1998.
*TC GV1599 .D393 1998*

**CORONARY ARTERIES - DISEASES.** *See* **CORONARY HEART DISEASE.**

**CORONARY ARTERIOSCLEROSIS.** *See* **CORONARY HEART DISEASE.**

**CORONARY DISEASE.** *See* **CORONARY HEART DISEASE.**

**CORONARY HEART DISEASE - ALTERNATIVE TREATMENT.**
DeFelice, Stephen L., 1936- The carnitine defense. [Emmaus, Pa.] : Rodale Press ; [New York] : Distributed to the book trade by St. Martin's Press, c1999.
*TC RC685.C6 D4235 1999*

**CORONARY HEART DISEASE - PREVENTION.**
DeFelice, Stephen L., 1936- The carnitine defense. [Emmaus, Pa.] : Rodale Press ; [New York] : Distributed to the book trade by St. Martin's Press, c1999.
*TC RC685.C6 D4235 1999*

**CORONARY THROMBOSIS.** *See* **CORONARY HEART DISEASE.**

**CORPORATE ACCOUNTABILITY.** *See* **SOCIAL RESPONSIBILITY OF BUSINESS.**

**CORPORATE CULTURE.**
Bazigos, Michael Nicholas. The relationship of upward feedback disparities to leader performance. 1999.
*TC 085 B33*

Collins, David, 1966- Organizational change. New York : Routledge, 1998.
*TC HD58.8 .C642 1998*

**CORPORATE EDUCATION.** *See* **EMPLOYER-SUPPORTED EDUCATION.**

**CORPORATE GIVING.** *See* **CORPORATIONS - CHARITABLE CONTRIBUTIONS.**

**CORPORATE INTELLIGENCE.** *See* **BUSINESS INTELLIGENCE.**

**CORPORATE MANAGEMENT.** *See* **INDUSTRIAL MANAGEMENT.**

**CORPORATE OFFICERS.** *See* **EXECUTIVES.**

**Corporate Productions.**
Bridges to independence [videorecording. Burbank, CA : RCA/Columbia Pictures Home Video ; [S.l.] : Distributed by] Rank Video Services Production, c1991.
*TC HV1646 .B7 1991*

Bright beginnings [videorecording. Burbank, CA : RCA/Columbia Pictures Home Video ; Toluca Lake, CA : [Distributed by] Corporate Productions, c1991.
*TC HV1642 .B67 1991*

Bright beginnings [videorecording. Burbank, CA : RCA/Columbia Pictures Home Video ; [S.l.] : Distributed by] Rank Video Services America, c1991.
*TC HV1642 .B67 1991*

Brighter visions [videorecording. Burbank, CA : RCA/Columbia Pictures Home Video ; Toluca Lake, CA : [Distributed by] Corporate Productions, c1991.
*TC HV1597.5 .B67 1991*

Touch 'n' go [videorecording. Burbank, Calif. : Columbia Tristar Home Video ; [S.l. : Distributed by] Rank Video Services Production, c1991.
*TC HV1626 .T6 1991*

**CORPORATE RESPONSIBILITY.** *See* **SOCIAL RESPONSIBILITY OF BUSINESS.**

**CORPORATE SOCIAL RESPONSIBILITY.** *See* **SOCIAL RESPONSIBILITY OF BUSINESS.**

**CORPORATION EXECUTIVES.** *See* **EXECUTIVES.**

**CORPORATIONS.** *See* **INTERNATIONAL BUSINESS ENTERPRISES.**

**CORPORATIONS - ART PATRONAGE.** *See* **ART PATRONAGE.**

**CORPORATIONS, BUSINESS.** *See* **CORPORATIONS.**

**CORPORATIONS - CHARITABLE CONTRIBUTIONS - UNITED STATES.**
Grants for schools. 4th ed. Gaithersburg, MD : Aspen Publishers, 2000.
*TC LB2825 .F46 2000*

**CORPORATIONS, INTERNATIONAL.** *See* **INTERNATIONAL BUSINESS ENTERPRISES.**

**CORPORATIONS - MANAGEMENT.** *See* **INDUSTRIAL MANAGEMENT.**

167

EDUCATION: 2000
Council of Church Boards of Education in the United States of America.

**CORPORATIONS, NONPROFIT.** See NONPROFIT ORGANIZATIONS.

**CORPORATIONS, NONPROFIT - UNITED STATES - MANAGEMENT.**
Crimmins, James C. Enterprise in the nonprofit sector. Washington, D.C. : Partners for Livable Places ; New York : Rockefeller Bros. Fund, c1983.
*TC HD62.6 .C74 1983*

**CORPORATIONS - PERSONNEL MANAGEMENT.** See PERSONNEL MANAGEMENT.

**CORPORATIONS, PUBLIC.** See CORPORATIONS.

**CORPORATIONS - SOCIAL RESPONSIBILITY.** See SOCIAL RESPONSIBILITY OF BUSINESS.

**Corporealities**
Defects. Ann Arbor : University of Michigan Press, c2000.
*TC HV1568.25.G7 D44 1999*

**CORPULENCE.** See OBESITY.

**CORRECTIONS.** See JUVENILE CORRECTIONS.

**CORRECTIVE TEACHING.** See REMEDIAL TEACHING.

**CORRELATION OF LANGUAGE ARTS WITH CONTENT SUBJECTS.** See LANGUAGE ARTS - CORRELATION WITH CONTENT SUBJECTS.

**CORRELATION (STATISTICS).** See CLUSTER ANALYSIS.

**CORRESPONDENCE.** See LETTERS.

**The correspondence of John Dewey. [computer file].**
Dewey, John, 1859-1952. Windows version. Charlottesville, VA : InteLex Corp., 1999- Computer data and program.
*TC B945.D44 A4 1999*

**The Corsini encyclopedia of psychology and behavioral science** / edited by W. Edward Craighead, Charles B. Nemeroff. 3rd ed. New York : Wiley, 2000. 4v. : ill. ; 29 cm. Rev. ed. of: Encyclopedia of psychology. 2nd. ed. c1994. Includes bibliographical references and indexes. ISBN 0-471-23949-6 (hardcover : set : alk. paper) DDC 150/.3
*1. Psychology - Encyclopedias. I. Craighead, W. Edward. II. Nemeroff, Charles B. III. Title: Encyclopedia of psychology.*
*TC BF31 .E52 2000*

**Corsini, Raymond J.** The dictionary of psychology / Raymond J. Corsini. Philadelphia, PA : Brunner/ Mazel, Taylor & Francis, c1999. xv, 1156 p. : ill. ; 27 cm. ISBN 1-58391-028-X (alk. paper) DDC 150/.3
*1. Psychology - Dictionaries. I. Title.*
*TC BF31 .C72 1999*

**Cortés, Carlos E.** The children are watching : how the media teach about diversity / Carlos E. Cortés. New York : Teachers College Press, c2000. xxi, 202 p. ; 24 cm. (Multicultural education series) Includes bibliographical references (p. 173-189) and index. ISBN 0-8077-3938-3 (cloth : alk. paper) ISBN 0-8077-3937-5 (paper : alk. paper) DDC 306
*1. Multiculturalism in mass media. 2. Multicultural education. 3. Mass media and education. I. Title. II. Series: Multicultural education series (New York, N.Y.)*
*TC P96.M83 C67 2000*

**CORTICAL EVOKED POTENTIALS.** See EVOKED POTENTIALS (ELECTROPHYSIOLOGY).

**Corwin, Miles.** And still we rise : a year in the life of gifted inner-city high school students / Miles Corwin. 1st ed. New York : Bard, 2000. xii, 418 p. ; 25 cm. "An Avon book." ISBN 0-380-97650-1 (hardcover : alk. paper) DDC 371.95/09794/94
*1. Gifted children - Education (Secondary) - United States - Case studies. 2. Socially handicapped children - Education (Secondary) - United States - Case studies. 3. Education, Urban - United States - Case studies. 4. Crenshaw High School (Los Angeles, Calif.) I. Title.*
*TC LC3993.9 .C678 2000*

**CORYNEBACTERIUM DISEASES.** See DIPHTHERIA.

**Corzo, Miguel Angel.**
Mortality immortality? Los Angeles : Getty Conservation Institute, c1999.
*TC N6485 .M67 1999*

**Cosgrave, John O'Hara, 1908-1968 illus.**
Diamant, Gertrude, 1901- The days of Ofelia, Boston, Houghton Mifflin company, 1942.
*TC F1210 .D5*

**Cosgrove, Art.**
A new history of Ireland. Oxford [England] : Clarendon Press ; New York : Oxford University Press, <1976-1986  >
*TC DA912 .N48*

**Cosgrove, Holli, 1964-.**
Encyclopedia of careers and vocational guidance. 11th ed. Chicago : Ferguson Pub. Co., 2000.
*TC HF5381 .E52 2000*

**Coslick, Ronald T.**
Baroody, Arthur J., 1947- Fostering children's mathematical power. Mahwah, N.J. : Lawrence Erlbaum Associates, 1998.
*TC QA135.5 .B2847 1998*

**COSMETIC SURGERY.** See SURGERY, PLASTIC.

**COSMETICS.** See PERFUMES.

**Cosmic alchemy.**
Stephen Hawking's universe [videorecording]. [Alexandria, Va.] : PBS Video; Burbank, CA : Distributed by Warner Home Video, c1997.
*TC QB982 .S7 1997*

**COSMOGONY.** See CREATION.

**COSMOGRAPHY.** See GEOGRAPHY.

**COSMOLOGY.** See also NAKED SINGULARITIES (COSMOLOGY).
Stephen Hawking's universe [videorecording]. [Alexandria, Va.] : PBS Video; Burbank, CA : Distributed by Warner Home Video, c1997.
*TC QB982 .S7 1997*

**COSMOLOGY - MATHEMATICS.**
Stephen Hawking's universe [videorecording]. [Alexandria, Va.] : PBS Video; Burbank, CA : Distributed by Warner Home Video, c1997.
*TC QB982 .S7 1997*

**COST BENEFIT ANALYSIS.**
Cost benefit analysis of heroin maintenance treatment. Basel : New York : Karger, c2000.
*TC RC568.H4 C67 2000*

**Cost benefit analysis of heroin maintenance treatment** / volume editors, Felix Gutzwiller, Thomas Steffen. Basel ; New York : Karger, c2000. ix, 133 p. : ill. ; 25 cm. (Medical prescription of narcotics ; vol. 2) Includes bibliographical references (p. 129-130) and index. ISBN 3-8055-6874-6 (hardcover : alk. paper) DDC 362.29/38
*1. Drug abuse - Treatment - Cost effectiveness. 2. Heroin habit - Treatment - Economic aspects. 3. Heroin Dependence - economics. 4. Cost Benefit Analysis. 5. Health Care Costs. 6. Heroin Dependence - therapy. 7. Prescriptions. Drug. I. Gutzwiller, Felix. II. Steffen, Thomas, Dr. III. Series.*
*TC RC568.H4 C67 2000*

**The cost-effectiveness of distance education for teacher training.**
Nielsen, H. Dean. Cambridge, Mass. : B.R.I.D.G.E.S. Basic Research and Implementation in Developing Education Systems, [1991].
*TC LB1731 .N43 1991*

**COSTA RICA.**
Biesanz, Mavis Hiltunen. The Ticos. Boulder, Colo. : Lynne Rienner Publishers, 1999.
*TC F1543 .B563 1999*

**Costello, Patrick J. M.** Thinking skills and early childhood education. London : David Fulton Publishers, 2000. xii, 164 p. ; 25 cm. ISBN 1-85346-551-8 DDC 370.1
*1. Critical thinking - Study and teaching (Elementary) - Great Britain.*
*TC LB1590.3 .C67 2000*

**COSTUME.** See CLOTHING AND DRESS; JEWELRY; UMBRELLAS AND PARASOLS.

**COSTUME - AFRICA, NORTH.**
Spring, Christopher. North African textiles. Washington, D.C. : Smithsonian Institution Press, c1995.
*TC NK8887.6 .S68 1995*

**COSTUME - SOCIAL ASPECTS.**
Cloth and human experience. Washington : Smithsonian Institution Press, c1989.
*TC GT525 .C57 1989*

**The COTA in the schools.**
Barlow, Tracie. San Antonio, Texas : Therapy Skill Builders, c1999.
*TC RM735 .B37 1999*

**Cotler, Amy.** The secret garden cookbook : recipes inspired by Frances Hodgson Burnett's Secret garden / Amy Cotler ; illustrations by Prudence See. 1st ed. New York : HarperCollins Publishers, c1999. 128 p. ; 23 cm. Includes index. SUMMARY: A compilation of recipes for foods served in England during the Victorian Era and inspired by characters and events in "The Secret Garden" by Frances Hodgson Burnett. ISBN 0-06-027740-8 DDC 394.1/0942
*1. Cookery, English - Juvenile literature. 2. Food habits - England - History - 19th century - Juvenile literature. 3. Cookery, English. 4. Food habits - England - History. 5. Literary cookbooks. I. See, Prudence, ill. II. Burnett, Frances Hodgson, 1849-1924. Secret garden. III. Title.*
*TC TX717 .C588 1999*

**COTTAGE INDUSTRIES.** See ARTISANS.

**Cotterall, Sara.**
Learner autonomy in language learning. Frankfurt am Main ; New York : Peter Lang, c1999.
*TC P53 .L378 1999*

**Cotton Noe, James Thomas, 1864- ed.**
Kentucky high school quarterly. Lexington, Ky. : Department of Education, State University of Kentucky, 1915-1927.

**Cottringer, Anne.** Movie magic : a star is born / written by Anne Cottringer. 1st American ed. New York : DK Pub., c1999. 48 p. : col. ill. ; 24 cm. (Eyewitness Level 3) "Grades 2 and 3--cover. SUMMARY: Follows a girl as she auditions for a part in a science fiction movie, spends a day filming at a movie studio, meets all the people involved in the making of a film, and attends the gala opening to see the results. ISBN 0-7894-3973-5 (hardcover) ISBN 0-7894-4008-3 (pbk.) DDC 791.43/023
*1. Motion pictures - Production and direction - Juvenile literature. 2. Motion pictures - Production and direction. I. Title. II. Series.*
*TC PN1995.9.P7 C66 1999*

**Coughlin, Debbie.** The mainstreaming handbook : how to be an advocate for your special-needs students / Deborah Coughlin ; [editor, Lois Bridges]. Portsmouth, NH : Heinemann, c2000. vi, 154 p. ; 23 cm. Includes bibliographical references and index. ISBN 0-325-00226-6 DDC 371.9/046
*1. Mainstreaming in education - United States - Case studies. 2. Handicapped children - Education (Elementary) - United States - Case studies. 3. Handicapped children - Legal status, laws, etc. - United States. I. Bird, Lois Bridges. II. Title.*
*TC LC1201 .C68 2000*

**Coulmas, Florian.**
Linguistic minorities and literacy. Berlin ; New York : Mouton Publishers, 1984.
*TC P119.315 .L56 1984*

**Couloumbis, Audrey.** Getting near to baby / Audrey Couloumbis. New York : Putnam, 1999. 211 p. ; 22 cm. SUMMARY: Although thirteen-year-old Willa Jo and her Aunt Patty seem to be constantly at odds, staying with her and Uncle Hob helps Willa Jo and her younger sister come to terms with the death of their family's baby. ISBN 0-399-23389-X DDC [Fic]
*1. Sisters - Fiction. 2. Grief - Fiction. 3. Death - Fiction. 4. Aunts - Fiction. I. Title.*
*TC PZ7.C8305 Gg 1999*

**Coulter, Angela.**
The global challenge of health care rationing. Buckingham [England] ; Philadelphia : Open University Press, 2000.
*TC RA394.9 .G56 2000*

**Council for Advancement and Support of Education.**
CASE currents. [Washington] Council for Advancement and Support of Education. 9 v. ill. 31 cm. Frequency: Monthly (except Aug.). Former frequency: Ceased with v. 9, no. 7 in 1983. v. 1- Sept. 1975- . Indexed selectively by: Current index to journals in education 0011-3565. Index for 1975-1984 in separate volume. Continued in Sept. 1983 by: Currents (Washington, D.C.) ISSN 0360-862X DDC 378/.005
*1. Education, Higher - Periodicals. I. Title. II. Title: Currents (Washington, D.C.)*

**Council for Children with Behavioral Disorders.**
Monograph in behavioral disorders. Severe behavior disorders of children and youth. Reston, Va. : Council for Children with Behavioral Disorders, c1978-1986.
*TC BF721 .M65*

**Council of Church Boards of Education in the United States of America.**
[Christian education (Chicago, Ill.)] Christian education. Chicago : [Council of Church Boards of Education in the United States of America,  -1952]

**Council of Europe.**
The challenges of the information and communication technologies facing history teaching. Strasbourg : Council of Europe Pub., c1999.
*TC D424 .C425 1999*

[Education newsletter (Strasbourg, France)] Education newsletter = Strasbourg [France] : Council of Europe, 1990-1995.
*TC LA620 .D6 1994*

Introducing learner autonomy in teacher education. Strasbourg : Council of Europe Pub., c1999.
*TC PB38.E8 I567 1999*

Learner autonomy. Strasbourg : Council of Europe Pub., c1999.
*TC PB38.E8 L424 1999*

Towards a pluralist and tolerant approach to teaching history. Strasbourg : Council of Europe Pub., c1999.
*TC D424 .T665 1999*

**Council of Europe. Council for Cultural Co-operation.** Bullying in schools : European teachers' seminar Bled, Slovenia, 16-19 April 1998 / Council for Cultural Co-operation In-Service Training Programme for Educational Staff. Strasbourg : Council of Europe Publishing, 1999. 60 p. ; 28 cm. (Education.) Includes bibliographical references. ISBN 92-871-3752-8
*1. Aggressiveness in children. 2. Behavioral assessment of children. 3. School discipline. 4. School psychology. I. Title. II. Series: Collection Education (Strasbourg, France).*
*TC BF637.B85 B842 1999*

The challenges of the information and communication technologies facing history teaching. Strasbourg : Council of Europe Pub., c1999.
*TC D424 .C425 1999*

Towards a pluralist and tolerant approach to teaching history. Strasbourg : Council of Europe Pub., c1999.
*TC D424 .T665 1999*

**Council of Europe. Council for Cultural Co-operation. Education Committee.**
The challenges of science education. Strasbourg : Council of Europe Pub., c1999.
*TC Q183.4.E85 C475 1999*

**COUNCIL OF EUROPE COUNTRIES.** *See* EUROPE.

**Council of Europe. Legislative Reform Programme for Higher Education.**
Groof, Jan de. Democracy and governance in higher education. The Hague ; Boston : Kluwer Law International, 1998.
*TC LB2341.8.E85 G76 1998*

**Council of State Governments.**
CSG state directory. Directory I, Elective officials. Lexington, Ky. : The Council, c1998-
*TC JK2403 .S69*

CSG state directory. Directory II, Legislative leadership, committees & staff. Lexington, Ky. : Council of State Governments, c1998-
*TC JK2495 .S688*

CSG state directory. Directory III, Administrative officials. Lexington, Ky. : The Council, c1998-
*TC JK2403 .B6*

**Council on Foreign Relations.**
Foreign affairs. New York : Council on Foreign Relations, 1922-

**COUNCILS, INDIAN.** *See* INDIAN COUNCILS.

**COUNSELING.** *See also* COUNSELORS; CROSS-CULTURAL COUNSELING; DRUG ABUSE COUNSELING; EDUCATIONAL COUNSELING; FAMILY COUNSELING; INTERVIEWING; MARRIAGE COUNSELING; MENTORING; SEX COUNSELING; SOCIAL CASE WORK; VOCATIONAL GUIDANCE.
Blocher, Donald H. 4th ed. New York : Wiley, c2000.
*TC BF637.C6 B48 2000*

**COUNSELING.**
Blocher, Donald H. Counseling. 4th ed. New York : Wiley, c2000.
*TC BF637.C6 B48 2000*

Brems, Christiane. Dealing with challenges in psychotherapy and counseling. Belmont, Calif. : Wadsworth Pub., Brooks/Cole, c2000.
*TC BF637.C6 B723 2000*

Burnard, Philip. Counselling skills for health professionals. 3rd ed. Cheltenham, U.K. : Stanley Thornes, 1999.

*TC BF637.C6 B82 1999*

Chaplin, Jocelyn. Feminist counselling in action. 2nd ed. Thousand Oaks, Calif. : SAGE, 1999.
*TC HQ1206 .C447 1999*

Clinical counselling in context. London ; New York : Routledge, 1999.
*TC RC466 .C55 1999*

Corey, Gerald. Theory and practice of counseling and psychotherapy. 6th ed. Stamford, Conn : Brooks/Cole, 2000.
*TC BF637.C6 C574 2000*

Drummond, Robert J. Appraisal procedures for counselors and helping professionals. 4th ed. Upper Saddle River, N.J. : Merrill, c2000.
*TC BF176 .D78 2000*

Epps, Susan. Empowered families, successful children. 1st ed. Washington, DC : American Psychological Association, c2000.
*TC BF637.C6 E66 2000*

Figler, Howard E. The career counselor's handbook. Berkeley, Calif. : Ten Speed Press, c1999.
*TC HF5549.5.C35 F54 1999*

Fransella, Fay. Personal construct counselling in action. 2nd ed. London ; Thousand Oaks, Calif. : Sage Publications, 2000.
*TC BF698.9.P47 F73 2000*

Handbook of counseling and psychotherapy with lesbian, gay, and bisexual clients. 1st ed. Washington, DC ; London : American Psychological Association, c2000.
*TC BF637.C6 H3125 2000*

Handbook of counseling psychology. 3rd ed. New York : J. Wiley, c2000.
*TC BF637.C6 H315 2000*

Hill, Clara E. Helping skills. 1st ed. Washington, DC : American Psychological Association, c1999.
*TC BF637.C6 H46 1999*

Howatt, William A. The human services counseling toolbox. Belmont, CA : Brooks/Cole-Wadsworth, c2000.
*TC BF637.C6 H677 2000*

Key readings in testing. 1st ed. Tucson, Ariz. : P. Juul Press, c1985.
*TC BF176 .K48 1985*

McLeod, John, 1951- An introduction to counselling. 2nd ed. Buckingham [England] ; Philadelphia, PA : Open University Press, 1998.
*TC BF637.C6 M379 1998*

Nystul, Michael S. Introduction to counseling. Boston : Allyn and Bacon, c1999.
*TC BF637.C6 N97 1999*

Patterson, Lewis E. The counseling process. 5th ed. Belmont, CA : Brooks/Cole : Wadsworth, 1999.
*TC BF637.C6 P325 1999*

The practice of counselling in primary care. London ; Thousand Oaks, Calif. : SAGE Publications, 1999.
*TC R727.4 .P733 1999*

Professional counseling. Springfield, Ill. : C.C. Thomas, Publishers, c1999.
*TC BF637.C6 D56 1999*

Salacuse, Jeswald W. The wise advisor. Westport, Conn. : Praeger, 2000.
*TC BF637.C56 .S26 2000*

Schapira, Sylvie K., 1940- Choosing a counselling or psychotherapy training. London ; New York : Routledge, 2000.
*TC BF637.C6 S355 2000*

Stewart, Ian, 1940- Transactional analysis counselling in action. 2nd ed. London : SAGE, 2000.
*TC RC489.T7 S74 2000*

Testing and assessment in counseling practice. 2nd ed. Mahwah, N.J. : L. Erlbaum Associates, 2000.
*TC BF176 .T423 2000*

Thorne, Brian, 1937- Person-centred counselling and Christian spirituality :. London : Whurr Publishers, 1998.
*TC BF637.C6 T496 1998*

Whiston, Susan C., 1953- Principles and applications of assessment in counseling. Australia ; U.S. : Brooks/Cole, c2000.
*TC BF637.C6 W467 2000*

**Counseling addicted women.**
Cohen, Monique. Thousand Oaks, Calif. : Sage Publications, c2000.

*TC HV4999.W65 C64 2000*

**Counseling and educational research.**
Houser, Rick. Thousand Oaks, Calif. : Sage Publications, c1998.
*TC Q180.A1 H595 1998*

**Counseling and human development.**
Focus on guidance. Denver, Love Publishing Co.

**Counseling and psychotherapy.**
Ivey, Allen E. 4th ed. Boston : Allyn and Bacon, c1997.
*TC BF637.C6 I93 1997*

**Counseling and psychotherapy with lesbian, gay, and bisexual clients.**
Handbook of counseling and psychotherapy with lesbian, gay, and bisexual clients. 1st ed. Washington, DC ; London : American Psychological Association, c2000.
*TC BF637.C6 H3125 2000*

**Counseling and the therapeutic state** / James J. Chriss, editor. New York : Aldine de Gruyter, c1999. ix, 207 p. ; 24 cm. (Social problems and social issues) Includes bibliographical references and index. ISBN 0-202-30623-2 (alk. paper) ISBN 0-202-30624-0 (pbk. : alk. paper) DDC 361/.02
*1. Counseling - Government policy - United States. 2. Psychotherapy - Government policy - United States. 3. Public welfare - United States. 4. Welfare state. I. Chriss, James J., 1955- II. Series.*
*TC HV95 .C675 1999*

**Counseling Asian families from a systems perspective** / edited by Kit S. Ng. Alexandria, Va. : American Counseling Ass., c1999. xiv, 177 p. ; 23 cm. (The family psychology and counseling series) Includes bibliographical references. ISBN 1-55620-203-2 (alk. paper) DDC 616.89/156/08995073
*1. Asian American families - Mental health. 2. Asian American families - Counseling of. 3. Family psychotherapy. I. Ng, Kit S. II. Series.*
*TC RC451.5.A75 C68 1999*

**COUNSELING ETHICS.** *See* COUNSELING - MORAL AND ETHICAL ASPECTS; COUNSELORS - PROFESSIONAL ETHICS.

**Counseling for hearing aid fittings** / edited by Robert W. Sweetow. San Diego : Singular Pub. Group, c1999. xvi, 353 p. : ill., forms ; 23 cm. + 1 computer disk (3 1/2 in.). (A singular audiology textbook) Includes bibliographical references and index. System requirements for computer disk: IBM-compatible PC; DOS; Windows 3.1 or higher; 1.4MB floppy disk drive. ISBN 1-56593-937-9 (alk. paper : soft cover) DDC 617.8/9
*1. Hearing aids - Fitting. 2. Hearing impaired - Counseling of. 3. Audiology. 4. Hearing Aids. 5. Audiology. 6. Counseling - methods. I. Sweetow, Robert W. II. Series: A Singular audiology text.*
*TC RF300 .C68 1999*

**COUNSELING - GOVERNMENT POLICY - UNITED STATES.**
Counseling and the therapeutic state. New York : Aldine de Gruyter, c1999.
*TC HV95 .C675 1999*

**COUNSELING - GREAT BRITAIN.**
Professionalism, boundaries, and the workplace. New York : Routledge, 2000.
*TC HV10.5 .P74 2000*

**COUNSELING IN ELEMENTARY EDUCATION - UNITED STATES.**
Schmidt, John J., 1946- Counseling in schools. 3rd ed. Boston : Allyn and Bacon, c1999.
*TC LB1027.5 .S2585 1999*

**COUNSELING IN HIGHER EDUCATION.** *See also* COLLEGE STUDENT DEVELOPMENT PROGRAMS.
Langer, Arthur Mark. Faculty assessment of mentoring roles at SUNY Empire State College. 1999.
*TC 06 no. 11138*

Love, Patrick G. Understanding and applying cognitive development theory. San Francisco : Jossey-Bass, c1999.
*TC LB2343 .L65 1999*

**COUNSELING IN HIGHER EDUCATION - UNITED STATES.**
Career counseling of college students. Washington, DC : American Psychological Association, c2000.
*TC LB2343 .C3273 2000*

Deegan, William L. Translating theory into practice. 1st ed. [Columbus, Ohio] : National Association of Student Personnel Administrators, c1985.

TC LB2343 .D356 1985
Powerful programming for student learning. San Francisco : Jossey-Bass, c2000.
*TC LB2343 .P643 2000*

**COUNSELING IN HIGHER EDUCATION - UNITED STATES - HANDBOOKS, MANUALS, ETC.**
Academic advising. 1st ed. San Francisco : Jossey-Bass, c2000.
*TC LB2343 .A29 2000*

**COUNSELING IN MIDDLE SCHOOL EDUCATION - UNITED STATES.**
Schmidt, John J., 1946- Counseling in schools. 3rd ed. Boston : Allyn and Bacon, c1999.
*TC LB1027.5 .S2585 1999*

**Counseling in schools.**
Schmidt, John J., 1946- 3rd ed. Boston : Allyn and Bacon, c1999.
*TC LB1027.5 .S2585 1999*

**COUNSELING IN SECONDARY EDUCATION.**
Johnson, Wanda Yvonne, 1936- Youth suicide. Bloomington, Ind. : Phi Delta Kappa Educational Foundation, c1999.
*TC HV6546 .J645 1999*

**COUNSELING IN SECONDARY EDUCATION - GREAT BRITAIN.**
King, Gail, 1949- Counselling skills for teachers. Buckingham [England] ; Philadelphia : Open University Press, 1999.
*TC LB1620.53.G7 K56 1999*

**COUNSELING IN SECONDARY EDUCATION - IRELAND - CASE STUDIES.**
Rethinking pastoral care. London ; New York : Routledge, 1999.
*TC LB1620.53.I73 R48 1999*

**COUNSELING IN SECONDARY EDUCATION - UNITED STATES.**
Schmidt, John J., 1946- Counseling in schools. 3rd ed. Boston : Allyn and Bacon, c1999.
*TC LB1027.5 .S2585 1999*

**COUNSELING - METHODS.**
Brief Alcohol Screening and Intervention for College Students (BASICS). New York : Guilford Press, c1999.
*TC HV5135 .B74 1998*

Counseling for hearing aid fittings. San Diego : Singular Pub. Group, c1999.
*TC RF300 .C68 1999*

**COUNSELING - MORAL AND ETHICAL ASPECTS.**
Cohen, Elliot D. The virtuous therapist. Belmont, CA : Brooks/Cole Wadworth, 1999.
*TC BF637.C6 C46 1999*

**COUNSELING - MORAL AND ETHICAL ASPECTS - CASE STUDIES.**
Cohen, Elliot D. The virtuous therapist. Belmont, CA : Brooks/Cole Wadworth, 1999.
*TC BF637.C6 C46 1999*

**COUNSELING, PASTORAL. See PASTORAL COUNSELING.**

**COUNSELING - PERIODICALS.**
Focus on guidance. Denver, Love Publishing Co.

International Association of Pupil Personnel Workers. The Journal. [Baton Rouge, La., etc.] International Association of Pupil Personnel Workers.

**The counseling process.**
Patterson, Lewis E. 5th ed. Belmont, CA : Brooks/Cole : Wadsworth, 1999.
*TC BF637.C6 P325 1999*

**COUNSELING - RELIGIOUS ASPECTS. See PASTORAL COUNSELING.**

**Counseling single parents.**
Maass, Vera Sonja. New York : Springer Pub. Co., c2000.
*TC HQ759.915 .M23 2000*

**Counseling the communicatively disabled and their families.**
Shames, George H., 1926- Boston ; London : Allyn and Bacon, c2000.
*TC RC428.8 .S53 2000*

**COUNSELING - UNITED STATES - HISTORY.**
Blocher, Donald H. The evolution of counseling psychology. New York : Springer, c2000.
*TC BF637.C6 .B473 2000*

**Counselling and helping carers.**
Noon, J. Mitchell. Leicester : BPS Books, 1999.
*TC R727.4 .N66 1999*

**Counselling and psychotherapy series.**
Thorne, Brian, 1937- Person-centred counselling and Christian spirituality :. London : Whurr Publishers, 1998.
*TC BF637.C6 T496 1998*

**Counselling couples and families.**
O'Leary, Charles J. London : SAGE, 1999.
*TC RC488.5 .O394 1999*

**Counselling in action.**
Chaplin, Jocelyn. Feminist counselling in action. 2nd ed. Thousand Oaks, Calif. : SAGE, 1999.
*TC HQ1206 .C447 1999*

Chaplin, Jocelyn. Feminist counselling in action. 2nd ed. Thousand Oaks, Calif. : SAGE, 1999.
*TC HQ1206 .C447 1999*

Fransella, Fay. Personal construct counselling in action. 2nd ed. London ; Thousand Oaks, Calif. : Sage Publications, 2000.
*TC BF698.9.P47 F73 2000*

Stewart, Ian, 1940- Transactional analysis counselling in action. 2nd ed. London : SAGE, 2000.
*TC RC489.T7 S74 2000*

**Counselling in schools.**
McGuiness, John. London ; New York : Cassell, 1998.
*TC LB1027.5 .M367 1998*

**Counselling skills for health professionals.**
Burnard, Philip. 3rd ed. Cheltenham, U.K. : Stanley Thornes, 1999.
*TC BF637.C6 B82 1999*

**Counselling skills for teachers.**
King, Gail, 1949- Buckingham [England] ; Philadelphia : Open University Press, 1999.
*TC LB1620.53.G7 K56 1999*

**Counselling supervision**
Proctor, Brigid. Group supervision. London ; Thousand Oaks : SAGE Publications, 2000.
*TC BF637.C6 P95176 2000*

**Counselling women in violent relationships.**
Lockley, Paul. London ; New York : Free Association Books, 1999.
*TC HV6626.23.G7 L624 1999*

**The counselor and the group.**
Trotzer, James P., 1943- 3rd ed. Philadelphia ; London : Accelerated Development, c1999.
*TC BF637.C6 T68 1999*

**COUNSELORS. See also STUDENT COUNSELORS.**
Blocher, Donald H. Counseling. 4th ed. New York : Wiley, c2000.
*TC BF637.C6 B48 2000*

**COUNSELORS - PROFESSIONAL ETHICS.**
Cohen, Elliot D. The virtuous therapist. Belmont, CA : Brooks/Cole Wadworth, 1999.
*TC BF637.C6 C46 1999*

**COUNSELORS - PROFESSIONAL ETHICS - GREAT BRITAIN.**
Professionalism, boundaries, and the workplace. New York : Routledge, 2000.
*TC HV10.5 .P74 2000*

**COUNSELORS - SUPERVISION OF.**
Proctor, Brigid. Group supervision. London ; Thousand Oaks : SAGE Publications, 2000.
*TC BF637.C6 P95176 2000*

Taking supervision forward. London : Sage, 2000.
*TC BF637.C6 T35 2000*

Taking supervision forward. London : Sage, 2000.
*TC BF637.C6 T35 2000*

**COUNSELORS - TRAINING OF.**
Schapira, Sylvie K., 1940- Choosing a counselling or psychotherapy training. London ; New York : Routledge, 2000.
*TC BF637.C6 S355 2000*

**Count-a-saurus.**
Blumenthal, Nancy. New York : Four Winds Press, c1989.
*TC QA113 .B57 1989*

**COUNTER CULTURE. See COMMUNAL LIVING; RADICALISM.**

**COUNTER-REFORMATION. See REFORMATION.**

**COUNTERGUERRILLA WARFARE. See COUNTERINSURGENCY.**

**COUNTERINSURGENCY - EL SALVADOR - HISTORY.**
Flores, Joaquín Evelio. Psychological effects of the civil war on children from rural communities of El Salvador.
*TC 083 F67*

**Counterpoints (New York, N.Y.)**
(vol. 103.) Curriculum in the postmodern condition. New York : P. Lang, c2000.
*TC LB2806.15 .C694 2000*

(vol. 104.) Paley, Nicholas. Questions of you and the struggle of collaborative life. New York : P. Lang, c2000.
*TC LB1028 .P233 2000*

(vol. 105.) Kennedy, Rosa L., 1938- A school for healing. New York : P. Lang, c1999.
*TC LC46.4 .K46 1999*

(vol. 107.) Black sons to mothers. New York ; Canterbury [England] : P. Lang, c2000.
*TC LC2731 .B53 2000*

(vol. 110.) Perspectives in critical thinking. New York : P. Lang, c2000.
*TC LB1590.3 .P476 2000*

(vol. 111.) Kincheloe, Joe L. The stigma of genius. New York ; Canterbury [England] : P. Lang, c1999.
*TC LB875.E562 K56 1999*

(vol. 114.) Burch, Kerry T., 1957- Eros as the educational principle of democracy. New York : P. Lang, c2000.
*TC LC196 .B75 2000*

(vol. 117.) Barone, Tom. Aesthetics, politics, and educational inquiry. New York : P. Lang, 2000.
*TC LB1028 .B345 2000*

(vol. 118) Thinking queer. New York : Peter Lang, c2000.
*TC LC192.6 .T55 2000*

(vol. 46.) Strangers in the land. New York : Peter Lang, c1999.
*TC E184.36.E84 S77 1999*

(vol. 64.) Harper, Helen J., 1957- Wild words- dangerous desires. New York : Peter Lang, c2000.
*TC LB1631 .H267 2000*

(vol. 70.) Contemporary curriculum discourses. New York : P. Lang, c1999.
*TC LB2806.15 .C6753 1999*

(vol. 72.) Hicks, D. Emily. Ninety-five languages and seven forms of intelligence. New York : P. Lang, c1999.
*TC LC196 .H53 1999*

(vol. 87.) Foster, Stuart J., 1960- Red alert!. New York ; Canterbury [England] : P. Lang, c2000.
*TC LC72.2 .F67 2000*

(vol. 89.) The postmodern educator. New York : P. Lang, c1999.
*TC LB1707 .P67 1999*

(vol. 98.) Chamberlin, J. Gordon (John Gordon) Upon whom we depend. New York : Peter Lang, c1999.
*TC HC110.P6 C326 1999*

(vol. 99.) Mirochnik, Elijah, 1952- Teaching in the first person. New York : P. Lang, c2000.
*TC LB1033 .M546 2000*

**Counterpoints (Oxford University Press)**
Cognition and emotion. Oxford ; New York : Oxford University Press, 2000.
*TC BF311 .C5477 2000*

**Countertransference and the treatment of trauma.**
Dalenberg, Constance J. 1st ed. Washington, D.C. : American Psychological Association, c2000.
*TC RC489.C68 D37 2000*

**COUNTERTRANSFERENCE (PSYCHOLOGY).**
Dalenberg, Constance J. Countertransference and the treatment of trauma. 1st ed. Washington, D.C. : American Psychological Association, c2000.
*TC RC489.C68 D37 2000*

**COUNTING.**
1 to 10 and back again. Los Angeles : J. Paul Getty Museum, c1999.
*TC QA113 .A14 1998*

Blumenthal, Nancy. Count-a-saurus. New York : Four Winds Press, c1989.

*TC QA113 .B57 1989*

Dana, Katharine Floyd, 1835-1886. Over in the meadow. New York : Scholastic, c1992
*TC PZ8.3.D2 Ov 1992*

Evans, Lezlie. Can you count ten toes? Boston, Mass. : Houghton Mifflin, 1999.
*TC QA113 .E84 1999*

Lesser, Carolyn. Spots. 1st ed. San Diego : Harcourt Brace, c1999.
*TC QA113 .L47 1999*

This old man. 1st American ed. Boston : Houghton Mifflin, 1990.
*TC PZ8.3 .T2965 1990b*

**COUNTING BOOKS.** *See* **COUNTING.**

**COUNTING - JUVENILE LITERATURE.**
1 to 10 and back again. Los Angeles : J. Paul Getty Museum, c1999.
*TC QA113 .A14 1998*

Blumenthal, Nancy. Count-a-saurus. New York : Four Winds Press, c1989.
*TC QA113 .B57 1989*

Evans, Lezlie. Can you count ten toes? Boston, Mass. : Houghton Mifflin, 1999.
*TC QA113 .E84 1999*

Lesser, Carolyn. Spots. 1st ed. San Diego : Harcourt Brace, c1999.
*TC QA113 .L47 1999*

**COUNTRY LIFE.** *See* **FARM LIFE.**

**COUNTRY LIFE - FICTION.**
Shelby, Anne. We keep a store. New York : Orchard Books, c1989.
*TC PZ7.S54125 We 1989*

Shelby, Anne. We keep a store. New York : Orchard Books, c1990.
*TC PZ7 .S54125We 1990*

**COUNTRY LIFE - GEORGIA.**
Foxfire 2: ghost stories, spring wild plant foods, spinning and weaving, midwifing, burial customs, corn shuckin's, wagon making and more affairs of plain living. Garden City, N.Y., Anchor Press/Doubleday, 1973.
*TC F291.2 .F62 1973*

Foxfire 2: ghost stories, spring wild plant foods, spinning and weaving, midwifing, burial customs, corn shuckin's, wagon making and more affairs of plain living. Garden City, N.Y., Anchor Press/Doubleday, 1973.
*TC F291.2 .F62 1973*

Foxfire 3. 1st ed. Garden City, N.Y. : Anchor Press, 1975.
*TC F291.2 .F622 1975*

**COUNTRY LIFE - GEORGIA. - JUVENILE LITERATURE.**
Foxfire 3. 1st ed. Garden City, N.Y. : Anchor Press, 1975.
*TC F291.2 .F622 1975*

**COUNTRY SCHOOLS.** *See* **RURAL SCHOOLS.**

Counts, George Sylvester, 1889- ed.
Frontiers of democracy. New York, Progressive Education Association, etc., 1934-

Counts, I. Wilmer (Ira Wilmer), 1931- A life is more than a moment : the desegregation of Little Rock's Central High / text and photographs by Will Counts ; with essays by Will Campbell, Ernest Dumas, and Robert S. McCord. Bloomington, IN : Indiana University Press, c1999. xviii, 76 p. : ill. ; 22 x 26 cm. ISBN 0-253-33637-6 (alk. paper)
*1. School integration - Arkansas - Little Rock - History - 20th century. 2. Afro-Americans - Civil rights - Arkansas. 3. Central High School (Little Rock, Ark.) - History. I. Campbell, Will D. II. Dumas, Ernest, 1937- III. McCord, Robert S. IV. Title.*
*TC LC214.23.L56 C68 1999*

**COUNTY LIBRARIES.** *See* **PUBLIC LIBRARIES.**

**COUP D'ETATS.** *See* **COUPS D'ÉTAT.**

**COUPLES.** *See* **MARRIED PEOPLE; UNMARRIED COUPLES.**

**COUPLES, DUAL-INCOME.** *See* **DUAL-CAREER FAMILIES.**

**Couples on the fault line** : new directions for therapists / edited by Peggy Papp. New York, NY : Guilford Press, 2000. xv, 344 p. ; 24 cm. Includes bibliographical references and index. ISBN 1-57230-536-3 (cloth) DDC 616.89/156
*1. Marital psychotherapy. I. Papp, Peggy.*

*TC RC488.5 .C6435 2000*

**COUPLES PSYCHOTHERAPY.** *See* **MARITAL PSYCHOTHERAPY.**

**COUPLES THERAPY.** *See* **MARITAL PSYCHOTHERAPY.**

**Couples therapy in managed care** : facing the crisis / Barbara Jo Brothers, editor. New York : Haworth Press, c1999. xiii, 130 p. ; 22 cm. "Co-published simultaneously as Journal of couples therapy, Volume 8, Numbers 3/4 1999." Includes bibliographical references and index. ISBN 0-7890-0788-6 (acid-free paper) ISBN 0-7890-0823-8 (acid-free paper) DDC 616.89/156
*1. Marital psychotherapy. 2. Managed care plans (Medical care) I. Brothers, Barbara Jo, 1940- II. Title: Journal of couples therapy.*
*TC RC488.5 .C64385 1999*

**COUPLES, TWO-CAREER.** *See* **DUAL-CAREER FAMILIES.**

**COUPS (COUPS D'ÉTAT).** *See* **COUPS D'ÉTAT.**

**COUPS D'ÉTAT - AFRICA.**
Onwumechili, Chuka. African democratization and military coups. Westport, Conn. : Praeger, 1998.
*TC JQ1873.5.C58 O58 1998*

**COURAGE.** *See* **HEROES.**

**COURAGE - FICTION.**
De Beer, Hans. [Kleine Eisbär und der Angsthase. English] Little Polar Bear and the brave little hare. New York : North-South Books, 1998.
*TC PZ7.D353 Liv 1998*

Mallat, Kathy. Brave bear. New York : Walker, 1999.
*TC PZ7.M29455 Br 1999*

**COURSES OF STUDY.** *See* **EDUCATION - CURRICULA.**

Courtenay, William J. Parisian scholars in the early fourteenth century : a social portrait / William J. Courtenay. Cambridge, U.K. ; New York, NY : Cambridge University Press, 1999. xix, 284 p. : maps ; 24 cm. (Cambridge studies in medieval life and thought ; 4th ser.) iTitle from cip record: a university of Paris in the early fourteenth century : a socialportrait. Includes bibliographical references (p. 255-261) and indexes. ISBN 0-521-64212-4 (hardback) DDC 378.44/361
*1. Université de Paris - History. 2. Education, Medieval - France - Paris. 3. Education, Higher - Social aspects - France - Paris - History. I. Title. II. Title: iTitle from cip record: a university of Paris in the early fourteenth century : a socialportrait III. Series.*
*TC LF2165 .C68 1999*

Courtland, Mary Clare.
Young adolescents meet literature. Vancouver : Pacific Education Press, 2000.
*TC LB1575.5.C3 Y68 2000*

**COURTS AND COURTIERS.** *See* **PRINCESSES.**

**COURTS - OFFICIALS AND EMPLOYEES.** *See* **JURORS.**

**COURTSHIP.** *See* **MARRIAGE.**

Couser, Cathy.
Jazz dance class [videorecording]. W. Long Branch, NJ : Kultur, [1992?]
*TC GV1784 .J3 1992*

**COVENANT HOUSE (NEW YORK, N.Y.).**
Starting over [videorecording]. [Charleston, W.V.] : Cambridge Educational, c1994.
*TC HV1435.C3 S7 1994*

Covenantal rights.
Novak, David, 1941- Princeton, N.J. : Princeton University Press, 2000.
*TC KC3 .N68 2000*

**COVENANTS NOT TO COMPETE.** *See* **COMPETITION.**

Coveney, John. Food, morals and meaning : the pleasure and anxiety of eating / John Coveney. London ; New York : Routledge, 2000. xiv, 206 p. ; 23 cm. Includes bibliographical references (p. [182]-197) and index. ISBN 0-415-20748-7 DDC 178
*1. Nutrition - Moral and ethical aspects. 2. Food - Moral and ethical aspects. 3. Nutrition - Social aspects. 4. Food - Social aspects. I. Title.*
*TC TX357 .C59 2000*

A covered wagon girl.
Hester, Sallie. Mankato, Minn. : Blue Earth Books, c2000.
*TC F593 .H47 2000*

Cowan, Carolyn Pape. When partners become parents : the big life change for couples / Carolyn Pape Cowan and Philip A. Cowan. Mahwah, NJ : Lawrence Erlbaum Associates, 1999. xxi, 258 p. ; 24 cm. Originally published: New York : BasicBooks, c1992. Includes bibliographical references (p. [223]-235) and index. ISBN 0-8058-3559-8 (p : alk. paper) DDC 306.874
*1. Parents - United States - Longitudinal studies. 2. Parenthood - United States - Longitudinal studies. I. Cowan, Philip A. II. Title.*
*TC HQ755.8 .C68 1999*

Cowan, John. 1932-.
George, Judith W. A handbook of techniques for formative evaluation :. London : Kogan Page, 1999.
*TC LB2333 .G46 1999*

Cowan, Philip A.
Cowan, Carolyn Pape. When partners become parents. Mahwah, NJ : Lawrence Erlbaum Associates, 1999.
*TC HQ755.8 .C68 1999*

**COWBOYS.**
Ancona, George. Charro. 1st ed. San Diego : Harcourt Brace, c1999.
*TC F1210 .A747 1999*

**COWBOYS - FICTION.**
Naylor, Phyllis Reynolds. Walker's Crossing. New York : Atheneum Books for Young Readers, c1999.
*TC PZ7.N24 Wai 1999*

Cowie, Anthony Paul. English dictionaries for foreign learners : a history / A.P. Cowie. Oxford : Clarendon Press : New York : Oxford University Press, 1999. xii, 232 p. : ill. ; 24 cm. Includes bibliographical references (p. [201]-215) and index. ISBN 0-19-823506-2 (acid-free paper) DDC 423/.028
*1. English language - Lexicography. 2. English language - Study and teaching - Foreign speakers - History. 3. English language - Textbooks for foreign speakers - History. 4. Encyclopedias and dictionaries - History and criticism. I. Title.*
*TC PE1611 .C58 1999*

Cowley, Joy. Agapanthus Hum and the eyeglasses / Joy Cowley ; illustrated by Jennifer Plecas. New York : Philomel Books, c1999. 44 p. : col. ill. ; 22 cm. SUMMARY: Agapanthus struggles to do handstands and other acrobatic tricks while wearing her eyeglasses, which have a tendency to fall off as she cavorts about. ISBN 0-399-23211-7 DDC [E]
*1. Eyeglasses - Fiction. 2. Acrobats - Fiction. I. Plecas, Jennifer, ill. II. Title.*
*TC PZ7.C8375 Ag 1999*

Cowley, William Harold, 1889- The personnel bibliographical index / [by] W. H. Cowley. Columbus, Ohio : The Ohio State University, 1932. v, 433 p. ; 24 cm. Annotated bibliography of student personnel administration with subject and author indexes. "Published by Bureau of Educational Research, Ohio State University."--p. [iv] DDC 016.378113
*1. Educational counseling - Bibliography. I. Ohio State University. Bureau of Educational Research. II. Title.*
*TC Z5814.P8 C8*

Cowne, Elizabeth A. The SENCO handbook : working within a whole-school approach / Elizabeth Cowne. 2nd ed. London : D. Fulton Publishers, 1998. vii, 131 p. : ill. ; 30 cm. Includes bibliographical references (p. 125-128) and index. ISBN 1-85346-552-6
*1. Special education - Great Britain - Administration - Handbooks, manuals, etc. I. Title.*
*TC LC3986.G7 C69 1998*

Cows, pigs, wars & witches.
Harris, Marvin, 1927- [1st ed.]. New York : Random House, c1974.
*TC GN320 .H328 1974*

Cows, pigs, wars and witches.
Harris, Marvin, 1927- Cows, pigs, wars & witches. [1st ed.], New York : Random House, c1974.
*TC GN320 .H328 1974*

Cox, Clinton. Come all you brave soldiers : Blacks in the Revolutionary War / Clinton Cox. 1st ed. New York : Scholastic Press, 1999. ix, 182 p. : ill. ; 22 cm. Includes bibliographical references (p. 173-175) and index. SUMMARY: Tells the story of the thousands of black men who served as soldiers fighting for independence from England during the American Revolutionary War. ISBN 0-590-47576-2 DDC 973.3/08996073
*1. United States - History - Revolution, 1775-1783 - Participation, Afro-American - Juvenile literature. 2. Afro-Americans - History - 18th century - Juvenile literature. 3. United States - History - Revolution, 1775-1783 - Participation, Afro-American. 4. Afro-American soldiers - History - 18th century. I. Title.*
*TC E269.N3 C69 1999*

**Cox, Dwayne, 1950-** The University of Louisville / Dwayne D. Cox and William J. Morison. [Lexington] : University Press of Kentucky, c2000. xii, 251 p. : ill. ; 29 cm. Includes bibliographical references (p. 213-238) and index. ISBN 0-8131-2142-6 (alk. paper) DDC 378.769/44
*1. University of Louisville - History. I. Morison, William James, 1943- II. Title.*
**TC LD3131.L42 C69 2000**

**Cox, Martha J.**
The transition to kindergarten. Baltimore : P.H. Brookes Pub., c1999.
**TC LB1205 .T72 1999**

**Cox, T. (Theodore).**
Combating educational disadvantage. London ; New York : Falmer Press, 2000.
**TC LC4065 .C66 1999**

**Coxwell, G. (Gloria).**
Educational competencies for graduates of associate degree nursing programs. [Rev.]. Sudbury, Mass. : Jones and Bartlett, 2000.
**TC RT74.5 .E38 2000**

**Coy, Patrick G.**
Social conflicts and collective identities. Lanham, Md. : Oxford : Rowman & Littlefield Publishers, c2000.
**TC HM1121 .S63 2000**

**Coyote.**
Swinburne, Stephen R. 1st ed. Honesdale, Pa. : Boyds Mill Press, c1999.
**TC QL737.C22 S9 1999**

**COYOTES - JUVENILE LITERATURE.**
Swinburne, Stephen R. Coyote :. 1st ed. Honesdale, Pa. : Boyds Mill Press, c1999.
**TC QL737.C22 S9 1999**

**COYOTES. <JUVENILE SUBJECT HEADING>.**
Swinburne, Stephen R. Coyote :. 1st ed. Honesdale, Pa. : Boyds Mill Press, c1999.
**TC QL737.C22 S9 1999**

**Cozic, Charles P., 1957-.**
Gangs. San Diego, CA : Greenhaven Press, c1996.
**TC HV6437 .G36 1996**

Welfare. San Diego, CA : Greenhaven Press, c1997.
**TC HV95 .W453 1997**

**CP review.**
Cerebral palsy review. Wichita, Kan., Institute of Logopedics.

**C.P. review   -Mar./Apr. 1965.**
Cerebral palsy journal. Wichita, Kan., Institute of Logopedics, inc.

**CPS (CHILD PROTECTIVE SERVICES). See CHILD WELFARE.**

**Crabbe, David.**
Learner autonomy in language learning. Frankfurt am Main ; New York : Peter Lang, c1999.
**TC P53 .L378 1999**

**Crabtree, Benjamin F.**
Doing qualitative research. 2nd ed. Thousand Oaks, Calif. : Sage Publications, c1999
**TC R853.S64 D65 1999**

**Cracking the GRE literature in English subject test.**
New York : Random House, 1996- v. : 28 cm. 1997 ed.- . Cracking the Graduate Record Examination literature in English subject test. Literature in English subject test. Cover title: Princeton Review cracking the GRE literature in English. Spine title: GRE literature.
*1. Graduate Record Examination - Study guides. 2. English literature - Examinations - Study guides. 3. American literature - Examinations - Study guides. I. Princeton Review (Firm) II. Title: Literature in English subject test III. Title: Princeton Review cracking the GRE literature in English IV. Title: GRE literature*
**TC LB2367.4 .L58**

**Craddock, George W.** Social disadvantagement and dependency: a community approach for the reduction of dependency through vocational rehabilitation [by] George W. Craddock, Calvin E. Davis [and] Jeanne L. Moore. Lexington, Mass., Heath Lexington Books [1970] xiii, 138 p. ; 23 cm. (Northeastern University studies in rehabilitation, no. 8) (Studies in social and economic process) Includes bibliographical references. DDC 331.86/8/ 0979463
*1. Vocational rehabilitation - Pittsburg, Calif. 2. Socially handicapped - Pittsburg, Calif. 3. Hard-core unemployed - Pittsburg, Calif. I. Davis, Calvin E., joint author. II. Moore, Jeanne L., joint author. III. Title. IV. Series.*
**TC HD7256.U6 C438**

**CRADLE SONGS. See LULLABIES.**

**CRAFTS (HANDICRAFTS). See HANDICRAFT.**

**CRAFTSMEN. See ARTISANS.**

**Crago, Patrick E.**
Biomechanics and neural control of posture and movement. New York : Springer, 2000.
**TC QP303 .B5684 2000**

**Craig, Robert J., 1941-** Interpreting personality tests : a clinical manual for the MMPI-2, MCMI-III, CPI-R, and 16PF / Robert J. Craig. New York : J. Wiley & Sons, c1999. 268 p. ; 24 cm. Includes bibliographical references (p. 257-258) and indexes. ISBN 0-471-34818-X (hardcover : alk. paper) DDC 155.2/83
*1. Personality tests. I. Title.*
**TC BF698.5 .C73 1999**

**Craig, Wendy (Wendy M.).**
Childhood social development. Malden, Mass. : Oxford : Blackwell Publishers, 2000.
**TC BF721 .C6675 2000**

**Craighead, W. Edward.**
The Corsini encyclopedia of psychology and behavioral science. 3rd ed. New York : Wiley, 2000.
**TC BF31 .E52 2000**

**Craik, Fergus I. M.**
The Oxford handbook of memory. Oxford ; New York : Oxford University Press, 2000.
**TC BF371 .O84 2000**

**Craik, Kenneth H.**
Person-environment psychology. 2nd ed. Mahwah, N.J. : L. Erlbaum, 2000.
**TC BF353 .P43 2000**

**Crain, Stephen.**
The development of binding. Hillsdale, N.J. : Lawrence Erlbaum , 1992.
**TC P158.2 .D5 1992**

**Crain, William C., 1943-** Theories of development : concepts and applications / William Crain. 4th ed. Uppder Saddle River, N.J. : Prentice Hall, c2000. xii, 420 p. ; 23 cm. Includes bibliographical references (p. 385-403) and indexes. ISBN 0-13-955402-5 DDC 155
*1. Developmental psychology. I. Title.*
**TC BF713 .C72 2000**

**Crainer, Stuart.** Gravy training : inside the business of business schools / Stuart Crainer, Des Dearlove. 1st ed. San Francisco : Jossey-Bass Publishers, c1999. xxii, 315 p. ; 24 cm. (The Jossey-Bass business & management series) Includes bibliographical references (p. 271-272) and indexes. CONTENTS: The business school phenomenon -- Building an engineer's paradise -- Business or ivory tower? -- The industrialization of the MBA -- The business of professorship -- Strings attached? -- Alumni associations -- Rankings on the line -- The new competition -- Uncertain futures -- Where now for business schools? ISBN 0-7879-4931-0 (acid-free paper) ISBN 0-7879-0858-4 DDC 650/.071/173
*1. Business schools. 2. Master of business administration degree. I. Dearlove, Des. II. Title. III. Series.*
**TC HF1111 .C7 1999**

**Cramer, Ronald L.** Creative power : the nature and nurture of children's writing / Ronald L. Cramer. New York ; London : Longman, c2001. xvii, 430 p. : ill. ; 24 cm. Includes bibliographical references (p. 395-409) and index. ISBN 0-321-04913-6 DDC 372.62/3
*1. English language - Composition and exercises - Study and teaching. 2. Children - Language. I. Title.*
**TC LB1576 .C758 2001**

The spelling connection : integrating reading, writing, and spelling instruction / Ronald L. Cramer. New York : Guilford Press, c1998. xx, 216 p. : ill. ; 27 cm. Includes bibliographical references and index. ISBN 1-57230-328-X (hardcover : alk. paper) ISBN 1-57230-329-8 (pbk. : alk. paper) DDC 372.63
*1. English language - Orthography and spelling - Study and teaching (Elementary) 2. English language - Composition and exercises - Study and teaching (Elementary) 3. Reading (Elementary) I. Title.*
**TC LB1574 .C65 1998**

**Cramond, Bonnie.**
Investigating creativity in youth. Cresskill, N.J. : Hampton Press, c1999.
**TC BF723.C7 I58 1999**

**Crane, Rochelle.**
Pierangelo, Roger. Complete guide to special education transition services. West Nyack, NY : Center for Applied Research in Education, c1997.
**TC HV1569.3.Y68 P55 1997**

Pierangelo, Roger. The special education yellow pages. Upper Saddle River, N.J. : Merrill, c2000.

**TC LC4031 .P488 2000**

**Crane, Susan A.**
Museums and memory. Stanford, Calif. : Stanford University Press, c2000.
**TC AM7 .M8815 2000**

**Craven, Rhonda.**
Teaching Aboriginal studies. St Leonards, N.S.W. : Allen & Unwin, 1999.
**TC GN666 .T43 1999**

**Crawford, Alan N.**
Gillet, Jean Wallace. Understanding reading problems. 5th ed. New York : Harlow, England : Longman, c2000.
**TC LB1050.46 .G55 2000**

**Crawford, Donna K.**
Bodine, Richard J. Developing emotional intelligence. Champaign, Ill : Research Press, c1999.
**TC BF561 .B6 1999**

**Crawford, George, 1937-** Philosophical & cultural values : applying ethics in schools / George Crawford, Janice Nicklaus. Larchmont, NY : Eye On Education, c2000. x, 129 p. : ill. ; 24 cm. (The School leadership library) Includes bibliographical references (p. 125-129). ISBN 1-88300-182-X DDC 371.2/012
*1. School principals - Professional ethics - United States. 2. Educational leadership - Moral and ethical aspects - United States. I. Nicklaus, Janice, 1949- II. Title. III. Title: Philosophical and cultural values IV. Series.*
**TC LB2831.92 .C72 2000**

**Crawford, Mary (Mary E.).**
Coming into her own. San Francisco, Calif. : Jossey-Bass, c1999.
**TC LC1503 .C65 1999**

**Crawford, Ray A. K., 1954-.**
Bolt, David B., 1954- Digital divide. New York : TV Books, c2000.
**TC LB1028.43 .B64 2000**

**Crawford, Tad, 1946-** The artist-gallery partnership : a practical guide to consigning art / Tad Crawford and Susan Mellon ; introduction by Daniel Grant. [2nd ed.]. New York : Allworth Press, c1998. xvii, 197 p. ; 23 cm. Includes bibliographical references (p. 187-188) and index. ISBN 1-88055-992-7 DDC 346.73/025
*1. Consignment sales - United States. 2. Artists' contracts - United States. I. Mellon, Susan. II. Title.*
**TC KF947 .C7 1998**

Business and legal forms for illustrators / Tad Crawford. Rev. ed. New York : Allworth Press, c1998. 160 p. : ill. ; 28 cm.+1 computer laser disc (4 3/4 in.). Includes index. ISBN 1-58115-008-3
*1. Illustrators - Legal status, laws. etc. - United States. 2. Artists' contracts - United States - Forms. I. Title.*
**TC KF390.A7 C7 1998**

Legal guide for the visual artist / Tad Crawford. 3rd ed. New York : Allworth Press : Copublished with the American Council for the Arts ; Cincinnati, Ohio : Distributor to the trade in the United States and Canada, North Light Books c1995. 255 p. : ill. ; 28 cm. "Revised 3rd expanded edition"--Cover. Includes bibliographical references (p. 247-248) and index. ISBN 0-927629-11-9
*1. Artists - Legal status, laws, etc. - United States. I. Title.*
**TC KF390.A7 C73 1995**

**CRAZES. See FADS.**

**CRC Press advanced and emerging communications technologies series**
Osso, Rafael. Handbook of emerging communications technologies. Boca Raton, Fla. : CRC Press, 2000.
**TC TK5105 .O62 2000**

**CRC series in exercise physiology**
Battinelli, Thomas. Physique, fitness, and performance. Boca Raton : CRC Press, c2000.
**TC QP301 .B364 2000**

Leutholtz, Brian C. Exercise and disease management. Boca Raton : CRC Press, c1999.
**TC RM725 .L45 1999**

McMurray, Robert G. Concepts in fitness programming. Boca Raton : CRC Press, c1999.
**TC QP301 .M3754 1999**

**The created self.**
Weber, Robert J. (Robert John), 1936- 1st ed. New York ; London : W.W. Norton, c2000.
**TC BF697.5.S44 W43 2000**

**Creating a catalyst for thinking.**
Mallery, Anne L. Boston : Allyn and Bacon, c2000.
**TC LB2806.15 .M34 2000**

**Creating a power web site.**
Junion-Metz, Gail, 1947- New York : Neal-Schuman, c1998.
*TC Z674.75.W67 J86 1998*

**Creating an education system for England and Wales.**
Phillips, Francis R. Lewiston, N.Y. : E. Mellen Press, 1992.
*TC LA633 .P48 1992*

**Creating caring and nurturing educational environments for African American children.**
Morris, Vivian Gunn, 1941- Westport, Conn. : London : Bergin & Garvey, 2000.
*TC LC2802.A2 M67 2000*

**Creating contexts for learning and self-authorship.**
Baxter Magolda, Marcia B., 1951- 1st ed. Nashville [Tenn.] : Vanderbilt University Press, 1999.
*TC LB1025.3 .B39 1999*

**Creating effective teams.**
Wheelan, Susan A. Thousand Oaks, Calif. : Sage Publications, c1999.
*TC HD66 .W485 1999*

**Creating equal.**
Connerly, Ward, 1939- San Francisco : Encounter Books, 2000.
*TC E185.97 .C74 2000*

**Creating hysteria.**
Acocella, Joan Ross. 1st ed. San Francisco : Jossey-Bass Publishers, c1999.
*TC RC569.5.M8 A28 1999*

**Creating integrated curriculum.**
Drake, Susan M., 1944- Thousand Oaks, Calif. : Corwin Press, c1998.
*TC LB1570 .D695 1998*

**CREATING JOBS.** *See* **JOB CREATION.**

**Creating literacy instruction for all children.**
Gunning, Thomas G. 3rd ed. Boston : Allyn and Bacon, c2000.
*TC LB1573 .G93 2000*

**Creating mind.**
Dowling, John E. 1st ed. New York : W.W. Norton, c1998.
*TC QP376 .D695 1998*

**Creating new schools :** how small schools are changing American education / Evans Clinchy, editor. New York ; London : Teachers College Press, c2000. xi, 226 p. ; 24 cm. Includes bibliographical references and index. ISBN 0-8077-3877-8 (cloth) ISBN 0-8077-3876-X (paper) DDC 371.01
*1. School improvement programs - United States. 2. Small schools - United States. I. Clinchy, Evans.*
*TC LB2822.82 .C76 2000*

**Creating successful partnerships between academic and student affairs** / John H. Schuh, Elizabeth J. Whitt, editors. San Francisco : Jossey-Bass Publishers, 1999. 97 p. : ill. ; 23 cm. (New directions for student services, no. 87.) "Fall 1999" Includes bibliographical references and index. CONTENTS: Partnerships: an imperative for enhancing student learning and institutional effectiveness / Charles C. Schroeder -- Partnerships for service learning / Barbara Jacoby -- Freshman interest groups: partnerships for promoting student success / Charles C. Schroeder, Frankie D. Minor, Theodore A. Tarkow -- Partnerships to connect in-and out-of-class experiences / Sarah B. Westfall -- The ursuline studies program: A collaborative core curriculum / Martin F. Larrey, Sandra M. Estanek -- Merging with academic affairs: a promotion or demotion for student affairs? / Jerry Price -- Guiding principles for evaluating student and academic affairs partnerships / John H. Schuh. ISBN 0-7879-4869-1
*1. Student affairs services - United States. 2. College student personnel administrators - United States. 3. Student activities - United States - Management. 4. Total quality management - Universities and colleges - United States. I. Schuh, John H. II. Whitt, Elizabeth J. III. Series: New directions for student services, no. 87.*
*TC LB2342.9 .C75 1999*

**Creating texts.**
Nash, Walter. London ; New York : Longman, 1997.
*TC PE1408 .N22 1997*

**Creating the early literacy classroom.**
Casey, Jean Marie. Englewood, Colo. : Libraries Unlimited, c2000.
*TC LB1576.7 .C38 2000*

**CREATION.** *See* **EVOLUTION.**

**CREATION - FOLKLORE.**
Bierhorst, John. The people with five fingers. New York : Marshall Cavendish, 2000.

*TC E78.C15 B523 2000*

**CREATION (LITERARY, ARTISTIC, ETC.).** *See also* **CREATIVE ABILITY; CREATIVE WRITING.**
Barnard, Malcolm, 1958- Art, design, and visual culture. New York : St. Martin's Press, 1998.
*TC N71 .B32 1998*

Carr, Richard John. The application of multimedia in arts-integrated curricula. 1998.
*TC 06 no. 10919*

Creativity. Huntington, NY : Nova Science Publishers, c2000.
*TC BF408 .C7547 2000*

Gangi, Robyn Joseph. A longitudinal case study of the musical/aesthetic experience of adolescent choral musicians. 1998.
*TC 06 no. 10932*

Khatena, Joe. Developing creative talent in art. Stamford, Conn. : Ablex Publ., c1999.
*TC NX164.C47 K53 1999*

Lowenfeld, Viktor. Creative and mental growth. Rev. ed. New York, Macmillan [1952]
*TC N350 .L62 1952*

**CREATION (LITERARY, ARTISTIC, ETC.) - JUVENILE LITERATURE.**
Kale, Shelly. My museum journal. Los Angeles, CA : J. Paul Getty Museum, c2000.
*TC N7440 .K35 2000*

**CREATION (LITERARY, ARTISTIC, ETC.) - PSYCHOLOGICAL ASPECTS.**
Brink, Andrew. The creative matrix. New York : Peter Lang, c2000.
*TC BF698.9.C74 B75 2000*

Wexler, Alice. The art of necessity. 1999.
*TC 06 no. 11072*

**CREATION (LITERARY, ARTISTIC, ETC.) - THERAPEUTIC USE.**
Wexler, Alice. The art of necessity. 1999.
*TC 06 no. 11072*

**CREATION - MYTHOLOGY.**
Bierhorst, John. The people with five fingers. New York : Marshall Cavendish, 2000.
*TC E78.C15 B523 2000*

**CREATIONISM.** *See* **CREATION.**

**CREATIVE ABILITY.** *See also* **CREATION (LITERARY, ARTISTIC, ETC.); CREATIVE THINKING; GENIUS.**
Creativity. Huntington, NY : Nova Science Publishers, c2000.
*TC BF408 .C7547 2000*

Creativity, spirituality, and transcendence. Stamford, Conn. : Ablex, c2000.
*TC BF411 .C76 2000*

Genius and eminence. 2nd ed. Oxford ; New York : Pergamon Press, 1992.
*TC BF412 .G43 1992*

Goleman, Daniel. The creative spirit. New York, N.Y., U.S.A. : Dutton, c1992.
*TC BF408 .G57 1992*

Handbook of creativity. Cambridge, U.K. ; New York : Cambridge University Press, 1999.
*TC BF408 .H285 1999*

Weiner, Robert, 1950- Creativity and beyond. Albany : State University of New York Press, 2000.
*TC BF408 .W384 2000*

**CREATIVE ABILITY (CHILD PSYCHOLOGY).** *See* **CREATIVE ABILITY IN CHILDREN.**

**CREATIVE ABILITY IN ADOLESCENCE.**
Boriss-Krimsky, Carolyn. The creativity handbook. Springfield, Ill. : C.C. Thomas, 1999.
*TC N350 .B656 1999*

**CREATIVE ABILITY IN ART.** *See* **CREATION (LITERARY, ARTISTIC, ETC.).**

**CREATIVE ABILITY IN BUSINESS.**
Creativity. Huntington, NY : Nova Science Publishers, c2000.
*TC BF408 .C7547 2000*

Denton, D. Keith. The toolbox for the mind. Milwaukee, WI : ASQ Quality Press, c1999.
*TC HD53 .D46 1999*

Leonard-Barton, Dorothy. When sparks fly. Boston, Mass. : Harvard Business School Press, 1999.

*TC HD53 .L46 1999*

**CREATIVE ABILITY IN CHILDREN.** *See also* **DRAWING ABILITY IN CHILDREN.**
Barnes, Barbara. Schools transformed for the 21st century. Torrance, Calif. : Griffin Pub. Group, c1999.
*TC LA217.2 .B39 1999*

Boriss-Krimsky, Carolyn. The creativity handbook. Springfield, Ill. : C.C. Thomas, 1999.
*TC N350 .B656 1999*

Creativity and giftedness in culturally diverse students. Cresskill, N.J. : Hampton Press, c2000.
*TC LC3993.2 .C74 2000*

Hafeli, Mary Claire. Drawing and painting in the middle school. 1999.
*TC 06 no. 11055*

Investigating creativity in youth. Cresskill, N.J. : Hampton Press, c1999.
*TC BF723.C7 I58 1999*

**CREATIVE ABILITY IN CHILDREN - TESTING.**
Khatena, Joe. Developing creative talent in art. Stamford, Conn. : Ablex Publ., c1999.
*TC NX164.C47 K53 1999*

**CREATIVE ABILITY IN SCIENCE.**
Creativity. Huntington, NY : Nova Science Publishers, c2000.
*TC BF408 .C7547 2000*

Miller, Arthur I. Insights of genius. 1st MIT Press pbk. ed. Cambridge, Mass. : MIT Press, 2000.
*TC QC6 .M44 2000*

**CREATIVE ABILITY IN TECHNOLOGY.** *See also* **INVENTIONS; TECHNOLOGICAL INNOVATIONS.**
Creativity. Huntington, NY : Nova Science Publishers, c2000.
*TC BF408 .C7547 2000*

Lienhard, John H., 1930- The engines of our ingenuity. Oxford ; New York : Oxford University Press, 2000.
*TC T14.5 .L52 2000*

**CREATIVE ABILITY (LINGUISTICS).** *See* **CREATIVITY (LINGUISTICS).**

**CREATIVE ABILITY - SOCIAL ASPECTS.**
Streznewski, Marylou Kelly, 1934- Gifted grownups. New York : J. Wiley, c1999.
*TC BF412 .S77 1999*

**CREATIVE ACTIVITIES AND SEAT WORK.** *See also* **ACTIVITY PROGRAMS IN EDUCATION.**
Gonsalves, Philip. Build it! festival. Berkeley, CA : Great Explorations in Math and Science (GEMS), Lawrence Hall of Science, University of California at Berkeley, c1995.
*TC QA462 .G66 1995*

**Creative and mental growth.**
Lowenfeld, Viktor Rev. ed. New York, Macmillan [1952]
*TC N350 .L62 1952*

**The creative classroom series**
(v. 1) Creativity in the classroom. Burbank, CA : Disney Learning Partnership, c1999.
*TC LB1062 .C7 1999*

**CREATIVE DRAMATICS (EDUCATION).** *See* **DRAMA IN EDUCATION.**

**Creative guide to designing and delivering faster, more effective training programs.**
Meier, Dave. The accelerated learning handbook. New York : McGraw Hill, c2000.
*TC LB1029.A22 M45 2000*

**The creative matrix.**
Brink, Andrew. New York : Peter Lang, c2000.
*TC BF698.9.C74 B75 2000*

**Creative nonfiction (Urbana, Ill.)**
Davis, Lennard J., 1949- My sense of silence. Urbana : University of Illinois Press, c2000.
*TC HQ759.912 .D38 2000*

**Creative physical activities & equipment.**
Davison, Bev, 1957- Creative physical activities and equipment. Champaign, IL : Human Kinetics, c1998.
*TC GV745 .D38 1998*

**Creative piano teaching.**
Lyke, James. 3rd ed. Champaign, Ill. : Stipes Pub. Co., c1996.
*TC MT220 .L95 1996*

**Creative power.**
Cramer, Ronald L. New York : London : Longman, c2001.
*TC LB1576 .C758 2001*

**Creative revolution.**
In search of human origins [videorecording]. [Boston, Mass.] : WGBH Educational Foundation, c1994.
*TC GN281 .I45 1994*

**The creative spirit.**
Goleman, Daniel. New York, N.Y., U.S.A. : Dutton, c1992.
*TC BF408 .G57 1992*

**Creative spirit (Television program).**
Goleman, Daniel. The creative spirit. New York, N.Y., U.S.A. : Dutton, c1992.
*TC BF408 .G57 1992*

**CREATIVE THINKING.**
Dodwell, P. C. Brave new mind. New York : Oxford University Press, 2000.
*TC BF311 .D568 2000*

Green, Andy. Creativity in public relations. London ; Dover, N.H. : Kogan Page, c1999.
*TC HD59 .G744 1999*

Handbook of creativity. Cambridge, U.K. ; New York : Cambridge University Press, 1999.
*TC BF408 .H285 1999*

Lamm, Sharon Lea. The connection between action reflection learning and transformative learning. 2000.
*TC 06 no. 11230*

Olson, Ivan, 1931- The arts and critical thinking in American education. Westport, Conn. : Bergin & Garvey, 2000.
*TC BH39 .O45 2000*

Perkins, David N. Archimedes' bathtub. 1st ed. New York : W.W. Norton, c2000.
*TC BF441 .P47 2000*

Root-Bernstein, Robert Scott. Sparks of genius. Boston, Mass. : Houghton Mifflin Co., 1999.
*TC BF408 R66 1999*

Weiner, Robert, 1950- Creativity and beyond. Albany : State University of New York Press, 2000.
*TC BF408 .W384 2000*

**CREATIVE THINKING (EDUCATION).** *See* **CREATIVE THINKING.**

**CREATIVE THINKING IN CHILDREN.**
Investigating creativity in youth. Cresskill, N.J. : Hampton Press, c1999.
*TC BF723.C7 I58 1999*

Khatena, Joe. Enhancing creativity of gifted children. Cresskill, N.J. : Hampton Press, c2000.
*TC LC3993 .K56 2000*

**CREATIVE THINKING - STUDY AND TEACHING.**
Creativity in the classroom. Burbank, CA : Disney Learning Partnership, c1999.
*TC LB1062 .C7 1999*

Johnson, Andrew P. Up and out :. Boston : Allyn and Bacon, c2000.
*TC LB1590.3 .J64 2000*

**CREATIVE THINKING - STUDY AND TEACHING (MIDDLE SCHOOL) - NEW YORK (STATE) - CASE STUDIES.**
Carr, Richard John. The application of multimedia in arts-integrated curricula. 1998.
*TC 06 no. 10919*

**CREATIVE WRITING (ELEMENTARY EDUCATION).**
Anderson, Carl, educator. How's it going? Portsmouth, NH : Heinemann, c2000.
*TC LB1576 .A6159 2000*

Tompkins, Gail E. Teaching writing. 3rd ed. Upper Saddle River, N.J. : Merrill, c2000.
*TC LB1576 .T66 2000*

Writers' workshop. Boston ; London : Allyn and Bacon, c2000.
*TC LB1576 .W734 2000*

**CREATIVE WRITING (HIGHER EDUCATION) - SOCIAL ASPECTS.**
Haake, Katharine. What our speech disrupts. Urbana, Ill. : National Council of Teachers of English, c2000.
*TC PE1404 .H3 2000*

**CREATIVE WRITING (MIDDLE SCHOOL).**
Writers' workshop. Boston ; London : Allyn and Bacon, c2000.

*TC LB1576 .W734 2000*

**CREATIVE WRITING (MIDDLE SCHOOL) - STUDY AND TEACHING.** *See* **CREATIVE WRITING (MIDDLE SCHOOL).**

**CREATIVE WRITING (SECONDARY EDUCATION).**
Noden, Harry R. Image grammar. Portsmouth, NH : Heinemann, 1999.
*TC LB1631 .N62 1999*

**CREATIVE WRITING (SECONDARY EDUCATION) - CASE STUDIES.**
Harper, Helen J., 1957- Wild words-dangerous desires. New York : Peter Lang, c2000.
*TC LB1631 .H267 2000*

**CREATIVE WRITING - STUDY AND TEACHING.**
Creativity in the classroom. Burbank, CA : Disney Learning Partnership, c1999.
*TC LB1062 .C7 1999*

Romano, Tom. Blending genre, altering style. Portsmouth, NH : Boynton/Cook ; Heinemann, c2000.
*TC PE1404 .R635 2000*

Writing across languages. Stamford, Conn. : Ablex Pub., c2000.
*TC PB36 .W77 2000*

**CREATIVE WRITING - STUDY AND TEACHING (ELEMENTARY).** *See* **CREATIVE WRITING (ELEMENTARY EDUCATION).**

**CREATIVE WRITING - STUDY AND TEACHING (HIGHER).** *See* **CREATIVE WRITING (HIGHER EDUCATION).**

**CREATIVE WRITING - STUDY AND TEACHING (MIDDLE SCHOOL).** *See* **CREATIVE WRITING (MIDDLE SCHOOL).**

**CREATIVE WRITING - STUDY AND TEACHING (SECONDARY).** *See* **CREATIVE WRITING (SECONDARY EDUCATION).**

**CREATIVE WRITING - THERAPEUTIC USE.**
Writing and healing. Urbana, Ill. : National Council of Teachers of English, c2000.
*TC RC489.W75 W756 2000*

**CREATIVENESS.** *See also* **CREATIVE ABILITY.**
Genius and eminence. 2nd ed. Oxford ; New York : Pergamon Press, 1992.
*TC BF412 .G43 1992*

**CREATIVITY.** *See* **CREATIVE ABILITY.**

**Creativity and beyond.**
Weiner, Robert, 1950- Albany : State University of New York Press, 2000.
*TC BF408 .W384 2000*

**Creativity and giftedness in culturally diverse students** / edited by Giselle B. Esquivel, John C. Houtz. Cresskill, N.J. : Hampton Press, c2000. xi, 276 p. ; 25 cm. (Perspectives on creativity) Includes bibliographical references and index. ISBN 1-57273-224-5 ISBN 1-57273-225-3 DDC 371.95
*1. Gifted children - Education - United States. 2. Children of minorities - Education - United States. 3. Creative ability in children. I. Esquivel, Giselle B. II. Houtz, John. III. Series.*
*TC LC3993.2 .C74 2000*

**Creativity :** being usefully innovative in solving diverse problems / Stuart Nagel (editor). Huntington, NY : Nova Science Publishers, c2000. xii, 254 p. : ill. ; 27 cm. Includes bibliographical references and index. ISBN 1-56072-837-X DDC 153.3/5
*1. Creative ability. 2. Creation (Literary, artistic, etc.) 3. Creative ability in technology. 4. Creative ability in business. 5. Creative ability in science. I. Nagel, Stuart S., 1934-*
*TC BF408 .C7547 2000*

**The creativity handbook.**
Boriss-Krimsky, Carolyn. Springfield, Ill. : C.C. Thomas, 1999.
*TC N350 .B656 1999*

**Creativity in public relations.**
Green, Andy. London ; Dover, N.H. : Kogan Page, c1999.
*TC HD59 .G744 1999*

**Creativity in the classroom :** an exploration / a production of Disney Learning Partnership in collaboration with Project Zero at the Harvard Graduate School of Education ; writer and producer, Ron Ritchhart. Burbank, CA : Disney Learning Partnership, c1999. 1 videocassette (45 min.) : sd., col. ; 1/2 in. + 1 educator's guide (90 p. ; 28 cm.) in container 32 x 29 x 5 cm. (The creative classroom series ; v. 1) (in a series ; v. 1) VHS. Catalogued from credits and container. Editor, Sandy Guthries; Carol Younman; graphic design and animation, Kerrin Bourque; music, Spin Music, Pierpaolo Tiano, Billy

White Acre. Footage originally produced for Disney's American Teachers Awards. For educators. SUMMARY: The video opens with 3 vignettes demonstrating a range of creativity: Roxann Rose-Duckworth teaching math to 4th and 5th graders at Alderwood Elementary School in Bellingham, Washington, using a concept called "Math around the Clock", a practical and fun approach to mathematics; Elba Marrero teaching a special needs class at P.S. 72 in Manhattan, using the idea of each child writing about and drawing a secret garden after visiting gardens and reading about them in literature; David Seiter teaching history to an 11th grade American History class in Northridge High School, in Layton, Utah, using skits, workshops and other activities that puts the student in the historical character's shoes. Glimpses of the creative approach to content, generating enthusiasm and creative practices are seen in other classrooms, where the activities range from visiting a historically preserved prairie, to studying animal visitors in the classroom.
*1. Creative thinking - Study and teaching. 2. Activity programs in education. 3. Group work in education. 4. Mathematics - Study and teaching. 5. Special education - Activity programs. 6. Creative writing - Study and teaching. 7. Drawing - Study and teaching. 8. United States - History - Study and teaching. I. Series. II. Series: in a series ; v. 1*
*TC LB1062 .C7 1999*

**CREATIVITY (LINGUISTICS).**
Kress, Gunther R. Early spelling. London ; New York : Routledge, 2000.
*TC P240.2 .K74 2000*

**Creativity, spirituality, and transcendence :** paths to integrity and wisdom in the mature self / edited by Melvin E. Miller & Susanne R. Cook-Greuter. Stamford, Conn. : Ablex, c2000. xxxiv, 261 p. : ill. ; 24 cm. (Publications in creativity research) Includes bibliographical references and indexes. ISBN 1-56750-460-4 (hbk.), ISBN 1-56750-461-2 (pbk.) DDC 153.3/5
*1. Creative ability. 2. Spirituality. 3. Maturation (Psychology) I. Miller, Melvin E. II. Cook-Greuter, Susanne R. III. Series.*
*TC BF411 .C76 2000*

**CRÈCHES (DAY NURSERIES).** *See* **DAY CARE CENTERS.**

**CREDULITY.** *See* **BELIEF AND DOUBT.**

**CREEKS.** *See* **RIVERS.**

**Creemers, Bert P. M.**
Enhancing educational excellence, equity, and efficiency. Dordrecht ; Boston : Kluwer Academic Publishers, c1999.
*TC LB2921 .E54 1999*

**Creese, Michael.** Improving schools and governing bodies : making a difference / Michael Creese and Peter Earley. London ; New York : Routledge, 1999. 133 p. : ill. ; 25 cm. Includes bibliographical references (p. [125]-128) and index. ISBN 0-415-20510-7 (hbk.) ISBN 0-415-20511-5 (pbk.) DDC 371.2/00941
*1. School improvement programs - Great Britain. 2. School boards - Great Britain. I. Earley, Peter. II. Title.*
*TC LB2822.84.G7 C75 1999*

**Crenshaw, Harry M., 1946-.**
Hoyle, John. Interpersonal sensitivity. Larchmont, NY : Eye on Education, c1997.
*TC LB2831.92.U6 H67 1997*

**CRENSHAW HIGH SCHOOL (LOS ANGELES, CALIF.).**
Corwin, Miles. And still we rise. 1st ed. New York : Bard, 2000.
*TC LC3993.9 .C678 2000*

**Crenson, Matthew A., 1943-** Building the invisible orphanage : a prehistory of the American welfare system / Matthew A. Crenson. Cambridge, Mass. : Harvard University Press, 1998. xii, 383 p. : ill. ; 24 cm. Includes bibliographical references (p. 333-374) and index. ISBN 0-674-46591-1 (alk. paper) DDC 362.7/0973
*1. Public welfare - United States - History. 2. United States - Social policy. 3. Child welfare - United States - History. 4. Welfare state. 5. Orphanages - United States - History. I. Title.*
*TC HV91 .C74 1998*

**Crenson, Matthew A., 1943- joint author.**
Greenberger, Martin, 1931- Models in the policy process. New York : Russell Sage Foundation : [distributed by Basic Books], c1976.
*TC H61 .G667*

**CREWS (GANGS).** *See* **GANGS.**

**Cribb, John T. E.**
Bennett, William J. (William John), 1943- The educated child. New York : Free Press, c1999.
*TC LB1048.5 .B45 1999*

**Crick, Bernard R.** Essays on citizenship / Bernard Crick. London ; New York : Continuum, 2000. xii, 210 p. : 1 ill. ; 22 cm. Includes bibliographical references. ISBN 0-

8264-4821-6 ISBN 0-8264-4812-7 (pbk.)
*1. Citizenship. I. Title.*
**TC JF801 .C75 2000**

**Crick, Joyce.**
Freud, Sigmund, 1856-1939 The interpretation of dreams. Oxford : New York : Oxford University Press, 1999.
**TC BF1078 .F72 1999**

**Cricket never does.**
Livingston, Myra Cohn. New York : Margaret K. McElderry Books, c1997.
**TC PS3562.I945 C75 1997**

**CRICKET - UNITED STATES - HISTORY.**
Melville, Tom. The tented field. Bowling Green, OH : Bowling Green State University Popular Press, c1998.
**TC GV928.U6 M45 1998**

**CRIES. See PEDDLERS AND PEDDLING.**

**Crighton, David A., 1964-.**
Towl, Graham J. The handbook of psychology for forensic practitioners. London ; New York : Routledge, 1996.
**TC RA1148 .T69 1996**

**CRIME. See CRIMINAL JUSTICE, ADMINISTRATION OF; JUVENILE DELINQUENCY; SEX CRIMES; VIOLENT CRIMES.**

**Crime & society (Boulder, Colo.)**
Chambliss, William J. Power, politics, and crime. Boulder, CO : Westview Press, c1999.
**TC HV6789 .C395 1999**

**CRIME AND AGE. See YOUTH - CRIMES AGAINST.**

**CRIME AND CRIMINALS. See CRIME.**

**CRIME - CONGRESSES.**
Genetics of criminal and antisocial behaviour. Chichester ; New York : Wiley, 1996.
**TC HV6047 .G46 1996**

**CRIME DETECTION. See CRIMINAL INVESTIGATION.**

**CRIME INVESTIGATION. See CRIMINAL INVESTIGATION.**

**CRIME - POLITICAL ASPECTS - UNITED STATES.**
Chambliss, William J. Power, politics, and crime. Boulder, CO : Westview Press, c1999.
**TC HV6789 .C395 1999**

**CRIME SCENES. See CRIMINAL INVESTIGATION.**

**CRIME SYNDICATES. See GANGS.**

**CRIMES. See CRIME.**

**CRIMES AGAINST HUMANITY. See GENOCIDE; MURDER; SLAVERY.**

**CRIMES AGAINST STUDENTS. See STUDENTS - CRIMES AGAINST.**

**CRIMES AGAINST YOUTH. See YOUTH - CRIMES AGAINST.**

**CRIMES OF VIOLENCE. See VIOLENT CRIMES.**

**CRIMES, VIOLENT. See VIOLENT CRIMES.**

**CRIMES WITHOUT VICTIMS. See DRUG ABUSE; SUBSTANCE ABUSE.**

**CRIMINAL ANTHROPOLOGY - PERIODICALS.**
The Journal of delinquency. Whittier, Calif. : Whittier State School, Dept. of Research, 1916-c1928.

**CRIMINAL ANTHROPOMETRY. See CRIMINAL ANTHROPOLOGY.**

**CRIMINAL ASSAULT. See RAPE.**

**CRIMINAL BEHAVIOR - GENETIC ASPECTS - CONGRESSES.**
Genetics of criminal and antisocial behaviour. Chichester ; New York : Wiley, 1996.
**TC HV6047 .G46 1996**

**CRIMINAL INVESTIGATION - FICTION.**
Cadnum, Michael. Rundown. New York : Viking, c1999.
**TC PZ7.C11724 Ru 1999**

**CRIMINAL INVESTIGATIONS. See CRIMINAL INVESTIGATION.**

**CRIMINAL JUSTICE, ADMINISTRATION OF. See CRIME; DISCRIMINATION IN CRIMINAL JUSTICE ADMINISTRATION; JUVENILE JUSTICE, ADMINISTRATION OF; POLICE.**

**CRIMINAL JUSTICE, ADMINISTRATION OF - POLITICAL ASPECTS - UNITED STATES.**
Chambliss, William J. Power, politics, and crime. Boulder, CO : Westview Press, c1999.
**TC HV6789 .C395 1999**

**CRIMINAL JUSTICE, ADMINISTRATION OF - STUDY AND TEACHING (HIGHER) - UNITED STATES.**
Nemeth, Charles P., 1951- A status report on contemporary criminal justice education. Lewiston, NY, USA : E. Mellen Press, c1989.
**TC HV7419.5 .N45 1989**

**CRIMINAL JUSTICE, ADMINISTRATION OF - UNITED STATES.**
Cole, David. No equal justice. New York : The New Press : Distributed by W. W. Norton, c1999.
**TC HV9950 .C65 1999**

**CRIMINAL JUSTICE PERSONNEL. See POLICE.**

**CRIMINAL LAW. See CONFIDENTIAL COMMUNICATIONS; CRIME; CRIMINAL JUSTICE, ADMINISTRATION OF; HOMICIDE; KIDNAPPING; RIOTS.**

**CRIMINAL PROCEDURE. See TRIAL PRACTICE.**

**CRIMINAL PSYCHOLOGY. See also CRIMINAL BEHAVIOR; PSYCHOLOGY, PATHOLOGICAL.**
Towl, Graham J. The handbook of psychology for forensic practitioners. London ; New York : Routledge, 1996.
**TC RA1148 .T69 1996**

**CRIMINALS. See CRIME; CRIMINAL JUSTICE, ADMINISTRATION OF; GANGS; MURDERERS; SEX OFFENDERS.**

**CRIMINALS - REHABILITATION. See ALTERNATIVES TO IMPRISONMENT.**

**CRIMINOLOGY. See CRIME.**

**Criminology studies**
(v. 7) Turk, William L. When juvenile crime comes to school. Lewiston, NY : E. Mellen Press, 1999.
**TC HV6250.4.S78 T87 1999**

**Crimmins, James C.** Enterprise in the nonprofit sector / James C. Crimmins and Mary Keil. Washington, D.C. : Partners for Livable Places ; New York : Rockefeller Bros. Fund, c1983. 141 p. ; 22 cm. Includes bibliographical references. ISBN 0-941182-03-7 (pbk.) DDC 658/.048
*1. Corporations, Nonprofit - United States - Management. I. Title.*
**TC HD62.6 .C74 1983**

**CRIPPLED. See PHYSICALLY HANDICAPPED.**

**The Crippled child.** Chicago [etc.] National Society for Crippled Children and Adults [etc.] 36 v. ill. 28 cm. V. 1-36, no. 2; Aug. 1923-Aug. 1958. Other title: Crippled child magazine. Issues for published under the association's earlier names: International Society for Crippled Children, Inc., later National Society for Crippled Children of the United States of America, Inc. DDC 362.7805
*1. Physically handicapped children - Periodicals. 2. Children - Diseases. I. National Society for Crippled Children and Adults.*

**CRIPPLED CHILDREN. See PHYSICALLY HANDICAPPED CHILDREN.**

**CRIPPLES. See PHYSICALLY HANDICAPPED.**

**CRISES, COMMERCIAL. See DEPRESSIONS.**

**Crisis intervention handbook :** assessment, treatment, and research / edited by Albert R. Roberts. 2nd ed. Oxford ; New York : Oxford University Press, 2000. xxix, 554 p. : ill. ; 24 cm. Includes bibliographical references and index. ISBN 0-19-513365-X (alk. paper) DDC 616.89/025
*1. Crisis intervention (Mental health services) - Handbooks, manuals, etc. 2. Community mental health services - Handbooks, manuals, etc. I. Roberts, Albert R.*
**TC RC480.6 .C744 2000**

**CRISIS INTERVENTION (MENTAL HEALTH SERVICES) - HANDBOOKS, MANUALS, ETC.**
Crisis intervention handbook. 2nd ed. Oxford ; New York : Oxford University Press, 2000.
**TC RC480.6 .C744 2000**

**CRISIS INTERVENTION (MENTAL HEALTH SERVICES) - UNITED STATES - EVALUATION.**
Violence in families. Washington, D.C. : National Academy Press, 1998.
**TC HV6626.2 .V56 1998**

**CRISIS MANAGEMENT. See CONFLICT MANAGEMENT; SCHOOL CRISIS MANAGEMENT.**

**The crisis of America's cities.**
Bartlett, Randall, 1945- Armonk, N.Y. : M.E. Sharpe, c1998.
**TC HT123 .B324 1998**

**Crissey, Brian L., joint author.**
Greenberger, Martin, 1931- Models in the policy process. New York : Russell Sage Foundation : [distributed by Basic Books], c1976.
**TC H61 .G667**

**CRITERION-REFERENCED TESTS. See CURRICULUM-BASED ASSESSMENT.**

**CRITICAL CARE - HISTORY - UNITED STATES.**
Fairman, Julie. Critical care nursing. Philadelphia : University of Pennsylvania Press, c1998.
**TC RT120.I5 F34 1998**

**CRITICAL CARE MEDICINE. See INTENSIVE CARE NURSING; TERMINAL CARE.**

**CRITICAL CARE NURSING. See also INTENSIVE CARE NURSING.**
Fairman, Julie. Philadelphia : University of Pennsylvania Press, c1998.
**TC RT120.I5 F34 1998**

**Critical challenges across the curriculum**
(#1) Critical challenges in social studies for junior high students. Burnaby, B.C. : Field Relations and Teacher In-Service Education, Faculty of Education, Simon Fraser University, 1996.
**TC D16.2 .C75 1996**

**Critical challenges across the curriculum series**
(2) McDiarmid, Tami, 1960- Critical challenges for primary students. Burnaby, B.C. : Field Relations and Teacher In-Service Education, Faculty of Education, Simon Fraser University, c1996.
**TC LB1590.3 .M36 1996**

(v. 3) Harrison, John, 1951- Critical challenges in social studies for upper elementary students. Vancouver : Critical Thinking Cooperative, 1999.
**TC LB1584.5.C3 H37 1999**

**Critical challenges for primary students.**
McDiarmid, Tami, 1960- Burnaby, B.C. : Field Relations and Teacher In-Service Education, Faculty of Education, Simon Fraser University, c1996.
**TC LB1590.3 .M36 1996**

**Critical challenges in social studies for junior high students** / Roland Case, LeRoi Daniels & Phyllis Schwartz (eds.) Burnaby, B.C. : Field Relations and Teacher In-Service Education, Faculty of Education, Simon Fraser University, 1996. xx, 145 p. ; 28 cm. (Critical challenges across the curriculum, 1205-9730 ; #1) Includes bibliographical references. Co-published by the Critical Thinking Cooperative. ISBN 0-86491-143-2 DDC 300/.71/2
*1. Social studies - Study and teaching (Secondary) I. Case, Roland, 1951- II. Daniels, LeRoi, 1930- III. Schwartz, Phyllis B. (Phyllis Benna) IV. Critical Thinking Cooperative. V. Simon Fraser University. Faculty of Education. Field Relations and Teacher In-Service Education. VI. Series.*
**TC D16.2 .C75 1996**

**Critical challenges in social studies for upper elementary students.**
Harrison, John, 1951- Vancouver : Critical Thinking Cooperative, 1999.
**TC LB1584.5.C3 H37 1999**

**Critical crosscurrents in education.**
Collins, Michael, 1939- Original ed. Malabar, Fla. : Krieger Pub. Co., 1998.
**TC LC196 .C65 1998**

**Critical education and ethics**
The academy and the possibility of belief. Cresskill, N.J. : Hampton Press, c2000.
**TC LB2324 .A27 2000**

**Critical education in the new information age** / Manuel Castells ... [et al.] ; introduction by Peter McLaren. Lanham, Md. : Rowman & Littlefield, c1999. v, 176 p. ; 23 cm. (Critical perspectives series) Includes bibliographical references and index. ISBN 0-8476-9011-3 (cloth : alk. paper) ISBN 0-8476-9010-5 (pbk. : alk. paper) DDC 370.11/5
*1. Critical pedagogy - United States. 2. Popular education - United States. 3. Education - Social aspects - United States. I. Castells, Manuel. II. Series.*
**TC LC196.5.U6 C745 1999**

**Critical ethnicity :** countering the waves of identity politics / edited by Robert H. Tai and Mary L. Kenyatta. Lanham, Md. : Rowman & Littlefield,

c1999. v. 213 p. ; 25 cm. (Critical perspectives series)
Includes bibliographical references and index. ISBN
0-8476-9113-6 (cloth : alk. paper) ISBN 0-8476-9114-4
(paper : alk. paper) DDC 370.11/5
*1. Discrimination in education - United States. 2. Multicultural
education - United States. 3. Minorities - Education - United
States. 4. Politics and education - United States. 5. Group
identity - Political aspects - United States. 6. Identity
(Psychology) - Political aspects - United States. 7. Ethnicity -
United States. 8. Critical pedagogy - United States. I. Tai,
Robert H., 1965- II. Kenyatta, Mary L., 1944- III. Series.*
**TC LC212.2 .C75 1999**

**Critical geographies**
(8) Children's geographies. London ; New York :
Routledge, 2000.
**TC HQ767.9 .C4559 2000**

**CRITICAL HUMANISM IN EDUCATION.** *See*
**CRITICAL PEDAGOGY.**

**Critical issues in educational leadership series**
Lensmire, Timothy J., 1961- Powerful writing/
responsible teaching. New York : Teachers College
Press, c2000.
**TC LB1576 .L42 2000**

**Critical issues in neuropsychology**
International handbook of neuropsychological
rehabilitation. New York : Kluwer Academic/Plenum
Publishers, c2000.
**TC RC387.5 .I478 2000**

Practitioner's guide to evaluating change with
neuropsychological assessment instruments. New
York : Kluwer Academic/Plenum Publishers, c2000.
**TC RC386.6.N48 P73 2000**

**Critical knowledge.**
Critical knowledge for diverse teachers & learners.
Washington, DC : AACTE : ERIC, c1997.
**TC LB1715 .C732 1997**

**Critical knowledge for diverse teachers & learners /**
edited by Jacqueline Jordan Irvine ; preface by James
Fraser. Washington, DC : AACTE : ERIC, c1997. x,
223 p. ; 22 cm. Includes bibliographical references. ISBN 0-
89333-149-X DDC 370/.71/0973
*1. Teachers - Training of - United States. 2. Teachers - In-
service training - United States. 3. Multicultural education -
United States. I. Irvine, Jacqueline Jordan. II. American
Association of Colleges for Teacher Education. III.
Educational Resources Information Center (U.S.) IV. Title:
Critical knowledge*
**TC LB1715 .C732 1997**

**Critical media studies**
Splichal, Slavko. Public opinion. Lanham, Md. :
Rowman & Littlefield, 1999.
**TC HM261 .S7515 1999**

**CRITICAL PEDAGOGY.** *See also* **POPULAR**
**EDUCATION.**
Wink, Joan. 2nd ed. New York : Longman, c2000.
**TC LC196.5.U6 W54 2000**

**CRITICAL PEDAGOGY.**
Armitage, Peter B., 1939- Political relationship and
narrative knowledge. Westport, Conn. : Bergin &
Garvey, 2000.
**TC LC93.G7 A86 2000**

Britzman, Deborah P., 1952- Lost subjects, contested
objects. Albany : State University of New York Press,
c1998.
**TC LB1060 .B765 1998**

Brown, Stephen Gilbert. Words in the wilderness.
Albany : State University of New York Press, c2000.
**TC E99.A86 B76 2000**

Burch, Kerry T., 1957- Eros as the educational
principle of democracy. New York : P. Lang, c2000.
**TC LC196 .B75 2000**

Chomsky, Noam. Chomsky on miseducation.
Lanham, Md. ; Oxford : Rowman & Littlefield
Publishers, c2000.
**TC LB885.C522 A3 2000**

Collins, Michael, 1939- Critical crosscurrents in
education. Original ed. Malabar, Fla. : Krieger Pub.
Co., 1998.
**TC LC196 .C65 1998**

Education policy. Cheltenham, UK : Northampton,
MA : Edward Elgar Pub., c1999.
**TC LC71 .E32 1999**

Flecha, Ramón. [Compartiendo palabras. English]
Sharing words. Lanham, Md. ; Oxford : Rowman &
Littlefield Publishers, c2000.

**TC LB1060 .F5913 2000**

Freire, Paulo, 1921- [Pedagogia de autonomia.
English] Pedagogy of freedom. Lanham : Rowman &
Littlefield Publishers, c1998.
**TC LC196 .F73713 1998**

Freirean pedagogy, praxis, and possibilities. New
York : Falmer Press, 2000.
**TC LC196 .F76 2000**

Globalization and education. New York : Routledge,
1999.
**TC LC191 .G545 1999**

Hicks, D. Emily. Ninety-five languages and seven
forms of intelligence. New York : P. Lang, c1999.
**TC LC196 .H53 1999**

Kincheloe, Joe L. The stigma of genius. New York :
Canterbury [England] : P. Lang, c1999.
**TC LB875.E562 K56 1999**

Lensmire, Timothy J., 1961- Powerful writing/
responsible teaching. New York : Teachers College
Press, c2000.
**TC LB1576 .L42 2000**

Making justice our project. Urbana, Ill. : National
Council of Teachers of English, c1999
**TC LB1576 .M3613 1999**

McLaren, Peter, 1948- Che Guevara, Paulo Freire,
and the pedagogy of revolution. Lanham [Md.] :
Rowman & Littlefield Publishers, c2000.
**TC LC196 .M29 2000**

Multicultural curriculum. New York : Routledge,
2000.
**TC LC1099 .M816 2000**

O'Sullivan, Edmund, 1938- Transformative learning.
London ; New York : Zed Books ; New York :
Distributed in USA exclusively by St. Martin's Press,
1999.
**TC LC196 .O7 1999**

Perspectives in critical thinking. New York : P. Lang,
c2000.
**TC LB1590.3 .P476 2000**

Roberts, Peter, 1963- Education, literacy, and
humanization. Westport, Conn. : Bergin & Garvey,
2000.
**TC LB880.F732 R62 2000**

Stories out of school. Stamford, Conn. : Ablex Pub.,
c2000.
**TC LC196 .S6994 2000**

Taught bodies. New York : P. Lang, c2000.
**TC LB14.7 .T38 2000**

Too, Yun Lee. The pedagogical contract. Ann Arbor:
University of Michigan Press, c2000.
**TC LB1033 .T66 2000**

Trifonas, Peter Pericles, 1960- The ethics of writing.
Lanham, Md. ; Oxford : Rowman & Littlefield, c2000.
**TC LB14.7 .T75 2000**

Trifonas, Peter Pericles, 1960- Revolutionary
pedagogies. New York : Routledge, 2000.
**TC LC196 .R48 2000**

**CRITICAL PEDAGOGY - AFRICA.**
Bassey, Magnus O. Western education and political
domination in Africa. Westport, CT : Bergin &
Garvey, 1999.
**TC LC95.A2 B37 1999**

**CRITICAL PEDAGOGY - AFRICA - CASE**
**STUDIES.**
Democratic teacher education reform in Africa.
Boulder, Colo. ; Oxford : Westview Press, 1999.
**TC LB1727.N3 D46 1999**

**CRITICAL PEDAGOGY - CANADA - CASE**
**STUDIES.**
Henry, Annette, 1955- Taking back control. Albany :
State University of New York Press, c1998.
**TC LB1775.4.C2 H45 1998**

Ryan, James, 1952 Oct. 18- Race and ethnicity in
multi-ethnic schools. Clevedon [England] ;
Philadelphia : Multilingual Matters, c1999.
**TC LC3734 .R93 1999**

**CRITICAL PEDAGOGY - EL SALVADOR - CASE**
**STUDIES.**
Purcell-Gates, Victoria. Now we read, we see, we
speak. Mahwah, N.J. : L. Erlbaum Associates,
Publishers, 2000.
**TC LC155.S22 P87 2000**

**CRITICAL PEDAGOGY - GREAT BRITAIN.**
Ozga, Jennifer. Policy research in educational

settings :. Buckingham [England] ; Philadelphia :
Open University Press, 2000.
**TC LB1028.25.G7 O93 2000**

**CRITICAL PEDAGOGY - NAMIBIA.**
Democratic teacher education reform in Africa.
Boulder, Colo. ; Oxford : Westview Press, 1999.
**TC LB1727.N3 D46 1999**

**CRITICAL PEDAGOGY - UNITED STATES.**
Apple, Michael W. Official knowledge. 2nd ed. New
York : Routledge, 2000.
**TC LC89 .A815 2000**

Bartolomé, Lilia I. The misteaching of academic
discourses. Boulder, Colo. : Westview Press, 1998.
**TC LB1033.5 .B37 1998**

Critical education in the new information age.
Lanham, Md. : Rowman & Littlefield, c1999.
**TC LC196.5.U6 C745 1999**

Critical ethnicity. Lanham, Md. : Rowman &
Littlefield, c1999.
**TC LC212.2 .C75 1999**

Education is politics. Portsmouth, NH : Boynton/
Cook, c1999.
**TC LC196.5.U6 E36 1999**

Eisler, Riane Tennenhaus. Tomorrow's children.
Boulder, Colo. ; Oxford : Westview Press, 2000.
**TC LC1023 .E57 2000**

Fletcher, Scott, 1959- Education and emancipation.
New York : Teachers College Press, c2000.
**TC LC191.4 .F54 2000**

From nihilism to possibility. Cresskill, N.J. : Hampton
Press, c2000.
**TC LC5141 .F76 1999**

Herideen, Penelope E., 1960- Policy, pedagogy, and
social inequality. Westport, Conn. : Bergin & Garvey,
1998.
**TC LB2328.15.U6 H47 1998**

Knowledge and power in the global economy.
Mahwah, N.J. : L. Erlbaum Associates, 2000.
**TC LC66 .K66 2000**

The literacy connection. Cresskill, N.J. : Hampton
Press, c1999.
**TC LC151 .L482 1999**

Macedo, Donaldo P. (Donaldo Pereira), 1950-
Dancing with bigotry. New York : St. Martin's Press,
1999.
**TC LC196.5.U6 D26 1999**

Powell, Rebecca, 1949- Literacy as a moral
imperative. Lanham, Md. : Rowman & Littlefield
Publishers, c1999.
**TC LC151 .P69 1999**

Reconceptualizing the literacies in adolescents' lives.
Mahwah, N.J. : L. Erlbaum Associates, 1998.
**TC LB1631 .R296 1998**

Robbins, Carol Braswell. An examination of critical
feminist pedagogy in practice. 1999.
**TC 06 no. 11067**

Strangers in the land. New York : Peter Lang, c1999.
**TC E184.36.E84 S77 1999**

Wink, Joan. Critical pedagogy. 2nd ed. New York :
Longman, c2000.
**TC LC196.5.U6 W54 2000**

**CRITICAL PEDAGOGY - UNITED STATES -**
**CASE STUDIES.**
Goodman, Greg S., 1949- Alternatives in education.
New York : P. Lang, c1999.
**TC LC46.4 .G66 1999**

**Critical perspectives on schooling and fertility in the**
**developing world /** Caroline H. Bledsoe ... [et al.]
editors ; Committee on Population, Commission on
Behavioral and Social Sciences and Education,
National Research Council. Washington, D.C. :
National Academy Press, 1999. x, 320 p. : ill ; 23 cm.
Includes bibliographical references and index. ISBN
0-309-06191-1 (pbk.) DDC 371.822
*1. Women - Education - Developing countries - Cross-cultural
studies. 2. Fertility, Human - Developing countries - Cross-
cultural studies. 3. Women - Developing countries - Social
conditions - Cross-cultural studies. I. Bledsoe, Caroline H. II.
National Research Council (U.S.). Committee on Population.
III. National Research Council (U.S.). Commission on
Behavioral and Social Sciences and Education.*
**TC LC2572 .C75 1998**

**Critical perspectives series.**
Chomsky, Noam. Chomsky on miseducation.
Lanham, Md. ; Oxford : Rowman & Littlefield
Publishers, c2000.

*TC LB885.C522 A3 2000*

Critical education in the new information age. Lanham, Md. : Rowman & Littlefield, c1999.
*TC LC196.5.U6 C745 1999*

Critical ethnicity. Lanham, Md. : Rowman & Littlefield, c1999.
*TC LC212.2 .C75 1999*

Flecha, Ramón. [Compartiendo palabras. English] Sharing words. Lanham, Md. : Oxford : Rowman & Littlefield Publishers, c2000.
*TC LB1060 .F5913 2000*

Freire, Paulo, 1921- [Pedagogia de autonomia. English] Pedagogy of freedom. Lanham : Rowman & Littlefield Publishers, c1998.
*TC LC196 .F73713 1998*

A sanctuary of their own. Lanham, Md. : Rowman & Littlefield, c2000.
*TC LC191.9 .S28 2000*

**Critical reflection and the foreign language classroom.**
Osborn, Terry A., 1966- Westport, Conn. ; London : Bergin & Garvey, 2000.
*TC P57.U7 O78 2000*

**Critical social thought**
McNeil, Linda M. Contradictions of school reform. New York : Routledge, 2000.
*TC LB3060.83 .M38 2000*

**Critical sociology :** selected readings / edited by Paul Connerton. Harmondsworth ; New York [etc.] : Penguin, 1976. 520 p. ; 18 cm. (Penguin education) (Penguin modern sociology readings) Bibliography: p. 498-509. Includes indexes. ISBN 0-14-080966-X DDC 301/.01
*1. Sociology. 2. Sociology - Germany (West) - History. 3. Frankfurt school of sociology - History. 4. Critical theory. I. Connerton, Paul.*
*TC HM24 .C74*

**Critical studies in education and culture series**
After the disciplines. Westport, Conn. : Bergin & Garvey, 1999.
*TC LB2362.N45 A48 1999*

Armitage, Peter B., 1939- Political relationship and narrative knowledge. Westport, Conn. : Bergin & Garvey, 2000.
*TC LC93.G7 A86 2000*

Becoming and unbecoming white. Westport, Conn. : Bergin & Garvey, 1999.
*TC E184.A1 B29 1999*

Herideen, Penelope E., 1960- Policy, pedagogy, and social inequality. Westport, Conn. : Bergin & Garvey, 1998.
*TC LB2328.15.U6 H47 1998*

Manning, Kathleen, 1954- Ritual, ceremonies, and cultural meaning in higher education. Westport, Conn. : Bergin & Garvey, 2000.
*TC LC191.9 .M26 2000*

Osborn, Terry A., 1966- Critical reflection and the foreign language classroom. Westport, Conn. ; London : Bergin & Garvey, 2000.
*TC P57.U7 O78 2000*

Peters, Michael (Michael A.), 1948- Wittgenstein. Westport, Conn. : Bergin & Garvey, 1999.
*TC B3376.W564 P388 1999*

Roberts, Peter, 1963- Education, literacy, and humanization. Westport, Conn. : Bergin & Garvey, 2000.
*TC LB880.F732 R62 2000*

**Critical technologies and competitiveness** / D. Malana (editor). Huntington, New York : Nova Science Publishers, c2000. 284 p. : ill. ; 26 cm. Includes bibliographical references and index. ISBN 1-56072-795-0
*1. Technological innovations - Economic aspects - United States. 2. Competition, International. I. Malana, D.*
*TC HC110.T4 C74 2000*

**CRITICAL THEORY.** See also **CRITICAL PEDAGOGY; FRANKFURT SCHOOL OF SOCIOLOGY; POPULAR EDUCATION.**
Armitage, Peter B., 1939- Political relationship and narrative knowledge. Westport, Conn. : Bergin & Garvey, 2000.
*TC LC93.G7 A86 2000*

Collins, Michael, 1939- Critical crosscurrents in education. Original ed. Malabar, Fla. : Krieger Pub. Co., 1998.
*TC LC196 .C65 1998*

Critical sociology. Harmondsworth ; New York [etc.] : Penguin, 1976.

*TC HM24 .C74*

Woodring, Carl, 1919- Literature. New York : Columbia University Press, 1999.
*TC PN70 .W66 1999*

**CRITICAL THEORY (SOCIOLOGY).** See **FRANKFURT SCHOOL OF SOCIOLOGY.**

**CRITICAL THINKING.**
Olson, Ivan, 1931- The arts and critical thinking in American education. Westport, Conn. : Bergin & Garvey, 2000.
*TC BH39 .O45 2000*

Rubenfeld, M. Gaie. Critical thinking in nursing. 2nd ed. Philadelphia : Lippincott, c1999.
*TC RT84.5 .R83 1999*

Schick, Theodore. How to think about weird things. 2nd ed. Mountain View, Calif. : Mayfield Pub., c1999.
*TC BC177 .S32 1999*

Sweeney, Jim, 1937- Judgment. Larchmont, NY : Eye on Education, c1997.
*TC LB2806 .S88 1997*

Thayer-Bacon, Barbara J., 1953- Transforming critical thinking. New York : Teachers College Press, c2000.
*TC BC177 .T45 2000*

**Critical Thinking Cooperative.**
Critical challenges in social studies for junior high students. Burnaby, B.C. : Field Relations and Teacher In-Service Education, Faculty of Education, Simon Fraser University, 1996.
*TC D16.2 .C75 1996*

Harrison, John, 1951- Critical challenges in social studies for upper elementary students. Vancouver : Critical Thinking Cooperative, 1999.
*TC LB1584.5.C3 H37 1999*

McDiarmid, Tami, 1960- Critical challenges for primary students. Burnaby, B.C. : Field Relations and Teacher In-Service Education, Faculty of Education, Simon Fraser University, c1996.
*TC LB1590.3 .M36 1996*

**Critical thinking in nursing.**
Rubenfeld, M. Gaie. 2nd ed. Philadelphia : Lippincott, c1999.
*TC RT84.5 .R83 1999*

**CRITICAL THINKING - STUDY AND TEACHING.**
Johnson, Andrew P. Up and out :. Boston : Allyn and Bacon, c2000.
*TC LB1590.3 .J64 2000*

Perspectives in critical thinking. New York : P. Lang, c2000.
*TC LB1590.3 .P476 2000*

Teaching critical thinking. Englewood Cliffs, N.J. : Prentice Hall, c1993.
*TC LB1590.3 .T4 1993*

**CRITICAL THINKING - STUDY AND TEACHING (ELEMENTARY) - GREAT BRITAIN.**
Costello, Patrick J. M. Thinking skills and early childhood education. London : David Fulton Publishers, 2000.
*TC LB1590.3 .C67 2000*

**CRITICAL THINKING - STUDY AND TEACHING (HIGHER) - UNITED STATES.**
Mentkowski, Marcia. Learning that lasts. 1st ed. San Francisco : Jossey-Bass, c2000.
*TC LB1060 .M464 2000*

**CRITICAL THINKING - STUDY AND TEACHING (PRIMARY).**
McDiarmid, Tami, 1960- Critical challenges for primary students. Burnaby, B.C. : Field Relations and Teacher In-Service Education, Faculty of Education, Simon Fraser University, c1996.
*TC LB1590.3 .M36 1996*

**CRITICAL THINKING - STUDY AND TEACHING (SECONDARY).**
Sharma, Martha B., 1945- Using internet primary sources to teach critical thinking skills in geography. Westport, Conn. ; London : Greenwood Press, 2000.
*TC G73 .S393 2000*

**Critical writings on graphic design.**
Looking closer 2. New York : Allworth Press : American Institute of Graphic Arts, c1997.
*TC NC997 .L632 1997*

**CRITICALLY ILL.** See **TERMINALLY ILL.**

**CRITICISM.** See also **AESTHETICS; ART CRITICISM; BOOKS - REVIEWS; LITERATURE - HISTORY AND CRITICISM.**

Jarrett, Michael, 1953- Drifting on a read. Albany, N.Y. : State University of New York Press, 1999.
*TC ML3849 .J39 1999*

Landow, George P. Hypertext 2.0. Rev., amplified ed. Baltimore : Johns Hopkins University Press, 1997.
*TC PN81 .L28 1997*

**CRITICISM - HISTORY - 20TH CENTURY.**
Young, R. V., 1947- At war with the word. Wilmington, Del. : ISI Books, 1999.
*TC PN94 .Y68 1999*

**CRITICISM - TECHNIQUE.** See **CRITICISM.**

**Crittenden, Patricia McKinsey.**
The organization of attachment relationships. New York : Cambridge University Press, 2000.
*TC BF575.A86.O74 2000*

**Critzer, John W., 1947-.**
Rai, Kul B. Affirmative action and the university. Lincoln : University of Nebraska Press, 2000.
*TC LC212.42 .R35 2000*

**CROCKERY.** See **POTTERY.**

**Crockett, Lisa J.**
Negotiating adolescence in times of social change. Cambridge, U.K. ; New York : Cambridge University Press, 2000.
*TC HQ796 .N415 2000*

**Croll, Paul.** Special needs in the primary school : one in five? / Paul Croll, Diana Moses. London : Cassell, 2000. viii, 167 p. ; 23 cm. (Special needs in ordinary schools) Includes bibliographical references ([160]-162) and index. ISBN 0-304-70563-2 ISBN 0-304-70564-0 (pbk.) DDC 371.90472
*1. Handicapped children - Education - England - Leicester. 2. Handicapped children - Rating of - England - Leicester. 3. Mainstreaming in education - England - Leicester. I. Moses, Diana. II. Title. III. Series.*
*TC LC4036.G6 C763 2000*

**Cromwell, Ellen, 1937-** Nurturing readiness in early childhood education : a whole-child curriculum for ages 2-5 / Ellen S. Cromwell. 2nd ed. Boston : Allyn & Bacon, c2000. x, 278 p. : ill. ; 24 cm. Rev. ed. of: Quality child care : a comprehensive guide for administrators and teachers. c1994. Includes bibliographical references and index. ISBN 0-205-28863-4 DDC 372.21
*1. Education, Preschool - United States - Curricula. 2. Day care centers - United States. 3. Child care - United States. 4. Child development - United States. I. Cromwell, Ellen, 1937- Quality child care.*
*TC LB1140.4 .C76 2000*

**Quality child care.**
Cromwell, Ellen, 1937- Nurturing readiness in early childhood education. 2nd ed. Boston : Allyn & Bacon, c2000.
*TC LB1140.4 .C76 2000*

**Cromwell Productions.**
Seurat [videorecording]. West Long Branch, NJ : Kultur, c1999.
*TC ND553.S5 S5 1999*

**Cronkite, Walter.**
Vietnam [videorecording]. Beverly Hills, CA : CBS/Fox Video, c1981.

Vietnam [videorecording]. [Beverly Hills, Calif.?] : CBS Fox Video : Distributed by Fox Video, c1993.
*TC DS557.7 .V53 1993*

**Crook, Thomas.**
Assessment in geriatric psychopharmacology. New Canaan, Conn. : Mark Powley Associates, 1983.
*TC WT150 .A846 1983*

**Crooks, Robert, 1941-** Our sexuality / Robert Crooks, Karla Baur. 7th ed. Pacific Grove, CA : Brooks/Cole Pub. Co., c1999. xxx, 706 p. : col. ill. ; 28 cm. Includes bibliographical references (p. 633-682) and indexes. ISBN 0-534-35467-X DDC 306.7
*1. Sex. 2. Sex customs - United States. I. Baur, Karla. II. Title.*
*TC HQ21 .C698 1999*

**Cropley, A. J.**
Knapper, Christopher. Lifelong learning in higher education. 3rd ed. London : Kogan Page, 2000.
*TC LC5215 .K593 2000*

**Cross cultural approaches to learning.**
Harrington, Charles C. New York : MSS Information, c1973.
*TC GN488.5 .H33 1973*

**CROSS-CULTURAL COMMUNICATION.** See **INTERCULTURAL COMMUNICATION.**

**Cross Cultural Communication Centre (Toronto, Ont.).**
Thomas, Barb, 1946- Combatting racism in the

workplace. Toronto : Cross Cultural Communication Centre, c1983.
*TC HD4903.5.C3 T56 1983*

**CROSS-CULTURAL COMPARISON.**
Intercultural therapy. [2nd ed.]. Oxford : Malden, MA : Blackwell Science, 2000.
*TC RC455.4.E8 I57 2000*

**CROSS-CULTURAL COUNSELING.**
Asian and Pacific Islander Americans :. Commack, N.Y. : Nova Science Publishers, 1999.
*TC RC451.5.A75 A83 1999*

Fukuyama, Mary A. Integrating spirituality into multicultural counseling. Thousand Oaks, Calif. : Sage Publications, c1999.
*TC BF637.C6 F795 1999*

Intercultural therapy. [2nd ed.]. Oxford ; Malden, MA : Blackwell Science, 2000.
*TC RC455.4.E8 I57 2000*

Ivey, Allen E. Counseling and psychotherapy. 4th ed. Boston : Allyn and Bacon, c1997.
*TC BF637.C6 I93 1997*

Robinson, Tracy L. The convergence of race, ethnicity, and gender. Upper Saddle River, N.J. : Merrill, c2000.
*TC BF637.C6 R583 2000*

**CROSS-CULTURAL COUNSELING - DICTIONARIES.**
Key words in multicultural interventions. Westport, Conn. : Greenwood Press, 1999.
*TC BF637.C6 K493 1999*

**CROSS-CULTURAL COUNSELING - GREAT BRITAIN.**
Banks, Nick. White counsellors--Black clients. Aldershot, Hants, England ; Brookfield, Vt. : Ashgate, c1999.
*TC HV3177.G7 B36 1999*

**CROSS-CULTURAL COUNSELING - UNITED STATES.**
Bridges to recovery. New York ; London : Free Press, c2000.
*TC HV5199.5 .B75 2000*

Pack-Brown, Sherlon P. Images of me. Boston : Allyn and Bacon, c1998.
*TC HV1445 .P33 1998*

Preparation, collaboration, and emphasis on the family in school counseling for the new millennium. Lewiston : E. Mellen Press, c2000.
*TC LB1027.5 .P6525 2000*

**Cross-cultural explorations.**
Goldstein, Susan B. Boston : Allyn and Bacon, c2000.
*TC HM258 .G63 2000*

**CROSS-CULTURAL MEDICAL CARE. See TRANSCULTURAL MEDICAL CARE.**

**CROSS-CULTURAL MEDICINE. See TRANSCULTURAL MEDICAL CARE.**

**CROSS-CULTURAL ORIENTATION. See INTERCULTURAL COMMUNICATION.**

**Cross-cultural perspectives on women**
([v. 22].) Contraception across cultures :. Oxford ; New York : Berg, 2000.
*TC RG136 .C574 2000*

**CROSS-CULTURAL PSYCHIATRY. See PSYCHIATRY, TRANSCULTURAL.**

**CROSS-CULTURAL PSYCHOLOGY. See ETHNOPSYCHOLOGY.**

**Cross-cultural psychology series**
(v. 2.) Aboud, Frances E. Health psychology in global perspective. Thousand Oaks : Sage Publications, c1998.
*TC R726.7 .A26 1998*

(v. 4) Social psychology and cultural context. Thousand Oaks, Calif. : Sage Publications, c1999.
*TC HM1033 .S64 1999*

**Cross-cultural risk perception :** a survey of empirical studies / edited by Ortwin Renn and Bernd Rohrmann. Dordrecht ; Boston : London : Kluwer Academic, c2000. 240 p. : ill. ; 25 cm. (Technology, risk, and society ; v. 13) Includes bibliographical references and index. ISBN 0-7923-7747-8 (hb : alk. paper) DDC 302/.12
*1. Risk - Sociological aspects. 2. Risk perception. 3. Risk perception - Cross-cultural studies. I. Renn, Ortwin. II. Rohrmann, Bernd. III. Series.*
*TC HM1101 .C76 2000*

**CROSS-CULTURAL STUDIES.** *See also* **PSYCHIATRY, TRANSCULTURAL.**
Goldstein, Susan B. Cross-cultural explorations. Boston : Allyn and Bacon, c2000.
*TC HM258 .G63 2000*

**CROSS-CULTURAL STUDIES - PERIODICALS.**
[International journal of intercultural relations (Online)] International journal of intercultural relations [computer file]. Oxford ; New York : Pergamon,
*TC EJOURNALS*

**Cross-functional teams.**
Parker, Glenn M., 1938- 1st ed. San Francisco, Calif. : Jossey-Bass, c1994.
*TC HD66 .P345 1994*

Parker, Glenn M., 1938- Cross-functional teams. 1st ed. San Francisco, Calif. : Jossey-Bass, c1994.
*TC HD66 .P345 1994*

**Cross, Máire.**
Gordon, Felicia. Early French feminisms, 1830-1940. Cheltenham, U.K. ; Brookfield, Vt. : Edward Elgar, c1996.
*TC HQ1615.A3 G67 1996*

**Cross, Michael.** Imagery of identity in South African education, 1880-1990 / Michael Cross. Durham, N.C. : Carolina Academic Press, c1999. xxix, 331 p. ; 23 cm. Includes bibliographical references (p. 301-331). ISBN 0-89089-727-1
*1. Afrikaners - Education - History - 19th century. 2. Afrikaners - Education - History - 20th century. 3. Afrikaners - Ethnic identity - History - 19th century. 4. Afrikaners - Ethnic identity - History - 20th century. 5. Blacks - Education - South Africa - History - 19th century. 6. Blacks - Education - South Africa - History - 20th century. 7. Blacks - Race identity - South Africa - History - 19th century. 8. Blacks - Race identity - South Africa - History - 20th century. 9. Colored people (South Africa) - Education - History - 19th century. 10. Colored people (South Africa) - Education - History - 20th century. 11. Colored people (South Africa) - Race identity - History - 19th century. 12. Colored people (South Africa) - Race identity - History - 20th century. 13. Nationalism and education - South Africa. I. Title.*
*TC LA1539 .C76 1999*

**Crossing.**
McCloskey, Deirdre N. Chicago, Ill. : University of Chicago Press, 1999.
*TC HQ77.8.M39 A3 1999*

**Crossing boundaries :** an international anthology of women's experiences in sport / Susan J. Bandy, Anne S. Darden, editors. Champaign, IL : Human Kinetics, c1999. xvi, 311 p. ; 23 cm. Includes bibliographical references. ISBN 0-7360-0088-7 DDC 808.8/0355
*1. Sports - Literary collections. 2. Women athletes - Literary collections. 3. Literature - Women authors. I. Bandy, Susan J. II. Darden, Anne S., 1963-*
*TC PN6071.S62 C76 1999*

**Crossing boundaries :** workbook. Teacher's ed. Lexington, Mass. : D.C. Heath and Company, c1983. 142 p. : ill. (some col.) ; 28 cm. (American readers ; 5) Includes index. ISBN 0-669-05061-x
*1. Readers (Elementary) 2. Reading (Elementary) I. Series.*
*TC PE1121 .C76 1983 Teacher's Ed. Workbook*

**Crossley, Michael** Educational development in the small states of the Commonwealth : retrospect and prospect. London : Commonwealth Secretariat, c1999. xii, 100 p. ; 21 cm. Includes bibliographical references and index. DDC 370.7
*1. Education and state - Commonwealth countries.*
*TC LC71 .C74 1999*

**Croteau, Jan Helling.** Perform it! : a complete guide to young people's theatre / Jan Helling Croteau. Portsmouth, NH : Heinemann, c2000. xiv, 96 p. : ill. ; 23 cm. Includes bibliographical references (p. 93). ISBN 0-325-00230-4 (pbk).
*1. Children's plays - Presentation. etc. I. Title.*
*TC PN3157 .C76 2000*

**Crouter, Ann C.**
Transitions to adulthood in a changing economy. Westport, Conn. : Praeger, c1999.
*TC HQ799.7 .T73 1999*

**Crow, Gary Monroe, 1947-** Leadership : a relevant and realistic role for principals / Gary M. Crow, L. Joseph Matthews, Lloyd E. McCleary. Princeton, NJ : Eye on Education, c1996. xvi, 144 p. ; 24 cm. (School leadership library) Includes bibliographical references. ISBN 1-88300-124-2 DDC 371.2/012
*1. School principals - United States. 2. Educational leadership - United States. I. Matthews, L. Joseph, 1950- II. McCleary, Lloyd E. (Lloyd Everald), 1924- III. Title. IV. Series.*

*TC LB2831.92 .C76 1996*

**CROW INDIANS - BIOGRAPHY.**
Snell, Alma Hogan. Grandmother's grandchild. Lincoln : University of Nebraska Press, c2000.
*TC E99.C92 S656 2000*

**CROW INDIANS - WOMEN. See CROW WOMEN.**

**CROW WOMEN - BIOGRAPHY.**
Snell, Alma Hogan. Grandmother's grandchild. Lincoln : University of Nebraska Press, c2000.
*TC E99.C92 S656 2000*

**CROWDS. See DEMONSTRATIONS; RIOTS.**

**The crucible of experience.**
Burston, Daniel, 1954- Cambridge, Mass. : Harvard University Press, c2000.
*TC RC438.6.L34 B86 2000*

**CRUELTY TO CHILDREN. See CHILD ABUSE.**

**Cruickshank, Donald R.** Preparing America's teachers / by Donald R. Cruickshank and associates, Deborah Bainer ... [et al.]. Bloomington, Ind. : Phi Delta Kappa Educational Foundation, c1996. 133 p. ; 23 cm. Includes bibliographical references. ISBN 0-87367-486-3 DDC 370/.71/0973
*1. Teachers - Training of - United States. 2. Educational change - United States. I. Title.*
*TC LB1715 .C86 1996*

**Cruikshank, Douglas E., 1941-.**
Sheffield, Linda Jensen, 1949- Teaching and learning elementary and middle school mathematics. 4th ed. New York : Wiley, c2000.
*TC QA135.5 .S48 2000*

**Crusher is coming!.**
Graham, Bob, 1942- New York, N.Y., U.S.A. : Puffin Books, 1990.
*TC PZ7.G751667 Cr 1990*

**Cruz Martinez, Alejandro, d. 1987.**
[Mujer que brillaba aún más que el sol. English & Spanish]
The woman who outshone the sun : the legend of Lucia Zenteno = La mujer que brillaba aún más que el sol : la leyenda de Lucía Zenteno / from a poem by/basado en el poema de Alejandro Cruz Martinez ; pictures by/ilustrado por Fernando Olivera ; story by/cuento por Rosalma Zubizarreta, Harriet Rohmer, David Schecter. San Francisco, Calif. : Children's Book Press, c1991. 30 p. : col. ill. ; 21 x 24 cm. SUMMARY: Retells the Zapotec legend of Lucia Zenteno, a beautiful woman with magical powers who is exiled from a mountain village and takes its water away in punishment. ISBN 0-89239-101-4 DDC 398.21/089976
*1. Zenteno, Lucia (Legendary character) - Legends. 2. Zapotec Indians - Folklore. 3. Zenteno, Lucia (Legendary character) - Legends. 4. Zapotec Indians - Folklore. 5. Indians of Mexico - Folklore. 6. Folklore - Mexico. 7. Spanish language materials - Bilingual. I. Olivera, Fernando, ill. II. Zubizarreta-Ada, Rosalma. III. Rohmer, Harriet. IV. Schecter, David. V. Title. VI. Title: Mujer que brillaba aún más que el sol.*
*TC F1221.Z3 C78 1991*

**Cruz, Ray.**
Viorst, Judith. Alexander, who used to be rich last Sunday. 1st ed. New York : Atheneum, 1978.
*TC PZ7.V816 Am 1978*

**Crying.**
Lutz, Tom. 1st ed. New York : London : W.W. Norton, c1999.
*TC BF575.C88 L87 1999*

**CRYING.**
Lutz, Tom. Crying. 1st ed. New York ; London : W.W. Norton, c1999.
*TC BF575.C88 L87 1999*

**CRYING - HISTORY.**
Lutz, Tom. Crying. 1st ed. New York ; London : W.W. Norton, c1999.
*TC BF575.C88 L87 1999*

**CRYPTOGAMS. See FUNGI.**

**CRYPTOGRAPHY.** *See also* **DATA ENCRYPTION (COMPUTER SCIENCE).**
Chacko, Mathew Vadakkan. Public key cryptosystems. 1998.
*TC 085 C35*

**Crystal, David, 1941-** Introduction to language pathology / David Crystal, Rosemary Varley. 4th ed. London : Whurr Publishers, c1998. xvii, 267 p. : ill. ; 24 cm. Includes bibliographical references (p. 252-253) and indexes. ISBN 1-86156-071-0
*1. Language disorders. I. Varley, Rosemary. II. Title.*
*TC RC423 .C76 1998*

**Csapó, Benő.**
Teaching and learning thinking skills. Lisse [Netherlands] ; Exton, PA : Swets & Zeitlinger, c1999.
*TC LB1590.3 .T36 1999*

**CSG state directory.** Directory I, Elective officials / The Council of State Governments. Lexington, Ky. : The Council, c1998- v. ; 28 cm. Frequency: Annual. 1998- . Elective officials. Directory I, Elective officials. Council of State Governments state directory. Directory I, Elective officials. Available also on CD-ROM. Continues: State leadership directory. Directory I, State elective officials ISSN: 1090-1159 (DLC)  96660100 (OCoLC)34276347. ISSN 1521-7272 DDC 352
*1. State governments - United States - Officials and employees - Directories. 2. Legislators - United States - States - Directories. I. Council of State Governments. II. Title: Elective officials III. Title: Directory I, Elective officials IV. Title: State leadership directory. Directory I. State elective officials*
*TC JK2403 .S69*

**CSG state directory.** Directory II, Legislative leadership, committees & staff. Lexington, Ky. : Council of State Governments, c1998- v. ; 28 cm. Frequency: Annual. 1998- . Council of State Governments state directory. Directory II, Legislative leadership. committees & staff. Legislative leadership, committees & staff. Legislative leadership, committees and staff. Directory II, Legislative leadership, committees & staff. Available also on CD-ROM. Continues: State leadership directory. Directory II, State legislative leadership, committees & staff (DLC)  96017181 (OCoLC)34672304.
*1. Legislative bodies - United States - States - Officials and employees - Directories. 2. Legislative bodies - United States - States - Committees - Directories. I. Council of State Governments. II. Title: Legislative leadership. committees & staff III. Title: Legislative leadership, committees and staff IV. Title: Directory II, Legislative leadership, committees & staff V. Title: State leadership directory. Directory II. State legislative leadership, committees & staff*
*TC JK2495 .S688*

**CSG state directory.** Directory III, Administrative officials / The Council of State Goverments. Lexington, Ky. : The Council, c1998- v. ; 28 cm. Frequency: Annual. 1998- . Council of State Governments state directory. Directory III, Administrative officials. Directory III, Administrative officials. Administrative officials. Available also on CD-ROM. Continues: State leadership directory. Directory III, State administrative officials classified by function ISSN: 1095-5097 (DLC)  97641446 (OCoLC)35031978. ISSN 1521-7264 DDC 353.9/32
*1. State governments - United States - Officials and employees - Directories. I. Council of State Governments. II. Title: Directory III, Administrative officials III. Title: Administrative officials IV. Title: State leadership directory. Directory III, State administrative officials classified by function*
*TC JK2403 .B6*

**Csikszentmihalyi, Mihaly.** Becoming adult : how teenagers prepare for the world of work / Mihaly Csikszentmihalyi and Barbara Schneider. New York : Basic Books, 2000. xx, 289 p. : ill. ; 25 cm. Includes bibliographical references and index. ISBN 0-465-01540-9 DDC 305.235/0973
*1. Teenagers - Vocational guidance - United States. 2. Teenagers - Employment - United States. 3. Teenagers - United States - Attitudes. I. Schneider, Barbara. II. Title.*
*TC HQ796 .C892 2000*

**Csóti, Márianna.** People skills for young adults / Márianna Csóti. London ; Philadelphia : Jessica Kingsley, 2000. 190 p. : ill. ; 25 cm. Includes bibliographical references (p. 190). ISBN 1-85302-716-2 (pb : alk. paper) DDC 302/.14/0835
*1. Young adults - United States - Psychology. 2. Young adults - United States - Life skills guides. 3. Self-esteem in young adults - United States. 4. Social skills - United States. I. Title.*
*TC HQ799.7 .C76 2000*

**CUBA - CIVILIZATION - AMERICAN INFLUENCES.**
Pérez, Louis A., 1943- On becoming Cuban. Chapel Hill : University of North Carolina Press, c1999.
*TC F1760 .P47 1999*

**CUBA - EMIGRATION AND IMMIGRATION.**
Gonzalez-Pando, Miguel. The Cuban Americans. Westport, Conn. : Greenwood Press, 1998.
*TC E184.C97 G64 1998*

**CUBA - RELATIONS - UNITED STATES.**
Pérez, Louis A., 1943- On becoming Cuban. Chapel Hill : University of North Carolina Press, c1999.
*TC F1760 .P47 1999*

**Cuba. Secretaria de Instrucción Publica.**
Cuba. Secretaría de Instrucción Pública y Bellas Artes. La Instrucción primaria; Havana.

**Cuba. Secretaría de Instrucción Pública y Bellas Artes.** La Instrucción primaria; revista quincenal. Havana. v. 1-11 (no.8); 1902-April 1913.
*1. Education - Cuba - Periodicals. I. Cuba. Secretaria de Instrucción Publica. II. Title.*

**The Cuban Americans.**
Gonzalez-Pando, Miguel. Westport, Conn. : Greenwood Press, 1998.
*TC E184.C97 G64 1998*

**CUBAN AMERICANS.**
Gonzalez-Pando, Miguel. The Cuban Americans. Westport, Conn. : Greenwood Press, 1998.
*TC E184.C97 G64 1998*

**Cuban, Larry.**
Reconstructing the common good in education. Stanford. Calif. : Stanford University Press, c2000.
*TC LA212 .R42 2000*

Urban school chiefs under fire / Larry Cuban. Chicago : University of Chicago Press, 1976. xiv, 223 p. ; 23 cm. Includes bibliographical references (p.209-215) and index. ISBN 0-226-12314-6 DDC 371.2/011/0973
*1. School superintendents. 2. Education, Urban. I. Title.*
*TC LB2831.7 .C82*

**CUBANACÁN (HAVANA, CUBA) - BUILDINGS, STRUCTURES, ETC.**
Loomis, John A., 1951- Revolution of forms. New York : Princeton Architectural Press, c1999.
*TC NA6602.A76 L66 1999*

**CUBISM.**
On pictures and paintings [videorecording]. Peasmarsh, East Sussex, Eng. ; Ho-Ho-kus, NJ : Roland Collection, 1992.
*TC ND195.O45 1992*

**Cucchiara, Anthony M.**
Roff, Sandra Shoiock. From the Free Academy to CUNY. New York : Fordham University Press, c2000.
*TC LD3835 .R64 2000*

**CUEBS news.**
Commission on Undergraduate Education in the Biological Sciences. [Washington, D.C.] Commission on Undergradute Education in the Biological Sciences.

**Cuéllar, Israel.**
Handbook of multicultural mental health :. San Diego : Academic Press, c2000.
*TC RC455.4 .H36 2000*

**CUIGH ULADH (NORTHERN IRELAND AND IRELAND).** *See* **ULSTER (NORTHERN IRELAND AND IRELAND).**

**CUISINE.** *See* **COOKERY.**

**Culkin, Mary L.**
Managing quality in young children's programs. New York : Teachers College Press, c2000.
*TC LB2822.6 .M36 2000*

**Culleton, Claire A.** Working class culture, women, and Britain, 1914-1921 / Claire A. Culleton. 1st ed. New York : St. Martin's Press, 2000. xii, 221 p. : ill. ; 22 cm. Includes bibliographical references (p. [201]-213) and index. ISBN 0-312-22541-5 DDC 940.3/082
*1. World War, 1914-1918 - Women - Great Britain. 2. Working class women - Great Britain - History - 20th century. I. Title.*
*TC D639.W7 C79 2000*

**Cullingford, Cedric.** The causes of exclusion : : home, school and the development of young criminals. / Cedric Cullingford. London : Kogan Page ; Sterling, VA : Stylus, 1999. x, 219 p. ; 24 cm. Includes bibliographical references and index. ISBN 0-7494-3039-7
*1. Home and school. 2. Education and crime. 3. Juvenile delinquency. I. Title.*
*TC HV6166 .C85 1999*

The human experience : the early years / Cedric Cullingford. Aldershot ; Brookfield, Vt. : Ashgate, c1999. xv, 298 p. ; 23 cm. Includes bibliographical references. ISBN 0-7546-1156-6 DDC 305.231
*1. Experience in children. 2. Child psychology. 3. Child development. I. Title.*
*TC BF723.E95 C84 1999*

An inspector calls :. London : Kogan Page, 1999.
*TC LB2900.5 .I58 1999*

**Cullum, Carolyn N.** The storytime sourcebook : a compendium of ideas and resources for storytellers / Carolyn N. Cullum. 2nd ed. New York ; London : Neal-Schuman Publishers, c1999. xix, 469 p. ; 28 cm. Includes bibliographical references (p. 331-399) and indexes. ISBN 1-55570-360-7 DDC 027.62/51
*1. Storytelling - United States. 2. Children's libraries - Activity programs - United States. I. Title.*

*TC Z718.3 .C85 1999*

**CULTIVATED WHEATS.** *See* **WHEAT.**

**Cultural amnesia.**
Bertman, Stephen. Westport, Conn. ; London : Praeger, 2000.
*TC HN59.2 .B474 2000*

**CULTURAL ANTHROPOLOGY.** *See* **ETHNOLOGY.**

**CULTURAL ASSIMILATION.** *See* **ASSIMILATION (SOCIOLOGY).**

**CULTURAL CHANGE.** *See* **SOCIAL CHANGE.**

**CULTURAL CHARACTERISTICS.**
Canino, Ian A. Culturally diverse children and adolescents. 2nd ed. New York : Guilford Press, c2000.
*TC RJ507.M54 C36 2000*

**Cultural conflict and struggle.**
Schmidt, Patricia Ruggiano, 1944- New York : P. Lang, c1998.
*TC LB1181 .S36 1998*

**Cultural diversity and education.**
Banks, James A. 4th ed. Boston ; London : Allyn & Bacon, c2001.
*TC LC3731 .B365 2001*

**CULTURAL DIVERSITY IN THE WORKPLACE.** *See* **DIVERSITY IN THE WORKPLACE.**

**CULTURAL DIVERSITY IN WORKFORCE.** *See* **DIVERSITY IN THE WORKPLACE.**

**CULTURAL DIVERSITY POLICY.** *See* **MULTICULTURALISM.**

**CULTURAL DIVERSITY - UNITED STATES.**
Clinical management of communication disorders in culturally diverse children. Boston : Allyn & Bacon, c2000.
*TC RJ496.C67 C556 2000*

**CULTURAL EXCHANGE PROGRAMS.** *See* **CULTURAL RELATIONS; INTELLECTUAL COOPERATION.**

**Cultural front (Series)**
Bad subjects. New York : New York University Press, c1998.
*TC E169.12 .B26 1998*

**CULTURAL GEOGRAPHY.** *See* **HUMAN GEOGRAPHY.**

**CULTURAL HERITAGE.** *See* **CULTURAL PROPERTY.**

**CULTURAL LAG.** *See* **COMPENSATORY EDUCATION.**

**CULTURAL LIFE.** *See* **INTELLECTUAL LIFE.**

**Cultural memory in the present**
Weber, Samuel M. [Freud-Legende. English] The legend of Freud. Expanded ed. Stanford, Calif. : Stanford University Press, 2000, c1982.
*TC BF173.F85 W2813 2000*

Winter, Sarah. Freud and the institution of psychoanalytic knowledge. Stanford, Calif. : Stanford University Press, 1999.
*TC BF173 .W5485 1999*

**The cultural one or the racial many.**
Camara, Evandro de Morais, 1946- Aldershot, Hants, England ; Brookfield, Vt., USA : Ashgate, c1997.
*TC HT1521 .C343 1997*

**The cultural origins of human cognition.**
Tomasello, Michael. Cambridge, Mass. ; London : Harvard University Press, 1999.
*TC BF311 .T647 1999*

**CULTURAL PATRIMONY.** *See* **CULTURAL PROPERTY.**

**CULTURAL PLURALISM POLICY.** *See* **MULTICULTURALISM.**

**CULTURAL POLICY.** *See* **ART AND STATE; CULTURAL PROPERTY - PROTECTION.**

**CULTURAL PROPERTY - PROTECTION - GOVERNMENT POLICY.** *See* **CULTURAL PROPERTY - PROTECTION.**

**CULTURAL PROPERTY - PROTECTION - HANDBOOKS, MANUALS, ETC.**
Building an emergency plan. Los Angeles, Calif. : Getty Conservation Institute, c1999.
*TC AM121 .B85 1999*

**CULTURAL PROPERTY, PROTECTION OF.** *See also* **CULTURAL PROPERTY - PROTECTION.**
Malaro, Marie C. Museum governance. Washington : Smithsonian Institution Press, c1994.
*TC AM121 .M35 1994*

**CULTURAL PSYCHIATRY.** *See also* **PSYCHIATRY, TRANSCULTURAL.**
Handbook of multicultural mental health :. San Diego : Academic Press, c2000.
*TC RC455.4 .H36 2000*

Intercultural therapy. [2nd ed.]. Oxford : Malden, MA : Blackwell Science, 2000.
*TC RC455.4.E8 I57 2000*

Seeley, Karen M. Cultural psychotherapy. Northvale, N.J. : Jason Aronson, c2000.
*TC RC455.4.E8 S44 2000*

**CULTURAL PSYCHIATRY - CROSS-CULTURAL STUDIES.** *See* **PSYCHIATRY, TRANSCULTURAL.**

**Cultural psychotherapy.**
Seeley, Karen M. Northvale, N.J. : Jason Aronson, c2000.
*TC RC455.4.E8 S44 2000*

**CULTURAL RELATIONS.**
Hansel, Bettina G. The exchange student survival kit. Yarmouth, ME : Intercultural Press, c1993.
*TC LB1696 .H36 1993*

**CULTURAL RELATIONS - HANDBOOKS, MANUALS, ETC.**
Kehoe, John W. A handbook for enhancing the multicultural climate of the school. [Vancouver, B.C.] : Western Education Development Group, Faculty of Education, University of British Colombia, c1984.
*TC LC1099 .K438 1984*

**CULTURAL RELATIONS - PERIODICALS.**
[International journal of intercultural relations (Online)] International journal of intercultural relations [computer file]. Oxford ; New York : Pergamon,
*TC EJOURNALS*

**CULTURAL RESOURCES MANAGEMENT.** *See* **CULTURAL PROPERTY - PROTECTION.**

**Cultural sitings**
Museums and memory. Stanford, Calif. : Stanford University Press, c2000.
*TC AM7 .M8815 2000*

**CULTURAL SOCIOLOGY.** *See* **CULTURE.**

**CULTURAL STUDIES.** *See* **CULTURE - STUDY AND TEACHING.**

**CULTURAL TRANSFORMATION.** *See* **SOCIAL CHANGE.**

**CULTURALLY DEPRIVED.** *See* **SOCIALLY HANDICAPPED.**

**CULTURALLY DISADVANTAGED.** *See* **SOCIALLY HANDICAPPED.**

**Culturally diverse children and adolescents.**
Canino, Ian A. 2nd ed. New York : Guilford Press, c2000.
*TC RJ507.M54 C36 2000*

**Culturally diverse videos, audios, and CD-ROMS for children and young adults** / [edited by] Irene Wood. New York : Neal-Schuman Publishers, 1999. xvii, 276p. ; 23 cm. Includes bibliographical references and indexes. ISBN 1-55570-377-1 DDC 011/.37
*1. Motion pictures for children - Catalogs. 2. Young adult films - Catalogs. 3. Video recordings - Catalogs. 4. CD-ROMs - Catalogs. I. Wood, Irene.*
*TC PN1998 .M85 1999*

**CULTURALLY HANDICAPPED.** *See* **SOCIALLY HANDICAPPED.**

**Culturally responsive teaching.**
Gay, Geneva. New York : Teachers College Press, c2000.
*TC LC1099.3 .G393 2000*

**Culturally speaking** : managing rapport through talk across cultures / edited by Helen Spencer-Oatey. London ; New York : Continuum ; [New York] : [Cassell], 2000. xv, 381 p. : ill. ; 25 cm. (Open linguistics series) Includes bibliographical references (p. [342]-369) and index. ISBN 0-304-70436-9 (hb) ISBN 0-304-70437-7 (pb) DDC 303.48/2
*1. Intercultural communication. 2. Interpersonal relations. 3. Language and culture. I. Spencer-Oatey, Helen, 1952- II. Series.*

*TC GN345.6 .C86 2000*

**CULTURE.** *See also* **CHRISTIANITY AND CULTURE; CIVILIZATION; COGNITION AND CULTURE; COMMUNICATION AND CULTURE; COMMUNISM AND CULTURE; CROSS-CULTURAL STUDIES; EDUCATION; EDUCATIONAL ANTHROPOLOGY; INTELLECTUAL LIFE; INTERCULTURAL COMMUNICATION; LANGUAGE AND CULTURE; LEARNING AND SCHOLARSHIP; MASS MEDIA AND CULTURE; MATERIAL CULTURE; PERSONALITY AND CULTURE; POLITICS AND CULTURE.**
Bertman, Stephen. Cultural amnesia. Westport, Conn. ; London : Praeger, 2000.
*TC HN59.2 .B474 2000*

Education for spiritual, moral, social and cultural development. London ; New York : Continuum, 2000.
*TC LC268 .E384 2000*

**Culture & power.**
Swartz, David, 1945- Chicago : University of Chicago Press, 1997.
*TC HM22.F8 S93 1997*

**CULTURE AND CHRISTIANITY.** *See* **CHRISTIANITY AND CULTURE.**

**CULTURE AND COGNITION.** *See* **COGNITION AND CULTURE.**

**Culture and cognition: readings in cross-cultural psychology.**
Berry, John W. comp. London, Methuen [1974]
*TC BF311 .B48*

**CULTURE AND COMMUNICATION.** *See* **COMMUNICATION AND CULTURE.**

**CULTURE AND COMMUNISM.** *See* **COMMUNISM AND CULTURE.**

**CULTURE AND EDUCATION.** *See* **EDUCATIONAL ANTHROPOLOGY.**

**Culture and education series**
McLaren, Peter, 1948- Che Guevara, Paulo Freire, and the pedagogy of revolution. Lanham [Md.] : Rowman & Littlefield Publishers, c2000.
*TC LC196 .M29 2000*

McLaren, Peter, 1948- Schooling as a ritual performance. 3rd ed. Lanham, Md. : Rowman & Littlefield, c1999.
*TC LC504.3.T67 M35 1999*

Owen, David, 1955- None of the above. Rev. and updated. Lanham, Md. : Rowman & Littlefield Publishers, c1999.
*TC LB2353.57 .O94 1999*

Powell, Rebecca, 1949- Literacy as a moral imperative. Lanham, Md. : Rowman & Littlefield Publishers, c1999.
*TC LC151 .P69 1999*

Trifonas, Peter Pericles, 1960- The ethics of writing. Lanham, Md. : Oxford : Rowman & Littlefield, c2000.
*TC LB14.7 .T75 2000*

**Culture and human development.**
Valsiner, Jaan. London ; Thousand Oaks, Calif. : Sage, 2000.
*TC BF713 .V35 2000*

**CULTURE AND MASS MEDIA.** *See* **MASS MEDIA AND CULTURE.**

**CULTURE AND PERSONALITY.** *See* **PERSONALITY AND CULTURE.**

**Culture and power.**
Swartz, David, 1945- Culture & power. Chicago : University of Chicago Press, 1997.
*TC HM22.F8 S93 1997*

**Culture and schooling.**
Thomas, Elwyn. Chichester, West Sussex, England ; New York : J. Wiley & Sons, c2000.
*TC LB45 .T476 2000*

**CULTURE CONFLICT.** *See also* **MARGINALITY, SOCIAL.**
Beverley, John. Subalternity and representation. Durham [N.C.] ; London : Duke University Press, 1999.
*TC HM1136 .B48 1999*

(Re)visioning composition textbooks. Albany : State University of New York Press, c1999.
*TC PE1404 .R46 1999*

**CULTURE CONFLICT - UNITED STATES.**
America, the West, and liberal education. Lanham, Md. : Rowman & Littlefield, c1999.
*TC LC1023 .A44 1999*

Kurin, Richard, 1950- Reflections of a culture broker. Washington, D.C. : Smithsonian Institution Press, c1997.
*TC GN36.U62 D5775 1997*

**CULTURE - DICTIONARIES, JUVENILE.**
A First dictionary of cultural literacy. Boston : Houghton Mifflin, 1989.
*TC AG105 .F43 1989*

**A culture for academic excellence.**
Freed, Jann E. Washington, D.C. : Graduate School of Education and Human Development, George Washington University, 1997.
*TC LB2341 .F688 1997*

**CULTURE - HISTORIOGRAPHY.**
Museums and memory. Stanford, Calif. : Stanford University Press, c2000.
*TC AM7 .M8815 2000*

**Culture in action.**
Derné, Steve, 1960- Albany : State University of New York Press, c1995.
*TC HQ670 .D46 1995*

**Culture in second language teaching and learning** / [edited by] Eli Hinkel. Cambridge, U.K. ; New York : Cambridge University Press, 1999. xi, 250 p. ; 24 cm. (Cambridge applied linguistics series) Includes bibliographical references (p. 221-244) and index. ISBN 0-521-64276-0 ISBN 0-521-64490-9 (pbk.) DDC 418/.007
*1. Language and languages - Study and teaching. 2. Second language acquisition. 3. Language and culture - Study and teaching. I. Hinkel, Eli. II. Series.*
*TC P53 .C77 1999*

**Culture in special education.**
Kalyanpur, Maya. Baltimore, Md. : P.H. Brookes Pub., c1999.
*TC LC3969 .K35 1999*

**Culture, literacy, and learning English** : voices from the Chinese classroom / edited by Kate Parry with Su Xiaojun. Portsmouth, NH : Boynton/Cook Publishers, c1998. xvii, 270 p. : ill. ;23 cm. Includes bibliographical references (p. 263-270). ISBN 0-86709-448-6 (acid-free paper) DDC 428/.007/051
*1. English language - Study and teaching - Chinese speakers. 2. English language - Study and teaching - China. 3. English language - Social aspects - China. 4. Language and culture - China. 5. Literacy - China. I. Parry, Kate. II. Su, Xiaojun.*
*TC PE1130.C4 C85 1998*

**The culture of American college radio.**
Sauls, Samuel J. 1st ed. Ames : Iowa State University Press, 2000.
*TC PN1991.67.C64 S38 2000*

**CULTURE - PHILOSOPHY.**
Pierre Bourdieu. Bern ; New York : P. Lang, c1999.
*TC HM621 .P54 1999*

Treichler, Paula A. How to have theory in an epidemic. Durham : Duke University Press, 1999.
*TC RA644.A25 T78 1999*

**CULTURE - POLITICAL ASPECTS.**
Giroux, Henry A. Stealing innocence. 1st ed. New York : St. Martin's Press, 2000.
*TC HM621 .G57 2000*

**CULTURE, POPULAR.** *See* **POPULAR CULTURE.**

**CULTURE - PSYCHOLOGICAL ASPECTS.**
Goldstein, Susan B. Cross-cultural explorations. Boston : Allyn and Bacon, c2000.
*TC HM258 .G63 2000*

**CULTURE - SOCIAL ASPECTS - INDIA.**
Culture, socialization and human development. New Delhi ; Thousand Oaks, CA : Sage Publications, c1999.
*TC HQ783 .C85 1999*

**Culture, socialization and human development** : theory, research, and applications in India / edited by T.S. Saraswathi. New Delhi ; Thousand Oaks, CA : Sage Publications, c1999. 438 p. ; 23 cm. Includes bibliographical references and indexes. ISBN 0-7619-9332-0 (c) DDC 303.3/2
*1. Socialization - India. 2. Child development - India. 3. Culture - Social aspects - India. 4. Social interaction in children - India. I. Saraswati, T. S.*
*TC HQ783 .C85 1999*

**CULTURE - STUDY AND TEACHING (HIGHER) - ACTIVITY PROGRAMS.**
Teaching about culture, ethnicity & diversity. Thousand Oaks : Sage Publications, c1998.

*TC HM101 .T38 1998*

**CULTURE - STUDY AND TEACHING (HIGHER) - NEW ZEALAND.**
After the disciplines. Westport, Conn. : Bergin & Garvey, 1999.
*TC LB2362.N45 A48 1999*

**CULTURE - STUDY AND TEACHING (HIGHER) - UNITED STATES.**
After the disciplines. Westport, Conn. : Bergin & Garvey, 1999.
*TC LB2362.N45 A48 1999*

**CULTURE - STUDY AND TEACHING - UNITED STATES - AUDIO-VISUAL AIDS.**
Hidden messages. Yarmouth, Me. : Intercultural Press, c1998.
*TC LC1099.3 .H53 1998*

**Cultures beginnings: from the heart of the country rice-planting songs.**
Heart of the country [videorecording]. [New York, NY : First Run/Icarus Films, 1998].
*TC LB1565.H6 H3 1998*

**Cultures of curriculum** / Pamela Bolotin Joseph ... [et al.]. Mahwah, N.J. ; London : L. Erlbaum Associates, 2000. xiii, 194 p. ; 23 cm. (Studies in curriculum theory) Includes bibliographical references and indexes. ISBN 0-8058-2274-7 (pbk. : alk. paper) DDC 374/.001
*1. Curriculum planning - United States. 2. Education - Curricula - Social aspects - United States. I. Joseph, Pamela Bolotin. II. Series.*
*TC LB2806.15 .C73 2000*

**Cummings, Janet L.**
Cummings, Nicholas A. The value of psychological treatment. Phoenix, AZ : Zeig, Tucker & Co., 1999.
*TC RA790.6 .C85 1999*

**Cummings, Nicholas A.** The value of psychological treatment : collected papers of Nicholas A. Cummings / edited by J. Lawrence Thomas and Janet L. Cummings. Phoenix, AZ : Zeig, Tucker & Co., 1999. xviii, 446 p. ; 24 cm. Includes bibliographical references and index. ISBN 1-89194-412-6 DDC 362.2/0973
*1. Mental health services - United States. 2. Managed mental health care - United States. 3. Mental health services - Utilization - United States. I. Thomas, J. Lawrence. II. Cummings, Janet L. III. Title.*
*TC RA790.6 .C85 1999*

**Cummings, Pat.** Clean your room, Harvey Moon! / by Pat Cummings. New York : Macmillan/McGraw-Hill School Pub. Co., c1991. 32 p. : col. ill. ; 46 x 34 cm. SUMMARY: Harvey tackles a big job: cleaning his room. ISBN 0-02-109107-2
*1. Orderliness - Fiction. 2. Hygiene - Fiction. 3. Afro-Americans - Fiction. I. Title.*
*TC PZ8.3.C898 Cl 1991*

Talking with artists. Volume three :. 1st ed. New York : Clarion Books, c1999.
*TC NC961.6 .T35 1999*

Talking with artists. Volume two :. 1st ed. New York : Simon & Schuster Books for Young Readers, c1995.
*TC NC975 .T34 1995*

**Cummings, Pat, ill.**
Caines, Jeannette Franklin. I need a lunch box. New York : Macmillan/McGraw-Hill, 1988.
*TC PZ7.C12 Iaan 1988*

**Cummins, Jim, 1949-** Language, power, and pedagogy : bilingual children in the crossfire / Jim Cummins. Clevedon [England] ; Buffalo [N.Y.] : Multilingual Matters, c2000. viii, 309 p. ; 24 cm. (Bilingual education and bilingualism ; 23) Includes bibliographical references (p. 284-306) and index. ISBN 1-85359-473-3 (pbk. : alk. paper) ISBN 1-85359-474-1 (hard : alk. paper) DDC 370.117/5
*1. Education, Bilingual - Social aspects. 2. Minorities - Education - Social aspects. I. Title. II. Series.*
*TC LC3719 .C86 2000*

**Cumulated subject index to Psychological abstracts.**
Cumulative subject index to Psychological abstracts. Washington, D.C. : American Psychological Association, 1971-
*TC BF1 .P652*

**Cumulative subject index to Psychological abstracts.**
Washington, D.C. : American Psychological Association, 1971- v. ; 36 cm. Frequency: Triennial. 1969/71- . Issued 1969/71- in two volumes. Continues: Cumulated subject index to Psychological abstracts. Psychological abstracts. ISSN 0277-0083
*1. Psychological abstracts - Indexes. 2. Psychology - Indexes. I. American Psychological Association. II. Title: Psychological abstracts. III. Title: Cumulated subject index to Psychological abstracts IV. Title: Psychological abstracts*

*TC BF1 .P652*

**Cunningham, George K.** Assessment in the classroom : constructing and interpreting texts / George K. Cunningham. London : Falmer, 1998. vii, 225 p. ; 24 cm. Bibliography: p. 214-217. ISBN 0-7507-0732-1 (pbk) ISBN 0-7507-0733-X (cased) DDC 371.26
*1. Educational tests and measurements. 2. Examinations - Design and construction. 3. Examinations - Validity. 4. Examinations - Interpretation. 5. Grading and marking (Students) I. Title.*
*TC LB3051 .C857 1998*

**CUNNINGHAM, MERCE.**
Vaughan, David, 1924- Merce Cunningham. 1st ed. New York, NY : Aperture, c1997.
*TC GV1785.C85 V38 1997*

**Cunningham, Patricia Marr.** Phonics they use : words for reading and writing / Patricia M. Cunningham. 3rd ed. New York : Longman, c2000. xii, 196 p. : ill. ; 24 cm. Includes bibliographical references and index. ISBN 0-321-02055-3 DDC 372.46/5
*1. Reading - Phonetic method. I. Title.*
*TC LB1573.3 .C86 2000*

Reading and writing in elementary classrooms. 4th ed. New York : Longman, c2000.
*TC LB1573 .R279 2000*

**Cunningham, William G.** Educational administration : a problem-based approach / William G. Cunningham, Paula A. Cordeiro. Boston ; London : Allyn & Bacon, c2000. xvii, 446 p. ; 25 cm. Includes bibliographical references (410-429) and indexes. ISBN 0-205-18459-6 DDC 371.2/071/1
*1. School management and organization - Study and teaching (Higher) - United States. 2. Problem-based learning - United States. 3. School administrators - Training of - United States. I. Cordeiro, Paula A. II. Title.*
*TC LB1738.5 .C86 2000*

**Cunninghame, Karen.**
Autism--a world apart [videorecording]. Boston, MA : Fanlight Productions, [1989, c1988].
*TC RJ506 .A98 1988*

**Cuomo, Celia, 1956-** In all probability : investigations in probability and statistics : teacher's guide / Celia Cuomo ; [illus., Carol Bevilacqua, Lisa Klofkorn ; photographs, Richard Hoyt] Berkeley, CA : Lawrence Hall of Science, University of California, Berkeley, c1998. [viii], 91 p., [9] p. : ill. ; 28 cm. "For grades 3-6." "Great explorations in math and science (GEMS)." Includes bibliographical references (p. 82). ISBN 0-912511-83-4 (pbk.)
*1. Probabilities - Study and teaching (Elementary). 2. Mathematical statistics - Study and teaching (Elementary). I. (GEMS) Project. II. Title.*
*TC QA276.18 .C866 1998*

**Cuomo, Chris J.**
Whiteness. Lanham, [Md.] : Rowman & Littlefield, c1999.
*TC E184.A1 W399 1999*

**CURATORS, MUSEUM. See MUSEUM CURATORS.**

**Curcio, John J.** Relationships among administrator personality, perceptions of feedback source credibility, and attitudes toward program feedback / John J. Curcio. 1999. vi, 129 leaves ; 29 cm. Issued also on microfilm. Includes tables. Thesis (Ph. D.)--Columbia University. Includes bibliographical references: (leaves 104-125)
*1. School management and organization - New York (State) - New York. 2. School administrators - New York (State) - New York - Attitudes. 3. Personality. 4. Educational evaluation - New York (State) - New York. 5. Public schools - New York (State) - New York - Administration. 6. Feedback (Psychology) I. Title.*
*TC 085 C92*

**CURE OF SOULS. See PASTORAL COUNSELING.**

**CURIOSITIES AND WONDERS.**
Schick, Theodore. How to think about weird things. 2nd ed. Mountain View, Calif. : Mayfield Pub., c1999.
*TC BC177 .S32 1999*

**CURIOSITY - FICTION.**
McBratney, Sam. The dark at the top of the stairs. 1st U.S. ed. Cambridge, Mass. : Candlewick Press, c1996.
*TC PZ7.M47826 DAr 1996*

**Curlee, Richard F. (Richard Frederick), 1935-.**
Stuttering and related disorders of fluency. 2nd ed. New York : Thieme Medical Publishers, 1999.
*TC RC424 .S768 1998*

**Current controversies.**
Guns and violence. San Diego : Greenhaven Press, c1999.
*TC HV7436 .G8774 1999*

Smoking. San Diego, CA : Greenhaven Press, c1997.
*TC HV5760 .S663 1997*

**Current history.**
Current history and Forum. New York [C-H Publishing Corporation: etc., etc., 1914-41]

**Current history & forum.**
[Current history (New York, N.Y. : 1916)] Current history. [New York : New York Times Co., 1916-1940]

**Current history and Forum.** New York [C-H Publishing Corporation; etc., etc., 1914-41] 53 v. illus., plates, ports., maps. 25-30 cm. Frequency: Monthly, Feb.-June 1941. Former frequency: Semimonthly, Dec. 1914-Jan. 1915. Former frequency: Monthly, Feb. 1915-Sept. 1940. Former frequency: Semimonthly, Oct. 1940-Jan. 1941. v. 1-53, no. 1; Dec. 1914-June 1941. Forum. Title varies: New York times current history; a monthly magazine. The European war Dec. 1914-Sept. 1915. Title varies: Current history ... Oct. 1915-June 1940. No numbers were issued for July and Aug. 1938. No more published. Published in New York by the New York Times Company, Dec. 1914-Apr. 1936; Current History, Inc., May 1936-Feb. 1939; C-H Publishing Corporation, Mar. 1939-June 1941. Absorbed Forum and Century, May 1940. United with Events, Sept. 1941, to form Current history; incorporating Events, Forum & Century. Absorbed: Forum May 1940. Absorbed: Century May 1940.
*1. History - Periodicals 2. World War, 1914-1918 - Periodicals. 3. World politics - Periodicals. I. Title: New York times. II. Title: Forum III. Title: Forum and Century IV. Title: Forum May 1940 V. Title: Century May 1940 VI. Title: Events Sept. 1941 VII. Title: Current history*

**[Current history (New York, N.Y. : 1916)]** Current history. [New York : New York Times Co., 1916-1940] 49 v. : ill. ; 24 cm. Frequency: Monthly. Vol. 3, no. 6 (Mar. 1916)-v. 51, no. 10 (June 1940). Title from caption. Suspended, July-Aug. 1938. Published: New York Times Co., Mar. 1916-Apr. 1936 ; Current History, Inc., May 1936-Feb. 1939 ; C-H Pub. Corp., Mar. 1939-June 1940. Merged with: Forum and century, to form: Current history & forum. Continues: New York times current history (DLC)sn 84044189 (OCoLC)6559523.
*1. World politics - Periodicals. I. Title: New York times. II. Title: New York times current history III. Title: Forum and century IV. Title: Current history & forum*

**Current index to journals in education.**
[ERIC (SilverPlatter International : Online)] The ERIC database [computer file]. WebSPIRS version 3.1. [Norwood, MA] : SilverPlatter International,
*TC NETWORKED RESOURCES*

**Current issues in developmental psychology :** biopsychological perspectives / edited by A.F. Kalverboer, M.L. Genta and J.B. Hopkins. Dordrecht : Boston : London : Kluwer Academic Publishers, c1999. 190 p. : ill. ; 25 cm. Includes bibliographical references and index. ISBN 0-7923-5902-X (hardcover : alk. paper) DDC 612.6/5
*1. Infants - Development. 2. Child development. 3. Developmental psychobiology. 4. Infant psychology. 5. Child psychology. I. Kalverboer, Alex Fedde. II. Genta, Maria Luisa. III. Hopkins, J. B.*
*TC RJ134 .C868 1999*

**Current problems in epilepsy**
(14) Childhood epilepsies and brain development. London : John Libbey, c1999.
*TC RJ496.E6 C45 1999*

**Current research in the semantics/pragmatics interface**
(v. 1) The semantics/pragmatics interface from different points of view. 1st ed. Oxford, UK ; New York : Elsevier, 1999.
*TC P325 .S3814 1999*

**The current state of interlanguage :** studies in honor of William E. Rutherford / edited by Lynn Eubank, Larry Selinker, Michael Sharwood Smith. Amsterdam : Philadelphia : J. Benjamins, c1995. vii, 293 p. : ill. ; 23 cm. Includes bibliographical references and index. ISBN 90-272-2152-9 (Eur. : alk. paper) ISBN 1-55619-506-0 (US : alk. paper) DDC 418
*1. Interlanguage (Language learning) 2. Second language acquisition. I. Rutherford, William E. II. Eubank, Lynn. III. Selinker, Larry, 1937- IV. Sharwood Smith, Michael, 1942-*
*TC P118.2 .C867 1995*

**Currents (Washington, D.C.).**
Council for Advancement and Support of Education. CASE currents. [Washington] Council for Advancement and Support of Education.

**CURRICULA (COURSES OF STUDY).** *See*
**EDUCATION - CURRICULA.**

**The curriculum.**
Foshay, Arthur Wellesley, 1912- New York ;
London : Teachers College Press, c2000.
*TC LB2806.15 .F66 2000*

**Curriculum.**
Marsh, Colin J. 2nd. ed. Upper Saddle River, N.J. :
Merrill, c1999.
*TC LB1570 .M3667 1999*

Ross, Alistair, 1946- London ; New York : Falmer
Press, 2000.
*TC LB1564.G7 R66 2000*

Sowell, Evelyn J. 2nd ed. Upper Saddle River, N.J. :
Merrill, c2000.
*TC LB2806.15 .S69 2000*

**CURRICULUM.**
Integrating community service into nursing education.
New York, NY : Springer Pub. Co., c1999.
*TC RT76 .I55 1999*

**Curriculum Advisory Service.**
CAS. Chicago : Curriculum Advisory Service, 1969-
1974.

**Curriculum Advisory Service quarterly.**
CAS. Chicago : Curriculum Advisory Service, 1969-
1974.

**Curriculum and consequence :** Herbert M. Kliebard
and the promise of schooling / edited by Barry M.
Franklin. New York : Teachers College Press, c2000.
ix, 208 p. ; 23 cm. (Reflective history series) Includes
bibliographical references and index. ISBN 0-8077-3951-0
(alk. paper) ISBN 0-8077-3950-2 (pbk. : alk. paper) DDC
375/.001/0973
*1. Education - United States - Curricula - History. 2.
Curriculum planning - United States - History. 3. Education -
United States - Philosophy - History. 4. Kliebard, Herbert M. I.
Kliebard, Herbert M. II. Franklin, Barry M. III. Series.*
*TC LB1570 .C88379 2000*

**Curriculum, assessment, and instruction for students
with disabilities.**
Bigge, June L. Belmont, CA : Wadsworth Pub.,
c1999.
*TC LC4031 .B46 1999*

**Curriculum-based assessment.**
Jones, Carroll J. Springfield, Ill. : C.C. Thomas,
Publisher, c1998.
*TC LB3060.32.C74 J66 1998*

**CURRICULUM-BASED ASSESSMENT - UNITED
STATES.**
Advanced applications of curriculum-based
measurement. New York : Guilford Press, c1998.
*TC LB3060.32.C74 A38 1998*

Howell, Kenneth W. Curriculum-based evaluation.
3rd ed. Belmont, CA. : Wadsworth, c2000.
*TC LB3060.32.C74 H68 2000*

Jones, Carroll J. Curriculum-based assessment.
Springfield, Ill. : C.C. Thomas, Publisher, c1998.
*TC LB3060.32.C74 J66 1998*

**Curriculum-based evaluation.**
Howell, Kenneth W. 3rd ed. Belmont, CA. :
Wadsworth, c2000.
*TC LB3060.32.C74 H68 2000*

**CURRICULUM CHANGE.**
Teaching in the 21st century. New York : Falmer
Press, 1999.
*TC PE1404 .T394 1999*

**CURRICULUM CHANGE - CROSS-CULTURAL
STUDIES.**
Curriculum politics, policy, practice. Albany : State
University of New York Press, c2000.
*TC LC71.3 .C87 2000*

The primary curriculum. New York ; London :
Routledge, 1998.
*TC LB1570 .P678 1998*

**CURRICULUM CHANGE - GREAT BRITAIN.**
Quicke, John, 1941- A curriculum for life.
Buckingham ; Philadelphia : Open University Press,
1999.
*TC LB1564.G7 Q85 1999*

**CURRICULUM CHANGE - UNITED STATES.**
Adams, Jacob E. Taking charge of curriculum. New
York : Teachers College Press, c2000.
*TC LB2806.15 .A35 2000*

Knowledge and power in the global economy.
Mahwah, N.J. : L. Erlbaum Associates, 2000.

**TC LC66 .K66 2000**
Marsh, Colin J. Curriculum. 2nd. ed. Upper Saddle
River, N.J. : Merrill, c1999.
*TC LB1570 .M3667 1999*

Queen, J. Allen. Curriculum practice in the
elementary and middle school. Upper Saddle River,
N.J. : Merrill, c1999.
*TC LB1570 .Q45 1999*

What's at stake in the K-12 standards wars. New
York : P. Lang, 2000.
*TC LB3060.83 .W53 2000*

**CURRICULUM CHANGE - UNITED STATES -
PHILOSOPHY.**
Contemporary curriculum discourses. New York : P.
Lang, c1999.
*TC LB2806.15 .C6753 1999*

**Curriculum, culture, and art education :** comparative
perspectives / edited by Kerry Freedman, Fernando
Hernández. Albany : State University of New York
Press, c1998. vii, 225 p. : ill. ; 24 cm. (SUNY series,
innovations in curriculum) Includes bibliographical references
(p. 193-212) and indexes. ISBN 0-7914-3773-6 (alk. paper)
ISBN 0-7914-3774-4 (pbk. : alk. paper) DDC 707
*1. Art - Study and teaching - Case studies. I. Freedman, Kerry
J. II. Hernández y Hernández, Fernando. III. Series.*
*TC N85 .C87 1998*

**Curriculum, cultures, and (homo)sexualities**
Queering elementary education. Lanham, Md. ;
Oxford : Rowman & Littlefield, c1999.
*TC LC192.6 .Q85 1999*

**CURRICULUM DEVELOPMENT.** *See*
**CURRICULUM PLANNING.**

**CURRICULUM ENRICHMENT.**
Graham, Sheila L. Urban minority gifted students.
1999.
*TC 06 no. 11119*

**CURRICULUM EVALUATION.**
Curriculum frameworks for mathematics and science.
Vancouver, Canada : Pacific Educational Press,
c1993.
*TC QA11 .C87 1993*

National contexts for mathematics & science
education. Vancouver : Pacific Educational Press,
1997.
*TC Q181 N37 1997*

Werner, Walter. Collaborative assessment of school-
based projects. Vancouver : Pacific Educational Press,
c1991.
*TC LB2822.8 .W47 1991*

**CURRICULUM EVALUATION - UNITED
STATES.**
Marsh, Colin J. Curriculum. 2nd. ed. Upper Saddle
River, N.J. : Merrill, c1999.
*TC LB1570 .M3667 1999*

**A curriculum for life.**
Quicke, John, 1941- Buckingham ; Philadelphia :
Open University Press, 1999.
*TC LB1564.G7 Q85 1999*

**Curriculum frameworks for mathematics and
science** / David F. Robitaille ... [et al.] ; general
editor, David F. Robitaille. Vancouver, Canada :
Pacific Educational Press, c1993. 102 p. : ill. ; 23 cm.
(TIMSS monograph ; no. 1) "The Third International
Mathematics and Science Study"--Cover. Includes
bibliographical references (p. 99-102). ISBN 0-88865-090-6
*1. Mathematics - Study and teaching. 2. Science - Study and
teaching. 3. Curriculum evaluation. I. Robitaille, David F. II.
Third International Mathematics and Science Study. III. Series.*
*TC QA11 .C87 1993*

**Curriculum in the postmodern condition** / Alicia de
Alba ... [et al.]. New York : P. Lang, c2000. 306 p. ; 23
cm. (Counterpoints ; vol. 103) Includes bibliographical
references (p. [263]-290) and index. ISBN 0-8204-4176-7 (alk.
paper) DDC 374/.001
*1. Curriculum planning - Social aspects. 2. Postmodernism and
education. 3. Postmodernism. I. Alba, Alicia de. II. Series:
Counterpoints (New York, N.Y.) ; vol. 103.*
*TC LB2806.15 .C694 2000*

**CURRICULUM LABORATORIES.** *See*
**INSTRUCTIONAL MATERIALS CENTERS.**

**CURRICULUM MATERIALS.** *See* **TEACHING -
AIDS AND DEVICES.**

**Curriculum models and strategies for educating
individuals with disabilities in inclusive
classrooms.**
Taylor, George R. Springfield, Ill. : C.C. Thomas,
Publisher, c1999.

**TC LC4031 .T33 1999**

**CURRICULUM PLANNING.** *See also*
**CURRICULUM CHANGE;
INTERDISCIPLINARY APPROACH IN
EDUCATION; STUDENT PARTICIPATION
IN CURRICULUM PLANNING.**
Classroom issues. London ; New York : Falmer Press,
2000.
*TC LC268 .C52 2000*

Interdisciplinary general education. New York, NY :
College Board Publications, c1999.
*TC LB2361 .I43 1999*

Kim, Eugene C. A resource guide for secondary
school teaching. 5th ed. New York : Macmillan Pub.
Co., c1991.
*TC LB1737.A3 K56 1991 5th ed.*

Sowell, Evelyn J. Curriculum. 2nd ed. Upper Saddle
River, N.J. : Merrill, c2000.
*TC LB2806.15 .S69 2000*

Stewig, John W. Language arts in the early childhood
classroom. Belmont [Calif.] : Wadsworth Pub. Co.,
c1995.
*TC LB1140.5.L3 S72 1995*

Trends in community college curriculum. San
Francisco : Jossey-Bass, c1999.
*TC LB2328.15.U6 T75 1999*

Wiltshire, Michael A. Integrating mathematics and
science for below average ninth grade students. 1997.
*TC 06 no. 10847*

**Curriculum planning :** a contemporary approach /
[compiled by] Forrest W. Parkay, Glen Hass. 7th ed.
Boston : Allyn and Bacon, c2000. xii, 548 p. : ill. ; 24
cm. Includes bibliographical references and index. ISBN
0-205-30710-8 (alk. paper) DDC 375/.001
*1. Curriculum planning - United States. 2. Child development -
United States. 3. Learning. 4. Educational psychology. I.
Parkay, Forrest W. II. Hass, Glen.*
*TC LB2806.15 .C868 2000*

**CURRICULUM PLANNING - CROSS-CULTURAL
STUDIES.**
The primary curriculum. New York ; London :
Routledge, 1998.
*TC LB1570 .P678 1998*

**CURRICULUM PLANNING - GREAT BRITAIN.**
Improving teaching and learning in the core
curriculum. London ; New York : Falmer Press, 2000.
*TC LB1564.G7 I475 2000*

**CURRICULUM PLANNING - GREAT BRITAIN -
CASE STUDIES.**
Woods, Peter, 1934- Multicultural children in the
early years. Clevedon ; Philadelphia : Multilingual
Matters Ltd, c1999.
*TC LC3736.G6 W66 1999*

**CURRICULUM PLANNING - HANDBOOKS,
MANUALS, ETC.**
Reid, Gavin, 1950- Dyslexia. Chichester ; New York :
J. Wiley, c1998.
*TC LC4708 .R45 1998*

**CURRICULUM PLANNING - MISCELLANEA.**
Fry, Edward Bernard, 1925- The reading teacher's
book of lists. 3rd ed. Englewood Cliffs, NJ : Prentice
Hall, c1993.
*TC LB1050.2 .F79 1993*

Fry, Edward Bernard, 1925- The reading teacher's
book of lists. 4th ed. Paramus, N.J. : Prentice Hall,
c2000.
*TC LB1050.2 .F79 2000*

**CURRICULUM PLANNING - SOCIAL ASPECTS.**
Curriculum in the postmodern condition. New York :
P. Lang, c2000.
*TC LB2806.15 .C694 2000*

Paradigm debates in curriculum and supervision.
Westport, Conn. ; London : Bergin & Garvey, 2000.
*TC LB2806.4 .P37 2000*

**CURRICULUM PLANNING - SOCIAL ASPECTS -
GREAT BRITAIN.**
Ross, Alistair, 1946- Curriculum. London ; New
York : Falmer Press, 2000.
*TC LB1564.G7 R66 2000*

**CURRICULUM PLANNING - UNITED STATES.**
Adams, Jacob E. Taking charge of curriculum. New
York : Teachers College Press, c2000.
*TC LB2806.15 .A35 2000*

Cultures of curriculum. Mahwah, N.J. ; London : L.
Erlbaum Associates, 2000.

*Curriculum planning - United States.*

*TC LB2806.15 .C73 2000*

Curriculum planning. 7th ed. Boston : Allyn and Bacon, c2000.
*TC LB2806.15 .C868 2000*

Designing mathematics or science curriculum programs. Washington, D.C. : National Academy Press, 1999.
*TC Q183.3.A1 D46 1999*

Foshay, Arthur Wellesley, 1912- The curriculum. New York : London : Teachers College Press, c2000.
*TC LB2806.15 .F66 2000*

Henderson, James George. Transformative curriculum leadership. 2nd ed. Upper Saddle River. N.J. : Merrill, c2000.
*TC LB1570 .H45 2000*

Mallery, Anne L. Creating a catalyst for thinking. Boston : Allyn and Bacon, c2000.
*TC LB2806.15 .M34 2000*

Marsh, Colin J. Curriculum. 2nd. ed. Upper Saddle River, N.J. : Merrill, c1999.
*TC LB1570 .M3667 1999*

Marshall, J. Dan. Turning points in curriculum. Upper Saddle River, N.J. : Merrill, c2000.
*TC LB1570 .M36675 2000*

Marzano, Robert J. Essential knowledge. Aurora, Colo. : McREL, 1999.
*TC LB3060.83 .M36 1999*

Morrow, Lesley Mandel. Literacy instruction in half- and whole-day kindergarten. Newark, Del. : International Reading Association ; Chicago, Ill. : National Reading Conference, c1998.
*TC LB1181.2 .M67 1998*

Queen, J. Allen. Curriculum practice in the elementary and middle school. Upper Saddle River, N.J. : Merrill, c1999.
*TC LB1570 .Q45 1999*

Reaching potentials. Washington, DC : National Association for the Education of Young Children, c1992-<1995>
*TC LB1140.23 .R36 1992*

Rogovin, Paula. Classroom interviews. Portsmouth, NH : Heinemann, c1998.
*TC LB1537 .R58 1998*

What your fifth grader needs to know. New York : Doubleday, c1993.
*TC LB1571 5th .W43 1993*

What your sixth grader needs to know. New York : Doubleday, c1993.
*TC LB1571 6th .W43 1993*

**CURRICULUM PLANNING - UNITED STATES - HANDBOOKS, MANUALS, ETC.**
Jackman, Hilda L. Sing me a story! Tell me a song!. Thousand Oaks, Calif. : Corwin Press, c1999.
*TC LB1139.35.A37 J33 1999*

**CURRICULUM PLANNING - UNITED STATES - HISTORY.**
Curriculum and consequence. New York : Teachers College Press, c2000.
*TC LB1570 .C88379 2000*

**CURRICULUM PLANNING - UNITED STATES - PHILOSOPHY.**
Contemporary curriculum discourses. New York : P. Lang, c1999.
*TC LB2806.15 .C6753 1999*

**Curriculum politics, policy, practice :** cases in comparative context / Catherine Cornbleth, editor. Albany : State University of New York Press, c2000. vi, 251 p. ; 24 cm. (SUNY series, innovations in curriculum) Includes bibliographical references and index. CONTENTS: 1. Viewpoints / Catherine Cornbleth -- 2. A Tale of Two Cultures and a Technology: A/musical Politics of Curriculum in Four Acts / Vivian Forssman and John Willinsky -- 3. Science for All Americans?: Critiquing Science Education Reform / Margery D. Osborne and Angela Calabrese-Barton -- 4. The Politics of Religious Knowledge in Singapore / Jason Tan -- 5. The Segregation of Stephen / Diana Lawrence-Brown -- 6. "They Don't Want to Hear it": Ways of Talking and Habits of the Heart in Multicultural Literature Classrooms / Suzanne Miller and Gina DeBlase Trzyna -- 7. Curriculum as a Site of Memory: The Struggle for History in South Africa / Nadine Dolby -- 8. Understanding Shifts in British Educational Discourses of Social Justice / Gaby Weiner -- 9. National Standards and Curriculum as Cultural Containment? / Catherine Cornbleth. ISBN 0-7914-4567-4 (hbk. : alk. paper) ISBN 0-7914-4568-2 (pbk. : alk. paper) DDC 379.1/55 DDC 379.1/55
*1. Education - Curricula - Political aspects - Cross-cultural*

studies. 2. Curriculum change - Cross-cultural studies. I. Cornbleth, Catherine. II. Series.
*TC LC71.3 .C87 2000*

**Curriculum practice in the elementary and middle school.**
Queen, J. Allen. Upper Saddle River, N.J. : Merrill, c1999.
*TC LB1570 .Q45 1999*

**CURRICULUM - STANDARDS.**
Educational competencies for graduates of associate degree nursing programs. [Rev.]. Sudbury, Mass. : Jones and Bartlett, 2000.
*TC RT74.5 .E38 2000*

**Curry, Barbara K.** Women in power : pathways to leadership in education / Barbara K. Curry ; foreword by Maxine Greene. New York : London : Teachers College Press, c2000. xi, 110 p. : 24 cm. (Athene series) Includes bibliographical references (p. 103-105) and index. ISBN 0-8077-3911-1 (hbk. : alk. paper) ISBN 0-8077-3910-3 (pbk. : alk. paper) DDC 371.2/011/082
*1. Women school administrators - United States. 2. Women educators - United States. 3. Educational leadership - United States. I. Title. II. Series.*
*TC LB2831.62 .C87 2000*

**Curry, Jane Louise.** A Stolen life / Jane Louise Curry. New York : McElderry Books, 1999. 198 p. ; 22 cm. SUMMARY: In 1758 in Scotland, teenaged Jamesina MacKenzie finds her courage and resolution severely tested when she is abducted by "spiriters" and, after a harrowing voyage across the Atlantic, sold as a bond slave to a Virginia planter. ISBN 0-689-82932-9 DDC [Fic]
*1. Indentured servants - Fiction. 2. Scotland - History - 18th century - Fiction. 3. Virginia - History - Colonial period, 1600-1775 - Fiction. I. Title.*
*TC PZ7.C936 St 1999*

**Curtis, A. Cheryl.**
Rasool, Joan. Multicultural education in middle and secondary classrooms. Belmont, CA : Wadsworth, c2000.
*TC LC1099.3 .R38 2000*

**Curtis, Christopher Paul.** Bud, not Buddy / Christopher Paul Curtis. New York : Delacorte Press, 1999. viii, 245 p. : ill. ; 22 cm. SUMMARY: Ten-year-old Bud, a motherless boy living in Flint, Michigan, during the Great Depression, escapes a bad foster home and sets out in search of the man he believes to be his father--the renowned bandleader, H.E. Calloway of Grand Rapids. ISBN 0-385-32306-9 DDC [Fic]
*1. Runaways - Fiction. 2. Afro-Americans - Fiction. 3. Depressions - 1929 - Fiction. I. Title.*
*TC PZ7.C94137 Bu 1999*

**Curtis, Sarah Ann.** Educating the faithful : religion, schooling, and society in nineteenth-century France / Sarah A. Curtis. DeKalb : Northern Illinois University Press, 2000. xii, 255 p. ; 24 cm. Includes bibliographical references (p. [227]-250) and index. ISBN 0-87580-262-1 (alk. paper) DDC 371.071/244
*1. Catholic church - Education - France - History - 19th century. 2. Catholic schools - France - History - 19th century. 3. Education, Primary - France - History - 19th century. I. Title.*
*TC LC506.F7 C87 2000*

**Curtiss, Deborah, 1937-.**
Spandorfer, Merle, 1934- Making art safely. New York : Van Nostrand Reinhold, c1993.
*TC RC963.6.A78 S62 1993*

**CURVES, PLANE. *See* CIRCLE.**

**Curzan, Anne.** First day to final grade : a graduate student's guide to teaching / Anne Curzan and Lisa Damour. Ann Arbor [Mich.] : University of Michigan Press, c2000. vii, 197 p. : ill. ; 24 cm. Includes bibliographical references and index. ISBN 0-472-09732-6 (cloth : alk. paper) ISBN 0-472-06732-X (paper : alk. paper) DDC 378.1/25
*1. Graduate teaching assistants - United States. 2. College teaching - United States. I. Damour, Lisa. II. Title.*
*TC LB2335.4 .C87 2000*

**Cusack, Sandra A.**
Glendenning, Frank. Teaching and learning in later life. Aldershot, Hants, Eng. : Burlington, Vt. : Ashgate / Arena, c2000.
*TC LC5457 .G54 2000*

**Cushman, Kathleen.**
Steinberg, Adria. Schooling for the real world. 1st ed. San Francisco : Jossey-Bass, c1999.
*TC LC1037.5 .S843 1999*

**Cutchin, Kay Lynch.** Landscapes and language : English for American academic discourse / Kay Lynch Cutchin, Gail Price Rottweiler, Ajanta Dutt. Cambridge, UK : New York, NY, USA : Cambridge

University Press, 1999. xix, 236 p. ; 23 cm. Originally published: New York : St. Martin's Press, c1998. Includes bibliographical references and index. ISBN 0-521-65766-0
*1. English language - Textbooks for foreign speakers. 2. English language - United States - Rhetoric - Problems, exercises, etc. 3. Academic writing - Problems, exercises, etc. 4. College readers. I. Rottweiler, Gail Price. II. Dutt, Ajanta, 1958- III. Title.*
*TC PE1128 .C88 1999*

**Cutler, Jill.**
Global visions. 1st ed. Boston : South End Press, c1993.
*TC HF1359 .G58 1993*

**Cutler, William W.** Parents and schools : the 150-year struggle for control in American education / William W. Cutler III. Chicago : University of Chicago Press, 2000. xiii, 290 p. : ill. ; 24 cm. Includes bibliographical references (p. [209]-272) and index. ISBN 0-226-13216-1 (cloth : alk. paper) DDC 371.19/2/0973
*1. Home and school - United States - History - 19th century. 2. Home and school - United States - History - 20th century. 3. Education - Parent participation - United States - History - 19th century. 4. Education - Parent participation - United States - History - 20th century. 5. Educational change - United States - History - 19th century. 6. Educational change - United States - History - 20th century. I. Title.*
*TC LC225.3 .C86 2000*

**The cybercultures reader** / edited by David Bell and Barbara M. Kennedy. London ; New York : Routledge, 2000. xxv, 768 p. : ill. ; 26 cm. Includes bibliographical references and index. ISBN 0-415-18378-2 ISBN 0-415-18379-0 (pbk.) DDC 306.1
*1. High technology - Social aspects. 2. Computers and civilization. 3. Cyberspace - Social aspects. I. Bell, David, 1965- II. Kennedy, Barbara M.*
*TC T14.5 .C934 2000*

**CYBERNETICS. *See also* COMPUTERS.**
Hayles, N. Katherine. How we became posthuman. Chicago, Ill. : University of Chicago Press, 1999.
*TC Q335 .H394 1999*

**Cyberpower.**
Jordan, Tim, 1959- London ; New York : Routledge, 1999.
*TC ZA4375 .J67 1999*

**Cyberpsychology** / edited by Ángel Gordo-López and Ian Parker. New York : Routledge, 1999. xii, 244 p. ; 23 cm. Includes bibliographical references and index. ISBN 0-415-92496-0 (hc) ISBN 0-415-92497-9 (pb)
*1. Human-computer interaction. I. Parker, Ian. 1956- II. Gordo-López, Angel.*
*TC HM1033 .C934 1999*

**Cyberseduction.**
Fink, Jeri. Amherst, N.Y. : Prometheus Books, 1999.
*TC QA76.9.P75 F53 1999*

**CYBERSPACE. *See also* COMPUTERS; TELEMATICS.**
Hakken, David. Cyborgs@cyberspace? New York : Routledge, 1999.
*TC QA76.9.C66 H34 1999*

Wertheim, Margaret. The pearly gates of cyberspace. 1st ed. New York : W.W. Norton, c1999.
*TC QA76.9.C66 W48 1999*

**CYBERSPACE - SOCIAL ASPECTS.**
The cybercultures reader. London ; New York : Routledge, 2000.
*TC T14.5 .C934 2000*

Jordan, Tim, 1959- Cyberpower. London ; New York : Routledge, 1999.
*TC ZA4375 .J67 1999*

Race in cyberspace. New York ; London : Routledge, 2000.
*TC HT1523 .R252 2000*

**Cyborgs at cyberspace?.**
Hakken, David. Cyborgs@cyberspace? New York : Routledge, 1999.
*TC QA76.9.C66 H34 1999*

**Cyborgs@cyberspace?.**
Hakken, David. New York : Routledge, 1999.
*TC QA76.9.C66 H34 1999*

**CYCLOPEDIAS. *See* ENCYCLOPEDIAS AND DICTIONARIES.**

**Cziko, Gary.** The things we do : using the lessons of Bernard and Darwin to understand the what, how, and why of our behavior / Gary Cziko. Cambridge, Mass. : MIT Press, c2000. xi, 290 p. : ill. ; 24 cm. "A Bradford book." Includes bibliographical references (p. [267]-277) and index. ISBN 0-262-03277-5 (hc : alk. paper) DDC 304

*1. Social psychology. 2. Sociobiology. 3. Behavior evolution. 4.
Social Darwinism. I. Title.*
**TC HM1033 .C95 2000**

**DA (INTERPERSONAL COMMUNICATION).** *See*
**DIALOGUE ANALYSIS.**

**Dabakis, Melissa.** Visualizing labor in American
sculpture : monuments, manliness, and the work ethic,
1880-1935 / Melissa Dabakis. New York : Cambridge
University Press, 1999. xvi, 296 p. : ill. ; 26 cm.
(Cambridge studies in American visual culture) Includes
bibliographical references (p. 273-286) and index. ISBN
0-521-46147-2 (hb) DDC 730/.973
*1. Labor in art. 2. Sculpture, American. 3. Sculpture, Modern -
19th century - United Sttes. 4. Sculpture, Modern - 20th
century - United States. I. Title. II. Series.*
**TC NB1952.L33 D24 1999**

**Dacey, John S.** Your anxious child : how parents and
teachers can relieve anxiety in children / John S.
Dacey, Lisa B. Fiore ; with contributions by G.T.
Ladd. 1st ed. San Francisco : Jossey-Bass, c2000. xi,
242 p. : ill. ; 24 cm. Includes bibliographical references (p.
227-232) and index. CONTENTS: What anxiety is and how it
can be alleviated -- Eight types of anxiety disorders in children
and adolescents -- Cope step one: calming the nervous
system -- Cope step two: originating an imaginative plan --
Cope step three: persisting in the face of obstacles and
failure -- Cope step four: evaluating and adjusting the plan --
How your parenting style can help ease your child's anxiety --
Appendix a: summary of all activities in this book and their
goals -- Appendix b: solutions to activity problems --
Appendix c: an annotated bibliography of books on self-
control -- Appendix d: an annotated bibliography of books on
anxiety. ISBN 0-7879-4997-3 (hard : alk. paper) DDC 649/.1
*1. Anxiety in children. 2. Anxiety in adolescence. 3. Stress
management in children. 4. Stress management in teenagers. 5.
Parenting. I. Fiore, Lisa B., 1970- II. Title.*
**TC BF723.A5 D33 2000**

**Dachler, Marvin W., 1942-.**
Chen, Zhe, 1964- Across the great divide. Oxford :
Blackwell, 2000.
**TC LB1103 .S6 v.65 no. 2**

**D'Acierno, Pellegrino, 1943-.**
The Italian American heritage. New York : Garland
Pub., 1999.
**TC E184.I8 I675 1999**

**DADAISM.** *See* **POP ART.**

**DADS.** *See* **FATHERS.**

**Dadzie, Stella, 1952-** Toolkit for tackling racism in
schools / Stella Dadzie. Stoke on Trent, Staffordshire,
England : Trentham Books, 2000. xviii, 102 p. : ill. ; 30
cm. Includes bibliographical references. ISBN 1-85856-188-4
*1. Discrimination in education - Great Britain. 2. Racism -
Great Britain. I. Title.*
**TC LC212.3.G7 D339 2000**

**DAHL, ROALD.**
**DANNY THE CHAMPION OF THE WORLD.**
Beech, Linda Ward. Danny the champion of the
world by Roald Dahl. New York : Scholastic,
c1997.
**TC LB11573 .B431 1997**

Beech, Linda Ward. Danny the champion of the
world by Roald Dahl. New York : Scholastic,
c1997.
**TC LB1573 .B431 1997**

**Dahlström, Lars, 1942-.**
Democratic teacher education reform in Africa.
Boulder, Colo. ; Oxford : Westview Press, 1999.
**TC LB1727.N3 D46 1999**

**Daily life in a Plains Indian village, 1868.**
Terry, Michael Bad Hand. 1st American ed. New
York : Clarion Books, c1999.
**TC E78.G73 T47 1999**

**Daines, Brian.** Psychodynamic approaches to sexual
problems / Brian Daines and Angelina Perrett.
Buckingham ; Philadelphia : Open University Press,
2000. ix, 177 p. : ill. ; 23 cm. Includes bibliographical
references (p. [163]-170) and index. ISBN 0-335-20160-1
(hardcover) ISBN 0-335-20159-8 (pbk.) DDC 616.85/830651
*1. Psychosexual disorders - Treatment. 2. Sex therapy. 3.
Psychodynamic psychotherapy. I. Perrett, Angelina, 1960- II.
Title.*
**TC RC557 .D35 2000**

**DAIRY PRODUCTS.** *See* **MILK.**

**DAKOTA INDIANS.** *See* **TETON INDIANS.**

**Dalenberg, Constance J.** Countertransference and the
treatment of trauma / Constance J. Dalenberg. 1st ed.
Washington, D.C. : American Psychological
Association, c2000. xii, 305 p. ; 24 cm. Includes

bibliographical references and index. ISBN 1-55798-687-8
(alk. paper) DDC 616.85/210651
*1. Countertransference (Psychology) 2. Psychic trauma -
Treatment. 3. Psychoanalysis. I. Title.*
**TC RC489.C68 D37 2000**

**Daley, Barbara J.**
Charting a course for continuing professional
education :. San Francisco : Jossey-Bass, c2000.
**TC LC1072.C56 C55 2000**

**Dallas Museum of Fine Arts.**
Cole, Herbert M. The arts of Ghana. Los Angeles :
Museum of Cultural History, University of California,
c1977.
**TC NX589.6.G5 C64**

**Dalton, Peggy.**
Fransella, Fay. Personal construct counselling in
action. 2nd ed. London ; Thousand Oaks, Calif. : Sage
Publications, 2000.
**TC BF698.9.P47 F73 2000**

**Dalton, Thomas Carlyle.**
Beyond heredity and environment. Boulder :
Westview Press, 1995.
**TC BF341 .B48 1995**

**Daly, Brenda O., 1941-** Authoring a life : a woman's
survival in and through literary studies / Brenda Daly.
Albany, NY : State University of New York Press,
c1998. xiii, 268 p. ; 24 cm. Includes bibliographical
references (p. 237-249) and index. ISBN 0-7914-3679-9 (hc :
alk. paper) ISBN 0-7914-3680-2 (pbk : alk. paper) DDC
616.85/83606
*1. Incest victims - Rehabilitation. 2. Bibliotherapy. 3.
Autobiography - Therapeutic use. 4. Incest in literature. I.
Title.*
**TC RC560.153 D35 1998**

**Damer, Mary.**
McEwan, Elaine K., 1941- Managing unmanageable
students. Thousand Oaks, Calif. : Corwin Press,
c2000.
**TC LC4801.5 .M39 2000**

**Damm, Robert J., 1964-** Repertoire, authenticity, and
instruction : the presentation of American Indian
music in Oklahoma's elementary schools / Robert J.
Damm. New York ; London : Garland Pub., 2000. xi,
131 p. ; 23 cm. (Native Americans) Includes bibliographical
references (p. 121-127) and index. ISBN 0-8153-3814-7 (alk.
paper) DDC 372.87/09766
*1. School music - Instruction and study - Oklahoma. 2. Indians
of North America - Music - History and criticism. 3. Indians
of North America - Education - Oklahoma. 4. Multicultural
education - Oklahoma. 5. Education, Elementary - Oklahoma.
I. Title. II. Series: Native Americans (Garland Publishing, Inc.)*
**TC MT3.U6 O53 2000**

**Damned if you do, damned if you don't.**
McMahon, Anthony. Aldershot, England : Brookfield,
USA : Ashgate, 1998.
**TC HV743.C5 M35 1998**

**Damour, Lisa.**
Curzan, Anne. First day to final grade. Ann Arbor
[Mich.] : University of Michigan Press, c2000.
**TC LB2335.4 .C87 2000**

**Dana, Katharine Floyd, 1835-1886.** Over in the
meadow : an old counting rhyme / based on the
original by Olive A. Wadsworth ; illustrated by David
Carter. New York : Scholastic, c1992 1 v. (unpaged) :
col. ill. ; 21 x 26 cm. SUMMARY: A variety of meadow
animals pursuing their daily activities introduce the numbers
one through ten. ISBN 0-590-44498-0 DDC [E]
*1. Nursery rhymes. 2. Children's poetry. 3. Nursery rhymes. 4.
Animals - Poetry. 5. Counting. I. Carter, David A., ill. II. Title.*
**TC PZ8.3.D2 Ov 1992**

**Dana, Richard H. (Richard Henry), 1927-.**
Handbook of cross-cultural and multicultural
personality assessment. Mahwah, N.J. ; London :
Lawrence Erlbaum Associates, 2000.
**TC RC473.P79 H36 2000**

**Danbury, Hazel, 1939-.**
Sharp, Mavis, 1945- The management of failing
DipSW students. Aldershot ; Brookfield, Vt. :
Ashgate, c1999.
**TC HV11.8.G7 S53 1999**

**DANCE.** *See* **BALLET; BALLROOM DANCING;
CHOREOGRAPHY; JAZZ DANCE; MODERN
DANCE; TAP DANCING.**

**The dance.**
Evans, Richard Paul. 1st ed. New York : Simon &
Schuster Books for Young Readers, c1999.
**TC PZ7.E89227 Dan 1999**

**Dance.**
International encyclopedia of dance. New York :
Oxford University Press, c1998.
**TC GV1585 .I586 1998**

**DANCE AND SOCIETY.** *See* **DANCE - SOCIAL
ASPECTS.**

**DANCE AS A PROFESSION.** *See* **DANCE -
VOCATIONAL GUIDANCE.**

**DANCE - CAMBODIA.**
Phim, Toni Samantha, 1957- Dance in Cambodia.
[Kuala Lampur] Malaysia ; Oxford ; New York :
Oxford University Press, 1999.
**TC GV1703.C3 P55 1999**

**DANCE - ENCYCLOPEDIAS.**
International encyclopedia of dance. New York :
Oxford University Press, c1998.
**TC GV1585 .I586 1998**

**Dance essays.**
Fleming, Bruce. Sex, art, and audience. New York ;
Canterbury [England] : P. Lang, c2000.
**TC GV1588.3 .F54 2000**

**DANCE - FICTION.**
Evans, Richard Paul. The dance. 1st ed. New York :
Simon & Schuster Books for Young Readers, c1999.
**TC PZ7.E89227 Dan 1999**

**DANCE - HISTORY.**
Williams, Drid, 1928- Anthropology and human
movement. Lanham, Md. ; London : Scarecrow Press,
2000.
**TC GV1595 .W53 2000**

**Dance in Cambodia.**
Phim, Toni Samantha, 1957- [Kuala Lampur]
Malaysia ; Oxford ; New York : Oxford University
Press, 1999.
**TC GV1703.C3 P55 1999**

**DANCE IN MOTION PICTURES, TELEVISION,
ETC.**
Jazz dance class [videorecording]. W. Long Branch,
NJ : Kultur, [1992?]
**TC GV1784 .J3 1992**

**DANCE IN TELEVISION.** *See* **DANCE IN
MOTION PICTURES, TELEVISION, ETC.**

**Dance instructional**
Ballet class for beginners [videorecording]. W. Long
Branch, NJ : Kultur, c1981.
**TC GV1589 .B3 1981**

Ballet class [videorecording]. W. Long Branch, NJ :
Kultur, c1984.
**TC GV1589 .B33 1984**

Ballroom dancing for beginners [videorecording]. W.
Long Branch, N.J. Kultur, c1993.
**TC GV1753.7 .B3 1993**

Ballroom dancing for beginners [videorecording]. W.
Long Branch, N.J. Kultur, c1993.
**TC GV1753.7 .B3 1993**

Jazz dance class [videorecording]. W. Long Branch,
NJ : Kultur, [1992?]
**TC GV1784 .J3 1992**

**Dance is the language of the gods.**
Nürnberger, Marianne, 1956- [Tanz ist die Sprache
der Götter. English] Amsterdam : VU University
Press, 1998.
**TC GV1703.S74 .N8713 1998**

**Dance, modernity, and culture.**
Thomas, Helen, 1947- London ; New York :
Routledge, 1995.
**TC GV1588.6 .T46 1995**

**The dance of change** : the challenges of sustaining
momentum in learning organizations / Peter Senge ...
[et al.]. 1st ed. New York : Currency/Doubleday,
1999. ix, 596 p. : ill. ; 23 cm. "A Fifth discipline resource."
Includes index. "A fifth discipline resource." DDC 658.4/06
*1. Organizational learning. 2. Organizational change. I. Senge,
Peter M.*
**TC HD58.82 .D36 1999**

**DANCE ON TELEVISION.** *See* **DANCE IN
MOTION PICTURES, TELEVISION, ETC.**

**Dance Perspectives Foundation.**
International encyclopedia of dance. New York :
Oxford University Press, c1998.
**TC GV1585 .I586 1998**

**DANCE - PHILOSOPHY.**
Fleming, Bruce. Sex, art, and audience. New York ;
Canterbury [England] : P. Lang, c2000.
**TC GV1588.3 .F54 2000**

**DANCE - REVIEWS.**
Denby, Edwin, 1903- Dance writings & poetry. New Haven [CT] : Yale University Press, c1998.
*TC GV1599 .D393 1998*

**DANCE - SOCIAL ASPECTS - UNITED STATES.**
Hanna, Judith Lynne. Partnering dance and education. Champaign, IL : Human Kinetics, c1999.
*TC GV1589 .H35 1999*

**DANCE - SOCIOLOGICAL ASPECTS.**
Thomas, Helen, 1947- Dance, modernity, and culture. London ; New York : Routledge, 1995.
*TC GV1588.6 .T46 1995*

**DANCE - SRI LANKA.**
Nürnberger, Marianne, 1956- [Tanz ist die Sprache der Götter. English] Dance is the language of the gods. Amsterdam : VU University Press, 1998.
*TC GV1703.S74 .N8713 1998*

**DANCE - SRI LANKA - RELIGIOUS ASPECTS.**
Nürnberger, Marianne, 1956- [Tanz ist die Sprache der Götter. English] Dance is the language of the gods. Amsterdam : VU University Press, 1998.
*TC GV1703.S74 .N8713 1998*

**DANCE - STUDY AND TEACHING (HIGHER) - UNITED STATES - HISTORY.**
Hagood, Thomas K. A history of dance in American higher education. Lewiston, N.Y. : E. Mellen Press, c2000.
*TC GV1589 .H33 2000*

**DANCE - STUDY AND TEACHING - UNITED STATES.**
Hanna, Judith Lynne. Partnering dance and education. Champaign, IL : Human Kinetics, c1999.
*TC GV1589 .H35 1999*

**DANCE - STUDY AND TEACHING - UNITED STATES - STATES - DIRECTORIES.**
Jones, Mark W. (Mark Walter), 1947- Dancer's resource. New York : Watson-Guptill Publications, c1999.
*TC GV1589 J65 1999*

**DANCE - UNITED STATES - PSYCHOLOGICAL ASPECTS.**
Hanna, Judith Lynne. Partnering dance and education. Champaign, IL : Human Kinetics, c1999.
*TC GV1589 .H35 1999*

**DANCE - VOCATIONAL GUIDANCE - UNITED STATES.**
Jones, Mark W. (Mark Walter), 1947- Dancer's resource. New York : Watson-Guptill Publications, c1999.
*TC GV1589 J65 1999*

**Dance writings & poetry.**
Denby, Edwin, 1903- New Haven [CT] : Yale University Press, c1998.
*TC GV1599 .D393 1998*

**Dance writings and poetry.**
Denby, Edwin, 1903- Dance writings & poetry. New Haven [CT] : Yale University Press, c1998.
*TC GV1599 .D393 1998*

**DANCERS.** *See* **BALLET DANCERS.**

**DANCERS - BIOGRAPHY.**
Mazo, Joseph H. Prime movers. 2nd revised edition. Princeton, NJ. : Princeton Book Co. Pub., c2000.
*TC GV1783 .M347 2000*

**Dancer's resource.**
Jones, Mark W. (Mark Walter), 1947- New York : Watson-Guptill Publications, c1999.
*TC GV1589 J65 1999*

**DANCERS - UNITED STATES - BIOGRAPHY.**
Limón, José. José Limón. Hanover, NH : University Press of New England, [1998?]
*TC GV1785.L515 A3 1998*

Vaughan, David, 1924- Merce Cunningham. 1st ed. New York, NY : Aperture, c1997.
*TC GV1785.C85 V38 1997*

**DANCES.** *See* **DANCE.**

**DANCING.** *See* **DANCE.**

**DANCING AND SOCIETY.** *See* **DANCE - SOCIAL ASPECTS.**

**DANCING, BALLET.** *See* **BALLET DANCING.**

**DANCING IN MOTION PICTURES, TELEVISION, ETC.** *See* **DANCE IN MOTION PICTURES, TELEVISION, ETC.**

**DANCING IN MOVING-PICTURES, TELEVISION, ETC.** *See* **DANCE IN MOTION PICTURES, TELEVISION, ETC.**

**DANCING - UNITED STATES - HISTORY.**
Mazo, Joseph H. Prime movers. 2nd revised edition. Princeton, NJ. : Princeton Book Co. Pub., c2000.
*TC GV1783 .M347 2000*

**Dancing with bigotry.**
Macedo, Donaldo P. (Donaldo Pereira), 1950- New York : St. Martin's Press, 1999.
*TC LC196.5.U6 D26 1999*

**Danforth, Scot.** Cases in behavior management / Scot Danforth, Joseph R. Boyle. Upper Saddle River, N.J. : Merrill, c2000. xii, 179 p. ; 24 cm. Includes bibliographical references. ISBN 0-13-755711-6 (pbk.) DDC 371.102/4
*1. Classroom management. 2. Behavior modification. I. Boyle, Joseph R. II. Title.*
*TC LB3013 .D34 2000*

**Dangerous desires.**
Harper, Helen J., 1957- Wild words-dangerous desires. New York : Peter Lang, c2000.
*TC LB1631 .H267 2000*

**Dangerous donations.**
Anderson, Eric, 1949- Columbia, Mo. : University of Missouri Press, c1999.
*TC LC2707 .A53 1999*

**The dangerous passion.**
Buss, David M. New York : Free Press, 2000.
*TC BF575.J4 B87 2000*

**Dangerous schools.**
Hyman, Irwin A. 1st ed. San Francisco : Jossey-Bass Publishers, c1999.
*TC LB3013 .H897 1999*

**Danhauer, Jeffrey L.**
Mendel, Lisa Lucks. Singular's pocket dictionary of audiology. San Diego : Singular Pub. Group, c1999.
*TC RF290 .M4642 1999*

**Daniel, Claire, 1936-** The great big book of fun phonics activities / by Claire Daniel, Deborah Eaton, and Carole Osterink. New York : Scholastic professional books, c1999. 352 p. : ill. ; 28 cm. ISBN 0-439-08247-1
*1. English language - Study and teaching (Primary) 2. Reading (Primary) 3. Reading (Elementary) - Phonetic method. I. Eaton, Deborah. II. Osterink, Carole. III. Title.*
*TC LB1525.3 .D36 1999*

**Daniel, Clifton, 1912-.**
20th century day by day. New York, NY : DK Pub., c1999.
*TC D422 .C53 1999*

**Daniels, Debbie.** Therapy with children : : children's rights, confidentiality and the law / Debbie Daniels and Peter Jenkins. London ; Thousand Oaks, Calif. : SAGE, 2000. 148 p. ; 22 cm. (Ethics in practice.) Includes bibliographical references (p. [137]-143) and index. ISBN 0-7619-5278-0 ISBN 0-7619-5279-9 (pbk.)
*1. Child psychotherapy. I. Jenkins, Peter. 1950- II. Title. III. Series.*
*TC RJ504 .D36 2000*

**Daniels, Harry.**
Special education re-formed. London : New York : Falmer Press, 2000.
*TC LC1203.G7 S72 1999*

**Daniels, Harvey, 1936-.**
Etching [videorecording]. Northbrook, Ill. ; Peasmarsh, East Sussex, Eng. : Roland Collection of Films on Art, c1990.
*TC NE2043 .E87 1990*

Screen printing [videorecording]. [Northbrook?], Ill. ; Peasmarsh, East Sussex, Eng. : Roland Collection of Films on Art, c1992.
*TC NE2238.G7 S4 1992*

Screen printing [videorecording]. [Northbrook?], Ill. ; Peasmarsh, East Sussex, Eng. : Roland Collection of Films on Art, c1992.
*TC NE2238.G7 S4 1992*

**Daniels, Harvey, 1947-** Methods that matter : six structures for best practice classrooms / Harvey Daniels and Marilyn Bizar. York, Me. : Stenhouse Publishers, c1998. xii, 260 p. : ill. ; 26 cm. Includes bibliographical references (p. [251]-256). ISBN 1-57110-082-2 (alk. paper) DDC 371.102
*1. Teaching. 2. Interdisciplinary approach in education. 3. Group work in education. 4. Educational tests and measurements. I. Bizar, Marilyn. II. Title.*
*TC LB1027 .D24 1998*

**Daniels, LeRoi, 1930-.**
Critical challenges in social studies for junior high students. Burnaby, B.C. : Field Relations and Teacher In-Service Education, Faculty of Education, Simon Fraser University, 1996.

*TC D16.2 .C75 1996*

**Danielson, Charlotte.** A collection of performance tasks and rubrics : primary school mathematics / Charlotte Danielson and Pia Hansen. Larchmont, NY : Eye On Education, c1999. xiv, 193 p. : ill. ; 23 cm. ISBN 1-88300-170-6 DDC 372.7
*1. Mathematics - Study and teaching (Primary) - Evaluation. I. Hansen, Pia. 1955- II. Title.*
*TC QA135.5 .D244 1999*

Teacher evaluation to enhance professional practice / Charlotte Danielson and Thomas L. McGreal. Alexandria, Va. : Association for Supervision and Curriculum Development, c2000, v, 156 p. ; 25 cm. Includes bibliographical references and index. "ASCD product no. 100219"--T.p. verso. ISBN 0-87120-380-4 (quality pbk.) DDC 371.14/4
*1. Teachers - Rating of - United States. 2. Teaching - United States - Evaluation. I. McGreal, Thomas L. II. Title.*
*TC LB2838 .D26 2000*

**Danish Conference of Activity Theory (2nd : 1991).**
The societal subject. Aarhus C, Denmark : Aarhus University Press, c1993.
*TC B105.A35 S68 1991*

**Danly, Susan.**
Pennsylvania Academy of the Fine Arts. Eakins and the photograph. Washington : Published for the Pennsylvania Academy of the Fine Arts by the Smithsonian Institution Press, c1994.
*TC TR652 .P46 1994*

**Dannells, Michael.** From discipline to development : rethinking student conduct in higher education / by Michael Dannells. Washington, DC : George Washington University, Graduate School of Education and Human Development, [1997] 159 p. ; 23 cm. (ASHE-ERIC higher education report ; v. 25, no. 2) Includes bibliographical references (p. 115-127) and index. CONTENTS: History of student discipline -- Present-day concerns about student misconduct and crime on campus -- The various definitions and purposes of student discipline -- Who misbehaves and why? -- Academic dishonesty -- Codes of conduct : legal issues and educational considerations -- Hoekema's model of student discipline -- The organization and administration of campus disciplinary/judicial systems -- Key legal issues in student discipline -- Student discipline and development theory -- The special issue and challenge of disciplinary counseling -- Conclusions and recommendations. ISBN 1-87838-074-5 DDC 378.1/95/0973
*1. College discipline - United States. 2. College students - United States - Attitudes. 3. College student development programs - United States. I. Title. II. Title: Rethinking student conduct in higher education III. Series: ASHE-ERIC higher education report ; vol. 25, no. 2.*
*TC LB2344 .D36 1997*

Linking theory to practice. 2nd ed. Philadelphia, Pa. : Taylor and Francis, 2000.
*TC LB2342.9 .L56 2000*

**Danny the champion of the world by Roald Dahl.**
Beech, Linda Ward. New York : Scholastic, c1997.
*TC LB11573 .B431 1997*

Beech, Linda Ward. New York : Scholastic, c1997.
*TC LB1573 .B431 1997*

**Danske selskab (Copenhagen, Denmark).**
Grundtvig's ideas in North America. Copenhagen, Denmark : Danske Selskab, 1983.
*TC LB675.G832 G79 1983*

**Dantas, Marcello.**
Processing the signal [videorecording]. Cicero, Ill. : Roland Collection of Films on Art, c1989.
*TC N6494.V53 P7 1989*

**Danto, Arthur Coleman, 1924-** The body/body problem : selected essays / Arthur C. Danto. Berkeley : University of California Press, c1999. xi, 262 p. ; 24 cm. Includes bibliographical references and index. ISBN 0-520-21282-7 (alk. paper) DDC 128/.6
*1. Representation (Philosophy) I. Title.*
*TC B105.R4 D36 1999*

Philosophizing art : selected essays / Arthur C. Danto. Berkeley : University of California Press, c1999. xv, 273 p. : ill. ; 24 cm. Includes bibliographical references and index. ISBN 0-520-21283-5 (alk. paper) DDC 701
*1. Art - Philosophy. I. Title.*
*TC N71 .D33 1999*

**Danziger, Sheldon.**
Securing the future. New York : Russell Sage Foundation, c2000.
*TC HV741 .S385 2000*

**Dar, Amit.**
Vocational education and training reform.

Washington, D.C. : World Bank/Oxford University Press, 2000.
*TC LC1044 .V62 2000*

**Darden, Anne S., 1963-.**
Crossing boundaries. Champaign, IL : Human Kinetics, c1999.
*TC PN6071.S62 C76 1999*

**Dare to discover** : teacher's planning guide. New York : Macmillan/McGraw-Hill, c1997. 1 v. (various pagings) : col. ill. ; 31 cm. (Spotlight on literacy ; Gr.6 l.12 u.2) (The road to independent reading) Includes index. ISBN 0-02-183195-5
*1. Language arts (Elementary) 2. Reading (Elementary) I. Series. II. Series: The road to independent reading*
*TC LB1576 .S66 1997 Gr.6 l.12 u.2*

**DARK AGES.** *See* **MIDDLE AGES.**

**The dark at the top of the stairs.**
McBratney, Sam. 1st U.S. ed. Cambridge, Mass. : Candlewick Press, c1996.
*TC PZ7.M47826 DAr 1996*

**DARK, FEAR OF THE.** *See* **FEAR OF THE DARK.**

**DARK MATTER (ASTRONOMY).**
Stephen Hawking's universe [videorecording]. [Alexandria, Va.] : PBS Video; Burbank, CA : Distributed by Warner Home Video, c1997.
*TC QB982 .S7 1997*

**Darling, Harold.** From Mother Goose to Dr. Seuss : children's book covers, 1860-1960 / by Harold Darling ; foreword by Seymour Chwast. San Francisco : Chronicle Books, c1999. 173 p. : col. ill. ; 25 cm. Includes index. ISBN 0-8118-1898-5 (sc) DDC 686.3/0941
*1. Bookbinding - Great Britain - History - 19th century. 2. Bookbinding - United States - History - 19th century. 3. Bookbinding - Great Britain - History - 20th century. 4. Bookbinding - United States - History - 20th century. 5. Children's books - Great Britain - History - 19th century. 6. Children's books - United States - History - 19th century. 7. Children's books - Great Britain - History - 20th century. 8. Children's books - United States - History - 20th century. I. Title. II. Title: From Mother Goose to Doctor Seuss*
*TC Z270.G7 D37 1999*

**Darling, Rosalyn Benjamin.** The partnership model in human services : sociological foundations and practices / Rosalyn Benjamin Darling. New York : Kluwer Academic/Plenum Publishers, c2000. xvi, 308 p. : ill. ; 24 cm. (Clinical sociology) Includes bibliographical references (p. 287-299) and index. ISBN 0-306-46274-5 (alk. paper) DDC 361.3
*1. Social case work. 2. Clinical sociology. 3. Interviewing in social work. 4. Social work education. I. Title. II. Series.*
*TC HV43 .D2 2000*

**DARPA INTERNET (COMPUTER NETWORK).** *See* **INTERNET (COMPUTER NETWORK).**

**DARTMOUTH COLLEGE.**
Miraculously builded in our hearts. Hanover : Dartmouth University Press, 1999.
*TC LD1438 .M573 1999*

**Dartmouth/Hitchcock Medical Center.**
Depression and manic depression [videorecording]. Boston, MA : Fanlight Productions, c1996.
*TC RC537 .D46 1996*

**Dartnall, Terry, 1943-.**
Perspectives on cognitive science. Stamford, Conn. : Ablex Pub. Corp., c1999.
*TC BF311 .P373 1999*

**Darton, F. J. Harvey (Frederick Joseph Harvey), 1878-1936.** Children's books in England : five centuries of social life / F.J. Harvey Darton. 3rd ed. / rev. by Brian Alderson. London : British Library ; New Castle, DE : Oak Knoll Press, 1982 [1999 printing] xviii, 398 p. : ill. ; 26 cm. Includes index. ISBN 0-7123-4606-6 (British Library) ISBN 1-88471-888-4 (Oak Knoll Press) DDC 028.5/0941
*1. Children's literature, English - History and criticism. 2. Children's literature - Publishing - England - History. 3. Children's literature, English - Bibliography. 4. Children - England - Books and reading. 5. England - Social life and customs. I. Alderson, Brian. II. Title.*
*TC PR990 .D3 1999*

**Darwiche, Chirine Hijazi.** The Beacons : an implementation evaluation / by Chirine Hijazi Darwiche. 1997. ix, 203 leaves ; 29 cm. Typescript; issued also on microfilm. Thesis (Ed.D.)--Teachers College, Columbia University, 1997. Includes bibliographical references (leaves 192-197).
*1. Junior high schools - New York (State) - New York - Case studies. 2. Community and school - New York (State) - New York - Evaluation. 3. Interorganizational relations - New York (State) - New York - Case studies - Evaluation. 4. Junior high*

school students - Attitudes. 5. Astoria (New York, N.Y.) - Social conditions. I. Title.
*TC 06 no. 10761*

**DARWIN, CHARLES, 1809-1882.**
Calvin, William H., 1939- Lingua ex machina. Cambridge, Mass. : London : MIT Press, c2000.
*TC QP399 .C35 2000*

**DARWINISM.** *See* **EVOLUTION (BIOLOGY).**

**Dasen, P. R., joint comp.**
Berry, John W. comp. Culture and cognition: readings in cross-cultural psychology, London, Methuen [1974]
*TC BF311 .B48*

**DATA COLLECTION - METHODS.**
Shelton, Patrick J. Measuring and improving patient satisfaction. Gaithersburg, Md. : Aspen Publishers, 2000.
*TC RA399.A1 S47 2000*

**DATA COMMUNICATION SYSTEMS.** *See* **DATA TRANSMISSION SYSTEMS.**

**DATA ENCODING (COMPUTER SCIENCE).** *See* **DATA ENCRYPTION (COMPUTER SCIENCE).**

**DATA ENCRYPTION (COMPUTER SCIENCE).**
Chacko, Mathew Vadakkan. Public key cryptosystems, 1998.
*TC 085 C35*

**DATA HIGHWAY.** *See* **INFORMATION SUPERHIGHWAY.**

**DATA LIBRARIES.** *See* **INFORMATION STORAGE AND RETRIEVAL SYSTEMS.**

**DATA MINING - CONGRESSES.**
MLDM'99 (1999 : Leipzig, Germany) Machine learning and data mining in pattern recognition. Berlin ; New York : Springer, c1999.
*TC Q327 .M56 1999*

**DATA NETWORKS, COMPUTER.** *See* **COMPUTER NETWORKS.**

**DATA PROCESSING.** *See* **ELECTRONIC DATA PROCESSING; INFORMATION STORAGE AND RETRIEVAL SYSTEMS.**

**DATA PROTECTION.** *See also* **COMPUTER SECURITY.**
Chacko, Mathew Vadakkan. Public key cryptosystems. 1998.
*TC 085 C35*

**DATA PROTECTION - LAW AND LEGISLATION.** *See* **PRIVACY, RIGHT OF.**

**DATA RETRIEVAL.** *See* **INFORMATION RETRIEVAL.**

**Data science, classification, and related methods.** International Federation of Classification Societies. Conference. 5th, 1996, Kobe, Japan. Tokyo ; New York : Springer, c1998.
*TC QA278 I53 1996*

**DATA STORAGE.** *See* **INFORMATION RETRIEVAL.**

**DATA STORAGE AND RETRIEVAL SYSTEMS.** *See* **INFORMATION STORAGE AND RETRIEVAL SYSTEMS.**

**DATA SUPERHIGHWAY.** *See* **INFORMATION SUPERHIGHWAY.**

**DATA TRANSMISSION SYSTEMS.** *See* **COMPUTER NETWORKS; LIBRARY INFORMATION NETWORKS.**

**DATA TRANSMISSION SYSTEMS - DICTIONARIES.**
Saigh, Robert A. The international dictionary of data communications. Chicago : Glenlake Pub. Co. ; New York : American Management Association, c1998.
*TC TK5102 .S25 1998*

**DATABASE MANAGEMENT.**
Balter, Alison. [Mastering Access 97 development] Alison Balter's Mastering Access 97 development. 2nd ed. Indianapolis, Ind. : Sams Pub., [c1997]
*TC QA76.9.D3 B32 1997*

**Database nation.**
Garfinkel, Simson. 1st ed. Beijing ; Cambridge : O'Reilly, c2000.
*TC JC596.2.U5 G37 2000*

**DATABASE SEARCHING.** *See* **DATA MINING.**

**DATE ABUSE.** *See* **DATING VIOLENCE.**

**DATE-BEATING.** *See* **DATING VIOLENCE.**

**DATE RAPE.** *See* **ACQUAINTANCE RAPE.**

**Date rape [videorecording] : behind closed doors.**
d·a·t·e rape [videorecording]. [Charleston, WV] : Cambridge Educational, c1994.
*TC RC560.R36 D3 1994*

**d·a·t·e rape** [videorecording] : behind closed doors / producers, Charlotte Angel, Matt Clark ; director, Matt Clark ; writer, Laura Kaminker. [Charleston, WV] : Cambridge Educational, c1994. 1 videocassette (35 min.) : sd., col. ; 1/2 in. VHS. Catalogued from credits and container. Narrator, Regina Newsome. Camera, Matt Clark, Greg Harpold; editor/graphics, Matt Clark. Adolescents through adult. SUMMARY: Explodes the myths about rape-- "She asked for it, the way she was dressed" or "He doesn't look like a rapist, she probably didn't say no". This video emphasizes that no one asks for it, that women can dress the way they want, that saying no is enough and everyone has a right to his or her body. Rape stems from anger, sadism and a need for power. It is a hate crime-- a crime of violence. Rape victims, male and female, discuss their ordeals and their recoveries. Counselors discuss the stages of recovery and the repercussions of the trauma. Advice is given on how to avoid rape and what to do if it happens to you or someone close to you.
*1. Acquaintance rape - United States - Psychological aspects. 2. Dating violence - United States - Psychological aspects. 3. Rape victims - Psychology. 4. Male rape victims - Psychology. 5. Rape trauma syndrome. 6. Acquaintance rape - United States - Prevention. 7. Dating violence - United States - Prevention. I. Newsome, Regina. II. Angel, Charlotte. III. Clark, Matt. IV. Kaminker, Laura. V. Cambridge Educational (Firm) VI. Title: Behind closed doors [videorecording] VII. Title: Date rape [videorecording] : behind closed doors*
*TC RC560.R36 D3 1994*

**DATING, BI-RACIAL.** *See* **INTERRACIAL DATING.**

**DATING, BIRACIAL.** *See* **INTERRACIAL DATING.**

**DATING, INTERRACIAL.** *See* **INTERRACIAL DATING.**

**DATING (SOCIAL CUSTOMS).** *See* **INTERRACIAL DATING; MAN-WOMAN RELATIONSHIPS.**

**DATING VIOLENCE.** *See* **ACQUAINTANCE RAPE.**

**DATING VIOLENCE - UNITED STATES - PREVENTION.**
d·a·t·e rape [videorecording]. [Charleston, WV] : Cambridge Educational, c1994.
*TC RC560.R36 D3 1994*

**DATING VIOLENCE - UNITED STATES - PSYCHOLOGICAL ASPECTS.**
d·a·t·e rape [videorecording]. [Charleston, WV] : Cambridge Educational, c1994.
*TC RC560.R36 D3 1994*

**Daub, Mervin, 1943-** Getting down to business : a history of business education at Queen's, 1889-1999 / Mervin Daub and P. Bruce Buchan. Montreal : Ithaca : McGill-Queen's University Press, c1999. xii, 129 p. : ill., ports. ; 24 cm. Includes bibliographical references (p. [121]-122) and index. ISBN 0-7735-2014-7
*1. Queen's University (Kingston, Ont.). - School of Business - History. 1. Buchan, P. Bruce (Peter Bruce), 1932- II. Title.*
*TC HF1134.Q442 D38 1999*

**DAUGHTERS.** *See* **FATHERS AND DAUGHTERS; MOTHERS AND DAUGHTERS.**

**DAUGHTERS AND FATHERS.** *See* **FATHERS AND DAUGHTERS.**

**DAUGHTERS AND MOTHERS.** *See* **MOTHERS AND DAUGHTERS.**

**Dautenhahn, Kerstin.**
Human cognition and social agent technology. Amsterdam ; Philadelphia : John Benjamins, c2000.
*TC BF311 .H766 2000*

**Davenier, Christine, ill.**
Millen, C. M. The low-down laundry line blues. Boston : Houghton Mifflin, 1999.
*TC PZ7.M6035 Lo 1999*

**Davenport, Horace Willard, 1912-.**
**Fifty years of medicine at the University of Michigan, 1891 1941.**
Davenport, Horace Willard, 1912- Not just any medical school. Ann Arbor : University of Michigan Press, c1999.
*TC R747.U6834 D38 1999*

**Davenport, Horace Willard, 1912**
Not just any medical school : the science, practice, and teaching of medicine at the University of Michigan, 1850-1941 / Horace W. Davenport. Ann Arbor : University of Michigan Press, c1999. xii, 382 p. : ill. ; 29 cm. Rev. ed. of: Fifty years of medicine at the University of Michigan, 1891-1941. 1986, c1987. Includes bibliographical references (p. 313-367) and index. ISBN 0-472-11076-4 (acid-free paper) DDC 610/.71/177435
*1. University of Michigan. - Medical School - History. 2. Medical colleges - Michigan - Ann Arbor - History. I. Davenport, Horace Willard, 1912- Fifty years of medicine at the University of Michigan, 1891-1941. II. Title.*
**TC R747.U6834 D38 1999**

**David, Anthony S.**
Insight and psychosis. New York : Oxford University Press, 1998.
**TC RC512 .I49 1998**

**David Filkin Enterprises.**
Stephen Hawking's universe [videorecording]. [Alexandria, Va.] : PBS Video; Burbank, CA : Distributed by Warner Home Video, c1997.
**TC QB982 .S7 1997**

**David, Jonathan.**
When the brain goes wrong [videorecording]. Short version. Boston, MA : Fanlight Productions [dist.], c1992.
**TC RC386 .W54 1992**

**Davidman, Lynn, 1955-** Motherloss / Lynn Davidman. Berkeley, Calif. : University of California Press, c2000. xiv, 293 p. ; 24 cm. Includes bibliographical references (p. [277]-282) and index. ISBN 0-520-22319-5 (hardcover : alk. paper) DDC 155.9/37
*1. Grief. 2. Bereavement - Psychological aspects. 3. Mothers - Death - Psychological aspects. 4. Loss (Psychology) I. Title.*
**TC BF575.G7 D37 2000**

**Davidson, Alan, 1924-** The Oxford companion to food / Alan Davidson ; illustrations by Soun Vannithone. Oxford : Oxford University Press, 1999. 892 p. : ill. ; 29 cm. Includes bibliographical references and index. ISBN 0-19-211579-0 DDC 641.3
*1. Food - Encyclopedias. 2. Cookery - Encyclopedias. 3. Food habits - Encyclopedias. 4. Food - Encyclopedias. 5. Cookery - Encyclopedias. 6. Food habits - Encyclopedias. I. Title.*
**TC TX349 .D38 1999**

**Davidson, James West.** The American nation : beginnings to 1877 / James West Davidson. Annotated teacher's ed. Upper Saddle River, N.J. : Prentice Hall, c1997. T30, xxx, 690 p. : ill., maps (some col.) ; 29 cm. Includes bibliographical references and index. ISBN 0-13-413048-0
*1. United States - History - Study and teaching (Secondary) I. Title.*
**TC E178.1 .D22 1997 Teacher's Ed.**

The American nation : beginnings to 1877 / James West Davidson. Upper Saddle River, N.J. : Prentice Hall, c1997. xxxiii, 690 p. : ill., maps (some col.) ; 27 cm. Includes bibliographical references and index. ISBN 0-13-411083-8
*1. United States - History - Juvenile literature. 2. United States - History. I. Title.*
**TC E178.1 .D22 1997**

The American nation / James West Davidson, Michael B. Stoff. Annotated teacher's ed. Upper Saddle River, N.J. : Prentice Hall, c1998. T30, xxxiv, 974 p. : ill., maps (some col.) ; 29 cm. Includes bibliographical references and index. SUMMARY: A textbook for United States history from earliest Indian civilizations to the present, with maps, charts, activities, study questions, and review chapters. ISBN 0-13-432212-6
*1. United States - History - Study and teaching (Secondary) I. Stoff, Michael B. II. Title.*
**TC E178.1 .D22 1998 Teacher's Ed.**

**Davidson, Kate M.** Cognitive therapy for personality disorders : : a guide for therapists / Kate M. Davidson. Oxford ; Boston : Butterworth-Heinemann, 2000. xi, 161 p. : ill. ; 24 cm. Includes bibliographical references and index. ISBN 0-7506-4488-5
*1. Personality disorders - Treatment. 2. Cognitive therapy. I. Title.*
**TC RC554 .D38 2000**

**Davidson, Prue.**
Art Gallery of New South Wales. Australian drawings from the gallery's collection. Sydney : Art Gallery of New South Wales, 1997.
**TC NC369 .A78 1997**

**Davidson, Richard J.**
Anxiety, depression, and emotion. Oxford ; New York : Oxford University Press, 2000.
**TC RC531 .A559 2000**

**Davidson, Susan, 1958-.**
Hopps, Walter. Robert Rauschenberg. New York : Guggenheim Museum, c1997.
**TC N6537.R27 H66 1997**

**Davie, Helen, ill.**
Goldin, Augusta R. Ducks don't get wet. Newly illustrated ed. New York : HarperCollinsPublishers, c1999.
**TC QL696.A52 G64 1999**

**Davie, Lynn.**
Livingstone, D. W. Public attitudes towards education in Ontario, 1996. Toronto : OISE/UT in association with University of Toronto Press, 1997.
**TC LA418.06 L58 1997**

**Davies, David, 1952-.**
Teare, Richard. The virtual university. London ; New York : Cassell, 1998.
**TC LC5215 .T42 1998**

**Davies, Dominic, 1959-.**
Therapeutic perspectives on working with lesbian, gay and bisexual clients. Buckingham [England] ; Philadelphia : Open University Press, 2000.
**TC RC451.4.G39 T476 2000**

**Davies, Gordon.**
IFIP TC3/WG3.3 & WG3.6 Joint Working Conference on the Virtual Campus: Trends for Higher Education and Training (1997 : Madrid, Spain) The virtual campus. 1st ed. London ; New York : Chapman & Hall on behalf of the International Federation for Information Processing (IFIP), 1998.
**TC LC5803.C65 I353 1997**

**Davies, Ian.**
Teaching the Holocaust :. London : Continuum, 2000.
**TC D804.33 .T43 2000**

**Davies, Ian, 1957-** Good citizenship and educational provision / Ian Davies, Ian Gregory, and Shirley Riley. London ; New York : Falmer Press, c1999. ix, 150 p. ; 24 cm. Includes bibliographical references (p. 135-144) and index. ISBN 0-7507-0959-6 (hard : alk. paper) ISBN 0-7507-0960-X (pbk.) DDC 372.83/2
*1. Citizenship - Study and teaching - Great Britain. 2. Teachers - Great Britain - Attitudes. I. Gregory, Ian, 1939- II. Riley, Shirley, 1949- III. Title.*
**TC LC1091 .D28 1999**

**Davies, John Graham.**
Challenge cases [videorecording]. Princeton, N.J. : Films for the Humanities & Sciences, 1998.
**TC RC455.2.C4 C4 1998**

Disorders due to psychoactive substance abuse [videorecording]. Princeton, N.J. : Films for the Humanities & Sciences, 1998.
**TC RC564 .D5 1998**

Mood disorders [videorecording]. Princeton, N.J. : Films for the Humanities & Sciences, 1998.
**TC RC537 .M6 1998**

Neurotic, stress-related, and somatoform disorders [videorecording]. Princeton, N.J. : Films for the Humanities & Sciences, 1998.
**TC RC530 .N4 1998**

Organic disorders [videorecording]. Princeton, N.J. : Films for the Humanities & Sciences, 1998.
**TC RC521 .O7 1998**

Personality disorders [videorecording]. Princeton, N.J. : Films for the Humanities & Sciences, 1998.
**TC RC554 .P4 1998**

Schizophrenia and delusional disorders [videorecording]. Princeton, N.J. : Films for the Humanities & Sciences, c1998.
**TC RC514 .S3 1998**

**Davis, Ann Castel.**
Vallecorsa, Ada, 1948- Students with mild disabilities in general education settings. Upper Saddle River, N.J. : Merrill, c2000.
**TC LC4705 .V35 2000**

**Davis, Brent.** Engaging minds : learning and teaching in a complex world / Brent Davis, Dennis Sumara, Rebecca Luce-Kapler. Mahwah, N.J. : L. Erlbaum Associates, 2000. xv, 282 p. : ill. ; 26 cm. Includes bibliographical references (p. [261]-272) and index. ISBN 0-8058-3785-X (pbk: alk. paper) DDC 370.15/23
*1. Learning. 2. Teaching. I. Sumara, Dennis J., 1958- II. Luce-Kapler, Rebecca. III. Title. IV. Title: Learning and teaching in a complex world*
**TC LB1060 .D38 2000**

**Davis, Calvin E., joint author.**
Craddock, George W. Social disadvantagement and dependency: Lexington, Mass., Heath Lexington Books [1970]

**TC HD7256.U6 C438**

**Davis, D. Diane (Debra Diane), 1963-** Breaking up (at) totality : a rhetoric of laughter / D. Diane Davis. Carbondale : Southern Illinois University Press, c2000. xv, 312 p. ; 24 cm. (Rhetorical philosophy and theory) Includes bibliographical references (p. 291-305) and index. ISBN 0-8093-2228-5 (cloth : alk. paper) ISBN 0-8093-2229-3 (pbk. : alk. paper) DDC 808/.042/07
*1. English language - Rhetoric - Study and teaching - Psychological aspects. 2. English language - Rhetoric - Study and teaching - Social aspects. 3. Report writing - Study and teaching - Psychological aspects. 4. Report writing - Study and teaching - Social aspects. 5. Laughter - Psychological aspects. 6. Laughter - Physiological aspects. 7. Laughter - Social aspects. 8. Feminist theory. I. Title. II. Series: Rhetorical philosophy and theory*
**TC PE1404 .D385 2000**

**Davis, Daniel Leifeld.** The aggressive adolescent : clinical and forensic issues / Daniel L. Davis. New York : Haworth Press, 1999. xv, 158 p. ; 22 cm. Includes bibliographical references and index. ISBN 0-7890-0863-7 (alk. paper) ISBN 0-7890-0910-2 (pbk. : alk. paper) DDC 616.85/82/00835
*1. Violence in adolescence. 2. Problem youth - Rehabilitation. I. Title.*
**TC RJ506.V56 D38 1999**

**Davis, G. Albyn (George Albyn), 1946-** Aphasiology : disorders and clinical practice / G. Albyn Davis. Boston : Allyn and Bacon, 2000. xii, 356 p. : ill. ; 25 cm. Includes bibliographical references and index. ISBN 0-205-29834-6 (hardcover)
*1. Aphasia. I. Title.*
**TC RC425 .D379 2000**

**Davis, James Earl, 1960-.**
Black sons to mothers. New York ; Canterbury [England] : P. Lang, c2000.
**TC LC2731 .B53 2000**

**Davis, Jessica Hoffmann, 1943-.**
Lawrence-Lightfoot, Sara, 1944- The art and science of portraiture. 1st ed. San Francisco : Jossey-Bass, c1997.
**TC H62 .L33 1997**

**Davis, Kevin M.**
Linn, Robert L. Measurement and assessment in teaching. 8th ed. Upper Saddle River, N.J. : Merrill, c2000.
**TC LB3051 .L545 2000**

**Davis, Lennard J., 1949-** My sense of silence : memoirs of a childhood with deafness / Lennard J. Davis. Urbana : University of Illinois Press, c2000. xi, 158 p. : ill. ; 22 cm. (Creative nonfiction) Includes bibliographical references. CONTENTS: The grain of sounds -- Language and the word of my father -- The two mothers -- Brother's keeper -- Honeymoon with mom -- Schooling -- Adolescence -- College and other awakenings. ISBN 0-252-02533-4 (cloth : alk. paper) DDC 306.874/092
*1. Davis, Lennard J.. - 1949- 2. Children of deaf parents - United States - Biography. 3. Deaf parents - United States - Biography. 4. Deaf - United States - Family relationships - Case studies. I. Title. II. Series: Creative nonfiction (Urbana, Ill.)*
**TC HQ759.912 .D38 2000**

**DAVIS, LENNARD J., 1949-.**
Davis, Lennard J., 1949- My sense of silence. Urbana : University of Illinois Press, c2000.
**TC HQ759.912 .D38 2000**

**Davis, Michael, 1943-** Ethics and the university / Michael Davis. London ; New York : Routledge, 1999. xii, 267 p. ; 23 cm. (Professional ethics) Includes bibliographical references (p. 255-265) and index. ISBN 0-415-18097-X (hard) ISBN 0-415-18098-8 (pbk.) DDC 174/.937
*1. Education, Higher - Moral and ethical aspects - United States. 2. Ethics - Study and teaching (Higher) - United States. 3. Research - Moral and ethical aspects - United States. 4. Sexual ethics - United States. I. Title. II. Series.*
**TC LB2324 .D38 1999**

**Davis Publications.**
Chapman, Laura H. Discover art. Worcester, Mass. : Davis Publications, c1985.
**TC N361 .C56 1985**

**Davis, Roger Dale.**
Millon, Theodore. Personality disorders in modern life. New York ; Chichester [England] : John Wiley & Sons, c2000.
**TC RC554 .M537 2000**

**Davis, Sara N., 1946-.**
Coming into her own. San Francisco, Calif. : Jossey-Bass, c1999.

*TC LC1503 .C65 1999*

**Davis, Thomas E., Ph. D.** The solution-focused school counselor : shaping professional practice / Thomas E. Davis, Cynthia J. Osborn. Philadelphia ; Hove [England] : Accelerated Development/Taylor & Francis Group, c2000. xvii, 114 p. : ill. ; 23 cm. Includes bibliographical references (p. 102-108) and index. ISBN 1-56032-862-2 (paper) DDC 371.4/6
*1. Educational counseling. 2. Solution-focused brief therapy. I. Osborn, Cynthia J. II. Title.*
*TC LB1027.5 .D335 2000*

**Davis, Trisha.**
Managing the licensing of electronic products. Washington, DC : Systems and Procedures Exchange Center, Office of Leadership and Management Service, Association of Research Libraries, c1999.

Managing the licensing of electronic products. Washington, DC : Systems and Procedures Exchange Center, Office of Leadership and Management Service, Association of Research Libraries, c1999.

Managing the licensing of electronic products. Washington, DC : Systems and Procedures Exchange Center, Office of Leadership and Management Service, Association of Research Libraries, c1999.
*TC HF5429.255 .M26 1999*

**Davison, Bev, 1957-** Creative physical activities and equipment / Bev Davison. Champaign, IL : Human Kinetics, c1998. xv, 111 p. : ill. ; 23 cm. Cover title: Creative physical activities & equipment. Includes bibliographical references (p. 107) and index. ISBN 0-88011-779-6 (pbk.) DDC 796/.028
*1. Sporting goods. 2. Physical education and training - Equipment and supplies. 3. Free material. I. Title: Creative physical activities & equipment*
*TC GV745 .D38 1998*

**Davison, Jon.**
Issues in English teaching. London ; New York : Routledge, 2000.
*TC LB1576 .I89 2000*

**Dawkins, John.**
Botel, Morton. Communicating. Lexington, Mass. : D. C. Heath, c1973.
*TC PE1121 .B67 1973 Bk A*

Botel, Morton. Communicating. Lexington, Mass. : D. C. Heath, c1973.
*TC PE1121 .B67 1973*

**Dawkins, Kevin.**
ADHD [videorecording]. New York, NY : Guilford Publications, Inc., c1992.
*TC RJ506.H9 A3 1992*

**Dawkins, Lee.**
ADHD [videorecording]. New York, NY : Guilford Publications, Inc., c1992.
*TC RJ506.H9 A3 1992*

**Dawson, Barry.**
Cooper, Ilay. Traditional buildings of India. New York : Thames and Hudson, c1998.
*TC NA1501 .C58 1998*

Street graphics India / Barry Dawson. London : Thames & Hudson, 1999. 112 p. : col. ill. ; 23 cm. ISBN 0-500-28095-9 DDC 741.60954
*1. Commercial art - India - Pictorial works. 2. Street decoration - India - Pictorial works. 3. India - Social life and customs - Pictorial works. 4. Commercial art - India - Pictorial works. 5. Street decoration - India - Pictorial works. 6. India - Social life and customs - Pictorial works. I. Title.*
*TC NC998.6.I6 D38 1999*

**Dawson, John E.**
Strang, Thomas J. K. Controlling museum fungal problems. Ottawa : Canadian Conservation Institute, Department of Communications, [1991]
*TC TH9031 .S75 1991*

**Dawson, Terry.**
Kirch, Olaf. Linux network administrator's guide. 2nd ed. Cambridge, Mass. : O'Reilly, 2000.
*TC QA76.76.O63 K566 2000*

**DAY.** *See* **NIGHT.**

**Day, Alexandra.** Carl's afternoon in the park / Alexandra Day. 1st ed. New York : Farrar, Straus & Giroux, 1991. 1 v. (unpaged) : chiefly col. ill. ; 28 cm. SUMMARY: Carl the rottweiler, in charge of a baby and a puppy, takes advantage of Mom's absence to lead them on a wild romp through the park. ISBN 0-374-31109-9 DDC [E]
*1. Dogs - Fiction. 2. Babies - Fiction. 3. Parks - Fiction. I. Title.*
*TC PZ7.D32915 Cars 1991*

Frank and Ernest on the road / by Alexandra Day. New York : Scholastic Inc., c1994. 1 v. (unpaged) : col.

ill. ; 29 cm. SUMMARY: While making a delivery for a friend, an elephant and a bear become familiar with the experiences and language of truck drivers. Includes a brief glossary of CB slang. ISBN 0-590-45048-4 DDC [E]
*1. Elephants - Fiction. 2. Bears - Fiction. 3. Citizens band radio - Slang - Fiction. 4. Truck drivers - Fiction. I. Title.*
*TC PZ7.D32915 Frn 1994*

**A day at Seagull beach.**
Wallace, Karen. 1st American ed. New York : DK Pub., 1999.
*TC PZ10.3.W1625 Se 1999*

**DAY CARE CENTERS.** *See* **NURSERY SCHOOLS.**

**DAY CARE CENTERS - JAPAN - HISTORY - 20TH CENTURY.**
Uno, Kathleen S., 1951- Passages to modernity. Honolulu : University of Hawai'i Press, c1999.
*TC HQ778.7.J3 U56 1999*

**DAY CARE CENTERS - UNITED STATES.**
Cromwell, Ellen, 1937- Nurturing readiness in early childhood education. 2nd ed. Boston : Allyn & Bacon, c2000.
*TC LB1140.4 .C76 2000*

**DAY CARE CENTERS - UNITED STATES - ADMINISTRATION.**
Click, Phyllis. Administration of schools for young children. 5th ed. Albany, NY : Delmar, 1999.
*TC LB2822.7 .C55 1999*

Shoemaker, Cynthia. Leadership and management of programs for young children. 2nd ed. Upper Saddle River, N.J. : Merrill, 2000.
*TC LB2822.6 .S567 2000*

**Day, Christopher, ACP.**
Leading schools in times of change. Buckingham [England] ; Philadelphia : Open University Press, 2000.
*TC LB2900.5 .L45 2000*

**DAY - FICTION.**
Uff, Caroline. Lulu's busy day. New York : Walker, 2000.
*TC PZ7.U285 Lu 2000*

**A day in the life of a museum curator.**
Tropea, Judith. Mahwah, N.J. : Troll Associates, c1991.
*TC QE22.E53 T76 1991*

**Day, Michael.**
The online writing classroom. Cresskill, N.J. : Hampton Press, c2000.
*TC PE1404 .O45 2000*

**Day, Monimalika.**
Harry, Beth. Building cultural reciprocity with families. Baltimore, Md. : P.H. Brookes Pub. Co., c1999.
*TC LC3969 .H377 1999*

**DAY NURSERIES.** *See* **DAY CARE CENTERS.**

**DAYS.** *See* **BIRTHDAYS; FESTIVALS; HOLIDAYS.**

**The days of Ofelia.**
Diamant, Gertrude, 1901- Boston, Houghton Mifflin company, 1942.
*TC F1210 .D5*

**D.B. Arts Films.**
Matisse, voyages [videorecording]. [Chicago, Ill.] : Home Vision : [S.l.] : Distributed worldwide by RM Associates, c1989.
*TC ND553.M37 M37 1989*

**De Beer, Hans.**
**[Kleine Eisbär und der Angsthase. English]**
Little Polar Bear and the brave little hare / written and illustrated by Hans de Beer : translated by J. Alison James. New York : North-South Books, 1998. 1 v. (unpaged) : col. ill. ; 30 cm. Originally published as an easy-to-read book. SUMMARY: After Lars the Little Polar Bear rescues a scared hare from a hole in the ice, the two new friends share an adventurous day, during which each discovers just how much courage he has. ISBN 0-7358-1011-7 (trade binding) ISBN 0-7358-1012-5 (library binding) DDC [Fic]
*1. Polar bear - Fiction. 2. Bears - Fiction. 3. Hares - Fiction. 4. Courage - Fiction. I. James, J. Alison. II. Title.*
*TC PZ7.D353 Liv 1998*

**De Groat, Diane, ill.**
Hahn, Mary Downing. Anna all year round. New York : Clarion Books, c1999.
*TC PZ7.H1256 An 1999*

**De Hart, Jane Sherron.**
Women's America. 5th ed. New York : Oxford University Press, 2000.

*TC HQ1426 .W663 2000*

**De Jesús, Joy.**
Growing up Puerto Rican. 1st ed. New York : Morrow, c1997.
*TC PS508.P84 G76 1997*

**De Koster, Katie, 1948-.**
Poverty. San Diego, CA : Greenhaven Press, c1994.
*TC HC110.P6 P63 1994*

**De la Rosa, Mario.**
Conducting drug abuse research with minority populations. New York : Haworth Press, c1999.
*TC HV5824.E85 C66 1999*

**De la Salle University. College of Education.**
[Tanglaw (Manila, Philippines)] Tanglaw. Manila : The College, 1992-

**De Montfort University. School of Education.**
Grugeon, Elizabeth. The art of storytelling for teachers and pupils. London : David Fulton, 2000.
*TC LB1042 .G78 2000*

**De Paola, Tomie.** 26 Fairmount Avenue / Tomie dePaola. New York : G.P. Putnam's Sons, c1999. 56 p. : ill. ; 23 cm. SUMMARY: Children's author-illustrator Tomie De Paola describes his experiences at home and in school when he was a boy. ISBN 0-399-23246-X DDC 813/.54
*1. De Paola, Tomie - Childhood and youth - Juvenile literature. 2. De Paola, Tomie - Homes and haunts - Connecticut - Meriden - Juvenile literature. 3. Authors, American - 20th century - Biography - Juvenile literature. 4. Meriden (Conn.) - Biography - Juvenile literature. 5. De Paola, Tomie - Childhood and youth. 6. Authors, American. 7. Illustrators. I. Title. II. Title: Twenty-six Fairmount Avenue*
*TC PS3554.E11474 Z473 1999*

The night of Las Posadas / written and illustrated by Tomie dePaola. New York : Putnam's, 1999. 1 v. (unpaged) : col. ill. ; 29 cm. SUMMARY: At the annual celebration of Las Posadas in old Santa Fe, the husband and wife slated to play Mary and Joseph are delayed by car trouble, but a mysterious couple seems perfect for the part. ISBN 0-399-23400-4 DDC [E]
*1. Posadas (Social custom) - Fiction. 2. Mary, Blessed Virgin, Saint - Fiction. 3. Joseph, Saint - Fiction. 4. Santa Fe (N.M.) - Fiction. I. Title.*
*TC PZ7.D439 Ni 1999*

**DE PAOLA, TOMIE - CHILDHOOD AND YOUTH.**
De Paola, Tomie. 26 Fairmount Avenue. New York : G.P. Putnam's Sons, c1999.
*TC PS3554.E11474 Z473 1999*

**DE PAOLA, TOMIE - CHILDHOOD AND YOUTH - JUVENILE LITERATURE.**
De Paola, Tomie. 26 Fairmount Avenue. New York : G.P. Putnam's Sons, c1999.
*TC PS3554.E11474 Z473 1999*

**DE PAOLA, TOMIE - HOMES AND HAUNTS - CONNECTICUT - MERIDEN - JUVENILE LITERATURE.**
De Paola, Tomie. 26 Fairmount Avenue. New York : G.P. Putnam's Sons, c1999.
*TC PS3554.E11474 Z473 1999*

**De Paola, Tomie, ill.**
Madrigal, Antonio Hernandez. Erandi's braids. New York : Putnam's, c1999.
*TC PZ7.M26575 Er 1999*

**De Pree, Max.** Leading without power : finding hope in serving community / Max De Pree. 1st ed. San Francisco, Calif. : Jossey-Bass, c1997. xiii, 192 p. ; 21 cm. ISBN 0-7879-1063-5 (acid-free paper) DDC 361.3/7
*1. Voluntarism - United States. 2. Nonprofit organizations - United States. 3. Community development - United States. I. Title.*
*TC HN90.V64 D4 1997*

**De Rivera, Joseph.** The psychological dimension of foreign policy. James N. Rosenau, consultant. Columbus, Ohio, C. E. Merrill Pub. Co. [1968] vi, 441 p. 24 cm. Bibliographical footnotes. DDC 327/.01/9
*1. International relations - Psychological aspects. I. Title.*
*TC JX1255 .D45*

**De Rôme, Denise.**
Lamping, Alwena. NTC's Italian grammar. Lincolnwood, Ill., U.S.A. : NTC Pub. Group, 1998.
*TC PC1112 .L34 1998*

**De Salvo, Donna M.** Past imperfect : a museum looks at itself / Donna De Salvo ; with essays by Maurice Berger, Alan Wallach ; and a contribution by Judith Barry. Southampton, N.Y. : Parrish Art Museum, in association with the New Press, New York, N.Y., c1993. 80 p. : ill. (some col.) ; 32 cm. "This publication documents the exhibition 'A museum looks at itself: mapping past and present at the Parrish Art Museum 1897-1992,' organized by the Parrish Art Museum, exhibition dates: August

*De Toledo, Sylvie.*

8-November 11, 1992"--Page opposite t.p. Bibliography: p. 78. ISBN 1-56584-166-2
*1. Parrish Art Museum - Exhibitions. 2. Art - New York (State) - Southampton - Exhibitions. I. Berger, Maurice. II. Wallach, Alan. V. Title. VI. Title: Museum looks at itself.*
**TC N750 .D4**

**De Toledo, Sylvie.** Grandparents as parents : a survival guide for raising a second family / Sylvie de Toledo, Deborah Edler Brown ; foreword by Ethel Dunn. New York : Guilford Press, c1995. xiv, 322 p. ; 24 cm. Includes bibliographical references (p. 307-314) and index. ISBN 1-57230-011-6 (acid-free paper) ISBN 1-57230-020-5 (pbk. : acid-free paper) DDC 649/.1
*1. Grandparent and child. 2. Child rearing. 3. Intergenerational relations. I. Brown, Deborah Edler. II. Title.*
**TC HQ759.9 .D423 1995**

**DE YOUNG, M. H. (MICHAEL H.) - JUVENILE FICTION.**
Frank, Phil. The ghost of the de Young Museum. [San Francisco : Fine Arts Museums of San Francisco, 1995]
**TC N739.5 .F72 1995**

**DEAF.** *See* **CHILDREN, DEAF.**

**Deaf American literature.**
Peters, Cynthia. Washington, D.C. : Gallaudet University Press, 2000.
**TC HV2471 .P38 2000**

**Deaf and hearing impaired pupils in mainstream schools.**
Watson, Linda R., 1950- London : David Fulton, c1999.
**TC LC1203.G7 W387 1999**

**The deaf child in the family and at school :** essays in honor of Kathryn P. Meadow-Orlans / [edited by] Patricia Elizabeth Spencer, Carol J. Erting, Marc Marschark. Mahwah, N.J. : Lawrence Erlbaum Associates, 2000. xix, 318 p. 24 cm. Includes bibliographical references. ISBN 0-8058-3220-3 (cloth : alk. paper) ISBN 0-8058-3221-1 (pbk. : alk. paper) DDC 362.4/23
*1. Deaf children - Family relationships. 2. Deaf children - Language. 3. Deaf children - Education. 4. Parents of deaf children. 5. Child development. 6. Socialization. I. Meadow-Orlans, Kathryn P. II. Spencer, Patricia Elizabeth. III. Erting, Carol. IV. Marschark, Marc.*
**TC HV2392.2 .D43 2000**

**DEAF CHILDREN.** *See* **CHILDREN, DEAF.**

**DEAF CHILDREN - CHINA.**
Callaway, Alison. Deaf children in China. Washington, D.C. : Gallaudet University Press, 2000.
**TC HV2888 .C35 2000**

**DEAF CHILDREN - CHINA - FAMILY RELATIONSHIPS.**
Callaway, Alison. Deaf children in China. Washington, D.C. : Gallaudet University Press, 2000.
**TC HV2888 .C35 2000**

**DEAF CHILDREN - EDUCATION.**
The deaf child in the family and at school. Mahwah, N.J. : Lawrence Erlbaum Associates, 2000.
**TC HV2392.2 .D43 2000**

**DEAF CHILDREN - EDUCATION - GREAT BRITAIN.**
Issues in deaf education. London : D. Fulton Publishers, 1998.
**TC HV2716 .I77 1998**

Knight, Pamela, 1940- The care and education of a deaf child. Clevedon [England] ; Buffalo [N.Y.] : Multilingual Matters, c1999.
**TC HV2716 .K65 1999**

**DEAF CHILDREN - FAMILY RELATIONSHIPS.**
The deaf child in the family and at school. Mahwah, N.J. : Lawrence Erlbaum Associates, 2000.
**TC HV2392.2 .D43 2000**

**DEAF CHILDREN - GREAT BRITAIN.**
Knight, Pamela, 1940- The care and education of a deaf child. Clevedon [England] ; Buffalo [N.Y.] : Multilingual Matters, c1999.
**TC HV2716 .K65 1999**

**DEAF CHILDREN - GREAT BRITAIN - LANGUAGE.**
Knight, Pamela, 1940- The care and education of a deaf child. Clevedon [England] ; Buffalo [N.Y.] : Multilingual Matters, c1999.
**TC HV2716 .K65 1999**

**Deaf children in China.**
Callaway, Alison. Washington, D.C. : Gallaudet University Press, 2000.

**TC HV2888 .C35 2000**

**DEAF CHILDREN - LANGUAGE.**
The deaf child in the family and at school. Mahwah, N.J. : Lawrence Erlbaum Associates, 2000.
**TC HV2392.2 .D43 2000**

Schirmer, Barbara R. Language and literacy development in children who are deaf. 2nd ed. Boston : Allyn and Bacon, 2000.
**TC HV2443 .S33 2000**

**DEAF - EDUCATION.**
Schirmer, Barbara R. Language and literacy development in children who are deaf. 2nd ed. Boston : Allyn and Bacon, 2000.
**TC HV2443 .S33 2000**

**DEAF - EDUCATION - ENGLISH LANGUAGE.**
Baker-Shenk, Charlotte Lee. American sign language. Silver Spring, Md. : T. J. Publishers, c1978, 1979 printing.
**TC HV2474 .B29**

**DEAF - EDUCATION - SPEECH.** *See* **DEAF - MEANS OF COMMUNICATION.**

**DEAF - EDUCATION - UNITED STATES - HISTORY.**
Buchanan, Robert (Robert M.) Illusions of equality. Washington, D.C. : Gallaudet University Press, 1999.
**TC HV2530 .B83 1999**

**DEAF - EMPLOYMENT - UNITED STATES - HISTORY.**
Buchanan, Robert (Robert M.) Illusions of equality. Washington, D.C. : Gallaudet University Press, 1999.
**TC HV2530 .B83 1999**

**DEAF, INTERPRETERS FOR.** *See* **INTERPRETERS FOR THE DEAF.**

**DEAF - MEANS OF COMMUNICATION.** *See also* **INTERPRETERS FOR THE DEAF.**
Gesture, speech, and sign. Oxford [England] ; New York : Oxford University Press, c1999.
**TC P117 .G469 1999**

Roots, James, 1955- The politics of visual language. Ottawa : Carleton University Press, 1999.
**TC HV2395 R66 1999**

**DEAF - MEANS OF COMMUNICATION - STUDY AND TEACHING (ELEMENTARY).**
Schirmer, Barbara R. Language and literacy development in children who are deaf. 2nd ed. Boston : Allyn and Bacon, 2000.
**TC HV2443 .S33 2000**

**DEAF - MEANS OF COMMUNICATION - UNITED STATES.**
Mindess, Anna. Reading between the signs. Yarmouth, Me. : Intercultural Press, c1999.
**TC HV2402 .M56 1999**

**DEAF-MUTES.** *See* **DEAF.**

**DEAF PARENTS - UNITED STATES - BIOGRAPHY.**
Davis, Lennard J., 1949- My sense of silence. Urbana : University of Illinois Press, c2000.
**TC HQ759.912 .D38 2000**

**DEAF - REHABILITATION.**
Rehabilitative audiology. 3rd ed. Philadelphia, PA : Lippincott Williams & Wilkins, c2000.
**TC RF297 .R44 2000**

**DEAF - SIGN LANGUAGE.** *See* **SIGN LANGUAGE.**

**DEAF - TRANSLATING SERVICES.** *See* **INTERPRETERS FOR THE DEAF.**

**DEAF - UNITED STATES - FAMILY RELATIONSHIPS - CASE STUDIES.**
Davis, Lennard J., 1949- My sense of silence. Urbana : University of Illinois Press, c2000.
**TC HQ759.912 .D38 2000**

**DEAFNESS.** *See* **HEARING.**

**DEAFNESS IN CHILDREN.** *See* **CHILDREN, DEAF.**

**DEAFNESS - PATIENTS.** *See* **DEAF.**

**DEAFNESS - REHABILITATION.**
Cochlear implants. Philadelphia : Lippincott Williams & Wilkins, c2000.
**TC RF305 .C6295 2000**

**DEAFNESS - SOCIAL ASPECTS.**
Roots, James, 1955- The politics of visual language. Ottawa : Carleton University Press, 1999.
**TC HV2395 R66 1999**

**Deal, Terrence E.** Shaping school culture : the heart of leadership / Terrence E. Deal, Kent D. Peterson. 1st ed. San Francisco : Jossey-Bass Publishers, c1999. xviii, 152 p. ; 24 cm. (The Jossey-Bass education series) Includes bibliographical references (p. 143-146) and index. CONTENTS: Introduction : the case for school culture -- Schools as tribes -- Vision and value : the bedrock of culture -- Ritual and ceremony : culture in action? -- History and stories : the importance of symbolic lore -- Architecture and artifacts : the potency of symbols and signs -- Putting it together : three schools -- Eight roles of symbolic leaders -- Pathways to successful culture -- Transforming toxic cultures -- Connecting school and community culture -- Conclusion : the future of schools. ISBN 0-7879-4342-8 (cloth : alk. paper) DDC 371.2
*1. Educational leadership. 2. School environment. 3. Educational change. 4. Educational leadership - Case studies. I. Peterson, Kent D. II. Title. III. Series.*
**TC LB2805 .D34 1999**

**DEALERS (RETAIL TRADE).** *See* **ART DEALERS.**

**Dealing with challenges in psychotherapy and counseling.**
Brems, Christiane. Belmont, Calif. : Wadsworth Pub., Brooks/Cole, c2000.
**TC BF637.C6 B723 2000**

**Dealing with drink.**
Thom, Betsy. London ; New York : Free Association Books, 1999.
**TC HV5283.G6 T56 1999**

**Dean, Alan Ph. D.** Complex life : nonmodernity and the emergence of cognition and culture / Alan Dean. Aldershot : Ashgate, c2000. vi, 149 p. ; 23 cm. Includes bibliographical references. ISBN 0-7546-1049-7 DDC 302.1
*1. Human beings. 2. Ethnophilosophy. 3. Behavior evolution. 4. Cognition and culture. I. Title.*
**TC BD450 .D43 2000**

**Dean, Geoff.**
Dean, Geoff. Teaching reading in secondary schools. London : David Fulton, 2000.
**TC LB1632 .D43 2000**

Teaching reading in secondary schools / Geoff Dean. London : David Fulton, 2000. iv, 122 p. : ill. ; 25 cm. Includes bibliographical references and index. ISBN 1-85346-661-1
*1. Reading (Secondary) - Great Britain. I. Dean, Geoff. II. Title.*
**TC LB1632 .D43 2000**

**Dean, Joan.** Improving children's learning : effective teaching in the primary school / Joan Dean. London ; New York : Routledge, 2000. 190 p. ; 24 cm. (Educational management series) Includes bibliographical references (p. 175-184) and index. ISBN 0-415-16896-1 (pbk. : alk. paper) DDC 372.1102
*1. Elementary school teaching - Great Britain. 2. Elementary school teachers - Training of - Great Britain. 3. Effective teaching - Great Britain. I. Title. II. Series.*
**TC LB1725.G6 D43 2000**

**Dean, Mitchell, 1955-** Governmentality : power and rule in modern society / Mitchell Dean. London ; Thousand Oaks, Calif. : Sage Publications, 1999. vi, 229 p. ; 24 cm. Includes bibliographical references (p. [213]-222) and index. ISBN 0-8039-7588-0 ISBN 0-8039-7589-9 (pbk.) DDC 303.3
*1. Power (Social sciences) 2. Social structure. 3. Foucault, Michel. 4. Foucault, Michel, - 1926-1984. 5. Social structure. 6. Power (Social sciences) I. Title.*
**TC HN49.P6 D43 1999**

**DEANS (EDUCATION).** *See also* **DEANS OF WOMEN; WOMEN DEANS (EDUCATION).**
Dimensions of managing academic affairs in the community college. San Francisco : Jossey-Bass, 2000.
**TC LB2341 .D56 2000**

**DEANS (EDUCATION) - GREAT BRITAIN.**
Bolton, Allan. Managing the academic unit. Buckingham [England] : Philadelphia : Open University Press, c2000.
**TC LB2341 .B583 2000**

Gledhill, John M., 1948- Managing students. Buckingham ; Philadelphia : Open University Press, 1999.
**TC LB2341.8.G7 G54 1996**

**DEANS (IN SCHOOLS).** *See* **DEANS (EDUCATION).**

**DEANS OF GIRLS.** *See* **DEANS OF WOMEN.**

**DEANS OF WOMEN - UNITED STATES - BIOGRAPHY.**
Nidiffer, Jana, 1957- Pioneering deans of women. New York ; London : Teachers College Press, c2000.

*TC LC1620 .N53 2000*

**Dear Juno.**
Pak, Soyung. New York : Viking, 1999.
*TC PZ7.P173 De 1999*

**Dear Mrs. Ryan, you're ruining my life.**
Jones, Jennifer B. New York : Walker & Co., 2000.
*TC PZ7.J7203 De 2000*

**Dearlove, Des.**
Crainer, Stuart. Gravy training. 1st ed. San Francisco : Jossey-Bass Publishers, c1999.
*TC HF1111 .C7 1999*

**DEATH.** *See* **BEREAVEMENT; CHILDREN - DEATH; MORTALITY; PARENTS - DEATH; TERMINAL CARE; TERMINALLY ILL.**

**DEATH (BIOLOGY).** *See* **MORTALITY.**

**DEATH CAMPS.** *See* **CONCENTRATION CAMPS.**

**DEATH - CAUSES.** *See* **DROWNING; SUICIDE.**

**DEATH - FICTION.**
Bunting, Eve, 1928- Blackwater. 1st ed. New York : Joanna Cotler Books, 1999.
*TC PZ7.B91527 Bne 1999*

Couloumbis, Audrey. Getting near to baby. New York : Putnam, 1999.
*TC PZ7.C8305 Gg 1999*

Recorvits, Helen. Goodbye, Walter Malinski. 1st ed. New York : Farrar, Straus and Giroux, c1999.
*TC PZ7.R24435 Go 1999*

Rodowsky, Colby F. The Turnabout Shop. 1st ed. New York : Farrar, Straus and Giroux, c1998.
*TC PZ7.R6185 Tu 1998*

Wild, Margaret, 1948- Toby. 1st American ed. New York : Ticknor & Fields, 1994.
*TC PZ7.W64574 To 1994*

**DEATH INSTINCT.**
Dufresne, Todd, 1966- Tales from the Freudian crypt. Stanford, Calif. : Stanford University Press, 2000.
*TC BF175.5.D4 D84 2000*

**Death** : medical, spiritual, and social care of the dying / editoral board, A.B.M.F. Karim, chairman ... [et al.]. Amsterdam : VU University Press, 1998. 246 p. ; 25 cm. Includes bibliographical references. ISBN 90-5383-601-2 DDC 362.1/75
*1. Terminally ill - Medical care. 2. Death - Social aspects. 3. Terminal care - Religious aspects. I. Karim, Abul Bashr Mohammed Fazlul.*
*TC R726.8 .D42 1998*

**DEATH, MERCY.** *See* **EUTHANASIA.**

**DEATH OF PARENTS.** *See* **PARENTS - DEATH.**

**DEATH - PHILOSOPHY.** *See* **DEATH.**

**DEATH - PROOF AND CERTIFICATION.**
The definition of death. Baltimore : Johns Hopkins University Press, 1999.
*TC RA1063 .D44 1999*

**DEATH - PSYCHOLOGICAL ASPECTS.**
Archer, John, 1944- The nature of grief. London ; New York : Routledge, 1999.
*TC BF575.G7 A73 1999*

Kastenbaum, Robert. Death, society, and human experience. 6th ed. Boston : Allyn and Bacon, c1998.
*TC BF789.D4 K36 1998*

**DEATH - SOCIAL ASPECTS.**
Death. Amsterdam : VU University Press, 1998.
*TC R726.8 .D42 1998*

Kastenbaum, Robert. Death, society, and human experience. 6th ed. Boston : Allyn and Bacon, c1998.
*TC BF789.D4 K36 1998*

**Death, society, and human experience.**
Kastenbaum, Robert. 6th ed. Boston : Allyn and Bacon, c1998.
*TC BF789.D4 K36 1998*

**Death, value, and meaning series**
Jevne, Ronna Fay. When dreams don't work. Amityville, N.Y. : Baywood Pub., c1998.
*TC BF481 .J48 1998*

**DEBATES AND DEBATING.** *See also* **FORUMS (DISCUSSION AND DEBATE).**
Felton, Mark Kenji. Metacognitive reflection and strategy development in argumentive discourse. 1999.
*TC 085 F34*

**Debates in psychology**
Models of cognitive aging. Oxford ; New York : Oxford University Press, 2000.

*TC BF724.55.C63 M63 2000*

Touch, representation, and blindness. Oxford : New York : Oxford University Press, 2000.
*TC BF275 .T68 2000*

**DeBello, Thomas C.**
Improved test scores, attitudes, and behaviors in America's schools. Westport, Conn. : Bergin & Garvey, 1999.
*TC LB2806.4 .I56 1999*

**DeBettencourt, Laurie Ungerleider.**
Vallecorsa, Ada, 1948- Students with mild disabilities in general education settings. Upper Saddle River, N.J. : Merrill, c2000.
*TC LC4705 .V35 2000*

**DeBoer, Peter P.** Origins of teacher education at Calvin College, 1900-1930 : and gladly teach / Peter P. DeBoer. Lewiston : E. Mellen Press, c1991. x, 105 p. : ill. ; 24 cm. (Mellen studies in education ; v. 18) Includes bibliographical references (p. [99]-102) and index. ISBN 0-7734-9670-X DDC 370[.7]/30977456
*1. Calvin College - History. 2. Teachers - Training of - Michigan - History. 3. Christian education - Michigan - History. I. Title. II. Series.*
*TC LD785 .D43 1991*

**DeBord, Kurt A.**
Handbook of counseling and psychotherapy with lesbian, gay, and bisexual clients. 1st ed. Washington, DC ; London : American Psychological Association, c2000.
*TC BF637.C6 H3125 2000*

**Debski, Robert.**
Worldcall. Lisse, Netherlands ; Abingdon [England] ; Exton, PA : Swets & Zeitlinger, c1999.
*TC P53.28 .W67 1999*

**DEBUSSY, CLAUDE, 1862-1918 - CRITICISM AND INTERPRETATION.**
Gingerich, Carol Joy. The French piano style of Fauré and Debussy. 1996.
*TC 06 no. 10644*

**Decade of reform.**
Finlayson, Geoffrey B. A. M. New York : Norton [1970]
*TC HN385 .F54 1970*

**DeCandido, GraceAnne A.** Transforming libraries : issues and innovations in service to users with disabilities / written by GraceAnne A. DeCandido ; editorial advisor, Julia Blixrud. Washington, D.C. : Association of Research Libraries, Office of Leadership and Management Services, c1999. 31 p. ; 28 cm. (SPEC kit, 0160-3582 ; 243. Transforming libraries ; 8) Cover title. Related material available on the world wide web at: http://arl.org/transform/ Includes bibliographical references (p. 30-31).
*1. Libraries and the handicapped - United States - Case studies. 2. Handicapped - Information services - United States - Case studies. I. Association of Research Libraries. Office of Leadership and Management Services. II. Blixrud. Julia C., 1954- III. Title. IV. Title: Issues and innovations in service to users with disabilities V. Title: Service to users with disabilities VI. Series: SPEC kit ; 243. VII. Series: Transforming libraries ; 8.*
*TC Z711.92.H3 D43 1999*

**DeCarrico, Jeanette S.** The structure of English : studies in form and function for language teaching / Jeanette S. DeCarrico. Ann Arbor, Mich. : University of Michigan Press ; Wantage : University Presses Marketing, 2000. 207 p. ; 26 cm. Includes bibliographical references. ISBN 0-472-08602-2 DDC 425
*1. English language - Grammar. 2. English language - Textbooks for foreign speakers. I. Title.*
*TC PE1112 .D43 2000*

**DECATUR (GA.) - CHURCH HISTORY - 20TH CENTURY.**
Stroupe, Nibs. While we run this race. Maryknoll, N.Y. : Orbis Books, c1995.
*TC BX8949.D43 S77 1995*

**DECATUR (GA.) - ETHNIC RELATIONS - HISTORY - 20TH CENTURY.**
Keating, Tom, 1941- Saturday school. Bloomington, Ind. : Phi Delta Kappa Educational Foundation, c1999.
*TC LC212.23.D43 K42 1999*

**DECATUR (GA.) - RACE RELATIONS.**
Stroupe, Nibs. While we run this race. Maryknoll, N.Y. : Orbis Books, c1995.
*TC BX8949.D43 S77 1995*

**DECENTRALIZATION IN EDUCATION.** *See* **SCHOOLS - DECENTRALIZATION.**

**DECENTRALIZATION IN GOVERNMENT.** *See* **PUBLIC ADMINISTRATION.**

**DECENTRALIZATION IN SCHOOLS.** *See* **SCHOOLS - DECENTRALIZATION.**

**Decentralization of education.**
Patrinos, Harry Anthony. Washington, D.C. : World Bank, c1997.
*TC LB2826.6.D44 P38 1997*

Welsh, Thomas. Paris : International Institute for Educational Planning (IIEP); Paris : UNESCO, 1999.
*TC LB5 .F85 v.64*

**DECIMAL FRACTIONS.**
Decimals [videorecording]. Princeton, N.J. : Video Tutor, 1988.
*TC QA117 .D4 1988*

Number concepts [videorecording]. Princeton, N.J. : Video Tutor, 1988.
*TC QA117 .N8 1988*

Number concepts [videorecording]. Princeton, N.J. : Video Tutor, 1988.
*TC QA117 .N8 1988*

**DECIMAL SYSTEM.**
Decimals [videorecording]. Princeton, N.J. : Video Tutor, 1988.
*TC QA117 .D4 1988*

**Decimals** [videorecording] / Video Tutor, Inc. Princeton, N.J. : Video Tutor, 1988. 1 videocassette (VHS) (ca. 31 min.) : sd., col. ; 1/2 in. + 1 student workbook & pre/post test system ([12] p. ; 19 cm.). (Video tutor instructional series) (A mathematics series) Title on container: Basic decimals [videorecording]. Title on voice-over: Video Tutor introduces decimals [videorecording]. Title on cassette label: Video Tutor Inc. presents basic decimals [videorecording]. VHS. Catalogued from credits, cassette label and container. John Hall, instructor. For grades 5-9 math classes. SUMMARY: Covers addition, subtraction, multiplication, and division of decimals.
*1. Decimal fractions. 2. Decimal system. I. Hall, John. II. Video Tutor. III. Title: Basic decimals [videorecording] IV. Title: Video Tutor introduces decimals [videorecording] V. Title: Video Tutor Inc. presents basic decimals [videorecording] VI. Series. VII. Series: A mathematics series*
*TC QA117 .D4 1988*

**DECISION-MAKING.** *See* **CHOICE (PSYCHOLOGY); CONSENSUS (SOCIAL SCIENCES); PROBLEM SOLVING.**

**DECISION MAKING.**
Cavalier, Robert P., 1933- Personal motivation. Westport, Conn. ; London : Praeger, 2000.
*TC BF503 .C39 2000*

Hammond, Kenneth R. Judgments under stress. New York : Oxford University Press, 2000.
*TC BF441 .H27 2000*

Judgment and decision making. 2nd ed. Cambridge, U.K. ; New York, NY : Cambridge University Press, 2000.
*TC BF441 .J79 2000*

Judgment and decision making. Mahwah, N.J. : L. Erlbaum Associates, 1999.
*TC BF448 .J83 1999*

Kepner, Charles Higgins, 1922- The new rational manager. Princeton, N.J. (P.O. Box 704, Research Rd., Princeton 08540) : Princeton Research Press, c1981.
*TC HD31 .K456 1981*

O'Toole, James. Leadership A to Z. 1st ed. San Francisco, CA : Jossey-Bass Publishers, c1999.
*TC HD57.7 .O87 1999*

**Decision making in health care.**
Chapman, Gretchen B., 1965- New York : Cambridge University Press, 2000.
*TC R723.5 .C48 2000*

**DECISION MAKING - UNITED STATES.**
Reed, Carol J., 1937- Teaching with power. New York : Teachers College Press, c2000.
*TC LB2806.45 .R44 2000*

**Decker, Eric, 1960-.**
Antioxidants in muscle foods. New York ; Chichester [England] : John Wiley, c2000.
*TC TX556.M4 A57 2000*

**Decolonization & independence in Kenya, 1940-93 /** [edited by] B.A. Ogot and W.R. Ochieng'. London : J. Currey ; Athens : Ohio University Press, 1995. xviii, 270 p. ; 23 cm. (Eastern African studies) Includes bibliographical references and index. ISBN 0-8214-1050-4 ISBN 0-8214-1051-2 (pbk.) DDC 967.62
*1. Kenya - Politics and government - 1963-1978. 2. Kenya -*

*Politics and government - 1978- 3. Kenya - Politics and government - To 1963. 4. Decolonization - Kenya - History - 20th century. 5. Kenya - Colonial influence. I. Ogot, Bethwell A. II. Ochieng'. William Robert. 1943- III. Title: Decolonization and independence in Kenya IV. Series: Eastern African studies (London. England)*

**TC DT433.58 .D4 1995**

**Decolonization and independence in Kenya.**
Decolonization & independence in Kenya, 1940-93. London : J. Currey ; Athens : Ohio University Press, 1995.

**TC DT433.58 .D4 1995**

**DECOLONIZATION IN LITERATURE - STUDY AND TEACHING.**
Teaching post-colonialism and post-colonial literatures. Aarhus, Denmark ; Oakville, Conn. : Aarhus University Press, c1997.

**TC PR9080.A53 T43 1997**

Teaching the literatures of early America. New York : Modern Language Association of America, 1999.

**TC PS186 .T43 1999**

**DECOLONIZATION - KENYA - HISTORY - 20TH CENTURY.**
Decolonization & independence in Kenya, 1940-93. London : J. Currey ; Athens : Ohio University Press, 1995.

**TC DT433.58 .D4 1995**

**DECONSTRUCTION.**
Trifonas, Peter Pericles, 1960- The ethics of writing. Lanham, Md. : Oxford : Rowman & Littlefield, c2000.

**TC LB14.7 .T75 2000**

Young, R. V., 1947- At war with the word. Wilmington, Del. : ISI Books, 1999.

**TC PN94 .Y68 1999**

**DECORATION AND ORNAMENT.** *See* ANTIQUES; DESIGN; FURNITURE; ILLUSTRATION OF BOOKS; MURAL PAINTING AND DECORATION; STREET DECORATION.

**DECORATIVE ARTS.** *See* ANTIQUES; COSTUME; FIGURINES; FOLK ART; FURNITURE; JEWELRY; PORCELAIN; POTTERY; TEXTILE FABRICS.

**DECORATIVE ARTS - UNITED STATES - CATALOGS.**
Renwick Gallery. Skilled work. Washington, D.C. : Smithsonian Institution Press, c1998.

**TC NK460.W3 R467 1998**

**DECORATIVE ARTS - WASHINGTON (D.C.) - CATALOGS.**
Renwick Gallery. Skilled work. Washington, D.C. : Smithsonian Institution Press, c1998.

**TC NK460.W3 R467 1998**

**DECRIMINALIZATION.** *See* DRUG LEGALIZATION.

**DECRIMINALIZATION OF ILLEGAL DRUGS.** *See* DRUG LEGALIZATION.

**Deculturalization and the struggle for equality.**
Spring, Joel H. 3rd ed. Boston : McGraw-Hill, c2001.

**TC LC3731 .S68 2001**

**DEDUCTION (LOGIC).** *See* LOGIC.

**DEDUCTIVE LOGIC.** *See* LOGIC.

**Deductive reasoning and strategies** / edited by Walter Schaeken ... [et al.]. Mahwah, N.J. : L. Erlbaum Associates, 2000. xiv, 321 p. : ill. ; 24 cm. "Emerged from the Workshop on Deductive Reasoning and Strategies which took place at the Royal Academy of Science, in Brussels, Belgium, March 20-21 1998"--Preface. Includes bibliographical references and indexes. ISBN 0-8058-3238-6 (cloth : alk. paper) DDC 153.4/3
*1. Reasoning (Psychology) I. Schaeken. Walter.*

**TC BF442 .D43 2000**

**Dee, Ruby.** Two ways to count to ten : a Liberian folktale / retold by Ruby Dee ; illustrated by Susan Meddaugh. New York : H. Holt., c1988. [32] p. : col. ill. ; 46 x 34 cm. SUMMARY: A retelling of a traditional Liberian tale in which King Leopard invites all the animals to a spear-throwing contest whose winner will marry his daughter and succeed him as king. ISBN 0-02-109108-0
*1. Folklore - Africa. I. Meddaugh. Susan, ill. II. Title.*

**TC PZ8.1.D378 Tw 1988**

Two ways to count to ten : a Liberian folktale / retold by Ruby Dee ; illustrated by Susan Meddaugh. New York : H. Holt., c1988. [32] p. : col. ill. ; 46 x 34 cm. SUMMARY: A retelling of a traditional Liberian tale in which King Leopard invites all the animals to a spear-throwing contest whose winner will marry his daughter and succeed him

as king. ISBN 0-02-109108-0
*1. Folklore - Africa. I. Meddaugh, Susan, ill. II. Title.*

**TC PZ8.1.D378 Tw 1988a**

Two ways to count to ten : a Liberian folktale / retold by Ruby Dee ; illustrated by Susan Meddaugh. 1st ed. New York : H. Holt., c1988. [32] p. : col. ill. ; 26 cm. SUMMARY: A retelling of a traditional Liberian tale in which King Leopard invites all the animals to a spear-throwing contest whose winner will marry his daughter and succeed him as king. ISBN 0-8050-0407-6 DDC 398.2/096; E
*1. Folklore - Africa. I. Meddaugh, Susan, ill. II. Title.*

**TC PZ8.1.D378 Tw 1988**

**Deegan, Mary Jo, 1946-.**
Mead, George Herbert, 1863-1931. Play, school, and society. New York : Peter Lang, c1999.

**TC HQ782 .M43 1999**

**Deegan, William L.** Translating theory into practice : implications of Japanese management theory for student personnel administrators / by William L. Deegan, Brenton H. Steele, Thomas B. Thielen. 1st ed. [Columbus, Ohio] : National Association of Student Personnel Administrators, c1985. 84 p. : ill. ; 23 cm. (NASPA monograph series ; v. 3) "March 1985." Bibliography: p. 82-84. ISBN 0-931654-03-3 (pbk.) DDC 378/.194
*1. Counseling in higher education - United States. 2. College student personnel administrators - United States. 3. Industrial management - Japan. I. Steele, Brenton H., 1942- II. Thielen, Thomas B., 1934- III. Title. IV. Series.*

**TC LB2343 .D356 1985**

**Deege, Robert.**
The salsa-riffic world of Spanish [videorecording]. [Arlington, Va.] : Cerebellum Corp., c1998.

**TC PC4112.7 .S25 1998**

**DEFAMATION AGAINST GROUPS.** *See* HATE SPEECH.

**DEFECTIVE AND DELINQUENT CLASSES - PERIODICALS.**
The Journal of delinquency. Whittier, Calif. : Whittier State School, Dept. of Research, 1916-c1928.

**DEFECTIVE SPEECH.** *See* SPEECH DISORDERS.

**Defects :** engendering the modern body / Helen Deutsch and Felicity Nussbaum, editors. Ann Arbor : University of Michigan Press, c2000. x, 332 p. : ill ; 25 cm. (Corporealities) Includes bibliographical references and index. ISBN 0-472-09698-2 (cloth : acid-free paper) ISBN 0-472-06698-6 (pbk. : acid-free paper) DDC 362.4/0941
*1. Disability studies - Great Britain - History - 17th century. 2. Disability studies - Great Britain - History - 18th century. 3. Disability studies - France - History - 17th century. 4. Disability studies - France - History - 18th century. I. Deutsch, Helen. 1961- II. Nussbaum, Felicity. III. Series.*

**TC HV1568.25.G7 D44 1999**

**DeFelice, Stephen L., 1936-** The carnitine defense : a nutraceutical formula to prevent and treat heart disease, the nation's #1 killer / Stephen L. DeFelice with Helen Kohl. [Emmaus, Pa.] : Rodale Press ; [New York] : Distributed to the book trade by St. Martin's Press, c1999. xxi, 266 p. : ill. ; 24 cm. Includes bibliographical references (p. 241-252) and index. ISBN 1-57954-133-X (hardcover : alk. paper) DDC 616.1/061
*1. Carnitine - Therapeutic use. 2. Coronary heart disease - Prevention. 3. Coronary heart disease - Alternative treatment. 4. Functional foods. 5. Carnitine - therapeutic use. 6. Dietary Supplements. 7. Heart Diseases - prevention & control. 8. Heart Diseases - therapy. I. Kohl, Helen. II. Title.*

**TC RC685.C6 D4235 1999**

**DEFENSE MECHANISMS.**
Wurmser, Leon. [Flucht vor dem Gewissen. English] The power of the inner judge. Northvale, N.J. : Jason Aronson Inc., c2000.

**TC RC530 .W8713 2000**

**DEFENSE MECHANISMS - IN INFANCY & CHILDHOOD - CONGRESSES.**
Developmental perspectives on trauma. Rochester, N.Y., USA : University of Rochester Press, 1997.

**TC RJ499 .D4825 1997**

**DEFENSE MECHANISMS (PSYCHOLOGY).** *See* ACTING OUT (PSYCHOLOGY); REPRESSION (PSYCHOLOGY).

**DEFENSIVENESS (PSYCHOLOGY).** *See* AGGRESSIVENESS (PSYCHOLOGY).

**DEFERENCE.** *See* RESPECT.

**Defiant children :** a clinician's manual for assessment and parent training.
Understanding the defiant child [videorecording]. New York : Guilford Publications, c1997.

**TC HQ755.7 .U63 1997**

**Defining the humanities.**
Proctor, Robert E., 1945- 2nd ed. Bloomington : Indiana University Press, c1998.

**TC AZ221 .P75 1998**

**DEFINITION (LOGIC).** *See* SEMANTICS (PHILOSOPHY).

**The definition of death :** contemporary controversies / edited by Stuart J. Youngner, Robert M. Arnold, and Renie Schapiro. Baltimore : Johns Hopkins University Press, 1999. xx, 346 p. ; 24 cm. Includes bibliographical references and index. ISBN 0-8018-5985-9 (alk. paper) DDC 614/.1
*1. Death - Proof and certification. 2. Brain death. I. Youngner, Stuart J. II. Arnold, Robert M., 1957- III. Schapiro, Renie.*

**TC RA1063 .D44 1999**

**Definitive guide to developing, marketing, and presenting school assembly programs.**
Heflick, David. How to make money performing in schools. Orient, Wash. : Silcox Productions, c1996.

**TC LB3015 .H428 1996**

**DeFleur, Melvin L. (Melvin Lawrence), 1923-**
Theories of mass communication / Melvin L. De Fleur. New York : D. McKay, c1966. xviii, 171 p. : ill. ; 20 cm. (McKay social science series) Includes bibliographical references (p. 159-166) and index. DDC 302.23
*1. Mass media - Social aspects - History. 2. Mass media - Social aspects - United States - History. I. Title. II. Series.*

**TC HM258 .D35 1966**

**Defying disaffection.**
Klein, Reva Staffordshire, England : Trentham Books, 1999.

**TC LC4091 .K53 1999**

**Degen, Bruce, ill.**
Yolen, Jane. Mouse's birthday. New York : Putnam's, c1993.

**TC PZ8.3.Y76 Mo 1993**

**Dégh, Linda.**
Traditional storytelling today. Chicago : Fitzroy Dearborn Publishers, 1999.

**TC GR72 .T73 1999**

**Degler, Stephen.**
Carling, M. Linux system administration. Indianapolis, IN : New Riders, c2000.

**TC QA76.76.O63 C3755 2000**

**DEGLUTITION DISORDERS - REHABILITATION.**
Neurogenic communication disorders. New York : Thieme, 2000.

**TC RC423 .N48 2000**

**DEGLUTITION DISORDERS - REHABILITATION.**
Neurogenic communication disorders. New York : Thieme, 2000.

**TC RC423 .N48 2000**

**DEGREE MILLS.** *See* DIPLOMA MILLS.

**DEGREES, ACADEMIC.** *See* DOCTOR OF PHILOSOPHY DEGREE.

**DEGREES, ACADEMIC - UNITED STATES.**
Adelman, Clifford. Answers in the tool box. Washington, DC : U.S. Dept. of Education, Office of Educational Research and Improvement, [1999]

**TC LB2390 .A34 1999**

**Degrees of distance.**
Clauss, Caroline Seay. 1999.

**TC 085 C58**

**DEINSTITUTIONALIZATION.** *See* INSTITUTIONAL CARE.

**DEISM.** *See* COSMOLOGY; RATIONALISM.

**Deiss, Joseph Jay.** The town of Hercules : a buried treasure trove / Joseph Jay Deiss. Rev. and expanded. Malibu, Calif. : J. Paul Getty Museum, c1995. 183 p. : ill. (some col.), col. maps ; 26 cm. Includes index. ISBN 0-89236-222-7 DDC 937/.7
*1. Herculaneum (Extinct city) - Juvenile literature. 2. Herculaneum (Extinct city) I. Title.*

**TC DG70.H5 D4 1995**

**Deixis, grammar, and culture.**
Perkins, Revere D. (Revere Dale) Amsterdam ; Philadelphia : J. Benjamins Pub. co., 1992.

**TC P35 .P47 1992**

**DEJECTION.** *See* DEPRESSION, MENTAL; MELANCHOLY.

**DELAMONT, SARA.** The doctoral experience : : success and failure in graduate school. London ; New York : Falmer Press, 2000. viii, 206 p. ; 24 cm. Includes

bibliographical references and indexes. ISBN 0-7507-0927-8
*1. Doctor of philosophy degree - Great Britain.*
**TC LB2386 .D45 2000**

**Delamont, Sara, 1947-.**
Qualitative research. Aldershot, Hants, England ;
Brookfield, Vt. : Avebury, c1996.
**TC H62 .Q355 1996**

**Delano, Monica.**
Snell, Martha E. Social relationships and peer support.
Baltimore, Md. ; London : Paul H. Brookes Pub. Co.,
c2000.
**TC LC4069 .S54 2000**

**Delaware Art Museum.**
Myth, magic and mystery. Boulder, Colo. : Roberts
Rinehart Publishers ; [Norfolk, Va.] : in cooperation
with the Chrysler Museum of Art, c1996.
**TC NC975 .M98 1996**

**DELAY, DOROTHY, 1917-.**
Sand, Barbara Lourie. Teaching genius. Portland, Or. :
Amadeus Press, 2000.
**TC ML423.D35 S36 2000**

**Delegation and empowerment.**
Ward, Michael E., 1953- Larchmont, NY : Eye on
Education, c1999.
**TC LB2831.92 .W37 1999**

**DELEGATION OF AUTHORITY.**
Ward, Michael E., 1953- Delegation and
empowerment. Larchmont, NY : Eye on Education,
c1999.
**TC LB2831.92 .W37 1999**

**DeLeone, Tina.**
Jazz dance class [videorecording]. W. Long Branch,
NJ : Kultur, [1992?]
**TC GV1784 .J3 1992**

**DELEUZE, GILLES - CONTRIBUTIONS IN
LOGIC.**
Olkowski, Dorothea. Gilles Deleuze and the ruin of
representation. Berkeley : University of California
Press, c1999.
**TC N6537.K42 O44 1999**

**Delgado-Campbell, Delores.**
Campbell, Duane E. Choosing democracy. 2nd ed.
Upper Saddle River, N.J. : Merrill, c2000.
**TC LC1099.3 .C36 2000**

**Delhi. Central Institute of Education. Alumni
Association.**
Educational forum. Delhi, Dept. of Extension
Services, Central Institute of Education.

**Delhi. Central Institute of Education. Dept. of
Extension Services.**
Educational forum. Delhi, Dept. of Extension
Services, Central Institute of Education.

**Delhi (India). National Institute of Education.
Central Bureau of Educational and Vocational
Guidance.**
Guidance review. [Delhi] Central Bureau of
Educational and Vocational Guidance, National
Council of Educational Research and Training.

**Delhi. National Institute of Audio Visual Education.**
Audio-visual education. [Delhi, Manager of
Publications]

**Delhi. National Institute of Education. Central
Bureau of Educational and Vocational Guidance.**
**Guidance news.**
Guidance review. [Delhi] Central Bureau of
Educational and Vocational Guidance, National
Council of Educational Research and Training.

**Delhi School of Economics. Centre for Development
Economics.**
Public report on basic education in India. New Delhi ;
Oxford : Oxford University Press, c1999.
**TC LA1151 .P83 1999**

**Deliagina, T. G.**
Orlovsky, G. N. (Grigoriĭ Nikolaevich) Neuronal
control of locomotion. Oxford ; New York : Oxford
University Press, 1999.
**TC QP303 .O75 1999**

**DELINQUENCY. See CRIME.**

**DELINQUENCY, JUVENILE. See JUVENILE
DELINQUENCY.**

**DELIRIUM. See DELIRIUM TREMENS.**

**DELIRIUM, DEMENTIA, AMNESTIC,
COGNITIVE DISORDERS - DIAGNOSIS.**
Lacks, Patricia. Bender Gestalt screening for brain
dysfunction. 2nd ed. New York : John Wiley & Sons,
c1999.

**TC RC386.6.B46 L3 1999**

**DELIRIUM - DIAGNOSIS.**
Organic disorders [videorecording]. Princeton, N.J. :
Films for the Humanities & Sciences, 1998.
**TC RC521 .O7 1998**

**DELIRIUM - PATIENTS.**
Organic disorders [videorecording]. Princeton, N.J. :
Films for the Humanities & Sciences, 1998.
**TC RC521 .O7 1998**

**DELIRIUM TREMENS - DIAGNOSIS.**
Disorders due to psychoactive substance abuse
[videorecording]. Princeton, N.J. : Films for the
Humanities & Sciences, 1998.
**TC RC564 .D5 1998**

**DELIRIUM TREMENS - PATIENTS.**
Disorders due to psychoactive substance abuse
[videorecording]. Princeton, N.J. : Films for the
Humanities & Sciences, 1998.
**TC RC564 .D5 1998**

**Delivering a course.**
Forsyth, Ian. The complete guide to teaching a course.
2nd ed. London : Kogan Page : Sterling, VA : Stylus
Publishing, 1999.
**TC LB1025.3 .F67 1999**

**Delivering digital images :** cultural heritage resources
for education. Los Angeles, Calif. : Getty Information
Institute, 1998. 1 v. : ill. (some col.) ; 28 cm. "MESL"--
Cover. Includes bibliographical references. ISBN
0-89236-508-0 (alk. paper) ISBN 0-89236-509-9 DDC
025.067
*1. Art - Computer network resources. 2. Museum Educational
Site Licensing Project. 3. Picture archiving and
communication systems - United States. 4. Pictures in
education - United States - Data processing.*
**TC N59 .D45 1998**

**Delivering digitally.**
Inglis, Alistair. London : Kogan Page, c1999.
**TC LB1044.87 .I545 1999**

**Delivering views :** distant cultures in early postcards /
edited by Christraud M. Geary and Virginia-Lee
Webb. Washington [D.C.] : Smithsonian Institution
Press, c1998. vii, 199 p. : ill. (some col.) ; 27 cm. Includes
bibliographical references (p. 179-184) and index. ISBN
1-56098-759-6 (cloth : alk. paper) DDC 741.6/83/09034
*1. Postcards - History - 19th century - Themes, motives. 2.
Postcards - History - 20th century - Themes, motives. I. Geary,
Christraud M. II. Webb, Virginia-Lee.*
**TC NC1872 .D46 1998**

**DELIVERY OF HEALTH CARE. See MEDICAL
CARE.**

**DELIVERY OF HEALTH CARE.**
Tulchinsky, Theodore H. The new public health. San
Diego, Calif. ; London : Academic Press, c2000.
**TC RA425 .T85 2000**

Vetter, Norman. Epidemiology and public health
medicine. Edinburgh ; New York : Churchill
Livingstone, 1999.
**TC RA427 .V48 1999**

**DELIVERY OF HEALTH CARE - ECONOMICS -
UNITED STATES.**
Health care and its costs. 1st ed. New York : Norton,
c1987.
**TC RA395.A3 H392 1987**

**DELIVERY OF HEALTH CARE - ECONOMICS -
UNITED STATES - NURSES' INSTRUCTION.**
Finkler, Steven A. Financial management for nurse
managers and executives. 2nd ed. Philadelphia ;
London : W.B. Saunders, c2000.
**TC RT86.7 .F46 2000**

**DELIVERY OF HEALTH CARE - UNITED
STATES.**
Andrulis, Dennis P. Managed care and the inner city.
San Francisco : Jossey-Bass, 1999.
**TC RA413.5.U5 A57 1999**

**DELIVERY OF MEDICAL CARE. See MEDICAL
CARE.**

**Della Sala, Sergio.**
Mind myths. Chichester, England ; New York : J.
Wiley & Sons, c1999.
**TC BF161 .M556 1999**

**DELSARTE SYSTEM. See EXPRESSION.**

**Delton, Judy.** Angel spreads her wings / Judy Delton.
Boston : Houghton Mifflin, 1999. 143 p. : ill. ; 22 cm.
SUMMARY: Angel, whose active imagination always causes
her to expect the worst, is given many new things to worry
about when her stepfather plans to move the family to Greece
for the summer. ISBN 0-395-91006-4 DDC [Fic]

*1. Stepfamilies - Fiction. 2. Greece - Fiction. 3. Vacations -
Fiction. 4. Imagination - Fiction. I. Title.*
**TC PZ7.D388 Anf 1999**

**DELUGE. See NOAH'S ARK.**

**DELUSIONAL BELIEFS. See DELUSIONS.**

**DELUSIONAL DISORDERS. See DELUSIONS.**

**DELUSIONS.**
Schizophrenia and delusional disorders
[videorecording]. Princeton, N.J. : Films for the
Humanities & Sciences, c1998.
**TC RC514 .S3 1998**

**DELUSIONS - CASE STUDIES.**
Challenge cases [videorecording]. Princeton, N.J. :
Films for the Humanities & Sciences, 1998.
**TC RC455.2.C4 C4 1998**

**DELUSIONS - CONGRESSES.**
Memory, brain, and belief. Cambridge, Mass. ;
London : Harvard University Press, 2000.
**TC QP406 .M44 2000**

**Demaine, Jack.**
Education policy and contemporary politics.
Basingstoke, Hampshire : Macmillan, 1999.
**TC LC93.G7 E382 1999**

**DEMAND (ECONOMIC THEORY). See
CONSUMPTION (ECONOMICS).**

**The demands of liberal education.**
Levinson, Meira. Oxford ; New York : Oxford
University Press, 1999.
**TC LC1091 .L38 1999**

**Demarest, Chris L.**
Italian picture dictionary. Princeton, NJ : Berlitz Kids,
c1997.
**TC PC1629 .I73 1997**

**Demarest, Chris L., ill.**
French picture dictionary. Princeton : Berlitz Kids,
Berlitz Pub. Co., c1997.
**TC PC2629 .F74 1997**

German picture dictionary. Princeton, NJ : Berlitz
Pub. Co., 1997.
**TC PF3629 .G47 1997**

What's on the menu? New York : Viking, 1992.
**TC PS595.F65 W48 1992**

**DEMENTIA. See also AIDS DEMENTIA
COMPLEX; PRESENILE DEMENTIA;
SENILE DEMENTIA.**
Mace, Nancy L. The 36-hour day. 3rd ed. Baltimore :
Johns Hopkins University Press, c1999.
**TC RC523 .M33 1999**

**DEMENTIA - DIAGNOSIS.**
Organic disorders [videorecording]. Princeton, N.J. :
Films for the Humanities & Sciences, 1998.
**TC RC521 .O7 1998**

**DEMENTIA - PATIENTS.**
Organic disorders [videorecording]. Princeton, N.J. :
Films for the Humanities & Sciences, 1998.
**TC RC521 .O7 1998**

**DEMENTIA PRAECOX. See SCHIZOPHRENIA.**

**DEMENTIAS. See DEMENTIA.**

**Demetriou, Andrew J.** Health care integration :
structural and legal issues / Andrew J. Demetriou,
Thomas E. Dutton. Washington, D.C. : Bureau of
National Affairs, Inc., c1996. 1 v. (loose-leaf) : forms ; 28
cm. (BNA's health law & business series) Includes
bibliographical references. ISBN 1-55871-338-7 ISSN 1087-
7185
*1. Vertical integration. 2. Health facilities - United States -
Business management. 3. Health facilities - Law and
legislation - United States. 4. Health services administration -
United States. I. Dutton, Thomas E. II. Bureau of National
Affairs (Washington, D.C.) III. Title. IV. Series.*
**TC KF3825 .D394 1996**

**DeMeulle, Lisa.**
Morrison, Gary R. Integrating computer technology
into the classroom. Upper Saddle River, N.J. : Merrill,
c1999.
**TC LB1028.5 .M6373 1999**

**Demi.** The donkey and the rock / Demi. New York :
Henry Holt, 1999. 1 v. (unpaged) : col. ill. ; 26 cm.
SUMMARY: In this version of a tale with many Asian
variations, a wise king, who rules a town full of foolish people
in the mountains of Tibet, puts a donkey and a rock on trial to
settle the dispute between two honest men. ISBN
0-8050-5959-8 (alk. paper) DDC 398.2/0951/502; E
*1. Folklore - China - Tibet. I. Title.*
**TC PZ8.1.D38 Do 1999**

*Demi.*

**[Opposites]**
Demi's opposites : an animal game book. New York : Grosset & Dunlap, c1987. [48] p. : chiefly col. ill. ; 26 cm. SUMMARY: Brief humorous verses and illustrations of animals engaged in a variety of activities demonstrate opposites such as curly/straight, inside/outside, and empty/full. ISBN 0-448-18995-X (lib. bdg.) DDC 428.1
*1. English language - Synonyms and antonyms - Juvenile literature. 2. Animals - Juvenile literature. 3. English language - Synonyms and antonyms. 4. Animals. I. Title. II. Title: Opposites.*
*TC PE1591 .D43 1987*

**Deming, W. Edwards (William Edwards), 1900-** The new economics : for industry, government, education / W. Edwards Deming. 2nd ed. Cambridge, Mass. ; London : MIT Press, 2000. xvi, 247 p. : ill. ; 23 cm. Originally published: Cambridge, Mass. : MIT, Center for Advanced Engineering Studies, 1994. Includes bibliographical references and index. ISBN 0-262-54116-5 (pbk. : alk. paper) DDC 658.4
*1. Total quality management. 2. Leadership. I. Title.*
*TC HD62.15 .D46 2000*

**Demi's opposites.**
Demi. [Opposites] New York : Grosset & Dunlap, c1987.
*TC PE1591 .D43 1987*

**DEMOCRACY.** *See also* **EQUALITY; LIBERTY.**
Digital democracy. Toronto ; New York : Oxford University Press, 1998.
*TC JC421 .D55 1998*

**Democracy & the arts** / edited by Arthur M. Melzer, Jerry Weinberger, M. Richard Zinman. Ithaca : Cornell University Press, c1999. viii, 220 p. ; 24 cm. Essays collected here were delivered as papers at a conference sponsored by the body Symposium on Science, Reason, and Modern Democracy, held in April 1995 at Michigan State University. Includes bibliographical references (p. [193]-206) and index. ISBN 0-8014-3541-2 (cloth : alk. paper) DDC 700/.1/03
*1. Arts and society - United States - History - Congresses. 2. Arts - Political aspects - United States - History - Congresses. 3. Democracy - United States - Congresses. 4. Politics and culture - United States - History - Congresses. I. Melzer, Arthur M. II. Weinberger, J. III. Zinman, M. Richard. IV. Symposium on Science, Reason, and Modern Democracy. V. Title: Democracy and the arts*
*TC NX180.S6 D447 1999*

**DEMOCRACY - AFRICA.**
Onwumechili, Chuka. African democratization and military coups. Westport, Conn. : Praeger, 1998.
*TC JQ1873.5.C58 O58 1998*

**Democracy and governance in higher education.**
Groof, Jan de. The Hague ; Boston : Kluwer Law International, 1998.
*TC LB2341.8.E85 G76 1998*

**Democracy and the arts.**
Democracy & the arts. Ithaca : Cornell University Press, c1999.
*TC NX180.S6 D447 1999*

**DEMOCRACY - MORAL AND ETHICAL ASPECTS.**
Edgoose, Julian Miles. Partnerships of possibility. 1999.
*TC 085 E117*

**DEMOCRACY - STUDY AND TEACHING.**
Burch, Kerry T., 1957- Eros as the educational principle of democracy. New York : P. Lang, c2000.
*TC LC196 .B75 2000*

**DEMOCRACY - STUDY AND TEACHING - GREAT BRITAIN.**
Quicke, John, 1941- A curriculum for life. Buckingham ; Philadelphia : Open University Press, 1999.
*TC LB1564.G7 Q85 1999*

**DEMOCRACY - STUDY AND TEACHING (HIGHER) - UNITED STATES.**
Higher education for democracy. New York : P. Lang, c1999.
*TC LD2001.G452 .S33 1999*

**DEMOCRACY - STUDY AND TEACHING - UNITED STATES.**
Rediscovering the democratic purposes of education. Lawrence : University Press of Kansas, c2000.
*TC LC89 .R43 2000*

**DEMOCRACY - UNITED STATES.**
Bertman, Stephen. Cultural amnesia. Westport, Conn. ; London : Praeger, 2000.
*TC HN59.2 .B474 2000*

**DEMOCRACY - UNITED STATES - CONGRESSES.**
Democracy & the arts. Ithaca : Cornell University Press, c1999.
*TC NX180.S6 D447 1999*

Nonprofits and government. Washington, DC : Urban Institute Press, 1999.
*TC HD62.6 .N694 1999*

**DEMOCRACY - UNITED STATES - HISTORY.**
Lorini, Alessandra, 1949- Rituals of race. Charlottesville : University Press of Virginia, 1999.
*TC E185.61 .L675 1999*

**Democratic dialogue with special needs students :** Mike Pezone & Alan Singer / produced by the Social Science Education Consortium. [Boulder, Colo.] : Social Science Education Consortium, c1997. 1 videocassette (25 min.) : sd., col. ; 1/2 in. VHS. Catalogued from credits and cassette label. Title from cassette label. Edited by Vicki Murray-Kurzban. For educators, especially teachers of "at-risk" students. SUMMARY: Mike Pezone, teacher at Russell Sage Junior High, discusses how he teaches "at-risk" kids, the "kids that no one invests in", kids with ADD, learning disabilities, hearing challenges, etc. He stresses learning self-worth and validation as human beings, over content, emphasizing his students' need to listen to each other, their need to speak and the importance of everyone's voice being heard. In this class the students evaluate themselves. We view his students in action during a democratic dialogue and later in a Social Studies discussion. CONTENTS: Russell Sage Junior High : democratic dialogue with special needs students -- Mike Pezone's "8B7" class with Alan Singer from Hofstra University -- Who are the 8B7? -- Outcomes/Rationale -- Set up for Project -- Practice/rehearsal for performance -- The dialogue -- Debriefing -- Effort or result : how should teachers grade? -- Russell Sage Junior High : Mike Pezone's 9-C Social Studies class discussion.
*1. Socially handicapped children - Education - United States. 2. Mentally handicapped children - Education - Aims and objectives - United States. 3. Socially handicapped children - United States - Attitudes. 4. Mentally handicapped children - 5. Social sciences - Study and teaching - United States. I. Pezone, Mike. II. Singer, Alan. III. Social Science Education Consortium.*
*TC LC4069.3 .D4 1997*

**DEMOCRATIC NATIONAL CONVENTION (1968 : CHICAGO, ILL.).**
Walker, Daniel, 1922- Rights in conflict; convention week in Chicago, August, 25-29, 1968; New York : Dutton, c1968.
*TC F548.52 .W3 1968c*

**Democratic teacher education reform in Africa :** the case of Namibia / [edited by] Ken Zeichner, Lars Dahlström. Boulder, Colo. ; Oxford : Westview Press, 1999. xix, 269 p. : ill. ; 24 cm. Includes bibliographical references and index. ISBN 0-8133-9062-1 (alk. paper) DDC 370/.71/1
*1. Teachers - Training of - Namibia. 2. Critical pedagogy - Namibia. 3. Teachers - Training of - Africa - Case studies. 4. Critical pedagogy - Africa - Case studies. I. Zeichner, Kenneth M. II. Dahlström, Lars, 1942-*
*TC LB1727.N3 D46 1999*

**DÉMOCRATIE.**
Digital democracy. Toronto ; New York : Oxford University Press, 1998.
*TC JC421 .D55 1998*

**DEMOCRATIZATION - AFRICA.**
Onwumechili, Chuka. African democratization and military coups. Westport, Conn. : Praeger, 1998.
*TC JQ1873.5.C58 O58 1998*

**Demographic differences in organizations.**
Tsui, Anne S. Lanham, MD : Lexington Books, 1999.
*TC HF5549.5.M5 T75 1999*

**DEMOGRAPHY.** *See* **FERTILITY, HUMAN; MORTALITY; POPULATION.**

**Demonstrating care.**
Libster, Martha. Albany, NY : Delmar Thomson Learning, 2000.
*TC RT86 .L535 2000*

**DEMONSTRATION CENTERS IN EDUCATION.** *See* **LABORATORY SCHOOLS.**

**DEMONSTRATION CENTERS IN EDUCATION - UNITED STATES.**
Taylor, Kathe. Children at the center. Portsmouth, NH : Heinemann, c1998.
*TC LB3060.57 .T39 1998*

**DEMONSTRATION SCHOOLS.** *See* **LABORATORY SCHOOLS.**

**DEMONSTRATIONS.** *See* **RIOTS.**

**DEMONSTRATIONS - YUGOSLAVIA - BELGRADE (SERBIA).**
[Ajmo, ajde, svi u šetnju. English.] Protest in Belgrade. Budapest, Hungary ; New York, NY, USA : Central European University Press, 1999.
*TC DR2044 .A3913 1999*

**Demos, Vasilikie.**
Social change for women and children. Stamford, Conn. : JAI Press, 2000.
*TC HQ1421 .S68 2000*

**Dempsey, Arthur D.**
Dempsey, Patricia Ann. Using nursing research. 5th ed. Baltimore, Md. : Lippincott, c2000.
*TC RT81.5 .D46 2000*

**Dempsey, Patricia Ann.**
**Nursing research**
Dempsey, Patricia Ann. Using nursing research. 5th ed. Baltimore, Md. : Lippincott, c2000.
*TC RT81.5 .D46 2000*

Using nursing research : process, critical evaluation, and utilization / Patricia Ann Dempsey, Arthur D. Dempsey. 5th ed. Baltimore, Md. : Lippincott, c2000. xx, 380 p. : ill. ; 24 cm. + 1 computer disk (3 1/2 in.). Rev. ed. of: Nursing research. 4th ed. c1996. Includes bibliographical references and index. System requirements for computer disk: IBM PC; DOS; an ASCII C compiler; high-density floppy disk drive and hard disk. ISBN 0-7817-1790-6 DDC 610.73/072
*1. Nursing - Research. 2. Nursing Research. I. Dempsey, Arthur D. II. Dempsey, Patricia Ann. Nursing research III. Title.*
*TC RT81.5 .D46 2000*

**Demystifying drugs.**
Goldberg, Ted. New York : St. Martin's Press, 1999.
*TC HV5801 .G633 1999*

**Den høgre skolen, 1864-1964.**
Husby, Egil, 1913- Kristiansund, 1966.

**DENATIONALIZATION.** *See* **PRIVATIZATION.**

**Denby, Edwin, 1903-** Dance writings & poetry / Edwin Denby ; edited by Robert Cornfield. New Haven [CT] : Yale University Press, c1998. xiv, 320 p. ; 22 cm. Includes bibliographical references (p. 307) and index. ISBN 0-300-07617-7 (cloth : alk. paper) ISBN 0-300-06985-5 (paper : alk. paper) DDC 793.3
*1. Dance - Reviews. I. Cornfield, Robert. II. Title. III. Title: Dance writings and poetry*
*TC GV1599 .D393 1998*

**Denco, Eze.**
Pre-primary education in Nigeria. Onitsha [Nigeria] : Lincel, 1998.
*TC LB1140.25.N6 P74 1998*

**DENDROLOGY.** *See* **TREES.**

**DENG, XIAOPING, 1904-.**
Reynolds, Barbara G. Reform and education. 1999.
*TC 06 no. 11166*

**Denim, Sue, 1966-** Make way for Dumb Bunnies / story by Sue Denim ; pictures by Dav Pilkey. New York : Blue Sky Press, c1996. 1 v. (unpaged) : col. ill. ; 22 cm. SUMMARY: The Dumb Bunnies have a very active day, during which they do many things backwards or wrong. ISBN 0-590-58286-0 (hc) DDC [E]
*1. Rabbits - Fiction. 2. Humorous stories. I. Pilkey, Dav, 1966- ill. II. Title.*
*TC PZ7.D4149 Mak 1996*

**Denmark, Vicki M., 1957-.**
Podsen, India, 1945- Coaching & mentoring first-year and student teachers. Larchmont, NY : Eye On Education, c2000.
*TC LB1731.4 .P63 2000*

**Denning, Patt, 1950-** Practicing harm reduction psychotherapy : an alternative approach to addictions / Patt Denning ; foreword by G. Alan Marlatt. New York : Guilford Press, 2000. xxv, 262 p. ; 24 cm. Includes bibliographical references (p. 239-246) and indexes. ISBN 1-57230-555-X DDC 616.86/0651
*1. Substance abuse - Complications - Prevention. 2. Psychotherapy. 3. Substance abuse - Treatment. 4. Substance abuse - Social aspects. I. Title.*
*TC RC564 .D44 2000*

**Dennis, James.**
Carling, M. Linux system administration. Indianapolis, IN : New Riders, c2000.
*TC QA76.76.O63 C3755 2000*

**DENOMINATIONAL COLLEGES.** *See* **CHURCH COLLEGES.**

**DENOMINATIONAL SCHOOLS.** *See* CHURCH SCHOOLS.

**DENOMINATIONS, RELIGIOUS.** *See* RELIGIONS.

**DENTISTRY.** *See* TEETH.

**DENTITION.** *See* TEETH.

**Denton, D. Keith.** The toolbox for the mind : finding and implementing creative solutions in the workplace / D. Keith Denton with contributions from Rebecca A. Denton. Milwaukee, WI : ASQ Quality Press, c1999. xix, 178 p. : ill. ; 27 cm. Includes bibliographical references and index. ISBN 0-87389-448-0 (alk. paper) DDC 153.4/3
*1. Creative ability in business. 2. Problem solving. 3. Product management. I. Denton, Rebecca A., 1969- II. Title.*
*TC HD53 .D46 1999*

**Denton, Rebecca A., 1969-.**
Denton, D. Keith. The toolbox for the mind. Milwaukee, WI : ASQ Quality Press, c1999.
*TC HD53 .D46 1999*

**Denver East High School State competition and Thunder Ridge Middle School non-competitive hearing 1997.**
We the people simulated congressional hearing [videorecording]. [Boulder, Colo.] : Social Science Education Consortium, c1997.
*TC KF4208.5.L3 W4 1997*

**Denzin, Norman K.**
Handbook of qualitative research. 2nd ed. Thousand Oaks, Calif. : Sage Publications, c2000.
*TC H62 .H2455 2000*

**DEONTOLOGY.** *See* ETHICS.

**Department & discipline.**
Abbott, Andrew. Chicago, IL : University of Chicago Press, c1999.
*TC HM22.U5 A23 1999*

**Department and discipline.**
Abbott, Andrew. Department & discipline. Chicago, IL : University of Chicago Press, c1999.
*TC HM22.U5 A23 1999*

**DEPARTMENT CHAIRMEN (UNIVERSITIES).** *See* DEPARTMENTAL CHAIRMEN (UNIVERSITIES).

**DEPARTMENTAL CHAIRMEN (COLLEGES).** *See* DEPARTMENTAL CHAIRMEN (UNIVERSITIES).

**DEPARTMENTAL CHAIRMEN (UNIVERSITIES).**
Lucas, Ann F. Leading academic change. 1st ed. San Francisco : Jossey-Bass, c2000.
*TC LB2341 .L82 2000*

**DEPARTMENTAL CHAIRMEN (UNIVERSITIES) - GREAT BRITAIN.**
Bolton, Allan. Managing the academic unit. Buckingham [England] ; Philadelphia : Open University Press, c2000.
*TC LB2341 .B583 2000*

**DEPARTMENTS, EXECUTIVE.** *See* EXECUTIVE DEPARTMENTS.

**DEPENDENCY (PSYCHOLOGY).** *See* AUTONOMY (PSYCHOLOGY).

**Depiction.**
Podro, Michael. New Haven, CT : Yale University Press, c1998.
*TC N71 .P64 1998*

**The deployment of educational innovation through foreign aid.**
Basile, Michael L., 1943- 1989.
*TC LD3234.M267 B32 1989*

**DePorter, Bobbi.** Quantum teaching : orchestrating student success / Bobbi DePorter, Mark Reardon, Sarah Singer-Nourie. Boston, Mass. : Allyn and Bacon, c1999. viii, 230 p. : ill. ; 28 cm. Includes bibliographical references (p. 220-224) and index. ISBN 0-205-28664-X
*1. Teaching. 2. Effective teaching. I. Reardon, Mark. II. Singer-Nourie, Sarah. III. Title.*
*TC LB1027 .D418 1999*

**DEPOSIT LIBRARIES.** *See* LIBRARIES, STORAGE.

**DEPOSITORY INSTITUTIONS.** *See* BANKS AND BANKING.

**DEPRESSED PEOPLE.** *See* DEPRESSED PERSONS.

**DEPRESSED PERSONS - PASTORAL COUNSELING OF.**
Stone, Howard W. Depression and hope. Minneapolis : Fortress Press, c1998.
*TC BV4461 .S76 1998*

**Depression and hope.**
Stone, Howard W. Minneapolis : Fortress Press, c1998.
*TC BV4461 .S76 1998*

**Depression and manic depression** [videorecording] / producer/writer, Jamie Guth. Boston, MA : Fanlight Productions, c1996. 1 videocassette (28 min.) : sd., col. ; 1/2 in. (The Doctor is in) VHS. Catalogued from credits and container; title from container. Presenter, Jamie Guth. Videographer/editor, Keven Siegert. "From the award-winning 'The Doctor is In' series, produced at Dartmouth-Hitchcock Medical [Center]".-- Container. For adolescents through adult. SUMMARY: Depression affects over 17 million Americans each year. This program explains the depression and manic-depression through the experiences of several people, including Mike Wallace, Kay Redfield Jamison, Lama Dejani, and Robert Boorstin. An overview of medications and therapy and a list of resources is also provided.
*1. Depression, Mental. 2. Manic-depressive illness. I. Guth, Jamie. II. Dartmouth/Hitchcock Medical Center. III. Fanlight Productions. IV. Series.*
*TC RC537 .D46 1996*

**DEPRESSION, BIPOLAR.** *See* MANIC-DEPRESSIVE ILLNESS.

**The depression hits home** [picture]. Amawalk, NY : Jackdaw Publications, c1997. 12 posters : b&w ; 43 x 56 cm. + 1 leaflet ([6] p. : ill. ; 28 cm.). (Jackdaw photo collections ; PC 101) Compiled by Enid Goldberg & Norman Itzkowitz. SUMMARY: 12 historical photo-posters depicting the depression in the urban and rural United States. CONTENTS: 1. The start: Black Tuesday, October 29, 1929 -- 2. The rural poor: woman with belongings in car -- 3. The Dust Bowl: a Kansas dust storm -- 4. The urban poor: breadline near the Brooklyn Bridge -- 5. Despair: woman with children in lean-to -- 6. Hitting bottom: men sleeping on a street in California -- 7. Earning money any way one can: selling apples -- 8. Alternatives for the out-of-work: dance marathons -- 9. Lending a hand: the soup kitchen -- 10. Contrasts in lifestyle: "Ride the Train" -- 11. Forgetting for a while: boys at a movie marquee -- 12. Trying to pull out: woman teaching children at home. ISBN 1-56696-157-2
*1. Depressions - 1929 - United States - Posters. 2. United States - Economic conditions - 1918-1945 - Posters. 3. United States - Social conditions - 1918-1932 - Posters. 4. United States - Social conditions - 1933-1945 - Posters. 5. United States - History - 1919-1933 - Posters. 6. United States - History - 1933-1945 - Posters. 7. Documentary photography - United States - Posters. I. Goldberg, Enid. II. Itzkowitz, Norman. III. Jackdaw Publications. IV. Series.*
*TC TR820.5 .D4 1997*

**DEPRESSION IN ADOLESCENCE - PERSONAL NARRATIVES.**
The Choice of a lifetime [videorecording]. Hohokus, NJ : New Day Films, c1996.
*TC RC569 .C45 1996*

**DEPRESSION IN ADOLESCENCE - UNITED STATES.**
Gallagher, Trish. Arousal patterns, emotion identification, and cognitive style in depressed and nondepressed inner-city adolescent Latinas. 1997.
*TC 085 G136*

**DEPRESSION IN CHILDREN - EL SALVADOR.**
Flores, Joaquín Evelio. Psychological effects of the civil war on children from rural communities of El Salvador.
*TC 083 F67*

**DEPRESSION IN CHILDREN - PERSONAL NARRATIVES.**
The Choice of a lifetime [videorecording]. Hohokus, NJ : New Day Films, c1996.
*TC RC569 .C45 1996*

**DEPRESSION IN OLD AGE.**
Depression in older adults [videorecording]. Boston, MA : Fanlight Productions : [Chicago, Ill.] : Distributed by Terra Nova Films, Inc., 1997.
*TC RC537.5 .D4 1997*

Grice, Marthe Jane. Attachment, race, and gender in late life. 1999.
*TC 085 G865*

**DEPRESSION IN OLD AGE - PERSONAL NARRATIVES.**
The Choice of a lifetime [videorecording]. Hohokus, NJ : New Day Films, c1996.
*TC RC569 .C45 1996*

**Depression in older adults** [videorecording] : the right to feel better / Produced by Educational Media Services, Duke University Medical Center; producer/director, Claiborne M. Clark. Boston, MA : Fanlight Productions ; [Chicago, Ill.] : Distributed by Terra Nova Films, Inc., 1997. 1 videocassette (VHS) (30 min.) : sd., col. ; 1/2 in. + 1 viewer's guide ([6] p. ; 22 cm.). VHS. Catalogued from credits, container and cassette label. Medical editor, Dan Blazer; videographers, Greg Hobbs, Mick Stewart; script consultants, Lisa Gwyther, Jim Vanden Bosch. Distributor from cassette label; publisher information from label mounted on container. For adults. SUMMARY: Presents the signs, causes, and treatment of depression in the elderly, with comments from Dan Blazer, M.D. Discusses the increase in suicide in the elderly, how it can be treated, and presents the signs of suicide risk to look for in the elderly.
*1. Depression in old age. I. Blazer, Dan G. (Dan German), 1944- II. Clark, Claiborne M. III. Duke University. Medical Center. Educational Media Services. IV. Terra Nova Films. V. Fanlight Productions. VI. Title: Right to feel better [videorecording]*
*TC RC537.5 .D4 1997*

**DEPRESSION IN THE AGED.** *See* DEPRESSION IN OLD AGE.

**DEPRESSION IN WOMEN.**
Newman, Stephanie. Self-silencing, depression, gender role, and gender role conflict in women and men. 1997.
*TC 085 N47*

**DEPRESSION IN WOMEN - SOCIAL ASPECTS.**
Stoppard, Janet M. (Janet Mary), 1945- Understanding depression. London ; New York : Routledge, 2000.
*TC RC537 .S82 2000*

**DEPRESSION, MANIC.** *See* MANIC-DEPRESSIVE ILLNESS.

**DEPRESSION, MENTAL.** *See also* DEPRESSION IN ADOLESCENCE; DEPRESSION IN CHILDREN; DEPRESSION IN OLD AGE; DEPRESSION IN WOMEN; MANIC-DEPRESSIVE ILLNESS; MELANCHOLY.
Ainsworth, Patricia, M.D. Understanding depression. Jackson : University Press of Mississippi, c2000.
*TC RC537 .A39 2000*

Clark, David A., 1954- Scientific foundations of cognitive theory and therapy of depression. New York : John Wiley, c1999.
*TC RC537 .C53 1999*

Depression and manic depression [videorecording]. Boston, MA : Fanlight Productions, c1996.
*TC RC537 .D46 1996*

Smith, Jeffery, 1961- Where the roots reach for water. New York : North Point Press, 1999.
*TC BF575.M44 S55 1999*

**DEPRESSION, MENTAL - CHEMOTHERAPY.** *See* ANTIDEPRESSANTS.

**DEPRESSION, MENTAL - CONGRESSES.**
Anxiety, depression, and emotion. Oxford ; New York : Oxford University Press, 2000.
*TC RC531 .A559 2000*

**DEPRESSION, MENTAL - DIAGNOSIS.**
Mood disorders [videorecording]. Princeton, N.J. : Films for the Humanities & Sciences, 1998.
*TC RC537 .M6 1998*

**DEPRESSION, MENTAL, IN CHILDREN.** *See* DEPRESSION IN CHILDREN.

**DEPRESSION, MENTAL, IN WOMEN.** *See* DEPRESSION IN WOMEN.

**DEPRESSION, MENTAL - PATIENTS.** *See also* DEPRESSED PERSONS.
Mood disorders [videorecording]. Princeton, N.J. : Films for the Humanities & Sciences, 1998.
*TC RC537 .M6 1998*

**DEPRESSION, MENTAL - PERSONAL NARRATIVES.**
The Choice of a lifetime [videorecording]. Hohokus, NJ : New Day Films, c1996.
*TC RC569 .C45 1996*

**DEPRESSION, MENTAL - POPULAR WORKS.**
Irwin, Cait. Conquering the beast within. New York : Times Books, 1999.
*TC RC537 .I77 1999*

**DEPRESSION, MENTAL - PSYCHOLOGICAL ASPECTS.**
Newman, Stephanie. Self-silencing, depression, gender role, and gender role conflict in women and men. 1997.

*TC 085 N47*

**DEPRESSION, MENTAL - RELIGIOUS ASPECTS - CHRISTIANITY.**
Stone, Howard W. Depression and hope. Minneapolis : Fortress Press, c1998.
*TC BV4461 .S76 1998*

**DEPRESSION, MENTAL - SOCIAL ASPECTS.**
Lippert, Robin Alissa. Conflating the self with the body. 1999.
*TC 085 L655*

Newman, Stephanie. Self-silencing, depression, gender role, and gender role conflict in women and men. 1997.
*TC 085 N47*

**DEPRESSION, UNIPOLAR.** *See* **DEPRESSION, MENTAL.**

**DEPRESSIONS - 1929.**
Uys, Errol Lincoln. Riding the rails. New York : TV Books ; c1999.
*TC HC106.3 U97 1999*

**DEPRESSIONS - 1929 - FICTION.**
Curtis, Christopher Paul. Bud, not Buddy. New York : Delacorte Press, 1999.
*TC PZ7.C94137 Bu 1999*

Littlesugar, Amy. Tree of hope. New York : Philomel Books, 1999.
*TC PZ7.L7362 Tr 1999*

Recorvits, Helen. Goodbye, Walter Malinski. 1st ed. New York : Farrar, Straus and Giroux, c1999.
*TC PZ7.R24435 Go 1999*

**DEPRESSIONS - 1929 - UNITED STATES - POSTERS.**
The depression hits home [picture]. Amawalk, NY : Jackdaw Publications, c1997.
*TC TR820.5 .D4 1997*

**DEPRESSIVE DISORDER.** *See* **DEPRESSION, MENTAL.**

**DEPRESSIVE PSYCHOSES.** *See* **DEPRESSION, MENTAL.**

**DEPRIVATION, PATERNAL.** *See* **PATERNAL DEPRIVATION.**

**Derby, Lara.**
The salsa-riffic world of Spanish [videorecording]. [Arlington, Va.] : Cerebellum Corp., c1998.
*TC PC4112.7 .S25 1998*

**Derné, Steve, 1960-** Culture in action : family life, emotion, and male dominance in Banaras, India / Steve Derné. Albany : State University of New York Press, c1995. xiii, 232 p. ; 24 cm. Includes bibliographical references (p. 199-220) and index. ISBN 0-7914-2425-1 (alk. paper) ISBN 0-7914-2426-X (pbk. : alk. paper) DDC 306.8/0954
*1. Family - India. 2. Marriage - India. 3. Marriage - Religious aspects - Hinduism. I. Title.*
*TC HQ670 .D46 1995*

**Derricott, R.**
Citizenship for the 21st century. [Rev. ed.]. London : Kogan Page, 2000.
*TC LC1091 .C575 2000*

**DERRIDA, JACQUES.**
Forrester, John. The seductions of psychoanalysis. 1st pbk. ed. Cambridge ; New York : Cambridge University Press, 1991 (1992 printing)
*TC RC504 .F63 1991*

Trifonas, Peter Pericles, 1960- The ethics of writing. Lanham, Md. : Oxford : Rowman & Littlefield, c2000.
*TC LB14.7 .T75 2000*

**DeSalle, Rob.**
Epidemic!. New York : The New Press ; New York : Distributed by W.W. Norton, c1999.
*TC RA651 .E596 1999*

**DESCARTES, RENÉ, 1596-1650 - CONTRIBUTIONS IN PHILOSOPHY OF MIND.**
Ostenfeld, Erik Nis. Ancient Greek psychology and the modern mind-body debate. Aarhus, Denmark : Aarhus University Press, 1987.
*TC BF161 .O88 1987*

**DESCENT.** *See* **GENEALOGY.**

**DESCENT AND DISTRIBUTION.** *See* **INHERITANCE AND SUCCESSION.**

**DESCENTS.** *See* **INHERITANCE AND SUCCESSION.**

A description and investigation of strategies for teaching classroom music improvisation.
Bitz, Michael Eric. 1998.
*TC 06 no. 11012*

**DESCRIPTIVE SOCIOLOGY.** *See* **SOCIAL HISTORY.**

**DESEGREGATION IN EDUCATION.** *See* **SCHOOL INTEGRATION.**

**DESERTION AND NON-SUPPORT.** *See* **PARENT AND CHILD (LAW).**

**Desforges, Charles.**
Hughes, Martin, 1949 May 15- Numeracy and beyond. Buckingham [England] ; Philadelphia : Open University Press, 2000.
*TC QA135.5 .H844 2000*

**DESIGN.** *See* **DESIGNERS; LANDSCAPE DESIGN.**

**Design approaches and tools in education and training** / edited by Jan van den Akker ... [et al.] ; in collaboration with Interuniversitair Centrum voor Onderwijskundig Onderzoek. Dordrecht ; Boston : Kluwer Academic Publishers, c1999. x, 296 p. : ill. ; 25 cm. ISBN 0-7923-6139-3 (alk. paper) DDC 371.33/4
*1. Instructional systems - Design. 2. Computer-assisted instruction. I. Akker, J. J. H. van den, 1950- II. Interuniversitair Centrum voor Onderwijskundig Onderzoek.*
*TC LB1028.38 .D46 1999*

**DESIGN - AUSTRALIA - HISTORY - 19TH CENTURY.**
Bogle, Michael. Design in Australia, 1880-1970. Sydney : Craftsman House : G+B Arts International, c1998.
*TC NK1490.A1 B64 1998*

**DESIGN - AUSTRALIA - HITORY - 20TH CENTURY.**
Bogle, Michael. Design in Australia, 1880-1970. Sydney : Craftsman House : G+B Arts International, c1998.
*TC NK1490.A1 B64 1998*

**Design culture :** an anthology of writing from the AIGA journal of graphic design / edited by Steven Heller and Marie Finamore. New York : Allworth Press : American Institute of Graphic Arts, c1997. xv, 303 p. ; 26 cm. Anthology of writing from the AIGA journal of graphic design. Includes bibliographical references and index. ISBN 1-88055-971-4
*1. AIGA journal of graphic design. 2. Graphic arts - United States. I. Heller, Steven. II. Finamore, Marie. III. American Institute of Graphic Arts. IV. Title: AIGA journal of graphic design. V. Title: Anthology of writing from the AIGA journal of graphic design*
*TC NC998.5.A1 D46 1997*

**Design dialogues** / [interviews conducted and edited by] Steven Heller and Elinor Pettit. New York : Allworth Press, c1998. ix, 261 p. ; ill. ; 25 cm. Includes index. ISBN 1-58115-007-5 DDC 745.4
*1. Designers - Interviews. 2. Design - History - 20th century. 3. Graphic arts - History - 20th century. I. Heller, Steven. II. Pettit, Elinor.*
*TC NK1390 .D473 1998*

**Design for a life.**
Bateson, P. P. G. (Paul Patrick Gordon), 1938- New York ; London : Simon & Schuster c2000.
*TC BF341 .B37 2000*

**DESIGN - HISTORY - 20TH CENTURY.**
Design dialogues. New York : Allworth Press, c1998.
*TC NK1390 .D473 1998*

**Design in Australia, 1880-1970.**
Bogle, Michael. Sydney : Craftsman House : G+B Arts International, c1998.
*TC NK1490.A1 B64 1998*

**DESIGN, INDUSTRIAL.** *See* **INDUSTRIAL DESIGNERS.**

**Design literacy.**
Heller, Steven. New York : Allworth Press, c1997.
*TC NC998 .H45 1997*

**DESIGN PERCEPTION.** *See* **PATTERN PERCEPTION.**

**DESIGN - STUDY AND TEACHING.**
The education of a graphic designer. New York : Allworth Press [in association with the] School of Visual Arts, c1998
*TC NC590 .E38 1998*

**DESIGN - STUDY AND TEACHING (ELEMENTARY) - GREAT BRITAIN.**
Bold, Christine. Progression in primary design and technology. London : David Fulton, 1999.
*TC LB1541 .B65 1999*

**DESIGNED GENETIC CHANGE.** *See* **GENETIC ENGINEERING.**

**DESIGNERS.** *See* **INDUSTRIAL DESIGNERS.**

**DESIGNERS - INTERVIEWS.**
Design dialogues. New York : Allworth Press, c1998.
*TC NK1390 .D473 1998*

**Designing a world wide web professional development resources for integration of music into elementary classrooms.**
Nord, Michael B. Music in the classroom (MITC). 1998.
*TC 06 no. 10974*

**Designing and teaching an on-line course.**
Schweizer, Heidi. Boston : Allyn & Bacon, c1999.
*TC LB1028.3 .S377 1999*

**Designing interactive worlds with words.**
Kaufer, David S. Mahwah, N.J. : Lawrence Erlbaum Associates, 2000.
*TC PE1404 .K38 2000*

**Designing learning environments for developing understanding of geometry and space** / edited by Richard Lehrer, Daniel Chazan. Mahwah, N.J. : Lawrence Erlbaum, c1998. xiii, 504 p : ill. ; 24 cm. (Studies in mathematical thinking and learning) Includes bibliographical references and indexes. ISBN 0-8058-1948-7 (alk. paper) ISBN 0-8058-1949-5 (pbk. : alk. paper) DDC 516/.0071
*1. Geometry - Study and teaching. I. Lehrer, Richard. II. Chazan, Daniel. III. Series.*
*TC QA461 .L45 1998*

**Designing mathematics or science curriculum programs :** a guide for using mathematics and science education standards / Committee on Science Education K-12 and the Mathematical Sciences Education Board, Center for Science, Mathematics, and Engineering Education, National Research Council Washington, D.C. : National Academy Press, 1999. xii, 56 p. : ill. ; 28 cm. Includes bibliographical references (p. 53-56). National Science Foundation. ESI-9355774 ISBN 0-309-06527-5
*1. Mathematics - Study and teaching - United States. 2. Science - Study and teaching - United States. 3. Education - Standards - United States. 4. Curriculum planning - United States. I. National Research Council (U.S.). Committee on Science Education K-12. II. National Research Council (U.S.). Mathematical Sciences Education Board. III. Title.*
*TC Q183.3.A1 D46 1999*

**Designing performance appraisal systems.**
Mohrman, Allan M. 1st ed. San Francisco : Jossey-Bass Publishers, 1989.
*TC HF5549.5.P35 M64 1989*

**Designing preschool interventions.**
Barnett, David W., 1946- New York : Guilford Press, 1999.
*TC LC4801 .B36 1999*

**Designing project-based science.**
Polman, Joseph L., 1965- New York ; London : Teachers College Press, c2000.
*TC Q181 .P4694 2000*

**Designing qualitative research.**
Marshall, Catherine. 3rd ed. Thousand Oaks, Calif. : Sage Publications, c1999.
*TC H62 .M277 1999*

**Designing successful professional meetings and conferences in education :** planning, implementing, and evaluating / Susan Mundry ... [et al.] ; National Institute for Science Education. Thousand Oaks, Calif. : Corwin Press, c2000. xv, 88 p. ; 27 cm. Includes bibliographical references (p. 83-84) and index. ISBN 0-7619-7632-9 (cloth : alk. paper) ISBN 0-7619-7633-7 (pbk. alk. paper) DDC 370/.68
*1. Forums (Discussion and debate) - Handbooks, manuals, etc. 2. Education - Congresses - Handbooks, manuals, etc. I. Mundry, Susan. II. National Institute for Science Education (U.S.).*
*TC LC6519 .D48 2000*

**Designing surveys that work!.**
Thomas, Susan J. Thousand Oaks, Calif. : Corwin Press, c1999.
*TC H62 .T447 1999*

**Designing women.**
Adams, Annmarie. Toronto : University of Toronto Press, c2000.
*TC NA1997 A32 2000*

DESIRABILITY, SOCIAL. *See* SOCIAL DESIRABILITY.

DESIRE IN LITERATURE.
Keroes, Jo. Tales out of school. Carbondale : Southern Illinois University Press, c1999.
*TC PS374.T43 K47 1999*

Desiring whiteness.
Seshadri-Crooks, Kalpana. London ; New York : Routledge, 2000.
*TC BF175.4.R34 S47 2000*

Desler, Mary K.
Barr, Margaret J. The handbook of student affairs administration. 2nd ed. San Francisco : Jossey-Bass, c2000.
*TC LB2342.92 .B37 2000*

Deslippe, Dennis A. (Dennis Arthur), 1961- Rights, not roses : unions and the rise of working-class feminism, 1945-80 / Dennis A. Deslippe. Urbana : University of Illinois Press, c2000. x, 259 p. : ill., ports., charts ; 24 cm. (The working class in American history) Includes bibliographical references (p. [197]-252) and index. CONTENTS: Beyond the doldrums : postwar organized labor and "women's issues," -- Prospects for equality : union women, equal pay legislation, and national politics, 1945-63 -- The roots of discontent : gender relations in the United Packinghouse Workers, 1945-63 -- Accounting for equality : gender relations in the International Union of Electrical Workers, 1945-63 -- Organized labor, national politics, and gender equality, 1964-74 -- Rank-and-file militancy in the service of anti-equality : Title VII and the United Packinghouse Workers, 1964-75 -- A genuine good faith effort : women and equal employment opportunity in the International Union of Electrical Workers, 1964-80 -- Conclusion : from equality to equity : working-class feminists in the AFL-CIO, 1975-80. ISBN 0-252-02519-9 (acid-free paper) ISBN 0-252-06834-3 (pbk. : acid-free paper)
*1. Women labor union members - United States. 2. Equal pay for equal work - United States. 3. Sex discrimination against women - United States. 4. Sex discrimination in employment - United States. I. Title. II. Title: Unions and the rise of working-class feminism 1945-80 III. Series.*
*TC HD6079.2.U5 D47 2000*

Desmarais, Jane Haville. The Beardsley industry : the critical reception in England and France, 1893-1914 / Jane Haville Desmarais. Aldershot, Hants, England ; Brookfield, Vt. : Ashgate, c1998. xviii, 166 p. : ill. ; 25 cm. Includes bibliographical references (p. [152]-159) and index. ISBN 1-84014-205-7 (hb : alk. paper) DDC 741.6/092
*1. Beardsley, Aubrey, - 1872-1898 - Criticism and interpretation. 2. Beardsley, Aubrey, - 1872-1898 - Appreciation - England. 3. Beardsley, Aubrey, - 1872-1898 - Appreciation - France. 4. Art criticism - England - History - 19th century. 5. Art criticism - England - History - 20th century. 6. Art criticism - France - History - 19th century. 7. Art criticism - France - History - 20th century. I. Title.*
*TC NC242.B3 D475 1998*

DESPAIR.
Handbook of hope. San Diego, Calif. : Academic, 2000.
*TC BF575.H56 H36 2000*

DeStefano, Lizanne.
Evaluation as a democratic process. San Francisco, CA : Jossey-Bass, c2000.
*TC LB2806 .E79 2000*

DESTITUTION. *See* POVERTY.

DESTRUCTION OF THE JEWS (1939-1945). *See* HOLOCAUST, JEWISH (1939-1945).

DETECTIVE AND MYSTERY STORIES.
White, Gillian, 1945- The plague stone. Large print ed. Thorndike, Me., USA : G.K. Hall ; Bath, Avon, England : Chivers Press, 1996, c1990.
*TC PR6073.H4925 P58 1996*

DETECTIVES. *See* CRIMINAL INVESTIGATION.

Detels, Claire Janice, 1953- Soft boundaries : re-visioning the arts and aesthetics in American education / Claire Detels. Westport, Conn. : Bergin & Garvey, 1999. xi, 181 p. ; 24 cm. Includes bibliographical references and index. ISBN 0-89789-666-1 (alk. paper) DDC 700/.71
*1. Arts - Study and teaching - United States. 2. Aesthetics - Study and teaching - United States. 3. Education - United States - Curricula. I. Title.*
*TC LB1591.5.U6 D48 1999*

DETENTION CAMPS. *See* CONCENTRATION CAMPS.

DETENTION OF PERSONS. *See* CONCENTRATION CAMPS.

DETROIT (MICH.) - RACE RELATIONS.
Hartigan, John, 1964- Racial situations. Princeton, N.J. : Princeton University Press, c1999.
*TC F574.D49 A1 1999*

Deubel, Robert.
Norman Rockwell's world -- an American dream [videorecording]. [Chicago, Ill] : Home Vision, 1987, c1972.
*TC ND237.R68 N6 1987*

Deuchar, M. (Margaret) Bilingual acquisition : theoretical implications of a case study / Margaret Deuchar and Suzanne Quay. Oxford ; New York : Oxford University Press, 2000. viii, 163 p. ; 24 cm. Includes bibliographical references. ISBN 0-19-823685-9 DDC 401/.93
*1. Language acquisition - Case studies. 2. Bilingualism in children - Case studies. I. Quay, Suzanne. II. Title.*
*TC P118 .D439 2000*

Deuschle, C. (Constance) Stop the bus : a handbook for assessing critical issues with students / C. Deuschle, C. Burreson, E. Bramlett-Jackson. Lanham, Md. : University Press of America, c2000. 122 p. : ill. ; 23 cm. Includes bibliographical references (p. 111-113) and index. ISBN 0-7618-1600-3 (pbk. : alk. paper)
*1. Educational counseling - United States - Handbooks, manuals, etc. 2. Student counselors - United States - Handbooks, manuals, etc. I. Burreson, C. (Cynthia) II. Bramlett-Jackson, E. (Elizabeth) III. Title. IV. Title: Handbook for assessing critical issues with students*
*TC LB1027.5 .D4567 2000*

Deutsch, Helen, 1961-.
Defects. Ann Arbor : University of Michigan Press, c2000.
*TC HV1568.25.G7 D44 1999*

Deutsche Kommission für Geistige Zusammenarbeit.
Hochschule und Ausland. Berlin : Kulturpolitische Gesellschaft, 1923-1937.

Deutscher Akademischer Austauschdienst.
Hochschule und Ausland. Berlin : Kulturpolitische Gesellschaft, 1923-1937.

DeVault, Marjorie L., 1950- Liberating method : feminism and social research / Marjorie L. DeVault. Philadelphia : Temple University Press, 1999. x, 275 p. ; 24 cm. Includes bibliographical references (p. 247-267) and index. ISBN 1-56639-697-2 (cloth : alk. paper) ISBN 1-56639-698-0 (pbk. : alk. paper) DDC 305.4/01
*1. Feminism - Research - Methodology. 2. Social sciences - Research - Methodology. 3. Feminist theory. 4. Interdisciplinary research. I. Title.*
*TC HQ1180 .D48 1999*

Developing adult learners.
Taylor, Kathleen, 1943- 1st ed. San Francisco : Jossey-Bass, c2000.
*TC LC5225.L42 T39 2000*

Developing an information literacy program K-12 : a how-to-do-it manual and CD-ROM package / developed by the Iowa City Community School District and edited by Mary Jo Langhorne. New York : Neal-Schuman, c1998. xii, 294 p. : ill. ; 28 cm. + 1 computer disc (4 3/4 in.). (How-to-do-it manuals for librarians ; no. 85) System requirements for accompanying computer disc: IBM-compatible and Macintosh formats, using Microsoft Word 6.0.1 for the Mac and Microsoft Word 7.0 for Windows. Includes bibliographical references (p. 277-279) and index. ISBN 1-55570-332-1 (pbk.) DDC 025.5/6
*1. Library orientation for school children - United States. 2. Library orientation for high school students - United States. 3. Information retrieval - Study and teaching (Elementary) - United States. 4. Information retrieval - Study and teaching (Secondary) - United States. I. Langhorne, Mary Jo. II. Iowa City Community School District (Iowa City, Iowa) III. Series: How-to-do-it manuals for libraries ; no. 85.*
*TC Z711.2 .D49 1998*

DEVELOPING COUNTRIES - ECONOMIC INTEGRATION.
Ripton, John R. Export agriculture and social crisis. 1997.
*TC 085 R48*

DEVELOPING COUNTRIES - POPULATION - CONGRESSES.
Conference on Population and Economic Change in Less Developed Countries (1976 : Philadelphia, Pa.) Population and economic change in developing countries. Chicago : University of Chicago Press, 1980.
*TC HB849 .C59 1976*

Developing creative talent in art.
Khatena, Joe. Stamford, Conn. : Ablex Publ., c1999.
*TC NX164.C47 K53 1999*

Developing emotional intelligence.
Bodine, Richard J. Champaign, Ill : Research Press, c1999.
*TC BF561 .B6 1999*

Developing health promotion programs.
Anspaugh, David J. Boston ; London : McGraw-Hill, c2000.
*TC RA427.8 .A57 2000*

Developing network organizations.
Chisholm, Rupert F. Reading, Mass. : Addison-Wesley, c1998.
*TC HD69.S8 C45 1998*

Developing numerical power.
Future basics. Golden, Colo. : National Council of Supervisors of Mathematics, c1998.
*TC QA141 .C43 1998*

Developing talent across the lifespan / edited by Cornelis F. M. van Lieshout, Peter G. Heymans. Hove [U.K.] : Psychology Press ; Philadelphia : Taylor & Francis, 2000. xviii, 333 p. : ill. ; 24 cm. Includes bibliographical references and index. ISBN 0-86377-556-X DDC 155
*1. Developmental psychology. I. Heymans, P. G. II. Lieshout, C. F. M. van.*
*TC BF713 .D48 2000*

Developing teacher education
Tickle, Les. Teacher induction. Buckingham [England] ; Philadelphia : Open University Press, 2000.
*TC LB1729 .T53 2000*

Development and the arts : critical perspectives / edited by Margery B. Franklin, Bernard Kaplan. Hillsdale, N.J. : L. Erlbaum Associates, 1994. xiv, 257 p. : ill. ; 24 cm. Includes bibliographical references and indexes. ISBN 0-8058-0487-0 (acid-free paper) DDC 701/.15
*1. Artists - Psychology. 2. Aesthetics. I. Franklin, Margery B. II. Kaplan, Bernard.*
*TC N71 .D495 1994*

DEVELOPMENT AND WOMEN. *See* WOMEN IN DEVELOPMENT.

DEVELOPMENT (BIOLOGY). *See* DEVELOPMENTAL BIOLOGY.

DEVELOPMENT, CAREER. *See* CAREER DEVELOPMENT.

DEVELOPMENT, CHILD. *See* CHILD DEVELOPMENT.

Development communication in action.
Moemeka, Andrew A. (Andrew Azukaego) Lanham, Md. : University Press of America, c2000.
*TC HD76 .M644 2000*

DEVELOPMENT, ECONOMIC. *See* ECONOMIC DEVELOPMENT.

DEVELOPMENT ECONOMICS. *See* ECONOMIC DEVELOPMENT.

The development of a common framework scale of language proficiency.
North, Brian, 1950- New York : P. Lang, c2000.
*TC P53.4 .N67 2000*

Development of a manual for practitioners creating web-based training programs.
Driscoll, Margaret M. The application of adult education principles in the development of a manual for practitioners creating web-based training programs. 1999.
*TC 06 no. 11106*

The development of a van Hiele-based summer geometry program and its impact on student van Hiele level and achievement in high school geometry.
Baynes, Joyce Frisby. 1998.
*TC 06 no. 10915*

The development of binding / Stephen Crain and Kenneth Wexler, guest editors. Hillsdale, N.J. : Lawrence Erlbaum , 1992. p. [255]-413 : ill. ; 22 cm. Language acquisition : a journal of developmental linguistics, v.2 no. 4, 1992. Includes bibliographical references. ISSN 1048-9223
*1. Government-binding theory (Linguistics) 2. Generative grammar. I. Crain, Stephen. II. Wexler, Kenneth. III. Title.*
*TC P158.2 .D5 1992*

The development of cognitive leadership frames among African American female college presidents.
Tobe, Dorothy Echols. 1999.
*TC 06 no. 11187*

**Development of education in India.**
Agrawal, S. P., 1929- New Delhi : Concept Pub. Co.,
1997.
*TC LA1150 .A39 1997*

**Development of mental representation** : theories and
applications / edited by Irving E. Sigel. Mahwah, NJ :
L. Erlbaum Associates, c1999. xiii, 489 p. : ill. ; 23 cm.
Includes bibliographical references and indexes. ISBN
0-8058-2228-3 (alk. paper) DDC 153.2
*1. Mental representation in children. 2. Connectionism. 3.
Knowledge, Theory of. I. Sigel, Irving E.*
*TC BF723.M43 T47 1999*

**The development of romantic relationships in
adolescence** / edited by Wyndol Furman, B. Bradford
Brown, Candice Feiring. Cambridge, U.K. ; New
York : Cambridge University Press. xvii, 443 p. ;
24 cm. (Cambridge studies in social and emotional
development) Includes indexes. Includes bibliographical
references. ISBN 0-521-59156-2 (hardcover) DDC 155.5/18
*1. Love in adolescence. I. Furman, Wyndol. II. Brown, B.
Bradford (Benson Bradford), 1949- III. Feiring, Candice. IV.
Series.*
*TC BF724.3.L68 D48 1999*

**DEVELOPMENT PROGRAMS, COLLEGE
STUDENT.** *See* **COLLEGE STUDENT
DEVELOPMENT PROGRAMS.**

**DEVELOPMENT PROJECTS, ECONOMIC.** *See*
**ECONOMIC DEVELOPMENT PROJECTS.**

**DEVELOPMENT (PSYCHOLOGY).** *See*
**DEVELOPMENTAL PSYCHOLOGY.**

**DEVELOPMENT, RURAL.** *See* **RURAL
DEVELOPMENT.**

**DEVELOPMENT, SUSTAINABLE.** *See*
**SUSTAINABLE DEVELOPMENT.**

**Developmental and clinical perspectives of the
Kestenberg Movement Profile.**
The meaning of movement. Amsterdam : Gordon and
Breach, c1999.
*TC RC473.K47 M4 1999*

**Developmental assets.**
Scales, Peter, 1949- Minneapolis : Search Institute,
c1999.
*TC BF724 .S327 1999*

**DEVELOPMENTAL BIOLOGY.** *See* **AGING;
CHILD DEVELOPMENT; GROWTH.**

**DEVELOPMENTAL BIOLOGY - CONGRESSES.**
Developmental science and the holistic approach.
Mahwah, N.J. ; London : Lawrence Erlbaum
Associates, 2000.
*TC BF712.5 .D485 2000*

**Developmental clinical psychology and psychiatry**
(v. 41.) Luthar, Suniya S. Poverty and children's
adjustment. Thousand Oaks, Calif. : Sage
Publications, c1999.
*TC HV741 .L88 1999*

(v. 42) Windle, Michael T. Alcohol use among
adolescents. Thousand Oaks : Sage Publications,
c1999.
*TC RJ506.A4 W557 1999*

**Developmental cognitive neuropsychology.**
Temple, Christine. Hove, East Sussex, UK :
Psychology Press, c1997.
*TC RC553.C64 T46 1997*

**Developmental cognitive styles.**
Hashway, Robert M. San Francisco : Austin &
Winfield Publishers, 1998.
*TC LB1060 .H373 1998*

**DEVELOPMENTAL DISABILITIES.** *See*
**AUTISM; CEREBRAL PALSY;
DEVELOPMENTALLY DISABLED;
EPILEPSY; MENTAL RETARDATION.**

**DEVELOPMENTAL DISABILITIES.**
Psychiatric and behavioural disorders in
developmental disabilities and mental retardation.
Cambridge, UK ; New York, NY, USA : Cambridge
University Press, 1999.
*TC RC451.4.M47 P77 1999*

**DEVELOPMENTAL DISABILITIES -
PREVENTION & CONTROL.**
Handbook of infant mental health. New York : Wiley,
c2000.
*TC RJ502.5 .H362 2000*

**Developmental disability and behaviour** / edited by
Christopher Gillberg and Gregory O'Brien. London,
England : Mac Keith Press, 2000. x, 189 p. : ill. ; 25 cm.
(Clinics in developmental medicine ; no. 149) Includes
bibliographical references and index. ISBN 1-89868-318-2

*1. Developmentally disabled children. 2. Behavior disorders in
children. I. Gillberg, Christopher, 1950- II. O'Brien, Gregory.
III. Series.*
*TC RJ506.D47 D48 2000*

**DEVELOPMENTAL DYSLEXIA.** *See* **DYSLEXIA.**

**DEVELOPMENTAL LINGUISTICS.** *See*
**LANGUAGE ACQUISITION.**

**DEVELOPMENTAL NEUROBIOLOGY.** *See*
**DEVELOPMENTAL NEUROPHYSIOLOGY.**

**DEVELOPMENTAL NEUROPHYSIOLOGY -
CONGRESSES.**
Developmental science and the holistic approach.
Mahwah, N.J. : London : Lawrence Erlbaum
Associates, 2000.
*TC BF712.5 .D485 2000*

**Developmental perspectives on trauma** : theory,
research, and intervention / edited by Dante
Cicchetti & Sheree L. Toth. Rochester, N.Y., USA :
University of Rochester Press, 1997. xvii, 613 p. : ill. ;
24 cm. (Rochester Symposium on Developmental
Psychopathology, 1056-6511 ; v. 8) Includes bibliographical
references and indexes. ISBN 1-87882-297-7 (acid-free paper)
DDC 618.92/89
*1. Child psychopathology - Congresses. 2. Child abuse -
Congresses. 3. Child development - Congresses. 4. Stress,
Psychological - in infancy & childhood - congresses. 5. Child
Development - congresses. 6. Wounds and Injuries -
psychology - congresses. 7. Child Abuse - congresses. 8. Life
Change Events - congresses. 9. Defense Mechanisms - in
infancy & childhood - congresses. I. Cicchetti, Dante. II. Toth,
Sheree L. III. Series: Rochester Symposium on Developmental
Psychopathology (Series) ; v. 8.*
*TC RJ499 .D4825 1997*

**The developmental process of positive attitudes and
mutual respect** : a multicultural approach to
advocating school safety / edited by Rose Duhon-
Sells, Sandra M. Cooley, and Gwendolyn Duhon.
Lewiston, N.Y. : E. Mellen Press, c1999. 250 p. ; 24 cm.
(Studies in world peace ; v. 11) ISBN 0-7734-7886-8 (hard)
DDC 371.2
*1. School improvement programs - United States. 2.
Educational leadership - United States. 3. Multicultural
education - United States. 4. Home and school - United States.
5. Self-esteem - Study and teaching - United States. 6. Peace -
Study and teaching - United States. I. Duhon-Sells, Rose M. II.
Cooley, Sandra M. III. Duhon, Gwendolyn M. IV. Series.*
*TC LB2822.82 .D49 1999*

**DEVELOPMENTAL PSYCHOBIOLOGY.** *See also*
**CHILD DEVELOPMENT;
DEVELOPMENTAL PSYCHOLOGY.**
Beyond heredity and environment. Boulder :
Westview Press, 1995.
*TC BF341 .B48 1995*

Current issues in developmental psychology.
Dordrecht : Boston ; London : Kluwer Academic
Publishers, c1999.
*TC RJ134 .C868 1999*

**DEVELOPMENTAL PSYCHOLINGUISTICS.** *See*
**LANGUAGE ACQUISITION.**

**DEVELOPMENTAL PSYCHOLOGY.** *See also*
**AGING - PSYCHOLOGICAL ASPECTS;
CHILD PSYCHOLOGY; LIFE CHANGE
EVENTS; MATURATION (PSYCHOLOGY).**
Andersen, Christopher Lawrence. A microgenetic
study of science reasoning in social context. 1998.
*TC 085 An2305*

Baxter Magolda, Marcia B., 1951- Creating contexts
for learning and self-authorship. 1st ed. Nashville
[Tenn.] : Vanderbilt University Press, 1999.
*TC LB1025.3 .B39 1999*

Crain, William C., 1943- Theories of development.
4th ed. Uppder Saddle River, N.J. : Prentice Hall,
c2000.
*TC BF713 .C72 2000*

Developing talent across the lifespan. Hove [U.K.] :
Psychology Press ; Philadelphia : Taylor & Francis,
2000.
*TC BF713 .D48 2000*

Developmental psychology. Philadelphia, PA :
Psychology Press, 1999.
*TC BF713 .D4646 1999*

The Developmental social psychology of gender.
Mahwah, N.J. : Lawrence Erlbaum, c2000.
*TC HQ1075 .D47 2000*

Felton, Mark Kenji. Metacognitive reflection and
strategy development in argumentive discourse. 1999.

*TC 085 F34*
Frontiers of developmental psychopathology. New
York : Oxford University Press, 1996.
*TC RC454.4 .F76 1996*

Learning activity and development. Aarhus : Aarhus
Universit #, 1999.
*TC LB1060 .L43 1999*

Oyama, Susan. Evolution's eye. Durham, NC : Duke
University Press, 2000.
*TC BF713 .O93 2000*

Paris, Joel, 1940- Myths of childhood. Philadelphia,
PA : Brunner/Mazel, c2000.
*TC BF713 .P37 2000*

Personality development. London : New York :
Routledge, 1999.
*TC BF175.45 .P47 1999*

Settersten, Richard A. Lives in time and place.
Amityville, N.Y. : Baywood Pub., c1999.
*TC BF713 .S48 1999*

Stevens, Anthony. On Jung. 2nd ed. Princeton, N.J. :
Princeton University Press, 1999.
*TC BF173 .S828 1999*

Thomas, R. Murray (Robert Murray), 1921- Human
development theories. Thousand Oaks : Sage
Publications, c1999.
*TC HQ783 .T57 1999*

Toward a feminist developmental psychology. New
York : Routledge, 2000.
*TC BF713 .T66 2000*

Variability in the social construction of the child. San
Francisco : Jossey-Bass, 2000.
*TC BF723.S62 .V37 2000*

Wachs, Theodore D., 1941- Necessary but not
sufficient. 1st ed. Washington, DC : American
Psychological Association, c2000.
*TC BF713 .W33 2000*

Waddell, Margot, 1946- Inside lives. New York :
Routledge, 1998.
*TC BF175.45 .W33 1998*

**Developmental psychology** : achievements and
prospects / edited by Mark Bennett. Philadelphia, PA :
Psychology Press, 1999. xvi, 338 p. : ill. : 23 cm. Includes
bibliographical references and indexes. ISBN 0-86377-577-2
(case : alk. paper) ISBN 0-86377-578-0 (pbk. : alk. paper)
DDC 155
*1. Developmental psychology. I. Bennett, Mark, 1956-*
*TC BF713 .D4646 1999*

**Developmental psychology and psychiatry;**
(v.10) Wolfe, David A. Child abuse. 2nd ed.
Thousands Oaks, Calif. : Sage Publications, 1999.
*TC HV6626.5 .W58 1999*

**DEVELOPMENTAL PSYCHOLOGY -
CONGRESSES.**
Developmental science and the holistic approach.
Mahwah, N.J. : London : Lawrence Erlbaum
Associates, 2000.
*TC BF712.5 .D485 2000*

**DEVELOPMENTAL PSYCHOLOGY - CROSS-
CULTURAL STUDIES.**
Valsiner, Jaan. Culture and human development.
London ; Thousand Oaks, Calif. : Sage, 2000.
*TC BF713 .V35 2000*

**DEVELOPMENTAL PSYCHOLOGY - HISTORY.**
A history of geropsychology in autobiography. 1st ed.
Washington, DC : London : American Psychological
Association, c2000.
*TC BF724.8 .H57 2000*

**The developmental psychology of personal
relationships.**
Mills, Rosemary S.L. Chichester ; New York : John
Wiley, c2000.
*TC BF723.I646 M55 2000*

**DEVELOPMENTAL PSYCHOLOGY -
PROBLEMS, EXERCISES, ETC.**
Straub, Richard O. (Richard Otto) Study guide. New
York : Worth Publishers, 1998.
*TC BF713 .B463 1998 Guide*

Straub, Richard O. (Richard Otto) Study guide. New
York : Worth Publishers, 1998.
*TC BF713 .B463 1998 Guide*

Straub, Richard O. (Richard Otto) Study guide. New
York : Worth Publishers, 1998.
*TC BF713 .B463 1998 guide*

## DEVELOPMENTAL PSYCHOLOGY - RESEARCH.

Embiricos, Anne-Marie T. The effects of content knowledge and strategies on memory development among 4- and 6-year-old children. 1998.
*TC 085 Em22*

Embiricos, Anne-Marie T. The effects of content knowledge and strategies on memory development among 4- and 6-year-old children. 1998.
*TC 085 Em22*

**Developmental psychopathology :** Epidemiology, diagnostics and treatment / edited by Cecilia Ahmoi Essau and Franz Petermann. Australia : Harwood Academic Publishers, c1997. xvii, 478 p. : ill. ; 24 cm. Includes bibliographical references and indexes. ISBN 90-5702-190-0 DDC 618.92/89
*1. Child psychopathology. 2. Child development. I. Essau, Cecilia Ahmoi. II. Petermann, Franz.*
*TC RJ499 .D48 1997*

## DEVELOPMENTAL READING.

O'Donnell, Michael P. Becoming a reader. 2nd ed. Boston : Allyn and Bacon, c1999.
*TC LB1050.53 .O35 1999*

Rasinski, Timothy V. Effective reading strategies. 2nd ed. Upper Saddle River, N.J. : Merrill, c2000.
*TC LB1050.5 .R33 2000*

**Developmental science and the holistic approach /** edited by Lars R. Bergman ... [et al.]. Mahwah, N.J. ; London : Lawrence Erlbaum Associates, 2000. x, 484 p. : ill. ; 24 cm. Includes bibliographical references and indexes. ISBN 0-8058-3374-9 (cloth : alk. paper) DDC 155
*1. Developmental psychology - Congresses. 2. Developmental biology - Congresses. 3. Developmental neurophysiology - Congresses. I. Bergman, Lars R.*
*TC BF712.5 .D485 2000*

**The Developmental social psychology of gender /** edited by Thomas Eckes, Hanns M. Trautner. Mahwah, N.J. : Lawrence Erlbaum, c2000. xiv, 470 p. ; 23 cm. Includes bibliographical references and indexes. ISBN 0-8058-3189-4 (cloth : alk. paper) ISBN 0-8058-3190-8 (pbk. : alk. paper) DDC 305.3
*1. Sex role. 2. Sex differences (Psychology) 3. Social psychology. 4. Developmental psychology. I. Eckes, Thomas. II. Trautner, Hanns Martin, 1943-*
*TC HQ1075 .D47 2000*

**Developmentally appropriate practice.**
Developmentally appropriate practice in early childhood programs. Rev. ed. Washington, D.C. : National Association for the Education of Young Children, 1997.
*TC LB1139.25 .D48 1997*

**Developmentally appropriate practice in early childhood programs /** Sue Bredekamp and Carol Copple, editors. Rev. ed. Washington, D.C. : National Association for the Education of Young Children, 1997. ix, 185 p. : ill. ; 28 cm. (NAEYC #234) Spine title: Developmentally appropriate practice. Rev. ed. of: Developmentally appropriate practice in early childhood programs serving children from birth through age 8. Includes bibliographical references and index. ISBN 0-935989-79-X
*1. Early childhood education - United States. 2. Child development - United States. I. Bredekamp, Sue. II. Copple, Carol. III. National Association for the Education of Young Children. IV. Title: Developmentally appropriate practice*
*TC LB1139.25 .D48 1997*

**DEVELOPMENTALLY DISABLED.** See DYSLEXICS; MENTALLY HANDICAPPED.

## DEVELOPMENTALLY DISABLED CHILDREN.
See also AUTISTIC CHILDREN; DYSLEXIC CHILDREN; MENTALLY ILL CHILDREN.
Developmental disability and behaviour. London, England : Mac Keith Press, 2000.
*TC RJ506.D47 D48 2000*

## DEVELOPMENTALLY DISABLED CHILDREN - GREAT BRITAIN - BIOGRAPHY.

Gregory, Jane, 1960- Bringing up a challenging child at home. London ; Philadelphia : Jessica Kingsley Publishers, 2000.
*TC HQ759.913 .G74 2000*

## DEVELOPMENTALLY DISABLED CHILDREN - IDENTIFICATION.

Interdisciplinary clinical assessment of young children with developmental disabilities. Baltimore : Paul H. Brookes Pub. Co., c2000.
*TC HV891 .I58 2000*

## DEVELOPMENTALLY DISABLED CHILDREN - NEW YORK (STATE) - NEW YORK - CASE STUDIES.

Flynn, Bernadette Marie. The teacher-child

relationship, temperament, and coping in children with developmental disabilities. 2000.
*TC 06 no. 11267*

## DEVELOPMENTALLY DISABLED CHILDREN - SERVICES FOR.

Interdisciplinary clinical assessment of young children with developmental disabilities. Baltimore : Paul H. Brookes Pub. Co., c2000.
*TC HV891 .I58 2000*

## DEVELOPMENTALLY DISABLED - LEGAL STATUS, LAWS, ETC. - UNITED STATES.

Field, Martha A. Equal treatment for people with mental retardation. Cambridge, Mass. ; London : Harvard University Press, 1999.
*TC KF480 .F54 1999*

**Developments in elementary mathematics teaching.**
Sawyer, Ann Elisabeth. Portsmouth, NH : Heinemann, c1995.
*TC QA135.5 .S278 1995*

**DEVIANT BEHAVIOR.** *See also* **CRIMINAL BEHAVIOR.**
Shoham, S. Giora, 1929- Personality and deviance. Westport, Conn. : Praeger, 2000.
*TC BF698 .S5186 2000*

**The devil knows Latin.**
Kopff, E. Christian. Wilmington, Del. : ISI Books, 1999.
*TC PA78.U6 K67 1999*

**Devlin, Keith J.** The math gene : how mathematical thinking evolved and why numbers are like gossip / Keith Devlin. [New York] : Basic Books, 2000. xvii, 328 p. : ill. ; 25 cm. Math gene. "First published in Great Britain in 2000 by Weidenfeld & Nicolson"--t.p. verso. Includes bibliographical references (p. [309]-315) and index. ISBN 0-465-01618-9
*1. Mathematical ability. 2. Mathematics - Philosophy. 3. Language and languages - Philosophy. I. Title. II. Title: Math gene III. Title: How mathematical thinking evolved and why numbers are like gossip*
*TC QA141 .D48 2000*

## DEVRIES, DIANE.

Frank, Gelya, 1948- Venus on wheels. Berkeley, Calif. : University of California Press, c2000.
*TC HV3021.W66 F73 2000*

**Dewey and European education :** general problems and case studies / edited by Jürgen Oelkers and Heinz Rhyn. Dordrecht : Kluwer Academic Publishers, c2000. 221 p. ; 25 cm. Includes bibliographical references. ISBN 0-7923-6389-2 (alk. paper) DDC 370/.1
*1. Dewey, John, - 1859-1952. 2. Education - Philosophy. 3. Education - Europe. I. Oelkers, Jürgen, 1947- II. Rhyn, Heinz, 1960-*
*TC LB875.D5 D47 2000*

**Dewey, Ariane.**
Ginsburg, Mirra. Mushroom in the rain. New York : Macmillan/McGraw-Hill, 1974.
*TC PZ10.3 .G455Mu 1974*

**Dewey, Ariane, ill.**
Sierra, Judy. Antarctic antics. 1st ed. San Diego : Harcourt Brace & Co., c1998.
*TC PS3569.I39 A53 1998*

**Dewey, John, 1859-1952.** The correspondence of John Dewey. [computer file] / general editor, Larry A. Hackman ; editors, Barbara Levine, Anne Sharpe, Harriet Furst Simon. Windows version. Charlottesville, VA : InteLex Corp., 1999- Computer data and program. computer optical discs : col. ; 4 3/4 in. user's guide (38 p. : ill. ; 22 cm). (Past masters.) Title on container: John Dewey correspondence. "The Center for Dewey Studies, Southern Illinois University at Carbondale"--Title screen. Includes bibliographical references. Text (Correspondence). "Folio infobase." SUMMARY: Transcriptions of the correspondence written or received by John Dewey, as well as selected letters about him. The text of each letter is fully searchable using the Folio Views software and includes notes on transcription provenance. Other searchable fields include date, writer, addressee, place, and source of the document. Also includes a chronology of Dewey's life and a few photographs. System requirements: IBM-compatible computer; Windows 3.1 or higher; CD-ROM drive; monitor. Also available in print edition. Issued with: The collected works of John Dewey, 1882-1953, electronic edition (ref. LB875 .D363 1997). PARTIAL CONTENTS: v. 1. 1871-1918. ISBN 1-57085-124-7 (cd-rom) ISBN 1-57085-019-4 (container) ISBN 1-57085-021-6 (user's guide)
*1. Dewey, John, - 1859-1952 - Correspondence. 2. Philosophers - United States - Correspondence. 3. Educators - United States - Correspondence. I. Hackman, Larry A. II. Center for Dewey Studies. III. InteLex Corporation. IV. Title.*

*V. Title: Folio infobase. VI. Title: John Dewey correspondence. VII. Series: Past masters (InteLex Corporation).*
*TC B945.D44 A4 1999*

How we think : a restatement of the relation of reflective thinking to the educative process / by John Dewey ; with a foreword by Maxine Greene. Boston : Houghton Mifflin, c1998. xxvi, 301 p. ; 19 cm. Includes index. ISBN 0-395-89754-8 (hardcover) DDC 153.4/2
*1. Thought and thinking. 2. Educational psychology. I. Title.*
*TC BF441 .D43 1998*

[Works.]
The collected works of John Dewey, 1882-1953. [computer file] : the electronic edition / John Dewey. Windows version. Charlottesville, VA : InteLex Corp, 1997, c1992. Computer program. 1 computer laser optical disc ; 4 3/4 in. user's guide. (Past masters.) Title from title screen. System requirements for Windows: IBM-compatible personal computer; 512K RAM; DOS 2.0 or higher; CD-ROM drive; monochrome or color monitor. Includes bibliographical references. Also available in print version. "Folio infobase." Library copy issued with: Correspondence of John Dewey (Ref. B945.D44 A4). ISBN 1-57085-118-2 (cd-rom) ISBN 1-57085-019-4 (container) ISBN 1-57085-021-6 (user's guide)
*1. Education - Philosophy. 2. Philosophy - Collected works. I. InteLex Corporation. II. Title. III. Title: Folio infobase. IV. Series: Past masters (InteLex Corporation).*
*TC LB875 .D363 1997*

## DEWEY, JOHN, 1859-1952.

Berube, Maurice R. Eminent educators. Westport, Conn. : Greenwood Press, 2000.
*TC LB875.D5 B47 2000*

Dewey and European education. Dordrecht : Kluwer Academic Publishers, c2000.
*TC LB875.D5 D47 2000*

Dunt, Lesley, 1944- Speaking worlds. Parkville, Vic. : History Department, The University of Melbourne, c1993.
*TC LA2101 .D96 1993*

Gordon, Mordechai. Toward an integrative conception of authority in education. 1997.
*TC 085 G656*

## DEWEY, JOHN, 1859-1952 - CORRESPONDENCE.

Dewey, John, 1859-1952. The correspondence of John Dewey. [computer file]. Windows version. Charlottesville, VA : InteLex Corp., 1999- Computer data and program.
*TC B945.D44 A4 1999*

**Deyhle, Donna.**
Race is-- race isn't. Boulder, CO : Westview Press, c1999.
*TC LC3731 .R27 1999*

**DeYoung, Sandra.**
Grodner, Michele. Foundations and clinical applications of nutrition. 2nd ed. St. Louis, Mo. : Mosby, c2000.
*TC RM216 .G946 2000*

**Dhingra, Koshi.** An ethnographic study of the construction of science on television. 1999. vii, 238 leaves : ill. ; 29 cm. Issued also on microfilm. Thesis (Ed.D.)--Teachers College, Columbia University, 1999. Includes tables. Includes bibliographical references (leaves 219-226).
*1. Science - Study and teaching. 2. Television in science education. 3. Constructivism (Education) 4. Science - Social aspects. 5. Television in science. 6. Television programs. I. Title.*
*TC 06 no. 11101*

**Di Pasquale, Mauro G.** Amino acids and proteins for the athlete : the anabolic edge / Mauro Di Pasquale. Boca Raton : CRC Press, c1997. 257 p. : ill. ; 26 cm. (Nutrition in exercise and sport) Includes bibliographical references (p. 187-243) and index. ISBN 0-8493-8193-2 (acid-free paper) DDC 612.3/98/088796
*1. Proteins in human nutrition. 2. Amino acids in human nutrition. 3. Athletes - Nutrition. 4. Dietary supplements. I. Title. II. Series.*
*TC QP551 .D46 1997*

**DIABETES MELLITUS.** See DIABETES.

**DIABETES - PATIENTS.** See DIABETICS.

## DIABETES - PATIENTS - EDUCATION - NEW YORK (STATE) - NEW YORK.

Mendoza, Maria Adalia. A study to compare inner city Black men and women completers and non-attenders of diabetes self-care classes. 1999.
*TC 06 no. 11206*

**DIABETIC ACIDOSIS.** See DIABETES.

## DIABETICS - NEW YORK (STATE) - NEW YORK - ATTITUDES.

Mendoza, Maria Adalia. A study to compare inner

*Diagnosis*

city Black men and women completers and non-attenders of diabetes self-care classes. 1999.
*TC 06 no. 11206*

**DIAGNOSIS.** *See* **DISABILITY EVALUATION.**

**DIAGNOSIS, DIFFERENTIAL.**
Challenge cases [videorecording]. Princeton, N.J. : Films for the Humanities & Sciences, 1998.
*TC RC455.2.C4 C4 1998*

Disorders due to psychoactive substance abuse [videorecording]. Princeton, N.J. : Films for the Humanities & Sciences, 1998.
*TC RC564 .D5 1998*

Mood disorders [videorecording]. Princeton, N.J. : Films for the Humanities & Sciences, 1998.
*TC RC537 .M6 1998*

Neurotic, stress-related, and somatoform disorders [videorecording]. Princeton, N.J. : Films for the Humanities & Sciences, 1998.
*TC RC530 .N4 1998*

Organic disorders [videorecording]. Princeton, N.J. : Films for the Humanities & Sciences, 1998.
*TC RC521 .O7 1998*

Personality disorders [videorecording]. Princeton, N.J. : Films for the Humanities & Sciences, 1998.
*TC RC554 .P4 1998*

Schizophrenia and delusional disorders [videorecording]. Princeton, N.J. : Films for the Humanities & Sciences, c1998.
*TC RC514 .S3 1998*

**Diagnosis in speech-language pathology** / edited by J. Bruce Tomblin, Hughlett L. Morris, D.C. Spriestersbach ; assistant to the editors, Juanita C. Limas. 2nd ed. San Diego : Singular, c2000. xxi, 513 p. : ill. ; 26 cm. Includes bibliographical references and index. ISBN 0-7693-0050-2 (softcover : alk. paper) DDC 616.85/5075
*1. Speech disorders - Diagnosis. 2. Language Disorders. 3. Speech Disorders. 4. Speech-Language Pathology. I. Tomblin, J. Bruce. II. Morris, Hughlett L. III. Spriestersbach, D. C.*
*TC RC423 .D473 2000*

**DIAGNOSTIC PSYCHOLOGICAL TESTING.** *See* **PSYCHODIAGNOSTICS.**

**Diagnostic teaching of reading.**
Walker, Barbara J., 1946- 4th ed. Upper Saddle River, NJ : Merrill, c2000.
*TC LB1050.5 .W35 2000*

**DIAGRAMS, STATISTICAL.** *See* **STATISTICS - CHARTS, DIAGRAMS, ETC.**

**DIALECTIC (LOGIC).** *See* **LOGIC.**

**DIALOGUE.** *See also* **DRAMA.**
Flecha, Ramón. [Compartiendo palabras. English] Sharing words. Lanham, Md. : Oxford : Rowman & Littlefield Publishers, c2000.
*TC LB1060 .F5913 2000*

**DIALOGUE ANALYSIS - JAPAN.**
Tanaka, Hiroko. Turn-taking in Japanese conversation. Amsterdam : Philadelphia, PA : John Benjamins Pub. Co., c1999.
*TC PL640.5 .T36 1999*

**Dialogue on early childhood science, mathematics, and technology education.** Washington, DC : American Association for the Advancement of Science/Project 2061, 1999. vi, 194 p. : ill. ; 18 cm. Papers commissioned by the American Association for the Advancement of Science for presentation at the Forum on Early Childhood Science, Mathematics, and Technology Education, held in Washington, D.C., February 1998. Includes bibliographical references and index. ISBN 0-87168-629-5 DDC 372.3/5
*1. Science - Study and teaching (Early childhood) - United States. 2. Technology - Study and teaching (Early childhood) - United States. 3. Mathematics - Study and teaching (Early childhood) - United States. I. Project 2061 (American Association for the Advancement of Science) II. Forum on Early Childhood Science, Mathematics, and Technology Education (1998 : Washington, D.C.)*
*TC LB1139.5.S35 D53 1999*

**DIAMANDOPOULOS, PETER.**
Lewis, Lionel S. (Lionel Stanley) When power corrupts. New Brunswick, NJ : Transaction Publishers, c2000.
*TC LD25.8 .L49 2000*

**Diamant, Gertrude, 1901-** The days of Ofelia, illustrated by John O'Hara Cosgrave II. Boston, Houghton Mifflin company, 1942. 226 p. illus., plates. 21 cm. At head of title: By Gertrude Diamant. DDC 917.2
*1. National characteristics, Mexican. 2. Mexico - Social life*

and customs. *I. Cosgrave, John O'Hara, 1908-1968 illus. II. Title.*
*TC F1210 .D5*

**Diamant, Neil Jeffrey, 1964-** Revolutionizing the family : politics, love, and divorce in urban and rural China, 1949-1968 / Neil J. Diamant. Berkeley : University of California Press, c2000. xviii, 440 p. : ill., maps ; 24 cm. Includes bibliographical references (p. 405-423) and index. ISBN 0-520-21720-9 (alk. paper) DDC 306.85/0951
*1. Family - China. 2. Family policy - China. 3. China - Social conditions - 1949-1976. I. Title. II. Title: Politics, love, and divorce in urban and rural China, 1949-1964*
*TC HQ684 .D53 2000*

**Diamond, C. T. Patrick.**
The postmodern educator. New York : P. Lang, c1999.
*TC LB1707 .P67 1999*

**Diana Hess at Denver High School 1997 [videorecording].**
Public issues discussion [videorecording] : Diana Hess at Denver High School 1997. [Boulder, Colo.] : Social Science Education Consortium, c1997.
*TC H62.3 .P4 1997*

**Dianetics.**
Hubbard, L. Ron (La Fayette Ron), 1911- Los Angeles, Calif. : Bridge Publications, c2000.
*TC BP605.S2 H7956 2000*

**DIANETICS.**
Hubbard, L. Ron (La Fayette Ron), 1911- Dianetics. Los Angeles, Calif. : Bridge Publications, c2000.
*TC BP605.S2 H7956 2000*

**DIAPHRAGM.** *See* **VOICE.**

**DIARIES.**
Berry, Carrie, b. 1854. A Confederate girl. Mankato, Minn. : Blue Earth Books, c2000.
*TC E605 .B5 2000*

Bircher, William, 1845-1917. A Civil War drummer boy. Mankato, Minn. : Blue Earth Books, c2000.
*TC E601 .B605 2000*

Forten, Charlotte L. A free Black girl before the Civil War. Mankato, Minn. : Blue Earth Books, c2000.
*TC F74.S1 F67 2000*

Gillespie, Sarah (Sarah L.) A pioneer farm girl. Mankato, Minn. : Blue Earth Books, c2000.
*TC F629.M28 G55 2000*

Hester, Sallie. A covered wagon girl. Mankato, Minn. : Blue Earth Books, c2000.
*TC F593 .H47 2000*

Jernegan, Laura, b. 1862. A whaling captain's daughter. Mankato, Minn. : Blue Earth Books, c2000.
*TC G545 .J47 2000*

Richards, Caroline Cowles, 1842-1913. A nineteenth-century schoolgirl. Mankato, Minn. : Blue Earth Books, c2000.
*TC F129.C2 R53 2000*

Wister, Sarah, 1761-1804. A colonial Quaker girl. Mankato, Minn. : Blue Earth Books, c2000.
*TC F158.44 .W75 2000*

**DIARIES - AUTHOSHIP.**
Moon, Jennifer A. Learning journals. London : Kogan Page, 1999.
*TC PE1408 .M66 1999*

**Diaries, letters, and memoirs**
Berry, Carrie, b. 1854. A Confederate girl. Mankato, Minn. : Blue Earth Books, c2000.
*TC E605 .B5 2000*

Bircher, William, 1845-1917. A Civil War drummer boy. Mankato, Minn. : Blue Earth Books, c2000.
*TC E601 .B605 2000*

Forten, Charlotte L. A free Black girl before the Civil War. Mankato, Minn. : Blue Earth Books, c2000.
*TC F74.S1 F67 2000*

Gillespie, Sarah (Sarah L.) A pioneer farm girl. Mankato, Minn. : Blue Earth Books, c2000.
*TC F629.M28 G55 2000*

Hester, Sallie. A covered wagon girl. Mankato, Minn. : Blue Earth Books, c2000.
*TC F593 .H47 2000*

Jernegan, Laura, b. 1862. A whaling captain's daughter. Mankato, Minn. : Blue Earth Books, c2000.
*TC G545 .J47 2000*

Richards, Caroline Cowles, 1842-1913. A nineteenth-century schoolgirl. Mankato, Minn. : Blue Earth Books, c2000.

Wister, Sarah, 1761-1804. A colonial Quaker girl. Mankato, Minn. : Blue Earth Books, c2000.
*TC F158.44 .W75 2000*

**Diary of a European tour, 1900.**
Addison, Margaret, 1868-1940. Montréal : McGill-Queen's University Press, c1999.
*TC LE3.T619 A33 1999*

**The diary of a young girl by Anne Frank.**
Beech, Linda Ward. New York : Scholastic, c1998.
*TC LB1573 .B433 1998*

**Diary of Charles Francis Adams.**
Adams, Charles Francis, 1807-1886. Cambridge : Belknap Press of Harvard University Press, 1964-68.
*TC KF367.A33 A3*

**Dias, Patrick.**
Worlds apart. Mahwah, N.J. : L. Erlbaum Associates, 1999.
*TC PE1404 .W665 1999*

**Díaz, Carlos (Carlos F.).**
Multicultural education for the 21st century. 1st ed. New York : Longman, 2001.
*TC LC1099.3 .M8163 2001*

**DiCenso, James, 1957-** The other Freud : religion, culture, and psychoanalysis / James J. DiCenso. London ; New York : Routledge, 1999. vi, 174 p. ; 25 cm. Includes bibliographical references (p. [149]-169) and index. ISBN 0-415-19658-2 (hardcover : alk. paper) ISBN 0-415-19659-0 (pbk. : alk. paper) DDC 150.19/52/092
*1. Psychoanalysis and religion. 2. Freud, Sigmund, - 1856-1939 - Religion. I. Title.*
*TC BF175.4.R44 D53 1999*

**Dichanz, Horst, 1937-** Changing traditions in Germany's public schools / by Horst Dichanz and John A. Zahorik. Bloomington, Ind. : Phi Delta Kappa Educational Foundation, c1998. 87 p. ; 23 cm. (Phi Delta Kappa international studies in education) Includes bibliographical references (p. 85-86). ISBN 0-87367-396-4 DDC 371.01/0943
*1. Public schools - Germany. 2. Education, Elementary - Germany. 3. Education, Secondary - Germany. I. Zahorik, John A. II. Title. III. Series.*
*TC LA723 .D53 1998*

**DICKERING.** *See* **NEGOTIATION.**

**Dickerson, Pless Moore.** Haitian students' perception of a school as a community of support : a case study at Westbury High School / by Pless Moore Dickerson. 1998. iv, 102 leaves ; 29 cm. Typescript; issued also on microfilm. Thesis (Ed.D.)--Teachers College, Columbia University. 1998. Includes bibliographical references (leaves 99-102).
*1. Haitians - New York (State) - Westbury. 2. High school students - Social conditions. 3. School environment - Evaluation. 4. Social integration. 5. Haitians - New York (State) - Westbury - Cultural assimilation. 6. Westbury Public Schools (Westbury, N.Y.) - Students - Attitude. I. Title.*
*TC 06 no. 11018*

Haitian students' perception of a school as a community of support : a case study at Westbury High School / by Pless Moore Dickerson. 1998. iv, 102 leaves ; 29 cm. Typescript; issued also on microfilm. Thesis (Ed.D.)--Teachers College, Columbia University. 1998. Includes bibliographical references (leaves 99-102).
*1. Haitians - New York (State) - Westbury. 2. High school students - Social conditions. 3. School environment - Evaluation. 4. Social integration. 5. Haitians - New York (State) - Westbury - Cultural assimilation. 6. Westbury Public Schools (Westbury, N.Y.) - Students - Attitude. I. Title.*
*TC 06 no. 11018*

Haitian students' perception of a school as a community of support : a case study at Westbury High School / by Pless Moore Dickerson. 1998. iv, 102 leaves ; 29 cm. Typescript; issued also on microfilm. Thesis (Ed.D.)--Teachers College, Columbia University. 1998. Includes bibliographical references (leaves 99-102).
*1. Haitians - New York (State) - Westbury. 2. High school students - Social conditions. 3. School environment - Evaluation. 4. Social integration. 5. Haitians - New York (State) - Westbury - Cultural assimilation. 6. Westbury Public Schools (Westbury, N.Y.) - Students - Attitude. I. Title.*
*TC 06 no. 11018*

**Dickinson College.** The Spahr lectures, Dickinson College, v.4, 1962-1969. Carlisle, Pa., : Dickinson College 1970. viii, 243 p. illus., ports. 22 cm. (The Boyd Lee Spahr lectures in Americana, 1962-1969.) Includes bibliographical references. CONTENTS.- S. Sack: Liberal education: what is it? I. Brant: The free, or not so free, air of Pennsylvania. D.J. D'Elia: Benjamin Rush, America's philosopher of revolutionary education. J.A. Bonar: We have aimed honestly at doing good: trusteeship at Dickinson, 1783-

1816. B.I. Wiley: Johnny Reb and Billy Yank. J. Bakeless: Captain Conrad's spy net. N.B. Wainwright: The loyal opposition in Civil War Philadelphia. L.D. Easton: Moncure Conway and German philosophy. W.S. Smith: Moncure Conway's journey back to earth.
*1. Dickinson College. 2. Conway. Moncure Daniel. - 1832-1907. 3. Dickinson College - History. 4. Pennsylvania - History. I. Title. II. Series: Boyd Lee Spahr lectures in Americana ; 1962-1969.*
**TC LD1663 .A5 1970**

**DICKINSON COLLEGE.**
Dickinson College. The Spahr lectures, Dickinson College, Carlisle, Pa., : Dickinson College 1970.
**TC LD1663 .A5 1970**

**DICKINSON COLLEGE - HISTORY.**
Dickinson College. The Spahr lectures, Dickinson College, Carlisle, Pa., : Dickinson College 1970.
**TC LD1663 .A5 1970**

**Dickinson, Thomas S.**
Promoting literacy in grades 4-9. Boston ; London : Allyn and Bacon, c2000.
**TC LB1576 .P76 2000**

**DiClemente, Ralph J.**
Handbook of health promotion and disease prevention. New York : Kluwer Academic/Plenum Publishers, c1999.
**TC RA427.8 .H36 1999**

Handbook of HIV prevention. New York : Kluwer/ Plenum, 2000.
**TC RA644.A25 H365 2000**

**DICTION.** *See* **VOCABULARY.**

**DICTIONARIES.** *See* **ENCYCLOPEDIAS AND DICTIONARIES.**

**Dictionary of confusable words** / [edited by] Adrian Room ; acquisition director, Anne-Lucie Norton. Chicago, IL : Fitzroy Dearborn Publ., 2000. viii, 251 p. ; 24 cm. ISBN 1-57958-271-0
*1. Homonyms. 2. English language - Usage. 3. English language - Errors of usage. I. Room, Adrian. II. Title: Confusable words*
**TC PE1591 .D53 2000**

**A dictionary of folklore.**
Pickering, David, 1958- New York, N.Y. : Facts on File, 1999.
**TC GR35 .P53 1999**

**Dictionary of hearing.**
Martin, Michael, OBE. London : Whurr, 1999.
**TC QP461 .M375 1999**

**Dictionary of philosophy.**
The Cambridge dictionary of philosophy. 2nd ed. Cambridge : New York : Cambridge University Press, 1999.
**TC B41 .C35 1999**

**The dictionary of psychology.**
Cardwell, Mike. London : Chicago : Fitzroy Dearborn Publishers, 1999, c1996.
**TC BF31 .C33 1999**

Corsini, Raymond J. Philadelphia, PA : Brunner/ Mazel, Taylor & Francis, c1999.
**TC BF31 .C72 1999**

**Dicum, Gregory.** The coffee book : anatomy of an industry from crop to the last drop / Gregory Dicum and Nina Luttinger. New York : New Press : Distributed by W.W. Norton, c1999. xi, 196 p. : ill. ; 18 cm. (The bazaar book series ; 2) Includes bibliographical references (p. 185-190) and index. ISBN 1-56584-452-1 ISBN 1-56584-508-0 DDC 338.1/7373
*1. Coffee industry. 2. Coffee. I. Luttinger, Nina. II. Title. III. Series: Bazaar book ; 2.*
**TC HD9199.A2 D53 1999**

**DIDACTIC FICTION, ENGLISH - HISTORY AND CRITICISM.**
Barney, Richard A., 1955- Plots of enlightenment. Stanford, Calif. : Stanford University Press, c1999.
**TC PR858.E38 B37 1999**

**DIDACTICS.** *See* **TEACHING.**

**Diderot, Denis, 1713-1784.**
[Selections. English. 1995]
Diderot on art / edited and translated by John Goodman ; introduction by Thomas Crow. New Haven : Yale University Press, 1995. v. <2 > : ill. ; 23 cm. Translated from the French. Includes 90 plates. Includes bibliographical references and indexes. CONTENTS: V. 1. The salon of 1765 and Notes on painting -- v. 2. The salon of 1767. ISBN 0-300-06248-6 (v. 1 : alk. paper) ISBN 0-300-06251-6 (v. 1 : pbk. : alk. paper) ISBN 0-300-06249-4 (v. 2 : alk. paper) ISBN 0-300-06252-4 (v. 2 : pbk. : alk. paper) DDC 759.4/09/033

*1. Art. French - Exhibitions. 2. Art. Modern - 17th-18th centuries - France - Exhibitions. 3. Salon (Exhibition : Paris. France) 4. Aesthetics - Early works to 1800. 5. Painting - Early works to 1800. I. Goodman. John. 1952 Sept. 19- II. Title.*
**TC N6846 .D4613 1995**

**Diderot on art.**
Diderot, Denis, 1713-1784. [Selections. English. 1995] New Haven : Yale University Press, 1995.
**TC N6846 .D4613 1995**

**Diebenkorn, Richard, 1922-.**
Livingston, Jane. The art of Richard Diebenkorn. New York : Whitney Museum of American Art ; Berkeley : University of California Press, c1997.
**TC N6537.D447 A4 1997**

**DIEBENKORN, RICHARD, 1922- - CRITICISM AND INTERPRETATION.**
Livingston, Jane. The art of Richard Diebenkorn. New York : Whitney Museum of American Art ; Berkeley : University of California Press, c1997.
**TC N6537.D447 A4 1997**

**DIEBENKORN, RICHARD, 1922- - EXHIBITIONS.**
Livingston, Jane. The art of Richard Diebenkorn. New York : Whitney Museum of American Art ; Berkeley : University of California Press, c1997.
**TC N6537.D447 A4 1997**

**Diego Rivera.**
Hamill, Pete, 1935- New York : Harry N. Abrams, 1999.
**TC ND259.R5 H28 1999**

**Diekema, Anthony J.** Academic freedom and Christian scholarship / Anthony J. Diekema. Grand Rapids, Mich. : Wm.B. Eerdmans Pub. Co., c2000. xviii, 214 p. ; 23 cm. Cover title: Academic freedom & Christian scholarship. Includes bibliographical references (p. 197-210) and index. ISBN 0-8028-4756-0 (alk. paper) DDC 378.1/21
*1. Academic freedom - United States. 2. Church colleges - United States - Curricula. 3. Church and education - United States. I. Title. II. Title: Academic freedom & Christian scholarship*
**TC LC72.2 .D54 2000**

**DIET.** *See also* **FOOD; FOOD HABITS; NUTRITION.**
Evolutionary aspects of nutrition and health. Basel ; New York : Karger, c1999.
**TC QP141 .E95 1999**

Goldfein, Juli Ann. The importance of shape and weight in normal-weight women with bulimia nervosa, restrained eaters (dieters), and normal controls (Non-dieters). 1997.
**TC 085 G5675**

The nutty, nougat-filled world of human nutrition [videorecording]. [Arlington, Va.] : Cerebellum Corp., c1998.
**TC QP141 .N8 1998**

**Diet and nutrition activities.**
Toner, Patricia Rizzo, 1952- West Nyack, N.Y. : Center for Applied Research in Education, c1993.
**TC QP143 .T65 1993**

**DIET - ATLASES.**
Human nutrition and obesity. Philadelphia : Current Medicine, 1999.
**TC RC620.5 .H846 1999**

**DIET - CHINA.**
Feeding China's little emperors. Stanford, Calif. : Stanford University Press, 2000.
**TC TX361.C5 F44 2000**

**DIET THERAPY.**
Grodner, Michele. Foundations and clinical applications of nutrition. 2nd ed. St. Louis, Mo. : Mosby, c2000.
**TC RM216 .G946 2000**

**DIET THERAPY.**
Nutritional aspects of HIV infection. London ; New York : Arnold : Co-published in the United States by Oxford University Press, 1999.
**TC RC607.A26 N895 1998**

**DIET THERAPY - METHODS - NURSES' INSTRUCTION.**
Grodner, Michele. Foundations and clinical applications of nutrition. 2nd ed. St. Louis, Mo. : Mosby, c2000.
**TC RM216 .G946 2000**

**DIETARIES.** *See* **FOOD.**

**DIETARY SUPPLEMENTS.**
DeFelice, Stephen L., 1936- The carnitine defense. [Emmaus, Pa.] : Rodale Press ; [New York] :

Distributed to the book trade by St. Martin's Press. c1999.
**TC RC685.C6 D4235 1999**

**DIETARY SUPPLEMENTS.**
Di Pasquale, Mauro G. Amino acids and proteins for the athlete. Boca Raton : CRC Press, c1997.
**TC QP551 .D46 1997**

Energy-yielding macronutrients and energy metabolism in sports nutrition. Boca Raton, Fla. : London : CRC Press, c2000.
**TC QP176 .E546 2000**

**DIETETICS.** *See also* **NUTRITION.**
Hudson, Nancy R. Management practice in dietetics. Australia : Belmont, Calif. : Wadsworth, c2000.
**TC TX911.3.M27 H83 2000**

**Dietrich, Eric.**
Cognitive dynamics. Mahwah, N.J. ; London : L. Erlbaum, 2000.
**TC BF316.6 .C64 2000**

**DIFFERENTIABLE DYNAMICAL SYSTEMS.** *See* **CHAOTIC BEHAVIOR IN SYSTEMS.**

**Differential diagnosis in psychiatry**
Challenge cases [videorecording]. Princeton, N.J. : Films for the Humanities & Sciences, 1998.
**TC RC455.2.C4 C4 1998**

Disorders due to psychoactive substance abuse [videorecording]. Princeton, N.J. : Films for the Humanities & Sciences, 1998.
**TC RC564 .D5 1998**

Mood disorders [videorecording]. Princeton, N.J. : Films for the Humanities & Sciences, 1998.
**TC RC537 .M6 1998**

Neurotic, stress-related, and somatoform disorders [videorecording]. Princeton, N.J. : Films for the Humanities & Sciences, 1998.
**TC RC530 .N4 1998**

Organic disorders [videorecording]. Princeton, N.J. : Films for the Humanities & Sciences, 1998.
**TC RC521 .O7 1998**

Personality disorders [videorecording]. Princeton, N.J. : Films for the Humanities & Sciences, 1998.
**TC RC554 .P4 1998**

Schizophrenia and delusional disorders [videorecording]. Princeton, N.J. : Films for the Humanities & Sciences, c1998.
**TC RC514 .S3 1998**

**Differential object representations in inpatients with narcissistic and borderline personality disorders and normal controls.**
Gutin, Nina J. 1997.
**TC 085 G975**

**Differentiated supervision.**
Glatthorn, Allan A., 1924- 2nd ed. Alexandria, Va. : Association for Supervision and Curriculum Development, c1997.
**TC LB2806.4 .G548 1997**

**DIFFERENTIATION (COGNITION).**
Eddy, Jennifer B.K. Multiple intelligences, styles, and proficiency. 1997.
**TC 085 E10**

**DIFFERENTIATION (EDUCATION).** *See* **INDIVIDUALIZED INSTRUCTION.**

**DIFFUSION.** *See* **ATMOSPHERIC DIFFUSION.**

**DIFFUSION OF INNOVATIONS.** *See* **TECHNOLOGY TRANSFER.**

**DIGESTION.** *See* **NUTRITION.**

**Digital communication**
Welch, Kathleen E. Electric rhetoric. Cambridge, Mass. : MIT Press, c1999.
**TC P301.5.D37 W45 1999**

**DIGITAL COMMUNICATIONS.** *See* **COMPUTER NETWORKS; DATA TRANSMISSION SYSTEMS; DIGITAL TELEVISION.**

**DIGITAL COMPUTER SIMULATION.** *See* **ARTIFICIAL INTELLIGENCE.**

**Digital democracy :** discourse and decision making in the Information Age / edited by Barry N. Hague and Brian D. Loader. London ; New York : Routledge, 1999. xvi, 277 p. : ill. ; 23 cm. Chiefly based on papers presented at a conference sponsored by the Community Informatics Research and Applications Unit, University of Teesside, UK. Includes bibliographical references (p. [245]-261) and index. ISBN 0-415-19737-6 (hbk.) ISBN 0-415-19738-4 (pbk.) DDC 351/.0285
*1. Public administration - Data processing - Congresses. 2.*

*Administrative agencies - Data processing - Congresses. 3. Information technology - Political aspects - Congresses. I. Hague, Barry N. II. Loader, Brian, 1958-*
**TC JF1525.A8 D54 1999**

**Digital democracy :** policy and politics in the wired world / edited by Cynthia J. Alexander and Leslie A. Pal. Toronto : New York : Oxford University Press, 1998. xv, 237 p. : ill. ; 23 cm. Includes bibliographical references. ISBN 0-19-541359-8 DDC 303.48/33
*1. Democracy. 2. Information technology - Political aspects. 3. Information society - Political aspects. 4. Communication - Political aspects. 5. Science politique. 6. Sciences de la politique. 7. Technologie de l'information - Aspect politique. 8. Communication - Aspect politique. 9. Démocratie. I. Alexander, Cynthia Jacqueline, 1960- II. Pal, Leslie Alexander, 1954-*
**TC JC421 .D55 1998**

**Digital dilemma.**
Van Dusen, Gerald C. San Francisco : Jossey-Bass, c2000.
**TC LC5805 .V35 2000**

**The digital dilemma :** intellectual property in the information age / Committee on Intellectual Property Rights and the Emerging Information Infrastructure, Computer Science and Telecommunications Board, Commission on Physical Sciences, Mathematics, and Applications, National Research Council. Washington, D.C. : National Academy Press, c2000. xxi, 340 p. : ill. ; 24 cm. Includes bibliographical references and index. Also available on the Internet at: http://books.nap.edu/html/digital%5Fdilemma. URL: http://books.nap.edu/html/digital%5Fdilemma ISBN 0-309-06499-6 (pbk.)
*1. Intellectual property - United States. 2. Copyright and electronic data processing - United States. 3. Information superhighway - Law and legislation - United States. I. National Research Council (U.S.). Committee on Intellectual Property Rights and the Emerging Information Infrastructure. II. National Research Council (U.S.). Computer Science and Telecommunications Board. III. National Research Council (U.S.). Commission on Physical Sciences, Mathematics, and Applications. IV. Title: Intellectual property in the information age.*
**TC KF2979 .D53 2000**

**Digital diversions :** youth culture in the age of multimedia / edited by Julian Sefton-Green. London : UCL Press, 1998. 179 p. : ill. ; 24 cm. Includes bibliographical references and index. ISBN 1-85728-856-4 (hard) ISBN 1-85728-857-2 (pbk.)
*1. Multimedia systems - Social aspects. 2. Computer games - Social aspects. 3. Internet (Computer network) - Social aspects. 4. Computers and children. 5. Subculture. I. Sefton-Green, Julian. II. Series: Media, education, culture.*
**TC QA76.575 .D536 1998**

**Digital divide.**
Bolt, David B., 1954- New York : TV Books, c2000.
**TC LB1028.43 .B64 2000**

**DIGITAL HIGHWAY.** *See* **INFORMATION SUPERHIGHWAY.**

**Digital imaging for libraries and archives.**
Kenney, Anne R., 1950- Moving theory into practice. Mountain View, CA : Research Libraries Group, 2000.
**TC Z681.3.D53 K37**

**DIGITAL LIBRARIES.** *See also* **INFORMATION STORAGE AND RETRIEVAL SYSTEMS.**
Borgman, Christine L., 1951- From Gutenberg to the global information infrastructure. Cambridge, Mass. : MIT Press, 2000.
**TC ZA3225 .B67 2000**

**Digital libraries and electronic publishing.**
Borgman, Christine L., 1951- From Gutenberg to the global information infrastructure. Cambridge, Mass. : MIT Press, 2000.
**TC ZA3225 .B67 2000**

**DIGITAL LIBRARIES - CONGRESSES.**
ECDL '99 (3rd : Paris, France) Research and advanced technology for digital libraries. Berlin ; New York : Springer, c1999.
**TC ZA4080 .E28 1999**

**DIGITAL LIBRARIES - EUROPE - CONGRESSES.**
ECDL '99 (3rd : 1999 : Paris, France) Research and advanced technology for digital libraries. Berlin ; New York : Springer, c1999.
**TC ZA4080 .E28 1999**

**DIGITAL LIBRARIES - GREAT BRITAIN - PLANNING.**
Towards the digital library. London : The British Library, 1998.

**TC Z664.B75 T683 1998**

**DIGITAL LIBRARIES - UNITED STATES.**
Borgman, Christine L., 1951- From Gutenberg to the global information infrastructure. Cambridge, Mass. : MIT Press, 2000.
**TC ZA3225 .B67 2000**

**DIGITAL MEDIA.**
Lunenfeld, Peter. Snap to grid. Cambridge, MA : MIT, 2000.
**TC QA76.9.C66 L86 2000**

**DIGITAL MEDIA - SOCIAL ASPECTS.**
Buckingham, David, 1954- After the death of childhood. Malden, MA : Polity Press, 2000.
**TC HQ784.M3 B83 2000**
Wolf, Mark J. P. Abstracting reality. Lanham, Md.: University Press of America, c2000.
**TC HM851 .W65 2000**

**DIGITAL PRESERVATION.**
Kenney, Anne R., 1950- Moving theory into practice. Mountain View, CA : Research Libraries Group, 2000.
**TC Z681.3.D53 K37**

**DIGITAL TELEVISION - ECONOMIC ASPECTS - UNITED STATES - FORECASTING.**
Owen, Bruce M. The Internet challenge to television. Cambridge, Mass. : Harvard University Press, 1999.
**TC HE8700.8 .O826 1999**

**DIGITAL VIDEO - ECONOMIC ASPECTS - UNITED STATES - FORECASTING.**
Owen, Bruce M. The Internet challenge to television. Cambridge, Mass. : Harvard University Press, 1999.
**TC HE8700.8 .O826 1999**

**DiGiulio, Robert C., 1949-** Positive classroom management : a step-by-step guide to successfully running the show without destroying student dignity / Robert DiGiulio. 2nd ed. Thousand Oaks, CA. : Corwin Press, c2000. xiv, 122 p. ; 24 cm. Includes bibliographical references (p. 113-118) and index. ISBN 0-8039-6815-9 (C : alk. paper) ISBN 0-8039-6816-7 (P : alk. paper) DDC 371.102/4/0973
*1. Classroom management - United States. I. Title.*
**TC LB3013 .D54 2000**

**Dignan, Mark B.**
Anspaugh, David J. Developing health promotion programs. Boston ; London : McGraw-Hill, c2000.
**TC RA427.8 .A57 2000**

**DIGS (ARCHAEOLOGY).** *See* **EXCAVATIONS (ARCHAEOLOGY).**

**Dillon, Diane, ill.**
Murphy, Shirley Rousseau. Wind child. New York, NY : HarperCollins, c1999.
**TC PZ8.M957 Wi 1999**

**Dillon, James J.**
Partnerships in research, clinical, and educational settings. Stamford, Conn. : Ablex Pub., c1999.
**TC HM1106 .P37 1999**

**Dillon, Leo, ill.**
Murphy, Shirley Rousseau. Wind child. New York, NY : HarperCollins, c1999.
**TC PZ8.M957 Wi 1999**

**Dilman, İlham.** Raskolnikov's rebirth : psychology and the understanding of good and evil / İlham Dilman. Chicago : Open Court, c2000. xxix, 214 p. ; 23 cm. Includes bibliographical references (p. 207-210) and index. ISBN 0-8126-9416-3 (paper : alk. paper) DDC 150/.1
*1. Ethics. 2. Good and evil. 3. Psychology. Religious. 4. Psychoanalysis. 5. Freud, Sigmund. - 1856-1939. I. Title.*
**TC BF47 .D55 2000**

**DiLorenzo, Thomas J.**
Bennett, James T. From pathology to politics. New Brunswick [N.J.] (U.S.A.) : Transaction Publishers, c2000.
**TC RA445 .B45 2000**

**DIMACS series in discrete mathematics and theoretical computer science**
(v. 36) Discrete mathematics in the schools. Providence, R.I. : American Mathematical Society, National Council of Teachers of Mathematics, c1997.
**TC QA11.A1 D57 1997**

**Dimeff, Linda A.**
Brief Alcohol Screening and Intervention for College Students (BASICS). New York : Guilford Press, c1999.
**TC HV5135 .B74 1998**

**Dimensions of managing academic affairs in the community college** / Douglas Robillard, Jr., editor. San Francisco : Jossey-Bass, 2000. 99 p. ; 23 cm. (New directions for community colleges, 0194-3081 ; no. 109 (spring 2000)) Spine title: Managing academic affairs. "Spring 2000" Includes bibliographic references and index. CONTENTS: Toward a definition of deaning / Douglas Robillard, Jr. -- The dean as chief academic officer / John Stuart Erwin -- The dean and the faculty / Hans A. Andrews -- The dean and the president / Hans J. Kuss -- Aspects of difficult decisions / George I. Findlen -- Conflict: the skeleton in academe's closet / Rose Ann Findlen -- Academic economics: the academic dean and financial management / Susan A. McBride -- Community college alchemists: turning data into information / George H. Johnston, Sharon A. R. Kristovich -- Preparing community college deans to lead change / Debra D. Bragg -- A dean's survival tool kit / George L. Findlen. ISBN 0-7879-5369-5
*1. Community colleges - United States - Administration. 2. Deans (Education) 3. Community colleges - Administration. 4. Community colleges - Faculty. I. Robillard, Douglas. II. Title: Managing academic affairs III. Series: New directions for community colleges no. 109.*
**TC LB2341 .D56 2000**

**The dimensions of nations.**
Rummel, R. J. (Rudolph J.), 1932- Beverly Hills, Sage Publications [1972]
**TC JX1291 .R84**

**The dimensions of time and the challenge of school reform** / edited by Patricia Gándara. Albany : State University of New York Press, c2000. vi, 260 p. : ill. ; 23 cm. (SUNY series, restructuring and school change) Includes bibliographical references and index. ISBN 0-7914-4357-4 (hc : alk. paper) ISBN 0-7914-4358-2 (pb : alk. paper) DDC 371.2/42
*1. Schedules, School - United States. 2. Time management - United States. 3. Educational change - United States. I. Gándara, Patricia C. II. Series.*
**TC LB3032 .D55 2000**

**Dindia, Kathryn.**
Communication and personal relationships. New York : Wiley, 2000.
**TC HM1116 .C65 2000**

**Dine, Jim, 1935-.**
Livingstone, Marco. Jim Dine. New York : Monacelli Press, 1998.
**TC N6537.D5 A4 1998**

**DINE, JIM, 1935- - CRITICISM AND INTERPRETATION.**
Livingstone, Marco. Jim Dine. New York : Monacelli Press, 1998.
**TC N6537.D5 A4 1998**

**DINE, JIM, 1935- - THEMES, MOTIVES.**
Livingstone, Marco. Jim Dine. New York : Monacelli Press, 1998.
**TC N6537.D5 A4 1998**

**DINERS (RESTAURANTS) - FICTION.**
Kirk, Daniel. Breakfast at the Liberty Diner. 1st ed. New York : Hyperion Books for Children, c1997.
**TC PZ7.K6339 Br 1997**

**DINING.** *See* **DINNERS AND DINING.**

**DINNERS AND DINING.** *See* **COOKERY; DRINKING CUSTOMS; FOOD.**

**DINNERS AND DINING - FICTION.**
Zamorano, Ana. Let's eat!. New York : Scholastic Press, 1997.
**TC PZ7.Z25455 Le 1997**

**DINOSAURIA.** *See* **DINOSAURS.**

**DINOSAURS.**
Blumenthal, Nancy. Count-a-saurus. New York : Four Winds Press, c1989.
**TC QA113 .B57 1989**
O'Brien, Patrick, 1960- Gigantic!. 1st ed. New York : Henry Holt, 1999.
**TC QE862.D5 O27 1999**

**DINOSAURS - FICTION.**
Carrick, Carol. Patrick's dinosaurs on the Internet. New York : Clarion Books, 1999.
**TC PZ7.C2344 Patf 1999**

**DINOSAURS - JUVENILE LITERATURE.**
Blumenthal, Nancy. Count-a-saurus. New York : Four Winds Press, c1989.
**TC QA113 .B57 1989**

**DINOSAURS - SIZE - JUVENILE LITERATURE.**
O'Brien, Patrick, 1960- Gigantic!. 1st ed. New York : Henry Holt, 1999.
**TC QE862.D5 O27 1999**

**Dinosaurs to dodos.**
Lessem, Don. 1st ed. New York : Scholastic Reference, 1999.
*TC QE842 .L47 1999*

**DIOCESAN SCHOOLS.** *See* **CHURCH SCHOOLS.**

**Dioguardi, Raffaele A.**
NTC's beginner's Italian and English dictionary. Lincolnwood, Ill. : NTC Pub. Group, c1995.
*TC PC1640 .N83 1995*

**DiPalma, Carolyn.**
Teaching introduction to women's studies. Westport, Conn. : Bergin & Garvey, 1999.
*TC HQ1181.U5 T43 1999*

**DIPHTHERIA - NEW YORK (STATE) - NEW YORK - HISTORY - 19TH CENTURY.**
Hammonds, Evelynn Maxine. Childhood's deadly scourge. Baltimore, Md. : Johns Hopkins University Press, c1999.
*TC RA644.D6 H36 1999*

**DIPHTHERIA - NEW YORK (STATE) - NEW YORK - HISTORY - 20TH CENTURY.**
Hammonds, Evelynn Maxine. Childhood's deadly scourge. Baltimore, Md. : Johns Hopkins University Press, c1999.
*TC RA644.D6 H36 1999*

**DIPLOMA FACTORIES.** *See* **DIPLOMA MILLS.**

**DIPLOMA MILLS - UNITED STATES.**
Misrepresentation in the marketplace and beyond. Washington, DC : American Association of Collegiate Registrars and Admissions Officers, 1996.
*TC LB2331.615.U6 M57 1996*

**DIPLOMATS.** *See* **AMBASSADORS.**

**DIPSOMANIA.** *See* **ALCOHOLISM.**

**DIPTERA.** *See* **FLIES.**

**DIRECT MARKETING.**
Stimolo, Bob. Introduction to school marketing. [Haddam], Conn. : School Market Research Institute, c1989.
*TC HF5415.122 .S75 1989*

**DIRECT SELLING.** *See* **PEDDLERS AND PEDDLING.**

**Directions in development (Washington, D.C.)**
Patrinos, Harry Anthony. Decentralization of education. Washington, D.C. : World Bank, c1997.
*TC LB2826.6.D44 P38 1997*

**DIRECTORS, MOTION PICTURE.** *See* **MOTION PICTURE PRODUCERS AND DIRECTORS.**

**DIRECTORS, MUSEUM.** *See* **MUSEUM DIRECTORS.**

**DIRECTORS OF MUSEUMS.** *See* **MUSEUM DIRECTORS.**

**DIRECTORS OF RELIGIOUS EDUCATION.**
Winings, Kathy. What has the church/synagogue to do with the academy. 1996.
*TC 06 no. 10718*

**Directory I, Elective officials.**
CSG state directory. Directory I, Elective officials. Lexington, Ky. : The Council, c1998-
*TC JK2403 .S69*

**Directory II, Legislative leadership, committees & staff.**
CSG state directory. Directory II, Legislative leadership, committees & staff. Lexington, Ky. : Council of State Governments, c1998-
*TC JK2495 .S688*

**Directory III, Administrative officials.**
CSG state directory. Directory III, Administrative officials. Lexington, Ky. : The Council, c1998-
*TC JK2403 .B6*

**Directory of American scholars.** 9th ed. / edited by Rita C. Velazquez. Detroit, Mich. : Gale Group, 1999. 5 v. ; 29 cm. Includes indexes. CONTENTS: v. 1. History -- v. 2. English, speech and drama -- v. 3. Foreign languages, linguistics and philology -- v. 4. Philosophy, religion and law -- v. 5. Indexes. ISBN 0-7876-3164-7 (set) ISBN 0-7876-3165-5 (volume 1) ISBN 0-7876-3166-3 (volume 2) ISBN 0-7876-3167-1 (volume 3) ISBN 0-7876-3168-X (volume 4) ISBN 0-7876-3859-5 (volume 5)
*1. Scholars, American - Directories. 2. Educators, American - Directories. 3. United States - Biography. I. Velazquez, Rita C. II. Jaques Cattell Press.*
*TC LA2311 .D57 1999*

**Directory of audiocassettes for children.**
Bowker's directory of audiocassettes for children. New Providence, N.J. : R.R. Bowker, c1998-

*TC ZA4750 .B69*

**Directory of financial aids for minorities.**
Financial aid for African Americans. El Dorado Hills, Calif. : Reference Service Press, c1997-
*TC LB2338 .F5643*

**Directory of grants for organizations serving people with disabilities.** Loxahatchee, Fla. : Research Grant Guides, c1993- v. : 26 cm. 8th ed.- . "A guide to funding sources in the United States for organizations serving people with disabilities." Editor: 1993- Richard M. Eckstein. Continues: Handicapped funding directory ISSN: 0733-4753 (DLC)  82642077 (OCoLC)4374073. ISSN 1077-3282 DDC 338.433624048//0973
*1. Handicapped - Services for - United States - Finance - Directories. 2. Federal aid to services for the handicapped - United States - Directories. 3. Economic assistance, Domestic - United States - Directories. 4. Fund raising - United States - Directories. 5. Endowments - United States - Directories. I. Eckstein, Richard M. II. Title: Handicapped funding directory*
*TC HV3006.A4 H35*

**Directory of internship and post-doctoral fellowships in clinical child/pediatric psychology, 1997** / Susan J. Simonian & Kenneth J. Tarnowski. [Mahwah, N.J. : Lawrence Erlbaum Associates, c1997]. i, 192 p. ; 28 cm. Title from cover. "Completed with the support of the Section on Clinical Child Psychology (Section I) and the Society of Pediatric Psychology (Section V) of the Division of Clinical Psychology of the American Psychological Association (APA)."--p. i. Includes indexes. ISBN 0-8058-2957-1
*1. Clinical child psychology - Study and teaching (Internship) - Directories. 2. Clinical child psychology - Scholarships, fellowships, etc. - Directories. I. Simonian, Susan J. II. Tarnowski, Kenneth J. III. American Psychological Association. Section on Clinical Child Psychology. IV. Society of Pediatric Psychology.*
*TC RJ503.3 .D57 1997*

**Directory of online education resources.**
Bigham, Vicki Smith. The Prentice Hall directory of online education resources. Paramus, N.J. : Prentice Hall, c1998.
*TC LB1044.87 .B54 1998*

**The directory of programs for students at risk.**
Williams, Thomas L., 1946- Larchmont, N.Y. : Eye on Education, c1999.
*TC LC4091 .W55 1999*

**Directory of schools for alternative and complementary health care** / edited by Karen Rappaport. 2nd ed. Phoenix, AZ : Oryx Press, 1999. xix, 330 p. ; 26 cm. Includes bibliographical references and index. ISBN 1-57356-294-7 (alk. paper) DDC 615.5/071/173
*1. Alternative medicine - Study and teaching - United States - Directories. 2. Alternative medicine - Study and teaching - Canada - Directories. I. Rappaport, Karen.*
*TC R733.D59 D59 1999*

**Directory of videocassettes for children.**
Bowker's directory of videocassettes for children. New Providence, N.J. : R.R. Bowker, c1998-
*TC PN1992.945 .B66*

**Disability.**
Marks, Deborah, 1964- London ; New York : Routledge, 1999.
*TC HV1568.2 .M37 1999*

**Disability and the family life cycle.**
Marshak, Laura E. New York : Basic Books, c1999.
*TC HV1568 .M277 1999*

**DISABILITY EVALUATION - UNITED STATES.**
Accommodations in higher education under the Americans with Disabilities Act (ADA) :. DeWitt, NY : GSI Publications, 2000.
*TC RA1055.5 A28 2000*

**DISABILITY EVALUATION - UNITED STATES.**
Accommodations in higher education under the Americans with Disabilities Act (ADA) :. DeWitt, NY : GSI Publications, 2000.
*TC RA1055.5 A28 2000*

**Disability, human rights, and society**
Thomas, Carol, 1958- Female forms. Philadelphia, Pa. : Open University Press, 1999.
*TC HV1568.25.G7 T46 1999*

**DISABILITY RATING.** *See* **DISABILITY EVALUATION.**

**DISABILITY, SOCIOLOGY OF.** *See* **SOCIOLOGY OF DISABILITY.**

**DISABILITY STUDIES.**
Marks, Deborah, 1964- Disability. London ; New York : Routledge, 1999.
*TC HV1568.2 .M37 1999*

**DISABILITY STUDIES - FRANCE - HISTORY - 17TH CENTURY.**
Defects. Ann Arbor : University of Michigan Press, c2000.
*TC HV1568.25.G7 D44 1999*

**DISABILITY STUDIES - FRANCE - HISTORY - 18TH CENTURY.**
Defects. Ann Arbor : University of Michigan Press, c2000.
*TC HV1568.25.G7 D44 1999*

**DISABILITY STUDIES - GREAT BRITAIN.**
Thomas, Carol, 1958- Female forms. Philadelphia, Pa. : Open University Press, 1999.
*TC HV1568.25.G7 T46 1999*

**DISABILITY STUDIES - GREAT BRITAIN - HISTORY - 17TH CENTURY.**
Defects. Ann Arbor : University of Michigan Press, c2000.
*TC HV1568.25.G7 D44 1999*

**DISABILITY STUDIES - GREAT BRITAIN - HISTORY - 18TH CENTURY.**
Defects. Ann Arbor : University of Michigan Press, c2000.
*TC HV1568.25.G7 D44 1999*

**DISABLED.** *See* **HANDICAPPED.**

**Disabled children.**
Middleton, Laura. Malden, Mass. : Blackwell Sciences, 1999.
*TC HV888 .M53 1999*

**DISABLED COLLEGE STUDENTS.** *See* **HANDICAPPED COLLEGE STUDENTS.**

**DISABLED, DEVELOPMENTALLY.** *See* **DEVELOPMENTALLY DISABLED.**

**DISABLED PARENTS.** *See* **HANDICAPPED PARENTS.**

**DISABLED PEOPLE.** *See* **HANDICAPPED.**

**DISABLED STUDENTS.** *See* **HANDICAPPED STUDENTS.**

**DISABLEMENT, SOCIOLOGY OF.** *See* **SOCIOLOGY OF DISABILITY.**

**DISADVANTAGED CHILDREN.** *See* **SOCIALLY HANDICAPPED CHILDREN.**

**DISADVANTAGED, CULTURALLY.** *See* **SOCIALLY HANDICAPPED.**

**DISADVANTAGED, SOCIALLY.** *See* **SOCIALLY HANDICAPPED.**

**Disadvantaged youth project** / [authors, Zsolt Bakos ... et al.]. Budapest : Ministry of Labour, 1998. 148 p. : ill. ; 24 cm.
*1. Socially handicapped children - Education - Hungary. 2. Vocational educational - Hungary. I. Bakos, Zsoltné.*
*TC LC4096.H9 D57 1998*

**DISAFFECTION (SOCIAL PSYCHOLOGY).** *See* **ALIENATION (SOCIAL PSYCHOLOGY).**

**DISARMAMENT.** *See* **MILITARISM; PEACE.**

**DISASTER PLANNING.** *See* **EMERGENCY MANAGEMENT.**

**DISASTER PREPAREDNESS.** *See* **EMERGENCY MANAGEMENT.**

**DISASTER PREVENTION.** *See* **EMERGENCY MANAGEMENT.**

**DISASTER RELIEF - PLANNING.** *See* **EMERGENCY MANAGEMENT.**

**DISASTER RELIEF - UNITED STATES - PLANNING.**
Baldwin, Harmon A. (Harmon Arthur), 1922- Planning for disaster. 2nd ed. Bloomington, Ind. : Phi Delta Kappa Educational Foundation, c1999.
*TC LB2864.5 .B35 1999*

**DISASTERS - PLANNING.** *See* **EMERGENCY MANAGEMENT.**

**DISASTERS - PREPAREDNESS.** *See* **EMERGENCY MANAGEMENT.**

**DISCIPLINARY POWER.** *See* **PARENT AND CHILD (LAW).**

**DISCIPLINE.** *See also* **COLLEGE DISCIPLINE; SCHOOL DISCIPLINE; SELF-CONTROL.**
Tucker, Gina Marie. 1998.
*TC 06 no. 10999*

**Discipline and democracy.**
Koshewa, Allen. Portsmouth, NH : Heinemann, c1999.

*TC LB3011 .K66 1999*

**Discipline by negotiation.**
Tomal, Daniel R. 1st ed. Lancaster, Pa. : Technomic Pub. Co., c1999.
*TC LB3011.5 .T66 1999*

**DISCIPLINE, COLLEGE.** *See* **COLLEGE DISCIPLINE.**

**The discipline of teamwork.**
Barker, James R. (James Robert), 1957- Thousand Oaks, Calif. : Sage Publications, Inc., c1999.
*TC HD66 .B364 1999*

**Disciplined minds.**
Schmidt, Jeff, 1946- Lanham, Md. : Oxford : Rowman & Littlefield, c2000.
*TC HT687 .S35 2000*

**DISCLOSURE, MEDICAL.** *See* **INFORMED CONSENT (MEDICAL LAW).**

**DISCOURSE ANALYSIS.** *See also* **SUBLANGUAGE; WRITTEN COMMUNICATION.**
Discourse and perspective in cognitive linguistics. Amsterdam : Philadelphia : J. Benjamins, c1997.
*TC P165 .D57 1997*

Felton, Mark Kenji. Metacognitive reflection and strategy development in argumentative discourse. 1999.
*TC 085 F34*

Hanks, William F. Intertexts. Lanham : Rowman & Littlefield Publishers, Inc., c2000.
*TC P35.5.M6 H36 2000*

Jones, Carl Mounsey. The film-audience relationship. 1997.
*TC 06 no. 10769*

Jones, Carl Mounsey. The film-audience relationship. 1997.
*TC 06 no. 10769*

Lopez, Marianne Exum, 1960- When discourses collide. New York : P. Lang, c1999.
*TC HQ792.U5 L665 1999*

A Rhetoric of doing. Carbondale : Southern Illinois University Press, c1992.
*TC PE1404 .R496 1992*

Riggenbach, Heidi. Discourse analysis in the language classroom. Ann Arbor : University of Michigan Press, c1999-
*TC P53.2965 .R54 1999*

The semantics/pragmatics interface from different points of view. 1st ed. Oxford, UK ; New York : Elsevier, 1999.
*TC P325 .S3814 1999*

Situated literacies. London ; New York : Routledge, 2000.
*TC LC149 .S52 2000*

Social constructionism, discourse, and realism. London ; Thousand Oaks, Calif. : SAGE Publications, 1998.
*TC HM251 .S671163 1998*

Stubbs, Michael, 1947- Text and corpus analysis. Oxford, OX, UK ; Cambridge, Mass., USA : Blackwell Publishers, c1996.
*TC P302 .S773 1996*

Talk, work, and institutional order. Berlin ; New York : Mouton de Gruyter, 1999.
*TC P95 .T286 1999*

**DISCOURSE ANALYSIS - DATA PROCESSING.**
Popping, Roel. Computer-assisted text analysis. Thousand Oaks, Calif. ; London : SAGE, c2000.
*TC P302 .P636 2000*

Stubbs, Michael, 1947- Text and corpus analysis. Oxford, OX, UK ; Cambridge, Mass., USA : Blackwell Publishers, c1996.
*TC P302 .S773 1996*

**Discourse analysis in the language classroom.**
Riggenbach, Heidi. Ann Arbor : University of Michigan Press, c1999-
*TC P53.2965 .R54 1999*

**DISCOURSE ANALYSIS, NARATIVE.**
Fleischer, Lee. Living in contradiction. 1998.
*TC 06 no. 11021*

**DISCOURSE ANALYSIS, NARRATIVE.** *See also* **NARRATION (RHETORIC).**
Golden, Joanne Marie, 1949- Storymaking in elementary and middle school classrooms. Mahwah, N.J. : L. Erlbaum Associates, 2000.

*TC LB1042 .G54 2000*

**DISCOURSE ANALYSIS - SOCIAL ASPECTS.**
Genre and institutions. London ; Washington : Cassell, 1997.
*TC P302.84 .G46 1997*

**DISCOURSE ANALYSIS - UNITED STATES - CASE STUDIES.**
Freeman, Rebecca D. (Rebecca Diane), 1960- Bilingual education and social change. Clevedon [England] ; Philadelphia : Multilingual Matters, c1998.
*TC LC3731 .F72 1998*

**Discourse and perspective in cognitive linguistics /** edited by Wolf-Andreas Liebert, Gisela Redeker, Linda Waugh. Amsterdam ; Philadelphia : J. Benjamins, c1997. xiii, 271 p. ; 23 cm. (Amsterdam studies in the theory and history of linguistic science. Series IV, Current issues in linguistic theory, 0304-0763 ; v. 151) Selected rev. papers read at the 4th bi-annual International Cognitive Linguistics Conference held in Albuquerque at the University of New Mexico, July 16-21, 1995. Includes bibliographical references and index. ISBN 1-55619-866-3 (alk. paper) DDC 415
*1. Cognitive grammar. 2. Discourse analysis. 3. Modality (Linguistics) 4. Metaphor. I. Liebert, Wolf-Andreas, 1959- II. Redeker, Gisela. III. Waugh, Linda R. IV. International Cognitive Linguistics Conference (4th : 1995 : Albuquerque, N.M.) V. Series.*
*TC P165 .D57 1997*

**DISCOURSE GRAMMAR.** *See* **DISCOURSE ANALYSIS.**

**Discover art.**
Chapman, Laura H. Worcester, Mass. : Davis Publications, c1987.
*TC N361 .C56 1987*

Chapman, Laura H. Worcester, Mass. : Davis Publications, c1985.
*TC N361 .C56 1985*

**Discover : Grade 1, level 1.5, [Themes 9 and 10].**
Cooper, J. David (James David), 1942- Boston : Houghton Mifflin, 1997.
*TC LB1575.8 .C6616 1997*

**DISCOVERIES IN SCIENCE.**
Klahr, David. Exploring science. Cambridge, Mass. : MIT Press, c2000.
*TC Q180.55.D57 K55 2000*

Wagman, Morton. Scientific discovery processes in humans and computers. Westport, CT : Praeger, 2000.
*TC Q180.55.D57 W34 2000*

**Discovering French. Bleu.**
Valette, Jean-Paul. Extended teacher's ed. Evanston, Ill. : McDougal Littell, c1997.
*TC PC1129.E5 V342 1997 Teacher's Ed.*

**Discovering French. Rouge.**
Valette, Jean-Paul. Evanston, Ill. : McDougal Littell, c1997.
*TC PC2129.E5 V342 1997*

Valette, Jean Paul. Lexington, Mass. : D.C. Heath and Co., c1997.
*TC PC2129.E5 V342 1997*

**Discovering me.**
Herod, Leslie. Boston, MA : Allyn and Bacon, c1999.
*TC BF724.3.S36 H47 1999*

**Discovery works.**
DiscoveryWorks. Parsippany, N.J. : Silver Burdett Ginn, c1996-
*TC LB1585 .D574 1996*

DiscoveryWorks. Parsippany, N.J. : Silver Burdett Ginn, c1996
*TC LB1585 .D574 1996 Teaching Guide Gr. 4*

DiscoveryWorks. Parsippany, N.J. : Silver Burdett Ginn, c1996
*TC LB1585 .D574 1996 Teaching Guide Gr. 5*

DiscoveryWorks. Parsippany, N.J. : Silver Burdett Ginn, c1996
*TC LB1585 .D574 1996 Teaching Guide Gr. 6*

DiscoveryWorks. Parsippany, N.J. : Silver Burdett Ginn, c1996
*TC LB1585 .D574 1996 Teaching Guide Gr. 1*

DiscoveryWorks. Parsippany, N.J. : Silver Burdett Ginn, c1996
*TC LB1585 .D574 1996 Teaching Guide Gr. 2*

DiscoveryWorks. Parsippany, N.J. : Silver Burdett Ginn, c1996

*TC LB1585 .D574 1996 Teaching Guide Gr. 3*

DiscoveryWorks. Parsippany, N.J. : Silver Burdett Ginn, c1996
*TC LB1585 .D574 1996 Teaching Guide Gr. K*

DiscoveryWorks. Parsippany, NJ : Silver Burdett Ginn, c1996-
*TC LB1585 .D574 1996*

DiscoveryWorks. Parsippany, N.J. : Silver Burdett Ginn, c1996-
*TC LB1585 .D574 1996 Workbook*

**DiscoveryWorks.** Parsippany, N.J. : Silver Burdett Ginn, c1996- 6 v. : col. ill. ; 31 cm. (Silver Burdett Ginn science) Includes index. ISBN 0-382-38858-5 (Gr. 1) ISBN 0-382-38857-7 (Gr. 2) ISBN 0-382-33383-7 (Gr. 3) ISBN 0-382-33384-5 (Gr. 4) ISBN 0-382-33385-3 (Gr. 5) ISBN 0-382-33386-1 (Gr. 6)
*1. Science - Study and teaching (Elementary) I. Silver Burdett Ginn (Firm) II. Title: Discovery works III. Series.*
*TC LB1585 .D574 1996*

**DiscoveryWorks :** teaching guide. Parsippany, N.J. : Silver Burdett Ginn, c1996 1 v. (various pagings) : col. ill. ; 31 cm. (Silver Burdett Ginn science) Cover title: DiscoveryWorks : teaching guide/4. Includes index. CONTENTS: (Unit A) Earth's land resources -- (Unit B) Properties of matter -- (Unit C) Animals -- (Unit D) Magnetism and electricity -- (Unit E) Weather and climate -- (Unit F) The body's delivery systems. ISBN 0-382-31983-4 ISBN 0-382-33469-8 (UNit A) ISBN 0-382-33470-1 (UNit B) ISBN 0-382-33472-8 (UNit C) ISBN 0-382-33473-6 (UNit D) ISBN 0-382-33474-4 (UNit E) ISBN 0-382-33475-2 (UNit F)
*1. Science - Study and teaching (Elementary) I. Silver Burdett Ginn (Firm) II. Title: DiscoveryWorks : teaching guide/4 III. Title: Discovery works IV. Series.*
*TC LB1585 .D574 1996 Teaching Guide Gr. 4*

**DiscoveryWorks :** teaching guide. Parsippany, N.J. : Silver Burdett Ginn, c1996 1 v. (various pagings) : col. ill. ; 31 cm. (Silver Burdett Ginn science) Cover title: DiscoveryWorks : teaching guide/5. Includes index. CONTENTS: (Unit A) Plants -- (Unit B) The solar system and beyond -- (Unit C) Energy, work, and machines -- (Unit D) Populations and ecosystems -- (Unit E) The solid earth -- (Unit F) Light and sound -- (Unit G) Movement and control. ISBN 0-382-31984-2 ISBN 0-382-33476-0 (Unit A) ISBN 0-382-33477-9 (Unit B) ISBN 0-382-33478-7 (Unit C) ISBN 0-382-33479-5 (Unit D) ISBN 0-382-33480-9 (Unit E) ISBN 0-382-33481-7 (Unit F) ISBN 0-382-33482-5 (Unit G)
*1. Science - Study and teaching (Elementary) I. Silver Burdett Ginn (Firm) II. Title: DiscoveryWorks : teaching guide/5 III. Title: Discovery works IV. Series.*
*TC LB1585 .D574 1996 Teaching Guide Gr. 5*

**DiscoveryWorks :** teaching guide. Parsippany, N.J. : Silver Burdett Ginn, c1996 1 v. (various pagings) : col. ill. ; 31 cm. (Silver Burdett Ginn science) Cover title: DiscoveryWorks : teaching guide/6. Includes index. CONTENTS: (Unit A) Cells and microbes -- (Unit B) The changing earth -- (Unit C) The nature of matter -- (Unit D) Contunuity of life -- (Unit E) Oceanography -- (Unit F) Forces and motion -- (Unit G) Growing up healthy. ISBN 0-382-31985-0 ISBN 0-382-33483-3 (Unit A) ISBN 0-382-33484-1 (Unit B) ISBN 0-382-33486-8 (Unit C) ISBN 0-382-33487-6 (Unit D) ISBN 0-382-33488-4 (Unit E) ISBN 0-382-33489-2 (Unit F) ISBN 0-382-33490-6 (Unit G)
*1. Science - Study and teaching (Elementary) I. Silver Burdett Ginn (Firm) II. Title: DiscoveryWorks : teaching guide/6 III. Title: Discovery works IV. Series.*
*TC LB1585 .D574 1996 Teaching Guide Gr. 6*

**DiscoveryWorks :** teaching guide/1. Parsippany, N.J. : Silver Burdett Ginn, c1996 5 v. : col. ill. ; 31 cm. (Silver Burdett Ginn science) Includes index. CONTENTS: [v. 1] Kinds of living things -- [v. 2] Weather and seasons -- [v. 3] Magnets -- [v. 4] Earth's land and water -- [v. 5] Keeping fit and healthy. ISBN 0-382-33446-9 [v. 1] ISBN 0-382-33447-7 [v. 2] ISBN 0-382-33448-5 [v. 3] ISBN 0-382-33449-3 [v. 4] ISBN 0-382-33450-7 [v. 5]
*1. Science - Study and teaching (Elementary) I. Silver Burdett Ginn (Firm) II. Title: Discovery works III. Series.*
*TC LB1585 .D574 1996 Teaching Guide Gr. 1*

**DiscoveryWorks :** teaching guide/2. Parsippany, N.J. : Silver Burdett Ginn, c1996 5 v. : col. ill. ; 31 cm. (Silver Burdett Ginn science) Includes index. CONTENTS: [v. 1] Interactions of living things -- [v. 2] Light and color -- [v. 3] Earth through time -- [v. 4] Solids, liquids, and gases -- [v. 5] What makes me sick. ISBN 0-382-33457-4 [v. 1] ISBN 0-382-33458-2 [v. 2] ISBN 0-382-33459-0 [v. 3] ISBN 0-382-33460-4 [v. 4] ISBN 0-382-33461-2 [v. 5]
*1. Science - Study and teaching (Elementary) I. Silver Burdett Ginn (Firm) II. Title: Discovery works III. Series.*
*TC LB1585 .D574 1996 Teaching Guide Gr. 2*

**DiscoveryWorks :** teaching guide/3. Parsippany, N.J. : Silver Burdett Ginn, c1996 1 v. (various pagings) : col. ill. ; 31 cm. (Silver Burdett Ginn science) Includes index.

CONTENTS: (Unit A) Life cycles -- (Unit B) Sun, moon, and earth -- (Unit C) Forms of energy -- (Unit D) Earth's water -- (Unit E) Roles of living things -- (Unit F) What's for lunch. ISBN 0-382-31982-6
1. *Science - Study and teaching (Elementary)* I. *Silver Burdett Ginn (Firm)* II. *Title: Discovery works* III. *Series.*
*TC LB1585 .D574 1996 Teaching Guide Gr. 3*

**DiscoveryWorks : teaching guide/4.** DiscoveryWorks. Parsippany, N.J. : Silver Burdett Ginn, c1996
*TC LB1585 .D574 1996 Teaching Guide Gr. 4*

**DiscoveryWorks : teaching guide/5.** DiscoveryWorks. Parsippany, N.J. : Silver Burdett Ginn, c1996
*TC LB1585 .D574 1996 Teaching Guide Gr. 5*

**DiscoveryWorks : teaching guide/6.** DiscoveryWorks. Parsippany, N.J. : Silver Burdett Ginn, c1996
*TC LB1585 .D574 1996 Teaching Guide Gr. 6*

**DiscoveryWorks : teaching guide/K.** Parsippany, N.J. : Silver Burdett Ginn, c1996 5 v. : col. ill. ; 31 cm. (Silver Burdett Ginn science) Includes index. CONTENTS: [v. 1] Characteristics of living things -- [v. 2] Exploring with the senses -- [v. 3] Looking at the sky -- [v. 4] Pushes and pulls -- [v. 5] Body parts. ISBN 0-382-33441-8 [v. 1] ISBN 0-382-33442-6 [v. 2] ISBN 0-382-33443-4 [v. 3] ISBN 0-382-33444-2 [v. 4] ISBN 0-382-33445-0 [v. 5]
1. *Science - Study and teaching (Elementary)* I. *Silver Burdett Ginn (Firm)* II. *Title: Discovery works* III. *Series.*
*TC LB1585 .D574 1996 Teaching Guide Gr. K*

**DiscoveryWorks :** teaching guide / [William Badders ... et al.]. Parsippany, NJ : Silver Burdett Ginn, c1996- v. : col. ill. ; 31 cm. (Silver Burdett Ginn science) Vol. 1 has title: Kinds of living things. Includes bibliographical references and indexes. Vol. <1> also called Teacher ed. ISBN 0-382-33446-9 (v. 1) ISBN 0-382-31982-6 (v. 3) ISBN 0-382-31984-2 (v. 5)
1. *Science - Study and teaching (Elementary)* I. *Badders, William.* II. *Silver Burdett Ginn (Firm)* III. *Title: Discovery works* IV. *Title: Kinds of living things* V. *Series.*
*TC LB1585 .D574 1996*

**DiscoveryWorks :** workbook. Parsippany, N.J. : Silver Burdett Ginn, c1996- 6 v. : ill. ; 31 cm. (Silver Burdett Ginn science) "Lesson reviews" on T.p. for Gr. K-2; "Investigation reviews" on T.p. for Gr. 3-6. ISBN 0-382-88863-1 (Gr. K) ISBN 0-382-88864-x (Gr. 1) ISBN 0-382-88865-8 (Gr. 2) ISBN 0-382-88866-6 (Gr. 3) ISBN 0-382-88867-4 (Gr. 4) ISBN 0-382-88868-2 (Gr. 5) ISBN 0-382-88869-0 (Gr. 6)
1. *Science - Study and teaching (Elementary)* I. *Silver Burdett Ginn (Firm)* II. *Title: Discovery works* III. *Series.*
*TC LB1585 .D574 1996 Workbook*

**Discrete mathematics in the schools** / Joseph G. Rosenstein, Deborah S. Franzblau, Fred S. Roberts, editors. Providence, R.I. : American Mathematical Society, National Council of Teachers of Mathematics, c1997. xxxiii, 452 p. : ill. ; 26 cm. (DIMACS series in discrete mathematics and theoretical computer science, 1052-1798 ; v. 36) Papers from a conference held at DIMACS at Rutgers University in Oct. 1992. "NSF Science and Technology Center in Discrete Mathematics and Theoretical Computer Science. A consortium of Rutgers University, Princeton University, AT&T Labs, Bell Labs, and Bellcore." Includes bibliographical references. ISBN 0-8218-0448-0 (hardcover : acid-free paper) DDC 511/.07/1
1. *Mathematics - Study and teaching - Congresses.* I. *Rosenstein, Joseph G.* II. *Franzblau, Deborah S., 1957-* III. *Roberts, Fred S.* IV. *NSF Science and Technology Center in Discrete Mathematics and Theoretical Computer Science.* V. *Series.*
*TC QA11.A1 D57 1997*

**DISCRIMINATION.** *See* **HOMOPHOBIA; MINORITIES; RACE DISCRIMINATION; REVERSE DISCRIMINATION.**

**DISCRIMINATION AGAINST DISABLED PERSONS.** *See* **DISCRIMINATION AGAINST THE HANDICAPPED.**

**DISCRIMINATION AGAINST HANDICAPPED PERSONS.** *See* **DISCRIMINATION AGAINST THE HANDICAPPED.**

**DISCRIMINATION AGAINST OVERWEIGHT PERSONS.** Solovay, Sondra, 1970- Tipping the scales of justice. Amherst, N.Y. : Prometheus Books, 2000.
*TC BF697.5.B63 S65 2000*

**DISCRIMINATION AGAINST THE DISABLED.** *See* **DISCRIMINATION AGAINST THE HANDICAPPED.**

**DISCRIMINATION AGAINST THE HANDICAPPED - UNITED STATES.** Frank, Gelya, 1948- Venus on wheels. Berkeley, Calif. : University of California Press, c2000.
*TC HV3021.W66 F73 2000*

**DISCRIMINATION AGAINST WOMEN.** *See* **SEX DISCRIMINATION AGAINST WOMEN.**

**DISCRIMINATION IN COLLEGES AND UNIVERSITIES.** *See* **DISCRIMINATION IN HIGHER EDUCATION.**

**DISCRIMINATION IN CRIMINAL JUSTICE ADMINISTRATION - UNITED STATES.** Cole, David. No equal justice. New York : The New Press ; Distributed by W. W. Norton, c1999.
*TC HV9950 .C65 1999*

**DISCRIMINATION IN EDUCATION.** *See also* **SEGREGATION IN EDUCATION; SEX DISCRIMINATION IN EDUCATION; TEST BIAS.** Education and racism :. Aldershot ; Brookfield, Vt. : Ashgate, c1999.
*TC LC212.3.G7E48 1999*

**DISCRIMINATION IN EDUCATION - CANADA.** Racism and education. Ottawa : Canadian Teachers' Federation, 1992.
*TC LC212.3.C3 R32 1992*

**DISCRIMINATION IN EDUCATION - CANADA - CASE STUDIES.** Ryan, James, 1952 Oct. 18- Race and ethnicity in multi-ethnic schools. Clevedon [England] ; Philadelphia : Multilingual Matters, c1999.
*TC LC3734 .R93 1999*

**DISCRIMINATION IN EDUCATION - GEORGIA - DECATUR - HISTORY - 20TH CENTURY.** Keating, Tom, 1941- Saturday school. Bloomington, Ind. : Phi Delta Kappa Educational Foundation, c1999.
*TC LC212.23.D43 K42 1999*

**DISCRIMINATION IN EDUCATION - GEORGIA - HISTORY - 20TH CENTURY.** O'Brien, Thomas V., 1958- The politics of race and schooling. Lanham, Md. : Lexington Books, c1999.
*TC LC212.22.G46 O37 1999*

**DISCRIMINATION IN EDUCATION - GREAT BRITAIN.** Dadzie, Stella, 1952- Toolkit for tackling racism in schools. Stoke on Trent, Staffordshire, England : Trentham Books, 2000.
*TC LC212.3.G7 D339 2000*

Promoting equality in secondary schools. London ; New York : Cassell, 1999.
*TC LC212.3.G7 P77 1999*

Richardson, Robin. Inclusive schools, inclusive society. Stoke on Trent, Staffordshire, England : Trentham Books, 1999.
*TC LC212.3.G7 R523 1999*

**DISCRIMINATION IN EDUCATION - ISRAEL.** Swirski, Shlomo. Politics and education in Israel. New York : Falmer Press, 1999.
*TC LC94.I75 S95 1999*

**DISCRIMINATION IN EDUCATION - SOUTH AFRICA - HISTORY.** Hlatshwayo, Simphiwe A. (Simphiwe Abner) Education and independence. Westport, Conn : Greenwood Press, 2000.
*TC LA1536 .H53 2000*

**DISCRIMINATION IN EDUCATION - UNITED STATES.** Charting terrains of Chicana(o)/Latina(o) education. Cresskill, N.J. : Hampton Press, c2000.
*TC LC2669 .C42 2000*

Critical ethnicity. Lanham, Md. : Rowman & Littlefield, c1999.
*TC LC212.2 .C75 1999*

Hyman, Irwin A. Dangerous schools. 1st ed. San Francisco : Jossey-Bass Publishers, c1999.
*TC LB3013 .H897 1999*

Race is-- race isn't. Boulder, CO : Westview Press, c1999.
*TC LC3731 .R27 1999*

**DISCRIMINATION IN EDUCATION - UNITED STATES - CASE STUDIES.** Educators healing racism. Reston, VA : Association of Teacher Educators ; Olney, MD : Association for Childhood Education International, c1999.
*TC LC212.2 .E38 1999*

**DISCRIMINATION IN EDUCATION - UNITED STATES - HISTORY.** Spring, Joel H. Deculturalization and the struggle for equality. 3rd ed. Boston : McGraw-Hill, c2001.
*TC LC3731 .S68 2001*

**DISCRIMINATION IN EMPLOYMENT.** *See* **AFFIRMATIVE ACTION PROGRAMS; EQUAL PAY FOR EQUAL WORK; SEX DISCRIMINATION IN EMPLOYMENT.**

**DISCRIMINATION IN EMPLOYMENT - CANADA.** Thomas, Barb, 1946- Combatting racism in the workplace. Toronto : Cross Cultural Communication Centre, c1983.
*TC HD4903.5.C3 T56 1983*

**DISCRIMINATION IN EMPLOYMENT - UNITED STATES.** Job creation. Washington, DC : Joint Center for Political and Economic Studies : Lanham, Md. ; Oxford : University Press of America, c1998.
*TC HD8081.A65 J63 1998*

**DISCRIMINATION IN HIGHER EDUCATION - GREAT BRITAIN.** Woodward, Diana, 1948- Managing equal opportunities in higher education. Buckingham [England] ; Philadelphia : Society for Research into Higher Education : Open University Press, 2000.
*TC LC213.3.G7 W66 2000*

**DISCRIMINATION IN HIGHER EDUCATION - UNITED STATES.** Grass roots and glass ceilings. Albany : State University of New York Press, c1999.
*TC LC212.42 .G73 1999*

Power, race, and gender in academe. New York : Modern Language Association, 2000.
*TC LC3727 .P69 2000*

Rai, Kul B. Affirmative action and the university. Lincoln : University of Nebraska Press, 2000.
*TC LC212.42 .R35 2000*

**DISCRIMINATION IN MEDICAL CARE - UNITED STATES.** Smith, David Barton. Health care divided. Ann Arbor : University of Michigan Press, 1999.
*TC RA448.5.N4 S63 1999*

**DISCRIMINATION IN MEDICAL EDUCATION - LAW AND LEGISLATION - UNITED STATES.** Ball, Howard. The Bakke case. Lawrence, Kan. : University Press of Kansas, 2000.
*TC KF228.B34 B35 2000*

**DISCRIMINATION, RACIAL.** *See* **RACE DISCRIMINATION.**

**DISCRIMINATION - RELIGIOUS ASPECTS - UNITED STATES.** Perlmutter, Philip. Legacy of hate. Armonk, N.Y. ; London : M.E. Sharpe, c1999.
*TC BF575.H3 P47 1999*

**DISCRIMINATION - STUDY AND TEACHING (ELEMENTARY) - UNITED STATES.** Teaching for a tolerant world, grades K-6. Urbana, Ill. : National Council of Teachers of English, c1999.
*TC HM1271 .T43 1999*

**DISCRIMINATION - UNITED STATES.** Affirmative action. San Diego, Calif. : Greenhaven Press, 2000.
*TC JC599.U5 A34685 2000*

**DISCURSIVE PSYCHOLOGY.** Gillett, Grant, 1950- The mind and its discontents. Oxford ; New York : Oxford University Press, c1999.
*TC BD418.3 .G555 1999*

Ochsner, Mindy Blaise. Something rad & risque'e. 1999.
*TC 06 no. 11208*

**DISCUSSION.** *See also* **FORUMS (DISCUSSION AND DEBATE); NEGOTIATION.** Bligh, Donald A. What's the point in discussion? Exeter, Eng. : Portland, OR : Intellect, 2000.
*TC LC6519 .B555 2000*

**DISCUSSIONxSTUDY AND TEACHING (SECONDARY) - COLORADO - DENVER - PROBLEMS, EXERCISES, ETC.** Public issues discussion [videorecording] : Diana Hess at Denver High School 1997. [Boulder, Colo.] : Social Science Education Consortium, c1997.
*TC H62.3 .P4 1997*

Socratic seminar [videorecording]. [Boulder, Colo.] : Social Science Education Consortium, c1997.

*Diseases*

**DISEASES.** *See* **HEALTH; MENTAL ILLNESS; NUTRITION DISORDERS; SICK.**

**DISEASES - CAUSES AND THEORIES OF CAUSATION.** *See also* **HEALTH BEHAVIOR; INFECTION.**
Chiozza, Luis A. Why do we fall ill? Madison, Conn. : Psychosocial Press, c1999.
*TC R726.7 .C48 1999*

**DISEASES, MENTAL.** *See* **MENTAL ILLNESS; PSYCHOLOGY, PATHOLOGICAL.**

**DISEASES OF CHILDREN.** *See* **CHILDREN - DISEASES.**

**DISEASES - PREVENTION.** *See* **MEDICINE, PREVENTIVE.**

**DiSessa, Andrea A.** Changing minds : computers, learning, and literacy / Andrea A. DiSessa. Cambridge, MA : MIT Press, c2000. xix, 271 p. : ill. ; 24 cm. Includes bibliographical references and index. ISBN 0-262-04180-4 (hc : alk. papr) DDC 370/.285
*1. Education - Data processing. 2. Learning, Psychology of. 3. Literacy. I. Title.*
*TC LB1028.43 .D57 2000*

**DISHONESTY.** *See* **HONESTY.**

**DISK OPERATING SYSTEMS.** *See* **OPERATING SYSTEMS (COMPUTERS).**

**Disordered mother or disordered diagnosis?.**
Allison, David B. Hillsdale, NJ : Analytic Press, 1998.
*TC RC569.5.M83 A38 1998*

**DISORDERLY CONDUCT.**
Behaving badly. 1st ed. Washington, D.C. : American Psychological Association, 2001.
*TC HM1106 .B45 2001*

**DISORDERS, AFFECTIVE.** *See* **AFFECTIVE DISORDERS.**

**DISORDERS, DELUSIONAL.** *See* **DELUSIONS.**

**DISORDERS, DISSOCIATIVE.** *See* **DISSOCIATIVE DISORDERS.**

**Disorders due to psychoactive substance abuse** [videorecording] / a presentation of Films for the Humanities & Sciences ; University of Sheffield ; produced and directed by Steve Collier ; written by Dr. Steve Peters : Sheffield University Television. Princeton, N.J. : Films for the Humanities & Sciences, 1998. 1 videocassette (34 min.) : sd., col. : 1/2 in. (Differential diagnosis in psychiatry) Series subtitle: Visual aid based on ICD 10. VHS. Catalogued from credits and container. Commentary: John Graham Davies. Sound: Ken Hardy; cameras: Jackie Jones, Mark Parkin, Gary Wraith; graphics: Sean Purcell. Originally produced 1995-1997 at the University of Sheffield. "Clinical features of myotonic dystrophy and Huntington's disease" included in list of complete series on container no longer part of series. For students of psychiatry, clinical psychology and social work, and counselling. SUMMARY: This program discusses psychoactive substance abuse, mainly with alcohol, but also including withdrawal from the Benzodiazepines, and amphetamine abuse. We see six patients. The first presents with dependence syndrome in alcohol use; the second presents with a withdrawal state from the Benzodiazepines, in this case, in this case, delirium tremens from alcohol withdrawal. The fourth are two cases of drug-induced psychotic disorder, one from amphetamines and the other from alcohol. The last is a case of Korsakov's syndrome.
*1. Drug abuse. 2. Alcoholic psychoses - Diagnosis. 3. Alcoholic psychoses - Patients. 4. Delirium tremens - Diagnosis. 5. Delirium tremens - Patients. 6. Psychoses - Diagnosis. 7. Psychoses - Patients. 8. Korsakoff's syndrome - Diagnosis. 9. Korsakoff's syndrome - Patients. 10. Drug withdrawal symptoms. 11. Diagnosis, Differential. I. Peters, Steve, Dr. II. Collier, Steve. III. Davies, John Graham. IV. University of Sheffield. V. Sheffield University Television. VI. Films for the Humanities (Firm) VII. Title: Visual aid based on ICD 10 VIII. Series.*
*TC RC564 .D5 1998*

**DISORDERS OF COMMUNICATION.** *See* **COMMUNICATIVE DISORDERS.**

**DISORDERS OF COMMUNICATION IN CHILDREN.** *See* **COMMUNICATIVE DISORDERS IN CHILDREN.**

**DISORDERS OF EATING.** *See* **EATING DISORDERS.**

**DISORDERS OF NUTRITION.** *See* **NUTRITION DISORDERS.**

**DISORDERS OF PERSONALITY.** *See* **PERSONALITY DISORDERS.**

**DISORDERS OF SPEECH.** *See* **SPEECH DISORDERS.**

**DISORDERS, PANIC.** *See* **PANIC DISORDERS.**

**DISORDERS, PSYCHOSEXUAL.** *See* **PSYCHOSEXUAL DISORDERS.**

**Dispatches from the Freud wars.**
Forrester, John. Cambridge, Mass. : Harvard University Press, 1997.
*TC BF175 .F646 1997*

**DISPLACED PERSONS.** *See* **REFUGEES.**

**DISPLAY TECHNIQUES.** *See* **MUSEUM EXHIBITS.**

**DISPLAYS IN EDUCATION.**
Skaggs, Gayle, 1952- On display. Jefferson, NC : McFarland, c1999.
*TC Z675.S3 S5975 1999*

**DISPLAYS, LIBRARY.** *See* **LIBRARY EXHIBITS.**

**DISPLAYS, MUSEUM.** *See* **MUSEUM EXHIBITS.**

**DISPOSABLE INCOME.** *See* **INCOME DISTRIBUTION.**

**DISPUTE PROCESSING.** *See* **DISPUTE RESOLUTION (LAW).**

**DISPUTE RESOLUTION (LAW).** *See also* **MEDIATION.**
Isenhart, Myra Warren. Collaborative approaches to resolving conflict. Thousand Oaks, Calif. : Sage Publications, c2000.
*TC HM1126 .I74 2000*

**DISPUTE SETTLEMENT.** *See* **CONFLICT MANAGEMENT; DISPUTE RESOLUTION (LAW).**

**DISRUPTIVE BEHAVIOR DISORDERS IN CHILDREN.** *See* **BEHAVIOR DISORDERS IN CHILDREN.**

**DISSECTION.** *See* **HUMAN DISSECTION.**

**Disseminating nursing research**
Key aspects of comfort. New York : Springer Pub. Co., c1989.
*TC RT87.P35 K48 1989*

**Disseminating Nursing Research Project.**
Key aspects of comfort. New York : Springer Pub. Co., c1989.
*TC RT87.P35 K48 1989*

**Dissent, injustice, and the meanings of America.**
Shiffrin, Steven H., 1941- Princeton, N.J. : Princeton University Press, c1999.
*TC KF4772 .S448 1999*

**DISSERTATIONS, ACADEMIC.**
Piantanida, Maria. The qualitative dissertation. Thousand Oaks, Calif. : Corwin Press, c1999.
*TC LB2369 .P48 1999*

Theses and dissertations. Lanham, Md. : University Press of America, 1997.
*TC LB2369 .T44 1997*

**DISSERTATIONS, ACADEMIC - HANDBOOKS, MANUALS, ETC.**
Elphinstone, Leonie. How to get a research degree. St. Leonards, Australia : Allen & Unwin, 1998.
*TC LB2371 .E46 1998*

Thomas, R. Murray (Robert Murray), 1921- Theses and dissertations. Westport, Conn. : Bergin & Garvey, 2000.
*TC LB2369 .T458 2000*

**DISSOCIATED PERSONALITY.** *See* **MULTIPLE PERSONALITY.**

**DISSOCIATION (PSYCHOLOGY).** *See* **DISSOCIATIVE DISORDERS.**

**Dissociation, trauma, memory, and hypnosis book series**
Healing from within. 1st ed. Washington, DC ; London : American Psychological Association, c2000.
*TC RC497 .H42 2000*

**DISSOCIATIVE DISORDERS.** *See* **FUGUE (PSYCHOLOGY); MULTIPLE PERSONALITY.**

**DISSOCIATIVE DISORDERS - CASE STUDIES.**
Goldberg, Arnold, 1929- Being of two minds. Hillsdale, NJ : Analytic Press, 1999.
*TC RC569.5.M8 G65 1999*

**DISSOCIATIVE DISORDERS - CASE STUDIES.**
Goldberg, Arnold, 1929- Being of two minds. Hillsdale, NJ : Analytic Press, 1999.

*TC RC569.5.M8 G65 1999*

**DISSOCIATIVE DISORDERS - DIAGNOSIS.**
Neurotic, stress-related, and somatoform disorders [videorecording]. Princeton, N.J. : Films for the Humanities & Sciences, 1998.
*TC RC530 .N4 1998*

**DISSOCIATIVE DISORDERS - PATIENTS.**
Challenge cases [videorecording]. Princeton, N.J. : Films for the Humanities & Sciences, 1998.
*TC RC455.2.C4 C4 1998*

Neurotic, stress-related, and somatoform disorders [videorecording]. Princeton, N.J. : Films for the Humanities & Sciences, 1998.
*TC RC530 .N4 1998*

**DISSOCIATIVE IDENTITY DISORDER.** *See* **MULTIPLE PERSONALITY.**

**Distance and campus universities.**
Guri-Rozenblit, Sarah. 1st ed. Oxford, UK ; New York, NY : Pergamon, published for IAU Press, 1999.
*TC LC5800 .G87 1999*

**DISTANCE EDUCATION.** *See also* **OPEN LEARNING; TELEVISION IN EDUCATION; UNIVERSITY EXTENSION.**
Hanson, Dan. 2nd ed. Washington, DC : Association for Educational Communications and Technology ; Ames, Iowa : Research Institute for Studies in Education, c1997.
*TC LC5800 .S3 1997*

**DISTANCE EDUCATION.**
Anderson, Dennis S. Mathematics and distance education on the internet. 1999.
*TC 085 An2317*

Kouki, Rafa. Telelearning via the Internet. Hershey, PA : Idea Group Pub., c1999.
*TC LC5800 .K68 1999*

McConnell, David, 1951- Implementing computer supported cooperative learning.. 2nd ed. London : Kogan Page, 2000.
*TC LB1032 .M38 2000*

Morgan, Chris. Assessing open and distance learners. London : Kogan Page ; Sterling, VA : Stylus Pub., 1999.
*TC LC5800 .M67 1999*

Nielsen, H. Dean. The cost-effectiveness of distance education for teacher training. Cambridge, Mass. : B.R.I.D.G.E.S. Basic Research and Implementation in Developing Education Systems, [1991].
*TC LB1731 .N43 1991*

Salmon, Gilly. E-moderating. London : Kogan Page ; Sterling, VA : Stylus, 2000.
*TC LB1044.87 .S25 2000*

Schweizer, Heidi. Designing and teaching an on-line course :. Boston : Allyn & Bacon, c1999.
*TC LB1028.3 .S377 1999*

Simpson, Ormond. Supporting students in open and distance learning. London : Kogan Page, 2000.
*TC LC5800 .S56 2000*

Staff development in open and flexible learning. London ; New York : Routledge, 1998.
*TC LC5800 .S83 1998*

Teaching and learning at a distance. Upper Saddle River, N.J. : Merrill, c2000.
*TC LC5800 .T43 2000*

**DISTANCE EDUCATION - BIBLIOGRAPHY.**
Hanson, Dan. Distance education :. 2nd ed. Washington, DC : Association for Educational Communications and Technology ; Ames, Iowa : Research Institute for Studies in Education, c1997.
*TC LC5800 .S3 1997*

**DISTANCE EDUCATION - COMPUTER-ASSISTED INSTRUCTION.**
Belanger, France, 1963- Evaluation and implementation of distance learning. Hershey, PA ; London : Idea Group Pub., c2000.
*TC LC5803.C65 B45 2000*

Distance learning technologies. Hershey, PA ; London : Idea Group Pub., c2000.
*TC LC5803.C65 D57 2000*

International perspectives on tele-education and virtual learning environments. Aldershot : Ashgate, 2000.
*TC LB1044.87 .I55 2000*

Virtual instruction. Englewood, Colo. : Libraries Unlimited, 1999.

*TC LC5803.C65 V57 1999*

## DISTANCE EDUCATION - COMPUTER-ASSISTED INSTRUCTION - CONGRESSES.
IFIP TC3 WG3.2/3.6 International Working Conference on Building University Electronic Educational Environments (1999 : Irvine, Calif.) Building university electronic educational environments. Boston : Kluwer Academic Publishers, c2000.
*TC LC5803.C65 .I352 2000*

IFIP TC3/WG3.3 & WG3.6 Joint Working Conference on the Virtual Campus: Trends for Higher Education and Training (1997 : Madrid, Spain) The virtual campus. 1st ed. London ; New York : Chapman & Hall on behalf of the International Federation for Information Processing (IFIP), 1998.
*TC LC5803.C65 I353 1997*

## DISTANCE EDUCATION - CROSS CULTURAL STUDIES.
Guri-Rozenblit, Sarah. Distance and campus universities. 1st ed. Oxford, UK ; New York, NY : Pergamon, published for IAU Press, 1999.
*TC LC5800 .G87 1999*

## DISTANCE EDUCATION - DEVELOPING COUNTRIES.
Perraton, H. D. Open and distance learning in the developing world. London ; New York : Routledge, 2000.
*TC LC5808.D48 P47 2000*

## DISTANCE EDUCATION - INDIA - CONGRESSES.
Open learning system. New Delhi : Lancer International, c1989.
*TC LC5808.I4 O64 1989*

## DISTANCE EDUCATION - UNITED STATES.
Van Dusen, Gerald C. Digital dilemma. San Francisco : Jossey-Bass, c2000.
*TC LC5805 .V35 2000*

## DISTANCE LEARNING.
International perspectives on tele-education and virtual learning environments. Aldershot : Ashgate, 2000.
*TC LB1044.87 .I55 2000*

**Distance learning technologies** : issues, trends and opportunities / [edited by] Linda K. Lau. Hershey, PA ; London : Idea Group Pub., c2000. i, 252 p. : ill. ; 25 cm. Includes bibliographical references and index. ISBN 1-87828-980-2 DDC 371.3/5
*1. Distance education - Computer-assisted instruction. 2. Educational technology. 3. World Wide Web. I. Lau, Linda, 1958-*
*TC LC5803.C65 D57 2000*

**Distinctively American** : the residential liberal arts college. New Brunswick [N.J.] : Transaction Publishers, [2000] xvi, 318 p. ; 23 cm. ISBN 0-7658-0721-1 DDC 378.0
*1. Universities and colleges - United States - History I. Koblik, Steven.*
*TC LA226 .D57 2000*

## DISTRIBUTION (ECONOMIC THEORY). See INCOME DISTRIBUTION.

## DISTRIBUTION OF INCOME. See INCOME DISTRIBUTION.

## DISTRIBUTION OF WEALTH. See WEALTH.

**Dittmer, Allan.**
Themes and issues in faculty development. Lanham, MD : University Press of America, 1999.
*TC LB1738 .T54 1999*

**Dive.**
Griffin, Adele. 1st ed. New York : Hyperion Books for Children, 1999.
*TC PZ7.G881325 Di 1999*

## DIVERS (BIRDS). See GREBES.

## DIVERSIFICATION, BIOLOGICAL. See BIOLOGICAL DIVERSITY.

**Diversification in higher education.**
Wasser, Henry Hirsch, 1919- Kassel : Wissenschaftliches Zentrum für Berufs- und Hochschulforschung der Gesamthochschule Kassel, 1999.
*TC LA622 .W37 1999*

**Diversity and distrust.**
Macedo, Stephen, 1957- Cambridge, Mass. ; London : Harvard University Press, 2000.
*TC LA217.2 .M33 2000*

## DIVERSITY, BIOLOGICAL. See BIOLOGICAL DIVERSITY.

## DIVERSITY, BIOTIC. See BIOLOGICAL DIVERSITY.

**Diversity in families.**
Zinn, Maxine Baca, 1942- 5th ed. New York : Longman, 1998.
*TC HQ536 .Z54 1998*

**Diversity in technology education** / editor Betty L. Rider. New York : Glencoe, c1998. xvi, 198 p. ; 24 cm. 1 computer laser optical disc (4 3/4 in.). (47th yearbook, 1998 / Council on Technology Teacher Education.) Includes bibliographical references and index. System requirements for accompanying computer disk: Windows/Mac compatible. CONTENTS: Chapter 1. Society, diversity, and technology education / Donna K. Trautman -- Chapter 2. Historical view of women's roles in technology education / Karen F. Zuga -- Chapter 3. Contributions of African-Americans to technology education / Michael L. Scott and Keith V. Johnson -- Chapter 4. Women as technology educators / Colleen E. Hill -- Chapter 5. Minority Students / Elazer J. Barnette -- Chapter 6. Reading, writing, and technology / Karen Coale Tracey -- Chapter 7. Mentors for women in technology / Daniel L. Householder -- Chapter 8. Effective leadership for all / Elizabeth Smith -- Chapter 9. Environmental and climate challenges in technology education / Jane A. Liedtke. -- Chapter 10. Diversity in technology education. Janet L. Robb. ISBN 0-02-831274-0
*1. Technology - Study and teaching. 2. Women in techology. 3. Minorities in technology. 4. Technology - Social aspects. I. Rider, Betty L. II. Series: Yearbook (Council on Technology Teacher Education (U.S.)), 47th, 1998.*
*TC T61 .A56 47th 1998*

**Diversity in technology education** / editor Betty L. Rider. New York : Glencoe, c1998. xvi, 198 p. ; 24 cm. 1 computer laser optical disc (4 3/4 in.). (47th yearbook, 1998 / Council on Technology Teacher Education.) Includes bibliographical references and index. System requirements for accompanying computer disk: Windows/Mac compatible. CONTENTS: Chapter 1. Society, diversity, and technology education / Donna K. Trautman -- Chapter 2. Historical view of women's roles in technology education / Karen F. Zuga -- Chapter 3. Contributions of African-Americans to technology education / Michael L. Scott and Keith V. Johnson -- Chapter 4. Women as technology educators / Colleen E. Hill -- Chapter 5. Minority Students / Elazer J. Barnette -- Chapter 6. Reading, writing, and technology / Karen Coale Tracey -- Chapter 7. Mentors for women in technology / Daniel L. Householder -- Chapter 8. Effective leadership for all / Elizabeth Smith -- Chapter 9. Environmental and climate challenges in technology education / Jane A. Liedtke. -- Chapter 10. Diversity in technology education. Janet L. Robb. ISBN 0-02-831274-0
*1. Technology - Study and teaching. 2. Women in techology. 3. Minorities in technology. 4. Technology - Social aspects. I. Rider, Betty L. II. Series: Yearbook (Council on Technology Teacher Education (U.S.)), 47th, 1998.*
*TC T61 .A56 47th 1998*

## DIVERSITY IN THE WORK PLACE. See DIVERSITY IN THE WORKPLACE.

## DIVERSITY IN THE WORKFORCE. See DIVERSITY IN THE WORKPLACE.

## DIVERSITY IN THE WORKPLACE.
Tsui, Anne S. Demographic differences in organizations. Lanham, MD : Lexington Books, 1999.
*TC HF5549.5.M5 T75 1999*

## DIVERSITY IN THE WORKPLACE - UNITED STATES.
Addressing cultural issues in organizations. Thousand Oaks, Calif. : Sage Publications, 2000.
*TC E184.A1 A337 2000*

**Diversity** [videorecording] / [produced by Herzog Associates] ; series producers, Shanta and Milan Herzog ; writer and co-producer, Janet Gonzales-Mena. Barrington, IL : Magna Systems, Inc., 1996. 4 videocassettes : sd., col. ; 1/2 in. (Early childhood training) At head of title: M Magna System, Inc. presents... [videorecording]. VHS. Cataloged from credits and cassette label; title from cassette label. Editor, Susan Jenkins ; camera, Estaban Ruiz and Richard Kehn ; music, Lou Wilson. Workbook applies to entire series. Includes credits and cassette label. For educators, parents, and developmental psychologists. SUMMARY: Presents information on a variety of topics designed for early childhood educators, caregivers and students.
*1. Early childhood education - United States. 2. Child development. 3. Multicultural education. I. Herzog, Shanta. II. Herzog, Milan. III. Gonzales-Mena, Janet. IV. Magna Systems. V. Herzog Associates. VI. Title: M Magna System, Inc. presents... [videorecording] VII. Series.*
*TC LB1139.25 .D5 1996*

**Divided we fall.**
Perlmutter, Philip. Legacy of hate. Armonk, N.Y. ; London : M.E. Sharpe, c1999.
*TC BF575.H3 P47 1999*

**DiVincenzo, Joe.** Group decision making : a tool kit for schools / [Joe DiVincenzo and Fred Ricci]. [S.l.] : NEA Professional Library : NEA Affiliate Capacity Building, c1999. 112 p. : ill. ; 28 cm. ISBN 0-8106-2010-3
*1. School management and organization - Decision making. 2. Group decision making. I. Ricci. Fred. II. NEA Professional Library (Association). III. National Education Association of the United States. IV. Title.*
*TC LB2806 .D58 1999*

## DIVINE HEALING. See CHRISTIAN SCIENCE.

## DIVISION - FICTION.
Dodds, Dayle Ann. The Great Divide. 1st ed. Cambridge, MA : Candlewick Press, 1999.
*TC PZ8.3.D645 Gr 1999*

## DIVISION OF LABOR. See SEXUAL DIVISION OF LABOR.

## DIVISION OF LABOR BY SEX. See SEXUAL DIVISION OF LABOR.

**DiVito, Anna, ill.**
German picture dictionary. Princeton, NJ : Berlitz Pub. Co., 1997.
*TC PF3629 .G47 1997*

## DIVORCE - FICTION.
Caseley, Judith. Losing Louisa. 1st ed. New York : Farrar, Straus and Giroux, c1999.
*TC PZ7.C2677 Lo 1999*

Cooney, Caroline B. Tune in anytime. New York : Delacorte Press, 1999.
*TC PZ7.C7834 Tu 1999*

Jones, Jennifer B. Dear Mrs. Ryan, you're ruining my life. New York : Walker & Co., 2000.
*TC PZ7.J7203 De 2000*

## DIVORCE - PSYCHOLOGICAL ASPECTS.
Ellis, Elizabeth M. Divorce wars. 1st ed. Washington, D.C. : American Psychological Association, c2000.
*TC RC488.6 .E45 2000*

## DIVORCE THERAPY.
Ellis, Elizabeth M. Divorce wars. 1st ed. Washington, D.C. : American Psychological Association, c2000.
*TC RC488.6 .E45 2000*

Isaacs, Marla Beth. [Difficult divorce] Therapy of the difficult divorce. Northvale, N.J. ; London : J. Aronson, c2000.
*TC RC488.6 .I83 2000*

## DIVORCE - UNITED STATES.
Ganong, Lawrence H. Changing families, changing responsibilities. Mahwah, N.J. : Lawrence Erlbaum Associates, 1999.
*TC HQ834 .G375 1999*

**Divorce wars.**
Ellis, Elizabeth M. 1st ed. Washington, D.C. : American Psychological Association, c2000.
*TC RC488.6 .E45 2000*

## DIVORCED PARENTS. See CHILDREN OF DIVORCED PARENTS; SINGLE PARENTS.

## DIVORCED PARENTS' CHILDREN. See CHILDREN OF DIVORCED PARENTS.

## DIVORCED PARENTS - UNITED STATES.
Ganong, Lawrence H. Changing families, changing responsibilities. Mahwah, N.J. : Lawrence Erlbaum Associates, 1999.
*TC HQ834 .G375 1999*

## DIVORCED PEOPLE. See DIVORCE; DIVORCED PARENTS.

**Dixon. Charlotte G.**
Professional counseling. Springfield, Ill. : C.C. Thomas, Publishers, c1999.
*TC BF637.C6 D56 1999*

**Dixon, Jerome C.** A qualitative study of perceptions of external factors that influence the persistence of Black males at a predominantly white four-year state college / by Jerome C. Dixon. 1999. viii, 180 leaves ; 29 cm. Typescript; issued also on microfilm. Thesis (Ed.D.)--Teachers College, Columbia University, 1999. Includes bibliographical references (leaves 136-142).
*1. Afro-American college graduates. 2. Afro-American men - Education (Higher) - Economic aspects. 3. Afro-American college students - Attitudes. 4. College environment - Evaluation. 5. Social interaction. 6. Persistence. 7. Success. I. Title.*
*TC 06 no. 11050*

**Dixon, Judith M.**
Mates, Barbara T. Adaptive technology for the Internet. Chicago, Ill. : American Library Association, 1999.
*TC Z675.B M38 1999*

**Dixson, Robert James.** Easy reading selections in English: with drills in conversation based on the reading selections. Rev. ed. [New York] Regents Pub. Co. [c1971] 137 p. illus. 22 cm. (Dixson English series)
*1. English language - Text-books for foreigners. 2. Readers - 1950- I. Title.*
*TC PE1128.A2 D5 1971*

**DK Publishing, Inc.**
Children's illustrated encyclopedia. [2nd] rev. ed. New York : DK Pub., 1998.
*TC AG5 .C535 1998*

Chronicle of the Olympics, 1896-2000. 1st American ed. New York : DK Pub., c1998.
*TC GV721.5 .C474 1998*

Henderson, Carolyn. Horse & pony breeds. 1st American ed. New York, N.Y. : DK Pub., 1999.
*TC SF291 .H365 1999*

Henderson, Carolyn. Horse & pony care. 1st American ed. New York : DK Pub., 1999.
*TC SF302 .H425 1999*

Henderson, Carolyn. Horse & pony shows & events. 1st American ed. New York, N.Y. : DK Pub., 1999.
*TC SF294.7 .H67 1999*

Henderson, Carolyn. Improve your riding skills. 1st American ed. New York, N.Y. : DK Pub., 1999.
*TC SF309.2 .H46 1999*

**DK riding club**
Henderson, Carolyn. Horse & pony breeds. 1st American ed. New York, N.Y. : DK Pub., 1999.
*TC SF291 .H365 1999*

Henderson, Carolyn. Horse & pony care. 1st American ed. New York : DK Pub., 1999.
*TC SF302 .H425 1999*

Henderson, Carolyn. Horse & pony shows & events. 1st American ed. New York, N.Y. : DK Pub., 1999.
*TC SF294.7 .H67 1999*

Henderson, Carolyn. Improve your riding skills. 1st American ed. New York, N.Y. : DK Pub., 1999.
*TC SF309.2 .H46 1999*

**Dober, Richard P.** Campus landscape : functions, forms, features / Richard P. Dober. New York : Wiley, c2000. xxvi, 259 p. : ill. ; 26 cm. Includes index. ISBN 0-471-35356-6 (alk. paper) DDC 712/.7
*1. Campus planning - United States. 2. Landscape design - United States. 3. Universities and colleges - United States.*
*TC LB3223.3 .D65 2000*

**Dobson, R. B. (Richard Barrie).**
The medieval church. Woodbridge, Suffolk : Rochester, NY : Published for the Ecclesiastical History Society by the Boydell Press, 1999.
*TC BR270 .M43 1999*

**Docherty, Linda Jones.**
Paris 1900. New Brunswick, N.J. : Rutgers University Press ; Montclair, N.J. : Montclair Art Museum, c1999.
*TC N6510 .P28 1999*

**Docking, Jim.**
New labour's policies for schools. London : David Fulton Publishers, c2000.
*TC LC93.G7 N59 2000*

**DOCTOR-ASSISTED SUICIDE.** *See* **ASSISTED SUICIDE.**

**The Doctor is in**
Depression and manic depression [videorecording]. Boston, MA : Fanlight Productions, c1996.
*TC RC537 .D46 1996*

**DOCTOR OF PHILOSOPHY DEGREE - GREAT BRITAIN.**
DELAMONT, SARA. The doctoral experience :. London : New York : Falmer Press, 2000.
*TC LB2386 .D45 2000*

**The doctor-patient relationship in pharmacotherapy.**
Tasman, Allan, 1947- New York : Guilford Press, c2000.
*TC RC483.3 .T375 2000*

**DOCTORS.** *See* **PHYSICIANS.**

**DOCTORS' DEGREES.** *See* **DEGREES, ACADEMIC.**

**DOCTORS OF MEDICINE.** *See* **PHYSICIANS.**

**DOCUMENTARIES (MOTION PICTURES).** *See* **DOCUMENTARY FILMS.**

**DOCUMENTARTY TELEVISION PROGRAMS.**
Changing lives [videorecording]. Princeton, NJ : Films for the Humanities & Sciences, c1998.
*TC RC564 .C54 1998*

**DOCUMENTARY FILMS.**
The Amish [videorecording]. Oak Forest, Ill. : MPI Home Video, c1988.
*TC BX8129.A5 A5 1988*

Andy Warhol [videorecording]. [Chicago, IL] : Home Vision [distributor],cc1987.
*TC N6537.W28 A45 1987*

Andy Warhol [videorecording]. [Chicago, IL] : Home Vision [distributor],cc1987.
*TC N6537.W28 A45 1987*

Between the lines [videorecording]. Boston, MA : Fanlight Productions,c1997.
*TC RC552.S4 B4 1997*

Children of the night [videorecording]. [Charleston, W.V.] : Cambridge Educational, c1994.
*TC HV1435.C3 C45 1994*

Children of the night [videorecording]. [Charleston, W.V.] : Cambridge Educational, c1994.
*TC HV1435.C3 C45 1994*

Children of the night [videorecording]. [Charleston, W.V.] : Cambridge Educational, c1994.
*TC HV1435.C3 C45 1994*

Comics, the 9th art [videorecording]. [S.l.] : EPISA : Cicero, Ill. : [Distributed by] The Roland Collection, 1990.
*TC PN6710 .C6 1990*

Georgia O'Keeffe [videorecording]. [Boston?] : Home Vision ; c1977.
*TC ND237.O5 G4 1977*

Impressionism [videorecording]. [London] : The National Gallery ; Tillingham, Peasmarsh, East Sussex, England : Ho-Ho-Kus, NJ : Distributed by The Roland Collection, c1990.
*TC ND547.5.I4 A7 1990*

Mary Cassatt [videorecording]. [Chicago, Ill.]: Home Vision ; c1977.
*TC ND237.C3 M37 1977*

Nevelson in process [videorecording]. Chicago, IL : Public Media Inc., 1977.
*TC NB237.N43 N43 1977*

Norman Rockwell's world -- an American dream [videorecording]. [Chicago, Ill] : Home Vision, 1987, c1972.
*TC ND237.R68 N6 1987*

Photomontage today, Peter Kennard [videorecording]. [London] : Art Council of Great Britain : Ho-Ho-Kus, N.J. : [distributed by] Anthony Roland Collection of Films on Art, c1982.
*TC TR685 .P45 1982*

Picasso [videorecording]. Chicago, IL : Home Vision, c1986.
*TC N6853.P5 P52 1986*

Processing the signal [videorecording]. Cicero, Ill. : Roland Collection of Films on Art, c1989.
*TC N6494.V53 P7 1989*

Starting over [videorecording]. [Charleston, W.V.] : Cambridge Educational, c1994.
*TC HV1435.C3 S7 1994*

Tassili N'Ajjer [videorecording]. [S.l.] : Editions Cinégraphiques ; Northbrook, Ill. : [distributed by] the Roland Collection, 1968.
*TC N5310.5.A4 T3 1968*

**DOCUMENTARY FILMS - GREAT BRITAIN.**
42 up. New York : The New Press : Distributed by W.W. Norton, c1998.
*TC HQ792.G7 A18 1998*

**DOCUMENTARY MASS MEDIA.** *See* **DOCUMENTARY TELEVISION PROGRAMS.**

**DOCUMENTARY PHOTOGRAPHY.**
The power of idea : [videorecording]. Minneapolis, Minn. : Media Loft, c1992.
*TC TR690 .P5 1992*

Sport photography today! [videorecording]. Minneapolis, Minn. : Media Loft, c1992.

*TC TR821 .S64 1992*

**DOCUMENTARY PHOTOGRAPHY - NEW YORK (STATE) - NEW YORK.**
Hine, Lewis Wickes, 1874-1940. The Empire State Building. Munich : New York : Prestel, c1998.
*TC TR820.5 .H5634 1998*

**DOCUMENTARY PHOTOGRAPHY - NEW YORK (STATE) - NEW YORK - HISTORY - 20TH CENTURY.**
Visual journal. Washington, DC : Smithsonian Institution Press, c1996.
*TC TR820.5 .V57 1996*

**DOCUMENTARY PHOTOGRAPHY - UNITED STATES.**
Child labor [picture]. Amawalk, NY : Jackdaw Publications, c1997.
*TC HD6250.U5 C4 1997*

Mills [picture]. Amawalk, NY : Jackdaw Publications, c1999.
*TC TR820.5 .M5 1999*

Roaring twenties [picture]. Amawalk, NY : Jackdaw Publications, c1997.
*TC E784 .R6 1997*

**DOCUMENTARY PHOTOGRAPHY - UNITED STATES - POSTERS.**
Civil war [picture]. Amawalk, NY : Jackdaw Publications, c1999.
*TC TR820.5 .C56 1999*

Civil war [picture]. Amawalk, NY : Jackdaw Publications, c1999.
*TC TR820.5 .C56 1999*

The depression hits home [picture]. Amawalk, NY : Jackdaw Publications, c1997.
*TC TR820.5 .D4 1997*

Ellis Island [picture]. Amawalk, NY : Jackdaw Publications, c1997.
*TC TR820.5 .E4 1997*

Holocaust children [picture]. Amawalk, NY : Jackdaw Publications, c1999.
*TC TR820.5 .H6 1999*

[Japanese-American internment picture. Amawalk, NY : Jackdaw Publications, c1999.
*TC TR820.5 .J3 1999*

World War II [picture]. Amawalk, NY : Jackdaw Publications, c1999.
*TC TR820.5 .W6 1999*

**DOCUMENTARY PHOTOGRAPHY - WASHINGTON (D.C.) - HISTORY - 20TH CENTURY.**
Visual journal. Washington, DC : Smithsonian Institution Press, c1996.
*TC TR820.5 .V57 1996*

**Documentary sources in contemporary art**
(v. 5) Talking visions. New York, N.Y. : New Museum of Contemporary Art ; Cambridge, Mass. : MIT Press, c1998.
*TC NX180.F4 T36 1998*

**DOCUMENTARY TELEVISION PROFRAMS - JAPAN - KANAYAMA.**
Heart of the country [videorecording]. [New York, NY : First Run/Icarus Films, 1998].
*TC LB1565.H6 H3 1998*

**DOCUMENTARY TELEVISION PROGRAMS.**
Africans in America [videorecording]. [Boston, Mass.] : WGBH Educational Foundation ; South Burlington, VT : WGBH Boston Video [distributor], c1998.
*TC E441 .A47 1998*

The Amish [videorecording]. Oak Forest, IL : MPI Home Video, 1988.

The blue planet [videorecording]. [New York, N.Y.?] : Unapix Entertainment, Inc. [distributor], c1996.
*TC QB631.2 .B5 1996*

Bright beginnings [videorecording. Burbank, CA : RCA/Columbia Pictures Home Video ; Toluca Lake, CA : [Distributed by] Corporate Productions, c1991.
*TC HV1642 .B67 1991*

Bright beginnings [videorecording. Burbank, CA : RCA/Columbia Pictures Home Video ; [S.l. : Distributed by] Rank Video Services America, c1991.
*TC HV1642 .B67 1991*

Brighter visions [videorecording. Burbank, CA : RCA/Columbia Pictures Home Video ; Toluca Lake, CA : [Distributed by] Corporate Productions, c1991.

*TC HV1597.5 .B67 1991*

The climate puzzle [videorecording]. [New York, N.Y.?] : Unapix Entertainment, Inc. [distributor], c1996.
*TC QB631.2 .C5 1996*

Education's big gamble [videorecording]. New York, NY : Merrow Report, c1997.
*TC LB2806.36 .E3 1997*

The filming of a television commercial [videorecording]. Minneapolis, Minn. : Media Loft, c1992.
*TC HF6146.T42 F5 1992*

Heroin [videorecording]. [Princeton, N.J.] : Films for the Humanities & Sciences, c1998.
*TC HV5822.H4 H4 1998*

In search of human origins [videorecording]. [Boston, Mass.] : WGBH Educational Foundation, c1994.
*TC GN281 .I45 1994*

The living machine [videorecording]. [New York, N.Y.?] : Unapix Entertainment, Inc. [distributor], c1996.
*TC QB631.2 .L5 1996*

Matisse, voyages [videorecording]. [Chicago, Ill.] : Home Vision : [S.l.] : Distributed worldwide by RM Associates, c1989.
*TC ND553.M37 M37 1989*

The next generation [videorecording]. Princeton, NJ : Films for the Humanities & Sciences, c1998.
*TC RC564 .N4 1998*

Fate of the earth [videorecording]. [New York, N.Y.?] : Unapix Entertainment, Inc. [distributor], c1996.
*TC QB631.2 .F3 1996*

Rabbit in the moon [videorecording]. San Francisco, Calif. : Wabi-Sabi Productions, 1999.
*TC D753.8 .R3 1999*

Roy Lichtenstein [videorecording]. [Chicago, IL] : Home Vision : [S.l.] : distributed worldwide by RM Asssociates, c1991.
*TC ND237.L627 R6 1991*

Gifts from the earth [videorecording]. [New York, N.Y.?] : Unapix Entertainment, Inc. [distributor], c1996.
*TC QB631.2 .G5 1996*

Sean's story [videorecording]. Princeton, N.J. : Films for the Humanities & Sciences ; [S.l. : distributed by] ABC Multimedia : Capital Cities/ABC, c1994.
*TC LC1203.M3 .S39 1994*

The solar sea [videorecording]. [New York, N.Y.?] : Unapix Entertainment, Inc. [distributor], c1996.
*TC QB631.2 .S6 1996*

Tales from other worlds [videorecording]. [New York, N.Y.?] : Unapix Entertainment, Inc. [distributor], c1996.
*TC QB631.2 .T3 1996*

Tales from other worlds [videorecording]. [New York, N.Y.?] : Unapix Entertainment, Inc. [distributor], c1996.
*TC QB631.2 .T3 1996*

Teen killers [videorecording]. Princeton, NJ : Films for the Humanities and Sciences, c1998-1999.
*TC HV9067.H6 T4 1999*

Teen violence [videorecording]. Princeton, NJ : Films for the Humanities & Sciences, c1998.
*TC RJ506.V56 T44 1998*

Touch 'n' go [videorecording. Burbank, Calif. : Columbia Tristar Home Video ; [S.l. : Distributed by] Rank Video Services Production, c1991.
*TC HV1626 .T6 1991*

Vietnam [videorecording]. [Beverly Hills, Calif.?] : CBS Fox Video : Distributed by Fox Video, c1993.
*TC DS557.7 .V53 1993*

Work sight [videorecording]. Burbank, Ca. : RCA/ Columbia Pictures Home Video, c1991.
*TC HV1652 .W6 1991*

## DOCUMENTARY TELEVISION PROGRAMS - POLAND.
Ecole 27 [videorecording]. Bruxelles : Paradise Films ; New York, N.Y. : [distributed by] First Run/ Icarus Films, 1997, c1996.
*TC LC746.P7 E2 1997*

**DOCUMENTARY VIDEOS.** *See* **DOCUMENTARY TELEVISION PROGRAMS.**

**DOCUMENTATION.** *See* **INFORMATION RETRIEVAL; LIBRARIES.**

**Documentation Centre for Education in Europe. News-letter - Documentation Centre for Education in Europe.**
[Documentation newsletter (Strasbourg, France)] Education newsletter = Strasbourg [France] : Council of Europe, 1990-1995.
*TC LA620 .D6 1994*

## DOCUMENTS IN MICROFORM.
Weber, Hartmut. Opto-electronic storage. Washington, DC : Commission on Preservation and Access, 1993.
*TC Z678.93.O7 W4315 1993*

## DOCUMENTS IN OPTICAL STORAGE.
Weber, Hartmut. Opto-electronic storage. Washington, DC : Commission on Preservation and Access, 1993.
*TC Z678.93.O7 W4315 1993*

**The Documents of 20th-century art**
Léger, Fernand, 1881-1955. [Fonctions de la peinture. English] Functions of painting, New York, Viking Press [1973]
*TC N70 .L45213 1973*

**Dodds, Dayle Ann.** The Great Divide / Dayle Ann Dodds ; illustrated by Tracy Mitchell. 1st ed. Cambridge, MA : Candlewick Press, 1999. 1v. (unpaged) : col. ill. ; 25 cm. SUMMARY: Eighty people begin to race in the Great Divide, but each new challenge divides the number of racers in half. ISBN 0-7636-0442-9 (alk. paper) DDC [E]
*1. Racing - Fiction. 2. Division - Fiction. 3. Stories in rhyme. 1. Mitchell, Tracy, ill. II. Title.*
*TC PZ8.3.D645 Gr 1999*

**Dodge, Diane Triste.**
Bickart, Toni S. Building the primary classroom. Washington, DC : Teaching Strategies : Portsmouth, NH : Heinemann, 1999.
*TC LB1507 .B53 1999*

## DODGE, GRACE H. (GRACE HOADLEY), 1856-1914.
Her heritage [computer file]. Cambridge, MA : Pilgrim New Media, c1994. Interactive multimedia.
*TC HQ1412 .A43 1994*

**Dodwell, P. C.** Brave new mind : a thoughtful inquiry into the nature and meaning of mental life / Peter Dodwell. New York : Oxford University Press, 2000. ix, 250 p. : ill. ; 24 cm. Includes bibliographical references (p. 219-231) and index. ISBN 0-19-508905-7 (alk. paper) DDC 153
*1. Cognitive science. 2. Creative thinking. 3. Consciousness. 4. Cognition - Social aspects. 1. Title.*
*TC BF311 .D568 2000*

**Doerr, Marilyn.**
Owen, David, 1955- None of the above. Rev. and updated. Lanham, Md. : Rowman & Littlefield Publishers, c1999.
*TC LB2353.57 .O94 1999*

**DOG.** *See* **DOGS.**

**Dog Donovan**
Hendry, Diana, 1941- 1st U.S. ed. Cambridge, Mass. : Candlewick Press, 1995.
*TC PZ7.H38586 Dm 1995*

**Doggett, Sandra L.** Beyond the book : technology integration into the secondary school library media curriculum / Sandra L. Doggett ; edited by Paula Kay Montgomery. Englewood, Colo. : Libraries Unlimited, 2000. xi, 177 p. : ill. ; 28 cm. (Library and information problem-solving skills series) Includes bibliographical references (p. 163-171) and index. ISBN 1-56308-584-4 DDC 025.04/071/273
*1. Electronic information resource literacy - Study and teaching (Secondary) - United States. 2. High school libraries - United States - Data processing. 3. Instructional materials centers - United States - Data processing. 4. High school libraries - Activity programs - United States. 5. Computer-assisted instruction - United States. I. Montgomery, Paula Kay. II. Title. III. Series.*
*TC ZA4065 .D64 2000*

## DOGS - FICTION.
Clement, Rod. Frank's great museum adventure. 1st American ed. [New York] : HarperCollins Publishers, 1999.
*TC PZ7.C59114 Fr 1999*

Day, Alexandra. Carl's afternoon in the park. 1st ed. New York : Farrar, Straus & Giroux, 1991.
*TC PZ7.D32915 Cars 1991*

Hendry, Diana, 1941- Dog Donovan. 1st U.S. ed. Cambridge, Mass. : Candlewick Press, 1995.

*TC PZ7.H38586 Dm 1995*

Moeyaert, Bart. [Blote handen. English] Bare hands. 1st ed. Asheville, N.C. : Front Street, 1998.
*TC PZ7.M7227 Bar 1998*

Rylant, Cynthia. Henry and Mudge and the wild wind. 1st ed. New York : Bradbury Press ; Toronto : Maxwell Macmillan Canada ; New York : Maxwell Macmillan International, c1993.
*TC PZ7.R982 Heb 1992*

Serfozo, Mary. What's what? a guessing game/ 1st ed. New York, NY : Margaret K. McElderry Books, c1996.
*TC PZ7.S482 Wg 1996*

Thompson, Colin (Colin Edward) Unknown. New York : Walker & Co., 2000.
*TC PZ7.T371424 Un 2000*

Wild, Margaret, 1948- Toby. 1st American ed. New York : Ticknor & Fields, 1994.
*TC PZ7.W64574 To 1994*

**Doherty, Robert Emmett, 1923-** Industrial and labor relations terms : a glossary / Robert E. Doherty. 5th ed., rev. Ithaca, NY : ILR Press, c1989. 36 p. ; 23 cm. (ILR bulletin ; 44) ISBN 0-87546-152-2 DDC 331/.03/21
*1. Industrial relations - Terminology. I. Title. II. Series: Bulletin (New York State School of Industrial and Labor Relations) ; no. 44.*
*TC HD4839 .D6 1989*

**Dohrenwend, Bruce Philip, 1927-.**
Adversity, stress, and psychopathology. New York : Oxford University Press, 1998.
*TC RC455.4.S87 A39 1998*

**Doing child and adolescent psychotherapy.**
Bromfield, Richard. Northvale, N.J. ; London : Jason Aronson, c1999.
*TC RJ504 .B753 1999*

**Doing engineering.**
Tang, Joyce, 1962- Lanham, Md. ; Oxford : Rowman & Littlefield Publishers, c2000.
*TC TA157 .T363 2000*

**Doing postgraduate research in Australia.**
Stevens, Kate. Melbourne : Melbourne University Press, 1999.
*TC LB2371.6.A7 S74 1999*

**Doing qualitative research** / Benjamin F. Crabtree and William L. Miller. editors. 2nd ed. Thousand Oaks, Calif. : Sage Publications, c1999 xvii, 406 p. : ill. ; 24 cm. Includes bibliographical references (p. 363-390) and index. ISBN 0-7619-1497-8 (acid-free paper) ISBN 0-7619-1498-6 (acid-free paper) DDC 362.1/072 DDC 362.1/072
*1. Primary care (Medicine) - Research - Methodology. 2. Social medicine - Research - Methodology. 3. Social sciences - Research - Methodology. I. Crabtree, Benjamin F. II. Miller, William L. (William Lloyd), 1949-*
*TC R853.S64 D65 1999*

**Doing qualitative research in educational settings**
Bassey, Michael. Case study research in educational settings. Buckingham [England] ; Philadelphia : Open University Press, 1999.
*TC LB1028.25.G7 B37 1999*

Ozga, Jennifer. Policy research in educational settings :. Buckingham [England] ; Philadelphia : Open University Press, 2000.
*TC LB1028.25.G7 O93 2000*

**Doing research that is useful for theory and practice** / Edward E. Lawler III ... [et al.]. Lanham, Md. ; Oxford : Lexington Books, c1999. liii, 371 : ill. ; 23 cm. Originally published: San Francisco : Jossey-Bass, 1985. Includes bibliographical references and index. ISBN 0-7391-0100-5 (pbk. : alk. paper) DDC 300/.7/2
*1. Organizational behavior - Research. 2. Organization - Research. I. Lawler, Edward E.*
*TC HD58.7 .D65 1999*

**Doing your research project.**
Bell, Judith, 1930- 3rd ed. Buckingham [England] ; Philadelphia : Open University Press, 1999.
*TC LB1028 .B394 1999*

**Doll, Mary Aswell.** Like letters in running water : a mythopoetics of curriculum / Mary Aswell Doll. Mahwah, N.J. ; London : L. Erlbaum Publishers, 2000. xix, 253 p. ; 24 cm. (Studies in curriculum theory) Includes bibliographical references (p. 218-238) and indexes. ISBN 0-8058-2984-9 (hbk. : alk. paper) ISBN 0-8058-2985-7 (pbk. : alk. paper) DDC 807.1
*1. Literature - Study and teaching. 2. Myth in literature. 3. Education - Curriculum - Philosophy. I. Title. II. Series.*
*TC LB1575 .D64 2000*

**Dollars, distance, and online education :** The New Economics of College Teaching and Learning / Martin J. Finkelstein ... [et al.]. Phoenix, Az. : Oryx Press, 2000. xviii, 373 p. : ill. ; 23 cm. Includes bibliographic references and index. ISBN 1-57356-395-1 (alk. paper) DDC 378/.00285
*1. Education, Higher - Effect of technological innovations on - United States. 2. Universities and colleges - United States - Data processing. 3. Information technology - United States - Finance. I. Finkelstein, Martin J., 1949-*
*TC LB2395.7 .M26 2000*

**DOLLS - FICTION.**
Pomerantz, Charlotte. The chalk doll. New York : Lippincott, c1989.
*TC PZ7.P77 Ch 1989*

**Dolphin (Arhus, Denmark)**
(no. 22.) Literary pedagogics after deconstruction. Aarhus, Denmark : Aarhus University Press, 1992.
*TC PR33 .L58 1992*

(no. 27.) Teaching post-colonialism and post-colonial literatures. Aarhus, Denmark : Oakville, Conn. : Aarhus University Press, c1997.
*TC PR9080.A53 T43 1997*

**Dombey, Henrietta.** Whole to part phonics : how children learn to read and spell / by Henrietta Dombey, Margaret Moustafa and the staff of the Centre for Language in Primary Education: Myra Barrs ... [et al.]. London : Centre for Language in Primary Education : Language Matters, c1998. 44 p. ; 21 x 30 cm. Includes bibliographical references. ISBN 1-87226-713-0 (pbk) ISBN 1-87226-713-0 DDC 372.465
*1. Reading - Phonetic method. I. Moustafa, Margaret. II. Barrs, Myra. III. Centre for Language in Primary Education (London, England) IV. Title.*
*TC LB1573.3 .D66 1998*

**Dombroski, Ann P.** Administrative problem solving : factors affecting expertise / by Ann P. Dombroski. 1999. ix, 224 leaves ; 29 cm. Includes tables. Issued also on microfilm. Thesis (Ed.D.) -- Teachers College, Columbia University, 1999. Includes bibliographical references (leaves 180-184).
*1. School management and organization. 2. Expertise. 3. Cognitive psychology. 4. Problem solving. 5. Educational administration. 6. Leadership. 7. A. 8. L. 9. R I. Title.*
*TC 06 no. 11104*

Administrative problem solving : factors affecting expertise / by Ann P. Dombroski. 1999. ix, 224 leaves : ill ; 29 cm. Includes tables. Issued also on microfilm. Thesis (Ed.D.) -- Teachers College, Columbia University, 1999. Includes bibliographical references (leaves 180-184)
*1. School management and organization. 2. Expertise. 3. Cognitive psychology. 4. Problem solving. 5. Leadership. 6. Sampling (Statistics) I. Title.*
*TC 06 no. 11104*

**DOMESTIC ANIMALS.** *See* **CATS; DOGS; HORSES.**

**DOMESTIC ANIMALS - DISEASES.** *See* **VETERINARY MEDICINE.**

**DOMESTIC ARCHITECTURE.** *See* **ARCHITECTURE, DOMESTIC.**

**The domestic domain.**
Pennartz, Paul. Aldershot, Hants, England : Brookfield, Vt. : Ashgate, c1999.
*TC HQ728 .P46 1999*

**DOMESTIC ECONOMY.** *See* **HOME ECONOMICS.**

**DOMESTIC EDUCATION.** *See* **TUTORS AND TUTORING.**

**DOMESTIC FICTION.**
Stegner, Wallace Earle, 1909- Angle of repose. New York : Modern Library, 2000.
*TC PS3537.T316 A8 2000*

**DOMESTIC PARTNERS.** *See* **UNMARRIED COUPLES.**

**DOMESTIC RABBIT.** *See* **RABBITS.**

**DOMESTIC RELATIONS.** *See* **FAMILY; GUARDIAN AND WARD; PARENT AND CHILD (LAW).**

**DOMESTIC RELATIONS - CRIMINAL PROVISIONS.** *See* **FAMILY VIOLENCE - LAW AND LEGISLATION.**

**DOMESTIC SCIENCE.** *See* **HOME ECONOMICS.**

**DOMESTIC VIOLENCE.** *See* **FAMILY VIOLENCE.**

**DOMESTIC VIOLENCE - UNITED STATES - LEGISLATION.**
Assessment of family violence. 2nd ed. New York : John Wiley, c1999.
*TC RC569.5.F3 A87 1999*

**Domesticating history.**
West, Patricia, 1958- Washington [D.C.] : Smithsonian Institution Press, c1999.
*TC E159 .W445 1999*

**DOMICILE.** *See* **CITIZENSHIP.**

**DOMICILES.** *See* **DWELLINGS.**

**Dominguez, Carmen.**
Comics, the 9th art [videorecording]. [S.l.] : EPISA ; Cicero, Ill. : [Distributed by] The Roland Collection, 1990.
*TC PN6710 .C6 1990*

**The Dominican Americans.**
Torres-Saillant, Silvio. Westport, Conn. : Greenwood Press, 1998.
*TC E184.D6 T67 1998*

**DOMINICAN AMERICANS.**
Torres-Saillant, Silvio. The Dominican Americans. Westport, Conn. : Greenwood Press, 1998.
*TC E184.D6 T67 1998*

**Dominicé, Pierre.** Learning from our lives : using educational biographies with adults / Pierre Dominice ; foreword by Alan B. Knox. 1st ed. San Francisco : Jossey-Bass, c2000. xxiii, 206 p. ; 24 cm. (Jossey-Bass higher and adult education series) Includes bibliographical references (p. 193-199) and index. CONTENTS: Essence of educational biography -- Educational biographies -- From life history to educational biography -- How adults educate themselves -- Understanding adults' ways of thinking -- Learners' needs, motivations, and dreams -- Helping learners put words to their lives and experiences -- Giving evaluation another meaning -- Creating conditions for successful learning in adult life. ISBN 0-7879-1031-7 (hardcover: alk. paper) DDC 374/.139
*1. Education - Biographical methods. 2. Adult education. 3. Adult learning. I. Title. II. Series.*
*TC LB1029.B55 D64 2000*

**DOMINIONS, BRITISH.** *See* **COMMONWEALTH COUNTRIES.**

**Donahue, Paul J.** Mental health consultation in early childhood / by Paul J. Donahue, Beth Falk, and Anne Gersony Provet. Baltimore, MD : Paul H. Brookes Publishing, 2000. xx, 282 p. ; 23 cm. Includes bibliographical references and index. ISBN 1-55766-449-8 (pbk.) DDC 618.92/89
*1. Child psychiatry. 2. Mental health consultation. 3. Child mental health services. I. Falk, Beth. II. Provet, Anne Gersony. III. Title.*
*TC RJ499 .D595 2000*

**Donahue, Roberta.**
The nutty, nougat-filled world of human nutrition [videorecording]. [Arlington, Va.] : Cerebellum Corp., c1998.
*TC QP141 .N8 1998*

**Donald, Aïda DiPace. ed.**
Adams, Charles Francis, 1807-1886. Diary of Charles Francis Adams. Cambridge : Belknap Press of Harvard University Press, 1964-68.
*TC KF367.A33 A3*

**Donald, David Herbert, 1920- ed.**
Adams, Charles Francis, 1807-1886. Diary of Charles Francis Adams. Cambridge : Belknap Press of Harvard University Press, 1964-68.
*TC KF367.A33 A3*

**Donatelli, Gary.**
Ballet class [videorecording]. W. Long Branch, NJ : Kultur, c1984.
*TC GV1589 .B33 1984*

**DONATIONS.** *See* **ENDOWMENTS; GIFTS.**

**Donchin, Anne.**
Embodying bioethics. Lanham : Rowman & Littlefield Publishers, c1999.
*TC QH332 .E43 1999*

**The donkey and the rock.**
Demi. New York : Henry Holt, 1999.
*TC PZ8.1.D38 Do 1999*

**Donna O'Neeshuck was chased by some cows.**
Grossman, Bill. 1st ed. [New York] : Harper & Row, c1988.
*TC PZ8.3.G914 Do 1988*

**Donnell Library Center.** Video : Donnell Media Center, the New York Public Library, the Branch Libraries. New York : New York Public Library, 1990. 323 p. ; 28 cm. + 1994 Supplement (342 p. ; 28 cm.) "All cataloging for this volume was done by Karla Kostick of Donnell Media Center."--Introduction to the video catalog, Marie Nesthus, Principal Librarian.
*1. Donnell Library Center - Catalogs. 2. Video recordings - Catalogs. I. Merena. Elizabeth. II. Kostick. Karla. III. Nesthus, Marie. IV. Title.*
*TC PN1992.95 .D66*

**DONNELL LIBRARY CENTER - CATALOGS.**
Donnell Library Center. Video. New York : New York Public Library, 1990.
*TC PN1992.95 .D66*

**DONOR INSEMINATION, HUMAN.** *See* **ARTIFICIAL INSEMINATION, HUMAN.**

**The dons.**
Annan, Noel Gilroy Annan, Baron, 1916- Chicago : University of Chicago Press ; London : HarperCollins Publishers, 1999.
*TC LB2331.74.G7 A55 1999*

**Don't just surf.**
Henninger, Maureen, 1940- 2nd ed. Sydney : UNSW Press, 1999.
*TC ZA4201 .H46 1999*

**Don't make me laugh.**
Stevenson, James, 1929- 1st ed. New York : Farrar, Straus and Giroux, c1999.
*TC PZ7.S84748 Do 1999*

**Dooling, Dave.**
Bell, Trudy E. Engineering tomorrow :. Piscataway, NJ : IEEE Press, c2000.
*TC T174 .B451 2000*

**The door in the dream.**
Wasserman, Elga R. (Elga Ruth) Washington, D.C. : Joseph Henry Press, c2000.
*TC QH26 .W375 2000*

**DOOR-TO-DOOR SELLING.** *See* **PEDDLERS AND PEDDLING.**

**Doorlag, Donald H.**
Lewis, Rena B. Teaching special students in general education classrooms. 5th ed. Upper Saddle River, N.J. : Merrill, c1999.
*TC LC1201 .L48 1999*

**Doosje, Bertjan.**
Social identity. Malden, MA : Blackwell Publishers, 1999.
*TC HM131 .S58433 1999*

**DOPAMINE - RESEARCH.**
The hijacked brain [videorecording]. Princeton, NJ : Films for the Humanities & Sciences, c1998.
*TC RC564 .H5 1998*

**DOPING IN SPORTS.**
Pharmacology in exercise and sports. Boca Raton : CRC Press, c1996.
*TC QP301 .P53 1996*

**DOPING IN SPORTS - CONGRESSES.**
Fundacion Dr. Antonio Esteve. Symposium (7th : 1996 : Sitges, Spain) The clinical pharmacology of sport and exercise. Amsterdam ; New York : Elsevier Science B.V., Excerpta Medica, 1997.
*TC RC1230 .F86 1996*

**DOPING IN SPORTS - CONGRESSES.**
Fundacion Dr. Antonio Esteve. Symposium (7th : 1996 : Sitges, Spain) The clinical pharmacology of sport and exercise. Amsterdam ; New York : Elsevier Science B.V., Excerpta Medica, 1997.
*TC RC1230 .F86 1996*

**Dorans, Neil J.**
Wainer, Howard. Computerized adaptive testing. 2nd ed. Mahwah, N.J. : Lawrence Erlbaum Associates, 2000.
*TC LB3060.32.C65 W25 2000*

**Dorge, Valerie, 1946-.**
Building an emergency plan. Los Angeles, Calif. : Getty Conservation Institute, c1999.
*TC AM121 .B85 1999*

**Doria, Joseph.**
The nutty, nougat-filled world of human nutrition [videorecording]. [Arlington, Va.] : Cerebellum Corp., c1998.
*TC QP141 .N8 1998*

**Dorn, Linda J.** Apprenticeship in literacy : transitions across reading and writing / Linda J. Dorn, Cathy French, Tammy Jones. York, Me. : Stenhouse Publishers, c1998. xiv, 177 p. : ill. ; 26 cm. Includes bibliographical references (p. 169-171) and index. ISBN 1-57110-088-1 (alk. paper) DDC 372.6
*1. Language arts (Early childhood) - United States. 2. Reading*

(Early childhood) - United States. 3. English language - Composition and exercises - Study and teaching (Early childhood) - United States. I. French, Cathy. II. Jones, Tammy (Tammy P.) III. Title.
*TC LB1139.5.L35 D67 1998*

**Dorothea Lange--a visual life** / edited by Elizabeth Partridge. Washington : Smithsonian Institution Press, c1994. xi, 168 p. : ill. ; 29 cm. Includes bibliographical references. ISBN 1-56098-350-7 (alk. paper) ISBN 1-56098-455-4 (pbk. : alk. paper) DDC 770/.92
*1. Lange, Dorothea. 2. Women photographers - United States - Biography. I. Lange, Dorothea. II. Partridge, Elizabeth. III. Title: Visual life.*
*TC TR140.L3 D67 1994*

**Dorrell, Peter G.**
Thornes, Robin. Introduction to Object ID. [Los Angeles] : Getty Information Institute, c1999.
*TC N3998 .T457 1999*

**DORRIS, MICHAEL.**
  **GUESTS.**
    Beech, Linda Ward. Guests by Michael Dorris. New York, NY : Scholastic, c1996.
    *TC LB1573 .B432 1996*

**Dorsey, John Morris, 1900-** Psychology of language; a local habitation and a name [by] John M. Dorsey. Detroit, Center for Health Education [1971] xxxiv, 145 p. 24 cm. Bibliography: p. 123-131. DDC 401/.9
*1. Psycholinguistics. I. Title.*
*TC P106 .D64*

**Dossey, Barbara Montgomery.** Florence Nightingale : mystic, visionary, healer / Barbara Montgomery Dossey. Springhouse, PA : Springhouse Corp., c2000. vii, 440 p. : ill. (some col.) ; 29 cm. Includes bibliographical references (p. 428-436) and index. ISBN 0-87434-984-2 (alk. paper) DDC 610.73/092
*1. Nightingale, Florence, - 1820-1910. 2. Nurses - England - Biography. I. Title.*
*TC RT37.N5 D67 2000*

**DOUBLE-BASS AND PIANO MUSIC (JAZZ).** *See* **JAZZ.**

**DOUBLE CONSCIOUSNESS.** *See* **MULTIPLE PERSONALITY.**

**"Double happiness," double jeopardy.**
Woo, Kimberley Ann. 1999.
*TC 06 no. 11075*

**DOUBLE PERSONALITY.** *See* **MULTIPLE PERSONALITY.**

**DOUBLE SHIFTS (PUBLIC SCHOOLS).** *See* **CLASS SIZE.**

**DOUBT.** *See* **BELIEF AND DOUBT.**

**Douglas, Gillian.**
Children's rights and traditional values. Aldershot ; Brookfield, USA : Ashgate/Dartmouth, c1998.
*TC K639 .A55 1998*

**DOUGLASS, FREDERICK, 1817?-1895. NARRATIVE OF THE LIFE OF FREDERICK DOUGLASS, AN AMERICAN SLAVE.**
Approaches to teaching Narrative of the life of Frederick Douglass. New York : Modern Language Association of America, 1999.
*TC E449.D75 A66 1999*

**Dove, Nah.** Afrikan mothers : bearers of culture, makers of social change / Nah Dove. Albany : State University of New York Press, c1998. xviii, 261 p. ; 24 cm. Includes bibliographical references (p. 245-250) and index. ISBN 0-7914-3881-3 (HC : acid-free paper) ISBN 0-7914-3882-1 (PB : acid-free paper) DDC 305.48/896
*1. Women, Black - Great Britain - Interviews. 2. Women, Black - United States - Interviews. 3. Afrocentrism - Philosophy. 4. Education - Africa - Philosophy. 5. Africa - Civilization - Western influences. I. Title.*
*TC HQ1593 .D68 1998*

**Dow, Arthur W. (Arthur Wesley), 1857-1922.**
Composition : a series of exercises in art structure for the use of students and teachers / by Arthur Wesley Dow ; with a new introduction by Joseph Masheck. Berkeley : University of California Press, 1997. 177 p. : ill. (some col.) ; 29 cm. Originally published: 13th ed., rev. and enl. Garden City : New York : Doubleday, 1920. ISBN 0-520-21156-1 (cloth : alk. paper) ISBN 0-520-20749-1 (pbk. : alk. paper) DDC 702/.8
*1. Composition (Art) 2. Art - Study and teaching. I. Title.*
*TC N7430 .D68 1997*

**DOW, ARTHUR W. (ARTHUR WESLEY), 1857-1922 - INFLUENCE - EXHIBITIONS.**
Ira Spanierman Gallery. Arthur Wesley Dow (1857-1922). New York : Spanierman Gallery, 1999.

---

*TC N44.D7442 I73 1999*

**Dow, Sherry Zunker.**
Jazz dance class [videorecording]. W. Long Branch, NJ : Kultur, [1992?]
*TC GV1784 .J3 1992*

**Dowd, John F.**
Gore, M. C. Taming the time stealers. Thousand Oaks, Calif. : Corwin Press, c1999.
*TC LB2838.8 .G67 1999*

**Dowd, Nancy E., 1949-** Redefining fatherhood / Nancy E. Dowd. New York : New York University Press, 2000. x, 279 p. ; 23 cm. Includes bibliographical references (p. 235-275) and index. CONTENTS: Introduction -- The context of fatherhood -- Fathers in practice : the conduct of fatherhood -- Fatherhood, work, and family -- Subgroups of fathers -- Summary -- Constitutional fathers -- Biological fathers -- Economic fathers -- A new model -- Gender challenges : masculinities and mothers -- Redefined fatherhood. ISBN 0-8147-1925-2 (cloth : alk. paper) DDC 306.874/2
*1. Fatherhood. 2. Fathers. I. Title.*
*TC HQ756 .D588 2000*

**Dowdeswell, W. H. (Wilfrid Hogarth)** The mechanism of evolution, by W. H. Dowdeswell. 3d ed. London, Heinemann, 1963 xi, 131 p. illus., map, plates. 19 cm. (The Scholarship series in biology) Bibliography: p. 120-125.
*1. Evolution (Biology) I. Title.*
*TC QH366 .D68 1963*

**Dowds, Barbara Noel.**
Partnerships in research, clinical, and educational settings. Stamford, Conn. : Ablex Pub., c1999.
*TC HM1106 .P37 1999*

**Dowdy, Carol Ammons.**
Attention-Deficit/Hyperactivity disorder in the classroom. Austin, Tex. : Pro-Ed, c1998.
*TC LC4713.4 .A89 1998*

**Dowling, Cornelia E.**
Recent progress in mathematical psychology. Mahwah, N.J. : L. Erlbaum, 1998.
*TC BF39 .R35 1998*

**Dowling, John E.** Creating mind : how the brain works / John E. Dowling. 1st ed. New York : W.W. Norton, c1998. xi, 212 p. : ill. ; 24 cm. Includes bibliographical references (p. [205]-206) and index. ISBN 0-393-02746-5 DDC 612.8/2
*1. Brain. 2. Neurosciences. I. Title.*
*TC QP376 .D695 1998*

**Down, down, down in the ocean.**
Markle, Sandra. New York : Walker, 1999.
*TC QH541.5.S3 M2856 1999*

**Down syndrome** : a review of current knowledge / edited by Jean A. Rondal, Juan Perera and Lynn Nadel. London : Whurr, 1999. xii, 242 p. ; 24 cm. Includes bibliographical references and index. ISBN 1-86156-062-1 DDC 616.858842
*1. Down syndrome - Congresses. 2. Down Syndrome - Congresses. I. Rondal, J. A. II. Perera, Juan. III. Nadel, Lynn. IV. World Congress on Down Syndrome (6th : 1997 : Madrid, Spain)*
*TC RC571 .D675 1999*

**DOWN SYNDROME - CONGRESSES.**
Down syndrome. London : Whurr, 1999.
*TC RC571 .D675 1999*

**DOWN SYNDROME - CONGRESSES.**
Down syndrome. London : Whurr, 1999.
*TC RC571 .D675 1999*

**DOWN SYNDROME - MARYLAND.**
Sean's story [videorecording]. Princeton, N.J. : Films for the Humanities & Sciences ; [S.l. : distributed by] ABC Multimedia : Capital Cities/ABC, c1994.
*TC LC1203.M3 .S39 1994*

**Downes, Toni.**
IFIP TC3 WG3.1/3.5 Open Conference on Communications and Networking in Education (1999 : Aulanko, Finland) Communications and networking in education. Boston : Kluwer Academic Publishers, 2000.
*TC LB1044.87 .I45 2000*

**Downing, Julie, ill.**
Reeves, Mona Rabun. I had a cat. 1st American ed. New York : Bradbury Press, c1989.
*TC PZ8.3.R263 Iah 1989*

**DOWN'S SYNDROME.** *See* **DOWN SYNDROME.**

**DOWNSIZING OF ORGANIZATIONS.**
Skiba, Michaeline. A naturalistic inquiry of the relationship between organizational change and informal learning in the workplace. 1999.

---

*TC 06 no. 11180*

**Doyle, Denis P.** Raising the standard : an eight-step action guide for schools and communities / Denis P. Doyle, Susan Pimentel ; [illustration, Tom Smith]. 2nd ed. Thousand Oaks, Calif. : Corwin Press, c1999. x, 190 p. : ill. ; 28 cm. 1 computer optical disc (4 3/4 in.). "Revised, with a new section on charter schools." Includes index. CONTENTS: Take the plunge : building public demand for standards and reform -- How good is good enough? : organizing around high academic standards -- The truth will set you free : conducting an academic analysis -- Seize the day : reorganizing for change and building staff capacity -- Measuring up : holding students accountable -- Holding your feet to the fire : school and district accountability -- So what's in it for me? : developing new partnerships -- There is no finish line : making continuous improvements -- Have you done this? : a checklist of action steps. ISBN 0-8039-6869-8 (pbk. : alk. paper) ISBN 0-8039-6868-X (cloth : alk. paper) DDC 371.2/07/0973
*1. School improvement programs - United States - Case studies. 2. Education - Standards - United States - Case studies. 3. Educational change - United States - Case studies. 4. Community and school - United States - Case studies. I. Pimentel, Susan. II. Title.*
*TC LB2822.82 .D69 1999*

**DOYLE, MILDRED E. (MILDRED ELOISE), 1904-1989.**
McGarrh, Kellie, d. 1995. Kellie McGarrh's hangin' in tough. New York : P. Lang, c2000.
*TC LA2317.D6185 M34 2000*

**Dr. Seuss kindergarten** [computer file] Windows / Macintosh CD-ROM ; v. 1.0. Novato, CA : Brøderbund, c1998. 1 computer optical disc : sd., col. ; 4 3/4 in. + user's manual (22 p. : ill. ; 12 cm.) + troubleshooting guide (8 p. ; 22 cm.). System requirements (Windows): Windows 3.1 or Windows 95 ; 66MHz 486DX or faster ; 8MB of RAM for Windows 3.1, 16 MB recommended ; 16 MB RAM for Windows95 ; minimum 20 MB hard disk space ; 2X CD-ROM drive or faster ; 640 x 480 display, 256 colors ; high and true color supported for Windows 95 ; Video and sound cards compatible with DirectX for Windows 95. System requirements (Macintosh): System 7.1 or higher ; 20 MHz 68040 processor or faster or PowerPC ; 68040 Macintosh requires 6.5 MB free ; PowerPC requires 8MB free ; minimum 20 MB hard disk space ; 2X CD-ROM drive or faster ; 640x480 display, 256 colors. Title from title screen. Issued in box (26 cm.). SUMMARY: "[The program] offers a full year of math, reading, and other essential kindergarten skills set in the wonderful and witty world of Dr. Seuss. Gerald McGrew is building a zoo in Seussville. As children help him find exotic animals, they will be learning math and reading."-- Container. ISBN 1-57135-401-8
*1. Kindergarten - Juvenile software. 2. Educational games - Juvenile software. 3. Kindergarten - Interactive multimedia. 4. Seuss, - Dr. - Juvenile software. I. Brøderbund.*
*TC LB1195 .D77 1998*

**DRAGONS - FICTION.**
Hill, T. L. Morris and the kingdom of Knoll. Malibu, Calif. : J. Paul Getty Museum and Children's Library Press, c1996.
*TC PZ7.H55744 Mo 1996*

**DRAGONS - JUVENILE FICTION.**
Gannett, Ruth Stiles. My father's dragon. New York : Random House, 1948.
*TC PZ7.G15 My 1948*

**Drake, Jim, 1955-** Computers and schools / Jim Drake. Des Plaines, Ill. : Heinemann Library, c1999. 32 p. : col. ill. ; 28 cm. (Log on to computers) Cover title: Computers and school. Includes bibliographical references (p. 32) and index. SUMMARY: A basic introduction to the use of computers in schools, describing word processing, desktop publishing, networks, computer-assisted learning, graphics, computer-produced music, and computer simulations. ISBN 1-57572-785-4 (lib. bdg.) DDC 372.133/4
*1. Computer-assisted instruction - Juvenile literature. 2. Education (Primary) - Data processing - Juvenile literature. 3. Computers - Juvenile literature. 4. Computers. I. Title. II. Title: Computers and school III. Series: Drake, Jim, 1955- Log on to computers.*
*TC LB1028.5 .D69 1999*

**Log on to computers.**
Drake, Jim, 1955- Computers and schools. Des Plaines, Ill. : Heinemann Library, c1999.
*TC LB1028.5 .D69 1999*

**Drake, Susan M., 1944-** Creating integrated curriculum : proven ways to increase student learning / Susan M. Drake. Thousand Oaks, Calif. : Corwin Press, c1998. xx, 236 p. : ill. ; 24 cm. Includes bibliographical references (p. 199-224) and index. CONTENTS: What is integrated curriculum and why is it important? -- Does integrated curriculum work? -- Creating multidisciplinary programs -- Using interdisciplinary

approaches -- Exploring transdisciplinary approaches -- Connecting standards to curriculum -- Aligning teaching, learning, and assessment -- Overcoming the obstacles and finding success. ISBN 0-8039-6716-0 (cloth : alk. paper) ISBN 0-8039-6717-9 (pbk. : alk. paper) DDC 374/.000973
*1. Interdisciplinary approach in education - United States. 2. Interdisciplinary approach in education - Canada. 3. Education - United States - Curricula. 4. Education - Canada - Curricula. 5. Education - Standards - United States. 6. Education - Standards - Canada. I. Title.*
**TC LB1570 .D695 1998**

**Drake, Thelbert L.** The principalship / Thelbert L. Drake, William H. Roe. 5th ed. Upper Saddle River, N.J. : Merrill, c1999. xiv, 482 p. : ill. ; 24 cm. Includes bibliographical references and index. ISBN 0-13-263260-8 DDC 371.2/012
*1. School principals - United States. I. Roe, William Henry, 1917- II. Title.*
**TC LB2831.92 .D73 1999**

**DRAMA.** *See* **ACTING; CHILDREN'S PLAYS; PSYCHODRAMA.**

**Drama & theatre.**
First stage. Lafayette, Ind. : Purdue University, c1961-c1967.

**DRAMA - 20TH CENTURY - PERIODICALS.**
First stage. Lafayette, Ind. : Purdue University, c1961-c1967.

**Drama and performance studies**
Rinehart, Robert E., 1951- Players all. Bloomington : Indiana University Press, c1998.
**TC GV706.5 .R56 1998**

**Drama and traditional story for the early years.**
Toye, Nigel, 1949- London ; New York : Routledge, 2000.
**TC PN3171 .T695 2000**

**DRAMA IN EDUCATION.**
Brown, Victoria (Victoria L.) The dramatic difference. Portsmouth, NH : Heinemann, c1999.
**TC PN3171 .B76 1999**

Clipson-Boyles, Suzi. Drama in primary English teaching. London : David Fulton, 1998.
**TC PN1701 .C556 1998**

Ewart, Franzeska G. Let the shadows speak. Stoke on Trent, Staffordshire, England : Trentham Books, 1998.
**TC PN1979.S5 E8 1998**

Fennessey, Sharon M. History in the spotlight. Portsmouth, NH : Heinemann, c2000.
**TC PN3171 .F46 2000**

Phillips, Sarah. Drama with children. Oxford : New York : Oxford University Press, c1999.
**TC PN3171 .P45 1999**

Teaching Shakespeare through performance. New York : Modern Language Association of America, 1999.
**TC PR2987 .T366 1999**

**DRAMA IN EDUCATION - GREAT BRITAIN.**
Toye, Nigel, 1949- Drama and traditional story for the early years. London ; New York : Routledge, 2000.
**TC PN3171 .T695 2000**

**Drama in primary English teaching.**
Clipson-Boyles, Suzi. London : David Fulton, 1998.
**TC PN1701 .C556 1998**

**Drama, literacy and moral education 5-11.**
Winston, Joe. London : David Fulton, 2000.
**TC LC268 .W667 2000**

**DRAMA, MODERN.** *See* **DRAMA; DRAMA - 20TH CENTURY.**

**The drama of everyday life.**
Scheibe, Karl E., 1937- Cambridge, Mass. : Harvard University Press, 2000.
**TC BF121 .S328 2000**

**DRAMA - PERIODICALS.**
[Theatre journal (Online)] Theatre journal [computer file]. Baltimore, Md. : Johns Hopkins University Press, c1996-
**TC EJOURNALS**

**DRAMA - PHILOSOPHY.** *See* **DRAMA.**

**DRAMA - STUDY AND TEACHING.**
Teaching Shakespeare through performance. New York : Modern Language Association of America, 1999.
**TC PR2987 .T366 1999**

**DRAMA - STUDY AND TEACHING (EARLY CHILDHOOD) - GREAT BRITAIN.**

Toye, Nigel, 1949- Drama and traditional story for the early years. London ; New York : Routledge, 2000.
**TC PN3171 .T695 2000**

**DRAMA - STUDY AND TEACHING (ELEMENTARY).**
Clipson-Boyles, Suzi. Drama in primary English teaching. London : David Fulton, 1998.
**TC PN1701 .C556 1998**

Winston, Joe. Beginning drama 4-11. London : David Fulton Publishers, 1998.
**TC PN1701 .W567 1998**

**DRAMA - STUDY AND TEACHING (ELEMENTARY) - GREAT BRITAIN.**
Winston, Joe. Drama, literacy and moral education 5-11. London : David Fulton, 2000.
**TC LC268 .W667 2000**

**DRAMA THERAPY.** *See* **PSYCHODRAMA.**

**Drama with children.**
Phillips, Sarah. Oxford ; New York : Oxford University Press, c1999.
**TC PN3171 .P45 1999**

**DRAMATHERAPY.** *See* **PSYCHODRAMA.**

**The dramatic difference.**
Brown, Victoria (Victoria L.) Portsmouth, NH : Heinemann, c1999.
**TC PN3171 .B76 1999**

**DRAMATIC EDUCATION.** *See* **ACTING - STUDY AND TEACHING.**

**DRAMATIC MUSIC.** *See* **MUSICALS.**

**Draper, Sharon M. (Sharon Mills)** Romiette and Julio / Sharon M. Draper. 1st ed. New York : Atheneum Books for Young Readers, 1999. 236 p. 22 cm. SUMMARY: Romiette, an African-American girl, and Julio, a Hispanic boy, discover that they attend the same high school after falling in love on the Internet, but are harassed by a gang whose members object to their interracial dating. ISBN 0-689-82180-8 DDC [Fic]
*1. Internet - Fiction. 2. Gangs - Fiction. 3. High schools - Fiction. 4. Schools - Fiction. 5. Hispanic Americans - Fiction. 6. Afro-Americans - Fiction. I. Title.*
**TC PZ7.D78325 Ro 1999**

Teaching from the heart : reflections, encouragement, and inspiration / Sharon M. Draper. Portsmouth, NH : Heinemann, c2000. x, 133 p. ; 23 cm. ISBN 0-325-00131-6 (alk. paper) DDC 371.1/00973
*1. Teachers - United States. 2. Teaching - United States. 3. Draper, Sharon M. - (Sharon Mills) 4. Teachers - United States - Biography. I. Title.*
**TC LB1775.2 .D72 2000**

**DRAPER, SHARON M. (SHARON MILLS).**
Draper, Sharon M. (Sharon Mills) Teaching from the heart. Portsmouth, NH : Heinemann, c2000.
**TC LB1775.2 .D72 2000**

**DRAWING.** *See also* **CHILDREN'S DRAWINGS; FIGURE DRAWING.**
What is a good drawing? [videorecording]. Peasmarsh, East Sussex, Eng. : Ho-Ho-Kus, NJ : Roland Collection, [1980-1986?].
**TC NC703 .W45 1980**

**DRAWING - 20TH CENTURY - AUSTRALIA - EXHIBITIONS.**
Art Gallery of New South Wales. Australian drawings from the gallery's collection. Sydney : Art Gallery of New South Wales, 1997.
**TC NC369 .A78 1997**

**DRAWING ABILITY IN CHILDREN - SEX DIFFERENCES.**
Tuman, Donna M. Gender difference in form and content. 1998.
**TC 06 no. 11000**

**Drawing and painting in the middle school.**
Hafeli, Mary Claire. 1999.
**TC 06 no. 11055**

**DRAWING - AUSTRALIA - SYDNEY (N.S.W.) - EXHIBITIONS.**
Art Gallery of New South Wales. Australian drawings from the gallery's collection. Sydney : Art Gallery of New South Wales, 1997.
**TC NC369 .A78 1997**

**DRAWING, AUSTRALIAN - EXHIBITIONS.**
Art Gallery of New South Wales. Australian drawings from the gallery's collection. Sydney : Art Gallery of New South Wales, 1997.
**TC NC369 .A78 1997**

**DRAWING - INSTRUCTION.**
Kaupelis, Robert. Learning to draw; New York, Watson-Guptill Publications [1966]

**TC NC730 .K36**

**DRAWING, PSYCHOLOGY OF - SEX DIFFERENCES.**
Tuman, Donna M. Gender difference in form and content. 1998.
**TC 06 no. 11000**

**DRAWING - STUDY AND TEACHING.**
Creativity in the classroom. Burbank, CA : Disney Learning Partnership, c1999.
**TC LB1062 .C7 1999**

**DRAWING - TECHNIQUE.**
What is a good drawing? [videorecording]. Peasmarsh, East Sussex, Eng. : Ho-Ho-Kus, NJ : Roland Collection, [1980-1986?].
**TC NC703 .W45 1980**

**DRAWINGS.** *See* **DRAWING.**

**DRAWINGS, CHILDREN'S.** *See* **CHILDREN'S DRAWINGS.**

**DREAM ANALYSIS.** *See* **DREAM INTERPRETATION.**

**DREAM INTERPRETATION.**
Bulkeley, Kelly, 1962- Visions of the night. Albany, NY : State University of New York Press, c1999.
**TC BF1091 .B94 1999**

Flanagan, Owen J. Dreaming souls. Oxford ; New York : Oxford University Press, 2000.
**TC BF1091 .F58 2000**

Freud, Sigmund, 1856-1939 The interpretation of dreams. Oxford ; New York : Oxford University Press, 1999.
**TC BF1078 .F72 1999**

Luke, Helen M., 1904- Such stuff as dreams are made on. New York : Parabola Books, c2000.
**TC BF1091 .L82 2000**

Wax, Murray Lionel, 1922- Western rationality and the angel of dreams. Lanham, Md. ; Oxford : Rowman & Littlefield, c1999.
**TC BF1078 .W38 1999**

**Dream, phantasy, and art.**
Segal, Hanna. London ; New York : Tavistock/ Routledge, 1991.
**TC BF1078 .S375 1991**

**Dream spaces.**
Kavanagh, Gaynor. New York : Leicester University Press, 2000.
**TC AM7 .K37 2000**

**DREAMING.** *See* **DREAMS.**

**Dreaming as delirium.**
Hobson, J. Allan, 1933- [Chemistry of conscious states] 1st MIT Press ed. Cambridge, Mass. : MIT Press, 1999.
**TC QP426 .H629 1999**

**Dreaming souls.**
Flanagan, Owen J. Oxford ; New York : Oxford University Press, 2000.
**TC BF1091 .F58 2000**

**Dreamings of the desert :** aboriginal dot paintings of the Western Desert / Art Gallery of South Australia, Adelaide ; [exhibition co-ordinated by Jane Hylton ; photography by Clayton Glen ; essay by Vivien Johnson]. Adelaide : The Gallery, c1996. 140 p. : ill. (some col.), map ; 29 cm. "Drawings of the desert : aboriginal dot paintings of the Western Desert is published to accompany the exhibition of the same title, featuring the Art Gallery of South Australia's entire collection of Western Desert art ..."-- T.p. verso. CONTENTS: Foreword / Ron Radford -- Dreamings of the desert: recognition of a movement / Jane Hylton -- Map of current distribution of Central Australian languages -- A history of Western Desert art 1971-1996 / Vivien Johnson -- Origins 1971-1975 -- Papunya Tula artists 1978-1988 -- The spread of the Western Desert art 1985-1989 -- Into the nineties -- Conclusion -- Notes -- Artists' biographies -- Abbreviations -- Western desert dot painting: development of a movement / collated by Jane Hylton -- Bibliography. ISBN 0-7308-3073-X DDC 759.99429/089/9915
*1. Painting, Australian aboriginal - Australia - Western Desert (W.A.) - Exhibitions. 2. Painting - Australia - Adelaide (S. Aust.) - Exhibitions. 3. Art Gallery of South Australia - Exhibitions. I. Johnson, Vivien. II. Hylton, Jane. 1950- III. Art Gallery of South Australia. IV. Title: Aboriginal dot paintings of the Western Desert*
**TC ND1101 .D74 1996**

**DREAMS.**
Bulkeley, Kelly, 1962- Visions of the night. Albany, NY : State University of New York Press, c1999.
**TC BF1091 .B94 1999**

Flanagan, Owen J. Dreaming souls. Oxford : New York : Oxford University Press, 2000.
**TC BF1091 .F58 2000**

Hobson, J. Allan, 1933- [Chemistry of conscious states] Dreaming as delirium. 1st MIT Press ed. Cambridge, Mass. : MIT Press, 1999.
**TC QP426 .H629 1999**

Luke, Helen M., 1904- Such stuff as dreams are made on. New York : Parabola Books, c2000.
**TC BF1091 .L82 2000**

Segal, Hanna. Dream, phantasy, and art. London : New York : Tavistock/Routledge, 1991.
**TC BF1078 .S375 1991**

Social dreaming @ work. London : Karnac Books, 1998.
**TC BF1078 .S55 1998**

Wax, Murray Lionel, 1922- Western rationality and the angel of dreams. Lanham, Md. ; Oxford : Rowman & Littlefield, c1999.
**TC BF1078 .W38 1999**

**Dreams 1900-2000 :** science, art, and the unconscious mind / edited by Lynn Gamwell. Binghamton : Cornell University Press : Binghamtom University Art Museum, State University of New York, 2000. 304 p. : ill. (some col.) ; 31 cm. (Cornell studies in the history of psychiatry) "Published in conjunction with the exhibition Dreams 1900-2000: science, art, and the unconscious mind, curated by Lynn Gamwell" Includes bibliographical references and index. CONTENTS: Dreams in pursuit of art / Lucy C. Daniels -- The muse is within / Lynn Gamwell. The psychology and physiology of dreaming / Ernest Hartmann -- From vision to dream / Donald Kuspit -- Gallery -- Dream archive. ISBN 0-8014-3730-X (alk. paper) DDC 154.6/3/074
*1. Dreams - Exhibitions. I. Gamwell, Lynn, 1943- II. Title: Dreams nineteen hundred to two thousand III. Title: Dreams nineteen hundred-two thousand IV. Series.*
**TC BF1078 .D729 2000**

**Dreams and reverie.**
Ravenhill, Philip L. Washington : Smithsonian Institution Press, c1996.
**TC NB1255.C85 R38 1996**

**DREAMS - EXHIBITIONS.**
Dreams 1900-2000. Binghamton : Cornell University Press : Binghamtom University Art Museum, State University of New York, 2000.
**TC BF1078 .D729 2000**

**DREAMS - FICTION.**
Brown, Ruth. Mad summer night's dream. 1st American ed. New York : Dutton Children's Books, 1999.
**TC PZ8.3.B8155 Mad 1999**

Nye, Naomi Shihab. Benito's dream bottle. 1st ed. New York : Simon & Schuster Books for Young Readers, c1995.
**TC PZ7.N976 Be 1995**

**Dreams nineteen hundred to two thousand.**
Dreams 1900-2000. Binghamton : Cornell University Press : Binghamtom University Art Museum, State University of New York, 2000.
**TC BF1078 .D729 2000**

**Dreams nineteen hundred-two thousand.**
Dreams 1900-2000. Binghamton : Cornell University Press : Binghamtom University Art Museum, State University of New York, 2000.
**TC BF1078 .D729 2000**

**DREAMS - RELIGIOUS ASPECTS.**
Bulkeley, Kelly, 1962- Visions of the night. Albany, NY : State University of New York Press, c1999.
**TC BF1091 .B94 1999**

**DREAMS - THERAPEUTIC USE.**
Stevens, Anthony. The two million-year-old self. New York : Fromm International Publishing, 1997.
**TC BF175.5.A72 S75 1997**

**Dreamweaver [computer file].**
Macromedia Dreamweaver 3 [computer file]. Version 3.0 ; Windows 95, Windows 98, Windows NT ; Education version. San Francisco, CA : Macromedia, c1999. Computer program.
**TC TK5105.8883 .M33 1999**

**DREAMWEAVER (COMPUTER FILE).**
Macromedia Dreamweaver 3 [computer file]. Version 3.0 ; Windows 95, Windows 98, Windows NT ; Education version. San Francisco, CA : Macromedia, c1999. Computer program.
**TC TK5105.8883 .M33 1999**

**Dreher, Mariam Jean.**
Engaging young readers. New York : Guilford Press, c2000.

**TC LB1573 .E655 2000**

**Dreifus, Claudia.** Interview. New York : Seven Stories ; London : Turnaround, 1999, 336 p. ; 23 cm. Originally published: 1997. ISBN 1-88836-390-8 DDC 081
*1. Celebrities - Interviews. I. Title.*
**TC PN4874.D74158 1999**

**DRESS.** *See* **CLOTHING AND DRESS.**

**Drever, Mina.** Teaching English in primary classrooms / Mina Drever, Susan Moule and Keith Peterson. Stoke on Trent, Staffordshire, England : Trentham Books, 1999. xvi, 190 p. : ill. ; 25 cm. Includes bibliographical references. ISBN 1-85856-178-7 ISBN 1-85856-177-9 (pbk.)
*1. Language arts (Elementary) - Great Britain. 2. English language - Study and teaching (Elementary) - Great Britain. I. Moule, Susan. II. Peterson, Keith. III. Title.*
**TC LB1576 .D749 1999**

**Drew, Clifford J., 1943-.**
Hardman, Michael L. Human exceptionality. 6th ed. Boston : Allyn and Bacon, c1999.
**TC HV1568 .H37 1999**

**Dreyer, Susan T.** Student perceptions of their educational experiences at Satellite Academy High School and their former schools / by Susan T. Dreyer. 1999. 288 leaves ; 29 cm. Typescript; issued also on microfilm. Thesis (Ed.D.)--Teachers College, Columbia University, 1999. Includes bibliographical references (leaves 271-277).
*1. High school students - New York (State) - New York - Attitudes. 2. High school teachers - New York (State) - New York - Attitudes. 3. High school dropouts - New York (State) - New York - Interviews. 4. Alternative schools - New York (State) - New York - Social aspects. 5. Teacher-students relationships. 6. Classroom management. 7. High schools - Decentralization - New York (State) - New York. I. Title.*
**TC 06 no. 11105**

**Drifting on a read.**
Jarrett, Michael, 1953- Albany, N.Y. : State University of New York Press, 1999.
**TC ML3849 .J39 1999**

**DRILL AND MINOR TACTICS - HISTORY.**
Penn, Alan, 1926- Targeting schools. London ; Portland, OR : Woburn Press, 1999.
**TC GV443 .P388 1999**

**DRINKERS, PROBLEM.** *See* **ALCOHOLICS.**

**Drinking, conduct disorder, and social change.**
Kunitz, Stephen J. Oxford ; New York : Oxford University Press, 2000.
**TC E99.N3 K88 2000**

**DRINKING CUSTOMS - CROSS-CULTURAL STUDIES.**
Heath, Dwight B. Drinking occasions. Philadelphia : Brunner/Mazel, c2000.
**TC GT2884 .H4 2000**

**Drinking occasions.**
Heath, Dwight B. Philadelphia : Brunner/Mazel, c2000.
**TC GT2884 .H4 2000**

**DRINKING OF ALCOHOLIC BEVERAGES.** *See* **ALCOHOLISM.**

**DRINKING OF ALCOHOLIC BEVERAGES - CROSS-CULTURAL STUDIES.**
Heath, Dwight B. Drinking occasions. Philadelphia : Brunner/Mazel, c2000.
**TC GT2884 .H4 2000**

**DRINKING OF ALCOHOLIC BEVERAGES - PSYCHOLOGICAL ASPECTS.**
Psychological theories of drinking and alcoholism. 2nd ed. New York : Guilford Press, c1999.
**TC HV5045 .P74 1999**

**DRINKING OF ALCOHOLIC BEVERAGES - SOCIAL ASPECTS.**
Alcohol and emerging markets. Philadelphia, Penn : Brunner/Mazel, 1998.
**TC HD9350.6 .A4 1998**

**DRINKING PROBLEM.** *See* **ALCOHOLISM; DRINKING OF ALCOHOLIC BEVERAGES.**

**DRINKS.** *See* **BEVERAGES.**

**Driscoll, Amy.**
Freiberg, H. Jerome. Universal teaching strategies. 3rd ed. Boston : Allyn and Bacon, c2000.
**TC LB1025.3 .F74 2000**

**Driscoll, Marcy Perkins.** Psychology of learning for instruction / Marcy P. Driscoll. 2nd ed. Boston ; London : Allyn and Bacon, c2000. xvi, 448 p. : ill. ; 24 cm. Includes bibliographical references (p. 405-439) and index. ISBN 0-205-26321-6 (alk. paper) DDC 370.15/23

*1. Learning, Psychology of. 2. Cognitive learning theory. 3. Teaching. I. Title.*
**TC LB1060 .D75 2000**

**Driscoll, Margaret M.** The application of adult education principles in the development of a manual for practitioners creating web-based training programs / by Margaret M. Driscoll. 1999. x, 214 leaves ; 29 cm. Vol. 2 has title: Web-based training: tactics and techniques for designing adult learning experiences. Typescript; issued also on microfilm. Thesis (Ed.D.)--Teachers College, Columbia University, 1999. Includes bibliographical references (leaves 296-329).
*1. Adult education. 2. Internet (Computer network) in education. 3. Education - Computer netwoek resources. I. Title. II. Title: Development of a manual for practitioners creating web-based training programs III. Title: Web-based training: tactics and techniques for designing adult learning experiences*
**TC 06 no. 11106**

**Driskell, Judy A. (Judy Anne).**
Energy-yielding macronutrients and energy metabolism in sports nutrition. Boca Raton, Fla. ; London : CRC Press, c2000.
**TC QP176 .E546 2000**

**Drive.**
Viney, John. 1st U.S. ed. New York, N.Y. : Bloomsbury, 1999.
**TC HD57.7 .V564 1999**

Wieler, Diana J. (Diana Jean), 1961- Toronto : Douglas & McIntyre, 1998.
**TC PS8595.I53143 D74 1998**

**DRIVE (PSYCHOLOGY).** *See* **MOTIVATION (PSYCHOLOGY).**

**Dronzek, Laura, ill.**
Henkes, Kevin. Oh!. New York : Greenwillow Books, 1999.
**TC PZ8.3.H4165 Oh 1999**

**DROP-OUTS.** *See* **DROPOUTS.**

**Dropout or diploma.**
Tannenbaum, Abraham. New York : Teachers College Press, 1966.
**TC 371.2913T15**

**DROPOUTS.** *See* **HIGH SCHOOL DROPOUTS.**

**DROPOUTS - PREVENTION.**
Promising practices in recruitment, remediation, and retention. San Francisco, Calif. : Jossey-Bass, c1999.
**TC LB2331.72 .N48 1999**

**DROPOUTS - UNITED STATES - PREVENTION.**
Lovitt, Thomas C. Preventing school failure. 2nd ed. Austin, Tex. : Pro-Ed. : c2000.
**TC LC146.6 .L68 2000**

**Drotar, Dennis.**
Handbook of research in pediatric and clinical child psychology. New York : Kluwer Academic/Plenum Publishers, c 2000.
**TC RJ499.3 .H367 2000**

**DROWNING - FICTION.**
Bunting, Eve, 1928- Blackwater. 1st ed. New York : Joanna Cotler Books, 1999.
**TC PZ7.B91527 Bne 1999**

**Druce, Arden.** Paper bag puppets / Arden Druce ; illustrated by Geraldine Hulbert ... [et al.]. Lanham, MD : Scarecrow Press, 1999. xiv, 200 p. : ill. ; 28 cm. (School library media series ; no. 15) Includes index. ISBN 0-8108-3400-6 (paper : alk. paper) DDC 027.62/51
*1. Children's libraries - Activity programs - United States. 2. Storytelling - United States. 3. Libraries and puppets - United States. 4. Puppet theater in education - United States. 5. Teaching - United States - Aids and devices. 6. Biography - Study and teaching. 7. United States - Biography - Study and teaching. I. Title. II. Series.*
**TC Z718.3 .D78 1999**

**Drucker, Peter Ferdinand, 1909-** Management challenges for the 21st century / Peter F. Drucker. 1st ed. New York : HarperBusiness, c1999. xi, 207 p. ; 25 cm. Includes index. ISBN 0-88730-998-4 DDC 658
*1. Management - Forecasting. 2. Twenty-first century - Forecasts. I. Title. II. Title: Management challenges for the twenty-first century*
**TC HD30.27 .D78 1999**

**DRUG ABUSE.** *See also* **NARCOTIC HABIT.**
Disorders due to psychoactive substance abuse [videorecording]. Princeton, N.J. : Films for the Humanities & Sciences, 1998.
**TC RC564 .D5 1998**

Goldberg, Ted. Demystifying drugs. New York : St. Martin's Press, 1999.

Drug abuse

TC HV5801 .G633 1999

When the brain goes wrong [videorecording]. Short version. Boston, MA : Fanlight Productions [dist.], c1992.
TC RC386 .W54 1992

**DRUG ABUSE COUNSELING.**
Cohen, Monique. Counseling addicted women. Thousand Oaks, Calif. : Sage Publications, c2000.
TC HV4999.W65 C64 2000

Miller, Geraldine A., 1955- Learning the language of addiction counseling. Boston : Allyn and Bacon, c1999.
TC RC564 .M536 1999

**DRUG ABUSE COUNSELING - UNITED STATES.**
Bridges to recovery. New York ; London : Free Press, c2000.
TC HV5199.5 .B75 2000

**DRUG ABUSE EDUCATION. See DRUG ABUSE - STUDY AND TEACHING.**

**DRUG ABUSE - ENCYCLOPEDIAS.**
O'Brien, Robert, 1932- The encyclopedia of understanding alcohol and other drugs. New York, NY : Facts on File, c1999.
TC HV5017 .O37 1999

**DRUG ABUSE - FLORIDA - ORLANDO.**
Heroin [videorecording]. [Princeton, N.J.] : Films for the Humanities & Sciences, c1998.
TC HV5822.H4 H4 1998

**DRUG ABUSE - FLORIDA - ORLANDO - PREVENTION.**
Heroin [videorecording]. [Princeton, N.J.] : Films for the Humanities & Sciences, c1998.
TC HV5822.H4 H4 1998

**DRUG ABUSE - GOVERNMENT POLICY - ARIZONA.**
The politics of addiction [videorecording]. Princeton, NJ : Films for the Humanities & Sciences, c1998.
TC RC564 .P59 1998

**DRUG ABUSE - GOVERNMENT POLICY - UNITED STATES.**
The politics of addiction [videorecording]. Princeton, NJ : Films for the Humanities & Sciences, c1998.
TC RC564 .P59 1998

**DRUG ABUSE - PHYSIOLOGICAL ASPECTS - RESEARCH.**
The hijacked brain [videorecording]. Princeton, NJ : Films for the Humanities & Sciences, c1998.
TC RC564 .H5 1998

**DRUG ABUSE - PHYSIOLOGICAL EFFECT - RESEARCH.**
The hijacked brain [videorecording]. Princeton, NJ : Films for the Humanities & Sciences, c1998.
TC RC564 .H5 1998

**DRUG ABUSE - PREVENTION.**
Adolescent relationships and drug use. Mahwah, N.J. ; London : Lawrence Erlbaum Associates, 2000.
TC HV5824.Y68 A315 2000

The next generation [videorecording]. Princeton, NJ : Films for the Humanities & Sciences, c1998.
TC RC564 .N4 1998

**DRUG ABUSE - PREVENTION - STUDY AND TEACHING (ELEMENTARY).**
Weinstein, Sanford. The educator's guide to substance abuse prevention. Mahwah, N.J. : Lawrence Erlbaum Publishers, 1999.
TC HV5808 .W45 1999

**DRUG ABUSE - PSYCHOLOGICAL ASPECTS.**
Portrait of addiction [videorecording]. Princeton, NJ : Films for the Humanities & Sciences, c1998.
TC HV5801 .P6 1998

Portrait of addiction [videorecording]. Princeton, NJ : Films for the Humanities & Sciences, c1998.
TC RC564 .P6 1998

**DRUG ABUSE - RESEARCH - UNITED STATES.**
Conducting drug abuse research with minority populations. New York : Haworth Press, c1999.
TC HV5824.E85 C66 1999

**DRUG ABUSE - SOCIAL ASPECTS - FLORIDA - ORLAND.**
Heroin [videorecording]. [Princeton, N.J.] : Films for the Humanities & Sciences, c1998.
TC HV5822.H4 H4 1998

**DRUG ABUSE - STUDY AND TEACHING - FLORIDA - ORLANDO.**
Heroin [videorecording]. [Princeton, N.J.] : Films for the Humanities & Sciences, c1998.

TC HV5822.H4 H4 1998

**DRUG ABUSE - TREATMENT.**
Changing lives [videorecording]. Princeton, NJ : Films for the Humanities & Sciences, c1998.
TC RC564 .C54 1998

Seivewright, Nicholas. Community treatment of drug misuse. Cambridge, UK : New York : Cambridge University Press, 2000.
TC RC564 .S45 2000

**DRUG ABUSE - TREATMENT - COST EFFECTIVENESS.**
Cost benefit analysis of heroin maintenance treatment. Basel : New York : Karger, c2000.
TC RC568.H4 C67 2000

**DRUG ABUSE - UNITED STATES.**
The next generation [videorecording]. Princeton, NJ : Films for the Humanities & Sciences, c1998.
TC RC564 .N4 1998

**DRUG ADDICTION. See DRUG ABUSE; NARCOTIC HABIT.**

**DRUG ADDICTS. See NARCOTIC ADDICTS.**

**DRUG DECRIMINALIZATION. See DRUG LEGALIZATION.**

**DRUG EDUCATION. See DRUG ABUSE - STUDY AND TEACHING.**

**DRUG HABIT. See DRUG ABUSE; NARCOTIC HABIT.**

**DRUG INTERACTIONS.**
Pharmacology in exercise and sports. Boca Raton : CRC Press, c1996.
TC QP301 .P53 1996

**DRUG LEGALIZATION - UNITED STATES.**
Keys, David Patrick, 1955- Confronting the drug control establishment. Albany, N.Y. : State University of New York Press, c2000.
TC HM1031.L56 K49 2000

**DRUG USE. See DRUG ABUSE.**

**DRUG WITHDRAWAL SYMPTOMS.**
Disorders due to psychoactive substance abuse [videorecording]. Princeton, N.J. : Films for the Humanities & Sciences, 1998.
TC RC564 .D5 1998

**DRUGS. See DOPING IN SPORTS; PSYCHOTROPIC DRUGS.**

**Drugs & society (New York, N.Y.).**
Conducting drug abuse research with minority populations. New York : Haworth Press, c1999.
TC HV5824.E85 C66 1999

**DRUGS - ADMINISTRATION.**
Brown, Ronald T. Medications for school-age children. New York : Guilford Press, c1998.
TC RJ560 .B76 1998

**DRUGS AND YOUTH. See YOUTH - DRUG USE.**

**DRUGS - DICTIONARIES.**
Agins, Alan P. Parent & educators' drug reference :. Cranston, R.I. : PRN Press, c1999.
TC RJ560 .A35 1999

**DRUGS - HANDBOOKS, MANUALS, ETC.**
Agins, Alan P. Parent & educators' drug reference :. Cranston, R.I. : PRN Press, c1999.
TC RJ560 .A35 1999

**DRUGS IN SPORTS. See DOPING IN SPORTS.**

**DRUGS - LAW AND LEGISLATION - UNITED STATES - HISTORY.**
Goodwin, Lorine Swainston, 1925- The pure food, drink, and drug crusaders, 1879-1914. Jefferson, N.C. : McFarland, 1999.
TC HD9000.9.U5 G66 1999

**DRUGS - LAWS AND LEGISLATION. See DRUGS - LAW AND LEGISLATION.**

**DRUGS OF ABUSE. See DRUG ABUSE; PSYCHOTROPIC DRUGS.**

**DRUGS - OVERDOSAGE. See DRUG ABUSE.**

**DRUGS - PSYCHOTROPIC EFFECTS. See PSYCHOPHARMACOLOGY.**

**DRUM. See SNARE DRUM.**

**Drum, Jan.** Global winners : 74 learning activities for inside and outside the classroom / Jan Drum, Steve Hughes, and George Otero. Yarmouth, Me. : Intercultural Press, c1994. xviii, 209 p. : ill. ; 26 cm. Includes bibliographical references (p. 201-204). ISBN 1-87786-418-8 DDC 370.11/5
*1. International education - United States. 2. International*

education - United States - Activity programs. I. Hughes, Steve. II. Otero, George G. III. Title.
TC LC1099.3 .D78 1994

**Drummond, Lee, 1944-** American dreamtime : a cultural analysis of popular movies and their implications for a science of humanity / Lee Drummond. Lanham, Md. : Littlefield Adams Books, 1996. xiii, 336 p. : ill. ; 24 cm. Includes bibliographical references and indexes. ISBN 0-8226-3046-X (alk. paper) ISBN 0-8226-3047-8 (pbk. : alk. paper) DDC 791.43/615
*1. Myth in motion pictures. 2. Heroes in motion pictures. 3. Motion pictures - Semiotics. I. Title.*
TC PN1995.9.M96 D78 1996

**Drummond, Robert J.** Appraisal procedures for counselors and helping professionals / Robert J. Drummond. 4th ed. Upper Saddle River, N.J. : Merrill, c2000. xx, 540 p. ; 25 cm. Includes bibliographical references (p. 495-507) and indexes. ISBN 0-13-080590-4 DDC 150/.28/7
*1. Psychological tests. 2. Educational tests and measurements. 3. Counseling. I. Title.*
TC BF176 .D78 2000

**The drums** [videorecording] / director, Todd Brinegar ; producer, Mark S. Arnett : a production of Aesthetic Artist Records and Brinegar Video/Film Productions, Inc. in association with Backstage Pass Instructional Video. Van Nuys, CA : Backstage Pass Productions ; Canoga Park, Calif. : [Distributed by] MVP Home Entertainment, c1998. 1 videocassette (56 min.) : sd., col. ; 1/2 in. + 1 instruction booklet (8 p. : music ; 18 cm.). (Maestro music instrument instructional video ... for) Title on container: Snare drums for beginners [videorecording]. VHS, Hi-Fi, Stereo. Cataloged from credits, cassette label and container. Instructor: Mat Britain. Audio, Mark S. Arnett. For beginners. SUMMARY: Mat Britain teaches the basics of learning to play the snare drum, from handling to rudimentary playing, and demonstrates the technique along with two of his pupils. He also introduces other percussion instruments. CONTENTS: Various instruments -- Starting at the top -- The stroke -- Hand to hand -- Hand exercises -- Stick control -- Drum accents -- Single strokes -- Mallet instruments -- Maintaining your drum -- Wrapping it up.
*1. Snare drum - Instruction and study. 2. Snare drum - Studies and exercises. I. Britain, Mat. II. Brinegar, Todd. III. Arnett, Mark S. IV. Backstage Pass Productions. V. Aesthetic Artist Records. VI. Brinegar Video/Film Productions, Inc. VII. MVP Home Entertainment (Firm) VIII. Title: Snare drums for beginners [videorecording] IX. Series.*
TC MT662.3 .S6 1998

**DRUNKARDS. See ALCOHOLICS.**

**DRUNKENNESS. See ALCOHOLISM.**

**DRUNKS. See ALCOHOLICS.**

**Drury, Nevill, 1947-.**
Contemporary aboriginal painting. East Roseville, Australia : Craftsmen House, c1993.
TC ND1101 .C66 1993

Fire and shadow : spirituality in contemporary Australian art / Nevill Drury and Anna Voigt. Roseville East, NWS : Craftsman House ; Australia ; United States : G + B Arts International [distributor], c1996. 184 p. : col. ill. ; 30 cm. Includes bibliographical references (p. 182-183) and index. ISBN 976-641-042-9
*1. Art, Australian. 2. Art, Modern - 20th century - Australia. 3. Spiritualism in art. I. Voigt, Anna. II. Title.*
TC N7400.2 .D78 1996

**Druss, Richard G., 1933-** Listening to patients : : relearning the art of healing in psychotherapy / Richard G. Druss. Oxford ; New York : Oxford University Press, 2000. viii, 133 p. ; 22 cm. Includes bibliographical references and index. ISBN 0-19-513593-8 (cloth : alk. paper)
*1. Psychotherapy - Methodology. 2. Body image. 3. Interpersonal relations. 4. Mental healing. I. Title.*
TC RC480.8 .D78 2000

**DRY-GOODS. See TEXTILE FABRICS.**

**Dryden, Caroline.** Being married, doing gender : a critical analysis of gender relationships in marriage / Caroline Dryden. London ; New York : Routledge, 1999. vi, 161 p. ; 24 cm. (Women and psychology) Includes bibliographical references (p. 153-156) and indexes. ISBN 0-415-16558-X (HB) ISBN 0-415-16559-8 (PB) DDC 306.85
*1. Marriage - Psychological aspects. 2. Man-woman relationships. 3. Sex role. 4. Feminist psychology. I. Title. II. Series.*
TC HQ734 .D848 1999

**DSCHAGGA (AFRICAN PEOPLE). See CHAGA (AFRICAN PEOPLE).**

**DSM-IV diagnosis in the schools.**
House, Alvin E. New York : Guilford Press, c1999

*TC RJ503.5 .H68 1999*

**D.T.'S.** *See* **DELIRIUM TREMENS.**

**DTS.** *See* **DELIRIUM TREMENS.**

**Du, Zuru.** Modeling conditional item dependencies with a three-parameter logistic testlet model / by Zuru Du. 1998. vii, 98 leaves ; 29 cm. Issued also on microfilm. Includes tables. Thesis (Ph.D.)--Columbia University, 1998. Includes bibliographical references (leaves 96-98).
*1. Item response theory. 2. Educational tests and measurements - Statistical methods. 3. Parameter estimation. 4. Educational statistics. 5. Mathematical statistics. 6. Psychometrics. I. Title.*
*TC 085 D84*

**DUAL-CAREER COUPLES.** *See* **DUAL-CAREER FAMILIES.**

**DUAL-CAREER FAMILIES.** *See* **WORK AND FAMILY.**

**DUAL-CAREER FAMILIES - UNITED STATES - HISTORY.**
Landry, Bart. Black working wives. Berkeley : University of California Press, c2000.
*TC HQ536 .L335 2000*

**DUAL-CAREER MARRIAGE.** *See* **DUAL-CAREER FAMILIES.**

**DUAL-INCOME COUPLES.** *See* **DUAL-CAREER FAMILIES.**

**DUAL PERSONALITY.** *See* **MULTIPLE PERSONALITY.**

**DUALISM.** *See* **MIND AND BODY.**

**DUALISM - HISTORY.**
Ostenfeld, Erik Nis. Ancient Greek psychology and the modern mind-body debate. Aarhus, Denmark : Aarhus University Press, 1987.
*TC BF161 .O88 1987*

**Duarte, Eduardo Manuel.**
Foundational perpectives in multiculural education. New York : Longman, c2000.
*TC LC1099.3 .F68 2000*

**DuBoff, Leonard D.** The law (in plain English) for galleries / Leonard D. DuBoff. 2nd ed. New York : Allworth Press, c1999. xiii, 209 p. : forms ; 24 cm. Law for galleries. Includes index. ISBN 1-58115-026-1
*1. Art galleries, Commercial - Law and legislation - United States. 2. Art dealers - Legal status, laws, etc. - United States. 3. Consignment sales - United States. I. Title. II. Title: Law for galleries*
*TC KF2042.A76 D836 1999*

**Dubowitz, Lilly M. S.** The neurological assessment of the preterm and full-term newborn infant / Lilly M.S. Dubowitz, Victor Dubowitz, Eugenio Merucuri. 2nd ed. London : Mac Keith, 1999. xii, 155 p. : ill. ; 25 cm. (Clinics in developmental medicine, 0069-4835 ; no.148) Previous ed.: London : Spastics International Medical, 1981. Includes bibliographical references. Five sheets of the Hammersmith neonatal neurological examination in plastic flap attached to inside back cover lining paper. ISBN 1-89868-315-8 DDC 618.92804754
*1. Pediatric neurology - Diagnosis. 2. Infants (Newborn) - Diseases - Diagnosis. 3. Infant, Premature. 4. Nervous System Diseases. 5. Neurologic Examination. I. Dubowitz, Victor. II. Mercuri, Eugenio. III. Title. IV. Series.*
*TC RJ486 .D85 1999*

**Dubowitz, Victor.**
Dubowitz, Lilly M. S. The neurological assessment of the preterm and full-term newborn infant. 2nd ed. London : Mac Keith, 1999.
*TC RJ486 .D85 1999*

**L'Éducation nationale.** Paris. v.in    . illus. 22-32 cm. Frequency: Frequency varies. Began publication in 1850. Cf. List of the serial publications of foreign governments. Title varies: Bulletin administratif du Ministère de l'instruction publique. 18 -June 1, 1932. Title varies: Bulletin administratif du Ministère de l'éducation nationale. June 15, 1932-Dec. 15, 1932. Title varies: Bulletin officiel du Ministère de l'éducation nationale. Oct. 1932-Apr. 25, 1946. Issues for Dec. 18, 1863- called nouv. sér. Publication suspended Jan. 1933-Sept. 1944. Includes special numbers. Beginning with 1946, the official part of the publication is issued as a supplement under title: Bulletin officiel de l'éducation nationale. Lois et règlements. "L'École publique," "Documents administratifs pour les enseignements supérieur, du second degré, technique" and other supplements accompany some years.
*1. Education - France - Periodicals.*

**Duck, Steve.**
Communication and personal relationships. New York : Wiley, 2000.
*TC HM1116 .C65 2000*

Mills, Rosemary S.L. The developmental psychology of personal relationships. Chichester : New York : John Wiley, c2000.
*TC BF723.I646 M55 2000*

**DUCKS.**
Goldin, Augusta R. Ducks don't get wet. Newly illustrated ed. New York : HarperCollinsPublishers, c1999.
*TC QL696.A52 G64 1999*

**Ducks don't get wet.**
Goldin, Augusta R. Newly illustrated ed. New York : HarperCollinsPublishers, c1999.
*TC QL696.A52 G64 1999*

**DUCKS - JUVENILE LITERATURE.**
Goldin, Augusta R. Ducks don't get wet. Newly illustrated ed. New York : HarperCollinsPublishers, c1999.
*TC QL696.A52 G64 1999*

**Duderstadt, James J., 1942-** Intercollegiate athletics and the American university : a university president's perspective / James J. Duderstadt. Ann Arbor [Mich.] : University of Michigan Press, c2000. xvi, 331 p. : ill. ; 24 cm. Includes bibliographical references (p. 319-325) and index. ISBN 0-472-11156-6 (cloth : alk. paper) DDC 796.04/3/0973
*1. College sports - Corrupt practices - United States. 2. College sports - United States - Management. 3. College sports - Social aspects - United States. 4. College sports - Moral and ethical aspects - United States. I. Title.*
*TC GV351 .D83 2000*

A university for the 21st century / James J. Duderstadt. Ann Arbor, MI : University of Michigan Press, c2000. xiv, 358 p. ; 25 cm. Includes bibliographical references (p. [335]-352) and index. ISBN 0-472-11091-8 (alk. paper) DDC 378.774/35
*1. University of Michigan - History. 2. Educational leadership - Michigan - Ann Arbor. 3. Educational change - Michigan - Ann Arbor. I. Title.*
*TC LD3280 .D83 2000*

**Due process and higher education.**
Stevens, Ed. Washington, DC : Graduate School of Education and Human Development, George Washington University, [1999]
*TC LB2344 .S73 1999*

**DUE PROCESS OF LAW.**
Stevens, Ed. Due process and higher education. Washington, DC : Graduate School of Education and Human Development, George Washington University, [1999]
*TC LB2344 .S73 1999*

**DUELING.** *See* **COMBAT.**

**Duet literature for female voices with piano, organ or unaccompanied.**
Newman, Marilyn Stephanie Mercedes, 1954- 1998.
*TC 06 no. 10897*

**Duff, Kevin, 1968-.**
Practitioner's guide to evaluating change with neuropsychological assessment instruments. New York : Kluwer Academic/Plenum Publishers, c2000.
*TC RC386.6.N48 P73 2000*

**Dufresne, Todd, 1966-** Tales from the Freudian crypt : the death drive in text and context / Todd Dufresne. Stanford, Calif. : Stanford University Press, 2000. xvi, 229 p. ; 24 cm. Includes bibliographical references (p. [187]-222) and index. ISBN 0-8047-3491-7 (hbk. : alk. paper) ISBN 0-8047-3885-8 (pbk. : alk. paper) DDC 150.19/52
*1. Death instinct. 2. Psychoanalysis. 3. Freud, Sigmund, - 1856-1939. I. Title.*
*TC BF175.5.D4 D84 2000*

**Dugan, JoAnn R.** Advancing the world of literacy : moving into the 21st century co-editors, JoAnn R. Dugan ... [et al.]. Carrollton, Ga. : College Reading Association, 1999. x, 281 p. : ill. ; 22 cm. Moving into the 21st century. "The twenty-first yearbook. A peer reviewed publication of the College Reading Association, 1999." Includes bibliographical references. CONTENTS: Outside of a dog, a book is man's best friend. Inside of a dog, it's too dark to read (with apologies to Groucho Marx) / Timothy V. Rasinski -- Are we trend spotters or tale spinners? A report from the field / Donna L. Alvermann -- How the SQ3R came to be / Walter Pauk -- A case study of a last-to-emerge-into-literacy first grade reader and the interplay of reader and contexts / Linda S. Wold -- Emergent readers and literature circle discussions / Brenda Greene Williams -- Preservice teachers constructing their meanings of literacy in a field-based program / Michael A. Martin, Sarah H. Martin, and Charles E. Martin -- Collaborative research, reflection and refinement : the evolution of literacy coursework in a professional development center / Mary Beth Sampson, Carole Walker, and Michelle Fazio -- The impact of school-university partnerships on

reading teacher educators : important conversations we must have / Donna L. Wiseman -- 'I just loved those projects!' Choice and voice in students' computer-based language arts activities : a case study / Sarah Nixon-Ponder -- Using literacy play centers to engage middle grade students in content area learning / Lynn Romeo & Susan A. Young -- 'No Somali! Only English!' A case study of an adult refugee's use of CONTENTS: appropriate materials when learning English and reading skills / Judy S. Richardson -- Teaching effective reserach strategies to elementary school students / Julie K. Kidd -- New directions for developmental reading programs : meeting diverse student needs / Jeanne L. Higbee -- Learning from experience : preservice teachers' perceptions of literature discussions / JoAnn Rubino Dugan -- Encouraging metacognitive awareness in preservice literacy courses / Jane Brady Matanzo and Deborah L. Harris -- Preservice teachers constructing personal understandings about culture / Janelle B. Mathis -- Traditional and response-based writing tasks in the literature classroom : a comparison of meaning-making / Evangeline Newton -- Movement and motif writing : relationships to language development / Heidi Allen, Timothy G. Morrison, Patrick Debenham, Pamela S. Musil, and Margery Baudin -- Improving preservice teachers' attitudes toward writing / Susan Davis Lenski and Sherrie Pardieck.
*1. Literacy. 2. Reading teachers. I. Title. II. Title: Moving into the 21st century. III. Series: Yearbook of the College Reading Association ; 21st.*
*TC LB2395 .C62 1999*

**Duguid, Paul, 1954-.**
Brown, John Seely. The social life of information. Boston : Harvard Business School Press, c2000.
*TC HM851 .B76 2000*

**Duhon, Gwendolyn M.**
The African-American male perspective of barriers to success. Lewiston, N.Y. : Edwin Mellen Press, c1999.
*TC LC2731 .A32 1999*

The developmental process of positive attitudes and mutual respect. Lewiston, N.Y. : E. Mellen Press, c1999.
*TC LB2822.82 .D49 1999*

Preparation, collaboration, and emphasis on the family in school counseling for the new millennium. Lewiston : E. Mellen Press, c2000.
*TC LB1027.5 .P6525 2000*

**Duhon-Ross, Alice.**
Reaching and teaching children who are victims of poverty. Lewiston, N.Y. : Lampeter, Wales : E. Mellen Press, c1999.
*TC LC4091 .R38 1999*

**Duhon-Sells, Rose M.**
The developmental process of positive attitudes and mutual respect. Lewiston, N.Y. : E. Mellen Press, c1999.
*TC LB2822.82 .D49 1999*

**Duke University. Medical Center. Educational Media Services.**
Depression in older adults [videorecording]. Boston, MA : Fanlight Productions ; [Chicago, Ill.] : Distributed by Terra Nova Films, Inc., 1997.
*TC RC537.5 .D4 1997*

**Duker, Jan, joint author.**
White, Mary Alice. Education; New York, Holt, Rinehart and Winston [1973]
*TC LB41 .W62*

**Dumas, Ernest, 1937-.**
Counts, I. Wilmer (Ira Wilmer), 1931- A life is more than a moment. Bloomington, IN : Indiana University Press, c1999.
*TC LC214.23.L56 C68 1999*

**Dumontet, S.**
Heidelberger Ernährungsforum (5th : 1998 : Heidelberg) Food quality, nutrition, and health. Berlin ; New York : Springer, 2000.
*TC RA784 .H42 2000*

**Duncan, Barry L.**
Murphy, John J. (John Joseph), 1955- Brief intervention for school problems. New York : Guilford Press, c1997.
*TC LC4802 .M87 1997*

**Duncan, Diane.** Becoming a primary school teacher : a study of mature women / Diane Duncan. Stoke on Trent, England : Trentham, 1999. x, 139 p. : 23 cm. Includes bibliographical references [p. 137-38] and index. ISBN 1-85856-104-3 DDC 372.11/00941
*1. Elementary school teachers - Training of - Great Britain. 2. Elementary school teaching - Vocational guidance - Great Britain. I. Title.*
*TC LB1776.4.G7 D86 1999*

**Duncan, Donna.** I-Search, you search, we all to learn to research : a how-to-do-it manual for teaching elementary school students to solve information problems / Donna Duncan, Laura Lockhart. New York : Neal-Schuman Publishers, 2000. xiv, 159 p. ; 28 cm. (How-to-do-it manuals for librarians ; no. 97) ISBN 1-55570-381-X (alk. paper) DDC 372.13/028/1
*1. Library orientation for school children - United States. 2. Report writing. I. Lockhart, Laura. II. Title. III. Series: How-to-do-it manuals for libraries ; no. 97.*
*TC Z711.2 .D86 2000*

**Duncan, John, Dr.**
Attention, space, and action. Oxford : New York : Oxford University Press, 1999.
*TC QP405 .A865 1999*

**Duncan, Neil, 1956-** Sexual bullying : gender conflict and pupil culture in secondary schools / Neil Duncan. London ; New York : Routledge, 1999. 179 p. ; 25 cm. Includes bibliographical references (p. [170]-176) and index. ISBN 0-415-19113-0 (alk. paper) DDC 371.5/8
*1. Sexual harassment in education - Great Britain - Case studies. 2. Bullying - Great Britain - Case studies. 3. Education, Secondary - Great Britain - Case studies. I. Title.*
*TC LC212.83.G7 D85 1999*

**Dunford, Helen.**
Phillips, Diane. Projects with young learners. Oxford ; New York : Oxford University Press, c1999.
*TC LB1576 .P577 1999*

**Dunford, J. E.**
State schools. London ; Portland, OR : Woburn Press, 1999.
*TC LC93.G7 S73 1999*

**Dunklee, Dennis R.** If you want to lead, not just manage : a primer for principals / by Dennis R. Dunklee. Thousand Oaks, Calif. : Corwin Press, c2000. xiii, 154 p. ; 23 cm. Includes bibliographical references and index. ISBN 0-7619-7646-9 (cloth : alk. paper) ISBN 0-7619-7647-7 (pbk. : alk. paper) DDC 371.2/012/0973
*1. School principals - United States - Handbooks, manuals, etc. 2. Educational leadership - United States - Handbooks, manuals, etc. 3. School management and organization - United States - Handbooks, manuals, etc. I. Title.*
*TC LB2831.92 .D85 2000*

You sound taller on the telephone : a practitioner's view of the principalship / Dennis R. Dunklee. Thousand Oaks, Calif. : Corwin Press, c1999. xvi, 264 p. ; 26 cm. Includes bibliographical references. ISBN 0-8039-6849-3 (cloth : acid-free paper) ISBN 0-8039-6850-7 (pbk. : acid-free paper) DDC 371.2/012
*1. School principals. 2. School management and organization. I. Title.*
*TC LB2831.9 .D85 1999*

**Dunlap, Barbara J.**
Roff, Sandra Shoiock. From the Free Academy to CUNY. New York : Fordham University Press, c2000.
*TC LD3835 .R64 2000*

**Dunlap, Katherine M.** Family empowerment : one outcome of parental participation in cooperative preschool education / Katherine M. Dunlap. New York ; London : Garland Pub., 2000. xii, 247 p. ; 23 cm. (Children of poverty) "A Garland series." Includes bibliographical references (p. 217-243) and index. ISBN 0-8153-3378-1 (alk. paper) DDC 372.21 DDC 372.21
*1. Education, Preschool - Parent participation - North Carolina - Charlotte - Case studies. 2. Socially handicapped children - Education - North Carolina - Charlotte - Case studies. I. Title. II. Series.*
*TC LB1140.35.P37 D86 2000*

**Dunn, Dana.** The practical researcher : a student guide to conducting psychological research / Dana S. Dunn. Boston : McGraw-Hill College, c1999. xiv, 390 p. : ill. ; 24 cm. Includes bibliographical references (p. 372-382) and index. ISBN 0-07-018323-6 (alk. paper) DDC 150/.7/2
*1. Psychology - Research - Methodology. 2. Psychology, Experimental. I. Title.*
*TC BF76.5 .D864 1999*

**Dunn, Rita Stafford, 1930-.**
Improved test scores, attitudes, and behaviors in America's schools. Westport, Conn. : Bergin & Garvey, 1999.
*TC LB2806.4 .I56 1999*

Practical approaches to using learning styles in higher education. Westport, Conn. : Bergin & Garvey, 2000.
*TC LB2395 .P69 2000*

**Dunn, Ross E.** World history : links across time and place / Ross E. Dunn. Evanston, Ill. : McDougal, Littell & Co. , c1988. xx, 828 p. : ill. (some col.), maps (some col.) ; 26 cm. Includes tables. ISBN 0-86609-633-7
*1. World history. I. Title.*

*TC D21 .D86 1988*

**Dunne, Elisabeth, 1952-.**
Bennett, Neville. Skills development in higher education and employment. Buckingham [England] ; Philadelphia : Society for Research into Higher Education & Open University Press, 2000.
*TC LB1027.47 .B46 2000*

**Dunne, Máiréad.**
Cooper, Barry, 1950- Assessing children's mathematical knowledge. Buckingham ; Philadelphia : Open University Press, 2000.
*TC QA135.5 .C5955 2000*

**Dunning, William V., 1933-** Changing images of pictorial space : a history of spatial illusion in painting / William V. Dunning. 1st ed. Syracuse : Syracuse University Press, 1991. xi, 254 p. : ill. ; 24 cm. Includes bibliographical references (p. 237-243) and index. ISBN 0-8156-2505-7 (cloth : alk. paper) ISBN 0-8156-2508-1 (pbk. : alk. paper) DDC 750/.1/8
*1. Composition (Art) 2. Space (Art) 3. Painting - Technique. 4. Visual perception. I. Title.*
*TC ND1475 .D86 1991*

**Dunphy, Madeleine.** Here is the African savanna / Madeleine Dunphy ; illustrated by Tom Leonard. 1st ed. New York : Hyperion Books for Children, c1999. 1 v. (unpaged) : ill. (some col.) ; 22 x 26 cm. SUMMARY: Cumulative text describes the interdependence among the plants and animals of an African savanna. ISBN 0-7868-0162-X (tr) ISBN 0-7868-2134-5 (lb) DDC 577.4/8/096
*1. Savanna ecology - Africa - Juvenile literature. 2. Savanna ecology - Africa. 3. Grasslands - Africa. 4. Ecology - Africa. I. Leonard, Thomas, 1955- ill. II. Title.*
*TC QH194 .D86 1999*

**Dunt, Lesley, 1944-** Speaking worlds : the Australian educators and John Dewey, 1890-1940 / Lesley Dunt. Parkville, Vic. : History Department, The University of Melbourne, c1993. viii, 141 p. ; 21 cm. (Melbourne University history monographs ; 17) Bibliography: p. 120-141. ISBN 0-7325-0342-6 DDC 370.994
*1. Dewey, John - 1859-1952. 2. Education - Australia - History. 3. Educators - Australia. 4. Educational sociology - Australia - History. I. University of Melbourne. Dept. of History. II. Title. III. Series.*
*TC LA2101 .D96 1993*

**DURATION OF COPYRIGHT.** *See* **COPYRIGHT - DURATION.**

**DURBAN (SOUTH AFRICA) - HISTORY.**
Freund, Bill. Insiders and outsiders. Portsmouth, NH : Heinemann, c1995.
*TC HD8801.Z8 D8725 1995*

**DURBAN (SOUTH AFRICA) - SOCIAL CONDITIONS.**
Freund, Bill. Insiders and outsiders. Portsmouth, NH : Heinemann, c1995.
*TC HD8801.Z8 D8725 1995*

**Durkin, Diane Bennett.**
Language issues. White Plains, N.Y. : Longman Publishers USA, c1995.
*TC P51 .L346 1995*

**Durocher, Elizabeth Antointette.** Leadership orientations of school administrators : a survey of nationally recognized school leaders / by Elizabeth Antoinette Durocher. 1995. xi, 145 p. : ill. ; 29 cm. Thesis (Ed.D.)--Teachers College, Columbia University, 1995. Includes bibliographical references (p. 124-134). Xerography. Ann Arbor, Mich. : University Microfilms International, 2000. 28 cm.
*1. School administrators - United States. 2. Educational leadership - United States. 3. Cognitive styles - United States. 4. Thought and thinking. I. Title. II. Title: Survey of nationally recognized school leaders*
*TC 06 no. 10583a*

**Duryea, E. D. (Edwin D.)** The academic corporation : a history of college and university governing boards / Edwin D. Duryea ; edited by Don Williams. New York : Falmer Press, 2000. xv, 274 p. ; 23 cm. (Garland reference library of social science ; 1416. Garland studies in higher education ; 23) Includes bibliographical references (p. 231-252) and index. ISBN 0-8153-3376-5 (alk. paper) DDC 378.73
*1. Universities and colleges - United States - Administration - History. 2. Universities and colleges - Europe - Administration - History. I. Williams, Donald T. II. Title. III. Title: History of college and university governing boards IV. Series: Garland reference library of social science ; v. 416. V. Series: Garland reference library of social science. Garland studies in higher education ; vol. 23.*
*TC LB2341 .D79 2000*

**Duska, Ronald F., 1937-.**
Education, leadership, and business ethics. Boston, MA : Kluwer Academic Publishers, c1998.
*TC HF5387 .E346 1998*

**DUTCH - SOUTH AFRICA.** *See* **AFRIKANERS.**

**Dutt, Ajanta, 1958-.**
Cutchin, Kay Lynch. Landscapes and language. Cambridge, UK : New York, NY, USA : Cambridge University Press, 1999.
*TC PE1128 .C88 1999*

**Dutton, Thomas E.**
Demetriou, Andrew J. Health care integration. Washington, D.C. : Bureau of National Affairs, Inc., c1996.
*TC KF3825 .D394 1996*

**Dutwin, Phyllis.**
Boulmetis, John. The ABCs of evaluation. 1st ed. San Francisco, Calif. : Jossey-Bass, c2000.
*TC HD31 .B633 2000*

**DuWors, George Manter, 1948-** White knuckles and wishful thinking : learning from the moment of relapse in alcoholism and other addictions / George Manter DuWors ; illustrations, Sylvane Despretz ; cover art, Don Wissusik. 2nd rev. & expanded ed. Seattle : Hogrefe & Huber Publishers, c2000. xviii, 393 p. : ill. Includes bibliographical references and index. ISBN 0-88937-224-1 DDC 616.86/106
*1. Alcoholism - Relapse - Prevention. 2. Alcoholics - Rehabilitation. I. Title.*
*TC RC565 .D79 2000*

**DWELLINGS.** *See* **ARCHITECTURE, DOMESTIC; HOUSING; TENTS.**

**DWELLINGS - CONSERVATION AND RESTORATION - UNITED STATES - HISTORY.**
West, Patricia, 1958- Domesticating history. Washington [D.C.] : Smithsonian Institution Press, c1999.
*TC E159 .W445 1999*

**DWELLINGS - SOCIAL ASPECTS.** *See* **HOUSING.**

**DWELLINGS - VIRGINIA.** *See* **MOUNT VERNON (VA. : ESTATE).**

**Dworkin, Robert H.**
Origins and development of schizophrenia. Washington, DC : American Psychological Association, c1998.
*TC RC514 .O75 1998*

**Dyches, Tina Taylor.**
Gibb, Gordon S. Guide to writing quality individualzed education programs :. Boston : Allyn and Bacon, c2000.
*TC LC4019 .G43 2000*

**Dyck, Noel.**
Games, sports and cultures. Oxford ; New York : Berg, 2000.
*TC GV706.5 .G36 2000*

**DYEING.** *See* **DYES AND DYEING.**

**Dyer, Karen M.** The intuitive principal : a guide to leadership / by Karen M. Dyer, Jacqueline Carothers. Thousand Oaks, Calif. : Corwin Press, c2000. xii, 58 p. ; 24 cm. Includes index. ISBN 0-7619-7531-4 (cloth : alk. paper) ISBN 0-7619-7532-2 (pbk. : alk. paper) DDC 371.2/012/0973
*1. School principals - United States. 2. Educational leadership - United States. 3. Intuition. I. Carothers, Jacqueline. II. Title.*
*TC LB2831.92 .D94 2000*

**DYES AND DYEING - PERIODICALS.**
Ciba review. Basle, Switzerland Ciba Limited.

**DYING.** *See* **DEATH.**

**Dying at home.**
Sankar, Andrea. Rev. and updated ed. Baltimore, Md.: Johns Hopkins University Press, 1999.
*TC R726.8 .S26 1999*

**Dying for growth :** global inequality and the health of the poor / edited by Jim Yong Kim ... [et al.]. Monroe, Me. : Common Courage Press, c2000. xix, 585 p. : ill., map ; 23 cm. (Series in health and social justice) Includes bibliographical references (p. 511-566) and index. ISBN 1-56751-161-9 (cloth) ISBN 1-56751-160-0 (pbk.) DDC 362.1/086/942
*1. Poor - Medical care - Case studies. 2. Poor - Health and hygiene - Case studies. 3. Poor - Medical care - Economic aspects - Developing countries - Case studies. 4. Poor - Developing countries - Health aspects - Case studies. I. Kim, Jim Yong. II. Series: Series in health and social justice*

*TC RA418.5.P6 D95 2000*

**DYING PERSONS.** *See* **TERMINALLY ILL.**

**Dying to live.**
Kendall, Marion D. Cambridge ; New York :
Cambridge University Press, c1998.
*TC QR181.7 .K46 1998*

**Dying to quit.**
Brigham, Janet. Washington, D.C. : Joseph Henry
Press, 1998.
*TC HV5740 .B75 1998*

**Dynamic memory revisited.**
Schank, Roger C., 1946- [2nd ed.]. Cambridge ; New
York : Cambridge University Press, 1999.
*TC BF371 .S365 1999*

**DYNAMIC METEOROLOGY.** *See*
**ATMOSPHERIC DIFFUSION.**

**DYNAMICS.** *See* **CHAOTIC BEHAVIOR IN
SYSTEMS; MATTER; PHYSICS.**

**Dynamics of character.**
Shapiro, David, 1926- New York : Basic Books,
c2000.
*TC RC455.5.T45 .S46 2000*

**The dynamics of conflict resolution.**
Mayer, Bernard S., 1946- 1st ed. San Francisco :
Jossey-Bass Publishers, c2000.
*TC BF637.I48 M39 2000*

**Dynamics of effective teaching** / William Wilen ... [et
al.]. 4th ed. New York ; Harlow, England : Longman,
c2000. xiv, 397 p. : ill., maps, forms ; 24 cm. Rev. ed. of:
Dynamics of effective teaching / Richard Kindsvatter, William
Wilen, Margaret Ishler. 3rd ed. c1996. Includes bibliographical
references and index. ISBN 0-8013-3067-X DDC 373.1102
*1. High school teaching - United States. 2. Classroom
management - United States. 3. Motivation in education -
United States. I. Wilen, William W. II. Kindsvatter, Richard.
Dynamics of effective teaching.*
*TC LB1737.U6 K56 2000*

**The dynamics of now** / edited by William Furlong,
Polly Gould and Paul Hetherington. London :
Wimbledon School of Art in association with Tate,
c2000. 213 p. ; 24 cm. (Issues in art and education ; 3rd v.)
"Papers submitted at conferences held at the Tate Gallery in
1995, 1996, 1997 and 1998, organised by the Wimbledon
School of Art in collaberation with the Tate Gallery." Includes
bibliographical references. ISBN 1-85437-270-X
*1. Art - Study and teaching - Great Britain - Congresses. 2. Art
in education - Great Britain - Congresses. I. Furlong, William,
1944- II. Gould, Polly III. Hetherington, Paul. IV. Tate
Gallery. V. Wimbledon School of Art. VI. Series: Issues in art
and education ; v. 3.*
*TC N185 .D96 2000*

**Dynamics of the high school algebra classroom.**
Chazan, Daniel. Beyond formulas in mathematics and
teaching. New York : Teachers College Press, c2000.
*TC QA159 .C48 2000*

**DYSARTHRIA - CHILD.**
Love, Russell J. Childhood motor speech disability.
2nd ed. Boston ; London : Allyn and Bacon, c2000.
*TC RJ496.S7 L68 2000*

**DYSFUNCTIONAL FAMILIES.** *See* **PROBLEM
FAMILIES.**

**Dyslexia.**
Miles, T. R. (Thomas Richard) 2nd ed. Philadelphia ;
Buckingham : Open University Press, 1999.
*TC RC394.W6 M55 1998*

Reid, Gavin, 1950- Chichester ; New York : J. Wiley,
c1998.
*TC LC4708 .R45 1998*

**DYSLEXIA.**
Converging methods for understanding reading and
dyslexia. Cambridge, Mass. ; London : MIT Press,
c1999.
*TC LB1050.5 .C662 1999*

Dyslexia. Dordrecht ; Boston, Mass : Kluwer
Academic, 1999.
*TC RC394 .D9525 1999*

Keates, Anita. Dyslexia and information and
communications technology. London : D. Fulton
Publishers, 2000.
*TC LC4708.5K43 2000*

Miles, T. R. (Thomas Richard) Dyslexia. 2nd ed.
Philadelphia ; Buckingham : Open University Press,
1999.
*TC RC394.W6 M55 1998*

Miles, T. R. (Thomas Richard) Dyslexia. 2nd ed.
Philadelphia ; Buckingham : Open University Press,
1999.
*TC RC394.W6 M55 1998*

Snowling, Margaret J. Dyslexia. 2nd ed. Malden,
MA : Blackwell Publishers, 2000.
*TC RJ496.A5 S65 2000*

Walton, Margaret. Teaching reading and spelling to
dyslexic children. London : D. Fulton, 1998.
*TC LC4708 .W35 1998*

**Dyslexia :** advances in theory and practice / edited by
Ingvar Lundberg, Finn Egil Tønnessen & Ingolv
Austad. Dordrecht ; Boston, Mass : Kluwer
Academic, 1999. viii, 291 p. : ill. ; 25 cm.
(Neuropsychology and cognition ; 16) ISBN 0-7923-5837-6
(hardcover : alk. paper) DDC 616.85/53
*1. Dyslexia. I. Lundberg, Ingvar. II. Tønnessen, Finn Egil. III.
Austad, Ingolv. IV. Series.*
*TC RC394 .D9525 1999*

**Dyslexia and information and communications
technology.**
Keates, Anita. London : D. Fulton Publishers, 2000.
*TC LC4708.5K43 2000*

**DYSLEXIA - CASE STUDIES.**
Case studies in the neuropsychology of reading. Hove,
East Sussex : Psychology Press, c2000.
*TC RC394.W6 .C37 2000*

**DYSLEXIA - PATIENTS.** *See* **DYSLEXICS.**

**DYSLEXIACS.** *See* **DYSLEXICS.**

**DYSLEXIC CHILDREN - ABILITY TESTING -
HANDBOOKS, MANUALS, ETC.**
Reid, Gavin, 1950- Dyslexia. Chichester ; New York :
J. Wiley, c1998.
*TC LC4708 .R45 1998*

**DYSLEXIC CHILDREN - EDUCATION.**
Keates, Anita. Dyslexia and information and
communications technology. London : D. Fulton
Publishers, 2000.
*TC LC4708.5K43 2000*

Walton, Margaret. Teaching reading and spelling to
dyslexic children. London : D. Fulton, 1998.
*TC LC4708 .W35 1998*

**DYSLEXIC CHILDREN - EDUCATION -
HANDBOOKS, MANUALS, ETC.**
Reid, Gavin, 1950- Dyslexia. Chichester ; New York :
J. Wiley, c1998.
*TC LC4708 .R45 1998*

**DYSLEXIC PERSONS.** *See* **DYSLEXICS.**

**DYSLEXICS.** *See* **DYSLEXIC CHILDREN.**

**DYSLEXICS - UNITED STATES - BIOGRAPHY.**
Bursak, George J., 1913- If I can do it, so can you.
[S.l.] : G.J. Bursak, c1999.
*TC RC394.W6 B87 1999*

**Dyson, Alan.**
Theorising special education. London ; New York :
Routledge, 1998.
*TC LC3986.G7 T54 1998*

**DYSPHAGIA.** *See* **DEGLUTITION DISORDERS.**

**DYSPHAGY.** *See* **DEGLUTITION DISORDERS.**

**DYSPHASIA.** *See* **LANGUAGE DISORDERS.**

**DYSPHONIA.** *See* **VOICE DISORDERS.**

**E & ITV <Jan. 1980>-Apr. 1981.**
Educational & industrial television. [Ridgefield,
Conn. : C.S. Tepfer Pub. Co.,    -c1983]

**E. and I.T.V.**
Educational & industrial television. [Ridgefield,
Conn. : C.S. Tepfer Pub. Co.,    -c1983]

**E-ITV.**
Educational & industrial television. [Ridgefield,
Conn. : C.S. Tepfer Pub. Co.,    -c1983]

**E-ITV Jan. 1981-May 1983.**
Educational & industrial television. [Ridgefield,
Conn. : C.S. Tepfer Pub. Co.,    -c1983]

**E-moderating.**
Salmon, Gilly. London : Kogan Page ; Sterling, VA :
Stylus, 2000.
*TC LB1044.87 .S25 2000*

**e-Sphere.**
Pelton, Joseph N. Westport, Conn. ; London : Quorum
Books, 2000.
*TC P96.I5 P33 2000*

**E-topia.**
Mitchell, William J. (William John), 1944-
Cambridge, Mass. : MIT Press, 1999.
*TC HE7631 .M58 1999*

**Each mind a kingdom.**
Satter, Beryl, 1959- Berkeley : University of
California Press, c1999.
*TC BF639 .S124 1999*

**Eagle Wing Productions.**
Get a grip [videorecording]. Racine, WI : S.C.
Johnson and Son, Inc., 1999, c1998.
*TC TD170 .G4 1999*

**Eakins and the photograph.**
Pennsylvania Academy of the Fine Arts. Washington :
Published for the Pennsylvania Academy of the Fine
Arts by the Smithsonian Institution Press, c1994.
*TC TR652 .P46 1994*

**EAKINS, THOMAS, 1844-1916 - CATALOGUES
RAISONNÉS.**
Pennsylvania Academy of the Fine Arts. Eakins and
the photograph. Washington : Published for the
Pennsylvania Academy of the Fine Arts by the
Smithsonian Institution Press, c1994.
*TC TR652 .P46 1994*

**Eames, Bill.**
Civil war [picture]. Amawalk, NY : Jackdaw
Publications, c1999.
*TC TR820.5 .C56 1999*

Civil war [picture]. Amawalk, NY : Jackdaw
Publications, c1999.
*TC TR820.5 .C56 1999*

Holocaust children [picture]. Amawalk, NY : Jackdaw
Publications, c1999.
*TC TR820.5 .H6 1999*

[Japanese-American internment picture. Amawalk,
NY : Jackdaw Publications, c1999.
*TC TR820.5 .J3 1999*

Mills [picture]. Amawalk, NY : Jackdaw Publications,
c1999.
*TC TR820.5 .M5 1999*

World War II [picture]. Amawalk, NY : Jackdaw
Publications, c1999.
*TC TR820.5 .W6 1999*

**EAR.** *See* **HEARING.**

**EAR - DISEASES.** *See* **DEAFNESS.**

**EAR - PATHOPHYSIOLOGY.**
Møller, Aage R. Hearing, its physiology and
pathophysiology. San Diego : Academic Press, c2000.
*TC QP461 .M65 2000*

**EAR - PHYSIOLOGY.**
Møller, Aage R. Hearing, its physiology and
pathophysiology. San Diego : Academic Press, c2000.
*TC QP461 .M65 2000*

**EARHART, AMELIA, 1897-1937 - FICTION.**
Ryan, Pam Muñoz. Amelia and Eleanor go for a ride.
New York : Scholastic Press, 1999.
*TC PZ7.R9553 Am 1999*

**EARHART, AMELIA, 1897-1937 - JUVENILE
FICTION.**
Ryan, Pam Muñoz. Amelia and Eleanor go for a ride.
New York : Scholastic Press, 1999.
*TC PZ7.R9553 Am 1999*

**Earlam, Carolyn.**
Brown, Sally A. 500 tips for teachers. 2nd ed.
London : Kogan Page ; Sterling, VA : Stylus Pub.,
1998.
*TC LB3013 .B76 1998*

**Earle, Jonathan.** The Routledge atlas of African
American history / Jonathan Earle. New York :
Routledge, 2000. 144 p. : col. ill. ; 25 cm. (Routledge atlases
of American history) Includes bibliographical references and
index. ISBN 0-415-92136-8 (acid-free paper) ISBN
0-415-92142-2 (pbk. : acid-free paper) DDC 973/.0496073
*1. Afro-Americans - History. 2. Afro-Americans - History -
Maps. I. Title. II. Title: Atlas of African American history III.
Series.*
*TC E185 .E125 2000*

**Earley, Peter.**
Creese, Michael. Improving schools and governing
bodies. London ; New York : Routledge, 1999.
*TC LB2822.84.G7 C75 1999*

**Early 3 Rs.**
Mountain, Lee Harrison. Mahwah, N.J. ; London : L.
Erlbaum Associates, 2000.
*TC LB1139.23 .M68 2000*

**Early childhood care and education in Canada.**
Vancouver : UBC Press, c2000. x, 323 p. ; 24 cm. ISBN
0-7748-0771-7 DDC 372.2
*1. Early childhood education - Canada. I. Prochner, Lawrence*
**TC LB1139.3.C2 E27 2000**

**Early childhood development.**
Trawick-Smith, Jeffrey W. 2nd ed. Upper Saddle
River, N.J. : Merrill, c2000.
**TC LB1115 .T73 2000**

**EARLY CHILDHOOD EDUCATION.** *See also*
EDUCATION, PRESCHOOL; EDUCATION,
PRIMARY; KINDERGARTEN.
Kim, Jinyoung. Effects of word type, context, and
vocal assistance on children's pitch-matching abilities.
1998.
**TC 06 no. 10954**

Mountain, Lee Harrison. Early 3 Rs. Mahwah, N.J. :
London : L. Erlbaum Associates, 2000.
**TC LB1139.23 .M68 2000**

Stewig, John W. Language arts in the early childhood
classroom. Belmont [Calif.] : Wadsworth Pub. Co.,
c1995.
**TC LB1140.5.L3 S72 1995**

Trawick-Smith, Jeffrey W. Early childhood
development. 2nd ed. Upper Saddle River, N.J. :
Merrill, c2000.
**TC LB1115 .T73 2000**

**EARLY CHILDHOOD EDUCATION - ACTIVITY
PROGRAMS.**
Brown, Victoria (Victoria L.) The dramatic difference.
Portsmouth, NH : Heinemann, c1999.
**TC PN3171 .B76 1999**

Entz, Susan. Picture this. Thousand Oaks, Calif. :
Corwin Press, c2000.
**TC LB1043.67 .E58 2000**

**EARLY CHILDHOOD EDUCATION - ACTIVITY
PROGRAMS - UNITED STATES -
HANDBOOKS, MANUALS, ETC.**
Jackman, Hilda L. Sing me a story! Tell me a song!.
Thousand Oaks, Calif. : Corwin Press, c1999.
**TC LB1139.35.A37 J33 1999**

**EARLY CHILDHOOD EDUCATION - CANADA.**
Early childhood care and education in Canada.
Vancouver : UBC Press, c2000.
**TC LB1139.3.C2 E27 2000**

**EARLY CHILDHOOD EDUCATION -
COMPUTER-ASSISTED INSTRUCTION.**
Campbell, Hope. Managing technology in the early
childhood classroom. Westminster, CA : Teacher
Created Materials, c1999.
**TC LB1139.35.C64 C36 1999**

**EARLY CHILDHOOD EDUCATION - CROSS-
CULTURAL STUDIES.**
Effective early education. New York : Falmer Press,
1999.
**TC LB1139.23 .E44 1999**

Families speak. Ypsilanti, Mich. : High/Scope Press,
c1994.
**TC LB1139.23 .F36 1994**

How nations serve young children. Ypsilanti, Mich. :
High/Scope Press, c1989.
**TC HQ778.5 .H69 1989**

Landscapes in early childhood education. New York :
P. Lang, 2000.
**TC LB1139.23 .L26 2000**

**EARLY CHILDHOOD EDUCATION - EUROPE.**
Early childhood services. Buckingham [England] ;
Philadelphia, PA : Open University Press, 2000.
**TC LB1139.3.E85 E35 2000**

**EARLY CHILDHOOD EDUCATION -
EVALUATION.**
Puckett, Margaret B. Authentic assessment of the
young child. 2nd ed. Upper Saddle River, N.J. :
Merrill, c2000.
**TC LB3051 .P69 2000**

**Early childhood education for a multicultural society.**
Chud, Gyda. [Vancouver] : Western Education
Development Group, Faculty of Education, The
University of British Columbia, c1985.
**TC LC1099 .C494 1985**

**EARLY CHILDHOOD EDUCATION - GREAT
BRITAIN.**
Anning, Angela, 1944- Promoting children's learning
from birth to five. Buckingham [England] ;
Philadelphia : Open University Press, 1999.
**TC LB1139.3.G7 A55 1999**

Early childhood services. Buckingham [England] ;
Philadelphia, PA : Open University Press, 2000.
**TC LB1139.3.E85 E35 2000**

Siraj-Blatchford, Iram. Supporting identity, diversity
and language in the early years. Buckingham
[England] ; Philadelphia : Open University Press,
2000.
**TC LB1139.3.G7 S57 2000**

**EARLY CHILDHOOD EDUCATION - GREAT
BRITAIN - CURRICULA.**
Anning, Angela, 1944- Promoting children's learning
from birth to five. Buckingham [England] ;
Philadelphia : Open University Press, 1999.
**TC LB1139.3.G7 A55 1999**

**EARLY CHILDHOOD EDUCATION - ILLINOIS -
CHICAGO.**
Reynolds, Arthur J. Success in early intervention.
Lincoln, Neb. : University of Nebraska Press, c2000.
**TC HV743.C5 R48 2000**

**EARLY CHILDHOOD EDUCATION - NEW
YORK (STATE) - NEW YORK -
CURRICULA - CASE STUDIES.**
Ryan, Sharon Kaye. Freedom to choice. 1998.
**TC 06 no. 11034**

**EARLY CHILDHOOD EDUCATION - NEW
YORK (STATE) - NEW YORK -
PHILOSOPHY - CASE STUDIES.**
Ryan, Sharon Kaye. Freedom to choice. 1998.
**TC 06 no. 11034**

**EARLY CHILDHOOD EDUCATION - PARENT
PARTICIPATION.**
Bright beginnings [videorecording. Burbank, CA :
RCA/Columbia Pictures Home Video ; Toluca Lake,
CA : [Distributed by] Corporate Productions, c1991.
**TC HV1642 .B67 1991**

Bright beginnings [videorecording. Burbank, CA :
RCA/Columbia Pictures Home Video ; [S.l. :
Distributed by] Rank Video Services America, c1991.
**TC HV1642 .B67 1991**

**EARLY CHILDHOOD EDUCATION - PARENT
PARTICIPATION - CASE STUDIES.**
Lava, Valerie Forkin. Early intervention. 1998.
**TC 06 no. 11140**

**EARLY CHILDHOOD EDUCATION - PARENT
PARTICIPATION - HANDBOOKS,
MANUALS, ETC.**
Ramey, Sharon L. Going to school. New York :
Goddard Press ; Lanham, MD : Distributed to the
trade by National Book Network, c1999.
**TC LB1139.35.P37 R26 1999**

**EARLY CHILDHOOD EDUCATION - PARENT
PARTICIPATION - ILLINOIS - CHICAGO.**
Reynolds, Arthur J. Success in early intervention.
Lincoln, Neb. : University of Nebraska Press, c2000.
**TC HV743.C5 R48 2000**

**EARLY CHILDHOOD EDUCATION - PARENT
PARTICIPATION - UNITED STATES -
HANDBOOKS, MANUALS, ETC.**
Bennett, William J. (William John), 1943- The
educated child. New York : Free Press, c1999.
**TC LB1048.5 .B45 1999**

**Early childhood education series**
Rodd, Jillian. Leadership in early childhood. 2nd
edition. New York : Teachers College Press, 1998.
**TC LB1776.4.A8 R63 1998**

**Early childhood education series (Teachers College
Press)**
Managing quality in young children's programs. New
York : Teachers College Press, c2000.
**TC LB2822.6 .M36 2000**

Wilson, Catherine S. Telling a different story. New
York ; London : Teachers College Press, c2000.
**TC LC5131 .W49 2000**

**EARLY CHILDHOOD EDUCATION - SOCIAL
ASPECTS.**
Johnson, Richard T., 1956- Hands off!. New York ;
Canterbury [England] : P. Lang, c2000.
**TC LB1033 .J63 2000**

**EARLY CHILDHOOD EDUCATION - UNITED
STATES.**
Click, Phyllis. Administration of schools for young
children. 5th ed. Albany, NY : Delmar, 1999.
**TC LB2822.7 .C55 1999**

Developmentally appropriate practice in early
childhood programs. Rev. ed. Washington, D.C. :
National Association for the Education of Young
Children, 1997.

**TC LB1139.25 .D48 1997**

Diversity [videorecording]. Barrington, IL : Magna
Systems, Inc., 1996.
**TC LB1139.25 .D5 1996**

Morrison, George S. Fundamentals of early childhood
education. 2nd ed. Upper Saddle River, N.J. : Merrill,
c2000.
**TC LB1139.25 .M67 2000**

**EARLY CHILDHOOD EDUCATION - UNITED
STATES - ADMINISTRATION.**
Managing quality in young children's programs. New
York : Teachers College Press, c2000.
**TC LB2822.6 .M36 2000**

Shoemaker, Cynthia. Leadership and management of
programs for young children. 2nd ed. Upper Saddle
River, N.J. : Merrill, 2000.
**TC LB2822.6 .S567 2000**

**EARLY CHILDHOOD EDUCATION - UNITED
STATES - CONGRESSES.**
The transition to kindergarten. Baltimore : P.H.
Brookes Pub., c1999.
**TC LB1205 .T72 1999**

**EARLY CHILDHOOD EDUCATION - UNITED
STATES - CURRICULA.**
Mardell, Ben. From basketball to the Beatles.
Portsmouth, NH : Heinemann, 1999.
**TC LB1139.4 .M27 1999**

Reaching potentials. Washington, DC : National
Association for the Education of Young Children,
c1992-<1995>
**TC LB1140.23 .R36 1992**

Sawyer, Walter. Growing up with literature. 3rd ed.
Albany, N.Y. : Delmar, c2000.
**TC LB1140.5.L3 S28 2000**

**EARLY CHILDHOOD EDUCATORS.** *See* **EARLY
CHILDHOOD TEACHERS.**

**EARLY CHILDHOOD EDUCATORS - TRAINING
OF - AUSTRALIA.**
Rodd, Jillian. Leadership in early childhood. 2nd
edition. New York : Teachers College Press, 1998.
**TC LB1776.4.A8 R63 1998**

**Early childhood experiences in language arts.**
Machado, Jeanne M. 6th ed. Albany, N.Y. : Delmar
Publishers, c1999.
**TC LB1139.5.L35 M335 1999**

**Early childhood language arts.**
Jalongo, Mary Renck. 2nd ed. Boston ; London :
Allyn and Bacon, c2000.
**TC LB1140.5.L3 J35 2000**

**Early childhood services :** theory, policy, and practice /
edited by Helen Penn. Buckingham [England] ;
Philadelphia, PA : Open University Press, 2000. vi,
201 p. : ill. ; 23 cm. Includes bibliographical references and
index. ISBN 0-335-20329-9 (pb) ISBN 0-335-20330-2 (hb)
DDC 371.21/094
*1. Early childhood education - Europe. 2. Early childhood
education - Great Britain. 3. Child care services - Europe. 4.
Child care services - Great Britain. I. Penn, Helen.*
**TC LB1139.3.E85 E35 2000**

**EARLY CHILDHOOD TEACHERS.**
Revisiting a progressive pedagogy. Albany : State
University of New York Press, c2000.
**TC LB1117 .R44 2000**

**EARLY CHILDHOOD TEACHERS - TRAINING
OF.**
Revisiting a progressive pedagogy. Albany : State
University of New York Press, c2000.
**TC LB1117 .R44 2000**

**EARLY CHILDHOOD TEACHERS - TRAINING
OF - GREAT BRITAIN.**
Anning, Angela, 1944- Promoting children's learning
from birth to five. Buckingham [England] ;
Philadelphia : Open University Press, 1999.
**TC LB1139.3.G7 A55 1999**

**Early childhood training**
Diversity [videorecording]. Barrington, IL : Magna
Systems, Inc., 1996.
**TC LB1139.25 .D5 1996**

**Early education.**
The Grade teacher. Boston, Mass. : Educational Pub.
Co., -c1972.

The Grade teacher. Boston, Mass. : Educational Pub.
Co., -c1972.

**Early experience and the life path.**
Clarke, Ann M. (Ann Margaret) London ;
Philadelphia : Jessica Kingsley, 2000.

TC BF721 .C5457 2000

**Early experiences implementing a managed care approach.**
United States. General Accounting Office. Child welfare. Washington, D.C. (P.O. Box 37050, Washington, D.C. 20013) : The Office, [1998]
*TC HV741 .U525 1998a*

**Early French feminisms, 1830-1940.**
Gordon, Felicia. Cheltenham, U.K. ; Brookfield, Vt. : Edward Elgar, c1996.
*TC HQ1615.A3 G67 1996*

**EARLY INFANTILE AUTISM.** *See* **AUTISM IN CHILDREN.**

**Early intervention.**
Lava, Valerie Forkin. 1998.
*TC 06 no. 11140*

**EARLY INTERVENTION (EDUCATION).**
Gerber, Sanford E. Etiology and prevention of communicative disorders. 2nd ed. San Diego : Singular Pub. Group, c1998.
*TC RJ496.C67 G47 1998*

Handbook of infant mental health. New York : Wiley, c2000.
*TC RJ502.5 .H362 2000*

**EARLY INTERVENTION (EDUCATION) - UNITED STATES.**
Clinical management of communication disorders in culturally diverse children. Boston : Allyn & Bacon, c2000.
*TC RJ496.C67 C556 2000*

**Early literacy.**
Casey, Jean Marie. Rev. ed. Englewood, Colo. : Libraries Unlimited, 2000.
*TC LB1139.5.L35 C37 2000*

**EARLY MAN.** *See* **PREHISTORIC PEOPLES.**

**Early, Margaret.**
American education. Chicago, Ill. : NSSE : Distributed by the University of Chicago Press, 2000.
*TC LB5 .N25 99th pt. 2*

Constructivism in education. Chicago, Ill. : NSSE : Distributed by the University of Chicago Press, 2000.
*TC LB5 .N25 99th pt. 1*

**EARLY MEMORIES.**
Howe, Mark L. The fate of early memories. Washington, DC : American Psychological Association, c2000.
*TC BF378.E17 H69 2000*

**EARLY SCHOOL LEAVERS.** *See* **DROPOUTS.**

**Early spelling.**
Kress, Gunther R. London ; New York : Routledge, 2000.
*TC P240.2 .K74 2000*

**Early textile workers [picture].**
Mills [picture]. Amawalk, NY : Jackdaw Publications, c1999.
*TC TR820.5 .M5 1999*

**Early three Rs.**
Mountain, Lee Harrison. Early 3 Rs. Mahwah, N.J. ; London : L. Erlbaum Associates, 2000.
*TC LB1139.23 .M68 2000*

**Early years (London, England).**
Rodger, Rosemary, 1946- Planning an appropriate curriculum for the under fives. London : David Fulton, 1999.
*TC LB1140.25.G7 R64 1999*

**EARTH.** *See also* **WATER.**
The blue planet [videorecording]. [New York, N.Y.?] : Unapix Entertainment, Inc. [distributor], c1996.
*TC QB631.2 .B5 1996*

The climate puzzle [videorecording]. [New York, N.Y.?] : Unapix Entertainment, Inc. [distributor], c1996.
*TC QB631.2 .C5 1996*

Fate of the earth [videorecording]. [New York, N.Y.?] : Unapix Entertainment, Inc. [distributor], c1996.
*TC QB631.2 .F3 1996*

Gifts from the earth [videorecording]. [New York, N.Y.?] : Unapix Entertainment, Inc. [distributor], c1996.
*TC QB631.2 .G5 1996*

The solar sea [videorecording]. [New York, N.Y.?] : Unapix Entertainment, Inc. [distributor], c1996.

TC QB631.2 .S6 1996

Tales from other worlds [videorecording]. [New York, N.Y.?] : Unapix Entertainment, Inc. [distributor], c1996.
*TC QB631.2 .T3 1996*

Tales from other worlds [videorecording]. [New York, N.Y.?] : Unapix Entertainment, Inc. [distributor], c1996.
*TC QB631.2 .T3 1996*

**Earth, air, fire & water : poems** / selected by Frances McCullough. Rev. ed. New York, N.Y. : Harper & Row, c1989. xvi, 140 p. ; 24 cm. "A Charlotte Zolotow book." Includes indexes. SUMMARY: This collection of poetry represents the work of eighty-one contemporary poets including Robert Creeley, Richard Brautigan, Charles Simic, LeRoi Jones, Bob Dylan, Allen Ginsberg, and Sylvia Plath. ISBN 0-06-024207-8 ISBN 0-06-024208-6 (lib. bdg.) DDC 808.81/935
*1. Poetry - Collections. 2. Poetry - Collections. I. McCullough, Frances Monson, 1939- II. Title: Earth, air, fire, and water.*
*TC PN6101 .E37 1989*

**Earth, air, fire, and water.**
Earth, air, fire & water. Rev. ed. New York, N.Y. : Harper & Row, c1989.
*TC PN6101 .E37 1989*

**EARTH - EFFECT OF HUMAN BEINGS ON.** *See* **NATURE - EFFECT OF HUMAN BEINGS ON.**

**EARTH - FICTION.**
Reiser, Lynn. Earthdance. New York : Greenwillow Books, 1999.
*TC PZ7.R27745 Ear 1999*

**EARTH - GLOBES.** *See* **GLOBES.**

**EARTH - JUVENILE POETRY.**
Livingston, Myra Cohn. Earth songs. 1st ed. New York : Holiday House, c1986.
*TC PS3562.I945 E3 1986*

**EARTH NUTS.** *See* **PEANUTS.**

**EARTH - POETRY.**
Livingston, Myra Cohn. Earth songs. 1st ed. New York : Holiday House, c1986.
*TC PS3562.I945 E3 1986*

**EARTH - SATELLITE.** *See* **MOON.**

**EARTH SCIENCES.** *See also* **GEOGRAPHY; GEOLOGY.**
The blue planet [videorecording]. [New York, N.Y.?] : Unapix Entertainment, Inc. [distributor], c1996.
*TC QB631.2 .B5 1996*

Brandwein, Paul F. (Paul Franz), 1912- Matter. Curie ed. New York : Harcourt Brace Jovanovich, 1980.
*TC Q161.2 .C66 1980*

Marshall, Robert H. AGS earth science. Circle Pines, Minn. : AGS, American Guidance Service, c1997.
*TC QE28 .M37 1997*

Marshall, Robert H. AGS earth science. Teacher's ed. Circle Pines, Minn. : AGS, American Guidance Service, c1997.
*TC QE28 .M37 1997 Teacher's Ed.*

Fate of the earth [videorecording]. [New York, N.Y.?] : Unapix Entertainment, Inc. [distributor], c1996.
*TC QB631.2 .F3 1996*

Ramsey, William L. Modern earth science. Austin, Tex. : Holt, Rinehart and Winston, Inc., c1989.
*TC QE28 .R35 1989*

Tales from other worlds [videorecording]. [New York, N.Y.?] : Unapix Entertainment, Inc. [distributor], c1996.
*TC QB631.2 .T3 1996*

Tales from other worlds [videorecording]. [New York, N.Y.?] : Unapix Entertainment, Inc. [distributor], c1996.
*TC QB631.2 .T3 1996*

**EARTH SCIENCES - STUDY AND TEACHING (ELEMENTARY).**
Marshall, Robert H. AGS earth science. Teacher's ed. Circle Pines, Minn. : AGS, American Guidance Service, c1997.
*TC QE28 .M37 1997 Teacher's Ed.*

**EARTH SCIENCES - STUDY AND TEACHING (SECONDARY).**
Ramsey, William L. Modern earth science. Austin, Tex. : Holt, Rinehart and Winston, Inc., c1989.
*TC QE28 .R35 1989 Teacher's Resource Book*

**Earth songs.**
Livingston, Myra Cohn. 1st ed. New York : Holiday House, c1986.
*TC PS3562.I945 E3 1986*

**Earthdance.**
Reiser, Lynn. New York : Greenwillow Books, 1999.
*TC PZ7.R27745 Ear 1999*

**EARTHENWARE.** *See* **POTTERY.**

**EARTHQUAKES.**
The living machine [videorecording]. [New York, N.Y.?] : Unapix Entertainment, Inc. [distributor], c1996.
*TC QB631.2 .L5 1996*

**EAST AND WEST.** *See* **INTERCULTURAL COMMUNICATION.**

**EAST ASIA - CIVILIZATION - PERIODICALS.**
The East Asian library journal. Princeton, N.J. : Gest Library of Princeton University, c1994-
*TC Z733.G47 G46*

**EAST ASIA - LIBRARY RESOURCES - PERIODICALS.**
The East Asian library journal. Princeton, N.J. : Gest Library of Princeton University, c1994-
*TC Z733.G47 G46*

**East Asia (New York, N.Y.)**
Lee, Yoonmi. Modern education, textbooks and the image of the nation. New York ; London : Garland Pub., 2000.
*TC LB3048.K6 L44 2000*

**The East Asian library journal.** Princeton, N.J. : Gest Library of Princeton University, c1994- v. : ill. ; 26 cm. Frequency: Semiannual. Vol. 7, no. 1 (spring 1994)- . Not published 1995-1997. Issued by: the Friends of the Gest Library. Issue for spring 1998 includes: Repair and binding of old Chinese books, an English translation by David Halliwell of: Chung-kuo ku chi chuang ting hsiu pu chi shu, by Chen-t'ang Hsiao and Yü Ting. Continues: Gest Library journal ISSN: 0891-0553 (DLC)  89648007 (OCoLC)14554217. ISSN 1079-8021 DDC 027
*1. Gest Oriental Library and East Asian Collections - Periodicals. 2. East Asia - Civilization - Periodicals. 3. East Asia - Library resources - Periodicals. 4. Printing - History - Periodicals. I. Hsiao, Chen-t'ang. Chung-kuo ku chi chuang ting hsiu pu chi shu. English. II. Friends of the Gest Library. III. Title: Repair and binding of old Chinese books. IV. Title: Gest Library journal*
*TC Z733.G47 G46*

**EAST (FAR EAST).** *See* **EAST ASIA.**

**EAST HARLEM (NEW YORK, N.Y.).**
Smith, Hawthorne Emery. Psychological detachment from school. 1999.
*TC 085 Sm586*

**EAST INDIAN AMERICAN TEENAGERS - NEW YORK (STATE) - NEW YORK - CULTURAL ASSIMILATION.**
Asher, Nina. Margins, center, and the spaces in-between. 1999.
*TC 06 no. 11080*

**EAST INDIAN AMERICAN TEENAGERS - NEW YORK (STATE) - NEW YORK - FAMILY RELATIONSHIPS.**
Asher, Nina. Margins, center, and the spaces in-between. 1999.
*TC 06 no. 11080*

**EAST INDIAN AMERICAN TEENAGERS - NEW YORK (STATE) - NEW YORK - INTERVIEWS.**
Asher, Nina. Margins, center, and the spaces in-between. 1999.
*TC 06 no. 11080*

**EAST INDIAN AMERICANS - EDUCATION (SECONDARY) - ATTITUDES.**
Asher, Nina. Margins, center, and the spaces in-between. 1999.
*TC 06 no. 11080*

**EAST INDIAN AMERICANS - NEW YORK (STATE) - NEW YORK - ETHNIC IDENTITY.**
Asher, Nina. Margins, center, and the spaces in-between. 1999.
*TC 06 no. 11080*

**EAST INDIAN AMERICANS - UNITED STATES.** *See* **EAST INDIAN AMERICANS.**

**EAST INDIANS - EMPLOYMENT - SOUTH AFRICA - DURBAN - HISTORY.**
Freund, Bill. Insiders and outsiders. Portsmouth, NH : Heinemann, c1995.
*TC HD8801.Z8 D8725 1995*

**EAST INDIANS - UNITED STATES.** *See* **EAST INDIAN AMERICANS.**

**EAST (MIDDLE EAST).** *See* **MIDDLE EAST.**

**Easterlin, Richard A., 1926-.**
Conference on Population and Economic Change in Less Developed Countries (1976 : Philadelphia, Pa.) Population and economic change in developing countries. Chicago : University of Chicago Press, 1980.
*TC HB849 .C59 1976*

**Eastern African studies (London, England)**
Decolonization & independence in Kenya, 1940-93. London : J. Currey ; Athens : Ohio University Press, 1995.
*TC DT433.58 .D4 1995*

**EASTERN HEMISPHERE.** *See* **AFRICA; ASIA; EUROPE.**

**EASTERN HORSEMANSHIP.** *See* **HORSEMANSHIP.**

**Eastern Illinois University.**
Grounded for life [videorecording]. Charleston, WV : Cambridge Research Group, Ltd., 1988.
*TC HQ759.4 .G7 1988*

**EASTERN MEDITERRANEAN.** *See* **MIDDLE EAST.**

**Eastern promise :** education and social renewal in London's Docklands / edited by Tim Butler. London : Lawrence and Wishart, 2000. 254 p. : ill., maps ; 22 cm. Education and social renewal in London's Docklands. Includes bibliographical references. ISBN 0-85315-898-3 DDC 378.10309421
*1. University of East London. 2. Urban renewal - England - London. I. Butler, Tim, 1949- II. Title: Education and social renewal in London's Docklands*
*TC LC238.4.G73 L66 2000*

**EASTERN QUESTION.** *See* **WORLD POLITICS.**

**EASTERN RIDING.** *See* **HORSEMANSHIP.**

**Eastland, Lynette S.**
Communication in recovery. Cresskill, N.J. : Hampton Press, c1999.
*TC HV4998 .C64 1999*

**Eastman Johnson.**
Carbone, Teresa A. New York : Brooklyn Museum of Art in association with Rizzoli International Publications, 1999.
*TC ND237.J7 A4 1999*

**Eastment, David.**
The Internet. Oxford ; New York : Oxford University Press, c2000.
*TC TK5105.875.I57 I57 2000*

**Easy reading selections in English.**
Dixson, Robert James. Rev. ed. [New York] Regents Pub. Co. [c1971]
*TC PE1128.A2 D5 1971*

**EATING.** *See* **DINNERS AND DINING; FOOD HABITS.**

**EATING DISORDERS.** *See also* **BULIMIA.**
Tobin, David L. Coping strategies therapy for bulimia nervosa. Washington, DC : American Psychological Association, c2000.
*TC RC552.B84 T63 2000*

**EATING DISORDERS - DIAGNOSIS.**
Goldfein, Juli Ann. The importance of shape and weight in normal-weight women with bulimia nervosa, restrained eaters (dieters), and normal controls (Non-dieters). 1997.
*TC 085 G5675*

**EATING DISORDERS IN ADOLESCENCE - PREVENTION - HANDBOOKS, MANUALS, ETC.**
Preventing eating disorders. Philadelphia, PA : Brunner/Mazel, c1999.
*TC RC552.E18 P744 1999*

**EATING DISORDERS IN CHILDREN - PREVENTION - HANDBOOKS, MANUALS, ETC.**
Preventing eating disorders. Philadelphia, PA : Brunner/Mazel, c1999.
*TC RC552.E18 P744 1999*

**EATING DISORDERS - PATIENTS - RELIGIOUS LIFE.**
Lelwica, Michelle Mary. Starving for salvation. New York : Oxford University Press, 1999.
*TC RC552.E18 L44 1999*

**EATING DISORDERS - PREVENTION.**
The management of eating disorders and obesity. Totowa, N.J. : Humana Press, c1999.
*TC RC552.E18 M364 1999*

The prevention of eating disorders. New York : New York University Press, 1998.
*TC RC552.E18 P74 1998*

Working with groups to explore food & body connections. Duluth, Minn. : Whole Person Associates, c1996.
*TC RC552.E18 W67 1996*

**EATING DISORDERS - PREVENTION - HANDBOOKS, MANUALS, ETC.**
Preventing eating disorders. Philadelphia, PA : Brunner/Mazel, c1999.
*TC RC552.E18 P744 1999*

**EATING DISORDERS - PREVENTION - LONGITUDINAL STUDIES.**
Wittenberg, Lauren G. Peer education in eating disorder prevention. 1999.
*TC RC552.E18 W56 1999*

**EATING DISORDERS - THERAPY.**
The management of eating disorders and obesity. Totowa, N.J. : Humana Press, c1999.
*TC RC552.E18 M364 1999*

**EATING DISORDERS - TREATMENT.**
Practice guideline for the treatment of patients with eating disorders. 2nd ed. Washington, D.C. : American Psychiatric Association, c2000.
*TC RC552.E18 P73 2000*

Wittenberg, Lauren G. Peer education in eating disorder prevention. 1999.
*TC RC552.E18 W56 1999*

**EATING DISORDERS - UNITED STATES.**
Berg, Francie M. Women afraid to eat. Hettinger, ND : Healthy Weight Network, c2000.
*TC RC552.O25 B47 2000*

**EATING DISTURBANCES.** *See* **EATING DISORDERS.**

**EATING DYSFUNCTIONS.** *See* **EATING DISORDERS.**

**EATING, PATHOLOGICAL.** *See* **EATING DISORDERS.**

**Eaton, Deborah.**
Daniel, Claire, 1936- The great big book of fun phonics activities. New York : Scholastic professional books, c1999.
*TC LB1525.3 .D36 1999*

**Eberwein, Robert T., 1940-** Sex ed : film, video, and the framework of desire / Robert Eberwein. New Brunswick, N.J. : Rutgers University Press, 1999. xii, 267 p. : ill. ; 24 cm. Filmography: p. 235-241. Includes bibliographical references and index. ISBN 0-8135-2636-1 (cloth : alk. paper) ISBN 0-8135-2637-X (pbk. : alk. paper) DDC 613.9/071/0973
*1. Sex instruction - United States - History. 2. Hygiene, Sexual - Study and teaching - United States - History. 3. Motion pictures in sex instruction - United States - History. 4. Video tapes in sex instruction - United States - History. I. Title.*
*TC HQ56 .E19 1999*

**EBONICS.** *See* **BLACK ENGLISH.**

**ECCLESIASTICAL BIOGRAPHY.** *See* **CHRISTIAN BIOGRAPHY.**

**ECCLESIASTICAL HISTORY.** *See* **CHURCH HISTORY.**

**ECCLESIASTICAL LAW - GERMANY - BAVARIA - PERIODICALS.**
Bavaria (Germany). Staatsministerium für Unterricht und Kultus. Amtsblatt des Staatsministeriums für Unterricht und Kultus. München : Das Ministerium, 1918-

**ECCLESIASTICAL RITES AND CEREMONIES.** *See* **RITES AND CEREMONIES.**

**ECDL '99 (3rd : 1999 : Paris, France)** Research and advanced technology for digital libraries : third European conference, ECDL'99, Paris, France, September 22-24, 1999 : proceedings / Serge Abiteboul. Anne-Marie Vercoustre (eds.). Berlin ; New York : Springer, c1999. xi, 494 p. : ill. ; 24 cm. (Lecture notes in computer science, 0302-9743 ; 1696) Includes bibliographical references and index. ISBN 3-540-66558-7 (pbk.) DDC 025/.00285
*1. Digital libraries - Congresses. 2. Digital libraries - Europe - Congresses. I. Abiteboul, S. (Serge) II. Vercoustre, Anne-Marie, 1946- III. Title. IV. Series.*
*TC ZA4080 .E28 1999*

**Echevarria, Jana, 1956-** Making content comprehensible for English language learners : the SIOP model / Jana Echevarria, MaryEllen Vogt, Deborah J. Short. Boston, MA : Allyn and Bacon, 2000. xii, 212 p. : ill. ; 24 cm. Includes bibliographical references (p.203-208) and index. ISBN 0-205-29017-5 DDC 428/.0071
*1. English language - Study and teaching - Foreign speakers. 2. Language arts - Correlation with content subjects. I. Vogt, MaryEllen. II. Short, Deborah. III. Title.*
*TC PE1128.A2 E24 2000*

**Eck, Diana L.** Encountering God : a spiritual journey from Bozeman to Banaras / Diana L. Eck. Boston : Beacon Press, c1993. viii, 259 p. ; 24 cm. Includes bibliographical references (p. [245]-251) and index. ISBN 0-8070-7302-4 DDC 291.1/72
*1. Christianity and other religions. 2. Religions - Relations. 3. Eck, Diana L. 4. Christianity and other religions - Hinduism. 5. Hinduism - Relations - Christianity. I. Title.*
*TC BR127 .E25 1993*

**ECK, DIANA L.**
Eck, Diana L. Encountering God. Boston : Beacon Press, c1993.
*TC BR127 .E25 1993*

**Eckel, Peter J.**
Moving beyond the gap between research and practice in higher education. San Francisco, Calif. : Jossey-Bass, c2000.
*TC LA227.4 .M68 2000*

**Eckes, Thomas.**
The Developmental social psychology of gender. Mahwah, N.J. : Lawrence Erlbaum, c2000.
*TC HQ1075 .D47 2000*

**Eckmann, Sabine.**
Exiles + emigrés. Los Angeles, Calif. : Los Angeles County Museum of Art ; New York : H.N. Abrams, c1997.
*TC N6512 .E887 1997*

**Eckstein, Richard M.**
Directory of grants for organizations serving people with disabilities. Loxahatchee, Fla. : Research Grant Guides, c1993-
*TC HV3006.A4 H35*

**ECLECTIC PSYCHOTHERAPY.**
Johnson, Lynn D. Psychotherapy in the age of accountability. 1st ed. New York : W.W. Norton & Co., c1995.
*TC RC480.55 .J64 1995*

**ECLECTICISM IN ARCHITECTURE - NEW YORK (STATE) - NEW YORK.**
Stern, Robert A. M. New York 1880. New York, N.Y. : Monacelli Press, 1999.
*TC NA735.N5 S727 1999*

**ECO-FEMINISM.** *See* **ECOFEMINISM.**

**ECOFEMINISM - CONGRESSES.**
Environmental education for the 21st century. New York : Peter Lang, c1997.
*TC GE70 .E5817 1997*

**Ecole 27** [videorecording] / Paradise-Films présente une coproduction des Paradise-Film, ZDF-Arte, RTBF-Liège avec l'aid du Centre du Cinéma et de l'audio-visuel de la communaute française de Belgique ; un film écrit par Szymon Zaleski et réalisé par Szymon Zaleski et Marilyn Watelet ; production, Marilyn Watelet, Piotr Strzelecki. Bruxelles : Paradise Films ; New York, N.Y. : [distributed by] First Run/Icarus Films, 1997, c1996. 1 videocassette (64 min.) : sd., b&w. with col. sequences ; 1/2 in. Title on container and cassette label: School 27 [videorecording]. VHS. Catalogued from credits, container and cassette label French or Polish with English subtitles. 1997 Competition Cinéma du Réel. For general audiences. SUMMARY: Richly chronicles, with archival footage, the daily life of some of the Jewish children of Holocaust survivors,in a Poland that is in the prime of communist power, during the years from 1959-1968. Marek, Simon Jerzy, Tadek, Jola, Beniek were among the last groups of students attending "School 27" and are interviewed as adults today.
*1. Jews - Education - Poland - Warsaw - History - 20th century. 2. Jewish students - Poland - Warsaw - Interviews. 3. Documentary television programs - Poland. I. Zaleski. Szymon. II. Watelet, Marilyn III. Strzelecki, Piotr. IV. Paradise Films. V. Zweites Deutsches Fernsehen. VI. Radio-Télévision belge de la communauté culturelle française. VII. Centre du cinéma et de l'audio-visuel de la communauté Française de Belgique. VIII. First Run Features (Film) IX. Title: School 27 [videorecording] X. Title: Ecole vingt-sept [videorecording] XI. Title: School twenty-seven [videorecording]*
*TC LC746.P7 E2 1997*

**Ecole vingt-sept [videorecording].**
Ecole 27 [videorecording]. Bruxelles : Paradise
Films ; New York, N.Y. : [distributed by] First Run/
Icarus Films, 1997, c1996.
*TC LC746.P7 E2 1997*

**An ecological approach to perceptual learning and
development.**
Gibson, Eleanor Jack. Oxford ; New York : Oxford
University Press, 2000.
*TC BF720.P47 G53 2000*

**ECOLOGICAL ENGINEERING.** *See* **HUMAN
ECOLOGY.**

**ECOLOGICAL FEMINISM.** *See* **ECOFEMINISM.**

**ECOLOGICAL HETEROGENEITY.** *See*
**BIOLOGICAL DIVERSITY.**

**ECOLOGICALLY SUSTAINABLE
DEVELOPMENT.** *See* **SUSTAINABLE
DEVELOPMENT.**

**ECOLOGY.** *See also* **HUMAN ECOLOGY; NICHE
(ECOLOGY); SAVANNA ECOLOGY.**
Markle, Sandra. Down, down, down in the ocean.
New York : Walker, 1999.
*TC QH541.5.S3 M2856 1999*

Fate of the earth [videorecording]. [New York,
N.Y.?] : Unapix Entertainment, Inc. [distributor],
c1996.
*TC QB631.2 .F3 1996*

People and the land. New York, Noble and Noble
[1974]
*TC GN330 .P445*

Wright-Frierson, Virginia. A North American rain
forest scrapbook. New York : Walker and Co., 1999.
*TC QH105.W2 W75 1999*

**ECOLOGY - AFRICA.**
Dunphy, Madeleine. Here is the African savanna. 1st
ed. New York : Hyperion Books for Children, c1999.
*TC QH194 .D86 1999*

**ECOLOGY - ANTARCTICA - FICTION.**
Robinson, Kim Stanley. Antarctica. New York :
Bantam Books, c1998.
*TC PS3568.O2893 A82 1998*

**ECOLOGY - POPULAR WORKS.**
Get a grip [videorecording]. Racine, WI : S.C.
Johnson and Son, Inc., 1999, c1998.
*TC TD170 .G4 1999*

**ECOLOGY - SOCIAL ASPECTS.** *See* **HUMAN
ECOLOGY.**

**ECOLOGY - STUDY AND TEACHING
(SECONDARY) - PUERTO RICO.**
Laborde, Ilia M. Rediscovering San Cristóbal Canyon.
1996.
*TC 06 no. 10660*

Laborde, Ilia M. Rediscovering San Cristóbal Canyon.
1996.
*TC 06 no. 10660*

**ECONOMETRICS.** *See* **STATISTICS.**

**The economic analysis of substance use and abuse :**
an integration of econometric and behavioral
economic research / edited by Frank J. Chaloupka ...
[et al.]. Chicago : University of Chicago Press, 1999.
xi, 385 p. : ill. ; 24 cm. (A National Bureau of Economic
Research conference report) This volume contains papers
presented at a conference held in Cambridge, Massachusetts,
on 27-28 March 1997. Includes bibliographical references and
indexes. ISBN 0-226-10047-2 (cloth : alk. paper) DDC 338.4/
33629/0973
*1. Substance abuse - Economic aspects - United States -
Congresses. I. Chaloupka, Frank J. II. Series: Conference
report (National Bureau of Economic Research)*
*TC HV4999.2 .E25 1999*

**The economic and environmental consequences of
nutrient management in agriculture.**
Huang, Wen-Yuan. Commack, N.Y. : Nova Science,
c1999.
*TC S651 .H826 1999*

**ECONOMIC ASSISTANCE.** *See also* **ECONOMIC
DEVELOPMENT PROJECTS.**
The paradox of plenty. Oakland, Calif. : Food First
Books, c1999.
*TC HD1542 .P37 1999*

**ECONOMIC ASSISTANCE, DOMESTIC.** *See*
**COMMUNITY DEVELOPMENT; GRANTS-
IN-AID.**

**ECONOMIC ASSISTANCE, DOMESTIC -
UNITED STATES.**
Poverty. San Diego, CA : Greenhaven Press, c1994.

*TC HC110.P6 P63 1994*

**ECONOMIC ASSISTANCE, DOMESTIC -
UNITED STATES - DIRECTORIES.**
Directory of grants for organizations serving people
with disabilities. Loxahatchee, Fla. : Research Grant
Guides, c1993-
*TC HV3006.A4 H35*

**ECONOMIC CONDITIONS.** *See* **ECONOMIC
HISTORY.**

**ECONOMIC DEPRESSIONS.** *See* **DEPRESSIONS.**

**ECONOMIC DEVELOPMENT.** *See also*
**DEVELOPING COUNTRIES; RURAL
DEVELOPMENT.**
Science, technology, and the economic future. New
York : New York Academy of Sciences, c1998.
*TC HD82 .S35 1998*

**ECONOMIC DEVELOPMENT - EFFECT OF
EDUCATION ON.**
Ainley, Patrick. Learning policy. Basingstoke,
Hampshire : Macmillan Press ; New York : St.
Martin's Press, 1999.
*TC LC93.G7 A76 1999*

Majasan, James. Qualitative education and
development. Ibadan : Spectrum Books Limited ;
Channel Islands, UK : In association with Safari
Books (Export) ; Oxford, UK : African Books
Collective Ltd. (Distributor), 1998.
*TC LC2605 .M32 1998*

Quist, Hubert Oswald. Secondary education and
nation-building. 1999.
*TC 085 Q52*

World Bank. Human Development Network.
Education sector strategy. Washington, D.C. : World
Bank Group, c1999.
*TC LC2607 .W66 1999*

**ECONOMIC DEVELOPMENT - EFFECT OF
EDUCATION ON - CASE STUDIES.**
The response of higher education institutions to
regional needs. Paris : Organisation for Economic
Co-operation and Development, 1999.
*TC LC237 .R47 1999*

**ECONOMIC DEVELOPMENT - EFFECT OF
EDUCATION ON - STATISTICS.**
Lieberman, Carl, 1941- Educational expenditures and
economic growth in the American states. Akron,
Ohio : Midwest Press Incorporated, 1998.
*TC LC66 .L45 1998*

**ECONOMIC DEVELOPMENT -
ENVIRONMENTAL ASPECTS.** *See also*
**SUSTAINABLE DEVELOPMENT.**
Towards sustainable development. New York, N.Y. :
St. Martin's Press, 1999.
*TC HD75.6 .T695 1999*

**Economic Development Institute (Washington, D.C.).**
Petkoski, Djordjija B. Learning together with clients.
Washington, D.C. : World Bank, c1997.
*TC HQ4420.8.P48 1997*

**ECONOMIC DEVELOPMENT PROJECTS -
DEVELOPING COUNTRIES.**
Petkoski, Djordjija B. Learning together with clients.
Washington, D.C. : World Bank, c1997.
*TC HQ4420.8.P48 1997*

**ECONOMIC DEVELOPMENT PROJECTS -
UGANDA.**
Our friends at the bank [videorecording]. New York,
NY : First Run/Icarus Films, 1997.
*TC HG3881.5.W57 087 1997*

**ECONOMIC DEVELOPMENT - SOCIAL
ASPECTS.**
Strengthening the family. Tokyo ; New York : United
Nations University Press, c1995.
*TC HQ727.9 .S77 1995*

**ECONOMIC DEVELOPMENT - SOCIOLOGICAL
ASPECTS.**
Comparative anomie research. Aldershot, Hants,
England ; Brookfield, Vt., USA : Ashgate, c1999.
*TC HM816 .C65 1999*

**ECONOMIC DEVELOPMENT, SUSTAINABLE.**
*See* **SUSTAINABLE DEVELOPMENT.**

**ECONOMIC GROWTH.** *See* **ECONOMIC
DEVELOPMENT.**

**ECONOMIC HISTORY.** *See* **QUALITY OF LIFE.**

**ECONOMIC HISTORY - PERIODICALS.**
American economic security. Washington, Chamber
of Commerce of the United States of America.

**ECONOMIC INDICATORS.** *See* **SOCIAL
INDICATORS.**

**ECONOMIC MAN.** *See* **ECONOMICS.**

**ECONOMIC NATIONALISM.** *See* **ECONOMIC
POLICY.**

**ECONOMIC PLANNING.** *See* **ECONOMIC
POLICY.**

**ECONOMIC POLICY.** *See also* **ECONOMIC
ASSISTANCE, DOMESTIC; ECONOMIC
DEVELOPMENT; FULL EMPLOYMENT
POLICIES; INTERNATIONAL ECONOMIC
RELATIONS; STRUCTURAL ADJUSTMENT
(ECONOMIC POLICY); URBAN POLICY.**
Science, technology, and the economic future. New
York : New York Academy of Sciences, c1998.
*TC HD82 .S35 1998*

**ECONOMIC POLICY, FOREIGN.** *See*
**INTERNATIONAL ECONOMIC
RELATIONS.**

**ECONOMIC POLICY - MATHEMATICAL
MODELS.**
Greenberger, Martin, 1931- Models in the policy
process. New York : Russell Sage Foundation :
[distributed by Basic Books], c1976.
*TC H61 .G667*

**ECONOMIC RELATIONS, FOREIGN.** *See*
**INTERNATIONAL ECONOMIC
RELATIONS.**

**ECONOMIC SANCTIONS.** *See* **INTERNATIONAL
ECONOMIC RELATIONS.**

**ECONOMIC SECURITY.** *See* **SOCIAL
SECURITY.**

**ECONOMIC SUSTAINABILITY.** *See*
**SUSTAINABLE DEVELOPMENT.**

**ECONOMIC THEORY.** *See* **ECONOMICS.**

**ECONOMICS.** *See also* **CAPITALISM;
ECONOMIC DEVELOPMENT; ECONOMIC
HISTORY; ECONOMIC POLICY;
EMPLOYMENT (ECONOMIC THEORY);
INDUSTRIES; POPULATION; RISK;
STATISTICS; WEALTH.**
Arendt, Hannah. The human condition. 2nd ed. /
introduction by Margaret Canovan. Chicago :
University of Chicago Press, 1998.
*TC HM211 .A7 1998*

Smith, Adam, 1723-1790. An inquiry into the nature
and causes of the wealth of nations. Chicago :
University of Chicago Press, 1976.
*TC HB161 .S65 1976*

**ECONOMICS, INTERNATIONAL.** *See*
**INTERNATIONAL ECONOMIC
RELATIONS.**

**ECONOMICS, MEDICAL.** *See also* **MEDICAL
ECONOMICS.**
Tulchinsky, Theodore H. The new public health. San
Diego, Calif. ; London : Academic Press, c2000.
*TC RA425 .T85 2000*

**Economics of education.**
Arai, Kazuhiro, 1949- [Kyōiku no keizaigaku.
English] Tōkyō ; New York : Springer, 1998.
*TC LC67.68.J3 A72 1998*

**Economics of education review.**
[Economics of education review (Online)] Economics
of education review [computer file]. Oxford ; New
York : Pergamon,
*TC EJOURNALS*

**[Economics of education review (Online)]** Economics
of education review [computer file]. Oxford ; New
York : Pergamon, Coverage as of Mar. 30, 1998: Vol. 16,
issue 1 (Feb. 1997)- . System requirements: Internet
connectivity, World Wide Web browser, and Adobe Acrobat
reader. Abstracts, tables of contents, and citation information
are HTML encoded; articles are available in portable document
format (PDF) and as Postscript Level 2 files. Subscription and
registration required for access. Online version of the print
title: Economics of education review. Mode of access: World
Wide Web. Description based on: Vol. 16, issue 1 (Feb. 1997);
title from general information screen (viewed Mar. 30, 1998).
URL: http://www.sciencedirect.com/science/journal/02727757
URL: http://www.columbia.edu/cu/libraries/indexes/science-
direct.html URL: http://www.sciencedirect.com/ URL: http://
www.elsevier.com/homepage/elecserv.htt Available in other
form: Economics of education review ISSN: 0272-7757
(DLC) 82642752 (OCoLC)6933446. ISSN 0272-7757
*1. Education - Economic aspects - Periodicals. I. Title:
Sciencedirect. II. Title: Economics of education review*

## TC EJOURNALS

**The economics of knowledge production.**
Geuna, Aldo, 1965- Cheltenham, UK : Northampton, MA : E. Elgar, c1999.
**TC Q180.E9 G48 1999**

**Economics of population.**
Schultz, T. Paul. Reading, MA : Addison-Wesley, c1981.
**TC HB849.41 .S38**

**The Economics of the arts** / edited by Mark Blaug. Boulder, Colo. : Westview Press, 1976. 272 p. : ill. ; 23 cm. Includes bibliographical references. ISBN 0-89158-613-X DDC 338.4/7/7
*1. Arts - United States - Finance. 2. Arts - Great Britain - Finance. I. Blaug, Mark.*
**TC NX705.5.U6 E27 1976**

**ECONOMICS - PSYCHOLOGICAL ASPECTS.**
Antonides, Gerrit, 1951- Psychology in economics and business. 2nd rev. ed. Dordrecht, Netherlands : Boston : Kluwer Academic, c1996.
**TC HB74.P8 A64 1996**

Wärneryd, Karl Erik, 1927- The psychology of saving. Northampton, Mass. : E. Elgar, c1999.
**TC HB822 .W37 1999**

**ECONOMICS - STUDY AND TEACHING (HIGHER) - CONGRESSES.**
Educational innovation in economics and business. IV, Learning in a changing environment. Boston, MA : Kluwer Academic Publishers, c1999.
**TC HB74.5 .E3333 1999**

**ECONOMICS - STUDY AND TEACHING (HIGHER) - SASKATCHEWAN - SASKATOON - HISTORY.**
Spafford, Shirley. No ordinary academics. Toronto : University of Toronto Press, 1999.
**TC HB74.9.C3 S62 1999**

**ECONOMICS - STUDY AND TEACHING (HIGHER) - UNITED STATES.**
Teaching economics to undergraduates. Cheltenham, UK : Northampton, MA, USA : E. Elgar, c1998.
**TC HB74.8 .T4 1998**

**ECONOMY, MIXED.** *See* **MIXED ECONOMY.**

**ÉCRIVAINS AMÉRICAINS - 20E SIÈCLE - BIOGRAPHIES.**
Gard, Robert E. (Robert Edward), 1910- Prairie visions. Ashland, Wis. : Heartland Press, c1987.
**TC PS3513.A612 P7 1987**

**Eddy, Jennifer B.K.** Multiple intelligences, styles, and proficiency : issues and application in adult second language learning and teaching / by Jennifer B.K. Eddy. 1999. v, 252 leaves ; 29 cm. Typescript; issued also on microfilm. Thesis (Ph.D.)--Columbia University, 1999. Includes bibliographical references (leaves 219-233)
*1. Learning, Psychology of. 2. Cognitive styles - Psychological aspects. 3. Multiple intelligences. 4. Adult learning - Philosophy - Evaluation. 5. Spanish language - Study and teaching (Higher) - English speakers. 6. Metacognition. 7. Self-perception. 8. Differentiation (Cognition) I. Title. II. Title: Issues and application in adult second language learning and teaching*
**TC 085 E10**

**Eddy, John, 1932-** International higher education systems / John P. Eddy, Stanley D. Murphy. New ed. Lanham, Md. : Oxford : University Press of America, c2000. x, 190 p. ; 23 cm. Includes bibliographical references. ISBN 0-7618-1748-4 (pbk. : alk. paper) DDC 378
*1. Education, Higher - Cross-cultural studies. 2. Higher education and state - Cross-cultural studies. 3. International education. I. Murphy, Stanley D. II. Title.*
**TC LB2322.2 .E33 2000**

**EDDY, MARY BAKER, 1821-1910.**
Satter, Beryl, 1959- Each mind a kingdom. Berkeley : University of California Press, c1999.
**TC BF639 .S124 1999**

**Edelman, Marian Wright.** Lanterns : a memoir of mentors / Marian Wright Edelman. Boston : Beacon Press, c1999. xxi, 180 p. : ill. ; 23 cm. Includes bibliographical references (p. 177-180). ISBN 0-8070-7214-1 (acid-free paper) DDC 362.7/092
*1. Edelman, Marian Wright. 2. Mentoring - United States. 3. Edelman, Marian Wright - Friends and associates. 4. Afro-American women social reformers - Biography. 5. Edelman, Marian Wright - Philosophy. 6. Conduct of life. 7. Children - United States - Conduct of life. I. Title.*
**TC E185.97.E33 A3 1999**

**EDELMAN, MARIAN WRIGHT.**
Edelman, Marian Wright. Lanterns. Boston : Beacon Press, c1999.

**TC E185.97.E33 A3 1999**

**EDELMAN, MARIAN WRIGHT - FRIENDS AND ASSOCIATES.**
Edelman, Marian Wright. Lanterns. Boston : Beacon Press, c1999.
**TC E185.97.E33 A3 1999**

**EDELMAN, MARIAN WRIGHT - PHILOSOPHY.**
Edelman, Marian Wright. Lanterns. Boston : Beacon Press, c1999.
**TC E185.97.E33 A3 1999**

**Edelsky, Carole.**
Making justice our project. Urbana, Ill. : National Council of Teachers of English, c1999
**TC LB1576 .M3613 1999**

Reflections and connections. Cresskill, N.J. : Hampton Press, c1999.
**TC P51 .R36 1999**

**Eden, Michael, 1955-** Slipware : contemporary approaches / Michael and Victoria Eden. London : A & C Black ; Philadelphia, Pa. : University of Pennslvania Press, 1999. 160 p. : ill. (some col.) ; 29 cm. Includes bibliographical references (p. 159) and index. ISBN 0-8122-3480-4 (alk. paper) DDC 738.3/7
*1. Slipware. I. Eden, Victoria. II. Title.*
**TC NK4285 .E33 1999**

**Eden online.**
Harvey, Kerric. Cresskill, N.J. : Hampton Press, c2000.
**TC T14.5 .H367 2000**

**Eden, Victoria.**
Eden, Michael, 1955- Slipware. London : A & C Black ; Philadelphia, Pa. : University of Pennslvania Press, 1999.
**TC NK4285 .E33 1999**

**EDENBOROUGH, ROBERT.** Using psychometrics : a practical guide to testing and assessment. 2nd ed. London ; Dover, NH : Kogan Page, 1999. xii, 210 p. ; 24 cm. Includes bibliographical references and index. ISBN 0-7494-3126-1 DDC 152.8
*1. Psychometrics*
**TC BF39 .E34 1999**

**Eder, Elizabeth K.**
Hidden messages. Yarmouth, Me. : Intercultural Press, c1998.
**TC LC1099.3 .H53 1998**

**Edge books**
Nash, Gary B. Forbidden love. 1st ed. New York : H. Holt, 1999.
**TC E184.M47 N47 1999**

**The edge, critical studies in educational theory**
Bartolomé, Lilia I. The misteaching of academic discourses. Boulder, Colo. : Westview Press, 1998.
**TC LB1033.5 .B37 1998**

**Edge, Julian, 1948-** Mistakes and correction / Julian Edge. London ; New York : Longman, 1989. viii, 70 p. : ill. ; 22 cm. (Longman keys to language teaching) Includes bibliographical references. ISBN 0-582-74626-4 DDC 428/.007
*1. English language - Study and teaching - Foreign speakers. 2. English language - Errors of usage. I. Title. II. Series.*
**TC PE1128.A2 E28 1989**

**Edge, Karen.**
Leithwood, Kenneth A. Educational accountability. Gütersloh : Bertelsmann Foundation Publishers, 1999.
**TC LB2806.22 .L45 1999**

**Edgell, Derek.** The movement for community control of New York City's schools, 1966-1970 : class wars / Derek Edgell. Lewiston, N.Y. : E. Mellen Press, c1998. xvi, 516 p. ; 24 cm. Includes bibliographical references (p. 491-508) and index. ISBN 0-7734-8262-8 (hard) DDC 379.1/535
*1. Schools - Decentralization - New York (State) - New York - History - 20th century. 2. School management and organization - Parent participation - New York (State) - New York - History - 20th century. 3. Community and school - New York (State) - New York - History - 20th century. 4. Racism - New York (State) - New York - History - 20th century. 5. New York (N.Y.) - Race relations - History - 20th century. 6. Afro-Americans - New York (State) - New York - Relations with Jews - History - 20th century. I. Title.*
**TC LB2862 .E35 1998**

**Edgoose, Julian Miles.** Partnerships of possibility : educating for hope, democracy and justice / by Julian Miles Edgoose. 1999. ii, 149 leaves ; 29 cm. Issued also on microfilm. Thesis (Ph.D.)--Columbia University, 1999. Includes bibliographical references (leaves 137-149)
*1. Education - Social aspects. 2. Education - Philosophy. 3. Democracy - Moral and ethical aspects. 4. Social justice. 5.*

*Education - Aims and objectives. 6. Teacher-student relationships. I. Title.*
**TC 085 E117**

**EDI case studies**
Petkoski, Djordjija B. Learning together with clients. Washington, D.C. : World Bank, c1997.
**TC HQ4420.8.P48 1997**

**The Edinburgh encyclopedia of Continental philosophy** / Simon Glendinning, general editor. Edinburgh : University Press, c1999. xiii, 685 p. ; 26 cm. Includes bibliographical references and indexes. CONTENTS: Introduction -- 1. Classical idealism. Introduction / Philip Stratton-Lake -- 2. Philosophy of existence. Introduction / Lewis R. Gordon -- 3. Philosophies of life and understanding. Introduction / Fiona Hughes -- 4. Phenomenology. Introduction / Gail Weiss -- 5. Politics, psychoanalysis and science. Introduction / Gillian Howie -- 6. The Frankfurt School and critical theory. Introduction / Simon Jarvis -- 7. Structuralism. Introduction / Jeremy Jennings -- 8. Post-structuralism. Introduction / John Protevi -- [Indexes]. ISBN 0-7486-0783-8
*1. Philosophy, European. I. Glendinning, Simon. II. Title: Encyclopedia of Continental philosophy*
**TC B831.2 E35 1999**

**Edinburgh working papers in cognitive science**
(v. 9) Functional categories, argument structure and parametric variation. Edinburgh : Centre for Cognitive Study, University of Edinburgh, c1994.
**TC P151 .F86 1994**

**EDINEB Conference (4th : 1997 : Edinburgh, Scotland).**
Educational innovation in economics and business. IV, Learning in a changing environment. Boston, MA : Kluwer Academic Publishers, c1999.
**TC HB74.5 .E3333 1999**

**Editions Cinégraphiques.**
Tassili N'Ajjer [videorecording]. [S.l.] : Editions Cinégraphiques ; Northbrook, Ill. : [distributed by] the Roland Collection, c1968.
**TC N5310.5.A4 T3 1968**

**EDITORIAL PHOTOGRAPHY.** *See* **PHOTOJOURNALISM.**

**Edkins, Diana.**
Marks, Carole. The power of pride. 1st ed. New York : Crown Publishers, c1999.
**TC E185.6 .M35 1999**

**Edmonds, Robert.** Scriptwriting for the audio-visual media / by Robert Edmonds. New York : Teachers College Press, c1978. 185 p. : ill. ; 26 cm. ISBN 0-8077-2508-0
*1. Radio authorship. 2. Moving-picture authorship. 3. Television authorship. I. Title.*
**TC PN1991.7 .E3**

**Edmund W. Gordon :** producing knowledge, pursuing understanding / edited by Carol Camp Yeakey. Stamford, Conn. : Jai Press, c2000. xx, 345 p. ; 24 cm. (Advances in education in diverse communities ; v. 1) Includes bibliographical references and index. ISBN 0-7623-0428-6 (alk. paper) DDC 302 DDC 302
*1. Social psychology - United States. 2. Educational sociology - United States. 3. Afro-American children - Social conditions. 4. Gordon, Edmund W. I. Yeakey, Carol Camp. II. Series: Advances in education in diverse communities ; 1.*
**TC HM1033 .E35 2000**

**EDP (DATA PROCESSING).** *See* **ELECTRONIC DATA PROCESSING.**

**Educamus.** Pretoria : Govt. Printer, [1978- v. : ill. ; 28 cm. Frequency: Ten no. a year. Vol. 24, no. 4 (Mei 1978)- . Title from cover. Issue for Sept. 1978 incorrectly called v. 27, no. 8, but constitutes v. 24, no. 8. Afrikaans and English. Official organ of the Dept. of Bantu Education, -Mei 1978; Dept. of Education and Training, June 1978- Indexes to v. <25-26> published separately. Continues: Bantoe-onderwysblad ISSN: 0005-5662 (DLC) 67057533 (OCoLC)2529071. ISSN 0250-152X
*1. Bantus - South Africa - Education - Periodicals. 2. South Africa. - Dept. of Bantu Education - Periodicals. 3. South Africa. - Dept. of Education and Training - Periodicals. 4. Education - South Africa - Periodicals. 5. Blacks - Education - South Africa - Periodicals. I. South Africa. Dept. of Bantu Education. II. South Africa. Dept. of Education and Training. III. Title: Bantoe-onderwysblad.*

**Educate.**
K-eight. [Philadelphia, American Pub. Co.]

**The educated child.**
Bennett, William J. (William John), 1943- New York : Free Press, c1999.
**TC LB1048.5 .B45 1999**

**L'Éducateur et bulletin corporatif.** Lausanne, 46 v. : ill. ; 25-30 cm. Frequency: Semimonthly, 71. Année (1935)-103. année (1966); Jan. 1967-Dec. 1980. "... de la Société pédagogique de la Suisse romande." Title from caption. Volume numbering ceased after 1966. Continues: Éducateur (Lausanne, Switzerland). Continued by: Éducateur (Lausanne, Switzerland : 1981).
*1. Education - Periodicals. 2. Education - Switzerland - Periodicals. I. Société pédagogique de la Suisse romande. II. Title: Éducateur (Lausanne, Switzerland) III. Title: Éducateur (Lausanne, Switzerland : 1981)*

**Éducateur (Lausanne, Switzerland).**
L'Éducateur et bulletin corporatif. Lausanne.

**Éducateur (Lausanne, Switzerland : 1981).**
L'Éducateur et bulletin corporatif. Lausanne.

**Educating Americans for tomorrow's world :** state initiatives in international education / Committee on International Trade and Foreign relations, National Governors' Association ; Gerald L. Baliles, chairman. [Washington D.C.] : NGA, [1987] 41 p. ; 28 cm. "July, 1987."
*1. International education - United States. 2. Education and state - United States. I. Baliles, Gerald L. II. National Governors' Association. Committee on International Trade and Foreign Relations.*
*TC LC1099 .E225 1987*

**Educating by design.**
Strange, Charles Carney. 1st ed. San Francisco : Jossey-Bass, c2001.
*TC LB2324 .S77 2001*

**Educating entrepreneurs for wealth creation** / edited by Michael G. Scott, Peter Rosa, Heinz Klandt. Aldershot, Hants, England ; Brookfield, USA : Ashgate, 1998. xiv, 249 p. : ill. ; 23 cm. "Selected from 66 papers presented at the 4th Internationalizing Entrepreneurship Education and Training Conference (IntEnt94) held at Stirling University on July 4th-6th 1994"--Page facing t.p. Includes bibliographical references. Table of Contents URL: http://lcweb.loc.gov/catdir/toc/98-70990.html ISBN 1-85972-185-0
*1. Business education - Congresses. 2. Businesspeople - Training of - Congresses. 3. Entrepreneurship - Congresses. I. Scott, Michael (Michael G.) II. Rosa, Peter. 1951- III. Klandt, Heinz. IV. Internationalizing Entrepreneurship Education and Training Conference (4th : 1994 : University of Stirling)*
*TC HF1106 .E378 1998*

**Educating for life.**
Groome, Thomas H. Allen, Tex. : T. More, c1998.
*TC BV1471.2 .G6874 1998*

**Educating homeless children.**
Newman, Rebecca. New York ; London : Garland, 1999.
*TC LC5144.22.C2 N49 1999*

**Educating homeless students :** promising practices / James H. Strong and Evelyn Reed-Victor, editors. Larchmont, N.Y. : Eye On Education, c2000. x, 269 p. ; 24 cm. Includes bibliographical references. ISBN 1-88300-189-7 DDC 371.826/942
*1. Homeless children - Education - United States. 2. Homeless youth - Education - United States. I. Strong, James H., 1950- II. Reed-Victor, Evelyn, 1947-*
*TC LC5144.2 .E385 2000*

**Educating language-minority children** / Rosalie Pedalino Porter, editor. New Brunswick (U.S.A.) : Transaction Publishers, c2000. 178 p. : ill. ; 23 cm. (READ perspectives, v. 6.) Includes bibliographical references. ISBN 0-7658-0669-X
*1. Linguistic minorities - Education - United States - Evaluation. 2. Education, Bilingual - United States - Evaluation. 3. English language - Study and teaching - United States - Evaluation. 4. Second language acquisition. I. Porter, Rosalie Pedalino. 1931- II. Series.*
*TC LC3731 .E374 2000*

**Educating Latino students :** a guide to successful practice / edited by María Luísa González, Ana Huerta-Macías, Josefina Villamil Tinajero. Lancaster, Pa. : Technomic Pub. Co., c1998. xix, 383 p. : ill. ; 24 cm. Includes bibliographical references and index. ISBN 1-56676-568-4
*1. Hispanic American students - Education. 2. Education, Bilingual - United States. I. González, María Luísa. II. Huerta-Macías, Ana. III. Villamil Tinajero, Josefina.*
*TC LC2669 .E37 1998*

**Educating professional psychologists.**
Peterson, Donald R. (Donald Robert), 1923- 1st ed. Washington, D.C. : American Psychological Association, c1997.
*TC BF80.7.U6 P48 1997*

**Educating the disadvantaged, 1971-1972.**
Flaxman, Erwin, comp. New York : AMS Press, [c1973]

*TC LC4091 .F52 1973*

**Educating the disadvantaged, 1972-1973 :** an AMS anthology / Edited, with an introd., by Erwin Flaxman. New York : AMS Press, c1976. 412 p. : ill. ; 24 cm. Includes bibliographical references. ISBN 0-404-15095-0
*1. Socially handicapped children - Education - United States. I. Flaxman, Erwin.*
*TC LC4091 .F52 1976*

**Educating the faithful.**
Curtis, Sarah Ann. DeKalb : Northern Illinois University Press, 2000.
*TC LC506.F7 C87 2000*

**EDUCATION.** *See also* **ADULT EDUCATION; AFFECTIVE EDUCATION; ART IN EDUCATION; BASIC EDUCATION; BUSINESS EDUCATION; CAREER EDUCATION; CASE METHOD; CHURCH AND EDUCATION; CLASSICAL EDUCATION; COEDUCATION; COMMUNICATION IN EDUCATION; COMMUNISM AND EDUCATION; COMPENSATORY EDUCATION; COMPETENCY BASED EDUCATION; CONSTRUCTIVISM (EDUCATION); CONSUMER EDUCATION; CONTINUING EDUCATION; CRITICAL PEDAGOGY; CULTURE; DISCRIMINATION IN EDUCATION; DISTANCE EDUCATION; DRAMA IN EDUCATION; EARLY CHILDHOOD EDUCATION; ECONOMIC DEVELOPMENT - EFFECT OF EDUCATION ON; EDUCATION, ELEMENTARY; EDUCATION, SECONDARY; EDUCATORS; EMPLOYER-SUPPORTED EDUCATION; ENVIRONMENTAL EDUCATION; FEMINISM AND EDUCATION; FOREIGN STUDY; FUNDAMENTAL EDUCATION; GROUP WORK IN EDUCATION; HEALTH EDUCATION; HIGH TECHNOLOGY AND EDUCATION; HOME AND SCHOOL; HOME SCHOOLING; HOMOSEXUALITY AND EDUCATION; INCLUSIVE EDUCATION; INDUSTRY AND EDUCATION; INSTRUCTIONAL SYSTEMS; INTERNATIONAL EDUCATION; INTERNET (COMPUTER NETWORK) IN EDUCATION; LABOR SUPPLY - EFFECT OF EDUCATION ON; LANGUAGE AND EDUCATION; LANGUAGE EXPERIENCE APPROACH IN EDUCATION; LEARNING; LEARNING AND SCHOLARSHIP; LEARNING, PSYCHOLOGY OF; LITERACY; MAINSTREAMING IN EDUCATION; MASS MEDIA IN EDUCATION; MENTORING IN EDUCATION; MORAL EDUCATION; MULTICULTURAL EDUCATION; NATIONALISM AND EDUCATION; NATIVE LANGUAGE AND EDUCATION; NATURE STUDY; OCCUPATIONAL TRAINING; PHYSICAL EDUCATION AND TRAINING; PICTURES IN EDUCATION; POSTSECONDARY EDUCATION; PRIVATIZATION IN EDUCATION; PROGRESSIVE EDUCATION; PROPOSAL WRITING IN EDUCATION; PUPPET THEATER IN EDUCATION; RELIGIOUS EDUCATION; SCHOOL CHOICE; SCHOOLS; SEX DIFFERENCES IN EDUCATION; SEXUAL HARASSMENT IN EDUCATION; SOCIALIZATION; SPECIAL EDUCATION; STUDENTS; TEACHERS; TEACHING; TECHNICAL EDUCATION; TELEVISION IN EDUCATION; TRAINING; UNIVERSITIES AND COLLEGES; UNIVERSITY EXTENSION; VOCATIONAL EDUCATION; WOMEN IN EDUCATION.**
O'Brien, Nancy P. Education, a guide to reference and information sources. 2nd ed. Englewood, Colo. : Libraries Unlimited, 2000.
*TC Z5811 .B89 2000*

White, Mary Alice. New York, Holt, Rinehart and Winston [1973]
*TC LB41 .W62*

**EDUCATION.**
Gordon, Mordechai. Toward an integrative conception of authority in education. 1997.
*TC 085 G656*

Hall, G. Stanley (Granville Stanley), 1844-1924. Educational problems, New York, London, D. Appleton and company, 1911.
*TC 370.4/H14*

Mead, George Herbert, 1863-1931. Play, school, and society. New York : Peter Lang, c1999.

*TC HQ782 .M43 1999*

The politics of professionalism. London : Continuum, 2000.
*TC LB1779 .M33 2000*

Raymont, Thomas, 1864- A history of the education of young children,. London ; New York : Longmans, Green and co., [1937]
*TC LA21 .R37*

Routledge international companion to education. London ; New York : Routledge, 2000.
*TC LB7 .R688 2000*

Ushinskiĭ, K. D. (Konstantin Dmitrievich), 1824-1870. [Selected works. English. 1975] K. D. Ushinsky. Moscow : Progress, 1975.
*TC LB675 .U8213 1975*

**Education, a guide to reference and information sources.**
O'Brien, Nancy P. 2nd ed. Englewood, Colo. : Libraries Unlimited, 2000.
*TC Z5811 .B89 2000*

**EDUCATION - ACTIVITY PROGRAMS.** *See* **ACTIVITY PROGRAMS IN EDUCATION.**

**EDUCATION - ADDRESSES, ESSAYS, LECTURES.**
White, Mary Alice. Education; New York, Holt, Rinehart and Winston [1973]
*TC LB41 .W62*

**EDUCATION - AFRICA, FRENCH-SPEAKING WEST - FRENCH INFLUENCES.**
Kelly, Gail Paradise. French colonial education. New York : AMS Press, c2000.
*TC LA1186 .K45 2000*

**EDUCATION - AFRICA, FRENCH-SPEAKING WEST - HISTORY.**
Kelly, Gail Paradise. French colonial education. New York : AMS Press, c2000.
*TC LA1186 .K45 2000*

**EDUCATION - AFRICA - HISTORY - 20TH CENTURY.**
Sivonen, Seppo. White-collar or hoe handle. Helsinki : Suomen Historiallinen Seura, [1995]
*TC LA1531 .S58 1995*

**EDUCATION - AFRICA - PHILOSOPHY.**
Dove, Nah. Afrikan mothers. Albany : State University of New York Press, c1998.
*TC HQ1593 .D68 1998*

**EDUCATION - AFRICA, SUB-SAHARAN.**
Schooling in sub-Saharan Africa. New York : Garland Pub., 1998.
*TC LA1501 .S35 1998*

**EDUCATION - AFRICA, SUB-SAHARAN - CURRICULA.**
Schooling in sub-Saharan Africa. New York : Garland Pub., 1998.
*TC LA1501 .S35 1998*

**EDUCATION - AFRICA - WESTERN INFLUENCES.**
Bassey, Magnus O. Western education and political domination in Africa. Westport, CT : Bergin & Garvey, 1999.
*TC LC95.A2 B37 1999*

**EDUCATION - AIMS AND OBJECTIVES.** *See also* **EDUCATIONAL EQUALIZATION; EDUCATIONAL SOCIOLOGY.**
The aims of education. London ; New York : Routledge, 1999.
*TC LB41 .A36353 1999*

Calfee, Robert C. Teach your children well. Stanford, CA : Stanford Alumni Association, c1995.
*TC LB2822.82 .C32 1995*

Edgoose, Julian Miles. Partnerships of possibility. 1999.
*TC 085 E117*

Everyone a teacher. Notre Dame, Ind. : University of Notre Dame Press, c2000.
*TC LB1025.3 .E87 2000*

Giroux, Henry A. Stealing innocence. 1st ed. New York : St. Martin's Press, 2000.
*TC HM621 .G57 2000*

Lawrence, Alexandria Teresa. Cooperating teachers' perceptions of the nature and quality of professional development in a professional development school collaboration. 1999.
*TC 06 no. 11141*

Lawrence, Alexandria Teresa. Cooperating teachers' perceptions of the nature and quality of professional

*Education - Aims and objectives*

development in a professional development school collaboration. 1999.
*TC 06 no. 11141*

Lawrence, Alexandria Teresa. Cooperating teachers' perceptions of the nature and quality of professional development in a professional development school collaboration. 1999.
*TC 06 no. 11141*

Learning communities in education. London ; New York : Routledge, 1999.
*TC LB14.7 .L43 1999*

Levinson, Meira. The demands of liberal education. Oxford ; New York : Oxford University Press, 1999.
*TC LC1091 .L38 1999*

Martinez, Michael E. Education as the cultivation of intelligence. Mahwah, N.J. ; London : Lawrence Erlbaum Associates, 2000.
*TC LB1060 .M337 2000*

McLaren, Peter, 1948- Schooling as a ritual performance. 3rd ed. Lanham, Md. : Rowman & Littlefield, c1999.
*TC LC504.3.T67 M35 1999*

Thayer, Vivian Trow, 1886- Reorganizing secondary education; New York, Appleton-Century [c1939]
*TC LB1607 .T5*

### EDUCATION - AIMS AND OBJECTIVES - AFRICA, SUB-SAHARAN.
Brock-Utne, Birgit, 1938- Whose education for all? New York ; London : Falmer Press, 2000.
*TC LC67.A435 B76 2000*

### EDUCATION - AIMS AND OBJECTIVES - DEVELOPING COUNTRIES.
Majasan, James. Qualitative education and development. Ibadan : Spectrum Books Limited ; Channel Islands, UK : In association with Safari Books (Export) ; Oxford, UK : African Books Collective Ltd. (Distributor), 1998.
*TC LC2605 .M32 1998*

### EDUCATION - AIMS AND OBJECTIVES - ENGLAND.
Black, P. J. (Paul Joseph), 1930- Testing, friend or foe? London ; Washington : Falmer Press, 1998.
*TC LB3056.E54 B53 1998*

### EDUCATION - AIMS AND OBJECTIVES - RUSSIA (FEDERATION).
Russia, education in the transition = [S.l.] : The World Bank, ECA Country Development III, Human Resources Division, 1995.
*TC LA839.2 .R87 1995*

### EDUCATION - AIMS AND OBJECTIVES - UNITED STATES.
Black, P. J. (Paul Joseph), 1930- Testing, friend or foe? London ; Washington : Falmer Press, 1998.
*TC LB3056.E54 B53 1998*

Boutwell, Clinton E. Shell game. Bloomington, Ind. : Phi Delta Kappa Educational Foundation, c1997.
*TC LC1085.2 .B68 1997*

Grote, John E. Paideia agonistes. Lanham, Md. : University Press of America, c2000.
*TC LC1011 .G76 2000*

Heath, Douglas H. Morale, culture, and character. 1st ed. Bryn Mawr, PA : Conrow Pub. House, c1999.
*TC LC311 .H43 1999*

Hirsch, E. D. (Eric Donald), 1928- The schools we need and why we don't have them. 1st Anchor Books ed. New York : Anchor Books/Doubleday, 1999.
*TC LA210 .H57 1999*

Marzano, Robert J. Essential knowledge. Aurora, Colo. : McREL, 1999.
*TC LB3060.83 .M36 1999*

Powell, Rebecca, 1949- Literacy as a moral imperative. Lanham, Md. : Rowman & Littlefield Publishers, c1999.
*TC LC151 .P69 1999*

Rediscovering the democratic purposes of education. Lawrence : University Press of Kansas, c2000.
*TC LC89 .R43 2000*

Reforming American education from the bottom to the top. Portsmouth, NH : Heinemann, c1999.
*TC LA210 .R44 1999*

Reid, Charles R. Education and evolution. Lanham, Md. ; Oxford : University Press of America, c2000.
*TC LC191.4 .R43 2000*

Schneider, Frank. Our public schools. Mobile, Ala. : Factor Press, 2000.

*TC LA217.2 .S34 2000*

**EDUCATION AND ANTHROPOLOGY.** *See* EDUCATIONAL ANTHROPOLOGY.

**EDUCATION AND BUSINESS.** *See* INDUSTRY AND EDUCATION.

**EDUCATION AND CHURCH.** *See* CHURCH AND EDUCATION.

**EDUCATION AND COMMUNISM.** *See* COMMUNISM AND EDUCATION.

### EDUCATION AND CRIME.
Cullingford, Cedric. The causes of exclusion :. London : Kogan Page ; Sterling, VA : Stylus, 1999.
*TC HV6166 .C85 1999*

### Education and emancipation.
Fletcher, Scott, 1959- New York : Teachers College Press, c2000.
*TC LC191.4 .F54 2000*

**EDUCATION AND EMPLOYMENT.** *See* LABOR SUPPLY - EFFECT OF EDUCATION ON.

### Education and evolution.
Reid, Charles R. Lanham, Md. ; Oxford : University Press of America, c2000.
*TC LC191.4 .R43 2000*

**EDUCATION AND FEMINISM.** *See* FEMINISM AND EDUCATION.

**EDUCATION AND HIGH TECHNOLOGY.** *See* HIGH TECHNOLOGY AND EDUCATION.

**EDUCATION AND HOMOSEXUALITY.** *See* HOMOSEXUALITY AND EDUCATION.

### Education and independence.
Hlatshwayo, Simphiwe A. (Simphiwe Abner) Westport, Conn : Greenwood Press, 2000.
*TC LA1536 .H53 2000*

**EDUCATION AND INDUSTRY.** *See* INDUSTRY AND EDUCATION.

**EDUCATION AND LIBRARIES.** *See* LIBRARIES AND EDUCATION.

**EDUCATION AND NATIONALISM.** *See* NATIONALISM AND EDUCATION.

**EDUCATION AND POLITICS.** *See* POLITICS AND EDUCATION.

### Education and psychology in interaction.
Norwich, Brahm. London ; New York : Routledge, 2000.
*TC LB1051 .N645 2000*

### Education and racism : : a cross national inventory of positive effects of education on ethnic tolerance /
edited by Louk Hagendoorn and Shervin Nekuee. Aldershot ; Brookfield, Vt. : Ashgate, c1999. xiv, 217 p. : ill. ; 23 cm. (Research in migration and ethnic relations series.) Includes bibliographies and index. ISBN 0-7546-1141-8
*1. Racism. 2. Multicultural education. 3. Discrimination in education. I. Nekuee, Shervin. II. Hagendoorn, Louk. 1945- III. Series. IV. Series: Research in migration and ethnic relations series.*
*TC LC212.3.G7E48 1999*

### Education and Skills
Centre for Educational Research and Innovation. Knowledge management in the learning society. Paris : Organisation for Economic Co-operation and Development, 2000.
*TC HD30.2 .C462 2000*

### Education and skills
Investing in education. Paris : Organisation for Economic Co-operation and Development; Paris : UNESCO, 2000.
*TC LB2846 .I68 2000*

Motivating students for lifelong learning. Paris : Organisation for Economic Co-operation and Development, c2000.
*TC LB1065 .M669 2000*

Organisation for Economic Co-operation and Development (Paris) From initial education to working life. Paris : Organisation for Economic Co-operation and Development, 2000.
*TC LC1037 .O74 2000*

### Education and Skills
Organisation for Economic Co-operation and Development (Paris) Measuring student knowledge and skills. Paris : Organisation for Economic Co-operation and Development, 2000.
*TC LB3051 .M44 2000*

### Education and social renewal in London's Docklands.
Eastern promise. London : Lawrence and Wishart, 2000.
*TC LC238.4.G73 L66 2000*

**EDUCATION AND SOCIOLOGY.** *See* EDUCATIONAL SOCIOLOGY.

### EDUCATION AND STATE. *See also* ART AND STATE; ART COMMISSIONS; COMMUNITY AND SCHOOL; ENDOWMENTS; HIGHER EDUCATION AND STATE; POLITICS AND EDUCATION.
Accuracy or advocacy. Thousand Oaks, Calif. : Corwin Press, c1999.
*TC LB1028 .A312 1999*

Brighouse, Harry. School choice and social justice. Oxford ; New York : Oxford University Press, 2000.
*TC LB1027.9 .B75 2000*

Combating educational disadvantage. London ; New York : Falmer Press, 2000.
*TC LC4065 .C66 1999*

Education policy. Cheltenham, UK : Northampton, MA : Edward Elgar Pub., c1999.
*TC LC71 .E32 1999*

Globalization and education. New York : Routledge, 1999.
*TC LC191 .G545 1999*

Levinson, Meira. The demands of liberal education. Oxford ; New York : Oxford University Press, 1999.
*TC LC1091 .L38 1999*

Nelson, Joan M. Reforming health and education. Washington, DC : Overseas Development Council ; Baltimore, MD : Distributed by the Johns Hopkins University Press, c1999.
*TC HG3881.5.W57 N447 1999*

Porter, James. Reschooling and the global future. Wallingford, U.K. : Symposium Books ; c1999.
*TC LB1029.G55 P67 1999*

Processes of transition in education systems. Wallingford : Symposium, 1998.
*TC LC71 .P7 1998*

The role of measurement and evaluation in education policy. Paris : Unesco Pub., 1999.
*TC LB3051 .R653 1999*

Tooley, James. Reclaiming education. London ; New York : Cassell, 2000.
*TC LC71 .T65 2000*

### EDUCATION AND STATE - AFRICA - HISTORY - 20TH CENTURY.
Sivonen, Seppo. White-collar or hoe handle. Helsinki : Suomen Historiallinen Seura, [1995]
*TC LA1531 .S58 1995*

### EDUCATION AND STATE - ASIA, SOUTHEASTERN - CASE STUDIES.
Ramesh, M., 1960- Welfare capitalism in southeast Asia. New York : St. Martin's Press, c2000.
*TC HN690.8.A8 R35 2000*

### EDUCATION AND STATE - CAMBODIA - HISTORY - 20TH CENTURY.
Ayres, David M., 1971- Anatomy of a crisis. Honolulu : University of Hawai'i Press, c2000.
*TC LC94.C16 A971 2000*

### EDUCATION AND STATE - CASE STUDIES.
Inclusive education at work. Paris : Organisation for Economic Co-operation and Development, 1999.
*TC LC4015 .I525 1999*

### EDUCATION AND STATE - COLORADO.
Clay, Cheryl D., 1947- Schooling at-risk Native American children. New York : Garland Pub., 1998.
*TC E99.U8 C53 1998*

### EDUCATION AND STATE - COMMONWEALTH COUNTRIES.
Crossley, Michael Educational development in the small states of the Commonwealth. London : Commonwealth Secretariat, c1999.
*TC LC71 .C74 1999*

### EDUCATION AND STATE - CONNECTICUT - NEW HAVEN METROPOLITAN AREA - CASE STUDIES.
McDermott, Kathryn A., 1969- Controlling public education. Lawrence : University Press of Kansas, c1999.
*TC LC213.23.N39 M34 1999*

### EDUCATION AND STATE - CROSS-CULTURAL STUDIES.

Educational knowledge. Albany : State University of New York Press, c2000.
*TC LC71 .L335 2000*

**EDUCATION AND STATE - DEVELOPING COUNTRIES.**
Gender, education, and development. London ; New York : Zed Books : New York : Distributed in USA exclusively by St. Martin's Press, c1999.
*TC LC2607 .G46 1998*

**EDUCATION AND STATE - DEVELOPING COUNTRIES - CASE STUDIES.**
Tooley, James. The global education industry. London : Institute of Economic Affairs ; Washington, DC : International Finance Corporation, World Bank, 1999.
*TC LC57.5 .T667 1999*

**EDUCATION AND STATE - ENGLAND.**
New labour's policies for schools. London : David Fulton Publishers, c2000.
*TC LC93.G7 N59 2000*

**EDUCATION AND STATE - ENGLAND - HISTORY - 19TH CENTURY.**
Phillips, Francis R. Creating an education system for England and Wales. Lewiston, N.Y. : E. Mellen Press, 1992.
*TC LA633 .P48 1992*

**EDUCATION AND STATE - ENGLAND - LONDON - CASE STUDIES.**
Gillborn, David. Rationing education. Buckingham [England] ; Philadelphia : Open University Press, 2000.
*TC LC213.3.G73 L664 2000*

**EDUCATION AND STATE - EUROPEAN UNION COUNTRIES.**
Snick, Anne. Women in educational [sic] policy-making. Leuven, Belgium : Leuven University Press, 1999.
*TC LC93.A2 S56 1999*

**EDUCATION AND STATE - GREAT BRITAIN.**
Ainley, Patrick. Learning policy. Basingstoke, Hampshire : Macmillan Press ; New York : St. Martin's Press, 1999.
*TC LC93.G7 A76 1999*

Beveridge, Sally. Special educational needs in schools. 2nd ed. London ; New York : Routledge, 1999.
*TC LC3986.G7 B48 1999*

Bottery, Mike. Teachers and the state. London ; New York : Routledge, c2000.
*TC LB1775.4.G7 B68 2000*

Hayton, Annette. Tackling disaffection and social exclusion. London : Kogan Page, 1999.
*TC LC93.G7 H39 1999*

Reid, Ken. Truancy and schools. London ; New York : Routledge, 1999.
*TC LB3081 .R45 1999*

State schools. London ; Portland, OR : Woburn Press, 1999.
*TC LC93.G7 S73 1999*

Teacher professionalism and the challenge of change. Stoke-on-Trent, Staffordshire, England : Trentham Books, 1999.
*TC LB1775.4.G7 T43 1999*

Tooley, James. Reclaiming education. London ; New York : Cassell, 2000.
*TC LC71 .T65 2000*

Vernon, Jeni. Maintaining children in school. London : National Children's Bureau Enterprises, c1998.
*TC LB3081 .V47 1998*

**EDUCATION AND STATE - INDIA.**
The Great Indian education debate. Richmond : Curzon, 1999.
*TC LA1151 .G743 1999*

**EDUCATION AND STATE - IRELAND - HISTORY - 20TH CENTURY.**
O'Donoghue, T. A. (Tom A.), 1953- The Catholic Church and the secondary school curriculum in Ireland, 1922-1962. New York : P. Lang, c1999.
*TC LC506.G72 I745 1999*

**EDUCATION AND STATE - ISRAEL.**
Swirski, Shlomo. Politics and education in Israel. New York : Falmer Press, 1999.
*TC LC94.I75 S95 1999*

**EDUCATION AND STATE - JAPAN - HISTORY - 20TH CENTURY.**

Japanese education since 1945. Armonk, N.Y. : M.E. Sharpe, c1994.
*TC LA1311.82 .J39 1994*

**EDUCATION AND STATE - NEW YORK (STATE) - PERIODICALS.**
[Inside education (Albany, N.Y.)] Inside education. Albany : New York State Education Dept., 1968-1983.

[Inside education (Albany, N.Y. : 1991)] Inside education. Albany, N.Y. : University of the State of New York, State Education Dept., 1991-

**EDUCATION AND STATE - NEW ZEALAND - CASE STUDIES.**
Fiske, Edward B. When schools compete. Washington, D.C. : Brookings Institution Press, c2000.
*TC LB2822.84.N45 F58 2000*

**EDUCATION AND STATE - PAKISTAN.**
Education and the state. Karachi : Oxford University Press, 1998.
*TC LA1156 .E36 1998*

**EDUCATION AND STATE - RESEARCH - GREAT BRITAIN - METHODOLOGY.**
Ozga, Jennifer. Policy research in educational settings :. Buckingham [England] ; Philadelphia : Open University Press, 2000.
*TC LB1028.25.G7 O93 2000*

**EDUCATION AND STATE - RUSSIA (FEDERATION).**
Webber, Stephen L., 1967- School, reform and society in the new Russia . Houndmills [England] : Macmillan Press ; New York : St. Martin's Press in association with Centre for Russian and East European Studies, University of Birmingham, 2000.
*TC LA839.2 .W4 2000*

**EDUCATION AND STATE - SCOTLAND.**
Scottish education. Edinburgh : Edinburgh University Press, c1999.
*TC LA652 .S34 1999*

**EDUCATION AND STATE - SOVIET UNION.**
Tokar, Inna. Schools for the mathematically talented in the former Soviet Union. 1999.
*TC 085 T572*

**EDUCATION AND STATE - UGANDA - CASE STUDIES.**
Paige, John Rhodes. Preserving order amid chaos. New York : Berghahn Books, 2000.
*TC LA1567 .P25 2000*

**EDUCATION AND STATE - UNITED STATES.**
Balancing local control and state responsibility for K-12 education. Larchmont, NY : Eye on Education, 2000.
*TC LC89 .B35 2000*

Educating Americans for tomorrow's world. [Washington D.C.] : NGA, [1987]
*TC LC1099 .E225 1987*

Educational leadership. Stamford, Conn. : Ablex Pub. Corp., c2000.
*TC LB2805 .E3475 2000*

Elliott, Judy L. Improving test performance of students with disabilities-- on district and state assessments. Thousands Oaks, Calif. : Corwin Press, c2000.
*TC LB3051 .E48 2000*

Gallagher, Karen S. Shaping school policy. Newbury Park, Calif. : Corwin Press, c1992.
*TC LC89 .G35 1992*

Grossman, Herbert, 1934- Achieving educational equality. Springfield, Ill. : C.C. Thomas, c1998.
*TC LC213.2 .G76 1998*

In defense of good teaching. York, Me. : Stenhouse Publishers, c1998.
*TC LB1050.35 .I5 1998*

Mintrom, Michael, 1963- Policy entrepreneurs and school choice. Washington, DC : Georgetown University Press, c2000.
*TC LB1027.9 .M57 2000*

Morken, Hubert. The politics of school choice. Lanham, Md. : Rowman & Littlefield Publishers, c1999.
*TC LB1027.9 .M68 1999*

National Research Council (U.S.). Committee on Embedding Common Test Items in State and District Assessments. Embedding questions. Washington, DC : National Academy Press, c1999.

*TC LB3051 .N319 1999*

New school order [videorecording]. New York : First Run/Icarus Films, 1996.
*TC LB2831.583.P4 N4 1996*

School choice and social controversy. Washington, D.C. : Brookings Institution Press, c1999.
*TC LB1027.9 .S352 1999*

Wong, Kenneth K., 1955- Funding public schools. Lawrence : University Press of Kansas, c1999.
*TC LB2825 .W56 1999*

**EDUCATION AND STATE - UNITED STATES - CASE STUDIES.**
Hill, Paul Thomas, 1943- It takes a city. Washington, D.C. : Brookings Institution Press, c2000.
*TC LC5131 .H48 2000*

**EDUCATION AND STATE - UNITED STATES - CONGRESSES.**
Brookings papers on education policy, 2000. Washington, D.C. : Brookings Institution Press, c2000.
*TC LC89 .B7472 2000*

**EDUCATION AND STATE - UNITED STATES - HISTORY - 1945-1953.**
Foster, Stuart J., 1960- Red alert!. New York ; Canterbury [England] : P. Lang, c2000.
*TC LC72.2 .F67 2000*

**EDUCATION AND STATE - UNITED STATES - STATES.**
Mitchell, Bruce M. Multicultural education in the U.S.. Westport, Conn. ; London : Greenwood Press, 2000.
*TC LC1099.3 .M59 2000*

**Education and the soul.**
Miller, John P., 1943- Albany : State University of New York Press, c2000.
*TC LC268 .M52 2000*

**Education and the state :** fifty years of Pakistan / edited by Pervez Hoodbhoy. Karachi : Oxford University Press, 1998. 349 p. : ill. ; 22 cm. Includes bibliographical references and index. ISBN 0-19-577825-1 DDC 379.5491
*1. Education - Pakistan. 2. Education and state - Pakistan. I. Hoodbhoy, Pervez.*
*TC LA1156 .E36 1998*

**Education and welfare reform.**
Baldwin, John. Bloomington, Ind. : Phi Delta Kappa Educational Foundation, c1993.
*TC LC4033.S61 B34 1993*

**Education and World Affairs.**
Intercultural education. New York, International Council for Educational Development.

**EDUCATION, ART.** *See* **ART - STUDY AND TEACHING.**

**Education as a humanitarian response** / edited by Gonzalo Retamal and Ruth Aedo-Richmond. London ; Herndon, VA : Cassell : [s.l.] : UNESCO International Bureau of Education, 1998. xxvii, 371 p. : ill., maps ; 25 cm. (Frontiers of international education) Includes bibliographical references and index. ISBN 0-304-70193-9
*1. Refugees - Education. 2. Humanitarian assistance. 3. War and education. I. Retamal, Gonzalo. II. Aedo-Richmond, Ruth. III. Series.*
*TC LC3719 .E37 1998*

**Education as the cultivation of intelligence.**
Martinez, Michael E. Mahwah, N.J. ; London : Lawrence Erlbaum Associates, 2000.
*TC LB1060 .M337 2000*

**Education at a glance** [computer file] : OECD database. Ottawa, Ont. : Ivation Datasystems Inc. ; Paris, France : OECD, : 1 computer optical disc : col. ; 4 3/4 in. + user manual (19 p. ; 13 cm.). Frequency: Irregular. Title from disc surface. System requirement: minimum of a PC 386 with 4 MB RAM and 10 Mbytes of free disk space ; runs on Windows (3.1, 95, NT). Description based on: 1999 Numeric data Mode of access: web browser (Microsoft Internet Explorer included on disc) and "Beyond 20/20," a statistical data viewer installed from the disc. SUMMARY: Provides access to a unique set of comparative statistics and indicators on educational systems and policies in OECD countries.
*1. Educational indicators - Cross-cultural studies - Databases - periodicals. 2. Education - Evaluation - Statistics - Cross-cultural studies - Databases - Periodicals. I. Organisation for Economic Co-operation and Development. II. Ivation Datasystems. III. Title: OECD database [computer file] IV. Title: OECD education indicators [computer file] V. Title: OECD education database [computer file] VI. Title: OECD indicators [computer file]*
*TC LB2846 .E2473*

**EDUCATION - AUSTRALIA.**
Australian education. Camberwell, Vic. : Australian Council for Educational Research, 1998.
*TC LA2102.7 .A87 1998*

**EDUCATION - AUSTRALIA - ADDRESSES, ESSAYS, LECTURES.**
Bourke, S. F. The mastery of literacy and numeracy. Canberra : Australian Govt. Pub. Service, 1977.
*TC LA2102 .B68 1977*

**EDUCATION - AUSTRALIA - EVALUATION.**
Literacy and numeracy in Australian schools. Canberra : Australian Gov. Pub. Service, 1976-
*TC LA2102 .L57 1976*

**EDUCATION - AUSTRALIA - HISTORY.**
Dunt, Lesley, 1944- Speaking worlds. Parkville, Vic. : History Department, The University of Melbourne, c1993.
*TC LA2101 .D96 1993*

**EDUCATION - BIBLIOGRAPHY.**
El-Hi textbooks in print. New York, N.Y. : Bowker, 1970-
*TC Z5813 .A51*

O'Brien, Nancy P. Education, a guide to reference and information sources. 2nd ed. Englewood, Colo. : Libraries Unlimited, 2000.
*TC Z5811 .B89 2000*

**EDUCATION - BIBLIOGRAPHY - PERIODICALS.**
Resources in education. Semiannual index. Phoenix, AZ : Oryx Press,
*TC Z5813 .R42*

**EDUCATION, BILINGUAL.** *See also* **MULTICULTURAL EDUCATION.**
Literacy assessment of second language learners. Boston ; London : Allyn and Bacon, c2001.
*TC P53.4 .L58 2001*

**EDUCATION, BILINGUAL - ASIA - CONGRESSES.**
Bilingualism Through the Classroom : Strategies and Practices (1995 : Universiti Brunei Darussalam) Bilingualism through the classroom : strategies and practices. [Bandar Seri Begawan : Universiti Brunei Darussalam, 1995]
*TC P115 .B57 1995*

**EDUCATION, BILINGUAL - CALIFORNIA - CASE STUDIES.**
Samway, Katharine Davies. Buddy reading. Portsmouth, NH : Heinemann, c1995.
*TC LB1031.5 .S36 1995*

**EDUCATION, BILINGUAL - CONGRESSES.**
Bilingualism Through the Classroom : Strategies and Practices (1995 : Universiti Brunei Darussalam) Bilingualism through the classroom : strategies and practices. [Bandar Seri Begawan : Universiti Brunei Darussalam, 1995]
*TC P115 .B57 1995*

**EDUCATION, BILINGUAL - CROSS-CULTURAL STUDIES.**
BLACKLEDGE, ADRIAN. Literacy, power and social justice. Stoke on Trent, Staffordshire, England : Trentham Books, 2000.
*TC LC149 .B53 2000*

**EDUCATION, BILINGUAL - GREAT BRITAIN.**
Thompson, Linda, 1949- Young bilingual children in nursery school. Clevedon, UK ; Buffalo, NY : Multilingual Matters, c2000.
*TC LC3723 .T47 2000*

**EDUCATION, BILINGUAL - GREAT BRITAIN - CASE STUDIES.**
Moore, Alex, 1947- Teaching multicultured students. London ; New York : Falmer Press, 1999.
*TC LC3736.G6 M66 1999*

Woods, Peter, 1934- Multicultural children in the early years. Clevedon ; Philadelphia : Multilingual Matters Ltd, c1999.
*TC LC3736.G6 W66 1999*

**EDUCATION, BILINGUAL - NEW YORK (STATE) - CASE STUDIES.**
Schmidt, Patricia Ruggiano, 1944- Cultural conflict and struggle. New York : P. Lang, c1998.
*TC LB1181 .S36 1998*

**EDUCATION, BILINGUAL - SOCIAL ASPECTS.**
Cummins, Jim, 1949- Language, power, and pedagogy. Clevedon [England] ; Buffalo [N.Y.] : Multilingual Matters, c2000.
*TC LC3719 .C86 2000*

**EDUCATION, BILINGUAL - SOCIAL ASPECTS - UNITED STATES - CASE STUDIES.**
Freeman, Rebecca D. (Rebecca Diane), 1960- Bilingual education and social change. Clevedon [England] ; Philadelphia : Multilingual Matters, c1998.
*TC LC3731 .F72 1998*

**EDUCATION, BILINGUAL - TEXAS - CRYSTAL CITY.**
Trujillo, Armando L. Chicano empowerment and bilingual education. New York : Garland Pub., c1998.
*TC LC2688.C79 T78 1998*

**EDUCATION, BILINGUAL - UNITED STATES.**
Brisk, Maria. Literacy and bilingualism. Mahwah, N.J. : L. Erlbaum Associates, c2000.
*TC LC3731 .B684 2000*

Educating Latino students. Lancaster, Pa. : Technomic Pub. Co., c1998.
*TC LC2669 .E37 1998*

The politics of multiculturalism and bilingual education. Boston : McGraw-Hill, c2000.
*TC LC1099.3 .P64 2000*

So much to say. New York : Teachers College Press, c1999.
*TC PE1128.A2 S599 1999*

The sociopolitics of English language teaching. Clevedon ; Buffalo [N.Y.] : Multilingual Matters, c2000.
*TC PE1128.A2 S5994 2000*

The teaching of reading in Spanish to the bilingual student = 2nd ed. Mahwah, N.J. : L. Erlbaum Associates, 1998.
*TC LB1573 .T365 1998*

Toohey, Kelleen, 1950- Learning English at school. Clevedon, [England] ; Buffalo : Multilingual Matters, 2000.
*TC PE1128.A2 T63 2000*

**EDUCATION, BILINGUAL - UNITED STATES - CASE STUDIES.**
Ballenger, Cynthia. Teaching other people's children. New York : Teachers College Press, c1999.
*TC LC3746 .B336 1999*

Paratore, Jeanne R. What should we expect of family literacy? Newark, Del. : International Reading Association ; Chicago , Ill. : National Reading Conference. c1999.
*TC LC151 .P37 1999*

**EDUCATION, BILINGUAL - UNITED STATES - EVALUATION.**
Educating language-minority children. New Brunswick (U.S.A.) : Transaction Publishers, c2000.
*TC LC3731 .E374 2000*

**EDUCATION - BIOGRAPHICAL METHODS.**
Dominicé, Pierre. Learning from our lives. 1st ed. San Francisco : Jossey-Bass, c2000.
*TC LB1029.B55 D64 2000*

**EDUCATION - BRITISH COLUMBIA - PERIODICALS.**
Education bulletin of the Faculty and College of Education: Vancouver : University of British Columbia.

**Education bulletin of the Faculty and College of Education:** Vancouver and Victoria. Vancouver : University of British Columbia. 2 no. 24 cm. No. 1 (Mar. 1957)-no. 2 (Mar. 1958). Includes bibliographical references. Includes some text in French. Available in other form:. Education bulletin of the Faculty of Education Vancouver ISSN: 0315-4963. Continued by: Journal of education of the Faculty and College of Education, Vancouver and Victoria ISSN: 0068-1768. ISSN 0315-4963
*1. Education - British Columbia - Periodicals. 2. Teaching - British Columbia - Periodicals. 3. University of British Columbia. - Faculty and College of Education - Periodicals. I. University of British Columbia. Faculty and College of Education. II. Title: Education bulletin of the Faculty of Education Vancouver III. Title: Journal of education of the Faculty and College of Education, Vancouver and Victoria*

**Education bulletin of the Faculty of Education Vancouver.**
Education bulletin of the Faculty and College of Education: Vancouver : University of British Columbia.

**EDUCATION, BUSINESS.** *See* **BUSINESS EDUCATION.**

**EDUCATION - CALIFORNIA - PERIODICALS.**
California education. [Sacramento : California State Dept. of Education, 1963-1966]

California education. [Sacramento : California State Dept. of Education, 1963-1966]

California education. [Sacramento : California State Dept. of Education, 1963-1966]

California review of adult education. [Los Angeles : California State Dept. of Education, 1936.

**EDUCATION - CANADA - CURRICULA.**
Drake, Susan M., 1944- Creating integrated curriculum. Thousand Oaks, Calif. : Corwin Press, c1998.
*TC LB1570 .D695 1998*

**EDUCATION - CASE STUDIES.**
Improving education. London ; New York : Cassell, 1999.
*TC LB7 .I48 1999*

**EDUCATION CHANGE.** *See* **EDUCATIONAL CHANGE.**

**EDUCATION, CHARACTER.** *See* **MORAL EDUCATION.**

**EDUCATION - CHINA - HISTORY - 20TH CENTURY.**
Reynolds, Barbara G. Reform and education. 1999.
*TC 06 no. 11166*

**EDUCATION - CHINA - PHILOSOPHY - HISTORY - 20TH CENTURY.**
Reynolds, Barbara G. Reform and education. 1999.
*TC 06 no. 11166*

**EDUCATION, CHRISTIAN.** *See* **CHRISTIAN EDUCATION.**

**EDUCATION, CLASSICAL.** *See* **CLASSICAL EDUCATION.**

**EDUCATION, COLLECTIVE.** *See* **COLLECTIVE EDUCATION.**

**Education Committees' year book 1939-1978.**
Education year book. [London, England] : Councils and Education Press, 1979-
*TC L915 .E4*

**EDUCATION, COMPARATIVE.** *See* **COMPARATIVE EDUCATION.**

**EDUCATION, COMPENSATORY.** *See* **COMPENSATORY EDUCATION.**

**EDUCATION, COMPULSORY.** *See* **EDUCATIONAL LAW AND LEGISLATION; EVENING AND CONTINUATION SCHOOLS.**

**EDUCATION, COMPULSORY - LAW AND LEGISLATION.** *See* **EDUCATIONAL LAW AND LEGISLATION.**

**Education** [computer file]: the complete encyclopedia / Torsten Husén... [et al.]. Version 1.1. [Oxford, Eng.] : Pergamon, c1998. Computer program. 1 computer optical disc : col. ; 4 3/4 in. System requirements: PC version: 80486 processor; pentium preferred; 16Mb RAM; VGA or SVGA monitor (+256 colors or more); Windows 3.1; Windows 95 preferred; dual speed CD-ROM drive ; 15Mb free hard-disk space (to run 32 bit software under Windows 3.1) ; 4Mb free hard-disk space (running under Windows 95). System requirements: Macintosh version: Motorola 68040 processor or above ; 16 Mb RAM ; color monitor (+256 colors or more) ; system 7.0 or above ; dual-speed CD-ROM drive ; 4Mb free hard-disk space. SUMMARY: Combines the full text of the International Encyclopedia of Education (2nd edition) and the Encyclopedia of Higher Education. Uses the full range of CD-ROM functions to locate terms across the entire data set of both encyclopedias; provides full range indexes for subject, title, theme, contributor's names, cited authors: in full text, global and detailed search, reference linked to ERIC abstracts, and search save.
*1. Education. Higher - Encyclopedias - Software. 2. Education - Encyclopedias - Software. I. Husén, Torsten, 1916- II. Title: The international encyclopedia of education. 1994. III. Title: The encyclopedia of higher education. 1992. IV. Title: Complete encyclopedia [computer file]*
*TC LB15 .E3 1998*

**EDUCATION - COMPUTER NETWOEK RESOURCES.**
Driscoll, Margaret M. The application of adult education principles in the development of a manual for practitioners creating web-based training programs. 1999.
*TC 06 no. 11106*

**EDUCATION - COMPUTER NETWORK RESOURCES.**
Barron, Ann E. The Internet and instruction. 2nd ed. Englewood, Colo. : Libraries Unlimited, 1998.
*TC LB1044.87 .B37 1998*

Joseph, Linda C., 1949- Net curriculum. Medford, N.J. : CyberAge Books, c1999.
*TC LB1044.87 .J67 1999*

Kouki, Rafa. Telelearning via the Internet. Hershey, PA : Idea Group Pub., c1999.
*TC LC5800 .K68 1999*

Net-working. Dunedin, N.Z. : University of Otago Press, 1999.
*TC LB1044.87 .N47 1999*

Web-based learning and teaching technologies. Hershey, PA : London : Idea Group Pub., c2000.
*TC LB1044.87 .W435 2000*

Williams, Bard. The Internet for teachers. 3rd ed. Foster City, CA : IDG Books Worldwide, c1999.
*TC LB1044.87 .W55 1999*

### EDUCATION - COMPUTER NETWORK RESOURCES - DIRECTORIES.
Bigham, Vicki Smith. The Prentice Hall directory of online education resources. Paramus, N.J. : Prentice Hall, c1998.
*TC LB1044.87 .B54 1998*

The School administrator's handbook of essential Internet sites. Fourth ed. Gaithersburg, MD : Aspen Publishers.
*TC TK5105.875.I57 S3 2000*

Sharp, Richard M. The best Web sites for teachers. 3rd ed. Eugene, OR : International Society for Technology in Education, 2000.
*TC LB1044.87 .S52 2000*

### EDUCATION - COMPUTER PROGRAMS.
Brownell, Gregg. A PC for the teacher. Belmont, CA : Wadsworth Pub. Co., c1999.
*TC LB1028.43 .B755 1999*

### EDUCATION - CONGRESSES - HANDBOOKS, MANUALS, ETC.
Designing successful professional meetings and conferences in education. Thousand Oaks, Calif. : Corwin Press, c2000.
*TC LC6519 .D48 2000*

### EDUCATION - CONNECTICUT.
Connecticut. Board of Education. Connecticut schools ... [Hartford.], Connecticut Board of Education.

Connecticut teacher. Hartford, Conn. : The Association, [1933-

### EDUCATION - CONNECTICUT - PERIODICALS.
Connecticut teacher. Hartford, Conn. : The Association, [1933-

### EDUCATION, COOPERATIVE. *See* COLLEGE STUDENTS - EMPLOYMENT; SCHOOL-TO-WORK TRANSITION.

### EDUCATION - CUBA - PERIODICALS.
Cuba. Secretaría de Instrucción Pública y Bellas Artes. La Instrucción primaria; Havana.

**Education, culture, and values**
(v. 1) Systems of education. London ; New York : Falmer Press, 2000.
*TC LC191 .S98 2000*

(v. 2) Institutional issues. London ; New York : Falmer Press, 2000.
*TC LC191 .I495 2000*

(v. 3) Classroom issues. London ; New York : Falmer Press, 2000.
*TC LC268 .C52 2000*

(v. 4) Moral education and pluralism. London ; New York : Falmer Press, 2000.
*TC LC268 .M683 2000*

(v. 5) Spiritual and religious education. London ; New York : Falmer Press, 2000.
*TC BL42 .S68 2000*

(v. 6) Politics, education and citizenship. London ; New York : Falmer Press, 2000.
*TC LC1091 .P54 2000*

**Education, cultures, and economics :** dilemmas for development / edited by Fiona E. Leach, Angela W. Little. New York : Falmer Press, 1999. xv, 403 p. : ill. ; 23 cm. (Garland reference library of social science ; vol. 1152. Reference books in international education ; vol. 48) Includes bibliographical references and index. ISBN 0-8153-2783-8 (alk. paper) DDC 306.43/09172/4
*1. Educational sociology - Developing countries - Cross-cultural studies. 2. Education - Economic aspects - Developing countries - Cross-cultural studies. I. Leach, Fiona E. II. Little, Angela. III. Series: Garland reference library of social science ; v. 1152. IV. Series: Garland reference library of*

social science. Reference books in international education ; vol. 48.
*TC LC191.8.D44 E38 1999*

### EDUCATION - CURRICULA. *See also* ARTICULATION (EDUCATION); CURRICULUM CHANGE; CURRICULUM PLANNING; DISABILITY STUDIES; GAY AND LESBIAN STUDIES; LESSON PLANNING; SCHEDULES, SCHOOL; TEACHER PARTICIPATION IN CURRICULUM PLANNING; WOMEN'S STUDIES.
General education in school and college. Cambridge : Harvard University Press, 1952.
*TC 372G28*

Miller, John P., 1943- Education and the soul. Albany : State University of New York Press, c2000.
*TC LC268 .M52 2000*

### EDUCATION - CURRICULA - BIBLIOGRAPHY.
Interdisciplinary education. New York, NY : College Entrance Examination Board, 1999.
*TC LB2361 .I58 1999*

### EDUCATION - CURRICULA - COMPUTER NETWORK RESOURCES.
Provenzo, Eugene F. The Internet and the World Wide Web for preservice teachers. Boston : Allyn & Bacon, c1999.
*TC LB1044.87 .P763 1999*

Schweizer, Heidi. Designing and teaching an on-line course :. Boston : Allyn & Bacon, c1999.
*TC LB1028.3 .S377 1999*

### EDUCATION - CURRICULA - PERIODICALS.
Building America. [New York : Published for the Dept. of Supervision and Curriculum Development by the Society for Curriculum Study, Inc. ; distributed by Americana Corporation, 1935-

CAS. Chicago : Curriculum Advisory Service, 1969-1974.

### EDUCATION - CURRICULA - PHILOSOPHY.
Foshay, Arthur Wellesley, 1912- The curriculum. New York ; London : Teachers College Press, c2000.
*TC LB2806.15 .F66 2000*

### EDUCATION - CURRICULA - POLITICAL ASPECTS - CROSS-CULTURAL STUDIES.
Curriculum politics, policy, practice. Albany : State University of New York Press, c2000.
*TC LC71.3 .C87 2000*

### EDUCATION - CURRICULA - SOCIAL ASPECTS - GREAT BRITAIN.
Ross, Alistair, 1946- Curriculum. London ; New York : Falmer Press, 2000.
*TC LB1564.G7 R66 2000*

### EDUCATION - CURRICULA - SOCIAL ASPECTS - UNITED STATES.
Cultures of curriculum. Mahwah, N.J. ; London : L. Erlbaum Associates, 2000.
*TC LB2806.15 .C73 2000*

### EDUCATION - CURRICULUM - PHILOSOPHY.
Doll, Mary Aswell. Like letters in running water. Mahwah, N.J. ; London : L. Erlbaum Publishers, 2000.
*TC LB1575 .D64 2000*

### EDUCATION - DATA PROCESSING. *See also* COMPUTER-ASSISTED INSTRUCTION.
Armstrong, Alison, 1955- The child and the machine. Beltsville, Md. : Robins Lane Press, c2000.
*TC LB1028.43 .A76 2000*

Armstrong, Alison, 1955- The child and the machine. Toronto, Ont. : Key Porter Books, c1998.
*TC LB1028.43 .A75 1998*

Brownell, Gregg. A PC for the teacher. Belmont, CA : Wadsworth Pub. Co., c1999.
*TC LB1028.43 .B755 1999*

DiSessa, Andrea A. Changing minds. Cambridge, MA : MIT Press, c2000.
*TC LB1028.43 .D57 2000*

Geisert, Paul. Teachers, computers, and curriculum. 3rd ed. Boston : Allyn and Bacon, c2000.
*TC LB1028.5 .G42 2000*

Kahn, Jessica L. Ideas and strategies for the one-computer classroom. Eugene, OR : International Society for Technology in Education, c1998.
*TC LB1028.5 .K25 1998*

McConnell, David, 1951- Implementing computer supported cooperative learning.. 2nd ed. London : Kogan Page, 2000.

*TC LB1032 .M38 2000*
Race, Philip. 500 computing tips for teachers and lecturers. 2nd ed. London : Kogan Page ; Sterling, VA : Stylus Pub., 1999.
*TC LB1028.43 .R33 1999*

Sharp, Vicki F. Computer education for teachers. 3rd ed. Boston, Mass. : McGraw-Hill College, c1999.
*TC LB1028.43 .S55 1999*

### EDUCATION - DATA PROCESSING - FINANCE.
Bauer, David G. Technology funding for schools. 1st ed. San Francisco : Jossey-Bass, c2000.
*TC LB1028.43 .B38 2000*

### EDUCATION - DATA PROCESSING - STUDY AND TEACHING (HIGHER).
Forcier, Richard C. The computer as an educational tool. 2nd ed. Upper Saddle River, N.J. : Merrill, c1999.
*TC LB1028.43 .F67 1999*

### EDUCATION - DEMOGRAPHIC ASPECTS. *See* SCHOOL ENROLLMENT.

### EDUCATION - DEVELOPING COUNTRIES.
Gender, education, and development. London ; New York : Zed Books ; New York : Distributed in USA exclusively by St. Martin's Press, c1999.
*TC LC2607 .G46 1998*

World Bank. Human Development Network. Education sector strategy. Washington, D.C. : World Bank Group, c1999.
*TC LC2607 .W66 1999*

### EDUCATION - DEVELOPING COUNTRIES - CROSS CULTURAL STUDIES.
Third World education. New York : Garland Pub., 2000.
*TC LC2607 .T55 2000*

### EDUCATION - DEVELOPING COUNTRIES - FINANCE.
Patrinos, Harry Anthony. Decentralization of education. Washington, D.C. : World Bank, c1997.
*TC LB2826.6.D44 P38 1997*

### EDUCATION - ECONOMIC ASPECTS. *See also* EDUCATION - FINANCE.
Education policy. Cheltenham, UK : Northampton, MA : Edward Elgar Pub., c1999.
*TC LC71 .E32 1999*

Globalization and education. New York : Routledge, 1999.
*TC LC191 .G545 1999*

Investing in education. Paris : Organisation for Economic Co-operation and Development; Paris : UNESCO, 2000.
*TC LB2846 .I68 2000*

Majasan, James. Qualitative education and development. Ibadan : Spectrum Books Limited : Channel Islands, UK : In association with Safari Books (Export) : Oxford, UK : African Books Collective Ltd. (Distributor), 1998.
*TC LC2605 .M32 1998*

Organisation for Economic Co-operation and Development (Paris) The appraisal of investments in educational facilities. Paris : Organisation for Economic Co-operation and Development, 2000.
*TC LB2342.3 .A7 2000*

O'Sullivan, Edmund, 1938- Transformative learning. London ; New York : Zed Books ; New York : Distributed in USA exclusively by St. Martin's Press, 1999.
*TC LC196 .O7 1999*

### EDUCATION - ECONOMIC ASPECTS - AFRICA, SUB-SAHARAN.
Brock-Utne, Birgit, 1938- Whose education for all? New York ; London : Falmer Press, 2000.
*TC LC67.A435 B76 2000*

### EDUCATION - ECONOMIC ASPECTS - DEVELOPING COUNTRIES - CROSS-CULTURAL STUDIES.
Education, cultures, and economics. New York : Falmer Press, 1999.
*TC LC191.8.D44 E38 1999*

### EDUCATION - ECONOMIC ASPECTS - ECONOMETRIC MODELS.
Baker, Bruce D. A comparison of statistical and neural network models for forecasting educational spending. 1997.
*TC 06 no. 10792*

### EDUCATION - ECONOMIC ASPECTS - EUROPE.
Problems and prospects in European education. Westport, Conn. : Praeger, 2000.

*Education - Economic aspects - India.*

TC LC191.8. E85 P86 2000

**EDUCATION - ECONOMIC ASPECTS - INDIA.**
Public report on basic education in India. New Delhi ;
Oxford : Oxford University Press, c1999.
*TC LA1151 .P83 1999*

**EDUCATION - ECONOMIC ASPECTS -
PERIODICALS.**
[Economics of education review (Online)] Economics
of education review [computer file]. Oxford ; New
York : Pergamon.
*TC EJOURNALS*

**EDUCATION - ECONOMIC ASPECTS - UNITED
STATES.**
Boutwell, Clinton E. Shell game. Bloomington, Ind. :
Phi Delta Kappa Educational Foundation, c1997.
*TC LC1085.2 .B68 1997*

Engel, Michael, 1944- The struggle for control of
public education. Philadelphia, Pa. : Temple
University Press, c2000.
*TC LA217.2 .E533 2000*

Knowledge and power in the global economy.
Mahwah, N.J. : L. Erlbaum Associates, 2000.
*TC LC66 .K66 2000*

**EDUCATION - ECONOMIC ASPECTS - UNITED
STATES - STATES - STATISTICS.**
Lieberman, Carl, 1941- Educational expenditures and
economic growth in the American States. Akron,
Ohio : Midwest Press Incorporated, 1998.
*TC LC66 .L45 1998*

**EDUCATION, ELEMENTARY.** *See also*
**COUNSELING IN ELEMENTARY
EDUCATION; ELEMENTARY SCHOOL
TEACHING; FIFTH GRADE (EDUCATION);
SIXTH GRADE (EDUCATION).**
Charles, C. M. Elementary classroom management.
2nd ed. White Plains, N.Y. : Longman, c1995.
*TC LB3013 .C465 1995*

Evertson, Carolyn M., 1935- Classroom management
for elementary teachers. 5th ed. Boston : Allyn and
Bacon, c2000.
*TC LB3013 .C528 2000*

**EDUCATION, ELEMENTARY - ACTIVITY
PROGRAMS.**
Landy, Joanne M. Ready-to-use fundamental motor
skills & movement activities for young children. West
Nyack, NY : Center for Applied Research in
Education, c1999.
*TC GV452 .L355 1999*

Peters, Dorothy. Taking cues from kids. Portsmouth,
NH : Heinemann, c2000.
*TC LB3013 .P43 2000*

**EDUCATION, ELEMENTARY - ACTIVITY
PROGRAMS - UNITED STATES.**
Griss, Susan. Minds in motion. Portsmouth, NH :
Heinemann, c1998.
*TC LB1592 .G75 1998*

**EDUCATION, ELEMENTARY - AIMS AND
OBJECTIVES - UNITED STATES.**
Powerful middle schools : teaching and learning for
young adolescents (2000) Powerful middle schools
[videorecording]. [Washington, D.C.?] : U.S. Dept. of
Education, [2000].
*TC LB1623 .P6 2000*

**EDUCATION, ELEMENTARY - CALIFORNIA -
EVALUATION - HANDBOOKS, MANUALS,
ETC.**
Assessing literacy with the Learning Record.
Portsmouth, NH : Heinemann, c1999.
*TC LB1029.P67 B37 1999b*

**EDUCATION, ELEMENTARY - CHINA - AIMS
AND OBJECTIONS - CURRICULA.**
Reynolds, Barbara G. Reform and education. 1999.
*TC 06 no. 11166*

**EDUCATION, ELEMENTARY - COMPUTER-
ASSISTED INSTRUCTION.**
Saltveit, Elin Kordahl, 1964- Hit enter. Portsmouth,
NH : Heinemann, c1999.
*TC LB1028.5 .S233 1999*

**EDUCATION, ELEMENTARY - COMPUTER
NETWORK RESOURCES.**
McLain, Tim, 1970- How to create successful Internet
projects. El Segundo, Calif. : Classroom Connect,
c1999.
*TC LB1044.87 .M35 1999*

**EDUCATION, ELEMENTARY - CURRICULA -
CROSS-CULTURAL STUDIES.**
The primary curriculum. New York ; London :
Routledge, 1998.

TC LB1570 .P678 1998

**EDUCATION, ELEMENTARY - CURRICULA -
HANDBOOKS, MANUALS, ETC.**
Keys to the classroom. 2nd ed. Thousand Oaks,
Calif. : Corwin Press, c2000.
*TC LB1555 .K49 2000*

**EDUCATION (ELEMENTARY) - ECONOMIC
ASPECTS - CAMEROON.**
Amin, Martin E. (Martin Efuetngu) Trends in the
demand for primary education in Cameroon. Lanham,
MD : University Press of America, 1999.
*TC LC137.C36 A55 1999*

**EDUCATION, ELEMENTARY - ENGLAND.**
Teaching in primary schools. London : Cassell, 1998.
*TC LB1776.T43 1998*

**EDUCATION, ELEMENTARY - ENGLAND -
ESSEX - ADMINISTRATION.**
Supporting improving primary schools. London : New
York : Falmer Press, 2000.
*TC LB2822.84.E64 S86 1999*

**EDUCATION, ELEMENTARY - ENGLAND -
HISTORY.**
Heathorn, Stephen J., 1965- For home, country, and
race. Toronto : University of Toronto Press, 1999.
*TC LC93.E5 H42 1999*

**EDUCATION, ELEMENTARY - ENGLAND -
HISTORY - 19TH CENTURY.**
Phillips, Francis R. Creating an education system for
England and Wales. Lewiston, N.Y. : E. Mellen Press,
1992.
*TC LA633 .P48 1992*

**EDUCATION, ELEMENTARY - GERMANY.**
Dichanz, Horst, 1937- Changing traditions in
Germany's public schools. Bloomington, Ind. : Phi
Delta Kappa Educational Foundation, c1998.
*TC LA723 .D53 1998*

**EDUCATION, ELEMENTARY - GREAT
BRITAIN.**
Farrell, Michael. Key issues for primary schools.
London ; New York : Routledge, 1999.
*TC LA633 .F37 1999*

Hayes, Denis, 1949- Foundations of primary teaching.
2nd ed. London : David Fulton, 1999.
*TC LB1555 .H43 1999*

Wintle, Mike. Coordinating assessment practice
across the primary school. London ; Philadelphia,
PA : Falmer Press, 1999.
*TC LB3060.37 .W56 1999*

**EDUCATION, ELEMENTARY - GREAT
BRITAIN - CASE STUDIES.**
Wallace, Mike. Senior management teams in primary
schools. London : New York : Routledge, 1999.
*TC LB2806.3 .W37 1999*

**EDUCATION, ELEMENTARY - GREAT
BRITAIN - CURRICULA.**
Improving teaching and learning in the core
curriculum. London ; New York : Falmer Press, 2000.
*TC LB1564.G7 I475 2000*

**EDUCATION, ELEMENTARY - GREAT
BRITAIN - HISTORY.**
Penn, Alan, 1926- Targeting schools. London ;
Portland, OR : Woburn Press, 1999.
*TC GV443 .P388 1999*

**EDUCATION, ELEMENTARY - JAPAN -
KANAYAMA.**
Heart of the country [videorecording]. [New York,
NY : First Run/Icarus Films, 1998].
*TC LB1565.H6 H3 1998*

**EDUCATION, ELEMENTARY - LAW AND
LEGISLATION.** *See* **EDUCATIONAL LAW
AND LEGISLATION.**

**EDUCATION, ELEMENTARY - NIGERIA -
EVALUATION.**
Francis, Paul A. Hard lessons. Washington, D.C. :
World Bank, c1998.
*TC LA1632 .F73 1998*

**EDUCATION, ELEMENTARY - NIGERIA -
RESEARCH.**
Research on schooling in Nigeria. Ondo [Nigeria] :
Centre for Research on Schooling, Adeyemi College
of Education, 1995.
*TC LB1028.25.N6 R477 1995*

**EDUCATION, ELEMENTARY - OKLAHOMA.**
Damm, Robert J., 1964- Repertoire, authenticity, and
instruction. New York ; London : Garland Pub., 2000.
*TC MT3.U6 O53 2000*

**EDUCATION, ELEMENTARY - PARENT
PARTICIPATION.**
Wollman-Bonilla, Julie. Family message journals.
Urbana, Ill. : National Council of Teachers of English,
c2000.
*TC LB1576 .W644 2000*

**EDUCATION, ELEMENTARY - PARENT
PARTICIPATION - UNITED STATES.**
Powerful middle schools : teaching and learning for
young adolescents (2000) Powerful middle schools
[videorecording]. [Washington, D.C.?] : U.S. Dept. of
Education, [2000].
*TC LB1623 .P6 2000*

**EDUCATION, ELEMENTARY - PARENT
PARTICIPATION - UNITED STATES -
HANDBOOKS, MANUALS, ETC.**
Bennett, William J. (William John), 1943- The
educated child. New York : Free Press, c1999.
*TC LB1048.5 .B45 1999*

**EDUCATION, ELEMENTARY - PERIODICALS.**
The Grade teacher. Boston, Mass. : Educational Pub.
Co., -c1972.

**EDUCATION (ELEMENTARY) - SOCIAL
ASPECTS - CAMEROON.**
Amin, Martin E. (Martin Efuetngu) Trends in the
demand for primary education in Cameroon. Lanham,
MD : University Press of America, 1999.
*TC LC137.C36 A55 1999*

**EDUCATION, ELEMENTARY - SOCIAL
ASPECTS - NIGERIA.**
Francis, Paul A. Hard lessons. Washington, D.C. :
World Bank, c1998.
*TC LA1632 .F73 1998*

**EDUCATION, ELEMENTARY - SOCIAL
ASPECTS - UNITED STATES.**
Queering elementary education. Lanham, Md. ;
Oxford : Rowman & Littlefield, c1999.
*TC LC192.6 .Q85 1999*

**EDUCATION, ELEMENTARY - SOVIET UNION -
HISTORY.**
Holmes, Larry E. (Larry Eugene), 1942- Stalin's
school. Pittsburgh, Pa. : University of Pittsburgh
Press, c1999.
*TC LF4435.M657 H65 1999*

**EDUCATION, ELEMENTARY - UNITED STATES.**
Education's big gamble [videorecording]. New York,
NY : Merrow Report, c1997.
*TC LB2806.36 .E3 1997*

Public charter schools : new choices in public
education (May 3, 2000 : Washington, D.C.) Public
charter schools [videorecording]. [Washington,
D.C.] : U.S. Dept. of Education, [2000].
*TC LB2806.36 .P9 2000*

Strickland, Kathleen. Making assessment elementary.
Portsmouth, NH : Heinemann, 2000.
*TC LB3051 .S873 1999*

**EDUCATION, ELEMENTARY - UNITED
STATES - CURRICULA.**
Griss, Susan. Minds in motion. Portsmouth, NH :
Heinemann, c1998.
*TC LB1592 .G75 1998*

Queen, J. Allen. Curriculum practice in the
elementary and middle school. Upper Saddle River,
N.J. : Merrill, c1999.
*TC LB1570 .Q45 1999*

Queering elementary education. Lanham, Md. ;
Oxford : Rowman & Littlefield, c1999.
*TC LC192.6 .Q85 1999*

**EDUCATION, ELEMENTARY - UNITED
STATES - EVALUATION.**
Taylor, Kathe. Children at the center. Portsmouth,
NH : Heinemann, c1998.
*TC LB3060.57 .T39 1998*

**EDUCATION, ELEMENTARY - WALES.**
Teaching in primary schools. London : Cassell, 1998.
*TC LB1776.T43 1998*

**EDUCATION, ELEMENTARY - WALES -
HISTORY - 19TH CENTURY.**
Phillips, Francis R. Creating an education system for
England and Wales. Lewiston, N.Y. : E. Mellen Press,
1992.
*TC LA633 .P48 1992*

Smith, Robert Schools, politics and society. Cardiff :
University of Wales Press, 1999.
*TC LA663 .S65 1999*

**EDUCATION, EMPLOYER-SUPPORTED.** *See* EMPLOYER-SUPPORTED EDUCATION.

**EDUCATION - ENCYCLOPEDIAS - SOFTWARE.**
Education [computer file]: Version 1.1. [Oxford, Eng.] : Pergamon, c1998. Computer program.
*TC LB15 .E3 1998*

**EDUCATION - ENGLAND.**
Promoting quality in learning. London : New York : Cassell, 2000.
*TC LA632.b.P76 2000*

**EDUCATION - ENGLAND - EVALUATION.**
Black, P. J. (Paul Joseph), 1930- Testing, friend or foe? London ; Washington : Falmer Press, 1998.
*TC LB3056.E54 B53 1998*

**EDUCATION - ENGLAND - HISTORY.**
Silver, Harold. English education and the radicals 1780-1850. London ; Boston : Routledge & Kegan Paul, 1975.
*TC LA631.7 .S45*

**EDUCATION - ENGLAND - HISTORY - 18TH CENTURY.**
Barney, Richard A., 1955- Plots of enlightenment. Stanford, Calif. : Stanford University Press, c1999.
*TC PR858.E38 B37 1999*

**EDUCATION, ETHICAL.** *See* MORAL EDUCATION.

**EDUCATION - EUROPE.**
Dewey and European education. Dordrecht : Kluwer Academic Publishers, c2000.
*TC LB875.D5 D47 2000*

**EDUCATION - EUROPE - PERIODICALS.**
[Education newsletter (Strasbourg, France)] Education newsletter = Strasbourg [France] : Council of Europe, 1990-1995.
*TC LA620 .D6 1994*

**EDUCATION - EUROPEAN UNION COUNTRIES - DECISION MAKING.**
Snick, Anne. Women in educational [sic] policy-making. Leuven, Belgium : Leuven University Press, 1999.
*TC LC93.A2 S56 1999*

**EDUCATION - EVALUATION - STATISTICS - CROSS-CULTURAL STUDIES - DATABASES - PERIODICALS.**
Education at a glance [computer file]. Ottawa, Ont. : Ivation Datasystems Inc. ; Paris, France : OECD.
*TC LB2846 .E2473*

**EDUCATION - EXPERIMENTAL METHODS.** *See also* ACTIVITY PROGRAMS IN EDUCATION; ALTERNATIVE EDUCATION; COLLECTIVE EDUCATION; EDUCATIONAL INNOVATIONS; NONGRADED SCHOOLS.
Eggen, Paul D., 1940- Strategies for teachers. 4th ed. Boston : Allyn and Bacon, 2001.
*TC LB1027.3 .E44 2001*

Finkel, Donald L., 1943- Teaching with your mouth shut. Portsmouth, NH Boynton/Cook Publishers, c2000.
*TC LB1026 .F49 2000*

[Group psychotherapy.] Psychodrama and sociodrama in American education. New York Beacon House, 1949.

Journal of emotional education. New York, Emotional Education Press.

**EDUCATION - EXPERIMENTAL METHODS - PERIODICALS.**
Bulletin of the New York Society for the Experimental Study of Education. [New York : The Society,

The Library-college experimenter: a clearinghouse. Norman, Okla., Library-College Associates, Inc.

**Education faits nouveaux.**
[Education newsletter (Strasbourg, France)] Education newsletter = Strasbourg [France] : Council of Europe, 1990-1995.
*TC LA620 .D6 1994*

**EDUCATION - FEDERAL AID.** *See* FEDERAL AID TO EDUCATION.

**EDUCATION - FINANCE.** *See also* COLLEGE COSTS; EDUCATIONAL VOUCHERS; FEDERAL AID TO EDUCATION; SCHOOL BONDS.
Organisation for Economic Co-operation and Development (Paris) The appraisal of investments in educational facilities. Paris : Organisation for Economic Co-operation and Development, 2000.

*TC LB2342.3 .A7 2000*

**EDUCATION - FINANCE - LAW AND LEGISLATION - UNITED STATES.**
New school order [videorecording]. New York : First Run/Icarus Films, 1996.
*TC LB2831.583.P4 N4 1996*

**EDUCATION - FINANCE - UNITED STATES.**
Baker, Bruce D. A comparison of statistical and neural network models for forecasting educational spending. 1997.
*TC 06 no. 10792*

Making money matter. Washington, D.C. : National Academy Press, c1999.
*TC LB2825 .M27 1999*

**EDUCATION - FLORIDA.**
Florida. Dept. of Education. Florida school bulletin ... Tallahassee [1938-

**Education for one world.**
[Open doors (New York, N.Y.)] Open doors. New York, N.Y. : Institute of International Education.
*TC LB2283 .I615*

**Education for special needs.**
Steiner, Rudolf, 1861-1925. [Heilpädagogischer Kurs. English] [New ed.]. London : Rudolf Steiner Press, 1998.
*TC LB1029.W34 S73 1998*

**Education for spiritual, moral, social and cultural development** / edited by Ron Best. London ; New York : Continuum, 2000. viii, 216 p. ; 24 cm. (Continuum studies in pastoral care and personal and social education) Includes bibliographical references and index. ISBN 0-8264-4802-X (pbk.)
*1. Moral education. 2. Spiritual formation. 3. Social skills in children. 4. Education - Social aspects. 5. Culture. I. Best, Ron. 1945- II. Series.*
*TC LC268 .E384 2000*

**Education for values :** morals, ethics and citizenship in contemporary teaching / edited by Roy Gardner, Jo Cairns and Denis Lawton. London ; Sterling, VA : Kogan Page, 2000. xi, 340 p. : ill. ; 24 cm. Includes bibliographical references and index. ISBN 0-7494-3065-6 DDC 370.114
*1. Moral education. I. Gardner, Roy. II. Cairns, Jo. III. Lawton, Denis, 1931-*
*TC LC268 .E38 2000*

**EDUCATION - FRANCE.**
Promoting quality in learning. London ; New York : Cassell, 2000.
*TC LA632.b.P76 2000*

**EDUCATION - FRANCE - PERIODICALS.**
L'Éducation nationale. Paris.

**EDUCATION - GEORGIA - PERIODICALS.**
Georgia education journal. Macon, Ga. : Georgia Education Association, 1926-1970.

Georgia educator. [Atlanta]

Home, school, and community. Atlanta, Ga. : Georgia Council of Social Agencies, 1923-1926.

**EDUCATION - GERMANY - BAVARIA - PERIODICALS.**
Bavaria (Germany). Staatsministerium für Unterricht, Kultus, Wissenschaft und Kunst. Amtsblatt des Bayerischen Staatsministeriums für Unterricht, Kultus, Wissenschaft und Kunst. München : J. Jehle,

Bavaria (Germany). Staatsministerium für Unterricht und Kultus. Amtsblatt des Staatsministeriums für Unterricht und Kultus. München : Das Ministerium, 1918-

**EDUCATION - GERMANY - PERIODICALS.**
Hochschule und Ausland. Berlin : Kulturpolitische Gesellschaft, 1923-1937.

**EDUCATION - GHANA - HISTORY.**
Quist, Hubert Oswald. Secondary education and nation-building. 1999.
*TC 085 Q52*

**EDUCATION - GHANA - PERIODICALS.**
Ghana teachers' journal. Accra. 1952-1968.

Ghana teachers' journal. London : Nelson and Sons, 1957-1968.

**EDUCATION - GOVERNMENT POLICY.** *See* EDUCATION AND STATE.

**EDUCATION - GREAT BRITAIN - COMPUTER NETWORK RESOURCES - CASE STUDIES.**
Learning to teach using ICT in the secondary school. London ; New York : Routledge, 1999.
*TC LB1028.5 .L3884 1999*

**EDUCATION - GREAT BRITAIN - CURRICULA.**
Quicke, John, 1941- A curriculum for life. Buckingham ; Philadelphia : Open University Press, 1999.
*TC LB1564.G7 Q85 1999*

**EDUCATION - GREAT BRITAIN - DIRECTORIES.**
Education year book. [London, England] : Councils and Education Press, 1979-
*TC L915 .E4*

**EDUCATION - GREAT BRITAIN - PHILOSOPHY.**
An introduction to the study of education. London : David Fulton, 1999.
*TC LA632 .I58 1999*

**EDUCATION - GREECE.** *See* EDUCATION, GREEK.

**EDUCATION, GREEK - PHILOSOPHY.**
Too, Yun Lee. The pedagogical contract. Ann Arbor: University of Michigan Press, c2000.
*TC LB1033 .T66 2000*

**[Education (Guilford, Conn.)]** Education. Guilford, Ct., Dushkin Pub. Group. v. : ill. ; 28 cm. Frequency: Annual. 7th (80/81)- . (Annual editions.) Cover title: Annual editions: Education <1980/81->. Continues: Annual editions. Readings in education ISSN: 0095-5787. ISSN 0272-5010 DDC 370/.973
*1. Education - United States - Periodicals. I. Title: Annual editions: Education <1980/81-> II. Title: Annual editions. Readings in education III. Series.*
*TC LB41 .A673*

**EDUCATION - HAWAII - PERIODICALS.**
Hawaii educational review. [Honolulu : Dept. of Public Instruction and the Extension Dept. of the College of Hawaii], 1913-1954.

**EDUCATION, HIGHER.** *See also* COUNSELING IN HIGHER EDUCATION; DISCRIMINATION IN HIGHER EDUCATION; HIGHER EDUCATION AND STATE; HOMOPHOBIA IN HIGHER EDUCATION; PROFESSIONAL EDUCATION; SEMINARS; SEX DISCRIMINATION IN HIGHER EDUCATION; TELECOMMUNICATION IN HIGHER EDUCATION; UNIVERSITIES AND COLLEGES; UNIVERSITY EXTENSION; WOMEN'S COLLEGES; WOMEN - EDUCATION (HIGHER).
Knapper, Christopher. Lifelong learning in higher education. 3rd ed. London : Kogan Page, 2000.
*TC LC5215 .K593 2000*

Martin, Elaine, 1948- Changing academic work. Buckingham ; Philadelphia : Society for Research into Higher Education : Open University Press, 1999.
*TC LA184 .M37 1999*

Practical approaches to using learning styles in higher education. Westport, Conn. : Bergin & Garvey, 2000.
*TC LB2395 .P69 2000*

Problem-based learning in higher education. Buckingham ; Philadelphia, PA : Society for Research into Higher Education : Open University Press, 2000.
*TC LB1027.42 .S28 2000*

Stevens, Ed. Due process and higher education. Washington, DC : Graduate School of Education and Human Development, George Washington University, [1999]
*TC LB2344 .S73 1999*

**EDUCATION, HIGHER - ADMINISTRATION.**
Ramsden, Paul. Learning to lead in higher education. London ; New York : Routledge, 1998.
*TC LB2341 .R32 1998*

**EDUCATION, HIGHER - AIMS AND OBJECTIVES.**
The academy and the possibility of belief. Cresskill, N.J. : Hampton Press, c2000.
*TC LB2324 .A27 2000*

Barnett, Ronald, 1947- Realizing the university in an age of supercomplexity. Philadelphia, PA : Society for Research into Higher Education & Open University Press, 1999.
*TC LB2322.2 .B37 1999*

Elliott, Geoffrey, Dr. Lifelong learning. London ; Philadelphia : Jessica Kingsley Publishers, c1999.
*TC LB1060 .E447 1999*

George, Judith W. A handbook of techniques for formative evaluation :. London : Kogan Page, 1999.
*TC LB2333 .G46 1999*

*Education, Higher - Aims and objectives.*

Heywood, John, 1930- Assessment in higher education. London ; Philadelphia : Jessica Kingsley Publishers, 2000.
*TC LB2366 .H49 2000*

Sporn, Barbara. Adaptive university structures. London ; Philadelphia : Jessica Kingsley, c1999.
*TC LB2322.2 .S667 1999*

Taylor, Peter G., 1951- Making sense of academic life. Philadelphia, PA : Open University Press, 1999.
*TC LB1778 .T39 1999*

The university in transformation. Westport, Conn. : London : Bergin & Garvey, 2000.
*TC LB2324 .U56 2000*

What kind of university? 1st ed. Buckingham ; Philadelphia, PA : Society for Research into Higher Education : Open University Press, 1999.
*TC LB2322.2 .W43 1999*

**EDUCATION, HIGHER - AIMS AND OBJECTIVES - CANADA.**
A new world of knowledge. Ottawa : International Development Research Centre, c1999.
*TC LC1090 N38 1999*

**EDUCATION, HIGHER - AIMS AND OBJECTIVES - GREAT BRITAIN.**
Bennett, Neville. Skills development in higher education and employment. Buckingham [England] ; Philadelphia : Society for Research into Higher Education & Open University Press, 2000.
*TC LB1027.47 .B46 2000*

**EDUCATION, HIGHER - AIMS AND OBJECTIVES - UNITED STATES.**
Aronowitz, Stanley. The knowledge factory. Boston : Beacon Press, c2000.
*TC LA227.4 .A76 2000*

Bogue, E. Grady (Ernest Grady), 1935- Exploring the heritage of American higher education. Phoenix, Ariz. : Oryx Press, 2000.
*TC LA227.4 .B66 2000*

Bracey, Earnest N. Prophetic insight. Lanham : University Press of America, c1999.
*TC LC2781 .B73 1999*

Civic responsibility and higher education. Phoenix, Az. : Oryx Press, 2000.
*TC LC1091 .C5289 2000*

Colleges and universities as citizens. Boston : Allyn and Bacon, c1999.
*TC LC220.5 .C644 1999*

Higher education in transition. Westport, Conn. : London : Bergin & Garvey, 2000.
*TC LA227.4 .H53 2000*

Kernan, Alvin B. In Plato's cave. New Haven : Yale University Press, c1999.
*TC LA227.4 .K468 1999*

Moving beyond the gap between research and practice in higher education. San Francisco, Calif. : Jossey-Bass, c2000.
*TC LA227.4 .M68 2000*

Neusner, Jacob, 1932- Reaffirming higher education. New Brunswick, U.S.A. : Transaction Publishers, c2000.
*TC LA227.4 .N47 2000*

A sanctuary of their own. Lanham, Md. : Rowman & Littlefield, c2000.
*TC LC191.9 .S28 2000*

**EDUCATION, HIGHER - BANGLADESH - HISTORY - 20TH CENTURY.**
Siddiqui, Zillur Rahman. Visions and revisions. Dhaka : University Press, 1997.
*TC LA1168 .S53 1997*

**EDUCATION, HIGHER - CASE STUDIES.**
Inspiring students :. London : Kogan Page, 1999.
*TC LB1065 .I57 1999*

**EDUCATION, HIGHER - CHINA - ARCHIVAL RESOURCES - CONGRESSES.**
International Symposium on Historical Archives of Pre-1949 Christian Higher Education in China (1993 : Hong Kong) Chung-kuo chiao hui ta hsüeh li shih wen hsien yen t'ao hui lun wen chi. Hsiang-kang : Chung wen ta hsüeh ch'u pan she, 1995.
*TC LC432.C5 I58 1995*

**EDUCATION, HIGHER - COMPUTER-ASSISTED INSTRUCTION.**
Issues in Web-based pedagogy. Westport, Conn. : Greenwood Press, 2000.
*TC LB1044.87 .I88 2000*

The online teaching guide :. Boston, Mass. : Allyn and Bacon, c2000.
*TC LB1044.87 .O45 1999*

Salmon, Gilly. E-moderating. London : Kogan Page : Sterling, VA : Stylus, 2000.
*TC LB1044.87 .S25 2000*

**EDUCATION, HIGHER - COMPUTER NETWORK RESOURCES.**
Issues in Web-based pedagogy. Westport, Conn. : Greenwood Press, 2000.
*TC LB1044.87 .I88 2000*

**EDUCATION, HIGHER - COSTS.**
Analyzing costs in higher education. San Francisco, Calif. : Jossey-Bass Publishers, c2000.
*TC LB2342 .A68 2000*

**EDUCATION, HIGHER - CROSS-CULTURAL STUDIES.**
The adult university. Buckingham [England] ; Philadelphia, PA : Society for Research into Higher Education & Open University Press, 1999.
*TC LC5219 .A35 1999*

Eddy, John, 1932- International higher education systems. New ed. Lanham, Md. ; Oxford : University Press of America, c2000.
*TC LB2322.2 .E33 2000*

**EDUCATION, HIGHER - CROSS CULTURAL STUDIES.**
Guri-Rozenblit, Sarah. Distance and campus universities. 1st ed. Oxford, UK ; New York, NY : Pergamon, published for IAU Press, 1999.
*TC LC5800 .G87 1999*

**EDUCATION, HIGHER - CROSS-CULTURAL STUDIES.**
Higher education and disabilities. Aldershot ; Brookfield, Vt. : Ashgate, c1998.
*TC LC4812 .H55 1998*

Local knowledge and wisdom in higher education. 1st ed. Oxford : Published for the IAU Press [by] Pergamon, 2000.
*TC GN380 .L63 2000*

**EDUCATION, HIGHER - CURRICULA.**
Interdisciplinary general education. New York, NY : College Board Publications, c1999.
*TC LB2361 .I43 1999*

What kind of university? 1st ed. Buckingham ; Philadelphia, PA : Society for Research into Higher Education : Open University Press, 1999.
*TC LB2322.2 .W43 1999*

**EDUCATION, HIGHER - DATA PROCESSING - CASE STUDIES.**
Cases studies on information technology in higher education. Hershey, PA : Idea Group Pub., c2000.
*TC LB2395.7 .C39 2000*

**EDUCATION, HIGHER - DEVELOPING COUNTRIES.**
The Task Force on Higher Education and Society. Peril and promise. Washington, DC: World Bank, 2000.
*TC LC2610 .I53 2000*

**EDUCATION, HIGHER - DEVELOPING COUNTRIES - FINANCE.**
Learning from experience. The Hague : Centre for the Study of Education in Developing Countries, c1995.
*TC LC2610 .L43 1995*

**EDUCATION, HIGHER - ECONOMIC ASPECTS - AFRICA.**
A thousand flowers. Trenton, NJ : Africa World Press, c2000, [1999].
*TC LC67.68.A35 T56 2000*

**EDUCATION, HIGHER - ECONOMIC ASPECTS - CASE STUDIES.**
The response of higher education institutions to regional needs. Paris : Organisation for Economic Co-operation and Development, 1999.
*TC LC237 .R47 1999*

**EDUCATION, HIGHER - ECONOMIC ASPECTS - CROSS-CULTURAL STUDIES.**
Experiential learning around the world. London ; Philadelphia : J. Kingsley Publishers, 2000.
*TC LB2324 .E95 2000*

**EDUCATION, HIGHER - ECONOMIC ASPECTS - JAPAN.**
Arai, Kazuhiro, 1949- [Kyōiku no keizaigaku. English] Economics of education. Tōkyō ; New York : Springer, 1998.
*TC LC67.68.J3 A72 1998*

**EDUCATION, HIGHER - ECONOMIC ASPECTS - UNITED STATES.**
A sanctuary of their own. Lanham, Md. : Rowman & Littlefield, c2000.
*TC LC191.9 .S28 2000*

Smith, Charles W., 1938- Market values in American higher education. Lanham, Md. ; Oxford : Rowman & Littlefield, 2000.
*TC LB2342 .S55 2000*

**EDUCATION, HIGHER - ECONOMIC ASPECTS - UNITED STATES - CONGRESSES.**
Postbaccalaureate futures. Phoenix, AZ : Oryx Press, 2000.
*TC LB2371.4 .P68 2000*

**EDUCATION, HIGHER - EFFECT OF TECHNOLOGICAL INNOVATIONS ON - UNITED STATES.**
Dollars, distance, and online education. Phoenix, Az. : Oryx Press, 2000.
*TC LB2395.7 .M26 2000*

**EDUCATION, HIGHER - ENCYCLOPEDIAS - SOFTWARE.**
Education [computer file]: Version 1.1. [Oxford, Eng.] : Pergamon, c1998. Computer program.
*TC LB15 .E3 1998*

**EDUCATION, HIGHER - EUROPE - ADMINISTRATION.**
From the eye of the storm. Dordrecht ; Boston ; London : Kluwer Academic Publishers, c1999.
*TC LB2341.8.E85 F76 1999*

Groof, Jan de. Democracy and governance in higher education. The Hague ; Boston : Kluwer Law International, 1998.
*TC LB2341.8.E85 G76 1998*

**EDUCATION, HIGHER - EUROPE - CROSS-CULTURAL STUDIES.**
Groof, Jan de. Democracy and governance in higher education. The Hague ; Boston : Kluwer Law International, 1998.
*TC LB2341.8.E85 G76 1998*

**EDUCATION, HIGHER - EUROPE, EASTERN - HISTORY - CONGRESSES.**
Academia in upheaval. Westport, Conn. : Bergin & Garvey, 2000.
*TC LA837 .A6 2000*

**EDUCATION, HIGHER - EUROPE - PERIODICALS.**
Hochschul-Nachrichten. München : Academischer Verlag,

**EDUCATION, HIGHER - EVALUATION.**
Heywood, John, 1930- Assessment in higher education. London : Philadelphia : Jessica Kingsley Publishers, 2000.
*TC LB2366 .H49 2000*

**EDUCATION, HIGHER - EVALUATION - SOCIAL ASPECTS.**
Audit cultures. London : New York : Routledge, 2000.
*TC LB2324 .A87 2000*

**EDUCATION, HIGHER - GREAT BRITAIN.**
Bligh, Donald, 1936- Understanding higher education. Oxford : Intellect, 1999.
*TC LA637 .B55 1999*

Lange, Thomas, 1967- Rethinking higher education. London : IEA Education and Training Unit, 1998.
*TC LB2342.2.G7 L364 1998*

Powell, Stuart, 1949- Returning to study. Buckingham ; Philadelphia : Open University Press, c1999.
*TC LC5256.G7 P66 1999*

Preece, Julia. Combating social exclusion in university adult education. Aldershot ; Brookfield, Vt. : Ashgate, c1999.
*TC LC5256.G7 P84 1999*

**EDUCATION, HIGHER - GREAT BRITAIN - ADMINISTRATION.**
Gledhill, John M., 1948- Managing students. Buckingham ; Philadelphia : Open University Press, 1999.
*TC LB2341.8.G7 G54 1996*

**EDUCATION, HIGHER - GREAT BRITAIN - HISTORY.**
Bligh, Donald, 1936- Understanding higher education. Oxford : Intellect, 1999.
*TC LA637 .B55 1999*

**EDUCATION, HIGHER - GREAT BRITAIN - MANAGEMENT.**
Watson, David, 1949- Managing strategy.

Buckingham [England] ; Philadelphia : Open University Press, 2000.
*TC LB2341.8.G7 W28 2000*

**EDUCATION, HIGHER - INDIA.**
Staff development in higher and distance education. New Delhi : Aravali Books International, 1997.
*TC LB2331 .S692 1997*

**EDUCATION, HIGHER - INDIA - PERIODICALS.**
The Journal of university education. Delhi, Published by A. Singh for Federation of Central Universities Teachers' Associations, Aligarh.

**EDUCATION, HIGHER - KOREA (SOUTH).**
Higher education in Korea. New York : Falmer Press, 2000.
*TC LA1333 .H54 2000*

**EDUCATION, HIGHER - LATIN AMERICA.**
Myth, reality, and reform. Washington, D.C. : Inter-American Development Bank, 2000.
*TC LA543 .M46 2000*

**EDUCATION, HIGHER - LAW AND LEGISLATION - UNITED STATES - HISTORY.**
Oliver, Frank H. Fellow beggars. 1999.
*TC 06 no.11157*

**EDUCATION, HIGHER - MORAL AND ETHICAL ASPECTS.**
Audit cultures. London ; New York : Routledge, 2000.
*TC LB2324 .A87 2000*

**EDUCATION, HIGHER - MORAL AND ETHICAL ASPECTS - UNITED STATES.**
Davis, Michael, 1943- Ethics and the university. London ; New York : Routledge, 1999.
*TC LB2324 .D38 1999*

Golding, Martin P. (Martin Philip), 1930- Free speech on campus. Lanham, Md. ; Oxford : Rowman & Littlefield Publishers, c2000.
*TC LC72.2 .G64 2000*

**EDUCATION, HIGHER - NEW YORK (STATE) - NEW YORK - HISTORY.**
Roff, Sandra Shoiock. From the Free Academy to CUNY. New York : Fordham University Press, c2000.
*TC LD3835 .R64 2000*

**EDUCATION, HIGHER - PERIODICALS.**
Change in higher education. [New York, Science and University Affairs for Educational Change, Inc.]

Council for Advancement and Support of Education. CASE currents. [Washington] Council for Advancement and Support of Education.

Higher education and research in the Netherlands. The Hague, Netherlands Foundation for International Cooperation.

The Journal of university education. Delhi, Published by A. Singh for Federation of Central Universities Teachers' Associations, Aligarh.

**EDUCATION, HIGHER - PHILOSOPHY.**
The university and the knowledge society. Bemmel [Netherlands] : Concorde Publishing House, 1998.
*TC LB2322.2 .U55 1998*

**EDUCATION, HIGHER - POLITICAL ASPECTS.**
Gorham, Eric B., 1960- The theater of politics. Lanham, Md. ; Oxford: Lexington Books, c2000.
*TC LC171 .G56 2000*

Knowledge and power in higher education. New York : London : Teachers College Press, c2000.
*TC LC171 .K62 2000*

Morley, Louise, 1954- Organising feminisms. New York : St. Martin's Press, 1999.
*TC LC197 .M67 1999*

**EDUCATION, HIGHER - POLITICAL ASPECTS - RUSSIA (FEDERATION) - SAINT PETERSBURG.**
Konecny, Peter, 1963- Builders and deserters. Montreal : McGill-Queen's University Press, 1999.
*TC LA839.5.L45 K65 1999*

**EDUCATION, HIGHER - POLITICAL ASPECTS - UNITED STATES.**
Parks, Stephen, 1963- Class politics. Urbana, Ill. : National Council of Teachers of English, c2000.
*TC PE1405.U6 P3 2000*

**EDUCATION, HIGHER - RESEARCH - CROSS-CULTURAL STUDIES.**
Higher education research. 1st ed. Oxford ; [New York] : Pergamon, published for the IAU Press, 2000.
*TC LB2326.3 .H548 2000*

**EDUCATION, HIGHER - RESEARCH - UNITED STATES.**
What is institutional research all about ? San Francisco, Calif. : Jossey-Bass Publishers, c1999.
*TC LB2326.3 .W43 1999*

**EDUCATION, HIGHER - RESEARCH - UNITED STATES - TECHNOLOGICAL INNOVATIONS.**
How technology is changing institutional research. San Francisco, Calif. : Jossey-Bass Publishers, c1999.
*TC LB2326.3 .H69 1999*

**EDUCATION, HIGHER - SOCIAL ASPECTS - CROSS-CULTURAL STUDIES - CONGRESSES.**
The universities' responsibilities to society. 1st ed. New York : Pergamon, published for the IAU Press, 2000.
*TC LC191.9 .U55 2000*

**EDUCATION, HIGHER - SOCIAL ASPECTS - FRANCE - PARIS - HISTORY.**
Courtenay, William J. Parisian scholars in the early fourteenth century. Cambridge, U.K. ; New York, NY : Cambridge University Press, 1999.
*TC LF2165 .C68 1999*

**EDUCATION, HIGHER - SOCIAL ASPECTS - NORWAY.**
Bleiklie, Ivar, 1948- Policy and practice in higher education. London ; Phildadelphia : J. Kingsley Publishers, 2000.
*TC LC178.N8 B44 2000*

**EDUCATION, HIGHER - SOCIAL ASPECTS - UNITED STATES.**
Aronowitz, Stanley. The knowledge factory. Boston : Beacon Press, c2000.
*TC LA227.4 .A76 2000*

Manning, Kathleen, 1954- Ritual, ceremonies, and cultural meaning in higher education. Westport, Conn. : Bergin & Garvey, 2000.
*TC LC191.9 .M26 2000*

A sanctuary of their own. Lanham, Md. : Rowman & Littlefield, c2000.
*TC LC191.9 .S28 2000*

The social worlds of higher education :. Thousand Oaks, Calif. : Pine Forge Press, [1999].
*TC LB2331 .S573 1999 sampler*

**EDUCATION, HIGHER - SOVIET UNION - HISTORY - CONGRESSES.**
Academia in upheaval. Westport, Conn. : Bergin & Garvey, 2000.
*TC LA837 .A6 2000*

**EDUCATION, HIGHER - STANDARDS - GREAT BRITAIN.**
Benchmarking and threshold standards in higher education. London : Kogan Page, c1999.
*TC LB2341.8.G7 B463 1999*

**EDUCATION, HIGHER - SWEDEN.**
Transforming universities. London ; Philadelphia : Jessica Kingsley Publishers, 1999.
*TC LA908 .T73 1999*

**EDUCATION, HIGHER - UNITED STATE - FINANCE - HISTORY.**
Oliver, Frank H. Fellow beggars. 1999.
*TC 06 no.11157*

**EDUCATION, HIGHER - UNITED STATES.**
Bogue, E. Grady (Ernest Grady), 1935- Exploring the heritage of American higher education. Phoenix, Ariz. : Oryx Press, 2000.
*TC LA227.4 .B66 2000*

The full-time faculty handbook. Thousand Oaks : Sage Publications, c1999.
*TC LB1778.2 .F85 1999*

Kimball, Roger, 1953- Tenured radicals. Rev. ed., with a new introd. by the author, 1st Elephant pbk. ed. Chicago : Elephant Paperbacks, 1998.
*TC LA1023 .K56 1998*

Rojstaczer, Stuart. Gone for good. Oxford : Oxford University Press, 1999.
*TC LA227.4 .R65 1999*

Shattuck, Roger. Candor and perversion. 1st ed. New York : W.W. Norton, c1999.
*TC PN52 .S53 1999*

**EDUCATION, HIGHER - UNITED STATES - ADMINISTRATION.**
Freed, Jann E. A culture for academic excellence. Washington, D.C. : Graduate School of Education and Human Development, George Washington University, 1997.

*TC LB2341 .F688 1997*

Lenington, Robert L. Managing higher education as a business. Phoenix, Ariz. : Oryx Press, 1996.
*TC LB2341 .L426 1996*

**EDUCATION, HIGHER - UNITED STATES - BUSINESS MANAGEMENT.**
Lenington, Robert L. Managing higher education as a business. Phoenix, Ariz. : Oryx Press, 1996.
*TC LB2341 .L426 1996*

**EDUCATION, HIGHER - UNITED STATES - CASE STUDIES.**
Chen, Sheying. Remedial education and grading. New York : the City University of New York, 1999.
*TC LB1029.R4 C54 1999*

**EDUCATION, HIGHER - UNITED STATES - CURRICULA.**
Core texts in conversation . Lanham, MD : University Press of America, 2000.
*TC LB2361.5 .C68 2000*

Mentkowski, Marcia. Learning that lasts. 1st ed. San Francisco : Jossey-Bass, c2000.
*TC LB1060 .M464 2000*

**EDUCATION, HIGHER - UNITED STATES - EFFECT OF TECHNOLOGICAL INNOVATION ON.**
Becker, Nancy Jane. Implementing technology in higher education. 1999.
*TC 06 no. 11082*

**EDUCATION, HIGHER - UNITED STATES - FINANCE.**
ASHE reader on finance in higher education. Needham Heights, MA : Ginn Press, c1986.
*TC LB2342 .A76 1990*

Smith, Charles W., 1938- Market values in American higher education. Lanham, Md. ; Oxford : Rowman & Littlefield, 2000.
*TC LB2342 .S55 2000*

A struggle to survive. Thousand Oaks, Calif. : Corwin Press, c1996.
*TC LB2342 .S856 1996*

**EDUCATION, HIGHER - UNITED STATES - HISTORY.**
Watersheds in higher education. Lewiston, N.Y. : E. Mellen Press, c1997.
*TC LA228 .W28 1997*

**EDUCATION, HIGHER - UNITED STATES - HISTORY - 19TH CENTURY.**
The American college in the nineteenth century. 1st ed. Nashville : Vanderbilt University Press, 2000.
*TC LA227.1 .A64 2000*

**EDUCATION, HIGHER - UNITED STATES - HISTORY - 20TH CENTURY.**
Quehl, Gary H. Fifty years of innovations in undergraduate education. Indianapolis, Ind : USA Group Foundation, c1999.
*TC LB1027.3 .Q43 1999*

**EDUCATION, HIGHER - UNITED STATES - MANAGEMENT.**
Birnbaum, Robert. Management fads in higher education. San Francisco : Jossey-Bass, 2000.
*TC LB2341 .B49 2000*

**EDUCATION, HIGHER - UNITED STATES - PERIODICALS.**
Alternative higher education. [New York, Human Sciences Press]

[Review of higher education (Online)] The review of higher education [computer file]. Baltimore, Md. : Johns Hopkins University Press, c1996-
*TC EJOURNALS*

**EDUCATION, HIGHER - UNITED STATES - PHILOSOPHY.**
America, the West, and liberal education. Lanham, Md. : Rowman & Littlefield, c1999.
*TC LC1023 .A44 1999*

Watersheds in higher education. Lewiston, N.Y. : E. Mellen Press, c1997.
*TC LA228 .W28 1997*

**EDUCATION, HIGHER$ZBRITISH COLUMBIA.**
McKellin, Karen, 1950- Maintaining the momentum. Victoria, B.C. : British Columbia Centre for International Education, c1998.
*TC LC1090 .M24 1998*

**EDUCATION - HISTORY.** *See also*
  **COMPARATIVE EDUCATION.**
Educational foundations. Upper Saddle River, N.J. : Merrill, c2000.

**TC LB17 .E393 2000**
Raymont, Thomas, 1864- A history of the education of young children.. London ; New York : Longmans, Green and co., [1937]
**TC LA21 .R37**

**EDUCATION - HISTORY - 17TH CENTURY.**
Helmer, Karl. Umbruch zur Moderne. 1. Aufl. Sankt Augustin : Academia, 1994.
**TC LA116 .H445 1994**

**EDUCATION - HISTORY - MEDIEVAL, 500-1500.**
*See* EDUCATION, MEDIEVAL.

**EDUCATION - HISTORY - PERIODICALS.**
History of education journal. [Ann Arbor, Mich., s.n.]

**EDUCATION, HOME.** *See* HOME SCHOOLING.

**EDUCATION, HUMANISTIC.** *See also*
CLASSICAL EDUCATION.
After the disciplines. Westport, Conn. : Bergin & Garvey, 1999.
**TC LB2362.N45 A48 1999**

Nelson, Michael, 1949- Alive at the core. 1st ed. San Francisco : Jossey-Bass, c2000.
**TC AZ183.U5 N45 2000**

Preparing humanistic teachers for troubled children. Syracuse, N.Y. : Division of Special Education and Rehabilitation, Syracuse University, [1974?]
**TC LC4801 .P73**

White, Patricia, 1937- Civic virtues and public schooling. New York : Teachers College Press, c1996.
**TC LC1011 .W48 1996**

**EDUCATION, HUMANISTIC - ADDRESSES, ESSAYS, LECTURES.**
Read, Donald A., comp. Humanistic education sourcebook. Englewood Cliffs, N.J. : Prentice-Hall, [1975]
**TC LC1011 .R38**

**EDUCATION, HUMANISTIC - UNITED STATES.**
America, the West, and liberal education. Lanham, Md. : Rowman & Littlefield, c1999.
**TC LC1023 .A44 1999**

Eisler, Riane Tennenhaus. Tomorrow's children. Boulder, Colo. : Oxford : Westview Press, 2000.
**TC LC1023 .E57 2000**

Grote, John E. Paideia agonistes. Lanham, Md. : University Press of America, c2000.
**TC LC1011 .G76 2000**

Kimball, Roger, 1953- Tenured radicals. Rev. ed., with a new introd. by the author, 1st Elephant pbk. ed. Chicago : Elephant Paperbacks, 1998.
**TC LC1023 .K56 1998**

Mannoia, V. James. Christian liberal arts. Lanham, Md. : Rowman & Littlefield, c2000.
**TC LC427 .M26 2000**

Proctor, Robert E., 1945- Defining the humanities. 2nd ed. Bloomington : Indiana University Press, c1998.
**TC AZ221 .P75 1998**

**EDUCATION, HUMANISTIC - UNITED STATES - HISTORY.**
Rabil, Alison. Content, context, and continuity. 1998.
**TC 06 no. 10901**

**EDUCATION - HUNGARY - HISTORY - SOURCES.**
Gegő, Elek, 1805-1844. Népoktató. Budapest : Országos Pedagógiai Könyvtár és Múzeum, [1997]
**TC LC227 .G44 1997**

**EDUCATION - ILLINOIS.**
Illinois education; Mount Morris, Ill. [etc.]

The Illinois teacher: Peoria, Ill., Nason.

University of Illinois (Urbana-Champaign campus). Bureau of Educational Research. Bulletin. Urbana, 1918-47.

**EDUCATION - ILLINOIS - CHICAGO - PERIODICALS.**
Chicago schools journal. Chicago, Board of Education.

Illinois schools journal. Chicago, Ill. : Illinois State Teachers College Chicago-South, 1967-

**EDUCATION - ILLINOIS - PERIODICALS.**
Illinois journal of education. [Springfield, Ill.] : Superintendent of Public Instruction, 1961-

Illinois schools journal. Chicago, Ill. : Illinois State Teachers College Chicago-South, 1967-

**Education in a changing world.**
Rajput, J. S. New Delhi : Vikas Pub. House : Distributors, UBS Publishers' Distributors, 1999.
**TC LA1151 .R343 1999**

**Education in a global society :** a comparative perspective / [edited by] Kas Mazurek, Margret A. Winzer, Czeslaw Majorek. Boston : Allyn and Bacon, c2000. vii, 421 p. : ill. ; 25 cm. Includes bibliographical references and index. ISBN 0-205-26752-1 DDC 370/.9
*1. Comparative education. 2. Education - Social aspects.I. Mazurek, Kas. II. Winzer, M. A. (Margret A.), 1940- III. Majorek, Czeslaw.*
**TC LB43 .E385 2000**

**Education in depth.**
California education. [Sacramento : California State Dept. of Education, 1963-1966]

California education. [Sacramento : California State Dept. of Education, 1963-1966]

California education. [Sacramento : California State Dept. of Education, 1963-1966]

**Education in Edge City.**
Hinely, Reg. 2nd ed. Mahwah, N.J. : L. Erlbaum Associates, 2000.
**TC LB1029.C37 H45 2000**

**EDUCATION IN LITERATURE.**
Barney, Richard A., 1955- Plots of enlightenment. Stanford, Calif. : Stanford University Press, c1999.
**TC PR858.E38 B37 1999**

Keroes, Jo. Tales out of school. Carbondale : Southern Illinois University Press, c1999.
**TC PS374.T43 K47 1999**

**EDUCATION IN MASS MEDIA.**
Conners, Gail A. Good news!, Thousand Oaks, Calif. : Corwin Press, c2000.
**TC LB2847 .C65 2000**

**Education in the transition.**
Russia, education in the transition = [S.l.] : The World Bank, ECA Country Development III, Human Resources Division, 1995.
**TC LA839.2 .R87 1995**

**EDUCATION - INDEXES.**
[ERIC (SilverPlatter International : Online)] The ERIC database [computer file]. WebSPIRS version 3.1. [Norwood, MA] : SilverPlatter International,
**TC NETWORKED RESOURCES**

[ERIC (SilverPlatter International : Online)] The ERIC database [computer file]. WebSPIRS version 3.1. [Norwood, MA] : SilverPlatter International,
**TC NETWORKED RESOURCES**

**EDUCATION - INDIA.**
Rajput, J. S. Education in a changing world. New Delhi : Vikas Pub. House : Distributors, UBS Publishers' Distributors, 1999.
**TC LA1151 .R343 1999**

**EDUCATION - INDIA - ABSTRACTS.**
Fifth survey of educational research, 1988-92. New Delhi : National Council of Educational Research and Training, 1997-
**TC LB1028 .F44 1997**

**EDUCATION - INDIA - HISTORY.**
Agrawal, S. P., 1929- Development of education in India. New Delhi : Concept Pub. Co., 1997.
**TC LA1150 .A39 1997**

**EDUCATION - INDIA - HISTORY - 19TH CENTURY.**
The Great Indian education debate. Richmond : Curzon, 1999.
**TC LA1151 .G743 1999**

**EDUCATION - INDIA - KARNATAKA - PERIODICALS.**
Journal of the Karnataka State Education Federation. [Bangalore, India] : The Federation, [1973?-

**EDUCATION - INDIA - PERIODICALS.**
Indian journal of educational research. Bombay, Asia Publishing House.

**EDUCATION - INDIANA - PERIODICALS.**
The Indiana teacher. Indianapolis, Ind. : Indiana State Teachers Association, 1924-1972.

**EDUCATION, INDUSTRIAL.** *See* MANUAL TRAINING.

**Education, information, and transformation :** essays on learning and thinking / [edited by] Jeffrey Kane. Upper Saddle River, N.J. : Merrill, c1999. xxi, 346 p. : 24 cm. Includes bibliographical references and index. ISBN 0-13-520594-8 (pbk.) DDC 153

*1. Thought and thinking. 2. Knowledge, Theory of. 3. Learning, Psychology of. I. Kane, Jeffrey, 1952-*
**TC BF441 .E25 1999**

**EDUCATION - INNOVATIONS.** *See* EDUCATIONAL INNOVATIONS.

**EDUCATION - INTEGRATION.** *See* SCHOOL INTEGRATION.

**EDUCATION, INTERNATIONAL.** *See* INTERNATIONAL EDUCATION.

**EDUCATION - INTERNATIONAL COOPERATION.**
Changing international aid to education. Paris : Unesco Pub./NORRAG, 1999.
**TC LC2607 .C42 1999**

**ÉDUCATION INTERNATIONALE - CANADA.**
A new world of knowledge. Ottawa : International Development Research Centre, c1999.
**TC LC1090 N38 1999**

**ÉDUCATION INTERNATIONALE - COLOMBIE-BRITANNIQUE.**
McKellin, Karen, 1950- Maintaining the momentum. Victoria, B.C. : British Columbia Centre for International Education, c1998.
**TC LC1090 .M24 1998**

**Education is politics :** critical teaching across differences, K-12 / edited by Ira Shor & Caroline Pari ; foreword by Bob Peterson. Portsmouth, NH : Boynton/Cook, c1999. xxii, 260 p. : ill. ; 23 cm. Includes bibliographical references. ISBN 0-86709-465-6 DDC 370.11/5
*1. Critical pedagogy - United States. 2. Multicultural education - United States. 3. Educational equalization - United States. I. Shor, Ira, 1945- II. Pari, Caroline.*
**TC LC196.5.U6 E36 1999**

**EDUCATION - JAPAN.**
Competitor or ally? New York : Falmer Press, 1999.
**TC LA1312 .C667 1999**

Outline of education in Japan, 1997. Tōkyō : Government of Japan, Ministry of Education, Science, Sports and Culture, 1996.
**TC LA1312 .O87 1996**

**EDUCATION - JAPAN - AIMS AND OBJECTIVES.**
Nihon Kyōshokuin Kumiai. Educational reform on people's own initiative. [Tokyo?] : Japan Teachers Union, 1984.
**TC LC210.8.N54 1984**

**EDUCATION - JAPAN - HISTORY - 20TH CENTURY.**
Japanese education since 1945. Armonk, N.Y. : M.E. Sharpe, c1994.
**TC LA1311.82 J39 1994**

**EDUCATION - JAPAN - HISTORY - 20TH CENTURY - SOURCES.**
Japanese education since 1945. Armonk, N.Y. : M.E. Sharpe, c1994.
**TC LA1311.82 J39 1994**

**EDUCATION - JAPAN - STATISTICS - PERIODICALS.**
Statistical abstract of education, science, and culture. [Tokyo] : Research and Statistics Division, Minister's Secretariat, Ministry of Education, Science, and Culture, Japan,
**TC LA1310 .S73**

Statistical abstract of education, science, sports, and culture. [Tokyo] : Research and Statistics Planning Division, Minister's Secretariat, Ministry of Education, Science, Sports, and Culture, 1996-
**TC LA1310 .S73**

**EDUCATION, JEWISH.** *See* JEWISH RELIGIOUS EDUCATION; JEWS - EDUCATION.

**EDUCATION - KANSAS - PERIODICALS.**
Bulletin of education. Lawrence, Kan. : Bureau of School Service and Research, University of Kansas, 1926-1969.

**EDUCATION - KENYA - PERIODICALS.**
Kenya education journal. Nairobi.

**EDUCATION - LATIN AMERICA.**
Pan American Union. Division of Intellectual Cooperation. Lectura para maestros. Washington, D.C., Oficina de Cooperación Intelectual, Unión Panamericana, 193 -

**Education law.**
Imber, Michael. 2nd ed. Mahwah, N.J. : Lawrence Erlbaum Associates, 2000.
**TC KF4118 .143 2000**

**EDUCATION - LAW AND LEGISLATION.** *See* **EDUCATIONAL LAW AND LEGISLATION.**

**Education Law Association (U.S.).**
Mawdsley, Ralph D. Legal problems of religious and private schools. 4th ed. Dayton, OH : Education Law Association, c2000.
*TC KF4124.5 .M38 2000*

**Education law digest.**
West's education law digest. St. Paul : West Pub. Co., c1983-
*TC KF4110.3 .W47*

**EDUCATION LEADERSHIP.** *See* **EDUCATIONAL LEADERSHIP.**

**Education, leadership, and business ethics :** essays on the work of Clarence Walton / edited by Ronald F. Duska. Boston, MA : Kluwer Academic Publishers, c1998. xviii, 323 p. ; 25 cm. (Issues in business ethics ; v. 11) Essays presented at a symposium held in May 1997. ISBN 0-7923-5279-3 DDC 174/.4
*1. Business ethics - Congresses. 2. Business ethics - Study and teaching - Congresses. 3. Business education - Congresses. 4. Social responsibility of business - Congresses. 5. United States - Civilization - Congresses. 6. Leadership - Moral and ethical aspects - Congresses. 7. Walton, Clarence Cyril. - 1915- . I. Walton, Clarence Cyril. 1915- II. Duska. Ronald F.. 1937- III. Series.*
*TC HF5387 .E346 1998*

**EDUCATION, LIBERAL.** *See* **EDUCATION, HUMANISTIC.**

**Education, literacy, and humanization.**
Roberts, Peter, 1963- Westport, Conn. : Bergin & Garvey, 2000.
*TC LB880.F732 R62 2000*

**EDUCATION - LOUISIANA - PERIODICALS.**
Journal of the Louisiana Teachers' Association. [Baton Rouge] : The Association, [1923-1932], (Baton Rouge, La. : Gladney's Print Shop)

**Education management series.**
Wallace, Mike. Senior management teams in primary schools. London ; New York : Routledge, 1999.
*TC LB2806.3 .W37 1999*

**EDUCATION - MASSACHUSETTS - BOSTON - HISTORY - 19TH CENTURY.**
Osgood, Robert L. For "children who vary from the normal type". Washington, D.C. : Gallaudet University Press, c2000.
*TC LC3983.B7 O84 2000*

**EDUCATION - MASSACHUSETTS - BOSTON - HISTORY - 20TH CENTURY.**
Osgood, Robert L. For "children who vary from the normal type". Washington, D.C. : Gallaudet University Press, c2000.
*TC LC3983.B7 O84 2000*

**EDUCATION, MEDICAL.** *See* **MEDICAL EDUCATION.**

**EDUCATION, MEDICAL - HISTORY - UNITED STATES.**
Ludmerer, Kenneth M. Time to heal. Oxford ; New York : Oxford University Press, 1999.
*TC R745 .L843 1999*

**EDUCATION, MEDIEVAL.**
The medieval church. Woodbridge, Suffolk ; Rochester, NY : Published for the Ecclesiastical History Society by the Boydell Press, 1999.
*TC BR270 .M43 1999*

**EDUCATION, MEDIEVAL - EUROPE - CONGRESSES.**
Learning institutionalized. Notre Dame, Ind. : University of Notre Dame Press, c2000.
*TC LA177 .L43 2000*

**EDUCATION, MEDIEVAL - FRANCE - PARIS.**
Courtenay, William J. Parisian scholars in the early fourteenth century. Cambridge, U.K. ; New York, NY : Cambridge University Press, 1999.
*TC LF2165 .C68 1999*

**EDUCATION - MEXICO - COLLECTED WORKS.**
[Folleto de divulgación (Centro de Estudios Educativos).] Folleto de divulgación. México : Centro de Estudios Educativos,

**EDUCATION - MICHIGAN - HAMTRAMCK - PERIODICALS.**
Hamtramck public school bulletin. Hamtramck, Mich. : Board of Education,

**EDUCATION, MORAL.** *See* **MORAL EDUCATION.**

**EDUCATION - MORAL AND ETHICAL ASPECTS.**
White, Patricia, 1937- Civic virtues and public schooling. New York : Teachers College Press, c1996.
*TC LC1011 .W48 1996*

**EDUCATION, MOVEMENT.** *See* **MOVEMENT EDUCATION.**

**EDUCATION, MUSICAL.** *See* **MUSIC - INSTRUCTION AND STUDY.**

**EDUCATION - NETHERLANDS - PERIODICALS.**
Higher education and research in the Netherlands. The Hague, Netherlands Foundation for International Cooperation.

**EDUCATION - NEW JERSEY - CURRICULA.**
Campbell, Delois. High school students' perceptions of the impact of block scheduling on instructional effectiveness. 1999.
*TC 06 no. 11089*

**EDUCATION - NEW YORK (STATE).**
University of the State of New York Bulletin to the schools ... Albany, The University of the State of New York Press [1928-

**EDUCATION - NEW YORK (STATE) - PERIODICALS.**
[Inside education (Albany, N.Y.)] Inside education. Albany : New York State Education Dept., 1968-1983.

[Inside education (Albany, N.Y. : 1991)] Inside education. Albany, N.Y. : University of the State of New York, State Education Dept., 1991-

**EDUCATION - NEW ZEALAND - FINANCE - LONGITUDINAL STUDIES.**
Trading in futures. Buckingham [England] ; Philadelphia : Open University Press, 1999.
*TC LB2826.6.N45 T73 1999*

**Education newsletter.**
[Education newsletter (Strasbourg, France)] Strasbourg [France] : Council of Europe, 1990-1995.
*TC LA620 .D6 1994*

**[Education newsletter (Strasbourg, France)]**
Education newsletter = Education faits nouveaux. Strasbourg [France] : Council of Europe, 1990-1995. v. ; 30 cm. Frequency: Five times a year. 2 & 3/90-1/95. Education faits nouveaux. Running title: Newsletter/faits nouveaux. Title from cover. Some numbers are combined. English and French. Continues: Documentation Centre for Education in Europe. News-letter - Documentation Centre for Education in Europe (DLC) 79647046 (OCoLC)3660213.
*1. Education - Europe - Periodicals. I. Council of Europe. II. Title. III. Title: Education faits nouveaux IV. Title: Newsletter/ faits nouveaux V. Title: Documentation Centre for Education in Europe. News-letter - Documentation Centre for Education in Europe*
*TC LA620 .D6 1994*

**EDUCATION - NIGERIA.**
Research on schooling in Nigeria. Ondo [Nigeria] : Centre for Research on Schooling, Adeyemi College of Education, 1995.
*TC LB1028.25.N6 R477 1995*

**EDUCATION - NIGERIA - EVALUATION - CONGRESSES.**
Issues on examination malpractices in Nigeria :. Ikere-Ekiti [Nigeria] : Ondo State College of Education, c1998.
*TC LB3058.N6 1848 1998*

**EDUCATION, NURSING.**
Gaberson, Kathleen B. Clinical teaching strategies in nursing. New York : Springer, c1999.
*TC RT73 .G26 1999*

Integrating community service into nursing education. New York, NY : Springer Pub. Co., c1999.
*TC RT76 .I55 1999*

Reflective practice in nursing. 2nd ed. Oxford ; Malden, MA : Blackwell Scientific, 2000.
*TC RT73 .R3461 2000*

**EDUCATION, NURSING, ASSOCIATE - STANDARDS.**
Educational competencies for graduates of associate degree nursing programs. [Rev.]. Sudbury, Mass. : Jones and Bartlett, 2000.
*TC RT74.5 .E38 2000*

**EDUCATION, NURSING, GRADUATE - UNITED STATES - DIRECTORIES.**
Annual guide to graduate nursing education programs. New York, N.Y. : National League for Nursing Press, c1995-
*TC RT75 .A5*

**EDUCATION, NURSING - METHODS.**
Ulrich, Deborah L. Interactive group learning. New York : Springer, c1999.
*TC RT76 .U46 1999*

**The education of a Christian society.**
Anglo-Dutch Historical Conference (13th : 1997) Aldershot, Hants, England ; Brookfield, Vt. : Ashgate, c1999.
*TC BR377 .E38 1999*

**The education of a graphic designer** / edited by Steven Heller. New York : Allworth Press [in association with] School of Visual Arts, c1998 xiii, 273 p. : ill. : 25 cm. Includes essays, interviews and course syllabi. Includes bibliographical references and index. ISBN 1-88055-999-4 DDC 741.6/071
*1. Graphic arts - Study and teaching. 2. Design - Study and teaching. 3. Commercial art - Study and teaching. I. Heller, Steven.*
*TC NC590 .E38 1998*

**EDUCATION OF ADULTS.** *See* **ADULT EDUCATION.**

**EDUCATION OF CHILDREN.** *See* **EDUCATION.**

**The education of children with medical conditions** / edited by Alison Closs ; [foreword by Philippa Russell]. London : D. Fulton Publishers, 2000. xviii, 206 p. ; 25 cm. Includes bibliographic references (p. [195]-204) and index. ISBN 1-85346-569-0
*1. Chronically ill children - Education - Great Britain. 2. Sick children - Education - Great Britain. 3. Special education - Great Britain. I. Closs, Alison.*
*TC LC4564.G7 E38 2000*

**EDUCATION OF GIRLS.** *See* **WOMEN - EDUCATION.**

**Education of Hispanics in the United States :** Politics, policies, and outcomes / Volume editors, Abbas Tashakkori, Salvador Hector Ochoa. New York : AMS Press, c1999. xxiv, 271 p. ; 24 cm. (Readings on equal education, 0270-1448 ; v. 16) Includes bibliographical references and index. ISBN 0-404-10116-X (Volume 16) ISBN 0-404-10100-3 (Set)
*1. Hispanic Americans - Education. I. Tashakkori. Abbas. II. Ochoa, Salvador Hector. III. Series.*
*TC LC4091 .R417 1999*

**Education of Hispanics in the United States :** Politics, policies, and outcomes / Volume editors, Abbas Tashakkori, Salvador Hector Ochoa. New York : AMS Press, c1999. xxiv, 271 p. ; 24 cm. (Readings on equal education, 0270-1448 ; v. 16) Includes bibliographical references and index. ISBN 0-404-10116-X (Volume 16) ISBN 0-404-10100-3 (Set)
*1. Hispanic Americans - Education. I. Tashakkori. Abbas. II. Ochoa, Salvador Hector. III. Series.*
*TC LC4091 .R417 1999*

**Education of Pakistan** Karachi

**EDUCATION OF THE AGED.** *See* **AGED - EDUCATION.**

**EDUCATION OF THE DEAF.** *See* **DEAF - EDUCATION.**

**EDUCATION OF WOMEN.** *See* **WOMEN - EDUCATION.**

**EDUCATION OF WORKERS.** *See* **WORKING CLASS - EDUCATION.**

**EDUCATION - OHIO - PERIODICALS.**
[Journal (Martha Holden Jennings Foundation)] Journal. [Cleveland : The Foundation, 1974-

**Education on the move**
Changing international aid to education. Paris : Unesco Pub./NORRAG, 1999.
*TC LC2607 .C42 1999*

**EDUCATION - ONTARIO - PUBLIC OPINION.**
Livingstone, D. W. Public attitudes towards education in Ontario, 1996. Toronto : OISE/UT in association with University of Toronto Press, 1997.
*TC LA418.06 L58 1997*

**EDUCATION - OREGON.**
The High school. Eugene, Ore.

**EDUCATION - PAKISTAN.**
Education and the state. Karachi : Oxford University Press, 1998.
*TC LA1156 .E36 1998*

**EDUCATION - PAKISTAN - PERIODICALS.**
The Jamia educational quarterly. Malir City, Karachi : Jamia Millia Institute of Education, 1960-1972.

**EDUCATION - PAKISTAN - STATISTICS - PERIODICALS.**
Pakistan education statistics. Islamabad : Bureau of

Educational Planning and Management and Central Bureau of Education, Ministry of Education,
*TC LA1155 .P37 1995*

**EDUCATION - PARENT PARTICIPATION.** *See also* **HOME SCHOOLING.**
Hornby, Garry. Improving parental involvement. London : Cassell, 2000.
*TC LC225 .H67 2000*

**EDUCATION - PARENT PARTICIPATION - GREAT BRITAIN.**
The contribution of parents to school effectiveness. London : David Fulton Publishers, c2000.
*TC LC225.33.G7 C66 2000*

**EDUCATION - PARENT PARTICIPATION - INDIANA - INDIANAPOLIS - CASE STUDIES.**
Rosier, Katherine Brown. Mothering inner-city children. New Brunswick, NJ : Rutgers University Press, 2000.
*TC HV1447.I53 R67 2000*

**EDUCATION - PARENT PARTICIPATION - PSYCHOLOGICAL ASPECTS.**
Ryan, Daniel Prentice. Gay/lesbian parents and school personnel. 1998.
*TC 06 no. 10988*

**EDUCATION - PARENT PARTICIPATION - UNITED STATES.**
Annual State of American Education Address (7th : February 22, 2000 : Durham, N.C.) The seventh annual state of American education address [videorecording. [Washington, D.C. : U.S. Dept. of Education], 2000.

Bempechat, Janine, 1956- Getting our kids back on track. 1st ed. San Francisco : Jossey-Bass, c2000.
*TC LC225.3 .B45 2000*

Berger, Eugenia Hepworth. Parents as partners in education. 5th ed. Upper Saddle River, N.J. : Merrill, c2000.
*TC LC225.3 .B47 2000*

Kralovec, Etta. The end of homework. Boston, Mass. : Beacon Press, c2000.
*TC LB1048 .K73 2000*

Power, Brenda Miller. Parent power. Portsmouth, NH : Heinemann, c1999.
*TC LC225.3 .P69 1999*

**EDUCATION - PARENT PARTICIPATION - UNITED STATES - HANDBOOKS, MANUALS, ETC.**
Ottenburg, Susan D. Education today. 2nd. ed. Boston : Educational Publishing Group, Education Today, c1996.
*TC LC225.3 .O88 1996*

**EDUCATION - PARENT PARTICIPATION - UNITED STATES - HISTORY - 19TH CENTURY.**
Cutler, William W. Parents and schools. Chicago : University of Chicago Press, 2000.
*TC LC225.3 .C86 2000*

**EDUCATION - PARENT PARTICIPATION - UNITED STATES - HISTORY - 20TH CENTURY.**
Cutler, William W. Parents and schools. Chicago : University of Chicago Press, 2000.
*TC LC225.3 .C86 2000*

**EDUCATION - PERIODICALS.**
American educational digest. [Crawfordsville, Ind. : Educational Digest Co., 1923-1928]

Bulletin of education. Lawrence, Kan. : Bureau of School Service and Research, University of Kansas, 1926-1969.

Bulletin of the American Association of Collegiate Registrars. Philadelphia, American Association of College Registrars.

California journal of elementary education. Sacramento, California, State Department of Education.
*TC L11 .C27*

California review of adult education. [Los Angeles : California State Dept. of Education, 1936.

Changing education. Detroit [etc.]

Chicago schools journal. Chicago, Board of Education.

Child life. London, G. Philip & Son.

Connecticut teacher. Hartford, Conn. : The Association, [1933-

L'Éducateur et bulletin corporatif. Lausanne,

Forum of education. London, Longmans Green.

Frontiers of democracy. New York, Progressive Education Association, etc., 1934-

Fundamental and adult education. [Paris : Unesco, 1952-1960]

Fundamental education. [Paris, France : Unesco, 1949-1952].

Georgia education journal. Macon, Ga. : Georgia Education Association, 1926-1970.

Georgia educator. [Atlanta]

The Grade teacher. Boston, Mass. : Educational Pub. Co., -c1972.

Hamtramck public school bulletin. Hamtramck, Mich. : Board of Education,

Haryana journal of education. Chandigarh, Haryana Education Dept.

High points in the work of the high schools of New York City. New York City : Board of Education, 1931-1966.

The High school. Eugene, Ore.

The Idaho journal of education. [Boise, Idaho, Idaho Education Association, 1930-1946]

Illinois education; Mount Morris, Ill. [etc.]

Illinois journal of education. [Springfield, Ill.] : Superintendent of Public Instruction, 1961-

The Illinois teacher: Peoria, Ill., Nason.

Independent education. New York [etc.] : Craft Publication Company [etc.], 1927-1929.

The Indiana teacher. Indianapolis, Ind. : Indiana State Teachers Association, 1924-1972.

Intellect. [New York, Society for the Advancement of Education]

[International journal of educational development (Online)] International journal of educational development [computer file]. Oxford ; New York : Pergamon,
*TC EJOURNALS*

**EDUCATION - PERIODICALS.**
[International journal of educational development (Online)] International journal of educational development [computer file]. Oxford ; New York : Pergamon,
*TC EJOURNALS*

**EDUCATION - PERIODICALS.**
Internationale Zeitschrift für Erziehungswissenschaft. Salzburg.

Internationale Zeitschrift für Erziehungswissenschaft = Köln : J.P. Bachem,

[Journal (Martha Holden Jennings Foundation)] Journal. [Cleveland : The Foundation, 1974-

Journal of emotional education. New York, Emotional Education Press.

Journal of open education. Cambridge, Mass., Institute of Open Education.

The journal of pedagogy. Syracuse, N.Y., [etc.],

Journal of the American Association of Collegiate Registrars. Athens, Ohio [etc.] American Association of College Registrars.

Journal of the Louisiana Teachers' Association. [Baton Rouge] : The Association, [1923-1932], (Baton Rouge, La. : Gladney's Print Shop)

The Junior high clearing house. Lebanon, Pa., Junior High School Clearing House.

The Kadelpian quarterly review . [S.l.] : The Council, 1926-

Kentucky high school quarterly. Lexington, Ky. : Department of Education, State University of Kentucky, 1915-1927.

Kindergarten primary magazine. Chicago [etc.], A. B. Stockham & Co., [etc.]

Kwartalnik pedagogiczny. [Warszawa] Państwowe Wydawn. Naukowe.

Majallat al-tarbiyah al-ḥadīthah. al-Qāhirah : al-Jāmi'ah al-Amrīkīyah bi-al-Qāhirah, 1928- .

The University of Michigan School of Education bulletin. [Ann Arbor] : The School, 1929-1964.

University of Pittsburgh. School of Education. Journal. [Lancaster, Pa. : The School, 1925-

University of the State of New York Bulletin to the schools ... Albany, The University of the State of New York Press [1928-

**EDUCATION - PERIODICALS - INDEXES.**
[ERIC (SilverPlatter International : Online)] The ERIC database [computer file]. WebSPIRS version 3.1. [Norwood, MA] : SilverPlatter International,
*TC NETWORKED RESOURCES*

[ERIC (SilverPlatter International : Online)] The ERIC database [computer file]. WebSPIRS version 3.1. [Norwood, MA] : SilverPlatter International,
*TC NETWORKED RESOURCES*

**EDUCATION - PHILIPPINES.**
[Tanglaw (Manila, Philippines)] Tanglaw. Manila : The College, 1992-

**EDUCATION - PHILIPPINES - PERIODICALS.**
Baguio tech journal. [Baguio City, Philippines : Baguio Tech.,

**EDUCATION - PHILOSOPHY.** *See also* **EDUCATIONAL ANTHROPOLOGY; PROGRESSIVE EDUCATION.**
Acker, Victor, 1940- Célestin Freinet. Westport, CT : Greenwood Press, 2000.
*TC LB775 .A255 2000*

The aims of education. London ; New York : Routledge, 1999.
*TC LB41 .A36353 1999*

Barone, Tom. Aesthetics, politics, and educational inquiry. New York : P. Lang, 2000.
*TC LB1028 .B345 2000*

Berube, Maurice R. Eminent educators. Westport, Conn. : Greenwood Press, 2000.
*TC LB875.D5 B47 2000*

Challenges and opportunities for education in the 21st century. Lewiston, NY : Edwin Mellen Press, c1999.
*TC LA209.2 .C45 1999*

Chomsky, Noam. Chomsky on miseducation. Lanham, Md. : Oxford : Rowman & Littlefield Publishers, c2000.
*TC LB885.C522 A3 2000*

Dewey and European education. Dordrecht : Kluwer Academic Publishers, c2000.
*TC LB875.D5 D47 2000*

Dewey, John, 1859-1952. [Works.] The collected works of John Dewey, 1882-1953. [computer file]. Windows version. Charlottesville, VA : InteLex Corp, 1997, c1992. Computer program.
*TC LB875 .D363 1997*

Edgoose, Julian Miles. Partnerships of possibility. 1999.
*TC 085 E117*

Freirean pedagogy, praxis, and possibilities. New York : Falmer Press, 2000.
*TC LC196 .F76 2000*

Gordon, Mordechai. Toward an integrative conception of authority in education. 1997.
*TC 085 G656*

Groome, Thomas H. Educating for life. Allen, Tex. : T. More, c1998.
*TC BV1471.2 .G6874 1998*

Improving education. London ; New York : Cassell, 1999.
*TC LB7 .I48 1999*

Kincheloe, Joe L. The stigma of genius. New York ; Canterbury [England] : P. Lang, c1999.
*TC LB875.E562 K56 1999*

Locke, John, 1632-1704. [Some thoughts concerning education] Some thoughts concerning education : Indianapolis : Hackett Pub. Co., c1996.
*TC LB475.L6 L63 1996*

Peters, Michael (Michael A.), 1948- Wittgenstein. Westport, Conn. : Bergin & Garvey, 1999.
*TC B3376.W564 P388 1999*

Philosophical documents in education. 2nd ed. New York : Longman, c2000.
*TC LB7 .P5432 2000*

Reitz, Charles. Art, alienation, and the humanities. Albany : State University of New York Press, c2000.
*TC B945.M2984 R45 2000*

Roberts, Peter, 1963- Education, literacy, and humanization. Westport, Conn. : Bergin & Garvey, 2000.

*TC LB880.F732 R62 2000*

Tarcov, Nathan. Locke's education for liberty. Lanham, Md. : Lexington Books, c1999.
*TC LB475.L72 T27 1999*

Taught bodies. New York : P. Lang, c2000.
*TC LB14.7 .T38 2000*

Trifonas, Peter Pericles, 1960- The ethics of writing. Lanham, Md. : Oxford : Rowman & Littlefield, c2000.
*TC LB14.7 .T75 2000*

Trifonas, Peter Pericles, 1960- Revolutionary pedagogies. New York : Routledge, 2000.
*TC LC196 .R48 2000*

**EDUCATION - PHILOSOPHY - CONGRESSES.**
Grundtvig's ideas in North America. Copenhagen, Denmark : Danske Selskab, 1983.
*TC LB675.G832 G79 1983*

**EDUCATION, PHYSICAL.** *See* **PHYSICAL EDUCATION AND TRAINING.**

**EDUCATION - PLANNING.** *See* **EDUCATIONAL PLANNING.**

**Education policy and contemporary politics** / edited by Jack Demaine. Basingstoke, Hampshire : Macmillan, 1999. x, 207 p. ; 23 cm. Includes bibliographical references (p. 180-196) and index. ISBN 0-333-68250-5
*1. Politics and education - Great Britain. I. Demaine, Jack.*
*TC LC93.G7 E382 1999*

**Education policy** / edited by James Marshall and Michael Peters. Cheltenham, UK : Northampton, MA : Edward Elgar Pub., c1999. xxxv, 828 p. : ill. ; 26 cm. (The international library of comparative public policy ; 12) (An Elgar reference collection) Includes bibliographical references and index. ISBN 1-85898-792-X DDC 379
*1. Education and state. 2. Educational sociology. 3. Education - Economic aspects. 4. Critical pedagogy. I. Marshall, James (James D.) II. Peters, Michael (Michael A.), 1948- III. Series. IV. Series: An Elgar reference collection*
*TC LC71 .E32 1999*

**EDUCATION - POLITICAL ASPECTS.**
Accuracy or advocacy. Thousand Oaks, Calif. : Corwin Press, c1999.
*TC LB1028 .A312 1999*

Trifonas, Peter Pericles, 1960- Revolutionary pedagogies. New York : Routledge, 2000.
*TC LC196 .R48 2000*

**EDUCATION - POLITICAL ASPECTS - UNITED STATES.**
Apple, Michael W. Official knowledge. 2nd ed. New York : Routledge, 2000.
*TC LC89 .A815 2000*

New school order [videorecording]. New York : First Run/Icarus Films, 1996.
*TC LB2831.583.P4 N4 1996*

**EDUCATION, PRESCHOOL.** *See also* **NURSERY SCHOOLS.**
Campbell, Robin, 1937- Literacy from home to school :. Stoke on Trent, Staffordshire, Eng. : Trentham Books, 1999.
*TC LB1140.2 .C35 1999*

Murphy, Lois Barclay, 1902- The individual child. Washington : Department of Health Education, and Welfare : for sale by the Supt. of Docs., U. S. Govt. Print. Off., 1973.

**EDUCATION, PRESCHOOL - 1965 - - CURRICULA.**
Lavatelli, Celia Stendler, 1911- Piaget's theory applied to an early childhood curriculum. [1st ed.]. Boston : American Science and Engineering, [c1970].
*TC LB1140.2 .L3*

**EDUCATION, PRESCHOOL - GREAT BRITAIN - CURRICULA.**
Rodger, Rosemary, 1946- Planning an appropriate curriculum for the under fives. London : David Fulton, 1999.
*TC LB1140.25.G7 R64 1999*

**EDUCATION, PRESCHOOL - JAPAN.**
Holloway, Susan D. Contested childhood. New York : Routledge, 2000.
*TC LB1140.25.J3 H69 2000*

**EDUCATION, PRESCHOOL - NIGERIA - CONGRESSES.**
Pre-primary education in Nigeria. Onitsha [Nigeria] : Lincel, 1998.
*TC LB1140.25.N6 P74 1998*

**EDUCATION, PRESCHOOL - PARENT PARTICIPATION - NORTH CAROLINA - CHARLOTTE - CASE STUDIES.**

Dunlap, Katherine M. Family empowerment. New York : London : Garland Pub., 2000.
*TC LB1140.35.P37 D86 2000*

**EDUCATION, PRESCHOOL - PARENT PARTICIPATION - UNITED STATES.**
Hillman, Carol. Before the school bell rings. Bloomington, Ind. : Phi Delta Kappa Educational Foundation, c1995.
*TC LB1140.23 .H54 1995*

**EDUCATION, PRESCHOOL - UNITED STATES.**
Hillman, Carol. Before the school bell rings. Bloomington, Ind. : Phi Delta Kappa Educational Foundation, c1995.
*TC LB1140.23 .H54 1995*

**EDUCATION, PRESCHOOL - UNITED STATES - CURRICULA.**
Cromwell, Ellen, 1937- Nurturing readiness in early childhood education. 2nd ed. Boston : Allyn & Bacon, c2000.
*TC LB1140.4 .C76 2000*

Mardell, Ben. From basketball to the Beatles. Portsmouth, NH : Heinemann, 1999.
*TC LB1139.4 .M27 1999*

**EDUCATION, PRIMARY.** *See also* **FIRST GRADE (EDUCATION); FOURTH GRADE (EDUCATION); SECOND GRADE (EDUCATION).**
Bickart, Toni S. Building the primary classroom. Washington, DC : Teaching Strategies : Portsmouth, NH : Heinemann, 1999.
*TC LB1507 .B53 1999*

**EDUCATION, PRIMARY - ACTIVITY PROGRAMS.**
Opitz, Michael F. Rhymes & reasons. Portsmouth, NH : Heinemann, c2000.
*TC LB1528 .O65 2000*

**EDUCATION (PRIMARY) - ACTIVITY PROGRAMS.**
Phonics review kit [kit]. Chicago, Ill. : Open Court Pub. Co., c1995.
*TC LB1573.3 .P45 1995*

Teacher toolbox [kit]. Chicago, Ill. : Open Court Pub. Co., c1995.
*TC LB1573.3 .T4 1995*

**EDUCATION, PRIMARY - ACTIVITY PROGRAMS - UNITED STATES.**
Rogovin, Paula. Classroom interviews. Portsmouth, NH : Heinemann, c1998.
*TC LB1537 .R58 1998*

Stull, Elizabeth Crosby. Let's read!. West Nyack, NY : Center for Applied Research in Education, c2000.
*TC LB1573 .S896 2000*

**EDUCATION, PRIMARY - ASIA - CASE STUDIES.**
Grass roots networking for primary education :. Bangkok : Unesco Regional Office for Education in Asia and the Pacific, 1985.
*TC LA1054 .G73 1985*

**EDUCATION, PRIMARY - CURRICULA.**
Bickart, Toni S. Building the primary classroom. Washington, DC : Teaching Strategies : Portsmouth, NH : Heinemann, 1999.
*TC LB1507 .B53 1999*

**EDUCATION (PRIMARY) - DATA PROCESSING - JUVENILE LITERATURE.**
Drake, Jim, 1955- Computers and schools. Des Plaines, Ill. : Heinemann Library, c1999.
*TC LB1028.5 .D69 1999*

**EDUCATION, PRIMARY - EXPERIMENTAL METHODS.**
Ryan, Sharon Kaye. Freedom to choice. 1998.
*TC 06 no. 11034*

**EDUCATION, PRIMARY - FRANCE - HISTORY - 19TH CENTURY.**
Curtis, Sarah Ann. Educating the faithful. DeKalb : Northern Illinois University Press, 2000.
*TC LC506.F7 C87 2000*

**EDUCATION, PRIMARY - SOCIAL ASPECTS - NEW YORK (STATE) - NEW YORK - CASE STUDIES.**
Ochsner, Mindy Blaise. Something rad & risqu'e. 1999.
*TC 06 no. 11208*

**EDUCATION, PRIMARY - ZIMBABWE.**
Ross, Kenneth N. (Kenneth Norman), 1947- Indicators of the quality of education. Paris : International Institute for Educational Planning, 1992.

*TC LA1592 .R67 1992*

**EDUCATION, PRIMITIVE.** *See* **EDUCATION.**

**EDUCATION, PRIMITIVE - ADDRESSES, ESSAYS, LECTURES.**
Harrington, Charles C. Cross cultural approaches to learning. New York : MSS Informationc c1973.
*TC GN488.5 .H33 1973*

**EDUCATION, PROFESSIONAL.** *See* **PROFESSIONAL EDUCATION.**

**EDUCATION PROFESSORS.** *See* **TEACHER EDUCATORS.**

**EDUCATION - PSYCHOLOGY.** *See* **EDUCATIONAL PSYCHOLOGY.**

**EDUCATION - QUOTATIONS, MAXIMS, ETC.**
Lordahl, Jo Ann. Reflections for busy educators. Thousand Oaks, Calif. : Corwin Press, c1995.
*TC PN6084.E38 L67 1995*

**EDUCATION - REFERENCE BOOKS - BIBLIOGRAPHY.**
O'Brien, Nancy P. Education, a guide to reference and information sources. 2nd ed. Englewood, Colo. : Libraries Unlimited, 2000.
*TC Z5811 .B89 2000*

**EDUCATION REFORM.** *See* **EDUCATIONAL CHANGE.**

**EDUCATION - RESEARCH.** *See also* **ACTION RESEARCH IN EDUCATION.**
Accuracy or advocacy. Thousand Oaks, Calif. : Corwin Press, c1999.
*TC LB1028 .A312 1999*

Bell, Judith, 1930- Doing your research project. 3rd ed. Buckingham [England] ; Philadelphia : Open University Press, 1999.
*TC LB1028 .B394 1999*

Gay, L. R. Educational research. 6th ed. Upper Saddle River, N.J. : Merrill, c2000.
*TC LB1028 .G37 2000*

The international handbook of school effectiveness research. London ; New York : Falmer Press, 2000.
*TC LB2822.75 .I59 2000*

Johnson, Burke. Educational research. Boston : Allyn and Bacon, c2000.
*TC LB1028 .J59 2000*

McMillan, James H. Educational research. 3rd ed. New York ; Harlow, England : Longman, c2000.
*TC LB1028 .M364 2000*

Wiersma, William. Research methods in education. 7th ed. Boston : Allyn and Bacon, c2000.
*TC LB1028 .W517 2000*

Working the ruins. New York ; London : Routledge, 2000.
*TC LC197 .W67 2000*

**EDUCATION - RESEARCH - ADDRESSES, ESSAYS, LECTURES.**
Research into classroom processes; New York, Teachers College Press, 1971.
*TC LB1028 .W488*

**EDUCATION - RESEARCH - AUSTRALIA.**
Australian education. Camberwell, Vic. : Australian Council for Educational Research, 1998.
*TC LA2102.7 .A87 1998*

**EDUCATION - RESEARCH - BIBLIOGRAPHY - PERIODICALS.**
Resources in education. Semiannual index. Phoenix, AZ : Oryx Press,
*TC Z5813 .R42*

**EDUCATION - RESEARCH - CASE STUDIES.**
Improving education. London ; New York : Cassell, 1999.
*TC LB7 .I48 1999*

Merriam, Sharan B. Qualitative research and case study applications in education. 2nd ed. San Francisco : Jossey-Bass Publishers, c1998.
*TC LB1028 .M396 1998*

**EDUCATION - RESEARCH - GREAT BRITAIN - METHODOLOGY.**
Bassey, Michael. Case study research in educational settings. Buckingham [England] ; Philadelphia : Open University Press, 1999.
*TC LB1028.25.G7 B37 1999*

Murray, Louis, 1944- Practitioner-based enquiry. London ; New York : Falmer Press, 2000.

*TC LB1028.24 .M87 2000*

Ozga, Jennifer. Policy research in educational settings :. Buckingham [England] ; Philadelphia : Open University Press, 2000.
*TC LB1028.25.G7 O93 2000*

**EDUCATION - RESEARCH - ILLINOIS.**
University of Illinois (Urbana-Champaign campus). Bureau of Educational Research. Bulletin. Urbana, 1918-47.

**EDUCATION - RESEARCH - INDEXES.**
[ERIC (SilverPlatter International : Online)] The ERIC database [computer file]. WebSPIRS version 3.1. [Norwood, MA] : SilverPlatter International,
*TC NETWORKED RESOURCES*

[ERIC (SilverPlatter International : Online)] The ERIC database [computer file]. WebSPIRS version 3.1. [Norwood, MA] : SilverPlatter International,
*TC NETWORKED RESOURCES*

**EDUCATION - RESEARCH - INDIA.**
Indian Journal of Educational Administration and Research. New Delhi

Fifth survey of educational research, 1988-92. New Delhi : National Council of Educational Research and Training, 1997-
*TC LB1028 .F44 1997*

**EDUCATION - RESEARCH - METHODOLOGY.**
Barone, Tom. Aesthetics, politics, and educational inquiry. New York : P. Lang, 2000.
*TC LB1028 .B345 2000*

Bell, Judith, 1930- Doing your research project. 3rd ed. Buckingham [England] ; Philadelphia : Open University Press, 1999.
*TC LB1028 .B394 1999*

Clandinin, D. Jean. Narrative inquiry. 1st ed. San Francisco : Jossey-Bass Inc., c2000.
*TC LB1028 .C55 2000*

Merriam, Sharan B. Qualitative research and case study applications in education. 2nd ed. San Francisco : Jossey-Bass Publishers, c1998.
*TC LB1028 .M396 1998*

Paley, Nicholas. Questions of you and the struggle of collaborative life. New York : P. Lang, c2000.
*TC LB1028 .P233 2000*

Scheurich, James Joseph, 1944- Research method in the postmodern. London ; Washington, DC : Falmer Press, 1997.
*TC LB1028 .S242 1997*

**EDUCATION - RESEARCH - PERIODICALS.**
Indian Journal of Educational Administration and Research. New Delhi

**EDUCATION - RESEARCH - PHILOSOPHY.**
Scheurich, James Joseph, 1944- Research method in the postmodern. London ; Washington, DC : Falmer Press, 1997.
*TC LB1028 .S242 1997*

**EDUCATION - RESEARCH - SOCIAL ASPECTS.**
Barone, Tom. Aesthetics, politics, and educational inquiry. New York : P. Lang, 2000.
*TC LB1028 .B345 2000*

**EDUCATION - RESEARCH - SOCIAL ASPECTS - UNITED STATES.**
Lagemann, Ellen Condliffe, 1945- An elusive science. Chicago : University of Chicago Press, 2000.
*TC LB1028.25.U6 L33 2000*

Multiple and intersecting identities in qualitative research. Mahwah, N.J. ; London : L. Erlbaum Associates, 2001.
*TC LB1028.25.U6 M85 2001*

**EDUCATION - RESEARCH - UNITED STATES.**
Improving student learning. Washington, D.C. : National Academy Press, c1999.
*TC LB1028.25.U6 I66 1999*

**EDUCATION - RESEARCH - UNITED STATES - HANDBOOKS, MANUALS, ETC.**
Hubbard, Ruth, 1950- The art of classroom inquiry. Portsmouth, N.H. : Heinemann, c1993.
*TC LB1028 .H78 1993*

**EDUCATION - RESEARCH - UNITED STATES - HISTORY.**
Lagemann, Ellen Condliffe, 1945- An elusive science. Chicago : University of Chicago Press, 2000.
*TC LB1028.25.U6 L33 2000*

**EDUCATION - RESEARCH - UNITED STATES - PERIODICALS.**
American education annual. Detroit : Gale, c1999-

*TC LB1028.25.U6 A44*

**EDUCATION, RURAL.** *See* **RURAL SCHOOLS.**

**EDUCATION - RUSSIA.**
Ushinskiĭ, K. D. (Konstantin Dmitrievich), 1824-1870. [Selected works. English. 1975] K. D. Ushinsky. Moscow : Progress, 1975.
*TC LB675 .U8213 1975*

**EDUCATION - RUSSIA (FEDERATION).**
Innovation in Russian schools. Bloomington, Ind. : Phi Delta Kappa Educational Foundation, c1997.
*TC LB1027 .I6575 1997*

Webber, Stephen L., 1967- School, reform and society in the new Russia . Houndmills [England] : Macmillan Press ; New York : St. Martin's Press in association with Centre for Russian and East European Studies, University of Birmingham, 2000.
*TC LA839.2 .W4 2000*

**EDUCATION, SCIENTIFIC.** *See* **SCIENCE - STUDY AND TEACHING.**

**EDUCATION - SCOTLAND.**
Scottish education. Edinburgh : Edinburgh University Press, c1999.
*TC LA652 .S34 1999*

**EDUCATION, SECONDARY.** *See also* **COUNSELING IN SECONDARY EDUCATION; EVENING AND CONTINUATION SCHOOLS; FOLK HIGH SCHOOLS; HIGH SCHOOLS; NINTH GRADE (EDUCATION); TWELFTH GRADE (EDUCATION).**
Emmer, Edmund T. Classroom management for secondary teachers. 5th ed. Boston : Allyn and Bacon, c2000.
*TC LB3013 .C53 2000*

Mosley, Jenny. Quality circle time in the secondary school :. London : David Fulton, 1999.
*TC LB1032 .M67 1999*

Thayer, Vivian Trow, 1886- Reorganizing secondary education; New York, Appleton-Century [c1939]
*TC LB1607 .T5*

**EDUCATION, SECONDARY - ACTIVITY PROGRAMS - PUERTO RICO.**
Laborde, Ilia M. Rediscovering San Cristóbal Canyon. 1996.
*TC 06 no. 10660*

Laborde, Ilia M. Rediscovering San Cristóbal Canyon. 1996.
*TC 06 no. 10660*

**EDUCATION, SECONDARY - ACTIVITY PROGRAMS - UNITED STATES.**
Golub, Jeffrey N., 1944- Making learning happen. Portsmouth, NH : Boynton/Cook Publishers, c2000.
*TC LB1631 .G623 2000*

Kessler, Rachael, 1946- The soul of education. Alexandria, Va. : Association for Supervision and Curriculum Development, c2000.
*TC LB1072 .K48 2000*

**EDUCATION, SECONDARY - CALIFORNIA - EVALUATION - HANDBOOKS, MANUALS, ETC.**
Barr, Mary A. (Mary Anderson) Assessing literacy with the Learning Record. Portsmouth, NH : Heinemann, c1999.
*TC LB1029.P67 B37 1999*

**EDUCATION, SECONDARY - CANADA - CASE STUDIES.**
Louden, William. Understanding teaching. New York : Cassell : Teachers College Press, Teachers College, Columbia University, 1991.
*TC LB1025.3 .L68 1991*

**EDUCATION, SECONDARY - COMPUTER NETWORK RESOURCES.**
McLain, Tim, 1970- How to create successful Internet projects. El Segundo, Calif. : Classroom Connect, c1999.
*TC LB1044.87 .M35 1999*

**EDUCATION, SECONDARY - ENGLAND - HISTORY.**
Vlaeminke, Meriel. The English higher grade schools. London ; Portland, OR : Woburn Press, 2000.
*TC LA634 .V52 2000*

**EDUCATION, SECONDARY - ENGLAND - LONDON - CROSS-CULTURAL STUDIES.**
Making spaces. New York : St. Martin's Press, 2000.
*TC LC208.4 .M35 2000*

**EDUCATION, SECONDARY - ENGLAND - LONDON - HISTORY - 19TH CENTURY.**
Elledge, Paul. Lord Byron at Harrow School. Baltimore : Johns Hopkins University Press, c2000.
*TC PR4382 .E36 2000*

**EDUCATION, SECONDARY - FINLAND - HELSINKI - CROSS-CULTURAL STUDIES.**
Making spaces. New York : St. Martin's Press, 2000.
*TC LC208.4 .M35 2000*

**EDUCATION, SECONDARY - GERMANY.**
Dichanz, Horst, 1937- Changing traditions in Germany's public schools. Bloomington, Ind. : Phi Delta Kappa Educational Foundation, c1998.
*TC LA723 .D53 1998*

**EDUCATION, SECONDARY - GHANA - HISTORY.**
Quist, Hubert Oswald. Secondary education and nation-building. 1999.
*TC 085 Q52*

**EDUCATION, SECONDARY - GREAT BRITAIN.**
Helsby, Gill. Changing teachers' work. Buckingham [England] ; Philadelphia : Open University Press, 1999.
*TC LA635 .H375 1999*

**EDUCATION, SECONDARY - GREAT BRITAIN - CASE STUDIES.**
Duncan, Neil, 1956- Sexual bullying. London ; New York : Routledge, 1999.
*TC LC212.83.G7 D85 1999*

**EDUCATION, SECONDARY - GREAT BRITAIN - CURRICULA.**
Gender in the secondary curriculum. London ; New York : Routledge, 1998.
*TC LC212.93.G7 G46 1998*

**EDUCATION, SECONDARY - GREAT BRITAIN - DATA PROCESSING - CASE STUDIES.**
Learning to teach using ICT in the secondary school. London : New York : Routledge, 1999.
*TC LB1028.5 .L3884 1999*

**EDUCATION, SECONDARY - IRELAND - CURRICULA - HISTORY - 20TH CENTURY.**
O'Donoghue, T. A. (Tom A.), 1953- The Catholic Church and the secondary school curriculum in Ireland, 1922-1962. New York : P. Lang, c1999.
*TC LC506.G72 I745 1999*

**EDUCATION, SECONDARY - JAPAN - CASE STUDIES.**
Whitman, Nancy C. A case study of Japanese middle schools, 1983-1998. Lanham, Md. : Oxford : University Press of America, c2000.
*TC LA1316 .W45 2000*

**EDUCATION, SECONDARY - NEW JERSEY.**
Campbell, Delois. High school students' perceptions of the impact of block scheduling on instructional effectiveness. 1999.
*TC 06 no. 11089*

**EDUCATION, SECONDARY - NIGERIA - HISTORY - 20TH CENTURY.**
Hubbard, James P. (James Patrick), 1945- Education under colonial rule. Lanham : University Press of America, 2000.
*TC LG483.K78 H83 2000*

**EDUCATION, SECONDARY - NIGERIA - RESEARCH.**
Research on schooling in Nigeria. Ondo [Nigeria] : Centre for Research on Schooling, Adeyemi College of Education, 1995.
*TC LB1028.25.N6 R477 1995*

**EDUCATION, SECONDARY - NORWAY - KRISTIANSUND.**
Husby, Egil, 1913- Den høgre skolen, 1864-1964. Kristiansund, 1966.

**EDUCATION, SECONDARY - PERIODICALS.**
California quarterly of secondary education. Berkeley, Cal. : The Society, 1925-

Educational forum. Delhi, Dept. of Extension Services, Central Institute of Education.

L'Enseignement secondaire au Canada; [Quebec]

The High school. Eugene, Ore.

The High school quarterly. Athens, Ga. : University of Georgia, 1912-[1936]

The High school teacher. Blanchester, The Brown Publishing Co.

Journal of secondary education. [Burlingame, Calif. : California Association of Secondary School Administrators, 1961-1971]

The Junior high clearing house. Lebanon, Pa., Junior High School Clearing House.

**EDUCATION, SECONDARY - SOCIAL ASPECTS - ENGLAND.**
Vlaeminke, Meriel. The English higher grade schools. London ; Portland, OR : Woburn Press, 2000.
*TC LA634 .V52 2000*

**EDUCATION, SECONDARY - SOCIAL ASPECTS - ENGLAND - LONDON - CASE STUDIES.**
Gillborn, David. Rationing education. Buckingham [England] ; Philadelphia : Open University Press, 2000.
*TC LC213.3.G73 L664 2000*

**EDUCATION, SECONDARY - UGANDA - KABAROLE DISTRICT - HISTORY - 20TH CENTURY.**
Paige, John Rhodes. Preserving order amid chaos. New York : Berghahn Books, 2000.
*TC LA1567 .P25 2000*

**EDUCATION, SECONDARY - UNITED STATES.**
Education's big gamble [videorecording]. New York, NY : Merrow Report, c1997.
*TC LB2806.36 .E3 1997*

Public charter schools : new choices in public education (May 3, 2000 : Washington, D.C.) Public charter schools [videorecording]. [Washington, D.C.] : U.S. Dept. of Education, [2000].
*TC LB2806.36 .P9 2000*

Snodgrass, Dawn M., 1955- Collaborative learning in middle and secondary schools. Larchmont, N.Y. : Eye On Education, 2000.
*TC LB1032 .S62 2000*

Wetzel, Roberta, 1946- Student-generated sexual harassment in secondary schools. Westport, Conn. ; London : Bergin & Garvey, 2000.
*TC LC212.82 .W47 2000*

**EDUCATION, SECONDARY - UNITED STATES - ADMINISTRATION.**
The new American high school. Thousand Oaks, Calif. : Corwin Press, c1999.
*TC LA222 .N49 1999*

**EDUCATION, SECONDARY - UNITED STATES - CASE STUDIES.**
Abowitz, Kathleen Knight. Making meaning of community in an American high school. Cresskill, N.J. : Hampton Press, c2000.
*TC LC311 .A36 2000*

**EDUCATION, SECONDARY - UNITED STATES - CURRICULA.**
The new American high school. Thousand Oaks, Calif. : Corwin Press, c1999.
*TC LA222 .N49 1999*

Rasool, Joan. Multicultural education in middle and secondary classrooms. Belmont, CA : Wadsworth, c2000.
*TC LC1099.3 .R38 2000*

**Education sector strategy.**
World Bank. Human Development Network. Washington, D.C. : World Bank Group, c1999.
*TC LC2607 .W66 1999*

**EDUCATION - SEGREGATION.** *See* **SEGREGATION IN EDUCATION.**

**EDUCATION, SEX DISCRIMINATION IN.** *See* **SEX DISCRIMINATION IN EDUCATION.**

**ÉDUCATION SEXUELLE.**
McKay, Alexander, 1962- Sexual ideology and schooling. London, Ont. : Althouse Press, 1998.
*TC HQ57.3 .M34 1998*

**EDUCATION - SIMULATION METHODS.** *See also* **EDUCATIONAL GAMES.**
Keegan, Mark. Scenario educational software. Englewood Cliffs, N.J. : Educational Technology Publications, c1995.
*TC LB1028.6 .K44 1995*

**EDUCATION - SOCIAL ASPECTS.**
Edgoose, Julian Miles. Partnerships of possibility. 1999.
*TC 085 E117*

Education for spiritual, moral, social and cultural development. London ; New York : Continuum, 2000.
*TC LC268 .E384 2000*

Education in a global society. Boston : Allyn and Bacon, c2000.

*TC LB43 .E385 2000*
Evaluation as a democratic process. San Francisco, CA : Jossey-Bass, c2000.
*TC LB2806 .E79 2000*

Globalization and education. New York : Routledge, 1999.
*TC LC191 .G545 1999*

Images of educational change. Buckingham [England] ; Philadelphia : Open University Press, 2000.
*TC LB2805 .I415 2000*

The structure of schooling. Mountain View, Calif. : Mayfield Pub. Co., 1999.
*TC LC189 .S87 1999*

Thinking queer. New York : Peter Lang, c2000.
*TC LC192.6 .T55 2000*

Trifonas, Peter Pericles, 1960- Revolutionary pedagogies. New York : Routledge, 2000.
*TC LC196 .R48 2000*

**EDUCATION - SOCIAL ASPECTS - CAMBODIA - HISTORY - 20TH CENTURY.**
Ayres, David M., 1971- Anatomy of a crisis. Honolulu : University of Hawai'i Press, c2000.
*TC LC94.C16 A971 2000*

**EDUCATION - SOCIAL ASPECTS - CHINA - CASE STUDIES.**
The ethnographic eye. New York : Falmer Press, 2000.
*TC LB45 .E837 2000*

**EDUCATION - SOCIAL ASPECTS - CROSS-CULTURAL STUDIES.**
Educational knowledge. Albany : State University of New York Press, c2000.
*TC LC71 .L335 2000*

**EDUCATION - SOCIAL ASPECTS - EUROPE.**
Problems and prospects in European education. Westport, Conn. : Praeger, 2000.
*TC LC191.8. E85 P86 2000*

**EDUCATION - SOCIAL ASPECTS - FRANCE - HISTORY - 19TH CENTURY.**
Knottnerus, J. David. The social worlds of male and female children in the nineteenth century French educational system. Lewiston, N.Y. : Lampeter, Wales : Edwin Mellen Press, c1999.
*TC LC191.8.F8 K66 1999*

**EDUCATION - SOCIAL ASPECTS - GEORGIA - HISTORY - 20TH CENTURY.**
O'Brien, Thomas V., 1958- The politics of race and schooling. Lanham, Md. : Lexington Books, c1999.
*TC LC212.22.G46 O37 1999*

**EDUCATION - SOCIAL ASPECTS - HISTORY - CONGRESSES.**
Silences & images. New York : P. Lang, c1999.
*TC LA128 .S55 1999*

**EDUCATION - SOCIAL ASPECTS - INDIA.**
Public report on basic education in India. New Delhi ; Oxford : Oxford University Press, c1999.
*TC LA1151 .P83 1999*

**EDUCATION - SOCIAL ASPECTS - NEW ZEALAND - CASE STUDIES.**
Fiske, Edward B. When schools compete. Washington, D.C. : Brookings Institution Press, c2000.
*TC LB2822.84.N45 F58 2000*

**EDUCATION - SOCIAL ASPECTS - ONTARIO - TORONTO - CASE STUDIES.**
McLaren, Peter, 1948- Schooling as a ritual performance. 3rd ed. Lanham, Md. : Rowman & Littlefield, c1999.
*TC LC504.3.T67 M35 1999*

**EDUCATION - SOCIAL ASPECTS - TANZANIA - KILIMANJARO REGION.**
Stambach, Amy, 1966- Lessons from Mount Kilimanjaro. New York : Routledge, 2000.
*TC LA1844.K54 S72 2000*

**EDUCATION - SOCIAL ASPECTS - UNITED STATES.**
Apple, Michael W. Official knowledge. 2nd ed. New York : Routledge, 2000.
*TC LC89 .A815 2000*

Campbell, Duane E. Choosing democracy. 2nd ed. Upper Saddle River, N.J. : Merrill, c2000.
*TC LC1099.3 .C36 2000*

Critical education in the new information age. Lanham, Md. : Rowman & Littlefield, c1999.

*TC LC196.5.U6 C745 1999*
Hirsch, E. D. (Eric Donald), 1928- The schools we need and why we don't have them. 1st Anchor Books ed. New York : Anchor Books/Doubleday, 1999.
*TC LA210 .H57 1999*

Hot buttons. Bloomington, Ind. : Phi Delta Kappa Educational Foundation, c1997.
*TC LA210 .H68 1997*

New school order [videorecording]. New York : First Run/Icarus Films, 1996.
*TC LB2831.583.P4 N4 1996*

Reconstructing the common good in education. Stanford, Calif. : Stanford University Press, c2000.
*TC LA212 .R42 2000*

Reid, Charles R. Education and evolution. Lanham, Md. ; Oxford : University Press of America, c2000.
*TC LC191.4 .R43 2000*

Strangers in the land. New York : Peter Lang, c1999.
*TC E184.36.E84 S77 1999*

**EDUCATION - SOCIAL ASPECTS - UNITED STATES - HISTORY - CONGRESSES.**
Silences & images. New York : P. Lang, c1999.
*TC LA128 .S55 1999*

**EDUCATION, SOCIAL WORK.** *See* **SOCIAL WORK EDUCATION.**

**EDUCATION - SOCIETIES.**
Connecticut teacher. Hartford, Conn. : The Association, [1933-

**EDUCATION - SOUTH AFRICA - HISTORY.**
Hlatshwayo, Simphiwe A. (Simphiwe Abner) Education and independence. Westport, Conn : Greenwood Press, 2000.
*TC LA1536 .H53 2000*

**EDUCATION - SOUTH AFRICA - PERIODICALS.**
Educamus. Pretoria : Govt. Printer, [1978-

**EDUCATION, SPECIAL - METHODS.**
Peeters, Theo. Autism. 2nd ed. London : Whurr Publishers, 1999.
*TC RJ506.A9 P44 1999*

**EDUCATION - STANDARDS - CANADA.**
Drake, Susan M., 1944- Creating integrated curriculum. Thousand Oaks, Calif. : Corwin Press, c1998.
*TC LB1570 .D695 1998*

**EDUCATION - STANDARDS - GREAT BRITAIN.**
Sammons, Pam. School effectiveness. Lisse, Netherlands : Abingdon [England] ; Exton, PA : Swets & Zeitlinger Publishers, c1999.
*TC LB2822.75 .S24 1999*

**EDUCATION - STANDARDS - NEW YORK (STATE) - NEW YORK.**
Ort, Suzanne Wichterle. Standards in practice. 1999.
*TC 06 no. 11210*

**EDUCATION - STANDARDS - UNITED STATES.**
A case study in teaching to civic standards using a portfolio approach 1996 : "Office of Citizen". [Boulder, Colo.] : Social Science Education Consortium, c1997.
*TC LC1091 .C37 1997*

Designing mathematics or science curriculum programs. Washington, D.C. : National Academy Press, 1999.
*TC Q183.3.A1 D46 1999*

Drake, Susan M., 1944- Creating integrated curriculum. Thousand Oaks, Calif. : Corwin Press, c1998.
*TC LB1570 .D695 1998*

Foreign language standards. Lincolnwood, Ill., U.S.A. : National Textbook Company in conjunction with the American Council on the Teaching of Foreign Languages, c1999.
*TC P53 .F674 1999*

Kearns, David T. A legacy of learning. Washington, D.C. : Brookings Institution Press, c2000.
*TC LA217.2 .K43 2000*

Kordalewski, John. Standards in the classroom. New York ; London : Teachers College Press, c2000.
*TC LB3060.83 .K67 2000*

Lockwood, Anne Turnbaugh. Standards. Thousand Oaks, Calif. : Corwin Press, c1998.
*TC LB3060.83 .L63 1998*

Marzano, Robert J. Essential knowledge. Aurora, Colo. : McREL, 1999.

*TC LB3060.83 .M36 1999*

McNeil, Linda M. Contradictions of school reform. New York : Routledge, 2000.
*TC LB3060.83 .M38 2000*

Democratic dialogue with special needs students. [Boulder, Colo.] : Social Science Education Consortium, c1997.

Powerful middle schools : teaching and learning for young adolescents (2000) Powerful middle schools [videorecording]. [Washington, D.C.?] : U.S. Dept. of Education, [2000].
*TC LB1623 .P6 2000*

Shannon, Ann. Keeping score. Washington, D.C. : National Academy Press, 1999.
*TC QA135.5 .S45 1999x*

What's at stake in the K-12 standards wars. New York : P. Lang, 2000.
*TC LB3060.83 .W53 2000*

Will standards save public education? Boston : Beacon Press, c2000.
*TC LB3060.83 .W55 2000*

### EDUCATION - STANDARDS - UNITED STATES - CASE STUDIES.
Doyle, Denis P. Raising the standard. 2nd ed. Thousand Oaks, Calif. : Corwin Press, c1999.
*TC LB2822.82 .D69 1999*

### EDUCATION - STANDARDS - UNITED STATES - CONGRESSES.
Brookings papers on education policy, 2000. Washington, D.C. : Brookings Institution Press, c2000.
*TC LC89 .B7472 2000*

### EDUCATION - STATISTICAL METHODS. *See* EDUCATIONAL STATISTICS.

### EDUCATION - STATISTICS. *See* EDUCATIONAL INDICATORS.

### EDUCATION - STATISTICS - PERIODICALS.
The progress of nations. New York, NY : UNICEF, 1993-
*TC RA407.A1 P76*

### EDUCATION - STUDY AND TEACHING (GRADUATE) - NEW YORK (STATE).
Sosin, Adrienne. Achieving styles preferences of students in an urban graduate teacher education program. 1996.
*TC 06 no. 10701*

### EDUCATION - STUDY AND TEACHING (HIGHER).
International narratives on becoming a teacher educator. Lewiston, N.Y. ; Lampeter, Wales : E. Mellen Press, c2000.
*TC LB1737.5 .I58 2000*

### EDUCATION - STUDY AND TEACHING (HIGHER) - GREAT BRITAIN.
An introduction to the study of education. London : David Fulton, 1999.
*TC LA632 .I58 1999*

### EDUCATION - STUDY AND TEACHING (HIGHER) - UNITED STATES.
Educational foundations. Upper Saddle River, N.J. : Merrill, c2000.
*TC LB17 .E393 2000*

### EDUCATION - STUDY AND TEACHING - INDIA.
The Indian journal of education. Calcutta [etc] All-India Federation of Educational Associations.

### EDUCATION - SWEDEN - PERIODICALS.
Folk-högskolan. Stockholm : Lärarförbundet, 1979-

### EDUCATION - SWITZERLAND - PERIODICALS.
L'Éducateur et bulletin corporatif. Lausanne,

### EDUCATION TEACHERS. *See* TEACHER EDUCATORS.

### EDUCATION, TECHNICAL. *See* TECHNICAL EDUCATION.

### EDUCATION - TECHNOLOGICAL INNOVATIONS. *See* EDUCATIONAL INNOVATIONS.

### EDUCATION - TECHNOLOGICAL INNOVATIONS - UNITED STATES.
Burbules, Nicholas C. Watch IT. Boulder, Colo. : Westview Press, 2000.
*TC LB1028.43 .B87 2000*

### Education today.
Ottenburg, Susan D. 2nd. ed. Boston : Educational Publishing Group, Education Today, c1996.

*TC LC225.3 .O88 1996*

### Education under colonial rule.
Hubbard, James P. (James Patrick), 1945- Lanham : University Press of America, 2000
*TC LG483.K78 H83 2000*

### EDUCATION - UNITED STATES. *See also* AFRO-AMERICANS - EDUCATION.
Bracey, Gerald W. (Gerald Watkins) The truth about America's schools. Bloomington, Ind. : Phi Delta Kappa Educational Foundation, c1997.
*TC LA217:2 .B75 1997*

Calfee, Robert C. Teach your children well. Stanford, CA : Stanford Alumni Association, c1995.
*TC LB2822.82 .C32 1995*

Challenges and opportunities for education in the 21st century. Lewiston, NY : Edwin Mellen Press, c1999.
*TC LA209.2 .C45 1999*

Competitor or ally? New York : Falmer Press, 1999.
*TC LA1312 .C667 1999*

Hot buttons. Bloomington, Ind. : Phi Delta Kappa Educational Foundation, c1997.
*TC LA210 .H68 1997*

McNergney, Robert F. Foundations of education. 3rd ed. Boston : London : Allyn and Bacon, c2001.
*TC LB1775.2 .M32 2001*

Michel, Patrick. Using action research for school restructuring and organizational change. 2000.
*TC 06 no. 11295*

Reconstructing the common good in education. Stanford, Calif. : Stanford University Press, c2000.
*TC LA212 .R42 2000*

Sadovnik, Alan R. Exploring education. Boston : Allyn and Bacon, c1994.
*TC LB17 .S113 1994*

Sadovnik, Alan R. Exploring education. 2nd ed. Boston : Allyn and Bacon, 2000.
*TC LA217.2 .S23 2000*

### EDUCATION - UNITED STATES - BIOGRAPHICAL METHODS.
Ritchie, Joy S. Teacher narrative as critical inquiry. New York : Teachers College Press, c2000.
*TC LA2311 .R58 2000*

### EDUCATION - UNITED STATES - CURRICULA.
Barnes, Barbara. Schools transformed for the 21st century. Torrance, Calif. : Griffin Pub. Group, c1999.
*TC LA217.2 .B39 1999*

Detels, Claire Janice, 1953- Soft boundaries. Westport, Conn. : Bergin & Garvey, 1999.
*TC LB1591.5.U6 D48 1999*

Drake, Susan M., 1944- Creating integrated curriculum. Thousand Oaks, Calif. : Corwin Press, c1998.
*TC LB1570 .D695 1998*

Henderson, James George. Transformative curriculum leadership. 2nd ed. Upper Saddle River, N.J. : Merrill, c2000.
*TC LB1570 .H45 2000*

Marsh, Colin J. Curriculum. 2nd. ed. Upper Saddle River, N.J. : Merrill, c1999.
*TC LB1570 .M3667 1999*

Martinello, Marian L. Interdisciplinary inquiry in teaching and learning. 2nd. ed. Upper Saddle River, N.J. : Merrill, c2000.
*TC LB1570 .M3675 2000*

Marzano, Robert J. Essential knowledge. Aurora, Colo. : McREL, 1999.
*TC LB3060.83 .M36 1999*

What principals should know about--. Springfield, Ill. : C.C. Thomas, c2000.
*TC LB2831.92 .W52 2000*

### EDUCATION - UNITED STATES - CURRICULA - HISTORY.
Curriculum and consequence. New York : Teachers College Press, c2000.
*TC LB1570 .C88379 2000*

### EDUCATION - UNITED STATES - CURRICULA - HISTORY - 20TH CENTURY.
Marshall, J. Dan. Turning points in curriculum. Upper Saddle River, N.J. : Merrill, c2000.
*TC LB1570 .M36675 2000*

### EDUCATION - UNITED STATES - DATA PROCESSING.
Bolt, David B., 1954- Digital divide. New York : TV Books, c2000.

*TC LB1028.43 .B64 2000*

The Jossey-Bass reader on technology and learning. 1st ed. San Francisco, Calif. : Jossey-Bass, c2000.
*TC LB1028.3 .J66 2000*

### EDUCATION - UNITED STATES - EVALUATION.
Black, P. J. (Paul Joseph), 1930- Testing, friend or foe? London : Washington : Falmer Press, 1998.
*TC LB3056.E54 B53 1998*

Good, Thomas L., 1943- The great school debate. Mahwah, N.J. : L. Erlbaum Associates, 2000.
*TC LB2806.36 .G66 2000*

### EDUCATION - UNITED STATES - EVALUATION - PERIODICALS.
American education annual. Detroit : Gale, c1999-
*TC LB1028.25.U6 A44*

### EDUCATION - UNITED STATES - EXPERIMENTAL METHODS - LONGITUDINAL STUDIES.
Smith, Darren James, 1960- Stepping inside the classroom through personal narratives. Lanham, Md. : University Press of America, 1999.
*TC LB1737.U6 S55 1999*

### EDUCATION - UNITED STATES - FINANCE.
Boschee, Floyd. School bond success. 1st ed. Lancaster, Pa. : Technomic Publishing Co., c1999.
*TC LB2825 .B63 1999*

Grants for schools. 4th ed. Gaithersburg, MD : Aspen Publishers, 2000.
*TC LB2825 .F46 2000*

Law and school reform. New Haven [Conn.] : Yale University Press, c1999.
*TC LC213.2 .L38 1999*

Rufo-Lignos, Patricia Marie. Towards a new topology of public and private schools. 1999.
*TC 06 no. 11170*

Rufo-Lignos, Patricia Marie. Towards a new typology of public and private schools. 1999.
*TC 06 no. 11170*

Where does the money go? Thousand Oaks, Calif. : Corwin Press, c1996.
*TC LB2825 .W415 1996*

Wong, Kenneth K., 1955- Funding public schools. Lawrence : University Press of Kansas, c1999.
*TC LB2825 .W56 1999*

### EDUCATION - UNITED STATES - FORECASTING.
Baker, Bruce D. A comparison of statistical and neural network models for forecasting educational spending. 1997.
*TC 06 no. 10792*

### EDUCATION - UNITED STATES - HISTORY.
Educational foundations. Upper Saddle River, N.J. : Merrill, c2000.
*TC LB17 .E393 2000*

Fenn, Patricia. Rewards of merit. [Schoharie, N.Y.] : Ephemera Society of America ; Charlottesville [Va.] : Distributed by Howell Press, Inc., c1994.
*TC LA230 .F46 1994*

Johnson, Clifton, 1865-1940. Old-time schools and school-books. Detroit : Omnigraphics, 1999.
*TC LA206 .J6 1999*

### EDUCATION - UNITED STATES - HISTORY - 20TH CENTURY.
American education. Chicago, Ill. : NSSE : Distributed by the University of Chicago Press, 2000.
*TC LB5 .N25 99th pt. 2*

Ravitch, Diane. Left back. New York : Simon & Schuster, c2000.
*TC LA216 .R28 2000*

### EDUCATION - UNITED STATES - HISTORY - DICTIONARIES.
Historical dictionary of American education. Westport, Conn. : Greenwood Press, 1999.
*TC LB15 .H57 1999*

### EDUCATION - UNITED STATES - INFORMATION SERVICES.
Short, Paula M. Information collection. Larchmont, NY : Eye on Education, c1998.
*TC LB1028.27.U6 S46 1998*

### EDUCATION - UNITED STATES - PARENT PARTICIPATION.
Otterbourg, Susan D. Using technology to strengthen employee and family involvement in education. [New York] : Conference Board, c1998.
*TC LB1028.3 .O88 1998*

## EDUCATION - UNITED STATES - PERIODICALS.
American educational digest. [Crawfordsville, Ind. : Educational Digest Co., 1923-1928]

[Education (Guilford, Conn.)] Education. Guilford, Ct., : Dushkin Pub. Group.
*TC LB41 .A673*

University of Pittsburgh. School of Education. Journal. [Lancaster, Pa. : The School, 1925-

## EDUCATION - UNITED STATES - PHILOSOPHY.
Apple, Michael W. Official knowledge. 2nd ed. New York : Routledge, 2000.
*TC LC89 .A815 2000*

Fletcher, Scott, 1959- Education and emancipation. New York : Teachers College Press, c2000.
*TC LC191.4 .F54 2000*

Hirsch, E. D. (Eric Donald), 1928- The schools we need and why we don't have them. 1st Anchor Books ed. New York : Anchor Books/Doubleday, 1999.
*TC LA210 .H57 1999*

Hutchinson, Jaylynne N., 1954- Students on the margins. Albany : State University of New York Press, c1999.
*TC LA210 .H88 1999*

Sadovnik, Alan R. Exploring education. Boston : Allyn and Bacon, c1994.
*TC LB17 .S113 1994*

Sadovnik, Alan R. Exploring education. 2nd ed. Boston : Allyn and Bacon, 2000.
*TC LA217.2 . S23 2000*

## EDUCATION - UNITED STATES - PHILOSOPHY - CONGRESSES.
Grundtvig's ideas in North America. Copenhagen, Denmark : Danske Selskab, 1983.
*TC LB675.G832 G79 1983*

## EDUCATION - UNITED STATES - PHILOSOPHY - HISTORY.
Curriculum and consequence. New York : Teachers College Press, c2000.
*TC LB1570 .C88379 2000*

## EDUCATION - UNITED STATES - STATES - FINANCE - STATISTICS.
Lieberman, Carl, 1941- Educational expenditures and economic growth in the American States. Akron, Ohio : Midwest Press Incorporated, 1998.
*TC LC66 .L45 1998*

## EDUCATION - UNITED STATES - STATISTICS.
Baker, Bruce D. A comparison of statistical and neural network models for forecasting educational spending. 1997.
*TC 06 no. 10792*

## EDUCATION - UNITED STATES - STATISTICS - PERIODICALS.
Health, education, and welfare indicators. Washington, D.C. : U.S. Dept. of Health, Education and Welfare : For sale by the Supt. of Docs., U.S. G.P.O., 1960-[1967]

## EDUCATION, URBAN. See also SCHOOLS - DECENTRALIZATION.
Cuban, Larry. Urban school chiefs under fire. Chicago : University of Chicago Press, 1976.
*TC LB2831.7 .C82*

Teaching and learning in cities. [S.l.] : Whitbread, 1993.
*TC LC5115 .T43 1993*

## EDUCATION, URBAN - GREAT BRITAIN.
Johnson, Martin. Failing school, failing city. Charlbury, Oxfordshire [England] : Jon Carpenter Publishing, 1999.
*TC LC5136.G7 J64 1999*

## EDUCATION, URBAN - NEW JERSEY.
V'elez Arias, Hiram Oscar. A multi-case study of physical education teachers and working conditions in inner-city schools /by Hiram Oscar V'elez Arias. 1998.
*TC 06 no. 11001*

## EDUCATION, URBAN - NEW JERSEY - NEWARK - CASE STUDIES.
Handel, Ruth D. Building family literacy in an urban community. New York : Teachers College Press, c1999.
*TC LC152.N58 H36 1999*

## EDUCATION, URBAN - NEW YORK (STATE) - NEW YORK.
City schools. Baltimore : Johns Hopkins University Press, c2000.

*TC LC5133.N4 C57 2000*

## EDUCATION, URBAN - PERIODICALS.
The Center forum. New York, Center for Urban Education.

## EDUCATION, URBAN - POLITICAL ASPECTS - UNITED STATES - CASE STUDIES.
Hill, Paul Thomas, 1943- It takes a city. Washington, D.C. : Brookings Institution Press, c2000.
*TC LC5131 .H48 2000*

Portz, John, 1953- City schools and city politics. Lawrence : University Press of Kansas, c1999.
*TC LC5131 .P67 1999*

## EDUCATION, URBAN - SOCIAL ASPECTS - UNITED STATES.
Challenges of urban education. Albany : State Unviersity of New York Press, c2000.
*TC LC5131 .C38 2000*

Kozol, Jonathan. Savage inequalities. 1st Harper Perennial ed. New York : HarperPerennial, 1992.
*TC LC4091 .K69 1992*

## EDUCATION, URBAN - TEXAS - HOUSTON - CASE STUDIES.
McAdams, Donald R. Fighting to save our urban schools-- and winning!. New York : Teachers College Press, c2000.
*TC LC5133.H8 M32 2000*

## EDUCATION, URBAN - UNITED STATES.
Behavioral management in the public schools. Westport, Conn. ; London : Praeger, 1999.
*TC LB1060.2 .B44 1999*

Caring as tenacity. Cresskill, N.J. : Hampton Press, c2000.
*TC LC5131 .C35 2000*

From nihilism to possibility. Cresskill, N.J. : Hampton Press, c1999.
*TC LC5141 .F76 1999*

Gill, Walter. A common sense guide to non-traditional urban education. Nashville, Tenn. : James C. Winston Publishing Co., Inc., c1998.
*TC LC5115 .G55 1998*

Talking across boundaries. [New York] : [Bruner Foundation], 1996.
*TC LB1623.5 .T35 1996*

## EDUCATION, URBAN - UNITED STATES - ADMINISTRATION - CASE STUDIES.
Hill, Paul Thomas, 1943- It takes a city. Washington, D.C. : Brookings Institution Press, c2000.
*TC LC5131 .H48 2000*

## EDUCATION, URBAN - UNITED STATES - CASE STUDIES.
Corwin, Miles. And still we rise. 1st ed. New York : Bard, 2000.
*TC LC3993.9 .C678 2000*

Wilson, Catherine S. Telling a different story. New York ; London : Teachers College Press, c2000.
*TC LC5131 .W49 2000*

## EDUCATION, URBAN - WISCONSIN - MILWAUKEE - CASE STUDIES.
Witte, John F. The market approach to education. Princeton, N.J. : Princeton University Press, c2000.
*TC LB2828.85.W6 W58 2000*

## EDUCATION - VIETNAM - FRENCH INFLUENCES.
Kelly, Gail Paradise. French colonial education. New York : AMS Press, c2000.
*TC LA1186 .K45 2000*

## EDUCATION - VIETNAM - HISTORY.
Kelly, Gail Paradise. French colonial education. New York : AMS Press, c2000.
*TC LA1186 .K45 2000*

## EDUCATION, VOCATIONAL. See VOCATIONAL EDUCATION.

## EDUCATION VOUCHERS. See EDUCATIONAL VOUCHERS.

## EDUCATION WITHIN INDUSTRY. See EMPLOYER-SUPPORTED EDUCATION.

**Education year book.** [London, England] : Councils and Education Press, 1979- v ; 22 cm. 1979- . Description based on: 1981 ed. Continues: Education Committees' year book 1939-1978 ISSN: 0070-9158.
*1. Education - Great Britain - Directories. 2. School boards - Great Britain. I. Title: Education Committees' year book 1939-1978*
*TC L915 .E4*

## Educational and industrial television.
Educational & industrial television. [Ridgefield, Conn. : C.S. Tepfer Pub. Co., -c1983]

**Educational & industrial television.** [Ridgefield, Conn. : C.S. Tepfer Pub. Co., -c1983] v. : ill. ; 28 cm. Frequency: Monthly. -[v. 15, no. 5] (May 1983). Began in 1972. Educational and industrial television. EITV. E. and I.T.V. Other title: E-ITV Jan. 1981-May 1983. Running title: E & ITV <Jan. 1980>-Apr. 1981. Description based on: Vol. 4, no. 11 (Nov. 1972); title from cover. Indexed selectively by: Predicasts. Indexed selectively by: Media review digest 0363-7778. Continued in June 1983 by: E-ITV. Continues: Educational television (DLC) 77002050 (OCoLC)1567623. ISSN 0046-1466 DDC 371.3/358/05 *1. Television in education - Periodicals. 2. Industrial television - Periodicals. I. Title: Educational and industrial television II. Title: EITV III. Title: E.I.T.V. IV. Title: E. and I.T.V. V. Title: E-ITV Jan. 1981-May 1983 VI. Title: E & ITV <Jan. 1980>-Apr. 1981 VII. Title: Educational television VIII. Title: E-ITV*

## EDUCATIONAL ACCELERATION.
Graham, Sheila L. Urban minority gifted students. 1999.
*TC 06 no. 11119*

## EDUCATIONAL ACCELERATION - UNITED STATES - HANDBOOKS, MANUALS, ETC.
Meier, Dave. The accelerated learning handbook. New York : McGraw Hill, c2000.
*TC LB1029.A22 M45 2000*

## EDUCATIONAL ACCOUNTABILITY. See also EDUCATIONAL INDICATORS; EDUCATIONAL PRODUCTIVITY.
Leithwood, Kenneth A. Gütersloh : Bertelsmann Foundation Publishers, 1999.
*TC LB2806.22 .L45 1999*

## EDUCATIONAL ACCOUNTABILITY.
Leithwood, Kenneth A. Educational accountability. Gütersloh : Bertelsmann Foundation Publishers, 1999.
*TC LB2806.22 .L45 1999*

## EDUCATIONAL ACCOUNTABILITY - GREAT BRITAIN.
Sammons, Pam. School effectiveness. Lisse, Netherlands ; Abingdon [England] ; Exton, PA : Swets & Zeitlinger Publishers, c1999.
*TC LB2822.75 .S24 1999*

## EDUCATIONAL ACCOUNTABILITY - IDAHO - TWIN FALLS.
Smith, Steven H. Schoolwide test preparation. [Arlington, Va.] : Educational Research Service, c2000.
*TC LB2806.22 .S65 2000*

## EDUCATIONAL ACCOUNTABILITY - KENTUCKY - CASE STUDIES.
Accountability, assessment, and teacher commitment. Albany, N.Y. : State University of New York Press, 2000.
*TC LB2806.22 .A249 2000*

## EDUCATIONAL ACCOUNTABILITY - NEW JERSEY - CASE STUDIES.
Fleck, Mary B. Elementary principals' use of student assessment information. 1999.
*TC 06 no. 11113*

## EDUCATIONAL ACCOUNTABILITY - NEW YORK (STATE).
Southworth, Robert A. Evidence of student learning and implications for alternative policies that support instructional use of assessment. 1999.
*TC 06 no. 11218*

## EDUCATIONAL ACCOUNTABILITY - SOCIAL ASPECTS.
Audit cultures. London ; New York : Routledge, 2000.
*TC LB2324 .A87 2000*

## EDUCATIONAL ACHIEVEMENT. See ACADEMIC ACHIEVEMENT.

## EDUCATIONAL ADMINISTRATION. See also SCHOOL MANAGEMENT AND ORGANIZATION; UNIVERSITIES AND COLLEGES - ADMINISTRATION.
Cunningham, William G. Boston ; London : Allyn & Bacon, c2000.
*TC LB1738.5 .C86 2000*

## EDUCATIONAL ADMINISTRATION.
Dombroski, Ann P. Administrative problem solving. 1999.
*TC 06 no. 11104*

## EDUCATIONAL AIMS AND OBJECTIVES. See EDUCATION - AIMS AND OBJECTIVES.

## Educational and industrial television.
Educational & industrial television. [Ridgefield, Conn. : C.S. Tepfer Pub. Co., -c1983]

**EDUCATIONAL ANTHROPOLOGY.**
Audit cultures. London ; New York : Routledge, 2000.
*TC LB2324 .A87 2000*

Harrington, Charles C. Psychological anthropology
and education. New York : AMS Press, c1979.
*TC GN502 .H37*

Harrington, Charles C. Readings for anthropology and
education 1- New York, MSS Educational Publishing
Co. [c1971-
*TC LB45 .H3*

Spindler, George Dearborn. Fifty years of
anthropology and education, 1950-2000. Mahwah,
N.J. L.Erlbaum Associates, 2000.
*TC LB45 .S66 2000*

Thomas, Elwyn. Culture and schooling. Chichester,
West Sussex, England ; New York : J. Wiley & Sons,
c2000.
*TC LB45 .T476 2000*

**EDUCATIONAL ANTHROPOLOGY -
ABSTRACTS.**
Harrington, Charles C. Psychological anthropology
and education. New York : AMS Press, c1979.
*TC GN502 .H37*

**EDUCATIONAL ANTHROPOLOGY - CHINA -
CASE STUDIES.**
The ethnographic eye. New York : Falmer Press,
2000.
*TC LB45 .E837 2000*

**EDUCATIONAL ANTHROPOLOGY - ONTARIO -
TORONTO - CASE STUDIES.**
McLaren, Peter, 1948- Schooling as a ritual
performance. 3rd ed. Lanham, Md. : Rowman &
Littlefield, c1999.
*TC LC504.3.T67 M35 1999*

**EDUCATIONAL ANTHROPOLOGY -
TANZANIA - KILIMANJARO REGION.**
Stambach, Amy, 1966- Lessons from Mount
Kilimanjaro. New York : Routledge, 2000.
*TC LA1844.K54 S72 2000*

**EDUCATIONAL ANTHROPOLOGY - UNITED
STATES.**
Burbules, Nicholas C. Watch IT. Boulder, Colo. :
Westview Press, 2000.
*TC LB1028.43 .B87 2000*

Manning, Kathleen, 1954- Ritual, ceremonies, and
cultural meaning in higher education. Westport,
Conn. : Bergin & Garvey, 2000.
*TC LC191.9 .M26 2000*

Multiple and intersecting identities in qualitative
research. Mahwah, N.J. ; London : L. Erlbaum
Associates, 2001.
*TC LB1028.25.U6 M85 2001*

**EDUCATIONAL ANTHROPOLOGY - UNITED
STATES - CASE STUDIES.**
Kalyanpur, Maya. Culture in special education.
Baltimore, Md. : P.H. Brookes Pub., c1999.
*TC LC3969 .K35 1999*

**EDUCATIONAL ASPIRATIONS. See STUDENT
ASPIRATIONS.**

**EDUCATIONAL ASSESSMENT.** *See*
**EDUCATIONAL EVALUATION;
EDUCATIONAL TESTS AND
MEASUREMENTS.**

**EDUCATIONAL ASSISTANCE.**
Learning from experience. The Hague : Centre for the
Study of Education in Developing Countries, c1995.
*TC LC2610 .L43 1995*

**EDUCATIONAL ASSISTANCE - AFRICA.**
Changing international aid to education. Paris :
Unesco Pub./NORRAG, 1999.
*TC LC2607 .C42 1999*

**EDUCATIONAL ASSISTANCE - AFRICA, SUB-
SAHARAN.**
Brock-Utne, Birgit, 1938- Whose education for all?
New York ; London : Falmer Press, 2000.
*TC LC67.A435 B76 2000*

**EDUCATIONAL ASSISTANCE - DEVELOPING
COUNTRIES.**
Changing international aid to education. Paris :
Unesco Pub./NORRAG, 1999.
*TC LC2607 .C42 1999*

World Bank. Human Development Network.
Education sector strategy. Washington, D.C. : World
Bank Group, c1999.

*TC LC2607 .W66 1999*

**Educational/awareness presentation.**
The filming of a television commercial
[videorecording]. Minneapolis, Minn. : Media Loft,
c1992.
*TC HF6146.T42 F5 1992*

The power of idea : [videorecording]. Minneapolis,
Minn. : Media Loft, c1992.
*TC TR690 .P5 1992*

Sport photography today! [videorecording].
Minneapolis, Minn. : Media Loft, c1992.
*TC TR821 .S64 1992*

The sight and insight of Ernst Haas [videorecording].
Minneapolis, Minn. : Media Loft, 1992.
*TC TR647.H3 S5 1992*

**Educational bimonthly.**
Chicago schools journal. Chicago, Board of
Education.

**Educational Broadcasting Corporation.**
Georgia O'Keeffe [videorecording]. [Boston?] : Home
Vision : c1977.
*TC ND237.05 G4 1977*

Mary Cassatt [videorecording]. [Chicago, Ill.]: Home
Vision ; c1977.
*TC ND237.C3 M37 1977*

**EDUCATIONAL CHANGE.** *See also*
**EDUCATIONAL INNOVATIONS.**
The aims of education. London ; New York :
Routledge, 1999.
*TC LB41 .A36353 1999*

Carnoy, Martin. Globalization and educational reform.
Paris : International Institute for Educational Planning
(IIEP), 1999.
*TC LB5 .F85 v.63*

Clarke, Paul, 1961- Learning schools, learning
systems. London ; New York : Continuum, 2000.
*TC LB1027 .C468 2000*

Combating educational disadvantage. London ; New
York : Falmer Press, 2000.
*TC LC4065 .C66 1999*

Deal, Terrence E. Shaping school culture. 1st ed. San
Francisco : Jossey-Bass Publishers, c1999.
*TC LB2805 .D34 1999*

Images of educational change. Buckingham
[England] ; Philadelphia : Open University Press,
2000.
*TC LB2805 .I415 2000*

Learning communities in education. London ; New
York : Routledge, 1999.
*TC LB14.7 .L43 1999*

Lucas, Ann F. Leading academic change. 1st ed. San
Francisco : Jossey-Bass, c2000.
*TC LB2341 .L82 2000*

Martin, Elaine, 1948- Changing academic work.
Buckingham ; Philadelphia : Society for Research into
Higher Education : Open University Press, 1999.
*TC LA184 .M37 1999*

Osguthorpe, Russell T. Balancing the tensions of
change. Thousand Oaks, Calif. : Corwin Press, c1998.
*TC LB2331.53 .O74 1998*

Readings in discipline-based art education. Reston,
Va. : National Art Education Assoc., c2000.
*TC N87 .R43 2000*

Reforming college composition. Westport, Conn. :
Greenwood Press, 2000.
*TC PE1404 .R383 2000*

Sowell, Evelyn J. Curriculum. 2nd ed. Upper Saddle
River, N.J. : Merrill, c2000.
*TC LB2806.15 .S69 2000*

Taylor, Peter G., 1951- Making sense of academic
life. Philadelphia, PA : Open University Press, 1999.
*TC LB1778 .T39 1999*

Tooley, James. Reclaiming education. London ; New
York : Cassell, 2000.
*TC LC71 .T65 2000*

The university in transformation. Westport, Conn. ;
London : Bergin & Garvey, 2000.
*TC LB2324 .U56 2000*

**Educational change and development series**
Gordon, June A., 1950- The color of teaching.
London ; New York : RoutledgeFalmer, c2000.
*TC LB2835.25 .G67 2000*

**EDUCATIONAL CHANGE - CASE STUDIES.**
Improving education. London ; New York : Cassell,
1999.
*TC LB7 .I48 1999*

**EDUCATIONAL CHANGE - CHINA - 20TH
CENTURY.**
Reynolds, Barbara G. Reform and education. 1999.
*TC 06 no. 11166*

**EDUCATIONAL CHANGE - CROSS-CULTURAL
STUDIES.**
The adult university. Buckingham [England] :
Philadelphia, PA : Society for Research into Higher
Education & Open University Press, 1999.
*TC LC5219 .A35 1999*

Educational knowledge. Albany : State University of
New York Press, c2000.
*TC LC71 .L335 2000*

Experiential learning around the world. London :
Philadelphia : J. Kingsley Publishers, 2000.
*TC LB2324 .E95 2000*

**EDUCATIONAL CHANGE - EUROPE.**
From the eye of the storm. Dordrecht ; Boston :
London: Kluwer Academic Publishers, c1999.
*TC LB2341.8.E85 F76 1999*

Sporn, Barbara. Adaptive university structures.
London ; Philadelphia : Jessica Kingsley, c1999.
*TC LB2322.2 .S667 1999*

**EDUCATIONAL CHANGE - GREAT BRITAIN.**
Harris, Alma, 1958- Teaching and learning in the
effective school. Aldershot, England ; Brookfield,
Vt. : Ashgate, c1999.
*TC LB2822.84.G7 H37 1999*

Helsby, Gill. Changing teachers' work. Buckingham
[England] ; Philadelphia : Open University Press,
1999.
*TC LA635 .H375 1999*

Hoy, Charles, 1939- Improving quality in education.
London ; New York : Falmer Press, 2000.
*TC LB2822.84.G7 H69 1999*

Leading schools in times of change. Buckingham
[England] ; Philadelphia : Open University Press,
2000.
*TC LB2900.5 .L45 2000*

Tooley, James. Reclaiming education. London ; New
York : Cassell, 2000.
*TC LC71 .T65 2000*

Walsh, Mike. Building a successful school. London :
Kogan Page, 1999.
*TC LB2900.5 .W37 1999*

Whatever happened to equal opportunities in schools?
Buckingham [England] : Philadelphia : Open
University Press, 2000.
*TC LC213.3.G7 W53 2000*

**EDUCATIONAL CHANGE - GREAT BRITAIN -
CASE STUDIES.**
Improving schools. Buckingham [England] :
Philadelphia : Open University Press, 1999.
*TC LB2822.84.G7 I68 1999*

Woods, Peter, 1934- Multicultural children in the
early years. Clevedon : Philadelphia : Multilingual
Matters Ltd., c1999.
*TC LC3736.G6 W66 1999*

**Educational Change, inc.**
Change in higher education. [New York, Science and
University Affairs for Educational Change, Inc.]

**EDUCATIONAL CHANGE - INDIA.**
Rajput, J. S. Education in a changing world. New
Delhi : Vikas Pub. House : Distributors, UBS
Publishers' Distributors, 1999.
*TC LA1151 .R343 1999*

**EDUCATIONAL CHANGE - ISRAEL.**
The transformation of collective education in the
kibbutz. Frankfurt am Main ; New York : P. Lang,
1999.
*TC LC1027.I75 T73 1999*

**EDUCATIONAL CHANGE - JAPAN.**
Holloway, Susan D. Contested childhood. New York :
Routledge, 2000.
*TC LB1140.25.J3 H69 2000*

**EDUCATIONAL CHANGE - JAPAN - 1945-.**
Nihon Kyōshokuin Kumiai. Educational reform on
people's own initiative. [Tokyo?] : Japan Teachers
Union, 1984.
*TC LC210.8.N54 1984*

**EDUCATIONAL CHANGE - JAPAN - HISTORY - 20TH CENTURY.**
Japanese education since 1945. Armonk, N.Y. : M.E. Sharpe, c1994.
*TC LA1311.82 .J39 1994*

**EDUCATIONAL CHANGE - LATIN AMERICA.**
Myth, reality, and reform. Washington, D.C. : Inter-American Development Bank, 2000.
*TC LA543 .M46 2000*

**EDUCATIONAL CHANGE - MICHIGAN - ANN ARBOR.**
Duderstadt, James J., 1942- A university for the 21st century. Ann Arbor, MI : University of Michigan Press, c2000.
*TC LD3280 .D83 2000*

**EDUCATIONAL CHANGE - NIGERIA.**
Francis, Paul A. Hard lessons. Washington, D.C. : World Bank, c1998.
*TC LA1632 .F73 1998*

**EDUCATIONAL CHANGE - NORWAY.**
Bleiklie, Ivar, 1948- Policy and practice in higher education. London ; Philadelphia : J. Kingsley Publishers, 2000.
*TC LC178.N8 B44 2000*

**EDUCATIONAL CHANGE - OECD COUNTRIES - CASE STUDIES.**
Motivating students for lifelong learning. Paris : Organisation for Economic Co-operation and Development, c2000.
*TC LB1065 .M669 2000*

**EDUCATIONAL CHANGE - POLITICAL ASPECTS - MARYLAND - BALTIMORE - CASE STUDIES.**
Orr, Marion, 1962- Black social capital. Lawrence : University Press of Kansas, c1999.
*TC LC2803.B35 O77 1999*

**EDUCATIONAL CHANGE - RESEARCH - UNITED STATES.**
An educators' guide to schoolwide reform. Arlington, Va. : Educational Research Service, c1999.
*TC LB2806.35 .E38 1999*

**EDUCATIONAL CHANGE - RUSSIA (FEDERATION).**
Webber, Stephen L., 1967- School, reform and society in the new Russia . Houndmills [England] : Macmillan Press ; New York : St. Martin's Press in association with Centre for Russian and East European Studies, University of Birmingham, 2000.
*TC LA839.2 .W4 2000*

**EDUCATIONAL CHANGE - RUSSIA (FEDERATION) - 1991-.**
Russia, education in the transition = [S.l.] : The World Bank, ECA Country Development III, Human Resources Division, 1995.
*TC LA839.2 .R87 1995*

**EDUCATIONAL CHANGE - SOCIAL ASPECTS - NEW ZEALAND - CASE STUDIES.**
Thrupp, Martin, 1964- Schools making a difference-- let's be realistic!. Buckingham [England] ; Philadelphia : Open University Press, 1999.
*TC LB2822.75 .T537 1999*

**EDUCATIONAL CHANGE - SWEDEN.**
Transforming universities. London ; Philadelphia : Jessica Kingsley Publishers, 1999.
*TC LA908 .T73 1999*

**EDUCATIONAL CHANGE - TENNESSEE.**
Reforming a college. New York : P. Lang, c2000.
*TC LD5293 .R44 2000*

**EDUCATIONAL CHANGE - TEXAS - HOUSTON - CASE STUDIES.**
McAdams, Donald R. Fighting to save our urban schools-- and winning!. New York : Teachers College Press, c2000.
*TC LC5133.H8 M32 2000*

**EDUCATIONAL CHANGE - UNITED STATES.**
Barnes, Barbara. Schools transformed for the 21st century. Torrance, Calif. : Griffin Pub. Group, c1999.
*TC LA217.2 .B39 1999*

Becoming good American schools. 1st ed. San Francisco : Jossey-Bass, c2000.
*TC LB2822.82 .B44 2000*

Berends, Mark, 1962- Assessing the progress of New American Schools. Santa Monica, CA : RAND, 1999.
*TC LB2822.82 .B45 1999*

Challenges and opportunities for education in the 21st century. Lewiston, NY : Edwin Mellen Press, c1999.

*TC LA209.2 .C45 1999*

Challenges of urban education. Albany : State Unviersity of New York Press, c2000.
*TC LC5131 .C38 2000*

Collaborative reform and other improbable dreams. Albany, N.Y. : State University of New York Press, 2000.
*TC LB2154.A3 C65 2000*

Conflicting missions? Washington, D.C. : Brookings Institution Press, c2000.
*TC LB2844.53.U62 C66 2000*

Cruickshank, Donald R. Preparing America's teachers. Bloomington, Ind. : Phi Delta Kappa Educational Foundation, c1996.
*TC LB1715 .C86 1996*

The dimensions of time and the challenge of school reform. Albany : State University of New York Press, c2000.
*TC LB3032 .D55 2000*

Eisler, Riane Tennenhaus. Tomorrow's children. Boulder, Colo. ; Oxford : Westview Press, 2000.
*TC LC1023 .E57 2000*

Grote, John E. Paideia agonistes. Lanham, Md. : University Press of America, c2000.
*TC LC1011 .G76 2000*

Herideen, Penelope E., 1960- Policy, pedagogy, and social inequality. Westport, Conn. : Bergin & Garvey, 1998.
*TC LB2328.15.U6 H47 1998*

Hirsch, E. D. (Eric Donald), 1928- The schools we need and why we don't have them. 1st Anchor Books ed. New York : Anchor Books/Doubleday, 1999.
*TC LA210 .H57 1999*

Hurd, Paul DeHart, 1905- Transforming middle school science education. New York : Teachers College Press, c2000.
*TC LB1585.3 .H89 2000*

Hutchinson, Jaylynne N., 1954- Students on the margins. Albany : State University of New York Press, c1999.
*TC LA210 .H88 1999*

Kearns, David T. A legacy of learning. Washington, D.C. : Brookings Institution Press, c2000.
*TC LA217.2 .K43 2000*

Knowledge and power in the global economy. Mahwah, N.J. : L. Erlbaum Associates, 2000.
*TC LC66 .K66 2000*

Kralovec, Etta. The end of homework. Boston, Mass. : Beacon Press, c2000.
*TC LB1048 .K73 2000*

Law and school reform. New Haven [Conn.] : Yale University Press, c1999.
*TC LC213.2. L38 1999*

Lieberman, Ann. Teachers--transforming their world and their work. New York : Teachers College Press ; Alexandria, Va. : Association for Supervision and Curriculum Development, c1999.
*TC LB1025.3 .L547 1999*

Making money matter. Washington, D.C. : National Academy Press, c1999.
*TC LB2825 .M27 1999*

Martin, Jane Roland, 1929- Coming of age in academe. New York ; London : Routledge, 2000.
*TC LC197 .M37 2000*

McEwan, Elaine K., 1941- Managing unmanageable students. Thousand Oaks, Calif. : Corwin Press, c2000.
*TC LC4801.5 .M39 2000*

Michel, Patrick. Using action research for school restructuring and organizational change. 2000.
*TC 06 no. 11295*

Michel, Patrick. Using action research for school restructuring and organizational change. 2000.
*TC 06 no. 11295*

The new American high school. Thousand Oaks, Calif. : Corwin Press, c1999.
*TC LA222 .N49 1999*

Newman, Judith, 1943- Tensions of teaching. New York ; London : Teachers College Press, c1998.
*TC LB1025.3 .N49 1998*

Ohanian, Susan. Standards, plain English, and The ugly duckling. [Bloomington, Ind.] : Published by the Phi Delta Kappa Educational Foundation in

cooperation with the John Dewey Project on Progressive Education, [Burlington, Vt.], c1998.
*TC LA217.2 .O33 1998*

Pankake, Anita M., 1947- Implementation. Larchmont, NY : Eye on Education, c1998.
*TC LB2805 .P32 1998*

Reconstructing the common good in education. Stanford, Calif. : Stanford University Press, c2000.
*TC LA212 .R42 2000*

Reed, Carol J., 1937- Teaching with power. New York : Teachers College Press, c2000.
*TC LB2806.45 .R44 2000*

Reforming American education from the bottom to the top. Portsmouth, NH : Heinemann, c1999.
*TC LA210 .R44 1999*

Research on professional development schools. Thousand Oaks, Calif. : Corwin Press, c1999.
*TC LB2154.A3 R478 1999*

Sands, Deanna J. Inclusive education for the 21st century. Belmont, CA : Wadsworth/Thomson Learning, 2000.
*TC LC1201 .S27 2000*

Schneider, Frank. Our public schools. Mobile, Ala. : Factor Press, 2000.
*TC LA217.2 .S34 2000*

Schwarz, Gretchen, 1952- Teacher lore and professional development for school reform. Westport, Conn : Bergin & Garvey, 1998.
*TC LB1775.2 .S38 1998*

The social worlds of higher education :. Thousand Oaks, Calif. : Pine Forge Press, [1999].
*TC LB2331 .S573 1999 sampler*

Sporn, Barbara. Adaptive university structures. London ; Philadelphia : Jessica Kingsley, c1999.
*TC LB2322.2 .S667 1999*

Tierney, William G. Building the responsive campus. Thousand Oaks, Calif. : Sage, c1999.
*TC LB2341 .T584 1999*

Tileston, Donna Walker. Ten best teaching practices. Thousand Oaks, Calif. : Corwin Press, c2000.
*TC LB1775.2 .T54 2000*

**EDUCATIONAL CHANGE - UNITED STATES - CASE STUDIES.**
Case studies for school administrators. 1st ed. Lancaster, PA : Technomic Pub. Co., c1999.
*TC LB2806 .C316 1999*

Doyle, Denis P. Raising the standard. 2nd ed. Thousand Oaks, Calif. : Corwin Press, c1999.
*TC LB2822.82 .D69 1999*

Hill, Paul Thomas, 1943- It takes a city. Washington, D.C. : Brookings Institution Press, c2000.
*TC LC5131 .H48 2000*

Improved test scores, attitudes, and behaviors in America's schools. Westport, Conn. : Bergin & Garvey, 1999.
*TC LB2806.4 .I56 1999*

Nolan, James F., 1950- Teachers and educational change. Albany : State University of New York Press, c2000.
*TC LB1777.2 .N64 2000*

Portz, John, 1953- City schools and city politics. Lawrence : University Press of Kansas, c1999.
*TC LC5131 .P67 1999*

**EDUCATIONAL CHANGE - UNITED STATES - CONGRESSES.**
Brookings papers on education policy, 2000. Washington, D.C. : Brookings Institution Press, c2000.
*TC LC89 .B7472 2000*

**EDUCATIONAL CHANGE - UNITED STATES - HISTORY - 19TH CENTURY.**
Cutler, William W. Parents and schools. Chicago : University of Chicago Press, 2000.
*TC LC225.3 .C86 2000*

**EDUCATIONAL CHANGE - UNITED STATES - HISTORY - 20TH CENTURY.**
Cutler, William W. Parents and schools. Chicago : University of Chicago Press, 2000.
*TC LC225.3 .C86 2000*

Ravitch, Diane. Left back. New York : Simon & Schuster, c2000.
*TC LA216 .R28 2000*

**Educational competencies for graduates of associate degree nursing programs** / Council of Associate Degree Nursing, Competencies Task Force, National

League for Nursing ; with support from the National Organization of Associate Degree Nursing ; edited and revised by G. Coxwell and H. Gillerman. [Rev.]. Sudbury, Mass. : Jones and Bartlett, 2000. xii, 19 p. ; 23 cm. At head of title: NLN Press. Rev. ed. of: Educational outcomes of associate degree nursing programs: roles and competencies. National League for Nursing, 1990. Includes bibliographical references (p. 17). ISBN 0-7637-1404-6
*1. Education. Nursing, Associate - standards. 2. Competency-Based Education. 3. Curriculum - standards. 4. Educational Measurement - standards. I. Coxwell. G. (Gloria) II. Gillerman, H. (Harriet Ann) III. National League for Nursing. Council of Associate Degree Nursing. Competencies Task Force. IV. Title: Educational outcomes of associate degree nursing programs.*
*TC RT74.5 .E38 2000*

**EDUCATIONAL COMPUTING.** See **EDUCATION - DATA PROCESSING.**

**Educational computing in the schools :** technology, communication, and literacy / Jay Blanchard, editor. New York : Haworth Press, 1999. 119 p. ; 23 cm. "Co-published simultaneously as Computers in the schools, volume 15, number 1, 1999." Includes bibliographical references and index. ISBN 0-7890-0779-7 (alk. paper) ISBN 0-7890-0814-9 (alk. paper) DDC 371.33
*1. Educational technology. 2. Literacy. 3. Internet (Computer network) in education. I. Blanchard. Jay S. II. Title: Computers in the schools.*
*TC LB1028.3 .E332 1999*

**EDUCATIONAL CONSULTANTS - UNITED STATES.**
Idol, Lorna. Collaborative consultation. 3rd ed. Austin, Tex. : PRO-ED, c2000.
*TC LC4019 .I35 2000*

Marks, Edward S. Entry strategies for school consultation. New York : Guilford Press, c1995.
*TC LB2799.2 .M36 1995*

Using consultants to improve teaching. San Francisco : Jossey-Bass, c1999.
*TC LB2799.2 .U83 1999*

**EDUCATIONAL COUNSELING.** See also **STUDENT ASSISTANCE PROGRAMS; TEACHER PARTICIPATION IN EDUCATIONAL COUNSELING; VOCATIONAL GUIDANCE.**
Davis, Thomas E., Ph. D. The solution-focused school counselor. Philadelphia ; Hove [England] : Accelerated Development/Taylor & Francis Group, c2000.
*TC LB1027.5 .D335 2000*

Winslade, John. Narrative counseling in schools. Thousand Oaks, Calif. : Corwin Press, c1999.
*TC LB1027.5 .W535 1999*

**EDUCATIONAL COUNSELING - BIBLIOGRAPHY.**
Cowley, William Harold, 1889- The personnel bibliographical index. Columbus, Ohio : The Ohio State University, 1932.
*TC Z5814.P8 C8*

**EDUCATIONAL COUNSELING - GREAT BRITAIN.**
McGuiness, John. Counselling in schools. London ; New York : Cassell, 1998.
*TC LB1027.5 .M367 1998*

**EDUCATIONAL COUNSELING - NEW YORK (STATE) - NEW YORK - CASE STUDIES.**
Fleischer, Lee. Living in contradiction. 1998.
*TC 06 no. 11021*

**EDUCATIONAL COUNSELING - PERIODICALS.**
Focus on guidance. Denver, Love Publishing Co.

Guidance review. [Delhi] Central Bureau of Educational and Vocational Guidance, National Council of Educational Research and Training.

International Association of Pupil Personnel Workers. The Journal. [Baton Rouge, La., etc.] International Association of Pupil Personnel Workers.

Journal of the National Association of Deans of Women. Washington, D.C. : The Association, the Dept. of Deans of the National Education Association of the United States of America, [1938-1956]

Journal of the National Association of Women Deans and Counselors. Washington, D.C. : The Association, 1956-1973.

Journal of vocational and educational guidance. [Bombay]

**EDUCATIONAL COUNSELING - UNITED STATES.**
Baker, Stanley B., 1935- School counseling for the

twenty-first century. 3rd ed. Upper Saddle River, N.J. : Merrill, c2000.
*TC LB1731.75 .B35 2000*

Kampwirth, Thomas J. Collaborative consultation in the schools. Upper Saddle River, N.J. : Merrill, c1999.
*TC LB1027.5 .K285 1999*

Marks, Edward S. Entry strategies for school consultation. New York : Guilford Press, c1995.
*TC LB2799.2 .M36 1995*

Preparation, collaboration, and emphasis on the family in school counseling for the new millennium. Lewiston : E. Mellen Press, c2000.
*TC LB1027.5 .P6525 2000*

Schmidt, John J., 1946- Counseling in schools. 3rd ed. Boston : Allyn and Bacon, c1999.
*TC LB1027.5 .S2585 1999*

Ward, Mary Ann, 1946- Student guidance and development. Larchmont, N.Y. : Eye On Education, c1998.
*TC LB1027.5 .W356 1998*

**EDUCATIONAL COUNSELING - UNITED STATES - CASE STUDIES.**
Murphy, John J. (John Joseph), 1955- Brief intervention for school problems. New York : Guilford Press, c1997.
*TC LC4802 .M87 1997*

**EDUCATIONAL COUNSELING - UNITED STATES - HANDBOOKS, MANUALS, ETC.**
Deuschle, C. (Constance) Stop the bus. Lanham, Md. : University Press of America, c2000.
*TC LB1027.5 .D4567 2000*

**EDUCATIONAL COUNSELING - UNITED STATES - PERIODICALS.**
Journal of the National Association of Deans of Women. Washington, D.C. : The Association, the Dept. of Deans of the National Education Association of the United States of America, [1938-1956]

Journal of the National Association of Women Deans and Counselors. Washington, D.C. : The Association, 1956-1973.

**Educational data processing.**
Journal of educational data processing. [Malibu, Calif., etc., Educational Systems Corp.]

**Educational digest.**
American educational digest. [Crawfordsville, Ind. : Educational Digest Co., 1923-1928]

**EDUCATIONAL DISCRIMINATION.** See **DISCRIMINATION IN EDUCATION.**

**EDUCATIONAL ENDOWMENTS.** See **ENDOWMENTS.**

**EDUCATIONAL EQUALIZATION.**
Brighouse, Harry. School choice and social justice. Oxford ; New York : Oxford University Press, 2000.
*TC LB1027.9 .B75 2000*

Morley, Louise, 1954- Organising feminisms. New York : St. Martin's Press, 1999.
*TC LC197 .M67 1999*

Thompson, Melvin R. The implementation of multicultural curricula in the New York City public elementary schools. 1999.
*TC 06 no. 11186*

**EDUCATIONAL EQUALIZATION - AFRICA, SUB-SAHARAN.**
Egbo, Benedicta, 1954- Gender, literacy, and life chances in Sub-Saharan Africa. Clevedon ; Buffalo : Multilingual Matters, c2000.
*TC LC2412 .E42 2000*

**EDUCATIONAL EQUALIZATION - CONNECTICUT - NEW HAVEN METROPOLITAN AREA - CASE STUDIES.**
McDermott, Kathryn A., 1969- Controlling public education. Lawrence : University Press of Kansas, c1999.
*TC LC213.23.N39 M34 1999*

**EDUCATIONAL EQUALIZATION - DEVELOPING COUNTRIES.**
Gender, education, and development. London ; New York : Zed Books ; New York : Distributed in USA exclusively by St. Martin's Press, c1999.
*TC LC2607 .G46 1998*

**EDUCATIONAL EQUALIZATION - DEVELOPING COUNTRIES - CROSS CULTURAL STUDIES.**
Third World education. New York : Garland Pub., 2000.

*TC LC2607 .T55 2000*

**EDUCATIONAL EQUALIZATION - ENGLAND - LONDON - CASE STUDIES.**
Gillborn, David. Rationing education. Buckingham [England] ; Philadelphia : Open University Press, 2000.
*TC LC213.3.G73 L664 2000*

**EDUCATIONAL EQUALIZATION - EUROPE.**
Gender, policy and educational change :. London ; New York : Routledge, 2000.
*TC LC213.3.G7 G48 2000*

**EDUCATIONAL EQUALIZATION - GREAT BRITAIN.**
Gender in the secondary curriculum. London ; New York : Routledge, 1998.
*TC LC212.93.G7 G46 1998*

Gender, policy and educational change :. London ; New York : Routledge, 2000.
*TC LC213.3.G7 G48 2000*

Promoting equality in secondary schools. London ; New York : Cassell, 1999.
*TC LC212.3.G7 P77 1999*

Siraj-Blatchford, Iram. Supporting identity, diversity and language in the early years. Buckingham [England] ; Philadelphia : Open University Press, 2000.
*TC LB1139.3.G7 S57 2000*

Whatever happened to equal opportunities in schools? Buckingham [England] ; Philadelphia : Open University Press, 2000.
*TC LC213.3.G7 W53 2000*

Woodward, Diana, 1948- Managing equal opportunities in higher education. Buckingham [England] ; Philadelphia : Society for Research into Higher Education : Open University Press, 2000.
*TC LC213.3.G7 W66 2000*

**EDUCATIONAL EQUALIZATION - NEW YORK (STATE).**
Mahammad, Hasna. Multicultural education. 1998.
*TC 06 no. 11033*

**EDUCATIONAL EQUALIZATION - UNITED STATES.**
Bolt, David B., 1954- Digital divide. New York : TV Books, c2000.
*TC LB1028.43 .B64 2000*

Charting terrains of Chicana(o)/Latina(o) education. Cresskill, N.J. : Hampton Press, c2000.
*TC LC2669 .C42 2000*

Education is politics. Portsmouth, NH : Boynton/Cook, c1999.
*TC LC196.5.U6 E36 1999*

Gay, Geneva. Culturally responsive teaching. New York : Teachers College Press, c2000.
*TC LC1099.3 .G393 2000*

Grossman, Herbert, 1934- Achieving educational equality. Springfield, Ill. : C.C. Thomas, c1998.
*TC LC213.2 .G76 1998*

Law and school reform. New Haven [Conn.] : Yale University Press, c1999.
*TC LC213.2. L38 1999*

Lynch, Sharon J. Equity and science education reform. Mahwah, N.J. ; London : L. Erlbaum Associates, 2000.
*TC LB1585.3 .L96 2000*

Making money matter. Washington, D.C. : National Academy Press, c1999.
*TC LB2825 .M27 1999*

McEwan, Barbara, 1946- The art of classroom management. Upper Saddle River, N.J. : Merrill, c2000.
*TC LB3013 .M383 2000*

Measuring up. Boston : Kluwer Academic Publishers, c1999.
*TC LB3051 .M4627 1999*

Reaching and teaching children who are victims of poverty. Lewiston, N.Y. ; Lampeter, Wales : E. Mellen Press, c1999.
*TC LC4091 .R38 1999*

A simple justice. New York : Teachers College Press, 2000.
*TC LC213.2 .S56 2000*

Teaching transformed. Boulder, Colo. ; Oxford : Westview Press, 2000.

*TC LB2822.82 .T44 2000*

Vernez, Georges. Closing the education gap. Santa
Monica, CA : RAND, 1999.
*TC LC213.2 .V47 1999*

Viteritti, Joseph P., 1946- Choosing equality.
Washington, D.C. : Brookings Institution Press,
c1999.
*TC LB1027.9 .V58 1999*

**EDUCATIONAL EQUALIZATION - UNITED
STATES - CASE STUDIES.**
Brodie, Laura Fairchild. Breaking out. 1st ed. New
York : Pantheon Books, c2000.
*TC LC212.862 .B75 2000*

Educators healing racism. Reston, VA : Association
of Teacher Educators ; Olney, MD : Association for
Childhood Education International, c1999.
*TC LC212.2 .E38 1999*

**EDUCATIONAL EVALUATION.** *See also*
**CURRICULUM EVALUATION;
EDUCATIONAL PRODUCTIVITY.**
Measuring student knowledge and skills. Paris :
Organisation for Economic Co-operation and
Development, c1999.
*TC LB3051 .M43 1999*

Organisation for Economic Co-operation and
Development (Paris) Measuring student knowledge
and skills. Paris : Organisation for Economic Co-
operation and Development, 2000.
*TC LB3051 .M44 2000*

Tanner, David Earl, 1948- Assessing academic
achievement. Boston ; London : Allyn and Bacon,
c2001.
*TC LB2822.75 .T36 2001*

Zersen, David John. Independent learning among
clergy. 1998.
*TC 06 no. 11008*

**EDUCATIONAL EVALUATION - CASE STUDIES.**
Heath, Douglas H. Assessing schools of hope. 1st ed.
Bryn Mawr, PA : Conrow Pub. House, c1999.
*TC LB2822.75 .H42 1999*

**EDUCATIONAL EVALUATION - CROSS-
CULTURAL STUDIES.**
Learning from others. Dordrecht [Netherlands] ;
Boston : Kluwer Academic Publishers, c2000.
*TC LB43 .L42 2000*

**EDUCATIONAL EVALUATION - GREAT
BRITAIN.**
Hoy, Charles, 1939- Improving quality in education.
London ; New York : Falmer Press, 2000.
*TC LB2822.84.G7 H69 1999*

Sammons, Pam. School effectiveness. Lisse,
Netherlands ; Abingdon [England] ; Exton, PA :
Swets & Zeitlinger Publishers, c1999.
*TC LB2822.75 .S24 1999*

**EDUCATIONAL EVALUATION - GREAT
BRITAIN - CASE STUDIES.**
Kushner, Saville. Personalizing evaluation. London ;
Thousand Oaks, Calif. : SAGE, 2000.
*TC LB2822.75 .K87 2000*

**EDUCATIONAL EVALUATION - IDAHO - TWIN
FALLS.**
Smith, Steven H. Schoolwide test preparation.
[Arlington, Va.] : Educational Research Service,
c2000.
*TC LB2806.22 .S65 2000*

**EDUCATIONAL EVALUATION - NEW JERSEY -
CASE STUDIES.**
Fleck, Mary B. Elementary principals' use of student
assessment information. 1999.
*TC 06 no. 11113*

**EDUCATIONAL EVALUATION - NEW YORK
(STATE) - NEW YORK.**
Curcio, John J. Relationships among administrator
personality, perceptions of feedback source
credibility, and attitudes toward program feedback.
1999.
*TC 085 C92*

**EDUCATIONAL EVALUATION - NEW
ZEALAND - CASE STUDIES.**
Thrupp, Martin, 1964- Schools making a difference--
let's be realistic!. Buckingham [England] ;
Philadelphia : Open University Press, 1999.
*TC LB2822.75 .T537 1999*

**EDUCATIONAL EVALUATION - RESEARCH.**
The international handbook of school effectiveness
research. London ; New York : Falmer Press, 2000.

*TC LB2822.75 .I59 2000*

**EDUCATIONAL EVALUATION - UNITED
STATES.**
Heath, Douglas H. Morale, culture, and character. 1st
ed. Bryn Mawr, PA : Conrow Pub. House, c1999.
*TC LC311 .H43 1999*

Shannon, Ann. Keeping score. Washington, D.C. :
National Academy Press, 1999.
*TC QA135.5 .S45 1999x*

**EDUCATIONAL EVALUATION - UNITED
STATES - HANDBOOKS, MANUALS, ETC.**
Sanders, James R. Evaluating school programs. 2nd
ed. Thousand Oaks, Calif. : Corwin Press, c2000.
*TC LB2822.75 .S26 2000*

**EDUCATIONAL EXCHANGES.** *See* **STUDENT
EXCHANGE PROGRAMS.**

**EDUCATIONAL EXCHANGES - GERMANY -
PERIODICALS.**
Hochschule und Ausland. Berlin : Kulturpolitische
Gesellschaft, 1923-1937.

**EDUCATIONAL EXCHANGES -
NETHERLANDS - PERIODICALS.**
Higher education and research in the Netherlands. The
Hague, Netherlands Foundation for International
Cooperation.

**EDUCATIONAL EXCHANGES - PERIODICALS.**
International educational and cultural exchange.
[Washington, U.S. Advisory Commission on
International Educational and Cultural Affairs; for
sale by the Supt. of Docs., U.S. Govt. Print. Off.]

**EDUCATIONAL EXCHANGES - SOCIAL
ASPECTS - JAPAN.**
McConnell, David L., 1959- Importing diversity.
Berkeley : University of California Press, c2000.
*TC LB2285.J3 M33 2000*

**EDUCATIONAL EXCHANGES - UNITED
STATES - STATISTICS.**
Open doors. [New York, N.Y.] : Institute of
International Education, 1954-
*TC LB2283 .I615*

**EDUCATIONAL EXCHANGES - UNITED
STATES - STATISTICS - PERIODICALS.**
[Open doors (New York, N.Y.)] Open doors. New
York, N.Y. : Institute of International Education,
*TC LB2283 .I615*

**Educational expenditures and economic growth in
the American States.**
Lieberman, Carl, 1941- Akron, Ohio : Midwest Press
Incorporated, 1998.
*TC LC66 .L45 1998*

**EDUCATIONAL FILMS.** *See* **MOTION
PICTURES IN EDUCATION.**

**Educational forum.** Delhi, Dept. of Extension Services,
Central Institute of Education. v. 24 cm. Vol. 19 repeated
in numbering. Vol. 20 omitted. Published   -Jan. 1974 by the
Alumni Association of the Central Institute of Education. ISSN
0013-1733
*1. Education. Secondary - Periodicals. I. Delhi. Central
Institute of Education. Dept. of Extension Services. II. Delhi.
Central Institute of Education. Alumni Association.*

**Educational foundations :** an anthology / edited by
Roselle K. Chartock. Upper Saddle River, N.J. :
Merrill, c2000. xvii, 344 p. : ill. ; 24 cm. Includes
bibliographical references and indexes. ISBN 0-13-660176-6
DDC 370/.71/1
*1. Education - Study and teaching (Higher) - United States. 2.
Educational sociology. 3. Education - History. 4. Education -
United States - History. 5. Teaching. I. Chartock, Roselle.*
*TC LB17 .E393 2000*

**EDUCATIONAL FREEDOM.** *See* **ACADEMIC
FREEDOM.**

**EDUCATIONAL FUND RAISING - UNITED
STATES.**
Bauer, David G. Technology funding for schools. 1st
ed. San Francisco : Jossey-Bass, c2000.
*TC LB1028.43 .B38 2000*

Ferguson, Jacqueline. Grants for special education and
rehabilitation. 4th ed. Gaithersburg, MD : Aspen
Publishers, Inc., 2000.
*TC LB2825 .F424 2000*

Grants for school technology. 3rd ed. Gaithersburg,
MD : Aspen Publishers, c2000.
*TC LB2336 .G76365 2000*

Grants for schools. 4th ed. Gaithersburg, MD : Aspen
Publishers, 2000.

*TC LB2825 .F46 2000*

**EDUCATIONAL GAMES.**
Lee, Carol K. Learning about books & libraries. Fort
Atkinson, Wis. : Alleyside Press, 2000.
*TC Z711.2 .L455 2000*

**EDUCATIONAL GAMES - JUVENILE
LITERATURE.**
Fleisher, Paul, 1951- Brain food. Tucson, AZ : Zephyr
Press, c1997.
*TC GV1480 .F54 1997*

**EDUCATIONAL GAMES - JUVENILE
SOFTWARE.**
Dr. Seuss kindergarten [computer file] Windows /
Macintosh CD-ROM : v. 1.0. Novato, CA :
Brøderbund, c1998.
*TC LB1195 .D77 1998*

**EDUCATIONAL GAMES - SOFTWARE.**
Carmen Sandiego [computer file]. Novato, Calif. :
Brøderbund Software, 1998. Computer data and
program.
*TC QA115 .C37 1998*

**EDUCATIONAL GAMES - UNITED STATES.**
Lee, Carol K. Learning about books & libraries. Fort
Atkinson, Wis. : Alleyside Press, 2000.
*TC Z711.2 .L455 2000*

**EDUCATIONAL GOALS.** *See* **EDUCATION -
AIMS AND OBJECTIVES.**

**EDUCATIONAL GUIDANCE.** *See*
**EDUCATIONAL COUNSELING.**

**EDUCATIONAL INDICATORS.** *See also*
**EDUCATIONAL ACCOUNTABILITY.**
Investing in education. Paris : Organisation for
Economic Co-operation and Development; Paris :
UNESCO, 2000.
*TC LB2846 .I68 2000*

**EDUCATIONAL INDICATORS - CROSS-
CULTURAL STUDIES - DATABASES -
PERIODICALS.**
Education at a glance [computer file]. Ottawa, Ont. :
Ivation Datasystems Inc. ; Paris, France : OECD,
*TC LB2846 .E2473*

**EDUCATIONAL INDICATORS - STATISTICS.**
*See* **EDUCATIONAL INDICATORS.**

**EDUCATIONAL INEQUALITY.** *See*
**EDUCATIONAL EQUALIZATION.**

**Educational innovation in economics and business.**
IV, Learning in a changing environment / edited by
Jeannette Hommes ... [et al.]. Boston, MA : Kluwer
Academic Publishers, c1999. xvii, 288 p. ; 25 cm. Papers
presented at the Fourth EDINEB Conference, held in
Edinburgh, Scotland, Sept. 1-3, 1997. Includes bibliographical
references and index. ISBN 0-7923-5855-4 (alk. paper) DDC
330/.071/1
*1. Economics - Study and teaching (Higher) - Congresses. 2.
Business education - Congresses. 3. Educational technology -
Congresses. I. Hommes, Jeannette. II. EDINEB Conference
(4th : 1997 : Edinburgh, Scotland) III. Title: Learning in a
changing environment*
*TC HB74.5 .E3333 1999*

**EDUCATIONAL INNOVATIONS.** *See also*
**ALTERNATIVE EDUCATION;
DEMONSTRATION CENTERS IN
EDUCATION; EDUCATION -
EXPERIMENTAL METHODS;
EDUCATIONAL CHANGE; EDUCATIONAL
TECHNOLOGY; NON-FORMAL
EDUCATION.**
Basile, Michael L., 1943- The deployment of
educational innovation through foreign aid. 1989.
*TC LD3234.M267 B32 1989*

Clarke, Paul, 1961- Learning schools, learning
systems. London ; New York : Continuum, 2000.
*TC LB1027 .C468 2000*

Managing evaluation and innovation in language
teaching. New York : Longman, 1998.
*TC P53.63 .M36 1998*

**EDUCATIONAL INNOVATIONS - ASIA - CASE
STUDIES.**
Grass roots networking for primary education :.
Bangkok : Unesco Regional Office for Education in
Asia and the Pacific, 1985.
*TC LA1054 .G73 1985*

**EDUCATIONAL INNOVATIONS - RESEARCH -
UNITED STATES.**
An educators' guide to schoolwide reform. Arlington,
Va. : Educational Research Service, c1999.
*TC LB2806.35 .E38 1999*

**EDUCATIONAL INNOVATIONS - RUSSIA (FEDERATION).**
Innovation in Russian schools. Bloomington, Ind. : Phi Delta Kappa Educational Foundation, c1997.
*TC LB1027 .I6575 1997*

Russia, education in the transition = [S.l.] : The World Bank, ECA Country Development III, Human Resources Division, 1995.
*TC LA839.2 .R87 1995*

**EDUCATIONAL INNOVATIONS - UNITED STATES.**
Michel, Patrick. Using action research for school restructuring and organizational change. 2000.
*TC 06 no. 11295*

Quehl, Gary H. Fifty years of innovations in undergraduate education. Indianapolis, Ind : USA Group Foundation, c1999.
*TC LB1027.3 .Q43 1999*

Restructuring education. Westport, Conn. : Praeger, 2000.
*TC LB2822.82 . R45 2000*

Tileston, Donna Walker. Ten best teaching practices. Thousand Oaks, Calif. : Corwin Press, c2000.
*TC LB1775.2 .T54 2000*

**Educational knowledge :** changing relationships between the state, civil society, and the educational community / edited by Thomas S. Popkewitz. Albany : State University of New York Press, c2000. xiv, 351 p. ; 23 cm. (SUNY series, frontiers in education) Includes bibliographical references and index. ISBN 0-7914-4403-1 (hbk. : alk. paper) ISBN 0-7914-4404-X (pbk. : alk. paper) DDC 379
*1. Education and state - Cross-cultural studies. 2. School management and organization - Cross-cultural studies. 3. Education - Social aspects - Cross-cultural studies. 4. Educational change - Cross-cultural studies. I. Popkewitz, Thomas S. II. Series.*
*TC LC71 .L335 2000*

**EDUCATIONAL LAW AND LEGISLATION.** *See* CHURCH SCHOOLS - LAW AND LEGISLATION; COLLEGE STUDENTS - LEGAL STATUS, LAWS, ETC.; DISCRIMINATION IN MEDICAL EDUCATION - LAW AND LEGISLATION; EDUCATION, HIGHER - LAW AND LEGISLATION; EDUCATION - FINANCE - LAW AND LEGISLATION; EVOLUTION - STUDY AND TEACHING - LAW AND LEGISLATION; GIFTED CHILDREN - EDUCATION - LAW AND LEGISLATION; PRIVATE SCHOOLS - LAW AND LEGISLATION; SCHOOL MANAGEMENT AND ORGANIZATION - LAW AND LEGISLATION; SEGREGATION IN EDUCATION - LAW AND LEGISLATION; SEX DISCRIMINATION IN HIGHER EDUCATION - LAW AND LEGISLATION; SPECIAL EDUCATION - LAW AND LEGISLATION; UNIVERSITIES AND COLLEGES - LAW AND LEGISLATION.

**EDUCATIONAL LAW AND LEGISLATION - GERMANY - BAVARIA - PERIODICALS.**
Bavaria (Germany). Staatsministerium für Unterricht, Kultus, Wissenschaft und Kunst. Amtsblatt des Bayerischen Staatsministeriums für Unterricht, Kultus, Wissenschaft und Kunst. München : J. Jehle,

Bavaria (Germany). Staatsministerium für Unterricht und Kultus. Amtsblatt des Staatsministeriums für Unterricht und Kultus. München : Das Ministerium, 1918-

**EDUCATIONAL LAW AND LEGISLATION - UNITED STATES.**
Law and school reform. New Haven [Conn.] : Yale University Press, c1999.
*TC LC213.2 .L38 1999*

Valente, William D. Law in the schools. 4th ed. Upper Saddle River, N.J. : Merrill, c1998.
*TC KF4119 .V28 1998*

**EDUCATIONAL LAW AND LEGISLATION - UNITED STATES - CASES.**
Imber, Michael. Education law. 2nd ed. Mahwah, N.J. : Lawrence Erlbaum Associates, 2000.
*TC KF4118 .I43 2000*

**EDUCATIONAL LAW AND LEGISLATION - UNITED STATES - DIGESTS.**
The bi-weekly school law letter. Laramie, Wyo. : Published by R.R. Hamilton, 1951-1955.

West's education law digest. St. Paul : West Pub. Co., c1983-

*TC KF4110.3 .W47*

**EDUCATIONAL LAW AND LEGISLATION - UNITED STATES - POPULAR WORKS.**
Kelly, Evelyn B. Legal basics. Bloomington, Ind. : Phi Delta Kappa Educational Foundation, c1998.
*TC KF390.E3 K45 1998*

**EDUCATIONAL LEADERSHIP.**
Becker, Nancy Jane. Implementing technology in higher education. 1999.
*TC 06 no. 11082*

Deal, Terrence E. Shaping school culture. 1st ed. San Francisco : Jossey-Bass Publishers, c1999.
*TC LB2805 .D34 1999*

Leithwood, Kenneth A. Changing leadership for changing times. Buckingham ; Philadelphia : Open University Press, 1999.
*TC LB2805 .L358 1999*

Ramsden, Paul. Learning to lead in higher education. London ; New York : Routledge, 1998.
*TC LB2341 .R32 1998*

Tobe, Dorothy Echols. The development of cognitive leadership frames among African American female college presidents. 1999.
*TC 06 no. 11187*

Values and educational leadership. Albany : State University of New York Press, c1999.
*TC LB2806 .V25 1999*

The values of educational administration. London : Falmer, 1999.
*TC LB2806 .V255 1999*

**Educational leadership and learning.**
Law, Sue. Buckingham [England] ; Philadelphia : Open University Press, 2000.
*TC LB2900.5 .L39 1999*

**EDUCATIONAL LEADERSHIP - AUSTRALIA.**
Rodd, Jillian. Leadership in early childhood. 2nd edition. New York : Teachers College Press, 1998.
*TC LB1776.4.A8 R63 1998*

**EDUCATIONAL LEADERSHIP - CASE STUDIES.**
Deal, Terrence E. Shaping school culture. 1st ed. San Francisco : Jossey-Bass Publishers, c1999.
*TC LB2805 .D34 1999*

**EDUCATIONAL LEADERSHIP - GREAT BRITAIN.**
Brighouse, Tim. How to improve your school. London ; New York : Routledge, 1999.
*TC LB2822.84.G7 B75 1999*

Field, Kit. Effective subject leadership. London ; New York : Routledge, 2000.
*TC LB2806.15 .F54 2000*

Law, Sue. Educational leadership and learning. Buckingham [England] ; Philadelphia : Open University Press, 2000.
*TC LB2900.5 .L39 1999*

Leading schools in times of change. Buckingham [England] ; Philadelphia : Open University Press, 2000.
*TC LB2900.5 .L45 2000*

Thody, Angela. Leadership of schools. London ; Herndon, Va. : Cassell, 1997.
*TC LB2831.726.G7 T56 1997*

**EDUCATIONAL LEADERSHIP - GREAT BRITAIN - CASE STUDIES.**
Wallace, Mike. Senior management teams in primary schools. London ; New York : Routledge, 1999.
*TC LB2806.3 .W37 1999*

**EDUCATIONAL LEADERSHIP - ILLINOIS - CASE STUDIES.**
Lyman, Linda L. How do they know you care? New York : Teachers College Press, c2000.
*TC LB2831.924.I3 L96 2000*

**EDUCATIONAL LEADERSHIP - MICHIGAN - ANN ARBOR.**
Duderstadt, James J., 1942- A university for the 21st century. Ann Arbor, MI : University of Michigan Press, c2000.
*TC LD3280 .D83 2000*

**EDUCATIONAL LEADERSHIP - MORAL AND ETHICAL ASPECTS - UNITED STATES.**
Crawford, George, 1937- Philosophical & cultural values. Larchmont, NY : Eye On Education, c2000.
*TC LB2831.92 .C72 2000*

Nelson, Stephen James, 1947- Leaders in the crucible. Westport, Conn. : Bergin & Garvey, 2000.

*TC LB2341 .N386 2000*

**EDUCATIONAL LEADERSHIP - NEW JERSEY - CASE STUDIES.**
Fleck, Mary B. Elementary principals' use of student assessment information. 1999.
*TC 06 no. 11113*

**Educational leadership :** policy dimensions in the 21st century / edited by Bruce Anthony Jones Stamford, Conn. : Ablex Pub. Corp., c2000. x, 176 p. : ill. ; 24 cm. (Educational policy in the 21st century ; v. 1) Includes bibliographical references and indexes. ISBN 1-56750-488-4 (cloth) ISBN 1-56750-489-2 (pbk.) DDC 379.73
*1. Educational leadership - United States. 2. Educational planning - United States. 3. Education and state - United States.1. Jones, Bruce Anthony. II. Series.*
*TC LB2805 .E3475 2000*

**EDUCATIONAL LEADERSHIP - UNITED STATES.**
Beach, Don M. Supervisory leadership. Boston : Allyn and Bacon, c2000.
*TC LB2806.4 .B433 2000*

Catholic school leadership. London ; New York : Falmer Press, 2000.
*TC LC501 .C3484 2000*

Crow, Gary Monroe, 1947- Leadership. Princeton, NJ : Eye on Education, c1996.
*TC LB2831.92 .C76 1996*

Curry, Barbara K. Women in power. New York ; London : Teachers College Press, c2000.
*TC LB2831.62 .C87 2000*

The developmental process of positive attitudes and mutual respect. Lewiston, N.Y. : E. Mellen Press, c1999.
*TC LB2822.82 .D49 1999*

Durocher, Elizabeth Antointette. Leadership orientations of school administrators. 1995.
*TC 06 no. 10583a*

Dyer, Karen M. The intuitive principal. Thousand Oaks, Calif. : Corwin Press, c2000.
*TC LB2831.92 .D94 2000*

Educational leadership. Stamford, Conn. : Ablex Pub. Corp., c2000.
*TC LB2805 .E3475 2000*

Henderson, James George. Transformative curriculum leadership. 2nd ed. Upper Saddle River. N.J. : Merrill, c2000.
*TC LB1570 .H45 2000*

Keefe, James W. Instruction and the learning environment. Larchmont, NY : Eye On Education, c1997.
*TC LB2806.4 .K44 1997*

Lashway, Larry. Measuring leadership. Eugene, OR : ERIC Clearinghouse on Educational Management, University of Oregon, 1999.
*TC LB2806 .L28 1999*

Managing colleges and universities. Westport, Conn. : Bergin & Garvey, 2000.
*TC LB2341 .M2779 2000*

Managing quality in young children's programs. New York : Teachers College Press, c2000.
*TC LB2822.6 .M36 2000*

Pankake, Anita M., 1947- Implementation. Larchmont, NY : Eye on Education, c1998.
*TC LB2805 .P32 1998*

Pellicer, Leonard O. Caring enough to lead. Thousand Oaks, Calif. : Corwin Press, c1999.
*TC LB2805 .P375 1999*

Rallis, Sharon F. Principals of dynamic schools. 2nd ed. Thousand Oaks, Calif. : Corwin Press, c2000.
*TC LB2831.92 .G65 2000*

Sergiovanni, Thomas J. The principalship. 4th ed. Boston : Allyn & Bacon, c2001.
*TC LB2831.92 .S47 2001*

Villani, Susan. Are you sure you're the principal? Thousand Oaks, Calif. : Corwin Press, c1999.
*TC LB2831.92 .V55 1999*

Weller, L. David. Quality human resources leadership :. Lanham, Md. : Scarecrow Press, 2000.
*TC LB2831.92 .W45 2000*

**EDUCATIONAL LEADERSHIP - UNITED STATES - CASE STUDIES.**
Hughes, Larry W., 1931- Public relations for school leaders. Boston ; London : Allyn and Bacon, c2000.
*TC LB2847 .H84 2000*

Portz, John, 1953- City schools and city politics. Lawrence : University Press of Kansas, c1999.
*TC LC5131 .P67 1999*

Smulyan, Lisa. Balancing acts. Albany : State University of New York Press, c2000.
*TC LB2831.92 .S58 2000*

## EDUCATIONAL LEADERSHIP - UNITED STATES - HANDBOOKS, MANUALS, ETC.
Dunklee, Dennis R. If you want to lead, not just manage. Thousand Oaks, Calif. : Corwin Press, c2000.
*TC LB2831.92 .D85 2000*

## EDUCATIONAL LEARDERSHIP - UNITED STATES.
What principals should know about--. Springfield, Ill. : C.C. Thomas, c2000.
*TC LB2831.92 .W52 2000*

## EDUCATIONAL LINGUISTICS. See LANGUAGE AND EDUCATION.

## EDUCATIONAL LITERATURE. See EDUCATION - BIBLIOGRAPHY.

**Educational management series**
Blandford, Sonia. Managing professional development in schools. London : New York : Routledge, 2000.
*TC LB1731 .B57 2000*

Dean, Joan. Improving children's learning. London ; New York : Routledge, 2000.
*TC LB1725.G6 D43 2000*

## EDUCATIONAL MEASUREMENT.
Nugent, Patricia Mary, 1944- Test success. 3rd ed. Philadelphia : F.A. Davis, c2000.
*TC RT55 .N77 2000*

**Educational measurement and evaluation.**
Collins, Harold W. [Glenview, Ill.], Scott, Foresman, [c1969].
*TC LB3051 .C645*

## EDUCATIONAL MEASUREMENT - STANDARDS.
Educational competencies for graduates of associate degree nursing programs. [Rev.]. Sudbury, Mass. : Jones and Bartlett, 2000.
*TC RT74.5 .E38 2000*

## EDUCATIONAL MEASUREMENTS. See EDUCATIONAL TESTS AND MEASUREMENTS.

## EDUCATIONAL MEDIA. See TEACHING - AIDS AND DEVICES.

## EDUCATIONAL MEDIA CENTERS. See INSTRUCTIONAL MATERIALS CENTERS.

## EDUCATIONAL MEDIA PROGRAMS. See MEDIA PROGRAMS (EDUCATION).

**Educational news bulletin.**
The Journal of Arkansas education. [Little Rock : Arkansas Educational Association, 1923-1975].

**Educational news-gleaner.**
Illinois school journal. Normal, Ill. : [s.n.], 1881/82-1889.

## EDUCATIONAL OBJECTIVES. See EDUCATION - AIMS AND OBJECTIVES.

**Educational outcomes of associate degree nursing programs.**
Educational competencies for graduates of associate degree nursing programs. [Rev.]. Sudbury, Mass. : Jones and Bartlett, 2000.
*TC RT74.5 .E38 2000*

**Educational performance of scheduled castes.**
Kinjaram, Ramaiah. New Delhi : APH Pub. Corp., [1998?]
*TC LC4097.14 K55 1998*

## EDUCATIONAL PLANNING. See also CAMPUS PLANNING; EDUCATIONAL CHANGE; EDUCATIONAL INNOVATIONS; SCHOOL MANAGEMENT AND ORGANIZATION.
Educational planning. Mankato, Minn. : International Society of Educational Planners.

## EDUCATIONAL PLANNING.
Abu-Duhou, Ibtisam. School-based management. Paris : International Institute for Educational Planning (IIEP) ; Paris : Unesco, 1999.
*TC LB5 .F85 1999*

Carnoy, Martin. Globalization and educational reform. Paris : International Institute for Educational Planning (IIEP), 1999.

*TC LB5 .F85 v.63*

Quong, Terry. Values based strategic planning :. Singapore ; New York : Prentice Hall, 1998.
*TC LB2806 .Q86 1998*

Welsh, Thomas. Decentralization of education. Paris : International Institute for Educational Planning (IIEP) ; Paris : UNESCO, 1999.
*TC LB5 .F85 v.64*

**Educational planning.** Mankato, Minn., International Society of Educational Planners. v. Continued in May 1974 by a publication with the same title published in Toronto. ISSN 0315-9388 DDC 379
*I. International Society of Educational Planners. II. Title: Educational planning*

## EDUCATIONAL PLANNING - AFRICA - HISTORY - 20TH CENTURY.
Sivonen, Seppo. White-collar or hoe handle. Helsinki : Suomen Historiallinen Seura, [1995]
*TC LA1531 .S58 1995*

## EDUCATIONAL PLANNING - UNITED STATES.
Challenges and opportunities for education in the 21st century. Lewiston, NY : Edwin Mellen Press, c1999.
*TC LA209.2 .C45 1999*

Educational leadership. Stamford, Conn. : Ablex Pub. Corp., c2000.
*TC LB2805 .E3475 2000*

Erlandson, David A. Organizational oversight. Princeton, NJ : Eye on Education, c1996.
*TC LB2805 .E75 1996*

Herman, Jerry John, 1930- School planning & personnel. Lancaster, Pa. : Technomic Pub. Co., c1999.
*TC LB2831.58 .H47 1999*

Otterbourg, Susan D. Using technology to strengthen employee and family involvement in education. [New York] : Conference Board, c1998.
*TC LB1028.3 .O88 1998*

Reforming American education from the bottom to the top. Portsmouth, NH : Heinemann, c1999.
*TC LA210 .R44 1999*

## EDUCATIONAL POLICY. See EDUCATION AND STATE.

**Educational policy in the 21st century**
(v. 1) Educational leadership. Stamford, Conn. : Ablex Pub. Corp., c2000.
*TC LB2805 .E3475 2000*

**Educational policy (Los Altos, Calif.).**
Accuracy or advocacy. Thousand Oaks, Calif. : Corwin Press, c1999.
*TC LB1028 .A312 1999*

**Educational private practice.**
Zuelke, Dennis C. Lancaster : Technomic Pub., c1996.
*TC LB2844.1.S86 Z84 1996*

**Educational problems.**
Hall, G. Stanley (Granville Stanley), 1844-1924. New York, London, D. Appleton and company, 1911.
*TC 370.4/H14*

## EDUCATIONAL PRODUCTIVITY. See EDUCATIONAL ACCOUNTABILITY.

## EDUCATIONAL PRODUCTIVITY - UNITED STATES.
Making money matter. Washington, D.C. : National Academy Press, c1999.
*TC LB2825 .M27 1999*

## EDUCATIONAL PROGRAM EVALUATION. See EDUCATIONAL EVALUATION.

## EDUCATIONAL PSYCHOLOGY. See also ACHIEVEMENT MOTIVATION; ATTENTION; CHILD PSYCHOLOGY; IMAGINATION; INTELLIGENCE LEVELS; LEARNING, PSYCHOLOGY OF; LISTENING; REWARDS AND PUNISHMENTS IN EDUCATION; THOUGHT AND THINKING.
Assessing science understanding :. San Diego, Calif. : London : Academic, 2000.
*TC Q181 .A87 2000*

## EDUCATIONAL PSYCHOLOGY.
Bruer, John T., 1949- The myth of the first three years. New York : Free Press, c1999.
*TC BF318 .B79 1999*

Curriculum planning. 7th ed. Boston : Allyn and Bacon, c2000.

*TC LB2806.15 .C868 2000*

Dewey, John, 1859-1952. How we think. Boston : Houghton Mifflin, c1998.
*TC BF441 .D43 1998*

Feldberg, Suzanne. A comparison of different types of mathematical problem-solving hints selected by concrete and formal operational subjects in a hypercard environment. 1998.
*TC 085 F316*

Learning activity and development. Aarhus : Aarhus Universit #, 1999.
*TC LB1060 .L43 1999*

Monograph in behavioral disorders. Severe behavior disorders of children and youth. Reston, Va. : Council for Children with Behavioral Disorders, c1978-1986.
*TC BF721 .M65*

Norwich, Brahm. Education and psychology in interaction. London ; New York : Routledge, 2000.
*TC LB1051 .N645 2000*

Ravenette, Tom. Personal construct theory in educational psychology :. London : Whurr, c1999.
*TC LB1027.55 .R38 1999*

Readings in educational psychology. 2nd ed. Boston : Allyn and Bacon, c1998.
*TC LB1051 .R386 1998*

Ting, Yenren, 1948- Learning English text by heart in a Chinese university. [New York : Columbia University], 1999.
*TC 085 T438*

## EDUCATIONAL PSYCHOLOGY - CASE STUDIES.
Readings in educational psychology. 2nd ed. Boston : Allyn and Bacon, c1998.
*TC LB1051 .R386 1998*

## EDUCATIONAL PSYCHOLOGY - PERIODICALS.
Forum of education. London, Longmans Green.

## EDUCATIONAL PSYCHOLOGY - RESEARCH.
Conceptual issues in research on intelligence. Stamford, Conn. : JAI Press , 1998.
*TC BF311 .A38 v. 5 1998*

**The educational psychology series**
Martinez, Michael E. Education as the cultivation of intelligence. Mahwah, N.J. : London : Lawrence Erlbaum Associates, 2000.
*TC LB1060 .M337 2000*

## EDUCATIONAL PURPOSES. See EDUCATION - AIMS AND OBJECTIVES.

**Educational rankings.**
Educational rankings annual. Detroit, MI : Gale Research, c1991-
*TC LB2331.63 .E34*

**Educational rankings annual.** Detroit, MI : Gale Research, c1991- v. ; 29 cm. Frequency: Annual. 1991- . Educational rankings. Other title: ERA. Published by the Gale Group, <1999-> ISSN 1053-1378 DDC 378.73
*1. Universities and colleges - United States - Evaluation - Directories. 2. Universities and colleges - United States - Graduate work - Evaluation - Directories. 3. Universities and colleges - United States - Curricula - Evaluation - Directories. I. Gale Group II. Title: Educational rankings III. Title: ERA*
*TC LB2331.63 .E34*

## EDUCATIONAL REFORM. See EDUCATIONAL CHANGE.

**Educational reform on people's own initiative.**
Nihon Kyōshokuin Kumiai. [Tokyo?] : Japan Teachers Union, 1984.
*TC LC210.8.N54 1984*

**Educational reform series**
(no. 1) Nihon Kyōshokuin Kumiai. Educational reform on people's own initiative. [Tokyo?] : Japan Teachers Union, 1984.
*TC LC210.8.N54 1984*

## EDUCATIONAL RESEARCH. See also EDUCATION - RESEARCH.
Gay, L. R. 6th ed. Upper Saddle River, N.J. : Merrill, c2000.
*TC LB1028 .G37 2000*

Johnson, Burke. Boston : Allyn and Bacon, c2000.
*TC LB1028 .J59 2000*

McMillan, James H. 3rd ed. New York ; Harlow, England : Longman, c2000.
*TC LB1028 .M364 2000*

**EDUCATIONAL - RESEARCH - PERIODICALS.**
Indian journal of educational research. Bombay, Asia
Publishing House.

**Educational research series**
(no. 38, 46) Parkyn, George W. Success and failure
at the university. Wellington, New Zealand Council
for Educational Research, 1959-67.
*TC LB1131 .P29*

**Educational Research Service (Arlington, Va.).**
Smith, Steven H. Schoolwide test preparation.
[Arlington, Va.] : Educational Research Service,
c2000.
*TC LB2806.22 .S65 2000*

Special days and weeks for planning the school
calendar. Arlington, Va. : Educational Research
Service,
*TC LB3525 .S63*

**EDUCATIONAL RESEARCH -
TECHNOLOGICAL INNOVATIONS.**
Information technology in educational research and
statistics. New York : Haworth Press, 1999.
*TC LB1028.3 .I51945 1999*

**Educational Resources Information Center
[computer file].**
[ERIC (SilverPlatter International : Online)] The
ERIC database [computer file]. WebSPIRS version
3.1. [Norwood, MA] : SilverPlatter International,
*TC NETWORKED RESOURCES*

[ERIC (SilverPlatter International : Online)] The
ERIC database [computer file]. WebSPIRS version
3.1. [Norwood, MA] : SilverPlatter International,
*TC NETWORKED RESOURCES*

**Educational Resources Information Center (U.S.).**
Critical knowledge for diverse teachers & learners.
Washington, DC : AACTE : ERIC, c1997.
*TC LB1715 .C732 1997*

[ERIC (SilverPlatter International : Online)] The
ERIC database [computer file]. WebSPIRS version
3.1. [Norwood, MA] : SilverPlatter International,
*TC NETWORKED RESOURCES*

[ERIC (SilverPlatter International : Online)] The
ERIC database [computer file]. WebSPIRS version
3.1. [Norwood, MA] : SilverPlatter International,
*TC NETWORKED RESOURCES*

**EDUCATIONAL SOCIOLOGY.** *See also*
**CLASSROOM ENVIRONMENT;
EDUCATION - AIMS AND OBJECTIVES;
SCHOOL ENVIRONMENT; SOCIALLY
HANDICAPPED CHILDREN - EDUCATION;
SOCIALLY HANDICAPPED - EDUCATION.**
Bernstein, Basil B. Pedagogy, symbolic control, and
identity. Lanham, Md. : Rowman & Littlefield, 2000.
*TC LC191 .B456 2000*

Bernstein, Basil B. The structuring of pedagogic
discourse. London ; New York : Routledge, 1990.
*TC P40 .B39 1990*

Education policy. Cheltenham, UK : Northampton,
MA : Edward Elgar Pub., c1999.
*TC LC71 .E32 1999*

Educational foundations. Upper Saddle River, N.J. :
Merrill, c2000.
*TC LB17 .E393 2000*

Feinberg, Walter, 1937- School and society. 3rd ed.
New York : Teachers College Press, c1998.
*TC LC191 .F4 1998*

Fleischer, Lee. Living in contradiction. 1998.
*TC 06 no. 11021*

Institutional issues. London ; New York : Falmer
Press, 2000.
*TC LC191 .I495 2000*

Learning communities in education. London ; New
York : Routledge, 1999.
*TC LB14.7 .L43 1999*

Pierre Bourdieu. Bern ; New York : P. Lang, c1999.
*TC HM621 .P54 1999*

Researching school experience. London ; New York :
Falmer Press, 1999.
*TC LB1027 .R453 1999*

Spindler, George Dearborn. Fifty years of
anthropology and education, 1950-2000. Mahwah,
N.J. L.Erlbaum Associates, 2000.
*TC LB45 .S66 2000*

The structure of schooling. Mountain View, Calif. :
Mayfield Pub. Co., 1999.

*TC LC189 .S87 1999*

Systems of education. London : New York : Falmer
Press, 2000.
*TC LC191 .S98 2000*

Thomas, Elwyn. Culture and schooling. Chichester,
West Sussex, England ; New York : J. Wiley & Sons,
c2000.
*TC LB45 .T476 2000*

Ting, Yenren, 1948- Learning English text by heart in
a Chinese university. [New York : Columbia
University], 1999.
*TC 085 T438*

**EDUCATIONAL SOCIOLOGY - AFRICA.**
Mosha, R. Sambuli. The heartbeat of indigenous
Africa. New York : London : Garland Publishing :
[Falmer Press], 2000.
*TC LC191.8.T29 M67 2000*

**EDUCATIONAL SOCIOLOGY - AUSTRALIA -
HISTORY.**
Dunt, Lesley, 1944- Speaking worlds. Parkville, Vic. :
History Department, The University of Melbourne,
c1993.
*TC LA2101 .D96 1993*

**EDUCATIONAL SOCIOLOGY - DEVELOPING
COUNTRIES - CROSS-CULTURAL STUDIES.**
Education, cultures, and economics. New York :
Falmer Press, 1999.
*TC LC191.8.D44 E38 1999*

**EDUCATIONAL SOCIOLOGY - ENGLAND.**
Stray, Christopher. Classics transformed. Oxford :
Clarendon Press ; New York : Oxford University
Press, 1998.
*TC PA78.E53 S87 1998*

**EDUCATIONAL SOCIOLOGY - ENGLAND -
HISTORY.**
Silver, Harold. English education and the radicals
1780-1850. London ; Boston : Routledge & Kegan
Paul, 1975.
*TC LA631.7 .S45*

**EDUCATIONAL SOCIOLOGY - HANDBOOKS,
MANUALS, ETC.**
Handbook of the sociology of education. New York :
Kluwer Academic/Plenum, c2000.
*TC LC191 .H254 2000*

**EDUCATIONAL SOCIOLOGY - NEW
ZEALAND - CASE STUDIES.**
Thrupp, Martin, 1964- Schools making a difference--
let's be realistic!. Buckingham [England] ;
Philadelphia : Open University Press, 1999.
*TC LB2822.75 .T537 1999*

**EDUCATIONAL SOCIOLOGY - PERIODICALS.**
The Journal of educational sociology. [New York :
American Viewpoint Society, Inc., 1927-1963]

[Journal of educational sociology (Online)] The
journal of educational sociology [computer file]. New
York, N.Y. : American Viewpoint Society, Inc.,
1927-1963.
*TC EJOURNALS*

**EDUCATIONAL SOCIOLOGY - TANZANIA.**
Mosha, R. Sambuli. The heartbeat of indigenous
Africa. New York : London : Garland Publishing :
[Falmer Press], 2000.
*TC LC191.8.T29 M67 2000*

**EDUCATIONAL SOCIOLOGY - UNITED
STATES.**
Brint, Steven G. Schools and societies. Thousand
Oaks : Pine Forge Press, c1998.
*TC LC191.4 .B75 1998*

Edmund W. Gordon. Stamford, Conn. : Jai Press,
c2000.
*TC HM1033 .E35 2000*

Fletcher, Scott, 1959- Education and emancipation.
New York : Teachers College Press, c2000.
*TC LC191.4 .F54 2000*

Sadovnik, Alan R. Exploring education. Boston :
Allyn and Bacon, c1994.
*TC LB17 .S113 1994*

Sadovnik, Alan R. Exploring education. 2nd ed.
Boston : Allyn and Bacon, 2000.
*TC LA217.2 .S23 2000*

**Educational Software Evaluation Consortium.**
The ... Educational software preview guide. Redwood
City, CA : California TECC Software Library &
Clearinghouse,
*TC LB1028.7 .E35*

The ... **Educational software preview guide** /
developed by the Educational Software Evaluation
Consortium at the California TECC Software
Evaluation Forum. Redwood City, CA : California
TECC Software Library & Clearinghouse, v. ; 22 x 28
cm. Frequency: Annual. Vols. for 1986-19uu loose-leaf;
<1990/1991-> softcover. Published by: Educational Software
Evaluation Consortium : Distributed by International Society
for Technology in Education, <c1991-> Description based on:
1986. Published for the University of the State of New York,
Center for Learning Technologies? On cover, 1986-19uu:
University of the State of New York, State Education Dept.,
Center for Learning Technologies. ISSN 0898-2694 DDC 370
*1. Computer-assisted instruction - Catalogs. 2. Computer
software - Catalogs. I. Educational Software Evaluation
Consortium. II. University of the State of New York. Center for
Learning Technologies.*
*TC LB1028.7 .E35*

**EDUCATIONAL STATISTICS.**
Du, Zuru. Modeling conditional item dependencies
with a three-parameter logistic testlet model. 1998.
*TC 085 D84*

**EDUCATIONAL STATISTICS - STUDY AND
TEACHING.**
Ravid, Ruth. Practical statistics for educators. 2nd ed.
Lanham, Md. : University Press of America, c2000.
*TC LB2846 .R33 2000*

**EDUCATIONAL STATISTICS -
TECHNOLOGICAL INNOVATIONS.**
Information technology in educational research and
statistics. New York : Haworth Press, 1999.
*TC LB1028.3 .I51945 1999*

**Educational studies and documents**
(69) The role of measurement and evaluation in
education policy. Paris : Unesco Pub., 1999.
*TC LB3051 .R653 1999*

**EDUCATIONAL SURVEYS.** *See also* **ADULT
EDUCATION - EVALUATION.**
The international academic profession. Princeton,
N.J. : Carnegie Foundation for the Advancement of
Teaching, c1996.
*TC LB1778 .I54 1996*

International Adult Literacy Survey. Literacy in the
information age. Paris : Organisation for Economic
Co-operation and Development; Ottawa : Statistics
Canada, 2000.
*TC LC149 .L59 2000*

**EDUCATIONAL SURVEYS - AUSTRALIA.**
Literacy and numeracy in Australian schools.
Canberra : Australian Gov. Pub. Service, 1976-
*TC LA2102 .L57 1976*

**EDUCATIONAL SURVEYS - CAMEROON.**
Amin, Martin E. (Martin Efuetngu) Trends in the
demand for primary education in Cameroon. Lanham,
MD : University Press of America, 1999.
*TC LC137.C36 A55 1999*

**EDUCATIONAL SURVEYS - GREAT BRITAIN.**
Improving literacy in the primary school. London ;
New York : Routledge, 1998.
*TC LB1573 .I56 1998*

**EDUCATIONAL SURVEYS - NEW YORK
(STATE) - HERKIMER COUNTY - CASE
STUDIES.**
O'Connor-Pirkle, Marilyn. Tracking systemic change
in an interagency partnership. 1996.
*TC 06 no. 10677*

O'Connor-Pirkle, Marilyn. Tracking systemic change
in an interagency partnership. 1996.
*TC 06 no. 10677*

**EDUCATIONAL SURVEYS - NIGERIA.**
Francis, Paul A. Hard lessons. Washington, D.C. :
World Bank, c1998.
*TC LA1632 .F73 1998*

**EDUCATIONAL SURVEYS - UNITED STATES.**
Gregory, Sheila T. Black women in the academy. Rev.
and updated ed. Lanham, Md. : University Press of
America, 1999.
*TC LC2781 .G74 1999*

Heath, Douglas H. Assessing schools of hope. 1st ed.
Bryn Mawr, PA : Conrow Pub. House, c1999.
*TC LB2822.75 .H42 1999*

**EDUCATIONAL TECHNOLOGY.** *See also*
**AUDIO-VISUAL EDUCATION;
COMPUTER-ASSISTED INSTRUCTION;
MEDIA PROGRAMS (EDUCATION);
PROGRAMMED INSTRUCTION;
TEACHING - AIDS AND DEVICES.**
Belanger, France, 1963- Evaluation and

implementation of distance learning. Hershey, PA ; London : Idea Group Pub., c2000.
*TC LC5803.C65 B45 2000*

Bowe, Frank. Universal design in education. Westport, Conn. : London : Bergin & Garvey, 2000.
*TC LB1028.38 .B69 2000*

Campbell, Hope. Managing technology in the early childhood classroom. Westminster, CA : Teacher Created Materials, c1999.
*TC LB1139.35.C64 C36 1999*

Casey, Jean Marie. Early literacy. Rev. ed. Englewood, Colo. : Libraries Unlimited, 2000.
*TC LB1139.5.L35 C37 2000*

Changing university teaching :. London : Kogan Page ; Sterling, VA : Stylus Pub., 2000.
*TC LB2331 .C53 2000*

Distance learning technologies. Hershey, PA : London : Idea Group Pub., c2000.
*TC LC5803.C65 D57 2000*

Educational computing in the schools. New York : Haworth Press, 1999.
*TC LB1028.3 .E332 1999*

Grants for school technology. 3rd ed. Gaithersburg, MD : Aspen Publishers, c2000.
*TC LB2336 .G76365 2000*

Hoffman, Eric. An introduction to teaching composition in an electronic environment. Needham Heights, Mass. : Allyn & Bacon, c2000.
*TC LB1028.3 .H63 2000*

Innovations in science and mathematics education. Mahwah, N.J. : L. Erlbaum, 2000.
*TC Q181 .I654 1999*

Learning sites. 1st ed. Amsterdam ; New York : Pergamon, 1999.
*TC LB1060 .L4245 1999*

Linking literacy and technology. Newark, Del. : International Reading Association, c2000.
*TC LB1576.7 .L56 2000*

Page to screen. London ; New York : Routledge, 1998.
*TC LC149.5 .P35 1998*

Plugging in :. Washington, D.C. : NEKIA Communications ; Oak Brook, Ill. : North Central Regional Educational Laboratory, [1995]. ([1999]).
*TC LB1028.3 .P584 1995*

Schweizer, Heidi. Designing and teaching an on-line course :. Boston : Allyn & Bacon, c1999.
*TC LB1028.3 .S377 1999*

Simpson, Ormond. Supporting students in open and distance learning. London : Kogan Page, 2000.
*TC LC5800 .S56 2000*

Weintraub, Robert Steven. Informal learning in the workplace through desktop technology. 1998.
*TC 06 no. 11003*

**EDUCATIONAL TECHNOLOGY - CASE STUDIES.**
Cases studies on information technology in higher education. Hershey, PA : Idea Group Pub., c2000.
*TC LB2395.7 .C39 2000*

**EDUCATIONAL TECHNOLOGY - CONGRESSES.**
Educational innovation in economics and business. IV, Learning in a changing environment. Boston, MA : Kluwer Academic Publishers, c1999.
*TC HB74.5 .E3333 1999*

**EDUCATIONAL TECHNOLOGY - GREAT BRITAIN.**
Issues in education and technology :. London : Commonwealth Secretariat, c2000.
*TC LB1028.3 .I77 2000*

**EDUCATIONAL TECHNOLOGY - HANDBOOKS, MANUALS, ETC.**
Brunner, Cornelia, Dr. The new media literacy handbook. New York : Anchor Books, 1999.
*TC LB1028.3 .B77 1999*

Gardner, Paul (Paul Henry) Managing technology in the middle school classroom. Huntington Beach, CA : Teacher Created Materials, c1996.
*TC LB1028.5 .C353 1996*

**EDUCATIONAL TECHNOLOGY - INDIA - CONGRESSES.**
Open learning system. New Delhi : Lancer International, c1989.
*TC LC5808.I4 O64 1989*

**EDUCATIONAL TECHNOLOGY - PLANNING.**
Instructional technology for teaching and learning. 2nd ed. Upper Saddle River, N.J. : Merrill, c2000.
*TC LB1028.38 .I587 2000*

**EDUCATIONAL TECHNOLOGY - PUERTO RICO.**
Laborde, Ilia M. Rediscovering San Cristóbal Canyon. 1996.
*TC 06 no. 10660*

Laborde, Ilia M. Rediscovering San Cristóbal Canyon. 1996.
*TC 06 no. 10660*

**EDUCATIONAL TECHNOLOGY - SOCIAL ASPECTS.**
International perspectives on tele-education and virtual learning environments. Aldershot : Ashgate, 2000.
*TC LB1044.87 .I55 2000*

**EDUCATIONAL TECHNOLOGY - SOUTH CAROLINA - PLANNING.**
South Carolina Educational Technology Plan. [Columbia, S.C.] : South Carolina State Dept. of Education, [1995]
*TC LB1028.3 .S628 1995*

**EDUCATIONAL TECHNOLOGY - STANDARDS - UNITED STATES.**
International Society for Technology in Education. National educational technology standards for students. Eugene, OR : The Society, c1998.
*TC LB1028.3 .I569 1998*

**EDUCATIONAL TECHNOLOGY - UNITED STATES.**
Birnbaum, Barry W. Connecting special education and technology for the 21st century. Lewiston, N.Y. ; Lampeter, Wales : E. Mellen Press, c1999.
*TC LC3969.5 .B57 1999*

Burbules, Nicholas C. Watch IT. Boulder, Colo. : Westview Press, 2000.
*TC LB1028.43 .B87 2000*

The Jossey-Bass reader on technology and learning. 1st ed. San Francisco, Calif. : Jossey-Bass, c2000.
*TC LB1028.3 .J66 2000*

Modernizing schools : technology and buildings for a new century (September 19, 2000 : Washington, D.C.) Modernizing schools [videorecording]. [Washington, D.C.] : U.S. Dept. of Education, [2000].
*TC LB3205 .M64 2000*

Modernizing schools : technology and buildings for a new century (September 19, 2000 : Washington, D.C.) Modernizing schools [videorecording]. [Washington, D.C.] : U.S. Dept. of Education, [2000].
*TC LB3205 .M64 2000*

Otterbourg, Susan D. Using technology to strengthen employee and family involvement in education. [New York] : Conference Board, c1998.
*TC LB1028.3 .O88 1998*

Teaching with technology. Washington, D.C. : National Education Association of the United States, 1999.
*TC LB1044.88 .T44 1999*

Van Dusen, Gerald C. Digital dilemma. San Francisco : Jossey-Bass, c2000.
*TC LC5805 .V35 2000*

**EDUCATIONAL TELEVISION.** *See also* **TELEVISION IN EDUCATION.**
Educational & industrial television. [Ridgefield, Conn. : C.S. Tepfer Pub. Co.,    -c1983]

**EDUCATIONAL TELEVISION STATIONS.** *See* **TELEVISION IN EDUCATION.**

**Educational testing and measurement.**
Kubiszyn, Tom. 6th ed. New York : J. Wiley & Sons, c2000.
*TC LB3051 .K8 2000*

**Educational Testing Service.** ETS builds a test / Educational Testing Service. Princeton, NJ : The Service, c1959. 24 p. ; 24 cm.
*1. Educational tests and measurements. 2. Educational Testing Service. I. Title.*
*TC LB3051 .E38 1959*

**EDUCATIONAL TESTING SERVICE.**
Educational Testing Service. ETS builds a test. Princeton, NJ : The Service, c1959.
*TC LB3051 .E38 1959*

**EDUCATIONAL TESTING SERVICE - HISTORY.**
Lemann, Nicholas. The big test :. 1st ed. New York : Farrar, Straus and Giroux, 1999.

*TC LB3051 .L44 1999*

**EDUCATIONAL TESTS AND MEASUREMENTS.**
*See also* **COMPETENCY BASED EDUCATIONAL TESTS; EXAMINATIONS; GRADING AND MARKING (STUDENTS); NORM-REFERENCED TESTS; PERSONALITY TESTS; PSYCHOLOGICAL TESTS; TEST BIAS.**
Aiken, Lewis R., 1931- comp. Readings in psychological and educational testing, Boston, Allyn and Bacon [1973]
*TC LB3051 .A5625*

Anderson, Lorin W. Assessing affective characteristics in the schools. 2nd ed. Mahwah, NJ : Lawrence Erlbaum, c2000.
*TC LB3051 .A698 2000*

Ardovino, Joan. Multiple measures. Thousand Oaks, Calif. : Corwin Press, c2000.
*TC LB3051 .A745 2000*

Assessing science understanding :. San Diego, Calif. London : Academic, 2000.
*TC Q181 .A87 2000*

Assessment as inquiry. Urbana, Ill. : National Council of Teachers of English, 1999.
*TC LB3051 .A76665 1999*

Cizek, Gregory J. Cheating on tests. Mahwah, N.J. ; London : L. Erlbaum Associates, 1999.
*TC LB3609 .C47 1999*

Collins, Harold W. Educational measurement and evaluation. [Glenview, Ill.], Scott, Foresman, [c1969].
*TC LB3051 .C645*

Cunningham, George K. Assessment in the classroom. London : Falmer, 1998.
*TC LB3051 .C857 1998*

Daniels, Harvey, 1947- Methods that matter. York, Me. : Stenhouse Publishers, c1998.
*TC LB1027 .D24 1998*

Drummond, Robert J. Appraisal procedures for counselors and helping professionals. 4th ed. Upper Saddle River, N.J. : Merrill, c2000.
*TC BF176 .D78 2000*

Educational Testing Service. ETS builds a test. Princeton, NJ : The Service, c1959.
*TC LB3051 .E38 1959*

Hopkins, Charles D. Classroom testing. 2nd ed. Itasca, Ill. : F. E. Peacock Publishers, c1989.
*TC LB3060.65 .H661 1989*

Huba, Mary E. Learner-centered assessment on college campuses. Boston ; London : Allyn and Bacon, c2000.
*TC LB2331 .H83 2000*

Linn, Robert L. Measurement and assessment in teaching. 8th ed. Upper Saddle River, N.J. : Merrill, c2000.
*TC LB3051 .L545 2000*

Organisation for Economic Co-operation and Development (Paris) Measuring student knowledge and skills. Paris : Organisation for Economic Co-operation and Development, 2000.
*TC LB3051 .M44 2000*

Popham, W. James. Modern educational measurement. 3rd ed. Boston : Allyn and Bacon, c2000.
*TC LB3051 .P6143 2000*

Puckett, Margaret B. Authentic assessment of the young child. 2nd ed. Upper Saddle River, N.J. : Merrill, c2000.
*TC LB3051 .P69 2000*

Rafoth, Mary Ann. Inspiring independent learning. Washington, DC : National Education Association of the United States, 1999.
*TC LB1049 .R35 1999*

Ravid, Ruth. Practical statistics for educators. 2nd ed. Lanham, Md. : University Press of America, c2000.
*TC LB2846 .R33 2000*

The role of measurement and evaluation in education policy. Paris : Unesco Pub., 1999.
*TC LB3051 .R653 1999*

Routman, Regie. Conversations. Portsmouth, NH : Heinemann, c2000.
*TC LB1576 .R757 1999*

Shapiro, Edward S. (Edward Steven), 1951- Academic skills problems workbook. New York : Guilford Press, c1996.

*TC LB1029.R4 S52 1996*

The Use of standardized ability tests in American secondary schools and their impact on students, teachers, and administrators New York] Russell Sage Foundation [1965]
*TC LB3051 .R914*

Yi, Qing. Simulating nonmodel-fitting responses in a CAT environment. Iowa City, Iowa : ACT, 1998.
*TC LB3051 .A3 no. 98-10*

### EDUCATIONAL TESTS AND MEASUREMENTS - AUSTRALIA.
Literacy and numeracy in Australian schools. Canberra : Australian Gov. Pub. Service, 1976-
*TC LA2102 .L57 1976*

### EDUCATIONAL TESTS AND MEASUREMENTS - CALIFORNIA - CASE STUDIES.
Underwood, Terry. The portfolio project. Urbana, Ill. : National Council of Teachers of English, c1999.
*TC LB1029.P67 U53 1999*

### EDUCATIONAL TESTS AND MEASUREMENTS - DATA PROCESSING.
Computer-assisted assessment in higher education. London : Kogan Page, 1999.
*TC LB2366 .C65 1999*

### EDUCATIONAL TESTS AND MEASUREMENTS - ENGLAND.
Black, P. J. (Paul Joseph), 1930- Testing, friend or foe? London ; Washington : Falmer Press, 1998.
*TC LB3056.E54 B53 1998*

### EDUCATIONAL TESTS AND MEASUREMENTS - GREAT BRITAIN.
TYMMS, PETER. Baseline assessment and monitoring in primary schools. London : David Fulton Publishers, 1999.
*TC LB3060.22 .T96 1999*

### EDUCATIONAL TESTS AND MEASUREMENTS - IDAHO - TWIN FALLS.
Smith, Steven H. Schoolwide test preparation. [Arlington, Va.] : Educational Research Service, c2000.
*TC LB2806.22 .S65 2000*

### EDUCATIONAL TESTS AND MEASUREMENTS - KENTUCKY - CASE STUDIES.
Accountability, assessment, and teacher commitment. Albany, N.Y. : State University of New York Press, 2000.
*TC LB2806.22 .A249 2000*

### EDUCATIONAL TESTS AND MEASUREMENTS - NEW YORK (STATE) - VALIDITY.
Ort, Suzanne Wichterle. Standards in practice. 1999.
*TC 06 no. 11210*

Southworth, Robert A. Evidence of student learning and implications for alternative policies that support instructional use of assessment. 1999.
*TC 06 no. 11218*

### EDUCATIONAL TESTS AND MEASUREMENTS - NIGERIA - CONGRESSES.
Issues on examination malpractices in Nigeria :. Ikere-Ekiti [Nigeria] : Ondo State College of Education, c1998.
*TC LB3058.N6 1848 1998*

### EDUCATIONAL TESTS AND MEASUREMENTS - OECD COUNTRIES.
Measuring student knowledge and skills. Paris : Organisation for Economic Co-operation and Development, c1999.
*TC LB3051 .M43 1999*

### EDUCATIONAL TESTS AND MEASUREMENTS - SOCIAL ASPECTS - UNITED STATES.
Measuring up. Boston : Kluwer Academic Publishers, c1999.
*TC LB3051 .M4627 1999*

### EDUCATIONAL TESTS AND MEASUREMENTS - STATISTICAL METHODS.
Du, Zuru. Modeling conditional item dependencies with a three-parameter logistic testlet model. 1998.
*TC 085 D84*

### EDUCATIONAL TESTS AND MEASUREMENTS - UNITED STATES.
Alper, Sandra K. Alternate assessment of students with disabilities in inclusive settings. Boston ; London : Allyn and Bacon, c2001.
*TC LC4031 .A58 2001*

Bigge, June L. Curriculum, assessment, and instruction for students with disabilities. Belmont, CA : Wadsworth Pub., c1999.

---

*TC LC4031 .B46 1999*

Black, P. J. (Paul Joseph), 1930- Testing, friend or foe? London ; Washington : Falmer Press, 1998.
*TC LB3056.E54 B53 1998*

Carey, Lou. Measuring and evaluating school learning. 2nd ed. Boston : Allyn and Bacon, c1994.
*TC LB3051 .C36 1994*

Carey, Lou. Measuring and evaluating school learning. 3rd ed. Boston : London : Allyn and Bacon, c2001.
*TC LB3051 .C36 2001*

Chen, Sheying. Remedial education and grading. New York : the City University of New York, 1999.
*TC LB1029.R4 C54 1999*

Elliott, Judy L. Improving test performance of students with disabilities-- on district and state assessments. Thousands Oaks, Calif. : Corwin Press, c2000.
*TC LB3051 .E48 2000*

Finley, Carmen J. The national assessment approach to exercise development [Ann Arbor, Mich.] National Assessment of Educational Progress [1970]
*TC LB3051 .F53*

Howell, Kenneth W. Curriculum-based evaluation. 3rd ed. Belmont, CA. : Wadsworth, c2000.
*TC LB3060.32.C74 H68 2000*

Jones, Carroll J. Curriculum-based assessment. Springfield, Ill. : C.C. Thomas, Publisher, c1998.
*TC LB3060.32.C74 J66 1998*

Kordalewski, John. Standards in the classroom. New York ; London : Teachers College Press, c2000.
*TC LB3060.83 .K67 2000*

Kubiszyn, Tom. Educational testing and measurement. 6th ed. New York : J. Wiley & Sons, c2000.
*TC LB3051 .K8 2000*

Mabry, Linda. Portfolios plus. Thousand Oaks, Calif. : Corwin Press, c1999.
*TC LB3051 .M4243 1999*

National Research Council (U.S.). Committee on Embedding Common Test Items in State and District Assessments. Embedding questions. Washington, DC : National Academy Press, c1999.
*TC LB3051 .N319 1999*

Portfolios across the curriculum and beyond. 2nd ed. Thousand Oaks, Calif. : Corwin Press, 2000.
*TC LB1029.P67 C65 2000*

Sacks, Peter. Standardized minds. Cambridge, Mass. : Perseus Books, c1999.
*TC LB4051 .S22 1999*

Snodgrass, Dawn M., 1955- Collaborative learning in middle and secondary schools. Larchmont, N.Y. : Eye On Education, 2000.
*TC LB1032 .S62 2000*

Strickland, Kathleen. Making assessment elementary. Portsmouth, NH : Heinemann, 2000.
*TC LB3051 .S873 1999*

Taylor, Kathe. Children at the center. Portsmouth, NH : Heinemann, c1998.
*TC LB3060.57 .T39 1998*

Taylor, Ronald L., 1949- Assessment of exceptional students. 5th ed. Boston : Allyn and Bacon, c2000.
*TC LC4031 .T36 2000*

Venn, John. Assessing students with special needs. 2nd ed. Upper Saddle River, N.J. : Merrill, c2000.
*TC LC4031 .V46 2000*

Will standards save public education? Boston : Beacon Press, c2000.
*TC LB3060.83 .W55 2000*

### EDUCATIONAL TESTS AND MEASUREMENTS - UNITED STATES - CASE STUDIES.
Simmons, Jay, 1947- You never asked me to read. Boston : Allyn and Bacon, c2000.
*TC LB1050.46 .S535 2000*

### EDUCATIONAL TESTS AND MEASUREMENTS - UNITED STATES - DATA PROCESSING.
Chang, Shun-Wen. A comparative study of item exposure control methods in computerized adaptive testing. Iowa City, IA : ACT, Inc., 1998.
*TC LB3051 .A3 no. 98-3*

### EDUCATIONAL TESTS AND MEASUREMENTS - UNITED STATES - HANDBOOKS, MANUALS, ETC.
Haladyna, Thomas M. A complete guide to student grading. Boston : Allyn and Bacon, c1999.

---

*TC LB3051 .H296 1999*

### EDUCATIONAL TESTS AND MEASUREMENTS - UNITED STATES - HISTORY - 20TH CENTURY.
Lemann, Nicholas. The big test :. 1st ed. New York : Farrar, Straus and Giroux, 1999.
*TC LB3051 .L44 1999*

### EDUCATIONAL TOYS.
Sills, Thomas W. Science fun with toys. 1st ed. Chicago : Dearborn Resources, c1999.
*TC LB1029.T6 S54 1999*

### EDUCATIONAL VOUCHERS - DEVELOPING COUNTRIES.
Patrinos, Harry Anthony. Decentralization of education. Washington, D.C. : World Bank, c1997.
*TC LB2826.6.D44 P38 1997*

### EDUCATIONAL VOUCHERS - UNITED STATES.
Good, Thomas L., 1943- The great school debate. Mahwah, N.J. : L. Erlbaum Associates, 2000.
*TC LB2806.36 .G66 2000*

### EDUCATIONAL VOUCHERS - WISCONSIN - MILWAUKEE - CASE STUDIES.
Witte, John F. The market approach to education. Princeton, N.J. : Princeton University Press, c2000.
*TC LB2828.85.W6 W58 2000*

### EDUCATIONAL WORKSHOPS. See DEMONSTRATION CENTERS IN EDUCATION; EDUCATION - CONGRESSES.

Education's big gamble [videorecording] : charter schools / a production of Learning Matters, Inc. and South Carolina ETV ; producer, James R. Spahr. New York, NY : Merrow Report, c1997. 1 videocassette (57 min.) : sd., col. ; 1/2 in. + 1 resource guide ([15] p. ; 19 cm.). (Merrow report) VHS. Color. Catalogued from credits and container. Presenter: John Merrow. Camera: John Clouse ... [et al.] ; sound, Scott Constans ... [et al.]. For educators, parents and students. SUMMARY: Presents the educational concept of the charter school, a public school that has been given freedom from bureaucratic control in return for promising both academic achievement and financial responsibility. Schools featured in video: Fenton Avenue Charter School, Lakeview Terrace, CA; Horizon Charter School, Phoenix, AZ; Minnesota New Country School, LeSueur, MN and Citizen 2000, Phoenix, AZ.
*1. Charter schools - United States. 2. Privatization in education - United States. 3. Education, Elementary - United States. 4. Education, Secondary - United States. 5. School management and organization - United States. 6. Fenton Avenue Charter School (Lakeview Terrace, Calif.) 7. Horizon Charter School (Phoenix, Ariz.) 8. Minnesota New Country School (LeSueur, Minn.) 9. Citizen 2000 (Phoenix, Ariz.) 10. Documentary television programs. I. Spahr, James R. II. Learning Matters, Inc. III. South Carolina Educational Television Network. IV. Title: Charter schools [videorecording] V. Series.*
*TC LB2806.36 .E3 1997*

**Educator-journal.**
The Indiana teacher. Indianapolis, Ind. : Indiana State Teachers Association, 1924-1972.

**EDUCATORS.** See DEANS (EDUCATION); EARLY CHILDHOOD EDUCATORS; TEACHERS; WOMEN EDUCATORS.

### EDUCATORS, AMERICAN - DIRECTORIES.
Directory of American scholars. 9th ed / edited by Rita C. Velazquez. Detroit, Mich. : Gale Group, 1999.
*TC LA2311 .D57 1999*

### EDUCATORS - AUSTRALIA.
Dunt, Lesley, 1944- Speaking worlds. Parkville, Vic. : History Department, The University of Melbourne, c1993.
*TC LA2101 .D96 1993*

### EDUCATORS - CHINA - BIOGRAPHY.
Reynolds, Barbara G. Reform and education. 1999.
*TC 06 no. 11166*

### EDUCATORS, EARLY CHILDHOOD. See EARLY CHILDHOOD EDUCATORS.

### EDUCATORS - FRANCE - BIOGRAPHY.
Acker, Victor, 1940- Célestin Freinet. Westport, CT : Greenwood Press, 2000.
*TC LB775 .A255 2000*

**An educators guide to difficult parents.**
Wilde, Jerry, 1962- Huntington, N.Y. : Kroshka Books, c2000.
*TC LC225.3 .W54 2000*

**An educators' guide to schoolwide reform.** Arlington, Va. : Educational Research Service, c1999. vi, 141, [ca. 150] ; 28 cm. "Prepared by: American Institutes for Research, under contract to: American Association of School

Administrators, American Federation of Teachers, National Association of Elementary School Principals, National Association of Secondary School Principals, National Education Association." Includes bibliographical references (p. 133-141) SUMMARY: A guide prepared for educators and others to use when investigating different approaches to school reform. It reviews the research on 24 whole-school, comprehensive, or schoolwide approaches. CONTENTS: Overview -- Profiles of 24 approaches: Accelerated schools -- America's choice -- ATLAS communities -- Audrey Cohen College: Purpose-centered education -- Basic schools network -- Coalition of essential schools -- Community for learning -- Co-NECT -- Core knowledge -- Different ways of knowing -- Direct instruction -- Expeditionary learning outward bound -- Foxfire Fund -- High schools that work -- High/Scope K-3 model -- League of Professional Schools -- Modern red schoolhouse -- Onward to excellence -- Paideia -- Roots and wings-- School development program -- Success for all -- Talent development high school with career academics -- Urban learning centers -- Catalogs and reviews of schoolwide approaches -- References -- Appendices.
*1. Educational change - Research - United States. 2. School improvement programs - Research - United States. 3. School management and organization - Research - United States. 4. Educational innovations - Research - United States. I. American Institutes for Research II. American Association of School Administrators III. American Federation of Teachers IV. National Association of Elementary School Principals (U.S.) V. National Association of Secondary School Principals (U.S.) VI. National Education Association of the United States VII. Title.*
**TC LB2806.35 .E38 1999**

**The educator's guide to substance abuse prevention.**
Weinstein, Sanford. Mahwah, N.J. : Lawrence Erlbaum Publishers, 1999.
**TC HV5808 .W45 1999**

**Educators healing racism** / edited by Nancy L. Quisenberry and D. John McIntyre. Reston, VA : Association of Teacher Educators ; Olney, MD : Association for Childhood Education International, c1999. 160 p. ; 28 cm. Includes bibliographical references. ISBN 0-87173-147-9 (pbk.) DDC 370.117
*1. Discrimination in education - United States - Case studies. 2. Racism - United States - Case studies. 3. United States - Race relations - Case studies. 4. Educational equalization - United States - Case studies. 5. Multicultural education - United States - Case studies. I. Quisenberry, Nancy L. II. McIntyre, D. John. III. Association of Teacher Educators. IV. Association for Childhood Education International.*
**TC LC212.2 .E38 1999**

**EDUCATORS - HUNGARY - BIOGRAPHY.**
Emlékezés Szokolszky Istvánra. [Budapest] : Magyar Pedagógiai Társaság, 1998.
**TC LA2375.H92 S9653 1998**

**EDUCATORS - LEGAL STATUS, LAWS, ETC. - UNITED STATES - POPULAR WORKS.**
Kelly, Evelyn B. Legal basics. Bloomington, Ind. : Phi Delta Kappa Educational Foundation, c1998.
**TC KF390.E3 K45 1998**

**EDUCATORS - UNITED STATES - BIOGRAPHY.**
Beineke, John A. And there were giants in the land. New York : P. Lang, c1998.
**TC LB875.K54 B44 1998**

Berube, Maurice R. Eminent educators. Westport, Conn. : Greenwood Press, 2000.
**TC LB875.D5 B47 2000**

Kernan, Alvin B. In Plato's cave. New Haven : Yale University Press, c1999.
**TC LA227.4 .K468 1999**

Micklethwait, David. Noah Webster and the American dictionary. Jefferson, N.C. : McFarland, c2000.
**TC PE65.W5 M53 2000**

Watersheds in higher education. Lewiston, N.Y. : E. Mellen Press, c1997.
**TC LA228 .W28 1997**

**EDUCATORS - UNITED STATES - BIOGRAPHY - DICTIONARIES.**
Historical dictionary of American education. Westport, Conn. : Greenwood Press, 1999.
**TC LB15 .H57 1999**

**EDUCATORS - UNITED STATES - CORRESPONDENCE.**
Dewey, John, 1859-1952. The correspondence of John Dewey. [computer file]. Windows version. Charlottesville, VA : InteLex Corp., 1999- Computer data and program.
**TC B945.D44 A4 1999**

**EDUCAUSE (Association).**
Preparing your campus for a networked future. 1st ed. San Francisco : Jossey-Bass, c2000.
**TC LB2395.7 .P74 2000**

**EDUCAUSE leadership strategies**
(no. 1) Preparing your campus for a networked future. 1st ed. San Francisco : Jossey-Bass, c2000.
**TC LB2395.7 .P74 2000**

**Edward Clark :** for the sake of the search / edited by Barbara Cavaliere and George R. N'Namdi. Belleville Lake, Mich. : Belleville Lake Press, c1997. 128 p. : ill. (some col.) ; 26 cm. Includes an interview with Ed Clark by Quincy Troupe. Includes bibliographical references (p. 124-126).
*1. Clark, Edward, - 1926- - Exhibitions. 2. Afro-American painters - New York (State) - New York. I. Cavaliere, Barbara. II. N'Namdi, George R. III. Title: For the sake of the search*
**TC ND237.C524 E393 1997**

**Edwardian ladies and imperial power.**
Bush, Julia. London ; New York : Leicester University Press, 2000.
**TC DA16 .B87 2000**

**Edwards, Anne, 1946-.**
Anning, Angela, 1944- Promoting children's learning from birth to five. Buckingham [England] ; Philadelphia : Open University Press, 1999.
**TC LB1139.3.G7 A55 1999**

**Edwards, David C.** Motivation & emotion : evolutionary, physiological, cognitive, and social influences / David C. Edwards. Thousand Oaks, Calif. : Sage, c1999. xviii, 467 p. : ill. ; 27 cm. (Advanced psychology texts ; v. 3) Includes bibliographical references (p. 433-460) and index. ISBN 0-7619-0832-3 (hardcover : alk. paper) DDC 153.8
*1. Motivation (Psychology) 2. Emotions. I. Title. II. Title: Motivation and emotion III. Series.*
**TC BF503 .E38 1999**

**Edwards, Jeanette, 1954-.**
Technologies of procreation. 2nd ed. New York : Routledge, 1999.
**TC HQ761 .T43 1999**

**Edwards, Pamela Duncan.** Wacky wedding : a book of alphabet antics / Pamela Duncan Edwards ; illustrated by Henry Cole. 1st ed. New York : Hyperion Books for Children, c1999. 1 v. (unpaged) : col. ill. ; 24 cm. SUMMARY: An alphabetical ant wedding, attended by the other animals, is beset by various disasters. ISBN 0-7868-0308-8 (hardcover) ISBN 0-7868-2248-1 (lib. bdg.) DDC [E]
*1. Weddings - Fiction. 2. Ants - Fiction. 3. Animals - Fiction. 4. Alphabet. I. Cole, Henry, 1955- ill. II. Title.*
**TC PZ7.E26365 Wac 1999**

**Edworthy, Ann, 1952-** Managing stress / Ann Edworthy. Buckingham [England] ; Philadelphia : Open University Press, 2000. ix, 102 p. : ill. ; 23 cm. (Managing universities and colleges) Includes bibliographical references (p. [92]-97) and index. ISBN 0-335-20404-6 (hbk.) ISBN 0-335-20405-8 (pbk.) DDC 155.9/042/02437
*1. College teachers - Job stress - Great Britain. 2. Stress management - Great Britain. I. Title. II. Series.*
**TC LB2333.3 .E39 2000**

**Effect of deliberation on juror reasoning.**
Flaton, Robin Anne. 1999.
**TC 085 F612**

**The effect of structured exercise and structured reminiscing on agitation and aggression in geriatric psychiatric patients.**
Smith, Irmhild Wrede. 1996.
**TC 06 no. 10700**

**Effective alternative education programs.**
Chalker, Christopher S. Lancaster, Pa. : Technomic, c1999.
**TC LC4091 .C5 1999**

**Effective brief therapies : :** a clinician's guide / edited by Michel Hersen and Maryka Biaggio. San Diego : Academic Press, c2000. xv, 458 p. : ill. ; 23 cm. (Practical resources for the mental health professional.) Includes bibliographical references and indexes. CONTENTS: Introduction -- Overview of assessment and treatment issues -- Treatment of specific disorders (DSM-IV diagnoses) -- Major depressive episode -- Alcohol abuse -- Panic disorder -- Specific phobia -- Social phobia -- Obsessive-compulsive disorder -- Posttraumatic stress disorder -- Generalized anxiety disorder -- Somatization disorder -- Pain disorder -- Sexual dysfunction -- Exhibitionism -- Bulimia nervosa -- Primary insomnia -- Pathological gambling -- Trichotillomania -- Borderline personality disorder -- Histrionic personality disorder -- Special issues -- Considerations for gay and lesbian clients -- Considerations for clients with marital dysfunction -- Considerations for ethnically diverse clients -- Considerations for older adults. ISBN 0-12-343530-7
*1. Brief psychotherapy. I. Hersen, Michel. II. Biaggio, Maryka. 1950- III. Series.*

**TC RC480.55 .E376 2000**

**Effective early education :** cross-cultural perspectives / edited by Lotty Eldering and Paul P.M. Leseman. New York : Falmer Press, 1999. ix, 345 p. : ill. ; 23 cm. (Garland reference library of social science ; v. 1120. Studies in education and culture ; v. 11) Includes bibliographical references and index. ISBN 0-8153-2444-8 (alk. paper) DDC 372.21
*1. Early childhood education - Cross-cultural studies. 2. Socially handicapped children - Education (Early childhood) - Cross-cultural studies. I. Eldering, Lotty, 1939- II. Leseman, Paul. III. Series: Garland reference library of social science ; v. 1120. IV. Series: Garland reference library of social science. Studies in education and culture ; vol. 11*
**TC LB1139.23 .E44 1999**

**Effective lecturing behaviour in English-medium instruction.**
Klaassen, R. G. Delft, Netherlands : Delft University Press, 1999.
**TC LB2393 .K53 1999**

**Effective reading strategies.**
Rasinski, Timothy V. 2nd ed. Upper Saddle River, N.J. : Merrill, c2000.
**TC LB1050.5 .R33 2000**

**Effective school interventions.**
Rathvon, Natalie. New York : Guilford Press, c1999.
**TC LC1201 .R38 1999**

**Effective subject leadership.**
Field, Kit. London ; New York : Routledge, 2000.
**TC LB2806.15 .F54 2000**

**EFFECTIVE TEACHING.** *See also* **TEACHER EFFECTIVENESS.**
Hunt, Gilbert. 3rd ed. Springfield, Ill. : C.C. Thomas Publisher, c1999.
**TC LB1025.3 .H86 1999**

**EFFECTIVE TEACHING.**
Babbage, Keen J. High-impact teaching. Lancaster, Pa. : Technomic Pub. Co., c1998.
**TC LB1065 .B23 1998**

Biggs, John B. (John Burville). Teaching for quality learning at university :. Buckingham, UK ; Philadelphia : Society for Research into Higher Education : Open University Press, 1999.
**TC LB2331 .B526 1999**

Borich, Gary D. Effective teaching methods. 4th ed. Upper Saddle River, N.J. : Merrill, c2000.
**TC LB1025.3 .B67 2000**

DePorter, Bobbi. Quantum teaching. Boston, Mass. : Allyn and Bacon, c1999.
**TC LB1027 .D418 1999**

Gore, M. C. Taming the time stealers. Thousand Oaks, Calif. : Corwin Press, c1999.
**TC LB2838.8 .G67 1999**

Hunt, Gilbert. Effective teaching. 3rd ed. Springfield, Ill. : C.C. Thomas Publisher, c1999.
**TC LB1025.3 .H86 1999**

Newton, Douglas P. Teaching for understanding. London ; New York : Routledge/Falmer, 2000.
**TC LB1025.3 .N495 2000**

Routman, Regie. Conversations. Portsmouth, NH : Heinemann, c2000.
**TC LB1576 .R757 1999**

Rutter, Alison Lee. Professional growth of two multidisciplinary teams within a professional development school. 1999.
**TC 06 no. 11171**

Salmon, Gilly. E-moderating. London : Kogan Page ; Sterling, Va : Stylus, 2000.
**TC LB1044.87 .S25 2000**

Scheidecker, David, 1950- Bringing out the best in students. Thousand Oaks, Calif. : Corwin Press, c1999.
**TC LB1065 .S344 1999**

Sullo, Robert A., 1951- The inspiring teacher. Washington, D.C. : National Education Association of the United States, c1999.
**TC LB1025.3 .S85 1999**

Teaching as decision making. Upper Saddle River, N.J. : Prentice Hall, c2000.
**TC LB1607.5 .T43 2000**

V'elez Arias, Hiram Oscar. A multi-case study of physical education teachers and working conditions in inner-city schools /by Hiram Oscar V'elez Arias. 1998.

*TC 06 no. 11001*

**EFFECTIVE TEACHING - GREAT BRITAIN.**
Dean, Joan. Improving children's learning. London ;
New York : Routledge, 2000.
*TC LB1725.G6 D43 2000*

Harris, Alma, 1958- Teaching and learning in the
effective school. Aldershot, England : Brookfield,
Vt. : Ashgate, c1999.
*TC LB2822.84.G7 H37 1999*

**Effective teaching in elementary social studies.**
Savage, Tom V. 4th ed. Upper Saddle River, N.J. :
Merrill, c2000.
*TC LB1584 .S34 2000*

**Effective teaching methods.**
Borich, Gary D. 4th ed. Upper Saddle River, N.J. :
Merrill, c2000.
*TC LB1025.3 .B67 2000*

**EFFECTIVE TEACHING - NETHERLANDS -
DELFT.**
Klaassen, R. G. Effective lecturing behaviour in
English-medium instruction. Delft, Netherlands : Delft
University Press, 1999.
*TC LB2393 .K53 1999*

**EFFECTIVE TEACHING - UNITED STATES.**
Multicultural education for the 21st century. 1st ed.
New York : Longman, 2001.
*TC LC1099.3 .M8163 2001*

Sullivan, Susan, 1943- Supervision that improves
teaching. Thousand Oaks, Calif. : Corwin Press,
c2000.
*TC LB2806.4 .S85 2000*

Tileston, Donna Walker. Ten best teaching practices.
Thousand Oaks, Calif. : Corwin Press, c2000.
*TC LB1775.2 .T54 2000*

**EFFECTIVE TEACHING - UNITED STATES -
CASE STUDIES.**
Orange, Carolyn. 25 biggest mistakes teachers make
and how to avoid them. Thousand Oaks Calif. :
Corwin Press, c2000.
*TC LB1033 .O73 2000*

**EFFECTIVE TEACHING - UNITED STATES -
EVALUATION.**
Friedman, Myles I., 1924- Handbook on effective
instructional strategies. Columbia, S.C. : The Institute
for Evidence-Based Decision-Making in Education,
1998.
*TC LB1028.35 .F75 1998*

**Effectiveness of medical, mental health and
community.**
Gordon, Judith S., 1958- Helping survivors of
domestic violence. New York : Garland Pub., 1998.
*TC HV6626.2 .G67 1998*

**EFFECTS, CONTEXT (PSYCHOLOGY).** *See*
**CONTEXT EFFECTS (PSYCHOLOGY).**

**The effects of content knowledge and strategies on
memory development among 4- and 6-year-old
children.**
Embiricos, Anne-Marie T. 1998.
*TC 085 Em22*

Embiricos, Anne-Marie T. 1998.
*TC 085 Em22*

**The effects of early adversity on neurobehavioral
development** / edited by Charles A. Nelson. Mahwah,
N.J. : L. Erlbaum Associates, 2000. ix, 345 p. : ill. ; 24
cm. (Minnesota symposia on child psychology ; v. 31) Includes
bibliographical references and indexes. ISBN 0-8058-3406-0
(cloth : alk. paper) DDC 618.92/89071
*1. Child psychopathology - Etiology. 2. Pediatric
neuropsychiatry. 3. Prenatal influences. 4. Stress in children. I.
Nelson, Charles A. (Charles Alexander) II. Series: Minnesota
symposia on child psychology (Series) ; v. 31.*
*TC RJ499 .E34 2000*

**The effects of training on theory of mind tasks with
children who are deaf.**
Cerruto, Audra. 1999.
*TC 085 C34*

**Effects of word type, context, and vocal assistance on
children's pitch-matching abilities.**
Kim, Jinyoung. 1998.
*TC 06 no. 10954*

**The efferent auditory system** : basic science and
clinical applications / edited by Charles I. Berlin. San
Diego : Singular Pub. Group, c1999. xi, 130 p. : ill. ; 24
cm. + 1 computer laser optical disc (4 3/4 in.). (A Singular
audiology textbook) Includes bibliographical references and
index. System requirements for computer laser optical disc: PC
with Windows or Macintosh. ISBN 0-7693-0013-8

(hardcover : alk. paper) DDC 617.8
*1. Auditory pathways - Congresses. 2. Efferent pathways -
Congresses. 3. Auditory Pathways - physiology - Congresses.
4. Efferent Pathways - physiology - Congresses. I. Berlin.
Charles I. II. Series: Singular audiology text*
*TC RF286.5 .E36 1999*

**EFFERENT PATHWAYS.**
Orlovsky, G. N. (Grigoriĭ Nikolaevich) Neuronal
control of locomotion. Oxford ; New York : Oxford
University Press, 1999.
*TC QP303 .O75 1999*

**EFFERENT PATHWAYS - CONGRESSES.**
The efferent auditory system. San Diego : Singular
Pub. Group, c1999.
*TC RF286.5 .E36 1999*

**EFFERENT PATHWAYS - PHYSIOLOGY -
CONGRESSES.**
The efferent auditory system. San Diego : Singular
Pub. Group, c1999.
*TC RF286.5 .E36 1999*

**EFG CURRICULUM COLLABORATIVE.**
Barnes, Barbara. Schools transformed for the 21st
century. Torrance, Calif. : Griffin Pub. Group, c1999.
*TC LA217.2 .B39 1999*

**EFL.** *See* **ENGLISH LANGUAGE - STUDY AND
TEACHING - FOREIGN SPEAKERS;
ENGLISH LANGUAGE - TEXTBOOKS FOR
FOREIGN SPEAKERS.**

**Egan, M. Winston.**
Hardman, Michael L. Human exceptionality. 6th ed.
Boston : Allyn and Bacon, c1999.
*TC HV1568 .H37 1999*

**Egbo, Benedicta, 1954-** Gender, literacy, and life
chances in Sub-Saharan Africa / Benedicta Egbo.
Clevedon ; Buffalo : Multilingual Matters, c2000. ix,
206 p. ; 22 cm. (The language and education library ; 16)
Includes bibliographical references (p. 189-201) and index.
ISBN 1-85359-464-4 (hb : alk. paper) DDC 371.822/0967
*1. Women - Education - Africa, Sub-Saharan. 2. Literacy -
Africa, Sub-Saharan. 3. Educational equalization - Africa,
Sub-Saharan. I. Title. II. Series.*
*TC LC2412 .E42 2000*

**Egendorf, Laura K., 1973-.**
Male/female roles. San Diego, Calif. : Greenhaven
Press, c2000.
*TC HQ1075 .M353 2000*

**Eggen, Paul D., 1940-** Strategies for teachers : teaching
content and thinking skills / Paul D. Eggen, Donald P.
Kauchak. 4th ed. Boston : Allyn and Bacon, 2001. viii,
376 p. : ill. ; 25 cm. Includes bibliographical references (p.
361-368) and index. ISBN 0-205-30808-2 DDC 371.102
*1. Teaching. 2. Education - Experimental methods. 3. Thought
and thinking - Study and teaching. 4. Learning, Psychology of.
I. Kauchak. Donald P., 1946- II. Title.*
*TC LB1027.3 .E44 2001*

**Egger, Garry.**
Health promotion strategies & methods. Rev. ed.
Sydney ; New York : McGraw-Hill, c1999.
*TC RA427.8 .H527 1999*

**Eggington, William.**
The sociopolitics of English language teaching.
Clevedon ; Buffalo [N.Y.] : Multilingual Matters,
c2000.
*TC PE1128.A2 S5994 2000*

**The ego and the id and other works.**
Freud, Sigmund, 1856-1939. London : Hogarth Press,
1957.
*TC BF173.F645 1957*

**EGO (PSYCHOLOGY).** *See* **AUTONOMY
(PSYCHOLOGY); IDENTITY
(PSYCHOLOGY).**

**Ehrlich, Anne H.**
Ehrlich, Paul R. The population explosion. New
York : Simon and Schuster, c1990.
*TC HB871 .E33 1990*

**Ehrlich, Paul R.** The population explosion / Paul R.
Ehrlich & Anne H. Ehrlich. New York : Simon and
Schuster, c1990. 320 p. ; 24 cm. Includes bibliographical
references (p. 263-304) and index. ISBN 0-671-68984-3 DDC
304.6
*1. Overpopulation. 2. Human ecology. I. Ehrlich. Anne H. II.
Title.*
*TC HB871 .E33 1990*

**Ehrlich, Thomas, 1934-.**
Civic responsibility and higher education. Phoenix,
Az. : Oryx Press, 2000.
*TC LC1091 .C5289 2000*

**Eich, Eric.**
Cognition and emotion. Oxford ; New York : Oxford
University Press, 2000.
*TC BF311 .C5477 2000*

**Eight ways of knowing.**
Lazear, David G. 3rd ed. Arlington Heights, Ill. :
SkyLight Training and Pub., c1999.
*TC LB1060 .L39 1999*

**EIGHTEENTH CENTURY.** *See*
**ENLIGHTENMENT.**

**Einhorn, Jay.**
Wren, Carol T. Hanging by a twig. 1st ed. New York ;
London : Norton, c2000.
*TC RC394.L37 W74 2000*

**Einreinhofer, Nancy.** The American art museum :
elitism and democracy / Nancy Einreinhofer. London ;
New York : Leicester University Press, 1997. xii, 225
p. : ill. ; 24 cm. (Contemporary issues in museum culture)
Includes bibliographical references (p. [208]-218) and index.
ISBN 0-7185-0042-3 DDC 708.13
*1. Art museums - United States. 2. Art and society - United
States. 3. Art patronage - United States. I. Title. II. Series.*
*TC N510 .E45 1997*

**EINSTEIN, ALBERT, 1879-1955.**
Stephen Hawking's universe [videorecording].
[Alexandria, Va.] : PBS Video; Burbank, CA :
Distributed by Warner Home Video, c1997.
*TC QB982 .S7 1997*

**EINSTEIN, ALBERT, 1879-1955 - VIEWS ON
EDUCATION.**
Kincheloe, Joe L. The stigma of genius. New York ;
Canterbury [England] : P. Lang, c1999.
*TC LB875.E562 K56 1999*

**Einzig, Hetty.**
Parenting education and support. London : David
Fulton, c1999.
*TC HQ755.7 .P374 1999*

**Eisaguirre, Lynne, 1951-** Affirmative action : a
reference handbook / Lynne Eisaguirre. Santa
Barbara, Calif. : ABC-CLIO, c1999. xiii, 222 p. : ill. ; 24
cm. (Contemporary world issues) Includes bibliographical
references and index. ISBN 0-87436-854-5 (alk. paper) DDC
331.13/3/0973
*1. Affirmative action programs - United States - History. 2.
Affirmative action programs - Law and legislation - United
States. I. Title. II. Series.*
*TC HF5549.5.A34 E39 1999*

**Eisenberger, Joanne, 1942-** Self efficacy : raising the
bar for students with learning needs / by Joanne
Eisenberger, Marcia Conti-D'Antonio, Robert
Bertrando. Larchmont, N.Y. : Eye On Education,
c2000. xvii, 204 p. ; 28 cm. Includes bibliographical
references. ISBN 1-88300-190-0 DDC 371.92/6
*1. Learning disabled children - Education - United States. 2.
Inclusive education - United States. 3. Independent study -
United States. I. Conti-D'Antonio, Marcia, 1953- II.
Bertrando. Robert. 1941- III. Title.*
*TC LC4705 .C67 2000*

**The Eisenhower Center for the Conservation of
Human Resources studies in the new economy**
Employee training and U.S. competitiveness.
Boulder : Westview Press, 1991.
*TC HF5549.5.T7 E46 1991*

**Eisikovits, Rivka Anne.** The anthropology of child and
youth care work / Rivka A. Eisikovits. New York :
Haworth Press, c1997. xvii, 102 p. ; 23 cm. (Child & youth
services series) "Has also been published as Child & Youth
services, volume 18, number 1, 1997"--T.p. verso. Includes
bibliographical references (p. 89-97) and index. ISBN
1-56024-848-3 (alk. paper) DDC 362.7
*1. Social work with children - Research - Methodology. 2.
Social work with youth - Research - Methodology. I. Title. II.
Series.*
*TC HV713 .E47 1997*

**Eisler, Riane Tennenhaus.** Tomorrow's children : a
blueprint for partnership education in the 21st
century / Riane Eisler. Boulder, Colo. : Oxford :
Westview Press, 2000. xx, 362 p. : ill. ; 24 cm. Includes
bibliographical references (p. 339-352) and index. ISBN
0-8133-9040-0 (alk. paper) DDC 370.11/5
*1. Education, Humanistic - United States. 2. Critical
pedagogy - United States. 3. Affective education - United
States. 4. Educational change - United States. I. Title.*
*TC LC1023 .E57 2000*

**EITV.**
Educational & industrial television. [Ridgefield,
Conn. : C.S. Tepfer Pub. Co., -c1983]

Educational & industrial television. [Ridgefield,
Conn. : C.S. Tepfer Pub. Co., -c1983]

**Eitzen, D. Stanley.** Fair and foul : beyond the myths and paradoxes of sport / D. Stanley Eitzen. Lanham, Md. : Rowman & Littlefield Publishers, c1999. vii, 185 p. ; 25 cm. Includes bibliographical references and index. ISBN 0-8476-9170-5 (cloth : alk. paper) ISBN 0-8476-9171-3 (pbk. : alk. paper) DDC 796
*1. Sports - Sociological aspects. 2. Sports - Psychological aspects. I. Title.*
*TC GV706.5 .E567 1999*

Zinn, Maxine Baca, 1942- Diversity in families. 5th ed. New York : Longman, 1998.
*TC HQ536 .Z54 1998*

**EJECTION (PSYCHOLOGY).** *See* **PERCEPTION.**

**Ekbatani, Glayol.**
Learner-directed assessment in ESL. Mahwah, N.J. : Lawrence Erlbaum Associates, 2000.
*TC PE1128.A2 L359 2000*

**Ekman, Richard.**
Technology and scholarly communication. Berkeley, Calif. : University of California Press ; [Pittsburgh?] : Published in association with the Andrew K. Mellon Foundation, c1999.
*TC Z479 .T43 1999*

**Ekwall, Eldon E.**
Shanker, James L. Locating and correcting reading difficulties. 7th ed. Upper Saddle River, N.J. : Merrill, c1998.
*TC LB1050.5 .E38 1998*

**El-Hi textbooks in print.** New York, N.Y. : Bowker, 1970- v. ; 28 cm. 1970- . Continues: Textbooks in print. ISSN 0070-9565
*1. Text-books - Bibliogrpahy. 2. Education - Bibliography. 3. Publishers and publishing - United States - Directories. I. Title: Textbooks in print.*
*TC Z5813 .A51*

**El indigena en la novela de la Revolucion Mexicana.** Guevara-Vázquez, Fabián. 1999.
*TC 085 G934*

**EL NIÑO CURRENT.**
The blue planet [videorecording]. [New York, N.Y.?] : Unapix Entertainment, Inc. [distributor], c1996.
*TC QB631.2 .B5 1996*

Broad, Kenneth. Climate, culture, and values. 1999.
*TC 085 B7775*

**EL SALVADOR - POLITICS AND GOVERNMENT - 1979-1992.**
Flores, Joaquín Evelio. Psychological effects of the civil war on children from rural communities of El Salvador.
*TC 083 F67*

**EL SALVADOR - RURAL CONDITIONS.**
Flores, Joaquín Evelio. Psychological effects of the civil war on children from rural communities of El Salvador.
*TC 083 F67*

**Elbow, Gary S.**
Sharma, Martha B., 1945- Using internet primary sources to teach critical thinking skills in geography. Westport, Conn. ; London : Greenwood Press, 2000.
*TC G73 .S393 2000*

**Elbow, Peter.** Everyone can write : essays toward a hopeful theory of writing and teaching writing / Peter Elbow. New York : Oxford University Press, 2000. xxiv, 475 p. : ill. ; 25 cm. Includes bibliographical references (p. 471-475). ISBN 0-19-510415-3 (clothbound) ISBN 0-19-510416-1 (pbk.). DDC 808/.042/07
*1. English language - Rhetoric - Study and teaching. 2. Report writing - Study and teaching. I. Title.*
*TC PE1404 .E42 2000*

**Elder, Glen H.** Children of the land : adversity and success in rural America / Glen H. Elder Jr. and Rand D. Conger ; with a foreword by Ross D. Parke, and with the collaboration of Stephen T. Russell ... [et al.]. Chicago : University of Chicago Press, 2000. xx, 373 p. : ill. ; 24 cm. (The John D. and Catherine T. MacArthur Foundation series on mental health and development. Studies on successful adolescent development) Includes bibliographical references (p. 343-360) and index. ISBN 0-226-20266-6 (alk. paper) DDC 305.235/0973/091734
*1. Urban youth - United States - Family relationships. 2. Parenting - United States. 3. United States - Rural conditions. 4. Success - United States. I. Conger, Rand. II. Title. III. Series.*
*TC HQ796 .E525 2000*

**ELDERCARE.** *See* **AGED - CARE.**

**Elderfield, John.**
Livingston, Jane. The art of Richard Diebenkorn. New

York : Whitney Museum of American Art : Berkeley : University of California Press, c1997.
*TC N6537.D447 A4 1997*

Modernstarts. New York : Museum of Modern Art : Distributed by Harry N. Abrams, c1999.
*TC N620.M9 M63 1999*

Whitfield, Sarah, 1942- Bonnard. New York, N.Y. : Harry N. Abrams, 1998.
*TC ND553.B65 W45 1998*

**Eldering, Lotty, 1939-.**
Effective early education. New York : Falmer Press, 1999.
*TC LB1139.23 .E44 1999*

**ELDERLY, FRAIL.** *See* **FRAIL ELDERLY.**

**ELDERLY MEN.** *See* **AGED MEN.**

**ELDERLY PERSONS.** *See* **AGED.**

**ELDERLY WOMEN.** *See* **AGED WOMEN.**

**ELDREDGE, NILES.**
Tropea, Judith. A day in the life of a museum curator. Mahwah, N.J. : Troll Associates, c1991.
*TC QE22.E53 T76 1991*

**ELDREDGE, NILES - JUVENILE LITERATURE.**
Tropea, Judith. A day in the life of a museum curator. Mahwah, N.J. : Troll Associates, c1991.
*TC QE22.E53 T76 1991*

**Elective officials.**
CSG state directory. Directory I, Elective officials. Lexington, Ky. : The Council, c1998-
*TC JK2403 .S69*

**ELECTRIC COMMUNICATION.** *See* **TELECOMMUNICATION.**

**Electric rhetoric.**
Welch, Kathleen E. Cambridge, Mass. : MIT Press, c1999.
*TC P301.5.D37 W45 1999*

**ELECTRICITY - EXPERIMENTS.**
Ward, Alan, 1932- Experimenting with batteries, bulbs, and wires. New York : Chelsea Juniors, c1991.
*TC QC527.2 .W37 1991*

**ELECTRICITY - EXPERIMENTS - JUVENILE LITERATURE.**
Ward, Alan, 1932- Experimenting with batteries, bulbs, and wires. New York : Chelsea Juniors, c1991.
*TC QC527.2 .W37 1991*

**ELECTROCONVULSIVE THERAPY.**
Mood disorders. Basel ; New York : Karger, c1997.
*TC RC483 .M6 1997*

**ELECTROENCEPHALOGRAPHY.** *See* **EVOKED POTENTIALS (ELECTROPHYSIOLOGY).**

**ELECTRONIC APPARATUS AND APPLIANCES.** *See* **COMPUTERS.**

**ELECTRONIC BRAINS.** *See* **ARTIFICIAL INTELLIGENCE; COMPUTERS.**

**ELECTRONIC CALCULATING-MACHINES.** *See* **COMPUTERS.**

**ELECTRONIC COMPUTERS.** *See* **COMPUTERS.**

**ELECTRONIC DATA PROCESSING.** *See* **ARTIFICIAL INTELLIGENCE; DATA TRANSMISSION SYSTEMS; ONLINE DATA PROCESSING.**

**ELECTRONIC DATA PROCESSING AND COPYRIGHT.** *See* **COPYRIGHT AND ELECTRONIC DATA PROCESSING.**

**ELECTRONIC DATA PROCESSING - DISTRIBUTED PROCESSING.** *See* **COMPUTER NETWORKS.**

**ELECTRONIC DATA PROCESSING IN PROGRAMMED INSTRUCTION.** *See* **COMPUTER-ASSISTED INSTRUCTION.**

**ELECTRONIC DATA PROCESSING - KEYBOARDING.**
Penso, Dorothy E. Keyboarding skills for children with disabilities. London ; Philadelphia, Pa. : Whurr, 1999.
*TC LC4024 .P467 1999*

**ELECTRONIC DIGITAL COMPUTERS - SECURITY MEASURES.** *See* **COMPUTER SECURITY.**

**ELECTRONIC GAMES.** *See* **COMPUTER GAMES.**

**ELECTRONIC GOVERNMENT INFORMATION - UNITED STATES - DIRECTORIES.**
Andriot, Laurie. Internet blue pages. 1999 ed. Medford, NJ : Information Today, c1998.
*TC ZA5075 .A53 1998*

Andriot, Laurie. Uncle Sam's K-12 Web. Medford, N.J. : CyberAge Books, 1999.
*TC ZA575 .A53 1999*

**ELECTRONIC INDUSTRIES.** *See* **COMPUTER INDUSTRY.**

**ELECTRONIC INFORMATION RESOURCE LITERACY - STUDY AND TEACHING (SECONDARY) - UNITED STATES.**
Doggett, Sandra L. Beyond the book. Englewood, Colo. : Libraries Unlimited, 2000.
*TC ZA4065 .D64 2000*

**ELECTRONIC INFORMATION RESOURCE SEARCHING - ENGLISH-SPEAKING COUNTRIES.**
Knapp, Sara D. The contemporary thesaurus of search terms and synonyms. 2nd ed. Phoenix, Ariz. : Oryx Press, 2000.
*TC ZA4060 .K58 2000*

**ELECTRONIC INFORMATION RESOURCES.** *See* **COMPUTER NETWORK RESOURCES; INFORMATION STORAGE AND RETRIEVAL SYSTEMS.**

**ELECTRONIC LIBRARIES.** *See* **DIGITAL LIBRARIES.**

**ELECTRONIC MAIL SYSTEMS.**
Morton, Jessica G. Kids on the 'Net. Portsmouth, NH : Heinemann, c1998.
*TC LB1044.87 .M67 1998*

**ELECTRONIC MAIL SYSTEMS IN EDUCATION.**
Anderson, Dennis S. Mathematics and distance education on the internet. 1999.
*TC 085 An2317*

**ELECTRONIC OFFICE MACHINES.** *See* **COMPUTERS.**

**ELECTRONIC PUBLICATIONS - LICENSES - UNITED STATES.**
Managing the licensing of electronic products. Washington, DC : Systems and Procedures Exchange Center, Office of Leadership and Management Service, Association of Research Libraries, c1999.

Managing the licensing of electronic products. Washington, DC : Systems and Procedures Exchange Center, Office of Leadership and Management Service, Association of Research Libraries, c1999.

Managing the licensing of electronic products. Washington, DC : Systems and Procedures Exchange Center, Office of Leadership and Management Service, Association of Research Libraries, c1999.
*TC HF5429.255 .M26 1999*

**ELECTRONIC SUPERHIGHWAY.** *See* **INFORMATION SUPERHIGHWAY.**

**ELECTRONIC SYSTEMS.** *See* **COMPUTER NETWORKS; COMPUTERS; DATA TRANSMISSION SYSTEMS; TELEVISION.**

**Electronic writing centers.**
Coogan, David. Stamford, Conn. : Ablex Pub. Corp., c1999.
*TC PE1404 .C6347 1999*

**ELECTROPHYSIOLOGY.** *See* **EVOKED POTENTIALS (ELECTROPHYSIOLOGY).**

**Elementary classroom management.**
Charles, C. M. 2nd ed. White Plains, N.Y. : Longman, c1995.
*TC LB3013 .C465 1995*

**ELEMENTARY EDUCATION.** *See* **EDUCATION, ELEMENTARY.**

**ELEMENTARY EDUCATION COUNSELING.** *See* **COUNSELING IN ELEMENTARY EDUCATION.**

**ELEMENTARY EDUCATION GUIDANCE.** *See* **COUNSELING IN ELEMENTARY EDUCATION.**

**ELEMENTARY EDUCATION OF ADULTS.** *See* **READING (ADULT EDUCATION).**

**Elementary literacy lessons.**
Richards, Janet C. Mahwah, N.J. : L. Erlbaum Associates, 2000.
*TC LB1576 .R517 2000*

**Elementary mathematics four.**
Payne, Joseph N. (Joseph Neal) Elementary mathematics 4. Teachers' ed. New York : Harcourt, Brace & World, 1966.
*TC QA107 .E43 1966 Teacher's Ed.*

**Elementary mathematics : patterns and structure.** New York : Holt, Rinehart and Winson, 1966. v. : ill. ; 24 cm.
Includes index.
*1. Mathematics.*
*TC QA107 .E53 1966*

**Elementary mathematics, patterns and structure; accelerated sequence. Teacher's ed.** [by] Eugene D. Nichols [and others] New York, Holt, Rinehart and Winston [c1966] 3 v. illus. 24 cm. Grades: 5-7, accelerated.
Includes index.
*1. Mathematics - Study and teaching (Elementary) 2. Mathematics - Study and teaching (Secondary) I. Nichols, Eugene Douglas, 1923-*

**Elementary principals' use of student assessment information.**
Fleck, Mary B. 1999.
*TC 06 no. 11113*

**ELEMENTARY READERS.** *See* **READERS (ELEMENTARY).**

**ELEMENTARY SCHOOL ADMINISTRATION - GREAT BRITAIN.**
Wintle, Mike. Coordinating assessment practice across the primary school. London ; Philadelphia, PA : Falmer Press, 1999.
*TC LB3060.37 .W56 1999*

**ELEMENTARY SCHOOL ADMINISTRATION - NEW YORK (STATE) - NEW YORK - CASE STUDIES.**
Harwayne, Shelley. Going public. Portsmouth, NH : Heinemann, c1999.
*TC LB2822.5 .H37 1999*

**ELEMENTARY SCHOOL ADMINISTRATION - UNITED STATES - HANDBOOKS, MANUALS, ETC.**
Callison, William. Elementary school principal's handbook. Lancaster, Pa. : Technomic, c1999.
*TC LB2822.5 .C34 1999*

**ELEMENTARY SCHOOL COUNSELING.** *See* **COUNSELING IN ELEMENTARY EDUCATION.**

**Elementary school English.**
Kirby, Anne. Teachers' ed. Palo Alto, Calif. : Addison-Wesley Publishing Company, 1967.
*TC PE1112 .K57 1967 Teachers' Ed.*

Kirby, Anne. Palo Alto, Calif. : Addison-Wesley Publishing Company, 1967.
*TC PE1112 .K57 1967*

**ELEMENTARY SCHOOL GUIDANCE.** *See* **COUNSELING IN ELEMENTARY EDUCATION.**

**ELEMENTARY SCHOOL LIBRARIES - BOOK SELECTION - UNITED STATES.**
Van Orden, Phyllis. Selecting books for the elementary school library media center. New York : Neal-Schuman Publishers, c2000.
*TC Z675.S3 V36 2000*

**ELEMENTARY SCHOOL LIBRARIES - PROBLEMS, EXERCISES, ETC.**
Lee, Carol K. Learning about books & libraries. Fort Atkinson, Wis. : Alleyside Press, 2000.
*TC Z711.2 .L455 2000*

**ELEMENTARY SCHOOL LIBRARIES - UNITED STATES.**
Exploring science in the library. Chicago : American Library Association, 2000.
*TC Z675.S3 E97 2000*

**ELEMENTARY SCHOOL LIBRARIES - UNITED STATES - PROBLEMS, EXERCISES, ETC.**
Lee, Carol K. Learning about books & libraries. Fort Atkinson, Wis. : Alleyside Press, 2000.
*TC Z711.2 .L455 2000*

**Elementary school principal's handbook.**
Callison, William. Lancaster, Pa. : Technomic, c1999.
*TC LB2822.5 .C34 1999*

**ELEMENTARY SCHOOL PRINCIPALS - HANDBOOKS, MANUALS, ETC.**
Callison, William. Elementary school principal's handbook. Lancaster, Pa. : Technomic, c1999.
*TC LB2822.5 .C34 1999*

**ELEMENTARY SCHOOL PRINCIPALS - JAPAN - KANAYAMA.**

Heart of the country [videorecording]. [New York, NY : First Run/Icarus Films, 1998].
*TC LB1565.H6 H3 1998*

**ELEMENTARY SCHOOL PRINCIPALS - NEW JERSEY - CASE STUDIES.**
Fleck, Mary B. Elementary principals' use of student assessment information. 1999.
*TC 06 no. 11113*

**ELEMENTARY SCHOOL STUDENTS.** *See* **SCHOOL CHILDREN.**

**ELEMENTARY SCHOOL STUDENTS - NEW JERSEY - RATING OF - CASE STUDIES.**
Fleck, Mary B. Elementary principals' use of student assessment information. 1999.
*TC 06 no. 11113*

**Elementary school teacher development.**
Seferoglu, Süleyman Sadi. 1996.
*TC 06 no. 10693*

**ELEMENTARY SCHOOL TEACHERS - ATTITUDES - TURKEY - ANKARA.**
Seferoglu, Süleyman Sadi. Elementary school teacher development. 1996.
*TC 06 no. 10693*

**ELEMENTARY SCHOOL TEACHERS - IN-SERVICE TRAINING - TURKEY - ANKARA.**
Seferoglu, Süleyman Sadi. Elementary school teacher development. 1996.
*TC 06 no. 10693*

**ELEMENTARY SCHOOL TEACHERS - TRAINING OF - GREAT BRITAIN.**
Dean, Joan. Improving children's learning. London ; New York : Routledge, 2000.
*TC LB1725.G6 D43 2000*

Duncan, Diane. Becoming a primary school teacher. Stoke on Trent, England : Trentham, 1999.
*TC LB1776.4.G7 D86 1999*

**ELEMENTARY SCHOOL TEACHERS - TURKEY - ANKARA.**
Seferoglu, Süleyman Sadi. Elementary school teacher development. 1996.
*TC 06 no. 10693*

**ELEMENTARY SCHOOL TEACHERS - UNITED STATES.**
Riner, Phillip S., 1950- Successful teaching in the elementary classroom. Upper Saddle River, N.J. : Merrill, c2000.
*TC LB1555 .R53 2000*

**ELEMENTARY SCHOOL TEACHERS - UNITED STATES - BIOGRAPHY.**
Carr, Janine Chappell. A child went forth. Portsmouth, NH : Heinemann, 1999.
*TC LB1576 .C31714 1999*

**ELEMENTARY SCHOOL TEACHERS - UNITED STATES - CASE STUDIES.**
Stone, Randi. Best classroom practices. Thousand Oaks, Calif. : Corwin Press, c1999.
*TC LB1776.2 .S86 1999*

**ELEMENTARY SCHOOL TEACHING.**
Teaching in primary schools. London : Cassell, 1998.
*TC LB1776.T43 1998*

**ELEMENTARY SCHOOL TEACHING - GREAT BRITAIN.**
Bell, Derek, 1950- Towards effective subject leadership in the primary school. Buckingham [England] ; Philadelphia : Open University Press, c1999.
*TC LB2832.4.G7 B45 1999*

Dean, Joan. Improving children's learning. London ; New York : Routledge, 2000.
*TC LB1725.G6 D43 2000*

Hayes, Denis, 1949- Foundations of primary teaching. 2nd ed. London : David Fulton, 1999.
*TC LB1555 .H43 1999*

O'Hara, Mark. Teaching 3-8 :. London ; New York : Continuum, 2000.
*TC LB1725.G7 O36 2000*

**ELEMENTARY SCHOOL TEACHING - HANDBOOKS, MANUALS, ETC.**
Keys to the classroom. 2nd ed. Thousand Oaks, Calif. : Corwin Press, c2000.
*TC LB1555 .K49 2000*

**ELEMENTARY SCHOOL TEACHING - UNITED STATES.**
Riner, Phillip S., 1950- Successful teaching in the elementary classroom. Upper Saddle River, N.J. : Merrill, c2000.

*TC LB1555 .R53 2000*

**ELEMENTARY SCHOOL TEACHING - UNITED STATES - CASE STUDIES.**
Stone, Randi. Best classroom practices. Thousand Oaks, Calif. : Corwin Press, c1999.
*TC LB1776.2 .S86 1999*

**ELEMENTARY SCHOOL TEACHING - VOCATIONAL GUIDANCE - GREAT BRITAIN.**
Duncan, Diane. Becoming a primary school teacher. Stoke on Trent, England : Trentham, 1999.
*TC LB1776.4.G7 D86 1999*

**ELEMENTARY SCHOOLS.** *See* **MIDDLE SCHOOLS.**

**ELEMENTARY SCHOOLS - ADMINISTRATION.** *See* **ELEMENTARY SCHOOL ADMINISTRATION.**

**ELEMENTARY SCHOOLS - CURRICULA - NEW YORK (STATE) - NEW YORK - CASE STUDIES.**
Nord, Michael B. Music in the classroom (MITC). 1998.
*TC 06 no. 10974*

**ELEMENTARY SCHOOLS - EXAMINATIONS.**
Hedges, William D. Evaluation in the elementary school New York, Holt, Rinehart and Winston [1969]
*TC LB3051 .H4*

**Elementary science methods.**
Martin, David Jerner. 2nd ed. Belmont, CA : Wadsworth, c2000.
*TC LB1585.3 .M37 2000*

**The elements of learning.**
Banner, James M., 1935- New Haven, Conn. : Yale University Press, c1999.
*TC LB1060 .B36 1999*

**ELEPHANTIDAE.** *See* **ELEPHANTS.**

**ELEPHANTS - FICTION.**
Day, Alexandra. Frank and Ernest on the road. New York : Scholastic Inc., c1994.
*TC PZ7.D32915 Frn 1994*

Hallensleben, Georg. Pauline. New York : Farrar, Straus & Giroux, c1999.
*TC PZ7.H15425 Pau 1999*

**ELEPHANTS - FICTION. <JUVENILE SUBJECT HEADING>.**
McKee, David. Hide-and-seek Elmer. 1st U.S. ed. New York : Lothrop, Lee & Shepard Books, c1998.
*TC PZ7.M19448 Hi 1998*

**Elephants swim.**
Riley, Linda Capus. Boston : Houghton Mifflin, 1995.
*TC QP310.S95 R55 1995*

**Elgaard, Berit.**
Research on socialization of young children in the Nordic countries. Aarhus : Aarhus University Press, c1989.
*TC Z7164.S678 R47 1989*

**An Elgar reference collection**
Education policy. Cheltenham, UK : Northampton, MA : Edward Elgar Pub., c1999.
*TC LC71 .E32 1999*

**ELIMINATION (IN EDUCATION).**
Tannenbaum, Abraham. Dropout or diploma. New York : Teachers College Press, 1966.
*TC 371.2913T15*

**ELITE (SOCIAL SCIENCES).**
Gendering elites. Houndmills, Basingstoke, Hampshire : Macmillan Press ; New York : St. Martin's Press, 2000.
*TC HM1261 .G46 2000*

**ELITE (SOCIAL SCIENCES) - AFRICA.**
Bassey, Magnus O. Western education and political domination in Africa. Westport, CT : Bergin & Garvey, 1999.
*TC LC95.A2 B37 1999*

**ELITE (SOCIAL SCIENCES) - FRANCE - HISTORY - 19TH CENTURY.**
Knottnerus, J. David. The social worlds of male and female children in the nineteenth century French educational system. Lewiston, N.Y. ; Lampeter, Wales : Edwin Mellen Press, c1999.
*TC LC191.8.F8 K66 1999*

**ELITE (SOCIAL SCIENCES) - NEW YORK (STATE) - NEW YORK.**
Ostrower, Francie. Why the wealthy give. Princeton, N.J. : Princeton University Press, c1995.

*TC HV99.N59 O85 1995*

**ELITE (SOCIAL SCIENCES) - UNITED STATES.**
Lemann, Nicholas. The big test :. 1st ed. New York : Farrar, Straus and Giroux, 1999.
*TC LB3051 .L44 1999*

**ELITE (SOCIAL SCIENCES) - WASHINGTON (D.C.) - HISTORY - 19TH CENTURY.**
Moore, Jacqueline M., 1965- Leading the race. Charlottesville : University Press of Virginia, 1999.
*TC E185.93.D6 M66 1999*

**ELITE (SOCIAL SCIENCES) - WASHINGTON (D.C.) - HISTORY - 20TH CENTURY.**
Moore, Jacqueline M., 1965- Leading the race. Charlottesville : University Press of Virginia, 1999.
*TC E185.93.D6 M66 1999*

**ELITES (SOCIAL SCIENCES).** *See* **ELITE (SOCIAL SCIENCES).**

**Elizabeth Catlett sculpture.**
Catlett, Elizabeth, 1915- [Purchase, N.Y.] : Neuberger Museum of Art, Purchase College, State University of New York ; Seattle : Distributed by University of Washington Press, c1998.
*TC NB259.C384 A4 1998*

**Elkins, James, 1955-** What painting is : how to think about oil painting, using the language of alchemy / James Elkins. New York : Routledge, 1999. x, 246 p. : col. ill. ; 21 cm. Includes bibliographical references and index. ISBN 0-415-92113-9 DDC 750/.1/8
*1. Painting. I. Title.*
*TC ND1135 .E44 1999*

**Elledge, Paul.** Lord Byron at Harrow School : speaking out, talking back, acting up, bowing out / Paul Elledge. Baltimore : Johns Hopkins University Press, c2000. xiii, 221 p., [16] p. of plates : ill. ; 24 cm. Includes bibliographical references (p. 207-215) and index. ISBN 0-8018-6343-0 (acid-free paper) DDC 821/.7
*1. Byron, George Gordon Byron, - Baron, - 1788-1824 - Childhood and youth. 2. Byron, George Gordon Byron, - Baron, - 1788-1824 - Knowledge and learning. 3. Byron, George Gordon Byron, - Baron, - 1788-1824 - Homes and haunts - England - London. 4. Harrow School - History. 5. Education, Secondary - England - London - History - 19th century. 6. Boarding schools - England - London - History - 19th century. 7. Poets, English - 19th century - Biography. I. Title.*
*TC PR4382 .E36 2000*

**Ellemers, Naomi.**
Social identity. Malden, MA : Blackwell Publishers, 1999.
*TC HM131 .S58433 1999*

**Elley, Warwick B.** How in the world do students read? : IEA study of reading literacy / Warwick B. Elley. Hamburg : The International Association for the Evaluation of Educational Achievement, [1992] xiii, 120 p. : ill. ; 24 cm. "July 1992." Includes bibliographical references (p. 89-91). CONTENTS: Preface -- Executive summary -- What is the study about? -- A word on international comparisons -- How well do nine-year-olds read around the world? -- How well do fourteen-year-olds read around the world? -- How do high-achieving countries differ from low-achieving countries? -- Differences in achievement by gender, home langauge and urban-rural location -- Other influences by location -- How does one become a good reader? -- Voluntary reading patterns.
*1. Reading - Research. I. International Association for the Evaluation of Educational Achievement. II. Title.*
*TC LB1050.6 .E55 1992*

**Elliot, Johnna.**
Janney, Rachel. Behavorial support. Baltimore, Md. ; London : Paul H. Brookes Pub., c2000.
*TC LB1060.2 .J26 2000*

Janney, Rachel. Modifying schoolwork. Baltimore, Md. : Paul H. Brookes Pub., c2000.
*TC LC1201 .J26 2000*

Snell, Martha E. Collaborative teaming. Baltimore : Paul H. Brookes Pub., c2000.
*TC LC1201 .S64 2000*

**Elliott, Geoffrey, Dr.** Lifelong learning : the politics of the new learning environment / Geoffrey Elliott. London ; Philadelphia : Jessica Kingsley Publishers, c1999. 144 p. ; 24 cm. (Higher education policy series ; 44) Includes bibliographic references (p. 133-139) and indexes. ISBN 1-85302-580-1
*1. Learning. 2. Education, Higher - Aims and objectives. I. Title. II. Title: Politics of the new learning environment III. Series.*
*TC LB1060 .E447 1999*

**Elliott, John, Dip. Phil. Ed.**
Images of educational change. Buckingham [England] : Philadelphia : Open University Press, 2000.
*TC LB2805 .I415 2000*

**Elliott, Judy L.** Improving test performance of students with disabilities-- on district and state assessments / Judy L. Elliott, Martha L. Thurlow. Thousands Oaks, Calif. : Corwin Press, c2000. xvi, 341 p. ; 30 cm. Includes bibliographical references and indexes. ISBN 0-7619-7558-6 (cloth : alk. paper) ISBN 0-7619-7559-4 (pbk. : alk. paper) DDC 371.9/043
*1. Educational tests and measurements - United States. 2. Handicapped children - Education - Ability testing - United States. 3. Education and state - United States. I. Thurlow, Martha L. II. Title.*
*TC LB3051 .E48 2000*

**Elliott, Mark, ill.**
Levine, Gail Carson. Princess Sonora and the long sleep. 1st ed. New York : HarperCollins Publishers, c1999.
*TC PZ8.L4793 Pq 1999*

**Elliott, Timothy R.**
Handbook of rehabilitation psychology. 1st ed. Washington, DC : American Psychological Association c2000.
*TC R726.7 .H366 2000*

**Ellis, Albert, ed.** The encyclopedia of sexual behavior, edited by Albert Ellis and Albert Abarbanel. [1st ed.]. New York, Hawthorn books [1961-1964] 2 v. (1059 p.) : diagrs. ; 27 cm. Includes index. Includes bibliographies. DDC 301.424
*1. Sex - Encyclopedias. I. Abarbanel, Albert, joint ed. II. Title.*
*TC HQ9 .E4*

**Ellis, Elizabeth M.** Divorce wars : interventions with families in conflict / Elizabeth M. Ellis. 1st ed. Washington, D.C. : American Psychological Association, c2000. viii, 401 p. ; 27 cm. Includes bibliographical references and index. ISBN 1-55798-679-7 DDC 616.89/156
*1. Divorce therapy. 2. Divorce - Psychological aspects. 3. Children of divorced parents - Mental health. I. Title.*
*TC RC488.6 .E45 2000*

**ELLIS ISLAND IMMIGRATION STATION (N.Y. AND N.J.) - POSTERS.**
Ellis Island [picture]. Amawalk, NY : Jackdaw Publications, c1997.
*TC TR820.5 .E4 1997*

**Ellis Island** [picture] : the immigrants' experience. Amawalk, NY : Jackdaw Publications, c1997. 12 posters : b&w ; 43 x 56 cm. + 1 leaflet ([6] p. : ill. ; 28 cm.). (Jackdaw photo collections ; PC 102) Compiled by Enid Goldberg & Norman Itzkowitz. SUMMARY: 12 historical photo-posters depicting Ellis Island and the immigrants' first experiences of the United States. CONTENTS: 1. "Give me your tired, your poor ..."-- The Statue of Liberty -- 2. Crowds of immigrants on deck of S.S. Amerika, 1907 -- 3. A view of Ellis Island from New York Harbor, 1905 -- 4. Immigrants on ferry in New York Harbor, 1905 -- 5. Gathering luggage, main building, Ellis Island -- 6. Endless lines await the immigrants-- the Great Hall, 1904 -- 7. The dreaded medical exam, Ellis Island, 1920 -- 8. Children being examined for typhus, 1911 -- 9. Detained immigrants, Ellis Island Dining Room, circa 1900 -- 10. Leaving Ellis Island for New York City, circa 1900 -- 11. Moving on by rail, 1905 (Insert: Immigrant Railway Ticket) -- 12. Making it: Irving Berlin, immigrant. ISBN 1-56696-158-0
*1. Ellis Island Immigration Station (N.Y. and N.J.) - Posters. 2. Statue of Liberty (New York, N.Y.) - Posters. 3. Immigrants - United States - History - Posters. 4. United States - Emigration and immigration - History - Posters. 5. Documentary photography - United States - Posters. I. Goldberg, Elizabeth. II. Itzkowitz, Norman. III. Jackdaw Publications. IV. Title: Immigrants' experience [picture] V. Series.*
*TC TR820.5 .E4 1997*

**Ellis, Rod.** Learning a second language through interaction / Rod Ellis ; with contributions from Sandra Fotos ... [et al.]. Amsterdam ; Philadelphia : J. Benjamins, c1999. x, 285 p. ; 23 cm. (Studies in bilingualism, 0928-1533 ; v. 17) Includes bibliographical references (p. [259]-280) and index. ISBN 90-272-4124-4 (Eur. : hbk. : alk. paper) ISBN 90-272-4125-2 (Eur. : pbk. : alk. paper) ISBN 1-55619-736-5 (US : hbk. : alk. paper) ISBN 1-55619-737-3 (US : pbk. : alk. paper) DDC 401/.93
*1. Second language acquisition. 2. Interaction analysis in education. I. Fotos, Sandra. II. Title. III. Series.*
*TC P118.2 .E38 1999*

**Elmore, Richard F.**
Testing, teaching, and learning. Washington, D.C. : National Academy Press, c1999.
*TC LC3981 .T4 1999*

**ELOCUTION.** *See* **ACTING; EXPRESSION; ORAL READING; READING; VOICE.**

**ELOQUENCE.** *See* **EXPRESSION.**

**Elowitz, Larry.**
Remy, Richard C. Government in the United States. New York : Scribner educational publishers, 1987.
*TC JK274 .R54 1987*

**Elphinstone, Leonie.** How to get a research degree : a survival guide / Leonie Elphinstone and Robert Schweitzer. St. Leonards, Australia : Allen & Unwin, 1998. x, 134 p. : ill. ; 20 cm. Includes bibliographical references (p. 130-132) and index. Tertiary students. ISBN 1-86448-560-4
*1. Graduate students. 2. Universities and colleges - Graduate work. 3. Study skills. 4. Dissertations, Academic - Handbooks, manuals, etc. I. Schweitzer, Robert, 1950- II. Title.*
*TC LB2371 .E46 1998*

**Elster, Jon, 1940-** Alchemies of the mind : rationality and the emotions / Jon Elster. Cambridge, U.K. ; New York : Cambridge University Press, 1999. xi, 450 p. ; 23 cm. Includes bibliographical references (p. 419-439) and index. ISBN 0-521-64279-5 (hardcover) ISBN 0-521-64487-9 (pbk.) DDC 152.4
*1. Emotions. 2. Emotions - Social aspects. 3. Emotions in literature. I. Title.*
*TC BF531 .E47 1999*

Strong feelings : emotion, addiction, and human behavior / Jon Elster. Cambridge, Mass. : MIT Press, c1999. xii, 252 p. : ill. ; 21 cm. (The Jean Nicod lectures ; 1997) "A Bradford book." Includes bibliographical references (p. [229]-245) and index. ISBN 0-262-05056-0 (alk. paper) DDC 616.86
*1. Emotions. 2. Addicts - Psychology. 3. Compulsive behavior - Etiology. 4. Substance abuse - Etiology. 5. Choice (Psychology) I. Title. II. Series.*
*TC BF531 .E475 1999*

Ulysses unbound : studies in rationality, precommitment, and constraints / Jon Elster. Cambridge, U.K. ; New York : Cambridge University Press, 2000. xi, 308 p. : ill. ; 24 cm. Includes bibliographical references (p. 283-300) and index. CONTENTS: I. Ulysses Revisited: How and Why People Bind Themselves. I.1. Introduction: Constraint Theory. I.2. Passion as a Reason for Self-Binding. I.3. Time-Inconsistency and Discounting. I.4. Time-Inconsistency and Strategic Behavior. I.5. Passion as a Device for Self-Binding. I.6. Variations on a Russian Nobleman. I.7. Addiction and Precommitment. I.8. Obstacles, Objections, and Alternatives -- II. Ulysses Unbound: Constitutions as Constraints. II.2. Disanalogies with Individual Precommitment. II.3. The Nature and Structure of Constitutions. II.4. Constraints on Constitution-Making. II.5. Two Levels of Constitutional Precommitment. II.6. Self-Binding in Athenian Politics. II.7. Interest and Passion in Philadelphia and Paris. II.8. Time-Inconsistency, Discounting, and Delays. II.9. Omnipotence, Strategic Behavior, and Separation of Powers. II.10. Efficiency. II.11. Obstacles and Objections. II.12. Ulysses Unbound -- III. Less Is More: Creativity and Constraints in the Arts. III.2. Daydreaming: Creativity Without Constraints. III.3. Constraints and Conventions in the Arts. III.4. Constraints, Value, and Creativity. III.5. Originality, Authenticity, and Creativity. III.6. The Hays Code. III.7. Lucien Leuwen as an Empty Set. III.8. Randomization in the Arts. III.9. Creativity and Constraints in Jazz. III.10. Obstacles and Objections. ISBN 0-521-66213-3 (hardback) ISBN 0-521-66561-2 (paperback) DDC 128/.4 DDC 128/.4
*1. Rationalism - Psychological aspects. 2. Reasoning (Psychology) 3. Psychology - Philosophy. I. Title.*
*TC BF441 .E45 2000*

**Elton, Georgina.**
Grugeon, Elizabeth. The art of storytelling for teachers and pupils. London : David Fulton, 2000.
*TC LB1042 .G78 2000*

**An elusive science.**
Lagemann, Ellen Condliffe, 1945- Chicago : University of Chicago Press, 2000.
*TC LB1028.25.U6 L33 2000*

**Elwood, William N.**
Power in the blood. Mahwah, N.J. : Erlbaum, 1999.
*TC RA644.A25 P69 1999*

**Ely, Mary L. (Mary Lillian).**
[Journal of adult education (New York, N.Y.)] Journal of adult education. New York : American Association for Adult Education, 1929-[1941]

**Elzey, Freeman F., joint author.**
Levine, Samuel, 1927- A programmed introduction to research Belmont, Calif., Wadsworth Pub. Co. [1968]
*TC BF76.5 .L44*

**EMANCIPATION.** *See* **LIBERTY.**

**EMANCIPATION OF WOMEN.** *See* **WOMEN'S RIGHTS.**

**EMBASSIES.** *See* **AMBASSADORS.**

**Embedding questions.**
National Research Council (U.S.). Committee on Embedding Common Test Items in State and District Assessments. Washington, DC : National Academy Press, c1999.
*TC LB3051 .N319 1999*

**Embiricos, Anne-Marie T.** The effects of content knowledge and strategies on memory development among 4- and 6-year-old children / by Anne-Marie T. Embiricos. 1998. vi, 90 leaves : ill. ; 29 cm. Typescript; issued also on microfilm. Thesis (Ph.D.)--Columbia University, 1998. Includes bibliographical references (leaves 74-80).
*1. Developmental psychology - Research. 2. Memory in children - Research. 3. Mnemonics. 4. Memory - Age factors - Research. 5. Concepts in children. I. Title.*
*TC 085 Em22*

The effects of content knowledge and strategies on memory development among 4- and 6-year-old children / by Anne-Marie T. Embiricos. 1998. vi, 90 leaves : ill. ; 29 cm. Typescript; issued also on microfilm. Thesis (Ph.D.)--Columbia University, 1998. Includes bibliographical references (leaves 74-80).
*1. Developmental psychology - Research. 2. Memory in children - Research. 3. Mnemonics. 4. Memory - Age factors - Research. 5. Concepts in children. I. Title.*
*TC 085 Em22*

**Embodying bioethics** : recent feminist advances / edited by Anne Donchin and Laura M. Purdy. Lanham : Rowman & Littlefield Publishers, c1999. ix, 286 p. : map ; 24 cm. (New feminist perspectives series) Direct outcome of a meeting sponsored by the International Association of Bioethics in 1992. Includes bibliographical references and index. ISBN 0-8476-8924-7 (cloth : alk. paper) ISBN 0-8476-8925-5 (pbk. : alk. paper) DDC 174/.2
*1. Bioethics. 2. Feminist theory. I. Donchin. Anne. II. Purdy, Laura Martha. III. International Association of Bioethics. IV. Series.*
*TC QH332 .E43 1999*

**Embretson, Susan E.** Item response theory for psychologists / Susan Embretson and Steve Reise. Mahwah, N.J. : Lawrence Erlbaum Associates, Publishers, 2000. xi, 371 p. : ill. ; 24 cm. (Multivariate applications) cip title: Psychometic methods : item response theory for psychologists. Includes bibliographical references and index. ISBN 0-8058-2818-4 (cloth : alk. paper) ISBN 0-8058-2819-2 (pbk. : alk. paper) DDC 150/.28/7
*1. Item response theory. 2. Psychometrics. I. Reise. Steve. II. Title. III. Title: Psychometic methods : item response theory for psychologists. IV. Series: Multivariate applications book series.*
*TC BF39 .E495 2000*

**Embroidering lives.**
Wilkinson-Weber, Clare M. Albany, N.Y. : State University of New York Press, c1999.
*TC HD6073.T42 I483 1999*

**EMBROIDERY.** *See* **WHITE WORK EMBROIDERY.**

**Emener, William G. (William George).**
Professional counseling. Springfield, Ill. : C.C. Thomas, Publishers, c1999.
*TC BF637.C6 D56 1999*

**The emergence of family into the 21st century** / [edited by] Patricia L. Munhall, Virginia M. Fitzsimons. Boston : Jones and Bartlett Publishers ; [New York] : NLN Press, c2001. xxiii, 339 p. ; 23 cm. Includes bibliographical references and index. ISBN 0-7637-1105-5 DDC 306.85/0973
*1. Family - United States. 2. Family life - United States. 3. Twenty-first century - Forecasts. I. Munhall, Patricia L. II. Fitzsimons, Virginia Macken. 1943-*
*TC HQ535 .E44 2001*

**The emergence of stability in the industrial city.**
Hewitt, Martin. Aldershot, England : Scolar Press ; Brookfield, Vt., USA : Ashgate Pub. Co., c1996.
*TC HN398.M27 H48 1996*

**The emergence of the speech capacity.**
Oller, D. Kimbrough. Mahwah, N.J. : Lawrence Erlbaum Associates, 2000.
*TC P118 .O43 2000*

**EMERGENCY MANAGEMENT.** *See* **DISASTER RELIEF.**

**EMERGENCY MANAGEMENT - HANDBOOKS, MANUALS, ETC.**
Building an emergency plan. Los Angeles, Calif. : Getty Conservation Institute, c1999.

*TC AM121 .B85 1999*

**EMERGENCY PLANNING.** *See* **EMERGENCY MANAGEMENT.**

**EMERGENCY PREPAREDNESS.** *See* **EMERGENCY MANAGEMENT.**

**EMERGENCY RELIEF.** *See* **DISASTER RELIEF.**

**The emerging arts.**
Jeffri. Joan. New York, N.Y. : Praeger, 1980.
*TC NX765 .J43*

**EMERGING NATIONS.** *See* **DEVELOPING COUNTRIES.**

**The emerging world of wireless communications.**
Nashville, TN : Institute for Information Studies, 1996. xxii, 173 p. : ill. ; 23 cm. (Annual review of The Institute for Information Studies, 1996.) A joint program of Nortel and The Aspen Institute. Includes bibliographical references. ISBN 0-89843-185-9
*1. Communication. 2. Telecommunication. I. Nortel North America. II. Aspen Institute. III. Series.*
*TC TK5103.2 .E44 1996*

**Emi, Frank.**
Rabbit in the moon [videorecording]. San Francisco, Calif. : Wabi-Sabi Productions, 1999.
*TC D753.8 .R3 1999*

**EMIGRANTS.** *See* **IMMIGRANTS.**

**EMIGRATION AND IMMIGRATION.** *See also* **ASSIMILATION (SOCIOLOGY).**
Review and appraisal of the progress made in achieving the goals and objectives of the Programme of Action of the International Conference on Population and Development. New York : United Nations, 1999.
*TC HB849 .R48 1999*

**EMIGRATION AND IMMIGRATION - FICTION.**
Figueredo, D. H., 1951- When this world was new. 1st ed. New York : Lee & Low Books, 1999.
*TC PZ7.F488 Wh 1999*

Rosenberg, Liz. The silence in the mountains. 1st American ed. New York : Orchard Books, c1999.
*TC PZ7.R71894 Si 1999*

**EMIGRATION AND IMMIGRATION - LAW AND LEGISLATION.** *See* **EMIGRATION AND IMMIGRATION LAW.**

**EMIGRATION AND IMMIGRATION LAW - UNITED STATES - CONGRESSES.**
National Legal Conference on Immigration and Refugee Policy (6th : 1983 : Washington, D.C.) Immigration and refugee policy. 1st ed. New York : Center for Migration Studies, 1984.
*TC KF4819.A2 N375 1983*

**EMIGRATION AND IMMIGRATION - RELIGIOUS ASPECTS - CATHOLIC CHURCH.**
Who are my sisters and brothers? Washington, D.C. : The Conference, c1996.
*TC BX1795.E44 W46 1996*

**EMIGRATION AND IMMIGRATION - SOCIAL ASPECTS.**
The challenge of diversity. Aldershot, England ; Brookfield, Vt. : Avebury, 1996.
*TC JV225 .C530 1996*

**Eminent educators.**
Berube, Maurice R. Westport, Conn. : Greenwood Press, 2000.
*TC LB875.D5 B47 2000*

**Emlékezés Szokolszky Istvánra** : élete és munkássága / összeállította és szerkesztette, Tatai Zoltán. [Budapest] : Magyar Pedagógiai Társaság, 1998. 263 p. : ill. ; 26 cm. Includes bibliographical references. "Kiadja a Magyar Pedagógiai Társaság Szokolszky István halálának 30. évfordulója alkalmából." "Szokolszky István irodalmi tevékenysége"--P. 250-255. ISBN 963-7644-79-2
*1. Szokolszky. István. - 1915-1968. 2. Educators - Hungary - Biography. I. Szokolszky. István. 1915-1968. II. Tatai. Zoltán.*
*TC LA2375.H92 S9653 1998*

**EMMANUEL COLLEGE (UNIVERSITY OF CAMBRIDGE) - HISTORY.**
Bendall, A. Sarah. A history of Emmanuel College, Cambridge. Woodbridge, Suffolk, UK ; Rochester, NY : Boydell Press, 1999.
*TC LF185 .B46 1999*

**Emmer, Edmund T.** Classroom management for secondary teachers / Edmund T. Emmer, Carolyn M. Evertson, Murray E. Worsham. 5th ed. Boston : Allyn and Bacon, c2000. xii, 236 p. : ill. ; 24 cm. Rev. ed. of: Classroom management for secondary teachers / Edmund T. Emmer ... [et al.]. 4th ed. c1997. Includes bibliographical

references (p. 227-231) and index. ISBN 0-205-30837-6 DDC 373.1102/4
*1. Classroom management. 2. Education. Secondary. I. Evertson, Carolyn M.. 1935- II. Worsham, Murray E. III. Title.*
*TC LB3013 .C53 2000*

Evertson, Carolyn M., 1935- Classroom management for elementary teachers. 5th ed. Boston : Allyn and Bacon, c2000.
*TC LB3013 .C528 2000*

**Emmons, Robert A.** The psychology of ultimate concerns : motivation and spirituality in personality / Robert A. Emmons. New York : Guilford Press, c1999. ix, 230 p. : ill. ; 23 cm. Includes bibliographical references (p. 201-223) and index. ISBN 1-57230-456-1 (hc) DDC 155.2/5
*1. Goal (Psychology) 2. Self-actualization (Psychology) 3. Happiness. 4. Motivation (Psychology) 5. Personality. 6. Personality - Religious aspects. I. Title.*
*TC BF505.G6 E58 1999*

**Emmons, Shirlee.** Power performance for singers : transcending the barriers / Shirlee Emmons, Alma Thomas. New York : Oxford University Press, 1998. xvi, 320 p. ; 24 cm. Includes bibliographical references (p. 313-316) and index. ISBN 0-19-511224-5 (acid-free paper) DDC 783/.043
*1. Singing - Psychological aspects. I. Thomas. Alma. 1939- II. Title.*
*TC MT892 .E55 1998*

**Emmorey, Karen.**
The signs of language revisited. Mahwah, N.J. : L.Erlbaum, 2000.
*TC HV2474 .S573 2000*

**EMOA INDIANS.** *See* **MACUNA INDIANS.**

**Emotion & social judgments.**
Emotion and social judgments. 1st ed. Oxford ; New York : Pergamon Press, 1991.
*TC BF531 .E4834 1991*

**Emotion and social judgments** / edited by Joseph P. Forgas. 1st ed. Oxford ; New York : Pergamon Press, 1991. viii, 301 p. : ill. ; 24 cm. (International series in experimental social psychology ; [v. 23]) Cover title: Emotion & social judgments. Includes bibliographical references and indexes. ISBN 0-08-040236-4 (hard) ISBN 0-08-040235-6 (soft) DDC 302/.12
*1. Affect (Psychology) 2. Mood (Psychology) 3. Emotions. 4. Social perception. I. Forgas. Joseph P. II. Title: Emotion & social judgments. III. Series.*
*TC BF531 .E4834 1991*

**Emotion, character, and responsibility.**
Sabini, John. 1947- New York : Oxford University Press, 1998.
*TC BF531 .S23 1998*

**EMOTIONAL HEALTH.** *See* **MENTAL HEALTH.**

**EMOTIONAL INTELLIGENCE.**
Bocchino, Rob. Emotional literacy. Thousand Oaks, Calif. : Sage Publications, c1999.
*TC BF576 .B63 1999*

Bodine, Richard J. Developing emotional intelligence. Champaign, Ill : Research Press, c1999.
*TC BF561 .B6 1999*

The handbook of emotional intelligence. 1st ed. San Francisco, Calif. : Jossey-Bass, c2000.
*TC BF576 .H36 2000*

**EMOTIONAL INTELLIGENCE TESTS.**
The handbook of emotional intelligence. 1st ed. San Francisco, Calif. : Jossey-Bass, c2000.
*TC BF576 .H36 2000*

**Emotional literacy.**
Bocchino, Rob. Thousand Oaks, Calif. : Sage Publications, c1999.
*TC BF576 .B63 1999*

**EMOTIONAL PROBLEMS - FICTION.**
Griffin, Adele. Dive. 1st ed. New York : Hyperion Books for Children, 1999.
*TC PZ7.G881325 Di 1999*

**EMOTIONAL STRESS.** *See* **STRESS (PSYCHOLOGY).**

**EMOTIONAL TRAUMA.** *See* **PSYCHIC TRAUMA.**

**The emotionally disturbed child.**
Gerard, Margaret Elizabeth Wilson, 1894-1954. New York, Child Welfare League of America [1956?]
*TC RJ499 .G4*

**EMOTIONALLY DISTURBED CHILDREN.** *See* **MENTALLY ILL CHILDREN.**

**EMOTIONS.** *See also* **AFFECT (PSYCHOLOGY); ANGER; ANXIETY; AUTONOMY (PSYCHOLOGY); BELIEF AND DOUBT; CONTROL (PSYCHOLOGY); CRYING; FEAR; GRIEF; GUILT; INTIMACY (PSYCHOLOGY); LAUGHTER; LOVE; MELANCHOLY; MOOD (PSYCHOLOGY); PAIN; PREJUDICES.**
Ben-Ze'ev, Aharon. The subtlety of emotions. Cambridge, Mass. : London : MIT Press, c2000.
*TC BF531 .B43 2000*

Berkowitz, Leonard, 1926- Causes and consequences of feelings. Cambridge, U.K. ; New York : Cambridge University Press ; Paris : Editions de la Maison des sciences de l'homme, 2000.
*TC BF531 .B45 2000*

Edwards, David C. Motivation & emotion. Thousand Oaks, Calif. : Sage, c1999.
*TC BF503 .E38 1999*

Elster, Jon, 1940- Alchemies of the mind. Cambridge, U.K. ; New York : Cambridge University Press, 1999.
*TC BF531 .E47 1999*

Elster, Jon, 1940- Strong feelings. Cambridge, Mass. : MIT Press, c1999.
*TC BF531 .E475 1999*

Emotion and social judgments. 1st ed. Oxford ; New York : Pergamon Press, 1991.
*TC BF531 .E4834 1991*

Feeling and thinking. Cambridge, U.K. ; New York : Cambridge University Press ; Paris : Editions de la Maison des Sciences de l'Homme, 2000.
*TC BF531 .F44 2000*

Greenfield, Susan. The private life of the brain. New York : John Wiley, c2000.
*TC BF515 G74 2000*

Handbook of emotions. 2nd ed. New York : Guilford Press, c2000.
*TC BF561 .H35 2000*

Lazarus, Richard S. Stress and emotion. New York : Springer Pub. Co., c1999.
*TC BF575.S75 L315 1999*

Planalp, Sally, 1950- Communicating emotion. Cambridge ; New York : Cambridge University Press ; Paris : Editions de la Maison des sciences de l'homme, 1999.
*TC BF591 .P57 1999*

Sabini, John, 1947- Emotion, character, and responsibility. New York : Oxford University Press, 1998.
*TC BF531 .S23 1998*

Turner, Jonathan H. On the origins of human emotions. Stanford, Calif. : Stanford University Press, c2000.
*TC BF531 .T87 2000*

**Emotions across languages and cultures.**
Wierzbicka, Anna. Cambridge : Cambridge University Press, 1999.
*TC BF531 .W54 1999*

**EMOTIONS AND COGNITION.**
Bocchino, Rob. Emotional literacy. Thousand Oaks, Calif. : Sage Publications, c1999.
*TC BF576 .B63 1999*

Cognition and emotion. Oxford ; New York : Oxford University Press, 2000.
*TC BF311 .C5477 2000*

Kövecses, Zoltán. Metaphor and emotion. Cambridge ; New York : Cambridge University Press ; Paris : Editions de la Maison des Sciences de l'Homme, 2000.
*TC BF582 .K68 2000*

Schutte, Nicola S. (Nicola Susanne) Measuring emotional intelligence and related constructs. Lewiston, N.Y. ; Lampeter, Wales : E. Mellen Press, c1999.
*TC BF576.3 .S38 1999*

**Emotions and social behavior**
Watson, David. Mood and temperament. New York ; London : Guilford Press, c2000.
*TC BF698.9.E45 W38 2000*

**EMOTIONS - CONGRESSES.**
Anxiety, depression, and emotion. Oxford ; New York : Oxford University Press, 2000.
*TC RC531 .A559 2000*

**EMOTIONS - CROSS-CULTURA STUDIES.**
Wierzbicka, Anna. Emotions across languages and

cultures. Cambridge : Cambridge University Press, 1999.
*TC BF531 .W54 1999*

**EMOTIONS - ENCYCLOPEDIAS.**
Encyclopedia of human emotions. New York : Macmillan Reference USA, c1999.
*TC BF531 .E55 1999*

**EMOTIONS - HEALTH ASPECTS.**
Newman, Stephanie. Self-silencing, depression, gender role, and gender role conflict in women and men. 1997.
*TC 085 N47*

**EMOTIONS IN ADOLESCENCE.** *See* **ANXIETY IN ADOLESCENCE.**

**EMOTIONS IN ADOLESCENCE - UNITED STATES.**
Gallagher, Trish. Arousal patterns, emotion identification, and cognitive style in depressed and nondepressed inner-city adolescent Latinas. 1997.
*TC 085 G136*

**EMOTIONS IN CHILDREN.**
Bocchino, Rob. Emotional literacy. Thousand Oaks, Calif. : Sage Publications, c1999.
*TC BF576 .B63 1999*

**EMOTIONS IN INFANTS.**
Janov, Arthur. The biology of love. Amherst, N.Y. : Prometheus Books, 2000.
*TC BF720.E45 .J36 2000*

Odent, Michel, 1930- The scientification of love. London ; New York : Free Association Books, 1999.
*TC BF575.L8 O33 1999*

**EMOTIONS IN LITERATURE.**
Elster, Jon, 1940- Alchemies of the mind. Cambridge, U.K. ; New York : Cambridge University Press, 1999.
*TC BF531 .E47 1999*

**EMOTIONS - MEASUREMENT.**
Schutte, Nicola S. (Nicola Susanne) Measuring emotional intelligence and related constructs. Lewiston, N.Y. ; Lampeter, Wales : E. Mellen Press, c1999.
*TC BF576.3 .S38 1999*

**EMOTIONS - PHYSIOLOGY.**
Biocultural approaches to the emotions. Cambridge, U.K. ; New York : Cambridge University Press, 1999.
*TC GN502 .B53 1999*

**EMOTIONS - RESEARCH.**
Qualitative research. Aldershot, Hants, England ; Brookfield, Vt. : Avebury, c1996.
*TC H62 .Q355 1996*

**EMOTIONS - SEX DIFFERENCES.**
Gender and emotion. New York : Cambridge University Press, 1999.
*TC BF591 .G45 1999*

**EMOTIONS - SOCIAL ASPECTS.**
Biocultural approaches to the emotions. Cambridge, U.K. ; New York : Cambridge University Press, 1999.
*TC GN502 .B53 1999*

Elster, Jon, 1940- Alchemies of the mind. Cambridge, U.K. ; New York : Cambridge University Press, 1999.
*TC BF531 .E47 1999*

Planalp, Sally, 1950- Communicating emotion. Cambridge ; New York : Cambridge University Press ; Paris : Editions de la Maison des sciences de l'homme, 1999.
*TC BF591 .P57 1999*

Schutte, Nicola S. (Nicola Susanne) Measuring emotional intelligence and related constructs. Lewiston, N.Y. ; Lampeter, Wales : E. Mellen Press, c1999.
*TC BF576.3 .S38 1999*

Turner, Jonathan H. On the origins of human emotions. Stanford, Calif. : Stanford University Press, c2000.
*TC BF531 .T87 2000*

**EMOTIONS - SOCIOLOGICAL ASPECTS.**
Handbook of emotions. 2nd ed. New York : Guilford Press, c2000.
*TC BF561 .H35 2000*

Kövecses, Zoltán. Metaphor and emotion. Cambridge ; New York : Cambridge University Press ; Paris : Editions de la Maison des Sciences de l'Homme, 2000.
*TC BF582 .K68 2000*

**EMOTIONS - STUDY AND TEACHING (SECONDARY) - UNITED STATES.**
Kessler, Rachael, 1946- The soul of education.

Alexandria, Va. : Association for Supervision and Curriculum Development, c2000.
*TC LB1072 .K48 2000*

**EMPATHY.**
Empathy and agency. Boulder, Colo. ; Oxford : Westview Press, 2000.
*TC BF64 .E67 2000*

Hoffman, Martin L. Empathy and moral development. Cambridge, U.K. ; New York : Cambridge University Press, 2000.
*TC BF723.M54 H64 2000*

**Empathy and agency :** the problem of understanding in the human sciences / edited by Hans Herbert Kögler, Karsten R. Stueber. Boulder, Colo. ; Oxford : Westview Press, 2000. ix, 318 p. ; 24 cm. Includes bibliographical references (p. 289-301) and indexes. ISBN 0-8133-9120-2 (hc : alk. paper) ISBN 0-8133-9119-9 (pb : alk. paper) DDC 128/.4
*1. Psychology - Philosophy. 2. Science and psychology. 3. Empathy. I. Kögler, Hans Herbert, 1960- II. Stueber, Karsten R.*
*TC BF64 .E67 2000*

**Empathy and moral development.**
Hoffman, Martin L. Cambridge, U.K. ; New York : Cambridge University Press, 2000.
*TC BF723.M54 H64 2000*

**EMPEROR PENGUIN - BEHAVIOR - JUVENILE LITERATURE.**
Jenkins, Martin. The emperor's egg. 1st U.S. ed. Cambridge, Mass. : Candlewick Press, 1999.
*TC QL696.S473 J45 1999*

**EMPEROR PENGUIN - HABITS AND BEHAVIOR.**
Jenkins, Martin. The emperor's egg. 1st U.S. ed. Cambridge, Mass. : Candlewick Press, 1999.
*TC QL696.S473 J45 1999*

**The emperor's egg.**
Jenkins, Martin. 1st U.S. ed. Cambridge, Mass. : Candlewick Press, 1999.
*TC QL696.S473 J45 1999*

**Emphasis art.**
Wachowiak, Frank. 7th ed. New York ; London : Longman, c2001.
*TC N350 .W26 2001*

**The Empire State Building.**
Hine, Lewis Wickes, 1874-1940. Munich ; New York : Prestel, c1998.
*TC TR820.5 .H5634 1998*

**EMPIRE STATE BUILDING (NEW YORK, N.Y.) - DESIGN AND CONSTRUCTION - PICTORIAL WORKS.**
Hine, Lewis Wickes, 1874-1940. The Empire State Building. Munich ; New York : Prestel, c1998.
*TC TR820.5 .H5634 1998*

**EMPIRE STATE BUILDING (NEW YORK, N.Y.) - FICTION.**
Wiesner, David. Sector 7. New York : Clarion Books, c1999.
*TC PZ7.W6367 Se 1999*

**Empire State College.**
Langer, Arthur Mark. Faculty assessment of mentoring roles at SUNY Empire State College. 1999.
*TC 06 no. 11138*

**EMPIRE STATE COLLEGE - FACULTY.**
Langer, Arthur Mark. Faculty assessment of mentoring roles at SUNY Empire State College. 1999.
*TC 06 no. 11138*

**Empire's children.**
Kutzer, M. Daphne. New York : Garland Pub., 2000.
*TC PR830.I54 K88 2000*

**Empirical perspectives on object relations theory /** edited by Joseph M. Masling and Robert F. Bornstein. 1st ed. Washington, DC : American Psychological Association, c1994. xxvi, 263 p. : ill. ; 24 cm. (Empirical studies of psychoanalytic theories ; vol. 5) Includes bibliographical references and indexes. ISBN 1-55798-256-2 (alk. paper) DDC 150.19/5
*1. Object relations (Psychoanalysis) 2. Object Attachment. I. Masling, Joseph M. II. Bornstein, Robert F. III. Series.*
*TC BF175.5.O24 E85 1994*

**Empirical studies of psychoanalytic theories** (vol. 5) Empirical perspectives on object relations theory. 1st ed. Washington, DC : American Psychological Association, c1994.
*TC BF175.5.O24 E85 1994*

**EMPIRICISM.**
Scruton, Roger. Art and imagination. South Bend, Ind. : St. Augustine's Press, 1998.

*TC BH301.J8 S37 1998*

**EMPLOYED MOTHERS.** *See* **WORKING MOTHERS.**

**EMPLOYEE DEVELOPMENT.** *See* **CAREER DEVELOPMENT; EMPLOYEES - TRAINING OF.**

**EMPLOYEE-EMPLOYER RELATIONS.** *See* **INDUSTRIAL RELATIONS.**

**EMPLOYEE FRINGE BENEFITS.** *See* **SOCIAL SECURITY.**

**EMPLOYEE TRAINING.** *See* **EMPLOYEES - TRAINING OF.**

**Employee training and US competitiveness.**
Employee training and U.S. competitiveness.
Boulder : Westview Press, 1991.
*TC HF5549.5.T7 E46 1991*

**Employee training and U.S. competitiveness :** lessons for the 1990s / Lauren Benton ... [et al.]. Boulder : Westview Press, 1991. vii, 115 p. ; 24 cm. (The Eisenhower Center for the Conservation of Human Resources studies in the new economy) Includes bibliographical references and index. ISBN 0-8133-8050-2 (alk. paper) DDC 331.25/92/0973
*1. Employees - Training of - United States. 2. Organizational change - United States. 3. Competition, International. 4. Textile industry - United States. 5. Retail trade - United States. 6. Banks and banking - United States. 7. Service industries - United States. 8. Technological innovations - United States. I. Benton, Lauren A. II. Title: Employee training and US competitiveness. III. Series.*
*TC HF5549.5.T7 E46 1991*

**EMPLOYEES.** *See* **INDUSTRIAL RELATIONS; PERSONNEL MANAGEMENT; PROFESSIONAL EMPLOYEES; TEXTILE WORKERS; WHITE COLLAR WORKERS.**

**EMPLOYEES - LEGAL STATUS, LAWS, ETC.** *See* **LABOR LAWS AND LEGISLATION.**

**EMPLOYEES, RATING OF.**
Mohrman, Allan M. Designing performance appraisal systems. 1st ed. San Francisco : Jossey-Bass Publishers, 1989.
*TC HF5549.5.P35 M64 1989*

**EMPLOYEES - RECRUITING.** *See* **EMPLOYMENT AGENCIES.**

**EMPLOYEES - SUPPLY AND DEMAND.** *See* **LABOR MARKET.**

**EMPLOYEES - TRAINING OF.** *See* **APPRENTICESHIP PROGRAMS.**

**EMPLOYEES, TRAINING OF.** *See* **EMPLOYEES - TRAINING OF.**

**EMPLOYEES - TRAINING OF.** *See also* **EMPLOYER-SUPPORTED EDUCATION; INTERNSHIP PROGRAMS.**
Garrick, John. Informal learning in the workplace. London ; New York : Routledge, 1998.
*TC HF5549.5.T7 G344 1998*

Raelin, Joseph A., 1948- Work based learning. Reading, MA : Addison-Wesley, 1999.
*TC HD30.4 .R33 1999*

Teare, Richard. The virtual university. London ; New York : Cassell, 1998.
*TC LC5215 .T42 1998*

The virtual learning organization. London ; New York : Continuum, 2000.
*TC LC5215 .V574 2000*

**EMPLOYEES - TRAINING OF - CONGRESSES.**
American Society for Training and Development. Issues in career and human resource development. Madison, Wisc. : American Society for Training and Development, c1980.
*TC HF5549.5.T7 A59 1980*

**EMPLOYEES - TRAINING OF - JAPAN.**
Vocational education in the industrialization of Japan. Tokyo : United Nations University, c1987.
*TC LC1047.J3 V63 1987*

**EMPLOYEES - TRAINING OF - UNITED STATES.**
Employee training and U.S. competitiveness. Boulder : Westview Press, 1991.
*TC HF5549.5.T7 E46 1991*

**EMPLOYER-EMPLOYEE RELATIONS.** *See* **INDUSTRIAL RELATIONS.**

**EMPLOYER-SPONSORED EDUCATION.** *See* **EMPLOYER-SUPPORTED EDUCATION.**

**EMPLOYER-SUPPORTED DAY CARE.** *See* **DAY CARE CENTERS.**

**EMPLOYER-SUPPORTED EDUCATION.** *See* **EMPLOYEES - TRAINING OF.**

**EMPLOYER-SUPPORTED EDUCATION - UNITED STATES.**
Hollenbeck, Kevin. Classrooms in the workplace. Kalamazoo, Mich. : W.E. Upjohn Institute for Employment Research, 1993.
*TC HF5549.5.T7 H598 1993*

**Employing the unemployed** / Eli Ginzberg, editor. New York : Basic Books, inc., c1980. x, 209 p. ; 24 cm. Includes bibliographical references and index. ISBN 0-465-01957-9 DDC 331.11/0973
*1. Manpower policy - United States - History - 20th century - Addresses, essays, lectures. I. Ginzberg, Eli, 1911-*
*TC HD5724 .E43 1980*

**EMPLOYMENT.**
American Nurses Association. Task Force on Staff Privileges. Guidelines for appointment of nurses for individual practice privileges in health care organizations. Kansas City, MO : American Nurses Association, Commission on Nursing Service, 1978.
*TC RT104 .A44 1978*

**EMPLOYMENT AGENCIES.** *See* **JOB HUNTING; JOB VACANCIES.**

**EMPLOYMENT AGENCIES - PERIODICALS.**
Journal of college placement. [Philadelphia, Pa. etc.], The College Placement Council, inc. [etc.]

**EMPLOYMENT AND EDUCATION.** *See* **LABOR SUPPLY - EFFECT OF EDUCATION ON.**

**Employment and health.**
Grimshaw, Jennie. London : British Library, 1999.
*TC HF5548.85 .G75 1999*

**EMPLOYMENT CREATION.** *See* **JOB CREATION.**

**EMPLOYMENT DISCRIMINATION.** *See* **DISCRIMINATION IN EMPLOYMENT.**

**EMPLOYMENT (ECONOMIC THEORY).** *See also* **DISCRIMINATION IN EMPLOYMENT; JOB VACANCIES; UNEMPLOYMENT.**
Vedder, Richard K. Out of work. New York : Holmes & Meier, 1993.
*TC HD7096.U5 V43 1993*

**EMPLOYMENT EXCHANGES.** *See* **EMPLOYMENT AGENCIES.**

**EMPLOYMENT INTERVIEWING.**
Pervola, Cindy, 1956- How to get a job if you're a teenager. Fort Atkinson, Wis. : Alleyside Press, 1998.
*TC HF5383 .P44 1998*

Pervola, Cindy, 1956- How to get a job if you're a teenager. Fort Atkinson, Wis. : Alleyside Press, 1998.
*TC HF5383 .P44 1998*

**EMPLOYMENT MANAGEMENT.** *See* **PERSONNEL MANAGEMENT.**

**EMPLOYMENT OF CHILDREN.** *See* **CHILDREN - EMPLOYMENT.**

**Employment of the mentally retarded in a competitive industrial setting, March 1, 1962 - February 28, 1967.**
Human Resources Center (N.Y.) Albertson, N.Y. [1967?]
*TC HV3005 .H85*

**EMPLOYMENT OF WOMEN.** *See* **WOMEN - EMPLOYMENT.**

**EMPLOYMENT OFFICES.** *See* **EMPLOYMENT AGENCIES.**

**EMPLOYMENT OPPORTUNITIES.** *See* **JOB VACANCIES.**

**EMPLOYMENT POLICY.** *See* **MANPOWER POLICY.**

**EMPLOYMENT PORTFOLIOS - UNITED STATES.**
Wyatt, Robert Lee, 1940- So you have to have a portfolio. Thousand Oaks, Calif. : Corwin Press, c1999.
*TC LB1728 .W93 1999*

**EMPLOYMENT SERVICES.** *See* **EMPLOYMENT AGENCIES.**

**EMPLOYMENT STABILIZATION.** *See* **FULL EMPLOYMENT POLICIES.**

**Empowered families, successful children.**
Epps, Susan. 1st ed. Washington, DC : American Psychological Association, c2000.

*TC BF637.C6 E66 2000*

**Empowering the powerless**
Empowering women of color. New York : Columbia University Press, c1999.
*TC HV1445 .E45 1999*

**Empowering women of color** / [edited by] Lorraine M. Gutiérrez and Edith A. Lewis. New York : Columbia University Press, c1999. xix, 272 p. ; 24 cm. (Empowering the powerless) Includes bibliographical references (p. [227]-253) and index. ISBN 0-231-10116-3 (cloth : acid-free paper) ISBN 0-231-10117-1 (pbk.) DDC 362.83
*1. Social work with women - United States. 2. Minority women - Services for - United States. 3. Minority women - United States - Psychology. 4. Self-esteem in women - United States. I. Gutiérrez, Lorraine M. (Lorraine Margot) II. Lewis, Edith Anne. III. Series.*
*TC HV1445 .E45 1999*

**Empowerment through health education.**
Ayim, Martin Ayong. 2nd ed. Ruston, LA : Vita Press International, c1998.
*TC RA441.5 .A95 1998*

**ENACTMENT (PSYCHOLOGY).** *See* **ACTING OUT (PSYCHOLOGY).**

**Encarta Africana.**
Microsoft encarta Africana [computer file]. Redmond, WA : Microsoft Corp., c1999. Computer data and programs.
*TC DT14 .M527 1999*

Microsoft encarta Africana [computer file]. Redmond, WA : Microsoft Corp., c1999. Computer data and programs.
*TC DT3 .M53 1999x*

**ENCEPHALITIS.** *See* **EPIDEMIC ENCEPHALITIS.**

**ENCEPHALITIS, EPIDEMIC.** *See* **EPIDEMIC ENCEPHALITIS.**

**ENCEPHALITIS EPIDEMICA.** *See* **EPIDEMIC ENCEPHALITIS.**

**ENCEPHALITIS LETHARGICA.** *See* **EPIDEMIC ENCEPHALITIS.**

**ENCHANTERS.** *See* **WIZARDS.**

**ENCLOSED COMMUNITIES.** *See* **GATED COMMUNITIES.**

**ENCOMENDEROS - COLOMBIA - HISTORY - 16TH CENTURY.**
Avellaneda Navas, José Ignacio. The conquerors of the New Kingdom of Granada. 1st ed. Albuquerque : University of New Mexico Press, c1995.
*TC F2272 .A84 1995*

**ENCOUNTER GROUPS.** *See* **GROUP RELATIONS TRAINING.**

**Encountering God.**
Eck, Diana L. Boston : Beacon Press, c1993.
*TC BR127 .E25 1993*

**ENCOUNTERS OF HUMANS WITH ALIENS.** *See* **HUMAN-ALIEN ENCOUNTERS.**

**ENCOUNTERS WITH UNIDENTIFIED FLYING OBJECTS.** *See* **UNIDENTIFIED FLYING OBJECTS - SIGHTINGS AND ENCOUNTERS.**

**ENCRYPTION OF DATA (COMPUTER SCIENCE).** *See* **DATA ENCRYPTION (COMPUTER SCIENCE).**

**ENCULTURATION.** *See* **SOCIALIZATION.**

**Encyclopedia of careers and vocational guidance** / Holli R. Cosgrove, editor-in-chief. 11th ed. Chicago : Ferguson Pub. Co., 2000. 4 v. : ill. ; 28 cm. Includes indexes. ISBN 0-89434-274-6 DDC 331.7/02
*1. Vocational guidance - Handbooks, manuals, etc. 2. Occupations - Handbooks, manuals, etc. I. Cosgrove, Holli, 1964-*
*TC HF5381 .E52 2000*

**Encyclopedia of Continental philosophy.**
The Edinburgh encyclopedia of Continental philosophy. Edinburgh : University Press, c1999.
*TC B831.2 E35 1999*

**Encyclopedia of food science and technology.** 2nd ed. / Frederick J. Francis [editor-in-chief]. New York : Wiley, c2000. 4 v. (xxi, 2768 p.) : ill. ; 29 cm. Cover title: Wiley encyclopedia of food science and technology. "A Wiley-Interscience publication." Includes bibliographical references and index. ISBN 0-471-19285-6 (set : cloth : alk. paper) ISBN 0-471-19255-4 (v. 1 : cloth : alk. paper) ISBN 0-471-19256-2 (v. 2 : cloth : alk. paper) ISBN 0-471-19257-0 (v. 3 : cloth : alk. paper) ISBN 0-471-19258-9 (v. 4 : cloth :

alk. paper) DDC 664/.003
1. *Food industry and trade - Encyclopedias. 1. Francis, F. J. (Frederick John). 1921- 11. Title: Wiley encyclopedia of food science and technology*
*TC TP368.2 .E62 2000*

**Encyclopedia of gun control and gun rights.**
Utter, Glenn H. Phoenix, Ariz. : Oryx Press, 2000.
*TC KF3941.A68 U88 2000*

**The encyclopedia of higher education. 1992.**
Education [computer file]: Version 1.1. [Oxford, Eng.] : Pergamon, c1998. Computer program.
*TC LB15 .E3 1998*

**Encyclopedia of human emotions** / edited by David Levinson, James J. Ponzetti, Jr., Peter F. Jorgensen. New York : Macmillan Reference USA, c1999. 2 v. (xviii, 768 p.) : ill., ports ; 29 cm. Includes bibliographical references and indexes. ISBN 0-02-864766-1 (set) ISBN 0-02-864768-8 (v. 1) ISBN 0-02-864767-X (v. 2) DDC 152.4/03
1. *Emotions - Encyclopedias. 2. Affect (Psychology) - Encyclopedias. 3. Mood (Psychology) - Encyclopedias. 1. Levinson, David, 1947- 11. Ponzetti, James J. 111. Jorgensen, Peter F.*
*TC BF531 .E55 1999*

**Encyclopedia of mental health** / editor-in-chief, Howard S. Friedman. San Diego : Academic Press, c1998. 3 v. : ill. ; 29 cm. Includes bibliographical references and index. SUMMARY: "Edited by Howard S. Friedman of the University of California/Riverside (called "the most cited psychologist" by the Social Science Citation Index), this work will be informative and accessible to college students and interested adults. In addition to discussing mental disorders, treatments, and personality attributes, articles focus on such subjects as burnout, caffeine, and commuting and mental health. Each article is formatted clearly with an outline describing its content and a short glossary to explain terminology. A complete table of contents for all volumes in the front of each, bibliographies for further reading at the end of every article, and an extensive index aid use".--"Outstanding Reference Sources : the 1999 Selection of New Titles", American Libraries, May 1999. Comp. by the Reference Sources Committee, RUSA, ALA. CONTENTS: Vol. 1. A-Di -- v. 2. Do-N -- v. 3. O-Z. Index. ISBN 0-12-226675-7 (set) ISBN 0-12-226676-5 (v. 1) ISBN 0-12-226677-3 (v. 2) ISBN 0-12-226678-1 (v. 3). Index. DDC 616.89/003
1. *Mental health - Dictionaries. 2. Psychology - Dictionaries. 3. Mental illness - Dictionaries. 4. Mental Health - encyclopedias. 5. Mental Disorders - encyclopedias. 6. Psychology - encyclopedias. 1. Friedman, Howard S.*
*TC RA790.5 .E53 1998*

**Encyclopedia of multicultural education.**
Mitchell, Bruce M. Westport, Conn. : Greenwood Press, 1999.
*TC LC1099.3 .M58 1999*

**Encyclopedia of nursing research.**
Nursing research digest. New York : Springer Pub. Co., c1999.
*TC RT81.5 .N8736 1999*

**Encyclopedia of people who changed the world.**
Philosophers and religious leaders. Phoenix, Ariz. : Oryx Press, 1999.
*TC B104 .P48 1999*

**Encyclopedia of psychology.**
The Corsini encyclopedia of psychology and behavioral science. 3rd ed. New York : Wiley, 2000.
*TC BF31 .E52 2000*

**Encyclopedia of psychology** / Alan E. Kazdin, editor in chief. Washington, D.C. : American Psychological Association, 2000. 8 v. : ill. ; 28 cm. Includes bibliographical references and index. ISBN 1-55798-650-9 (v. 1 : alk. paper) ISBN 1-55798-187-6 (set : alk. paper) DDC 150/.3
1. *Psychology - Encyclopedias. 1. Kazdin, Alan E.*
*TC BF31 .E52 2000*

**The encyclopedia of sexual behavior.**
Ellis, Albert, ed. [1st ed.]. New York, Hawthorn books [1961-1964]
*TC HQ9 .E4*

**Encyclopedia of smoking and tobacco.**
Hirschfelder, Arlene B. Phoenix, AZ : Oryx Press, 1999.
*TC HV5760 .H57 1999*

**Encyclopedia of special education :** a reference for the education of the handicapped and other exceptional children and adults/ edited by, Cecil R. Reynolds and Elaine Fletcher-Janzen. 2nd ed. New York : J. Wiley & Sons, c2000. 3 v. (xxvii, 1998 p.) : ill. ; 29 cm. Includes bibliographical references and indexes. ISBN 0-471-25309-X (set : alk. paper) ISBN 0-471-25323-5 (v. 1 : alk. paper) ISBN 0-471-25324-3 (v. 2 : alk. paper) ISBN

0-471-25325-1 (v. 3 : alk. paper) DDC 371.9/03
1. *Handicapped children - Education - United States - Encyclopedias. 2. Special education - United States - Encyclopedias. 3. Handicapped - Education - United States - Encyclopedias. 1. Reynolds, Cecil R., 1952- 11. Fletcher-Janzen, Elaine.*
*TC LC4007 .E53 2000*

**Encyclopedia of sports medicine**
Nutrition in sport. Osney Mead, Oxford ; Malden, MA : Blackwell Science, 2000.
*TC QP141 .N793 2000*

**The encyclopedia of understanding alcohol and other drugs.**
O'Brien, Robert, 1932- New York, NY : Facts on File, c1999.
*TC HV5017 .O37 1999*

**ENCYCLOPEDIAS AND DICTIONARIES.** *See* HANDBOOKS, VADE-MECUMS, ETC.; QUESTIONS AND ANSWERS.

**ENCYCLOPEDIAS AND DICTIONARIES, ENGLISH.** *See* ENCYCLOPEDIAS AND DICTIONARIES.

**ENCYCLOPEDIAS AND DICTIONARIES - HISTORY AND CRITICISM.**
Cowie, Anthony Paul. English dictionaries for foreign learners. Oxford : Clarendon Press ; New York : Oxford University Press, 1999.
*TC PE1611 .C58 1999*

Micklethwait, David. Noah Webster and the American dictionary. Jefferson, N.C. : McFarland, c2000.
*TC PE65.W5 M53 2000*

**ENCYCLOPEDIAS AND DICTIONARIES - JUVENILE FILMS.**
Exploring the English language [videorecording]. [Princeton, N.J.] : Video Tutor ; [Chesterton, Ind.? : Distributed by] Griffin Media Design, 1988, c1986.

**ENCYCLOPEDIAS AND DICTIONARIES. <JUVENILE SUBJECT HEADING>.**
Children's illustrated encyclopedia. [2nd] rev. ed. New York : DK Pub., 1998.
*TC AG5 .C535 1998*

**The end of homework.**
Kralovec, Etta. Boston, Mass. : Beacon Press, c2000.
*TC LB1048 .K73 2000*

**Ender, Steven C.** Students helping students : a guide for peer educators on college campuses / Steven C. Ender, Fred B. Newton. 1st ed. San Francisco : Jossey-Bass Publishers, c2000. xvii, 254 p. ; 23 cm. (The Jossey-Bass higher and adult education series) Adaptation of: Students helping students / Steven C. Ender, Sue Saunders McCaffrey, Theodore K. Miller. c1979. Includes bibliographical references (p. 241-245) and index. ISBN 0-7879-4459-9 (alk. paper) DDC 371.4/047
1. *Peer counseling of students. 2. Peer-group tutoring of students. 1. Newton, Fred B. 11. Title. 111. Series.*
*TC LB1027.5 .E52 2000*

**ENDOCRINE GLANDS - DISEASES.** *See* DIABETES.

**ENDOWED CHARITIES.** *See* CHARITIES; ENDOWMENTS.

**ENDOWMENT OF RESEARCH.** *See* EDUCATION AND STATE; SCHOLARSHIPS.

**ENDOWMENTS.** *See* CHARITIES.

**ENDOWMENTS - SOUTHERN STATES - HISTORY.**
Anderson, Eric, 1949- Dangerous donations. Columbia, Mo. : University of Missouri Press, c1999.
*TC LC2707 .A53 1999*

**ENDOWMENTS - UNITED STATES.**
Lagemann, Ellen Condliffe, 1945- The politics of knowledge. 1st ed. Middletown, Conn. : Wesleyan University Press, c1989.
*TC HV97.C3 L34 1989*

Panas, Jerold. Megagifts. Chicago, Ill. : Pluribus Press, c1984.
*TC HV41 .P34 1984*

**ENDOWMENTS - UNITED STATES - DIRECTORIES.**
Directory of grants for organizations serving people with disabilities. Loxahatchee, Fla. : Research Grant Guides, c1993-
*TC HV3006.A4 H35*

Grants for school technology. 3rd ed. Gaithersburg, MD : Aspen Publishers, c2000.

*TC LB2336 .G76365 2000*

**ENDOWMENTS - UNITED STATES - HISTORY.**
Oliver, Frank H. Fellow beggars. 1999.
*TC 06 no.11157*

**ENDURANCE, PHYSICAL.** *See* PHYSICAL FITNESS.

**Energetics of human activity** / W.A. Sparrow, editor. Champaign, IL : Human Kinetics, c2000. vi, 306 p. : ill. ; 24 cm. Includes bibliographical references and index. ISBN 0-88011-787-7 DDC 612.7/6
1. *Human locomotion. 2. Energy metabolism. 3. Human mechanics. 1. Sparrow, William Anthony, 1955-*
*TC QP301 .E568 2000*

**ENERGIZERS, PSYCHIC.** *See* ANTIDEPRESSANTS.

**Energy balance, weight control, metabolism.**
The nutty, nougat-filled world of human nutrition [videorecording]. [Arlington, Va.] : Cerebellum Corp., c1998.
*TC QP141 .N8 1998*

**An energy field more intense than war.**
True, Michael. 1st ed. Syracuse, N.Y. : Syracuse University Press, 1995.
*TC PS169.N65 T78 1995*

**ENERGY METABOLISM.**
Energetics of human activity. Champaign, IL : Human Kinetics, c2000.
*TC QP301 .E568 2000*

Energy-yielding macronutrients and energy metabolism in sports nutrition. Boca Raton, Fla. ; London : CRC Press, c2000.
*TC QP176 .E546 2000*

Exercise metabolism. Champaign, IL : Human Kinetics, c1995.
*TC QP301 .E967 1995*

**ENERGY METABOLISM.**
Exercise metabolism. Champaign, IL : Human Kinetics, c1995.
*TC QP301 .E967 1995*

**ENERGY METABOLISM.**
Exercise physiology. 3rd ed. Mountain View, Calif. : Mayfield Pub., c2000.
*TC QP301 .B885 2000*

Nutrition in sport. Osney Mead, Oxford : Malden, MA : Blackwell Science, 2000.
*TC QP141 .N793 2000*

Wildman, Robert E. C., 1964- Advanced human nutrition. Boca Raton : CRC Press, c2000.
*TC QP141 .W512 2000*

**ENERGY METABOLISM.**
Wildman, Robert E. C., 1964- Advanced human nutrition. Boca Raton : CRC Press, c2000.
*TC QP141 .W512 2000*

**Energy-yielding macronutrients and energy metabolism in sports nutrition** / edited by Judy A. Driskell, Ira Wolinsky. Boca Raton, Fla. ; London : CRC Press, c2000. 337 p. ; 27 cm. (Nutrition in exercise and sport) Includes bibliographical references and index. ISBN 0-8493-0755-4 (alk. paper) DDC 612.3/9/088796
1. *Energy metabolism. 2. Athletes - Nutrition. 3. Dietary supplements. 4. Nutrition. 1. Driskell, Judy A. (Judy Anne) 11. Wolinsky, Ira. 111. Series.*
*TC QP176 .E546 2000*

**ENFANTS - MORALE PRATIQUE - OUVRAGES AVANT 1800.**
Jocelin, Elizabeth, 1596-1622. The mothers legacy to her vnborn [i.e. unborn] childe [i.e. child]. Toronto : University of Toronto Press, 2000.
*TC BV4570 .J62 2000*

**ENFANTS - VIE RELIGIEUSE - OUVRAGES AVANT 1800.**
Jocelin, Elizabeth, 1596-1622. The mothers legacy to her vnborn [i.e. unborn] childe [i.e. child]. Toronto : University of Toronto Press, 2000.
*TC BV4570 .J62 2000*

**Eng, Thomas R.**
Institute of Medicine (U.S.). Committee on Prevention and Control of Sexually Transmitted Diseases. The hidden epidemic. Washington, D.C. : National Academy Press, 1997.
*TC RA644.V4 I495 1997*

**Engaging minds.**
Davis, Brent. Mahwah, N.J. : L. Erlbaum Associates, 2000.
*TC LB1060 .D38 2000*

**Engaging young readers :** promoting achievement and motivation / edited by Linda Baker, Mariam Jean Dreher, John T. Guthrie. New York : Guilford Press, c2000. xv, 331 p. ; 24 cm. (Solving problems in the teaching of literacy) Includes bibliographical references and index. ISBN 1-57230-554-1 (hc. : alk. paper) ISBN 1-57230-535-5 (pbk. : alk. paper) DDC 428.4
*1. Reading (Elementary) - United States. 2. Academic achievement - United States. 3. Motivation in education - United States. I. Baker, Linda. II. Dreher, Mariam Jean. III. Guthrie, John T. IV. Series.*
*TC LB1573 .E655 2000*

**Engel, Michael, 1944-** The struggle for control of public education : market ideology vs. democratic values / Michael Engel. Philadelphia, Pa. : Temple University Press, c2000. xi, 223 p. ; 22 cm. Includes bibliographical references and index. ISBN 1-56639-740-5 (cloth : alk. paper) ISBN 1-56639-741-3 (pbk. : alk. paper) DDC 371.01/0973
*1. Public schools - United States. 2. Politics and education - United States. 3. Education - Economic aspects - United States. 4. School choice - United States. 5. Charter schools - United States. I. Title.*
*TC LA217.2 .E533 2000*

**Engelkamp, Johannes.**
[Erinnern eigener Handlungen. English]
Memory for actions / Johannes Engelkamp. Hove, East Sussex, UK : Psychology Press, c1998. vii, 166 p. : ill. ; 24 cm. (Essays in cognitive psychology, 0959-4779) Includes bibliographical references (p. 147-158) and indexes. ISBN 0-86377-765-1 DDC 153.1/2
*1. Memory. I. Title. II. Series.*
*TC BF371 .E5413 1998*

**Engelsted, Niels.**
Essays in general psychology. Aarhus : Aarhus University Press, c1989.
*TC BF38 .E78 1989*

The societal subject. Aarhus C, Denmark : Aarhus University Press, c1993.
*TC B105.A35 S68 1991*

**ENGINEERING - AUTHORSHIP.** *See* TECHNICAL WRITING.

**ENGINEERING - FORECASTING.**
Bell, Trudy E. Engineering tomorrow :. Piscataway, NJ : IEEE Press, c2000.
*TC T174 .B451 2000*

**ENGINEERING, GENETIC.** *See* GENETIC ENGINEERING.

**ENGINEERING - STUDY AND TEACHING - GREAT BRITAIN.**
McCormick, Kevin, 1944- Engineers in Japan and Britain. London ; New York : Routledge, 2000.
*TC T155 .M37 2000*

**ENGINEERING - STUDY AND TEACHING - JAPAN.**
McCormick, Kevin, 1944- Engineers in Japan and Britain. London ; New York : Routledge, 2000.
*TC T155 .M37 2000*

**Engineering tomorrow.**
Bell, Trudy E. Piscataway, NJ : IEEE Press, c2000.
*TC T174 .B451 2000*

**ENGINEERS.** *See* INVENTORS; LOCOMOTIVE ENGINEERS.

**ENGINEERS - EMPLOYMENT - UNITED STATES.**
Tang, Joyce, 1962- Doing engineering. Lanham, Md. ; Oxford : Rowman & Littlefield Publishers, c2000.
*TC TA157 .T363 2000*

**Engineers in Japan and Britain.**
McCormick, Kevin, 1944- London ; New York : Routledge, 2000.
*TC T155 .M37 2000*

**ENGINEERS - TRAINING OF - GREAT BRITAIN.**
McCormick, Kevin, 1944- Engineers in Japan and Britain. London ; New York : Routledge, 2000.
*TC T155 .M37 2000*

**ENGINEERS - TRAINING OF - JAPAN.**
McCormick, Kevin, 1944- Engineers in Japan and Britain. London ; New York : Routledge, 2000.
*TC T155 .M37 2000*

**ENGINEERS - VOCATIONAL GUIDANCE.**
Enhancing the postdoctoral experience for scientists and engineers. Washington, DC : National Academy Press, 2000.
*TC Q147 .E53 2000*

**The engines of our ingenuity.**
Lienhard, John H., 1930- Oxford ; New York : Oxford University Press, 2000.

*TC T14.5 .L52 2000*

**ENGLAND - CIVILIZATION - CLASSICAL INFLUENCES.**
Stray, Christopher. Classics transformed. Oxford : Clarendon Press ; New York : Oxford University Press, 1998.
*TC PA78.E53 S87 1998*

**ENGLAND - FICTION.**
Rowling, J. K. Harry Potter and the Chamber of Secrets. New York : Arthur A. Levine Books, 1999.
*TC PZ7.R7968 Har 1999*

Rowling, J. K. Harry Potter and the prisoner of Azkaban. New York : Arthur A. Levine Books, 1999.
*TC PZ7.R79835 Ham 1999*

Rowling, J. K. Harry Potter and the sorcerer's stone. 1st American ed. New York : A.A. Levine Books, 1998.
*TC PZ7.R79835 Har 1998*

**ENGLAND - HISTORY.** *See* GREAT BRITAIN - HISTORY.

**ENGLAND - KINGS AND RULERS.** *See* GREAT BRITAIN - KINGS AND RULERS.

**ENGLAND - POLITICS AND GOVERNMENT.** *See* GREAT BRITAIN - POLITICS AND GOVERNMENT.

**ENGLAND - SOCIAL CONDITIONS - 19TH CENTURY.**
Finlayson, Geoffrey B. A. M. Decade of reform; New York, Norton [1970]
*TC HN385 .F54 1970*

Stray, Christopher. Classics transformed. Oxford : Clarendon Press ; New York : Oxford University Press, 1998.
*TC PA78.E53 S87 1998*

**ENGLAND - SOCIAL CONDITIONS - 20TH CENTURY.**
Stray, Christopher. Classics transformed. Oxford : Clarendon Press ; New York : Oxford University Press, 1998.
*TC PA78.E53 S87 1998*

**ENGLAND - SOCIAL LIFE AND CUSTOMS.**
Darton, F. J. Harvey (Frederick Joseph Harvey), 1878-1936. Children's books in England. 3rd ed. / rev. by Brian Alderson. London : British Library ; New Castle, DE : Oak Knoll Press, 1982 (1999 printing)
*TC PR990 .D3 1999*

**England's last chance.**
The American Revolution. [videorecording]. New York, N.Y. : A&E Home Video, c1994.
*TC E208 .A447 1994*

**ENGLISH AESTHETICS.** *See* AESTHETICS, BRITISH.

**ENGLISH AS A FOREIGN LANGUAGE.** *See* ENGLISH LANGUAGE - STUDY AND TEACHING - FOREIGN SPEAKERS; ENGLISH LANGUAGE - TEXTBOOKS FOR FOREIGN SPEAKERS.

**ENGLISH AS A SECOND LANGUAGE.** *See* ENGLISH LANGUAGE - STUDY AND TEACHING - FOREIGN SPEAKERS; ENGLISH LANGUAGE - TEXTBOOKS FOR FOREIGN SPEAKERS.

**English as a second language (Roslyn Heights, N.Y.)**
Basic English [videorecording]. [Roslyn Heights, N.Y.] : Video Aided Instruction, [c1995].
*TC PE1128 .B3 1995*

Intermediate English [videorecording]. [Roslyn Heights, N.Y.] : Video Aided Instruction, [c1995].
*TC PE1128 .I5 1995*

**ENGLISH AUTHORS.** *See* AUTHORS, ENGLISH.

**ENGLISH BIBLE STORIES.** *See* BIBLE STORIES, ENGLISH.

**ENGLISH CHILDREN'S LITERATURE.** *See* CHILDREN'S LITERATURE, ENGLISH.

**ENGLISH CHILDREN'S STORIES.** *See* CHILDREN'S STORIES, ENGLISH.

**The English common reader.**
Altick, Richard Daniel, 1915- 2nd ed. Columbus : Ohio State University Press, [1998], c1957.
*TC Z1003.5.G7 A53 1998*

**ENGLISH COOKERY.** *See* COOKERY, ENGLISH.

**English dictionaries for foreign learners.**
Cowie, Anthony Paul. Oxford : Clarendon Press ; New York : Oxford University Press, 1999.

*TC PE1611 .C58 1999*

**ENGLISH DIDACTIC FICTION.** *See* DIDACTIC FICTION, ENGLISH.

**English education and the radicals 1780-1850.**
Silver, Harold. London ; Boston : Routledge & Kegan Paul, 1975.
*TC LA631.7 .S45*

**ENGLISH FICTION.** *See* CHILDREN'S STORIES, ENGLISH; DIDACTIC FICTION, ENGLISH; PSYCHOLOGICAL FICTION, ENGLISH.

**ENGLISH FICTION - 18TH CENTURY - HISTORY AND CRITICISM.**
Barney, Richard A., 1955- Plots of enlightenment. Stanford, Calif. : Stanford University Press, c1999.
*TC PR858.E38 B37 1999*

**ENGLISH FICTION - HISTORY AND CRITICISM.**
Keroes, Jo. Tales out of school. Carbondale : Southern Illinois University Press, c1999.
*TC PS374.T43 K47 1999*

**ENGLISH FICTION - STORIES, PLOTS, ETC.**
Herald, Diana Tixier. Genreflecting. 5th ed. Englewood, CO : Libraries Umlimited, 2000.
*TC PS374.P63 H47 2000*

**English for specific purposes (New York, N.Y.).**
[English for specific purposes (New York, N.Y. : Online)] English for specific purposes [computer file]. Oxford ; New York : Pergamon,
*TC EJOURNALS*

**[English for specific purposes (New York, N.Y. : Online)]** English for specific purposes [computer file]. Oxford ; New York : Pergamon, Coverage as of Apr. 3, 1998: Vol. 16, issue 1 (1997)- . Mode of access: World Wide Web. Abstracts, tables of contents, and citation information are HTML encoded; articles are available in portable document format (PDF) and as Postscript Level 2 files. Subscription and registration required for access. System requirements: Internet connectivity, World Wide Web browser, and Adobe Acrobat reader. Online version of the print title: English for specific purposes. Description based on: Vol. 16, issue 1 (1997); title from general information screen (viewed Apr. 3, 1998). URL: http://www.sciencedirect.com/science/journal/08894906 URL: http://www.columbia.edu/cu/libraries/indexes/science-direct.html URL: http://www.sciencedirect.com/ URL: http://www.elsevier.com/homepage/elecserv.htt Available in other form: English for specific purposes (New York, N.Y.) ISSN: 0889-4906 (DLC) 87658058 (OCoLC)13909329. ISSN 0889-4906
*1. English language - Study and teaching - Foreign speakers - Periodicals. 2. English language - Business English - Study and teaching - Periodicals. 3. English language - Technical English - Study and teaching - Periodicals. I. Title: ScienceDirect. II. Title: English for specific purposes (New York, N.Y.)*
*TC EJOURNALS*

**The English higher grade schools.**
Vlaeminke, Meriel. London ; Portland, OR : Woburn Press, 2000.
*TC LA634 .V52 2000*

**ENGLISH HORSEMANSHIP.** *See* HORSEMANSHIP.

**English in the digital age.**
Goodwyn, Andrew. London : Cassell, 2000.
*TC PR35 .E65 2000*

**English, June, 1955-** Scholastic encyclopedia of the United States at war / June English, Thomas D. Jones. New York : Scholastic, 1998. 188 p. : col. ill. ; 28 cm. Includes index. SUMMARY: Discusses all of the major wars in which the United States has participated beginning with the American Revolution and concluding with the Gulf War of 1991. ISBN 0-590-59959-3 DDC 973
*1. United States - History, Military - Encyclopedias, Juvenile. 2. United States - History, Military - Encyclopedias. I. Jones, Thomas D. II. Title. III. Title: Scholastic encyclopedia of U.S. at war*
*TC E181 .E64 1998*

**English, Karen.** Nadia's hands / by Karen English ; illustrated by Jonathan Weiner. 1st ed. Honesdale, PA : Boyds Mills Press, 1999. [32] p. : col. ill. ; 29 cm. SUMMARY: A Pakistani-American girl takes part in her aunt's traditional Pakistani wedding. ISBN 1-56397-667-6
*1. Weddings - Juvenile fiction. 2. Pakistan - Social life and customs - Juvenile fiction. I. Weiner, Jonathan. ill. II. Title.*
*TC PZ7.E7232 Na 1999*

**ENGLISH LANGUAGE - ABILITY TESTING.**
Assessment of writing. New York : Modern Language Association of America, 1996.
*TC PE1404 .A88 1996*

Learner-directed assessment in ESL. Mahwah, N.J. : Lawrence Erlbaum Associates, 2000.
*TC PE1128.A2 L359 2000*

**ENGLISH LANGUAGE - ALPHABET - JUVENILE LITERATURE.**
Bea, Holly, 1956- My spiritual alphabet book. Tiburon, Calif. : H.J. Kramer, c2000.
*TC BL625.5 .B43 1999*

J. Paul Getty Museum. A is for artist. Los Angeles : J. Paul Getty Museum, c1997.
*TC N582.M25 A513 1997*

**ENGLISH LANGUAGE - AMERICANISMS.** *See* AMERICANISMS.

**ENGLISH LANGUAGE - ANALYSIS AND PARSING.** *See* ENGLISH LANGUAGE - GRAMMAR.

**ENGLISH LANGUAGE - ANTONYMS.** *See* ENGLISH LANGUAGE - SYNONYMS AND ANTONYMS.

**The English language arts handbook.**
Tchudi, Susan J. (Susan Jane), 1945- 2nd ed. Portsmouth, NH : Boynton/Cook, c1999.
*TC LB1576 .T358 1999*

**ENGLISH LANGUAGE - BUSINESS ENGLISH.**
Knox, Carolyn W. AGS English for the world of work. Circle Pines, Minn. : American Guidance Service, c1997.
*TC PE1127.W65 K66 1997*

Knox, Carolyn W. AGS English for the world of work. Teacher's ed. Circle Pines, Minn. : American Guidance Service, c1997.
*TC PE1127.W65 K66 1997 Teacher's Ed.*

**ENGLISH LANGUAGE - BUSINESS ENGLISH - STUDY AND TEACHING - PERIODICALS.**
[English for specific purposes (New York, N.Y. : Online)] English for specific purposes [computer file]. Oxford ; New York : Pergamon,
*TC EJOURNALS*

**ENGLISH LANGUAGE - CHRESTOMATHIES.** *See* READERS.

**ENGLISH LANGUAGE - COMPOSITION AND EXERCISES.** *See also* ENGLISH LANGUAGE - GRAMMAR.
Babin, Edith H. Contemporary composition studies. Westport, Conn. : Greenwood Press, 1999.
*TC PE1404 .B23 1999*

Botel, Morton. Communicating. Lexington, Mass. : D. C. Heath, c1973.
*TC PE1121 .B67 1973*

Campbell, Cherry. Teaching second-language writing. Pacific Grove : Heinle & Heinle, c1998.
*TC PE1128.A2 C325 1998*

Christ, Henry I. (Henry Irving), 1915- Modern English in action. Lexington, Mass. : D. C. Heath, 1978
*TC PE1112 .C47 1978*

Christ, Henry I. (Henry Irving), 1915- Modern English in action. Lexington, Mass. : D. C. Heath, 1975
*TC PE1112 .C47 1975*

Christ, Henry I. (Henry Irving), 1915- Modern English in action. Teacher's ed. Lexington, Mass. : D. C. Heath, 1975
*TC PE1112 .C47 1975 Teacher's Ed.*

Christ, Henry I. (Henry Irving), 1915- Modern English in action. Teacher's ed. Lexington, Mass. : D. C. Heath, 1978
*TC PE1112 .C47 1978 Teacher's ed.*

Christ, Henry I. (Henry Irving), 1915- Modern English in action. Teacher's ed. Lexington, Mass. : D. C. Heath, 1978
*TC PE1112 .C47 1978 Teacher's Ed.*

Christ, Henry I. (Henry Irving), 1915- Modern English in action. Teacher's ed. Lexington, Mass. : D. C. Heath, 1978
*TC PE1112 .C47 1978 Teacher's Ed.*

History, reflection, and narrative. Stamford, Conn. : Ablex Pub., c1999.
*TC PE1405.U6 H56 1999*

Issues and trends in literacy education. 2nd ed. Boston : Allyn and Bacon, c2000.
*TC LB1576 .I87 2000*

Kirby, Anne. Elementary school English. Teachers' ed. Palo Alto, Calif. : Addison-Wesley Publishing Company, 1967.

*TC PE1112 .K57 1967 Teachers' Ed.*

Kirby, Anne. Elementary school English. Palo Alto, Calif. : Addison-Wesley Publishing Company, 1967.
*TC PE1112 .K57 1967*

Roberts, Paul. The Roberts English series. Teacher's ed. New York : Harcourt, Brace & World c<1966- >
*TC PE1112 .R6 Teacher's edition*

Roberts, Paul. The Roberts English series. Teacher's ed. New York : Harcourt, Brace & World c<1966- >
*TC PE1112 .R6 Teacher's edition*

Taylor, Denny, 1947- Family literacy. Portsmouth, NH : Heinemann, c1998.
*TC LC149 .T37 1998*

Trautman, Barbara A. AGS English to use. Teacher's ed. Circle Pines, Minn. : AGS, American Guidance Service, c1998.
*TC PE1121 .T72 1998 Teacher's Ed.*

Trautman, Barbara A. AGS English to use. Circle Pines, Minn. : AGS, American Guidance Service, c1998.
*TC PE1121 .T72 1998*

Walker, Bonnie L. AGS basic English composition. Circle Pines, Minn. : American Guidance Service, c1997.
*TC PE1408 .W34 1997*

Walker, Bonnie L. AGS basic English composition. Teacher's ed. Circle Pines, Minn. : American Guidance Service, c1997.
*TC PE1408 .W34 1997 Teacher's Ed.*

Walker, Bonnie L. AGS basic English composition. Teacher's ed. Circle Pines, Minn. : American Guidance Service, c1997.
*TC PE1408 .W34 1997 Teacher's Ed.*

Walker, Bonnie L. AGS basic English composition. Teacher's ed. Circle Pines, Minn. : American Guidance Service, c1997.
*TC PE1408 .W34 1997 Teacher's Ed.*

Walker, Bonnie L. AGS basic English grammar. Circle Pines, Minn. : AGS, American Guidance Service, c1997.
*TC PE1112 .W34 1997*

Walker, Bonnie L. AGS basic English grammar. Teacher's ed. Circle Pines, Minn. : AGS, American Guidance Service, c1997.
*TC PE1112 .W34 1997 Teacher's Ed.*

**ENGLISH LANGUAGE - COMPOSITION AND EXERCISES - ABILITY TESTING.**
Speck, Bruce W. Grading students' classroom writing. Washington, DC : Graduate School of Education and Human Development, The George Washington University, 2000.
*TC LB1576 .S723 2000*

**ENGLISH LANGUAGE - COMPOSITION AND EXERCISES - DATA PROCESSING.**
Coogan, David. Electronic writing centers. Stamford, Conn. : Ablex Pub. Corp., c1999.
*TC PE1404 .C6347 1999*

Passions, pedagogies, and 21st century technologies. Logan : Utah State University Press ; Urbana, Ill. : National Council of Teachers of English, c1999.
*TC PE1404 .P38 1999*

**ENGLISH LANGUAGE - COMPOSITION AND EXERCISES - RESEARCH.**
Williams, James D. (James Dale), 1949- Preparing to teach writing. 2nd ed. Mahwah, N.J. : Lawrence Erlbaum Associates, 1998.
*TC PE1404 .W54 1998*

**ENGLISH LANGUAGE - COMPOSITION AND EXERCISES - STUDY AND TEACHING.**
Cava, Margaret T. Second language learner strategies and the unsuccessful second language writer. 1999.
*TC 085 C295*

Cramer, Ronald L. Creative power. New York ; London : Longman, c2001.
*TC LB1576 .C758 2001*

Lensmire, Timothy J., 1961- Powerful writing/responsible teaching. New York : Teachers College Press, c2000.
*TC LB1576 .L42 2000*

**ENGLISH LANGUAGE - COMPOSITION AND EXERCISES - STUDY AND TEACHING - BIBLIOGRAPHY - PERIODICALS.**
CCCC bibliography of composition and rhetoric. Carbondale : Southern Illinois University Press, c1990-

*TC Z5818.E5 L66*

**ENGLISH LANGUAGE - COMPOSITION AND EXERCISES - STUDY AND TEACHING (EARLY CHILDHOOD).**
Children achieving. Newark, Del. : International Reading Association, c1998.
*TC LB1139.5.R43 C55 1998*

McCarrier, Andrea. Interactive writing. Portsmouth, NH : Heinemann, c2000.
*TC LB1139.5.L35 M39 2000*

**ENGLISH LANGUAGE - COMPOSITION AND EXERCISES - STUDY AND TEACHING (EARLY CHILDHOOD) - GREAT BRITAIN.**
MALLETT, MARGARET. Young researchers. London : New York : Routledge, 1999.
*TC LB1576 .M3627 1999*

**ENGLISH LANGUAGE - COMPOSITION AND EXERCISES - STUDY AND TEACHING (EARLY CHILDHOOD) - UNITED STATES.**
Dorn, Linda J. Apprenticeship in literacy. York, Me. : Stenhouse Publishers, c1998.
*TC LB1139.5.L35 D67 1998*

**ENGLISH LANGUAGE - COMPOSITION AND EXERCISES - STUDY AND TEACHING (ELEMENTARY).**
Anderson, Carl, educator. How's it going? Portsmouth, NH : Heinemann, c2000.
*TC LB1576 .A6159 2000*

Cramer, Ronald L. The spelling connection. New York : Guilford Press, c1998.
*TC LB1576 .C65 1998*

Grugeon, Elizabeth. The art of storytelling for teachers and pupils. London : David Fulton, 2000.
*TC LB1042 .G78 2000*

Gunning, Thomas G. Creating literacy instruction for all children. 3rd ed. Boston : Allyn and Bacon, c2000.
*TC LB1573 .G93 2000*

Reading and writing in elementary classrooms. 4th ed. New York : Longman, c2000.
*TC LB1573 .R279 2000*

Tompkins, Gail E. Teaching writing. 3rd ed. Upper Saddle River, N.J. : Merrill, c2000.
*TC LB1576 .T66 2000*

Wollman-Bonilla, Julie. Family message journals. Urbana, Ill. : National Council of Teachers of English, c2000.
*TC LB1576 .W644 2000*

Writers' workshop. Boston ; London : Allyn and Bacon, c2000.
*TC LB1576 .W734 2000*

**ENGLISH LANGUAGE - COMPOSITION AND EXERCISES - STUDY AND TEACHING (ELEMENTARY) - GREAT BRITAIN.**
MALLETT, MARGARET. Young researchers. London : New York : Routledge, 1999.
*TC LB1576 .M3627 1999*

**ENGLISH LANGUAGE - COMPOSITION AND EXERCISES - STUDY AND TEACHING (ELEMENTARY) - UNITED STATES.**
Brusko, Mike. Writing rules!. Portsmouth, NH : Heinemann, c1999.
*TC LB1576 .B876 1999*

Carr, Janine Chappell. A child went forth. Portsmouth, NH : Heinemann, 1999.
*TC LB1576 .C31714 1999*

Fraser, Jane. On their way. Portsmouth, NH : Heinemann, c1994.
*TC LB1576 .F72 1994*

**ENGLISH LANGUAGE - COMPOSITION AND EXERCISES - STUDY AND TEACHING (MIDDLE SCHOOL).**
Winning ways of coaching writing. Boston ; London : Allyn and Bacon, c2001.
*TC LB1631 .W55 2001*

Writers' workshop. Boston ; London : Allyn and Bacon, c2000.
*TC LB1576 .W734 2000*

**ENGLISH LANGUAGE - COMPOSITION AND EXERCISES - STUDY AND TEACHING (SECONDARY).**
Winning ways of coaching writing. Boston ; London : Allyn and Bacon, c2001.
*TC LB1631 .W55 2001*

**ENGLISH LANGUAGE - COMPOSITION AND EXERCISES - STUDY AND TEACHING - UNITED STATES.**

Miller, Wilma H. Ready-to-use activities & materials for improving content reading skills. West Nyack, NY : Center For Applied Research in Education, c1999.
*TC LB1576 .M52 1999*

**ENGLISH LANGUAGE - COMPOUND WORDS - JUVENILE FILMS.**
Exploring the English language [videorecording]. [Princeton, N.J.] : Video Tutor ; [Chesterton, Ind.? : Distributed by] Griffin Media Design, 1988, c1986.

**ENGLISH LANGUAGE - COMPUTER-ASSISTED INSTRUCTION.**
Casey, Jean Marie. Creating the early literacy classroom. Englewood, Colo. : Libraries Unlimited, c2000.
*TC LB1576.7 .C38 2000*

Coogan, David. Electronic writing centers. Stamford, Conn. : Ablex Pub. Corp., c1999.
*TC PE1404 .C6347 1999*

Feminist cyberscapes. Stamford, Conn. : Ablex Pub., c1999.
*TC PE1404 .F39 1999*

Goodwyn, Andrew. English in the digital age. London : Cassell, 2000.
*TC PR35 .E65 2000*

Goodwyn, Andrew. English in the digital age. London : Cassell, 2000.
*TC PR35 .E65 2000*

Language learning online. Austin : Labyrinth Publications, c1998.
*TC PE1128.A2 L2955 1998*

The online writing classroom. Cresskill, N.J. : Hampton Press, c2000.
*TC PE1404 .O45 2000*

Taking flight with OWLs. Mahwah, N.J. : Lawrence Erlbaum Associates, Publishers, 2000.
*TC PE1404 .T24 2000*

Transitions. Greenwich, Conn. : Ablex Pub. Corp., c1998.
*TC PE1404 .T74 1998*

**ENGLISH LANGUAGE - COMPUTER-ASSISTED INSTRUCTION FOR FOREIGN SPEAKERS.**
Quann, Steve. Learning computers, speaking English. Ann Arbor : University of Michigan Press, c2000.
*TC PE1128.A2 .Q83 2000*

**ENGLISH LANGUAGE - DIAGRAMING. See ENGLISH LANGUAGE - GRAMMAR.**

**ENGLISH LANGUAGE - DIALECTS - UNITED STATES. See AMERICANISMS.**

**ENGLISH LANGUAGE - DICTIONARIES. See also PICTURE DICTIONARIES, ENGLISH.**
The American Heritage dictionary of the English language. 4th ed. Boston : Houghton Mifflin, 2000.
*TC PE1628 .A623 2000*

**ENGLISH LANGUAGE - DICTIONARIES - GERMAN.**
1,000 German words. Princeton, N.J. : Berlitz Kids, c1998.
*TC PF3629 .A14 1998*

**ENGLISH LANGUAGE - DICTIONARIES - HISTORY AND CRITICISM. See ENGLISH LANGUAGE - LEXICOGRAPHY.**

**ENGLISH LANGUAGE - DICTIONARIES - ITALIAN.**
NTC's beginner's Italian and English dictionary. Lincolnwood, Ill. : NTC Pub. Group, c1995.
*TC PC1640 .N83 1995*

**ENGLISH LANGUAGE - DICTIONARIES - JUVENILE FILMS.**
Exploring the English language [videorecording]. [Princeton, N.J.] : Video Tutor ; [Chesterton, Ind.? : Distributed by] Griffin Media Design, 1988, c1986.

**ENGLISH LANGUAGE - DICTIONARIES, JUVENILE - FRENCH.**
French picture dictionary. Princeton : Berlitz Kids, Berlitz Pub. Co., c1997.
*TC PC2629 .F74 1997*

**ENGLISH LANGUAGE - DICTIONARIES, JUVENILE - GERMAN.**
German picture dictionary. Princeton, NJ : Berlitz Pub. Co., 1997.
*TC PF3629 .G47 1997*

**ENGLISH LANGUAGE - DICTIONARIES, JUVENILE - ITALIAN.**
Italian picture dictionary. Princeton, NJ : Berlitz Kids, c1997.

*TC PC1629 .I73 1997*

**ENGLISH LANGUAGE - DICTIONARIES, JUVENILE - SPANISH.**
Inglés. Princeton [NJ] : Berlitz Pub. Co., 1997.
*TC PE1628.5 .I54 1997*

Spanish picture dictionary. Princeton [N.J.] : Berlitz Kids, c1997.
*TC PC4629 .S63 1997*

**ENGLISH LANGUAGE - DICTIONARIES - SPANISH.**
Inglés. Princeton [NJ] : Berlitz Pub. Co., 1997.
*TC PE1628.5 .I54 1997*

**ENGLISH LANGUAGE - DISCOURSE ANALYSIS - DATA PROCESSING.**
Lorenz, Gunter R. Adjective intensification--learners versus native speakers. Amsterdam ; Atlanta, GA : Rodopi, 1999.
*TC PE1074.5 .L67 1999*

Partington, Alan. Patterns and meanings. Amsterdam ; Philadelphia : J. Benjamins Pub., c1998.
*TC PE1074.5 .P37 1998*

**ENGLISH LANGUAGE - ERRORS OF USAGE.**
Dictionary of confusable words. Chicago, IL : Fitzroy Dearborn Publ., 2000.
*TC PE1591 .D53 2000*

Edge, Julian, 1948- Mistakes and correction. London ; New York : Longman, 1989.
*TC PE1128.A2 E28 1989*

O'Riordan, Mary. Strategic use of transfer and explicit linguistic knowledge. 1998.
*TC 06 no. 10975*

**ENGLISH LANGUAGE - EXAMINATIONS. See TEST OF ENGLISH AS A FOREIGN LANGUAGE.**

**ENGLISH LANGUAGE - EXAMINATIONS, QUESTIONS, ETC.**
Folse, Keith S. 100 clear grammar tests. Ann Arbor : University of Michigan Press, c2000.
*TC PE1128.A2 F646 2000*

**ENGLISH LANGUAGE - EXERCISES. See ENGLISH LANGUAGE - COMPOSITION AND EXERCISES.**

**ENGLISH LANGUAGE - FILMS FOR FOREIGN SPEAKERS.**
Connect with English [videorecording]. S. Burlington, Vt. : The Annenberg/CPB Collection, c1997.
*TC PE1128 .C66 1997*

**ENGLISH LANGUAGE - FOREIGN COUNTRIES.**
From testing to assessment. London ; New York : Longman, 1994.
*TC PE1128.A2 F778 1994*

**ENGLISH LANGUAGE - FOREIGN SPEAKERS.**
Li, Duan-Duan. Expressing needs and wants in a second language. 1998.
*TC 06 no. 10958*

**ENGLISH LANGUAGE - GLOSSARIES, VOCABULARIES, ETC. - JUVENILE LITERATURE.**
1,000 French words. Princeton, N.J. : Berlitz Kids, Berlitz Pub. Co., 1998.
*TC PC2680 .A15 1998*

1,000 palabras en inglés. Princeton : Berlitz Kids, c1998.
*TC PC4680 .A12 1998*

1,000 Spanish words. Princeton, N.J. : Berlitz Kids, c1998.
*TC PC4680 .A13 1998*

**ENGLISH LANGUAGE - GRAMMAR.**
Basic English [videorecording]. [Roslyn Heights, N.Y.] : Video Aided Instruction, [c1995].
*TC PE1128 .B3 1995*

DeCarrico, Jeanette S. The structure of English. Ann Arbor, Mich. : University of Michigan Press ; Wantage : University Presses Marketing, 2000.
*TC PE1112 .D43 2000*

Intermediate English [videorecording]. [Roslyn Heights, N.Y.] : Video Aided Instruction, [c1995].
*TC PE1128 .I5 1995*

Measham, D. C. English now and then. Cambridge [Eng.] University Press, 1965.
*TC PE1112 .M4*

Quigley, Jean. The grammar of autobiography. Mahwah, N.J. : Lawrence Erlbaum Associates, c2000.
*TC PE1112 .M4*

*TC PE1315.M6 Q54 2000*

Walker, Bonnie L. AGS basic English composition. Circle Pines, Minn. : American Guidance Service, c1997.
*TC PE1408 .W34 1997*

Walker, Bonnie L. AGS basic English composition. Teacher's ed. Circle Pines, Minn. : American Guidance Service, c1997.
*TC PE1408 .W34 1997 Teacher's Ed.*

Walker, Bonnie L. AGS basic English composition. Teacher's ed. Circle Pines, Minn. : American Guidance Service, c1997.
*TC PE1408 .W34 1997 Teacher's Ed.*

Walker, Bonnie L. AGS basic English composition. Teacher's ed. Circle Pines, Minn. : American Guidance Service, c1997.
*TC PE1408 .W34 1997 Teacher's Ed.*

Walker, Bonnie L. AGS basic English grammar. Circle Pines, Minn. : AGS, American Guidance Service, c1997.
*TC PE1112 .W34 1997*

Walker, Bonnie L. AGS basic English grammar. Teacher's ed. Circle Pines, Minn. : AGS, American Guidance Service, c1997.
*TC PE1112 .W34 1997 Teacher's Ed.*

**ENGLISH LANGUAGE - GRAMMAR - 1950-.**
Roberts, Paul. The Roberts English series. Teacher's ed. New York : Harcourt, Brace & World c<1966- >
*TC PE1112 .R6 Teacher's edition*

Roberts, Paul. The Roberts English series. Teacher's ed. New York : Harcourt, Brace & World c<1966- >
*TC PE1112 .R6 Teacher's edition*

**ENGLISH LANGUAGE - GRAMMAR - JUVENILE FILMS.**
Exploring the English language [videorecording]. [Princeton, N.J.] : Video Tutor ; [Chesterton, Ind.? : Distributed by] Griffin Media Design, 1988, c1986.

**ENGLISH LANGUAGE - GRAMMAR - PROBLEMS, EXERCISES, ETC.**
Christ, Henry I. (Henry Irving), 1915- Modern English in action. Lexington, Mass. : D. C. Heath, 1978
*TC PE1112 .C47 1978*

Christ, Henry I. (Henry Irving), 1915- Modern English in action. Lexington, Mass. : D. C. Heath, 1975
*TC PE1112 .C47 1975*

Christ, Henry I. (Henry Irving), 1915- Modern English in action. Teacher's ed. Lexington, Mass. : D. C. Heath, 1975
*TC PE1112 .C47 1975 Teacher's Ed.*

Christ, Henry I. (Henry Irving), 1915- Modern English in action. Teacher's ed. Lexington, Mass. : D. C. Heath, 1978
*TC PE1112 .C47 1978 Teacher's ed.*

Christ, Henry I. (Henry Irving), 1915- Modern English in action. Teacher's ed. Lexington, Mass. : D. C. Heath, 1978
*TC PE1112 .C47 1978 Teacher's Ed.*

Christ, Henry I. (Henry Irving), 1915- Modern English in action. Teacher's ed. Lexington, Mass. : D. C. Heath, 1978
*TC PE1112 .C47 1978 Teacher's Ed.*

Kirby, Anne. Elementary school English. Teachers' ed. Palo Alto, Calif. : Addison-Wesley Publishing Company, 1967.
*TC PE1112 .K57 1967 Teachers' Ed.*

Kirby, Anne. Elementary school English. Palo Alto, Calif. : Addison-Wesley Publishing Company, 1967.
*TC PE1112 .K57 1967*

**ENGLISH LANGUAGE - GRAMMAR - STUDY AND TEACHING (SECONDARY).**
Noden, Harry R. Image grammar. Portsmouth, NH : Heinemann, 1999.
*TC LB1631 .N62 1999*

**ENGLISH LANGUAGE - GREAT BRITAIN - COMPOSITION AND EXERCISES.**
Literacy in the secondary school. London : David Fulton, 2000.
*TC LB1632 .L587 2000*

**ENGLISH LANGUAGE - HISTORY.**
Measham, D. C. English now and then. Cambridge [Eng.] University Press, 1965.
*TC PE1112 .M4*

**ENGLISH LANGUAGE IN THE UNITED STATES.** *See* ENGLISH LANGUAGE - UNITED STATES.

**ENGLISH LANGUAGE - LEXICOGRAPHY.**
Cowie, Anthony Paul. English dictionaries for foreign learners. Oxford : Clarendon Press ; New York : Oxford University Press, 1999.
*TC PE1611 .C58 1999*

**ENGLISH LANGUAGE - LEXICOGRAPHY - HISTORY.**
Micklethwait, David. Noah Webster and the American dictionary. Jefferson, N.C. : McFarland, c2000.
*TC PE65.W5 M53 2000*

**ENGLISH LANGUAGE - MODALITY.**
Quigley, Jean. The grammar of autobiography. Mahwah, N.J. : Lawrence Erlbaum Associates, c2000.
*TC PE1315.M6 Q54 2000*

Stubbs, Michael, 1947- Text and corpus analysis. Oxford, OX, UK ; Cambridge, Mass., USA : Blackwell Publishers, c1996.
*TC P302 .S773 1996*

**ENGLISH LANGUAGE - MORPHOLOGY.** *See* ENGLISH LANGUAGE - WORD FORMATION.

**ENGLISH LANGUAGE - NETHERLANDS - DELFT.**
Klaassen, R. G. Effective lecturing behaviour in English-medium instruction. Delft, Netherlands : Delft University Press, 1999.
*TC LB2393 .K53 1999*

**ENGLISH LANGUAGE - ORTHOGRAPHY AND SPELLING.**
Vos Savant, Marilyn, 1946- The art of spelling. New York : W.W. Norton, 2000.
*TC PE1143 .V67 2000*

Words their way. 2nd ed. Upper Saddle River, N.J. : Merrill, c2000.
*TC LB1050.44 .B43 2000*

**ENGLISH LANGUAGE - ORTHOGRAPHY AND SPELLING - STUDY AND TEACHING.**
Pinnell, Gay Su. Word matters. Portsmouth, NH : Heinemann, c1998.
*TC LB1573.3 .P55 1998*

**ENGLISH LANGUAGE - ORTHOGRAPHY AND SPELLING - STUDY AND TEACHING (ELEMENTARY).**
Cramer, Ronald L. The spelling connection. New York : Guilford Press, c1998.
*TC LB1574 .C65 1998*

Gentry, J. Richard Spelling connections. Columbus, Ohio : Zaner Bloser, c1996.
*TC LB1574 .G46 1996 Gr. 1*

Gentry, J. Richard Spelling connections. Columbus, Ohio : Zaner Bloser, c1996.
*TC LB1574 .G46 1996 Gr. 3*

Gentry, J. Richard Spelling connections. Columbus, Ohio : Zaner Bloser, c1996.
*TC LB1574 .G46 1996 Gr. 5*

Hughes, Margaret, 1941- The violent E and other tricky sounds. York, Me. : Stenhouse Publishers ; Markham, Ontario : Pembroke Publishers Limited, c1997.
*TC LB1574 .H84 1997*

Rosencrans, Gladys. The spelling book. Newark, Del. : International Reading Association, c1998.
*TC LB1574 .R654 1998*

Westwood, Peter S. Spelling :. Camberwell, Vic. : ACER Press, 1999.
*TC LB1574 .W47 1999*

**ENGLISH LANGUAGE - ORTHOGRAPHY AND SPELLING - STUDY AND TEACHING (ELEMENTARY) - UNITED STATES.**
Gunning, Thomas G. Building words. Boston : London : Allyn and Bacon, c2001.
*TC LB1573.3 .G83 2001*

**ENGLISH LANGUAGE - ORTHOGRAPHY AND SPELLING - STUDY AND TEACHING (SECONDARY).**
Gentry, J. Richard Spelling connections. Columbus, Ohio : Zaner Bloser, c1996.
*TC LB1574 .G46 1996 Gr. 1*

Gentry, J. Richard Spelling connections. Columbus, Ohio : Zaner Bloser, c1996.
*TC LB1574 .G46 1996 Gr. 3*

Gentry, J. Richard Spelling connections. Columbus, Ohio : Zaner Bloser, c1996.

*TC LB1574 .G46 1996 Gr. 5*

**ENGLISH LANGUAGE - PARTS OF SPEECH - JUVENILE FILMS.**
Exploring the English language [videorecording]. [Princeton, N.J.] : Video Tutor ; [Chesterton, Ind.? : Distributed by] Griffin Media Design, 1988, c1986.

**ENGLISH LANGUAGE - PHONEMICS - STUDY AND TEACHING (PRIMARY).**
Phonics review kit [kit]. Chicago, Ill. : Open Court Pub. Co., c1995.
*TC LB1573.3 .P45 1995*

Teacher toolbox [kit]. Chicago, Ill. : Open Court Pub. Co., c1995.
*TC LB1573.3 .T4 1995*

**ENGLISH LANGUAGE - PHONETICS.** *See* READING - PHONETIC METHOD.

**ENGLISH LANGUAGE - PHONETICS - STUDY AND TEACHING (EARLY CHILDHOOD).**
Blachman, Benita A. Road to the code. Baltimore : Paul H. Brookes, c2000.
*TC LB1139.L3 B53 2000*

**ENGLISH LANGUAGE - PHONETICS - STUDY AND TEACHING (ELEMENTARY).**
Goldsworthy, Candace L. Sourcebook of phonological awareness activities. San Diego : Singular Pub. Group, c1998.
*TC LB1050.5 .G66 1998*

**ENGLISH LANGUAGE - PHONETICS - STUDY AND TEACHING (PRESCHOOL).**
Goldsworthy, Candace L. Sourcebook of phonological awareness activities. San Diego : Singular Pub. Group, c1998.
*TC LB1050.5 .G66 1998*

**ENGLISH LANGUAGE - PROBLEMS, EXERCISES, ETC.**
Botel, Morton. Communicating. Lexington, Mass. : D. C. Heath, c1973.
*TC PE1121 .B67 1973 Bk A*

Ramírez de Mellor, Elva Fun with English. Pupil's ed. Mexico : McGraw-Hill c1987
*TC PE1129.S8 .R35 1987*

Richards, J. C. (Jack Croft), 1943- Passages. Cambridge : Cambridge University Press, 2000.
*TC PE1128 .R4599 2000*

Richards, Jack C. Passages. Cambridge, U.K. ; New York : Cambridge University Press, 2000.
*TC PE1128 .R4599 2000*

**ENGLISH LANGUAGE - PROBLEMS, EXERCISES, ETC. - JUVENILE FILMS.**
Exploring the English language [videorecording]. [Princeton, N.J.] : Video Tutor ; [Chesterton, Ind.? : Distributed by] Griffin Media Design, 1988, c1986.

**ENGLISH LANGUAGE - PROVINCIALISMS - UNITED STATES.** *See* AMERICANISMS.

**ENGLISH LANGUAGE - READERS.** *See* READERS.

**ENGLISH LANGUAGE - RESEARCH - DATA PROCESSING.**
Lorenz, Gunter R. Adjective intensification--learners versus native speakers. Amsterdam ; Atlanta, GA : Rodopi, 1999.
*TC PE1074.5 .L67 1999*

Partington, Alan. Patterns and meanings. Amsterdam ; Philadelphia : J. Benjamins Pub., c1998.
*TC PE1074.5 .P37 1998*

**ENGLISH LANGUAGE - REVERSE DICTIONARIES.** *See* ENGLISH LANGUAGE - SYNONYMS AND ANTONYMS.

**ENGLISH LANGUAGE - RHETORIC.** *See also* ENGLISH LANGUAGE - COMPOSITION AND EXERCISES.
Measham, D. C. English now and then, Cambridge [Eng.] : University Press, 1965.
*TC PE1112 .M4*

Moon, Jennifer A. Learning journals. London : Kogan Page, 1999.
*TC PE1408 .M66 1999*

Nash, Walter. Creating texts. London ; New York : Longman, 1997.
*TC PE1408 .N22 1997*

**ENGLISH LANGUAGE - RHETORIC - COMPUTER NETWORK RESOURCES.**
The online writing classroom. Cresskill, N.J. : Hampton Press, c2000.

**ENGLISH LANGUAGE - RHETORIC - PROBLEMS, EXERCISES, ETC.**
Literacies. 2nd ed. New York : W.W. Norton, c2000.
*TC PE1417 .L62 2000*

**ENGLISH LANGUAGE - RHETORIC - STUDY AND TEACHING.**
The Allyn & Bacon sourcebook for college writing teachers. Boston : London : Allyn and Bacon, 2000.
*TC PE1404 .A45 2000*

Assessment of writing. New York : Modern Language Association of America, 1996.
*TC PE1404 .A88 1996*

Babin, Edith H. Contemporary composition studies. Westport, Conn. : Greenwood Press, 1999.
*TC PE1404 .B23 1999*

Comp tales. New York : Longman, c2000.
*TC PE1404 .C617 2000*

Elbow, Peter. Everyone can write. New York : Oxford University Press, 2000.
*TC PE1404 .E42 2000*

Flower, Linda. Learning to rival. Mahwah, New Jersey : Lawrence Erlbaum Associates, c2000.
*TC PE1404 .F59 2000*

Kaufer, David S. Designing interactive worlds with words. Mahwah, N.J. : Lawrence Erlbaum Associates, 2000.
*TC PE1404 .K38 2000*

Reforming college composition. Westport, Conn. : Greenwood Press, 2000.
*TC PE1404 .R383 2000*

A Rhetoric of doing. Carbondale : Southern Illinois University Press, c1992.
*TC PE1404 .R496 1992*

Romano, Tom. Blending genre, altering style. Portsmouth, NH : Boynton/Cook ; Heinemann, c2000.
*TC PE1404 .R635 2000*

Roskelly, Hephzibah. Reason to believe. Albany : State University of New York Press, c1998.
*TC PE1404 .R67 1998*

Self-assessment and development in writing. Cresskill, N.J. : Hampton Press, c2000.
*TC PE1404 .S37 2000*

A sourcebook for responding to student writing. Cresskill, N.J. : Hampton Press, c1999.
*TC PE1404 .S683 1999*

Stories from the center. Urbana, Ill. National Council of Teachers of English, c2000.
*TC PE1404 .S834 2000*

Student writing in higher education. Philadelphia, Pa. : Open University Press, c2000.
*TC PE1404 .S84 2000*

Teaching in the 21st century. New York : Falmer Press, 1999.
*TC PE1404 .T394 1999*

Transitions. Greenwich, Conn. : Ablex Pub. Corp., c1998.
*TC PE1404 .T74 1998*

Working with student writers. New York : P. Lang, c1999.
*TC PE1404 .W66 1999*

Worlds apart. Mahwah, N.J. : L. Erlbaum Associates, 1999.
*TC PE1404 .W665 1999*

The writing teacher's sourcebook. 4th ed. New York : Oxford University Press, 2000.
*TC PE1404 .W74 2000*

**ENGLISH LANGUAGE - RHETORIC - STUDY AND TEACHING - BIBLIOGRAPHY - PERIODICALS.**
CCCC bibliography of composition and rhetoric. Carbondale : Southern Illinois University Press, c1990-
*TC Z5818.E5 L66*

**ENGLISH LANGUAGE - RHETORIC - STUDY AND TEACHING - DATA PROCESSING.**
Coogan, David. Electronic writing centers. Stamford, Conn. : Ablex Pub. Corp., c1999.
*TC PE1404 .C6347 1999*

Feminist cyberscapes. Stamford, Conn. : Ablex Pub., c1999.
*TC PE1404 .F39 1999*

The online writing classroom. Cresskill, N.J. : Hampton Press, c2000.

*TC PE1404 .O45 2000*

Passions, pedagogies, and 21st century technologies. Logan : Utah State University Press ; Urbana, Ill. : National Council of Teachers of English, c1999.
*TC PE1404 .P38 1999*

Taking flight with OWLs. Mahwah, N.J. : Lawrence Erlbaum Associates, Publishers, 2000.
*TC PE1404 .T24 2000*

**ENGLISH LANGUAGE - RHETORIC - STUDY AND TEACHING - GREAT BRITAIN.**
Students writing in the university. Amsterdam ; Philadelphia : John Benjamins Pub., c1999.
*TC PE1405.G7 S78 1999*

**ENGLISH LANGUAGE - RHETORIC - STUDY AND TEACHING (HIGHER) - PERIODICALS.**
Trends & issues in postsecondary English studies. Urbana, Ill. : National Council of Teachers of English, c1999-
*TC PE65 .T75*

**ENGLISH LANGUAGE - RHETORIC - STUDY AND TEACHING (HIGHER) - UNITED STATES.**
Comp tales. New York : Longman, c2000.
*TC PE1404 .C617 2000*

**ENGLISH LANGUAGE - RHETORIC - STUDY AND TEACHING - MORAL AND ETHICAL ASPECTS.**
Ethical issues in college writing. New York ; Canterbury [England] : Peter Lang, c1999.
*TC PE1404 .E84 1999*

**ENGLISH LANGUAGE - RHETORIC - STUDY AND TEACHING - POLITICAL ASPECTS.**
(Re)visioning composition textbooks. Albany : State University of New York Press, c1999.
*TC PE1404 .R46 1999*

**ENGLISH LANGUAGE - RHETORIC - STUDY AND TEACHING - POLITICAL ASPECTS - UNITED STATES.**
Parks, Stephen, 1963- Class politics. Urbana, Ill. : National Council of Teachers of English, c2000.
*TC PE1405.U6 P3 2000*

**ENGLISH LANGUAGE - RHETORIC - STUDY AND TEACHING - PSYCHOLOGICAL ASPECTS.**
Davis, D. Diane (Debra Diane), 1963- Breaking up (at) totality. Carbondale : Southern Illinois University Press, c2000.
*TC PE1404 .D385 2000*

**ENGLISH LANGUAGE - RHETORIC - STUDY AND TEACHING - RESEARCH.**
Williams, James D. (James Dale), 1949- Preparing to teach writing. 2nd ed. Mahwah, N.J. : Lawrence Erlbaum Associates, 1998.
*TC PE1404 .W54 1998*

**ENGLISH LANGUAGE - RHETORIC - STUDY AND TEACHING - SOCIAL ASPECTS.**
Davis, D. Diane (Debra Diane), 1963- Breaking up (at) totality. Carbondale : Southern Illinois University Press, c2000.
*TC PE1404 .D385 2000*

Haake, Katharine. What our speech disrupts. Urbana, Ill. : National Council of Teachers of English, c2000.
*TC PE1404 .H3 2000*

(Re)visioning composition textbooks. Albany : State University of New York Press, c1999.
*TC PE1404 .R46 1999*

**ENGLISH LANGUAGE - RHETORIC - STUDY AND TEACHING - TECHNOLOGICAL INNOVATIONS.**
Passions, pedagogies, and 21st century technologies. Logan : Utah State University Press ; Urbana, Ill. : National Council of Teachers of English, c1999.
*TC PE1404 .P38 1999*

Transitions. Greenwich, Conn. : Ablex Pub. Corp., c1998.
*TC PE1404 .T74 1998*

**ENGLISH LANGUAGE - RHETORIC - STUDY AND TEACHING - TERMINOLOGY.**
Babin, Edith H. Contemporary composition studies. Westport, Conn. : Greenwood Press, 1999.
*TC PE1404 .B23 1999*

**ENGLISH LANGUAGE - RHETORIC - STUDY AND TEACHING - UNITED STATES - HISTORY - 20TH CENTURY.**
History, reflection, and narrative. Stamford, Conn. : Ablex Pub., c1999.

*TC PE1405.U6 H56 1999*

**ENGLISH LANGUAGE - RHETORIC - TEXTBOOKS - HISTORY - 20TH CENTURY.**
(Re)visioning composition textbooks. Albany : State University of New York Press, c1999.
*TC PE1404 .R46 1999*

**ENGLISH LANGUAGE - RHETORIC - TEXTBOOKS - PUBLISHING.**
(Re)visioning composition textbooks. Albany : State University of New York Press, c1999.
*TC PE1404 .R46 1999*

**ENGLISH LANGUAGE - RHYME - DICTIONARIES.**
Young, Sue, 1932- The Scholastic rhyming dictionary. New York : Scholastic Reference, c1994.
*TC PE1519 .Y684 1994*

**ENGLISH LANGUAGE - RHYME - DICTIONARIES, JUVENILE.**
Young, Sue, 1932- The Scholastic rhyming dictionary. New York : Scholastic Reference, c1994.
*TC PE1519 .Y684 1994*

**ENGLISH LANGUAGE - RHYME - STUDY AND TEACHING (PRIMARY).**
Teacher toolbox [kit]. Chicago, Ill. : Open Court Pub. Co., c1995.
*TC LB1573.3 .T4 1995*

**ENGLISH LANGUAGE - RIME.** *See* **ENGLISH LANGUAGE - RHYME.**

**ENGLISH LANGUAGE - SCIENTIFIC ENGLISH.** *See* **ENGLISH LANGUAGE - TECHNICAL ENGLISH.**

**ENGLISH LANGUAGE - SELF-INSTRUCTION.**
Basic English [videorecording]. [Roslyn Heights, N.Y.] : Video Aided Instruction, [c1995].
*TC PE1128 .B3 1995*

Connect with English [videorecording]. S. Burlington, Vt. : The Annenberg/CPB Collection, c1997.
*TC PE1128 .C66 1997*

Intermediate English [videorecording]. [Roslyn Heights, N.Y.] : Video Aided Instruction, [c1995].
*TC PE1128 .I5 1995*

**ENGLISH LANGUAGE - SENTENCES - JUVENILE FILMS.**
Exploring the English language [videorecording]. [Princeton, N.J.] : Video Tutor : [Chesterton, Ind.? : Distributed by] Griffin Media Design, 1988, c1986.

**English language series**
(20) Nash, Walter. Creating texts. London ; New York : Longman, 1997.
*TC PE1408 .N22 1997*

**ENGLISH LANGUAGE - SOCIAL ASPECTS - CHINA.**
Culture, literacy, and learning English. Portsmouth, NH : Boynton/Cook Publishers, c1998.
*TC PE1130.C4 C85 1998*

**ENGLISH LANGUAGE - SOCIAL ASPECTS - UNITED STATES.**
Rickford, John R., 1949- Spoken soul. New York ; Chichester [England] : Wiley, c2000.
*TC PE3102.N42 R54 2000*

**ENGLISH LANGUAGE - SPELLING.** *See* **ENGLISH LANGUAGE - ORTHOGRAPHY AND SPELLING.**

**ENGLISH LANGUAGE - SPELLING - FICTION.**
Falwell, Cathryn. Word wizard. New York : Clarion Books, c1998.
*TC PZ7.F198 Wo 1998*

**ENGLISH LANGUAGE - SPOKEN ENGLISH - EXAMINATIONS.**
Folse, Keith S. 100 clear grammar tests. Ann Arbor : University of Michigan Press, c2000.
*TC PE1128.A2 F646 2000*

**ENGLISH LANGUAGE - SPOKEN ENGLISH - MODALITY.**
Kunz, Linda Ann. English modals in American talk shows. 1999.
*TC 06 no. 11136*

**ENGLISH LANGUAGE - SPOKEN ENGLISH - UNITED STATES.**
Kunz, Linda Ann. English modals in American talk shows. 1999.
*TC 06 no. 11136*

Rickford, John R., 1949- Spoken soul. New York ; Chichester [England] : Wiley, c2000.

*TC PE3102.N42 R54 2000*

**ENGLISH LANGUAGE - STANDARDIZATION.**
Milroy, James. Authority in language. 3rd ed. London [England] ; New York : Routledge, 1999.
*TC P368 .M54 1999*

**ENGLISH LANGUAGE - STUDY AND TEACHING.**
Mellgren, Lars. New horizons in English, [workbooks]. Reading, Mass. : Addison-Wesley Pub. Co., 1973-c1978.
*TC PE1128 .M38*

Multiliteracies. London ; New York : Routledge, 2000.
*TC LC149 .M85 2000*

Tchudi, Susan J. (Susan Jane), 1945- The English language arts handbook. 2nd ed. Portsmouth, NH : Boynton/Cook, c1999.
*TC LB1576 .T358 1999*

**ENGLISH LANGUAGE - STUDY AND TEACHING - AFRO-AMERICAN STUDENTS.** *See* **BLACK ENGLISH.**

**ENGLISH LANGUAGE - STUDY AND TEACHING - ASIA - CONGRESSES.**
Bilingualism Through the Classroom : Strategies and Practices (1995 : Universiti Brunei Darussalam) Bilingualism through the classroom : strategies and practices. [Bandar Seri Begawan : Universiti Brunei Darussalam, 1995]
*TC P115 .B57 1995*

**ENGLISH LANGUAGE - STUDY AND TEACHING - AUDIO-VISUAL AIDS.**
Connect with English [videorecording]. S. Burlington, Vt. : The Annenberg/CPB Collection, c1997.
*TC PE1128 .C66 1997*

Goodwyn, Andrew. English in the digital age. London : Cassell, 2000.
*TC PR35 .E65 2000*

**ENGLISH LANGUAGE - STUDY AND TEACHING - CHINA.**
Culture, literacy, and learning English. Portsmouth, NH : Boynton/Cook Publishers, c1998.
*TC PE1130.C4 C85 1998*

Ting, Yenren, 1948- Learning English text by heart in a Chinese university. [New York : Columbia University], 1999.
*TC 085 T438*

**ENGLISH LANGUAGE - STUDY AND TEACHING - CHINA - CHINESE SPEAKERS.**
Ting, Yenren, 1948- Learning English text by heart in a Chinese university. [New York : Columbia University], 1999.
*TC 085 T438*

**ENGLISH LANGUAGE - STUDY AND TEACHING - CHINESE SPEAKERS.**
Culture, literacy, and learning English. Portsmouth, NH : Boynton/Cook Publishers, c1998.
*TC PE1130.C4 C85 1998*

**ENGLISH LANGUAGE - STUDY AND TEACHING - CHINESE SPEAKERS - TAIWAN - CASE STUDIES.**
Tian, Shiau-ping. TOEFL reading comprehension. 2000.
*TC 06 no. 11316*

**ENGLISH LANGUAGE - STUDY AND TEACHING - COMPUTER-ASSISTED INSTRUCTION.**
The Internet. Oxford ; New York : Oxford University Press, c2000.
*TC TK5105.875.I57 I57 2000*

**ENGLISH LANGUAGE - STUDY AND TEACHING - CONGRESSES.**
Bilingualism Through the Classroom : Strategies and Practices (1995 : Universiti Brunei Darussalam) Bilingualism through the classroom : strategies and practices. [Bandar Seri Begawan : Universiti Brunei Darussalam, 1995]
*TC P115 .B57 1995*

**ENGLISH LANGUAGE - STUDY AND TEACHING - DATA PROCESSING.**
Partington, Alan. Patterns and meanings. Amsterdam ; Philadelphia : J. Benjamins Pub., c1998.
*TC PE1074.5 .P37 1998*

**ENGLISH LANGUAGE - STUDY AND TEACHING (ELEMENTARY).**
Christ, Henry I. (Henry Irving), 1915- Modern English in action. Teacher's ed. Lexington, Mass. : D. C. Heath, 1975

*TC PE1112 .C47 1975 Teacher's Ed.*

Christ, Henry I. (Henry Irving), 1915- Modern
English in action. Teacher's ed. Lexington, Mass. : D.
C. Heath, 1978
*TC PE1112 .C47 1978 Teacher's ed.*

Christ, Henry I. (Henry Irving), 1915- Modern
English in action. Teacher's ed. Lexington, Mass. : D.
C. Heath, 1978
*TC PE1112 .C47 1978 Teacher's Ed.*

Christ, Henry I. (Henry Irving), 1915- Modern
English in action. Teacher's ed. Lexington, Mass. : D.
C. Heath, 1978
*TC PE1112 .C47 1978 Teacher's Ed.*

Kirby, Anne. Elementary school English. Teachers'
ed. Palo Alto, Calif. : Addison-Wesley Publishing
Company, 1967.
*TC PE1112 .K57 1967 Teachers' Ed.*

Phillips, Diane. Projects with young learners. Oxford ;
New York : Oxford University Press, c1999.
*TC LB1576 .P577 1999*

Ragno, Nancy N. World of language. [Teacher ed.].
Morristown, NJ : Silver Burdett & Ginn, c1990.

Ragno, Nancy N. World of language. [Teacher ed.].
Morristown, NJ : Silver Burdett & Ginn, c1990.

Ragno, Nancy N. World of language. [Teacher ed.].
Morristown, NJ : Silver Burdett & Ginn, c1990.

Ragno, Nancy Nickell. World of language. Needham,
Ma. : Silver Burdett Ginn, c1996.
*TC LB1576 .S4471 1996*

Ragno, Nancy Nickell. World of language. Needham,
Mass. : Silver Burdett Ginn, c1996.
*TC LB1576 .S4471 1996*

Ramírez de Mellor, Elva Fun with english. Mexico :
McGraw-Hill c1987
*TC PE1129.S8 .R35 1987*

Roberts, Paul. The Roberts English series. Teacher's
ed. New York : Harcourt, Brace & World c<1966- >
*TC PE1112 .R6 Teacher's edition*

Roberts, Paul. The Roberts English series. Teacher's
ed. New York : Harcourt, Brace & World c<1966- >
*TC PE1112 .R6 Teacher's edition*

World of language. Needham, Mass. : Silver Burdett
Ginn, c1996.
*TC LB1576 .S4471 1996*

World of language. Teacher ed. Needham, Mass. :
Silver Burdett Ginn, c1996.
*TC LB1576 .S4471 1996 Teacher Ed.*

### ENGLISH LANGUAGE - STUDY AND TEACHING (ELEMENTARY) - ACTIVITY PROGRAMS.
Phillips, Sarah. Drama with children. Oxford ; New
York : Oxford University Press, c1999.
*TC PN3171 .P45 1999*

### ENGLISH LANGUAGE - STUDY AND TEACHING (ELEMENTARY) - ENGLAND.
Issues in English teaching. London ; New York :
Routledge, 2000.
*TC LB1576 .I89 2000*

### ENGLISH LANGUAGE - STUDY AND TEACHING (ELEMENTARY) - GREAT BRITAIN.
Drever, Mina. Teaching English in primary
classrooms. Stoke on Trent, Staffordshire, England :
Trentham Books, 1999.
*TC LB1576 .D749 1999*

An Introduction to oracy. London : Cassell, 1998.
*TC P95.4.G7 I58 1998*

Use of language across the primary curriculum.
London ; New York : Routledge, 1998.
*TC LB1576 U74 1998*

Wilson, Angela. Language knowledge for primary
teachers :. London : David Fulton, 1999.
*TC LB1576 .W557 1999*

### ENGLISH LANGUAGE - STUDY AND TEACHING (ELEMENTARY) - WALES.
Issues in English teaching. London ; New York :
Routledge, 2000.
*TC LB1576 .I89 2000*

### ENGLISH LANGUAGE - STUDY AND TEACHING - EUROPE.
English teacher education in Europe. Frankfurt am
Main ; New York : P. Lang, 1999.
*TC PE1128.A2 E547 1999*

### ENGLISH LANGUAGE - STUDY AND TEACHING - FOREIGN SPEAKERS.
Arias, Rafael. Analysis of discourse in an ESL peer-
mentoring teacher group. 1999.
*TC 06 no. 10791*

Campbell, Cherry. Teaching second-language writing.
Pacific Grove : Heinle & Heinle, c1998.
*TC PE1128.A2 C325 1998*

Canagarajah, A. Suresh. Resisting linguistic
imperialism in English teaching. Oxford : Oxford
University Press, 1999.
*TC PE1068.S7 C36 1999*

Cava, Margaret T. Second language learner strategies
and the unsuccessful second language writer. 1999.
*TC 085 C295*

Connect with English [videorecording]. S. Burlington,
Vt. : The Annenberg/CPB Collection, c1997.
*TC PE1128 .C66 1997*

Echevarria, Jana, 1956- Making content
comprehensible for English language learners.
Boston, MA : Allyn and Bacon, 2000.
*TC PE1128.A2 E24 2000*

Edge, Julian, 1948- Mistakes and correction. London ;
New York : Longman, 1989.
*TC PE1128.A2 E28 1989*

English teacher education in Europe. Frankfurt am
Main ; New York : P. Lang, 1999.
*TC PE1128.A2 E547 1999*

Folse, Keith S. 100 clear grammar tests. Ann Arbor :
University of Michigan Press, c2000.
*TC PE1128.A2 F646 2000*

From testing to assessment. London ; New York :
Longman, 1994.
*TC PE1128.A2 F778 1994*

Learner-directed assessment in ESL. Mahwah, N.J. :
Lawrence Erlbaum Associates, 2000.
*TC PE1128.A2 L359 2000*

Quann, Steve. Learning computers, speaking English.
Ann Arbor : University of Michigan Press, c2000.
*TC PE1128.A2 .Q83 2000*

The sociopolitics of English language teaching.
Clevedon ; Buffalo [N.Y.] : Multilingual Matters,
c2000.
*TC PE1128.A2 S5994 2000*

Supervising postgraduates from non-English speaking
backgrounds. Buckingham ; Philadelphia : Society for
Research into Higher Education : Open University
Press, 1999.
*TC LB2343 .S86 1999*

Toohey, Kelleen, 1950- Learning English at school.
Clevedon, [England] ; Buffalo : Multilingual Matters,
2000.
*TC PE1128.A2 T63 2000*

### ENGLISH LANGUAGE - STUDY AND TEACHING - FOREIGN SPEAKERS - AUDIO-VISUAL AIDS.
Basic English [videorecording]. [Roslyn Heights,
N.Y.] : Video Aided Instruction, [c1995].
*TC PE1128 .B3 1995*

Intermediate English [videorecording]. [Roslyn
Heights, N.Y.] : Video Aided Instruction, [c1995].
*TC PE1128 .I5 1995*

### ENGLISH LANGUAGE - STUDY AND TEACHING - FOREIGN SPEAKERS - DATA PROCESSING.
Language learning online. Austin : Labyrinth
Publications, c1998.
*TC PE1128.A2 L2955 1998*

### ENGLISH LANGUAGE - STUDY AND TEACHING - FOREIGN SPEAKERS - HISTORY.
Cowie, Anthony Paul. English dictionaries for foreign
learners. Oxford : Clarendon Press ; New York :
Oxford University Press, 1999.
*TC PE1611 .C58 1999*

### ENGLISH LANGUAGE - STUDY AND TEACHING - FOREIGN SPEAKERS - PERIODICALS.
[English for specific purposes (New York, N.Y. :
Online)] English for specific purposes [computer file].
Oxford ; New York : Pergamon,
*TC EJOURNALS*

### ENGLISH LANGUAGE - STUDY AND TEACHING - FOREIGN STUDENTS. *See* ENGLISH LANGUAGE - STUDY AND TEACHING - FOREIGN SPEAKERS.

### ENGLISH LANGUAGE - STUDY AND TEACHING - FOREIGN STUDENTS - PERIODICALS.
Journal of English as a second language. [New York,
American Language Institute, New York University]

### ENGLISH LANGUAGE - STUDY AND TEACHING (HIGHER) - FOREIGN SPEAKERS.
Kasper, Loretta F. (Loretta Frances), 1951- Content-
based college ESL instruction. Mahwah, N.J. :
Lawrence Erlbaum Associates, 2000.
*TC PE1128.A2 K376 2000*

### ENGLISH LANGUAGE - STUDY AND TEACHING (HIGHER) - JAPANESE SPEAKERS.
Sasaki, Miyuki, 1959- Second language proficiency,
foreign language aptitude, and intelligence. New
York : P. Lang, c1999.
*TC P53.4 .S27 1999*

### ENGLISH LANGUAGE - STUDY AND TEACHING (HIGHER) - PERIODICALS.
Trends & issues in postsecondary English studies.
Urbana, Ill. : National Council of Teachers of English,
c1999-
*TC PE65 .T75*

### ENGLISH LANGUAGE - STUDY AND TEACHING (HIGHER) - SPANISH SPEAKERS.
O'Riordan, Mary. Strategic use of transfer and
explicit linguistic knowledge. 1998.
*TC 06 no. 10975*

### ENGLISH LANGUAGE - STUDY AND TEACHING (HIGHER) - UNITED STATES.
Kasper, Loretta F. (Loretta Frances), 1951- Content-
based college ESL instruction. Mahwah, N.J. :
Lawrence Erlbaum Associates, 2000.
*TC PE1128.A2 K376 2000*

### ENGLISH LANGUAGE - STUDY AND TEACHING - NORTH AMERICA - FOREIGN SPEAKERS.
Richards, J. C. (Jack Croft), 1943- Passages.
Cambridge : Cambridge University Press, 2000.
*TC PE1128 .R4599 2000*

### ENGLISH LANGUAGE - STUDY AND TEACHING - POLITICAL ASPECTS - SRI LANKA.
Canagarajah, A. Suresh. Resisting linguistic
imperialism in English teaching. Oxford : Oxford
University Press, 1999.
*TC PE1068.S7 C36 1999*

### ENGLISH LANGUAGE - STUDY AND TEACHING - POLITICAL ASPECTS - UNITED STATES.
The sociopolitics of English language teaching.
Clevedon ; Buffalo [N.Y.] : Multilingual Matters,
c2000.
*TC PE1128.A2 S5994 2000*

### ENGLISH LANGUAGE - STUDY AND TEACHING (PRIMARY).
Daniel, Claire, 1936- The great big book of fun
phonics activities. New York : Scholastic professional
books, c1999.
*TC LB1525.3 .D36 1999*

Ragno, Nancy N. World of language. [Teacher ed.].
Morristown, NJ : Silver Burdett & Ginn, c1990.

Ragno, Nancy N. World of language. [Teacher ed.].
Morristown, NJ : Silver Burdett & Ginn, c1990.

Ragno, Nancy N. World of language. [Teacher ed.].
Morristown, NJ : Silver Burdett & Ginn, c1990.

Ragno, Nancy Nickell. World of language. Needham,
Ma. : Silver Burdett Ginn, c1996.
*TC LB1576 .S4471 1996*

Ragno, Nancy Nickell. World of language. Needham,
Mass. : Silver Burdett Ginn, c1996.
*TC LB1576 .S4471 1996*

World of language. Needham, Mass. : Silver Burdett
Ginn, c1996.
*TC LB1576 .S4471 1996*

World of language. Teacher ed. Needham, Mass. :
Silver Burdett Ginn, c1996.
*TC LB1576 .S4471 1996 Teacher Ed.*

World of language. Morristown, N.J. : Silver Burdett
Ginn, c1996.
*TC LB1576 .S4471 1996 Pict. Bks.*

### ENGLISH LANGUAGE - STUDY AND TEACHING (SECONDARY).
Knox, Carolyn W. AGS English for the world of

work. Teacher's ed. Circle Pines, Minn. : American Guidance Service, c1997.
*TC PE1127.W65 K66 1997 Teacher's Ed.*

Trautman, Barbara A. AGS English to use. Teacher's ed. Circle Pines, Minn. : AGS, American Guidance Service, c1998.
*TC PE1121 .T72 1998 Teacher's Ed.*

Walker, Bonnie L. AGS basic English composition. Teacher's ed. Circle Pines, Minn. : American Guidance Service, c1997.
*TC PE1408 .W34 1997 Teacher's Ed.*

Walker, Bonnie L. AGS basic English composition. Teacher's ed. Circle Pines, Minn. : American Guidance Service, c1997.
*TC PE1408 .W34 1997 Teacher's Ed.*

Walker, Bonnie L. AGS basic English composition. Teacher's ed. Circle Pines, Minn. : American Guidance Service, c1997.
*TC PE1408 .W34 1997 Teacher's Ed.*

**ENGLISH LANGUAGE - STUDY AND TEACHING (SECONDARY) - ENGLAND.**
Issues in English teaching. London ; New York : Routledge, 2000.
*TC LB1576 .I89 2000*

**ENGLISH LANGUAGE - STUDY AND TEACHING (SECONDARY) - FOREIGN SPEAKERS.**
So much to say. New York : Teachers College Press, c1999.
*TC PE1128.A2 S599 1999*

**ENGLISH LANGUAGE - STUDY AND TEACHING (SECONDARY) - GREAT BRITAIN.**
Literacy in the secondary school. London : David Fulton, 2000.
*TC LB1632 .L587 2000*

**ENGLISH LANGUAGE - STUDY AND TEACHING (SECONDARY) - UNITED STATES.**
Golub, Jeffrey N., 1944- Making learning happen. Portsmouth, NH : Boynton/Cook Publishers, c2000.
*TC LB1631 .G623 2000*

Proett, Jackie, 1926- The writing process in action. Urbana, Ill. : National Council of Teachers of English, c1986.
*TC LB1631 .P697 1986*

So much to say. New York : Teachers College Press, c1999.
*TC PE1128.A2 S599 1999*

**ENGLISH LANGUAGE - STUDY AND TEACHING (SECONDARY) - UNITED STATES - CONGRESSES.**
A middle mosaic. Urbana, Ill. : National Council of Teachers of English, c2000.
*TC LB1631 .A2 2000*

**ENGLISH LANGUAGE - STUDY AND TEACHING (SECONDARY) - WALES.**
Issues in English teaching. London ; New York : Routledge, 2000.
*TC LB1576 .I89 2000*

**ENGLISH LANGUAGE - STUDY AND TEACHING - SOCIAL ASPECTS.**
Toohey, Kelleen, 1950- Learning English at school. Clevedon, [England] ; Buffalo : Multilingual Matters, 2000.
*TC PE1128.A2 T63 2000*

**ENGLISH LANGUAGE - STUDY AND TEACHING - SOCIAL ASPECTS - SRI LANKA.**
Canagarajah, A. Suresh. Resisting linguistic imperialism in English teaching. Oxford : Oxford University Press, 1999.
*TC PE1068.S7 C36 1999*

**ENGLISH LANGUAGE - STUDY AND TEACHING - SOCIAL ASPECTS - UNITED STATES.**
The sociopolitics of English language teaching. Clevedon : Buffalo [N.Y.] : Multilingual Matters, c2000.
*TC PE1128.A2 S5994 2000*

**ENGLISH LANGUAGE - STUDY AND TEACHING - SRI LANKA.**
Canagarajah, A. Suresh. Resisting linguistic imperialism in English teaching. Oxford : Oxford University Press, 1999.
*TC PE1068.S7 C36 1999*

**ENGLISH LANGUAGE - STUDY AND TEACHING - UNITED STATES.**
Christenbury, Leila. Making the journey. 2nd ed. Portsmouth, NH : Boynton/Cook Publishers, c2000.
*TC LB1631 .C4486 2000*

Folse, Keith S. 100 clear grammar tests. Ann Arbor : University of Michigan Press, c2000.
*TC PE1128.A2 F646 2000*

**ENGLISH LANGUAGE - STUDY AND TEACHING - UNITED STATES - EVALUATION.**
Educating language-minority children. New Brunswick (U.S.A.) : Transaction Publishers, c2000.
*TC LC3731 .E374 2000*

**ENGLISH LANGUAGE - STUDY AND TEACHING - UNITED STATES - FOREIGN SPEAKERS.**
Brisk, Maria. Literacy and bilingualism. Mahwah, N.J. : L. Erlbaum Associates, c2000.
*TC LC3731 .B684 2000*

**ENGLISH LANGUAGE - STUDY AND TEACHING - UNITED STATES - SPANISH SPEAKERS - CASE STUDIES.**
Paratore, Jeanne R. What should we expect of family literacy? Newark, Del. : International Reading Association ; Chicago , Ill. : National Reading Conference, c1999.
*TC LC151 .P37 1999*

**ENGLISH LANGUAGE - STYLE.**
Romano, Tom. Blending genre, altering style. Portsmouth, NH : Boynton/Cook ; Heinemann, c2000.
*TC PE1404 .R635 2000*

**ENGLISH LANGUAGE - SYNONYMS AND ANTONYMS.**
Demi. [Opposites] Demi's opposites. New York : Grosset & Dunlap, c1987.
*TC PE1591 .D43 1987*

The Facts on File student's thesaurus. 2nd ed. New York : Facts on File, 2000.
*TC PE1591 .H45 2000*

The Facts on File student's thesaurus. 2nd ed. New York : Facts on File, 2000.
*TC PE1591 .H45 2000*

**ENGLISH LANGUAGE - SYNONYMS AND ANTONYMS - FICTION.**
Serfozo. Mary. What's what? a guessing game/ 1st ed. New York, NY : Margaret K. McElderry Books, c1996.
*TC PZ7.S482 Wg 1996*

**ENGLISH LANGUAGE - SYNONYMS AND ANTONYMS - JUVENILE LITERATURE.**
Demi. [Opposites] Demi's opposites. New York : Grosset & Dunlap, c1987.
*TC PE1591 .D43 1987*

**ENGLISH LANGUAGE - TEACHER TRAINING.** *See* ENGLISH TEACHERS - TRAINING OF.

**ENGLISH LANGUAGE - TECHNICAL ENGLISH - STUDY AND TEACHING - PERIODICALS.**
[English for specific purposes (New York, N.Y. : Online)] English for specific purposes [computer file]. Oxford ; New York : Pergamon,
*TC EJOURNALS*

**ENGLISH LANGUAGE - TECHNICAL ENGLISH - STUDY AND TEACHING - THAILAND.**
Pupipat, Apisak. Scientific writing and publishing in English in Thailand. 1998.
*TC 06 no. 10981*

**ENGLISH LANGUAGE - TERMS AND PHRASES.**
Knapp, Sara D. The contemporary thesaurus of search terms and synonyms. 2nd ed. Phoenix, Ariz. : Oryx Press, 2000.
*TC ZA4060 .K58 2000*

**ENGLISH LANGUAGE - TEXT-BOOKS.** *See* ENGLISH LANGUAGE - TEXTBOOKS.

**ENGLISH LANGUAGE - TEXT-BOOKS FOR FOREIGN SPEAKERS.** *See* ENGLISH LANGUAGE - TEXTBOOKS FOR FOREIGN SPEAKERS.

**ENGLISH LANGUAGE - TEXT-BOOKS FOR FOREIGNERS.** *See also* ENGLISH LANGUAGE - TEXTBOOKS FOR FOREIGN SPEAKERS.
Dixson, Robert James. Easy reading selections in English; Rev. ed. [New York] Regents Pub. Co. [c1971]

*TC PE1128.A2 D5 1971*

**ENGLISH LANGUAGE - TEXTBOOKS.** *See* ENGLISH LANGUAGE - TEXTBOOKS FOR FOREIGN SPEAKERS.

**ENGLISH LANGUAGE - TEXTBOOKS - CHINA.**
Ting, Yenren, 1948- Learning English text by heart in a Chinese university. [New York : Columbia University], 1999.
*TC 085 T438*

**ENGLISH LANGUAGE - TEXTBOOKS FOR FOREIGN SPEAKERS.**
Cutchin, Kay Lynch. Landscapes and language. Cambridge, UK : New York, NY, USA : Cambridge University Press, 1999.
*TC PE1128 .C88 1999*

DeCarrico, Jeanette S. The structure of English. Ann Arbor, Mich. : University of Michigan Press : Wantage : University Presses Marketing, 2000.
*TC PE1112 .D43 2000*

Huizenga, Jann. Writing workout. Glenview, Ill. : Scott, Foresman and Co.,cc1990.
*TC PE1128 .H84 1990*

New immigrants in the United States. Cambridge, U.K. ; New York : Cambridge University Press, 2000.
*TC PE1128 .N384 1999*

Ramírez de Mellor, Elva Fun with English. Pupil's ed. Mexico : McGraw-Hill c1987
*TC PE1129.S8 .R35 1987*

Ramírez de Mellor, Elva Fun with english. Mexico : McGraw-Hill c1987
*TC PE1129.S8 .R35 1987*

Richards, Jack C. Passages. Cambridge, U.K. ; New York : Cambridge University Press, 2000.
*TC PE1128 .R4599 2000*

**ENGLISH LANGUAGE - TEXTBOOKS FOR FOREIGN SPEAKERS - HISTORY.**
Cowie, Anthony Paul. English dictionaries for foreign learners. Oxford : Clarendon Press ; New York : Oxford University Press, 1999.
*TC PE1611 .C58 1999*

**ENGLISH LANGUAGE - UNITED STATES.** *See* AMERICANISMS; BLACK ENGLISH.

**ENGLISH LANGUAGE - UNITED STATES - COMPOSITION AND EXERCISES.**
Proett, Jackie. 1926- The writing process in action. Urbana, Ill. : National Council of Teachers of English, c1986.
*TC LB1631 .P697 1986*

**ENGLISH LANGUAGE - UNITED STATES - COMPOSITION AND EXERCISES - CONGRESSES.**
A middle mosaic. Urbana, Ill. : National Council of Teachers of English, c2000.
*TC LB1631 .A2 2000*

**ENGLISH LANGUAGE - UNITED STATES - ERRORS OF USAGE.**
Kovacs, George. Literal literacy II. Lewiston, NY : E. Mellen Press, c1993.
*TC PE2827 .K682 1993*

**ENGLISH LANGUAGE - UNITED STATES - GLOSSARIES, VOCABULARIES, ETC.**
Smitherman, Geneva, 1940- Black talk. Rev. ed. Boston : Houghton Mifflin, 2000.
*TC PE3102.N4 S65 2000*

**ENGLISH LANGUAGE - UNITED STATES - LEXICOGRAPHY - HISTORY.**
Micklethwait, David. Noah Webster and the American dictionary. Jefferson, N.C. : McFarland, c2000.
*TC PE65.W5 M53 2000*

**ENGLISH LANGUAGE - UNITED STATES - RHETORIC - PROBLEMS, EXERCISES, ETC.**
Cutchin, Kay Lynch. Landscapes and language. Cambridge, UK : New York, NY, USA : Cambridge University Press, 1999.
*TC PE1128 .C88 1999*

**ENGLISH LANGUAGE - UNITED STATES - SLANG - DICTIONARIES.**
Smitherman, Geneva, 1940- Black talk. Rev. ed. Boston : Houghton Mifflin, 2000.
*TC PE3102.N4 S65 2000*

**ENGLISH LANGUAGE - UNITED STATES - USAGE.**
Kovacs, George. Literal literacy II. Lewiston, NY : E. Mellen Press, c1993.
*TC PE2827 .K682 1993*

**ENGLISH LANGUAGE - USAGE.**
Dictionary of confusable words. Chicago, IL : Fitzroy Dearborn Publ., 2000.
*TC PE1591 .D53 2000*

Trautman, Barbara A. AGS English to use. Teacher's ed. Circle Pines, Minn. : AGS, American Guidance Service, c1998.
*TC PE1121 .T72 1998 Teacher's Ed.*

Trautman, Barbara A. AGS English to use. Circle Pines, Minn. : AGS, American Guidance Service, c1998.
*TC PE1121 .T72 1998*

**ENGLISH LANGUAGE - VARIATION.**
Milroy, James. Authority in language. 3rd ed. London [England] ; New York : Routledge, 1999.
*TC P368 .M54 1999*

**ENGLISH LANGUAGE - VOCABULARIES.** *See* **ENGLISH LANGUAGE - GLOSSARIES, VOCABULARIES, ETC.**

**ENGLISH LANGUAGE - VOCABULARY.** *See* **VOCABULARY.**

**ENGLISH LANGUAGE - WORD FORMATION - JUVENILE FILMS.**
Exploring the English language [videorecording]. [Princeton, N.J.] : Video Tutor ; [Chesterton, Ind.? : Distributed by] Griffin Media Design, 1988, c1986.

**ENGLISH LANGUAGE - WRITING - PROBLEMS, EXERCISES, ETC.**
Huizenga, Jann. Writing workout. Glenview, Ill. : Scott, Foresman and Co.,cc1990.
*TC PE1128 .H84 1990*

**ENGLISH LANGUAGE - WRITTEN ENGLISH - HISTORY.**
Baron, Naomi S. Alphabet to email. London ; New York : Routledge, 2000.
*TC PE1075 .B28 2000*

**ENGLISH LANGUAGE - WRITTEN ENGLISH - THAILAND.**
Pupipat, Apisak. Scientific writing and publishing in English in Thailand. 1998.
*TC 06 no. 10981*

**English, Leona M. 1963-.**
Addressing the spiritual dimensions of adult learning :. San Francisco : Jossey Bass, 2000.
*TC LC5219 .A25 2000*

**ENGLISH LITERATURE.** *See* **CHILDREN'S LITERATURE, ENGLISH; ENGLISH FICTION; ENGLISH POETRY; ENGLISH PROSE LITERATURE; YOUNG ADULT LITERATURE, ENGLISH.**

**ENGLISH LITERATURE - 20TH CENTURY - STUDY AND TEACHING.**
Teaching post-colonialism and post-colonial literatures. Aarhus, Denmark ; Oakville, Conn. : Aarhus University Press, c1997.
*TC PR9080.A53 T43 1997*

**ENGLISH LITERATURE - COMMONWEALTH AUTHORS.** *See* **COMMONWEALTH LITERATURE (ENGLISH).**

**ENGLISH LITERATURE - COMMONWEALTH OF NATIONS AUTHORS.** *See* **COMMONWEALTH LITERATURE (ENGLISH).**

**ENGLISH LITERATURE - EARLY MODERN, 1500-1700 - HISTORY AND CRITICISM.**
Wheale, Nigel. Writing and society. London ; New York : Routledge, 1999.
*TC PR438.P65 W75 1999*

**ENGLISH LITERATURE - EXAMINATIONS - STUDY GUIDES.**
Cracking the GRE literature in English subject test. New York : Random House, 1996-
*TC LB2367.4 .L58*

**ENGLISH LITERATURE - HISTORY AND CRITICISM - THEORY, ETC.**
Caughie, Pamela L., 1953- Passing and pedagogy. Urbana : University of Illinois Press, c1999.
*TC PN61 .C38 1999*

**ENGLISH LITERATURE - STUDY AND TEACHING.**
Goodwyn, Andrew. English in the digital age. London : Cassell, 2000.
*TC PR35 .E65 2000*

Literary pedagogics after deconstruction. Aarhus, Denmark : Aarhus University Press, 1992.

*TC PR33 .L58 1992*

**ENGLISH LITERATURE - STUDY AND TEACHING - GREAT BRITAIN.**
Benton, Michael, 1939- Studies in the spectator role. London ; New York : Routledge, 2000.
*TC PR51.G7 B46 2000*

**ENGLISH LITERATURE - STUDY AND TEACHING (HIGHER) - PERIODICALS.**
Trends & issues in postsecondary English studies. Urbana, Ill. : National Council of Teachers of English, c1999-
*TC PE65 .T75*

**ENGLISH LITERATURE - STUDY AND TEACHING (SECONDARY) - GREAT BRITAIN.**
Teaching literature 11-18. London & New York : Continuum, 2000.
*TC PR51.G7 T43 2000*

**English modals in American talk shows.**
Kunz, Linda Ann. 1999.
*TC 06 no. 11136*

**English now and then.**
Measham, D. C. Cambridge [Eng.] University Press, 1965.
*TC PE1112 .M4*

**ENGLISH PERIODICALS.**
Guidance review. [Delhi] Central Bureau of Educational and Vocational Guidance, National Council of Educational Research and Training.

**ENGLISH PHILOLOGY - STUDY AND TEACHING.**
Lesbian and gay studies and the teaching of English. Urbana, Ill. : National Council of Teachers of English, 2000.
*TC PE66 .L45 2000*

**ENGLISH PHILOLOGY - STUDY AND TEACHING (GRADUATE) - NEW YORK (STATE) - ALBANY.**
North, Stephen M. Refiguring the Ph.D. in English studies. Urbana, Ill. : National Council of Teachers of English, c2000.
*TC PE69.A47 N67 2000*

**ENGLISH PHILOLOGY - STUDY AND TEACHING - HANDBOOKS, MANUALS, ETC.**
Burke, Jim, 1961- The English teachers' companion. Portsmouth, NH : Boynton/Cook, c1999.
*TC PE65 .B87 1999*

**ENGLISH PHILOLOGY - STUDY AND TEACHING (HIGHER) - PERIODICALS.**
Trends & issues in postsecondary English studies. Urbana, Ill. : National Council of Teachers of English, c1999-
*TC PE65 .T75*

**ENGLISH PHILOLOGY - STUDY AND TEACHING (HIGHER) - UNITED STATES.**
Preparing a nation's teachers. New York : Modern Language Association of America, 1999.
*TC PE68.U5 P74 1999*

**ENGLISH PHILOLOGY - STUDY AND TEACHING - POLITICAL ASPECTS.**
Lesbian and gay studies and the teaching of English. Urbana, Ill. : National Council of Teachers of English, 2000.
*TC PE66 .L45 2000*

**ENGLISH PHILOLOGY - STUDY AND TEACHING - UNITED STATES - VOCATIONAL GUIDANCE.**
Christenbury, Leila. Making the journey. 2nd ed. Portsmouth, NH : Boynton/Cook Publishers, c2000.
*TC LB1631 .C4486 2000*

**ENGLISH PICTURE DICTIONARIES.** *See* **PICTURE DICTIONARIES, ENGLISH.**

**ENGLISH POETRY.**
Simon, Francesca. Calling all toddlers. 1st American ed. New York : Orchard Books, 1999.
*TC PZ8.3.S5875 Cal 1999*

**ENGLISH POETRY - COLLECTIONS.**
Poems for fathers. 1st ed. New York : Holiday House, c1989.
*TC PS595.F39 P64 1989*

**ENGLISH POETRY - STUDY AND TEACHING (SECONDARY).**
Osakwe, Mabel. Poetrymate 1. Enugu, Nigeria : Fourth Dimension Publishing Co., 1996.
*TC PN1101 .O73 1996*

**ENGLISH POETS.** *See* **POETS, ENGLISH.**

**ENGLISH PROSE LITERATURE - 18TH CENTURY - HISTORY AND CRITICISM.**
Pearson, Jacqueline, 1949- Women's reading in Britain, 1750-1835. Cambridge, UK : New York : Cambridge University Press, 1999.
*TC PR756.W65 P43 1999*

**ENGLISH PROSE LITERATURE - 19TH CENTURY - HISTORY AND CRITICISM.**
Pearson, Jacqueline, 1949- Women's reading in Britain, 1750-1835. Cambridge, UK ; New York : Cambridge University Press, 1999.
*TC PR756.W65 P43 1999*

**ENGLISH PSYCHOLOGICAL FICTION.** *See* **PSYCHOLOGICAL FICTION, ENGLISH.**

**ENGLISH RIDING.** *See* **HORSEMANSHIP.**

**English teacher education in Europe :** new trends and developments / [edited by] Pamela Faber ... [et al.]. Frankfurt am Main ; New York : P. Lang, 1999. 261 p. ; 21 cm. (Foreign language teaching in Europe ; vol. 1) Includes bibliographical references. ISBN 0-8204-4321-2 ISBN 3-631-34653-0 DDC 428/.007
*1. English language - Study and teaching - Foreign speakers. 2. English language - Study and teaching - Europe. 3. English teachers - Training of - Europe. I. Faber, Pamela B., 1950- II. Series.*
*TC PE1128.A2 E547 1999*

**ENGLISH TEACHERS - ATTITUDES.**
Stories from the center. Urbana, Ill. National Council of Teachers of English, c2000.
*TC PE1404 .S834 2000*

**The English teachers' companion.**
Burke, Jim, 1961- Portsmouth, NH : Boynton/Cook, c1999.
*TC PE65 .B87 1999*

**English teacher's guide to performance tasks and rubrics, high school.**
Benjamin, Amy, 1951- Larchmont, N.Y. : Eye On Education, 2000.
*TC LB1631 .B383 2000*

**ENGLISH TEACHERS - IN-SERVICE TRAINING.**
Arias, Rafael. Analysis of discourse in an ESL peer-mentoring teacher group. 1999.
*TC 06 no. 10791*

**ENGLISH TEACHERS - TRAINING OF.**
Christenbury, Leila. Making the journey. 2nd ed. Portsmouth, NH : Boynton/Cook Publishers, c2000.
*TC LB1631 .C4486 2000*

Williams, James D. (James Dale), 1949- Preparing to teach writing. 2nd ed. Mahwah, N.J. : Lawrence Erlbaum Associates, 1998.
*TC PE1404 .W54 1998*

**ENGLISH TEACHERS - TRAINING OF - EUROPE.**
English teacher education in Europe. Frankfurt am Main ; New York : P. Lang, 1999.
*TC PE1128.A2 E547 1999*

**ENGLISH TEACHERS - TRAINING OF - UNITED STATES.**
Preparing a nation's teachers. New York : Modern Language Association of America, 1999.
*TC PE68.U5 P74 1999*

**ENGLISH TEACHERS - TRAINING OF - UNITED STATES - HISTORY - 20TH CENTURY.**
History, reflection, and narrative. Stamford, Conn. : Ablex Pub., c1999.
*TC PE1405.U6 H56 1999*

**ENGLISH TEACHERS - UNITED STATES - BIOGRAPHY.**
Comp tales. New York : Longman, c2000.
*TC PE1404 .C617 2000*

**ENGLISH TO SPEAKERS OF OTHER LANGUAGES.** *See* **ENGLISH LANGUAGE - STUDY AND TEACHING - FOREIGN SPEAKERS; ENGLISH LANGUAGE - TEXTBOOKS FOR FOREIGN SPEAKERS.**

**ENGLISH YOUNG ADULT LITERATURE.** *See* **YOUNG ADULT LITERATURE, ENGLISH.**

**ENGRAVING.** *See* **ETCHING.**

**Engs, Ruth C.** Clean living movements : American cycles of health reform / Ruth Clifford Engs. Westport, Conn. ; London : Praeger, 2000. xiv, 312 p. ; 25 cm. Includes bibliographical references (p. [269]-303) and index. ISBN 0-275-95994-5 (alk. paper) DDC 613/.0973
*1. Health promotion - United States - History. 2. Health reformers - United States - History. 3. Health behavior - United States - History. I. Title.*

**TC RA427.8 .E54 2000**

**Enhanced photography.**
Luciana, James. The art of enhanced photography :.
Gloucester, Mass. : Rockport Publishers, c1999.
**TC TR654 .L83 1999**

**Enhancing creativity of gifted children.**
Khatena, Joe. Cresskill, N.J. : Hampton Press, c2000.
**TC LC3993 .K56 2000**

**Enhancing education in heterogeneous schools :**
theory and application ; studies in memory of Yehuda
Amir / edited by Rachel Ben-Ari, Yisrael Rich.
Ramat-Gan : Bar-Ilan University Press, [1997] 359 p. :
ill. ; 25 cm. Includes bibliographical references and index.
ISBN 9652261831
*1. School integration. 2. Intergroup relations. 3. Group work in
education. 4. Multicultural education. 5. Minorities -
Education. I. Amir, Yehuda. II. Ben-Ari, Rachel. III. Rich,
Yisrael.*
**TC LC214 .E54 1997**

**Enhancing educational excellence, equity, and
efficiency :** evidence from evaluations of systems and
schools in change / edited by Roel J. Bosker, Bert
P.M. Creemers, and Sam Stringfield ; in collaboration
with Interuniversitair Centrum voor Onderwijskundig
Onderzoek (ICO). Dordrecht ; Boston : Kluwer
Academic Publishers, c1999. x, 259 p. : ill. ; 25 cm.
Includes bibliographical references and index. ISBN
0-7923-6138-5 (alk. paper) DDC 317.2
*1. School management and organization - Netherlands -
Cross-cultural studies. 2. School management and
organization - Great Britain - Cross-cultural studies. 3. School
management and organization - United States - Cross-cultural
studies. I. Bosker, R. J. (Roel J.) II. Creemers, Bert P. M. III.
Stringfield, Sam. IV. Interuniversitair Centrum voor
Onderwijskundig Onderzoek.*
**TC LB2921 .E54 1999**

**Enhancing program quality in science and
mathematics /** by Joyce S. Kaser, ... [et al.].
Thousand Oaks, Calif. : Corwin Press, c1999. xv, 222
p. : ill. ; 26 cm. Includes bibliographical references and index.
ISBN 0-8039-6857-4 (acid-free paper) ISBN 0-8039-6858-2
(acid-free paper) DDC 507.1
*1. Science - Study and teaching - United States. 2.
Mathematics - Study and teaching - United States. 3. Science
teachers - In-service training - United States. 4. Mathematics
teachers - In-service training - United States. 5. Action
research in education - United States. I. Kaser, Joyce S.*
**TC LB1585.3 .E55 1999**

**Enhancing the postdoctoral experience for scientists
and engineers :** a guide for postdoctoral scholars,
advisers, institutions, funding organizations, and
disciplinary societies / Committee on Science,
Engineering, and Public Policy, National Academy of
Sciences, National Academy of Engineering, Institute
of Medicine. Washington, DC : National Academy
Press, 2000. xxvi, 184 p. : ill. ; 23 cm. Includes
bibliographical references (p. 110-112). ISBN 0-309-06996-3
*1. Scientists - Vocational guidance. 2. Engineers - Vocational
guidance. 3. Mentoring in the professions. I. Committee on
Science, Engineering, and Public Policy (U.S.) II. Title: Guide
for postdoctoral scholars, advisers, institutions, funding
organizations, and disciplinary societies*
**TC Q147 .E53 2000**

**The enigma of the oceanic feeling.**
Parsons, William Barclay, 1955- New York : Oxford
University Press, 1999.
**TC BF175.4.R44 P37 1999**

**ENLIGHTENMENT.**
Maxwell, Kenneth, 1941- Pombal, paradox of the
Enlightenment. Cambridge [England] ; New York,
NY : Cambridge University Press, 1995.
**TC DP641 .M39 1995**

**ENLIGHTENMENT - ENGLAND.**
Barney, Richard A., 1955- Plots of enlightenment.
Stanford, Calif. : Stanford University Press, c1999.
**TC PR858.E38 B37 1999**

**ENLIGHTENMENT - EUROPE.**
Gascoigne, John, Ph. D. Science, politics, and
universities in Europe, 1600-1800. Aldershot
[England] ; Brookfield, Vt. : Ashgate, c1998.
**TC LA621.5 .G37 1998**

**Enoch, Yvonne.**
Lyke, James. Creative piano teaching. 3rd ed.
Champaign, Ill. : Stipes Pub. Co., c1996.
**TC MT220 .L95 1996**

**Enomoto, Ernestine, 1949-.**
Gardiner, Mary E., 1953- Coloring outside the lines.
Albany : State University of New York Press, c2000.
**TC LB2831.82 .G37 2000**

**Enriching early scientific learning.**
Johnston, Jane, 1954- Philadelphia : Open University
Press, 1999.
**TC Q181 .J58 1999**

**Enriching the primary curriculum--child, teacher,
context**
Cook, Deirdre, 1943- Interactive children,
communicative teaching. Buckingham [England] ;
Philadelphia : Open University Press, 1999.
**TC LB1028.46 .C686 1999**

**ENROLLMENT, SCHOOL.** *See* **SCHOOL
ENROLLMENT.**

**ENSEIGNEMENT COMMERCIAL - CANADA -
HISTOIRE.**
Capitalizing knowledge. Toronto : University of
Toronto Press, c2000.
**TC HF1131 .C36 2000**

**L'Enseignement des sciences.** [Paris] 2 v. Absorbed by:
Sciences et L'Enseignement des sciences.
*1. Science - Periodicals. 2. Study and teaching - Periodicals. I.
Title: Sciences et L'Enseignement des sciences*

**ENSEIGNEMENT PRIMAIRE - ANGLETERRE -
HISTOIRE.**
Heathorn, Stephen J., 1965- For home, country, and
race. Toronto : University of Toronto Press, 1999.
**TC LC93.E5 H42 1999**

**ENSEIGNEMENT - RÉFORME - ÉVALUATION.**
Werner, Walter. Collaborative assessment of school-
based projects. Vancouver : Pacific Educational Press,
c1991.
**TC LB2822.8 .W47 1991**

**Enseignement secondaire au Canada.**
L'Enseignement secondaire au Canada; [Quebec]

**L'Enseignement secondaire au Canada;** revue
officielle des maisons d'enseignement secondaire
affiliées aux Universités Laval, Quebec, et de
Montréal, Montréal, P.Q. [Quebec] v. 1-46; 1916-67.
Vols. 1-20, 1915-41. 1 v. Vols. 21-30, 1941-1951. 1 v.
*1. Catholic Church in Canada - Education - Periodicals. 2.
Education. Secondary - Periodicals. 3. French periodicals I.
Title: Enseignement secondaire au Canada*

**ENSEIGNEMENT SUPÉRIEUR - COLOMBIE-
BRITANNIQUE.**
McKellin, Karen, 1950- Maintaining the momentum.
Victoria, B.C. : British Columbia Centre for
International Education, c1998.
**TC LC1090 .M24 1998**

**ENSEIGNEMENT SUPÉRIEUR - FINALITÉS -
CANADA.**
A new world of knowledge. Ottawa : International
Development Research Centre, c1999.
**TC LC1090 N38 1999**

**ENSEIGNEMENT UNIVERSITAIRE -
COLOMBIE-BRITANNIQUE -
PROGRAMMES D'ÉTUDES.**
McKellin, Karen, 1950- Maintaining the momentum.
Victoria, B.C. : British Columbia Centre for
International Education, c1998.
**TC LC1090 .M24 1998**

**Enseñanza de la lectura en español para el estudiante
bilingüe.**
The teaching of reading in Spanish to the bilingual
student = 2nd ed. Mahwah, N.J. : L. Erlbaum
Associates, 1998.
**TC LB1573 .T365 1998**

**Enterprise in the nonprofit sector.**
Crimmins, James C. Washington, D.C. : Partners for
Livable Places ; New York : Rockefeller Bros. Fund,
c1983.
**TC HD62.6 .C74 1983**

**ENTERPRISES.** *See* **BUSINESS ENTERPRISES.**

**ENTERTAINERS.** *See* **DANCERS; MUSICIANS.**

**ENTERTAINERS' CONTRACTS.** *See* **ARTISTS'
CONTRACTS.**

**ENTERTAINERS - TAXATION - UNITED
STATES - HANDBOOKS, MANUALS, ETC.**
Chadwick, Annie. Showbiz bookkeeper. Dorset,
Vermont : Theatre Directories, 1992, c1991.
**TC HF5686.P24 C53 1991**

**ENTERTAINING.** *See* **DINNERS AND DINING.**

**ENTERTAINING - FICTION.**
Gould, Deborah Lee. Brendan's best-timed birthday.
New York : Bradbury Press, 1988.
**TC PZ7.G723 Br 1988**

**Entertainment industry economics.**
Vogel, Harold L. (Harold Leslie), 1946- 4th ed.
Cambridge [England] ; New York, NY, USA :
Cambridge University Press, 1998.
**TC PN1590.F55 V6 1998**

**Entrancing relationships.**
Feeney, Don J., 1948- Westport, Conn. : Praeger,
1999.
**TC RC552.R44 F44 1999**

**ENTREPRENEUR.** *See* **ENTREPRENEURSHIP.**

**ENTREPRENEURS.** *See* **BUSINESSPEOPLE.**

**ENTREPRENEURS, WOMEN.** *See*
**BUSINESSWOMEN.**

**ENTREPRENEURSHIP - CONGRESSES.**
Educating entrepreneurs for wealth creation.
Aldershot, Hants, England ; Brookfield, USA :
Ashgate, 1998.
**TC HF1106 .E378 1998**

**Entry strategies for school consultation.**
Marks, Edward S. New York : Guilford Press, c1995.
**TC LB2799.2 .M36 1995**

**Entz, Susan.** Picture this : digital and instant
photography activites for early childhood learning /
Susan Entz Sheri Lyn Galarza. Thousand Oaks,
Calif. : Corwin Press, c2000. xvi, 204 p. ; 28 cm.
Includes index. ISBN 0-8039-6886-8 (cloth : acid-free paper)
ISBN 0-8039-6887-6 (pbk. : acid-free paper) DDC 371.33/52
*1. Pictures in education. 2. Early childhood education -
Activity programs. 3. Photography. I. Galarza, Sheri Lyn. II.
Title.*
**TC LB1043.67 .E58 2000**

**ENVIRONMENT.** *See* **ECOLOGY.**

**The environment and mental health :** a guide for
clinicians / edited by Ante Lundberg. Mahwah, N.J. :
Lawrence Erlbaum Associates, c1998. xi, 233 p. ; 24 cm.
Includes bibliographical references and indexes. ISBN
0-8058-2907-5 (c : alk. paper) DDC 616.89/071
*1. Mental illness - Environmental aspects. 2. Mental health -
Environmental aspects. 3. Environmentally induced diseases.
4. Mental Disorders - etiology. 5. Environmental Exposure -
adverse effects. 6. Environmental Illness. I. Lundberg, Ante.*
**TC RC455.4.E58 E528 1998**

**ENVIRONMENT AND STATE.** *See*
**ENVIRONMENTAL POLICY.**

**ENVIRONMENT AND TEENAGERS -
CALIFORNIA - CASE STUDIES.**
Childress, Herb, 1958- Landscapes of betrayal,
landscapes of joy. Albany [N.Y.] : State University of
New York Press, c2000.
**TC HQ796 .C458237 2000**

**ENVIRONMENT (ART).** *See* **INSTALLATIONS
(ART).**

**ENVIRONMENT, CLASSROOM.** *See*
**CLASSROOM ENVIRONMENT.**

**ENVIRONMENT, COLLEGE.** *See* **COLLEGE
ENVIRONMENT.**

**ENVIRONMENT, EFFECT OF HUMAN BEINGS
ON.** *See* **NATURE - EFFECT OF HUMAN
BEINGS ON.**

**ENVIRONMENT, HUMAN.** *See* **HUMAN
ECOLOGY.**

**ENVIRONMENT, SCHOOL.** *See* **SCHOOL
ENVIRONMENT.**

**ENVIRONMENTAL AUDITING.** *See*
**ENVIRONMENTAL POLICY.**

**ENVIRONMENTAL BIOLOGY.** *See* **ECOLOGY.**

**ENVIRONMENTAL CONTROL.** *See*
**ENVIRONMENTAL POLICY.**

**ENVIRONMENTAL EDUCATION -
BIBLIOGRAPHY.**
Roberts, Patricia, 1936- Language arts and
environmental awareness. New Haven, Conn. : Linnet
Professional Publications, 1998.
**TC Z5863.E55 R63 1998**

**ENVIRONMENTAL EDUCATION -
CONGRESSES.**
Environmental education for the 21st century. New
York : Peter Lang, c1997.
**TC GE70 .E5817 1997**

**Environmental education for the 21st century :**
international and interdisciplinary perspectives /
Patricia J. Thompson, editor ; with an introduction by
Ricardo Fernández. New York : Peter Lang, c1997.
xxvii, 356 p. : ill. ; 23 cm. "In cooperation with the Office of
Media Relations and Publications at Lehman College, Anne D.

Perryman, director." Includes bibliographical references. ISBN 0-8204-3749-2 (alk. paper) DDC 333.7/071
*1. Environmental education - Congresses. 2. Environmental policy - Congresses. 3. Environmental ethics - Congresses. 4. Ecofeminism - Congresses. I. Thompson, Patricia J. II. Title: Environmental education for the twenty-first century*
*TC GE70 .E5817 1997*

**Environmental education for the twenty-first century.**
Environmental education for the 21st century. New York : Peter Lang, c1997.
*TC GE70 .E5817 1997*

**ENVIRONMENTAL EDUCATION - UNITED STATES.**
Barnes, Barbara. Schools transformed for the 21st century. Torrance, Calif. : Griffin Pub. Group, c1999.
*TC LA217.2 .B39 1999*

**ENVIRONMENTAL ENGINEERING.** *See* **ENVIRONMENTAL HEALTH; ENVIRONMENTAL PROTECTION.**

**ENVIRONMENTAL ETHICS - CONGRESSES.**
Environmental education for the 21st century. New York : Peter Lang, c1997.
*TC GE70 .E5817 1997*

**ENVIRONMENTAL EXPOSURE - ADVERSE EFFECTS.**
The environment and mental health. Mahwah, N.J. : Lawrence Erlbaum Associates, c1998.
*TC RC455.4.E58 E528 1998*

**ENVIRONMENTAL HEALTH.** *See also* **SANITATION.**
Moore, Gary S. Living with the earth. Boca Raton, Fla. : Lewis Publishers, c1999.
*TC RA565 .M665 1999*

**ENVIRONMENTAL HEALTH - COMPUTER-ASSISTED INSTRUCTION.**
Moore, Gary S. Living with the earth. Boca Raton, Fla. : Lewis Publishers, c1999.
*TC RA565 .M665 1999*

**ENVIRONMENTAL HEALTH - DICTIONARIES.**
Lewis' dictionary of occupational and environmental safety and health. Boca Raton : Lewis Publishers, c2000.
*TC T55 .L468 2000*

**ENVIRONMENTAL ILLNESS.**
The environment and mental health. Mahwah, N.J. : Lawrence Erlbaum Associates, c1998.
*TC RC455.4.E58 E528 1998*

**ENVIRONMENTAL ILLNESS - EPIDEMIOLOGY.**
Vetter, Norman. Epidemiology and public health medicine. Edinburgh ; New York : Churchill Livingstone, 1999.
*TC RA427 .V48 1999*

**ENVIRONMENTAL IMPACT ANALYSIS.**
Brown, Lester Russell, 1934- Vital signs 2000 :. New York : Norton, c2000.
*TC HD75.6 .B768 2000*

Sosin, Adrienne. Achieving styles preferences of students in an urban graduate teacher education program. 1996.
*TC 06 no. 10701*

**Environmental impacts of food production practices.**
Bissonnette, Madeline Monaco. Adolescents' perspectives about the environmental impacts of food production practices. 1999.
*TC 06 no. 11084*

**Environmental influences:** proceedings of a conference under the auspices of Russell Sage Foundation and the Rockefeller University. David C. Glass, editor. New York, Rockefeller University Press ; Russell Sage Foundation, 1968. ix, 304 p. : ill. ; 25 cm. (Biology and behavior) Conference held Apr. 21-22, 1967. Includes bibliographical references (p. 267-288) and index. DDC 155.9
*1. Environmental psychology. 2. Psychobiology. I. Glass, David C. II. Russell Sage Foundation. III. Rockefeller University. IV. Series.*
*TC BF353 .E5*

**Environmental justice** : a middle-school mathematics unit / MMAP. Menlo Park, Calif. : Institute for Research on Learning, c1998. 199 p. : ill. ; 30 cm. + 2 computer discs (3 1/2 in.)
*1. Mathematics - Study and teaching (Elementary) I. Middle-school Mathematics through Applications Project.*
*TC QA135.5 .E68 1998*

**ENVIRONMENTAL POLICY.** *See* **ENVIRONMENTAL PROTECTION.**

**ENVIRONMENTAL POLICY - CONGRESSES.**
Environmental education for the 21st century. New York : Peter Lang, c1997.
*TC GE70 .E5817 1997*

**ENVIRONMENTAL PROTECTION.** *See* **ENVIRONMENTAL POLICY.**

**ENVIRONMENTAL PROTECTION - FICTION. <JUVENILE SUBJECT HEADING>.**
Burningham, John. Whaddayamean. 1st American ed. New York : Crown Publishers, 1999.
*TC PZ7.B936 We 1999*

**ENVIRONMENTAL PROTECTION - POPULAR WORKS.**
Get a grip [videorecording]. Racine, WI : S.C. Johnson and Son, Inc., 1999, c1998.
*TC TD170 .G4 1999*

**ENVIRONMENTAL PSYCHOLOGY.**
Environmental influences: New York, Rockefeller University Press ; Russell Sage Foundation, 1968.
*TC BF353 .E5*

Fullilove, Mindy Thompson. The house of Joshua. Lincoln, NE : University of Nebraska Press, c1999.
*TC BF353 .F85 1999*

Kahn, Peter H. The human relationship with nature. Cambridge, Mass. : MIT Press, c1999.
*TC BF353.5.N37 K34 1999*

Metzner, Ralph. Green psychology. Rochester, Vt. : Park Street Press, c1999.
*TC BF353.5.N37 M47 1999*

Person-environment psychology. 2nd ed. Mahwah, N.J. : L. Erlbaum, 2000.
*TC BF353 .P43 2000*

Walters, Glenn D. Beyond behavior. Westport, Conn. : London : Praeger, 2000.
*TC BF353 .W356 2000*

**ENVIRONMENTAL QUALITY.** *See* **ENVIRONMENTAL PROTECTION.**

**ENVIRONMENTAL QUALITY - GOVERNMENT POLICY.** *See* **ENVIRONMENTAL POLICY.**

**ENVIRONMENTAL QUALITY - HEALTH ASPECTS.** *See* **ENVIRONMENTAL HEALTH.**

**ENVIRONMENTAL QUALITY MANAGEMENT.** *See* **ENVIRONMENTAL PROTECTION.**

**ENVIRONMENTAL QUALITY - MORAL AND ETHICAL ASPECTS.** *See* **ENVIRONMENTAL ETHICS.**

**ENVIRONMENTAL SCIENCE.** *See* **ENVIRONMENTAL SCIENCES.**

**ENVIRONMENTAL SCIENCES.** *See* **EARTH SCIENCES; ECOLOGY; ENVIRONMENTAL PROTECTION.**

**ENVIRONMENTAL SCIENCES - STUDY AND TEACHING (ELEMENTARY) - BIBLIOGRAPHY.**
Roberts, Patricia, 1936- Language arts and environmental awareness. New Haven, Conn. : Linnet Professional Publications, 1998.
*TC Z5863.E55 R63 1998*

**ENVIRONMENTALISM.**
Baskin, Yvonne. The work of nature. Washington, D.C. : Island Press, 1997.
*TC GE195 .B36 1997*

O'Sullivan, Edmund, 1938- Transformative learning. London ; New York : Zed Books ; New York : Distributed in USA exclusively by St. Martin's Press, 1999.
*TC LC196 .O7 1999*

**ENVIRONMENTALISM - POPULAR WORKS.**
Get a grip [videorecording]. Racine, WI : S.C. Johnson and Son, Inc., 1999, c1998.
*TC TD170 .G4 1999*

**ENVIRONMENTALISM - PSYCHOLOGICAL ASPECTS.**
Metzner, Ralph. Green psychology. Rochester, Vt. : Park Street Press, c1999.
*TC BF353.5.N37 M47 1999*

**ENVIRONMENTALISM - SCHOLARSHIPS, FELLOWSHIPS, ETC. - DIRECTORIES.**
Weinstein, Miriam (Miriam H.) Making a difference. Rev. & exp. 2nd ed. Gabriola Island, BC, Can. : New Society Publishers, 2000.
*TC LB2338 W45 2000*

**ENVIRONMENTALLY INDUCED DISEASES.**
The environment and mental health. Mahwah, N.J. : Lawrence Erlbaum Associates, c1998.

*TC RC455.4.E58 E528 1998*

**EPHEMERA, PRINTED.** *See* **PRINTED EPHEMERA.**

**Ephemera Society of America.**
Fenn, Patricia. Rewards of merit. [Schoharie, N.Y.] : Ephemera Society of America ; Charlottesville [Va.] : Distributed by Howell Press, Inc., c1994.
*TC LA230 .F46 1994*

**EPHEMERAL PRINTING.** *See* **PRINTED EPHEMERA.**

**EPIDEMIC ENCEPHALITIS - MASSACHUSETTS - SALEM - HISTORY - 17TH CENTURY.**
Carlson, Laurie M., 1952- A fever in Salem. Chicago : I.R. Dee, 1999.
*TC BF1576 .C37 1999*

**Epidemic!** : the world of infectious diseases / Rob DeSalle, editor. New York : The New Press ; New York : Distributed by W.W. Norton, c1999. 246 p. : ill. ; 24 cm. "Published in conjunction with the American Museum of Natural History." Includes bibliographical references and index. ISBN 1-56584-546-3 DDC 614.4
*1. Epidemiology. 2. Communicable diseases. 3. Epidemics. I. DeSalle, Rob. II. American Museum of Natural History.*
*TC RA651 .E596 1999*

**EPIDEMICS.**
Epidemic!. New York : The New Press ; New York : Distributed by W.W. Norton, c1999.
*TC RA651 .E596 1999*

**EPIDEMIOLOGIC METHODS.**
Vetter, Norman. Epidemiology and public health medicine. Edinburgh ; New York : Churchill Livingstone, 1999.
*TC RA427 .V48 1999*

**EPIDEMIOLOGIC STUDIES.**
Vetter, Norman. Epidemiology and public health medicine. Edinburgh ; New York : Churchill Livingstone, 1999.
*TC RA427 .V48 1999*

**EPIDEMIOLOGY.** *See also* **DISEASES.**
Epidemic!. New York : The New Press ; New York : Distributed by W.W. Norton, c1999.
*TC RA651 .E596 1999*

Vetter, Norman. Epidemiology and public health medicine. Edinburgh ; New York : Churchill Livingstone, 1999.
*TC RA427 .V48 1999*

**Epidemiology and public health medicine.**
Vetter, Norman. Edinburgh ; New York : Churchill Livingstone, 1999.
*TC RA427 .V48 1999*

**EPILEPSY.** *See also* **TEMPORAL LOBE EPILEPSY.**
When the brain goes wrong [videorecording]. Short version. Boston, MA : Fanlight Productions [dist.], c1992.
*TC RC386 .W54 1992*

**EPILEPSY IN CHILDREN.**
Childhood epilepsies and brain development. London : John Libbey, c1999.
*TC RJ496.E6 C45 1999*

**EPILEPSY - PERIODICALS.**
Journal of psycho-asthenics. Faribault, Minn. : Association of American Institutions for Feeble-Minded, [1896-1918]

**EPISA (Firm).**
Comics, the 9th art [videorecording]. [S.l.] : EPISA ; Cicero, Ill. : [Distributed by] The Roland Collection, 1990.
*TC PN6710 .C6 1990*

**EPISTEMOLOGY.** *See* **KNOWLEDGE, THEORY OF.**

**Epling, W. Frank.**
Pierce, W. David. Behavior analysis and learning. 2nd ed. Upper Saddle River, N.J. : Prentice Hall, c1999.
*TC BF199 .P54 1999*

**Eppridge, Bill.**
Sport photography today! [videorecording]. Minneapolis, Minn. : Media Loft, c1992.
*TC TR821 .S64 1992*

**Epps, Susan.** Empowered families, successful children : early intervention programs that work / Susan Epps and Barbara J. Jackson. 1st ed. Washington, DC : American Psychological Association, c2000. ix, 287 p. : ill. ; 26 cm. Includes bibliographical references and index. ISBN 1-55798-659-2 (alk. paper) DDC 362.7

*1. Children - Counseling of. 2. Infants - Counseling of. 3. Counseling. I. Jackson. Barbara. 1952- II. Title.*
**TC BF637.C6 E66 2000**

**EPSEWASSON (VA.).** *See* **MOUNT VERNON (VA. : ESTATE).**

**EQUAL EDUCATION.** *See* **EDUCATIONAL EQUALIZATION.**

**EQUAL EDUCATIONAL OPPORTUNITY.** *See* **EDUCATIONAL EQUALIZATION.**

**EQUAL EMPLOYMENT OPPORTUNITY.** *See* **AFFIRMATIVE ACTION PROGRAMS; DISCRIMINATION IN EMPLOYMENT.**

**EQUAL OPPORTUNITY IN EMPLOYMENT.** *See* **AFFIRMATIVE ACTION PROGRAMS; DISCRIMINATION IN EMPLOYMENT.**

**EQUAL PAY FOR EQUAL WORK.** *See* **WOMEN - EMPLOYMENT.**

**EQUAL PAY FOR EQUAL WORK - UNITED STATES.**
Deslippe, Dennis A. (Dennis Arthur), 1961- Rights, not roses. Urbana : University of Illinois Press, c2000.
**TC HD6079.2.U5 D47 2000**

**EQUAL RIGHTS AMENDMENTS.** *See* **SEX DISCRIMINATION AGAINST WOMEN - LAW AND LEGISLATION.**

**Equal treatment for people with mental retardation.**
Field, Martha A. Cambridge, Mass. ; London : Harvard Unviersity Press, 1999.
**TC KF480 .F54 1999**

**EQUALITY.** *See* **LIBERTY; SOCIAL JUSTICE.**

**EQUALITY - CONGRESSES.**
Freedom, equality, and social change. Lewiston : E. Mellen Press, c1989.
**TC HM216 .F83 1989**

**EQUALIZATION, EDUCATIONAL.** *See* **EDUCATIONAL EQUALIZATION.**

**EQUATORIAL FOREST ECOLOGY.** *See* **RAIN FOREST ECOLOGY.**

**EQUESTRIAN CENTERS.** *See* **HORSEMANSHIP.**

**EQUESTRIANISM.** *See* **HORSEMANSHIP.**

**EQUIPMENT DESIGN.**
Venema, Ted. Compression for clinicians. San Diego, Calif. : Singular Pub. Group, c1998.
**TC RF300 .V46 1998**

**EQUITATION.** *See* **HORSEMANSHIP.**

**Equity & excellence.**
Integrated education. [Amherst, Mass., etc., Center for Equal Education, School of Education, University of Massachusetts, etc.]

**Equity and science education reform.**
Lynch, Sharon J. Mahwah, N.J. ; London : L. Erlbaum Associates, 2000.
**TC LB1585.3 .L96 2000**

**EQUUS.** *See* **HORSES.**

**EQUUS CABALLUS.** *See* **HORSES.**

**ERA.**
Educational rankings annual. Detroit, MI : Gale Research, c1991-
**TC LB2331.63 .E34**

**Erandi's braids.**
Madrigal, Antonio Hernandez. New York : Putnam's, c1999.
**TC PZ7.M26575 Er 1999**

**ERCOLANO (EXTINCT CITY).** *See* **HERCULANEUM (EXTINCT CITY).**

**E.R.D.C. report**
(no. 13.) Bourke, S. F. The mastery of literacy and numeracy. Canberra : Australian Govt. Pub. Service, 1977.
**TC LA2102 .B68 1977**

(no. 8-.) Literacy and numeracy in Australian schools. Canberra : Australian Gov. Pub. Service, 1976-
**TC LA2102 .L57 1976**

**ERECT POSITION OF HUMAN BEINGS.** *See* **POSTURE.**

**ERIC Clearinghouse on Higher Education.**
Aguirre, Adalberto. Women and minority faculty in the academic workplace. San Francisco, Calif. : Jossey-Bass c2000.
**TC LB2332.3 .A35 2000**

Alstete, Jeffrey W. Posttenure faculty development. San Fransisco, [Calif.] : Jossey-Bass c2000.
**TC LB2335.7 .A47 2000**

Austin, Ann E. Academic workplace. Washington, D.C. : Association for the Study of Higher Education, 1983.
**TC LB2331.7 .A96 1983**

Freed, Jann E. A culture for academic excellence. Washington, D.C. : Graduate School of Education and Human Development, George Washington University, 1997.
**TC LB2341 .F688 1997**

Speck, Bruce W. Grading students' classroom writing. Washington, DC : Graduate School of Education and Human Development, The George Washington University, 2000.
**TC LB1576 .S723 2000**

Stevens, Ed. Due process and higher education. Washington, DC : Graduate School of Education and Human Development, George Washington University, [1999]
**TC LB2344 .S73 1999**

Van Dusen, Gerald C. Digital dilemma. San Francisco : Jossey-Bass, c2000.
**TC LC5805 .V35 2000**

**ERIC Clearinghouse on Urban Education.**
Flaxman, Erwin. Youth mentoring. New York, N.Y. : ERIC Clearinghouse on Urban Education, 1988.
**TC LC4065 .F53 1988**

**The ERIC database [computer file].**
[ERIC (SilverPlatter International : Online)] WebSPIRS version 3.1. [Norwood, MA] : SilverPlatter International,
**TC NETWORKED RESOURCES**

[ERIC (SilverPlatter International : Online)] WebSPIRS version 3.1. [Norwood, MA] : SilverPlatter International,
**TC NETWORKED RESOURCES**

[ERIC (SilverPlatter International : Online)] The ERIC database [computer file]. WebSPIRS version 3.1. [Norwood, MA] : SilverPlatter International, 1982- . Other title: Educational Resources Information Center [computer file]. Description based on search screen viewed 2000-05-17. Producer: Educational Resources Information Center. Access restricted to institutional subscribers. SUMMARY: Consists of two files: the Resources in Education (RIE) file of document citations and the Current Index to Journals in Education (CIJE) file of journal article citations from over 750 professional journals. Mode of access: Online access via Internet. Also available on CD-ROM. URL: http://webspirs3.silverplatter.com/cgi-bin/waldo.cgi/ER
*1. Education - Indexes. 2. Education - Periodicals - Indexes. 3. Education - Research - Indexes. I. SilverPlatter International. II. Educational Resources Information Center (U.S.) III. Title. IV. Title: WebSPIRS. V. Title: Educational Resources Information Center [computer file]*
**TC NETWORKED RESOURCES**

[ERIC (SilverPlatter International : Online)] The ERIC database [computer file]. WebSPIRS version 3.1. [Norwood, MA] : SilverPlatter International, 1982- . Other title: Educational Resources Information Center [computer file]. Description based on search screen viewed 2000-05-17. Producer: Educational Resources Information Center. Access restricted to institutional subscribers. SUMMARY: Consists of two files: the Resources in Education (RIE) file of document citations and the Current Index to Journals in Education (CIJE) file of journal article citations from over 750 professional journals. Mode of access: Online access via Internet. Also available on CD-ROM. Search software: WebSPIRS. URL: http://webspirs3.silverplatter.com/cgi-bin/waldo.cgi/ER
*1. Education - Indexes. 2. Education - Periodicals - Indexes. 3. Education - Research - Indexes. I. SilverPlatter International. II. Educational Resources Information Center (U.S.) III. Title. IV. Title: WebSPIRS. V. Title: Resources in education. VI. Title: Current index to journals in education. VII. Title: Educational Resources Information Center [computer file]*
**TC NETWORKED RESOURCES**

**Erich Fromm.**
Funk, Rainer. New York : Continuum, 2000.
**TC BF109.F76 F8413 2000**

**Ericksen, Julia A., 1941-** Kiss and tell : surveying sex in the twentieth century / Julia A. Ericksen with Sally A. Steffen. Cambridge, Mass. : Harvard University Press, 1999. ix, 270 p. ; 24 cm. Includes bibliographical references (p. [231-260) and index. ISBN 0-674-50535-2 (alk. paper) DDC 306.7/0973/0904
*1. Sexual behavior surveys - United States. 2. Sexology - United States - History - 20th century. 3. Sex customs - United States. I. Steffen, Sally A. II. Title.*

**TC HQ18.U5 E75 1999**

**ERICKSON, MILTON H. - CONGRESSES.**
Ericksonian approaches to hypnosis and psychotherapy. New York : Brunner/Mazel, c1982.
**TC RC490.5.E75 E75**

**Ericksonian approaches to hypnosis and psychotherapy** / edited by Jeffrey K. Zeig. New York : Brunner/Mazel, c1982. xxvi, 518 p. : ill. ; 24 cm. Proceedings of the International Congress on Ericksonian Approaches to Hypnosis and Psychotherapy, held Dec. 3-8, 1980, in Phoenix, Ariz. Includes bibliographies and index. ISBN 0-87630-276-2 DDC 616.89/14
*1. Erickson, Milton H. - Congresses. 2. Hypnotism - Therapeutic use - Congresses. 3. Psychotherapy - Congresses. 4. Hypnosis - Congresses. 5. Psychotherapy - Congresses. I. Zeig. Jeffrey K.. 1947- II. International Congress on Ericksonian Approaches to Hypnosis and Psychotherapy (1980 : Phoenix, Ariz.)*
**TC RC490.5.E75 E75**

**Erin, Charles A.**
HIV and AIDS. Oxford ; New York ; Oxford University Press, 1999.
**TC RA644.A25 H57855 1999**

**Erkkila, Linda.**
Reforming the Electoral College [videorecording]. [Boulder, Colo.? : Social Science Education Consortium?], c1996.
**TC H62.5.U5 R4 1996**

**Erlandson, David A.** Organizational oversight : planning and scheduling for effectiveness / David Erlandson, Peggy L. Stark, Sharon M. Ward. Princeton, NJ : Eye on Education, c1996. xvi, 156 p. : ill. ; 24 cm. (School leadership library) Includes bibliographical references (p 155-156). ISBN 1-88300-126-9 DDC 371.2
*1. School management and organization - United States. 2. Educational planning - United States. 3. Scheduling - United States. 4. School principals - United States. I. Stark, Peggy L., 1949- II. Ward, Sharon M., 1938- III. Title. IV. Series.*
**TC LB2805 .E75 1996**

**Ernest, Ivan.** Faculty evaluation of post-tenure review at a research university / by Ivan Ernest. 1999. viii, 211 leaves ; 29 cm. Typescript; issued also on microfilm. Thesis (Ed.D.)--Teachers College, Columbia University, 1999. Includes bibliographical references (leaves 161-166).
*1. College teachers - New Jersey - Tenure. 2. College teachers - Tenure - Evaluation. 3. Rutgers University - Faculty - Case studies. 4. Academic freedom - United States. 5. Universities and colleges - Faculty - United States - Professional ethics. I. Title.*
**TC 06 no. 11110**

**Ernest, Paul.** Mathematics for primary teachers. London ; New York : Routledge, 2000.
**TC QA135.5 .K67 2000**

**Ernst Haas : to dream with open eyes [videorecording].**
The sight and insight of Ernst Haas [videorecording]. Minneapolis, Minn. : Media Loft, 1992.
**TC TR647.H3 S5 1992**

**Eros as the educational principle of democracy.**
Burch, Kerry T., 1957- New York : P. Lang, c2000.
**TC LC196 .B75 2000**

**ERS information aid.**
Special days and weeks for planning the school calendar. Arlington, Va. : Educational Research Service,
**TC LB3525 .S63**

Special days and weeks for planning the school calendar. Arlington, Va. : Educational Research Service,
**TC LB3525 .S63**

**ERS monograph**
Smith, Steven H. Schoolwide test preparation. [Arlington, Va.] : Educational Research Service, c2000.
**TC LB2806.22 .S65 2000**

**Erting, Carol.**
The deaf child in the family and at school. Mahwah, N.J. : Lawrence Erlbaum Associates, 2000.
**TC HV2392.2 .D43 2000**

**ERUDITION.** *See* **LEARNING AND SCHOLARSHIP.**

**Eruptions**
(vol. 1) McWilliam, Erica. Pedagogical pleasures. New York ; Canterbury [England] : P. Lang, c1999.
**TC LB1775 .M319 1999**

(vol. 2) Johnson, Richard T., 1956- Hands off!.
New York : Canterbury [England] : P. Lang, c2000.
*TC LB1033 .J63 2000*

(vol. 5) Taught bodies. New York : P. Lang, c2000.
*TC LB14.7 .T38 2000*

**Ervin, Naomi E.**
Simms, Lillian M. (Lillian Margaret) The professional
practice of nursing administration. 3rd ed. Albany,
NY : Delmar Publishers, c2000.
*TC RT89 .S58 2000*

**ESKIMAUAN INDIANS.** *See* **ESKIMOS.**

**ESKIMOS - FICTION.**
George, Jean Craighead, 1919- Snow Bear. 1st ed.
New York : Hyperion Books for Children, 1999.
*TC PZ7.G2933 Sn 1999*

**ESL.** *See* **ENGLISH LANGUAGE - STUDY AND
TEACHING - FOREIGN SPEAKERS;
ENGLISH LANGUAGE - TEXTBOOKS FOR
FOREIGN SPEAKERS.**

**ESL [videorecording].**
Basic English [videorecording]. [Roslyn Heights,
N.Y.] : Video Aided Instruction, [c1995].
*TC PE1128 .B3 1995*

Intermediate English [videorecording]. [Roslyn
Heights, N.Y.] : Video Aided Instruction, [c1995].
*TC PE1128 .I5 1995*

**ESOL.** *See* **ENGLISH LANGUAGE - STUDY AND
TEACHING - FOREIGN SPEAKERS;
ENGLISH LANGUAGE - TEXTBOOKS FOR
FOREIGN SPEAKERS.**

**ESOPHAGUS - DISEASES.** *See* **DEGLUTITION
DISORDERS.**

**Espace Video Europeén.**
On pictures and paintings [videorecording].
Peasmarsh, East Sussex, Eng. ; Ho-Ho-kus, NJ :
Roland Collection, 1992.
*TC ND195.O45 1992*

**El español al día.**
Turk, Laurel Herbert, 1903- 5th ed. Lexington, Mass. :
D.C. Heath, c1979.
*TC PC4111 .T87 1979*

Turk, Laurel Herbert, 1903- Revised ed. Lexington,
Mass. : D.C. Heath, c1974.
*TC PC4111 .T87 1974*

Turk, Laurel Herbert, 1903- 4th ed. Lexington, Mass.,
Heath [1973]
*TC PC4112 .T766 1973 Teacher's Ed.*

**ESPIONAGE, BUSINESS.** *See* **BUSINESS
INTELLIGENCE.**

**ESPIONAGE, INDUSTRIAL.** *See* **BUSINESS
INTELLIGENCE.**

**Esprit international.**
L'Esprit international.

**L'Esprit international.** The international mind. v. 26 cm.
Frequency: Quarterly. Seal on t.-p.: Dotation Carnegie. Centre
europeén. French text.
*I. Title: Esprit international II. Title: International mind.*

**ESQUIMAUX.** *See* **ESKIMOS.**

**Esquivel, Giselle B.**
Creativity and giftedness in culturally diverse
students. Cresskill, N.J. : Hampton Press, c2000.
*TC LC3993.2 .C74 2000*

**Essau, Cecilia Ahmoi.**
Developmental psychopathology. Australia : Harwood
Academic Publishers, c1997.
*TC RJ499 .D48 1997*

**Essays in cognitive psychology**
Engelkamp, Johannes. [Erinnern eigener Handlungen.
English] Memory for actions. Hove, East Sussex,
UK : Psychology Press, c1998.
*TC BF371 .E5413 1998*

**Essays in developmental psychology.**
Pérez Pereira, Miguel. Language development and
social interaction in blind children. Hove, UK :
Psychology Press, c1999.
*TC P118 .P37 1999*

**Essays in general psychology :** seven Danish
contributions presented to Henrik Poulsen / edited by
Niels Engelsted, Lars Hem and Jens Mammen.
Aarhus : Aarhus University Press, c1989. 146 p. : ill. ;
22 cm. Includes bibliographical references. Errata slip inserted.
ISBN 87-7288-277-8
*1. Psychology - Philosophy. 2. Psychology - Methodology. 3.
Psychology - Denmark I. Engelsted, Niels. II. Hem, Lars. III.
Mammen, Jens. IV. Title.*

*TC BF38 .E78 1989*

**Essays in social psychology**
Sorrentino, Richard M. The uncertain mind.
Philadelphia : Psychology Press, c2000.
*TC BF697 .S674 2000*

**Essays on citizenship.**
Crick, Bernard R. London ; New York : Continuum,
2000.
*TC JF801 .C75 2000*

**Essays on contemporary photography.**
Over exposed. New York : New Press, c1999.
*TC TR642 .O94 1999*

**Essays on Historical Archives of Christian Higher
Education in China.**
International Symposium on Historical Archives of
Pre-1949 Christian Higher Education in China (1993 :
Hong Kong) Chung-kuo chiao hui ta hsüeh li shih wen
hsien yen t'ao hui lun wen chi. Hsiang-kang : Chung
wen ta hsüeh ch'u pan she, 1995.
*TC LC432.C5 I58 1995*

**Essays on the academic history of QCG/UCG/NUI,
Galway.**
From Queen's College to National University. Dublin,
Ireland : Four Courts Press, c1999.
*TC LF933 .F76 1999*

**Essays on the history of Trinity College Library,
Dublin** / Vincent Kinane & Anne Walsh, editors.
Dublin : Four Courts, c2000. 206 p., 16 p. of plates : ill. ;
25 cm. Includes bibliographical references and index.
CONTENTS: The librarians of Trinity College / Peter Fox --
Custodes librorum : service, staff and salaries, 1601-1855 /
Lydia Ferguson -- The function of the library in the early
seventeenth century / Elizabethanne Boran -- The Long Room
survey of sixteenth- and seventeenth-century books of the first
collections / Anthony Cains -- The library buildings up to
1970 / Brendan Grimes -- A guide to the manuscript sources in
TCD for the history of the library / Jane Maxwell -- John
Madden's manuscripts / William O'Sullivan -- Lost and
found : a stray of the thirteenth century from Trinity College
Library / Bernard Meehan -- Legal deposit, 1801-1922 /
Vincent Kinane -- The library as revealed in the Parliamentary
Commission Report of 1853 / Anne Walsh -- The study of
German in TCD and the acquisition of German language works
by the library in the nineteenth century / Veronika Koeper-
Saul -- A select bibliography of the library / Ciaran Nicholson
and Ann O'Brien -- A selection of published illustrations
relating to the library : buildings, people, and some artifacts /
Ciaran Nicholson -- A select chronology / Isolde Harpur. ISBN
1-85182-467-7
*1. Trinity College (Dublin, Ireland). - Library - History. I.
Kinane, Vincent. II. Walsh, Anne.*
*TC Z792.5.T75 E87 2000*

**ESSENCES AND ESSENTIAL OILS.** *See*
**PERFUMES.**

**Essential knowledge.**
Marzano, Robert J. Aurora, Colo. : McREL, 1999.
*TC LB3060.83 .M36 1999*

**Essential psychology for nurses and other health
professionals.**
Russell, Graham, 1954- London ; New York :
Routledge, c1999.
*TC R726.7 .R87 1999*

**Essential readings in developmental psychology**
Adolescent development. Oxford ; Malden, Mass. :
Blackwell Publishers, 2000.
*TC BF724 .A275 2000*

Childhood cognitive development. Malden, Mass. :
Blackwell, 2000.
*TC BF723.C5 C487 2000*

Childhood social development. Malden, Mass. ;
Oxford : Blackwell Publishers, 2000.
*TC BF721 .C6675 2000*

The nature-nurture debate. Oxford ; Malden, Mass. :
Blackwell, 1999.
*TC BF341 .N39 1999*

**Essentials of Bayley scales of infant development - II
assessment.**
Black, Maureen M. New York : Wiley, c2000.
*TC RJ151.D48 B52 2000*

**Essentials of Myers-Briggs type indicator assessment.**
Quenk, Naomi L., 1936- New York : J. Wiley & Sons,
2000.
*TC BF698.8.M94 Q45 1999*

**Essentials of psychological assessment series**
Black, Maureen M. Essentials of Bayley scales of
infant development--II assessment. New York :
Wiley, c2000.
*TC RJ151.D48 B52 2000*

Kaufman, Alan S. Essentials of WISC-III and
WPPSI-R assessment. New York ; Chichester
[England] : Wiley, c2000.
*TC BF432.5.W42 K36 2000*

Quenk, Naomi L., 1936- Essentials of Myers-Briggs
type indicator assessment. New York : J. Wiley &
Sons, 2000.
*TC BF698.8.M94 Q45 1999*

**Essentials of WISC-III and WPPSI-R assessment.**
Kaufman, Alan S. New York : Chichester [England] :
Wiley, c2000.
*TC BF432.5.W42 K36 2000*

**Esser, Heribert.**
Schenker, Heinrich, 1868-1935. [Kunst des Vortrags.
English] The art of performance. New York : Oxford
University Press, 2000.
*TC MT220 .S24513 2000*

**ESSEX (AIRCRAFT CARRIER).**
Streb, Richard W. Life and death aboard the U.S.S.
Essex. Pittsburgh, Pa. : Dorrance Pub. Co., c1999.
*TC D774.E7 S77 1999*

**ESSEX PRIMARY SCHOOL IMPROVEMENT
RESEARCH AND DEVELOPMENT
PROGRAMME.**
Supporting improving primary schools. London ; New
York : Falmer Press, 2000.
*TC LB2822.84.E64 S86 1999*

**ESTATES (SOCIAL ORDERS).** *See*
**LEGISLATIVE BODIES; SOCIAL CLASSES.**

**ESTEEM.** *See* **RESPECT.**

**Esterly, David.** Grinling Gibbons and the art of
carving / David Esterly. New York : H.N. Abrams,
1998. 223 p. : ill. (some col.) ; 29 cm. Includes bibliographical
references (p. 220) and index. ISBN 0-8109-4142-2
(hardcover) DDC 730/.092
*1. Gibbons, Grinling, - 1648-1721 - Criticism and
interpretation. 2. Wood-carving - England. I. Title.*
*TC NK9798.G5 E88 1998*

**ESTHETICS.** *See* **AESTHETICS.**

**ESTIMATION OF DISABILITY.** *See* **DISABILITY
EVALUATION.**

**ESTRANGEMENT (SOCIAL PSYCHOLOGY).** *See*
**ALIENATION (SOCIAL PSYCHOLOGY).**

**ETCHING.** *See* **AQUATINT.**

**ETCHING - 20TH CENTURY - ENGLAND.**
Etching [videorecording]. Northbrook, Ill. ;
Peasmarsh, East Sussex, Eng. : Roland Collection of
Films on Art, c1990.
*TC NE2043 .E87 1990*

**ETCHING, BRITISH.**
Etching [videorecording]. Northbrook, Ill. ;
Peasmarsh, East Sussex, Eng. : Roland Collection of
Films on Art, c1990.
*TC NE2043 .E87 1990*

**ETCHING - TECHNIQUE.**
Etching [videorecording]. Northbrook, Ill. ;
Peasmarsh, East Sussex, Eng. : Roland Collection of
Films on Art, c1990.
*TC NE2043 .E87 1990*

**Etching** [videorecording] / produced and directed by
Gavin Nettleton ; written by Gavin Nettleton,
Terrence Gravett with help from Harvey Daniels.
Northbrook, Ill. ; Peasmarsh, East Sussex, Eng. :
Roland Collection of Films on Art, c1990. 1
videocassette (47 min.) : sd., col. ; 1/2 in. At head of title:
Anthony Roland Collection of Films on Art. VHS. Catalogued
from credits, cassette label and container. Narrator, Barbara
Myers. Music by Sam Hayden; production team: John Warr,
Bob Seago. Addresses of the Roland Collection on container:
Ho-Ho-Kus, N.J. and Peasmarsh, East Sussex, Eng. For
students of intaglio, aquatint, engraving, drypoint and other
metal plate processes. SUMMARY: Follows the artist, Sandy
Sykes, with Terry Gravett, as she prepares and prints from an
engraved metal plate, step by step in a method that has not
changed much since the 17th century. Sykes also uses an
aquatint plate in creating her work of art.
*1. Etching - Technique. 2. Lithography - Metal plate
processes - Technique. 3. Etching - 20th century - England. 4.
Etching, British. 5. Aquatint - Technique. 6. Prints -
Technique. 7. Prints - 20th century - England. 8. Art, Modern - 20th
century - England. I. Myers, Barbara. II. Sykes, Sandy. III.
Gravett, Terry. IV. Daniels, Harvey, 1936- V. Nettleton, Gavin.
VI. Anthony Roland Collection of Film on Art. VII. Brighton
Polytechnic. Media Services. VIII. Title: Anthony Roland
Collection of Films on Art*
*TC NE2043 .E87 1990*

**ETCHINGS.** *See* ETCHING.

**ETHANOL.** *See* ALCOHOL.

**An ethic for health promotion.**
Buchanan, David Ross. New York ; Oxford : Oxford University Press, 2000.
*TC RA427.8 .B83 2000*

**ETHIC, WORK.** *See* WORK ETHIC.

**Ethical conflicts in psychology** / Donald N. Bersoff.
2nd ed. Washington, DC : American Psychological Association, c1999. xxiv, 597 p. ; 29 cm. Includes bibliographical references and index. ISBN 1-55798-599-5 (pbk. : alk. paper) ISBN 1-55798-591-X (hardcover : alk. paper) DDC 174/.915
*1. Psychology - Moral and ethical aspects. 2. Psychologists - Professional ethics.I. Bersoff, Donald N.*
*TC BF76.4 .E814 1999*

**ETHICAL EDUCATION.** *See* MORAL EDUCATION; RELIGIOUS EDUCATION.

**Ethical issues in college writing** / edited by Fredric G. Gale, Phillip Sipiora, and James L. Kinneavy. New York ; Canterbury [England] : Peter Lang, c1999. xix, 249 p. ; 23 cm. (Studies in composition and rhetoric, 1080-5397 ; vol. 1) Includes bibliographical references and index. ISBN 0-8204-3072-2 (alk. paper) DDC 808/.042/0711
*1. English language - Rhetoric - Study and teaching - Moral and ethical aspects. 2. Report writing - Study and teaching (Higher) - Moral and ethical aspects. 3. College teaching - Moral and ethical aspects. 4. Rhetoric - Moral and ethical aspects. I. Gale, Fredric G., 1933- II. Kinneavy, James L., 1920- III. Sipiora, Phillip. IV. Series.*
*TC PE1404 .E84 1999*

**Ethical know-how.**
Varela, Francisco J., 1945- [Know-how per l'etica. English] Stanford, Calif. : Stanford University Press, 1999.
*TC BJ1012 .V3813 1999*

**ETHICS.** *See also* CHARACTER; CONDUCT OF LIFE; ENVIRONMENTAL ETHICS; EXAMPLE; GUILT; MORAL EDUCATION; PEACE; RESPONSIBILITY; SECULARISM; SELF-REALIZATION; SEXUAL ETHICS; SOCIAL ETHICS; VALUES; WORK ETHIC.
Hartmann, Nicolai, 1882-1950. London, G. Allen & Unwin ltd,; New York, The Macmillan company [1932]
*TC BJ1114 .H3C6 1932*

**ETHICS.**
Britzman, Deborah P., 1952- Lost subjects, contested objects. Albany : State University of New York Press, c1998.
*TC LB1060 .B765 1998*

Dilman, İlham. Raskolnikov's rebirth. Chicago : Open Court, c2000.
*TC BF47 .D55 2000*

Hartmann, Nicolai, 1882-1950. Ethics, London, G. Allen & Unwin ltd,; New York, The Macmillan company [1932]
*TC BJ1114 .H3C6 1932*

Malaro, Marie C. Museum governance. Washington : Smithsonian Institution Press, c1994.
*TC AM121 .M35 1994*

Varela, Francisco J., 1945- [Know-how per l'etica. English] Ethical know-how. Stanford, Calif. : Stanford University Press, 1999.
*TC BJ1012 .V3813 1999*

**Ethics and community in the health care professions** / edited by Michael Parker. London ; New York : Routledge, 1999. x, 207 p. ; 23 cm. (Professional ethics) Includes bibliographical references (p. 188-200) and index. ISBN 0-415-15027-2 (hc.) ISBN 0-415-15028-0 (pbk.) DDC 174/.2
*1. Medical ethics - Social aspects. 2. Communitarianism - Health aspects. 3. Medical personnel - Moral and ethical aspects. 4. Professional ethics.I. Parker, Michael, 1958- II. Series.*
*TC R725.5 .E87 1999*

**Ethics and electronic information in the twenty-first century** / edited by Lester J. Pourciau. West Lafayette, Ind. : Purdue University Press, c1999. xi, 334 p. ; 25 cm. Title from pre-cip information: Ethics and information in the twenty-first century. Includes bibliographical references and index. ISBN 1-55753-138-2 (cloth : alk. paper) DDC 174/.90904
*1. Information technology - Moral and ethical aspects. I. Pourciau, Lester J., 1936- II. Title: Ethics and information in the twenty-first century*
*TC T58.5 .E77 1999*

**Ethics and information in the twenty-first century.**
Ethics and electronic information in the twenty-first century. West Lafayette, Ind. : Purdue University Press, c1999.
*TC T58.5 .E77 1999*

**ETHICS AND SOCIAL SCIENCES.** *See* SOCIAL SCIENCES AND ETHICS.

**Ethics and the university.**
Davis, Michael, 1943- London ; New York : Routledge, 1999.
*TC LB2324 .D38 1999*

**ETHICS, BUSINESS.** *See* BUSINESS ETHICS.

**ETHICS, COMMERCIAL.** *See* BUSINESS ETHICS.

**Ethics in plain English.**
Nagy, Thomas F. 1st ed. Washington, DC ; London : American Psychological Association, c2000.
*TC BF76.4 .N34 2000*

**Ethics in practice.**
Daniels, Debbie. Therapy with children :. London ; Thousand Oaks, Calif. : SAGE, 2000.
*TC RJ504 .D36 2000*

**ETHICS, MEDICAL.** *See also* MEDICAL ETHICS.
HIV and AIDS. Oxford ; New York ; Oxford University Press, 1999.
*TC RA644.A25 H57855 1999*

**ETHICS, NURSING.**
Bandman, Elsie L. Nursing ethics through the life span. 3rd ed. Norwalk, Conn. : Appleton & Lange, c1995.
*TC RT85 .B33 1995*

Bishop, Anne H., 1935- Nursing ethics. 2nd ed. Sudbury, Mass. : Jones and Bartlett, c2001.
*TC RT85 .B57 2001*

Nurse's legal handbook. 4th ed. Springhouse, Pa. : Springhouse Corp., c2000.
*TC RT86.7 .N88 2000*

Streubert, Helen J. Qualitative research in nursing. 2nd ed. Philadelphia : Lippincott, c1999.
*TC RT81.5 .S78 1999*

**The ethics of everyday life**
Everyone a teacher. Notre Dame, Ind. : University of Notre Dame Press, c2000.
*TC LB1025.3 .E87 2000*

**The ethics of writing.**
Trifonas, Peter Pericles, 1960- Lanham, Md. ; Oxford : Rowman & Littlefield, c2000.
*TC LB14.7 .T75 2000*

**ETHICS, PRACTICAL.** *See* CONDUCT OF LIFE.

**ETHICS, PRIMITIVE.** *See* ETHICS.

**ETHICS, SEXUAL.** *See* SEXUAL ETHICS.

**ETHICS - STUDY AND TEACHING (HIGHER) - UNITED STATES.**
Davis, Michael, 1943- Ethics and the university. London : New York : Routledge, 1999.
*TC LB2324 .D38 1999*

**Ethics under siege.**
Misrepresentation in the marketplace and beyond. Washington, DC : American Association of Collegiate Registrars and Admissions Officers, 1996.
*TC LB2331.615.U6 M57 1996*

**ETHIOPIA - FICTION.**
Kurtz, Jane. Faraway home. San Diego : Harcourt, c2000.
*TC PZ7.K9626 Far 2000*

**ETHNIC ART - UNITED STATES.** *See* AFRO-AMERICAN ART; INDIAN ART - NORTH AMERICA.

**ETHNIC ATTITUDES.** *See* RACE AWARENESS.

**ETHNIC ATTITUDES - UNITED STATES.**
Gabaccia, Donna R., 1949- We are what we eat. Cambridge, Mass. : Harvard University Press, 1998.
*TC GT2853.U5 G33 1998*

**ETHNIC CLEANSING.** *See* GENOCIDE.

**ETHNIC CONFLICT.** *See* ETHNIC RELATIONS.

**ETHNIC DIVERSITY.** *See* PLURALISM (SOCIAL SCIENCES).

**ETHNIC DIVERSITY POLICY.** *See* MULTICULTURALISM.

**ETHNIC FOOD INDUSTRY - UNITED STATES.**
Gabaccia, Donna R., 1949- We are what we eat. Cambridge, Mass. : Harvard University Press, 1998.

*TC GT2853.U5 G33 1998*

**ETHNIC GROUPS.** *See* ETHNIC RELATIONS; MINORITIES.

**ETHNIC GROUPS IN LITERATURE - BIBLIOGRAPHY.**
Peck, David R. American ethnic literatures. Pasadena, Calif. : Salem Press, c1992.
*TC Z1229.E87 P43 1992*

**ETHNIC GROUPS - PSYCHOLOGY.** *See* ETHNOPSYCHOLOGY.

**ETHNIC GROUPS - PSYCHOLOGY.**
Canino, Ian A. Culturally diverse children and adolescents. 2nd ed. New York : Guilford Press, c2000.
*TC RJ507.M54 C36 2000*

**ETHNIC GROUPS - UNITED STATES - LITERARY COLLECTIONS.**
Coming of age in America. New York : New Press : Distributed by W.W. Norton, c1994.
*TC PS509.M5 C66 1994*

**ETHNIC HANDICAPPED.** *See* MINORITY HANDICAPPED.

**ETHNIC IDENTITY.** *See* ETHNICITY.

**ETHNIC LITERATURE (AMERICAN).** *See* AMERICAN LITERATURE - MINORITY AUTHORS.

**ETHNIC MINORITIES.** *See* MINORITIES.

**ETHNIC POLITICS.** *See* ETHNIC RELATIONS - POLITICAL ASPECTS.

**ETHNIC PSYCHOLOGY.** *See* ETHNOPSYCHOLOGY.

**ETHNIC RELATIONS.** *See also* ETHNIC ATTITUDES; MINORITIES; RACE RELATIONS.
Camara, Evandro de Morais, 1946- The cultural one or the racial many. Aldershot, Hants, England ; Brookfield, Vt., USA : Ashgate, c1997.
*TC HT1521 .C343 1997*

**ETHNIC RELATIONS - POLITICAL ASPECTS.**
Ethnicity and intra-state conflict. Aldershot, Hants, England ; Brookfield, Vt., USA : Ashgate, c1999.
*TC GN495.6 .E83 1999*

**ETHNIC RELATIONS - POLITICAL ASPECTS - CONGRESSES.**
Ethnicity and intra-state conflict. Aldershot, Hants, England ; Brookfield, Vt., USA : Ashgate, c1999.
*TC GN495.6 .E83 1999*

**ETHNICITY.** *See also* BLACKS - RACE IDENTITY; ETHNICITY IN CHILDREN; MULTICULTURALISM; PLURALISM (SOCIAL SCIENCES).
Fenton, Steve, 1942- Lanham, Md. : Rowman & Littlefield, c1999.
*TC GN495.6 .F46 1999x*

**ETHNICITY.**
Ethnicity and intra-state conflict. Aldershot, Hants, England ; Brookfield, Vt., USA : Ashgate, c1999.
*TC GN495.6 .E83 1999*

Fenton, Steve, 1942- Ethnicity. Lanham, Md. : Rowman & Littlefield, c1999.
*TC GN495.6 .F46 1999x*

Woo, Kimberley Ann. "Double happiness," double jeopardy. 1999.
*TC 06 no. 11075*

**Ethnicity and intra-state conflict** / edited by Hakan Wiberg, Christian P. Scherrer. Aldershot, Hants, England ; Brookfield, Vt., USA : Ashgate, c1999. ix, 327 p. : ill. ; 22 cm. Includes bibliographical references and index. Most chapters are revised versions of the authors' presentations at a May 1997 symposium convened by the Copenhagen Peace Research Institute's (COPRI) research program, Intra-State Conflict: Causes and Peace Strategies (CONF)--Introd. ISBN 1-84014-713-X DDC 305.8
*1. Ethnicity - Congresses. 2. War and society - Congresses. 3. World politics - 1945- - Congresses 4. International relations - Congresses. 5. Ethnic relations - Political aspects - Congresses. 6. Human territoriality - Political aspects - Congresses. 7. Ethnicity. 8. War and society. 9. World politics - 1945- 10. International relations. 11. Ethnic relations - Political aspects. 12. Human territoriality - Political aspects.I. Wiberg, Hakan, 1942- II. Scherrer, Christian P.*
*TC GN495.6 .E83 1999*

**ETHNICITY - CANADA - CASE STUDIES.**
Ryan, James, 1952 Oct. 18- Race and ethnicity in multi-ethnic schools. Clevedon [England] ; Philadelphia : Multilingual Matters, c1999.

*TC LC3734 .R93 1999*

**ETHNICITY - CONGRESSES.**
Ethnicity and intra-state conflict. Aldershot, Hants,
England : Brookfield, Vt., USA : Ashgate, c1999.
*TC GN495.6 .E83 1999*

**ETHNICITY - HANDBOOKS, MANUALS, ETC.**
Handbook of language & ethnic identity. New York :
Oxford University Press, 1999.
*TC P35 .H34 1999*

**ETHNICITY IN CHILDREN - UNITED STATES -
JUVENILE LITERATURE.**
Nash, Renea D. Everything you need to know about
being a biracial/biethnic teen. 1st ed. New York :
Rosen Pub. Group, 1995.
*TC HQ77.9 .N39 1995*

**ETHNICITY - RESEARCH - UNITED STATES.**
Gender, culture, and ethnicity. Mountain View,
Calif. : Mayfield Pub. Co., c1999.
*TC HQ1181.U5 G45 1999*

**ETHNICITY - STUDY AND TEACHING
(HIGHER) - ACTIVITY PROGRAMS.**
Teaching about culture, ethnicity & diversity.
Thousand Oaks : Sage Publications, c1998.
*TC HM101 .T38 1998*

**ETHNICITY - UNITED STATES.**
Clauss, Caroline Seay. Degrees of distance. 1999.
*TC 085 C58*

Critical ethnicity. Lanham, Md. : Rowman &
Littlefield, c1999.
*TC LC212.2 .C75 1999*

Interracial relationships. San Diego : Greenhaven
Press, c2000.
*TC HQ1031 .I59 2000*

**ETHNOCENTRISM.** *See* **AFROCENTRISM.**

**ETHNOCIDE.** *See* **GENOCIDE.**

**Ethnographic alternatives book series**
(v. 2) Angrosino, Michael V. Opportunity house.
Walnut Creek, CA : AltaMira Press, c1998.
*TC HV3006.A4 A48 1998*

**The ethnographic eye :** interpretive studies of
education in China / edited by Judith Liu, Heidi A.
Ross, and Donald P. Kelly. New York : Falmer Press,
2000. viii, 210 p. ; 22 cm. (Garland reference library of social
science ; v. 922. Reference books in international education ; v.
47) Includes bibliographical references and index. ISBN 0-
8153-1471-X (alk. paper) DDC 306.43
*1. Educational anthropology - China - Case studies. 2.
Education - Social aspects - China - Case studies. I. Liu,
Judith, 1950- II. Ross, Heidi A., 1954- III. Kelly, Donald P. IV.
Title: Interpretive studies of education in China V. Series:
Garland reference library of social science ; v. 922. VI. Series:
Garland reference library of social science. Reference books in
international education ; vol. 47.*
*TC LB45 .E837 2000*

**Ethnographic eyes.**
Frank, Carolyn. Portsmouth, NH : Heinemann, c1999.
*TC LB1027.28 .F73 1999*

**Ethnographic study of Chinese immigrant women's
requesting behavior.**
Li, Duan-Duan. Expressing needs and wants in a
second language. 1998.
*TC 06 no. 10958*

**An ethnographic study of the construction of science
on television.**
Dhingra, Koshi. 1999.
*TC 06 no. 11101*

**ETHNOGRAPHY.** *See* **ETHNOLOGY.**

**Ethnography in nursing research.**
Roper, Janice M. Thousand Oaks, Calif. : Sage
Publications, c2000.
*TC RT81.5 .R66 2000*

**ETHNOLOGY.** *See also* **BLACKS; ETHNIC
GROUPS; ETHNIC RELATIONS;
FOLKLORE; HUMAN TERRITORIALITY;
INDIGENOUS PEOPLES; LANGUAGE AND
LANGUAGES; RACE RELATIONS; WHITES.**
Kuper, Adam. Among the anthropologists. London :
New Brunswick, NJ : Athlone Press : Somerset, N.J. :
Distributed in the United States by Transaction
Publishers, 1999.
*TC GN325 .K89 1999*

People and the land. New York, Noble and Noble
[1974]
*TC GN330 .P445*

Researching school experience. London ; New York :
Falmer Press, 1999.

*TC LB1027 .R453 1999*
Roper, Janice M. Ethnography in nursing research.
Thousand Oaks, Calif. : Sage Publications, c2000.
*TC RT81.5 .R66 2000*

**ETHNOLOGY - ADDRESSES, ESSAYS,
LECTURES.**
Harrington, Charles C. Cross cultural approaches to
learning. New York : MSS Informationc c1973.
*TC GN488.5 .H33 1973*

**ETHNOLOGY - AFRICA, SOUTHERN.**
Kuper, Adam. Among the anthropologists. London ;
New Brunswick, NJ : Athlone Press : Somerset, N.J. :
Distributed in the United States by Transaction
Publishers, 1999.
*TC GN325 .K89 1999*

**ETHNOLOGY - AFRICA, WEST.** *See* **MANDINGO
(AFRICAN PEOPLE).**

**ETHNOLOGY - AMERICA.** *See* **INDIANS.**

**ETHNOLOGY - AUSTRALIA.** *See* **AUSTRALIAN
ABORIGINES; TORRES STRAIT
ISLANDERS.**

**ETHNOLOGY - BENIN.** *See* **YORUBA (AFRICAN
PEOPLE).**

**ETHNOLOGY - BIBLIOGRAPHY -
PERIODICALS.**
International bibliography of anthropology = London ;
New York : Routledge, 1999-
*TC Z7161 .I593*

**ETHNOLOGY - CHINA.** *See* **CHINESE;
KAZAKHS.**

**ETHNOLOGY - GREAT BRITAIN.** *See* **BRITISH.**

**ETHNOLOGY - HAITI.** *See* **HAITIANS.**

**ETHNOLOGY - INDIA.** *See* **EAST INDIANS;
INDIA - SCHEDULED TRIBES.**

**ETHNOLOGY - INDONESIA - BAYUNG GEDÉ
(BALI) - FIELD WORK.**
Sullivan, Gerald. Margaret Mead, Gregory Bateson,
and Highland Bali. Chicago, IL : University of
Chicago Press, 1999.
*TC GN635.I65 S948 1999*

**ETHNOLOGY - ISRAEL.** *See* **JEWS.**

**ETHNOLOGY - JUVENILE LITERATURE.**
People and the land. New York, Noble and Noble
[1974]
*TC GN330 .P445*

**ETHNOLOGY - KAZAKHSTAN.** *See* **KAZAKHS.**

**ETHNOLOGY - METHODOLOGY.** *See* **CROSS-
CULTURAL STUDIES.**

**ETHNOLOGY - MEXICO - MEXQUITIC.**
Behar, Ruth, 1956- Translated woman. Boston :
Beacon Press, c1993.
*TC HQ1465.M63 B44 1993*

**ETHNOLOGY - MISCELLANEA.**
Harris, Marvin, 1927- Cows, pigs, wars & witches.
[1st ed.]. New York : Random House, c1974.
*TC GN320 .H328 1974*

**ETHNOLOGY - NEW ZEALAND.** *See* **MAORI
(NEW ZEALAND PEOPLE).**

**ETHNOLOGY - NIGERIA.** *See* **YORUBA
(AFRICAN PEOPLE).**

**ETHNOLOGY - PUERTO RICO.** *See* **PUERTO
RICANS.**

**ETHNOLOGY - RUSSIA (FEDERATION) -
SIBERIA.**
Oakes, Jill E. (Jill Elizabeth), 1952- Spirit of Siberia.
Washington, D.C. : Smithsonian Institution Press,
c1998.
*TC DK758 .O24 1998*

**ETHNOLOGY - RUSSIAN S.F.S.R.** *See*
**ETHNOLOGY - RUSSIA (FEDERATION).**

**ETHNOLOGY - SCANDINAVIA.** *See*
**NORTHMEN.**

**ETHNOLOGY - SOUTH AFRICA.** *See*
**AFRIKANERS; COLORED PEOPLE (SOUTH
AFRICA).**

**ETHNOLOGY - SPAIN.** *See* **SPANIARDS.**

**ETHNOLOGY - TANZANIA.** *See* **CHAGA
(AFRICAN PEOPLE).**

**ETHNOLOGY - UGANDA.** *See* **GANDA
(AFRICAN PEOPLE).**

**ETHNOLOGY - UNITED STATES.** *See also*
**AFRO-AMERICANS; ASIAN AMERICANS;
CHINESE AMERICANS; EAST INDIAN
AMERICANS; FINNISH AMERICANS;
GREEK AMERICANS; HAITIAN
AMERICANS; HISPANIC AMERICANS;
HUNGARIAN AMERICANS; IRISH
AMERICANS; ITALIAN AMERICANS;
JAPANESE AMERICANS; KOREAN
AMERICANS; MEXICAN AMERICANS;
PACIFIC ISLANDER AMERICANS; POLISH
AMERICANS.**
Angrosino, Michael V. Opportunity house. Walnut
Creek, CA : AltaMira Press, c1998.
*TC HV3006.A4 A48 1998*

**ETHNOLOGY - UNITED STATES -
PHILOSOPHY.**
Trencher, Susan R. Mirrored images. Westport, CT :
Bergin & Garvey, 2000.
*TC GN17.3.U6 T74 2000*

**ETHNOLOGY - UNITED STATES - STATISTICS.**
Heaton, Tim B. Statistical handbook on racial groups
in the United States. Phoenix, AZ : Oryx Press, 2000.
*TC E184.A1 H417 2000*

**ETHNOMUSICOLOGY.**
Blacking, John. Music, culture, & experience.
Chicago : University of Chicago Press, c1995.
*TC ML60 .B63 1995*

**ETHNOPHILOSOPHY.** *See also* **COGNITION
AND CULTURE.**
Dean, Alan Ph. D. Complex life. Aldershot : Ashgate,
c2000.
*TC BD450 .D43 2000*

**ETHNOPSYCHOLOGY.** *See also* **COGNITION
AND CULTURE; PERSONALITY AND
CULTURE; RACE AWARENESS.**
Bar-Tal, Daniel. Shared beliefs in a society. Thousand
Oaks, Calif. : Sage Publications, c2000.
*TC HM1041 .B37 2000*

Biocultural approaches to the emotions. Cambridge,
U.K. : New York : Cambridge University Press, 1999.
*TC GN502 .B53 1999*

Handbook of cross-cultural and multicultural
personality assessment. Mahwah, N.J. ; London :
Lawrence Erlbaum Associates, 2000.
*TC RC473.P79 H36 2000*

Handbook of cross-cultural psychology. 2nd ed.
Boston : Allyn and Bacon, c1997.
*TC GN502 .H36 1997*

Handbook of multicultural mental health :. San
Diego : Academic Press, c2000.
*TC RC455.4 .H36 2000*

Harrington, Charles C. Psychological anthropology
and education. New York : AMS Press, c1979.
*TC GN502 .H37*

Intercultural therapy. [2nd ed.]. Oxford ; Malden,
MA : Blackwell Science, 2000.
*TC RC455.4.E8 I57 2000*

Justman, Stewart. The psychological mystique.
Evanston, Ill. : Northwestern University Press, 1998.
*TC BF38 .J87 1998*

Seeley, Karen M. Cultural psychotherapy. Northvale,
N.J. : Jason Aronson, c2000.
*TC RC455.4.E8 S44 2000*

Social psychology and cultural context. Thousand
Oaks, Calif. : Sage Publications, c1999.
*TC HM1033 .S64 1999*

Valsiner, Jaan. Culture and human development.
London ; Thousand Oaks, Calif. : Sage, 2000.
*TC BF713 .V35 2000*

**ETHNOPSYCHOLOGY - ABSTRACTS.**
Harrington, Charles C. Psychological anthropology
and education. New York : AMS Press, c1979.
*TC GN502 .H37*

**ETHNOPSYCHOLOGY - AFRICA, SOUTHERN.**
Holdstock, T. Len. Re-examining psychology.
London ; New York : Routledge, 2000.
*TC BF108.A3 .H65 2000*

**ETHNOSCIENCE.**
What is indigenous knowledge? New York : Falmer
Press, 1999.
*TC GN476 .W47 1999*

**ETHOLOGY.** *See* **CHARACTER; ETHICS;
HUMAN BEHAVIOR.**

**ETHOLOGY, COMPARATIVE.** *See*
PSYCHOLOGY, COMPARATIVE.

**ETHYL ALCOHOL.** *See* ALCOHOL.

**Etiology and prevention of communicative disorders.**
Gerber, Sanford E. 2nd ed. San Diego : Singular Pub.
Group, c1998.
*TC RJ496.C67 G47 1998*

**ETIQUETTE.** *See* DINNERS AND DINING;
ENTERTAINING.

**ETS builds a test.**
Educational Testing Service. Princeton, NJ : The
Service, c1959.
*TC LB3051 .E38 1959*

**ETV (EDUCATIONAL TELEVISION).** *See*
TELEVISION IN EDUCATION.

**Eubank, Lynn.**
The current state of interlanguage. Amsterdam ;
Philadelphia : J. Benjamins, c1995.
*TC P118.2 .C867 1995*

**EUCLID'S ELEMENTS.** *See* GEOMETRY.

**EUGENIC STERILIZATION.** *See*
STERILIZATION, EUGENIC.

**Eugenical news.**
Eugenics quarterly. New York : American Eugenics
Society, [1954]-c1968.

**EUGENICS.** *See* CONTRACEPTION;
STERILIZATION, EUGENIC.

**EUGENICS - PERIODICALS.**
Eugenics quarterly. New York : American Eugenics
Society, [1954]-c1968.

**Eugenics quarterly.** New York : American Eugenics
Society, [1954]-c1968. 15 v. : ill. ; 25 cm. Frequency:
Quarterly. Vol. 1, no. 1 (Mar. 1954)-v. 15, no. 4 (Dec. 1968).
"To further knowledge of the biological and sociocultural
forces affecting human populations." Eugenical news ISSN:
0361-7769. Continued by: Social biology ISSN: 0037-766X.
ISSN 0097-2762 DDC 613.94; 301.323
*1. Eugenics - Periodicals. 2. Birth control - Periodicals. I.
American Eugenics Society. II. Title: Eugenical news III. Title:
Social biology*

**Eugenie, ill.**
Munsch, Robert N., 1945- Ribbon rescue. New York :
Scholastic, 1999.
*TC PZ7.M927 Ri 1999*

**EURASIA.** *See* ASIA; EUROPE.

**Eureka :** teacher's planning guide. New York :
Macmillan/McGraw-Hill, c1997. 1 v. (various pagings) :
col. ill. ; 31 cm. (Spotlight on literacy : Gr.2 L6 u.2) (The road
to independent reading) Includes index. ISBN 0-02-181159-8
*1. Language arts (Primary) 2. Reading (Primary) I. Series. II.
Series: The road to independent reading*
*TC LB1576 .S66 1997 Gr.2 L6 u.2*

**EURINDIANS (LATIN AMERICA).** *See*
MESTIZOS.

**EUROPE - CIVILIZATION.**
Barzun, Jacques, 1907- From dawn to decadence. 1st
ed. New York : HarperCollins, c2000.
*TC CB245 .B365 2000*

**EUROPE - CIVILIZATION - 476-1492.** *See*
CIVILIZATION, MEDIEVAL.

**EUROPE - DESCRIPTION AND TRAVEL.**
Addison, Margaret, 1868-1940. Diary of a European
tour, 1900. Montréal : McGill-Queen's University
Press, c1999.
*TC LE3.T619 A33 1999*

**EUROPE - DESCRIPTIONS ET VOYAGES.**
Addison, Margaret, 1868-1940. Diary of a European
tour, 1900. Montréal : McGill-Queen's University
Press, c1999.
*TC LE3.T619 A33 1999*

**EUROPE - HISTORY.**
Riker, Thad Weed, 1880-1952. The story of modern
Europe. Boston : Houghton, Mifflin, 1942.
*TC D209 .R48*

**EUROPE - HISTORY - 20TH CENTURY - STUDY
AND TEACHING - EUROPE - CONGRESSES.**
The challenges of the information and communication
technologies facing history teaching. Strasbourg :
Council of Europe Pub., c1999.
*TC D424 .C425 1999*

Towards a pluralist and tolerant approach to teaching
history. Strasbourg : Council of Europe Pub., c1999.

*TC D424 .T665 1999*

**EUROPE - HISTORY - 476-1492.** *See* MIDDLE
AGES - HISTORY.

**EUROPE - INTELLECTUAL LIFE.**
Barzun, Jacques, 1907- From dawn to decadence. 1st
ed. New York : HarperCollins, c2000.
*TC CB245 .B365 2000*

**EUROPE - INTELLECTUAL LIFE - 17TH
CENTURY.**
Gascoigne, John, Ph. D. Science, politics, and
universities in Europe, 1600-1800. Aldershot
[England] ; Brookfield, Vt. : Ashgate, c1998.
*TC LA621.5 .G37 1998*

**EUROPE - INTELLECTUAL LIFE - 18TH
CENTURY.**
Gascoigne, John, Ph. D. Science, politics, and
universities in Europe, 1600-1800. Aldershot
[England] ; Brookfield, Vt. : Ashgate, c1998.
*TC LA621.5 .G37 1998*

**EUROPE - LANGUAGES - HANDBOOKS,
MANUALS, ETC.**
Allen, C. G. (Charles Geoffry) A manual of European
languages for librarians. 2nd ed. New Providence,
NJ : Bowker-Saur, c1999.
*TC P380 .A4 1999*

**EUROPE - STATISTICS - HISTORY.**
Mitchell, B. R. (Brian R.) International historical
statistics. 4th ed. London : Macmillan Reference ;
New York, N.Y. : Grove's dictionaries [division of
Stockton Press], 1998.
*TC HA1107 .M53 1998*

**European Association for Research on Adolescence.**
Spruijt-Metz, Donna. Adolescence, affect and health.
Hove : Psychology Press, for the European
Association for Research on Adolescence, 1999.
*TC RJ47.53 .S67 1999*

**European Association for Research on Learning and
Instruction.**
Learning sites. 1st ed. Amsterdam ; New York :
Pergamon, 1999.
*TC LB1060 .L4245 1999*

New perspectives on conceptual change. 1st ed.
Amsterdam ; New York ; Oxford : Pergamon, 1999.
*TC LB1062 .N49 1999*

**European Association of Social Anthropologists
(Series)**
Audit cultures. London ; New York : Routledge, 2000.
*TC LB2324 .A87 2000*

**European Centre for Modern Languages.**
Introducing learner autonomy in teacher education.
Strasbourg : Council of Europe Pub., c1999.
*TC PB38.E8 I567 1999*

Learner autonomy. Strasbourg : Council of Europe
Pub., c1999.
*TC PB38.E8 L424 1999*

**European Centre for Social Welfare Policy and
Research.**
The challenge of diversity. Aldershot, England ;
Brookfield, Vt. : Avebury, 1996.
*TC JV225 .C530 1996*

**European Communities Biologists Association.**
Heidelberger Ernährungsforum (5th : 1998 :
Heidelberg) Food quality, nutrition, and health.
Berlin ; New York : Springer, 2000.
*TC RA784 .H42 2000*

**European modernism :** 1900-1940 / Art Education for
the Blind & Paula Gerson, with Virginia Hooper. New
York, N.Y. : OpticalTouch Systems ; Louisville, Ky. :
American Printing House for the Blind, c1998-1999.
71 p. of print and braille : ill. (some col.) ; 29 cm. + 7 sound
cassettes (analog ; 7 1/2 ips) + 1 braille sheet (28 cm.) + 1
computer disk (3 1/2 in.) and manual (34 x 29 x 6 cm.). (Art
history through touch & sound) Series subtitle on container and
manual: Multisensory guide for the blind and visually
impaired. Title and statement of responsibility from container.
"An Art Education for the Blind Book"-- Container and manual
cover. Computer disk is teacher's supplement. ISBN
1-89011-607-6 (container) ISBN 1-89011-606-8
(audiocassettes) ISBN 1-89011-605-x (manual) ISBN
1-89011-610-6 (teacher's suppl. disk)
*1. Art, Modern - 20th century - Europe. 2. Blind - Books and
reading. 3. Visually handicapped - Books and reading. I.
Gerson, Paul Lieber. II. Hooper, Virginia. III. Art Education
for the Blind. IV. Title: Multisensory guide for the blind and
visually impaired V. Series.*
*TC N6758 .A7 1999*

**EUROPEAN WAR, 1914-1918.** *See* WORLD WAR,
1914-1918.

**EUROPEAN WAR, 1939-1945.** *See* WORLD WAR,
1939-1945.

**EUTHANASIA.** *See* ASSISTED SUICIDE.

**EUTHANASIA - MORAL AND ETHICAL
ASPECTS.**
Lederer, Jane. Participation in active euthanasia and
assisted suicide and attitudes and interpersonal values
of physicians and nurses. 1996.
*TC 06 no. 10849*

Prado, C. G. The last choice. 2nd ed. Westport,
Conn. : Greenwood Press, 1998.
*TC HV6545.2 .P7 1998*

**EUTHENICS.** *See* EUGENICS.

**EVACUATION AND RELOCATION OF
JAPANESE AMERICANS, 1942-1945.** *See*
JAPANESE AMERICANS - EVACUATION
AND RELOCATION, 1942-1945.

**Evaluating a course.**
Forsyth, Ian. The complete guide to teaching a course.
2nd ed. London : Kogan Page ; Sterling, VA : Stylus
Publishing, 1999.
*TC LB1025.3 .F67 1999*

**Evaluating health promotion :** practice and methods /
edited by Margaret Thorogood and Yolande Coombes.
Oxford ; New York : Oxford University Press, 2000.
x, 174 p. ; 22 cm. Includes bibliographical references and
index. ISBN 0-19-263169-1 (acid-free paper) DDC 613/.068
*1. Health promotion - Evaluation. 2. Health Promotion -
standards. 3. Program Evaluation - methods. I. Thorogood,
Margaret. II. Coombes, Yolande.*
*TC RA427.8 .E95 2000*

**Evaluating, improving, and judging faculty
performance in two-year colleges.**
Miller, Richard I. Westport, Conn. ; London :
Bergin & Garvey, 2000.
*TC LB2333 .M49 2000*

**Evaluating school programs.**
Sanders, James R. 2nd ed. Thousand Oaks, Calif. :
Corwin Press, c2000.
*TC LB2822.75 .S26 2000*

**Evaluating teachers for professional growth.**
Beerens, Daniel R. Thousand Oaks, Calif. ; London :
Corwin Press, c2000.
*TC LB2838 .B44 2000*

**EVALUATION.** *See also* DISABILITY
EVALUATION; EDUCATIONAL
EVALUATION; EVALUATION RESEARCH
(SOCIAL ACTION PROGRAMS).
Rossi, Peter Henry, 1921- 6th ed. Thousand Oaks,
Calif. : Sage Publications, c1999.
*TC H62 .R666 1999*

**Evaluation and implementation of distance learning.**
Belanger, France, 1963- Hershey, PA ; London : Idea
Group Pub., c2000.
*TC LC5803.C65 B45 2000*

**Evaluation as a democratic process :** promoting
inclusion, dialogue, and deliberation / Katherine E.
Ryan, Lizanne DeStefano, editors. San Francisco,
CA : Jossey-Bass, c2000. 111 p. ; 23 cm. (New directions
for evaluation, 0197-6736 ; no. 85) (Jossey-Bass education
series) "Spring 2000" Includes bibliographical references and
index. ISBN 0-7879-5371-7
*1. Evaluation - Education. 2. Education - Social aspects. I.
Ryan, Katherine E. II. DeStefano, Lizanne. III. Series. IV.
Series: New directions for evaluation ; no.85*
*TC LB2806 .E79 2000*

**EVALUATION - EDUCATION.**
Evaluation as a democratic process. San Francisco,
CA : Jossey-Bass, c2000.
*TC LB2806 .E79 2000*

**Evaluation in education and human services**
Measuring up. Boston : Kluwer Academic Publishers,
c1999.
*TC LB3051 .M4627 1999*

**Evaluation in the elementary school.**
Hedges, William D. New York, Holt, Rinehart and
Winston [1969]
*TC LB3051 .H4*

**EVALUATION - MORAL AND ETHICAL
ASPECTS.**
Information technologies in evaluation. San Francisco,
Calif. : Jossey-Bass, 1999.
*TC H62 .I54 1999*

**EVALUATION OF CURRICULUM.** *See* CURRICULUM EVALUATION.

**EVALUATION OF LITERATURE.** *See* BOOKS AND READING; CRITICISM; LITERATURE - HISTORY AND CRITICISM.

**EVALUATION OF SOCIAL ACTION PROGRAMS.** *See* EVALUATION RESEARCH (SOCIAL ACTION PROGRAMS).

**Evaluation of the interaction between users of screen reading technology and graphical user interface elements.**
Barnicle, Katherine Ann. 1999.
*TC 085 B265*

**An evaluation of the National Conference on Teacher Education 1986.**
Tamakloe, E. K. Accra : Ghana Universities Press, 1997.
*TC LB1727.G5 T36 1997*

**Evaluation quarterly 1977-1979.**
Evaluation review. [Beverly Hills] Sage Publications.

**EVALUATION RESEARCH IN EDUCATION.** *See* EDUCATIONAL EVALUATION.

**Evaluation research: methods of assessing program effectiveness.**
Weiss, Carol H. Englewood Cliffs, N.J., Prentice-Hall [1972]
*TC H62 .W3962*

**EVALUATION RESEARCH (SOCIAL ACTION PROGRAMS).**
How and why language matters in evaluation. San Francisco, CA : Jossey-Bass, c2000.
*TC H62 .H67 2000*

Rossi, Peter Henry, 1921- Evaluation. 6th ed. Thousand Oaks, Calif. : Sage Publications, c1999.
*TC H62 .R666 1999*

Weiss, Carol H. Evaluation research: methods of assessing program effectiveness Englewood Cliffs, N.J., Prentice-Hall [1972]
*TC H62 .W3962*

**EVALUATION RESEARCH (SOCIAL ACTION PROGRAMS) - MORAL AND ETHICAL ASPECTS.**
Information technologies in evaluation. San Francisco, Calif. : Jossey-Bass, 1999.
*TC H62 .I54 1999*

**EVALUATION RESEARCH (SOCIAL ACTION PROGRAMS) - PERIODICALS.**
Evaluation review. [Beverly Hills] Sage Publications.

**EVALUATION RESEARCH (SOCIAL ACTION PROGRAMS) - UNITED STATES.**
Violence in families. Washington, D.C. : National Academy Press, 1998.
*TC HV6626.2 .V56 1998*

**EVALUATION RESEARCH (SOCIAL ACTION PROGRAMS) - UNITED STATES - ADDRESSES, ESSAYS, LECTURES.**
Utilization of evaluative information. San Francisco : Jossey-Bass, 1980.
*TC H62.5.U5 U86*

**Evaluation review.** [Beverly Hills] Sage Publications. v. 22 cm. Frequency: Six no. a year, 1980- . Former frequency: Quarterly, 1977-1979. v. 1- Feb. 1977- . Title varies: Evaluation quarterly 1977-1979. "A journal of applied social research." ISSN 0193-841X
*1. Evaluation research (Social action programs) - Periodicals. I. Title: Evaluation quarterly 1977-1979*

**Evaluative research in recreation, park, and sport settings.**
Riddick, Carol Cutler. [Champaign, Ill.? : Sagamore Publishing], c1999.
*TC GV181.46 .R533 1999*

**EVALUATIVE RESEARCH (SOCIAL ACTION PROGRAMS).** *See* EVALUATION RESEARCH (SOCIAL ACTION PROGRAMS).

**EVANGELICAL RELIGION.** *See* EVANGELICALISM.

**EVANGELICAL REVIVAL.** *See* EVANGELICALISM.

**EVANGELICALISM.** *See* FUNDAMENTALISM.

**EVANGELICALISM - UNITED STATES - HISTORY.**
Ladd, Tony. Muscular Christianity. Grand Rapids, Mich. : Baker Books, c1999.
*TC GV706.42 .L34 1999*

**Evans, Janet.**
What's in the picture? London : P. Chapman Pub. Ltd., c1998.
*TC LB1044.9.P49 W52 1998*

**Evans, Karen, 1949-** Learning and work in the risk society : lessons for the labour markets of Europe from Eastern Germany / Karen Evans, Martina Behrens, Jens Kaluza. New York : St. Martin's Press, 2000. xiv, 188 p. : ill. ; 23 cm. Includes bibliographical references and index. ISBN 0-312-23160-1 (cloth) DDC 331.11/423/09431
*1. College graduates - Employment - Germany (East) 2. Labor supply - Effect of education on - Germany (East) 3. Occupational training - Germany (East) 4. Vocational education - Germany (East) I. Behrens. Martina. II. Kaluza. Jens. III. Title.*
*TC HD6278.G4 E93 2000*

**Evans, Karin.** The lost daughters of China : abandoned girls, their journey to America and the search for a missing past / Karin Evans. New York : J.P. Tarcher/Putnam, c2000. xi, 270 p. : ill. ; 22 cm. Includes bibliographical references (p. 261-264). ISBN 1-58542-026-3 (acid-free paper) DDC 362.73/4/0820951
*1. Orphanages - China. 2. Abandoned children - China. 3. Chinese - United States. 4. Intercountry adoption - Case studies. I. Title.*
*TC HV1317 .E93 2000*

**Evans, Kim.**
Andy Warhol [videorecording]. [Chicago, IL] : Home Vision [distributor],cc1987.
*TC N6537.W28 A45 1987*

Andy Warhol [videorecording]. [Chicago, IL] : Home Vision [distributor],cc1987.
*TC N6537.W28 A45 1987*

Jackson Pollock [videorecording]. [Chicago, Ill.] : Home Vision : [S.l.] : Distributed Worldwide by RM Associates, c1987.
*TC ND237.P73 J3 1987*

Marc Chagall [videorecording]. [Chicago, Ill.] : Home Vision [distributor], c1985.
*TC ND699.C5 C5 1985*

**Evans, Lezlie.** Can you count ten toes? : count to 10 in 10 different languages / Lezlie Evans ; illustrated by Denis Roche. Boston. Mass. : Houghton Mifflin, 1999. 1 v. (unpaged) : col. ill. ; 22 cm. SUMMARY: Rhyming verses instruct the reader to count different objects in one of ten languages, including Spanish, Japanese, Russian, Tagalog, and Hebrew. ISBN 0-395-90499-4 DDC 513.2/11; E
*1. Counting - Juvenile literature. 2. Counting. 3. Polyglot materials. I. Roche, Denis. ill. II. Title.*
*TC QA113 .E84 1999*

**Evans, Nancy J., 1947-.**
Toward acceptance. Lanham, Md. : University Press of America, 1999.
*TC LC192.6 .T69 1999*

**Evans, Norman, 1923-.**
Experiential learning around the world. London ; Philadelphia : J. Kingsley Publishers, 2000.
*TC LB2324 .E95 2000*

**Evans, Richard I. (Richard Isadore), 1922-.**
Jung on film [videorecording]. [Chicago, Ill.?] : Public Media Video, c1990.
*TC BF109.J8 J4 1990*

Jung on film [videorecording]. [Chicago, Ill.?] : Public Media Video, c1990.
*TC BF109.J8 J4 1990*

**Evans, Richard Paul.** The dance / Richard Paul Evans ; illustrations by Jonathan Linton. 1st ed. New York : Simon & Schuster Books for Young Readers, c1999. 1 v. (unpaged) : col. ill. ; 31 cm. SUMMARY: A father watches his daughter dance through various stages of her life. ISBN 0-689-82351-7 DDC [E]
*1. Fathers and daughters - Fiction. 2. Dance - Fiction. I. Linton, Jonathan, ill. II. Title.*
*TC PZ7.E89227 Dan 1999*

**Evans, Terry D. (Terry Denis).**
Changing university teaching :. London : Kogan Page : Sterling, VA : Stylus Pub., 2000.
*TC LB2331 .C53 2000*

**EVENING AND CONTINUATION SCHOOLS - LOUISIANA - SHREVEPORT.**
Baldwin, John. Education and welfare reform. Bloomington, Ind. : Phi Delta Kappa Educational Foundation, c1993.
*TC LC4033.S61 B34 1993*

**EVENING COLLEGES.** *See* EVENING AND CONTINUATION SCHOOLS.

**EVENING SCHOOLS.** *See* EVENING AND CONTINUATION SCHOOLS.

**Evensen, Dorothy H.**
Problem-based learning. Mahwah, N.J. : L. Erlbaum Associates, 2000.
*TC LB1027.42 .P78 2000*

**EVENT-RELATED BRAIN POTENTIALS.** *See* EVOKED POTENTIALS (ELECTROPHYSIOLOGY).

**EVENT-RELATED POTENTIALS (ELECTROPHYSIOLOGY).** *See* EVOKED POTENTIALS (ELECTROPHYSIOLOGY).

**EVENTS, LIFE CHANGE.** *See* LIFE CHANGE EVENTS.

**Events Sept. 1941.**
Current history and Forum. New York [C-H Publishing Corporation; etc., etc., 1914-41]

**Everett, Craig A.** Family therapy for ADHD : treating children, adolescents, and adults / Craig A. Everett, Sandra Volgy Everett. New York : Guilford Press, 1999. xiv, 270 p. : ill. ; 24 cm. Includes bibliographical references and index. ISBN 1-57230-438-3 DDC 616.85/89
*1. Attention-deficit hyperactivity disorder. 2. Attention-deficit disorder in adolescence. 3. Attention-deficit disorder in adults. 4. Hyperactive children - Family relationships. 5. Attention-deficit disordered children - Family relationships. 6. Attention-deficit disordered youth - Family relationships. 7. Attention-deficit disordered adults - Family relationships. 8. Family psychotherapy. 9. Attention Deficit Disorders with Hyperactivity - in adolescence. 10. Attention Deficit Disorders with Hyperactivity - in adulthood. 11. Family Therapy. I. Volgy. Sandra Everett. II. Title. III. Title: Family therapy for attention-deficit hyperactivity disorder*
*TC RJ506.H9 E94 1999*

Nichols, William C. Systemic family therapy. New York : Guilford Press, c1986.
*TC RC488.5 .N535 1986*

**Everitt, Brian.** Chance rules : an informal guide to probability, risk, and statistics / Brian S. Everitt. New York : Copernicus, c1999. xiv, 202 p. : ill. ; 24 cm. Includes bibliographical references (p. 193-194) and index. ISBN 0-387-98776-2 (alk. paper) ISBN 0-387-98768-1 (pbk. : alk. paper)
*1. Probabilities. 2. Chance. 3. Mathematical statistics. I. Title.*
*TC QA273 .E84 1999*

**Evertson, Carolyn M., 1935-** Classroom management for elementary teachers / Carolyn M. Evertson, Edmund T. Emmer, Murray E. Worsham. 5th ed. Boston : Allyn and Bacon, c2000. xii, 244 p. : ill. ; 21 cm. Rev. ed. of: Classroom management for elementary teachers / Carolyn M. Evertson ... [et al.]. 4th ed. c1997. Includes bibliographical references (p. 235-238) and index. ISBN 0-205-30838-4 DDC 372.1102/4
*1. Classroom management. 2. Education, Elementary. I. Emmer, Edmund T. II. Worsham, Murray E. III. Title.*
*TC LB3013 .C528 2000*

Emmer, Edmund T. Classroom management for secondary teachers. 5th ed. Boston : Allyn and Bacon, c2000.
*TC LB3013 .C53 2000*

**Everybody's children.**
Gormley, William T., 1950- Washington, D.C. : Brookings Institution, c1995.
*TC HQ778.63 .G674 1995*

**Everyone a teacher** / edited by Mark Schwehn. Notre Dame, Ind. : University of Notre Dame Press, c2000. xii, 380 p. : ill. ; 25 cm. (The ethics of everyday life) Includes bibliographical references. ISBN 0-268-04209-8 (hbk. : alk. paper) ISBN 0-268-04210-1 (pbk. : alk. paper) DDC 371.102
*1. Teaching. 2. Learning. 3. Teachers. 4. Education - Aims and objectives. I. Schwehn. Mark R.. 1945- II. Series.*
*TC LB1025.3 .E87 2000*

**Everyone can write.**
Elbow, Peter. New York : Oxford University Press, 2000.
*TC PE1404 .E42 2000*

**Everything you need to know about being a biracial/biethnic teen.**
Nash, Renea D. 1st ed. New York : Rosen Pub. Group, 1995.
*TC HQ77.9 .N39 1995*

**Evetts-Secker, Josephine.** Father and son tales / retold by Josephine Evetts-Secker ; illustrated by Helen Cann. Richmond Hill, Ont. : Scholastic Canada, 1998. 80 p. : col. ill. ; 27 cm. ISBN 0-590-03873-7 DDC 398.27
*1. Fathers and sons - Folklore. 2. Tales. I. Cann, Helen. II. Title.*
*TC GR469 E93 1998*

**Evidence-based assessment of the scientific research literature on reading and its implications for reading instruction.**
National Reading Panel (U.S.) Report of the National Reading Panel : teaching children to read. [Washington, D.C.?] : National Institute of Child Health and Human Development, National Institutes of Health, [2000]
*TC LB1050 .N335 2000*

**EVIDENCE-BASED MEDICINE.**
Reconciling empirical knowledge and clinical experience. 1st ed. Washington, DC : American Psychological Association, c1999.
*TC RC480 .R395 1999*

**EVIDENCE-BASED MEDICINE.**
Reconciling empirical knowledge and clinical experience. 1st ed. Washington, DC : American Psychological Association, c1999.
*TC RC480 .R395 1999*

**EVIDENCE, EXPERT - UNITED STATES.**
Pope, Kenneth S. The MMPI, MMPI-2, & MMPI-A in court. 2nd ed. Washington, DC : American Psychological Association, 2000.
*TC KF8965 .P66 1999*

**EVIDENCE (LAW).** See **CONFIDENTIAL COMMUNICATIONS.**

**Evidence of student learning and implications for alternative policies that support instructional use of assessment.**
Southworth, Robert A. 1999.
*TC 06 no. 11218*

**Evocative images :** the thematic apperception test and the art of projection / edited by Lon Gieser and Morris I. Stein. 1st ed. Washington, DC : American Psychological Association, c1999. xv, 231 p. ; 27 cm. Includes bibliographical references (p.219-221) and index. ISBN 1-55798-579-0 (hardcover : alk. paper) DDC 155.2/844
*1. Thematic Apperception Test. I. Gieser, Lon. II. Stein, Morris Isaac, 1921-*
*TC BF698.8.T5 E96 1999*

**EVOKED CORTICAL POTENTIALS.** See **EVOKED POTENTIALS (ELECTROPHYSIOLOGY).**

**EVOKED POTENTIALS (ELECTROPHYSIOLOGY).**
Learning. Berlin ; New York : Walter de Gruyter, 1999.
*TC QP408 .L44 1999*

**EVOLUTION.** See also **CREATION; EVOLUTION (BIOLOGY).**
Evolutionary aspects of nutrition and health. Basel ; New York : Karger, c1999.
*TC QP141 .E95 1999*

**EVOLUTION (BIOLOGY).**
Dowdeswell, W. H. (Wilfrid Hogarth) The mechanism of evolution, 3d ed. London, Heinemann, 1963
*TC QH366 .D68 1963*

**EVOLUTION (BIOLOGY) - PHILOSOPHY.**
Ruse, Michael. Mystery of mysteries. Cambridge, Mass. : Harvard University Press, 1999.
*TC QH360.5 .R874 1999*

**Evolution in mind.**
Plotkin, H. C. (Henry C.) Cambridge, Mass. : Harvard University Press, 1998.
*TC BF701 .P57 1998*

**The evolution of cognition** / edited by Cecilia Heyes and Ludwig Huber. Cambridge, Mass. : MIT Press, c2000. viii, 386 p. : ill. ; 23 cm. (Vienna series in theoretical biology) "A Bradford book." Includes bibliographical references and indexes. ISBN 0-262-08286-1 (pbk. : alk. paper) DDC 156/.3
*1. Genetic psychology. 2. Psychology, Comparative. I. Heyes, Cecilia M. II. Huber, Ludwig, 1950- III. Series.*
*TC BF701 .E598 2000*

**The evolution of counseling psychology.**
Blocher, Donald H. New York : Springer, c2000.
*TC BF637.C6 .B473 2000*

**EVOLUTION - STUDY AND TEACHING - LAW AND LEGISLATION - UNITED STATES.**
Larson, Edward J. (Edward John) Summer for the gods. New York : BasicBooks, c1997.
*TC KF224.S3 L37 1997*

**Evolutionary aspects of nutrition and health :** diet, exercise, genetics, and chronic disease / volume editor, A.P. Simopoulos. Basel ; New York : Karger, c1999. xiv, 145 p. : ill., map ; 25 cm. (World review of nutrition and dietetics ; vol. 84) Includes bibliographical

references and index. ISBN 3-8055-6827-4 (hardcover) DDC 612.3
*1. Nutrition. 2. Human evolution. 3. Human genetics. 4. Nutritionally induced diseases. 5. Chronic diseases. 6. Diet 7. Evolution 8. Exercise 9. Nutrition Disorders - etiology 10. Nutrition 11. Variation (Genetics) I. Series.*
*TC QP141 .E95 1999*

**Evolutionary principles of human adolescence.**
Weisfeld, Glenn, 1943- New York, NY : Basic Books, 1999.
*TC BF724 .W35 1999*

**Evolution's eye.**
Oyama, Susan. Durham, NC : Duke University Press, 2000.
*TC BF713 .O93 2000*

**Evolving role of the guardian ad litem.**
Clark, Alison. The child in focus. London : National Children's Bureau Enterprise, c1999.
*TC KD785 .C43 1999*

**Ewart, Franzeska G.** Let the shadows speak : developing children's language through shadow puppetry / Franzeska G. Ewart. Stoke on Trent, Staffordshire, England : Trentham Books, 1998. x, 122 p. : ill. ; 25 cm. Includes bibliographical references (p. 119) and index. ISBN 1-85856-099-3
*1. Drama in education. 2. Shadow puppets. 3. Shadow shows. 4. Language arts (Elementary) I. Title.*
*TC PN1979.S5 E8 1998*

**Ewing, Patrick Aloysius, 1962-.**
Milbank Memorial Library story hour [videorecording]. [New York : Milbank Memorial Library, 1999]
*TC Z718.3 .M5 1999 Series 3 Prog. 6*

**EX-MILITARY PERSONNEL.** See **VETERANS.**

**EX-SERVICE MEN.** See **VETERANS.**

**EX-SLAVES.** See **FREEDMEN.**

**An examination of critical feminist pedagogy in practice.**
Robbins, Carol Braswell. 1999.
*TC 06 no. 11067*

**EXAMINATIONS.** See also **EDUCATIONAL TESTS AND MEASUREMENTS; NORM-REFERENCED TESTS.**
Ardovino, Joan. Multiple measures. Thousand Oaks, Calif. : Corwin Press, c2000.
*TC LB3051 .A745 2000*

**EXAMINATIONS - DESIGN AND CONSTRUCTION.**
Ardovino, Joan. Multiple measures. Thousand Oaks, Calif. : Corwin Press, c2000.
*TC LB3051 .A745 2000*

Cunningham, George K. Assessment in the classroom. London : Falmer, 1998.
*TC LB3051 .C857 1998*

Hopkins, Charles D. Classroom testing. 2nd ed. Itasca, Ill. : F. E. Peacock Publishers, c1989.
*TC LB3060.65 .H661 1989*

Yi, Qing. Simulating nonmodel-fitting responses in a CAT environment. Iowa City, Iowa : ACT, 1998.
*TC LB3051 .A3 no. 98-10*

**EXAMINATIONS - EVALUATION.**
Chang, Shun-Wen. A comparative study of item exposure control methods in computerized adaptive testing. Iowa City, IA : ACT, Inc., 1998.
*TC LB3051 .A3 no. 98-3*

**EXAMINATIONS - INTERPRETATION.** See also **EXAMINATIONS - VALIDITY; GRADING AND MARKING (STUDENTS).**
Cunningham, George K. Assessment in the classroom. London : Falmer, 1998.
*TC LB3051 .C857 1998*

**EXAMINATIONS - NIGERIA - CONGRESSES.**
Issues on examination malpractices in Nigeria :. Ikere-Ekiti [Nigeria] : Ondo State College of Education, c1998.
*TC LB3058.N6 1848 1998*

**EXAMINATIONS - UNITED STATES.**
Strickland, Kathleen. Making assessment elementary. Portsmouth, NH : Heinemann, 2000.
*TC LB3051 .S873 1999*

**EXAMINATIONS - UNITED STATES - SCORING.**
Mabry, Linda. Portfolios plus. Thousand Oaks, Calif. : Corwin Press, c1999.
*TC LB3051 .M4243 1999*

**EXAMINATIONS - VALIDITY.** See also **TEST BIAS.**
Ardovino, Joan. Multiple measures. Thousand Oaks, Calif. : Corwin Press, c2000.
*TC LB3051 .A745 2000*

Cunningham, George K. Assessment in the classroom. London : Falmer, 1998.
*TC LB3051 .C857 1998*

**EXAMINATIONS - VALIDITY - UNITED STATES.**
Mabry, Linda. Portfolios plus. Thousand Oaks, Calif. : Corwin Press, c1999.
*TC LB3051 .M4243 1999*

**Examining pedagogical content knowledge :** the construct and its implications for science education / edited by Julie Gess-Newsome and Norman G. Lederman. Dordrecht ; London : Kluwer Academic, c1999. xii, 306 p. : ill. ; 25 cm. (Science & technology education library ; v. 6) Published in cooperation with the Association for the Education of Teachers in Science. Includes bibliographical references and index. ISBN 0-7923-5903-8 DDC 507.12
*1. Science - Study and teaching. 2. Science teachers - Training of. I. Gess-Newsome, Julie. II. Lederman, Norman G. III. Association for the Education of Teachers in Science. IV. Series.*
*TC Q181 .E93 1999*

**Examining science teaching in elementary school from the perspective of a teacher and learner.**
Osborne, Margery D. New York : Falmer Press, 1999.
*TC LB1585 .O77 1999*

**EXAMPLE.** See **INFLUENCE (PSYCHOLOGY).**

**EXAMPLE - PSYCHOLOGICAL ASPECTS.**
Loase, John Frederick, 1947- Sigfluence III. Lanham, Md. : University Press of America, c1996.
*TC BF774 .L63 1996*

**The example school portfolio :** a companion to The school portfolio, a comprehensive framework for school improvement / by Victoria L. Bernhardt. Larchmont, N.Y. : Eye On Education, 2000. xv, 287, p. : ill. ; 28 cm. Includes bibliographical references. ISBN 1-88300-192-7 DDC 371.2
*1. School improvement programs - United States. 2. Portfolios in education - United States. I. Bernhardt, Victoria L., 1952- II. Bernhardt, Victoria L., 1952-. School portfolio.*
*TC LB2822.82 .E92 2000*

**EXCAVATION SITES (ARCHAEOLOGY).** See **EXCAVATIONS (ARCHAEOLOGY).**

**EXCAVATIONS (ARCHAEOLOGY) - NORTH CAROLINA - WINSTON-SALEM.**
South, Stanley A. Historical archaeology in Wachovia. New York : Kluwer Academic/Plenum Publishers, c1999.
*TC F264.W8 S66 1999*

**EXCEPTIONAL CHILDREN.** See also **ATTENTION-DEFICIT-DISORDERED CHILDREN; GIFTED CHILDREN; HANDICAPPED CHILDREN; HYPERACTIVE CHILDREN; PARENTS OF EXCEPTIONAL CHILDREN.**
Heward, William L., 1949- 6th ed. Upper Saddle River, N.J. : Merrill, c2000.
*TC LC3981 .H49 2000*

**EXCEPTIONAL CHILDREN.**
Hardman, Michael L. Human exceptionality. 6th ed. Boston : Allyn and Bacon, c1999.
*TC HV1568 .H37 1999*

Kirk, Samuel Alexander, 1904- 10 years of research at the Institute for Research on Exceptional Children, University of Illinois, 1952-1962. [Urbana : s.n.], 1964.
*TC HQ773.7 .I4 1964*

**Exceptional children and youth, an introduction.**
Special education & student disability. 4th ed. Denver, Colo. : Love Pub. Co., c1995.
*TC LC3965 .E87 1995*

**EXCEPTIONAL CHILDREN - EDUCATION.** See **SPECIAL EDUCATION.**

**EXCEPTIONAL CHILDREN - UNITED STATES.**
Heward, William L., 1949- Exceptional children. 6th ed. Upper Saddle River, N.J. : Merrill, c2000.
*TC LC3981 .H49 2000*

**EXCEPTIONAL PARENTS.** See **HANDICAPPED PARENTS.**

**EXCHANGE OF PERSONS PROGRAMS.** See **EDUCATIONAL EXCHANGES; STUDENT EXCHANGE PROGRAMS.**

**EXCHANGE OF PRISONERS OF WAR.** *See* PRISONERS OF WAR.

**EXCHANGE OF STUDENTS.** *See* STUDENT EXCHANGE PROGRAMS.

**EXCHANGE PROGRAMS, STUDENT.** *See* STUDENT EXCHANGE PROGRAMS.

**The exchange student survival kit.**
Hansel, Bettina G. Yarmouth, ME : Intercultural Press, c1993.
*TC LB1696 .H36 1993*

**EXCHANGE THEORY (SOCIOLOGY).** *See* POWER (SOCIAL SCIENCES); SOCIAL INTERACTION.

**EXCHANGES, EDUCATIONAL.** *See* EDUCATIONAL EXCHANGES.

**EXCURSIONS, SCHOOL.** *See* SCHOOL FIELD TRIPS.

**EXECUTIVE ABILITY.**
Bell, Lisa M. Frontal lobe dysfunction in first episode Schizophrenia. 1998.
*TC 085 B3995*

Judge, William Q. The leader's shadow. Thousand Oaks, Calif. : Sage Publications, c1999.
*TC HD57.7 .J83 1999*

O'Toole, James. Leadership A to Z. 1st ed. San Francisco, CA : Jossey-Bass Publishers, c1999.
*TC HD57.7 .O87 1999*

Ulrich, David, 1953- Results-based leadership. Boston : Harvard Business School Press, 1999.
*TC HD57.7 .U45 1999*

**EXECUTIVE AGENCIES.** *See* ADMINISTRATIVE AGENCIES.

**EXECUTIVE DEPARTMENTS - EVALUATION.**
Building effective evaluation capacity. New Brunswick, N.J. : Transaction Publishers, c1999.
*TC JF1351 .B83 1999*

**EXECUTIVE NURSES.** *See* NURSE ADMINISTRATORS.

**EXECUTIVE POWER.** *See* CIVIL-MILITARY RELATIONS; MONARCHY.

**EXECUTIVE TRAINING.** *See* EXECUTIVES - TRAINING OF.

**EXECUTIVES - ATTITUDES.**
Skiba, Michaeline. A naturalistic inquiry of the relationship between organizational change and informal learning in the workplace. 1999.
*TC 06 no. 11180*

**EXECUTIVES, TRAINING OF.** *See* EXECUTIVES - TRAINING OF.

**EXECUTIVES - TRAINING OF.**
Raelin, Joseph A., 1948- Work based learning. Reading, MA : Addison-Wesley, 1999.
*TC HD30.4 .R33 1999*

**EXECUTIVES - TRAINING OF - CASE STUDIES.**
Business-driven action learning. New York : St. Martin's Press, 2000.
*TC HD58.82 .B87 2000*

**EXECUTIVES - TRAINING OF - PERIODICALS.**
Management learning. London ; Thousand Oaks, CA : Sage Publications, c1994-

**EXEMPLA.** *See* EXAMPLE; LEGENDS.

**EXERCISE.** *See also* PHYSICAL EDUCATION AND TRAINING; PHYSICAL FITNESS.
Evolutionary aspects of nutrition and health. Basel ; New York : Karger, c1999.
*TC QP141 .E95 1999*

Foss, Merle L., 1936- Fox's physiological basis for exercise and sport. 6th ed. / Merle L. Foss, Steven J. Keteyian. Boston, Mass. : WCB/McGraw-Hill, c1998.
*TC RC1235 .F65 1998*

Leutholtz, Brian C. Exercise and disease management. Boca Raton : CRC Press, c1999.
*TC RM725 .L45 1999*

McMurray, Robert G. Concepts in fitness programming. Boca Raton : CRC Press, c1999.
*TC QP301 .M3754 1999*

Rowell, Loring B. Human cardiovascular control. New York : Oxford University Press, 1993.
*TC QP109 .R68 1993*

White, Timothy P. The wellness guide to lifelong fitness. New York : Rebus : Distributed by Random House, c1993.

*TC RA781 .W47 1993*

**Exercise and circulation in health and disease** / Bengt Saltin ... [et al.], editors. Champaign, IL : Leeds, U.K. : Human Kinetics, c2000. xiv, 345 p. : ill. ; 29 cm. Includes bibliographical references and index. ISBN 0-88011-632-3 DDC 612/.044
*1. Exercise - Physiological aspects. 2. Cardiovascular system - Physiology. 3. Blood - Circulation. I. Saltin, Bengt, 1935-*
*TC QP301 .E9346 2000*

**Exercise and disease management.**
Leutholtz, Brian C. Boca Raton : CRC Press, c1999.
*TC RM725 .L45 1999*

**EXERCISE FOR THE AGED.**
Shephard, Roy J. Aging, physical activity, and health. Champaign, IL : Human Kinetics, c1997.
*TC QP86 .S478 1997*

**EXERCISE FOR THE AGED - UNITED STATES.**
Active older adults. Champaign, IL : Human Kinetics, c1999.
*TC GV482.6 .A38 1999*

**EXERCISE - HEALTH ASPECTS.**
Leutholtz, Brian C. Exercise and disease management. Boca Raton : CRC Press, c1999.
*TC RM725 .L45 1999*

**EXERCISE - IMMUNOLOGICAL ASPECTS.**
Mackinnon, Laurel T., 1953- Advances in exercise immunology. Champaign, IL : Human Kinetics, c1999.
*TC QP301 .M159 1999*

Nutrition and exercise immunology. Boca Raton, Fla. ; London : CRC Press, c2000.
*TC QP301 .N875 2000*

**Exercise immunology.**
Mackinnon, Laurel T., 1953- Advances in exercise immunology. Champaign, IL : Human Kinetics, c1999.
*TC QP301 .M159 1999*

**Exercise metabolism** / Mark Hargreaves, editor. Champaign, IL : Human Kinetics, c1995. viii, 263 p. : ill. ; 24 cm. Includes bibliographical references and index. ISBN 0-87322-453-1 (hardcover) DDC 612/.044
*1. Exercise - Physiological aspects. 2. Energy metabolism. 3. Metabolism. 4. Energy Metabolism. 5. Exertion. 6. Muscle. Skeletal - metabolism. I. Hargreaves, Mark, 1961-*
*TC QP301 .E967 1995*

**EXERCISE - PHYSIOLOGICAL ASPECTS.**
Battinelli, Thomas. Physique, fitness, and performance. Boca Raton : CRC Press, c2000.
*TC QP301 .B364 2000*

Exercise and circulation in health and disease. Champaign, IL ; Leeds, U.K. : Human Kinetics, c2000.
*TC QP301 .E9346 2000*

Exercise metabolism. Champaign, IL : Human Kinetics, c1995.
*TC QP301 .E967 1995*

Exercise physiology. 3rd ed. Mountain View, Calif. : Mayfield Pub., c2000.
*TC QP301 .B885 2000*

Foss, Merle L., 1936- Fox's physiological basis for exercise and sport. 6th ed. / Merle L. Foss, Steven J. Keteyian. Boston, Mass. : WCB/McGraw-Hill, c1998.
*TC RC1235 .F65 1998*

Houston, Michael E., 1941- Biochemistry primer for exercise science. Champaign, IL : Human Kinetics, c1995.
*TC QP514.2 .H68 1995*

Karlsson, Jan, 1940- Antioxidants and exercise. Champaign, IL : Human Kinetics, c1997.
*TC RB170 .K37 1997*

Muller, Susan. Student study guide to accompany Fox's physiological basis for exercise and sport. 6th ed. Boston, Mass. : WCB/McGraw-Hill, c1998.
*TC RC1235 .F65 1998 guide*

Nutrition in sport. Osney Mead, Oxford : Malden, MA : Blackwell Science, 2000.
*TC QP141 .N793 2000*

Pharmacology in exercise and sports. Boca Raton : CRC Press, c1996.
*TC QP301 .P53 1996*

**EXERCISE - PHYSIOLOGICAL ASPECTS - CONGRESSES.**
Fundacion Dr. Antonio Esteve. Symposium (7th : 1996 : Sitges, Spain) The clinical pharmacology of sport and exercise. Amsterdam ; New York : Elsevier Science B.V., Excerpta Medica, 1997.

*TC RC1230 .F86 1996*

The physiology and pathophysiology of exercise tolerance. New York : Plenum Press, c1996.
*TC QP301 .P576 1996*

**EXERCISE - PHYSIOLOGICAL EFFECT.** *See* EXERCISE - PHYSIOLOGICAL ASPECTS.

**EXERCISE PHYSIOLOGY.** *See* EXERCISE - PHYSIOLOGICAL ASPECTS.

**EXERCISE - PHYSIOLOGY.**
Karlsson, Jan, 1940- Antioxidants and exercise. Champaign, IL : Human Kinetics, c1997.
*TC RB170 .K37 1997*

Mackinnon, Laurel T., 1953- Advances in exercise immunology. Champaign, IL : Human Kinetics, c1999.
*TC QP301 .M159 1999*

Pharmacology in exercise and sports. Boca Raton : CRC Press, c1996.
*TC QP301 .P53 1996*

**EXERCISE - PHYSIOLOGY - CONGRESSES.**
The physiology and pathophysiology of exercise tolerance. New York : Plenum Press, c1996.
*TC QP301 .P576 1996*

**Exercise physiology** : human bioenergetics and its applications / George A. Brooks ... [et al.]. 3rd ed. Mountain View, Calif. : Mayfield Pub., c2000. xxi, 851 p. : ill. ; 25 cm. Second ed. gives Brooks as main entry. Includes bibliographical references and index. ISBN 0-7674-1024-6 DDC 612/.044
*1. Exercise - Physiological aspects. 2. Energy metabolism. 3. Bioenergetics. I. Brooks, George A. (George Austin), 1944-*
*TC QP301 .B885 2000*

**EXERCISE - PSYCHOLOGICAL ASPECTS.**
Hays, Kate F. Working it out. 1st ed. Washington, DC : American Psychological Association, c1999.
*TC RC489.E9 H39 1999*

**EXERCISE TESTS.** *See* EXERCISE - PHYSIOLOGICAL ASPECTS.

**EXERCISE THERAPY.**
Hays, Kate F. Working it out. 1st ed. Washington, DC : American Psychological Association, c1999.
*TC RC489.E9 H39 1999*

**EXERCISE THERAPY.**
Hays, Kate F. Working it out. 1st ed. Washington, DC : American Psychological Association, c1999.
*TC RC489.E9 H39 1999*

Leutholtz, Brian C. Exercise and disease management. Boca Raton : CRC Press, c1999.
*TC RM725 .L45 1999*

**EXERCISE THERAPY.**
Leutholtz, Brian C. Exercise and disease management. Boca Raton : CRC Press, c1999.
*TC RM725 .L45 1999*

**EXERCISE THERAPY FOR THE AGED - NEW JERSEY.**
Smith, Irmhild Wrede. The effect of structured exercise and structured reminiscing on agitation and aggression in geriatric psychiatric patients. 1996.
*TC 06 no. 10700*

**EXERCISE TOLERANCE - PHYSIOLOGY - CONGRESSES.**
The physiology and pathophysiology of exercise tolerance. New York : Plenum Press, c1996.
*TC QP301 .P576 1996*

**EXERTION.**
Exercise metabolism. Champaign, IL : Human Kinetics, c1995.
*TC QP301 .E967 1995*

**EXHAUSTION.** *See* FATIGUE.

**Exhibiting dilemmas** : issues of representation at the Smithsonian / edited by Amy Henderson and Adrienne L. Kaeppler. Washington, D.C. : Smithsonian Insitution Press, c1997. vi, 285 p. : ill. ; 24 cm. Includes bibliographical references and index. ISBN 1-56098-690-5 (alk. paper) ISBN 1-56098-444-9 DDC 069/.09753
*1. Exhibitions - Washington (D.C.) 2. Smithsonian Institution. I. Henderson, Amy. II. Kaeppler, Adrienne Lois.*
*TC AM151 .E96 1997*

**EXHIBITIONS.** *See* LIBRARY EXHIBITS; MUSEUM EXHIBITS.

**Exhibitions in museums.**
Belcher, Michael. Washington, D.C. : Smithsonian Institution Press, c1991.
*TC AM7 .B3 1991*

## EXHIBITIONS - POLITICAL ASPECTS - UNITED STATES - HISTORY.
Lorini, Alessandra, 1949- Rituals of race. Charlottesville : University Press of Virginia, 1999.
**TC E185.61 .L675 1999**

## EXHIBITIONS - WASHINGTON (D.C.).
Exhibiting dilemmas. Washington, D.C. : Smithsonian Insitution Press, c1997.
**TC AM151 .E96 1997**

## EXHIBITS. *See* EXHIBITIONS.

**Exiles + emigrés :** the flight of European artists from Hitler / Stephanie Barron with Sabine Eckmann ; contributions by Matthew Affron ... [et al.]. Los Angeles, Calif. : Los Angeles County Museum of Art ; New York : H.N. Abrams, c1997. 432 p. : ill. (some col.), maps ; 31 cm. Catalog of an exhibition organized by and held at the Los Angeles County Museum of Art, Feb. 23-May 11, 1997; the Montreal Museum of Fine Arts, June 19-Sept. 7, 1997; and the Neue Nationalgalerie, Berlin, Oct. 9, 1997-Jan. 4, 1998. Includes bibliographical references (p. 408-413) and index. ISBN 0-8109-3271-7 (cloth) ISBN 0-87587-178-X (paper) DDC 704/.03/034073
*1. Expatriate artists - United States - Exhibitions. 2. Artists - Europe - Exhibitions. 3. Art, Modern - 20th century - United States - Exhibitions. 4. Art, Modern - 20th century - Europe - Exhibitions. 5. Political refugees - United States - Exhibitions. 6. Exiles - United States - Exhibitions. I. Barron, Stephanie, 1950- II. Eckmann, Sabine. III. Affron, Matthew, 1963- IV. Los Angeles County Museum of Art. V. Montreal Museum of Fine Arts. VI. Neue Nationalgalerie (Germany) VII. Title: Exiles and emigrés*
**TC N6512 .E887 1997**

**Exiles and emigrés.**
Exiles + emigrés. Los Angeles, Calif. : Los Angeles County Museum of Art ; New York : H.N. Abrams, c1997.
**TC N6512 .E887 1997**

## EXILES - UNITED STATES - EXHIBITIONS.
Exiles + emigrés. Los Angeles, Calif. : Los Angeles County Museum of Art ; New York : H.N. Abrams, c1997.
**TC N6512 .E887 1997**

## EXISTENTIAL PHENOMENOLOGY.
Pathways into the Jungian world. London : New York : Routledge, 2000.
**TC BF175 .P29 2000**

## EXISTENTIAL PSYCHOTHERAPY.
Burston, Daniel, 1954- The crucible of experience. Cambridge, Mass. : Harvard University Press, c2000.
**TC RC438.6.L34 B86 2000**

## EXOCRINE GLANDS - SECRETIONS. *See* MILK.

**Expanding photgraphic vision [videorecording].**
The sight and insight of Ernst Haas [videorecording]. Minneapolis, Minn. : Media Loft, 1992.
**TC TR647.H3 S5 1992**

**EXPANDING UNIVERSE.**
Stephen Hawking's universe [videorecording]. [Alexandria, Va.] : PBS Video; Burbank, CA : Distributed by Warner Home Video, c1997.
**TC QB982 .S7 1997**

## EXPANSION (UNITED STATES POLITICS). *See* IMPERIALISM.

## EXPATRIATE ARTISTS - UNITED STATES - EXHIBITIONS.
Exiles + emigrés. Los Angeles, Calif. : Los Angeles County Museum of Art ; New York : H.N. Abrams, c1997.
**TC N6512 .E887 1997**

## EXPATRIATE PAINTERS - FRANCE - BIOGRAPHY.
Tomkins, Calvin, 1925- Living well is the best revenge. 1998 Modern Library ed. New York : Modern Library, c1998.
**TC ND237.M895 T66 1998**

## EXPECTANT MOTHERS. *See* PREGNANT WOMEN.

## EXPECTATION (PSYCHOLOGY).
How expectancies shape experience. 1st ed. Washington, DC : American Psychological Association, c1999.
**TC BF323.E8 H69 1999**

## EXPERIENCE. *See* EXPERIENTIAL LEARNING; LIFE CHANGE EVENTS.

## EXPERIENCE-BASED LEARNING. *See* EXPERIENTIAL LEARNING.

## EXPERIENCE IN CHILDREN.
The child's world. Camberwell, Vic. : ACER Press, 2000.
**TC BF723.C5 C467 2000**

Cullingford, Cedric. The human experience. Aldershot ; Brookfield, Vt. : Ashgate, c1999.
**TC BF723.E95 C84 1999**

## EXPERIENCES, STRESSFUL LIFE. *See* LIFE CHANGE EVENTS.

**Experiential activities for intercultural learning** / H. Ned Seelye, editor. Yarmouth, Me., USA : Intercultural Press, c1996- v. <1 > : ill. ; 26 cm. Includes bibliographical references. ISBN 1-87786-433-1 (v. 1) DDC 370.19/6
*1. Multicultural education - United States - Activity programs. 2. Interpersonal communication - United States. I. Seelye, H. Ned.*
**TC LC1099.3 .E97 1996**

## EXPERIENTIAL LEARNING. *See also* ACTIVE LEARNING.
Garrick, John. Informal learning in the workplace. London ; New York : Routledge, 1998.
**TC HF5549.5.T7 G344 1998**

Hess, J. Daniel (John Daniel), 1937- Studying abroad/learning abroad. Yarmouth, Me., USA : Intercultural Press, c1997.
**TC LB2375 .H467 1997**

Lamm, Sharon Lea. The connection between action reflection learning and transformative learning. 2000.
**TC 06 no. 11230**

Martin, Robert J. A study of the reflective practices of physical education student teachers. 1998.
**TC 06 no. 11031**

**Experiential learning around the world :** employability and the global economy / edited by Norman Evans. London ; Philadelphia : J. Kingsley Publishers, 2000. 222 p. ; 24 cm. (Higher education policy series ; 52) Includes bibliographical references and indexes. ISBN 1-85302-736-7 (alk. paper) DDC 374
*1. Experiential learning - Cross-cultural studies. 2. Education, Higher - Economic aspects - Cross-cultural studies. 3. Educational change - Cross-cultural studies. 4. Higher education and state - Economic aspects - Cross-cultural studies. I. Evans, Norman, 1923- II. Series.*
**TC LB2324 .E95 2000**

## EXPERIENTIAL LEARNING - CROSS-CULTURAL STUDIES.
Experiential learning around the world. London ; Philadelphia : J. Kingsley Publishers, 2000.
**TC LB2324 .E95 2000**

## EXPERIMENTAL DESIGN. *See* ANALYSIS OF VARIANCE.

## EXPERIMENTAL LITERATURE. *See* LITERATURE, EXPERIMENTAL.

## EXPERIMENTAL METHODS IN EDUCATION. *See* EDUCATION - EXPERIMENTAL METHODS.

## EXPERIMENTATION ON HUMANS, PSYCHOLOGICAL. *See* HUMAN EXPERIMENTATION IN PSYCHOLOGY.

**Experimenting with batteries, bulbs, and wires.**
Ward, Alan, 1932- New York : Chelsea Juniors, c1991.
**TC QC527.2 .W37 1991**

## EXPERIMENTS.
Ward, Alan, 1932- Experimenting with batteries, bulbs, and wires. New York : Chelsea Juniors, c1991.
**TC QC527.2 .W37 1991**

## EXPERT SYSTEMS (COMPUTER SCIENCE).
Innovative teaching and learning. Heidelberg [Germany] ; New York : Physica-Verlag, c2000.
**TC QA76.76.E95 I54 2000**

Pfeifer, Rolf, 1947- Understanding intelligence. Cambridge, Mass. : MIT Press, c1999.
**TC Q335 .P46 1999**

## EXPERTISE. *See also* ABILITY.
Dombroski, Ann P. Administrative problem solving. 1999.
**TC 06 no. 11104**

Dombroski, Ann P. Administrative problem solving. 1999.
**TC 06 no. 11104**

## EXPERTISE - ENVIRONMENTAL ASPECTS.
Yang, Fang-Ying. An analysis of 12th grade students' reasoning styles and competencies when presented with an environmental problem in a social and scientific context. 1999.
**TC 06 no. 11076**

**Expertise, research and applications**
Cognitive task analysis. Mahwah, N.J. : L. Erlbaum Associates, 2000.
**TC BF311 .C55345 2000**

## EXPERTISE - SOCIAL ASPECTS.
Yang, Fang-Ying. An analysis of 12th grade students' reasoning styles and competencies when presented with an environmental problem in a social and scientific context. 1999.
**TC 06 no. 11076**

## EXPLANATION.
Explanation and cognition. Cambridge, Mass. : MIT Press, c2000.
**TC BF311 .E886 2000**

**Explanation and cognition** / edited by Frank C. Keil and Robert A. Wilson. Cambridge, Mass. : MIT Press, c2000. x, 396 p. : ill. ; 24 cm. "A Bradford book." Includes bibliographical references and index. ISBN 0-262-11249-3 (alk. paper) DDC 153
*1. Cognition. 2. Explanation. I. Keil, Frank C., 1952- II. Wilson, Robert A. (Robert Andrew)*
**TC BF311 .E886 2000**

**The explicit teaching of reading** / Joelie Hancock, editor. Newark, Del. : International Reading Association, c1999. x, 139 p. : ill. ; 26 cm. Includes bibliographical references and index. ISBN 0-87207-253-3 DDC 372.41/6
*1. Reading. 2. Literacy - Social aspects. I. Hancock, Joelie. II. International Reading Association.*
**TC LB1573 .E96 1999**

**An exploration of school belongingness.**
Schlanger, Dean J. 1998.
**TC 06 no. 10993**

**Explorations in sociology**
Practising identities. New York : St. Martin's Press, 1999.
**TC HM131 .P677 1999**

## EXPLORATORY BEHAVIOR. *See* CURIOSITY.

**Exploring disability.**
Barnes, Colin, 1946- Cambridge, UK : Polity Press ; Malden, MA : Blackwell Publishers, 1999.
**TC HV1568 .B35 1999**

**Exploring education.**
Sadovnik, Alan R. Boston : Allyn and Bacon, c1994.
**TC LB17 .S113 1994**

Sadovnik, Alan R. 2nd ed. Boston : Allyn and Bacon, 2000.
**TC LA217.2 . S23 2000**

**Exploring leadership.**
Komives, Susan R., 1946- 1st ed. San Francisco : Jossey-Bass Publishers, c1998.
**TC LB3605 .K64 1998**

**Exploring science.**
Klahr, David. Cambridge, Mass. : MIT Press, c2000.
**TC Q180.55.D57 K55 2000**

**Exploring science in early childhood.**
Lind, Karen. 3rd ed. Albany, NY ; London : Delmar/Thomson Learning, c2000.
**TC LB1532 .L47 2000**

**Exploring science in early childhood education.**
Lind, Karen. Exploring science in early childhood. 3rd ed. Albany, NY ; London : Delmar/Thomson Learning, c2000.
**TC LB1532 .L47 2000**

**Exploring science in the library :** resources and activities for young people / edited by Maria Sosa and Tracy Gath. Chicago : American Library Association, 2000. x, 236 p. : ill. ; 23 cm. Includes bibliographical references and index. ISBN 0-8389-0768-7 DDC 027.8/222
*1. Elementary school libraries - United States. 2. Libraries - United States - Special collections - Science. 3. Science - Study and teaching (Elementary) - United States. I. Sosa, Maria. II. Gath, Tracy.*
**TC Z675.S3 E97 2000**

**Exploring the English language** [videorecording] / produced & directed by Harry J. Karabel ; written by Edward B. Jenkinson, Harry J. Karabel, Michael J. Griffin ; a Video Tutor videotext production. [Princeton, N.J.] : Video Tutor ; [Chesterton, Ind.? : Distributed by] Griffin Media Design, 1988, c1986. 8 videocassettes (ca. 480 min.) : sd., col. ; 1/2 in. At head of title on container: Video Tutor : exploring the English language [videorecording]. VHS. Catalogued from credits, container and cassette label for tape 1. Title from container; copyright date from cassette label for tape 1. Art director, Gregory Burke;

artist, Gregory Burke ... [et al.] ; cameras, Mike Fisher ... [et al.] ; audio, Doug Ballard, Randy Johns. For grades 2-8, as well as high school remedial, ESL, and literacy curriculums. SUMMARY: A supplemental instructional device teaching parts of speech, compound sentences, dictionary skills, vocabulary, etc. Includes exercises. CONTENTS: Tape 1. Fun with words -- Tape 2. Writing basic sentences -- Tape 3. Compounding sentences and recognizing parts of speech -- Tape 4. Writing complex sentences -- Tape 5-6. Dictionaries and their meanings -- Tape 7. Forming words and building vocabularies -- Tape 8. Naming people, places, and things. *1. English language - Grammar - Juvenile films. 2. English language - Parts of speech - Juvenile films. 3. English language - Sentences - Juvenile films. 4. English language - Word formation - Juvenile films. 5. English language - Compound words - Juvenile films. 6. Encyclopedias and dictionaries - Juvenile films. 7. English language - Dictionaries - Juvenile films. 8. Vocabulary - Juvenile films. 9. Library orientation - Juvenile films. 10. English language - Problems, exercises, etc. - Juvenile films. 11. Video recordings for children. I. Karabel, Harry J. II. Jenkinson, Edward B. III. Griffin, Michael J. IV. Video Tutor, Inc. V. Griffin Media Design, Inc. VI. Title: Video Tutor : exploring the English language [videorecording]*

**Exploring the heritage of American higher education.**
Bogue, E. Grady (Ernest Grady), 1935- Phoenix, Ariz. : Oryx Press, 2000.
*TC LA227.4 .B66 2000*

**Exploring ways in which ethnicity, gender, and high school influence the social construction of identity in Chinese American girls.**
Woo, Kimberley Ann. "Double happiness," double jeopardy. 1999.
*TC 06 no. 11075*

**Exploring world art.**
Belloli, Andrea P. A. Los Angeles, Calif. : J. Paul Getty Museum, 1999.
*TC N7440 .B35 1999*

**Export agriculture and social crisis.**
Ripton, John R. 1997.
*TC 085 R48*

**EXPOSED CHILDREN.** See **ABANDONED CHILDREN.**

**EXPOSITION UNIVERSELLE INTERNATIONALE DE 1900 (PARIS, FRANCE).**
Paris 1900. New Brunswick, N.J. : Rutgers University Press ; Montclair, N.J. : Montclair Art Museum, c1999.
*TC N6510 .P28 1999*

**EXPOSITIONS.** See **EXHIBITIONS.**

**Expressing needs and wants in a second language.**
Li, Duan-Duan. 1998.
*TC 06 no. 10958*

**EXPRESSION.** See also **ACTING; FACIAL EXPRESSION; RHETORIC.**
Planalp, Sally, 1950- Communicating emotion. Cambridge ; New York : Cambridge University Press ; Paris : Editions de la Maison des sciences de l'homme, 1999.
*TC BF591 .P57 1999*

Speaking of emotions. Berlin : New York : Mouton de Gruyter, 1998.
*TC BF591. S64 1998*

**EXPRESSION - SEX DIFFERENCES.**
Gender and emotion. New York : Cambridge University Press, 1999.
*TC BF591 .G45 1999*

**EXPRESSIONISM (ART) - FRANCE - PARIS - EXHIBITIONS.**
Kleeblatt, Norman L. An expressionist in Paris. Munich ; New York : Jewish Museum, c1998.
*TC ND553.S7 A4 1998*

**An expressionist in Paris.**
Kleeblatt, Norman L. Munich ; New York : Jewish Museum, c1998.
*TC ND553.S7 A4 1998*

**Expressions of identity.**
Hetherington, Kevin. London ; Thousand Oaks, Calif. : Sage Publications, 1998.
*TC HM131 .H3995 1998*

**EXPRESSIVE BEHAVIOR.** See **EXPRESSION.**

**Expressive therapy with troubled children.**
Klorer, P. Gussie. Northvale, NJ : Jason Aronson, 2000.
*TC RJ505.A7 K56 2000*

**EXPURGATED BOOKS.** See **CENSORSHIP.**

**EXTENSION EDUCATION.** See **UNIVERSITY EXTENSION.**

**EXTERMINATION, JEWISH (1939-1945).** See **HOLOCAUST, JEWISH (1939-1945).**

**EXTERNAL TRADE.** See **INTERNATIONAL TRADE.**

**EXTERNALISM (PHILOSOPHY OF MIND).**
Rowlands, Mark. The body in mind. Cambridge, U.K. ; New York : Cambridge University Press, 1999.
*TC BD418.3 .R78 1999*

**EXTINCT ANIMALS.** See also **EXTINCTION (BIOLOGY).**
Lessem, Don. Dinosaurs to dodos. 1st ed. New York : Scholastic Reference, 1999.
*TC QE842 .L47 1999*

**EXTINCT ANIMALS - ENCYCLOPEDIAS, JUVENILE.**
Lessem, Don. Dinosaurs to dodos. 1st ed. New York : Scholastic Reference, 1999.
*TC QE842 .L47 1999*

**EXTINCT CITIES - ITALY.** See **HERCULANEUM (EXTINCT CITY).**

**EXTINCT LANGUAGES.** See **ALPHABET; WRITING.**

**EXTINCTION (BIOLOGY).** See also **EXTINCT ANIMALS.**
Lessem, Don. Dinosaurs to dodos. 1st ed. New York : Scholastic Reference, 1999.
*TC QE842 .L47 1999*

**EXTRA-CURRICULAR ACTIVITIES.** See **STUDENT ACTIVITIES.**

**EXTRACHROMOSOMAL DNA.** See **VIRUSES.**

**EXTRAPYRAMIDAL DISORDERS.** See **CEREBRAL PALSY.**

**EXTRATERRESTRIAL BEINGS.**
Brooks, Philip, 1955- Invaders from outer space. 1st American ed. New York : DK, 1999.
*TC TL789.2 .B76 1999*

**EXTRATERRESTRIAL BEINGS - FICTION.**
Camp, Lindsay. Why? New York : Putnam, c1998.
*TC PZ7.C1475 Wf 1998*

**EXTRATERRESTRIAL ENCOUNTERS WITH HUMANS.** See **HUMAN-ALIEN ENCOUNTERS.**

**The extreme searcher's guide to Web search engines.**
Hock, Randolph, 1944- Medford, NJ : CyberAge Books, c1999.
*TC ZA4226 .H63 1998*

**EXTREMISM, POLITICAL.** See **RADICALISM.**

**Eye, Alexander von.**
Growing up in times of social change. New York : Walter de Gruyter, 1999.
*TC HQ799.G5 G76 1999*

Regression analysis for social sciences / Alexander von Eye, Christof Schuster. San Diego, Calif. : Academic Press, c1998. xv, 386 p. : ill. ; 24 cm. Includes bibliographical references (p. 373-380) and index. ISBN 0-12-724955-9 DDC 300/.01/519536
*1. Social sciences - Statistical methods. 2. Regression analysis. I. Schuster, Christof. II. Title.*
*TC HA31.3 .E94 1998*

**The eye expanded :** life and the arts in Greco-Roman antiquity / edited by Frances B. Titchener and Richard F. Moorton. Berkeley : University of California Press, c1999. xiii, 294 p. : ill. ; 24 cm. "Includes bibliographical works by Peter M. Green" (p. 267-271). Includes bibliographical references and index. ISBN 0-520-21029-8 (alk. paper) DDC 938
*1. Greece - Civilization. 2. Rome - Civilization. 3. Civilization, Western - Classical influences. I. Titchener, Frances B., 1954- II. Moorton, Richard F.*
*TC DE59 .E93 1999*

**The eye of the beholder.**
Housen, Abigail. 1983.
*TC BH39 .H68 1983*

**EYEGLASSES - FICTION.**
Cowley, Joy. Agapanthus Hum and the eyeglasses. New York : Philomel Books, c1999.
*TC PZ7.C8375 Ag 1999*

**Eyewitness readers. Level 1**
Wallace, Karen. A day at Seagull beach. 1st American ed. New York : DK Pub., 1999.
*TC PZ10.3.W1625 Se 1999*

**Eyewitness readers. Level 2**
Grindley, Sally. The little ballerina. 1st American ed. New York : DK Pub., 1999.
*TC GV1787.5 .G75 1999*

Walker-Hodge, Judith. Animal hospital. 1st American ed. New York : DK Pub., 1999.
*TC SF604.55 .H63 1999*

**Eyewitness readers. Level 3**
Brooks, Philip, 1955- Invaders from outer space. 1st American ed. New York : DK, 1999.
*TC TL789.2 .B76 1999*

Cottringer, Anne. Movie magic. 1st American ed. New York : DK Pub., c1999.
*TC PN1995.9.P7 C66 1999*

**Eyewitness readers. Level 4**
Petty, Kate. Horse heroes. 1st American ed. New York : DK Pub., c1999.
*TC SF302 .P47 1999*

**Faber, Pamela B., 1950-.**
English teacher education in Europe. Frankfurt am Main : New York : P. Lang, 1999.
*TC PE1128.A2 E547 1999*

**Fables of La Fontaine.**
La Fontaine, Jean de, 1621-1695. [Fables. English. Selections] Marc Chagall. New York : New Press : Distributed by W.W. Norton, [1997]
*TC PQ1811.E3 W6 1997*

**FABRICS.** See **TEXTILE FABRICS.**

**FACE - EXPRESSION.** See **FACIAL EXPRESSION.**

**FACETIAE.** See **WIT AND HUMOR.**

**FACIAL EXPRESSION - CROSS-CULTURAL STUDIES.**
Wierzbicka, Anna. Emotions across languages and cultures. Cambridge : Cambridge University Press, 1999.
*TC BF531 .W54 1999*

**FACIAL EXPRESSION - TESTING - SEX DIFFERENCES - RESEARCH.**
Gender and the interpretation of emotion [videorecording]. Princeton, NJ : Films for the Humanities & Sciences, c1997.
*TC BF592.F33 G4 1997*

**The facilitative leader.**
Ray, R. Glenn. Upper Saddler River, NJ : Prentice Hall, c1999.
*TC HD66 .R3918 1999*

**FACILITIES, HEALTH.** See **HEALTH FACILITIES.**

**Facing the consequences :** using TIMSS for a closer look at U.S. mathematics and science education / edited by William H. Schmidt ... [et al.] ; with the collaboration of David E. Wiley ... [et al.]. Dordrecht ; Boston : Kluwer Academic Publishers, c1999. 236 p. : ill. (some col.) ; 25 cm. "In association with the US National Research Center for the Third International Mathematics and Science Study (TIMSS), Michigan State University." Includes bibliographical references. ISBN 0-7923-5567-9 (hc. : alk. paper) ISBN 0-7923-5568-7 (pbk.)
*1. Third International Mathematics and Science Study. 2. Mathematics - Study and teaching - United States. 3. Science - Study and teaching - United States. I. Schmidt, William H.*
*TC QA13 .F33 1999*

**FACTOR ANALYSIS.** See also **PSYCHOLOGY - MATHEMATICAL MODELS.**
Butler, John M. Quantitative naturalistic research; Englewood Cliffs, N.J., Prentice-Hall [1963]
*TC BF39 .B83*

Felton, Mark Kenji. Metacognitive reflection and strategy development in argumentive discourse. 1999.
*TC 085 F34*

Rummel, R. J. (Rudolph J.), 1932- The dimensions of nations Beverly Hills, Sage Publications [1972]
*TC JX1291 .R84*

**FACTORIES - FICTION.**
Weeks, Sarah. Little factory. 1st ed. [New York] : Laura Geringer book, c1998.
*TC PZ7.W4125 Li 1998*

**Factors affecting parental attitudes toward a child's therapist and therapy.**
Nevas, Debra Baron. 1997.
*TC 085 N401*

**Factors influencing the sexual and contraceptive behavior of sexually abused adolescents of color.**
Richardson, Bonnie. 1999.

TC 06 no. 11167

**Factors relating to Hispanic and non-Hispanic White Americans' willingness to seek psychotherapy.**
Tiago de Melo, Janine. 1969- 1998.
*TC 085 T43*

**FACTORY BUILDINGS.** *See* FACTORIES.

**FACTORY SCHOOLS.** *See* EVENING AND CONTINUATION SCHOOLS.

**FACTORY SYSTEM.** *See* FACTORIES.

**FACTS, MISCELLANEOUS.** *See* HANDBOOKS, VADE-MECUMS, ETC.; QUESTIONS AND ANSWERS.

**Facts on File, Inc.**
Pickering, David, 1958- A dictionary of folklore. New York, N.Y. : Facts on File, 1999.
*TC GR35 .P53 1999*

**The Facts on File student's thesaurus** / [edited by] Marc McCutcheon. 2nd ed. New York : Facts on File, 2000. vi, 504 p. ; 25 cm. SUMMARY: Provides synonyms and antonyms for more than 7000 words listed in alphabetical order. ISBN 0-8160-4058-3 (alk. paper) DDC 423/.1
*1. English language - Synonyms and antonyms. 2. English language - Synonyms and antonyms. I. McCutcheon. Marc.*
*TC PE1591 .H45 2000*

**FACULTY ADVISORS.**
Supervising postgraduates from non-English speaking backgrounds. Buckingham : Philadelphia : Society for Research into Higher Education : Open University Press, 1999.
*TC LB2343 .S86 1999*

**FACULTY ADVISORS - UNITED STATES - HANDBOOKS, MANUALS, ETC.**
Academic advising. 1st ed. San Francisco : Jossey-Bass, c2000.
*TC LB2343 .A29 2000*

**Faculty assessment of mentoring roles at SUNY Empire State College.**
Langer, Arthur Mark. 1999.
*TC 06 no. 11138*

**Faculty diversity at American independent schools.**
Orsini, Alfonso J. The color of excellence. 1999.
*TC 06 no. 11209*

**FACULTY (EDUCATION).** *See* COLLEGE TEACHERS; EDUCATORS; TEACHERS; UNIVERSITIES AND COLLEGES - FACULTY.

**Faculty evaluation of post-tenure review at a research university.**
Ernest, Ivan. 1999.
*TC 06 no. 11110*

**FACULTY INTEGRATION.**
Rutter, Alison Lee. Professional growth of two multidisciplinary teams within a professional development school. 1999.
*TC 06 no. 11171*

**Faculty meetings with Rudolf Steiner.**
Steiner, Rudolf, 1861-1925. [Konferenzen mit den Lehrern der Freien Waldorfschule in Stuttgart. English] Hudson, NY : Anthroposophic Press, c1998.
*TC LF3195.S834 S8413 1998*

**Faculty of color in academe.**
Turner, Caroline Sotello Viernes. Boston : Allyn and Bacon, c2000.
*TC LB2332.72 .T87 2000*

**FACULTY PARTICIPATION IN ADMINISTRATION.** *See* TEACHER PARTICIPATION IN ADMINISTRATION.

**FACULTY-PRINCIPAL RELATIONSHIPS.** *See* TEACHER-PRINCIPAL RELATIONSHIPS.

**Faculty productivity** : : facts, fictions and issues / edited by william G. Tierney. New York : Falmer Press, 1999. xviii, 186 p. : ill. ; 22 cm. (Garland studies in higher education, v. 15.) (Garland reference library of social science, v. 1396.) Includes bibliographical references and index. ISBN 0-8153-3220-3
*1. College teachers - United States - Workload. 2. College teaching - United States - Evaluation. 3. Universities and colleges - United States - Faculty - Research. 4. Universities and colleges - United States - Faculty - Statistics. I. Tierney, William G. II. Series: Garland reference library of social science, v. 1396. III. Series: Garland studies in higher education, vol. 15.*
*TC LB2331.7 .F33 1999*

**FADS - UNITED STATES.**
Birnbaum, Robert. Management fads in higher education. San Francisco : Jossey-Bass, 2000.

*TC LB2341 .B49 2000*

**Fagg, William Buller.** Yoruba, sculpture of West Africa / text by William Fagg ; descriptive catalogue by John Pemberton 3rd ; edited by Bryce Holcombe. 1st ed. New York : Knopf : Distributed by Random House, 1982. xiii, 209 p. : ill. (some col.) ; 32 cm. Bibliography: p. 201-208. ISBN 0-394-52358-X ISBN 0-394-71039-8 (pbk.) DDC 732/.2/0966
*1. Sculpture, Yoruba. 2. Sculpture, Primitive - Nigeria. 3. Sculpture, Primitive - Togo. 4. Sculpture, Primitive - Ghana. I. Pemberton. John. 1928- II. Holcombe, Bryce. III. Title.*
*TC NB1099.N5 F34*

**Fahey, Kathleen R.** Language development, differences, and disorders : a perspective for general and special education teachers and classroom-based speech-language pathologists / Kathleen R. Fahey and D. Kim Reid. Austin, Tex. : PRO-ED, c2000. xviii, 515 p. : ill. ; 24 cm. Includes bibliographical references and indexes. ISBN 0-89079-822-2 (hardcover) DDC 418
*1. Children - Language. 2. Language acquisition. 3. Language disorders in children. 4. Speech therapy for children. 5. Language arts - Remedial teaching. I. Reid, D. Kim. II. Title.*
*TC LB1139.L3 F35 2000*

**Fahimian, Nima.**
Rabow, Jerome. Tutoring matters. Philadelphia : Temple University Press, 1999.
*TC LC41 .R33 1999*

**Fahlman, Ruth.**
Chud, Gyda. Early childhood education for a multicultural society. [Vancouver] : Western Education Development Group, Faculty of Education, The University of British Columbia, c1985.
*TC LC1099 .C494 1985*

**Fail-safe.**
Burdick, Eugene. 1st Ecco ed. Hopewell, N.J. : Ecco Press ; New York, NY : Distributed by W.W. Norton, 1999.
*TC PS3552.U7116 F35 1999*

**Failing school, failing city.**
Johnson, Martin. Charlbury, Oxfordshire [England] : Jon Carpenter Publishing, 1999.
*TC LC5136.G7 J64 1999*

**Failing teachers?** / E.C. Wragg ... [et al.]. London ; New York : Routledge, 2000. x, 239 p. ; 24 cm. Includes bibliographical references (p. [231]-233) and index. ISBN 0-415-22021-1 (hard) ISBN 0-415-22022-X (pbk.) DDC 371.14/4/0941
*1. Teacher effectiveness - Great Britain - Case studies. I. Wragg, E. C. (Edward Conrad)*
*TC LB1775.4.G7 F35 2000*

**FAILURE (PSYCHOLOGY).** *See* SCHOOL FAILURE; SUCCESS.

**FAILURE, SCHOOL.** *See* SCHOOL FAILURE.

**Fair and foul.**
Eitzen, D. Stanley. Lanham, Md. : Rowman & Littlefield Publishers, c1999.
*TC GV706.5 .E567 1999*

**FAIR EMPLOYMENT PRACTICE.** *See* DISCRIMINATION IN EMPLOYMENT.

**FAIR USE (COPYRIGHT).** *See* COPYRIGHT AND ELECTRONIC DATA PROCESSING.

**FAIR USE (COPYRIGHT) - UNITED STATES - POPULAR WORKS.**
Talab, R. S., 1948- Commonsense copyright. 2nd ed. Jefferson, N.C. : McFarland & Co., 1999.
*TC KF2994 .T36 1999*

**The fairies.**
Scalora, Suza. New York : Joanna Cotler Books, c1999.
*TC PZ7.S27915 Fai 1999*

**FAIRIES - FICTION.**
Scalora, Suza. The fairies. New York : Joanna Cotler Books, c1999.
*TC PZ7.S27915 Fai 1999*

**Fairman, Julie.** Critical care nursing : a history / Julie Fairman and Joan E. Lynaugh ; with a foreword by Gladys M. Campbell and Barbara Siebelt. Philadelphia : University of Pennsylvania Press, c1998. x, 175 p. : ill. ; 23 cm. (Studies in health, illness, and caregiving) Includes bibliographical references (p. [149]-166) and index. ISBN 0-8122-3258-5 (alk. paper) DDC 610.73/61
*1. Intensive care nursing - History. 2. History of Nursing - United States. 3. Critical Care - history - United States. I. Lynaugh, Joan E. II. Title. III. Series.*
*TC RT120.I5 F34 1998*

**FAIRS.** *See* EXHIBITIONS.

**Fairweather, Peter G.**
Gibbons, Andrew S. Computer-based instruction. Englewood Cliffs, N.J. : Educational Technology Publications, c1998.
*TC LB1028.5 .G487 1998*

**FAIRY TALES.**
Aylesworth, Jim. The full belly bowl. 1st ed. New York : Atheneum Books for Young Readers, c1998.
*TC PZ8.A95 Fu 1998*

Levine, Gail Carson. Princess Sonora and the long sleep. 1st ed. New York : HarperCollins Publishers, c1999.
*TC PZ8.L4793 Pq 1999*

Mayer, Marianna. Iron John. New York : Morrow Junior Books, 1998.
*TC PZ8.M4514 Ir 1998*

Murphy, Shirley Rousseau. Wind child. New York, NY : HarperCollins, c1999.
*TC PZ8.M957 Wi 1999*

Steer, Dugald. Just one more story. New York : Dutton Children's Books, 1999.
*TC PZ7.S81534 Ju 1999*

**FAIRY TALES - HISTORY AND CRITICISM.**
Cashdan, Sheldon. The witch must die. New York : Basic Books, 1999.
*TC GR550 .C39 1999*

**FAIRY TALES - SOCIAL ASPECTS.**
Cashdan, Sheldon. The witch must die. New York : Basic Books, 1999.
*TC GR550 .C39 1999*

**Falk, Beth.**
Donahue, Paul J. Mental health consultation in early childhood. Baltimore, MD : Paul H. Brookes Publishing, 2000.
*TC RJ499 .D595 2000*

**Fallen, Nancy H.**
**Young children with special needs.**
Umansky, Warren. Young children with special needs. 3rd ed. Upper Saddle River, N.J. : Merrill, c1998.
*TC LC4031 .U425 1998*

**Fallows, Stephen J.**
Inspiring students :. London : Kogan Page, 1999.
*TC LB1065 .I57 1999*

**FALSE CERTIFICATION - UNITED STATES.**
Misrepresentation in the marketplace and beyond. Washington, DC : American Association of Collegiate Registrars and Admissions Officers, 1996.
*TC LB2331.615.U6 M57 1996*

**FALSE MEMORIES.** *See* FALSE MEMORY SYNDROME.

**False-memory creation in children and adults** : theory, research, and implications / edited by David F. Bjorklund. Mahwah, N.J. ; London : L. Erlbaum, 2000. x, 254 p. : ill. ; 24 cm. Includes bibliographical references and indexes. ISBN 0-8058-3169-X (cloth : alk. paper) DDC 616.85/8369
*1. False memory syndrome. I. Bjorklund, David F., 1949-*
*TC RC455.2.F35 F34 2000*

**FALSE MEMORY SYNDROME.**
Acocella, Joan Ross. Creating hysteria. 1st ed. San Francisco : Jossey-Bass Publishers, c1999.
*TC RC569.5.M8 A28 1999*

False-memory creation in children and adults. Mahwah, N.J. ; London : L. Erlbaum, 2000.
*TC RC455.2.F35 F34 2000*

Prager, Jeffrey, 1948- Presenting the past. Cambridge, Mass. : Harvard University Press, 1998.
*TC BF175.4.C84 P73 1998*

**FALSE MEMORY SYNDROME - CASE STUDIES.**
Prager, Jeffrey, 1948- Presenting the past. Cambridge, Mass. : Harvard University Press, 1998.
*TC BF175.4.C84 P73 1998*

**Faltis, Christian, 1950-.**
So much to say. New York : Teachers College Press, c1999.
*TC PE1128.A2 S599 1999*

**Falwell, Cathryn.** Word wizard / by Cathryn Falwell. New York : Clarion Books, c1998. 31 p. : col. ill. ; 26 cm. SUMMARY: Using her magical spoon to make new words by changing letters around, Anna embarks on a series of adventures with a lost little boy. ISBN 0-395-85580-2 DDC [E]
*1. English language - Spelling - Fiction. 2. Imagination - Fiction. I. Title.*
*TC PZ7.F198 Wo 1998*

**Falwell, Cathryn, ill.**
Heide, Florence Parry. It's about time!. New York : Clarion Books, c1999.
*TC PS3558.E427 I77 1999*

**FAME.**
Giles, David, 1964- Illusions of immortality. Houndmills [England] : Macmillan Press ; New York : St. Martin's Press, 2000.
*TC BJ1470.5 .G55 2000*

**FAME - PSYCHOLOGICAL ASPECTS.**
Giles, David, 1964- Illusions of immortality. Houndmills [England] : Macmillan Press ; New York : St. Martin's Press, 2000.
*TC BJ1470.5 .G55 2000*

**Familial and neighborhood influences on children's achievement.**
Leventhal, Tama. Poverty and turbulence. 1999.
*TC 085 L5515*

**FAMILIAL BEHAVIOR IN ANIMALS.** *See* **ANIMALS - INFANCY; PARENTAL BEHAVIOR IN ANIMALS.**

**FAMILIES.** *See* **FAMILY.**

**FAMILIES, AFRO-AMERICAN.** *See* **AFRO-AMERICAN FAMILIES.**

**Families and communes.**
Smith, William L., 1956- Thousand Oaks, Calif. : Sage Publications, c1999.
*TC HQ971 .S55 1999*

**Families and teachers of individuals with disabilities :** collaborative orientations and responsive practices / Dorothy J. O'Shea ... [et al.]. Boston ; London : Allyn and Bacon, c2001. xv, 301 p. : ill. ; 24 cm. Includes bibliographical references and index. ISBN 0-205-15131-0 (alk. paper) DDC 371.9
*1. Special education teachers - United States. 2. Parent-teacher relationships - United States. 3. Family - United States. 4. Handicapped students - United States - Family relationships. I. O'Shea, Dorothy J.*
*TC LC3969 .F34 2001*

**FAMILIES, ASIAN AMERICAN.** *See* **ASIAN AMERICAN FAMILIES.**

**Families at school.**
Thomas, Adele, 1942- Newark, Del. : International Reading Association, c1999.
*TC LC151 .T56 1999*

Thomas, Adele, 1942- Newark, Del. : International Reading Association, c1999.
*TC LC151 .T563 1999*

**Families, children, and the quest for a global ethic.**
Rapoport, Robert N. Aldershot ; Brookfield, Vt. : Ashgate, c1997.
*TC HQ518 .R36 1997*

**FAMILIES, DUAL-CAREER.** *See* **DUAL-CAREER FAMILIES.**

**Families speak :** early childhood care and education in 11 countries / edited by Patricia P. Olmsted, David P. Weikart, with national research coordinators Joaquim Bairrão ... [et al.] ; with commentaries by Çiğdem Kağitçibaşi ... [et al.]. Ypsilanti, Mich. : High/Scope Press, c1994. xxii, 380 p. : ill. ; 26 cm. At head of title: The IEA Preprimary Project--Phase 1. Includes bibliographical references. ISBN 0-929816-89-7 DDC 372.21
*1. Early childhood education - Cross-cultural studies. 2. Child care services - Cross-cultural studies. I. Olmsted, Patricia P. II. Weikart, David P. III. IEA Preprimary Study. IV. High/Scope Educational Research Foundation.*
*TC LB1139.23 .F36 1994*

**FAMILIES WITH PROBLEMS.** *See* **PROBLEM FAMILIES.**

**FAMILY.** *See also* **AUNTS; BROTHERS AND SISTERS; CHILDREN; DIVORCE; DUAL-CAREER FAMILIES; HOME; MARRIAGE; PARENT AND CHILD; PARENTHOOD; PARENTS; PROBLEM FAMILIES; STEPFAMILIES; UNCLES; WORK AND FAMILY.**
Cavan, Ruth (Shonle) 1896- ed. Marriage and family in the modern world, 2d ed. New York, Crowell [1965]
*TC HQ734 .C382 1965*

[Family (New York, N.Y. : 1984)] The family. New York : United Nations, 1984-

Fivaz-Depeursinge, Elisabeth. The primary triangle :. New York : Basic Books, c1999.
*TC HQ755.85 .F583 1999*

Nichols, William C. Systemic family therapy. New York : Guilford Press, c1986.

*TC RC488.5 .N535 1986*

Pennartz, Paul. The domestic domain :. Aldershot, Hants, England : Brookfield, Vt. : Ashgate, c1999.
*TC HQ728 .P46 1999*

Rapoport, Robert N. Families, children, and the quest for a global ethic. Aldershot ; Brookfield, Vt. : Ashgate, c1997.
*TC HQ518 .R36 1997*

**Family album :** teacher's planning guide. New York : Macmillan/McGraw-Hill, c1997. 1 v. (various pagings) : col. ill. ; 31 cm. (Spotlight on literacy) (The road to independent reading) Includes index. ISBN 0-02-181167-9
*1. Language arts (Primary) 2. Reading (Primary) I. Series. II. Series: The road to independent reading*
*TC LB1576 .S66 1997 Gr.3 L8 u.3*

**Family and child mental health journal.**
Issues in child mental health. [New York, Human Sciences Press]

**Family and child mental health journal :** journal of the Jewish Board of Family and Children's Services. New York, NY : Human Sciences Press, [c1980-c1982] 3 v. ; 23 cm. Frequency: Semiannual. Vol. 6, no. 1 (spring/summer 1980)-v. 8, no. 1 & 2 (fall/winter 1982). Title from cover. Indexed selectively by: Sociological abstracts 0038-0202. Indexed selectively by: Social welfare, social planning/policy & social development 0195-7988. Indexed selectively by: Psychological abstracts 0033-2887 1980-. Continues: Issues in child mental health ISSN: 0362-403X (DLC) 76021890 (OCoLC)3455637. ISSN 0190-230X DDC 618.92/89/005
*1. Child psychiatry - Periodicals. 2. Child mental health - Periodicals. 3. Family psychotherapy - Periodicals. 4. Child Health Services - periodicals. 5. Family Health - periodicals. 6. Family Therapy - periodicals. 7. Mental Health Services - periodicals. I. Jewish Board of Family and Children's Services (New York, N.Y.) II. Title: Issues in child mental health*

**The family and inheritance.**
Sussman, Marvin B. New York, Russell Sage Foundation, 1970.
*TC KFO142 .S9*

**Family and peers :** linking two social worlds / edited by Kathryn A. Kerns, Josefina M. Contreras, and Angela M. Neal-Barnett. Westport, Conn. : Praeger, 2000. xi, 267 p. : ill. ; 25 cm. (Praeger series in applied psychology) "This book is published in connection with the Tenth Kent State Psychology Forum"--P. x. Includes bibliographical references and index. ISBN 0-275-96506-6 (alk. paper) DDC 306.874
*1. Parent and child. 2. Child rearing. 3. Interpersonal relations in children. 4. Interpersonal relations in adolescence. 5. Social interaction in children. 6. Social interaction in adolescence. I. Kerns, Kathryn A., 1961- II. Contreras, Josefina M., 1960- III. Neal-Barnett, Angela M., 1960- IV. Series.*
*TC HQ755.85 .F365 2000*

**FAMILY AND STATE.** *See* **FAMILY POLICY.**

**FAMILY AND WORK.** *See* **WORK AND FAMILY.**

**FAMILY CAREGIVERS.** *See* **CAREGIVERS.**

**FAMILY CASE WORK.** *See* **FAMILY SOCIAL WORK.**

**FAMILY-CENTERED NURSING.** *See* **FAMILY NURSING.**

**FAMILY - CHINA.**
Diamant, Neil Jeffrey, 1964- Revolutionizing the family. Berkeley : University of California Press, c2000.
*TC HQ684 .D53 2000*

**FAMILY - COLLECTED WORKS.**
[Family (New York, N.Y. : 1984)] The Family. New York : United Nations, 1984-

**FAMILY - CONGRESSES.**
The changing family and child development. Aldershot : Ashgate, c2000.
*TC HQ518 .C478 2000*

**Family coordinator.**
The Family life coordinator. Eugene, Ore. : E. C. Brown Trust Foundation.

**The Family coordinator.** Minneapolis, Minn. : National Council on Family Relations, c1968- 12 v. ; 26 cm. Frequency: Quarterly. Vol. 17, no. 1 (Jan. 1968)- . Ceased publication in 1979. "Journal of education, counseling, and services." Title from cover. Indexed selectively by: Social welfare, social planning/policy & social development 0195-7988. Indexed selectively by: Women studies abstracts 0049-7835. Indexed selectively by: Social work research & abstracts 0148-0847. Indexed by: International bibliography of sociology. Indexed selectively by: Sociological abstracts 0038-0202. Indexed selectively by: Psychological abstracts 0033-2887 1968-1979. Continued in 1980 by: Family relations

Continues: Family life coordinator ISSN: 0886-0394 (DLC) 61022699 (OCoLC)1781607. ISSN 0014-7214
*1. Family life education - United States - Periodicals. 2. Family - United States - Periodicals. 3. Marriage - United States - Periodicals. I. National Council on Family Relations. II. Title: Family life coordinator III. Title: Family relations*

**FAMILY COUNSELING.**
O'Leary, Charles J. Counselling couples and families. London : SAGE, 1999.
*TC RC488.5 .O394 1999*

O'Leary, Charles J. Counselling couples and families. London : SAGE, 1999.
*TC RC488.5 .O394 1999*

**FAMILY COUNSELING - HANDBOOKS, MANUALS, ETC.**
Handbook of family development and intervention. New York : Wiley, c2000.
*TC RC489.F33 .H36 2000*

**Family culture.**
Familyculture. Boston, Mass. : [s.n.],

**FAMILY - DEVELOPING COUNTRIES.**
Strengthening the family. Tokyo ; New York : United Nations University Press, c1995.
*TC HQ727.9 .S77 1995*

**Family diversity and family policy.**
Lerner, Richard M. Boston ; London : Kluwer Academic, c1999.
*TC HQ535 .L39 1999*

**FAMILY - ECONOMIC ASPECTS - UNITED STATES.**
Williams, Joan, 1952- Unbending gender. Oxford ; New York : Oxford University Press, c2000.
*TC HD4904.25 .W55 2000*

**FAMILY - ECONOMIC CONDITIONS.** *See* **FAMILY - ECONOMIC ASPECTS.**

**Family empowerment.**
Dunlap, Katherine M. New York : London : Garland Pub., 2000.
*TC LB1140.35.P37 D86 2000*

**The family encyclopedia of health.**
Sharma, R. (Rajendra), 1959- Boston : Element Books, 1999.
*TC RC81.A2 S53 1999*

**Family ethnicity :** strength in diversity / Harriette Pipes McAdoo, editor. 2nd ed. Thousand Oaks, Calif. : Sage Publications, c1999. xvi, 400 p. ; 24 cm. Includes bibliographical references (p. 325-369) and indexes. ISBN 0-7619-1856-6 (cloth : alk. paper) ISBN 0-7619-1857-4 (pbk. : alk. paper) DDC 305.8/00973
*1. Minorities - United States. 2. Family - United States. 3. United States - Social conditions - 1980- I. McAdoo, Harriette Pipes.*
*TC E184.A1 F33 1999*

**Family experiences with mental illness.**
Tessler, Richard C. Westport, Conn. ; London : Auburn House, 2000.
*TC RC455.4.F3 T46 2000*

**FAMILY - FRANCE - HISTORY.**
Gager, Kristin Elizabeth. Blood ties and fictive ties. Princeton, N.J. : Princeton University Press, c1996.
*TC HV875.58.F8 G34 1996*

**Family fun:** teacher's planning guide. New York : Macmillan/McGraw-Hill, c1997. 1 v. (various pagings) : col. ill. ; 31 cm. (Spotlight on literacy ; Gr.2 L6 u.1) (The road to independent reading) Includes index. ISBN 0-02-181158-x
*1. Language arts (Primary) 2. Reading (Primary) I. Series. II. Series: The road to independent reading*
*TC LB1576 .S66 1997 Gr.2 L6 u.1*

**FAMILY GROUP THERAPY.** *See* **FAMILY PSYCHOTHERAPY.**

**FAMILY - HEALTH AND HYGIENE.** *See also* **FAMILY PSYCHOTHERAPY.**
Stress, coping, and health in families. Thousand Oaks, Calif. : Sage Publications, c1998.
*TC RC455.4.F3 S79 1998*

**FAMILY HEALTH - NEW YORK - STATISTICS.**
Maternal, child and adolescent health profile. Albany, N.Y. : New York State Dept. of Health, 1996.
*TC HV742.N7 B83 1996*

**FAMILY HEALTH - PERIODICALS.**
Family and child mental health journal. New York, NY : Human Sciences Press, [c1980-c1982]

**FAMILY HISTORY.** *See* **GENEALOGY.**

**FAMILY - INDIA.**
Derné, Steve, 1960- Culture in action. Albany : State University of New York Press, c1995.

TC HQ670 .D46 1995

**FAMILY LEAVE.** *See* **PARENTAL LEAVE.**

**Family life coordinator.**
The Family coordinator. Minneapolis, Minn. :
National Council on Family Relations, c1968-

**The Family life coordinator.** Eugene, Ore. : E. C.
Brown Trust Foundation. 9 v. ; 26 cm. v. 8-16; 1959-67.
Official organ of the Pacific Northwest Council of Family
Relations; and, 1959-60, of the Oregon Coordinating Council
of Social Hygiene and Family Life. Indexed by: International
bibliography of sociology. Bibliographie internationale de
sociologie 0085-2606. Issued 1959-60 by Oregon Coordinating
Council on Social Hygiene and Family Life; 1961-67, by the E.
C. Brown Trust Foundation. Vols. 1-7 of Coordinator and v.
7-10, 1952-61. 1 v; v. 1-7 of Coordinator and v. 8-16, 1952-67.
1 v. Continues: Coordinator. Continued by: Family coordinator
ISSN: 0014-7214.
*1. Family - Periodicals. I. Oregon Coordinating Council of
Social Hygiene and Family Life. II. Pacific Northwest Council
of Family Relations. III. Title: Coordinator IV. Title: Family
coordinator*

**FAMILY LIFE EDUCATION.** *See* **HOME
ECONOMICS; PARENTING - STUDY AND
TEACHING; SEX INSTRUCTION.**

**FAMILY LIFE EDUCATION - UNITED STATES -
PERIODICALS.**
The Family life coordinator. Minneapolis, Minn. :
National Council on Family Relations, c1968-

**FAMILY LIFE - FICTION.**
Recorvits, Helen. Goodbye, Walter Malinski. 1st ed.
New York : Farrar, Straus and Giroux, c1999.
*TC PZ7.R24435 Go 1999*

Reid, Barbara. The party. New York : Scholastic
Press, 1999.
*TC PZ8.3.R2665 Pat 1999*

Rosenberg, Liz. The silence in the mountains. 1st
American ed. New York : Orchard Books, c1999.
*TC PZ7.R71894 Si 1999*

Turner, Ann Warren. Red flower goes West. 1st ed.
New York : Hyperion Books for Children, c1999.
*TC PZ7.T8535 Rf 1999*

Vail, Rachel. If you only knew. 1st ed. New York :
Scholastic, c1998.
*TC PZ7.V1916 If 1998*

Zamorano, Ana. Let's eat!. New York : Scholastic
Press, 1997.
*TC PZ7.Z25455 Le 1997*

**FAMILY LIFE - MARYLAND - BALTIMORE -
FICTION.**
Hahn, Mary Downing. Anna all year round. New
York : Clarion Books, c1999.
*TC PZ7.H1256 An 1999*

**FAMILY LIFE - NEW JERSEY - FICTION.**
Karr, Kathleen. Man of the family. 1st ed. New York :
Farrar, Straus and Giroux, 1999.
*TC PZ7.K149 Man 1999*

**FAMILY LIFE SURVEYS - UNITED STATES -
LONGITUDINAL STUDIES.**
Leventhal, Tama. Poverty and turbulence. 1999.
*TC 085 L5515*

**FAMILY LIFE - UNITED STATES.**
The emergence of family into the 21st century.
Boston : Jones and Bartlett Publishers ; [New York] :
NLN Press, c2001.
*TC HQ535 .E44 2001*

**FAMILY LIFE - VIRGINIA - FICTION.**
Ransom, Candice F., 1952- The promise quilt. New
York : Walker and Co., 1999.
*TC PZ7.R1743 Pr 1999*

**Family literacy.**
Taylor, Denny, 1947- Portsmouth, NH : Heinemann,
c1998.
*TC LC149 .T37 1998*

**FAMILY LITERACY PROGRAMS - NEW
JERSEY - NEWARK - CASE STUDIES.**
Handel, Ruth D. Building family literacy in an urban
community. New York : Teachers College Press,
c1999.
*TC LC152.N58 H36 1999*

**FAMILY LITERACY PROGRAMS - UNITED
STATES.**
Talan, Carole. Founding and funding family literacy
programs. New York : Neal-Schuman, c1999.
*TC Z716.45 .T35 1999*

Thomas, Adele, 1942- Families at school. Newark,
Del. : International Reading Association, c1999.

TC LC151 .T56 1999

Thomas, Adele, 1942- Families at school. Newark,
Del. : International Reading Association, c1999.
*TC LC151 .T563 1999*

**FAMILY LITERACY PROGRAMS - UNITED
STATES - CASE STUDIES.**
Paratore, Jeanne R. What should we expect of family
literacy? Newark, Del. : International Reading
Association ; Chicago , Ill. : National Reading
Conference, c1999.
*TC LC151 .P37 1999*

**FAMILY MEDICINE.** *See* **FAMILY NURSING.**

**FAMILY - MENTAL HEALTH.**
Stress, coping, and health in families. Thousand Oaks,
Calif. : Sage Publications, c1998.
*TC RC455.4.F3 S79 1998*

Walsh, Froma. Strengthening family resilience. New
York : Guilford Press, c1998.
*TC RC489.F33 W34 1998*

**Family message journals.**
Wollman-Bonilla, Julie. Urbana, Ill. : National
Council of Teachers of English, c2000.
*TC LB1576 .W644 2000*

**FAMILY - MORAL AND ETHICAL ASPECTS.**
Rapoport, Robert N. Families, children, and the quest
for a global ethic. Aldershot ; Brookfield, Vt. :
Ashgate, c1997.
*TC HQ518 .R36 1997*

[Family (New York, N.Y. : 1984)] The family /
Department of International Economic and Social
Affairs, Centre for Social Development and
Humanitarian Affairs. New York : United Nations,
1984- v. ; 30 cm. [No. 1]- . No. 1 lacks numbering.
*1. Family. I. Centre for Social Development and Humanitarian
Affairs (United Nations)*

[Family (New York, N.Y. : 1984)] The Family /
Department of International Economic and Social
Affairs, Centre for Social Development and
Humanitarian Affairs. New York : United Nations,
1984- v. ; 30 cm. [No. 1]- . Each issue has also a distinctive
title. Vol. 1 lacks numbering.
*1. Family - Collected works. I. Centre for Social Development
and Humanitarian Affairs (United Nations)*

**Family nurse practitioner certification review /**
[edited by] Pamela S. Kidd, Denise L. Robinson. St.
Louis : Mosby, c1999. xxi, 745 p. ; 26 cm. Includes
bibliographical references and index. ISBN 0-8151-5581-6
DDC 610.73/076
*1. Family nursing - Examinations, questions, etc. 2. Nurse
practitioners - Examinations, questions, etc. 3. Nurse
Practitioners - examination questions. 4. Family Practice -
nurses' instruction - examination questions. I. Kidd, Pamela
Stinson. II. Robinson, Denise L.*
*TC RT120.F34 F353 1998*

**FAMILY NURSING - EXAMINATIONS,
QUESTIONS, ETC.**
Family nurse practitioner certification review. St.
Louis : Mosby, c1999.
*TC RT120.F34 F353 1998*

**FAMILY - PERIODICALS.**
The Family life coordinator. Eugene, Ore. : E. C.
Brown Trust Foundation.

Familyculture. Boston, Mass. : [s.n.],

**FAMILY PLANNING.** *See* **BIRTH CONTROL.**

**FAMILY POLICY.** *See* **CHILD WELFARE.**

**FAMILY POLICY - CHINA.**
Diamant, Neil Jeffrey, 1964- Revolutionizing the
family. Berkeley : University of California Press,
c2000.
*TC HQ684 .D53 2000*

**FAMILY POLICY - DEVELOPING COUNTRIES.**
Strengthening the family. Tokyo : New York : United
Nations University Press, c1995.
*TC HQ727.9 .S77 1995*

**FAMILY POLICY - UNITED STATES.**
Lerner, Richard M. Family diversity and family
policy. Boston ; London : Kluwer Academic, c1999.
*TC HQ535 .L39 1999*

**FAMILY PRACTICE - NURSES' INSTRUCTION -
EXAMINATION QUESTIONS.**
Family nurse practitioner certification review. St.
Louis : Mosby, c1999.
*TC RT120.F34 F353 1998*

**FAMILY PROBLEMS - FICTION.**
Cooney, Caroline B. Tune in anytime. New York :
Delacorte Press, 1999.

TC PZ7.C7834 Tu 1999

Griffin, Adele. Dive. 1st ed. New York : Hyperion
Books for Children, 1999.
*TC PZ7.G881325 Di 1999*

Moeyaert, Bart. [Blote handen. English] Bare hands.
1st ed. Asheville, N.C. : Front Street, 1998.
*TC PZ7.M7227 Bar 1998*

**FAMILY - PSYCHOLOGICAL ASPECTS.**
Boss, Pauline. Ambiguous loss. Cambridge, Mass. :
Harvard University Press, 1999.
*TC BF575.D35 B67 1999*

Fullilove, Mindy Thompson. The house of Joshua.
Lincoln, NE : University of Nebraska Press, c1999.
*TC BF353 .F85 1999*

Woodruff, Debra, 1967- General family functioning,
parental bonding, and attachment style. 1998.
*TC 085 W858*

**FAMILY - PSYCHOLOGICAL ASPECTS -
HANDBOOKS, MANUALS, ETC.**
Handbook of family development and intervention.
New York : Wiley, c2000.
*TC RC489.F33 .H36 2000*

**The family psychology and counseling series**
Counseling Asian families from a systems
perspective. Alexandria, Va. : American Counseling
Ass., c1999.
*TC RC451.5.A75 C68 1999*

**FAMILY PSYCHOTHERAPY.** *See also* **MARITAL
PSYCHOTHERAPY.**
The adolescent in group and family therapy. 2nd ed.
Northvale, NJ : Jason Aronson, 1999.
*TC RJ505.G7 A36 1999*

Boyd-Franklin, Nancy. Reaching out in family
therapy. New York : Guilford Press, 2000.
*TC RC488.5 .B678 2000*

Children in therapy. New York : W.W. Norton, 2000.
*TC RC488.5 .C468 2000*

Counseling Asian families from a systems
perspective. Alexandria, Va. : American Counseling
Ass., c1999.
*TC RC451.5.A75 C68 1999*

Everett, Craig A. Family therapy for ADHD. New
York : Guilford Press, 1999.
*TC RJ506.H9 E94 1999*

Feminism, community, and communication. New
York ; London : Haworth Press, c2000.
*TC RC488.5 .F43 2000*

Handbook of psychotherapies with children and
families. New York ; London : Kluwer Academic/
Plenum Publishers, c1999.
*TC RJ504 .H3619 1999*

Isaacs, Marla Beth. [Difficult divorce] Therapy of the
difficult divorce. Northvale, N.J. ; London : J.
Aronson, c2000.
*TC RC488.6 .I83 2000*

Nichols, William C. Systemic family therapy. New
York : Guilford Press, c1986.
*TC RC488.5 .N535 1986*

Stein, Joan W The family as a unit of study and
treatment, [Seattle] Regional Rehabilitation Research
Institute, University of Washington, School of Social
Work [1970]
*TC RC488.5 .S88*

Theraplay. Northvale, N.J. : J. Aronson, c2000.
*TC RJ505.P6 T485 2000*

Walsh, Froma. Strengthening family resilience. New
York : Guilford Press, c1998.
*TC RC489.F33 W34 1998*

**FAMILY PSYCHOTHERAPY - CASE STUDIES.**
Casebook in family therapy. Belmont : Brooks/Cole,
c1999.
*TC RC488.5 .C369 1999*

**FAMILY PSYCHOTHERAPY - HANDBOOKS,
MANUALS, ETC.**
Handbook of family development and intervention.
New York : Wiley, c2000.
*TC RC489.F33 .H36 2000*

Preventive approaches in couples therapy.
Philadelphia : Brunner/Mazel, 1999.
*TC RC488.5 .P74 1999*

**FAMILY PSYCHOTHERAPY - PERIODICALS.**
Family and child mental health journal. New York,
NY : Human Sciences Press, [c1980-c1982]

**FAMILY PSYCHOTHERAPY - TECHNIQUE.**
McGoldrick, Monica. Genograms. 2nd ed. New
York : W.W. Norton, 1999.
*TC RC488.5 .M395 1999*

**FAMILY PSYCHOTHERAPY - UNITED STATES.**
Bridges to recovery. New York : London : Free Press,
c2000.
*TC HV5199.5 .B75 2000*

**FAMILY RECREATION.**
Lipkin, Lisa. Bringing the story home. New York :
W.W. Norton & Co., c2000.
*TC LB1042 .L515 2000*

**Family relations.**
The Family coordinator. Minneapolis, Minn. :
National Council on Family Relations, c1968-

**FAMILY RELATIONSHIPS.** *See* **FAMILY.**

**FAMILY - RESEARCH.**
Strengthening the family. Tokyo ; New York : United
Nations University Press, c1995.
*TC HQ727.9 .S77 1995*

**FAMILY REUNIONS.** *See* **FAMILY.**

**Family secrets.**
Kuhn, Annette. London : New York : Verso, 1995.
*TC CT274 .K84 1995*

**FAMILY SERVICES.** *See* **FAMILY SOCIAL
WORK; LIBRARIES - SERVICES TO
FAMILIES.**

**FAMILY - SERVICES FOR.** *See* **FAMILY
SERVICES.**

**FAMILY SERVICES - UNITED STATES.**
Scheinfeld, Daniel, 1933- Strengthening refugee
families. Chicago, Ill. : Lyceum Books, c1997.
*TC HV640.4.U54 S34 1997*

**FAMILY SIZE.** *See* **BIRTH CONTROL.**

**FAMILY - SOCIAL ASPECTS.** *See* **FAMILY.**

**FAMILY - SOCIAL CONDITIONS.** *See* **FAMILY.**

**FAMILY SOCIAL WORK.**
Walsh, Froma. Strengthening family resilience. New
York : Guilford Press, c1998.
*TC RC489.F33 W34 1998*

**FAMILY SOCIAL WORK - UNITED STATES.**
The challenge of permanency planning in a
multicultural society. New York : Haworth Press,
c1997.
*TC HV741 .C378 1997*

**FAMILY - STUDY AND TEACHING.** *See* **FAMILY
LIFE EDUCATION.**

**FAMILY THERAPY.** *See* **FAMILY
PSYCHOTHERAPY.**

**FAMILY THERAPY.**
Adolescent siblings in stepfamilies. Chicago, Ill. :
University of Chicago Press, 1999.
*TC LB1103.S6 v.64 no. 4*

Everett, Craig A. Family therapy for ADHD. New
York : Guilford Press, 1999.
*TC RJ506.H9 E94 1999*

Nichols, William C. Systemic family therapy. New
York : Guilford Press, c1986.
*TC RC488.5 .N535 1986*

**Family therapy for ADHD.**
Everett, Craig A. New York : Guilford Press, 1999.
*TC RJ506.H9 E94 1999*

**Family therapy for attention-deficit hyperactivity
disorder.**
Everett, Craig A. Family therapy for ADHD. New
York : Guilford Press, 1999.
*TC RJ506.H9 E94 1999*

**FAMILY THERAPY - METHODS.**
Handbook of psychotherapies with children and
families. New York ; London : Kluwer Academic/
Plenum Publishers, c1999.
*TC RJ504 .H3619 1999*

**FAMILY THERAPY - PERIODICALS.**
Family and child mental health journal. New York,
NY : Human Sciences Press, [c1980-c1982]

**FAMILY TREES.** *See* **GENEALOGY.**

**FAMILY - UGANDA.**
Gitta, Cosmas. International human rights. 1998.
*TC 085 G4398*

**FAMILY - UNITED STATES.** *See also* **AFRO-
AMERICAN FAMILIES; ASIAN AMERICAN
FAMILIES.**
The emergence of family into the 21st century.

Boston : Jones and Bartlett Publishers : [New York] :
NLN Press, c2001.
*TC HQ535 .E44 2001*

Families and teachers of individuals with disabilities.
Boston : London : Allyn and Bacon, c2001.
*TC LC3969 .F34 2001*

Family ethnicity. 2nd ed. Thousand Oaks, Calif. :
Sage Publications, c1999.
*TC E184.A1 F33 1999*

Hoffman, Lois Norma Wladis, 1929- Mothers at
work. Cambridge ; New York : Cambridge University
Press, 1999.
*TC HQ759.48 .H63 1999*

Lerner, Richard M. Family diversity and family
policy. Boston ; London : Kluwer Academic, c1999.
*TC HQ535 .L39 1999*

Primers for prudery. Updated ed. Baltimore : Johns
Hopkins University Press, 2000.
*TC HQ18.U5 P75 2000*

Resilience across contexts. Mahwah, NJ : Lawrence
Erlbaun, 2000.
*TC HQ535 .R47 2000*

Zinn, Maxine Baca, 1942- Diversity in families. 5th
ed. New York : Longman, 1998.
*TC HQ536 .Z54 1998*

**FAMILY - UNITED STATES - HISTORY.**
Primers for prudery. Updated ed. Baltimore : Johns
Hopkins University Press, 2000.
*TC HQ18.U5 P75 2000*

Smith, William L., 1956- Families and communes.
Thousand Oaks, Calif. : Sage Publications, c1999.
*TC HQ971 .S55 1999*

**FAMILY - UNITED STATES - HISTORY - 20TH
CENTURY.**
Coontz, Stephanie. The way we never were. New
York, NY : BasicBooks, c1992.
*TC HQ535 .C643 1992*

**FAMILY - UNITED STATES - PERIODICALS.**
The Family coordinator. Minneapolis, Minn. :
National Council on Family Relations, c1968-

**FAMILY - U.S.**
Cavan, Ruth Shonle, 1896- The American family. 3d
ed. New York, Crowell [1963]
*TC HQ535 .C33 1963*

**FAMILY VIOLENCE.** *See also* **CHILD ABUSE;
VICTIMS OF FAMILY VIOLENCE.**
Assessment of family violence. 2nd ed. New York :
John Wiley, c1999.
*TC RC569.5.F3 A87 1999*

Rossman, B. B. Robbie. Children and interparental
violence. Philadelphia, Pa. : London : Brunner/Mazel,
c2000.
*TC HQ784.V55 R675 2000*

**FAMILY VIOLENCE - GREAT BRITAIN.**
Lockley, Paul. Counselling women in violent
relationships. London ; New York : Free Association
Books, 1999.
*TC HV6626.23.G7 L624 1999*

**FAMILY VIOLENCE - LAW AND
LEGISLATION - UNITED STATES.**
Assessment of family violence. 2nd ed. New York :
John Wiley, c1999.
*TC RC569.5.F3 A87 1999*

**FAMILY VIOLENCE - PREVENTION.**
Rossman, B. B. Robbie. Children and interparental
violence. Philadelphia, Pa. ; London : Brunner/Mazel,
c2000.
*TC HQ784.V55 R675 2000*

**FAMILY VIOLENCE - UNITED STATES -
PREVENTION - EVALUATION.**
Violence in families. Washington, D.C. : National
Academy Press, 1998.
*TC HV6626.2 .V56 1998*

**FAMILY VIOLENCE VICTIMS.** *See* **VICTIMS OF
FAMILY VIOLENCE.**

**FAMILY WELFARE - UNITED STATES.**
Schorr, Alvin Louis, 1921- Filial responsibility in the
modern American family. [Washington] U.S. Dept. of
Health, Education, and Welfare, Social Security
Administration, Division of Program Research [1960]
*TC HV75 .S36 1960*

**Familyculture.** Boston, Mass. : [s.n.], 1 v. Vol. 1, no. 1
(Mar. 1896)-v. 1, no. 12 (Feb. 1897). Family culture. Caption
title. No more published?
*1. Family - Periodicals. 2. Marriage - Periodicals. I. Title:
Family culture. II. Series: History of women. periodicals.*

**FAMOUS PEOPLE.** *See* **CELEBRITIES.**

**FAMOUS PERSONS.**
Genius and eminence. 2nd ed. Oxford : New York :
Pergamon Press, 1992.
*TC BF412 .G43 1992*

**Famous problems and their mathematicians.**
Johnson, Art, 1946- Englewood, Colo. : Teacher Ideas
Press, 1999.
*TC QA43 .J56 1999*

**FANCY DRESS.** *See* **COSTUME.**

**FANCY WORK.** *See* **WHITE WORK
EMBROIDERY.**

**Fanlight Productions.**
Autism--a world apart [videorecording]. Boston, MA :
Fanlight Productions, [1989, c1988].
*TC RJ506 .A98 1988*

Between the lines [videorecording]. Boston, MA :
Fanlight Productions, c1997.
*TC RC552.S4 B4 1997*

Break throughs [videorecording]. Boston, MA :
Fanlight Productions, c1998.
*TC LC4717.5 .B7 1998*

Depression and manic depression [videorecording].
Boston, MA : Fanlight Productions, c1996.
*TC RC537 .D46 1996*

Depression in older adults [videorecording]. Boston,
MA : Fanlight Productions ; [Chicago, Ill.] :
Distributed by Terra Nova Films, Inc., 1997.
*TC RC537.5 .D4 1997*

First break [videorecording]. Boston, MA : Fanlight
Productions, c1997.
*TC RC465 .F5 1997*

First break [videorecording]. Boston, MA : Fanlight
Productions, c1997.
*TC RC465 .F5 1997*

First break [videorecording]. Boston, MA : Fanlight
Productions, c1997.
*TC RC465 .F5 1997*

Step on a crack [videorecording]. Boston, MA :
Fanlight Productions, 1996.
*TC RC533 .S7 1996*

When the brain goes wrong [videorecording]. Short
version. Boston, MA : Fanlight Productions [dist.],
c1992.
*TC RC386 .W54 1992*

**Fanshel, Susan.**
Nevelson in process [videorecording]. Chicago, IL :
Public Media Inc., 1977.
*TC NB237.N43 N43 1977*

**FANTASY.**
Freeman, Don. Corduroy. Harmondsworth,
Middlesex ; New York : Puffin Books, 1976.
*TC PZ8.9.F85 C5 1976*

Segal, Hanna. Dream, phantasy, and art. London ;
New York : Tavistock/Routledge, 1991.
*TC BF1078 .S375 1991*

**FANTASY IN ART.**
Sci-fi aesthetics. London : Academy Group Ltd. ;
Lanham, Md. : Distributed in the USA by National
Book Network, c1997.
*TC N8217.F28 S34 1994*

**FAR EAST.** *See* **EAST ASIA.**

**FAR NORTH.** *See* **ARCTIC REGIONS.**

**FAR WEST (U.S.).** *See* **WEST (U.S.).**

**Faraway home.**
Kurtz, Jane. San Diego : Harcourt, c2000.
*TC PZ7.K9626 Far 2000*

**Fariss, Linda K., 1951-.**
Pauwels, Colleen Kristl, 1946- Legal research.
Bloomington, Ind. : Phi Delta Kappa Educational
Foundation, c1999.
*TC KF240 .P38 1999*

**FARM BUILDINGS.** *See* **BARNS.**

**FARM LIFE.** *See* **RANCH LIFE.**

**FARM LIFE - IOWA - MANCHESTER REGION -
JUVENILE LITERATURE.**
Gillespie, Sarah (Sarah L.) A pioneer farm girl.
Mankato, Minn. : Blue Earth Books, c2000.
*TC F629.M28 G55 2000*

**Farmer, Lesley S. J.** Go figure! : mathematics through
sports / Lesley S.J. Farmer. Englewood, Colo. :
Teacher Ideas Press, 1999. xiv, 170 p. : ill. ; cm. Includes
bibliographical references (p. 163-166) and index. ISBN

1-56308-708-1 (softbound) DDC 510
*1. Mathematics. I. Title.*
**TC QA39.2 .F373 1999**

**Farmer, Nancy.** Casey Jones's fireman : the story of
Sim Webb / Nancy Farmer ; pictures by James
Bernardin. 1st ed. New York : Phyllis Fogelman
Books, c1998. 1 v. (unpaged) : col. ill. ; 22 x 27 cm.
SUMMARY: Even though the railroad fireman senses danger
ahead, he follows his engineer's command to increase the
train's power so that the mysterious whistle blows. ISBN
0-8037-1929-9 (trade) DDC 398.2; E
*1. Jones, Casey. - 1863-1900 - Legends. 2. Webb, Sim -
Legends. 3. Jones, Casey. - 1863-1900 - Legends. 4. Webb,
Sim - Legends. 5. Afro-Americans - Folklore. 6. Folklore -
United States. I. Bernardin, James, ill. II. Title.*
**TC PZ8.1.F2225 Cas 1998**

**FARMING.** *See* **AGRICULTURE.**

**Farndon, John.** Volcanoes / written by John Farndon ;
[special photographers, Philip Dowell ... et al. ;
illustrators, David Ashby ... et al.]. 1st American ed.
New York : DK Pub., 1998. 128 p. : ill. (some col.) ; 13
cm. (Pockets) Includes index. ISBN 0-7894-3416-4 DDC
551.21
*1. Volcanoes. 2. Volcanism. I. Title. II. Series.*
**TC QE522 .F37 1998**

**Farooq, R. A.**
Rugh, Andrea B. Teaching practices to increase
student achievement. Cambridge, Mass. :
B.R.I.D.G.E.S. Basic Research and Implementation in
Developing Education Systems, [1991].
**TC LB1025.2 .R83 1991**

**Farr, Dennis, 1929-** Francis Bacon : a retrospective /
guest curator, Dennis Farr ; co-curator, Massimo
Martino ; with essays by Dennis Farr, Michael
Peppiatt, Sally Yard. New York : Harry N. Abrams in
association with the Trust for Museum Exhibitions,
1999. 239 p. : ill. (some col.) ; 29 cm. Some pages fold-out to
reveal other illustrations. Catalog of an exhibition held at the
Yale Center for British Art, Jan. 25-Mar. 21, 1999 ... [et al.].
Includes bibliographical references (p. 235-236) and index.
ISBN 0-8109-4011-6 (hardcover) DDC 759.2
*1. Bacon, Francis. - 1909- - Exhibitions. I. Martino, Massimo.
II. Bacon, Francis. 1909- III. Peppiatt, Michael. IV. Yard,
Sally. V. Trust for Museum Exhibitions. VI. Yale Center for
British Art. VII. Title.*
**TC ND497.B16 A4 1999**

**Farrell, Michael.** Key issues for primary schools /
Michael Farrell. London : New York : Routledge,
1999. xiv, 210 p. ; 24 cm. Includes bibliographical references
(p. [206]-210). ISBN 0-415-18262-X DDC 372.941
*1. Education. Elementary - Great Britain. I. Title.*
**TC LA633 .F37 1999**

**FARRIERY.** *See* **HORSES; VETERINARY
MEDICINE.**

**FASHION.** *See* **CLOTHING AND DRESS;
COSTUME.**

**FASHION (FAD).** *See* **FADS.**

**FASHIONABLE SOCIETY.** *See* **UPPER CLASS.**

**Fass, Paula S.**
Childhood in America. New York : New York
University Press, c2000.
**TC HQ792.U5 C4199 1999**

**Fast forward.**
Sikes, Alfred C. 1st ed. New York : William Morrow,
2000.
**TC HM851 .S545 2000**

**Fastback**
(355.) Baldwin, John. Education and welfare
reform. Bloomington, Ind. : Phi Delta Kappa
Educational Foundation, c1993.
**TC LC4033.S61 B34 1993**

(361.) Fersh, Seymour. Integrating the trans-
national/cultural dimension. Bloomington, Ind. : Phi
Delta Kappa Educational Foundation, c1993.
**TC LC1090 .F47 1993**

(431.) Baker, Justine C. A neural network guide to
teaching. Bloomington, Ind. : Phi Delta Kappa
Educational Foundation, c1998.
**TC LB1057 .B35 1998**

**FASTS AND FEASTS.** *See* **CHRISTMAS;
FESTIVALS; HOLIDAYS; THANKSGIVING
DAY.**

**Fat talk.**
Nichter, Mimi. Cambridge, Mass. : Harvard
University Press, 2000.
**TC RJ399.C6 N53 2000**

**FATALLY ILL.** *See* **TERMINALLY ILL.**

**The fate of early memories.**
Howe, Mark L. Washington, DC : American
Psychological Association, c2000.
**TC BF378.E17 H69 2000**

**FATHER AND CHILD.** *See also* **FATHERS AND
DAUGHTERS; FATHERS AND SONS.**
Fivaz-Depeursinge, Elisabeth. The primary triangle :.
New York : Basic Books, c1999.
**TC HQ755.85 .F583 1999**

**FATHER AND CHILD - FICTION.**
Guettier, Bénédicte. The father who had ten children.
1st ed. New York : Dial Books for Young Readers,
1999.
**TC PZ7.G93824 Fat 1999**

**FATHER AND CHILD - UNITED STATES.**
The role of the father in child development. 3rd ed.
New York : Wiley, c1997.
**TC HQ756 .R64 1997**

**Father and son tales.**
Evetts-Secker, Josephine. Richmond Hill, Ont. :
Scholastic Canada, 1998.
**TC GR469 E93 1998**

**FATHER-CHILD RELATIONSHIP.** *See* **FATHER
AND CHILD.**

**FATHER CHRISTMAS.** *See* **SANTA CLAUS.**

**FATHER-SEPARATED CHILDREN.** *See*
**PATERNAL DEPRIVATION.**

**The father who had ten children.**
Guettier, Bénédicte. 1st ed. New York : Dial Books
for Young Readers, 1999.
**TC PZ7.G93824 Fat 1999**

**FATHERHOOD.**
Dowd, Nancy E., 1949- Redefining fatherhood. New
York : New York University Press, 2000.
**TC HQ756 .D588 2000**

**FATHERS.**
Dowd, Nancy E., 1949- Redefining fatherhood. New
York : New York University Press, 2000.
**TC HQ756 .D588 2000**

The role of the father in child development. 3rd ed.
New York : Wiley, c1997.
**TC HQ756 .R64 1997**

**FATHERS AND DAUGHTERS - FICTION.**
Camp, Lindsay. Why? New York : Putnam, c1998.
**TC PZ7.C1475 Wf 1998**

Cole, Brock. Buttons. 1st ed. New York : Farrar
Straus Giroux, 2000.
**TC PZ7.C67342 Bu 2000**

Conrad, Pam. Blue willow. New York : Philomel
Books, c1999.
**TC PZ7.C76476 Bl 1999**

Evans, Richard Paul. The dance. 1st ed. New York :
Simon & Schuster Books for Young Readers, c1999.
**TC PZ7.E89227 Dan 1999**

Kurtz, Jane. Faraway home. San Diego : Harcourt,
c2000.
**TC PZ7.K9626 Far 2000**

Ross, Alice. Jezebel's spooky spot. 1st ed. New
York : Dutton Children's Books, 1999.
**TC PZ7.R719694 Jf 1999**

**FATHERS AND SONS - FICTION.**
Figueredo, D. H., 1951- When this world was new. 1st
ed. New York : Lee & Low Books, 1999.
**TC PZ7.F488 Wh 1999**

Karr, Kathleen. Man of the family. 1st ed. New York :
Farrar, Straus and Giroux, 1999.
**TC PZ7.K149 Man 1999**

Many, Paul. My life, take two. New York : Walker &
Co., 2000.
**TC PZ7.M3212 My 2000**

Schmidt, Gary D. Anson's way. New York : Clarion
Books, c1999.
**TC PZ7.S3527 An 1999**

**FATHERS AND SONS - FOLKLORE.**
Evetts-Secker, Josephine. Father and son tales.
Richmond Hill, Ont. : Scholastic Canada, 1998.
**TC GR469 E93 1998**

**FATHERS AND SONS - JUVENILE FICTION.**
Krumgold, Joseph, 1908- Onion John. New York,
N.Y. : Thomas Y. Crowell Company, 1959.
**TC XFK942**

**FATHERS - JUVENILE POETRY.**
Poems for fathers. 1st ed. New York : Holiday House,
c1989.
**TC PS595.F39 P64 1989**

**FATHERS - POETRY.**
Poems for fathers. 1st ed. New York : Holiday House,
c1989.
**TC PS595.F39 P64 1989**

**FATHERS - UNITED STATES - EMPLOYMENT.**
Levine, James A. Working fathers. Reading, Mass. :
Addison-Wesley, c1997.
**TC HQ756 .L474 1997**

**FATHERS - UNITED STATES - PSYCHOLOGY.**
Levine, James A. Working fathers. Reading, Mass. :
Addison-Wesley, c1997.
**TC HQ756 .L474 1997**

**FATIGUE - CONGRESSES.**
The physiology and pathophysiology of exercise
tolerance. New York : Plenum Press, c1996.
**TC QP301 .P576 1996**

**FATIGUE - NURSING.**
Key aspects of comfort. New York : Springer Pub.
Co., c1989.
**TC RT87.P35 K48 1989**

**FATNESS.** *See* **OBESITY.**

**Fatty acids in foods and their health implications** /
edited by Ching Kuang Chow. 2nd ed., rev. and
expanded. New York : M. Dekker, c2000. xii, 1045 p. :
ill. ; 26 cm. (Food science and technology ; 96) Includes
bibliographical references and index. ISBN 0-8247-6782-9
(alk. paper) DDC 612.3/97
*1. Fatty acids in human nutrition. 2. Food - Fat content. 3.
Fatty acids - Metabolism. I. Chow, Ching Kuang, 1940- II.
Series: Food science and technology (Marcel Dekker, Inc.) ;
96.*
**TC QP752.F35 F38 2000**

**FATTY ACIDS IN HUMAN NUTRITION.**
Fatty acids in foods and their health implications. 2nd
ed., rev. and expanded. New York : M. Dekker,
c2000.
**TC QP752.F35 F38 2000**

**FATTY ACIDS - METABOLISM.**
Fatty acids in foods and their health implications. 2nd
ed., rev. and expanded. New York : M. Dekker,
c2000.
**TC QP752.F35 F38 2000**

**Faulkner, Dorothy.**
Making sense of social development. London ; New
York : Routledge in association with the Open
University, 1999.
**TC HQ783 .L57 1999**

**FAULKNER, SHANNON - TRIALS, LITIGATION,
ETC.**
Manegold, Catherine S. In glory's shadow. 1st ed.
New York : Alfred A. Knopf, 1999.
**TC KF228.C53 M36 1999**

**FAUNA.** *See* **ANIMALS; ZOOLOGY.**

**FAURÉ GABRIEL, 1845-1924 - CRITICISM AND
INTERPRETATION.**
Gingerich, Carol Joy. The French piano style of Fauré
and Debussy. 1996.
**TC 06 no. 10644**

**Faustman, Cameron, 1960-.**
Antioxidants in muscle foods. New York ; Chichester
[England] : John Wiley, c2000.
**TC TX556.M4 A57 2000**

**Fauvel, John.**
Oxford figures. Oxford ; New York : Oxford
University Press, 2000.
**TC QA14.G73 O947 2000**

**Fayer, Steve, 1935-.**
Africans in America [videorecording]. [Boston,
Mass.] : WGBH Educational Foundation : South
Burlington, VT : WGBH Boston Video [distributor],
c1998.
**TC E441 .A47 1998**

**Fazio, Lynn.**
Thomas, Adele, 1942- Families at school. Newark,
Del. : International Reading Association, c1999.
**TC LC151 .T56 1999**

Thomas, Adele, 1942- Families at school. Newark,
Del. : International Reading Association, c1999.
**TC LC151 .T563 1999**

**FEAR.** *See* **ANXIETY; PHOBIAS.**

**FEAR - FICTION.**
Figueredo, D. H., 1951- When this world was new. 1st ed. New York : Lee & Low Books, 1999.
*TC PZ7.F488 Wh 1999*

Hendry, Diana, 1941- Dog Donovan. 1st U.S. ed. Cambridge, Mass. : Candlewick Press, 1995.
*TC PZ7.H38586 Dm 1995*

Ross, Alice. Jezebel's spooky spot. 1st ed. New York : Dutton Children's Books, 1999.
*TC PZ7.R719694 Jf 1999*

**FEAR IN CHILDREN.** *See* **FEAR OF THE DARK.**

**FEAR OF BEING ALONE.** *See* **AGORAPHOBIA.**

**FEAR OF FAILURE.**
Miller, Estelle L. Fears expressed by female reentry students at an urban community college : qualitative study. 1997.
*TC 06 no. 10864*

**Fear of intimacy.**
Firestone, Robert. 1st ed. Washington, DC : American Psychological Association, c1999.
*TC BF575.I5 F57 1999*

**FEAR OF OPEN SPACE.** *See* **AGORAPHOBIA.**

**FEAR OF OPEN SPACES.** *See* **AGORAPHOBIA.**

**FEAR OF SUCCESS.** *See* **SUCCESS.**

**FEAR OF THE DARK - FICTION.**
Apple, Margot. Brave Martha. Boston : Houghton Mifflin, 1999.
*TC PZ7.A6474 Br 1999*

**Fears expressed by female reentry students at an urban community college : qualitative study.**
Miller, Estelle L. 1997.
*TC 06 no. 10864*

**FEATURE FILMS - HISTORY AND CRITICISM.** *See* **MOTION PICTURES.**

**Fed up.**
Manton, Catherine, 1942- Westport, Conn. : Bergin & Garvey, 1999.
*TC HQ1410 .M355 1999*

**FEDERAL AID.** *See* **ECONOMIC ASSISTANCE, DOMESTIC.**

**FEDERAL AID TO DEPRESSED AREAS.** *See* **ECONOMIC ASSISTANCE, DOMESTIC.**

**FEDERAL AID TO EDUCATION - DEVELOPING COUNTRIES.**
Patrinos, Harry Anthony. Decentralization of education. Washington, D.C. : World Bank, c1997.
*TC LB2826.6.D44 P38 1997*

**FEDERAL AID TO EDUCATION - UNITED STATES.**
Ferguson, Jacqueline. Grants for special education and rehabilitation. 4th ed. Gaithersburg, MD : Aspen Publishers, Inc., 2000.
*TC LB2825 .F424 2000*

Grants for schools. 4th ed. Gaithersburg, MD : Aspen Publishers, 2000.
*TC LB2825 .F46 2000*

**FEDERAL AID TO HANDICAPPED SERVICES.** *See* **FEDERAL AID TO SERVICES FOR THE HANDICAPPED.**

**FEDERAL AID TO SERVICES FOR THE HANDICAPPED - UNITED STATES - DIRECTORIES.**
Directory of grants for organizations serving people with disabilities. Loxahatchee, Fla. : Research Grant Guides, c1993-
*TC HV3006.A4 H35*

**FEDERAL AID TO THE ARTS - PHILOSOPHY.**
Schwartz, David T. Art, education, and the democratic commitment. Dordrecht ; Boston : Kluwer Academic Publishers, c2000.
*TC NX720 .S33 2000*

**FEDERAL AID TO THE ARTS - UNITED STATES.**
Levy, Alan Howard. Government and the arts. Lanham, MD : University Press of America, c1997.
*TC NX735 .L48 1997*

Nancy Hanks lecture on arts and public policy. [New York, NY] : American Council for the Arts, <1988->
*TC NX730 .N25*

**FEDERAL AID TO THE ARTS - UNITED STATES - BIBLIOGRAPHY.**
Kalfatovic, Martin R., 1961- The New Deal fine arts projects. Metuchen, N.J. : Scarecrow Press, 1994.

*TC Z5961.U5 K36 1994*

**FEDERAL EMPLOYEES (U.S.).** *See* **UNITED STATES - OFFICIALS AND EMPLOYEES.**

**FEDERAL GOVERNMENT.** *See* **STATE GOVERNMENTS.**

**FEDERAL GRANTS.** *See* **GRANTS-IN-AID.**

**FEDERAL GRANTS FOR EDUCATION.** *See* **FEDERAL AID TO EDUCATION.**

**FEDERAL HOSPITALS.** *See* **PUBLIC HOSPITALS.**

**Federation for Child Study (U.S.).**
[Child study (New York, N.Y.)] Child study. [New York City] : Federation for Child Study, 1925-1960.

**Federation notes.** [Arlington, Va., : Wing Publications.]
Official publication of the Virginia Federation of Business and Professional Women's Clubs, inc. ISSN 0191-524X
*I. Virginia Federation of Business and Professional Women's Clubs.*

**Federation of Associations for Cripples (U.S.).**
American journal of care for cripples. New York : Douglas McMurtie, 1914-1919.

**Federation of Central Universities Teachers' Associations.**
The Journal of university education. Delhi, Published by A. Singh for Federation of Central Universities Teachers' Associations, Aligarh.

**Federici, Silvia.**
A thousand flowers. Trenton, NJ : Africa World Press, c2000, [1999].
*TC LC67.68.A35 T56 2000*

**Fee, Dwight.**
Pathology and the postmodern. London ; Thousand Oaks : SAGE, 2000.
*TC BF636 .P38 2000*

**FEEBLE-MINDED.** *See* **MENTALLY HANDICAPPED.**

**Feed all my sheep.**
Clark, Doris C., 1938- 1st ed. Louisville, Ky. : Geneva Press, c2000.
*TC BV1615.M37 C53 2000*

**FEEDBACK (PSYCHOLOGY).**
Curcio, John J. Relationships among administrator personality, perceptions of feedback source credibility, and attitudes toward program feedback. 1999.
*TC 085 C92*

Handbook of self-regulation. San Diego : Academic, 2000.
*TC BF632 .H254 2000*

**Feeding China's little emperors :** food, children, and social change / edited by Jun Jing. Stanford, Calif. : Stanford University Press, 2000. xiii, 279 p. : ill. ; 23 cm. Includes bibliographical references (p. [241]-266) and index. ISBN 0-8047-3133-0 (cloth : alk. paper) ISBN 0-8047-3134-9 (pbk. : alk. paper) DDC 363.8/083/0951
*1. Nutrition policy - China. 2. Diet - China. 3. Food habits - China. 4. Children - China - Nutrition. 5. Advertising and children - China. I. Jing, Jun, 1957-*
*TC TX361.C5 F44 2000*

**FEELING.** *See* **PERCEPTION; TOUCH.**

**Feeling and thinking :** the role of affect in social cognition / edited by Joseph P. Forgas. Cambridge, U.K. ; New York : Cambridge University Press ; Paris : Editions de la Maison des Sciences de l'Homme, 2000. xvi, 421 p. : ill. ; 24 cm. (Studies in emotion and social interaction. Second series) Includes bibliographical references and indexes. ISBN 0-521-64223-X (hardcover) ISBN 2-7351-0830-9 (France) DDC 152.4
*1. Affect (Psychology). 2. Mood (Psychology) 3. Emotions. 4. Social perception. I. Forgas, Joseph P. II. Series: Studies in emotion and social interaction. Second series*
*TC BF531 .F44 2000*

**FEELINGS.** *See* **EMOTIONS.**

**Feeney, Don J., 1948-** Entrancing relationships : exploring the hypnotic framework of addictive relationships / Don J. Feeney, Jr. Westport, Conn. : Praeger, 1999. xii, 238 p. : ill. ; 24 cm. Includes bibliographical references (p. [225]-229) and index. ISBN 0-275-96415-9 (alk. paper) DDC 616.86
*1. Relationship addiction. 2. Hypnotism. I. Title.*
*TC RC552.R44 F44 1999*

**Feetham, Suzanne.**
Handbook of clinical nursing research. Thousand Oaks, Calif. : Sage Publications, c1999.
*TC RT81.5 .H25 1999*

**Fegan, Claudia.**
Armstrong, Pat, 1945- Universal health care. New York : New Press : Distributed by W.W. Norton, c1998.
*TC RA412.5.C3 A76 1998*

**Fehr, Dennis Earl, 1952-.**
Real-world readings in art education. New York : Falmer Press, c2000.
*TC N353 .R43 2000*

**Feiman-Nemser, Sharon.**
Guiding teacher learning. Washington. DC : AACTE, c1997.
*TC LB1731 .G85 1997*

**Feinberg, Sandra, 1946-.**
Including families of children with special needs. New York : Neal Schuman Publishers, c1999.
*TC Z711.92.H3 I6 1999*

**Feinberg, Walter, 1937-** School and society / Walter Feinberg, Jonas F. Soltis. 3rd ed. New York : Teachers College Press, c1998. ix, 155 p. ; 23 cm. (Thinking about education series) Includes bibliographical references (p. 151-155). ISBN 0-8077-3802-6 (paper : alk. paper) DDC 306.43
*1. Educational sociology. I. Soltis, Jonas F. II. Title. III. Series.*
*TC LC191 .F4 1998*

**Feiring, Candice.**
The development of romantic relationships in adolescence. Cambridge, U.K. ; New York : Cambridge University Press, 1999.
*TC BF724.3.L68 D48 1999*

**Feistritzer, C. Emily.** Alternative teacher certification : a state-by-state analysis 2000 / C. Emily Feistritzer, David T. Chester. Washington, D.C. : National Center for Education Information, c2000. 422 p. ; 28 cm.
*1. Teachers - Certification - United States. 2. Teachers - Certification - United States - Statistics. I. Chester, David. II. National Center for Education Information (Washington, D.C.) III. Title.*
*TC LB1771 .A47 2000*

**Feisty females :** inspiring girls to think mathematically / Karen Karp ... [et al.]. Portsmouth, NH : Heinemann, c1998. x, 149 p. : ill. ; 24 cm. Includes bibliographical references. ISBN 0-325-00009-3 (acid-free paper) DDC 372.7/044
*1. Mathematics - Study and teaching. 2. Literature in mathematics education. 3. Women in mathematics. 4. Mathematical ability - Sex differences. I. Karp, Karen, 1951-*
*TC QA11 .F44 1998*

**Feldberg, Suzanne.** A comparison of different types of mathematical problem-solving hints selected by concrete and formal operational subjects in a hypercard environment / Suzanne Feldberg. 1998. vii, 178 leaves : ill. ; 29 cm. Issued also on microfilm. Includes tables. Thesis (Ph.D.)--Columbia University, 1998. Includes bibliographical references (leaves 95-103)
*1. Piaget, Jean. - 1896- 2. HyperCard (Computer file) 3. Cognition in children. 4. Mathematics - Study and teaching (Elementary) 5. Educational psychology. 6. Problem solving - Study and teaching. 7. Mathematical ability - Testing. I. Title.*
*TC 085 F316*

**Feldman, Alan, 1947-.**
Network science, a decade later. Mahwah, N.J. : Lawrence Erlbaum, 2000.
*TC LB1583.3 .N48 2000*

**Feldman, Lynne B.** A sense of place : Birmingham's Black middle-class community, 1890-1930 / Lynne B. Feldman. Tuscaloosa, Ala. ; London : University of Alabama Press, c1999. xvi, 326 p. : ill., maps ; 24 cm. Includes bibliographical references (p. 195-312) and index. CONTENTS: Acknowledgments -- Introduction -- The birth of a community -- Smithfield : the suburb -- Steps toward building the home sphere -- Leadership, the Black elite, and the business community -- Institution building : the creation of schools and their significance in the community -- Men seeking an identity : involvement in churches, clubs, and civic associations -- Women seeking an identity : improving the social and political environment -- Conclusion -- Notes -- Bibliography -- Index. ISBN 0-8173-0967-5 (cloth : alk. paper) ISBN 0-8173-0969-1 (paper : alk. paper) DDC 976.1/ 7810496073
*1. Afro-Americans - Alabama - Birmingham - History. 2. Middle class - Alabama - Birmingham - History. 3. Birmingham (Ala.) - History. I. Title.*
*TC F334.B69 N437 1999*

**Feldman, Robert S. (Robert Stephen), 1947-.**
The social context of nonverbal behavior. Cambridge, U.K. ; New York : Cambridge University Press ; Paris : Editions de la Maison des Sciences de l'Homme, 1999.
*TC BF637.N66 S63 1999*

**FELIDAE - AFRICA.**
Hall-Martin, Anthony. Cats of Africa. Washington,
D.C. : Smithsonian Institution Press, 1998.
*TC QL737.C23 H335 1997*

**FELIDAE - AFRICA - PICTORIAL WORKS.**
Hall-Martin, Anthony. Cats of Africa. Washington,
D.C. : Smithsonian Institution Press, 1998.
*TC QL737.C23 H335 1997*

**FELIS.** *See* **CATS.**

**FELIS CATUS.** *See* **CATS.**

**FELIS DOMESTICA.** *See* **CATS.**

**FELIS SILVESTRIS CATUS.** *See* **CATS.**

**Felkai, László.** Zsidó iskolázás Magyarországon, 1780-
1990 / Felkai László. Budapest : Országos Pedagógiai
Könyvtár és Múzeum, [1998] 157 p. ; 25 cm. Errata slip
inserted. Includes bibliographical references. ISBN 963-7644-
82-2
*1. Jews - Hungary - Education - History. 2. Jewish day
schools - Hungary - History. 3. Jewish religious schools -
Hungary - History. I. Országos Pedagógiai Könyvtár és
Múzeum. II. Title.*
*TC LC746.H8 F455 1998*

**Fellow beggars.**
Oliver, Frank H. 1999.
*TC 06 no.11157*

**FELLOWSHIPS.** *See* **SCHOLARSHIPS.**

**FELLOWSHIPS AND SCHOLARSHIPS - UNITED
STATES - DIRECTORIES.**
Financial aid for African Americans. El Dorado Hills,
Calif. : Reference Service Press, c1997-
*TC LB2338 .F5643*

**FELONIES.** *See* **CRIME.**

**Felson, Richard B.**
Psychological perspectives on self and identity. 1st ed.
Washington, DC : American Psychological
Association, c2000.
*TC BF697 .P765 2000*

**Feltham, Colin.**
Taking supervision forward. London : Sage, 2000.
*TC BF637.C6 T35 2000*

**Felton, Mark Kenji.** Metacognitive reflection and
strategy development in argumentive discourse / Mark
Kenji Felton. 1999. x, 176 leaves : ill. ; 29 cm. Issued also
on microfilm. Includes tables. Thesis (Ph. D.)--Columbia
University, 1999. Includes bibliographical references (leaves
148-156)
*1. Discourse analysis. 2. Metacognition. 3. Developmental
psychology. 4. Factor analysis. 5. Debates and debating. 6.
Reasoning. I. Title.*
*TC 085 F34*

**Female forms.**
Thomas, Carol, 1958- Philadelphia, Pa. : Open
University Press, 1999.
*TC HV1568.25.G7 T46 1999*

**FEMALE HOMOSEXUALS.** *See* **LESBIANS.**

**FEMALE-MALE RELATIONSHIPS.** *See* **MAN-
WOMAN RELATIONSHIPS.**

**FEMALE STUDIES.** *See* **WOMEN'S STUDIES.**

**FEMALES.** *See* **WOMEN.**

**FEMININE BEAUTY (AESTHETICS).**
Beauty matters. Bloomington : Indiana University
Press, c2000.
*TC HQ1219 .B348 2000*

**FEMININITY.** *See also* **WOMEN.**
André, Serge. [Que veut un femme? English] What
does a woman want? New York : Other Press, c1999.
*TC BF175 .A69613 1999*

**FEMINISM.** *See also* **ECOFEMINISM; FEMINIST
THEORY; FEMINIST THERAPY;
FEMINISTS; SEX DISCRIMINATION
AGAINST WOMEN; WOMEN - SOCIAL
CONDITIONS.**
Practicing feminist ethics in psychology. 1st ed.
Washington, DC : American Psychological
Association, c2000.
*TC BF201.4 .P73 2000*

Rosser, Sue Vilhauer. Women, science, and society.
New York : Teachers College Press, c2000.
*TC QH305.5 .R67 2000*

**FEMINISM AND ART.**
Olkowski, Dorothea. Gilles Deleuze and the ruin of
representation. Berkeley : University of California
Press, c1999.
*TC N6537.K42 O44 1999*

**FEMINISM AND ART - AUSTRALIA.**
Kirby, Sandy. Sight lines. Tortola, BVI : Craftsman
House in association with Gordon and Breach : New
York : Distributed in the USA by STBS Ltd., 1992.
*TC N72.F45 K57 1992*

**FEMINISM AND EDUCATION.**
Burch, Kerry T., 1957- Eros as the educational
principle of democracy. New York : P. Lang, c2000.
*TC LC196 .B75 2000*

Feminist cyberscapes. Stamford, Conn. : Ablex Pub.,
c1999.
*TC PE1404 .F39 1999*

Gontarczyk, Ewa. Kobiecość i męskość jako kategorie
społeczno-kulturowe w studiach feministycznych.
Poznań : Eruditus, 1995.
*TC HQ1181.P7 G66 1995*

Haake, Katharine. What our speech disrupts. Urbana,
Ill. : National Council of Teachers of English, c2000.
*TC PE1404 .H3 2000*

Hayes, Elisabeth. Women as learners. 1st ed. San
Francisco : Jossey-Bass Publishers, c2000.
*TC LC5225.L42 H39 2000*

Kelly, Deirdre M. Pregnant with meaning. New York :
P. Lang, c2000.
*TC LC4094.2.B8 K45 2000*

McGarrh, Kellie, d. 1995. Kellie McGarrh's hangin'
in tough. New York : P. Lang, c2000.
*TC LA2317.D6185 M34 2000*

McWilliam, Erica. Pedagogical pleasures. New York ;
Canterbury [England] : P. Lang, c1999.
*TC LB1775 .M319 1999*

Morley, Louise, 1954- Organising feminisms. New
York : St. Martin's Press, 1999.
*TC LC197 .M67 1999*

Ochsner, Mindy Blaise. Something rad & risqu'e.
1999.
*TC 06 no. 11208*

Working the ruins. New York ; London : Routledge,
2000.
*TC LC197 .W67 2000*

**FEMINISM AND EDUCATION - GREAT
BRITAIN.**
Gender in the secondary curriculum. London ; New
York : Routledge, 1998.
*TC LC212.93.G7 G46 1998*

**FEMINISM AND EDUCATION - UNITED
STATES.**
Coming into her own. San Francisco, Calif. : Jossey-
Bass, c1999.
*TC LC1503 .C65 1999*

Herideen, Penelope E., 1960- Policy, pedagogy, and
social inequality. Westport, Conn. : Bergin & Garvey,
1998.
*TC LB2328.15.U6 H47 1998*

Martin, Jane Roland, 1929- Coming of age in
academe. New York ; London : Routledge, 2000.
*TC LC197 .M37 2000*

Weiler, Jeanne. Codes and contradictions. Albany :
State University of New York Press, c2000.
*TC LC1755 .W45 2000*

Wise women. New York ; London : Routledge, 2000.
*TC LB2837 .W58 2000*

**FEMINISM AND EDUCATION - UNITED
STATES - CASE STUDIES.**
Brodie, Laura Fairchild. Breaking out. 1st ed. New
York : Pantheon Books, c2000.
*TC LC212.862 .B75 2000*

Gardiner, Mary E., 1953- Coloring outside the lines.
Albany : State University of New York Press, c2000.
*TC LB2831.82 .G37 2000*

**FEMINISM AND LITERATURE.**
Moi, Toril. What is a woman? Oxford ; New York :
Oxford University Press, 1999.
*TC HQ1190 .M64 1999*

**FEMINISM AND THE ARTS.** *See also* **FEMINISM
AND ART.**
Krauss, Rosalind E. Bachelors. Cambridge, Mass. :
MIT Press, c1999.
*TC NX180.F4 K73 1999*

Talking visions. New York, N.Y. : New Museum of
Contemporary Art ; Cambridge, Mass. : MIT Press,
c1998.
*TC NX180.F4 T36 1998*

**Feminism and the biological body.**
Birke, Lynda I. A. New Brunswick, N.J. : Rutgers
University Press, 2000.
*TC HQ1190 .B56 2000*

**FEMINISM - BIBLIOGRAPHY.** *See* **FEMINIST
LITERATURE.**

**Feminism, community, and communication** / Mary E.
Olson, editor. New York ; London : Haworth Press,
c2000. 162 p. ; 23 cm. "Co-published simultaneously as
Journal of feminist family therapy, volume 11, number 4,
2000." Includes bibliographical references and index. ISBN
0-7890-1151-4 (hbk. : alk. paper) ISBN 0-7890-1152-2 (pbk. :
alk. paper) DDC 616.89/156
*1. Family psychotherapy. 2. Feminist therapy. I. Olson, Mary
E. II. Title: Journal of feminist family therapy v. 11, no. 4.*
*TC RC488.5 .F43 2000*

**FEMINISM - DEVELOPING COUNTRIES.**
Feminist visions of development. London ; New
York : Routledge, c1998.
*TC HQ1240 .F464 1998*

**FEMINISM - EGYPT - HISTORY.**
Badran, Margot. Feminists, Islam, and nation.
Princeton, N.J. : Princeton University Press, c1995.
*TC HQ1793 .B33 1995*

**FEMINISM - ENCYCLOPEDIAS.**
Women's studies encyclopedia. Rev. and expanded
ed. Westport, Conn. : Greenwood Press, c1999.
*TC HQ1115 .W645 1999*

**FEMINISM - FRANCE - HISTORY.**
Gordon, Felicia. Early French feminisms, 1830-1940.
Cheltenham, U.K. ; Brookfield, Vt. : Edward Elgar,
c1996.
*TC HQ1615.A3 G67 1996*

**FEMINISM - PHILOSOPHY.** *See* **FEMINIST
THEORY.**

**FEMINISM - PSYCHOLOGICAL ASPECTS.**
Montagu, Ashley, 1905- The natural superiority of
women. 5th ed. Walnut Creek, Calif. : AltaMira Press,
c1999.
*TC HQ1206 .M65 1999*

**FEMINISM - RESEARCH - METHODOLOGY.**
Bloom, Leslie Rebecca. Under the sign of hope.
Albany, N.Y. : State University of New York Press,
c1998.
*TC HQ1185 .B56 1998*

DeVault, Marjorie L., 1950- Liberating method.
Philadelphia : Temple University Press, 1999.
*TC HQ1180 .D48 1999*

**FEMINISM - SOUTH ASIA - HISTORY - 20TH
CENTURY.**
Robinson, Catherine A. Tradition and liberation. New
York : St. Martin's Press, 1999.
*TC HQ1735.3 .R63 1999*

**FEMINISM - UNITED STATES.**
Chinn, Peggy L. Peace and power. 5th ed. Boston :
Jones and Bartlett Publishers, c2001.
*TC HQ1426 .W454 2001*

Robbins, Carol Braswell. An examination of critical
feminist pedagogy in practice. 1999.
*TC 06 no. 11067*

**FEMINISM - UNITED STATES - HISTORY.**
Satter, Beryl, 1959- Each mind a kingdom. Berkeley :
University of California Press, c1999.
*TC BF639 .S124 1999*

**FEMINISM - UNITED STATES - HISTORY -
SOURCES.**
Women's America. 5th ed. New York : Oxford
University Press, 2000.
*TC HQ1426 .W663 2000*

**FEMINIST ANTHROPOLOGY.**
Situated lives. New York : Routledge, 1997.
*TC GN479.65 .S57 1997*

**FEMINIST ART CRITICISM.**
Solomon-Godeau, Abigail. Male trouble :. London :
Thames and Hudson, c1997.
*TC N6847.5.N35 S64 1997*

**Feminist counseling in action.**
Chaplin, Jocelyn. Feminist counselling in action. 2nd
ed. Thousand Oaks, Calif. : SAGE, 1999.
*TC HQ1206 .C447 1999*

**Feminist counselling in action.**
Chaplin, Jocelyn. 2nd ed. Thousand Oaks, Calif. :
SAGE, 1999.
*TC HQ1206 .C447 1999*

**Feminist cyberscapes :** mapping gendered academic spaces / edited by Kristine Blair and Pamela Takayoshi. Stamford, Conn. : Ablex Pub., c1999. xiv, 458 p. : ill. ; 23 cm. (New directions in computers & composition studies) Includes bibliographical references and indexes. ISBN 1-56750-438-8 (cloth) ISBN 1-56750-439-6 (paper) DDC 808/.042/0285
*1. English language - Rhetoric - Study and teaching - Data processing. 2. Academic writing - Study and teaching - Data processing. 3. English language - Computer-assisted instruction. 4. Internet (Computer network) in education. 5. Academic writing - Sex differences. 6. Women - Education (Higher) 7. Feminism and education. I. Blair, Kristine. II. Takayoshi, Pamela. III. Series: New Directions in computers and composition studies.*
*TC PE1404 .F39 1999*

**FEMINIST ECOLOGY.** *See* ECOFEMINISM.

**FEMINIST LITERATURE - STUDY AND TEACHING (SECONDARY) - CASE STUDIES.**
Harper, Helen J., 1957- Wild words-dangerous desires. New York : Peter Lang, c2000.
*TC LB1631 .H267 2000*

**Feminist perspective on the body.**
Brook, Barbara, 1949- New York : Longman, 1999.
*TC GT495 .B76 1999*

**Feminist perspectives series**
Brook, Barbara, 1949- Feminist perspective on the body. New York : Longman, 1999.
*TC GT495 .B76 1999*

**Feminist poststructuralist study of gender in an urban kindergarten classroom.**
Ochsner, Mindy Blaise. Something rad & risqu'e. 1999.
*TC 06 no. 11208*

**FEMINIST PSYCHOLOGY.**
Chaplin, Jocelyn. Feminist counselling in action. 2nd ed. Thousand Oaks, Calif. : SAGE, 1999.
*TC HQ1206 .C447 1999*

Dryden, Caroline. Being married, doing gender. London ; New York : Routledge, 1999.
*TC HQ734 .D848 1999*

Practicing feminist ethics in psychology. 1st ed. Washington, DC : American Psychological Association, c2000.
*TC BF201.4 .P73 2000*

Roszak, Theodore, 1933- The gendered atom. Berkeley, Calif. : Conari Press, 1999.
*TC BF64 .R69 1999*

Stoppard, Janet M. (Janet Mary), 1945- Understanding depression. London ; New York : Routledge, 2000.
*TC RC537 .S82 2000*

Toward a feminist developmental psychology. New York : Routledge, 2000.
*TC BF713 .T66 2000*

Unger, Rhoda Kesler. Resisting gender. London ; Thousand Oaks, Calif. : Sage Publications, 1998.
*TC BF201.4 .U544 1998*

**FEMINIST PSYCHOTHERAPY.** *See* FEMINIST THERAPY.

**FEMINIST SOCIOLOGY.** *See* FEMINIST THEORY.

**FEMINIST STUDIES.** *See* WOMEN'S STUDIES.

**FEMINIST THEORY.**
Birke, Lynda I. A. Feminism and the biological body. New Brunswick, N.J. : Rutgers University Press, 2000.
*TC HQ1190 .B56 2000*

Brook, Barbara, 1949- Feminist perspective on the body. New York : Longman, 1999.
*TC GT495 .B76 1999*

Davis, D. Diane (Debra Diane), 1963- Breaking up (at) totality. Carbondale : Southern Illinois University Press, c2000.
*TC PE1404 .D385 2000*

DeVault, Marjorie L., 1950- Liberating method. Philadelphia : Temple University Press, 1999.
*TC HQ1180 .D48 1999*

Embodying bioethics. Lanham : Rowman & Littlefield Publishers, c1999.
*TC QH332 .E43 1999*

Gender and qualitative research. Aldershot, Hants, England ; Brookfield, Vt., USA : Avebury, c1996.

*TC HQ1075 .G4617 1996*

Gendering the city. Lanham [Md.] : Rowman & Littlefield, c2000.
*TC HT166 .G4614 2000*

Moi, Toril. What is a woman? Oxford ; New York : Oxford University Press, 1999.
*TC HQ1190 .M64 1999*

Ochsner, Mindy Blaise. Something rad & risqu'e. 1999.
*TC 06 no. 11208*

Race, rhetoric, and the postcolonial. Albany : State University of New York Press, c1999.
*TC P301.5.P67 R33 1999*

Thayer-Bacon, Barbara J., 1953- Transforming critical thinking. New York : Teachers College Press, c2000.
*TC BC177 .T45 2000*

Vital signs. Edinburgh : Edinburgh University Press, c1998.
*TC HQ1190 .V56 1998*

Vital signs. Edinburgh : Edinburgh University Press, c1998.
*TC HQ1190 .V56 1998*

**FEMINIST THEORY - GREAT BRITAIN.**
Thomas, Carol, 1958- Female forms. Philadelphia, Pa. : Open University Press, 1999.
*TC HV1568.25.G7 T46 1999*

**FEMINIST THEORY - UNITED STATES.**
Robbins, Carol Braswell. An examination of critical feminist pedagogy in practice. 1999.
*TC 06 no. 11067*

Whiteness. Lanham, [Md.] : Rowman & Littlefield, c1999.
*TC E184.A1 W399 1999*

**FEMINIST THERAPY.**
Children's rights, therapists' responsibilities. New York : Harrington Park Press, c1997.
*TC RJ504 .C486 1997*

Feminism, community, and communication. New York ; London : Haworth Press, c2000.
*TC RC488.5 .F43 2000*

Learning from our mistakes. New York : Haworth Press, c1998.
*TC RC489.F45 L43 1998*

**FEMINIST THERAPY - MISCELLANEA.**
For love or money. New York : Haworth Press, c1999.
*TC RC489.F45 F67 1999*

**Feminist visions of development :** gender analysis and policy / edited by Cecile Jackson and Ruth Pearson. London ; New York : Routledge, c1998. ix, 294 p. ; 24 cm. Includes bibliographical references and index. ISBN 0-415-14234-2 ISBN 0-415-15790-0 (pbk.) DDC 305.42
*1. Women in development. 2. Sex role - Developing countries. 3. Feminism - Developing countries. I. Jackson, Cecile, 1952- II. Pearson, Ruth.*
*TC HQ1240 .F464 1998*

**FEMINISTS - FRANCE - BIOGRAPHY.**
Gordon, Felicia. Early French feminisms, 1830-1940. Cheltenham, U.K. ; Brookfield, Vt. : Edward Elgar, c1996.
*TC HQ1615.A3 G67 1996*

**Feminists, Islam, and nation.**
Badran, Margot. Princeton, N.J. : Princeton University Press, c1995.
*TC HQ1793 .B33 1995*

**Fenichel, Ann.** The relationship between health care clinicians' relational abilities and psychosocial orientation to patient care, and patient adherence with medical treatment / by Ann Fenichel. 1999. xii, 164 leaves ; 29 cm. Typescript; issued also on microfilm. Thesis (Ph.D.)--Columbia University. Includes bibliographical references: (leaves 119-137).
*1. Bronx Veterans Affairs Medical Center (Bronx, N.Y.) 2. Nurse practitioners - Psychology. 3. Physicians - Psychology. 4. Medical personnel and patient - Psychological aspects. 5. Social medicine. 6. Patient compliance. 7. Interpersonal relations. I. Title.*
*TC 085 F352*

**Fenn, Patricia.** Rewards of merit : tokens of a child's progress and a teacher's esteem as an enduring aspect of American religious and secular education / by Patricia Fenn & Alfred P. Malpa. [Schoharie, N.Y.] : Ephemera Society of America ; Charlottesville [Va.] : Distributed by Howell Press, Inc., c1994. 224 p. : ill. (some col.), facsims. (some col.) ; 22 x 29 cm. Includes bibliography and index. ISBN 0-943231-68-X
*1. Education - United States - History. 2. Printed ephemera -*

*United States - History. 3. Awards - United States - History. 4. Reward (Psychology) in children - United States - History. 5. Sunday schools - United States - History. I. Malpa, Alfred P. II. Ephemera Society of America. III. Title.*
*TC LA230 .F46 1994*

**Fennessey, Sharon M.** History in the spotlight : creative drama and theatre practices for the social studies classroom / Sharon M. Fennessey. Portsmouth, NH : Heinemann, c2000. xii, 172 p. : ill. ; 24 cm. Includes bibliographical references. ISBN 0-325-00161-8 DDC 372.139/9
*1. Drama in education. 2. Social sciences - Study and teaching (Elementary) I. Title.*
*TC PN3171 .F46 2000*

**Fennimore, Beatrice Schneller.** Talk matters : refocusing the language of public schooling / Beatrice S. Fennimore ; foreword by James W. Fraser. New York ; London : Teachers College Press, c2000. xiv, 175 p. ; 24 cm. Includes bibliographical references (p. 155-162) and index. ISBN 0-8077-3903-0 (cloth : alk. paper) ISBN 0-8077-3902-2 (paper : alk. paper) DDC 370/.1/4
*1. Communication in education. 2. Public schools - Social aspects - United States. 3. Sociolinguistics - United States. I. Title.*
*TC LB1033.5 F46 2000*

**Fenton, Ann D.**
Peterson, Carolyn Sue, 1938- Story programs. 2nd ed. Lanham, Md. : Scarecrow Press, 2000.
*TC LB1042 .P47 2000*

**FENTON AVENUE CHARTER SCHOOL (LAKEVIEW TERRACE, CALIF.).**
Education's big gamble [videorecording]. New York, NY : Merrow Report, c1997.
*TC LB2806.36 .E3 1997*

**Fenton, Mark B.**
Business education and training. Lanham, Md. : University Press of America, c1997-<c2000 >
*TC LC1059 .B87*

**Fenton, Steve, 1942-** Ethnicity : racism, class and culture / Steve Fenton. Lanham, Md. : Rowman & Littlefield, c1999. xii, 260 p. : 22 cm. Includes bibliographical references (p. 239-254) and indexes. ISBN 0-8476-9528-X ISBN 0-8476-9529-8 (pbk.)
*1. Ethnicity. 2. Minorities - Social conditions. I. Title.*
*TC GN495.6 .F46 1999x*

**Feo, Luciano de.**
Intercine. Rome.

**Ferber, Linda S.** Masters of color and light : Homer, Sargent, and the American watercolor movement / Linda S. Ferber and Barbara Dayer Gallati. Washington : Brooklyn Museum of Art in Association with Smithsonian Institution Press, c1998. xiii, 223 p. : ill. (some col.) ; 29 cm. Includes bibliographical references and indexes. ISBN 1-56098-572-0 (cloth : alk. paper) DDC 751.42/2/097307474723
*1. Watercolor painting, American - Exhibitions. 2. Watercolor painting - 19th century - United States - Exhibitions. 3. Homer, Winslow, - 1836-1910 - Exhibitions. 4. Sargent, John Singer, - 1856-1925 - Exhibitions. 5. Watercolor painting - New York (State) - New York - Exhibitions. 6. Brooklyn Museum of Art - Exhibitions. I. Gallati, Barbara Dayer II. Brooklyn Museum of Art III. Title.*
*TC ND1807 .F47 1998*

**Ferguson, Ann Arnett, 1940-** Bad boys : public schools in the making of black masculinity / Ann Arnett Ferguson. Ann Arbor : University of Michigan Press, c2000. xi, 256 p. ; 24 cm. (Law, meaning, and violence) Includes bibliographical references (p. 237-241) and index. CONTENTS: Don't believe the Hype. Field note : a field trip -- The punishing room. Field note : first impressions -- School rules. Field note : self-description -- Naughty by nature. A shift in perspective -- The real world. Field note : mothering -- Getting in trouble. Field note : odd symptoms -- Unreasonable circumstances. Field note : promotion exercises -- Dreams. ISBN 0-472-11103-5 (cloth : acid-free paper) DDC 371.82996/073
*1. Afro-American boys - Education - Social aspects. 2. Masculinity. I. Title. II. Title: Public schools in the making of black masculinity III. Series.*
*TC LC2771 .F47 2000*

**Ferguson, Jacqueline.**
**Grants for schools.**
Grants for schools, 4th ed. Gaithersburg, MD : Aspen Publishers, 2000.
*TC LB2825 .F46 2000*

Grants for special education and rehabilitation : how to find and win funds for research, training and services / introduction by Jacqueline Ferguson. 4th ed. Gaithersburg, MD : Aspen Publishers, 2000. xxviii, 215 p. ; 28 cm. Includes index. ISBN 0-8342-1785-6
*1. Federal aid to education - United States. 2. Educational*

*fund raising - United States. 3. Grants-in-aid - United States. 4. Special education - United States - Finance. 5. Proposal writing for grants - United States. 6. Proposal writing in education - United States. I. Title.*
**TC LB2825 .F424 2000**

**Ferrari, M. D.** Self-awareness. New York : Guilford Press, c1998.
**TC BF697.5.S43 S434 1998**

**Ferrie, Richard.** The world turned upside down : George Washington and the Battle of Yorktown / Richard Ferrie. 1st ed. New York : Holiday House, c1999. 168 p. : ill., maps ; 27 cm. Includes bibliographical references (p. 161-162) and index. SUMMARY: This examination of the events surrounding the pivotal Revolutionary War battle that led to the defeat of the British forces at Yorktown, Virginia, focuses on the central role of General George Washington. ISBN 0-8234-1402-7 DDC 973.3/37
*1. Washington, George. - 1732-1799 - Military leadership - Juvenile literature. 2. Yorktown (Va.) - History - Siege, 1781 - Juvenile literature. 3. Washington, George. - 1732-1799. 4. Yorktown (Va.) - History - Siege, 1781. I. Title.*
**TC E241.Y6 F45 1999**

**Ferrini, Armeda F.** Health in the later years / Armeda Ferrini, Rebecca Ferrini. 3rd ed. Boston : McGraw-Hill, c2000. ix, 502 p. : ill. ; 24 cm. Includes bibliographical references and index. ISBN 0-697-26263-4 (acid-free paper) DDC 613/.0438
*1. Aged - Health and hygiene. 2. Health. I. Ferrini, Rebecca L. II. Title.*
**TC RA777.6 .F46 2000**

**Ferrini, Rebecca L.** Ferrini, Armeda F. Health in the later years. 3rd ed. Boston : McGraw-Hill, c2000.
**TC RA777.6 .F46 2000**

**Ferris, Steven.** Assessment in geriatric psychopharmacology. New Canaan, Conn. : Mark Powley Associates, 1983.
**TC WT150 .A846 1983**

**Ferro, Marc.** Towards a pluralist and tolerant approach to teaching history. Strasbourg : Council of Europe Pub., c1999.
**TC D424 .T665 1999**

**Fersh, Seymour.** Integrating the trans-national/cultural dimension / by Seymour Fersh. Bloomington, Ind. : Phi Delta Kappa Educational Foundation, c1993. 37 p. : port. ; 18 cm. (Fastback, 361.) Includes bibliographical references (p. 31-33, 38-39). ISBN 0-87367-361-1 (pbk.)
*1. International education. 2. Intercultural education. 3. Global method of teaching. 4. Social sciences - Study and teaching. I. Phi Delta Kappa. Educational Foundation. II. Title. III. Series.*
**TC LC1090 .F47 1993**

**FERTILE CRESCENT.** *See* **MIDDLE EAST.**

**FERTILITY, HUMAN - DEVELOPING COUNTRIES - CROSS-CULTURAL STUDIES.** Critical perspectives on schooling and fertility in the developing world. Washington, D.C. : National Academy Press, 1999.
**TC LC2572 .C75 1998**

**FERTILIZERS.** *See* **NITROGEN FERTILIZERS.**

**FESTIVALS.** *See also* **PAGEANTS.** Gilchrist, Cherry. Calendar of festivals. Kingswood, Bristol, U.K. : Barefoot Books, c1998.
**TC GT3932 .G54 1998**

**FESTIVALS - POLITICAL ASPECTS - UNITED STATES - HISTORY.** Lorini, Alessandra, 1949- Rituals of race. Charlottesville : University Press of Virginia, 1999.
**TC E185.61 .L675 1999**

**FETUS - DISEASES - DIAGNOSIS.** *See* **AMNIOCENTESIS.**

**Feurzeig, W.** Modeling and simulation in science and mathematics education. New York : Springer, c1999.
**TC Q181 .M62 1999**

**A fever in Salem.** Carlson, Laurie M., 1952- Chicago : I.R. Dee, 1999.
**TC BF1576 .C37 1999**

**Fever pitch.** Moffatt, Tracey. Tracey Moffatt. Annandale, N.S.W., Australia : Piper Press, c1995.
**TC TR647 .M843 1995**

**Feyten, Carine M.** Virtual instruction. Englewood, Colo. : Libraries Unlimited, 1999.
**TC LC5803.C65 V57 1999**

**FIBERS.** *See* **PAPER.**

**Fibonacci Association.** The Fibonacci quarterly. [St. Mary's College, Calif., Fibonacci Association]

**FIBONACCI NUMBERS - PERIODICALS.** The Fibonacci quarterly. [St. Mary's College, Calif., Fibonacci Association]

**The Fibonacci quarterly.** [St. Mary's College, Calif., Fibonacci Association] v. 26 cm. v. 1- Feb. 1963- . "The official journal of the Fibonacci Association." ISSN 0015-0517
*1. Mathematics - Periodicals. 2. Fibonacci numbers - Periodicals. I. Fibonacci Association.*

**FIBONACCI SEQUENCE.** *See* **FIBONACCI NUMBERS.**

**FICTION.** *See* **CHILDREN'S STORIES; FICTION GENRES; LEGENDS; ROMANTICISM; YOUNG ADULT FICTION.**

**FICTION - BIBLIOGRAPHY.** Herald, Diana Tixier. Genreflecting. 5th ed. Englewood, CO : Libraries Umlimited, 2000.
**TC PS374.P63 H47 2000**

**FICTION GENRES - BIBLIOGRAPHY.** Herald, Diana Tixier. Genreflecting. 5th ed. Englewood, CO : Libraries Umlimited, 2000.
**TC PS374.P63 H47 2000**

**Fiction, literature and media** / edited by Mary Kooy, Tanja Janssen and Ken Watson. Amsterdam : Amsterdam University Press, c1999. 95 p. : ports. ; 24 cm. (Studies in language & literature) ISBN 90-5356-392-X DDC 372.6
*1. Native language and education. 2. Literature - Study and teaching. 3. Language arts. 4. Native language and education. I. Kooy, Mary. II. Jansse, Tanya. III. Watson, Ken (Ken D.) IV. Series.*
**TC LB1575.8 .F53 1999**

**FICTION - PHILOSOPHY.** *See* **FICTION.**

**FICTION - TECHNIQUE.** McCallum, Robyn. Ideologies of identity in adolescent fiction. New York : Garland Pub., 1999.
**TC PN3443 .M38 1999**

**FIDDLE.** *See* **VIOLIN.**

**Fiddler, Morris.** Taylor, Kathleen, 1943- Developing adult learners. 1st ed. San Francisco : Jossey-Bass, c2000.
**TC LC5225.L42 T39 2000**

**Fidler, Brian.** Poorly performing staff and how to manage them. London ; New York : Routledge, 1999.
**TC LB2832.4.G7 P66 1999**

**Fiedler, Craig R.** Making a difference : advocacy competencies for special education professionals / Craig R. Fiedler. Boston ; London : Allyn and Bacon, c2000. xiii, 258 p. ; 24 cm. Includes bibliographical references (p. 243-252) and index. ISBN 0-205-30629-2 DDC 371.91
*1. Handicapped children - Education - United States. 2. Handicapped children - Services for - United States. 3. Special education - Law and legislation - United States. I. Title.*
**TC LC4031 .F52 2000**

**Field experience.** Posner, George J. 5th ed. New York : Longman, c2000.
**TC LB2157.A3 P6 2000**

**A field guide for the sight-impaired reader.** Leibs, Andrew. Westport, Conn. ; London : Greenwood Press, 1999.
**TC HV1731 .L45 1999**

**Field, Kit.** Effective subject leadership / Kit Field, Phil Holden, and Hugh Lawlor. London ; New York : Routledge, 2000. xi, 287 p. : ill. ; 24 cm. Includes bibliographical references (p. [262]-278) and index. ISBN 0-415-20303-1 (hbk. : alk. paper) ISBN 0-415-20295-7 (pbk. : alk. paper) DDC 374/.001
*1. Teacher participation in curriculum planning - Great Britain. 2. Educational leadership - Great Britain. 3. School improvement programs - Great Britain. I. Holden, Phil, 1950- II. Lawlor, Hugh. III. Title.*
**TC LB2806.15 .F54 2000**

**Field, Martha A.** Equal treatment for people with mental retardation : having and raising children / Martha A. Field, Valerie A. Sanchez. Cambridge, Mass. ; London : Harvard University Press, 1999. xii, 439 p. ; 25 cm. Includes bibliographical references (p. 347-424) and index. ISBN 0-674-80086-9 (alk. paper) DDC 342.73/087
*1. Developmentally disabled - Legal status, laws, etc. - United States. 2. Handicapped parents - Legal status, laws, etc. -*

*United States. 3. Parent and child (Law) - United States. 4. Sterilization. Eugenic - Law and legislation - United States. 5. Informed consent (Medical law) - United States. I. Sanchez, Valerie A., 1960- II. Title.*
**TC KF480 .F54 1999**

**Field Museum of Natural History.** Portraits of native Americans. New York : New Press ; Distributed by W.W. Norton, c1994.
**TC TR140.C388 C48**

**FIELD SPORTS.** *See* **SPORTS.**

**FIELD TRIPS, SCHOOL.** *See* **SCHOOL FIELD TRIPS.**

**FIELD WORK (EDUCATIONAL METHOD).** *See* **PROJECT METHOD IN TEACHING; SCHOOL FIELD TRIPS.**

**Fields, Ed.** Sean's story [videorecording]. Princeton, N.J. : Films for the Humanities & Sciences ; [S.l. : distributed by] ABC Multimedia : Capital Cities/ABC, c1994.
**TC LC1203.M3 .S39 1994**

**Fiels, Keith Michael.** Cohn, John M. Writing and updating technology plans. New York : Neal-Schuman Publishers, 2000.
**TC Z678.9.A4 U623 2000**

**Fife, Brian L.** Higher education in transition. Westport, Conn. ; London : Bergin & Garvey, 2000.
**TC LA227.4 .H53 2000**

**Fife, Jonathan D.** Freed, Jann E. A culture for academic excellence. Washington, D.C. : Graduate School of Education and Human Development, George Washington University, 1997.
**TC LB2341 .F688 1997**

**FIFTH GENERATION COMPUTERS.** *See* **ARTIFICIAL INTELLIGENCE.**

**FIFTH GRADE (EDUCATION) - UNITED STATES - CURRICULA.** What your fifth grader needs to know. New York : Doubleday, c1993.
**TC LB1571 5th .W43 1993**

**Fifth survey of educational research, 1988-92.** New Delhi : National Council of Educational Research and Training, 1997- v. ; 28 cm. Previous survey issued under title: Fourth survey of research in education, 1983-1988. Includes bibliographical references. PARTIAL CONTENTS: v. 1. Trend reports.
*1. Education - India - Abstracts. 2. Education - Research - India. I. National Council of Educational Research and Training (India) II. Title: Survey of educational research. 1988-92 III. Title: Survey of research in education*
**TC LB1028 .F44 1997**

**Fifty years of anthropology and education, 1950-2000.** Spindler, George Dearborn. Mahwah, N.J. L.Erlbaum Associates, 2000.
**TC LB45 .S66 2000**

Spindler, George Dearborn. Fifty years of anthropology and education, 1950-2000. Mahwah, N.J. L.Erlbaum Associates, 2000.
**TC LB45 .S66 2000**

**Fifty years of innovations in undergraduate education.** Quehl, Gary H. Indianapolis, Ind : USA Group Foundation, c1999.
**TC LB1027.3 .Q43 1999**

**FIGHTING.** *See* **COMBAT; WAR.**

**FIGHTING (PSYCHOLOGY).** *See* **AGGRESSIVENESS (PSYCHOLOGY).**

**Fighting to save our urban schools - and winning!.** McAdams, Donald R. New York : Teachers College Press, c2000.
**TC LC5133.H8 M32 2000**

**Figler, Howard E.** The career counselor's handbook / by Howard Figler and Richard N. Bolles. Berkeley, Calif. : Ten Speed Press, c1999. xi, 306 p. : ill. ; 23 cm. (The parachute library.) Includes bibliographical references and index. ISBN 1-58008-157-6 (pbk.)
*1. Vocational guidance. 2. Counseling. I. Bolles, Richard Nelson. II. Title. III. Series: Bolles, Richard Nelson. / Parachute library.*
**TC HF5549.5.C35 F54 1999**

**Figueredo, D. H., 1951-** When this world was new / by D.H. Figueredo ; illustrated by Enrique O. Sanchez. 1st ed. New York : Lee & Low Books, 1999. 1 v. (unpaged) : col. ill. ; 27 cm. SUMMARY: When his father leads him on a magical trip of discovery through new fallen

snow, a young boy who emigrated from his warm island home overcomes fears about living in New York. ISBN 1-88000-086-5 (hardcover) DDC [E]
*1. Emigration and immigration - Fiction. 2. Fear - Fiction. 3. Snow - Fiction. 4. Fathers and sons - Fiction. I. Sanchez, Enrique O., 1942- ill. II. Title.*
**TC PZ7.F488 Wh 1999**

**FIGURE DRAWING - PSYCHOLOGICAL ASPECTS - SEX DIFFERENCES.**
Tuman, Donna M. Gender difference in form and content. 1998.
**TC 06 no. 11000**

**FIGURE-GROUND PERCEPTION.** *See* **PATTERN PERCEPTION.**

**FIGURINES.** *See* **DOLLS.**

**FIGURINES - JUVENILE LITERATURE.**
Sohi, Morteza E. Look what I did with a shell!. New York : Walker & Co., 2000.
**TC TT862 .S64 2000**

**File, Karen.**
Prince, Russ Alan, 1958- The seven faces of philanthropy. 1st ed. San Francisco : Jossey-Bass, c1994.
**TC HV41.9.U5 P74 1994**

**Filial responsibility in the modern American family.**
Schorr, Alvin Louis, 1921- [Washington] U.S. Dept. of Health, Education, and Welfare, Social Security Administration, Division of Program Research [1960]
**TC HV75 .S36 1960**

**Filip, V. (Vaclav).**
Basic and clinical science of mental and addictive disorders. Basel ; New York : Karger, c1997.
**TC RC327 .B37 1997**

**Filkin, David.**
Stephen Hawking's universe [videorecording]. [Alexandria, Va.] : PBS Video; Burbank, CA : Distributed by Warner Home Video, c1997.
**TC QB982 .S7 1997**

**Film and audio-visual communication.**
Audio-visual communications. [New York : United Business Publications, 1967-c1989.

**The film answers back.**
Robson, Emanuel W., 1897- London : John Lane, [1947]
**TC PN1993.5.A1 R6 1947**

**The film-audience relationship.**
Jones, Carl Mounsey. 1997.
**TC 06 no. 10769**

Jones, Carl Mounsey. 1997.
**TC 06 no. 10769**

**FILM DIRECTORS.** *See* **MOTION PICTURE PRODUCERS AND DIRECTORS.**

**Film forum review** / Institute of Adult Education, Teachers College, Columbia University in cooperation with National Committee on Film Forums. [New York, N.Y.] : The Institute, 1946- v. ; 24 cm. Vol. 1, no. 1 (spring 1946)- . "Devoted to the use of motion pictures in adult education." Title from cover. No more published. Published by the Institute of Adult Education, Teachers College, Columbia University in cooperation with National Committee on Film Forums. Absorbed by: Adult education journal Jan. 1949. DDC 371.3352305
*1. Motion pictures in education - Periodicals. 2. Adult education - Periodicals. I. Columbia University. Teachers College. Institute of Adult Education. II. National Committee on Film Forums. III. Title: Adult education journal Jan. 1949*

**Film heritage.** Dayton, Ohio, University of Dayton. 12 v. ill. 22 cm. v. 1-12, no.3; fall 1965-spring 1977. No more published. ISSN 0015-1270 DDC 791.43/05
*1. Motion pictures - Periodicals*

**FILM PRODUCERS.** *See* **MOTION PICTURE PRODUCERS AND DIRECTORS.**

**Filming a television commercial [videorecording] : Klaus Lucka directing : an inside view of the production.**
The filming of a television commercial [videorecording]. Minneapolis, Minn. : Media Loft, c1992.
**TC HF6146.T42 F5 1992**

**The filming of a television commercial**
[videorecording] / the Saab "Deer" spot by LuckaFilm, New York for Ally G. Gargano Advertising, New York ; producer: R. Smith Schuneman ; script, edit and mix: Everett LaBuda ; a video documentary by MediaLoft ; produced by Media Loft, Inc. Minneapolis, Minn. : Media Loft, c1992. 1 videocassette (30 min.) : sd., col. ; 1/2 in. (Great

photographers ; v.8) (Educational awareness presentation) Title on cassette label and container: Filming a television commercial [videorecording] : Klaus Lucka directing : an inside view of the production. VHS. Catalogued from credits and cassette label and container. Narrated by Klaus Lucka. Videography, Everett LaBuda; location audio, R. Smith Schuneman. "TV-24-VHS"--Container. For general audiences. SUMMARY: An inside view of the making of a national TV commercial for Saab automobiles, from the beginning of the decision making process about location and the various shots, atmospheric conditions, etc., through the training of the deer and the coordination all the shots, to the finished product. a masterpiece of creativity, planning and long, hard, repetitive work. ISBN 1-88238-608-6
*1. Television advertising. 2. Television commercial films. 3. Television advertising directors - United States. 4. Lucka, Klaus. 5. Documentary television programs. I. Lucka, Klaus. II. Schuneman, R. Smith. III. LaBuda, Everett. IV. LuckaFilm (Firm) V. Ally G. Gargano Advertising (Firm) VI. Media Loft (Firm) VII. Title: Filming a television commercial [videorecording] : Klaus Lucka directing : an inside view of the production VIII. Title: Klaus Lucka directing [videorecording] IX. Title: Inside view of the production [videorecording] X. Series. XI. Series: Educational/awareness presentation.*
**TC HF6146.T42 F5 1992**

**FILMS.** *See* **MOTION PICTURES.**

**Films for the Humanities (Firm).**
Aging and saging [videorecording]. Princeton, NJ : Films for the Humanities & Sciences : Distributed by Canadian Broadcasting Corporation, 1998.
**TC BF724.55.A35 A35 1998**

Challenge cases [videorecording]. Princeton, N.J. : Films for the Humanities & Sciences, 1998.
**TC RC455.2.C4 C4 1998**

Changing lives [videorecording]. Princeton, NJ : Films for the Humanities & Sciences, c1998.
**TC RC564 .C54 1998**

Disorders due to psychoactive substance abuse [videorecording]. Princeton, N.J. : Films for the Humanities & Sciences, 1998.
**TC RC564 .D5 1998**

Gender and the interpretation of emotion [videorecording]. Princeton, NJ : Films for the Humanities & Sciences, c1997.
**TC BF592.F33 G4 1997**

**Films for the Humanities (firm).**
Heroin [videorecording]. [Princeton, N.J.] : Films for the Humanities & Sciences, c1998.
**TC HV5822.H4 H4 1998**

**Films for the Humanities (Firm).**
The hijacked brain [videorecording]. Princeton, NJ : Films for the Humanities & Sciences, c1998.
**TC RC564 .H5 1998**

Juvenile sex offenders [videorecording]. Princeton, N.J. : Films for the Humanities & Sciences, c1998.
**TC HV9067.S48 J8 1998**

Mood disorders [videorecording]. Princeton, N.J. : Films for the Humanities & Sciences, 1998.
**TC RC537 .M6 1998**

Neurotic, stress-related, and somatoform disorders [videorecording]. Princeton, N.J. : Films for the Humanities & Sciences, 1998.
**TC RC530 .N4 1998**

The next generation [videorecording]. Princeton, NJ : Films for the Humanities & Sciences, c1998.
**TC RC564 .N4 1998**

Organic disorders [videorecording]. Princeton, N.J. : Films for the Humanities & Sciences, 1998.
**TC RC521 .O7 1998**

Personality disorders [videorecording]. Princeton, N.J. : Films for the Humanities & Sciences, 1998.
**TC RC554 .P4 1998**

The politics of addiction [videorecording]. Princeton, NJ : Films for the Humanities & Sciences, c1998.
**TC RC564 .P59 1998**

Portrait of addiction [videorecording]. Princeton, NJ : Films for the Humanities & Sciences, c1998.
**TC HV5801 .P6 1998**

Portrait of addiction [videorecording]. Princeton, NJ : Films for the Humanities & Sciences, c1998.
**TC RC564 .P6 1998**

Schizophrenia and delusional disorders [videorecording]. Princeton, N.J. : Films for the Humanities & Sciences, c1998.

**TC RC514 .S3 1998**

**Films for the Humanities (firm).**
Sean's story [videorecording]. Princeton, N.J. : Films for the Humanities & Sciences ; [S.l. : distributed by] ABC Multimedia : Capital Cities/ABC, c1994.
**TC LC1203.M3 .S39 1994**

**Films for the Humanities (Firm).**
Summerhill at 70 [videorecording]. Princeton, N.J. : Films for the Humanities, c1992.
**TC LF795.L692953 S9 1992**

Teen killers [videorecording]. Princeton, NJ : Films for the Humanities and Sciences, c1998-1999.
**TC HV9067.H6 T4 1999**

Teen violence [videorecording]. Princeton, NJ : Films for the Humanities & Sciences, c1998.
**TC RJ506.V56 T44 1998**

**FILMS FOR YOUNG ADULTS.** *See* **YOUNG ADULT FILMS.**

**Films Incorporated.**
Jung on film [videorecording]. [Chicago, Ill.?] : Public Media Video, c1990.
**TC BF109.J8 J4 1990**

Jung on film [videorecording]. [Chicago, Ill.?] : Public Media Video, c1990.
**TC BF109.J8 J4 1990**

**Finamore, Marie.**
Design culture. New York : Allworth Press ; American Institute of Graphic Arts, c1997.
**TC NC998.5.A1 D46 1997**

**FINANCE.** *See* **BANKS AND BANKING; FINANCE, PERSONAL; WEALTH.**

**FINANCE, PERSONAL - FICTION.**
Viorst, Judith. Alexander, who used to be rich last Sunday. 1st ed. New York : Atheneum, 1978.
**TC PZ7.V816 Am 1978**

**FINANCE, PERSONAL - PLANNING.** *See* **FINANCE, PERSONAL.**

**FINANCIAL AID ADMINISTRATION, STUDENT.** *See* **STUDENT FINANCIAL AID ADMINISTRATION.**

**Financial aid for African Americans.** El Dorado Hills, Calif. : Reference Service Press, c1997- v. ; 29 cm. Frequency: Biennial. 1st ed. (1997-1999)- . "A list of: scholarships, fellowships, loans, grants, awards, and internships open primarily or exclusively to African Americans." Continues in part: Directory of financial aids for minorities ISSN: 0738-4122 (DLC)  85645355 (OCoLC)9599894. ISSN 1099-906X DDC 378
*1. Afro-American college students - Scholarships, fellowships, etc. - United States - Directories. 2. Student aid - United States - Directories. 3. Afro-Americans - Scholarships, fellowships, etc. - United States - Directories. 4. Internship programs - United States - Directories. 5. Financial Support - United States - directories. 6. Blacks - education - United States - directories. 7. Fellowships and Scholarships - United States - directories. I. Reference Service Press (El Dorado Hills, Calif.) II. Title: Directory of financial aids for minorities*
**TC LB2338 .F5643**

**FINANCIAL AID, STUDENT.** *See* **STUDENT AID.**

**FINANCIAL AID TO STUDENTS.** *See* **STUDENT AID.**

**FINANCIAL INSTITUTIONS.** *See* **BANKS AND BANKING.**

**Financial management for nurse managers and executives.**
Finkler, Steven A. 2nd ed. Philadelphia ; London : W.B. Saunders, c2000.
**TC RT86.7 .F46 2000**

**FINANCIAL MANAGEMENT - METHODS - UNITED STATES - NURSES' INSTRUCTION.**
Finkler, Steven A. Financial management for nurse managers and executives. 2nd ed. Philadelphia ; London : W.B. Saunders, c2000.
**TC RT86.7 .F46 2000**

**FINANCIAL SUPPORT - UNITED STATES - DIRECTORIES.**
Financial aid for African Americans. El Dorado Hills, Calif. : Reference Service Press, c1997-
**TC LB2338 .F5643**

**FINANCIERS.** *See* **CAPITALISTS AND FINANCIERS.**

**Financing America's schools.**
Making money matter. Washington, D.C. : National Academy Press, c1999.
**TC LB2825 .M27 1999**

**Fincham, H. W. (Henry Walter)** Artists and engravers of British and American book plates : a book of reference for book plate and print collectors / by Henry W. Fincham. New York : Dodd, Mead, and Company, 1897. xvi, 135 p. [21] leaves of plates : ill. ; 30 cm. "This edition is limited to 1050 copies for England and America." Includes index.
*1. Bookplates, English. 2. Bookplates, American. I. Title.*
*TC Z993 .F49 1897*

**Finding places.** Teacher's ed. New York, N.Y. : American Book Company, c1980. xvi, 344 p. : ill. (some col.) ; 28 cm. (American readers ; P) Includes index. ISBN 0-278-45844-0
*1. Readers (Primary) 2. Reading (Primary) I. Series.*
*TC PE1119 .F56 1980 Teacher's Ed.*

**Finding places.** New York, NY : American Book Company, c1980. 176 p. : col. ill. ; 24 cm. (American readers ; P) ISBN 0-278-45811-4
*1. Readers (Primary) I. Series.*
*TC PE1119 .F56 1980*

**Finding places.** Lexington, Mass. : D.C. Heath and Company, c1983. 184 p. : ill. ; 24 cm. (American readers ; P) ISBN 0-669-04936-0
*1. Readers (Primary) I. Series.*
*TC PE1119 .F56 1983*

**Finding places.** Teacher's ed. Lexington, Mass. : D.C. Heath and Company, c1983. xxxii, 361 p. : ill. (some col.) ; 28 cm. (American readers ; P) Includes index. ISBN 0-669-04938-7
*1. Readers (Primary) 2. Reading (Primary) I. Series.*
*TC PE1119 .F56 1983 Teacher's Ed.*

**Finding places.** Teacher's ed. Lexington, Mass. : D.C. Heath and Company, c1986. T32, 390 p. : ill. (some col.) ; 28 cm. (Heath American readers ; P) Includes index. ISBN 0-669-08047-0
*1. Readers (Primary) 2. Reading (Primary) I. Series.*
*TC PE1119 .F56 1986 Teacher's Ed.*

**Finding places** : workbook. Teacher's ed. New York, N.Y. : American Book Company, c1980. 176 p. : col. ill. ; 28 cm. (American readers ; P) Includes index. ISBN 0-278-45924-2
*1. Readers (Primary) 2. Reading (Primary) I. Series.*
*TC PE1119 .F56 1980 Teacher's Ed. Workbook*

**Finding places** : workbook. Teacher's ed. Lexington, Mass. : D.C. Heath and Company, c1983. 128 p. : col. ill. ; 28 cm. (American readers ; P) Includes index. ISBN 0-669-04943-3
*1. Readers (Primary) 2. Reading (Primary) I. Series.*
*TC PE1119 .F56 1983 Teacher's Ed. Workbook*

**FINE ARTS.** *See* ART; ARTS.

**Fine Arts Museums of San Francisco.**
Frank, Phil. The ghost of the de Young Museum. [San Francisco : Fine Arts Museums of San Francisco, 1995]
*TC N739.5 .F72 1995*

The New painting. San Francisco, CA : Fine Arts Museums of San Francisco, c1996.
*TC ND547.5.I4 N38 1996*

**Fine, Michell.**
Talking across boundaries. [New York] : [Bruner Foundation], 1996.
*TC LB1623.5 .T35 1996*

**FINE PRINTS.** *See* PRINTS.

**Fingarette, Herbert.** Self-deception / Herbert Fingarette. Berkeley, Calif. : London : University of California Press, 2000. 189 p. ; 21 cm. Originally published: London : Routledge & K. Paul, 1969. Includes bibliographical references (p. 179-182) and index. ISBN 0-520-22052-8 (alk. paper) DDC 126
*1. Self-deception. I. Title.*
*TC BF697 .F47 2000*

**FINGER CALCULATION.**
Pai, Hang Young. Chisanbop finger calculation method. New York : McCormick-Mathers Pub. Co., 1981.
*TC QA115 .P23 1981*

Pai, Hang Young. Chisanbop. Teacher's annotated ed. New York : American Book Co., 1980.
*TC QA115 .P23 1980 Teacher's Ed.*

Pai, Hang Young. Chisanbop. New York : American Book Co., 1980.
*TC QA115 .P23 1980*

Pai, Hang Young. Chisanbop. New York : American Book Co., 1980.
*TC QA115 .P231 1980*

Pai, Hang Young. Chisanbop. Teacher's annotated ed. New York : American Book Co., 1980.

*TC QA115 .P231 1980 Teacher's Ed.*

**Finger calculation method : manual for subtraction and division.**
Pai, Hang Young. Chisanbop finger calculation method. New York : McCormick-Mathers Pub. Co., 1981.
*TC QA115 .P23 1981*

**FINGER PLAY.**
Briggs, Diane. 101 fingerplays, stories, and songs to use with finger puppets. Chicago : American Library Association, 1999.
*TC GV1218.F5 B74 1999*

**FINGER PUPPETS.**
Briggs, Diane. 101 fingerplays, stories, and songs to use with finger puppets. Chicago : American Library Association, 1999.
*TC GV1218.F5 B74 1999*

**Finger, Stanley.** Minds behind the brain : a history of the pioneers and their discoveries / Stanley Finger. Oxford : New York : Oxford University Press, 2000. xii, 364 p. : ill. ; 26 cm. Includes bibliographical references (p. [311]-347) and index. ISBN 0-19-508571-X DDC 612.8/2/072
*1. Brain - Research - History. 2. Neurosciences - History. I. Title.*
*TC QP353 .F549 2000*

**Fink, Dale Borman, 1949-** Making a place for kids with disabilities / Dale Borman Fink. Westport, Conn. : Praeger, 2000. xviii, 204 p. ; 25 cm. Includes bibliographical references (p. [195]-199) and index. ISBN 0-275-96565-1 (alk. paper) DDC 790.1/96
*1. Handicapped children - Recreation - United States. 2. Handicapped youth - Recreation - United States. 3. Sports for the handicapped - United States. I. Title.*
*TC GV183.6 .F56 2000*

**Fink, Dean, 1936-** Good schools/real schools : why school reform doesn't last / Dean Fink. New York : Teachers College Press, c2000. xvii, 192 p. ; 24 cm. (The series on school reform) Includes bibliographical references (p. 173-184) and index. ISBN 0-8077-3945-6 (cloth) ISBN 0-8077-3944-8 (pbk.) DDC 373.713
*1. Lord Byron High School. 2. School improvement programs - Canada - Ontario - Case studies. 3. School management and organization - Canada - Ontario - Case studies. 4. Schools - Canada - Ontario - Sociological aspects - Case studies. I. Series.*
*TC LB2822.84.C2 F56 2000*

**Fink, Jeri.** Cyberseduction : reality in the age of psychotechnology / Jeri Fink. Amherst, N.Y. : Prometheus Books, 1999. 308 p. ; 24 cm. Includes bibliographical references and index. ISBN 1-57392-743-0 (hardcover : alk. paper) DDC 004/.01/9
*1. Computers - Psychological aspects. 2. Human-computer interaction. 3. Virtual reality. I. Title.*
*TC QA76.9.P75 F53 1999*

**Fink, Seymour.** Mastering piano technique : a guide for students, teachers, and performers / Seymour Fink ; with illustrations by Donald G. Bell. Portland, Or. : Amadeus Press, c1992. 187 p. : ill. ; 29 cm. Includes bibliographical references (p. 183-184) and index. ISBN 0-931340-46-2 DDC 786.2/193
*1. Piano - Instruction and study. I. Title.*
*TC MT220 .F44 1992*

**Finkel, Donald L., 1943-** Teaching with your mouth shut / Donald L. Finkel. Portsmouth, NH Boynton/Cook Publishers, c2000. xviii, 180 p. ; 23 cm. Includes bibliographical references (p. 173-174) and index. ISBN 0-86709-469-9 DDC 371.102
*1. Teaching. 2. Education - Experimental methods. 3. Learning, Psychology of. I. Title.*
*TC LB1026 .F49 2000*

**Finkelstein, Barbara, 1937-.**
Hidden messages. Yarmouth, Me. : Intercultural Press, c1998.
*TC LC1099.3 .H53 1998*

**Finkelstein, Martin J., 1949-.**
Dollars, distance, and online education. Phoenix, Az. : Oryx Press, 2000.
*TC LB2395.7 .M26 2000*

**Finkler, Steven A.** Financial management for nurse managers and executives / Steven A. Finkler, Christine T. Kovner. 2nd ed. Philadelphia ; London : W.B. Saunders, c2000. xxiv, 518 p. : ill. ; 27 cm. Includes bibliographical references and index. ISBN 0-7216-7714-2 DDC 362.1/73/0681
*1. Nursing services - Business management. 2. Health facilities - Business management. 3. Financial Management - methods - United States - Nurses' Instruction. 4. Delivery of Health Care - economics - United States - Nurses' Instruction. 5. Nurse Administrators - United States. I. Kovner, Christine Tassone. II. Title.*

*TC RT86.7 .F46 2000*

**Finlay, Ann, 1944-** The National Literacy Trust's international annotated bibliography of books on literacy / Ann Finlay and Jo Weinberger. Stoke-on-Trent : Trentham Books, 1999. xii, 64 p. ; 21 cm. Includes bibliographical references and indexes. ISBN 1-85856-164-7 (pbk.) ISBN 1-85856-164-7 DDC 016.3022244
*1. Literacy - Bibliographies. I. Weinberger, Jo. II. National Literacy Trust (Great Britain) III. Title.*
*TC LC149 .F565 1999*

**Finlayson, Geoffrey B. A. M.** Decade of reform; England in the eighteen thirties, by Geoffrey B. A. M. Finlayson. New York, Norton [1970] ix, 115 p. 21 cm. (Foundations of modern history) Includes bibliographical references and index. ISBN 0-393-05406-3 DDC 309.1/42
*1. Social reformers - Great Britain. 2. England - Social conditions - 19th century. I. Title.*
*TC HN385 .F54 1970*

**Finlayson, Helen, 1945-.**
Cook, Deirdre, 1943- Interactive children, communicative teaching. Buckingham [England] ; Philadelphia : Open University Press, 1999.
*TC LB1028.46 .C686 1999*

**Finley, Carmen J.** The national assessment approach to exercise development [by] Carmen J. Finley and Frances S. Berdie. [Ann Arbor, Mich.] National Assessment of Educational Progress [1970] ii, 135 p. ; 23 cm. Bibliography: p. 135. DDC 371.2/6/0973
*1. Educational tests and measurements - United States. I. Berdie, Frances S., joint author. II. Title.*
*TC LB3051 .F53*

**Finley, Charles.**
Miller, Richard I. Evaluating, improving, and judging faculty performance in two-year colleges. Westport, Conn. : London : Bergin & Garvey, 2000.
*TC LB2333 .M49 2000*

**Finn, Chester E., 1944-.**
Bennett, William J. (William John), 1943- The educated child. New York : Free Press, c1999.
*TC LB1048.5 .B45 1999*

Charter schools in action : renewing public education / Chester E. Finn, Bruno V. Manno, Gregg Vanourek. Princeton, N.J. : Princeton University Press, c2000. x, 290 p. ; 25 cm. Includes bibliographical references and index. ISBN 0-691-00480-3 (cloth : alk. paper) DDC 371.01
*1. Charter schools - United States. I. Manno, Bruno V. II. Vanourek, Gregg. III. Title.*
*TC LB2806.36 .F527 2000*

**FINNISH AMERICANS - FICTION.**
Holm, Jennifer L. Our only May Amelia. 1st ed. New York : HarperCollinsPublishers, c1999.
*TC PZ7.H732226 Ou 1999*

**FINNISH AMERICANS - UNITED STATES.** *See* FINNISH AMERICANS.

**FINNS - UNITED STATES.** *See* FINNISH AMERICANS.

**Fiore, Lisa B., 1970-.**
Dacey, John S. Your anxious child. 1st ed. San Francisco : Jossey-Bass, c2000.
*TC BF723.A5 D33 2000*

**Fire and shadow.**
Drury, Nevill, 1947- Roseville East, NWS : Craftsman House :Australia ; United States : G + B Arts International [distributor], c1996.
*TC N7400.2 .D78 1996*

**A fire in the bones.**
Raboteau, Albert J. Boston : Beacon Press, c1995.
*TC BR563.N4 R24 1995*

**FIREARMS.** *See* GUN CONTROL.

**FIREARMS CONTROL.** *See* FIREARMS - LAW AND LEGISLATION; GUN CONTROL.

**FIREARMS - LAW AND LEGISLATION - UNITED STATES.**
Guns and violence. San Diego : Greenhaven Press, c1999.
*TC HV7436 .G8774 1999*

**FIREARMS - LAW AND LEGISLATION - UNITED STATES - ENCYCLOPEDIA.**
Utter, Glenn H. Encyclopedia of gun control and gun rights. Phoenix, Ariz. : Oryx Press, 2000.
*TC KF3941.A68 U88 2000*

**FIREARMS - LAWS AND REGULATIONS.** *See* FIREARMS - LAW AND LEGISLATION.

**FIREARMS OWNERSHIP - UNITED STATES.**
Guns and violence. San Diego : Greenhaven Press, c1999.

***TC HV7436 .G8774 1999***

**Firestone, Robert.** Fear of intimacy / Robert W. Firestone and Joyce Catlett. 1st ed. Washington, DC : American Psychological Association, c1999. xvi, 358 p. : ill. ; 26 cm. Includes bibliographical references (p. 315-340) and indexes. ISBN 1-55798-605-3 DDC 158.2
*1. Intimacy (Psychology) I. Catlett, Joyce. II. Title.*
***TC BF575.I5 F57 1999***

**FIREWORKS - FICTION.**
Moeyaert, Bart. [Blote handen. English] Bare hands. 1st ed. Asheville, N.C. : Front Street, 1998.
***TC PZ7.M7227 Bar 1998***

**FIRMS.** *See* **BUSINESS ENTERPRISES.**

**First break** [videorecording] / co-directors, Adrienne Amato and Derek Rogers ; producer, Silva Basmajian ; a National Film Board of Canada production. Boston, MA : Fanlight Productions, c1997. 1 videocassette (51 min.) : sd., col. ; 1/2 in. At head of title: NFB ONF... The National Film Board of Canada presents... VHS. Catalogued from credits and container. Simon, Ariadne and Shely and their families Cinematographer, Derek Rogers; original music, Ken Myhr; editor, Caroline Christie. For adolescents through adult. SUMMARY: Three young adults, Simon, Ariadne and Shely, and their families and loved ones, openly and honestly discuss their lives over a one-year period after a psychotic break with reality. Simon received a diagnosis of schizophrenia, Ariadne, manic-depressive disorder, and Shely, a hopefully isoldated, undiagnosable incidence of psychosis. They describe their symptoms, their illnesses, and the impact it has had on their self-identities and family relationships. The ending offers a message of hope to the mentally ill as Simon, Ariadne and Shely slowly put their lives back together.
*1. Mental illness. 2. Mentally ill - Case studies. 3. Mentally ill - Interviews. 4. Mentally ill - Family relationships. 5. Youth - Mental health. 6. Young adults - Mental health. I. Amato, Adrienne. II. Rogers, Derek. III. Basmajian, Silva. IV. National Film Board of Canada. V. Fanlight Productions. VI. Title: NFB ONF... The National Film Board of Canada presents...*
***TC RC465 .F5 1997***

**First break** [videorecording] / co-directors, Adrienne Amato and Derek Rogers ; producer, Silva Basmajian ; a National Film Board of Canada production. Boston, MA : Fanlight Productions, c1997. 1 videocassette (51 min.) : sd., col. ; 1/2 in. At head of title: NFB ONF... The National Film Board of Canada presents... VHS. Catalogued from credits and container. Simon, Ariadne and Shely and their families Cinematographer, Derek Rogers; original music, Ken Myhr; editor, Caroline Christie. For adolescents through adult. SUMMARY: Three young adults, Simon, Ariadne and Shely, and their families and loved ones, openly and honestly discuss their lives over a one-year period after a psychotic break with reality. Simon received a diagnosis of schizophrenia, Ariadne, manic-depressive disorder, and Shely, a hopefully isoldated, undiagnosable incidence of psychosis. They describe their symptoms, their illnesses, and the impact it has had on their self-identities and family relationships. The ending offers a message of hope to the mentally ill as Simon, Ariadne and Shely slowly put their lives back together.
*1. Mental illness. 2. Mentally ill - Case studies. 3. Mentally ill - Interviews. 4. Mentally ill - Family relationships. 5. Schizohrenia. 6. Schizophrenics - Case studies. 7. Schizophrenics - Interviews. 8. Schizophrenics - Family relationships. 9. Manic-depression. 10. Manic-depressive persons - Case studies. 11. Manic-depressive persons - Interviews. 12. Manic-depressive persons - Family relationships. 13. Youth - Mental health. 14. Young adults - Mental health. I. Amato, Adrienne. II. Rogers, Derek. III. Basmajian, Silva. IV. National Film Board of Canada. V. Fanlight Productions. VI. Title: NFB ONF... The National Film Board of Canada presents... VII. Title: 1st break [videorecording]*
***TC RC465 .F5 1997***

**First break** [videorecording] / co-directors, Adrienne Amato and Derek Rogers ; producer, Silva Basmajian ; a National Film Board of Canada production. Boston, MA : Fanlight Productions, c1997. 1 videocassette (51 min.) : sd., col. ; 1/2 in. At head of title: NFB ONF... The National Film Board of Canada presents... VHS. Catalogued from credits and container. Simon, Ariadne and Shely and their families Cinematographer, Derek Rogers; original music, Ken Myhr; editor, Caroline Christie. For adolescents through adult. SUMMARY: Three young adults, Simon, Ariadne and Shely, and their families and loved ones, openly and honestly discuss their lives over a one-year period after a psychotic break with reality. Simon received a diagnosis of schizophrenia, Ariadne, manic-depressive disorder, and Shely, a hopefully isoldated, undiagnosable incidence of psychosis. They describe their symptoms, their illnesses, and the impact it has had on their self-identities and family relationships. The ending offers a message of hope to the mentally ill as Simon, Ariadne and Shely slowly put their lives back together.
*1. Mental illness. 2. Mentally ill - Case studies. 3. Mentally ill - Interviews. 4. Mentally ill - Family relationships. 5. Schizohrenia. 6. Schizophrenics - Case studies. 7. Schizophrenics - Interviews. 8. Schizophrenics - Family relationships. 9. Manic-depression. 10. Manic-depressive persons - Case studies. 11. Manic-depressive persons - Interviews. 12. Manic-depressive persons - Family relationships. 13. Youth - Mental health. 14. Young adults - Mental health. I. Amato, Adrienne. II. Rogers, Derek. III. Basmajian, Silva. IV. National Film Board of Canada. V. Fanlight Productions. VI. Title: NFB ONF... The National Film Board of Canada presents... VII. Title: 1st break [videorecording]*
***TC RC465 .F5 1997***

**First day to final grade.**
Curzan, Anne. Ann Arbor [Mich.] : University of Michigan Press, c2000.
***TC LB2335.4 .C87 2000***

**A First dictionary of cultural literacy :** what our children need to know / edited by E.D. Hirsch, Jr. ; associate editors, William G. Rowland, Jr. & Michael Stanford. Boston : Houghton Mifflin, 1989. xv, 271 p. : ill. ; 25 cm. Includes index. Bibliography: p. 249-254. SUMMARY: Presents an outline of the knowledge that, according to the Cultural Literacy Foundation, should be acquired by the end of sixth grade, in such categories as literature, religion and philosophy, history, geography, mathematics, science, and technology. ISBN 0-395-51040-6
*1. Handbooks, vade-mecums, etc. - Juvenile literature. 2. Culture - Dictionaries, Juvenile. I. Hirsch, E. D. (Eric Donald) 1928- II. Rowland, William G. III. Stanford, Michael. 1923-*
***TC AG105 .F43 1989***

**FIRST GENERATION CHILDREN.** *See* **CHILDREN OF IMMIGRANTS.**

**FIRST GRADE (EDUCATION) - PERIODICALS.**
The Kindergarten and first grade. Springfield, Mass. : Milton Bradley Co., 1916-[1924]

**FIRST LOVES.** *See* **LOVE.**

**First Run Features (Film).**
Ecole 27 [videorecording]. Bruxelles : Paradise Films ; New York, N.Y. : [distributed by] First Run/ Icarus Films, 1997, c1996.
***TC LC746.P7 E2 1997***

**First-Run Features (Firm).**
Heart of the country [videorecording]. [New York, NY : First Run/Icarus Films, 1998].
***TC LB1565.H6 H3 1998***

**First Run/Icarus Films.**
New school order [videorecording]. New York : First Run/Icarus Films, 1996.
***TC LB2831.583.P4 N4 1996***

Our friends at the bank [videorecording]. New York, NY : First Run/Icarus Films, 1997.
***TC HG3881.5.W57 O87 1997***

**First stage.** Lafayette, Ind. : Purdue University, c1961-c1967. 6 v. : ill., ports. ; 28 cm. Frequency: Quarterly. Vol. 1, no. 1 (winter 1961-62)-v. 6, no. 4 (winter 1967-68). Indexed selectively by: Annual bibliography of English language and literature 0066-3786. Available also on microfilm. Continued by: Drama & theatre ISSN: 0012-5954 (OCoLC)1566932 (DLC) 65035279. ISSN 0885-047X DDC 808.82/04 DDC 792 DDC 810
*1. Drama - 20th century - Periodicals. 2. Theater - Periodicals. I. Purdue University. II. Title: Drama & theatre*

**FIRST WORLD WAR.** *See* **WORLD WAR, 1914-1918.**

**First year Latin.**
Jenney, Charles. Jenney's first year Latin. Needham, Mass. : Prentice Hall, c1990.
***TC PA2087.5 .J46 1990***

**First year Latin workbook.**
Jenney, Charles. Newton, Mass. : Allyn and Bacon, c1987.
***TC PA2087.5 .J46 1987***

**FIRST YEAR TEACHERS - ATTITUDES.**
Reflections of first-year teachers on school culture. San Francisco : Jossey-Bass Inc., 1999.
***TC LB2844.1.N4 R44 1999***

**FIRST YEAR TEACHERS - HANDBOOKS, MANUALS, ETC.**
Keys to the classroom. 2nd ed. Thousand Oaks, Calif. : Corwin Press, c2000.
***TC LB1555 .K49 2000***

**FIRST YEAR TEACHERS - SUPERVISION OF - GREAT BRITAIN.**
Bleach, Kevan. The induction and mentoring of newly qualified teachers :. London : David Fulton, 1999.
***TC LB1729 .B584 1999***

**FIRST YEAR TEACHERS - TRAINING OF.**
Tickle, Les. Teacher induction. Buckingham [England] ; Philadelphia : Open University Press, 2000.
***TC LB1729 .T53 2000***

**FIRST YEAR TEACHERS - UNITED STATES.**
A better beginning. Alexandria, Va. : Association for Supervision and Curriculum Development, c1999.
***TC LB2844.1.N4 B48 1999***

Podsen, India, 1945- Coaching & mentoring first-year and student teachers. Larchmont, NY : Eye On Education, c2000.
***TC LB1731.4 .P63 2000***

**Fiscella, Joan B.**
Interdisciplinary education. New York, NY : College Entrance Examination Board, 1999.
***TC LB2361 .I58 1999***

**Fischer, Agneta, 1958-.**
Gender and emotion. New York : Cambridge University Press, 1999.
***TC BF591 .G45 1999***

**Fischer, Diane Pietrucha.**
Paris 1900. New Brunswick, N.J. : Rutgers University Press ; Montclair, N.J. : Montclair Art Museum, c1999.
***TC N6510 .P28 1999***

**Fischer, Joel.**
Corcoran, Kevin (Kevin J.) Measures for clinical practice. 3rd ed. New York ; London : Free Press, c2000.
***TC BF176 .C66 2000***

**Fischer, Martin A. (Martin Alan), 1950-.**
Bridging the family-professional gap. Springfield, Ill. : Charles C. Thomas, c1999.
***TC HV888.5 .B74 1999***

**Fischer, Steven R.** A history of language / Steven Roger Fischer. London : Reaktion Books, 1999. 240 p. : ill., maps ; 24 cm. (Globalities) Includes bibliographical references (p. 232-235) and index. ISBN 1-86189-051-6
*1. Historical linguistics. 2. Sociolinguistics. 3. Linguistic change. 4. Linguistic change - Social aspects. I. Title. II. Series: Globalities*
***TC P140 .F57 1999***

**Fischetti, Mark.**
Berners-Lee, Tim. Weaving the Web. 1st ed. San Francisco : HarperSanFrancisco, c1999.
***TC TK5105.888 .B46 1999***

**FISH.** *See* **FISHES.**

**Fishbein, Martin.**
Readings in attitude theory and measurement. New York: Wiley, 1967.
***TC BF323.C5 F5***

**Fishel, Elizabeth.** Reunion : the girls we used to be, the women we became / Elizabeth Fishel. 1st ed. New York : Random House, c2000. xii, 282 p. ; 24 cm. ISBN 0-679-44983-3 (alk. paper) DDC 373.747/1
*1. Brearley School. - Class of 1968. 2. Brearley School - Alumni and alumnae - Biography. I. Title.*
***TC LD7501.N494 F575 2000***

**Fisher, Bobbi.** Perspectives on shared reading : planning and practice / Bobbi Fisher and Emily Fisher Medvic. Portsmouth, NH : Heinémann, c2000. xiv, 81 p. : ill. ; 23 cm. Includes bibliographical references (p.81). ISBN 0-325-00215-0 DDC 372.4
*1. Reading (Elementary) 2. Reading - Parent participation. I. Medvic, Emily Fisher. II. Title.*
***TC LB1573 .F528 2000***

**Fisher, James C.**
The welfare-to-work challenge for adult literacy educators. San Francisco, CA : Jossey-Bass Publishers, 1999.
***TC LC149.7 .W43 1999***

**Fisher, Jane E. (Jane Ellen) 1957-.**
Management and administration skills for the mental health professional. San Diego, Calif. London : Academic, c1999.
***TC RA790 .M325 1999***

**Fisher, Leonard Everett.** Look around : a book about shapes / by Leonard Everett Fisher. New York, N.Y., U.S.A. : Viking Kestrel, 1987. [30] p. : col. ill. ; 24 cm. SUMMARY: Presents basic geometrical shapes in familiar scenes for the reader to identify. ISBN 0-670-80869-5 DDC 516/.15
*1. Geometry - Juvenile literature. 2. Shape. 3. Geometry. I. Title.*
***TC QA447 .F5 1987***

**Fisher, Leonard Everett, ill.**
Livingston, Myra Cohn. Celebrations. 1st ed. New York : Holiday House, c1985.
*TC PS3562.I945 C4 1985*

Livingston, Myra Cohn. Earth songs. 1st ed. New York : Holiday House, c1986.
*TC PS3562.I945 E3 1986*

Livingston, Myra Cohn. Sea songs. 1st ed. New York : Holiday House, c1986.
*TC PS3562.I945 S4 1986*

Livingston, Myra Cohn. Sky songs. 1st ed. New York : Holiday House, c1984.
*TC PS3562.I945 S5 1984*

Livingston, Myra Cohn. Up in the air. 1st ed. New York : Holiday House, c1989.
*TC PS3562.I945 U6 1989*

**Fisher, Miles Mark, 1899-** Negro slave songs in the United States / by Miles Mark Fisher ; with a foreword by Ray Allen Billington. Secaucus, N.J. : Citadel Press, c1953. xv, 223 p. ; 21 cm. Includes bibliographical references (p. 193-213) and index.
*1. Afro-Americans - Music - History and criticism. I. Title.*
*TC ML3556 .F58 1953*

**Fisher, Robert, 1943-.**
Unlocking literacy. London : David Fulton, 2000.
*TC LC149 .U485 2000*

**Fisher, S. (Shirley)** Stress and strategy / Shirley Fisher. London ; Hillsdale, N.J. : Lawrence Erlbaum Associates, c1986. viii, 272 p. : ill. ; 24 cm. Cover title: Stress & strategy. Includes bibliographical references( p.245-262) and index. ISBN 0-86377-031-2 DDC 155.9
*1. Stress (Psychology) 2. Control (Psychology) I. Title. II. Title: Stress & strategy.*
*TC BF575.S75 F52 1986*

**Fisher, Simon, 1948-.**
Working with conflict. New York : Zed Books ; Birmingham, UK : In association with Responding to Conflict ; New York : Distributed in the USA exclusively by St. Martin's Press, 2000.
*TC HM1126 .W67 2000*

**Fisher, Steven P.**
Friedman, Myles I., 1924- Handbook on effective instructional strategies. Columbia, S.C. : The Institute for Evidence-Based Decision-Making in Education, 1998.
*TC LB1028.35 .F75 1998*

**FISHERIES. See FISHES; WHALING.**

**FISHERIES - CHILE - CLIMATIC FACTORS.**
Broad, Kenneth. Climate, culture, and values. 1999.
*TC 085 B7775*

**FISHERIES - PERU - CLIMATIC FACTORS.**
Broad, Kenneth. Climate, culture, and values. 1999.
*TC 085 B7775*

**FISHERY INDUSTRY. See FISHERIES.**

**FISHERY METHODS. See FISHERIES.**

**FISHES. See FISHERIES.**

**FISHES - FICTION.**
Gomi, Tarō. [Kingyo ga nigeta. English] Where's the fish? New York : William Morrow, [1986], c1977.
*TC PZ7.G586 Wh 1977*

**FISHING. See FISHES.**

**FISHING INDUSTRY. See FISHERIES.**

**Fishkin, Anne S.**
Investigating creativity in youth. Cresskill, N.J. : Hampton Press, c1999.
*TC BF723.C7 I58 1999*

**Fishman, David.**
Stern, Robert A. M. New York 1880. New York, N.Y. : Monacelli Press, 1999.
*TC NA735.N5 S727 1999*

**Fishman, Gideon, 1945-.**
Schwartz, Ira M. Kids raised by the government. Westport, Conn. : Praeger, 1999.
*TC HV741 .S367 1999*

**Fishman, Joshua A.**
Handbook of language & ethnic identity. New York : Oxford University Press, 1999.
*TC P35 .H34 1999*

The multilingual Apple. Berlin ; New York : Mouton de Gruyter, 1997.
*TC P40.5.L56 M8 1997*

**Fishman, Stephen M.** Unplayed tapes : a personal history of collaborative teacher research / Stephen M. Fishman & Lucille McCarthy. Urbana, Ill. : National Council of Teachers of English ; New York : Teachers College Press, c2000. xi, 300 p. ; 23 cm. (The practitioner inquiry series) Includes bibliographical references (p. 277-287). ISBN 0-8141-5573-1 (acid-free paper) DDC 370./7/2
*1. Action research in education - United States - Case studies. I. McCarthy, Lucille Parkinson, 1944- II. Title. III. Series.*
*TC LB1028.24 .F52 2000*

**Fiske, Edward B.**
Champions of change. Washington, DC : Arts Education Partnership : President's Committee on the Arts and the Humanities, [1999]
*TC NX304.A1 C53 1999*

When schools compete : a cautionary tale / Edward B. Fiske and Helen F. Ladd. Washington, D.C. : Brookings Institution Press, c2000. xvii, 342 p. : ill. ; 24 cm. Includes index. Bibliography: p. 323-328. ISBN 0-8157-2836-0 ISBN 0-8157-2835-2 (pbk.) DDC 379.93
*1. School improvement programs - New Zealand - Case studies. 2. Education - Social aspects - New Zealand - Case studies. 3. Education and state - New Zealand - Case studies. I. Ladd, Helen F. II. Title.*
*TC LB2822.84.N45 F58 2000*

**FITNESS, PHYSICAL. See PHYSICAL FITNESS.**

**Fitzgerald, Hiram E.**
Handbook of infant mental health. New York : Wiley, c2000.
*TC RJ502.5 .H362 2000*

Infancy and culture. New York : Falmer Press, 1999.
*TC GN482 .I53 1999*

**Fitzgibbon, Marian.**
From maestro to manager. Dublin : Oak Tree Press in association with the Graduate School of Business, University College Dublin, c1997.
*TC NX770.E85 F76 1997*

**Fitzgrald Kit.**
Processing the signal [videorecording]. Cicero, Ill. : Roland Collection of Films on Art, c1989.
*TC N6494.V53 P7 1989*

**Fitzpatrick, Joyce J., 1944-.**
Nursing research digest. New York : Springer Pub. Co., c1999.
*TC RT81.5 .N8736 1999*

**Fitzpatrick, Ray.**
Handbook of social studies in health and medicine. London ; Thousand Oaks, Calif. : Sage Publications, 2000.
*TC RA418 .H36 2000*

**FITZSIMMONS, ELLEN.** Teach me : an ethnography of adolescent learning : cultural shopping and student lore in urban America. Lanham [Md.] : International Scholars Publications, c1999. viii, 269 p. ; 24 cm. Includes bibliographical references and index. ISBN 1-57309-400-5 DDC 305.2
*1. High school students - Chicago - Social life and customs - Case studies.*
*TC HQ796 .F58 1999*

**Fitzsimmons, Phil.**
Geekie, Peter. Understanding literacy development. Stoke on Trent, England : Trentham Books, 1999.
*TC LC149 .G44 1999*

**Fitzsimmons, Virginia Macken, 1943-.**
The emergence of family into the 21st century. Boston : Jones and Bartlett Publishers ; [New York] : NLN Press, c2001.
*TC HQ535 .E44 2001*

**Fivaz-Depeursinge, Elisabeth.** The primary triangle : : a developmental view of mothers, fathers and children / Elisabeth Fivaz-Depeursinge and Antoinette Corboz-Warnery. New York : Basic Books, c1999. xlvi, 208 p. : ill. ; 24 cm. Includes bibliographical references and index. ISBN 0-465-09582-8
*1. Family. 2. Mother and child. 3. Father and child. I. Corboz-Warnery, Antoinette. II. Title.*
*TC HQ755.85 .F583 1999*

**The five biggest ideas in science.**
Wynn, Charles M. New York : Wiley, c1997.
*TC Q163 .W99 1997*

**Five hundred computing tips for teachers and lecturers.**
Race, Philip. 500 computing tips for teachers and lecturers. 2nd ed. London : Kogan Page ; Sterling, VA : Stylus Pub., 1999.
*TC LB1028.43 .R33 1999*

**Five hundred tips for teachers.**
Brown, Sally A. 500 tips for teachers. 2nd ed. London : Kogan Page ; Sterling, VA : Stylus Pub., 1998.

*TC LB3013 .B76 1998*

**Five hundred tips on group learning.**
Race, Phil. 500 tips on group learning. London : Kogan Page, 2000.
*TC LB1032 .A15 2000*

**Five women build a number system.**
Speiser, R. (Robert) Stamford, Conn. : Ablex Pub., c2000.
*TC QA135.5 .S5785 2000*

**FIXED IDEAS. See OBSESSIVE-COMPULSIVE DISORDER.**

**FIXED WING AIRCRAFT. See AIRPLANES.**

**Flamm, Jacqueline, 1940-.**
Ramírez de Mellor, Elva Fun with English. Pupil's ed. Mexico : McGraw-Hill c1987
*TC PE1129.S8 .R35 1987*

Ramírez de Mellor, Elva Fun with english. Mexico : McGraw-Hill c1987
*TC PE1129.S8 .R35 1987*

**Flammer, August.**
Control of human behavior, mental processes, and consciousness. Mahwah, N.J. : Lawrence Erlbaum Associates, c2000.
*TC BF611 .C67 2000*

**Flanagan, Dawn P.** The Wechsler intelligence scales and Gf-Gc theory : a contemporary approach to interpretation / Dawn P. Flanagan, Kevin S. McGrew, Samuel O. Ortiz ; foreword by Alan S. Kaufman. Boston ; London : Allyn and Bacon, c2000. xx, 424 : ill. ; 25 cm. Includes bibliographical references (p. 392-417) and index. ISBN 0-205-29271-2 DDC 153.9/32
*1. Wechsler Adult Intelligence Scale. 2. Intelligence tests. 3. Intellect. I. McGrew, Kevin S. II. Ortiz, Samuel O., 1958- III. Title.*
*TC BF432.5.W4 F53 2000*

**Flanagan, Owen J.** Dreaming souls : sleep, dreams, and the evolution of the conscious mind / Owen Flanagan. Oxford ; New York : Oxford University Press, 2000. xii, 210 p. : ill. ; 24 cm. (Philosophy of mind series) Includes bibliographical references (p. [197]-203) and index. ISBN 0-19-512687-4 (alk. paper) DDC 154.6/3
*1. Dreams. 2. Dream interpretation. 3. Philosophy of mind. I. Title. II. Series.*
*TC BF1091 .F58 2000*

**Flannery, Daniele D., 1942-.**
Hayes, Elisabeth. Women as learners. 1st ed. San Francisco : Jossey-Bass Publishers, c2000.
*TC LC5225.L42 H39 2000*

**Flaton, Robin Anne.** Effect of deliberation on juror reasoning / Robin Anne Flaton. 1999. xiii, 207 leaves : ill. ; 29 cm. Issued also on microfilm. Includes tables. Thesis (Ph. D.)--Columbia University, 1999. Includes bibliographical references (leaves 151-157)
*1. Jury - United States - Decision making. 2. Trial practice - United States. 3. Reasoning. 4. Verdicts - United States. 5. Jurors - United States. 6. Social interaction - United States. I. Title.*
*TC 085 F612*

**Flax, Zena, ill.**
Ward, Alan, 1932- Experimenting with batteries, bulbs, and wires. New York : Chelsea Juniors, c1991.
*TC QC527.2 .W37 1991*

**Flaxman, Erwin.**
Educating the disadvantaged, 1972-1973. New York : AMS Press, c1976.
*TC LC4091 .F52 1976*

Youth mentoring: programs and practices / Erwin Flaxman, Carol Ascher, Charles Harrington. New York, N.Y. : ERIC Clearinghouse on Urban Education, 1988. iv, 63 p. ; 28 cm. (Urban diversity series ; no. 97) "December 1988." Includes bibliographical references (p. 53-60).
*1. Mentors in education. 2. Socially handicapped youth. 3. Socialization. 4. Poor children - Education. I. Ascher, Carol, 1941- II. Harrington, Charles C. III. ERIC Clearinghouse on Urban Education. IV. Title. V. Series.*
*TC LC4065 .F53 1988*

**Flaxman, Erwin, comp.** Educating the disadvantaged, 1971-1972 : an AMS anthology / Edited, with an introd., by Erwin Flaxman. New York : AMS Press, [c1973] 498 p. : ill. ; 24 cm. Includes bibliographies. ISBN 0-404-10104-6 ISBN 0-404-10156-9 (pbk.) DDC 371.9/67/0973
*1. Socially handicapped children - Education - United States. I. Title.*
*TC LC4091 .F52 1973*

**Flecha, Ramón.**
[Compartiendo palabras. English]
Sharing words : theory and practice of dialogic learning / Ramón Flecha. Lanham, Md. : Oxford : Rowman & Littlefield Publishers, c2000. x, 133 p. ; 24 cm. (Critical perspectives series) Includes bibliographical references (p. 26-29) and index. ISBN 0-8476-9595-6 (cloth : alk. paper) ISBN 0-8476-9596-4 (paper : alk. paper) DDC 370.15/23
*1. Learning - Social aspects. 2. Critical pedagogy. 3. Dialogue. 4. Group reading. 5. Communication in education. I. Title. II. Series.*
**TC LB1060 .F5913 2000**

**Fleck, Mary B.** Elementary principals' use of student assessment information / by Mary B. Fleck. 1999. xiii, 150 leaves ; 29 cm. Issued also on microfilm. Thesis (Ed.D.)--Teachers College, Columbia University. Includes bibliographical references (leaves 132-137).
*1. Elementary school principals - New Jersey - Case studies. 2. Elementary school students - New Jersey - Rating of - Case studies. 3. Educational leadership - New Jersey - Case studies. 4. Educational accountability - New Jersey - Case studies. 5. Organizational effectiveness - New Jersey - Case studies. 6. Educational evaluation - New Jersey - Case studies. I. Title.*
**TC 06 no. 11113**

**Fleckner, Uwe.**
The treasure chests of mnemosyne. Dresden : Verlag der Kunst, 1998.
**TC BF371 .T7413 1998**

**Fleischer, Lee.** Living in contradiction : stories of special education students / by Lee Elliot Fleischer. 1998. xv, 217 leaves : ill. ; 29 cm. Issued also on microfilm. Thesis (Ed.D.)--Teachers College, Columbia University, 1998. Includes bibliographical references (leaves 244-291).
*1. Special education - New York (State) - New York - Case studies. 2. High school students - New York (State) - New York - Case studies. 3. Educational counseling - New York (State) - New York - Case studies. 4. Discourse analysis, Narative. 5. Educational sociology. I. Title.*
**TC 06 no. 11021**

**Fleisher, Paul, 1951-** Brain food : games that make kids think / Paul Fleisher ; illustrated by Patricia Keeler. Tucson, AZ : Zephyr Press, c1997. iv, 198, [2] p. : ill. ; 28 cm. Includes bibliographical references (p. [199]) and index. SUMMARY: A compilation of thinking games requiring intelligence skills, in such categories as "Spatial Orientation and Strategy Games," "Alignment Games," "Capture Games," "Maze Games," "Mathematical Games," and "Word Games." ISBN 1-56976-072-1 DDC 793.7
*1. Educational games - Juvenile literature. 2. Games. I. Keeler, Patricia A., ill. II. Title.*
**TC GV1480 .F54 1997**

**Fleming, Bruce.** Sex, art, and audience : dance essays / Bruce E. Fleming. New York ; Canterbury [England] : P. Lang, c2000. xi, 316 p. ; 23 cm. (New studies in aesthetics ; vol. 30) Includes index. ISBN 0-8204-4476-6 DDC 792.8
*1. Dance - Philosophy. 2. Movement, Aesthetics of. 3. Modern dance. 4. Sex in dance. I. Title. II. Title: Dance essays III. Series.*
**TC GV1588.3 .F54 2000**

**Fleming, Candace.** When Agnes caws / written by Candace Fleming ; illustrated by Giselle Potter. 1st ed. New York : Atheneum Books for Young Readers, 1999. 1 v. (unpaged) : col. ill. ; 26 cm. "An Anne Schwartz book." SUMMARY: When eight-year-old Agnes Peregrine, an accomplished birdcaller, travels with her parents to the Himalayas in search of the elusive pink-headed duck, she encounters a dastardly foe. ISBN 0-689-81471-2 DDC [E]
*1. Birdsongs - Fiction. 2. Birds - Fiction. 3. Humorous stories. I. Potter, Giselle, ill. II. Title.*
**TC PZ7.F59936 Wh 1999**

**Fleming, Inez.**
Stroupe, Nibs. While we run this race. Maryknoll, N.Y. : Orbis Books, c1995.
**TC BX8949.D43 S77 1995**

**FLEMING, INEZ.**
Stroupe, Nibs. While we run this race. Maryknoll, N.Y. : Orbis Books, c1995.
**TC BX8949.D43 S77 1995**

**Fleming, John.**
Honour, Hugh. The visual arts. 5th ed. New York : Henry N. Abrams, 1999.
**TC N5300 .H68 1999**

**Fletcher-Janzen, Elaine.**
Encyclopedia of special education. 2nd ed. New York : J. Wiley & Sons, c2000.
**TC LC4007 .E53 2000**

**Fletcher, Melba.**
Robles de Melendez, Wilma J. Teaching social studies

in early education. Albany, NY : Delmar Thomson Learning, c2000.
**TC LB1139.5.S64 R62 2000**

**Fletcher, Scott, 1959-** Education and emancipation : theory and practice in a new constellation / Scott Fletcher. New York : Teachers College Press, c2000. xii, 211 p. ; 24 cm. Includes bibliographical references (p. 195-202) and index. ISBN 0-8077-3927-8 (pbk.) ISBN 0-8077-3928-6 (cloth) DDC 371.11/5
*1. Educational sociology - United States. 2. Critical pedagogy - United States. 3. Education - United States - Philosophy. I. Title.*
**TC LC191.4 .F54 2000**

**Fletcher, Todd V.**
Helping individuals with disabilities and their families. Tempe, Ariz. : Bilingual Review/Press, c1999.
**TC LC4035.M6 H45 1999**

**Fleury, Julie.**
Keller, Colleen, 1949- Health promotion for the elderly. Thousand Oaks, Calif. ; London : Sage Publications, c2000.
**TC RA564.8 .K438 2000**

**Flew, Antony, 1923-**
[Thinking about thinking]
How to think straight : an introduction to critical reasoning / Antony Flew. 2nd ed. Amherst, N.Y. : Prometheus Books, 1998. 164 p. ; 23 cm. "Originally published in the United Kingdom as Thinking about thinking and later reissued in the United States of America as Thinking straight"--Foreword. Includes bibliographical references (p. 147-151) and indexes. ISBN 1-57392-239-0 (pbk. : alk. paper) DDC 160
*1. Thought and thinking. I. Title.*
**TC BF455 .F614 1998**

**FLEXIBILITY (PSYCHOLOGY).** *See* **ADAPTABILITY (PSYCHOLOGY).**

**FLEXIBLE LEARNING.** *See* **OPEN LEARNING.**

**FLEXISTUDY.** *See* **OPEN LEARNING.**

**FLIES - JUVENILE POETRY.**
Michelson, Richard. A book of flies. New York : Cavendish Children's Books, 1999.
**TC PS3563.I34 B66 1999**

**FLIES - POETRY.**
Michelson, Richard. A book of flies. New York : Cavendish Children's Books, 1999.
**TC PS3563.I34 B66 1999**

**Flight.**
Burleigh, Robert. New York : Philomel Books, c1991.
**TC TL540.L5 B83 1991**

**FLIGHT - JUVENILE POETRY.**
Livingston, Myra Cohn. Up in the air. 1st ed. New York : Holiday House, c1989.
**TC PS3562.I945 U6 1989**

**FLIGHT - POETRY.**
Livingston, Myra Cohn. Up in the air. 1st ed. New York : Holiday House, c1989.
**TC PS3562.I945 U6 1989**

**Flights of fancy and other poems.**
Livingston, Myra Cohn. 1st ed. New York : M.K. McElderry Books ; Toronto : Maxwell Macmillan Canada ; New York : Maxwell Macmillan International, c1994.
**TC PS3562.I945 F58 1994**

**FLIGHTS, TRANSATLANTIC.** *See* **TRANSATLANTIC FLIGHTS.**

**Flinders, David J., 1955-.**
Block scheduling. Bloomington, IN : Phi Delta Phi International, c1999.
**TC LB3032.2 .B47 1999**

**Flint, Kate.** The Victorians and the visual imagination / Kate Flint. Cambridge, U.K. ; New York : Cambridge University Press, 2000. xvi, 427 p. : ill. ; 26 cm. Includes bibliographical references (p. 313-415) and index. ISBN 0-521-77026-2 DDC 701/.15/094109034
*1. Visual perception. 2. Art, Victorian - Psychological aspects. 3. Aesthetics, British - 19th century. I. Title.*
**TC N6767 .F58 2000**

**Flippen, Annette Rose.** Similarity versus motive as explanations for ingroup bias / by Annette Rose Flippen. 1996. iii, 46 leaves ; 29 cm. Includes tables. Thesis (Ph.D.)--Columbia University, 1996. Includes bibliographical references (leaves 39-42).
*1. Similarity (Psychology) 2. Stereotype (Psychology) 3. Prejudice. 4. Social groups. 5. Group identity. 6. Intergroup relations. I. Title.*
**TC 085 F65**

**Flippo, Rona F.**
Handbook of college reading and study strategy research. Mahwah, N.J. : Lawrence Erlbaum Associates, c2000.
**TC LB2395.3 .H36 2000**

**Flood, Raymond.**
Oxford figures. Oxford ; New York : Oxford University Press, 2000.
**TC QA14.G73 O947 2000**

**FLOOR COVERINGS.** *See* **RUGS.**

**Flora and fauna in Mughal art** / edited by Som Prakash Verma. [Bombay] : Marg Publications, c1999. 164 p. : ill., facsims. ; 33 cm. Includes bibliographical references. ISBN 81-85026-43-2
*1. Animals in art. 2. Plants in art. 3. Art, Mogul. I. Verma, Som Prakash, 1942-*
**TC N7302 .F567 1999**

**FLORAL PRODUCTS.** *See* **FLOWERS.**

**Florence Nightingale.**
Dossey, Barbara Montgomery. Springhouse, PA : Springhouse Corp., c2000.
**TC RT37.N5 D67 2000**

**Flores, Joaquín Evelio.** Psychological effects of the civil war on children from rural communities of El Salvador / by Joaquín Evelio Flores. viii, 177 leaves ; 29 cm. Issued also on microfilm. Includes tables. Thesis (Ph. D.)--Columbia University, 1999. Includes bibliographical references (leaves 113-125).
*1. Children - El Salvador - Social conditions. 2. Insurgency - El Salvador - History. 3. Counterinsurgency - El Salvador - History. 4. Post-traumatic stress disorder in children - El Salvador. 5. Anxiety in children - El Salvador. 6. Depression in children - El Salvador. 7. El Salvador - Rural conditions. 8. El Salvador - Politics and government - 1979-1992. I. Title.*
**TC 083 F67**

**Florida. Department of public instruction.**
Florida school exponent Miami, Fla.,

**Florida. Dept. of Education.** Florida school bulletin ... Tallahassee [1938- v. 23 cm. v. 1- Oct. 15, 1938- .
*1. Education - Florida. I. Title.*

**Florida education.**
Florida Education Association. Journal of the Florida Education Association. Tallahassee, the Association.

**Florida education.** [Jacksonville] v. in illus. 30 cm. Frequency: monthly (except June-Aug.). Began publication with Sept. 1923 issue. Union list of serials. List of serials. Title varies: Florida Education Association. Journal. Official journal of the Florida Education Association. ISSN 0015-4016 DDC 649
*I. Florida Education Association. II. Title: Florida Education Association. Journal.*

**Florida Education Association.**
Florida education. [Jacksonville]

Journal of the Florida Education Association. Tallahassee, the Association. v. ill. Frequency: Frequency varies. v. 1- ; Sept. 1923- . Ceased with: v. 37?, 1959. Continued by: Florida education.
*I. Title. II. Title: Florida education*

**Florida Education Association. Journal.**
Florida education. [Jacksonville]

**Florida educational association.**
Florida school exponent Miami, Fla.,

**Florida school bulletin ...**
Florida. Dept. of Education. Tallahassee [1938-

**Florida school exponent** Miami, Fla., v. illus. 30 cm. Frequency: Monthly except July and August. Official organ of the Florida educational association and of the state Department of public instruction.
*I. Carpenter, Hattie H., ed. II. Florida educational association. III. Florida. Department of public instruction.*

**Floridi, Luciano, 1964-** Philosophy and computing : an introduction / Luciano Floridi. London ; New York: Routledge, 1999. xiv, 242 p. : ill. ; 24 cm. Includes bibliographical references and index. ISBN 0-415-18024-4 (hardbound) ISBN 0-415-18025-2 (pbk.) DDC 004/.01
*1. Computer science - Philosophy. I. Title.*
**TC QA76.167 .F56 1999**

**Flower, Linda.** Learning to rival : a literate practice for intercultural inquiry / Linda Flower, Elenore Long, Lorraine Higgins. Mahwah, New Jersey : Lawrence Erlbaum Associates, c2000. xii, 332 p. : ill. ; 24 cm. Includes bibliographical references (p. 309-315) and indexes. DDC 808/.042/07
*1. English language - Rhetoric - Study and teaching. 2. Academic writing - Study and teaching. 3. Communication, Intercultural. 4. Minority college students. I. Long, Elenore. II. Higgins, Lorraine. III. Title.*

**TC PE1404 .F59 2000**

**FLOWERING PLANTS.** *See* **FLOWERS.**

**FLOWERS - FICTION.**
Turner, Ann Warren. Red flower goes West. 1st ed.
New York : Hyperion Books for Children, c1999.
**TC PZ7.T8535 Rf 1999**

**Flowers, Toni.** Reaching the child with autism through
art : practical, fun activities to enhance motor skills
and improve tactile and concept awareness / by Toni
Flowers. Arlington, TX : Future Education, c1992. 124
p. : ill. ; 28 cm. ISBN 1-88547-723-6 DDC 618.928
*1. Autistic children - Education. 2. Autistic children -
Rehabilitation. I. Title. II. Title: Practical fun activities to
enhance motor skills and improve tactile and concept
awareness*
**TC LC4717 .F56 2000**

**Floyd, Samuel A.**
International dictionary of black composers. Chicago ;
London : Fitzroy Dearborn, c1999.
**TC ML105 .I5 1999**

**Fluency and its teaching.**
Guillot, Marie-Noëlle, 1955- Clevedon, England ;
Philadelphia, Pa. : Multilingual Matters, c1999.
**TC P53.6 .G85 1999**

**Fluitman, Fred.**
Vocational education and training reform.
Washington, D.C. : World Bank/Oxford University
Press, 2000.
**TC LC1044 .V62 2000**

**Flute for beginners.**
The flute [videorecording]. Van Nuys, CA : Backstage
Pass Productions ; Canoga Park, Calif. : [Distributed
by] MVP, c1995.
**TC MT345 .F6 1995**

**The flute** [videorecording] / director, Todd Brinegar ;
producer, Mark S. Arnett ; a production of Aesthetic
Artist Records and Brinegar Video/Film Productions,
Inc. in association with Backstage Pass Instructional
Video. Van Nuys, CA : Backstage Pass Productions ;
Canoga Park, Calif. : [Distributed by] MVP, c1995. 1
videocassette (55 min.) : sd., col. ; 1/2 in. + 1 instruction
booklet (6 p. ; 18 cm.). (Maestro music instrument instructional
video ... for) Title on container: Flute for beginners. VHS, Hi-
Fi, Stereo. Cataloged from credits, cassette label and container.
Instructor: Rebecca Magg. Audio, Mark S. Arnett. For
beginners. SUMMARY: Rebecca Magg teaches the basics of
learning to play the flute, from handling to rudimentary
playing, and demonstrates the technique along with two of her
pupils. CONTENTS: Getting started -- Flute assembly -- Forty
notes -- Different flutes -- How flutes work -- Making a
sound -- Learning articulation -- Fingering notes -- Reading
music -- Wrapping it up.
*1. Flutes - Instruction and study. 2. Flutes - Studies and
exercises. I. Magg. Rebecca. II. Brinegar, Todd. III. Arnett,
Mark S. IV. Backstage Pass Productions. V. Aesthetic Artist
Records. VI. Brinegar Video/Film Productions, Inc. VII. MVP
Home Entertainment (Firm) VIII. Title: Flute for beginners IX.
Series.*
**TC MT345 .F6 1995**

**FLUTES - INSTRUCTION AND STUDY.**
The flute [videorecording]. Van Nuys, CA : Backstage
Pass Productions ; Canoga Park, Calif. : [Distributed
by] MVP, c1995.
**TC MT345 .F6 1995**

**FLUTES - STUDIES AND EXERCISES.**
The flute [videorecording]. Van Nuys, CA : Backstage
Pass Productions ; Canoga Park, Calif. : [Distributed
by] MVP, c1995.
**TC MT345 .F6 1995**

**FLUXIONS (MATHEMATICS).** *See* **CALCULUS.**

**FLY.** *See* **FLIES.**

**FLYING.** *See* **FLIGHT.**

**FLYING-MACHINES.** *See* **AIRPLANES.**

**FLYING SAUCERS.** *See* **UNIDENTIFIED FLYING
OBJECTS.**

**Flynn, Bernadette Marie.** The teacher-child
relationship, temperament, and coping in children
with developmental disabilities / by Bernadette Marie
Flynn. 2000. xii, 170 leaves ; 29 cm. Issued also on
microfilm. Thesis (Ed.D.)--Teachers College, Columbia
University, 1999. Includes bibliographical references (leaves
119-128).
*1. Developmentally disabled children - New York (State) - New
York - Case studies. 2. Preschool children - New York (State) -
New York - Psychology. 3. Temperament in children. 4.
Teacher-student relationships. 5. Interaction analysis in
education. 6. Parent and child - Psychological aspects. I. Title.*

**TC 06 no. 11267**

**Flynn, Suzanne.**
The generative study of second language acquisition.
Mahwah, N.J. : L. Erlbaum, 1998.
**TC P118.2 .G46 1998**

**Focus groups.**
Krueger, Richard A. 3rd ed. Thousand Oaks, Calif. :
Sage Publications, c2000.
**TC H61.28 .K78 2000**

**Focus groups as qualitative research / David L.
Morgan.**
Morgan, David L. 2nd ed. Thousand Oaks, Calif. :
Sage Publications, c1997.
**TC H61.28 .M67 1997**

**Focus on central america.**
Third world peoples, a Gospel perspective. Maryknoll,
NY : Maryknoll Fathers and Brothers, c1987.
**TC F1439.T54 1987**

**FOCUS ON FAMILIES (PROGRAM).**
The next generation [videorecording]. Princeton, NJ :
Films for the Humanities & Sciences, c1998.
**TC RC564 .N4 1998**

**Focus on guidance.** Denver. Love Publishing Co. 9 v. 28
cm. Frequency: Monthly (except July and Aug.). v. 1-9; Sept.
1968-June 1977. Continued by: Counseling and human
development ISSN: 0193-7375 (OCoLC)3393635. ISSN
0015-5136
*1. Student counselors - Periodicals. 2. Counseling -
Periodicals. 3. Educational counseling - Periodicals. I. Title:
Counseling and human development*

**FOCUSED GROUP INTERVIEWING.**
Krueger, Richard A. Focus groups. 3rd ed. Thousand
Oaks, Calif. : Sage Publications, c2000.
**TC H61.28 .K78 2000**

Morgan, David L. Focus groups as qualitative
research / David L. Morgan. 2nd ed. Thousand Oaks,
Calif. : Sage Publications, c1997.
**TC H61.28 .M67 1997**

**Foerstel, Herbert N.** Freedom of information and the
right to know : the origins and applications of the
freedom of information act / Herbert N. Foerstel.
Westport, Conn. : Greenwood Press, 1999. vii, 219 p. ;
24 cm. Includes bibliographical references and index. ISBN
0-313-28546-2 (alk. paper) DDC 342.73/0662
*1. Government information - United States. 2. Public records -
Law and legislation - United States. 3. Freedom of
information - United States. 4. United States. - Freedom of
Information Act. I. Title.*
**TC KF5753 .F64 1999**

**Fogg Art Museum.**
Panzer, Mary. Mathew Brady and the image of
history. Washington, D.C. : Smithsonian Institution
Press for the National Portrait Gallery, c1997.
**TC TR140.B7 P36 1997**

**Földiák, Peter, 1963-.**
Information theory and the brain. Cambridge
[England] ; New York : Cambridge University Press,
2000.
**TC QP363.3 .I54 2000**

**Foley, Griff.**
Understanding adult education and training. 2nd ed.
St. Leonards, NSW, Australia : Allen & Unwin, 2000.
**TC LC5259 U53 2000**

**Foley, Jeana Kae.**
Panzer, Mary. Mathew Brady and the image of
history. Washington, D.C. : Smithsonian Institution
Press for the National Portrait Gallery, c1997.
**TC TR140.B7 P36 1997**

**Foley, Tadhg.**
From Queen's College to National University. Dublin,
Ireland : Four Courts Press, c1999.
**TC LF933 .F76 1999**

**Folgarait, Leonard.** Mural painting and social
revolution in Mexico, 1920-1940 : art of the new
order / Leonard Folgarait. Cambridge ; New York,
NY : Cambridge University Press, 1998. xiv, 256 p. : ill.
(some col.) ; 29 cm. Includes bibliographical references (p.
237-251) and index. ISBN 0-521-58147-8 (hardback) DDC
751.7/3/097209041
*1. Mural painting and decoration. Mexican. 2. Art and
revolution - Mexico. 3. Mural painting and decoration -
Mexico - History - 20th century. 4. Orozco. José Clemente. -
1883-1949 - Criticism and interpretation. 5. Rivera, Diego, -
1886-1957 - Criticism and interpretation. 6. Siqueiros, David
Alfaro - Criticism and interpretation. I. Title.*
**TC ND2644 .F63 1998**

**Folio infobase.**
Dewey, John, 1859-1952. The correspondence of John
Dewey. [computer file]. Windows version.
Charlottesville, VA : InteLex Corp., 1999- Computer
data and program.
**TC B945.D44 A4 1999**

Dewey, John, 1859-1952. [Works.] The collected
works of John Dewey, 1882-1953. [computer file].
Windows version. Charlottesville, VA : InteLex Corp,
1997, c1992. Computer program.
**TC LB875 .D363 1997**

**FOLK ARCHITECTURE.** *See* **VERNACULAR
ARCHITECTURE.**

**FOLK ART.** *See* **DECORATIVE ARTS.**

**FOLK ART - AUSTRALIA.**
Thomas, Nicholas. Possessions. New York, N.Y. :
Thames and Hudson, c1999.
**TC N5313 .T46 1999**

**FOLK ART - NEW ZEALAND.**
Thomas, Nicholas. Possessions. New York, N.Y. :
Thames and Hudson, c1999.
**TC N5313 .T46 1999**

**FOLK BELIEFS.** *See* **FOLKLORE.**

**FOLK HIGH SCHOOLS - CONGRESSES.**
Grundtvig's ideas in North America. Copenhagen,
Denmark : Danske Selskab, 1983.
**TC LB675.G832 G79 1983**

**Folk-högskolan :** Organ för Svenska folkhögskolans
lärarförbund. Stockholm : Lärarförbundet, 1979- v. :
ill. ; 24 cm. Frequency: Eight issues a year. Årg. 60, nr 1
(1979)- . Continues: Tidskrift för svenska folkhögskolan
*1. Adult education - Sweden - Periodicals. 2. Education -
Sweden - Periodicals. I. Svenska folkhögskolans
lärarförbundet. II. Title: Tidskrift för svenska folkhögskolan*

**FOLK LITERATURE.** *See* **FOLK SONGS;
LEGENDS; TALES.**

**FOLK LITERATURE - THEMES, MOTIVES.**
Traditional storytelling today. Chicago : Fitzroy
Dearborn Publishers, 1999.
**TC GR72 .T73 1999**

**FOLK-LORE.** *See* **FOLKLORE.**

**FOLK MUSIC.** *See* **FOLK SONGS.**

**FOLK MUSIC - HISTORY AND CRITICISM.**
Blacking, John. Music, culture, & experience.
Chicago : University of Chicago Press, c1995.
**TC ML60 .B63 1995**

**FOLK MUSIC - UNITED STATES.** *See* **BLUES
(MUSIC).**

**FOLK POETRY, AFRICAN - STUDY AND
TEACHING (SECONDARY).**
Osakwe, Mabel. Poetrymate 1. Enugu, Nigeria :
Fourth Dimension Publishing Co., 1996.
**TC PN1101 .O73 1996**

**FOLK-PSYCHOLOGY.** *See*
**ETHNOPSYCHOLOGY.**

**FOLK SONGS.**
Stevens, Janet. Animal fair. New York : Holiday
House, c1981.
**TC PZ8.3.S844 An**

This old man. 1st American ed. Boston : Houghton
Mifflin, 1990.
**TC PZ8.3 .T2965 1990b**

**FOLK SONGS, ENGLISH.**
This old man. 1st American ed. Boston : Houghton
Mifflin, 1990.
**TC PZ8.3 .T2965 1990b**

**FOLK SONGS - TEXTS.**
Stevens, Janet. Animal fair. New York : Holiday
House, c1981.
**TC PZ8.3.S844 An**

**FOLK TALES.** *See also* **LEGENDS; TALES.**

**FOLKLORE.** *See also* **FAIRIES; FOLK
LITERATURE; FOLK MUSIC; MATERIAL
CULTURE; MYTHOLOGY.**
Levine, Gail Carson. Princess Sonora and the long
sleep. 1st ed. New York : HarperCollins Publishers,
c1999.
**TC PZ8.L4793 Pq 1999**

Mayer, Marianna. Women warriors. New York :
Morrow Junior Books, 1999.
**TC PZ8.1.M46 Wo 1999**

Traditional storytelling today. Chicago : Fitzroy
Dearborn Publishers, 1999.

TC GR72 .T73 1999

**FOLKLORE - AFRICA.**
Dee, Ruby. Two ways to count to ten. New York : H. Holt., c1988.
*TC PZ8.1.D378 Tw 1988*

Dee, Ruby. Two ways to count to ten. New York : H. Holt., c1988.
*TC PZ8.1.D378 Tw 1988a*

Dee, Ruby. Two ways to count to ten. 1st ed. New York : H. Holt., c1988.
*TC PZ8.1.D378 Tw 1988*

Haley, Gail E. A story, a story. 2nd Aladdin Books ed. New York : Aladdin Books, 1988, c1970.
*TC PZ8.1.H139 St 1988*

Swann, Brian. The house with no door. 1st ed. San Diego : Harcourt Brace & Company., c1998.
*TC PS3569.W256 H6 1998*

Swann, Brian. The house with no door. 1st ed. San Diego : Harcourt Brace & Company., c1998.
*TC PS3569.W256 H6 1998*

**FOLKLORE AND CHILDREN.**
Barchers, Suzanne I. Multicultural folktales. Englewood, Colo. : Teacher Ideas Press, 2000.
*TC GR43.C4 B39 2000*

Kraus, Anne Marie. Folktale themes and activities for children. Englewood, Colo. : Teacher Ideas Press, c1998-1999.
*TC GR45 .K73 1998*

**FOLKLORE - APPALACHIAN REGION.**
Johnson, Paul Brett. Old Dry Frye. New York : Scholastic Press, 1999.
*TC PZ8.1.J635 Ol 1999*

**FOLKLORE - CALIFORNIA.**
Bierhorst, John. The people with five fingers. New York : Marshall Cavendish, 2000.
*TC E78.C15 B523 2000*

**FOLKLORE - CHINA - TIBET.**
Demi. The donkey and the rock. New York : Henry Holt, 1999.
*TC PZ8.1.D38 Do 1999*

**FOLKLORE - DICTIONARIES.**
Pickering, David, 1958- A dictionary of folklore. New York, N.Y. : Facts on File, 1999.
*TC GR35 .P53 1999*

**FOLKLORE - GERMANY.**
Mayer, Marianna. Iron John. New York : Morrow Junior Books, 1998.
*TC PZ8.M4514 Ir 1998*

**FOLKLORE - GREAT BRITAIN.** *See* **ROBIN HOOD (LEGENDARY CHARACTER); SHERIFF OF NOTTINGHAM (LEGENDARY CHARACTER).**

**FOLKLORE - JAPAN.**
Uchida, Yoshiko. The two foolish cats. New York : M.K. McElderry Books, c1987.
*TC PZ8.1.U35 Tw 1987*

**FOLKLORE - MEXICO.** *See also* **ZENTENO, LUCIA (LEGENDARY CHARACTER).**
Cruz Martinez, Alejandro, d. 1987. [Mujer que brillaba aún más que el sol. English & Spanish] The woman who outshone the sun. San Francisco, Calif. : Children's Book Press, c1991.
*TC F1221.Z3 C78 1991*

**FOLKLORE - PERFORMANCE.** *See* **STORYTELLING.**

**FOLKLORE - UNITED STATES.**
Farmer, Nancy. Casey Jones's fireman. 1st ed. New York : Phyllis Fogelman Books, c1998.
*TC PZ8.1.F2225 Cas 1998*

**Folkskollärarnas tidning :** organ för Sverges folkskollärarförbund. Stockholm : Folkskollärarförbund, v. Frequency: Weekly. Description based on: Arg. 24, nr. 44 (30 okt. 1943); title from caption.
*I. Sveriges folkskollärarförbund.*

**FOLKSONGS.** *See* **FOLK SONGS.**

**Folktale themes and activities for children.**
Kraus, Anne Marie. Englewood, Colo. : Teacher Ideas Press, c1998-1999.
*TC GR45 .K73 1998*

**FOLKTALES.** *See* **TALES.**

**Folleto de divulgación.**
[Folleto de divulgación (Centro de Estudios Educativos).] México : Centro de Estudios Educativos,

**[Folleto de divulgación (Centro de Estudios Educativos).]** Folleto de divulgación. México : Centro de Estudios Educativos, v. ; 23 cm. Began with: 1 (1964). Description based on: 2 (1964). Each issue has a distinctive title. ISSN 0577-2354
*1. Education - Mexico - Collected works. I. Centro de Estudios Educativos. II. Title.*

**Follett Social Studies**
Ball, Grant T. Civics. Fifth edition. Chicago, Ill. : Follett Pub. Co., c1978.
*TC H62 .B34 1978*

**Fölling-Albers, Maria.**
The transformation of collective education in the kibbutz. Frankfurt am Main ; New York : P. Lang, 1999.
*TC LC1027.I75 T73 1999*

**Fölling, Werner, 1944-.**
The transformation of collective education in the kibbutz. Frankfurt am Main ; New York : P. Lang, 1999.
*TC LC1027.I75 T73 1999*

**Folse, Keith S.** 100 clear grammar tests : reproducible grammar tests for beginning to intermediate ESL/EFL classes / Keith S. Folse ...[et al.]. Ann Arbor : University of Michigan Press, c2000. xi, 198 p. ; 28 cm. "Intended to accompany Clear grammar 1, 2, and 3."--P. [v]. Includes index. ISBN 0-472-08654-5
*1. English language - Study and teaching - Foreign speakers. 2. English language - Examinations, questions, etc. 3. English language - Spoken English - Examinations. 4. English language - Study and teaching - United States. I. Folse, Keith S. Clear grammar. II. Title. III. Title: One hundred clear grammar tests.*
*TC PE1128.A2 F646 2000*

**Clear grammar.**
Folse, Keith S. 100 clear grammar tests. Ann Arbor : University of Michigan Press, c2000.
*TC PE1128.A2 F646 2000*

**Fonseca, Peter.**
Ballet class [videorecording]. W. Long Branch, NJ : Kultur, c1984.
*TC GV1589 .B33 1984*

**FOOD.** *See also* **BEVERAGES; COOKERY; DIET; NUTRITION.**
Gross, Ruth Belov. What's on my plate? 1st American ed. New York : Macmillan, c1990.
*TC TX355 .G795 1990*

Rinzler, Carol Ann. The new complete book of food. New York : Facts on File, c1999.
*TC TX353 .R525 1999*

**Food & body connections.**
Working with groups to explore food & body connections. Duluth, Minn. : Whole Person Associates, c1996.
*TC RC552.E18 W67 1996*

**Food & feasts**
Martell, Hazel. Food & feasts with the Vikings. Parsippany, N.J. : New Discovery Books, c1995.
*TC DL65 .M359 1995*

**Food & feasts with the Vikings.**
Martell, Hazel. Parsippany, N.J. : New Discovery Books, c1995.
*TC DL65 .M359 1995*

**FOOD - ADULTERATION.** *See* **FOOD ADULTERATION AND INSPECTION.**

**FOOD ADULTERATION AND INSPECTION - LAW AND LEGISLATION - UNITED STATES - HISTORY.**
Goodwin, Lorine Swainston, 1925- The pure food, drink, and drug crusaders, 1879-1914. Jefferson, N.C. : McFarland, 1999.
*TC HD9000.9.U5 G66 1999*

**FOOD ADULTERATION AND INSPECTION - UNITED STATES - HISTORY.**
Goodwin, Lorine Swainston, 1925- The pure food, drink, and drug crusaders, 1879-1914. Jefferson, N.C. : McFarland, 1999.
*TC HD9000.9.U5 G66 1999*

**Food and body connections.**
Working with groups to explore food & body connections. Duluth, Minn. : Whole Person Associates, c1996.
*TC RC552.E18 W67 1996*

**Food and feasts with the Vikings.**
Martell, Hazel. Food & feasts with the Vikings. Parsippany, N.J. : New Discovery Books, c1995.
*TC DL65 .M359 1995*

**Food and society in classical antiquity.**
Garnsey, Peter. Cambridge, U.K. ; New York : Cambridge University Press, 1999.
*TC GT2853.G8 G37 1999*

**FOOD BINGE-PURGE BEHAVIOR.** *See* **BULIMIA.**

**FOOD CONTROL.** *See* **FOOD SUPPLY.**

**FOOD CROPS.** *See also* **VEGETABLES.**
Vaughan, J. G. (John Griffith) The new Oxford book of food plants. Oxford ; New York : Oxford University Press, 1997.
*TC SB175 .V38 1997*

**FOOD CUSTOMS.** *See* **FOOD HABITS.**

**FOOD - ENCYCLOPEDIAS.**
Davidson, Alan, 1924- The Oxford companion to food. Oxford : Oxford University Press, 1999.
*TC TX349 .D38 1999*

Davidson, Alan, 1924- The Oxford companion to food. Oxford : Oxford University Press, 1999.
*TC TX349 .D38 1999*

**FOOD - FAT CONTENT.**
Fatty acids in foods and their health implications. 2nd ed., rev. and expanded. New York : M. Dekker, c2000.
*TC QP752.F35 F38 2000*

Sims, Laura S., 1943- The politics of fat. Armonk, N.Y. : M.E. Sharpe, c1998.
*TC TX360.U6 S58 1998*

**Food for thought.**
Food for thought. Toronto, The Canadian Association for Adult Education.

**Food for thought.** Toronto, The Canadian Association for Adult Education. 21 v. 22-27 cm. no. 1-v.21; Jan. 1940-Nov./Dec. 1961. Organ of the Canadian Association for Adult Education. Also available on microfilm from: Ann Arbor, Mich. : University Microfilms. Available in other form: Food for thought ISSN: 0383-9540. Adult learning. ISSN: 0701-3507. Superseded by: Continuous learning. ISSN: 0010-7778. ISSN 0383-9540
*I. Canadian Association for Adult Education. II. Title: Food for thought III. Title: Adult learning. IV. Title: Continuous learning.*

**FOOD, FORTIFIED - CONGRESSES.**
Fundacion Dr. Antonio Esteve. Symposium (7th : 1996 : Sitges, Spain) The clinical pharmacology of sport and exercise. Amsterdam ; New York : Elsevier Science B.V., Excerpta Medica, 1997.
*TC RC1230 .F86 1996*

**FOOD HABITS.** *See also* **DIET; FOOD PREFERENCES; NUTRITION.**
Barer-Stein, Thelma. You eat what you are. 2nd ed. Toronto : Firefly Books, 1999.
*TC GT2850 .B37 1999*

Bissonnette, Madeline Monaco. Adolescents' perspectives about the environmental impacts of food production practices. 1999.
*TC 06 no. 11084*

The nutty, nougat-filled world of human nutrition [videorecording]. [Arlington, Va.] : Cerebellum Corp., c1998.
*TC QP141 .N8 1998*

Working with groups to explore food & body connections. Duluth, Minn. : Whole Person Associates, c1996.
*TC RC552.E18 W67 1996*

**FOOD HABITS - CHINA.**
Feeding China's little emperors. Stanford, Calif. : Stanford University Press, 2000.
*TC TX361.C5 F44 2000*

**FOOD HABITS - ENCYCLOPEDIAS.**
Davidson, Alan, 1924- The Oxford companion to food. Oxford : Oxford University Press, 1999.
*TC TX349 .D38 1999*

Davidson, Alan, 1924- The Oxford companion to food. Oxford : Oxford University Press, 1999.
*TC TX349 .D38 1999*

**FOOD HABITS - ENGLAND - HISTORY.**
Cotler, Amy. The secret garden cookbook. 1st ed. New York : HarperCollins Publishers, c1999.
*TC TX717 .C588 1999*

**FOOD HABITS - ENGLAND - HISTORY - 19TH CENTURY - JUVENILE LITERATURE.**
Cotler, Amy. The secret garden cookbook. 1st ed. New York : HarperCollins Publishers, c1999.
*TC TX717 .C588 1999*

**FOOD HABITS - GREECE - HISTORY.**
Garnsey, Peter. Food and society in classical
antiquity. Cambridge, U.K. ; New York : Cambridge
University Press, 1999.
*TC GT2853.G8 G37 1999*

**FOOD HABITS - HISTORY - TO 1500 - JUVENILE
LITERATURE.**
Martell, Hazel. Food & feasts with the Vikings.
Parsippany, N.J. : New Discovery Books, c1995.
*TC DL65 .M359 1995*

**FOOD HABITS - ROME - HISTORY.**
Garnsey, Peter. Food and society in classical
antiquity. Cambridge, U.K. ; New York : Cambridge
University Press, 1999.
*TC GT2853.G8 G37 1999*

**FOOD HABITS - SCANDINAVIA.**
Martell, Hazel. Food & feasts with the Vikings.
Parsippany, N.J. : New Discovery Books, c1995.
*TC DL65 .M359 1995*

**FOOD HABITS - UNITED STATES.**
Gabaccia, Donna R., 1949- We are what we eat.
Cambridge, Mass. : Harvard University Press, 1998.
*TC GT2853.U5 G33 1998*

Manton, Catherine, 1942- Fed up. Westport, Conn. :
Bergin & Garvey, 1999.
*TC HQ1410 .M355 1999*

**FOOD INDUSTRY AND TRADE.** See also **ETHNIC
FOOD INDUSTRY.**
Shiva, Vandana. Stolen harvest. Cambridge, MA :
South End Press, c2000.
*TC HD9000.5 .S454 2000*

**FOOD INDUSTRY AND TRADE -
ENCYCLOPEDIAS.**
Encyclopedia of food science and technology. 2nd
ed. / Frederick J. Francis [editor-in-chief]. New York :
Wiley, c2000.
*TC TP368.2 .E62 2000*

**FOOD INDUSTRY AND TRADE -
ENVIRONMENTAL ASPECTS.**
Bissonnette, Madeline Monaco. Adolescents'
perspectives about the environmental impacts of food
production practices. 1999.
*TC 06 no. 11084*

**FOOD INDUSTRY AND TRADE - LAW AND
LEGISLATION.** See **FOOD LAW AND
LEGISLATION.**

**FOOD - INSPECTION.** See **FOOD
ADULTERATION AND INSPECTION.**

**FOOD INSPECTION.** See **FOOD
ADULTERATION AND INSPECTION.**

**FOOD - JUVENILE LITERATURE.**
Gross, Ruth Belov. What's on my plate? 1st American
ed. New York : Macmillan, c1990.
*TC TX355 .G795 1990*

**FOOD - JUVENILE POETRY.**
What's on the menu? New York : Viking, 1992.
*TC PS595.F65 W48 1992*

**FOOD LAW AND LEGISLATION.** See **FOOD
ADULTERATION AND INSPECTION - LAW
AND LEGISLATION.**

**FOOD - LAW AND LEGISLATION.** See **FOOD
LAW AND LEGISLATION.**

**FOOD LAW AND LEGISLATION - UNITED
STATES - HISTORY.**
Goodwin, Lorine Swainston, 1925- The pure food,
drink, and drug crusaders, 1879-1914. Jefferson,
N.C. : McFarland, 1999.
*TC HD9000.9.U5 G66 1999*

**FOOD - MORAL AND ETHICAL ASPECTS.**
Coveney, John. Food, morals and meaning. London ;
New York : Routledge, 2000.
*TC TX357 .C59 2000*

**Food, morals and meaning.**
Coveney, John. London ; New York : Routledge,
2000.
*TC TX357 .C59 2000*

**FOOD OF ANIMAL ORIGIN.** See **MEAT.**

**FOOD - PERIODICALS.**
Food research. Champaign, Ill. : The Institute, -
c1960.

**FOOD - POETRY.**
What's on the menu? New York : Viking, 1992.
*TC PS595.F65 W48 1992*

**FOOD POLICY.** See **NUTRITION POLICY.**

**FOOD PREFERENCES - SOCIAL ASPECTS.**
Bissonnette, Madeline Monaco. Adolescents'
perspectives about the environmental impacts of food
production practices. 1999.
*TC 06 no. 11084*

**FOOD PREPARATION.** See **COOKERY; FOOD
INDUSTRY AND TRADE.**

**FOOD PREPARATION INDUSTRY.** See **FOOD
INDUSTRY AND TRADE.**

**FOOD PROCESSING.** See **FOOD INDUSTRY AND
TRADE.**

**FOOD PROCESSING INDUSTRY.** See **FOOD
INDUSTRY AND TRADE.**

**FOOD, PURE.** See **FOOD ADULTERATION AND
INSPECTION; FOOD LAW AND
LEGISLATION.**

**FOOD QUALITY.** See **FOOD - QUALITY.**

**FOOD - QUALITY.**
Ford, Brian J. (Brian John), 1939- The future of food.
London : Thames & Hudson, c2000.
*TC RA601 .F65 2000*

**FOOD - QUALITY - CONGRESSES.**
Heidelberger Ernährungsforum (5th : 1998 :
Heidelberg) Food quality, nutrition, and health.
Berlin : New York : Springer, 2000.
*TC RA784 .H42 2000*

**Food quality, nutrition, and health.**
Heidelberger Ernährungsforum (5th : 1998 :
Heidelberg) Berlin ; New York : Springer, 2000.
*TC RA784 .H42 2000*

**Food research** : an official publication of the Institute of
Food Technologists. Champaign, Ill. : The
Institute, -c1960. 25 v. : ill. (part col.) ; 27 cm. Frequency:
Bimonthly. -v. 25, no. 6 (Nov.-Dec. 1960). Began with: Vol. 1
(Jan./Feb. 1936). Continued by: Journal of food science ISSN:
0022-1147 (DLC)a 39000649 (OCoLC)1680911. ISSN 0095-
974X
*1. Food - Periodicals. 2. Food - Research - Periodicals. I.
Institute of Food Technologists. II. Title: Journal of food
science*

**FOOD - RESEARCH - PERIODICALS.**
Food research. Champaign, Ill. : The Institute, -
c1960.

**Food science and technology (Marcel Dekker, Inc.)**
(96.) Fatty acids in foods and their health
implications. 2nd ed., rev. and expanded. New
York : M. Dekker, c2000.
*TC QP752.F35 F38 2000*

**FOOD SELECTION.** See **FOOD PREFERENCES.**

**FOOD SERVICE MANAGEMENT.**
Hudson, Nancy R. Management practice in dietetics.
Australia ; Belmont, Calif. : Wadsworth, c2000.
*TC TX911.3.M27 H83 2000*

**FOOD - SOCIAL ASPECTS.**
Coveney, John. Food, morals and meaning. London ;
New York : Routledge, 2000.
*TC TX357 .C59 2000*

Interpreting weight. New York : Aldine de Gruyter,
c1999.
*TC RA645.O23 I55 1999*

Weighty issues. Hawthorne, N.Y. : Aldine de Gruyter,
c1999.
*TC RA645.O23 W45 1999*

**FOOD - SOCIAL ASPECTS - UNITED STATES.**
Manton, Catherine, 1942- Fed up. Westport, Conn. :
Bergin & Garvey, 1999.
*TC HQ1410 .M355 1999*

**FOOD - SOCIAL ASPECTS - UNITED STATES -
HISTORY - 20TH CENTURY.**
Witt, Doris. Black hunger. New York : Oxford
University Press, 1999.
*TC E185.86 .W58 1999*

**FOOD SUPPLY.** See also **AGRICULTURE.**
Shiva, Vandana. Stolen harvest. Cambridge, MA :
South End Press, c2000.
*TC HD9000.5 .S454 2000*

**FOOD SUPPLY - DEVELOPING COUNTRIES.**
Foster, Phillips, 1931- The world food problem. 2nd
ed. Boulder : Lynne Rienner Publishers, 1999.
*TC HD9018.D44 F68 1999*

The paradox of plenty. Oakland, Calif. : Food First
Books, c1999.

*TC HD1542 .P37 1999*

**FOOD SUPPLY - DEVELOPING COUNTRIES -
INTERNATIONAL COOPERATION.**
Foster, Phillips, 1931- The world food problem. 2nd
ed. Boulder : Lynne Rienner Publishers, 1999.
*TC HD9018.D44 F68 1999*

**FOOD SUPPLY - GOVERNMENT POLICY -
DEVELOPING COUNTRIES.**
Foster, Phillips, 1931- The world food problem. 2nd
ed. Boulder : Lynne Rienner Publishers, 1999.
*TC HD9018.D44 F68 1999*

**FOOD SUPPLY - GREECE - HISTORY.**
Garnsey, Peter. Food and society in classical
antiquity. Cambridge, U.K. ; New York : Cambridge
University Press, 1999.
*TC GT2853.G8 G37 1999*

**FOOD SUPPLY - ROME - HISTORY.**
Garnsey, Peter. Food and society in classical
antiquity. Cambridge, U.K. ; New York : Cambridge
University Press, 1999.
*TC GT2853.G8 G37 1999*

**FOOD - TERMINOLOGY.**
Barer-Stein, Thelma. You eat what you are. 2nd ed.
Toronto : Firefly Books, 1999.
*TC GT2850 .B37 1999*

**FOOD TRADE.** See **FOOD INDUSTRY AND
TRADE.**

**FOODS.** See **FOOD.**

**FOODWAYS.** See **FOOD HABITS.**

**FOOT WEAR.** See **FOOTWEAR.**

**FOOTBALL.** See also **SOCCER.**
Giulianotti, Richard, 1966- Cambridge, UK : Polity
Press ; Malden, MA : Blackwell Publishers, 1999.
*TC GV943.9.S64 G576 1999*

**FOOTBALL (SOCCER).** See **SOCCER.**

**Footer, Jacquie.**
Impressionism [videorecording]. [London] : The
National Gallery ; Tillingham, Peasmarsh, East
Sussex, England : Ho-Ho-Kus, NJ : Distributed by
The Roland Collection, c1990.
*TC ND547.5.I4 A7 1990*

**FOOTWEAR - RUSSIA (FEDERATION) -
SIBERIA.**
Oakes, Jill E. (Jill Elizabeth), 1952- Spirit of Siberia.
Washington, D.C. : Smithsonian Institution Press,
c1998.
*TC DK758 .O24 1998*

**For "children who vary from the normal type".**
Osgood, Robert L. Washington, D.C. : Gallaudet
University Press, c2000.
*TC LC3983.B7 O84 2000*

**--For dummies**
Williams, Bard. The Internet for teachers. 3rd ed.
Foster City, CA : IDG Books Worldwide, c1999.
*TC LB1044.87 .W55 1999*

**For home, country, and race.**
Heathorn, Stephen J., 1965- Toronto : University of
Toronto Press, 1999.
*TC LC93.E5 H42 1999*

**For love or money** : the fee in feminist therapy / Marcia
Hill, Ellyn Kaschak, editors. New York : Haworth
Press, c1999. 113 p. ; 21 cm. "For love or money : the fee in
feminist therapy has been co-published simultaneously as
Women & therapy, Volume 22, number 3, 1999." Includes
bibliographical references and index. ISBN 0-7890-0955-2
(alk. paper) ISBN 0-7890-0956-0 (alk. paper) DDC 616.89/
14/082
*1. Feminist therapy - Miscellanea. 2. Psychotherapists - Fees.
3. Psychotherapist and patient. I. Hill, Marcia. II. Kaschak,
Ellyn, 1943-*
*TC RC489.F45 F67 1999*

**For the love of it.**
Booth, Wayne C. Chicago : University of Chicago
Press, c1999.
*TC ML418.B49 A3 1999*

**For the love of literature.**
Savage, John F., 1938- Boston : McGraw-Hill, c2000.
*TC LB1575 .S28 2000*

**For the sake of the search.**
Edward Clark. Belleville Lake, Mich. : Belleville
Lake Press, c1997.
*TC ND237.C524 E393 1997*

**For theater artists, dance artists, singers,
instrumentalists, mimes, speakers, puppeteers,
storytellers.**

Heflick, David. How to make money performing in schools. Orient, Wash. : Silcox Productions, c1996.
*TC LB3015 .H428 1996*

**Forbidden love.**
Nash, Gary B. 1st ed. New York : H. Holt, 1999.
*TC E184.M47 N47 1999*

**The force of character.**
Hillman, James. 1st ed. New York : Random House, c1999.
*TC BF724.85.S45 H535 1999b*

**Forces of nature :** teacher's planning guide. New York : Macmillan/McGraw-Hill, c1997. 1 v. (various pagings) : col. ill. ; 31 cm. (Spotlight on literacy : Gr.3 l.9 u.2) (The road to independent reading) Includes index. ISBN 0-02-181169-5
*1. Language arts (Primary) 2. Reading (Primary) I. Series. II. Series: The road to independent reading*
*TC LB1576 .S66 1997 Gr.3 L.9 u.2*

**Forcey, Linda Rennie.**
Peacebuilding for adolescents. New York : P. Lang, c1999.
*TC JZ5534 .P43 1999*

**Forcier, Richard C.**
**Computer as a productivity tool in education.**
Forcier, Richard C. The computer as an educational tool. 2nd ed. Upper Saddle River, N.J. : Merrill, c1999.
*TC LB1028.43 .F67 1999*

The computer as an educational tool : productivity and problem solving / Richard C. Forcier. 2nd ed. Upper Saddle River, N.J. : Merrill, c1999. xvi, 383 p. : ill. ; 24 cm. Rev. ed. of: The computer as a productivity tool in education. Includes bibliographical references and index. ISBN 0-13-741968-6 DDC 371.33/4
*1. Education - Data processing - Study and teaching (Higher) 2. Computers - Study and teaching (Higher) 3. Computer managed instruction. 4. Computer-assisted instruction. I. Forcier, Richard C. Computer as a productivity tool in education. II. Title.*
*TC LB1028.43 .F67 1999*

**Ford, Brian J. (Brian John), 1939-** The future of food / Brian J. Ford. London : Thames & Hudson, c2000. 120 p. ; 22 cm. (Prospects for tomorrow.) Includes bibliographical references and index. ISBN 0-500-28075-4
*1. Food - Quality. 2. Nutrition policy. 3. Health - Nutritional aspects. I. Title. II. Series.*
*TC RA601 .F65 2000*

**The Ford Foundation series on asset building**
Securing the future. New York : Russell Sage Foundation, c2000.
*TC HV741 .S385 2000*

**Ford, Karen.**
Hinely, Reg. Education in Edge City. 2nd ed. Mahwah, N.J. : L. Erlbaum Associates, 2000.
*TC LB1029.C37 H45 2000*

**Ford, Richard B., 1935-** Tradition and change in four societies; an inquiry approach. New York, Holt, Rinehart and Winston, 1968. xvii, 349 p. : col. ill. ; 24 cm. (Holt social studies curriculum) Includes bibliographies and index. CONTENTS: Unit 1. Race relations in the Republic of South Africa. The development of society in the Republic of South Africa. Contemporary South Africa.--Unit 2. Race relations in Brazil. The beginnings of interracial contact in Brazil. Race relations in modern Brazil.--Unit 3. Economic development in India. The traditional society. The development of a modern society.--Unit 4. Totalitarian government in China. China: the traditional society. China under the Communists.
*1. Race discrimination - South Africa. 2. Brazil - Race question. 3. India - Economic conditions. 4. China - Politics and government. I. Title.*
*TC HT1521 .F6 1968*

**Ford, Terry.** Becoming multicultural : : personal and social construction through critical teaching / by Terry Ford. New York : Falmer Press, 1999. xiii, 229 p. ; 23 cm. (Critical education practice, v. 19.) (Garland reference library of social science, v. 1079.) Includes bibliographical references (p. 217-223) and index. CONTENTS: ch. 1. Defining perspectives -- ch. 2. Being and becoming multicultural -- ch. 3. Constructing a critical context -- ch. 4. Constructing self as object: salient autobiographical experiences -- ch. 5. Deconstructing self as object -- ch. 6. (Re)Presenting self as subject -- ch. 7. Lived truth and distorted honesty -- ch. 8. Implications for critical teaching. ISBN 0-8153-2199-6
*1. Multicultural education. 2. Minorities - Education. I. Title. II. Series. III. Series: Garland reference library of social science. Critical education practice, vol. 19.*
*TC LC1099 .F674 1999*

**Forecast for home economics.** Teacher edition of Co-ed. Dayton, Ohio, Scholastic Magazine. 20 v. ill. 29 cm. Frequency: Monthly (Sept.-May/June). v. 12-31; Sept. 1966-

May/June 1986. Indexed by: Education index 0013-1385. SUMMARY: The Sept. issue contains the annual Teaching aids Section. Continues: Practical/Forecast for home economics 1963-66. Continued by: Forecast for the home economist. ISSN 0015-7090
*1. Home economics - Periodicals I. Title: Practical/Forecast for home economics 1963-66 II. Title: Forecast for the home economist*

**Forecast for the home economist.**
Forecast for home economics. Teacher edition of Co-ed. Dayton, Ohio, Scholastic Magazine.

**FORECASTING.**
Scanning the future. New York : Thames & Hudson, c1999.
*TC CB161 .S44 1999*

**FORECASTING, POPULATION.** *See* POPULATION FORECASTING.

**FOREIGN AFFAIRS.** *See also* INTERNATIONAL RELATIONS.

**Foreign affairs.** New York : Council on Foreign Relations, 1922- v. : maps (part fold.) ; 26 cm. Frequency: Five issues yearly, fall 1978- . Former frequency: Quarterly, 1922-July 1978. Vol. 1, no. 1 (Sept. 15, 1922)- . An American quarterly review. SUMMARY: Includes sections "Recent books on international relations" and "Source material." Separately paged supplements accompany some numbers. "An American quarterly review," 1922-1977. Vols. 1 (1922)-50 (1972) in 1 v. Continues: Journal of international relations ISSN: 0148-8937. ISSN 0015-7120 DDC 327/.05
*1. World politics - 20th century - Periodicals. 2. International relations - Periodicals. 3. International relations - Bibliography - Periodicals. I. Council on Foreign Relations. II. Title: Recent books on international relations. III. Title: Journal of international relations*

**FOREIGN AID TO EDUCATION.** *See* EDUCATIONAL ASSISTANCE.

**FOREIGN-BORN POPULATION.** *See* IMMIGRANTS.

**FOREIGN COMMERCE.** *See* INTERNATIONAL TRADE.

**FOREIGN ECONOMIC POLICY.** *See* INTERNATIONAL ECONOMIC RELATIONS.

**FOREIGN ECONOMIC RELATIONS.** *See* INTERNATIONAL ECONOMIC RELATIONS.

**Foreign education digest.** [Berkeley, Calif., S. W. Downs] 31 v. 26 cm. v.1-31; 1936-Apr./June 1967.

**FOREIGN EDUCATIONAL AID.** *See* EDUCATIONAL ASSISTANCE.

**Foreign language standards :** linking research, theories, and practices / June K. Phillips, editor ; Robert M. Terry, associate editor ; <contributions by> Joanne Burnett ... <et al.>. Lincolnwood, Ill., U.S.A. : National Textbook Company in conjunction with the American Council on the Teaching of Foreign Languages, c1999, v, 266 p. : ill. ; 23 cm. (The ACTFL foreign language education series) Includes bibliographical references and indexes. ISBN 0-8442-9375-X
*1. Language and languages - Study and teaching - Standards - United States. 2. Language and languages - Study and teaching - Research. 3. Language and culture - Study and teaching - Standards - United States. 4. Education - Standards - United States. I. Phillips, June K. II. Terry, Robert M. (Robert Meredith) III. Burnett, Joanne, 1961- IV. American Council on the Teaching of Foreign Languages. V. Series.*
*TC P53 .F674 1999*

**FOREIGN LANGUAGE STUDY.** *See* LANGUAGE AND LANGUAGES - STUDY AND TEACHING.

**Foreign language teaching in Europe**
(vol. 1) English teacher education in Europe. Frankfurt am Main ; New York : P. Lang, 1999.
*TC PE1128.A2 E547 1999*

**FOREIGN LANGUAGES.** *See* LANGUAGE AND LANGUAGES; LANGUAGES, MODERN.

**FOREIGN LICENSING AGREEMENTS.** *See* TECHNOLOGY TRANSFER.

**FOREIGN POLICY.** *See* INTERNATIONAL RELATIONS.

**FOREIGN POPULATION.** *See* IMMIGRANTS; MINORITIES.

**FOREIGN RELATIONS.** *See* INTERNATIONAL RELATIONS.

**FOREIGN STUDENTS.** *See* STUDENTS, FOREIGN.

**FOREIGN STUDENTS' SPOUSES.** *See* STUDENTS, FOREIGN.

**FOREIGN STUDY.** *See also* STUDENTS, FOREIGN.
Hess, J. Daniel (John Daniel), 1937- Studying abroad/learning abroad. Yarmouth, Me., USA : Intercultural Press, c1997.
*TC LB2375 .H467 1997*

**FOREIGN STUDY - UNITED STATES.**
Hansel, Bettina G. The exchange student survival kit. Yarmouth, ME : Intercultural Press, c1993.
*TC LB1696 .H36 1993*

**FOREIGN TEACHERS.** *See* TEACHERS, FOREIGN.

**FOREIGN TRADE.** *See* INTERNATIONAL TRADE.

**FOREIGNERS.** *See* IMMIGRANTS.

**Foreman, Grant, 1869-1953.** Advancing the frontier, 1830-1860 / Grant Foreman. Norman : University of Oklahoma Press, 1968 printing, c1933. 363 p., [4] leaves of plates, : ill., 3 folded maps, plans, ports. ; 23 cm. (Civilization of the American Indian [4]) Includes bibliographical references (p. [331]-337) and index.
*1. Indians of North America - Government relations - 1789-1869. 2. Indians of North America - West (U.S.) 3. Indians of North America - Indian Territory. 4. Indian councils - West (U.S.) 5. Indians of North America - Wars - 1815-1875. 6. Military bases - United States. 7. Indians of North America - History - 19th century. 8. Indians of North America - Social life and customs. I. Title. II. Series: Civilization of the American Indian series ; v. 4.*
*TC E93 .F67 1968*

**FORENSIC NEUROPSYCHOLOGY.**
Bell, Lisa M. Frontal lobe dysfunction in first episode Schizophrenia. 1998.
*TC 085 B3995*

**FORENSIC SCIENCES.** *See* CRIMINAL INVESTIGATION.

**FOREST ECOLOGY.** *See* RAIN FOREST ECOLOGY.

**Foresta, Merry A.**
National Museum of American Art (U.S.) American photographs. Washington, D.C. : National Museum of American Art, Smithsonian Institution : Smithsonian Institution Press, c1996.
*TC TR645.W18 N37 1996*

**FORESTS AND FORESTRY.** *See* RAIN FORESTS; TREES.

**Forgas, Joseph P.**
Emotion and social judgments. 1st ed. Oxford ; New York : Pergamon Press, 1991.
*TC BF531 .E4834 1991*

Feeling and thinking. Cambridge, U.K. ; New York : Cambridge University Press ; Paris : Editions de la Maison des Sciences de l'Homme, 2000.
*TC BF531 .F44 2000*

The message within. Philadelphia, Pa. : Psychology Press, 2000.
*TC BF697 .M457 2000*

**FORGERY.** *See* FALSE CERTIFICATION.

**FORGIVENESS.**
Forgiveness. New York : Guilford Press, c1999.
*TC BF637.F67 F67 1999*

**Forgiveness :** theory, research, and practice / edited by Michael E. McCullough, Kenneth I. Pargament, Carl E. Thoresen. New York : Guilford Press, c1999. xviii, 334 p. : ill. ; 24 cm. Includes bibliographical references and indexes. ISBN 1-57230-510-X DDC 155.9/2
*1. Forgiveness. I. McCullough, Michael E. II. Pargament, Kenneth I. (Kenneth Ira), 1950- III. Thoresen, Carl E.*
*TC BF637.F67 F67 1999*

**The forgotten mourners.**
Smith, Susan C. 2nd ed. London ; Philadelphia : Jessica Kingsley Publishers, 1999.
*TC BF723.G75 P46 1999*

**FORM LETTERS - HANDBOOKS, MANUALS, ETC.**
Grady, Marilyn L. 124 high-impact letters for busy principals. Thousand Oaks, Calif. : Corwin Press, c2000.
*TC LB2831.9 .G72 2000*

**FORM PERCEPTION.** *See* PATTERN PERCEPTION.

**FORM PERCEPTION IN CHILDREN - SEX DIFFERENCES.**
Tuman, Donna M. Gender difference in form and content. 1998.
*TC 06 no. 11000*

**Formaçao.** Rio de Janeiro, Brazil. v. ano 1- agto. 1938- .
"Mens'ario sôbre educaçao e sua t'ecnica."

**FORMAL DISCIPLINE.** *See* **MEMORY.**

**FORMAL SEMANTICS.** *See* **SEMANTICS.**

**FORMATS, MARC.** *See* **MARC FORMATS.**

**FORMICIDAE.** *See* **ANTS.**

**Formicola, Jo Renee, 1941-.**
Morken, Hubert. The politics of school choice. Lanham, Md. : Rowman & Littlefield Publishers, c1999.
*TC LB1027.9 .M68 1999*

**Forrester, John.** Dispatches from the Freud wars : psychoanalysis and its passions / John Forrester. Cambridge, Mass. : Harvard University Press, 1997. 309 p. ; 24 cm. Includes bibliographical references (p. 259-296) and index. ISBN 0-674-53960-5 (alk. paper) DDC 150.19/5
*1. Psychoanalysis. 2. Psychoanalysis - History. 3. Psychoanalytic interpretation. 4. Freud, Sigmund. - 1856-1939. I. Title.*
*TC BF175 .F646 1997*

The seductions of psychoanalysis : Freud, Lacan and Derrida / John Forrester. 1st pbk. ed. Cambridge ; New York : Cambridge University Press, 1991 (1992 printing) xii, 421 p. ; 21 cm. (Cambridge studies in French) Includes bibliographical references (p. 386-404) and index. ISBN 0-521-42466-6 (pbk.) ISBN 0-521-37243-7
*1. Freud, Sigmund. - 1856-1939. 2. Lacan, Jacques. - 1901-3. Derrida, Jacques. 4. Psychoanalysis. I. Title. II. Series.*
*TC RC504 .F63 1991*

**Forrester, Michael A.** Psychology of the image / Michael Forrester. London ; Philadelphia : Routledge, 2000. 208 p. : ill. ; 25 cm. Includes bibliographical references (p. [181]-201) and index. CONTENTS: 1. Outlining a psychology of the image -- Theme I. Images of what is 'inside' or internal. 2. Seeing, visualising and mental imagery. 3. Sound imagery. 4. Dream images and conceptions of the unconscious -- Theme II. Interdependent images: inside and out, or outside and in? 5. The developing self. 6. Self-image and social identity. 7. The gendered image -- Theme III. External images and all that is 'out there'. 8. The mass media of the moving image: television and film. 9. Virtual semiotics and electronic images. 10. Photography and the photographic image. 11. Postscript to a psychology of the image. ISBN 0-415-16515-6 DDC 153.3/2 DDC 153.3/2
*1. Imagery (Psychology) I. Title.*
*TC BF367 .F675 2000*

**Forsberg, Rolf.**
Headline stories of the century [videorecording]. Chicago, IL. : Distributed by Questar Video, Inc., c1992.
*TC D743 .H42 1992*

**Forsyth, Ian.** The complete guide to teaching a course : practical strategies for teachers, lecturers and trainers / Ian Forsyth, Alan Jolliffe and David Stevens. 2nd ed. London : Kogan Page ; Sterling, VA : Stylus Publishing, 1999. 4 v. : ill. ; 22 cm. Includes bibliographical references and indexes. PARTIAL CONTENTS: [1] Planning a course -- [2] Preparing a course -- [3] Delivering a course -- [4] Evaluating a course. ISBN 0-7494-2807-4 (1 : pbk) ISBN 0-7494-2808-2 (2 : pbk) ISBN 0-7494-2809-0 (3 : pbk) ISBN 0-7494-2810-4 (4 : pbk)
*1. Teaching - Handbooks, manuals, etc. 2. Instructional systems - Design - Handbooks, manuals, etc. I. Jolliffe, Alan. II. Stevens, David. III. Title. IV. Title: Planning a course V. Title: Preparing a course VI. Title: Delivering a course VII. Title: Evaluating a course*
*TC LB1025.3 .F67 1999*

**FORT ONTARIO EMERGENCY REFUGEE SHELTER - FICTION.**
Bat-Ami, Miriam. Two suns in the sky. 1st ed. [Chicago, IL] : Front Street/Cricket Books, 1999.
*TC PZ7.B2939 Tw 1999*

**FORT ONTARIO EMERGENCY REFUGEE SHELTER - JUVENILE FICTION.**
Bat-Ami, Miriam. Two suns in the sky. 1st ed. [Chicago, IL] : Front Street/Cricket Books, 1999.
*TC PZ7.B2939 Tw 1999*

**Forten, Charlotte L.** A free Black girl before the Civil War : the diary of Charlotte Forten, 1854 / edited by Christy Steele with Kerry Graves ; foreword by Suzanne Bunkers ; [illustrator, Linda Clavel]. Mankato, Minn. : Blue Earth Books, c2000. 32 p. : ill. (some col.) ; 24 cm. (Diaries, letters, and memoirs) Includes bibliographical references and index. SUMMARY: The diary of a sixteen-year-old free African American who lived in Massachusetts in 1854 records her schooling, participation in the antislavery movement, and concern for an arrested fugitive slave. Includes sidebars, activities, and a timeline related to this era. ISBN 0-7368-0345-9 DDC 974.4/5
*1. Forten, Charlotte L. - Diaries - Juvenile literature. 2. Afro-American teenage girls - Massachusetts - Salem - Diaries - Juvenile literature. 3. Free Afro-Americans - Massachusetts - Salem - Diaries - Juvenile literature. 4. Salem (Mass.) - Race relations - Juvenile literature. 5. Salem (Mass.) - Social life and customs - Juvenile literature. 6. Antislavery movements - Massachusetts - History - 19th century - Juvenile literature. 7. Forten, Charlotte L. 8. Massachusetts - Race relations. 9. Massachusetts - Social life and customs. 10. Antislavery movements. 11. Afro-Americans - History. 12. Diaries. 13. Afro-Americans - Biography. 14. Women - Biography. I. Steele. Christy. II. Graves. Kerry. III. Clavel, Linda, ill. IV. Title. V. Series.*
*TC F74.S1 F67 2000*

Forten, Charlotte L. A free Black girl before the Civil War. Mankato, Minn. : Blue Earth Books, c2000.
*TC F74.S1 F67 2000*

**FORTEN, CHARLOTTE L. - DIARIES - JUVENILE LITERATURE.**
Forten, Charlotte L. A free Black girl before the Civil War. Mankato, Minn. : Blue Earth Books, c2000.
*TC F74.S1 F67 2000*

**Fortfürhungsnachweis zur bereinigten Sammlung der Verwaltungsvorschriften des Bayerischen Staatsministeriums für Unterricht und Kultus (BayBSVK) für die Zeit von 1865 bis ...**
Bavaria (Germany). Staatsministerium für Unterricht und Kultus. Amtsblatt des Staatsministeriums für Unterricht und Kultus. München : Das Ministerium, 1918-

**Fortress America.**
Blakely, Edward James, 1938- Washington, D.C. : Brookings Institution Press, c1997.
*TC HT169.59.U6 B53 1997*

**FORTUNE.** *See* **SUCCESS.**

**FORTUNES.** *See* **WEALTH.**

**The fortunes of the humanities.**
Gilman, Sander L. Stanford, Calif. : Stanford University Press, c2000.
*TC AZ183.U5 G55 2000*

**Forty-two up.**
42 up. New York : The New Press : Distributed by W.W. Norton, c1998.
*TC HQ792.G7 A18 1998*

**Forum.**
Current history and Forum. New York [C-H Publishing Corporation; etc., etc., 1914-41]

**Forum and Century.**
Current history and Forum. New York [C-H Publishing Corporation; etc., etc., 1914-41]

**Forum and century.**
[Current history (New York, N.Y. : 1916)] Current history. [New York : New York Times Co., 1916-1940]

**Forum May 1940.**
Current history and Forum. New York [C-H Publishing Corporation; etc., etc., 1914-41]

**Forum of education.** London, Longmans Green. 8v. ill. 25cm. v. 1-8 (new series) Feb. 1923-Nov. 1930. Issued by Training College Association. Journal of experimental pedagogy and training college record. Superseded by: British Journal of educational psychology.
*1. Education - Periodicals. 2. Educational psychology - Periodicals. I. Training College Association (Great Britain) II. Title: Journal of experimental pedagogy and training college record III. Title: British Journal of educational psychology*

**Forum on Biodiversity (1997 : National Academy of Sciences)** Nature and human society : the quest for a sustainable world : proceedings of the 1997 Forum on Biodiversity / Board on Biology, National Research Council. Washington, D.C. : National Academy Press, 2000. xii, 625 p. : ill. ; 24 cm. Includes bibliographical references and index. ISBN 0-309-06555-0 (hardcover) DDC 333.95/11
*1. Biological diversity - Congresses. 2. Nature - Effect of human beings on - Congresses. 3. Human ecology - Congresses. 4. Sustainable development - Congresses. I. National Research Council (U.S.). Board on Biology. II. Title.*
*TC QH541.15.B56 F685 1997*

**Forum on Early Childhood Science, Mathematics, and Technology Education (1998 : Washington, D.C.).**
Dialogue on early childhood science, mathematics, and technology education. Washington, DC : American Association for the Advancement of Science/Project 2061, 1999.
*TC LB1139.5.S35 D53 1999*

**FORUM, OPEN.** *See* **FORUMS (DISCUSSION AND DEBATE).**

**FORUMS (DISCUSSION AND DEBATE).** *See also* **GROUP READING; SEMINARS.**
Bligh, Donald A. What's the point in discussion? Exeter, Eng. ; Portland, OR : Intellect, 2000.
*TC LC6519 .B555 2000*

**FORUMS (DISCUSSION AND DEBATE) - HANDBOOKS, MANUALS, ETC.**
Designing successful professional meetings and conferences in education. Thousand Oaks, Calif. : Corwin Press, c2000.
*TC LC6519 .D48 2000*

**Forward trends.** London, National Council for Special Education [etc.] 17 v. ill. irreg. v. 1-17, no. 3; 1956-March 1974. Superseded by: Special education: forward trends.
*1. Mentally handicapped children - Education - Periodicals. I. National Council for Special Education. II. Title: Special education: forward trends*

**Fosha, Diana.** The transforming power of affect : a model for accelerated change / Diana Fosha. 1st ed. New York : BasicBooks, 2000. xi, 376 p. ; 25 cm. Includes bibliographical references and index. ISBN 0-465-09567-4 DDC 616.8914
*1. Change (Psychology) 2. Self-actualization (Psychology) I. Title.*
*TC BF637.C4 F67 2000*

**Foshay, Arthur Wellesley, 1912-** The curriculum : purpose, substance, practice / Arthur Wellesley Foshay ; foreword by O.L. Davis, Jr. New York ; London : Teachers College Press, c2000. xvii, 92 p. ; 24 cm. Includes bibliographical references (p. 81-85) and index. ISBN 0-8077-3936-7 (cloth) ISBN 0-8077-3935-9 (paper) DDC 375/.001/0973
*1. Curriculum planning - United States. 2. Education - Curricula - Philosophy. I. Title.*
*TC LB2806.15 .F66 2000*

**Foss, Kathleen E.**
Lathrop, Ann. Student cheating and plagiarism in the Internet era. Englewood, Colo. : Libraries Unlimited, 2000.
*TC LB3609 .L28 2000*

**Foss, Merle L., 1936-** Fox's physiological basis for exercise and sport. 6th ed. / Merle L. Foss, Steven J. Keteyian. Boston, Mass. : WCB/McGraw-Hill, c1998. xix, 620 p. : ill. (some col.), col. map ; 29 cm. Rev. ed. of: The physiological basis for exercise and sport / Edward L. Fox, Richard W. Bowers, Merle L. Foss. 5th ed. c1993. First through 4th eds. published under title: The physiological basis of physical education and athletics. Includes bibliographical references and index. ISBN 0-697-25904-8 (acid-free paper) DDC 612/.044
*1. Sports - Physiological aspects. 2. Exercise - Physiological aspects. 3. Sports. 4. Sports Medicine. 5. Physical Education and Training. 6. Exercise. I. Keteyian, Steven J. II. Fox, Edward L. Physiological basis for exercise and sport. III. Fox, Edward L. Physiological basis of physical education and athletics. IV. Title. V. Title: Physiological basis for exercise and sport*
*TC RC1235 .F65 1998*

**Foss, Merle L. 1936-.**
Muller, Susan. Student study guide to accompany Fox's physiological basis for exercise and sport. 6th ed. Boston, Mass. : WCB/McGraw-Hill, c1998.
*TC RC1235 .F65 1998 guide*

**FOSTER CARE, HOME.** *See* **FOSTER HOME CARE.**

**FOSTER CHILDREN - MICHIGAN.**
Schwartz, Ira M. Kids raised by the government. Westport, Conn. : Praeger, 1999.
*TC HV741 .S367 1999*

**FOSTER CHILDREN - UNITED STATES.**
The challenge of permanency planning in a multicultural society. New York : Haworth Press, c1997.
*TC HV741 .C378 1997*

Schwartz, Ira M. Kids raised by the government. Westport, Conn. : Praeger, 1999.
*TC HV741 .S367 1999*

**FOSTER DAY CARE.** *See* **DAY CARE CENTERS.**

**FOSTER FAMILY CARE.** *See* **FOSTER HOME CARE.**

**FOSTER HOME CARE.** *See* **ADOPTION.**

**FOSTER HOME CARE - FICTION.**
Polacco, Patricia. Welcome Comfort. New York :
Philomel Books, 1999.
*TC PZ7.P75186 Wg 1999*

**Foster, Phillips, 1931-** The world food problem :
tackling the causes of undernutrition in the Third
World / Phillips Foster, Howard D. Leathers. 2nd ed.
Boulder : Lynne Rienner Publishers, 1999. xiv, 411 p. :
ill. ; 23 cm. Includes bibliographical references (p. 377-402)
and index. ISBN 1-55587-703-6 (pbk. : alk. paper) DDC
363.8//09172/4
*1. Food supply - Developing countries. 2. Poor - Developing
countries - Nutrition. 3. Malnutrition - Developing countries.
4. Food supply - Government policy - Developing countries. 5.
Nutrition policy - Developing countries. 6. Food supply -
Developing countries - International cooperation. I. Leathers,
Howard D. II. Title.*
*TC HD9018.D44 F68 1999*

**Foster, Stuart J., 1960-** Red alert! : educators confront
the Red Scare in American public schools, 1947-
1954 / Stuart J. Foster with a foreword by O.L. Davis,
Jr. New York ; Canterbury [England] : P. Lang,
c2000. xiv, 274 p. ; 23 cm. (Counterpoints ; vol. 87) Includes
bibliographical references (p. [211]-263) and index. ISBN 0-
8204-4050-7 DDC 371.1/04
*1. Academic freedom - United States - History - 1945-1953. 2.
National Education Association of the United States - History -
1945-1953. 3. Anti-communist movements - United States -
History - 1945-1953. 4. Education and state - United States -
History - 1945-1953. 5. Public schools - United States -
History - 1945-1953. I. Title. II. Series: Counterpoints (New
York, N.Y.) ; vol. 87.*
*TC LC72.2 .F67 2000*

**Fostering children's mathematical power.**
Baroody, Arthur J., 1947- Mahwah, N.J. : Lawrence
Erlbaum Associates, 1998.
*TC QA135.5 .B2847 1998*

**Fostering emotional well-being in the classroom.**
Page, Randy M. 2nd ed. Sudbury, Mass. ; London :
Jones and Bartlett Publishers, c2000.
*TC LB3430 .P34 2000*

**Fotos, Sandra.**
Ellis, Rod. Learning a second language through
interaction. Amsterdam ; Philadelphia : J. Benjamins,
c1999.
*TC P118.2 .E38 1999*

**Fouad, Nadya A.**
Swanson, Jane Laurel. Career theory and practice.
Thousand Oaks, Calif. : Sage Publications, c1999.
*TC HF5381 .S937 1999*

**FOUCAULT, MICHEL.**
**FOLIE ET DÉRAISON.**
LaCapra, Dominick, 1939- History and reading.
Toronto : University of Toronto Press, c2000.
*TC DC36.9.L32 1999*

LaCapra, Dominick, 1939- History and reading.
Toronto : University of Toronto Press, c2000.
*TC DC36.9.L32 1999*

**FOUCAULT, MICHEL.**
Dean, Mitchell, 1955- Governmentality. London ;
Thousand Oaks, Calif. : Sage Publications, 1999.
*TC HN49.P6 D43 1999*

**FOUCAULT, MICHEL, 1926-1984.**
Dean, Mitchell, 1955- Governmentality. London ;
Thousand Oaks, Calif. : Sage Publications, 1999.
*TC HN49.P6 D43 1999*

**FOUCAULT, MICHEL - CONTRIBUTIONS IN
FEMINIST THEORY.**
Preece, Julia. Using Foucault and feminist theory to
explain why some adults are excluded from British
university education. Lewiston, N.Y. : E. Mellen
Press, c1999.
*TC LC6256.G7 P74 1999*

**Fouchet, Max-Pol.**
Tassili N'Ajjer [videorecording]. [S.l.] : Editions
Cinégraphiques ; Northbrook, Ill. : [distributed by] the
Roland Collection, c1968.
*TC N5310.5.A4 T3 1968*

**Fouke, Janie.**
Bell, Trudy E. Engineering tomorrow :. Piscataway,
NJ : IEEE Press, c2000.
*TC T174 .B451 2000*

**Foulkes, David, 1935-** Children's dreaming and the
development of consciousness / David Foulkes.
Cambridge, Mass. : Harvard University Press, 1999.
viii, 187 p. ; 22 cm. Includes bibliographical references (p.
173-181) and index. ISBN 0-674-11620-8 (hardcover : alk.

paper) DDC 154.6/3/083
*1. Children's dreams. 2. Consciousness. I. Title.*
*TC BF1099.C55 F67 1999*

**Foundation Center.**
Geever, Jane C. The Foundation Center's guide to
proposal writing. Rev. ed. New York : Foundation
Center, c1997.
*TC HG177.5.U6 G44 1997*

Renz, Loren. Arts funding. 3rd ed. [New York, N.Y.] :
Foundation Center, c1998.
*TC NX711.U5 R4 1998*

**The Foundation Center's guide to proposal writing.**
Geever, Jane C. Rev. ed. New York : Foundation
Center, c1997.
*TC HG177.5.U6 G44 1997*

**Foundational perpectives in multicultural education /**
[edited by] Eduardo Manuel Duarte, Stacy Smith.
New York : Longman, c2000. viii, 374 p. ; 24 cm.
Includes bibliographical references (p. ) and index. ISBN 0-
321-02345-5 DDC 370.117
*1. Multicultural education - United States. I. Duarte, Eduardo
Manuel. II. Smith, Stacy, 1968-*
*TC LC1099.3 .F68 2000*

**Foundations and clinical applications of nutrition.**
Grodner, Michele. 2nd ed. St. Louis, Mo. : Mosby,
c2000.
*TC RM216 .G946 2000*

**FOUNDATIONS (ENDOWMENTS).** *See*
**ENDOWMENTS.**

**Foundations in social studies**
Tumin, Melvin Marvin, 1919- Male and female in
today's world. New York : Harcourt Brace
Jovanovich, c1980.
*TC GN479.65 .T95 1980*

**Foundations of education.**
McNergney, Robert F. 3rd ed. Boston ; London :
Allyn and Bacon, c2001.
*TC LB1775.2 .M32 2001*

**Foundations of ethical practice, research, and
teaching in psychology.**
Kitchener, Karen S. Mahwah, N.J. : L. Erlbaum, 2000.
*TC BF76.4 .K58 2000*

**Foundations of experimental research.**
Plutchik, Robert. New York, Harper & Row [1968]
*TC BF181 .P56*

**Foundations of language;** international journal of
language and philosophy. Dordrecht, Holland, Reidel.
14 v. illus. Frequency: Bimonthly, 1972-1976. Former
frequency: Quarterly, 1965-1971. v. 1-14;  1965-1976. Text
mainly in English; some articles in German, French, or
Russian.
*1. Language and languages - Periodicals. 2. Philosophy,
Modern - Periodicals.*

**Foundations of primary teaching.**
Hayes, Denis, 1949- 2nd ed. London : David Fulton,
1999.
*TC LB1555 .H43 1999*

**Foundations of psychodrama.**
Blatner, Adam. 4th ed. New York : Springer Pub. Co,.
c2000.
*TC RC489.P7 B475 2000*

**Foundations of Waldorf education**
(8) Steiner, Rudolf, 1861-1925. [Konferenzen mit
den Lehrern der Freien Waldorfschule in Stuttgart.
English] Faculty meetings with Rudolf Steiner.
Hudson, NY : Anthroposophic Press, c1998.
*TC LF3195.S834 S8413 1998*

**Founders Society.**
The frescoes of Diego Rivera [videorecording].
[Detroit, Mich.] : Founders Society, Detroit Institute
of Arts ; [Chicago, Ill.?] : Home Vision [distributor],
c1986.
*TC ND259.R5 F6 1986*

**Founding and funding family literacy programs.**
Talan, Carole. New York : Neal-Schuman, c1999.
*TC Z716.45 .T35 1999*

**FOUNTAINS - AUSTRALIA.**
Hedger, Michael. Public sculpture in Australia.
Roseville East, NSW : Distributed by Craftsman
House ; United States : G+B Arts International,
c1995.
*TC NB1100 .H44 1995*

**Fountas, Irene C.** Matching books to readers : : using
leveled books in guided reading, K-3 / Irene C.
Fountas and Gay Su Pinnell. Portsmouth, NH :
Heinemann, c1999. xvii, 400 p. : ill. ; 28 cm. Includes
bibliographical references (p. 395-400) and index.

SUMMARY: Compiles more than seven thousand caption
books, natural language texts, series books, and childrens
literature for kindergarten through grade three. ISBN 0-325-
00193-6
*1. Reading (Elementary). I. Pinnell. Gay Su. II. Title. III. Title:
Using leveled books in guided reading. K-3.*
*TC LB1573 .F68*

McCarrier, Andrea. Interactive writing. Portsmouth,
NH : Heinemann, c2000.
*TC LB1139.5.L35 M39 2000*

Pinnell, Gay Su. Word matters. Portsmouth, NH :
Heinemann, c1998.
*TC LB1573.3 .P55 1998*

**Fountoukidis, Dona, 1938-.**
Fry, Edward Bernard, 1925- The reading teacher's
book of lists. 3rd ed. Englewood Cliffs, NJ : Prentice
Hall, c1993.
*TC LB1050.2 .F79 1993*

Fry, Edward Bernard, 1925- The reading teacher's
book of lists. 4th ed. Paramus, N.J. : Prentice Hall,
c2000.
*TC LB1050.2 .F79 2000*

**The four pillars of healing.**
Galland, Leo. 1st ed. New York : Random House,
c1997.
*TC R733 .G35 1997*

**FOURTH GRADE (EDUCATION) - UNITED
STATES.**
Servis, Joan. Celebrating the fourth. Portsmouth, NH :
Heinemann, c1999.
*TC LB1571 4th .S47 1999*

**FOURTH WORLD.** *See* **DEVELOPING
COUNTRIES.**

**FOX.** *See* **FOXES.**

**Fox, Barbara J.**
**Strategies for word identification.**
Fox, Barbara J. Word identification strategies. 2nd
ed. Upper Saddle River, N.J. : Merrill, c2000.
*TC LB1050.34 .F69 2000*

Word identification strategies : phonics from a new
perspective / Barbara J. Fox. 2nd ed. Upper Saddle
River, N.J. : Merrill, c2000. x, 260 p. : ill. ; 24 cm. Rev.
ed. of: Strategies for word identification, c1996. Includes
bibliographical references and index. ISBN 0-13-020342-4
DDC 372.4/145
*1. Reading - Phonetic method - Study and teaching (Higher) I.
Fox, Barbara J. Strategies for word identification. II. Title.*
*TC LB1050.34 .F69 2000*

**FOX, BOB.** Using ICT in primary mathematics :
practice and possibilities. London : D. Fulton, 2000.
vi, 153 p. ; 25 cm. Includes bibliographical references and
index. ISBN 1-85346-647-6 DDC 510.7
*1. Mathematics - Study and teaching - Computer-assisted
instruction.*
*TC QA20.C65 F69 2000*

**Fox, Edward L.**
**Physiological basis for exercise and sport.**
Foss, Merle L., 1936- Fox's physiological basis for
exercise and sport. 6th ed. / Merle L. Foss, Steven
J. Keteyian. Boston, Mass. : WCB/McGraw-Hill,
c1998.
*TC RC1235 .F65 1998*

Muller, Susan. Student study guide to accompany
Fox's physiological basis for exercise and sport. 6th
ed. Boston, Mass. : WCB/McGraw-Hill, c1998.
*TC RC1235 .F65 1998 guide*

**Physiological basis of physical education and
athletics.**
Foss, Merle L., 1936- Fox's physiological basis for
exercise and sport. 6th ed. / Merle L. Foss, Steven
J. Keteyian. Boston, Mass. : WCB/McGraw-Hill,
c1998.
*TC RC1235 .F65 1998*

Muller, Susan. Student study guide to accompany
Fox's physiological basis for exercise and sport. 6th
ed. Boston, Mass. : WCB/McGraw-Hill, c1998.
*TC RC1235 .F65 1998 guide*

**Fox, Glenys.** A handbook for learning support
assistants : teachers and assistants working together /
Glenys Fox. London : D. Fulton Publishers, 1998. vii,
87 p. : ill. ; 30 cm. Includes bibliographical references (p. 86-
87). ISBN 1-85346-475-9
*1. Teachers' assistants - Great Britain - Handbooks, manuals,
etc. 2. Special education - Great Britain - Handbooks,
manuals, etc. I. Title.*
*TC LB2844.1.A8 F68 1998*

**Fox, Lise.**
Westling, David L. Teaching students with severe disabilities. 2nd ed. Upper Saddle River, N.J. : Merrill, c2000.
*TC LC4031 .W47 2000*

**Fox, Roy F.**
UpDrafts. Urbana, Ill. : National Council of Teachers of English, c2000.
*TC LB1775.2 .U63 2000*

**Fox Video (Firm).**
Vietnam [videorecording]. [Beverly Hills, Calif.?] : CBS Fox Video : Distributed by Fox Video, c1993.
*TC DS557.7 .V53 1993*

**FOXES - FICTION.**
Taylor, Harriet Peck. Ulaq and the northern lights. 1st ed. New York : Farrar Straus Girous, 1998.
*TC PZ7.T2135 Ul 1998*

**Foxfire.**
Foxfire 2: ghost stories, spring wild plant foods, spinning and weaving, midwifing, burial customs, corn shuckin's, wagon making and more affairs of plain living. Garden City, N.Y., Anchor Press/ Doubleday, 1973.
*TC F291.2 .F62 1973*

Foxfire 3. 1st ed. Garden City, N.Y. : Anchor Press, 1975.
*TC F291.2 .F622 1975*

**Foxfire 2: ghost stories, spring wild plant foods, spinning and weaving, midwifing, burial customs, corn shuckin's, wagon making and more affairs of plain living.** Edited with an introd. by Eliot Wigginton. Garden City, N.Y., Anchor Press/ Doubleday, 1973. 410 p. : ill. ; 24 cm. SUMMARY: Interviews and essays describe the way of life and crafts of pioneer America still surviving in the Appalachian region. ISBN 0-385-02267-0 DDC 975.8/123
*1. Georgia - Social life and customs. 2. Country life - Georgia. 3. Handicraft - Georgia. 4. Country life - Georgia. 5. Handicraft. I. Wigginton, Eliot, ed. II. Title: Foxfire.*
*TC F291.2 .F62 1973*

**Foxfire 3 :** animal care, banjos and dulcimers, hide tanning, summer and fall wild plant foods, butter churns, ginseng, and still more affairs of plain living / edited with an introd. by Eliot Wigginton. 1st ed. Garden City, N.Y. : Anchor Press, 1975. 511 p. : ill. ; 25 cm. Includes "Cumulative index for the Foxfire book, Foxfire 2, and Foxfire 3." SUMMARY: Interviews and essays describe the way of life and crafts of pioneer America still surviving in the Appalachian region. ISBN 0385022654. ISBN 0-385-02272-7 (pbk.) DDC 975.8/123
*1. Georgia - Social life and customs. 2. Country life - Georgia. - Juvenile literature. 3. Handicraft - Georgia. - Juvenile literature. 4. Country life - Georgia. 5. Handicraft. I. Wigginton, Eliot, ed. II. Title: Foxfire.*
*TC F291.2 .F622 1975*

**Fox's physiological basis for exercise and sport.**
Foss, Merle L., 1936- 6th ed. / Merle L. Foss, Steven J. Keteyian. Boston, Mass. : WCB/McGraw-Hill, c1998.
*TC RC1235 .F65 1998*

**Foye, Stephanie Diane.** Using item response theory methods to explore the effect of item wording on Likert data / Stephanie Diane Foye. 1997. ix, 190 leaves : ill. ; 29 cm. Issued also on microfilm. Includes tables. Thesis (Ph. D.)--Columbia University, 1997. Includes bibliographical references (leaves 136-141).
*1. Item response theory. 2. Scale analysis (Psychology). 3. Attitude (Psychology) - Testing. 4. Likert scale. 5. Scaling (Social sciences) 6. Social psychology - Research. I. Title.*
*TC 085 F82*

**FRACTIONS.**
Fractions [videorecording]. Princeton, N.J. : Video Tutor, 1988.
*TC QA117 .F7 1988*

Number concepts [videorecording]. Princeton, N.J. : Video Tutor, 1988.
*TC QA117 .N8 1988*

Number concepts [videorecording]. Princeton, N.J. : Video Tutor, 1988.
*TC QA117 .N8 1988*

**FRACTIONS - STUDY AND TEACHING (ELEMENTARY).**
Lamon, Susan J., 1949- More. Mahwah, N.J. : L. Erlbaum Associates, 1999.
*TC QA137 .L34 1999*

**Fractions** [videorecording] / Video Tutor, Inc. Princeton, N.J. : Video Tutor, 1988. 1 videocassette (VHS) (64 min.) : sd., col. ; 1/2 in. + 1 student workbook & pre/post test system ([24] p. ; 19 cm.). (Video tutor instructional series) (A mathematics series) Title on container: Basic fractions [videorecording]. Title on voice-over: Video Tutor introduces fractions [videorecording]. VHS. Catalogued from credits, cassette label and container. John Hall, instructor. For grades 5-9 math classes. SUMMARY: Reducing fractions, finding common denominators, adding and subtracting fractions and mixed numbers.
*1. Fractions. I. Hall, John. II. Video Tutor. III. Title: Basic fractions [videorecording] IV. Title: Video Tutor introduces fractions [videorecording] V. Series. VI. Series: A mathematics series*
*TC QA117 .F7 1988*

**FRAGRANCES.** *See* ODORS.

**FRAIL ELDERLY - CARE - UNITED STATES.**
Pearce, Benjamin W. Senior living communities. Baltimore : Johns Hopkins University Press, 1998.
*TC HD7287.92.U54 P4 1998*

**Fralic, Maryann F.**
Staffing management and methods. San Francisco : Jossey-Bass, 2000.
*TC RT89.3 .S72 2000*

**FRANCE - COLONIES - AFRICA - HISTORY.**
Kelly, Gail Paradise. French colonial education. New York : AMS Press, c2000.
*TC LA1186 .K45 2000*

**FRANCE - COLONIES - ASIA - HISTORY.**
Kelly, Gail Paradise. French colonial education. New York : AMS Press, c2000.
*TC LA1186 .K45 2000*

**FRANCE - CULTURAL POLICY - HISTORY - 19TH CENTURY.**
Lehning, James R., 1947- Peasant and French. Cambridge [England] ; New York : Cambridge University Press, 1995.
*TC DC34 .L5 1995*

**FRANCE - ÉTUDE ET ENSEIGNEMENT.**
LaCapra, Dominick, 1939- History and reading. Toronto : University of Toronto Press, c2000.
*TC DC36.9.L32 1999*

**FRANCE - HISTORIOGRAPHIE.**
LaCapra, Dominick, 1939- History and reading. Toronto : University of Toronto Press, c2000.
*TC DC36.9.L32 1999*

**FRANCE - HISTORIOGRAPHY.**
LaCapra, Dominick, 1939- History and reading. Toronto : University of Toronto Press, c2000.
*TC DC36.9.L32 1999*

**FRANCE - HISTORY - CHARLES VII, 1422-1461.**
Hodges, Margaret, 1911- Joan of Arc. 1st ed. New York : Holiday House, c1999.
*TC DC103.5 .H64 1999*

**FRANCE - HISTORY - CHARLES VII, 1422-1461 - JUVENILE LITERATURE.**
Hodges, Margaret, 1911- Joan of Arc. 1st ed. New York : Holiday House, c1999.
*TC DC103.5 .H64 1999*

**FRANCE - HISTORY - GERMAN OCCUPATION, 1940-1945 - FICTION.**
Maguire, Gregory. The good liar. New York : Clarion Books, c1999.
*TC PZ7.M2762 Go 1999*

**FRANCE - LITERATURES.** *See* FRENCH LITERATURE.

**FRANCE - STUDY AND TEACHING.**
LaCapra, Dominick, 1939- History and reading. Toronto : University of Toronto Press, c2000.
*TC DC36.9.L32 1999*

**Francis Bacon.**
Farr, Dennis, 1929- New York : Harry N. Abrams in association with the Trust for Museum Exhibitions, 1999.
*TC ND497.B16 A4 1999*

**Francis, F. J. (Frederick John), 1921-.**
Encyclopedia of food science and technology. 2nd ed. / Frederick J. Francis [editor-in-chief]. New York : Wiley, c2000.
*TC TP368.2 .E62 2000*

**Francis, Paul A.** Hard lessons : primary schools, community, and social capital in Nigeria / Paul A. Francis with S.P.I. Agi ... [et al.]. Washington, D.C. : World Bank, c1998. xv, 66 p. : ill., 1 col. map ; 28 cm. (World Bank technical paper ; no. 420. Africa region series) Includes bibliographical references (p. 65-66). ISBN 0-8213-4333-5 DDC 372.9669
*1. Education, Elementary - Nigeria - Evaluation. 2. Community and school - Nigeria. 3. Education, Elementary - Social aspects - Nigeria. 4. Educational change - Nigeria. 5. Educational surveys - Nigeria. I. World Bank. II. Title. III.*
*Series: World Bank technical paper ; no. 420. IV. Series: World Bank technical paper. Africa region series.*
*TC LA1632 .F73 1998*

**Francis, Robert Jay.** Motor characteristics of the mentally retarded, by Robert J. Francis and G. Lawrence Rarick. [Washington] U.S. Dept. of Health, Education, and Welfare, Office of Education [1960] viii, 40 p. diagrs., tables. 23 cm. (United States. Office of Education. Cooperative research monograph no. 1) "OE-35005." Bibliography: p. 39-40. DDC 136.776
*1. Movement. Psychology of I. Rarick, G. Lawrence (George Lawrence), 1911- joint author. II. Title.*
*TC RJ499 .F7 1960*

**Francis Thompson, Inc.**
The frescoes of Diego Rivera [videorecording]. [Detroit, Mich.] : Founders Society, Detroit Institute of Arts ; [Chicago, Ill.?] : Home Vision [distributor], c1986.
*TC ND259.R5 F6 1986*

**Franco, Barbara.**
Ideas and images. Walnut Creek, CA : AltaMira Press, 1997.
*TC E172 .I34 1997*

**Frank and Ernest on the road.**
Day, Alexandra. New York : Scholastic Inc., c1994.
*TC PZ7.D32915 Frn 1994*

**FRANK, ANNE, 1929-1945. ACHTERHUIS. ENGLISH.**
Beech, Linda Ward. The diary of a young girl by Anne Frank. New York : Scholastic, c1998.
*TC LB1573 .B433 1998*

**Frank, Barbara E.** Mande potters & leatherworkers : art and heritage in West Africa / Barbara E. Frank. Washington, D.C. : Smithsonian Institution Press, 1998. xvi, 192 p. : ill. (some col.) ; 29 cm. Includes bibliographical references and index. ISBN 1-56098-794-4 (cloth : alk. paper) DDC 738/.089/96345
*1. Pottery, Mandingo. 2. Leatherwork, Mandingo. 3. Mandingo (African people) - Industries. 4. Art, West African. 5. Sex role - Africa, West. 6. Sexual division of labor - Africa, West. 7. Sex role in art. I. Title. II. Title: Mande potters and leatherworkers*
*TC DT474.6.M36 F73 1998*

**Frank, Carolyn.** Ethnographic eyes : a teacher's guide to classroom observation / Carolyn Frank ; foreword by Judith L. Green and Carol N. Dixon ; [editor, Lois Bridges]. Portsmouth, NH : Heinemann, c1999. xiii, 111 p. : ill. ; 24 cm. Includes bibliographical references (p. 103-106) and index. ISBN 0-325-00201-0 (alk. paper) DDC 371.39
*1. Observation (Educational method) 2. Teaching - Social aspects - United States. 3. Classroom management - United States. 4. Teachers - Training of - United States. I. Bird, Lois Bridges. II. Title.*
*TC LB1027.28 .F73 1999*

**Frank, Ellen, 1944-.**
Gender and its effects on psychopathology. Washington, DC : American Psychiatric Press, c2000.
*TC RC455.4.S45 G465 2000*

**Frank, Gelya, 1948-** Venus on wheels : two decades of dialogue on disability, biography, and being female in America / Gelya Frank. Berkeley, Calif. : University of California Press, c2000. xv, 284 p. : ill. ; 24 cm. Includes bibliographical references (p. 229-266) and index. ISBN 0-520-21715-2 (alk. paper) ISBN 0-520-21716-0 (pbk. : alk. paper) DDC 362.4/3/092
*1. DeVries, Diane. 2. Physically handicapped women - United States - Social conditions. 3. Physically handicapped women - United States - Biography. 4. Handicapped women - United States - Biography. 5. Handicapped - United States - Psychology. 6. Sociology of disability - United States. 7. Discrimination against the handicapped - United States. I. Title.*
*TC HV3021.W66 F73 2000*

**Frank, Phil.** The ghost of the de Young Museum : Farley, Irene, and Olive-- one San Francisco family's unusual visit to the museum / [text and artwork] by Phil Frank for the Fine Arts Museums of San Francisco. [San Francisco : Fine Arts Museums of San Francisco, 1995] [24] p. : col. ill. ; 26 cm. Cover title. SUMMARY: In comic book style presentation, the ghost of the de Young Museum's founder, Michael H. de Young, gives a little girl a tour and history lesson she won't soon forget.
*1. De Young, M. H. (Michael H.) - Juvenile fiction. 2. M.H. de Young Memorial Museum - Juvenile fiction. 3. M.H. de Young Memorial Museum - History - Juvenile fiction. 4. Art museums - California - San Francisco - Juvenile fiction. I. Fine Arts Museums of San Francisco. II. Title.*
*TC N739.5 .F72 1995*

**Frank, Robert G., 1952-.**
Handbook of rehabilitation psychology. 1st ed. Washington, DC : American Psychological Association c2000.

**FRANK W. BALLOU SENIOR HIGH SCHOOL (WASHINGTON, D.C.) - STUDENTS - BIOGRAPHY.**
Suskind, Ron. A hope in the unseen. 1st ed. New York : Broadway Books, c1998.
*TC LC2803.W3 S87 1998*

**FRANKFURT AM MAIN (GERMANY) - POLITICS AND GOVERNMENT.**
Palmowski, Jan. Urban liberalism in imperial Germany. Oxford ; New York : Oxford University Press, 1999.
*TC DD901.F78 P35 1999*

**FRANKFURT SCHOOL. See FRANKFURT SCHOOL OF SOCIOLOGY.**

**FRANKFURT SCHOOL OF SOCIOLOGY - HISTORY.**
Critical sociology. Harmondsworth ; New York [etc.] : Penguin, 1976.
*TC HM24 .C74*

**FRANKFURT SOCIOLOGISTS. See FRANKFURT SCHOOL OF SOCIOLOGY.**

**Franklin, Barry M.**
Curriculum and consequence. New York : Teachers College Press, c2000.
*TC LB1570 .C88379 2000*

**Franklin Institute (Philadelphia, Pa.).**
When the brain goes wrong [videorecording]. Short version. Boston, MA : Fanlight Productions [dist.], c1992.
*TC RC386 .W54 1992*

**Franklin, Margery B.**
Development and the arts. Hillsdale, N.J. : L. Erlbaum Associates, 1994.
*TC N71 .D495 1994*

**Franklin, Phyllis.**
Preparing a nation's teachers. New York : Modern Language Association of America, 1999.
*TC PE68.U5 P74 1999*

**Franklin, Stephen D.**
IFIP TC3 WG3.2/3.6 International Working Conference on Building University Electronic Educational Environments (1999 : Irvine, Calif.) Building university electronic educational environments. Boston : Kluwer Academic Publishers, c2000.
*TC LC5803.C65 .I352 2000*

**Frank's great museum adventure.**
Clement, Rod. 1st American ed. [New York] : HarperCollinsPublishers, 1999.
*TC PZ7.C59114 Fr 1999*

**Fransella, Fay.** Personal construct counselling in action / Fay Fransella and Peggy Dalton. 2nd ed. London : Thousand Oaks, Calif. : Sage Publications, 2000. xi, 162 p. : ill. ; 23 cm. (Counselling in action) Includes bibliographical references (p. 155-157) and index. ISBN 0-7619-6614-5 ISBN 0-7619-6615-3 (pbk.) DDC 158/.3
*1. Personal construct theory. 2. Counseling. 3. Personal construct therapy. I. Dalton, Peggy. II. Title. III. Series.*
*TC BF698.9.P47 F73 2000*

**Franzblau, Deborah S., 1957-.**
Discrete mathematics in the schools. Providence, R.I. : American Mathematical Society, National Council of Teachers of Mathematics, c1997.
*TC QA11.A1 D57 1997*

**Frasconi, Antonio, ill.**
If the owl calls again. 1st ed. New York : M.K. McElderry Books ; Toronto : Collier Macmillan ; New York : Maxwell Macmillan, c1990.
*TC PN6109.97 .I3 1990*

**Fraser, Celeste.**
Baerwald, Thomas John. Prentice Hall world geography. Englewood Cliffs, N.J. : Prentice Hall, c1992.
*TC G128 .B34 1992*

**Fraser, D. A. S. (Donald Alexander Stuart), 1925-**
Nonparametric methods in statistics. New York, Wiley [1957] 299 p. : ill. ; 24 cm. (A Wiley publication in mathematical statistics) DDC 519
*1. Nonparametric statistics. I. Title. II. Series.*
*TC QA276 .F66 1957*

**Fraser, Jane.** On their way : celebrating second graders as they read and write / Jane Fraser & Donna Skolnick. Portsmouth, NH : Heinemann, c1994. xix, 190 p. : ill. ; 22 cm. (Teacher to teacher) Includes bibliographical references. ISBN 0-435-08830-0 (acid-free paper) DDC 372.6
*1. Language arts (Elementary) - United States. 2. Reading*
*(Elementary) - United States. 3. English language - Composition and exercises - Study and teaching (Elementary) - United States. 4. Second grade (Education) - United States. I. Skolnick, Donna. II. Title. III. Series: Teacher to teacher series.*
*TC LB1576 .F72 1994*

**Fraser, Mary Ann.** Where are the night animals? / Mary Ann Fraser. 1st ed. New York : HarperCollins Publishers, c1999. 29 p. : col. ill. ; 21 x 27 cm. (Let's-read-and-find-out science. Stage 1) SUMMARY: Describes various nocturnal animals and their nighttime activities, including the opossum, brown bat, and tree frog. ISBN 0-06-027717-3 ISBN 0-06-027718-1 (lib. bdg) ISBN 0-06-445176-3 (pbk.) DDC 591.5/18
*1. Nocturnal animals - Juvenile literature. 2. Nocturnal animals. I. Title. II. Series.*
*TC QL755.5 .F735 1999*

**FRATERCULA. See PUFFINS.**

**Frattali, Carol.**
Measuring outcomes in speech-language pathology. New York : Thieme, 1998.
*TC RC423 .M39 1997*

Neurogenic communication disorders. New York : Thieme, 2000.
*TC RC423 .N48 2000*

**Frattura, Elise.**
Capper, Colleen A., 1960- Meeting the needs of students of all abilities. Thousand Oaks, Calif. : Corwin Press, c2000.
*TC LC1201 .C36 2000*

**FRAUD. See DIPLOMA MILLS; FALSE CERTIFICATION.**

**Frazier, Anthony.**
Get a grip [videorecording]. Racine, WI : S.C. Johnson and Son, Inc., 1999, c1998.
*TC TD170 .G4 1999*

**Fredenburg, Aldene.**
The multiage handbook. Peterborough, NH : Society for Developmental Education, c1996.
*TC LB1029.N6 M754 1996*

**Frederick S. Wight Art Gallery.**
Cole, Herbert M. The arts of Ghana. Los Angeles : Museum of Cultural History, University of California, c1977.
*TC NX589.6.G5 C64*

**Fredericks, Anthony D.** More social studies through children's literature : an integrated approach / Anthony D. Fredericks ; illustrated by Rebecca N. Fredericks. Englewood, Colo. : Teacher Ideas Press, 2000. xix, 225 p. : ill. ; 28 cm. Includes bibliographical references (p. 195-206) and index. ISBN 1-56308-761-8 DDC 372.83044
*1. Social sciences - Study and teaching (Elementary) - United States. 2. Children's literature - Study and teaching (Elementary) - United States. 3. Language experience approach in education - United States. I. Title.*
*TC LB1584 .F659 2000*

Science discoveries on the net : an integrated approach / Anthony D. Fredericks. Englewood, Colo. : Libraries Unlimited, 2000. xiv, 313 p. : ill. ; 28 cm. Includes bibliographical references and index. ISBN 1-56308-823-1 (softbound) DDC 025.06/5
*1. Science - Study and teaching - Computer network resources. 2. Internet in education. I. Title.*
*TC Q182.7 .F73 2000*

Social studies discoveries on the net : an integrated approach / Anthony D. Fredericks. Englewood, Colo. : Libraries Unlimited, 2000. xii, 275 p. ; 28 cm. Includes bibliographical references and index. ISBN 1-56308-824-X (softbound) DDC 372.83/044
*1. Social sciences - Study and teaching (Elementary) - United States - Computer network resources. 2. Social sciences - Study and teaching (Elementary) - Computer network resources. 3. Internet in education - United States. I. Title.*
*TC LB1584 .F6597 2000*

**FREE AFRO-AMERICANS - MASSACHUSETTS - BOSTON - BIOGRAPHY.**
Paul, Susan, fl. 1837. Memoir of James Jackson, the attentive and obedient scholar, who died in Boston, October 31, 1833, aged six years and eleven months. Cambridge, MA : Harvard University Press, 2000.
*TC F73.9.N4 P38 2000*

**FREE AFRO-AMERICANS - MASSACHUSETTS - SALEM - DIARIES - JUVENILE LITERATURE.**
Forten, Charlotte L. A free Black girl before the Civil War. Mankato, Minn. : Blue Earth Books, c2000.
*TC F74.S1 F67 2000*

**A free Black girl before the Civil War.**
Forten, Charlotte L. Mankato, Minn. : Blue Earth Books, c2000.
*TC F74.S1 F67 2000*

**FREE BLACKS - UNITED STATES. See FREE AFRO-AMERICANS.**

**FREE ENTERPRISE.**
Giroux, Henry A. Stealing innocence. 1st ed. New York : St. Martin's Press, 2000.
*TC HM621 .G57 2000*

**FREE LOVE. See UNMARRIED COUPLES.**

**FREE MARKETS - NEW ZEALAND - LONGITUDINAL STUDIES.**
Trading in futures. Buckingham [England] ; Philadelphia : Open University Press, 1999.
*TC LB2826.6.N45 T73 1999*

**FREE MATERIAL. See also GIFTS.**
Davison, Bev, 1957- Creative physical activities and equipment. Champaign, IL : Human Kinetics, c1998.
*TC GV745 .D38 1998*

**FREE RADICAL REACTIONS. See FREE RADICALS (CHEMISTRY).**

**FREE RADICALS (CHEMISTRY) - PATHOPHYSIOLOGY.**
Karlsson, Jan, 1940- Antioxidants and exercise. Champaign, IL : Human Kinetics, c1997.
*TC RB170 .K37 1997*

**FREE RADICALS - METABOLISM.**
Karlsson, Jan, 1940- Antioxidants and exercise. Champaign, IL : Human Kinetics, c1997.
*TC RB170 .K37 1997*

**FREE SCHOOLS - ENGLAND - LEISTON.**
Summerhill at 70 [videorecording]. Princeton, N.J. : Films for the Humanities, c1992.
*TC LF795.L692953 S9 1992*

**FREE SPEECH. See FREEDOM OF SPEECH.**

**Free speech on campus.**
Golding, Martin P. (Martin Philip), 1930- Lanham, Md. : Oxford : Rowman & Littlefield Publishers, c2000.
*TC LC72.2 .G64 2000*

**FREE THOUGHT. See RATIONALISM.**

**FREE TIME (LEISURE). See LEISURE.**

**Freed, Alice F., 1946-.**
Rethinking language and gender research. London ; New York : Longman, 1996.
*TC P120.S48 R48 1996*

**Freed, Jann E.** A culture for academic excellence : implementing the quality principles in higher education / Jann E. Freed, Marie R. Klugman, and Jonathan D. Fife ; prepared by ERIC Clearinghouse on Higher Education, the George Washington University in cooperation with ASHE, Association for the Study of Higher Education. Washington, D.C. : Graduate School of Education and Human Development, George Washington University, 1997. xv, 191 p. : ill. ; 23 cm. (ASHE-ERIC higher education report, 0884-0040 ; vol. 25, no. 1) Includes bibliographical references (p. 147-162) and index. ISBN 1-87838-073-7
*1. Education, Higher - United States - Administration. 2. Total quality management - United States. 3. Universities and colleges - United States - Evaluation. I. Klugman, Marie R. II. Fife, Jonathan D. III. ERIC Clearinghouse on Higher Education. IV. Association for the Study of Higher Education. V. Title. VI. Series.*
*TC LB2341 .F688 1997*

Huba, Mary E. Learner-centered assessment on college campuses. Boston ; London : Allyn and Bacon, c2000.
*TC LB2331 .H83 2000*

**FREED SLAVES. See FREEDMEN.**

**Freedman, Joseph S.** Philosophy and the arts in Central Europe, 1500-1700 : teaching and texts at schools and universities / Joseph S. Freedman. Aldershot : Ashgate, 1999. 1 v. various pagings : ill., ports. ; 23 cm. (Variorum collected studies series ; CS626) ISBN 0-86078-780-X DDC 190
*1. Arts - Study and teaching - Europe, Central - History. 2. Philosophy - Study and teaching - Europe, Central - History. I. Title. II. Series: Collected studies ; CS626.*
*TC B52.3.C36 F74 1999*

**Freedman, Kerry J.**
Curriculum, culture, and art education. Albany : State University of New York Press, c1998.
*TC N85 .C87 1998*

**FREEDMEN - MARYLAND - HISTORY.**
Fuke, Richard Paul, 1940- Imperfect equality. New York : Fordham University Press, 1999.
*TC E185.93.M2 F85 1999*

**FREEDOM.** *See* **LIBERTY.**

**FREEDOM, ACADEMIC.** *See* **ACADEMIC FREEDOM.**

**Freedom, equality, and social change** / edited by Creighton Peden and James P. Sterba. Lewiston : E. Mellen Press, c1989. 400 p. : ill. ; 24 cm. (Studies in social and political theory ; v. 3) (Social philosophy today ; no. 2) "Most of the material presented here came out of the First International Conference on Social Philosophy held at Colorado Springs in 1985 and sponsored by North American Society"--Pref. Includes bibliographical references. ISBN 0-88946-103-1 ISBN 0-88946-100-7 (ser.) DDC 170
*1. Social ethics - Congresses. 2. Liberty - Congresses. 3. Equality - Congresses. 4. Social change - Congresses. I. Peden, Creighton, 1935- II. Sterba, James P. III. International Conference on Social Philosophy (1st : 1985 : Colorado Springs, Colo.) IV. Series. V. Series: Social philosophy today ; no. 2*
*TC HM216 .F83 1989*

**FREEDOM OF INFORMATION.** *See* **ACADEMIC FREEDOM; FREEDOM OF SPEECH; RADIO BROADCASTING.**

**Freedom of information and the right to know.**
Foerstel, Herbert N. Westport, Conn. : Greenwood Press, 1999.
*TC KF5753 .F64 1999*

**FREEDOM OF INFORMATION - UNITED STATES.**
Foerstel, Herbert N. Freedom of information and the right to know. Westport, Conn. : Greenwood Press, 1999.
*TC KF5753 .F64 1999*

**FREEDOM OF SPEECH.** *See* **FREEDOM OF INFORMATION.**

**FREEDOM OF SPEECH - UNITED STATES.**
Golding, Martin P. (Martin Philip), 1930- Free speech on campus. Lanham, Md. : Oxford : Rowman & Littlefield Publishers, c2000.
*TC LC72.2 .G64 2000*

Shiffrin, Steven H., 1941- Dissent, injustice, and the meanings of America. Princeton, N.J. : Princeton University Press, c1999.
*TC KF4772 .S448 1999*

**FREEDOM OF TEACHING.** *See* **TEACHING, FREEDOM OF.**

**FREEDOM (PSYCHOLOGY).** *See* **AUTONOMY (PSYCHOLOGY).**

**Freedom to choice.**
Ryan, Sharon Kaye. 1998.
*TC 06 no. 11034*

**Freedom to practise.**
Binnie, Alison. Oxford ; Boston : Butterworth-Heinemann, 1999.
*TC RT41 .B56 1999*

**Freedom Writers.** The Freedom Writers diary : how a teacher and 150 teens used writing to change themselves and the world around them / the Freedom Writers with Erin Gruwell ; foreword by Zlata Filipovic. 1st ed. New York : Doubleday, c1999. xvii, 280 p. : ill. ; 21 cm. ISBN 0-385-49422-X (pbk) DDC 305.235
*1. Teenagers - United States - Diaries. 2. Toleration - United States. I. Gruwell, Erin.*
*TC HQ796 .F76355 1999*

**Freeman, Don.** Corduroy / story and pictures by Don Freeman. Harmondsworth, Middlesex ; New York : Puffin Books, 1976. 1 v. (unpaged) : col. ill. ; 19 x 23 cm. Reprint. Originally published: New York : Viking, 1968. SUMMARY: A toy bear in a department store wants number of things, but when a little girl finally buys him he finds what he has always wanted most of all. ISBN 0-14-050173-8 (pbk)
*1. Toys - Fiction. 2. Fantasy. I. Title.*
*TC PZ8.9.F85 C5 1976*

**Freeman, Howard E.**
Rossi, Peter Henry, 1921- Evaluation. 6th ed. Thousand Oaks, Calif. : Sage Publications, c1999.
*TC H62 .R666 1999*

**Freeman, Phyllis R.**
Wise women. New York : London : Routledge, 2000.
*TC LB2837 .W58 2000*

**Freeman, Rebecca D. (Rebecca Diane), 1960-**
Bilingual education and social change / Rebecca D. Freeman. Clevedon [England] ; Philadelphia : Multilingual Matters, c1998. ix, 262 p. ; 25 cm. (Bilingual

education and bilingualism ; 14) Includes bibliographical references (p. 249-257) and index. ISBN 1-85359-419-9 (hbk. : alk. paper) ISBN 1-85359-418-0 (pbk. : alk. paper) DDC 370.117/5/0973
*1. Education. Bilingual - Social aspects - United States - Case studies. 2. Linguistic minorities - Education - Social aspects - United States - Case studies. 3. Discourse analysis - United States - Case studies. I. Title. II. Series.*
*TC LC3731 .F72 1998*

**Freeman, William, 1951-.**
Scheidecker, David, 1950- Bringing out the best in students. Thousand Oaks, Calif. : Corwin Press, c1999.
*TC LB1065 .S344 1999*

**Freer Gallery of Art.**
Twelve centuries of Japanese art from the Imperial collections. Washington, DC : Freer Gallery of Art and the Arthur M. Sackler Gallery, Smithsonian Institution Press, c1997.
*TC ND1457.J32 W377 1997*

**Freestone, Ian.**
Pottery in the making. Washington, D.C. : Smithsonian Institution Press, c1997.
*TC NK3780 .P68 1997*

**Freiberg, H. Jerome.**
Beyond behaviorism. Boston : Allyn and Bacon, c1999.
*TC LB3013 .B42 1999*

School climate. London ; Philadelphia : Falmer Press, 1999.
*TC LC210 .S35 1999*

Universal teaching strategies / H. Jerome Freiberg, Amy Driscoll. 3rd ed. Boston : Allyn and Bacon, c2000. xv, 480 p. : ill. ; 24 cm. Includes bibliographical references and indexes. ISBN 0-205-30285-8 DDC 371.102
*1. Teaching. 2. Classroom management. I. Driscoll, Amy. II. Title.*
*TC LB1025.3 .F74 2000*

**FREIE WALDORFSCHULE.**
Steiner, Rudolf, 1861-1925. [Konferenzen mit den Lehrern der Freien Waldorfschule in Stuttgart. English] Faculty meetings with Rudolf Steiner. Hudson, NY : Anthroposophic Press, c1998.
*TC LF3195.S834 S8413 1998*

**FREIE WALDORFSCHULE - FACULTY.**
Steiner, Rudolf, 1861-1925. [Konferenzen mit den Lehrern der Freien Waldorfschule in Stuttgart. English] Faculty meetings with Rudolf Steiner. Hudson, NY : Anthroposophic Press, c1998.
*TC LF3195.S834 S8413 1998*

**FREINET, CÉLESTIN.**
Acker, Victor, 1940- Célestin Freinet. Westport, CT : Greenwood Press, 2000.
*TC LB775 .A255 2000*

**Freire, Paulo, 1921-**
**[Pedagogia de autonomia. English]**
Pedagogy of freedom : ethics, democracy, and civic courage / Paulo Freire ; translated by Patrick Clarke ; foreword by Donaldo Macedo ; introduction by Stanley Aronowitz. Lanham : Rowman & Littlefield Publishers, c1998. xxxii, 144 p. ; 23 cm. (Critical perspectives series) Includes bibliographical references (p. 131-134) and index. ISBN 0-8476-9046-6 (cloth : alk. paper) ISBN 0-8476-9047-4 (pbk. : alk. paper) DDC 370.11/5
*1. Popular education. 2. Critical pedagogy. 3. Teaching. I. Title. II. Series.*
*TC LC196 .F73713 1998*

Freirean pedagogy, praxis, and possibilities. New York : Falmer Press, 2000.
*TC LC196 .F76 2000*

McLaren, Peter, 1948- Che Guevara, Paulo Freire, and the pedagogy of revolution. Lanham [Md.] : Rowman & Littlefield Publishers, c2000.
*TC LC196 .M29 2000*

Purcell-Gates, Victoria. Now we read, we see, we speak. Mahwah, N.J. : L. Erlbaum Associates, Publishers, 2000.
*TC LC155.S22 P87 2000*

Robbins, Carol Braswell. An examination of critical feminist pedagogy in practice. 1999.
*TC 06 no. 11067*

Roberts, Peter, 1963- Education, literacy, and humanization. Westport, Conn. : Bergin & Garvey, 2000.
*TC LB880.F732 R62 2000*

**Freirean pedagogy, praxis, and possibilities :** projects for the new millennium / edited by Stanley F. Steiner ... [et al.]. New York : Falmer Press, 2000. xvi, 289 p. ; 23 cm. (Garland reference library of social science ; v. 1417. Critical education practice ; v. 19) Includes bibliographical references and index. ISBN 0-8153-3377-3 (alk. paper) DDC 370.11/5
*1. Critical pedagogy. 2. Freire, Paulo - 1921- 3. Education - Philosophy. I. Steiner, Stanley F. II. Series: Garland reference library of social science ; v. 1417. III. Series: Garland reference library of social science. Critical education practice ; vol. 19.*
*TC LC196 .F76 2000*

**FRENCH ART.** *See* **ART, FRENCH.**

**French, Cathy.**
Dorn, Linda J. Apprenticeship in literacy. York, Me. : Stenhouse Publishers, 1998.
*TC LB1139.5.L35 D67 1998*

**French, Chris.**
Anastos, Phillip. Illegal. New York : Rizzoli, 1991.
*TC F392.R5 A53 1991*

**French colonial education.**
Kelly, Gail Paradise. New York : AMS Press, c2000.
*TC LA1186 .K45 2000*

**French, Fiona.** King Tree. London, Oxford University Press, 1973. [38] p. : chiefly col. ill. ; 29 cm. ISBN 0-19-279687-9
*I. Title.*
*TC PZ7.F8887 Ki3*

**FRENCH LANGUAGE - DICTIONARIES, JUVENILE - ENGLISH.**
French picture dictionary. Princeton : Berlitz Kids, Berlitz Pub. Co., c1997.
*TC PC2629 .F74 1997*

**FRENCH LANGUAGE - GLOSSARIES, VOCABULARIES, ETC. - JUVENILE LITERATURE.**
1,000 French words. Princeton, N.J. : Berlitz Kids, Berlitz Pub. Co., 1998.
*TC PC2680 .A15 1998*

**FRENCH LANGUAGE MATERIALS - BILINGUAL.**
1,000 French words. Princeton, N.J. : Berlitz Kids, Berlitz Pub. Co., 1998.
*TC PC2680 .A15 1998*

French picture dictionary. Princeton : Berlitz Kids, Berlitz Pub. Co., c1997.
*TC PC2629 .F74 1997*

**FRENCH LANGUAGE - PRONUNCIATION.**
Adams, David, 1950- A handbook of diction for singers. New York : Oxford University Press, 1999.
*TC MT883 .A23 1999*

**FRENCH LANGUAGE - TEXT-BOOKS FOR FOREIGN SPEAKERS.** *See* **FRENCH LANGUAGE - TEXTBOOKS FOR FOREIGN SPEAKERS.**

**FRENCH LANGUAGE - TEXTBOOKS FOR FOREIGN SPEAKERS - ENGLISH.**
Valette, Jean-Paul. Discovering French. Bleu. Extended teacher's ed. Evanston, Ill. : McDougal Littell, c1997.
*TC PC1129.E5 V342 1997 Teacher's Ed.*

Valette, Jean-Paul. Discovering French. Rouge. Evanston, Ill. : McDougal Littell, c1997.
*TC PC2129.E5 V342 1997*

Valette, Jean Paul. Discovering French. Rouge. Lexington, Mass. : D.C. Heath and Co., c1997.
*TC PC2129.E5 V342 1997*

**French, Lillie Hamilton, 1854- ed.**
National Institute of Social Sciences. Journal of the National Institute of Social Sciences. [New York]

**FRENCH LITERATURE - 19TH CENTURY - HISTORY AND CRITICISM.**
Balakian, Anna Elizabeth, 1915- The symbolist movement. 1977 ed. New York : New York University Press, 1977
*TC PN56.S9 .B3 1977*

**FRENCH LITERATURE - HISTORY AND CRITICISM.**
Shattuck, Roger. Candor and perversion. 1st ed. New York : W.W. Norton, c1999.
*TC PN52 .S53 1999*

**French music of to-day.**
Jean-Aubry, G. (Georges), 1882-1950. [Musique française d'aujourd'hui. English] 4th ed. London, K. Paul, Trench, Trubner, 1926.

*TC ML60.A82 E8 1926*

**French, Nancy K.**
Sands, Deanna J. Inclusive education for the 21st century. Belmont, CA : Wadsworth/Thomson Learning, 2000.
*TC LC1201 .S27 2000*

**FRENCH PAINTING.** *See* **PAINTING, FRENCH.**

**FRENCH PERIODICALS.**
L'Enseignement secondaire au Canada; [Quebec]

**The French piano style of Fauré and Debussy.**
Gingerich, Carol Joy. 1996.
*TC 06 no. 10644*

**French picture dictionary** / [illustrations by Chris L. Demarest]. Princeton : Berlitz Kids, Berlitz Pub. Co., c1997. 128 p. : col. ill. ; 32 cm. Includes index. SUMMARY: Learn basic foreign words such as colors, shapes, numbers and animals. Each word has a picture, a translation and a simple sentence. A beginner's conversation section is also included. ISBN 2-8315-6254-6 DDC 443/.21
*1. Picture dictionaries, French. 2. Picture dictionaries, English. 3. French language - Dictionaries, Juvenile - English. 4. English language - Dictionaries, Juvenile - French. 5. Picture dictionaries, French. 6. Picture dictionaries. 7. French language materials - Bilingual. I. Demarest, Chris L., ill. II. Berlitz Publishing Company.*
*TC PC2629 .F74 1997*

**French, Sally.**
Therapy and learning difficulties. Boston, Mass : Butterworth-Heinemann, 1999.
*TC HV3008.G7 T48 1999*

**Frendo, Henry.**
Towards a pluralist and tolerant approach to teaching history. Strasbourg : Council of Europe Pub., c1999.
*TC D424 .T665 1999*

**FRESCO PAINTING.** *See* **MURAL PAINTING AND DECORATION.**

**The frescoes of Diego Rivera** [videorecording] / produced by Michael Camerini Inc., Francis Thompson, Inc. in collaboration with Stanton L. Catlin ; written by Michael Camerini, Stanton L. Catlin ; produced and directed by Michael Camerini. [Detroit, Mich.] : Founders Society, Detroit Institute of Arts ; [Chicago, Ill.?] : Home Vision [distributor], c1986. 1 videocassette (35 min.) : sd., col. with b&w sequences ; 1/2 in. (Portrait of an artist) At head of title: Home Vision... presents... [videorecording]. Title on container: Rivera [videorecording]. VHS. Catalogued from credits and container. Narrator, Michael Moriarity. Dirk Bakker, photography; Paul Marcus, editor. For adolescent through adult. SUMMARY: Explores Rivera's evolution as an artist, his use of the fresco technique, and his politics. Looks at the murals Rivera created for public buildings in the U.S. and Mexico. "These frescoes unite themes of nature and revolution, drawing a parallel between the evolution of life and the struggle for human dignity."--Container. ISBN 0-7800-0137-0
*1. Rivera, Diego, - 1886-1957. 2. Mural painting and decoration, Mexican. 3. Painting, Modern - 20th century - Mexico. I. Rivera, Diego, 1886-1957. II. Camerini, Michael. III. Moriarity, Michael. IV. Catlin, Stanton L. (Stanton Loomis) V. Michael Camerini, Inc. VI. Francis Thompson, Inc. VII. Founders Society. VIII. Home Vision (Firm) IX. Title: Home Vision... presents... [videorecording] X. Title: Rivera [videorecording] XI. Series.*
*TC ND259.R5 F6 1986*

**FRESHMAN CLASS (HIGH SCHOOL).** *See* **NINTH GRADE (EDUCATION).**

**Fressola, Maria C.** How nurse executives learned to become leaders / by Maria C. Fressola. 1998. vi, 261 leaves : ill. ; 29 cm. Includes tables. Issued also on microfilm. Thesis (Ed.D.) -- Teachers College, Columbia University, 1998. Includes bibliographical references (leaves 229-243)
*1. Nurse administrators - United States. 2. Nursing services - Administration. 3. Health services administration - United States. 4. Leadership. 5. Medical care - United States. 6. Interpersonal relations - United States. I. American Organization of Nurse Executives. II. Title.*
*TC 06 no. 11115*

How nurse executives learned to become leaders / Maria C. Fressola. 1998. vi, 261 leaves : ill. ; 29 cm. Includes tables. Issued also on microfilm. Thesis (Ed.D.) -- Teachers College, Columbia University, 1998. Includes bibliographical references (leaves 229-243)
*1. Nurse administrators - United States. 2. Nursing services - Administration. 3. Health services administration - United States. 4. Leadership. 5. Medical care - United States. 6. Interpersonal relations - United States. I. American Organization of Nurse Executives. II. Title.*
*TC 06 no. 11115*

**Freud and the institution of psychoanalytic knowledge.**
Winter, Sarah. Stanford, Calif. : Stanford University Press, 1999.
*TC BF173 .W5485 1999*

**Freud and the question of pseudoscience.**
Cioffi, Frank. Chicago : Open Court, c1998.
*TC BF173 .C495 1998*

**Freud, psychoanalysis, and symbolism.**
Petocz, Agnes. Cambridge ; New York : Cambridge University Press, 1999.
*TC BF109.F74 P48 1999*

**Freud, Sigmund, 1856-1939.** The ego and the id and other works / Sigmund Freud ; authorized translation by Joan Riviere. London : Hogarth Press, 1957. 88 p. ; 23 cm. (Th international psycho-analytical library, no.12.) DDC 131.341
*1. Psychoanalysis. I. Riviere, Joan, trans. II. Title.*
*TC BF173.F645 1957*

The interpretation of dreams / Sigmund Freud ; translated by Joyce Crick, with an introduction and notes by Ritchie Robertson. Oxford ; New York : Oxford University Press, 1999. liv, 458 p. ; 23 cm. ISBN 0-19-210049-1 DDC 154.6
*1. Dream interpretation I. Crick, Joyce. II. Robertson, Ritchie.*
*TC BF1078 .F72 1999*

**[Sammlung kleiner schriften zur neurosenlehre. eng]**
Collected papers. Authorized translation under the supervision of Joan Riviere. 1st American ed. New York : Basic Books, 1959. <v. 3> ; 22 cm. (The International psycho-analytical library : no. 9) Vol. III: Authorized translation by Alix and James Strachey. Vol. 5 ed. by James Strachey. Includes bibliographical references. CONTENTS: --III. Case histories -- .
*1. Psychoanalysis. I. Riviere, Joan. II. Strachey, Alix, tr. III. Strachey, James, tr. IV. Title. V. Series.*
*TC BF173 .F672 1959*

**VIEWS ON SURGERY.**
Stepansky, Paul E. Freud, surgery, and the surgeons. Hillsdale, NJ : Analytic Press, 1999.
*TC RC506 .S733 1999*

**FREUD, SIGMUND, 1856-1939.**
The analytic Freud. London ; New York : Routledge, 2000.
*TC BF109.F74 A84 2000*

Billig, Michael. Freudian repression. New York : Cambridge University Press, 1999.
*TC BF175.5.R44 B55 1999*

Buse, William Joseph. The alternate session. 1999.
*TC 085 B9603*

Cioffi, Frank. Freud and the question of pseudoscience. Chicago : Open Court, c1998.
*TC BF173 .C495 1998*

Dilman, İlham. Raskolnikov's rebirth. Chicago : Open Court, c2000.
*TC BF47 .D55 2000*

Dufresne, Todd, 1966- Tales from the Freudian crypt. Stanford, Calif. : Stanford University Press, 2000.
*TC BF175.5.D4 D84 2000*

Forrester, John. Dispatches from the Freud wars. Cambridge, Mass. : Harvard University Press, 1997.
*TC BF175 .F646 1997*

Forrester, John. The seductions of psychoanalysis. 1st pbk. ed. Cambridge ; New York : Cambridge University Press, 1991 (1992 printing)
*TC RC504 .F63 1991*

Jung on film [videorecording]. [Chicago, Ill.?] : Public Media Video, c1990.
*TC BF109.J8 J4 1990*

Jung on film [videorecording]. [Chicago, Ill.?] : Public Media Video, c1990.
*TC BF109.J8 J4 1990*

MacIntyre, Alasdair C. The unconscious. Bristol, England : Thoemmes Press, 1997, c1958.
*TC BF315 .M23 1997*

Moorjani, Angela B. Beyond fetishism and other excursions in psychopragmatics. New York : St. Martin's Press, 2000.
*TC BF175.4.C84 M663 2000*

Noland, Richard W. Sigmund Freud revisited. New York : Twayne Publishers, c1999.
*TC BF109.F74 N65 1999*

Parsons, William Barclay, 1955- The enigma of the oceanic feeling. New York : Oxford University Press, 1999.

Petocz, Agnes. Freud, psychoanalysis, and symbolism. Cambridge ; New York : Cambridge University Press, 1999.
*TC BF109.F74 P48 1999*

Smith, David Livingstone, 1953- Freud's philosophy of the unconscious. Dordrecht : Boston : Kluwer, 1999.
*TC BF173.F85 S615 1999*

Stepansky, Paul E. Freud, surgery, and the surgeons. Hillsdale, NJ : Analytic Press, 1999.
*TC RC506 .S733 1999*

Wax, Murray Lionel, 1922- Western rationality and the angel of dreams. Lanham, Md. : Oxford : Rowman & Littlefield, c1999.
*TC BF1078 .W38 1999*

Weber, Samuel M. [Freud-Legende. English] The legend of Freud. Expanded ed. Stanford, Calif. : Stanford University Press, 2000, c1982.
*TC BF173.F85 W2813 2000*

Winter, Sarah. Freud and the institution of psychoanalytic knowledge. Stanford, Calif. : Stanford University Press, 1999.
*TC BF173 .W5485 1999*

**FREUD, SIGMUND, 1856-1939 - CONGRESSES.**
The Hartmann era. New York : Other Press, 2000.
*TC BF173 .B4675 2000*

**FREUD, SIGMUND, 1856-1939 - INFLUENCE.**
Caper, Robert. Immaterial facts. London ; New York : Routledge, 2000.
*TC BF173 .C35 2000*

**FREUD, SIGMUND, 1856-1939 - RELIGION.**
DiCenso, James, 1957- The other Freud. London ; New York : Routledge, 1999.
*TC BF175.4.R44 D53 1999*

**Freud, surgery, and the surgeons.**
Stepansky, Paul E. Hillsdale, NJ : Analytic Press, 1999.
*TC RC506 .S733 1999*

**Freudian analysts/feminist issues.**
Hughes, Judith M. New Haven [Conn.] : Yale University Press, c1999.
*TC BF175.4.F45 H84 1999*

**Freudian repression.**
Billig, Michael. New York : Cambridge University Press, 1999.
*TC BF175.5.R44 B55 1999*

**Freud's philosophy of the unconscious.**
Smith, David Livingstone, 1953- Dordrecht ; Boston : Kluwer, 1999.
*TC BF173.F85 S615 1999*

**Freund, Bill.** Insiders and outsiders : the Indian working class of Durban, 1910-1990 / Bill Freund. Portsmouth, NH : Heinemann, c1995. xv, 133 p. : ill. ; 23 cm. (Social history of Africa) Includes bibliographical references (p. 93-127) and index. ISBN 0-435-08959-5 (cloth) ISBN 0-435-08961-7 (pbk.) DDC 331.6/2154068455
*1. East Indians - Employment - South Africa - Durban - History. 2. Durban (South Africa) - Social conditions. 3. Durban (South Africa) - History. I. Title. II. Series.*
*TC HD8801.Z8 D8725 1995*

**Freundlich, Irwin, joint author.**
Friskin, James, 1886-1967. Music for the piano; New York, Dover Publications [1973]
*TC ML128.P3 F7 1973*

**Frey, James H.**
Nixon, Howard L., 1944- A sociology of sport. Belmont : Wadsworth Pub. Co., c1996.
*TC GV706.5 .N58 1996*

**FRICK, HENRY CLAY, 1849-1919.**
Sanger, Martha Frick Symington. Henry Clay Frick. 1st ed. New York : Abbeville Press Publishers, c1998.
*TC HC102.5.F75 S32 1998*

**Friedberg, Felix.** Caveat homo sapiens : the furtive mind / Felix Friedberg. Lanham, Md. ; Oxford : University Press of America, c2000. vi, 74 p. ; 23 cm. Includes bibliographical references. ISBN 0-7618-1681-X (cloth : alk. paper) DDC 150
*1. Psychology. I. Title.*
*TC BF41 .F75 2000*

**Friederici, Angela D.**
Learning. Berlin ; New York : Walter de Gruyter, 1999.
*TC QP408 .L44 1999*

**Friedman, Barbara, 1947-** Connecting generations : integrating aging education and intergenerational programs with elementary and middle grades curricula / Barbara M. Friedman ; foreword by Robert N. Butler. Boston : Allyn and Bacon, c1999. xxi, 212 p. : ill. ; 28 cm. Includes bibliographical references and index. "Annotated book list (books not cited within chapters)": p. 195-209. ISBN 0-205-27513-3 DDC 305.26/071
*1. Aging - Study and teaching (Elementary) - United States. 2. Intergenerational relations - Study and teaching (Elementary) - United States. 3. Children and adults - Study and teaching (Elementary) - United States. I. Title.*
*TC HQ1064.U5 F755 1999*

**Friedman, Howard S.**
Encyclopedia of mental health. San Diego : Academic Press, c1998.
*TC RA790.5 .E53 1998*

**Friedman, Myles I., 1924-** Handbook on effective instructional strategies : evidence for decision-making / Myles I. Friedman and Steven P. Fisher. Columbia, S.C. : The Institute for Evidence-Based Decision-Making in Education, 1998. xxv, 312 p. : ill. ; 27 cm. Includes bibliographical references and indexes. ISBN 0-9666588-0-9
*1. Instructional systems - United States - Evaluation. 2. Effective teaching - United States - Evaluation. I. Fisher, Steven P. II. Title.*
*TC LB1028.35 .F75 1998*

**Friedman, Reva C.**
Talents unfolding. 1st ed. Washington, DC : American Psychological Association, c2000.
*TC BF723.G5 T35 2000*

**Friend, Marilyn Penovich, 1953-** Interactions : collaboration skills for school professionals / Marilyn Friend, Lynne Cook. 3rd ed. New York : Longman, 1999. xviii, 318 p. : ill. ; 24 cm. Includes bibliographical references (p.297-310) and index. ISBN 0-8013-3065-3 (alk. paper) DDC 371.9
*1. Special education teachers - Training of. 2. Interpersonal relations. 3. Communication in education. I. Cook, Lynne. II. Title.*
*TC LC3969.45 .F75 1999*

**FRIENDLINESS. See FRIENDSHIP.**

**FRIENDLY VISITING. See SOCIAL CASE WORK.**

**FRIENDS. See QUAKERS.**

**Friends of the Gest Library.**
The East Asian library journal. Princeton, N.J. : Gest Library of Princeton University, c1994-
*TC Z733.G47 G46*

**FRIENDS (QUAKERS). See QUAKERS.**

**FRIENDSHIP. See also LOVE.**
Close relationships. Thousand Oaks, Calif. : Sage Publications, c2000.
*TC HM1106 .C55 2000*

**FRIENDSHIP - CROSS-CULTURAL STUDIES.**
The anthropology of friendship. Oxford ; New York : Berg, 1999.
*TC GN486.3 .A48 1999*

**FRIENDSHIP - FICTION.**
Graham, Bob, 1942- Crusher is coming!. New York, N.Y., U.S.A. : Puffin Books, 1990.
*TC PZ7.G751667 Cr 1990*

Hallensleben, Georg. Pauline. New York : Farrar, Straus & Giroux, c1999.
*TC PZ7.H15425 Pau 1999*

Jones, Jennifer B. Dear Mrs. Ryan, you're ruining my life. New York : Walker & Co., 2000.
*TC PZ7.J7203 De 2000*

McDonald, Megan. The night Iguana left home. 1st ed. New York : DK Ink, 1999.
*TC PZ7.M478419 Ni 1999*

Sharmat, Marjorie Weinman. The 329th friend. New York : Four Winds Press, c1979.
*TC PZ7.S5299 Tk 1979*

Vail, Rachel. If you only knew. 1st ed. New York : Scholastic, c1998.
*TC PZ7.V1916 If 1998*

Vail, Rachel. Please, please, please. New York : Scholastic, c1998.
*TC PZ7.V1916 Pl 1998*

**FRIENDSHIP - JUVENILE FICTION.**
Krumgold, Joseph, 1908- Onion John. New York, N.Y. : Thomas Y. Crowell Company, 1959.
*TC XFK942*

**Fries, Peter Howard.**
Lockwood, David G. Functional approaches to language, culture, and cognition. Amsterdam ; Philadelphia : J. Benjamins, c2000.
*TC P147 .L63 1998*

**FRIGHT. See FEAR.**

**Friskin, James, 1886-1967.** Music for the piano: a handbook of concert and teaching material from 1580 to 1952, by James Friskin and Irwin Freundlich. New York, Dover Publications [1973] ix, 434 p. 22 cm. "This Dover edition ... is an unabridged, slightly corrected republication of the work originally published as volume V of the series entitled The field of music, ... by Holt, Rinehart and Winston, Inc., in 1954. A new preface by Irwin Freundlich and a new biographical appendix have been added ... " ISBN 0-486-22918-1 DDC 016.7864/05
*1. Piano music - Bibliography. I. Freundlich, Irwin, joint author. II. Title.*
*TC ML128.P3 F7 1973*

**FROEBEL SYSTEM OF EDUCATION. See KINDERGARTEN.**

**From another angle :** children's strengths and school standards : the Prospect Center's descriptive review of the child / edited by Margaret Himley with Patricia F. Carini. New York : Teachers College Press, c2000. x, 230 p. : ill. ; 24 cm. (The Practitioner inquiry series) Includes bibliographical references (p. 219-223) and index. ISBN 0-8077-3931-6 (paper) ISBN 0-8077-3932-4 (cloth) DDC 371.8/09743/8
*1. Prospect School (North Bennington, Vt.) 2. Child development - Vermont - Bennington. 3. School children - Vermont - Bennington. 4. Schools - Standards - Vermont - Bennington. I. Himley, Margaret. II. Carini, Patricia F. III. Prospect Archives and Center for Education and Research. IV. Series.*
*TC LB1117 .F735 2000*

**From basketball to the Beatles.**
Mardell, Ben. Portsmouth, NH : Heinemann, 1999.
*TC LB1139.4 .M27 1999*

**From clinic to classroom.**
Radest, Howard B., 1928- Westport, Conn. ; London : Praeger, 2000.
*TC R725.5 .R33 2000*

**From cognition to being.**
McHenry, Henry Davis. Ottawa : University of Ottawa Press, c1999.
*TC LB1025.3 .M36 1999*

**From dawn to decadence.**
Barzun, Jacques, 1907- 1st ed. New York : HarperCollins, c2000.
*TC CB245 .B365 2000*

**From discipline to development.**
Dannells, Michael. Washington, DC : George Washington University, Graduate School of Education and Human Development, [1997]
*TC LB2344 .D36 1997*

**From Gutenberg to the global information infrastructure.**
Borgman, Christine L., 1951- Cambridge, Mass. : MIT Press, 2000.
*TC ZA3225 .B67 2000*

**From infancy to childhood.**
Smith, Richard Mason, 1881- Boston : Atlantic monthly press, [c1925]
*TC RJ61 .S675*

**From initial education to working life.**
Organisation for Economic Co-operation and Development (Paris) Paris : Organisation for Economic Co-operation and Development, 2000.
*TC LC1037 .O74 2000*

**From maestro to manager :** critical issues in arts and culture management / edited by Marian Fitzgibbon, Anne Kelly. Dublin : Oak Tree Press in association with the Graduate School of Business, University College Dublin, c1997. xii, 452 p. ; 24 cm. (Irish studies in management) Includes bibliographies and index. ISBN 1-86076-041-4 (pbk)
*1. Arts - Management - Europe. I. Fitzgibbon, Marian. II. Kelly, Anne. III. Series.*
*TC NX770.E85 F76 1997*

**From Mother Goose to Doctor Seuss.**
Darling, Harold. From Mother Goose to Dr. Seuss. San Francisco : Chronicle Books, c1999.
*TC Z270.G7 D37 1999*

**From Mother Goose to Dr. Seuss.**
Darling, Harold. San Francisco : Chronicle Books, c1999.
*TC Z270.G7 D37 1999*

**From mythic to linear.**
Nikolajeva, Maria. Lanham, Md. : Children's Literature Association : Scarecrow Press, 2000.
*TC PN1009.5.T55 N55 2000*

**From nihilism to possibility :** democratic transformations for the inner city / edited by Frederick Yeo, Barry Kanpol. Cresskill, N.J. : Hampton Press, c1999. vii, 215 p. ; 24 cm. (Understanding education and policy) Includes bibliographical references and indexes. ISBN 1-57273-212-1 (hbk.) ISBN 1-57273-213-X (pbk.) DDC 370/.9173/2
*1. Education, Urban - United States. 2. Critical pedagogy - United States. I. Yeo, Frederick L. II. Kanpol, Barry. III. Series.*
*TC LC5141 .F76 1999*

**From pathology to politics.**
Bennett, James T. New Brunswick [N.J.] (U.S.A.) : Transaction Publishers, c2000.
*TC RA445 .B45 2000*

**From Queen's College to National University :** essays on the academic history of QCG/UCG/NUI, Galway / Tadhg Foley, editor. Dublin, Ireland : Four Courts Press, c1999. xii, 440 p. : ill., ports. ; 26 cm. Includes bibliographical references and index. ISBN 1-85182-527-4
*1. University College, Galway - History. I. Foley, Tadhg. II. Title: Essays on the academic history of QCG/UCG/NUI, Galway*
*TC LF933 .F76 1999*

**From reading research to practice**
(v. 5) Biemiller, Andrew, 1939- Language and reading success. Cambridge, Mass. : Brookline Books, c1999.
*TC LB1139.L3 B48 1999*

**From testing to assessment :** English as an international language / edited by Clifford Hill and Kate Parry. London ; New York : Longman, 1994. viii, 283 p. : ill. ; 22 cm. (Applied linguistics and language study.) Includes bibliographical references (p. 272-278) and index. ISBN 0-582-21885-3 (pbk.) DDC 428/.0071
*1. English language - Study and teaching - Foreign speakers. 2. English language - Foreign countries. 3. Communication, International. I. Hill, Clifford. II. Parry, Kate. III. Series.*
*TC PE1128.A2 F778 1994*

**From the Emerald Isle to the promise land [videorecording].**
The Irish in America [videorecording]. [New York, N.Y.] : A&E Home Video ; New York, N.Y. : Distributed by the New Video Group, 1997.
*TC E184.16 I6 1997*

**From the eye of the storm :** higher education's changing institution / edited by Ben Jongbloed, Peter Maassen and Guy Neave. Dordrecht ; Boston ; London : Kluwer Academic Publishers, c1999. xvi, 316 p. : ill. ; 25 cm. Includes bibliographical references. ISBN 0-7923-6065-6 (alk. paper) DDC 378.4
*1. Education, Higher - Europe - Administration. 2. Educational change - Europe. I. Jongbloed, B. W. A. II. Maassen, Peter A. M. III. Neave, Guy R. IV. Centrum voor Studies van het Hoger Onderwijsbeleid (Enschede, Netherlands)*
*TC LB2341.8.E85 F76 1999*

**From the Free Academy to CUNY.**
Roff, Sandra Shoiock. New York : Fordham University Press, c2000.
*TC LD3835 .R64 2000*

**From whence cometh my help.**
Smith, Ethel Morgan, 1952- Columbia ; London : University of Missouri Press, c2000.
*TC F234.H65 S55 2000*

**FROMM, ERICH, 1900-.**
Funk, Rainer. Erich Fromm. New York : Continuum, 2000.
*TC BF109.F76 F8413 2000*

**Frontal lobe dysfunction in first episode Schizophrenia.**
Bell, Lisa M. 1998.
*TC 085 B3995*

**FRONTAL LOBES - DISEASES.**
Bell, Lisa M. Frontal lobe dysfunction in first episode Schizophrenia. 1998.
*TC 085 B3995*

**FRONTIER AND PIONEER LIFE. See OVERLAND JOURNEYS TO THE PACIFIC; RANCH LIFE.**

**FRONTIER AND PIONEER LIFE - FICTION.**
Thomas, Joyce Carol. I have heard of a land. 1st ed. [New York] : HarperCollins Publishers, c1998.
*TC PZ7.T36696 Iae 1998*

**FRONTIER AND PIONEER LIFE - HISTORY.** *See* FRONTIER AND PIONEER LIFE.

**FRONTIER AND PIONEER LIFE - IOWA.**
Gillespie, Sarah (Sarah L.) A pioneer farm girl. Mankato, Minn. : Blue Earth Books, c2000.
*TC F629.M28 G55 2000*

**FRONTIER AND PIONEER LIFE - WASHINGTON (STATE) - FICTION.**
Holm, Jennifer L. Our only May Amelia. 1st ed. New York : HarperCollinsPublishers, c1999.
*TC PZ7.H732226 Ou 1999*

**FRONTIER AND PIONEER LIFE - WEST (U.S.).**
Hester, Sallie. A covered wagon girl. Mankato, Minn. : Blue Earth Books, c2000.
*TC F593 .H47 2000*

**FRONTIER AND PIONEER LIFE - WEST (U.S.) - EXHIBITIONS.**
White, Richard, 1947- The frontier in American culture. Chicago : The Library ; Berkeley : University of California Press, c1994.
*TC F596 .W562 1994*

**FRONTIER AND PIONEER LIFE - WEST (U.S.) - JUVENILE LITERATURE.**
Hester, Sallie. A covered wagon girl. Mankato, Minn. : Blue Earth Books, c2000.
*TC F593 .H47 2000*

**FRONTIER CHILDREN.** *See* PIONEER CHILDREN.

**The frontier in American culture.**
White, Richard, 1947- Chicago : The Library ; Berkeley : University of California Press, c1994.
*TC F596 .W562 1994*

**Frontiers of democracy.** New York, Progressive Education Association, etc., 1934- v. 31 cm. Frequency: Monthly during the academic year. v. 1- Oct. 1934- . Title varies: Social frontier; a journal of educational criticism and reconstruction Oct. 1934-June 1939. Editors: Oct. 1934-June 1937, G.S. Counts and others.--Oct. 1937-June 1939, g.W. Hartmann and others.--Oct. 1939- W.H. Kilpatrick and others. Includes section "The teacher's bookshelf."
*1. Socialism - Periodicals. 2. Sociology - Periodicals. 3. Education - Periodicals. I. Counts, George Sylvester, 1889- ed. II. Hartmann, George W. (George Wilfried), 1904-1955 ed. III. Kilpatrick, William Heard, 1871-1965. ed. IV. Progressive Education Association. V. Title: Teacher's bookshelf.*

**Frontiers of developmental psychopathology** / edited by Mark F. Lenzenweger, Jeffrey J. Haugaard. New York : Oxford University Press, 1996. viii, 241 p. : ill. ; 25 cm. Includes bibliographical references and index. ISBN 0-19-509001-2 (alk. paper) DDC 616.89/071
*1. Mental illness - Etiology. 2. Developmental psychology. 3. Mental Disorders. 4. Models, Psychological. I. Lenzenweger, Mark F. II. Haugaard, Jeffrey J., 1951-*
*TC RC454.4 .F76 1996*

**Frontiers of industrial and organizational psychology**
Multilevel theory, research, and methods in organizations. 1st ed. San Francisco : Jossey-Bass, c2000.
*TC HF5548.8 .M815 2000*

**Frontiers of international education**
Education as a humanitarian response. London ; Herndon, VA : Cassell ; [s.l.] : UNESCO International Bureau of Education, 1998.
*TC LC3719 .E37 1998*

**Frosch, Mary.**
Coming of age in America. New York : New Press : Distributed by W.W. Norton, c1994.
*TC PS509.M5 C66 1994*

**Frosh, Stephen.** The politics of psychoanalysis : an introduction to Freudian and post-Freudian theory / Stephen Frosh. 2nd ed. New York : New York University Press, 1999. xii, 336 p. ; 23 cm. Includes bibliographical references (p. 318-324) and index. ISBN 0-8147-2699-2 (cloth : alk. paper) ISBN 0-8147-2700-X (pbk. : alk. paper) DDC 150.19/5
*1. Psychoanalysis. 2. Social sciences and psychoanalysis. 3. Women and psychoanalysis. I. Title.*
*TC BF173 .F92 1999*

**Froyen, Len A.**
**Classroom management.**
Froyen, Len A. Schoolwide and classroom management. 3rd ed. Upper Saddle River, N.J. : Merrill, c1999.
*TC LB3013 .F783 1999*

Schoolwide and classroom management : the reflective educator-leader / Len A. Froyen, Annette M. Iverson. 3rd ed. Upper Saddle River, N.J. : Merrill, c1999. xix, 395 p. : ill. ; 24 cm. Rev. ed. of: Classroom management. c1988. Includes bibliographical references and

indexes. ISBN 0-13-573205-0 DDC 371.102/4
*1. Classroom management. I. Iverson, Annette M., 1950- II. Froyen, Len A. Classroom management. III. Title.*
*TC LB3013 .F783 1999*

**FROZEN STARS.** *See* BLACK HOLES (ASTRONOMY).

**Fry, Edward Bernard, 1925-** The reading teacher's book of lists / Edward Bernard Fry, Jacqueline E. Kress, Dona Lee Fountoukidis. 3rd ed. Englewood Cliffs, NJ : Prentice Hall, c1993. xvi, 391 p. : ill. ; 28 cm. Includes bibliographical references and index. ISBN 0-13-762014-4 ISBN 0-13-034893-7 DDC 428.4
*1. Reading - Miscellanea. 2. Curriculum planning - Miscellanea. 3. Tutors and tutoring - Miscellanea. 4. Handbooks, vade-mecums, etc. I. Kress, Jacqueline E. II. Fountoukidis, Dona, 1938- III. Title. IV. Title: Book of lists.*
*TC LB1050.2 .F79 1993*

The reading teacher's book of lists / Edward Bernard Fry, Jacqueline E. Kress, Dona Lee Fountoukidis. 4th ed. Paramus, N.J. : Prentice Hall, c2000. xv, 464 p. : ill. ; 28 cm. Includes bibliographical references and index. ISBN 0-13-028185-9 (pbk.) ISBN 0-13-088406-5 (spiral wire) DDC 428.4
*1. Reading - Miscellanea. 2. Curriculum planning - Miscellanea. 3. Tutors and tutoring - Miscellanea. 4. Handbooks, vade-mecums, etc. I. Kress, Jacqueline E. II. Fountoukidis, Dona, 1938- III. Title. IV. Title: Book of lists*
*TC LB1050.2 .F79 2000*

**Fry, Heather.**
A handbook for teaching and learning in higher education. London : Kogan Page, 1999.
*TC LB2331 .H29 1999*

**Fry, Roger Eliot, 1866-1934.** Art and the market : Roger Fry on commerce in art / selected writings, edited and with an interpretation by Craufurd D. Goodwin. Ann Arbor, Mich. : University of Michigan Press, 1999. xii, 222 p. : ill. ; 24 cm. Includes bibliographical references and index. ISBN 0-472-10902-2 (cloth : alk. paper) DDC 701/.03
*1. Art - Marketing. 2. Fry, Roger Eliot, - 1866-1934. I. Goodwin, Craufurd D. W. II. Title.*
*TC N8600 .F78 1999*

**FRY, ROGER ELIOT, 1866-1934.**
Fry, Roger Eliot, 1866-1934. Art and the market. Ann Arbor, Mich. : University of Michigan Press, 1999.
*TC N8600 .F78 1999*

**Frye, L. Thomas.**
Ideas and images. Walnut Creek, CA : AltaMira Press, 1997.
*TC E172 .I34 1997*

**Fu, Freddie H.**
Proprioception and neuromuscular control in joint stability. [Champaign, IL] : Human Kinetics, c2000.
*TC QP454 .P77 2000*

**Fuchs, Bernie, ill.**
Bodkin, Odds. Ghost of the Southern Belle. 1st ed. Boston : Little, Brown, 1999.
*TC PZ7.B6355 Gh 1999*

**Fuchshuber, Annegert.**
**[Karlinchen. English]**
Carly / Annegert Fuchshuber ; translated by Florence Howe and Heidi Kirk. 1st ed. New York : The Feminist Press, c1997. 1 v. (unpaged) : col. ill. ; 27 cm. SUMMARY: A homeless girl wanders the land searching for food and shelter, but no one will help her until she meets a Fool, who is kinder than all the others. ISBN 1-55861-177-0 (alk. paper) DDC [E]
*1. Homeless persons - Fiction. 2. Prejudices - Fiction. 3. Kindness - Fiction. I. Howe, Florence. II. Kirk, Heidi. III. Title.*
*TC PZ7.F94 Car 1997*

**FUGITIVE SLAVES IN LITERATURE.**
Mensh, Elaine, 1924- Black, white, and Huckleberry Finn. Tuscaloosa : University of Alabama Press, c2000.
*TC PS1305 .M46 2000*

**Fuglei, Kate.**
Paris [videorecording]. New York, NY : V.I.E.W. Video, c1996.
*TC DC707 .P3 1996*

**FUGUE (PSYCHOLOGY) - CASE STUDIES.**
Hacking, Ian. Mad travelers. Charlottesville, Va. : University Press of Virginia, 1998.
*TC RC553.F83 H33 1998*

**Fuhrer, Ronald.** Israeli painting / Ronald Fuhrer. Woodstock, N.Y. : Overlook Press in association with Ronald Lauder, 1998. 260 p. : col. ill. ; 30 cm. "The elephant's eye book." Includes bibliographical references (p. 256-258) and index. ISBN 0-87951-822-7 DDC 759.95694
*1. Painting, Israeli - Themes, motives. 2. Painting, Israeli -*

Foreign influences. 3. Painting, Modern - 20th century - Israel - Themes, motives. I. Title.
*TC ND977 .F85 1998*

**Fuke, Richard Paul, 1940-** Imperfect equality : African Americans and the confines of white racial attitudes in post-emancipation Maryland / Richard Paul Fuke. New York : Fordham University Press, 1999. xxv, 307 p. : ill. ; 24 cm. (Reconstructing America ; no. 2) Includes bibliographical references (p. [253]-294) and index. ISBN 0-8232-1962-3 (hardcover) ISBN 0-8232-1963-1 (pbk.) DDC 305.896/0730752
*1. Afro-Americans - Civil rights - Maryland - History - 19th century. 2. Freedmen - Maryland - History. 3. Whites - Maryland - Attitudes - History - 19th century. 4. Reconstruction - Maryland. 5. Maryland - Race relations. I. Title. II. Series: Reconstructing America (Series) ; no. 2.*
*TC E185.93.M2 F85 1999*

**Fukuyama, Mary A.** Integrating spirituality into multicultural counseling / Mary A. Fukuyama, Todd D. Sevig. Thousand Oaks, Calif. : Sage Publications, c1999. xvii, 182 p. : ill. ; 23 cm. (Multicultural aspects of counseling series ; 13) Includes bibliographical references and index. ISBN 0-7619-1583-4 ISBN 0-7619-1584-2 DDC 158/.3
*1. Cross-cultural counseling. 2. Spirituality. 3. Pluralism (Social sciences) - Religious aspects. 4. Transpersonal psychology. 5. Religion and culture. I. Sevig, Todd D. II. Title. III. Series: Multicultural aspects of counseling series ; v. 13.*
*TC BF637.C6 F795 1999*

**FULFILLMENT (ETHICS).** *See* SELF-REALIZATION.

**The full belly bowl.**
Aylesworth, Jim. 1st ed. New York : Atheneum Books for Young Readers, c1998.
*TC PZ8.A95 Fu 1998*

**FULL-DAY KINDERGARTEN - UNITED STATES.**
Morrow, Lesley Mandel. Literacy instruction in half- and whole-day kindergarten. Newark, Del. : International Reading Association ; Chicago, Ill. : National Reading Conference, c1998.
*TC LB1181.2 .M67 1998*

**FULL EMPLOYMENT POLICIES.** *See* JOB CREATION; UNEMPLOYMENT.

**FULL EMPLOYMENT POLICIES - UNITED STATES.**
Job creation. Washington, DC : Joint Center for Political and Economic Studies ; Lanham, Md. : Oxford : University Press of America, c1998.
*TC HD8081.A65 J63 1998*

**The full-time faculty handbook** / edited by Virginia Bianco-Mathis, Neal Chalofsky. Thousand Oaks : Sage Publications, c1999. xv, 229 p. : ill. ; 24 cm. Includes bibliographical references and index. CONTENTS: Administration and management / Nyla Carney and Teresa Long -- Teaching and learning / James J. Fletcher and Sondra K. Patrick -- Student advising / Rosemarie Bosler and Sharon L. Levin -- Academic research / Sharon Ahern Fechter -- University service / William J. A. Marshall -- Professional service / Karen L. Medsker -- Professional development and advancement / Rhonda J. Malone -- New learning approaches / Sharon Johnson Confessore -- Technology / Theodore E. Stone -- Diversity in higher education / Mary Hartwood Futrell and Walter A. Brown. ISBN 0-7619-1222-3 (cloth : acid-free paper) ISBN 0-7619-1223-1 (pbk. : acid-free paper) DDC 378.1/2
*1. Universities and colleges - United States - Faculty. 2. College teachers - United States - Social conditions. 3. College teaching - Vocational guidance - United States. 4. Education, Higher - United States. I. Bianco-Mathis, Virginia. II. Chalofsky, Neal, 1945-*
*TC LB1778.2 .F85 1999*

**Fuller, Kenneth G.**
Upton, Clifford Brewster. 1877- American Arithmetic. 2nd ed. New York, N.Y. : American Book Company, 1963.
*TC QA103 .U67 1963*

**Fullilove, Mindy Thompson.** The house of Joshua : meditations on family and place / Mindy Thompson Fullilove. Lincoln, NE : University of Nebraska Press, c1999. xv, 160 p. : ill. ; 25 cm. (Texts and contexts) Includes bibliographical references (p. [155]-160). ISBN 0-8032-2007-3 (hardcover) DDC 155.9/092
*1. Environmental psychology. 2. Home - Psychological aspects. 3. Public spaces - Psychological aspects. 4. Family - Psychological aspects. 5. Afro-Americans - Psychology. I. Title. II. Series: Texts and contexts (Unnumbered)*
*TC BF353 .F85 1999*

**Fully exposed.**
Cooper, Emmanuel. 2nd ed. London ; New York : Routledge, c1995.
*TC TR674 .C66 1995*

**Fun with english.**
Ramírez de Mellor, Elva Mexico : McGraw-Hill
c1987
*TC PE1129.S8 .R35 1987*

**FUNCTIONAL ANALYSIS (LINGUISTICS).** *See*
FUNCTIONALISM (LINGUISTICS).

**Functional analysis of problem behavior :** from
effective assessment to effective support / [edited by]
Alan C. Repp, Robert H. Horner. Belmont, CA :
Wadsworth Pub. Co., c1999. xvi, 416 p. : ill. ; 23 cm. (The
Wadsworth special educator series) Includes bibliographic
references and index. ISBN 0-534-34850-5 (pbk.) DDC 371.92
*1. Behavior assessment. 2. Handicapped - Functional
assessment. 3. Behavior disorders in children - Diagnosis. I.
Repp, Alan C. II. Horner, Robert H. III. Series.*
*TC RC473.B43 F85 1999*

**Functional approaches to language, culture, and
cognition.**
Lockwood, David G. Amsterdam ; Philadelphia : J.
Benjamins, c2000.
*TC P147 .L63 1998*

**Functional categories, argument structure and
parametric variation** / edited by Rhys, C.S., Adger,
D., von Klopp, A. Edinburgh : Centre for Cognitive
Study, University of Edinburgh, c1994. viii, 179 p. : ill. ;
30 cm. (Edinburgh working papers in cognitive science ; v. 9)
"Research in the Principles and Parameters framework that was
presented at the Workshop on Parametric Variation and
Grammar Specification at the Centre for Cognitive Science in
1992."--Pref. Includes bibliographical references.
*1. Grammar, Comparative and general - Grammatical
catagories. 2. Functionalism (Linguistics) 3. Language and
languages - Variation. 4. Principles and parameters
(Linguistics) 5. Generative grammar. I. Rhys, C. S. II. Adger,
D. III. Von Klopp, A. IV. University of Edinburgh. Centre for
Cognitive Science. V. Workshop on Parametric Variation and
Grammar Specification (1992 : Edinburgh, Scotland) VI.
Series.*
*TC P151 .F86 1994*

**FUNCTIONAL FOODS.**
DeFelice, Stephen L., 1936- The carnitine defense.
[Emmaus, Pa.] : Rodale Press ; [New York] :
Distributed to the book trade by St. Martin's Press,
c1999.
*TC RC685.C6 D4235 1999*

**FUNCTIONAL ILLITERACY.** *See* FUNCTIONAL
LITERACY.

**FUNCTIONAL LINGUISTICS.** *See*
FUNCTIONALISM (LINGUISTICS).

**FUNCTIONAL LITERACY.** *See also*
WORKPLACE LITERACY.
The future of literacy in a changing world. Rev. ed.
Cresskill, N.J. : Hampton Press, c1998.
*TC LC149 .F87 1998*

Rassool, Naz, 1949- Literacy for sustainable
development in the age of information. Clevedon
[England] ; Philadelphia : Multilingual Matters,
c1999.
*TC LC149 .R37 1999*

**FUNCTIONAL LITERACY - EL SALVADOR -
CASE STUDIES.**
Purcell-Gates, Victoria. Now we read, we see, we
speak. Mahwah, N.J. : L. Erlbaum Associates,
Publishers, 2000.
*TC LC155.S22 P87 2000*

**FUNCTIONAL LITERACY - STATISTICS.**
International Adult Literacy Survey. Literacy in the
information age. Paris : Organisation for Economic
Co-operation and Development; Ottawa : Statistics
Canada, 2000.
*TC LC149 .L59 2000*

**FUNCTIONAL-STRUCTURAL ANALYSIS
(LINGUISTICS).** *See* FUNCTIONALISM
(LINGUISTICS).

**FUNCTIONALISM (LINGUISTICS).**
Functional categories, argument structure and
parametric variation. Edinburgh : Centre for Cognitive
Study, University of Edinburgh, c1994.
*TC P151 .F86 1994*

Lockwood, David G. Functional approaches to
language, culture, and cognition. Amsterdam ;
Philadelphia : J. Benjamins, c2000.
*TC P147 .L63 1998*

Researching language in schools and communities.
London ; Washington [D.C.] : Cassell, 2000.
*TC P53 .R463 2000*

**FUNCTIONS.** *See* CALCULUS.

**Functions of painting.**
Léger, Fernand, 1881-1955. [Fonctions de la peinture.
English] New York, Viking Press [1973]
*TC N70 .L45213 1973*

**FUNCTIONS OF REAL VARIABLES.**
Stahl, Saul. Real analysis. New York : J. Wiley,
c1999.
*TC QA300 .S882 1999*

**Fund for Adult Education (U.S.).**
Learning for living series. [Toronto]

**FUND RAISERS (PERSONS).** *See* FUND RAISING.

**FUND RAISING.** *See* EDUCATIONAL FUND
RAISING.

**FUND RAISING - LAW AND LEGISLATION -
UNITED STATES.**
Seltzer, Michael, 1947- Securing your organization's
future. New York, N.Y. : Foundation Center, 1987.
*TC HV41.9.U5 S45 1987*

**FUND RAISING - UNITED STATES.**
Mixer, Joseph R., 1923- Principles of professional
fundraising. 1st ed. San Francisco : Jossey-Bass,
c1993.
*TC HV41.9.U5 M58 1993*

Prince, Russ Alan, 1958- The seven faces of
philanthropy. 1st ed. San Francisco : Jossey-Bass,
c1994.
*TC HV41.9.U5 P74 1994*

Seltzer, Michael, 1947- Securing your organization's
future. New York, N.Y. : Foundation Center, 1987.
*TC HV41.9.U5 S45 1987*

Shaw, Sondra C., 1936- Reinventing fundraising. 1st
ed. San Francisco : Jossey-Bass Publishers, c1995.
*TC HV41.9.U5 S53 1995*

**FUND RAISING - UNITED STATES -
DIRECTORIES.**
Directory of grants for organizations serving people
with disabilities. Loxahatchee, Fla. : Research Grant
Guides, c1993-
*TC HV3006.A4 H35*

**FUND RAISING - UNITED STATES - HISTORY.**
Oliver, Frank H. Fellow beggars. 1999.
*TC 06 no.11157*

**Fundacion Dr. Antonio Esteve. Symposium (7th :
1996 : Sitges, Spain)** The clinical pharmacology of
sport and exercise : proceedings of the Esteve
Foundation Symposium VII, Sitges, Spain, 2-5
October 1996 / editors, Thomas Reilly and Michael
Orme. Amsterdam ; New York : Elsevier Science
B.V., Excerpta Medica, 1997. xv, 308 p. : ill. ; 25 cm.
(International congress series ; no. 1125) Includes
bibliographical references and indexes. ISBN 0-444-82454-5
(alk. paper) DDC 362.29/088/796
*1. Doping in sports - Congresses. 2. Exercise - Physiological
aspects - Congresses. 3. Doping in Sports - congresses. 4.
Sports Medicine - congresses. 5. Food, Fortified - congresses.
6. Sports - physiology - congresses. I. Reilly, Thomas, 1941- II.
Orme, Michael, 1940- III. Title. IV. Series.*
*TC RC1230 .F86 1996*

**Fundamental and adult education.**
Fundamental education. [Paris, France : Unesco,
1949-1952].

**Fundamental and adult education.** [Paris : Unesco,
1952-1960] 9 v. : ill. ; 25 cm. Frequency: Quarterly. Vol. 4,
no. 3 (July 1952)-v. 12, no. 4 (1960). Title from cover.
Continues: Fundamental education (DLC)sn 89038694
(OCoLC)5320097. Continued by: International journal of adult
and youth education (DLC)sn 89038693 (OCoLC)8867065.
*1. Education - Periodicals. 2. Adult education - Periodicals. 3.
Fundamental education - Periodicals. I. Unesco. II. Title:
Fundamental education III. Title: International journal of
adult and youth education*

**FUNDAMENTAL EDUCATION.** *See also*
COMPETENCY BASED EDUCATION.
Fundamental and adult education. [Paris : Unesco,
1952-1960]

**FUNDAMENTAL EDUCATION.**
The future of literacy in a changing world. Rev. ed.
Cresskill, N.J. : Hampton Press, c1998.
*TC LC149 .F87 1998*

**Fundamental education :** a quarterly bulletin. [Paris,
France : Unesco, 1949-1952]. 4 v. : ill. ; 25 cm.
Frequency: Quarterly. Vol. 1, no. 4 (Oct. 1949)-v. 4, no. 2
(Apr. 1952). Vol. 3 (1951)-v. 4 (1952), in Fundamental and
adult education, v. 5. Continues: Quarterly bulletin of
fundamental education (OCoLC)9022908. Continued by:
Fundamental and adult education (DLC)sn 89038692

(OCLC)8867086.
*1. Education - Periodicals. 2. Fundamental education -
Periodicals. I. Unesco. II. Title: Quarterly bulletin of
fundamental education III. Title: Fundamental and adult
education*

**FUNDAMENTAL EDUCATION - PERIODICALS.**
Fundamental and adult education. [Paris : Unesco,
1952-1960]

Fundamental education. [Paris, France : Unesco,
1949-1952].

**Fundamental motor skills & movement activities for
young children.**
Landy, Joanne M. Ready-to-use fundamental motor
skills & movement activities for young children. West
Nyack, NY : Center for Applied Research in
Education, c1999.
*TC GV452 .L355 1999*

**FUNDAMENTAL RIGHTS.** *See* CIVIL RIGHTS.

**FUNDAMENTALISM.** *See* EVANGELICALISM.

**FUNDAMENTALISM - POLITICAL ASPECTS -
UNITED STATES.**
New school order [videorecording]. New York : First
Run/Icarus Films, 1996.
*TC LB2831.583.P4 N4 1996*

**FUNDAMENTALISMS, RELIGIOUS.** *See*
RELIGIOUS FUNDAMENTALISM.

**FUNDAMENTALIST MOVEMENTS, RELIGIOUS.**
*See* RELIGIOUS FUNDAMENTALISM.

**Fundamentals of early childhood education.**
Morrison, George S. 2nd ed. Upper Saddle River,
N.J. : Merrill, c2000.
*TC LB1139.25 .M67 2000*

**Fundamentals of educational planning**
(61.) Bray, Mark. The shadow education system :.
Paris : Unesco, International Institute for
Educational Planning, 1999.
*TC LC41 .B73 1999*

(62) Abu-Duhou, Ibtisam. School-based
management. Paris : International Institute for
Educational Planning (IIEP); Paris : Unesco, 1999.
*TC LB5 .F85 1999*

(63) Carnoy, Martin. Globalization and educational
reform. Paris : International Institute for
Educational Planning (IIEP), 1999.
*TC LB5 .F85 v.63*

(64) Welsh, Thomas. Decentralization of education.
Paris : International Institute for Educational
Planning (IIEP); Paris : UNESCO, 1999.
*TC LB5 .F85 v.64*

**Funding public schools.**
Wong, Kenneth K., 1955- Lawrence : University
Press of Kansas, c1999.
*TC LB2825 .W56 1999*

**FUNDRAISING.** *See* FUND RAISING.

**FUNDS, SCHOLARSHIP.** *See* SCHOLARSHIPS.

**FUNGI.** *See* MUSHROOMS.

**FUNGI-BACTERIA RELATIONSHIPS.** *See*
BACTERIA.

**FUNGI - CONTROL.**
Strang, Thomas J. K. Controlling museum fungal
problems. Ottawa : Canadian Conservation Institute,
Department of Communications, [1991]
*TC TH9031 .S75 1991*

**Funk, Rainer.** Erich Fromm : his life and ideas : an
illustrated biography / Rainer Funk ; translated by Ian
Portman. New York : Continuum, 2000. 175 p. : ill. ; 29
cm. Includes bibliographical references (p. 166-168) and index.
ISBN 0-8264-1224-6 (hardcover) DDC 150.19/57/092
*1. Fromm, Erich, - 1900- 2. Psychoanalysts - United States -
Biography. I. Title.*
*TC BF109.F76 F8413 2000*

**Funk, Sandra G.**
Key aspects of comfort. New York : Springer Pub.
Co., c1989.
*TC RT87.P35 K48 1989*

**Funnell, Elaine.**
Case studies in the neuropsychology of reading. Hove,
East Sussex : Psychology Press, c2000.
*TC RC394.W6 .C37 2000*

**FUNNIES.** *See* COMIC BOOKS, STRIPS, ETC.

**Furlong, William, 1944-.**
The dynamics of now. London : Wimbledon School of
Art in association with Tate, c2000.

**TC N185 .D96 2000**

**Furman, Wyndol.**
The development of romantic relationships in adolescence. Cambridge, U.K. : New York : Cambridge University Press, 1999.
**TC BF724.3.L68 D48 1999**

**Furneaux, Barbara.** The special child.
Harmondsworth : Penguin, 1969. 208 p. ; 19 cm. (Penguin education special) (Penguin education.) Includes bibliographical references (p. [205]-208). ISBN 0-14-080092-1 DDC 371.9
*1. Mentally handicapped children - Education. I. Title.*
**TC LC4661 .F87**

**FURNITURE.** *See also* **SCHOOLS - FURNITURE, EQUIPMENT, ETC.**
1 to 10 and back again. Los Angeles : J. Paul Getty Museum, c1999.
**TC QA113 .A14 1998**

**FURNITURE - FRANCE - JUVENILE LITERATURE.**
1 to 10 and back again. Los Angeles : J. Paul Getty Museum, c1999.
**TC QA113 .A14 1998**

**FUSION WEAPONS.** *See* **NUCLEAR WEAPONS.**

**Futrell, Mynga K.**
Geisert, Paul. Teachers, computers, and curriculum. 3rd ed. Boston : Allyn and Bacon, c2000.
**TC LB1028.5 .G42 2000**

**Future basics :** developing numerical power / Randall Charles, Joanne Lobato. Golden, Colo. : National Council of Supervisors of Mathematics, c1998. 43 p. : ill. ; 28 cm. (Monograph of the National Council of Supervisors of Mathematics) Developing numerical power. Cover title. Includes bibliographical references (p. 42-43)
*1. Mathematics - Study and teaching. 2. Numeration - Study and teaching. I. Lobato, Joanne (Joanne Elizabeth) II. Title. III. Title: Developing numerical power IV. Series.*
**TC QA141 .C43 1998**

**The future of education from 14+**
Apprenticeship. London : Kogan Page, c1999.
**TC HD4885.G7 A67 1999**

Hayton, Annette. Tackling disaffection and social exclusion. London : Kogan Page, 1999.
**TC LC93.G7 H39 1999**

**The future of food.**
Ford, Brian J. (Brian John), 1939- London : Thames & Hudson, c2000.
**TC RA601 .F65 2000**

**The future of literacy in a changing world** / edited by Daniel A. Wagner. Rev. ed. Cresskill, N.J. : Hampton Press, c1998. xxx, 417 p. ; 23 cm. (Series on literacy) Includes bibliographical references and indexes. ISBN 1-57273-082-X (cloth) ISBN 1-57273-083-8 (pbk.) DDC 302.2/244
*1. Literacy. 2. Functional literacy. 3. Fundamental education. 4. Comparative education. I. Wagner, Daniel A., 1946- II. Series.*
**TC LC149 .F87 1998**

**Future organizational design.**
Groth, Lars. Chichester ; New York : Wiley, c1999.
**TC HD30.2 .G76 1999**

**G. Schirmer's editions of oratorios and cantatas**
Mendelssohn-Bartholdy, Felix, 1809-1847. [Paulus. Vocal score. English] Saint Paul; New York, G. Schirmer [19--]
**TC M2003.M53 S35**

**Gabaccia, Donna R., 1949-** We are what we eat : ethnic food and the making of Americans / Donna R. Gabaccia ; [illustrations by Susan Keller]. Cambridge, Mass. : Harvard University Press, 1998. 278 p. : ill. ; 24 cm. Includes bibliographical references (p. [243]-267) and index. ISBN 0-674-94860-2 DDC 394.1/2/0973
*1. Food habits - United States. 2. Ethnic food industry - United States. 3. Ethnic attitudes - United States. 4. United States - Social life and customs. I. Title.*
**TC GT2853.U5 G33 1998**

**Gabbard, David.**
Knowledge and power in the global economy. Mahwah, N.J. : L. Erlbaum Associates, 2000.
**TC LC66 .K66 2000**

**Gaberson, Kathleen B.** Clinical teaching strategies in nursing / Kathleen B. Gaberson, Marilyn H. Oermann. New York : Springer, c1999. xi, 241 p. : ill., forms ; 24 cm. (Springer series on the teaching of nursing) Includes bibliographical references and index. ISBN 0-8261-1278-1 (hardcover) DDC 610.73/071
*1. Nursing - Study and teaching. 2. Education, Nursing. 3.*

Teaching - methods. I. Oermann. Marilyn H. II. Title. III. Series.
**TC RT73 .G26 1999**

**GAD (GENDER AND DEVELOPMENT).** *See* **WOMEN IN DEVELOPMENT.**

**Gaddy, Barbara B., 1953-.**
Marzano, Robert J. Essential knowledge. Aurora, Colo. : McREL, 1999.
**TC LB3060.83 .M36 1999**

**Gade, Rune, 1964-.**
Symbolic imprints. Aarhus : Aarhus University Press, c1999.
**TC TR145 .S96 1999**

**Gadfly <Oct. 1964-Apr. 1968>.**
The classroom teacher. Berkeley, Calif., Berkeley Federation of Teachers Local 1078.

**Gaffney, Janet S.**
Stirring the waters. Portsmouth, NH : Heinemann, c1999.
**TC LB1139.5.L35 S85 1999**

**Gafner, George, 1947-** Handbook of hypnotic inductions / George Gafner, Sonja Benson. New York : W. W. Norton, 2000. x, 177 p. ; 25 cm. "A Norton professional book." Includes bibliographical references and index. ISBN 0-393-70324-X DDC 615.8/512
*1. Hypnotism - Therapeutic use - Handbooks, manuals. etc. I. Benson, Sonja, 1968- II. Title.*
**TC RC495 .G27 2000**

**Gage, John.**
Weiss, Jeffrey. Mark Rothko. Washington : National Gallery of Art ; New Haven, Conn. : Yale University Press, c1998.
**TC N6537.R63 A4 1998**

**Gager, Kristin Elizabeth.** Blood ties and fictive ties : adoption and family life in early modern France / Kristin Elizabeth Gager. Princeton, N.J. : Princeton University Press, c1996. 197 p. ; 25 cm. Includes bibliographical references (p. [173]-190) and index. ISBN 0-691-02984-9 (cl. : alk. paper) DDC 362.7/34/0944
*1. Adoption - France - History. 2. Adopted children - France - History. 3. Family - France - History. I. Title.*
**TC HV875.58.F8 G34 1996**

**GAIA HYPOTHESIS.**
Fate of the earth [videorecording]. [New York, N.Y.?] : Unapix Entertainment, Inc. [distributor], c1996.
**TC QB631.2 .F3 1996**

**Gaimster, David R. M.**
Pottery in the making. Washington, D.C. : Smithsonian Institution Press, c1997.
**TC NK3780 .P68 1997**

**Gaither, Gerald H.**
Promising practices in recruitment, remediation, and retention. San Francisco, Calif. : Jossey-Bass, c1999.
**TC LB2331.72 .N48 1999**

**Galarza, Sheri Lyn.**
Entz, Susan. Picture this. Thousand Oaks, Calif. : Corwin Press, c2000.
**TC LB1043.67 .E58 2000**

**GALAXIES.** *See* **STARS.**

**Galaxy series**
Phillips, James B. Accent. Glenview, Ill. : Scott, Foresman, 1972.
**TC PE1121 .P54 1972**

**Gale, Fredric G., 1933-.**
Ethical issues in college writing. New York ; Canterbury [England] : Peter Lang, c1999.
**TC PE1404 .E84 1999**

(Re)visioning composition textbooks. Albany : State University of New York Press, c1999.
**TC PE1404 .R46 1999**

**Gale Group.**
Educational rankings annual. Detroit, MI : Gale Research, c1991-
**TC LB2331.63 .E34**

Junior edition [computer file] [Farmington Hills, Mi.] : The Gale Group, c1999. Computer data.

Kids edition [computer file] [Farmington Hills, Mi.] : The Gale Group, c1999. Computer data.

**Gale Research Inc.**
American education annual. Detroit : Gale, c1999-
**TC LB1028.25.U6 A44**

**Gale, Xin Liu, 1952-.**
(Re)visioning composition textbooks. Albany : State University of New York Press, c1999.

**TC PE1404 .R46 1999**

**Galinsky, Maeda J.**
Support groups. New York : Haworth Press, c1995.
**TC HV45 .S896 1995**

**Gallagher, Donald R., 1929-.**
Bagin, Don, 1938- The school and community relations. 7th ed. Boston ; London : Allyn and Bacon, c2001.
**TC LC221 .G35 2001**

**Gallagher, Karen S.** Shaping school policy : guide to choices, politics, and community relations / Karen S. Gallagher. Newbury Park, Calif. : Corwin Press, c1992. xiii, 97 p. : ill. ; 22 cm. (Successful schools ; v. 2) Includes bibliographical references. ISBN 0-8039-6022-0 (pbk.) DDC 379.1/54/0973
*1. Education and state - United States. 2. School boards - United States. 3. School administrators - United States. I. Title. II. Series.*
**TC LC89 .G35 1992**

**Gallagher, S. Saelig, ill.**
Conrad, Pam. Blue willow. New York : Philomel Books, c1999.
**TC PZ7.C76476 Bl 1999**

**Gallagher, Trish.** Arousal patterns, emotion identification, and cognitive style in depressed and nondepressed inner-city adolescent Latinas / Trish Gallagher. 1997. x, 183 leaves ; 29 cm. Issued also on microfilm. Includes tables. Thesis (Ph.D.)--Columbia University, 1997. Includes bibliographical references (leaves 117-132).
*1. Emotions in adolescence - United States. 2. Cognitive styles - United States. 3. Inner cities - United States. 4. Hispanic American teenagers - United States - Psychology. 5. Depression in adolescence - United States. 6. Psychiatric rating scales - United States. I. Title.*
**TC 085 G136**

**Galland, Leo.** The four pillars of healing : how the new integrated medicine-- the best of conventional and alternative approaches-- can cure you / Leo Galland. 1st ed. New York : Random House, c1997. xix, 330 p. ; 24 cm. Includes bibliographical references (p. [269]-321) and index. ISBN 0-679-44888-8 DDC 610
*1. Holistic medicine. 2. Medicine - Philosophy. I. Title.*
**TC R733 .G35 1997**

**Gallati, Barbara Dayer.**
Ferber, Linda S. Masters of color and light. Washington : Brooklyn Museum of Art in Association with Smithsonian Institution Press, c1998.
**TC ND1807 .F47 1998**

**Gallaway, Lowell E. (Lowell Eugene), 1930-.**
Vedder, Richard K. Out of work. New York : Holmes & Meier, 1993.
**TC HD7096.U5 V43 1993**

**GALLERIES, ART.** *See* **ART MUSEUMS.**

**Galliher, John F.**
Keys, David Patrick, 1955- Confronting the drug control establishment. Albany, N.Y. : State University of New York Press, c2000.
**TC HM1031.L56 K49 2000**

**Gallin, Alice.** Negotiating identity : Catholic higher education since 1960 / Alice Gallin. Notre Dame, Ind. : University of Notre Dame Press, c2000. xiii, 269 p. ; 24 cm. Errata label pasted on t.p. verso. Includes bibliographical references (p. 196-243) and index. ISBN 0-268-01489-2 (cloth : alk. paper) DDC 378/.071/273
*1. Catholic universities and colleges - United States - History - 20th century. I. Title.*
**TC LC501 .G36 2000**

**Gallois, Cynthia.**
Wilson, Keithia. Assertion and its social context. 1st ed. Oxford ; New York : Pergamon Press, 1993.
**TC BF575.A85 W55 1993**

**GALVANISM.** *See* **ELECTRICITY.**

**Galvin, Matthew.**
Stilwell, Barbara M. Right vs. wrong--. Bloomington : Indiana University Press, c2000.
**TC BJ1471 .S69 2000**

**Gamache, Gail, 1938-.**
Tessler, Richard C. Family experiences with mental illness. Westport, Conn. : London : Auburn House, 2000.
**TC RC455.4.F3 T46 2000**

**Gambell, Trevor J.**
Young adolescents meet literature. Vancouver : Pacific Education Press, 2000.
**TC LB1575.5.C3 Y68 2000**

**GAMES.** *See also* **EDUCATIONAL GAMES; PLAY; RHYMING GAMES; SCHOOLS - EXERCISES AND RECREATIONS; SPORTS.**
Fleisher, Paul, 1951- Brain food. Tucson, AZ : Zephyr Press, c1997.
*TC GV1480 .F54 1997*

Kirchner, Glenn. Children's games from around the world. 2nd ed. Boston : Allyn and Bacon, c2000.
*TC GV1203 .K65 2000*

Lichtman, Brenda, 1948- More innovative games. Champaign, IL : Human Kinetics, c1999.
*TC GV443 .L516 1999*

**GAMES, COMPUTER ADVENTURE.** *See* **COMPUTER ADVENTURE GAMES.**

**GAMES IN MATHEMATICS EDUCATION.**
Math around the world. Berkeley, CA : Lawrence Hall of Science, University of California at Berkeley, c1995.
*TC QA20.G35 M384 1995*

**GAMES, OLYMPIC.** *See* **OLYMPICS.**

**Games, Richard.**
Colleges and universities as citizens. Boston : Allyn and Bacon, c1999.
*TC LC220.5 .C644 1999*

**Games, sports and cultures** / edited by Noel Dyck. Oxford ; New York : Berg, 2000. viii, 246 p. : ill. ; 25 cm. Includes bibliographical references and index. CONTENTS: Games, bodies, celebrations and boundaries / Noel Dyck -- Why should an anthropologist sutdy sports in China? / Susan Brownell -- Society, body, and style / George Mentore -- Kabaddi, a national sport of India / Joseph S. Alter -- Soccer and the politics of culture in Western Australia / Philip Moore -- Parents, kids and coaches / Noel Dyck -- Reflections on the social and cultural dimensions of children's elite sport in Sweden / Yngve Georg Lithman -- Culture, context and content analysis / Melford S. Weiss -- "America" in Takamiya / Charles Fruehling Springwood -- Sport, celebrity and liminality / Synthia Sydnor. ISBN 1-85973-312-3 ISBN 1-85973-317-4 (pbk.) DDC 306.483
*1. Sports - Anthropological aspects. 2. Sports - Sociological aspects. 3. Sports - Cross-cultural studies. I. Dyck, Noel.*
*TC GV706.5 .G36 2000*

**GAMES WITH RHYMES.** *See* **RHYMING GAMES.**

**Gamson, Zelda F.**
Austin, Ann E. Academic workplace. Washington, D.C. : Association for the Study of Higher Education, 1983.
*TC LB2331.7 .A96 1983*

**Gamwell, Lynn, 1943-.**
Dreams 1900-2000. Binghamton : Cornell University Press : Binghamtom University Art Museum, State University of New York, 2000.
*TC BF1078 .D729 2000*

**GANDA (AFRICAN PEOPLE) - POLITICS AND GOVERNMENT.**
Gitta, Cosmas. International human rights. 1998.
*TC 085 G4398*

**GANDA (AFRICAN PEOPLE) - SOCIAL CONDITIONS.**
Gitta, Cosmas. International human rights. 1998.
*TC 085 G4398*

**Gandara, Patricia C.**
The dimensions of time and the challenge of school reform. Albany : State University of New York Press, c2000.
*TC LB3032 .D55 2000*

**Gangi, Robyn Joseph.** A longitudinal case study of the musical/aesthetic experience of adolescent choral musicians / by Robyn Joseph Gangi. 1998. 2 v. (489 leaves) ; 29 cm. Issued also on microfilm. Thesis (Ed.D.)-- Teachers College, Columbia University, 1998. Includes bibliographical references (leaves 178-184).
*1. Choral singing - Psychological aspects - Case studies. 2. High school students. 3. Choral music - Analysis, appreciation - Longitudinal studies. 4. Music - Philosophy and aesthetics. 5. Aesthetics - Psychological aspects. 6. Creation (Literary, artistic, etc.) I. Title. II. Title: Musical/aesthetic experience of adolescent choral musicians*
*TC 06 no. 10932*

**GANGS.**
Gangs. San Diego, CA : Greenhaven Press, c1996.
*TC HV6437 .G36 1996*

Rosen, Sidney M. Toward a gang solution. [Norman, Okla.?] NRC Youth Services, 1996.
*TC HV6439.U7 R67 1996*

**GANGS - FICTION.**
Draper, Sharon M. (Sharon Mills) Romiette and Julio. 1st ed. New York : Atheneum Books for Young Readers. 1999.
*TC PZ7.D78325 Ro 1999*

**GANGS - HAWAII - CASE STUDIES.**
Rosen, Sidney M. Toward a gang solution. [Norman, Okla.?] NRC Youth Services, 1996.
*TC HV6439.U7 R67 1996*

**Gangs** : opposing viewpoints / Charles P. Cozic, book editor. San Diego, CA : Greenhaven Press, c1996. 191 p. : ill. ; 23 cm. (Opposing viewpoints series) Includes bibliographical references (p. 183-185) and index. ISBN 1-56510-363-7 (lib. ed. : alk. paper) ISBN 1-56510-362-9 (pbk. : alk. paper) DDC 364.1/06/6
*1. Gangs. I. Cozic, Charles P., 1957- II. Series: Opposing viewpoints series (Unnumbered)*
*TC HV6437 .G36 1996*

**Gannett, Ruth Chrisman. ill.**
Gannett, Ruth Stiles. My father's dragon. New York : Random House, 1948.
*TC PZ7.G15 My 1948*

**Gannett, Ruth Stiles.** My father's dragon / story by Ruth Stiles Gannett ; illustrations by Ruth Chrisman Gannett. New York : Random House, 1948. 86 p. : ill. ; 22 cm. Map on lining papers. SUMMARY: A young boy determines to rescue a poor baby dragon who is being used by a group of lazy wild animals to ferry them across the river on Wild Island. To do so, he evades the more dangerous animals, solving their personal problems by giving each one what it needs.
*1. Animals - Juvenile fiction. 2. Dragons - Juvenile fiction. 3. Human-animal relationships - Juvenile fiction. I. Gannett, Ruth Chrisman, ill. II. Title.*
*TC PZ7.G15 My 1948*

**Ganong, Lawrence H.** Changing families, changing responsibilities : family obligations following divorce and remarriage / Lawrence H. Ganong and Marilyn Coleman. Mahwah, N.J. : Lawrence Erlbaum Associates, 1999. viii, 203 p. ; 24 cm. Includes bibliographical references (p. 184-196) and indexes. ISBN 0-8058-2691-2 (alk. paper) DDC 306.89
*1. Divorce - United States. 2. Remarriage - United States. 3. Divorced parents - United States. 4. Children of divorced parents - United States. 5. Intergenerational relations - United States. I. Coleman, Marilyn. II. Title.*
*TC HQ834 .G375 1999*

**Ganter, Susan L.**
Calculus renewal. New York : Kluwer Academic/ Plenum Publishers, c2000.
*TC QA303.3 .C34 2000*

**Garafola, Lynn.**
Limón, José. José Limón. Hanover, NH : University Press of New England, [1998?]
*TC GV1785.L515 A3 1998*

**GARATTI, VITTORIO, 1927-.**
Loomis, John A., 1951- Revolution of forms. New York : Princeton Architectural Press, c1999.
*TC NA6602.A76 L66 1999*

**Garbarino, James.** Lost boys : why our sons turn violent and how we can save them / James Garbarino. New York : Free Press, c1999. xiii, 274 p. ; 25 cm. Includes bibliographical references (p. 251-265) and index. ISBN 0-684-85908-4 DDC 303.6/0835
*1. Youth and violence - United States. 2. Violence - United States - Prevention. I. Title.*
*TC HQ799.2.V56 G37 1999*

**Garber, Zev, 1941-.**
Academic approaches to teaching Jewish studies. Lanham, Md. : University Press of America, c2000.
*TC BM71 .A33 2000*

**García, Jorge G.**
Psychological interventions and research with Latino populations. Boston : Allyn and Bacon, c1997.
*TC RC451.5.H57 P77 1997*

**García, Mildred.**
Succeeding in an academic career. Westport, Conn. : Greenwood Press, 2000.
*TC LB2331.72 .S83 2000*

**García, Ofelia.**
The multilingual Apple. Berlin ; New York : Mouton de Gruyter, 1997.
*TC P40.5.L56 M8 1997*

**Garcia, Ricardo L.** Teaching for diversity / Ricardo L. Garcia. Bloomington, Ind. : Phi Delta Kappa Educational Foundation, 1998. 141 p. : ill. ; 23 cm. Includes bibliographical references (p. 135-139). ISBN 0-87367-807-9 (pbk).
*1. Multicultural education - United States. 2. Multicultural*

education - Canada. 3. Minorities - Education - United States. 4. Minorities - Education - Canada. 5. Pluralism (Social sciences) - Study and teaching. I. Title.
*TC LC1099.3 .G367 1998*

**Gard, Robert E. (Robert Edward), 1910-** Prairie visions : a personal search for the springs of regional art and folklife / by Robert Gard. Ashland, Wis. : Heartland Press, c1987. 319 p. ; 24 cm. ISBN 0-942802-54-3 DDC 818/.5409
*1. Gard, Robert E. (Robert Edward), - 1910- - Biography. 2. Authors, American - 20th century - Biography. 3. Prairies - Biography. 4. Prairies - Social life and customs. 5. Gard, Robert E. - (Robert Edward), - 1910- - Biographie. 6. Écrivains américains - 20e siècle - Biographies. 7. Prairies - Biographies. 8. Prairies - Moeurs et coutumes. I. Title.*
*TC PS3513.A612 P7 1987*

**GARD, ROBERT E. (ROBERT EDWARD), 1910- - BIOGRAPHIE.**
Gard, Robert E. (Robert Edward), 1910- Prairie visions. Ashland, Wis. : Heartland Press, c1987.
*TC PS3513.A612 P7 1987*

**GARD, ROBERT E. (ROBERT EDWARD), 1910- - BIOGRAPHY.**
Gard, Robert E. (Robert Edward), 1910- Prairie visions. Ashland, Wis. : Heartland Press, c1987.
*TC PS3513.A612 P7 1987*

**GARDEN FOUNTAINS.** *See* **FOUNTAINS.**

**Gärdenfors, Peter.** Conceptual spaces : the geometry of thought / Peter Gärdenfors. Cambridge, Mass. ; London : MIT Press, c2000. x, 307 p. : ill. ; 24 cm. "A Bradford book." Includes bibliographical references (p. [263]- 298) and index. ISBN 0-262-07199-1 (alk. paper) DDC 006.3
*1. Artificial intelligence. 2. Cognitive science. I. Title.*
*TC Q335 .G358 2000*

**GARDENING - FICTION.**
O'Malley, Kevin, 1961- Bud. New York : Walker, 2000.
*TC PZ7.O526 Bu 2000*

**Gardiner, Mary E., 1953-** Coloring outside the lines : mentoring women into school leadership / Mary E. Gardiner, Ernestine Enomoto, and Margaret Grogan. Albany : State University of New York Press, c2000. xii, 249 p. ; 24 cm. (SUNY series in women in education) Includes bibliographical references (p. 233-242) and index. ISBN 0-7914-4581-X (hc : acid free) ISBN 0-7914-4582-8 (pb : acid free) DDC 371.2/011/082
*1. Women school administrators - United States - Interviews. 2. Feminism and education - United States - Case studies. 3. Mentoring in education - United States - Case studies. I. Enomoto, Ernestine, 1949- II. Grogan, Margaret, 1952- III. Title. IV. Series.*
*TC LB2831.82 .G37 2000*

**Gardner, E. Ty.**
Grounded for life [videorecording]. Charleston, WV : Cambridge Research Group, Ltd., 1988.
*TC HQ759.4 .G7 1988*

**Gardner, Howard.** Leading minds : an anatomy of leadership / Howard Gardner ; in collaboration with Emma Laskin. New York, NY : BasicBooks, c1995. xi, 400 p. ; ill. ; 24 cm. Includes bibliographical references (p. [367]-380) and indexes. ISBN 0-465-08279-3 DDC 303.3/4
*1. Leadership. 2. Leadership - Case studies. I. Laskin, Emma. II. Title.*
*TC HM141 .G35 1995*

**GARDNER, HOWARD.**
Berube, Maurice R. Eminent educators. Westport, Conn. : Greenwood Press, 2000.
*TC LB875.D5 B47 2000*

**Gardner, Janet.**
Children of the night [videorecording]. [Charleston, W.V.] : Cambridge Educational, c1994.
*TC HV1435.C3 C45 1994*

Children of the night [videorecording]. [Charleston, W.V.] : Cambridge Educational, c1994.
*TC HV1435.C3 C45 1994*

Children of the night [videorecording]. [Charleston, W.V.] : Cambridge Educational, c1994.
*TC HV1435.C3 C45 1994*

Starting over [videorecording]. [Charleston, W.V.] : Cambridge Educational, c1994.
*TC HV1435.C3 S7 1994*

**Gardner, Paul.**
Grugeon, Elizabeth. The art of storytelling for teachers and pupils. London : David Fulton, 2000.
*TC LB1042 .G78 2000*

**Gardner, Paul (Paul Henry)** Managing technology in the middle school classroom / author, Paul Gardner ; illustrator, Howard Chaney ; editor, Dorinda Mas.

Huntington Beach, CA : Teacher Created Materials, c1996. 288 p. : ill. ; 29 cm. Includes bibliographical references (p. 279). ISBN 1-55734-667-4 DDC 373.133/4
*1. Computer-assisted instruction - Handbooks. manuals. etc. 2. Educational technology - Handbooks. manuals. etc. 3. Middle schools - Data processing - Handbooks. manuals. etc. I. Mas, Dorinda. II. Title.*
*TC LB1028.5 .C353 1996*

**Gardner, Richard A.** Developmental conflicts and diagnostic evaluation in adolescent psychotherapy / Richard A. Gardner. Northvale, N.J. : J. Aronson, c1999. xix, 377 p. ; 23 cm. (Psychotherapy with adolescents ; v. 1) "The hardcover edition was entitled Psychotherapy with adolescents"--T.p. verso. Includes bibliographical references (p. 369-372) and indexes. ISBN 0-7657-0206-1 (softcover : alk. paper) DDC 616.89/14/0835
*1. Adolescent psychotherapy. 2. Behavior disorders in children - Treatment. 3. Mental Disorders - in adolescence. 4. Mental Disorders - diagnosis. 5. Psychotherapy - in adolescence. I. Series: Gardner. Richard A. Psychotherapy with adolescents ; v. 1.*
*TC RJ503 .G376 1999*

**Psychotherapy with adolescents**
(v. 1.) Gardner, Richard A. Developmental conflicts and diagnostic evaluation in adolescent psychotherapy. Northvale, N.J. : J. Aronson, c1999.
*TC RJ503 .G376 1999*

**Gardner, Roy.**
Education for values. London ; Sterling, VA : Kogan Page, 2000.
*TC LC268 .E38 2000*

**Garey, Anita Ilta, 1947-** Weaving work and motherhood / Anita Ilta Garey. Philadelphia, PA : Temple University Press, 1999. xi, 239 p. ; 24 cm. (Women in the political economy) Includes bibliographical references and index. ISBN 1-56639-699-9 (cloth : alk. paper) ISBN 1-56639-700-6 (paper : alk. paper) DDC 331.4/4/0973
*1. Working mothers - United States - Case studies. 2. Mothers - Employment - United States - Case studies. 3. Hospitals - United States - Staff - Case studies. 4. Work and family - United States - Case studies. I. Title. II. Series.*
*TC HQ759.48 .G37 1999*

**Garfinkel, Simson.** Database nation : the death of privacy in the 21st century / Simson Garfinkel. 1st ed. Beijing ; Cambridge : O'Reilly, c2000. vii, 312 p. : ill. ; 24 cm. Includes bibliographical references (p. 273-292) and index. ISBN 1-56592-653-6 (alk. paper) DDC 323.44/8/0973
*1. Privacy, Right of - United States. 2. Computer security - United States. I. Title.*
*TC JC596.2.U5 G37 2000*

**Garland reference library of social science**
(v. 1013.) Higher education in Korea. New York : Falmer Press, 2000.
*TC LA1333 .H54 2000*

(v. 1043.) MacCann, Donnarae. White supremacy in children's literature. New York : Garland Pub., 1998.
*TC PS173.N4 M33 1998*

(v. 1079.) Ford, Terry. Becoming multicultural :. New York : Falmer Press, 1999.
*TC LC1099 .F674 1999*

(v. 1094.) McCallum, Robyn. Ideologies of identity in adolescent fiction. New York : Garland Pub., 1999.
*TC PN3443 .M38 1999*

(v. 1120.) Effective early education. New York : Falmer Press, 1999.
*TC LB1139.23 .E44 1999*

(v. 1140.) Osborne, Margery D. Examining science teaching in elementary school from the perspective of a teacher and learner. New York : Falmer Press, 1999.
*TC LB1585 .O77 1999*

(v. 1152.) Education, cultures, and economics. New York : Falmer Press, 1999.
*TC LC191.8.D44 E38 1999*

(v. 1168.) Infancy and culture. New York : Falmer Press, 1999.
*TC GN482 .I53 1999*

(v. 1188.) Sissel, Peggy A. Staff, parents, and politics in Head Start. New York ; London : Falmer Press, 2000.
*TC LC4091 .S49 2000*

(v. 1189.) Teaching in the 21st century. New York : Falmer Press, 1999.
*TC PE1404 .T394 1999*

(v. 1191.) What is indigenous knowledge? New York : Falmer Press, 1999.

**TC GN476 .W47 1999**
(v. 1193.) Practicing what we preach. New York : Falmer Press, 1999.
*TC LB1735.5 .P73 1999*

(v. 1195.) Two-year colleges for women and minorities. New York : Falmer Press, 1999.
*TC LB2328.15.U6 T96 1999*

(v. 1396.) Faculty productivity :. New York : Falmer Press, 1999.
*TC LB2331.7 .F33 1999*

(v. 1407) Competitor or ally? New York : Falmer Press, 1999.
*TC LA1312 .C667 1999*

(v. 1417.) Freirean pedagogy, praxis, and possibilities. New York : Falmer Press, 2000.
*TC LC196 .F76 2000*

(v. 1442.) Mosha, R. Sambuli. The heartbeat of indigenous Africa. New York ; London : Garland Publishing : [Falmer Press], 2000.
*TC LC191.8.T29 M67 2000*

(v. 1444.) Real-world readings in art education. New York : Falmer Press, c2000.
*TC N353 .R43 2000*

(v. 1445.) Brock-Utne, Birgit, 1938- Whose education for all? New York ; London : Falmer Press, 2000.
*TC LC67.A435 B76 2000*

(v. 416.) Duryea, E. D. (Edwin D.) The academic corporation. New York : Falmer Press, 2000.
*TC LB2341 .D79 2000*

(v. 911.) Third World education. New York : Garland Pub., 2000.
*TC LC2607 .T55 2000*

(v. 922.) The ethnographic eye. New York : Falmer Press, 2000.
*TC LB45 .E837 2000*

(v. 946.) Swirski, Shlomo. Politics and education in Israel. New York : Falmer Press, 1999.
*TC LC94.I75 S95 1999*

(v. 952.) Schooling in sub-Saharan Africa. New York : Garland Pub., 1998.
*TC LA1501 .S35 1998*

(v. 996) Teacher education in the Asia-Pacific region. New York : Falmer Press, c2000.
*TC LB1727.A69 T42 2000*

**Garland reference library of social science. Children's literature and culture series**
(v. 4.) MacCann, Donnarae. White supremacy in children's literature. New York : Garland Pub., 1998.
*TC PS173.N4 M33 1998*

(v. 8.) McCallum, Robyn. Ideologies of identity in adolescent fiction. New York : Garland Pub., 1999.
*TC PN3443 .M38 1999*

**Garland reference library of social science. Critical education practice**
(vol. 18.) Osborne, Margery D. Examining science teaching in elementary school from the perspective of a teacher and learner. New York : Falmer Press, 1999.
*TC LB1585 .O77 1999*

(vol. 19.) Ford, Terry. Becoming multicultural :. New York : Falmer Press, 1999.
*TC LC1099 .F674 1999*

(vol. 19.) Freirean pedagogy, praxis, and possibilities. New York : Falmer Press, 2000.
*TC LC196 .F76 2000*

**Garland reference library of social science. Cultural studies in the classroom**
(v. 1.) Teaching in the 21st century. New York : Falmer Press, 1999.
*TC PE1404 .T394 1999*

**Garland reference library of social science. Garland studies in higher education**
(vol. 15.) Faculty productivity :. New York : Falmer Press, 1999.
*TC LB2331.7 .F33 1999*

(vol. 16.) Two-year colleges for women and minorities. New York : Falmer Press, 1999.
*TC LB2328.15.U6 T96 1999*

(vol. 17.) Higher education in Korea. New York : Falmer Press, 2000.

**TC LA1333 .H54 2000**
(vol. 23.) Duryea, E. D. (Edwin D.) The academic corporation. New York : Falmer Press, 2000.
*TC LB2341 .D79 2000*

**Garland reference library of social science. Indigenous knowledge and schooling**
(v. 2.) What is indigenous knowledge? New York : Falmer Press, 1999.
*TC GN476 .W47 1999*

(v. 3.) Mosha, R. Sambuli. The heartbeat of indigenous Africa. New York ; London : Garland Publishing : [Falmer Press], 2000.
*TC LC191.8.T29 M67 2000*

**Garland reference library of social science. Reference books in international education**
(v. 45.) Competitor or ally? New York : Falmer Press, 1999.
*TC LA1312 .C667 1999*

(vol. 41.) Schooling in sub-Saharan Africa. New York : Garland Pub., 1998.
*TC LA1501 .S35 1998*

(vol. 44.) Third World education. New York : Garland Pub., 2000.
*TC LC2607 .T55 2000*

(vol. 47.) The ethnographic eye. New York : Falmer Press, 1999.
*TC LB45 .E837 2000*

(vol. 48.) Education, cultures, and economics. New York : Falmer Press, 1999.
*TC LC191.8.D44 E38 1999*

(vol. 48) Teacher education in the Asia-Pacific region. New York : Falmer Press, c2000.
*TC LB1727.A69 T42 2000*

**Garland reference library of social science. Source books on education**
(vol. 56.) Practicing what we preach. New York : Falmer Press, 1999.
*TC LB1735.5 .P73 1999*

**Garland reference library of social science. Studies in education and culture**
(vol. 11) Effective early education. New York : Falmer Press, 1999.
*TC LB1139.23 .E44 1999*

**Garland reference library of social science. Studies in education/politics**
(vol. 3.) Swirski, Shlomo. Politics and education in Israel. New York : Falmer Press, 1999.
*TC LC94.I75 S95 1999*

(vol. 4.) Sissel, Peggy A. Staff, parents, and politics in Head Start. New York ; London : Falmer Press, 2000.
*TC LC4091 .S49 2000*

(vol. 6.) Brock-Utne, Birgit, 1938- Whose education for all? New York ; London : Falmer Press, 2000.
*TC LC67.A435 B76 2000*

**Garland reference library of social science. Thinking and teaching**
(v. 1.) Real-world readings in art education. New York : Falmer Press, c2000.
*TC N353 .R43 2000*

**Garland reference library of the humanities**
(v. 2126) McGillis, Roderick. Voices of the other. New York : Garland Publishing., Inc., c2000.
*TC PN344 .M35 2000*

(vol. 1473.) The Italian American heritage. New York : Garland Pub., 1999.
*TC E184.I8 I675 1999*

(vol. 1625) Protest, power, and change. New York : Garland Pub., 1997.
*TC HM278 .P76 1997*

(vol. 1975.) Stephens, John, 1944- Retelling stories, framing culture. New York : Garland Pub., 1998.
*TC PN1009.A1 S83 1998*

(vol. 2005.) Kutzer, M. Daphne. Empire's children. New York : Garland Pub., 2000.
*TC PR830.I54 K88 2000*

(vol. 2152.) Transcending boundaries. New York : Garland, 1999.
*TC PN1009.A1 T69 1999*

(vol. 2165) Wojcik-Andrews, Ian, 1952- Children's films. New York : Garland Pub., 2000.
*TC PN1995.9.C45 W59 2000*

**Garland reference library of the humanities. Children's literature and culture**
(v. 12) Wojcik-Andrews, Ian, 1952- Children's films. New York : Garland Pub., 2000.
***TC PN1995.9.C45 W59 2000***

(v. 13.) Transcending boundaries. New York : Garland, 1999.
***TC PN1009.A1 T69 1999***

(v. 16.) Kutzer, M. Daphne. Empire's children. New York : Garland Pub., 2000.
***TC PR830.I54 K88 2000***

(v. 5.) Stephens, John, 1944- Retelling stories, framing culture. New York : Garland Pub., 1998.
***TC PN1009.A1 S83 1998***

**Garman, Noreen B.**
Piantanida, Maria. The qualitative dissertation. Thousand Oaks, Calif. : Corwin Press, c1999.
***TC LB2369 .P48 1999***

**GARMENTS.** *See* **CLOTHING AND DRESS.**

**Garmer, Amy Korzick.**
Investing in diversity. Washington, D.C. : Aspen Institute, Communications and Society Program, c1998.
***TC P94.5.M552 U647 1997***

**Garne, S. T.** By a blazing blue sea / written by S.T. Garne ; illustrated by Lori Lohstoeter. San Diego : Harcourt Brace & Co., 1999. 1 v. (unpaged) : col. ill. ; 22 x 26 cm. "Gulliver books" SUMMARY: A rhyming description of the simple and colorful life of a Caribbean fisherman. ISBN 0-15-201780-1 DDC [E]
*1. Caribbean Area - Juvenile fiction. 2. Caribbean Area - Fiction. 3. Color - Fiction. 4. Stories in rhyme. I. Lohstoeter, Lori, ill. II. Title.*
***TC PZ8.3.G1866 By 1999***

**Garner, Bryan A.**
Black, Henry Campbell, 1860-1927. Black's law dictionary. 7th ed. / Bryan A. Garner, editor in chief. St. Paul, MN : West Group, 1999.
***TC KF156 .B53 1999***

**Garnsey, Peter.** Food and society in classical antiquity / Peter Garnsey. Cambridge, U.K. ; New York : Cambridge University Press, 1999. xiv, 175 p. : ill. ; 24 cm. (Key themes in ancient history) Includes bibliographical references (p. 149-168) and index. ISBN 0-521-64182-9 (hardback) ISBN 0-521-64588-3 (paperback) DDC 394.1/2/0937
*1. Food habits - Greece - History. 2. Food habits - Rome - History. 3. Food supply - Greece - History. 4. Food supply - Rome - History. 5. Civilization, Classical. I. Title. II. Series.*
***TC GT2853.G8 G37 1999***

**Garoian, Charles R., 1943-** Performing pedagogy : toward an art of politics / Charles R. Garoian. Albany, N.Y. : State University of New York Press, 1999. xii, 248 p. : ill. ; 23 cm. (SUNY series, interruptions -- border testimony(ies) and critical discourse/s) (SUNY series, innovations in curriculum) Includes bibliographical references and index. ISBN 0-7914-4323-X (hc. : alk. paper) ISBN 0-7914-4324-8 (pbk. : alk. paper) DDC 370/.1
*1. Performance art - United States. 2. Artists - United States - Psychology. 3. Arts - Study and teaching - Methodology. 4. Communication in education - United States. I. Title. II. Series: SUNY series. Interruptions -- Border testimony(ies) and Critical Discourse/s III. Series: SUNY series, innovations in curriculum*
***TC NX504 .G37 1999***

**Garrick, John.** Informal learning in the workplace : unmasking human resource development / John Garrick. London ; New York : Routledge, 1998. xi, 212 p. : ill. ; 23 cm. Includes bibliographical references (p. [182]-198) and index. ISBN 0-415-18527-0 (hc.) ISBN 0-415-18528-9 (pbk.) DDC 331.25/92
*1. Employees - Training of. 2. Occupational training. 3. Experiential learning. I. Title.*
***TC HF5549.5.T7 G344 1998***

**Garrin, Paul.**
Processing the signal [videorecording]. Cicero, Ill. : Roland Collection of Films on Art, c1989.
***TC N6494.V53 P7 1989***

**Garrod, Andrew, 1937-.**
Learning disabilities and life stories. Boston : Allyn and Bacon, c2001.
***TC LC4818.38 .L42 2001***

Souls looking back. New York : Routledge, 1999.
***TC E185.625 .S675 1999***

**Garson, G. David.**
Social dimensions of information technology. Hershey, Pa. : Ideas Group Pub., 2000.
***TC HM851 .S63 2000***

**Gartner, Richard B.** Betrayed as boys : psychodynamic treatment of sexually abused men / Richard B. Gartner. New York : Guilford Press, c1999. xii, 356 p. ; 24 cm. Includes bibliographical references (p. 326-346) and index. ISBN 1-57230-467-7 (hard) DDC 616.85/83690651
*1. Adult child sexual abuse victims. 2. Male sexual abuse victims. 3. Psychodynamic psychotherapy. 4. Psychotherapy - in adulthood. 5. Child Abuse, Sexual - therapy. 6. Men - psychology. I. Title.*
***TC RC569.5.A28 G37 1999***

**Garvin, David A.** Learning in action : a guide to putting the learning organization to work / David A. Garvin. Boston, Mass. : Harvard Business School Press, 2000. xvi, 256 p. ; 24 cm. Includes bibliographical references and index. ISBN 1-57851-251-4 (alk. paper) DDC 658.4/06
*1. Organizational learning. 2. Organizational learning - Case studies. I. Title.*
***TC HD58.82 .G37 2000***

**Gascoigne, John, Ph. D.** Science, politics, and universities in Europe, 1600-1800 / John Gascoigne. Aldershot [England] ; Brookfield, Vt. : Ashgate, c1998. 1 v. (various pagings) : ill. ; 24 cm. (Variorum collected studies series ; CS636) Essays and articles originally published between 1984 and 1995; one essay published here for the first time. Includes bibliographical references and index. ISBN 0-86078-767-2 (hard : alk. paper) DDC 378.4
*1. Universities and colleges - Europe - Sociological aspects - History - 17th century. 2. Universities and colleges - Europe - Sociological aspects - History - 18th century. 3. University of Cambridge - History - 17th century. 4. University of Cambridge - History - 18th century. 5. Europe - Intellectual life - 17th century. 6. Europe - Intellectual life - 18th century. 7. Scientists - Europe - Biography. 8. Enlightenment - Europe. I. Title. II. Series: Collected studies ; CS636.*
***TC LA621.5 .G37 1998***

**Gass, Robert H.** Persuasion, social influence, and compliance gaining / Robert H. Gass, John S. Seiter. Boston : Allyn and Bacon, c1999. xiv, 354 p. : ill. ; 23 cm. Includes bibliographical references and indexes. ISBN 0-205-26352-6 (pbk.) DDC 303.3/42
*1. Persuasion (Psychology) 2. Influence (Psychology) 3. Manipulative behavior. I. Seiter, John S. II. Title.*
***TC BF637.P4 G34 1999***

**Gass, Susan M.**
Language transfer in language learning. Rev. ed. with corrections. Amsterdam ; Philadelphia : J. Benjamins Pub. Co., 1994.
***TC P118.25 .L36 1994***

**GASTROINTESTINAL DISEASES - COMPLICATIONS.**
Nutritional aspects of HIV infection. London ; New York : Arnold : Co-published in the United States by Oxford University Press, 1999.
***TC RC607.A26 N895 1998***

**GASTROINTESTINAL SYSTEM - DISEASES.** *See* **NAUSEA.**

**GASTRONOMY.** *See* **COOKERY; DINNERS AND DINING; FOOD.**

**GATED COMMUNITIES - UNITED STATES.**
Blakely, Edward James, 1938- Fortress America. Washington, D.C. : Brookings Institution Press, c1997.
***TC HT169.59.U6 B53 1997***

**Gates, Bill, 1955-** Business @ the speed of thought : using a digital nervous system / Bill Gates with Collins Hemingway. New York, NY : Warner Books, c1999. xxii, 470 p. : ill. ; 23 cm. Includes bibliographical references and index. CONTENTS: pt. 1. Information flow is your lifeblood -- ch. 1. Manage with the force of facts -- ch. 2. Can your digital nervous system do this? -- ch. 3. Create a paperless office -- pt. 2. Commerce: the Internet changes everything -- ch. 4. Ride the inflection rocket -- ch. 5. The Middleman must add value -- ch. 6. Touch your customers -- ch. 7. Adopt the web lifestyle -- ch. 8. Change the boundaries of business -- ch. 9. Get to market first -- pt. 3. Manage knowledge to improve strategic thought -- ch. 10. Bad news must travel fast -- ch. 11. Convert bad news to good -- ch. 12. Know your numbers -- ch. 13. Shift people into thinking work -- ch. 14. Raise your corporate IQ -- ch. 15. Big wins require big risks -- pt. 4. Bring insight to business operations -- ch. 16. Develop processes that empower people -- ch. 17. Information technology enables reengineering -- ch. 18. Treat it as a strategic resource -- pt. 5. Special enterprises -- ch. 19. No health care system is an island -- ch. 20. Take government to the people -- ch. 21. When reflex is a matter of life and death -- ch. 22. Create connected learning communities -- pt. 6. Expect the unexpected -- ch. 23. Prepare for the digital future. ISBN 0-446-52568-5
*1. Business enterprises - Computer networks. 2. Business enterprises - Communication systems. I. Hemingway, Collins. II. Title. III. Title: Using a digital nervous system*
***TC HD30.37 .G38 1999***

**Gates, Henry Louis.**
Microsoft encarta Africana [computer file]. Redmond, WA : Microsoft Corp., c1999. Computer data and programs.
***TC DT14 .M527 1999***

Microsoft encarta Africana [computer file]. Redmond, WA : Microsoft Corp., c1999. Computer data and programs.
***TC DT3 .M53 1999x***

The Norton anthology of African American literature. 1st ed. New York : W.W. Norton & Co., c1997.
***TC PS508.N3 N67 1996***

**Gateways to democracy :** six urban community college systems / Raymond C. Bowen, Gilbert H. Miller, editors. San Francisco : Jossey-Bass, 1999. 101 p. ; 23 cm. (New directions for community colleges, 0194-3081 ; no. 107) Six urban community college systems. "Fall 1999" Includes bibliographical references and index. CONTENTS: Urban America and the community college imperative: the importance of open access and opportunity / Joshua L. Smith, Fayyaz A. Vellani-- Miami-Dade community college forging new urban partnerships / Eduardo J. Padron, Theodore Levitt -- CUNY's community colleges: democratic education on trial / Joanne Reitano -- Seattle community colleges: centered on the urban student / Julie Yearsley Hungar -- The Los Angeles community colleges: pathways to urban change / Jack Fujimoto -- Profiles in Urban challenges: confronting Maricopa"s social and economic agenda / Paul A. Elsner -- Baltmore county: a college and community in transition / Irving Pressley McPhail, Rondald C. Heacock -- Sources and information about urban community colleges / Dana Scott Peterman, Carol A. Kozeracki. ISBN 0-7879-4848-9
*1. Community colleges. 2. Organizational change. I. Bowen, Raymond C. II. Muller, Gilbert H. III. Title: Six urban community college systems IV. Series: New directions for community colleges ; no.107*
***TC LB2328.N53 1999***

**Gath, Tracy.**
Exploring science in the library. Chicago : American Library Association, 2000.
***TC Z675.S3 E97 2000***

**Gatter, Philip.** Identity and sexuality : AIDS in Britain in the 1990s / Philip Gatter. New York : Cassell, 1999. vi, 186 p. ;c23 cm. Includes bibliographical references (p.175-182) and index. ISBN 0-304-33341-7 DDC 305.3/09421
*1. Sex role - England - London. 2. Gender identity - England - London. 3. Gays - England - London - Identity. 4. AIDS (Disease) - Patients - England - London. 5. HIV infections - Patients - England - London. 6. Community life - England - London. 7. London (England) - Social conditions. 8. London (England) - Politics and government I. Title.*
***TC HQ1075.5.G7 G37 1999***

**Gauch, Patricia Lee.** Poppy's puppet / Patricia Lee Gauch ; illustrations by David Christiana. 1st ed. New York : Holt, 1999. 1 v. (unpaged) : col. ill. ; 26 cm. SUMMARY: Poppy carves wonderful marionettes from pieces of wood, listening to each piece to see just what he should make, but when he finds a silent piece and decides to make it into a ballerina, things do not turn out as planned. ISBN 0-8050-5291-7 (hc : alk. paper) DDC [E]
*1. Puppets - Fiction. 2. Toymakers - Fiction. 3. Self-realization - Fiction. I. Christiana, David, ill. II. Title.*
***TC PZ7.G2315 Po 1999***

Presenting Tanya, the Ugly Duckling / by Patricia Lee Gauch ; illustrated by Satomi Ichikawa. New York : Philomel Books, c1999. 1 v. (unpaged) : col. ill. ; 23 x 25 cm. SUMMARY: When she has trouble mastering her dance steps in the part of the Ugly Duckling for the spring ballet recital, Tanya is discouraged and fears that she has much in common with the character. ISBN 0-399-23200-1 DDC [E]
*1. Ballet dancing - Fiction. 2. Self-perception - Fiction. I. Ichikawa, Satomi, ill. II. Title.*
***TC PZ7.G2315 Pr 1999***

**Gauchet, Marcel.**
**[La pratique de l'esprit humain. English]**
Madness and democracy : the modern psychiatric universe / Marcel Gauchet and Gladys Swain ; translated by Catherine Porter ; with a foreword by Jerrold Seigel. Princeton, N.J. : Princeton University Press, c1999. xxvi, 323 p. ; 25 cm. (New French thought) Includes bibliographical references (p. [311]-315) and index. ISBN 0-691-03372-2 (cl : alk. paper) DDC 362.2/1
*1. Psychiatric hospital care. 2. Power (Social sciences) 3. Mental illness - Social aspects. 4. Mental Disorders - therapy. 5. Hospitals, Psychiatric. 6. Power (Psychology) 7. Psychotherapy - methods. I. Swain, Gladys, 1945- II. Title. III. Series.*
***TC RC439 .G2813 1999***

**GAUCHOS.** *See* **COWBOYS.**

**Gauntlett, David.** TV Living : television, culture and everyday life / David Gauntlett and Annette Hill. London ; New York : Routledge, 1999. xi. 315 p. ; 25 cm. "Published in association with British Film Institute." "Erratum slip inserted." Includes bibliographical references (p. [297]-305) and index. ISBN 0-415-18485-1 (alk. paper) ISBN 0-415-18486-X (pbk. : alk. paper) DDC 302.23/45/0941
*1. Television viewers - Great Britain - Attitudes. 2. Television - Social aspects - Great Britain. I. Hill, Annette. II. Title.*
*TC PN1992.55 .G38 1999*

**Gaweł-Luty, Elżbieta.** Przetwarzanie informacji społecznych dla ocen moralnych u uczniów klas młodszoszkolnych / Elżbieta Gaweł-Luty. Słupsk : Wyższa Szkoła Pedagogiczna w Słupsku, 1996. 184 p. ; 21 cm. Includes bibliographical references (p. 170-182). ISBN 83-87006-01-7
*1. Moral education (Elementary) - Poland. I. Title.*
*TC LC314.P7 G37 1996*

**GAY AND LESBIAN STUDIES.**
Lesbian and gay studies and the teaching of English. Urbana, Ill. : National Council of Teachers of English, 2000.
*TC PE66 .L45 2000*

Reader's guide to lesbian and gay studies. Chicago : Fitzroy Dearborn Publishers, 2000.
*TC HQ75.15 .R43 2000*

**GAY AND LESBIAN STUDIES - BIBLIOGRAPHY.**
Reader's guide to lesbian and gay studies. Chicago : Fitzroy Dearborn Publishers, 2000.
*TC HQ75.15 .R43 2000*

**GAY COLLEGE STUDENTS.** *See* **LESBIAN COLLEGE STUDENTS.**

**GAY COLLEGE STUDENTS - UNITED STATES - BIOGRAPHY.**
Out & about campus. 1st ed. Los Angeles : Alyson Books, 2000.
*TC LC2574.6 .O87 2000*

**GAY COLLEGE STUDENTS - UNITED STATES - SOCIAL CONDITIONS.**
Toward acceptance. Lanham, Md. : University Press of America, 1999.
*TC LC192.6 .T69 1999*

**Gay, Geneva.** Culturally responsive teaching : theory, research, and practice / Geneva Gay. New York : Teachers College Press, c2000. xx, 251 p. ; 24 cm. (Multicultural education series) Includes bibliographical references and index. ISBN 0-8077-3955-3 ISBN 0-8077-3954-5 (pbk.) DDC 370.117
*1. Multicultural education - United States. 2. Educational equalization - United States. 3. Teaching - Social aspects - United States. I. Title. II. Series: Multicultural education series (New York, N.Y.)*
*TC LC1099.3 . G393 2000*

**Gay, Geri.**
Information technologies in evaluation. San Francisco, Calif. : Jossey-Bass, 1999.
*TC H62 .I54 1999*

**Gay, L. R.** Educational research : competencies for analysis and application / L.R. Gay, Peter Airasian. 6th ed. Upper Saddle River, N.J. : Merrill, c2000. xxv, 661 p. ; ill. (some col.) ; 27 cm. Includes bibliographical references and indexes. ISBN 0-13-096103-5 DDC 370./7/2
*1. Education - Research. I. Airasian, Peter W. II. Title.*
*TC LB1028 .G37 2000*

**Gay/lesbian parents and school personnel.**
Ryan, Daniel Prentice. 1998.
*TC 06 no. 10988*

**Gay-lesbian parents and school personnel.**
Ryan, Daniel Prentice. Gay/lesbian parents and school personnel. 1998.
*TC 06 no. 10988*

**GAY LIB.** *See* **GAY LIBERATION MOVEMENT.**

**GAY LIBERATION MOVEMENT - UNITED STATES.**
Andriote, John-Manuel. Victory deferred. Chicago : The University of Chicago Press, c1999.
*TC RA644.A25 A523 1999*

**GAY MEN IN LITERATURE.**
Lesbian and gay studies and the teaching of English. Urbana, Ill. : National Council of Teachers of English, 2000.
*TC PE66 .L45 2000*

**GAY MEN - STUDY AND TEACHING.** *See* **GAY AND LESBIAN STUDIES.**

**GAY MEN - UNITED STATES.**
Rogers, Richard Randall. The impact of gay identity and perceived milieu toward gay employees on job involvement and organizational commitment of gay men. 1998.
*TC 085 R635*

**GAY MEN - UNITED STATES - DISEASES.**
Andriote, John-Manuel. Victory deferred. Chicago : The University of Chicago Press, c1999.
*TC RA644.A25 A523 1999*

**GAY PARENTS.** *See also* **CHILDREN OF GAY PARENTS.**
Golombok, Susan. Parenting. London ; Philadelphia : Routledge, 2000.
*TC HQ755.8 .G655 2000*

**GAY PARENTS' CHILDREN.** *See* **CHILDREN OF GAY PARENTS.**

**GAY PARENTS - UNITED STATES.**
Ryan, Daniel Prentice. Gay/lesbian parents and school personnel. 1998.
*TC 06 no. 10988*

**GAY PEOPLE.** *See* **GAYS.**

**GAY PERSONS.** *See* **GAYS.**

**GAY RIGHTS MOVEMENT.** *See* **GAY LIBERATION MOVEMENT.**

**GAY STUDENTS - UNITED STATES.**
School experiences of gay and lesbian youth. New York : Harrington Park Press, c1997.
*TC LC2575 .S36 1997*

**GAY STUDIES.** *See* **GAY AND LESBIAN STUDIES.**

**GAY TEACHERS.** *See* **LESBIAN TEACHERS.**

**GAY TEACHERS - FLORIDA - INTERVIEWS.**
Sanlo, Ronni L., 1947- Unheard voices. Westport, Conn. ; London : Bergin & Garvey, 1999.
*TC LB2844.1.G39 S36 1999*

**GAY WOMEN.** *See* **LESBIANS.**

**GAYS.** *See* **GAY MEN; LESBIANS.**

**GAYS - COUNSELING OF.**
Handbook of counseling and psychotherapy with lesbian, gay, and bisexual clients. 1st ed. Washington, DC ; London : American Psychological Association, c2000.
*TC BF637.C6 H3125 2000*

Therapeutic perspectives on working with lesbian, gay and bisexual clients. Buckingham [England] ; Philadelphia : Open University Press, 2000.
*TC RC451.4.G39 T476 2000*

**GAYS - ENGLAND - LONDON - IDENTITY.**
Gatter, Philip. Identity and sexuality. New York : Cassell, 1999.
*TC HQ1075.5.G7 G37 1999*

**GAYS, FEMALE.** *See* **LESBIANS.**

**GAYS - IDENTITY.**
Thinking queer. New York : Peter Lang, c2000.
*TC LC192.6 .T55 2000*

**GAYS, MALE.** *See* **GAY MEN.**

**GAYS - STUDY AND TEACHING.** *See* **GAY AND LESBIAN STUDIES.**

**GAYS' WRITINGS - STUDY AND TEACHING.**
Lesbian and gay studies and the teaching of English. Urbana, Ill. : National Council of Teachers of English, 2000.
*TC PE66 .L45 2000*

**Gazzaniga, Michael S.**
Cognitive neuroscience. Malden, Mass. ; Oxford : Blackwell, 2000.
*TC QP360.5 .C639 2000*

**Geary, Christraud M.**
Delivering views. Washington [D.C.] : Smithsonian Institution Press, c1998.
*TC NC1872 .D46 1998*

**Geddes, Marion.**
Individualisation. Oxford : Modern English Publications, 1982.
*TC LC32 .I53 1982*

**Gedeon, Lucinda H.**
Catlett, Elizabeth, 1915- Elizabeth Catlett sculpture. [Purchase, N.Y.] : Neuberger Museum of Art, Purchase College, State University of New York ; Seattle : Distributed by University of Washington Press, c1998.
*TC NB259.C384 A4 1998*

**Geekie, Peter.** Understanding literacy development / Peter Geekie, Brian Cambourne and Phil Fitzsimmons. Stoke on Trent, England : Trentham Books, 1999. v, 233 p. : facsims. ; 23 cm. Includes bibliographical references (p. 225-229) and index. ISBN 1-85856-086-1
*1. Literacy - Study and teaching. I. Cambourne. Brian. II. Fitzsimmons, Phil. III. Title.*
*TC LC149 .G44 1999*

**GEESE - FICTION.**
Braun, Trudi. My goose Betsy. 1st U.S. ed. Cambridge, MA : Candlewick Press, 1999.
*TC PZ10.3.B745 My 1998*

**GEESE - JUVENILE FICTION.**
Braun, Trudi. My goose Betsy. 1st U.S. ed. Cambridge, MA : Candlewick Press, 1999.
*TC PZ10.3.B745 My 1998*

**Geever, Jane C.** The Foundation Center's guide to proposal writing / Jane C. Geever, Patricia McNeill. Rev. ed. New York : Foundation Center, c1997. xviii, 213 p. ; 24 cm. Includes bibliographical references. ISBN 0-87954-703-0 DDC 658.15/224
*1. Proposal writing for grants - United States - Handbooks, manuals, etc. I. McNeill, Patricia, 1941- II. Foundation Center. III. Title. IV. Title: Guide to proposal writing*
*TC HG177.5.U6 G44 1997*

**Gegő, Elek, 1805-1844.** Népoktató : új esztendei ajándék a köznép számára : 1840 / Gegő Elek ; [a szöveget kiadásra előkészítette, a tanulmányt és a jegyzeteket írta D. Mátai Mária]. Budapest : Országos Pedagógiai Könyvtár és Múzeum, [1997] 108 p. : ill. ; 20 cm. Includes bibliographical references. ISBN 963-7644-57-1
*1. Teachers and community - Hungary. 2. Education - Hungary - History - Sources. I. Mátai, Mária D. II. Title.*
*TC LC227 .G44 1997*

**Geiger, Keith.**
Randall, Ruth E. School choice. Bloomington, Ind. : National Educational Service, 1991.
*TC LB1027.9 .R36 1991*

**Geiger, Roger L., 1943-.**
The American college in the nineteenth century. 1st ed. Nashville : Vanderbilt University Press, 2000.
*TC LA227.1 .A64 2000*

**Geisert, Paul.** Teachers, computers, and curriculum : microcomputers in the classroom / Paul G. Geisert, Mynga K. Futrell. 3rd ed. Boston : Allyn and Bacon, c2000. xxi, 358 p. : ill. ; 24 cm. Includes bibliographical references and index. ISBN 0-205-28855-3 (alk. paper) DDC 371.33/4
*1. Computer-assisted instruction. 2. Microcomputers - Study and teaching. 3. Education - Data processing. 4. Computer managed instruction. I. Futrell, Mynga K. II. Title.*
*TC LB1028.5 .G42 2000*

**Geisler, Eliezer, 1942-** The metrics of science and technology / Eliezer Geisler. Westport, Conn. : Quorum Books, 2000. xvi, 380 p. ; 24 cm. Includes bibliographical references (p. [371]-375) and index. ISBN 1-56720-213-6 (alk. paper) DDC 303.48/3
*1. Science - Social aspects. 2. Technology - Social aspects. I. Title.*
*TC Q175.5 .G43 2000*

**Geissler, Catherine.**
Vaughan, J. G. (John Griffith) The new Oxford book of food plants. Oxford ; New York : Oxford University Press, 1997.
*TC SB175 .V38 1997*

**Geist der Zeit.**
Hochschule und Ausland. Berlin : Kulturpolitische Gesellschaft, 1923-1937.

**Gelernter, Mark, 1951-** A history of American architecture : buildings in their cultural and technological context / Mark Gelernter. Hanover, NH ; London : University Press of New England, c1999. xxii, 346 p. : ill., maps, plans ; 25 cm. Includes bibliographical references (p. [330]-337) and index. ISBN 0-87451-940-3 (cloth) DDC 720/.973
*1. Architecture - United States. 2. Architecture and society - United States. I. Title.*
*TC NA705 .G35 1999*

**Gelfand, Stanley A., 1948-** Hearing : an introduction to psychological and physiological acoustics / Stanley A. Gelfand. 3rd ed., rev. and expanded. New York : Marcel Dekker, c1998. viii, 470 p. : ill. ; 26 cm. Includes bibliographical references and indexes. ISBN 0-8247-0143-7 (acid-free paper) DDC 152.1/5
*1. Hearing. 2. Psychoacoustics. I. Title.*
*TC QP461 .G28 1998*

**Gemeindeschreiberverband des Kantons Luzern.**
Korrespondenz-blatt. Luzern : Luzerner
Staatspersonalverband, 1947-

**(GEMS) Project.**
Cuomo, Celia, 1956- In all probability. Berkeley, CA :
Lawrence Hall of Science, University of California,
Berkeley, c1998.
*TC QA276.18 .C866 1998*

**GEMS (Project).**
Gonsalves, Philip. Build it! festival. Berkeley, CA :
Great Explorations in Math and Science (GEMS),
Lawrence Hall of Science, University of California at
Berkeley, c1995.
*TC QA462 .G66 1995*

Goodman, Jan M. Group solutions : : [Teacher's
guide]. Rev. Berkeley, Calif. : Lawrence Hall of
Science, University of California, 1997, c1992.
*TC QA8.7 .G5 1997*

Math around the world. Berkeley, CA : Lawrence Hall
of Science, University of California at Berkeley,
c1995.
*TC QA20.G35 M384 1995*

**GENDARMES.** *See* **POLICE.**

**Gender & work.**
Handbook of gender & work. Thousand Oaks, CA :
Sage Publications, Inc., c1999.
*TC HQ1233 .H33 1999*

**GENDER AND DEVELOPMENT.** *See* **WOMEN IN
DEVELOPMENT.**

**Gender and emotion :** social psychological
perspectives / [edited by] Agneta H. Fischer. New
York : Cambridge University Press, 1999. xi, 331 p. ; 23
cm. (Studies in emotion and social interaction. Second series)
Includes bibliographical references and index. ISBN 0-521-
63015-0 ISBN 0-521-63986-7 (pbk.) DDC 155.3/3
*1. Expression - Sex differences. 2. Emotions - Sex differences. I.
Fischer, Agneta, 1958- II. Series.*
*TC BF591 .G45 1999*

**Gender and its effects on psychopathology** / edited by
Ellen Frank. Washington, DC : American Psychiatric
Press, c2000. xvi, 315 p. : ill. ; 24 cm. "American
Psychopathological Association." Includes bibliographical
references and index. ISBN 0-88048-798-4 DDC 616.89
*1. Mental illness - Sex factors. 2. Sex differences (Psychology)
3. Psychology, Pathological. 4. Mental Disorders. 5. Sex
Factors. I. Frank, Ellen, 1944-*
*TC RC455.4.S45 G465 2000*

**Gender and mental health.**
Prior, Pauline. New York : New York University
Press, 1999.
*TC RC455.4.S45 P75 1999*

**Gender and psychology**
Unger, Rhoda Kesler. Resisting gender. London ;
Thousand Oaks, Calif. : Sage Publications, 1998.
*TC BF201.4 .U544 1998*

**Gender and qualitative research** / edited by Jane
Pilcher, Amanda Coffey. Aldershot, Hants, England :
Brookfield, Vt., USA : Avebury, c1996. ix, 163 p. ; 22
cm. (Cardiff papers in qualitative research) Includes
bibliographical references. CONTENTS: Masculinity in
prison / Keith Carter -- Coping with pit closure in the 1990s :
women's perspectives / Bella Dicks -- From "honorary chap"
to mother : combining work in the professions with
motherhood / Janet Stephens -- Childish things : men, ageing
and violence / Julie Owen -- Chance to choice : two
generations of reproductive decision making / Evelyn P.
Parsons -- In the company of other women : a case study of
menopause support groups / Trish Harding -- Focus groups,
young people and sex education / Lesley Pugsley -- Men and
feminist research / Mark Jones -- Time for feminist approaches
to technology, "nature" and work / Barbara Adam. ISBN 1-
85972-199-0 DDC 305.3/07/2
*1. Gender identity - Research. 2. Sex role - Research. 3.
Sexology - Research. 4. Feminist theory. I. Pilcher, Jane. II.
Coffey, Amanda, 1967- III. Series.*
*TC HQ1075 .G4617 1996*

**Gender and society :** essays based on Herbert Spencer
lectures given in the University of Oxford / edited by
Colin Blakemore, Susan Iversen. Oxford ; New York :
Oxford University Press, 2000. viii, 205 p. : ill. ; 23 cm.
Includes bibliographical references (p. 187-199) and index.
ISBN 0-19-829792-0 DDC 305.3
*1. Sex role. 2. Sex differences. 3. Women - Social conditions. I.
Blakemore, Colin. II. Iversen, Susan D., 1940-*
*TC HQ1075 .G4619 2000*

**Gender and the interpretation of emotion**
[videorecording] / [Open University]. Princeton, NJ :
Films for the Humanities & Sciences, c1997. 1
videocassette (25 min.) : sd., col. ; 1/2 in. VHS. Catalogued

from credits and container. Statement of responsibility from
container. Narrator, Carol Vorderman. Location sound, Paul
Roberts, Linton Howell-Hughes, Wilf Eynon ; camera, Tony
Sturman ; academic consultant, Kevin McConway. Originally
produced by Open University and the BBC in 1995. For
college through adult. SUMMARY: Describes research on
gauging emotions from still photographs of facial expressions,
and of eyes only, done at Cambridge University under
controlled laboratory conditions, and under uncontrolled
conditions, in the streets, in a newspaper feature and on a
nationally televised program. Researchers were looking for
gender differences in the perception of thoughts and feelings
they "read" on other peoples' faces. Sample sizes, the
advantages and disadvantages of controlled and uncontrolled
conditions, and cultural differences are discussed, as well as,
the implications of the research on understanding the
predominantly male condition of autism.
*1. Facial expression - Testing - Sex differences - Research. 2.
Judgment - Sex differences - Research. 3. Perception - Sex
differences - Research. 4. Thought and thinking - Sex
differences - Research. 5. Autism. I. Vorderman, Carol. II.
Law, Andrew. III. British Broadcasting Corporation. IV. Open
University. V. Films for the Humanities (Firm)*
*TC BF592.F33 G4 1997*

**Gender and work.**
Handbook of gender & work. Thousand Oaks, CA :
Sage Publications, Inc., c1999.
*TC HQ1233 .H33 1999*

**Gender, change and identity.**
Merrill, Barbara. Aldershot, Hants, England ;
Brookfield, Vt. : Ashgate, c1999.
*TC LC2046 .M477 1999*

**Gender, culture, and ethnicity :** current research about
women and men / [edited by] Letitia Anne Peplau ...
[et al.]. Mountain View, Calif. : Mayfield Pub. Co.,
c1999. xii, 363 p. ; 24 cm. Includes bibliographical
references. ISBN 0-7674-0521-8 (pbk.) DDC 305.3/07/073
*1. Women - Research - United States. 2. Women - United
States - Psychology. 3. Men - Research - United States. 4. Sex
role - Research - United States. 5. Ethnicity - Research -
United States. I. Peplau, Letitia Anne.*
*TC HQ1181.U5 G45 1999*

**Gender difference in form and content.**
Tuman, Donna M. 1998.
*TC 06 no. 11000*

**Gender, education & development.**
Gender, education, and development. London ; New
York : Zed Books ; New York : Distributed in USA
exclusively by St. Martin's Press, c1998.
*TC LC2607 .G46 1998*

**Gender, education, and development :** beyond access
to empowerment / edited by Christine Heward and
Sheila Bunwaree. London ; New York : Zed Books ;
New York : Distributed in USA exclusively by St.
Martin's Press, c1999. xii, 223 p. : ill. ; 22 cm. Cover title:
Gender, education & development. Includes bibliographical
references and index. ISBN 1-85649-631-7 (hardcover) ISBN
1-85649-632-5 (pbk.) DDC 371.822
*1. Education - Developing countries. 2. Women - Education -
Developing countries. 3. Women in development - Developing
countries. 4. Educational equalization - Developing countries.
5. Education and state - Developing countries. I. Heward,
Christine. II. Bunwaree, Sheila S. III. Title: Gender,
education & development*
*TC LC2607 .G46 1998*

**Gender, ethnicity, and health research.**
Loue, Sana. New York : Kluwer Academic/Plenum
Publishers, c1999.
*TC RA448.4 .L68 1999*

**GENDER IDENTITY.**
Golden, Valerie. Significant others' perceptions of the
effects of their partners' psychotherapy. 1998.
*TC 085 G566*

Masculinities at school. Thousand Oaks, Calif. :
SAGE, c2000.
*TC LC1390 .M37 2000*

Newman, Stephanie. Self-silencing, depression,
gender role, and gender role conflict in women and
men. 1997.
*TC 085 N47*

Woo, Kimberley Ann. "Double happiness," double
jeopardy. 1999.
*TC 06 no. 11075*

**GENDER IDENTITY DISORDERS.** *See*
**TRANSSEXUALISM.**

**GENDER IDENTITY - ENGLAND - LONDON.**
Gatter, Philip. Identity and sexuality. New York :
Cassell, 1999.
*TC HQ1075.5.G7 G37 1999*

**GENDER IDENTITY IN ART.**
Talking visions. New York, N.Y. : New Museum of
Contemporary Art ; Cambridge, Mass. : MIT Press,
c1998.
*TC NX180.F4 T36 1998*

**GENDER IDENTITY IN LITERATURE.**
Keroes, Jo. Tales out of school. Carbondale : Southern
Illinois University Press, c1999.
*TC PS374.T43 K47 1999*

**GENDER IDENTITY - RESEARCH.**
Gender and qualitative research. Aldershot, Hants,
England : Brookfield, Vt., USA : Avebury, c1996.
*TC HQ1075 .G4617 1996*

**GENDER IDENTITY - UNITED STATES -
PSYCHOLOGICAL ASPECTS.**
McCloskey, Deirdre N. Crossing. Chicago, Ill. :
University of Chicago Press, 1999.
*TC HQ77.8.M39 A3 1999*

**Gender in the secondary curriculum :** balancing the
books / edited by Ann Clark and Elaine Millard.
London ; New York : Routledge, 1998. xiii, 259 p. : ill. ;
24 cm. Includes bibliographical references and index. ISBN 0-
415-16701-9 ISBN 0-415-16702-7 (pbk.) DDC 306.43
*1. Sex differences in education - Great Britain. 2. Education,
Secondary - Great Britain - Curricula. 3. Feminism and
education - Great Britain. 4. Educational equalization - Great
Britain. I. Clark, Ann, 1961- II. Millard, Elaine.*
*TC LC212.93.G7 G46 1998*

**Gender inequalities in health** / edited by Ellen
Annandale and Kate Hunt. Buckingham [England] ;
Philadelphia : Open University Press, 2000. ix, 214 p. :
ill. ; 24 cm. Includes bibliographical references and index.
ISBN 0-335-20365-5 (hbk.) ISBN 0-335-20364-7 (pbk.) DDC
362.1
*1. Health - Sex differences. 2. Medical care - Utilization - Sex
differences. 3. Sex discrimination in medicine. I. Annandale,
Ellen. II. Hunt, Kate, 1959-*
*TC RA564.85 .G4653 2000*

**Gender, literacy, and life chances in Sub-Saharan
Africa.**
Egbo, Benedicta, 1954- Clevedon ; Buffalo :
Multilingual Matters, c2000.
*TC LC2412 .E42 2000*

**Gender mainstreaming in education.**
Leo-Rhynie, Elsa. London : Commonwealth
Secretariat, c1999.
*TC LC2572 .L46 1999*

**Gender management system series**
Leo-Rhynie, Elsa. Gender mainstreaming in
education. London : Commonwealth Secretariat,
c1999.
*TC LC2572 .L46 1999*

**Gender, policy & educational change.**
Gender, policy and educational change :. London ;
New York : Routledge, 2000.
*TC LC213.3.G7 G48 2000*

**Gender, policy and educational change : :** shifting
agendas in the UK and Europe / edited by Jane
Salisbury and Sheila Riddell. London ; New York :
Routledge, 2000. xxii, 315 p. : ill. ; 24 cm. Cover title:
Gender, policy & educational change. Includes bibliographical
references and index. ISBN 0-415-19433-4 (hard) ISBN
0-415-19434-2 (pbk.)
*1. Educational equalization - Great Britain. 2. Sex
discrimination in education - Great Britain. 3. Educational
equalization - Europe. 4. Sex discrimination in education -
Europe. I. Salisbury, Jane. II. Riddell, Sheila. III. Title:
Gender, policy & educational change.*
*TC LC213.3.G7 G48 2000*

**Gender, politics and communication** / edited by
Annabelle Sreberny, Liesbet van Zoonen. Cresskill,
N.J. : Hampton Press, c2000. ix, 348 p. ; 24 cm. (The
Hampton Press communication series. Political
communication) Includes bibliographical references and
indexes. ISBN 1-57273-241-5 (hbk.) ISBN 1-57273-242-3
(pbk.) DDC 302.23/082
*1. Women in mass media. 2. Women in politics. 3. Mass
media - Political aspects. I. Sreberny, Annabelle. II. Zoonen,
Liesbet van, 1959- III. Series.*
*TC P94.5.W65 G46 2000*

**GENDER ROLE.** *See* **SEX ROLE.**

**GENDER (SEX).** *See* **SEX.**

**The gendered atom.**
Roszak, Theodore, 1933- Berkeley, Calif. : Conari
Press, 1999.
*TC BF64 .R69 1999*

**Gendered missions :** women and men in missionary
discourse and practice / edited by Mary Taylor Huber
and Nancy C. Lutkehaus. Ann Arbor : University of

Michigan Press, c1999. x, 252 p. : ill., map ; 24 cm.
Includes bibliographical references and index. CONTENTS:
Introduction: gendered missions at home and abroad / Mary
Taylor Huber and Nancy C. Lutkehaus -- Missionary-imperial
feminism / Susan Thorne -- Piety and patriarchy: contested
gender regimes in nineteenth-century evangelical missions /
Line Nyhagen Predelli and Jon Miller -- Altruism and
domesticity: images of missionizing women among the church
missionary society in nineteenth-century East Africa / T. O.
Beidelman -- Why can't a woman be more like a man?
bureaucratic contradictions in the Dutch missionary society /
Rita Smith Kipp -- The dangers of immorality: dignity and
disorder in gender relations in a northern New Guinea diocese /
Mary taylor Huber -- Missionary maternalism: gendered
images of the Holy Spirit sisters in colonial New Guinea /
Nancy C. Lutkehaus. ISBN 0-472-10987-1 (alk. paper) DDC
266/.0082
*1. Women in missionary work - History. 2. Women
missionaries - History. 3. Missions - History. I. Huber, Mary
Taylor, 1944- II. Lutkehaus, Nancy.*
*TC BV2610 .G46 1999*

**Gendering elites** : economic and political leadership in
27 industrialised societies / coordinated and edited by
Mino Vianello and Gwen Moore ; foreword by
Cynthia Fuchs Epstein. Houndmills, Basingstoke,
Hampshire : Macmillan Press ; New York : St.
Martin's Press, 2000. xxv, 304 p. : ill. ; 23 cm. (Advances
in political science) Includes bibliographical references (p.
289-300) and index. ISBN 0-333-77697-6 (hc.) ISBN
0-333-77698-4 (pbk.) ISBN 0-312-23213-6 (U.S.) DDC
303.3/4
*1. Leadership. 2. Elite (Social sciences) 3. Power (Social
sciences) 4. Women in public life. I. Vianello, Mino, 1927- II.
Moore, Gwen, 1944- III. Series: Advances in political science
(New York, N.Y.)*
*TC HM1261 .G46 2000*

**Gendering the city** : women, boundaries, and visions of
urban life / edited by Kristine B. Miranne & Alma H.
Young. Lanham [Md.] : Rowman & Littlefield, c2000.
ix, 229 p. ; 24 cm. Includes bibliographical references and
index. ISBN 0-8476-9450-X (cloth : alk. paper) ISBN
0-8476-9451-8 (pbk. : alk. paper) DDC 307.1/216/082
*1. Women and city planning. 2. Urban ecology. 3. Urban
women - Social conditions. 4. Feminist theory. I. Miranne,
Kristine B. II. Young, Alma H.*
*TC HT166 .G4614 2000*

**GENE SPLICING.** *See* **GENETIC ENGINEERING.**

**GENEALOGICAL RESEARCH.** *See*
**GENEALOGY.**

**GENEALOGY.** *See* **BIOGRAPHY.**

**GENEALOGY - HANDBOOKS, MANUALS, ETC.**
*See* **GENEALOGY.**

**GENEALOGY - RESEARCH.** *See* **GENEALOGY.**

**GENEALOGY - STUDY AND TEACHING
(ELEMENTARY) - UNITED STATES.**
History comes home. York, Me. : Stenhouse
Publishers, c2000.
*TC CS49 .H57 2000*

**General catalogue issue <1972-1973>.**
Harvard University. The Harvard University
catalogue. Cambridge : Published for the University
by C.W. Sever, 1873-c1975.

**GENERAL EDUCATION.** *See* **LITERACY.**

**General education in school and college** / a committee
report by members of the faculties of Andover,
Exeter, Lawrenceville, Harvard, Princeton and Yale.
Cambridge : Harvard University Press, 1952. v, 142 p. ;
22 cm. DDC 373
*1. Education - Curricula. 2. Articulation (Education) 3.
Universities and colleges - Curricula. I. Phillips Academy.*
*TC 372G28*

**General family functioning, parental bonding, and
attachment style.**
Woodruff, Debra, 1967- 1998.
*TC 085 W858*

**The General Teaching Council.**
Sayer, John, 1931- London : Cassell, 2000.
*TC LB1775.4.G7 S39 2000*

**GENERAL TEACHING COUNCIL FOR
ENGLAND.**
Sayer, John, 1931- The General Teaching Council.
London : Cassell, 2000.
*TC LB1775.4.G7 S39 2000*

**GENERAL TEACHING COUNCIL FOR WALES.**
Sayer, John, 1931- The General Teaching Council.
London : Cassell, 2000.
*TC LB1775.4.G7 S39 2000*

**A general theory of love.**
Lewis, Thomas. New York : Random House, 2000.
*TC BF575.L8 L49 2000*

**GENERAL WILL.** *See* **CONSENSUS (SOCIAL
SCIENCES).**

**Generations at risk** : reproductive health and the
environment / Ted Schettler ... [et al.]. Cambridge,
Mass. : MIT Press, c1999. xviii, 417 p. : ill. ; 24 cm.
Includes bibliographical references (p. [337]-396) and index.
ISBN 0-262-19413-9 (alk. paper) DDC 615.9/02/09744
*1. Reproductive toxicology. 2. Reproduction. 3. Toxicology. I.
Schettler, Ted.*
*TC RA1224.2 .G46 1999*

**GENERATIVE GRAMMAR.** *See also*
**GOVERNMENT-BINDING THEORY
(LINGUISTICS); MINIMALIST THEORY
(LINGUISTICS); OPTIMALITY THEORY
(LINGUISTICS); PRINCIPLES AND
PARAMETERS (LINGUISTICS).**
Cook, V. J. (Vivian James), 1940- Chomsky's
universal grammar. 2nd [updated] ed. Oxford, OX,
UK ; Cambridge, Mass., USA : Blackwell Publishers,
1996.
*TC P85.C47 C66 1996*

The development of binding. Hillsdale, N.J. :
Lawrence Erlbaum , 1992.
*TC P158.2 .D5 1992*

Functional categories, argument structure and
parametric variation. Edinburgh : Centre for Cognitive
Study, University of Edinburgh, c1994.
*TC P151 .F86 1994*

Nida, Eugène Albert, 1914- Componential analysis of
meaning. The Hague : Mouton, 1975.
*TC P325 .N5*

**GENERATIVE GRAMMAR - CONGRESSES.**
The generative study of second language acquisition.
Mahwah, N.J. : L. Erlbaum, 1998.
*TC P118.2 .G46 1998*

**GENERATIVE ORGANS, FEMALE - DISEASES.**
*See* **GYNECOLOGY.**

**The generative study of second language acquisition** /
edited by Suzanne Flynn, Gita Martohardjono, Wayne
O'Neil. Mahwah, N.J. : L. Erlbaum, 1998. xiv, 366 p. :
ill. ; 24 cm. Papers presented at a conference held Jan. 1993,
Massachusetts Institute of Technology. Includes
bibliographical references and indexes. ISBN 0-8058-1553-8
(alk. paper) ISBN 0-8058-1554-6 (pbk. : alk. paper) DDC 418
*1. Second language acquisition - Congresses. 2. Generative
grammar - Congresses. I. Flynn, Suzanne. II. Martohardjono,
Gita, 1956- III. O'Neil, Wayne A.*
*TC P118.2 .G46 1998*

**GENEROSITY.** *See* **GIFTS.**

**GENEROSITY - FICTION.**
Munsch, Robert N., 1945- Ribbon rescue. New York :
Scholastic, 1999.
*TC PZ7.M927 Ri 1999*

**GENETIC ENGINEERING.** *See* **CLONING.**

**GENETIC ENGINEERING - FICTION.**
Lasky, Kathryn. Star split. 1st ed. New York :
Hyperion Books for Children, 1999.
*TC PZ7.L3274 St 1999*

**GENETIC INTERVENTION.** *See* **GENETIC
ENGINEERING.**

**GENETIC PSYCHOLOGY.** *See also*
**INTELLIGENCE LEVELS; MATURATION
(PSYCHOLOGY).**
The evolution of cognition. Cambridge, Mass. : MIT
Press, c2000.
*TC BF701 .E598 2000*

McNamara, Patrick, 1956- Mind and variability.
Westport, Conn. : Praeger, 1999.
*TC BF371 .M385 1999*

Oyama, Susan. Evolution's eye. Durham, NC : Duke
University Press, 2000.
*TC BF713 .O93 2000*

Plotkin, H. C. (Henry C.) Evolution in mind.
Cambridge, Mass. : Harvard University Press, 1998.
*TC BF701 .P57 1998*

Wright, Robert, 1957- The moral animal. 1st Vintage
books ed. New York : Vintage Books, 1995, c1994.
*TC GN365.9 .W75 1995*

**GENETIC RECOMBINATION.** *See* **GENETIC
ENGINEERING.**

**GENETIC SURGERY.** *See* **GENETIC
ENGINEERING.**

**GENETIC VECTORS.** *See* **VIRUSES.**

**GENETICS, BEHAVIORAL - CONGRESSES.**
Genetics of criminal and antisocial behaviour.
Chichester ; New York : Wiley, 1996.
*TC HV6047 .G46 1996*

**GENETICS, MEDICAL.**
McConkey, Edwin H. Human genetics. Boston : Jones
and Bartlett Publishers, c1993.
*TC QH431 .M3298 1993*

**GENETICS, MEDICAL - NURSES'
INSTRUCTION.**
Lashley, Felissa R., 1941- Clinical genetics in nursing
practice. 2nd ed. New York : Springer, c1998.
*TC RB155 .L37 1998*

**Genetics of criminal and antisocial behaviour.**
Chichester ; New York : Wiley, 1996. viii, 283 p. [1]
folded leaf of plates : ill., map ; 24 cm. (Ciba foundation
symposium ; 194) Based on the Symposium on Genetics of
Criminal and Antisocial Behaviour, held at the Ciba
Foundation, London, Feb. 14-16, 1995. Editors: Gregory R.
Bock and Jamie A. Goode. Includes bibliographical references
and indexes. ISBN 0-471-95719-4 DDC 364.2/4
*1. Criminal behavior - Genetic aspects - Congresses. 2.
Antisocial personality disorders - Genetic aspects -
Congresses. 3. Behavioral genetics - Congresses. 4. Genetics,
Behavioral - congresses. 5. Crime - congresses. 6. Social
Behavior Disorders - genetics - congresses. I. Bock, Gregory.
II. Goode, Jamie. III. Symposium on Genetics of Criminal and
Antisocial Behaviour (1995 : Ciba Foundation) IV. Series.*
*TC HV6047 .G46 1996*

**GENIUS.** *See also* **CREATION (LITERARY,
ARTISTIC, ETC.).**
Genius and eminence. 2nd ed. Oxford ; New York :
Pergamon Press, 1992.
*TC BF412 .G43 1992*

Howe, Michael J. A., 1940- Genius explained.
Cambridge, U.K. ; New York : Cambridge University
Press, 1999.
*TC BF416.A1 H68 1999*

Kincheloe, Joe L. The stigma of genius. New York ;
Canterbury [England] : P. Lang, c1999.
*TC LB875.E562 K56 1999*

**Genius and eminence** / edited by Robert S. Albert. 2nd
ed. Oxford ; New York : Pergamon Press, 1992. xviii,
410 p. : ill., maps ; 24 cm. (International series in experimental
social psychology) Includes bibliographical references and
indexes. ISBN 0-08-037764-5 (HC) ISBN 0-08-037765-3 (FC)
DDC 153.9/8
*1. Genius. 2. Creative ability. 3. Nature and nurture. 4.
Achievement. 5. Creativeness. 6. Famous Persons. 7.
Psychology, Social. I. Albert, Robert S. II. Series.*
*TC BF412 .G43 1992*

**GENIUS - CASE STUDIES.**
Howe, Michael J. A., 1940- Genius explained.
Cambridge, U.K. ; New York : Cambridge University
Press, 1999.
*TC BF416.A1 H68 1999*

**Genius explained.**
Howe, Michael J. A., 1940- Cambridge, U.K. ; New
York : Cambridge University Press, 1999.
*TC BF416.A1 H68 1999*

**GENIUSES.** *See* **GIFTED PERSONS.**

**GENOCIDE.** *See* **HOLOCAUST, JEWISH (1939-
1945).**

**GENOCIDE - STUDY AND TEACHING
(ELEMENTARY) - UNITED STATES.**
Teaching for a tolerant world, grades K-6. Urbana,
Ill. : National Council of Teachers of English, c1999.
*TC HM1271 .T43 1999*

**Genograms.**
McGoldrick, Monica. 2nd ed. New York : W.W.
Norton, 1999.
*TC RC488.5 .M395 1999*

**Genre and institutions** : social processes in the
workplace and school / edited by Frances Christie and
J.R. Martin. London ; Washington : Cassell, 1997. 270
p. : ill. ; 24 cm. (Open linguistics series) Includes
bibliographical references and index. ISBN 0-304-33766-8
ISBN 0-8264-4740-6 (softcover) DDC 401/.41
*1. Discourse analysis - Social aspects. 2. Language and
education. I. Christie, Frances. II. Martin, J. R. III. Series.*
*TC P302.84 .G46 1997*

**GENRE FICTION.** *See* **FICTION GENRES.**

**Genreflecting.**
Herald, Diana Tixier. 5th ed. Englewood, CO :
Libraries Unlimited, 2000.
*TC PS374.P63 H47 2000*

**Genreflecting advisory series**
Herald, Diana Tixier. Genreflecting. 5th ed. Englewood, CO : Libraries Umlimited, 2000.
*TC PS374.P63 H47 2000*

**Genta, Maria Luisa.**
Current issues in developmental psychology. Dordrecht : Boston : London : Kluwer Academic Publishers, c1999.
*TC RJ134 .C868 1999*

**Gentlemen, scientists, and doctors.**
Weatherall, Mark. Woodbridge, Suffolk ; Rochester, N.Y. : Boydell Press : Cambridge University Library, 2000.
*TC R487 .W43 2000*

**Gentry, J. Richard** Spelling connections : words into language / J. Richard Gentry. Columbus, Ohio : Zaner Bloser, c1996. 3 v. : ill. (some col.) ; 30 cm. In the pocket of [v. 3] there are: 1) Word-list sample transparency, 2) Spelling progress chart, 3) The writing progress. Grade 1. CONTENTS: [v. 1. Student text] -- [v. 2] Teacher ed. -- [v. 3] Teacher materials resource book. ISBN 0-88085-773-0 [v. 1] ISBN 0-88085-789-7 [v. 2]
*1. English language - Orthography and spelling - Study and teaching (Elementary) 2. English language - Orthography and spelling - Study and teaching (Secondary) 3. Spellers.*
*TC LB1574 .G46 1996 Gr. 1*

Spelling connections : words into language / J. Richard Gentry. Columbus, Ohio : Zaner Bloser, c1996. 3 v. : ill. (some col.) ; 30 cm. In the pocket of [v. 3] there are: 1) Word-list sample transparency, 2) Spelling progress chart, 3) The writing progress, 4) Blackline masters for alternative word lists. Grade 3. CONTENTS: [v. 1. Student text] -- [v. 2] Teacher ed. -- [v. 3] Teacher materials resource book. ISBN 0-88085-775-7 [v. 1] ISBN 0-88085-791-9 [v. 2] ISBN 0-88309-485-1 [v. 3 Word Lists]
*1. English language - Orthography and spelling - Study and teaching (Elementary) 2. English language - Orthography and spelling - Study and teaching (Secondary) 3. Spellers.*
*TC LB1574 .G46 1996 Gr. 3*

Spelling connections : words into language / J. Richard Gentry. Columbus, Ohio : Zaner Bloser, c1996. 3 v. : ill. (some col.) ; 30 cm. [v. 3] includes 1) Word-list sample transparency, 2) Spelling progress chart, 3) The writing progress, 4) Blackline masters for alternative word lists. Grade 5. CONTENTS: [v. 1. Student text] -- [v. 2] Teacher ed. -- [v. 3] Teacher materials resource book. ISBN 0-88085-777-3 [v. 1] ISBN 0-88085-793-5 [v. 2] ISBN 0-88309-487-8 [v. 3 Word lists]
*1. English language - Orthography and spelling - Study and teaching (Elementary) 2. English language - Orthography and spelling - Study and teaching (Secondary) 3. Spellers.*
*TC LB1574 .G46 1996 Gr. 5*

**Genuis, Mark.**
The changing family and child development. Aldershot : Ashgate, c2000.
*TC HQ518 .C478 2000*

**GEODETIC ASTRONOMY.** *See* **TIME.**

**GEOGNOSY.** *See* **GEOLOGY.**

**[Geografiía v shkole (Moscow, Russia)]** Geografiía v shkole / Upravlenie nachal'noĭ i sredneĭ shkoly Narkomprosa RSFSR. Moskva : Gos. ucheb.-pedagog. izd-vo, 1934- v. : ill. ; 26 cm. Frequency: Bimonthly, 1935- . Former frequency: 4 no. a year, 1934. 1934, no 1- . Publisher: izd-vo "Prosveshchenie," 1964-Sept./Oct. 1969; Izd-vo "Pedagogika," Nov./Dec. 1969-1992, 3/4; "Shkola-Press," 1992, 4/5- "Zhurnal dlía uchiteleĭ nachal'noĭ i sredneĭ shkoly," <1934->. Issues 1992, 2/3-    lack monthly designation. Publication suspended July 1941-1945. Organ of: Narkompros RSFSR, <1934->; Ministerstvo prosveshcheniía RSFSR, <1934->-1967; Ministerstvo prosveshcheniía SSSR, 1968-Mar./Apr. 1988; Gosudarstvennyĭ komitet SSSR po narodnomu obrazovaniíu, May/June 1988-Dec. 1991; Ministerstvo obrazovaniía Rossiĭskoĭ Federatsii, '92, 2/3- ISSN 0016-7207
*1. Geography - Periodicals. I. Upravlenie nachal'noi i srednei shkoly Narkomprosa RSFSR. II. Russian S.F.S.R. Narodnyĭ komissariat prosveshcheniia. III. Russian S.F.S.R. Ministerstvo prosveshcheniia. IV. Soviet Union. Ministerstvo prosveshcheniia. V. Soviet Union. Gosudarstvennyĭ komitet po narodnomu obrazovaniíu. VI. Russia (Federation). Ministerstvo obrazovaniia.*

**GEOGRAPHICAL DISTRIBUTION OF HUMANS.** *See* **HUMAN GEOGRAPHY.**

**GEOGRAPHICAL PERCEPTION.** *See* **ORIENTATION (PSYCHOLOGY).**

**GEOGRAPHY.** *See* **HUMAN GEOGRAPHY; MAPS.**

**GEOGRAPHY - PERIODICALS.**
[Geografiía v shkole (Moscow, Russia)] Geografiía v shkole. Moskva : Gos. ucheb.-pedagog. izd-vo, 1934-

**GEOGRAPHY - STUDY AND TEACHING.**
Baerwald, Thomas John. Prentice Hall world geography. Englewood Cliffs, N.J. : Prentice Hall, c1992.
*TC G128 .B34 1992*

**GEOGRAPHY - STUDY AND TEACHING - INDIA - PERIODICALS.**
The geography teacher, India. Madras : The Society for the Promotion of Education in India, 1965-

**GEOGRAPHY - STUDY AND TEACHING (SECONDARY).**
Silver, James F. Ready-to-use world geography activities for grades 5-12. West Nyack, N.Y. : Center for Applied Research in Education, 1992.
*TC G73 .S45 1992*

**GEOGRAPHY - STUDY AND TEACHING (SECONDARY) - COMPUTER NETWORK RESOURCES.**
Sharma, Martha B., 1945- Using internet primary sources to teach critical thinking skills in geography. Westport, Conn. ; London : Greenwood Press, 2000.
*TC G73 .S393 2000*

**Geography teacher.**
The geography teacher, India. Madras : The Society for the Promotion of Education in India, 1965-

**The geography teacher, India.** Madras : The Society for the Promotion of Education in India, 1965- v. : ill. ; 22 cm. Frequency: Bimonthly. Vol. 1, no. 1 (June 1965)- . Running title: Geography teacher. Title from cover. Oct.-Nov. 1966-    Official journal of the Association of Geography Teachers of India.
*1. Geography - Study and teaching - India - Periodicals. I. Society for the Promotion of Education in India. II. Association of Geography Teachers of India. III. Title: Geography teacher*

**GEOLINGUISTICS.** *See* **AREAL LINGUISTICS.**

**GEOLOGISTS.** *See* **PALEONTOLOGISTS.**

**GEOLOGY.**
The blue planet [videorecording]. [New York, N.Y.?] : Unapix Entertainment, Inc. [distributor], c1996.
*TC QB631.2 .B5 1996*

Fate of the earth [videorecording]. [New York, N.Y.?] : Unapix Entertainment, Inc. [distributor], c1996.
*TC QB631.2 .F3 1996*

Ramsey, William L. Modern earth science. Austin, Tex. : Holt, Rinehart and Winston, Inc., c1989.
*TC QE28 .R35 1989*

Tales from other worlds [videorecording]. [New York, N.Y.?] : Unapix Entertainment, Inc. [distributor], c1996.
*TC QB631.2 .T3 1996*

Tales from other worlds [videorecording]. [New York, N.Y.?] : Unapix Entertainment, Inc. [distributor], c1996.
*TC QB631.2 .T3 1996*

**GEOLOGY - STUDY AND TEACHING (SECONDARY).**
Ramsey, William L. Modern earth science. Austin, Tex. : Holt, Rinehart and Winston, Inc., c1989.
*TC QE28 .R35 1989 Teacher's Resource Book*

**GEOMETRICAL DRAWING.** *See* **DESIGN.**

**GEOMETRY.** *See also* **RATIO AND PROPORTION; TOPOLOGY.**
Fisher, Leonard Everett. Look around. New York, N.Y., U.S.A. : Viking Kestrel, 1987.
*TC QA447 .F5 1987*

The high school proficiency test [videorecording]. Princeton, N.J. : Video Tutor, 1988.
*TC QA445 .H5 1988*

**GEOMETRY, INFINITESIMAL.** *See* **CALCULUS.**

**GEOMETRY - JUVENILE LITERATURE.**
Fisher, Leonard Everett. Look around. New York, N.Y., U.S.A. : Viking Kestrel, 1987.
*TC QA447 .F5 1987*

**GEOMETRY - JUVENILE LITERATURE - BIBLIOGRAPHY.**
Cooper, Cathie Hilterbran, 1953- Color and shape books for all ages. Lanham, Md. ; London : Scarecrow Press, 2000.
*TC QC496 .C66 2000*

**The geometry of visual phonology.**
Uyechi, Linda, 1957- Stanford, Calif. : CSLI Publications, 1996.
*TC HV2474 .U88 1996*

**GEOMETRY, PLANE.** *See* **CIRCLE.**

**GEOMETRY - PROBLEMS, EXERCISES, ETC.**
Baynes, Joyce Frisby. The development of a van Hiele-based summer geometry program and its impact on student van Hiele level and achievement in high school geometry. 1998.
*TC 06 no. 10915*

**GEOMETRY - STUDY AND TEACHING.**
Designing learning environments for developing understanding of geometry and space. Mahwah, N.J. : Lawrence Erlbaum, c1998.
*TC QA461 .L45 1998*

**GEOMETRY - STUDY AND TEACHING (ELEMENTARY).**
Gonsalves, Philip. Build it! festival. Berkeley, CA : Great Explorations in Math and Science (GEMS), Lawrence Hall of Science, University of California at Berkeley, c1995.
*TC QA462 .G66 1995*

**GEOMETRY - STUDY AND TEACHING (ELEMENTARY) - ACTIVITY PROGRAMS - UNITED STATES.**
Cooper, Cathie Hilterbran, 1953- Color and shape books for all ages. Lanham, Md. ; London : Scarecrow Press, 2000.
*TC QC496 .C66 2000*

**GEOMETRY - STUDY AND TEACHING (SECONDARY).**
Bumby, Douglas R. Mathematics. 2nd ed. Columbus, Ohio : C.E. Merrill, c1982-<1986.>
*TC QA154.2 .B8 1982*

**GEOMETRY - STUDY AND TEACHING (SECONDARY) - ACTIVITY PROGRAMS.**
Baynes, Joyce Frisby. The development of a van Hiele-based summer geometry program and its impact on student van Hiele level and achievement in high school geometry. 1998.
*TC 06 no. 10915*

**Geometry [videorecording].**
The high school proficiency test [videorecording]. Princeton, N.J. : Video Tutor, 1988.
*TC QA445 .H5 1988*

**GEOPHYSICS.**
The living machine [videorecording]. [New York, N.Y.?] : Unapix Entertainment, Inc. [distributor], c1996.
*TC QB631.2 .L5 1996*

**GEOPOLITICS.** *See* **WORLD POLITICS.**

**GEOPOLITICS - HISTORY.**
Hugill, Peter J. Global communications since 1844. Baltimore, Md. : Johns Hopkins University Press, c1999.
*TC TK5102.2 .H84 1999*

**George, Carol.**
Attachment disorganization. New York ; London : Guilford Press, c1999.
*TC RJ507.A77 A87 1999*

**The George Gund Foundation imprint in African American studies.**
Landry, Bart. Black working wives. Berkeley : University of California Press, c2000.
*TC HQ536 .L335 2000*

**GEORGE, JEAN CRAIGHEAD, 1919- /. JULIE OF THE WOLVES.**
Beech, Linda Ward. Julie of the wolves by Jean Craighead George. New York : Scholastic, c1996.
*TC LB1573 .B434 1996*

Snow Bear / Jean Craighead George ; paintings by Wendell Minor. 1st ed. New York : Hyperion Books for Children, 1999. 1 v. (unpaged) : col. ill. ; 26 cm. SUMMARY: Bessie and a polar bear cub named Snow Bear play on the ice, while her older brother and the mother bear watch to make sure that everyone is safe. ISBN 0-7868-0456-4 DDC [E]
*1. Polar bear - Fiction. 2. Bears - Fiction. 3. Play - Fiction. 4. Eskimos - Fiction. 5. Arctic regions - Fiction. I. Minor, Wendell, ill. II. Title.*
*TC PZ7.G2933 Sn 1999*

**George, Judith W.** A handbook of techniques for formative evaluation : : mapping the student's learning experience / Judith George, John Cowan. London : Kogan Page, 1999. 136 p. : ill. ; 24 cm. Includes bibliographical references (p. 124-130) and index. ISBN 0-7494-3063-X
*1. College students - Rating of - Handbooks, manuals, etc. 2. College teaching - Evaluation - Handbooks, manuals, etc. 3. Education, Higher - Aims and objectives. I. Cowan, John, 1932- II. Title.*

TC LB2333 .G46 1999

**George, Kristine O'Connell.** Old Elm speaks : tree poems / by Kristine O'Connell George ; illustrated by Kate Kiesler. New York : Clarion Books, c1998. 48 p. : col. ill. ; 26 cm. SUMMARY: A collection of short, simple poems which present images relating to trees in various circumstances and throughout the seasons. ISBN 0-395-87611-7 DDC 811/.54
*1. Trees - Juvenile poetry. 2. Children's poetry, American. 3. Trees - Poetry. 4. American poetry. I. Kiesler, Kate, ill. II. Title.*
TC PS3557.E488 O4 1998

**George Washington University.**
Alstete, Jeffrey W. Posttenure faculty development. San Francisco, [Calif.] : Jossey-Bass c2000.
TC LB2335.7 .A47 2000

**George Washington University. Graduate School of Education and Human Development.**
Aguirre, Adalberto. Women and minority faculty in the academic workplace. San Francisco, Calif. : Jossey-Bass c2000.
TC LB2332.3 .A35 2000

Van Dusen, Gerald C. Digital dilemma. San Francisco : Jossey-Bass, c2000.
TC LC5805 .V35 2000

**Georgetown University. Center for Personalized Instruction.**
Journal of personalized instruction. [Washington] Center for Personalized Instruction [Georgetown University]

**Georgia Association of Educators.**
Georgia educator. [Atlanta]

**GEORGIA - CHURCH HISTORY - 20TH CENTURY.**
Stroupe, Nibs. While we run this race. Maryknoll, N.Y. : Orbis Books, c1995.
TC BX8949.D43 S77 1995

**Georgia College Association.**
The High school quarterly. Athens, Ga. : University of Georgia, 1912-[1936]

**Georgia Congress of Parents and Teachers.**
Home, school, and community. Atlanta, Ga. : Georgia Council of Social Agencies, 1923-1926.

**Georgia Council of Social Agencies.**
Home, school, and community. Atlanta, Ga. : Georgia Council of Social Agencies, 1923-1926.

**Georgia Education Association.**
Georgia education journal. Macon, Ga. : Georgia Education Association, 1926-1970.

Home, school, and community. Atlanta, Ga. : Georgia Council of Social Agencies, 1923-1926.

**Georgia education journal.**
Georgia educator. [Atlanta]

Home, school, and community. Atlanta, Ga. : Georgia Council of Social Agencies, 1923-1926.

**Georgia education journal.** Macon, Ga. : Georgia Education Association, 1926-1970. 46 v. : ill. ; 24-29 cm. Frequency: Monthly (except June-Aug.). Vol. 18, no. 6 (Sept. 1926)-v. 63, no. 8 (May 1970). Title from cover. Imprint varies. Issue for Jan. 1927 called v. 18, no 10 but constitutes v. 19, no. 1. Continues: Home, school, and community (DLC)sn 95029884. Continued in part by: Georgia educator (DLC) 79018882 (OCoLC)5924738. DDC 370/.9758
*1. Education - Periodicals. 2. Education - Georgia - Periodicals. I. Georgia Education Association. II. Title: Home, school, and community III. Title: Georgia educator*

**Georgia educator.**
Georgia education journal. Macon, Ga. : Georgia Education Association, 1926-1970.

**Georgia educator.** [Atlanta] v. ill. 29 cm. Frequency: 8 no. a year. v. 1-4, no. 4, Sept. 1970-Feb./Mar. 1974; fall 1979- . Suspended Apr. 1974-summer 1979. Issues for 1979- lack vol. designation. Official publication of the Georgia Association of Educators. Georgia education journal (DLC) 11024627 (OCoLC)1446537. DDC 370/.5
*1. Education - Periodicals. 2. Education - Georgia - Periodicals. I. Georgia Association of Educators. II. Title: Georgia education journal*

**Georgia O'Keeffe** [videorecording] / a production of WNET/13 ; produced and directed by Perry Miller Adato. [Boston?] : Home Vision ; c1977. 1 videocassette (60 min.) : sd., col. with b&w sequences ; 1/2 in. VHS. (Portrait of an artist) (Women in art) Title on container: O'Keeffe. At head of title: Home Vision... presents, from New York, WNET presents... [videorecording]. VHS. Cataloged from credits and container. Camera, Don Lenzer ; sound, Kay Armstrong, Jay Freund, Charles Peck ; film editors, Muriel

Balash, Suzanne Bauman ; music composed and conducted by John Morris. "Produced by WNET/Thirteen for Women in art."--Container. "OKE 01"--Container. Produced by Educational Broadcasting Corporation in 1977. Adolescent through adult. SUMMARY: This sensitive presentation looks behind the O'Keeffe legend to reveal a woman who was also full of warmth, humor and practical wisdom. For the first time, O'Keeffe appeared on film to talk candidly about her work and life, especially her marriage to photographer Alfred Stieglitz. Her paintings also figure prominently here, showing her wide range of style and how nature continually inspired her.
*1. O'Keeffe, Georgia, - 1887-1986. 2. Artists - United States - Biography. 3. Stieglitz, Alfred, - 1864-1946. 4. Documentary films. 5. Biographical films. I. O'Keeffe, Georgia, 1887-1986. II. WNET (Television station : New York, N.Y.) III. Home Vision (Firm) IV. Educational Broadcasting Corporation. V. Title: O'Keeffe VI. Title: Home Vision... presents, from New York, WNET presents... [videorecording] VII. Series. VIII. Series: Women in art*
TC ND237.O5 G4 1977

**GEORGIA - RACE RELATIONS.**
Stroupe, Nibs. While we run this race. Maryknoll, N.Y. : Orbis Books, c1995.
TC BX8949.D43 S77 1995

**GEORGIA - SOCIAL LIFE AND CUSTOMS.**
Foxfire 2: ghost stories, spring wild plant foods, spinning and weaving, midwifing, burial customs, corn shuckin's, wagon making and more affairs of plain living. Garden City, N.Y., Anchor Press/Doubleday, 1973.
TC F291.2 .F62 1973

Foxfire 3. 1st ed. Garden City, N.Y. : Anchor Press, 1975.
TC F291.2 .F622 1975

**Georgia State High School Association.**
The High school quarterly. Athens, Ga. : University of Georgia, 1912-[1936]

**GEOSCIENCE.** *See* GEOLOGY.

**GEOSCIENCES.** *See* EARTH SCIENCES.

**GER Bulletin.**
Schurer, Heinz. [London, German educational reconstruction, 1946]

**Gerard, Margaret Elizabeth Wilson, 1894-1954.** The emotionally disturbed child; papers on diagnosis, treatment, and care. New York, Child Welfare League of America [1956?] 168 p. : ill. ; 24 cm. 1957 printing.
*1. Child psychiatry. I. Title.*
TC RJ499 .G4

**Gerber, Linda L.**
Haines, B. Joan E. (Beatrice Joan Elizabeth), 1920- Leading young children to music. 6th ed. Upper Saddle River, NJ : Merrill, c2000.
TC MT1 .H13 2000

**Gerber, Rodney.**
The child's world. Camberwell, Vic. : ACER Press, 2000.
TC BF723.C5 C467 2000

**Gerber, Sanford E.** Etiology and prevention of communicative disorders / Sanford E. Gerber. 2nd ed. San Diego : Singular Pub. Group, c1998. xiii, 310 p. : ill. ; 26 cm. (A Singular audiology text) Rev. ed. of: Prevention : the etiology of communicative disorders in children. c1990. Includes bibliographical references and index. ISBN 1-56593-947-6 (soft cover : alk. paper) DDC 618.92/855
*1. Communicative disorders in children - Etiology. 2. Communicative disorders in children - Prevention. 3. Communicative disorders. 4. Communication Disorders - in infancy & childhood. 5. Communication Disorders - prevention & control. 6. Communication Disorders - etiology. 7. Early Intervention (Education) I. Gerber, Sanford E. Prevention. II. Title. III. Series.*
TC RJ496.C67 G47 1998

**Prevention.**
Gerber, Sanford E. Etiology and prevention of communicative disorders. 2nd ed. San Diego : Singular Pub. Group, c1998.
TC RJ496.C67 G47 1998

**Gerdeman, Bernice K.**
Stemple, Joseph C. Clinical voice pathology. 3rd ed. San Diego : Singular Pub. Group, c2000.
TC RF510 .S74 2000

**Geriatric audiology.**
Weinstein, Barbara E. New York : Thieme, 2000.
TC RF291.5.A35 W44 2000

**GERIATRIC EXERCISE THERAPY.** *See* EXERCISE THERAPY FOR THE AGED.

**GERIATRIC PSYCHIATRY.** *See also* DEPRESSION IN OLD AGE.
Assessment in geriatric psychopharmacology. New Canaan, Conn. : Mark Powley Associates, 1983.
TC WT150 .A846 1983

Hartz, Gary W. Psychosocial intervention in long-term care. New York : Haworth Press, c1997.
TC RC451.4.N87 H37 1997

Psychological problems of ageing. Chichester ; New York : Wiley, c1999.
TC RC451.4.A5 P7774 1999

Smith, Irmhild Wrede. The effect of structured exercise and structured reminiscing on agitation and aggression in geriatric psychiatric patients. 1996.
TC 06 no. 10700

**GERIATRIC PSYCHIATRY - HANDBOOKS, MANUALS, ETC.**
Handbook of assessment in clinical gerontology. New York : Wiley, 1999.
TC RC451.4.A5 H358 1999

**GERIATRICS.** *See* AGED - MEDICAL CARE; GERONTOLOGY.

**GERIATRICS - HISTORY - PERSONAL NARRATIVES.**
A history of geropsychology in autobiography. 1st ed. Washington, DC ; London : American Psychological Association, c2000.
TC BF724.8 .H57 2000

**Germaine, Kevin P., 1953-.**
Managing evaluation and innovation in language teaching. New York : Longman, 1998.
TC P53.63 .M36 1998

**German educational reconstruction. Publications.**
(No.5.) Schurer, Heinz. GER Bulletin [London, German educational reconstruction, 1946]

**German, J. Bruce.**
Nutrition and immunology. Totowa, N.J. : Humana Press, c2000.
TC QP141 .N7767 2000

**GERMAN LANGUAGE - DICTIONARIES - ENGLISH.**
1,000 German words. Princeton, N.J. : Berlitz Kids, c1998.
TC PF3629 .A14 1998

**GERMAN LANGUAGE - DICTIONARIES, JUVENILE - ENGLISH.**
German picture dictionary. Princeton, NJ : Berlitz Pub. Co., 1997.
TC PF3629 .G47 1997

**GERMAN LANGUAGE - GRAMMAR.**
Komm mit. Austin, Tex. : Holt, Rinehart and Winston, c1995-96.
TC PF3111 .K65 1998

Komm mit. Teacher's ed. Austin, Tex. : Holt, Rinehart and Winston, 1995-96.
TC PF3111 .K65 1995-96 Teacher's Ed.

Komm mit. Austin, Tex. : Holt, Rinehart and Winston, c1995.
TC PF3111 .K653 1995

**GERMAN LANGUAGE MATERIALS - BILINGUAL.**
1,000 German words. Princeton, N.J. : Berlitz Kids, c1998.
TC PF3629 .A14 1998

German picture dictionary. Princeton, NJ : Berlitz Pub. Co., 1997.
TC PF3629 .G47 1997

**GERMAN LANGUAGE - PRONUNCIATION.**
Adams, David, 1950- A handbook of diction for singers. New York : Oxford University Press, 1999.
TC MT883 .A23 1999

**GERMAN LANGUAGE - STUDY AND TEACHING - FOREIGN SPEAKERS.**
Komm mit. Teacher's ed. Austin, Tex. : Holt, Rinehart and Winston, 1995-96.
TC PF3111 .K65 1995-96 Teacher's Ed.

**GERMAN LANGUAGE - TEXTBOOKS FOR FOREIGN SPEAKERS - ENGLISH.**
Komm mit. Austin, Tex. : Holt, Rinehart and Winston, c1995-96.
TC PF3111 .K65 1998

Komm mit. Teacher's ed. Austin, Tex. : Holt, Rinehart and Winston, 1995-96.

**TC PF3111 .K65 1995-96 Teacher's Ed.**

Komm mit. Austin, Tex. : Holt, Rinehart and Winston, c1995.
*TC PF3111 .K653 1995*

**German picture dictionary** / [illustrations by Chris Demarest, Anna DiVito, Claude Martinot]. Princeton, NJ : Berlitz Pub. Co., 1997. 128 p. : col. ill. ; 32 cm. At head of title on cover: Berlitz Kids. Text in English and German. Includes word list. "A Child's First German Dictionary Over 1,000 Words and Phrases"--Cover. Includes index. ISBN 2-8315-6255-4
*1. Picture dictionaries, German. 2. Picture dictionaries. English. 3. German language - Dictionaries, Juvenile - English. 4. English language - Dictionaries, Juvenile - German. 5. Picture dictionaries, German. 6. Picture dictionaries. 7. German language materials - Bilingual. I. Demarest, Chris L., ill. II. DiVito, Anna, ill. III. Martinot. Claude, ill. IV. Title: Berlitz Kids German picture dictionary*
*TC PF3629 .G47 1997*

**GERMANIC LANGUAGES.** *See* **ENGLISH LANGUAGE; GERMAN LANGUAGE.**

**GERMANIC PHILOLOGY.** *See* **ENGLISH PHILOLOGY.**

**GERMANY - FOREIGN RELATIONS - 1933-1945.**
Robbins, Keith. Appeasement. Oxford, UK ; New York, NY, USA : B. Blackwell, 1988.
*TC DA47.2 .R62 1988*

**GERMANY - FOREIGN RELATIONS - GREAT BRITAIN.**
Robbins, Keith. Appeasement. Oxford, UK ; New York, NY, USA : B. Blackwell, 1988.
*TC DA47.2 .R62 1988*

**GERMANY - HISTORY - UNIFICATION, 1990.**
Growing up in times of social change. New York : Walter de Gruyter, 1999.
*TC HQ799.G5 G76 1999*

**GERMS.** *See* **BACTERIA.**

**Germs make me sick!.**
Berger, Melvin. 1st ed. New York : Crowell, c1985.
*TC QR57 .B47 1985*

**The gerontological prism :** developing interdisciplinary bridges / edited by Jeffrey Michael Clair and Richard M. Allman. Amityville, N.Y. : Baywood Pub., c2000. xi, 338 p. : ill. ; 24 cm. (Society and aging series) Includes bibliographical references and index. ISBN 0-89503-201-5 (cloth) DDC 305.26
*1. Gerontology. 2. Aged - Medical care. I. Clair, Jeffrey M., 1958- II. Allman, Richard M., 1955- III. Series.*
*TC HQ1061 .G416 2000*

**GERONTOLOGY.** *See also* **AGING; GERIATRICS.**
The gerontological prism. Amityville, N.Y. : Baywood Pub., c2000.
*TC HQ1061 .G416 2000*

The many dimensions of aging. New York : Springer Pub., c2000.
*TC HQ1061 .M337 2000*

The self and society in aging processes. New York : Springer Pub., c1999.
*TC HQ1061 .S438 1999*

**GERONTOLOGY - RESEARCH.**
Handbook of theories of aging. New York : Springer Pub. Co., c1999.
*TC HQ1061 .H3366 1999*

**GERONTOPSYCHIATRY.** *See* **GERIATRIC PSYCHIATRY.**

**GEROPSYCHIATRY.** *See* **GERIATRIC PSYCHIATRY.**

**Geropsychology in autobiography.**
A history of geropsychology in autobiography. 1st ed. Washington, DC ; London : American Psychological Association, c2000.
*TC BF724.8 .H57 2000*

**Gershwin, M. Eric, 1946-.**
Nutrition and immunology. Totowa, N.J. : Humana Press, c2000.
*TC QP141 .N7767 2000*

**Gerson, Paul Lieber.**
European modernism. New York, N.Y. : OpticalTouch Systems ; Louisville, Ky. : American Printing House for the Blind, c1998-1999.
*TC N6758 .A7 1999*

**Gerson, Randy.**
McGoldrick, Monica. Genograms. 2nd ed. New York : W.W. Norton, 1999.

**TC RC488.5 .M395 1999**

**Gerstein, Mordicai.** Noah and the great flood / Mordicai Gerstein. 1st ed. New York : Simon & Schuster for Young Readers, c1999. 1 v. (unpaged) : col. ill. ; 28 cm. SUMMARY: A retelling of the Old Testament story of how Noah and his family were saved, along with two of every living creature, when God destroyed the wicked of the world with a devastating flood. ISBN 0-689-81371-6 (hc) DDC 222/.1109505
*1. Noah - (Biblical figure) - Juvenile literature. 2. Noah's ark - Juvenile literature. 3. Bible stories. English - O.T. - Genesis. 4. Noah - (Biblical figure) 5. Noah's ark. 6. Bible stories - O.T. I. Title.*
*TC BS580.N6 G47 1999*

**Gersten, Russell Monroe, 1947-.**
Contemporary special education research. Mahwah, N.J. : Lawrence Erlbaum, c2000.
*TC LC4019 .C575 2000*

**Gess-Newsome, Julie.**
Examining pedagogical content knowledge. Dordrecht ; London : Kluwer Academic, c1999.
*TC Q181 .E93 1999*

**Gest Library journal.**
The East Asian library journal. Princeton, N.J. : Gest Library of Princeton University, c1994-
*TC Z733.G47 G46*

**GEST ORIENTAL LIBRARY AND EAST ASIAN COLLECTIONS - PERIODICALS.**
The East Asian library journal. Princeton, N.J. : Gest Library of Princeton University, c1994-
*TC Z733.G47 G46*

**GESTALT PSYCHOLOGY.** *See* **ATTRIBUTION (SOCIAL PSYCHOLOGY).**

**GESTATION.** *See* **PREGNANCY.**

**GESTURE.** *See also* **SIGN LANGUAGE.**
Gesture, speech, and sign. Oxford [England] ; New York : Oxford University Press, c1999.
*TC P117 .G469 1999*

**GESTURE LANGUAGE.** *See* **DEAF - MEANS OF COMMUNICATION; SIGN LANGUAGE.**

**Gesture, speech, and sign** / edited by Lynn S. Messing and Ruth Campbell. Oxford [England] ; New York : Oxford University Press, c1999. xxv, 227 p. : ill. ; 24 cm. Includes bibliographical references and index. ISBN 0-19-852451-X DDC 419
*1. Gesture. 2. Speech. 3. Sign language. 4. Deaf - Means of communication. 5. Human-computer interaction. I. Messing, Lynn S. II. Campbell, Ruth, 1944-*
*TC P117 .G469 1999*

**Gestwicki, Carol, 1940-** Home, school, and community relations : a guide to working with families / Carol Gestwicki. 4th ed. Albany, NY : Delmar Publishers, c2000. xiv, 521 p. : ill. ; 24 cm. Includes bibliographical references (p. 503-514) and index. ISBN 0-7668-0356-2 DDC 372.119
*1. Home and school - United States. 2. Parent-teacher relationships - United States. I. Title.*
*TC LC225.3 .G47 2000*

**Gesunde Ernährung**
Heidelberger Ernährungsforum (5th : 1998 : Heidelberg) Food quality, nutrition, and health. Berlin ; New York : Springer, 2000.
*TC RA784 .H42 2000*

**Get a grip** [videorecording] / John Marshall High School ; Eagle Wing Productions ; Anthony Frazier, director/off-line editor ; Sharonda Hunter, writer/ director ; Jonathan Tillman, producer ; Tracey Coleman, writer. Racine, WI : S.C. Johnson and Son, Inc., 1999, c1998. 1 videocassette (ca. 13 min.) : sd., col. ; 1/2 in. + 4 lesson plans (4 sheets ; 28 cm.). VHS. Catalogued from credits, cassette label, and container. Music, Frank Sensabaugh; sound effects, Michael Starks; videographers: Casey Hardy, Marquis Graves. "This video is a product of a school-to-work transition partnership with the John Marshall High School and S.C. Johnson and Son, Inc. The teaching materials are courtesy of Keep America Beautiful."--Container. SUMMARY: For general audiences. The environmental concept of "eco-efficiency" is explained and explored in this video produced by John Marshall High School at the request of Johnson's Wax. Ways of "doing more with less," "zero-impact," and "sustainability" are discussed as today's children show concern for tomorrow's generation. Recycling, reusability, packaging, chemical content, refillability and availability in concentrated form are the criteria for judging eco-efficiency.
*1. Environmentalism - Popular works. 2. Ecology - Popular works. 3. Environmental protection - Popular works. I. Frazier, Anthony. II. Hunter, Sharonda. III. Tillman, Jonathan. IV. Coleman, Tracey. V. John Marshall High School (Racine.*

*Wis.) VI. Eagle Wing Productions. VII. Keep American Beautiful, Inc. VIII. Johnson Wax.*
*TC TD170 .G4 1999*

**Getting acquainted in conversation.**
Svennevig, Jan. Amsterdam ; Philadelphia : J. Benjamins Pub. Co., c1999.
*TC P95.45 .S89 1999*

**Getting along in Spanish.**
Jarvis, Ana C. Lexington, Mass. : D.C. Heath, c1984.
*TC PC4121 .J37 1984*

**Getting down to business.**
Daub, Mervin, 1943- Montreal ; Ithaca : McGill-Queen's University Press, c1999.
*TC HF1134.Q442 D38 1999*

**Getting near to baby.**
Couloumbis, Audrey. New York : Putnam, 1999.
*TC PZ7.C8305 Gg 1999*

**Getting our kids back on track.**
Bempechat, Janine, 1956- 1st ed. San Francisco : Jossey-Bass, c2000.
*TC LC225.3 .B45 2000*

**Getting real.**
Gray, Kenneth C. Thousand Oaks, Calif. : Corwin Press, c2000.
*TC HF5382.5.U5 G676 2000*

**Getting to know you :** teacher's planning guide. New York : Macmillan/McGraw-Hill, c1997. 1 v. (various pagings) : col. ill. ; 31 cm. (Spotlight on literacy ; Gr.5 l.11 u.4) (The road to independent reading) Includes index. ISBN 0-02-181182-2
*1. Language arts (Elementary) 2. Reading (Elementary) I. Series. II. Series: The road to independent reading*
*TC LB1576 .S66 1997 Gr.5 l.11 u.4*

**Getting your act together**
Jones, Mark W. (Mark Walter), 1947- Dancer's resource. New York : Watson-Guptill Publications, c1999.
*TC GV1589 .J65 1999*

**GETTY CENTER FOR EDUCATION IN THE ARTS.**
Readings in discipline-based art education. Reston, Va. : National Art Education Assoc., c2000.
*TC N87 .R43 2000*

**GETTY CENTER (LOS ANGELES, CALIF.).**
Seibold, J.otto. Going to the Getty. Los Angeles : J. Paul Getty Museum, c1997.
*TC NA6813.U6 L678 1997*

**GETTY CENTER (LOS ANGELES, CALIF.) - JUVENILE LITERATURE.**
Seibold, J.otto. Going to the Getty. Los Angeles : J. Paul Getty Museum, c1997.
*TC NA6813.U6 L678 1997*

**Getty Conservation Institute.**
Building an emergency plan. Los Angeles, Calif. : Getty Conservation Institute, c1999.
*TC AM121 .B85 1999*

Mortality immortality? Los Angeles : Getty Conservation Institute, c1999.
*TC N6485 .M67 1999*

**Getzels, Harriet Gordon.**
Summerhill at 70 [videorecording]. Princeton, N.J. : Films for the Humanities, c1992.
*TC LF795.L692953 S9 1992*

**Getzels, Peter.**
Summerhill at 70 [videorecording]. Princeton, N.J. : Films for the Humanities, c1992.
*TC LF795.L692953 S9 1992*

**Geuna, Aldo, 1965-** The economics of knowledge production : funding and the structure of university research / Aldo Geuna. Cheltenham, UK ; Northampton, MA : E. Elgar, c1999. xix, 205 p. : ill. ; 24 cm. (New horizons in the economics of innovation) Includes bibliographical references (p. 177-197) and index. ISBN 1-84064-028-6 DDC 507/.204
*1. Research - Europe. 2. Science and state - Europe. 3. Universities and colleges - Europe. I. Title. II. Series.*
*TC Q180.E9 G48 1999*

**Gewirtz, Abigail Hadassah.** Coping strategies and stage of change among Vietnam combat veterans diagnosed with posttraumatic stress disorder and comorbid substance use disorders / Abigail Hadassah Gewirtz. 1997. v, 139 leaves ; 29 cm. Includes tables. Thesis (Ph.D.)--Columbia University, 1997. Includes bibliographical references (leaves 106-114).
*1. Vietnamese Conflict, 1961-1975 - Veterans - United States. 2. Post-traumatic stress disorder - United States. 3. Veterans - Mental health - United States. 4. Narcotic habit - Treatment. 5.*

*Adjustment (Psychology)* 6. *Substance abuse - Treatment - United States.* I. *Title.*
**TC 085 G338**

Coping strategies and stage of change among Vietnam combat veterans diagnosed with posttraumatic stress disorder and comorbid substance use disorders [microform] / Abigail Hadassah Gewirtz. 1997. v, 139 leaves. Thesis (Ph.D.)--Columbia University, 1997. Includes bibliographical references (leaves 106-114). Department: Education (Psychology). Microfilm. Ann Arbor, Mich. : University Microfilms International, 1997. 1 microfilm reel ; 35 mm. 97-28,204.
*1. Title.*

**Ghana. Dept. of Education.**
Ghana teachers' journal. London : Nelson and Sons, 1957-1968.

**GHANA - HISTORY.**
Boahen, A. Adu. Mfantsipim and the making of Ghana. Accra, Ghana : Sankofa Educational Publishers, c1996.
**TC LG497.M42 B62 1996**

**Ghana journal of education.**
Ghana teachers' journal. Accra. 1952-1968.

Ghana teachers' journal. London : Nelson and Sons, 1957-1968.

**Ghana. Ministry of Education.**
Ghana teachers' journal. Accra. 1952-1968.

Ghana teachers' journal. London : Nelson and Sons, 1957-1968.

**GHANA - POLITICS AND GOVERNMENT.**
Quist, Hubert Oswald. Secondary education and nation-building. 1999.
**TC 085 Q52**

**Ghana teachers' journal.** Accra. 1952-1968. 60 no. May 1952- . Ceased in 1968. Title varies: Gold Coast Education May 1952- . Title varies: Gold Coast teacher's journal 1955-Apr. 1957. Vols. for May 1952-Sept. 1954 issued by the University College of the Gold Coast, Institute of Education; 1955-Apr. 1957 by the Gold Coast Education Dept.; July 1957- by the Ghana Dept. of Education; 1958- by the Ghana Ministry of Education. Continues: Gold Coast teacher's journal. Continued by: Ghana journal of education.
*1. Education - Ghana - Periodicals. 2. Teachers - Ghana - Periodicals. I. Ghana. Ministry of Education. II. Title: Gold Coast Education May 1952- III. Title: Gold Coast teacher's journal 1955-Apr. 1957 IV. Title: Gold Coast teacher's journal V. Title: Ghana journal of education*

**Ghana teachers' journal.** London : Nelson and Sons, 1957-1968. v. : ill. ; 21 cm. Frequency: Quarterly. July 1957-Oct. 1968. Numbered also within year; issues for Apr. 1958-Oct. 1968 called also no. 18-60. Published for Dept. of Education, July 1957-Oct. 1957; by Ministry of Education, 1958- Continues: Gold Coast teachers' journal. Continued by: Ghana journal of education ISSN: 0534-0349.
*1. Education - Ghana - Periodicals. I. Ghana. Dept. of Education. II. Ghana. Ministry of Education. III. Title: Gold Coast teachers' journal IV. Title: Ghana journal of education*

**GHANAIAN ARTS.** *See* **ARTS, GHANAIAN.**

**GHETTOS, INNER CITY.** *See* **INNER CITIES.**

**The ghost of the de Young Museum.**
Frank, Phil. [San Francisco : Fine Arts Museums of San Francisco, 1995]
**TC N739.5 .F72 1995**

**Ghost of the Southern Belle.**
Bodkin, Odds. 1st ed. Boston : Little, Brown, 1999.
**TC PZ7.B6355 Gh 1999**

**GHOSTS - FICTION.**
Bodkin, Odds. Ghost of the Southern Belle. 1st ed. Boston : Little, Brown, 1999.
**TC PZ7.B6355 Gh 1999**

**Giacobbe, Mary Ellen.**
Pinnell, Gay Su. Word matters. Portsmouth, NH : Heinemann, c1998.
**TC LB1573.3 .P55 1998**

**Giangrande, Gregory.** The liberal arts advantage : how to turn your degree into a great job / Gregory Giangrande. New York : Avon Books, c1998. xviii, 184 p. ; 21 cm. ISBN 0-380-79567-1 DDC 650.14
*1. Job hunting. 2. Vocational guidance. I. Title.*
**TC HF5382.7 .G53 1998**

**GIANTS - FICTION.**
Root, Phyllis. Soup for supper. 1st ed. New York : Harper & Row, c1986.
**TC PZ7.R6784 So 1986**

**Gibaldi, Joseph, 1942-.**
Gibaldi, Joseph, 1942- The MLA style manual. New

York : Modern Language Association of America, 1985.
**TC PN147 .G53 1998**

The MLA style manual / Walter S. Achtert, Joseph Gibaldi. New York : Modern Language Association of America, 1985. viii, 271 p. ; 24 cm. Includes index. ISBN 0-87352-699-6
*1. Authorship - Style manuals. I. Gibaldi. Joseph. 1942- II. Modern Language Association of America. III. Title.*
**TC PN147 .G53 1998**

**Gibb, Blair, 1947-.**
Schwartz, Peter, 1946- When good companies do bad things. New York : John Wiley, c1999.
**TC HD60 .S39 1999**

**Gibb, Gordon S.** Guide to writing quality individualzed education programs : : what's best for students with disabilities? / Gordon S. Gibb, Tina Taylor Dyches. Boston : Allyn and Bacon, c2000. viii, 79 p. : ill. ; 28 cm. CONTENTS: Introduction: individualized education programs -- 1. Describe the student -- 2. Describe the student's present levels of educational performance -- 3. Writ the student's annual goals, with benchmarks or short-term objectives -- 4. Describe the special education and realted services needed to achieve the goals -- 5. Describe the extent to which the student will not participate in the general curriculum -- 6. Explain the student's participation in statewide and district assessments -- 7. Describe ways that the student's parents will be regualarly informed of progress toward goals -- Summary -- Appendix: Sample blank IEP form. Completed sample IEP form. Resources. ISBN 0-205-31692-1
*1. Individualized education programs. 2. Handicapped children - Education. 3. Special education. I. Dyches, Tina Taylor. II. Title. III. Title: Writing quality individualized education programs : what's best for students with disabilities?*
**TC LC4019 .G43 2000**

**Gibbons, Andrew S.** Computer-based instruction : design and development / Andrew S. Gibbons, Peter G. Fairweather. Englewood Cliffs, N.J. : Educational Technology Publications, c1998. xiii, 543 p. : ill. ; 27 cm. Includes bibliographical references and index. ISBN 0-87778-300-4 (hardcover) ISBN 0-87778-301-2 (softcover) DDC 371.33/4
*1. Computer-assisted instruction. 2. Instructional systems - Design. I. Fairweather, Peter G. II. Title.*
**TC LB1028.5 .G487 1998**

**Gibbons, Gail.** Say woof! : the day of a country veterinarian / [written and illustrated] by Gail Gibbons. 1st ed. New York : Macmillan ; Toronto : Maxwell Macmillan Canada ; New York : Maxwell Macmillan International, c1992. 1 v. (unpaged) : col. ill. ; 22 cm. SUMMARY: Describes the work of a veterinarian and some of the procedures and instruments he uses to treat animals in his office and on farms. Also tells how to take good care of pets. ISBN 0-02-736781-9 DDC 636.089
*1. Veterinarians - Juvenile literature. 2. Veterinary medicine - Vocational guidance - Juvenile literature. 3. Veterinary medicine. 4. Veterinarians. 5. Occupations. I. Title.*
**TC SF756 .G53 1992**

**GIBBONS, GRINLING, 1648-1721 - CRITICISM AND INTERPRETATION.**
Esterly, David. Grinling Gibbons and the art of carving. New York : H.N. Abrams, 1998.
**TC NK9798.G5 E88 1998**

**Gibbs, Raymond W.** Intentions in the experience of meaning / Raymond W. Gibbs, Jr. New York : Cambridge University Press, 1999. vii, 414 p. ; 24 cm. Includes bibliographical references (p. 339-399) and index. ISBN 0-521-57245-2 (hardcover) ISBN 0-521-57630-X (pbk.) DDC 121/.68
*1. Meaning (Psychology) 2. Intentionalism. I. Title.*
**TC BF463.M4 G53 1999**

**Gibson, Eleanor Jack.** An ecological approach to perceptual learning and development / Eleanor J. Gibson, Anne D. Pick. Oxford ; New York : Oxford University Press, 2000. vi, 238 p. : ill. ; 24 cm. Includes bibliographical references (p. 203-226) and indexes. ISBN 0-19-511825-1 (alk. paper) DDC 155.4/137
*1. Perception in infants. 2. Perceptual learning. 3. Infant psychology. I. Pick, Anne D. II. Title.*
**TC BF720.P47 G53 2000**

**Gidley, Jennifer.**
The university in transformation. Westport, Conn. ; London : Bergin & Garvey, 2000.
**TC LB2324 .U56 2000**

**Gieser, Lon.**
Evocative images. 1st ed. Washington, DC : American Psychological Association, c1999.
**TC BF698.8.T5 E96 1999**

**Gifford, Susan.**
Mathematics in the primary school. 2nd ed. London : D. Fulton, 1999.
**TC QA135.5 .M36934 1999**

**GIFTED ADULTS.** *See* **GIFTED PERSONS.**

**Gifted books, gifted readers.**
Polette, Nancy. Englewood, Colo. : Libraries Unlimited, 2000.
**TC LB1575.5.U5 P64 2000**

**GIFTED CHILDREN.** *See also* **EDUCATIONAL ACCELERATION.**
Howe, Michael J. A., 1940- The psychology of high abilities. New York : New York University Press, 1999.
**TC BF723.A25 H69 1999**

Talents unfolding. 1st ed. Washington, DC : American Psychological Association, c2000.
**TC BF723.G5 T35 2000**

**Gifted children and legal issues.**
Karnes, Frances A. Scottsdale, AZ : Gifted Psychology Press, 2000.
**TC KF4209.5 .K369 2000**

**Gifted children and legal issues in education :** parents' stories of hope / [edited by] Frances A. Karnes and Ronald G. Marquardt. Dayton, Ohio : Ohio Psychology Press, c1991. xxiv, 191 p. ; 23 cm. Includes bibliographical references (p. 156). ISBN 0-910707-16-2 DDC 344.73/07915; 347.3047915
*1. Gifted children - Education - Law and legislation - United States. 2. Gifted children - Legal status, laws, etc. - United States. I. Karnes, Frances A. II. Marquardt, Ronald G., 1939-*
**TC KF4209.5 .G54 1991**

**Gifted children and the law.**
Karnes, Frances A. Dayton, Ohio : Ohio Psychology Press, c1991.
**TC KF4209.5 .K37 1991**

**GIFTED CHILDREN - EDUCATION.** *See also* **TEACHERS OF GIFTED CHILDREN.**
Cleveland Board of Education (Ohio). Cleveland's plan for gifted children. [Cleveland] : Cleveland Board of Education, c1956.
**TC LC3983.C5 A3**

Khatena, Joe. Enhancing creativity of gifted children. Cresskill, N.J. : Hampton Press, c2000.
**TC LC3993 .K56 2000**

Kincheloe, Joe L. The stigma of genius. New York ; Canterbury [England] : P. Lang, c1999.
**TC LB875.E562 K56 1999**

**GIFTED CHILDREN - EDUCATION (ELEMENTARY) - UNITED STATES.**
Polette, Nancy. Gifted books, gifted readers. Englewood, Colo. : Libraries Unlimited, 2000.
**TC LB1575.5.U5 P64 2000**

**GIFTED CHILDREN - EDUCATION - LAW AND LEGISLATION - UNITED STATES.**
Gifted children and legal issues in education. Dayton, Ohio : Ohio Psychology Press, c1991.
**TC KF4209.5 .G54 1991**

Karnes, Frances A. Gifted children and legal issues. Scottsdale, AZ : Gifted Psychology Press, 2000.
**TC KF4209.5 .K369 2000**

Karnes, Frances A. Gifted children and the law. Dayton, Ohio : Ohio Psychology Press, c1991.
**TC KF4209.5 .K37 1991**

**GIFTED CHILDREN - EDUCATION (SECONDARY) - UNITED STATES - CASE STUDIES.**
Corwin, Miles. And still we rise. 1st ed. New York : Bard, 2000.
**TC LC3993.9 .C678 2000**

**GIFTED CHILDREN - EDUCATION - SOVIET UNION.**
Tokar, Inna. Schools for the mathematically talented in the former Soviet Union. 1999.
**TC 085 T572**

**GIFTED CHILDREN - EDUCATION - UNITED STATES.**
Creativity and giftedness in culturally diverse students. Cresskill, N.J. : Hampton Press, c2000.
**TC LC3993.2 .C74 2000**

**GIFTED CHILDREN - IDENTIFICATION.**
Khatena, Joe. Developing creative talent in art. Stamford, Conn. : Ablex Publ., c1999.
**TC NX164.C47 K53 1999**

**GIFTED CHILDREN - LEGAL STATUS, LAWS, ETC. - UNITED STATES.**

Gifted children and legal issues in education. Dayton, Ohio : Ohio Psychology Press, c1991.
*TC KF4209.5 .G54 1991*

Karnes, Frances A. Gifted children and legal issues. Scottsdale, AZ : Gifted Psychology Press, 2000.
*TC KF4209.5 .K369 2000*

Karnes, Frances A. Gifted children and the law. Dayton, Ohio : Ohio Psychology Press, c1991.
*TC KF4209.5 .K37 1991*

**GIFTED CHILDREN - NEW YORK (STATE) - NEW YORK.**
Graham, Sheila L. Urban minority gifted students. 1999.
*TC 06 no. 11119*

**GIFTED CHILDREN - PSYCHOLOGY - AUSTRALIA.**
The many faces of giftedness. Belmont, CA : Wadsworth Pub. Co., c1999.
*TC BF723.G5 M36 1999*

**GIFTED CHILDREN - PSYCHOLOGY - CASE STUDIES.**
The many faces of giftedness. Belmont, CA : Wadsworth Pub. Co., c1999.
*TC BF723.G5 M36 1999*

**GIFTED CHILDREN - PSYCHOLOGY - UNITED STATES.**
The many faces of giftedness. Belmont, CA : Wadsworth Pub. Co., c1999.
*TC BF723.G5 M36 1999*

**GIFTED CHILDREN, TEACHERS OF.** See **TEACHERS OF GIFTED CHILDREN.**

**GIFTED CHILDREN - UNITED STATES - BOOKS AND READING.**
Polette, Nancy. Gifted books, gifted readers. Englewood, Colo. : Libraries Unlimited, 2000.
*TC LB1575.5.U5 P64 2000*

**Gifted grownups.**
Streznewski, Marylou Kelly, 1934- New York : J. Wiley, c1999.
*TC BF412 .S77 1999*

**GIFTED PERSONS.** See also **GIFTED CHILDREN.**
Streznewski, Marylou Kelly, 1934- Gifted grownups. New York : J. Wiley, c1999.
*TC BF412 .S77 1999*

Talents unfolding. 1st ed. Washington, DC : American Psychological Association, c2000.
*TC BF723.G5 T35 2000*

**GIFTED PERSONS - CASE STUDIES.**
Streznewski, Marylou Kelly, 1934- Gifted grownups. New York : J. Wiley, c1999.
*TC BF412 .S77 1999*

**GIFTED STUDENTS.**
Cohen, Joseph W., ed. The superior student in American higher education. New York : McGraw-Hill, [c1966]
*TC 371.95C66*

**GIFTS - UNITED STATES.**
Panas, Jerold. Megagifts. Chicago, Ill. : Pluribus Press, c1984.
*TC HV41 .P34 1984*

**Gigantic!.**
O'Brien, Patrick, 1960- 1st ed. New York : Henry Holt, 1999.
*TC QE862.D5 O27 1999*

**Gilbert, Douglas, 1889-1948.** American vaudeville, its life and times. New York, Dover Publications [c1940, c1968] x, 428 p. front., ill., ports. ; 22 cm. Reprint of the 1940 ed. published by Whittlesey House. Includes music.
*1. Vaudeville - United States. 2. Musicals - United States - History and criticism. I. Title.*
*TC PN1967 .G5 1968*

**Gilbert, Elliot M.**
Nellist, John G. Understanding modern telecommunications and the information superhighway. Boston, Mass. : Artech House, 1999.
*TC TK5105.5 .N45 1999*

**Gilbert, Glen G. (Glen Gordon), 1946-** Health education : creating strategies for school and community health / Glen G. Gilbert, Robin G. Sawyer. 2nd ed. Sudbury, Mass. : Jones and Bartlett, c2000. xix, 346 p. : ill. ; 23 cm. Includes bibliographical references and index. ISBN 0-7637-1334-1 DDC 613/.071/073
*1. Health education - United States. I. Sawyer, Robin G. II. Title.*
*TC RA440.5 .G48 2000*

**Gilbert, Martin, 1936-** A history of the twentieth century / Martin Gilbert. 1st U.S. ed. New York : W. Morrow, c1997- v. <1-2  > : ill., maps ; 25 cm. Includes bibliographical references and indexes. PARTIAL CONTENTS: v. 1. 1900-1933. -- v. 2. 1933-1951 ISBN 0-688-10064-3 (v. 1) ISBN 0-688-10065-1 (v. 2) DDC 909.82
*1. History, Modern - 20th century. I. Title.*
*TC D421 .G55 1997*

**Gilchrist, Cherry.** Calendar of festivals / retold by Cherry Gilchrist ; illustrated by Helen Cann. Kingswood, Bristol, U.K. : Barefoot Books, c1998. 80 p. : col. ill. ; 28 cm. Includes bibliographic references (p. 80) SUMMARY: A collection of eight holiday tales from around the world. ISBN 1-901223-68-X
*1. Festivals. I. Cann, Helen, ill.*
*TC GT3932 .G54 1998*

**Gilchrist, Jan Spivey.**
Greenfield, Eloise. Water, water. [New York?] : HarperFestival, c1999.
*TC GB662.3 .G7 1999*

**Giles, David, 1964-** Illusions of immortality : a psychology of fame and celebrity / David Giles. Houndmills [England] : Macmillan Press ; New York : St. Martin's Press, 2000. viii, 187 p. ; 23 cm. Includes bibliographical references (p. 177-183) and index. ISBN 0-333-75449-2 (Macmillan : hbk.) ISBN 0-333-75450-6 (Macmillan : pbk.) ISBN 0-312-22943-7 (St. Martin's : hbk.) DDC 306.4
*1. Fame. 2. Celebrities - Psychology. 3. Fame - Psychological aspects. I. Title.*
*TC BJ1470.5 .G55 2000*

**Gilhooley, James.** Using peer mediation in classrooms and schools : strategies for teachers, counselors, and administrators / James Gilhooley and Nannette S. Scheuch. Thousand Oaks, Calif. : Corwin Press, c2000. xii, 88 p. ; 27 cm. Includes index. ISBN 0-7619-7650-7 (cloth: alk. paper) ISBN 0-7619-7651-5 (pbk. : alk. paper) DDC 371.4/047
*1. Peer counseling of students. 2. Mediation. 3. Conflict management - Study and teaching. I. Scheuch, Nannette S. II. Title.*
*TC LB1027.5 .G48 2000*

**Gill, Indermit Singh, 1961-.**
Vocational education and training reform. Washington, D.C. : World Bank/Oxford University Press, 2000.
*TC LC1044 .V62 2000*

**Gill, Kenneth Joseph.** Social psychological artifacts in the measurement of consumer satisfaction with health care / Kenneth Joseph Gill. 1996. v, 109 leaves : ill. ; 29 cm. Issued also on microfilm. Includes tables. Thesis (Ph.D.)--Columbia University, 1996. Includes bibliographical references (leaves 85-90)
*1. Consumer satisfaction. 2. Medical care - Evaluation. 3. Social desirability - Testing. 4. Analysis of variance - Data processing. 5. Patient satisfaction - Testing. 6. Medical personnel and patient. I. Title.*
*TC 085 G396*

**Gill, Kent, 1928-.**
Proett, Jackie, 1926- The writing process in action. Urbana, Ill. : National Council of Teachers of English, c1986.
*TC LB1631 .P697 1986*

**Gill, Walter.** A common sense guide to non-traditional urban education / Walter Gill, foreword by James M. Mcphartland; introduction by Molefi Kate Asante Nashville, Tenn. : James C. Winston Publishing Co., Inc., c1998. xix, 358 p. : ill. ; 24 cm. Includes bibliographical references (p. 303-350) ISBN 1-55523-814-9
*1. Education, Urban - United States. 2. Afro-Americans - Education. 3. Minorities - Education - United States. I. James C. Winston Publishing Company (Nashville, Tenn.) II. Title.*
*TC LC5115 .G55 1998*

**Gillam, Ronald B. (Ronald Bradley), 1955-.**
Communication sciences and disorders. San Diego : Singular Pub. Group/Thomson Learning, c2000.
*TC RC423 .C647 2000*

**Gillberg, Christopher, 1950-.**
Developmental disability and behaviour. London, England : Mac Keith Press, 2000.
*TC RJ506.D47 D48 2000*

Peeters, Theo. Autism. 2nd ed. London : Whurr Publishers, 1999.
*TC RJ506.A9 P44 1999*

**Gillborn, David.** Rationing education : policy, practice, reform and equity / David Gillborn and Deborah Youdell. Buckingham [England] ; Philadelphia : Open University Press, 2000. xiii, 253 p. : ill. ; 24 cm. Includes bibliographical references (p. [233]-244) and indexes. ISBN 0-335-20361-2 (hbk.) ISBN 0-335-20360-4 (pbk.) DDC

379.421/2
*1. Educational equalization - England - London - Case studies. 2. Education and state - England - London - Case studies. 3. Education, Secondary - Social aspects - England - London - Case studies. I. Youdell, Deborah, 1970- II. Title.*
*TC LC213.3.G73 L664 2000*

**Gillen, Marie A.**
Addressing the spiritual dimensions of adult learning :. San Francisco : Jossey Bass, 2000.
*TC LC5219 .A25 2000*

**Gillerman, H. (Harriet Ann).**
Educational competencies for graduates of associate degree nursing programs. [Rev.]. Sudbury, Mass. : Jones and Bartlett, 2000.
*TC RT74.5 .E38 2000*

**Gilles Deleuze and the ruin of representation.**
Olkowski, Dorothea. Berkeley : University of California Press, c1999.
*TC N6537.K42 O44 1999*

**Gillespie, John Thomas, 1928-.**
Best books for young teen readers, grades 7 to 10. New Providence, N.J. : R.R. Bowker, 2000.
*TC Z1037 .B55 2000*

Characters in young adult literature / [compiled by] John T. Gillespie, Corinne J. Naden. Detroit : Gale Research, c1997. xiv, 535 p. : ill. ; 25 cm. Includes bibliographical references and index. ISBN 0-7876-0401-1 (alk. paper) DDC 809.3/00835
*1. Young adult literature - Stories, plots, etc. 2. Characters and characteristics in literature. 3. Young adult literature - Book reviews. 4. Youth - Books and reading. I. Naden, Corinne J. II. Title.*
*TC Z1037.A1 G47 1997*

**Gillespie, Paula.** The Allyn and Bacon guide to peer tutoring / Paula Gillespie, Neal Lerner. Boston : Allyn & Bacon, c2000. x, 182 p. ; 24 cm. Includes bibliographical references (p. 171-178) and index. ISBN 0-205-29766-8 DDC 371.39/4
*1. Peer-group tutoring of students. 2. Tutors and tutoring. 3. Writing centers. I. Lerner, Neal. II. Title. III. Title: Guide to peer tutoring*
*TC LB1031.5 .G55 2000*

**Gillespie, Sarah (Sarah L.)** A pioneer farm girl : the diary of Sarah Gillespie, 1877-1878 / edited by Suzanne L. Bunkers with Ann Hodgson ; foreword by Suzanne L. Bunkers. Mankato, Minn. : Blue Earth Books, c2000. 32 p. : ill. (some col.) ; 24 cm. (Diaries, letters, and memoirs) Includes bibliographical references (p. 31) and index. SUMMARY: Excerpts from the diary of Sarah Gillispie, a pioneer in Iowa in the nineteenth century. Includes sidebars, activities, and a timeline related to the era. ISBN 0-7368-0347-5 DDC 977.7/385
*1. Gillespie, Sarah - (Sarah L.) - Diaries - Juvenile literature. 2. Girls - Iowa - Manchester Region - Diaries - Juvenile literature. 3. Manchester Region (Iowa) - Juvenile literature. 4. Manchester Region (Iowa) - Social life and customs - Juvenile literature. 5. Farm life - Iowa - Manchester Region - Juvenile literature. 6. Gillespie, Sarah (Sarah L.) 7. Frontier and pioneer life - Iowa. 8. Diaries. 9. Women - Biography. I. Bunkers, Suzanne L. II. Hodgson, Ann. III. Title. IV. Series.*
*TC F629.M28 G55 2000*

**GILLESPIE, SARAH (SARAH L.).**
Gillespie, Sarah (Sarah L.) A pioneer farm girl. Mankato, Minn. : Blue Earth Books, c2000.
*TC F629.M28 G55 2000*

**GILLESPIE, SARAH (SARAH L.) - DIARIES - JUVENILE LITERATURE.**
Gillespie, Sarah (Sarah L.) A pioneer farm girl. Mankato, Minn. : Blue Earth Books, c2000.
*TC F629.M28 G55 2000*

**Gillet, Jean Wallace.** Understanding reading problems : assessment and instruction / Jean Wallace Gillet, Charles Temple, with Alan N. Crawford, Samuel R. Mathews II, Josephine Peyton Young. 5th ed. New York ; Harlow, England : Longman, 2000. xiv, 498 p. : ill., forms ; 25 cm. Includes bibliographical references and index. ISBN 0-321-01333-6 DDC 372.48
*1. Reading - Ability testing. 2. Reading - Remedial teaching. I. Temple, Charles A., 1947- II. Crawford, Alan N. III. Mathews, Samuel R. IV. Young, Josephine Peyton. V. Title.*
*TC LB1050.46 .G55 2000*

**Gillett, Grant, 1950-** The mind and its discontents : an essay in discursive psychiatry / Grant Gillett. Oxford ; New York : Oxford University Press, c1999. xvi, 445 p. ; 24 cm. Includes bibliographical references (p. [428]-440) and index. ISBN 0-19-852313-0
*1. Philosophy of mind. 2. Psychiatry - Philosophy 3. Brain 4. Personality 5. Discursive psychology I. Title.*
*TC BD418.3 .G555 1999*

**Gilley, Jerry W.** Organizational learning, performance, and change : an introduction to strategic human resource development / [by] Jerry W. Gilley and Ann Maycunich. Cambridge, Mass. : Perseus, c2000. xix, 488 p. : ill. ; 25 cm. Includes bibliographical references (p. 453-468) and index. ISBN 0-7382-0248-7
*1. Manpower policy. 2. Organizational effectiveness. 3. Organizational learning. 4. Organizational change. I. Maycunich, Ann. II. Title. III. Title: Introduction to strategic human resource development*
**TC HF5549.5.M3 G555 2000**

**GILLIGAN, CAROL, 1936-.**
Berube, Maurice R. Eminent educators. Westport, Conn. : Greenwood Press, 2000.
**TC LB875.D5 B47 2000**

**Gilliland, Judith Heide.**
Heide, Florence Parry. It's about time!. New York : Clarion Books, c1999.
**TC PS3558.E427 I77 1999**

**Gilman, Sander L.** The fortunes of the humanities : thoughts for after the year 2000 / Sander L. Gilman. Stanford, Calif. : Stanford University Press, c2000. xiii, 127 p. ; 22 cm. Includes bibliographical references. ISBN 0-8047-3263-9 (acid-free paper) ISBN 0-8047-3264-7 (pbk. : acid-free paper) DDC 001.3/071/173
*1. Humanities - Study and teaching (Higher) - United States. 2. Humanities - Philosophy. 3. Learning and scholarship - United States - History. I. Title.*
**TC AZ183.U5 G55 2000**

**Gilpin, Sue.**
Parr, Susie, 1953- Talking about aphasia. Buckingham ; Philadelphia : Open University Press, 1997.
**TC RC425 .P376 1997**

**Gilreath, James, 1947-.**
Thomas Jefferson and the education of a citizen. Washington, DC : Library of Congress, 1999.
**TC Z663 .T425 1999**

**Gingerich, Carol Joy.** The French piano style of Fauré and Debussy : cultural aesthetics, performance style characteristics, and pedagogical implications / by Carol Joy Gingerich. 1996. 262 leaves : ill., music ; 29 cm. Typescript; issued also on microfilm. Thesis (Ed.D.)--Teachers College, Columbia University, 1996. Includes bibliographical references (leaves 256-262).
*1. Fauré Gabriel, - 1845-1924 - Criticism and interpretation. 2. Debussy, Claude, - 1862-1918 - Criticism and interpretation. 3. Music - France - 20th century. 4. Music - France - Philosophy and aesthetics. 5. Music - Effect of multiculturalism on - France. 6. Performance practice (Music) - France - 20th century. 7. Piano - Studies and exercises. I. Title.*
**TC 06 no. 10644**

**Ginsberg, Allen, 1926-** Howl and other poems / by Allen Ginsberg ; [introduction by William Carlos Williams]. San Francisco : City Lights Books, [1996] 57 p. ; 17 cm. (The pocket poets series ; no. 4) ISBN 0-87286-310-7 DDC 811/.54
*I. Title.*
**TC PS3513.I74 H6 1996**

**Ginsburg, Mirra.** Mushroom in the rain / by Mirra Ginsburg ; adapted from the Russian of V. Suteyev ; pictures by Jose Aruego & Ariane Dewey. New York : Macmillan/McGraw-Hill, 1974. [32] p. : col. ill. ; 38 x 46 cm. SUMMARY: How can an ant, butterfly, mouse, sparrow, and rabbit all take shelter from the rain under the same mushroom? ISBN 0-02-178450-7
*1. Animals - Fiction. 2. Mushrooms - Fiction. I. Suteev, Vladimir Grigor'evich. Pod gribom. II. Aruego, Jose. III. Dewey, Ariane. IV. Title.*
**TC PZ10.3 .G455Mu 1974**

**Ginzberg, Eli, 1911-.**
Employing the unemployed. New York : Basic Books, inc., c1980.
**TC HD5724 .E43 1980**

**Giordano, Gus.**
Jazz dance class [videorecording]. W. Long Branch, NJ : Kultur, [1992?]
*TC GV1784 .J3 1992*

**Giordano, Nan.**
Jazz dance class [videorecording]. W. Long Branch, NJ : Kultur, [1992?]
**TC GV1784 .J3 1992**

**Gipe, Joan P.**
Richards, Janet C. Elementary literacy lessons. Mahwah, N.J. : L. Erlbaum Associates, 2000.
**TC LB1576 .R517 2000**

**Girl Scouts of America. Report.**
Boy Scouts of America. Annual report of the Boy Scouts of America. Washington, D.C., Govt. Print. Off.
**TC HS3313.B7 A15**

**GIRLS. See FATHERS AND DAUGHTERS; MOTHERS AND DAUGHTERS; TEENAGE GIRLS; YOUNG WOMEN.**

**GIRLS - BOOKS AND READING.**
Girls, boys, books, toys. Baltimore : Johns Hopkins University Press, 1999.
**TC PN1009.5.S48 G57 1999**

O'Keefe, Deborah. Good girl messages. New York : Continuum, 2000.
**TC PS374.G55 O44 2000**

**Girls, boys, books, toys :** gender in children's literature and culture / edited by Beverly Lyon Clark and Margaret R. Higonnet. Baltimore : Johns Hopkins University Press, 1999. 296 p. : ill. ; 24 cm. Includes bibliographical references (p. [259]-281) and index. ISBN 0-8018-6053-9 (alk. paper) DDC 305.3/09
*1. Children's literature - History and criticism. 2. Sexism in literature. 3. Girls - Books and reading. 4. Boys - Books and reading. 5. Play - Social aspects. 6. Toys - Social aspects. 7. Sexism. I. Clark, Beverly Lyon. II. Higonnet, Margaret R.*
**TC PN1009.5.S48 G57 1999**

**Girls can succeed in science!.**
Samuels, Linda S. Thousand Oaks, Calif. : Corwin Press, c1999.
**TC Q181 .S19 1999**

**GIRLS - DIARIES - JUVENILE LITERATURE.**
Jernegan, Laura, b. 1862. A whaling captain's daughter. Mankato, Minn. : Blue Earth Books, c2000.
**TC G545 .J47 2000**

**GIRLS - EDUCATION. See WOMEN - EDUCATION.**

**GIRLS - EMPLOYMENT. See CHILDREN - EMPLOYMENT.**

**GIRLS - ETHNIC IDENTITY.**
Woo, Kimberley Ann. "Double happiness," double jeopardy. 1999.
**TC 06 no. 11075**

**GIRLS - GEORGIA - ATLANTA - DIARIES - JUVENILE LITERATURE.**
Berry, Carrie, b. 1854. A Confederate girl. Mankato, Minn. : Blue Earth Books, c2000.
**TC E605 .B5 2000**

**GIRLS IN LITERATURE.**
O'Keefe, Deborah. Good girl messages. New York : Continuum, 2000.
**TC PS374.G55 O44 2000**

**GIRLS - IOWA - MANCHESTER REGION - DIARIES - JUVENILE LITERATURE.**
Gillespie, Sarah (Sarah L.) A pioneer farm girl. Mankato, Minn. : Blue Earth Books, c2000.
**TC F629.M28 G55 2000**

**GIRLS - NEW YORK (STATE) - CANANDAIGUA - DIARIES - JUVENILE LITERATURE.**
Richards, Caroline Cowles, 1842-1913. A nineteenth-century schoolgirl. Mankato, Minn. : Blue Earth Books, c2000.
**TC F129.C2 R53 2000**

**GIRLS - WEST (U.S.) - DIARIES - JUVENILE LITERATURE.**
Hester, Sallie. A covered wagon girl. Mankato, Minn. : Blue Earth Books, c2000.
**TC F593 .H47 2000**

**Giroux, Henry A.** Channel surfing : race talk and the destruction of today's youth / Henry A. Giroux. 1st ed. New York : St. Martin's Press, 1997. 248 p. ; 22 cm. Includes bibliographical references (p. [217]-244) and index. ISBN 0-312-16265-0 DDC 305.235
*1. Youth - United States. 2. Mass media - Social aspects - United States. 3. Racism - United States. 4. Popular culture - United States. I. Title.*
**TC HQ799.7 .G57 1997**

Stealing innocence : youth. corporate power, and the politics of culture / Henry A. Giroux. 1st ed. New York : St. Martin's Press, 2000. 197 p. ; 22 cm. Includes bibliographical references (p. [173]-192) and index. ISBN 0-312-22440-0 DDC 306
*1. Culture - Political aspects. 2. Politics and culture. 3. Children and adults. 4. Education - Aims and objectives. 5. Free enterprise. 6. Industries - Social aspects. 7. Civil society. I. Title.*
**TC HM621 .G57 2000**

**Gitelman, Lisa.** Scripts, grooves, and writing machines : representing technology in the Edison era / Lisa Gitelman. Stanford, Calif. : Stanford University Press, c1999. vii, 282 p. : ill. ; 23 cm. Includes bibliographical references (p. 257-275) and index. ISBN 0-8047-3270-1 (cl. : alk. paper) ISBN 0-8047-3872-6 (pa. : alk. paper) DDC 302.2/0973
*1. Communication and technology - United States - History. 2. Literacy - Technological innovations - United States - History. I. Title.*
**TC P96.T422 U6343**

**Gitta, Cosmas.** International human rights : an imperial imposition? (A case study of Buganda, 1856-1955) / Cosmas Gitta. 1998. vii, 242 leaves : map ; 29 cm. Issued also on microfilm. Thesis (Ph.D.)--Columbia University, 1998. Includes bibliographical references (leaves 231-241).
*1. Human rights - Uganda - Case study. 2. Ganda (African people) - Politics and government. 3. Ganda (African people) - Social conditions. 4. Social structure - Uganda. 5. Marriage - Uganda. 6. Family - Uganda. 7. Uganda - History. I. Title.*
**TC 085 G4398**

**Giulianotti, Richard, 1966-** Football : a sociology of the global game / Richard Giulianotti. Cambridge, UK : Polity Press ; Malden, MA : Blackwell Publishers, 1999. xvi, 218 p. ; 24 cm. Includes bibliographical references (p. [185]-207) and index. ISBN 0-7456-1768-9 (hbk. : alk. paper) ISBN 0-7456-1769-7 (pbk. : alk. paper) DDC 306.4/83
*1. Soccer - Social aspects. 2. Soccer - History. 3. Sports - Sociological aspects. I. Title.*
**TC GV943.9.S64 G576 1999**

**Give sorrow words.**
Judd, Dorothy. 2nd ed. New York : Haworth Press, 1995.
**TC RJ249 .J83 1995**

**GIVING. See GENEROSITY.**

**Glaberman, Martin.**
James, C. L. R. (Cyril Lionel Robert), 1901- Marxism for our times. Jackson, Miss: University Press of Mississippi, c1999.
**TC HX44 .J25 1999**

**Gladding, Samuel T.** Group work : a counseling specialty / Samuel T. Gladding. 3rd ed. Upper Saddle River, N.J. : Merrill, c1999. xix, 524 p. : ill. ; 25 cm. Includes bibliographical references and indexes. ISBN 0-13-875543-4 DDC 158/.35
*1. Group counseling. I. Title.*
**TC BF637.C6 G5334 1999**

**GLADNESS. See CONTENTMENT.**

**Glander, Timothy Richard, 1960-** Origins of mass communications research during the American Cold War : educational effects and contemporary implications / Timothy Glander. Mahwah, N.J. ; London : L. Erlbaum, 2000. xiv, 237 p. ; 24 cm. (Sociocultural, political, and historical studies in education) Includes bibliographical references (p. 219-232) and index. ISBN 0-8058-2734-X (hbk.) ISBN 0-8058-2735-8 (pbk.) DDC 302.23/07/2073
*1. Mass media - Research - United States - History. 2. Mass media in education - United States. I. Title. II. Series.*
**TC P91.5.U5 G57 2000**

**Glanz, Jeffrey.**
Paradigm debates in curriculum and supervision. Westport, Conn. ; London : Bergin & Garvey, 2000.
**TC LB2806.4 .P37 2000**

Sullivan, Susan, 1943- Supervision that improves teaching. Thousand Oaks, Calif. : Corwin Press, c2000.
**TC LB2806.4 .S85 2000**

**Glanz, Karen.**
Health behavior and health education. 2nd ed. San Francisco : Jossey-Bass, 1997.
**TC RA776.9 .H434 1997**

**Glas, Cees A. W.**
Computerized adaptive testing. Dordrecht ; Boston : Kluwer Academic, c2000.
**TC LB3060.32.C65 C66 2000**

**Glass, David C.**
Environmental influences: New York, Rockefeller University Press ; Russell Sage Foundation, 1968.
**TC BF353 .E5**

**Glass, Laurie.** Read! read! read! : training effective reading partners / by Laurie Glass, Beth Pike, Linda Peist. Thousand Oaks, Calif. : Corwin Press, c2000. xi, 115 p. : ill. ; 28 cm. Includes bibliographical references and index. ISBN 0-7619-7634-5 (cloth: acid-free paper) ISBN 0-7619-7635-3 (pbk.: acid-free paper) DDC 372.42/5
*1. Reading - Parent participation - United States - Case studies. 2. Books Pals (Program) 3. Home and school - United States - Case studies. I. Pike, Beth. II. Peist, Linda. III. Title.*
**TC LB1050.2 .G54 2000**

**GLASSES, EYE.** *See* **EYEGLASSES.**

**Glassie, Henry H.**
**Material culture.**
Glassie, Henry H. The potter's art. Philadelphia :
Material Culture ; Bloomington : Indiana
University Press, 1999.
*TC NK4235 .G54 1999*

Material culture / Henry Glassie ; photographs,
drawings, and design by the author. Bloomington :
Indiana University Press, 1999. 413 p. : ill. ; 24 cm.
Includes bibliographical references (p. 385-404) and index.
ISBN 0-253-33574-4 (cloth : alk. paper) DDC 306
*1. Material culture I. Title.*
*TC GN406 .G53 1999*

The potter's art / Henry Glassie ; photography and
design by the author. Philadelphia : Material Culture ;
Bloomington : Indiana University Press, 1999. 149 p. :
ill. (some col.) ; 23 cm. (Material culture ; 1) "Expanded
revision of the fourth chapter of Henry Glassie's Material
culture, published by the Indiana University Press in 1999"--
T.p. verso. Includes bibliographical references (p. 139-144)
and index. ISBN 0-253-33732-1 (cl : alk. paper) ISBN
0-253-21356-8 (pbk. : alk. paper) DDC 738/.09
*1. Pottery - Cross-cultural studies. I. Glassie, Henry H.*
*Material culture. II. Title. III. Series: Material culture (Indiana*
*University, Bloomington) ; 1.*
*TC NK4235 .G54 1999*

**Glatthorn, Allan A., 1924-** Differentiated supervision /
Allan A. Glatthorn. 2nd ed. Alexandria, Va. :
Association for Supervision and Curriculum
Development, c1997. 105 p. : ill. ; 23 cm. Includes
bibliographical references. CONTENTS: The foundations of
differentiated supervision -- A rationale for and an overview of
differentiated supervision -- Developing the foundations for
differentiated supervision -- Fostering the learning-centered
classroom -- The developmental options of differentiated
supervision -- Providing intensive development -- Fostering
cooperative professional development -- Facilitating self-
directed development -- The evaluative options in a
differentiated system -- Providing evaluative options --
Building homegrown differentiated models -- Developing the
local model. ISBN 0-87120-275-1 DDC 371.2/03/0973
*1. School supervision - United States. 2. Teachers - In-service*
*training - United States. I. Title.*
*TC LB2806.4 .G548 1997*

**Glaze, Leslie E.**
Stemple, Joseph C. Clinical voice pathology. 3rd ed.
San Diego : Singular Pub. Group, c2000.
*TC RF510 .S74 2000*

**Glazer, Joan I.** Literature for young children / Joan I.
Glazer. 4th ed. Upper Saddle River, N.J. : Merrill,
2000. vi, 329 p. : ill. ; 24 cm. Includes bibliographical
references and index. ISBN 0-13-010987-8 DDC 028.5/5
*1. Children - Books and reading - United States. 2. Children's*
*literature - Study and teaching (Early childhood) - United*
*States. I. Title.*
*TC Z1037.A1 G573 2000*

**GLAZES.**
Wood, Nigel. Chinese glazes. Philadelphia, Pa. :
University of Pennylvania Press, 1999.
*TC TP812 .W65 1999*

**Gledhill, John M., 1948-** Managing students / John M.
Gledhill. Buckingham ; Philadelphia : Open
University Press, 1999. xiii, 140 p. ; 22 cm. (Managing
colleges and universities) Includes bibliographical references
and index. ISBN 0-335-20257-8 (hardbound) ISBN 0-335-
20256-X (pbk) DDC 378.1/01
*1. Education, Higher - Great Britain - Administration. 2.*
*Deans (Education) - Great Britain 3. Student affairs services -*
*Great Britain - Administration. I. Title. II. Series.*
*TC LB2341.8.G7 G54 1996*

**Gleitman, Henry.**
Perception, cognition, and language. Cambridge,
Mass. : MIT, c2000.
*TC BF455 .P389 2000*

**GLEITMAN, HENRY.**
Perception, cognition, and language. Cambridge,
Mass. : MIT, c2000.
*TC BF455 .P389 2000*

**Gleitman, Lila R.**
Perception, cognition, and language. Cambridge,
Mass. : MIT, c2000.
*TC BF455 .P389 2000*

**Glendenning, Frank.** Teaching and learning in later
life : theoretical implications / Frank Glendenning ;
with contributions from Sandra Cusack ... [et al.].
Aldershot, Hants, Eng. ; Burlington, Vt. : Ashgate /
Arena, c2000. xii, 118 p. ; 23 cm. (Studies in educational
gerontology ; 4) Includes bibliographical references (p. 103-
114) and index. ISBN 1-84014-802-0 (cloth) DDC 374.00846

*1. Aged - Education. 2. Aged - Education - Social aspects. 3.*
*Learning, Psychology of. in old age. I. Cusack, Sandra A. II.*
*Title. III. Series.*
*TC LC5457 .G54 2000*

**Glendinning, Simon.**
The Edinburgh encyclopedia of Continental
philosophy. Edinburgh : University Press, c1999.
*TC B831.2 E35 1999*

**Glendon, Kellie J.**
Ulrich, Deborah L. Interactive group learning. New
York : Springer, c1999.
*TC RT76 .U46 1999*

**Glenn, Charles Leslie, 1938-** The ambiguous embrace :
government and faith-based schools and social
agencies / Charles L. Glenn ; with a foreword by Peter
L. Berger. Princeton, N.J. : Princeton University
Press, c2000. xii, 315 p. ; 25 cm. (New forum books)
Includes bibliographical references (p. [297]-310) and index.
ISBN 0-691-04852-5 (alk. paper) DDC 361.7/5/0973
*1. Human services - Contracting out - United States. 2. Human*
*services - Contracting out - Europe. 3. Civil society - United*
*States. 4. Civil society - Europe. 5. Church and state - United*
*States. 6. Church and state - Europe. 7. Church charities -*
*United States. 8. Church charities - Europe. 9. Church*
*schools - United States. 10. Church schools - Europe. I. Title.*
*II. Series.*
*TC HV95 .G54 2000*

**Gliner, Jeffrey A.** Research methods in applied
settings : an integrated approach to design and
analysis / Jeffrey A. Gliner and George A. Morgan.
Mahwah, N.J. : Lawrence Erlbaum, 2000. x, 465 p. :
ill. ; 27 cm. Includes bibliographical references (p. 441-448)
and indexes. ISBN 0-8058-2992-X (alk. paper) DDC 300/.7/2
*1. Social sciences - Research. I. Morgan, George A. (George*
*Arthur), 1936- II. Title.*
*TC H62 .G523 2000*

**Glisan, Eileen W.**
Shrum, Judith L. Teacher's handbook. 2nd ed. Boston,
Mass. : Heinle & Heinle, c2000.
*TC P51 .S48 2000*

**The global challenge of health care rationing** / edited
by Angela Coulter and Chris Ham. Buckingham
[England] ; Philadelphia : Open University Press,
2000. xii, 267 p. : ill. ; 23 cm. (State of health series)
Includes bibliographical references (p. [251]-264) and index. ISBN
0-335-20464-3 (hb.) ISBN 0-335-20463-5 (pb.) DDC 362.1
*1. Health care rationing. 2. Medical economics - Moral and*
*ethical aspects. 3. Health planning - Moral and ethical aspects.*
*I. Coulter, Angela. II. Ham, Christopher. III. Series: State of*
*health series*
*TC RA394.9 .G56 2000*

**GLOBAL COMMERCE.** *See* **INTERNATIONAL
TRADE.**

**Global communication and world politics.**
Tehranian, Majid. Boulder, Colo. : Lynne Rienner
Publishers, 1999.
*TC P95.8 .T44 1999*

**Global communications since 1844.**
Hugill, Peter J. Baltimore, Md. : Johns Hopkins
University Press, c1999.
*TC TK5102.2 .H84 1999*

**GLOBAL CORPORATIONS.** *See*
**INTERNATIONAL BUSINESS
ENTERPRISES.**

**GLOBAL EDUCATION.** *See* **INTERNATIONAL
EDUCATION.**

**The global education industry.**
Tooley, James. London : Institute of Economic
Affairs ; Washington, DC : International Finance
Corporation, World Bank, 1999.
*TC LC57.5 .T667 1999*

**GLOBAL ENVIRONMENTAL CHANGE.**
Broad, Kenneth. Climate, culture, and values. 1999.
*TC 085 B7775*

**Global estimates and projections of population by sex
and age.**
World population prospects. New York : United
Nations, 1985-
*TC HA154 .W6*

**GLOBAL INFORMATION INFRASTRUCTURE.**
*See* **INFORMATION SUPERHIGHWAY.**

**Global literacies and the World-Wide Web** / edited by
Gail E. Hawisher and Cynthia L. Selfe. London ;
New York : Routledge, 2000. x, 299 p. : ill. ; 24 cm.
(Literacies) Includes bibliographical references and index.
ISBN 0-415-18941-1 (hbk.) ISBN 0-415-18942-X (pbk.) DDC
303.48/33
*1. Communication and culture. 2. Communication and*

*technology. 3. World Wide Web - Social aspects. 4. Written*
*communication - Social aspects. I. Hawisher, Gail E. II. Selfe,*
*Cynthia L., 1951- III. Series.*
*TC P94.6 .G58 2000*

**GLOBAL METHOD OF TEACHING.**
Fersh, Seymour. Integrating the trans-national/cultural
dimension. Bloomington, Ind. : Phi Delta Kappa
Educational Foundation, c1993.
*TC LC1090 .F47 1993*

Porter, James. Reschooling and the global future.
Wallingford, U.K. : Symposium Books ; c1999.
*TC LB1029.G55 P67 1999*

**Global perspectives for local action :** using TIMSS to
improve U.S. mathematics and science education / a
joint project of the Committee on Science Education
K-12 and the Mathematical Sciences Education
Board ; Continuing to Learn from TIMSS Committee,
Center for Science, Mathematics, and Engineering
Education, National Research Council. Washington,
D.C. : National Academy Press, 1999. xii, 90 p. : ill. ; 28
cm. "This study was conducted by the Continuing to Learn
from TIMSS Committee through a grant from the U.S.
Department of Education (grant number R215U970015) to the
National Academy of Sciences/National Research Council"--
T.p. verso. Includes bibliographical references (p. 87-90) ISBN
0-309-06530-5
*1. Third International Mathematics and Science Study. 2.*
*Mathematics - Study and teaching - United States. 3. Science*
*- Study and teaching - United States. 4. Academic achievement -*
*United States. I. National Research Council (U.S.). Committee*
*on Science Education K-12. II. National Research Council*
*(U.S.). Mathematical Sciences Education Board.*
*TC LB1583.3 .G56 1999*

**Global public goods :** international cooperation in the
21st century / edited by Inge Kaul, Isabelle Grunberg,
Marc A. Stern. New York : Oxford University Press,
1999. xxxviii, 546 p. : ill. ; 24 cm. Includes bibliographical
references (p. 512-516) and index. ISBN 0-19-513051-0
(cloth) ISBN 0-19-513052-9 (paper) DDC 363
*1. Public goods. 2. International cooperation. I. Kaul, Inge. II.*
*Grunberg, Isabelle. III. Stern, Marc A.*
*TC HB846.5 .G55 1999*

**GLOBAL TRADE.** *See* **INTERNATIONAL
TRADE.**

**Global visions :** beyond the new world order / edited by
Jeremy Brecher, John Brown Childs, and Jill Cutler.
1st ed. Boston : South End Press, c1993. xxvi, 317 p. ;
22 cm. Includes bibliographical references and index. ISBN
0-89608-460-4 (pbk. : alk. paper) ISBN 0-89608-461-2 (cloth)
DDC 337
*1. International economic relations. 2. International*
*cooperation. 3. Social movements. I. Brecher, Jeremy. II.*
*Childs, John Brown. III. Cutler, Jill.*
*TC HF1359 .G58 1993*

**GLOBAL WARMING.**
The climate puzzle [videorecording]. [New York,
N.Y.?] : Unapix Entertainment, Inc. [distributor],
c1996.
*TC QB631.2 .C5 1996*

**Global winners.**
Drum, Jan. Yarmouth, Me. : Intercultural Press,
c1994.
*TC LC1099.3 .D78 1994*

**Globalisation and pedagogy :** space, place, and
identity / Richard Edwards and Robin Usher. London ;
New York : Routledge, 2000. 179 p. ; 25 cm. Includes
bibliographical references (p. [158]-169) and index. ISBN
0-415-19114-9 (hard) DDC 370.116
*1. International education. 2. Internationalism. I. Usher,*
*Robin, 1944- II. Title.*
*TC LC1090 .E33 2000*

**Globalities**
Fischer, Steven R. A history of language. London :
Reaktion Books, 1999.
*TC P140 .F57 1999*

**Globalization and education :** critical perspectives /
Nicholas C. Burbules and Carlos Alberto Torres, eds.
New York : Routledge, 1999. 376 p. ; 23 cm. (Social
theory, education, and cultural change) Includes
bibliographical references and index. ISBN 0-415-92048-5
(hard) ISBN 0-415-92047-7 (pbk.) DDC 370.11/5
*1. Education - Social aspects. 2. Education - Economic*
*aspects. 3. Education and state. 4. International economic*
*relations. 5. International education. 6. Critical pedagogy. I.*
*Burbules, Nicholas C. II. Torres, Carlos Alberto. III. Series.*
*TC LC191 .G545 1999*

**Globalization and educational reform.**
Carnoy, Martin. Paris : International Institute for
Educational Planning (IIEP), 1999.

TC LB5 .F85 v.63

**GLOBES - JUVENILE LITERATURE.**
Knowlton, Jack. Maps & globes. New York :
HarperCollins, c1985.
*TC GA105.6 .K58 1985*

**GLOBES, TERRESTRIAL.** *See* GLOBES.

**GLORY.** *See* FAME.

**The glory and the power.**
Marty, Martin E., 1928- Boston : Beacon Press,
c1992.
*TC BL238 .M37 1992*

**Glory and the power (Radio program).**
Marty, Martin E., 1928- The glory and the power.
Boston : Beacon Press, c1992.
*TC BL238 .M37 1992*

**Glory and the power (Television program).**
Marty, Martin E., 1928- The glory and the power.
Boston : Beacon Press, c1992.
*TC BL238 .M37 1992*

**GLOTTOPOLITICS.** *See* LANGUAGE POLICY.

**Glover, Derek.**
Law, Sue. Educational leadership and learning.
Buckingham [England] ; Philadelphia : Open
University Press, 2000.
*TC LB2900.5 .L39 1999*

**Glover, Judith, 1949-** Women and scientific
employment / Judith Glover ; consultant editor, Jo
Campling. Houndmills [England] : Macmillan Press ;
New York : St. Martin's Press, 2000. xi, 190 p. : ill. ; 23
cm. Includes bibliographical references and index. ISBN
0-333-68318-8 (Macmillan : cloth) ISBN 0-312-22928-3 (St.
Martin's : cloth) DDC 305.43/0941
*1. Women scientists - Employment - Great Britain. 2. Women
scientists - Employment - United States. 3. Women scientists -
Employment - France. I. Title.*
*TC Q130 .G64 2000*

**GLYCOSYLATED HEMOGLOBIN.** *See*
DIABETES.

**Glynn, Ian.** An anatomy of thought : the origin and
machinery of mind / Ian Glynn. Oxford ; New York :
Oxford University Press, [1999], viii, 456 p. : ill. ; 25 cm.
"First published in Great Britain in 1999 by Weidenfeld &
Nicholson"--T.p. verso. Includes bibliographical references (p.
[415]-448) and index. ISBN 0-19-513696-9 (hardcover : alk.
paper) DDC 612.8/2
*1. Neuropsychology. 2. Philosophy of mind. 3. Brain. 4.
Cognition. I. Title.*
*TC QP360 .G595 1999*

**Go figure!.**
Farmer, Lesley S. J. Englewood, Colo. : Teacher Ideas
Press, 1999.
*TC QA39.2 .F373 1999*

**GOAL-DIRECTED ACTION.** *See* ACTION
THEORY.

**GOAL-DIRECTED BEHAVIOR.** *See* ACTION
THEORY.

**GOAL (PSYCHOLOGY).**
Emmons, Robert A. The psychology of ultimate
concerns. New York : Guilford Press, c1999.
*TC BF505.G6 E58 1999*

Handbook of self-regulation. San Diego : Academic,
2000.
*TC BF632 .H254 2000*

Katz, Tal Y. Self-construal as a moderator of the
effects of task and reward interdependence of group
performance. 1999.
*TC 085 K1524*

**GOALS, EDUCATIONAL.** *See* EDUCATION -
AIMS AND OBJECTIVES.

**The goat in the rug.**
Blood, Charles L., 1929- New York : Four Winds
Press, 1976.
*TC PZ7.B6227 Go 1976*

**GOD.** *See also* RELIGION.
Bea, Holly, 1956- My spiritual alphabet book.
Tiburon, Calif. : H.J. Kramer, c2000.
*TC BL625.5 .B43 1999*

**GOD - FICTION. <JUVENILE SUBJECT
HEADING>.**
Burningham, John. Whaddayamean. 1st American ed.
New York : Crown Publishers, 1999.
*TC PZ7.B936 We 1999*

**GODDARD COLLEGE.**
Higher education for democracy. New York : P. Lang,
c1999.

TC LD2001.G452 .S33 1999

**Goddard parenting guides**
Ramey, Sharon L. Going to school. New York :
Goddard Press : Lanham, MD : Distributed to the
trade by National Book Network, c1999.
*TC LB1139.35.P37 R26 1999*

**GODDESSES, GREEK.** *See* ATHENA (GREEK
DEITY).

**"Godless communists".**
Husband, William. DeKalb : Northern Illinois
University Press, 2000.
*TC BL2765.S65 H87 2000*

**Godly things :** museums, objects, and religion /
edited by Crispin Paine. New York : Leicester University
Press, 2000. xvii, 235 p. : ill. ; 24 cm. (Leicester museum
studies) Includes bibliographical references and index. ISBN
0-7185-0153-5 (hardback) DDC 200/.75
*1. Religion - Museums. 2. Religious articles - Museums. I.
Paine, Crispin. II. Series: Leicester museum studies series.*
*TC BL45 .G63 2000*

**Godmillow, Jill.**
Nevelson in process [videorecording]. Chicago, IL :
Public Media Inc., 1977.
*TC NB237.N43 N43 1977*

**GODS.** *See* MYTHOLOGY; RELIGIONS.

**Goembel, Ponder, ill.**
McDonald, Megan. The night Iguana left home. 1st
ed. New York : DK Ink, 1999.
*TC PZ7.M478419 Ni 1999*

**Goethals, M. Serra, 1934-** Student teaching : a process
approach to reflective practice : a guide for student,
intern, and beginning teachers / M. Serra Goethals,
Rose A. Howard ; foreword by Ken Zeichner ; [editor,
Debra A. Stollenwerk]. Upper Saddle River, N.J. :
Merrill, c2000. xvi, 223 p. : ill. ; 28 cm. Includes
bibliographical references and index. ISBN 0-13-920125-4
DDC 370/.71
*1. Student teaching - Handbooks, manuals, etc. 2. Teachers -
Training of - Handbooks, manuals, etc. I. Howard, Rose A. II.
Stollenwerk, Debra A. III. Title.*
*TC LB2157.A3 G57 2000*

**Goffin, Richard D., 1956-.**
Problems and solutions in human assessment.
Boston : Kluwer Academic Publishers, c2000.
*TC BF698.4 .P666 2000*

**Goffman and social organization :** studies in a
sociological legacy / edited by Greg Smith. London ;
New York : Routledge, 1999. vi, 229 p. ; 23 cm.
(Routledge studies in social and political thought ; 17) Includes
bibliographical references (p. [198]-215) and index. ISBN 0-
415-11204-4 DDC 301
*1. Goffman, Erving. 2. Social structure. 3. Social interaction. 4.
Social groups. 5. Social role. I. Smith, Greg, M. A. II. Series.*
*TC HM291 .G57 1999*

**GOFFMAN, ERVING.**
Goffman and social organization. London ; New
York : Routledge, 1999.
*TC HM291 .G57 1999*

**Goggin, Maureen Daly.**
Inventing a discipline. Urbana, Ill. : National Council
of Teachers of English, c2000.
*TC PN175 .I58 2000*

**Going far.** New York, N.Y. : American Book Company,
c1980. 95 p. : col. ill. ; 23x22 cm. (American readers ; PP-3)
ISBN 0-278-45809-2
*1. Readers (Primary) I. Series.*
*TC PE1119 .G64 1980*

**Going public.**
Harwayne, Shelley. Portsmouth, NH : Heinemann,
c1999.
*TC LB2822.5 .H37 1999*

**Going to school.**
Ramey, Sharon L. New York : Goddard Press ;
Lanham, MD : Distributed to the trade by National
Book Network, c1999.
*TC LB1139.35.P37 R26 1999*

**Going to the Getty.**
Seibold, J.otto. Los Angeles : J. Paul Getty Museum,
c1997.
*TC NA6813.U6 L678 1997*

**Golan, Romy.**
Kleeblatt, Norman L. An expressionist in Paris.
Munich ; New York : Jewish Museum, c1998.
*TC ND553.S7 A4 1998*

**Gold Coast Education May 1952-.**
Ghana teachers' journal. Accra. 1952-1968.

**Gold Coast teacher's journal.**
Ghana teachers' journal. Accra. 1952-1968.

**Gold Coast teachers' journal.**
Ghana teachers' journal. London : Nelson and Sons,
1957-1968.

**Gold Coast teacher's journal   1955-Apr. 1957.**
Ghana teachers' journal. Accra. 1952-1968.

**GOLD DISCOVERIES.** *See* GOLD MINES AND
MINING.

**Gold fever.**
Kay, Verla. New York : Putnam's, c1999.
*TC PZ8.3.K225 Go 1999*

**Gold, Jodi.**
Just sex. Lanham, MD : Rowman & Littlefield, 2000.
*TC HQ21 .J87 1999*

**Gold, Michael Evan.** An introduction to labor law /
Michael Evan Gold. 2nd ed. Ithaca : ILR Press,
c1998. viii, 72 p. ; 23 cm. (ILR bulletin ; 66) Includes index.
ISBN 0-8014-8477-4 (acid-free paper) DDC 344.7301
*1. Labor laws and legislation - United States. I. Title. II.
Series: Bulletin (New York State School of Industrial and
Labor Relations) ; no. 66.*
*TC KF3319 .G62 1998*

**GOLD MINES AND MINING - FICTION.**
Kay, Verla. Gold fever. New York : Putnam's, c1999.
*TC PZ8.3.K225 Go 1999*

**GOLD RUSH.** *See* GOLD MINES AND MINING.

**GOLD RUSHES.** *See* GOLD MINES AND
MINING.

**Goldberg, Arnold, 1929-** Being of two minds : the
vertical split in psychoanalysis and psychotherapy /
Arnold Goldberg. Hillsdale, NJ : Analytic Press, 1999.
ix, 185 p. ; 24 cm. Includes bibliographical references (p. 173-
178) and index. ISBN 0-88163-308-9 DDC 616.85/236
*1. Multiple personality - Case studies. 2. Dissociative
disorders - Case studies. 3. Dissociative Disorders - case
studies. 4. Personality Disorders - case studies. 5.
Psychoanalytic Therapy - case studies. I. Title.*
*TC RC569.5.M8 G65 1999*

**Goldberg, David P.**
Mental health in our future cities. Hove, England :
Psychology Press, c1998.
*TC RA790.5 .M4196 1998*

**Goldberg, Elizabeth.**
Ellis Island [picture]. Amawalk, NY : Jackdaw
Publications, c1997.
*TC TR820.5 .E4 1997*

**Goldberg, Enid.**
Child labor [picture]. Amawalk, NY : Jackdaw
Publications, c1997.
*TC HD6250.U5 C4 1997*

The depression hits home [picture]. Amawalk, NY :
Jackdaw Publications, c1997.
*TC TR820.5 .D4 1997*

Roaring twenties [picture]. Amawalk, NY : Jackdaw
Publications, c1997.
*TC E784 .R6 1997*

**Goldberg, Ken.**
The Robot in the garden. Cambridge, Mass. : MIT
Press, 2000.
*TC TJ211 .R537 2000*

**Goldberg, Marilee C.** The art of the question : a guide
to short-term question-centered therapy / Marilee C.
Goldberg. New York : Wiley, c1998. xvi, 352 p. : ill. ;
24 cm. (Wiley series in couples and family dynamics and
treatment) Includes bibliographical references (p. [346]-348)
and index. ISBN 0-471-12387-0 (acid-free paper) DDC
616.89/14
*1. Neurolinguistic programming. 2. Questioning - Therapeutic
use. 3. Psychotherapy. I. Title. II. Series.*
*TC RC489.N47 G65 1998*

**Goldberg, Melissa.**
Headline stories of the century [videorecording].
Chicago, IL. : Distributed by Questar Video, Inc.,
c1992.
*TC D743 .H42 1992*

**Goldberg, Ted.** Demystifying drugs : a psychosocial
perspective / Ted Goldberg. New York : St. Martin's
Press, 1999. vii, 291 p. ; 22 cm. Includes bibliographical
references (p. 269-277) and index. ISBN 0-312-22312-9
(cloth) DDC 362.29
*1. Drug abuse. 2. Narcotic addicts. 3. Narcotics, Control of. I.
Title.*
*TC HV5801 .G633 1999*

**Golden, Joanne Marie, 1949-** Storymaking in elementary and middle school classrooms : constructing and interpreting narrative texts / Joanne M. Golden. Mahwah, N.J. : L. Erlbaum Associates, 2000. xiii, 163 p. ; 23 cm. Includes bibliographical references (p. 152-156) and indexes. ISBN 0-8058-3287-4 (pbk. : alk. paper) DDC 372.67/7
*1. Storytelling. 2. Discourse analysis. Narrative. 3. Reading (Elementary) 4. Reading (Middle school) I. Title.*
**TC LB1042 .G54 2000**

**Golden, Valerie.** Significant others' perceptions of the effects of their partners' psychotherapy / Valerie Golden. 1998. iv, 123 leaves ; 29 cm. Issued also on microfilm. Includes tables. Thesis (Ph.D.)--Columbia University, 1998. Includes bibliographical references (leaves 99-107).
*1. Psychotherapy. 2. Interpersonal communication. 3. Psychotherapist and patient. 4. Behavioral assessment. 5. Object relations (Psychoanalysis) 6. Gender identity. I. Title.*
**TC 085 G566**

**Goldfarb, Roz.** Careers by design : a headhunter's secrets for success and survival in graphic design / by Roz Goldfarb. Rev. ed. New York, NY : Allworth Press Council, c1997. 223 p. ; 26 cm. Includes bibliographical references (p. 211-213) and index. ISBN 1-88055-957-9
*1. Commercial art - Vocational guidance - United States. I. Title.*
**TC NC1001 .G65 1997**

**Goldfein, Juli Ann.** The importance of shape and weight in normal-weight women with bulimia nervosa, restrained eaters (dieters), and normal controls (Non-dieters) / by Juli Ann Goldfein. 1997. vii, 172 leaves ; 29 cm. Includes tables. Thesis (Ph.D.)--Columbia University, 1997. Includes bibliographical references (leaves 127-136).
*1. Physical fitness for women. 2. Eating disorders - Diagnosis. 3. Bulimia. 4. Nutrition. 5. Body image. 6. Diet. I. Title.*
**TC 085 G5675**

**Goldin, Augusta R.** Ducks don't get wet / by Augusta Goldin ; illustrated by Helen K. Davie. Newly illustrated ed. New York : HarperCollins Publishers, c1999. 32 p. : col. ill. ; 21 x 26 cm. (Let's-read-and-find-out science. Stage 1) "Ages 3-6"--Jacket. SUMMARY: Describes the behavior of different kinds of ducks and, in particular, discusses how all ducks use preening to keep their feathers dry. ISBN 0-06-027881-1 ISBN 0-06-445187-9 (pbk.) ISBN 0-06-027882-X (lib. bdg.) DDC 598.4/1
*1. Ducks - Juvenile literature. 2. Ducks. I. Davie, Helen, ill. II. Title. III. Series.*
**TC QL696.A52 G64 1999**

**Golding, Martin P. (Martin Philip), 1930-** Free speech on campus / Martin P. Golding. Lanham, Md. ; Oxford : Rowman & Littlefield Publishers, c2000. ix, 118 p. ; 24 cm. (Issues in academic ethics) Includes bibliographical references and index. ISBN 0-8476-8791-0 (hbk. : alk. paper) ISBN 0-8476-8792-9 (pbk. : alk. paper) DDC 378.1/012
*1. Academic freedom - United States. 2. Freedom of speech - United States. 3. College students - Civil rights - United States. 4. Education, Higher - Moral and ethical aspects - United States. I. Title. II. Series.*
**TC LC72.2 .G64 2000**

**Golding, Stephen.** Photomontage : : a step-by-step guide to building pictures / written and illustrated by Stephen Golding. Rockport, Massachusetts : Rockport Pub. Cincinnati, Ohio : North Light Books [distributor], c1997. 144 p. : col. ill. ; 24 cm. Includes index. ISBN 1-56496-289-X (hc.)
*1. Photomontage. I. Title.*
**TC TR685 .G64 1997**

**Goldman, Linda, 1946-** Life & loss : a guide to help grieving children / Linda Goldman. 2nd ed. Philadelphia : Accelerated Development, c2000. xvii, 203 p. : ill., forms ; 28 cm. Includes bibliographical references (p. 167-195) and index. ISBN 1-56032-861-4 (pbk. : alk. paper) DDC 155.9/37/083
*1. Grief in children. 2. Loss (Psychology) in children. 3. Children - Counseling of. I. Title. II. Title: Life and loss*
**TC BF723.G75 G65 2000**

**Goldman, Marlene.** Women and health / edited by Marlene Goldman, Maureen Hatch. San Diego, Calif. : Academic, c2000. 1276 p., [4] p. of plates : ill., maps ; 29 cm. ISBN 0-12-288145-1 DDC 613.04244
*1. Women - Health and hygiene. 2. Women's Health. I. Hatch, Maureen. II. Title.*
**TC RA564.85 .G66 2000**

**Goldring, Ellen B. (Ellen Borish), 1957-.**
**Principals of dynamic schools.**
Rallis, Sharon F. Principals of dynamic schools. 2nd ed. Thousand Oaks, Calif. : Corwin Press, c2000.

**TC LB2831.92 .G65 2000**

Rallis, Sharon F. Principals of dynamic schools. 2nd ed. Thousand Oaks, Calif. : Corwin Press, c2000.
**TC LB2831.92 .G65 2000**

**Goldsmith, Marshall.**
Leading beyond the walls. 1st ed. San Francisco : Jossey-Bass, c1999.
**TC HD57.7 .L4374 1999**

**Goldstein, Arnold P.** The Prepare Curriculum : teaching prosocial competencies / Arnold P. Goldstein. Revised ed. Champaign, Ill. : Research Press, c1999. ix, 899 p. : ill. ; 23 cm. Includes bibliographical references (p. 845-874) and indexes. ISBN 0-87822-419-x
*1. Social skills - Study and teaching. 2. Interpersonal relations - Study and teaching. I. Title. II. Title: Teaching prosocial competencies*
**TC HM299 .G65 1999**

**Goldstein, Bobbye S.**
What's on the menu? New York : Viking, 1992.
**TC PS595.F65 W48 1992**

**Goldstein, David J. (David Joel), 1947-.**
The management of eating disorders and obesity. Totowa, N.J. : Humana Press, c1999.
**TC RC552.E18 M364 1999**

**Goldstein, Gerald, 1931-.**
Handbook of psychological assessment. 3rd ed. Amsterdam ; New York : Pergamon, 2000.
**TC BF39 .H2645 2000**

**Goldstein, Lewis P.**
The Artificial larynx handbook. New York : Grune & Stratton, c1978.
**TC RF538 .A77**

**Goldstein, Susan B.** Cross-cultural explorations : activities in culture and psychology / Suan Goldstein. Boston : Allyn and Bacon, c2000. xii, 387 p. : 28 cm. Includes bibliographical references. ISBN 0-205-28520-1
*1. Culture - Psychological aspects. 2. Cross-cultural studies. 3. Intercultural communication - Problems, exercises, etc. I. Title.*
**TC HM258 .G63 2000**

**Goldsworthy, Candace L.** Sourcebook of phonological awareness activities : children's classic literature / Candace L. Goldsworthy. San Diego : Singular Pub. Group, c1998. viii, 206 p. : ill. ; 28 cm. Includes bibliographical references (p. 205-206). ISBN 1-56593-797-X (pbk.) DDC 371.91/44
*1. Reading disability. 2. Reading - Remedial teaching. 3. English language - Phonetics - Study and teaching (Preschool) 4. English language - Phonetics - Study and teaching (Elementary) 5. Speech therapy for children. 6. Language acquisition. 7. Speech Therapy - methods. 8. Phonetics. 9. Awareness. 10. Literature. I. Title. II. Title: Phonological awareness activities III. Title: Children's classic literature*
**TC LB1050.5 .G66 1998**

**Goleman, Daniel.** The creative spirit / Daniel Goleman, Paul Kaufman, Michael Ray. New York, N.Y., U.S.A. : Dutton, c1992. 185 p. : ill. (some col.) ; 25 cm. "The Creative spirit television series, a production of WETA, Washington D.C., for broadcast on PBS and funded by IBM"--T.p. verso. Includes index. ISBN 0-525-93354-9 DDC 153.3/5
*1. Creative ability. I. Kaufman, Paul, 1935- II. Ray, Michael L. III. Title. IV. Title: Creative spirit (Television program)*
**TC BF408 .G57 1992**

**Gollifer, Sue.**
Screen printing [videorecording]. [Northbrook?], Ill. ; Peasmarsh, East Sussex, Eng. : Roland Collection of Films on Art, c1992.
**TC NE2238.G7 S4 1992**

**Golombok, Susan.** Parenting : what really counts? / Susan Golombok. London ; Philadelphia : Routledge, 2000. xiii, 124 p. ; 25 cm. Includes bibliographical references (p. [105]-118) and indexes. ISBN 0-415-22715-1 (hbk.) ISBN 0-415-22716-X (pbk.) DDC 649/.1
*1. Parenting. 2. Parent and child. 3. Parents - Psychology. 4. Single parents. 5. Gay parents. 6. Child psychology. I. Title.*
**TC HQ755.8 .G655 2000**

**Golper, Lee Ann C., 1948-** Sourcebook for medical speech pathology / Lee Ann C. Golper. 2nd ed. San Diego, Calif. : Singular Pub. Group, c1998. xiii, 436 p. : ill. ; 23 cm. (Clinical competence series) Includes bibliographical references (p. 427-428) and index. ISBN 1-56593-861-5 DDC 616.85/5
*1. Speech therapy. 2. Internal medicine. 3. Medicine - Terminology. 4. Speech therapists. 5. Speech-Language Pathology - handbooks. 6. Nomenclature - handbooks. 7. Clinical Medicine - handbooks. I. Title. II. Series.*
**TC RC423 .G64 1998**

**Golub, Jeffrey N., 1944-** Making learning happen : strategies for an interactive classroom / Jeffrey N. Golub. Portsmouth, NH : Boynton/Cook Publishers, c2000. xvi, 112 p. : ill. ; 24 cm. Includes bibliographical references and index. ISBN 0-86709-493-1 DDC 428/.0071/273
*1. English language - Study and teaching (Secondary) - United States. 2. Education, Secondary - Activity programs - United States. I. Title.*
**TC LB1631 .G623 2000**

**Gombash, Laurie L.**
Barlow, Tracie. The COTA in the schools. San Antonio, Texas : Therapy Skill Builders, c1999.
**TC RM735 .B37 1999**

**Gombrich, E. H. (Ernst Hans), 1909-** The uses of images : studies in the social function of art and visual communication / E.H. Gombrich. London : Phaidon, 1999. 304 p. : ill. ; 26 cm. Includes bibliographical references (p. 274-292) and index. ISBN 0-7148-3655-9
*1. Art and society. 2. Art - Psychology. I. Title.*
**TC N72.S6 G66 1999**

**Gomi, Tarō.**
**[Kingyo ga nigeta. English]**
Where's the fish? / by Taro Gomi. New York : William Morrow, [1986], c1977. [25] p. : chiefly col. ill. ; 22 cm. Translation of: Kingyo ga nigeta. SUMMARY: The reader is invited to find the fish in pictures where it is well camouflaged. ISBN 0-688-06241-5 ISBN 0-688-06242-3 (lib. bdg.) DDC [E]
*1. Fishes - Fiction. I. Title.*
**TC PZ7.G586 Wh 1977**

**Gone for good.**
Rojstaczer, Stuart. Oxford : Oxford University Press, 1999.
**TC LA227.4 .R65 1999**

**Gonsalves, Philip.** Build it! festival : teacher's guide : grades K-6 ... / by Philip Gonsalves and Jaine Kopp. Berkeley, CA : Great Explorations in Math and Science (GEMS), Lawrence Hall of Science, University of California at Berkeley, c1995. viii, 216 p. : ill. ; 28 cm. Includes bibliographical references (p. 205-212). ISBN 0-912511-88-5 DDC 372.7
*1. Geometry - Study and teaching (Elementary) 2. Creative activities and seat work. I. Kopp, Jaine. II. GEMS (Project) III. Title.*
**TC QA462 .G66 1995**

**Gontarczyk, Ewa.** Kobiecość i męskość jako kategorie społeczno-kulturowe w studiach feministycznych : perspektywa socjologiczno-pedagogiczna / Ewa Gontarczyk. Poznań : Eruditus, 1995. 166 p. ; 21 cm. (Poznańska drukarnia naukowa) Includes bibliographical references (p. 153-[167]). ISBN 83-86142-07-3
*1. Women's studies - Poland. 2. Feminism and education. 3. Women - Poland - Social conditions. I. Title. II. Series.*
**TC HQ1181.P7 G66 1995**

**Gonzales-Mena, Janet.**
Diversity [videorecording]. Barrington, IL : Magna Systems, Inc., 1996.
**TC LB1139.25 .D5 1996**

**González, Maria del Carmen.**
Modernstarts. New York : Museum of Modern Art : Distributed by Harry N. Abrams, c1999.
**TC N620.M9 M63 1999**

**González, María Luísa.**
Educating Latino students. Lancaster, Pa. : Technomic Pub. Co., c1998.
**TC LC2669 .E37 1998**

**Gonzalez-Pando, Miguel.** The Cuban Americans / Miguel Gonzalez-Pando. Westport, Conn. : Greenwood Press, 1998. xv, 185 p. : ill. ; 24 cm. (The new Americans, 1092-6364) Includes bibliographical references (p. [175]-178) and index. ISBN 0-313-29824-6 (alk. paper) DDC 975.9/3004687291
*1. Cuban Americans. 2. Political refugees - United States. 3. Cuba - Emigration and immigration. 4. United States - Emigration and immigration. I. Title. II. Series: New Americans (Westport, Conn.)*
**TC E184.C97 G64 1998**

**González, Roberto Cortéz.**
Peterson, Nadene. The role of work in people's lives. Australia ; Belmont, Calif. : Wadsworth Pub. Co., c2000.
**TC HF5381 .P483 2000**

**GOOBERS. See PEANUTS.**

**GOOD AND EVIL. See also GUILT.**
Dilman, İlham. Raskolnikov's rebirth. Chicago : Open Court, c2000.

TC BF47 .D55 2000

**Good citizenship and educational provision.**
Davies, Ian, 1957- London : New York : Falmer Press, c1999.
*TC LC1091 .D28 1999*

**Good girl messages.**
O'Keefe, Deborah. New York : Continuum, 2000.
*TC PS374.G55 O44 2000*

**"Good guys don't wear hats".**
Tobin, Joseph Jay. New York : Teachers College Press, c2000.
*TC HQ784.M3 T63 2000*

**The good liar.**
Maguire, Gregory. New York : Clarion Books, c1999.
*TC PZ7.M2762 Go 1999*

**Good news!.**
Conners, Gail A. Thousand Oaks, Calif. : Corwin Press, c2000.
*TC LB2847 .C65 2000*

**Good thinking :** teacher's planning guide. New York : Macmillan/McGraw-Hill, c1997. 1 v. (various pagings) : col. ill. ; 31 cm. (Spotlight on literacy ; Gr.3 l.8 u.1) (The road to independent reading) Includes index. ISBN 0-02-181165-2
*1. Language arts (Primary) 2. Reading (Primary) I. Series. II. Series: The road to independent reading*
*TC LB1576 .S66 1997 Gr.3 l.8 u.1*

**Good, Thomas L., 1943-.**
American education. Chicago, Ill. : NSSE : Distributed by the University of Chicago Press, 2000.
*TC LB5 .N25 99th pt. 2*

The great school debate : choice, vouchers, and charters / Thomas L. Good, Jennifer S. Braden. Mahwah, N.J. : L. Erlbaum Associates, 2000. xvii, 273 p. : ill. ; 24 cm. Includes bibliographical references and indexes. ISBN 0-8058-3691-8 (cloth : acid-free paper) ISBN 0-8058-3551-2 (paper : acid-free paper) DDC 379.3/2/0973
*1. Privatization in education - United States. 2. School choice - United States. 3. Educational vouchers - United States. 4. Charter schools - United States. 5. Education - United States - Evaluation. I. Braden, Jennifer S. II. Title.*
*TC LB2806.36 .G66 2000*

McCaslin, Mary M. Listening in classrooms. 1st ed. New York : HarperCollins College Publishers, c1996.
*TC LB1033 .M34 1996*

**Goodbye, Walter Malinski.**
Recorvits, Helen. 1st ed. New York : Farrar, Straus and Giroux, c1999.
*TC PZ7.R24435 Go 1999*

**Goode, Jamie.**
Genetics of criminal and antisocial behaviour. Chichester ; New York : Wiley, 1996.
*TC HV6047 .G46 1996*

**Goodman, Greg S., 1949-** Alternatives in education : critical pedagogy for disaffected youth / Greg S. Goodman. New York : P. Lang, c1999. viii, 115 p. ; 23 cm. Includes bibliographical references and index. ISBN 0-8204-4430-8 (pbk. : alk. paper) DDC 371.04/0973
*1. Alternative education - United States - Case studies. 2. Alternative schools - United States - Case studies. 3. Critical pedagogy - United States - Case studies. 4. Problem youth - Education - United States - Case studies. I. Title.*
*TC LC46.4 .G66 1999*

**Goodman, Jan M.** Group solutions : : cooperative logic activities. [Teacher's guide] / by Jan M. Goodman. Rev. Berkeley, Calif. : Lawrence Hall of Science, University of California, 1997, c1992. 148 p., [3] folded leaves of plates : ill. ; 28 cm. (Great explorations in math and science (GEMS).) Includes bibliographical references (p. 27-29). Grades K-4. ISBN 0-912511-81-8 (pbk.)
*1. Group problem solving - Study and teaching (Elementary). 2. Problem solving in children. I. Lawrence Hall of Science. II. GEMS (Project). III. Title. IV. Series.*
*TC QA8.7 .G5 1997*

**Goodman, John, 1952 Sept. 19-.**
Diderot, Denis, 1713-1784. [Selections. English. 1995] Diderot on art. New Haven : Yale University Press, 1995.
*TC N6846 .D4613 1995*

**Goodman, Kenneth S.**
In defense of good teaching. York, Me. : Stenhouse Publishers, c1998.
*TC LB1050.35 .I5 1998*

Reflections and connections. Cresskill, N.J. : Hampton Press, c1999.
*TC P51 .R36 1999*

**GOODMAN, KENNETH S. - INFLUENCE.**
Reflections and connections. Cresskill, N.J. : Hampton Press, c1999.
*TC P51 .R36 1999*

**Goodman, Roger.**
Sean's story [videorecording]. Princeton, N.J. : Films for the Humanities & Sciences : [S.l. : distributed by] ABC Multimedia : Capital Cities/ABC, c1994.
*TC LC1203.M3 .S39 1994*

**Goodwill towards peoples in the development of international relations.**
National Institute of Social Sciences. Journal of the National Institute of Social Sciences. [New York]

**Goodwin, Craufurd D. W.**
Fry, Roger Eliot, 1866-1934. Art and the market. Ann Arbor, Mich. : University of Michigan Press, 1999.
*TC N8600 .F78 1999*

**Goodwin, Lorine Swainston, 1925-** The pure food, drink, and drug crusaders, 1879-1914 / by Lorine Swainston Goodwin. Jefferson, N.C. : McFarland, 1999. viii, 352 p. ; 24 cm. Includes bibliographical references (p. 297-340) and index. Table of Contents URL: http://lcweb.loc.gov/catdir/toc/99028286.html ISBN 0-7864-0618-6 (lib. bdg. : alk. paper) DDC 363.19/0973
*1. Food adulteration and inspection - United States - History. 2. Consumer protection - United States - History. 3. Women social reformers - United States - History. 4. Food adulteration and inspection - Law and legislation - United States - History. 5. Food law and legislation - United States - History. 6. Beverages - Law and legislation - United States - History. 7. Drugs - Law and legislation - United States - History. 8. United States. - Food and Drugs Act - History. I. Title.*
*TC HD9000.9.U5 G66 1999*

**Goodwyn, Andrew.** English in the digital age : information and communications technology (ICT) and the teaching of English / edited by Andrew Goodwyn. London : Cassell, 2000. xiv, 141 p. : ill. ; 24 cm. Includes bibliographical references and index. ISBN 0-304-70623-X DDC 420.785
*1. English literature - Study and teaching. 2. English language - Computer-assisted instruction. 3. English language - Computer-assisted instruction. 4. English language - Study and teaching - Audio-visual aids. I. Title.*
*TC PR35 .E65 2000*

**Goodyear, Rodney K.**
Scientist-practitioner perspectives on test interpretation. Boston, Mass. : Allyn and Bacon, c1999.
*TC BF176 .S37 1999*

**Goonen, Norma M.** Higher education administration : a guide to legal, ethical, and practical issues / Norma M. Goonen and Rachel S. Blechman. Westport, Conn. ; London : Greenwood Press, 1999. x, 231 p. ; 24 cm. (The Greenwood educators' reference collection, 1056-2192) Includes bibliographical references (p. [221]-224) and index. ISBN 0-313-30304-5 (alk. paper) DDC 378.73
*1. Universities and colleges - United States - Administration. 2. Universities and colleges - Administration - Law and legislation - United States. 3. Universities and colleges - Administration - Moral and ethical aspects - United States. I. Blechman, Rachel S., 1938- II. Title. III. Series.*
*TC LB2341 .G573 1999*

**GOOSE.** *See* **GEESE.**

**Gopnik, Alison.** The scientist in the crib : minds, brains, and how children learn / Alison Gopnik, Andrew N. Meltzoff, Patricia K. Kuhl. New York : William Morrow & Co., 1999. xv, 279 p. ; 24 cm. Includes bibliographical references and index. ISBN 0-688-15988-5 DDC 155.4/13
*1. Cognition. 2. Cognition in children. 3. Learning, Psychology of. I. Meltzoff, Andrew N. II. Kuhl, Patricia K. (Patricia Katherine), 1946- III. Title.*
*TC BF311 .G627 1999*

**Gorbach, Sherwood L., 1934-.**
Nutritional aspects of HIV infection. London ; New York : Arnold : Co-published in the United States by Oxford University Press, 1999.
*TC RC607.A26 N895 1998*

**Gordo-López, Angel.**
Cyberpsychology. New York : Routledge, 1999.
*TC HM1033 .C934 1999*

**Gordon, Amy, 1949-** When JFK was my father / Amy Gordon. Boston : Houghton Mifflin, 1999. 202 p. ; 22 cm. SUMMARY: Feeling neglected by her father in Brazil and her mother in Washington, D.C., Georgia Hughes tries to cope with life at a boarding school in Connecticut by imagining relationships with John Kennedy and Miss Beard, the ghost of the former headmistress of the school. ISBN 0-395-91364-0 DDC [Fic]
*1. Boarding schools - Fiction. 2. Schools - Fiction. 3. Self-perception - Fiction. 4. Parent and child - Fiction. I. Title.*
*TC PZ7.G65 Wh 1999*

**GORDON, EDMUND W.**
Edmund W. Gordon. Stamford, Conn. : Jai Press, c2000.
*TC HM1033 .E35 2000*

**Gordon, Felicia.** Early French feminisms, 1830-1940 : a passion for liberty / by Felicia Gordon and Máire Cross. Cheltenham, U.K. ; Brookfield, Vt. : Edward Elgar, c1996. vii, 287 p. : ill. ; 25 cm. Includes bibliographical references (p. 267-278) and index. ISBN 1-85278-969-7 DDC 305.42/092/244
*1. Feminists - France - Biography. 2. Feminism - France - History. 3. Women socialists - France - Biography. 4. Socialism - France - History. I. Cross, Máire. II. Title.*
*TC HQ1615.A3 G67 1996*

**Gordon, Jacob U.** Black leadership for social change / Jacob U. Gordon ; foreword by Samuel DuBois Cook. Westport, Conn. : Greenwood Press, 2000. xviii, 242 p. ; 24 cm. (Contributions in Afro-American and African studies, 0069-9624 ; no. 200) Includes bibliographical references and index. ISBN 0-313-31396-2 (alk. paper) DDC 303.3/4/08996073
*1. Afro-American leadership. 2. Social change - United States. 3. Afro-Americans - Politics and government. 4. Afro-Americans - Social conditions. I. Title. II. Series.*
*TC E185.615 .G666 2000*

**Gordon, Judith S., 1958-** Helping survivors of domestic violence : the effectiveness of medical, mental health, and community services / Judith S. Gordon. New York : Garland Pub., 1998. xiii, 159 p. ; 23 cm. (Health care policy in the United States) Includes bibliographical references and index. ISBN 0-8153-3330-7 (alk. paper) DDC 362.82/92
*1. Abused women - United States - Psychology. 2. Abused women - United States - Health aspects. 3. Abused women - United States - Family relationships. 4. Abused women - Counseling of - United States. 5. Victims of family violence - United States. 6. Women - Abuse of - United States - Prevention. 7. Battered woman syndrome - United States. I. Title. II. Title: Effectiveness of medical, mental health and community. III. Series.*
*TC HV6626.2 .G67 1998*

**Gordon, June A., 1950-** The color of teaching / June A. Gordon. London ; New York : RoutledgeFalmer, c2000. xii, 128 p. ; 25 cm. (Educational change and development series) Includes bibliographical references (p. 110-121) and index. ISBN 0-7507-0997-9 (hc) ISBN 0-7507-0996-0 (pbk.) DDC 331.7/613711
*1. Minority teachers - Recruiting - United States. 2. Minorities - Education - Social aspects - United States. 3. Teaching - Social aspects - United States. I. Title. II. Series.*
*TC LB2835.25 .G67 2000*

**Gordon, Linda.** The great Arizona orphan abduction / Linda Gordon. Cambridge, Mass. : Harvard University Press, 1999. xii, 416 p. : ill., maps ; 24 cm. Includes bibliographical references (p. [321]-404) and index. ISBN 0-674-36041-9 (cloth : alk. paper) DDC 305.8/009791/51
*1. Clifton (Ariz.) - Race relations. 2. Orphans - Arizona - Clifton - History - 20th century. 3. Kidnapping - Arizona - Clifton - History - 20th century. 4. Catholic Church - Arizona - Clifton - History - 20th century. 5. Mexican Americans - Arizona - Clifton - History - 20th century. 6. Whites - Arizona - Clifton - History - 20th century. 7. Vigilantes - Arizona - Clifton - History - 20th century. I. Title.*
*TC F819.C55 G67 1999*

**Gordon, Michael. Ph. D.**
Accommodations in higher education under the Americans with Disabilities Act (ADA) :. DeWitt, NY : GSI Publications, 2000.
*TC RA1055.5 A28 2000*

**Gordon, Mordechai.** Toward an integrative conception of authority in education : a comparison of Hannah Arendt and John Dewey's views on authority / by Mordechai Gordon. 1997. iii, 225 p. ; 29 cm. Issued also on microfilm. Thesis (Ed.D.) -- Teachers College, Columbia University, 1997. Includes bibliographical references (leaves 218-225)
*1. Authority. 2. Education. I. Title.*
*TC 085 G656*

Toward an integrative conception of authority in education : a comparison of Hannah Arendt's and John Dewey's views on authority / Mordechai Gordon. 1997. iii, 225 leaves; 29 cm. Issued also on microfilm. Thesis (Ph.D.)--Columbia University, 1997. Includes bibliographical references (leaves 218-225).
*1. Arendt, Hannah. 2. Dewey, John, - 1859-1952. 3. Lyotard, Jean François. 4. Teaching - United States. 5. Authority. 6. Education - Philosophy. 7. Liberalism - United States. 8. Teachers - Training of - United States. I. Title. II. Title: Comparison of Hannah Arendt's and John Dewey's views on authority*

**TC 085 G656**

**Gordon, Peter, 1927-** Royal education : past, present, and future / Peter Gordon and Denis Lawton. London ; Portland, OR : Frank Cass, 1999. xiii, 286 p. : ill. ; 25 cm. Includes bibliographical references (p. 257-271) and index. ISBN 0-7146-5014-5 (cloth) DDC 371.826/21
*1. Upper class - Education - Great Britain - History. 2. Great Britain - Kings and rulers - Education - History. I. Lawton, Denis. II. Title.*
**TC LC4945.G72 G67 1999**

**Gordon, Ruth, 1933-.**
Time is the longest distance. 1st ed. New York, NY : HarperCollins, c1991.
**TC PN6109.97 .T56 1991**

**Gordon, Sol, 1923-** Personal issues in human sexuality / Sol Gordon, Craig W. Snyder. Boston : Allyn and Bacon, 1986. viii, 328 p. : ill. ; 24 cm. Includes bibliographical records (p314-317) and index. "EDP 7987366"--Cover. ISBN 0-205-08736-1 (pbk.) DDC 613.9/5
*1. Sex instruction. 2. College students - Sexual behavior. 3. Hygiene, Sexual. 4. Sex. 5. Sex. Behavior. I. Snyder, Craig W. II. Title.*
**TC HQ35.2 .G67 1986**

**Gordon, Tatiana.** Russian language directives / by Tatiana Gordon. 1998. vii, 181 leaves ; 29 cm. Issued also on microfilm. Thesis (Ed.D.)--Teachers College, Columbia University, 1998. Includes bibliographical references (leaves 165-173).
*1. Russian language - Discourse analysis. 2. Speech acts (Linguistics). 3. Language and culture. 4. Oral communication - Social aspects. 5. Psycholinguistics. 6. Persuasion (Rhetoric). I. Title.*
**TC 06 no. 10940**

**Gordon, Tuula.**
Making spaces. New York : St. Martin's Press, 2000.
**TC LC208.4 .M35 2000**

**Gordon, Virginia N.**
Academic advising. 1st ed. San Francisco : Jossey-Bass, c2000.
**TC LB2343 .A29 2000**

**Gore, M. C.** Taming the time stealers : tricks of the trade from organized teachers / M.C. Gore, John F. Dowd. Thousand Oaks, Calif. : Corwin Press, c1999. x, 162 p. : ill. ; 26 cm. Includes bibliographical references (p. 161-162). CONTENTS: Organizing your time and memory. First-generation organizational aids. Second-generation organizational aids -- Buried under administrative paperwork? Streamlining daily tasks. Accomodating occasional administrative tasks. Organizing student data. Setting up the classroom library. Creating the paperless classroom -- Mananging instructional print material. Streamlining print resources and planning. Organizing student work print. Transporting materials. Organizing for substitute teachers -- Corralling nonprint materials. Containers. Containers for small items. Storing small but relatively flat items. Storing bulletin board materials. Organizing tools. Organizing physical education equipment. Moving nonprint materials -- "Dejunking" : taking the cure. Basic dejunking. Minimizing memento junk. Weaning yourself away from junk -- Decisions : from simple to complex. Quick and easy decision-making techniques. More complete decision-making techniques. The best and most complete model of decision making -- Organizing your teaching. The content. The lesson-planning process. The teaching act. Improving standardized testing -- Helping students learn to organize themselves. Materials. Time and memory. Learning behavior -- Teaching for students with special needs. Establishing the behavioral environment. Organizing the learning environment. Developing the support system communication -- Working with parents. Writing to parents. Parent conference. The CONTENTS: parent conference. Parent involvement -- Requesting assistance. Deciding what kind of help you need. Organizing to get the help you need -- Organizational strategies for your soul. ISBN 0-8039-6843-4 (cloth : acid-free paper) ISBN 0-8039-6844-2 (pbk. : acid-free paper) DDC 371.102
*1. Teachers - Time management. 2. Effective teaching. 3. Teaching - Decision making. 4. Classroom environment. I. Dowd, John F. II. Title.*
**TC LB2838.8 .G67 1999**

**GORGE-PURGE SYNDROME.** *See* **BULIMIA.**

**Gorham, Eric B., 1960-** The theater of politics : Hannah Arendt, political science, and higher education / Eric B. Gorham. Lanham, Md. ; Oxford: Lexington Books, c2000. xvi, 235 p. ; 24 cm. Includes bibliographical references (p. [219]-229) and index. ISBN 0-7391-0048-3 (cl. : alk. paper) ISBN 0-7391-0049-1 (pa. : alk. paper) DDC 378/.01
*1. Education, Higher - Political aspects. 2. Arendt, Hanna - Contributions in political science. I. Title.*
**TC LC171 .G56 2000**

**Gorman, Jack M.**
Nathan, Peter E. Treating mental disorders. New York : Oxford University Press, 1999.
**TC RC480.515 .N38 1999**

**Gormley, William T., 1950-** Everybody's children : child care as a public problem / William T. Gormley, Jr. Washington, D.C. : Brookings Institution, c1995. ix, 243 p. : ill. ; 24 cm. Includes bibliographical references (p. 197-236) and index. ISBN 0-8157-3224-4 (alk. paper) ISBN 0-8157-3223-6 (pbk. : alk. paper) DDC 362.7/0973
*1. Child care - United States. 2. Child care - Government policy - United States. 3. Child care services - Government policy - United States. I. Title.*
**TC HQ778.63 .G674 1995**

**Gormlie, Chris.**
Seurat [videorecording]. West Long Branch, NJ : Kultur, c1999.
**TC ND553.S5 S5 1999**

**Gorski, Paul.**
Professional development guide for educators. Washington, D.C. : National Education Association of the United States, 2000.
**TC LC1099.3 .P755 1999**

**Gosselin, Laurent A.**
Grounded for life [videorecording]. Charleston, WV : Cambridge Research Group, Ltd., 1988.
**TC HQ759.4 .G7 1988**

**GOSSIP.**
Behaving badly. 1st ed. Washington, D.C. : American Psychological Association, 2001.
**TC HM1106 .B45 2001**

**GOTHIC REVIVAL (ARCHITECTURE).** *See* **ARCHITECTURE, VICTORIAN.**

**Goto, Scott, ill.**
Ketteman, Helen. Shoeshine Whittaker. New York : Walker & Co., 1999.
**TC PZ7.K494 Sh 1999**

**GOTTARDI, ROBERTO, 1927-.**
Loomis, John A., 1951- Revolution of forms. New York : Princeton Architectural Press, c1999.
**TC NA6602.A76 L66 1999**

**Gottesman, Barbara Little.** Peer coaching for educators / Barbara Gottesman. 2nd ed. Lanham, Md. : Scarecrow Press, 2000. xiv, 161 p. ; 23 cm. Includes bibliographical references (p. 157-159). ISBN 0-8108-3745-5 (paper : alk. paper) DDC 371.14/8
*1. Teaching teams - United States. 2. Mentoring in education - United States. I. Title.*
**TC LB1029.T4 G68 2000**

**Gottman, John Mordechai.** Why marriages succeed or fail : : --and how you can make yours last / John Gottman, with Nan Silver. 1st Fireside ed. New York : Fireside, 1995. 234 p. ; 25 cm. "Gift from Professor Maxine Greene" (c.2) ISBN 0-671-86748-2 ISBN 0-684-80241-4 (pbk.)
*1. Marriage - United States. 2. Communication in marriage - United States. I. Silver, Nan. II. Title.*
**TC HQ536 .G68 1994**

**Gottsegen, Gloria B., joint author.**
Blank, Leonard. Confrontation; New York, Macmillan [1971]
**TC HM132 .B55**

**Gottsegen, Monroe G., joint author.**
Blank, Leonard. Confrontation; New York, Macmillan [1971]
**TC HM132 .B55**

**Götz, Stephan, 1960-**
**[New Yorker Künstler in ihren Ateliers. English]**
American artists in their New York studios : conversations about the creation of contemporary art / Stephan Götz ; edited by Craigen W. Bowen and Katherine Olivier. Cambridge [Mass.] : Center for Conservation and Technical Studies, Harvard University Art Museums ; Stuttgart : Daco-Verlag Günter Bläse, c1992. 176 p. : col. ill. ; 28 cm. ISBN 3-87135-006-0
*1. Art, American - New York (State) - New York. 2. Art, Modern - 20th century - New York (State) - New York. 3. Artists - New York (State) - New York - Interviews. I. Bowen, Craigen W. II. Olivier, Katherine. III. Title.*
**TC N6535.N5 G6813 1992**

**Gough, Stephen.**
Clamp, Cynthia G. L. Resources for nursing research. 3rd ed. London ; Thousand Oaks, Calif. : Sage, 1999.
**TC Z6675.N7 C53 1999**

**GOUIN, FRANÇOIS, 1831-1896.**
Roberts, J. T. (John T.) Two French language teaching reformers reassessed. Lewiston [N.Y.] : E. Mellen Press, c1999.

**TC PB35 .R447 1999**

**Gould, Deborah Lee.** Brendan's best-timed birthday / by Deborah Gould ; illustrated by Jacqueline Rogers. New York : Bradbury Press, 1988. [32] p. : col. ill. ; 21 x 26 cm. SUMMARY: Brendan has a wonderful birthday party, highlighted by sharing his father's gift of a digital watch with a stopwatch with his friends who time every activity. ISBN 0-02-109115-3
*1. Clocks and watches - Fiction. 2. Birthdays - Fiction. 3. Entertaining - Fiction. I. Rogers, Jackie, ill. II. Title.*
**TC PZ7.G723 Br 1988**

**Gould, Polly.**
The dynamics of now. London : Wimbledon School of Art in association with Tate, c2000.
**TC N185 .D96 2000**

**Govan, Jennifer Lee.**
Milbank Memorial Library story hour [videorecording]. [New York : Milbank Memorial Library, 1999].
**TC Z718.3 .M5 1999 Series 3 Prog. 11**

**Sing Along Christmas.**
Milbank Memorial Library story hour [videorecording]. [New York : Milbank Memorial Library, 1999].
**TC Z718.3 .M5 1999 Series 3 Prog. 11**

**Governing childhood** / edited with an introduction by Anne McGillivray. Aldershot, England ; Brookfield, Vt. : Dartmouth, c1997. ix, 259 p. ; 23 cm. (Issues in law and society) Includes bibliographical references. ISBN 1-85521-833-X ISBN 1-85521-840-2 (pbk.) DDC 305.23
*1. Children - Government policy. 2. Juvenile justice, Administration of. 3. Children - Legal status, laws, etc. I. McGillivray, Anne. II. Series.*
**TC HQ789 .G68 1997**

**GOVERNMENT.** *See* **POLITICAL SCIENCE.**

**GOVERNMENT AGENCIES.** *See* **ADMINISTRATIVE AGENCIES.**

**GOVERNMENT AID TO EDUCATION - UNITED STATES.**
Kane, Thomas J. The price of admission. Washington, D.C. : Brookings Institution Press ; New York : Russell Sage Foundation, c1999.
**TC LB2342 .K35 1999**

**GOVERNMENT AID TO HIGHER EDUCATION - UNITED STATES.**
A struggle to survive. Thousand Oaks, Calif. : Corwin Press, c1996.
**TC LB2342 .S856 1996**

**GOVERNMENT AND BINDING (LINGUISTICS).** *See* **GOVERNMENT-BINDING THEORY (LINGUISTICS).**

**Government and the arts.**
Levy, Alan Howard. Lanham, Md. : University Press of America, c1997.
**TC NX735 .L48 1997**

**GOVERNMENT ASSISTANCE.** *See* **ECONOMIC ASSISTANCE, DOMESTIC.**

**GOVERNMENT-BINDING THEORY (LINGUISTICS).**
Cook, V. J. (Vivian James), 1940- Chomsky's universal grammar. 2nd [updated] ed. Oxford, OX, UK ; Cambridge, Mass. : USA : Blackwell Publishers, 1996.
**TC P85.C47 C66 1996**

The development of binding. Hillsdale, N.J. : Lawrence Erlbaum , 1992.
**TC P158.2 .D5 1992**

**GOVERNMENT HOSPITALS.** *See* **PUBLIC HOSPITALS.**

**Government in the United States.**
Remy, Richard C. New York : Scribner educational publishers, 1987.
**TC JK274 .R54 1987**

**GOVERNMENT INFORMATION.** *See* **PUBLIC RECORDS.**

**GOVERNMENT INFORMATION - UNITED STATES.**
Foerstel, Herbert N. Freedom of information and the right to know. Westport, Conn. : Greenwood Press, 1999.
**TC KF5753 .F64 1999**

**Government, markets and vocational qualifications.**
Raggatt, Peter C. M. London ; New York : Falmer Press, 1999.
**TC HF5381.6 .R34 1999**

**GOVERNMENT MINISTRIES.** *See* EXECUTIVE DEPARTMENTS.

**GOVERNMENT OWNERSHIP.** *See* PRIVATIZATION.

**GOVERNMENT PUBLICITY.** *See* RADIO BROADCASTING.

**GOVERNMENT PUBLICITY - UNITED STATES.**
Schachter, Hindy Lauer. Reinventing government or reinventing ourselves. Albany : State University of New York Press, c1997.
*TC JK1764 .S35 1997*

**GOVERNMENT RECORDS.** *See* PUBLIC RECORDS.

**GOVERNMENT, RESISTANCE TO.** *See* ANARCHISM; COUPS D'ÉTAT; INSURGENCY.

**Government versus private railroads.**
National Institute of Social Sciences. Journal of the National Institute of Social Sciences. [New York]

**GOVERNMENTAL INVESTIGATIONS.** *See* LEGISLATIVE HEARINGS.

**Governmentality.**
Dean, Mitchell, 1955- London ; Thousand Oaks, Calif. : Sage Publications, 1999.
*TC HN49.P6 D43 1999*

**Grace, Kay Sprinkel.** Beyond fund raising : new strategies for nonprofit innovation and investment / Kay Sprinkel Grace. New York : Wiley, c1997. xvi, 288 p. ; 24 cm. (The NSFRE/Wiley fund development series) Includes bibliographical references (p.280) and index. ISBN 0-471-16232-9 (alk. paper) DDC 658.15
*1. Nonprofit organizations - Finance I. Title. II. Series.*
*TC HG4027.65 .G73 1997*

**The grad school handbook.**
Jerrard, Richard. 1st ed. New York : Berkley Pub. Group, 1998.
*TC LB2371.4 .J47 1998*

**GRADE SCHOOLS.** *See* ELEMENTARY SCHOOLS.

**The Grade teacher.** Boston, Mass. : Educational Pub. Co., -c1972. 44 v. : ill. ; 30 cm. Frequency: Monthly (except July-Aug.). Vol. 46, no. 7 (June [1929])-v. 89, no. 9 (May/June 1972). Absorbed: Primary education, popular educator; and: Early education. Title from caption. Continued by: Teacher (Greenwich, Conn.). (IEN)AAM4700. Continued by: Teacher (Greenwich, Conn.).
*1. Education - Periodicals. 2. Education, Elementary - Periodicals. I. Title: Primary education, popular educator. II. Title: Early education. III. Title: Primary education, popular educator. IV. Title: Early education. V. Title: Teacher (Greenwich, Conn.). VI. Title: Teacher (Greenwich, Conn.).*

**Graded Italian reader.**
Cioffari, Angelina Grimaldi, 1913- 2nd ed. Lexington, Mass. : D.C. Heath, c1984.
*TC PC1113 .C48 1984*

Cioffari, Vincenzo, 1905- 3rd ed. Lexington, Mass. : D.C. Heath, c1991.
*TC PC1113 .C5 1991*

**GRADED SCHOOLS.** *See* GRADING AND MARKING (STUDENTS).

**GRADING AND MARKING (STUDENTS).**
Cunningham, George K. Assessment in the classroom. London : Falmer, 1998.
*TC LB3051 .C857 1998*

Hedges, William D. Evaluation in the elementary school New York, Holt, Rinehart and Winston [1969]
*TC LB3051 .H4*

A sourcebook for responding to student writing. Cresskill, N.J. : Hampton Press, c1999.
*TC PE1404 .S683 1999*

Speck, Bruce W. Grading students' classroom writing. Washington, DC : Graduate School of Education and Human Development, The George Washington University, 2000.
*TC LB1576 .S723 2000*

**GRADING AND MARKING (STUDENTS) - GREAT BRITAIN.**
Sharp, Mavis, 1945- The management of failing DipSW students. Aldershot ; Brookfield, Vt. : Ashgate, c1999.
*TC HV11.8.G7 S53 1999*

Wintle, Mike. Coordinating assessment practice across the primary school. London : Philadelphia, PA : Falmer Press, 1999.

---

*TC LB3060.37 .W56 1999*

**GRADING AND MARKING (STUDENTS) - GREAT BRITAIN - PROBLEMS, EXERCISES, ETC.**
Sharp, Mavis, 1945- The management of failing DipSW students. Aldershot ; Brookfield, Vt. : Ashgate, c1999.
*TC HV11.8.G7 S53 1999*

**GRADING AND MARKING (STUDENTS) - NEW YORK (STATE) - EVALUATION.**
Ort, Suzanne Wichterle. Standards in practice. 1999.
*TC 06 no. 11210*

Southworth, Robert A. Evidence of student learning and implications for alternative policies that support instructional use of assessment. 1999.
*TC 06 no. 11218*

**GRADING AND MARKING (STUDENTS) - UNITED STATES - CASE STUDIES.**
Chen, Sheying. Remedial education and grading. New York : the City University of New York, 1999.
*TC LB1029.R4 C54 1999*

**GRADING AND MARKING (STUDENTS) - UNITED STATES - HANDBOOKS, MANUALS, ETC.**
Haladyna, Thomas M. A complete guide to student grading. Boston : Allyn and Bacon, c1999.
*TC LB3051 .H296 1999*

**Grading students' classroom writing.**
Speck, Bruce W. Washington, DC : Graduate School of Education and Human Development, The George Washington University, 2000.
*TC LB1576 .S723 2000*

**GRADUATE NURSING EDUCATION.** *See* NURSING - STUDY AND TEACHING (GRADUATE).

**GRADUATE RECORD EXAMINATION - STUDY GUIDES.**
Cracking the GRE literature in English subject test. New York : Random House, 1996-
*TC LB2367.4 .L58*

**GRADUATE STUDENTS.** *See also* GRADUATE TEACHING ASSISTANTS; WOMEN GRADUATE STUDENTS.
Elphinstone, Leonie. How to get a research degree. St. Leonards, Australia : Allen & Unwin, 1998.
*TC LB2371 .E46 1998*

**GRADUATE STUDENTS - AUSTRALIA - HANDBOOKS, MANUALS, ETC.**
Stevens, Kate. Doing postgraduate research in Australia. Melbourne : Melbourne University Press, 1999.
*TC LB2371.6.A7 S74 1999*

**GRADUATE STUDENTS - COUNSELING OF.**
Supervising postgraduates from non-English speaking backgrounds. Buckingham ; Philadelphia : Society for Research into Higher Education : Open University Press, 1999.
*TC LB2343 .S86 1999*

**GRADUATE STUDENTS - EMPLOYMENT - UNITED STATES - HANDBOOKS, MANUALS, ETC.**
Vesilind, P. Aarne. So you want to be a professor? Thousand Oaks, Calif. : Sage Publications, c2000.
*TC LB1778.2 .V47 2000*

**GRADUATE STUDENTS - SCHOLARSHIPS, FELLOWSHIPS, ETC.**
GrantFinder. Arts and humanities. New York, NY : St. Martin's Press, 2000.
*TC LB2337.2 .G72*

GrantFinder : Social sciences. New York, NY : St. Martin's Press, 2000.
*TC LB2337.2 .G7 2000*

**GRADUATE STUDENTS - SCHOLARSHIPS, FELLOWSHIPS, ETC. - DIRECTORIES.**
GrantFinder. Science. New York : St. Martin's Press, c2000.
*TC LB2338 .G652 2000*

GrantFinder : Arts and humanities. New York, NY : St. Martin's Press, 2000.
*TC LB2337.2 .G72*

GrantFinder : Medicine. New York, NY : St. Martin's Press,
*TC LB2337.2 .G73*

**GRADUATE STUDENTS - UNITED STATES - HANDBOOKS, MANUALS, ETC.**
Jerrard, Richard. The grad school handbook. 1st ed. New York : Berkley Pub. Group, 1998.

---

*TC LB2371.4 .J47 1998*

**[Graduate study in psychology (1992)]** Graduate study in psychology. Washington, D.C. : American Psychological Association, c1992- v. : 28 cm. Frequency: Annual. 1992- . Continues: Graduate study in psychology and associated fields (OCoLC)9907952 (DLC) 84641215.
*1. Psychology - Study and teaching (Graduate) - United States - Directories. 2. Psychology - Study and teaching (Graduate) - Canada - Directories. I. American Psychological Association. II. Title: Graduate study in psychology and associated fields*
*TC BF77 .G73*

**Graduate study in psychology and associated fields.**
[Graduate study in psychology (1992)] Graduate study in psychology. Washington, D.C. : American Psychological Association, c1992-
*TC BF77 .G73*

**GRADUATE TEACHING ASSISTANTS - UNITED STATES.**
Curzan, Anne. First day to final grade. Ann Arbor [Mich.] : University of Michigan Press, c2000.
*TC LB2335.4 .C87 2000*

**GRADUATE TEACHING ASSISTANTS - UNITED STATES - HANDBOOKS, MANUALS, ETC.**
Sarkisian, Ellen. Teaching American students. Rev. ed. Cambridge, Mass. : The President and Fellows of Harvard University, Derek Bok Center for Teaching and Learning, 1997, c1990.
*TC LB1738 .S371 1997*

**GRADUATE WORK IN PSYCHOLOGY.** *See* PSYCHOLOGY - STUDY AND TEACHING (GRADUATE).

**GRADUATES, COLLEGE.** *See* COLLEGE GRADUATES.

**GRADUATES, HIGH SCHOOL.** *See* HIGH SCHOOL GRADUATES.

**Grady, Marilyn L.** 124 high-impact letters for busy principals : a guide to handling difficult correspondence / Marilyn L. Grady. Thousand Oaks, Calif. : Corwin Press, c2000. xiii, 151 p. ; 30 cm. + 1 computer optical disc (4 3/4 in.). ISBN 0-7619-7663-9 (cloth : alk. paper) ISBN 0-7619-7664-7 (pbk. : alk. paper) DDC 651.7/52
*1. School principals - Correspondence - Handbooks, manuals, etc. 2. Form letters - Handbooks, manuals, etc. I. Title. II. Title: One hundred twenty-four high-impact letters for busy principals*
*TC LB2831.9 .G72 2000*

Brock, Barbara L. Rekindling the flame. Thousand Oaks, Calif. : Corwin Press, c2000.
*TC LB2840.2 .B76 2000*

**GRAFFITI.** *See* STREET ART.

**Graham, Barbara, 1947 Aug. 3-.**
Ali, Lynda, 1946- Moving on in your career. London ; New York : RoutledgeFalmer, 2000.
*TC LB1778.4.G7 A45 2000*

**Graham, Bob, 1942-** Crusher is coming! / Bob Graham. New York, N.Y., U.S.A. : Puffin Books, 1990. [32] p. : col. ill. ; 26 cm. Reprint. Originally published: New York : Viking Kestrel, 1988, c1987. "Ages 3-8"--P. 4 of cover. SUMMARY: When Pete brings home his friend Crusher, the school's tough football hero, he's worried that his baby sister Claire will be a nuisance. ISBN 0-14-050826-0 DDC [E]
*1. Friendship - Fiction. 2. Brothers and sisters - Fiction. 3. Humorous stories. I. Title.*
*TC PZ7.G751667 Cr 1990*

**Graham, George, 1945-.**
When self-consciousness breaks. Cambridge, Mass. : MIT Press, c2000.
*TC RC553.A84 S74 2000*

**Graham, Jim. 1946-.**
Teacher professionalism and the challenge of change. Stoke-on-Trent, Staffordshire, England : Trentham Books, 1999.
*TC LB1775.4.G7 T43 1999*

**Graham, John R. (John Robert), 1940-** MMPI-2 : assessing personality and psychopathology / John R. Graham. 3rd ed. New York : Oxford University Press, 1999. xvii, 510 p. : ill. ; 25 cm. Title page dated 2000. Includes bibliographical references (p. 386-426) and indexes. ISBN 0-19-511481-7 (alk. paper) DDC 155.2/83
*1. Minnesota Multiphasic Personality Inventory. I. Title.*
*TC RC473.M5 G73 1999*

MMPI-2 correlates for outpatient community mental health settings / John R. Graham, Yossef S. Ben-Porath, and John L. McNulty ; foreword by James N. Butcher. Minneapolis : University of Minnesota Press, c1999. xx, 598 p. : ill. ; 26 cm. Includes bibliographical

references (p. 107-112) and index. ISBN 0-8166-2564-6
(hardcover) DDC 616.89/075
*1. Minnesota Multiphasic Personality Inventory. 2. Minnesota
Multiphasic Personality Inventory - Validity. 3. Community
Mental Health Services. 4. MMPI. I. Ben-Porath, Yossef S. II.
McNulty, John L. III. Title.*
*TC RC473.M5 G733 1999*

**Graham, Sheila L.** Urban minority gifted students :
perspectives of the graduates of the Mott Hall School /
by Sheila L. Graham. 1999. ix, 158 leaves ; 29 cm.
Typescript; issued also on microfilm. Thesis (Ed.D.)--Teachers
College, Columbia University, 1999. Includes bibliographical
references (leaves 132-142).
*1. Children of minorities - Education (Middle school) - New
York (State) - New York. 2. Gifted children - New York (State) -
New York. 3. Curriculum enrichment. 4. Educational
acceleration. 5. Mott Hall School (New York, N.Y.) 6. School
environment. 7. Mott Hall School (New York, N.Y.) - Students -
Attitudes. I. Title.*
*TC 06 no. 11119*

**GRAMMAR.** *See* **GRAMMAR, COMPARATIVE
AND GENERAL.**

**GRAMMAR, COMPARATIVE AND GENERAL.**
*See also* **GENERATIVE GRAMMAR;
LANGUAGE AND LANGUAGES;
PRINCIPLES AND PARAMETERS
(LINGUISTICS).**
Cook, V. J. (Vivian James), 1940- Chomsky's
universal grammar. 2nd [updated] ed. Oxford, OX,
UK ; Cambridge, Mass., USA : Blackwell Publishers,
1996.
*TC P85.C47 C66 1996*

Lillo-Martin, Diane C. (Diane Carolyn), 1959-
Universal grammar and American sign language.
Dordrecht ; Boston : Kluwer Academic Publishers,
c1991.
*TC HV2474 .L55 1991*

Loritz, Donald, 1947- How the brain evolved
language. New York : Oxford University Press, 1999.
*TC P116 .L67 1999*

**GRAMMAR, COMPARATIVE AND GENERAL -
DEIXIS.** *See also* **INDEXICALS
(SEMANTICS).**
Perkins, Revere D. (Revere Dale) Deixis, grammar,
and culture. Amsterdam ; Philadelphia : J. Benjamins
Pub. co., 1992.
*TC P35 .P47 1992*

**GRAMMAR, COMPARATIVE AND GENERAL -
DERIVATION.** *See* **GENERATIVE
GRAMMAR.**

**GRAMMAR, COMPARATIVE AND GENERAL -
GRAMMATICAL CATAGORIES.**
Functional categories, argument structure and
parametric variation. Edinburgh : Centre for Cognitive
Study, University of Edinburgh, c1994.
*TC P151 .F86 1994*

**GRAMMAR, COMPARATIVE AND GENERAL -
PHONOLOGY.**
Uyechi, Linda, 1957- The geometry of visual
phonology. Stanford, Calif. : CSLI Publications, 1996.
*TC HV2474 .U88 1996*

**GRAMMAR, COMPARATIVE AND GENERAL -
SENTENCES.**
Alston, William P. Illocutionary acts and sentence
meaning. Ithaca : Cornell University Press, 2000.
*TC P95.55 .A47 2000*

**GRAMMAR, GENERATIVE.** *See* **GENERATIVE
GRAMMAR.**

**The grammar of autobiography.**
Quigley, Jean. Mahwah, N.J. : Lawrence Erlbaum
Associates, c2000.
*TC PE1315.M6 Q54 2000*

**GRAMMAR, PHILOSOPHICAL.** *See* **GRAMMAR,
COMPARATIVE AND GENERAL.**

**GRAMMAR SCHOOLS.** *See* **PUBLIC SCHOOLS.**

**GRAMMAR, TRANSFORMATIONAL.** *See*
**GENERATIVE GRAMMAR.**

**GRAMMAR, UNIVERSAL.** *See* **GRAMMAR,
COMPARATIVE AND GENERAL.**

**GRAND-MOTHERS.** *See* **GRANDMOTHERS.**

**Grand Palais (Paris, France).**
Tinterow, Gary. Origins of impressionism. New
York : Metropolitan Museum of Art : Distributed by
H.N. Abrams, c1994.
*TC ND547.5.I4 L6913 1994*

**The grand resort hotels of the White Mountains.**
Tolles, Bryant Franklin, 1939- 1st ed. Boston : D.R.
Godine, 1995.
*TC TX909 .T58 1995*

**GRANDFATHERS - FICTION.**
Jones, Joy. Tambourine moon. New York : Simon &
Schuster, 1999.
*TC PZ7.J72025 Tam 1999*

Michelson, Richard. Grandpa's gamble. New York :
Marshall Cavendish, 1999.
*TC PZ7.M581915 Gr 1999*

O'Malley, Kevin, 1961- Bud. New York : Walker,
2000.
*TC PZ7.O526 Bu 2000*

Rosenberg, Liz. The silence in the mountains. 1st
American ed. New York : Orchard Books, c1999.
*TC PZ7.R71894 Si 1999*

**GRANDMAS.** *See* **GRANDMOTHERS.**

**GRANDMOTHERS - FICTION.**
Nye, Naomi Shihab. Benito's dream bottle. 1st ed.
New York : Simon & Schuster Books for Young
Readers, c1995.
*TC PZ7.N976 Be 1995*

Pak, Soyung. Dear Juno. New York : Viking, 1999.
*TC PZ7.P173 De 1999*

Rosen, Michael, 1946- A Thanksgiving wish. New
York : Blue Sky Press, c1999.
*TC PZ7.R71867 Tf 1999*

**Grandmother's grandchild.**
Snell, Alma Hogan. Lincoln : University of Nebraska
Press, c2000.
*TC E99.C92 S656 2000*

**GRANDPARENT AND CHILD.**
De Toledo, Sylvie. Grandparents as parents. New
York : Guilford Press, c1995.
*TC HQ759.9 .D423 1995*

Handbook on grandparenthood. Westport, Conn. :
Greenwood Press, 1998.
*TC HQ759.9 .H36 1998*

**GRANDPARENTING.**
Handbook on grandparenthood. Westport, Conn. :
Greenwood Press, 1998.
*TC HQ759.9 .H36 1998*

**GRANDPARENTS.** *See* **GRANDFATHERS;
GRANDMOTHERS.**

**Grandparents as parents.**
De Toledo, Sylvie. New York : Guilford Press, c1995.
*TC HQ759.9 .D423 1995*

**GRANDPARENTS - FICTION.**
Stegner, Wallace Earle, 1909- Angle of repose. New
York : Modern Library, 2000.
*TC PS3537.T316 A8 2000*

**GRANDPARENTS - SOCIAL CONDITIONS.**
Handbook on grandparenthood. Westport, Conn. :
Greenwood Press, 1998.
*TC HQ759.9 .H36 1998*

**Grandpa's gamble.**
Michelson, Richard. New York : Marshall Cavendish,
1999.
*TC PZ7.M581915 Gr 1999*

**Grandpa's soup.**
Kadono, Eiko. Grand Rapids, MI : Eerdmans Books
for Young Readers, 1999.
*TC PZ7.K1167 Gr 1999*

**GrandPré, Mary, ill.**
Rowling, J. K. Harry Potter and the sorcerer's stone.
1st American ed. New York : A.A. Levine Books,
1998.
*TC PZ7.R79835 Har 1998*

**Granfield, Robert, 1955-** Coming clean : overcoming
addiction without treatment / Robert Granfield and
William Cloud ; foreword by Stanton Peele. New
York ; London : New York University Press, c1999.
xxi, 296 p. ; 22 cm. Includes bibliographical references (p.
[251]-287) and index. ISBN 0-8147-1581-8 (cloth : alk. paper)
ISBN 0-8147-1582-6 (paper : alk. paper) DDC 616.86/06
*1. Recovering addicts. 2. Self-care, Health. 3. Self-management
(Psychology) 4. Alcoholics - Rehabilitation. 5. Narcotic
addicts - Rehabilitation. I. Cloud, William, 1947- II. Title.*
*TC HV4998 .G73 1999*

**The Grannyman.**
Schachner, Judith Byron. 1st ed. New York : Dutton
Children's Books, c1999.
*TC PZ7.S3286 Gr 1999*

**Gransow, Bettina.**
Comparative anomie research. Aldershot, Hants,
England : Brookfield, Vt., USA : Ashgate, c1999.
*TC HM816 .C65 1999*

**Grant, Ann Boyle.** Nursing leadership, management &
research / Ann Boyle Grant, Veta H. Massey.
Springhouse, Pa. : Springhouse Corp., c1999. vi. 249
p. : col. ill. ; 23 cm. (Springhouse notes) Includes
bibliographical references and index. ISBN 0-87434-968-0
(alk. paper) DDC 362.1/73/068
*1. Nursing services - Administration - Outline. syllabi. etc. 2.
Leadership - Outline. syllabi. etc. 3. Nursing - Research -
Outline. syllabi. etc. 4. Nursing - organization &
administration - outlines. 5. Leadership - nurses' instruction.
6. Nursing Research - outlines. I. Massey, Veta H. II. Title. III.
Title: Nursing leadership, management, and research IV.
Series.*
*TC RT89 .G727 1999*

**Grant, Brian W., 1939-** The condition of madness /
Brian Grant. Lanham, Md : University Press of
America, 1999. v, 232 p. 23 cm. ISBN 0-7618-1443-4
(cloth : alk. paper) ISBN 0-7618-1444-2 (pbk. : alk. paper)
DDC 616.89/001
*1. Mental illness - Philosophy. 2. Psychiatry - Philosophy. I.
Title.*
*TC RC437.5 .G73 1999*

**Grant finder. Arts and humanities.**
GrantFinder. Arts and humanities. New York, NY :
St. Martin's Press, 2000.
*TC LB2337.2 .G72*

GrantFinder : Arts and humanities. New York, NY :
St. Martin's Press, 2000.
*TC LB2337.2 .G72*

**Grant finder. Arts and humanities.**
GrantFinder : Arts and humanities. New York, NY :
St. Martin's Press, 2000.
*TC LB2337.2 .G72*

**Grant finder. Medicine.**
GrantFinder. Medicine. New York, NY : St. Martin's
Press.
*TC LB2337.2 .G73*

**Grant finder. Medicine.**
GrantFinder : Medicine. New York, NY : St. Martin's
Press.
*TC LB2337.2 .G73*

**Grant finder. Science.**
GrantFinder. Science. New York : St. Martin's Press,
c2000.
*TC LB2338 .G652 2000*

**Grant finder : the complete guide to postgraduate
funding worldwide. Arts and humanities.**
GrantFinder : Arts and humanities. New York, NY :
St. Martin's Press, 2000.
*TC LB2337.2 .G72*

**Grant finder : the complete guide to postgraduate
funding worldwide. Medicine.**
GrantFinder : Medicine. New York, NY : St. Martin's
Press.
*TC LB2337.2 .G73*

**Grant finder : the complete guide to postgraduate
funding worldwide. Social sciences.**
GrantFinder : Social sciences. New York, NY : St.
Martin's Press.
*TC LB2337.2 .G7 2000*

**Grant, Jim, 1942-.**
The multiage handbook. Peterborough, NH : Society
for Developmental Education, c1996.
*TC LB1029.N6 M754 1996*

**Grant, Kirsty.**
National Gallery of Victoria. In relief. Melbourne :
National Gallery of Victoria, c1997.
*TC NE1190.25 .G72 1997*

**GRANT-MAINTAINED SCHOOLS.** *See*
**CHARTER SCHOOLS.**

**Grant, Marcus.**
Alcohol and emerging markets. Philadelphia, Penn :
Brunner/Mazel, 1998.
*TC HD9350.6 .A4 1998*

**GRANT PROPOSAL WRITING.** *See* **PROPOSAL
WRITING FOR GRANTS.**

**Grant, Ruth Weissbourd, 1951-.**
Locke, John, 1632-1704. [Some thoughts concerning
education] Some thoughts concerning education ;
Indianapolis : Hackett Pub. Co., c1996.
*TC LB475.L6 L63 1996*

**GRANT WRITING.** See **PROPOSAL WRITING FOR GRANTS.**

**GrantFinder. Arts and humanities.**
GrantFinder : Arts and humanities. New York, NY :
St. Martin's Press, 2000.
*TC LB2337.2 .G72*

**GrantFinder. Arts and humanities.**
GrantFinder : Arts and humanities. New York, NY :
St. Martin's Press, 2000.
*TC LB2337.2 .G72*

**GrantFinder.** Arts and humanities. New York, NY : St.
Martin's Press, 2000. vii, 466 p. ; 26 cm. Frequency:
Biennial. Grant finder. Arts and humanities. Arts and
humanities. Includes index. ISBN 0-312-22893-7
*1. Student aid. 2. Graduate students - Scholarships,
fellowships, etc. 3. Arts - Research grants. 4. Humanities -
Research grants. I. Title: Grant finder. Arts and humanities II.
Title: Arts and humanities*
*TC LB2337.2 .G72*

**GrantFinder. Medicine.**
GrantFinder : Medicine. New York, NY : St. Martin's
Press,
*TC LB2337.2 .G73*

**GrantFinder. Medicine.**
GrantFinder : Medicine. New York, NY : St. Martin's
Press,
*TC LB2337.2 .G73*

**GrantFinder.** Science : the complete guide to
postgraduate funding worldwide. New York : St.
Martin's Press, c2000. vii, 458 p. ; 26 cm. Developed from
the Grants register. Includes indexes. ISBN 0-312-22895-3 (St.
Martin's) ISBN 0-333-77728-X (Macmillan)
*1. Student aid - Directories. 2. Graduate students -
Scholarships, fellowships, etc. - Directories. 3. Science -
Research grants - Directories. I. Title: Grants register. II.
Title: Grant finder. Science*
*TC LB2338 .G652 2000*

**GrantFinder :** the complete guide to postgraduate
funding worldwide. Arts and humanities. New York,
NY : St. Martin's Press, 2000. vii, 466 p. ; 26 cm.
Frequency: Biennial. Grant finder : the complete guide to
postgraduate funding worldwide. Arts and humanities. Spine
title: GrantFinder. Arts and humanities. Includes index. ISBN
0-312-22893-7
*1. Student aid - Directories. 2. Graduate students -
Scholarships, fellowships, etc. - Directories. 3. Arts -
Scholarships, fellowships, etc. - Directories. 4. Arts - Research
grants - Directories. 5. Humanities - Scholarships, fellowships,
etc. - Directories. 6. Humanities - Research grants -
Directories. I. Title: Grant finder : the complete guide to
postgraduate funding worldwide. Arts and humanities II. Title:
GrantFinder. Arts and humanities III. Title: Grant finder. Arts
and humanities IV. Title: Grant finder. Arts and humanities V.
Title: GrantFinder. Arts and humanities VI. Title: Arts and
humanities VII. Title: Complete guide to postgraduate funding
worldwide*
*TC LB2337.2 .G72*

**GrantFinder :** the complete guide to postgraduate
funding worldwide. Medicine. New York, NY : St.
Martin's Press, 2000. v. Frequency: Biennial. Grant finder : the
complete guide to postgraduate funding worldwide. Medicine.
Spine title: GrantFinder. Medicine. ISSN 1526-0925
*1. Student aid - Directories. 2. Graduate students -
Scholarships, fellowships, etc. - Directories. 3. Medicine -
Scholarships, fellowships, etc. - Directories. 4. Medicine -
Research grants - Directories. I. Title: Grant finder : the
complete guide to postgraduate funding worldwide. Medicine
II. Title: GrantFinder. Medicine III. Title: Grant finder.
Medicine IV. Title: Grant finder. Medicine V. Title:
GrantFinder. Medicine VI. Title: Medicine VII. Title:
Complete guide to postgraduate funding worldwide*
*TC LB2337.2 .G73*

**GrantFinder :** the complete guide to postgraduate
funding worldwide. Social sciences. New York, NY :
St. Martin's Press, v. Frequency: Biennial. Grant finder : the
complete guide to postgraduate funding worldwide. Social
sciences. Social sciences. Includes indexes. ISSN 1526-0909
*1. Student aid - Directories. 2. Graduate students -
Scholarships, fellowships, etc. 3. Social sciences - Research
grants. I. Title: Grant finder : the complete guide to
postgraduate funding worldwide. Social sciences II. Title:
Social sciences III. Title: Complete guide to postgraduate
funding worldwide*
*TC LB2337.2 .G7 2000*

**Grantmakers in the Arts.**
Renz, Loren. Arts funding. 3rd ed. [New York, N.Y.] :
Foundation Center, c1998.
*TC NX711.U5 R4 1998*

**GRANTS.** See **GRANTS-IN-AID.**

**Grants for school technology :** a guide to federal and
private funding / Health & Administration
Development Group. 3rd ed. Gaithersburg, MD :
Aspen Publishers, c2000. viii, 221 p. ; 28 cm. "A
GrantScape annual guidebook." Includes index. ISBN 0-8342-
1786-4
*1. Endowments - United States - Directories. 2. Educational
technology. 3. Educational fund raising - United States. 4.
Grants-in-aid - United States - Directories. I. Health and
Administration Development Group (Aspen Publishers)*
*TC LB2336 .G76365 2000*

**Grants for schools :** how to find and win funds for K-12
programs / Health & Administration Development
Group ; [introduction by Jacqueline Ferguson]. 4th ed.
Gaithersburg, MD : Aspen Publishers, 2000. xlvii, 285
p. ; 28 cm. (A GrantScape annual guidebook) Rev. ed. of:
Grants for schools / Jacqueline Ferguson. 2nd ed. c1993.
Includes bibliographical references (p. 267-269) and index.
ISBN 0-8342-1788-0 DDC 371.2/06
*1. Educational fund raising - United States. 2. Federal aid to
education - United States. 3. Grants-in-aid - United States. 4.
Education - United States - Finance. 5. Corporations -
Charitable contributions - United States. I. Ferguson,
Jacqueline. Grants for schools. II. Health and Administration
Development Group (Aspen Publishers) III. Title. IV. Series*
*TC LB2825 .F46 2000*

**Grants for special education and rehabilitation.**
Ferguson, Jacqueline. 4th ed. Gaithersburg, MD :
Aspen Publishers, Inc., 2000.
*TC LB2825 .F424 2000*

**GRANTS-IN-AID.** See **ECONOMIC ASSISTANCE,
DOMESTIC; FEDERAL AID TO
EDUCATION; FEDERAL AID TO SERVICES
FOR THE HANDICAPPED; FEDERAL AID
TO THE ARTS.**

**GRANTS-IN-AID - UNITED STATES.**
Ferguson, Jacqueline. Grants for special education and
rehabilitation. 4th ed. Gaithersburg, MD : Aspen
Publishers, Inc., 2000.
*TC LB2825 .F424 2000*

Grants for schools. 4th ed. Gaithersburg, MD : Aspen
Publishers, 2000.
*TC LB2825 .F46 2000*

**GRANTS-IN-AID - UNITED STATES -
DIRECTORIES.**
Grants for school technology. 3rd ed. Gaithersburg,
MD : Aspen Publishers, c2000.
*TC LB2336 .G76365 2000*

**Grants register.**
GrantFinder. Science. New York : St. Martin's Press,
c2000.
*TC LB2338 .G652 2000*

**A GrantScape annual guidebook**
Grants for schools. 4th ed. Gaithersburg, MD : Aspen
Publishers, 2000.
*TC LB2825 .F46 2000*

**GRANTSMANSHIP.** See **PROPOSAL WRITING
FOR GRANTS.**

**GRANTWRITING.** See **PROPOSAL WRITING
FOR GRANTS.**

**Grapes, Bryan J.**
Affirmative action. San Diego, Calif. : Greenhaven
Press, 2000.
*TC JC599.U5 A34685 2000*

Interracial relationships. San Diego : Greenhaven
Press, c2000.
*TC HQ1031 .I59 2000*

**GRAPHIC ARTS.** See also **COMMERCIAL ART;
DRAWING; PAINTING; PICTURE BOOKS;
PRINTING; PRINTS.**
Looking closer 2. New York : Allworth Press :
American Institute of Graphic Arts, c1997.
*TC NC997 .L632 1997*

Looking closer. New York : Allworth Press :
American Institute of Graphic Arts ; Saint Paul, MN :
Distributor, Consortium Book Sales & Distribution,
c1994.
*TC NC997 .L63 1994*

**GRAPHIC ARTS - HISTORY.**
Heller, Steven. Design literacy. New York : Allworth
Press, c1997.
*TC NC998 .H45 1997*

**GRAPHIC ARTS - HISTORY - 20TH CENTURY.**
Design dialogues. New York : Allworth Press, c1998.
*TC NK1390 .D473 1998*

**GRAPHIC ARTS - STUDY AND TEACHING.**
The education of a graphic designer. New York :

Allworth Press [in association with the] School of
Visual Arts, c1998
*TC NC590 .E38 1998*

**GRAPHIC ARTS - UNITED STATES.**
Design culture. New York : Allworth Press :
American Institute of Graphic Arts, c1997.
*TC NC998.5.A1 D46 1997*

**GRAPHIC DESIGN (GRAPHIC ARTS).** See
**GRAPHIC ARTS.**

**GRAPHICAL USER INTERFACES (COMPUTER
SYSTEMS).**
Barnicle, Katherine Ann. Evaluation of the interaction
between users of screen reading technology and
graphical user interface elements. 1999.
*TC 085 B265*

Pfaffenberger, Bryan, 1949- Mastering GNOME. San
Francisco, CA : Sybex, Inc., 1999.
*TC QA76.9.U83 P453 1999*

**GRAPHICS.** See **GRAPHIC ARTS.**

**GRAPHOLOGY.** See **DRAWING, PSYCHOLOGY
OF.**

**GRASS NUTS.** See **PEANUTS.**

**Grass roots and glass ceilings :** African American
administrators in predominantly white colleges and
universities / edited by William B. Harvey. Albany :
State University of New York Press, c1999. vii, 169 p. ;
24 cm. (SUNY series, frontiers in education) Includes index.
ISBN 0-7914-4163-6 (hardcover : alk. paper) ISBN
0-7914-4164-4 (pbk. : alk. paper) DDC 378.1/11/08996073
*1. Discrimination in higher education - United States. 2. Afro-
American college administrators. I. Harvey, William B.
(William Bernard) II. Series*
*TC LC212.42 .G73 1999*

**Grass roots networking for primary education : :**
case studies, Thailand, Sri Lanka, Philippines, Japan.
Bangkok : Unesco Regional Office for Education in
Asia and the Pacific, 1985. 39 p. : ill. ; 28 cm. At head of
title: APEID, Asia and the Pacific Programme of Educational
Innovation for Development. "BKA/85/OPE/383-1200"--T.p.
verso.
*1. Education, Primary - Asia - Case studies. 2. Educational
innovations - Asia - Case studies. I. Unesco. Regional Office
for Education in Asia and the Pacific. II. Asia and the Pacific
Programme of Educational Innovation for Development*
*TC LA1054 .G73 1985*

**GRASSES.** See **GRASSLANDS; WHEAT.**

**GRASSLANDS.** See **PRAIRIES.**

**GRASSLANDS - AFRICA.**
Dunphy, Madeleine. Here is the African savanna. 1st
ed. New York : Hyperion Books for Children, c1999.
*TC QH194 .D86 1999*

**Grattan-Guinness, I.**
**[Fontana history of the mathematical sciences]**
The Norton history of the mathematical sciences :
the rainbow of mathematics / Ivor Grattan-
Guinness. 1st American ed. New York : W.W.
Norton, 1998. 817 p. : ill. ; 25 cm. (Norton history of
science) Originally published: The Fontana history of the
mathematical sciences. London : Fontana Press, 1997.
Includes bibliographical references (p.[763]-788 ) and
index. ISBN 0-393-04650-8 DDC 510/.9
*1. Mathematics - History. I. Title. II. Title: Rainbow of
mathematics III. Series*
*TC QA21 .G695 1998*

**Graves, Kerry.**
Forten, Charlotte L. A free Black girl before the Civil
War. Mankato, Minn. : Blue Earth Books, c2000.
*TC F74.S1 F67 2000*

Richards, Caroline Cowles, 1842-1913. A nineteenth-
century schoolgirl. Mankato, Minn. : Blue Earth
Books, c2000.
*TC F129.C2 R53 2000*

**Graves, Michael F.**
Reading for meaning. New York ; London : Teachers
College Press, c2000.
*TC LB1050.45 .R443 2000*

**Gravett, Terry.**
Etching [videorecording]. Northbrook, Ill. :
Peasmarsh, East Sussex, Eng. : Roland Collection of
Films on Art, c1990.
*TC NE2043 .E87 1990*

Screen printing [videorecording]. [Northbrook?], Ill. :
Peasmarsh, East Sussex, Eng. : Roland Collection of
Films on Art, c1992.
*TC NE2238.G7 S4 1992*

*Gravett, Terry.*

Screen printing [videorecording]. [Northbrook?], Ill. : Peasmarsh, East Sussex, Eng. : Roland Collection of Films on Art, c1992.
*TC NE2238.G7 S4 1992*

**GRAVIDA.** *See* **PREGNANT WOMEN.**

**GRAVITATION.** *See* **MATTER.**

**GRAVITATIONAL COLLAPSE.** *See also* **BLACK HOLES (ASTRONOMY).**
Stephen Hawking's universe [videorecording]. [Alexandria, Va.] : PBS Video; Burbank, CA : Distributed by Warner Home Video, c1997.
*TC QB982 .S7 1997*

**Gravy training.**
Crainer, Stuart. 1st ed. San Francisco : Jossey-Bass Publishers, c1999.
*TC HF1111 .C7 1999*

**Gray, Adelaide, 1973-.**
Johnston, Jane, 1954- Enriching early scientific learning. Philadelphia : Open University Press, 1999.
*TC Q181 .J58 1999*

**Gray, Barry, 1944-** Lifemaps of people with learning difficulties / Barry Gray and Geoff Ridden. London ; Philadelphia : Jessica Kingsley, 1999. 138 p. : ill. ; 23 cm. Includes bibliographical references. ISBN 1-85302-690-5 (pbk. : alk. paper) DDC 362.3/092/2
*1. Social work with the mentally handicapped - Psychological aspects. 2. Mentally handicapped - Biography. 3. Mentally handicapped - Psychology. 4. Learning disabled - Biography. 5. Learning disabled - Psychology. 6. Psychology - Biographical methods. I. Ridden, G. M. II. Title. III. Title: Lifemaps of people with learning disabilities*
*TC HV3004 .G73 1999*

**Gray, Betty G.**
Ragno, Nancy N. World of language. [Teacher ed.]. Morristown, NJ : Silver Burdett & Ginn, c1990.

Ragno, Nancy N. World of language. [Teacher ed.]. Morristown, NJ : Silver Burdett & Ginn, c1990.

Ragno, Nancy N. World of language. [Teacher ed.]. Morristown, NJ : Silver Burdett & Ginn, c1990.

Ragno, Nancy Nickell. World of language. Needham, Ma. : Silver Burdett Ginn, c1996.
*TC LB1576 .S4471 1996*

Ragno, Nancy Nickell. World of language. Needham, Mass. : Silver Burdett Ginn, c1996.
*TC LB1576 .S4471 1996*

World of language. Needham, Mass. : Silver Burdett Ginn, c1996.
*TC LB1576 .S4471 1996*

World of language. Teacher ed. Needham, Mass. : Silver Burdett Ginn, c1996.
*TC LB1576 .S4471 1996 Teacher Ed.*

**Gray, John (John Michael), 1948-.**
Improving schools. Buckingham [England] : Philadelphia : Open University Press, 1999.
*TC LB2822.84.G7 I68 1999*

**Gray, Kenneth C.** Getting real : helping teens find their future / Kenneth Gray. Thousand Oaks, Calif. : Corwin Press, c2000. xiii, 138 p. ; 23 cm. Includes bibliographical references (p. 129-132) and index. ISBN 0-7619-7514-4 (alk. paper) ISBN 0-7619-7515-2 (pbk. : alk. paper) DDC 331.7/0233
*1. Vocational guidance - United States. 2. High school graduates - Employment - United States. 3. High school students - Vocational guidance - United States. 4. Postsecondary education - United States. I. Title.*
*TC HF5382.5.U5 G676 2000*

**Gray, Libba Moore.** When Uncle took the fiddle / by Libba Moore Gray ; illustrated by Lloyd Bloom. New York : Orchard Books, 1999. 1 v. (unpaged) : col. ill. ; 29 cm. SUMMARY: Uncle's inspired playing of the fiddle causes sleepy family members to pick up other instruments and join him, while the neighbors come to join the celebration. ISBN 0-531-30137-0 (trade) ISBN 0-531-33137-7 (lib. bdg.) DDC [E]
*1. Violin - Fiction. 2. Music - Fiction. I. Bloom, Lloyd, ill. II. Title.*
*TC PZ7.G7793 Wh 1999*

**Gray, Maryann Jacobi.**
Combining service and learning in higher education. Santa Monica, CA : RAND Education, 1999.
*TC LC220.5 .C646 1999*

**GRAY WOLVES.** *See* **WOLVES.**

**Graywolf forum**
(3) The business of memory. Saint Paul, Minn. : Graywolf Press, c1999.
*TC BF378.A87 B87 1999*

**GRE (EDUCATIONAL TEST).** *See* **GRADUATE RECORD EXAMINATION.**

**GRE literature.**
Cracking the GRE literature in English subject test. New York : Random House, 1996-
*TC LB2367.4 .L58*

**Grealy, Madeleine A.**
International Conference on Perception and Action (10th : 1999 : Edinburgh, Scotland) Studies in perception and action V. Mahwah, N.J. : L. Erlbaum Associates, 1999.
*TC BF295 .I57 1999*

**The great Arizona orphan abduction.**
Gordon, Linda. Cambridge, Mass. : Harvard University Press, 1999.
*TC F819.C55 G67 1999*

**The great artists**
Seurat [videorecording]. West Long Branch, NJ : Kultur, c1999.
*TC ND553.S5 S5 1999*

**The great big book of fun phonics activities.**
Daniel, Claire, 1936- New York : Scholastic professional books, c1999.
*TC LB1525.3 .D36 1999*

**GREAT BOOKS PROGRAM.** *See* **GROUP READING.**

**GREAT BRITAIN - CHURCH HISTORY - 16TH CENTURY.**
Anglo-Dutch Historical Conference (13th : 1997) The education of a Christian society. Aldershot, Hants, England : Brookfield, Vt. : Ashgate, c1999.
*TC BR377 .E38 1999*

**GREAT BRITAIN - COLONIES - AFRICA - ADMINISTRATION.**
Mungazi, Dickson A. The last British liberals in Africa. Westport, Conn. : Praeger, 1999.
*TC DT2979.T63 M86 1999*

**GREAT BRITAIN - COLONIES - AFRICA - ADMINISTRATION - HISTORY - 20TH CENTURY.**
Hubbard, James P. (James Patrick), 1945- Education under colonial rule. Lanham : University Press of America, 2000.
*TC LG483.K78 H83 2000*

**GREAT BRITAIN - COLONIES - AFRICA - HISTORY - 20TH CENTURY.**
Sivonen, Seppo. White-collar or hoe handle. Helsinki : Suomen Historiallinen Seura, [1995]
*TC LA1531 .S58 1995*

**GREAT BRITAIN - COLONIES - POLITICS AND GOVERNMENT.**
Bush, Julia. Edwardian ladies and imperial power. London : New York : Leicester University Press, 2000.
*TC DA16 .B87 2000*

**Great Britain. Department for Education and Employment.**
Morgan, Sally, 1951- Care about education. London : DfEE, 1999.
*TC HV59 .M67 1999*

**Great Britain. Department of Health.**
Morgan, Sally, 1951- Care about education. London : DfEE, 1999.
*TC HV59 .M67 1999*

**GREAT BRITAIN - FOREIGN RELATIONS - 1936-1945.**
Robbins, Keith. Appeasement. Oxford, UK ; New York, NY, USA : B. Blackwell, 1988.
*TC DA47.2 .R62 1988*

**GREAT BRITAIN - FOREIGN RELATIONS - GERMANY.**
Robbins, Keith. Appeasement. Oxford, UK ; New York, NY, USA : B. Blackwell, 1988.
*TC DA47.2 .R62 1988*

**GREAT BRITAIN - FOREIGN RELATIONS - UNITED STATES.**
Hendrick, Burton Jesse, 1870-1949. The life and letters of Walter H. Page. Garden City, N.Y. : Doubleday, Page & Co., 1925.
*TC E664.P15 H45 1925*

**GREAT BRITAIN - HISTORY - RICHARD I, 1189-1199 - FICTION.**
Cadnum, Michael. In a dark wood. New York : Orchard Books, c1998.
*TC PZ7.C11724 In 1998*

**GREAT BRITAIN - HISTORY - RICHARD I, 1189-1199 - JUVENILE FICTION.**
Cadnum, Michael. In a dark wood. New York : Orchard Books, c1998.
*TC PZ7.C11724 In 1998*

**GREAT BRITAIN - HISTORY - VICTORIA, 1837-1901.**
Black, Barbara J., 1962- On exhibit. Charlottesville ; London : University Press of Virginia, 2000.
*TC AM43.L6 B53 2000*

Brock, W. H. (William Hodson) Science for all. Brookfield, VT : Variorum, 1996.
*TC Q127.G5 B76 1996*

**GREAT BRITAIN - KINGS AND RULERS - EDUCATION - HISTORY.**
Gordon, Peter, 1927- Royal education. London ; Portland, OR : Frank Cass, 1999.
*TC LC4945.G72 G67 1999*

**GREAT BRITAIN. OFFICE FOR STANDARDS IN EDUCATION.**
An inspector calls :. London : Kogan Page, 1999.
*TC LB2900.5 .I58 1999*

**GREAT BRITAIN - POLITICS AND GOVERNMENT - 1603-1714.**
Wheale, Nigel. Writing and society. London ; New York : Routledge, 1999.
*TC PR438.P65 W75 1999*

**GREAT BRITAIN - POLITICS AND GOVERNMENT - 1901-1910.**
Bush, Julia. Edwardian ladies and imperial power. London ; New York : Leicester University Press, 2000.
*TC DA16 .B87 2000*

**GREAT BRITAIN - POPULAR CULTURE.** *See* **POPULAR CULTURE - GREAT BRITAIN.**

**GREAT BRITAIN - SOCIAL POLICY.**
Ainley, Patrick. Learning policy. Basingstoke, Hampshire : Macmillan Press ; New York : St. Martin's Press, 1999.
*TC LC93.G7 A76 1999*

**The Great Divide.**
Dodds, Dayle Ann. 1st ed. Cambridge, MA : Candlewick Press, 1999.
*TC PZ8.3.D645 Gr 1999*

**Great explorations in math and science (GEMS).**
Goodman, Jan M. Group solutions : : [Teacher's guide]. Rev. Berkeley, Calif. : Lawrence Hall of Science, University of California, 1997, c1992.
*TC QA8.7 .G5 1997*

**The great fire by Jim Murphy.**
Beech, Linda Ward. New York : Scholastic, c1996.
*TC LB11573 .B437 1996*

Beech, Linda Ward. New York : Scholastic, c1996.
*TC LB1573 .B437 1996*

**The great Gilly Hopkins by Katherine Paterson.**
Beech, Linda Ward. New York : Scholastic, c1998.
*TC LB1573 .B439 1998*

**Great ideas for teaching about Africa** / edited by Misty L. Bastian and Jane L. Parpart. Boulder : Lynne Rienner, 1999. x, 243 p. ; 24 cm. Includes bibliographical references and index. ISBN 1-55587-815-6 (hardcover : alk. paper) ISBN 1-55587-816-4 (pbk. : alk. paper) DDC 960./07/073
*1. Africa - Study and teaching - United States. I. Bastian, Misty L., 1955- II. Parpart, Jane L.*
*TC DT19.9.U5 G74 1999*

**The Great Indian education debate :** documents relating to the Orientalist-Anglicist controversy, 1781-1843 / edited by Lynn Zastoupil and Martin Moir. Richmond : Curzon, 1999. xvi, 357 ; 23 cm. (London studies on South Asia ; no. 18) Includes bibliographical references (p. 345-351) and index. ISBN 0-7007-1181-3
*1. Education - India - History - 19th century. 2. Education and state - India. I. Zastoupil, Lynn, 1953- II. Moir, Martin. III. Series: London studies on South Asia ; no. 18*
*TC LA1151 .G743 1999*

**Great photographers**
(v.10) The power of idea : [videorecording]. Minneapolis, Minn. : Media Loft, c1992.
*TC TR690 .P5 1992*

(v.2) The sight and insight of Ernst Haas [videorecording]. Minneapolis, Minn. : Media Loft, 1992.
*TC TR647.H3 S5 1992*

(v.3) Sport photography today! [videorecording]. Minneapolis, Minn. : Media Loft, c1992.

TC TR821 .S64 1992

(v.8) The filming of a television commercial [videorecording]. Minneapolis, Minn. : Media Loft, c1992.
**TC HF6146.T42 F5 1992**

**The great school debate.**
Good, Thomas L., 1943- Mahwah, N.J. : L. Erlbaum Associates, 2000.
**TC LB2806.36 .G66 2000**

**Great scouts!.**
Paul, Nora. Medford, NJ : Information Today, c1999.
**TC ZA4201 .P38 1999**

**The great transformation.**
Marsh, Robert Mortimer. Armonk, N.Y. : M.E. Sharpe, c1996.
**TC HN749.T35 M37 1996**

**GREBES - FICTION.**
Jennings, Patrick. Putnam and Pennyroyal. 1st ed. New York : Scholastic Press, 1999.
**TC PZ7.J4298715 Co 1999**

**GREECE - CIVILIZATION.**
The eye expanded. Berkeley : University of California Press, c1999.
**TC DE59 .E93 1999**

**GREECE - CIVILIZATION - EGYPTIAN INFLUENCES.**
Berlinerblau, Jacques. Heresy in the University. New Brunswick, N.J. : Rutgers University Press, c1999.
**TC DF78.B3983 B47 1999**

**GREECE - CIVILIZATION - PHOENICIAN INFLUENCES.**
Berlinerblau, Jacques. Heresy in the University. New Brunswick, N.J. : Rutgers University Press, c1999.
**TC DF78.B3983 B47 1999**

**GREECE - FICTION.**
Bunting, Eve, 1928- I have an olive tree. 1st ed. New York : HarperCollins Publishers, c1999.
**TC PZ7.B91527 Iaar 1999**

Delton, Judy. Angel spreads her wings. Boston : Houghton Mifflin, 1999.
**TC PZ7.D388 Anf 1999**

**GREECE - HISTORIOGRAPHY.**
Berlinerblau, Jacques. Heresy in the University. New Brunswick, N.J. : Rutgers University Press, c1999.
**TC DF78.B3983 B47 1999**

**GREEK AMERICANS - FICTION.**
Bunting, Eve, 1928- I have an olive tree. 1st ed. New York : HarperCollins Publishers, c1999.
**TC PZ7.B91527 Iaar 1999**

**GREEK AMERICANS - JUVENILE FICTION.**
Bunting, Eve, 1928- I have an olive tree. 1st ed. New York : HarperCollins Publishers, c1999.
**TC PZ7.B91527 Iaar 1999**

**GREEK AMERICANS - UNITED STATES.** See **GREEK AMERICANS.**

**GREEK EDUCATION.** See **EDUCATION, GREEK.**

**GREEK LANGUAGE.** See **CLASSICAL PHILOLOGY.**

**GREEK LETTER SOCIATIES - HISTORY.**
Tolliver, Joseph A. Administratively mandated change at Amherst College. 1997.
**TC 06 no. 10871**

**GREEK LITERATURE.** See **CLASSICAL PHILOLOGY.**

**GREEK MUSIC.** See **MUSIC, GREEK AND ROMAN.**

**GREEK PHILOLOGY.** See **CLASSICAL PHILOLOGY.**

**GREEKS - UNITED STATES.** See **GREEK AMERICANS.**

**Green, Andy.** Creativity in public relations / Andy Green ; illustrations by Ihor Tymchak. London ; Dover, N.H. : Kogan Page, c1999. xvi, 200 p. : ill. ; 22 cm. (The Institute of Public relations / PR in practice series) Includes bibliographical references (p. 190-193) and index. ISBN 0-7494-2938-0
*1. Public relations. 2. Creative thinking. I. Title. II. Series: PR in practice series*
**TC HD59 .G744 1999**

**Green, Bert F.**
National Research Council (U.S.). Committee on Embedding Common Test Items in State and District Assessments. Embedding questions. Washington, DC : National Academy Press, c1999.

TC LB3051 .N319 1999

**Green, Charles.** Peripheral vision : contemporary Australian Art, 1970-1994 / by Charles Green. Roseville East, N.S.W. : Craftsman House, 1995. 153 p. : ill. (some col.) ; 30 cm. ISBN 976-641-026-7 DDC 709/.94/09045
*1. Art, Australian. 2. Art, Modern - 20th century - Australia. I. Title.*
**TC N7400.2 .G74 1995**

**Green College lecture series**
LaCapra, Dominick, 1939- History and reading. Toronto : University of Toronto Press, c2000.
**TC DC36.9.L32 1999**

**GREEN FEMINISM.** See **ECOFEMINISM.**

**Green, Joanne.** Neuropsychological evaluation of the older adult : a clinician's guidebook. San Diego : Academic Press, c2000. xiv, 311 p. ; 24 cm. Includes bibliographical references and index. ISBN 0-12-298190-1 DDC 616.8
*1. Neurologic examination 2. Neurologic Examination*
**TC RC348 .G74 2000**

**Green, Joseph P. (Joseph Patrick).**
Healing from within. 1st ed. Washington, DC ; London : American Psychological Association, c2000.
**TC RC497 .H42 2000**

**Green, Lawrence W.**
Settings for health promotion. Thousand Oaks, Calif. : Sage Publications, Inc., c2000.
**TC RA427.8 .S48 2000**

**Green, Martha.**
Professional development guide for educators. Washington, D.C. : National Education Association of the United States, 2000.
**TC LC1099.3 .P755 1999**

**Green, Nancy E.**
Ira Spanierman Gallery. Arthur Wesley Dow (1857-1922). New York : Spanierman Gallery, 1999.
**TC N44.D7442 I73 1999**

**Green psychology.**
Metzner, Ralph. Rochester, Vt. : Park Street Press, c1999.
**TC BF353.5.N37 M47 1999**

**Green, Thomas F.** Voices : the educational formation of conscience / Thomas F. Green. Notre Dame, Ind. : University of Notre Dame Press, c1999. xiv, 214 p. : ill. ; 24 cm. Includes bibliographical references (p. 197-210) and index. ISBN 0-268-01924-X (alk. paper) DDC 370.11/4
*1. Moral education. I. Title.*
**TC LC268 .G667 1999**

**Green Umbrella Ltd.**
In search of human origins [videorecording]. [Boston, Mass.] : WGBH Educational Foundation, c1994.
**TC GN281 .I45 1994**

**Greenberg, Daniel S., 1931-** The politics of pure science / Daniel S. Greenberg. New ed. / with introductory essays by John Maddox and Steven Shapin and a new afterword by the author. Chicago : University of Chicago Press, 1999. xxvii, 311 p. ; 23 cm. Includes bibliographical references and index. ISBN 0-226-30631-3 (cloth : alk. paper) ISBN 0-226-30632-1 (paper : alk. paper) DDC 509/.73
*1. Science and state - United States. 2. Science - Political aspects - United States. I. Title.*
**TC Q127.U6 G68 1999**

**Greenberger, Martin, 1931-** Models in the policy process : public decision making in the computer era / Martin Greenberger, Matthew A. Crenson, Brian L. Crissey. New York : Russell Sage Foundation ; [distributed by Basic Books], c1976. xx, 355 p. : ill. ; 24 cm. Includes bibliographical references and index. DDC 309.2
*1. Policy sciences - Mathematical models. 2. Economic policy - Mathematical models. I. Crenson, Matthew A., 1943- joint author. II. Crissey, Brian L., joint author. III. Title.*
**TC H61 .G667**

**Greene, Carol.** Sunflower Island / by Carol Greene ; pictures by Leonard Jenkins. 1st ed. New York : HarperCollins, 1999. 1 v. (unpaged) : col. ill. ; 21 x 26 cm. SUMMARY: A young girl sees a sidewheeler run aground and over many years describes how the river makes the remains of the wreck into an island and then washes it away again. Based on a true story. ISBN 0-06-027326-7 ISBN 0-06-027327-5 (lib. bdg.) DDC [Fic]
*1. Shipwrecks - Fiction. 2. Rivers - Fiction. I. Jenkins, Leonard, ill. II. Title.*
**TC PZ7.G82845 Sl 1999**

**Greene, James.**
Matisse, voyages [videorecording]. [Chicago, Ill.] : Home Vision ; [S.l.] : Distributed worldwide by RM Associates, c1989.

TC ND553.M37 M37 1989

**GREENE, JOHN MORTON, 1830-1919.**
Quesnell, Quentin. The strange disappearance of Sophia Smith. Northampton [Mass.] : Smith College, c1999.
**TC LD7152.65.S45 Q84 1999**

**Greene, Maxine.** Active learning and aesthetic encounters : talks at the Lincoln Center Institute, 1994 / Maxine Greene. New York : NCREST, 1995. v, 22 p. ; 28 cm. "March 1995"--t.p. Includes bibliographical references (p. 21-22)
*1. Aesthetics. 2. Active learning. 3. Art in education. I. Title.*
**TC BH39 .G74 1995**

**Greene, Roger L.** The MMPI-2 : an interpretive manual / Roger L. Greene. 2nd ed. Boston : Allyn and Bacon, c2000. vii, 696 p. ; 25 cm. Rev. ed. of: The MMPI-2/MMPI. c1991. Includes bibliographical references (p. 654-687) and indexes. ISBN 0-205-28416-7 DDC 155.2/83
*1. Minnesota Multiphasic Personality Inventory. I. Greene, Roger L. MMPI-2/MMPI. II. Title.*
**TC BF698.8.M5 G74 2000**

**MMPI 2/MMPI.**
Greene, Roger L. The MMPI-2. 2nd ed. Boston : Allyn and Bacon, c2000.
**TC BF698.8.M5 G74 2000**

**Greenfield, Eloise.** Water, water / Eloise Greenfield ; pictures by Jan Spivey Gilchrist. [New York?] : HarperFestival, c1999. 1 v. (unpaged) : col. ill. ; 23 cm. "Harper growing tree"--Spine. ISBN 0-694-01247-5
*1. Water - Juvenile literature. I. Gilchrist, Jan Spivey. II. Title.*
**TC GB662.3 .G7 1999**

**Greenfield, Susan.** The private life of the brain : emotions, consciousness, and the secret of the self / Susan Greenfield. New York : John Wiley, c2000. xi, 258 p. ; 25 cm. Includes bibliographical references (p. 233-250) and index. ISBN 0-471-18343-1 (alk. paper) DDC 152.4/2
*1. Pleasure. 2. Emotions. I. Title.*
**TC BF515 G74 2000**

**Greenspan, Stanley I.** Building healthy minds : the six experiences that create intelligence and emotional growth in babies and young children / Stanley I. Greenspan and Nancy Breslau Lewis. Cambridge, MA : Perseus, 1999. 398 p. : ill. ; 25 cm. "A Merloyd Lawrence book." CONTENTS: Introduction : how minds grow -- 1. Stage 1 : becoming calm, attentive, and interested in the world -- 2. Stage 2 : falling in love -- 3. Stage 3 : becoming a two-way communicator -- 4. Stage 4 : solving problems and forming a sense of self -- 5. Stage 5 : discovering a world of ideas -- 6. Stage 6 : building bridges between ideas -- 7. Floor-time : nurturing all six levels of intelligence and emotional health at the same time -- 8. Giving more and expecting more -- Appendix I. The functional developmental growth chart and questionnaire -- Appendix II. The six essential developmental stages and growth of the brain -- Appendix III. Ten ways to environmentally childproof your home. ISBN 0-7382-0063-8 DDC 305.231
*1. Parenting. 2. Child development. I. Lewis, Nancy Breslau. II. Title.*
**TC HQ772 .G672 1999**

**The Greenwood educators' reference collection**
Goonen, Norma M. Higher education administration. Westport, Conn. ; London : Greenwood Press, 1999.
**TC LB2341 .G573 1999**

Issues in Web-based pedagogy. Westport, Conn. : Greenwood Press, 2000.
**TC LB1044.87 .I88 2000**

Kohn, Daniel B., 1963- Practical pedagogy for the Jewish classroom. Westport, Conn. : Greenwood Press, 1999.
**TC BM108 .K65 1999**

Succeeding in an academic career. Westport, Conn. : Greenwood Press, 2000.
**TC LB2331.72 .S83 2000**

**Greenwood professional guides in school librarianship**
Sharma, Martha B., 1945- Using internet primary sources to teach critical thinking skills in geography. Westport, Conn. ; London : Greenwood Press, 2000.
**TC G73 .S393 2000**

**Greer, W. Dwaine.** Art as a basic : the reformation in art education / W. Dwaine Greer. Bloomington, Ind. : Phi Delta Kappa Education Foundation, c1997. 133 p. : ill. ; 23 cm. Includes bibliographical references (p. 125-133). ISBN 0-87367-497-9
*1. Art - Study and teaching - United States - History - 20th century. I. Title.*
**TC N108 .G74 1997**

**Gregory, Gayle.**
Robbins, Pamela. Thinking inside the block schedule. Thousand Oaks, Calif. : Corwin Press, c2000.
*TC LB3032.2 .R63 2000*

**Gregory, Ian, 1939-.**
Davies, Ian. 1957- Good citizenship and educational provision. London : New York : Falmer Press, c1999.
*TC LC1091 .D28 1999*

**Gregory, Jane, 1960-** Bringing up a challenging child at home : when love is not enough / Jane Gregory. London : Philadelphia : Jessica Kingsley Publishers, 2000. 188 p. ; 24 cm. Includes bibliographical references (p. 183-188). ISBN 1-85302-874-6 (alk. paper) DDC 649/.15/092
*1. Gregory, Jane. - 1960- 2. Parents of exceptional children - Great Britain - Biography. 3. Developmentally disabled children - Great Britain - Biography. 4. Learning disabled children - Great Britain - Biography. I. Title.*
*TC HQ759.913 .G74 2000*

**GREGORY, JANE, 1960-.**
Gregory, Jane, 1960- Bringing up a challenging child at home. London : Philadelphia : Jessica Kingsley Publishers, 2000.
*TC HQ759.913 .G74 2000*

**Gregory, Sheila T.** Black women in the academy : the secrets to success and achievement / Sheila T. Gregory. Rev. and updated ed. Lanham, Md. : University Press of America, 1999. xx, 213 p. ; 21 cm. Includes bibliographical references and index. ISBN 0-7618-1412-4 (alk. paper) DDC 378/.0089/96073
*1. Afro-American women - Education (Higher) 2. Afro-American college students. 3. Afro-American college graduates. 4. Afro-American women college teachers. 5. Academic achievement - United States. 6. Educational surveys - United States. I. Title.*
*TC LC2781 .G74 1999*

**Gregory, Susan, 1945-.**
Issues in deaf education. London : D. Fulton Publishers, 1998.
*TC HV2716 .I77 1998*

Watson, Linda R., 1950- Deaf and hearing impaired pupils in mainstream schools. London : David Fulton, c1999.
*TC LC1203.G7 W387 1999*

**Gregory, Vicki L., 1950-** Multicultural resources on the Internet. The United States and Canada / Vicki L. Gregory, Marilyn H. Karrenbrock Stauffer, Thomas W. Keene, Jr. Englewood, Colo. : Libraries Unlimited, 1999. ix, 366 p. ; 26 cm. Includes bibliographical references and index. ISBN 1-56308-676-X (softbound) DDC 973/.04/0285
*1. Minorities - United States - Computer network resources - Directories. 2. United States - Civilization - Computer network resources - Directories. 3. Pluralism (Social sciences) - United States - Computer network resources - Directories. 4. Minorities - Canada - Computer network resources - Directories. 5. Canada - Civilization - Computer network resources - Directories. 6. Pluralism (Social sciences) - Canada - Computer network resources - Directories. I. Stauffer, Marilyn H. Karrenbrock. 1936- II. Keene, Thomas W. III. Title.*
*TC E184.A1 G874 1999*

**Greif, Gary F.** The tragedy of the self : individual and social disintegration viewed through the self psychology of Heinz Kohut / Gary F. Greif. Lanham, Md. ; Oxford : University Press of America, c2000. xiv, 132 p. ; 24 cm. Includes bibliographical references (p. [121]-128) and index. ISBN 0-7618-1623-2 (hardcover : alk. paper) DDC 150.19/5/092
*1. Self psychology. 2. Kohut, Heinz. 3. Social psychology. I. Title.*
*TC BF175.5.S44 G74 2000*

**Grenfell, Michael, 1953-** Modern languages and learning strategies : in theory and practice / Michael Grenfell and Vee Harris. London ; New York : Routledge, 1999. 165 p. ; 24 cm. Includes bibliographical references (p. <153>-159) and index. ISBN 0-415-21340-1 (hc. : alk. paper) ISBN 0-415-17868-1 (pbk. : alk. paper) DDC 418/.0071/2
*1. Languages, Modern - Study and teaching. I. Harris, Vee, 1949- II. Title.*
*TC PB35 .G783 1999*

Pierre Bourdieu. Bern ; New York : P. Lang, c1999.
*TC HM621 .P54 1999*

Training teachers in practice / Michael Grenfell. Clevedon, UK ; Philadelphia : Multilingual Matters, c1998. iv, 187 p. : ill. ; 22 cm. (Modern languages in practice ; 9) Includes bibliographical references (p. 181-185) and index. ISBN 1-85359-400-8 (hbk : alk. paper) ISBN 1-85359-399-0 (pbk : alk. paper) DDC 418/.007
*1. Language teachers - Training of. I. Title. II. Series.*

*TC P53.85 .G74 1998*

**Grey, Alex.** The mission of art / Alex Grey : foreword by Ken Wilber. 1st ed. Boston : Shambhala, 1998. xv, 255 p. : ill. ; 23 cm. Includes bibliographical references (p. 243-247) and index. ISBN 1-57062-396-1 (cloth) DDC 759.13
*1. Grey, Alex - Philosophy. 2. Grey, Alex - Criticism and interpretation. I. Title.*
*TC N6537.G718 A4 1998*

**GREY, ALEX - CRITICISM AND INTERPRETATION.**
Grey, Alex. The mission of art. 1st ed. Boston : Shambhala, 1998.
*TC N6537.G718 A4 1998*

**GREY, ALEX - PHILOSOPHY.**
Grey, Alex. The mission of art. 1st ed. Boston : Shambhala, 1998.
*TC N6537.G718 A4 1998*

**Grey, Duncan.** The internet in school / Duncan Grey. London ; New York : Cassell Academic, 1999. 155 p. : ill. ; 24 cm. (Cassell education.) Includes bibliographical references (p. [152]) and index. ISBN 0-304-70531-4
*1. Internet (Computer network) in education - Great Britain. 2. Internet (Computer network) - Study and teaching - Great Britain. I. Title. II. Series.*
*TC LB1044.87 .G74 1999*

**Greystone Communications.**
The American Revolution. [videorecording]. New York, N.Y. : A&E Home Video, c1994.
*TC E208 .A447 1994*

The Irish in America [videorecording]. [New York, N.Y.] : A&E Home Video ; New York, N.Y. : Distributed by the New Video Group, 1997.
*TC E184.I6 I6 1997*

**Grice, Marthe Jane.** Attachment, race, and gender in late life : relationships to depression, anxiety, and self-efficacy / Marthe Jane Grice. 1999. vi, 162 leaves : ill. ; 29 cm. Includes tables. Thesis (Ph. D.)--Columbia University, 1999. Includes bibliographical references (leaves 118-132).
*1. Attachment behavior. 2. Depression in old age. 3. Self-efficacy. 4. Sex differences (Psychology) 5. Anxiety in old age. 6. Aged - Psychology. 7. African American aged - United States. 8. Whites - United States. I. Title.*
*TC 085 G865*

**Grief.**
Sanders, Catherine M. 2nd ed. New York : J. Wiley, c1999.
*TC BF575.G7 S26 1999*

**GRIEF.**
Archer, John, 1944- The nature of grief. London ; New York : Routledge, 1999.
*TC BF575.G7 A73 1999*

Boss, Pauline. Ambiguous loss. Cambridge, Mass. : Harvard University Press, 1999.
*TC BF575.D35 B67 1999*

Davidman, Lynn, 1955- Motherloss. Berkeley, Calif. : University of California Press, c2000.
*TC BF575.G7 D37 2000*

Loss and trauma. Philadelphia, PA : Brunner-Routledge, c2000.
*TC BF575.D35 L67 2000*

Rosenblatt, Paul C. Parent grief. Philadelphia ; Hove [England] : Brunner/Mazel, c2000.
*TC BF575.G7 R673 2000*

Sanders, Catherine M. Grief. 2nd ed. New York : J. Wiley, c1999.
*TC BF575.G7 S26 1999*

**GRIEF - FICTION.**
Couloumbis, Audrey. Getting near to baby. New York : Putnam, 1999.
*TC PZ7.C8305 Gg 1999*

Kadono, Eiko. Grandpa's soup. Grand Rapids, MI : Eerdmans Books for Young Readers, 1999.
*TC PZ7.K1167 Gr 1999*

Rodowsky, Colby F. The Turnabout Shop. 1st ed. New York : Farrar, Straus and Giroux, c1998.
*TC PZ7.R6185 Tu 1999*

**GRIEF IN ADOLESCENCE.**
Christ, Grace Hyslop. Healing children's grief. New York ; Oxford : Oxford University Press, 2000.
*TC BF723.G75 C58 2000*

**GRIEF IN CHILDREN.**
Christ, Grace Hyslop. Healing children's grief. New York ; Oxford : Oxford University Press, 2000.
*TC BF723.G75 C58 2000*

Goldman, Linda, 1946- Life & loss. 2nd ed. Philadelphia : Accelerated Development, c2000.
*TC BF723.G75 G65 2000*

Smith, Susan C. The forgotten mourners. 2nd ed. London ; Philadelphia : Jessica Kingsley Publishers, 1999.
*TC BF723.G75 P46 1999*

**Griffin, Adele.** Dive / Adele Griffin. 1st ed. New York : Hyperion Books for Children, 1999. 155 p. ; 22 cm. SUMMARY: Young Ben finds that he is happy in the stable life provided by his stepfather despite his uncertain relationship with his moody and troubled stepbrother and his mother's growing restlessness in her new marriage. ISBN 0-7868-0440-8 (trade : alk. paper) ISBN 0-7868-2389-5 (lib. : alk. paper) DDC [Fic]
*1. Stepfamilies - Fiction. 2. Family problems - Fiction. 3. Emotional problems - Fiction. 4. Interpersonal relations - Fiction. 5. Parent and child - Fiction. I. Title.*
*TC PZ7.G881325 Di 1999*

**Griffin Media Design, Inc.**
Exploring the English language [videorecording]. [Princeton, N.J.] : Video Tutor ; [Chesterton, Ind.? : Distributed by] Griffin Media Design, 1988, c1986.

**Griffin, Michael J.**
Exploring the English language [videorecording]. [Princeton, N.J.] : Video Tutor ; [Chesterton, Ind.? : Distributed by] Griffin Media Design, 1988, c1986.

**Griffiths, Jenny, 1943-.**
Study to teach. London ; New York : Routledge, 2000.
*TC LB1707 .S88 2000*

**Griggs, Shirley A.**
Practical approaches to using learning styles in higher education. Westport, Conn. : Bergin & Garvey, 2000.
*TC LB2395 .P69 2000*

**Grigsby, Jim.** Neurodynamics of personality / Jim Grigsby, David Stevens. New York : Guilford Press, 2000. xii, 436 p. : ill. ; 24 cm. Includes bibliographical references and index. ISBN 1-57230-547-9 (hard)
*1. Personality - Physiological aspects. 2. Brain - Physiology. 3. Neuropsychology. 4. Personality - physiology. 5. Brain - physiology. 6. Mental Processes - physiology. 7. Neuropsychology. 8. Psychological Theory. I. Stevens, David, 1954- II. Title.*
*TC BF698.9.B5 G741 2000*

**Grillner, Sten, 1941-.**
Orlovsky, G. N. (Grigoriĭ Nikolaevich) Neuronal control of locomotion. Oxford ; New York : Oxford University Press, 1999.
*TC QP303 .O75 1999*

**Grimme, L. H.**
Heidelberger Ernährungsforum (5th : 1998 : Heidelberg) Food quality, nutrition, and health. Berlin ; New York : Springer, 2000.
*TC RA784 .H42 2000*

**Grimshaw, Jennie.** Employment and health : psychosocial stress in the workplace / by Jennie Grimshaw. London : British Library, 1999. xx, 418 p. ; 23 cm. (Social policy) "British Library, Science Technology and Business"--Cover. Includes bibliographical references and indexes. ISBN 0-7123-0847-4 DDC 158.72
*1. Job stress. 2. Work - Psychological aspects. 3. Stress (Psychology) - Social aspects. I. British Library. Science Technology and Business. II. Title. III. Series: Social policy*
*TC HF5548.85 .G75 1999*

**Grin, John.**
Vision assessment. New York : Springer, 2000.
*TC T174.5 V57 2000*

**Grindley, Sally.** The little ballerina / written by Sally Grindley. 1st American ed. New York : DK Pub., 1999. 32 p. : col. ill. ; 24 cm. (Eyewitness readers. Level 2) SUMMARY: Follows the activities of a group of young students in their ballet class as they prepare for a show. ISBN 0-7894-4005-9 (hard) ISBN 0-7894-4004-0 (pbk.) DDC 792.8
*1. Ballet - Juvenile literature. 2. Ballet dancing - Juvenile literature. 3. Ballet. 4. Ballet dancing. I. Title. II. Series.*
*TC GV1787.5 .G75 1999*

**Grinling Gibbons and the art of carving.**
Esterly, David. New York : H.N. Abrams, 1998.
*TC NK9798.G5 E88 1998*

**Gripsrud, Jostein, 1952-.**
Television and common knowledge. New York : Routledge, 1999.
*TC PN1992.6 .T379 1999*

**Grishin, Sasha.** Australian printmaking in the 1990s : artist printmakers, 1990-1995 / Sasha Grishin. Sydney, NSW : Craftsman House : G+B Arts International, c1997. 336 p. : ill. (some col.) ; 32 cm. Includes bibliographical references. ISBN 90-5703-391-7 DDC 769.994/09/049

*1. Prints, Australian - Themes, motives. 2. Prints - 20th century - Australia - Themes, motives. 3. Printmakers - Australia - Biography - History and criticism. I. Title.*
***TC NE789.4 .G74 1997***

**Griss, Susan.** Minds in motion : a kinesthetic approach to teaching elementary curriculum / Susan Griss : [editor, Victoria Merecki]. Portsmouth, NH : Heinemann, c1998. xiii, 130 p. : ill. ; 22 cm. (Teacher to teacher) Includes bibliographical references (p. 128-130). ISBN 0-325-00034-4 (alk. paper) DDC 372.19
*1. Education, Elementary - Activity programs - United States. 2. Education, Elementary - United States - Curricula. 3. Movement education - United States. 4. Interdisciplinary approach in education - United States. I. Merecki, Victoria. II. Title. III. Series: Teacher to teacher series.*
***TC LB1592 .G75 1998***

**Gritton, Joy L.**
Shared visions. 1st New Press ed. New York : New Press : Distributed by Norton, [1993], c1991.
***TC N6538.A4 A7 1993***

**Grob, Alexander, 1958-.**
Control of human behavior, mental processes, and consciousness. Mahwah, N.J. : Lawrence Erlbaum Associates, c2000.
***TC BF611 .C67 2000***

**Grodner, Michele.** Foundations and clinical applications of nutrition : a nursing approach / Michele Grodner, Sara Long Anderson, Sandra DeYoung. 2nd ed. St. Louis, Mo. : Mosby, c2000. xix, 868 p. : ill. (chiefly col.), ports. (chiefly col.) ; 28 cm. Includes bibliographical references and index. ISBN 0-323-00390-7 (pbk.)
*1. Diet therapy. 2. Nutrition. 3. Nursing. 4. Nutrition - nurses' instruction. 5. Diet Therapy - methods - nurses' instruction. 6. Nursing Process. I. Anderson, Sara Long. II. DeYoung, Sandra. III. Title. IV. Title: Nutrition*
***TC RM216 .G946 2000***

**Groff, James L.** Advanced nutrition and human metabolism / James L. Groff, Sareen S. Gropper. 3rd ed. Belmont, CA : West/Wadsworth, c2000. xii, 584 p. : ill. ; 29 cm. Includes bibliographical references and index. ISBN 0-534-55521-7 DDC 612.3/9
*1. Nutrition. 2. Metabolism. I. Gropper, Sareen Annora Stepnick. II. Title.*
***TC QP141 .G76 2000***

**Grogan, Margaret, 1952-.**
Gardiner, Mary E., 1953- Coloring outside the lines. Albany : State University of New York Press, c2000.
***TC LB2831.82 .G37 2000***

**Grogan, Sarah, 1959-** Body image : understanding body dissatisfaction in men, women, and children / Sarah Grogan. London ; New York : Routledge, 1999. xii, 225 p. : ill. ; 22 cm. Includes bibliographical references (p. [196]-210) and indexes. ISBN 0-415-14784-0 (hardcover) ISBN 0-415-14785-9 (pbk.) DDC 155.9/1
*1. Body image - Social aspects - United States. 2. Body image - Social aspects - Great Britain. I. Title.*
***TC BF697.5.B63 G76 1999***

**Gröning, Karl.** Body decoration : a world survey of body art / Karl Gröning. New York : Vendome Press : Distributed in the USA by Rizzoli, 1998. 256 p. : col. ill., maps ; 33 cm. Includes bibliographical references (p. 248-249) and index. ISBN 0-86565-997-4 DDC 391.6
*1. Body marking. 2. Body painting. I. Title.*
***TC GT2343 .G76 1998***

**Gronlund, Norman Edward, 1920-.**
Linn, Robert L. Measurement and assessment in teaching. 8th ed. Upper Saddle River, N.J. : Merrill, c2000.
***TC LB3051 .L545 2000***

**Groof, Jan de.** Democracy and governance in higher education / Jan De Groof, Guy Neave, Juraj Švec. The Hague ; Boston : Kluwer Law International, 1998. xiv, 401 p. ; 25 cm. (Legislating for higher education in Europe ; v. 2) "Legislative Reform Programme for Higher Education and Research, Council of Europe." Includes bibliographical references and index. ISBN 90-411-0575-1 (hardcover : alk. paper) DDC 378.1/01/0973
*1. Education, Higher - Europe - Administration. 2. University autonomy - Europe. 3. Higher education and state - Europe. 4. Community and college - Europe. 5. Education, Higher - Europe - Cross-cultural studies. I. Neave, Guy R. II. Švec, Juraj. III. Council of Europe. Legislative Reform Programme for Higher Education. IV. Title. V. Series.*
***TC LB2341.8.E85 G76 1998***

**Groome, Thomas H.** Educating for life : a spiritual vision for every teacher and parent / Thomas H. Groome. Allen, Tex. : T. More, c1998. 472 p. ; 24 cm. Includes bibliographical references (p. [467]-472) and index. ISBN 0-88347-383-6 DDC 268/.82
*1. Christian education. 2. Education - Philosophy. 3. Catholic Church - Education. I. Title. II. Title: Spiritual vision for every teacher and parent*
***TC BV1471.2 .G6874 1998***

**Gropper, Sareen Annora Stepnick.**
Groff, James L. Advanced nutrition and human metabolism. 3rd ed. Belmont, CA : West/Wadsworth, c2000.
***TC QP141 .G76 2000***

**Gross, Clifford M.** The new idea factory : expanding technology companies with university intellectual capital / Clifford M. Gross, Uwe Reischl, Paul Abercrombie. Columbus, OH : Battelle Press, c2000. xiv, 169 p. : ill. ; 23 cm. Includes bibliographical references (p. 99-100) and index. ISBN 1-57477-090-X (softcover : alk. paper) DDC 658
*1. Intellectual capital - United States. 2. High technology industries - United States. 3. Industry and education - United States. 4. Technology transfer - United States. I. Reischl, Uwe, 1945- II. Abercrombie, Paul, 1968- III. Title.*
***TC HD53 .G75 2000***

**Gross, Martin L. (Martin Louis), 1925-** The conspiracy of ignorance : the failure of American public schools / Martin L. Gross. New York : HarperCollins, c1999. x, 291 p. ; 25 cm. Includes bibliographical references (p. 255-276) and index. ISBN 0-06-019458-8 DDC 371.01/0973
*1. Public schools - United States - Evaluation. 2. School failure - United States. I. Title.*
***TC LA217.2 .G76 1999***

**Gross, Ruth Belov.** What's on my plate? / by Ruth Belov Gross ; illustrated by Isadore Seltzer. 1st American ed. New York : Macmillan, c1990. [32] p. : col. ill. ; 27 cm. SUMMARY: Describes, in simple text and illustrations, where some of the common things we eat originate. ISBN 0-02-737000-3 DDC 641.3
*1. Food - Juvenile literature. 2. Food. I. Seltzer, Isadore, ill. II. Title.*
***TC TX355 .G795 1990***

**Grossman, Bill.** Donna O'Neeshuck was chased by some cows / by Bill Grossman ; illustrated by Sue Truesdell. 1st ed. [New York] : Harper & Row, c1988. [38] p. : col. ill. ; 21 x 26 cm. SUMMARY: Donna O'Neeshuck cannot understand why she is being chased by cows, mooses, gooses, and a host of others, until she discovers that her head pats are irresistible. ISBN 0-06-022158-5 ISBN 0-06-022159-3 (lib. bdg.) DDC [E]
*1. Animals - Fiction. 2. Stories in rhyme. I. Truesdell, Sue, ill. II. Title.*
***TC PZ8.3.G914 Do 1988***

**Grossman, Frances Kaplan, 1939-.**
With the phoenix rising. 1st ed. San Francisco : Jossey-Bass, c1999.
***TC RC569.5.A28 W57 1999***

**Grossman, Herbert, 1934-** Achieving educational equality : assuring all students an equal opportunity in school / by Herbert Grossman. Springfield, Ill. : C.C. Thomas, c1998. xii, 217 p. ; 27 cm. Includes bibliographical references (p. 210-217). ISBN 0-398-06884-4 (cloth) ISBN 0-398-06885-2 (pbk.) DDC 379.2/6/0973
*1. Educational equalization - United States. 2. Children of minorities - Education - United States. 3. Socially handicapped children - Education - United States. 4. Sex differences in education - United States. 5. Teachers - Training of - United States. 6. Education and state - United States. I. Title.*
***TC LC213.2 .G76 1998***

**Grossman, James R.**
White, Richard, 1947- The frontier in American culture. Chicago : The Library ; Berkeley : University of California Press, c1994.
***TC F596 .W562 1994***

**Grossman, Leigh.**
The adult student's guide. Berkley trade pbk. ed. New York, N.Y. : Berkley Books, 1999.
***TC L901 .A494 1999***

**Grossman, Seth.**
Millon, Theodore. Personality-guided psychotherapy. New York : J. Wiley, c1999.
***TC RC480.5 .M54 1999***

**Grossman, Sheila.** The new leadership challenge : creating the future of nursing / Sheila C. Grossman, Theresa M. Valiga. Philadelphia : F.A. Davis, c2000. xxvi, 241 p. : ill. ; 23 cm. Includes bibliographical references and index. ISBN 0-8036-0594-3 DDC 362.1/73/068
*1. Nursing services - Administration. 2. Leadership. 3. Nursing, Supervisory. 4. Leadership. 5. Nurse Administrators. I. Valiga, Theresa M. II. Title.*
***TC RT89 .G77 2000***

**Grossman, Wynne, 1950-.**
Collaborating to improve community health. San Francisco : Jossey-Bass Publishers, c1996.
***TC RA427 .C59 1996***

**Grossnickle, Foster E.**
Brueckner, Leo J. Moving ahead in arithmetic. New York, N.Y. : Holt, Rinehart and Winston, 1963.
***TC QA107 .B78 1963***

Brueckner, Leo J. Moving ahead in arithmetic. New York, N.Y. : Holt, Rinehart and Winston, 1963.
***TC QA107 .B78 1963***

Brueckner, Leo J. Moving ahead in arithmetic. New York : Holt, Rinehart and Winston, 1963.
***TC QA107 .B78 1963***

Brueckner, Leo J. Moving ahead in arithmetic. New York : Holt, Rinehart and Winston, 1963.
***TC QA107 .B78 1963***

**Grosvenor, Ian.**
An introduction to the study of education. London : David Fulton, 1999.
***TC LA632 .I58 1999***

Silences & images. New York : P. Lang, c1999.
***TC LA128 .S55 1999***

**Grote, John E.** Paideia agonistes : the lost soul of modern education / John E. Grote. Lanham, Md. : University Press of America, c2000. ix, 220 p. ; 23 cm. Includes bibliographical references and index. ISBN 0-7618-1726-3 (pbk. : alk. paper) DDC 370.11/2
*1. Education, Humanistic - United States. 2. Education - Aims and objectives - United States. 3. Educational change - United States. I. Title. II. Title: Lost soul of modern education*
***TC LC1011 .G76 2000***

**GROTESQUE IN ART - JUVENILE LITERATURE.**
Barr, Beryl. Wonders, warriors, and beasts abounding. [1st ed.]. Garden City, N.Y., Doubleday [1967]
***TC N8217.G8 B33***

**Groth, Lars.** Future organizational design : the scope for the IT-based enterprise / Lars Groth. Chichester ; New York : Wiley, c1999. xxviii, 448 p. : ill. ; 24 cm. (Wiley series in information systems) Includes bibliographical references (p. [427]-434) and indexes. ISBN 0-471-98893-6
*1. Information technology - Management. 2. Organizational change - Data processing. I. Title.*
***TC HD30.2 .G76 1999***

**Groth-Marnat, Gary.**
Neuropsychological assessment in clinical practice. New York : Wiley, c2000.
***TC RC386.6.N48 N474 2000***

**GROUND-NUTS.** *See* **PEANUTS.**

**Grounded for life** [videorecording] : (afraid to say no!) / produced by WEIU-TV, Eastern Illinois Univ. [and] ... Lyon Video, Inc. ; produced and edited by John L. Beabout, Laurent A. Gosselin ; videography and directed by John L. Beabout ; written by E. Ty Gardner, James M. Blackwell. Charleston, WV : Cambridge Research Group, Ltd., 1988. 1 videocassette (39 min.) : sd., col. ; 1/2 in. Title on container: Grounded for life [videorecording] : teenage pregnancy : afraid to say no! At head of title: Cambridge Career Products. VHS. Catalogued from credits and container and cassette label. Host, Cheryl Brown; narrator, Heidi Hoover. Edited by Robert S. Lyon. "Cambridge Educational"--Container spine, cassette label. For teens and their parents. SUMMARY: Students discuss teen pregnancy and the reasons they were afraid to say no to sexual activity.
*1. Teenage mothers. 2. Single parents. 3. Teenage parents. I. Brown, Cheryl. II. Hoover, Heidi. III. Beabout, John L. IV. Gosselin, Laurent A. V. Gardner, E. Ty. VI. Blackwell, James M. VII. Cambridge Research Group, Ltd. VIII. Cambridge Educational (Firm) IX. Cambridge Career Products (Firm) X. WEIU-TV (Television Station : Charleston, Ill.) XI. Eastern Illinois University. XII. Lyon Video Inc. XIII. Title: Grounded for life [videorecording] : teenage pregnancy : afraid to say no! XIV. Title: Teenage pregnancy [videorecording] : afraid to say no! XV. Title: Afraid to say no! [videorecording] XVI. Title: Cambridge Career Products*
***TC HQ759.4 .G7 1988***

**Grounded for life [videorecording] : teenage pregnancy : afraid to say no!.**
Grounded for life [videorecording]. Charleston, WV : Cambridge Research Group, Ltd., 1988.
***TC HQ759.4 .G7 1988***

**GROUNDNUTS.** *See* **PEANUTS.**

**The group context.**
Thompson, Sheila. London ; Philadelphia : Jessica Kingsley Publishers, 1999.
***TC BF637.C6 T49 1999***

**GROUP COUNSELING.** *See also* **SELF-HELP GROUPS.**

Gladding, Samuel T. Group work. 3rd ed. Upper Saddle River, N.J. : Merrill, c1999.
*TC BF637.C6 G5334 1999*

Johnson, Toni Cavanagh. Sexual, physical, and emotional abuse in out-of-home care. New York : The Haworth Maltreatment and Trauma Press, c1997.
*TC RJ507.A29 J64 1997*

Smead, Rosemarie, 1943- Skills for living. Champaign, IL : Research Press, c1990.
*TC BF637.C6 M67 1990*

Thompson, Sheila. The group context. London ; Philadelphia : Jessica Kingsley Publishers, 1999.
*TC BF637.C6 T49 1999*

Trotzer, James P., 1943- The counselor and the group. 3rd ed. Philadelphia ; London : Accelerated Development, c1999.
*TC BF637.C6 T68 1999*

Working with groups to explore food & body connections. Duluth, Minn. : Whole Person Associates, c1996.
*TC RC552.E18 W67 1996*

## GROUP COUNSELING FOR CHILDREN.
Johnson, Toni Cavanagh. Sexual, physical, and emotional abuse in out-of-home care. New York : The Haworth Maltreatment and Trauma Press, c1997.
*TC RJ507.A29 J64 1997*

**Group decision making.**
DiVincenzo, Joe. [S.l.] : NEA Professional Library : NEA Affiliate Capacity Building, c1999.
*TC LB2806 .D58 1999*

DiVincenzo, Joe. Group decision making. [S.l.] : NEA Professional Library : NEA Affiliate Capacity Building, c1999.
*TC LB2806 .D58 1999*

Lipman-Blumen, Jean. Hot groups. New York : Oxford University Press, 1999.
*TC HD58.9 .L56 1999*

## GROUP DECISION-MAKING - HANDBOOKS, MANUALS, ETC.
The consensus building handbook. Thousand Oaks, Calif. : Sage Publications, c1999.
*TC HM746 .C66 1999*

## GROUP DEFAMATION. See HATE SPEECH.

## GROUP DISCUSSION. See FORUMS (DISCUSSION AND DEBATE).

## GROUP DYNAMICS. See SOCIAL GROUPS.

**Group exercises for adolescents.**
Carrell, Susan. 2nd ed. Thousand Oaks : Sage Publications, c2000.
*TC RJ505.G7 C37 2000*

## GROUP FACILITATION.
Ray, R. Glenn. The facilitative leader. Upper Saddler River, NJ : Prentice Hall, c1999.
*TC HD66 .R3918 1999*

**Group for the Advancement of Psychiatry.**
(no. 62) Group for the Advancement of Psychiatry. Committee on Child Psychiatry. Psychopathological disorders in childhood; [New York, 1966]
*TC RJ499 .G76*

**Group for the Advancement of Psychiatry. Committee on Child Psychiatry.**
In the long run--longitudinal studies of psychopathology in children. Washington, DC : American Psychiatric Press, c1999.
*TC RC321 .G7 no. 143*

Psychopathological disorders in childhood: theoretical considerations and a proposed classification. [New York, 1966] 173-343 p. 23 cm. (Group for the Advancement of Psychiatry. Report no. 62) Includes bibliographies.
*1. Child psychiatry. I. Title.*
*TC RJ499 .G76*

## GROUP HOMES. See FOSTER HOME CARE.

## GROUP IDENTITY. See also ETHNICITY.
Flippen, Annette Rose. Similarity versus motive as explanations for ingroup bias. 1996.
*TC 085 F65*

Hetherington, Kevin. Expressions of identity. London ; Thousand Oaks, Calif. : Sage Publications, 1998.
*TC HM131 .H3995 1998*

Practising identities. New York : St. Martin's Press, 1999.

*TC HM131 .P677 1999*

Social identity. Malden, MA : Blackwell Publishers, 1999.
*TC HM131 .S58433 1999*

## GROUP IDENTITY - CASE STUDIES.
Social conflicts and collective identities. Lanham, Md. : Oxford : Rowman & Littlefield Publishers, c2000.
*TC HM1121 .S63 2000*

## GROUP IDENTITY, ETHNIC. See ETHNICITY.

## GROUP IDENTITY - POLITICAL ASPECTS - UNITED STATES.
Critical ethnicity. Lanham, Md. : Rowman & Littlefield, c1999.
*TC LC212.2 .C75 1999*

## GROUP IDENTITY - UNITED STATES.
Calderwood, Patricia E., 1954- Learning community. New York : Teachers College Press, c2000.
*TC LB1032 .C34 2000*

## GROUP LIBEL. See HATE SPEECH.

## GROUP METHOD IN TEACHING. See GROUP WORK IN EDUCATION.

## GROUP PROBLEM SOLVING.
Katz, Tal Y. Self-construal as a moderator of the effects of task and reward interdependence of group performance. 1999.
*TC 085 K1524*

## GROUP PROBLEM SOLVING - STUDY AND TEACHING (ELEMENTARY).
Goodman, Jan M. Group solutions : : [Teacher's guide]. Rev. Berkeley, Calif. : Lawrence Hall of Science, University of California, 1997, c1992.
*TC QA8.7 .G5 1997*

**Group processes.**
Brown, Rupert, 1950- 2nd ed. Oxford ; Malden, Mass. : Blackwell Publishers, 2000.
*TC HM131 .B726 2000*

## GROUP PROCESSES.
The process of group psychotherapy. Washington, DC : American Psychological Association, c2000.
*TC RC488 .P75 2000*

## GROUP PSYCHOANALYSIS.
Acting out in groups. Minneapolis, Minn. ; London : University of Minnesota Press, c1999.
*TC RC569.5.A25 A28 1999*

## GROUP PSYCHOTHERAPY. See FAMILY PSYCHOTHERAPY; PSYCHODRAMA.

[Group psychotherapy.] Psychodrama and sociodrama in American education. New York Beacon House, 1949. xii, 251 p. 24 cm. Bibliography: p. 246.
*1. Psychodrama 2. Education - Experimental methods I. Haas, Robert Bartlett. ed. II. Title.*

## GROUP PSYCHOTHERAPY.
The adolescent in group and family therapy. 2nd ed. Northvale, NJ : Jason Aronson, 1999.
*TC RJ505.G7 A36 1999*

Changing lives [videorecording]. Princeton, NJ : Films for the Humanities & Sciences, c1998.
*TC RC564 .C54 1999*

Group psychotherapy for psychological trauma. New York : Guilford Press, c2000.
*TC RC552.P67 G76 2000*

The process of group psychotherapy. Washington, DC : American Psychological Association, c2000.
*TC RC488 .P75 2000*

Thompson, Sheila. The group context. London ; Philadelphia : Jessica Kingsley Publishers, 1999.
*TC BF637.C6 T49 1999*

**Group psychotherapy for psychological trauma /**
Robert H. Klein, Victor L. Schermer, editors ; foreword by K. ROy MacKenzie. New York : Guilford Press, c2000. xx, 364 p. ; 23 cm. Includes bibliographical references and index. ISBN 1-57230-557-6 (hc : alk. paper) DDC 616.85/210651
*1. Post-traumatic stress disorder - Treatment. 2. Group psychotherapy. 3. Psychic trauma - Treatment. I. Klein, Robert H. II. Schermer, Victor L.*
*TC RC552.P67 G76 2000*

## GROUP PSYCHOTHERAPY FOR TEENAGERS - PROBLEMS, EXERCISES, ETC.
Carrell, Susan. Group exercises for adolescents. 2nd ed. Thousand Oaks : Sage Publications, c2000.
*TC RJ505.G7 C37 2000*

## GROUP PSYCHOTHERAPY - UNITED STATES.
Pack-Brown, Sherlon P. Images of me. Boston : Allyn and Bacon, c1998.
*TC HV1445 .P33 1998*

## GROUP READING.
Flecha, Ramón. [Compartiendo palabras. English] Sharing words. Lanham, Md. ; Oxford : Rowman & Littlefield Publishers, c2000.
*TC LB1060 .F5913 2000*

## GROUP READING - UNITED STATES.
Calkins, Lucy McCormick. The art of teaching reading. 1st ed. New York ; London : Longman, c2001.
*TC LB1573 .C185 2001*

## GROUP RELATIONS TRAINING.
Blank, Leonard. Confrontation; New York, Macmillan [1971]
*TC HM132 .B55*

Race, Phil. 500 tips on group learning. London : Kogan Page, 2000.
*TC LB1032 .A15 2000*

## GROUP RELATIONS TRAINING - UNITED STATES.
Hoyle, John. Interpersonal sensitivity. Larchmont, NY : Eye on Education, c1997.
*TC LB2831.92.U6 H67 1997*

**Group solutions : : [Teacher's guide].**
Goodman, Jan M. Rev. Berkeley, Calif. : Lawrence Hall of Science, University of California, 1997, c1992.
*TC QA8.7 .G5 1997*

## GROUP STRUCTURE.
Ulrich, Deborah L. Interactive group learning. New York : Springer, c1999.
*TC RT76 .U46 1999*

**Group supervision.**
Proctor, Brigid. London : Thousand Oaks : SAGE Publications, 2000.
*TC BF637.C6 P95176 2000*

## GROUP TEACHING. See GROUP WORK IN EDUCATION.

## GROUP THEORY.
Peatling, John H. Career development. Muncie, Ind. : Accelerated Development, c1977.
*TC BF697 .P384*

## GROUP THEORY - CONGRESSES.
Algebra, K-theory, groups, and education. Providence, R.I. : American Mathematical Society, c1999.
*TC QA150 .A419 1999*

## GROUP THERAPY. See GROUP PSYCHOTHERAPY.

**Group work.**
Gladding, Samuel T. 3rd ed. Upper Saddle River, N.J. : Merrill, c1999.
*TC BF637.C6 G5334 1999*

## GROUP WORK IN EDUCATION. See also TEAM LEARNING APPROACH IN EDUCATION.
Bligh, Donald A. What's the point in discussion? Exeter, Eng. ; Portland, OR : Intellect, 2000.
*TC LC6519 .B555 2000*

Creativity in the classroom. Burbank, CA : Disney Learning Partnership, c1999.
*TC LB1062 .C7 1999*

Daniels, Harvey, 1947- Methods that matter. York, Me. : Stenhouse Publishers, c1998.
*TC LB1027 .D24 1998*

Enhancing education in heterogeneous schools. Ramat-Gan : Bar-Ilan University Press, [1997]
*TC LC214 .E54 1997*

Light, Paul. Social processes in children's learning. Cambridge, U.K. ; New York : Cambridge University Press, 1999.
*TC LB1060 .L533 1999*

McCaslin, Mary M. Listening in classrooms. 1st ed. New York : HarperCollins College Publishers, c1996.
*TC LB1033 .M34 1996*

McConnell, David, 1951- Implementing computer supported cooperative learning.. 2nd ed. London : Kogan Page, 2000.
*TC LB1032 .M38 2000*

Race, Phil. 500 tips on group learning. London : Kogan Page, 2000.
*TC LB1032 .A15 2000*

Ryan, Sharon Kaye. Freedom to choice. 1998.

TC 06 no. 11034

**GROUP WORK IN EDUCATION - SPAIN.**
Sauquet, Alfonso. Conflict and team learning:. 2000.
*TC 06 no. 11308*

**GROUP WORK IN EDUCATION - UNITED STATES.**
Bess, James L. Teaching alone, teaching together. 1st ed. San Francisco : Jossey-Bass, c2000.
*TC LB2331 .B48 2000*

Calderwood, Patricia E., 1954- Learning community. New York : Teachers College Press, c2000.
*TC LB1032 .C34 2000*

Kampwirth, Thomas J. Collaborative consultation in the schools. Upper Saddle River, N.J. : Merrill, c1999.
*TC LB1027.5 .K285 1999*

Learning circles. Thousand Oaks, Calif. : Corwin Press, c1998.
*TC LB1032 .L355 1998*

Snodgrass, Dawn M., 1955- Collaborative learning in middle and secondary schools. Larchmont, N.Y. : Eye On Education, 2000.
*TC LB1032 .S62 2000*

**GROUP WORK IN EDUCATION - UNITED STATES - CASE STUDIES.**
Linn, Marcia C. Computers, teachers, peers. Mahwah, N.J. : L. Erlbaum Associates, 2000.
*TC LB1585.3 .L56 2000*

**GROUP WORK IN RESEARCH.**
Collaborative inquiry in practice. Thousand Oaks [Calif.] : Sage Publications, c2000.
*TC H62 .C5657 2000*

**GROUP WORK, SOCIAL.** *See* **SOCIAL GROUP WORK.**

**GROUPS, ETHNIC.** *See* **ETHNIC GROUPS.**

**GROUPS, SELF-HELP.** *See* **SELF-HELP GROUPS.**

**GROUPS, SOCIAL.** *See* **SOCIAL GROUPS.**

**GROUPS, THEORY OF.** *See* **GROUP THEORY.**

**Grover, Iqbal S.**
Guru Nanak Dev University. Guru Nanak Dev University. Amritsar : The University, 1994.
*TC LG169.A62 G87 1994*

**Groves, Ernest Rutherford, 1878-1946.** Wholesome childhood, by Ernest R. Groves and Gladys Hoagland Groves. Boston, Houghton Mifflin Company, 1924.
xxi, 183p. ; 19cm. Includes index. "Books of value to parents": p.[177]-178. DDC 649.1/G92
*1. Child rearing 2. Children - Health and hygiene 3. Infants - Health and hygiene I. Groves, Gladys (Hoagland. joint author II. Title.*
*TC HQ772 .G75*

**Groves, Gladys (Hoagland. joint author.**
Groves, Ernest Rutherford, 1878-1946. Wholesome childhood, Boston, Houghton Mifflin Company, 1924.
*TC HQ772 .G75*

**Growing up girls :** popular culture and the construction of identity / edited by Sharon R. Mazzarella and Norma Odom Pecora. New York : P. Lang, c1999. viii, 228 p. ; 23 cm. (Adolescent cultures, school & society ; vol. 9) Includes bibliographical references. ISBN 0-8204-4021-3 (alk. paper) DDC 305.235
*1. Teenage girls - Psychology. 2. Teenage girls - Attitudes. 3. Teenage girls in popular culture. 4. Adolescent psychology. 5. Identity (Psychology) 6. Stereotype (Psychology) in mass media. I. Mazzarella, Sharon R. II. Pecora, Norma Odom. III. Series.*
*TC HQ798 .G76 1999*

**Growing up in times of social change** / edited by Rainer K. Silbereisen, Alexander von Eye. New York : Walter de Gruyter, 1999. xvi, 343 p. : ill. ; 25 cm. (International studies on childhood and adolescence ; 7) Includes bibliographical references. ISBN 3-11-016500-7 (cloth : alk. paper) DDC 305.235/0943
*1. Teenagers - Germany. 2. Germany - History - Unification, 1990. I. Silbereisen. R. K. (Rainer K.), 1944- II. Eye, Alexander von. III. Series.*
*TC HQ799.G5 G76 1999*

**Growing up Puerto Rican :** an anthology / edited and with an introduction by Joy L. De Jesús ; foreword by Ed Vega. 1st ed. New York : Morrow, c1997. xxi, 233 p. ; 25 cm. ISBN 0-688-13740-7 (alk. paper) DDC 813
*1. American literature - Puerto Rican authors. 2. Puerto Ricans - United States - Literary collections. 3. Puerto Rican children - Literary collections. 4. Puerto Rican youth - Literary collections. I. De Jesús, Joy.*
*TC PS508.P84 G76 1997*

**Growing up with literature.**
Sawyer, Walter. 3rd ed. Albany, N.Y. : Delmar, c2000.
*TC LB1140.5.L3 S28 2000*

**GROWN-UP ABUSED CHILDREN.** *See* **ADULT CHILD ABUSE VICTIMS.**

**GROWTH.** *See* **DEVELOPMENTAL BIOLOGY.**

**GROWTH - FICTION.**
Shavick, Andrea. You'll grow soon, Alex. New York : Walker, 2000.
*TC PZ7.S5328 Yo 2000*

**GROWTH, PERSONAL.** *See* **SELF-ACTUALIZATION (PSYCHOLOGY).**

**GROWTH (PSYCHOLOGY).** *See* **MATURATION (PSYCHOLOGY); SUCCESS.**

**Groza, Victor, 1956-** Clinical and practice issues in adoption : bridging the gap between adoptees placed as infants and as older children / written and edited by Victor Groza and Karen F. Rosenberg. Westport, Conn. : Praeger, 1998. ix, 175 p. ; 24 cm. Includes bibliographical references and index. ISBN 0-275-95816-7 (alk. paper) DDC 155.44/5
*1. Adoption - Psychological aspects. 2. Adopted children - Psychology. I. Rosenberg, Karen F. II. Title.*
*TC HV875 .G776 1998*

**Grubb, W. Norton.** The roles of evaluation for vocational education and training : plain talk on the field of dreams / W. Norton Grubb, Paul Ryan. London : Kogan Page ; Sterling, VA : Distributed in the US by Stylus Pub. Inc., 1999. xi, 195 p. ; 25.cm. Includes bibliographical references (p. 167-185) and index. ISBN 0-7494-3070-2
*1. Vocational education - Evaluation. 2. Occupational training - Evaluation. I. Ryan. Paul, 1947- II. Title. III. Title: Vocational education and training*
*TC LC1044 .G78 1999*

**Gruenberg, Benjamin Charles, 1875-** ed.
Child Study Association of America. Guidance of childhood and youth; New York, Macmillan, 1926.
*TC HQ772 .C45*

**Grugeon, Elizabeth.** The art of storytelling for teachers and pupils : using stories to develop literacy in primary classrooms / Elizabeth Grugeon and Paul Gardner ; with contributions from members of the Primary Team in The School of Education, De Montfort University, Bedford: Georgina Elton ... [et al.] London : David Fulton, 2000. xiii, 128 p. : ill. ; 22 cm. Includes bibliographical references and index. ISBN 1-85346-617-4
*1. Storytelling. 2. Reading (Elementary) 3. English language - Composition and exercises - Study and teaching (Elementary) I. Gardner. Paul. II. Elton. Georgina. III. De Montfort University. School of Education. IV. Title.*
*TC LB1042 .G78 2000*

**Grunberg, Isabelle.**
Global public goods. New York : Oxford University Press, 1999.
*TC HB846.5 .G55 1999*

**Grundtvig, N. F. S. (Nicolai Frederik Severin), 1783-1872.**
Grundtvig's ideas in North America. Copenhagen, Denmark : Danske Selskab, 1983.
*TC LB675.G832 G79 1983*

**GRUNDTVIG, N. F. S. (NICOLAI FREDERIK SEVERIN), 1783-1872 - CONGRESSES.**
Grundtvig's ideas in North America. Copenhagen, Denmark : Danske Selskab, 1983.
*TC LB675.G832 G79 1983*

**Grundtvig's ideas in North America :** influences and parallels : workshop / sponsored by Scandinavian Seminar College, Holte, Denmark, 1983 ; edited and published by Det Danske Selskab. Copenhagen, Denmark : Danske Selskab, 1983. 173 p. : ill. ; 24 cm. Includes bibliographical references. ISBN 87-7429-052-5 DDC 370/.1
*1. Grundtvig, N. F. S. - (Nicolai Frederik Severin). - 1783-1872 - Congresses. 2. Education - Philosophy - Congresses. 3. Education - United States - Philosophy - Congresses. 4. Folk high schools - Congresses. I. Grundtvig, N. F. S. (Nicolai Frederik Severin), 1783-1872. II. Scandinavian Seminar College. III. Danske selskab (Copenhagen, Denmark)*
*TC LB675.G832 G79 1983*

**Grunwald, Armin.**
Vision assessment. New York : Springer, 2000.
*TC T174.5 V57 2000*

**Grusin, Richard.**
Bolter, J. David, 1951- Remediation. Cambridge, Mass. : MIT Press, c1999.

TC P96.T42 B59 1998

**Gruwell, Erin.**
Freedom Writers. The Freedom Writers diary. 1st ed. New York : Doubleday, c1999.
*TC HQ796 .F76355 1999*

**Gryning, Sven-Erik.**
Air pollution modeling and its application XII. New York : Plenum Press, c1998.
*TC TD881 .A47523 1998*

**GUANGZHOU (CHINA) - ECONOMIC CONDITIONS.**
Ikels, Charlotte. The return of the god of wealth. Stanford, Calif. : Stanford University Press, c1996.
*TC HC428.C34 I38 1996*

**GUANGZHOU (CHINA) - ECONOMIC POLICY.**
Ikels, Charlotte. The return of the god of wealth. Stanford, Calif. : Stanford University Press, c1996.
*TC HC428.C34 I38 1996*

**GUARDIAN AND WARD.** *See* **PARENT AND CHILD (LAW).**

**GUARDIAN AND WARD - GREAT BRITAIN.**
Clark, Alison. The child in focus. London : National Children's Bureau Enterprise, c1999.
*TC KD785 .C43 1999*

**GUARDIANSHIPS.** *See* **GUARDIAN AND WARD.**

**GUATEMALA - LANGUAGES.** *See* **MAYA LANGUAGE.**

**Gubrium, Jaber F.**
Holstein, James A. The self we live by. New York : Oxford University Press, 2000.
*TC BF697.5.S65 H65 2000*

**GUERRILLA WARFARE.** *See* **COUNTERINSURGENCY.**

**Guest, Ken.**
Photomontage today, Peter Kennard [videorecording]. [London] : Art Council of Great Britain ; Ho-Ho-Kus, N.J. : [distributed by] Anthony Roland Collection of Films on Art, c1982.
*TC TR685 .P45 1982*

**GUESTS.** *See* **ENTERTAINING.**

**Guests by Michael Dorris.**
Beech, Linda Ward. New York, NY : Scholastic, c1996.
*TC LB1573 .B432 1996*

**Guettier, Bénédicte.** The father who had ten children / story and pictures by Benedicte Guettier. 1st ed. New York : Dial Books for Young Readers, 1999. 1 v. (unpaged) : col. ill. ; 31 cm. SUMMARY: After working hard to take care of his ten children, a devoted father plans to get away by himself--until he decides that something is missing. ISBN 0-8037-2446-2 (hc. : trade) DDC [E]
*1. Father and child - Fiction. I. Title.*
*TC PZ7.G93824 Fat 1999*

**GUEVARA, ERNESTO, 1928-1967.**
McLaren, Peter, 1948- Che Guevara, Paulo Freire, and the pedagogy of revolution. Lanham [Md.] : Rowman & Littlefield Publishers, c2000.
*TC LC196 .M29 2000*

**Guevara-Vázquez, Fabián.** El indigena en la novela de la Revolucion Mexicana : el fracaso de su representacion / by Fabián Guevara-Vázquez. 1999. x, 308 leaves ; 29 cm. Issued also on microfilm. Thesis (Ph.D.)--Columbia University, 1999. Includes bibliographical references: (leaves 286-294) Introduction and conclusion in both Spanish and English.
*1. Azuela, Mariano, - 1873-1952. - Los de abajo. 2. Magdaleno, Mauricio, - 1906- 3. López y Fuentes, Gregorio, - 1897-1966. - Indio. 4. Menéndez, Miguel Angel. 5. Literature, Modern - 20th century - History and criticism. 6. Indians of Mexico - Social life and customs. 7. Characters and characteristics in literature. 8. Social change - Mexico. 9. Mexico - History - Revolution, 1910-1920 - Fiction. 10. Mexico - Literatures. I. Title.*
*TC 085 G934*

**Guggenheim Museum Soho.**
Antipodean currents. New York : Guggenheim Museum, c1995.
*TC N7404 .A58 1995*

**GUIDANCE COUNSELORS.** *See* **STUDENT COUNSELORS.**

**GUIDANCE, EDUCATIONAL.** *See* **EDUCATIONAL COUNSELING.**

**GUIDANCE IN ELEMENTARY EDUCATION.** *See* **COUNSELING IN ELEMENTARY EDUCATION.**

**GUIDANCE IN HIGHER EDUCATION.** See
COUNSELING IN HIGHER EDUCATION.

**GUIDANCE IN MIDDLE SCHOOL EDUCATION.**
See COUNSELING IN MIDDLE SCHOOL
EDUCATION.

**GUIDANCE IN SECONDARY EDUCATION.** See
COUNSELING IN SECONDARY
EDUCATION.

**Guidance of childhood and youth.**
Child Study Association of America. New York,
Macmillan, 1926.
*TC HQ772 .C45*

**Guidance review.** [Delhi] Central Bureau of
Educational and Vocational Guidance, National
Council of Educational Research and Training. v. 25
cm. Frequency: Quarterly. v. 1- Jan. 1963- . Delhi.
National Institute of Education. Central Bureau of
Educational and Vocational Guidance. Guidance news.
*1. Educational counseling - Periodicals. 2. English periodicals
I. Delhi (India). National Institute of Education. Central
Bureau of Educational and Vocational Guidance. II. Title:
Delhi. National Institute of Education. Central Bureau of
Educational and Vocational Guidance. Guidance news*

**GUIDANCE, SCHOOL.** See EDUCATIONAL
COUNSELING.

**GUIDANCE, STUDENT.** See EDUCATIONAL
COUNSELING; VOCATIONAL GUIDANCE.

**GUIDANCE, VOCATIONAL.** See VOCATIONAL
GUIDANCE.

**Guide for music methods classes.**
Hall, Louis O. Strategies for teaching. Reston, VA :
Music Educators National Conference, c1997.
*TC MT1.H136 S77 1997*

**Guide for postdoctoral scholars, advisers,
institutions, funding organizations, and
disciplinary societies.**
Enhancing the postdoctoral experience for scientists
and engineers. Washington, DC : National Academy
Press, 2000.
*TC Q147 .E53 2000*

**Guide to analysis of language transcripts.**
Retherford, Kristine S., 1950- 2nd ed. Eau Claire,
WI : Thinking Publications, 1993.
*TC RJ496.L35 S84 1993*

**Guide to nursing management and leadership.**
Marriner-Tomey, Ann, 1943- 6th ed. St. Louis, Mo. :
Mosby, 2000.
*TC RT89.3 M37 2000*

**Guide to peer tutoring.**
Gillespie, Paula. The Allyn and Bacon guide to peer
tutoring. Boston : Allyn & Bacon, c2000.
*TC LB1031.5 .G55 2000*

**Guide to poetry teaching and learning for junior
secondary schools.**
Osakwe, Mabel. Poetrymate 1. Enugu, Nigeria :
Fourth Dimension Publishing Co., 1996.
*TC PN1101 .O73 1996*

**Guide to proposal writing.**
Geever, Jane C. The Foundation Center's guide to
proposal writing. Rev. ed. New York : Foundation
Center, c1997.
*TC HG177.5.U6 G44 1997*

**Guide to publishing in psychology journals** / edited by
Robert J. Sternberg. Cambridge, U.K. ; New York :
Cambridge University Press, 2000. viii, 214 p. ; 24 cm.
Includes bibliographical references and index. ISBN 0-521-
59447-2 ISBN 0-521-59460-X (pbk.) DDC 808/.06615
*1. Psychology - Authorship. I. Sternberg, Robert J.*
*TC BF76.8 .G85 2000*

**Guide to reprints.** Munich : K.G. Saur, 2000- v. ; 28 cm.
2000- . "An international directory of available facsimile
reprints." Issued in 2 parts, Author/Title and Subject. Previous
editions were published by Guide to Reprints, Inc., 1967-1998.
ISSN 1439-2755
*1. Reprints (Publications) - Bibliography. 2. Out-of-print
books - Bibliography.*
*TC Z1036 .G8*

**Guide to suicide assessment and intervention.**
The Harvard Medical School guide to suicide
assessment and intervention. 1st ed. San Francisco :
Jossey-Bass, c1999.
*TC RC569 .H37 1999*

**Guide to writing quality individualzed education
programs.**
Gibb, Gordon S. Boston : Allyn and Bacon, c2000.
*TC LC4019 .G43 2000*

**Guidelines for appointment of nurses for individual
practice privileges in health care organizations.**
American Nurses Association. Task Force on Staff
Privileges. Kansas City, MO : American Nurses
Association, Commission on Nursing Service, 1978.
*TC RT104 .A44 1978*

**Guiding children's learning of mathematics.**
Kennedy, Leonard M. 9th ed. Belmont, CA :
Wadsworth/Thomson Learning, c2000.
*TC QA135.5 .K43 2000*

**Guiding teacher learning :** insider studies of classroom
work with prospective & practicing teachers / edited
by Sharon Feiman-Nemser & Cheryl Rosaen.
Washington. DC : AACTE, c1997. 113 p. ; 22 cm.
Includes bibliographical references.
*1. Teachers - In-service training - United States. 2. Mentoring
in education - United States. 3. Student teachers - Training of -
United States - Case studies. I. Feiman-Nemser, Sharon. II.
Rosaen. Cheryl L.*
*TC LB1731 .G85 1997*

**The Guilford family therapy series**
Nichols, William C. Systemic family therapy. New
York : Guilford Press, c1986.
*TC RC488.5 .N535 1986*

Walsh, Froma. Strengthening family resilience. New
York : Guilford Press, c1998.
*TC RC489.F33 W34 1998*

**Guilford Press (New York, N.Y.).**
ADHD [videorecording]. New York, NY : Guilford
Publications, Inc., c1992.
*TC RJ506.H9 A3 1992*

**Guilford Publications, Inc.**
ADHD [videorecording]. New York, NY : Guilford
Publications, Inc., c1992.
*TC RJ506.H9 A3 1992*

Understanding the defiant child [videorecording].
New York : Guilford Publications, c1997.
*TC HQ755.7 .U63 1997*

**The Guilford school practitioner series**
Advanced applications of curriculum-based
measurement. New York : Guilford Press, c1998.
*TC LB3060.32.C74 A38 1998*

Barnett, David W., 1946- Designing preschool
interventions. New York : Guilford Press, 1999.
*TC LC4801 .B36 1999*

Brown, Ronald T. Medications for school-age
children. New York : Guilford Press, c1998.
*TC RJ560 .B76 1998*

Conducting school-based assessments of child and
adolescent behavior. New York : Guilford Press,
c2000.
*TC LB1124 .C66 2000*

House, Alvin E. DSM-IV diagnosis in the schools.
New York : Guilford Press, c1999
*TC RJ503.5 .H68 1999*

Marks, Edward S. Entry strategies for school
consultation. New York : Guilford Press, c1995.
*TC LB2799.2 .M36 1995*

Murphy, John J. (John Joseph), 1955- Brief
intervention for school problems. New York :
Guilford Press, c1997.
*TC LC4802 .M87 1997*

Rathvon, Natalie. Effective school interventions. New
York : Guilford Press, c1999.
*TC LC1201 .R38 1999*

Shapiro, Edward S. (Edward Steven), 1951-
Academic skills problems workbook. New York :
Guilford Press, c1996.
*TC LB1029.R4 S52 1996*

**The Guilford substance abuse series**
Psychological theories of drinking and alcoholism.
2nd ed. New York : Guilford Press, c1999.
*TC HV5045 .P74 1999*

**Guillot, Marie-Noëlle, 1955-** Fluency and its teaching /
Marie Noëlle Guillot. Clevedon, England ;
Philadelphia, Pa. : Multilingual Matters, c1999. viii,
184 p. ; 22 cm. (Modern languages in practice ; 11) (Includes
bibliographical references and index.) ISBN 1-85359-440-7
(alk. paper) ISBN 1-85359-439-3 (pbk. : alk. paper) DDC
418/.007
*1. Language and languages - Study and teaching. 2. Oral
communication - Study and teaching. I. Title. II. Series. III.
Series: Includes bibliographical references and index.*
*TC P53.6 .G85 1999*

**GUILT - FICTION.**
Bunting, Eve, 1928- Blackwater. 1st ed. New York :
Joanna Cotler Books, 1999.

*TC PZ7.B91527 Bne 1999*

**GUIS (COMPUTER SYSTEMS).** See GRAPHICAL
USER INTERFACES (COMPUTER
SYSTEMS).

**GULLS - FICTION.**
Wallace, Karen. A day at Seagull beach. 1st American
ed. New York : DK Pub., 1999.
*TC PZ10.3.W1625 Se 1999*

**GULLS - JUVENILE FICTION.**
Wallace, Karen. A day at Seagull beach. 1st American
ed. New York : DK Pub., 1999.
*TC PZ10.3.W1625 Se 1999*

**GUN CONTROL - GOVERNMENT POLICY.** See
GUN CONTROL.

**GUN CONTROL - LAW AND LEGISLATION.** See
FIREARMS - LAW AND LEGISLATION.

**GUN CONTROL - UNITED STATES.**
Guns and violence. San Diego : Greenhaven Press,
c1999.
*TC HV7436 .G8774 1999*

**GUN CONTROL - UNITED STATES -
ENCYCLOPEDIA.**
Utter, Glenn H. Encyclopedia of gun control and gun
rights. Phoenix, Ariz. : Oryx Press, 2000.
*TC KF3941.A68 U88 2000*

**GUN OWNERSHIP.** See FIREARMS
OWNERSHIP.

**Gunning, Thomas G.** Best books for building literacy
for elementary school children / Thomas G. Gunning.
Boston : Allyn and Bacon, 2000. 299 p. : ill. ; 24 cm.
Includes bilbiographical references and indexes. ISBN 0-205-
28625-9 DDC 372.4
*1. Reading (Elementary) - United States. 2. Children - Books
and reading - United States. 3. Children's literature.
American - Bibliography. I. Title.*
*TC LB1573 .B47 2000*

Building words : a resource manual for teaching word
analysis and spelling strategies / Thomas G. Gunning ;
illustrated by Norma Kable. Boston ; London : Allyn
and Bacon, c2001. xiii, 321 p. : ill., forms ; 28 cm. Includes
bibliographical references (p. 313-315) and index. ISBN 0-
205-30922-4 DDC 372.46/5
*1. Reading - Phonetic method - United States. 2. English
language - Orthography and spelling - Study and teaching
(Elementary) - United States. I. Title.*
*TC LB1573.3 .G83 2001*

Creating literacy instruction for all children / Thomas
G. Gunning. 3rd ed. Boston : Allyn and Bacon, c2000.
xvi, 592 p. : ill. ; 25 cm. Rev. ed. of: Creating reading
instruction for all children. 2nd ed. c1996. Includes
bibliographical references (p. 555-576) and index. ISBN 0-
205-28793-X DDC 372.41
*1. Reading (Elementary) 2. English language - Composition
and exercises - Study and teaching (Elementary) I. Gunning,
Thomas G. Creating reading instruction for all children. II.
Title.*
*TC LB1573 .G93 2000*

**Creating reading instruction for all children.**
Gunning, Thomas G. Creating literacy instruction
for all children. 3rd ed. Boston : Allyn and Bacon,
c2000.
*TC LB1573 .G93 2000*

Phonological awareness and primary phonics /
Thomas G. Gunning ; illustrated by Norma Kable.
Boston : Allyn and Bacon, c2000. vi, 202 p. : ill. ; 28 cm.
Includes bibliographical references (p. 163-164) and index.
ISBN 0-205-32323-5
*1. Phonetics. 2. Reading - Phonetic method. I. Title.*
*TC P221 .G85 2000*

**GUNS.** See FIREARMS.

**Guns and violence** / Henny H. Kim, book editor. San
Diego : Greenhaven Press, c1999. 219 p. ; 25 cm.
(Current controversies.) Includes bibliographical references (p.
205-207) and index. ISBN 0-7377-0065-3 (lib. bdg. : alk.
paper) ISBN 0-7377-0064-5 (pbk. : alk. paper)
*1. Gun control - United States. 2. Firearms ownership - United
States. 3. Firearms - Law and legislation - United States. 4.
Violence - United States. 5. Violent crimes - United States. I.
Kim, Henny H. 1968- II. Series.*
*TC HV7436 .G8774 1999*

**Gunter, Barrie.** Psychology of the home / Barrie
Gunter ; consulting editor Adrian Furnham. London ;
Philadelphia : Whurr, c2000. xi, 191 p. : ill. ; 24 cm.
Includes bibliographical references and index. ISBN 1-86156-
146-6 DDC 155.945
*1. Home - Psychological aspects. I. Title.*
*TC GT165.5 .G86 2000*

**Gunton, Michael.**
In search of human origins [videorecording]. [Boston, Mass.] : WGBH Educational Foundation, c1994.
*TC GN281 .I45 1994*

**Guppies :** a middle-school mathematics unit / MMAP. Menlo Park, Calif. : Institute for Research on Learning, c1997. 312 p. : ill. ; 30 cm. + 1 computer disc (3 1/2 in.). Library copy is a draft copy.
*1. Mathematics - Study and teaching (Elementary) I. Middle-school Mathematics through Applications Project.*
*TC QA135.5 .G86 1997*

**Guralnick, Michael J.**
Interdisciplinary clinical assessment of young children with developmental disabilities. Baltimore : Paul H. Brookes Pub. Co., c2000.
*TC HV891 .I58 2000*

**Guri-Rozenblit, Sarah.** Distance and campus universities : tensions and interactions : a comparative study of five countries / Sarah Guri-Rosenblit. 1st ed. Oxford, UK ; New York, NY : Pergamon, published for IAU Press, 1999. xxii, 290 p. : ill. ; 24 cm. (Issues in higher education) Includes bibliographical references (p.265-290) and index. ISBN 0-08-043066-X (hard) DDC 378.1/75
*1. Distance education - Cross cultural studies. 2. Education, Higher - Cross cultural studies. I. Title. II. Series: Issues in higher education (Oxford, England)*
*TC LC5800 .G87 1999*

**Gurin, Joel, 1953-.**
The Horizons of health. Cambridge, Mass. : Harvard University Press, 1977.
*TC R850 .H67*

**Guru Nanak Dev University.**
Guru Nanak Dev University. Amritsar : The University, 1994.
*TC LG169.A62 G87 1994*

Guru Nanak Dev University : a profile / editorial board [I.S. Grover ... et al.]. Amritsar : The University, 1994. 188 p. ; 22 cm. "Silver jubilee, 1994." "Books published by faculty": P. [133]-160. "University publications other than those of faculty": P. [161]-162.
*1. Guru Nanak Dev University. I. Grover, Iqbal S. II. Title.*
*TC LG169.A62 G87 1994*

**GURU NANAK DEV UNIVERSITY.**
Guru Nanak Dev University. Guru Nanak Dev University. Amritsar : The University, 1994.
*TC LG169.A62 G87 1994*

**Gusterson, Hugh.** Nuclear rites : a weapons laboratory at the end of the Cold War / Hugh Gusterson. "First paperback printing 1998". Berkeley : University of California Press, 1998. xviii, 351 p. : ill., map ; 24 cm. Includes bibliographical references (p. 291-344) and index. ISBN 0-520-21373-4 (pbk.)
*1. Nuclear weapons - Research - Social aspects - California - Livermore. 2. Lawrence Livermore National Laboratory - Employees. 3. Antinuclear movement - Social aspects. I. Title. II. Title: Weapons laboratory at the end of the Cold War*
*TC U264.4.C2 G87 1998*

**Guston, David H.** Between politics and science : assuring the integrity and productivity of research / David H. Guston. Cambridge, U.K. ; New York, NY : Cambridge University Press, 2000. xvii, 213 p. : ill. ; 24 cm. Includes bibliographical references (p. 185-205) and index. ISBN 0-521-65318-5 DDC 338.973/06
*1. Science and state - United States. I. Title.*
*TC Q127.U6 G87 2000*

**Gutek, Barbara A.**
Tsui, Anne S. Demographic differences in organizations. Lanham, MD : Lexington Books, 1999.
*TC HF5549.5.M5 T75 1999*

**Guth, Jamie.**
Depression and manic depression [videorecording]. Boston, MA : Fanlight Productions, c1996.
*TC RC537 .D46 1996*

**Guthrie, John T.**
Engaging young readers. New York : Guilford Press, c2000.
*TC LB1573 .E655 2000*

**Guthrie, Victoria L.**
Love, Patrick G. Understanding and applying cognitive development theory. San Francisco : Jossey-Bass, c1999.
*TC LB2343 .L65 1999*

**Gutiérrez, Lorraine M. (Lorraine Margot).**
Empowering women of color. New York : Columbia University Press, c1999.
*TC HV1445 .E45 1999*

**Gutin, Nina J.** Differential object representations in inpatients with narcissistic and borderline personality disorders and normal controls / by Nina J. Gutin.

1997. vii, 136 leaves ; 29 cm. Issued also on microfilm. Includes tables. Thesis (Ph.D.)--Columbia University. Includes bibliographical references: (leaves 111-117)
*1. Borderline personality disorder. 2. Hospital patients - Psychology. 3. Narcissism. 4. Mental health. 5. Thematic Apperception Test. 6. Psychological tests. I. Title.*
*TC 085 G975*

**Gutner, Howard.** Caddie Woodlawn by Carol Ryrie Brink / written by Howard Gutner. New York : Scholastic, c1997. 16 p. : ill. ; 28 cm. (Scholastic literature guide. Grades 4-8.) "Author biography, chapter summaries, discussion questions, vocabulary builders, assessment strategies, reproducibles, cross-curricular activities for students of all learning styles."--Cover. ISBN 0-590-37359-5
*1. Brink, Carol Ryrie, - 1895- / - Caddie Woodlawn. 2. Children's literature - Study and teaching. 3. Reading (Elementary) I. Title. II. Series.*
*TC LB1573 .G87 1997*

**Gutzwiller, Felix.**
Cost benefit analysis of heroin maintenance treatment. Basel : New York : Karger, c2000.
*TC RC568.H4 C67 2000*

**Guy, Talmadge C.**
Providing culturally relevant adult education. San Francisco : Jossey Bass, c1999.
*TC LC5219 .P76 1999*

**GYMNASTICS.** See PHYSICAL EDUCATION AND TRAINING; SCHOOLS - EXERCISES AND RECREATIONS.

**GYMNASTS.** See ACROBATS.

**GYNECOLOGY - PERIODICALS.**
Clinical obstetrics and gynecology. [New York] Hoeber Medical Division, Harper & Row.

**H. Eugene and Lillian Youngs Lehman series**
Pérez, Louis A., 1943- On becoming Cuban. Chapel Hill : University of North Carolina Press, c1999.
*TC F1760 .P47 1999*

**H is for history.**
Singleton, Laurel R., 1950- Boulder, Colo. : Social Science Education Consortium, 1995.
*TC LB1582.U6 S56 1995*

**Haaften, A. W. van (A. Wouter), 1941-.**
Moral sensibilities and education. Bemmel : Concorde Pub. House, 1999-
*TC BF723.M54 M684 1999*

**Haaften, A. W. van. (A. Wouter) 1941-.**
The university and the knowledge society. Bemmel [Netherlands] : Concorde Publishing House, 1998.
*TC LB2322.2 .U55 1998*

**Haags Gemeentemuseum.**
Piet Mondrian, 1872-1944. Milan : Leonardo Arte, 1994.
*TC N6953.M64 A4 1994*

**Haake, Katharine.** What our speech disrupts : feminism and creative writing studies / Katharine Haake. Urbana, Ill. : National Council of Teachers of English, c2000. x, 285 p. ; 26 cm. Includes bibliographical references (p. 275-278) and index. ISBN 0-8141-5671-1 (pbk.) DDC 808/.042/071
*1. English language - Rhetoric - Study and teaching - Social aspects. 2. Creative writing (Higher education) - Social aspects. 3. Authorship - Sex differences. 4. Women - Education (Higher) 5. Feminism and education. I. Title.*
*TC PE1404 .H3 2000*

**Haas, Ernst, 1921-.**
The sight and insight of Ernst Haas [videorecording]. Minneapolis, Minn. : Media Loft, 1992.
*TC TR647.H3 S5 1992*

**HAAS, ERNST, 1921-.**
The sight and insight of Ernst Haas [videorecording]. Minneapolis, Minn. : Media Loft, 1992.
*TC TR647.H3 S5 1992*

**Haas, Linda.**
Organizational change & gender equity. Thousand Oaks : Sage Publications, c2000.
*TC HD58.8 .O7289 2000*

**Haas, Robert Bartlett. ed.**
[Group psychotherapy.] Psychodrama and sociodrama in American education. New York Beacon House, 1949.

**Haass, Richard.** The bureaucratic entrepreneur : how to be effective in any unruly organization / Richard N. Haass. Washington, D.C. : Brookings Institution, c1999. xix, 198 p. ; 23 cm. Rev. ed. of: Power to persuade. Includes bibliographical references.
*1. Public administration. 2. Bureaucracy. 3. Performance. 4. Persuasion (Psychology) 5. Office politics. 6. Administrative*

agencies - United States - Management. I. Haass, Richard. Power to persuade. II. Title.
*TC JF1351 .H2 1999*

**Power to persuade.**
Haass, Richard. The bureaucratic entrepreneur. Washington, D.C. : Brookings Institution, c1999.
*TC JF1351 .H2 1999*

**HABIT.** *See also* FOOD HABITS; HEALTH BEHAVIOR; NARCOTIC HABIT; TOBACCO HABIT.
Rachlin, Howard, 1935- The science of self-control. Cambridge, Mass. : Harvard University Press, 2000.
*TC BF632 .R3 2000*

**HABITAT (ECOLOGY).** *See* NICHE (ECOLOGY).

**Habley, Wesley R.**
Academic advising. 1st ed. San Francisco : Jossey-Bass, c2000.
*TC LB2343 .A29 2000*

**Hacking, Ian.** Mad travelers : reflections on the reality of transient mental illnesses / Ian Hacking. Charlottesville, Va. : University Press of Virginia, 1998. x, 239 p. : ill., maps ; 24 cm. "Page-Barbour lectures for 1997." Includes bibliographical references (p. 223-234) and index. ISBN 0-8139-1823-5 (acid-free paper) DDC 616.85/232
*1. Fugue (Psychology) - Case studies. 2. Tissié, Philippe. - 1852-1925. 3. Social psychiatry. 4. Niche (Ecology) I. Title.*
*TC RC553.F83 H33 1998*

**Hackman, Larry A.**
Dewey, John, 1859-1952. The correspondence of John Dewey. [computer file]. Windows version. Charlottesville, VA : InteLex Corp., 1999- Computer data and program.
*TC B945.D44 A4 1999*

**Hackmann, Willem Dirk.**
Learning, language, and invention. Aldershot, Hampshire, Great Britain : Variorum ; Brookfield, Vt., USA : Ashgate Pub. Co. ; Paris, France : Société internationale de l'Astrolabe, 1994.
*TC AC5 .L38 1994*

**Hackney Downs :** the school that dared to fight. London ; New York : Cassell, 1999. xix, 266 p. ; 22 cm. ISBN 0-304-70710-4 DDC 373
*1. High schools - England - London - History. I. O'Connor, Maureen*
*TC LF795.L66 H33 1999*

**Haenisch, Siegfried** AGS algebra / by Siegfried Haenisch. Circle Pines, Minn. : AGS, American Guidance Service, c1998. xi, 484 p. : ill. (some col.) ; 25 cm. Includes index. ISBN 0-7854-1457-6
*1. Algebra. I. Title. II. Title: American Guidance Service algebra*
*TC QA152.2 .H33 1998*

AGS algebra / by Siegfried Haenisch. Teacher's ed. Circle Pines, Minn. : AGS, American Guidance Service, c1998. T19, xii, 502 p. : ill. (some col.) ; 28 cm. Includes index. ISBN 0-7854-1458-4
*1. Algebra. I. Title. II. Title: American Guidance Service algebra*
*TC QA152.2 .H33 1998 Teacher's Ed.*

AGS algebra / by Siegfried Haenisch. Teacher's ed. Circle Pines, Minn. : AGS, American Guidance Service, c1998. T19, xii, 502 p. : ill. (some col.) ; 28 cm. Includes index. ISBN 0-7854-1458-4
*1. Algebra. I. Title. II. Title: American Guidance Service algebra*
*TC QA152.2 .H33 1998 Teacher's Ed.*

AGS algebra / by Siegfried Haenisch. Teacher's ed. Circle Pines, Minn. : AGS, American Guidance Service, c1998. T19, xii, 502 p. : ill. (some col.) ; 28 cm. Includes index. ISBN 0-7854-1458-4
*1. Algebra. I. Title. II. Title: American Guidance Service algebra*
*TC QA152.2 .H33 1998 Teacher's Ed.*

AGS pre-algebra / by Siegfried Haenisch. Circle Pines, Minn. : AGS, American Guidance Service, c1998. xi, 483 p. : col. ill. ; 25 cm. Includes index. ISBN 0-7854-1451-7
*1. Mathematics. I. Title. II. Title: American Guidance Service pre-algebra*
*TC QA107 .H33 1998*

AGS pre-algebra / by Siegfried Haenisch. Teacher's ed. Circle Pines, Minn. : AGS, American Guidance Service, c1998. T20, xii, 504 p. : col. ill. ; 28 cm. Includes index. ISBN 0-7854-1452-5
*1. Mathematics. I. Title. II. Title: American Guidance Service pre-algebra*
*TC QA107 .H33 1998 Teacher's Ed.*

AGS pre-algebra / by Siegfried Haenisch. Teacher's ed. Circle Pines, Minn. : AGS, American Guidance

Service, c1998. T20, xii, 504 p. : col. ill. ; 28 cm. Includes index. ISBN 0-7854-1452-5
*1. Mathematics. I. Title. II. Title: American Guidance Service pre-algebra*
**TC QA107 .H33 1998 Teacher's Ed.**

AGS pre-algebra / by Siegfried Haenisch. Teacher's ed. Circle Pines, Minn. : AGS, American Guidance Service, c1998. T20, xii, 504 p. : col. ill. ; 28 cm. Includes index. ISBN 0-7854-1452-5
*1. Mathematics. I. Title. II. Title: American Guidance Service pre-algebra*
**TC QA107 .H33 1998 Teacher's Ed.**

**Hafeli, Mary Claire.** Drawing and painting in the middle school : intentions, decisions and judgments of students and their teachers / by Mary Claire Hafeli. 1999. 283 leaves : ill. (some col.) ; 29 cm. Typescript; issued also on microfilm. Thesis (Ed.D.)--Teachers College, Columbia University, 1999. Includes bibliographical references (leaves 247-260).
*1. Art - Study and teaching (Middle school) 2. Aesthetics - Study and teaching (Middle school) 3. Children's drawings - Psychological aspects. 4. Creative ability in children. I. Title.*
**TC 06 no. 11055**

**Hafner, Marylin, ill.**
Berger, Melvin. Germs make me sick!. 1st ed. New York : Crowell, c1985.
**TC QR57 .B47 1985**

**Hagberg, Garry, 1952-** Art as language : Wittgenstein, meaning, and aesthetic theory / G.L. Hagberg. Ithaca : Cornell University Press, c1995. xi, 196 p. ; 24 cm. Includes bibliographical references and index. ISBN 0-8014-3040-2 (alk. paper) DDC 111/.85/092
*1. Wittgenstein, Ludwig, - 1889-1951. 2. Aesthetics, Modern - 20th century. I. Title.*
**TC B3376.W564 H25 1995**

**Hagedorn, Linda Serra.**
What contributes to job satisfaction among faculty and staff. San Francisco, Calif. : Jossey-Bass Publishers, c2000.
**TC LB2331.7 .W45 2000**

**Hagendoorn, Louk. 1945-.**
Education and racism :. Aldershot ; Brookfield, Vt. : Ashgate, c1999.
**TC LC212.3.G7E48 1999**

**HAGGLING. See NEGOTIATION.**

**Hagood, Margaret C.**
Alvermann, Donna E. Popular culture in the classroom. Newark, Del. : International Reading Association ; Chicago, Ill. : National Reading Conference, c1999.
**TC P91.3 .A485 1999**

**Hagood, Thomas K.** A history of dance in American higher education : dance and the American university / Thomas K. Hagood. Lewiston, N.Y. : E. Mellen Press, c2000. xii, 399 p. : ill. ; 24 cm. (Studies in dance, 077347742X ; v. 1) Includes bibliographical references (p. 354-378) and index. ISBN 0-7734-7799-3 DDC 792.8/071/173
*1. Dance - Study and teaching (Higher) - United States - History. I. Title. II. Series.*
**TC GV1589 .H33 2000**

**Hagoort, Peter.**
The neurocognition of language. Oxford : New York : Oxford University Press, 1999.
**TC QP399 .N483 1999**

**Hague, Barry N.**
Digital democracy. London ; New York : Routledge, 1999.
**TC JF1525.A8 D54 1999**

**Hahn, Mary Downing.** Anna all year round / by Mary Downing Hahn ; illustrated by Diane deGroat. New York : Clarion Books, c1999. 133 p. : ill. ; 22 cm. SUMMARY: Eight-year-old Anna experiences a series of episodes, some that are funny, others sad, involving friends and family during a year in Baltimore just before World War I. ISBN 0-395-86975-7 DDC [Fic]
*1. Family life - Maryland - Baltimore - Fiction. 2. Baltimore (Md.) - Fiction. I. De Groat, Diane, ill. II. Title.*
**TC PZ7.H1256 An 1999**

**HAIKU.**
Livingston, Myra Cohn. Cricket never does. New York : Margaret K. McElderry Books, c1997.
**TC PS3562.I945 C75 1997**

**HAIKU, AMERICAN.**
Livingston, Myra Cohn. Cricket never does. New York : Margaret K. McElderry Books, c1997.
**TC PS3562.I945 C75 1997**

**Haines, B. Joan E. (Beatrice Joan Elizabeth), 1920-**
Leading young children to music / B. Joan E. Haines, Linda L. Gerber. 6th ed. Upper Saddle River, NJ : Merrill, c2000. xvi, 300 p. : ill. ; 28 cm. Includes bibliographical references (p. 285-288) and indexes. ISBN 0-13-976275-2 DDC 372.87/044
*1. School music - Instruction and study. I. Gerber, Linda L. II. Title.*
**TC MT1 .H13 2000**

**Haines, Betty M.** Parchment : the physical and chemical characteristics of parchment and the materials used in its conservation / by Betty M. Haines. Northampton [England] : Leather Conservation Centre, 1999. 33 p. : ill. : 30 cm. Includes bibliographical reference (p. 33) ISBN 0-946072-05-1
*1. Parchment. 2. Parchment - Conservation and restoration. I. Title. II. Title: Physical and chemical characteristics of parchment and the materials used in its conservation*
**TC TS1165 .H35 1999**

**Haines, Dawn Denham.** Writing together : how to transform your writing in a writing group / Dawn Denham Haines, Susan Newcomer, Jacqueline Raphael. 1st ed. New York : Berkley Pub. Group, 1997. xv, 222 p. ; 21 cm. "A Perigee book." Includes bibliographical references (p. 203-214) and index. ISBN 0-399-52338-3 DDC 808/.02
*1. Authorship. I. Newcomer, Susan. II. Raphael, Jacqueline. III. Title.*
**TC PN145 .H28 1997**

**HAIR - FICTION.**
Hooks, Bell. Happy to be nappy. 1st ed. New York : Hyperion Books for Children, 1999.
**TC PZ7.H7663 Hap 1999**

Madrigal, Antonio Hernandez. Erandi's braids. New York : Putnam's, c1999.
**TC PZ7.M26575 Er 1999**

**HAITIAN AMERICAN TEENAGERS - NEW YORK (STATE) - NEW YORK - EDUCATION.**
Chrispin, Marie C. Resilient adaptation of church-affiliated young Haitian immigrants. 1998.
**TC 06 no. 11015**

**HAITIAN AMERICAN TEENAGERS - NEW YORK (STATE) - NEW YORK - ETHNIC IDENTITY.**
Chrispin, Marie C. Resilient adaptation of church-affiliated young Haitian immigrants. 1998.
**TC 06 no. 11015**

**HAITIAN AMERICAN TEENAGERS - NEW YORK (STATE) - NEW YORK - RELIGIOUS LIFE.**
Chrispin, Marie C. Resilient adaptation of church-affiliated young Haitian immigrants. 1998.
**TC 06 no. 11015**

**HAITIAN AMERICANS - EDUCATION (PRESCHOOL) - UNITED STATES - CASE STUDIES.**
Ballenger, Cynthia. Teaching other people's children. New York : Teachers College Press, c1999.
**TC LC3746 .B336 1999**

**HAITIAN AMERICANS - NEW YORK (STATE) - NEW YORK - CULTURAL ASSIMILATION.**
Chrispin, Marie C. Resilient adaptation of church-affiliated young Haitian immigrants. 1998.
**TC 06 no. 11015**

**HAITIAN AMERICANS - UNITED STATES. See HAITIAN AMERICANS.**

**Haitian students' perception of a school as a community of support.**
Dickerson, Pless Moore. 1998.
**TC 06 no. 11018**

Dickerson, Pless Moore. 1998.
**TC 06 no. 11018**

Dickerson, Pless Moore. 1998.
**TC 06 no. 11018**

**HAITIANS - NEW YORK (STATE) - WESTBURY.**
Dickerson, Pless Moore. Haitian students' perception of a school as a community of support. 1998.
**TC 06 no. 11018**

Dickerson, Pless Moore. Haitian students' perception of a school as a community of support. 1998.
**TC 06 no. 11018**

Dickerson, Pless Moore. Haitian students' perception of a school as a community of support. 1998.
**TC 06 no. 11018**

**HAITIANS - NEW YORK (STATE) - WESTBURY - CULTURAL ASSIMILATION.**

Dickerson, Pless Moore. Haitian students' perception of a school as a community of support. 1998.
**TC 06 no. 11018**

Dickerson, Pless Moore. Haitian students' perception of a school as a community of support. 1998.
**TC 06 no. 11018**

Dickerson, Pless Moore. Haitian students' perception of a school as a community of support. 1998.
**TC 06 no. 11018**

**HAITIANS - UNITED STATES. See HAITIAN AMERICANS.**

**Hakim, Simon.**
Restructuring education. Westport, Conn. : Praeger, 2000.
**TC LB2822.82 . R45 2000**

**Hakken, David.** Cyborgs@cyberspace? : an ethnographer looks at the future / David Hakken. New York : Routledge, 1999. xi, 264 p. ; 24 cm. Includes bibliographical references (p. [229]-244) and index. ISBN 0-415-91558-9 (hc. : alk. paper) ISBN 0-415-91559-7 (pbk. : alk. paper) DDC 303.48/34
*1. Computers and civilization. 2. Computers - Social aspects. 3. Cyberspace. I. Title. II. Title: Cyborgs at cyberspace?*
**TC QA76.9.C66 H34 1999**

**Haladyna, Thomas M.** A complete guide to student grading / Thomas M. Haladyna. Boston : Allyn and Bacon, c1999. xiii, 178 p. ; 24 cm. Includes bibliographical references (p. 171-175) and index. ISBN 0-205-27259-2 (alk. paper) DDC 371.27/2
*1. Grading and marking (Students) - United States - Handbooks, manuals, etc. 2. Educational tests and measurements - United States - Handbooks, manuals, etc. I. Title.*
**TC LB3051 .H296 1999**

**Halbert, Debora J. (Debora Jean)** Intellectual property in the information age : the politics of expanding ownership rights / Debora J. Halbert. Westport, Conn. : Quorum, 1999. xvii, 186 p. ; 24 cm. Includes bibliographical references (p. [165]-179) and index. ISBN 1-56720-254-3 (acid-free paper) DDC 346.7304/8
*1. Intellectual property - United States. 2. Information superhighway - Law and legislation - United States. I. Title.*
**TC KF2979 .H35 1999**

**Haldane, Suzanne, ill.**
Left Hand Bull, Jacqueline. Lakota hoop dancer. 1st ed. New York : Dutton Children's Books, c1999.
**TC E99.T34 L43 1999**

**Haley, Gail E.** A story, a story : an African tale / retold and illustrated by Gail E. Haley. 2nd Aladdin Books ed. New York : Aladdin Books, 1988, c1970. [36] p. : col. ill. ; 23 cm. SUMMARY: Recounts how most African folk tales came to be called "Spider Stories." ISBN 0-689-71201-4 (pbk.) DDC 398.2/096; v.1
*1. Folklore - Africa. I. Title.*
**TC PZ8.1.H139 St 1988**

**Hall, C. Margaret (Constance Margaret)** Heroic self : sociological dimensions of clinical practice / by C. Margaret Hall. Springfield, Ill. : C.C. Thomas, c1998. xiii, 153 p. : 26 cm. Includes bibliographical references (p. 135-142) and indexes. ISBN 0-398-06864-X (cloth) ISBN 0-398-06865-8 (paper) DDC 158
*1. Self-actualization (Psychology) - Social aspects. 2. Social participation. 3. Identity (Psychology) 4. Clinical sociology. I. Title.*
**TC RC489.S62 H35 1998**

**Hall, Christine, 1951-.**
Coles, Martin, 1952- Children's reading choices. London ; New York : Routledge, 1999.
**TC Z1037.A1 C59 1999**

**Hall, David D.**
The colonial book in the Atlantic world. Cambridge, U.K. ; New York : Cambridge University Press, 2000.
**TC Z473 .C686 1999**

**Hall, G. Stanley (Granville Stanley), 1844-1924.**
Educational problems, by G. Stanley Hall .. New York, London, D. Appleton and company, 1911. 2 v. diagrs. 25 cm. CONTENTS: v. 1. The pedagogy of the kindergarten. The educational value of dancing and pantomime. The pedagogy of music. The religious training of children and the Sunday-school. Moral education. Children's lies: their psychology and pedagogy. The pedagogy of sex. Industrial education.--v. 2. The budding girl. Missionary pedagogy. Special child-welfare agencies outside the school. Preventive and constructive movements. Sunday observance. The German teacher teaches. Pedagogy of modern languages. Pedagogy of history. Pedagogy and the press. The pedagogy of elementary mathematics. Pedagogy of reading: how and what? Pedagogy of drawing. School geography. Some defects of our public schools. The American high school. Civic education.

DDC 370.4/H14
1. Education. I. Title.
TC 370.4/H14

**Hall, James C., 1960-.**
Approaches to teaching Narrative of the life of Frederick Douglass. New York : Modern Language Association of America, 1999.
TC E449.D75 A66 1999

**Hall, Joan Kelly.**
The sociopolitics of English language teaching. Clevedon ; Buffalo [N.Y.] : Multilingual Matters, c2000.
TC PE1128.A2 S5994 2000

**Hall, Jody S.** Organizing wonder : making inquiry science work in the elementary school / Jody S. Hall with Carol Callahan ... [et al.]. Portsmouth, NH : Heinemann, c1998. xvii, 110 p. : ill. ; 23 cm. Includes bibliographical references (p. 107-110). ISBN 0-325-00045-X (alk. paper) DDC 372.3/5/044
1. Science - Study and teaching (Elementary) - United States. I. Title.
TC LB1585.3 .H35 1998

**Hall, John.**
Decimals [videorecording]. Princeton, N.J. : Video Tutor, 1988.
TC QA117 .D4 1988

Fractions [videorecording]. Princeton, N.J. : Video Tutor, 1988.
TC QA117 .F7 1988

The high school proficiency test [videorecording]. Princeton, N.J. : Video Tutor, 1988.
TC QA445 .H5 1988

Number concepts [videorecording]. Princeton, N.J. : Video Tutor, 1988.
TC QA117 .N8 1988

Number concepts [videorecording]. Princeton, N.J. : Video Tutor, 1988.
TC QA117 .N8 1988

Percents [videorecording]. Princeton, N.J. : Video Tutor, 1988.
TC QA117.P4 1988

Pre-algebra [videorecording]. Princeton, N.J. : Video Tutor, 1988.
TC QA152.2 .P6 1988

Word problems [videorecording]. Princeton, N.J. : Video Tutor, 1988.
TC QA139 .W6 1988

**Hall, John A., 1949-** Is America breaking apart? / John A. Hall and Charles Lindholm. Princeton, NJ : Princeton University Press, c1999. xi, 162 p. ; 23 cm. Includes bibliographical references and index. ISBN 0-691-00410-2 (cl : alk. paper) DDC 306/.0973
1. United States - Social conditions - 1980- 2. Social values - United States. 3. National characteristics, American. 4. Sociology - United States. 5. United States - Politics and government - Philosophy. I. Lindholm, Charles, 1946- II. Title.
TC HN59.2 .H34 1999

**Hall, Kim Q., 1965-.**
Whiteness. Lanham, [Md.] : Rowman & Littlefield, c1999.
TC E184.A1 W399 1999

**Hall, Louis O.** Strategies for teaching : guide for music methods classes / compiled and edited by Louis O. Hall ... [et al.]. Reston, VA : Music Educators National Conference, c1997. v, 229 p. ; 28 cm. (Strategies for teaching) Lessons and resources for teaching general and choral music in grades K-12, and instrumental music in grades 5-12. "Your key to implementing the national standards for music education." Includes bibliographical references.
1. School music - Instruction and study - United States. I. Music Educators National Conference (U.S.) II. Title. III. Title: Guide for music methods classes IV. Series: MENC's strategies for teaching series.
TC MT1.H136 S77 1997

**Hall-Martin, Anthony.** Cats of Africa / text by Anthony Hall-Martin ; paintings and drawings by Paul Bosman. Washington, D.C. : Smithsonian Institution Press, 1998. 152 p. : ill. (some col.), maps (some col.) ; 29 cm. Includes bibliographical references (p. 146-147) and index. ISBN 1-56098-760-X DDC 599.75/096
1. Felidae - Africa. 2. Felidae - Africa - Pictorial works. I. Bosman, Paul. II. Title.
TC QL737.C23 H335 1997

**Hall, Perry A., 1947-** In the vineyard : working in African American studies / Perry A. Hall. 1st ed. Knoxville : University of Tennessee Press, c1999. xii,

247 p. ; 25 cm. Includes bibliographical references (p. [231]-237) and index. CONTENTS: Struggle outward: barricades and ivory towers -- Struggle inward: whither, then, and how? -- Afrocentrism: more or less -- Alternative approaches in African American studies -- Systematic and thematic principles -- Conceptualizing Black identity -- The songs of Black folks -- Crisis, culture, and literacy in the community. ISBN 1-57233-054-6 (alk. paper) DDC 305.896073/071
1. Afro-Americans - Study and teaching - History - 20th century. 2. Afro-Americans - Historiography. I. Title.
TC E184.7 .H24 1999

**Hallensleben, Georg.** Pauline / Georg Hallensleben. New York : Farrar, Straus & Giroux, c1999. 1 v. (unpaged) : col. ill. ; 31 cm. 1st ed. "Frances Foster books." SUMMARY: Pauline the weasel has an imaginative plan to rescue her elephant friend who has been trapped by hunters. ISBN 0-374-35758-7 DDC [E]
1. Weasels - Fiction. 2. Elephants - Fiction. 3. Friendship - Fiction. I. Title.
TC PZ7.H15425 Pau 1999

**Hallinan, Maureen T.**
Handbook of the sociology of education. New York : Kluwer Academic/Plenum, c2000.
TC LC191 .H254 2000

**Halliwell, Martin.** Romantic science and the experience of self : transatlantic crosscurrents from William James to Oliver Sacks / Martin Halliwell. Aldershot, Hants : Brookfield, Vt. : Ashgate, c1999. viii, 283 p. ; 24 cm. (Studies in European cultural transition ; v. 2) Includes bibliographical references (p. [259]-276) and index. ISBN 1-84014-626-5 (hc.) DDC 150/.9
1. Self - History - 20th century. 2. Psychology - History - 20th century. 3. Romanticism - Influence. I. Title. II. Series.
TC BF697 R6375 1999

**HALLOW-EVE.** *See* HALLOWEEN.

**HALLOWEEN - JUVENILE POETRY.**
Hubbell, Patricia. Boo!. 1st ed. New York : Marshall Cavendish, 1998.
TC PS3558.U22 B66 1998

**Halloween poems and limericks.**
Hubbell, Patricia. Boo!. 1st ed. New York : Marshall Cavendish, 1998.
TC PS3558.U22 B66 1998

**HALLUCINATIONS AND ILLUSIONS.** *See also* DELUSIONS.
Schizophrenia and delusional disorders [videorecording]. Princeton, N.J. : Films for the Humanities & Sciences, c1998.
TC RC514 .S3 1998

**Halperin, Jane Carol.** The influence of causal attributions on the psychological adjustment of post-treatment adolescent cancer survivors / Jane Carol Halperin. 1999. v, 124 leaves ; 29 cm. Thesis (Ph. D.)--Columbia University, 1999. Includes bibliographical references (leaves 77-87). Issued also on microfilm. Includes tables.
1. Causation. 2. Attribution (Social psychology) 3. Cancer - Patients - Rehabilitation. 4. Adjustment (Psychology) 5. Social desirability in adolescence - Testing. 6. Control (Psychology) I. Title.
TC 085 H155

**Halperin, Wendy Anderson, ill.**
Aylesworth, Jim. The full belly bowl. 1st ed. New York : Atheneum Books for Young Readers, c1998.
TC PZ8.A95 Fu 1998

**Halpern, Diane F.** Sex differences in cognitive abilities / Diane F. Halpern. 3rd ed. Mahwah, N.J. : L. Erlbaum Associates, 2000. xviii, 420 p. ; ill ; 24 cm. Includes bibliographical references (p. 335-376) and indexes. ISBN 0-8058-2791-9 (hardcover : alk. paper) ISBN 0-8058-2792-7 (pbk. : alk. paper) DDC 155.3/3
1. Cognition. 2. Sex differences (Psychology) 3. Sex role. I. Title.
TC BF311 .H295 2000

**Halpern, John, 1957- ill.**
Tropea, Judith. A day in the life of a museum curator. Mahwah, N.J. : Troll Associates, c1991.
TC QE22.E53 T76 1991

**Halwell, Brian.**
Brown, Lester Russell, 1934- Vital signs 2000 :. New York : Norton, c2000.
TC HD75.6 .B768 2000

**Ham, Christopher.**
The global challenge of health care rationing. Buckingham [England] ; Philadelphia : Open University Press, 2000.
TC RA394.9 .G56 2000

**Hamdan, Laureen.**
Hawkins, Robert P., 1931- Measuring behavioral

health outcomes. New York : Kluwer Academic/Plenum Publishers, c1999.
TC RJ503.5 .H39 1999

**Hamernyck, Leo A., 1929-.**
Banff International Conference on Behavior Modification, 4th, 1972. Behavior change. Champaign, Ill. : Research Press, 1974, c1973.
TC BF637.B4 B354 1972

**Hameroff, Stuart R.**
Toward a science of consciousness III. Cambridge, Mass. : MIT Press, c1999.
TC BF311 .T67 1999

**Hamers, J. H. M. (Jo H. M.), 1945-.**
Teaching and learning thinking skills. Lisse [Netherlands] ; Exton, PA : Swets & Zeitlinger, c1999.
TC LB1590.3 .T36 1999

**Hamers, Josiane F.** Bilinguality and bilingualism / Josiane F. Hamers and Michel H.A. Blanc. 2nd ed. Cambridge, England ; New York, NY : Cambridge University Press, 2000. xiv, 468 p. : ill. ; 24 cm. Includes bibliographical references (p. 377-432) and indexes. ISBN 0-521-64049-0 (hb) ISBN 0-521-64843-2 (pb) DDC 404/.2
1. Bilingualism. I. Blanc, Michel, sociolinguiste. II. Title.
TC P115 .H3613 2000

**Hamill, Pete, 1935-** Diego Rivera / Pete Hamill. New York : Harry N. Abrams, 1999. 208 p. : ill. (some col.), ports. ; 26 cm. Includes bibliographical references (p. 204-205) and index. ISBN 0-8109-3234-2 DDC 759.972
1. Rivera, Diego, - 1886-1957. 2. Painters - Mexico - Biography. I. Title.
TC ND259.R5 H28 1999

**Hamilton, Carole L., 1951-.**
Short stories in the classroom. Urbana, Ill. : National Council of Teachers of English, c1999.
TC PS374.S5 S48 1999

**Hamilton, Mary, 1949-.**
Situated literacies. London ; New York : Routledge, 2000.
TC LC149 .S52 2000

**Hamm, Mary.**
Adams, Dennis M. Media and literacy. 2nd ed. Springfield, Ill. : C.C. Thomas, c2000.
TC LB1043 .A33 2000

**Hammersley, Martyn.**
Researching school experience. London ; New York : Falmer Press, 1999.
TC LB1027 .R453 1999

Taking sides in social research : essays on partisanship and bias / Martyn Hammersley. London ; New York : Routledge, 2000. 196 p. : ill. ; 24 cm. Includes bibliographical references (p. [167]-184) and index. ISBN 0-415-20286-8 (hbk.) ISBN 0-415-20287-6 (pbk.) DDC 300/.7/2
1. Social sciences - Research. 2. Social sciences - Methodology. 3. Values. I. Title.
TC H62 .H2338 2000

**Hammond, Kenneth R.**
Judgment and decision making. 2nd ed. Cambridge, U.K. ; New York, NY : Cambridge University Press, 2000.
TC BF441 .J79 2000

Judgments under stress / Kenneth R. Hammond. New York : Oxford University Press, 2000. xii, 242 p. ; 24 cm. Includes index. Bibliography: 218-233. ISBN 0-19-513143-6 DDC 153.8/3
1. Decision making. 2. Judgment. 3. Stress (Psychology) I. Title.
TC BF441 .H27 2000

**Hammonds, Evelynn Maxine.** Childhood's deadly scourge : the campaign a control diphtheria in New York City, 1880-1930 / Evelynn Maxine Hammonds. Baltimore, Md. : Johns Hopkins University Press, c1999. ix, 299 p. : map ; 24 cm. Includes bibliographical references (p. [229]-288) and index. ISBN 0-8018-5978-6 (alk. paper) DDC 614.5/123/097471
1. Diphtheria - New York (State) - New York - History - 19th century. 2. Diphtheria - New York (State) - New York - History - 20th century. I. Title.
TC RA644.D6 H36 1999

**Hamner, Candace J.**
Chamberlain, Kathryn A. The JCAHO mock survey made simple. 1998 ed. Marblehead, MA : Opus Communications, c1998.
TC RA981.A2 C45 1999

**Hampton Press communication series**
Organizational communication and change. Cresskill, N.J. : Hampton Press, 1999.

*TC HD30.3 .O722 1999*

**The Hampton Press communication series. Political communication**
Gender, politics and communication. Cresskill, N.J. : Hampton Press, c2000.
*TC P94.5.W65 G46 2000*

Harvey, Kerric. Eden online. Cresskill, N.J. : Hampton Press, c2000.
*TC T14.5 .H367 2000*

**Hamtramck (Mich.). Board of Education.**
Hamtramck public school bulletin. Hamtramck, Mich. : Board of Education,

**Hamtramck public school bulletin.** Hamtramck, Mich. : Board of Education, v. : ill. ; 22 cm. Frequency: Monthly (except July and Aug.). Description based on: Vol. 3, no. 1 (Sept. 1929); title from cover.
*1. Public schools - Michigan - Hamtramck - Periodicals. 2. Education - Michigan - Hamtramck - Periodicals. 3. Education - Periodicals. I. Hamtramck (Mich.). Board of Education.*

**Hancock, Joelie.**
The explicit teaching of reading. Newark, Del. : International Reading Association, c1999.
*TC LB1573 .E96 1999*

**Hancock, Marjorie R.** A celebration of literature and response : children, books, and teachers in K-8 classrooms / Marjorie R. Hancock. Upper Saddle River, N.J. : Merrill, c2000. xviii, 430 p. : ill. ; 24 cm. Includes bibliographical references and indexes. ISBN 0-13-740291-0 DDC 372.64/044
*1. Children's literature - Study and teaching (Elementary) 2. Reader-response criticism. 3. Children - Books and reading. I. Title.*
*TC LB1575 .H36 2000*

**Hancock, Peter J. B., 1958-.**
Information theory and the brain. Cambridge [England] ; New York : Cambridge University Press, 2000.
*TC QP363.3 .I54 2000*

**Hancock, Ralph C., 1951-.**
America, the West, and liberal education. Lanham, Md. : Rowman & Littlefield, c1999.
*TC LC1023 .A44 1999*

**HAND BELL RINGING.** *See* **HANDBELL RINGING.**

**Hand in hand :** essentials of communication and orientation and mobility for your students who are deaf-blind : a trainer's manual / Jeanne Glidden Prickett ... [et al.]. New York : AFB Press, c1995. x, 134 p. 28 cm. ISBN 0-89128-940-2 (pbk.) DDC 371.91/1
*1. Blind-deaf children - Study and teaching. 2. Blind-deaf children - Orientation and mobility. 3. Blind-deaf children - Means of communication. 4. Teachers of the blind-deaf - Training of. I. Prickett, Jeanne Glidden.*
*TC HV1597.2 .H342 1995*

**Hand in hand :** essentials of communication and orientation and mobility for your students who are deaf-blind / Kathleen Mary Heubner ... [et al.] editors. New York : AFB Press, c1995. 2v. : ill, 28 cm. Includes bibliographical references and index. ISBN 0-89128-937-2 (set : pbk.) DDC 371.91/1
*1. Blind-deaf children - Study and teaching. 2. Blind-deaf children - Orientation and mobility. 3. Blind-deaf children - Means of communication. 4. Teachers of the blind-deaf - Training of. I. Heubner, Kathleen Mary.*
*TC HV1597.2 .H34 1995*

**Hand in hand :** teacher's planning guide. New York : Macmillan/McGraw-Hill, c1997. 1 v. (various pagings) : col. ill. ; 31 cm. (Spotlight on literacy ; Gr.2 l.7 u.2) (The road to independent reading) Includes index. ISBN 0-02-181162-8
*1. Language arts (Primary) 2. Reading (Primary) I. Series. II. Series: The road to independent reading*
*TC LB1576 .S66 1997 Gr.2 l.7 u.2*

**Hand in hand** [videorecording] : it can be done! / AFB Deaf-Blind Project, Video Development Staff ; producer, Janice Reynolds ; director/editor, Kim Schneider. New York, N.Y. : AFB Press, c1995. 1 videocassette (68 min.) : sd., col. ; 1/2 in. + 1 discussion guide (27 p. ; 21 cm.). At head of title: American Foundation for the Blind presents ... VHS. Catalogued from credits and container and cassette label. Closed-captioned for the hearing impaired. Narrator, Jack Jones. Project director, Kathleen Mary Huebner. For those who work with visually impaired, hearing impaired and multiply disabled children. SUMMARY: An instructive film for those working with the visually impaired, the hearing impaired, those with multiple handicaps-- parents, teachers, administrators, counselors, special education students, etc. It features many deaf-blind people, their families and teachers. CONTENTS: Section 1. Learn from your students -- Section 2. Every child is a communicator -- Section 3. No turning back -- Section 4. It can be done. ISBN 0-89128-281-5
*1. Blind-deaf children - Education. 2. Blind-deaf children - Rehabilitation. 3. Blind-deaf children - Psychology. 4. Blind-deaf children - Language. 5. Children, Blind - Education. 6. Children, Blind - Rehabilitation. 7. Children, Blind - Psychology. 8. Children, Blind - Language. 9. Children, Deaf - Education. 10. Children, Deaf - Rehabilitation. 11. Children, Deaf - Psychology. 12. Children, Deaf - Language. 13. Handicapped children - Education. 14. Handicapped children - Rehabilitation. 15. Handicapped children - Psychology. 16. Handicapped children - Language. 17. Special education. 18. Special education - Parent participation. 19. Video recordings for the hearing impaired. I. Jones, Jack. II. Reynolds, Janice. III. Schneider, Kim. IV. American Foundation for the Blind. V. AFB Deaf-Blind Project. Video Development Staff. VI. AFB Press. VII. Title: It can be done! [videorecording] VIII. Title: American Foundation for the Blind presents ...*
*TC HV1597.2 .H3 1995*

**HAND WEAVING.**
Alexander, Marthann. Weaving on cardboard; New York, Taplinger Pub. Co. [1972]
*TC TT848 .A67*

Alexander, Marthann. Weaving on cardboard; New York, Taplinger Pub. Co. [1972]
*TC TT848 .A67*

**HAND WEAVING - BIBLIOGRAPHY.**
Buschman, Isabel, 1927- Handweaving. Metuchen, N.J. : Scarecrow Press, 1991.
*TC Z6153.T4 B87 1991*

**HAND WEAVING - FICTION.**
Blood, Charles L., 1929- The goat in the rug. New York : Four Winds Press, 1976.
*TC PZ7.B6227 Go 1976*

**HANDBELL RINGING - STANDARDS.**
McBride, Michael B. Meeting the national standards with handbells and handchimes. Lanham, MD : Scarecrow Press, 2000.
*TC MT711 .M35 2000*

**HANDBELLS.** *See* **HANDCHIMES.**

**HANDBELLS - INSTRUCTION AND STUDY.**
McBride, Michael B. Meeting the national standards with handbells and handchimes. Lanham, MD : Scarecrow Press, 2000.
*TC MT711 .M35 2000*

**Handbook for assessing critical issues with students.**
Deuschle, C. (Constance) Stop the bus. Lanham, Md. : University Press of America, c2000.
*TC LB1027.5 .D4567 2000*

**A handbook for enhancing the multicultural climate of the school.**
Kehoe, John W. [Vancouver, B.C.] : Western Education Development Group, Faculty of Education, University of British Colombia, c1984.
*TC LC1099 .K438 1984*

**A handbook for learning support assistants.**
Fox, Glenys. London : D. Fulton Publishers, 1998.
*TC LB2844.1.A8 F68 1998*

**Handbook for literacy tutors.**
Adams, Arlene. Springfield, Ill. : C.C. Thomas, Publisher, c1999.
*TC LB1576 .A3893 1999*

**A handbook for teaching and learning in higher education :** enhancing academic practice / [editors] Heather Fry, Steve Ketteridge, Stephanie Marshall. London : Kogan Page, 1999. viii, 408 p. ; 25 cm. Includes bibliographical references and index. ISBN 0-7494-2948-8
*1. College teaching - Handbooks, manuals, etc. 2. College teachers. 3. Lecture method in teaching. I. Fry, Heather. II. Ketteridge, Steve. III. Marshall, Stephanie.*
*TC LB2331 .H29 1999*

**Handbook for teaching statistics and research methods** / edited by Mark E. Ware, Charles L. Brewer. 2nd ed. Mahwah, N.J. : Lawrence Erlbaum Associates, c1999. viii, 287 p. ; 28 cm. Includes bibliographical references and indexes. ISBN 0-8058-3049-9 (pbk. : alk. paper) DDC 001.4/2
*1. Statistics - Study and teaching. 2. Research - Study and teaching. I. Ware, Mark E. II. Brewer, Charles L.*
*TC QA276.18 .H36 1999*

**Handbook of assessment in clinical gerontology** / edited by Peter A. Lichtenberg. New York : Wiley, 1999. ix, 662 p. : ill. ; 26 cm. (Wiley series on adulthood and aging) Includes bibliographic references and indexes. ISBN 0-471-28300-2 (cloth : alk. paper) DDC 618.97/689075
*1. Geriatric psychiatry - Handbooks, manuals, etc. 2. Aged - Psychological testing - Handbooks, manuals, etc. 3. Psychodiagnostics - Handbooks, manuals, etc. I. Lichtenberg, Peter A. II. Series.*
*TC RC451.4.A5 H358 1999*

**Handbook of attachment interventions.**
Levy, Terry M. San Diego, Calif. : Academic, c2000.
*TC RJ507.A77 L47 2000*

**Handbook of clinical nursing research** / editors, Ada Sue Hinshaw, Suzanne L. Feetham, Joan L.F. Shaver. Thousand Oaks, Calif. : Sage Publications, c1999. xvi, 696 p. : ill. ; 29 cm. Includes bibliographical references and index. ISBN 0-8039-5784-X (acid-free paper) DDC 610.73/072
*1. Nursing - Research - Handbooks, manuals, etc. I. Hinshaw, Ada Sue. II. Feetham, Suzanne. III. Shaver, Joan.*
*TC RT81.5 .H25 1999*

**Handbook of college reading and study strategy research** / edited by Rona F. Flippo, David C. Caverly. Mahwah, N.J. : Lawrence Erlbaum Associates, c2000. xx, 509 p. : ill. ; 27 cm. Includes bibliographical references (p. 460-472) and indexes. ISBN 0-8058-3003-0 (cloth : alk. paper) ISBN 0-8058-3004-9 (paper : alk. paper) DDC 428.4/071/1
*1. Reading (Higher education) - United States - Handbooks, manuals, etc. 2. Study skills - United States - Handbooks, manuals, etc. I. Flippo, Rona F. II. Caverly, David C.*
*TC LB2395.3 .H36 2000*

**Handbook of community psychology** / edited by Julian Rappaport and Edward Seidman. New York ; London : Kluwer Academic/Plenum, c2000. xxi, 1011 p. : ill. ; 26 cm. Includes bibliographical references and index. ISBN 0-306-46160-9 DDC 362.2
*1. Community psychology - Handbooks, manuals, etc. I. Rappaport, Julian. II. Seidman, Edward.*
*TC RA790.55 .H36 2000*

**Handbook of contemporary learning theories** / edited by Robert R. Mowrer, Stephen B. Klein. Mahwah, N.J. ; London : Lawrence Erlbaum Associates, 2001. x, 622 p. : ill. ; 24 cm. Includes bibliographical references and indexes. ISBN 0-8058-3334-X (cloth : alk. paper) DDC 370.15/23
*1. Learning. 2. Learning, Psychology of. 3. Cognition. I. Mowrer, Robert R., 1956- II. Klein, Stephen B. III. Title: Contemporary learning theories*
*TC LB1060 .H3457 2001*

**Handbook of counseling and psychotherapy with lesbian, gay, and bisexual clients** / [edited by] Ruperto M. Perez, Kurt A. DeBord, Kathleen J. Bieschke. 1st ed. Washington, DC ; London : American Psychological Association, c2000. xvi, 484 p. ; 27 cm. Includes bibliographical references and indexes. ISBN 1-55798-610-X (alk. paper) DDC 158/.3/0866
*1. Counseling. 2. Psychotherapy. 3. Lesbians - Counseling of. 4. Gays - Counseling of. 5. Bisexuals - Counseling of. I. Perez, Ruperto M. II. DeBord, Kurt A. III. Bieschke, Kathleen J. IV. Title: Counseling and psychotherapy with lesbian, gay, and bisexual clients*
*TC BF637.C6 H3125 2000*

**Handbook of counseling psychology** / edited by Steven D. Brown, Robert W. Lent. 3rd ed. New York : J. Wiley, c2000. xiii, 865 p. : ill. ; 28 cm. Includes bibliographical references and indexes. ISBN 0-471-25458-4 (alk. paper) DDC 158/.3
*1. Counseling. 2. Psychology, Applied. I. Brown, Steven D. (Steven Douglas), 1947- II. Lent, Robert W. (Robert William), 1953-*
*TC BF637.C6 H315 2000*

**Handbook of creativity** / edited by Robert J. Sternberg. Cambridge, U.K. ; New York : Cambridge University Press, 1999. ix, 490 p. : ill. ; 25 cm. Includes bibliographical references and indexes. ISBN 0-521-57285-1 ISBN 0-521-57604-0 (pbk.) DDC 153.3/5
*1. Creative ability. 2. Creative thinking. I. Sternberg, Robert J.*
*TC BF408 .H285 1999*

**Handbook of cross-cultural and multicultural personality assessment** / edited by Richard H. Dana. Mahwah, N.J. ; London : Lawrence Erlbaum Associates, 2000. xviii, 719 p. : ill. ; 24 cm. (The LEA series in personality and clinical psychology) Includes bibliographical references and indexes. ISBN 0-8058-2789-7 (cloth : alk. paper) DDC 616.89/075/089
*1. Minorities - Psychological testing. 2. Personality assessment. 3. Ethnopsychology. I. Dana, Richard H. (Richard Henry), 1927- II. Series.*
*TC RC473.P79 H36 2000*

**Handbook of cross-cultural psychology.** 2nd ed. Boston : Allyn and Bacon, c1997. 3 v. : ill. ; 24 cm. Includes bibliographical references and indexes. CONTENTS: v. 1. Theory and method / edited by John W. Berry, Ype H. Poortinga, Janak Pandey -- v. 2. Basic processes and human development / edited by John W. Berry, Pierre R. Dasen, T.S. Saraswathi -- v. 3. Social behavior and applications / edited by John W. Berry, Marshall H. Segall, Cigdem Kagitçibasi. ISBN 0-205-16074-3 (v. 1) ISBN 0-205-16075-1 (v. 2) ISBN 0-205-

16076-x (V. 3) DDC 155.82
1. Ethnopsychology. I. Berry, John W. II. Poortinga, Ype H., 1939- III. Pandey, Janak, 1945-
**TC GN502 .H36 1997**

**Handbook of demonstrations and activities in the teaching of psychology** / edited by Mark E. Ware, David E. Johnson. 2nd ed. Mahwah, N.J. : Lawrence Erlbaum Associates, c2000. 3 v. : ill. ; 28 cm. Includes bibliographical references and indexes. CONTENTS: v. 1. Introductory, statistics, research methods, and history -- v. 2. Physiological-comparative, perception, learning, cognitive, and developmental -- v. 3. Personality, abnormal, clinical-counseling, and social. ISBN 0-8058-3048-0 (set : alk. paper) ISBN 0-8058-3045-6 (v. 1 : alk. paper) ISBN 0-8058-3046-4 (v. 2 : alk. paper) ISBN 0-8058-3047-2 (v. 3 : alk. paper) DDC 150/.71/1
1. Psychology - Study and teaching (Higher) 2. Psychology - Study and teaching - Activity programs. 3. Psychology - Study and teaching - Simulation methods. 4. Psychology - Study and teaching - Audio-visual methods. I. Ware, Mark E. II. Johnson, David E., 1953-
**TC BF77 .H265 2000**

**A handbook of diction for singers.**
Adams, David, 1950- New York : Oxford University Press, 1999.
**TC MT883 .A23 1999**

**Handbook of emerging communications technologies.**
Osso, Rafael. Boca Raton, Fla. : CRC Press, 2000.
**TC TK5105 .O62 2000**

**The handbook of emotional intelligence** : theory, development, assessment, and application at home, school, and in the workplace / Reuven Bar-On, James D.A. Parker, editors. 1st ed. San Francisco, Calif. : Jossey-Bass, c2000. xv, 528 p. : ill. ; 25 cm. Includes bibliographical references and indexes. ISBN 0-7879-4984-1 (hardcover : alk. paper) DDC 152.4
1. Emotional intelligence. 2. Emotional intelligence tests. I. Bar-On, Reuven, 1944- II. Parker, James D. A. (James Donald Alexander), 1959-
**TC BF576 .H36 2000**

**Handbook of emotions** / edited by Michael Lewis, Jeannette M. Haviland-Jones. 2nd ed. New York : Guilford Press, c2000. xvi, 720 p. : ill. ; 26 cm. Includes bibliographical references and indexes. ISBN 1-57230-529-0 (hardcover : alk. paper) DDC 152.4
1. Emotions. 2. Emotions - Sociological aspects. I. Lewis, Michael, 1937 Jan. 10- II. Haviland-Jones, Jeannette M.
**TC BF561 .H35 2000**

**Handbook of family development and intervention** / edited by William C. Nichols ... [et al.]. New York : Wiley, c2000. xxii, 482 p. : ill. ; 26 cm. (Wiley series in couples and family dynamics and treatment) Includes bibliographical references and index. ISBN 0-471-29967-7 (cloth) DDC 616.89/156
1. Family psychotherapy - Handbooks, manuals, etc. 2. Family - Psychological aspects - Handbooks, manuals, etc. 3. Family counseling - Handbooks, manuals, etc. I. Nichols, William C. II. Series.
**TC RC489.F33 .H36 2000**

**Handbook of gender & work** / Gary N. Powell, editor. Thousand Oaks, CA : Sage Publications, Inc., c1999. xx, 651 p. : ill. ; 26 cm. Includes bibliographical references (p. 495-596) and indexes. ISBN 0-7619-1355-6 (alk. paper) DDC 306.3/615
1. Leadership in women. 2. Women executives. 3. Sex role in the work environment. 4. Leadership. 5. Women - Employment. I. Powell, Gary N. II. Title: Handbook of gender and work III. Title: Gender & work IV. Title: Gender and work
**TC HQ1233 .H33 1999**

**Handbook of gender and work.**
Handbook of gender & work. Thousand Oaks, CA : Sage Publications, Inc., c1999.
**TC HQ1233 .H33 1999**

**Handbook of health promotion and disease prevention** / edited by James M. Raczynski and Ralph J. DiClemente. New York : Kluwer Academic/ Plenum Publishers, c1999. xvi, 669 p. : ill. ; 26 cm. (The Plenum series in behavioral psychophysiology and medicine) Includes bibliographical references and index. ISBN 0-306-46140-4 DDC 613
1. Health promotion - Handbooks, manuals, etc. 2. Medicine, Preventive - Handbooks, manuals, etc. 3. Preventive Medicine. 4. Health Promotion. I. Raczynski, James M. II. DiClemente, Ralph J. III. Series.
**TC RA427.8 .H36 1999**

**Handbook of HIV prevention** / edited by John L. Peterson and Ralph J. DiClemente. New York : Kluwer/Plenum, 2000. xvi, 337 p. ; 26 cm. (AIDS prevention and mental health) Includes bibliographical references and index. ISBN 0-306-46223-0 DDC 616.97/9205

1. AIDS (Disease) - Prevention - Handbooks, manuals, etc. I. Peterson, John L. II. DiClemente, Ralph J. III. Series.
**TC RA644.A25 H365 2000**

**Handbook of hope** : theory, measures, & applications / editor, C.R. Snyder. San Diego, Calif. : Academic, 2000. xxv, 440 p. : ill. ; 24 cm. Includes bibliographical references and indexes. ISBN 0-12-654050-0
1. Hope. 2. Despair. I. Snyder, C. R. (Charles Richard)
**TC BF575.H56 H36 2000**

**Handbook of human resource management.**
The IEBM handbook of human resource management. 1st ed. London : Boston : International Thomson Business Press, 1998.
**TC HF5549.17 .I33 1998**

**Handbook of hypnotic inductions.**
Gafner, George, 1947- New York : W. W. Norton, 2000.
**TC RC495 .G27 2000**

**Handbook of infant mental health** / World Association for Infant Mental Health ; Joy D. Osofsky and Hiram E. Fitzgerald, editors. New York : Wiley, c2000. 4 v. : ill. ; 26 cm. Cover title: WAIMH handbook of infant mental health. Includes bibliographical references and indexes. At head of title: WAIMH. CONTENTS: v. 1. Perspectives of infant mental health -- v. 2. Early intervention, evaluation, and assessment -- v. 3. Parenting and child care -- v. 4. Infant mental health in groups at high risk. ISBN 0-471-18988-X (set : alk. paper) ISBN 0-471-18941-3 (v. 1 : cloth : alk. paper) ISBN 0-471-18944-8 (v. 2 : cloth : alk. paper) ISBN 0-471-18946-4 (v. 3 : cloth : alk. paper) ISBN 0-471-18947-2 (v. 4 : cloth : alk. paper) DDC 618.92/89
1. Infants - Mental health - Handbooks, manuals, etc. 2. Infant psychiatry - Handbooks, manuals, etc. 3. Child psychopathology - Prevention - Hanbooks, manuals, etc. 4. Child Development. 5. Infant. 6. Child Psychology. 7. Parenting. 8. Early Intervention (Education) 9. Developmental Disabilities - prevention & control. I. Osofsky, Joy D. II. Fitzgerald, Hiram E. III. World Association for Infant Mental Health. IV. Title: WAIMH handbook of infant mental health
**TC RJ502.5 .H362 2000**

**Handbook of intelligence** / edited by Robert J. Sternberg. Cambridge ; New York : Cambridge University Press, 2000. xiii, 677 p. ; 26 cm. Includes indexes. ISBN 0-521-59371-9 (hardcover) ISBN 0-521-59648-3 (pbk.) DDC 153.9
1. Intellect. 2. Intelligence levels. 3. Intelligence tests. 4. Psychology, Comparative. I. Sternberg, Robert J.
**TC BF431 .H31865 2000**

**Handbook of language & ethnic identity** / edited by Joshua A. Fishman. New York : Oxford University Press, 1999. xii, 468 p. : maps ; 24 cm. Includes bibliographical references and index. ISBN 0-19-512428-6 DDC 306.44/089
1. Language and culture - Handbooks, manuals, etc. 2. Ethnicity - Handbooks, manuals, etc. 3. Areal linguistics - Handbooks, manuals, etc. I. Fishman, Joshua A. II. Title: Handbook of language and ethnic identity
**TC P35 .H34 1999**

**Handbook of language and ethnic identity.**
Handbook of language & ethnic identity. New York : Oxford University Press, 1999.
**TC P35 .H34 1999**

**Handbook of multicultural mental health** : : assessment and treatment of diverse populations / edited by Israel Cuéllar, Freddy A. Paniagua. San Diego : Academic Press, c2000. xxx, 486 p. : ill. ; 24 cm. Includes bibliographical references and index. CONTENTS: Overview theory, models, and demographics -- Culture and mental health: an introduction and overview of foundations, concepts, and issues -- Cultural models of health and illness -- Acculturation and mental health: ecological transactional relations of adjustment -- Gender as subculture: the first division of multicultural diversity -- Multicultural demographic developments: current and future trends -- Methodology -- Culture and methodology in personality assessment -- Test translation and cultural equivalence methodologies for use with diverse populations -- Assessment and treatment -- Culture-bound syndromes, cultural variations, and psychopathology -- Assessing and treating Asian Americans: recent advances -- Mental health assessment and treatment of African Americans: a multicultural perspective -- Assessing and treating Latinos: overview of research -- Assessing and treating American Indians and Alaska natives -- Multicultural issues in treating clients with HIV/AIDS from the African American, American Indian, Asian, and Hispanic populations -- History: current status, and future of multicultural psychotherapy -- Conducting the cross-cultural clinical interview -- Mental health of culturally diverse elderly: research and clinical issues -- Race, ethnicity, and the epidemiology of mental disorders in adults -- Depression and suicidal behaviors among adolescents: the role of ethnicity -- Culturally competent use of CONTENTS: the Minnesota multiphasic personality inventory-2 with

minorities -- Neuropsychological assessment of ethnic minorities: clinical issues -- Training in cultural competence -- Limitations of the multicultural approach to psychotherapy with diverse clients -- Responding to the challenge: preparing mental health professionals for the new Millennium. ISBN 0-12-199370-1
1. Psychiatry, Transcultural - United States. 2. Cultural psychiatry. 3. Ethnopsychology. I. Cuéllar, Israel. II. Paniagua, Freddy A. III. Title: Multicultural mental health.
**TC RC455.4 .H36 2000**

**Handbook of nonprofit leadership and management.**
The Jossey-Bass handbook of nonprofit leadership and management. 1st ed. San Francisco : Jossey-Bass, c1994.
**TC HD62.6 .J67 1994**

**Handbook of personality** : theory and research / edited by Lawrence A. Pervin, Oliver P. John. 2nd ed. New York : Guilford Press, c1999. xiii, 738 p. : ill. 26 cm. Includes bibliographical references and indexes. ISBN 1-57230-483-9 DDC 155.2
1. Personality. I. Pervin, Lawrence A. II. John, Oliver P.
**TC BF698 .H335 1999**

**Handbook of psychological assessment** / edited by Gerald Goldstein, Michel Hersen. 3rd ed. Amsterdam ; New York : Pergamon, 2000. vi, 627 p. : ill. ; 26 cm. Includes bibliographical references and indexes. ISBN 0-08-043645-5 (hardcover) DDC 150/.28/7
1. Psychometrics. 2. Psychological tests. I. Goldstein, Gerald, 1931- II. Hersen, Michel.
**TC BF39 .H2645 2000**

**Handbook of psychological assessment in primary care settings** / edited by Mark E. Maruish. Mahwah, NJ : Lawrence Erlbaum Associates, Publishers, 2000. xiv, 848 p. : ill. ; 27 cm. Includes bibliographical references and index. ISBN 0-8058-2999-7 (cloth : alk. paper) DDC 616.89/075
1. Psychodiagnostics - Handbooks, manuals, etc. 2. Primary care (Medicine) I. Maruish, Mark E. (Mark Edward)
**TC RC469 .H374 2000**

**Handbook of psychological change** : : psychotherapy processes & practices for the 21st century / edited by C.R. Snyder & Rick E. Ingram. New York : John Wiley & Sons, c2000. xvi, 768 p. : ill. Other title: Psychological change. Includes bibliographical references and indexes. ISBN 0-471-24191-1 (alk. paper)
1. Psychotherapy. 2. Psychotherapy - Methodology. I. Snyder, C. R. II. Ingram, Rick E.
**TC RC480 .H2855 2000**

**The handbook of psychological testing.**
Kline, Paul. 2nd ed. London : New York : Routledge, 2000.
**TC BF176 .K575 2000**

**The handbook of psychology for forensic practitioners.**
Towl, Graham J. London ; New York : Routledge, 1996.
**TC RA1148 .T69 1996**

**Handbook of psychophysiology** / edited by John T. Cacioppo, Louis G. Tassinary, Gary G. Berntson. 2nd ed. Cambridge, UK ; New York, NY, USA : Cambridge University Press, 2000. xiii, 1039 p. : ill. ; 29 cm. Rev. ed. of: Principles of psychophysiology. 1990. Includes bibliographical references and index. ISBN 0-521-62634-X (hardback) DDC 612.8
1. Psychophysiology - Handbooks, manuals, etc. 2. Psychophysiology. I. Cacioppo, John T. II. Tassinary, Louis G. III. Berntson, Gary G. IV. Title: Principles of psychophysiology.
**TC QP360 .P7515 2000**

**Handbook of psychotherapies with children and families** / edited by Sandra W. Russ and Thomas H. Ollendick. New York ; London : Kluwer Academic/ Plenum Publishers, c1999. xviii, 584 p. : ill. ; 26 cm. (Issues in clinical child psychology) Includes bibliographical references and indexes. ISBN 0-306-46098-X DDC 618.92/ 8914
1. Child psychotherapy. 2. Family psychotherapy. 3. Psychotherapy - methods - Adolescence. 4. Psychotherapy - methods - Child. 5. Family Therapy - methods. I. Russ, Sandra Walker. II. Ollendick, Thomas H. III. Series.
**TC RJ504 .H3619 1999**

**Handbook of qualitative research** / Norman K. Denzin, Yvonna S. Lincoln, editors. 2nd ed. Thousand Oaks, Calif. : Sage Publications, c2000. 1 v. (various pagings) ; 26 cm. Includes bibliographical references and indexes. CONTENTS: Introduction: The discipline and practice of qualitative research / Norman K. Denzin and Yvonna S. Lincoln -- Qualitative methods: their history in sociology and anthropology / Arthur J. Vidich and Stanford M. Lyman -- Reconstructing the relationship between universities and society through action research / Davydd J.

Greenwood and Morten Levin -- For whom? qualitative research, representations, and social responsibilities / Michelle Fine ... [et al.] -- Ethics and politics in qualitative research / Clifford G. Christians -- Paradigmatic controversies, contradictions, and emerging confluences / Yvonna CONTENTS: S. Lincoln and Egon G. Guba -- Three epistemological stances for qualitative inquiry: interpretivism, hermeneutics, and social constructionism / Thomas A. Schwandt -- Feminisms and qualitative research at and into the millennium / Virgina L. Olesen -- Racialized discourses and ethnic epistemologies / Gloria Ladson-Billings -- Rethinking critical theory and qualitative research / Joe L. Kincheloe and Peter McLaren -- Cultural studies / John Frow and Meaghan Morris -- Sexualities, queer theory, and qualitative research / Joshua Gamson -- The choreography of qualitative research design: CONTENTS: minuets, improvisations, and crystallization / Valerie J. Janesick -- An untold story? Doing funded qualitative research / Julianne Cheek -- Performance ethnography: a brief history and some advice / Michael M. McCall -- Case studies / Robert E. Stake -- Ethnography and ethnographic representation / Barbara Tedlock -- Analyzing interpretive practice / Jaber F. Gubrium and James A. Holstein -- Grounded theory: objectivist and constructivist methods / Kathy Charmaz -- Undaunted courage: life history and the postmodern challenge / William G. Tierney -- Testimonio, subalternity, CONTENTS: and narrative authority / John Beverley -- Participatory action research / Stephen Kemmis and Robin McTaggart -- Clinical research / William L. Miller and Benjamin F. Crabtree -- The interview: from structured questions to negotiated text / Andrea Fontana and James H. Frey -- Rethinking observation: from method to context / Michael V. Angrosino and Kimberly A. Mays de Pérez -- The interpretation of documents and material culture / Ian Hodder -- Reimagining visual methods: Galileo to Neuromancer / Douglas Harper -- Autoethnography, personal narrative, reflexivity: researcher as subject / CONTENTS: Carolyn Ellis and Arthur P. Bochner -- Data management and analysis methods / Gery W. Ryan and H. Russell Bernard -- Software and qualitative research / Eben A. Weitzman -- Analyzing talk and text / David Silverman -- Focus groups in feminist research / Esther Madriz -- Applied ethnography / Erve Chambers -- The problem of criteria in the age of relativism / John K. Smith and Deborah K. Deemer -- The practices and politics of interpretation / Norman K. Denzin -- Writing: a method of inquiry / Laurel Richardson -- Anthropological poetics / Ivan Brady -- Understanding social CONTENTS: programs through evaluation / Jennifer C. Greene -- Influencing the policy process with qualitative research / Ray C. Rist -- Qualitative inquiry: tensions and transformations / Mary M. Gergen and Kenneth J. Gergen -- The seventh moment: out of the past / Yvonna S. Lincoln and Norman K. Denzin. ISBN 0-7619-1512-5 (acid free paper) DDC 300/.7/2
*1. Social sciences - Research. 2. Social Sciences. 3. Research. I. Denzin, Norman K. II. Lincoln, Yvonna S. III. Title. IV. Title: Qualitative research*
***TC H62 .H2455 2000***

**Handbook of reading research** / editor, P. David Pearson [and] section editors, Rebecca Barr, Michael L. Kamil, Peter Mosenthal. New York : Longman, c1984-<2000 > v. <1-3 > : ill. ; 26 cm. Vol. 2 edited by Rebecca Barr and others. Vol. 3 published by L. Erlbaum Associates, Mahwah, N.J., and edited by Michael L. Kamil and others. Vol. 1 lacks volume numbering. Includes bibliographies and indexes. ISBN 0-582-28119-9 (v. 1) ISBN 0-8013-0292-7 (v. 2) ISBN 0-8058-2398-0 (v. 3 : cloth) ISBN 0-8058-2399-9 (v. 3 : pbk.) DDC 428.4/072
*1. Reading. 2. Reading - Research - Methodology. I. Pearson, P. David. II. Barr, Rebecca. III. Kamil, Michael L. IV. Title: Reading research.*
***TC LB1050 .H278 2000***

**Handbook of rehabilitation psychology** / edited by Robert G. Frank and Timothy R. Elliott. 1st ed. Washington, DC : American Psychological Association c2000. xiv, 727 p. : ill. ; 27 cm. Includes bibliographical references and indexes. ISBN 1-55798-644-4 (alk. paper) DDC 617/.03/019
*1. Clinical health psychology - Handbooks, manuals, etc. 2. Medical rehabilitation - Psychological aspects - Handbooks, manuals, etc. I. Frank, Robert G., 1952- II. Elliott, Timothy R.*
***TC R726.7 .H366 2000***

**Handbook of research design in mathematics and science education** / edited by Anthony E. Kelly and Richard Lesh. Mahwah, N.J. : Lawrence Erlbaum, 1999. 993 p. : ill. ; 26 cm. Includes bibliographical references and index. ISBN 0-8058-3281-5 (cloth : alk. paper) DDC 507.1
*1. Mathematics - Study and teaching - Research. 2. Science - Study and teaching - Research. I. Kelly, Anthony E. II. Lesh, Richard A.*
***TC QA11 .H256 1999***

**Handbook of research in pediatric and clinical child psychology : practical strategies and methods** / edited by Dennis Drotar. New York : Kluwer Academic/ Plenum Publishers, c 2000. xiii, 557 p. : ill. ; 26 cm. (Issues in clinical child psychology) Other title: Research in pediatric and clinical child psychology. Includes bibliographical references and index. ISBN 0-306-46229-X
*1. Child Psychology. 2. Psychology, Clinical - Child. 3. Research - methods. I. Drotar, Dennis. II. Series.*
***TC RJ499.3 .H367 2000***

**Handbook of research methods in social and personality psychology** / edited by Harry T. Reis, Charles M. Judd. Cambridge, U.K. ; New York : Cambridge University Press, 2000. xii, 558 p. : ill. ; 26 cm. Includes bibliographical references and indexes. ISBN 0-521-55128-5 (hardback) ISBN 0-521-55903-0 (paperback) DDC 302/.07/2
*1. Social psychology - Research - Methodology. 2. Personality - Research - Methodology. I. Reis, Harry T. II. Judd, Charles M.*
***TC HM1019 .H36 2000***

**Handbook of school health.**
Medical Officers of Schools Association. 18th ed. Stoke-on-Trent : Trentham, 1998.
***TC LB3409.G7 H36 1998***

**Handbook of self-regulation** / edited by Monique Boekaerts, Paul R. Pintrich and Moshe Zeidner. San Diego : Academic, 2000. xxix, 783 p. : ill. ; 24 cm. Includes bibliographical references and index. ISBN 0-12-109890-7 DDC 153.8
*1. Learning. 2. Self-control. 3. Goal (Psychology) 4. Feedback (Psychology) 5. Self-determination. 6. Will. I. Zeidner, Moshe. II. Pintrich, Paul R. III. Boekaerts, Monique.*
***TC BF632 .H254 2000***

**Handbook of social studies in health and medicine** / edited by Gary L. Albrecht, Ray Fitzpatrick and Susan C. Scrimshaw. London ; Thousand Oaks, Calif. : Sage Publications, 2000. xxvii, 545 p. : ill. ; 26 cm. Includes bibliographical references and indexes. ISBN 0-7619-5617-4 DDC 362.1042
*1. Social medicine. I. Albrecht, Gary L. II. Fitzpatrick, Ray. III. Scrimshaw, Susan.*
***TC RA418 .H36 2000***

**The handbook of student affairs administration.**
Barr, Margaret J. 2nd ed. San Francisco : Jossey-Bass, c2000.
***TC LB2342.92 .B37 2000***

**A handbook of techniques and strategies for coaching student teachers.**
Pelletier, Carol Marra. 2nd ed. Boston : Allyn and Bacon, 1999.
***TC LB2157.U5 P38 1999***

**A handbook of techniques for formative evaluation.**
George, Judith W. London : Kogan Page, 1999.
***TC LB2333 .G46 1999***

**Handbook of the sociology of education** / edited by Maureen T. Hallinan. New York : Kluwer Academic/Plenum, c2000. xv, 588 p. : ill. ; 26 cm. (Handbooks of sociology and social research) Includes bibliographical references and indexes. ISBN 0-306-46238-9 DDC 306.43
*1. Educational sociology - Handbooks, manuals, etc. I. Hallinan, Maureen T. II. Series.*
***TC LC191 .H254 2000***

**Handbook of the sociology of mental health** / edited by Carol S. Aneshensel and Jo C. Phelan. New York : Kluwer Academic/Plenum Publishers, c1999. xix, 628 p. : ill. ; 26 cm. (Handbooks of sociology and social research) Includes bibliographical references and index. ISBN 0-306-46069-6 DDC 362.2
*1. Social psychiatry. 2. Mental illness - Social aspects. I. Aneshensel, Carol S. II. Phelan, Jo C. III. Series.*
***TC RC455 .H2874 1999***

**Handbook of theories of aging** / Vern L. Bengtson and K. Warner Schaie, editors. New York : Springer Pub. Co., c1999. xviii, 516 p. : ill. ; 24 cm. Includes bibliographical references and indexes. ISBN 0-8261-1234-X DDC 305.26/07/2
*1. Aging - Research. 2. Gerontology - Research. I. Bengtson, Vern L. II. Schaie, K. Warner (Klaus Warner), 1928-*
***TC HQ1061 .H3366 1999***

**Handbook on effective instructional strategies.**
Friedman, Myles I., 1924- Columbia, S.C. : The Institute for Evidence-Based Decision-Making in Education, 1998.
***TC LB1028.35 .F75 1998***

**Handbook on ethical issues in aging** / edited by Tanya Fusco Johnson. Westport, Conn. : Greenwood Press, 1999. xii,420 p. ; 24 cm. Includes bibliographical references (p. [351]-391) and indexes. ISBN 0-313-28726-0 (alk. paper) DDC 174/.2
*1. Aged - Care - Moral and ethical aspects. 2. Aging - Moral and ethical aspects. I. Johnson, Tanya F.*
***TC HV1451 .H35 1999***

**Handbook on grandparenthood** / edited by Maximiliane E. Szinovacz. Westport, Conn. : Greenwood Press, 1998. viii, 364 p. : ill. ; 25 cm. Includes bibliographical references (p. [289]-336) and index. ISBN 0-313-29886-6 (alk. paper) DDC 306.874/5
*1. Grandparents - Social conditions. 2. Grandparenting. 3. Grandparent and child. I. Szinovácz, Maximiliane.*
***TC HQ759.9 .H36 1998***

**Handbooks of sociology and social research**
Handbook of the sociology of education. New York : Kluwer Academic/Plenum, c2000.
***TC LC191 .H254 2000***

Handbook of the sociology of mental health. New York : Kluwer Academic/Plenum Publishers, c1999.
***TC RC455 .H2874 1999***

**HANDBOOKS, VADE-MECUMS, ETC.** *See also* **TEXTBOOKS.**
Fry, Edward Bernard, 1925- The reading teacher's book of lists. 3rd ed. Englewood Cliffs, NJ : Prentice Hall, c1993.
***TC LB1050.2 .F79 1993***

Fry, Edward Bernard, 1925- The reading teacher's book of lists. 4th ed. Paramus, N.J. : Prentice Hall, c2000.
***TC LB1050.2 .F79 2000***

**HANDBOOKS, VADE-MECUMS, ETC. - JUVENILE LITERATURE.**
A First dictionary of cultural literacy. Boston : Houghton Mifflin, 1989.
***TC AG105 .F43 1989***

**HANDCHIMES - INSTRUCTION AND STUDY.**
McBride, Michael B. Meeting the national standards with handbells and handchimes. Lanham, MD : Scarecrow Press, 2000.
***TC MT711 .M35 2000***

**HANDCRAFT.** *See* **HANDICRAFT.**

**Handel, Ruth D.** Building family literacy in an urban community / Ruth D. Handel. New York : Teachers College Press, c1999. ix, 179 p. ; 24 cm. (Language and literacy series) Includes bibliographical references (p. 157-167) and index. ISBN 0-8077-3895-6 (cloth : alk. paper) ISBN 0-8077-3894-8 (pbk. : alk. paper) DDC 302.2/244/0974932
*1. Family literacy programs - New Jersey - Newark - Case studies. 2. Education, Urban - New Jersey - Newark - Case studies. I. Title. II. Series: Language and literacy series (New York, N.Y.)*
***TC LC152.N58 H36 1999***

**HANDGUN CONTROL.** *See* **GUN CONTROL.**

**HANDICAPPED.** *See also* **DEVELOPMENTALLY DISABLED; DISCRIMINATION AGAINST THE HANDICAPPED; HANDICAPPED PARENTS; HANDICAPPED STUDENTS; LIBRARIES AND THE HANDICAPPED; MENTALLY HANDICAPPED; MINORITY HANDICAPPED; PHYSICALLY HANDICAPPED; SICK; SOCIALLY HANDICAPPED; SOCIOLOGY OF DISABILITY.**
Hardman, Michael L. Human exceptionality. 6th ed. Boston : Allyn and Bacon, c1999.
***TC HV1568 .H37 1999***

Marks, Deborah, 1964- Disability. London : New York : Routledge, 1999.
***TC HV1568.2 .M37 1999***

**HANDICAPPED AND LIBRARIES.** *See* **LIBRARIES AND THE HANDICAPPED.**

**HANDICAPPED CHILDREN.** *See also* **DEVELOPMENTALLY DISABLED CHILDREN; HANDICAPPED YOUTH; LIBRARIES AND HANDICAPPED CHILDREN; MENTALLY HANDICAPPED CHILDREN; PARENTS OF HANDICAPPED CHILDREN; PHYSICALLY HANDICAPPED CHILDREN; SOCIALLY HANDICAPPED CHILDREN.**
Berel, Marianne. Musical play sessions. [S.l. : s.n.], 1994.
***TC ML3920 .B45 1994***

**HANDICAPPED CHILDREN AND LIBRARIES.** *See* **LIBRARIES AND HANDICAPPED CHILDREN.**

**HANDICAPPED CHILDREN - EDUCATION.** *See also* **TEACHERS OF HANDICAPPED CHILDREN.**
Gibb, Gordon S. Guide to writing quality individualzed education programs :. Boston : Allyn and Bacon, c2000.

TC LC4019 .G43 2000

Hand in hand [videorecording]. New York, N.Y. : AFB Press, c1995.
*TC HV1597.2 .H3 1995*

Seligman, Milton, 1937- Conducting effective conferences with parents of children with disabilities. New York : Guilford Press, c2000.
*TC LC4019 .S385 2000*

Special education & student disability. 4th ed. Denver, Colo. : Love Pub. Co., c1995.
*TC LC3965 .E87 1995*

Steiner, Rudolf, 1861-1925. [Heilpädagogischer Kurs. English] Education for special needs. [New ed.]. London : Rudolf Steiner Press, 1998.
*TC LB1029.W34 S73 1998*

Trawick-Smith, Jeffrey W. Early childhood development. 2nd ed. Upper Saddle River, N.J. : Merrill, c2000.
*TC LB1115 .T73 2000*

**HANDICAPPED CHILDREN - EDUCATION - ABILITY TESTING - UNITED STATES.**
Elliott, Judy L. Improving test performance of students with disabilities-- on district and state assessments. Thousands Oaks, Calif. : Corwin Press, c2000.
*TC LB3051 .E48 2000*

**HANDICAPPED CHILDREN - EDUCATION - ART.**
Henley, David R. Exceptional children: exceptional art. Worcester, Mass. : Davis Publications, c1992.
*TC RJ505.A7 H46 1992*

**HANDICAPPED CHILDREN - EDUCATION - CASE STUDIES.**
Inclusive education at work. Paris : Organisation for Economic Co-operation and Development, 1999.
*TC LC4015 .I525 1999*

**HANDICAPPED CHILDREN - EDUCATION - CROSS-CULTURAL STUDIES.**
Inclusive education. London ; Philadelphia : Falmer Press, 1999.
*TC LC1200 .I53 1999*

**HANDICAPPED CHILDREN - EDUCATION (EARLY CHILDHOOD).**
Lava, Valerie Forkin. Early intervention. 1998.
*TC 06 no. 11140*

Making the most of early communication [videorecording]. New York, NY : Distributed by AFB Press, c1997.
*TC HV1597.2 .M3 1997*

**HANDICAPPED CHILDREN - EDUCATION (ELEMENTARY) - MARYLAND.**
Sean's story [videorecording]. Princeton, N.J. : Films for the Humanities & Sciences ; [S.l. : distributed by] ABC Multimedia : Capital Cities/ABC, c1994.
*TC LC1203.M3 .S39 1994*

**HANDICAPPED CHILDREN - EDUCATION (ELEMENTARY) - UNITED STATES - CASE STUDIES.**
Coughlin, Debbie. The mainstreaming handbook. Portsmouth, NH : Heinemann, c2000.
*TC LC1201 .C68 2000*

**HANDICAPPED CHILDREN - EDUCATION - ENGLAND - LEICESTER.**
Croll, Paul. Special needs in the primary school. London : Cassell, 2000.
*TC LC4036.G6 C763 2000*

**HANDICAPPED CHILDREN - EDUCATION - GREAT BRITAIN.**
Special needs and the beginning teacher. London ; New York : Continuum, 2000.
*TC LC4036.G7 S684 2000*

**HANDICAPPED CHILDREN - EDUCATION - MEXICO.**
Helping individuals with disabilities and their families. Tempe, Ariz. : Bilingual Review/Press, c1999.
*TC LC4035.M6 H45 1999*

**HANDICAPPED CHILDREN - EDUCATION - PERIODICALS.**
Annual distinguished lectures in special education and rehabilitation. Los Angeles, Dept. of Exceptional Children, University of Southern California.
*TC LC4019 .D57*

**HANDICAPPED CHILDREN - EDUCATION (PRESCHOOL).**
Cook, Ruth E. Adapting early childhood curricula for

children in inclusive settings. 5th ed. Englewood Cliffs, N.J. : Merrill, c2000.
*TC LC4019.2 .C66 2000*

**HANDICAPPED CHILDREN - EDUCATION (PRESCHOOL) - CURRICULA.**
Cook, Ruth E. Adapting early childhood curricula for children in inclusive settings. 5th ed. Englewood Cliffs, N.J. : Merrill, c2000.
*TC LC4019.2 .C66 2000*

**HANDICAPPED CHILDREN - EDUCATION (PRIMARY) - UNITED STATES.**
Turner, Nancy D'Isa. Children's literature for the primary inclusive classroom. Albany, N.Y. : Delmar Publishers, c2000.
*TC LC4028 .T87 2000*

**HANDICAPPED CHILDREN - EDUCATION - SOCIAL ASPECTS - GREAT BRITAIN.**
Mittler, Peter J. Working towards inclusive education. London : D. Fulton Publishers, 2000.
*TC LC1203.G7 M58 2000*

**HANDICAPPED CHILDREN - EDUCATION - UNITED STATES.**
Alper, Sandra K. Alternate assessment of students with disabilities in inclusive settings. Boston ; London : Allyn and Bacon, c2001.
*TC LC4031 .A58 2001*

Behavioral assessment in schools. 2nd ed. New York : Guilford Press, c2000.
*TC LB1124 .B435 2000*

Fiedler, Craig R. Making a difference. Boston ; London : Allyn and Bacon, c2000.
*TC LC4031 .F52 2000*

Helping individuals with disabilities and their families. Tempe, Ariz. : Bilingual Review/Press, c1999.
*TC LC4035.M6 H45 1999*

Instruction of students with severe disabilities. 5th ed. Upper Saddle River, N.J. : Merrill, c2000.
*TC LC4031 .I572 2000*

MacCuspie, P. Ann (Patricia Ann), 1950- Promoting acceptance of children with disabilities. Halifax, N.S. : Atlantic Provinces Special Education Authority, c1996.
*TC LC4301 .M33 1996*

Successful inclusive teaching. 3rd ed. Boston : Allyn and Bacon, c2000.
*TC LC1201 .S93 2000*

Taylor, Ronald L., 1949- Assessment of exceptional students. 5th ed. Boston : Allyn and Bacon, c2000.
*TC LC4031 .T36 2000*

Umansky, Warren. Young children with special needs. 3rd ed. Upper Saddle River, N.J. : Merrill, c1998.
*TC LC4031 .U425 1998*

Vallecorsa, Ada, 1948- Students with mild disabilities in general education settings. Upper Saddle River, N.J. : Merrill, c2000.
*TC LC4705 .V35 2000*

Vaughn, Sharon, 1952- Teaching exceptional, diverse, and at-risk students in the general education classroom. 2nd ed. Boston : Allyn and Bacon, 2000.
*TC LC3981 .V28 2000*

Venn, John. Assessing students with special needs. 2nd ed. Upper Saddle River, N.J. : Merrill, c2000.
*TC LC4031 .V46 2000*

Westling, David L. Teaching students with severe disabilities. 2nd ed. Upper Saddle River, N.J. : Merrill, c2000.
*TC LC4031 .W47 2000*

**HANDICAPPED CHILDREN - EDUCATION - UNITED STATES - CASE STUDIES.**
Inclusive education. Mahwah, N.J. : L. Erlbaum Associates, c2000.
*TC LC1201 .I527 2000*

Meese, Ruth Lyn. Teaching learners with mild disabilities. 2nd ed. Belmont, CA : Wadsworth/ Thomson Learning, c2001.
*TC LC4031 .M44 2001*

**HANDICAPPED CHILDREN - EDUCATION - UNITED STATES - CURRICULA.**
Bigge, June L. Curriculum, assessment, and instruction for students with disabilities. Belmont, CA : Wadsworth Pub., c1999.
*TC LC4031 .B46 1999*

Taylor, George R. Curriculum models and strategies for educating individuals with disabilities in inclusive

classrooms. Springfield, Ill. : C.C. Thomas, Publisher, c1999.
*TC LC4031 .T33 1999*

**HANDICAPPED CHILDREN - EDUCATION - UNITED STATES - ENCYCLOPEDIAS.**
Encyclopedia of special education. 2nd ed. New York : J. Wiley & Sons, c2000.
*TC LC4007 .E53 2000*

**HANDICAPPED CHILDREN - EDUCATION - UNITED STATES - HANDBOOKS, MANUALS, ETC.**
Kochhar, Carol. Successful inclusion. 2nd ed. Upper Saddle River, NJ : Prentice Hall, c2000.
*TC LC1201 .K63 2000*

**HANDICAPPED CHILDREN - EDUCATION - UNITED STATES - PLANNING.**
Janney, Rachel. Modifying schoolwork. Baltimore, Md. : Paul H. Brookes Pub., c2000.
*TC LC1201 .J26 2000*

**HANDICAPPED CHILDREN - FAMILY RELATIONSHIPS - CASE STUDIES.**
Lava, Valerie Forkin. Early intervention. 1998.
*TC 06 no. 11140*

**HANDICAPPED CHILDREN - LANGUAGE.**
Hand in hand [videorecording]. New York, N.Y. : AFB Press, c1995.
*TC HV1597.2 .H3 1995*

Making the most of early communication [videorecording]. New York, NY : Distributed by AFB Press, c1997.
*TC HV1597.2 .M3 1997*

**HANDICAPPED CHILDREN - LEGAL STATUS, LAWS, ETC. - UNITED STATES.**
Coughlin, Debbie. The mainstreaming handbook. Portsmouth, NH : Heinemann, c2000.
*TC LC1201 .C68 2000*

**HANDICAPPED CHILDREN - NEW YORK (STATE) - NEW YORK - CASE STUDIES.**
Wexler, Alice. The art of necessity. 1999.
*TC 06 no. 11072*

**HANDICAPPED CHILDREN - PSYCHOLOGICAL TESTING - UNITED STATES.**
Taylor, Ronald L., 1949- Assessment of exceptional students. 5th ed. Boston : Allyn and Bacon, c2000.
*TC LC4031 .T36 2000*

Venn, John. Assessing students with special needs. 2nd ed. Upper Saddle River, N.J. : Merrill, c2000.
*TC LC4031 .V46 2000*

**HANDICAPPED CHILDREN - PSYCHOLOGY.**
Hand in hand [videorecording]. New York, N.Y. : AFB Press, c1995.
*TC HV1597.2 .H3 1995*

Making the most of early communication [videorecording]. New York, NY : Distributed by AFB Press, c1997.
*TC HV1597.2 .M3 1997*

**HANDICAPPED CHILDREN - RATING OF - ENGLAND - LEICESTER.**
Croll, Paul. Special needs in the primary school. London : Cassell, 2000.
*TC LC4036.G6 C763 2000*

**HANDICAPPED CHILDREN - RECREATION - UNITED STATES.**
Fink, Dale Borman, 1949- Making a place for kids with disabilities. Westport, Conn. : Praeger, 2000.
*TC GV183.6 .F56 2000*

**HANDICAPPED CHILDREN - REHABILITATION.**
Hand in hand [videorecording]. New York, N.Y. : AFB Press, c1995.
*TC HV1597.2 .H3 1995*

Making the most of early communication [videorecording]. New York, NY : Distributed by AFB Press, c1997.
*TC HV1597.2 .M3 1997*

**HANDICAPPED CHILDREN - SERVICES FOR.**
Middleton, Laura. Disabled children. Malden, Mass. : Blackwell Sciences, 1999.
*TC HV888 .M53 1999*

**HANDICAPPED CHILDREN - SERVICES FOR - CASE STUDIES.**
Lava, Valerie Forkin. Early intervention. 1998.
*TC 06 no. 11140*

**HANDICAPPED CHILDREN - SERVICES FOR - UNITED STATES.**
Bridging the family-professional gap. Springfield, Ill. : Charles C. Thomas, c1999.

*TC HV888.5 .B74 1999*

Fiedler, Craig R. Making a difference. Boston : London : Allyn and Bacon, c2000.
*TC LC4031 .F52 2000*

**HANDICAPPED CHILDREN - SERVICES FOR - UNITED STATES - DIRECTORIES.**
Pierangelo, Roger. The special education yellow pages. Upper Saddle River, N.J. : Merrill, c2000.
*TC LC4031 .P488 2000*

**HANDICAPPED CHILDREN - SOCIAL CONDITIONS.**
Middleton, Laura. Disabled children. Malden, Mass. : Blackwell Sciences, 1999.
*TC HV888 .M53 1999*

**HANDICAPPED CHILDREN, TEACHERS OF.** *See* **TEACHERS OF HANDICAPPED CHILDREN.**

**HANDICAPPED CHILDREN - TESTING.** *See* **HANDICAPPED CHILDREN - PSYCHOLOGICAL TESTING.**

**HANDICAPPED COLLEGE STUDENTS - LEGAL STATUS, LAWS, ETC. - UNITED STATES.**
Accommodations in higher education under the Americans with Disabilities Act (ADA) :. DeWitt, NY : GSI Publications, 2000.
*TC RA1055.5 A28 2000*

**HANDICAPPED COLLEGE STUDENTS - SERVICES FOR - CROSS-CULTURAL STUDIES.**
Higher education and disabilities. Aldershot ; Brookfield, Vt. : Ashgate, c1998.
*TC LC4812 .H55 1998*

**HANDICAPPED - EDUCATION.**
Bowe, Frank. Universal design in education. Westport, Conn. ; London : Bergin & Garvey, 2000.
*TC LB1028.38 .B69 2000*

**HANDICAPPED - EDUCATION (HIGHER) - CROSS-CULTURAL STUDIES.**
Higher education and disabilities. Aldershot ; Brookfield, Vt. : Ashgate, c1998.
*TC LC4812 .H55 1998*

**HANDICAPPED - EDUCATION - RESEARCH - UNITED STATES - METHODOLOGY.**
Contemporary special education research. Mahwah, N.J. : Lawrence Erlbaum, c2000.
*TC LC4019 .C575 2000*

**HANDICAPPED - EDUCATION (SECONDARY) - LOUISIANA - SHREVEPORT.**
Baldwin, John. Education and welfare reform. Bloomington, Ind. : Phi Delta Kappa Educational Foundation, c1993.
*TC LC4033.S61 B34 1993*

**HANDICAPPED - EDUCATION - TECHNOLOGICAL INNOVATIONS.**
King, Thomas W. Modern Morse code in rehabilitation and education. Boston : Allyn and Bacon, c2000.
*TC HV1569.5 .K55 2000*

**HANDICAPPED - EDUCATION - UNITED STATES.**
Accommodations in higher education under the Americans with Disabilities Act (ADA) :. DeWitt, NY : GSI Publications, 2000.
*TC RA1055.5 A28 2000*

Idol, Lorna. Collaborative consultation. 3rd ed. Austin, Tex. : PRO-ED, c2000.
*TC LC4019 .I35 2000*

**HANDICAPPED - EDUCATION - UNITED STATES - ENCYCLOPEDIAS.**
Encyclopedia of special education. 2nd ed. New York : J. Wiley & Sons, c2000.
*TC LC4007 .E53 2000*

**HANDICAPPED - EMPLOYMENT.** *See* **VOCATIONAL GUIDANCE FOR THE HANDICAPPED; VOCATIONAL REHABILITATION.**

**HANDICAPPED - FAMILY RELATIONSHIPS.**
Marshak, Laura E. Disability and the family life cycle. New York : Basic Books, c1999.
*TC HV1568 .M277 1999*

**HANDICAPPED - FUNCTIONAL ASSESSMENT.**
Functional analysis of problem behavior. Belmont, CA : Wadsworth Pub. Co., c1999.
*TC RC473.B43 F85 1999*

**Handicapped funding directory.**
Directory of grants for organizations serving people with disabilities. Loxahatchee, Fla. : Research Grant Guides, c1993-

*TC HV3006.A4 H35*

**HANDICAPPED - GOVERNMENT POLICY.**
Barnes, Colin, 1946- Exploring disability. Cambridge, UK : Polity Press : Malden, MA : Blackwell Publishers, 1999.
*TC HV1568 .B35 1999*

**HANDICAPPED - HOME CARE.**
Marshak, Laura E. Disability and the family life cycle. New York : Basic Books, c1999.
*TC HV1568 .M277 1999*

**HANDICAPPED IN LITERATURE - HISTORY AND CRITICISM.**
Klages, Mary. Woeful afflictions. Philadelphia : University of Pennsylvania Press, c1999.
*TC HV1553 .K53 1999*

**HANDICAPPED IN MASS MEDIA - HISTORY.**
Klages, Mary. Woeful afflictions. Philadelphia : University of Pennsylvania Press, c1999.
*TC HV1553 .K53 1999*

**HANDICAPPED - INFORMATION SERVICES - UNITED STATES - CASE STUDIES.**
DeCandido, GraceAnne A. Transforming libraries. Washington, D.C. : Association of Research Libraries, Office of Leadership and Management Services, c1999.
*TC Z711.92.H3 D43 1999*

**HANDICAPPED - MEANS OF COMMUNICATION.**
Augmentative and alternative communication. London : Whurr, 1999.
*TC RC429 .A94 1999*

**HANDICAPPED PARENTS - LEGAL STATUS, LAWS, ETC. - UNITED STATES.**
Field, Martha A. Equal treatment for people with mental retardation. Cambridge, Mass. ; London : Harvard University Press, 1999.
*TC KF480 .F54 1999*

**HANDICAPPED PEOPLE.** *See* **HANDICAPPED.**

**HANDICAPPED - PERIODICALS.**
American journal of care for cripples. New York : Douglas McMurtie, 1914-1919.

**HANDICAPPED - RECREATION.** *See* **SPORTS FOR THE HANDICAPPED.**

**HANDICAPPED - REHABILITATION - TECHNOLOGICAL INNOVATIONS.**
King, Thomas W. Modern Morse code in rehabilitation and education. Boston : Allyn and Bacon, c2000.
*TC HV1569.5 .K55 2000*

**HANDICAPPED - RESEARCH.**
Barnes, Colin, 1946- Exploring disability. Cambridge, UK : Polity Press : Malden, MA : Blackwell Publishers, 1999.
*TC HV1568 .B35 1999*

**HANDICAPPED SERVICES.** *See* **HANDICAPPED - SERVICES FOR.**

**HANDICAPPED - SERVICES FOR.**
Hardman, Michael L. Human exceptionality. 6th ed. Boston : Allyn and Bacon, c1999.
*TC HV1568 .H37 1999*

**HANDICAPPED - SERVICES FOR - FEDERAL AID.** *See* **FEDERAL AID TO SERVICES FOR THE HANDICAPPED.**

**HANDICAPPED - SERVICES FOR - FINANCE.** *See* **FEDERAL AID TO SERVICES FOR THE HANDICAPPED.**

**HANDICAPPED - SERVICES FOR - UNITED STATES.**
Westling, David L. Teaching students with severe disabilities. 2nd ed. Upper Saddle River, N.J. : Merrill, c2000.
*TC LC4031 .W47 2000*

**HANDICAPPED - SERVICES FOR - UNITED STATES - FINANCE - DIRECTORIES.**
Directory of grants for organizations serving people with disabilities. Loxahatchee, Fla. : Research Grant Guides, c1993-
*TC HV3006.A4 H35*

**HANDICAPPED STUDENTS.** *See* **HANDICAPPED COLLEGE STUDENTS.**

**HANDICAPPED STUDENTS - EDUCATION - UNITED STATES.**
MacCuspie, P. Ann (Patricia Ann), 1950- Promoting acceptance of children with disabilities. Halifax, N.S. : Atlantic Provinces Special Education Authority, c1996.

*TC LC4301 .M33 1996*

Sands, Deanna J. Inclusive education for the 21st century. Belmont, CA : Wadsworth/Thomson Learning, 2000.
*TC LC1201 .S27 2000*

**HANDICAPPED STUDENTS - UNITED STATES - FAMILY RELATIONSHIPS.**
Families and teachers of individuals with disabilities. Boston ; London : Allyn and Bacon, c2001.
*TC LC3969 .F34 2001*

**HANDICAPPED - STUDY AND TEACHING.** *See* **DISABILITY STUDIES.**

**HANDICAPPED TEENAGERS.** *See* **MENTALLY HANDICAPPED TEENAGERS; PHYSICALLY HANDICAPPED TEENAGERS.**

**HANDICAPPED - UNITED STATES - HISTORY - 19TH CENTURY.**
Klages, Mary. Woeful afflictions. Philadelphia : University of Pennsylvania Press, c1999.
*TC HV1553 .K53 1999*

**HANDICAPPED - UNITED STATES - PSYCHOLOGY.**
Frank, Gelya, 1948- Venus on wheels. Berkeley, Calif. : University of California Press, c2000.
*TC HV3021.W66 F73 2000*

**HANDICAPPED - UNITED STATES - PUBLIC OPINION.**
Klages, Mary. Woeful afflictions. Philadelphia : University of Pennsylvania Press, c1999.
*TC HV1553 .K53 1999*

**HANDICAPPED WOMEN.** *See* **PHYSICALLY HANDICAPPED WOMEN; SOCIALLY HANDICAPPED WOMEN.**

**HANDICAPPED WOMEN - GREAT BRITAIN.**
Thomas, Carol, 1958- Female forms. Philadelphia, Pa. : Open University Press, 1999.
*TC HV1568.25.G7 T46 1999*

**HANDICAPPED WOMEN - UNITED STATES - BIOGRAPHY.**
Frank, Gelya, 1948- Venus on wheels. Berkeley, Calif. : University of California Press, c2000.
*TC HV3021.W66 F73 2000*

**HANDICAPPED WOMEN X INTERNATIONAL COOPERATION.**
Loud, proud & passionate. 1st ed. Eugene, OR : Mobility International USA, 1997.
*TC HV1569.3.W65 L68 1997*

**HANDICAPPED YOUTH.** *See* **SOCIALLY HANDICAPPED YOUTH.**

**HANDICAPPED YOUTH - EDUCATION (MIDDLE SCHOOL) - UNITED STATES.**
Hughes, Carolyn, 1946- The transition handbook. Baltimore : P.H. Brookes Pub., c2000.
*TC LC4019 .H84 2000*

**HANDICAPPED YOUTH - EDUCATION (SECONDARY) - UNITED STATES.**
Hughes, Carolyn, 1946- The transition handbook. Baltimore : P.H. Brookes Pub., c2000.
*TC LC4019 .H84 2000*

**HANDICAPPED YOUTH - EDUCATION - UNITED STATES.**
Lovitt, Thomas C. Preventing school failure. 2nd ed. Austin, Tex. : Pro-Ed. : c2000.
*TC LC146.6 .L68 2000*

Westling, David L. Teaching students with severe disabilities. 2nd ed. Upper Saddle River, N.J. : Merrill, c2000.
*TC LC4031 .W47 2000*

**HANDICAPPED YOUTH - RECREATION - UNITED STATES.**
Fink, Dale Borman, 1949- Making a place for kids with disabilities. Westport, Conn. : Praeger, 2000.
*TC GV183.6 .F56 2000*

**HANDICAPPED YOUTH - SERVICES FOR - UNITED STATES.**
Hughes, Carolyn, 1946- The transition handbook. Baltimore : P.H. Brookes Pub., c2000.
*TC LC4019 .H84 2000*

Pierangelo, Roger. Complete guide to special education transition services. West Nyack, NY : Center for Applied Research in Education, c1997.
*TC HV1569.3.Y68 P55 1997*

**HANDICAPPED YOUTH - VOCATIONAL EDUCATION - UNITED STATES.**
Pierangelo, Roger. Complete guide to special

education transition services. West Nyack, NY : Center for Applied Research in Education, c1997.
_TC HV1569.3.Y68 P55 1997_

**HANDICRAFT.** _See also_ **INDUSTRIAL ARTS; MANUAL TRAINING; OCCUPATIONS; SHELLCRAFT.**
Alexander, Marthann. Weaving on cardboard; New York, Taplinger Pub. Co. [1972]
_TC TT848 .A67_

Foxfire 2: ghost stories, spring wild plant foods, spinning and weaving, midwifing, burial customs, corn shuckin's, wagon making and more affairs of plain living. Garden City, N.Y., Anchor Press/Doubleday, 1973.
_TC F291.2 .F62 1973_

Foxfire 3. 1st ed. Garden City, N.Y. : Anchor Press, 1975.
_TC F291.2 .F622 1975_

Sohi, Morteza E. Look what I did with a shell!. New York : Walker & Co., 2000.
_TC TT862 .S64 2000_

**Handicraft Feb. 1914.**
Industrial arts magazine. Milwaukee [etc.] Bruce Publishing Co.

**HANDICRAFT - GEORGIA.**
Foxfire 2: ghost stories, spring wild plant foods, spinning and weaving, midwifing, burial customs, corn shuckin's, wagon making and more affairs of plain living. Garden City, N.Y., Anchor Press/Doubleday, 1973.
_TC F291.2 .F62 1973_

**HANDICRAFT - GEORGIA. - JUVENILE LITERATURE.**
Foxfire 3. 1st ed. Garden City, N.Y. : Anchor Press, 1975.
_TC F291.2 .F622 1975_

**Hands in clay.**
Speight, Charlotte F., 1919- 4th ed. Mountain View, Calif. : Mayfield, c1999.
_TC TT920 .S685 1999_

**Hands off!.**
Johnson, Richard T., 1956- New York ; Canterbury [England] : P. Lang, c2000.
_TC LB1033 .J63 2000_

**Handweaving.**
Buschman, Isabel, 1927- Metuchen, N.J. : Scarecrow Press, 1991.
_TC Z6153.T4 B87 1991_

**HANDWRITING.** _See_ **WRITING.**

**Handy, Lee C.**
Banff International Conference on Behavior Modification, 4th, 1972. Behavior change. Champaign, Ill. : Research Press, 1974, c1973.
_TC BF637.B4 B354 1972_

**Hane, Paula.**
Paul, Nora. Great scouts!. Medford, NJ : Information Today, c1999.
_TC ZA4201 .P38 1999_

**Hangin' in tough.**
McGarrh, Kellie, d. 1995. Kellie McGarrh's hangin' in tough. New York : P. Lang, c2000.
_TC LA2317.D6185 M34 2000_

**Hanging by a twig.**
Wren, Carol T. 1st ed. New York ; London : Norton, c2000.
_TC RC394.L37 W74 2000_

**Hanhardt, John G.**
Processing the signal [videorecording]. Cicero, Ill. : Roland Collection of Films on Art, c1989.
_TC N6494.V53 P7 1989_

**Hanks, William F.** Intertexts : writings on language, utterance, and context / William F. Hanks. Lanham : Rowman & Littlefield Publishers, Inc., c2000. v, 327 p. : ill. ; 24 cm. Collection of previously published (1986-1996) articles and essays. Includes bibliographical references and index. ISBN 0-8476-8740-6 (alk. paper) ISBN 0-8476-8741-4 (pbk. : alk. paper) DDC 306.44/089/971452
_1. Language and culture - Mexico - Yucátan (State) 2. Discourse analysis. 3. Indexicals (Semantics) 4. Maya language - Social aspects. I. Title._
_TC P35.5.M6 H36 2000_

**Hanley, Teresa Carrera.**
Valette, Jean Paul. Spanish for mastery. Lexington, Mass. : D.C. Heath, c1980.
_TC PC4112 .V29 1980_

**Hanna, Judith Lynne.** Partnering dance and education : intelligent moves for changing times / Judith Lynne Hanna. Champaign, IL : Human Kinetics, c1999. xv, 255 p. : ill. ; 23 cm. Includes bibliographical references (p. 225-248) and index. ISBN 0-88011-511-4 DDC 792.8/071/073
_1. Dance - Study and teaching - United States. 2. Interdisciplinary approach in education - United States. 3. Dance - Social aspects - United States. 4. Dance - United States - Psychological aspects. I. Title._
_TC GV1589 .H35 1999_

**Hannah, Mo Therese.**
Preventive approaches in couples therapy. Philadelphia : Brunner/Mazel, 1999.
_TC RC488.5 .P74 1999_

**Hannum, Wallace H.**
Jonassen, David H., 1947- Task analysis methods for instructional design. Mahwah, N.J. : L. Erlbaum Associates, 1999.
_TC LB1028.38 .J65 1999_

**HANSCOM, ELIZABETH DEERING, 1865-1960. SOPHIA SMITH AND THE BEGINNINGS OF SMITH COLLEGE.**
Quesnell, Quentin. The strange disappearance of Sophia Smith. Northampton [Mass.] : Smith College, c1999.
_TC LD7152.65.S45 Q84 1999_

**Hansel, Bettina G.** The exchange student survival kit / Bettina Hansel. Yarmouth, ME : Intercultural Press, c1993. xx, 128 p. ; 23 cm. Includes bibliographical references (p. 123-124) and index. ISBN 1-87786-417-X DDC 370.19/62
_1. Foreign study - United States. 2. Student exchange programs - United States. 3. Cultural relations. 4. High school students - United States - Attitudes. I. Title._
_TC LB1696 .H36 1993_

**Hansen, Janet S.**
Making money matter. Washington, D.C. : National Academy Press, c1999.
_TC LB2825 .M27 1999_

**Hansen, Joyce.** The heart calls home / Joyce Hansen. New York : Walker & Company, 1999. viii, 175 p. 22 cm. Sequel to: Out from this place. SUMMARY: After the Civil War, former slave Obi Booker tries to make a new life on a South Carolina island while waiting to be joined by his beloved Easter, who is studying in the North. ISBN 0-8027-8636-7 DDC [Fic]
_1. Afro-Americans - Juvenile fiction. 2. Reconstruction - Juvenile fiction. 3. United States - History - 1865-1898 - Juvenile fiction. 4. Afro-Americans - Fiction. 5. Reconstruction - Fiction. 6. United States - History - 1865-1898 - Fiction. 7. Islands - Fiction. 8. South Carolina - Fiction. I. Title._
_TC PZ7.H19825 He 1999_

**Hansen, Pia, 1955-.**
Danielson, Charlotte. A collection of performance tasks and rubrics. Larchnmont, NY : Eye On Education, c1999.
_TC QA135.5 .D244 1999_

**Hanson, Dan.** Distance education : : review of the literature / Dan Hanson ... [et al.]. 2nd ed. Washington, DC : Association for Educational Communications and Technology ; Ames, Iowa : Research Institute for Studies in Education, c1997. 61 p. ; 28 cm. "This monograph was written for the research group of the Iowa Distance Education Alliance ..." Includes bibliographical references. ISBN 0-89240-106-0
_1. Distance education - Bibliography. I. Iowa Distance Education Alliance. II. Title._
_TC LC5800 .S3 1997_

**HAPLORHINI.** _See_ **MONKEYS.**

**HAPPENING (ART).** _See_ **PERFORMANCE ART.**

**HAPPINESS.** _See also_ **CONTENTMENT; MENTAL HEALTH.**
Emmons, Robert A. The psychology of ultimate concerns. New York : Guilford Press, c1999.
_TC BF505.G6 E58 1999_

**Happy birthday, Lulu!.**
Uff, Caroline. New York : Walker & Company, 2000.
_TC PZ7.U285 Hap 2000_

**Happy to be nappy.**
Hooks, Bell. 1st ed. New York : Hyperion Books for Children, 1999.
_TC PZ7.H7663 Hap 1999_

**HAPTIC SENSE.** _See_ **TOUCH.**

**HAPTICS.** _See_ **TOUCH.**

**HARASSMENT.** _See_ **SEXUAL HARASSMENT.**

**HARD-CORE UNEMPLOYED - PITTSBURG, CALIF.**
Craddock, George W. Social disadvantagement and

dependency: Lexington, Mass., Heath Lexington Books [1970]
_TC HD7256.U6 C438_

**Hard lessons.**
Francis, Paul A. Washington, D.C. : World Bank, c1998.
_TC LA1632 .F73 1998_

**HARD-OF-HEARING.** _See_ **HEARING IMPAIRED.**

**Hard truths.**
Tye, Barbara Benham, 1942- New York : Teachers College Press, c2000.
_TC LB2822.82 .T94 2000_

**Hardcastle, William J., 1943-.**
Coarticulation. Cambridge, U.K. ; New York : Cambridge University Press, 1999.
_TC QP306 .C68 1999_

**HARDCORE UNEMPLOYED.** _See_ **HARD-CORE UNEMPLOYED.**

**Harding, Anne S.** Milestones in health and medicine / by Anne S. Harding. Phoenix : Oryx Press, 2000. xii, 267 p. :bill. ; 29 cm. Includes bibliographical references and index. ISBN 1-57356-140-1 DDC 610/.9
_1. Medicine - History. I. Title._
_TC R133 .H36 2000_

**Harding, F.**
Milk quality. 1st ed. London ; New York : Blackie, 1995.
_TC SF251 .M65 1995_

**Hardisty, David.**
The Internet. Oxford ; New York : Oxford University Press, c2000.
_TC TK5105.875.I57 I57 2000_

**Hardman, Michael L.** Human exceptionality : society, school, and family / Michael L. Hardman, Clifford J. Drew, M. Winston Egan. 6th ed. Boston : Allyn and Bacon, c1999. xviii, 615 p. : col. ill. ; 27 cm. Includes bibliographical references (p. 555-588) and indexes. ISBN 0-205-28039-0 DDC 362
_1. Handicapped. 2. Exceptional children. 3. Handicapped - Services for. 4. Learning disabilities. I. Drew, Clifford J., 1943- II. Egan, M. Winston. III. Title._
_TC HV1568 .H37 1999_

**HARDWARE, COMPUTER.** _See_ **COMPUTERS.**

**Hardy, Colin A.**
Learning and teaching in physical education. London ; Philadelphia, PA : Falmer Press, 1999.
_TC GV361 .L42 1999_

**HARES - FICTION.**
De Beer, Hans. [Kleine Eisbär und der Angsthase. English] Little Polar Bear and the brave little hare. New York : North-South Books, 1998.
_TC PZ7.D353 Liv 1998_

**Hargis, Charles H.** Teaching and testing in reading : a practical guide for teachers and parents / by Charles H. Hargis. Springfield, Ill. : C.C. Thomas, c1999. ix, 154 p. ; 24 cm. Includes bibliographical references (p. 147-149) and index. ISBN 0-398-06925-5 (cloth) ISBN 0-398-06926-3 (pbk.) DDC 372.41/6
_1. Reading - United States. 2. Reading - Ability testing - United States. I. Title._
_TC LB1050 .H29 1999_

**Hargraves, Martha A.**
Minority health in America. Baltimore, Md. : Johns Hopkins University Press, 2000.
_TC RA448.4 .M566 2000_

**Hargreaves, Linda.**
The primary curriculum. New York ; London : Routledge, 1998.
_TC LB1570 .P678 1998_

**Hargreaves, Mark, 1961-.**
Exercise metabolism. Champaign, IL : Human Kinetics, c1995.
_TC QP301 .E967 1995_

**Harkness, Sara.**
Variability in the social construction of the child. San Francisco : Jossey-Bass, 2000.
_TC BF723.S62 .V37 2000_

**Harlan, Jean Durgin.** Science experiences for the early childhood years : an integrated approach / Jean D. Harlan, Mary S. Rivkin. 7th ed. Upper Saddle River, N.J. : Merrill, c2000. xvi, 351 p. ; 24 cm. Includes bibliographical references and index. ISBN 0-13-099957-1 DDC 372.3/5
_1. Science - Study and teaching (Early childhood) I. Rivkin, Mary S. II. Title._
_TC LB1139.5.S35 H37 2000_

**Harlem Horizon Art Studio.**
Wexler, Alice. The art of necessity. 1999.
*TC 06 no. 11072*

**HARLEM HORIZON ART STUDIO.**
Wexler, Alice. The art of necessity. 1999.
*TC 06 no. 11072*

**HARLEM (NEW YORK, N.Y.) - FICTION.**
Littlesugar, Amy. Tree of hope. New York : Philomel
Books, 1999.
*TC PZ7.L7362 Tr 1999*

**HARLEM (NEW YORK, N.Y.) - HISTORY.**
Harlem on my mind : cultural capital of Black
America, 1900-1968. New York : New Press :
Distributed by W.W. Norton & Co., c1995.
*TC F128.68.H3 S3 1995*

**HARLEM (NEW YORK, N.Y.) - HISTORY - 20TH
CENTURY - PICTORIAL WORKS.**
Visual journal. Washington, DC : Smithsonian
Institution Press, c1996.
*TC TR820.5 .V57 1996*

**HARLEM (NEW YORK, N.Y.) - INTELLECTUAL
LIFE - SOURCES.**
Marks, Carole. The power of pride. 1st ed. New
York : Crown Publishers, c1999.
*TC E185.6 .M35 1999*

**HARLEM (NEW YORK, N.Y.) - SOCIAL
CONDITIONS.**
Wright, Stanley Nathaniel. The Beacon model. 1998.
*TC 06 no. 11007*

**Harlem on my mind : cultural capital of Black
America, 1900-1968** / edited & with a new
introduction by Allon Schoener ; and with a new
foreword by Henry Louis Gates, Jr. New York : New
Press : Distributed by W.W. Norton & Co., c1995. 258
p. : ill. ; 28 cm. Originally published: New York : Random
House, 1968. Includes index. ISBN 1-56584-266-9 DDC
974.7/1
*1. Harlem (New York, N.Y.) - History. 2. Afro-Americans - New
York (State) - New York - History. 3. New York (N.Y.) -
History. 4. Afro-American arts - New York (State) - New York -
History. I. Schoener, Allon.*
*TC F128.68.H3 S3 1995*

**Harlem renaissance.**
Huggins, Nathan Irvin, 1927- London ; New York :
Oxford University Press, 1973, c1971.
*TC NX511.N5 H89 1973*

**HARLEM RENAISSANCE.**
Huggins, Nathan Irvin, 1927- Harlem renaissance.
London ; New York : Oxford University Press, 1973,
c1971.
*TC NX511.N5 H89 1973*

Marks, Carole. The power of pride. 1st ed. New
York : Crown Publishers, c1999.
*TC E185.6 .M35 1999*

**Harlen, Wynne.**
Assessment in primary school science. London :
Commonwealth Secretariat, c1998.
*TC LB1585 .A87 1998*

**Harnessing science and technology for America's
economic future :** national and regional priorities /
Office of Special Projects, Policy Division, National
Research Council. Washington, D.C. : National
Academy Press, c1999. viii, 165 p. : ill. ; 23 cm. (National
forum on science and technology goals) Includes
bibliographical references. ISBN 0-309-06538-0 DDC
338.973/06
*1. Science and state - United States. 2. Science - United States -
Economic aspects. 3. Technology and state - United States. 4.
Technology - United States - Economic aspects. I. National
Research Council (U.S.). Office of Special Projects. II. Series.*
*TC Q127.U5 H37 1999*

**Harper, Helen J., 1957-** Wild words-dangerous
desires : high school girls and feminist avant-garde
writing / Helen J. Harper. New York : Peter Lang,
c2000. 186 p. ; 23 cm. (Counterpoints ; vol. 64) Includes
bibliographical references (p. [173]-183). ISBN 0-8204-3861-8
(alk. paper) DDC 808/.042/0712
*1. Creative writing (Secondary education) - Case studies. 2.
Feminist literature - Study and teaching (Secondary) - Case
studies. 3. Literature, Experimental - Study and teaching
(Secondary) - Case studies. 4. Teenage girls - Education -
Case studies. I. Title. II. Title: Wild words III. Title:
Dangerous desires IV. Series: Counterpoints (New York,
N.Y.) ; vol. 64.*
*TC LB1631 .H267 2000*

**Harrington, Charles C.** Cross cultural approaches to
learning / edited by Charles Harrington. New York :
MSS Information c1973. 293 p. : ill. ; 24 cm. Includes
bibliographical references. CONTENTS: Barry, H., Bacon,

M.K., and Child, I.L. / A cross-cultural survey of some sex
differences in socialization -- Brown, J. / A cross cultural study
of female initiation rites -- Burton, R. and Whiting, J. / The
absent father and cross sex identity -- Foster, G.M. / Peasant
society and the image of limited good -- Bumpert, P. and
Harrington, C. / Intellect and cultural deprivation --
Harrington, C. / Pupils, peers, and politics -- Harrington, C. /
Sexual differentiation in socialization and some male genital
mutilations -- Harrington, C. and Whiting, J. / Socialization
process and personality -- Homans, G. / Anxiety and ritual --
Hostetler, J. / Persistence and change patterns in Amish
society -- Jayawardena, C. / Ideology and conflict in lower
class communities -- Lee, D. / Lineal and non-lineal
codification of reality -- Levine, R. / The internalization of
political values in stateless societies -- Roberts, J. and Sutton-
Smith, B. / Child training and game involvement -- Washburn,
S.L. The study of race. ISBN 0-8422-0287-0 DDC 301.15/7
*1. Education, Primitive - Addresses, essays, lectures. 2.
Socialization - Cross-cultural studies - Addresses, essays,
lectures. 3. Ethnology - Addresses, essays, lectures. I. Title.*
*TC GN488.5 .H33 1973*

Flaxman, Erwin. Youth mentoring: New York, N.Y. :
ERIC Clearinghouse on Urban Education, 1988.
*TC LC4065 .F53 1988*

Psychological anthropology and education : a
delineation of a field of inquiry / Charles Harrington.
New York : AMS Press, c1979. xii, 232 p. ; 23 cm.
Bibliography. p. 129-222. Includes index. ISBN 0-404-16012-
3 DDC 155.8
*1. Ethnopsychology. 2. Educational anthropology. 3.
Personality and culture. 4. Ethnopsychology - Abstracts. 5.
Educational anthropology - Abstracts. 6. Personality and
culture - Abstracts. I. Title.*
*TC GN502 .H37*

Readings for anthropology and education 1- Edited by
Charles Harrington. New York, MSS Educational
Publishing Co. [c1971- v. illus. "... a custom made book of
readings prepared for the courses taught by the editor."
Includes bibliography.
*1. Educational anthropology. I. Title.*
*TC LB45 .H3*

**Harrington, Helen L.**
Who learns what from cases and how? Mahwah, N.J. :
L. Erlbaum Associates, 1999.
*TC LB1029.C37 W56 1999*

**Harrington, Jeff.**
Sport photography today! [videorecording].
Minneapolis, Minn. : Media Loft, c1992.
*TC TR821 .S64 1992*

**Harrington, Margaret M.**
Brisk, Maria. Literacy and bilingualism. Mahwah,
N.J. : L. Erlbaum Associates, c2000.
*TC LC3731 .B684 2000*

**Harrington, Patricia A.**
Integrating community service into nursing education.
New York, NY : Springer Pub. Co., c1999.
*TC RT76 .I55 1999*

**Harrington, Susanmarie.**
The online writing classroom. Cresskill, N.J. :
Hampton Press, c2000.
*TC PE1404 .O45 2000*

**Harris, Albert Josiah.** How to increase reading ability,
a guide to individualized and remedial methods /
Albert J. Harris ... 2d ed., rev. and enl. London ; New
York[etc.] : Longmans, Green and Co., 1947. xxi, 582
p., incl. : illus., (incl. facsims.), forms, diagrs ; 22 cm. "First
edition January 1940...Second edition January 1947." Printed
in the United States of America. Includes bibliographies. DDC
372.4
*1. Reading (Elementary). 2. Remedial teaching. 3. Reading,
Psychology of. I. Title.*
*TC 372.4H2421*

**Harris, Alma, 1958-** Teaching and learning in the
effective school / Alma Harris. Aldershot, England ;
Brookfield, Vt. : Ashgate, c1999. xix, 116 p. : ill. ; 23 cm.
Includes bibliographical references (p. 97-110) and index.
ISBN 1-85742-412-3 (hardcover) DDC 371.2/00941
*1. School improvement programs - Great Britain. 2. Effective
teaching - Great Britain. 3. Teacher effectiveness - Great
Britain. 4. Classroom management - Great Britain. 5.
Educational change - Great Britain. I. Title.*
*TC LB2822.84.G7 H37 1999*

**Harris, Hal.**
The trombone [videorecording]. Van Nuys, CA :
Backstage Pass Productions ; Canoga Park, Calif. :
[Distributed by] MVP, c1998.
*TC MT465 .T7 1998*

**Harris, Ian M., 1943-.**
Peacebuilding for adolescents. New York : P. Lang,
c1999.

*TC JZ5534 .P43 1999*

**Harris, John.**
J. Paul Getty Museum. A is for artist. Los Angeles : J.
Paul Getty Museum, c1997.
*TC N582.M25 A513 1997*

**Harris, Marvin, 1927-** Cows, pigs, wars & witches : the
riddles of culture. [1st ed.]. New York : Random
House, c1974. viii, 276 p. ; 22 cm. Includes bibliographical
references. ISBN 0-394-48338-3 DDC 392
*1. Ethnology - Miscellanea. 2. Witchcraft. I. Title. II. Title:
Riddles of culture [videorecording] III. Title: Cows, pigs, wars
and witches.*
*TC GN320 .H328 1974*

**Harris, Mary B. (Mary Bierman), 1943-.**
School experiences of gay and lesbian youth. New
York : Harrington Park Press, c1997.
*TC LC2575 .S36 1997*

**Harris, Melissa.**
Vaughan, David, 1924- Merce Cunningham. 1st ed.
New York, NY : Aperture, c1997.
*TC GV1785.C85 V38 1997*

**Harris, Neil, 1938-** The artist in American society : the
formative years, 1790-1860 / Neil Harris. Phoenix ed.,
with a new pref. Chicago : University of Chicago
Press, 1982. xvi, 432 p., [16] p. of plates : ill. ; 24 cm.
Originally published: New York : G. Braziller, 1966. Includes
bibliographical references (p.317-324) and index. ISBN
0-226-31754-4 (pbk.) DDC 701/.03
*1. Art and Society - United States. 2. Artists - United States -
Psychology. 3. Art, American. 4. Art, Modern - 19th century -
United States. I. Title.*
*TC N6507 .H27 1982*

Building lives : constructing rites and passages / Neil
Harris. New Haven [Conn.] ; London : Yale
University Press, c1999. ix, 198 p. : ill. ; 26 cm. Includes
bibliographical references (p. 167-187) and index. ISBN
0-300-07045-4 (alk. paper) DDC 720
*1. Architecture and society - United States. 2. Architecture,
American - History - 19th century. 3. Architecture, American -
History - 20th century. 4. Rites and ceremonies - United States.
5. United States - Social life and customs. I. Title.*
*TC NA2543.S6 H37 1999*

**Harris, Paul L.** The work of the imagination / Paul L.
Harris. Oxford : Blackwell Publishers, 2000. xii, 222
p. : ill. ; 22 cm. (Understanding children's worlds) Includes
bibliographical references and index.
*1. Imagination in children. I. Title. II. Series.*
*TC BF723.I5 H37a 2000*

**Harris, Scott L.**
Philosophers and religious leaders. Phoenix, Ariz. :
Oryx Press, 1999.
*TC B104 .P48 1999*

**Harris, Sidney, ill.**
Wynn, Charles M. The five biggest ideas in science.
New York : Wiley, c1997.
*TC Q163 .W99 1997*

**Harris, Vee, 1949-.**
Grenfell, Michael, 1953- Modern languages and
learning strategies. London ; New York : Routledge,
1999.
*TC PB35 .G783 1999*

**Harris, Whitney G.**
The African-American male perspective of barriers to
success. Lewiston, N.Y. : Edwin Mellen Press, c1999.
*TC LC2731 .A32 1999*

**Harrison, Barbara.**
Public charter schools : new choices in public
education (May 3, 2000 : Washington, D.C.) Public
charter schools [videorecording]. [Washington,
D.C.] : U.S. Dept. of Education, [2000].
*TC LB2806.36 .P9 2000*

**Harrison, Charles, 1942-.**
On pictures and paintings [videorecording].
Peasmarsh, East Sussex, Eng. ; Ho-Ho-kus, NJ :
Roland Collection, 1992.
*TC ND195.O45 1992*

**Harrison, Jennifer, 1949-** Sex education in secondary
schools / Jennifer K. Harrison. Buckingham
[England] ; Philadelphia : Open University Press,
2000. xvi, 192 p. : ill. ; 24 cm. Includes bibliographical
references (p. [182]-186) and index. ISBN 0-335-20108-3
(hbk.) ISBN 0-335-20107-5 (pbk.) DDC 613.9/071/241
*1. Sex instruction - Great Britain. 2. Hygiene, Sexual - Study
and teaching (Secondary) - Great Britain. 3. Sexual ethics -
Study and teaching (Secondary) - Great Britain. 4. Health
education (Secondary) - Great Britain. I. Title.*
*TC HQ57.6.G7 H37 2000*

**Harrison, John, 1951-** Critical challenges in social studies for upper elementary students / John Harrison, Neil Smith, Ian Wright. Vancouver : Critical Thinking Cooperative, 1999. xx, 144 p. ; 28 cm. (Critical challenges across the curriculum series, 1205-9730 ; v. 3) Copublished by: Field Relations and Teacher In-Service Education, Faculty of Education, Simon Fraser University. ISBN 0-86491-192-0 DDC 372.83/044
*1. Social sciences - Study and teaching (Elementary) I. Smith, Neil. II. Wright, Ian, 1941- III. Critical Thinking Cooperative. IV. Simon Fraser University. Faculty of Education. Field Relations and Teacher In-Service Education. V. Title. VI. Series.*
*TC LB1584.5.C3 H37 1999*

**Harrison, Kimberly.**
Babin, Edith H. Contemporary composition studies. Westport, Conn. : Greenwood Press, 1999.
*TC PE1404 .B23 1999*

**Harrison, Mark, lecturer.** Climates & constitutions : : health, race, environment and British imperialism in India 1600-1850 / Mark Harrison. New Delhi ; New York : Oxford University Press, c1999. xii, 263 p. : maps ; 23 cm. Includes bibliographical references (p. [225]-254) and index. ISBN 0-19-564657-6
*1. Public health - India - History. I. Title: Climates and constitutions.*
*TC RA395.I5 H37 1999*

**Harrison, Mike. (Mike A.).**
Wintle, Mike. Coordinating assessment practice across the primary school. London ; Philadelphia, PA : Falmer Press, 1999.
*TC LB3060.37 .W56 1999*

**Harrison, Patricia M.** Racial identification and self-concept issues in biracial Black/White adolescent girls / by Patricia M. Harrison. 1997. viii, 216 leaves ; 29 cm. Typescript; issued also on microfilm. Thesis (Ph.D.)--Columbia University, 1997. Includes bibliographical references (leaves 160-179). Photocopy. Ann Arbor, Mich. : UMI Dissertation Services.
*1. Racially mixed people - United States - Race identity. 2. Racially mixed people - United States - Psychology. 3. Teenage girls - United States - Psychology. 4. Self-perception in adolescence - United States. I. Title. II. Title: Racial identification and self-concept issues in biracial adolescent girls*
*TC 085 H247*

**HARROW SCHOOL - HISTORY.**
Elledge, Paul. Lord Byron at Harrow School. Baltimore : Johns Hopkins University Press, c2000.
*TC PR4382 .E36 2000*

**Harry, Beth.** Building cultural reciprocity with families : case studies in special education / by Beth Harry, Maya Kalyanpur, and Monimalika Day. Baltimore, Md. : P.H. Brookes Pub. Co., c1999. xix, 227 p. : ill. ; 23 cm. "The book was supported in part by the Consortium for Collaborative Research on Social Relationships of Children and Youth with Diverse Abilities, Cooperative Agreement No. H086A20003"--T.p. verso. Includes bibliographical references. ISBN 1-55766-377-7 DDC 371.9/04
*1. Special education - Parent participation - United States - Case studies. 2. Minority handicapped - Education - United States - Case studies. 3. Parent-teacher relationships - United States - Case studies. I. Kalyanpur, Maya. II. Day, Monimalika. III. Title.*
*TC LC3969 .H377 1999*

Kalyanpur, Maya. Culture in special education. Baltimore, Md. : P.H. Brookes Pub., c1999.
*TC LC3969 .K35 1999*

**Harry Potter and the Chamber of Secrets.**
Rowling, J. K. New York : Arthur A. Levine Books, 1999.
*TC PZ7.R7968 Har 1999*

**Harry Potter and the prisoner of Azkaban.**
Rowling, J. K. New York : Arthur A. Levine Books, 1999.
*TC PZ7.R79835 Ham 1999*

**Harry Potter and the sorcerer's stone.**
Rowling, J. K. 1st American ed. New York : A.A. Levine Books, 1998.
*TC PZ7.R79835 Har 1998*

**Hart, D. G. (Darryl G.)** The university gets religion : religious studies in American higher education / D.G. Hart. Baltimore, Md. : Johns Hopkins University Press, 1999. xi, 321 p. ; 24 cm. Includes bibliographical references and index. ISBN 0-8018-6210-8 (hardcover : alk. paper) DDC 200/.71/173
*1. Religion - Study and teaching (Higher) - United States - History. 2. Universities and colleges - United States - Religion. I. Title.*

*TC BL41 .H38 1999*

**Hart, D. J., 1948-.**
Livingstone, D, W. Public attitudes towards education in Ontario, 1996. Toronto : OISE/UT in association with University of Toronto Press, 1997.
*TC LA418.06 L58 1997*

**Hart-Hewins, Linda.** Better books! Better readers! : how to choose, use, and level books for children in the primary grades / Linda Hart-Hewins, Jan Wells. York, Me. : Stenhouse Publishers ; Markham, Ont. : Pembroke Publishers, c1999. 151 p. : ill. ; 25 cm. Includes bibliographical references (p. 150-151). ISBN 1-57110-305-8 ISBN 1-55138-105-2 (Pembroke) DDC 372.4
*1. Reading (Primary) 2. Children - Books and reading. 3. Book selection. I. Wells, Jan, 1948- II. Title.*
*TC LB1525 .H26 1999*

**Hart, Susan.** Thinking through teaching : a framework for enhancing participation and learning / Susan Hart with contributions from Niv Culora... [et al.]. London : David Fulton, 2000. viii, 152 p. : ill. ; 25 cm. Includes bibliographical references and index. ISBN 1-85346-628-X DDC 371.102
*1. Teaching - Great Britain. 2. Learning, Psychology of. I. Title.*
*TC LB1025.3 .H37 2000*

**Hartigan, John, 1964-** Racial situations : class predicaments of whiteness in Detroit / John Hartigan, Jr. Princeton, N.J. : Princeton University Press, c1999. xii, 354 p. : ill., map ; 24 cm. Includes bibliographical references (p. [285]-345) and index. ISBN 0-691-02886-9 (alk. paper) ISBN 0-691-02885-0 (pbk. : alk. paper) DDC 977.4/34004034
*1. Whites - Michigan - Detroit - Ethnic identity. 2. Detroit (Mich.) - Race relations. I. Title.*
*TC F574.D49 A1 1999*

**Hartley, James, Ph. D.**
The applied psychologist. 2nd ed. Buckingham [England] ; Philadelphia : Open University Press, 2000.
*TC BF76 .A63 2000*

**Hartley, James, Ph. D.** Learning and studying : a research perspective / James Hartley. London ; New York : Routledge, 1998. xii, 179 p. : ill. ; 22 cm. (Psychology focus) Includes bibliographical references (p. 153-172) and index. ISBN 0-415-16851-1 (hardcover) ISBN 0-415-16852-X (pbk.) DDC 153.1/5
*1. Learning, Psychology of. 2. Study skills. I. Title. II. Series.*
*TC BF318 .H365 1998*

**Hartley, Peter, 1946-** Interpersonal communication / Peter Hartley. 2nd ed. London ; New York : Routledge, 1999. vi, 254 p. : ill. ; 22 cm. Includes bibliographical references (p. [230]-246) and index. ISBN 0-415-18107-0 (pbk. : alk. paper) ISBN 0-415-20793-2 DDC 153.6
*1. Interpersonal communication. I. Title.*
*TC BF637.C45 H35 1999*

**The Hartmann era** / editor, Martin S. Bergmann. New York : Other Press, 2000. x, 373 p. ; 23 cm. "Conference proceedings, October 18-19, 1997, New York, N.Y." Includes bibliographical references and index. ISBN 1-89274-622-0 DDC 150.19/52/09
*1. Psychoanalysis - History - Congresses. 2. Freud, Sigmund, -1856-1939 - Congresses. 3. Hartmann, Heinz - Congresses. I. Bergmann, Martin S., 1913-*
*TC BF173 .B4675 2000*

**Hartmann, George W. (George Wilfried), 1904-1955 ed.**
Frontiers of democracy. New York, Progressive Education Association, etc., 1934-

**HARTMANN, HEINZ - CONGRESSES.**
The Hartmann era. New York : Other Press, 2000.
*TC BF173 .B4675 2000*

**Hartmann, Nicolai, 1882-1950.** Ethics, by Nicolai Hartmann ... translated by Stanton Coit (authorized version) introduction by J.H. Miurhead. London, G. Allen & Unwin ltd.; New York, The Macmillan company [1932] 3 v. ; 22 cm. (Library of philosophy, ed. by J. H. Miurhead) The German original "Ethik" was published in 1926. Includes bibliographical footnotes and index. Issued with various prinitng dates. Library lacks v. 2. CONTENTS: I. Moral phenomena.--II. Moral values.--III. Moral freedom.
*1. Ethics. I. Coit, Stanton, 1857-1944 tr. II. Title.*
*TC BJ1114 .H3C6 1932*

**Hartsell, Thomas L. (Thomas Lee), 1955-.**
Bernstein, Barton E. The portable lawyer for mental health professionals. New York : J. Wiley, c1998.
*TC KF3828.Z9 B47 1998*

**Hartung, Susan Kathleen, ill.**
Pak, Soyung. Dear Juno. New York : Viking, 1999.

*TC PZ7.P173 De 1999*

**Hartz, Gary W.** Psychosocial intervention in long-term care : an advanced guide / Gary W. Hartz, D. Michael Splain. New York : Haworth Press, c1997. xvi, 219 p. : ill. ; 22 cm. Includes bibliographical references and index. ISBN 0-7890-0114-4 (hc : alk. paper) ISBN 0-7890-0189-6 (pbk. : alk. paper) DDC 362.1/6
*1. Nursing home patients - Mental health. 2. Geriatric psychiatry. I. Splain, D. Michael. II. Title.*
*TC RC451.4.N87 H37 1997*

**Harvard business review book series**
Kotter, John P., 1947- John P. Kotter on what leaders really do. Boston : Harvard Business School Press, c1999.
*TC HD57.7 .K665 1999*

**Harvard Medical School.**
The Harvard Medical School guide to suicide assessment and intervention. 1st ed. San Francisco : Jossey-Bass, c1999.
*TC RC569 .H37 1999*

**The Harvard Medical School guide to suicide assessment and intervention** / Douglas G. Jacobs, editor. 1st ed. San Francisco : Jossey-Bass, c1999. xiv, 704 p. : ill. ; 24 cm. Includes bibliographical references (p. 593-667) and indexes. ISBN 0-7879-4303-7 (cloth : acid-free paper) DDC 616.85/8445
*1. Suicide. 2. Suicide - Prevention. I. Jacobs, Douglas. II. Harvard Medical School. III. Title: Guide to suicide assessment and intervention IV. Title: Suicide assessment and intervention*
*TC RC569 .H37 1999*

**Harvard University.** The Harvard University catalogue. Cambridge : Published for the University by C.W. Sever, 1873-c1975. v. ; 19-24 cm. Frequency: Annual. 1872-73-Oct. 1975. (<1966/67>: Official register of Harvard University) Catalogue. Cover title: General catalogue issue <1972-1973>. Continues: Harvard University. Catalogue of the officers and students of the University in Cambridge (DLC)sn 90039249 (OCoLC)11748631. Continued by: Harvard University. Harvard University general catalogue ISSN: 1052-9357 (DLC)sc 83007022 (OCoLC)7255650. DDC 378.744/4
*1. Harvard University - Periodicals. I. Title. II. Title: Catalogue III. Title: General catalogue issue <1972-1973> IV. Title: Harvard University. Catalogue of the officers and students of the University in Cambridge V. Title: Harvard University. Harvard University general catalogue*

**The Harvard University catalogue.**
Harvard University. Cambridge : Published for the University by C.W. Sever, 1873-c1975.

**Harvard University. Catalogue of the officers and students of the University in Cambridge.**
Harvard University. The Harvard University catalogue. Cambridge : Published for the University by C.W. Sever, 1873-c1975.

**Harvard University. Derek Bok Center for Teaching and Learning.**
Sarkisian, Ellen. Teaching American students. Rev. ed. Cambridge, Mass. : The President and Fellows of Harvard University, Derek Bok Center for Teaching and Learning, 1997, c1990.
*TC LB1738 .S371 1997*

**Harvard University. Graduate School of Education. International Network of Principals' Centers.**
Partners in progress. San Francisco, Calif. : Jossey-Bass Inc., c1999.
*TC LC3981 .P27 1999*

Reflections of first-year teachers on school culture. San Francisco : Jossey-Bass Inc., 1999.
*TC LB2844.1.N4 R44 1999*

**Harvard University. Harvard University general catalogue.**
Harvard University. The Harvard University catalogue. Cambridge : Published for the University by C.W. Sever, 1873-c1975.

**HARVARD UNIVERSITY - PERIODICALS.**
Harvard University. The Harvard University catalogue. Cambridge : Published for the University by C.W. Sever, 1873-c1975.

**Harvel, Lonnie.**
Unix and Windows 2000 handbook. Upper Saddle River, NJ : Prentice Hall, 2000.
*TC QA76.76.O63 U58 2000*

**HARVEST FESTIVALS.** *See* **THANKSGIVING DAY.**

**Harvey, Cynthia.**
Ballet class [videorecording]. W. Long Branch, NJ : Kultur, c1984.

*TC GV1589 .B33 1984*

**Harvey, James.**
Hill, Paul Thomas, 1943- It takes a city. Washington, D.C. : Brookings Institution Press, c2000.
*TC LC5131 .H48 2000*

**Harvey, James, 1944-.**
Kearns, David T. A legacy of learning. Washington, D.C. : Brookings Institution Press, c2000.
*TC LA217.2 .K43 2000*

**Harvey, John H., 1943-.**
Loss and trauma. Philadelphia, PA : Brunner-Routledge, c2000.
*TC BF575.D35 L67 2000*

**Harvey, Kerric.** Eden online : re-inventing humanity in a technological universe / Kerric Harvey. Cresskill, N.J. : Hampton Press, c2000. xix, 267 p. ; 24 cm. (The Hampton Press communication series. Political communication) Includes bibliographical references (p. 247-260) and indexes. ISBN 1-57273-189-3 (hbk.) ISBN 1-57273-190-7 (pbk.) DDC 303.48/3
*1. Technology - Social aspects. I. Title. II. Series.*
*TC T14.5 .H367 2000*

**Harvey, William B. (William Bernard).**
Grass roots and glass ceilings. Albany : State University of New York Press, c1999.
*TC LC212.42 .G73 1999*

**Harwayne, Shelley.** Going public : priorities and practice at the Manhattan New School / Shelley Harwayne. Portsmouth, NH : Heinemann, c1999. xxiii, 338 p. : ill. ; 20 cm. Includes bibliographical references (p. 329) and index. ISBN 0-325-00175-8 DDC 372.9747/1
*1. Elementary school administration - New York (State) - New York - Case studies. 2. Manhattan New School (New York, N.Y.) I. Title.*
*TC LB2822.5 .H37 1999*

Lifetime guarantees : toward ambitious literacy teaching / Shelley Harwayne. Portsmouth, NH : Heinemann, c2000. xvi, 384 p. : ill. ; 24 cm. Includes bibliographical references (p. B1-B8) and index. ISBN 0-325-00241-X DDC 372.6/044
*1. Language arts - United States. 2. Literacy - United States. 3. Activity programs in education - United States. 4. Manhattan New School (New York, N.Y.) I. Title.*
*TC LB1575 .H38 2000*

**Haryana (India). Education Dept.**
Haryana journal of education. Chandigarh, Haryana Education Dept.

**Haryana journal of education.** Chandigarh, Haryana Education Dept. v. ill. 25 cm. Vol. 9, nos. 2-3 not published. ISSN 0017-825X
*1. Education - Periodicals. I. Haryana (India). Education Dept.*

**HAS.**
Joint Commission on Accreditation of Healthcare Organizations. Hospital accreditation standards : HAS. Oakbrook Terrace, Ill. : The Commission, c1996-
*TC RA981.A2 J59a*

**Hasan, Mushirul.** Legacy of a Divided Nation : India's Muslims since independence / Mushirul Hasan. Boulder, Colo. : WestviewPress, c1997. xv, 383 p. ; 23 cm. Inlcudes bibliographical references (p. 352-367) and index. ISBN 0-8133-3339-3 (hc) ISBN 0-8133-3340-7 (pbk.) DDC 954.03/088/2971
*1. Muslims - India - Politics and government. 2. Islam and politics - India. 3. India - Politics and government - 1857-1919. 4. India - Politics and government - 1919-1947.*
*TC DS479 .L36 1997*

**Hashway, Robert M.** Developmental cognitive styles : a primer to the literature including an introduction to the theory of developmentalism / Robert Michael Hashway. San Francisco : Austin & Winfield Publishers, 1998. viii, 172 p. : ill. ; 22 cm. Includes bibliographical references and index. ISBN 1-57292-087-4 (hardcover : alk. paper) ISBN 1-57292-086-6 (pbk. : alk. paper) DDC 370.15/23
*1. Learning, Psychology of. 2. Cognitive styles in children. 3. Child development. I. Title.*
*TC LB1060 .H373 1998*

**Haskell, Barbara.** The American century : art & culture, 1900-1950 / Barbara Haskell. New York : Whitney Museum of American Art in association with W.W. Norton, c1999. 408 p. : ill. (some col.) ; 29 cm. Published on the occasion of the exhibition .... held at the Whitney Museum of American Art, part I, 1900-1950 is on view from April 23 to August 22, 1999 and part II, 1950-2000 is on view from September 26, 1999 to January 23, 2000. Includes bibliographical references (p. 385-392) and index. ISBN 0-393-04723-7 (Norton cloth) ISBN 0-87427-122-3 (Whitney pbk.) DDC 709/.73/0747471

*1. Art, American - Exhibitions. 2. Art, Modern - 20th century - United States - Exhibitions. 3. Arts, American - Exhibitions. 4. Arts, Modern - 20th century - United States - Exhibitions. I. Whitney Museum of American Art. II. Title.*
*TC N6512 .H355 1999*

**Haskins, James, 1941-** Bayard Rustin : behind the scenes of the civil rights movement / James Haskins. 1st ed. New York : Hyperion Books for Children, c1997. 121 p. : ill. ; 24 cm. Includes bibliographical references (p. 115) and index. SUMMARY: A biography of Bayard Rustin, a skillful organizer behind the scenes of the American civil rights movement whose ideas stongly influenced Martin Luther King, Jr. ISBN 0-7868-0168-9 (trade) ISBN 0-7868-2140-X (library) DDC 323/.092
*1. Rustin, Bayard. - 1912-1987 - Juvenile literature. 2. Civil rights workers - United States - Biography - Juvenile literature. 3. Afro-Americans - Civil rights - Juvenile literature. 4. Civil rights movements - United States - History - 20th century - Juvenile literature. 5. Rustin, Bayard. - 1912-1987. 6. Civil rights workers. 7. Afro-Americans - Biography. 8. Afro-Americans - Civil rights. I. Title.*
*TC E185.97.R93 H37 1997*

**Haslett, Julia.**
Connect with English [videorecording]. S. Burlington, Vt. : The Annenberg/CPB Collection, c1997.
*TC PE1128 .C66 1997*

**Haspels, Nelien.**
Action against child labour. Geneva : International Labour Office, c2000.
*TC HD6231 .A28 2000*

**Hass, Glen.**
Curriculum planning. 7th ed. Boston : Allyn and Bacon, c2000.
*TC LB2806.15 .C868 2000*

**Hastie, Cécile A.**
Milbank Memorial Library story hour [videorecording]. [New York : Milbank Memorial Library, 1999].
*TC Z718.3 .M5 1999 Series 3 Prog. 11*

**Hastings Center studies in ethics**
Promoting healthy behavior. Washington, D.C. : Georgetown University Press, c2000.
*TC RA427.8 .P766 2000*

**Hastings, Penny.** Sports for her : a reference guide for teenage girls / Penny Hastings. Westport, Conn. ; London : Greenwood Press, 1999. ix, 254 p. : ill. ; 24 cm. SUMMARY: Discusses issues related to girls' participation in sports and provides information on the rules, equipment, training, and more for eight sports which high school girls are most likely to play. Includes bibliographical references (p. [241]-247) and index. CONTENTS: 1. Girls Get a Kick Out of Sports -- 2. Basketball -- 3. Field Hockey -- 4. Soccer -- 5. Softball -- 6. Swimming and Diving -- 7. Tennis -- 8. Track and Field -- 9. Volleyball -- 10. Other Sports to Try -- 11. Breaking the Barriers: Male-Dominated Sports -- 12. The Young Female Athlete: Dealing with Special Issues -- 13. Pursuing Sports Beyond High School. ISBN 0-313-30551-X (alk. paper) DDC 796/.082 DDC 796/.082
*1. Sports for women - United States - Juvenile literature. 2. School sports - United States - Juvenile literature. 3. Sports for women. I. Title.*
*TC GV709.18.U6 H37 1999*

**Haswell, Richard H.**
Comp tales. New York : Longman, c2000.
*TC PE1404 .C617 2000*

**Hatch, Laurie Russell.** Beyond gender differences : adaptation to aging in life course perspective / Laurie Russell Hatch. Amityville, N.Y. : Baywood Pub., c2000. vii, 268 p. ; 24 cm. (Society and aging series) Includes bibliographical references (p. 193-237) and index. ISBN 0-89503-210-4 (cloth : alk. paper) DDC 305.26
*1. Aging - Social aspects. 2. Aging - Psychological aspects. 3. Sex role. 4. Adaptability (Psychology) in old age. 5. Sex differences (Psychology) in old age. 6. Adjustment (Psychology) in old age. I. Title. II. Series.*
*TC HQ1061 .H375 2000*

**Hatch, Maureen.**
Goldman, Marlene. Women and health. San Diego, Calif. : Academic, c2000.
*TC RA564.85 .G66 2000*

**Hatchet by Gary Paulsen.**
Beech, Linda Ward. New York : Scholastic, c1998.
*TC LB1573 .B4310 1998*

**HATE SPEECH - UNITED STATES.**
Shiffrin, Steven H., 1941- Dissent, injustice, and the meanings of America. Princeton, N.J. : Princeton University Press, c1999.
*TC KF4772 .S448 1999*

**HATE - UNITED STATES.**
Perlmutter, Philip. Legacy of hate. Armonk, N.Y. : London : M.E. Sharpe, c1999.
*TC BF575.H3 P47 1999*

**HATRED.** *See* HATE.

**Haug, M. (Marc).**
Animal models of human emotion and cognition. 1st ed. Washington, DC : American Psychological Association, c1999.
*TC BF671 .A55 1999*

**Haugaard, Jeffrey J., 1951-.**
Frontiers of developmental psychopathology. New York : Oxford University Press, 1996.
*TC RC454.4 .F76 1996*

**Haunted children.**
Roemmelt, Arthur F., 1944- Albany : State University of New York Press, c1998.
*TC RJ504 .R64 1998*

**HAUNTED PLACES.** *See* GHOSTS.

**Haviland-Jones, Jeannette M.**
Handbook of emotions. 2nd ed. New York : Guilford Press, c2000.
*TC BF561 .H35 2000*

**Hawaii. Dept. of Public Instruction.**
Hawaii educational review. [Honolulu : Dept. of Public Instruction and the Extension Dept. of the College of Hawaii], 1913-1954.

**Hawaii educational review.** [Honolulu : Dept. of Public Instruction and the Extension Dept. of the College of Hawaii], 1913-1954. 42 v. : ill. ; 28 cm. Frequency: Monthly (except July and Aug.). Former frequency: Monthly. Vol. 1, no. 1 (Jan. 1913)- . Ceased with v. 42, no. 10 (June 1954). Title from caption. Vol. 3, no. 9, Dec. 1915 not published.
*1. Education - Hawaii - Periodicals. I. Hawaii. Dept. of Public Instruction. II. College of Hawaii. Extension Dept.*

**HAWAII - HISTORY - JUVENILE LITERATURE.**
Linnea, Sharon. Princess Ka'iulani. Grand Rapids, Mich. : Eerdmans Books for Young Readers, 1999.
*TC DU627.17.K3 L56 1999*

**Hawisher, Gail E.**
Global literacies and the World-Wide Web. London ; New York : Routledge, 2000.
*TC P94.6 .G58 2000*

Passions, pedagogies, and 21st century technologies. Logan : Utah State University Press ; Urbana, Ill. : National Council of Teachers of English, c1999.
*TC PE1404 .P38 1999*

**Hawke, Constance S., 1952-** Computer and Internet use on campus : a legal guide to issues of intellectual property, free speech, and privacy / Constance S. Hawke. 1st ed. San Francisco : Jossey-Bass, c2001. xix, 172 p. ; 22 cm. (The Jossey-Bass higher and adult education series) Includes bibliographical references (p. 159-163) and indexes. ISBN 0-7879-5516-7 (alk. paper) DDC 343.7309/944
*1. Computer networks - Law and legislation - United States. 2. Computers - Law and legislation - United States. 3. College students - Legal status, laws, etc. - United States. 4. Internet. I. Title. II. Series.*
*TC KF390.5.C6 H39 2001*

**HAWKERS AND HAWKING.** *See* PEDDLERS AND PEDDLING.

**Hawking, S. W. (Stephen W.).**
Stephen Hawking's universe [videorecording]. [Alexandria, Va.] : PBS Video; Burbank, CA : Distributed by Warner Home Video, c1997.
*TC QB982 .S7 1997*

**HAWKING, S. W. (STEPHEN W.).**
Stephen Hawking's universe [videorecording]. [Alexandria, Va.] : PBS Video; Burbank, CA : Distributed by Warner Home Video, c1997.
*TC QB982 .S7 1997*

**Hawkins, Anne Hunsaker, 1944-** A small, good thing : stories of children with HIV and those who care for them / Anne Hunsaker Hawkins. New York : W.W. Norton, 2000. xv, 286 p. : ill. ; 22 cm. Includes bibliographical references. ISBN 0-393-04944-2 DDC 362.1/98929792
*1. AIDS (Disease) in children - Patients - Biography. 2. AIDS (Disease) in children - Popular works. I. Title.*
*TC RJ387.A25 H39 2000*

**Hawkins, Robert P., 1931-** Measuring behavioral health outcomes : a practical guide / Robert P. Hawkins, Judith R. Mathews, and Laureen Hamdan. New York : Kluwer Academic/Plenum Publishers, c1999. xiv, 191 p. : ill. ; 24 cm. (Clinical child psychology library) Includes bibliographical references (p. 141-143) and

index. ISBN 0-306-46080-7 (hardbound) ISBN 0-306-46081-5 (pbk.) DDC 618.92/89/0072
*1. Behavioral assessment of children - Handbooks, manuals, etc. 2. Behavioral assessment - Handbooks, manuals, etc. 3. Outcome assessment (Medical care) - Handbooks, manuals, etc. 4. Child psychology - Methodology - Handbooks, manuals, etc. I. Mathews, Judith R. II. Hamdan, Laureen. III. Title. IV. Series.*
**TC RJ503.5 .H39 1999**

**Hawksworth, Hamilton.**
Photomontage today, Peter Kennard [videorecording]. [London] : Art Council of Great Britain : Ho-Ho-Kus, N.J. : [distributed by] Anthony Roland Collection of Films on Art, c1982.
**TC TR685 .P45 1982**

**Hawthorne, Richard D.**
Henderson, James George. Transformative curriculum leadership. 2nd ed. Upper Saddle River, N.J. : Merrill, c2000.
**TC LB1570 .H45 2000**

**Hayashi, Chikio, 1918-.**
International Federation of Classification Societies. Conference. 5th, 1996, Kobe, Japan. Data science, classification, and related methods :. Tokyo ; New York : Springer, c1998.
**TC QA278 I53 1996**

**Hayden, Jacqueline, 1952-.**
Landscapes in early childhood education. New York : P. Lang, 2000.
**TC LB1139.23 .L26 2000**

**Haydn, Terry, 1951-** Learning to teach history in the secondary school : a companion to school experience / Terry Haydn, James Arthur and Martin Hunt. London ; New York : Routledge, 1997. xii, 301 p. : ill. ; 24 cm. (Learning to teach subjects in the secondary school series) Includes bibliographical references (p. [280]-293) and index. ISBN 0-415-15453-7 (pbk. : alk. paper) DDC 907.1/2
*1. History - Study and teaching (Secondary) I. Arthur, James, 1957- II. Hunt, Martin, 1936- III. Title. IV. Title: History V. Series.*
**TC D16.25 .H38 1997**

**Haydon, Geoffrey.**
Lyke, James. Creative piano teaching. 3rd ed. Champaign, Ill. : Stipes Pub. Co., c1996.
**TC MT220 .L95 1996**

**Haydon, Graham.** Values, virtues and violence : education and the public understanding of morality / Graham Haydon. Oxford ; Malden, MA : Blackwell Publishers, 1999. xii, 184 p. ; 23 cm. Special issue of The journal of philosophy of education. Includes bibliographical references (p. [175]-179) and index. ISBN 0-631-21532-8 DDC 370.11/4
*1. Moral education. 2. Values - Study and teaching. I. Title. II. Title: Journal of philosophy of education. Special issue.*
**TC LC268 .H294 1999**

**Hayes, Bartlett H., 1904- joint ed.**
Hofmann, Hans, 1880-1966. Search for the real, [Rev. ed.]. Cambridge, Mass., M.I.T. Press [c1967]
**TC N7445 .H76 1967**

Hofmann, Hans, 1880-1966. Search for the real, [Rev. ed.]. Cambridge, Mass., M.I.T. Press [c1967]
**TC N7445 .H76 1967**

**Hayes, Denis, 1949-** Foundations of primary teaching / Denis Hayes. 2nd ed. London : David Fulton, 1999. vi, 234 p. : ill. ; 25 cm. Previous ed.: 1996. Includes bibliographical references and index. ISBN 1-85346-563-1
*1. Education, Elementary - Great Britain. 2. Elementary school teaching - Great Britain. I. Title.*
**TC LB1555 .H43 1999**

**Hayes, Elisabeth.** Women as learners : the significance of gender in adult learning / Elisabeth Hayes and Daniele D. Flannery ; with Ann K. Brooks, Elizabeth J. Tisdell, and Jane M. Hugo. 1st ed. San Francisco : Jossey-Bass Publishers, c2000. xxiii, 280 p. ; 24 cm. (The Jossey-Bass higher and adult education series) Includes bibliographical references (p. 253-269) and index. ISBN 0-7879-0920-3 (alk. paper) DDC 374/.0082
*1. Adult learning. 2. Women - Education. 3. Feminism and education. I. Flannery, Daniele D., 1942- II. Title. III. Series: Jossey-Bass higher and adult education series.*
**TC LC5225.L42 H39 2000**

**Hayes, William, 1938-** Real-life case studies for school administrators / William Hayes. Lanham, Md. : Scarecrow Press, c2000. viii, 135 p. ; 23 cm. ISBN 0-8108-3742-0 (paper : alk. paper) DDC 371.2/00973
*1. School administrators - United States - Case studies. 2. School management and organization - United States - Case studies. I. Title.*
**TC LB2806 .H39 2000**

Real-life case studies for teachers / William Hayes. Lanham, Md. : Scarecrow Press, 2000. viii, 135 p. ; 23 cm. "Technomic books." ISBN 0-8108-3748-X (pbk. : alk. paper) DDC 371.102
*1. Teachers - United States - Case studies. 2. Teaching - United States - Case studies. I. Title.*
**TC LB1775.2 .H39 2000**

**Hayles, N. Katherine.** How we became posthuman : virtual bodies in cybernetics, literature, and informatics / N. Katherine Hayles. Chicago, Ill. : University of Chicago Press, 1999. xiv, 350 p. ; 23 cm. Includes bibliographical references and index. ISBN 0-226-32145-2 (cloth : alk. paper) ISBN 0-226-32146-0 (pbk. :alk. paper) DDC 003/.5
*1. Artificial intelligence. 2. Cybernetics. 3. Computer science. 4. Virtual reality. 5. Virtual reality in literature. I. Title.*
**TC Q335 .H394 1999**

**Haynes, Stephen N.** Principles and practice of behavioral assessment / Stephen N. Haynes and William Hayes O'Brien. New York ; London : Kluwer Academic/Plenum, c2000. xviii, 348 p. : ill. ; 26 cm. (Applied clinical psychology) Includes bibliographical references (p. 317-335) and indexes. ISBN 0-306-46221-4 DDC 150/.287
*1. Behavioral assessment. I. O'Brien, William Hayes. II. Title. III. Series.*
**TC BF176.5 .H39 2000**

**Hays, Kate F.** Working it out : using exercise in psychotherapy / Kate F. Hays. 1st ed. Washington, DC : American Psychological Association, c1999. xxi, 281 p. ; 27 cm. Includes indexes. Includes bibliographical references (p. 247-266). ISBN 1-55798-592-8 (case)
*1. Book 2. Exercise Therapy 3. Psychotherapy - methods 4. Exercise therapy. 5. Exercise - Psychological aspects. 6. Mental health promotion. I. American Psychological Association. II. Title. III. Title: Using exercise in psychotherapy*
**TC RC489.E9 H39 1999**

**Hayton, Annette.** Tackling disaffection and social exclusion : education perspectives and policies / edited by Annette Hayton. London : Kogan Page, 1999. viii, 226 p. : ill. ; 24 cm. (The future of education from 14+) Includes bibliographical references and index. ISBN 0-7494-2889-9
*1. Social isolation - Great Britain. 2. Education and state - Great Britain. I. Title. II. Series.*
**TC LC93.G7 H39 1999**

**Hazen-Hammond, Susan.** Thunder Bear and Ko : the Buffalo nation and Nambe Pueblo / text and photography by Susan Hazen-Hammond. 1st ed. New York : Dutton Children's Books, 1999. 1 v. (unpaged) : col. ill. ; 26 cm. SUMMARY: Describes the life of Thunder Bear Yates and his family in Nambe Pueblo, where they are trying to preserve the traditions of their ancestors as well as the buffalo that are sacred to their people. ISBN 0-525-46013-6 (hc) DDC 978.9/56
*1. Nambe Pueblo (N.M.) - Juvenile literature. 2. Tewa Indians - Juvenile literature. 3. American bison - Juvenile literature. 4. Pueblo Indians - Juvenile literature. 5. Pueblo Indians. 6. Indians of North America - New Mexico. 7. Nambe Pueblo (N.M.) 8. Bison. I. Title.*
**TC E99.T35 H36 1999**

**HBO original programming.**
Teen killers [videorecording]. Princeton, NJ : Films for the Humanities and Sciences, c1998-1999.
**TC HV9067.H6 T4 1999**

**HEAD.** *See* **BRAIN; EAR; HAIR.**

**Head, John (John O.)** Understanding the boys : issues of behaviour and achievement / John Head. New York : Falmer Press, 1999. 120 p. ; 24 cm. Includes bibliographical references (p. [109]-118) and index. ISBN 0-7507-0867-0 (hardback : alk. paper) ISBN 0-7507-0866-2 (pbk. : alk. paper) DDC 373.18235/1
*1. Teenage boys - Education - Great Britain. 2. Teenage boys - Great Britain - Psychology. 3. Teenage boys - Great Britain - Physiology. 4. Academic achievement - Great Britain. 5. Teenage boys - Great Britain - Social conditions. I. Title.*
**TC LC1390 .H43 1999**

**HEAD MASTERS.** *See* **SCHOOL PRINCIPALS.**

**HEAD MISTRESSES.** *See* **SCHOOL PRINCIPALS.**

**HEAD NURSES.** *See* **NURSE ADMINISTRATORS.**

**Head Start National Research Conference (4th : 1998 : Washington, D.C.)** Children and families in an era of rapid change : creating a shared agenda for researchers, practitioners and policy makers : summary of conference proceedings July 9-12, 1998 Washington, D.C. New York : Columbia University's Joseph L. Mailman School of Public Health Center for Population and Family Health ; Ann Arbor, Mich. :

Society for Research in Child Development, 1999. v, 721 p. ; 26 cm. Includes bibliographical references.
*1. Head Start Program (U.S.) - Congresses.*
**TC LC4069.2 .H43 1998**

**HEAD START PROGRAM (U.S.).**
Lacy, Gary L. Head start social services. New York : Garland Pub., 1999.
**TC HV699 .L33 1999**

Sissel, Peggy A. Staff, parents, and politics in Head Start. New York ; London : Falmer Press, 2000.
**TC LC4091 .S49 2000**

**HEAD START PROGRAM (U.S.) - CONGRESSES.**
Head Start National Research Conference (4th : 1998 : Washington, D.C.) Children and families in an era of rapid change. New York : Columbia University's Joseph L. Mailman School of Public Health Center for Population and Family Health ; Ann Arbor, Mich. : Society for Research in Child Development, 1999.
**TC LC4069.2 .H43 1998**

**HEAD START PROGRAMS - COLORADO.**
Clay, Cheryl D., 1947- Schooling at-risk Native American children. New York : Garland Pub., 1998.
**TC E99.U8 C53 1998**

**HEAD START PROGRAMS - UNITED STATES.**
Lacy, Gary L. Head start social services. New York : Garland Pub., 1999.
**TC HV699 .L33 1999**

**HEAD START PROGRAMS - UNITED STATES - CASE STUDIES.**
Sissel, Peggy A. Staff, parents, and politics in Head Start. New York ; London : Falmer Press, 2000.
**TC LC4091 .S49 2000**

Wilson, Catherine S. Telling a different story. New York : London : Teachers College Press, c2000.
**TC LC5131 .W49 2000**

**Head start social services.**
Lacy, Gary L. New York : Garland Pub., 1999.
**TC HV699 .L33 1999**

**HEAD TEACHERS.** *See* **SCHOOL PRINCIPALS.**

**HEADACHE.**
When the brain goes wrong [videorecording]. Short version. Boston, MA : Fanlight Productions [dist.], c1992.
**TC RC386 .W54 1992**

**Headline stories of the century** [videorecording] : a newsreel library of World War II / original footage provided by Hearst Entertainment, Ashley Entertainment ; [produced by: Hearst Entertainment and Questar Video, Inc.] ; assistant producer, Melissa Goldberg ; writers, Walter De Hoog, Rolf Forsberg. Chicago, IL. : Distributed by Questar Video, Inc., c1992. 1 videocassette (90 min.) : sd., b&w with color sequences ; 1/2 in. VHS. Catalogued from credits and container. Narration: Phil Tonken, Howard Reig. For high school and adult audiences. SUMMARY: "Covering the most documented war in history, this video presents 84 carefully edited, black-and-white Hearst newsreels from dramatic combat footage, most filmed by the Signal Corps, Coast Guard, Air Force, and Navy photographers.-- Container. ISBN 0-927992-69-8
*1. World War, 1939-1945 - Motion pictures and the war. 2. Motion picture journalism - United States. 3. Newsreels. I. Goldberg, Melissa. II. Hoog, Walter de. III. Forsberg, Rolf. IV. Tonken, Phil. V. Reig, Howard. VI. Questar Video, Inc. VII. Hearst Entertainment (Firm) VIII. Ashley Entertainment. IX. Title: Newsreel library of World War II*
**TC D743 .H42 1992**

**HEADMASTERS.** *See* **SCHOOL PRINCIPALS.**

**HEADMISTRESSES.** *See* **SCHOOL PRINCIPALS.**

**HEADS OF HOUSEHOLDS.** *See* **WOMEN HEADS OF HOUSEHOLDS.**

**HEADTEACHERS.** *See* **SCHOOL PRINCIPALS.**

**Healey, E. Charles.**
Stuttering research and practice. Mahwah, N.J. : Erlbaum, 1999.
**TC RC424 .S786 1999**

**HEALING.** *See* **MENTAL HEALING.**

**Healing children's grief.**
Christ, Grace Hyslop. New York ; Oxford : Oxford University Press, 2000.
**TC BF723.G75 C58 2000**

**Healing from within** : the use of hypnosis in women's health care / edited by Lynne M. Hornyak and Joseph P. Green. 1st ed. Washington, DC : London : American Psychological Association, c2000. xiii, 285 p. ; 27 cm. (Dissociation, trauma, memory, and hypnosis book series) Includes bibliographical references and indexes. ISBN

1-55798-647-9 (cloth : alk. paper) DDC 615.8/512/082
*1. Hypnotism - Therapeutic use. 2. Women - Diseases -
Treatment. I. Hornyak, Lynne M. II. Green, Joseph P. (Joseph
Patrick) III. Series.*
**TC RC497 .H42 2000**

**HEALING SYSTEMS.** *See* **ALTERNATIVE
MEDICINE.**

**Healing the whole person.**
McNeilly, Robert B. New York : Chichester
[England] : John Wiley & Sons, c2000.
**TC RC489.S65 M38 2000**

**HEALTH.** *See also* **DIET; DISEASES; EXERCISE;
HEALTH ATTITUDES; HEALTH STATUS
INDICATORS; HYGIENE; MENTAL
HEALTH; NUTRITION; PHYSICAL
FITNESS; PUBLIC HEALTH; STRESS
MANAGEMENT.**
Children's understanding of biology and health. 1st
ed. Cambridge, U.K. ; New York : Cambridge
University Press, 1999.
**TC BF723.C5 C514 1999**

Ferrini, Armeda F. Health in the later years. 3rd ed.
Boston : McGraw-Hill, c2000.
**TC RA777.6 .F46 2000**

Jonas, Steven. Talking about health and wellness with
patients. New York : Springer, c2000.
**TC RA427.8 .J66 2000**

**HEALTH ADMINISTRATION.** *See* **HEALTH
SERVICES ADMINISTRATION.**

**Health and Administration Development Group
(Aspen Publishers).**
Grants for school technology. 3rd ed. Gaithersburg,
MD : Aspen Publishers, c2000.
**TC LB2336 .G76365 2000**

Grants for schools. 4th ed. Gaithersburg, MD : Aspen
Publishers, 2000.
**TC LB2825 .F46 2000**

**Health and healthcare in the United States :** county
and metro area data / editor, Richard K. Thomas. 1st
ed. Lanham, MD : Bernan Press : Nationshealth
Corp., c1999. xiv, 437 p. : maps ; 28 cm. + 1 computer laser
optical disc (4 3/4 in.). SUMMARY : Compendium of health-
related statistics presented for each county and metropolitan
area in the United States. Includes data on demographics, vital
statistics, healthcare resources, and medicare. System
requirements for CD-Rom: PC with Pentium 133 or higher;
Microsoft Windows 95, Windows NT, version 4.0 or higher;
32 MB of Ram; 40 MB of hard disk space; CD-ROM dirve;
VGA or higher monitor; mouse. ISBN 0-89059-188-1
*1. United States - Statistics. 2. Public health - United States -
Statistics. I. Thomas, Richard K., 1944- II. Title.*
**TC HA214 .H435 1999**

**Health and healthcare in the United States :** county
and metro area data / editor, Richard K. Thomas. 1st
ed. Lanham, MD : Bernan Press : Nationshealth
Corp., c1999. xiv, 437 p. : maps ; 28 cm. + 1 computer laser
optical disc (4 3/4 in.). SUMMARY : Compendium of health-
related statistics presented for each county and metropolitan
area in the United States. Includes data on demographics, vital
statistics, healthcare resources, and medicare. System
requirements for CD-Rom: PC with Pentium 133 or higher;
Microsoft Windows 95, Windows NT, version 4.0 or higher;
32 MB of Ram; 40 MB of hard disk space; CD-ROM dirve;
VGA or higher monitor; mouse. ISBN 0-89059-188-1
*1. United States - Statistics. 2. Public health - United States -
Statistics. I. Thomas, Richard K., 1944- II. Title.*
**TC HA214 .H435 1999**

**HEALTH ATTITUDES.** *See also* **HEALTH
BEHAVIOR; PATIENT SATISFACTION.**
Shucksmith, Janet, 1953- Health issues and
adolescents. London ; New York : Routledge, 1998.
**TC RJ47.53 .S455 1998**

**HEALTH ATTITUDES - SCOTLAND.**
Shucksmith, Janet, 1953- Health issues and
adolescents. London ; New York : Routledge, 1998.
**TC RJ47.53 .S455 1998**

**HEALTH BEHAVIOR.** *See also* **HEALTH
ATTITUDES.**
Health behavior and health education. 2nd ed. San
Francisco : Jossey-Bass, 1997.
**TC RA776.9 .H434 1997**

**Health behavior and health education :** theory,
research, and practice / Karen Glanz, Frances Marcus
Lewis, Barbara K. Rimer, editors ; foreword by J.
Michael McGinnis. 2nd ed. San Francisco : Jossey-
Bass, 1997. xxx, 496 p. : ill. ; 24 cm. (Jossey-Bass health
series) Includes bibliographical references and indexes. ISBN
0-7879-0310-8 (hardcover : alk. paper) DDC 613

*1. Health behavior. 2. Health education. I. Glanz, Karen. II.
Lewis, Frances Marcus. III. Rimer, Barbara K. IV. Series.*
**TC RA776.9 .H434 1997**

**HEALTH BEHAVIOR - ECONOMIC ASPECTS.**
Reframing health behavior change with behavioral
economics. Mahwah, N.J. ; London : Lawrence
Erlbaum. 2000.
**TC RA776.9 .R433 2000**

**HEALTH BEHAVIOR IN ADOLESCENCE.**
Shucksmith, Janet, 1953- Health issues and
adolescents. London ; New York : Routledge, 1998.
**TC RJ47.53 .S455 1998**

**HEALTH BEHAVIOR IN ADOLESCENCE -
SCOTLAND.**
Shucksmith, Janet, 1953- Health issues and
adolescents. London ; New York : Routledge, 1998.
**TC RJ47.53 .S455 1998**

**HEALTH BEHAVIOR - PSYCHOLOGICAL
ASPECTS.**
Mendoza, Maria Adalia. A study to compare inner
city Black men and women completers and non-
attenders of diabetes self-care classes. 1999.
**TC 06 no. 11206**

**HEALTH BEHAVIOR - SOCIAL ASPECTS.**
Mendoza, Maria Adalia. A study to compare inner
city Black men and women completers and non-
attenders of diabetes self-care classes. 1999.
**TC 06 no. 11206**

**HEALTH BEHAVIOR - UNITED STATES -
HISTORY.**
Engs, Ruth C. Clean living movements. Westport,
Conn. ; London : Praeger, 2000.
**TC RA427.8 .E54 2000**

**HEALTH CARE.** *See* **MEDICAL CARE.**

**HEALTH CARE ADMINISTRATION.** *See*
**HEALTH SERVICES ADMINISTRATION.**

**Health care and its costs** / Carl J. Schramm, editor. 1st
ed. New York : Norton, c1987. x, 301 p. ; 22 cm. At head
of title: The American Assembly, Columbia University.
Includes bibliographies and index. ISBN 0-393-02437-7 ISBN
0-393-95671-7 (pbk.) DDC 338.4/73621/0973
*1. Medical care - United States. 2. Medical care - United
States - Finance. 3. Delivery of Health Care - economics -
United States. I. Schramm, Carl J. II. American Assembly.*
**TC RA395.A3 H392 1987**

**HEALTH CARE COSTS.**
Cost benefit analysis of heroin maintenance treatment.
Basel ; New York : Karger, c2000.
**TC RC568.H4 C67 2000**

**HEALTH CARE DELIVERY.** *See* **MEDICAL
CARE.**

**Health care divided.**
Smith, David Barton. Ann Arbor : University of
Michigan Press, 1999.
**TC RA448.5.N4 S63 1999**

**HEALTH CARE ETHICS.** *See* **MEDICAL
ETHICS.**

**HEALTH CARE FACILITIES.** *See* **HEALTH
FACILITIES.**

**Health care in the new millennium.**
Morrison, J. Ian, 1952- 1st ed. San Francisco :
Jossey-Bass Publishers, c2000.
**TC RA395.A3 M675 2000**

**HEALTH CARE INSTITUTIONS.** *See* **HEALTH
FACILITIES.**

**Health care integration.**
Demetriou, Andrew J. Washington, D.C. : Bureau of
National Affairs, Inc., c1996.
**TC KF3825 .D394 1996**

**HEALTH CARE MANAGEMENT.** *See* **HEALTH
SERVICES ADMINISTRATION.**

**HEALTH CARE NEED.** *See* **MEDICAL CARE -
NEEDS ASSESSMENT.**

**HEALTH CARE NEEDS.** *See* **MEDICAL CARE -
NEEDS ASSESSMENT.**

**HEALTH CARE PERSONNEL.** *See* **MEDICAL
PERSONNEL.**

**HEALTH CARE PLANNING.** *See* **HEALTH
PLANNING.**

**HEALTH CARE POLICY.** *See* **MEDICAL
POLICY.**

**Health care policy and politics A to Z.**
Rovner, Julie. Washington, DC : CQ Press, 2000.

**TC RA395.A3 R685 1999**

**Health care policy in the United States**
Gordon, Judith S., 1958- Helping survivors of
domestic violence. New York : Garland Pub., 1998.
**TC HV6626.2 .G67 1998**

**HEALTH CARE RATIONING.**
The global challenge of health care rationing.
Buckingham [England] ; Philadelphia : Open
University Press, 2000.
**TC RA394.9 .G56 2000**

**HEALTH CARE REFORM - UNITED STATES.**
Health policy reform in America. 2nd ed. Armonk,
N.Y. : M.E. Sharpe, c1997.
**TC RA395.A3 H42564 1997**

O'Brien, Lawrence J. Bad medicine. Amherst, N.Y. :
Prometheus Books, c1999.
**TC RA395.A3 O28 1999**

Rushefsky, Mark E., 1945- Politics, power & policy
making. Armonk, N.Y. : M.E. Sharpe, c1998.
**TC RA395.A3 R855 1998**

**HEALTH CARE REFORM - UNITED STATES -
STATES.**
Health policy reform in America. 2nd ed. Armonk,
N.Y. : M.E. Sharpe, c1997.
**TC RA395.A3 H42564 1997**

**Health, civilization, and the state.**
Porter, Dorothy, 1953- London ; New York :
Routledge, 1999.
**TC RA424 .P67 1999**

**Health communication (Cresskill, N.J.)**
Communication in recovery. Cresskill, N.J. : Hampton
Press, c1999.
**TC HV4998 .C64 1999**

**HEALTH COUNSELING.** *See also* **ALCOHOLISM
COUNSELING; DRUG ABUSE
COUNSELING.**
Noon, J. Mitchell. Counselling and helping carers.
Leicester : BPS Books, 1999.
**TC R727.4 .N66 1999**

The practice of counselling in primary care. London ;
Thousand Oaks, Calif. : SAGE Publications, 1999.
**TC R727.4 .P733 1999**

**HEALTH ECOLOGY.** *See* **ENVIRONMENTAL
HEALTH.**

**HEALTH - ECONOMIC ASPECTS.** *See* **MEDICAL
ECONOMICS.**

**HEALTH ECONOMICS.** *See* **MEDICAL
ECONOMICS.**

**HEALTH EDUCATION.** *See also* **HEALTH
PROMOTION.**
Gilbert, Glen G. (Glen Gordon), 1946- 2nd ed.
Sudbury, Mass. : Jones and Bartlett, c2000.
**TC RA440.5 .G48 2000**

**HEALTH EDUCATION.**
Health behavior and health education. 2nd ed. San
Francisco : Jossey-Bass, 1997.
**TC RA776.9 .H434 1997**

**Health, education, and welfare indicators** / Office of
Program Analysis, Office of the Secretary, United
States Department of Health, Education, and Welfare.
Washington, D.C. : U.S. Dept. of Health, Education
and Welfare : For sale by the Supt. of Docs., U.S.
G.P.O., 1960-[1967] v. : ill., diagrs. ; 26 cm. Frequency:
Monthly. Began in 1958; ceased publication in 1967. "First
public issue Sept. 1960" To be used in conjunction with the
annual Health, education, and welfare trends. Has supplement:
Health, education, and welfare trends ISSN: 0082-9897.
*1. Education - United States - Statistics - Periodicals. 2. Public
health - United States - Statistics - Periodicals. 3. Public
welfare - United States - Statistics - Periodicals. I. United
States. Dept. of Health, Education, and Welfare. Office of the
Secretary. II. United States. Dept. of Health, Education, and
Welfare. Office of Program Analysis. III. Title: Health,
education, and welfare trends*

**Health, education, and welfare trends.**
Health, education, and welfare indicators.
Washington, D.C. : U.S. Dept. of Health, Education
and Welfare : For sale by the Supt. of Docs., U.S.
G.P.O., 1960-[1967]

**HEALTH EDUCATION - AUSTRALIA.**
Health promotion strategies & methods. Rev. ed.
Sydney ; New York : McGraw-Hill, c1999.
**TC RA427.8 .H527 1999**

**HEALTH EDUCATION - AUSTRALIA.**
Health promotion strategies & methods. Rev. ed.
Sydney ; New York : McGraw-Hill, c1999.

TC RA427.8 .H527 1999

**HEALTH EDUCATION - CASE STUDIES.**
Pridmore, Pat, 1947- Children as partners for health.
London ; New York : Zed Books ; New York :
Distributed exclusively in the USA by St. Martin's
Press, 2000.
*TC LB1587.A3 P75 2000*

**HEALTH EDUCATION - DEVELOPING
COUNTRIES - CROSS-CULTURAL STUDIES.**
Ayim, Martin Ayong. Empowerment through health
education. 2nd ed. Ruston, LA : Vita Press
International, c1998.
*TC RA441.5 .A95 1998*

**HEALTH EDUCATION (ELEMENTARY) -
UNITED STATES.**
Teaching children about health. Englewood, Colo. :
Morton Pub., 1999.
*TC LB1587.A3 T43 1999*

**HEALTH EDUCATION OF WOMEN.** *See*
**WOMEN - HEALTH AND HYGIENE.**

**HEALTH EDUCATION - PERIODICALS.**
International journal of health education. [Geneva,
Studer, 1958-1981]

**HEALTH EDUCATION - PERIODICALS.**
International journal of health education. [Geneva,
Studer, 1958-1981]

**HEALTH EDUCATION (SECONDARY).**
Spruijt-Metz, Donna. Adolescence, affect and health.
Hove : Psychology Press, for the European
Association for Research on Adolescence, 1999.
*TC RJ47.53 .S67 1999*

**HEALTH EDUCATION (SECONDARY) - GREAT
BRITAIN.**
Harrison, Jennifer, 1949- Sex education in secondary
schools. Buckingham [England] ; Philadelphia : Open
University Press, 2000.
*TC HQ57.6.G7 H37 2000*

**HEALTH EDUCATION (SECONDARY) - UNITED
STATES - PROBLEMS, EXERCISES, ETC.**
Toner, Patricia Rizzo, 1952- Consumer health and
safety activities. West Nyack, N.Y. : Center for
Applied Research in Education, c1993.
*TC RA440.3.U5 T66 1993*

**HEALTH EDUCATION - UNITED STATES.**
Gilbert, Glen G. (Glen Gordon), 1946- Health
education. 2nd ed. Sudbury, Mass. : Jones and
Bartlett, c2000.
*TC RA440.5 .G48 2000*

Meeks, Linda Brower. Comprehensive school health
education. 2nd edition. Blacklick, OH : Meeks Heit
Pub. Co., c1996.
*TC RA440.3.U5 M445 1996*

**HEALTH EDUCATION - UNITED STATES -
CURRICULA.**
Teaching children about health. Englewood, Colo. :
Morton Pub., 1999.
*TC LB1587.A3 T43 1999*

**HEALTH - ENCYCLOPEDIAS.**
Sharma, R. (Rajendra), 1959- The family
encyclopedia of health. Boston : Element Books,
1999.
*TC RC81.A2 S53 1999*

**HEALTH - ENVIRONMENTAL ASPECTS.** *See*
**ENVIRONMENTAL HEALTH.**

**HEALTH FACILITIES.** *See* **HOSPITALS.**

**HEALTH FACILITIES - ADMINISTRATION.** *See*
**HEALTH FACILITIES - AFFILIATIONS.**

**HEALTH FACILITIES - AFFILIATIONS.** *See*
**MULTIHOSPITAL SYSTEMS.**

**HEALTH FACILITIES - AFFILIATIONS -
UNITED STATES.**
Remaking health care in America. 1st ed. San
Francisco : Jossey-Bass Publishers, c1996.
*TC RA395.A3 R46 1996*

**HEALTH FACILITIES - BUSINESS
MANAGEMENT.**
Finkler, Steven A. Financial management for nurse
managers and executives. 2nd ed. Philadelphia ;
London : W.B. Saunders, c2000.
*TC RT86.7 .F46 2000*

**HEALTH FACILITIES - LAW AND
LEGISLATION - UNITED STATES.**
Demetriou, Andrew J. Health care integration.
Washington, D.C. : Bureau of National Affairs, Inc.,
c1996.

TC KF3825 .D394 1996

**HEALTH FACILITIES - NEW YORK (CITY) -
DIRECTORIES.**
The CARES directory in electronic form [computer
file] Maywood, NJ : ACIT.
*TC HV99.N59 S58*

**HEALTH FACILITIES - NEW YORK
METROPOLITAN AREA - DIRECTORIES.**
The CARES directory in electronic form [computer
file] Maywood, NJ : ACIT.
*TC HV99.N59 S58*

**HEALTH FACILITIES - RELATIONSHIPS.** *See*
**HEALTH FACILITIES - AFFILIATIONS.**

**HEALTH FACILITIES - UNITED STATES -
BUSINESS MANAGEMENT.**
Demetriou, Andrew J. Health care integration.
Washington, D.C. : Bureau of National Affairs, Inc.,
c1996.
*TC KF3825 .D394 1996*

**HEALTH HABITS.** *See* **HEALTH BEHAVIOR.**

**Health hazards manual for artists.**
McCann, Michael, 1943- 4th rev. and augm. ed. New
York, NY : Lyons & Burford, c1994.
*TC RC963.6.A78 M324 1994*

**Health in the later years.**
Ferrini, Armeda F. 3rd ed. Boston : McGraw-Hill,
c2000.
*TC RA777.6 .F46 2000*

**HEALTH INDICATORS.** *See* **HEALTH STATUS
INDICATORS.**

**HEALTH INSTITUTIONS.** *See* **HEALTH
FACILITIES.**

**Health issues and adolescents.**
Shucksmith, Janet, 1953- London ; New York :
Routledge, 1998.
*TC RJ47.53 .S455 1998*

**HEALTH MAINTENANCE ORGANIZATIONS.**
American Nurses Association. Task Force on Staff
Privileges. Guidelines for appointment of nurses for
individual practice privileges in health care
organizations. Kansas City, MO : American Nurses
Association, Commission on Nursing Service, 1978.
*TC RT104 .A44 1978*

**HEALTH MANPOWER.** *See* **MEDICAL
PERSONNEL.**

**[Health news (Albany, N.Y. : 1916)]** Health news /
New York State Dept. of Health. Albany, N.Y. : The
Dept., 1916-1916. 1 v. : 23 cm. Frequency: Semimonthly.
Vol. 1, no. 1 (Jan. 1, 1916)-v. 1, no. 7 (Apr. 1, 1916). Title
from caption. Continued by: Official bulletin (New York
(State). Dept. of Health).
*1. New York (State). Dept. of Health. II. Title: Official bulletin
(New York (State). Dept. of Health)*

**HEALTH - NUTRITIONAL ASPECTS.**
Ford, Brian J. (Brian John), 1939- The future of food.
London : Thames & Hudson, c2000.
*TC RA601 .F65 2000*

**HEALTH - NUTRITIONAL ASPECTS -
CONGRESSES.**
Heidelberger Ernährungsforum (5th : 1998 :
Heidelberg) Food quality, nutrition, and health.
Berlin ; New York : Springer, 2000.
*TC RA784 .H42 2000*

**HEALTH OCCUPATIONS SCHOOLS.** *See*
**MEDICAL COLLEGES; NURSING
SCHOOLS.**

**HEALTH OF CHILDREN.** *See* **CHILDREN -
HEALTH AND HYGIENE.**

**HEALTH OF WOMEN.** *See* **WOMEN - HEALTH
AND HYGIENE.**

**HEALTH PERSONNEL.** *See* **MEDICAL
PERSONNEL.**

**HEALTH PLANNING.** *See also* **HEALTH
SERVICES ADMINISTRATION; MEDICAL
CARE - NEEDS ASSESSMENT.**
Collaborating to improve community health. San
Francisco : Jossey-Bass Publishers, c1996.
*TC RA427 .C59 1996*

**HEALTH PLANNING - MORAL AND ETHICAL
ASPECTS.**
The global challenge of health care rationing.
Buckingham [England] ; Philadelphia : Open
University Press, 2000.
*TC RA394.9 .G56 2000*

**HEALTH PLANNING - PERIODICALS.**
American journal of health planning. [Alexandria,
Va., American Association for Comprehensive Health
Planning]

**HEALTH PLANNING - PHILOSOPHY.**
Anspaugh, David J. Developing health promotion
programs. Boston : London : McGraw-Hill, c2000.
*TC RA427.8 .A57 2000*

**HEALTH POLICY.** *See* **MEDICAL POLICY.**

**HEALTH POLICY.**
Tulchinsky, Theodore H. The new public health. San
Diego, Calif. ; London : Academic Press, c2000.
*TC RA425 .T85 2000*

**Health policy reform in America :** innovations from
the states / Howard M. Leichter, editor. 2nd ed.
Armonk, N.Y. : M.E. Sharpe, c1997. xiv, 266 p. : ill. ; 24
cm. Includes bibliographical references and index. ISBN
1-56324-899-9 (c : alk. paper) ISBN 1-56324-900-6 (p : alk.
paper) DDC 362.1/0973
*1. Medical policy - United States. 2. Health care reform -
United States. 3. Medical policy - United States - States. 4.
Health care reform - United States - States. I. Leichter,
Howard M.*
*TC RA395.A3 H42564 1997*

**Health Policy Tracking Service.** Major health care
policies : fifty state profiles, 1999 / by Health Policy
Tracking Service, National Conference of State
Legislatures. 8th ed. Washington, D.C. : Health Policy
Tracking Service, 2000. v, 454 p. : ill., maps ; 28 cm.
"January 2000." Includes bibliographical references.
Continues: Major state health care policies.
*1. Medical policy - United States - States. I. National
Conference of State Legislatures. II. Title. III. Title: Major
state health care policies.*
*TC KF3821 .H4 2000*

**HEALTH POLICY - UNITED STATES.**
Institute of Medicine (U.S.). Committee on Prevention
and Control of Sexually Transmitted Diseases. The
hidden epidemic. Washington, D.C. : National
Academy Press, 1997.
*TC RA644.V4 I495 1997*

Rovner, Julie. Health care policy and politics A to Z.
Washington, DC : CQ Press, 2000.
*TC RA395.A3 R685 1999*

**HEALTH PROFESSIONS.** *See* **MEDICAL
PERSONNEL.**

**Health progress (Saint Louis, Mo.).**
Hospital progress. St. Louis [etc.] Catholic Health
Association of the United States [etc.]

**HEALTH PROMOTION.** *See* **HEALTH
EDUCATION.**

**HEALTH PROMOTION.**
Handbook of health promotion and disease
prevention. New York : Kluwer Academic/Plenum
Publishers, c1999.
*TC RA427.8 .H36 1999*

**HEALTH PROMOTION.**
Jonas, Steven. Talking about health and wellness with
patients. New York : Springer, c2000.
*TC RA427.8 .J66 2000*

Keller, Colleen, 1949- Health promotion for the
elderly. Thousand Oaks, Calif. ; London : Sage
Publications, c2000.
*TC RA564.8 .K438 2000*

**HEALTH PROMOTION.**
Russell, Graham, 1954- Essential psychology for
nurses and other health professionals. London ; New
York : Routledge, c1999.
*TC R726.7 .R87 1999*

**HEALTH PROMOTION.**
Settings for health promotion. Thousand Oaks, Calif. :
Sage Publications, c2000.
*TC RA427.8 .S48 2000*

**HEALTH PROMOTION.**
Settings for health promotion. Thousand Oaks, Calif. :
Sage Publications, Inc., c2000.
*TC RA427.8 .S48 2000*

**HEALTH PROMOTION - AUSTRALIA.**
Health promotion strategies & methods. Rev. ed.
Sydney ; New York : McGraw-Hill, c1999.
*TC RA427.8 .H527 1999*

**HEALTH PROMOTION - DEVELOPING
COUNTRIES - CROSS-CULTURAL STUDIES.**
Ayim, Martin Ayong. Empowerment through health
education. 2nd ed. Ruston, LA : Vita Press
International, c1998.

TC RA441.5 .A95 1998

**HEALTH PROMOTION - EVALUATION.**
Evaluating health promotion. Oxford ; New York :
Oxford University Press, 2000.
*TC RA427.8 .E95 2000*

**Health promotion for the elderly.**
Keller, Colleen, 1949- Thousand Oaks, Calif. :
London : Sage Publications, c2000.
*TC RA564.8 .K438 2000*

**HEALTH PROMOTION - HANDBOOKS,
MANUALS, ETC.**
Handbook of health promotion and disease
prevention. New York : Kluwer Academic/Plenum
Publishers, c1999.
*TC RA427.8 .H36 1999*

**HEALTH PROMOTION - METHODS -
AUSTRALIA.**
Health promotion strategies & methods. Rev. ed.
Sydney : New York : McGraw-Hill, c1999.
*TC RA427.8 .H527 1999*

**HEALTH PROMOTION - MORAL AND
ETHICAL ASPECTS.**
Buchanan, David Ross. An ethic for health promotion.
New York ; Oxford : Oxford University Press, 2000.
*TC RA427.8 .B83 2000*

Promoting healthy behavior. Washington, D.C. :
Georgetown University Press, c2000.
*TC RA427.8 .P766 2000*

**HEALTH PROMOTION - PHILOSOPHY.**
Anspaugh, David J. Developing health promotion
programs. Boston ; London : McGraw-Hill, c2000.
*TC RA427.8 .A57 2000*

Buchanan, David Ross. An ethic for health promotion.
New York ; Oxford : Oxford University Press, 2000.
*TC RA427.8 .B83 2000*

**HEALTH PROMOTION PROGRAMS.** *See*
**HEALTH PROMOTION.**

**HEALTH PROMOTION - RESEARCH.**
Researching health promotion. London ; New York :
Routledge, 2000.
*TC RA427.8 .R47 2000*

**HEALTH PROMOTION SERVICES.** *See* **HEALTH
PROMOTION.**

**HEALTH PROMOTION - SOCIAL ASPECTS.**
Promoting healthy behavior. Washington, D.C. :
Georgetown University Press, c2000.
*TC RA427.8 .P766 2000*

**HEALTH PROMOTION - STANDARDS.**
Evaluating health promotion. Oxford ; New York :
Oxford University Press, 2000.
*TC RA427.8 .E95 2000*

**Health promotion strategies & methods** / Garry
Egger ... [et al.]. Rev. ed. Sydney ; New York :
McGraw-Hill, c1999. xi, 199 p. : ill. ; 23 cm. Includes
bibliographical references and index. ISBN 0-07-470483-4
DDC 613.0994
*1. Health promotion - Australia. 2. Health education -
Australia. 3. Preventive health services - Australia -
Marketing. 4. Health Promotion - methods - Australia. 5.
Health Education - Australia. I. Egger. Garry. II. Title: Health
promotion strategies and methods*
*TC RA427.8 .H527 1999*

**Health promotion strategies and methods.**
Health promotion strategies & methods. Rev. ed.
Sydney ; New York : McGraw-Hill, c1999.
*TC RA427.8 .H527 1999*

**HEALTH PROMOTION - UNITED STATES.**
Promoting health in multicultural populations.
Thousand Oaks, Calif. : Sage Publications, c1999.
*TC RA448.4 .P76 1999*

**HEALTH PROMOTION - UNITED STATES -
HISTORY.**
Engs, Ruth C. Clean living movements. Westport,
Conn. ; London : Praeger, 2000.
*TC RA427.8 .E54 2000*

**HEALTH PSYCHOLOGY.** *See* **CLINICAL
HEALTH PSYCHOLOGY.**

**HEALTH PSYCHOLOGY, CLINICAL.** *See*
**CLINICAL HEALTH PSYCHOLOGY.**

**Health psychology in global perspective.**
Aboud, Frances E. Thousand Oaks : Sage
Publications, c1998.
*TC R726.7 .A26 1998*

**HEALTH - PUBLIC OPINION.** *See* **HEALTH
ATTITUDES.**

**HEALTH REFORM.** *See* **HEALTH CARE
REFORM.**

**HEALTH REFORMERS - UNITED STATES -
HISTORY.**
Engs, Ruth C. Clean living movements. Westport,
Conn. ; London : Praeger, 2000.
*TC RA427.8 .E54 2000*

**HEALTH - RESEARCH - CROSS-CULTURAL
STUDIES.**
Loue, Sana. Gender, ethnicity, and health research.
New York : Kluwer Academic/Plenum Publishers,
c1999.
*TC RA448.4 .L68 1999*

**HEALTH RISK ASSESSMENT.** *See*
**ENVIRONMENTAL HEALTH.**

**HEALTH SCIENCES ADMINISTRATION.** *See*
**HEALTH SERVICES ADMINISTRATION.**

**HEALTH SCIENCES PERSONNEL.** *See*
**MEDICAL PERSONNEL.**

**HEALTH SERVICES.** *See* **MEDICAL CARE;
PUBLIC HEALTH.**

**HEALTH SERVICES.**
Vetter, Norman. Epidemiology and public health
medicine. Edinburgh ; New York : Churchill
Livingstone, 1999.
*TC RA427 .V48 1999*

**HEALTH SERVICES ADMINISTRATION.** *See*
**HEALTH PLANNING; NURSING
SERVICES - ADMINISTRATION.**

**HEALTH SERVICES ADMINISTRATION -
UNITED STATES.**
Demetriou, Andrew J. Health care integration.
Washington, D.C. : Bureau of National Affairs, Inc.,
c1996.
*TC KF3825 .D394 1996*

Fressola, Maria C. How nurse executives learned to
become leaders. 1998.
*TC 06 no. 11115*

Fressola, Maria C. How nurse executives learned to
become leaders. 1998.
*TC 06 no. 11115*

Remaking health care in America. 1st ed. San
Francisco : Jossey-Bass Publishers, c1996.
*TC RA395.A3 R46 1996*

**HEALTH SERVICES ADMINISTRATORS.** *See*
**NURSE ADMINISTRATORS.**

**HEALTH SERVICES FOR THE AGED.**
Weinstein, Barbara E. Geriatric audiology. New
York : Thieme, 2000.
*TC RF291.5.A35 W44 2000*

**HEALTH SERVICES MANAGEMENT.** *See*
**HEALTH SERVICES ADMINISTRATION.**

**HEALTH SERVICES NEEDS.** *See* **MEDICAL
CARE - NEEDS ASSESSMENT.**

**HEALTH SERVICES NEEDS AND DEMAND -
CONGRESSES.**
Unmet need in psychiatry. Cambridge, U.K. ; New
York, NY : Cambridge University Press, 2000.
*TC RA790.5 .U565 2000*

**HEALTH SERVICES - NEW YORK (CITY) -
DIRECTORIES.**
The CARES directory in electronic form [computer
file] Maywood, NJ : ACIT,
*TC HV99.N59 S58*

**HEALTH SERVICES PERSONNEL.** *See*
**MEDICAL PERSONNEL.**

**HEALTH SERVICES PLANNING.** *See* **HEALTH
PLANNING.**

**Health services reports.**
United States. Health Services and Mental Health
Administration. Rockville, Md.

**HEALTH SERVICES, SCHOOL.** *See* **SCHOOL
HEALTH SERVICES.**

**HEALTH - SEX DIFFERENCES.**
Gender inequalities in health. Buckingham [England] ;
Philadelphia : Open University Press, 2000.
*TC RA564.85 .G4653 2000*

**HEALTH STATUS INDEXES.** *See* **HEALTH
STATUS INDICATORS.**

**HEALTH STATUS INDICATORS.**
Individual quality of life. Amsterdam : Harwood
Academic, c1999.
*TC RA407 .I54 1999*

**HEALTH STATUS INDICATORS -
PERIODICALS.**
The progress of nations. New York, NY : UNICEF,
1993-
*TC RA407.A1 P76*

**HEALTH - STUDY AND TEACHING.** *See*
**HEALTH EDUCATION.**

**HEALTH SURVEYS.** *See* **HEALTH STATUS
INDICATORS.**

**HEALTH SURVEYS - NEW YORK (STATE).**
Maternal, child and adolescent health profile. Albany,
N.Y. : New York State Dept. of Health, 1996.
*TC HV742.N7 B83 1996*

**HEALTH SURVEYS - UNITED STATES.**
Minority health in America. Baltimore, Md. : Johns
Hopkins University Press, 2000.
*TC RA448.4 .M566 2000*

**HEALTH SYSTEM REFORM.** *See* **HEALTH
CARE REFORM.**

**HEALTH THOUGHTS.** *See* **MENTAL HEALING.**

**HEALTHS, DRINKING OF.** *See* **DRINKING
CUSTOMS.**

**Heard, James.**
Impressionism [videorecording]. [London] : The
National Gallery ; Tillingham, Peasmarsh, East
Sussex, England : Ho-Ho-Kus, NJ : Distributed by
The Roland Collection, c1990.
*TC ND547.5.I4 A7 1990*

Italian painting before 1400 [videorecording].
[London] : The National Gallery, c1989.

Italian painting before 1400 [videorecording].
[London] : The National Gallery, c1989.
*TC ND1575 .I87 1989*

**Heard Museum.**
Shared visions. 1st New Press ed. New York : New
Press : Distributed by Norton, [1993], c1991.
*TC N6538.A4 A7 1993*

**HEARING.** *See also* **AUDIOLOGY; AUDITORY
PATHWAYS; AUDITORY PERCEPTION;
DEAFNESS; EAR; LISTENING.**
Gelfand, Stanley A., 1948- 3rd ed., rev. and expanded.
New York : Marcel Dekker, c1998.
*TC QP461 .G28 1998*

**HEARING.**
Broadbent, Donald E. (Donald Eric) Perception and
communication. New York, Pergamon Press, 1958.
*TC BF38 .B685*

Gelfand, Stanley A., 1948- Hearing. 3rd ed., rev. and
expanded. New York : Marcel Dekker, c1998.
*TC QP461 .G28 1998*

Møller, Aage R. Hearing, its physiology and
pathophysiology. San Diego : Academic Press, c2000.
*TC QP461 .M65 2000*

**HEARING AIDS.**
Counseling for hearing aid fittings. San Diego :
Singular Pub. Group, c1999.
*TC RF300 .C68 1999*

Venema, Ted. Compression for clinicians. San Diego,
Calif. : Singular Pub. Group, c1998.
*TC RF300 .V46 1998*

**HEARING AIDS.**
Vonlanthen, A. (Andy), 1961- Hearing instrument
technology for the hearing healthcare professional.
2nd ed. San Diego : Singular Pub. Group, c2000.
*TC RF300 .V66 2000*

**HEARING AIDS.**
Vonlanthen, A. (Andy), 1961- Hearing instrument
technology for the hearing healthcare professional.
2nd ed. San Diego : Singular Pub. Group, c2000.
*TC RF300 .V66 2000*

**HEARING AIDS - DESIGN AND
CONSTRUCTION.**
Venema, Ted. Compression for clinicians. San Diego,
Calif. : Singular Pub. Group, c1998.
*TC RF300 .V46 1998*

**HEARING AIDS - FITTING.**
Counseling for hearing aid fittings. San Diego :
Singular Pub. Group, c1999.
*TC RF300 .C68 1999*

Venema, Ted. Compression for clinicians. San Diego,
Calif. : Singular Pub. Group, c1998.
*TC RF300 .V46 1998*

**HEARING AIDS, MECHANICAL.** *See* **HEARING
AIDS.**

**HEARING - DICTIONARIES.**
Martin, Michael, OBE. Dictionary of hearing.
London : Whurr, 1999.
*TC QP461 .M375 1999*

Martin, Michael, OBE. Dictionary of hearing.
London : Whurr, 1999.
*TC QP461 .M375 1999*

**HEARING DISORDERS.** *See also* **DEAFNESS.**
Vonlanthen, A. (Andy), 1961- Hearing instrument technology for the hearing healthcare professional. 2nd ed. San Diego : Singular Pub. Group, c2000.
*TC RF300 .V66 2000*

**HEARING DISORDERS - AGED.**
Weinstein, Barbara E. Geriatric audiology. New York : Thieme, 2000.
*TC RF291.5.A35 W44 2000*

**HEARING DISORDERS IN CHILDREN.** *See also* **CHILDREN, DEAF; HEARING IMPAIRED CHILDREN.**
Making the most of early communication [videorecording]. New York, NY : Distributed by AFB Press, c1997.
*TC HV1597.2 .M3 1997*

**HEARING DISORDERS - PATIENTS.** *See* **HEARING IMPAIRED.**

**HEARING IMPAIRED.** *See* **DEAF.**

**HEARING IMPAIRED - BIOGRAPHY.**
Merker, Hannah. Listening. 1st Southern Methodist Univ. Press ed. Dallas, Tex. : Southern Methodist University Press, 2000.
*TC BF323.L5 M37 2000*

**HEARING IMPAIRED CHILDREN.** *See* **CHILDREN, DEAF.**

**HEARING IMPAIRED CHILDREN - CHINA - FAMILY RELATIONSHIPS.**
Callaway, Alison. Deaf children in China. Washington, D.C. : Gallaudet University Press, 2000.
*TC HV2888 .C35 2000*

**HEARING IMPAIRED CHILDREN - EDUCATION (EARLY CHILDHOOD).**
Making the most of early communication [videorecording]. New York, NY : Distributed by AFB Press, c1997.
*TC HV1597.2 .M3 1997*

**HEARING IMPAIRED CHILDREN - EDUCATION - GREAT BRITAIN.**
Watson, Linda R., 1950- Deaf and hearing impaired pupils in mainstream schools. London : David Fulton, c1999.
*TC LC1203.G7 W387 1999*

**HEARING IMPAIRED CHILDREN - LANGUAGE.**
Making the most of early communication [videorecording]. New York, NY : Distributed by AFB Press, c1997.
*TC HV1597.2 .M3 1997*

**HEARING IMPAIRED CHILDREN - PSYCHOLOGY.**
Making the most of early communication [videorecording]. New York, NY : Distributed by AFB Press, c1997.
*TC HV1597.2 .M3 1997*

**HEARING IMPAIRED CHILDREN - REHABILITATION.**
Making the most of early communication [videorecording]. New York, NY : Distributed by AFB Press, c1997.
*TC HV1597.2 .M3 1997*

**HEARING IMPAIRED - COUNSELING OF.**
Counseling for hearing aid fittings. San Diego : Singular Pub. Group, c1999.
*TC RF300 .C68 1999*

**HEARING IMPAIRED - REHABILITATION.**
Rehabilitative audiology. 3rd ed. Philadelphia, PA : Lippincott Williams & Wilkins, c2000.
*TC RF297 .R44 2000*

**HEARING IMPAIRED - UNITED STATES - BIOGRAPHY.**
Stenross, Barbara, 1946- Missed connections. Philadelphia : Temple University Press, 1999.
*TC RF291 .S74 1999*

**Hearing instrument technology.**
Vonlanthen, A. (Andy), 1961- Hearing instrument technology for the hearing healthcare professional. 2nd ed. San Diego : Singular Pub. Group, c2000.
*TC RF300 .V66 2000*

**Hearing instrument technology for the hearing healthcare professional.**
Vonlanthen, A. (Andy), 1961- 2nd ed. San Diego : Singular Pub. Group, c2000.
*TC RF300 .V66 2000*

**Hearing, its physiology and pathophysiology.**
Møller, Aage R. San Diego : Academic Press, c2000.
*TC QP461 .M65 2000*

**HEARING LOSS.** *See* **DEAFNESS.**

**HEARING - PERIODICALS.**
International audiology. Leiden, Netherlands : International Society of Audiology, 1962-1970.

**HEARING - PHYSIOLOGY - AGED.**
Weinstein, Barbara E. Geriatric audiology. New York : Thieme, 2000.
*TC RF291.5.A35 W44 2000*

**HEARINGS, LEGISLATIVE.** *See* **LEGISLATIVE HEARINGS.**

**Hearn, Michael Patrick.**
Myth, magic and mystery. Boulder, Colo. : Roberts Rinehart Publishers ; [Norfolk, Va.] : in cooperation with the Chrysler Museum of Art, c1996.
*TC NC975 .M98 1996*

**Hearst Entertainment (Firm).**
Headline stories of the century [videorecording]. Chicago, IL. : Distributed by Questar Video, Inc., c1992.
*TC D743 .H42 1992*

**The heart calls home.**
Hansen, Joyce. New York : Walker & Company, 1999.
*TC PZ7.H19825 He 1999*

**HEART - DISEASES.** *See* **CORONARY HEART DISEASE.**

**HEART DISEASES - PREVENTION & CONTROL.**
DeFelice, Stephen L., 1936- The carnitine defense. [Emmaus, Pa.] : Rodale Press ; [New York] : Distributed to the book trade by St. Martin's Press, c1999.
*TC RC685.C6 D4235 1999*

**HEART DISEASES - THERAPY.**
DeFelice, Stephen L., 1936- The carnitine defense. [Emmaus, Pa.] : Rodale Press ; [New York] : Distributed to the book trade by St. Martin's Press, c1999.
*TC RC685.C6 D4235 1999*

**HEART MOUNTAIN RELOCATION CENTER (WYO.).**
Rabbit in the moon [videorecording]. San Francisco, Calif. : Wabi-Sabi Productions, 1999.
*TC D753.8 .R3 1999*

**Heart of the country** [videorecording] / presented by the Alaska Center for Documentary Film, University of Alaska Museum in collaboration with the community of Kanayama, Hokkaido, Japan ; written and directed by Leonard Kamerling ; produced by Leonard Kamerling, William Parrett. [New York, NY : First Run/Icarus Films, 1998]. 1 videocassette (92 min.) : sd., col. ; 1/2 in. At head of title: Cultures beginnings: from the heart of the country rice-planting songs. Japanese with English subtitles, title and credits in English. VHS. Catalogued from credits and container. Photography and editing: Leonard Kamerling; sound recorded by Toshifumi Kono ... [et al.]. "This film is dedicated to the memory of Takahiko Sato, Kanayama Elementary School student and friend." For general audiences. SUMMARY: Story of Shinichi Yasutomo, principal of a rural elementary school in Kanayama, Hokkaido. Follows Yasutomo, his teachers and staff, students and their families over the course of one entire year. Golden Apple Award, 1998 National Educational Media Network Competition; Judge's Award, 1997 Northwest Film Festival (Portland); Special Exhibition, 1998 Cinéma du Réel (Paris, France).
*1. Education, Elementary - Japan - Kanayama. 2. Documentary television proframs - Japan - Kanayama. 3. Yasutomo, Shinichi. 4. Elementary school principals - Japan - Kanayama. 5. Kanayama Elementary School. I. Kamerling, Leonard. II. Parrett, William. III. Sato, Takahiko. IV. University of Alaska Museum. V. First-Run Features (Firm) VI. Title: Cultures beginnings: from the heart of the country rice-planting songs*
*TC LB1565.H6 H3 1998*

**Heart to heart.**
Toft, Robert. Oxford ; New York : Oxford University Press, 2000.
*TC MT823 .T64 2000*

**The heartbeat of indigenous Africa.**
Mosha, R. Sambuli. New York ; London : Garland Publishing : [Falmer Press], 2000.

*TC LC191.8.T29 M67 2000*

**Heartfield, John, 1891-1968.**
Photomontage today. Peter Kennard [videorecording]. [London] : Art Council of Great Britain : Ho-Ho-Kus, N.J. : [distributed by] Anthony Roland Collection of Films on Art, c1982.
*TC TR685 .P45 1982*

**Heath American readers**
Making choices. Lexington, Mass. : D.C. Heath & co., c1986.
*TC PE1121 .M34 1986*

Making choices. Lexington, Mass. : D.C. Heath & co., c1986.
*TC PE1121 .M34 1986 Activity Pad*

Making choices. Lexington, Mass. : D.C. Heath & Co., c1986.
*TC PE1121 .M34 1986 Skills Pad*

Making choices. Lexington, Mass. : D.C. Heath & co., c1986.
*TC PE1121 .M34 1986 Resource Binder*

Making choices. Teacher's ed. Lexington, Mass. : D.C. Heath & co., c1986.
*TC PE1121 .M34 1986 Teacher's Ed. Workbook*

Moving on. Lexington, Mass. : D.C. Heath, c1983.
*TC PE1119 .M68 1986 Teacher's Ed.*

(2-1) Marching along. Teacher's ed. Lexington, Mass. : D.C. Heath and Company, c1986.
*TC PE1119 .M37 1986 Teacher's Ed.*

(2-2) Turning corners. Teacher's ed. Lexington, Mass. : D.C. Heath and Company, c1986.
*TC PE1119 .T87 1986 Teacher's Ed.*

(3-1) Building dreams. Teacher's ed. Lexington, Mass. : D.C. Heath and Company, c1986.
*TC PE1119 .B84 1986 Teacher's Ed.*

(3-2) Catching glimpses. Teacher's ed. Lexington, Mass. : D.C. Heath & co., c1986.
*TC PE1119 .C37 1986 Teacher's Ed.*

(6) Making choices. Teacher's ed. Lexington, Mass. : D.C. Heath & co., c1986.
*TC PE1121 .M34 1986 Teacher's Ed.*

(8) Meeting challenges. Teacher's ed. Lexington, Mass. : D.C. Heath and Company, c1986.
*TC PE1121 .M43 1986 Teacher's Ed.*

(8) Meeting challenges. Lexington, Mass. : D.C. Heath and Company, c1986.
*TC PE1121 .M43 1986*

**Heath American Readers**
(8) Meeting challenges. Lexington, Mass. : D. C. Heath and Company, c1986.
*TC PE1121 .M43 1986 Skills Pad*

**Heath American readers**
(8) Meeting challenges. Teacher's ed. Lexington, Mass. : D.C. Heath and Company, c1986.
*TC PE1121 .M43 1986 Teacher's Ed. Workbook*

(K-1) Warming up. Teacher's ed. Lexington, Mass. : D.C. Heath and Company, c1986.
*TC PE1119 .W37 1986 Teacher's Ed.*

(P) Finding places. Teacher's ed. Lexington, Mass. : D.C. Heath and Company, c1986.
*TC PE1119 .F56 1986 Teacher's Ed.*

(PP1-2-3) Looking out. Climbing up. Going far. Teacher's ed. Lexington, Mass. : D.C. Heath and Cpmpany, c1986.
*TC PE1119 .L66 1986 Teacher's Ed.*

(R) Starting off. Teacher's ed. Lexington, Mass. : D.C. Heath and Company, c1986.
*TC PE1119 .S82 1986 Teacher's Ed.*

**Heath, Douglas H.** Assessing schools of hope : methods, norms, and case studies / Douglas H. Heath. 1st ed. Bryn Mawr, PA : Conrow Pub. House, c1999. ix, 166 p. ; 28 cm. Includes index. ISBN 0-9641727-4-7
*1. Educational evaluation - Case studies. 2. Students - United States - Attitudes. 3. Educational surveys - United States. I. Title.*
*TC LB2822.75 .H42 1999*

Morale, culture, and character : assessing schools of hope / Douglas H. Heath. 1st ed. Bryn Mawr, PA : Conrow Pub. House, c1999. xvi, 290 p. ; 24 cm. Includes bibliographical references (p. 273-277) and index. ISBN 0-9641727-2-0 (hardcover) ISBN 0-9641727-3-9 (paper)
*1. Moral education - United States. 2. Education - Aims and objectives - United States. 3. Educational evaluation - United States. 4. Self-actualization (Psychology) I. Title.*

*TC LC311 .H43 1999*

**Heath, Dwight B.** Drinking occasions : comparative perspectives on alcohol and culture / Dwight B. Heath. Philadelphia : Brunner/Mazel, c2000. xv, 240 p. : ill. ; 24 cm. (Series on alcohol in society) Includes bibliographical references (p. 199-216) and index. ISBN 1-58391-047-6 (alk. paper) DDC 394.1/3
*1. Drinking customs - Cross-cultural studies. 2. Drinking of alcoholic beverages - Cross-cultural studies. I. Title. II. Series.*
*TC GT2884 .H4 2000*

**Heath English series**
Botel, Morton. Communicating. Lexington, Mass. : D. C. Heath, c1973.
*TC PE1121 .B67 1973 Bk A*

Botel, Morton. Communicating. Lexington, Mass. : D. C. Heath, c1973.
*TC PE1121 .B67 1973*

**Heath, Richard A.** Nonlinear dynamics : techniques and applications in psychology / Richard A. Heath. Mahwah, N.J. ; London : L. Erlbaum Associates, 2000. ix, 379 p. : ill. ; 24 cm. Includes bibliographical references (p. [335]-357) and indexes. ISBN 0-8058-3199-1 (hbk. : alk. paper) ISBN 0-8058-3200-9 (pbk. : alk. paper) DDC 150/.1//515
*1. Psychometrics. I. Title.*
*TC BF39 .H35 2000*

**Heathorn, Stephen J., 1965-** For home, country, and race : constructing gender, class, and Englishness in the elementary school, 1880-1914 / Stephen Heathorn. Toronto : University of Toronto Press, 1999. xii, 300 p. ; 24 cm. (Studies in gender and history series) Includes bibliographical references and index. ISBN 0-8020-4436-0 (bound) DDC 306.43
*1. Nationalism and education - England - History. 2. Nationalism - Study and teaching (Elementary) - England - History. 3. Working class - Education - England - History. 4. Education, Elementary - England - History. 5. Nationalisme et éducation - Angleterre - Histoire. 6. Nationalisme - Étude et enseignement (Primaire) - Angleterre - Histoire. 7. Travailleurs - Éducation - Angleterre - Histoire. 8. Enseignement primaire - Angleterre - Histoire. I. Title. II. Series.*
*TC LC93.E5 H42 1999*

**Heaton, Tim B.** Statistical handbook on racial groups in the United States / by Tim B. Heaton, Bruce A. Chadwick, and Cardell K. Jacobson. Phoenix, AZ : Oryx Press, 2000. xix, 355 p. ; 29 cm. Includes bibliographical references and index. ISBN 1-57356-266-1 (alk. paper) DDC 305.8/00973/021
*1. Ethnology - United States - Statistics. 2. United States - Population - Statistics. I. Chadwick, Bruce A. II. Jacobson, Cardell K., 1941- III. Title.*
*TC E184.A1 H417 2000*

**Heber, David.**
Human nutrition and obesity. Philadelphia : Current Medicine, 1999.
*TC RC620.5 .H846 1999*

**Hébert, Yvonne M., 1942-.**
Kehoe, John W. A handbook for enhancing the multicultural climate of the school. [Vancouver, B.C.] : Western Education Development Group, Faculty of Education, University of British Colombia, c1984.
*TC LC1099 .K438 1984*

**HEBREW DAY SCHOOLS.** *See* **JEWISH DAY SCHOOLS.**

**HEBREWS.** *See* **JEWS.**

**Hedberg, Betsy.**
Teaching government and citizenship using the Internet. Rev. ed. viii, 112 p. : ill. ; 28 cm.
*TC H61.95 .T43 2000*

**Hedegaard, Mariane.**
International Society for Activity Theory and Cultural Research. Congress (4th : 1998 : Aarhus, Denmark) Activity theory and social practice. Aarhus : Aarhus University Press, c1999.
*TC B105.A35 I57 1998*

International Society for Activity Theory and Cultural Research. Congress (4th : 1998 : Aarhus, Denmark) Activity theory and social practice. Aarhus : Aarhus University Press, c1999.
*TC B105.A35 I57 1998*

**Hedegaard, Mariane.**
Learning activity and development. Aarhus : Aarhus Universit #, 1999.
*TC LB1060 .L43 1999*

**Hedger, Michael.** Public sculpture in Australia / Michael Hedger. Roseville East, NSW : Distributed by Craftsman House ; United States : G+B Arts

International, c1995. 132 p. : ill. (some col.) ; 30 cm. Includes bibliographical references (p. [123]-125) and index. ISBN 976-8097-79-5 DDC 731/.76/0994
*1. Public sculpture - Australia. 2. Sculpture - Australia. 3. Fountains - Australia. 4. War memorials - Australia. I. Title.*
*TC NB1100 .H44 1995*

**Hedges, William D.** Evaluation in the elementary school [by] William D. Hedges. New York. Holt, Rinehart and Winston [1969] iv, 220 p. illus. 24 cm. Bibliographical footnotes. ISBN 0-03-063520-9 DDC 372.1/2/7
*1. Elementary schools - Examinations. 2. Grading and marking (Students) I. Title.*
*TC LB3051 .H4*

**Heflick, David.** How to make money performing in schools : the definitive guide to developing, marketing, and presenting school assembly programs / David Heflick. Orient, Wash. : Silcox Productions, c1996. 190 p. ; 22 cm. On cover: For theater artists, dance artists, singers, instrumentalists, mimes, speakers, puppeteers, storytellers. Includes bibliographical references (p. 182) and index. ISBN 0-9638705-8-0
*1. Schools - Exercises and recreations - United States. 2. Student activities - United States. 3. Small business - Management. I. Heflick, David. How to make money performing in the public schools. II. Title. III. Title: Make money performing in schools IV. Title: Definitive guide to developing, marketing, and presenting school assembly programs V. Title: For theater artists, dance artists, singers, instrumentalists, mimes, speakers, puppeteers, storytellers*
*TC LB3015 .H428 1996*

**How to make money performing in the public schools.**
Heflick, David. How to make money performing in schools. Orient, Wash. : Silcox Productions, c1996.
*TC LB3015 .H428 1996*

**Hefling, Stephen E.** Mahler, Das Lied von der Erde = (The song of the earth) / Stephen E. Hefling. Cambridge, UK ; New York : Cambridge University Press, c2000. iv, 159 p. : ill. ; 23 cm. (Cambridge music handbooks) Includes bibliographical references (p. 149-153) and index. ISBN 0-521-47534-1 (hardback) ISBN 0-521-47558-9 (pbk.) DDC 782.4/7
*1. Mahler, Gustav, - 1860-1911.- Lied von der Erde. I. Title. II. Title: Lied von der Erde III. Title: Song of the earth IV. Series.*
*TC MT121.M34 H44 2000*

**HEGEL, GEORG WILHELM FRIEDRICH, 1770-1831 - AESTHETICS.**
Wyss, Beat, 1947- [Trauer der Vollendung. English] Hegel's art history and the critique of modernity. Cambridge, U.K. ; New York : Cambridge University Press, c1999.
*TC BH151 .W9713 1999*

**Hegel's art history and the critique of modernity.**
Wyss, Beat, 1947- [Trauer der Vollendung. English] Cambridge, U.K. ; New York : Cambridge University Press, c1999.
*TC BH151 .W9713 1999*

**Heide, Florence Parry.** It's about time! : poems / by Florence Parry Heide, Judith Heide Gilliland & Roxanne Heide Pierce ; illustrated by Cathryn Falwell. New York : Clarion Books, c1999. 32 p. : col. ill. ; 28 cm. SUMMARY: A collection of poems about the many aspects of time, including "The Time Machine," "Wasting Time," and "Time Zones." ISBN 0-395-86612-X DDC 811/.54
*1. Children's poetry, American. 2. Time - Juvenile poetry. 3. Time - Poetry. 4. American poetry - Collections. I. Gilliland, Judith Heide. II. Pierce, Roxanne Heide. III. Falwell, Cathryn, ill. IV. Title. V. Title: It is about time!*
*TC PS3558.E427 I77 1999*

**Heidelberger Ernährungsforum (5th : 1998 : Heidelberg)** Food quality, nutrition, and health : 5th Heidelberg Nutrition Forum : proceedings of the ECBA - symposium and workshop, February 27-March 1, 1998 in Heidelberg, Germany / L.H. Grimme, S. Dumontet (eds.). Berlin ; New York : Springer, 2000. xi, 214 p. ; 24 cm. (Gesunde Ernährung) Includes bibliographical references and index. ISBN 3-540-65997-8 (hardcover : alk. paper) DDC 613.2
*1. Health - Nutritional aspects - Congresses. 2. Food - Quality - Congresses. 3. Nutrition - Social aspects - Congresses. I. Grimme, L. H. II. Dumontet, S. III. European Communities Biologists Association. IV. Title. V. Series.*
*TC RA784 .H42 2000*

**Heine, Ralph W.** Psychotherapy [by] Ralph W. Heine. Englewood Cliffs, N.J., Prentice-Hall [1971] x, 170 p. 24 cm. (Lives in disorder series) Bibliography: p. 157-163. ISBN 0-13-736801-1 DDC 616.89/14
*1. Psychotherapy. I. Title.*
*TC RC480 .H42*

**Heinzerling, Barbara M.**
Chandler, Tomasita M. Children and adolescents in the market place. Ann Arbor, Mich. : Pierian Press, 1999.
*TC HF5822 .C43 1999*

**HEIRS.** *See* **INHERITANCE AND SUCCESSION.**

**Heit, Philip.**
Meeks, Linda Brower. Comprehensive school health education. 2nd edition. Blacklick, OH : Meeks Heit Pub. Co., c1996.
*TC RA440.3.U5 M445 1996*

**Helen Dwight Reid Educational Foundation.**
Improving college and university teaching. [Corvallis : Graduate School, Oregon State College,

**Heller, Agnes.**
The challenge of diversity. Aldershot, England : Brookfield, Vt. : Avebury, 1996.
*TC JV225 .C530 1996*

**Heller, Julek, ill.**
Mayer, Marianna. Women warriors. New York : Morrow Junior Books, 1999.
*TC PZ8.1.M46 Wo 1999*

**Heller, Morton A.**
Touch, representation, and blindness. Oxford ; New York : Oxford University Press, 2000.
*TC BF275 .T68 2000*

**Heller, Steven.**
Design culture. New York : Allworth Press : American Institute of Graphic Arts, c1997.
*TC NC998.5.A1 D46 1997*

Design dialogues. New York : Allworth Press, c1998.
*TC NK1390 .D473 1998*

Design literacy : understanding graphic design / Steven Heller and Karen Pomeroy. New York : Allworth Press, c1997. x, 277 p. ; 25 cm. Includes bibliographical references (p. 269-272) and index. ISBN 1-88055-976-5
*1. Graphic arts - History. 2. Commercial art - History. I. Pomeroy, Karen. II. Title.*
*TC NC998 .H45 1997*

The education of a graphic designer. New York : Allworth Press [in association with the] School of Visual Arts, c1998.
*TC NC590 .E38 1998*

**Hellums, Duane.**
Red Hat Linux :. Indianapolis, Ind. : Que : Macmillan USA, c2000.
*TC QA76.76.O63 R43 2000*

**Helmer, Karl.** Umbruch zur Moderne : Studien zur Bildungsgeschichte im 17. Jahrhundert / Karl Helmer. 1. Aufl. Sankt Augustin : Academia, 1994. 195 p. ; 22 cm. Includesent/pargraphical references (p. 169-183) and indexes. ISBN 3-88345-443-5
*1. Education - History - 17th century. I. Title. II. Title: Studien zur Bildungsgeschichte im 17. Jahrhundert*
*TC LA116 .H445 1994*

**Helmes, Edward, 1949-.**
Problems and solutions in human assessment. Boston : Kluwer Academic Publishers, c2000.
*TC BF698.4 .P666 2000*

**Help! It's an indoor recess day.**
Novak, Dori E. Thousand Oaks, Calif. : Corwin Press, c2000.
*TC LB3033 .N68 2000*

**HELP-SEEKING BEHAVIOR.**
Tiago de Melo, Janine, 1969- Factors relating to Hispanic and non-Hispanic White Americans' willingness to seek psychotherapy. 1998.
*TC 085 T43*

**Helping adolescents in school.**
Branwhite, Tony. Westport, Conn. ; London : Praeger, 2000.
*TC LB1027.55 .B72 2000*

**HELPING BEHAVIOR.** *See also* **COUNSELING.**
Hill, Clara E. Helping skills. 1st ed. Washington, DC : American Psychological Association, c1999.
*TC BF637.C6 H46 1999*

Salacuse, Jeswald W. The wise advisor. Westport, Conn. : Praeger, 2000.
*TC BF637.C56 .S26 2000*

**Helping individuals with disabilities and their families :** Mexican and U.S. perspectives / edited by Todd V. Fletcher and Candace S. Bos. Tempe, Ariz. : Bilingual Review/Press, c2000. xviii, 214 p. : ill. ; 26 cm. Includes bibliographical references. ISBN 0-927534-84-3 (alk. paper) DDC 371.91/07
*1. Handicapped children - Education - Mexico. 2.*

*Handicapped children - Education - United States. 3. Parents
of handicapped children - Services for - Mexico. 4. Parents of
handicapped children - Services for - United States. I. Fletcher,
Todd V. II. Bos, Candace S., 1950-*
**TC LC4035.M6 H45 1999**

**Helping skills.**
Hill, Clara E. 1st ed. Washington, DC : American
Psychological Association, c1999.
**TC BF637.C6 H46 1999**

**Helping survivors of domestic violence.**
Gordon, Judith S., 1958- New York : Garland Pub.,
1998.
**TC HV6626.2 .G67 1998**

**Helsby, Gill.** Changing teachers' work : the 'reform' of
secondary schooling / Gill Helsby. Buckingham
[England] ; Philadelphia : Open University Press,
1999. x, 196 p. ; 24 cm. (Changing education) Includes
bibliographical references (p. [176]-188) and indexes. ISBN
0-335-19939-9 (hbk.) ISBN 0-335-19938-0 (pbk.) DDC
373.41
*1. Education, Secondary - Great Britain. 2. High school
teaching - Great Britain. 3. School management and
organization - Great Britain. 4. Educational change - Great
Britain. I. Title. II. Series.*
**TC LA635 .H375 1999**

The politics of professionalism. London : Continuum,
2000.
**TC LB1779 .M33 2000**

**Hem, Lars.**
Essays in general psychology. Aarhus : Aarhus
University Press, c1989.
**TC BF38 .E78 1989**

**Hemelrijk, Emily Ann, 1953-** Matrona docta : educated
women in the Roman élite from Cornelia to Julia
Domna / Emily A. Hemelrijk. London ; New York :
Routledge, 1999. xvi, 382 p. : ill. ; 24 cm. "Routledge
classical monographs"--Jacket. Includes bibliographical
references (p. 360-372) and indexes. ISBN 0-415-19693-0
DDC 305.4/09456/32
*1. Upper class women - Rome - History. 2. Upper class
women - Education - Rome - History. 3. Upper class women -
Rome - Intellectual life. 4. Rome - Civilization. 5. Rome -
Social life and customs. I. Title.*
**TC HQ1136 .H45 1999**

**Hemingway, Collins.**
Gates, Bill, 1955- Business @ the speed of thought.
New York, NY : Warner Books, c1999.
**TC HD30.37 .G38 1999**

**HEMODYNAMICS.** *See also* **BLOOD PRESSURE.**
Rowell, Loring B. Human cardiovascular control.
New York : Oxford University Press, 1993.
**TC QP109 .R68 1993**

**Henderson, Amy.**
Exhibiting dilemmas. Washington, D.C. : Smithsonian
Insitution Press, c1997.
**TC AM151 .E96 1997**

**Henderson, Carolyn.** Horse & pony breeds / Carolyn
Henderson. 1st American ed. New York, N.Y. : DK
Pub., 1999. 48 p. : col. ill. ; 24 cm. (DK riding club) Includes
index. SUMMARY: An illustrated guide to horse and pony
breeds, their history, physical characteristics, and uses. ISBN
0-7894-4267-1 (pbk.) ISBN 0-7894-4268-X (hardcover) DDC
636.1
*1. Horse breeds - Juvenile literature. 2. Horses - Juvenile
literature. 3. Ponies - Juvenile literature. 4. Horses. 5. Ponies.
I. DK Publishing, Inc. II. Title. III. Title: Horse and pony
breeds IV. Series.*
**TC SF291 .H365 1999**

Horse & pony care / by Carolyn Henderson. 1st
American ed. New York : DK Pub., 1999. 48 p. : col.
ill. ; 24 cm. (DK riding club) Includes index. SUMMARY: An
illustrated introduction for young riders to caring for a horse or
pony. ISBN 0-7894-4269-8 (pbk.) ISBN 0-7894-4270-1
(hardcover) DDC 636.1/083
*1. Horses - Juvenile literature. 2. Ponies - Juvenile literature.
3. Horses. 4. Ponies. I. DK Publishing, Inc. II. Title. III. Title:
Horse and pony care IV. Series.*
**TC SF302 .H425 1999**

Horse & pony shows & events / Carolyn Henderson ;
foreword by Carl Hester. 1st American ed. New York,
N.Y. : DK Pub., 1999. 48 p. : col. ill. ; 24 cm. (DK riding
club) Includes index. SUMMARY: A completely illustrated
guide to horse and pony shows, competitions, and other events.
ISBN 0-7894-4265-5 (pbk.) ISBN 0-7894-4266-3 (hc) DDC
798.2/4
*1. Horse shows - Juvenile literature. 2. Horsemanship -
Juvenile literature. 3. Horse shows. 4. Horsemanship. I. DK
Publishing, Inc. II. Title. III. Title: Horse and pony shows and
events IV. Series.*

---

**TC SF294.7 .H67 1999**

Improve your riding skills / Carolyn Henderson ;
foreword by Lynn Russell. 1st American ed. New
York, N.Y. : DK Pub., 1999. 48 p. : col. ill. ; 24 cm. (DK
riding club) Includes index. SUMMARY: Basic riding skills
completely illustrated for the young horse enthusiast. ISBN
0-7894-4263-9 (pbk.) ISBN 0-7894-4264-7 (hardcover) DDC
798.2
*1. Horsemanship - Juvenile literature. 2. Horsemanship. I. DK
Publishing, Inc. II. Title. III. Series.*
**TC SF309.2 .H46 1999**

**Henderson, Charles, 1923-.**
Ullman, B. L. (Berthold Louis), 1882-1965. Latin for
Americans. First book. 7th ed. Woodland Hills,
Calif. : Glencoe, c1990.
**TC PA2087.5 .U339 1990**

Ullman, B. L. (Berthold Louis), 1882-1965. Latin for
Americans. First book. 7th ed. Woodland Hills,
Calif. : Glencoe, c1990.
**TC PA2087.5 .U339 1990 First Book**

Ullman, B. L. (Berthold Louis), 1882-1965. Latin for
Americans. Second book. 7th ed. Mission Hills,
Calif. : Glencoe, c1990.
**TC PA2087.5 .U339 1990 Teacher's Guide**

Ullman, B. L. (Berthold Louis), 1882-1965. Latin for
Americans. Second book. 7th ed. Mission Hills,
Calif. : Glencoe, c1990.
**TC PA2087.5 .U339 1990**

Ullman, B. L. (Berthold Louis), 1882-1965. Latin for
Americans. Second book. 7th ed. Mission Hills,
Calif. : Glencoe, c1990.
**TC PA2087.5 .U339 1990 Third Book**

Ullman, B. L. (Berthold Louis), 1882-1965. Latin for
Americans. Second book. 7th ed. Mission Hills,
Calif. : Glencoe, c1990.
**TC PA2087.5 .U339 1990 Second Book**

**Henderson, James George.** Transformative curriculum
leadership / James G. Henderson, Richard D.
Hawthorne ; [editor, Debra A. Stollenwerk ;
illustrations, Stellarvisions]. 2nd ed. Upper Saddle
River, N.J. : Merrill, c2000. xiii, 209 p. : ill. ; 23 cm.
Includes bibliographical references and index. ISBN 0-13-
081075-4 DDC 375/.000973
*1. Education - United States - Curricula. 2. Curriculum
planning - United States. 3. Educational leadership - United
States. I. Hawthorne, Richard D. II. Stollenwerk, Debra A. III.
Title.*
**TC LB1570 .H45 2000**

**Henderson, Katharine Rhodes.** The public leadership
of women of faith / by Katharine Rhodes Henderson.
2000. 2 v. (xiv, 519 leaves) ; 29 cm. Issued also on microfilm.
Thesis (Ed.D.)--Teachers College, Columbia University, 2000.
Includes bibliographical references (leaves 496-502).
*1. Women in public life - United States - Case studies. 2.
Women and religion - United States - Case studies. 3.
Leadership in women - United States - Case studies. 4.
Religion and politics. 5. Leadership - United States - Religious
aspects. 6. Women social reformers - United States - Case
studies. 7. Women in the professions - United States - Case
studies. 8. Women - United States - Attitudes - Case studies. I.
Title.*
**TC 06 no. 11276**

**Henderson, Sandra H.**
Adolescent siblings in stepfamilies. Chicago, Ill. :
University of Chicago Press, 1999.
**TC LB1103.S6 v.64 no. 4**

**Henderson, Scott, 1935-.**
Unmet need in psychiatry. Cambridge, U.K. ; New
York, NY : Cambridge University Press, 2000.
**TC RA790.5 .U565 2000**

**Hendrick, Burton Jesse, 1870-1949.** The life and
letters of Walter H. Page / by Burton J. Hendrick.
Garden City, N.Y. : Doubleday, Page & Co., 1925. xi,
436, [1] leaf of plates, 437 p., [12] p. of plates : front., ports.,
facsims. ; 24 cm. This one-volume edition does not include the
letters to President Wilson. Includes index. Includes
bibliographical footnotes.
*1. Page, Walter Hines, - 1855-1918. 2. United States - Foreign
relations - Great Britain. 3. Great Britain - Foreign relations -
United States. I. Title.*
**TC E664.P15 H45 1925**

**Hendrick, Clyde.**
Close relationships. Thousand Oaks, Calif. : Sage
Publications, c2000.
**TC HM1106 .C55 2000**

**Hendrick, Susan, 1944-.**
Close relationships. Thousand Oaks, Calif. : Sage
Publications, c2000.

---

**TC HM1106 .C55 2000**

**Hendriks, Jean Harris.** When father kills mother :
guiding children through trauma and grief / Jean
Harris-Hendriks, Dora Black, and Tony Kaplan. 2nd
ed. London ; Philadelphia : Routledge, 2000. xii, 281
p. ; 25 cm. Includes bibliographical references (p. [254]-266)
and indexes. ISBN 0-415-19627-2 (hbk) ISBN 0-415-19628-0
(pbk.) DDC 618.92/858220651
*1. Children of uxoricides - Rehabilitation. 2. Children of
uxoricides - Mental health. I. Black, Dora. II. Kaplan, Tony.
III. Title.*
**TC RJ506.U96 .B53 2000**

**Hendry, Diana, 1941-** Dog Donovan / by Diana
Hendry ; illustrated by Margaret Chamberlain. 1st
U.S. ed. Cambridge, Mass. : Candlewick Press, 1995.
1 v. (unpaged) : col. ill. ; 27 cm. SUMMARY: The Donovans
are afraid of so many things that the family gets a dog from the
animal shelter to protect them. ISBN 1-56402-537-3 DDC [E]
*1. Fear - Fiction. 2. Dogs - Fiction. I. Chamberlain, Margaret,
ill. II. Title.*
**TC PZ7.H38586 Dm 1995**

**Hendry, Leo B.**
Shucksmith, Janet, 1953- Health issues and
adolescents. London ; New York : Routledge, 1998.
**TC RJ47.53 .S455 1998**

**Henkes, Kevin.** Oh! / words by Kevin Henkes ; pictures
by Laura Dronzek. New York : Greenwillow Books,
1999. 1 v. (unpaged) : ill. ; 21 cm. SUMMARY: The morning
after a snowfall finds animals and children playing. ISBN
0-688-17053-6 (trade : alk. paper) ISBN 0-688-17054-4 (lib.
bdg. : alk. paper) DDC [E]
*1. Snow - Fiction. 2. Animals - Play behavior - Fiction. 3.
Play - Fiction. 4. Stories in rhyme. I. Dronzek, Laura, ill. II.
Title.*
**TC PZ8.3.H4165 Oh 1999**

**Henle, R. J. (Robert John), 1909-** The American
Thomistic revival in the philosophical papers of R.J.
Henle, S.J. : from the writings of R.J. Henle. St.
Louis, Mo. : Saint Louis University Press, c1999. xvi,
397 p. ; 23 cm. Includes bibliographical references and index.
ISBN 0-9652929-2-4 DDC 149/.91/0973
*1. Neo-Scholasticism. I. Title.*
**TC B839 .H46 1999**

**Henley, David R.** Exceptional children: exceptional art :
teaching art to special needs / David R. Henley.
Worcester, Mass. : Davis Publications, c1992. 280 p. :
ill. ; 26 cm. Includes index. Bibliography: p. 276-277. ISBN
0-87192-238-X
*1. Special education - Art. 2. Handicapped children -
Education - United States. I. Title.*
**TC RJ505.A7 H46 1992**

**Henninger, Maureen, 1940-** Don't just surf : effective
research strategies for the net / Maureen Henninger.
2nd ed. Sydney : UNSW Press, 1999. v, 189 p. : ill. ; 20
cm. Includes bibliographical references (p. [180]-184) and
index. ISBN 0-86840-656-2
*1. Internet (Computer network) 2. Research - Methodology. 3.
Research - Computer network resources. 4. Computer network
resources. I. Title.*
**TC ZA4201 .H46 1999**

**Henri Matisse [videorecording].**
Matisse, voyages [videorecording]. [Chicago, Ill.] :
Home Vision ; [S.l.] : Distributed worldwide by RM
Associates, c1989.
**TC ND553.M37 M37 1989**

**Henry and Mudge and the wild wind.**
Rylant, Cynthia. 1st ed. New York : Bradbury Press ;
Toronto : Maxwell Macmillan Canada ; New York :
Maxwell Macmillan International, c1993.
**TC PZ7.R982 Heb 1992**

**Henry, Annette, 1955-** Taking back control : African
Canadian women teachers' lives and practice /
Annette Henry. Albany : State University of New
York Press, c1998. xii, 211 p. ; 24 cm. (SUNY series,
identities in the classroom) Includes bibliographical references
(p. 175-205) and index. ISBN 0-7914-3837-6 (hardcover : alk.
paper) ISBN 0-7914-3838-4 (pbk. : alk. paper) DDC 371.1/
00896071
*1. Women teachers, Black - Canada - Social conditions - Case
studies. 2. Black Carib women - Canada - Social conditions -
Case studies. 3. Children, Black - Education (Elementary) -
Social aspects - Canada - Case studies. 4. Literacy - Canada -
Case studies. 5. Critical pedagogy - Canada - Case studies. I.
Title. II. Series.*
**TC LB1775.4.C2 H45 1998**

**Henry Clay Frick.**
Sanger, Martha Frick Symington. 1st ed. New York :
Abbeville Press Publishers, c1998.
**TC HC102.5.F75 S32 1998**

**Henry Hobson Richardson and the small public library in America.**
Breisch, Kenneth A. Cambridge, Mass. : MIT Press, c1997.
*TC Z679.2.U54 B74 1997*

**Henry, Norman E.**
Ullman, B. L. (Berthold Louis), 1882-1965. Latin for Americans. First book. 7th ed. Woodland Hills, Calif. : Glencoe, c1990.
*TC PA2087.5 .U339 1990*

Ullman, B. L. (Berthold Louis), 1882-1965. Latin for Americans. First book. 7th ed. Woodland Hills, Calif. : Glencoe, c1990.
*TC PA2087.5 .U339 1990 First Book*

Ullman, B. L. (Berthold Louis), 1882-1965. Latin for Americans. Second book. 7th ed. Mission Hills, Calif. : Glencoe, c1990.
*TC PA2087.5 .U339 1990 Teacher's Guide*

Ullman, B. L. (Berthold Louis), 1882-1965. Latin for Americans. Second book. 7th ed. Mission Hills, Calif. : Glencoe, c1990.
*TC PA2087.5 .U339 1990*

Ullman, B. L. (Berthold Louis), 1882-1965. Latin for Americans. Second book. 7th ed. Mission Hills, Calif. : Glencoe, c1990.
*TC PA2087.5 .U339 1990 Third Book*

Ullman, B. L. (Berthold Louis), 1882-1965. Latin for Americans. Second book. 7th ed. Mission Hills, Calif. : Glencoe, c1990.
*TC PA2087.5 .U339 1990 Second Book*

**Her heritage** [computer file] : a biographical encyclopedia of famous American women / Pilgrim New Media ; biographical profiles, Merriam Webster ; edited by Robert McHenry. Cambridge, MA : Pilgrim New Media, c1994. Interactive multimedia. 1 computer optical disc : sd., col. ; 4 3/4 in. + 1 user guide. SUMMARY: Multimedia entries for more than 1,000 women who changed America, including movie clips, newsreels, interviews, photographs and text. Includes a biographical entry on Grace Hoadley Dodge (1856-1914). Disc characteristics: CD-ROM. Title from disc label. "Merriam Webster knowledgebase." System requirements: Macintosh or Power Macintosh; 4MB of available memory; System 7 operating system; color monitor with at least 640x480 pixel resolution, CD-ROM drive (double speed recommended), Quick Time v. 2.0. System requirements: Windows 95/Windows 3.1; 80486 or Pentium; 4MB RAM (8MB recommended); VGA+ color monitor with 640x480 pixel display; CD-ROM drive (double speed recommended); MS DOS v. 6.0+ with Microsoft CD ROM extensions (MSCDEX); Quick Time for Windows v. 2.0 ISBN 1-88521-307-7
*1. Women - United States - Biography - Encyclopedias. 2. Dodge, Grace H. (Grace Hoadley), 1856-1914. I. McHenry, Robert. II. Pilgrim New Media, Inc. III. Merriam-Webster, Inc. IV. Title: Biographical encyclopedia of famous American women [computer file]*
*TC HQ1412 .A43 1994*

**Herald, Diana Tixier.** Genreflecting : a guide to reading interests in genre fiction / Diana Tixier Herald. 5th ed. Englewood, CO : Libraries Umlimited, 2000. xxiii, 553 p. ; 27 cm. (Genreflecting advisory series) Includes bibliographical references and indexes. ISBN 1-56308-638-7 DDC 016.813009
*1. American fiction - Stories, plots, etc. 2. Popular literature - Stories, plots, etc. 3. English fiction - Stories, plots, etc. 4. Fiction genres - Bibliography. 5. Fiction - Bibliography. 6. Reading interests. I. Title. II. Series.*
*TC PS374.P63 H47 2000*

**HERALDRY.** *See* **GENEALOGY.**

**Herber, Harold L.**
Nelson, Joan Meeting challenges. Lexington, Mass. : D. C. Heath and Company, c1983.
*TC PE1121 .M43 1983*

**Herbert, Joanne M.**
McNergney, Robert F. Foundations of education. 3rd ed. Boston ; London : Allyn and Bacon, c2001.
*TC LB1775.2 .M32 2001*

**Herbst, Philip.** The color of words : an encyclopaedic dictionary of ethnic bias in the United States / Philip H. Herbst. Yarmouth, Me., USA : Intercultural Press, [1997] xxi, 259 p. ; 24 cm. Includes bibliographical references (p. 243-259). ISBN 1-87786-442-0 DDC 305.8/00973
*1. Racism - United States - Dictionaries. 2. United States - Ethnic relations - Dictionaries. 3. Racism in language - Dictionaries. I. Title.*
*TC E184.A1 H466 1997*

**HERCULANEUM (ANCIENT CITY).** *See* **HERCULANEUM (EXTINCT CITY).**

**HERCULANEUM (EXTINCT CITY).**
Deiss, Joseph Jay. The town of Hercules. Rev. and expanded. Malibu, Calif. : J. Paul Getty Museum, c1995.
*TC DG70.H5 D4 1995*

**HERCULANEUM (EXTINCT CITY) - JUVENILE LITERATURE.**
Deiss, Joseph Jay. The town of Hercules. Rev. and expanded. Malibu, Calif. : J. Paul Getty Museum, c1995.
*TC DG70.H5 D4 1995*

**HERDERS.** *See* **COWBOYS.**

**Herdman, Paul.**
Hill, Paul Thomas, 1943- It takes a city. Washington, D.C. : Brookings Institution Press, c2000.
*TC LC5131 .H48 2000*

**Here is the African savanna.**
Dunphy, Madeleine. 1st ed. New York : Hyperion Books for Children, c1999.
*TC QH194 .D86 1999*

**HEREDITARY DISEASES - NURSES' INSTRUCTION.**
Lashley, Felissa R., 1941- Clinical genetics in nursing practice. 2nd ed. New York : Springer, c1998.
*TC RB155 .L37 1998*

**HEREDITARY SUCCESSION.** *See* **INHERITANCE AND SUCCESSION.**

**HEREDITY.** *See* **EUGENICS.**

**HERESIES AND HERETICS.** *See* **HERESIES, CHRISTIAN.**

**HERESIES, CHRISTIAN - HISTORY - MIDDLE AGES, 600-1500.**
The medieval church. Woodbridge, Suffolk ; Rochester, NY : Published for the Ecclesiastical History Society by the Boydell Press, 1999.
*TC BR270 .M43 1999*

**HERESY.** *See* **HERESIES, CHRISTIAN.**

**Heresy in the University.**
Berlinerblau, Jacques. New Brunswick, N.J. : Rutgers University Press, c1999.
*TC DF78.B3983 B47 1999*

**Herideen, Penelope E., 1960-** Policy, pedagogy, and social inequality : community college student realities in post-industrial America / Penelope E. Herideen. Westport, Conn. : Bergin & Garvey, 1998. x, 146 p. ; 25 cm. (Critical studies in education and culture series, 1064-8615) Includes bibliographical references (p. [131]-141) and index. ISBN 0-89789-593-2 (alk. paper) DDC 306.43/2
*1. Community colleges - United States - Sociological aspects. 2. Feminism and education - United States. 3. Critical pedagogy - United States. 4. Educational change - United States. I. Title. II. Series.*
*TC LB2328.15.U6 H47 1998*

**HERITAGE PROPERTY.** *See* **CULTURAL PROPERTY.**

**HERKIMER COUNTY (N.Y.).**
O'Connor-Pirkle, Marilyn. Tracking systemic change in an interagency partnership. 1996.
*TC 06 no. 10677*

O'Connor-Pirkle, Marilyn. Tracking systemic change in an interagency partnership. 1996.
*TC 06 no. 10677*

**Herman, Janice L.**
Herman, Jerry John, 1930- School planning & personnel. Lancaster, Pa. : Technomic Pub. Co., c1999.
*TC LB2831.58 .H47 1999*

**Herman, Jerry John, 1930-** School planning & personnel : a resource guide to effective administration / Jerry J. Herman, Janice L. Herman. Lancaster, Pa. : Technomic Pub. Co., c1999. xx, 320 p. : ill. ; 23 cm. Includes bibliographical references (p. 309-314) and index. ISBN 1-56676-657-5 (softcover : acid-free paper) DDC 371.2/01
*1. School personnel management - United States. 2. Educational planning - United States. I. Herman, Janice L. II. Title. III. Title: School planning and personnel*
*TC LB2831.58 .H47 1999*

**Herman, Robert D., 1946-.**
The Jossey-Bass handbook of nonprofit leadership and management. 1st ed. San Francisco : Jossey-Bass, c1994.
*TC HD62.6 .J67 1994*

**Hernandez, Donald J.**
Children of immigrants. Washington, D.C. : National Academy Press, c1999.

*TC HV741 .C536157 1999*

**HERNÁNDEZ, ESPERANZA.**
Behar, Ruth, 1956- Translated woman. Boston : Beacon Press, c1993.
*TC HQ1465.M63 B44 1993*

**Hernández, Ramona.**
Torres-Saillant, Silvio. The Dominican Americans. Westport, Conn. : Greenwood Press, 1998.
*TC E184.D6 T67 1998*

**Hernández y Hernández, Fernando.**
Curriculum, culture, and art education. Albany : State University of New York Press, c1998.
*TC N85 .C87 1998*

**Herndon, Lynne.**
Robbins, Pamela. Thinking inside the block schedule. Thousand Oaks, Calif. : Corwin Press, c2000.
*TC LB3032.2 .R63 2000*

**Herndon, Sandra L.**
Communication in recovery. Cresskill, N.J. : Hampton Press, c1999.
*TC HV4998 .C64 1999*

**Herne, Steve, 1950-.**
Study to teach. London ; New York : Routledge, 2000.
*TC LB1707 .S88 2000*

**HERNHUTTERS.** *See* **MORAVIANS.**

**Herod, Leslie.** Discovering me : a guide to teaching health and building adolescents' self-esteem / Leslie Herod ; illustrated by Meg Biddle, Leslie Herod. Boston, MA : Allyn and Bacon, c1999. xx, 364 p. : ill. ; 28 cm. Includes bibliographical references. ISBN 0-205-27474-9 (alk. paper) DDC 373.17/1
*1. Self-esteem in adolescence - Study and teaching (Secondary) I. Title.*
*TC BF724.3.S36 H47 1999*

**HEROES.** *See* **COURAGE; WOMEN HEROES.**

**HEROES - FICTION.**
Pilkey, Dav, 1966- Captain Underpants and the invasion of the incredibly naughty cafeteria ladies from outer space .... New York : Blue Sky Press, c1999.
*TC PZ7.P63123 Cat 1999*

**HEROES - FOLKLORE.**
Mayer, Marianna. Women warriors. New York : Morrow Junior Books, 1999.
*TC PZ8.1.M46 Wo 1999*

**HEROES IN MOTION PICTURES.**
Drummond, Lee, 1944- American dreamtime. Lanham, Md. : Littlefield Adams Books, 1996.
*TC PN1995.9.M96 D78 1996*

**Heroic self.**
Hall, C. Margaret (Constance Margaret) Springfield, Ill. : C.C. Thomas, c1998.
*TC RC489.S62 H35 1998*

**HEROIN DEPENDENCE - ECONOMICS.**
Cost benefit analysis of heroin maintenance treatment. Basel ; New York : Karger, c2000.
*TC RC568.H4 C67 2000*

**HEROIN DEPENDENCE - THERAPY.**
Cost benefit analysis of heroin maintenance treatment. Basel ; New York : Karger, c2000.
*TC RC568.H4 C67 2000*

**HEROIN DEPENDENCY.** *See* **HEROIN HABIT.**

**HEROIN HABIT - FLORIDA - ORLANDO.**
Heroin [videorecording]. [Princeton, N.J.] : Films for the Humanities & Sciences, c1998.
*TC HV5822.H4 H4 1998*

**HEROIN HABIT - PHYSIOLOGICAL ASPECTS - RESEARCH.**
The hijacked brain [videorecording]. Princeton, NJ : Films for the Humanities & Sciences, c1998.
*TC RC564 .H5 1998*

**HEROIN HABIT - PHYSIOLOGICAL EFFECT - RESEARCH.**
The hijacked brain [videorecording]. Princeton, NJ : Films for the Humanities & Sciences, c1998.
*TC RC564 .H5 1998*

**HEROIN HABIT - PSYCHOLOGICAL ASPECTS.**
Portrait of addiction [videorecording]. Princeton, NJ : Films for the Humanities & Sciences, c1998.
*TC HV5801 .P6 1998*

Portrait of addiction [videorecording]. Princeton, NJ : Films for the Humanities & Sciences, c1998.
*TC RC564 .P6 1998*

EDUCATION: 2000

**HEROIN HABIT - TREATMENT - ECONOMIC ASPECTS.**
Cost benefit analysis of heroin maintenance treatment.
Basel : New York : Karger, c2000.
*TC RC568.H4 C67 2000*

**Heroin** [videorecording] : the new high school high /
ABC News ; producer, Jonathan Talmadge : a
presentation of Films for the Humanities & Sciences.
[Princeton, N.J.] : Films for the Humanities &
Sciences, c1998. 1 videocassette (42 min.) : sd., col. ; 1/2 in.
VHS. Catalogued from credits and container. Originally
broadcast as an episode of the ABC News television
program, Turning Point, on March 6, 1997. Host: Diane
Sawyer. Editors: Collin Hill, Nobuko Oganesoff. For
elementary school children through adult. SUMMARY:
Focuses on drug use, especially heroin use, in teenagers in
Orlando, Florida. Follows the lives of two teenage friends--
both drug users. Jonathan Goodwin, an honor student gifted
with looks and popularity, and a surfing enthusiast, dies of a
heroin overdose. Lee Anna McCollum, the daughter of two
missionaries, finds herself in a drug rehab center at age 15,
after running away from home at 14 and being arrested.
Neither fits the long-held stereotype of a heroin user. Lee Anna
McCollum describes the downhill spiral their lives took. The
program proclaims heroin as the "chic" drug of choice today--
so pure that it no longer has to be cooked or injected-- the "fast
food" drug of choice among more and more of our younger and
younger children-- as readily available as a pack of gum.
Experts discuss the difficulties heroin users face in quitting.
*1. Drug abuse - Florida - Orlando. 2. Heroin habit - Florida -
Orlando. 3. Drug abuse - Social aspects - Florida - Orland. 4.
Drug abuse - Study and teaching - Florida - Orlando. 5.
Narcotic habit - Florida - Orlando. 6. Narcotic habit -
Compications - Florida - Orlando. 7. Drug abuse - Florida -
Orlando - Prevention. 8. Documentary television programs. I.
Sawyer, Diane, 1945- II. Talmadge, Jonathan. III. ABC News.
IV. Films for the Humanities (firm) V. Title: Turning point
(Television program) VI. Title: New high school high
[videorecording]*
*TC HV5822.H4 H4 1998*

**HEROINES.** *See* WOMEN HEROES.

**HEROISM.** *See* COURAGE; HEROES.

**Herrera-Sobek, María.**
Power, race, and gender in academe. New York :
Modern Language Association, 2000.
*TC LC3727 .P69 2000*

**Herriot, Sarah T.** The Slow learner project: The
secondary school "slow learner" in mathematics.
[Stanford, Calif.: Leland Stanford Junior University;
1967] 164 p. ; 25 cm. (SMSG Reports, no. 5.)
*1. Mathematics - Study and teaching. I. Title. II. Series.*
*TC QA11 .S25 no.5*

**HERRNHUTER.** *See* MORAVIANS.

**Hersen, Michel.**
Assessment of family violence. 2nd ed. New York :
John Wiley, c1999.
*TC RC569.5.F3 A87 1999*

Effective brief therapies :. San Diego : Academic
Press, c2000.
*TC RC480.55 .E376 2000*

Handbook of psychological assessment. 3rd ed.
Amsterdam : New York : Pergamon, 2000.
*TC BF39 .H2645 2000*

**Herzenberg, Caroline L., 1932-.**
Howes, Ruth (Ruth Hege) Their day in the sun.
Philadelphia, PA : Temple University Press, 1999.
*TC QC773.3.U5 H68 1999*

**Herzog Associates.**
Diversity [videorecording]. Barrington, IL : Magna
Systems, Inc., 1996.
*TC LB1139.25 .D5 1996*

**Herzog, Milan.**
Diversity [videorecording]. Barrington, IL : Magna
Systems, Inc., 1996.
*TC LB1139.25 .D5 1996*

**Herzog, Shanta.**
Diversity [videorecording]. Barrington, IL : Magna
Systems, Inc., 1996.
*TC LB1139.25 .D5 1996*

**Hess, Diana.**
Public issues discussion [videorecording] : Diana
Hess at Denver High School 1997. [Boulder, Colo.] :
Social Science Education Consortium, c1997.
*TC H62.3 .P4 1997*

Socratic seminar [videorecording]. [Boulder, Colo.] :
Social Science Education Consortium, c1997.

**Hess, J. Daniel (John Daniel), 1937-** Studying abroad/
learning abroad : an abridged edition of The whole
world guide to culture learning / J. Daniel Hess.
Yarmouth, Me., USA : Intercultural Press, c1997. xii,
147 p. : ill. ; 22 cm. Includes bibliographical references (p.
141-147). ISBN 1-87786-450-1 DDC 370.116
*1. Foreign study. 2. American students - Foreign countries. 3.
International education. 4. Experiential learning. 5. Returned
students - United States. I. Hess, J. Daniel (John Daniel).
1937- Whole world guide to culture learning. II. Title.*
*TC LB2375 .H467 1997*

**Whole world guide to culture learning.**
Hess, J. Daniel (John Daniel), 1937- Studying
abroad/learning abroad. Yarmouth, Me., USA :
Intercultural Press, c1997.
*TC LB2375 .H467 1997*

**Hessel, Dieter.**
Hessel, Ingo. Inuit art. New York : Harry N. Abrams,
1998.
*TC E99.E7 H493 1998*

**Hessel, Ingo.** Inuit art : an introduction / Ingo Hessel ;
photography by Dieter Hessel ; with a foreword by
George Swinton. New York : Harry N. Abrams, 1998.
x, 198 p. : ill. (some col.) ; 29 cm. Includes bibliographical
references (p.194-196) and index. ISBN 0-8109-3476-0
(hardcover) DDC 704.03/9712
*1. Inuit art - Canada. I. Hessel, Dieter. II. Title.*
*TC E99.E7 H493 1998*

**Hesselbein, Frances.**
Leading beyond the walls. 1st ed. San Francisco :
Jossey-Bass, c1999.
*TC HD57.7 .L4374 1999*

**Hester, Sallie.** A covered wagon girl : the diary of Sallie
Hester, 1849-1850 / edited by Christy Steele with Ann
Hodgson ; foreword by Suzanne L. Bunkers.
Mankato, Minn. : Blue Earth Books, c2000. 32 p. : ill.
(some col.) ; 24 cm. (Diaries, letters, and memoirs) Includes
bibliographical references (p. 31) and index. SUMMARY:
Excerpts from the diary of a fourteen-year-old girl tell of her
family's journey along the Oregon-California Trail during
1849-1850. Includes sidebars, activities, and a timeline related
to the era. ISBN 0-7368-0344-0 DDC 978/.02/092
*1. Hester, Sallie - Diaries - Juvenile literature. 2. Pioneer
children - West (U.S.) - Diaries - Juvenile literature. 3. Girls -
West (U.S.) - Diaries - Juvenile literature. 4. Overland
journeys to the Pacific - Juvenile literature. 5. Frontier and
pioneer life - West (U.S.) - Juvenile literature. 6. West (U.S.) -
Description and travel - Juvenile literature. 7. Hester, Sallie. 8.
Overland journeys to the Pacific. 9. Frontier and pioneer life -
West (U.S.) 10. West (U.S.) - Description and travel. 11.
Diaries. 12. Women - Biography I. Steele, Christy. II.
Hodgson, Ann. III. Title. IV. Series.*
*TC F593 .H47 2000*

**HESTER, SALLIE.**
Hester, Sallie. A covered wagon girl. Mankato,
Minn. : Blue Earth Books, c2000.
*TC F593 .H47 2000*

**HESTER, SALLIE - DIARIES - JUVENILE
LITERATURE.**
Hester, Sallie. A covered wagon girl. Mankato,
Minn. : Blue Earth Books, c2000.
*TC F593 .H47 2000*

**Heston, Charlton.**
Brighter visions [videorecording. Burbank, CA :
RCA/Columbia Pictures Home Video ; Toluca Lake,
CA : [Distributed by] Corporate Productions, c1991.
*TC HV1597.5 .B67 1991*

**HETEROSEXISM.** *See* HOMOPHOBIA.

**Hetherington, E. Mavis.**
Adolescent siblings in stepfamilies. Chicago, Ill. :
University of Chicago Press, 1999.
*TC LB1103.S6 v.64 no. 4*

**Hetherington, E. Mavis (Eileen Mavis), 1926-** Child
psychology : a contemporary viewpoint / E. Mavis
Hetherington, Ross D. Parke ; revised by Ross D.
Parke and Virginia Otis Locke. 5th ed. Boston :
McGraw-Hill College, c1999. 1 v. (various pagings) : col.
ill. ; 29 cm. Includes bibliographical references and indexes.
ISBN 0-07-028469-5 (hardcover : alk. paper) ISBN 0-07-
115728-X (ISE) DDC 155.4
*1. Child psychology. I. Parke, Ross D. II. Locke, Virginia O.
III. Title.*
*TC BF721 .H418 1999*

Reiss, David, 1937- The relationship code.
Cambridge, Mass. ; London : Harvard University
Press, c2000.
*TC BF724 .R39 2000*

**Hetherington, Kevin.** Expressions of identity : space,
performance, politics / Kevin Hetherington. London ;
Thousand Oaks, Calif. : Sage Publications, 1998. 181

p. ; 25 cm. (Theory, culture & society) Includes bibliographical
references (p. [161]-173) and index. ISBN 0-8039-7876-6
ISBN 0-8039-7877-4 (pbk.)
*1. Group identity. 2. Social movements. I. Title. II. Series:
Theory, culture & society (Unnumbered)*
*TC HM131 .H3995 1998*

**Hetherington, Paul.**
The dynamics of now. London : Wimbledon School of
Art in association with Tate, c2000.
*TC N185 .D96 2000*

**Heubert, Jay Philip.**
Law and school reform. New Haven [Conn.] : Yale
University Press, c1999.
*TC LC213.2. L38 1999*

**Heubner, Kathleen Mary.**
Hand in hand. New York : AFB Press, c1995.
*TC HV1597.2 .H34 1995*

**Heusinkveld, Paula Rae.**
Pathways to culture. Yarmouth, ME : Intercultural
Press, c1997.
*TC P53 .P37 1997*

**Heward, Christine.**
Gender, education, and development. London ; New
York : Zed Books ; New York : Distributed in USA
exclusively by St. Martin's Press, c1999.
*TC LC2607 .G46 1998*

**Heward, William L., 1949-** Exceptional children : an
introduction to special education / William L. Heward.
6th ed. Upper Saddle River, N.J. : Merrill, c2000. 1 v.
(various pagings) : ill. (chiefly col.) ; 26 cm. Includes
bibliographical references and indexes. ISBN 0-13-012938-0
DDC 371.9/0973
*1. Special education - United States. 2. Exceptional children -
United States. I. Title.*
*TC LC3981 .H49 2000*

**Hewett, Dave.**
Challenging behaviour. London : D. Fulton, 1998.
*TC RC451.4.M47 C492 1998*

**Hewitt, Martin.** The emergence of stability in the
industrial city : Manchester, 1832-67 / Martin Hewitt.
Aldershot, England : Scolar Press ; Brookfield, Vt.,
USA : Ashgate Pub. Co., c1996. xii, 335 p. : maps ; 24
cm. Includes bibliographical references (p. [305]-327) and
index. ISBN 1-85928-276-8 (cloth) DDC 306/.09427/33
*1. Manchester (England) - Social conditions. 2. Manchester
(England) - Politics and government. 3. Industries - England -
Manchester - History - 19th century. 4. Working class -
England - Manchester - History - 19th century. I. Title.*
*TC HN398.M27 H48 1996*

**Hewlett, Nigel.**
Coarticulation. Cambridge, U.K. ; New York :
Cambridge University Press, 1999.
*TC QP306 .C68 1999*

**Heycock, Caroline B., 1960-.**
Language acquisition. 1st ed. Amsterdam ; New
York : North-Holland, 1999.
*TC P118 .L2539 1999*

**Heyes, Cecilia M.**
The evolution of cognition. Cambridge, Mass. : MIT
Press, c2000.
*TC BF701 .E598 2000*

**Heymans, P. G.**
Developing talent across the lifespan. Hove [U.K.] :
Psychology Press ; Philadelphia : Taylor & Francis,
2000.
*TC BF713 .D48 2000*

**Heywood, John, 1930-** Assessment in higher
education : student learning, teaching, programmes
and institutions / John Heywood ; foreword by
Thomas Angelo. London ; Philadelphia : Jessica
Kingsley Publishers, 2000. 448 p. : ill. ; 25 cm. (Higher
education policy series ; 56) Includes bibliographical
references (p. 405-434) and indexes. ISBN 1-85302-831-2 (alk.
paper) DDC 378.1/664
*1. Universities and colleges - Examinations. 2. College
teaching - Evaluation. 3. Education, Higher - Evaluation. 4.
Education, Higher - Aims and objectives. I. Title. II. Series.*
*TC LB2366 .H49 2000*

**Hibbard, K. Michael.** Performance-based learning and
assessment in middle school science / K. Michael
Hibbard. Larchmont, NY : Eye On Education, 2000.
214 p. ; 28 cm. ISBN 1-88300-181-1 DDC 507/.1273
*1. Science - Study and teaching (Middle school) - United
States. 2. Competency based education - United States. I. Title.*
*TC Q181 .H52 2000*

**Hickey, Dona J.**
Learning literature in an era of change. Sterling, Va. :
Stylus Pub., c2000.

*Hicks, D. Emily.*

*TC PN59 .L39 2000*

**Hicks, D. Emily.** Ninety-five languages and seven forms of intelligence : education in the twenty-first century / D. Emily Hicks. New York : P. Lang, c1999. viii, 187 p. ; 23 cm. (Counterpoints ; vol. 72) Includes bibliographical references (p. [159]-176) and index. ISBN 0-8204-3909-6 (alk. paper) DDC 370.11/5
*1. Critical pedagogy. 2. Postmodernism and education. 3. Multicultural education. I. Title. II. Title: 95 languages and 7 forms of intelligence III. Title: 95 languages and seven forms of intelligence IV. Series: Counterpoints (New York, N.Y.) ; vol. 72.*
*TC LC196 .H53 1999*

**The hidden epidemic.**
Institute of Medicine (U.S.). Committee on Prevention and Control of Sexually Transmitted Diseases. Washington, D.C. : National Academy Press, 1997.
*TC RA644.V4 I495 1997*

**Hidden messages :** instructional materials for investigating culture / Barbara Finkelstein and Elizabeth K. Eder, editors. Yarmouth, Me. : Intercultural Press, c1998. xi, 178 p. : ill. ; 26 cm. Includes bibliographical references. ISBN 1-87786-456-0 DDC 370.117/0973
*1. Multicultural education - United States - Audio-visual aids. 2. Multicultural education - United States - Curricula. 3. Culture - Study and teaching - United States - Audio-visual aids. 4. Language and culture - United States - Audio-visual aids. I. Finkelstein, Barbara, 1937- II. Eder, Elizabeth K.*
*TC LC1099.3 .H53 1998*

**Hide-and-seek Elmer.**
McKee, David. 1st U.S. ed. New York : Lothrop, Lee & Shepard Books, c1998.
*TC PZ7.M19448 Hi 1998*

**HIDES AND SKINS.** *See* **LEATHER; PARCHMENT.**

**Hiebert, Elfrieda.**
Ragno, Nancy N. World of language. [Teacher ed.]. Morristown, NJ : Silver Burdett & Ginn, c1990.

Ragno, Nancy N. World of language. [Teacher ed.]. Morristown, NJ : Silver Burdett & Ginn, c1990.

Ragno, Nancy N. World of language. [Teacher ed.]. Morristown, NJ : Silver Burdett & Ginn, c1990.

Ragno, Nancy Nickell. World of language. Needham, Ma. : Silver Burdett Ginn, c1996.
*TC LB1576 .S4471 1996*

Ragno, Nancy Nickell. World of language. Needham, Mass. : Silver Burdett Ginn, c1996.
*TC LB1576 .S4471 1996*

World of language. Needham, Mass. : Silver Burdett Ginn, c1996.
*TC LB1576 .S4471 1996*

World of language. Teacher ed. Needham, Mass. : Silver Burdett Ginn, c1996.
*TC LB1576 .S4471 1996 Teacher Ed.*

**Hiele, Pierre M. van.**
Baynes, Joyce Frisby. The development of a van Hiele-based summer geometry program and its impact on student van Hiele level and achievement in high school geometry. 1998.
*TC 06 no. 10915*

**HIELE, PIERRE M. VAN.**
Baynes, Joyce Frisby. The development of a van Hiele-based summer geometry program and its impact on student van Hiele level and achievement in high school geometry. 1998.
*TC 06 no. 10915*

**HIEROGLYPHICS.** *See* **ALPHABET.**

**Higgins, Lorraine.**
Flower, Linda. Learning to rival. Mahwah, New Jersey : Lawrence Erlbaum Associates, c2000.
*TC PE1404 .F59 2000*

**HIGGLING.** *See* **NEGOTIATION.**

**Higgs, Eric S.**
Technology and the good life? Chicago ; London : University of Chicago Press, 2000.
*TC T14 .T386 2000*

**HIGH ACHIEVERS.** *See* **SUCCESSFUL PEOPLE.**

**High-impact teaching.**
Babbage, Keen J. Lancaster, Pa. : Technomic Pub. Co., c1998.
*TC LB1065 .B23 1998*

**High, Linda Oatman.** Barn savers / by Linda Oatman High ; illustrated by Ted Lewin. 1st ed. Honesdale, Pa. : Caroline House/Boyds Mills Press, 1999. 1 v. (unpaged) : col. ill. ; 29 cm. SUMMARY: A young boy helps his father recycle a 19th-century barn. ISBN 1-56397-403-7
*1. Barns - United States - History - Juvenile fiction. 2. Barns - United States - Conservation and restoration - Juvenile literature. 3. Barns - United States - History. I. Lewin, Ted, ill. II. Title.*
*TC PZ7.H543968 Bar 1999*

**High-minded and low-down.**
Tawa, Nicholas E. Boston : Northeastern University Press, c2000.
*TC ML3917.U6 T39 2000*

**High points.**
High points in the work of the high schools of New York City. New York City : Board of Education, 1931-1966.

**High points in the New York City public schools.**
High points in the work of the high schools of New York City. New York City : Board of Education, 1931-1966.

**High points in the work of the high schools of New York City.** New York City : Board of Education, 1931-1966. 36 v. ; 22 cm. Frequency: Monthly (except July and Aug.). Vol. 13, no. 6 (June 1931)-v. 48, no. 9 (Dec. 1966). High points. Title from cover. Continues: Bulletin of high points in the work of the high schools of New York City (OCoLC)7627151 (DLC) 92649269. Continued by: High points in the New York City public schools (OCoLC)7664237 (DLC) 92649270. DDC 373.747
*1. Education - Periodicals. 2. High schools - New York (State) - New York - Periodicals. I. New York (N.Y.) Board of Education. II. Title: High points III. Title: Bulletin of high points in the work of the high schools of New York City IV. Title: High points in the New York City public schools*

**High-risk sexual behavior.**
Becker, Evvie. New York : Plenum Press, c1998.
*TC HQ60.7.U6 B43 1998*

**HIGH RISK STUDENTS.**
Chalker, Christopher S. Effective alternative education programs. Lancaster, Pa. : Technomic, c1999.
*TC LC4091 .C5 1999*

**High school.**
The High school teacher. Blanchester, The Brown Publishing Co.

**The High school.** Eugene, Ore. 9 v. 26 cm. Frequency: Frequency varies. v. 1-9; 1923-Apr. 1932. "Published by the School of Education of the University of Oregon in the interests of secondary education in Oregon and the Northwest." V. 2, no. 4; v. 3 no. 2; v. 5 no. 4 never published. Four nos. a year. v. 1; 3 nos. a year, v. 2; 4 nos. a year, v. 3-4; 3 nos. a year, v. 5; 4 nos. a year, v. 6; 5 nos. a year, v. 7; 6 nos. a year, v. 8-9. "Authorized by the State Board of Higher Education." SUMMARY: Includes sections: "New books received"; "Recent publications." Vol. 2, no. 3 called v. 2, no. 2. Vols. 5-9 paged continuously.
*1. High schools - Periodicals. 2. Education - Periodicals. 3. Education, Secondary - Periodicals. 4. Education - Oregon. I. University of Oregon. School of Education. II. Oregon. State Board of Higher Education.*

**HIGH SCHOOL ATTENDANCE - BERMUDA ISLANDS.**
Tucker, Gina Marie. Discipline. 1998.
*TC 06 no. 10999*

**HIGH SCHOOL-COLLEGE COOPERATION.** *See* **COLLEGE-SCHOOL COOPERATION.**

**HIGH SCHOOL COUNSELING.** *See* **COUNSELING IN SECONDARY EDUCATION.**

**HIGH SCHOOL DROPOUTS - EDUCATION - UNITED STATES - CASE STUDIES.**
Kennedy, Rosa L., 1938- A school for healing. New York : P. Lang, c1999.
*TC LC146.4 .K46 1999*

**HIGH SCHOOL DROPOUTS - NEW YORK (STATE) - NEW YORK - INTERVIEWS.**
Dreyer, Susan T. Student perceptions of their educational experiences at Satellite Academy High School and their former schools. 1999.
*TC 06 no. 11105*

**HIGH SCHOOL EDUCATION.** *See* **EDUCATION, SECONDARY.**

**HIGH SCHOOL GRADUATES - EMPLOYMENT - UNITED STATES.**
Gray, Kenneth C. Getting real. Thousand Oaks, Calif. : Corwin Press, c2000.
*TC HF5382.5.U5 G676 2000*

**HIGH SCHOOL GUIDANCE.** *See* **COUNSELING IN SECONDARY EDUCATION.**

**HIGH SCHOOL LIBRARIES - ACTIVITY PROGRAMS - UNITED STATES.**
Doggett, Sandra L. Beyond the book. Englewood, Colo. : Libraries Unlimited, 2000.
*TC ZA4065 .D64 2000*

**HIGH SCHOOL LIBRARIES - UNITED STATES - DATA PROCESSING.**
Doggett, Sandra L. Beyond the book. Englewood, Colo. : Libraries Unlimited, 2000.
*TC ZA4065 .D64 2000*

**The high school principal's calendar.**
Ricken, Robert. Thousand Oaks, Calif. : Corwin Press, c2000.
*TC LB3032 .R53 2000*

**HIGH SCHOOL PRINCIPALS - UNITED STATES - HANDBOOKS, MANUALS, ETC.**
Ricken, Robert. The high school principal's calendar. Thousand Oaks, Calif. : Corwin Press, c2000.
*TC LB3032 .R53 2000*

**The high school proficiency test** [videorecording] : geometry / Video Tutor, Inc. Princeton, N.J. : Video Tutor, 1988. 1 videocassette (VHS) (62 min.) : sd., col. ; 1/2 in. + 1 student workbook & pre/post test system ([12] p. ; 19 cm.). (Video tutor instructional series) (A mathematics series) Title on container: Basic geometry [videorecording]. VHS. Catalogued from credits, cassette label and container. John Hall, instructor. For grades 5-9 math classes. SUMMARY: Clear explanation of such basic geometry concepts as angles, areas, volumes and perimeters.
*1. Geometry. I. Hall, John. II. Video Tutor. III. Title: Basic geometry [videorecording] IV. Title: Geometry [videorecording] V. Series. VI. Series: A mathematics series*
*TC QA445 .H5 1988*

**The high school quarterly.** Athens, Ga. : University of Georgia, 1912-[1936] 24 v. : ill. ; 22 cm. Vol. 1, no. 1 (Oct. 1912)-v. 24 (July 1936). Official organ of the Georgia High School Association and, from Jan. 1914, of the Commission on Accredited Schools of the Southern Association of Colleges and Secondary Schools, and, from Oct. 1917, of the Georgia College Association and the National High School Inspectors' Association. Title from cover. Continued by: School & college.
*1. High schools - Georgia - Periodicals. 2. Education. Secondary - Periodicals. I. University of Georgia. II. Georgia State High School Association. III. Georgia College Association. IV. National High School Inspectors' Association. V. Southern Association of Colleges and Secondary Schools. Commission on Accredited Schools of the Southern States. VI. Title: School & college*

**HIGH SCHOOL SENIORS - NEW YORK (STATE) - NUTRITION.**
Bissonnette, Madeline Monaco. Adolescents' perspectives on the environmental impacts of food production practices. 1999.
*TC 06 no. 11084*

**HIGH SCHOOL SPORTS.** *See* **SCHOOL SPORTS.**

**HIGH SCHOOL STUDENTS.** *See also* **HIGH SCHOOL DROPOUTS; HIGH SCHOOL SENIORS; LIBRARY ORIENTATION FOR HIGH SCHOOL STUDENTS.**
Gangi, Robyn Joseph. A longitudinal case study of the musical/aesthetic experience of adolescent choral musicians. 1998.
*TC 06 no. 10932*

**HIGH SCHOOL STUDENTS - ATTITUDES - NEW YORK (STATE) - NEW YORK.**
Smith, Hawthorne Emery. Psychological detachment from school. 1999.
*TC 085 Sm586*

**HIGH SCHOOL STUDENTS - BERMUDA ISLANDS - DISCIPLINE.**
Tucker, Gina Marie. Discipline. 1998.
*TC 06 no. 10999*

**HIGH SCHOOL STUDENTS - CHICAGO - SOCIAL LIFE AND CUSTOMS - CASE STUDIES.**
FITZSIMMONS, ELLEN. Teach me. Lanham [Md.] : International Scholars Publications, c1999.
*TC HQ796 .F58 1999*

**HIGH SCHOOL STUDENTS - COUNSELING OF.** *See* **COUNSELING IN SECONDARY EDUCATION.**

**HIGH SCHOOL STUDENTS - EDUCATION - NEW JERSEY - ATTITUDES.**
Campbell, Delois. High school students' perceptions of the impact of block scheduling on instructional effectiveness. 1999.
*TC 06 no. 11089*

**HIGH SCHOOL STUDENTS - ENGLAND - LONDON - SOCIAL CONDITIONS - CROSS-CULTURAL STUDIES.**
Making spaces. New York : St. Martin's Press, 2000.
*TC LC208.4 .M35 2000*

**HIGH SCHOOL STUDENTS - FINLAND - HELSINKI - SOCIAL CONDITIONS - CROSS-CULTURAL STUDIES.**
Making spaces. New York : St. Martin's Press, 2000.
*TC LC208.4 .M35 2000*

**HIGH SCHOOL STUDENTS - INTERVIEWS.**
Baynes, Joyce Frisby. The development of a van Hiele-based summer geometry program and its impact on student van Hiele level and achievement in high school geometry. 1998.
*TC 06 no. 10915*

Tsai, Chin-Chung. The interrelationships between junior high school students' scientific epistemologicl beliefs, learning environment preferences and their cognitive structure outcomes. 1996.
*TC 06 no. 10713*

**HIGH SCHOOL STUDENTS - LIBRARY ORIENTATION. See LIBRARY ORIENTATION FOR HIGH SCHOOL STUDENTS.**

**HIGH SCHOOL STUDENTS - NEW YORK (STATE) - NEW YORK.**
Asher, Nina. Margins, center, and the spaces in-between. 1999.
*TC 06 no. 11080*

**HIGH SCHOOL STUDENTS - NEW YORK (STATE) - NEW YORK - ATTITUDES.**
Dreyer, Susan T. Student perceptions of their educational experiences at Satellite Academy High School and their former schools. 1999.
*TC 06 no. 11105*

**HIGH SCHOOL STUDENTS - NEW YORK (STATE) - NEW YORK - CASE STUDIES.**
Fleischer, Lee. Living in contradiction. 1998.
*TC 06 no. 11021*

**HIGH SCHOOL STUDENTS - NEW ZEALAND - SOCIAL CONDITIONS - CASE STUDIES.**
Thrupp, Martin, 1964- Schools making a difference-- let's be realistic!. Buckingham [England] ; Philadelphia : Open University Press, 1999.
*TC LB2822.75 .T537 1999*

**High school students' perceptions of the impact of block scheduling on instructional effectiveness.**
Campbell, Delois. 1999.
*TC 06 no. 11089*

**HIGH SCHOOL STUDENTS - SOCIAL CONDITIONS.**
Dickerson, Pless Moore. Haitian students' perception of a school as a community of support. 1998.
*TC 06 no. 11018*

Dickerson, Pless Moore. Haitian students' perception of a school as a community of support. 1998.
*TC 06 no. 11018*

Dickerson, Pless Moore. Haitian students' perception of a school as a community of support. 1998.
*TC 06 no. 11018*

**HIGH SCHOOL STUDENTS - SOCIAL LIFE AND CUSTOMS.**
Woo, Kimberley Ann. "Double happiness," double jeopardy. 1999.
*TC 06 no. 11075*

**HIGH SCHOOL STUDENTS - UNITED STATES - ATTITUDES.**
Hansel, Bettina G. The exchange student survival kit. Yarmouth, ME : Intercultural Press, c1993.
*TC LB1696 .H36 1993*

**HIGH SCHOOL STUDENTS - VOCATIONAL GUIDANCE - UNITED STATES.**
Gray, Kenneth C. Getting real. Thousand Oaks, Calif. : Corwin Press, c2000.
*TC HF5382.5.U5 G676 2000*

**The High school teacher.** Blanchester, The Brown Publishing Co. 11 v. v. 1-11; 1925-June 1935. "A national journal of secondary education." Superseded by: High school.
*1. Education, Secondary - Periodicals. I. Title: High school*

**HIGH SCHOOL TEACHERS - BERMUDA ISLANDS - ATTITUDES.**
Tucker, Gina Marie. Discipline. 1998.
*TC 06 no. 10999*

**HIGH SCHOOL TEACHERS - NEW YORK (STATE) - NEW YORK - ATTITUDES.**
Dreyer, Susan T. Student perceptions of their

educational experiences at Satellite Academy High School and their former schools. 1999.
*TC 06 no. 11105*

**HIGH SCHOOL TEACHERS - UNITED STATES - CASE STUDIES.**
Nolan, James F., 1950- Teachers and educational change. Albany : State University of New York Press, c2000.
*TC LB1777.2 .N64 2000*

**HIGH SCHOOL TEACHING.**
Clark, Leonard H. Secondary and middle school teaching methods. 7th ed. Englewood Cliffs, N.J. : Merrill, c1996.
*TC LB1737.A3 C53 1996*

Kim, Eugene C. A resource guide for secondary school teaching. 5th ed. New York : Macmillan Pub. Co., c1991.
*TC LB1737.A3 K56 1991 5th ed.*

**HIGH SCHOOL TEACHING - GREAT BRITAIN.**
Helsby, Gill. Changing teachers' work. Buckingham [England] ; Philadelphia : Open University Press, 1999.
*TC LA635 .H375 1999*

McNamara, Eddie. Positive pupil management and motivation :. London : David Fulton, 1999.
*TC LB3013 .M336 1999*

**HIGH SCHOOL TEACHING - HANDBOOKS, MANUALS, ETC.**
Learning to teach in the secondary school. 2nd ed. London ; New York : Routledge, 1999.
*TC LB1737.A3 L43 1999*

**HIGH SCHOOL TEACHING - NEW JERSEY - EVALUATION.**
Campbell, Delois. High school students' perceptions of the impact of block scheduling on instructional effectiveness. 1999.
*TC 06 no. 11089*

**HIGH SCHOOL TEACHING - UNITED STATES.**
Allan, Karen Kuelthau. Literacy and learning. Boston : Houghton Mifflin, c2000.
*TC LB1631 .A37 2000*

Dynamics of effective teaching. 4th ed. New York ; Harlow, England : Longman, c2000.
*TC LB1737.U6 K56 2000*

**HIGH SCHOOL TEACHING - UNITED STATES - DECISION MAKING.**
Teaching as decision making. Upper Saddle River, N.J. : Prentice Hall, c2000.
*TC LB1607.5 .T43 2000*

**HIGH SCHOOL TEACHING - UNITED STATES - LONGITUDINAL STUDIES.**
Smith, Darren James, 1960- Stepping inside the classroom through personal narratives. Lanham, Md. : University Press of America, 1999.
*TC LB1737.U6 S55 1999*

**HIGH SCHOOLS. See CATHOLIC HIGH SCHOOLS; EDUCATION, SECONDARY.**

**HIGH SCHOOLS - ALUMNI AND ALUMNAE. See HIGH SCHOOL GRADUATES.**

**HIGH SCHOOLS - BERMUDA ISLANDS - ADMINISTRATION.**
Tucker, Gina Marie. Discipline. 1998.
*TC 06 no. 10999*

**HIGH SCHOOLS - DECENTRALIZATION - NEW YORK (STATE) - NEW YORK.**
Dreyer, Susan T. Student perceptions of their educational experiences at Satellite Academy High School and their former schools. 1999.
*TC 06 no. 11105*

**HIGH SCHOOLS - ENGLAND - LONDON - HISTORY.**
Hackney Downs. London ; New York : Cassell, 1999.
*TC LF795.L66 H33 1999*

**HIGH SCHOOLS - FICTION.**
Draper, Sharon M. (Sharon Mills) Romiette and Julio. 1st ed. New York : Atheneum Books for Young Readers, 1999.
*TC PZ7.D78325 Ro 1999*

Sheldon, Dyan. Confessions of a teenage drama queen. 1st ed. Cambridge, Mass. : Candlewick Press, 1999.
*TC PZ7.S54144 Co 1999*

**HIGH SCHOOLS - GEORGIA - PERIODICALS.**
The High school quarterly. Athens, Ga. : University of Georgia, 1912-[1936]

**HIGH SCHOOLS, JUNIOR. See JUNIOR HIGH SCHOOLS.**

**HIGH SCHOOLS - KENTUCKY - PERIODICALS.**
Kentucky high school quarterly. Lexington, Ky. : Department of Education, State University of Kentucky, 1915-1927.

**HIGH SCHOOLS - NEW YORK (STATE) - NEW YORK - PERIODICALS.**
High points in the work of the high schools of New York City. New York City : Board of Education, 1931-1966.

**HIGH SCHOOLS - NEW ZEALAND - SOCIOLOGICAL ASPECTS - CASE STUDIES.**
Thrupp, Martin, 1964- Schools making a difference-- let's be realistic!. Buckingham [England] ; Philadelphia : Open University Press, 1999.
*TC LB2822.75 .T537 1999*

**HIGH SCHOOLS - PERIODICALS.**
The High school. Eugene, Ore.

Kentucky high school quarterly. Lexington, Ky. : Department of Education, State University of Kentucky, 1915-1927.

**HIGH SCHOOLS, RURAL. See RURAL SCHOOLS.**

**HIGH SCHOOLS - SCHEDULES. See SCHEDULES, SCHOOL.**

**HIGH SCHOOLS - UNITED STATES.**
Ikeda, Keiko. A room full of mirrors. Stanford, Calif. : Stanford University Press; 1998.
*TC LB3618 .I54 1998*

The new American high school. Thousand Oaks, Calif. : Corwin Press, c1999.
*TC LA222 .N49 1999*

**High/Scope Educational Research Foundation.**
Families speak. Ypsilanti, Mich. : High/Scope Press, c1994.
*TC LB1139.23 .F36 1994*

**HIGH SOCIETY. See UPPER CLASS.**

**HIGH TECH. See HIGH TECHNOLOGY.**

**High tech heretic.**
Stoll, Clifford. 1st ed. New York : Doubleday, c1999.
*TC LB1028.5 .S77 1999*

**HIGH TECHNOLOGY AND EDUCATION - UNITED STATES - FINANCE.**
Bauer, David G. Technology funding for schools. 1st ed. San Francisco : Jossey-Bass, c2000.
*TC LB1028.43 .B38 2000*

**HIGH TECHNOLOGY INDUSTRIES - UNITED STATES.**
Gross, Clifford M. The new idea factory. Columbus, OH : Battelle Press, c2000.
*TC HD53 .G75 2000*

**HIGH TECHNOLOGY - SOCIAL ASPECTS.**
The cybercultures reader. London : New York : Routledge, 2000.
*TC T14.5 .C934 2000*

**Higher ed**
(vol. 1) Higher education for democracy. New York : P. Lang, c1999.
*TC LD2001.G452 .S33 1999*

(vol. 4) Reforming a college. New York : P. Lang, c2000.
*TC LD5293 .R44 2000*

**HIGHER EDUCATION. See EDUCATION, HIGHER.**

**Higher education administration.**
Goonen, Norma M. Westport, Conn. ; London : Greenwood Press, 1999.
*TC LB2341 .G573 1999*

**Higher education and disabilities :** international approaches / edited by Alan Hurst. Aldershot ; Brookfield, Vt. : Ashgate, c1998. xi, 234 p. ; 23 cm. Includes bibliographical references. ISBN 1-85972-508-2
*1. Handicapped - Education (Higher) - Cross-cultural studies. 2. Handicapped college students - Services for - Cross-cultural studies. 3. Education, Higher - Cross-cultural studies. 4. Higher education and state - Cross-cultural studies. I. Hurst, Alan, 1944-*
*TC LC4812 .H55 1998*

**Higher education and research in the Netherlands.**
The Hague, Netherlands Foundation for International Cooperation. 26 v. ill. 24 cm. Frequency: 2 no. a year, - 1982. Former frequency: Quarterly, 1957- . v. 1-26; Mar. 1957-summer/autumn 1982. Indexed selectively by:

Sociological abstracts 0038-0202. Indexed selectively by: Social welfare, social planning/policy & social development 0195-7988. English and Spanish. Bulletin of the Netherlands Universities Foundation for International Co-operation. Vols. 1-5, 1957-61, with v. 5; vols. 6-10, 1962-66, with v. 10. ISSN 0018-1587
*1. Learning and scholarship - Netherlands - Periodicals. 2. Universities and colleges - Netherlands - Periodicals. 3. Education, Higher - Periodicals. 4. Education - Netherlands - Periodicals. 5. Research - Netherlands - Periodicals. 6. Educational exchanges - Netherlands - Periodicals. I. Stichting voor Internationale Samenwerking der Nederlandse Universiteiten en Hogescholen.*

## HIGHER EDUCATION AND STATE.
Knowledge and power in higher education. New York : London : Teachers College Press, c2000.
*TC LC171 .K62 2000*

Towards a new model of governance for universities? London ; Philadelphia : Jessica Kingsley, c1999.
*TC LC171 .T683 1999*

## HIGHER EDUCATION AND STATE - CROSS-CULTURAL STUDIES.
Eddy, John, 1932- International higher education systems. New ed. Lanham, Md. ; Oxford : University Press of America, c2000.
*TC LB2322.2 .E33 2000*

Higher education and disabilities. Aldershot ; Brookfield, Vt. : Ashgate, c1998.
*TC LC4812 .H55 1998*

Higher education research. 1st ed. Oxford ; [New York] : Pergamon, published for the IAU Press, 2000.
*TC LB2326.3 .H548 2000*

## HIGHER EDUCATION AND STATE - CROSS-CULTURAL STUDIES - CONGRESSES.
The universities' responsibilities to society. 1st ed. New York : Pergamon, published for the IAU Press, 2000.
*TC LC191.9 .U55 2000*

## HIGHER EDUCATION AND STATE - ECONOMIC ASPECTS - CROSS-CULTURAL STUDIES.
Experiential learning around the world. London ; Philadelphia : J. Kingsley Publishers, 2000.
*TC LB2324 .E95 2000*

## HIGHER EDUCATION AND STATE - EUROPE.
Groof, Jan de. Democracy and governance in higher education. The Hague ; Boston : Kluwer Law International, 1998.
*TC LB2341.8.E85 G76 1998*

## HIGHER EDUCATION AND STATE - GREAT BRITAIN.
Bligh, Donald, 1936- Understanding higher education. Oxford : Intellect, 1999.
*TC LA637 .B55 1999*

Lange, Thomas, 1967- Rethinking higher education. London : IEA Education and Training Unit, 1998.
*TC LB2342.2.G7 L364 1998*

## HIGHER EDUCATION AND STATE - NORWAY.
Bleiklie, Ivar, 1948- Policy and practice in higher education. London ; Phildadelphia : J. Kingsley Publishers, 2000.
*TC LC178.N8 B44 2000*

## HIGHER EDUCATION AND STATE - SOVIET UNION - HISTORY.
Konecny, Peter, 1963- Builders and deserters. Montreal : McGill-Queen's University Press, 1999.
*TC LA839.5.L45 K65 1999*

## HIGHER EDUCATION AND STATE - SWEDEN.
Transforming universities. London ; Philadelphia : Jessica Kingsley Publishers, 1999.
*TC LA908 .T73 1999*

## HIGHER EDUCATION AND STATE - UNITED STATES.
ASHE reader on finance in higher education. Needham Heights, MA : Ginn Press, c1986.
*TC LB2342 .A76 1990*

Bogue, E. Grady (Ernest Grady), 1935- Exploring the heritage of American higher education. Phoenix, Ariz. : Oryx Press, 2000.
*TC LA227.4 .B66 2000*

Higher education in transition. Westport, Conn. ; London : Bergin & Garvey, 2000.
*TC LA227.4 .H53 2000*

## HIGHER EDUCATION COUNSELING. See COUNSELING IN HIGHER EDUCATION.

**Higher education for democracy :** experiments in progressive pedagogy at Goddard College / edited by Steven A. Schapiro. New York : P. Lang, c1999. x, 292 p. : ill. ; 23 cm. (Higher ed ; vol. 1) Includes bibliographical references. ISBN 0-8204-4107-4 (pbk. : alk. paper) DDC 378.743/4
*1. Goddard College. 2. Progressive education - United States. 3. Democracy - Study and teaching (Higher) - United States. I. Schapiro, Steven A., 1950- II. Series.*
*TC LD2001.G452 .S33 1999*

## HIGHER EDUCATION GUIDANCE. See COUNSELING IN HIGHER EDUCATION.

**Higher education in Korea :** tradition and adaptation / edited by John C. Weidman and Namgi Park. New York : Falmer Press, 2000. xii, 264 p. ; 23 cm. (Garland reference library of social science ; v. 1013. Garland studies in higher education ; v. 17) Includes bibliographical references and index. ISBN 0-8153-1957-6 (alk. paper) DDC 378.5195
*1. Education, Higher - Korea (South) I. Weidman, John C., 1945- II. Park, Namgi. III. Series: Garland reference library of social science ; v. 1013. IV. Series: Garland reference library of social science. Garland studies in higher education ; vol. 17.*
*TC LA1333 .H54 2000*

**Higher education in transition :** the challenges of the new millennium / edited by Joseph Losco, Brian L. Fife. Westport, Conn. ; London : Bergin & Garvey, 2000. x, 222 p. : ill. ; 25 cm. Includes bibliographical references and index. ISBN 0-89789-637-8 (alk. paper) DDC 378.73
*1. Education, Higher - Aims and objectives - United States. 2. Higher education and state - United States. I. Losco, Joseph. II. Fife, Brian L.*
*TC LA227.4 .H53 2000*

## HIGHER EDUCATION OF WOMEN. See WOMEN - EDUCATION (HIGHER).

**Higher education policy series**
(44) Elliott, Geoffrey, Dr. Lifelong learning. London ; Philadelphia : Jessica Kingsley Publishers, c1999.
*TC LB1060 .E447 1999*

(48) Transforming universities. London ; Philadelphia : Jessica Kingsley Publishers, 1999.
*TC LA908 .T73 1999*

(49) Bleiklie, Ivar, 1948- Policy and practice in higher education. London ; Philadelphia : J. Kingsley Publishers, 2000.
*TC LC178.N8 B44 2000*

(52) Experiential learning around the world. London ; Philadelphia : J. Kingsley Publishers, 2000.
*TC LB2324 .E95 2000*

(53) Towards a new model of governance for universities? London ; Philadelphia : Jessica Kingsley, c1999.
*TC LC171 .T683 1999*

(56) Heywood, John, 1930- Assessment in higher education. London ; Philadelphia : Jessica Kingsley Publishers, 2000.
*TC LB2366 .H49 2000*

**Higher education research :** its relationship to policy and practice / edited by Ulrich Teichler and Jan Sadlak. 1st ed. Oxford ; [New York] : Pergamon, published for the IAU Press, 2000. xvi, 192 p. : ill. ; 24 cm. (Issues in higher education) "UNESCO." Includes bibliographical references (p. 175-187) and indexes. ISBN 0-08-043452-5 DDC 378/.007/2
*1. Education, Higher - Research - Cross-cultural studies. 2. Higher education and state - Cross-cultural studies. I. Teichler, Ulrich. II. Sadlak, Jan. III. Unesco. IV. Series: Issues in higher education (Oxford, England)*
*TC LB2326.3 .H548 2000*

**Higher education series**
(54.) Sporn, Barbara. Adaptive university structures. London ; Philadelphia : Jessica Kingsley, c1999.
*TC LB2322.2 .S667 1999*

**Higher ground.**
Latimer, Leah Y. New York : Avon Books, c1999.
*TC LC2781 .L27 1999*

## HIGHWAY TRANSPORT WORKERS. See TRUCK DRIVERS.

**Higonnet, Margaret R.**
Girls, boys, books, toys. Baltimore : Johns Hopkins University Press, 1999.
*TC PN1009.5.S48 G57 1999*

**The hijacked brain** [videorecording] / a presentation of Films for the Humanities & Sciences ; a production of Public Affairs Television, Inc. ; a presentation of

Thirteen/WNET New York ; produced and directed by Gail Pellett. Princeton, NJ : Films for the Humanities & Sciences, c1998. 1 videocassette (57 min.) : sd., col. ; 1/2 in. (The Moyers collection) (Close to home. Moyers on addiction) Title on cassette label: Close to home, the hijacked brain [videorecording]. VHS. Catalogued from credits and cassette label and container. Host, Bill Moyers. Editor, Vanessa Procopio ; camera, Bob Achs ... [et al.] ; music, Richard Fiocca ; audio, Paul Bang ... [et al.]. "FFH 7860"--Cassette label. For adolescents through adult. SUMMARY: Scientists are making dramatic discoveries about how addiction affects the brain. Moyers goes into the laboratory to follow researchers engaged in charting an "image of desire in the brain." Discusses how drugs change the biochemical processing in the brain and initially increase the dopamine system and then stop, creating the need for the drug of choice just to feel "normal". Discusses the increased risks of addiction facing children of alcoholics who have an initial low response to alcohol.
*1. Drug abuse - Physiological effect - Research. 2. Drug abuse - Physiological aspects - Research. 3. Substance abuse - Physiological effect - Research. 4. Substance abuse - Physiological aspects - Research. 5. Alcohol - Physiological effect - Research. 6. Alcoholism - Physiological aspects - Research. 7. Narcotic habit - Physiological aspects - Research. 8. Narcotic habit - Physiological effect - Research. 9. Heroin habit - Physiological aspects - Research. 10. Heroin habit - Physiological effect - Research. 11. Cocaine habit - Physiological aspects - Research. 12. Cocaine habit - Physiological effect - Research. 13. Brain mapping - Research. 14. Dopamine - Research. 15. Alcoholics - Interviews. 16. Narcotic addicts - Interviews. I. Moyers, Bill D. II. Pellett, Gail. III. Public Affairs Television (Firm) IV. WNET (Television station : New York, N.Y.) V. Films for the Humanities (Firm) VI. Title: Close to home. the hijacked brain [videorecording] VII. Series: Close to home (Series)*
*TC RC564 .H5 1998*

**Hijirida, Kyoko, 1937-.**
New trends & issues in teaching Japanese language & culture. Honolulu ; Second Language Teaching and Curriculum, University of Hawai'i at Manoa, 1997.
*TC PL519 .N45 1997*

## HIKING.
Olien, Rebecca. Walk this way!. Portsmouth, NH : Heinemann, c1998.
*TC LB1047 .O55 1998*

**Hill, Annette.**
Gauntlett, David. TV Living. London ; New York : Routledge, 1999.
*TC PN1992.55 .G38 1999*

**Hill, Clara E.** Helping skills : facilitating exploration, insight, and action / Clara E. Hill, Karen M. O'Brien. 1st ed. Washington, DC : American Psychological Association, c1999. xix, 401 p. : ill. ; 27 cm. Includes bibliographical references (p. 347-362) and indexes. ISBN 1-55798-572-3 (hardcover : alk. paper) ISBN 1-55798-576-6 (pbk. : alk. paper) DDC 158/.3
*1. Counseling. 2. Helping behavior. I. O'Brien, Karen M. II. Title.*
*TC BF637.C6 H46 1999*

**Hill, Clifford.** Children and reading tests / Clifford Hill and Eric Larsen. Stamford, Conn. : Ablex Pub. Corp., c2000. xix, 425 p. : ill. ; 24 cm. (Advances in discourse processes ; v. 65) Includes bibliographical references (p. 413-418) and indexes. ISBN 1-56750-444-2 (hbk. : alk. paper) ISBN 1-56750-445-0 (pbk. : alk. paper) DDC 372.48
*1. Reading - Ability testing. 2. Reading comprehension - Ability testing. 3. Children - Books and reading. I. Larsen, Eric. II. Title. III. Series.*
*TC LB1050.46 .H55 2000*

From testing to assessment. London : New York : Longman, 1994.
*TC PE1128.A2 F778 1994*

**Hill, Dave, 1945-.**
Promoting equality in secondary schools. London ; New York : Cassell, 1999.
*TC LC212.3.G7 P77 1999*

**Hill, Fran, 1950-** Teamwork in the management of emotional and behavioural difficulties : developing peer support systems for teachers in mainstream and special school / Fran Hill and Lynne Parsons. London : David Fulton, 2000. iv, 74 p. ; 30 cm. (Resource materials for teachers.) Includes bibliographical references (p. 71-72) and index. ISBN 1-85346-619-0 (paper)
*1. Problem children - Education - Great Britain - Management. 2. Teachers of problem children - Training of - Great Britain. I. Parsons, Lynne. II. Title. III. Series.*
*TC LC4803.G7 H54 2000*

**Hill, Marcia.**
Children's rights, therapists' responsibilities. New York : Harrington Park Press, c1997.

*TC RJ504 .C486 1997*

For love or money. New York : Haworth Press, c1999.
*TC RC489.F45 F67 1999*

Learning from our mistakes. New York : Haworth Press, c1998.
*TC RC489.F45 L43 1998*

**Hill, Paul Thomas, 1943-** It takes a city : getting serious about urban school reform / Paul T. Hill, Christine Campbell, James Harvey ; with Paul Herdman ... [et al.]. Washington, D.C. : Brookings Institution Press, c2000. xvii, 205 p. : ill. ; 23 cm. Includes bibliographical references (193-198) and index. CONTENTS: The realities of urban school reform -- Lessons from six cities -- Beneath the surface : theories of action -- From wishful thinking to the realities of reform -- Holding a strategy in place -- Local politics of reform -- Getting started. ISBN 0-8157-3639-8 (pbk. : alk. paper) DDC 370/.9173/2
*1. Education, Urban - United States - Administration - Case studies. 2. Education, Urban - Political aspects - United States - Case studies. 3. Educational change - United States - Case studies. 4. Education and state - United States - Case studies. I. Campbell, Christine. II. Harvey, James. III. Herdman, Paul. IV. Title.*
*TC LC5131 .H48 2000*

**Hill, Peter C., 1953-.**
Baker encyclopedia of psychology & counseling. 2nd ed. Grand Rapids, Mich. : Baker Books, c1999.
*TC BF31 .B25 1999*

**Hill, Sam S.**
Psychologists' desk reference. New York : Oxford University Press, 1998.
*TC RC467.2 .P78 1998*

**Hill, Shirley A. (Shirley Ann), 1947-** African American children : socialization and development in families / Shirley A. Hill. Thousand Oaks, Calif. : Sage Publications, c1999. xxiii, 192 p. ; 24 cm. (Understanding families ; v. 14) Includes bibliographical references (p. 173-184) and index. ISBN 0-7619-0433-6 (cloth : acid-free paper) ISBN 0-7619-0434-4 (pbk. : acid-free paper) DDC 306.85/089/96073
*1. Afro-American children. 2. Socialization - United States. 3. Afro-American families. 4. Parenting - United States. I. Title. II. Series.*
*TC E185.86 .H665 1999*

**Hill, T. L.** Morris and the kingdom of Knoll / story by T.L. Hill ; illustrations by Jeff Colson. Malibu, Calif. : J. Paul Getty Museum and Children's Library Press, c1996. 1 v. (unpaged) : col. ill. ; 27 cm. SUMMARY: When Morris the dragon keeps crashing through the kingdom of Knoll tearing things up, the villagers go to the king for a solution. ISBN 0-89236-341-X DDC [E]
*1. Dragons - Fiction. 2. Work - Fiction. I. Colson, Jeff, ill. II. Title.*
*TC PZ7.H55744 Mo 1996*

**Hillman, Carol.** Before the school bell rings / by Carol B. Hillman. Bloomington, Ind. : Phi Delta Kappa Educational Foundation, c1995. 77 p. : ill. ; 23 cm. Includes bibliographical references (p. 77). ISBN 0-87367-476-6 (pbk.) DDC 372.21
*1. Education, Preschool - United States. 2. Child care - United States. 3. Education, Preschool - Parent participation - United States. 4. Child development - United States. I. Title.*
*TC LB1140.23 .H54 1995*

**Hillman, James.** The force of character : and the lasting life / James Hillman. 1st ed. New York : Random House, c1999. xxx, 236 p. ; 25 cm. Includes bibliographical references (p. 213-221) and index. ISBN 0-375-50120-7 DDC 155.67/1825
*1. Self-actualization (Psychology) in old age. 2. Character. 3. Adulthood - Psychological aspects. 4. Aged - Psychology. I. Title.*
*TC BF724.85.S45 H535 1999b*

**Hillman, Jennifer L.** Clinical perspectives on elderly sexuality / Jennifer L. Hillman. New York : Kluwer Academic/Plenum Publishers, c2000. ix, 206 p. ; 26 cm. (Issues in the practice of psychology) Includes bibliographical references (p. 191-200) and index. ISBN 0-306-46335-0 DDC 306.7/0846
*1. Aged - Sexual behavior. 2. Sexology - Research. I. Title. II. Series.*
*TC HQ30 .H55 2000*

**Hills, Patricia.**
Carbone, Teresa A. Eastman Johnson. New York : Brooklyn Museum of Art in association with Rizzoli International Publications, 1999.
*TC ND237.J7 A4 1999*

**Hilton, Mary, 1946-.**
Practical visionaries. Harlow, England ; New York : Longman, 2000.

*TC LC2042 .P72 2000*

**Hilweg, Werner, 1950-.**
[Kindheit und Trauma. English.] Childhood and trauma. Aldershot, Hants, UK ; Brookfield, Vt., USA : Ashgate, c1999.
*TC RJ506.P66 K613 1999*

**Himley, Margaret.**
From another angle. New York : Teachers College Press, c2000.
*TC LB1117 .F735 2000*

**Hindle, Debbie, 1949-.**
Personality development. London ; New York : Routledge, 1999.
*TC BF175.45 .P47 1999*

**Hinds, Pamela S.**
Quality of life from nursing and patient perspectives. Sudbury, Mass. ; London : Jones and Bartlett, c1998.
*TC RC262 .Q34 1998*

**HINDUISM.** *See* WOMEN IN HINDUISM.

**HINDUISM AND POLITICS - INDIA - HISTORY.**
Robinson, Catherine A. Tradition and liberation. New York : St. Martin's Press, 1999.
*TC HQ1735.3 .R63 1999*

**HINDUISM - POLITICAL ASPECTS.** *See* HINDUISM AND POLITICS.

**HINDUISM - RELATIONS - CHRISTIANITY.**
Eck, Diana L. Encountering God. Boston : Beacon Press, c1993.
*TC BR127 .E25 1993*

**Hine, Lewis Wickes, 1874-1940.** The Empire State Building / Lewis W. Hine ; with an introduction by Freddy Langer. Munich ; New York : Prestel, c1998. 103 p. : ill. ; 31 cm. ISBN 3-7913-1996-5 (alk. paper) DDC 779/.969
*1. Documentary photography - New York (State) - New York. 2. Construction workers - Pictorial works. 3. Hine, Lewis Wickes, - 1874-1940. 4. Empire State Building (New York, N.Y.) - Design and construction - Pictorial works. I. Langer, Freddy, 1957- II. Title.*
*TC TR820.5 .H5634 1998*

Hine, Lewis Wickes, 1874-1940. The Empire State Building. Munich ; New York : Prestel, c1998.
*TC TR820.5 .H5634 1998*

**Hinely, Reg.** Education in Edge City : cases for reflection and action / Reg Hinely, Alexandra G. Leavell, Karen Ford. 2nd ed. Mahwah, N.J. : L. Erlbaum Associates, 2000. xviii, 207 p. ; 28 cm. Includes bibliographical references and index. ISBN 0-8058-2852-4 (pb : alk. paper) DDC 371.39
*1. Case method. 2. Teaching. 3. Teachers - Training of. I. Leavell, Alexandra G. II. Ford, Karen. III. Title.*
*TC LB1029.C37 H45 2000*

**Hingano, Pasimi V.**
Rosen, Sidney M. Toward a gang solution. [Norman, Okla.?] NRC Youth Services, 1996.
*TC HV6439.U7 R67 1996*

**Hinkel, Eli.**
Culture in second language teaching and learning. Cambridge, U.K. ; New York : Cambridge University Press, 1999.
*TC P53 .C77 1999*

**Hinshaw, Ada Sue.**
Handbook of clinical nursing research. Thousand Oaks, Calif. : Sage Publications, c1999.
*TC RT81.5 .H25 1999*

**Hinton, Alexander Laban.**
Biocultural approaches to the emotions. Cambridge, U.K. ; New York : Cambridge University Press, 1999.
*TC GN502 .B53 1999*

**HINTON, KENNETH H.**
Lyman, Linda L. How do they know you care? New York : Teachers College Press, c2000.
*TC LB2831.924.13 L96 2000*

**HIP-HOP.**
Wimsatt, William Upski. No more prisons. [New York] : Soft Skull Press, [2000?]
*TC HV9276.5 .W567x 2000*

**HIPPOLOGY.** *See* HORSES.

**Hirabayashi, James.**
Rabbit in the moon [videorecording]. San Francisco, Calif. : Wabi-Sabi Productions, 1999.
*TC D753.8 .R3 1999*

**Hirabayashi, Moritoku, 1933-.**
Twelve centuries of Japanese art from the Imperial collections. Washington, DC : Freer Gallery of Art

and the Arthur M. Sackler Gallery, Smithsonian Institution Press, c1997.
*TC ND1457.J32 W377 1997*

**Hirsch, E. D. (Eric Donald), 1928-** Books to build on : a grade-by-grade resource guide for parents and teachers / edited by John Holdren and E.D. Hirsch, Jr. New York : Delta, 1996. xvi, 361 p. ; 24 cm. (The core knowledge series) Hirsch's name is prominently displayed on t.p. Includes index. ISBN 0-385-31640-2 DDC 011.62
*1. Children - United States - Books and reading. I. Holdren, John. II. Title. III. Series.*
*TC Z1037 .H646 1996*

**Hirsch, E. D. (Eric Donald) 1928-.**
A First dictionary of cultural literacy. Boston : Houghton Mifflin, 1989.
*TC AG105 .F43 1989*

**Hirsch, E. D. (Eric Donald), 1928-** The schools we need and why we don't have them / E.D. Hirsch, Jr. 1st Anchor Books ed. New York : Anchor Books/Doubleday, 1999. xv111, 317 p. ; 24 cm. Includes bibliographical references and index. ISBN 0-385-49524-2 (alk. paper) DDC 370/.973
*1. Education - Aims and objectives - United States. 2. Education - United States - Philosophy. 3. Educational change - United States. 4. Education - Social aspects - United States. I. Title. II. Title: Schools we need*
*TC LA210 .H57 1999*

What your fifth grader needs to know. New York : Doubleday, c1993.
*TC LB1571 5th .W43 1993*

What your sixth grader needs to know. New York : Doubleday, c1993.
*TC LB1571 6th .W43 1993*

**Hirsch, Pam.**
Practical visionaries. Harlow, England ; New York : Longman, 2000.
*TC LC2042 .P72 2000*

**Hirschfelder, Arlene B.** Encyclopedia of smoking and tobacco / Arlene B. Hirschfelder. Phoenix, AZ : Oryx Press, 1999. xviii, 411 p. : ill. ; 26 cm. Includes bibliographical references (p. 383-388) and index. ISBN 1-57356-202-5 (alk. paper) DDC 362.29/6/097303
*1. Tobacco habit - United States - Encyclopedias. 2. Smoking - United States - Encyclopedias. 3. Tobacco industry - United States - Encyclopedias. I. Title.*
*TC HV5760 .H57 1999*

**Hirshler, Erica E.**
Cassatt, Mary, 1844-1926. Mary Cassatt, modern woman. 1st ed. New York : Art Institute of Chicago in association with H.N. Abrams, c1998.
*TC N6537.C35 A4 1998*

**[His**
(v. 1)] Rummel, R. J. (Rudolph J.), 1932- The dimensions of nations Beverly Hills, Sage Publications [1972]
*TC JX1291 .R84*

**HISPANIC AMERICAN CHILDREN - EDUCATION.**
Manning, M. Lee. Multicultural education of children and adolescents. 3rd ed. Boston : Allyn and Bacon, c2000.
*TC LC1099.3 .M36 2000*

**HISPANIC AMERICAN CHILDREN - EDUCATION (ELEMENTARY) - CASE STUDIES.**
Paratore, Jeanne R. What should we expect of family literacy? Newark, Del. : International Reading Association ; Chicago , Ill. : National Reading Conference, c1999.
*TC LC151 .P37 1999*

**HISPANIC AMERICAN COLLEGE TEACHERS - SELECTION AND APPOINTMENT.**
Turner, Caroline Sotello Viernes. Faculty of color in academe. Boston : Allyn and Bacon, c2000.
*TC LB2332.72 .T87 2000*

**HISPANIC AMERICAN STUDENTS - EDUCATION.**
Educating Latino students. Lancaster, Pa. : Technomic Pub. Co., c1998.
*TC LC2669 .E37 1998*

The teaching of reading in Spanish to the bilingual student = 2nd ed. Mahwah, N.J. : L. Erlbaum Associates, 1998.
*TC LB1573 .T365 1998*

**HISPANIC AMERICAN TEENAGERS - SEXUAL BEHAVIOR.**
Richardson, Bonnie. Factors influencing the sexual and contraceptive behavior of sexually abused adolescents of color. 1999.

*TC 06 no. 11167*

**HISPANIC AMERICAN TEENAGERS - UNITED STATES - PSYCHOLOGY.**
Gallagher, Trish. Arousal patterns, emotion identification, and cognitive style in depressed and nondepressed inner-city adolescent Latinas. 1997.
*TC 085 G136*

**HISPANIC AMERICAN YOUTH - MENTAL HEALTH.**
Koss-Chioino, Joan. Working with Latino youth. 1st ed. San Francisco : Jossey-Bass, c1999.
*TC RC451.5.H57 K67 1999*

**HISPANIC AMERICAN YOUTH - MENTAL HEALTH SERVICES.**
Koss-Chioino, Joan. Working with Latino youth. 1st ed. San Francisco : Jossey-Bass, c1999.
*TC RC451.5.H57 K67 1999*

**HISPANIC AMERICANS.** *See* **PUERTO RICANS - UNITED STATES.**

**HISPANIC AMERICANS - EDUCATION.**
Education of Hispanics in the United States. New York : AMS Press, c1999.
*TC LC4091 .R417 1999*

Education of Hispanics in the United States. New York : AMS Press, c1999.
*TC LC4091 .R417 1999*

**HISPANIC AMERICANS - EDUCATION (HIGHER) - UNITED STATES.**
Capeheart-Meningall, Jennifer. Quality of students of color efort on a predominantly white college and the internal environmental elements that influence involvement. 1998.
*TC 06 no. 10874*

**HISPANIC AMERICANS - EDUCATION - SOCIAL ASPECTS.**
Charting terrains of Chicana(o)/Latina(o) education. Cresskill, N.J. : Hampton Press, c2000.
*TC LC2669 .C42 2000*

**HISPANIC AMERICANS - FICTION.**
Draper, Sharon M. (Sharon Mills) Romiette and Julio. 1st ed. New York : Atheneum Books for Young Readers, 1999.
*TC PZ7.D78325 Ro 1999*

**HISPANIC AMERICANS - HEALTH RISK ASSESSMENT.**
Psychological interventions and research with Latino populations. Boston : Allyn and Bacon, c1997.
*TC RC451.5.H57 P77 1997*

**HISPANIC AMERICANS IN LITERATURE - BIBLIOGRAPHY.**
Peck, David R. American ethnic literatures. Pasadena, Calif. : Salem Press, c1992.
*TC Z1229.E87 P43 1992*

**HISPANIC AMERICANS - MENTAL HEALTH.**
Tiago de Melo, Janine, 1969- Factors relating to Hispanic and non-Hispanic White Americans' willingness to seek psychotherapy. 1998.
*TC 085 T43*

**HISPANIC AMERICANS - MENTAL HEALTH SERVICES.**
Psychological interventions and research with Latino populations. Boston : Allyn and Bacon, c1997.
*TC RC451.5.H57 P77 1997*

**HISPANIC AMERICANS - PSYCHOLOGY.**
Psychological interventions and research with Latino populations. Boston : Allyn and Bacon, c1997.
*TC RC451.5.H57 P77 1997*

Tiago de Melo, Janine, 1969- Factors relating to Hispanic and non-Hispanic White Americans' willingness to seek psychotherapy. 1998.
*TC 085 T43*

**HISPANIC AMERICANS - UNITED STATES.** *See* **HISPANIC AMERICANS.**

**HISPANO-INDIANS (LATIN AMERICA).** *See* **MESTIZOS.**

**HISPANOS.** *See* **MEXICAN AMERICANS.**

**HISTOIRE - MÉTHODOLOGIE.**
LaCapra, Dominick, 1939- History and reading. Toronto : University of Toronto Press, c2000.
*TC DC36.9.L32 1999*

**Histonium.** Buenos Aires : [s.n.], 1939-1972. 398 v. : ill. ; 29 cm. Frequency: Monthly. No. 1 (mayo 1939)-no. 397/398 (jun./jul. 1972). Revista mensual de cultura e información mundial. No. 1 (mayo 1939)-no. 397/398 (jun./jul. 1972) also called = Año 1-año 33. Editor: Carlos della Penna. Continued by: Histonium en su nueva dimensión (OCoLC)1788325. ISSN

0018-2265
*1. Argentina - Periodicals. I. Title: Histonium en su nueva dimensión*

**Histonium en su nueva dimensión.**
Histonium. Buenos Aires : [s.n.], 1939-1972.

**HISTORIANS - UNITED STATES - BIOGRAPHY.**
Buhle, Paul, 1944- William Appleman Williams. New York : Routledge, 1995.
*TC E175.5.W55 B84 1995*

**HISTORIC BUILDINGS.** *See* **HISTORIC SITES.**

**HISTORIC BUILDINGS - FRANCE - PARIS.**
Paris [videorecording]. New York, NY : V.I.E.W. Video, c1996.
*TC DC707 .P3 1996*

**HISTORIC BUILDINGS - MASSACHUSETTS - ANDOVER.**
Montgomery, Susan J., 1947- Phillips Academy. New York : Princeton Architectural Press, 2000.
*TC LD7501.A5 M65 2000*

**HISTORIC HOUSES, ETC.** *See* **HISTORIC BUILDINGS.**

**HISTORIC PRESERVATION.** *See* **CULTURAL PROPERTY - PROTECTION.**

**Historic Scotland.**
Ralston, Nicola L. Parchment/vellum conservation survey and bibliography. Edinburgh : Historic Scotland : Crown Copyright, c2000.
*TC Z701.4.I5 R35 2000*

**Historic Scotland technical advice notes**
Ralston, Nicola L. Parchment/vellum conservation survey and bibliography. Edinburgh : Historic Scotland : Crown Copyright, c2000.
*TC Z701.4.I5 R35 2000*

**HISTORIC SITE INTERPRETATION.** *See* **HISTORIC SITES - INTERPRETIVE PROGRAMS.**

**HISTORIC SITES.** *See* **HISTORIC BUILDINGS; MONUMENTS.**

**HISTORIC SITES - INTERPRETIVE PROGRAMS - UNITED STATES.**
Ideas and images. Walnut Creek, CA : AltaMira Press, 1997.
*TC E172 .I34 1997*

**HISTORIC SITES - UNITED STATES.**
Loewen, James W. Lies across America. New York : New Press : Distributed by W.W. Norton, c1999.
*TC E159 .L64 1999*

**Historical appreciation of the cinema.**
Robson, Emanuel W., 1897- The film answers back. London : John Lane, [1947]
*TC PN1993.5.A1 R6 1947*

**HISTORICAL ARCHAEOLOGY.** *See* **ARCHAEOLOGY AND HISTORY.**

**Historical archaeology in Wachovia.**
South, Stanley A. New York : Kluwer Academic/Plenum Publishers, c1999.
*TC F264.W8 S66 1999*

**Historical Association studies**
Robbins, Keith. Appeasement. Oxford, UK ; New York, NY, USA : B. Blackwell, 1988.
*TC DA47.2 .R62 1988*

**Historical choices of the twenty-first century.**
Wallerstein, Immanuel Maurice, 1930- Utopistics, or, Historical choices of the twenty-first century. New York : New Press, 1998.
*TC D860 .W35 1998*

**HISTORICAL CRITICISM.** *See* **HISTORIOGRAPHY.**

**Historical dictionary of American education** / edited by Richard J. Altenbaugh. Westport, Conn. : Greenwood Press, 1999. xvi, 499 p. ; 25 cm. Includes bibliographical references (p. [393]-444) and index. ISBN 0-313-28590-X (alk. paper) DDC 370/.9
*1. Education - United States - History - Dictionaries. 2. Educators - United States - Biography - Dictionaries. I. Altenbaugh, Richard J.*
*TC LB15 .H57 1999*

**Historical dictionary of quotations in cognitive science :** a treasury of quotations in psychology, philosophy, and artificial intelligence / compiled by Morton Wagman. Westport, Conn. : Greenwood Press, 2000. ix, 271 p. ; 25 cm. Includes bibliographical references (p. [241]-258) and indexes. ISBN 0-313-31284-2 (alk. paper) DDC 153
*1. Cognitive science - Quotations, maxims, etc. 2. Artificial intelligence - Quotations, maxims, etc. 3. Psychology -*

*Quotations, maxims, etc. 4. Philosophy - Quotations, maxims, etc. I. Wagman, Morton.*
*TC PN6084.C545 H57 2000*

**Historical encyclopedia of nursing.**
Snodgrass, Mary Ellen. Santa Barbara, Calif. : ABC-CLIO, 1999.
*TC RT31 .S66 1999*

**HISTORICAL JUDAISM.** *See* **CONSERVATIVE JUDAISM.**

**HISTORICAL LINGUISTICS.** *See also* **LINGUISTIC CHANGE.**
Fischer, Steven R. A history of language. London : Reaktion Books, 1999.
*TC P140 .F57 1999*

Lockwood, David G. Functional approaches to language, culture, and cognition. Amsterdam ; Philadelphia : J. Benjamins, c2000.
*TC P147 .L63 1998*

**HISTORICAL MONUMENTS.** *See* **MONUMENTS.**

**HISTORICAL MUSEUMS - HISTORY.**
Making histories in museums. London ; New York : Leicester University Press, 1996.
*TC AM7 .M35 1996*

**HISTORICAL MUSEUMS - UNITED STATES.**
Ideas and images. Walnut Creek, CA : AltaMira Press, 1997.
*TC E172 .I34 1997*

**HISTORICAL MUSEUMS - UNITED STATES - HISTORY.**
West, Patricia, 1958- Domesticating history. Washington [D.C.] : Smithsonian Institution Press, c1999.
*TC E159 .W445 1999*

**Historical outlook :** a journal for readers, students and teachers of history. Philadelphia, Pa. : McKinley Pub. Co., c1918-c1933. 16 v. : ill. ; 27 cm. Frequency: Monthly (bimonthly June, July, Aug. and Sept.). Vol. 9, no. 7 (Oct. 1918)-v. 24, no. 8 (Dec. 1933). Journal for readers, students and teachers of history. Subtitle varies. Title from cover. Edited under the supervision of the American Historical Association (with the cooperation of the National Board for Historical Service, Jan. 1918-Jan. 1920; the National Council for the Social Studies, June 1923- Continues: History teacher's magazine (DLC) 99100519 (OCoLC)1752167. Continued by: Social studies ISSN: 0037-7996 (DLC) 12025956 (OCoLC)1775420.
*1. Social sciences - Study and teaching - Periodicals. 2. History - Study and teaching - Periodicals. I. American Historical Association. II. National Board for Historical Service. III. National Council for the Social Studies. IV. Title: Journal for readers, students and teachers of history V. Title: History teacher's magazine VI. Title: Social studies*

**HISTORICAL SITES.** *See* **HISTORIC SITES.**

**HISTORICAL SOCIOLOGY.** *See* **CULTURE.**

**HISTORICAL TELEVISION PROGRAMS.**
Africans in America [videorecording]. [Boston, Mass.] : WGBH Educational Foundation : South Burlington, VT : WGBH Boston Video [distributor], c1998.
*TC E441 .A47 1998*

**HISTORIOGRAPHERS.** *See* **HISTORIANS.**

**HISTORIOGRAPHY.** *See also* **MILITARY HISTORY; PSYCHOHISTORY.**
Osokura, Israel O. (Israel Olu). Writing and teaching history. Ibadan : Laurel Educational Publishers, 1996.
*TC D13 .O86 1996*

**HISTORIOGRAPHY - HISTORY.**
Making histories in museums. London ; New York : Leicester University Press, 1996.
*TC AM7 .M35 1996*

**HISTORIOGRAPHY, MILITARY.** *See* **MILITARY HISTORY.**

**HISTORIOMETRY.** *See* **PSYCHOHISTORY.**

**HISTORY.** *See also* **ARCHAEOLOGY; ARCHAEOLOGY AND HISTORY; BIOGRAPHY; CHURCH HISTORY; COUPS D'ÉTAT; GENEALOGY; HISTORIC SITES; MILITARY HISTORY; RIOTS; SOCIAL HISTORY; WORLD HISTORY.**
Haydn, Terry, 1951- Learning to teach history in the secondary school. London ; New York : Routledge, 1997.
*TC D16.25 .H38 1997*

**History and reading.**
LaCapra, Dominick, 1939- Toronto : University of Toronto Press, c2000.

TC DC36.9.L32 1999

**HISTORY - AUTHORSHIP.** *See* HISTORIOGRAPHY.

**HISTORY - BIOGRAPHY.** *See* BIOGRAPHY.

**History Channel (Firm).**
The American Revolution. [videorecording]. New York, N.Y. : A&E Home Video, c1994.
*TC E208 .A447 1994*

**History Channel presents the American Revolution.**
The American Revolution. [videorecording]. New York, N.Y. : A&E Home Video, c1994.
*TC E208 .A447 1994*

**HISTORY, CHURCH.** *See* CHURCH HISTORY.

**History comes home :** family stories across the curriculum / Steven Zemelman ... [et al.]. York, Me. : Stenhouse Publishers, c2000. ix, 164 p. : ill. ; 24 cm. Includes bibliographical references (p. 163-164). ISBN 1-57110-308-2 (acid-free paper) DDC 929/.1/071273
*1. Genealogy - Study and teaching (Elementary) - United States. I. Zemelman, Steven.*
*TC CS49 .H57 2000*

**HISTORY - COMPUTER-ASSISTED INSTRUCTION - UNITED STATES.**
History.edu. Armonk, N.Y. ; London : M.E. Sharpe, c2001.
*TC D16.3 .H53 2001*

**HISTORY - CRITICISM.** *See* HISTORIOGRAPHY.

**HISTORY, ECCLESIASTICAL.** *See* CHURCH HISTORY.

**HISTORY, ECONOMIC.** *See* ECONOMIC HISTORY.

**HISTORY - HISTORIOGRAPHY.** *See* HISTORIOGRAPHY.

**HISTORY IN LITERATURE.**
Singleton, Laurel R., 1950- H is for history. Boulder, Colo. : Social Science Education Consortium, 1995.
*TC LB1582.U6 S56 1995*

**History in the spotlight.**
Fennessey, Sharon M. Portsmouth, NH : Heinemann, c2000.
*TC PN3171 .F46 2000*

**HISTORY, MEDIEVAL.** *See* MIDDLE AGES - HISTORY.

**HISTORY - METHODOLOGY.**
LaCapra, Dominick, 1939- History and reading. Toronto : University of Toronto Press, c2000.
*TC DC36.9.L32 1999*

Making histories in museums. London ; New York : Leicester University Press, 1996.
*TC AM7 .M35 1996*

Memory and methodology. Oxford ; New York : Berg, 2000.
*TC BD181.7 .M46 2000*

Memory and methodology. Oxford ; New York : Berg, 2000.
*TC BD181.7 .M46 2000*

**HISTORY, MILITARY.** *See* MILITARY HISTORY.

**HISTORY, MODERN.**
Riker, Thad Weed, 1880-1952. The story of modern Europe. Boston : Houghton, Mifflin, 1942.
*TC D209 .R48*

**HISTORY, MODERN - 20TH CENTURY.** *See also* WORLD WAR, 1914-1918; WORLD WAR, 1939-1945.
Gilbert, Martin, 1936- A history of the twentieth century. 1st U.S. ed. New York : W. Morrow, c1997-
*TC D421 .G55 1997*

**HISTORY, MODERN - 20TH CENTURY - CHRONOLOGY.**
20th century day by day. New York, NY : DK Pub., c1999.
*TC D422 .C53 1999*

**HISTORY - MUSEUMS.** *See* HISTORICAL MUSEUMS.

**HISTORY, NATURAL.** *See* NATURAL HISTORY.

**A history of American architecture.**
Gelernter, Mark, 1951- Hanover, NH ; London : University Press of New England, c1999.
*TC NA705 .G35 1999*

**History of childhood quarterly.** [Broadway, N.Y., Atcom] 3 v. ill. 23 cm. v. 1-3; summer 1973-spring 1976. "The journal of psychohistory." Indexed selectively by: Social work research & abstracts 0148-0847. Indexed selectively by: Psychological abstracts 0033-2887 1973-1976. Indexed by: Child development abstracts and bibliography. Indexed selectively by: Sociological abstracts 0038-0202. Indexed by: Historical abstracts 0018-2435. Indexed by: America, history and life 0002-7065. Available on microfilm from University Microfilms. Continued by: Journal of psychohistory ISSN: 0145-3378. ISSN 0091-4266 DDC 350.2/3/05
*1. Child rearing - History - Periodicals. 2. Children - History - Periodicals. 3. Psychohistory - Periodicals. I. Title: Journal of psychohistory*

**History of college and university governing boards.**
Duryea, E. D. (Edwin D.) The academic corporation. New York : Falmer Press, 2000.
*TC LB2341 .D79 2000*

**A history of dance in American higher education.**
Hagood, Thomas K. Lewiston, N.Y. : E. Mellen Press, c2000.
*TC GV1589 .H33 2000*

**History of education journal.** [Ann Arbor, Mich., s.n.] 10 v. ill. 23 cm. Frequency: Quarterly. v. 1-10; autumn 1949-1959. Indexed selectively by: America, history and life 0002-7065 1954-1959. Indexed selectively by: Historical abstracts. Part A. Modern history abstracts 0363-2717 1954-1959. Indexed selectively by: Historical abstracts. Part B. Twentieth century abstracts 0363-2725 1954-1959. Superseded by: History of education quarterly ISSN: 0018-2680 (DLC) 6324253 (OCoLC)1752162. ISSN 0162-8607
*1. Education - History - Periodicals. I. Title: History of education quarterly*

**History of education quarterly.**
History of education journal. [Ann Arbor, Mich., s.n.]

**A history of Emmanuel College, Cambridge.**
Bendall, A. Sarah. Woodbridge, Suffolk, UK ; Rochester, NY : Boydell Press, 1999.
*TC LF185 .B46 1999*

**History of fund raising campaigning in U.S higher education.**
Oliver, Frank H. Fellow beggars. 1999.
*TC 06 no.11157*

**A history of geropsychology in autobiography** / edited by James E. Birren and Johannes J.F. Schroots. 1st ed. Washington, DC ; London : American Psychological Association, c2000. vii, 363 p. : ill. ; 26 cm. Includes bibliographical references and index. ISBN 1-55798-631-2 (alk. paper) DDC 155.67
*1. Aging - Psychological aspects - Study and teaching - History. 2. Aged - Psychology - Study and teaching - History. 3. Developmental psychology - History. 4. Psychologists - Biography. 5. Geriatrics - history - Personal Narratives. 6. Aged - psychology. 7. Psychology - history - Personal Narratives. I. Birren. James E. II. Schroots, J. J. F. III. Title: Geropsychology in autobiography*
*TC BF724.8 .H57 2000*

**A history of Irish emigrant and missionary education.**
Murphy, Daniel. Dublin, Ireland ; Portland, Ore. : Four Courts Pres, c2000.
*TC BV2630.M87 2000*

**A history of language.**
Fischer, Steven R. London : Reaktion Books, 1999.
*TC P140 .F57 1999*

**A history of madness in sixteenth-century Germany.**
Midelfort, H. C. Erik Stanford, Calif. : Stanford University Press, c1999.
*TC RC450.G3 M528 1999*

**HISTORY OF MEDICINE, 17TH CENT. - UNITED STATES.**
Reiss, Oscar, 1925- Medicine in colonial America. Lanham : University Press of America, 2000.
*TC RC151 .R44 2000*

**HISTORY OF MEDICINE, 18TH CENT. - UNITED STATES.**
Reiss, Oscar, 1925- Medicine in colonial America. Lanham : University Press of America, 2000.
*TC RC151 .R44 2000*

**HISTORY OF MEDICINE, 20TH CENT. - UNITED STATES.**
Ludmerer, Kenneth M. Time to heal. Oxford ; New York : Oxford University Press, 1999.
*TC R745 .L843 1999*

**HISTORY OF NURSING - UNITED STATES.**
Fairman, Julie. Critical care nursing. Philadelphia : University of Pennsylvania Press, c1998.
*TC RT120.I5 F34 1998*

**A history of psychology.**
Leahey, Thomas Hardy. 5th ed. Upper Saddle River, N.J. : Prentice Hall, c2000.
*TC BF81 .L4 2000*

**History of psychotherapy and psychoanalysis.**
Bromberg, Walter, 1900- The mind of man. Harper colophon ed. New York : Harper & Row, 1963.
*TC RC480 .B7 1963*

**History of schools and schooling**
(v. 3.) McGarrh, Kellie, d. 1995. Kellie McGarrh's hangin' in tough. New York : P. Lang, c2000.
*TC LA2317.D6185 M34 2000*

(v. 5.) Beineke, John A. And there were giants in the land. New York : P. Lang, c1998.
*TC LB875.K54 B44 1998*

(v. 7.) Silences & images. New York : P. Lang, c1999.
*TC LA128 .S55 1999*

(v. 9) Miller-Bernal, Leslie, 1946- Separate by degree. New York : P. Lang, c2000.
*TC LC1601 .M55 2000*

**History of the American people.**
Risjord, Norman K. New York : Holt, Rinehart, and Winston, c1986.
*TC E178.1 .R597 1986*

**History of the book in America**
(v. 1.) The colonial book in the Atlantic world. Cambridge, U.K. ; New York : Cambridge University Press, 2000.
*TC Z473 .C686 1999*

**A history of the education of young children,.**
Raymont, Thomas, 1864- London ; New York : Longmans, Green and co., [1937]
*TC LA21 .R37*

**History of the International Union of Psychological Science (IUPsyS)** / Mark R. Rosenzweig ... [et al.]. Hove, East Sussex : Psychology Press, 2000. xiii, 290 p. : ill. ; 23 cm. Includes bibliographical references and index. ISBN 1-84169-197-6
*1. International Union of Psychological Science - History. I. Rosenzweig, Mark R.*
*TC BF11 .H57 2000*

**History of the Internet :** a chronology, 1843 to the present / Christos J.P. Moschovitis ... [et al.]. Santa Barbara, Calif. : ABC-CLIO, c1999. xviii, 312 p. : ill. ; 27 cm. Includes bibliographical references (p. 282-292) and index. ISBN 1-57607-118-9 (alk. paper) DDC 004.67/8/09
*1. Internet (Computer network) 2. Telecommunication - History. I. Moschovitis, Christos J. P.*
*TC TK5105.875.I57 H58 1999*

**A history of the twentieth century.**
Gilbert, Martin, 1936- 1st U.S. ed. New York : W. Morrow, c1997-
*TC D421 .G55 1997*

**History of the United States.**
Conlin, Joseph Robert. Our land, our time. Annotated teacher's ed. San Diego : Coronado Publishers, c1987.
*TC E178.1 .C762 1987*

**History of the University of Cambridge. Texts and studies**
(3) Weatherall, Mark. Gentlemen, scientists, and doctors. Woodbridge, Suffolk ; Rochester, N.Y. : Boydell Press : Cambridge University Library, 2000.
*TC R487 .W43 2000*

**A history of the U.S. Army Nurse Corps.**
Sarnecky, Mary T. Philadelphia : University of Pennsylvania Press, c1999.
*TC UH493 .S27 1999*

**History of women and business in the United States.**
Kwolek-Folland, Angel. Incorporating women. New York : Twayne Publishers, 1998.
*TC HD6095 .K85 1998*

**History of women at the University of Delaware.**
Hoffecker, Carol E. Beneath thy guiding hand. Newark, Del. : University of Delaware, c1994.
*TC LD1483 .H64 1994*

**History of women in the sciences :** readings from Isis / edited by Sally Gregory Kohlstedt. Chicago, Ill. : University of Chicago Press, c1999. 379 p. : ill. ; 27 cm. Includes bibliographical references and index. ISBN 0-226-45069-4 ISBN 0-226-45070-8 (pbk.) DDC 500/.82
*1. Women in science. I. Kohlstedt, Sally Gregory, 1943- II. Title: Isis.*
*TC Q130 .H58 1999*

*History of women, periodicals.*

**History of women, periodicals.**
Familyculture. Boston, Mass. : [s.n.],

**HISTORY - PERIODICALS.**
Current history and Forum. New York [C-H Publishing Corporation; etc., etc., 1914-41]

**HISTORY - PHILOSOPHY.**
Museums and memory. Stanford, Calif. : Stanford University Press, c2000.
*TC AM7 .M8815 2000*

**HISTORY - PSYCHOLOGICAL ASPECTS.** *See* PSYCHOHISTORY.

**History, reflection, and narrative :** the professionalization of composition, 1963-1983 / edited by Mary Rosner, Beth Boehm, Debra Journet. Stamford, Conn. : Ablex Pub., c1999. xxiii, 352 p. : ill. ; 24 cm. (Perspectives on writing ; v. 3) Includes bibliographical references and indexes. ISBN 1-56750-397-7 (cloth) ISBN 1-56750-398-5 (paper) DDC 808/.042/07/073
*1. English language - Rhetoric - Study and teaching - United States - History - 20th century. 2. English teachers - Training of - United States - History - 20th century. 3. Report writing - Study and teaching - United States - History. 4. English language - Composition and exercises. I. Rosner, Mary. II. Boehm, Beth. III. Journet, Debra. IV. Series.*
*TC PE1405.U6 H56 1999*

**HISTORY - STUDY AND TEACHING**
Osokoya, Israel O. (Israel Olu). Writing and teaching history. Ibadan : Laurel Educational Publishers, 1996.
*TC D13 .O86 1996*

**HISTORY - STUDY AND TEACHING (ELEMENTARY).**
Issues in history teaching. London ; New York : Routledge, 2000.
*TC D16.2 .I88 2000*

**HISTORY - STUDY AND TEACHING (ELEMENTARY) - UNITED STATES.**
Singleton, Laurel R., 1950- H is for history. Boulder, Colo. : Social Science Education Consortium, 1995.
*TC LB1582.U6 S56 1995*

**HISTORY - STUDY AND TEACHING - EUROPE.**
The challenges of the information and communication technologies facing history teaching. Strasbourg : Council of Europe Pub., c1999.
*TC D424 .C425 1999*

Towards a pluralist and tolerant approach to teaching history. Strasbourg : Council of Europe Pub., c1999.
*TC D424 .T665 1999*

**HISTORY - STUDY AND TEACHING - PERIODICALS.**
Historical outlook. Philadelphia, Pa. : McKinley Pub. Co., c1918-c1933.

**HISTORY - STUDY AND TEACHING (SECONDARY).**
Haydn, Terry, 1951- Learning to teach history in the secondary school. London ; New York : Routledge, 1997.
*TC D16.25 .H38 1997*

Issues in history teaching. London ; New York : Routledge, 2000.
*TC D16.2 .I88 2000*

**HISTORY - STUDY AND TEACHING - UNITED STATES.**
History.edu. Armonk, N.Y. ; London : M.E. Sharpe, c2001.
*TC D16.3 .H53 2001*

**History teacher's magazine.**
Historical outlook. Philadelphia, Pa. : McKinley Pub. Co., c1918-c1933.

**HISTORY - YEARBOOKS.** *See* HISTORY - PERIODICALS.

**History.edu :** essays on teaching with technology / Dennis A. Trinkle, Scott A. Merriman, editors. Armonk, N.Y. ; London : M.E. Sharpe, c2001. xviii, 266 p. : ill., maps ; 24 cm. Includes bibliographical references and index. ISBN 0-7656-0549-X (alk. paper) DDC 907.1/073
*1. History - Study and teaching - United States. 2. History - Computer-assisted instruction - United States. I. Trinkle, Dennis A., 1968- II. Merriman, Scott A., 1968-*
*TC D16.3 .H53 2001*

**HISTRIONICS.** *See* ACTING; THEATER.

**Hit enter.**
Saltveit, Elin Kordahl, 1964- Portsmouth, NH : Heinemann, c1999.
*TC LB1028.5 .S233 1999*

**Hitchcock, Susan Tyler.** The University of Virginia : a pictorial history / Susan Tyler Hitchcock. Charlottesville : University Press of Virginia and

University of Virginia Bookstore, 1999. ix, 246 p. : ill., ports (some Color) ; 31 cm. Includes bibliographical references and index. ISBN 0-8139-1902-9 (cl. : alk. paper) DDC 378.755/481
*1. University of Virginia - History. 2. University of Virginia - Pictorial works. I. Title.*
*TC LD5678 .H58 1999*

**The Hite report.**
Hite, Shere. New York : Dell, 1987.
*TC HQ29 .H57 1987*

**The Hite report on male sexuality.**
Hite, Shere. 1st Ballantine Book ed. New York : Ballantine Books, 1982.
*TC HQ28 .H57 1982*

**Hite, Shere.** The Hite report : a nationwide study of female sexuality / Shere Hite. New York : Dell, 1987. 664 p. ; 18 cm. Includes bibliographical references. ISBN 0-440-13690-3
*1. Women - Sexual behavior - United States. 2. Sexual behavior surveys - United States. 3. Orgasm, Female. I. Title.*
*TC HQ29 .H57 1987*

The Hite report on male sexuality / Shere Hite. 1st Ballantine Book ed. New York : Ballantine Books, 1982. xxxiv, 1054 p. : ill. ; 18 cm. Includes index. ISBN 0-345-35248-3
*1. Men - United States - Sexual behavior. 2. Intercourse. 3. Orgasm. 4. Sex (Psychology) I. Title.*
*TC HQ28 .H57 1982*

**HIV and AIDS :** testing, screening, and confidentiality / edited by Rebecca Bennett and Charles A. Erin. Oxford ; New York ; Oxford University Press, 1999. xvi, 285 p. : ill. ; 23 cm. (Issues in biomedical ethics) Includes bibliographical references (p. [271]-279) and index. ISBN 0-19-823801-0 (alk. paper) DDC 362.1/969792075
*1. HIV infections - Diagnosis - Moral and ethical aspects. 2. HIV infections - Law and legislation. 3. HIV infections - Diagnosis - Social aspects. 4. Confidential communications - Physicians. 5. HIV Infections - diagnosis. 6. AIDS Serodiagnosis. 7. Mass Screening. 8. Ethics, Medical. 9. Confidentiality. I. Bennett, Rebecca, 1969- II. Erin, Charles A. III. Series.*
*TC RA644.A25 H57855 1999*

**HIV COGNITIVE-MOTOR COMPLEX.** *See* AIDS DEMENTIA COMPLEX.

**HIV DEMENTIA.** *See* AIDS DEMENTIA COMPLEX.

**HIV INFECTIONS.** *See* AIDS (DISEASE).

**HIV INFECTIONS.**
Schoub, B. D. AIDS & HIV in perspective. 2nd ed. Cambridge ; New York, NY : Cambridge University Press, 1999.
*TC RC607.A26 S3738 1999*

**HIV INFECTIONS - COMPLICATIONS.**
Nutritional aspects of HIV infection. London : New York : Arnold : Co-published in the United States by Oxford University Press, 1999.
*TC RC607.A26 N895 1998*

**HIV INFECTIONS - DIAGNOSIS.**
HIV and AIDS. Oxford ; New York ; Oxford University Press, 1999.
*TC RA644.A25 H57855 1999*

**HIV INFECTIONS - DIAGNOSIS - MORAL AND ETHICAL ASPECTS.**
HIV and AIDS. Oxford ; New York ; Oxford University Press, 1999.
*TC RA644.A25 H57855 1999*

**HIV INFECTIONS - DIAGNOSIS - SOCIAL ASPECTS.**
HIV and AIDS. Oxford ; New York ; Oxford University Press, 1999.
*TC RA644.A25 H57855 1999*

**HIV INFECTIONS - LAW AND LEGISLATION.**
HIV and AIDS. Oxford ; New York ; Oxford University Press, 1999.
*TC RA644.A25 H57855 1999*

**HIV INFECTIONS - PATIENTS - ENGLAND - LONDON.**
Gatter, Philip. Identity and sexuality. New York : Cassell, 1999.
*TC HQ1075.5.G7 G37 1999*

**HIV-POSITIVE PERSONS.** *See* AIDS (DISEASE) - PATIENTS.

**HIV (VIRUSES) INFECTIONS.** *See* HIV INFECTIONS.

**HJELHOLT, GUNNAR.**
Madsen, Benedicte, 1943- Survival in the

organization. Aarhus [Denmark] : Oakville, Conn. : Aarhus University Press, c1996.
*TC D805.G3 M24 1996*

**Hjorth, Linda S.**
Technology and society. Upper Saddle River, NJ : Prentice Hall, 2000.
*TC T14.5 .T44168 2000*

**Hlatshwayo, Simphiwe A. (Simphiwe Abner)**
Education and independence : education in South Africa, 1658-1988 / Simphiwe A. Hlatshwayo. Westport, Conn : Greenwood Press, 2000. x, 132 p. ; 25 cm. (Contributions in Afro-American and African studies, 0069-9624 ; no. 196) Includes bibliographical references (p. [121]-130) and index. ISBN 0-313-30056-9 (alk. paper) DDC 370/.973/0903
*1. Education - South Africa - History. 2. Discrimination in education - South Africa - History. 3. South Africa - Social conditions. I. Title. II. Series.*
*TC LA1536 .H53 2000*

**Hmelo, Cindy E.**
Problem-based learning. Mahwah, N.J. : L. Erlbaum Associates, 2000.
*TC LB1027.42 .P78 2000*

**Hoban, Tana.** Of colors and things / Tana Hoban. 1st Tupelo Board Book ed. New York : Tupelo Books, 1998. 1 v. (unpaged) : all col. ill. ; 13 x 16 cm. SUMMARY: Photographs of toys, food, and other common objects are grouped on each page according to color. ISBN 0-688-16389-0
*1. Color - Pictorial works - Juvenile literature. 2. Color. I. Title.*
*TC QC495.5 .H62 1998*

**Hobbs, Dave (Dave J.).**
International perspectives on tele-education and virtual learning environments. Aldershot : Ashgate, 2000.
*TC LB1044.87 .I55 2000*

**Hobbs, Sandy.** Child labor : a world history companion / Sandy Hobbs, Jim McKechnie, and Michael Lavalette. Santa Barbara, Calif. : ABC-CLIO, 1999. xx, 292 p. : ill. ; 26 cm. Includes bibliographical references (p. 273-284) and index. ISBN 0-87436-956-8 (alk. paper) DDC 331.3/1
*1. Child labor - History. I. McKechnie, Jim. II. Lavalette, Michael. III. Title.*
*TC HD6231 .H63 1999*

**Hobgood, Debby, 1964-.**
Pervola, Cindy, 1956- How to get a job if you're a teenager. Fort Atkinson, Wis. : Alleyside Press, 1998.
*TC HF5383 .P44 1998*

**Hobson, J. Allan, 1933-**
**[Chemistry of conscious states]**
Dreaming as delirium : how the brain goes out of its mind / J. Allan Hobson. 1st MIT Press ed. Cambridge, Mass. : MIT Press, 1999. xvii, 300 p. ; 23 cm. "A Bradford book." Originally published: The chemistry of conscious states. Boston : Little, Brown, c1994. Includes index. ISBN 0-262-58179-5 (pbk. : alk. paper) DDC 612.8/2
*1. Dreams. 2. Consciousness. 3. Neuropsychology. I. Title.*
*TC QP426 .H629 1999*

**Hochschul-Nachrichten** / herausgegeben von Paul von Salvisberg. München : Academische Verlag, v. : ill. ; 29 cm. Frequency: Monthly (Aug.-Sept. issues combined). Began publication with Oct. 1890 issue. Description based on: 13. Jahrg., Nr. 1 (Okt. 1902) = Heft 145; title from caption. Absorbed: Academische Revue (DLC) 26019541 (OCoLC)7564566.
*1. Universities and colleges - Europe - Periodicals. 2. Education, Higher - Europe - Periodicals. I. Salvisberg, Paul von, 1855-1925. II. Title: Academische Revue*

**Hochschule und Ausland.** Berlin : Kulturpolitische Gesellschaft, 1923-1937. 15 v. ; 25 cm. Frequency: Monthly. -15. Jahrg., Heft 3 (März 1937). Began in 1923. Cf. Union list of serials. Description based on: Jahrg. 12, Heft 3 (März 1934) Organ of both: Deutscher Akademischer Austauschdienst, and: Deutsche Kommission für Geistige Zusammenarbeit, 193 -1935; 1936-1937, organ of: Deutscher Akademischer Austauschdienst. Continued by: Geist der Zeit (OCoLC)7700004.
*1. Education - Germany - Periodicals. 2. Educational exchanges - Germany - Periodicals. I. Deutscher Akademischer Austauschdienst. II. Deutsche Kommission für Geistige Zusammenarbeit. III. Title: Geist der Zeit*

**Hock, Randolph, 1944-** The extreme searcher's guide to Web search engines : a handbook for the serious searcher / Randolph Hock ; foreword by Paula Berinstein. Medford, NJ : CyberAge Books, c1999. xxiii, 212 p. : ill. ; 24 cm. Includes index. ISBN 0-910965-26-9 (pbk.) DDC 025.04
*1. Web search engines. I. Title. II. Title: Web search engines*

*TC ZA4226 .H63 1998*

**Hodge, Alison, 1959-.**
Twentieth century actor training. London ; New York : Routledge, 2000.
*TC PN2075 .T94 2000*

**Hodges, Margaret, 1911-** Joan of Arc : the lily maid / by Margaret Hodges ; illustrated by Robert Rayevsky. 1st ed. New York : Holiday House, c1999. [32] p. : col. ill. ; 29 cm. SUMMARY: A biography of the fifteenth-century peasant girl who led a French army to victory against the English, witnessed the crowning of King Charles VII, and was later burned at the stake for witchcraft. ISBN 0-8234-1424-8 DDC 944/.026/092
*1. Joan, - of Arc, Saint, - 1412-1431 - Juvenile literature. 2. Christian saints - France - Biography - Juvenile literature. 3. France - History - Charles VII, 1422-1461 - Juvenile literature. 4. Women soldiers - France - Biography - Juvenile literature. 5. Joan, - of Arc, Saint, - 1412-1431. 6. Saints. 7. Women - Biography. 8. France - History - Charles VII, 1422-1461. I. Rayevsky, Robert, ill. II. Title.*
*TC DC103.5 .H64 1999*

**Hodgson, Ann.**
Gillespie, Sarah (Sarah L.) A pioneer farm girl. Mankato, Minn. : Blue Earth Books, c2000.
*TC F629.M28 G55 2000*

Hester, Sallie. A covered wagon girl. Mankato, Minn. : Blue Earth Books, c2000.
*TC F593 .H47 2000*

**Hoffecker, Carol E.** Beneath thy guiding hand : a history of women at the University of Delaware / Carol E. Hoffecker. Newark, Del. : University of Delaware, c1994. xv, 145 p. : ill. ; 23 cm. Includes bibliographical references (p. 139-145).
*1. University of Delaware - History. 2. Women college students - Delaware - Newark - History. 3. Women graduate students - Delaware - Newark - History. 4. Women in education - Delaware - Newark - History. I. Title. II. Title: History of women at the University of Delaware.*
*TC LD1483 .H64 1994*

**Hoffer, Alan R.** I can! : math activity program . Teacher's guide / Alan R. Hoffer ... [et al.]. New York : Macmillan/McGraw-Hill School Publishing Co., 1996. 3 v. : col. ill. ; 31 cm. (Mathematics in action.) For use with grades K-2. Includes bibliographical references and indexes. ISBN 0-02-109245-1 (Gr. K) ISBN 0-02-109246-x (Gr. 1) ISBN 0-02-109247-8 (Gr. 2)
*1. Mathematics - Study and teaching (Primary). 2. Mathematics - Study and teaching - Activity programs. I. Series.*
*TC QA139 .H63 1996*

I can! : math activity program . Teacher's guide / Alan R. Hoffer ... [et al.]. New York : Macmillan/ McGraw-Hill School Publishing Co., 1996. 3 v. : col. ill. ; 31 cm. (Mathematics in action.) For use with grades K-2. Includes bibliographical references and indexes. ISBN 0-02-109245-1 (Gr. K) ISBN 0-02-109246-x (Gr. 1) ISBN 0-02-109247-8 (Gr. 2)
*1. Mathematics - Study and teaching (Primary). 2. Mathematics - Study and teaching - Activity programs. I. Title: I can : math activity program . Teacher's guide. II. Series.*
*TC QA139 .H63 1996*

**Hoffert, Bernard.**
Art in diversity. 2nd. ed. Melbourne : Longman, c1995.
*TC N5300 .A78 1995*

**Hoffman, Allan M. (Allan Michael).**
Managing colleges and universities. Westport, Conn. : Bergin & Garvey, 2000.
*TC LB2341 .M2779 2000*

**Hoffman, Eric.** An introduction to teaching composition in an electronic environment / Eric Hoffman [and] Carol Scheidenhelm. Needham Heights, Mass. : Allyn & Bacon, c2000. 257 p. : ill. ; 27 cm. Includes bibliographical references (p. 252-256). ISBN 0-205-29715-3
*1. Composition (Language arts). 2. Educational technology. I. Scheidenhelm, Carol. II. Title.*
*TC LB1028.3 .H63 2000*

**Hoffman, Irwin Z.** Ritual and spontaneity in the psychoanalytic process : a dialectical-constructivist view / Irwin Z. Hoffman. Hillsdale, NJ : Analytic Press, c1998. xxxii, 310 p. ; 24 cm. Includes bibliographical references (p. 275-291) and index. ISBN 0-88163-172-8 DDC 616.89/17
*1. Psychoanalytic counseling. 2. Psychoanalysis. I. Title.*
*TC BF175.4.C68 H64 1998*

**Hoffman, James V.** Balancing principles for teaching elementary reading / James V. Hoffman, James F. Baumann, Peter Afflerbach, with Ann M. Duffy-Hester, Sarah J. McCarthey, Jennifer R. Moon. Mahwah, N.J. : L. Erlbaum Associates, c2000. x, 115 p. : ill. ; 24 cm. Includes bibliographical references and indexes. ISBN 0-8058-2912-1 (cloth : alk. paper) ISBN 0-8058-2913-X (pbk. : alk. paper) DDC 372.4
*1. Reading (Elementary) I. Baumann, James F. II. Afflerbach, Peter. III. Title.*
*TC LB1573 . H459 2000*

**Hoffman, Lois Norma Wladis, 1929-** Mothers at work : effects on children's well-being / Lois W. Hoffman, Lise M. Youngblade with Rebekah Levine Coley, Allison Sidle Fuligni, Donna Dumm Kovacs. Cambridge ; New York : Cambridge University Press, 1999. xiii, 338 p. : ill. ; 24 cm. (Cambridge studies in social and emotional development) Includes bibliographical references (p. 313-326) and indexes. ISBN 0-521-57289-4 (hardback) ISBN 0-521-66896-4 (pbk.) DDC 306.87
*1. Working mothers - United States. 2. Children of working mothers - United States. 3. Family - United States. 4. Parenting - United States. I. Youngblade, Lise M. (Lise Marie) II. Title. III. Series.*
*TC HQ759.48 .H63 1999*

**Hoffman, Martin L.** Empathy and moral development : implications for caring and justice / Martin L. Hoffman. Cambridge, U.K. ; New York : Cambridge University Press, 2000. x, 331 p. ; 23 cm. Includes bibliographical references (p. 299-317) and indexes. ISBN 0-521-58034-X DDC 155.2/5
*1. Moral development. 2. Empathy. I. Title.*
*TC BF723.M54 H64 2000*

**Hoffman, Mary, 1945-** Three wise women / Mary Hoffman ; pictures by Lynne Russell. 1st ed. New York : Phyllis Fogelman Books, 1999. 1 v. (unpaged) : col. ill. ; 29 cm. SUMMARY: Three wise women follow a bright star to find a very special newborn baby in a stable, where each of them is able in her own way to give the child a gift. ISBN 0-8037-2466-7 DDC [Fic]
*1. Jesus Christ - Nativity - Juvenile fiction. 2. Jesus Christ - Nativity - Fiction. I. Russell, Lynne, ill. II. Title.*
*TC PZ7.H67562 Th 1999*

**Hofmann, Hans, 1880-1966.** Search for the real, and other essays. edited by Sara T. Weeks and Bartlett H. Hayes. [Rev. ed.]. Cambridge, Mass., M.I.T. Press [c1967] xiii, 72 p.: ill., (part col.); 21 cm. "Based on an exhibition, covering a half century of the art of Hans Hofmann, held at the Addison Gallery of American Art, Phillips Academy, Andover, January 2-February 22, 1948." DDC 700.8
*1. Art. 2. Art - Study and teaching. I. Weeks, Sarah T., 1926- ed. II. Hayes, Bartlett H., 1904- joint ed. III. Phillips Academy, Andover, Mass. Addison Gallery of American Art. IV. Title.*
*TC N7445 .H76 1967*

Search for the real, and other essays. edited by Sara T. Weeks and Bartlett H. Hayes. [Rev. ed.]. Cambridge, Mass., M.I.T. Press [c1967] xiii, 72 p.: ill., (part col.); 21 cm. "Based on an exhibition, covering a half century of the art of Hans Hofmann, held at the Addison Gallery of American Art, Phillips Academy, Andover, January 2-February 22, 1948." DDC 700.8
*1. Art. 2. Art - Study and teaching. I. Weeks, Sarah T., 1926- ed. II. Hayes, Bartlett H., 1904- joint ed. III. Phillips Academy, Andover, Mass. Addison Gallery of American Art. IV. Title.*
*TC N7445 .H76 1967*

**Hogarth, William, 1697-1764.** The analysis of beauty / William Hogarth ; edited with an introduction and notes by Ronald Paulson. New Haven, Conn. : Published for the Paul Mellon Centre for Britsh Art by Yale University Press, c1997. lxii, 162 p., 26 p. of plates (some folded) : ill. ; 23 cm. "The present edition is based on the first (and only) edition published during Hogarth's lifetime, incorporating his errata in the text, and correcting obvious errors."--Pref. Includes bibliographical references (p. [143]-155) and index. ISBN 0-300-07335-6 (cloth : alk. paper) ISBN 0-300-07346-1 (pbk. : alk. paper) DDC 111/.85
*1. Aesthetics - Early works to 1800. I. Paulson, Ronald. II. Title.*
*TC BH181 .H6 1997*

**Hogben, Lancelot Thomas,d1895-** Science for the citizen; a self-educator based on the social background of scientific discovery; illustrated by J. F. Horrabin. [2d ed.]. New York, W. W. Norton & Co. c1938. xiii, 1082, xxvi p. illus., diagrs. 25 cm. "Answers to examples (edited by Mr. Richard Palmer)": p. 1077-1082. "Selected references" at end of each part except part IV.
*1. Science 2. Science - History 3. Civilization I. Horrabin, James Francis, 1884-1962. II. Palmer, Richard. ed. III. Title.*
*TC Q162 .H7 1938*

**Hoge, Robert D.** Assessing adolescents in educational, counseling, and other settings / Robert D. Hoge. Mahwah, N.J. : Lawrence Erlbaum Associates, 1999. viii, 318 p. : ill. ; 24 cm. Includes bibliographical references (p. 266-291) and indexes. ISBN 0-8058-3094-4 (alk. paper) DDC 155.5/028/7
*1. Teenagers - Psychological testing. 2. Youth - Psychological testing. I. Title.*
*TC BF724.25 .H64 1999*

**Hogg, Michael A., 1954-.**
Attitudes, behavior, and social context. Mahwah, N.J. : L. Erlbaum Associates, 2000.
*TC HM132 .B48 1998*

**Den Høgre skolen** Oslo, Steenske forlag. 23-25 cm. 41. arg., nr. 13,-74. arg.; 1 sept. 1939-1975. Cover title. Some issues have subtitle: Tidsskrift for Norsk lektorlag. Continues: Høiere skole. Continued by: Skoleforum 75.- arg.; 1976- ISSN: 0332-7167.
*I. Norsk lektorlag. II. Title: Høiere skole III. Title: Skoleforum 75.- arg.; 1976-*

**Hogue, Carol J. R.**
Minority health in America. Baltimore, Md. : Johns Hopkins University Press, 2000.
*TC RA448.4 .M566 2000*

**Høiere skole.**
Den Høgre skolen Oslo, Steenske forlag.

**Holcombe, Bryce.**
Fagg, William Buller. Yoruba, sculpture of West Africa. 1st ed. New York : Knopf : Distributed by Random House, 1982.
*TC NB1099.N5 F34*

**Holden, Phil, 1950-.**
Field, Kit. Effective subject leadership. London ; New York : Routledge, 2000.
*TC LB2806.15 .F54 2000*

**Holderness, Jackie.**
An Introduction to oracy. London : Cassell, 1998.
*TC P95.4.G7 I58 1998*

**Holdren, John.**
Hirsch, E. D. (Eric Donald), 1928- Books to build on. New York : Delta, 1996.
*TC Z1037 .H646 1996*

**Holdstock, T. Len.** Re-examining psychology : critical perspectives and African insights / T. Len Holdstock. London ; New York : Routledge, 2000. xi, 255 p. ; 24 cm. Includes bibliographical references and indexes. ISBN 0-415-18792-3 DDC 155.8
*1. Psychology - Africa, Sub-Saharan. 2. Racism in psychology. 3. Ethnopsychology - Africa, Southern. I. Title.*
*TC BF108.A3 .H65 2000*

**HOLIDAYS.** *See* **CHRISTMAS; MAY DAY; NEW YEAR; SCHOOLS - EXERCISES AND RECREATIONS; THANKSGIVING DAY; VACATIONS.**

**HOLIDAYS - JUVENILE POETRY.**
Livingston, Myra Cohn. Celebrations. 1st ed. New York : Holiday House, c1985.
*TC PS3562.I945 C4 1985*

**HOLIDAYS - POETRY.**
Livingston, Myra Cohn. Celebrations. 1st ed. New York : Holiday House, c1985.
*TC PS3562.I945 C4 1985*

**HOLIDAYS - UNITED STATES - CHRONOLOGY.**
Special days and weeks for planning the school calendar. Arlington, Va. : Educational Research Service,
*TC LB3525 .S63*

**HOLISTIC MEDICINE.** *See also* **HEALTH; MIND AND BODY.**
Galland, Leo. The four pillars of healing. 1st ed. New York : Random House, c1997.
*TC R733 .G35 1997*

**HOLISTIC NURSING.**
Bishop, Anne H., 1935- Nursing ethics. 2nd ed. Sudbury, Mass. : Jones and Bartlett, c2001.
*TC RT85 .B57 2001*

**Holladay, Sharlene.**
The nutty, nougat-filled world of human nutrition [videorecording]. [Arlington, Va.] : Cerebellum Corp., c1998.
*TC QP141 .N8 1998*

**Holland, Janet.**
Making spaces. New York : St. Martin's Press, 2000.
*TC LC208.4 .M35 2000*

**Holland, John L.** Making vocational choices : a theory of vocational personalities and work environments / John L. Holland. 3rd ed. Odessa, Fla. : Psychological Assessment Resources, c1997. xiv, 303 p. : ill. ; 26 cm. Includes bibliographical references (p. 219-261) and indexes. ISBN 0-911907-27-0 DDC 331.7/02
*1. Vocational guidance. I. Title.*
*TC HF5381 .H5668 1997*

**Hollander, Edwin Paul, 1927-** Leaders, groups, and influence [by] E. P. Hollander. New York, Oxford University Press, 1964. xiv, 256 p. 22 cm. Bibliography: p.

239-248. DDC 301.155
*1. Leadership - Addresses, essays, lectures. 2. Social interaction. 3. Conformity. I. Title.*
**TC HM141 .H58**

**Hollands, William D.** Teaching the Internet to library staff and users : 10 ready-to-go workshops that work / by William D. Hollands. New York : Neal-Schuman, c1999. ix, 208 p. ; 28 cm. (Neal-Schuman netguide series) Includes bibliographical references (p. [202]) and index. ISBN 1-55570-349-6 DDC 025.04/071
*1. Computer network resources - Study and teaching (Continuing education) - United States. I. Title. II. Series: Neal-Schuman net-guide series.*
**TC ZA4201 .H65 1999**

**Holleman, Frank.**
Public charter schools : new choices in public education (May 3, 2000 : Washington, D.C.) Public charter schools [videorecording]. [Washington, D.C.] : U.S. Dept. of Education, [2000].
**TC LB2806.36 .P9 2000**

**Hollenbeck, Kevin.** Classrooms in the workplace : workplace literacy programs in small and medium-sized firms / Kevin Hollenbeck. Kalamazoo, Mich. : W.E. Upjohn Institute for Employment Research, 1993. x, 137 p. : ill. ; 24 cm. Includes bibliographical references (p. 131) and index. ISBN 0-88099-146-1 ISBN 0-88099-145-3 (pbk.) DDC 658.3/1244
*1. Employer-supported education - United States. 2. Workplace literacy - United States. 3. Adult education - United States. 4. Small business - United States. I. Title. II. Title: Classrooms in the work place.*
**TC HF5549.5.T7 H598 1993**

**Hollingsworth, John, 1949-.**
Ardovino, Joan. Multiple measures. Thousand Oaks, Calif. : Corwin Press, c2000.
**TC LB3051 .A745 2000**

**HOLLINS COLLEGE - BIOGRAPHY.**
Smith, Ethel Morgan, 1952- From whence cometh my help. Columbia ; London : University of Missouri Press, c2000.
**TC F234.H65 S55 2000**

**HOLLINS COLLEGE - HISTORY.**
Smith, Ethel Morgan, 1952- From whence cometh my help. Columbia ; London : University of Missouri Press, c2000.
**TC F234.H65 S55 2000**

**HOLLINS (VA.) - HISTORY.**
Smith, Ethel Morgan, 1952- From whence cometh my help. Columbia ; London : University of Missouri Press, c2000.
**TC F234.H65 S55 2000**

**HOLLINS (VA.) - RACE RELATIONS.**
Smith, Ethel Morgan, 1952- From whence cometh my help. Columbia ; London : University of Missouri Press, c2000.
**TC F234.H65 S55 2000**

**Holloway, Sarah, 1970-.**
Children's geographies. London ; New York : Routledge, 2000.
**TC HQ767.9 .C4559 2000**

**Holloway, Susan D.** Contested childhood : diversity and change in Japanese preschools / Susan D. Holloway. New York : Routledge, 2000. xi, 240 p. : ill. ; 24 cm. Includes bibliographical references (p. 225-236) and index. ISBN 0-415-92458-8 (hb) ISBN 0-415-92459-6 (pb) DDC 372.21/0952
*1. Education, Preschool - Japan. 2. Educational change - Japan. I. Title.*
**TC LB1140.25.J3 H69 2000**

**Holm, Jennifer L.** Our only May Amelia / by Jennifer L. Holm. 1st ed. New York : HarperCollinsPublishers, c1999. 253 p. : ill., map ; 22 cm. SUMMARY: As the only girl in a Finnish American family of seven brothers, May Amelia Jackson resents being expected to act like a lady while growing up in Washington state in 1899. ISBN 0-06-027822-6 DDC [Fic]
*1. Frontier and pioneer life - Washington (State) - Fiction. 2. Brothers and sisters - Fiction. 3. Sex role - Fiction. 4. Finnish Americans - Fiction. 5. Washington (State) - Fiction. I. Title.*
**TC PZ7.H732226 Ou 1999**

**Holmes Group (U.S.).**
Lawrence, Alexandria Teresa. Cooperating teachers' perceptions of the nature and quality of professional development in a professional development school collaboration. 1999.
**TC 06 no. 11141**

**HOLMES GROUP (U.S.).**
Lawrence, Alexandria Teresa. Cooperating teachers' perceptions of the nature and quality of professional

development in a professional development school collaboration. 1999.
**TC 06 no. 11141**

Lawrence, Alexandria Teresa. Cooperating teachers' perceptions of the nature and quality of professional development in a professional development school collaboration. 1999.
**TC 06 no. 11141**

**Holmes, Larry E. (Larry Eugene), 1942-** Stalin's school : Moscow's model School No. 25, 1931-1937 / Larry E. Holmes. Pittsburgh, Pa. : University of Pittsburgh Press, c1999. x, 228 p. : ill. ; 24 cm. (Pitt series in Russian and East European studies) Includes bibliographical references (p. 215-222) and index. ISBN 0-8229-4101-5 DDC 372.947
*1. Model School no. 25 (Moscow, Russia) - History. 2. Education, Elementary - Soviet Union - History. 3. Communism and education - Soviet Union - History. 4. Communism and culture - Soviet Union - History. I. Title. II. Series: Series in Russian and East European studies.*
**TC LF4435.M657 H65 1999**

**Holmes, Robert L.**
Nonviolence in theory and practice. Belmont, Calif. : Wadsworth Pub. Co., c1990.
**TC HM278 .N67 1990**

**Holmes, Robina F.**
Niebrand, Chris. The pocket mentor. Boston, Mass. : Allyn and Bacon, 2000.
**TC LB1775.2 .N54 2000**

**Holmqvist, Berit.**
The Computer as medium. Cambridge [England] ; New York : Cambridge University Press, 1993.
**TC QA76.5 .C612554 1993**

**Holocaust children** [picture]. Amawalk, NY : Jackdaw Publications, c1999. 12 posters : b&w ; 43 x 56 cm. + 1 leaflet ([6] p. : ill. ; 28 cm.). (Jackdaw photo collections ; PC 105) Compiled by Bill Eames. SUMMARY: 12 historical photo-posters depicting the tragic children of the Holocaust. CONTENTS: 1. Mother and son wearing the "Jew" label -- 2. Jewish refugee children arrive in England before World War II -- 3. Warsaw ghetto beggars: "They sat everywhere... and begged." -- 4. Jewish children board train to Treblinka Concentration Camp -- 5. After the Warsaw Ghetto uprising, soldiers march captured Jews away -- 6. Women and children march to death camp train -- 7. Gypsy prisoners awaiting fate at concentration camp -- 8. Hungarian Jews walk to gassing -- 9. Buchenwald survivor: "He saw it all" -- 10. At a roll call, a young survivor waits for freedom -- 11. Youthful Jews after liberation from death camp -- 12. Gaunt death camp survivors face liberators' cameras. ISBN 1-56696-162-9
*1. Jewish children in the Holocaust - Posters. 2. Holocaust, Jewish - Posters. 3. Holocaust survivors - Posters. 4. Documentary photography - United States - Posters. I. Eames, Bill. II. Jackdaw Publications. III. Series.*
**TC TR820.5 .H6 1999**

**HOLOCAUST, JEWISH (1939-1945).** See **JEWISH CHILDREN IN THE HOLOCAUST; WORLD WAR, 1939-1945 - JEWS.**

**HOLOCAUST, JEWISH (1939-1945) - STUDY AND TEACHING.**
Teaching the Holocaust :. London : Continuum, 2000.
**TC D804.33 .T43 2000**

**HOLOCAUST, JEWISH - POSTERS.**
Civil war [picture]. Amawalk, NY : Jackdaw Publications, c1999.
**TC TR820.5 .C56 1999**

Holocaust children [picture]. Amawalk, NY : Jackdaw Publications, c1999.
**TC TR820.5 .H6 1999**

**HOLOCAUST SURVIVORS - FICTION.**
Bat-Ami, Miriam. Two suns in the sky. 1st ed. [Chicago, IL] : Front Street/Cricket Books, 1999.
**TC PZ7.B2939 Tw 1999**

**HOLOCAUST SURVIVORS - POSTERS.**
Civil war [picture]. Amawalk, NY : Jackdaw Publications, c1999.
**TC TR820.5 .C56 1999**

Holocaust children [picture]. Amawalk, NY : Jackdaw Publications, c1999.
**TC TR820.5 .H6 1999**

**HOLOCAUST SURVIVORS - UNITED STATES - JUVENILE FICTION.**
Bat-Ami, Miriam. Two suns in the sky. 1st ed. [Chicago, IL] : Front Street/Cricket Books, 1999.
**TC PZ7.B2939 Tw 1999**

**Holstein, James A.** The self we live by : narrative identity in a postmodern world / James A. Holstein, Jaber F. Gubrium. New York : Oxford University Press, 2000. xi, 268 p. ; 24 cm. Includes bibliographical

references (p. 248-262) and indexes. ISBN 0-19-511928-2 (hardcover : alk. paper) ISBN 0-19-511929-0 (pbk. : alk. paper) DDC 155.2
*1. Self. 2. Self - Social aspects. 3. Identity (Psychology) I. Gubrium, Jaber F. II. Title.*
**TC BF697.5.S65 H65 2000**

**Holt, Carleton R.**
Boschee, Floyd. School bond success. 1st ed. Lancaster, Pa. : Technomic Publishing Co., c1999.
**TC LB2825 .B63 1999**

**Holt science** / Abruscato ... [et al.]. New York : Holt, Rinehart and Winston, c1986. vii, 288 p. : ill. ; 25 cm. For grades K-6. Includes bibliographical references and index. ISBN 0-03-003078-1
*1. Science - Study and teaching (Elementary) I. Abruscato, Joseph.*
**TC Q161.2 .A27 1986**

**Holt science** / Abruscato ... [et al.]. New York : Holt, Rinehart and Winston, c1986. vii, 288 p. : ill. ; 25 cm. For grades K-6. Includes bibliographical references and index. ISBN 0-03-003078-1
*1. Science - Study and teaching (Elementary) I. Abruscato, Joseph.*
**TC Q161.2 .A27 1986**

**Holtzman, Linda, 1949-** Media messages : what film, television, and popular music teach us about race, class, gender, and sexual orientation / Linda Holtzman. Armonk, NY : M.E. Sharpe, 2000. xiv, 346 p. : ill. ; 24 cm. Includes bibliographical references and index. ISBN 0-7656-0336-5 (hardcover : alk. paper) DDC 302.23
*1. Mass media and race relations - United States. 2. Mass media and sex - United States. 3. Mass media - Social aspects - United States. 4. Popular culture - United States. 5. Social classes - United States. 6. United States - Social conditions - 1980- I. Title.*
**TC P94.5.M552 U646 2000**

**HOME.** See **FAMILY; HOME ECONOMICS; MARRIAGE.**

**HOME AND SCHOOL.** See also **PARENT-TEACHER RELATIONSHIPS.**
Cullingford, Cedric. The causes of exclusion :. London : Kogan Page ; Sterling, VA : Stylus, 1999.
**TC HV6166 .C85 1999**

Hornby, Garry. Improving parental involvement. London : Cassell, 2000.
**TC LC225 .H67 2000**

McCaslin, Mary M. Listening in classrooms. 1st ed. New York : HarperCollins College Publishers, c1996.
**TC LB1033 .M34 1996**

Revisiting a progressive pedagogy. Albany : State University of New York Press, c2000.
**TC LB1117 .R44 2000**

**Home and school--a working alliance**
Parenting education and support. London : David Fulton, c1999.
**TC HQ755.7 .P374 1999**

**HOME AND SCHOOL - GREAT BRITAIN - CASE STUDIES.**
Woods, Peter, 1934- Multicultural children in the early years. Clevedon ; Philadelphia : Multilingual Matters Ltd, c1999.
**TC LC3736.G6 W66 1999**

**HOME AND SCHOOL - HANDBOOKS, MANUALS, ETC.**
Ramey, Sharon L. Going to school. New York : Goddard Press ; Lanham, MD : Distributed to the trade by National Book Network, c1999.
**TC LB1139.35.P37 R26 1999**

**HOME AND SCHOOL - UNITED STATES.**
Bempechat, Janine, 1956- Getting our kids back on track. 1st ed. San Francisco : Jossey-Bass, c2000.
**TC LC225.3 .B45 2000**

Berger, Eugenia Hepworth. Parents as partners in education. 5th ed. Upper Saddle River, N.J. : Merrill, c2000.
**TC LC225.3 .B47 2000**

Black sons to mothers. New York : Canterbury [England] : P. Lang, c2000.
**TC LC2731 .B53 2000**

The developmental process of positive attitudes and mutual respect. Lewiston, N.Y. : E. Mellen Press, c1999.
**TC LB2822.82 .D49 1999**

Gestwicki, Carol, 1940- Home, school, and community relations. 4th ed. Albany, NY : Delmar Publishers, c2000.

*TC LC225.3 .G47 2000*

Kralovec, Etta. The end of homework. Boston, Mass. : Beacon Press, c2000.
*TC LB1048 .K73 2000*

Lopez, Marianne Exum, 1960- When discourses collide. New York : P. Lang, c1999.
*TC HQ792.U5 L665 1999*

Power, Brenda Miller. Parent power. Portsmouth, NH : Heinemann, c1999.
*TC LC225.3 .P69 1999*

Powerful middle schools : teaching and learning for young adolescents (2000) Powerful middle schools [videorecording]. [Washington, D.C.?] : U.S. Dept. of Education, [2000].
*TC LB1623 .P6 2000*

Preparation, collaboration, and emphasis on the family in school counseling for the new millennium. Lewiston : E. Mellen Press, c2000.
*TC LB1027.5 .P6525 2000*

Ryan, Daniel Prentice. Gay/lesbian parents and school personnel, 1998.
*TC 06 no. 10988*

Snell, Martha E. Collaborative teaming. Baltimore : Paul H. Brookes Pub., c2000.
*TC LC1201 .S64 2000*

Thomas, Adele, 1942- Families at school. Newark, Del. : International Reading Association, c1999.
*TC LC151 .T56 1999*

Thomas, Adele, 1942- Families at school. Newark, Del. : International Reading Association, c1999.
*TC LC151 .T563 1999*

**HOME AND SCHOOL - UNITED STATES - CASE STUDIES.**
Ballenger, Cynthia. Teaching other people's children. New York : Teachers College Press, c1999.
*TC LC3746 .B336 1999*

Glass, Laurie. Read! read! read!. Thousand Oaks, Calif. : Corwin Press, c2000.
*TC LB1050.2 .G54 2000*

**HOME AND SCHOOL - UNITED STATES - HANDBOOKS, MANUALS, ETC.**
Bennett, William J. (William John), 1943- The educated child. New York : Free Press, c1999.
*TC LB1048.5 .B45 1999*

Ottenburg, Susan D. Education today. 2nd. ed. Boston : Educational Publishing Group, Education Today, c1996.
*TC LC225.3 .O88 1996*

**HOME AND SCHOOL - UNITED STATES - HISTORY - 19TH CENTURY.**
Cutler, William W. Parents and schools. Chicago : University of Chicago Press, 2000.
*TC LC225.3 .C86 2000*

**HOME AND SCHOOL - UNITED STATES - HISTORY - 20TH CENTURY.**
Cutler, William W. Parents and schools. Chicago : University of Chicago Press, 2000.
*TC LC225.3 .C86 2000*

**Home at last.**
Sayre, April Pulley. 1st ed. New York : Holt, 1998.
*TC QL754 .S29 1998*

**HOME-BASED EDUCATION.** *See* **HOME SCHOOLING.**

**Home Box Office (Firm).**
Teen killers [videorecording]. Princeton, NJ : Films for the Humanities and Sciences, c1998-1999.
*TC HV9067.H6 T4 1999*

**HOME CARE SERVICES.**
Caregiving systems. Hillsdale, N.J. : L. Erlbaum Associates, 1993.
*TC HV1451 .C329 1993*

**HOME CARE SERVICES - HANDBOOKS, MANUALS, ETC.**
Pierce, Roberta B. Speech-language pathologist's guide to home health care. San Diego : Academic Press, c2000.
*TC RC423 .P54 2000*

**HOME CARE SERVICES - UNITED STATES.**
Brown, Gloria M. Post-hospital care for the elderly. 1997.
*TC 06 no. 10759*

**HOME COMPUTERS.** *See* **MICROCOMPUTERS.**

**HOME DESIGN.** *See* **ARCHITECTURE, DOMESTIC.**

**HOME ECONOMICS.** *See* **CONSUMER EDUCATION; COOKERY; ENTERTAINING; FOOD.**

**Home economics news.** Peoria, Ill. : Published by the Manual Arts Press, [1930-1932]. 3 v. : ill. ; 31 cm. Frequency: Monthly. Vol. 1, no. 1 (Jan. 1930)-v. 3, no. 10 (Oct. 1932). Absorbed by: Practical home economics.
*1. Title: Practical home economics*

**HOME ECONOMICS - PERIODICALS.**
The Boston Cooking School magazine of culinary science and domestic economics. Boston : Boston Cooking-School Magazine, [1896]-1914.

Forecast for home economics. Teacher edition of Co-ed. Dayton, Ohio, Scholastic Magazine.

**HOME ECONOMICS - STUDY AND TEACHING (SECONDARY) - CANADA, WESTERN.**
Peterat, Linda, 1946- Making textile studies matter. Vancouver : Pacific Educational Press, 1999.
*TC TX340 .P47 1999*

**HOME EDUCATION.** *See* **HOME SCHOOLING.**

**HOME - FICTION.**
Blake, Quentin. Clown. 1st American ed. New York : H. Holt, 1996.
*TC PZ7.B56 Cl 1996*

McCarty, Peter. Little bunny on the move. 1st ed. New York : Holt, 1999.
*TC PZ7.M47841327 Li 1999*

**HOME - GREAT BRITAIN - HISTORY - 20TH CENTURY.**
Webster, Wendy. Imagining home. London ; Bristol, Pa. : UCL Press, 1998.
*TC HQ1593 .W43 1998*

**HOME HEALTH AGENCIES.** *See* **HOME CARE SERVICES.**

**HOME HEALTH CARE.** *See* **HOME CARE SERVICES.**

**HOME HEALTH CAREGIVERS.** *See* **CAREGIVERS.**

**HOME INSTRUCTION.** *See* **HOME SCHOOLING.**

**HOME - JUVENILE POETRY.**
Wherever home begins. New York : Orchard Books, c1995.
*TC PS595.H645 W48 1995*

**HOME MOVIES.** *See* **CINEMATOGRAPHY.**

**HOME NURSING.**
Caregiving systems. Hillsdale, N.J. : L. Erlbaum Associates, 1993.
*TC HV1451 .C329 1993*

Mace, Nancy L. The 36-hour day. 3rd ed. Baltimore : Johns Hopkins University Press, c1999.
*TC RC523 .M33 1999*

**HOME - POETRY.**
Wherever home begins. New York : Orchard Books, c1995.
*TC PS595.H645 W48 1995*

**HOME - PSYCHOLOGICAL ASPECTS.**
Fullilove, Mindy Thompson. The house of Joshua. Lincoln, NE : University of Nebraska Press, c1999.
*TC BF353 .F85 1999*

Gunter, Barrie. Psychology of the home. London ; Philadelphia : Whurr, c2000.
*TC GT165.5 .G86 2000*

**Home, school, and community.**
Georgia education journal. Macon, Ga. : Georgia Education Association, 1926-1970.

**Home, school, and community.** Atlanta, Ga. : Georgia Council of Social Agencies, 1923-1926. 4 v. : ill. ; 28 cm. Frequency: Monthly. Vol. 15, no. 12 (Dec. 1923)-v. 18, no. 5 (May 1926). Title from cover. Some issues combined. SUMMARY: "Journal of motives in education and public welfare." Published: Georgia Council of Social Agencies, 1923-June 1924; Georgia Education Association, July 1924-1926; the Georgia Branch of the Congress of Parents and Teachers, July 1924- ; Georgia Congress of Parents and Teachers, <1926> Continues: School and home (Atlanta, Ga.) (DLC)sn 95029882. Continued by: Georgia education journal (DLC) 11024627 (OCoLC)1446537.
*1. Education - Georgia - Periodicals. I. Georgia Council of Social Agencies. II. Georgia Education Association. III. National Congress of Parents and Teachers. Georgia Branch. IV. Georgia Congress of Parents and Teachers. V. Title: School and home (Atlanta, Ga.) VI. Title: Georgia education journal*

**Home, school, and community relations.**
Gestwicki, Carol, 1940- 4th ed. Albany, NY : Delmar Publishers, c2000.
*TC LC225.3 .G47 2000*

**HOME SCHOOLING.** *See* **EDUCATION - PARENT PARTICIPATION.**

**HOME SCHOOLING - UNITED STATES.**
Wimsatt, William Upski. No more prisons. [New York] : Soft Skull Press, [2000?]
*TC HV9276.5 .W567x 2000*

**HOME TEACHING BY PARENTS.** *See* **HOME SCHOOLING.**

**Home Vision ... presents an RM Arts production... [videorecording].**
Marc Chagall [videorecording]. [Chicago, Ill.] : Home Vision [distributor], c1985.
*TC ND699.C5 C5 1985*

**Home Vision a Films Incorporated Company presents .**
Jung on film [videorecording]. [Chicago, Ill.?] : Public Media Video, c1990.
*TC BF109.J8 J4 1990*

**Home Vision (Firm).**
Andy Warhol [videorecording]. [Chicago, IL] : Home Vision [distributor],cc1987.
*TC N6537.W28 A45 1987*

Andy Warhol [videorecording]. [Chicago, IL] : Home Vision [distributor],cc1987.
*TC N6537.W28 A45 1987*

The frescoes of Diego Rivera [videorecording]. [Detroit, Mich.] : Founders Society, Detroit Institute of Arts ; [Chicago, Ill.?] : Home Vision [distributor], c1986.
*TC ND259.R5 F6 1986*

Georgia O'Keeffe [videorecording]. [Boston?] : Home Vision ; c1977.
*TC ND237.O5 G4 1977*

Jackson Pollock [videorecording]. [Chicago, Ill.] : Home Vision ; [S.l.] : Distributed Worldwide by RM Associates, c1987.
*TC ND237.P73 J3 1987*

Jung on film [videorecording]. [Chicago, Ill.?] : Public Media Video, c1990.
*TC BF109.J8 J4 1990*

Jung on film [videorecording]. [Chicago, Ill.?] : Public Media Video, c1990.
*TC BF109.J8 J4 1990*

Marc Chagall [videorecording]. [Chicago, Ill.] : Home Vision [distributor], c1985.
*TC ND699.C5 C5 1985*

Mary Cassatt [videorecording]. [Chicago, Ill.]: Home Vision, c1977.
*TC ND237.C3 M37 1977*

Matisse, voyages [videorecording]. [Chicago, Ill.] : Home Vision ; [S.l.] : Distributed worldwide by RM Associates, c1989.
*TC ND553.M37 M37 1989*

Monsieur René Magritte [videorecording]. [Chicago, Ill.] : Home Vision [distributor], c1978.
*TC ND673.M35 M6 1978*

Nevelson in process [videorecording]. Chicago, IL : Public Media Inc., 1977.
*TC NB237.N43 N43 1977*

Norman Rockwell's world -- an American dream [videorecording]. [Chicago, Ill] : Home Vision, 1987, c1972.
*TC ND237.R68 N6 1987*

Picasso [videorecording]. Chicago, IL : Home Vision, c1986.
*TC N6853.P5 P52 1986*

Roy Lichtenstein [videorecording]. [Chicago, IL] : Home Vision ; [S.l.] : distributed worldwide by RM Asssociates, c1991.
*TC ND237.L627 R6 1991*

**Home Vision... presents an RM Arts production... [videorecording].**
Andy Warhol [videorecording]. [Chicago, IL] : Home Vision [distributor],cc1987.
*TC N6537.W28 A45 1987*

Andy Warhol [videorecording]. [Chicago, IL] : Home Vision [distributor],cc1987.

*TC N6537.W28 A45 1987*

**Home Vision... presents an RM Arts Production... [videorecording].**
Jackson Pollock [videorecording]. [Chicago, Ill.] : Home Vision : [S.l.] : Distributed Worldwide by RM Associates, c1987.
*TC ND237.P73 J3 1987*

**Home Vision... presents an RM ARTS Production... [videorecording].**
Matisse, voyages [videorecording]. [Chicago, Ill.] : Home Vision : [S.l.] : Distributed worldwide by RM Associates, c1989.
*TC ND553.M37 M37 1989*

**Home Vision... presents an RM Arts Production [videorecording].**
Roy Lichtenstein [videorecording]. [Chicago, IL] : Home Vision : [S.l.] : distributed worldwide by RM Asssociates, c1991.
*TC ND237.L627 R6 1991*

**Home Vision... presents, from New York, WNET presents... [videorecording].**
Georgia O'Keeffe [videorecording]. [Boston?] : Home Vision : c1977.
*TC ND237.O5 G4 1977*

**Home Vision... presents... [videorecording].**
The frescoes of Diego Rivera [videorecording]. [Detroit, Mich.] : Founders Society, Detroit Institute of Arts ; [Chicago, Ill.?] : Home Vision [distributor], c1986.
*TC ND259.R5 F6 1986*

Monsieur René Magritte [videorecording]. [Chicago, Ill.] : Home Vision [distributor], c1978.
*TC ND673.M35 M6 1978*

**Home Vision... presents... [videorecording].**
Nevelson in process [videorecording]. Chicago, IL : Public Media Inc., 1977.
*TC NB237.N43 N43 1977*

**HOMELESS ADULTS.** *See* **HOMELESS PERSONS.**

**Homeless and working youth around the world :**
exploring developmental issues / Marcela Raffaelli, Reed W. Larson, editors. San Francisco : Jossey-Bass, 1999. 90 p. : ill. ; 23 cm. (New directions for child and adolescent development, 1520-3247 ; no. 85 (Fall 1999)) (Jossey-Bass education series) Includes bibliographical references and index. CONTENTS: Socializations for survival: developmental issues among working street children in India / Suman Verma -- Daily reality on the streets of Campinas, Brazil / Marcelo Diversi, Ney Moraes filho., Margareth Morelli -- Street children in Nairobi: gender differences in mental health / Lewis Aptekar, Lynda M Ciano-Federpff -- Homeless youth in the United States: description and developmental issues / Jazqueline Smollar -- Methodological and ethical issues in research with street children / Claudio S. Hutz, Silvia H. Koller -- Children at the margins of society: research and practice / Felton CONTENTS: Earls, Nata Carlson. ISBN 0-7879-1252-2
*1. Homeless children. 2. Homeless youth. 3. Social psychology. 4. Street children - Social conditions. 5. Youth - Housing. 6. Homelessness. I. Raffaelli, Marcela, 1960- II. Larson, Reed W. III. Series. IV. Series: New directions for child and adolescent development ; no.85*
*TC HV4493 .H655 1999*

**HOMELESS CHILDREN.** *See also* **ABANDONED CHILDREN.**
Homeless and working youth around the world. San Francisco : Jossey-Bass, 1999.
*TC HV4493 .H655 1999*

**HOMELESS CHILDREN - EDUCATION - CALIFORNIA - CASE STUDIES.**
Newman, Rebecca. Educating homeless children. New York ; London : Garland, 1999.
*TC LC5144.22.C2 N49 1999*

**HOMELESS CHILDREN - EDUCATION - UNITED STATES.**
Educating homeless students. Larchmont, N.Y. : Eye On Education, c2000.
*TC LC5144.2 .E385 2000*

**HOMELESS PEOPLE.** *See* **HOMELESS PERSONS.**

**HOMELESS PERSONS.** *See* **HOMELESS CHILDREN; HOMELESS YOUTH.**

**HOMELESS PERSONS - FICTION.**
Fuchshuber, Annegert. [Karlinchen. English] Carly. 1st ed. New York : The Feminist Press, c1997.
*TC PZ7.F94 Car 1997*

**HOMELESS YOUTH.**
Homeless and working youth around the world. San Francisco : Jossey-Bass, 1999.
*TC HV4493 .H655 1999*

**HOMELESS YOUTH - CALIFORNIA - LOS ANGELES.**
Children of the night [videorecording]. [Charleston, W.V.] : Cambridge Educational, c1994.
*TC HV1435.C3 C45 1994*

Children of the night [videorecording]. [Charleston, W.V.] : Cambridge Educational, c1994.
*TC HV1435.C3 C45 1994*

Children of the night [videorecording]. [Charleston, W.V.] : Cambridge Educational, c1994.
*TC HV1435.C3 C45 1994*

Starting over [videorecording]. [Charleston, W.V.] : Cambridge Educational, c1994.
*TC HV1435.C3 S7 1994*

**HOMELESS YOUTH - DRUG USE - UNITED STATES.**
Children of the night [videorecording]. [Charleston, W.V.] : Cambridge Educational, c1994.
*TC HV1435.C3 C45 1994*

Starting over [videorecording]. [Charleston, W.V.] : Cambridge Educational, c1994.
*TC HV1435.C3 S7 1994*

**HOMELESS YOUTH - EDUCATION - UNITED STATES.**
Educating homeless students. Larchmont, N.Y. : Eye On Education, c2000.
*TC LC5144.2 .E385 2000*

**HOMELESS YOUTH - EMPLOYMENT - UNITED STATES.**
Starting over [videorecording]. [Charleston, W.V.] : Cambridge Educational, c1994.
*TC HV1435.C3 S7 1994*

**HOMELESS YOUTH - FLORIDA - FORT LAUDERDALE.**
Starting over [videorecording]. [Charleston, W.V.] : Cambridge Educational, c1994.
*TC HV1435.C3 S7 1994*

**HOMELESS YOUTH - NEW YORK (STATE) - NEW YORK.**
Children of the night [videorecording]. [Charleston, W.V.] : Cambridge Educational, c1994.
*TC HV1435.C3 C45 1994*

Children of the night [videorecording]. [Charleston, W.V.] : Cambridge Educational, c1994.
*TC HV1435.C3 C45 1994*

Children of the night [videorecording]. [Charleston, W.V.] : Cambridge Educational, c1994.
*TC HV1435.C3 C45 1994*

Starting over [videorecording]. [Charleston, W.V.] : Cambridge Educational, c1994.
*TC HV1435.C3 S7 1994*

**HOMELESS YOUTH - UNITED STATES.**
Whitbeck, Les B. Nowhere to grow. New York : Aldine de Gruyer, 1999.
*TC HV4505 .W43 1999*

**HOMELESSNESS.** *See also* **HOMELESS PERSONS.**
Homeless and working youth around the world. San Francisco : Jossey-Bass, 1999.
*TC HV4493 .H655 1999*

**HOMEMAKERS.** *See* **HOUSEWIVES.**

**Homer, Winslow, 1836-1910.**
Cikovsky, Nicolai. Winslow Homer. Washington, D.C. : National Gallery of Art, 1995.
*TC N6537.H58 A4 1995*

**HOMER, WINSLOW, 1836-1910 - EXHIBITIONS.**
Cikovsky, Nicolai. Winslow Homer. Washington, D.C. : National Gallery of Art, 1995.
*TC N6537.H58 A4 1995*

Ferber, Linda S. Masters of color and light. Washington : Brooklyn Museum of Art in Association with Smithsonian Institution Press, c1998.
*TC ND1807 .F47 1998*

**HOMES.** *See* **DWELLINGS; HOUSING.**

**HOMES (INSTITUTIONS).** *See* **INSTITUTIONAL CARE.**

**HOMESCHOOLING.** *See* **HOME SCHOOLING.**

**HOMESTEADING.** *See* **FRONTIER AND PIONEER LIFE.**

**Homework.**
Hong, Eunsook. Westport, Conn. : Bergin & Garvey, 2000.
*TC LB1048 .H69 2000*

**HOMEWORK - PSYCHOLOGICAL ASPECTS.**
Hong, Eunsook. Homework. Westport, Conn. : Bergin & Garvey, 2000.
*TC LB1048 .H69 2000*

**HOMEWORK - SOCIAL ASPECTS - UNITED STATES.**
Kralovec, Etta. The end of homework. Boston, Mass. : Beacon Press, c2000.
*TC LB1048 .K73 2000*

**HOMICIDE.** *See* **EUTHANASIA; JUVENILE HOMICIDE; MURDER; SUICIDE.**

**HOMICIDE OFFENDERS.** *See* **MURDERERS.**

**HOMICIDE - PSYCHOLOGICAL ASPECTS.**
Bourke, Joanna. An intimate history of killing. [New York, NY] : Basic Books, c1999.
*TC U22.3 .B68 1999*

**HOMICIDE - STATISTICS.**
Richardson, Lewis Fry, 1881-1953. Statistics of deadly quarrels. Pacific Grove, Ca. Boxwood Press [1960]
*TC U21.7 .R5 1960*

**HOMICIDE - UNITED STATES.**
Teen killers [videorecording]. Princeton, NJ : Films for the Humanities and Sciences, c1998-1999.
*TC HV9067.H6 T4 1999*

**HOMICULTURE.** *See* **EUGENICS.**

**HOMILETICAL ILLUSTRATIONS.** *See* **LEGENDS.**

**HOMINIDS.** *See* **HUMAN BEINGS.**

**Hommes, Jeannette.**
Educational innovation in economics and business. IV, Learning in a changing environment. Boston, MA : Kluwer Academic Publishers, c1999.
*TC HB74.5 .E3333 1999*

**HOMO SAPIENS.** *See* **HUMAN BEINGS.**

**HOMOLOGY THEORY.** *See* **K-THEORY.**

**HOMONYMS.**
Dictionary of confusable words. Chicago, IL : Fitzroy Dearborn Publ., 2000.
*TC PE1591 .D53 2000*

**HOMOPHILE MOVEMENT.** *See* **GAY LIBERATION MOVEMENT.**

**HOMOPHILE STUDIES.** *See* **GAY AND LESBIAN STUDIES.**

**HOMOPHOBIA IN HIGHER EDUCATION - UNITED STATES.**
Toward acceptance. Lanham, Md. : University Press of America, 1999.
*TC LC192.6 .T69 1999*

**HOMOPHOBIA - UNITED STATES.**
School experiences of gay and lesbian youth. New York : Harrington Park Press, c1997.
*TC LC2575 .S36 1997*

**HOMOPLASY.** *See* **EVOLUTION (BIOLOGY).**

**HOMOSEXUAL LIBERATION MOVEMENT.** *See* **GAY LIBERATION MOVEMENT.**

**HOMOSEXUAL PARENTS.** *See* **GAY PARENTS.**

**HOMOSEXUALITY.** *See* **PSYCHOANALYSIS AND HOMOSEXUALITY.**

**HOMOSEXUALITY AND EDUCATION.**
Thinking queer. New York : Peter Lang, c2000.
*TC LC192.6 .T55 2000*

**HOMOSEXUALITY AND EDUCATION - UNITED STATES.**
Queering elementary education. Lanham, Md. ; Oxford : Rowman & Littlefield, c1999.
*TC LC192.6 .Q85 1999*

Toward acceptance. Lanham, Md. : University Press of America, 1999.
*TC LC192.6 .T69 1999*

**HOMOSEXUALITY AND EDUCATION - UNITED STATES - CASE STUDIES.**
Out & about campus. 1st ed. Los Angeles : Alyson Books, 2000.
*TC LC2574.6 .O87 2000*

**HOMOSEXUALITY AND LITERATURE - STUDY AND TEACHING.**
Lesbian and gay studies and the teaching of English.

Urbana, Ill. : National Council of Teachers of English, 2000.
*TC PE66 .L45 2000*

**HOMOSEXUALITY AND PSYCHOANALYSIS. See PSYCHOANALYSIS AND HOMOSEXUALITY.**

**HOMOSEXUALITY IN THE WORKPLACE - UNITED STATES.**
Rogers, Richard Randall. The impact of gay identity and perceived milieu toward gay employees on job involvement and organizational commitment of gay men. 1998.
*TC 085 R635*

**HOMOSEXUALITY, MALE - STUDY AND TEACHING. See GAY AND LESBIAN STUDIES.**

**HOMOSEXUALITY - MORAL AND ETHICAL ASPECTS.**
Stein, Edward, 1965- The mismeasure of desire. Oxford ; New York : Oxford University Press, 1999.
*TC HQ76.25 .S69 1999*

**HOMOSEXUALITY - PHILOSOPHY.**
Stein, Edward, 1965- The mismeasure of desire. Oxford ; New York : Oxford University Press, 1999.
*TC HQ76.25 .S69 1999*

**HOMOSEXUALITY - RESEARCH.**
Stein, Edward, 1965- The mismeasure of desire. Oxford ; New York : Oxford University Press, 1999.
*TC HQ76.25 .S69 1999*

**HOMOSEXUALITY - STUDY AND TEACHING. See also GAY AND LESBIAN STUDIES.**
Lesbian and gay studies and the teaching of English. Urbana, Ill. : National Council of Teachers of English, 2000.
*TC PE66 .L45 2000*

**HOMOSEXUALS. See GAYS.**

**HOMOSEXUALS, FEMALE. See LESBIANS.**

**HOMOSEXUALS, MALE. See GAY MEN.**

**HOMOSEXUALS' WRITINGS. See GAYS' WRITINGS.**

Honan, Linda. Picture the Middle Ages : the Middle Ages resource book / [written by Linda Honan ; illustrated by Ellen Kosmer ; music and dance by Karen Hastie-Wilson]. Amawalk, N.Y. : Golden Owl Pub. Co. : Higgins Armory Museum, c1994. 106 p. : ill., maps, music ; 29 cm. Includes bibliographical references (p. 102-103). SUMMARY: Presents an overview of medieval history and daily life as depicted in the imaginary town of Higginswold. ISBN 1-56696-025-8 DDC 940.1
*1. Civilization, Medieval - Juvenile literature. 2. Middle Ages - History - Juvenile literature. 3. Middle Ages - Study and teaching (Elementary). 4. Civilization, Medieval - Study and teaching (Elementary) I. Kosmer, Ellen Virginia, ill. II. Title.*
*TC CB351 .H58 1994*

**HONESTY. See CHEATING (EDUCATION).**

**HONESTY - FICTION.**
Cadnum, Michael. Rundown. New York : Viking, c1999.
*TC PZ7.C11724 Ru 1999*

**HONESTY - STUDY AND TEACHING - UNITED STATES.**
Annual State of American Education Address (7th : February 22, 2000 : Durham, N.C.) The seventh annual state of American education address [videorecording. [Washington, D.C. : U.S. Dept. of Education], 2000.

**Honey for a child's heart.**
Hunt, Gladys M. 3rd ed. Grand Rapids, Mich. : Zondervan Books, c1989.
*TC Z1037 .H945 1989*

**Honeycutt, James M.** Cognition, communication, and romantic relationships / James M. Honeycutt, James G. Cantrill. Mahwah, N.J. ; London : L. Erlbaum Associates, 2001. xxiii, 198 p. : ill. ; 23 cm. (LEA's series in personal relationships) Includes bibliographical references (p. 179-192) and indexes. ISBN 0-8058-3577-6 (pbk. : alk. paper) DDC 158.2
*1. Intimacy (Psychology) 2. Interpersonal relations. 3. Love. 4. Interpersonal communication. 5. Cognition. I. Cantrill, James G. (James Gerard), 1955- II. Title. III. Series: LEA's series on personal relationships.*
*TC BF575.I5 H66 2001*

**Honeyman, David Smith.**
A struggle to survive. Thousand Oaks, Calif. : Corwin Press, c1996.
*TC LB2342 .S856 1996*

**HONEYMOONS. See MARRIAGE.**

**Hong, Eunsook.** Homework : motivation and learning preference / Eunsook Hong and Roberta M. Milgram. Westport, Conn. : Bergin & Garvey, 2000. xv, 191 p. ; 25 cm. Includes bibliographical references (p. [171]-186) and index. ISBN 0-89789-585-1 (alk. paper) DDC 370.15/4
*1. Homework - Psychological aspects. 2. Motivation in education. I. Milgram, Roberta M. II. Title.*
*TC LB1048 .H69 2000*

**HONG KONG (CHINA) - SOCIAL CONDITIONS.**
Lam-Chan, Gladys Lan Tak. Parenting in stepfamilies. Aldershot ; Brookfield USA : Ashgate, c1999.
*TC HQ759.92 .L34 1999*

**HONORARY DEGREES. See DEGREES, ACADEMIC.**

**Honour, Hugh.** The visual arts : a history / Hugh Honour, John Fleming. 5th ed. New York : Henry N. Abrams, 1999. 928 p. : ill. (some col.) ; 29 cm. Includes bibliographical references (p. [900]-909) and index. ISBN 0-8109-3935-5 DDC 709
*1. Art - History. I. Fleming, John. II. Title.*
*TC N5300 .H68 1999*

**HOOD, ROBIN (LEGENDARY CHARACTER). See ROBIN HOOD (LEGENDARY CHARACTER).**

**Hoodbhoy, Pervez.**
Education and the state. Karachi : Oxford University Press, 1998.
*TC LA1156 .E36 1998*

**HOODLUMS. See GANGS.**

**Hoog, Walter de.**
Headline stories of the century [videorecording]. Chicago, IL. : Distributed by Questar Video, Inc., c1992.
*TC D743 .H42 1992*

**Hooks, Bell.** Art on my mind : visual politics / Bell Hooks. New York : New Press : Distributed by W.W. Norton, c1995. xvi, 224 p. : ill. (some col.) ; 21 cm. Includes bibliographical references and index. ISBN 1-56584-263-4 DDC 704/.0396073
*1. Hooks, Bell - Philosophy. 2. Afro-American art - Political aspects. I. Title.*
*TC N6537.H585 A2 1995*

Happy to be nappy / bell hooks ;[illustrated by] Chris Raschka. 1st ed. New York : Hyperion Books for Children, 1999. 1 v. : col. ill. ; 27 cm. SUMMARY: Celebrates the joy and beauty of nappy hair. ISBN 0-7868-0427-0 (trade) ISBN 0-7868-2377-1 (lb) DDC [E]
*1. Hair - Fiction. 2. Afro-Americans - Fiction. I. Raschka, Christopher, ill. II. Title.*
*TC PZ7.H7663 Hap 1999*

Yearning : race, gender, and cultural politics / Bell Hooks. Boston, MA : South End Press, c1990. 236 p. ; 23 cm. Includes bibliographical references (p. 231-236). ISBN 0-89608-386-1 ISBN 0-89608-385-3 (pbk.) DDC 305.896/073
*1. Afro-Americans - Intellectual life. 2. Afro-Americans - Race identity. I. Title.*
*TC E185.86 .H742 1990*

**HOOKS, BELL - PHILOSOPHY.**
Hooks, Bell. Art on my mind. New York : New Press : Distributed by W.W. Norton, c1995.
*TC N6537.H585 A2 1995*

**HOOP DANCE.**
Left Hand Bull, Jacqueline. Lakota hoop dancer. 1st ed. New York : Dutton Children's Books, c1999.
*TC E99.T34 L43 1999*

**HOOP DANCE - SOUTH DAKOTA - JUVENILE LITERATURE.**
Left Hand Bull, Jacqueline. Lakota hoop dancer. 1st ed. New York : Dutton Children's Books, c1999.
*TC E99.T34 L43 1999*

**HOOP OF PEACE DANCE. See HOOP DANCE.**

**Hooper, Don W.**
Hughes, Larry W., 1931- Public relations for school leaders. Boston ; London : Allyn and Bacon, c2000.
*TC LB2847 .H84 2000*

**Hooper, Stephen R.**
Umansky, Warren. Young children with special needs. 3rd ed. Upper Saddle River, N.J. : Merrill, c1998.
*TC LC4031 .U425 1998*

**Hooper, Virginia.**
European modernism. New York, N.Y. : OpticalTouch Systems ; Louisville, Ky. : American Printing House for the Blind, c1998-1999.

*TC N6758 .A7 1999*

**Hoover, Heidi.**
Grounded for life [videorecording]. Charleston, WV : Cambridge Research Group, Ltd., 1988.
*TC HQ759.4 .G7 1988*

**HOPE.**
Handbook of hope. San Diego, Calif. : Academic, 2000.
*TC BF575.H56 H36 2000*

**Hope fulfilled for at-risk and violent youth.**
Barr, Robert D. 2nd ed. Boston ; London : Allyn and Bacon, c2001.
*TC LC4802 .B37 2001*

**A hope in the unseen.**
Suskind, Ron. 1st ed. New York : Broadway Books, c1998.
*TC LC2803.W3 S87 1998*

**Hopkins, Charles D.** Classroom testing : construction / Charles D. Hopkins, Richard L. Antes. 2nd ed. Itasca, Ill. : F. E. Peacock Publishers, c1989. x, 193 p. : ill. ; 23 cm. Includes index. Bibliography: p. 183-184. ISBN 0-87581-334-8
*1. Examinations - Design and construction. 2. Educational tests and measurements. I. Antes, Richard L. II. Title.*
*TC LB3060.65 .H661 1989*

**Hopkins, Christine.**
Mathematics in the primary school. 2nd ed. London : D. Fulton, 1999.
*TC QA135.5 .M36934 1999*

**Hopkins, David, 1949-.**
Joyce, Bruce R. The new structure of school improvement. Buckingham [England] ; Philadelphia : Open University Press, 1999.
*TC LB2822.84.G7 J69 1999*

**Hopkins, Dianne McAfee.**
Zweizig, Douglas. Lessons from library power. Englewood, Colo. : Libraries Unlimited, 1999.
*TC Z675.S3 Z94 1999*

**Hopkins, J. B.**
Current issues in developmental psychology. Dordrecht ; Boston ; London : Kluwer Academic Publishers, c1999.
*TC RJ134 .C868 1999*

**Hopkins, Lee Bennett.**
My mane catches the wind. 1st ed. New York : Harcourt Brace Jovanovich, c1979.
*TC PN6110.H7 M9*

The sky is full of song. 1st ed. New York : Harper & Row, c1983.
*TC PS595.S42 S5 1983*

To the zoo. 1st ed. Boston : Little, Brown, c1992.
*TC PS595.Z66 T6 1992*

**Hopps, Walter.** Robert Rauschenberg : a retrospective / Walter Hopps and Susan Davidson ; with essays by Trisha Brown ... [et al.]. New York : Guggenheim Museum, c1997. 629 p. : ill. (some col.) ; 31 cm. Catalog of an exhibition held at the Solomon R. Guggenheim Museum, Guggenheim Museum SoHo, and Guggenheim Museum at Ace Gallery, New York, September 19, 1997-January 7, 1998, and at three other museums through March 7, 1999. Includes chronology (p. 550-587). Includes bibliographical references (p. 619-626) and index. ISBN 0-8109-6903-3 (cloth)
*1. Rauschenberg, Robert, - 1925- - Exhibitions. I. Rauschenberg, Robert, 1925- II. Davidson, Susan, 1958- III. Brown, Trisha. IV. Solomon R. Guggenheim Museum. V. Title.*
*TC N6537.R27 H66 1997*

**Hopson, Rodney K.**
How and why language matters in evaluation. San Francisco, CA : Jossey-Bass, c2000.
*TC H62 .H67 2000*

**Horenczyk, Gabriel, 1954-.**
National variations in Jewish identity. Albany, N.Y. : State University of New York Press, 1999.
*TC DS143 .N27 1999*

**Horgan, John, 1953-** The undiscovered mind : how the human brain defies replication, medication, and explanation / John Horgan. New York : Free Press, c1999. 325 p. ; 25 cm. Includes bibliographical references (p. [269]-312) and index. ISBN 0-684-85075-3 DDC 612.8/2
*1. Neurosciences - Popular works. I. Title.*
*TC RC343 .H636 1999*

**HORIZON CHARTER SCHOOL (PHOENIX, ARIZ.).**
Education's big gamble [videorecording]. New York, NY : Merrow Report, c1997.
*TC LB2806.36 .E3 1997*

**Horizon Film and Video (Firm).**
Teen violence [videorecording]. Princeton, NJ : Films for the Humanities & Sciences, c1998.
*TC RJ506.V56 T44 1998*

**The Horizons of health** / edited by Henry Wechsler, Joel Gurin, George F. Cahill, Jr. Cambridge, Mass. : Harvard University Press, 1977. xvi, 412 p. : ill. ; 24 cm. Includes bibliographical references (p.393-398) and index. ISBN 0-674-40630-3 DDC 610/.7/2
*1. Medicine - Research. 2. Medicine - Research - United States. 3. Research - Popular works. I. Wechsler, Henry, 1932- II. Gurin, Joel, 1953- III. Cahill, George F., 1927-*
*TC R850 .H67*

**The horizontal organization.**
Ostroff, Frank. New York : Oxford University Press, 1999.
*TC HD66 .O68 1999*

**Hormones, health, and behavior :** a socio-ecological and lifespan perspective / edited by C. Panter-Brick and C.M. Worthman. Cambridge ; New York : Cambridge University Press, 1999. ix, 290 p. : ill. ; 24 cm. Includes bibliographical references and index. ISBN 0-521-57332-7 DDC 306.4/61
*1. Psychoneuroendocrinology. 2. Physical anthropology. 3. Clinical health psychology. 4. Human ecology. I. Panter-Brick, Catherine, 1959- II. Worthman, C. M. (Carol M.), 1948-*
*TC QP356.45 .H67 1999*

**Horn, Elizabeth.**
Niebrand, Chris. The pocket mentor. Boston, Mass. : Allyn and Bacon, 2000.
*TC LB1775.2 .N54 2000*

**Horn, Rebecca, 1944-** Rebecca Horn : la lune rebelle. [Stuttgart] : Edition Cantz, 1993. 84 p. : ill. (some col.) ; 26 cm. ISBN 3-89322-548-X (English ed.) ISBN 3-89322-547-1 (German ed.)
*1. Horn, Rebecca. - 1944- I. Title. II. Title: Lune rebelle.*
*TC NB573.H78 H785 1993*

**HORN, REBECCA, 1944-.**
Horn, Rebecca, 1944- Rebecca Horn. [Stuttgart] : Edition Cantz, 1993.
*TC NB573.H78 H785 1993*

**Hornby, Garry.** Improving parental involvement / Gary Hornby. London : Cassell, 2000. ix, 166 p. ; 24 cm. Includes bibliographical references (p. [156]-162) and indexes. ISBN 0-304-70551-9 ISBN 0-304-70552-7 (pbk.)
*1. Home and school. 2. Parent-teacher relationships. 3. Education - Parent participation. I. Title.*
*TC LC225 .H67 2000*

**Horner, Abigail.**
Brooks, Nigel. Town mouse house. New York : Walker & Co., 2000.
*TC PZ7.B7977 To 2000*

**Horner, Robert H.**
Functional analysis of problem behavior. Belmont, CA : Wadsworth Pub. Co., c1999.
*TC RC473.B43 F85 1999*

**Horney, Karen, 1885-1952.** The therapeutic process : essays and lectures / Karen Horney ; edited with an introduction by Bernard J. Paris. New Haven : Yale University Press, c1999. xviii, 272 p. ; 24 cm. "Writings of Karen Horney": p. 259-266. Includes bibliographical references (p. 257-258) and index. ISBN 0-300-07527-8 (c : alk. paper) DDC 616.89/17
*1. Psychoanalysis. I. Paris, Bernard J. II. Title.*
*TC RC509 .H674 1999*

**HORNEY, KAREN, 1885-1952.**
The unknown Karen Horney. New Haven : Yale University Press, c2000.
*TC BF173 .U55 2000*

**Horning, Alice S.**
The literacy connection. Cresskill, N.J. : Hampton Press, c1999.
*TC LC151 .L482 1999*

**Hornyak, Lynne M.**
Healing from within. 1st ed. Washington, DC ; London : American Psychological Association, c2000.
*TC RC497 .H42 2000*

**HOROLOGY.** *See* **CLOCKS AND WATCHES; TIME.**

**Horowitz, Mardi Jon, 1934-** Stress response syndromes : PTSD, grief, and adjustment disorders / Mardi Jon Horowitz. 3rd ed. Northvale, N.J. : J. Aronson, c1997. xx, 358 p. : ill. ; 24 cm. Includes bibliographical references (p. 327-347) and index. ISBN 0-7657-0025-5 DDC 616.85/21
*1. Post-traumatic stress disorder. 2. Post-traumatic stress disorder - Case studies. I. Title.*
*TC RC552.P67 H67 1997*

**Horrabin, James Francis, 1884-1962.**
Hogben, Lancelot Thomas, d1895- Science for the citizen: [2d ed.]. New York, W. W. Norton & Co. c1938.
*TC Q162 .H7 1938*

**HORROR.** *See* **FEAR.**

**HORSE.** *See* **HORSES.**

**Horse & pony breeds.**
Henderson, Carolyn. 1st American ed. New York, N.Y. : DK Pub., 1999.
*TC SF291 .H365 1999*

**Horse & pony care.**
Henderson, Carolyn. 1st American ed. New York : DK Pub., 1999.
*TC SF302 .H425 1999*

**Horse & pony shows & events.**
Henderson, Carolyn. 1st American ed. New York, N.Y. : DK Pub., 1999.
*TC SF294.7 .H67 1999*

**Horse and pony breeds.**
Henderson, Carolyn. Horse & pony breeds. 1st American ed. New York, N.Y. : DK Pub., 1999.
*TC SF291 .H365 1999*

**Horse and pony care.**
Henderson, Carolyn. Horse & pony care. 1st American ed. New York : DK Pub., 1999.
*TC SF302 .H425 1999*

**Horse and pony shows and events.**
Henderson, Carolyn. Horse & pony shows & events. 1st American ed. New York, N.Y. : DK Pub., 1999.
*TC SF294.7 .H67 1999*

**HORSE BREEDS - JUVENILE LITERATURE.**
Henderson, Carolyn. Horse & pony breeds. 1st American ed. New York, N.Y. : DK Pub., 1999.
*TC SF291 .H365 1999*

**Horse heroes.**
Petty, Kate. 1st American ed. New York : DK Pub., c1999.
*TC SF302 .P47 1999*

**HORSE RIDING.** *See* **HORSEMANSHIP.**

**HORSE SHOWS.**
Henderson, Carolyn. Horse & pony shows & events. 1st American ed. New York, N.Y. : DK Pub., 1999.
*TC SF294.7 .H67 1999*

**HORSE SHOWS - JUVENILE LITERATURE.**
Henderson, Carolyn. Horse & pony shows & events. 1st American ed. New York, N.Y. : DK Pub., 1999.
*TC SF294.7 .H67 1999*

**HORSEBACK RIDING.** *See* **HORSEMANSHIP.**

**HORSEMANSHIP.**
Henderson, Carolyn. Horse & pony shows & events. 1st American ed. New York, N.Y. : DK Pub., 1999.
*TC SF294.7 .H67 1999*

Henderson, Carolyn. Improve your riding skills. 1st American ed. New York, N.Y. : DK Pub., 1999.
*TC SF309.2 .H46 1999*

**HORSEMANSHIP - JUVENILE LITERATURE.**
Henderson, Carolyn. Horse & pony shows & events. 1st American ed. New York, N.Y. : DK Pub., 1999.
*TC SF294.7 .H67 1999*

Henderson, Carolyn. Improve your riding skills. 1st American ed. New York, N.Y. : DK Pub., 1999.
*TC SF309.2 .H46 1999*

**HORSEMEN AND HORSEWOMEN.** *See* **CHARROS; COWBOYS.**

**HORSES.** *See also* **HORSE BREEDS; PONIES.**
Henderson, Carolyn. Horse & pony breeds. 1st American ed. New York, N.Y. : DK Pub., 1999.
*TC SF291 .H365 1999*

Henderson, Carolyn. Horse & pony care. 1st American ed. New York : DK Pub., 1999.
*TC SF302 .H425 1999*

Petty, Kate. Horse heroes. 1st American ed. New York : DK Pub., c1999.
*TC SF302 .P47 1999*

**HORSES - BIOGRAPHY - JUVENILE LITERATURE.**
Petty, Kate. Horse heroes. 1st American ed. New York : DK Pub., c1999.
*TC SF302 .P47 1999*

**HORSES - BREEDS.** *See* **HORSE BREEDS.**

**HORSES - JUVENILE LITERATURE.**
Henderson, Carolyn. Horse & pony breeds. 1st American ed. New York, N.Y. : DK Pub., 1999.

*TC SF291 .H365 1999*

Henderson, Carolyn. Horse & pony care. 1st American ed. New York : DK Pub., 1999.
*TC SF302 .H425 1999*

**HORSES - JUVENILE POETRY.**
My mane catches the wind. 1st ed. New York: Harcourt Brace Jovanovich, c1979.
*TC PN6110.H7 M9*

**HORSES - POETRY.**
My mane catches the wind. 1st ed. New York: Harcourt Brace Jovanovich, c1979.
*TC PN6110.H7 M9*

**Horsman, Jenny.** Too scared to learn : women, violence, and education / Jenny Horsman. Mahwah, N.J. : L. Erlbaum Associates, Publishers, 2000. xxii, 362 p. ; 23 cm. Includes bibliographical references (p. 345-352) and index. ISBN 0-8058-3658-6 (alk. paper) ISBN 0-8058-3659-4 (pbk. : alk. paper) DDC 371.822
*1. Abused women - Education. 2. Language arts. 3. Literacy - Social aspects. I. Title.*
*TC LC1481 . H67 2000*

**HORTICULTURAL CROPS.** *See* **VEGETABLES.**

**HORTICULTURAL PRODUCTS.** *See* **VEGETABLES.**

**HORTICULTURE.** *See* **GARDENING.**

**Hosp World.**
The Hospital world. Toronto : [Canadian Hospital Association?], 1912-1923.

**HOSPITAL ACCREDITATION.** *See* **HOSPITALS - ACCREDITATION.**

**Hospital accreditation standards : HAS.**
Joint Commission on Accreditation of Healthcare Organizations. Oakbrook Terrace, Ill. : The Commission, c1996-
*TC RA981.A2 J59a*

**HOSPITAL CARE - NEW YORK (STATE) - NEW YORK - HISTORY - 20TH CENTURY.**
Opdycke, Sandra. No one was turned away. New York : Oxford University Press, 1999.
*TC RA982.N49 O63 1999*

**Hospital medical and nursing world.** Toronto. v. v. 25-36; 1924-1929.

**Hospital, medical, and nursing world 1924?-1929 (not owned).**
The Hospital world. Toronto : [Canadian Hospital Association?], 1912-1923.

**HOSPITAL PATIENTS.** *See* **PSYCHIATRIC HOSPITAL PATIENTS.**

**HOSPITAL PATIENTS - MEDICAL CARE.** *See* **HOSPITAL CARE.**

**HOSPITAL PATIENTS - PSYCHOLOGY.**
Gutin, Nina J. Differential object representations in inpatients with narcissistic and borderline personality disorders and normal controls. 1997.
*TC 085 G975*

**Hospital progress.** St. Louis [etc.] Catholic Health Association of the United States [etc.] 65 v. ill. 30 cm. v. 1-65, no. 7; May 1920-July/Aug. 1984. Indexed selectively by: Hospital literature index 0018-5736. Indexed selectively by: Excerpta medica. Indexed selectively by: Energy information abstracts 0147-6521. Indexed selectively by: Environment abstracts 0093-3287. Indexed selectively by: Cumulative index to nursing & allied health literature 0146-5554. Indexed selectively by: Social work research & abstracts 0148-0847. Indexed selectively by: Energy research abstracts 0160-3604. Indexed selectively by: Catholic periodical and literature index 0008-8285. The special directory number was issued as one of the monthly numbers of v. 11-17, 42- (1930-36, 1943- ) and as an extra number of v. 18- (1937- ). Official magazine of the Catholic Hospital Association of the United States and Canada, 1920- ; of the Catholic Hospital Association, 19 - ; of the Catholic Health Association of the United States, 19 - Continued by: Health progress (Saint Louis, Mo.) ISSN: 0882-1577 (DLC) 85645984 (OCoLC)11228094. ISSN 0018-5817 DDC 362.05
*1. Hospitals - Periodicals. 2. Hospitals - United States. 3. Hospitals - Canada. 4. Nursing - Periodicals. 5. Hospitals - Directories. 6. Nursing - Directories. 7. Hospitals - periodicals. 8. Nursing - periodicals. I. Catholic Health Association of the United States. II. Catholic Hospital Association of the United States and Canada. III. Catholic Hospital Association. IV. Title: Health progress (Saint Louis, Mo.)*

**HOSPITAL SOCIAL WORK.** *See* **MEDICAL SOCIAL WORK.**

365

EDUCATION: 2000

How and why language matters in evaluation / Rodney K. Hopson, editor.

HOSPITAL SYSTEMS, MULTI-INSTITUTIONAL. See MULTIHOSPITAL SYSTEMS.

HOSPITAL TRAINING-SCHOOLS. See NURSING SCHOOLS.

The Hospital world. Toronto : [Canadian Hospital Association?], 1912-1923. 24 v. : ill. ; 26 cm. Vol. 1, no. 1 (Jan. 1912)-v. 24 (1923). "An international journal published in the interests of hospitals, sanatoria, asylums, and public charitable institutions through out America, Great Britain and her colonies." Absorbed: Journal of preventive medicine and sociology 1906-1914 (not owned). Continued by: Hospital, medical, and nursing world (not owned).
*1. Serial 2. Periodical I. Title: Hosp World II. Title: Journal of preventive medicine and sociology 1906-1914 (not owned) III. Title: Hospital, medical, and nursing world 1924?-1929 (not owned)*

HOSPITALITY INDUSTRY. See HOTELS.

HOSPITALIZED PATIENTS. See HOSPITAL PATIENTS.

HOSPITALS. See MULTIHOSPITAL SYSTEMS; PUBLIC HOSPITALS; VETERINARY HOSPITALS.

HOSPITALS - ACCREDITATION - STANDARDS - UNITED STATES - PERIODICALS.
Joint Commission on Accreditation of Healthcare Organizations. Hospital accreditation standards : HAS. Oakbrook Terrace, Ill. : The Commission, c1996-
*TC RA981.A2 J59a*

HOSPITALS - ACCREDITATION - UNITED STATES - PROBLEMS, EXERCISES, ETC.
Chamberlain, Kathryn A. The JCAHO mock survey made simple. 1998 ed. Marblehead, MA : Opus Communications, c1998.
*TC RA981.A2 C45 1999*

HOSPITALS - CANADA.
Hospital progress. St. Louis [etc.] Catholic Health Association of the United States [etc.]

HOSPITALS - DIRECTORIES.
Hospital progress. St. Louis [etc.] Catholic Health Association of the United States [etc.]

HOSPITALS, FEDERAL. See PUBLIC HOSPITALS.

HOSPITALS FOR ANIMALS. See VETERINARY HOSPITALS.

HOSPITALS, GOVERNMENT. See PUBLIC HOSPITALS.

HOSPITALS, NATIONAL. See PUBLIC HOSPITALS.

HOSPITALS - PATIENTS. See HOSPITAL PATIENTS.

HOSPITALS - PERIODICALS.
Hospital progress. St. Louis [etc.] Catholic Health Association of the United States [etc.]

HOSPITALS - PERIODICALS.
Hospital progress. St. Louis [etc.] Catholic Health Association of the United States [etc.]

HOSPITALS, PSYCHIATRIC.
Gauchet, Marcel. [La pratique de l'esprit humain. English] Madness and democracy. Princeton, N.J. : Princeton University Press, c1999.
*TC RC439 .G2813 1999*

HOSPITALS, PUBLIC. See PUBLIC HOSPITALS.

HOSPITALS - STANDARDS - UNITED STATES - PERIODICALS.
Joint Commission on Accreditation of Healthcare Organizations. Hospital accreditation standards : HAS. Oakbrook Terrace, Ill. : The Commission, c1996-
*TC RA981.A2 J59a*

HOSPITALS - STANDARDS - UNITED STATES - PROBLEMS, EXERCISES, ETC.
Chamberlain, Kathryn A. The JCAHO mock survey made simple. 1998 ed. Marblehead, MA : Opus Communications, c1998.
*TC RA981.A2 C45 1999*

HOSPITALS - UNITED STATES.
Hospital progress. St. Louis [etc.] Catholic Health Association of the United States [etc.]

HOSPITALS - UNITED STATES - HOME CARE PROGRAMS.
Brown, Gloria M. Post-hospital care for the elderly. 1997.
*TC 06 no. 10759*

HOSPITALS - UNITED STATES - STAFF - CASE STUDIES.
Garey, Anita Ilta, 1947- Weaving work and motherhood. Philadelphia, PA : Temple University Press, 1999.
*TC HQ759.48 .G37 1999*

Høstaker, Roar.
Bleiklie, Ivar, 1948- Policy and practice in higher education. London ; Phildadelphia : J. Kingsley Publishers, 2000.
*TC LC178.N8 B44 2000*

HOSTILITIES. See WAR.

Hot buttons / edited by Donovan R. Walling. Bloomington, Ind. : Phi Delta Kappa Educational Foundation, c1997. 268 p. ; 23 cm. Subtitle on cover: Unraveling 10 controversial issues in education. Includes bibliographical references. ISBN 0-87367-495-2 DDC 370/.973
*1. Education - United States. 2. Education - Social aspects - United States. I. Walling, Donovan R., 1948- II. Title: Unraveling 10 controversial issues in education*
*TC LA210 .H68 1997*

Hot groups.
Lipman-Blumen, Jean. New York : Oxford University Press, 1999.
*TC HD58.9 .L56 1999*

Hot topics series
Block scheduling. Bloomington, IN : Phi Delta Phi International, c1999.
*TC LB3032.2 .B47 1999*

Time and learning :. Bloomington, IN : Phi Delta Kappa International, c1998.
*TC LB3032 .T562 1998*

([no. 17]) Preventing student violence. Bloomington, IN (P.O. Box 789, Bloomington 47402-0789) : Phi Delta Kappa International, c1999.
*TC LB3013.3 .P755 1999*

(no. 17) Preventing student violence. Bloomington, IN (P.O. Box 789, Bloomington 47402-0789) : Phi Delta Kappa International, c1999.
*TC LB3013.3 .P755 1999*

HOTELS, TAVERNS, ETC. See HOTELS.

HOTELS - WHITE MOUNTAINS (N.H. AND ME.) - HISTORY.
Tolles, Bryant Franklin, 1939- The grand resort hotels of the White Mountains. 1st ed. Boston : D.R. Godine, 1995.
*TC TX909 .T58 1995*

Houghton Mifflin teacher's book: a resource for planning and teaching.
Cooper, J. David (James David), 1942- Discover : Grade 1, level 1.5, [Themes 9 and 10]. Boston : Houghton Mifflin, 1997.
*TC LB1575.8 .C6616 1997*

HOURS OF LABOR. See HOLIDAYS; LEAVE OF ABSENCE.

HOURS (TIME). See TIME.

House, Alvin E. DSM-IV diagnosis in the schools / Alvin E. House. New York : Guilford Press, c1999 ix, 230 p. ; 24 cm. (The Guilford school practitioner series) Includes bibliographical references (p. 205-223) and index. ISBN 1-57230-346-8 DDC 618.92/890075
*1. Mental illness - Diagnosis. 2. Child psychopathology. 3. School children - Mental health. I. Title. II. Series.*
*TC RJ503.5 .H68 1999*

HOUSE DRAINAGE. See SANITATION.

HOUSE FURNISHINGS. See CLOCKS AND WATCHES; FURNITURE; POTTERY.

The house of Joshua.
Fullilove, Mindy Thompson. Lincoln, NE : University of Nebraska Press, c1999.
*TC BF353 .F85 1999*

HOUSE-RAISING PARTIES. See DWELLINGS.

The house with no door.
Swann, Brian. 1st ed. San Diego : Harcourt Brace & Company., c1998.
*TC PS3569.W256 H6 1998*

HOUSEHOLD ECOLOGY. See DWELLINGS.

HOUSEHOLD MANAGEMENT. See HOME ECONOMICS.

HOUSEHOLD SCIENCE. See HOME ECONOMICS.

HOUSEHOLD VIOLENCE. See FAMILY VIOLENCE.

HOUSEHOLDS. See also FAMILY; HOME ECONOMICS.
Pennartz, Paul. The domestic domain :. Aldershot, Hants, England : Brookfield, Vt. : Ashgate, c1999.
*TC HQ728 .P46 1999*

HOUSEHUSBANDS. See FATHERS.

Housen, Abigail. The eye of the beholder : measuring aesthetic development / by Abigail Housen. 1983. xii, 333 leaves. ; ill. ; 28 cm. Thesis (Ph. D.)--Harvard University, 1983. Bibliography: leaves 319-332. Photocopy. Ann Arbor, Mich. : University Microfilms International, 1983. 29 cm. s1983   miu na
*1. Aesthetics. 2. Art - Philosophy. I. Title.*
*TC BH39 .H68 1983*

Houser, Rick. Counseling and educational research : evaluation and application / Rick Houser. Thousand Oaks, Calif. : Sage Publications, c1998. xiv, 266 p. : ill. ; 24 cm. Includes bibliographical references (p. 245-252) and indexes. ISBN 0-7619-0739-4 (hardcover : acid-free paper) ISBN 0-7619-0740-8 (pbk. : acid-free paper) DDC 507.2
*1. Science - Research - Study and teaching. I. Title.*
*TC Q180.A1 H595 1998*

HOUSES. See ARCHITECTURE, DOMESTIC; DWELLINGS; HOUSING.

HOUSEWIVES. See MOTHERS.

HOUSEWIVES - GREAT BRITAIN - HISTORY.
Robertson, Una A. An illustrated history of the housewife, 1650-1950. New York : St. Martin's Press, 1997.
*TC HD8039.H842 G77 1997*

HOUSING. See CONGREGATE HOUSING; DWELLINGS; SLUMS.

HOUSING, COOPERATIVE. See COMMUNAL LIVING.

HOUSING NEEDS. See HOUSING.

HOUSING POLICY - UNITED STATES.
Affordable housing and urban redevelopment in the United States. Thousand Oaks, Calif. : Sage Publications, c1997.
*TC HD7293 .A55 1997*

HOUSING - SOCIAL ASPECTS. See HOUSING.

HOUSING - UNITED STATES.
Affordable housing and urban redevelopment in the United States. Thousand Oaks, Calif. : Sage Publications, c1997.
*TC HD7293 .A55 1997*

HOUSTON INDEPENDENT SCHOOL DISTRICT - HISTORY.
Kellar, William Henry, 1952- Make haste slowly. 1st ed. College Station : Texas A&M University Press, c1999.
*TC LC214.23.H68 K45 1999*

Houston, Michael E., 1941- Biochemistry primer for exercise science / Michael E. Houston. Champaign, IL : Human Kinetics, c1995. viii, 135 p. : ill. ; 28 cm. Includes bibliographical references (p. 129) and index. ISBN 0-87322-577-5 DDC 574.19/2
*1. Biochemistry. 2. Exercise - Physiological aspects. I. Title.*
*TC QP514.2 .H68 1995*

Houtz, John.
Creativity and giftedness in culturally diverse students. Cresskill, N.J. : Hampton Press, c2000.
*TC LC3993.2 .C74 2000*

How and why language matters in evaluation / Rodney K. Hopson, editor. San Francisco, CA : Jossey-Bass, c2000. 115 p. ; 23 cm. (New directions for evaluation ; no. 86) Includes bibliographical references and index. CONTENTS: Overview : language matters / Michael Quinn Patton -- Language in defining social problems and in evaluating social programs / Anna Marie Madison -- HIV/AIDS talk : implications for prevention intervention and evaluation / Rodney K. Hopson, Kenya J. Lucas, James A. Peterson -- Translating evaluation findings into "policy language" / Kenneth Cabatoff -- Sociolinguistic dynamics of gender in focus groups / Courtney L. Brown -- Beyond the literal : metaphors and why they matter / Alexis Kaminsky -- Dialogue for learning : evaluator as critical friend / Sharon F. Rallis, Gretchen B. Rossman -- Border lessons : linguistic "rich points" and evaluative understanding / Michael Agar. ISBN 0-7879-5430-6
*1. Evaluation research (Social action programs) 2. Sociolinguistics. I. Hopson, Rodney K. II. Series: New directions for education ; no. 86*
*TC H62 .H67 2000*

**How children learn the meanings of words.**
Bloom, Paul, 1963- Cambridge, MA : MIT Press, c2000.
*TC P118 .B623 2000*

**How children understand war and peace :** a call for international peace education / Amiram Raviv, Louis Oppenheimer, Daniel Bar-Tal, editors. 1st ed. San Francisco : Jossey-Bass, c1999. x, 342 p. ; 24 cm. Includes bibliographical references and indexes. ISBN 0-7879-4169-7 (acid-free paper) DDC 303.6/6
*1. Peace - Study and teaching. 2. Children and peace. I. Raviv, Amiram. II. Oppenheimer, Louis. III. Bar-Tal, Daniel.*
*TC JZ5534 .H69 1999*

**How clients make therapy work.**
Bohart, Arthur C. 1st ed. Washington, DC : American Psychological Association, c1999.
*TC RC480.5 .B64 1999*

**How do they know you care?.**
Lyman, Linda L. New York : Teachers College Press, c2000.
*TC LB2831.924.13 L96 2000*

**How expectancies shape experience** / edited by Irving Kirsch. 1st ed. Washington, DC : American Psychological Association, c1999. xiv, 431 p. : ill. ; 27 cm. Includes bibliographical references and indexes. ISBN 1-55798-586-3 (hardcover : alk. paper) DDC 150
*1. Expectation (Psychology) 2. Self-fulfilling prophecy. 3. Medicine, Psychosomatic. I. Kirsch, Irving, 1943-*
*TC BF323.E8 H69 1999*

**How I paint.**
Buechner, Thomas S. New York : Harry N. Abrams, 2000.
*TC ND237.B8827 A4 2000*

**How in the world do students read?.**
Elley, Warwick B. Hamburg : The International Association for the Evaluation of Educational Achievement, [1992]
*TC LB1050.6 .E55 1992*

**How language and literacy come togethe, k-2.**
McCarrier, Andrea. Interactive writing. Portsmouth, NH : Heinemann, c2000.
*TC LB1139.5.L35 M39 2000*

**How mathematical thinking evolved and why numbers are like gossip.**
Devlin, Keith J. The math gene. [New York] : Basic Books, 2000.
*TC QA141 .D48 2000*

**How much is enough?.**
Murdin, Lesley. London ; New York : Routledge, 2000.
*TC RC489.T45 M87 2000*

**How nations serve young children :** profiles of child care and education in 14 countries / edited by Patricia P. Olmsted, David P. Weikart ; with an afterword by Lilian G. Katz. Ypsilanti, Mich. : High/Scope Press, c1989. xxiv, 409 p. : ill. ; 24 cm. Includes bibliographical references. ISBN 0-929816-07-2 DDC 362.7
*1. Child care services - Cross-cultural studies. 2. Early childhood education - Cross-cultural studies. I. Olmsted, Patricia P. II. Weikart, David P.*
*TC HQ778.5 .H69 1989*

**How nurse executives learned to become leaders.**
Fressola, Maria C. 1998.
*TC 06 no. 11115*

Fressola, Maria C. 1998.
*TC 06 no. 11115*

**How people learn :** brain, mind, experience, and school / John D. Bransford ... [et al.], editors ; Committee on Developments in the Science of Learning and Committee on Learning Research and Educational Practice, Commission on Behavioral and Social Sciences and Education, National Research Council. Expanded ed. Washington, D.C. : National Academy Press, c2000. x, 374 p. : ill. ; 27 cm. Includes bibliographical references (p. 285-348) and index.
CONTENTS: Learning : from speculation to science -- How experts differ from novices -- Learning and transfer -- How children learn -- Mind and brain -- The design of learning environments -- Effective teaching : examples in history, mathematics, and science -- Teaching learning -- Technology to support learning -- Conclusions -- Next Steps for Research.
ISBN 0-309-07036-8 (pbk.) DDC 370.15/23
*1. Learning, Psychology of. 2. Learning - Social aspects. I. Bransford, John. II. National Research Council (U.S.). Committee on Developments in the Science of Learning. III. National Research Council (U.S.). Committee on Learning Research and Educational Practice.*
*TC LB1060 .H672 2000*

**How should education in Japan be reformed now.**
Nihon Kyōshokuin Kumiai. Educational reform on people's own initiative. [Tokyo?] : Japan Teachers Union, 1984.
*TC LC210.8.N54 1984*

**How special do you need to be to find yourself in a special school?.**
Phtiaka, Helen. Special kids for special treatment?, or, How special do you need to be to find yourself in a special school? London ; Washington, D.C. : Falmer Press, 1997.
*TC LC4803.G7 P58 1998*

**How technology is changing institutional research** / Liz Sanders, editor. San Francisco, Calif. : Jossey-Bass Publishers, c1999. 105 p. ; 23 cm. (New directions for institutional research, no. 103, Fall 1999.) (New directions for higher and adult education series.) Includes bibliographies and index. ISBN 0-7879-5240-0
*1. Education, Higher - Research - United States - Technological innovations. 2. Research - United States - Technological innovations. I. Sanders, Liz. II. Series. III. Series: New directions for institutional research, v.103.*
*TC LB2326.3 .H69 1999*

**How the brain evolved language.**
Loritz, Donald, 1947- New York : Oxford University Press, 1999.
*TC P116 .L67 1999*

**How to create successful Internet projects.**
McLain, Tim, 1970- El Segundo, Calif. : Classroom Connect, c1999.
*TC LB1044.87 .M35 1999*

**How-to-do-it manuals for libraries**
(no. 85.) Developing an information literacy program K-12. New York : Neal-Schuman, c1998.
*TC Z711.2 .D49 1998*

(no. 88.) Including families of children with special needs. New York : Neal Schuman Publishers, c1999.
*TC Z711.92.H3 I6 1999*

(no. 92.) Talan, Carole. Founding and funding family literacy programs. New York : Neal-Schuman, c1999.
*TC Z716.45 .T35 1999*

(no. 97.) Duncan, Donna. I-Search, you search, we all to learn to research. New York : Neal-Schuman Publishers, 2000.
*TC Z711.2 .D86 2000*

**How to get a job if you're a teenager.**
Pervola, Cindy, 1956- Fort Atkinson, Wis. : Alleyside Press, 1998.
*TC HF5383 .P44 1998*

**How to get a research degree.**
Elphinstone, Leonie. St. Leonards, Australia : Allen & Unwin, 1998.
*TC LB2371 .E46 1998*

**How to get a teaching job.**
Moffatt, Courtney W. Boston ; London : Allyn and Bacon, c2000.
*TC LB1780 .M64 2000*

**How to have theory in an epidemic.**
Treichler, Paula A. Durham : Duke University Press, 1999.
*TC RA644.A25 T78 1999*

**How to improve your school.**
Brighouse, Tim. London ; New York : Routledge, 1999.
*TC LB2822.84.G7 B75 1999*

**How to increase reading ability, a guide to individualized and remedial methods.**
Harris, Albert Josiah. 2d ed., rev. and enl. London ; New York[etc.] : Longmans, Green and Co., 1947.
*TC 372.4H2421*

**How to make money performing in schools.**
Heflick, David. Orient, Wash. : Silcox Productions, c1996.
*TC LB3015 .H428 1996*

**How to reach students with autism [videorecording].**
Break throughs [videorecording]. Boston, MA : Fanlight Productions, c1998.
*TC LC4717.5 .B7 1998*

**How to read and why.**
Bloom, Harold. New York : Scribner, c2000.
*TC LB1050 .B56 2000*

**HOW TO STUDY.** *See* **STUDY SKILLS.**

**How to succeed in academics.**
McCabe, Linda. San Diego, Calif. : Academic, c2000.

*TC LB2331.7 .M34 2000*

**How to think about weird things.**
Schick, Theodore. 2nd ed. Mountain View, Calif. : Mayfield Pub., c1999.
*TC BC177 .S32 1999*

**How to think straight.**
Flew, Antony, 1923- [Thinking about thinking] 2nd ed. Amherst, N.Y. : Prometheus Books, 1998.
*TC BF455 .F614 1998*

**How we became posthuman.**
Hayles, N. Katherine. Chicago, Ill. : University of Chicago Press, 1999.
*TC Q335 .H394 1999*

**How we think.**
Dewey, John, 1859-1952. Boston : Houghton Mifflin, c1998.
*TC BF441 .D43 1998*

**Howard, David.**
Ballet class for beginners [videorecording]. W. Long Branch, NJ : Kultur, c1981.
*TC GV1589 .B3 1981*

Ballet class [videorecording]. W. Long Branch, NJ : Kultur, c1984.
*TC GV1589 .B33 1984*

**Howard-Hamilton, Mary F.**
Robinson, Tracy L. The convergence of race, ethnicity, and gender. Upper Saddle River, N.J. : Merrill, c2000.
*TC BF637.C6 R583 2000*

**Howard, John R., 1933-** The shifting wind : the Supreme Court and civil rights from Reconstruction to Brown / John R. Howard. Albany : State University of New York Press, c1999. vii, 393 p. ; 24 cm. (SUNY series in Afro-American studies) Includes bibliographical references (p. 377-384) and index. ISBN 0-7914-4089-3 (hc : alk. paper) ISBN 0-7914-4090-7 (pbk. : alk. paper) DDC 342.73/085
*1. Afro-Americans - Civil rights - History. 2. Civil rights - United States - History. 3. United States. - Supreme Court - History. I. Title. II. Series.*
*TC KF4757 .H69 1999*

**Howard, Kim, 1971-.**
Out & about campus. 1st ed. Los Angeles : Alyson Books, 2000.
*TC LC2574.6 .O87 2000*

**Howard, Kim, ill.**
Bea, Holly, 1956- My spiritual alphabet book. Tiburon, Calif. : H.J. Kramer, c2000.
*TC BL625.5 .B43 1999*

**Howard, Rose A.**
Goethals, M. Serra, 1934- Student teaching. Upper Saddle River, N.J. : Merrill, c2000.
*TC LB2157.A3 G57 2000*

**Howard, Sara.**
New directions in language development and disorders. New York : Kluwer Academic/Plenum Publishers, c2000.
*TC P118 .N49 2000*

**Howatt, William A.** The human services counseling toolbox : theory, development, technique, and resources / William A. Howatt. Belmont, CA : Brooks/Cole-Wadsworth, c2000. xvi, 317 p. ; 24 cm. Includes bibliographical references and indexes. ISBN 0-534-35932-9 (alk. paper) DDC 361/.06
*1. Counseling. 2. Psychotherapy. I. Title.*
*TC BF637.C6 H677 2000*

**Howe, Florence.**
Fuchshuber, Annegert. [Karlinchen. English] Carly. 1st ed. New York : The Feminist Press, c1997.
*TC PZ7.F94 Car 1997*

**Howe, Mark L.** The fate of early memories : developmental science and the retention of childhood experiences / Mark L. Howe. Washington, DC : American Psychological Association, c2000. xvii, 219 p. ; 27 cm. Includes bibliographical references (p. 163-198) and indexes. ISBN 1-55798-628-2 (cloth : alk. paper) DDC 153.1/2
*1. Early memories. 2. Memory in children. I. Title.*
*TC BF378.E17 H69 2000*

**Howe, Michael J. A., 1940-** Genius explained / Michael J.A. Howe. Cambridge, U.K. ; New York : Cambridge University Press, 1999. ix, 221 p. ; 23 cm. Includes bibliographical references (p. 212-215) and index. ISBN 0-521-64018-0 (hardbound) ISBN 0-521-64968-4 (pbk.) DDC 153.9/8
*1. Genius. 2. Genius - Case studies. I. Title.*
*TC BF416.A1 H68 1999*

The psychology of high abilities / Michael J.A. Howe. New York : New York University Press, 1999. x, 198

p. ; 23 cm. Includes bibliographical references (p. 183-193) and index. ISBN 0-8147-3612-2 (alk. paper) DDC 153.9/8
*1. Ability in children. 2. Gifted children. 3. Nature and nurture. I. Title.*
*TC BF723.A25 H69 1999*

**Howell, Kenneth W.** Curriculum-based evaluation : teaching and decision making / Kenneth W. Howell, Victor Nolet. 3rd ed. Belmont, CA. : Wadsworth, c2000. xviii, 565 p. : ill. ; 25 cm. Includes bibliographical references (p. 524-548) and indexes. ISBN 0-534-34370-8 DDC 371.26/4
*1. Curriculum-based assessment - United States. 2. Educational tests and measurements - United States. I. Nolet, Victor. II. Title.*
*TC LB3060.32.C74 H68 2000*

**Howell, Ron.** One hundred jobs :b a panorama of work in the American city / Ron Howell ; photographs by Ozier Muhammad. New York : New Press : Distributed by W.W. Norton, 1999. 223 p. : ill. ; 21 cm. Subtitle on cip record: paoroma of work in the American city. ISBN 1-56584-430-0 (pbk.) DDC 331.7/02/09747
*1. Vocational guidance - New York (State) - New York. 2. Occupations - New York (State) - New York - Case studies. I. Title. II. Title: paorama of work in the American city. III. Title: Panorama of work in the American city.*
*TC HF5382.5.U6 N37 1999*

**Howes, Ruth (Ruth Hege)** Their day in the sun : women of the Manhattan Project / Ruth H. Howes and Caroline L. Herzenberg ; foreword by Ellen C. Weaver. Philadelphia, PA : Temple University Press, 1999. viii, 264 p. : ill. ; 24 cm. (Labor and social change) Includes bibliographical references (p. 237-251) and index. ISBN 1-56639-719-7 (cloth : alk. paper) DDC 355.8/25119/0922
*1. Manhattan Project (U.S.) - History. 2. Women scientists - United States. I. Herzenberg, Caroline L., 1932- II. Title. III. Series.*
*TC QC773.3.U5 H68 1999*

**Howl and other poems.**
Ginsberg, Allen, 1926- San Francisco : City Lights Books, [1996]
*TC PS3513.I74 H6 1996*

**How's it going?.**
Anderson, Carl, educator. Portsmouth, NH : Heinemann, c2000.
*TC LB1576 .A6159 2000*

**Hoy, Charles, 1939-** Improving quality in education / Charles Hoy, Colin Bayne-Jardine and Margaret Wood ; with an introduction by Maurice Holt. London ; New York : Falmer Press, 2000. xi, 157 p. : ill. ; 24 cm. Includes bibliographical references and index. ISBN 0-7507-0941-3 (alk. paper) ISBN 0-7507-0940-5 (pbk. : alk. paper) DDC 371.2/00941
*1. School improvement programs - Great Britain. 2. Educational change - Great Britain. 3. Educational evaluation - Great Britain. I. Bayne-Jardine, Colin Charles. II. Wood, Margaret, 1957- III. Title.*
*TC LB2822.84.G7 H69 1999*

**Hoyle, John.** Interpersonal sensitivity / John R. Hoyle and Harry M. Crenshaw, II. Larchmont, NY : Eye on Education, c1997. xvii, 142 p. : ill. ; 24 cm. (The school leadership library) Includes bibliographical references (p. 139-142). ISBN 1-88300-129-3 DDC 302/.14
*1. School principals - United States - Attitudes. 2. Interpersonal relations - United States. 3. School environment - United States. 4. Group relations training - United States. I. Crenshaw, Harry M., 1946- II. Title. III. Series.*
*TC LB2831.92.U6 H67 1997*

**Høyrup, Jens.** Human sciences : reappraising the humanities through history and philosophy / Jens Høyrup. Albany, NY : State University of New York Press, c2000. xi, 448 p. ; 24 cm. Includes bibliographical references (p. 395-413) and indexes. ISBN 0-7914-4603-4 (alk. paper) ISBN 0-7914-4604-2 (pbk. : alk. paper) DDC 001.3/01
*1. Humanities - Philosophy. 2. Humanities - History. 3. Science and the humanities. I. Title.*
*TC AZ103 .H69 2000*

**Hoyt, Dan R., 1949-.**
Whitbeck, Les B. Nowhere to grow. New York : Aldine de Gruyter, 1999.
*TC HV4505 .W43 1999*

**Hrdy, Sarah Blaffer, 1946-** Mother nature : a history of mothers, infants, and natural selection / Sarah Blaffer Hrdy. 1st ed. New York : Pantheon Books, c1999. xix, 723 p. : ill. (some col.) ; 25 cm. Includes bibliographical references (p. 603-690) and index. ISBN 0-679-44265-0 DDC 306.874/3
*1. Mother and child. 2. Motherhood - Psychological aspects. 3. Natural selection. 4. Parental behavior in animals. 5. Working mothers. I. Title.*

*TC HQ759 .H784 1999*

**Hsi, Sherry.**
Linn, Marcia C. Computers, teachers, peers. Mahwah, N.J. : L. Erlbaum Associates, 2000.
*TC LB1585.3 .L56 2000*

**Hsiao, Chen-t'ang.**
**Chung kuo ku chi chuang ting hsiu pu chi shu. English.**
The East Asian library journal. Princeton, N.J. : Gest Library of Princeton University, c1994-
*TC Z733.G47 G46*

**Hsu, John S. J., 1955-.**
Leonard, Thomas, 1948- Bayesian methods. Cambridge, U.K. : New York : Cambridge University Press, 1999.
*TC QA279.5 .L45 1999*

**HTLV-III INFECTIONS. See HIV INFECTIONS.**

**HTLV-III-LAV INFECTIONS. See HIV INFECTIONS.**

**Huang, Wen-Yuan.** The economic and environmental consequences of nutrient management in agriculture / Wen-yuan Huang and Noel D. Uri. Commack, N.Y. : Nova Science, c1999. viii, 174 p. ; 27 cm. Includes bibliographical references and index. ISBN 1-56072-754-3 DDC 631.8/4
*1. Nitrogen fertilizers. 2. Nitrogen fertilizers - Environmental aspects. I. Uri, Noel D. II. Title.*
*TC S651 .H826 1999*

**Huba, Mary E.** Learner-centered assessment on college campuses : shifting the focus from teaching to learning / Mary E. Huba, Jann E. Freed. Boston ; London : Allyn and Bacon, c2000. xviii, 286 p. : ill. ; 23 cm. Includes bibliographical references and index. ISBN 0-205-28738-7 DDC 378.1/25
*1. College teaching. 2. College students - Rating of. 3. Learning - Evaluation. 4. Educational tests and measurements. I. Freed, Jann E. II. Title.*
*TC LB2331 .H83 2000*

**Hubbard, James P. (James Patrick), 1945-** Education under colonial rule : a history of Katsina College, 1921-1942 / James P. Hubbard. Lanham : University Press of America, 2000 306 p. ; 24 cm. Includes bibliographical references (p.285-293) and index. ISBN 0-7618-1589-9 (cloth) DDC 373.669/76
*1. Katsina College - History - 20th century. 2. Education, Secondary - Nigeria - History - 20th century. 3. Great Britain - Colonies - Africa - Administration - History - 20th century. I. Title.*
*TC LG483.K78 H83 2000*

**Hubbard, L. Ron (La Fayette Ron), 1911-** Dianetics : the modern science of mental health / L. Ron Hubbard. Los Angeles, Calif. : Bridge Publications, c2000. ix, 601 p. : ill. ; 24 cm. "A Hubbard publication." Includes index. CONTENTS: The goal of man -- The single source of all inorganic mental and organic psychosomatic ills -- Therapy. ISBN 0-88404-416-5
*1. Dianetics. 2. Alternative Medicine. I. Title.*
*TC BP605.S2 H7956 2000*

**Hubbard, Merle.**
Ballet class for beginners [videorecording]. W. Long Branch, NJ : Kultur, c1981.
*TC GV1589 .B3 1981*

**Hubbard, Nick.**
Woods, Peter, 1934- Multicultural children in the early years. Clevedon ; Philadelphia : Multilingual Matters Ltd, c1999.
*TC LC3736.G6 W66 1999*

**Hubbard, Ruth.** Living the art of classroom inquiry : a handbook for teacher-researchers / by Ruth Shagoury Hubbard, Brenda Miller Power. Portsmouth, N.H. : Heinemann, c1993. xviii, 165 p. : ill. ; 24 cm. Includes bibliographical references (p. 161-165). ISBN 0-435-08762-2 DDC 370.78
*1. Education - Research - United States - Handbooks, manuals, etc. 2. Teaching - Case studies. I. Power, Brenda Miller. II. Title.*
*TC LB1028 .H78 1993*

**Hubbell, Patricia.** Boo! : Halloween poems and limericks / Patricia Hubbell ; illustrations by Jeff Spackman. 1st ed. New York : Marshall Cavendish, 1998. 40 p. : col. ill. ; 29 cm. SUMMARY: A collection of limericks and other poems about Halloween, including "Halloween Scarecrow," "There Once Was a Witch from North Dublin," and "Pumpkin Surprise." ISBN 0-7614-5023-8 DDC 811/.54
*1. Halloween - Juvenile poetry. 2. Children's poetry, American. 3. Limericks, Juvenile. I. Spackman, Jeff, ill. II. Title. III. Title: Halloween poems and limericks*
*TC PS3558.U22 B66 1998*

**HUBBLE, EDWIN POWELL, 1889-1953.**
Stephen Hawking's universe [videorecording]. [Alexandria, Va.] : PBS Video ; Burbank, CA : Distributed by Warner Home Video, c1997.
*TC QB982 .S7 1997*

**Huber, Diane.** Leadership and nursing care management / Diane Huber. 2nd ed. Philadelphia : W.B. Saunders, c2000. xi, 708 p. : ill. ; 23 cm. Includes bibliographical references and index. ISBN 0-7216-7699-5 DDC 362.1/73/068
*1. Nursing services - Administration. 2. Nursing services - United States - Administration. 3. Nursing Services - organization & administration - Leadership. 4. Nursing, Supervisory - Leadership. I. Title.*
*TC RT89 .H83 2000*

**Huber, Ludwig, 1950-.**
The evolution of cognition. Cambridge, Mass. : MIT Press, c2000.
*TC BF701 .E598 2000*

**Huber, Mary Taylor, 1944-.**
Gendered missions. Ann Arbor : University of Michigan Press, c1999.
*TC BV2610 .G46 1999*

**Huck, Charlotte S.**
Children's literature in the elementary school. 7th ed. Dubuque, IA : McGraw-Hill, c2001.
*TC LB1575.5.U5 H79 2001*

**The Huckabuck family and how they raised popcorn in Nebraska and quit and came back.**
Sandburg, Carl, 1878-1967. 1st ed. New York : Farrar Strauss Giroux, c1999.
*TC PZ7.S1965 Hu 1999*

**Huckman, Lynda, 1943-.**
Wallace, Mike. Senior management teams in primary schools. London ; New York : Routledge, 1999.
*TC LB2806.3 .W37 1999*

**HUCKSTERS. See PEDDLERS AND PEDDLING.**

**Hudson Institute.**
Kahn, Herman, 1922- The year 2000. New York : Macmillan, c1967.
*TC CB160 .K3 1967*

**Hudson, Julie.**
Spring, Christopher. North African textiles. Washington, D.C. : Smithsonian Institution Press, c1995.
*TC NK8887.6 .S68 1995*

**Hudson, Nancy R.** Management practice in dietetics / Nancy R. Hudson. Australia ; Belmont, Calif. : Wadsworth, c2000. xvii 510 p. : ill. ; 24 cm. Includes bibliographical references (p. 467-469) and index. ISBN 0-534-54504-1 DDC 647.95/068
*1. Food service management. 2. Dietetics. I. Title.*
*TC TX911.3.M27 H83 2000*

**Hudson, Stephen M.**
Remaking relapse prevention with sex offenders. Thousand Oaks, Calif. : Sage Publications, c2000.
*TC RC560.S47 R46 2000*

**Huerta-Macías, Ana.**
Educating Latino students. Lancaster, Pa. : Technomic Pub. Co., c1998.
*TC LC2669 .E37 1998*

**Huff, Robert M.**
Promoting health in multicultural populations. Thousand Oaks, Calif. : Sage Publications, c1999.
*TC RA448.4 .P76 1999*

**Huggins, Nathan Irvin, 1927-** Harlem renaissance / Nathan Irvin Huggins. London ; New York : Oxford University Press, 1973, c1971. ix, 343 p., [16] p. of plates : ill., ports. ; 21 cm. "1st issued as an Oxford University Press paperback." Includes bibliographical references and index. ISBN 0-19-501665-3 (pbk.)
*1. Afro-American arts - New York State - New York. 2. Harlem Renaissance. I. Title.*
*TC NX511.N5 H89 1973*

**Hughes, Carolyn, 1946-** The transition handbook : strategies high school teachers use that work! / by Carolyn Hughes and Erik W. Carter. Baltimore : P.H. Brookes Pub., c2000. xxii, 416 p. : ill. ; 28 cm. Includes bibliographical references and indexes. ISBN 1-55766-439-0 DDC 371.9/0473
*1. Handicapped youth - Education (Secondary) - United States. 2. Handicapped youth - Education (Middle school) - United States. 3. Handicapped youth - Services for - United States. 4. School-to-work transition - United States. 5. Community and school - United States. I. Carter, Erik W. II. Title.*
*TC LC4019 .H84 2000*

**Hughes, David, 1944-.**
Trading in futures. Buckingham [England] :
Philadelphia : Open University Press, 1999.
*TC LB2826.6.N45 T73 1999*

**Hughes, Honore M.**
Rossman, B. B. Robbie. Children and interparental
violence. Philadelphia, Pa. : London : Brunner/Mazel,
c2000.
*TC HQ784.V55 R675 2000*

**Hughes, James W.**
America's demographic tapestry. New Brunswick,
N.J. : Rutgers University Press, c1999.
*TC HB3505 .A683 1999*

**Hughes, Judith M.** Freudian analysts/feminist issues /
Judith M. Hughes. New Haven [Conn.] : Yale
University Press, c1999. x, 222 p. ; 25 cm. Includes
bibliographical references (p. [186]-211) and index. ISBN
0-300-07524-3 (alk. paper) DDC 150.19/5/082
*1. Psychoanalysis and feminism. I. Title.*
*TC BF175.4.F45 H84 1999*

**Hughes, Kathleen.**
The next generation [videorecording]. Princeton, NJ :
Films for the Humanities & Sciences, c1998.
*TC RC564 .N4 1998*

**Hughes, Larry W., 1931-** Public relations for school
leaders / Larry W. Hughes, Don W. Hooper. Boston ;
London : Allyn and Bacon, c2000. x, 230 p. : ill. ; 25 cm.
Includes bibliographical references and index. ISBN 0-205-
30623-3 DDC 659.2/9371
*1. Schools - Public relations - United States - Case studies. 2.*
*Community and school - United States - Case studies. 3.*
*School administrators - United States - Case studies. 4.*
*Educational leadership - United States - Case studies. I.*
*Hooper, Don W. II. Title.*
*TC LB2847 .H84 2000*

**Hughes, Margaret, 1941-** The violent E and other
tricky sounds : learning to spell from kindergarten
through grade 6 / Margaret Hughes and Dennis Searle.
York, Me. : Stenhouse Publishers ; Markham,
Ontario : Pembroke Publishers Limited, c1997. ix, 188
p. : ill. ; 23 cm. Includes bibliographical references (p. 187-
188). ISBN 1-57110-034-2 (pbk. : alk. paper) DDC 372.63/2/
044
*1. English language - Orthography and spelling - Study and*
*teaching (Elementary) I. Searle, Dennis. II. Title.*
*TC LB1574 .H84 1997*

**Hughes, Martin, 1949 May 15-** Numeracy and beyond :
applying mathematics in the primary school / Martin
Hughes, Charles Desforges and Christine Mitchell
with Clive Carré. Buckingham [England] :
Philadelphia : Open University Press, 2000. 126 p. :
ill. ; 24 cm. Includes bibliographical references (p. [120]-121)
and index. ISBN 0-335-20130-X (hb) ISBN 0-335-20129-6
(pb) DDC 372.7/2/0941
*1. Mathematics - Study and teaching (Primary) - Great Britain.*
*2. Mathematics - Study and teaching (Primary) - Japan. I.*
*Desforges, Charles. II. Mitchell, Christine. III. Title.*
*TC QA135.5 .H844 2000*

**Hughes, Steve.**
Drum, Jan. Global winners. Yarmouth, Me. :
Intercultural Press, c1994.
*TC LC1099.3 .D78 1994*

**Hugill, Peter J.** Global communications since 1844 :
geopolitics and technology / Peter J. Hugill.
Baltimore, Md. : Johns Hopkins University Press,
c1999. xvii, 277 p. : ill. ; 26 cm. Includes bibliographical
references and indexes. ISBN 0-8018-6039-3 (alk. paper)
ISBN 0-8018-6074-1 (pbk. : alk. paper) DDC 384/.09
*1. Telecommunication - History. 2. Geopolitics - History. I.*
*Title.*
*TC TK5102.2 .H84 1999*

**Huizenga, Jann.** Writing workout : a program for new
students of English / Jann Huizenga [and] Maria
Thomas-Ružić. Glenview, Ill. : Scott, Foresman and
Co.,cc1990. vi, 186 p. : ill. ; 26 cm. Includes index. ISBN 0-
673-24574-8
*1. English language - Textbooks for foreign speakers. 2.*
*English language - Writing - Problems, exercises, etc. I.*
*Thomas-Ružić, Maria. II. Title.*
*TC PE1128 .H84 1990*

**HULL HOUSE (CHICAGO, ILL.) - HISTORY.**
Jackson, Shannon, 1967- Lines of activity. Ann
Arbor : University of Michigan Press, c2000.
*TC HV4196.C4 J33 2000*

**Hull, Mary.** Censorship in America : a reference
handbook / Mary E. Hull. Santa Barbara, Calif. :
ABC-CLIO, c1999. xii, 233 p. : ill. ; 24 cm. (Contemporary
world issues) Includes bibliographical references and index.
ISBN 1-57607-057-3 (alk. paper) DDC 363.3/1
*1. Censorship - United States. I. Title. II. Series.*

---

*TC Z658.U5 H84 1999*

**Hulls, Brian.**
Photomontage today, Peter Kennard [videorecording].
[London] : Art Council of Great Britain ; Ho-Ho-Kus,
N.J. : [distributed by] Anthony Roland Collection of
Films on art, c1982.
*TC TR685 .P45 1982*

**Hulse, John.** Teachable movies for elementary and
middle school classrooms / selected and compiled
John Hulse. Bloomington, Ind. : Phi Delta Kappa
Educational Foundation, c1998. 243 p. ; 23 cm.
Filmography: p. 239. ISBN 0-87367-804-4
*1. Motion pictures - Catalogs. 2. Motion pictures - Moral and*
*ethical aspects. 3. Motion pictures in education. I. Title. II.*
*Title: Movies for elementary and middle school classrooms*
*TC PN1998 .H76 1998*

**HUMAN ACTION.** *See* **HUMAN BEHAVIOR.**

**HUMAN-ALIEN CONTACTS.** *See* **HUMAN-**
**ALIEN ENCOUNTERS.**

**HUMAN-ALIEN ENCOUNTERS - JUVENILE**
**LITERATURE.**
Brooks, Philip, 1955- Invaders from outer space. 1st
American ed. New York : DK, 1999.
*TC TL789.2 .B76 1999*

**HUMAN ANATOMY.** *See* **BODY, HUMAN.**

**HUMAN ANATOMY - HISTORY - 16TH**
**CENTURY.**
Carlino, Andrea, 1960- [Fabbrica del corpo. English]
Books of the body. Chicago : University of Chicago
Press, c1999.
*TC QM33.4 .C3613 1999*

**HUMAN-ANIMAL RELATIONSHIPS.** *See*
**ANIMALS.**

**HUMAN-ANIMAL RELATIONSHIPS - JUVENILE**
**FICTION.**
Gannett, Ruth Stiles. My father's dragon. New York :
Random House, 1948.
*TC PZ7.G15 My 1948*

**HUMAN ARTIFICIAL INSEMINATION.** *See*
**ARTIFICIAL INSEMINATION, HUMAN.**

**HUMAN ASSETS.** *See* **HUMAN CAPITAL.**

**Human attachment.**
Colin, Virginia L. Philadelphia : Temple University
Press, c1996.
*TC BF575.A86 C65 1996*

**HUMAN BEHAVIOR.** *See also* **BEHAVIOR**
**MODIFICATION; HEALTH BEHAVIOR;**
**LIFESTYLES; PSYCHOLOGY,**
**COMPARATIVE; WORK.**
Perspectives on behavioral self-regulation. Mahwah,
N.J. : Lawrence Erlbaum Associates, 1999.
*TC HM291 A345 1999*

Smith, John L., 1945- The psychology of action. New
York : St. Martin's Press, 2000.
*TC BF121 .S56 2000*

Wright, Robert, 1957- The moral animal. 1st Vintage
books ed. New York : Vintage Books, 1995, c1994.
*TC GN365.9 .W75 1995*

**HUMAN BEHAVIOR - ANIMAL MODELS.**
Animal models of human emotion and cognition. 1st
ed. Washington, DC : American Psychological
Association, c1999.
*TC BF671 .A55 1999*

**HUMAN BEINGS.** *See also* **ANTHROPOLOGY;**
**ETHNOLOGY; NATURE - EFFECT OF**
**HUMAN BEINGS ON; PREHISTORIC**
**PEOPLES; WOMEN.**
Dean, Alan Ph. D. Complex life. Aldershot : Ashgate,
c2000.
*TC BD450 .D43 2000*

Mead, Margaret, 1901-1978. Male and female.
London : Victor Gollancz, c1949.
*TC HQ21 .M464 1949*

Mead, Margaret, 1901-1978. Male and female.
London : Victor Gollancz, c1949.
*TC HQ21 .M464 1949*

**HUMAN BEINGS AND ANIMALS.** *See* **HUMAN-**
**ANIMAL RELATIONSHIPS.**

**HUMAN BEINGS - ATTITUDE AND**
**MOVEMENT.** *See* **MOVEMENT**
**EDUCATION; POSTURE.**

**HUMAN BEINGS - CONSTITUTION.** *See* **BODY,**
**HUMAN; TEMPERAMENT.**

---

**HUMAN BEINGS - DISEASES.** *See* **DISEASES.**

**HUMAN BEINGS - ECOLOGY.** *See* **HUMAN**
**ECOLOGY.**

**HUMAN BEINGS - ECONOMIC VALUE.** *See*
**HUMAN CAPITAL.**

**HUMAN BEINGS - EFFECT OF ENVIRONMENT**
**ON.** *See* **HUMAN ECOLOGY.**

**HUMAN BEINGS - FOOD HABITS.** *See* **FOOD**
**HABITS.**

**HUMAN BEINGS IN ART - EXHIBITIONS.**
Modernstarts. New York : Museum of Modern Art :
Distributed by Harry N. Abrams, c1999.
*TC N620.M9 M63 1999*

**HUMAN BEINGS - INFLUENCE ON NATURE.**
*See* **NATURE - EFFECT OF HUMAN BEINGS**
**ON.**

**HUMAN BEINGS - ORIGIN.**
In search of human origins [videorecording]. [Boston,
Mass.] : WGBH Educational Foundation, c1994.
*TC GN281 .I45 1994*

**HUMAN BIOLOGY.** *See* **HUMAN ANATOMY;**
**HUMAN BEHAVIOR; MEDICINE;**
**PSYCHOLOGY.**

**HUMAN BODY.** *See* **BODY, HUMAN.**

**HUMAN CAPITAL.** *See also* **INTELLECTUAL**
**CAPITAL; LABOR SUPPLY.**
Human capital investment. Paris : Organisation for
Economic Co-operation and Development, c1998.
*TC HD4904.7 .H843 1998*

**HUMAN CAPITAL - GOVERNMENT POLICY.**
Human capital investment. Paris : Organisation for
Economic Co-operation and Development, c1998.
*TC HD4904.7 .H843 1998*

**Human capital investment :** an international
comparison / Centre for Educational Research and
Innovation. Paris : Organisation for Economic Co-
operation and Development, c1998. 113 p. : col. ill. ; 28
cm. At head of title: Centre for Educational Research and
Innovation. Includes bibliographical references. Other editions
available: L'investissement dans le capital humain : une
comparaison internationale 9264260676. ISBN 92-64-16067-1
*1. Human capital. 2. Human capital - Government policy. 3.*
*Human capital - Management. I. Centre for Educational*
*Research and Innovation. II. Title: L'investissement dans le*
*capital humain : une comparaison internationale*
*TC HD4904.7 .H843 1998*

**HUMAN CAPITAL - MANAGEMENT.**
Human capital investment. Paris : Organisation for
Economic Co-operation and Development, c1998.
*TC HD4904.7 .H843 1998*

**Human cardiovascular control.**
Rowell, Loring B. New York : Oxford University
Press, 1993.
*TC QP109 .R68 1993*

**HUMAN CHROMOSOME 21.** *See* **DOWN**
**SYNDROME.**

**HUMAN CHROMOSOME ABNORMALITIES.** *See*
**DOWN SYNDROME.**

**Human cognition and social agent technology** / edited
by Kerstin Dautenhahn. Amsterdam : Philadelphia :
John Benjamins, c2000. xxiv, 447 p. : ill. ; 22 cm.
(Advances in consciousness research, 1381-589x ; v. 19)
Includes bibliographical references and indexes. ISBN
90-272-5139-8 (Eur. : pbk. : alk. paper) ISBN 1-55619-435-8
(U.S. : pbk. : alk. paper) DDC 153
*1. Cognition. 2. Learning, Psychology of. 3. Socialization. 4.*
*Artificial intelligence. 5. Technology - Psychological aspects. I.*
*Dautenhahn, Kerstin. II. Series.*
*TC BF311 .H766 2000*

**HUMAN COMFORT.** *See also* **QUALITY OF LIFE.**
Key aspects of comfort. New York : Springer Pub.
Co., c1989.
*TC RT87.P35 K48 1989*

**HUMAN-COMPUTER INTERACTION.** *See also*
**USER INTERFACES (COMPUTER**
**SYSTEMS).**
Cyberpsychology. New York : Routledge, 1999.
*TC HM1033 .C934 1999*

Fink, Jeri. Cyberseduction. Amherst, N.Y. :
Prometheus Books, 1999.
*TC QA76.9.P75 F53 1999*

Gesture, speech, and sign. Oxford [England] ; New
York : Oxford University Press, c1999.

*TC P117 .G469 1999*
Nord, Michael B. Music in the classroom (MITC).
1998.
*TC 06 no. 10974*

**The human condition.**
Arendt, Hannah. 2nd ed. / introduction by Margaret
Canovan. Chicago : University of Chicago Press,
1998.
*TC HM211 .A7 1998*

**HUMAN CONTACTS WITH ALIENS.** *See*
**HUMAN-ALIEN ENCOUNTERS.**

**Human development theories.**
Thomas, R. Murray (Robert Murray), 1921- Thousand
Oaks : Sage Publications, c1999.
*TC HQ783 .T57 1999*

**Human differences.**
Aiken, Lewis R., 1931- Mahwah, N.J. : L. Erlbaum
Associates, 1999.
*TC BF697 .A55 1999*

**HUMAN DISSECTION - HISTORY - 16TH
CENTURY.**
Carlino, Andrea, 1960- [Fabbrica del corpo. English]
Books of the body. Chicago : University of Chicago
Press, c1999.
*TC QM33.4 .C3613 1999*

**HUMAN DONOR INSEMINATION.** *See*
**ARTIFICIAL INSEMINATION, HUMAN.**

**HUMAN ECOLOGY.** *See also* **COMMUNITY
LIFE; ECOFEMINISM; HUMAN
GEOGRAPHY; NATURE - EFFECT OF
HUMAN BEINGS ON; POPULATION;
QUALITY OF LIFE; SOCIAL
PSYCHOLOGY.**
Baskin, Yvonne. The work of nature. Washington,
D.C. : Island Press, 1997.
*TC GE195 .B36 1997*

Ehrlich, Paul R. The population explosion. New
York : Simon and Schuster, c1990.
*TC HB871 .E33 1990*

Hormones, health, and behavior. Cambridge ; New
York : Cambridge University Press, 1999.
*TC QP356.45 .H67 1999*

Gifts from the earth [videorecording]. [New York,
N.Y.?] : Unapix Entertainment, Inc. [distributor],
c1996.
*TC QB631.2 .G5 1996*

Symposium on Issues in Human Development (1967 :
Philadelphia) Issues in human development;
Washington, For sale by the Supt. of Docs., U. S.
Govt. Print. Off. [1970?]
*TC RJ131.A1 S93 1967*

**HUMAN ECOLOGY - CONGRESSES.**
Forum on Biodiversity (1997 : National Academy of
Sciences) Nature and human society. Washington,
D.C. : National Academy Press, 2000.
*TC QH541.15.B56 F685 1997*

**HUMAN ECOLOGY - JUVENILE LITERATURE.**
People and the land. New York, Noble and Noble
[1974]
*TC GN330 .P445*

**HUMAN ECOLOGY - MORAL AND ETHICAL
ASPECTS.** *See* **ENVIRONMENTAL ETHICS.**

**HUMAN ECOLOGY - RELIGIOUS ASPECTS.**
Metzner, Ralph. Green psychology. Rochester, Vt. :
Park Street Press, c1999.
*TC BF353.5.N37 M47 1999*

**HUMAN ECOLOGY - STUDY AND TEACHING.**
*See* **NATURE STUDY.**

**HUMAN ENCOUNTERS WITH ALIENS.** *See*
**HUMAN-ALIEN ENCOUNTERS.**

**HUMAN ENGINEERING.** *See also* **HUMAN-
MACHINE SYSTEMS.**
Johnson, Robert R., 1951- User-centered technology.
Albany : State University of New York Press, c1998.
*TC QA76.9.U83 J64 1998*

**HUMAN ENVIRONMENT.** *See* **HUMAN
ECOLOGY.**

**HUMAN EVOLUTION.**
Evolutionary aspects of nutrition and health. Basel ;
New York : Karger, c1999.
*TC QP141 .E95 1999*

In search of human origins [videorecording]. [Boston,
Mass.] : WGBH Educational Foundation, c1994.

*TC GN281 .I45 1994*
Jolly, Alison. Lucy's legacy. Cambridge, Mass. ;
London : Harvard University Press, 1999.
*TC GN281 .J6 1999*

Loritz, Donald, 1947- How the brain evolved
language. New York : Oxford University Press, 1999.
*TC P116 .L67 1999*

Ridley, Matt. The Red Queen :. New York : Penguin
Books, 1995.
*TC GN365.9 .R53 1995*

**Human evolution, behavior, and intelligence**
McNamara, Patrick, 1956- Mind and variability.
Westport, Conn. : Praeger, 1999.
*TC BF371 .M385 1999*

**Human exceptionality.**
Hardman, Michael L. 6th ed. Boston : Allyn and
Bacon, c1999.
*TC HV1568 .H37 1999*

**The human experience.**
Cullingford, Cedric. Aldershot ; Brookfield, Vt. :
Ashgate, c1999.
*TC BF723.E95 C84 1999*

**HUMAN EXPERIMENTATION IN
PSYCHOLOGY - DATA PROCESSING.**
Psychological experiments on the Internet. San
Diego : Academic Press, c2000.
*TC BF198.7 .P79 2000*

**HUMAN EXPERIMENTATION IN
PSYCHOLOGY - MORAL AND ETHICAL
ASPECTS.**
Protecting human subjects. 1st ed. Washington, DC :
American Psychological Association, c1999.
*TC BF181 .P65 1999*

**HUMAN FEMALES.** *See* **WOMEN.**

**HUMAN FERTILITY.** *See* **FERTILITY, HUMAN.**

**HUMAN FIGURE IN ART.** *See* **FIGURE
DRAWING.**

**Human genetics.**
McConkey, Edwin H. Boston : Jones and Bartlett
Publishers, c1993.
*TC QH431 .M3298 1993*

**HUMAN GENETICS.**
Evolutionary aspects of nutrition and health. Basel ;
New York : Karger, c1999.
*TC QP141 .E95 1999*

McConkey, Edwin H. Human genetics. Boston : Jones
and Bartlett Publishers, c1993.
*TC QH431 .M3298 1993*

**HUMAN GEOGRAPHY.** *See also* **HUMAN
ECOLOGY; HUMAN TERRITORIALITY.**
Ajmera, Maya. Children from Australia to Zimbabwe.
Watertown, Mass. : Charlesbridge, c1997.
*TC GF48 .A45 1997*

Children's geographies. London ; New York :
Routledge, 2000.
*TC HQ767.9 .C4559 2000*

**HUMAN GEOGRAPHY - JUVENILE
LITERATURE.**
Ajmera, Maya. Children from Australia to Zimbabwe.
Watertown, Mass. : Charlesbridge, c1997.
*TC GF48 .A45 1997*

**HUMAN GEOGRAPHY - PICTORIAL WORKS -
JUVENILE LITERATURE.**
Ajmera, Maya. Children from Australia to Zimbabwe.
Watertown, Mass. : Charlesbridge, c1997.
*TC GF48 .A45 1997*

**HUMAN INFORMATION PROCESSING.** *See also*
**SELECTIVITY (PSYCHOLOGY).**
Ableman, Paul. The secret of consciousness. London ;
New York : Marion Boyars, 1999.
*TC BF311 .A195 1999*

Control of human behavior, mental processes, and
consciousness. Mahwah, N.J. : Lawrence Erlbaum
Associates, c2000.
*TC BF611 .C67 2000*

Kinnamon, James C. A comparison of structural
knowledge in eighth graders and college students.
1999.
*TC 085 K6194*

Looking at looking. Thousand Oaks, Calif. ; London :
Sage Publications, c2001.
*TC BF241 .L64 2001*

Perspectives on fundamental processes in intellectual
functioning. Stamford, Conn. : Ablex Pub. Corp.,
c1998-

*TC BF444 .P42 1998*

**HUMAN INFORMATION PROCESSING IN
CHILDREN.**
Chen, Zhe, 1964- Across the great divide. Oxford :
Blackwell, 2000.
*TC LB1103 .S6 v.65 no. 2*

**HUMAN INTELLIGENCE.** *See* **INTELLECT.**

**HUMAN INTERACTION.** *See* **SOCIAL
INTERACTION.**

**Human Kinetics (Organization).**
Sammann, Patricia, 1951- Active youth. Champaign,
IL : Human Kinetics, c1998.
*TC GV443 .A27 1998*

**HUMAN LOCOMOTION.** *See also* **SWIMMING.**
Energetics of human activity. Champaign, IL : Human
Kinetics, c2000.
*TC QP301 .E568 2000*

**HUMAN LOCOMOTION - CONGRESSES.**
Peripheral and spinal mechanisms in the neural
control of movement. Amsterdam ; Oxford : Elsevier,
1999.
*TC QP376.A1 P7 1999*

**HUMAN LOCOMOTION - MATHEMATICAL
MODELS.**
Biomechanics and neural control of posture and
movement. New York : Springer, 2000.
*TC QP303 .B5684 2000*

**HUMAN-MACHINE SYSTEMS.** *See* **USER
INTERFACES (COMPUTER SYSTEMS).**

**HUMAN-MACHINE SYSTEMS - UNITED
STATES - HISTORY.**
Oldenziel, Ruth, 1958- Making technology masculine.
Amsterdam : Amsterdam University Press, c1999.
*TC HD8072 .O57 1999*

**HUMAN MECHANICS.** *See also* **HUMAN
LOCOMOTION.**
Energetics of human activity. Champaign, IL : Human
Kinetics, c2000.
*TC QP301 .E568 2000*

**HUMAN MECHANICS - MATHEMATICAL
MODELS.**
Biomechanics and neural control of posture and
movement. New York : Springer, 2000.
*TC QP303 .B5684 2000*

**Human memory.**
Jones, Janet L. The psychotherapist's guide to human
memory. New York : Basic Books, c1999.
*TC BF371 .J66 1999*

**The human mind according to artificial intelligence.**
Wagman, Morton. Westport, Conn. : Praeger, 1999.
*TC Q335 .W342 1999*

**HUMAN MOLECULAR GENETICS.**
McConkey, Edwin H. Human genetics. Boston : Jones
and Bartlett Publishers, c1993.
*TC QH431 .M3298 1993*

**HUMAN MOVEMENTS.** *See* **HUMAN
MECHANICS.**

**Human nature and the social order.**
Thorndike, Edward L. (Edward Lee), 1874-1949.
Cambridge, Mass., M.I.T. Press [1969]
*TC BF121 .T442*

**Human nutrition and obesity** / [edited by] David
Heber. Philadelphia : Current Medicine, 1999. xiii, 226
p.: ill. ; 32 cm. (Atlas of clinical endocrinology ; 5) Includes
bibliographical references and index. ISBN 0-632-04401-2
DDC 616.3/9
*1. Nutrition disorders - Atlases. 2. Obesity - Atlases. 3.
Nutrition - Atlases. 4. Nutrition - Atlases. 5. Diet - Atlases. 6.
Obesity - Atlases. I. Heber, David. II. Series.*
*TC RC620.5 .H846 1999*

**Human nutrition [videorecording].**
The nutty, nougat-filled world of human nutrition
[videorecording]. [Arlington, Va.] : Cerebellum Corp.,
c1998.
*TC QP141 .N8 1998*

**HUMAN OPERATORS (SYSTEMS
ENGINEERING).** *See* **HUMAN-MACHINE
SYSTEMS.**

**HUMAN PHYSIOLOGY.** *See also* **BODY, HUMAN;
HUMAN MECHANICS; HUMAN
REPRODUCTION.**
The nutty, nougat-filled world of human nutrition
[videorecording]. [Arlington, Va.] : Cerebellum Corp.,
c1998.

*TC QP141 .N8 1998*

**HUMAN POPULATION.** *See* **POPULATION.**

**HUMAN POPULATIONS.** *See* **POPULATION.**

**Human protein metabolism.**
Welle, Stephen. New York : Springer, c1999.
*TC QP551 .W43 1999*

**HUMAN RACE.** *See* **HUMAN BEINGS.**

**HUMAN RELATIONS.** *See* **INTERPERSONAL RELATIONS.**

**Human relations materials for the school, church & community.**
B'nai B'rith. Anti-defamation League. [New York : Anti-defamation League of B'nai B'rith, [1981?]
*TC Z7204.S67 A5 1981*

**The human relationship with nature.**
Kahn, Peter H. Cambridge, Mass. : MIT Press, c1999.
*TC BF353.5.N37 K34 1999*

**HUMAN REPRODUCTION.** *See also* **FERTILITY, HUMAN.**
Brook, Barbara, 1949- Feminist perspective on the body. New York : Longman, 1999.
*TC GT495 .B76 1999*

**HUMAN REPRODUCTION - SOCIAL ASPECTS.**
Technologies of procreation. 2nd ed. New York : Routledge, 1999.
*TC HQ761 .T43 1999*

**HUMAN REPRODUCTIVE TECHNOLOGY.** *See* **ARTIFICIAL INSEMINATION, HUMAN.**

**HUMAN RESILIENCE.** *See* **RESILIENCE (PERSONALITY TRAIT).**

**HUMAN RESOURCE DEVELOPMENT.** *See* **EDUCATION; MANPOWER POLICY.**

**The human resource function in educational administration.**
Castetter, William Benjamin, 1914- 7th ed. Upper Saddle River, N.J. : Merrill, c2000.
*TC LB2831.58 .C37 2000*

**HUMAN RESOURCE MANAGEMENT.** *See* **PERSONNEL MANAGEMENT.**

**Human resource management :** gaining a competitive advantage / Raymond A. Noe ... [et al.]. 3rd ed. Boston : Irwin/McGraw-Hill, 2000. xxxiv, 637 p. : ill. ; 26 cm. Includes bibliographical references and index. ISBN 0-07-228518-4 (alk. paper) DDC 658.3
*1. Personnel management - United States. I. Noe, Raymond A.*
*TC HF5549.2.U5 H8 2000*

**HUMAN RESOURCES.** *See* **HUMAN CAPITAL.**

**Human resources administration in education.**
Rebore, Ronald W. 6th ed. Boston ; London : Allyn and Bacon, c2001.
*TC LB2831.58 .R43 2001*

**Human Resources Center (N.Y.)** Employment of the mentally retarded in a competitive industrial setting, March 1, 1962 - February 28, 1967. Albertson, N.Y. [1967?] ix, 222 p. illus. 28 cm. Includes bibliographies. DDC 331.5/9
*1. Mentally handicapped - Employment - United States. 2. Mentally handicapped - Rehabilitation - United States. I. Title.*
*TC HV3005 .H85*

**HUMAN RIGHTS.** *See also* **CIVIL RIGHTS; WOMEN'S RIGHTS.**
Language, a right and a resource. Budapest, Hungary ; New York : Central European University Press, c1999.
*TC P119.3 .L277 1999*

Rights to language. Mahwah, N.J. : L. Erlbaum Associates, 2000.
*TC P119.3 .R54 2000*

Skutnabb-Kangas, Tove. Linguistic genocide in education, or worldwide diversity and human rights? Mahwah, N.J. : L. Erlbaum Associates, 2000.
*TC P40.8 .S58 2000*

**HUMAN RIGHTS - CONGRESSES.**
Rights, justice, and community. Lewiston, N.Y., USA : Edwin Mellen Press, c1992.
*TC HM216 .R56 1992*

**Human rights :** new dimensions and challenges / edited by Janusz Symonides. Aldershot, England ; Brookfield, VT : Ashgate/Dartmouth ; Paris : UNESCO Publishing, 1998. xiv, 318 p. ; 24 cm. ISBN 1-84014-426-2 ISBN 92-3-103582-7 (UNESCO) DDC 323
*1. Human rights - Study and teaching. I. Symonides, Janusz. II. Unesco.*
*TC JC571 .H76967 1998*

**HUMAN RIGHTS - RELIGIOUS ASPECTS - JUDAISM - HISTORY OF DOCTRINES.**
Novak, David, 1941- Covenantal rights. Princeton, N.J. : Princeton University Press, 2000.
*TC KC3 .N68 2000*

**HUMAN RIGHTS - STUDY AND TEACHING.**
Human rights. Aldershot, England : Brookfield, VT : Ashgate/Dartmouth ; Paris : UNESCO Publishing, 1998.
*TC JC571 .H76967 1998*

Spring, Joel H. The universal right to education. Mahwah, N.J. ; London : Lawrence Erlbaum Associates, 2000.
*TC LC213 .S67 2000*

**HUMAN RIGHTS - UGANDA - CASE STUDY.**
Gitta, Cosmas. International human rights. 1998.
*TC 085 G4398*

**HUMAN SCIENCES.** *See also* **SOCIAL SCIENCES.**
Høyrup, Jens. Albany, NY : State University of New York Press, c2000.
*TC AZ103 .H69 2000*

**Human Sciences Research Council.**
[Humanitas (Pretoria, South Africa)] Humanitas. [Pretoria, South African Human Sciences Research Council]

**HUMAN SERVICES.** *See* **DISASTER RELIEF; FAMILY SERVICES; PUBLIC HEALTH; PUBLIC WELFARE; SOCIAL SERVICE.**

**HUMAN SERVICES - CONTRACTING OUT - EUROPE.**
Glenn, Charles Leslie, 1938- The ambiguous embrace. Princeton, N.J. : Princeton University Press, c2000.
*TC HV95 .G54 2000*

**HUMAN SERVICES - CONTRACTING OUT - UNITED STATES.**
Glenn, Charles Leslie, 1938- The ambiguous embrace. Princeton, N.J. : Princeton University Press, c2000.
*TC HV95 .G54 2000*

**The human services counseling toolbox.**
Howatt, William A. Belmont, CA : Brooks/Cole-Wadsworth, c2000.
*TC BF637.C6 H677 2000*

**HUMAN SERVICES - GOVERNMENT POLICY - UNITED STATES.**
Kahn, Alfred J., 1919- Big cities in the welfare transition. New York City : Cross-National Studies Research Program, Columbia University School of Social Work, 1998.
*TC HV91 .K27 1998*

**HUMAN SERVICES PERSONNEL.** *See* **SOCIAL WORKERS.**

**HUMAN SERVICES PERSONNEL - PROFESSIONAL ETHICS - GREAT BRITAIN.**
Professionalism, boundaries, and the workplace. New York : Routledge, 2000.
*TC HV10.5 .P74 2000*

**HUMAN SERVICES WORKERS.** *See* **HUMAN SERVICES PERSONNEL.**

**HUMAN SETTLEMENTS.** *See* **CITIES AND TOWNS; COMMUNITY; HOUSING.**

**HUMAN SUBSYSTEMS (SYSTEMS ENGINEERING).** *See* **HUMAN-MACHINE SYSTEMS.**

**HUMAN T-LYMPHOTROPIC VIRUS III INFECTIONS.** *See* **HIV INFECTIONS.**

**HUMAN TERRITORIALITY - POLITICAL ASPECTS.**
Ethnicity and intra-state conflict. Aldershot, Hants, England : Brookfield, Vt., USA : Ashgate, c1999.
*TC GN495.6 .E83 1999*

**HUMAN TERRITORIALITY - POLITICAL ASPECTS - CONGRESSES.**
Ethnicity and intra-state conflict. Aldershot, Hants, England : Brookfield, Vt., USA : Ashgate, c1999.
*TC GN495.6 .E83 1999*

**HUMANE SOCIETIES.** *See* **CHILD WELFARE.**

**HUMANISM.** *See also* **CLASSICAL EDUCATION; CLASSICAL PHILOLOGY; HUMANITIES; LEARNING AND SCHOLARSHIP.**
Humanism and early modern philosophy. London ; New York : Routledge, 2000.
*TC B821 .H657 2000*

**Humanism and early modern philosophy** / edited by Jill Kraye and M.W.F. Stone. London ; New York : Routledge, 2000. xiii, 270 p. : ill. ; 23 cm. (London studies

in the history of philosophy) Includes bibliographical references and index. ISBN 0-415-18616-1 DDC 144
*1. Humanism. 2. Philosophy, Modern. I. Kraye, Jill. II. Stone, M. W. F. (Martin William Francis), 1965- III. Series.*
*TC B821 .H657 2000*

**HUMANISM - GREAT BRITAIN.**
Anglo-Dutch Historical Conference (13th : 1997) The education of a Christian society. Aldershot, Hants, England : Brookfield, Vt. : Ashgate, c1999.
*TC BR377 .E38 1999*

**HUMANISM - NETHERLANDS.**
Anglo-Dutch Historical Conference (13th : 1997) The education of a Christian society. Aldershot, Hants, England : Brookfield, Vt. : Ashgate, c1999.
*TC BR377 .E38 1999*

**The Humanist educator.** [Washington, American Personnel and Guidance Association] v. 23 cm. "Official publication of the Association for Humanistic Education and Development." Continues: Student Personnel Association for Teacher Education. Journal ISSN: 0036-1. ISSN 0362-9783
*1. Teachers, Training of - Periodicals. I. Association for Humanistic Education and Development. II. American Personnel and Guidance Association. III. Title: Student Personnel Association for Teacher Education. Journal*

**HUMANISTIC EDUCATION.** *See* **EDUCATION, HUMANISTIC.**

**Humanistic education sourcebook.**
Read, Donald A., comp. Englewood Cliffs, N.J. : Prentice-Hall, [1975]
*TC LC1011 .R38*

**HUMANISTIC PSYCHOLOGY.** *See* **SELF-ACTUALIZATION (PSYCHOLOGY).**

**HUMANITARIAN ASSISTANCE.**
Education as a humanitarian response. London ; Herndon, VA : Cassell ; [s.l.] : UNESCO International Bureau of Education, 1998.
*TC LC3719 .E37 1998*

**HUMANITARIANS.** *See* **PHILANTHROPISTS.**

**[Humanitas (Pretoria, South Africa)]** Humanitas. [Pretoria, South African Human Sciences Research Council]] v. 30 cm. Two no. a year. Afrikaans or English. Ceased with v. 9, no. 4. Vol. 7, no. 4 not published. Subtitle also in English. Published by the South African Human Sciences Research Council.
*1. Social sciences - Periodicals. I. Human Sciences Research Council.*

**HUMANITIES.** *See* **ARTS; CLASSICAL EDUCATION; EDUCATION, HUMANISTIC; PHILOSOPHY.**

**HUMANITIES - COMPUTER NETWORK RESOURCES - DIRECTORIES.**
Millhorn, Jim, 1953- Student's companion to the World Wide Web. Lanham, Md. ; London : Scarecrow Press, 1999.
*TC H61.95 .M55 1999*

**HUMANITIES - DATA PROCESSING.**
Information technology and scholarship. Oxford : Oxford University Press for the British Academy, c1999.
*TC AZ186 .I556 1999*

Information technology and scholarship. Oxford : Oxford University Press for the British Academy, c1999.
*TC AZ186 .I556 1999*

**HUMANITIES - HISTORY.**
Høyrup, Jens. Human sciences. Albany, NY : State University of New York Press, c2000.
*TC AZ103 .H69 2000*

**HUMANITIES - PHILOSOPHY.**
Gilman, Sander L. The fortunes of the humanities: Stanford, Calif. : Stanford University Press, c2000.
*TC AZ183.U5 G55 2000*

Høyrup, Jens. Human sciences. Albany, NY : State University of New York Press, c2000.
*TC AZ103 .H69 2000*

**HUMANITIES - RESEARCH GRANTS.**
GrantFinder. Arts and humanities. New York, NY : St. Martin's Press, 2000.
*TC LB2337.2 .G72*

**HUMANITIES - RESEARCH GRANTS - DIRECTORIES.**
GrantFinder : Arts and humanities. New York, NY : St. Martin's Press, 2000.
*TC LB2337.2 .G72*

**HUMANITIES - SCHOLARSHIPS, FELLOWSHIPS, ETC. - DIRECTORIES.**

GrantFinder : Arts and humanities. New York, NY : St. Martin's Press, 2000.
*TC LB2337.2 .G72*

**HUMANITIES - STUDY AND TEACHING (ELEMENTARY) - GREAT BRITAIN.**
Improving teaching and learning in the humanities. London : Falmer ; New York : Published in the USA and Canada by Garland, 1999.
*TC LB1564.G7 147 1999*

**HUMANITIES - STUDY AND TEACHING (HIGHER) - UNITED STATES.**
Gilman, Sander L. The fortunes of the humanities: Stanford, Calif. : Stanford University Press, c2000.
*TC AZ183.U5 G55 2000*

Nelson, Michael, 1949- Alive at the core. 1st ed. San Francisco : Jossey-Bass, c2000.
*TC AZ183.U5 N45 2000*

Roberts, Jon H. The sacred and the secular university. Princeton, N.J. : Princeton University Press, c2000.
*TC LA636.7 .R62 2000*

**HUMANITIES - STUDY AND TEACHING - UNITED STATES.**
Proctor, Robert E., 1945- Defining the humanities. 2nd ed. Bloomington : Indiana University Press, c1998.
*TC AZ221 .P75 1998*

**HUMANITY. See KINDNESS.**

**HUMANITY (HUMAN BEINGS). See HUMAN BEINGS.**

**HUMANIZATION OF WORK LIFE. See QUALITY OF WORK LIFE.**

**HUMANKIND. See HUMAN BEINGS.**

**HUMANS. See HUMAN BEINGS.**

**HUMANS IN ART. See HUMAN BEINGS IN ART.**

**Hume, Clephane.**
Penso, Dorothy E. Keyboarding skills for children with disabilities. London ; Philadelphia, Pa. : Whurr, 1999.
*TC LC4024 .P467 1999*

**Humes, Walter M.**
Scottish education. Edinburgh : Edinburgh University Press, c1999.
*TC LA652 .S34 1999*

**Humfrey, Christine, 1947-** Managing international students : recruitment to graduation / Christine Humfrey. Philadelphia, Penn : Society for Research into Higher Education & Open University Press, 1999. xx, 164 p. ; 22 cm. (Managing colleges and universities) Includes bibliographical references (p.[159]-161) and index. ISBN 0-335-20308-6 (hard) ISBN 0-335-20307-8 (pbk.) DDC 378.1/9826/91
*1. Students, Foreign - Great Britain. 2. College students - Recruiting - Great Britain. 3. International education - Great Britain. I. Title. II. Series.*
*TC LB2376.6.G7 H86 1999*

**HUMOR. See WIT AND HUMOR.**

**Humor and psyche :** psychoanalytic perspectives / edited by James W. Barron. Hillsdale, NJ : Analytic Press, c1999. xi, 232 p. : music ; 23 cm. Includes bibliographical references and index. ISBN 0-88163-257-0 DDC 152.4/3
*1. Psychoanalysis. 2. Wit and humor - Psychological aspects. I. Barron, James W., 1944-*
*TC BF175 .H85 1999*

**HUMOROUS STORIES.**
Cole, Brock. Buttons. 1st ed. New York : Farrar Straus Giroux, 2000.
*TC PZ7.C67342 Bu 2000*

Denim, Sue, 1966- Make way for Dumb Bunnies. New York : Blue Sky Press, c1996.
*TC PZ7.D4149 Mak 1996*

Fleming, Candace. When Agnes caws. 1st ed. New York : Atheneum Books for Young Readers, 1999.
*TC PZ7.F59936 Wh 1999*

Graham, Bob, 1942- Crusher is coming!. New York, N.Y., U.S.A. : Puffin Books, 1990.
*TC PZ7.G751667 Cr 1990*

Pilkey, Dav, 1966- Captain Underpants and the invasion of the incredibly naughty cafeteria ladies from outer space .... New York : Blue Sky Press, c1999.
*TC PZ7.P63123 Cat 1999*

Sachar, Louis, 1954- Sideways stories from Wayside School. New York : Morrow Junior Books, 1998.

*TC PZ7.S1185 Si 1998*

Sandburg, Carl, 1878-1967. The Huckabuck family and how they raised popcorn in Nebraska and quit and came back. 1st ed. New York : Farrar Strauss Giroux, c1999.
*TC PZ7.S1965 Hu 1999*

Viorst, Judith. Alexander, who used to be rich last Sunday. 1st ed. New York : Atheneum, 1978.
*TC PZ7.V816 Am 1978*

**Humphrey, James Harry, 1911-** Stress in college athletics : causes, consequences, coping / James H. Humphrey, Deborah A. Yow, William W. Bowden. New York : Haworth Press, c2000. xiii, 183 p. ; 23 cm. Includes bibliographical references (p. 169-176) and index. ISBN 0-7890-0934-X (hb : alk. paper) ISBN 0-7890-0935-8 (pbk. : alk. paper) DDC 796/.01
*1. College athletes - Psychology. 2. Stress (Psychology) I. Yow, Deborah A. II. Bowden, William W. III. Title.*
*TC GV347 .H86 2000*

**Humphreys, Glyn W.**
Attention, space, and action. Oxford ; New York : Oxford University Press, 1999.
*TC QP405 .A865 1999*

**HUNGARIAN AMERICANS - FICTION.**
Karr, Kathleen. Man of the family. 1st ed. New York : Farrar, Straus and Giroux, 1999.
*TC PZ7.K149 Man 1999*

**HUNGARIAN AMERICANS - JUVENILE FICTION.**
Karr, Kathleen. Man of the family. 1st ed. New York : Farrar, Straus and Giroux, 1999.
*TC PZ7.K149 Man 1999*

**HUNGARIAN AMERICANS - UNITED STATES. See HUNGARIAN AMERICANS.**

**HUNGARIANS - UNITED STATES. See HUNGARIAN AMERICANS.**

**HUNGARY - POLITICS AND GOVERNMENT - 1989-.**
Adolescent development and rapid social change. Albany : State University of New York Press, c2000.
*TC HQ799.H8 A35 2000*

**Hungler, Bernadette P.**
Polit-O'Hara, Denise. Nursing research. 6th ed. Philadelphia : Lippincott, c1999.
*TC RT81.5 .P64 1999*

**Hunt, Chris.**
Roy Lichtenstein [videorecording]. [Chicago, IL] : Home Vision ; [S.l.] : distributed worldwide by RM Asssociates, c1991.
*TC ND237.L627 R6 1991*

**Hunt, Gilbert.** Effective teaching : preparation and implementation / by Gilbert H. Hunt, Timothy J. Touzel, Dennis G. Wiseman. 3rd ed. Springfield, Ill. : C.C. Thomas Publisher, c1999. xi, 254 p. ; 26 cm. Rev. ed. of: Effective teaching / Lance E. Bedwell ... [et al.]. 2nd ed. c1991. Includes bibliographical references (p. 233-244) and index. ISBN 0-398-06995-6 (cloth) ISBN 0-398-06996-4 (pbk.) DDC 371.102
*1. Effective teaching. 2. Teachers - Psychology. 3. Teacher-student relationships. 4. Behavior modification. 5. Students - Rating of. I. Touzel, Timothy J. II. Wiseman, Dennis. III. Title.*
*TC LB1025.3 .H86 1999*

**Hunt, Gladys M.** Honey for a child's heart : the imaginative use of books in family life / Gladys Hunt. 3rd ed. Grand Rapids, Mich. : Zondervan Books, c1989. 224 p. : ill. ; 21 cm. Includes bibliographical references (p. 125-210). ISBN 0-310-26381-6 DDC 011.62
*1. Children - Books and reading. 2. Children - Religious life. I. Title.*
*TC Z1037 .H945 1989*

**Hunt, Kate, 1959-.**
Gender inequalities in health. Buckingham [England] ; Philadelphia : Open University Press, 2000.
*TC RA564.85 .G4653 2000*

**Hunt, Martin, 1936-.**
Haydn, Terry, 1951- Learning to teach history in the secondary school. London ; New York : Routledge, 1997.
*TC D16.25 .H38 1997*

**Hunt, Peter, 1945-.**
Understanding children's literature. London ; New York : Routledge, 1999.
*TC PN1009.A1 U44 1999*

**Hunt, Thomas C., 1930-.**
Catholic school leadership. London ; New York : Falmer Press, 2000.
*TC LC501 .C3484 2000*

**Hunter, Nan D.**
AIDS agenda. 1st ed. New York : New Press, c1992.
*TC RA644.A25 A33214 1992*

**Hunter, Sharonda.**
Get a grip [videorecording]. Racine, WI : S.C. Johnson and Son, Inc., 1999, c1998.
*TC TD170 .G4 1999*

**HUNTING, JOB. See JOB HUNTING.**

**HURBAN (1939-1945). See HOLOCAUST, JEWISH (1939-1945).**

**HURBN (1939-1945). See HOLOCAUST, JEWISH (1939-1945).**

**Hurd, Paul DeHart, 1905-** Transforming middle school science education / Paul DeHart Hurd ; foreword by James J. Gallagher. New York : Teachers College Press, c2000. x, 99 p. ; 24 cm. (Ways of knowing in science series) Includes bibliographical references and index. ISBN 0-8077-3923-5 (cloth : alk. paper) ISBN 0-8077-3922-7 (pbk. : alk. paper) DDC 507.1/2
*1. Science - Study and teaching (Middle School) - United States. 2. Adolescence - United States. 3. Educational change - United States. I. Title. II. Series.*
*TC LB1585.3 .H89 2000*

**Hurh, Won Moo.** The Korean Americans / Won Moo Hurh. Westport, Conn. : Greenwood Press, c1998. xvi, 190 p. : ill. ; 25 cm. (The new Americans, 1092-6364) Includes bibliographical references (P. [173]-186) and index. ISBN 0-313-29741-X (alk. paper) DDC 973/.04957
*1. Korean Americans. I. Title. II. Series: New Americans (Westport, Conn.)*
*TC E184.K6 H875 1998*

**Hurley, Sandra Rollins.**
Literacy assessment of second language learners. Boston ; London : Allyn and Bacon, c2001.
*TC P53.4 .L58 2001*

**Hurst, Alan, 1944-.**
Higher education and disabilities. Aldershot ; Brookfield, Vt. : Ashgate, c1998.
*TC LC4812 .H55 1998*

**Husband, William.** "Godless communists" : atheism and society in Soviet Russia, 1917-1932 / William B. Husband. DeKalb : Northern Illinois University Press, 2000. xvii, 241 p. ; 22 cm. Includes bibliographical references (p. [217]-233) and index. ISBN 0-87580-257-5 (alk. paper) DDC 211/.8/0947
*1. Atheism - Soviet Union - History. 2. Soviet Union - Religion. I. Title.*
*TC BL2765.S65 H87 2000*

**HUSBANDRY. See AGRICULTURE.**

**Husby, Egil, 1913-** Den høgre skolen, 1864-1964. Bernstorffskolen og Borgerskolen, 1795-1864. Utg. av Forstanderskapet for Kristiansund off. høgre almenskole. Kristiansund, 1966. 237 p. illus., ports. 26 cm. Bibliography : p. 228-231.
*1. Education, Secondary - Norway - Kristiansund. 2. Kristiansund, Norway. - Offentlige høgre allmennskole. I. Title.*

**Husén, Torsten, 1916-.**
Education [computer file]: Version 1.1. [Oxford, Eng.] : Pergamon, c1998. Computer program.
*TC LB15 .E3 1998*

**HUSSITES. See MORAVIANS.**

**Hutcheon, Pat Duffy.** Building character and culture / Pat Duffy Hutcheon. Westport, Conn. : Praeger, 1999. xvi, 286 p. ; 25 cm. Includes bibliographical references and index. "Annotated bibliography of research on the effects of media portrayals of violence and pornography on human development": p. [237]-275. ISBN 0-275-96381-0 (alk. paper) ISBN 0-275-96469-8 (pbk. : alk. paper) DDC 303.3/2
*1. Socialization. 2. Character. 3. Moral education. I. Title.*
*TC HQ783 .H88 1999*

**Hutchins, Pat, 1942-** Changes, changes. New York, Macmillan c1971. [30] p. : col. ill. ; 38 x 45 cm. SUMMARY: Two wooden dolls rearrange wooden building blocks to form various objects. ISBN 0-02-109106-4
*1. Stories without words. I. Title.*
*TC PZ8.9 .H95 1971*

Changes, changes. New York, Macmillan c1971. [30] p. : col. ill. ; 38 x 45 cm. SUMMARY: Two wooden dolls rearrange wooden building blocks to form various objects. ISBN 0-02-109106-4
*1. Stories without words. I. Title.*
*TC PZ8.9.H95 Ch 1971*

**Hutchins, Trova K     ed.**
Stein, Joan W The family as a unit of study and treatment, [Seattle] Regional Rehabilitation Research Institute, University of Washington, School of Social Work [1970]

**Hutchinson, Helene D.** Mixed bag : artifacts from the contemporary culture [by] Helene D. Hutchinson. [Glenview, Ill.] Scott, Foresman [1970] 318 p. illus. (part col.) 23 cm. Includes bibliographical references. DDC 810.8/005
*1. College readers. I. Title.*
*TC PE1122 .H85*

**Hutchinson, Jaylynne N., 1954-** Students on the margins : education, stories, dignity / Jaylynne N. Hutchinson. Albany : State University of New York Press, c1999. xvi, 166 p. ; 25 cm. (SUNY series, urban voices, urban visions) Includes bibliographical references (p. 155-160) and index. ISBN 0-7914-4165-2 (alk. paper) ISBN 0-7914-4166-0 (pbk. : alk. paper) DDC 370/.1
*1. Education - United States - Philosophy. 2. Educational change - United States. 3. Moral education - United States. 4. Students - United States. I. Title. II. Series.*
*TC LA210 .H88 1999*

**Huttenlocher, Janellen.**
Newcombe, Nora S. Making space. Cambridge, Mass. : MIT Press, 2000.
*TC BF723.S63 N49 2000*

**Hwang, Philip O.**
Organizational change & gender equity. Thousand Oaks : Sage Publications, c2000.
*TC HD58.8 .O7289 2000*

**HYDRAULIC STRUCTURES.** *See* **FOUNTAINS.**

**HYDROLOGY.** *See* **WATER.**

**Hygie.**
International journal of health education. [Geneva, Studer, 1958-1981]

**HYGIENE.** *See* **HEALTH; HYGIENE, SEXUAL; SANITATION.**

**HYGIENE - ECONOMIC ASPECTS.** *See* **MEDICAL ECONOMICS.**

**HYGIENE - FICTION.**
Cummings, Pat. Clean your room, Harvey Moon!. New York : Macmillan/McGraw-Hill School Pub. Co., c1991.
*TC PZ8.3.C898 Cl 1991*

**HYGIENE, PUBLIC.** *See* **PUBLIC HEALTH.**

**HYGIENE - PUBLIC OPINION.** *See* **HEALTH ATTITUDES.**

**HYGIENE, SEXUAL.** *See also* **BIRTH CONTROL; CONTRACEPTION; SEX INSTRUCTION; SEXUALLY TRANSMITTED DISEASES.**
Gordon, Sol, 1923- Personal issues in human sexuality. Boston : Allyn and Bacon, 1986.
*TC HQ35.2 .G67 1986*

**HYGIENE, SEXUAL - PERIODICALS.**
Journal of social hygiene. New York : American Social Hygiene Association,

**HYGIENE, SEXUAL - STUDY AND TEACHING (SECONDARY) - GREAT BRITAIN.**
Harrison, Jennifer, 1949- Sex education in secondary schools. Buckingham [England] ; Philadelphia : Open University Press, 2000.
*TC HQ57.6.G7 H37 2000*

**HYGIENE, SEXUAL - STUDY AND TEACHING - UNITED STATES - HISTORY.**
Eberwein, Robert T., 1940- Sex ed. New Brunswick, N.J. : Rutgers University Press, 1999.
*TC HQ56 .E19 1999*

**HYGIENE, SEXUAL - UNITED STATES.**
Becker, Evvie. High-risk sexual behavior. New York : Plenum Press, c1998.
*TC HQ60.7.U6 B43 1998*

**HYGIENE, SOCIAL.** *See* **HYGIENE, SEXUAL; PUBLIC HEALTH.**

**HYGIENE - STUDY AND TEACHING.** *See* **HEALTH EDUCATION.**

**Hylton, Jane, 1950-.**
Dreamings of the desert. Adelaide : The Gallery, c1996.
*TC ND1101 .D74 1996*

**Hyman, Ira E.**
Memory observed. 2nd ed. New York : Worth Publishers, c2000.
*TC BF371 .M455 2000*

**Hyman, Irwin A.** Dangerous schools : what we can do about the physical and emotional abuse of our children / Irwin A. Hyman, Pamela A. Snook. 1st ed. San Francisco : Jossey-Bass Publishers, c1999. ix, 267 p. ; 24 cm. Includes bibliographical references (p. [251]-256)

and index. CONTENTS: Physical maltreatment in the classroom -- Psychological maltreatment in the classroom -- Attacks on children's senses of justice and democracy -- Drugs, dogs and discipline : double messages in the schoolhouse -- Morality, sex, and censorship -- Toxic punishments, laws, and litigation -- Taking stand : what to do if your child is maltreated in school -- Taking action : understanding the playing field and how to make it even -- How can schools be democratic and stop maltreatment? ISBN 0-7879-4363-0 (acid-free paper) DDC 371.7/8
*1. School violence - United States. 2. School discipline - United States. 3. Students - Violence against - United States. 4. Child abuse - United States. 5. School violence - United States. 6. Discrimination in education - United States. 7. Schools - United States - Safety measures. I. Snook, Pamela A. II. Title.*
*TC LB3013 .H897 1999*

**Hyman, Jane Wegscheider.** Women living with self-injury / Jane Wegscheider Hyman. Philadelphia : Temple University Press, 1999. x, 214 p. ; 24 cm. Includes bibliographical references (p. 195-210) and index. ISBN 1-56639-720-0 (cloth : alk. paper) ISBN 1-56639-721-9 (paper : alk. paper) DDC 616.85/82/0082
*1. Self-mutilation. 2. Women - Mental health. 3. Self-injurious behavior. I. Title.*
*TC RC552.S4 H95 1999*

**Hyman, Trina Schart, ill.**
Updike, John. A child's calendar. <Rev. ed.>. New York : Holiday House, 1999.
*TC PS3571.P4 C49 1999*

**Hymel, Shelley.**
Lonliness in childhood and adolescence. New York : Cambridge University Press, 1999.
*TC BF723.L64 L64 1999*

**HYMENOPTERA.** *See* **ANTS.**

**HYPERACTIVE CHILD SYNDROME.** *See* **ATTENTION-DEFICIT HYPERACTIVITY DISORDER.**

**HYPERACTIVE CHILDREN.** *See also* **ATTENTION-DEFICIT-DISORDERED CHILDREN.**
ADHD [videorecording]. New York, NY : Guilford Publications, Inc., c1992.
*TC RJ506.H9 A3 1992*

**HYPERACTIVE CHILDREN - FAMILY RELATIONSHIPS.**
Everett, Craig A. Family therapy for ADHD. New York : Guilford Press, 1999.
*TC RJ506.H9 E94 1999*

**HYPERCARD (COMPUTER FILE).**
Feldberg, Suzanne. A comparison of different types of mathematical problem-solving hints selected by concrete and formal operational subjects in a hypercard environment. 1998.
*TC 085 F316*

**HYPERKINESIA IN CHILDREN.** *See* **ATTENTION-DEFICIT HYPERACTIVITY DISORDER.**

**HYPERKINETIC CHILDREN.** *See* **HYPERACTIVE CHILDREN.**

**HYPERKINETIC SYNDROME.** *See* **ATTENTION-DEFICIT HYPERACTIVITY DISORDER.**

**HYPERMEDIA SYSTEMS.** *See* **INTERACTIVE MULTIMEDIA.**

**HYPERSTUDIO.**
Idzal, June M. Multimedia authoring tools and teacher training. 1997.
*TC 06 no. 10816*

**Hypertext 2.0.**
Landow, George P. Rev., amplified ed. Baltimore : Johns Hopkins University Press, 1997.
*TC PN81 .L28 1997*

**HYPERTEXT SYSTEMS.** *See also* **WORLD WIDE WEB (INFORMATION RETRIEVAL SYSTEM).**
Landow, George P. Hypertext 2.0. Rev., amplified ed. Baltimore : Johns Hopkins University Press, 1997.
*TC PN81 .L28 1997*

Page to screen. London ; New York : Routledge, 1998.
*TC LC149.5 .P35 1998*

**Hypertext two point zero.**
Landow, George P. Hypertext 2.0. Rev., amplified ed. Baltimore : Johns Hopkins University Press, 1997.
*TC PN81 .L28 1997*

**HYPERTHYROIDISM - DIAGNOSIS.**
Organic disorders [videorecording]. Princeton, N.J. : Films for the Humanities & Sciences, 1998.
*TC RC521 .O7 1998*

**HYPERTHYROIDISM - PATIENTS.**
Organic disorders [videorecording]. Princeton, N.J. : Films for the Humanities & Sciences, 1998.
*TC RC521 .O7 1998*

**HYPNOANALYSIS.** *See* **HYPNOTISM - THERAPEUTIC USE.**

**HYPNOSIS.** *See* **HYPNOTISM.**

**HYPNOSIS - CONGRESSES.**
Ericksonian approaches to hypnosis and psychotherapy. New York : Brunner/Mazel, c1982.
*TC RC490.5.E75 E75*

**HYPNOTHERAPY.** *See* **HYPNOTISM - THERAPEUTIC USE.**

**HYPNOTISM.**
Feeney, Don J., 1948- Entrancing relationships. Westport, Conn. : Praeger, 1999.
*TC RC552.R44 F44 1999*

**HYPNOTISM - THERAPEUTIC USE.**
Healing from within. 1st ed. Washington, DC ; London : American Psychological Association, c2000.
*TC RC497 .H42 2000*

**HYPNOTISM - THERAPEUTIC USE - CONGRESSES.**
Ericksonian approaches to hypnosis and psychotherapy. New York : Brunner/Mazel, c1982.
*TC RC490.5.E75 E75*

**HYPNOTISM - THERAPEUTIC USE - HANDBOOKS, MANUALS, ETC.**
Gafner, George, 1947- Handbook of hypnotic inductions. New York : W. W. Norton, 2000.
*TC RC495 .G27 2000*

**HYPOMANIA - DIAGNOSIS.**
Mood disorders [videorecording]. Princeton, N.J. : Films for the Humanities & Sciences, 1998.
*TC RC537 .M6 1998*

**HYPOMANIA - PATIENTS.**
Mood disorders [videorecording]. Princeton, N.J. : Films for the Humanities & Sciences, 1998.
*TC RC537 .M6 1998*

**I can do it** : practice book. Teacher's ed. New York : Macmillan/McGraw-Hill School Publishing Co., 1994. v. : ill. ; 28 cm. (Mathematics in action.) "Contains full-sized annotated worksheets of the I can do it! Practice book. The practice book pages provide additional practice exercises to accompany the activities the children do in the Macmillan/McGraw-Hill I can! Math activity program". ISBN 0-02-109125-0 (Gr. K) ISBN 0-02-109127-7 (Gr. 1) ISBN 0-02-109129-3 (Gr. 2)
*1. Mathematics - Study and teaching (Primary) 2. Mathematics - Study and teaching - Activity programs. I. Series.*
*TC QA139 .H63 1994 Teacher's Ed.*

**I can do it** : practice book. New York : Macmillan/ McGraw-Hill School Publishing Co., 1994. v. : ill. ; 28 cm. (Mathematics in action.) "Contains worksheets that provide additional practice exercises to accompany the activities the children do in the Macmillan/McGraw-Hill I can! Math activity program". ISBN 0-02-109123-4 (Gr. K) ISBN 0-02-109128-5 (Gr. 2)
*1. Mathematics. I. Series.*
*TC QA139 .M37 1994*

**I can! Math activity program.**
Math anthology. New York : Macmillan/McGraw-Hill Pub. Co., c1993.
*TC QA141.3 .M37 1993*

Math anthology. New York : Macmillan/McGraw-Hill Pub. Co., c1993.
*TC QA141.3 .M37 1993*

**I can : math activity program . Teacher's guide.**
Hoffer, Alan R. I can! : Teacher's guide. New York : Macmillan/McGraw-Hill School Publishing Co., 1996.
*TC QA139 .H63 1996*

**I had a cat.**
Reeves, Mona Rabun. 1st American ed. New York : Bradbury Press, c1989.
*TC PZ8.3.R263 Iah 1989*

**I have an olive tree.**
Bunting, Eve, 1928- 1st ed. New York : HarperCollins Publishers, c1999.
*TC PZ7.B91527 Iaar 1999*

**I have heard of a land.**
Thomas, Joyce Carol. 1st ed. [New York] : HarperCollins Publishers, c1998.
*TC PZ7.T36696 Iae 1998*

**I hear America reading** : why we read, what we read / [compiled by] Jim Burke ; foreword by John Y. Cole. Portsmouth, NH : Heinemann, c1999. xii, 116 p. ; 23 cm. ISBN 0-325-00134-0 DDC 028/.9/0973
*1. Books and reading - United States. I. Burke, Jim, 1961-*
*TC Z1003.2 .I34 1999*

**I know how we fight germs.**
Rowan, Kate. Cambridge, Mass. : Candlewick Press, 1999.
*TC QR57 .R69 1999*

**I need a lunch box.**
Caines, Jeannette Franklin. New York : Macmillan/ McGraw-Hill, 1988.
*TC PZ7.C12 Iaan 1988*

**I once was a monkey.**
Lee, Jeanne M. 1st ed. New York : Farrar, Straus and Giroux, 1999.
*TC BQ1462.E5 L44 1999*

**I-Search, you search, we all to learn to research.**
Duncan, Donna. New York : Neal-Schuman Publishers, 2000.
*TC Z711.2 .D86 2000*

**I shop, therefore I am** : compulsive buying and the search for self / edited by April Lane Benson. Northvale, NJ : Jason Aronson, c2000. xxxvii, 528 p. ; 24 cm. Includes bibliographical references and index. ISBN 0-7657-0242-8 (alk. paper) DDC 616.85/84
*1. Compulsive shopping. I. Benson, April Lane.*
*TC RC569.5.S56 I12 2000*

**I spy treasure hunt.**
Wick, Walter. New York : Scholastic, c1999.
*TC GV1507.P47 W5296 1999*

**I-WAY (INFORMATION SUPERHIGHWAY).** *See* **INFORMATION SUPERHIGHWAY.**

**Iambic Productions (Firm).**
Roy Lichtenstein [videorecording]. [Chicago, IL] : Home Vision ; [S.l.] : distributed worldwide by RM Asssociates, c1991.
*TC ND237.L627 R6 1991*

**IATROGENIC DISEASES.** *See* **FALSE MEMORY SYNDROME.**

**Ichikawa, Satomi, ill.**
Gauch, Patricia Lee. Presenting Tanya, the Ugly Duckling. New York : Philomel Books, c1999.
*TC PZ7.G2315 Pr 1999*

Kadono, Eiko. Grandpa's soup. Grand Rapids, MI : Eerdmans Books for Young Readers, 1999.
*TC PZ7.K1167 Gr 1999*

**ICHTHYOLOGY.** *See* **FISHES.**

**ICONOGRAPHY.** *See* **ART.**

**Iconography of power.**
Bonnell, Victoria E. Berkeley : University of California Press, c1997.
*TC DK266.3 .B58 1997*

**Idaho Congress of Parents and Teachers.**
The Idaho journal of education. [Boise, Idaho, Idaho Education Association, 1930-1946]

**Idaho Education Association.**
The Idaho journal of education. [Boise, Idaho, Idaho Education Association, 1930-1946]

**Idaho journal of education.**
Idaho teacher. Boise, Idaho.

**The Idaho journal of education.** [Boise, Idaho, Idaho Education Association, 1930-1946] v. illus. 25-29 cm. Frequency: Monthly (except June-August). v.   , 1929/30-1945/46. Official Organ of the Idaho Education Association, and of the Idaho Congress of Parents and Teachers.
*1. Education - Periodicals. I. Idaho Education Association. II. Idaho Congress of Parents and Teachers.*

**Idaho State Teachers' Association.**
Idaho teacher. Boise, Idaho.

**Idaho teacher.** Boise, Idaho. v. ill. Frequency: Monthly (Sept.-June). Published 1919-Sept. 1927. Official organ of the Idaho State Teachers' Association. Continued by: Idaho journal of education.
*1. Idaho State Teachers' Association. II. Title: Idaho journal of education*

**IDDM (DISEASE).** *See* **DIABETES.**

**IDEAL BEAUTIFUL WOMEN.** *See* **FEMININE BEAUTY (AESTHETICS).**

**IDEALISM.** *See* **DUALISM.**

**IDEALS (PSYCHOLOGY).** *See* **EXAMPLE.**

**Ideas & strategies for the one-computer classroom.**
Kahn, Jessica L. Ideas and strategies for the one-computer classroom. Eugene, OR : International Society for Technology in Education, c1998.
*TC LB1028.5 .K25 1998*

**Ideas and images** : developing interpretive history exhibits / Kenneth L. Ames, Barbara Franco, and L. Thomas Frye, editors. Walnut Creek, CA : AltaMira Press, 1997. viii, 336 p. : ill., plans ; 23 cm. (American Association for State and Local History book series) Originally published: Nashville, Tenn. : American Association for State and Local History, c1992. "Published in cooperation with the American Association for State and Local History." Includes bibliographical references and index. ISBN 0-7619-8932-3 (alk. paper) DDC 973/.075
*1. Historical museums - United States. 2. Historic sites - Interpretive programs - United States. 3. United States - History, Local - Exhibitions - Handbooks, manuals, etc. I. Ames, Kenneth L. II. Franco, Barbara. III. Frye, L. Thomas. IV. American Association for State and Local History. V. Series.*
*TC E172 .I34 1997*

**Ideas and strategies for the one-computer classroom.**
Kahn, Jessica L. Eugene, OR : International Society for Technology in Education, c1998.
*TC LB1028.5 .K25 1998*

**Ideas for action.**
Active older adults. Champaign, IL : Human Kinetics, c1999.
*TC GV482.6 .A38 1999*

**IDENTITY.**
Bernstein, Basil B. Pedagogy, symbolic control, and identity. Lanham, Md. : Rowman & Littlefield, 2000.
*TC LC191 .B456 2000*

**Identity and sexuality.**
Gatter, Philip. New York : Cassell, 1999.
*TC HQ1075.5.G7 G37 1999*

**IDENTITY, COLLECTIVE.** *See* **GROUP IDENTITY.**

**IDENTITY, COMMUNITY.** *See* **GROUP IDENTITY.**

**IDENTITY - FICTION.**
Mills, Claudia. You're a brave man, Julius Zimmerman. 1st ed. New York : Farrar Straus Giroux, c1999.
*TC PZ7.M63963 Yo 1999*

Schmidt, Gary D. Anson's way. New York : Clarion Books, c1999.
*TC PZ7.S3527 An 1999*

Sheldon, Dyan. Confessions of a teenage drama queen. 1st ed. Cambridge, Mass. : Candlewick Press, 1999.
*TC PZ7.S54144 Co 1999*

Vail, Rachel. Please, please, please. New York : Scholastic, c1998.
*TC PZ7.V1916 Pl 1998*

Weeks, Sarah. Regular Guy. 1st ed. New York : Laura Geringer Book, c1999.
*TC PZ7.W42215 Rg 1999*

**IDENTITY, GROUP.** *See* **GROUP IDENTITY.**

**IDENTITY, JEWISH.** *See* **JEWS - IDENTITY.**

**IDENTITY, NATIONAL.** *See* **NATIONALISM.**

**IDENTITY (PSYCHOLOGY).** *See also* **GENDER IDENTITY; GROUP IDENTITY; PASSING (IDENTITY); STIGMA (SOCIAL PSYCHOLOGY).**
Abel, Chris. Architecture and identity. 2nd ed. Oxford ; Boston : Architectural Press, 2000.
*TC NA2500 .A392 2000*

Growing up girls. New York : P. Lang, c1999.
*TC HQ798 .G76 1999*

Hall, C. Margaret (Constance Margaret) Heroic self. Springfield, Ill. : C.C. Thomas, c1998.
*TC RC489.S62 H35 1998*

Holstein, James A. The self we live by. New York : Oxford University Press, 2000.
*TC BF697.5.S65 H65 2000*

McNamara, Patrick, 1956- Mind and variability. Westport, Conn. : Praeger, 1999.
*TC BF371 .M385 1999*

Practising identities. New York : St. Martin's Press, 1999.

*TC HM131 .P677 1999*

**IDENTITY (PSYCHOLOGY) IN ADOLESCENCE - SOCIAL ASPECTS.**
Woo, Kimberley Ann. "Double happiness," double jeopardy. 1999.
*TC 06 no. 11075*

**IDENTITY (PSYCHOLOGY) IN CHILDREN.**
Ochsner, Mindy Blaise. Something rad & risqu'e. 1999.
*TC 06 no. 11208*

**IDENTITY (PSYCHOLOGY) IN LITERATURE.**
McCallum, Robyn. Ideologies of identity in adolescent fiction. New York : Garland Pub., 1999.
*TC PN3443 .M38 1999*

**IDENTITY (PSYCHOLOGY) - POLITICAL ASPECTS - UNITED STATES.**
Critical ethnicity. Lanham, Md. : Rowman & Littlefield, c1999.
*TC LC212.2 .C75 1999*

**IDENTITY, SOCIAL.** *See* **GROUP IDENTITY.**

**IDEOLOGICAL EXTREMISM.** *See* **RADICALISM.**

**Ideologies of desire**
Stein, Edward, 1965- The mismeasure of desire. Oxford ; New York : Oxford University Press, 1999.
*TC HQ76.25 .S69 1999*

**Ideologies of identity in adolescent fiction.**
McCallum, Robyn. New York : Garland Pub., 1999.
*TC PN3443 .M38 1999*

**IDIOCY.** *See* **MENTAL RETARDATION.**

**Idol, Lorna.** Collaborative consultation / Lorna Idol, Ann Nevin, Phyllis Paolucci-Whitcomb. 3rd ed. Austin, Tex. : PRO-ED, c2000. xiii, 345 p. ; 24 cm. Includes bibliographical references (p. 295-325) and indexes. ISBN 0-89079-823-0 (alk. paper) DDC 371.91
*1. Handicapped - Education - United States. 2. Teachers of handicapped children - United States. 3. Teaching teams - United States. 4. Educational consultants - United States. 5. Mainstreaming in education - United States. I. Nevin, Ann. II. Paolucci-Whitcomb, Phyllis. III. Title.*
*TC LC4019 .I35 2000*

**IDP (DATA PROCESSING).** *See* **ELECTRONIC DATA PROCESSING.**

**Idzal, June M.** Multimedia authoring tools and teacher training : does it change instructional outlook and behavior. 1997. xiii, 258 leaves : ill. ; 29 cm. Typescript; issued also on microfilm. Includes tables. Thesis (Ed.D.)-- Teachers College, Columbia University, 1997. Includes bibliographical references (leaves 199-208).
*1. ToolBook. 2. HyperStudio. 3. Microsoft PowerPoint (Computer file) 4. Teachers - Training of - Computer-assisted instruction. 5. Multimedia systems. 6. Interactive multimedia. 7. Teaching - Aids and devices. 8. Instructional systems. 9. Internet (Computer network) in education. I. Title.*
*TC 06 no. 10816*

**IEA Preprimary Study.**
Families speak. Ypsilanti, Mich. : High/Scope Press, c1994.
*TC LB1139.23 .F36 1994*

**IEA studies in education**
(no. 7) Tooley, James. The global education industry. London : Institute of Economic Affairs ; Washington, DC : International Finance Corporation, World Bank, 1999.
*TC LC57.5 .T667 1999*

**The IEBM handbook of human resource management** / edited by Michael Poole and Malcolm Warner. 1st ed. London ; Boston : International Thomson Business Press, 1998. xviii, 974 p. : ill. ; 26 cm. (IEBM handbook series) Cover title: Handbook of human resource management. Includes bibliographical references and index. ISBN 1-86152-166-9
*1. Personnel management - Handbooks, manuals, etc. I. Poole, Michael. II. Warner, Malcolm. III. Title: Handbook of human resource management IV. Title: International encyclopedia of business and management handbook of human resource management V. Series: IEBM handbook series.*
*TC HF5549.17 .I33 1998*

**IEBM handbook series.**
The IEBM handbook of human resource management. 1st ed. London ; Boston : International Thomson Business Press, 1998.
*TC HF5549.17 .I33 1998*

**Ierley, Merritt.** Open house : a guided tour of the American home, 1637-present / Merritt Ierley. 1st ed. New York : Henry Holt and Co., 1999. xiv, 317 p. : ill. ; 25 cm. Includes bibliographical references (p. [299]-306) and index. ISBN 0-8050-4837-5 (hc : acid-free paper) DDC 728/

.0973
*1. Architecture, Domestic - United States. I. Title.*
***TC NA7205 .I35 1999***

**If...**
Perry, Sarah. Malibu, Calif. : J.P. Getty Museum ; Venice, Calif. : Children's Library Press, c1995.
***TC PZ7.P43595 If 1995***

**If I can do it, so can you.**
Bursak, George J., 1913- [S.l.] : G.J. Bursak, c1999.
***TC RC394.W6 B87 1999***

**If the owl calls again :** a collection of owl poems / selected by Myra Cohn Livingston ; woodcuts by Antonio Frasconi. 1st ed. New York : M.K. McElderry Books ; Toronto : Collier Macmillan ; New York : Maxwell Macmillan, c1990. 114 p. : ill. ; 22 cm. Includes indexes. SUMMARY: A collection of poems about owls by many different authors. ISBN 0-689-50501-9 DDC 808.81/936
*1. Owls - Juvenile poetry. 2. Owls - Poetry. 3. Poetry - Collections. I. Livingston, Myra Cohn. II. Frasconi, Antonio, ill.*
***TC PN6109.97 .I3 1990***

**If you only knew.**
Vail, Rachel. 1st ed. New York : Scholastic, c1998.
***TC PZ7.V1916 If 1998***

**If you want to lead, not just manage.**
Dunklee, Dennis R. Thousand Oaks, Calif. : Corwin Press, c2000.
***TC LB2831.92 .D85 2000***

**IFIP TC3 WG3.1/3.5 Open Conference on Communications and Networking in Education (1999 : Aulanko, Finland)** Communications and networking in education : learning in a networked society : IFIP TC3 WG3.1/3.5 Open Conference on Communications and Networking in Education, June 13-18, 1999, Aulanko, Finland / edited by Deryn Watson, Toni Downes. Boston : Kluwer Academic Publishers, 2000. xiv, 331 p. : ill. ; 24 cm. (International Federation for Information Processing ; 35) Includes bibliographical references and index. ISBN 0-7923-7760-5 DDC 371.33/4
*1. Internet in education - Congresses. 2. Computer-assisted instruction - Congresses. 3. Information technology - Congresses. I. Watson, Deryn. II. Downes, Toni. III. International Federation for Information Processing. IV. Title. V. Series: International Federation for Information Processing (Series) ; 35.*
***TC LB1044.87 .I45 2000***

**IFIP TC3 WG3.2/3.6 International Working Conference on Building University Electronic Educational Environments (1999 : Irvine, Calif.)** Building university electronic educational environments : IFIP TC3 WG3.2/3.6 International Working Conference on Building University Electronic Educational Environments, August 4-6, 1999, Irvine, California, USA / edited by Stephen D. Franklin, Ellen Strenski. Boston : Kluwer Academic Publishers, c2000. xvi, 273 p. : ill. ; 25 cm. (IFIP ; 38) Includes bibliographical references. ISBN 0-7923-7831-8 (alk. paper) DDC 378.1/75
*1. Distance education - Computer-assisted instruction - Congresses. 2. Telecommunication in higher education - Congresses. 3. Internet in education - Congresses. 4. World Wide Web - Congresses. I. Franklin, Stephen D. II. Strenski, Ellen, 1942- III. International Federation for Information Processing. IV. Title. V. Series: International Federation for Information Processing (Series) ; 38.*
***TC LC5803.C65 .I352 2000***

**IFIP TC3/WG3.3 & WG3.6 Joint Working Conference on the Virtual Campus: Trends for Higher Education and Training (1997 : Madrid, Spain)** The virtual campus : trends for higher education and training ; IFIP TC3/WG3.3 & WG3.6 Joint Working Conference on the Virtual Campus : Trends for Higher Education and Training, 27-29 November 1997, Madrid, Spain / edited by Felisa Verdejo and Gordon Davies. 1st ed. London ; New York : Chapman & Hall on behalf of the International Federation for Information Processing (IFIP), 1998. vi, 303 p. : ill. ; 24 cm. Includes bibliographical references and indexes. ISBN 0-412-83550-9 (acid-free paper)
*1. Distance education - Computer-assisted instruction - Congresses. 2. Telecommunication in higher education - Congresses. 3. Internet (Computer network) in education - Congresses. I. Verdejo, Maria Feliza. II. Davies, Gordon. III. International Federation for Information Processing. IV. Title.*
***TC LC5803.C65 I353 1997***

**IGBO ART.** *See* **ART, IGBO.**

**Igboabuchi, B. O.**
Pre-primary education in Nigeria. Onitsha [Nigeria] : Lincel, 1998.
***TC LB1140.25.N6 P74 1998***

**IGUANAS - FICTION.**
McDonald, Megan. The night Iguana left home. 1st ed. New York : DK Ink, 1999.
***TC PZ7.M478419 Ni 1999***

**IGUANIDAE.** *See* **IGUANAS.**

**Ihde, Don, 1934-** Technology and the lifeworld : from garden to earth / by Don Ihde. Bloomington : Indiana University Press, c1990. xiv, 226 p.: ill. ; 25 cm. (The Indiana series in the philosophy of technology) Includes bibliographical references. ISBN 0-253-32900-0 (alk. paper) ISBN 0-253-20560-3 (pbk. : alk. paper) DDC 601
*1. Technology - Philosophy. I. Title. II. Series.*
***TC T14 .I353 1990***

**Iheoma, E. O.** The philosophy of religious education : an introduction / Eugene O. Iheoma. Enugu, Nigeria : Fourth Dimension Pub., 1997. ix, 100 p. ; 21 cm. Includes bibliographical references (p. 93-95) and index. ISBN 978-156-440-7 DDC 268/.01
*1. Religious education - Philosophy. I. Title.*
***TC BV1464 .I44 1997***

**IIEP research report**
(96.) Ross, Kenneth N. (Kenneth Norman), 1947- Indicators of the quality of education. Paris : International Institute for Educational Planning, 1992.
***TC LA1592 .R67 1992***

**IJIR.**
[International journal of intercultural relations (Online)] International journal of intercultural relations [computer file]. Oxford ; New York : Pergamon,
***TC EJOURNALS***

**Ikeda, Keiko.** A room full of mirrors : high school reunions in middle America / Keiko Ikeda. Stanford, Calif. : Stanford University Press; 1998. x, 205 p. : ill. ; 23 cm. Includes bibliographical references (p. [185]-197) and index. ISBN 0-8047-3435-6 (alk. paper) DDC 371.8/9
*1. Class reunions - United States. 2. High schools - United States. I. Title.*
***TC LB3618 .I54 1998***

**Ikels, Charlotte.** The return of the god of wealth : the transition to a market economy in urban China / Charlotte Ikels. Stanford, Calif. : Stanford University Press, c1996. viii, 311 p. : ill., maps ; 24 cm. Includes bibliographical references (p. [297]-304) and index. ISBN 0-8047-2580-2 (alk. paper) ISBN 0-8047-2581-0 (pbk. : alk. paper)
*1. Guangzhou (China) - Economic policy. 2. Guangzhou (China) - Economic conditions. 3. Mixed economy - China - Guangzhou. I. Title. II. Title: Transition to a market economy in urban China*
***TC HC428.C34 I38 1996***

**Ilan pasin** = This is our way : Torres Strait art / exhibition curator, Tom Mosby : research and development, Brian Robinson. Queensland : Cairns Regional Gallery, [1998?]. 151 p. : col. ill., map ; 31 cm. "Published in conjunction with an exhibition organised by Cairns Regional Gallery"--T.p. verso. Includes bibliographical references. ISBN 0-9586858-4-3
*1. Art, Australian - Australia - Torres Strait Islands (Qld.) - Exhibitions. 2. Art, Modern - 20th century - Australia - Torres Strait Islands (Qld.) - Exhibitions. 3. Torres Strait Islanders - Social life and customs - Exhibitions. I. Mosby, Tom, 1969- II. Cairns Regional Gallery. III. Title: This is our way IV. Title: Torres Strait art*
***TC DU125.T67 I53 1998***

**Illegal.**
Anastos, Phillip. New York : Rizzoli, 1991.
***TC F392.R5 A53 1991***

**ILLEGAL ALIENS - TEXAS - LOWER RIO GRANDE VALLEY - PICTORIAL WORKS.**
Anastos, Phillip. Illegal. New York : Rizzoli, 1991.
***TC F392.R5 A53 1991***

**Illinois Education Association.**
Illinois education; Mount Morris, Ill. [etc.]

Illinois education; Mount Morris, Ill. [etc.]

The Illinois teacher: Peoria, Ill., Nason.

**Illinois education;** official publication, Illinois education association. Mount Morris, Ill. [etc.] v. illus., ports. 22-29 cm. Frequency: Monthly (except June-Aug.) v. 27- . Former frequency: Monthly (except July-Aug.) v. -26. Former frequency: Monthly vols. 1- . v. 1- Apr. 1913- . Title varies: Illinois teacher Apr. 1913-May 1940. Title varies: Illinois education Sept. 1940- . Vols. 1-25, 1913-1936 issued under the earlier name of the association: Illinois state teachers' association.
*1. Education - Periodicals. 2. Education - Illinois. I. Illinois Education Association. II. Illinois Education Association.*

**Illinois educational press bulletin.**
Illinois journal of education. [Springfield, Ill.] : Superintendent of Public Instruction, 1961-

**Illinois journal of education.** [Springfield, Ill.] : Superintendent of Public Instruction, 1961- v. : ill. ; 23 cm. Frequency: Monthly (except Jan., Apr., June-Aug.). Vol. 52, no. 4 (Sept. 1961)- = whole no. 499- . Title from cover. Continues: Illinois educational press bulletin (DLC)sn 88029286.
*1. Education - Periodicals. 2. Education - Illinois - Periodicals. I. Illinois. Office of the Superintendent of Public Instruction. II. Title: Illinois educational press bulletin*

**Illinois. Office of the Superintendent of Public Instruction.**
Illinois journal of education. [Springfield, Ill.] : Superintendent of Public Instruction, 1961-

**Illinois school journal.**
Chicago schools journal. Chicago, Board of Education.

**Illinois school journal :** a monthly magazine for teachers and school officers. Normal, Ill. : [s.n.], 1881/82-1889. 8 v. : ill. ; 26 cm. Vol. 1, [no. 1] (May 1881)-v. 8, no. 10 (June 1889) = -whole no. 94. Subtitle varies: Devoted to the theory and art of school teaching. Imprint varies: Bloomington, Ill., Geo. P. Brown. Continues in part: Educational news-gleaner. Continued by: Public-school journal.
*1. Title: Educational news-gleaner II. Title: Public-school journal*

**Illinois schools journal.** Chicago, Ill. : Illinois State Teachers College Chicago-South, 1967- v. ; 24 cm. Frequency: Semi-annual, <1993->. Former frequency: Quarterly, spring 1967-v. 67, no. 2 (1987). Vol. 47, no. 1 (spring 1967)- . Title from cover. Indexed selectively by: Current index to journals in education 0011-3565. Indexed selectively by: Sociological abstracts 0038-0202. Indexed by: Current contents education. Issued also on microfilm by University Microfilms International. Vols. for fall 1967-summer 1971 published by the Chicago State College; fall 1971- by the Chicago State University. Continues: Chicago schools journal (DLC) 4631967 (OCoLC)1554185. ISSN 0019-2236 DDC 370
*1. Education - Illinois - Chicago - Periodicals. 2. Education - Illinois - Periodicals. I. Illinois Teachers College Chicago South. II. Chicago State College. III. Chicago State University. IV. Title: Chicago schools journal*

**The Illinois teacher:** devoted to education, science and free schools. Peoria, Ill., Nason. 18 v. ill. 22 cm. v. 1-18; Feb. 1855-Dec. 1872. Subtitle varies. Vol. 1, no. 11 (Dec. 1855) incorrectly numbered v. 1, no. 10; v. 2 consists of 11 numbers; v. 5 incorrectly numbered v. 4 on t.p. SUMMARY: Vols. 1, 3-15, 17-18 contain Proceedings of the 1st-5th, 17th-18th annual meetings of the Illinois state teachers' association, 1854-1871. Vol. 1 published by Merriman & Morris, Bloomington, Ill. v. 1-4 (1855-1858), organ of the State teachers' association.
*1. Education - Periodicals. 2. Education - Illinois. I. Illinois Education Association.*

**Illinois Teachers College Chicago South.**
Illinois schools journal. Chicago, Ill. : Illinois State Teachers College Chicago-South, 1967-

**ILLINOIS. UNIVERSITY. INSTITUTE FOR RESEARCH ON EXCEPTIONAL CHILDREN.**
Kirk, Samuel Alexander, 1904- 10 years of research at the Institute for Research on Exceptional Children, University of Illinois, 1952-1962. [Urbana : s.n.], 1964.
***TC HQ773.7 .I4 1964***

**ILLITERACY.** *See* **LITERACY.**

**ILLNESS.** *See* **DISEASES.**

**ILLNESSES.** *See* **DISEASES.**

**Illocutionary acts and sentence meaning.**
Alston, William P. Ithaca : Cornell University Press, 2000.
***TC P95.55 .A47 2000***

**ILLOCUTIONARY ACTS (LINGUISTICS).** *See* **SPEECH ACTS (LINGUISTICS).**

**ILLUMINATI.** *See* **ENLIGHTENMENT.**

**ILLUMINATION OF BOOKS AND MANUSCRIPTS, MEDIEVAL.**
Kendrick, Laura. Animating the letter. Columbus, Ohio : Ohio State University Press, c1999.
***TC NK3610 .K46 1999***

**Illusions of equality.**
Buchanan, Robert (Robert M.) Washington, D.C. : Gallaudet University Press, 1999.
***TC HV2530 .B83 1999***

**Illusions of immortality.**
Giles, David, 1964- Houndmills [England] :
Macmillan Press : New York : St. Martin's Press,
2000.
*TC BJ1470.5 .G55 2000*

**ILLUSTRATED BOOKS.** *See* **ILLUSTRATED CHILDREN'S BOOKS.**

**ILLUSTRATED BOOKS, CHILDREN'S.** *See* **ILLUSTRATED CHILDREN'S BOOKS.**

**ILLUSTRATED CHILDREN'S BOOKS.** *See* **PICTURE BOOKS FOR CHILDREN; TOY AND MOVABLE BOOKS.**

**ILLUSTRATED CHILDREN'S BOOKS - JUVENILE LITERATURE.**
Wings of an artist. New York : Harry N. Abrams,
1999.
*TC NC965 .W56 1999*

**ILLUSTRATED CHILDREN'S BOOKS - UNITED STATES - EXHIBITIONS.**
Myth, magic and mystery. Boulder, Colo. : Roberts
Rinehart Publishers ; [Norfolk, Va.] : in cooperation
with the Chrysler Museum of Art, c1996.
*TC NC975 .M98 1996*

**Illustrated dictionary of speech-language pathology.**
Singh, Sadanand. San Diego : Singular Pub. Group,
c2000.
*TC RC423 .S533 2000*

**An illustrated history of American psychology.**
Popplestone, John A. 2nd ed. Akron, Ohio : The
University of Akron Press, c1999.
*TC BF108.U5 P67 1999*

**An illustrated history of the housewife, 1650-1950.**
Robertson, Una A. New York : St. Martin's Press,
1997.
*TC HD8039.H842 G77 1997*

**ILLUSTRATION OF BOOKS.** *See* **DRAWING.**

**ILLUSTRATION OF BOOKS - 20TH CENTURY - JUVENILE LITERATURE.**
Wings of an artist. New York : Harry N. Abrams,
1999.
*TC NC965 .W56 1999*

**ILLUSTRATION OF BOOKS - 20TH CENTURY - UNITED STATES -        EXHIBITIONS.**
Myth, magic and mystery. Boulder, Colo. : Roberts
Rinehart Publishers ; [Norfolk, Va.] : in cooperation
with the Chrysler Museum of Art, c1996.
*TC NC975 .M98 1996*

**ILLUSTRATORS.**
De Paola, Tomie. 26 Fairmount Avenue. New York :
G.P. Putnam's Sons, c1999.
*TC PS3554.E11474 Z473 1999*

Morrison, Taylor. Civil War artist. Boston : Houghton
Mifflin, 1999.
*TC E468.9 .M86 1999*

Wings of an artist. New York : Harry N. Abrams,
1999.
*TC NC965 .W56 1999*

**ILLUSTRATORS - JUVENILE LITERATURE.**
Wings of an artist. New York : Harry N. Abrams,
1999.
*TC NC965 .W56 1999*

**ILLUSTRATORS - LEGAL STATUS, LAWS, ETC. - UNITED STATES.**
Crawford, Tad, 1946- Business and legal forms for
illustrators. Rev. ed. New York : Allworth Press,
c1998.
*TC KF390.A7 C7 1998*

**ILLUSTRATORS - UNITED STATES - BIOGRAPHY - JUVENILE LITERATURE.**
Talking with artists. Volume three :. 1st ed. New
York : Clarion Books, c1999.
*TC NC961.6 .T35 1999*

Talking with artists. Volume two :. 1st ed. New York :
Simon & Schuster Books for Young Readers, c1995.
*TC NC975 .T34 1995*

**ILLUSTRATORS - UNITED STATES - HISTORY - 19TH CENTURY - JUVENILE LITERATURE.**
Morrison, Taylor. Civil War artist. Boston : Houghton
Mifflin, 1999.
*TC E468.9 .M86 1999*

**ILLUSTRATORS - UNITED STATES - STUDY AND TEACHING (ELEMENTARY).**
Walmsley, Bonnie Brown. Teaching with favorite
Marc Brown books. New York : Scholastic
Professional Books, c1998.

*TC LB1576 .W258 1998*

**ILLUSTRIOUS PEOPLE.** *See* **CELEBRITIES.**

**I'm chocolate, you're vanilla.**
Wright, Marguerite A. 1st paperback ed. San
Francisco : Jossey-Bass, 2000.
*TC BF723.R3 W75 2000*

**IMAGE, BODY.** *See* **BODY IMAGE.**

**Image grammar.**
Noden, Harry R. Portsmouth, NH : Heinemann, 1999.
*TC LB1631 .N62 1999*

**IMAGE PROCESSING.** *See also* **PICTURE ARCHIVING AND COMMUNICATION SYSTEMS.**
Looking at looking. Thousand Oaks, Calif. ; London :
Sage Publications, c2001.
*TC BF241 .L64 2001*

**IMAGE PROCESSING - CONGRESSES.**
MLDM'99 (1999 : Leipzig, Germany) Machine
learning and data mining in pattern recognition.
Berlin ; New York : Springer, c1999.
*TC Q327 .M56 1999*

**IMAGE PROCESSING - DIGITAL TECHNIQUES.**
Brinkman, Ronald. The art and science of digital
compositing. San Diego : Morgan Kaufmann ;
Academic Press, 1999.
*TC T385 .B75 1999*

Kenney, Anne R., 1950- Moving theory into practice.
Mountain View, CA : Research Libraries Group,
2000.
*TC Z681.3.D53 K37*

**Image - the journal of nursing scholarship.**
Journal of nursing scholarship. Indianapolis, IN : JNS
Publication Office, 2000-
*TC RT1 .142*

**IMAGERY, MENTAL.** *See* **IMAGERY (PSYCHOLOGY); IMAGINATION.**

**Imagery of identity in South African education, 1880-1990.**
Cross, Michael. Durham, N.C. : Carolina Academic
Press, c1999.
*TC LA1539 .C76 1999*

**IMAGERY (PSYCHOLOGY).** *See also* **ARCHETYPE (PSYCHOLOGY); BODY IMAGE.**
Forrester, Michael A. Psychology of the image.
London ; Philadelphia : Routledge, 2000.
*TC BF367 .F675 2000*

Tsamasiros, Katherine V. Using interactive
multimedia software to improve cognition of complex
imagery in adolescents. 1998.
*TC 06 no. 10905*

**IMAGERY (PSYCHOLOGY) IN ART.**
Podro, Michael. Depiction. New Haven, CT : Yale
University Press, c1998.
*TC N71 .P64 1998*

**IMAGERY (PSYCHOLOGY) IN CHILDREN - SEX DIFFERENCES.**
Tuman, Donna M. Gender difference in form and
content. 1998.
*TC 06 no. 11000*

**IMAGES, MENTAL.** *See* **IMAGERY (PSYCHOLOGY); IMAGINATION.**

**Images of Asia**
Phim, Toni Samantha, 1957- Dance in Cambodia.
[Kuala Lampur] Malaysia ; Oxford ; New York :
Oxford University Press, 1999.
*TC GV1703.C3 P55 1999*

**Images of educational change** / edited by Herbert
Altrichter and John Elliott. Buckingham [England] ;
Philadelphia : Open University Press, 2000. x, 229 p. :
ill. ; 24 cm. Includes bibliographical references and index.
ISBN 0-335-20188-1 (pb.) ISBN 0-335-20189-X (hb.) DDC
371.2
*1. Educational change. 2. School management and
organization. 3. Education - Social aspects. 1. Altrichter,
Herbert. II. Elliott, John, Dip. Phil. Ed.*
*TC LB2805 .1415 2000*

**Images of me.**
Pack-Brown, Sherlon P. Boston : Allyn and Bacon,
c1998.
*TC HV1445 .P33 1998*

**IMAGINATION.** *See* **CREATION (LITERARY, ARTISTIC, ETC.); IMAGERY (PSYCHOLOGY).**

**IMAGINATION - FICTION.**
Delton, Judy. Angel spreads her wings. Boston :
Houghton Mifflin, 1999.
*TC PZ7.D388 Anf 1999*

Falwell, Cathryn. Word wizard. New York : Clarion
Books, c1998.
*TC PZ7.F198 Wo 1998*

Perry, Sarah. If.... Malibu, Calif. : J.P. Getty
Museum ; Venice, Calif. : Children's Library Press,
c1995.
*TC PZ7.P43595 If 1995*

**IMAGINATION IN CHILDREN.**
Harris, Paul. L. The work of the imagination. Oxford :
Blackwell Publishers, 2000.
*TC BF723.I5 H37a 2000*

**Imaging sound.**
Wade, Bonnie C. Chicago : University of Chicago
Press, c1998.
*TC ML338 .W318 1998*

**Imagining home.**
Webster, Wendy. London ; Bristol, Pa. : UCL Press,
1998.
*TC HQ1593 .W43 1998*

**IMBECILITY.** *See* **MENTALLY HANDICAPPED.**

**Imber, Michael.** Education law / Michael Imber and
Tyll van Geel. 2nd ed. Mahwah, N.J. : Lawrence
Erlbaum Associates, 2000. xx, 520 p. ; 26 cm. Includes
index. ISBN 0-8058-3277-7 (cloth : alk. paper) DDC 344.73/
07
*1. Educational law and legislation - United States - Cases. 2.
School management and organization - Law and legislation -
United States - Cases. I. Van Geel, Tyll. II. Title.*
*TC KF4118 .143 2000*

**Imel, Susan.**
Addressing the spiritual dimensions of adult
learning :. San Francisco : Jossey Bass, 2000.
*TC LC5219 .A25 2000*

**IMITATION.** *See also* **EXAMPLE.**
Bitz, Michael Eric. A description and investigation of
strategies for teaching classroom music improvisation.
1998.
*TC 06 no. 11012*

**Immaterial facts.**
Caper, Robert. London ; New York : Routledge, 2000.
*TC BF173 .C35 2000*

**Immigrant mothers.**
Irving, Katrina. Urbana : University of Illinois Press,
c2000.
*TC HQ1419 .175 2000*

**IMMIGRANT TEENAGERS.** *See* **TEENAGE IMMIGRANTS.**

**Immigrant women's health :** problems and solutions /
Elizabeth J. Kramer, Susan L. Ivey, and Yu-Wen
Ying, editors. 1st ed. San Francisco : Jossey-Bass,
c1999. xxiv, 438 p. ; 24 cm. Includes bibliographical
references (p. 343-395) and indexes. ISBN 0-7879-4294-4
(cloth : acid-free paper) DDC 613/.04244/08691
*1. Women immigrants - Health and hygiene - United States. 1.
Kramer, Elizabeth Jane. II. Ivey, Susan L. III. Ying, Yu-Wen.*
*TC RA448.5.144 144 1999*

**IMMIGRANTS.** *See also* **CHILDREN OF IMMIGRANTS; TEENAGE IMMIGRANTS; WOMEN IMMIGRANTS.**
The Irish in America [videorecording]. [New York,
N.Y.] : A&E Home Video ; New York, N.Y. :
Distributed by the New Video Group, 1997.
*TC E184.16 16 1997*

**IMMIGRANTS' CHILDREN.** *See* **CHILDREN OF IMMIGRANTS.**

**Immigrants' experience [picture].**
Ellis Island [picture]. Amawalk, NY : Jackdaw
Publications, c1997.
*TC TR820.5 .E4 1997*

**IMMIGRANTS - FICTION.**
Michelson, Richard. Grandpa's gamble. New York :
Marshall Cavendish, 1999.
*TC PZ7.M581915 Gr 1999*

Ó Flatharta, Antoine. The prairie train. New York :
Crown Publishers, 1997.
*TC PZ7.O331275 Pr 1997*

**IMMIGRANTS IN LITERATURE - HISTORY.**
Irving, Katrina. Immigrant mothers. Urbana :
University of Illinois Press, c2000.
*TC HQ1419 .175 2000*

**IMMIGRANTS - LEGAL STATUS, LAWS, ETC.**
*See* **EMIGRATION AND IMMIGRATION LAW.**

**IMMIGRANTS - SOCIAL CONDITIONS.**
The challenge of diversity. Aldershot, England ; Brookfield, Vt. : Avebury, 1996.
*TC JV225 .C530 1996*

**IMMIGRANTS - UNITED STATES - HISTORY - POSTERS.**
Ellis Island [picture]. Amawalk, NY : Jackdaw Publications, c1997.
*TC TR820.5 .E4 1997*

**IMMIGRANTS - UNITED STATES - PROBLEMS, EXERCISES, ETC.**
New immigrants in the United States. Cambridge, U.K. : New York : Cambridge University Press, 2000.
*TC PE1128 .N384 1999*

**IMMIGRATION.** *See* **EMIGRATION AND IMMIGRATION.**

**Immigration and refugee policy.**
National Legal Conference on Immigration and Refugee Policy (6th : 1983 : Washington, D.C.) 1st ed. New York : Center for Migration Studies, 1984.
*TC KF4819.A2 N375 1983*

**IMMIGRATION LAW.** *See* **EMIGRATION AND IMMIGRATION LAW.**

**IMMUNE SYSTEM - POPULAR WORKS.**
Kendall, Marion D. Dying to live. Cambridge ; New York : Cambridge University Press, c1998.
*TC QR181.7 .K46 1998*

**IMMUNITY.**
Mackinnon, Laurel T., 1953- Advances in exercise immunology. Champaign, IL : Human Kinetics, c1999.
*TC QP301 .M159 1999*

Nutrition and immunology. Totowa, N.J. : Humana Press, c2000.
*TC QP141 .N7767 2000*

**IMMUNITY - JUVENILE LITERATURE.**
Rowan, Kate. I know how we fight germs. Cambridge, Mass. : Candlewick Press, 1999.
*TC QR57 .R69 1999*

**IMMUNITY - NUTRITIONAL ASPECTS.**
Nutrition and immunology. Totowa, N.J. : Humana Press, c2000.
*TC QP141 .N7767 2000*

**IMMUNOLOGIC DISEASES IN CHILDREN.** *See* **AIDS (DISEASE) IN CHILDREN.**

**IMMUNOLOGICAL DEFICIENCY SYNDROMES.** *See* **AIDS (DISEASE).**

**IMMUNOLOGICAL SYSTEM.** *See* **IMMUNE SYSTEM.**

**IMMUNOLOGY.** *See* **IMMUNE SYSTEM; IMMUNITY.**

**Impact of block scheduling on instructional effectiveness.**
Campbell, Delois. High school students' perceptions of the impact of block scheduling on instructional effectiveness. 1999.
*TC 06 no. 11089*

**The impact of gay identity and perceived milieu toward gay employees on job involvement and organizational commitment of gay men.**
Rogers, Richard Randall. 1998.
*TC 085 R635*

**The impact of secondary school testing.**
The Use of standardized ability tests in American secondary schools and their impact on students, teachers, and administrators New York] Russell Sage Foundation [1965]
*TC LB3051 .R914*

**IMPAIRMENT, SOCIOLOGY OF.** *See* **SOCIOLOGY OF DISABILITY.**

**IMPENNES.** *See* **PENGUINS.**

**Imperfect equality.**
Fuke, Richard Paul, 1940- New York : Fordham University Press, 1999.
*TC E185.93.M2 F85 1999*

**IMPERIALISM.** *See* **COLONIES; DECOLONIZATION; MILITARISM.**

**IMPERIALISM IN LITERATURE.**
Kutzer, M. Daphne. Empire's children. New York : Garland Pub., 2000.
*TC PR830.I54 K88 2000*

**IMPERIALISM - SOCIAL ASPECTS - GREAT BRITAIN - HISTORY - 20TH CENTURY.**
Bush, Julia. Edwardian ladies and imperial power. London ; New York : Leicester University Press, 2000.
*TC DA16 .B87 2000*

**Implementation.**
Pankake, Anita M., 1947- Larchmont, NY : Eye on Education, c1998.
*TC LB2805 .P32 1998*

**The implementation of multicultural curricula in the New York City public elementary schools.**
Thompson, Melvin R. 1999.
*TC 06 no. 11186*

**Implementing computer supported cooperative learning.**
McConnell, David, 1951- 2nd ed. London : Kogan Page, 2000.
*TC LB1032 .M38 2000*

**Implementing standards-based mathematics instruction :** a casebook for professional development / Mary Kay Stein ... [et al.] ; foreword by Deborah Loewenberg Ball. New York : Teachers College Press, c2000. xv, 146 p. : ill. ; 23 cm. (Ways of knowing in science series) Includes bibliographical references (p. 137-139) and index. ISBN 0-8077-3908-1 (cloth) ISBN 0-8077-3907-3 (pbk.) DDC 510/.71/2
*1. Mathematics - Study and teaching (Middle school) - Case studies. I. Stein, Mary Kay. II. Series.*
*TC QA135.5 .I525 2000*

**Implementing technology in higher education.**
Becker, Nancy Jane. 1999.
*TC 06 no. 11082*

**The importance of shape and weight in normal-weight women with bulimia nervosa, restrained eaters (dieters), and normal controls (Non-dieters).**
Goldfein, Juli Ann. 1997.
*TC 085 G5675*

**Importing diversity.**
McConnell, David L., 1959- Berkeley : University of California Press, c2000.
*TC LB2285.J3 M33 2000*

**IMPOVERISHED PEOPLE.** *See* **POOR.**

**Impressionism.**
Art in the making, Impressionism. London : National Gallery, in association with Yale University Press, c1991.
*TC ND547.5.I4 I4472 1991*

**IMPRESSIONISM (ART) - EXHIBITIONS.**
Cassatt, Mary, 1844-1926. Mary Cassatt, modern woman. 1st ed. New York : Art Institute of Chicago in association with H.N. Abrams, c1998.
*TC N6537.C35 A4 1998*

**IMPRESSIONISM (ART) - FRANCE.**
Adams, Steven. The Barbizon school & the origins of impressionism. 1st ed. London : Phaidon, c1994.
*TC N6847.5.B3 A28 1994*

Impressionism [videorecording]. [London] : The National Gallery ; Tillingham, Peasmarsh, East Sussex, England : Ho-Ho-Kus, NJ : Distributed by The Roland Collection, c1990.
*TC ND547.5.I4 A7 1990*

**IMPRESSIONISM (ART) - FRANCE - EXHIBITIONS.**
Art in the making, Impressionism. London : National Gallery, in association with Yale University Press, c1991.
*TC ND547.5.I4 I4472 1991*

The New painting. San Francisco, CA : Fine Arts Museums of San Francisco, c1996.
*TC ND547.5.I4 N38 1996*

Tinterow, Gary. Origins of impressionism. New York : Metropolitan Museum of Art : Distributed by H.N. Abrams, c1994.
*TC ND547.5.I4 L6913 1994*

**IMPRESSIONISM (ART) - TECHNIQUE.**
Art in the making, Impressionism. London : National Gallery, in association with Yale University Press, c1991.
*TC ND547.5.I4 I4472 1991*

**IMPRESSIONISM (ART) - UNITED STATES.**
Mary Cassatt [videorecording]. [Chicago, Ill.]: Home Vision, c1977.
*TC ND237.C3 M37 1977*

**Impressionism** [videorecording] / written and presented by James Heard ; produced by Jacquie Footer ... [et al.]. [London] : The National Gallery ; Tillingham,

Peasmarsh, East Sussex, England : Ho-Ho-Kus, NJ : Distributed by The Roland Collection, c1990. 1 videocassette (22 min.) : sd., col. ; 22 cm. (Art in the making) Title on cassette label: Art in the making [videorecording] : impressionisn. At head of title: Anthony Roland Collection of Films on Art. VHS. Catalogued from credits, cassette label and container. Presenter: James Heard. Music by Poulenc performed by Maria Hayward. "Sponsored by Esso UK." For high school and adult audiences. SUMMARY: A documentary film which discusses the traditional education of the Impressionist artists and their work outside of the annual French salon. This leads to a discussion of the artists' materials and the introduction of new artificial pigments which changed the palette and color theory. Includes examples of work by Claude Monet, Camille Pissarro, and Auguste Renoir. Discusses the philosophy of painting from nature while seeking to capture the transitory.
*1. Impressionism (Art) - France. 2. Painting, Modern - 19th century - France. 3. Renoir, Auguste. - 1841-1919. 4. Monet, Claude. - 1840-1926. 5. Pissarro, Camille. - 1830-1903. 6. Documentary films. I. Heard, James. II. Footer, Jacquie. III. National Gallery (Great Britain) IV. Anthony Roland Collection of Film on Art. V. Title: Art in the making [videorecording] : impressionism VI. Title: Anthony Roland Collection of Films on Art VII. Series.*
*TC ND547.5.I4 A7 1990*

**Impressionist from Philadelphia [videorecording].**
Mary Cassatt [videorecording]. [Chicago, Ill.]: Home Vision, c1977.
*TC ND237.C3 M37 1977*

**The Impressionists**
Seurat [videorecording]. West Long Branch, NJ : Kultur, c1999.
*TC ND553.S5 S5 1999*

**IMPRISONMENT ALTERNATIVES.** *See* **ALTERNATIVES TO IMPRISONMENT.**

**Improve your riding skills.**
Henderson, Carolyn. 1st American ed. New York, N.Y. : DK Pub., 1999.
*TC SF309.2 .H46 1999*

**Improved test scores, attitudes, and behaviors in America's schools :** supervisors' success stories / edited by Rita Dunn and Thomas C. DeBello. Westport, Conn. : Bergin & Garvey, 1999. xiv, 228 p. : ill. ; 25 cm. Includes bibliographical references and index. ISBN 0-89789-687-4 (alk. paper) DDC 371.2/00973
*1. School supervision - United States - Case studies. 2. School supervisors - United States - Case studies. 3. Individualized instruction - United States - Case studies. 4. Academic achievement - United States - Case studies. 5. Educational change - United States - Case studies. I. Dunn, Rita Stafford, 1930- II. DeBello, Thomas C.*
*TC LB2806.4 .I56 1999*

**IMPROVEMENT PROGRAMS, SCHOOL.** *See* **SCHOOL IMPROVEMENT PROGRAMS.**

**Improving children's learning.**
Dean, Joan. London ; New York : Routledge, 2000.
*TC LB1725.G6 D43 2000*

**Improving classroom questions.**
Chuska, Kenneth R. Bloomington, Ind. : Phi Delta Kappa Educational Foundation, 1995.
*TC LB1027.44 .C58 1995*

**Improving college and university teaching.**
[Corvallis : Graduate School, Oregon State College, v. : ill. ; 27 cm. Frequency: Quarterly. -v. 32, no. 4 (fall 1984). Began with: Vol. 1, no. 1 (Feb. 1953). Description based on: Vol. 6, no. 1 (winter 1958); title from contents t.p. Indexed by: Biological abstracts. Indexed in its entirety by: Education index 0013-1385. Indexed selectively by: Current index to journals in education 0011-3565. Issued by: Graduate School, Oregon State College, Feb. 1953-winter 1961; Graduate School, Oregon State University, spring 1961-autumn 1977; Helen Dwight Reid Educational Foundation, winter 1978- Published: Washington, D.C. : Heldref Publications, winter 1978- Vols. 1 (1953)-10 (1962), 1 v. Continued by: College teaching ISSN: 8756-7555 (DLC) 85642200 (OCoLC)11658781. ISSN 0019-3089
*1. College teaching - Periodicals. I. Oregon State College. Graduate School. II. Oregon State University. Graduate School. III. Helen Dwight Reid Educational Foundation. IV. Title: College teaching*

**Improving college and university teaching yearbook.**
Corvallis, Ore., Oregon State University Press. v. 28 cm. 1975- . ISSN 0363-2598 DDC 378.1/2
*1. College teaching - Yearbooks.*

**Improving education :** realist approaches to method and research / edited by Joanna Swann and John Pratt. London ; New York : Cassell, 1999. xii, 196 p. ; 24 cm. (Cassell education) Includes bibliographical references (p. [181]-191) and index. ISBN 0-304-70553-5 ISBN 0-304-70554-3 (pbk.) DDC 370/.7/2

*1. Education - Research - Case studies. 2. Education - Case studies. 3. Popper, Karl Raimund, - Sir, - 1902- 4. Education - Philosophy. 5. Educational change - Case studies. I. Swann, Joanna. II. Pratt, John, 1945- III. Title. IV. Series.*
***TC LB7 .148 1999***

**Improving human performance.** Washington, National Society for Performance and Instruction [etc.] 3 v. ill. 23 cm. Frequency: Quarterly, <fall 1974>. Former frequency: Monthly. v. 1-3, no. 3; Mar. 1972-fall 1974. Vols. 1-2 issued by the National Society for Programmed Instruction; v. 3 by the National Society for Performance and Instruction. With: National Society for Programmed Instruction. NSPI newsletter, supersedes: National Society for Programmed Instruction. NSPI journal. Continued by: Improving human performance quarterly (DLC)sc 78000082 ISSN: 0146-3756 (OCoLC)2921859. DDC 371.3/9442/05
*1. Performance - Periodicals. 2. Programmed instruction - Periodicals. I. National Society for Programmed Instruction. II. National Society for Performance and Instruction. III. Title: National Society for Programmed Instruction. NSPI journal IV. Title: Improving human performance quarterly*

**Improving human performance quarterly.**
Improving human performance. Washington, National Society for Performance and Instruction [etc.]

**Improving literacy in the primary school** / E.C. Wragg ... [et al.]. London ; New York : Routledge, 1998. xi, 290 p. ; 24 cm. Includes bibliographical references (p. 277-284) and index. ISBN 0-415-17287-X (hbk. : alk. paper) ISBN 0-415-17288-8 (pbk. : alk. paper) DDC 372.4/0941
*1. Reading (Elementary) - Great Britain. 2. Educational surveys - Great Britain. 3. Literacy - Great Britain. I. Wragg, E. C. (Edward Conrad)*
***TC LB1573 .I56 1998***

**Improving parental involvement.**
Hornby, Garry. London : Cassell, 2000.
***TC LC225 .H67 2000***

**Improving quality in education.**
Hoy, Charles, 1939- London ; New York : Falmer Press, 2000.
***TC LB2822.84.G7 H69 1999***

**Improving schools and governing bodies.**
Creese, Michael. London ; New York : Routledge, 1999.
***TC LB2822.84.G7 C75 1999***

**Improving schools :** performance and potential / John Gray ... [et al.]. Buckingham [England] ; Philadelphia : Open University Press, 1999. viii, 168 p. : ill. ; 23 cm. Includes bibliographical references (p. [153]-160) and indexes. ISBN 0-335-20399-X (hbk.) ISBN 0-335-20398-1 (pbk.) DDC 371.2/00941
*1. School improvement programs - Great Britain - Case studies. 2. Academic achievement - Great Britain - Case studies. 3. School management and organization - Great Britain - Case studies. 4. Educational change - Great Britain - Case studies. I. Gray, John (John Michael), 1948-*
***TC LB2822.84.G7 I68 1999***

**Improving student learning :** a strategic plan for education research and its utilization / Committee on a Feasibility Study for a Strategic Education Research Program, Commission on Behavioral and Social Sciences and Education, National Research Council. Washington, D.C. : National Academy Press, c1999. x, 76 p. ; 26 cm. Includes bibliographical references (p. 67-76). ISBN 0-309-06489-9 (pbk.) DDC 370/.7/20973
*1. Education - Research - United States. 2. School improvement programs - United States. I. National Research Council (U.S.). Committee on a Feasibility Study for a Strategic Education Research Program.*
***TC LB1028.25.U6 I66 1999***

**Improving teaching and learning in the core curriculum** / edited by Kate Ashcroft and John Lee. London ; New York : Falmer Press, 2000. ix, 180 p. : ill. ; 25 cm. (Looking afresh at the primary curriculum series) Includes bibliographical references and index. ISBN 0-7507-0813-1 (pbk. : alk. paper) DDC 372.19/0941
*1. Education, Elementary - Great Britain - Curricula. 2. Curriculum planning - Great Britain. I. Ashcroft, Kate. II. Lee, John, 1944- III. Series.*
***TC LB1564.G7 I475 2000***

**Improving teaching and learning in the humanities** / edited by Martin Ashley. London : Falmer ; New York : Published in the USA and Canada by Garland, 1999. xi, 234 p. ; 25 cm. (Looking afresh at the primary curriculum series) Includes bibliographical references and index. ISBN 0-7507-0801-8
*1. Humanities - Study and teaching (Elementary) - Great Britain. 2. Moral education (Elementary) - Great Britain. I. Ashley, Martin. II. Title. III. Series.*
***TC LB1564.G7 I47 1999***

**Improving test performance of students with disabilities - on district and state assessments.**
Elliott, Judy L. Thousands Oaks, Calif. : Corwin Press, c2000.
***TC LB3051 .E48 2000***

**IMPROVISATION (MUSIC).**
Bitz, Michael Eric. A description and investigation of strategies for teaching classroom music improvisation. 1998.
***TC 06 no. 11012***

**IMPULSE.** *See* **COMPULSIVE BEHAVIOR.**

**In a dark wood.**
Cadnum, Michael. New York : Orchard Books, c1998.
***TC PZ7.C11724 In 1998***

**in a series**
(v. 1) Creativity in the classroom. Burbank, CA : Disney Learning Partnership, c1999.
***TC LB1062 .C7 1999***

**In all probability.**
Cuomo, Celia, 1956- Berkeley, CA : Lawrence Hall of Science, University of California, Berkeley, c1998.
***TC QA276.18 .C866 1998***

**In defense of good teaching :** what teachers need to know about the "reading wars" / edited by Kenneth S. Goodman. York, Me. : Stenhouse Publishers, c1998. iv, 195 p. ; 23 cm. Includes bibliographical references. ISBN 1-57110-086-5 (alk. paper) DDC 372.4
*1. Reading - United States - Language experience approach. 2. Politics and education - United States. 3. Reading - United States - Language experience approach - Religious aspects. 4. Education and state - United States. I. Goodman, Kenneth S. II. Title: What teachers need to know about the "reading wars"*
***TC LB1050.35 .I5 1998***

**In defense of the alien**
(v. 6.) National Legal Conference on Immigration and Refugee Policy (6th : 1983 : Washington, D.C.) Immigration and refugee policy. 1st ed. New York : Center for Migration Studies, 1984.
***TC KF4819.A2 N375 1983***

**In glory's shadow.**
Manegold, Catherine S. 1st ed. New York : Alfred A. Knopf, 1999.
***TC KF228.C53 M36 1999***

**In good hands.**
McLeod, Ellen Mary Easton, 1945- Montreal ; Ithaca : Published for Carleton University by McGill-Queen's University Press, c1999.
***TC NK841 .M38 1999***

**IN-LINE DATA PROCESSING.** *See* **ONLINE DATA PROCESSING.**

**In Plato's cave.**
Kernan, Alvin B. New Haven : Yale University Press, c1999.
***TC LA227.4 .K468 1999***

**In relief.**
National Gallery of Victoria. Melbourne : National Gallery of Victoria, c1997.
***TC NE1190.25 .G72 1997***

**In search of human origins** [videorecording] / with Don Johanson ; a Nova production by Green Umbrella Ltd. and the WGBH Science Unit in association with the Institute of Human Origins ... [et al.] ; presented by Don Johanson ; series producer, Peter Jones. [Boston, Mass.] : WGBH Educational Foundation, c1994. 3 videocassettes (180 min.) : sd., col. ; 1/2 in. VHS. Catalogued from credits for Episode 1 and containers. Host: Don Johanson. Editor, Dick Bartlett ; camera, Richard Ganniclifft, Brian McDairmant ; original music by Ray Loring. Originally broadcast on the PBS television series, Nova. Accompanying book: Ancestors : in search of human origins / Don Johanson, Lenora Johanson. SUMMARY: For general audiences. Controversial fossil hunter Don Johanson involves the viewer in his quest to unravel the mystery of human origin. Episode 1 tells the story of Lucy, the almost 3 million year old fossil and our oldest human ancestor. The discovery of Lucy stunned the world of paleoanthropolgy by showing that what separated man from the ape was walking upright and not a larger brain as previously supposed. In Episode 2, Johanson disproves the theory that man's larger brain and reliance on technology are by-products of the ability to hunt. Instead he sets out to find food in a journey across the Serengeti savanna of East Africa by scavenging off the leftovers of predators--lions and leopards-- not by hunting, thus proving cunning and intelligence were needed to steal a meal without becoming one. In Episode 3, Johanson sets out to solve the mystery of the sudden transformation of hunter-gatherers fifty thousand generations ago, to beings who began to paint, carve, talk, travel, trade, and bury their dead-- a topic of many heated debates some explain away as mass genocide by a group of superior human beings. CONTENTS: Episode 1. The story of Lucy / written and produced by Michael Gunton (60 min.) -- Episode 2. Surviving in Africa / written and produced by Lenora Carey Johanson (60 min.) -- Episode 3. The creative revolution / written and produced by Lauren Seeley Aguirre (60 min.).
*1. Prehistoric peoples. 2. Human beings - Origin. 3. Human evolution. 4. Documentary television programs. I. Johanson, Donald C. hst II. Gunton, Michael. III. Johanson, Lenora. IV. Aguirre, Lauren Seeley. V. Jones, Peter, 1929- VI. Johanson, Donald C. Ancestors : in search of human origins. VII. Johanson, Lenora. Ancestors : in search of human origins. VIII. Green Umbrella Ltd. IX. WGBH (Television station : Boston, Mass.). Science Unit. X. Institute of Human Origins. XI. Title: Nova (Television program) XII. Title: Story of Lucy. XIII. Title: Surviving in Africa. XIV. Title: Creative revolution.*
***TC GN281 .I45 1994***

**IN-SERVICE TRAINING.** *See* **EMPLOYEES - TRAINING OF.**

**In the lap of tigers.**
Cleverley, John F. Lanham, Md. ; Oxford : Rowman & Littlefield, c2000.
***TC S539.C6 C64 2000***

**In the long run--longitudinal studies of psychopathology in children** / formulated by the Committee on Child Psychiatry, Group for the Advancement of Psychiatry. Washington, DC : American Psychiatric Press, c1999. 183 p. ; 23 cm. (Report ; no. 143) Includes bibliographical references and index. ISBN 0-87318-211-1 (alk. paper) DDC 618.92/89
*1. Child psychopathology - Longitudinal studies. 2. Mentally ill children - Longitudinal studies. 3. Mental Disorders - in infancy & childhood. 4. Longitudinal Studies - in infancy & childhood. I. Group for the Advancement of Psychiatry. Committee on Child Psychiatry. II. Series: Report (Group for the Advancement of Psychiatry : 1984) ; no. 143.*
***TC RC321 .G7 no. 143***

**In the New England fashion.**
Kelly, Catherine E. Ithaca, N.Y. : Cornell University Press, 1999.
***TC HQ1438.N35 K45 1999***

**In the vineyard.**
Hall, Perry A., 1947- 1st ed. Knoxville : University of Tennessee Press, c1999.
***TC E184.7 .H24 1999***

**Inayatullah, Sohail, 1958-.**
The university in transformation. Westport, Conn. ; London : Bergin & Garvey, 2000.
***TC LB2324 .U56 2000***

**Inc.**
The Inc. [Los Angeles, CA : Inc. Publishing,

The Inc. [Los Angeles, CA : Inc. Publishing,

**The Inc.** [Los Angeles, CA : Inc. Publishing, v. : ill. ; 28 cm. The International Council of Nurses. Special issue, included in the numbering, of: Inc. Supplement to: Inc.
*1. Nursing I. Title: Inc. II. Title: The International Council of Nurses III. Title: Inc.*

**INCAPACITY, ESTIMATION OF.** *See* **DISABILITY EVALUATION.**

**The incarnate ground of Christian faith.**
Martin, Robert K., 1959- Lanham, Md. : University Press of America, c1998.
***TC BV1464 .M37 1998***

**INCENTIVE (PSYCHOLOGY).** *See* **REWARDS AND PUNISHMENTS IN EDUCATION.**

**INCENTIVES IN EDUCATION.** *See* **REWARDS AND PUNISHMENTS IN EDUCATION.**

**INCEST IN LITERATURE.**
Daly, Brenda O., 1941- Authoring a life. Albany, NY : State University of New York Press, c1998.
***TC RC560.I53 D35 1998***

**INCEST - UNITED STATES - PSYCHOLOGICAL ASPECTS.**
Juvenile sex offenders [videorecording]. Princeton, N.J. : Films of the Humanities & Sciences, c1998.
***TC HV9067.S48 J8 1998***

**INCEST VICTIMS - MENTAL HEALTH.**
Woodruff, Debra, 1967- General family functioning, parental bonding, and attachment style. 1998.
***TC 085 W858***

**INCEST VICTIMS - REHABILITATION.**
Daly, Brenda O., 1941- Authoring a life. Albany, NY : State University of New York Press, c1998.
***TC RC560.I53 D35 1998***

**Inch, Dennis.**
Keefe, Laurence E. The life of a photograph. 2nd ed. Boston : Focal Press, c1990.

**TC TR465 .K44 1990**

**Incidents in the life of a slave girl : written by herself.**
Jacobs, Harriet A. (Harriet Ann), 1813-1897.
Cambridge, Mass. : Harvard University Press, 2000.
**TC E444.J17 A3 2000c**

**Includes bibliographical references and index.**
Guillot, Marie-Noëlle, 1955- Fluency and its teaching.
Clevedon, England ; Philadelphia, Pa. : Multilingual
Matters, c1999.
**TC P53.6 .G85 1999**

**Including families of children with special needs : a**
how-to-do-it manual for librarians / Sandra
Feinberg ... [et al.]. New York : Neal Schuman
Publishers, c1999. x, 208 p. ; 28 cm. (How-to-do-it manuals
for librarians ; no. 88) Includes bibliographical references (p.
[175]-183) and index. ISBN 1-55570-339-9
*1. Libraries and handicapped children - United States. 2.*
*Libraries - Services to families - United States. 3. Libraries -*
*Services to preschool children - United States. I. Feinberg,*
*Sandra, 1946- II. Series: How-to-do-it manuals for libraries ;*
*no. 88.*
**TC Z711.92.H3 I6 1999**

**Inclusion 101.**
Bauer, Anne M. Baltimore, Md. : P.H. Brookes Pub.,
c1999.
**TC LC1201 .B38 1999**

**INCLUSION (EDUCATION).** *See* **INCLUSIVE**
**EDUCATION.**

**Inclusion one hundred and one.**
Bauer, Anne M. Inclusion 101. Baltimore, Md. : P.H.
Brookes Pub., c1999.
**TC LC1201 .B38 1999**

**Inclusion one hundred one.**
Bauer, Anne M. Inclusion 101. Baltimore, Md. : P.H.
Brookes Pub., c1999.
**TC LC1201 .B38 1999**

**Inclusion practices with special needs students :**
theory, research, and application / Steven I. Pfeiffer,
Linda A. Reddy, editors. New York : Haworth Press,
c1999. 210 p. ; 22 cm. "Co-published simultaneously as
Special services in the schools, volume 15, numbers 1/2 1999."
Includes bibliographical references and index. ISBN
0-7890-0843-2 (alk. paper) ISBN 0-7890-0954-4 (alk. paper)
DDC 371.9/046
*1. Inclusive education - United States. 2. Mainstreaming in*
*education - United States. I. Pfeiffer, Steven I. II. Reddy, Linda*
*A.*
**TC LC1201 .I538 1999**

**INCLUSIVE EDUCATION.** *See*
**MAINSTREAMING IN EDUCATION.**

**Inclusive education :** a casebook and readings for
prospective and practicing teachers / edited by
Suzanne E. Wade. Mahwah, N.J. : L. Erlbaum
Associates, c2000. xv, 223 p. ; 24 cm. "A companion
volume--Preparing teachers for inclusive education : case
pedagogies and curricula for teacher educators--is available to
accompany this book"--Pref. Includes bibliographical
references and indexes. ISBN 0-8058-2508-8 (pbk. : alk.
paper) DDC 371.9/046
*1. Inclusive education - United States - Case studies. 2.*
*Handicapped children - Education - United States - Case*
*studies. 3. Teachers of handicapped children - United States -*
*Case studies. I. Wade, Suzanne E.*
**TC LC1201 .I527 2000**

**Inclusive education at work :** students with disabilities
in mainstream schools. Paris : Organisation for
Economic Co-operation and Development, 1999. 375
p. : ill. ; 23 cm. At head of title: Centre for Educational
Research and Innovation. Includes bibliographical references.
ISBN 92-64-17121-5
*1. Mainstreaming in education - Case studies. 2. Handicapped*
*children - Education - Case studies. 3. Education and state -*
*Case studies. I. Organisation for Economic Co-operation and*
*Development. II. Centre for Educational Research and*
*Innovation.*
**TC LC4015 .I525 1999**

**INCLUSIVE EDUCATION - CASE STUDIES.**
Janney, Rachel. Behavorial support. Baltimore, Md. ;
London : Paul H. Brookes Pub., c2000.
**TC LB1060.2 .J26 2000**

**INCLUSIVE EDUCATION - CROSS-CULTURAL**
**STUDIES.**
Inclusive education. London ; Philadelphia : Falmer
Press, 1999.
**TC LC1200 .I53 1999**

**Inclusive education for the 21st century.**
Sands, Deanna J. Belmont, CA : Wadsworth/Thomson
Learning, 2000.

**TC LC1201 .S27 2000**

**Inclusive education for the twenty-first century.**
Sands, Deanna J. Inclusive education for the 21st
century. Belmont, CA : Wadsworth/Thomson
Learning, 2000.
**TC LC1201 .S27 2000**

**INCLUSIVE EDUCATION - GREAT BRITAIN.**
Special education re-formed. London ; New York :
Falmer Press, 2000.
**TC LC1203.G7 S72 1999**

**INCLUSIVE EDUCATION - GREAT BRITAIN -**
**CASE STUDIES.**
Moore, Alex, 1947- Teaching multicultured students.
London ; New York : Falmer Press, 1999.
**TC LC3736.G6 M66 1999**

**Inclusive education :** international voices on disability
and justice / edited by Keith Ballard. London ;
Philadelphia : Falmer Press, 1999. ix, 189 p. ; 25 cm.
(Studies in inclusive education series) Includes bibliographical
references and index. ISBN 0-7507-0935-9 (cased : alk. paper)
ISBN 0-7507-0934-0 (pbk : alk. paper) DDC 371.9/046
*1. Inclusive education - Cross-cultural studies. 2.*
*Mainstreaming in education - Cross-cultural studies. 3.*
*Handicapped children - Education - Cross-cultural studies. I.*
*Ballard, Keith. II. Series: Studies in inclusive education series*
**TC LC1200 .I53 1999**

**INCLUSIVE EDUCATION - MARYLAND.**
Sean's story [videorecording]. Princeton, N.J. : Films
for the Humanities & Sciences ; [S.l. : distributed by]
ABC Multimedia : Capital Cities/ABC, c1994.
**TC LC1203.M3 .S39 1994**

**INCLUSIVE EDUCATION - SOCIAL ASPECTS -**
**GREAT BRITAIN.**
Mittler, Peter J. Working towards inclusive education.
London : D. Fulton Publishers, 2000.
**TC LC1203.G7 M58 2000**

**INCLUSIVE EDUCATION - STUDY AND**
**TEACHING - UNITED STATES -**
**CURRICULA.**
Preparing teachers for inclusive education. Mahwah,
N.J. : L. Erlbaum Associates, 2000.
**TC LC1201 .P74 2000**

**INCLUSIVE EDUCATION - UNITED STATES.**
Alper, Sandra K. Alternate assessment of students
with disabilities in inclusive settings. Boston ;
London : Allyn and Bacon, c2001.
**TC LC4031 .A58 2001**

Bauer, Anne M. Inclusion 101. Baltimore, Md. : P.H.
Brookes Pub., c1999.
**TC LC1201 .B38 1999**

Capper, Colleen A., 1960- Meeting the needs of
students of all abilities. Thousand Oaks, Calif. :
Corwin Press, c2000.
**TC LC1201 .C36 2000**

Collaboration for inclusive education. Boston :
London : Allyn and Bacon, c2000.
**TC LC1201 .C63 1999**

Eisenberger, Joanne, 1942- Self efficacy. Larchmont,
N.Y. : Eye On Education, c2000.
**TC LC4705 .C67 2000**

Inclusion practices with special needs students. New
York : Haworth Press, c1999.
**TC LC1201 .I538 1999**

Lewis, Rena B. Teaching special students in general
education classrooms. 5th ed. Upper Saddle River,
N.J. : Merrill, c1999.
**TC LC1201 .L48 1999**

McGregor, Gail Inclusive schooling practices. [S.l.] :
Allegheny University of Health Sciences ; Balitmore :
Distributed exclusively by Paul H. Brookes
Publishing, c1998.
**TC LC4031 .M394 1998**

Rathvon, Natalie. Effective school interventions. New
York : Guilford Press, c1999.
**TC LC1201 .R38 1999**

Sands, Deanna J. Inclusive education for the 21st
century. Belmont, CA : Wadsworth/Thomson
Learning, 2000.
**TC LC1201 .S27 2000**

Snell, Martha E. Collaborative teaming. Baltimore :
Paul H. Brookes Pub., c2000.
**TC LC1201 .S64 2000**

Snell, Martha E. Social relationships and peer support.
Baltimore, Md. ; London : Paul H. Brookes Pub. Co.,
c2000.

**TC LC4069 .S54 2000**

Successful inclusive teaching. 3rd ed. Boston : Allyn
and Bacon, c2000.
**TC LC1201 .S93 2000**

Taylor, George R. Curriculum models and strategies
for educating individuals with disabilities in inclusive
classrooms. Springfield, Ill. : C.C. Thomas, Publisher,
c1999.
**TC LC4031 .T33 1999**

Teaching transformed. Boulder, Colo. ; Oxford :
Westview Press, 2000.
**TC LB2822.82 .T44 2000**

Turner, Nancy D'Isa. Children's literature for the
primary inclusive classroom. Albany, N.Y. : Delmar
Publishers, c2000.
**TC LC4028 .T87 2000**

Vaughn, Sharon, 1952- Teaching exceptional, diverse,
and at-risk students in the general education
classroom. 2nd ed. Boston : Allyn and Bacon, 2000.
**TC LC3981 .V28 2000**

**INCLUSIVE EDUCATION - UNITED STATES -**
**CASE STUDIES.**
Inclusive education. Mahwah, N.J. : L. Erlbaum
Associates, c2000.
**TC LC1201 .I527 2000**

Preparing teachers for inclusive education. Mahwah,
N.J. : L. Erlbaum Associates, 2000.
**TC LC1201 .P74 2000**

**INCLUSIVE EDUCATION - UNITED STATES -**
**HANDBOOKS, MANUALS, ETC.**
Kochhar, Carol. Successful inclusion. 2nd ed. Upper
Saddle River, NJ : Prentice Hall, c2000.
**TC LC1201 .K63 2000**

**INCLUSIVE EDUCATION - UNITED STATES -**
**PLANNING.**
Janney, Rachel. Modifying schoolwork. Baltimore,
Md. : Paul H. Brookes Pub., c2000.
**TC LC1201 .J26 2000**

**Inclusive schooling practices.**
McGregor, Gail [S.l.] : Allegheny University of
Health Sciences : Baltimore : Distributed exclusively
by Paul H. Brookes Publishing, c1998.
**TC LC4031 .M394 1998**

**Inclusive schools, inclusive society.**
Richardson, Robin. Stoke on Trent, Staffordshire,
England : Trentham Books, 1999.
**TC LC212.3.G7 R523 1999**

**INCLUSIVE SCHOOLS MOVEMENT.** *See*
**INCLUSIVE EDUCATION.**

**INCOME DISTRIBUTION - DEVELOPING**
**COUNTRIES.**
The paradox of plenty. Oakland, Calif. : Food First
Books, c1999.
**TC HD1542 .P37 1999**

**INCOME DISTRIBUTION - UNITED STATES.**
Stanback, Thomas M. Cities in transition. Totowa,
N.J. : Allanheld, Osmun, 1982.
**TC HD5724 .S649 1982**

**INCOME DISTRIBUTION - UNITED STATES -**
**STATISTICS.**
The society and population health reader. Volume I.
New York, N.Y. : The New Press, c1999.
**TC RA418 .S6726 1999**

**Income inequality and health.**
The society and population health reader. Volume I.
New York, N.Y. : The New Press, c1999.
**TC RA418 .S6726 1999**

**INCOME MAINTENANCE PROGRAMS.** *See*
**SOCIAL SECURITY.**

**Incorporating women.**
Kwolek-Folland, Angel. New York : Twayne
Publishers, 1998.
**TC HD6095 .K85 1998**

**INCULTURATION (CHRISTIAN THEOLOGY).**
*See* **CHRISTIANITY AND CULTURE.**

**INCUNABULA.** *See* **PRINTING - HISTORY.**

**Indangasi, Henry.**
American studies in eastern Africa. Nairobi : Nairobi
University Press, 1993.
**TC E172.9 .A47 1993**

**INDENTURED SERVANTS - FICTION.**
Curry, Jane Louise. A Stolen life. New York :
McElderry Books, 1999.
**TC PZ7.C936 St 1999**

**INDEPENDENCE (PSYCHOLOGY).** *See* AUTONOMY (PSYCHOLOGY).

**Independent education.** New York [etc.] : Craft Publication Company [etc.], 1927-1929. 3 v. : ill. ; 30 cm. Frequency: Monthly (except July and Aug.) Sept.-Dec. 1929. Former frequency: Monthly (Oct.-June) Oct. 1927-June 1929. Vol. 1, no. 1 (Oct. 1927)-v. 3, no. 4 (Dec. 1929). Subtitle varies.
*1. Education - Periodicals.*

**Independent learning among clergy.**
Zersen, David John. 1998.
*TC 06 no. 11008*

**Independent projects, step by step.**
Wee, Patricia Hachten, 1948- Lanham, MD : Scarecrow Press, c2000.
*TC LB1620 .W42 2000*

**Independent scholar in 20th century America.**
Bornet, Vaughn Davis, 1917- An independent scholar in twentieth century America. Talent, Or. : Bornet Books, 1995.
*TC H59.B63 A3 1995*

**An independent scholar in twentieth century America.**
Bornet, Vaughn Davis, 1917- Talent, Or. : Bornet Books, 1995.
*TC H59.B63 A3 1995*

**INDEPENDENT SCHOOLS.** *See* **PRIVATE SCHOOLS.**

**Independent studies in political economy**
Vedder, Richard K. Out of work. New York : Holmes & Meier, 1993.
*TC HD7096.U5 V43 1993*

**INDEPENDENT STUDY.** *See also* **OPEN LEARNING.**
Anderson, Dennis S. Mathematics and distance education on the internet. 1999.
*TC 085 An2317*

Bell, Judith, 1930- Doing your research project. 3rd ed. Buckingham [England] ; Philadelphia : Open University Press, 1999.
*TC LB1028 .B394 1999*

Rafoth, Mary Ann. Inspiring independent learning. Washington, DC : National Education Association of the United States, 1999.
*TC LB1049 .R35 1999*

Zersen, David John. Independent learning among clergy. 1998.
*TC 06 no. 11008*

**INDEPENDENT STUDY - UNITED STATES.**
Eisenberger, Joanne, 1942- Self efficacy. Larchmont, N.Y. : Eye On Education, c2000.
*TC LC4705 .C67 2000*

Kent, Richard Burt. Beyond room 109. Portsmouth, NH : Heinemann, 2000.
*TC LB1049 .K45 2000*

**INDEPENDENT STUDY - UNITED STATES - HANDBOOKS, MANUALS, ETC.**
Wee, Patricia Hachten, 1948- Independent projects, step by step. Lanham, MD : Scarecrow Press, c2000.
*TC LB1620 .W42 2000*

**INDEXES.** *See* PERIODICALS - INDEXES.

**INDEXES, HEALTH STATUS.** *See* HEALTH STATUS INDICATORS.

**INDEXICALITY (SEMANTICS).** *See* INDEXICALS (SEMANTICS).

**INDEXICALS (SEMANTICS).**
Hanks, William F. Intertexts. Lanham : Rowman & Littlefield Publishers, Inc., c2000.
*TC P35.5.M6 H36 2000*

**INDIA - ECONOMIC CONDITIONS.**
Ford, Richard B., 1935- Tradition and change in four societies; New York, Holt, Rinehart and Winston, 1968.
*TC HT1521 .F6 1968*

**India International Centre.**
Open learning system. New Delhi : Lancer International, c1989.
*TC LC5808.I4 O64 1989*

**INDIA - POLITICS AND GOVERNMENT - 1857-1919.**
Hasan, Mushirul. Legacy of a Divided Nation. Boulder, Colo. : WestviewPress, c1997.
*TC DS479 .L36 1997*

**INDIA - POLITICS AND GOVERNMENT - 1919-1947.**
Hasan, Mushirul. Legacy of a Divided Nation. Boulder, Colo. : WestviewPress, c1997.
*TC DS479 .L36 1997*

**INDIA - SCHEDULED TRIBES - EDUCATION.**
Kinjaram, Ramaiah. Educational performance of scheduled castes. New Delhi : APH Pub. Corp., [1998?]
*TC LC4097.I4 K55 1998*

**INDIA - SOCIAL LIFE AND CUSTOMS - PICTORIAL WORKS.**
Dawson, Barry. Street graphics India. London : Thames & Hudson, 1999.
*TC NC998.6.I6 D38 1999*

Dawson, Barry. Street graphics India. London : Thames & Hudson, 1999.
*TC NC998.6.I6 D38 1999*

**Indian American high school students' lives at home and school.**
Asher, Nina. Margins, center, and the spaces in-between. 1999.
*TC 06 no. 11080*

**INDIAN ART - BRITISH COLUMBIA - PACIFIC COAST.**
Wyatt, Gary, 1958- Mythic beings. Vancouver : Douglas & McIntyre ; Seattle : University of Washington Press, c1999.
*TC E78.B9 W93 1999*

**INDIAN ART - CANADA.**
Ryan, Allan J. The trickster shift. Vancouver, BC : UBC Press ; Seattle : University of Washington Press, c1999.
*TC E78.C2 R93 1999*

**INDIAN ART - COLLECTORS AND COLLECTING - NORTH AMERICA - HISTORY - 20TH CENTURY.**
Native American art in the twentieth century. London ; New York : Routledge, 1999.
*TC E98.A7 R89 1999*

**INDIAN ART, MODERN.** *See* **INDIAN ART.**

**INDIAN ART - NORTH AMERICA.**
Sullivan, Missy. The Native American look book. New York : The New Press, 1996.
*TC E98.A7 S93 1996*

**INDIAN ART - NORTH AMERICA - ENCYCLOPEDIAS.**
Werness, Hope B. The Continuum encyclopedia of native art. New York : Continuum, 2000.
*TC E98.A7 W49 2000*

**INDIAN ART - NORTH AMERICA - HISTORY - 20TH CENTURY.**
Native American art in the twentieth century. London ; New York : Routledge, 1999.
*TC E98.A7 R89 1999*

**INDIAN ART - NORTH AMERICA - JUVENILE LITERATURE.**
Sullivan, Missy. The Native American look book. New York : The New Press, 1996.
*TC E98.A7 S93 1996*

**INDIAN ART - NORTH AMERICA - THEMES, MOTIVES.**
Native American art in the twentieth century. London ; New York : Routledge, 1999.
*TC E98.A7 R89 1999*

**INDIAN COUNCILS - WEST (U.S.).**
Foreman, Grant, 1869-1953. Advancing the frontier, 1830-1860. Norman : University of Oklahoma Press, 1968 printing, c1933.
*TC E93 .F67 1968*

**INDIAN DANCE - NORTH AMERICA.** *See* HOOP DANCE.

**The Indian historian.** [San Francisco, American Indian Historical Society] 16 v. ill. 28 cm. Frequency: Quarterly. v. 1-4, no. 3; Oct. 1964-fall 1967; new ser. v. 1-12; Dec. 1967-1979. New ser. v. 2, no. 4 never published. Merged with: Wassaja (San Francisco, Calif. : 1973), to form: Wassaja, the Indian historian. ISSN 0019-4840
*1. Indians of North America - Periodicals. I. American Indian Historical Society. II. Title: Wassaja (San Francisco, Calif. : 1973) III. Title: Wassaja, the Indian historian*

**INDIAN INSPECTORS.** *See* **INDIANS OF NORTH AMERICA - GOVERNMENT RELATIONS.**

**Indian Institute of Education.**
Indian journal of educational research. Bombay, Asia Publishing House.

**The Indian journal of education.** Calcutta [etc] All-India Federation of Educational Associations. v. 25 cm. Frequency: Quarterly. Former frequency: Twelve issues a year 1936- . v.1-   ; 1936-   .
*1. Education - Study and teaching - India. I. All India Federation of Educational Associations.*

**Indian journal of educational research.** Bombay, Asia Publishing House. Frequency: Quarterly. v. 1-4, no. 1; June 1950-June 1952. "Edited by the Indian Institute of Education."
*1. Educational - Research - Periodicals. 2. Education - India - Periodicals. 3. Periodicals I. Indian Institute of Education.*

**INDIAN MYTHOLOGY - BRITISH COLUMBIA - PACIFIC COAST.**
Wyatt, Gary, 1958- Mythic beings. Vancouver : Douglas & McIntyre ; Seattle : University of Washington Press, c1999.
*TC E78.B9 W93 1999*

**INDIAN PAINTINGS - CANADA.**
Ryan, Allan J. The trickster shift. Vancouver, BC : UBC Press ; Seattle : University of Washington Press, c1999.
*TC E78.C2 R93 1999*

**The Indian teacher.**
Singh, Rajendra Pal, 1932- Delhi, National [Pub. House, 1969]

**INDIAN TEXTILE FABRICS - SOUTHWEST, NEW - FICTION.**
Blood, Charles L., 1929- The goat in the rug. New York : Four Winds Press, 1976.
*TC PZ7.B6227 Go 1976*

**The Indiana series in the philosophy of technology**
Ihde, Don, 1934- Technology and the lifeworld. Bloomington : Indiana University Press, c1990.
*TC T14 .I353 1990*

**Indiana State Teachers Association.**
The Indiana teacher. Indianapolis, Ind. : Indiana State Teachers Association, 1924-1972.

**The Indiana teacher.** Indianapolis, Ind. : Indiana State Teachers Association, 1924-1972. 50 v. : ill. ; 29 cm. Frequency: Quarterly, fall 1967-summer 1972. Former frequency: Monthly (except July and Aug.), May 1924-June 1924. Former frequency: Monthly (except June, July and Aug.), Sept. 1924-May 1964. Former frequency: Bimonthly (except July and August), Sept./Oct. 1964-May/June 1967. Vol. 1, no. 1 (May 1924)-v. 1, no. 2 (June 1924) ; Vol. 69, no. 1 (Sept. 1924)-v. 117, no. 2 (winter 1972). Title from cover. Beginning in Sept. 1924 numbered vol. 69, no. 1-v. 117, no. 2 in continuation of the combined numbering of Indiana school journal, and Educator-journal. Official publication of the Indiana State Teachers Association. Continues: Educator-journal (OCoLC)8936616.
*1. Teachers - Indiana - Periodicals. 2. Education - Periodicals. 3. Education - Indiana - Periodicals. I. Indiana State Teachers Association. II. Title: Educator-journal*

**Indiana University. Center on Philanthropy.**
American Assembly (93rd : 1998 : Los Angeles, Calif.) Trust, service, and the common purpose. Indianapolis, IN : Indiana University Center on Philanthropy ; New York, NY : American Assembly, [1998]
*TC HD62.6 .A44 1998*

**Indiana University. Research Center for the Language Sciences.**
Language sciences. Bloomington, Indiana University Research Center for the Language Sciences.

**INDIANS - ART.** *See* INDIAN ART.

**INDIANS - CIVILIZATION.** *See* INDIANS.

**INDIANS, EAST.** *See* EAST INDIANS.

**INDIANS IN LITERATURE - BIBLIOGRAPHY.**
Peck, David R. American ethnic literatures. Pasadena, Calif. : Salem Press, c1992.
*TC Z1229.E87 P43 1992*

**INDIANS - MIXED DESCENT.** *See* MESTIZOS.

**INDIANS OF MEXICO.** *See* ZAPOTEC INDIANS.

**INDIANS OF MEXICO - ETHNOLOGY.** *See* ETHNOLOGY - MEXICO; INDIANS OF MEXICO.

**INDIANS OF MEXICO - FOLKLORE.**
Cruz Martinez, Alejandro, d. 1987. [Mujer que brillaba aún más que el sol. English & Spanish] The woman who outshone the sun. San Francisco, Calif. : Children's Book Press, c1991.
*TC F1221.Z3 C78 1991*

**INDIANS OF MEXICO - SOCIAL LIFE AND CUSTOMS.**
Guevara-Vázquez, Fabián. El indigena en la novela de la Revolucion Mexicana. 1999.

*TC 085 G934*

**INDIANS OF NORTH AMERICA.** *See* **ESKIMOS.**

**INDIANS OF NORTH AMERICA -
ANTIQUITIES - JUVENILE POETRY.**
When the rain sings. New York : Simon & Schuster
Books for Young Readers, 1999.
*TC PS591.I55 W48 1999*

**INDIANS OF NORTH AMERICA - ARIZONA.** *See*
**TEWA INDIANS.**

**INDIANS OF NORTH AMERICA - ART.** *See*
**INDIAN ART - NORTH AMERICA.**

**INDIANS OF NORTH AMERICA - ART -
EXHIBITIONS.**
Shared visions. 1st New Press ed. New York : New
Press : Distributed by Norton, [1993], c1991.
*TC N6538.A4 A7 1993*

**INDIANS OF NORTH AMERICA - CALIFORNIA -
FOLKLORE.**
Bierhorst, John. The people with five fingers. New
York : Marshall Cavendish, 2000.
*TC E78.C15 B523 2000*

Bierhorst, John. The people with five fingers. New
York : Marshall Cavendish, 2000.
*TC E78.C15 B523 2000*

**INDIANS OF NORTH AMERICA - COUNCILS.**
*See* **INDIAN COUNCILS.**

**INDIANS OF NORTH AMERICA - CULTURE.** *See*
**INDIANS OF NORTH AMERICA.**

**INDIANS OF NORTH AMERICA - CUSTOMS.** *See*
**INDIANS OF NORTH AMERICA - SOCIAL
LIFE AND CUSTOMS.**

**INDIANS OF NORTH AMERICA - EDUCATION.**
Manning, M. Lee. Multicultural education of children
and adolescents. 3rd ed. Boston : Allyn and Bacon,
c2000.
*TC LC1099.3 .M36 2000*

**INDIANS OF NORTH AMERICA - EDUCATION
(HIGHER) - UNITED STATES.**
Capeheart-Meningall, Jennifer. Quality of students of
color efort on a predominantly white college and the
internal environmental elements that influence
involvement. 1998.
*TC 06 no. 10874*

**INDIANS OF NORTH AMERICA - EDUCATION -
OKLAHOMA.**
Damm, Robert J., 1964- Repertoire, authenticity, and
instruction. New York ; London : Garland Pub., 2000.
*TC MT3.U6 O53 2000*

**INDIANS OF NORTH AMERICA - ETHNIC
IDENTITY.**
Partial recall. 1st ed. New York : New Press :
Distributed by W.W. Norton & Co., Inc., 1992.
*TC E89 .P33 1992*

**INDIANS OF NORTH AMERICA - ETHNOLOGY.**
*See* **INDIANS OF NORTH AMERICA.**

**INDIANS OF NORTH AMERICA -
GOVERNMENT POLICY.** *See* **INDIANS OF
NORTH AMERICA - GOVERNMENT
RELATIONS.**

**INDIANS OF NORTH AMERICA -
GOVERNMENT RELATIONS - 1789-1869.**
Foreman, Grant, 1869-1953. Advancing the frontier,
1830-1860. Norman : University of Oklahoma Press,
1968 printing, c1933.
*TC E93 .F67 1968*

**INDIANS OF NORTH AMERICA - GREAT
PLAINS.** *See also* **CROW INDIANS; TETON
INDIANS.**
Terry, Michael Bad Hand. Daily life in a Plains Indian
village, 1868. 1st American ed. New York : Clarion
Books, c1999.
*TC E78.G73 T47 1999*

**INDIANS OF NORTH AMERICA - GREAT
PLAINS - HISTORY - JUVENILE
LITERATURE.**
Terry, Michael Bad Hand. Daily life in a Plains Indian
village, 1868. 1st American ed. New York : Clarion
Books, c1999.
*TC E78.G73 T47 1999*

**INDIANS OF NORTH AMERICA - GREAT
PLAINS - SOCIAL LIFE AND CUSTOMS -
JUVENILE LITERATURE.**
Terry, Michael Bad Hand. Daily life in a Plains Indian
village, 1868. 1st American ed. New York : Clarion
Books, c1999.

*TC E78.G73 T47 1999*

**INDIANS OF NORTH AMERICA - HISTORY.** *See*
**INDIANS OF NORTH AMERICA - WARS.**

**INDIANS OF NORTH AMERICA - HISTORY -
19TH CENTURY.**
Foreman, Grant, 1869-1953. Advancing the frontier,
1830-1860. Norman : University of Oklahoma Press,
1968 printing, c1933.
*TC E93 .F67 1968*

**INDIANS OF NORTH AMERICA - INDIAN
TERRITORY.**
Foreman, Grant, 1869-1953. Advancing the frontier,
1830-1860. Norman : University of Oklahoma Press,
1968 printing, c1933.
*TC E93 .F67 1968*

**INDIANS OF NORTH AMERICA - MATERIAL
CULTURE - GREAT PLAINS - JUVENILE
LITERATURE.**
Terry, Michael Bad Hand. Daily life in a Plains Indian
village, 1868. 1st American ed. New York : Clarion
Books, c1999.
*TC E78.G73 T47 1999*

**INDIANS OF NORTH AMERICA - MONTANA.**
*See* **CROW INDIANS.**

**INDIANS OF NORTH AMERICA - MUSIC -
HISTORY AND CRITICISM.**
Damm, Robert J., 1964- Repertoire, authenticity, and
instruction. New York ; London : Garland Pub., 2000.
*TC MT3.U6 O53 2000*

**INDIANS OF NORTH AMERICA - NEW
MEXICO.** *See also* **TEWA INDIANS.**
Hazen-Hammond, Susan. Thunder Bear and Ko. 1st
ed. New York : Dutton Children's Books, 1999.
*TC E99.T35 H36 1999*

**INDIANS OF NORTH AMERICA -
PERIODICALS.**
The Indian historian. [San Francisco, American Indian
Historical Society]

**INDIANS OF NORTH AMERICA - PICTORIAL
WORKS.**
Partial recall. 1st ed. New York : New Press :
Distributed by W.W. Norton & Co., Inc., 1992.
*TC E89 .P33 1992*

Portraits of native Americans. New York : New
Press : Distributed by W.W. Norton, c1994.
*TC TR140.C388 C48*

Spirit capture. Washington : Smithsonian Institution
Press in association with the National Museum of the
American Indian, Smithsonian Institution, c1998.
*TC E77.5 .S65 1998*

**INDIANS OF NORTH AMERICA - POETRY.**
When the rain sings. New York : Simon & Schuster
Books for Young Readers, 1999.
*TC PS591.I55 W48 1999*

**INDIANS OF NORTH AMERICA - POLITICS
AND GOVERNMENT.** *See* **INDIAN
COUNCILS.**

**INDIANS OF NORTH AMERICA - PORTRAITS.**
Partial recall. 1st ed. New York : New Press :
Distributed by W.W. Norton & Co., Inc., 1992.
*TC E89 .P33 1992*

**INDIANS OF NORTH AMERICA - SCHOOLS.** *See*
**INDIANS OF NORTH AMERICA -
EDUCATION.**

**INDIANS OF NORTH AMERICA - SOCIAL LIFE
AND CUSTOMS.**
Foreman, Grant, 1869-1953. Advancing the frontier,
1830-1860. Norman : University of Oklahoma Press,
1968 printing, c1933.
*TC E93 .F67 1968*

Sullivan, Missy. The Native American look book.
New York : The New Press, 1996.
*TC E98.A7 S93 1996*

**INDIANS OF NORTH AMERICA - SOCIAL LIFE
AND CUSTOMS - ENCYCLOPEDIAS.**
Werness, Hope B. The Continuum encyclopedia of
native art. New York : Continuum, 2000.
*TC E98.A7 W49 2000*

**INDIANS OF NORTH AMERICA - SOUTH
DAKOTA.**
Left Hand Bull, Jacqueline. Lakota hoop dancer. 1st
ed. New York : Dutton Children's Books, c1999.
*TC E99.T34 L43 1999*

**INDIANS OF NORTH AMERICA - SOUTHWEST,
NEW.** *See* **NAVAJO INDIANS; PUEBLO
INDIANS.**

**INDIANS OF NORTH AMERICA - SOUTHWEST,
NEW - FICTION.**
Blake, Robert J. Yudonsi. New York : Philomel
Books, 1999.
*TC PZ7.B564 Yu 1999*

**INDIANS OF NORTH AMERICA - SOUTHWEST,
NEW - TEXTILE INDUSTRY AND FABRICS.**
*See* **INDIAN TEXTILE FABRICS -
SOUTHWEST, NEW.**

**INDIANS OF NORTH AMERICA - UNITED
STATES.** *See* **INDIANS OF NORTH
AMERICA.**

**INDIANS OF NORTH AMERICA - WARS - 1815-
1875.**
Foreman, Grant, 1869-1953. Advancing the frontier,
1830-1860. Norman : University of Oklahoma Press,
1968 printing, c1933.
*TC E93 .F67 1968*

**INDIANS OF NORTH AMERICA - WEST (U.S.).**
Foreman, Grant, 1869-1953. Advancing the frontier,
1830-1860. Norman : University of Oklahoma Press,
1968 printing, c1933.
*TC E93 .F67 1968*

**INDIANS OF NORTH AMERICA - WYOMING.**
*See* **CROW INDIANS.**

**INDIANS OF SOUTH AMERICA - BRAZIL.** *See*
**MACUNA INDIANS.**

**INDIANS OF SOUTH AMERICA - COLOMBIA.**
*See* **MACUNA INDIANS.**

**INDIANS OF THE UNITED STATES.** *See*
**INDIANS OF NORTH AMERICA.**

**INDIANS - PERIODICALS.**
América indígena. México.

**INDIANS - PICTORIAL WORKS.**
Spirit capture. Washington : Smithsonian Institution
Press in association with the National Museum of the
American Indian, Smithsonian Institution, c1998.
*TC E77.5 .S65 1998*

**INDIANS - RELIGION AND MYTHOLOGY.** *See*
**INDIAN MYTHOLOGY.**

**INDIANS - TEXTILE INDUSTRY AND FABRICS.**
*See* **INDIAN TEXTILE FABRICS.**

**INDICATORS, HEALTH STATUS.** *See* **HEALTH
STATUS INDICATORS.**

**Indicators of the quality of education.**
Ross, Kenneth N. (Kenneth Norman), 1947- Paris :
International Institute for Educational Planning, 1992.
*TC LA1592 .R67 1992*

**INDICES (SEMANTICS).** *See* **INDEXICALS
(SEMANTICS).**

**INDIGENIZATION (CHRISTIAN THEOLOGY).**
*See* **CHRISTIANITY AND CULTURE.**

**INDIGENOUS ARCHITECTURE.** *See*
**VERNACULAR ARCHITECTURE.**

**Indigenous art, colonial culture.**
Thomas, Nicholas. Possessions. New York, N.Y. :
Thames and Hudson, c1999.
*TC N5313 .T46 1999*

**Indigenous community-based education** / edited by
Stephen May. Clevedon [England] ; Philadelphia :
Multilingual Matters, c1999. 180 p. ; 26 cm. "This book is
also available as vol. 11, no. 3, of the journal Language,
culture, and curriculum"--T.p. verso. Includes bibliographic
references. ISBN 1-85359-450-4 (hbk.) DDC 371/.0086/93
*1. Community education. 2. Indigenous peoples - Education. 3.
Language and languages - Study and teaching. I. May,
Stephen, 1962- II. Title: Language, culture, and curriculum.*
*TC LC1036 .I43 1999*

**Indigenous educational models for contemporary
practice** : in our mother's voice / edited by Maenette
Kapeàhiokalani Padeken Ah Nee-Benham with
Joanne Elizabeth Cooper. Mahwah, N.J. : L. Erlbaum
Associates, 2000. xxi, 204 p. : ill. ; 24 cm. (Sociocultural,
political, and historical studies in education) Includes
bibliographical references and index. ISBN 0-8058-3461-3
(cloth : alk. paper) ISBN 0-8058-3462-1 (pbk. : alk. paper)
DDC 371.829/97
*1. Indigenous peoples - Education - Social aspects - Case
studies. 2. Native language and education - Case studies. I.
Nee-Benham, Maenette K. P. II. Cooper, Joanne E. III. Series.*
*TC LC3719 .I53 2000*

**INDIGENOUS PEOPLES - COLONIZATION.**
Thomas, Nicholas. Possessions. New York, N.Y. :
Thames and Hudson, c1999.
*TC N5313 .T46 1999*

**INDIGENOUS PEOPLES - EDUCATION.**
Indigenous community-based education. Clevedon
|England| : Philadelphia : Multilingual Matters,
c1999.
*TC LC1036 .I43 1999*

**INDIGENOUS PEOPLES - EDUCATION
(HIGHER).**
Local knowledge and wisdom in higher education. 1st
ed. Oxford : Published for the IAU Press |by|
Pergamon, 2000.
*TC GN380 .L63 2000*

**INDIGENOUS PEOPLES - EDUCATION -
SOCIAL ASPECTS - CASE STUDIES.**
Indigenous educational models for contemporary
practice. Mahwah, N.J. : L. Erlbaum Associates, 2000.
*TC LC3719 .I53 2000*

**INDIGENOUS PEOPLES - ETHNIC IDENTITY.**
Thomas, Nicholas. Possessions. New York, N.Y. :
Thames and Hudson, c1999.
*TC N5313 .T46 1999*

**INDIGENOUS PEOPLES - GOVERNMENT
RELATIONS.** *See* **INDIGENOUS PEOPLES.**

**INDIGENOUS PEOPLES - MATERIAL
CULTURE - RUSSIA (FEDERATION) -
SIBERIA.**
Oakes, Jill E. (Jill Elizabeth), 1952- Spirit of Siberia.
Washington, D.C. : Smithsonian Institution Press,
c1998.
*TC DK758 .O24 1998*

**INDIGENOUS PEOPLES - PSYCHOLOGY.** *See*
**ETHNOPSYCHOLOGY.**

**INDIGENOUS PEOPLES - RUSSIA
(FEDERATION) - SIBERIA.**
Oakes, Jill E. (Jill Elizabeth), 1952- Spirit of Siberia.
Washington, D.C. : Smithsonian Institution Press,
c1998.
*TC DK758 .O24 1998*

**INDIGENOUS POPULATIONS.** *See* **INDIGENOUS
PEOPLES.**

**INDIGNATION.** *See* **ANGER.**

**The individual child.**
Murphy, Lois Barclay, 1902- Washington :
Department of Health Education, and Welfare : for
sale by the Supt. of Docs., U. S. Govt. Print. Off.,
1973.

**INDIVIDUAL DIFFERENCES.**
Aiken, Lewis R., 1931- Human differences. Mahwah,
N.J. : L. Erlbaum Associates, 1999.
*TC BF697 .A55 1999*

International perspectives on individual differences.
Stamford, Conn. : Ablex, 2000-
*TC BF697 .I58 2000*

Sorrentino, Richard M. The uncertain mind.
Philadelphia : Psychology Press, c2000.
*TC BF697 .S674 2000*

**INDIVIDUAL INSTRUCTION.** *See*
**INDIVIDUALIZED INSTRUCTION.**

**Individual psychology.**
Wexberg, Erwin, 1889- New York, Cosmopolitan
Book Corporation, 1929.
*TC BF175 .W48*

**Individual quality of life :** approaches to
conceptualisation and assessment / edited by C.R.B.
Joyce, Hannah M. McGee and Ciaran A. O'Boyle.
Amsterdam : Harwood Academic, c1999. xii, 234 p. :
ill. : 25 cm. Includes bibliographical references and index.
ISBN 90-5702-425-X
*1. Quality of life. 2. Quality of life - Evaluation. 3. Health
status indicators. I. Joyce, C. R. B. (Charles Richard
Boddington), 1923- II. McGee, Hannah M., 1959- III. O'Boyle,
Ciaran A.*
*TC RA407 .I54 1999*

**Individualisation /** edited by Marion Gedders and Gill
Sturtridge. Oxford : Modern English Publications,
1982. 83 p. : ill. ; 25 cm. Includes bibliographical references.
ISBN 0-906149-21-5
*1. Self-culture. 2. Study skills. 3. Learning strategies. I.
Geddes, Marion. II. Sturtridge, Gill.*
*TC LC32 .I53 1982*

**INDIVIDUALISM.**
Moessinger, Pierre. |Irrationalité individuelle et ordre
social. English| The paradox of social order. New
York : Aldine de Gruyter, c2000.
*TC HM1276 .M6413 2000*

**INDIVIDUALITY.** *See* **IDENTITY;
PERSONALITY; SELF.**

**INDIVIDUALIZED EDUCATION PROGRAMS.**
Gibb, Gordon S. Guide to writing quality
individualzed education programs :. Boston : Allyn
and Bacon, c2000).
*TC LC4019 .G43 2000*

**INDIVIDUALIZED INSTRUCTION.** *See*
**MASTERY LEARNING.**

**INDIVIDUALIZED INSTRUCTION -
PERIODICALS.**
Journal of personalized instruction. |Washington|
Center for Personalized Instruction |Georgetown
University|

**INDIVIDUALIZED INSTRUCTION - UNITED
STATES.**
Personalized instruction. Larchmont, N.Y. : Eye on
Education, c2000).
*TC LB1031 .K383 2000*

**INDIVIDUALIZED INSTRUCTION - UNITED
STATES - CASE STUDIES.**
Improved test scores, attitudes, and behaviors in
America's schools. Westport, Conn. : Bergin &
Garvey, 1999.
*TC LB2806.4 .I56 1999*

**INDIVIDUALIZED READING INSTRUCTION.**
O'Donnell, Michael P. Becoming a reader. 2nd ed.
Boston : Allyn and Bacon, c1999.
*TC LB1050.53 .O35 1999*

Walker, Barbara J., 1946- Diagnostic teaching of
reading. 4th ed. Upper Saddle River, NJ : Merrill,
c2000.
*TC LB1050.5 .W35 2000*

**The induction and mentoring of newly qualified
teachers.**
Bleach, Kevan. London : David Fulton, 1999.
*TC LB1729 .B584 1999*

**INDUSTRIAL ACCIDENTS.** *See* **DISABILITY
EVALUATION.**

**INDUSTRIAL ACCIDENTS - PREVENTION.** *See*
**INDUSTRIAL SAFETY.**

**INDUSTRIAL ADMINISTRATION.** *See*
**INDUSTRIAL MANAGEMENT.**

**Industrial and labor relations terms.**
Doherty, Robert Emmett, 1923- 5th ed., rev. Ithaca,
NY : ILR Press, c1989.
*TC HD4839 .D6 1989*

**Industrial and organizational psychology.**
Spector, Paul E. 2nd ed. New York : John Wiley,
2000.
*TC HF5548.8 .S625 2000*

**Industrial and organizational psychology :** linking
theory with practice / edited by Cary L. Cooper,
Edwin A. Locke. Oxford, UK ; Malden, Mass. :
Blackwell Business, 2000). xiv, 356 p. : ill. ; 26 cm.
Includes bibliographical references and indexes. ISBN
0-631-20991-3 (hc : alk. paper) ISBN 0-631-20992-1 (pb : alk.
paper) DDC 158.7
*1. Psychology, Industrial. 2. Organizational behavior -
Psychological aspects. I. Cooper, Cary L. II. Locke, Edwin A.*
*TC HF5548.8 .I5233 2000*

**INDUSTRIAL ARTS.** *See* **AGRICULTURE;
ENGINEERING; MANUAL TRAINING;
TECHNOLOGY.**

**Industrial arts and vocational education June 1930-
May/June 1972.**
Industrial arts magazine. Milwaukee |etc.| Bruce
Publishing Co.

**Industrial arts and vocational education June1930-
May/June 1972.**
Industrial education. Greenwich, Conn., Macmillan
Professional Magazines.

**INDUSTRIAL ARTS - EXHIBITIONS.** *See*
**EXHIBITIONS.**

**Industrial arts magazine.** Milwaukee |etc.| Bruce
Publishing Co. 19 v. ill. 29 cm. v. 1-19, no. 5; 1914-May
1930. Microfilm. Ann Arbor, Mich. ; University Microfilms,
1975. 4 microfilm reels ; 4 in., 35 mm. Absorbed Handicraft in
Feb. 1914 and Arts and crafts magazine in May 1914.
Continued by: Industrial arts and vocational education June
1930-May/June 1972 ISSN: 0019-8005.
*1. Technical education - Periodicals. 2. Manual training -
Periodicals. 3. Industrial arts - Periodicals. 4. Art industries
and trade - Study and teaching - Periodicals. I. Title:
Handicraft Feb. 1914 II. Title: Arts and crafts magazine May
1914 III. Title: Industrial arts and vocational education June
1930-May/June 1972*

**INDUSTRIAL ARTS - PERIODICALS.**
Industrial arts magazine. Milwaukee |etc.| Bruce
Publishing Co.

**INDUSTRIAL BUILDINGS.** *See* **FACTORIES.**

**INDUSTRIAL CERAMICS.** *See* **CERAMICS.**

**INDUSTRIAL CHEMISTRY.** *See* **CHEMISTRY,
TECHNICAL.**

**INDUSTRIAL COMMUNICATION.** *See*
**BUSINESS COMMUNICATION.**

**INDUSTRIAL CONCENTRATION.** *See*
**COMPETITION.**

**INDUSTRIAL DESIGNERS - UNITED STATES -
BIOGRAPHY.**
Bursak, George J., 1913- If I can do it, so can you.
|S.l.| : G.J. Bursak, c1999.
*TC RC394.W6 B87 1999*

**INDUSTRIAL EDUCATION.** *See also* **MANUAL
TRAINING.**

**Industrial education.** Greenwich, Conn., Macmillan
Professional Magazines. v. ill. 29 cm. Frequency: Monthly
(except July and Aug.; May/June combined issue). v. 61, no.
6- Sept. 1972- . Indexed by: Education index 0013-1385.
Continues: Industrial arts and vocational education June1930-
May/June 1972 1642387. ISSN 0091-8601
*1. Technical education - Periodicals. 2. Manual training -
Periodicals. I. Title: Industrial arts and vocational education
June1930-May/June 1972*

**Industrial education magazine.** Chicago, Ill. : The
University of Chicago Press, 1899-1939. 41 v. : ill. ;
26-31 cm. Vol. 1 (Oct. 1899)-v. 41 (Nov. 1939). Title varies:
Manual training magazine Oct. 1899-June 1914, Sept. 1916-
June 1922. Title varies: Manual training and vocational
eduation Sept. 1914-June 1916. Absorbed: Vocational
education Sept. 1914.
*1. Manual training - Periodicals. 2. Vocational education -
Periodicals. I. Title: Manual training magazine Oct. 1899-June
1914, Sept. 1916-June 1922 II. Title: Manual training and
vocational eduation Sept. 1914-June 1916 III. Title: Vocational
education Sept. 1914*

**INDUSTRIAL EFFICIENCY.**
Lipman-Blumen, Jean. Hot groups. New York :
Oxford University Press, 1999.
*TC HD58.9 .L56 1999*

**INDUSTRIAL ENGINEERING.** *See*
**PSYCHOLOGY, INDUSTRIAL.**

**INDUSTRIAL ESPIONAGE.** *See* **BUSINESS
INTELLIGENCE.**

**INDUSTRIAL EXHIBITIONS.** *See* **EXHIBITIONS.**

**INDUSTRIAL HYGIENE.**
Moore, Gary S. Living with the earth. Boca Raton,
Fla. : Lewis Publishers, c1999.
*TC RA565 .M665 1999*

**INDUSTRIAL LAWS AND LEGISLATION.** *See*
**LABOR LAWS AND LEGISLATION.**

**INDUSTRIAL MANAGEMENT.** *See* **BUSINESS
INTELLIGENCE.**

**INDUSTRIAL MANAGEMENT - JAPAN.**
Deegan, William L. Translating theory into practice.
1st ed. |Columbus, Ohio| : National Association of
Student Personnel Administrators, c1985.
*TC LB2343 .D356 1985*

**INDUSTRIAL MANAGEMENT - JAPAN -
HISTORY.**
Cole, Robert E. Managing quality fads. New York :
Oxford University Press, 1999.
*TC HD66 .C539 1999*

**INDUSTRIAL MANAGEMENT - STUDY AND
TEACHING - PERIODICALS.**
Management learning. London ; Thousand Oaks, CA :
Sage Publications, c1994-

**INDUSTRIAL MANAGEMENT - UNITED
STATES - HISTORY.**
Cole, Robert E. Managing quality fads. New York :
Oxford University Press, 1999.
*TC HD66 .C539 1999*

**INDUSTRIAL MENTAL HEALTH.** *See*
**INDUSTRIAL PSYCHIATRY.**

**Industrial nursing.** |Chicago : Industrial Medicine Pub.
Co., v. : ill. ; 22 cm. Frequency: Monthly. Description based
on: Vol. 4, no. 1 (Jan. 1945); title from cover. Vol. 1-3
published in v. 10-13 of Industrial medicine. Official
publication of: American Association of Industrial Nurses.
Absorbed by: Trained nurse and hospital review (DLC)ca
06001365 (OCoLC)1767687.

1. *Industrial nursing - Periodicals.* I. American Association of Industrial Nurses. II. Title: Trained nurse and hospital review

**INDUSTRIAL NURSING - PERIODICALS.**
Industrial nursing. [Chicago : Industrial Medicine Pub. Co.,

**INDUSTRIAL ORGANIZATION.** See **INDUSTRIAL MANAGEMENT.**

**INDUSTRIAL PLANTS.** See **FACTORIES.**

**INDUSTRIAL PRODUCTION.** See **INDUSTRIES.**

**INDUSTRIAL PROJECT MANAGEMENT.** See **ECONOMIC DEVELOPMENT PROJECTS.**

**INDUSTRIAL PSYCHIATRY - CONGRESSES.**
Work and well-being. Washington, DC : American Psychological Association, c1992.
*TC RC967.5 .W67 1992*

**INDUSTRIAL PSYCHOLOGISTS.** See **PSYCHOLOGY, INDUSTRIAL.**

**INDUSTRIAL PSYCHOLOGY.** See **PSYCHOLOGY, INDUSTRIAL.**

**INDUSTRIAL RELATIONS.** See also **COLLECTIVE BARGAINING; EMPLOYEES; MANAGEMENT.**
Anstey, Mark. Managing change. 2nd ed. Kenwyn : Juta, 1999.
*TC HD42 .A57 1999*

**INDUSTRIAL RELATIONS - TERMINOLOGY.**
Doherty, Robert Emmett, 1923- Industrial and labor relations terms. 5th ed., rev. Ithaca, NY : ILR Press, c1989.
*TC HD4839 .D6 1989*

**INDUSTRIAL SAFETY.**
Moore, Gary S. Living with the earth. Boca Raton, Fla. : Lewis Publishers, c1999.
*TC RA565 .M665 1999*

**INDUSTRIAL SAFETY - DICTIONARIES.**
Lewis' dictionary of occupational and environmental safety and health. Boca Raton : Lewis Publishers, c2000.
*TC T55 .L468 2000*

**INDUSTRIAL SCHOOLS.** See **MANUAL TRAINING; REFORMATORIES; TRADE SCHOOLS.**

**INDUSTRIAL SOCIOLOGY.** See **INDUSTRIES - SOCIAL ASPECTS; SEX ROLE IN THE WORK ENVIRONMENT.**

**INDUSTRIAL TELEVISION - PERIODICALS.**
Educational & industrial television. [Ridgefield, Conn. : C.S. Tepfer Pub. Co.,    -c1983]

**INDUSTRIALIZATION.** See **DEVELOPING COUNTRIES.**

**INDUSTRIES.** See **HIGH TECHNOLOGY INDUSTRIES; SERVICE INDUSTRIES.**

**INDUSTRIES - ENGLAND - MANCHESTER - HISTORY - 19TH CENTURY.**
Hewitt, Martin. The emergence of stability in the industrial city. Aldershot, England : Scolar Press ; Brookfield, Vt., USA : Ashgate Pub. Co., c1996.
*TC HN398.M27 H48 1996*

**INDUSTRIES - SIZE.** See **SMALL BUSINESS.**

**INDUSTRIES - SOCIAL ASPECTS.** See also **SOCIAL RESPONSIBILITY OF BUSINESS.**
Giroux, Henry A. Stealing innocence. 1st ed. New York : St. Martin's Press, 2000.
*TC HM621 .G57 2000*

**INDUSTRIES - SOCIAL ASPECTS - UNITED STATES.**
Meeting human needs, toward a new public philosophy. Washington : American Enterprise Institute for Public Policy Research, c1982.
*TC HD60.5.U5 M427 1982*

**INDUSTRIES - SOCIAL RESPONSIBILITY.** See **SOCIAL RESPONSIBILITY OF BUSINESS.**

**INDUSTRY.** See **INDUSTRIES.**

**INDUSTRY AND COLLEGES.** See **INDUSTRY AND EDUCATION.**

**INDUSTRY AND EDUCATION - GREAT BRITAIN.**
Bennett, Neville. Skills development in higher education and employment. Buckingham [England] ; Philadelphia : Society for Research into Higher Education & Open University Press, 2000.
*TC LB1027.47 .B46 2000*

**INDUSTRY AND EDUCATION - UNITED STATES.**
Boutwell, Clinton E. Shell game. Bloomington, Ind. : Phi Delta Kappa Educational Foundation, c1997.
*TC LC1085.2 .B68 1997*

Gross, Clifford M. The new idea factory. Columbus, OH : Battelle Press, c2000.
*TC HD53 .G75 2000*

Otterbourg, Susan D. Using technology to strengthen employee and family involvement in education. [New York] : Conference Board, c1998.
*TC LB1028.3 .O88 1998*

**INDUSTRY (PSYCHOLOGY).** See **WORK.**

**INDUSTRY-SPONSORED EDUCATION.** See **EMPLOYER-SUPPORTED EDUCATION.**

**INEBRIATES.** See **ALCOHOLICS.**

**INEBRIETY.** See **ALCOHOLISM.**

**INEQUALITY.** See **EQUALITY.**

**INEQUALITY OF INCOME.** See **INCOME DISTRIBUTION.**

**INFANCY.** See **INFANTS.**

**Infancy and culture :** an international review and source book / edited by Hiram E. Fitzgerald ... [et al.]. New York : Falmer Press, 1999. 159 p. ; 23 cm. (Garland reference library of the social sciences ; v. 1168) (Reference books on family issues ; v. 27) Includes bibliographical references and indexes. ISBN 0-8153-2838-9 (alk. paper) DDC 305.23
1. *Children - Cross-cultural studies.* 2. *Child development - Cross-cultural studies.* 3. *Child psychology - Cross-cultural studies.* I. *Fitzgerald, Hiram E.* II. *Series.* III. *Series: Garland reference library of social science ; v. 1168.*
*TC GN482 .I53 1999*

**INFANCY OF ANIMALS.** See **ANIMALS - INFANCY.**

**INFANT.**
Handbook of infant mental health. New York : Wiley, c2000.
*TC RJ502.5 .H362 2000*

**INFANT ANIMALS.** See **ANIMALS - INFANCY.**

**INFANT CARE.**
Shore, Rima. Rethinking the brain. New York : Families and Work Institute, c1997.
*TC RJ486.5 .S475 1997*

**INFANT CARE LEAVE.** See **PARENTAL LEAVE.**

**INFANT EDUCATION.** See **EDUCATION, PRESCHOOL.**

**INFANT, PREMATURE.**
Dubowitz, Lilly M. S. The neurological assessment of the preterm and full-term newborn infant. 2nd ed. London : Mac Keith, 1999.
*TC RJ486 .D85 1999*

**INFANT PSYCHIATRY - HANDBOOKS, MANUALS, ETC.**
Handbook of infant mental health. New York : Wiley, c2000.
*TC RJ502.5 .H362 2000*

**INFANT PSYCHOLOGY.** See also **INFANT PSYCHIATRY.**
Current issues in developmental psychology. Dordrecht ; Boston ; London : Kluwer Academic Publishers, c1999.
*TC RJ134 .C868 1999*

Gibson, Eleanor Jack. An ecological approach to perceptual learning and development. Oxford ; New York : Oxford University Press, 2000.
*TC BF720.P47 G53 2000*

**INFANT PSYCHOLOGY - PERIODICALS.**
Progress in infancy research. Mahwah, NJ : Lawrence Erlbaum Associates, 2000-
*TC BF719 .P76*

**INFANTICIDE IN ANIMALS.** See **ANIMALS - INFANCY.**

**INFANTILE AUTISM.** See **AUTISM IN CHILDREN.**

**Infants & toddlers :** the best resources to help you parent / Julie Soto, editor. 2nd ed. Seattle, Wash. : Resourse Pathways, 1999. 361 p. ; 28 cm. (Resource Pathways guidebook) Includes index. ISBN 1-89214-810-2 DDC 016.6491
1. *Child care - Bibliography.* 2. *Parenting - Bibliography.* I. *Soto, Julie.* II. *Title: Infants and toddlers* III. *Series.*
*TC HQ755.8 .I54 1999*

**Infants and toddlers.**
Infants & toddlers. 2nd ed. Seattle, Wash. : Resourse Pathways, 1999.
*TC HQ755.8 .I54 1999*

**INFANTS - CARE AND HYGIENE.** See **INFANTS - HEALTH AND HYGIENE.**

**INFANTS - COUNSELING OF.**
Epps, Susan. Empowered families, successful children. 1st ed. Washington, DC : American Psychological Association, c2000.
*TC BF637.C6 E66 2000*

**INFANTS - DEVELOPMENT.** See also **INFANT PSYCHOLOGY.**
Current issues in developmental psychology. Dordrecht ; Boston ; London : Kluwer Academic Publishers, c1999.
*TC RJ134 .C868 1999*

Shore, Rima. Rethinking the brain. New York : Families and Work Institute, c1997.
*TC RJ486.5 .S475 1997*

**INFANTS - HEALTH AND HYGIENE.**
Groves, Ernest Rutherford, 1878-1946. Wholesome childhood. Boston, Houghton Mifflin Company, 1924.
*TC HQ772 .G75*

**INFANTS - MENTAL HEALTH - HANDBOOKS, MANUALS, ETC.**
Handbook of infant mental health. New York : Wiley, c2000.
*TC RJ502.5 .H362 2000*

**INFANTS (NEWBORN) - DISEASES - DIAGNOSIS.**
Dubowitz, Lilly M. S. The neurological assessment of the preterm and full-term newborn infant. 2nd ed. London : Mac Keith, 1999.
*TC RJ486 .D85 1999*

**INFANTS (NEWBORN) - PSYCHOLOGY.**
Janov, Arthur. The biology of love. Amherst, N.Y. : Prometheus Books, 2000.
*TC BF720.E45 .J36 2000*

Odent, Michel, 1930- The scientification of love. London : New York : Free Association Books, 1999.
*TC BF575.L8 O33 1999*

**INFANTS (NEWBORN) - WOUNDS AND INJURIES.**
Janov, Arthur. The biology of love. Amherst, N.Y. : Prometheus Books, 2000.
*TC BF720.E45 .J36 2000*

**INFANTS - PSYCHOLOGY.** See **INFANT PSYCHOLOGY.**

**INFANTS' SUPPLIES.** See **TOYS.**

**INFANTS - UNITED STATES - INTELLIGENCE TESTING - LONGITUDINAL STUDIES.**
Leventhal, Tama. Poverty and turbulence. 1999.
*TC 085 L5515*

**INFECTION - JUVENILE LITERATURE.**
Rowan, Kate. I know how we fight germs. Cambridge, Mass. : Candlewick Press, 1999.
*TC QR57 .R69 1999*

**INFECTIOUS DISEASES.** See **INFECTION.**

**INFERENCE.**
Andersen, Christopher Lawrence. A microgenetic study of science reasoning in social context. 1998.
*TC 085 An2305*

**INFERTILITY.** See **FERTILITY, HUMAN.**

**Infinite potential.**
Peat, F. David, 1938- Reading, Mass. : Addison Wesley, c1997.
*TC QC16.B627 P43 1997*

**INFINITESIMAL CALCULUS.** See **CALCULUS.**

**INFIRMARIES.** See **HOSPITALS.**

**INFLATIONARY UNIVERSE.**
Stephen Hawking's universe [videorecording]. [Alexandria, Va.] : PBS Video; Burbank, CA : Distributed by Warner Home Video, c1997.
*TC QB982 .S7 1997*

**INFLORESCENCES.** See **FLOWERS.**

**The influence of causal attributions on the psychological adjustment of post-treatment adolescent cancer survivors.**
Halperin, Jane Carol. 1999.
*TC 085 H155*

**Influence of Deng Xiaoping's ideas on current primary education policy, curricula and textbooks**

in China.
Reynolds, Barbara G. Reform and education. 1999.
*TC 06 no. 11166*

**Influence of depression, gender, gender role, perfectionism, and self-silencing on body esteem.**
Lippert, Robin Alissa. Conflating the self with the body. 1999.
*TC 085 L655*

**INFLUENCE (PSYCHOLOGY).** *See also*
**EXAMPLE; PERSUASION (PSYCHOLOGY).**
Gass, Robert H. Persuasion, social influence, and compliance gaining. Boston : Allyn and Bacon, c1999.
*TC BF637.P4 G34 1999*

Loase, John Frederick, 1947- Sigfluence III. Lanham, Md. : University Press of America, c1996.
*TC BF774 .L63 1996*

Wheeler, Ladd, 1937- Interpersonal influence. Boston, Allyn and Bacon [1970]
*TC HM291 .W35*

**INFOBAHN.** *See* **INFORMATION SUPERHIGHWAY.**

**INFOPIKE.** *See* **INFORMATION SUPERHIGHWAY.**

**INFORMAL CAREGIVERS.** *See* **CAREGIVERS.**

**Informal learning in the workplace.**
Garrick, John. London ; New York : Routledge, 1998.
*TC HF5549.5.T7 G344 1998*

**Informal learning in the workplace through desktop technology.**
Weintraub, Robert Steven. 1998.
*TC 06 no. 11003*

**Information collection.**
Short, Paula M. Larchmont, NY : Eye on Education, c1998.
*TC LB1028.27.U6 S46 1998*

**INFORMATION, FREEDOM OF.** *See* **FREEDOM OF INFORMATION.**

**INFORMATION HIGHWAY.** *See* **INFORMATION SUPERHIGHWAY.**

**INFORMATION INFRASTRUCTURE.** *See* **INFORMATION SUPERHIGHWAY.**

**Information literacy series**
Small, Ruth V. Turning kids on to research. Englewood, Colo. : Libraries Unlimited, 2000.
*TC LB1065 .S57 2000*

Stanley, Deborah B. Practical steps to the research process for high school. Englewood, Colo. : Libraries Unlimited, 1999.
*TC Z711.2 .S72 1999*

**INFORMATION NETWORKS.** *See also*
**COMPUTER NETWORKS; INFORMATION SUPERHIGHWAY; LIBRARY INFORMATION NETWORKS.**
Castells, Manuel. The rise of the network society. 2nd ed. Malden, MA : Blackwell Publishers, 2000.
*TC HC79.I55 C373 2000*

**INFORMATION NETWORKS, LIBRARY.** *See* **LIBRARY INFORMATION NETWORKS.**

**INFORMATION PROCESSING.**
Stratification in cognition and consciousness. Amsterdam ; Philadelphia : J. Benjamins, c1999.
*TC BF444 .S73 1999*

**INFORMATION PROCESSING SYSTEMS.** *See* **INFORMATION STORAGE AND RETRIEVAL SYSTEMS.**

**INFORMATION RESOURCE MANAGEMENT.** *See* **INFORMATION RESOURCES MANAGEMENT.**

**INFORMATION RESOURCES.** *See* **REFERENCE SOURCES.**

**INFORMATION RESOURCES MANAGEMENT - UNITED STATES.**
Becker, Nancy Jane. Implementing technology in higher education. 1999.
*TC 06 no. 11082*

**INFORMATION RETRIEVAL.** *See also*
**CATALOGING; INFORMATION STORAGE AND RETRIEVAL SYSTEMS.**
Whitson, Donna L. Accessing information in a technological age. Original ed. Malabar, Fla. : Krieger Pub. Co., 1997.

*TC ZA3075 .W48 1997*

**INFORMATION RETRIEVAL - STUDY AND TEACHING.**
Small, Ruth V. Turning kids on to research. Englewood, Colo. : Libraries Unlimited, 2000.
*TC LB1065 .S57 2000*

**INFORMATION RETRIEVAL - STUDY AND TEACHING (ELEMENTARY) - UNITED STATES.**
Developing an information literacy program K-12. New York : Neal-Schuman, c1998.
*TC Z711.2 .D49 1998*

**INFORMATION RETRIEVAL - STUDY AND TEACHING (SECONDARY) - UNITED STATES.**
Developing an information literacy program K-12. New York : Neal-Schuman, c1998.
*TC Z711.2 .D49 1998*

**INFORMATION RETRIEVAL SYSTEMS.** *See* **INFORMATION STORAGE AND RETRIEVAL SYSTEMS.**

**INFORMATION SCIENCE.** *See* **INFORMATION RETRIEVAL.**

**INFORMATION SCIENTISTS.** *See* **LIBRARIANS.**

**INFORMATION SERVICES.** *See* **RESEARCH.**

**INFORMATION SERVICES - USER EDUCATION.** *See* **LIBRARY ORIENTATION.**

**INFORMATION SOCIETY.** *See also*
**INFORMATION SUPERHIGHWAY.**
Brown, John Seely. The social life of information. Boston : Harvard Business School Press, c2000.
*TC HM851 .B76 2000*

Castells, Manuel. The rise of the network society. 2nd ed. Malden, MA : Blackwell Publishers, 2000.
*TC HC79.I55 C373 2000*

Michel, Patrick. Using action research for school restructuring and organizational change. 2000.
*TC 06 no. 11295*

Robins, Kevin. Times of the technoculture. London ; New York : Routledge, 1999.
*TC T58.5 .R65 1999*

Slevin, James. The internet and society. Malden, MA : Polity Press, 2000.
*TC HM851 .S58 2000*

Social dimensions of information technology. Hershey, Pa. : Ideas Group Pub., 2000.
*TC HM851 .S63 2000*

Stefik, Mark. The Internet edge. Cambridge, Mass. : MIT Press, c1999.
*TC HM851 .S74 1999*

The university and the knowledge society. Bemmel [Netherlands] : Concorde Publishing House, 1998.
*TC LB2322.2 .U55 1998*

**INFORMATION SOCIETY - POLITICAL ASPECTS.**
Digital democracy. Toronto ; New York : Oxford University Press, 1998.
*TC JC421 .D55 1998*

**INFORMATION STORAGE.** *See* **INFORMATION RETRIEVAL.**

**INFORMATION STORAGE AND RETRIEVAL.** *See* **INFORMATION RETRIEVAL.**

**INFORMATION STORAGE AND RETRIEVAL SYSTEMS.** *See also* **COMPUTERS; DIGITAL LIBRARIES; EXPERT SYSTEMS (COMPUTER SCIENCE); INFORMATION RETRIEVAL; MULTIMEDIA SYSTEMS; PICTURE ARCHIVING AND COMMUNICATION SYSTEMS.**
Weil, Ulric. Information systems in the 80's. Englewood Cliffs, N.J. : Prentice-Hall, c1982.
*TC HD9696.C63 U5954 1982*

**INFORMATION STORAGE AND RETRIEVAL SYSTEMS - EDUCATION - PERIODICALS.**
AEDS journal. Washington, Association for Educational Data Systems.

**INFORMATION STORAGE AND RETRIEVAL SYSTEMS - EDUCATION - UNITED STATES.**
Short, Paula M. Information collection. Larchmont, NY : Eye on Education, c1998.
*TC LB1028.27.U6 S46 1998*

**INFORMATION STORAGE AND RETRIEVAL SYSTEMS - PERIODICALS.**
Online information review. Bradford, West Yorkshire : MCB University Press, 2000-

**INFORMATION SUPERHIGHWAY.** *See also*
**INFORMATION SOCIETY; INFORMATION TECHNOLOGY.**
Borgman, Christine L., 1951- From Gutenberg to the global information infrastructure. Cambridge, Mass. : MIT Press, 2000.
*TC ZA3225 .B67 2000*

Nellist, John G. Understanding modern telecommunications and the information superhighway. Boston, Mass. : Artech House, 1999.
*TC TK5105.5 .N45 1999*

**INFORMATION SUPERHIGHWAY IN EDUCATION.**
Inglis, Alistair. Delivering digitally. London : Kogan Page, c1999.
*TC LB1044.87 .I545 1999*

**INFORMATION SUPERHIGHWAY - LAW AND LEGISLATION - UNITED STATES.**
The digital dilemma. Washington, D.C. : National Academy Press, c2000.
*TC KF2979 .D53 2000*

Halbert, Debora J. (Debora Jean) Intellectual property in the information age. Westport, Conn. : Quorum, 1999.
*TC KF2979 .H35 1999*

**INFORMATION SUPERHIGHWAY - SOCIAL ASPECTS.**
Mitchell, William J. (William John), 1944- E-topia. Cambridge, Mass. : MIT Press, 1999.
*TC HE7631 .M58 1999*

**INFORMATION SUPERHIGHWAY - UNITED STATES.**
Borgman, Christine L., 1951- From Gutenberg to the global information infrastructure. Cambridge, Mass. : MIT Press, 2000.
*TC ZA3225 .B67 2000*

**Information systems in the 80's.**
Weil, Ulric. Englewood Cliffs, N.J. : Prentice-Hall, c1982.
*TC HD9696.C63 U5954 1982*

**INFORMATION SYSTEMS MANAGEMENT.** *See* **INFORMATION RESOURCES MANAGEMENT.**

**Information technologies in evaluation :** social, moral, epistemological, and practice implications / Geri Gay, Tammy L. Bennington, editors. San Francisco, Calif. : Jossey-Bass, 1999. 109 p. ; 23 cm. (New directions for evaluation, 0197-6736 ; no. 84, Winter 1999) "Winter" Includes bibliographical references and index. ISBN 0-7879-4904-3
*1. Evaluation - Moral and ethical aspects. 2. Evaluation research (Social action programs) - Moral and ethical aspects. I. Gay, Geri. II. Bennington, Tammy L. III. Series: New directions for evaluation ; no. 84.*
*TC H62 .I54 1999*

**INFORMATION TECHNOLOGY.** *See also*
**INFORMATION SUPERHIGHWAY.**
Cook, Deirdre, 1943- Interactive children, communicative teaching. Buckingham [England] ; Philadelphia : Open University Press, 1999.
*TC LB1028.46 .C686 1999*

Information technology in educational research and statistics. New York : Haworth Press, 1999.
*TC LB1028.3 .I51945 1999*

Passions, pedagogies, and 21st century technologies. Logan : Utah State University Press ; Urbana, Ill. : National Council of Teachers of English, c1999.
*TC PE1404 .P38 1999*

Transitions. Greenwich, Conn. : Ablex Pub. Corp., c1998.
*TC PE1404 .T74 1998*

Walton, Richard E. Up and running. Boston, Mass. : Harvard Business School Press, c1989.
*TC T58.6 .W345 1989*

**Information technology and scholarship :**
Applications in the humanities and social sciences / edited by Terry Coppock. Oxford : Oxford University Press for the British Academy, c1999. vi, 343 p. : ill. ; 25 cm. pbk. Includes bibliographical references. ISBN 0-19-726205-8 DDC 001.30285
*1. Humanities - Data processing. 2. Social sciences - Data processing. 3. Learning and scholarship - Technological innovations. 4. Humanities - Data processing. 5. Social sciences - Data processing. 6. Learning and scholarship - Technological innovations.*
*TC AZ186 .I556 1999*

**INFORMATION TECHNOLOGY - CASE STUDIES.**
Cases studies on information technology in higher education. Hershey, PA : Idea Group Pub., c2000.
*TC LB2395.7 .C39 2000*

**INFORMATION TECHNOLOGY - CONGRESSES.**
IFIP TC3 WG3.1/3.5 Open Conference on Communications and Networking in Education (1999 : Aulanko, Finland) Communications and networking in education. Boston : Kluwer Academic Publishers, 2000.
*TC LB1044.87 .I45 2000*

**INFORMATION TECHNOLOGY - ECONOMIC ASPECTS.**
Castells, Manuel. The rise of the network society. 2nd ed. Malden, MA : Blackwell Publishers, 2000.
*TC HC79.I55 C373 2000*

**INFORMATION TECHNOLOGY - EUROPE - CONGRESSES.**
The challenges of the information and communication technologies facing history teaching. Strasbourg : Council of Europe Pub., c1999.
*TC D424 .C425 1999*

**Information technology for schools.**
Bucher, Katherine Toth, 1947- 2nd ed. Worthington, Ohio : Linworth Pub., c1998.
*TC Z675.S3 B773 1998*

**INFORMATION TECHNOLOGY - GREAT BRITAIN - CASE STUDIES.**
Learning to teach using ICT in the secondary school. London ; New York : Routledge, 1999.
*TC LB1028.5 .L3884 1999*

**Information technology in educational research and statistics** / Leping Liu, D. LaMont Johnson, Cleborne D. Maddux, editors. New York : Haworth Press, 1999. 241 p. : ill. ; 22 cm. "...Co-published simultaneously as Computers in the schools, volume 15, numbers 3/4 & volume 16, number 1 1999." Includes bibliographical references and index. ISBN 0-7890-0958-7 (alk. paper) ISBN 0-7890-0976-5 (alk. paper) DDC 370/.7/2
*1. Educational research - Technological innovations. 2. Educational statistics - Technological innovations. 3. Information technology. I. Liu, Leping. II. Johnson, D. LaMont (Dee LaMont), 1939- III. Maddux, Cleborne D., 1942- IV. Title: Computers in the schools.*
*TC LB1028.3 .I51945 1999*

**INFORMATION TECHNOLOGY - MANAGEMENT.**
Groth, Lars. Future organizational design. Chichester ; New York : Wiley, c1999.
*TC HD30.2 .G76 1999*

**INFORMATION TECHNOLOGY - MORAL AND ETHICAL ASPECTS.**
Ethics and electronic information in the twenty-first century. West Lafayette, Ind. : Purdue University Press, c1999.
*TC T58.5 .E77 1999*

**INFORMATION TECHNOLOGY - POLITICAL ASPECTS.**
Digital democracy. Toronto ; New York : Oxford University Press, 1998.
*TC JC421 .D55 1998*

**INFORMATION TECHNOLOGY - POLITICAL ASPECTS - CONGRESSES.**
Digital democracy. London ; New York : Routledge, 1999.
*TC JF1525.A8 D54 1999*

**INFORMATION TECHNOLOGY - SOCIAL ASPECTS.**
Brown, John Seely. The social life of information. Boston : Harvard Business School Press, c2000.
*TC HM851 .B76 2000*

Castells, Manuel. The rise of the network society. 2nd ed. Malden, MA : Blackwell Publishers, 2000.
*TC HC79.I55 C373 2000*

Michel, Patrick. Using action research for school restructuring and organizational change. 2000.
*TC 06 no. 11295*

Michel, Patrick. Using action research for school restructuring and organizational change. 2000.
*TC 06 no. 11295*

Rassool, Naz, 1949- Literacy for sustainable development in the age of information. Clevedon [England] ; Philadelphia : Multilingual Matters, c1999.
*TC LC149 .R37 1999*

Robins, Kevin. Times of the technoculture. London ; New York : Routledge, 1999.

*TC T58.5 .R65 1999*
Social dimensions of information technology. Hershey, Pa. : Ideas Group Pub., 2000.
*TC HM851 .S63 2000*

**INFORMATION TECHNOLOGY - UNITED STATES.**
Becker, Nancy Jane. Implementing technology in higher education. 1999.
*TC 06 no. 11082*

Burbules, Nicholas C. Watch IT. Boulder, Colo. : Westview Press, 2000.
*TC LB1028.43 .B87 2000*

Van Dusen, Gerald C. Digital dilemma. San Francisco : Jossey-Bass, c2000.
*TC LC5805 .V35 2000*

**INFORMATION TECHNOLOGY - UNITED STATES - FINANCE.**
Dollars, distance, and online education. Phoenix, Az. : Oryx Press, 2000.
*TC LB2395.7 .M26 2000*

**INFORMATION THEORY.** *See* **DATA TRANSMISSION SYSTEMS; LANGUAGE AND LANGUAGES; SEMANTICS; TELECOMMUNICATION.**

**Information theory and the brain** / edited by Roland Baddeley, Peter Hancock, Peter Földiák. Cambridge [England] ; New York : Cambridge University Press, 2000. xiii, 344 p. : ill. ; 25 cm. Includes bibliographical references (p. 318-340) and index. ISBN 0-521-63197-1 (hbk.) DDC 612.8/2
*1. Neural networks (Neurobiology) 2. Neural networks (Computer science) 3. Information theory in biology. I. Baddeley, Roland, 1965- II. Hancock, Peter J. B., 1958- III. Földiák, Peter, 1963-*
*TC QP363.3 .I54 2000*

**INFORMATION THEORY IN BIOLOGY.**
Information theory and the brain. Cambridge [England] ; New York : Cambridge University Press, 2000.
*TC QP363.3 .I54 2000*

**INFORMATION THEORY IN PSYCHOLOGY.**
Broadbent, Donald E. (Donald Eric) Perception and communication. New York, Pergamon Press, 1958.
*TC BF38 .B685*

**Informational picture books for children.**
Cianciolo, Patricia J. Chicago : American Library Association, 2000.
*TC Z1037.A1 C54 1999*

**INFORMED CONSENT (MEDICAL LAW) - UNITED STATES.**
Field, Martha A. Equal treatment for people with mental retardation. Cambridge, Mass. ; London : Harvard University Press, 1999.
*TC KF480 .F54 1999*

**InfoTrac.**
Junior edition [computer file] [Farmington Hills, Mi.] : The Gale Group, c1999. Computer data.

Kids edition [computer file] [Farmington Hills, Mi.] : The Gale Group, c1999. Computer data.

**INFRASTRUCTURE, INFORMATION.** *See* **INFORMATION SUPERHIGHWAY.**

**INGESTION DISORDERS.** *See* **DEGLUTITION DISORDERS.**

**Ingham, Roger J., 1945-.**
Treatment efficacy for stuttering. San Diego, Calif. : Singular Pub. Group, c1998.
*TC RC424 .T698 1998*

**Inglés diccionario ilustrado.**
Inglés. Princeton [NJ] : Berlitz Pub. Co., 1997.
*TC PE1628.5 .I54 1997*

**Inglés : diccionario ilustrado.** Princeton [NJ] : Berlitz Pub. Co., 1997. 128 p. : col. ill. ; 32 cm. Subtitle from cover Primer diccionario de inglés para niños más de 1.000 palabras y frases. At head of title on cover : Berlitz kids. Parallel English and Spanish text. ISBN 2-8315-6253-8 DDC 423/.61
*1. English language - Dictionaries, Juvenile - Spanish. 2. English language - Dictionaries - Spanish. 3. Picture dictionaries. Spanish. 4. Picture dictionaries. 5. Spanish language materials - Bilingual. I. Title: Inglés diccionario ilustrado II. Title: Berlitz kids ingles diccionario ilustrado*
*TC PE1628.5 .I54 1997*

**Inglis, Alistair.** Delivering digitally : managing the transition to the knowledge media / Alistair Inglis, Peter Ling, Vera Joosten. London : Kogan Page, c1999. xiv, 210 p. : ill. ; 24 cm. (Open and distance learning series.) Includes bibliographical references (p. 203-205) and index. ISBN 0-7494-2933-X DDC 371.334467

*1. Information superhighway in education. 2. Open learning - Computer network resources. 3. World Wide Web. I. Ling, Peter. II. Joosten, Vera. III. Title. IV. Series.*
*TC LB1044.87 .I545 1999*

**Ingram, Rick E.**
Handbook of psychological change :. New York : John Wiley & Sons, c2000.
*TC RC480 .H2855 2000*

**Ingres, Jean-Auguste-Dominique, 1780-1867.** Portraits by Ingres : image of an epoch / edited by Gary Tinterow and Philip Conisbee ; drawings entries by Hans Naef ; with contributions by Philip Conisbee ... [et al.]. New York : Metropolitan Museum of Art : Distributed by Harry N. Abrams, c1999. xii, 596 p. : ill. (some col.) ; 32 cm. Catalog of an exhibition held at the National Gallery, London, Jan. 27-Apr. 25, 1999, the National Gallery of Art, Washington, D.C., May 23-Aug. 22, 1999, and the Metropolitan Museum of Art, New York, Sept. 28, 1999-Jan. 2, 2000. Includes bibliographical references (p. 557-585) and index. ISBN 0-87099-890-0 (hc) ISBN 0-8109-6536-4 (Abrams) ISBN 0-87099-891-9 (pbk. : alk. paper) DDC 759.4
*1. Ingres, Jean-Auguste-Dominique, - 1780-1867 - Exhibitions. I. Tinterow, Gary. II. Conisbee, Philip. III. Naef, Hans, 1920- IV. National Gallery (Great Britain) V. National Gallery of Art (U.S.) VI. Metropolitan Museum of Art (New York, N.Y.) VII. Title.*
*TC ND1329.I53 A4 1999*

**INGRES, JEAN-AUGUSTE-DOMINIQUE, 1780-1867 - EXHIBITIONS.**
Ingres, Jean-Auguste-Dominique, 1780-1867. Portraits by Ingres. New York : Metropolitan Museum of Art : Distributed by Harry N. Abrams, c1999.
*TC ND1329.I53 A4 1999*

**Ingulsrud, John E.** Learning to read in China : sociolinguistic perspectives on the acquisition of literacy / John E. Ingulsrud and Kate Allen. Lewiston, N.Y. ; Lampeter, Wales : Mellen, c1999. xi, 169 p., [4] leaves of plates : col. ill. ; 24 cm. Includes bibliographical references (p. 151-162) and index. ISBN 0-7734-7961-9 DDC 372.4/0951
*1. Chinese language - Study and teaching (Elementary) - China. 2. Reading (Elementary) - China. 3. Chinese characters - Study and teaching (Elementary) - China. 4. Sociolinguistics. I. Allen, Kate, 1950- II. Title.*
*TC LB1577.C48 I54 1999*

**INHERITANCE AND SUCCESSION - OHIO.**
Sussman, Marvin B. The family and inheritance New York, Russell Sage Foundation, 1970.
*TC KFO142 .S9*

**INITIALS.**
Kendrick, Laura. Animating the letter. Columbus, Ohio : Ohio State University Press, c1999.
*TC NK3610 .K46 1999*

**Initiatives (Washington, D.C.).**
National Association for Women Deans, Administrators & Counselors. Journal. [Washington, D.C. : National Association for Women Deans, Administrators, & Counselors]

**INK PAINTING, JAPANESE - EXHIBITIONS.**
Twelve centuries of Japanese art from the Imperial collections. Washington, DC : Freer Gallery of Art and the Arthur M. Sackler Gallery, Smithsonian Institution Press, c1997.
*TC ND1457.J32 W377 1997*

**Inman, James A.**
Taking flight with OWLs. Mahwah, N.J. : Lawrence Erlbaum Associates, Publishers, 2000.
*TC PE1404 .T24 2000*

**INNER CITIES - PENNSYLVANIA - PHILADELPHIA.**
Anderson, Elijah. Code of the street. 1st ed. New York : W.W Norton, c1999.
*TC F158.9.N4 A52 1999*

**INNER CITIES - UNITED STATES.**
Gallagher, Trish. Arousal patterns, emotion identification, and cognitive style in depressed and nondepressed inner-city adolescent Latinas. 1997.
*TC 085 G136*

Violence and childhood in the inner city. Cambridge, UK ; New York : Cambridge University Press, 1997.
*TC HN90.V5 V532 1997*

Wimsatt, William Upski. No more prisons. [New York] : Soft Skull Press, [2000?]
*TC HV9276.5 .W567x 2000*

**INNER CITY EDUCATION.** *See* **EDUCATION, URBAN.**

**INNER CITY GHETTOS.** *See* **INNER CITIES.**

**INNER CITY PROBLEMS.** *See* **INNER CITIES.**

**INNER PLANETS.** *See* **EARTH.**

**Inner vision.**
Zeki, Semir. Oxford ; New York : Oxford University Press, c1999.
*TC N71 .Z45 1999*

**Innovation in Russian schools** / edited by Z.I. Batioukova and T.D. Shaposhnikova ; translated by Maria Korolov. Bloomington, Ind. : Phi Delta Kappa Educational Foundation, c1997. vii, 76 p. ; 23 cm. (Phi Delta Kappa international studies in education) Includes bibliographical references (p. vi-vii). ISBN 0-87367-496-0 DDC 370/.947
*1. Educational innovations - Russia (Federation) 2. Education - Russia (Federation) I. Batioukova, Z. I. II. Shaposhnikova, T. D. III. Series.*
*TC LB1027 .I6575 1997*

**INNOVATION RELAY CENTERS.** *See* **TECHNOLOGICAL INNOVATIONS.**

**INNOVATIONS, AGRICULTURAL.** *See* **AGRICULTURAL INNOVATIONS.**

**INNOVATIONS, EDUCATIONAL.** *See* **EDUCATIONAL INNOVATIONS.**

**Innovations in science and mathematics education :** advanced designs for technologies of learning / edited by Michael J. Jacobson, Robert B. Kozma. Mahwah, N.J. : L. Erlbaum, 2000. xiv, 430 p. : ill. ; 23 cm. Includes bibliographical references and indexes. ISBN 0-8058-2846-X (acid-free paper) DDC 507/.12
*1. Science - Study and teaching - Technological innovations. 2. Mathematics - Study and teaching - Technological innovations. 3. Educational technology. I. Jacobson, Michael J. II. Kozma, Robert B.*
*TC Q181 .I654 1999*

**Innovations in science education and technology**
Science, technology, and society. New York : Kluwer Academic/Plenum, c2000.
*TC Q181 .S38225 1999*

**INNOVATIONS, INDUSTRIAL.** *See* **TECHNOLOGICAL INNOVATIONS.**

**INNOVATIONS, TECHNOLOGICAL.** *See* **TECHNOLOGICAL INNOVATIONS.**

**Innovative higher education.**
Alternative higher education. [New York, Human Sciences Press]

**Innovative interventions in child and adolescent therapy.**
Innovative psychotherapy techniques in child and adolescent therapy. 2nd ed. New York : Wiley, c1999.
*TC RJ504 .I57 1999*

**Innovative practices for teaching sign language interpreters** / Cynthia B. Roy, editor. Washington, D.C. : Gallaudet University Press, 2000. xviii, 181 p. : ill. ; 24 cm. Includes bibliographical references and index. ISBN 1-56368-088-2 DDC 419
*1. Interpreters for the deaf - Training of - United States. 2. Sign language - Study and teaching - United States. 3. American Sign Language - Study and teaching. I. Roy, Cynthia B., 1950-*
*TC HV2402 .I56 2000*

**Innovative psychotherapy techniques in child and adolescent therapy** / edited by Charles E. Schaefer. 2nd ed. New York : Wiley, c1999. xii, 514 p. : ill. ; 25 cm. Rev. ed. of: Innovative interventions in child and adolescent therapy / edited by Charles E. Schaefer. c1988. Includes bibliographical references and indexes. ISBN 0-471-24404-X (cloth : alk. paper) DDC 618.92/8914
*1. Child psychotherapy. 2. Adolescent psychotherapy. 3. Psychotherapy - in infancy & childhood. 4. Psychotherapy - in adolescence. 5. Psychotherapy - methods. I. Schaefer, Charles E. II. Title: Innovative interventions in child and adolescent therapy.*
*TC RJ504 .I57 1999*

**Innovative teaching and learning :** knowledge-based paradigms / Lakhmi C. Jain (editor). Heidelberg [Germany] ; New York : Physica-Verlag, c2000. xii, 334 p. : ill. ; 24 cm. (Studies in fuzziness and soft computing ; vol. 36) Includes bibliographical references and index. ISBN 3-7908-1246-3 (hard : alk. paper) DDC 006.3/3
*1. Expert systems (Computer science) 2. Artificial intelligence. 3. Computer-aided instruction. I. Jain, L. C. II. Series.*
*TC QA76.76.E95 I54 2000*

**INNS.** *See* **HOTELS.**

**Inquiries in social construction**
Pathology and the postmodern. London ; Thousand Oaks, CA : SAGE, 2000.
*TC BF636 .P38 2000*

Social constructionism, discourse, and realism. London : Thousand Oaks, Calif. : SAGE Publications, 1998.
*TC HM251 .S671163 1998*

**Inquiry and the National Science Education Standards :** a guide for teaching and learning / Committee on Development of an Addendum to the National Science Education Standards on Scientific Inquiry, Center for Science, Mathematics, and Engineering Education, National Research Council. Washington, D.C. : National Academy Press, c2000. xviii, 202 p. : ill. ; 28 cm. Includes bibliographical references (p. 153-158) and index. CONTENTS: Inquiry in science and in classrooms -- Inquiry in the National Science Education Standards -- Images of inquiry in K-12 classrooms -- Classroom assessment and inquiry -- Preparing teachers for inquiry-based teaching -- Making the case for inquiry -- Frequently asked questions about inquiry -- Supporting inquiry-based teaching and learning. ISBN 0-309-06476-7 (pbk.) DDC 507.1/073
*1. Science - Study and teaching - Standards - United States. 2. Inquiry (Theory of knowledge) I. Center for Science, Mathematics, and Engineering Education. Committee on Development of an Addendum to the National Science Education Standards on Scientific Inquiry.*
*TC LB1585.3 .I57 2000*

**An inquiry into the nature and causes of the wealth of nations.**
Smith, Adam, 1723-1790. Chicago : University of Chicago Press, 1976.
*TC HB161 .S65 1976*

**INQUIRY (THEORY OF KNOWLEDGE).**
Inquiry and the National Science Education Standards. Washington, D.C. : National Academy Press, c2000.
*TC LB1585.3 .I57 2000*

Reagan, Timothy G. Becoming a reflective educator. 2nd ed. Thousand Oaks Calif. : Sage Publications, c2000.
*TC LB1025.3 .R424 2000*

**INQUISITIVENESS.** *See* **CURIOSITY.**

**INSANE - LEGAL STATUS, LAWS, ETC.** *See* **MENTAL HEALTH LAWS.**

**INSANITY.** *See* **PSYCHIATRY; PSYCHOLOGY, PATHOLOGICAL.**

**INSECT SOCIETIES.** *See* **ANTS; TERMITES.**

**INSECTS.** *See* **ANTS; FLIES; TERMITES.**

**INSERVICE TRAINING.** *See* **EMPLOYEES - TRAINING OF.**

**[Inside education (Albany, N.Y.)]** Inside education. Albany : New York State Education Dept., 1968-1983. 15 v. : ill. ; 28-55 cm. Frequency: Monthly (except July, Aug. and Dec.) <1981>. Former frequency: Bimonthly, Sept. 1968- . Vol. 55, no. 1 (Oct. 1968)-v. 69, no.3 (Spring/summer 1983). Title from caption. Indexed selectively by: Public Affairs Information Service bulletin 0033-3409. Sept. 1968 issued as pilot issue. of annual report. Absorbed: University of the State of New York. Annual report. Continued in part by: University of the State of New York. Annual report. Continues: University of the State of New York. Bulletin to the schools Oct. 1914-June 1968 (DLC)sn 39039821 OCoLC)1641025. Continued by: Learning in New York (Albany, N.Y.) (DLC)sn 85062661 (OCoLC)10120612. ISSN 0020-1855 DDC 370/.9747
*1. Education - New York (State) - Periodicals. 2. Education and state - New York (State) - Periodicals. I. University of the State of New York. II. Title: University of the State of New York. Annual report III. Title: University of the State of New York. Bulletin to the schools Oct. 1914-June 1968 IV. Title: Learning in New York (Albany, N.Y.) V. Title: University of the State of New York. Annual report*

**[Inside education (Albany, N.Y. : 1991)]** Inside education / published by the New York State Education Department's Office of Communications. Albany, N.Y. : University of the State of New York, State Education Dept., 1991- v. : ill. ; 28-55 cm. Jan. 1991- . Title from caption. " A newsletter to the New York State Legislature." None published in 1992.
*1. Education - New York (State) - Periodicals. 2. Education and state - New York (State) - Periodicals. I. University of the State of New York. Office of Communications.*

**Inside lives.**
Waddell, Margot, 1946- New York : Routledge, 1998.
*TC BF175.45 .W33 1998*

**Inside picture books.**
Spitz, Ellen Handler, 1939- New Haven : Yale University Press, c1999.
*TC BF456.R2 S685 1999*

**Inside view of the production [videorecording].**
The filming of a television commercial [videorecording]. Minneapolis, Minn. : Media Loft, c1992.
*TC HF6146.T42 F5 1992*

**Insiders and outsiders.**
Freund, Bill. Portsmouth, NH : Heinemann, c1995.
*TC HD8801.Z8 D8725 1995*

**INSIGHT.** *See also* **INTUITION.**
Insight and psychosis. New York : Oxford University Press, 1998.
*TC RC512 .I49 1998*

**Insight and psychosis** / edited by Xavier F. Amador, Anthony S. David. New York : Oxford University Press, 1998. xviii, 366 p. : ill. ; 25 cm. Includes bibliographical references and index. ISBN 0-19-508497-7 (alk. paper) DDC 616.89
*1. Psychoses - Diagnosis. 2. Insight. 3. Mental status examination. 4. Psychotic Disorders - psychology. 5. Awareness. I. Amador, Xavier Francisco. II. David, Anthony S.*
*TC RC512 .I49 1998*

**Insights of genius.**
Miller, Arthur I. 1st MIT Press pbk. ed. Cambridge, Mass. : MIT Press, 2000.
*TC QC6 .M44 2000*

**INSPECTION OF FOOD.** *See* **FOOD ADULTERATION AND INSPECTION.**

**INSPECTION OF SCHOOLS.** *See* **SCHOOL MANAGEMENT AND ORGANIZATION.**

**An inspector calls : :** Ofsted and its effect on school standards / edited by Cedric Cullingford. London : Kogan Page, 1999. viii, 227 p. : ill. ; 24 cm. Includes bibliographical references and index. ISBN 0-7494-3053-2
*1. Great Britain - Office for Standards in Education. 2. School management and organization - Great Britain. I. Cullingford, Cedric.*
*TC LB2900.5 .I58 1999*

**INSPIRATION.** *See also* **CREATION (LITERARY, ARTISTIC, ETC.).**
Perkins, David N. Archimedes' bathtub. 1st ed. New York : W.W. Norton, c2000.
*TC BF441 .P47 2000*

**Inspired classroom series**
Rafoth, Mary Ann. Inspiring independent learning. Washington, DC : National Education Association of the United States, 1999.
*TC LB1049 .R35 1999*

**The inspired classroom series**
Sullo, Robert A., 1951- The inspiring teacher. Washington, D.C. : National Education Association of the United States, c1999.
*TC LB1025.3 .S85 1999*

**Inspiring independent learning.**
Rafoth, Mary Ann. Washington, DC : National Education Association of the United States, 1999.
*TC LB1049 .R35 1999*

**Inspiring students : :** case studies in motivating the learner / [edited by] Stephen Fallows and Kemal Ahmet. London : Kogan Page, 1999. xii, 180 p. : ill. ; 24 cm. (Staff and educational development series.) Includes bibliographical references and index. CONTENTS: Inspiring students: an introduction / Stephen Fallows and Kemal Ahmet -- Experiential learning through practicals / Kemal Ahmet and Stephen Fallows -- Teaching science to non-science students using a student-centered classroom / Calvin S. Kalman -- Problem-based learning / Peter Ommundsen -- Enhancing motivation and learning through collaboration and the use of problems / John R. Savery -- Simulation in management education / Mark W. Teale -- Inspiring students in a health studies programme / Andrea Riesch Toepell -- Introducing computing and information systems / Jonathan Lean, Terry Mangles and Jonathan Moizer -- Introducing communication skills / Susan Nichols -- Library and information skills for the reluctant student / Carol Primrose -- Communications skills using legal, ethical and professional issues / AC Lynn Zelmer -- Mathematics appreciation / Josefina Alvarez -- Working with students to enhance an unpopular course / Anne Arnold and John Truran -- Student-led investigations to introduce statistics / Graham Clarke -- Work-based assessments to improve learning / John Flynn -- The biology of numbers / Philip Hammond [et al] -- Introducing an interdisciplinary course / Balasubramanyam Chandramohan -- The 'art' in introducing technology to non-technologists / Ian McPherson. ISBN 0-7494-2872-4
*1. Motivation in education - Case studies. 2. Education, Higher - Case studies. I. Fallows, Stephen J. II. Ahmet, Kemal. III. Series.*
*TC LB1065 .I57 1999*

**The inspiring teacher.**
Sullo, Robert A., 1951- Washington, D.C. : National Education Association of the United States, c1999.
*TC LB1025.3 .S85 1999*

**Installation art.**
Oliveira, Nicolas de. London : Thames and Hudson, 1994.
*TC N6494.E O4 1994*

**INSTALLATIONS (ART).**
Oliveira, Nicolas de. Installation art. London : Thames and Hudson, 1994.
*TC N6494.E O4 1994*

**INSTINCT.** *See* ORIENTATION (PHYSIOLOGY); ORIENTATION (PSYCHOLOGY); PSYCHOLOGY, COMPARATIVE.

**Institute for Community Development and the Arts.**
Resource development handbook. [Washington, D.C.] : National Assembly of Local Arts Agencies, Institute for Community Development and the Arts, 1995.
*TC NX110 .R47 1995*

**Institute for Emotional Education.**
Journal of emotional education. New York, Emotional Education Press.

**Institute for Sex Research.**
Sexual behavior in the human female. Bloomington, Ind. : Indiana University Press, [1998]
*TC HQ29 .S487 1998*

**Institute of Economic Affairs. Education and Training Unit.**
Lange, Thomas, 1967- Rethinking higher education. London : IEA Education and Training Unit, 1998.
*TC LB2342.2.G7 L364 1998*

**Institute of Food Technologists.**
Food research. Champaign, Ill. : The Institute, - c1960.

**Institute of Human Origins.**
In search of human origins [videorecording]. [Boston, Mass.] : WGBH Educational Foundation, c1994.
*TC GN281 .I45 1994*

**Institute of International Education (New York, N.Y.).**
[Open doors (New York, N.Y.)] Open doors. New York, N.Y. : Institute of International Education,
*TC LB2283 .I615*

Open doors. [New York, N.Y.] : Institute of International Education, 1954-
*TC LB2283 .I615*

**Institute of International Education (New York, N.Y.). Education for one world; annual census of foreign students in the United States.**
Open doors. [New York, N.Y.] : Institute of International Education, 1954-
*TC LB2283 .I615*

**Institute of Logopedics.**
Cerebral palsy journal. Wichita, Kan., Institute of Logopedics, inc.

Cerebral palsy review. Wichita, Kan., Institute of Logopedics.

**Institute of Medicine (U.S.). Committee on Prevention and Control of Sexually Transmitted Diseases.** The hidden epidemic : confronting sexually transmitted diseases / Thomas R. Eng and William T. Butler, editors ; Committee on Prevention and Control of Sexually Transmitted Diseases, Institute of Medicine, Division of Health Promotion and Disease Prevention. Washington, D.C. : National Academy Press, 1997. xii, 432 p. : ill. ; 24 cm. Includes bibliographical references and index. ISBN 0-309-05495-8 DDC 614.5/47/0973
*1. Sexually transmitted diseases - United States. 2. Sexually Transmitted Diseases - prevention & control - United States. 3. Sexually Transmitted Diseases - epidemiology - United States. 4. Health Policy - United States. I. Eng, Thomas R. II. Butler, William T. III. Title.*
*TC RA644.V4 I495 1997*

**Institute of Paper Conservation.** Modern works, modern problems? : conference papers / edited by Alison Richmond. [England] : Institute of Paper Conservation, c1994. 180 p. : ill. (some col.) ; 30 cm. Conference held at the Tate Gallery, London, 3-5 March 1994. Conference committee: Sofia Fairclough, Camilla Baskcomb, Heather Norville-Day. Includes bibliographical references. ISBN 0-9507268-5-0
*1. Art - Conservation and restoration - Congresses. 2. Paper - Conservation and restoration - Congresses. I. Richmond, Alison. II. Tate Gallery. III. Title.*

*TC N8560 .I59 1994*

**INSTITUTIONAL CARE.** *See* HOSPITAL CARE.

**INSTITUTIONAL CARE - GREAT BRITAIN.**
Morgan, Sally, 1951- Care about education. London : DfEE, 1999.
*TC HV59 .M67 1999*

**Institutional issues :** pupils, schools and teacher education / edited by Mal Leicester, Celia Modgil and Sohan Modgil. London ; New York : Falmer Press, 2000. vi, 237 p. : ill. ; 29 cm. (Education, culture and values ; v. 2) Includes bibliographical references and index. ISBN 0-7507-1003-9 (hard) DDC 306.43
*1. Educational sociology. 2. Values - Study and teaching. 3. Multiculturalism. 4. Teachers - Training of. I. Leicester, Mal. II. Modgil, Celia. III. Modgil, Sohan. IV. Series.*
*TC LC191 .I495 2000*

**INSTITUTIONAL LINGUISTICS.** *See* LANGUAGE POLICY.

**INSTITUTIONAL RESEARCH (EDUCATION).** *See* EDUCATION, HIGHER - RESEARCH.

**INSTITUTIONS, ASSOCIATIONS, ETC.** *See* ASSOCIATIONS, INSTITUTIONS, ETC.

**INSTITUTIONS, CHARITABLE AND PHILANTHROPIC.** *See* CHARITIES.

**INSTITUTIONS, HEALTH.** *See* HEALTH FACILITIES.

**INSTITUTIONS, INTERNATIONAL.** *See* INTERNATIONAL AGENCIES; INTERNATIONAL COOPERATION.

**La Instrucción primaria.**
Cuba. Secretaría de Instrucción Pública y Bellas Artes. Havana.

**INSTRUCTION.** *See* EDUCATION; TEACHING.

**Instruction and the learning environment.**
Keefe, James W. Larchmont, NY : Eye On Education, c1997.
*TC LB2806.4 .K44 1997*

**INSTRUCTION, HOME.** *See* HOME SCHOOLING.

**Instruction of students with severe disabilities /** [edited by] Martha E. Snell, Fredda Brown. 5th ed. Upper Saddle River, N.J. : Merrill, c2000. xiii, 683 p. : ill. ; 26 cm. Includes bibliographical references and indexes. ISBN 0-13-014247-6 DDC 371.91/0973
*1. Handicapped children - Education - United States. 2. Special education - United States. I. Snell, Martha E. II. Brown, Fredda.*
*TC LC4031 .I572 2000*

**Instructional and cognitive impacts of Web-based education /** Beverly Abbey. Hershey, PA : Idea Group Pub., c2000. iv, 270 p. : ill. ; 26 cm. Includes bibliographical references and index. ISBN 1-87828-905-4 (s/c) DDC 371.33/44678
*1. Internet in education - Psychological aspects. 2. World Wide Web. 3. Instructional systems - Design. I. Abbey, Beverly, 1944-*
*TC LB1044.87 .I545 2000*

**Instructional and information technology**
The online writing classroom. Cresskill, N.J. : Hampton Press, c2000.
*TC PE1404 .O45 2000*

**INSTRUCTIONAL CHANGE.** *See* CURRICULUM CHANGE.

**INSTRUCTIONAL DESIGN.** *See* INSTRUCTIONAL SYSTEMS - DESIGN.

**INSTRUCTIONAL EFFECTIVENESS.** *See* EFFECTIVE TEACHING.

**INSTRUCTIONAL IMPROVEMENT PROGRAMS.** *See* SCHOOL IMPROVEMENT PROGRAMS.

**INSTRUCTIONAL MATERIALS.** *See also* TEACHING - AIDS AND DEVICES.
Audiovisual instruction. Washington, D.C : Dept. of Audiovisual Instruction, NEA, 1956-1978.

**Instructional materials.** [Washington, D.C.] : Dept. of Audio Visual Instruction, NEA, 1956. 1 v. : ill. ; 29 cm. Frequency: Monthly (except July, Aug., and Sept.). Vol. 1, issue 1 (Feb. 1956)-v. 1, issue 4 (June 1956). Title from cover. Continued by: Audiovisual instruction ISSN: 0004-7635 (OCoLC)5053653 (DLC)  59030807.
*1. Audio-visual education - Periodicals. I. National Education Association of the United States. Dept. of Audiovisual Instruction. II. Title: Audiovisual instruction*

**INSTRUCTIONAL MATERIALS CENTERS.** *See* SCHOOL LIBRARIES.

**INSTRUCTIONAL MATERIALS CENTERS - BOOK SELECTION - UNITED STATES.**
Van Orden, Phyllis. Selecting books for the elementary school library media center. New York : Neal-Schuman Publishers, c2000.
*TC Z675.S3 V36 2000*

**INSTRUCTIONAL MATERIALS CENTERS - SERVICES TO THE HANDICAPPED.** *See* LIBRARIES AND THE HANDICAPPED.

**INSTRUCTIONAL MATERIALS CENTERS - UNITED STATES - DATA PROCESSING.**
Bucher, Katherine Toth, 1947- Information technology for schools. 2nd ed. Worthington, Ohio : Linworth Pub., c1998.
*TC Z675.S3 B773 1998*

Doggett, Sandra L. Beyond the book. Englewood, Colo. : Libraries Unlimited, 2000.
*TC ZA4065 .D64 2000*

**INSTRUCTIONAL MATERIALS CENTERS - USER EDUCATION.** *See* LIBRARY ORIENTATION.

**INSTRUCTIONAL MATERIALS INDUSTRY.**
Stimolo, Bob. Introduction to school marketing. [Haddam], Conn. : School Market Research Institute, c1989.
*TC HF5415.122 .S75 1989*

**INSTRUCTIONAL MATERIALS PERSONNEL.** *See* AUDIO-VISUAL EDUCATION.

**INSTRUCTIONAL MATERIALS PROGRAMS.** *See* MEDIA PROGRAMS (EDUCATION).

**INSTRUCTIONAL MEDIA CENTERS.** *See* INSTRUCTIONAL MATERIALS CENTERS.

**Instructional models for physical education.**
Metzler, Michael W., 1952- Boston : Allyn and Bacon, c2000.
*TC GV363 .M425 2000*

**INSTRUCTIONAL OBJECTIVES.** *See* EDUCATION - AIMS AND OBJECTIVES.

**Instructional Objectives Exchange.** American history, grades 7-12 / Instructional Objectves Exchange. Los Angeles : The Exchange, [1968?] xi [i.e. xiv], 63 p. : ill. ; 23 cm.
*1. United States - History - Study and teaching (Secondary). I. Title.*
*TC E175.8.I56*

**INSTRUCTIONAL SUPERVISION.** *See* SCHOOL SUPERVISION.

**INSTRUCTIONAL SYSTEMS.** *See also* EDUCATION - CURRICULA; EDUCATIONAL TECHNOLOGY; TEACHING.
Idzal, June M. Multimedia authoring tools and teacher training. 1997.
*TC 06  no. 10816*

**INSTRUCTIONAL SYSTEMS ANALYSIS.** *See* EDUCATIONAL EVALUATION.

**INSTRUCTIONAL SYSTEMS - DESIGN.** *See also* CURRICULUM PLANNING.
Belanger, France, 1963- Evaluation and implementation of distance learning. Hershey, PA ; London : Idea Group Pub., c2000.
*TC LC5803.C65 B45 2000*

Bowe, Frank. Universal design in education. Westport, Conn. ; London : Bergin & Garvey, 2000.
*TC LB1028.38 .B69 2000*

Bruning, Roger H. Cognitive psychology and instruction. 3rd ed. Upper Saddle River, N.J. : Merrill, c1999.
*TC LB1060 .B786 1999*

Design approaches and tools in education and training. Dordrecht ; Boston : Kluwer Academic Publishers, c1999.
*TC LB1028.38 .D46 1999*

Gibbons, Andrew S. Computer-based instruction. Englewood Cliffs, N.J. : Educational Technology Publications, c1998.
*TC LB1028.5 .G487 1998*

Instructional and cognitive impacts of Web-based education. Hershey, PA : Idea Group Pub., c2000.
*TC LB1044.87 .I545 2000*

Instructional technology for teaching and learning. 2nd ed. Upper Saddle River, N.J. : Merrill, c2000.

*TC LB1028.38 .I587 2000*

Jonassen, David H., 1947- Task analysis methods for instructional design. Mahwah, N.J. : L. Erlbaum Associates, 1999.
*TC LB1028.38 .J65 1999*

Keegan, Mark. Scenario educational software. Englewood Cliffs, N.J. : Educational Technology Publications, c1995.
*TC LB1028.6 .K44 1995*

MORRISON, GARY R. Designing effective instruction. 3rd ed. New York : John Wiley, c2001.
*TC LB1028.38 .K46 2001*

Morrison, Gary R. Integrating computer technology into the classroom. Upper Saddle River, N.J. : Merrill, c1999.
*TC LB1028.5 .M6373 1999*

Nord, Michael B. Music in the classroom (MITC). 1998.
*TC 06 no. 10974*

Osborne, Margery D. Examining science teaching in elementary school from the perspective of a teacher and learner. New York : Falmer Press, 1999.
*TC LB1585 .O77 1999*

Piskurich, George M. Rapid instructional design. San Francisco, Calif. : Jossey-Bass, c2000.
*TC LB1028.38 .P57 2000*

Queen, J. Allen. Curriculum practice in the elementary and middle school. Upper Saddle River, N.J. : Merrill, c1999.
*TC LB1570 .Q45 1999*

**INSTRUCTIONAL SYSTEMS - DESIGN - HANDBOOKS, MANUALS, ETC.**
Forsyth, Ian. The complete guide to teaching a course. 2nd ed. London : Kogan Page ; Sterling, VA : Stylus Publishing, 1999.
*TC LB1025.3 .F67 1999*

**INSTRUCTIONAL SYSTEMS - UNITED STATES.**
Barnes, Barbara. Schools transformed for the 21st century. Torrance, Calif. : Griffin Pub. Group, c1999.
*TC LA217.2 .B39 1999*

**INSTRUCTIONAL SYSTEMS - UNITED STATES - EVALUATION.**
Friedman, Myles I., 1924- Handbook on effective instructional strategies. Columbia, S.C. : The Institute for Evidence-Based Decision-Making in Education, 1998.
*TC LB1028.35 .F75 1998*

**INSTRUCTIONAL TECHNOLOGY.** *See* **EDUCATIONAL TECHNOLOGY.**

**Instructional technology for teaching and learning :** designing instruction, integrating computers, and using media / Timothy J. Newby ... [et al.]. 2nd ed. Upper Saddle River, N.J. : Merrill, c2000. xxi, 313 p. : ill. (some col.), col. map ; 28 cm. Includes bibliographical references (p. 301-304) and indexes. ISBN 0-13-914052-2 (pbk.) DDC 371.3
*1. Instructional systems - Design. 2. Educational technology - Planning. 3. Computer-assisted instruction. I. Newby, Timothy J.*
*TC LB1028.38 .I587 2000*

**INSTRUCTIONS TO JURIES.** *See* **VERDICTS.**

**INSTRUCTIVE GAMES.** *See* **EDUCATIONAL GAMES.**

**INSTRUCTIVE TOYS.** *See* **EDUCATIONAL TOYS.**

**INSTRUCTORS.** *See* **COLLEGE TEACHERS.**

**INSTRUMENTALISTS.** *See* **ORGANISTS; VIOLONCELLISTS.**

**INSTRUMENTS, PERCUSSION.** *See* **PERCUSSION INSTRUMENTS.**

**INSULIN-DEPENDENT DIABETES.** *See* **DIABETES.**

**INSURANCE, ACCIDENT.** *See* **DISABILITY EVALUATION.**

**INSURANCE, HEALTH.** *See* **HEALTH CARE REFORM; INSURANCE, LONG-TERM CARE; MANAGED CARE PLANS (MEDICAL CARE); MEDICAL CARE.**

**INSURANCE, HEALTH - LONG-TERM CARE.** *See* **INSURANCE, LONG-TERM CARE.**

**INSURANCE, LONG-TERM CARE - UNITED STATES.**
Public and private responsibilities in long-term care. Baltimore : Johns Hopkins University Press, 1998.

*TC RA644.6 .P8 1998*

**INSURANCE, MENTAL HEALTH.** *See* **MANAGED MENTAL HEALTH CARE.**

**INSURANCE, SOCIAL.** *See* **SOCIAL SECURITY.**

**INSURANCE, STATE AND COMPULSORY.** *See* **SOCIAL SECURITY.**

**INSURANCE, WORKING-MEN'S.** *See* **SOCIAL SECURITY.**

**INSURGENCY.** *See* **COUNTERINSURGENCY; PEASANT UPRISINGS.**

**INSURGENCY - EL SALVADOR - HISTORY.**
Flores, Joaquín Evelio. Psychological effects of the civil war on children from rural communities of El Salvador.
*TC 083 F67*

**Int Audiol.**
International audiology. Leiden, Netherlands : International Society of Audiology, 1962-1970.

**INTANGIBLE PROPERTY.** *See* **COPYRIGHT; INTELLECTUAL PROPERTY.**

**INTEGRATED CURRICULUM.** *See* **INTERDISCIPLINARY APPROACH IN EDUCATION.**

**INTEGRATED DATA PROCESSING.** *See* **ELECTRONIC DATA PROCESSING.**

**Integrated education.** [Amherst, Mass., etc., Center for Equal Education, School of Education, University of Massachusetts, etc.] 22 v. ill., maps. 19-28 cm. Frequency: Bimonthly. v. 1-22; Jan. 1963-Jan./June 1984. Cover title: Integrateducation May/June 1973- . Includes bibliographies. Indexed in its entirety by: Current index to journals in education 0011-3565 1984. Indexed by: Education administration abstracts 1984. Indexed in its entirety by: Education index 0013-1385 1984. Indexed by: Index to periodical articles by and about Negroes 0073-5973 1984. Indexed by: Public affairs information service 1984. Vol. <2, no. 1 (Feb./Mar. 1964)>-v. 22, no. 1-3 (Jan./June 1984) also called issue <7>-issues 127-129. Some issues have two different dates; one is the chronological designation and the other is the date of publication (e.g. vol. 19, no. 1-2 (Jan./Apr. 1981) published Jan. 1982.) Also issued in microform from UMI. Issues for Jan.-Dec. 1963/Jan. 1964 published by Teachers for Integrated Schools; <1975-> by Integrated Education Associates; <, Nov./Dec. 1978-> by the Center for Equal Education, School of Education, University of Massachusetts. Continued by: Equity & excellence ISSN: 0894-0681 (DLC) 89662154 (OCoLC)15037564. ISSN 0020-4862 DDC 370.19/344
*1. Segregation in education - Periodicals. I. University of Massachusetts at Amherst. Center for Equal Education. II. Teachers for Integrated Schools. III. Integrated Education Associates. IV. Title: Integrateducation May/June 1973- V. Title: Equity & excellence*

**Integrated Education Associates.**
Integrated education. [Amherst, Mass., etc., Center for Equal Education, School of Education, University of Massachusetts, etc.]

**INTEGRATED RURAL DEVELOPMENT.** *See* **RURAL DEVELOPMENT.**

**Integrateducation May/June 1973-.**
Integrated education. [Amherst, Mass., etc., Center for Equal Education, School of Education, University of Massachusetts, etc.]

**Integrating community service into nursing education :** a guide to service-learning / Patricia A. Bailey, Dona Rinaldi Carpenter, Patricia A. Harrington, editors. New York, NY : Springer Pub. Co., c1999. xviii, 126 p. ; 24 cm. (Springer series, the teaching of nursing) Includes bibliographical references and index. ISBN 0-8261-1268-4 (hardcover) DDC 610.73/071/55
*1. Nurses - In-service training. 2. Nursing - Study and teaching (Continuing education) 3. Social service. 4. Education, Nursing. 5. Altruism. 6. Community-Institutional Relations. 7. Curriculum. 8. Voluntary Workers. I. Bailey, Patricia A. (Patricia Ann) II. Carpenter, Dona Rinaldi. III. Harrington, Patricia A. IV. Series: Springer series on the teaching of nursing.*
*TC RT76 .I55 1999*

**Integrating computer technology into the classroom.**
Morrison, Gary R. Upper Saddle River, N.J. : Merrill, c1999.
*TC LB1028.5 .M6373 1999*

**Integrating literature and the arts throughout the curriculum.**
Cornett, Claudia E. The arts as meaning makers. Upper Saddle River, N.J. : Merrill, 1999.
*TC LB1591 .C67 1999*

**Integrating mathematics and science for below average ninth grade students.**
Wiltshire, Michael A. 1997.
*TC 06 no. 10847*

**Integrating quantitative and qualitative methods in research** / George R. Taylor [editor]. Lanham, Md. ; Oxford : University Press of America, c2000. v, 245 p. : ill. ; 24 cm. Includes bibliographical references. ISBN 0-7618-1644-5 (cloth : alk. paper) ISBN 0-7618-1645-3 (paper : alk. paper) DDC 001.4/2
*1. Research - Methodology. I. Taylor, George R.*
*TC Q175 .I513 2000*

**Integrating spirituality into multicultural counseling.**
Fukuyama, Mary A. Thousand Oaks, Calif. : Sage Publications, c1999.
*TC BF637.C6 F795 1999*

**Integrating spirituality into treatment :** resources for practitioners / edited by William R. Miller. 1st ed. Washington, DC : American Psychological Association, c1999. xix, 293 p. : 27 cm. Includes bibliographical references and index. ISBN 1-55798-581-2 (casebound : alk. paper) DDC 616.89/14
*1. Psychotherapy - Religious aspects. 2. Spirituality. I. Miller, William R.*
*TC RC489.R46 I58 1999*

**Integrating the trans-national/cultural dimension.**
Fersh, Seymour. Bloomington, Ind. : Phi Delta Kappa Educational Foundation, c1993.
*TC LC1090 .F47 1993*

**INTEGRATION IN EDUCATION.** *See* **SCHOOL INTEGRATION.**

**INTEGRATION, RACIAL.** *See* **RACE RELATIONS.**

**INTEGRITY.** *See* **HONESTY.**

**InteLex Corporation.**
Dewey, John, 1859-1952. The correspondence of John Dewey. [computer file]. Windows version. Charlottesville, VA : InteLex Corp., 1999- Computer data and program.
*TC B945.D44 A4 1999*

Dewey, John, 1859-1952. [Works.] The collected works of John Dewey, 1882-1953. [computer file]. Windows version. Charlottesville, VA : InteLex Corp., 1997, c1992. Computer program.
*TC LB875 .D363 1997*

**INTELLECT.** *See also* **COGNITIVE STYLES; CREATION (LITERARY, ARTISTIC, ETC.); IMAGINATION; KNOWLEDGE, THEORY OF; LOGIC; MEMORY; MENTAL RETARDATION; PERCEPTION; THOUGHT AND THINKING.**
Flanagan, Dawn P. The Wechsler intelligence scales and Gf-Gc theory. Boston ; London : Allyn and Bacon, c2000.
*TC BF432.5.W4 F53 2000*

Handbook of intelligence. Cambridge ; New York : Cambridge University Press, 2000.
*TC BF431 .H31865 2000*

Locke, John, 1632-1704. [Some thoughts concerning education] Some thoughts concerning education ; Indianapolis : Hackett Pub. Co., c1996.
*TC LB475.L6 L63 1996*

Mind myths. Chichester, England ; New York : J. Wiley & Sons, c1999.
*TC BF161 .M556 1999*

Mind myths. Chichester, England ; New York : J. Wiley & Sons, c1999.
*TC BF161 .M556 1999*

Perspectives on fundamental processes in intellectual functioning. Stamford, Conn. : Ablex Pub. Corp., c1998-
*TC BF444 .P42 1998*

Practical intelligence in everyday life. Cambridge, UK ; New York, NY : Cambridge University Press, 2000.
*TC BF431 .P64 2000*

Sasaki, Miyuki, 1959- Second language proficiency, foreign language aptitude, and intelligence. New York : P. Lang, c1999.
*TC P53.4 .S27 1999*

**Intellect.** [New York, Society for the Advancement of Education] 6 v. ill. 26 cm. Frequency: Monthly (except bimonthly May-Oct.). v. 101-106 (no. 2343-2397); Oct. 1972-June 1978. Indexed by: Readers' guide to periodical literature 0034-0464. Indexed by: Social sciences citation index 0091-3707. Indexed by: Current contents: social & behavioral sciences. Indexed by: Women studies abstracts 0049-7835.

Indexed by: Index to periodical articles related to law. Indexed by: Education index 0013-1385. Indexed by: Education administration abstracts. Indexed by: Current index to journals in education 0011-3565. Indexed by: College student personnel abstracts. Available on microfilm to subscribers only from University Microfilms; available on microfiche from Bell & Howell Micro Photo Division or Johnson Associates.
Continues: School & society ISSN: 0036-6455
(DLC)  17001407 (OCoLC)1608100. Continued by: USA today ISSN: 0161-7389 (DLC)  78645500 (OCoLC)4014217. ISSN 0149-0095 DDC 370/.5
*1. Education - Periodicals. I. Society for the Advancement of Education. II. Title: School & society III. Title: USA today*

## INTELLECT - GENETIC ASPECTS.
Valencia, Richard R. Intelligence testing and minority students. Thousand Oaks, Calif. : Sage Publications, [2000]
*TC BF431.5.U6 V35 2000*

## INTELLECTRONICS. *See* ARTIFICIAL INTELLIGENCE.

## INTELLECTUAL CAPITAL - UNITED STATES.
Gross, Clifford M. The new idea factory. Columbus, OH : Battelle Press, c2000.
*TC HD53 .G75 2000*

## INTELLECTUAL COOPERATION. *See* CONGRESSES AND CONVENTIONS; CULTURAL RELATIONS; EDUCATIONAL EXCHANGES; INTERNATIONAL EDUCATION.

## INTELLECTUAL COOPERATION - BIBLIOGRAPHY - PERIODICALS.
League of Nations. Bulletin de la coopération intellectuelle. Paris : Institut international de coopération intellectuelle, [1931?-1932?]

## INTELLECTUAL COOPERATION - PERIODICALS.
League of Nations. Bulletin de la coopération intellectuelle. Paris : Institut international de coopération intellectuelle, [1931?-1932?]

[Open doors (New York, N.Y.)] Open doors. New York, N.Y. : Institute of International Education,
*TC LB2283 .I615*

## INTELLECTUAL COOPERATION - STATISTICS.
Open doors. [New York, N.Y.] : Institute of International Education, 1954-
*TC LB2283 .I615*

## INTELLECTUAL FREEDOM. *See* ACADEMIC FREEDOM; CENSORSHIP; FREEDOM OF INFORMATION; FREEDOM OF SPEECH; TEACHING, FREEDOM OF.

## INTELLECTUAL LIFE. *See* LEARNING AND SCHOLARSHIP; POPULAR CULTURE.

## INTELLECTUAL LIFE - STATISTICS - PERIODICALS.
[Statistical yearbook (Unesco)] Statistical yearbook = [Paris : Unesco], 1987-
*TC AZ361 .U45*

## INTELLECTUAL PROPERTY. *See also* COPYRIGHT.
Perspectives on plagiarism and intellectual property in a postmodern world. Albany : State University of New York Press, c1999.
*TC PN167 .P47 1999*

**Intellectual property in the information age.**
The digital dilemma. Washington, D.C. : National Academy Press, c2000.
*TC KF2979 .D53 2000*

Halbert, Debora J. (Debora Jean) Westport, Conn. : Quorum, 1999.
*TC KF2979 .H35 1999*

## INTELLECTUAL PROPERTY - UNITED STATES.
The digital dilemma. Washington, D.C. : National Academy Press, c2000.
*TC KF2979 .D53 2000*

Halbert, Debora J. (Debora Jean) Intellectual property in the information age. Westport, Conn. : Quorum, 1999.
*TC KF2979 .H35 1999*

## INTELLECTUALS, AFRO-AMERICAN. *See* AFRO-AMERICAN INTELLECTUALS.

## INTELLECTUALS - INTERVIEWS.
Race, rhetoric, and the postcolonial. Albany : State University of New York Press, c1999.
*TC P301.5.P67 R33 1999*

## INTELLECTUALS - UNITED STATES. *See* AFRO-AMERICAN INTELLECTUALS.

## INTELLECTUALS - UNITED STATES - BIOGRAPHY.
Pioneers in popular culture studies. Bowling Green, OH : Bowling Green State University Popular Press, c1999.
*TC E169.04 .P563 1999*

## INTELLIGENCE. *See also* INTELLECT.
Jolly, Alison. Lucy's legacy. Cambridge, Mass. : London : Harvard University Press, 1999.
*TC GN281 .J6 1999*

Martinez, Michael E. Education as the cultivation of intelligence. Mahwah, N.J. ; London : Lawrence Erlbaum Associates, 2000.
*TC LB1060 .M337 2000*

## INTELLIGENCE, ARTIFICIAL. *See* ARTIFICIAL INTELLIGENCE.

## INTELLIGENCE, BUSINESS. *See* BUSINESS INTELLIGENCE.

## INTELLIGENCE, CORPORATE. *See* BUSINESS INTELLIGENCE.

## INTELLIGENCE LEVELS. *See also* GENIUS.
Bell, Lisa M. Frontal lobe dysfunction in first episode Schizophrenia. 1998.
*TC 085 B3995*

Handbook of intelligence. Cambridge ; New York : Cambridge University Press, 2000.
*TC BF431 .H31865 2000*

## INTELLIGENCE LEVELS - RESEARCH.
Conceptual issues in research on intelligence. Stamford, Conn. : JAI Press , 1998.
*TC BF311 .A38 v. 5 1998*

## INTELLIGENCE LEVELS - TESTING. *See* INTELLIGENCE TESTS.

## INTELLIGENCE LEVELS - UNITED STATES.
Valencia, Richard R. Intelligence testing and minority students. Thousand Oaks, Calif. : Sage Publications, [2000]
*TC BF431.5.U6 V35 2000*

## INTELLIGENCE OF ANIMALS. *See* PSYCHOLOGY, COMPARATIVE.

## INTELLIGENCE QUOTIENT. *See* INTELLIGENCE LEVELS.

## INTELLIGENCE TESTING. *See* INTELLIGENCE TESTS.

**Intelligence testing and minority students.**
Valencia, Richard R. Thousand Oaks, Calif. : Sage Publications, [2000]
*TC BF431.5.U6 V35 2000*

## INTELLIGENCE TESTS.
Flanagan, Dawn P. The Wechsler intelligence scales and Gf-Gc theory. Boston : London : Allyn and Bacon, c2000.
*TC BF432.5.W4 F53 2000*

Handbook of intelligence. Cambridge ; New York : Cambridge University Press, 2000.
*TC BF431 .H31865 2000*

## INTELLIGENCE TESTS - UNITED STATES.
Valencia, Richard R. Intelligence testing and minority students. Thousand Oaks, Calif. : Sage Publications, [2000]
*TC BF431.5.U6 V35 2000*

## INTELLIGENCE TESTS - UNITED STATES - HISTORY - 20TH CENTURY.
Lemann, Nicholas. The big test :. 1st ed. New York : Farrar, Straus and Giroux, 1999.
*TC LB3051 .L44 1999*

## INTELLIGENT MACHINES. *See* ARTIFICIAL INTELLIGENCE.

**Intelligent multimedia information retrieval** / edited by Mark T. Maybury ; [foreword by Karen Spärck Jones]. Menlo Park, Calif. : AAAI Press ; Cambridge, Mass. : MIT Press, c1997. xxxiii, 478 p. : ill. ; 23 cm.
Includes bibliographical references and index. ISBN 0-262-63179-2 (pb : acid-free paper) DDC 025.04
*1. Multimedia systems. 2. User interfaces (Computer systems) 3. Artificial intelligence. I. Maybury, Mark T.*
*TC QA76.575 .I577 1997*

## INTELLIGENTSIA. *See* INTELLECTUALS.

## INTEMPERANCE. *See* ALCOHOLISM.

## INTENSION (PHILOSOPHY). *See* SEMANTICS (PHILOSOPHY).

## INTENSIVE CARE NURSING - HISTORY.
Fairman, Julie. Critical care nursing. Philadelphia : University of Pennsylvania Press, c1998.

*TC RT120.I5 F34 1998*

## INTENSIVE PROGRAMS IN EDUCATION. *See* EDUCATIONAL ACCELERATION.

## INTENTIONALISM.
Gibbs, Raymond W. Intentions in the experience of meaning. New York : Cambridge University Press, 1999.
*TC BF463.M4 G53 1999*

## INTENTIONALITY (PHILOSOPHY).
Wilton, Richard. Consciousness, free will, and the explanation of human behavior. Lewiston, N.Y. : E. Mellen Press, c2000.
*TC BF161 .W495 2000*

**Intentions in the experience of meaning.**
Gibbs, Raymond W. New York : Cambridge University Press, 1999.
*TC BF463.M4 G53 1999*

## INTER-AMERICAN DEVELOPMENT BANK.
Nelson, Joan M. Reforming health and education. Washington, DC : Overseas Development Council ; Baltimore, MD : Distributed by the Johns Hopkins University Press, c1999.
*TC HG3881.5.W57 N447 1999*

**Inter-American Indian Institute.**
América indígena. México.

## INTER-CULTURAL STUDIES. *See* CROSS-CULTURAL STUDIES.

## INTER-VARSITY CHRISTIAN FELLOWSHIP.
Bramadat, Paul A. The church on the world's turf. Oxford ; New York : Oxford University Press, 2000.
*TC BV970.I6 B73 2000*

## INTERACTION ANALYSIS IN EDUCATION.
Arias, Rafael. Analysis of discourse in an ESL peer-mentoring teacher group. 1999.
*TC 06 no. 10791*

Ellis, Rod. Learning a second language through interaction. Amsterdam : Philadelphia : J. Benjamins, c1999.
*TC P118.2 .E38 1999*

Flynn, Bernadette Marie. The teacher-child relationship, temperament, and coping in children with developmental disabilities. 2000.
*TC 06 no. 11267*

Jones, Vernon F., 1945- Comprehensive classroom management. 6th ed. Boston : Allyn and Bacon, c2001.
*TC LB3013 .J66 2001*

Martin, Robert J. A study of the reflective practices of physical education student teachers. 1998.
*TC 06 no. 11031*

O'Neil, Judith Ann. The role of the learning advisor in action learning. 1999.
*TC 06 no. 11156*

## INTERACTION ANALYSIS IN EDUCATION - ADDRESSES, ESSAYS, LECTURES.
Research into classroom processes: New York, Teachers College Press, 1971.
*TC LB1028 .W488*

## INTERACTION ANALYSIS IN EDUCATION - AUDIO-VISUAL AIDS.
Carr, Richard John. The application of multimedia in arts-integrated curricula. 1998.
*TC 06 no. 10919*

## INTERACTION ANALYSIS IN EDUCATION - CASE STUDIES.
Mirochnik, Elijah, 1952- Teaching in the first person. New York : P. Lang, c2000.
*TC LB1033 .M546 2000*

Orange, Carolyn. 25 biggest mistakes teachers make and how to avoid them. Thousand Oaks Calif. : Corwin Press, c2000.
*TC LB1033 .O73 2000*

## INTERACTION PROCESS ANALYSIS IN EDUCATION. *See* INTERACTION ANALYSIS IN EDUCATION.

## INTERACTION, SOCIAL. *See* SOCIAL INTERACTION.

**Interactional perspectives on LSP** / edited by Inger Lassen. Aalborg Øst, Denmark : Centre for Languages and Intercultural Studies, Aalborg University, 1997. 94 p. : ill. ; 21 cm. (Language and cultural contact, 0908-777X ; 22) Papers presented at the 3rd annual symposium, Intercultural Communication and National Identity, held in November 1996 at Aalborg University. Includes bibliographical references. ISBN 87-7307-602-3 (pbk.)

*1. Sublanguage - Congresses. I. Lassen, Inger. II. Series: Sprog og kulturmøde ; 22.*
*TC P120.S9 I58 1997*

**Interactions.**
Friend, Marilyn Penovich, 1953- 3rd ed. New York : Longman, 1999.
*TC LC3969.45 .F75 1999*

## INTERACTIVE ANALYSIS IN EDUCATION.
Asher, James J. (James John), 1929- Learning another language through actions. 4th ed. Los Gatos, Calif. : Sky Oaks Productions, 1993.
*TC PB36 .A8 1993*

**Interactive children, communicative teaching.**
Cook, Deirdre, 1943- Buckingham [England] : Philadelphia : Open University Press, 1999.
*TC LB1028.46 .C686 1999*

**Interactive group learning.**
Ulrich, Deborah L. New York : Springer, c1999.
*TC RT76 .U46 1999*

### INTERACTIVE MEDIA. *See* INTERACTIVE MULTIMEDIA.

### INTERACTIVE MULTIMEDIA.
The Computer as medium. Cambridge [England] : New York : Cambridge University Press, 1993.
*TC QA76.5 .C612554 1993*

Idzal, June M. Multimedia authoring tools and teacher training. 1997.
*TC 06 no. 10816*

International perspectives on tele-education and virtual learning environments. Aldershot : Ashgate, 2000.
*TC LB1044.87 .I55 2000*

Teare, Richard. The virtual university. London ; New York : Cassell, 1998. ·
*TC LC5215 .T42 1998* ·

### INTERACTIVE MULTIMEDIA - HANDBOOKS, MANUALS, ETC.
Brunner, Cornelia, Dr. The new media literacy handbook. New York : Anchor Books, 1999.
*TC LB1028.3 .B77 1999*

### INTERACTIVE MULTIMEDIA - SOCIAL ASPECTS.
International perspectives on tele-education and virtual learning environments. Aldershot : Ashgate, 2000.
*TC LB1044.87 .I55 2000*

### INTERACTIVE TELEVISION.
Interactive television. Aalborg, Denmark : Aalborg University Press, 1999.
*TC HE8700.95 .I57 1999*

**Interactive television : TV of the future or the future of TV? /** edited by Jens F. Jensen & Cathy Toscan. Aalborg, Denmark : Aalborg University Press, 1999. 278 p. : ill. ; 25 cm. (Media & cultural studies ; 1) Includes bibliographical references. CONTENTS: Introduction / Jens F. Jensen & Cathy Toscan -- The concept of interactivity / Jens F. Jenson -- Interactive television and virtual culture / David Tafler -- Interactive television - a shattered dream? / Gerhard Fuchs --Digital TV and public service in the Nordic countries / Rolf Brandrud -- New media change / Terje Rasmussen -- A new approach to radio and television broadcasting over the Internet / Borko Furht, Raymond Westwater & Jeffrey Ice --As viewers become consumer-users / Derek Nicoll -- Interactive television at home / James Stewart -- A new generation of audiences for the 21st century / Cathy Toscan. ISBN 87-7307-625-2
*1. Interactive television. I. Jensen, Jens F. II. Toscan, Cathy. III. Series.*
*TC HE8700.95 .I57 1999*

### INTERACTIVE TELEVISION - UNITED STATES - HANDBOOKS, MANUALS, ETC.
Lawyer-Brook, Dianna, 1949- Shifting focus. Lanham, Md. ; London : Scarecrow Press, 2000.
*TC LB1044.7 .L313 2000*

**Interactive writing.**
McCarrier, Andrea. Portsmouth, NH : Heinemann, c2000.
*TC LB1139.5.L35 M39 2000*

**Interactive writing : language and literacy and how it all comes together.**
McCarrier, Andrea. Interactive writing. Portsmouth, NH : Heinemann, c2000.
*TC LB1139.5.L35 M39 2000*

### INTERCHANGE OF STUDENTS. *See* STUDENT EXCHANGE PROGRAMS.

**Intercine.** Rome. v. ill. 28 cm. (v. 1: 23 cm.). v. 1- ; July 1929-Dec. 1935. Title varies: International review of educational cinematography; July 1929-Dec. 1934. Published in 5 editions: English, French, Italian, Spanish and German. Includes section "Bibliography." Issued by the International Educational Cinematographic Institute, League of Nations. Also called The International Institute of Eduational Cinematography. Superseded by: Cinéma. DDC 371.335
*1. Moving-pictures in education. 2. Moving-pictures - Periodicals. I. Feo, Luciano de. II. International Educational Cinematographic Institute. III. Title: International review of educational cinematography; July 1929-Dec. 1934 IV. Title: Cinéma*

### INTERCOLLEGIATE ATHLETICS. *See* COLLEGE SPORTS.

**Intercollegiate athletics and the American university.**
Duderstadt, James J., 1942- Ann Arbor [Mich.] : University of Michigan Press, c2000.
*TC GV351 .D83 2000*

### INTERCOLLEGIATE SPORTS. *See* COLLEGE SPORTS.

### INTERCOUNTRY ADOPTION - CASE STUDIES.
Evans, Karin. The lost daughters of China. New York : J.P. Tarcher/Putnam, c2000.
*TC HV1317 .E93 2000*

### INTERCOURSE.
Hite, Shere. The Hite report on male sexuality. 1st Ballantine Book ed. New York : Ballantine Books, 1982.
*TC HQ28 .H57 1982*

### INTERCULTURAL COMMUNICATION.
Culturally speaking. London ; New York : Continuum ; [New York] : [Cassell], 2000.
*TC GN345.6 .C86 2000*

### INTERCULTURAL COMMUNICATION - FOREIGN COUNTRIES.
Pollock, David C. The third culture kid experience. Yarmouth, Me. : Intercultural Press, c1999.
*TC HQ784.S56 P65 1999*

### INTERCULTURAL COMMUNICATION - NEW YORK (STATE) - CASE STUDIES.
Schlanger, Dean J. An exploration of school belongingness. 1998.
*TC 06 no. 10993*

### INTERCULTURAL COMMUNICATION - PERIODICALS.
[International journal of intercultural relations (Online)] International journal of intercultural relations [computer file]. Oxford ; New York : Pergamon.
*TC EJOURNALS*

### INTERCULTURAL COMMUNICATION - PROBLEMS, EXERCISES, ETC.
Goldstein, Susan B. Cross-cultural explorations. Boston : Allyn and Bacon, c2000.
*TC HM258 .G63 2000*

### INTERCULTURAL COMMUNICATION - STUDY AND TEACHING (HIGHER) - ACTIVITY PROGRAMS.
Teaching about culture, ethnicity & diversity. Thousand Oaks : Sage Publications, c1998.
*TC HM101 .T38 1998*

### INTERCULTURAL COMMUNICATION - UNITED STATES.
Clauss, Caroline Seay. Degrees of distance. 1999.
*TC 085 C58*

Mindess, Anna. Reading between the signs. Yarmouth, Me. : Intercultural Press, c1999.
*TC HV2402 .M56 1999*

### INTERCULTURAL EDUCATION. *See also* MULTICULTURAL EDUCATION.
Fersh, Seymour. Integrating the trans-national/cultural dimension. Bloomington, Ind. : Phi Delta Kappa Educational Foundation, c1993.
*TC LC1090 .F47 1993*

Math around the world. Berkeley, CA : Lawrence Hall of Science, University of California at Berkeley, c1995.
*TC QA20.G35 M384 1995*

**Intercultural education.** New York, International Council for Educational Development. v. 26 cm. Frequency: Irregular. v. 1-2, no. 6; 1969-May 1971. "An information service of the International Council for Educational Development." Vol. 1, no. 1-9 issued by the council under its earlier name: Education and World Affairs. ISSN 0020-532X DDC 370.19/6
*1. Multicultural education - Periodicals. I. International*

Council for Educational Development. II. Education and World Affairs.

### INTERCULTURAL EDUCATION - CANADA.
Chud, Gyda. Early childhood education for a multicultural society. [Vancouver] : Western Education Development Group, Faculty of Education, The University of British Columbia, c1985.
*TC LC1099 .C494 1985*

Thomas, Barb, 1946- Combatting racism in the workplace. Toronto : Cross Cultural Communication Centre, c1983.
*TC HD4903.5.C3 T56 1983*

### INTERCULTURAL EDUCATION - CANADA - CURRICULA - HANDBOOKS, MANUALS, ETC.
Kehoe, John W. A handbook for enhancing the multicultural climate of the school. [Vancouver, B.C.] : Western Education Development Group, Faculty of Education, University of British Colombia, c1984.
*TC LC1099 .K438 1984*

### INTERCULTURAL EDUCATION - CANADA - HANDBOOKS, MANUALS, ETC.
Kehoe, John W. A handbook for enhancing the multicultural climate of the school. [Vancouver, B.C.] : Western Education Development Group, Faculty of Education, University of British Colombia, c1984.
*TC LC1099 .K438 1984*

### INTERCULTURAL RELATIONS. *See* CULTURAL RELATIONS.

### INTERCULTURAL STUDIES. *See* CROSS-CULTURAL STUDIES.

**Intercultural therapy /** edited by Jafar Kareem and Roland Littlewood. [2nd ed.]. Oxford ; Malden, MA : Blackwell Science, 2000. xiv, 278 p. : ill. ; 24 cm. Includes bibliographical references (p. 252-272) and index. ISBN 0-632-05224-4 DDC 616.89/14
*1. Cultural psychiatry. 2. Cross-cultural counseling. 3. Psychiatry, Transcultural. 4. Cross-Cultural Comparison 5. Psychotherapy 6. Ethnopsychology I. Kareem, Jafar. II. Littlewood. Roland.*
*TC RC455.4.E8 I57 2000*

### INTERDEPENDENCE OF NATIONS. *See* INTERNATIONAL COOPERATION; INTERNATIONAL ECONOMIC RELATIONS; INTERNATIONAL RELATIONS.

### INTERDICTION (CIVIL LAW). *See* GUARDIAN AND WARD.

### INTERDISCIPLINARITY IN EDUCATION. *See* INTERDISCIPLINARY APPROACH IN EDUCATION.

### INTERDISCIPLINARY APPROACH IN EDUCATION. *See also* LANGUAGE ARTS - CORRELATION WITH CONTENT SUBJECTS.
Chatton, Barbara. Blurring the edges. Portsmouth, NH : Heinemann, c1999.
*TC LB1576 .C46 1999*

Cornett, Claudia E. The arts as meaning makers. Upper Saddle River, N.J. : Merrill, 1999.
*TC LB1591 .C67 1999*

Daniels, Harvey, 1947- Methods that matter. York, Me. : Stenhouse Publishers, c1998.
*TC LB1027 .D24 1998*

Interdisciplinary general education. New York, NY : College Board Publications, c1999.
*TC LB2361 .I43 1999*

Kasper, Loretta F. (Loretta Frances), 1951- Content-based college ESL instruction. Mahwah, N.J. : Lawrence Erlbaum Associates, 2000.
*TC PE1128.A2 K376 2000*

Math around the world. Berkeley, CA : Lawrence Hall of Science, University of California at Berkeley, c1995.
*TC QA20.G35 M384 1995*

Parks, Stephen, 1963- Class politics. Urbana, Ill. : National Council of Teachers of English, c2000.
*TC PE1405.U6 P3 2000*

Student writing in higher education. Philadelphia, Pa. : Open University Press, c2000.
*TC PE1404 .S84 2000*

Teaching children about health. Englewood, Colo. : Morton Pub., 1999.

*TC LB1587.A3 T43 1999*

Teaching critical thinking. Englewood Cliffs, N.J. : Prentice Hall, c1993.
*TC LB1590.3 .T4 1993*

Teaching in the 21st century. New York : Falmer Press, 1999.
*TC PE1404 .T394 1999*

Wiltshire, Michael A. Integrating mathematics and science for below average ninth grade students. 1997.
*TC 06 no. 10847*

### INTERDISCIPLINARY APPROACH IN EDUCATION - BIBLIOGRAPHY.
Interdisciplinary education. New York, NY : College Entrance Examination Board, 1999.
*TC LB2361 .I58 1999*

### INTERDISCIPLINARY APPROACH IN EDUCATION - CANADA.
Drake, Susan M., 1944- Creating integrated curriculum. Thousand Oaks, Calif. : Corwin Press, c1998.
*TC LB1570 .D695 1998*

### INTERDISCIPLINARY APPROACH IN EDUCATION - CASE STUDIES.
Carr, Richard John. The application of multimedia in arts-integrated curricula. 1998.
*TC 06 no. 10919*

### INTERDISCIPLINARY APPROACH IN EDUCATION - GREAT BRITAIN.
Use of language across the primary curriculum. London : New York : Routledge, 1998.
*TC LB1576 U74 1998*

### INTERDISCIPLINARY APPROACH IN EDUCATION - NEW YORK (STATE) - NEW YORK - CASE STUDIES.
Nord, Michael B. Music in the classroom (MITC). 1998.
*TC 06 no. 10974*

### INTERDISCIPLINARY APPROACH IN EDUCATION - PUERTO RICO.
Laborde, Ilia M. Rediscovering San Cristóbal Canyon. 1996.
*TC 06 no. 10660*

Laborde, Ilia M. Rediscovering San Cristóbal Canyon. 1996.
*TC 06 no. 10660*

### INTERDISCIPLINARY APPROACH IN EDUCATION - UNITED STATES.
Art works!. Portsmouth, NH : Heinemann, c1999.
*TC LB1628.5 .A78 1999*

Drake, Susan M., 1944- Creating integrated curriculum. Thousand Oaks, Calif. : Corwin Press, c1998.
*TC LB1570 .D695 1998*

Griss, Susan. Minds in motion. Portsmouth, NH : Heinemann, c1998.
*TC LB1592 .G75 1998*

Hanna, Judith Lynne. Partnering dance and education. Champaign, IL : Human Kinetics, c1999.
*TC GV1589 .H35 1999*

Mallery, Anne L. Creating a catalyst for thinking. Boston : Allyn and Bacon, c2000.
*TC LB2806.15 .M34 2000*

Martinello, Marian L. Interdisciplinary inquiry in teaching and learning. 2nd. ed. Upper Saddle River, N.J. : Merrill, c2000.
*TC LB1570 .M3675 2000*

Strategies for energizing large classes : from small groups to learning communities. San Francisco, Calif. : Jossey-Bass, 2000.
*TC LB2361.5 .S77 2000*

### INTERDISCIPLINARY APPROACH TO KNOWLEDGE.
Martinello, Marian L. Interdisciplinary inquiry in teaching and learning. 2nd. ed. Upper Saddle River, N.J. : Merrill, c2000.
*TC LB1570 .M3675 2000*

**Interdisciplinary clinical assessment of young children with developmental disabilities** / edited by Michael J. Guralnick. Baltimore : Paul H. Brookes Pub. Co., c2000. xv, 471 p. : ill. ; 24 cm. (International issues in early intervention.) Includes bibliographical references and index. ISBN 1-55766-450-1 (hardcover)
*1. Developmentally disabled children - Services for. 2. Developmentally disabled children - Identification. 3. Social work with handicapped children. I. Guralnick, Michael J. II. Series.*

*TC HV891 .I58 2000*

**Interdisciplinary education** : a guide to resources / Joan B. Fiscella and Stacey E. Kimmel, editors. New York, NY : College Entrance Examination Board, 1999. 343 p. ; 23 cm. Includes bibliographical references and index. "The editors have gathered and annotated a comprehensive bibliography and organized it in such a way that both practitioners and students of interdisciplinarity will be able to find their way through the thickets."--Foreword. ISBN 0-87447-632-1 (pbk.)
*1. Interdisciplinary approach in education - Bibliography. 2. Education - Curricula - Bibliography. I. Fiscella. Joan B. II. Kimmel, Stacey E.*

*TC LB2361 .I58 1999*

**Interdisciplinary general education** : questioning outside the lines : University of Hartford all-university curriculum / Marcia Bundy Seabury, editor. New York, NY : College Board Publications, c1999. xxix, 366 p. ; 22 cm. Cover title: University of Hartford experience. ISBN 0-87447-639-9
*1. Interdisciplinary approach in education. 2. Education. Higher - Curricula. 3. Curriculum planning. 4. University of Hartford - Curricula. I. Seabury, Marcia Bundy. II. Title: Questioning outside the lines III. Title: University of Hartford experience*

*TC LB2361 .I43 1999*

**Interdisciplinary inquiry in teaching and learning.** Martinello, Marian L. 2nd. ed. Upper Saddle River, N.J. : Merrill, c2000.
*TC LB1570 .M3675 2000*

### INTERDISCIPLINARY RESEARCH.
DeVault, Marjorie L., 1950- Liberating method. Philadelphia : Temple University Press, 1999.
*TC HQ1180 .D48 1999*

**Interdisciplinary research series in ethnic, gender, and class relations**
Banks, Nick. White counsellors--Black clients. Aldershot, Hants, England ; Brookfield, Vt. : Ashgate, c1999.
*TC HV3177.G7 B36 1999*

**Interdisciplinary research series in ethnic, gender and class relations**
Preece, Julia. Combating social exclusion in university adult education. Aldershot ; Brookfield, Vt. : Ashgate, c1999.
*TC LC5256.G7 P84 1999*

### INTERDISCIPLINARY STUDIES. *See* INTERDISCIPLINARY APPROACH IN EDUCATION.

### INTEREST (PSYCHOLOGY). *See* ATTENTION; CURIOSITY.

### INTERETHNIC RELATIONS. *See* ETHNIC RELATIONS.

### INTERFACES, USER (COMPUTER SYSTEMS). *See* USER INTERFACES (COMPUTER SYSTEMS).

### INTERFERENCE (LINGUISTICS).
Pupipat, Apisak. Scientific writing and publishing in English in Thailand. 1998.
*TC 06 no. 10981*

### INTERGENERATIONAL RELATIONS. *See also* CHILDREN AND ADULTS.
Bhattacharya, Diya. The college experience and the construction of cultural identity among first generation Indian American undergraduates. 1999.
*TC 06 no. 11083*

De Toledo, Sylvie. Grandparents as parents. New York : Guilford Press, c1995.
*TC HQ759.9 .D423 1995*

Woo, Kimberley Ann. "Double happiness," double jeopardy. 1999.
*TC 06 no. 11075*

### INTERGENERATIONAL RELATIONS - STUDY AND TEACHING (ELEMENTARY) - UNITED STATES.
Friedman, Barbara, 1947- Connecting generations. Boston : Allyn and Bacon, c1999.
*TC HQ1064.U5 F755 1999*

### INTERGENERATIONAL RELATIONS - UNITED STATES.
Ganong, Lawrence H. Changing families, changing responsibilities. Mahwah, N.J. : Lawrence Erlbaum Associates, 1999.
*TC HQ834 .G375 1999*

### INTERGOVERNMENTAL FISCAL RELATIONS. *See* GRANTS-IN-AID.

### INTERGROUP CONFLICT. *See* INTERGROUP RELATIONS.

### INTERGROUP RELATIONS. *See also* INTERORGANIZATIONAL RELATIONS.
Brown, Rupert, 1950- Group processes. 2nd ed. Oxford ; Malden, Mass. : Blackwell Publishers, 2000.
*TC HM131 .B726 2000*

Enhancing education in heterogeneous schools. Ramat-Gan : Bar-Ilan University Press, [1997]
*TC LC214 .E54 1997*

Flippen, Annette Rose. Similarity versus motive as explanations for ingroup bias. 1996.
*TC 085 F65*

Kinloch, Graham Charles. The comparative understanding of intergroup realtions [i.e. relations]. Boulder, CO : Westview Press, 1999.
*TC HM131 .K495 1999*

Parker, Glenn M., 1938- Cross-functional teams. 1st ed. San Francisco, Calif. : Jossey-Bass, c1994.
*TC HD66 .P345 1994*

Social identity. Malden, MA : Blackwell Publishers, 1999.
*TC HM131 .S58433 1999*

### INTERGROUP RELATIONS - PERIODICALS.
[Journal of intergroup relations (1970)] Journal of intergroup relations. Louisville, KY : National Association of Human Rights Workers,

### INTERIOR DECORATION. *See* FURNITURE; MURAL PAINTING AND DECORATION.

### INTERLANGUAGE (LANGUAGE LEARNING).
The current state of interlanguage. Amsterdam ; Philadelphia : J. Benjamins, c1995.
*TC P118.2 .C867 1995*

Language transfer in language learning. Rev. ed. with corrections. Amsterdam ; Philadelphia : J. Benjamins Pub. Co., 1994.
*TC P118.25 .L36 1994*

Li, Duan-Duan. Expressing needs and wants in a second language. 1998.
*TC 06 no. 10958*

O'Riordan, Mary. Strategic use of transfer and explicit linguistic knowledge. 1998.
*TC 06 no. 10975*

### INTERMARRIAGE. *See* INTERRACIAL MARRIAGE.

### INTERMARRIAGE, RACIAL. *See* INTERRACIAL MARRIAGE.

### INTERMARRIAGE - UNITED STATES.
Interracial relationships. San Diego : Greenhaven Press, c2000.
*TC HQ1031 .I59 2000*

**Intermediate English: English as a second language [videorecording].**
Intermediate English [videorecording]. [Roslyn Heights, N.Y.] : Video Aided Instruction, [c1995].
*TC PE1128 .I5 1995*

**Intermediate English** [videorecording] : ESL / [presented by] Video Aided Instruction, Inc. ; produced & directed by Peter Lanzer, Mona E. Lanzer. [Roslyn Heights, N.Y.] : Video Aided Instruction, [c1995]. 2 videocassettes (240 min.) : sd., col. ; 1/2 in. + 1 exercise booklet (62 p. ; 19 cm.). (English as a second language series) Title from container: Intermediate English: English as a second language [videorecording]. At head of title: Video Aided Instruction, Inc. presents Intermediate English [videorecording]. VHS. Catalogued from credits and container. Instructor, William W. Jex. For intermediate English-as-a-second-language students. SUMMARY: Twenty-five lessons in intermediate English with more advanced vocabulary and grammar. The emphasis is placed on everyday language used in everyday situations-- in the restaurant, the airport, the bank, etc. Designed for native speakers of other languages who want to learn English correctly and easily. ISBN 1-57385-002-0 (vols. 1 and 2)
*1. English language - Self-instruction. 2. English language - Study and teaching - Foreign speakers - Audio-visual aids. 3. English language - Grammar. I. Lanzer, Peter. II. Lanzer, Mona E. III. Jex, William W. IV. Video Aided Instruction, Inc. V. Title: ESL [videorecording] VI. Title: Intermediate English: English as a second language [videorecording] VII. Title: Video Aided Instruction, Inc. presents Intermediate English [videorecording] VIII. Series: English as a second language (Roslyn Heights, N.Y.)*

*TC PE1128 .I5 1995*

### INTERMEDIATE SANCTIONS. *See* ALTERNATIVES TO IMPRISONMENT.

**INTERMEDIATE SCHOOL DISTRICTS.** *See* SCHOOL DISTRICTS.

**INTERMEDIATE SCHOOL TEACHING.** *See* MIDDLE SCHOOL TEACHING.

**INTERMEDIATE SCHOOLS.** *See* JUNIOR HIGH SCHOOLS; MIDDLE SCHOOLS.

**INTERNAL MEDICINE.**
Golper, Lee Ann C., 1948- Sourcebook for medical speech pathology. 2nd ed. San Diego, Calif. : Singular Pub. Group, c1998.
*TC RC423 .G64 1998*

**INTERNAL SECURITY.** *See* INSURGENCY.

**The international academic profession** : portraits of fourteen countries / edited by Philip G. Altbach ; with a foreword by Ernest L. Boyer. Princeton, N.J. : Carnegie Foundation for the Advancement of Teaching, c1996. xxii, 762 p. ; 25 cm. (A special report) Includes bibliographical references (p. [709]-741) and index. ISBN 0-931050-53-7 (alk. paper) DDC 378.12
*1. College teachers - Attitudes - Cross-cultural studies. 2. College teaching - Cross-cultural studies. 3. Educational surveys. I. Altbach, Philip G. II. Carnegie Foundation for the Advancement of Teaching. III. Series: Special report (Carnegie Foundation for the Advancement of Teaching)*
*TC LB1778 .I54 1996*

**International Academy for Biomedical and Drug Research (Series)**
(vol. 12.) New therapeutic indications of antidepressants. Basel ; New York : Karger, c1997.
*TC RM332 .N475 1997*

**INTERNATIONAL ADMINISTRATION.** *See* INTERNATIONAL AGENCIES.

**INTERNATIONAL ADOPTION.** *See* INTERCOUNTRY ADOPTION.

**International Adult Literacy Survey.**
International Adult Literacy Survey. Literacy in the information age. Paris : Organisation for Economic Co-operation and Development; Ottawa : Statistics Canada, 2000.
*TC LC149 .L59 2000*

Literacy in the information age : final report of the International Adult Literacy Survey. Paris : Organisation for Economic Co-operation and Development; Ottawa : Statistics Canada, 2000. xvi, 185 p. : ill. ; 27 cm. ISBN 92-64-17654-3 DDC 302.2/244 DDC 300
*1. Functional literacy - Statistics. 2. Literacy - Statistics. 3. Literacy - Economic aspects - Statistics. 4. Literacy - Government policy - Statistics. 5. Educational surveys. I. Statistics Canada. II. International Adult Literacy Survey. III. Organisation for Economic Co-operation and Development.*
*TC LC149 .L59 2000*

**International African Institute.**
Museums & archaeology in West Africa. Washington : Smithsonian Institution Press ; Oxford : J. Currey, c1997.
*TC AM91.A358 M85 1997*

**INTERNATIONAL AGENCIES - PERIODICALS.**
International transnational associations. [Bruxelles, Union of International Associations]

**INTERNATIONAL AGENCIES - PERIODICALS.**
International transnational associations. [Bruxelles, Union of International Associations]

**International Association for Computing in Education.**
AEDS journal. Washington, Association for Educational Data Systems.

**International Association for the Evaluation of Educational Achievement.**
Civic education across countries. Amsterdam, the Netherlands : International Association for the Evaluation of Educational Achievement, c1999.
*TC JA86 .C6 1999*

Elley, Warwick B. How in the world do students read? Hamburg : The International Association for the Evaluation of Educational Achievement, [1992]
*TC LB1050.6 .E55 1992*

**International Association of Bioethics.**
Embodying bioethics. Lanham : Rowman & Littlefield Publishers, c1999.
*TC QH332 .E43 1999*

**International Association of Pupil Personnel Workers.** The Journal. [Baton Rouge, La., etc.] International Association of Pupil Personnel Workers. 36 v. ill. 27 cm. Frequency: Quarterly. v. 1-36, no. 2; Nov. 1956-summer 1992. Title varies slightly. Continued by: Journal for truancy and dropout prevention (DLC)sn 93029252

(OCoLC)27606987. ISSN 0020-6016
*1. Educational counseling - Periodicals. 2. Counseling - Periodicals. I. Title: Journal for truancy and dropout prevention*

**International Association of Universities.**
The universities' responsibilities to society. 1st ed. New York : Pergamon, published for the IAU Press, 2000.
*TC LC191.9 .U55 2000*

**INTERNATIONAL ASSOCIATIONS.** *See also* INTERNATIONAL AGENCIES.
International transnational associations. [Bruxelles, Union of International Associations]

**International audiology.** Leiden, Netherlands : International Society of Audiology, 1962-1970. 9 v. ; 25 cm. Vol. 1 (1962)-v. 9 (1970). Other title: Audiologie internationale. Issued by the Executive Committee of the International Society of Audiology. Vols. 1 (1962)-9 (1970). 1 v. Continued by: Audiology 1971-1995 77S404L.
*1. Serial 2. Periodical 3. Hearing - periodicals I. International Society of Audiology. II. Title: Int Audiol III. Title: Audiologie internationale IV. Title: Audiology 1971-1995*

**International bibliography of anthropology** = Bibliographie internationale d'anthropologie. London ; New York : Routledge, 1999- v. ; 24 cm. Frequency: Annual. Vol. 44 (1998)- . (International bibliography of the social sciences = Bibliographies internationales de sciences sociales) Bibliographie internationale d'anthropologie. At head of title on cover: BLPES. English and French. Prepared by the British Library of Political and Economic Science with the support of the International Committee for Social Science Information and Documentation, and the assistance of UNESCO. Continues: International bibliography of social and cultural anthropology ISSN: 0085-2074 (DLC)   58004366 (OCoLC)1753416.
*1. Anthropology - Bibliography - Periodicals. 2. Ethnology - Bibliography - Periodicals. 3. Sociology - Bibliography - Periodicals. I. International Committee for Social Science Information and Documentation. II. Unesco. III. British Library of Political and Economic Science. IV. Title: Bibliographie internationale d'anthropologie V. Title: BLPES VI. Title: International bibliography of social and cultural anthropology VII. Series: International bibliography of the social sciences.*
*TC Z7161 .I593*

**International bibliography of social and cultural anthropology.**
International bibliography of anthropology = London ; New York : Routledge, 1999-
*TC Z7161 .I593*

**International bibliography of the social sciences.**
International bibliography of anthropology = London ; New York : Routledge, 1999-
*TC Z7161 .I593*

**INTERNATIONAL BUSINESS ENTERPRISES.**
Schwartz, Peter, 1946- When good companies do bad things. New York : John Wiley, c1999.
*TC HD60 .S39 1999*

University curriculum on transnational corporations. New York : United Nations, 1991.
*TC HD2755.5 .U55 1991*

**INTERNATIONAL BUSINESS ENTERPRISES - MANAGEMENT - STUDY AND TEACHING - CASE STUDIES.**
Business-driven action learning. New York : St. Martin's Press, 2000.
*TC HD58.82 .B87 2000*

**International Business Machines Corporation.**
Weintraub, Robert Steven. Informal learning in the workplace through desktop technology. 1998.
*TC 06 no. 11003*

**INTERNATIONAL BUSINESS MACHINES CORPORATION - EMPLOYEES - TRAINING OF.**
Weintraub, Robert Steven. Informal learning in the workplace through desktop technology. 1998.
*TC 06 no. 11003*

**International Center of Photography.**
Panzer, Mary. Mathew Brady and the image of history. Washington, D.C. : Smithsonian Institution Press for the National Portrait Gallery, c1997.
*TC TR140.B7 P36 1997*

**International Cognitive Linguistics Conference (4th : 1995 : Albuquerque, N.M.).**
Discourse and perspective in cognitive linguistics. Amsterdam ; Philadelphia : J. Benjamins, c1997.
*TC P165 .D57 1997*

**International Colloquium on Cognitive Science (5th : 1997 : San Sebastián, Spain).**
Cognition, agency, and rationality. Boston : Kluwer Academic, 1999.
*TC BC177 .C45 1999*

**International Committee for Social Science Information and Documentation.**
International bibliography of anthropology = London ; New York : Routledge, 1999-
*TC Z7161 .I593*

**International Committee on Christian Literature for Africa.**
Books for Africa. London, International Committee on Christian Literature for Africa.

**International Committee on Computational Linguistics.**
Language and automation. Washington, Center for Applied Linguistics.

**International Conference on Perception and Action (10th : 1999 : Edinburgh, Scotland)** Studies in perception and action V / Tenth International Conference on Perception and Action : Aug. 8-13, 1999, Edinburgh, Scotland / edited by Madeleine A. Grealy, James A. Thomson. Mahwah, N.J. : L. Erlbaum Associates, 1999. xxv, 346 p. : ill. ; 24 cm. Includes bibliographical references and indexes. ISBN 0-8058-3257-2 (pbk. : alk. paper) DDC 153.7
*1. Perceptual-motor processes - Congresses. 2. Perception - Congresses. I. Grealy, Madeleine A. II. Thomson, James A. (James Alick), 1951- III. Title.*
*TC BF295 .I57 1999*

**INTERNATIONAL CONFERENCE ON POPULATION AND DEVELOPMENT (1994 : CAIRO, EGYPT).**
Review and appraisal of the progress made in achieving the goals and objectives of the Programme of Action of the International Conference on Population and Development. New York : United Nations, 1999.
*TC HB849 .R48 1999*

**International Conference on Social Philosophy (1st : 1985 : Colorado Springs, Colo.).**
Freedom, equality, and social change. Lewiston : E. Mellen Press, c1989.
*TC HM216 .F83 1989*

**INTERNATIONAL CONFERENCES, CONGRESSES AND CONVENTIONS.** *See* CONGRESSES AND CONVENTIONS.

**International congress calendar.**
International transnational associations. [Bruxelles, Union of International Associations]

**International congress calendar. Supplement.**
International transnational associations. [Bruxelles, Union of International Associations]

**International Congress of Mathematicians (new series) (7th : 1954 : Amsterdam)** Proceedings of the International Congress of Mathematicians, 1954, [held at] Amsterdam, September 2-September 9 [under the auspices of the Wiskundig Genootschap. Editorial Committee: Johan C. H. Gerretsen, Johannes de Groot] Groningen, E. P. Noordhoff, 1954-1957. 3 v. 25 cm. "Volume II ... printed before the Congress, contains the abstracts of those communications in the sections which reached the Editorial Committee in time." English, French or German.
*1. Mathematics - Congresses.*
*TC QA2 .I612 1954*

**International Congress on Ericksonian Approaches to Hypnosis and Psychotherapy (1980 : Phoenix, Ariz.).**
Ericksonian approaches to hypnosis and psychotherapy. New York : Brunner/Mazel, c1982.
*TC RC490.5.E75 E75*

**International Congress on the Changing Family and Child Development (1st : 1997 : University of Calgary).**
The changing family and child development. Aldershot : Ashgate, c2000.
*TC HQ518 .C478 2000*

**International congress series**
(no. 1125) Fundacion Dr. Antonio Esteve. Symposium (7th : 1996 : Sitges, Spain) The clinical pharmacology of sport and exercise. Amsterdam ; New York : Elsevier Science B.V., Excerpta Medica, 1997.
*TC RC1230 .F86 1996*

**INTERNATIONAL COOPERATION.** *See also* CONGRESSES AND CONVENTIONS; INTELLECTUAL COOPERATION;

**INTERNATIONAL AGENCIES; INTERNATIONAL EDUCATION.**
Global public goods. New York : Oxford University Press, 1999.
*TC HB846.5 .G55 1999*

Global visions. 1st ed. Boston : South End Press, c1993.
*TC HF1359 .G58 1993*

**INTERNATIONAL COOPERATION - PERIODICALS.**
International transnational associations. [Bruxelles, Union of International Associations]

**INTERNATIONAL COOPERATION - PERIODICALS.**
International transnational associations. [Bruxelles, Union of International Associations]

**INTERNATIONAL CORPORATIONS.** *See* **INTERNATIONAL BUSINESS ENTERPRISES.**

**International Council for Educational Development.**
Intercultural education. New York, International Council for Educational Development.

**International Council of Scientific Unions. Scientific Committee on Problems of the Environment.**
Baskin, Yvonne. The work of nature. Washington, D.C. : Island Press, 1997.
*TC GE195 .B36 1997*

**International Development Research Centre (Canada).**
A new world of knowledge. Ottawa : International Development Research Centre, c1999.
*TC LC1090 N38 1999*

**International dictionary of black composers** / editor Samuel A. Floyd Jr. Chicago : London : Fitzroy Dearborn, c1999. 2 v. : ports. ; 29 cm. At head of title: Center for Black Music Research. Includes bibliographical references. ISBN 1-88496-427-3 DDC 780/.92/396
*1. Afro-American composers - Bio-bibliography - Dictionaries. 2. Composers, Black - Bio-bibliography - Dictionaries. I. Floyd, Samuel A. II. Columbia College (Chicago, Ill.). Center for Black Music Research.*
*TC ML105 .I5 1999*

**The international dictionary of data communications.**
Saigh, Robert A. Chicago : Glenlake Pub. Co. : New York : American Management Association, c1998.
*TC TK5102 .S25 1998*

**INTERNATIONAL ECONOMIC POLICY.** *See* **INTERNATIONAL ECONOMIC RELATIONS.**

**INTERNATIONAL ECONOMIC RELATIONS.** *See also* **INTERNATIONAL TRADE.**
Global visions. 1st ed. Boston : South End Press, c1993.
*TC HF1359 .G58 1993*

Globalization and education. New York : Routledge, 1999.
*TC LC191 .G545 1999*

**INTERNATIONAL ECONOMIC RELATIONS - HISTORY.**
Abu-Lughod, Janet L. New York, Chicago, Los Angeles. Minneapolis : University of Minnesota Press, c1999.
*TC HT123 .A613 1999*

**INTERNATIONAL ECONOMICS.** *See* **INTERNATIONAL ECONOMIC RELATIONS.**

**INTERNATIONAL EDUCATION.** *See also* **INTELLECTUAL COOPERATION; STUDENT EXCHANGE PROGRAMS.**
Eddy, John, 1932- International higher education systems. New ed. Lanham, Md. ; Oxford : University Press of America, c1999.
*TC LB2322.2 .E33 2000*

Fersh, Seymour. Integrating the trans-national/cultural dimension. Bloomington, Ind. : Phi Delta Kappa Educational Foundation, c1993.
*TC LC1090 .F47 1993*

Globalisation and pedagogy. London ; New York : Routledge, 2000.
*TC LC1090 .E33 2000*

Globalization and education. New York : Routledge, 1999.
*TC LC191 .G545 1999*

Hess, J. Daniel (John Daniel), 1937- Studying abroad/learning abroad. Yarmouth, Me., USA : Intercultural Press, c1997.

*TC LB2375 .H467 1997*

**INTERNATIONAL EDUCATION - BRITISH COLUMBIA.**
McKellin, Karen, 1950- Maintaining the momentum. Victoria, B.C. : British Columbia Centre for International Education, c1998.
*TC LC1090 .M24 1998*

**INTERNATIONAL EDUCATION - CANADA.**
A new world of knowledge. Ottawa : International Development Research Centre, c1999.
*TC LC1090 N38 1999*

**INTERNATIONAL EDUCATION - GREAT BRITAIN.**
Humfrey, Christine, 1947- Managing international students. Philadelphia, Penn : Society for Research into Higher Education & Open University Press, 1999.
*TC LB2376.6.G7 H86 1999*

**INTERNATIONAL EDUCATION - PERIODICALS.**
International educational and cultural exchange. [Washington, U.S. Advisory Commission on International Educational and Cultural Affairs; for sale by the Supt. of Docs., U.S. Govt. Print. Off.]

**International education review.**
Internationale Zeitschrift für Erziehungswissenschaft = Köln : J.P. Bachem,

**INTERNATIONAL EDUCATION - STUDY AND TEACHING.**
Regional studies series. Englewood Cliffs, N.J. : Globe Book Co., c1993.
*TC LC1090 .R43 1993*

**INTERNATIONAL EDUCATION - UNITED STATES.**
Drum, Jan. Global winners. Yarmouth, Me. : Intercultural Press, c1994.
*TC LC1099.3 .D78 1994*

Educating Americans for tomorrow's world. [Washington D.C.] : NGA, [1987]
*TC LC1099 .E225 1987*

**INTERNATIONAL EDUCATION - UNITED STATES - ACTIVITY PROGRAMS.**
Drum, Jan. Global winners. Yarmouth, Me. : Intercultural Press, c1994.
*TC LC1099.3 .D78 1994*

**International educational and cultural exchange.**
[Washington, U.S. Advisory Commission on International Educational and Cultural Affairs; for sale by the Supt. of Docs., U.S. Govt. Print. Off.] 14 v. 24 cm. v. 1-14, no. 1; summer 1965-summer 1978. ISSN 0020-6601 DDC 370.19/6/05
*1. International education - Periodicals. 2. Educational exchanges - Periodicals. I. United States. Advisory Commission on International Educational and Cultural Affairs.*

**International Educational Cinematographic Institute.**
Intercine. Rome.

**INTERNATIONAL EDUCATIONAL EXCHANGES.** *See* **EDUCATIONAL EXCHANGES.**

**International encyclopedia of business and management handbook of human resource management.**
The IEBM handbook of human resource management. 1st ed. London ; Boston : International Thomson Business Press, 1998.
*TC HF5549.17 .I33 1998*

**International encyclopedia of dance :** a project of Dance Perspectives Foundation, Inc. / founding editor, Selma Jeanne Cohen ; area editors, George Dorris ... [et al.] ; consultants, Thomas F. Kelly ... [et al.]. New York : Oxford University Press, c1998. 6 v. : ill. ; 29 cm. Includes bibliographical references and index. SUMMARY: "Exciting and fascinating, this reference work succeeds in its goal of bringing "joy as well as enlightenment" about all forms of dance in all countries of the world. An extremely useful synoptic outline of contents" with nine sections (including "Ritual and Religion" and "Popular Entertainment") enables the user to explore dance in its cultural and social aspects, while topical essays complement the 2,000-plus entries. Heavily illustrated with black-and-white photographs, the encyclopedia captures the fluid movement of dance; with its depth and scope, this outstanding work has carved a well-deserved niche".--"Outstanding Reference Sources : the 1999 Selection of New Titles", American Libraries, May 1999. Comp. by the Reference Sources Committee, RUSA, ALA. ISBN 0-19-509462-X (set) ISBN 0-19-512305-0 (v. 1) ISBN 0-19-512306-9 (v. 2) ISBN 0-19-512307-7 (v. 3) ISBN 0-19-512308-5 (v. 4) ISBN 0-19-512309-3 (v. 5) ISBN 0-19-512310-7 (v. 6) DDC 792.8/03

*1. Dance - Encyclopedias. 2. Ballet - Encyclopedias. I. Cohen, Selma Jeanne. 1920- II. Dance Perspectives Foundation. III. Title: Dance*
*TC GV1585 .I586 1998*

**The international encyclopedia of education. 1994.**
Education [computer file]: Version 1.1. [Oxford, Eng.] : Pergamon, c1998. Computer program.
*TC LB15 .E3 1998*

**International exchange news. Washington International Center of the American Council of Education.** Washington.

**INTERNATIONAL EXCHANGE OF STUDENTS.** *See* **STUDENT EXCHANGE PROGRAMS.**

**INTERNATIONAL EXHIBITIONS.** *See* **EXHIBITIONS.**

**International Federation for Information Processing.**
IFIP TC3 WG3.1/3.5 Open Conference on Communications and Networking in Education (1999 : Aulanko, Finland) Communications and networking in education. Boston : Kluwer Academic Publishers, 2000.
*TC LB1044.87 .I45 2000*

IFIP TC3 WG3.2/3.6 International Working Conference on Building University Electronic Educational Environments (1999 : Irvine, Calif.) Building university electronic educational environments. Boston : Kluwer Academic Publishers, c2000.
*TC LC5803.C65 .I352 2000*

IFIP TC3/WG3.3 & WG3.6 Joint Working Conference on the Virtual Campus: Trends for Higher Education and Training (1997 : Madrid, Spain) The virtual campus. 1st ed. London ; New York : Chapman & Hall on behalf of the International Federation for Information Processing (IFIP), 1998.
*TC LC5803.C65 1353 1997*

**International Federation for Information Processing (Series)**
(35.) IFIP TC3 WG3.1/3.5 Open Conference on Communications and Networking in Education (1999 : Aulanko, Finland) Communications and networking in education. Boston : Kluwer Academic Publishers, 2000.
*TC LB1044.87 .I45 2000*

(38.) IFIP TC3 WG3.2/3.6 International Working Conference on Building University Electronic Educational Environments (1999 : Irvine, Calif.) Building university electronic educational environments. Boston : Kluwer Academic Publishers, c2000.
*TC LC5803.C65 .I352 2000*

**International Federation of Classification Societies. Conference. 5th, 1996, Kobe, Japan.** Data science, classification, and related methods : : proceedings of the fifth Conference of the International Federation of Classification Societies (IFCS-96), Kobe, Japan, March 27-30, 1996 / C. Hayashi ... [et al.]. Tokyo ; New York : Springer, c1998. xv, 780 p. : ill. ; 25 cm. (Studies in classification, data analysis, and knowledge organization.) Includes bibliographical references and name index. ISBN 4-431-70208-3
*1. Cluster analysis - Congresses. 2. Pattern perception - Congresses. 3. Classification - Congresses. I. Hayashi, Chikio, 1918-. II. Title. III. Series.*
*TC QA278 I53 1996*

**International Federation of Sports Medicine.**
Nutrition in sport. Osney Mead, Oxford ; Malden, MA : Blackwell Science, 2000.
*TC QP141 .N793 2000*

**International handbook of neuropsychological rehabilitation** / edited by Anne-Lise Christensen and B.P. Uzzell. New York : Kluwer Academic/Plenum Publishers, c2000. xv, 381 p., [2] p. of plates : ill. (some col.) ; 26 cm. (Critical issues in neuropsychology) Includes bibliographical references and index. ISBN 0-306-46174-9 DDC 616.8/043
*1. Brain damage - Patients - Rehabilitation - Handbooks, manuals, etc. 2. Clinical neuropsychology - Handbooks, manuals, etc. 3. Brain Injuries - rehabilitation. 4. Neuropsychological Tests. I. Christensen, Anne-Lise. II. Uzzell, Barbara P. III. Series.*
*TC RC387.5 .I478 2000*

**The international handbook of school effectiveness research** / [edited by] Charles Teddlie and David Reynolds. London ; New York : Falmer Press, 2000. xiii, 411 p. ; 25 cm. Includes bibliographical references (p. 345-396) and index. CONTENTS: The historical and intellectual foundations of school effectiveness research. An introduction to school effectiveness research / David Reynolds ... [et al.]. Current topics and approaches in school

effectiveness research : the contemporary field / Charles Teddlie and David Reynolds, with Sharon Pol -- The knowledge base of school effectiveness research. The methodology and scientific properties of school effectiveness research / Charles Teddlie, David Reynolds, and Pam Sammons. The processes of school effectiveness / David Reynolds and Charles Teddlie. Context issues within school effectiveness research / Charles Teddlie, Sam Stringfield, and David Reynolds -- The cutting edge issues of school effectiveness research. Some methodological issues in school effectiveness research / Eugene Kennedy and Garrett Mandeville. Linking school effectiveness and school improvement / David Reynolds ... [et al.]. School effectiveness : the international dimension / David Reynolds. School effectiveness and education indicators / Carol Fitz-Gibbon and Susan Kochan. Theory development in school effectiveness research / Bert Creemers, Jaap Scheerens and David Reynolds -- The future of school effectiveness research. School effectiveness research and the social and behavioural sciences / Charles Teddlie and David Reynolds. The future agenda for school effectiveness research / David Reynolds and Charles Teddlie. ISBN 0-7507-0607-4 (pbk.) DDC 371/.0072
*1. Educational evaluation - Research. 2. Schools - Evaluation - Research. 3. Education - Research. I. Teddlie. Charles. II. Reynolds, David, 1949-*
*TC LB2822.75 .I59 2000*

### International higher education systems.
Eddy, John, 1932- New ed. Lanham, Md. ; Oxford : University Press of America, c2000.
*TC LB2322.2 .E33 2000*

### International historical statistics.
Mitchell, B. R. (Brian R.) 4th ed. London : Macmillan Reference ; New York, N.Y. : Grove's dictionaries [division of Stockton Press], 1998.
*TC HA1107 .M53 1998*

Mitchell, B. R. (Brian R.) 4th ed. London : Macmillan Reference ; New YorkGrove Dictionaries[division of : Stockton Press], 1998.
*TC HA1107 .M55 1998*

### International historical statistics, Africa, Asia & Oceania, 1750-1993.
Mitchell, B. R. (Brian R.) 3rd ed. London : Macmillan Reference ; New York : Ggrove's Dictionaries[division of Stockton Press], 1998.
*TC HA1107 .M54 1998*

### International human rights.
Gitta, Cosmas. 1998.
*TC 085 G4398*

### International Institute of Differing Civilizations.
Civilisations. Bruxelles, Institut International des Civilisations Différentes.

### International Institute of Intellectual Co-operation.
League of Nations. Bulletin de la coopération intellectuelle. Paris : Institut international de coopération intellectuelle, [1931?-1932?]

INTERNATIONAL INSTITUTIONS. *See* INTERNATIONAL AGENCIES; INTERNATIONAL COOPERATION.

### International issues in early intervention.
Interdisciplinary clinical assessment of young children with developmental disabilities. Baltimore : Paul H. Brookes Pub. Co., c2000.
*TC HV891 .I58 2000*

### International journal of adult and youth education.
Fundamental and adult education. [Paris : Unesco, 1952-1960]

### International journal of continuing education and training.
Journal of continuing education and training. [Farmingdale, N.Y.] Baywood Pub. Co.

### International journal of educational development.
[International journal of educational development (Online)] International journal of educational development [computer file]. Oxford ; New York : Pergamon,
*TC EJOURNALS*

[International journal of educational development (Online)] International journal of educational development [computer file]. Oxford ; New York : Pergamon, Coverage as of Apr. 16, 1998: Vol. 17, issue 1 (Jan. 1997)- . Mode of access: World Wide Web. Abstracts, tables of contents, and citation information are HTML encoded; articles are available in portable document format (PDF) and as Postscript Level 2 files. Subscription and registration required for access. Online version of the print title: International journal of educational development. System requirements: Internet connectivity, World Wide Web browser, and Adobe Acrobat reader. Description based on: Vol. 17, issue 1 (Jan. 1997); title from general information screen (viewed Apr. 16, 1998). URL: http://www.sciencedirect.com/

science/journal/07380593 URL: http://www.columbia.edu/cu/ libraries/indexes/science-direct.html URL: http:// www.sciencedirect.com/ URL: http://www.elsevier.com/ homepage/elecserv.htt Available in other form: International journal of educational development ISSN: 0738-0593 (DLC) 84640824 (OCoLC)8660698. ISSN 0738-0593
*1. Education - Periodicals. 2. Education - periodicals. I. Title: Sciencedirect. II. Title: International journal of educational development*
*TC EJOURNALS*

### International journal of health education. [Geneva,
Studer, 1958-1981] 24 v. ill. 24 cm. Frequency: Quarterly. [Vol. 1, no. 1 (Jan. 1958)]-v. 3, no. 4 (Oct. 1960) ; 1961/1-1981/4. Title from cover. Indexed in its entirety by: Excerpta medica. Indexed by: Biological abstracts 0006-3169. Issues for 1961-81 called also v. 4-13. Supplements accompany some numbers. Also available on microfilm Official organ of the International Union for Health Education of the Public, Jan. 1958-Oct. 1960; of the International Union for Health Education, 1961-1981. Issued also in French and German editions. Continued by: Hygie (OCoLC)8832140. ISSN 0020-7306
*1. Health education - Periodicals. 2. Health Education - periodicals. I. International Union for Health Education of the Public. II. International Union for Health Education. III. Title: Hygie*

### [International journal of intercultural relations (Online)] International journal of intercultural
relations [computer file] : IJIR. Oxford ; New York : Pergamon, Frequency: Quarterly. Coverage as of March 13, 2000: Vol. 19, issue 1 (Winter 1995)- . IJIR. Mode of access: ScienceDirect via World Wide Web. Subscription required for access. Description based on: Vol. 19, issue 1 (Winter 1995); title from general information screen (viewed March 13, 2000). Indexed selectively by: Psychological abstracts 0033-2887 1977-1980. Indexed selectively by: Social welfare, social planning/policy & social development 0195-7988. Indexed selectively by: Sociological abstracts 0038-0202. Also available by subscription via the World Wide Web. Official publication of the Society for Intercultural Education, Training, and Research. URL: http://www.sciencedirect.com/science/ journal/01471767 URL: http://www.columbia.edu/cu/ libraries/indexes/sciencedirect.html URL: http:// www.sciencedirect.com/ ISSN 0147-1767
*1. Intercultural communication - Periodicals. 2. Cultural relations - Periodicals. 3. Cross-cultural studies - Periodicals. I. Society for Intercultural Education, Training, and Research. II. Title: IJIR*
*TC EJOURNALS*

### International Labour Office.
Action against child labour. Geneva : International Labour Office, c2000.
*TC HD6231 .A28 2000*

### The international library of comparative public policy
(12) Education policy. Cheltenham, UK : Northampton, MA : Edward Elgar Pub., c1999.
*TC LC71 .E32 1999*

### The international library of group analysis
(7) Thompson, Sheila. The group context. London ; Philadelphia : Jessica Kingsley Publishers, 1999.
*TC BF637.C6 T49 1999*

### International library of psychology
Children's peer relations. London ; New York : Routledge, 1998.
*TC BF723.I646 C47 1998*

### International library of psychology, philosophy, and scientific method.
Piaget, Jean, 1896-1980. [Représentation du monde chez l'enfant. English] The child's conception of the world. Translated by Joan and Andrew Tomlinson. Paterson, N.J., Littlefield, Adams, 1960.
*TC BF721 .P513 1960*

INTERNATIONAL MIGRATION. *See* EMIGRATION AND IMMIGRATION.

### International mind.
L'Esprit international.

### International narratives on becoming a teacher educator : pathways to a profession / edited by
George A. Churukian and Corey R. Lock. Lewiston, N.Y. : Lampeter,Wales : E. Mellen Press, c2000. iii, 172 p. ; 24 cm. (Mellen studies in education ; v. 42) ISBN 0-7734-8015-3 DDC 370/.71/1
*1. Teacher educators - Biography. 2. Teacher educators - Training of. 3. Education - Study and teaching (Higher) I. Churukian, George Allen, 1932- II. Lock, Corey. III. Series: Mellen Studies in education ; v.42*
*TC LB1737.5 .I58 2000*

### International Network for Innovative School Systems.

Leithwood, Kenneth A. Educational accountability. Gütersloh : Bertelsmann Foundation Publishers, 1999.
*TC LB2806.22 .L45 1999*

### International obligations.
National Institute of Social Sciences. Journal of the National Institute of Social Sciences. [New York]

### INTERNATIONAL OLYMPIC COMMITTEE - HISTORY.
Senn, Alfred Erich. Power, politics, and the Olympic Games. Champaign, IL : Human Kinetics, c1999.
*TC GV721.5 .S443 1999*

INTERNATIONAL ORGANIZATION. *See* INTERNATIONAL AGENCIES; INTERNATIONAL COOPERATION; WORLD POLITICS.

INTERNATIONAL ORGANIZATIONS. *See* INTERNATIONAL AGENCIES.

### International perspectives on individual differences /
edited by Richard J. Riding and Stephen G. Rayner. Stamford, Conn. : Ablex, 2000- v. : ill. ; 24 cm. Includes bibliographical references and indexes. PARTIAL CONTENTS: v.1 Cognitive styles. ISBN 1-56750-458-2 (v.1)
*1. Individual differences.*
*TC BF697 .I58 2000*

### International perspectives on tele-education and virtual learning environments / edited by Graham
Orange and Dave Hobbs. Aldershot : Ashgate, 2000. xv, 182 p. : ill. ; 23 cm. ISBN 0-7546-1202-3 DDC 371.358
*1. Internet in education. 2. Interactive multimedia. 3. Telecommunication in education. 4. Distance education - Computer-assisted instruction. 5. Distance learning. 6. Educational technology - Social aspects. 7. Interactive multimedia - Social aspects. 8. Computer-assisted instruction - Social aspects. I. Orange, Graham. II. Hobbs, Dave (Dave J.)*
*TC LB1044.87 .I55 2000*

### International political economy series
Ramesh, M., 1960- Welfare capitalism in southeast Asia. New York : St. Martin's Press, c2000.
*TC HN690.8.A8 R35 2000*

INTERNATIONAL POLITICS. *See* WORLD POLITICS.

### The International psycho-analytical library :
(no. 9) Freud, Sigmund, 1856-1939. [Sammlung kleiner schriften zur neurosenlehre. eng] Collected papers. 1st American ed. New York : Basic Books, 1959.
*TC BF173 .F672 1959*

### International questions.
National Institute of Social Sciences. Journal of the National Institute of Social Sciences. [New York]

### International Reading Association.
The changing face of whole language. Newark, Del. : International Reading Association ; Victoria, Australia : Australian Literacy Educators' Association, c1997.
*TC LB1050.35 .C43 1997*

Children achieving. Newark, Del. : International Reading Association, c1998.
*TC LB1139.5.R43 C55 1998*

The explicit teaching of reading. Newark, Del. : International Reading Association, c1999.
*TC LB1573 .E96 1999*

Key, Daphne. Literacy shutdown. Newark, Del. : International Reading Association : Chicago, Ill. : National Reading Conference, c1998.
*TC LC1752 .K49 1998*

Literacy instruction for culturally and linguistically diverse students. Newark, Del. : International Reading Association, c1998.
*TC LC3731 .L566 1998*

Reading assessment. Newark, Del. : International Reading Association, c1999.
*TC LB1573 .R2793 1999*

INTERNATIONAL RELATIONS. *See also* CONGRESSES AND CONVENTIONS; CULTURAL RELATIONS; INTERNATIONAL COOPERATION; INTERNATIONAL ECONOMIC RELATIONS; NATIONALISM; PEACE; WAR; WORLD POLITICS.
Ethnicity and intra-state conflict. Aldershot, Hants, England : Brookfield, Vt., USA : Ashgate, c1999.
*TC GN495.6 .E83 1999*

### INTERNATIONAL RELATIONS - BIBLIOGRAPHY - PERIODICALS.
Foreign affairs. New York : Council on Foreign Relations, 1922-

## INTERNATIONAL RELATIONS - CONGRESSES.
Ethnicity and intra-state conflict. Aldershot, Hants, England ; Brookfield, Vt., USA : Ashgate, c1999.
*TC GN495.6 .E83 1999*

## INTERNATIONAL RELATIONS - FICTION.
Lederer, William J., 1912- The ugly American. 1st ed. New York : Norton, 1958.
*TC PS3523 .E27U35 1958*

## INTERNATIONAL RELATIONS LITERATURE.
*See* INTERNATIONAL RELATIONS - BIBLIOGRAPHY.

## INTERNATIONAL RELATIONS - PERIODICALS.
Foreign affairs. New York : Council on Foreign Relations, 1922-

## INTERNATIONAL RELATIONS - PSYCHOLOGICAL ASPECTS.
De Rivera, Joseph. The psychological dimension of foreign policy. Columbus, Ohio, C. E. Merrill Pub. Co. [1968]
*TC JX1255 .D45*

## INTERNATIONAL RELATIONS - RESEARCH.
Rummel, R. J. (Rudolph J.), 1932- The dimensions of nations Beverly Hills, Sage Publications [1972]
*TC JX1291 .R84*

Smith, Clagett G., 1930- comp. Conflict resolution: contributions of the behavioral sciences. Notre Dame [Ind.] University of Notre Dame Press [1971]
*TC JX1291 .S45*

**International review of community development.**
Centro sociale. Roma.

**International review of educational cinematography; July 1929-Dec. 1934.**
Intercine. Rome.

**International School of Biocybernetics (1997 : Naples, Italy)** Neuronal bases and psychological aspects of consiousness : proceedings of the International School of Biocybernetics, Casamicciola, Napoli, Italy, 13-18 October 1997 / edited by C. Taddei-Ferretti, C. Musio. Singapore ; River Edge, N.J : World Scientific, c1999. xi, 587 p. : ill. ; 23 cm. (Series on biophysics and biocybernetics ; vol. 8, biocybernetics.) Includes bibliographical references. ISBN 981-02-3597-6
*1. Consciousness - Congresses. 2. Consciousness - physiology - Congresses. 3. Neuropsychology - Congresses. 4. Brain - physiology - Congresses. 5. Neural Networks (Computer) - Congresses. I. Taddei-Ferretti, C. (Cloe) II. Musio, Carlo. III. Title. IV. Series: Series on biophysics and biocybernetics ; vol. 8.*
*TC QP411 .I56 1997*

**International series in experimental social psychology**
Genius and eminence. 2nd ed. Oxford ; New York : Pergamon Press, 1992.
*TC BF412 .G43 1992*

Wilson, Keithia. Assertion and its social context. 1st ed. Oxford ; New York : Pergamon Press, 1993.
*TC BF575.A85 W55 1993*

([v. 23]) Emotion and social judgments. 1st ed. Oxford ; New York : Pergamon Press, 1991.
*TC BF531 .E4834 1991*

**International Society for Activity Theory and Cultural Research. Congress (4th : 1998 : Aarhus, Denmark)** Activity theory and social practice : cultural-historical approaches / edited by Seth Chaiklin, Mariane Hedegaard and Uffe Juul Jensen. Aarhus : Aarhus University Press, c1999. 381 p. ; 25 cm. Includes bibliographical references and index. ISBN 87-7288-811-3
*1. Act (Philosophy) - Congresses. 2. Action theory - Congresses. I. Chaiklin, Seth. II. Hedegaard, Mariane. III. Jensen, Uffe Juul. IV. Title.*
*TC B105.A35 I57 1998*

Activity theory and social practice : cultural-historical approaches / edited by Seth Chaiklin, Mariane Hedegaard and Uffe Juul Jensen. Aarhus : Aarhus University Press, c1999. 381 p. ; 25 cm. Includes bibliographical references and index. ISBN 87-7288-811-3
*1. Act (Philosophy) - Congresses. 2. Action theory - Congresses. I. Chaiklin, Seth. II. Hedegaard, Mariane. III. Jensen, Uffe Juul. IV. Title.*
*TC B105.A35 I57 1999*

**International Society for Paediatric Neurosurgery.**
Child's brain. Basel, New York, Karger.

**International Society for Technology in Education.**
Kahn, Jessica L. Ideas and strategies for the one-computer classroom. Eugene, OR : International Society for Technology in Education, c1998.

*TC LB1028.5 .K25 1998*
National educational technology standards for students / International Society for Technology in Education. Eugene, OR : The Society, c1998. 19 p. : ill. ; 28 cm. Cover title.
*1. Educational technology - Standards - United States. 2. Computer literacy - Standards - United States. I. Title.*
*TC LB1028.3 .I569 1998*

**International Society of Audiology.**
International audiology. Leiden, Netherlands : International Society of Audiology, 1962-1970.

**International Society of Educational Planners.**
Educational planning. Mankato, Minn., International Society of Educational Planners.

## INTERNATIONAL STANDARD BOOK NUMBERS. *See* BOOKS.

## INTERNATIONAL STUDENTS. *See* STUDENTS, FOREIGN.

**International studies on childhood and adolescence**
(7) Growing up in times of social change. New York : Walter de Gruyter, 1999.
*TC HQ799.G5 G76 1999*

**International Symposium on Attention and Performance (11th : 1984 : Eugene, Or.)** Attention and performance XI / edited by Michael I. Posner, Oscar S. M. Marin. Hillsdale, N.J. : L. Erlbaum Associates, 1985. xxiii, 675 p. : ill. ; 24 cm. Other title: Attention and performance eleven. Other title: Attention and performance 11. "Proceedings of the Eleventh International Symposium on Attention and Performance, Eugene, Oregon, July 1-8, 1984"--P. [i]. Includes bibliographies and indexes. ISBN 0-89859-639-4 DDC 153.7/33
*1. Attention - Congresses. 2. Performance - Congresses. 3. Selectivity (Psychology) - Congresses. 4. Orientation (Psychology) - Congresses. I. Posner, Michael I. II. Marin, Oscar. III. Title: Attention and performance eleven IV. Title: Attention and performance 11*
*TC BF321 .A82 1985*

**International Symposium on Historical Archives of Pre-1949 Christian Higher Education in China (1993 : Hong Kong)** Chung-kuo chiao hui ta hsüeh li shih wen hsien yen tʻao hui lun wen chi / Wu Tzu-ming pien. Hsiang-kang : Chung wen ta hsüeh chʻu pan she, 1995. xxiii, 605 p. ; 21 cm. Colophon title: Essays on Historical Archives of Christian Higher Education in China. ISBN 962-201-674-X
*1. Church colleges - China - Archival resources - Congresses. 2. Education, Higher - China - Archival resources - Congresses. I. Wu, Tzu-ming. II. Title. III. Title: Essays on Historical Archives of Christian Higher Education in China*
*TC LC432.C5 I58 1995*

**International Symposium on the Physiology and Pathophysiology of Exercise Tolerance (1994 : Ulm, Germany).**
The physiology and pathophysiology of exercise tolerance. New York : Plenum Press, c1996.
*TC QP301 .P576 1996*

## INTERNATIONAL TRADE - MORAL AND ETHICAL ASPECTS.
The paradox of plenty. Oakland, Calif. : Food First Books, c1999.
*TC HD1542 .P37 1999*

**International transnational associations.** Associations transnationales internationales. [Bruxelles, Union of International Associations] 9 v. ill. 30 cm. Frequency: 6 no. a year, 1981- . Former frequency: Ten no. a year. 29th year (Jan./Feb. 1977)-37th year, no 6 (nov./déc. 1985). Associations transnationales internationales. Running title: Transnational associations <1977, 1984>. Running title: Associations transnationales <1977, 1984>. "The review of international associations and meetings." SUMMARY: Includes monthly supplements to: International congress calendar. English and French. Issued with: International congress calendar (OCoLC)1635938. Continues: International associations ISSN: 0020-6059 (DLC) 52039082 (OCoLC)4272898. Continued by: Transnational associations (DLC) 866647184 (OCoLC)14578454. ISSN 0250-4928 DDC 050
*1. International agencies - Periodicals. 2. International Agencies - periodicals. 3. International cooperation - Periodicals. 4. International Cooperation - periodicals. 5. Associations, institutions, etc. - Periodicals. 6. Congresses and conventions - Periodicals. I. Union of International Associations. II. Title: International congress calendar. Supplement. III. Title: Associations transnationales internationales <1977, 1984> V. Title: Associations transnationales <1977, 1984> VI. Title: International congress calendar VII. Title: International associations VIII. Title: Transnational associations*

## INTERNATIONAL TRAVEL REGULATIONS. *See* EMIGRATION AND IMMIGRATION LAW.

**International Union for Health Education.**
International journal of health education. [Geneva, Studer, 1958-1981]

**International Union for Health Education of the Public.**
International journal of health education. [Geneva, Studer, 1958-1981]

## INTERNATIONAL UNION OF PSYCHOLOGICAL SCIENCE - HISTORY.
History of the International Union of Psychological Science (IUPsyS). Hove, East Sussex : Psychology Press, 2000.
*TC BF11 .H57 2000*

## INTERNATIONAL UNIONS. *See* INTERNATIONAL AGENCIES.

**International Young Men's Christian Association Training School (Springfield, Mass.)**
The Association outlook. [Springfield, Mass. : International Young Men's Christian Association Training School, -1900.]

**Internationale Zeitschrift für Erziehung.**
Internationale Zeitschrift für Erziehungswissenschaft. Salzburg.

Internationale Zeitschrift für Erziehungswissenschaft = Köln : J.P. Bachem,

**Internationale Zeitschrift für Erziehungswissenschaft.** Salzburg. v. 4-6; Apr. 1947-51. Continues the vol. numbering of Internationale Zeitschrift für Erziehung v. 1-3 which the same editor issued 1931-34. cf. Union list of serials.
*1. Education - Periodicals. I. Title: Internationale Zeitschrift für Erziehung*

**Internationale Zeitschrift für Erziehungswissenschaft** = International education review = Revue internationale de pédagogie. Köln : J.P. Bachem, 3 v. : ill. ; 25 cm. Frequency: Quarterly. 1. Jahrg., 1. Heft (1931/32)-3. Jahrg., 4. Heft (1933/34). International education review. Revue internationale de pédagogie. SUMMARY: Includes section: "Literarische Übersichten und Buchbesprechungen. Literary reviews and notices of books. Aperçus bibliographiques et analyses critiques." Continued by: Internationale Zeitschrift für Erziehung.
*1. Education - Periodicals. I. Title: International education review II. Title: Revue internationale de pédagogie III. Title: Internationale Zeitschrift für Erziehung*

## INTERNATIONALISM. *See also* INTERNATIONAL EDUCATION; NATIONALISM.
Globalisation and pedagogy. London ; New York : Routledge, 2000.
*TC LC1090 .E33 2000*

**Internationalizing Entrepreneurship Education and Training Conference (4th : 1994 : University of Stirling).**
Educating entrepreneurs for wealth creation. Aldershot, Hants, England ; Brookfield, USA : Ashgate, 1998.
*TC HF1106 .E378 1998*

## INTERNET.
Burwell, Helen P. Online competitive intelligence. Tempe, AZ : Facts on Demand Press, c1999.
*TC HD38.7 .B974 1999*

Hawke, Constance S., 1952- Computer and Internet use on campus. 1st ed. San Francisco : Jossey-Bass, c2001.
*TC KF390.5.C6 H39 2001*

**Internet & personal computing abstracts : IPCA.** Medford, N.J. : Information Today, Inc., c2000- v. ; 28 cm. Frequency: Quarterly. Vol. 21, no. 1 (Mar. 2000)- . Internet and personal computing abstracts. Issue for March 2000, vol. 21, no. 1 has title Internet & personal computers abstracts on title page. IPCA. Dec. issue includes a cumulative index. Continues: Microcomputer abstracts ISSN: 1074-3995 (DLC) 94659108 (OCoLC)29690201. ISSN 1529-7705 DDC 016
*1. Microcomputers - Abstracts - Periodicals. 2. Internet - Indexes - Periodicals. 3. Internet - Abstracts - Periodicals. 4. Microcomputers - Indexes - Periodicals. I. Title: Internet and personal computing abstracts. II. Title: Issue for March 2000, vol. 21, no. 1 has title Internet & personal computers abstracts on title page. III. Title: IPCA IV. Title: Microcomputer abstracts*
*TC QA75.5 .M5*

## INTERNET - ABSTRACTS - PERIODICALS.
Internet & personal computing abstracts. Medford, N.J. : Information Today, Inc., c2000-

*TC QA75.5 .M5*

**INTERNET ACCESS FOR LIBRARY USERS - UNITED STATES.**
Smith, Mark, 1956- Neal-Schuman Internet policy handbook for libraries. New York : Neal-Schuman, c1999.
*TC Z692.C65 S66 1999*

**The Internet and instruction.**
Barron, Ann E. 2nd ed. Englewood, Colo. : Libraries Unlimited, 1998.
*TC LB1044.87 .B37 1998*

**Internet and personal computing abstracts.**
Internet & personal computing abstracts. Medford, N.J. : Information Today, Inc., c2000-
*TC QA75.5 .M5*

**The internet and society.**
Slevin, James. Malden, MA : Polity Press, 2000.
*TC HM851 .S58 2000*

**The Internet and the World Wide Web for preservice teachers.**
Provenzo, Eugene F. Boston : Allyn & Bacon, c1999.
*TC LB1044.87 .P763 1999*

**Internet blue pages.**
Andriot, Laurie. 1999 ed. Medford, NJ : Information Today, c1998.
*TC ZA5075 .A53 1998*

**The Internet challenge to television.**
Owen, Bruce M. Cambridge, Mass. : Harvard University Press, 1999.
*TC HE8700.8 .O826 1999*

**INTERNET (COMPUTER NETWORK).** *See also* **WORLD WIDE WEB (INFORMATION RETRIEVAL SYSTEM).**
Ameis, Jerry A. Mathematics on the Internet. Upper Saddle River, N.J. : Merrill, 2000.
*TC QA41.6 .A64 2000*

Barnicle, Katherine Ann. Evaluation of the interaction between users of screen reading technology and graphical user interface elements. 1999.
*TC 085 B265*

Bergan, Helen, 1937- Where the information is. Alexandria, VA : BioGuide Press, c1996.
*TC HD62.6 .B47 1996*

Henninger, Maureen, 1940- Don't just surf. 2nd ed. Sydney : UNSW Press, 1999.
*TC ZA4201 .H46 1999*

History of the Internet. Santa Barbara, Calif. : ABC-CLIO, c1999.
*TC TK5105.875.I57 H58 1999*

Shiva, V. A. Arts and the Internet. New York : Allworth Press, c1996.
*TC NX260 .S55 1996*

Wertheim, Margaret. The pearly gates of cyberspace. 1st ed. New York : W.W. Norton, c1999.
*TC QA76.9.C66 W48 1999*

**INTERNET (COMPUTER NETWORK) AND CHILDREN - UNITED STATES.**
Calvert, Sandra L. Children's journeys through the information age. 1st ed. Boston : McGraw-Hill College, c1999.
*TC HQ784.T4 C24 1999*

**INTERNET (COMPUTER NETWORK) IN EDUCATION.**
Anderson, Dennis S. Mathematics and distance education on the internet. 1999.
*TC 085 An2317*

Barron, Ann E. The Internet and instruction. 2nd ed. Englewood, Colo. : Libraries Unlimited, 1998.
*TC LB1044.87 .B37 1998*

Driscoll, Margaret M. The application of adult education principles in the development of a manual for practitioners creating web-based training programs. 1999.
*TC 06 no. 11106*

Educational computing in the schools. New York : Haworth Press, 1999.
*TC LB1028.3 .E332 1999*

Feminist cyberscapes. Stamford, Conn. : Ablex Pub., c1999.
*TC PE1404 .F39 1999*

Idzal, June M. Multimedia authoring tools and teacher training. 1997.
*TC 06 no. 10816*

Joseph, Linda C., 1949- Net curriculum. Medford, N.J. : CyberAge Books, c1999.

*TC LB1044.87 .J67 1999*
Kouki, Rafa. Telelearning via the Internet. Hershey, PA : Idea Group Pub., c1999.
*TC LC5800 .K68 1999*

McConnell, David, 1951- Implementing computer supported cooperative learning.. 2nd ed. London : Kogan Page, 2000.
*TC LB1032 .M38 2000*

Morton, Jessica G. Kids on the 'Net. Portsmouth, NH : Heinemann, c1998.
*TC LB1044.87 .M67 1998*

Provenzo, Eugene F. The Internet and the World Wide Web for preservice teachers. Boston : Allyn & Bacon, c1999.
*TC LB1044.87 .P763 1999*

Schweizer, Heidi. Designing and teaching an on-line course :. Boston : Allyn & Bacon, c1999.
*TC LB1028.3 .S377 1999*

Stoll, Clifford. High tech heretic. 1st ed. New York : Doubleday, c1999.
*TC LB1028.5 .S77 1999*

Surfing social studies. Washington, DC : National Council for the Social Studies, c1999.
*TC LB1044.87 .S97 1999*

Teaching government and citizenship using the Internet. Rev. ed. viii, 112 p. : ill. ; 28 cm.
*TC H61.95 .T43 2000*

Web-based learning and teaching technologies. Hershey, PA : London : Idea Group Pub., c2000.
*TC LB1044.87 .W435 2000*

**INTERNET (COMPUTER NETWORK) IN EDUCATION - CONGRESSES.**
IFIP TC3/WG3.3 & WG3.6 Joint Working Conference on the Virtual Campus: Trends for Higher Education and Training (1997 : Madrid, Spain) The virtual campus. 1st ed. London ; New York : Chapman & Hall on behalf of the International Federation for Information Processing (IFIP), 1998.
*TC LC5803.C65 I353 1997*

**INTERNET (COMPUTER NETWORK) IN EDUCATION - DIRECTORIES.**
Bigham, Vicki Smith. The Prentice Hall directory of online education resources. Paramus, N.J. : Prentice Hall, c1998.
*TC LB1044.87 .B54 1998*

**INTERNET (COMPUTER NETWORK) IN EDUCATION - GREAT BRITAIN.**
Grey, Duncan. The internet in school. London ; New York : Cassell Academic, 1999.
*TC LB1044.87 .G74 1999*

**INTERNET (COMPUTER NETWORK) IN EDUCATION - STUDY AND TEACHING.**
The Internet. Oxford ; New York : Oxford University Press, c2000.
*TC TK5105.875.I57 I57 2000*

**INTERNET (COMPUTER NETWORK) IN EDUCATION - UNITED STATES.**
Buzzeo, Toni. Terrific connections with authors, illustrators, and storytellers. Englewood, Colo. : Libraries Unlimited, 1999.
*TC LB1575.5.U5 B87 1999*

Network science, a decade later. Mahwah, N.J. : Lawrence Erlbaum, 2000.
*TC LB1583.3 .N48 2000*

Preparing your campus for a networked future. 1st ed. San Francisco : Jossey-Bass, c2000.
*TC LB2395.7 .P74 2000*

**INTERNET (COMPUTER NETWORK) IN EDUCATION - UNITED STATES - DIRECTORIES.**
Andriot, Laurie. Uncle Sam's K-12 Web. Medford, N.J. : CyberAge Books, 1999.
*TC ZA575 .A53 1999*

**INTERNET (COMPUTER NETWORK) IN EDUCATION - UNITED STATES - FINANCE.**
Bauer, David G. Technology funding for schools. 1st ed. San Francisco : Jossey-Bass, c2000.
*TC LB1028.43 .B38 2000*

**INTERNET (COMPUTER NETWORK) IN EXPERIMENTAL PSYCHOLOGY.**
Psychological experiments on the Internet. San Diego : Academic Press, c2000.
*TC BF198.7 .P79 2000*

**INTERNET (COMPUTER NETWORK) LITERACY - UNITED STATES.**

Librarians as learners, librarians as teachers. Chicago : Association of College and Research Libraries, 1999.
*TC Z675.U5 L415 1999*

**INTERNET (COMPUTER NETWORK) - PSYCHOLOGICAL ASPECTS.**
Wallace, Patricia M. The psychology of the Internet. Cambridge ; New York : Cambridge University Press, 1999.
*TC BF637.C45 W26 1999*

**INTERNET (COMPUTER NETWORK) - SOCIAL ASPECTS.**
Digital diversions. London : UCL Press, 1998.
*TC QA76.575 .D536 1998*

Jordan, Tim, 1959- Cyberpower. London : New York : Routledge, 1999.
*TC ZA4375 .J67 1999*

Race in cyberspace. New York : London : Routledge, 2000.
*TC HT1523 .R252 2000*

Sikes, Alfred C. Fast forward. 1st ed. New York : William Morrow, 2000.
*TC HM851 .S545 2000*

Slevin, James. The internet and society. Malden, MA : Polity Press, 2000.
*TC HM851 .S58 2000*

Stefik, Mark. The Internet edge. Cambridge, Mass. : MIT Press, c1999.
*TC HM851 .S74 1999*

**INTERNET (COMPUTER NETWORK) - STUDY AND TEACHING.**
The Internet. Oxford ; New York : Oxford University Press, c2000.
*TC TK5105.875.I57 I57 2000*

McLain, Tim, 1970- How to create successful Internet projects. El Segundo, Calif. : Classroom Connect, c1999.
*TC LB1044.87 .M35 1999*

**INTERNET (COMPUTER NETWORK) - STUDY AND TEACHING - GREAT BRITAIN.**
Grey, Duncan. The internet in school. London ; New York : Cassell Academic, 1999.
*TC LB1044.87 .G74 1999*

**INTERNET (COMPUTER NETWORK) IN EDUCATION.**
The Internet in action for math & science 7-12 [videorecording]. [New York] : Thirteen-WNET : [Alexandria, Va. : distributed by] PBS Video, c1997.
*TC LB1044.87 .I453 1997*

The Internet in action for math & science K-6 [videorecording]. [New York] : Thirteen-WNET : [Alexandria, Va. : distributed by] PBS Video, c1998.
*TC LB1044.87 .I45 1998*

**The Internet edge.**
Stefik, Mark. Cambridge, Mass. : MIT Press, c1999.
*TC HM851 .S74 1999*

**INTERNET - FICTION.**
Draper, Sharon M. (Sharon Mills) Romiette and Julio. 1st ed. New York : Atheneum Books for Young Readers, 1999.
*TC PZ7.D78325 Ro 1999*

**The Internet for teachers.**
Williams, Bard. 3rd ed. Foster City, CA : IDG Books Worldwide, 1999.
*TC LB1044.87 .W55 1999*

**The Internet in action for math & science 7-12**
[videorecording] / a production of Thirteen/WNET Educational Resources Center ; senior producer, Maura Kelly ; [producer, Pam Newman Pooley] ; directed by Wayne Palmer. [New York] : Thirteen-WNET ; [Alexandria, Va. : distributed by] PBS Video, c1997. 3 videocassettes (ca. 200 mins.) : sd., col. ; 1/2 in. + 1 guide (102 p. : ill. ; 28 cm.). Title on container: Internet in action for math and science 7-12 : a professional development series for middle and high school math and science teachers [videorecording]. VHS. Catalogued from credits and container for Cassette 1 and accompanying material. Set designer, Frank Lopez; title & graphic design, B.T. Whitehall. "For information, resources and links, visit the Internet primer at www.wnet.org/wnetschool."-- Containers. For middle and high school math and science teachers. SUMMARY: A professional development series for middle and high school math and science teachers. Three cassettes divided into 15 segments cover topics like visionary views, how to get connected, how to do a smart search, amazing sites, the student-scientist partnership, how to create a web page, looking to the future, the Internet and your curriculum, Internet classroom applications, and technology equity. URL: http://www.wnet.org/wnetschool/ntti CONTENTS: Tape 1. The

student computer squad; Smart searching; Internet-ize your lessons; Super science site; Worldwide classroom (65 min.) -- Tape 2. Virtual dinosaurs; Virtual expeditions; Global projects ; Online communications; Amazing Math site (75 min.) -- Tape. 3. The real world; Create a Web site 1; Create a Web site 2: Ohio SchoolNet: a statewide model; wNetSChool and lesson plans (60 min.).

*1. Internet (Comupter network) in education. 2. Mathematics - Study and teaching (Secondary) - Computer network resources. 3. Science - Study and teaching (Secondary) - Computer network resources. 4. Mathematics - Study and teaching (Middle school) - Computer network resources. 5. Science - Study and teaching (Middle school) - Computer network resources. I. Kelly, Maura. II. Pooley, Pam Newman. III. Morris, Bob. IV. WNET (Television station : New York, N.Y.) V. WNET (Television station : New York, N.Y.) Educational Resources Center. VI. National Teacher Training Institute. VII. Title: Internet in action for math and science seventh-twelfth grade [videorecording] VIII. Title: Internet in action for math and science 7-12 : a professional development series for middle and high school math and science teachers [videorecording] IX. Title: Professional development series for middle and high school math and science teachers [videorecording]*

**TC LB1044.87 .I453 1997**

**The Internet in action for math & science K-6**
[videorecording] / a production of Thirteen/WNET Educational Resources Center ; senior producer, Maura Kelly ; producer, Pam Newman Pooley ; directed by Wayne Palmer. [New York] : Thirteen-WNET ; [Alexandria, Va. : distributed by] PBS Video, c1998. 3 videocassettes (ca. 220 mins.) : sd., col. ; 1/2 in. + 1 guide (71 p. : ill. ; 28 cm.). Title on container: Internet in action for math and science K-6 : a professional development series for elementary and middle school math and science teachers [videorecording]. VHS. Catalogued from credits and container for Cassette 1 and accompanying material. Editor, Kerry Soloway; title & graphic design, B.T. Whitehall. "For information, resources and links, visit the Internet primer at www.wnet.org/wnetschool."-- Containers. For elementary and middle school math and science teachers. SUMMARY: A professional development series for elementary and middle school math and science teachers. Three cassettes divided into 16 segments cover topics like Internet classroom applications, using the Internet for lessons, great Websites, virtual expeditions, creating a website and more. URL: http://www.wnet.org/wnetschool CONTENTS: Tape 1. Visionary views; How to get connected; How to do a smart search; Amazing Science sites; Amazing Math sites; Real-time data sheet (70 min.) -- Tape 2. The Internet and your curriculum; Internet classroom applications #1; Internet classroom applications #2; Internet classroom applications #3; Technology equity (75 min.) -- Tape. 3. The student-scientist partnership; How to create a Web page [3 segments]; Looking to the future (75 min.).

*1. Internet (Comupter network) in education. 2. Mathematics - Study and teaching (Elementary) - Computer network resources. 3. Science - Study and teaching (Elementary) - Computer network resources. 4. Mathematics - Study and teaching (Middle school) - Computer network resources. 5. Science - Study and teaching (Middle school) - Computer network resources. I. Kelly, Maura. II. Pooley, Pam Newman. III. Palmer, Wayne. IV. WNET (Television station : New York, N.Y.) V. WNET (Television station : New York, N.Y.) Educational Resources Center. VI. National Teacher Training Institute. VII. Title: Internet in action for math and science kindergarten-six [videorecording] VIII. Title: Internet in action for math and science kindergarten-sixth grade [videorecoridng] IX. Title: Internet in action for math and science K-6 : a professional development series for elementary and middle school math and science teachers [videorecording] X. Title: Professional development series for elementary and middle school math and science teachers [videorecording]*

**TC LB1044.87 .I45 1998**

**Internet in action for math and science 7-12 : a professional development series for middle and high school math and science teachers [videorecording].**
The Internet in action for math & science 7-12 [videorecording]. [New York] : Thirteen-WNET ; [Alexandria, Va. : distributed by] PBS Video, c1997.

**TC LB1044.87 .I453 1997**

**Internet in action for math and science K-6 : a professional development series for elementary and middle school math and science teachers [videorecording].**
The Internet in action for math & science K-6 [videorecording]. [New York] : Thirteen-WNET ; [Alexandria, Va. : distributed by] PBS Video, c1998.

**TC LB1044.87 .I45 1998**

**Internet in action for math and science kindergarten-six [videorecording].**
The Internet in action for math & science K-6

[videorecording]. [New York] : Thirteen-WNET ; [Alexandria, Va. : distributed by] PBS Video, c1998.

**TC LB1044.87 .I45 1998**

**Internet in action for math and science kindergarten-sixth grade [videorecoridng].**
The Internet in action for math & science K-6 [videorecording]. [New York] : Thirteen-WNET ; [Alexandria, Va. : distributed by] PBS Video, c1998.

**TC LB1044.87 .I45 1998**

**Internet in action for math and science seventh-twelfth grade [videorecording].**
The Internet in action for math & science 7-12 [videorecording]. [New York] : Thirteen-WNET ; [Alexandria, Va. : distributed by] PBS Video, c1997.

**TC LB1044.87 .I453 1997**

**INTERNET IN EDUCATION.**
Fredericks, Anthony D. Science discoveries on the net. Englewood, Colo. : Libraries Unlimited, 2000.
**TC Q182.7 .F73 2000**

International perspectives on tele-education and virtual learning environments. Aldershot : Ashgate, 2000.
**TC LB1044.87 .I55 2000**

Issues in Web-based pedagogy. Westport, Conn. : Greenwood Press, 2000.
**TC LB1044.87 .I88 2000**

Lathrop, Ann. Student cheating and plagiarism in the Internet era. Englewood, Colo. : Libraries Unlimited, 2000.
**TC LB3609 .L28 2000**

Net-working. Dunedin, N.Z. : University of Otago Press, 1999.
**TC LB1044.87 .N47 1999**

Salmon, Gilly. E-moderating. London : Kogan Page ; Sterling, VA : Stylus, 2000.
**TC LB1044.87 .S25 2000**

The School administrator's handbook of essential Internet sites. Fourth ed. Gaithersburg, MD : Aspen Publishers.
**TC TK5105.875.I57 S3 2000**

Sharma, Martha B., 1945- Using internet primary sources to teach critical thinking skills in geography. Westport, Conn. ; London : Greenwood Press, 2000.
**TC G73 .S393 2000**

Williams, Bard. The Internet for teachers. 3rd ed. Foster City, CA : IDG Books Worldwide, c1999.
**TC LB1044.87 .W55 1999**

**INTERNET IN EDUCATION - CONGRESSES.**
IFIP TC3 WG3.1/3.5 Open Conference on Communications and Networking in Education (1999 : Aulanko, Finland) Communications and networking in education. Boston : Kluwer Academic Publishers, 2000.
**TC LB1044.87 .I45 2000**

IFIP TC3 WG3.2/3.6 International Working Conference on Building University Electronic Educational Environments (1999 : Irvine, Calif.) Building university electronic educational environments. Boston : Kluwer Academic Publishers, c2000.
**TC LC5803.C65 .I352 2000**

**INTERNET IN EDUCATION - DIRECTORIES.**
Sharp, Richard M. The best Web sites for teachers. 3rd ed. Eugene, OR : International Society for Technology in Education, 2000.
**TC LB1044.87 .S52 2000**

**INTERNET IN EDUCATION - PSYCHOLOGICAL ASPECTS.**
Instructional and cognitive impacts of Web-based education. Hershey, PA : Idea Group Pub., c2000.
**TC LB1044.87 .I545 2000**

**INTERNET IN EDUCATION - UNITED STATES.**
Fredericks, Anthony D. Social studies discoveries on the net. Englewood, Colo. : Libraries Unlimited, 2000.
**TC LB1584 .F6597 2000**

**The internet in school.**
Grey, Duncan. London ; New York : Cassell Academic, 1999.
**TC LB1044.87 .G74 1999**

**INTERNET - INDEXES - PERIODICALS.**
Internet & personal computing abstracts. Medford, N.J. : Information Today, Inc., c2000-
**TC QA75.5 .M5**

**The Internet kids & family yellow pages.**
Polly, Jean Armour. Millenium ed. Berkeley, Calif. : Osborne McGraw-Hill, c2000.

**TC ZA4226 .P6 2000**

**Internet kids and family yellow pages.**
Polly, Jean Armour. The Internet kids & family yellow pages. Millenium ed. Berkeley, Calif. : Osborne McGraw-Hill, c2000.
**TC ZA4226 .P6 2000**

**Internet policy handbook for libraries.**
Smith, Mark, 1956- Neal-Schuman Internet policy handbook for libraries. New York : Neal-Schuman, c1999.
**TC Z692.C65 S66 1999**

**Internet power searching.**
Bradley, Phil, 1959- New York : Neal-Schuman Publishers, 1999.
**TC ZA4201 .B69 1999**

**INTERNET RESOURCES.** *See* **COMPUTER NETWORK RESOURCES.**

**The Internet** / Scott Windeatt, David Hardisty, and David Eastment. Oxford ; New York : Oxford University Press, c2000. vii, 136 p. : ill. ; 25 cm. (Resource books for teachers) ISBN 0-19-437223-5
*1. Internet (Computer network) - Study and teaching. 2. Internet (Computer network) in education - Study and teaching. 3. World Wide Web (Information retrieval system) - Study and teaching. 4. English language - Study and teaching - Computer-assisted instruction. I. Windeatt, Scott. II. Hardisty, David. III. Eastment, David. IV. Series.*
**TC TK5105.875.I57 I57 2000**

**INTERNET SEARCHING.**
Bradley, Phil, 1959- Internet power searching. New York : Neal-Schuman Publishers, 1999.
**TC ZA4201 .B69 1999**

Paul, Nora. Great scouts!. Medford, NJ : Information Today, c1999.
**TC ZA4201 .P38 1999**

**INTERNMENT CAMPS.** *See* **CONCENTRATION CAMPS.**

**INTERNMENT OF JAPANESE AMERICANS, 1942-1945.** *See* **JAPANESE AMERICANS - EVACUATION AND RELOCATION, 1942-1945.**

**INTERNSHIP PROGRAMS - UNITED STATES - DIRECTORIES.**
Financial aid for African Americans. El Dorado Hills, Calif. : Reference Service Press, c1997-
**TC LB2338 .F5643**

**INTERNSHIPS.** *See* **INTERNSHIP PROGRAMS.**

**INTERORGANIZATIONAL RELATIONS.** *See also* **BUREAUCRACY; COLLEGE-SCHOOL COOPERATION; COMMUNITY ORGANIZATION; HEALTH FACILITIES - AFFILIATIONS; INTERNATIONAL AGENCIES.**
Osguthorpe, Russell T. Balancing the tensions of change. Thousand Oaks, Calif. : Corwin Press, c1998.
**TC LB2331.53 .O74 1998**

Parker, Glenn M., 1938- Cross-functional teams. 1st ed. San Francisco, Calif. : Jossey-Bass, c1994.
**TC HD66 .P345 1994**

**INTERORGANIZATIONAL RELATIONS - NEW YORK (STATE) - NEW YORK.**
Wright, Stanley Nathaniel. The Beacon model. 1998.
**TC 06 no. 11007**

**INTERORGANIZATIONAL RELATIONS - NEW YORK (STATE) - NEW YORK - CASE STUDIES - EVALUATION.**
Darwiche, Chirine Hijazi. The Beacons. 1997.
**TC 06 no. 10761**

**INTERPERSONAL COMMUNICATION.** *See also* **DIALOGUE ANALYSIS.**
Hartley, Peter, 1946- 2nd ed. London ; New York : Routledge, 1999.
**TC BF637.C45 H35 1999**

**INTERPERSONAL COMMUNICATION.**
Bridges not walls. 7th ed. Boston : McGraw Hill College, c1999.
**TC BF637.C45 B74 1999**

Communication and aging. 2nd ed. Mahwah, NJ : London : L. Erlbaum, 2000.
**TC HQ1064.U5 C5364 2000**

Communication and personal relationships. New York : Wiley, 2000.
**TC HM1116 .C65 2000**

Golden, Valerie. Significant others' perceptions of the effects of their partners' psychotherapy. 1998.

*TC 085 G566*

Hartley, Peter, 1946- Interpersonal communication. 2nd ed. London : New York : Routledge, 1999.
*TC BF637.C45 H35 1999*

Honeycutt, James M. Cognition, communication, and romantic relationships. Mahwah, N.J. : London : L. Erlbaum Associates, 2001.
*TC BF575.I5 H66 2001*

Penman, Robyn. Reconstructing communicating. Mahwah, N.J. : London : Lawrence Erlbaum Associates, 2000.
*TC BF637.C45 P435 2000*

Planalp, Sally, 1950- Communicating emotion. Cambridge ; New York : Cambridge University Press : Paris : Editions de la Maison des sciences de l'homme, 1999.
*TC BF591. .P57 1999*

Podesta, Connie. Life would be easy if it weren't for other people. Thousand Oaks, Calif. : Corwin Press, c1999.
*TC BF637.I48 P63 1999*

Wilson, Keithia. Assertion and its social context. 1st ed. Oxford ; New York : Pergamon Press, 1993.
*TC BF575.A85 W55 1993*

Young, Robert L. (Robert Louis), 1949- Understanding misunderstandings. 1st ed. Austin : University of Texas Press, 1999.
*TC BF637.C45 Y69 1999*

**INTERPERSONAL COMMUNICATION IN CHILDREN.** *See also* **CHILDREN - LANGUAGE; LANGUAGE ACQUISITION.**
Communication. Stamford, Conn. : Ablex Pub. Corp., c2000.
*TC BF712 .A36 v.19*

Peterson, Susan Louise, 1960- Why children make up stories. San Francisco ; London : International Scholars Publications, 1999.
*TC BF723.C57 P47 1999*

**INTERPERSONAL COMMUNICATION IN INFANTS.**
Communication. Stamford, Conn. : Ablex Pub. Corp., c2000.
*TC BF712 .A36 v.19*

**INTERPERSONAL COMMUNICATION - STUDY AND TEACHING (SECONDARY).**
Toner, Patricia Rizzo, 1952- Relationships and communication activities. West Nyack, N.Y. : Center for Applied Research in Education, c1993.
*TC HM132 .T663 1993*

**INTERPERSONAL COMMUNICATION - UNITED STATES.**
Experiential activities for intercultural learning. Yarmouth, Me., USA : Intercultural Press, c1996-
*TC LC1099.3 .E97 1996*

**INTERPERSONAL COMPETENCE.** *See* **SOCIAL SKILLS.**

**INTERPERSONAL CONFLICT.** *See also* **SOCIAL CONFLICT.**
Behaving badly. 1st ed. Washington, D.C. : American Psychological Association, 2001.
*TC HM1106 .B45 2001*

Close relationships. Thousand Oaks, Calif. : Sage Publications, c2000.
*TC HM1106 .C55 2000*

Lulofs, Roxane Salyer. Conflict. 2nd ed. Boston : Allyn and Bacon, c2000.
*TC BF637.I48 L85 2000*

Mayer, Bernard S., 1946- The dynamics of conflict resolution. 1st ed. San Francisco : Jossey-Bass Publishers, c2000.
*TC BF637.I48 M39 2000*

Podesta, Connie. Life would be easy if it weren't for other people. Thousand Oaks, Calif. : Corwin Press, c1999.
*TC BF637.I48 P63 1999*

Wilde, Jerry, 1962- An educators guide to difficult parents. Huntington, N.Y. : Kroshka Books, c2000.
*TC LC225.3 .W54 2000*

**INTERPERSONAL CONFLICT IN ADOLESCENCE - UNITED STATES - PREVENTION.**
Promoting nonviolence in early adolescence. New York : Kluwer Academic/Plenum Publishers, c2000.
*TC HM1126 .P76 2000*

**INTERPERSONAL CONFRONTATION.**
Blank, Leonard. Confrontation: New York, Macmillan [1971]
*TC HM132 .B55*

**Interpersonal influence.**
Wheeler, Ladd, 1937- Boston, Allyn and Bacon [1970]
*TC HM291 .W35*

**INTERPERSONAL PERCEPTION.** *See* **SOCIAL PERCEPTION.**

**INTERPERSONAL PSYCHOTHERAPY.**
Interpersonal psychotherapy for group. New York : Basic Books, 2000.
*TC RC489.I55 I584 2000*

**Interpersonal psychotherapy for group** / Denise E. Wilfley ... [et al.]. New York : Basic Books, 2000. xv, 237 p. ; 24 cm. (Basic behavioral science) Includes bibliographical references and index. ISBN 0-465-09569-0 DDC 616.89/14
1. Interpersonal psychotherapy. I. Wilfley, Denise E., 1960- II. Series.
*TC RC489.I55 I584 2000*

**INTERPERSONAL RELATIONS.** *See also* **DISCRIMINATION; FRIENDSHIP; GROUP RELATIONS TRAINING; INTERGENERATIONAL RELATIONS; INTERPERSONAL COMMUNICATION; INTIMACY (PSYCHOLOGY); MAN-WOMAN RELATIONSHIPS; OBJECT RELATIONS (PSYCHOANALYSIS); PARENT AND CHILD; SOCIAL PERCEPTION; SOCIAL SKILLS; TEACHER-STUDENT RELATIONSHIPS.**
Adolescent relationships and drug use. Mahwah, N.J. ; London : Lawrence Erlbaum Associates, 2000.
*TC HV5824.Y68 A315 2000*

Attitudes, behavior, and social context. Mahwah, N.J. : L. Erlbaum Associates, 2000.
*TC HM132 .B48 1998*

Balancing the secrets of private disclosures. Mahwah, N.J. : Lawrence Erlbaum Associates, Publishers, 2000.
*TC BF697.5.S427 B35 2000*

Behaving badly. 1st ed. Washington, D.C. : American Psychological Association, 2001.
*TC HM1106 .B45 2001*

Bennett, Joel B. Time and intimacy. Mahwah, N.J. ; London : Lawrence Erlbaum Associates, 2000.
*TC BF575.I5 B45 2000*

Boss, Pauline. Ambiguous loss. Cambridge, Mass. : Harvard University Press, 1999.
*TC BF575.D35 B67 1999*

Brown, Rupert, 1950- Group processes. 2nd ed. Oxford ; Malden, Mass. : Blackwell Publishers, 2000.
*TC HM131 .B726 2000*

Close relationships. Thousand Oaks, Calif. : Sage Publications, c2000.
*TC HM1106 .C55 2000*

Communication and personal relationships. New York : Wiley, 2000.
*TC HM1116 .C65 2000*

Culturally speaking. London ; New York : Continuum ; [New York] : [Cassell], 2000.
*TC GN345.6 .C86 2000*

Druss, Richard G., 1933- Listening to patients :. Oxford ; New York : Oxford University Press, 2000.
*TC RC480.8 .D78 2000*

Fenichel, Ann. The relationship between health care clinicians' relational abilities and psychosocial orientation to patient care, and patient adherence with medical treatment. 1998.
*TC 085 F352*

Friend, Marilyn Penovich, 1953- Interactions. 3rd ed. New York : Longman, 1999.
*TC LC3969.45 .F75 1999*

Honeycutt, James M. Cognition, communication, and romantic relationships. Mahwah, N.J. ; London : L. Erlbaum Associates, 2001.
*TC BF575.I5 H66 2001*

Nevas, Debra Baron. Factors affecting parental attitudes toward a child's therapist and therapy. 1997.
*TC 085 N401*

Partnerships in research, clinical, and educational settings. Stamford, Conn. : Ablex Pub., c1999.
*TC HM1106 .P37 1999*

Podesta, Connie. Life would be easy if it weren't for other people. Thousand Oaks, Calif. : Corwin Press, c1999.
*TC BF637.I48 P63 1999*

Social dreaming @ work. London : Karnac Books, 1998.
*TC BF1078 .S55 1998*

Tobe, Dorothy Echols. The development of cognitive leadership frames among African American female college presidents. 1999.
*TC 06 no. 11187*

Viney, John. Drive. 1st U.S. ed. New York, N.Y. : Bloomsbury, 1999.
*TC HD57.7 .V564 1999*

Winslade, John. Narrative counseling in schools. Thousand Oaks, Calif. : Corwin Press, c1999.
*TC LB1027.5 .W535 1999*

Zachary, Lois J. The mentor's guide. 1st ed. San Francisco : Jossey-Bass Publishers, c2000.
*TC LB1731.4 .Z23 2000*

**INTERPERSONAL RELATIONS - AUDIOVISUAL AIDS - CATALOGS.**
B'nai B'rith. Anti-defamation League. Human relations materials for the school, church & community. [New York : Anti-defamation League of B'nai B'rith, [1981?]
*TC Z7204.S67 A5 1981*

**INTERPERSONAL RELATIONS - BIBLIOGRAPHY - CATALOGS.**
B'nai B'rith. Anti-defamation League. Human relations materials for the school, church & community. [New York : Anti-defamation League of B'nai B'rith, [1981?]
*TC Z7204.S67 A5 1981*

**INTERPERSONAL RELATIONS - CALIFORNIA - CASE STUDIES.**
Samway, Katharine Davies. Buddy reading. Portsmouth, NH : Heinemann, c1995.
*TC LB1031.5 .S36 1995*

**INTERPERSONAL RELATIONS - FICTION.**
Griffin, Adele. Dive. 1st ed. New York : Hyperion Books for Children, 1999.
*TC PZ7.G881325 Di 1999*

Sheldon, Dyan. Confessions of a teenage drama queen. 1st ed. Cambridge, Mass. : Candlewick Press, 1999.
*TC PZ7.S54144 Co 1999*

Vail, Rachel. If you only knew. 1st ed. New York : Scholastic, c1998.
*TC PZ7.V1916 If 1998*

**INTERPERSONAL RELATIONS IN ADOLESCENCE.**
Family and peers. Westport, Conn. : Praeger, 2000.
*TC HQ755.85 .F365 2000*

**INTERPERSONAL RELATIONS IN ADOLESCENCE - STATISTICAL METHODS.**
Recent advances in the measurement of acceptance and rejection in the peer system. San Francisco : Jossey-Bass Publishers, c2000.
*TC BF723.I65 R4 2000*

**INTERPERSONAL RELATIONS IN CHILDREN.**
Children's peer relations. London ; New York : Routledge, 1998.
*TC BF723.I646 C47 1998*

Family and peers. Westport, Conn. : Praeger, 2000.
*TC HQ755.85 .F365 2000*

Mills, Rosemary S.L. The developmental psychology of personal relationships. Chichester ; New York : John Wiley, c2000.
*TC BF723.I646 M55 2000*

**INTERPERSONAL RELATIONS IN CHILDREN - STATISTICAL METHODS.**
Recent advances in the measurement of acceptance and rejection in the peer system. San Francisco : Jossey-Bass Publishers, c2000.
*TC BF723.I65 R4 2000*

**INTERPERSONAL RELATIONS - NEW YORK (STATE) - CASE STUDIES.**
Schlanger, Dean J. An exploration of school belongingness. 1998.
*TC 06 no. 10993*

**INTERPERSONAL RELATIONS - PSYCHOLOGICAL ASPECTS - CASE STUDIES.**
Brown, Gloria M. Post-hospital care for the elderly. 1997.

*TC 06 no. 10759*

**INTERPERSONAL RELATIONS - STUDY AND TEACHING.**
Goldstein, Arnold P. The Prepare Curriculum. Revised ed. Champaign, Ill. : Research Press, c1999.
*TC HM299 .G65 1999*

**INTERPERSONAL RELATIONS - STUDY AND TEACHING (SECONDARY).**
Toner, Patricia Rizzo, 1952- Relationships and communication activities. West Nyack, N.Y. : Center for Applied Research in Education, c1993.
*TC HM132 .T663 1993*

**INTERPERSONAL RELATIONS - TURKEY - ANKARA.**
Seferoglu, Süleyman Sadi. Elementary school teacher development. 1996.
*TC 06 no. 10693*

**INTERPERSONAL RELATIONS - UNITED STATES.**
Calderwood, Patricia E., 1954- Learning community. New York : Teachers College Press, c2000.
*TC LB1032 .C34 2000*

Fressola, Maria C. How nurse executives learned to become leaders. 1998.
*TC 06 no. 11115*

Fressola, Maria C. How nurse executives learned to become leaders. 1998.
*TC 06 no. 11115*

Hoyle, John. Interpersonal sensitivity. Larchmont, NY : Eye on Education, c1997.
*TC LB2831.92.U6 H67 1997*

Komives, Susan R., 1946- Exploring leadership. 1st ed. San Francisco : Jossey-Bass Publishers, c1998.
*TC LB3605 .K64 1998*

**Interpersonal sensitivity.**
Hoyle, John. Larchmont, NY : Eye on Education, c1997.
*TC LB2831.92.U6 H67 1997*

**INTERPLANETARY VOYAGES - FICTION.**
Carrick, Carol. Patrick's dinosaurs on the Internet. New York : Clarion Books, 1999.
*TC PZ7.C2344 Patf 1999*

**Interplay, arts, history, theory**
Nochlin, Linda. Representing women. New York : Thames and Hudson, 1999.
*TC ND1460.W65 N63 1999*

Thomas, Nicholas. Possessions. New York, N.Y. : Thames and Hudson, c1999.
*TC N5313 .T46 1999*

**INTERPRETATION, DREAM.** *See* **DREAM INTERPRETATION.**

**INTERPRETATION IN PSYCHOANALYSIS.** *See* **PSYCHOANALYTIC INTERPRETATION.**

**INTERPRETATION OF CULTURAL AND NATURAL RESOURCES.** *See* **HISTORIC SITES - INTERPRETIVE PROGRAMS.**

**INTERPRETERS FOR THE DEAF.**
Peters, Cynthia. Deaf American literature. Washington, D.C. : Gallaudet University Press, 2000.
*TC HV2471 .P38 2000*

**INTERPRETERS FOR THE DEAF - TRAINING OF - UNITED STATES.**
Innovative practices for teaching sign language interpreters. Washington, D.C. : Gallaudet University Press, 2000.
*TC HV2402 .I56 2000*

**INTERPRETERS FOR THE DEAF - UNITED STATES.**
Mindess, Anna. Reading between the signs. Yarmouth, Me. : Intercultural Press, c1999.
*TC HV2402 .M56 1999*

**Interpreting personality tests.**
Craig, Robert J., 1941- New York : J. Wiley & Sons, c1999.
*TC BF698.5 .C73 1999*

**Interpreting weight :** the social management of fatness and thinness / Jeffery Sobal and Donna Maurer, editors. New York : Aldine de Gruyter, c1999. x, 264 p. : ill. ; 24 cm. (Social problems and social issues) Includes bibliographical references and index. ISBN 0-202-30577-5 (alk. paper) ISBN 0-202-30578-3 (pbk. : alk. paper) DDC 306.4/61
*1. Obesity - Social aspects. 2. Food - Social aspects. 3. Nutrition - Social aspects. I. Sobal, Jeffery, 1950- II. Maurer, Donna, 1961- III. Series.*

*TC RA645.O23 I55 1999*

**INTERPRETIVE DANCING.** *See* **MODERN DANCE.**

**INTERPRETIVE PROGRAMS OF HISTORIC SITES.** *See* **HISTORIC SITES - INTERPRETIVE PROGRAMS.**

**Interpretive studies of education in China.**
The ethnographic eye. New York : Falmer Press, 2000.
*TC LB45 .E837 2000*

**INTERPROFESSIONAL RELATIONS.** *See* **PROFESSIONS.**

**INTERPROFESSIONAL RELATIONS.**
Traynor, Michael, 1956- Managerialism and nursing. London ; New York : Routledge, 1999.
*TC RT86.45 .T73 1999*

**INTERPROFESSIONAL RELATIONS - GREAT BRITAIN.**
Traynor, Michael, 1956- Managerialism and nursing. London ; New York : Routledge, 1999.
*TC RT86.45 .T73 1999*

**INTERPROFESSIONAL RELATIONS - UNITED STATES.**
Collaborative practice. Westport, Conn. ; London : Praeger, 1999.
*TC HV741 .C5424 1999*

**INTERRACIAL ADOPTION.** *See* **INTERCOUNTRY ADOPTION.**

**INTERRACIAL DATING - MARYLAND - PRINCE GEORGE'S COUNTY.**
Kohn, Howard. We had a dream. New York : Simon & Schuster, 1998.
*TC F187.P9 K64 1998*

**INTERRACIAL MARRIAGE - FICTION.**
McGill, Alice. Molly Bannaky. Boston, Mass. : Houghton Mifflin, 1999.
*TC PZ7.M478468 Mol 1999*

**INTERRACIAL MARRIAGE - MARYLAND - PRINCE GEORGE'S COUNTY.**
Kohn, Howard. We had a dream. New York : Simon & Schuster, 1998.
*TC F187.P9 K64 1998*

**INTERRACIAL MARRIAGE - UNITED STATES.**
Interracial relationships. San Diego : Greenhaven Press, c2000.
*TC HQ1031 .I59 2000*

**Interracial relationships** / Bryan J. Grapes, editor. San Diego : Greenhaven Press, c2000. 80 p. ; 24 cm. (At issue) Includes bibliographical references (p. 75-76) and index. ISBN 0-7377-0155-2 (lib. : alk. paper) ISBN 0-7377-0154-4 (pbk. : alk. paper) DDC 306.84/6
*1. Intermarriage - United States. 2. Interracial marriage - United States. 3. Ethnicity - United States. 4. United States - Race relations. I. Grapes, Bryan J. II. Series: At issue (San Diego, Calif.)*
*TC HQ1031 .I59 2000*

**The interrelationships between junior high school students' scientific epistemologicl beliefs, learning environment preferences and their cognitive structure outcomes.**
Tsai, Chin-Chung. 1996.
*TC 06 no. 10713*

**INTERROGATION.** *See* **QUESTIONING.**

**Interruptions.**
Jarrett, Michael, 1953- Drifting on a read. Albany, N.Y. : State University of New York Press, 1999.
*TC ML3849 .J39 1999*

**INTERSCHOLASTIC ATHLETICS.** *See* **SCHOOL SPORTS.**

**INTERSTELLAR MATTER.** *See also* **DARK MATTER (ASTRONOMY).**
Stephen Hawking's universe [videorecording]. [Alexandria, Va.] : PBS Video; Burbank, CA : Distributed by Warner Home Video, c1997.
*TC QB982 .S7 1997*

**INTERSUBJECTIVITY.**
Shaddock, David. Contexts and connections. New York : Basic Books, 2000.
*TC RC488.5 .S483 2000*

**Intertexts.**
Hanks, William F. Lanham : Rowman & Littlefield Publishers, Inc., c2000.
*TC P35.5.M6 H36 2000*

**Interuniversitair Centrum voor Onderwijskundig Onderzoek.**
Design approaches and tools in education and

training. Dordrecht ; Boston : Kluwer Academic Publishers, c1999.
*TC LB1028.38 .D46 1999*

Enhancing educational excellence, equity, and efficiency. Dordrecht ; Boston : Kluwer Academic Publishers, c1999.
*TC LB2921 .E54 1999*

**INTERVENTION (CIVIL PROCEDURE).**
Rosen, Sidney M. Toward a gang solution. [Norman, Okla.?] NRC Youth Services, 1996.
*TC HV6439.U7 R67 1996*

**Intervention planning for adults with communication problems : Volume 2.**
Klein, Harriet B. Boston : Allyn and Bacon, c1999.
*TC RC423 .K57 1999*

**Interview.**
Dreifus, Claudia. New York : Seven Stories ; London : Turnaround, 1999.
*TC PN4874.D74158 1999*

**INTERVIEW, PSYCHOLOGICAL.**
Clinician's guide to neuropsychological assessment. 2nd ed. Mahwah, N.J. : Lawrence Erlbaum Associates, c2000.
*TC RC386.6.N48 G85 2000*

**INTERVIEW, PSYCHOLOGICAL - METHODS.**
Sommers-Flanagan, Rita, 1953- Clinical interviewing. 2nd ed. New York : Wiley, c1999.
*TC RC480.7 .S66 1999*

**INTERVIEW, PSYCHOLOGICAL - METHODS - ADOLESCENCE - HANDBOOKS.**
Cepeda, Claudio, 1942- Concise guide to the psychiatric interview of children and adolescents. Washington, DC : American Psychiatric Press, c2000.
*TC RJ503.6 .C46 2000*

**INTERVIEW, PSYCHOLOGICAL - METHODS - CHILD - HANDBOOKS.**
Cepeda, Claudio, 1942- Concise guide to the psychiatric interview of children and adolescents. Washington, DC : American Psychiatric Press, c2000.
*TC RJ503.6 .C46 2000*

**INTERVIEW, PSYCHOLOGICAL - METHODS - CHILD, PRESCHOOL - HANDBOOKS.**
Cepeda, Claudio, 1942- Concise guide to the psychiatric interview of children and adolescents. Washington, DC : American Psychiatric Press, c2000.
*TC RJ503.6 .C46 2000*

**INTERVIEWING.** *See also* **COUNSELING; INTERVIEWS; SOCIAL CASE WORK.**
O'Neil, Judith Ann. The role of the learning advisor in action learning. 1999.
*TC 06 no. 11156*

**INTERVIEWING IN ADOLESCENT PSYCHIATRY - HANDBOOKS, MANUALS, ETC.**
Cepeda, Claudio, 1942- Concise guide to the psychiatric interview of children and adolescents. Washington, DC : American Psychiatric Press, c2000.
*TC RJ503.6 .C46 2000*

**INTERVIEWING IN CHILD PSYCHIATRY - HANDBOOKS, MANUALS, ETC.**
Cepeda, Claudio, 1942- Concise guide to the psychiatric interview of children and adolescents. Washington, DC : American Psychiatric Press, c2000.
*TC RJ503.6 .C46 2000*

**INTERVIEWING IN MENTAL HEALTH.**
Sommers-Flanagan, Rita, 1953- Clinical interviewing. 2nd ed. New York : Wiley, c1999.
*TC RC480.7 .S66 1999*

**INTERVIEWING IN PSYCHIATRY.**
Sommers-Flanagan, Rita, 1953- Clinical interviewing. 2nd ed. New York : Wiley, c1999.
*TC RC480.7 .S66 1999*

**INTERVIEWING IN RADIO.** *See* **TALK SHOWS.**

**INTERVIEWING IN SOCIAL WORK.**
Darling, Rosalyn Benjamin. The partnership model in human services. New York : Kluwer Academic/ Plenum Publishers, c2000.
*TC HV43 .D2 2000*

**INTERVIEWING IN TELEVISION.** *See* **TALK SHOWS.**

**INTERVIEWING - STUDY AND TEACHING (PRIMARY) - UNITED STATES.**
Rogovin, Paula. Classroom interviews. Portsmouth, NH : Heinemann, c1998.
*TC LB1537 .R58 1998*

**INTERVIEWS.** *See* **INTERVIEWING.**

**INTERVIEWS - UNITED STATES.**
Rosenzweig, Roy. The presence of the past. New York : Columbia University Press, c1998.
*TC E179.5 .R67 1998*

**INTESTACY.** *See* **INHERITANCE AND SUCCESSION.**

**INTESTATE SUCCESSION.** *See* **INHERITANCE AND SUCCESSION.**

**Intimacy** / edited by Lauren Berlant. Chicago : University of Chicago Press, c2000. 455 p. : ill. (some col.) ; 23 cm. Includes bibliographical references and index. ISBN 0-226-38441-1 ISBN 0-226-38443-8 (pbk.) DDC 302
*1. Intimacy (Psychology) I. Berlant, Lauren Gail, 1957-*
*TC BF575.I5 I57 2000*

**INTIMACY (PSYCHOLOGY).** *See also* **LOVE.**
Bennett, Joel B. Time and intimacy. Mahwah, N.J. ; London : Lawrence Erlbaum Associates, 2000.
*TC BF575.I5 B45 2000*

Brown, Norman M., 1942- Love and intimate relationships. Philadelphia ; Hove [England] : Brunner/Mazel, c2000.
*TC BF575.L8 B75 2000*

Firestone, Robert. Fear of intimacy. 1st ed. Washington, DC : American Psychological Association, c1999.
*TC BF575.I5 F57 1999*

Honeycutt, James M. Cognition, communication, and romantic relationships. Mahwah, N.J. ; London : L. Erlbaum Associates, 2001.
*TC BF575.I5 H66 2001*

Intimacy. Chicago : University of Chicago Press, c2000.
*TC BF575.I5 I57 2000*

Wilson, John, 1928- Learning to love. Houndmills [England] : Macmillan Press ; New York : St. Martin's Press, 2000.
*TC BF575.L8 .W555 2000*

**INTIMACY (PSYCHOLOGY) - HEALTH ASPECTS.**
The psychology of couples and illness. 1st ed. Washington, D.C. : American Psychological Association, c2000.
*TC R726.5 .P785 2000*

**An intimate history of killing.**
Bourke, Joanna. [New York, NY] : Basic Books, c1999.
*TC U22.3 .B68 1999*

**Into the enchanted forest** : language, drama and science in primary schools. Stoke on Trent, Staffordshire : Trentham Books, 1999. xx, 123 p. ; 25 cm. Includes bibliographical references. ISBN 1-85856-132-9 ISBN 1-85856-131-0 (hb) DDC 372.6
*1. Language arts (Primary) - Great Britain. I. Brock, Avril.*
*TC LB1528 .I68 1999*

**INTOXICANTS.** *See* **ALCOHOL; ALCOHOLIC BEVERAGES.**

**INTOXICATION.** *See* **ALCOHOLISM; NARCOTIC HABIT.**

**INTRAFAMILY VIOLENCE.** *See* **FAMILY VIOLENCE.**

**Intramural law review (Winston-Salem, N.C.).**
Wake Forest law review. [Winston-Salem, N.C., Wake Forest Law Review Association, etc.]
*TC K27 .A36*

**INTRAPRENEUR.** *See* **ENTREPRENEURSHIP.**

**INTRAPSYCHIC CONFLICT.** *See* **CONFLICT (PSYCHOLOGY).**

**Introducing Canada** : content backgrounders, strategies, and resources for educators / edited by William W. Joyce and Richard Beach. Washington, D.C. : National Council for the Social Studies in association with National Consortium for Teaching Canada, c1997. 192 p. : ill. ; 24 cm. (NCSS bulletin ; 94) Includes bibliographical references. CONTENTS: Foreword / by Michael S. Bittner -- Introduction / by Jeanne Kissner and Marion Salinger -- An introduction to the history of Canada / by Victor Howard -- Geography of Canada / by Michael J. Broadway -- Canadian government and politics / by George Sherman -- Canada and the world / by Donald K. Alper and Matthew Sparke -- The Canadian economy / by Anthony Cicerone and Mark J. Kasoff -- Canadian culture in the late 1990s / by William Metcalfe -- Quebec, past and present / by Richard Beach -- Canada within the social studies / by William W. Joyce -- Instructional activities / by Janet Alleman -- Resources for learning and teaching about Canada / by Gail F.

Curry Yvon -- Technology in the classroom / by Matthew Smith and John Preston. ISBN 0-87986-075-8 DDC 971
*1. Canada - Study and teaching. I. Joyce, William W. II. Beach, Richard (J. Richard) III. Series: Bulletin (National Council for the Social Studies) ; 94.*
*TC F1025 .I59 1997*

**Introducing learner autonomy in teacher education** / compiled and edited by A. Camilleri. Strasbourg : Council of Europe Pub., c1999. 75 p. ; 24 cm. "European Centre for Modern Languages." Includes bibliographical references (p. 73-75) ISBN 92-871-4006-5
*1. Languages, Modern - Study and teaching - Europe. I. Camilleri, George. II. European Centre for Modern Languages. III. Council of Europe.*
*TC PB38.E8 I567 1999*

**Introduction to counseling.**
Nystul, Michael S. Boston : Allyn and Bacon, c1999.
*TC BF637.C6 N97 1999*

**An introduction to counselling.**
McLeod, John, 1951- 2nd ed. Buckingham [England] ; Philadelphia, PA : Open University Press, 1998.
*TC BF637.C6 M379 1998*

**Introduction to education**
Promoting equality in secondary schools. London ; New York : Cassell, 1999.
*TC LC212.3.G7 P77 1999*

**An introduction to labor law.**
Gold, Michael Evan. 2nd ed. Ithaca : ILR Press, c1998.
*TC KF3319 .G62 1998*

**Introduction to language pathology.**
Crystal, David, 1941- 4th ed. London : Whurr Publishers, c1998.
*TC RC423 .C76 1998*

**Introduction to nutrition.**
The nutty, nougat-filled world of human nutrition [videorecording]. [Arlington, Va.] : Cerebellum Corp., c1998.
*TC QP141 .N8 1998*

**Introduction to Object ID.**
Thornes, Robin. [Los Angeles] : Getty Information Institute, c1999.
*TC N3998 .T457 1999*

**An Introduction to oracy** : frameworks for talk / edited by Jackie Holderness and Barbara Lalljee. London : Cassell, 1998. xi, 242 p. : ill. ; 26 cm. (Cassell education) Includes bibliographical references (p. [234]-235) and index. ISBN 0-304-33949-0 (hbk.) ISBN 0-304-33950-4 (pbk.) DDC 372.62/2044/0941
*1. Oral communication - Study and teaching (Elementary) - Great Britain. 2. English language - Study and teaching (Elementary) - Great Britain. I. Holderness, Jackie. II. Lalljee, Barbara. III. Series.*
*TC P95.4.G7 I58 1998*

**Introduction to problem solving.**
O'Connell, Susan. Portsmouth, NH : Heinemann, c2000.
*TC QA63 .O36 2000*

**Introduction to school marketing.**
Stimolo, Bob. [Haddam], Conn. : School Market Research Institute, c1989.
*TC HF5415.122 .S75 1989*

**Introduction to special education.**
Smith, Deborah Deutsch. 4th ed. Boston : Allyn and Bacon, c2001.
*TC LC3981 .S56 2001*

**Introduction to strategic human resource development.**
Gilley, Jerry W. Organizational learning, performance, and change. Cambridge, Mass. : Perseus, c2000.
*TC HF5549.5.M3 G555 2000*

**An introduction to teaching composition in an electronic environment.**
Hoffman, Eric. Needham Heights, Mass. : Allyn & Bacon, c2000.
*TC LB1028.3 .H63 2000*

**An introduction to the study of education** / edited by David Matheson and Ian Grosvenor. London : David Fulton, 1999. vii, 184 p. : ill. ; 25 cm. Includes bibliographical references and index. ISBN 1-85346-612-3
*1. Education - Great Britain - Philosophy. 2. Education - Study and teaching (Higher) - Great Britain. I. Grosvenor, Ian. II. Matheson, David.*
*TC LA632 .I58 1999*

**Introduction to work and organizational psychology** : a European perspective / edited by Nik Chmiel. Malden, Mass. : Blackwell, 1999. viii, 518 p. : ill. ; 25 cm. Includes bibliographical references and index. ISBN 0-631-20675-2 (alk. paper) ISBN 0-631-20676-0 (pbk. : alk. paper) DDC 158/.7
*1. Psychology, Industrial - Europe. 2. Organizational behavior - Europe. I. Chmiel, Nik.*
*TC HF5548.8 .I576 1999*

**INTROSPECTION (THEORY OF KNOWLEDGE).** *See* **SELF-KNOWLEDGE, THEORY OF.**

**INTUITION.**
Dyer, Karen M. The intuitive principal. Thousand Oaks, Calif. : Corwin Press, c2000.
*TC LB2831.92 .D94 2000*

The intuitive practitioner. Buckingham [England] ; Philadelphia : Open University Press, 2000.
*TC LB1025.3 .I59 2000*

**INTUITION - MORAL AND ETHICAL ASPECTS.**
Wilson, James Q. Moral intuitions. New Brunswick, N.J. : Transaction Publishers, c2000.
*TC BJ1472 .W55 2000*

**INTUITION (PSYCHOLOGY).** *See* **PERCEPTION.**

**INTUITIONALISM.** *See* **INTUITION.**

**The intuitive practitioner** : on the value of not always knowing what one is doing / edited by Terry Atkinson and Guy Claxton. Buckingham [England] ; Philadelphia : Open University Press, 2000. ix, 278 p. : ill. ; 24 cm. Includes bibliographical references and index. ISBN 0-335-20363-9 (hbk.) ISBN 0-335-20362-0 (pbk.) DDC 371.102
*1. Teaching - Psychological aspects. 2. Intuition. I. Atkinson, Terry, 1948- II. Claxton, Guy.*
*TC LB1025.3 .I59 2000*

**The intuitive principal.**
Dyer, Karen M. Thousand Oaks, Calif. : Corwin Press, c2000.
*TC LB2831.92 .D94 2000*

**INUIT - ART.** *See* **INUIT ART.**

**Inuit art.**
Hessel, Ingo. New York : Harry N. Abrams, 1998.
*TC E99.E7 H493 1998*

**INUIT ART - CANADA.**
Hessel, Ingo. Inuit art. New York : Harry N. Abrams, 1998.
*TC E99.E7 H493 1998*

**Invaders from outer space.**
Brooks, Philip, 1955- 1st American ed. New York : DK, 1999.
*TC TL789.2 .B76 1999*

**INVALIDS.** *See* **HANDICAPPED.**

**INVALIDS - OCCUPATIONS.** *See* **OCCUPATIONAL THERAPY.**

**INVASION OF PRIVACY.** *See* **PRIVACY, RIGHT OF.**

**INVECTIVE.**
Behaving badly. 1st ed. Washington, D.C. : American Psychological Association, 2001.
*TC HM1106 .B45 2001*

**Inventing a discipline** : rhetoric scholarship in honor of Richard E. Young / edited by Maureen Daly Goggin. Urbana, Ill. : National Council of Teachers of English, c2000. xxviii, 457 p. : ill. ; 23 cm. Includes bibliographical references and index. ISBN 0-8141-2375-9 (pbk.) DDC 808
*1. Rhetoric. I. Goggin, Maureen Daly. II. Young, Richard E. (Richard Emerson), 1932-*
*TC PN175 .I58 2000*

**INVENTIONS.** *See also* **INVENTORS; TECHNOLOGICAL INNOVATIONS; TECHNOLOGY TRANSFER.**
Learning, language, and invention. Aldershot, Hampshire, Great Britain : Variorum ; Brookfield, Vt., USA : Ashgate Pub. Co. ; Paris, France : Société internationale de l'Astrolabe, 1994.
*TC AC5 .L38 1994*

**INVENTIONS - HISTORY - 20TH CENTURY.**
Singer, Edward. 20th century revolutions in technology. Commack, NY : Nova Science Pub., 1998.
*TC T173.8 .S568 1998*

**INVENTORS.** *See* **ENGINEERS.**

**INVENTORS - UNITED STATES - BIOGRAPHY - JUVENILE LITERATURE.**
Matthews, Tom, 1949- Always inventing. Washington, D.C. : National Geographic Society, c1999.

*TC TK6143.B4 M37 1999*

**Investigating creativity in youth :** research and methods / edited by Anne S. Fishkin, Bonnie Cramond, Paula Olszewski-Kubilius. Cresskill, N.J. : Hampton Press, c1999. xi, 449 p. : ill. ; 24 cm. (Perspectives on creativity) Includes bibliographical references and indexes. ISBN 1-57273-126-5 (hbk.) ISBN 1-57273-127-3 (pbk.) DDC 155.4/1335
*1. Creative ability in children. 2. Creative thinking in children. I. Fishkin, Anne S. II. Cramond, Bonnie. III. Olszewski-Kubilius, Paula. IV. Series.*
*TC BF723.C7 I58 1999*

**An investigation of the relative effectiveness of the composite approach and the phenomenological method for enhancing self-esteem in adults with mental retardation.**
Yamusah, Salifu. 1998.
*TC 085 Y146*

**INVESTIGATIONS. See CRIMINAL INVESTIGATION.**

**Investing in diversity :** advancing opportunities for minorities and the media / Amy Korzick Garmer, editor. Washington, D.C. : Aspen Institute, Communications and Society Program, c1998. xi, 248 p. ; 23 cm. "A report of The Aspen Institute Forum on Diversity and the Media." Includes bibliographical references. ISBN 0-89843-240-5
*1. Mass media and minorities - United States. 2. Minorities in mass media - United States. I. Garmer, Amy Korzick. II. Communications and Society Program (Aspen Institute)*
*TC P94.5.M552 U647 1997*

**Investing in education :** Analysis of the 1999 world education indicators. Paris : Organisation for Economic Co-operation and Development; Paris : UNESCO, 2000. 189 p. ; 24 cm. (Education and skills) ISBN 92-64-17183-5 DDC 330
*1. Education - Economic aspects. 2. Educational indicators. I. Series.*
*TC LB2846 .I68 2000*

**INVESTORS. See CAPITALISTS AND FINANCIERS.**

**The invisible man and other cases.**
Simon, Seymour. Rev. ed. New York : Morrow Junior Books, c1998.
*TC PZ7.S60573 In 1998*

**Invisible privilege.**
Rothenberg, Paula S., 1943- Lawrence : University Press of Kansas, c2000.
*TC E185.615 .R68 2000*

**Invitations to literacy**
Cooper, J. David (James David), 1942- Discover : Grade 1, level 1.5, [Themes 9 and 10]. Boston : Houghton Mifflin, 1997.
*TC LB1575.8 .C6616 1997*

**INVOLUNTARY STERILIZATION. See STERILIZATION, EUGENIC.**

**INVOLUNTARY TREATMENT. See INFORMED CONSENT (MEDICAL LAW); STERILIZATION, EUGENIC.**

**Involving commuter students in learning** / Barbara Jacoby, editor. San Francisco, Calif. : Jossey-Bass, 2000. 93 p. : ill. ; 23 cm. (New directions for higher education, 0271-0560 ; no. 109, Spring 2000) (Jossey-Bass higher and adult education series) Includes bibliographical references and index. CONTENTS: Why involve commuter students in learning? / Barbara Jacoby -- Curricular learning communities / Jodi H. Levine, Nancy S. Shapiro -- Creating community within individual courses / Arthur W. Chickering -- The collegium: community as gathering place / Carla Erickson Orlando -- Developing community through experiential education / Sharon Rubin -- Teamwork and research at the frontiers of learning / Robert Yuan, Spencer Benson -- Using information technology to create communities of learners / Kevin Kruger --Welcoming commuter students into living-learning programs / Richard A. CONTENTS: Stevens Jr. -- Involving commuter students in learning: moving from rhetoric to reality / Barbara Jacoby. ISBN 0-7879-5340-7
*1. Commuting college students. 2. Student learning. I. Jacoby, Barbara. II. Series. III. Series: New directions for higher education ; no. 109.*
*TC LB2343.6 .I68 2000*

**IOC Medical Commission.**
Nutrition in sport. Osney Mead, Oxford ; Malden, MA : Blackwell Science, 2000.
*TC QP141 .N793 2000*

**Iowa City Community School District (Iowa City, Iowa).**
Developing an information literacy program K-12. New York : Neal-Schuman, c1998.

*TC Z711.2 .D49 1998*

**Iowa Distance Education Alliance.**
Hanson, Dan. Distance education :. 2nd ed. Washington, DC : Association for Educational Communications and Technology ; Ames, Iowa : Research Institute for Studies in Education, c1997.
*TC LC5800 .S3 1997*

**Ipaye, J. B. (J. Babatunde).**
Research on schooling in Nigeria. Ondo [Nigeria] : Centre for Research on Schooling, Adeyemi College of Education, 1995.
*TC LB1028.25.N6 R477 1995*

**IPCA.**
Internet & personal computing abstracts. Medford, N.J. : Information Today, Inc., c2000-
*TC QA75.5 .M5*

**IQ. See INTELLIGENCE LEVELS.**

**IQ TESTS. See INTELLIGENCE TESTS.**

**Ira Spanierman Gallery.** Arthur Wesley Dow (1857-1922) : his art and his influence : November 9, 1999-January 15, 2000 / essays by Nancy E. Green ... [et al.]. New York : Spanierman Gallery, 1999. 272 p. : ill. (some col.), ports. ; 33 cm. Cover title: Arthur Wesley Dow : his art and his influence. Price list (6 p.), press release (2 p.) and errata slip inserted. Includes bibliographical references and index. ISBN 0-945936-24-9
*1. Dow, Arthur W. - (Arthur Wesley), - 1857-1922 - Influence - Exhibitions. I. Green, Nancy E. II. Title. III. Title: Arthur Wesley Dow : his art and his influence*
*TC N44.D7442 I73 1999*

**IRAN - KINGS AND RULERS - BIOGRAPHY.**
Amanat, Abbas. Pivot of the universe. Berkeley : University of California Press, c1997.
*TC DS307.N38 A63 1997*

**Ireland, Chris.**
Parr, Susie, 1953- Talking about aphasia. Buckingham ; Philadelphia : Open University Press, 1997.
*TC RC425 .P376 1997*

**IRELAND - HISTORY.**
A new history of Ireland. Oxford [England] : Clarendon Press ; New York : Oxford University Press, <1976-1986 >
*TC DA912 .N48*

**IRELAND - HISTORY - 18TH CENTURY - FICTION.**
Schmidt, Gary D. Anson's way. New York : Clarion Books, c1999.
*TC PZ7.S3527 An 1999*

**IRELAND - HISTORY - 18TH CENTURY - JUVENILE FICTION.**
Schmidt, Gary D. Anson's way. New York : Clarion Books, c1999.
*TC PZ7.S3527 An 1999*

**IRISH AMERICANS.**
The Irish in America [videorecording]. [New York, N.Y.] : A&E Home Video ; New York, N.Y. : Distributed by the New Video Group, 1997.
*TC E184.16 I6 1997*

**IRISH AMERICANS - HISTORY.**
The Irish in America [videorecording]. [New York, N.Y.] : A&E Home Video ; New York, N.Y. : Distributed by the New Video Group, 1997.
*TC E184.16 I6 1997*

**IRISH AMERICANS - UNITED STATES. See IRISH AMERICANS.**

**IRISH FREE STATE. See IRELAND.**

**Irish in America [videorecording] : from the Emerald Isle to the promise land.**
The Irish in America [videorecording]. [New York, N.Y.] : A&E Home Video ; New York, N.Y. : Distributed by the New Video Group, 1997.
*TC E184.16 I6 1997*

**The Irish in America** [videorecording] / produced by Greystone Communications, Inc. for A&E Network ; produced by Rhys Thomas. [New York, N.Y.] : A&E Home Video ; New York, N.Y. : Distributed by the New Video Group, 1997. 2 videocassettes (100 min.) : sd., col. with b&w sequences ; 1/2 in. Title on cassette case: Irish in America [videorecording] : from the Emerald Isle to the promise land. VHS. Catalogued from credits and cassette case. Editor, Kevin Browne ; director of photography, John Sorapure. Narrator: Aidan Quinn. For general audiences. SUMMARY: This program follows the nation's first immigrant group on their journey to the American dream. From war hero and President Andrew Jackson to union organizer Mother Jones, you'll meet the colorful Irish-Americans who fought and worked their way past oppression

and into history. ISBN 0-7670-0078-1 (box) ISBN 0-7670-0079-X (v. 1) ISBN 0-7670-0080-3 (v. 2)
*1. Irish Americans. 2. Irish Americans - History. 3. Immigrants. I. Thomas. Rhys. II. Quinn, Aidan. III. Greystone Communications. IV. Arts and Entertainment Network. V. A&E Home Video (Firm) VI. New Video Group. VII. Title: Irish in America [videorecording] : from the Emerald Isle to the promise land VIII. Title: From the Emerald Isle to the promise land [videorecording]*
*TC E184.16 I6 1997*

**IRISH POTATOES. See POTATOES.**

**Irish studies in management**
From maestro to manager. Dublin : Oak Tree Press in association with the Graduate School of Business, University College Dublin, c1997.
*TC NX770.E85 F76 1997*

**Irish studies (New York, N.Y.)**
(vol. 5.) O'Donoghue, T. A. (Tom A.), 1953- The Catholic Church and the secondary school curriculum in Ireland, 1922-1962. New York : P. Lang, c1999.
*TC LC506.G72 I745 1999*

**IRISH TRAVELERS (NOMADIC PEOPLE). See IRISH TRAVELLERS (NOMADIC PEOPLE).**

**IRISH TRAVELLERS (NOMADIC PEOPLE) - EDUCATION (SECONDARY) - IRELAND.**
Kenny, Máirín. The routes of resistance. Aldershot, Hants, England ; Brookfield, Vt. : Ashgate, c1997.
*TC LC3650.I74 K45 1997*

**IRISH TRAVELLING PEOPLE (NOMADIC PEOPLE). See IRISH TRAVELLERS (NOMADIC PEOPLE).**

**IRISH - UNITED STATES. See IRISH AMERICANS.**

**IRM. See INFORMATION RESOURCES MANAGEMENT.**

**Iron horses.**
Kay, Verla. New York : Putnam, c1999.
*TC PZ8.3.K225 Ir 1999*

**Iron John.**
Mayer, Marianna. New York : Morrow Junior Books, 1998.
*TC PZ8.M4514 Ir 1998*

**IRRELIGION. See ATHEISM; SECULARISM.**

**Irvine, Jacqueline Jordan.**
Critical knowledge for diverse teachers & learners. Washington, DC : AACTE : ERIC, c1997.
*TC LB1715 .C732 1997*

**Irving, Katrina.** Immigrant mothers : narratives of race and maternity, 1890-1925 / Katrina Irving. Urbana : University of Illinois Press, c2000. x, 148 p. : ill. ; 24 cm. Includes bibliographical references (p. [113]-142) and index. CONTENTS: Introduction : amazing racial hybrids and ethnic horrors : race and the immigrant woman, 1890-1925 -- Rediscovered problem : engendering the new immigrant -- Flouting the racial border : nativism, eugenics, and the sexualized immigrant woman -- President Roosevelt and Ellis Island : racial economics and biological parsimony -- Sentimental ambitions : Americanization and the "isolated and alien" mother -- Eternal mothers : cultural pluralism, primitivism, and the triumph of difference. ISBN 0-252-02534-2 (cloth : alk. paper) DDC 305.48/9691
*1. Women immigrants - United States - Public opinion - History. 2. Mothers - United States - Public opinion - History. 3. Xenophobia - United States - History. 4. Immigrants in literature - History. 5. United States - Emigration and immigration - Public opinion - History. 6. United States - Ethnic relations - History. I. Title.*
*TC HQ1419 .I75 2000*

**Irwin, Cait.** Conquering the beast within : how I fought depression adn won--and how you can, too / written and illustrated by Cait Irwin. New York : Times Books, 1999. 105 p. : coll. ill. ; 23 cm. ISBN 0-8129-3247-1 DDC 616.85/27
*1. Depression. Mental - Popular works. I. Title.*
*TC RC537 .I77 1999*

**Is America breaking apart?.**
Hall, John A., 1949- Princeton, NJ : Princeton University Press, c1999.
*TC HN59.2 .H34 1999*

**Isaacs, Marla Beth.**
[Difficult divorce]
Therapy of the difficult divorce : managing crises, reorienting warring couples, working with the children, and expediting court processes / Marla Beth Isaacs, Braulio Montalvo, David Abelsohn. Northvale, N.J. ; London : J. Aronson, c2000. xvi, 302 p. : ill. ; 24 cm. Originally published: The difficult

divorce. New York : Basic Books, 1986. With new pref. Includes bibliographical references (p. [289]-[290]) and index. ISBN 0-7657-0212-6 DDC 616.89/156
1. *Divorce therapy. 2. Family psychotherapy. I. Isaacs, Marla Beth. The difficult divorce. II. Montalvo, Braulio. III. Abelsohn, David. IV. Title.*
*TC RC488.6 .I83 2000*

**The difficult divorce.**
Isaacs, Marla Beth. [Difficult divorce] Therapy of the difficult divorce. Northvale, N.J. ; London : J. Aronson, c2000.
*TC RC488.6 .I83 2000*

**ISCHEMIC HEART DISEASE.** *See* **CORONARY HEART DISEASE.**

**ISCPES book series**
Sport and physical education in China. London ; New York : Routledge, 1999.
*TC GV651 .S655 1999*

**Isenhart, Myra Warren.** Collaborative approaches to resolving conflict / by Myra Warren Isenhart, Michael Spangle. Thousand Oaks, Calif. : Sage Publications, c2000. xiv, 242 p. : ill. ; 26 cm. Includes bibliographical references and index. ISBN 0-7619-1929-5 ISBN 0-7619-1930-9 (pbk. : acid-free paper) DDC 303.6/9
1. *Conflict management. 2. Dispute resolution (Law) I. Spangle, Michael. II. Title.*
*TC HM1126 .I74 2000*

**Isis.**
History of women in the sciences. Chicago, Ill. : University of Chicago Press, c1999.
*TC Q130 .H58 1999*

**ISLAM AND POLITICS - ASIA, CENTRAL.**
Khalid, Adeeb, 1964- The politics of Muslim cultural reform. Berkeley : University of California Press, c1998.
*TC BP63.A34 K54 1998*

**ISLAM AND POLITICS - INDIA.**
Hasan, Mushirul. Legacy of a Divided Nation. Boulder, Colo. : WestviewPress, c1997.
*TC DS479 .L36 1997*

**ISLAM AND POLITICS - PAKISTAN.**
Malik, Jamal. Colonization of Islam. New Delhi : Manohar, 1996.
*TC BP173.25 .M34 1996*

**ISLAM AND STATE - ASIA, CENTRAL.**
Khalid, Adeeb, 1964- The politics of Muslim cultural reform. Berkeley : University of California Press, c1998.
*TC BP63.A34 K54 1998*

**ISLAM - ASIA, CENTRAL.**
Khalid, Adeeb, 1964- The politics of Muslim cultural reform. Berkeley : University of California Press, c1998.
*TC BP63.A34 K54 1998*

**ISLAM - PAKISTAN.**
Malik, Jamal. Colonization of Islam. New Delhi : Manohar, 1996.
*TC BP173.25 .M34 1996*

**ISLAM - POLITICAL ASPECTS.** *See* **ISLAM AND POLITICS.**

**ISLAM - SOCIAL ASPECTS - ASIA, CENTRAL.**
Khalid, Adeeb, 1964- The politics of Muslim cultural reform. Berkeley : University of California Press, c1998.
*TC BP63.A34 K54 1998*

**ISLAM - SOCIAL ASPECTS - PAKISTAN.**
Malik, Jamal. Colonization of Islam. New Delhi : Manohar, 1996.
*TC BP173.25 .M34 1996*

**ISLAMIC LAW - PAKISTAN.**
Malik, Jamal. Colonization of Islam. New Delhi : Manohar, 1996.
*TC BP173.25 .M34 1996*

**ISLAMIC TEXTILE FABRICS.** *See* **TEXTILE FABRICS, ISLAMIC.**

**ISLAMIC WOMEN.** *See* **MUSLIM WOMEN.**

**ISLAMISM.** *See* **ISLAM.**

**Island of the blue dolphins by Scott O'Dell.**
Beech, Linda Ward. New York : Scholastic, c1997.
*TC LB1573 .B438 1997*

**ISLANDS - CARIBBEAN AREA.** *See* **WEST INDIES.**

**ISLANDS - FICTION.**
Hansen, Joyce. The heart calls home. New York : Walker & Company, 1999.

*TC PZ7.H19825 He 1999*

**ISLANDS OF THE ATLANTIC.** *See* **WEST INDIES.**

**ISLANDS OF THE CARIBBEAN.** *See* **WEST INDIES.**

**ISLANDS OF THE PACIFIC.** *See* **OCEANIA.**

**ISLANDS - SOUTH PACIFIC OCEAN.** *See* **OCEANIA.**

**ISLES.** *See* **ISLANDS.**

**ISLETS.** *See* **ISLANDS.**

**ISOKINETIC EXERCISE.**
Isokinetics in human performance. Champaign, Ill. : Human Kinetics, 2000.
*TC QP303 .I82 2000*

**Isokinetics in human performance** / Lee E. Brown, editor. Champaign, Ill. : Human Kinetics, 2000. xvi, 456 p. : ill. ; 24 cm. Includes bibliographical references and index. ISBN 0-7360-0005-4 DDC 613.7/149
1. *Isokinetic exercise. I. Brown, Lee E., 1956-*
*TC QP303 .I82 2000*

**ISOLATION, FEAR OF.** *See* **AGORAPHOBIA.**

**ISOLATION, SOCIAL.** *See* **SOCIAL ISOLATION.**

**ISOPTERA.** *See* **TERMITES.**

**ISRAELI PAINTING.** *See also* **PAINTING, ISRAELI.**
Fuhrer, Ronald. Woodstock, N.Y. : Overlook Press in association with Ronald Lauder, 1998.
*TC ND977 .F85 1998*

**ISRAELITES.** *See* **JEWS.**

**Issue for March 2000, vol. 21, no. 1 has title Internet & personal computers abstracts on title page.**
Internet & personal computing abstracts. Medford, N.J. : Information Today, Inc., c2000-
*TC QA75.5 .M5*

**Issues and application in adult second language learning and teaching.**
Eddy, Jennifer B.K. Multiple intelligences, styles, and proficiency. 1999.
*TC 085 E10*

**Issues and innovations in service to users with disabilities.**
DeCandido, GraceAnne A. Transforming libraries. Washington, D.C. : Association of Research Libraries, Office of Leadership and Management Services, c1999.
*TC Z711.92.H3 D43 1999*

**Issues and trends in literacy education** / edited by Richard D. Robinson, Michael C. McKenna, Judy M. Wedman. 2nd ed. Boston : Allyn and Bacon, c2000. x, 342 p. : ill. ; 24 cm. Includes bibliographical references and index. ISBN 0-205-29651-3 DDC 372.6/044
1. *Language arts. 2. Reading. 3. English language - Composition and exercises. 4. Literacy. I. Robinson, Richard David, 1940- II. McKenna, Michael C. III. Wedman, Judy M., 1943-*
*TC LB1576 .I87 2000*

**Issues in academic ethics**
Golding, Martin P. (Martin Philip), 1930- Free speech on campus. Lanham, Md. ; Oxford : Rowman & Littlefield Publishers, c2000.
*TC LC72.2 .G64 2000*

**Issues in art and education**
(v. 3.) The dynamics of now. London : Wimbledon School of Art in association with Tate, c2000.
*TC N185 .D96 2000*

**Issues in biomedical ethics**
HIV and AIDS. Oxford ; New York ; Oxford University Press, 1999.
*TC RA644.A25 H57855 1999*

**Issues in business ethics**
(v. 11) Education, leadership, and business ethics. Boston, MA : Kluwer Academic Publishers, c1998.
*TC HF5387 .E346 1998*

**Issues in career and human resource development.**
American Society for Training and Development. Madison, Wisc. : American Society for Training and Development, c1980.
*TC HF5549.5.T7 A59 1980*

**Issues in child mental health.**
Family and child mental health journal. New York, NY : Human Sciences Press, [c1976-c1982]

**Issues in child mental health.** [New York, Human Sciences Press] 1 v. ill. 23 cm. v. 5; fall 1977-spring/

summer 1978. "Journal of the Jewish Board of Guardians". Includes bibliographical references. Indexed by: Community mental health review 0363-1605. Indexed by: Current literature/social work in health care. Indexed by: Public health reviews. Indexed by: Chicorel abstracts to reading and learning disabilities 0149-533X. Indexed selectively by: Psychological abstracts 0033-2887 1977-1978. Continues: Psychosocial process ISSN: 0556-431X. Continued by: Family and child mental health journal ISSN: 0190-230X (DLC) 81645955 (OCoLC)4676318. ISSN 0362-403X DDC 618.92/8/9005
1. *Child psychiatry - Periodicals. 2. Child health services - periodicals. 3. Child Psychology - periodicals. 4. Mental Health Services - periodicals. I. Jewish Board of Guardians. II. Title: Psychosocial process III. Title: Family and child mental health journal*

**Issues in clinical child psychology**
Handbook of psychotherapies with children and families. New York ; London : Kluwer Academic/ Plenum Publishers, c1999.
*TC RJ504 .H3619 1999*

Handbook of research in pediatric and clinical child psychology. New York : Kluwer Academic/Plenum Publishers, c 2000.
*TC RJ499.3 .H367 2000*

**Issues in deaf education** / edited by Susan Gregory ... [et al.]. London : D. Fulton Publishers, 1998. xi, 292 p. : ill. ; 25 cm. Includes bibliographical references (p. [255]-283) and index. ISBN 1-85346-512-7 (pbk.) DDC 371.91/2/0041
1. *Deaf children - Education - Great Britain. I. Gregory, Susan, 1945-*
*TC HV2716 .I77 1998*

**Issues in education & technology.**
Issues in education and technology :. London : Commonwealth Secretariat, c2000.
*TC LB1028.3 .I77 2000*

**Issues in education and technology : :** policy guidelines and strategies / edited by Cream Wright. London : Commonwealth Secretariat, c2000. 167 p. : ill. ; 26 cm. Cover title: Issues in education & technology. Includes bibliographical references. ISBN 0-85092-622-X
1. *Educational technology - Great Britain. I. Wright, Cream A. H. II. Title: Issues in education & technology.*
*TC LB1028.3 .I77 2000*

**Issues in English teaching** / edited by Jon Davison and John Moss. London ; New York : Routledge, 2000. xiv, 289 p. ; 24 cm. (Issues in subject teaching) Includes bibliographical references (p. [260]-277) and index. ISBN 0-415-20664-2 (hardcover) ISBN 0-415-20665-0 (pbk.) DDC 428/.0071/041
1. *English language - Study and teaching (Elementary) - England. 2. English language - Study and teaching (Elementary) - Wales. 3. English language - Study and teaching (Secondary) - England. 4. English language - Study and teaching (Secondary) - Wales. I. Davison, Jon. II. Moss, John, 1957- III. Series.*
*TC LB1576 .I89 2000*

**Issues in higher education (Oxford, England)**
Guri-Rozenblit, Sarah. Distance and campus universities. 1st ed. Oxford, UK ; New York, NY : Pergamon, published for IAU Press, 1999.
*TC LC5800 .G87 1999*

Higher education research. 1st ed. Oxford ; [New York] : Pergamon, published for the IAU Press, 2000.
*TC LB2326.3 .H548 2000*

Local knowledge and wisdom in higher education. 1st ed. Oxford : Published for the IAU Press [by] Pergamon, 2000.
*TC GN380 .L63 2000*

The universities' responsibilities to society. 1st ed. New York : Pergamon, published for the IAU Press, 2000.
*TC LC191.9 .U55 2000*

**Issues in history teaching** / edited by James Arthur and Robert Phillips. London ; New York : Routledge, 2000. xviii, 241 p. ; 24 cm. Includes bibliographical references (p. [220]-234) and index. ISBN 0-415-20668-5 (hb. : alk. paper) ISBN 0-415-20669-3 (pbk. : alk. paper) DDC 907.1/2
1. *History - Study and teaching (Secondary) 2. History - Study and teaching (Elementary) I. Arthur, James, 1959- II. Phillips, Robert, 1959-*
*TC D16.2 .I88 2000*

**Issues in human development.**
Symposium on Issues in Human Development (1967 : Philadelphia) Washington, For sale by the Supt. of Docs., U. S. Govt. Print. Off. [1970?]
*TC RJ131.A1 S93 1967*

**Issues in law and society**
Governing childhood. Aldershot, England ;
Brookfield, Vt. : Dartmouth, c1997.
*TC HQ789 .G68 1997*

**Issues in psychiatry**
Psychiatry and religion. 1st ed. Washington, DC :
American Psychiatric Press, c2000.
*TC RC455.4.R4 P755 2000*

**Issues in science education.**
Rhoton, Jack Arlington, Va. National Science
Teachers Association:   National Science Education
Leadership Association, c1997.
*TC Q181 .R56 1996*

**Issues in subject teaching**
Issues in English teaching. London ; New York :
Routledge, 2000.
*TC LB1576 .I89 2000*

**Issues in teaching numeracy in primary schools /**
edited by Ian Thompson. Buckingham [England] ;
Philadelphia : Open University Press, 1999. xiii, 209
p. : ill. ; 23 cm. Includes bibliographical references and index.
ISBN 0-335-20325-6 (hbk.) ISBN 0-335-20324-8 (pbk.) DDC
372.7/2/0973
*1. Mathematics - Study and teaching (Primary) - United States.
I. Thompson, Ian (Frederick Ian)*
*TC QA135.5 .I77 1999*

**Issues in the practice of psychology**
Hillman, Jennifer L. Clinical perspectives on elderly
sexuality. New York : Kluwer Academic/Plenum
Publishers, c2000.
*TC HQ30 .H55 2000*

**Issues in Web-based pedagogy :** a critical primer /
edited by Robert A. Cole. Westport, Conn. :
Greenwood Press, 2000. xii, 414 p. ; 25 cm. (The
Greenwood educators' reference collection, 1056-2192)
Includes bibliographical references and index. ISBN
0-313-31226-5 (alk. paper) DDC 378.1/73/4
*1. Education, Higher - Computer network resources. 2.
Internet in education. 3. Education, Higher - Computer-
assisted instruction. I. Cole. Robert A.. 1958- II. Series.*
*TC LB1044.87 .I88 2000*

**ISSUES MANAGEMENT.** *See* **SOCIAL
RESPONSIBILITY OF BUSINESS.**

**Issues on examination malpractices in Nigeria : :** a
book of readings / edited by Akin Adegboye,
Omotayo Olutoye, and Joseph Oyekayode
Adetunberu. Ikere-Ekiti [Nigeria] : Ondo State
College of Education, c1998. 234 p. ; 21 cm. Papers of the
National Conference on Examination Malpractice in Nigerian
Institutions of Learning, organized by the Ondo State College
of Education, August 29-September 1, 1995. Includes
bibliographical references.
*1. Examinations - Nigeria - Congresses. 2. Educational tests
and measurements - Nigeria - Congresses. 3. Education -
Nigeria - Evaluation - Congresses. I. Adegboye. Akin. II.
Olutoye, Qmotayo. III. Adetunberu. Joseph Oyekayode. IV.
Ondo State College of Education. V. National Conference on
Examination Malpractice in Nigerian Institutions of Learning.
(1995 : Ondo State College of Education).*
*TC LB3058.N6 I848 1998*

**Issues (Topeka, Kan.).**
The Kansas teacher. Topeka, Kansas-NEA.

**It can be done! [videorecording].**
Hand in hand [videorecording]. New York, N.Y. :
AFB Press, c1995.
*TC HV1597.2 .H3 1995*

**It is about time!.**
Heide, Florence Parry. It's about time!. New York :
Clarion Books, c1999.
*TC PS3558.E427 I77 1999*

**It is the story that counts.**
Whitin, David Jackman, 1947- It's the story that
counts. Portsmouth, NH : Heinemann, c1995.
*TC QA135.5 .W465 1995*

**It takes a city.**
Hill, Paul Thomas, 1943- Washington, D.C. :
Brookings Institution Press, c2000.
*TC LC5131 .H48 2000*

**ITALIAN AMERICAN ARTS.**
The Italian American heritage. New York : Garland
Pub., 1999.
*TC E184.I8 I675 1999*

**The Italian American heritage :** a companion to
literature and arts / Pellegrino D'Acierno, editor. New
York : Garland Pub., 1999. liv, 790 p. : ill. (some col.) ; 24
cm. (Garland reference library of the humanities ; v. 1473)
Includes bibliographical references and index. ISBN
0-8153-0380-7 (alk. paper) DDC 305.851073
*1. Italian Americans - Intellectual life. 2. Italian Americans -*

*Social life and customs. 3. American literature - Italian
American authors - History and criticism. 4. Italian Americans
in literature. 5. Italian American arts. I. D'Acierno. Pellegrino,
1943- II. Series: Garland reference library of the humanities ;
vol. 1473.*
*TC E184.I8 I675 1999*

**ITALIAN AMERICAN LITERATURE (ENGLISH).**
*See* **AMERICAN LITERATURE - ITALIAN
AMERICAN AUTHORS.**

**ITALIAN AMERICANS IN LITERATURE.**
The Italian American heritage. New York : Garland
Pub., 1999.
*TC E184.I8 I675 1999*

**ITALIAN AMERICANS - INTELLECTUAL LIFE.**
The Italian American heritage. New York : Garland
Pub., 1999.
*TC E184.I8 I675 1999*

**ITALIAN AMERICANS - SOCIAL LIFE AND
CUSTOMS.**
The Italian American heritage. New York : Garland
Pub., 1999.
*TC E184.I8 I675 1999*

**ITALIAN AMERICANS - UNITED STATES.** *See*
**ITALIAN AMERICANS.**

**Italian grammar.**
Lamping, Alwena. NTC's Italian grammar.
Lincolnwood, Ill., U.S.A. : NTC Pub. Group, 1998.
*TC PC1112 .L34 1998*

**ITALIAN LANGUAGE - DICTIONARIES.** *See*
**PICTURE DICTIONARIES, ITALIAN.**

**ITALIAN LANGUAGE - DICTIONARIES -
ENGLISH.**
NTC's beginner's Italian and English dictionary.
Lincolnwood, Ill. : NTC Pub. Group, c1995.
*TC PC1640 .N83 1995*

**ITALIAN LANGUAGE - DICTIONARIES,
JUVENILE - ENGLISH.**
Italian picture dictionary. Princeton, NJ : Berlitz Kids,
c1997.
*TC PC1629 .I73 1997*

**ITALIAN LANGUAGE - GRAMMAR -
HANDBOOKS, MANUALS, ETC.**
Lamping, Alwena. NTC's Italian grammar.
Lincolnwood, Ill., U.S.A. : NTC Pub. Group, 1998.
*TC PC1112 .L34 1998*

**ITALIAN LANGUAGE - PRONUNCIATION.**
Adams, David, 1950- A handbook of diction for
singers. New York : Oxford University Press, 1999.
*TC MT883 .A23 1999*

**ITALIAN LANGUAGE - READERS.**
Cioffari, Angelina Grimaldi, 1913- Graded Italian
reader. 2nd ed. Lexington, Mass. : D.C. Heath, c1984.
*TC PC1113 .C48 1984*

Cioffari, Vincenzo, 1905- Graded Italian reader. 3rd
ed. Lexington, Mass. : D.C. Heath, c1991.
*TC PC1113 .C5 1991*

**Italian painting before 1400** [videorecording] / The
National Gallery ; written & narrated by James
Heard ; production, Neil Aberdeen, Joan Lane, Carol
McFadyen. [London] : The National Gallery, c1989. 1
videocassette (20 min.) : sd., col. ; 1/2 in. (Art in the making.)
Title on cassette label: Art in the making [videorecording] :
Itlian painting before 1400. At head of title: Anthony Roland
Collection of Films on Art. VHS. Catalogued from credits,
cassette label and container. Presenter: James Heard.
"Sponsored by Esso, UK." SUMMARY: Begins with a capsule
history of artists and painting in Trecento Tuscany, particularly
in Florence and Siena. A discussion of altarpieces leads to a
demonstration of how they were composed and constructed as
well as the methods and materials used in painting them. The
preparation of the wood surface for gesso, the application of
layers of gesso, the grinding of color pigments, the use of egg
tempera and the two types of background gilding, water gilding
and mordant gilding are discussed.
*1. Artists' materials. 2. Painting - Technique. 3. Panel
painting, Italian - Italy - Tuscany. 4. Panel painting.
Medieval - Italy - Tuscany. I. Heard. James. II. Aberdeen. Neil.
III. Lane. Joan. IV. McFadyen. Carol. V. National Gallery
(Great Britain) VI. Anthony Roland Collection of Film on Art.
VII. Title: Italian painting before fourteen hundred
[videorecording] VIII. Title: Art in the making
[videorecording] : Itlian painting before 1400 IX. Title:
Anthony Roland Collection of Films on Art X. Series.*
*TC ND1575 .I87 1989*

**Italian painting before 1400** [videorecording] / The
National Gallery ; written & narrated by James
Heard ; production, Neil Aberdeen, Joan Lane, Carol
McFadyen. [London] : The National Gallery, c1989. 1
videocassette (20 min.) : sd., col. ; 1/2 in. (Art in the making.)
Title on cassette label: Art in the making [videorecording] :

Itlian painting before 1400. At head of title: Anthony Roland
Collection of Films on Art. VHS. Catalogued from credits,
cassette label and container. Presenter: James Heard.
"Sponsored by Esso, UK." SUMMARY: Begins with a capsule
history of artists and painting in Trecento Tuscany, particularly
in Florence and Siena. A discussion of altarpieces leads to a
demonstration of how they were composed and constructed as
well as the methods and materials used in painting them. The
preparation of the wood surface for gesso, the application of
layers of gesso, the grinding of color pigments, the use of egg
tempera and the two types of background gilding, water gilding
and mordant gilding are discussed.
*1. Artists' materials. 2. Painting - Technique. 3. Panel
painting. Italian - Italy - Tuscany. 4. Panel painting.
Medieval - Italy - Tuscany. I. Heard. James. II. Aberdeen. Neil.
III. Lane. Joan. IV. McFayden. Carol. V. National Gallery
(Great Britain) VI. Anthony Roland Collection of Film on Art.
VII. Title: Italian painting before fourteen hundred
[videorecording] VIII. Title: Art in the making
[videorecording] : Itlian painting before 1400 IX. Title:
Anthony Roland Collection of Films on Art X. Series.*
*TC ND1575 .I87 1989*

**Italian painting before fourteen hundred
[videorecording].**
Italian painting before 1400 [videorecording].
[London] : The National Gallery, c1989.

Italian painting before 1400 [videorecording].
[London] : The National Gallery, c1989.
*TC ND1575 .I87 1989*

**ITALIAN PANEL PAINTING.** *See* **PANEL
PAINTING, ITALIAN.**

**ITALIAN PASTE PRODUCTS.** *See* **PASTA
PRODUCTS.**

**ITALIAN PICTURE DICTIONARIES.** *See*
**PICTURE DICTIONARIES, ITALIAN.**

**Italian picture dictionary /** [illustrations by Chris L.
Demarest]. Princeton, NJ : Berlitz Kids, c1997. 128 p. :
col. ill. ; 32 X 27 cm. In English and Italian. Includes index.
Up to age 9. SUMMARY: Learn useful basic foreign words such as
colors, shapes, numbers and animals. Each word has a picture,
a translation, and a simple sentence. A beginner's conversation
section is also included. ISBN 2-8315-6256-2
*1. Picture dictionaries, Italian - Juvenile literature. 2. Italian
language - Dictionaries. Juvenile - English. 3. English
language - Dictionaries. Juvenile - Italian. I. Demarest, Chris
L.*
*TC PC1629 .I73 1997*

**ITALIANS - UNITED STATES.** *See* **ITALIAN
AMERICANS.**

**ITALIC LANGUAGES AND DIALECTS.** *See*
**LATIN LANGUAGE.**

**ITALY - ANTIQUITIES.** *See* **HERCULANEUM
(EXTINCT CITY).**

**ITEM RESPONSE THEORY.**
Du, Zuru. Modeling conditional item dependencies
with a three-parameter logistic testlet model. 1998.
*TC 085 D84*

Embretson, Susan E. Item response theory for
psychologists. Mahwah, N.J. : Lawrence Erlbaum
Associates, Publishers. 2000.
*TC BF39 .E495 2000*

Foye, Stephanie Diane. Using item response theory
methods to explore the effect of item wording on
Likert data. 1997.
*TC 085 F82*

**Item response theory for psychologists.**
Embretson, Susan E. Mahwah, N.J. : Lawrence
Erlbaum Associates, Publishers, 2000.
*TC BF39 .E495 2000*

**iTitle from cip record: a university of Paris in the
early fourteenth century : a socialportrait.**
Courtenay, William J. Parisian scholars in the early
fourteenth century. Cambridge, U.K. ; New York,
NY : Cambridge University Press, 1999.
*TC LF2165 .C68 1999*

**Ito, Leslie A.**
Okihiro, Gary Y., 1945- Stories lives. Seattle :
University of Washington Press, 1999.
*TC D753.8 .O38 1999*

**IT'S A WONDERFUL LIFE (MOTION PICTURE).**
Loase, John Frederick, 1947- Sigfluence III. Lanham,
Md. : University Press of America, c1996.
*TC BF774 .L63 1996*

**It's about time!.**
Heide, Florence Parry. New York : Clarion Books,
c1999.
*TC PS3558.E427 I77 1999*

**It's the story that counts.**
Whitin, David Jackman, 1947- Portsmouth, NH :
Heinemann, c1995.
*TC QA135.5 .W465 1995*

**Itzkowitz, Norman.**
Child labor [picture]. Amawalk, NY : Jackdaw
Publications, c1997.
*TC HD6250.U5 C4 1997*

The depression hits home [picture]. Amawalk, NY :
Jackdaw Publications, c1997.
*TC TR820.5 .D4 1997*

Ellis Island [picture]. Amawalk, NY : Jackdaw
Publications, c1997.
*TC TR820.5 .E4 1997*

Roaring twenties [picture]. Amawalk, NY : Jackdaw
Publications, c1997.
*TC E784 .R6 1997*

**Ivanič, Roz.**
Situated literacies. London ; New York : Routledge,
2000.
*TC LC149 .S52 2000*

**Ivation Datasystems.**
Education at a glance [computer file]. Ottawa, Ont. :
Ivation Datasystems Inc. ; Paris, France : OECD,
*TC LB2846 .E2473*

**Ivers, Karen S.**
Barron, Ann E. The Internet and instruction. 2nd ed.
Englewood, Colo. : Libraries Unlimited, 1998.
*TC LB1044.87 .B37 1998*

**Iversen, Susan D., 1940-.**
Gender and society. Oxford ; New York : Oxford
University Press, 2000.
*TC HQ1075 .G4619 2000*

**Iverson, Annette M., 1950-.**
Froyen, Len A. Schoolwide and classroom
management. 3rd ed. Upper Saddle River, N.J. :
Merrill, c1999.
*TC LB3013 .F783 1999*

**Ivey, Allen E.** Counseling and psychotherapy : a
multicultural perspective / Allen E. Ivey, Mary
Bradford Ivey, Lynn Simek-Morgan ; with
contributions from Harold E. Cheatham ... [et al.]. 4th
ed. Boston : Allyn and Bacon, c1997. xv, 429 p. : ill. ; 25
cm. Includes bibliographical references and indexes. ISBN
0-205-19890-2 (hardcover) DDC 158/.3
*1. Cross-cultural counseling. 2. Psychotherapy - Cross-
cultural studies. I. Ivey, Mary Bradford. II. Simek-Morgan,
Lynn. III. Title.*
*TC BF637.C6 I93 1997*

**Ivey, Mary Bradford.**
Ivey, Allen E. Counseling and psychotherapy. 4th ed.
Boston : Allyn and Bacon, c1997.
*TC BF637.C6 I93 1997*

**Ivey, Susan L.**
Immigrant women's health. 1st ed. San Francisco :
Jossey-Bass, c1999.
*TC RA448.5.I44 I44 1999*

**Ivimey, John W. (John William), b. 1868.**
[Complete version of ye Three blind mice]
Three blind mice : the classic nursery rhyme /
illustrated by Lorinda Bryan Cauley. New York :
G.P. Putnam's Sons, c1991. [32] p. : col. ill. ; 25 cm.
Originally published: Complete version of ye Three blind
mice. SUMMARY: Three small mice in search of fun
become hungry, scared, blind, wise, and finally happy.
Includes music. ISBN 0-399-21775-4 (lib. bdg.) DDC 821/
.912
*1. Nursery rhymes. 2. Children's poetry. 3. Nursery rhymes. I.
Cauley, Lorinda Bryan, ill. II. Title.*
*TC PZ8.3.I83 Th 1991*

**J. Paul Getty Museum.**
1 to 10 and back again. Los Angeles : J. Paul Getty
Museum, c1999.
*TC QA113 .A14 1998*

Bruegel, Jan, 1568-1625. Where's the bear? Los
Angeles : J. Paul Getty Museum, c1997.
*TC QL49 .B749 1997*

A is for artist : a Getty Museum alphabet / [John
Harris, writer and editor]. Los Angeles : J. Paul Getty
Museum, c1997. 1 v. (unpaged) : col. ill. ; 21 cm.
SUMMARY: An alphabet books illustrated with details taken
from paintings in the J. Paul Getty Museum. ISBN 0-89236-
377-0 DDC 708.194/93
*1. English language - Alphabet - Juvenile literature. 2.
Painting - California - Malibu - Juvenile literature. 3. J. Paul
Getty Museum - Juvenile literature. 4. Alphabet. 5. J. Paul
Getty Museum. I. Harris, John.*

*TC N582.M25 A513 1997*

Kale, Shelly. My museum journal. Los Angeles, CA :
J. Paul Getty Museum, c2000.
*TC N7440 .K35 2000*

**J. PAUL GETTY MUSEUM.**
J. Paul Getty Museum. A is for artist. Los Angeles : J.
Paul Getty Museum, c1997.
*TC N582.M25 A513 1997*

**J. PAUL GETTY MUSEUM - JUVENILE
LITERATURE.**
J. Paul Getty Museum. A is for artist. Los Angeles : J.
Paul Getty Museum, c1997.
*TC N582.M25 A513 1997*

Kale, Shelly. My museum journal. Los Angeles, CA :
J. Paul Getty Museum, c2000.
*TC N7440 .K35 2000*

Kale, Shelly. My museum journal. Los Angeles, CA :
J. Paul Getty Museum, c2000.
*TC N7440 .K35 2000*

**Jablon, Judy R.**
Bickart, Toni S. Building the primary classroom.
Washington, DC : Teaching Strategies ; Portsmouth,
NH : Heinemann, 1999.
*TC LB1507 .B53 1999*

**Jacinto, Gary.**
Ballet class [videorecording]. W. Long Branch, NJ :
Kultur, c1984.
*TC GV1589 .B33 1984*

**Jack, Dana Crowley.** Behind the mask : destruction and
creativity in women's aggression / Dana Crowley
Jack. Cambridge, Mass. ; London : Harvard
University Press, 1999. 321 p. ; 24 cm. Includes
bibliographical references (p. 285-310) and index. ISBN
0-674-06485-2 (alk. paper) DDC 155.6/33
*1. Women - Psychology. 2. Aggressiveness (Psychology) I.
Title.*
*TC HQ1206 .J26 1999*

**Jackdaw photo collections**
(PC 100) Child labor [picture]. Amawalk, NY :
Jackdaw Publications, c1997.
*TC HD6250.U5 C4 1997*

(PC 101) The depression hits home [picture].
Amawalk, NY : Jackdaw Publications, c1997.
*TC TR820.5 .D4 1997*

(PC 102) Ellis Island [picture]. Amawalk, NY :
Jackdaw Publications, c1997.
*TC TR820.5 .E4 1997*

(PC 104) Civil war [picture]. Amawalk, NY :
Jackdaw Publications, c1999.
*TC TR820.5 .C56 1999*

(PC 104) Civil war [picture]. Amawalk, NY :
Jackdaw Publications, c1999.
*TC TR820.5 .C56 1999*

(PC 105) Holocaust children [picture]. Amawalk,
NY : Jackdaw Publications, c1999.
*TC TR820.5 .H6 1999*

(PC 106) [Japanese-American internment picture.
Amawalk, NY : Jackdaw Publications, c1999.
*TC TR820.5 .J3 1999*

(PC 107) Mills [picture]. Amawalk, NY : Jackdaw
Publications, c1999.
*TC TR820.5 .M5 1999*

(PC 109) World War II [picture]. Amawalk, NY :
Jackdaw Publications, c1999.
*TC TR820.5 .W6 1999*

(S-PC 103) Roaring twenties [picture]. Amawalk,
NY : Jackdaw Publications, c1997.
*TC E784 .R6 1997*

**Jackdaw Publications.**
Child labor [picture]. Amawalk, NY : Jackdaw
Publications, c1997.
*TC HD6250.U5 C4 1997*

Civil war [picture]. Amawalk, NY : Jackdaw
Publications, c1999.
*TC TR820.5 .C56 1999*

Civil war [picture]. Amawalk, NY : Jackdaw
Publications, c1999.
*TC TR820.5 .C56 1999*

The depression hits home [picture]. Amawalk, NY :
Jackdaw Publications, c1997.
*TC TR820.5 .D4 1997*

Ellis Island [picture]. Amawalk, NY : Jackdaw
Publications, c1997.

*TC TR820.5 .E4 1997*

Holocaust children [picture]. Amawalk, NY : Jackdaw
Publications, c1999.
*TC TR820.5 .H6 1999*

[Japanese-American internment picture. Amawalk,
NY : Jackdaw Publications, c1999.
*TC TR820.5 .J3 1999*

Mills [picture]. Amawalk, NY : Jackdaw Publications,
c1999.
*TC TR820.5 .M5 1999*

Roaring twenties [picture]. Amawalk, NY : Jackdaw
Publications, c1997.
*TC E784 .R6 1997*

World War II [picture]. Amawalk, NY : Jackdaw
Publications, c1999.
*TC TR820.5 .W6 1999*

**Jackman, Hilda L.** Sing me a story! Tell me a song! :
creative curriculum activities for teachers of young
children / Hilda L. Jackman. Thousand Oaks, Calif. :
Corwin Press, c1999. ix, 307 p. : ill. ; 28 cm. + 1 computer
laser optical disc (4 3/4 in.). Includes bibliographical
references. CONTENTS: My body -- My friends -- My
family -- My self -- My home -- My community -- Seeing --
Hearing -- Tasting -- Smelling -- Touching -- Fall -- Winter --
Spring -- Summer -- Colors in our world -- Shapes in our
world -- Oceans and lakes -- Forests -- Zoo -- Farm -- Pets --
Insects and spiders -- Fish -- Birds -- Circus -- Dinosaurs --
Cars, trucks, and buses -- Airplanes -- Trains and tracks. ISBN
0-8039-6797-7 (pbk. : acid-free paper) DDC 372.13
*1. Early childhood education - Activity programs - United
States - Handbooks, manuals, etc. 2. Curriculum planning -
United States - Handbooks, manuals, etc. 3. Project method in
teaching - United States - Handbooks, manuals, etc. I. Title.*
*TC LB1139.35.A37 J33 1999*

**Jackson, Alan, 1957-.**
Reforming college composition. Westport, Conn. :
Greenwood Press, 2000.
*TC PE1404 .R383 2000*

**Jackson, Barbara, 1952-.**
Epps, Susan. Empowered families, successful
children. 1st ed. Washington, DC : American
Psychological Association, c2000.
*TC BF637.C6 E66 2000*

**Jackson, Carlton.** Two centuries of progress / Carlton
L. Jackson, Vito Perrone. 3rd ed. Mission Hills, CA :
Glencoe/McGraw-Hill, 1991. xvi, 797 p. : ill. (some col.),
col. maps ; 25 cm. Includes bibliographical references (p. 759-
765) and index. ISBN 0-02-650001-9
*1. United States - History. I. Perrone, Vito. II. Title.*
*TC E178.1 .J321 1991*

**Jackson, Cecile, 1952-.**
Feminist visions of development. London ; New
York : Routledge, c1998.
*TC HQ1240 .F464 1998*

**Jackson, Claire W.**
A challenge to change. New York : College Entrance
Examination Board, 1999.
*TC P51 .C427 1999*

**Jackson, Douglas Northrop, 1929-.**
Problems and solutions in human assessment.
Boston : Kluwer Academic Publishers, c2000.
*TC BF698.4 .P666 2000*

**Jackson, Eve, 1949-** Learning disability in focus : the
use of photography in the care of people with a
learning disability / Eve and Neil Jackson. London ;
Philadelphia : Jessica Kingsley, c1999. 74 p. ; 24 cm.
ISBN 1-85302-693-X (pb : alk. paper) DDC 616.85/88906
*1. Photography - Therapeutic use. 2. Learning disabilities -
Treatment - Miscellanea. 3. Mentally handicapped - Services
for. I. Jackson, Neil, 1951- II. Title.*
*TC RC489.P56 J33 1999*

**JACKSON, JAMES, 1826-1833.**
Paul, Susan, fl. 1837. Memoir of James Jackson, the
attentive and obedient scholar, who died in Boston,
October 31, 1833, aged six years and eleven months.
Cambridge, MA : Harvard University Press, 2000.
*TC F73.9.N4 P38 2000*

**Jackson, Neil, 1951-.**
Jackson, Eve, 1949- Learning disability in focus.
London ; Philadelphia : Jessica Kingsley, c1999.
*TC RC489.P56 J33 1999*

**Jackson Pollock.**
Varnedoe, Kirk, 1946- New York : Museum of
Modern Art ; Distributed in the U.S. and Canada by
Harry N. Abrams, c1998.
*TC ND237.P73 A4 1998*

**Jackson Pollock** [videorecording] / produced & directed by Kim Evans. [Chicago, Ill.] : Home Vision : [S.l.] : Distributed Worldwide by RM Associates, c1987. 1 videocassette (ca. 52 min.) : sd., col. with b&w sequences ; 1/2 in. (Portrait of an artist) At head of title: Home Vision... presents an RM Arts Production... [videorecording]. VHS. Catalogued from credits and container. Title from container. Edited and presented by Melvyn Bragg ; consultant, Jeffrey Potter ; photography, Paul Bond ; film researcher, Michael Gavey ; researcher, Mary Harron ; film editor, Jonathan Cooke ; sound, Trevor Carless. Biographical documentary in 2 parts. Originally presented on the television program "South Bank Show" by London Weekend Television in 1987. A London Weekend "South Bank Show" co-produced with RM Arts.-- Container. "A Public Media Incorporated release." -- Container. "POL020."--Container. For adolescent through adult. SUMMARY: Presents a documentary portrait of abstract expressionist painter Jackson Pollock who died in a car crash at the age of 44. Combines archival footage of his life and work with reminiscences from his contemporaries. ISBN 0-7800-0762-X
*1. Pollock, Jackson. - 1912-1956. 2. Abstract expressionism - United States. 3. Painters - United States - Biography. I. Pollock, Jackson, 1912-1956. II. Bragg, Melvyn. III. Evans, Kim. IV. Home Vision (Firm) V. RM Arts (Firm) VI. Public Media Incorporated (Wilmette, Ill.) VII. London Weekend Television, ltd. VIII. Reiner Moritz Associates. IX. Title: South Bank show (Television program) X. Title: Home Vision... presents an RM Arts Production... [videorecording] XI. Series.*
*TC ND237.P73 J3 1987*

**Jackson, Shannon, 1967-** Lines of activity : performance, historiography, Hull-House domesticity / Shannon Jackson. Ann Arbor : University of Michigan Press, c2000. viii, 371 p. : ill., plans ; 25 cm. Includes bibliographical references (p. [315]-366) and index. ISBN 0-472-11112-4 (cloth : alk. paper) DDC 362.84/009773/11
*1. Hull House (Chicago, Ill.) - History. 2. Social settlements - Illinois - Chicago - History. 3. Addams, Jane, - 1860-1935. I. Title.*
*TC HV4196.C4 J33 2000*

**Jacobs, Donald H.**
Marshall, Robert H. AGS physical science. Circle Pines, Minn. : AGS, American Guidance Service, c1997.
*TC QC23 .M37 1997*

Marshall, Robert H. AGS physical science. Teacher's ed. Circle Pines, Minn. : AGS, American Guidance Service, c1997.
*TC QC23 .M37 1997 Teacher's Ed.*

Treff, August V. AGS basic math skills. Circle Pines, Minn. : AGS, American Guidance Service, c1997.
*TC QA107 .T73 1997*

Treff, August V. AGS basic math skills. Teacher's ed. Circle Pines, Minn. : AGS, American Guidance Service, c1997.
*TC QA107 .T73 1997 Teacher's Ed.*

**Jacobs, Douglas.**
The Harvard Medical School guide to suicide assessment and intervention. 1st ed. San Francisco : Jossey-Bass, c1999.
*TC RC569 .H37 1999*

**Jacobs, Harriet A. (Harriet Ann), 1813-1897.**
Incidents in the life of a slave girl : written by herself / by Harriet A. Jacobs ; edited by L. Maria Child. Now with A true tale of slavery / by John S. Jacobs ; [both] edited and with an introduction by Jean Fagan Yellin. Cambridge, Mass. : Harvard University Press, 2000. xli, 336 p. : ill. ; 24 cm. Includes bibliographical references and index. ISBN 0-674-00278-4 ISBN 0-674-00271-7 (pbk.) DDC 305.5/67/092
*1. Jacobs, Harriet A. - (Harriet Ann). - 1813-1897. 2. Slaves - United States - Biography. 3. Women slaves - United States - Biography. 4. Slaves - United States - Social conditions. 5. Jacobs, Harriet A. - 1813-1897. I. Child, Lydia Maria Francis, 1802-1880. II. Yellin, Jean Fagan. III. Jacobs, John S., 1815-1875. True tale of slavery. 2000. IV. Title.*
*TC E444.J17 A3 2000c*

**JACOBS, HARRIET A. (HARRIET ANN), 1813-1897.**
Jacobs, Harriet A. (Harriet Ann), 1813-1897. Incidents in the life of a slave girl : written by herself. Cambridge, Mass. : Harvard University Press, 2000.
*TC E444.J17 A3 2000c*

**JACOBS, HARRIET ANN, 1813-1897.**
Jacobs, Harriet A. (Harriet Ann), 1813-1897. Incidents in the life of a slave girl : written by herself. Cambridge, Mass. : Harvard University Press, 2000.
*TC E444.J17 A3 2000c*

**Jacobs, James S., 1945-.**
Tunnell, Michael O. Children's literature, briefly. 2nd ed. Upper Saddle River, N.J. : Merrill, c2000.
*TC PN1008.8 .J33 2000*

**Jacobs, John S., 1815-1875.**
**True tale of slavery. 2000.**
Jacobs, Harriet A. (Harriet Ann), 1813-1897. Incidents in the life of a slave girl : written by herself. Cambridge, Mass. : Harvard University Press, 2000.
*TC E444.J17 A3 2000c*

**Jacobs, Leland B. (Leland Blair), 1907-** Just around the corner : poems about the seasons / Leland B. Jacobs : pictures by Jeff Kaufman. New York : H. Holt, 1993. 32 p. : col. ill. ; 26 cm. "A Bill Martin book." SUMMARY: A collection of twenty-five poems celebrating seasonal highlights such as the autumn leaves, snow prints, flying kites, and beaches. ISBN 0-8050-2676-2 DDC 811/.54
*1. Seasons - Juvenile poetry. 2. Children's poetry, American. 3. Seasons - Poetry. 4. American poetry. I. Kaufman, Jeff, ill. II. Title.*
*TC PS3560.A2545 J87 1993*

**Jacobs, Leland B. (Leland Blair), 1907- / joint author.**
Johnson, Eleanor M. (Eleanor Murdoch), 1892-1987. Treat shop. Columbus, Ohio : Charles E. Merrill, c1954.
*TC PE1119 .J63 1954*

**Jacobson, Cardell K., 1941-.**
Heaton, Tim B. Statistical handbook on racial groups in the United States. Phoenix, AZ : Oryx Press, 2000.
*TC E184.A1 H417 2000*

**Jacobson, Michael J.**
Innovations in science and mathematics education. Mahwah, N.J. : L. Erlbaum, 2000.
*TC Q181 .I654 1999*

**Jacobson, Willard J.** Science for children : a book for teachers / Willard J. Jacobson, Abby Barry Bergman. Englewood Cliffs, N.J. : Prentice-Hall, c1980. xxx, 494 p. : ill. ; 24 cm. Includes bibliographies and index. ISBN 0-13-794784-4 DDC 372.3/5/044
*1. Science - Study and teaching (Elementary) - Handbook, manuals, etc. I. Bergman, Abby Barry, joint author. II. Title.*
*TC LB1585 .J32*

**Jacoby, Barbara.**
Involving commuter students in learning. San Francisco, Calif. : Jossey-Bass, 2000.
*TC LB2343.6 .I68 2000*

**Jacoway, Elizabeth, 1944-.**
Understanding the Little Rock crisis. Fayetteville, Ark : University of Arkansas Press, 1999.
*TC LC214.23.L56 U53 1999*

**JACQUERIE, 1358.** *See* PEASANTRY - FRANCE.

**Jacques Lacan and the question of psychoanalytic training.**
Safouan, Moustafa. [Jacques Lacan et la question de la formation des analystes. English] New York : St. Martin's Press, 2000.
*TC BF173.L15 S2414 2000*

**Jacyna, L. S.** Lost words : narratives of language and the brain, 1825-1926 / L.S. Jacyna. Princeton, N.J. ; Oxford : Princeton University Press, c2000. vi, 241 p. : ill. ; 25 cm. Includes bibliographical references and index. ISBN 0-691-00413-7 (CL : alk. paper) DDC 616.85/52/009
*1. Aphasia - History. I. Title.*
*TC RC425 .J33 2000*

**JAGGA (AFRICAN PEOPLE).** *See* CHAGA (AFRICAN PEOPLE).

**Jagodzinski, Jan, 1953-** Postmodern dilemmas : outrageous essays in art & art education / Jan Jagodzinski. Mahwah, N.J. : Lawrence Erlbaum Associates, 1997. xvi, 270 p. : ill. ; 29 cm. (Studies in curriculum theory) Includes bibliographical references (p. 241-259) and indexes. ISBN 0-8058-2604-1 (cloth : alk. paper) ISBN 0-8058-2605-X (pbk. : alk. paper) DDC 709/.04/5
*1. Art, Modern - 20th century. 2. Art - Study and teaching - History - 20th century. 3. Postmodernism. I. Title. II. Series.*
*TC N7445.2 .J34 1997*

**Jain, L. C.**
Innovative teaching and learning. Heidelberg [Germany] ; New York : Physica-Verlag, c2000.
*TC QA76.76.E95 I54 2000*

**Jalongo, Mary Renck.** Early childhood language arts / Mary Renck Jalongo. 2nd ed. Boston ; London : Allyn and Bacon, c2000. xv, 352 p. : ill., facsims. ; 24 cm. Includes bibliographical references (p. 317-342) and index. ISBN 0-205-27377-7 DDC 372.6
*1. Language arts (Preschool) I. Title.*
*TC LB1140.5.L3 J35 2000*

**JAMAICA - FICTION.**
Pomerantz, Charlotte. The chalk doll. New York : Lippincott, c1989.
*TC PZ7.P77 Ch 1989*

**JAMAICA - HISTORY.**
Sherlock, Philip Manderson, Sir. The story of the Jamaican people. Kingston, Jamaica : I. Randle Publishers ; Princeton, N.J. : M. Wiener Publishers, 1998.
*TC F1881 .S5 1998*

**James, Allison.**
Research with children. New York : Falmer Press, 2000.
*TC HQ767.85 .R48 1999*

**James, C. L. R. (Cyril Lionel Robert), 1901-** Marxism for our times : C.L.R. James on revolutionary organization / by C.L.R. James ; edited and with an introduction by Martin Glaberman. Jackson, Miss. : University Press of Mississippi, c1999. xxvii, 206 p. ; 24 cm. Includes bibliographical references and index. ISBN 1-57806-150-4 (cloth : alk. paper) ISBN 1-57806-151-2 (pbk. : alk. paper) DDC 335.4
*1. Communism. 2. Socialism. 3. Revolutions and socialism. I. Glaberman, Martin. II. Title.*
*TC HX44 .J25 1999*

**James C. Winston Publishing Company (Nashville, Tenn.).**
Gill, Walter. A common sense guide to non-traditional urban education. Nashville, Tenn. : James C. Winston Publishing Co., Inc., c1998.
*TC LC5115 .G55 1998*

**James, J. Alison.**
De Beer, Hans. [Kleine Eisbär und der Angsthase. English] Little Polar Bear and the brave little hare. New York : North-South Books, 1998.
*TC PZ7.D353 Liv 1998*

**James, Oliver, 1953-.**
Teen violence [videorecording]. Princeton, NJ : Films for the Humanities & Sciences, c1998.
*TC RJ506.V56 T44 1998*

**James, Phoebe L.** Accompaniments for rhythmic expressions : children's music for children ; primary and upper grades. [Los Angeles? : s.n.], c1946. ix, 30 p. ; 28 cm. Spiral binding.
*1. Musico-callisthenics. 2. Children's songs. 3. Piano music, Juvenile. I. Title: Children's music for children*
*TC M1993.J18 A3*

**The Jamia educational quarterly.** Malir City, Karachi : Jamia Millia Institute of Education, 1960-1972. 13 v. ; 22 cm. -v. 13, no. 3 (July 1972). Began publication in 1960. Cf. New serial titles. Issues for Oct. 1970-July 1972 published: Jamia Millia Teachers College. Description based on: vol. 11, no. 1 (Jan. 1970). ISSN 0021-4191
*1. Education - Pakistan - Periodicals. I. Karachi. Jamia Institute of Education. II. Jamia Millia Teachers College (Karachi, Pakistan).*

**Jamia Millia Teachers College (Karachi, Pakistan).**
The Jamia educational quarterly. Malir City, Karachi : Jamia Millia Institute of Education, 1960-1972.

**Jamison, Kay R.** Night falls fast : understanding suicide / Kay Redfield Jamison. 1st ed. New York : Knopf ; Distributed by Random House, 1999. x, 432 p. : ill. ; 23 cm. Includes bibliographical references (p. 319-414) and index. ISBN 0-375-40145-8 (hc) DDC 616.85/8445/00973
*1. Suicide - United States. 2. Children - Suicidal behavior - United States. 3. Youth - Suicidal behavior - United States. I. Title.*
*TC RC569 .J36 1999*

**Janeczko, Paul B.**
Wherever home begins. New York : Orchard Books, c1995.
*TC PS595.H645 W48 1995*

**Jankanish, M.**
Action against child labour. Geneva : International Labour Office, c2000.
*TC HD6231 .A28 2000*

**Janney, Rachel.** Behavioral support / by Rachel Janney and Martha E. Snell with contributions from Johnna Elliot ... [et al.]. Baltimore, Md. ; London : Paul H. Brookes Pub., c2000. ix, 102 p. : ill., forms ; 26 cm. (Teachers' guides to inclusive practices) Includes bibliographical references (p. 77-79) and index. ISBN 1-55766-355-6 DDC 370.15/3
*1. Behavior modification - Case studies. 2. Inclusive education - Case studies. I. Snell, Martha E. II. Elliot, Johnna. III. Title.*
*TC LB1060.2 .J26 2000*

Modifying schoolwork / by Rachel Janney and Martha E. Snell with contributions from Johnna Elliot ... [et al.]. Baltimore, Md. : Paul H. Brookes Pub., c2000. ix, 93 p. : ill., forms ; 26 cm. (Teachers' guides to inclusive practices) Includes bibliographical references and index. ISBN 1-55766-354-8
*1. Inclusive education - United States - Planning. 2. Handicapped children - Education - United States - Planning. 3. Classroom management - United States. I. Snell, Martha E. II. Elliot, Johnna. III. Title. IV. Series.*
**TC LC1201 .J26 2000**

Snell, Martha E. Collaborative teaming. Baltimore : Paul H. Brookes Pub., c2000.
**TC LC1201 .S64 2000**

**Janov, Arthur.** The biology of love / Arthur Janov. Amherst, N.Y. : Prometheus Books, 2000. 364 p. : ill. ; 24 cm. Includes bibliographical references and index. ISBN 1-57392-829-1 DDC 152.4/1
*1. Emotions in infants. 2. Affect (Psychology) 3. Love. 4. Love - Physiological aspects. 5. Infants (Newborn) - Psychology. 6. Prenatal influences. 7. Infants (Newborn) - Wounds and injuries. I. Title.*
**TC BF720.E45 .J36 2000**

**Jansse, Tanya.**
Fiction, literature and media. Amsterdam : Amsterdam University Press, c1999.
**TC LB1575.8 .F53 1999**

**Jantzi, Doris.**
Leithwood, Kenneth A. Changing leadership for changing times. Buckingham ; Philadelphia : Open University Press, 1999.
**TC LB2805 .L358 1999**

Leithwood, Kenneth A. Educational accountability. Gütersloh : Bertelsmann Foundation Publishers, 1999.
**TC LB2806.22 .L45 1999**

**January, Brendan, 1972-** The New York Public Library amazing mythology : a book of answers for kids / Brendan January. New York : Wiley, 2000. 168 p. : ill. ; 23 cm. Includes bibliographical references. SUMMARY: Over 200 questions and answers introduce myths from many ancient cultures, including Egyptian, Greek, Roman, Celtic, Norse, and Native American. ISBN 0-471-33205-4 (paper) DDC 291.1/3
*1. Mythology - Miscellanea - Juvenile literature. 2. Mythology - Miscellanea. 3. Questions and answers. I. Title. II. Title: Amazing mythology*
**TC BL311 .J36 2000**

**Janus, Raizi Abby.** Mapping careers with LD and ADD clients : guidebook and case studies / Raizi Abby Janus. New York : Columbia University Press, c1999. x, 388 p. ; 24 cm. Includes bibliographical references (p. [373]-380) and index. ISBN 0-231-10978-4 (alk. paper) DDC 362.4/0484
*1. Vocational guidance for the handicapped. 2. Learning disabled - Vocational guidance. 3. Attention-deficit-disordered adults - Vocational guidance. 4. Vocational interests. 5. Vocational qualifications. 6. Vocational interests. 7. Vocational qualifications. 8. Learning disabled - Vocational guidance. 9. Vocational guidance for the handicapped. 10. Attention-deficit-disordered adults - Vocational guidance. I. Title.*
**TC HV1568.5 .J36 1999**

**Januszczak, Waldemar.**
Picasso [videorecording]. Chicago, IL : Home Vision, c1986.
**TC N6853.P5 P52 1986**

**JAPAN - HANDBOOKS, MANUALS, ETC.**
A Teacher's & textbook writers' handbook on Japan. 5th., rev. printing. Tokyo : International Society for Educational Information, c1993.
**TC DS806 .T34 1993**

**JAPAN. KUNAICHŌ - ART COLLECTIONS - EXHIBITIONS.**
Twelve centuries of Japanese art from the Imperial collections. Washington, DC : Freer Gallery of Art and the Arthur M. Sackler Gallery, Smithsonian Institution Press, c1997.
**TC ND1457.J32 W377 1997**

**JAPAN - LITERATURES.** *See* **JAPANESE LITERATURE.**

**Japan. Monbushō. Daijin Kanbō. Chōsa Tōkei Kikakuka.**
Statistical abstract of education, science, sports, and culture. [Tokyo] : Research and Statistics Planning Division, Minister's Secretariat, Ministry of Education, Science, Sports, and Culture, 1996-
**TC LA1310 .S73**

**Japan. Monbushō. Daijin Kanbō. Chōsa Tōkeika.**
Statistical abstract of education, science, and culture. [Tokyo] : Research and Statistics Division, Minister's

Secretariat, Ministry of Education, Science, and Culture, Japan,
**TC LA1310 .S73**

**JAPAN - SOCIAL CONDITIONS - 1945-.**
Morley, Patricia A. The mountain is moving. Washington Square, N.Y. : New York University Press, 1999.
**TC HQ1762 .M64 1999**

**JAPAN - STATISTICS - PERIODICALS.**
Statistical abstract of education, science, and culture. [Tokyo] : Research and Statistics Division, Minister's Secretariat, Ministry of Education, Science, and Culture, Japan,
**TC LA1310 .S73**

Statistical abstract of education, science, sports, and culture. [Tokyo] : Research and Statistics Planning Division, Minister's Secretariat, Ministry of Education, Science, Sports, and Culture, 1996-
**TC LA1310 .S73**

**JAPANESE AMERICAN CITIZENS' LEAGUE.**
Rabbit in the moon [videorecording]. San Francisco, Calif. : Wabi-Sabi Productions, 1999.
**TC D753.8 .R3 1999**

**JAPANESE AMERICAN COLLEGE STUDENTS - ECONOMIC CONDITIONS.**
Okihiro, Gary Y., 1945- Stories lives. Seattle : University of Washington Press, 1999.
**TC D753.8 .O38 1999**

**JAPANESE AMERICAN COLLEGE STUDENTS - SOCIAL CONDITIONS.**
Okihiro, Gary Y., 1945- Stories lives. Seattle : University of Washington Press, 1999.
**TC D753.8 .O38 1999**

[**Japanese-American internment** picture : life in the camps]. Amawalk, NY : Jackdaw Publications, c1999. 12 posters : b&w ; 43 x 56 cm. + 1 leaflet ([6] p. : ill. ; 28 cm.). (Jackdaw photo collections ; PC 106) Title from accompanying material. Compiled by Bill Eames. SUMMARY: 12 historical photo-posters depicting Japanese life in the American relocation camps. CONTENTS: 1. Flag-raising at Relocation Camp -- 2. Heart Mountain, Wyoming -- 3. Nisei football in Utah -- 4. Agricultural workers in Idaho -- 5. Night school for internees -- 6. A skating rink in Wyoming -- 7. Relocation camp mural tells the story -- 8. Community enterprise store in Wyoming -- 9. Baber shop in Idaho -- 10. Communal dining at Tule Lake Relocation Center -- 11. Easter egg hunt in Arkansas -- 12. Family of five in their barracks home. ISBN 1-56696-163-7
*1. Japanese Americans - Evacuation and relocation, 1942-1945. 2. Concentration camps - United States - Posters. 3. Documentary photography - United States - Posters. I. Eames, Bill. II. Jackdaw Publications. III. Title: Life in the camps [picture] IV. Series.*
**TC TR820.5 .J3 1999**

**JAPANESE AMERICANS - EVACUATION AND RELOCATION, 1942-1945.**
[Japanese-American internment picture. Amawalk, NY : Jackdaw Publications, c1999.
**TC TR820.5 .J3 1999**

Rabbit in the moon [videorecording]. San Francisco, Calif. : Wabi-Sabi Productions, 1999.
**TC D753.8 .R3 1999**

**JAPANESE AMERICANS - EVACUATION AND RELOCATION, 1942-1945 - PERSONAL NARRATIVES.**
Rabbit in the moon [videorecording]. San Francisco, Calif. : Wabi-Sabi Productions, 1999.
**TC D753.8 .R3 1999**

**JAPANESE AMERICANS - EVACUATION AND RELOCATION, 1942-1945 - PSYCHOLOGICAL ASPECTS.**
Rabbit in the moon [videorecording]. San Francisco, Calif. : Wabi-Sabi Productions, 1999.
**TC D753.8 .R3 1999**

**JAPANESE AMERICANS - UNITED STATES.** *See* **JAPANESE AMERICANS.**

**JAPANESE CALLIGRAPHY.** *See* **CALLIGRAPHY, JAPANESE.**

**Japanese education since 1945 :** a documentary study / [Edward R. Beauchamp, James M. Vardaman,Jr., editors]. Armonk, N.Y. : M.E. Sharpe, c1994. xii, 351 p. ; 24 cm. Chiefly documents previously published in various sources and translated from Japanese. "An East gate book." Includes bibliographical references (p. 30-33) and index. ISBN 0-87332-561-3 (alk. paper) DDC 370/.952/0904
*1. Education - Japan - History - 20th century. 2. Education - Japan - History - 20th century - Sources. 3. Education and state - Japan - History - 20th century. 4. Educational change -*

Japan - History - 20th century. I. Beauchamp, Edward R., 1933- II. Vardaman, James M., 1947-
**TC LA1311.82 .J39 1994**

**JAPANESE INK PAINTING.** *See* **INK PAINTING, JAPANESE.**

**JAPANESE LANGUAGE - CONNECTIVES.**
Mori, Junko. Negotiating agreement and disagreement in Japanese. Amsterdam ; Philadelphia, Pa. : J. Benjamins Pub. Co., c1999.
**TC PL611.C6 M67 1999**

**JAPANESE LANGUAGE - DISCOURSE ANALYSIS.**
Mori, Junko. Negotiating agreement and disagreement in Japanese. Amsterdam ; Philadelphia, Pa. : J. Benjamins Pub. Co., c1999.
**TC PL611.C6 M67 1999**

Tanaka, Hiroko. Turn-taking in Japanese conversation. Amsterdam ; Philadelphia, PA : John Benjamins Pub. Co., c1999.
**TC PL640.5 .T36 1999**

**JAPANESE LANGUAGE - STUDY AND TEACHING (HIGHER) - UNITED STATES - ENGLISH SPEAKERS.**
New trends & issues in teaching Japanese language & culture. Honolulu ; Second Language Teaching and Curriculum, University of Hawai'i at Manoa, 1997.
**TC PL519 .N45 1997**

**JAPANESE LITERATURE - STUDY AND TEACHING (HIGHER) - UNITED STATES.**
New trends & issues in teaching Japanese language & culture. Honolulu ; Second Language Teaching and Curriculum, University of Hawai'i at Manoa, 1997.
**TC PL519 .N45 1997**

**JAPANESE MANAGEMENT.** *See* **INDUSTRIAL MANAGEMENT - JAPAN.**

**JAPANESE PAINTING.** *See* **PAINTING, JAPANESE.**

**JAPANESE SCROLLS.** *See* **SCROLLS, JAPANESE.**

**JAPANESE - UNITED STATES.** *See* **JAPANESE AMERICANS.**

**Jaques Cattell Press.**
Directory of American scholars. 9th ed. / edited by Rita C. Velazquez. Detroit, Mich. : Gale Group, 1999.
**TC LA2311 .D57 1999**

**Jarrett, Michael, 1953-** Drifting on a read : jazz as a model for writing / Michael Jarrett. Albany, N.Y. : State University of New York Press, 1999. xiv, 227 p. : ill. ; 24 cm. (SUNY series, interruptions -- border testimony(ies) and critical discourse/s) Includes bibliographical references and index. ISBN 0-7914-4097-4 (hc. : alk. paper) ISBN 0-7914-4098-2 (pbk. : alk. paper) ISBN 0-7914-4104-0 (pbk. : alk. paper) DDC 781.65/11
*1. Written communication. 2. Jazz - History and criticism. 3. Popular culture. 4. Criticism. I. Title. II. Series: Interruptions.*
**TC ML3849 .J39 1999**

**Jarvis, Ana C.** Getting along in Spanish / Ana C. Jarvis, Raquel Lebredo. Lexington, Mass. : D.C. Heath, c1984. vi, 223 p. : ill. ; 28 cm. "Designed for use with the core text, Basic Spanish Grammar, Second Edition"--Pref. ISBN 0-669-06711-3
*1. Spanish language - Textbooks for foreign speakers - English. 2. Spanish language - Grammar - 1950- I. Lebredo, Raquel. II. Title.*
**TC PC4121 .J37 1984**

**Jasper Johns.**
Varnedoe, Kirk, 1946- New York : Museum of Modern Art : Distributed by Harry N. Abrams, c1996.
**TC N6537.J6 A4 1996**

**JATAKA STORIES.**
Lee, Jeanne M. I once was a monkey. 1st ed. New York : Farrar, Straus and Giroux, 1999.
**TC BQ1462.E5 L44 1999**

**JATAKA STORIES, ENGLISH.**
Lee, Jeanne M. I once was a monkey. 1st ed. New York : Farrar, Straus and Giroux, 1999.
**TC BQ1462.E5 L44 1999**

**Jauregi Ondarra, Kristi.** Collaborative negotiation of meaning : a longitudinal approach / Kristi Jauregi Ondarra. Amsterdam ; Atlanta, GA : Rodopi, 1997. 492 p. : ill. ; 23 cm. (Utrecht studies in language and communication ; 11) Includes bibliographical references (p. [472]-489) and index. ISBN 90-420-0116-X
*1. Second language acquisition - Research. 2. Oral communication. I. Title. II. Series.*
**TC P118.2 .J38 1997**

**Jaworski, Barbara.**
Comparing standards internationally. Wallingford :
Symposium, 1999.
*TC QA11 .C64 1999*

**Jay, Leah.**
Paris [videorecording]. New York, NY : V.I.E.W.
Video, c1996.
*TC DC707 .P3 1996*

**JAZZ.**
Weatherford, Carole Boston, 1956- The sound that
jazz makes. New York : Walker & Co., c2000.
*TC ML3506 .W42 2000*

**The jazz cadence of American culture** / edited by
Robert G. O'Meally. New York : Columbia
University Press, c1998. xvi, 665 p. : ill. ; 26 cm. Thirty-
five essays. Includes bibliographical references and index.
CONTENTS: What is jazz? -- One nation under a groove, or,
The United States of jazzocracy -- Jazz lines and colors : the
sound I saw -- Jazz is a dance : jazz art in motion -- Tell the
story : jazz, history, memory -- Writing the blues, writing jazz.
ISBN 0-231-10448-0 (cloth : alk. paper) ISBN 0-231-10449-9
(pbk. : alk. paper) DDC 781.65
*1. Jazz - History and criticism. 2. Blues (Music) - History and
criticism. 3. Afro-Americans - Music - History and criticism. I.
O'Meally, Robert G., 1948-*
*TC ML3508 .J38 1998*

**Jazz Dance Chicago (Organization).**
Jazz dance class [videorecording]. W. Long Branch,
NJ : Kultur, [1992?]
*TC GV1784 .J3 1992*

**Jazz dance class** [videorecording] : with Gus Giordano /
[presented by] All Night Moving Pictures ; produced
by Wendell F. Moody ... [et al.] ; directed by James
F. Robinson. W. Long Branch, NJ : Kultur, [1992?] 1
videocassette (63 min.) : sd., col. ; 1/2 in. (Dance instructional)
VHS, Hi-fi, Stereo, Mono-Compatible, Dolby System.
Catalogued from credits and container. Narrator: Cathy
Couser; host/instructor: Gus Giordano; Jazz Dance Chicago:
Debbie Chalifoux, Kenneth Comstock, Tina DeLeone, Tuni
Lewis, Nan Giordano, Jimmy Locust, Jeffrey Mildenstein,
Susan Quinn, Sam Watson, Michael Williams, Sherry Zunker.
Photography, Michael Smith ; music, Michael Morales ; editor,
Midge Noznebour. "A James F. Robinson videotape."
Originally produced as instructional video by Robinson in
1984. For aspiring jazz dancers. SUMMARY: Gus Giordano
and his dance troupe Jazz Dance Chicago present a workshop
in jazz dance techniques and exercises. Giordano is also
interviewed. CONTENTS: Chapter 1. The Warm-up -- Chapter
2. Basic jazz technique -- Chapter 3. Jazz walks -- Chapter 4.
Centre barre -- Chapter 5. The professional dancer. ISBN 1-
56127-207-8
*1. Jazz dance - Study and teaching. 2. Dance in motion
pictures, television, etc. I. Giordano, Gus. II. Robinson, James
F. III. Moody, Wendell F. IV. Couser, Cathy. V. Chalifoux,
Debbie. VI. Comstock, Kenneth. VII. DeLeone, Tina. VIII.
Lewis, Tuni. IX. Giordano, Nan. X. Locust, Jimmy. XI.
Mildenstein, Jeffrey, 1957-1989. XII. Quinn, Susan. XIII.
Watson, Sam. XIV. Williams, Michael. XV. Dow, Sherry
Zunker. XVI. Jazz Dance Chicago (Organization) XVII. All
Night Moving Pictures. XVIII. Kultur International Films. XIX.
Series.*
*TC GV1784 .J3 1992*

**JAZZ DANCE - STUDY AND TEACHING.**
Jazz dance class [videorecording]. W. Long Branch,
NJ : Kultur, [1992?]
*TC GV1784 .J3 1992*

**JAZZ DUETS.** *See* **JAZZ.**

**JAZZ ENSEMBLES.** *See* **JAZZ.**

**JAZZ - HISTORY AND CRITICISM.**
Cassidy, Donna. Painting the musical city.
Washington, DC : Smithsonian Institution Press,
c1997.
*TC ML85 .C37 1997*

Jarrett, Michael, 1953- Drifting on a read. Albany,
N.Y. : State University of New York Press, 1999.
*TC ML3849 .J39 1999*

The jazz cadence of American culture. New York :
Columbia University Press, c1998.
*TC ML3508 .J38 1998*

**JAZZ - HISTORY AND CRITICISM - JUVENILE
LITERATURE.**
Weatherford, Carole Boston, 1956- The sound that
jazz makes. New York : Walker & Co., c2000.
*TC ML3506 .W42 2000*

**JAZZ MUSIC.** *See* **JAZZ.**

**JAZZ NONETS.** *See* **JAZZ.**

**JAZZ OCTETS.** *See* **JAZZ.**

**JAZZ QUARTETS.** *See* **JAZZ.**

**JAZZ QUINTETS.** *See* **JAZZ.**

**JAZZ SEPTETS.** *See* **JAZZ.**

**JAZZ SEXTETS.** *See* **JAZZ.**

**JAZZ TRIOS.** *See* **JAZZ.**

**JAZZ - UNITED STATES.** *See* **JAZZ.**

**The JCAHO mock survey made simple.**
Chamberlain, Kathryn A. 1998 ed. Marblehead, MA :
Opus Communications, c1998.
*TC RA981.A2 C45 1999*

**JCT.**
Contemporary curriculum discourses. New York : P.
Lang, c1999.
*TC LB2806.15 .C6753 1999*

**JEALOUSY.**
Buss, David M. The dangerous passion. New York :
Free Press, 2000.
*TC BF575.J4 B87 2000*

**Jean-Aubry, G. (Georges), 1882-1950.**
**[Musique française d'aujourd'hui. English]**
French music of to-day / by G. Jean-Aubry ; with a
preface by Gabriel Fauré ; translated by Edwin
Evans. 4th ed. London, K. Paul, Trench, Trubner,
1926. xxxii, 262 p. ; 19 cm. (Library of music and
musicians) Translation of: Musique française d'aujourd'hui.
"Articles et lectures." Includes index.
*1. Music - France - History and criticism. 2. Musicians -
France - Biography. I. Title. II. Series.*
*TC ML60.A82 E8 1926*

**The Jean Nicod lectures**
(1997) Elster, Jon, 1940- Strong feelings.
Cambridge, Mass. : MIT Press, c1999.
*TC BF531 .E475 1999*

**Jeanrenaud, Claude.**
Valuing the cost of smoking. Boston : Kluwer
Academic Publishers, 1999.
*TC HV5735 .V35 1999*

**JEFFERSON, THOMAS, 1743-1826 - VIEWS ON
CITIZENSHIP - CONGRESSES.**
Thomas Jefferson and the education of a citizen.
Washington, DC : Library of Congress, 1999.
*TC Z663 .T425 1999*

**Jeffri, Joan.** The emerging arts : management, survival,
and growth / Joan Jeffri. New York, N.Y. : Praeger,
1980. ix, 245 p. ; 25 cm. Includes bibliographical references
(p.214-22) and index. ISBN 0-03-056707-6 DDC 700/.68
*1. Arts - United States - Management. 2. Arts - United States -
Finance. I. Title.*
*TC NX765 .J43*

**JELLINEK'S DISEASE.** *See* **ALCOHOLISM.**

**Jenkins, Adelbert H.** Psychology and African
Americans : a humanistic approach / Adelbert H.
Jenkins. 2nd ed. Boston : Allyn and Bacon, 1995. xxi,
328 p. ; 24 cm. Previous ed. published under title: The
psychology of the Afro-American. "A Longwood Professional
book". Includes bibliographical references (p. 281-306) and
indexes. ISBN 0-205-16488-9 ISBN 0-205-16489-7 (pbk.)
DDC 155.8/496073
*1. Afro-Americans - Psychology. 2. Afro-Americans - Race
identity. I. Jenkins, Adelbert H. Psychology of the Afro-
American. II. Title.*
*TC E185.625 .J47 1995*

**Psychology of the Afro American.**
Jenkins, Adelbert H. Psychology and African
Americans. 2nd ed. Boston : Allyn and Bacon,
1995.
*TC E185.625 .J47 1995*

**Jenkins, E. W. (Edgar William).**
Learning from others. Dordrecht [Netherlands] ;
Boston : Kluwer Academic Publishers, c2000.
*TC LB43 .L42 2000*

**Jenkins, John M.**
Keefe, James W. Instruction and the learning
environment. Larchmont, NY : Eye On Education,
c1997.
*TC LB2806.4 .K44 1997*

Personalized instruction. Larchmont, N.Y. : Eye on
Education, c2000.
*TC LB1031 .K383 2000*

**Jenkins, Leonard, ill.**
Greene, Carol. Sunflower Island. 1st ed. New York :
HarperCollins, c1999.
*TC PZ7.G82845 Sl 1999*

**Jenkins, Martin.** The emperor's egg / Martin Jenkins ;
illustrated by Jane Chapman. 1st U.S. ed. Cambridge,
Mass. : Candlewick Press, 1999. 29 p. : col. ill. ; 28 cm.
SUMMARY: Describes the parental behavior of Emperor
penguins, focusing on how the male keeps the egg warm until
it hatches and how the parents care for the chick after it is born.
ISBN 0-7636-0557-3 (alk. paper) DDC 598.47
*1. Emperor penguin - Behavior - Juvenile literature. 2.
Parental behavior in animals - Juvenile literature. 3. Emperor
penguin - Habits and behavior. 4. Penguins - Habits and
behavior. 5. Parental behavior in animals. I. Chapman, Jane,
1970- ill. II. Title.*
*TC QL696.S473 J45 1999*

**Jenkins, Peter. 1950-.**
Daniels, Debbie. Therapy with children :. London ;
Thousand Oaks, Calif. : SAGE, 2000.
*TC RJ504 .D36 2000*

**Jenkins, Steve, 1952- ill.**
Riley, Linda Capus. Elephants swim. Boston :
Houghton Mifflin, 1995.
*TC QP310.S95 R55 1995*

**Jenkinson, Edward B.**
Exploring the English language [videorecording].
[Princeton, N.J.] : Video Tutor ; [Chesterton, Ind.? :
Distributed by] Griffin Media Design, 1988, c1986.

**Jenney, Charles.** First year Latin workbook / Charles
Jenney, Jr., Rogers V. Scudder, Eric C. Baade.
Newton, Mass. : Allyn and Bacon, c1987. 252 p. ; 28
cm. ISBN 0-205-08725-6
*1. Latin language - Grammar. I. Baade, Eric C. II. Scudder,
Rogers V. III. Title.*
*TC PA2087.5 .J46 1987*

Fourth year Latin : teacher's guide / Charles Jenney,
Jr.,Rogers V. Scudder, David D. Coffin. Needham,
Mass. : Prentice Hall, c1990. 109 p. ; 22 cm. (Prentice
Hall Latin) ISBN 0-13-329939-2
*1. Latin language - Grammar. I. Scudder, Rogers V. II. Coffin,
David D. III. Title: Jenney's fourth year Latin IV. Series.*
*TC PA2087.5 .J463 1990*

Jenney's first year Latin / Charles Jenney, Jr., Eric C.
Baade, Thomas K. Burgess. Needham, Mass. :
Prentice Hall, c1990. xxviii, 579 p. : col. ill., maps ; 24 cm.
Includes index. ISBN 0-13-319328-4
*1. Latin language - Grammar. I. Baade, Eric C. II. Burgess,
Thomas K. III. Title. IV. Title: First year Latin*
*TC PA2087.5 .J46 1990*

Jenney's second year Latin / Charles Jenney, Jr. ... [et
al.]. Newton, Mass. : Allyn and Bacon, c1987. ix, 470
p. : ill. (some col.) ; maps (some col.) ; 25 cm. (The Allyn and
Bacon Latin program) ISBN 0-205-08726-4
*1. Latin language - Grammar. I. Title. Second year Latin II.
Series.*
*TC PA2087.5 .J461 1987*

Third year Latin / Charles Jenney, Jr., Rogers V.
Scudder, David D. Coffin. Newton, Mass. : Allyn and
Bacon, c1987. v. 552 p., [2] p. of plates : ill. ; 23 cm. (The
Allyn and Bacon Latin program) Includes index. ISBN 0-205-
08729-9
*1. Latin language - Readers. 2. Rome - Civilization - Problems,
exercises, etc. I. Scudder, Rogers V. II. Coffin, David D. III.
Title. IV. Title: Jenney's third year Latin V. Series.*
*TC PA2087.5 .J462 1987*

**Jenney's first year Latin.**
Jenney, Charles. Needham, Mass. : Prentice Hall,
c1990.
*TC PA2087.5 .J46 1990*

**Jenney's fourth year Latin.**
Jenney, Charles. Fourth year Latin. Needham, Mass. :
Prentice Hall, c1990.
*TC PA2087.5 .J463 1990*

**Jenney's third year Latin.**
Jenney, Charles. Third year Latin. Newton, Mass. :
Allyn and Bacon, c1987.
*TC PA2087.5 .J462 1987*

**JENNINGS, CEDRIC LAVAR - CHILDHOOD
AND YOUTH.**
Suskind, Ron. A hope in the unseen. 1st ed. New
York : Broadway Books, c1998.
*TC LC2803.W3 S87 1998*

**JENNINGS, CEDRIC LAVAR - KNOWLEDGE
AND LEARNING.**
Suskind, Ron. A hope in the unseen. 1st ed. New
York : Broadway Books, c1998.
*TC LC2803.W3 S87 1998*

**Jennings, Patrick.** Putnam and Pennyroyal / by Patrick
Jennings , pictures by Jon J. Muth. 1st ed. New York :
Scholastic Press, 1999. 163 p. 22 cm. SUMMARY: While
listening to her uncle as he tells a story about grebes, nine-
year-old Cora Lee realizes that he is revealing something about
himself through the characters he creates. ISBN 0-439-07965-9
(alk. paper) DDC [Fic]

*1. Grebes - Fiction. 2. Storytelling - Fiction. 3. Uncles - Fiction. 4. Birds - Fiction. I. Muth, Jon J. ill. II. Title.*
**TC PZ7.J4298715 Co 1999**

**Jenoure, Terry.** Navigators : African American musicians, dancers, and visual artists in academe / Theresa Jenoure. Albany, NY : State University of New York Press, c2000. xix, 225 p. : port. : 24 cm. (SUNY series, the social context of education) Discography: p. 221. Includes bibliographical references and index. ISBN 0-7914-4353-1 (alk. paper) ISBN 0-7914-4354-X (pbk. : alk. paper) DDC 700/.92/396073
*1. Afro-Ameican artists as teachers. 2. Afro-American artists - Interviews. 3. Afro-American arts. I. Title. II. Series: SUNY series, the social context of education.*
**TC NX396.5 .J45 2000**

**Jensen, Jens F.**
The Computer as medium. Cambridge [England] ; New York : Cambridge University Press, 1993.
**TC QA76.5 .C612554 1993**

Interactive television. Aalborg, Denmark : Aalborg University Press, 1999.
**TC HE8700.95 .I57 1999**

**Jensen, Lars.**
Teaching post-colonialism and post-colonial literatures. Aarhus, Denmark ; Oakville, Conn. : Aarhus University Press, c1997.
**TC PR9080.A53 T43 1997**

**Jensen, Uffe Juul.**
International Society for Activity Theory and Cultural Research. Congress (4th : 1998 : Aarhus, Denmark) Activity theory and social practice. Aarhus : Aarhus University Press, c1999.
**TC B105.A35 I57 1998**

International Society for Activity Theory and Cultural Research. Congress (4th : 1998 : Aarhus, Denmark) Activity theory and social practice. Aarhus : Aarhus University Press, c1999.
**TC B105.A35 I57 1999**

**Jernegan, Laura, b. 1862.** A whaling captain's daughter : the diary of Laura Jernegan, 1868-1871 / edited by Megan O'Hara ; foreword by Suzanne L. Bunkers ; content consultant, Judy Downey. Mankato, Minn. : Blue Earth Books, c2000. 32 p. : col. ill., map ; 24 cm. (Diaries, letters, and memoirs) Includes bibliographical references (p. 31) and index. SUMMARY: The diary of a young girl who traveled with her family on her father's whaling ship in the 1860s records her schooling, dangerous whale hunts, and the activities of her baby brother. Includes sidebars, activities, and a timeline related to this era. ISBN 0-7368-0346-7 DDC 910.4/5/092
*1. Jernegan, Laura, - b. 1862 - Diaries - Juvenile literature. 2. Jernegan, Laura, - b. 1862 - Journeys - Juvenile literature. 3. Girls - Diaries - Juvenile literature. 4. Seafaring life - Juvenile literature. 5. Whaling - Juvenile literature. 6. Jernegan, Laura, - b. 1862. 7. Seafaring life. 8. Whaling. 9. Diaries. 10. Women - Biography. I. O'Hara, Megan. II. Title. III. Series.*
**TC G545 .J47 2000**

**JERNEGAN, LAURA, B. 1862.**
Jernegan, Laura, b. 1862. A whaling captain's daughter. Mankato, Minn. : Blue Earth Books, c2000.
**TC G545 .J47 2000**

**JERNEGAN, LAURA, B. 1862 - DIARIES - JUVENILE LITERATURE.**
Jernegan, Laura, b. 1862. A whaling captain's daughter. Mankato, Minn. : Blue Earth Books, c2000.
**TC G545 .J47 2000**

**JERNEGAN, LAURA, B. 1862 - JOURNEYS - JUVENILE LITERATURE.**
Jernegan, Laura, b. 1862. A whaling captain's daughter. Mankato, Minn. : Blue Earth Books, c2000.
**TC G545 .J47 2000**

**Jerrard, Margot.**
Jerrard, Richard. The grad school handbook. 1st ed. New York : Berkley Pub. Group, 1998.
**TC LB2371.4 .J47 1998**

**Jerrard, Richard.** The grad school handbook : an insider's guide to getting in and succeeding / Richard Jerrard and Margot Jerrard. 1st ed. New York : Berkley Pub. Group, 1998. 259 p. ; 21 cm. "A Perigee book." Includes bibliographical references (p. [233]-239) and index. ISBN 0-399-52416-9 DDC 371.55/0973
*1. Universities and colleges - United States - Graduate work - Handbooks, manuals, etc. 2. Universities and colleges - United States - Graduate work - Admission - Handbooks, manuals, etc. 3. Graduate students - United States - Handbooks, manuals, etc. I. Jerrard, Margot. II. Title.*
**TC LB2371.4 .J47 1998**

**Jessel, John.**
Study to teach. London ; New York : Routledge, 2000.

**TC LB1707 .S88 2000**

**JESTS. See WIT AND HUMOR.**

**JESUS CHRIST - NATIVITY - FICTION.**
Hoffman, Mary, 1945- Three wise women. 1st ed. New York : Phyllis Fogelman Books, 1999.
**TC PZ7.H67562 Th 1999**

**JESUS CHRIST - NATIVITY - JUVENILE FICTION.**
Hoffman, Mary, 1945- Three wise women. 1st ed. New York : Phyllis Fogelman Books, 1999.
**TC PZ7.H67562 Th 1999**

**JET PUROGURAMU.**
McConnell, David L., 1959- Importing diversity. Berkeley : University of California Press, c2000.
**TC LB2285.J3 M33 2000**

**Jett-Simpson, Mary, 1938-.**
Stewig, John W. Language arts in the early childhood classroom. Belmont [Calif.] : Wadsworth Pub. Co., c1995.
**TC LB1140.5.L3 S72 1995**

**Jevne, Ronna Fay.** When dreams don't work : professional caregivers and burnout / Ronna F. Jevne and Donna Reilly Williams. Amityville, N.Y. : Baywood Pub., c1998. vi, 193 p. : ill. ; 24 cm. (Death, value, and meaning series) Includes bibliographical references and index. ISBN 0-89503-179-5 (hardcover : alk. paper) DDC 158.7/23
*1. Burn out (Psychology) 2. Work - Psychological aspects. I. Williams, Donna Reilly, 1945- II. Title. III. Title: When dreams do not work IV. Series.*
**TC BF481 .J48 1998**

**JEWELERS - AUSTRALIA - BIOGRAPHY.**
Anderson, Patricia, 1950- Contemporary jewellery in Australia and New Zealand. North Ryde, Sydney : Craftsman House, c1998.
**TC NK7390.A1 A53 1998**

**JEWELERS - NEW ZEALAND - BIOGRAPHY.**
Anderson, Patricia, 1950- Contemporary jewellery in Australia and New Zealand. North Ryde, Sydney : Craftsman House, c1998.
**TC NK7390.A1 A53 1998**

**Jewell, Nancy.** Sailor Song / by Nancy Jewell ; illustrated by Stefano Vitale. New York : Clarion Books, c1999. 1 v. (unpaged) : col. ill. ; 21 cm. SUMMARY: A mother sings her child a song that describes how a sailor makes his way home from the sea to his family. ISBN 0-395-82511-3 DDC [E]
*1. Mother and child - Fiction. 2. Songs - Fiction. 3. Sailors - Fiction. I. Vitale, Stefano, ill. II. Title.*
**TC PZ7.J55325 Sai 1999**

**JEWELLERY. See JEWELRY.**

**JEWELRY - AUSTRALIA - HISTORY - 20TH CENTURY.**
Anderson, Patricia, 1950- Contemporary jewellery in Australia and New Zealand. North Ryde, Sydney : Craftsman House, c1998.
**TC NK7390.A1 A53 1998**

**JEWELRY - NEW ZEALAND - HISTORY - 20TH CENTURY.**
Anderson, Patricia, 1950- Contemporary jewellery in Australia and New Zealand. North Ryde, Sydney : Craftsman House, c1998.
**TC NK7390.A1 A53 1998**

**JEWELRY, PRIMITIVE. See JEWELRY.**

**JEWELS. See JEWELRY.**

**Jewish Board of Family and Children's Services (New York, N.Y.).**
Family and child mental health journal. New York, NY : Human Sciences Press, [c1980-c1982]

**Jewish Board of Guardians.**
Issues in child mental health. [New York, Human Sciences Press]

**JEWISH CATASTROPHE (1939-1945). See HOLOCAUST, JEWISH (1939-1945).**

**JEWISH CHILDREN IN THE HOLOCAUST - POSTERS.**
Civil war [picture]. Amawalk, NY : Jackdaw Publications, c1999.
**TC TR820.5 .C56 1999**

Holocaust children [picture]. Amawalk, NY : Jackdaw Publications, c1999.
**TC TR820.5 .H6 1999**

**JEWISH COLLEGE STUDENTS.**
Winings, Kathy. What has the church/synagogue to do with the academy. 1996.

**TC 06 no. 10718**

**JEWISH DAY SCHOOLS. See JEWISH RELIGIOUS SCHOOLS.**

**JEWISH DAY SCHOOLS - HUNGARY - HISTORY.**
Felkai, László. Zsidó iskolázás Magyarországon, 1780-1990. Budapest : Országos Pedagógiai Könyvtár és Múzeum, [1998]
**TC LC746.H8 F455 1998**

**JEWISH HOLOCAUST (1939-1945). See HOLOCAUST, JEWISH (1939-1945).**

**JEWISH IDENTITY. See JEWS - IDENTITY.**

**JEWISH LAW. See CIVIL RIGHTS (JEWISH LAW); JEWS - IDENTITY.**

**Jewish Museum (New York, N.Y.).**
Kleeblatt, Norman L. An expressionist in Paris. Munich ; New York : Jewish Museum, c1998.
**TC ND553.S7 A4 1998**

**JEWISH NATIONALISM. See JEWS - IDENTITY.**

**JEWISH REFUGEES. See REFUGEES, JEWISH.**

**JEWISH RELIGIOUS EDUCATION. See JEWISH DAY SCHOOLS; JEWISH RELIGIOUS SCHOOLS.**

**JEWISH RELIGIOUS EDUCATION OF TEENAGERS.**
Kohn, Daniel B., 1963- Practical pedagogy for the Jewish classroom. Westport, Conn. : Greenwood Press, 1999.
**TC BM108 .K65 1999**

**JEWISH RELIGIOUS EDUCATION - TEACHING METHODS.**
Kohn, Daniel B., 1963- Practical pedagogy for the Jewish classroom. Westport, Conn. : Greenwood Press, 1999.
**TC BM108 .K65 1999**

**JEWISH RELIGIOUS SCHOOLS. See JEWISH DAY SCHOOLS.**

**JEWISH RELIGIOUS SCHOOLS - HUNGARY - HISTORY.**
Felkai, László. Zsidó iskolázás Magyarországon, 1780-1990. Budapest : Országos Pedagógiai Könyvtár és Múzeum, [1998]
**TC LC746.H8 F455 1998**

**JEWISH SCHOOLS. See JEWISH DAY SCHOOLS; JEWISH RELIGIOUS SCHOOLS.**

**JEWISH SECTS. See CONSERVATIVE JUDAISM.**

**JEWISH STUDENTS - POLAND - WARSAW - INTERVIEWS.**
Ecole 27 [videorecording]. Bruxelles : Paradise Films ; New York, N.Y. : [distributed by] First Run/ Icarus Films, 1997, c1996.
**TC LC746.P7 E2 1997**

**JEWISH TEACHERS - UNITED STATES - ATTITUDES.**
Strangers in the land. New York : Peter Lang, c1999.
**TC E184.36.E84 S77 1999**

**JEWISH THEOLOGICAL SEMINARY OF AMERICA - HISTORY.**
Tradition renewed. 1st ed. New York, N.Y. : The Seminary, 1997.
**TC BM90.J56 T83 1997**

**JEWISH WOMEN - UNITED STATES - BIOGRAPHY.**
Rothenberg, Paula S., 1943- Invisible privilege. Lawrence : University Press of Kansas, c2000.
**TC E185.615 .R68 2000**

**JEWS. See JUDAISM.**

**JEWS - CIVILIZATION. See UNITED STATES - CIVILIZATION - JEWISH INFLUENCES.**

**JEWS - EDUCATION. See JEWISH DAY SCHOOLS; JEWISH RELIGIOUS EDUCATION; JEWISH RELIGIOUS SCHOOLS.**

**JEWS - EDUCATION - POLAND - WARSAW - HISTORY - 20TH CENTURY.**
Ecole 27 [videorecording]. Bruxelles : Paradise Films ; New York, N.Y. : [distributed by] First Run/ Icarus Films, 1997, c1996.
**TC LC746.P7 E2 1997**

**JEWS - EDUCATION - UNITED STATES - PHILOSOPHY.**
Strangers in the land. New York : Peter Lang, c1999.
**TC E184.36.E84 S77 1999**

**JEWS - ETHNIC IDENTITY.** *See* **JEWS - IDENTITY.**

**JEWS - GEORGIA - DECATUR - HISTORY - 20TH CENTURY.**
Keating, Tom, 1941- Saturday school. Bloomington, Ind. : Phi Delta Kappa Educational Foundation, c1999.
*TC LC212.23.D43 K42 1999*

**JEWS - HUNGARY - EDUCATION - HISTORY.**
Felkai, László. Zsidó iskolázás Magyarországon, 1780-1990. Budapest : Országos Pedagógiai Könyvtár és Múzeum, [1998]
*TC LC746.H8 F455 1998*

**JEWS - IDENTITY - CONGRESSES.**
National variations in Jewish identity. Albany, N.Y. : State University of New York Press, 1999.
*TC DS143 .N27 1999*

**JEWS - ISRAEL - IDENTITY - CONGRESSES.**
National variations in Jewish identity. Albany, N.Y. : State University of New York Press, 1999.
*TC DS143 .N27 1999*

**JEWS - LEGAL STATUS, LAWS, ETC.** *See* **JEWS - IDENTITY.**

**JEWS - MIGRATIONS.** *See* **REFUGEES, JEWISH.**

**JEWS - NAZI PERSECUTION.** *See* **HOLOCAUST, JEWISH (1939-1945).**

**JEWS - NEW YORK (STATE) - OSWEGO - JUVENILE FICTION.**
Bat-Ami, Miriam. Two suns in the sky. 1st ed. [Chicago, IL] : Front Street/Cricket Books, 1999.
*TC PZ7.B2939 Tw 1999*

**JEWS - PERSECUTIONS.** *See* **HOLOCAUST, JEWISH (1939-1945).**

**JEWS - POLITICAL AND SOCIAL CONDITIONS.** *See* **JEWS - POLITICS AND GOVERNMENT.**

**JEWS - POLITICS AND GOVERNMENT - PHILOSOPHY.**
Novak, David, 1941- Covenantal rights. Princeton, N.J. : Princeton University Press, 2000.
*TC KC3 .N68 2000*

**JEWS - RACE IDENTITY.** *See* **JEWS - IDENTITY.**

**JEWS - RELIGION.** *See* **JUDAISM.**

**JEWS - RELIGIOUS EDUCATION.** *See* **JEWISH RELIGIOUS EDUCATION.**

**JEWS - RESCUE, 1939-1945.** *See* **WORLD WAR, 1939-1945 - JEWS - RESCUE.**

**JEWS - RUSSIA - FICTION.**
Schur, Maxine. [Shnook the peddler] The peddler's gift. 1st ed. New York : Dial Books for Young Readers, 1999.
*TC PZ7.S3964 Pe 1999*

**JEWS - UNITED STATES - ENCYCLOPEDIAS.**
American Jewish desk reference. 1st ed. New York : Random House, 1999.
*TC E184.35 .A44 1999*

**JEWS - UNITED STATES - FICTION.**
Bat-Ami, Miriam. Two suns in the sky. 1st ed. [Chicago, IL] : Front Street/Cricket Books, 1999.
*TC PZ7.B2939 Tw 1999*

Michelson, Richard. Grandpa's gamble. New York : Marshall Cavendish, 1999.
*TC PZ7.M581915 Gr 1999*

**JEWS - UNITED STATES - IDENTITY.**
Strangers in the land. New York : Peter Lang, c1999.
*TC E184.36.E84 S77 1999*

**JEWS - UNITED STATES - IDENTITY - CONGRESSES.**
National variations in Jewish identity. Albany, N.Y. : State University of New York Press, 1999.
*TC DS143 .N27 1999*

**JEWS - UNITED STATES - INTELLECTUAL LIFE.**
Strangers in the land. New York : Peter Lang, c1999.
*TC E184.36.E84 S77 1999*

**Jex, William W.**
Basic English [videorecording]. [Roslyn Heights, N.Y.] : Video Aided Instruction, [c1995].
*TC PE1128 .B3 1995*

Intermediate English [videorecording]. [Roslyn Heights, N.Y.] : Video Aided Instruction, [c1995].
*TC PE1128 .I5 1995*

**Jezebel's spooky spot.**
Ross, Alice. 1st ed. New York : Dutton Children's Books, 1999.

*TC PZ7.R719694 Jf 1999*

**Języki obce w szkole.** Warszawa : Wydawn. Szkolne i Pedagogiczne, v. ; 24 cm. Frequency: Bimonthly. "Czasopismo dla nauczycieli" Description based on: R.19, nr 2 (mar.-kwiec. 1975) = Nr 93; title from cover. Texts in Polish, English, French and Latin. Issued by: Ministerstwo Oświaty i Wychowania.
*1. Language and languages - Study and teaching - Periodicals. I. Poland. Ministerstwo Oświaty i Wychowania.*

**J.G. Ferguson Publishing Company.**
Career discovery encyclopedia. 4th ed. Chicago : Ferguson Pub. Co., 2000.
*TC HF5381.2 .C37 2000*

**JHI.**
[Journal of the history of ideas (Online)] Journal of the history of ideas [computer file]. Baltimore, MD : Journal of the History of Ideas, Inc., c1996-
*TC EJOURNALS*

**JIGGERMEN.** *See* **POTTERS.**

**Jim Dine.**
Livingstone, Marco. New York : Monacelli Press, 1998.
*TC N6537.D5 A4 1998*

**Jing, Jun, 1957-.**
Feeding China's little emperors. Stanford, Calif. : Stanford University Press, 2000.
*TC TX361.C5 F44 2000*

**Jipson, Janice.**
Paley, Nicholas. Questions of you and the struggle of collaborative life. New York : P. Lang, c2000.
*TC LB1028 .P233 2000*

**Joan of Arc.**
Hodges, Margaret, 1911- 1st ed. New York : Holiday House, c1999.
*TC DC103.5 .H64 1999*

**JOAN, OF ARC, SAINT, 1412-1431.**
Hodges, Margaret, 1911- Joan of Arc. 1st ed. New York : Holiday House, c1999.
*TC DC103.5 .H64 1999*

**JOAN, OF ARC, SAINT, 1412-1431 - JUVENILE LITERATURE.**
Hodges, Margaret, 1911- Joan of Arc. 1st ed. New York : Holiday House, c1999.
*TC DC103.5 .H64 1999*

**JOB BIAS.** *See* **DISCRIMINATION IN EMPLOYMENT.**

**JOB CREATION - GOVERNMENT POLICY - UNITED STATES.**
Job creation. Washington, DC : Joint Center for Political and Economic Studies ; Lanham, Md. ; Oxford : University Press of America, c1998.
*TC HD8081.A65 J63 1998*

**Job creation** : prospects & strategies / edited by Wilhelmina A. Leigh & Margaret C. Simms. Washington, DC : Joint Center for Political and Economic Studies ; Lanham, Md. ; Oxford : University Press of America, c1998. xi, 201 p. ; 24 cm. (Black worker in the 21st century ; v. 1) Includes bibliographical references. ISBN 0-7618-1349-7 (hbk. : alk. paper) ISBN 0-7618-1350-0 (pbk. : alk. paper) DDC 331.6/396073
*1. Afro-Americans - Employment. 2. Afro-Americans - Economic conditions. 3. Job creation - Government policy - United States. 4. Full employment policies - United States. 5. Labor market - United States. 6. Discrimination in employment - United States. I. Leigh, Wilhelmina. II. Simms, Margaret C. III. Series: Black worker in the 21st century.*
*TC HD8081.A65 J63 1998*

**JOB DISCRIMINATION.** *See* **DISCRIMINATION IN EMPLOYMENT.**

**JOB ENRICHMENT.** *See also* **JOB SATISFACTION.**
Rogers, Richard Randall. The impact of gay identity and perceived milieu toward gay employees on job involvement and organizational commitment of gay men. 1998.
*TC 085 R635*

**JOB HUNTING.**
Giangrande, Gregory. The liberal arts advantage. New York : Avon Books, c1998.
*TC HF5382.7 .G53 1998*

Pervola, Cindy, 1956- How to get a job if you're a teenager. Fort Atkinson, Wis. : Alleyside Press, 1998.
*TC HF5383 .P44 1998*

Pervola, Cindy, 1956- How to get a job if you're a teenager. Fort Atkinson, Wis. : Alleyside Press, 1998.

*TC HF5383 .P44 1998*

**JOB HUNTING - GREAT BRITAIN.**
Ali, Lynda, 1946- Moving on in your career. London : New York : RoutledgeFalmer, 2000.
*TC HF1778.4.G7 A45 2000*

**JOB HUNTING - UNITED STATES.**
On the market. 1st Riverhead ed. New York : Riverhead Books, 1997.
*TC LB2331.72 .O5 1997*

**Job involvement and organizational commitment of gay men.**
Rogers, Richard Randall. The impact of gay identity and perceived milieu toward gay employees on job involvement and organizational commitment of gay men. 1998.
*TC 085 R635*

**JOB MOBILITY.** *See* **OCCUPATIONAL MOBILITY.**

**JOB OPENINGS.** *See* **JOB VACANCIES.**

**JOB REQUIREMENTS.** *See* **VOCATIONAL QUALIFICATIONS.**

**JOB SAFETY.** *See* **INDUSTRIAL SAFETY.**

**JOB SATISFACTION.** *See also* **BURN OUT (PSYCHOLOGY); COLLEGE TEACHERS - JOB SATISFACTION.**
Rogers, Richard Randall. The impact of gay identity and perceived milieu toward gay employees on job involvement and organizational commitment of gay men. 1998.
*TC 085 R635*

**Job satisfaction among faculty and staff.**
What contributes to job satisfaction among faculty and staff. San Francisco, Calif. : Jossey-Bass Publishers, c2000.
*TC LB2331.7 .W45 2000*

**JOB SATISFACTION - UNITED STATES.**
What contributes to job satisfaction among faculty and staff. San Francisco, Calif. : Jossey-Bass Publishers, c2000.
*TC LB2331.7 .W45 2000*

**JOB SEARCHING.** *See* **JOB HUNTING.**

**JOB STRESS.** *See also* **BURN OUT (PSYCHOLOGY).**
Grimshaw, Jennie. Employment and health. London : British Library, 1999.
*TC HF5548.85 .G75 1999*

Professional burnout. Washington, DC : Taylor & Francis, c1993.
*TC BF481 .P77 1993*

**JOB STRESS - CONGRESSES.**
Work and well-being. Washington, DC : American Psychological Association, c1992.
*TC RC967.5 .W67 1992*

**JOB STRESS - HEALTH ASPECTS.**
Stress and health. Amsterdam : Harwood Academic ; Abingdon : Marston, 2000.
*TC RA785 .S774 2000*

**JOB TRAINING.** *See* **OCCUPATIONAL TRAINING.**

**JOB VACANCIES - UNITED STATES - CONGRESSES.**
Transitions to adulthood in a changing economy. Westport, Conn. : Praeger, c1999.
*TC HQ799.7 .T73 1999*

**Jobe, Ron.** Reluctant readers : connecting students and books for successful reading experiences / Ron Jobe, Mary Dayton-Sakari. Markham, Ont. : Pembroke Pub., 1999. 160 p. ; 24 cm. Includes bibliographical references and index. ISBN 1-55138-106-0 DDC 372.4
*1. Reading (Elementary) 2. Children - Books and reading. I. Sakari, Mary Dayton, 1941- II. Title.*
*TC LB1573 .J58 1999*

**JOBLESSNESS.** *See* **UNEMPLOYMENT.**

**JOBS.** *See* **OCCUPATIONS; PROFESSIONS.**

**Jocelin, Elizabeth, 1596-1622.** The mothers legacy to her vnborn [i.e. unborn] childe [i.e. child] / Elizabeth Joscelin ; edited with introduction and notes by Jean LeDrew Metcalfe. Toronto : University of Toronto Press, 2000. x, 135 p. : ill. ; 24 cm. Includes bibliographical references and index. ISBN 0-8020-4694-0 (bound) DDC 248.8/2
*1. Children - Religious life - Early works to 1800. 2. Children - Conduct of life - Early works to 1800. 3. Enfants - Vie religieuse - Ouvrages avant 1800. 4. Enfants - Morale pratique - Ouvrages avant 1800. I. Metcalfe, Jean D. LeDrew. II. Title. III. Title: The mothers legacy to her unborn child*

**TC BV4570 .J62 2000**

**Jody, Marilyn, 1932-.**
**Computer conversations.**
Jody, Marilyn, 1932- Using computers to teach literature. 2nd ed. Urbana, Ill. : National Council of Teachers of English, c1998.
**TC LB1050.37 .J63 1998**

Using computers to teach literature : a teacher's guide / Marilyn Jody, Marianne Saccardi. 2nd ed. Urbana, Ill. : National Council of Teachers of English, c1998. xix, 220 p. : ill. ; 24 cm. Rev. ed. of: Computer conversations. c1996. Includes bibliographical references (p. 189-217). ISBN 0-8141-0825-3 DDC 428.4/0285
*1. Reading - Computer-assisted instruction. 2. Language arts - Computer-assisted instruction. 3. Children - United States - Books and reading. 4. World Wide Web. I. Saccardi, Marianne. II. Jody, Marilyn, 1932- Computer conversations. III. Title.*
**TC LB1050.37 .J63 1998**

**Joffe, Hélène.** Risk and 'the other' / Hélène Joffe. Cambridge, U.K. ; New York : Cambridge University Press, 1999. ix, 165 p. ; 24 cm. Includes bibliographical references (p. 146-160) and index. ISBN 0-521-66009-2 (hbk.) ISBN 0-521-66969-3 (pbk.) DDC 302/.12
*1. Risk perception. 2. Social psychology. 3. Other minds (Theory of knowledge) I. Title.*
**TC HM256 .J63 1999**

**Johansen, John H.**
Collins, Harold W. Educational measurement and evaluation, [Glenview, Ill.], Scott, Foresman, [c1969].
**TC LB3051 .C645**

**Johanson, Donald C.**
**Ancestors : in search of human origins.**
In search of human origins [videorecording]. [Boston, Mass.] : WGBH Educational Foundation, c1994.
**TC GN281 .I45 1994**

**Johanson, Donald C. hst.**
In search of human origins [videorecording]. [Boston, Mass.] : WGBH Educational Foundation, c1994.
**TC GN281 .I45 1994**

**Johanson, Lenora.**
**Ancestors : in search of human origins.**
In search of human origins [videorecording]. [Boston, Mass.] : WGBH Educational Foundation, c1994.
**TC GN281 .I45 1994**

In search of human origins [videorecording]. [Boston, Mass.] : WGBH Educational Foundation, c1994.
**TC GN281 .I45 1994**

**John Dewey correspondence.**
Dewey, John, 1859-1952. The correspondence of John Dewey. [computer file]. Windows version. Charlottesville, VA : InteLex Corp., 1999- Computer data and program.
**TC B945.D44 A4 1999**

**John F. Kennedy Center for the Performing Arts (U.S.).**
Antipodean currents. New York : Guggenheim Museum, c1995.
**TC N7404 .A58 1995**

**The John Harvard library**
Paul, Susan, fl. 1837. Memoir of James Jackson, the attentive and obedient scholar, who died in Boston, October 31, 1833, aged six years and eleven months. Cambridge, MA : Harvard University Press, 2000.
**TC F73.9.N4 P38 2000**

**John Marshall High School (Racine, Wis.).**
Get a grip [videorecording]. Racine, WI : S.C. Johnson and Son, Inc., 1999, c1998.
**TC TD170 .G4 1999**

**John, Oliver P.**
Handbook of personality. 2nd ed. New York : Guilford Press, c1999.
**TC BF698 .H335 1999**

**John P. Kotter on what leaders really do.**
Kotter, John P., 1947- Boston : Harvard Business School Press, c1999.
**TC HD57.7 .K665 1999**

**The John Robert Seeley lectures**
Nussbaum, Martha Craven, 1947- Women and human development. Cambridge, U.K. ; New York : Cambridge University Press, 2000.
**TC HQ1240 .N87 2000**

**John Singer Sargent.**
Sargent, John Singer, 1856-1925. Princeton : Princeton University Press, 1998.
**TC ND237.S3 A4 1998a**

**A Johns Hopkins Press health book**
Mace, Nancy L. The 36-hour day. 3rd ed. Baltimore : Johns Hopkins University Press, c1999.
**TC RC523 .M33 1999**

Marr, Lisa. Sexually transmitted diseases. Baltimore, Md : The Johns Hopkins University Press, 1998.
**TC RC200.2 .M27 1998**

**Johns, Jasper, 1930-.**
Varnedoe, Kirk, 1946- Jasper Johns. New York : Museum of Modern Art : Distributed by Harry N. Abrams, c1996.
**TC N6537.J6 A4 1996**

**JOHNS, JASPER, 1930- - EXHIBITIONS.**
Varnedoe, Kirk, 1946- Jasper Johns. New York : Museum of Modern Art : Distributed by Harry N. Abrams, c1996.
**TC N6537.J6 A4 1996**

**Johnson, Andrew P.** Up and out : : using creative and critical thinking skills to enhance learning / Andrew P. Johnson. Boston : Allyn and Bacon, c2000. vii, 165 p. : ill., forms ; 24 cm. Includes bibliographical references and index. ISBN 0-205-29731-5
*1. Thought and thinking - Study and teaching. 2. Critical thinking - Study and teaching. 3. Creative thinking - Study and teaching. 4. Learning. I. Title. II. Title: Using creative and critical thinking skills to enhance learning.*
**TC LB1590.3 .J64 2000**

**Johnson, Art, 1946-** Famous problems and their mathematicians / Art Johnson. Englewood, Colo. : Teacher Ideas Press, 1999. xvi, 179 p. : ill. ; 28 cm. Includes bibliographical references (p. xiii) and index. ISBN 1-56308-446-5 (pbk.) DDC 510/.76
*1. Mathematics - Problems, exercises, etc. 2. Mathematics - History. I. Title.*
**TC QA43 .J56 1999**

**JOHNSON, BONNIE.**
Robbins, Carol Braswell. An examination of critical feminist pedagogy in practice. 1999.
**TC 06 no. 11067**

**Johnson, Burke.** Educational research : quantitative and qualitative approaches / Burke Johnson, Larry Christensen. Boston : Allyn and Bacon, c2000. xxi, 517 p. : ill. ; 25 cm. Includes bibliographical references and index. ISBN 0-205-26659-2 DDC 370/.7/2
*1. Education - Research. I. Christensen, Larry B., 1941- II. Title.*
**TC LB1028 .J59 2000**

**Johnson, Clifton, 1865-1940.** Old-time schools and school-books / by Clifton Johnson ; with many illustrations collected by the author. Detroit : Omnigraphics, 1999. xx1, 381 p. : ill. ;c22 cm. Originally published: New York : Macmillan, 1904. ISBN 1-55888-205-7 (lib. bdg. : alk. paper) DDC 372.973
*1. Education - United States - History. 2. Textbooks - United States. I. Title.*
**TC LA206 .J6 1999**

**Johnson, D. LaMont (Dee LaMont), 1939-.**
Information technology in educational research and statistics. New York : Haworth Press, 1999.
**TC LB1028.3 .I51945 1999**

**Johnson, David E., 1953-.**
Handbook of demonstrations and activities in the teaching of psychology. 2nd ed. Mahwah, N.J. : Lawrence Erlbaum Associates, c2000.
**TC BF77 .H265 2000**

**Johnson, Eastman, 1824-1906.**
Carbone, Teresa A. Eastman Johnson. New York : Brooklyn Museum of Art in association with Rizzoli International Publications, 1999.
**TC ND237.J7 A4 1999**

**JOHNSON, EASTMAN, 1824-1906 - EXHIBITIONS.**
Carbone, Teresa A. Eastman Johnson. New York : Brooklyn Museum of Art in association with Rizzoli International Publications, 1999.
**TC ND237.J7 A4 1999**

**Johnson, Eleanor M. (Eleanor Murdoch), 1892-1987.**
Treat shop / selected and edited by Eleanor M. Johnson and Leland B. Jacobs. Columbus, Ohio : Charles E. Merrill, c1954. 264 p. : col. ill. ; 22 cm. (Treasury of literature ; Readtext series) Includes index.
*1. Children's poetry. 2. Children's stories. I. Jacobs, Leland B. (Leland Blair), 1907- / joint author. II. Title. III. Series.*
**TC PE1119 .J63 1954**

**Johnson, Geraldine A.**
Sculpture and photography. Cambridge, [England] ; New York : Cambridge University Press, 1998.
**TC TR658.3 .S38 1998**

**Johnson, James A.**
Collins, Harold W. Educational measurement and evaluation, [Glenview, Ill.], Scott, Foresman, [c1969].
**TC LB3051 .C645**

**Johnson, Judith.**
Powerful middle schools : teaching and learning for young adolescents (2000) Powerful middle schools [videorecording]. [Washington, D.C.?] : U.S. Dept. of Education, [2000].
**TC LB1623 .P6 2000**

Public charter schools : new choices in public education (May 3, 2000 : Washington, D.C.) Public charter schools [videorecording]. [Washington, D.C.] : U.S. Dept. of Education, [2000].
**TC LB2806.36 .P9 2000**

**Johnson, Katherine, 1958-.**
Staines, Gail M., 1961- Social sciences research. Lanham, Md. ; London : Scarecrow Press, 2000.
**TC H62 .S736 2000**

**Johnson, Kathryn, 1947-.**
Collaborating to improve community health. San Francisco : Jossey-Bass Publishers, c1996.
**TC RA427 .C59 1996**

**Johnson, Kelley, 1947-.**
Women with intellectual disabilities. London ; Philadelphia : Jessica Kingsley Publishers, 2000.
**TC HV3009.5.W65 W66 2000**

**Johnson, Lynn D.** Psychotherapy in the age of accountability / Lynn D. Johnson. 1st ed. New York : W.W. Norton & Co., c1995. xiv, 257 p. ; 25 cm. "A Norton professional book." Includes bibliographical references (p. [233]-243) and index. ISBN 0-393-70209-X DDC 616.89/14
*1. Brief psychotherapy. 2. Eclectic psychotherapy. 3. Managed mental health care. 4. Therapeutic alliance. I. Title.*
**TC RC480.55 .J64 1995**

**Johnson, Martin.** Failing school, failing city : the reality of inner city education / Martin Johnson. Charlbury, Oxfordshire [England] : Jon Carpenter Publishing, 1999. 185 p. ; 24 cm. Includes index. ISBN 1-89776-641-6
*1. Education, Urban - Great Britain. I. Title.*
**TC LC5136.G7 J64 1999**

**Johnson, Norine G.**
Beyond appearance. 1st ed. Washington, DC : American Psychological Association, c1999.
**TC HQ798 .B43 1999**

**Johnson, Orval G., 1917-** Tests and measurements in child development: a handbook [by] Orval G. Johnson [and] James W. Bommarito. [1st ed.]. San Francisco, Jossey-Bass, 1971. xiii, 518 p. 27 cm. (Jossey-Bass behavioral science series) Includes bibliographies. ISBN 0-87589-090-3 DDC 155.41
*1. Psychological tests for children. I. Bommarito, James W., 1922- joint author. II. Title.*
**TC BF722 .J64**

**Johnson, Paul Brett.** Old Dry Frye / by Paul Brett Johnson. New York : Scholastic Press, 1999. 1v. (unpaged) : col. ill. ; 29 cm. SUMMARY: A humorous retelling of an Appalachian folktale about a preacher who chokes on a chicken bone. ISBN 0-590-37658-6 (alk. paper) DDC 398.2/0974/02
*1. Folklore - Appalachian Region. I. Title.*
**TC PZ8.1.J635 O1 1999**

**Johnson, Ralph H.** Manifest rationality : a pragmatic theory of argument / Ralph H. Johnson. Mahwah, N.J. ; London : Lawrence Erlbaum Associates, 2000. xiii, 391 p. : ill. ; 24 cm. Includes bibliographical references (p. 371-380) and indexes. ISBN 0-8058-2173-2 (cloth : alk. paper) ISBN 0-8058-2174-0 (paper : alk. paper) DDC 153.4/3
*1. Reasoning. I. Title.*
**TC BC177 .J54 2000**

**Johnson, Richard T., 1956-** Hands off! : the disappearance of touch in the care of children / Richard T. Johnson. New York : Canterbury [England] : P. Lang, c2000. xviii, 122 p. : ill. ; 23 cm. (Eruptions ; vol. 2) Includes bibliographical references (p. [97]-115) and index. ISBN 0-8204-3983-5 DDC 372.1102/3
*1. Teacher-student relationships. 2. Early childhood education - Social aspects. 3. Child care - Social aspects. 4. Child sexual abuse - Prevention. I. Title. II. Series.*
**TC LB1033 .J63 2000**

**Johnson, Robert R., 1951-** User-centered technology : a rhetorical theory for computers and other mundane artifacts / Robert R. Johnson. Albany : State University of New York Press, c1998. xviii, 195 p. : ill. ; 24 cm. (SUNY series, Studies in scientific and technical communication) Includes bibliographical references (p. 171-187) and index. ISBN 0-7914-3931-3 DDC 808/.0666

*1. User interfaces (Computer systems) 2. Human engineering. 3. Technology - Social aspects. I. Title. II. Series.*
**TC QA76.9.U83 J64 1998**

**Johnson, Tanya F.**
Handbook on ethical issues in aging. Westport, Conn. : Greenwood Press, 1999.
**TC HV1451 .H35 1999**

**Johnson, Tim, 1947-.**
Spirit capture. Washington : Smithsonian Institution Press in association with the National Museum of the American Indian, Smithsonian Institution, c1998.
**TC E77.5 .S65 1998**

**Johnson, Toni Cavanagh.** Sexual, physical, and emotional abuse in out-of-home care : prevention skills for at-risk children / Toni Cavanagh Johnson and associates. New York : The Haworth Maltreatment and Trauma Press, c1997. xii, 118 p. ; 23 cm. Includes bibliographical references (p. 83) and index. ISBN 0-7890-0088-1 (hardcover : alk. paper) ISBN 0-7890-0193-4 (pbk) DDC 618.92/858223
*1. Child abuse - Prevention - Problems, exercises, etc. 2. Children - Institutional care. 3. Group counseling for children. 4. Group counseling. I. Title.*
**TC RJ507.A29 J64 1997**

**Johnson, Tony W.**
Philosophical documents in education. 2nd ed. New York : Longman, c2000.
**TC LB7 .P5432 2000**

**Johnson, Vivien.**
Dreamings of the desert. Adelaide : The Gallery, c1996.
**TC ND1101 .D74 1996**

**Johnson, Wanda Yvonne, 1936-** Youth suicide : the school's role in prevention and response / [Wanda Y. Johnson]. Bloomington, Ind. : Phi Delta Kappa Educational Foundation, c1999. 89 p. ; 23 cm. Includes bibliographical references (p. 79-85). ISBN 0-87367-812-5
*1. Youth - Suicidal behavior - Prevention. 2. Suicide - Prevention. 3. Counseling in secondary education. I. Title.*
**TC HV6546 .J645 1999**

**Johnson Wax.**
Get a grip [videorecording]. Racine, WI : S.C. Johnson and Son, Inc., 1999, c1998.
**TC TD170 .G4 1999**

**Johnston, Jane, 1954-** Enriching early scientific learning / Jane Johnston and Adelaide Gray. Philadelphia : Open University Press, 1999. 100 p. : ill. ; 27 cm. Includes bibliographical references and index. ISBN 0-335-20393-0 (pbk) DDC 372.3/5044
*1. Science - Study and teaching. 2. Science - Study and teaching (Early childhood) 3. Science - Study and teaching (Early childhood) - Activity programs. 4. Learning, Psychology of. 5. Science teachers - Training of. I. Gray, Adelaide. 1973- II. Title.*
**TC Q181 .J58 1999**

**Johnston, Marilyn, 1942-.**
Collaborative reform and other improbable dreams. Albany, N.Y. : State University of New York Press, 2000.
**TC LB2154.A3 C65 2000**

**Johnston, Peter H.**
Running records. York, Me. : Stenhouse Publishers , 2000.
**TC LB1525 R75 2000**

**Johnston-Wilder, Sue.**
Learning to teach mathematics in the secondary school. New York : Routledge, 1999.
**TC QA13 .L4 1999**

**JOINDER OF PARTIES. See INTERVENTION (CIVIL PROCEDURE).**

**Joiner, Thomas E.**
Suicide science. Boston ; London : Kluwer Academic Publishers, c2000.
**TC RC569 .S9368 2000**

**Joint Commission on Accreditation of Healthcare Organizations.** Hospital accreditation standards : HAS / standards, intents : HAS / Joint Commission. Oakbrook Terrace, Ill. : The Commission, c1996- v. ; 23 cm. 1997- . HAS. Includes "the glossary from the Comprehensive accreditation manual for hospitals: the official handbook (CAMH)." Also issued as part of: Comprehensive accreditation manual for hospitals. Continues: Joint Commission on Accreditation of Healthcare Organizations. Accreditation manual for hospitals. Volume I, Standards ISSN: 1083-1762 (DLC) 96647179 (OCoLC)32724565. Comprehensive accreditation manual for hospitals ISSN: 1076-5638 (DLC) 94641130 (OCoLC)30534608. DDC 362.1/1/021873
*1. Hospitals - Accreditation - Standards - United States -*

*Periodicals. 2. Accreditation - standards - United States - periodicals. 3. Hospitals - standards - United States - periodicals. I. Title. II. Title: HAS III. Title: Joint Commission on Accreditation of Healthcare Organizations. Accreditation manual for hospitals. Volume I. Standards IV. Title: Comprehensive accreditation manual for hospitals*
**TC RA981.A2 J59a**

**Joint Commission on Accreditation of Healthcare Organizations. Accreditation manual for hospitals. Volume I, Standards.**
Joint Commission on Accreditation of Healthcare Organizations. Hospital accreditation standards : HAS. Oakbrook Terrace, Ill. : The Commission, c1996-
**TC RA981.A2 J59a**

**JOINT VENTURES. See INTERNATIONAL BUSINESS ENTERPRISES.**

**JOINTS - PATHOPHYSIOLOGY.**
Proprioception and neuromuscular control in joint stability. [Champaign, IL] : Human Kinetics, c2000.
**TC QP454 .P77 2000**

**JOKES. See WIT AND HUMOR.**

**JOKING. See PRACTICAL JOKES; WIT AND HUMOR.**

**Jolliffe, Alan.**
Forsyth, Ian. The complete guide to teaching a course. 2nd ed. London : Kogan Page ; Sterling, VA : Stylus Publishing, 1999.
**TC LB1025.3 .F67 1999**

**Jolly, Alison.** Lucy's legacy : sex and intelligence in human evolution / Alison Jolly. Cambridge, Mass. : London : Harvard University Press, 1999. 518 p. : ill. ; 25 cm. Includes bibliographical references (p. 437-499) and index. ISBN 0-674-00069-2 (alk. paper) DDC 599.93/8
*1. Human evolution. 2. Social evolution. 3. Women - Evolution. 4. Intelligence. I. Title.*
**TC GN281 .J6 1999**

**Jonas, Ann.** Where can it be? / Ann Jonas. 1st ed. New York : Greenwillow Books, c1986. [32] p. : col. ill. ; 21 cm. SUMMARY: A child looks all over the house for her missing blanket. Uses flaps to reveal what the child finds behind closed doors. ISBN 0-688-05169-3 ISBN 0-688-05246-0 (lib. bdg.) DDC [E]
*1. Toy and movable books - Specimens. 2. Lost and found possessions - Fiction. 3. Toy and movable books. I. Title.*
**TC PZ7.J664 Wi 1986**

**Jonas, Steven.** Talking about health and wellness with patients : integrating health promotion and disease prevention into your practice / Steven Jonas. New York : Springer, c2000. xv, 144 p. ; 23 cm. Includes bibliographical references (p. 131-137) and index. ISBN 0-8261-1338-9 (sc) DDC 613
*1. Health promotion. 2. Medicine, Preventive. 3. Clinical health psychology. 4. Health. I. Title.*
**TC RA427.8 .J66 2000**

**Jonassen, David H., 1947-** Task analysis methods for instructional design / David H. Jonassen, Martin Tessmer, Wallace H. Hannum. Mahwah, N.J. : L. Erlbaum Associates, 1999. viii, 275 p. : ill. ; 25 cm. Includes bibliographical references and index. ISBN 0-8058-3085-5 (alk. paper) DDC 370.15/23
*1. Instructional systems - Design. 2. Task analysis in education. I. Tessmer, Martin. II. Hannum, Wallace H. III. Title.*
**TC LB1028.38 J65 1999**

**Joncas, Richard, 1953-** Stanford University / Richard Joncas, David J. Neuman, and Paul V. Turner. 1st ed. New York : Princeton Architectural Press, 1999. ix, 175 p. : ill. (some col.), maps (some col.) ; 26 cm. (The campus guide) Maps of campus on endpapers. Includes bibliographical references (p. 160-168) and index. ISBN 1-56898-169-4 (alk. paper) DDC 378.794/73
*1. Stanford University - Guidebooks. 2. Stanford University - Buildings. 3. Stanford University - Buildings - Pictorial works. 4. Stanford University - Buildings - History. I. Neuman, David J. II. Turner, Paul Venable. III. Title. IV. Series: Campus guide (New York, N.Y.)*
**TC LD3031 .J65 1999**

**The Jones and Bartlett series in biology**
McConkey, Edwin H. Human genetics. Boston : Jones and Bartlett Publishers, c1993.
**TC QH431 .M3298 1993**

**The Jones and Bartlett series in health sciences**
Page, Randy M. Fostering emotional well-being in the classroom. 2nd ed. Sudbury, Mass. ; London : Jones and Bartlett Publishers, c2000.
**TC LB3430 .P34 2000**

**Jones and Bartlett series in oncology**
Quality of life from nursing and patient perspectives. Sudbury, Mass. ; London : Jones and Bartlett, c1998.
**TC RC262 .Q34 1998**

**Jones, Beau Fly.**
Plugging in :. Washington, D.C. : NEKIA Communications ; Oak Brook, Ill. : North Central Regional Educational Laboratory, [1995]. ([1999]).
**TC LB1028.3 .P584 1995**

**Jones, Bruce Anthony.**
Educational leadership. Stamford, Conn. : Ablex Pub. Corp., c2000.
**TC LB2805 .E3475 2000**

**Jones, Carl Mounsey.** The film-audience relationship : laughter at a comic film / Carl Mounsey Jones. 1997. v, 112 leaves : ill ; 29 cm. Typescript; issued also on microfilm. Thesis (Ed.D.)--Teachers College, Columbia University, 1997. Includes bibliographical references (leaves 109-112).
*1. Discourse analysis. 2. Conversation analysis. 3. Comedy films. 4. Mass media - Audiences. 5. Communication. 6. Laughter - Data processing. I. Title.*
**TC 06 no. 10769**

The film-audience relationship : laughter at a comic film / Carl Mounsey Jones. 1997. v, 112 leaves : ill ; 29 cm. Typescript; issued also on microfilm. Thesis (Ed.D.)--Teachers College, Columbia University, 1997. Includes bibliographical references (leaves 109-112).
*1. Discourse analysis. 2. Conversation analysis. 3. Comedy films. 4. Mass media - Audiences. 5. Communication. 6. Laughter - Data processing. I. Title.*
**TC 06 no. 10769**

**Jones, Carol, ill.**
This old man. 1st American ed. Boston : Houghton Mifflin, 1990.
**TC PZ8.3 .T2965 1990b**

**Jones, Carroll J.** Curriculum-based assessment : the easy way / Carroll J. Jones. Springfield, Ill. : C.C. Thomas, Publisher, c1998. xix, 156 p. : ill. ; 28 cm. Includes bibliographical references (p. 155-156). ISBN 0-398-06896-8 (pbk.) DDC 371.26/4
*1. Curriculum-based assessment - United States. 2. Educational tests and measurements - United States. 3. Learning disabled children - Education - United States. I. Title.*
**TC LB3060.32.C74 J66 1998**

**Jones, Carys.**
Students writing in the university. Amsterdam ; Philadelphia : John Benjamins Pub., c1999.
**TC PE1405.G7 S78 1999**

**JONES, CASEY, 1863-1900 - LEGENDS.**
Farmer, Nancy. Casey Jones's fireman. 1st ed. New York : Phyllis Fogelman Books, c1998.
**TC PZ8.1.F2225 Cas 1998**

Farmer, Nancy. Casey Jones's fireman. 1st ed. New York : Phyllis Fogelman Books, c1998.
**TC PZ8.1.F2225 Cas 1998**

**Jones, Charlotte Foltz.** Yukon gold : the story of the Klondike Gold Rush / Charlotte Foltz Jones. 1st ed. New York : Holiday House, c1999. 99 p. : ill., maps ; 24 cm. Includes bibliographical references (p. 91-92) and index. SUMMARY: Recounts the quest for gold that took place in the late 1890s in the Klondike region of the Yukon Territory of northwestern Canada. ISBN 0-8234-1403-5 (alk. paper) DDC 971.9/1
*1. Klondike River Valley (Yukon) - Gold discoveries - Juvenile literature. 2. Klondike River Valley (Yukon) - Gold discoveries. I. Title.*
**TC F1095.K5 J66 1999**

**Jones, Clare B.**
Parent articles about ADHD. San Antonio, Texas : Communication Skill Builders, c1999.
**TC RJ506.H9 P37 1999**

**Jones, Jack.**
Hand in hand [videorecording]. New York, N.Y. : AFB Press, c1995.
**TC HV1597.2 .H3 1995**

Making the most of early communication [videorecording]. New York, NY : Distributed by AFB Press, c1997.
**TC HV1597.2 .M3 1997**

**Jones, Janet L.** The psychotherapist's guide to human memory / Janet L. Jones. New York : Basic Books, c1999. vii, 296 p. : ill. ; 25 cm. (Basic behavioral science) Includes bibliographical references (p. 263-281) and index. ISBN 0-465-08517-2
*1. Memory. 2. Psychotherapy. I. Title. II. Title: Human memory*
**TC BF371 .J66 1999**

**Jones, Jennifer B.** Dear Mrs. Ryan, you're ruining my life / Jennifer B. Jones. New York : Walker & Co., 2000. 122 p. ; 22 cm. SUMMARY: In an effort to get his

mother to stop writing about him in her books, fifth-grader Harvey and his best friend decide to try to make a romantic connection between her and their school principal. ISBN 0-8027-8728-2 (HC) DDC [Fic]
*1. Mothers and sons - Fiction. 2. School stories. 3. Authors - Fiction. 4. Divorce - Fiction. 5. Friendship - Fiction. 6. Baseball - Fiction. I. Title.*
**TC PZ7.J7203 De 2000**

**Jones, John Charles.** Learning [by] J. Charles Jones. New York, Harcourt, Brace & World [1967] xi, 179 p. illus. 22 cm. (Professional education for teachers series) Includes bibliographies. DDC 370.15
*1. Learning. I. Title.*
**TC LB1051 .J59 1967**

**Jones, Joy.** Tambourine moon / Joy Jones ; illustrated by Terry Widener. New York : Simon & Schuster, 1999. 1 v. (unpaged) : col. ill. ; 26 cm. SUMMARY: Noni is afraid as she and her grandaddy walk home, until he tells her how he met her Granma Ismay one dark night in Alabama and how the big yellow moon came to light up the sky. ISBN 0-689-80648-5 DDC [E]
*1. Night - Fiction. 2. Grandfathers - Fiction. 3. Moon - Fiction. 4. Afro-Americans - Fiction. I. Widener, Terry. ill. II. Title.*
**TC PZ7.J72025 Tam 1999**

**Jones, Kathleen W.** Taming the troublesome child : American families, child guidance, and the limits of psychiatric authority / Kathleen W. Jones. Cambridge, Mass : Harvard University Press, 1999. x, 310, ; 25 cm. Includes bibliographical references and index. ISBN 0-674-86811-0 (alk. paper) DDC 362.2/083/0973
*1. Child mental health services - United States - History - 20th century. 2. Child guidance clinics - United States - History - 20th century. 3. Problem children - United States - History - 20th century. 4. Problem youth - United States - History - 20th century. I. Title.*
**TC RJ501.A2 J64 1999**

**Jones, Ken, 1949-.** Accountability, assessment, and teacher commitment. Albany, N.Y. : State University of New York Press, 2000.
**TC LB2806.22 .A249 2000**

**Jones, Louise S., 1949-.** Jones, Vernon F., 1945- Comprehensive classroom management. 6th ed. Boston : Allyn and Bacon, c2001.
**TC LB3013 .J66 2001**

**Jones, Mark W. (Mark Walter), 1947-** Dancer's resource : the Watson-Guptill guide to academic programs, internships and apprentice programs, residential and artist-in-residence programs, studio schools and private teachers, workshops and festivals / Mark W. Jones. New York : Watson-Guptill Publications, c1999. 208 p. : ill. ; 24 cm. (Getting your act together) Includes bibliographical references (p. 189-190) and index. ISBN 0-8230-7656-3 (pbk) DDC 792.8/071/073
*1. Dance - Study and teaching - United States - States - Directories. 2. Dance - Vocational guidance - United States. I. Watson-Guptill Publications. II. Title. III. Series.*
**TC GV1589 .J65 1999**

**Jones, Peter, 1929-.** In search of human origins [videorecording]. [Boston, Mass.] : WGBH Educational Foundation, c1994.
**TC GN281 .I45 1994**

**Jones, Reginald Lanier, 1931-.** Advances in African American psychology. Hampton, VA : Cobb & Henry, 1999.
**TC E185.625 .A36 1999**

**Jones, Robin R., 1946-.** Portz, John, 1953- City schools and city politics. Lawrence : University Press of Kansas, c1999.
**TC LC5131 .P67 1999**

**Jones, Robin (Robin E.).** Sport and physical education in China. London ; New York : Routledge, 1999.
**TC GV651 .S655 1999**

**Jones, Sharon L., 1961-.** Building an emergency plan. Los Angeles, Calif. : Getty Conservation Institute, c1999.
**TC AM121 .B85 1999**

**Jones, Tammy (Tammy P.).** Dorn, Linda J. Apprenticeship in literacy. York, Me. : Stenhouse Publishers, c1998.
**TC LB1139.5.L35 D67 1998**

**Jones, Thomas D.** English, June, 1955- Scholastic encyclopedia of the United States at war. New York : Scholastic, 1998.
**TC E181 .E64 1998**

**Jones, Vernon F., 1945-** Comprehensive classroom management : creating communities of support and solving problems / Vernon F. Jones with Louise S. Jones. 6th ed. Boston : Allyn and Bacon, c2001. xvi, 463 p. : ill. ; 25 cm. Includes bibliographical references (p. 440-450) and indexes. ISBN 0-205-31850-9 (alk. paper) DDC 371.5/3
*1. Classroom management. 2. Interaction analysis in education. 3. Motivation in education. 4. School discipline. I. Jones. Louise S., 1949- II. Title.*
**TC LB3013 . J66 2001**

**Jongbloed, B. W. A.** From the eye of the storm. Dordrecht ; Boston ; London: Kluwer Academic Publishers, c1999.
**TC LB2341.8.E85 F76 1999**

**Jooss, Walter.** Sport photography today! [videorecording]. Minneapolis, Minn. : Media Loft, c1992.
**TC TR821 .S64 1992**

**Joosten, Vera.** Inglis, Alistair. Delivering digitally. London : Kogan Page, c1999.
**TC LB1044.87 .I545 1999**

**Jordan, Dianne H., 1950-.** Belanger, France, 1963- Evaluation and implementation of distance learning. Hershey, PA ; London : Idea Group Pub., c2000.
**TC LC5803.C65 B45 2000**

**Jordan, Tim, 1959-** Cyberpower : the culture and politics of cyberspace and the Internet / Tim Jordan. London ; New York : Routledge, 1999. vii, 254 p. : ill. ; 24 cm. Includes bibliographical references (p. [233]-247) and index. ISBN 0-415-17077-X (hbk) ISBN 0-415-17078-8 (pbk.) DDC 303.48/33
*1. Cyberspace - Social aspects. 2. Telematics - Social aspects. 3. Power (Social sciences) 4. Internet (Computer network) - Social aspects. I. Title.*
**TC ZA4375 .J67 1999**

**Jordan, Van.** The nutty, nougat-filled world of human nutrition [videorecording]. [Arlington, Va.] : Cerebellum Corp., c1998.
**TC QP141 .N8 1998**

**Jorgensen, Peter F.** Encyclopedia of human emotions. New York : Macmillan Reference USA, c1999.
**TC BF531 .E55 1999**

**José Limón.** Limón, José. Hanover, NH : University Press of New England, [1998?]
**TC GV1785.L515 A3 1998**

**Joseph had a little overcoat.** Taback, Simms. New York : Viking, 1999.
**TC PZ7.T1115 Jo 1999**

**Joseph, Linda C., 1949-** Net curriculum : an educator's guide to using the Internet / by Linda C. Joseph. Medford, N.J. : CyberAge Books, c1999. xvi, 193 p. : ill. ; 24 cm. Includes indexes. ISBN 0-910965-30-7 (pbk.) DDC 371.33/44678
*1. Teaching - Computer network resources. 2. Education - Computer network resources. 3. Internet (Computer network) in education. I. Title.*
**TC LB1044.87 J67 1999**

**Joseph, Pamela Bolotin.** Cultures of curriculum. Mahwah, N.J. ; London : L. Erlbaum Associates, 2000.
**TC LB2806.15 .C73 2000**

**Joseph Rowntree Foundation.** Vernon, Jeni. Maintaining children in school. London : National Children's Bureau Enterprises, c1998.
**TC LB3081 .V47 1998**

**Joseph, Russell.** Stress free teaching : : a practical guide to tackling stress in teaching, lecturing and tutoring / Russell Joseph. London ; Sterling, VA : Kogan Page, 2000. xi, 144 p. ; 22 cm. Includes index. ISBN 0-7494-3114-8
*1. Teachers - Job stress. 2. Stress management. I. Title.*
**TC LB2840.2 .J67 2000**

**JOSEPH, SAINT - FICTION.** De Paola, Tomie. The night of Las Posadas. New York : Putnam's, 1999.
**TC PZ7.D439 Ni 1999**

**Joslyn Museum of Art.** Kinsey, Joni. Plain pictures. Washington, : Published for the University of Iowa Museum of Art by the Smithsonian Institution Press, 1996.
**TC N8214.5.U6 K56 1996**

**The Jossey-Bass business & management series** Crainer, Stuart. Gravy training. 1st ed. San Francisco : Jossey-Bass Publishers, c1999.
**TC HF1111 .C7 1999**

**Jossey-Bass business & management series** Multilevel theory, research, and methods in organizations. 1st ed. San Francisco : Jossey-Bass, c2000.
**TC HF5548.8 .M815 2000**

**The Jossey-Bass education series** Deal, Terrence E. Shaping school culture. 1st ed. San Francisco : Jossey-Bass Publishers, c1999.
**TC LB2805 .D34 1999**

**Jossey-Bass education series** Evaluation as a democratic process. San Francisco, CA : Jossey-Bass, c2000.
**TC LB2806 .E79 2000**

**The Jossey-Bass education series** Homeless and working youth around the world. San Francisco : Jossey-Bass, 1999.
**TC HV4493 .H655 1999**

**The Jossey-Bass education series** The Jossey-Bass reader on technology and learning. 1st ed. San Francisco, Calif. : Jossey-Bass, c2000.
**TC LB1028.3 .J66 2000**

**Jossey-Bass education series.** Merriam, Sharan B. Qualitative research and case study applications in education. 2nd ed. San Francisco : Jossey-Bass Publishers, c1998.
**TC LB1028 .M396 1998**

**The Jossey-Bass education series** Reading for understanding. 1st ed. San Francisco, Calif. : Jossey-Bass Publishers, c1999.
**TC LB1632 .R357 1999**

Steinberg, Adria. Schooling for the real world. 1st ed. San Francisco : Jossey-Bass, c1999.
**TC LC1037.5 .S843 1999**

**Jossey-Bass education series** Variability in the social construction of the child. San Francisco : Jossey-Bass, 2000.
**TC BF723.S62 .V37 2000**

**The Jossey-Bass handbook of nonprofit leadership and management** / Robert D. Herman and associates. 1st ed. San Francisco : Jossey-Bass, c1994. xxvi, 653 p. : ill. ; 26 cm. (The Jossey-Bass nonprofit sector series) Includes bibliographical references and index. ISBN 1-55542-651-4 DDC 658/.048
*1. Nonprofit organizations - Management. I. Herman, Robert D., 1946- II. Title: Handbook of nonprofit leadership and management. III. Series.*
**TC HD62.6 .J67 1994**

**Jossey-Bass health care series** Morrison, J. Ian, 1952- Health care in the new millennium. 1st ed. San Francisco : Jossey-Bass Publishers, c2000.
**TC RA395.A3 M675 2000**

**Jossey-Bass health series** Health behavior and health education. 2nd ed. San Francisco : Jossey-Bass, 1997.
**TC RA776.9 .H434 1997**

Sherman, V. Clayton. Raising standards in American health care. 1st ed. San Francisco : Jossey-Bass, c1999.
**TC RA395.A3 S483 1999**

**The Jossey-Bass higher and adult education series** Academic advising. 1st ed. San Francisco : Jossey-Bass, c2000.
**TC LB2343 .A29 2000**

**Jossey-Bass Higher and adult Education Series.** Analyzing costs in higher education. San Francisco, Calif. : Jossey-Bass Publishers, c2000.
**TC LB2342 .A68 2000**

**The Jossey-Bass higher and adult education series** Barr, Margaret J. The handbook of student affairs administration. 2nd ed. San Francisco : Jossey-Bass, c2000.
**TC LB2342.92 .B37 2000**

Bess, James L. Teaching alone, teaching together. 1st ed. San Francisco : Jossey-Bass, c2000.
**TC LB2331 .B48 2000**

**Jossey-Bass higher and adult education series** Dominicé, Pierre. Learning from our lives. 1st ed. San Francisco : Jossey-Bass, c2000.
**TC LB1029.B55 D64 2000**

**The Jossey-Bass higher and adult education series** Ender, Steven C. Students helping students. 1st ed. San Francisco : Jossey-Bass Publishers, c2000.

**TC LB1027.5 .E52 2000**

Hawke, Constance S., 1952- Computer and Internet use on campus. 1st ed. San Francisco : Jossey-Bass, c2001.
**TC KF390.5.C6 H39 2001**

**Jossey-Bass higher and adult education series.**
Hayes, Elisabeth. Women as learners. 1st ed. San Francisco : Jossey-Bass Publishers, c2000.
**TC LC5225.L42 H39 2000**

Involving commuter students in learning. San Francisco, Calif. : Jossey-Bass, 2000.
**TC LB2343.6 .I68 2000**

**The Jossey-Bass higher and adult education series**
Lucas, Ann F. Leading academic change. 1st ed. San Francisco : Jossey-Bass, c2000.
**TC LB2341 .L82 2000**

Mentkowski, Marcia. Learning that lasts. 1st ed. San Francisco : Jossey-Bass, c2000.
**TC LB1060 .M464 2000**

**Jossey-Bass higher and adult education series.**
Merriam, Sharan B. Qualitative research and case study applications in education. 2nd ed. San Francisco : Jossey-Bass Publishers, c1998.
**TC LB1028 .M396 1998**

Nelson, Michael, 1949- Alive at the core. 1st ed. San Francisco : Jossey-Bass, c2000.
**TC AZ183.U5 N45 2000**

Powerful programming for student learning. San Francisco : Jossey-Bass, c2000.
**TC LB2343 .P643 2000**

**The Jossey-Bass higher and adult education series**
Strange, Charles Carney. Educating by design. 1st ed. San Francisco : Jossey-Bass, c2001.
**TC LB2324 .S77 2001**

Taylor, Kathleen, 1943- Developing adult learners. 1st ed. San Francisco : Jossey-Bass, c2000.
**TC LC5225.L42 T39 2000**

**Jossey-Bass higher and adult education series**
Trends in community college curriculum. San Francisco : Jossey-Bass, c1999.
**TC LB2328.15.U6 T75 1999**

Understanding the work and career paths of midlevel administrators. San Francisco : Jossey-Bass, 2000.
**TC LB2341 .N5111 2000**

Using consultants to improve teaching. San Francisco : Jossey-Bass, c1999.
**TC LB2799.2 .U83 1999**

**The Jossey-Bass higher and adult education series**
Vella, Jane Kathryn, 1931- Taking learning to task. San Francisco, Calif. : Jossey-Bass, c2000.
**TC LC5225.L42 V43 2000**

Zachary, Lois J. The mentor's guide. 1st ed. San Francisco : Jossey-Bass Publishers, c2000.
**TC LB1731.4 .Z23 2000**

**Jossey-Bass Inc.**
The Jossey-Bass reader on technology and learning. 1st ed. San Francisco, Calif. : Jossey-Bass, c2000.
**TC LB1028.3 .J66 2000**

**The Jossey-Bass management series**
Mohrman, Allan M. Designing performance appraisal systems. 1st ed. San Francisco : Jossey-Bass Publishers, 1989.
**TC HF5549.5.P35 M64 1989**

Parker, Glenn M., 1938- Cross-functional teams. 1st ed. San Francisco, Calif. : Jossey-Bass, c1994.
**TC HD66 .P345 1994**

**The Jossey-Bass nonprofit sector series**
The Jossey-Bass handbook of nonprofit leadership and management. 1st ed. San Francisco : Jossey-Bass, c1994.
**TC HD62.6 .J67 1994**

Mixer, Joseph R., 1923- Principles of professional fundraising. 1st ed. San Francisco : Jossey-Bass, c1993.
**TC HV41.9.U5 M58 1993**

Prince, Russ Alan, 1958- The seven faces of philanthropy. 1st ed. San Francisco : Jossey-Bass, c1994.
**TC HV41.9.U5 P74 1994**

Shaw, Sondra C., 1936- Reinventing fundraising. 1st ed. San Francisco : Jossey-Bass Publishers, c1995.
**TC HV41.9.U5 S53 1995**

**The Jossey-Bass reader on technology and learning /** introduction by Roy D. Pea. 1st ed. San Francisco, Calif. : Jossey-Bass, c2000. xxv, 341 p. ; 23 cm. (The Jossey-Bass education series) Includes bibliographical references. ISBN 0-7879-5282-6 DDC 371.33/4
*1. Educational technology - United States. 2. Computer-assisted instruction - United States. 3. Education - United States - Data processing. I. Jossey-Bass Inc. II. Series.*
**TC LB1028.3 .J66 2000**

**Jossey-Bass social and behavioral science series.**
Multilevel theory, research, and methods in organizations. 1st ed. San Francisco : Jossey-Bass, c2000.
**TC HF5548.8 .M815 2000**

**Journal.**
University of Pittsburgh. School of Education. [Lancaster, Pa. : The School, 1925-

**Journal canadien des sciences appliquées au sport.**
Canadian journal of applied sport sciences = Windsor, Ont. : Canadian Association of Sports Sciences,

**Journal de mathématiques élémentaires.** [Paris : s.n., v. : ill. ; 28 cm. Frequency: Semimonthly. Began publication with janv. 1877.
*1. Mathematics - Periodicals.*

**Journal for readers, students and teachers of history.**
Historical outlook. Philadelphia, Pa. : McKinley Pub. Co., c1918-c1933.

**Journal for truancy and dropout prevention.**
International Association of Pupil Personnel Workers. The Journal. [Baton Rouge, La., etc.] International Association of Pupil Personnel Workers.

**[Journal (Martha Holden Jennings Foundation)]**
Journal / The Martha Holden Jennings Foundation. [Cleveland : The Foundation, 1974- v. : ill. ; 22 cm. Frequency: Twice a year. Vol. 1, no. 1 (Feb. 1974)- . Other title: Martha Holden Jennings journal. Description based on: v. 4, no. 1 (winter 1978); title from caption. "Summary : reports from the Martha Holden Jennings Foundation."
*1. Education - Ohio - Periodicals. 2. Education - Periodicals. 3. Teaching - Periodicals. I. Martha Holden Jennings Foundation. II. Title: Martha Holden Jennings journal*

**[Journal of adult education (New York, N.Y.)]** Journal of adult education. New York : American Association for Adult Education, 1929-[1941] 13 v. : ill. ; 26 cm. Frequency: Four times a year. [Vol. 1, no. 1] (Feb. 1929)-v. 13, no. 4 (Oct. 1941). Issues for 1934-35 include: Bulletin of the Adult Education Department of the National Education Association, which is published separately beginning with 1936 as Adult education bulletin. Edited by M. A. Cartwright (with Mary L. Ely, 1929-Jan. 1937, Oct. 1938-1941; with R. A. Beals, Apr. 1937-June 1928) June issues (Oct. in 1940) includes the Annual report of the director of the American Association for Adult Education for the preceding year. Continues: Journal of the American Association for Adult Education (DLC) 30000415 (OCoLC)9980813. Continued by: Adult education journal ISSN: 0888-5060 (DLC) 44003576 (OCoLC)1461121. American Association for Adult Education. Annual report of the director (OCoLC)2056152. ISSN 0888-5044 DDC 374
*1. Adult education - Periodicals. I. Cartwright, Morse A. (Morse Adams), 1890- II. Ely, Mary L. (Mary Lillian) III. Beals, Ralph A. (Ralph Albert) IV. American Association for Adult Education. V. Title: Bulletin of Adult Education Department. VI. Title: Journal of the American Association for Adult Education VII. Title: Adult education bulletin VIII. Title: Adult education journal IX. Title: American Association for Adult Education. Annual report of the director*

**Journal of adult education (New York, N.Y.).**
Journal of the American Association for Adult Education. New York, N.Y. : The Association, [1926-1928]

**Journal of animal behavior.**
The Journal of comparative and physiological psychology. Baltimore, 1921-82.

**The Journal of animal behavior.** Cambridge, Mass., H. Holt and Company; [etc., etc., 1911-17] 7 v. ill., plates, diagrs. 26 cm. v. 1-7; Jan./Feb. 1911-Nov./Dec. 1917. In Feb. 1921 united with Psychobiology to form the Journal of comparative psychology. ISSN 0095-9928
*1. Animals, Habits and behavior of - Periodicals. 2. Psychology, Comparative - Periodicals. I. Yerkes, Robert Mearns, 1876- ed. II. Title: Psychobiology 1921-1946 III. Title: Journal of comparative psychology*

**Journal of anthropology (Online).**
[Journal of the Anthropological Institute of Great Britain and Ireland (Online)] The journal of the Anthropological Institute of Great Britain and Ireland [computer file]. London [England] : Published for the Anthropological Institute of Great Britain and Ireland by Trübner & Co., 1872-1906.
**TC EJOURNALS**

**The Journal of Arkansas education.** [Little Rock : Arkansas Educational Association, 1923-1975]. 53 v. : ill. ; 26 cm. Frequency: Monthly (except July-Aug.). Began with: v. 1 (Jan. 1923); ceased with: v. [53], in 1975. Description based on: v. 3, no. 7 (Mar. 1925); title from cover. Volume numbers irregular: v. 10, nos. 6-7/8 incorrectly numbered 5-6; v. 12 numbered v. 10; 1956/57 and 1957/58 both called v. 30. Vols. for Sept. 1935-1975 called v. 9-47, but constitute v. 14-53. Official organ: Arkansas Education Association. Combining and continuing the Arkansas teacher, the Journal of the Arkansas Education Association, the Educational news bulletin.
*1. Tucker, Everett Brackin, ed. II. Lambert, H.L., ed. III. Arkansas Education Association. IV. Title: Arkansas teacher V. Title: Arkansas Education Association. Journal VI. Title: Educational news bulletin*

**Journal of Association of Principals of Technical Institutions.**
Association of Principals of Technical Institutions (India). Delhi, The Association.

**Journal of broadcasting.** Phila., Pa.[etc.] Association for Professional Broadcasting Education. 23 cm. Frequency: Quarterly. V.1-28 ; Winter 1956/57-1984. Vol. 1-25, 1956-1981. 1v. Continued by: Journal of broadcasting & electronic media.
*1. Radio broadcasting - Periodicals. 2. Television broadcasting - Periodicals. I. Title: Journal of broadcasting & electronic media*

**Journal of broadcasting & electronic media.**
Journal of broadcasting. Phila., Pa.[etc.] Association for Professional Broadcasting Education.

**The Journal of business education** New York City, The Haire Publishing Company. v. illus., ports. 31 cm. Frequency: Monthly. Vol. 1, nos. 1-6 have title: Business school journal. Absorbed the Journal of commercial education in March 1929.
*1. Business education - Periodicals. I. Title: Business school journal II. Title: Journal of commercial education*

**The Journal of child psychiatry.** New York : Child Care Publications, 1947-1956. 3 v. : ill. ; 26 cm. Frequency: Three sect. per vol., v. 1- . v. 1-3, no. 2 (1947-Aug. 1956). DDC 618.92
*1. Child psychiatry. 2. Child Psychiatry - periodicals.*

**The Journal of childhood and adolescence.** Ed. by Albert H. Yoder. Seattle. 3 v. illus., plates, diagrs. Frequency: Quarterly. Former frequency: Monthly, v. 1. v. 1-3, no. 1; Sept. 1900-April, 1903. Title varies: Journal of adolescence v. 1, no. 1-6. Vol. 1, no. 1-6 published in Oak Park, Ill. Available in other form: Journal of childhood and adolescence microfilm (ICU)781213.
*1. Child study - Periodicals. I. Title: Journal of childhood and adolescence microfilm*

**Journal of childhood and adolescence microfilm.**
The Journal of childhood and adolescence. Seattle.

**Journal of college placement.** [Philadelphia, Pa. etc.], The College Placement Council, inc. [etc.] illus., ports. 29 cm. Frequency: 4 no. a year. v.12 (Oct.1951)- . Title varies: School and college placement 1940-Dec.1951. Supplements accompany occasional volumes. University placement review. ISSN 0021-9770
*1. Service in education - Periodicals. 2. Employment agencies - Periodicals. 3. Vocational guidance - Periodicals. I. College Placement Council. II. Title. III. Title: School and college placement 1940-Dec.1951 IV. Title: University placement review*

**Journal of commercial education.**
The Journal of business education New York City, The Haire Publishing Company.

**The Journal of comparative and physiological psychology.** Baltimore, 1921-82. v. ill. Frequency: Bimonthly. v. 1-96; 1921-1982. Indexed by: Chemical abstracts 0009-2258. Indexed by: Biological abstracts 0006-3169. Indexed by: Psychological abstracts 0033-2887. Indexed by: Nuclear science abstracts 0029-5612. Indexed by: Index medicus 0019-3879. Indexed by: Bibliography of agriculture, 0006-1530. Monograph supplement issued and bound with some numbers. Microfilm. reels. 35 mm. Title varies: v. 1-39, 1921-46, Journal of comparative psychology. Split into: Behavioral neuroscience, and: Journal of comparative psychology (Washington, D.C. : 1983). Formed by the union of: Psychobiology. and Journal of animal behavior.
*1. Psychology, Comparative - Periodicals. I. Title: Journal of comparative psychology 1921-46 II. Title: Psychobiology III. Title: Journal of animal behavior IV. Title: Behavioral neuroscience V. Title: Journal of comparative psychology (Washington, D.C. : 1983)*

**Journal of comparative psychology.**
The Journal of animal behavior. Cambridge, Mass., H. Holt and Company; [etc., etc., 1911-17]

**Journal of comparative psychology 1921-46.**
The Journal of comparative and physiological psychology. Baltimore, 1921-82.

**Journal of comparative psychology (Washington, D.C. : 1983).**
The Journal of comparative and physiological psychology. Baltimore, 1921-82.

**Journal of consulting and clinical psychology.**
Journal of consulting psychology. [Lancaster, Pa., etc.] American Psychological Association.

**Journal of consulting psychology.** [Lancaster, Pa., etc.] American Psychological Association. 31 v. plates, ports. 26 cm. Frequency: Bimonthly. v. 1-31; Jan./Feb. 1937-Nov./Dec. 1967. Indexed selectively by: Psychological abstracts 0033-2887 1937-1967. Indexed by: Social sciences and humanities index. Issued 1937-38 by the Association of Consulting Psychologists; 1939-45 by the American Association for Applied Psychology; 1946-67 by the American Psychological Association. Author index: Vols. 1-10, 1937-46, in v. 10. Continued by: Journal of consulting and clinical psychology ISSN: 0022-006X (DLC) 80648904. ISSN 0095-8891 DDC 150.5
*1. Clinical psychology - Periodicals. 2. Psychology - Periodicals. I. American Psychological Association. II. Association of Consulting Psychologists. III. American Association for Applied Psychology. IV. Title: Journal of consulting and clinical psychology*

**Journal of continuing education and training.**
[Farmingdale, N.Y.] Baywood Pub. Co. 1 v. 23 cm. v. 1, no. 1-4; May 1971-May 1972. Continued by: International journal of continuing education and training ISSN: 0090-0966 (OCoLC)1784696. ISSN 0047-2344
*1. Continuing education - Periodicals. I. Title: International journal of continuing education and training*

**Journal of couples therapy.**
Couples therapy in managed care. New York : Haworth Press, c1999:
***TC RC488.5 .C64385 1999***

**The Journal of delinquency.** Whittier, Calif. : Whittier State School, Dept. of Research, 1916-c1928. 12 v. : ill. ; 25 cm. Frequency: Quarterly 1927-28. Former frequency: Bimonthly 1916-26. Vol. 1, no. 1 (Mar. 1916)-v. 12, no. 2 (June 1928). "Devoted to the scientific study of problems related to social conduct." Title from cover. Publication suspended during 1924. Issued 1916-20 by the Whittier State School, Dept. of Research; 192 -1928 by the California Bureau of Juvenile Research, Dept. of Research. Continued by: Journal of juvenile research (OCoLC)7663860.
*1. Defective and delinquent classes - Periodicals. 2. Juvenile delinquency - Periodicals. 3. Criminal anthropology - Periodicals. I. California. Bureau of Juvenile Research. Dept. of Research. II. Whittier State School (Calif.). Dept. of Research. III. Title: Journal of juvenile research*

**Journal of developmental reading.**
Journal of developmental reading. [Layfayette, Ind. : Dept. of English, Purdue University], c1957-1964.

**Journal of developmental reading.** [Layfayette, Ind. : Dept. of English, Purdue University], c1957-1964. 7 v. : ill. ; 23 cm. Frequency: Quarterly. Vol. 1, no. 1 (autumn 1957)-v. 7, no. 4 (summer 1964). Title from cover. Available on microfilm. Available in other form: Journal of developmental reading (OCoLC)7371901. Continued by: Journal of reading ISSN: 0022-4103 (OCoLC)1754770 (DLC) 64032293. ISSN 0731-3667
*1. Reading - Periodicals. I. Purdue University. Dept. of English. II. Title: Journal of developmental reading III. Title: Journal of reading*

**Journal of education of the Faculty and College of Education, Vancouver and Victoria.**
Education bulletin of the Faculty and College of Education: Vancouver : University of British Columbia.

The Journal of education of the Faculty of Education Vancouver. Vancouver, University of British Columbia, Faculty of Education.

**Journal of education of the Faculty of Education Vancouver.**
The Journal of education of the Faculty of Education Vancouver. Vancouver, University of British Columbia, Faculty of Education.

**The Journal of education of the Faculty of Education Vancouver.** Vancouver, University of British Columbia, Faculty of Education. 13 no. 24 cm. no. 9-21; Jan. 1964-Mar. 1975. Includes bibliographies and bibliographical references. Also available on microfilm from: Toronto : Micromedia. Published by the Faculty under its earlier name: Faculty and College of Education, 1959-1963. Indexes: 1957-1967, in no. 14. Available in other form: Journal of education of the Faculty of Education Vancouver ISSN: 0068-1768. Continues: Journal of education of the Faculty and College of Education, Vancouver and Victoria ISSN: 0068-1768. ISSN 0068-1768
*I. University of British Columbia. Faculty of Education. II. Title: Journal of education of the Faculty of Education Vancouver III. Title: Journal of education of the Faculty and College of Education. Vancouver and Victoria*

**Journal of educational data processing.** [Malibu, Calif., etc., Educational Systems Corp.] v. ill. 23 cm. v. 2- winter 1964/65- . Educational data processing. ISSN 0022-0647
*1. Schools - Data processing - Periodicals. I. Title. II. Title: Educational data processing*

**Journal of educational sociology.**
[Journal of educational sociology (Online)] The journal of educational sociology [computer file]. New York, N.Y. : American Viewpoint Society, Inc., 1927-1963.
***TC EJOURNALS***

**The Journal of educational sociology :** a magazine of theory and practice. [New York : American Viewpoint Society, Inc., 1927-1963] 36 v. : ill. ; 24 cm. Frequency: Monthly, from Sept. to May. Vol. 1, no. 1 (Sept. 1927)-v. 36, no. 9 (May 1963). Title from cover. Indexed selectively by: Psychological abstracts 0033-2887 1929-1963. Scanned images of issues are also available via the World Wide Web to subscribers of JSTOR. Vols. for Sept. 1941-May 1963 issued by the Payne Educational Society Foundation, inc. URL: http://www.jstor.org/journals/08853525.html Continued by: Sociology of education ISSN: 0038-0407 (DLC) 30008323 (OCoLC)1765952. ISSN 0885-3525 DDC 370
*1. Educational sociology - Periodicals. I. American Viewpoint Society. II. Payne Educational Sociology Foundation. III. Title: Sociology of education*

**[Journal of educational sociology (Online)]** The journal of educational sociology [computer file]. New York, N.Y. : American Viewpoint Society, Inc., 1927-1963. Frequency: Monthly (Sept.-May). Vol. 1, no. 1 (Sept. 1927)-v. 36, no. 9 (May 1963). Publisher varies: American Viewpoint Society, Inc., 1927-June 1931; Journal of Educational Sociology, Sept. 1931-May 1941; Payne Educational Sociology Foundation, Inc., Sept. 1941-May 1963. Description based on JSTOR World Wide Web homepage; title from title screen (viewed on Feb. 12, 1999). Restricted to institutions with a site license to the JSTOR collection. Bit-mapped images; PDF, PostScript, and TIFF formats available for printing SUMMARY: Provides image and full-text online access to back issues. Consult the online table of contents for specific holdings. Online version of the print publication. Mode of access: World Wide Web (URL: http://www.jstor.org/journals/08853525.html). System requirements: Graphical World Wide Web browser software; appropriate software is needed to print PDF, PostScript, and TIFF formats. Digitized and made available by: JSTOR. URL: http://www.jstor.org/journals/08853525.html Available in other form: Journal of educational sociology ISSN: 0885-3525 (DLC) 89648923 (OCoLC)1642390. Continued by: Sociology of education (Online) ISSN: 0038-0407 (DLC)sn 99023365 (OCoLC)40777440. ISSN 0885-3525
*1. Educational sociology - Periodicals. I. American Viewpoint Society. II. Payne Educational Sociology Foundation. III. JSTOR (Organization) IV. Title: Journal of educational sociology V. Title: Sociology of education (Online)*
***TC EJOURNALS***

**Journal of educational technology 1970.**
British journal of educational technology. London, Councils and Education Press.

**Journal of emotional education.** New York, Emotional Education Press. Frequency: Quarterly. v. 1- Jan. 1961- . Journal of the Institute for Emotional Education. Title varies: v. 1-6, no. 6, 1961-66, Institute of Applied Psychology, Inc., New York. Review.
*1. Education - Experimental methods 2. Education - Periodicals. 3. American periodicals I. Institute for Emotional Education*

**Journal of English as a second language.** [New York, American Language Institute, New York University] 4 v. in 2. Frequency: Two no. a year. v. 1-4; 1965/66-1969. Title varies: Occasional papers v. 1-2, no. 1, 1965/66-1967.
*1. English language - Study and teaching - Foreign students - Periodicals. 2. American periodicals*

**Journal of experimental pedagogy and training college record.**
Forum of education. London, Longmans Green.

**Journal of feminist family therapy v. 11, no. 4.**
Feminism, community, and communication. New York ; London : Haworth Press, c2000.
***TC RC488.5 .F43 2000***

**Journal of food science.**
Food research. Champaign, Ill. : The Institute, -c1960.

**Journal of gay & lesbian social services, v. 7, no. 4.**
School experiences of gay and lesbian youth. New York : Harrington Park Press, c1997.
***TC LC2575 .S36 1997***

**The Journal of health and physical education.** Ann Arbor, Mich., : American Physical Education Association, 19 v. : ill. ; 30 cm. Frequency: Monthly (Sept.-June). Vol. 1, no. 1 (Jan. 1930)- . Ceased with Vol. 19 in 1948. Title from cover. Indexed by: Biography index 0006-3053. Indexed by: Education index 0013-1385. Published Jan. 1930-Sept. 1937 by the American Physical Education Association; Oct. 1937-Sept. 1938 by the American Association for Health and Physical Education. Formed by the union of: Pentathlon (OCoLC)1643924, and American physical education review (OCLC)1480564. Continued by: Journal of the American Association for Health, Physical Education, and Recreation (OCLC)7980094.
*1. Physical education and training - Periodicals. I. American Association for Health, Physical Education, and Recreation. II. American Physical Education Association. III. Title: Pentathlon IV. Title: American physical education review V. Title: Journal of the American Association for Health, Physical Education, and Recreation*

**Journal of intergroup relations.**
[Journal of intergroup relations (1970)] Journal of intergroup relations. Louisville, KY : National Association of Human Rights Workers,

**[Journal of intergroup relations (1970)]** Journal of intergroup relations. Louisville, KY : National Association of Human Rights Workers, v. ; 23 cm. Frequency: Quarterly. Began with vol. 1 in fall 1970. First issue of each year includes the conference papers of the National Association of Human Rights Workers, <1984-> Description based on: Vol. 4, no. 2 (May 1975); title from cover. Indexed selectively by: America, history and life 0002-7065 1970-. Indexed selectively by: Current index to journals in education 0011-3565. Indexed selectively by: Historical abstracts. Part A. Modern history abstracts 0363-2717 1970-. Indexed selectively by: Historical abstracts. Part B. Twentieth century abstracts 0363-2725 1970-. Vol. for 1970 issued by the National Association of Intergroup Relations Officials; for <1972-1982> by the National Association of Human Rights Workers. Continues: Journal of intergroup relations ISSN: 0047-2492 (DLC) 65044615 (OCoLC)1643420. ISSN 0047-2492 DDC 305
*1. United States - Social conditions - Periodicals. 2. Intergroup relations - Periodicals. I. National Association of Human Rights Workers. II. National Association of Intergroup Relations Officials. III. Title: Journal of intergroup relations*

**Journal of international relations.**
Foreign affairs. New York : Council on Foreign Relations, 1922-

**Journal of juvenile research.**
The Journal of delinquency. Whittier, Calif. : Whittier State School, Dept. of Research, 1916-c1928.

**Journal of mathematical psychology.** New York, Academic Press. v. 24 cm. Frequency: Quarterly <, Mar. 1983->. Former frequency: Bimonthly. v. 1- Feb. 1964- . Indexed selectively by: Biological abstracts 0006-3169. Indexed selectively by: Computer & control abstracts 0036-8113 1992-. Indexed selectively by: Electrical & electronics abstracts 0036-8105 1992-. Indexed selectively by: Physics abstracts 0036-8091 1992-. Indexed selectively by: International aerospace abstracts 0020-5842. Indexed selectively by: Life sciences collection. Indexed selectively by: Mathematical reviews 0025-5629. Indexed selectively by: Psychological abstracts 0033-2887 1964-. Indexed by: Nuclear science abstracts 0029-5612. ISSN 0022-2496
*1. Psychometrics - Periodicals. 2. Psychology - Mathematical models - Periodicals.*

**Journal of memory and language 1985-.**
Journal of verbal learning and verbal behavior. New York, Academic Press.

**Journal of modern education.**
Majallat al-tarbiyah al-ḥadīthah. al-Qāhirah : al-Jāmiʻah al-Amrīkīyah bi-al-Qāhirah, 1928- .

**Journal of nursing scholarship :** an official publication of Sigma Theta Tau International Honor Society of Nursing. Indianapolis, IN : JNS Publication Office, 2000- v. : ill. ; 28 cm. Frequency: Quarterly. Vol. 32, no. 1 (first quarter 2000)- . Title from cover. Continues: Image--the journal of nursing scholarship ISSN: 0743-5150 (DLC)sn 84008169 (OCoLC)9629646. ISSN 1527-6546
*1. Nursing - Periodicals. 2. Nursing - United States - Periodicals. 3. Nursing - Periodicals. 4. Societies. Nursing - United States - Periodicals. I. Sigma Theta Tau International. II. Title: Image--the journal of nursing scholarship*
***TC RT1 .I42***

**Journal of open education.** Cambridge, Mass., Institute of Open Education. v. ill. 28 cm. Frequency: Three issues

yearly. v. 1- Fall 1972- .
*1. Education - Periodicals.*

**The journal of pedagogy.** Syracuse, N.Y., [etc.]. v. 1-20, no.2; 1887-June 1910. Suspended Jan. 1908-May 1910.
*1. Education - Periodicals. I. Title.*

**Journal of personality.**
Character and personality. Durham, N.C. : Duke Univ. Press, 1932-1945.

**Journal of personality assessment.**
Journal of projective techniques & personality assessment. Glendale, Calif.

**Journal of personalized instruction.** [Washington] Center for Personalized Instruction [Georgetown University] v. 28 cm. v. 1- Mar. 1976- . Indexed selectively by: Psychological abstracts 0033-2887 1976-. ISSN 0363-2628 DDC 371.39/4
*1. Individualized instruction - Periodicals. I. Georgetown University. Center for Personalized Instruction.*

**Journal of personnel research :** official publication of Personnel Research Federation. Baltimore : Williams & Wilkins Co., -1927. 5 v. : ill. ; 24 cm. Frequency: Monthly. Began with: Vol. 1, no. 1 (May 1922). -v. 5, no. 12 (Apr. 1927). Includes section "Book reviews". Description based on: Vol. 5, no. 12 (Apr. 1927); title from cover. Includes bibliographies. Indexed selectively by: Psychological abstracts 0033-2887 1926-1927. Continued by: Personnel journal ISSN: 0031-5745 (DLC) 24019564 (OCoLC)1605910. ISSN 0886-750X DDC 658.3/005
*1. Personnel management - Periodicals. I. Personnel Research Federation (U.S.) II. Title: Personnel journal*

**Journal of philosophy of education. Special issue.**
Haydon, Graham. Values, virtues and violence. Oxford ; Malden, MA : Blackwell Publishers, 1999.
***TC LC268 .H294 1999***

**Journal of preventive medicine and sociology 1906-1914 (not owned).**
The Hospital world. Toronto : [Canadian Hospital Association?], 1912-1923.

**Journal of projective techniques.** Glendale, Calif. : Society for Projective Techniques and Rorschach Institute, 1950-c1963. 14 v. : ill. ; 23 cm. Frequency: Quarterly. Vol. 14, no. 1 (Mar. 1950)-v. 27, no. 1 (Mar. 1963). Title from cover. Indexed selectively by: CIS abstracts 0302-7651. Issued -Mar. 1963 by: the Society for Projective Techniques. Vols. 11-14 in v. 14; Vols. 11-20 in v. 21. Continues: Rorschach research exchange and journal of projective techniques ISSN: 1068-3402 (OCoLC)1778178 (DLC)sf 84007106. Continued by: Journal of projective techniques & personality assessment ISSN: 0091-651X (OCoLC)1754755 (DLC)sc 85007065. ISSN 0885-3126 DDC 155.2/84/05
*1. Personality - Periodicals. 2. Rorschach Test - Periodicals. I. Society for Projective Techniques and Rorschach Institute. II. Society for Projective Techniques. III. Title: Rorschach research exchange and journal of projective techniques IV. Title: Journal of projective techniques & personality assessment*

**Journal of projective techniques & personality assessment.**
Journal of projective techniques. Glendale, Calif. : Society for Projective Techniques and Rorschach Institute, 1950-c1963.

**Journal of projective techniques & personality assessment.** Glendale, Calif. 34 v. in 25. 23 cm. v. 1-34; Sept. 1936-70. Title varies: Sept. 1936-1946, Rorschach research exchange; 1947-49, Rorschach research exchange and journal of projective techniques; 1950-Mar. 1963, Journal of projective techniques. Published by the Society for Projective Techniques. Continued by: Journal of personality assessment, ISSN: 0022-3891 (IEN)AAN4249. ISSN 0091-651X
*1. Rorschach Test - Periodicals. 2. Personality tests - Periodicals. I. Society for Projective Techniques. II. Title: Rorschach research exchange, Sept. 1936-1946. III. Title: Rorschach research exchange and journal of projective techniques, 1947-1949. IV. Title: Journal of projective techniques, 1950-Mar. 1963. V. Title: Journal of personality assessment.*

**Journal of projective techniques, 1950-Mar. 1963.**
Journal of projective techniques & personality assessment. Glendale, Calif.

**Journal of psychiatric nursing.**
Journal of psychiatric nursing. [Bordentown, N.J., etc., S. James Pub. Co., etc.]

**Journal of psychiatric nursing.** [Bordentown, N.J., etc., S. James Pub. Co., etc.] 4 v. ill., ports. 20 cm. v. 1-4; 1963-1966. Microfilm. Ann Arbor,Mich., University Microfilms, 1963-66. reels. 35 mm. Available in other form: Journal of psychiatric nursing ISSN: 0022-3948. Continued by: Journal of psychiatric nursing and mental health services ISSN: 0360-5973. ISSN 0022-3948
*1. Psychiatric nursing - Periodicals. 2. Nursing - Periodicals. I. Title: Journal of psychiatric nursing II. Title: Journal of psychiatric nursing and mental health services*

**Journal of psychiatric nursing and mental health services.**
Journal of psychiatric nursing. [Bordentown, N.J., etc., S. James Pub. Co., etc.]

**Journal of psycho-asthenics.** Faribault, Minn. : Association of American Institutions for Feeble-Minded. [1896-1918] 22 v. : ill., ports. ; 26 cm. Frequency: Quarterly. Vol. 1, no. 1 (Sept. 1896)-v. 22, no. 3 and 4 (Mar. and June 1918). "Devoted to the care, training, and treatment of the feeble-minded and of the epileptic." Title from cover. Issued by: American Association for the Study of the Feeble-Minded, <1906>-1918. Vols. 1 (1896)-5 (1901) with v. 1-4; vols. 11 (1906)-15 (1911), in v. 15, no. 3-4. Continued in part by: American Association for the Study of the Feeble-Minded. Proceedings and addresses (OCoLC)1781334.
*1. Epilepsy - Periodicals. 2. Psychiatry - Periodicals. 3. Mentally handicapped - Periodicals. 4. Mentally handicapped - Education - United States - Periodicals. I. Association of Medical Officers of American Institutions for Idiotic and Feeble-Minded Persons. II. American Association for the Study of the Feeble-Minded. III. Title: American Association for the Study of the Feeble-Minded. Proceedings and addresses*

**Journal of psychohistory.**
History of childhood quarterly. [Broadway, N.Y., Atcom]

**Journal of reading.**
Journal of developmental reading. [Layfayette, Ind. : Dept. of English, Purdue University], c1957-1964.

**Journal of research on computing in education.**
AEDS journal. Washington, Association for Educational Data Systems.

**Journal of secondary education.** [Burlingame, Calif. : California Association of Secondary School Administrators, 1961-1971] 11 v. ; 24 cm. Frequency: Monthly (Oct.-May). Vol. 36, no. 1 (Jan. 1961)-v. 46, no. 5 (May 1971). Title from cover. Indexed by: Education index. Continues: California journal of secondary education (OCoLC)1552561 (DLC) sc83002383. ISSN 0022-4464
*1. Education, Secondary - Periodicals. I. California Association of Secondary School Administrators. II. Title: California journal of secondary education*

**Journal of social hygiene.** New York : American Social Hygiene Association, 33 v. : ill. ; 26 cm. Frequency: Monthly (except July-Sept.), Jan. 1923-Dec. 1954. Former frequency: Quarterly, 1922. Vol. 8, no. 1 (Jan. 1922)-v. 40, no. 9 (Dec. 1954). Title from cover. Supplements accompany some numbers. Official periodical of the American Social Hygiene Association. Continues: Social hygiene ISSN: 0741-7934 (DLC)sf 83005051 (OCoLC)1715948. Absorbed in part by: Social hygiene news (DLC) 30034061 (OCoLC)2267765. Continued in part by: Social hygiene papers (DLC) 57025845 (OCoLC)12491668. ISSN 0741-9996 DDC 306.7/05
*1. Hygiene, Sexual - Periodicals. 2. Social problems - Periodicals. 3. Sex instruction - Periodicals. I. American Social Hygiene Association. II. Title: Social hygiene III. Title: Social hygiene news IV. Title: Social hygiene papers*

**Journal of the American Association for Adult Education.**
[Journal of adult education (New York, N.Y.)] Journal of adult education. New York : American Association for Adult Education, 1929-[1941]

**Journal of the American Association for Adult Education.** New York, N.Y. : The Association, [1926-1928] 2 v. ; 25 cm. Frequency: Irregular. Began with v. 1, in Dec. 1926. -v. 2, nos. 4 and 5 (June 12, 1928). Description based on: Vol. 1, no. 2 (Jan. 31, 1927); title from caption. Continued by: Journal of adult education (New York, N.Y.) ISSN: 0888-5044 (DLC) 30033107 (OCoLC)1645883.
*1. Adult education - Periodicals. I. American Association for Adult Education. II. Title: Journal of adult education (New York, N.Y.)*

**Journal of the American Association for Health, Physical Education, and Recreation.**
The Journal of health and physical education. Ann Arbor, Mich., : American Physical Education Association,

**Journal of the American Association of Collegiate Registrars.** Athens, Ohio [etc.] American Association of College Registrars. 10 v. 23 cm. Frequency: Quarterly. v. 13-22; Oct. 1937-July 1947. Indexed by: Education index. FOR HOLDINGS AND LOCATIONS SEE SERIALS SHELFLIST Continues: American Association of Collegiate Registrars. Bulletin of the American Association of Collegiate Registrars (OCoLC)4107270. Continued by: College and university ISSN: 0010-0889 (OCoLC)6168802.
*1. Education - Periodicals. 2. Universities and colleges - United States - Periodicals. I. American Association of Collegiate Registrars and Admissions Officers. II. Title. III. Title: American Association of Collegiate Registrars. Bulletin of the American Association of Collegiate Registrars IV. Title: College and university*

**Journal of the American Physical Therapy Association.** [New York, N.Y.] : The Association, [1962-1963] 2 v. : ill. ; 27 cm. Frequency: Monthly. [Vol. 42, no. 1] (Jan. 1962)-[v. 43, no. 12] (Dec. 1963). Title from cover. Continues: Physical therapy review (OCoLC)1778354. Continued by: Physical therapy ISSN: 0031-9023 (OCoLC)1762333 (DLC) 72620955.
*1. American Physical Therapy Association (1921- ) II. Title: Physical therapy review III. Title: Physical therapy*

**Journal of the American Social Science Association.**
National Institute of Social Sciences. Journal of the National Institute of Social Sciences. [New York]

**Journal of the Anthropological Institute of Great Britain and Ireland.**
[Journal of the Anthropological Institute of Great Britain and Ireland (Online)] The journal of the Anthropological Institute of Great Britain and Ireland [computer file]. London [England] : Published for the Anthropological Institute of Great Britain and Ireland by Trübner & Co., 1872-1906.
***TC EJOURNALS***

**[Journal of the Anthropological Institute of Great Britain and Ireland (Online)]** The journal of the Anthropological Institute of Great Britain and Ireland [computer file]. London [England] : Published for the Anthropological Institute of Great Britain and Ireland by Trübner & Co., 1872-1906. Vol. 1 (1872)- . Ceased with v. 36 (July/Dec. 1906). Published by: the Anthropological Institute of Great Britain and Ireland, 1900-1906. Vol. 1 (1872)-v. 30 (1900) are digital reproductions of the reprint ed. published: [S.l.] : Johnson Reprint Corp. ; Kraus Reprint Co., 1971. Description based on JSTOR World Wide Web homepage; title from title screen (viewed on Nov. 24, 1999). Restricted to institutions with a site license to the JSTOR collection. Bit-mapped images; PDF, PostScript, and TIFF formats available for printing SUMMARY: Provides image and full-text online access to back issues. Consult the online table of contents for specific holdings. Online version of the print publication. Mode of access: World Wide Web (URL: http://www.jstor.org/journals/09595295.html). System requirements: Graphical World Wide Web browser software; appropriate software is needed to print PDF, PostScript, and TIFF formats. Digitized and made available by: JSTOR. Formed by the union of: Journal of the Ethnological Society of London, and: Journal of anthropology. URL: http://www.jstor.org/journals/09595295.html Available in other form: Journal of the Anthropological Institute of Great Britain and Ireland ISSN: 0959-5295 (DLC)sn 90023020 (OCoLC)4409384. Continued by: Journal of the Royal Anthropological Institute of Great Britain and Ireland (Online) ISSN: 0307-3114 (DLC)sn 99023446 (OCoLC)42882494. ISSN 0959-5295
*1. Anthropology - Periodicals. I. Anthropological Institute of Great Britain and Ireland. II. JSTOR (Organization) III. Title: Journal of the Anthropological Institute of Great Britain and Ireland IV. Title: Journal of the Ethnological Society of London (1869 : Online) V. Title: Journal of anthropology (Online) VI. Title: Journal of the Royal Anthropological Institute of Great Britain and Ireland (Online)*
***TC EJOURNALS***

**Journal of the Anthropological Institute of Great Britain and Ireland (Online).**
[Journal of the Royal Anthropological Institute of Great Britain and Ireland (Online)] The journal of the Royal Anthropological Institute of Great Britain and Ireland [computer file]. London [England] : The Institute, 1907-1965.
***TC EJOURNALS***

**Journal of the College of Education.**
[Tanglaw (Manila, Philippines)] Tanglaw. Manila : The College, 1992-

**Journal of the Ethnological Society of London (1869 : Online).**
[Journal of the Anthropological Institute of Great Britain and Ireland (Online)] The journal of the Anthropological Institute of Great Britain and Ireland [computer file]. London [England] : Published for the Anthropological Institute of Great Britain and Ireland by Trübner & Co., 1872-1906.
***TC EJOURNALS***

**Journal of the Florida Education Association.**
Florida Education Association. Tallahassee, the Association.

**Journal of the history of ideas.**
[Journal of the history of ideas (Online)] Journal of the history of ideas [computer file]. Baltimore, MD : Journal of the History of Ideas, Inc., c1996-
***TC EJOURNALS***

**[Journal of the history of ideas (Online)]** Journal of the history of ideas [computer file]. Baltimore, MD : Journal of the History of Ideas, Inc., c1996- Frequency: Quarterly. 57.1 (Jan. 1996)- . Other title: JHI. Title from title screen. Restricted to institutions with a site license to the Project Muse collection. Text (electronic journal) Also available in a print ed. Mode of access: Internet via the World Wide Web. System requirements: World Wide Web browswer software. Digitized and made available by: Project Muse. URL: http://muse.jhu.edu/journals/journ al%5Fof%5Fthe%5Fhistory%5Fof%5Fideas/ Available in other form: Journal of the history of ideas ISSN: 0022-5037 (DLC) 42051802 (OCoLC)1591903. ISSN 1086-3222 DDC 105
*1. Philosophy - Periodicals. I. Project Muse. II. Title: JHI III. Title: Journal of the history of ideas*
***TC EJOURNALS***

**Journal of the Karnataka State Education Federation.** [Bangalore, India] : The Federation, [1973?- v. : ports. ; 25 cm. Frequency: Monthly (irregular). Vol. 27, no. 8 (Nov. 1973)- . Title from cover. English with occasional articles in Kannada. Continues: Journal of the Mysore State Education Federation (OCoLC)4588138. DDC 370/.954/87
*1. Education - India - Karnataka - Periodicals. I. Karnataka State Education Federation. II. Title: Journal of the Mysore State Education Federation*

**Journal of the Louisiana Teachers' Association.** [Baton Rouge] : The Association, [1923-1932], (Baton Rouge, La. : Gladney's Print Shop) 9 v. : ill. ; 24-30 cm. Frequency: Monthly (except June-Aug.). Vol. 1, no. 1 (May 1923)-v. 9, no. 9 (May 1932). Title from cover. Continued in Sept. 1932 by: Louisiana schools. Continues: Southern school work (OCoLC)6074808.
*1. Education - Periodicals. 2. Education - Louisiana - Periodicals. I. Louisiana Teachers' Association. II. Title: Southern school work III. Title: Louisiana schools*

**Journal of the Mysore State Education Federation.** Journal of the Karnataka State Education Federation. [Bangalore, India] : The Federation, [1973?-

**Journal of the National Association for Women Deans, Administrators & Counselors.** Journal of the National Association of Women Deans and Counselors. Washington, D.C. : The Association, 1956-1973.

**Journal of the National Association of Deans of Women.** Journal of the National Association of Women Deans and Counselors. Washington, D.C. : The Association, 1956-1973.

**Journal of the National Association of Deans of Women.** Washington, D.C. : The Association, the Dept. of Deans of the National Education Association of the United States of America, [1938-1956] 19 v. ; 26 cm. Frequency: Four no. a year. Vol. 1, no. 1 (June 1938)-v. 19, no. 4 (June 1956). Each issue has also a distinctive title. The June number contains the proceedings of the annual meeting of the Association. Title from cover. Continues: National Association of Deans of Women (U.S.). Bulletin, and: National Association of Deans of Women (U.S.). Meeting. Proceedings of the ... Annual Meeting of the National Association of Deans of Women, Department of Superintendence, National Education Association. Continued by: Journal of the National Association of Women Deans and Counselors ISSN: 0027-870X (DLC) 57027106 (OCoLC)4629275. DDC 378.11
*1. Women in education - Periodicals. 2. Women in education - United States - Periodicals. 3. Educational counseling - Periodicals. 4. Educational counseling - United States - Periodicals. I. National Association of Deans of Women (U.S.) II. Title: National Association of Deans of Women (U.S.). Bulletin III. Title: National Association of Deans of Women (U.S.). Meeting. Proceedings of the ... Annual Meeting of the National Association of Deans of Women, Department of Superintendence, National Education Association IV. Title: Journal of the National Association of Women Deans and Counselors*

**Journal of the National Association of Women Deans and Counselors.** Journal of the National Association of Deans of Women. Washington, D.C. : The Association, the Dept. of Deans of the National Education Association of the United States of America, [1938-1956]

**Journal of the National Association of Women Deans and Counselors.** Washington, D.C. : The Association, 1956-1973. 16 v. ; 26 cm. Frequency: Quarterly. Vol. 20, no. 1 (Oct. 1956)-v. 36, no. 4 (summer 1973). Title from cover. Each issue has also a distinctive title. Indexed in its entirety by: Current index to journals in education 0011-3565. Continues: Journal of the National Association of Deans of Women (DLC) 89657321 (OCoLC)2394781. Continued by: Journal of the National Association for Women Deans, Administrators & Counselors ISSN: 0094-3460 (DLC) 74644948 (OCoLC)1794158. ISSN 0027-870X DDC 378.11
*1. Women in education - Periodicals. 2. Women in education - United States - Periodicals. 3. Educational counseling - Periodicals. 4. Educational counseling - United States - Periodicals. I. National Association of Women Deans and Counselors. II. Title: Journal of the National Association of Deans of Women III. Title: Journal of the National Association for Women Deans, Administrators & Counselors*

**Journal of the reading specialist.** The Journal of the reading specialist. Bethlehem, Pa. : The Association, c1962-

**The Journal of the reading specialist** / the College Reading Association. Bethlehem, Pa. : The Association, c1962- 10 v. ; 23 cm. Frequency: Quarterly. Vol. 2, no. 1 (Sept. 1962)- . Ceased with: Vol. 11, no. 1 in 1971. Imprint varies: Rochester, N.Y. <, May 1966->; Syracuse, N.Y. <, May 1970->. Indexed selectively by: Psychological abstracts 0033-2887 1969-1971. Available on microfilm from University Microfilms. Official organ of the College Reading Association. Available in other form: Journal of the reading specialist ISSN: 0022-5126 (OCoLC)7558292. Continues: Newsletter (College Reading Association) (OCoLC)11961897. Continued by: Reading world ISSN: 0149-0117 (DLC) 72622936 (OCoLC)1589523. ISSN 0022-5126 DDC 428.4/05
*1. Reading - Periodicals. I. College Reading Association. II. Title: Journal of the reading specialist III. Title: Newsletter (College Reading Association) IV. Title: Reading world*

**Journal of the Royal Anthropological Institute of Great Britain and Ireland.** [Journal of the Royal Anthropological Institute of Great Britain and Ireland (Online)] The journal of the Royal Anthropological Institute of Great Britain and Ireland [computer file]. London [England] : The Institute, 1907-1965.
***TC EJOURNALS***

**Journal of the Royal Anthropological Institute of Great Britain and Ireland (Online).** [Journal of the Anthropological Institute of Great Britain and Ireland (Online)] The journal of the Anthropological Institute of Great Britain and Ireland [computer file]. London [England] : Published for the Anthropological Institute of Great Britain and Ireland by Trübner & Co., 1872-1906.
***TC EJOURNALS***

**[Journal of the Royal Anthropological Institute of Great Britain and Ireland (Online)]** The journal of the Royal Anthropological Institute of Great Britain and Ireland [computer file]. London [England] : The Institute, 1907-1965. Frequency: Semiannual. Vol. 37 (Jan./June 1907)-v. 95, pt. 2 (July/Dec. 1965). Description based on JSTOR World Wide Web homepage; title from title screen (viewed on Nov. 24, 1999). Restricted to institutions with a site license to the JSTOR collection. Issues for 1907-1944 called also new ser., v. 10-47. Bit-mapped images; PDF, PostScript, and TIFF formats available for printing SUMMARY: Provides image and full-text online access to back issues. Consult the online table of contents for specific holdings. Online version of the print publication. Mode of access: World Wide Web (URL: http://www.jstor.org/journals/03073114.html). System requirements: Graphical World Wide Web browser software; appropriate software is needed to print PDF, PostScript, and TIFF formats. Digitized and made available by: JSTOR. URL: http://www.jstor.org/journals/03073114.html Available in other form: Journal of the Royal Anthropological Institute of Great Britain and Ireland ISSN: 0307-3114 (DLC)sn 79006341 (OCoLC)1334521. Continues: Journal of the Anthropological Institute of Great Britain and Ireland (Online) ISSN: 0959-5295 (DLC)sn 99023445 (OCoLC)42882487. Absorbed in part by: Man (London, England : 1901 : Online) ISSN: 0025-1496 (DLC)sn 99023436 (OCoLC)42646610. ISSN 0307-3114
*1. Anthropology - Periodicals. I. Royal Anthropological Institute of Great Britain and Ireland. II. JSTOR (Organization) III. Title: Journal of the Royal Anthropological Institute of Great Britain and Ireland IV. Title: Journal of the Anthropological Institute of Great Britain and Ireland (Online) V. Title: Man (London, England : 1901 : Online)*
***TC EJOURNALS***

**Journal of the SMPTE.** New York, N.Y. : SMPTE, 1956-1975. 20 v. : ill. ; 29 cm. Frequency: Monthly. Vol. 65, no. 1 (Jan. 1956)-v. 84, no. 12 (Dec. 1975). Other title: Journal of the Society of Motion Picture and Television Engineers. Title from cover. Published: Scarsdale, N.Y., -1975. Indexed selectively by: Computer & control abstracts 0036-8113 1968-1971. Indexed selectively by: Electrical & electronics abstracts 0036-8105 1968-1971. Indexed selectively by: Physics abstracts 0036-8091 1968-1971. Continues: SMPTE journal (1955) ISSN: 0898-0438 (OCoLC)9724007 (DLC) 90642423. Continued by: SMPTE journal ISSN: 0036-1682 (DLC) 82645680 (OCoLC)2093452. ISSN 0361-4573 DDC 778
*1. Cinematography - Periodicals. 2. Television - Periodicals. I. Society of Motion Picture and Television Engineers. II. Title: Journal of the Society of Motion Picture and Television Engineers III. Title: SMPTE journal (1955) IV. Title: SMPTE journal*

**Journal of the Society of Motion Picture and Television Engineers.** Journal of the SMPTE. New York, N.Y. : SMPTE, 1956-1975.

**The Journal of university education.** Delhi, Published by A. Singh for Federation of Central Universities Teachers' Associations, Aligarh. 5 v. 23 cm. Frequency: Three no. a year. v. 1-5, no. 2; Sept. 1962-Dec. 1966. Published by the Federation of Central Universities Teachers' Associations.
*1. Education, Higher - Periodicals. 2. Education, Higher - India - Periodicals. I. Federation of Central Universities Teachers' Associations.*

**Journal of verbal learning and verbal behavior.** New York, Academic Press. 23v. 26 cm. v. 1-23;July 1962-Dec.1984. Indexed selectively by: MLA international bibliography of books and articles on the modern languages and literatures (Complete edition) 0024-8215. Indexed selectively by: Life sciences collection. Indexed selectively by: LLBA, language and language behavior abstracts 0023-8295. Indexed selectively by: International aerospace abstracts 0020-5842. Indexed selectively by: Language teaching 0261-4448. Indexed selectively by: Current index to journals in education 0011-3565. Indexed selectively by: Psychological abstracts 0033-2887 1962-. Indexed in its entirety by: Social sciences index 0094-4920. Continued by: Journal of memory and language ISSN: 0749-596X 1985-. ISSN 0022-5371
*1. Verbal behavior - Periodicals. 2. Verbal learning - Periodicals. I. Title: Journal of memory and language 1985-*

**Journal of vocational and educational guidance.** [Bombay] 25 cm. Began publication with Jan. 1954 issue. Cf. New serial titles, 1950-60. Vols. for <Aug.-Nov. 1963> issued by All India Educational and Vocational Association. ISSN 0449-332X
*1. Educational counseling - Periodicals. I. All India Educational and Vocational Association.*

**JOURNALISM.** *See also* **MOTION PICTURE JOURNALISM; PERIODICALS; PHOTOJOURNALISM.**
Morrison, Taylor. Civil War artist. Boston : Houghton Mifflin, 1999.
***TC E468.9 .M86 1999***

**JOURNALISM, CAMERA.** *See* **PHOTOJOURNALISM.**

**JOURNALISTIC PHOTOGRAPHY.** *See* **PHOTOJOURNALISM.**

**JOURNALS (DIARIES).** *See* **DIARIES.**

**Journals in psychology :** a resource listing for authors. 5th ed. Washington, D.C. : American Psychological Association, c1997. iv, 257 p. ; 28 cm. Includes index. ISBN 1-55798-438-7
*1. Psychology - Authorship. 2. Psychology - Periodicals - Publishing - Directories. 3. Psychology - United States - Authorship. 4. Psychology - Periodicals - Publishing - United States - Directories. I. American Psychological Association.*
***TC BF76.8 J655 1997***

**JOURNALS (PERIODICALS).** *See* **PERIODICALS.**

**Journet, Debra.**
History, reflection, and narrative. Stamford, Conn. : Ablex Pub., c1999.
***TC PE1405.U6 H56 1999***

**A journey through time in verse and rhyme** / poems collected by Heather Thomas. Rev. ed. Edinburgh : Floris Books, 1998. 366 p. ; 24 cm. Originally published in 1987. Includes index. "The poems in this book have been published in response to requests from teachers who are beginning their work in Rudolf Steiner or Waldorf Education, and who are looking for poems and verses to enrigh the experience of the main lesson and other suject lessons"--Introd. ISBN 0-86315-271-6
*1. Poetry - Collections. 2. Children's poetry. I. Thomas, Heather.*
***TC PN6109.97 .J68 1998***

**Joyce, Bruce R.** The new structure of school improvement : inquiring schools and achieving students / Bruce Joyce, Emily Calhoun, and David Hopkins. Buckingham [England] ; Philadelphia : Open University Press, 1999. xiv, 257 p. : ill ; 24 cm. Includes bibliographical references (p.228-254) and index. ISBN 0-335-20294-2 (pbk.) DDC 371.2
*1. School improvement programs - Great Britain. 2. School improvement programs - United States. 3. School-based management - Great Britain. 4. School-based management -*

United States. I. Calhoun, Emily. II. Hopkins, David. 1949- III. Title.
TC LB2822.84.G7 J69 1999

**Joyce, C. R. B. (Charles Richard Boddington), 1923-.**
Individual quality of life. Amsterdam : Harwood Academic, c1999.
TC RA407 .I54 1999

**Joyce, Michael, 1945-.**
Page to screen. London ; New York : Routledge, 1998.
TC LC149.5 .P35 1998

**Joyce, William.** Rolie Polie Olie / by William Joyce. 1st ed. New York : Laura Geringer Book, c1999. 1 v. (unpaged) : col. ill. ; 26 cm. SUMMARY: Rolie Polie Olie, a round robot living on a planet where everything is round, enjoys a busy day with his family and then is too wired to go to bed at night. ISBN 0-06-027163-9 ISBN 0-06-027164-7 (lib. bdg.) DDC [E]
*1. Robots - Fiction. 2. Circle - Fiction. 3. Stories in rhyme. I. Title.*
TC PZ8.3.J835 Ro 1999

**Joyce, William W.**
Introducing Canada. Washington, D.C. : National Council for the Social Studies in association with National Consortium for Teaching Canada, c1997.
TC F1025 .I59 1997

**JSTOR (Organization).**
[Journal of educational sociology (Online)] The journal of educational sociology [computer file]. New York, N.Y. : American Viewpoint Society, Inc., 1927-1963.
*TC EJOURNALS*

[Journal of the Anthropological Institute of Great Britain and Ireland (Online)] The journal of the Anthropological Institute of Great Britain and Ireland [computer file]. London [England] : Published for the Anthropological Institute of Great Britain and Ireland by Trübner & Co., 1872-1906.
*TC EJOURNALS*

[Journal of the Royal Anthropological Institute of Great Britain and Ireland (Online)] The journal of the Royal Anthropological Institute of Great Britain and Ireland [computer file]. London [England] : The Institute, 1907-1965.
*TC EJOURNALS*

**JUDAICA.** *See* JEWS.

**JUDAISM.** *See* CONSERVATIVE JUDAISM; JEWS.

**JUDAISM, CONSERVATIVE.** *See* CONSERVATIVE JUDAISM.

**JUDAISM - EDUCATION.** *See* JEWS - EDUCATION.

**JUDAISM - STUDY AND TEACHING.** *See* JEWISH RELIGIOUS EDUCATION.

**JUDAISM - STUDY AND TEACHING (HIGHER).**
Academic approaches to teaching Jewish studies. Lanham, Md. : University Press of America, c2000.
TC BM71 .A33 2000

**JUDAISM - UNITED STATES - ENCYCLOPEDIAS.**
American Jewish desk reference. 1st ed. New York : Random House, 1999.
TC E184.35 .A44 1999

**Judd, Charles M.**
Handbook of research methods in social and personality psychology. Cambridge, U.K. ; New York : Cambridge University Press, 2000.
TC HM1019 .H36 2000

**Judd, Dorothy.** Give sorrow words : working with a dying child / Dorothy Judd ; foreword by Dora Black. 2nd ed. New York : Haworth Press, 1995. xix, 242 p. : ill. ; 24 cm. Includes bibliographical references (p. 224-235) and index. ISBN 0-7890-6020-5 DDC 155.9/37
*1. Children and death. 2. Terminally ill children. 3. Attitude to Death - in infancy & childhood. 4. Terminal Care - in infancy & childhood. 5. Terminal Care - psychology. I. Title.*
TC RJ249 .J83 1995

**Judd, Lewis L.**
Basic and clinical science of mental and addictive disorders. Basel ; New York : Karger, c1997.
TC RC327 .B37 1997

New therapeutic indications of antidepressants. Basel ; New York : Karger, c1997.
TC RM332 .N475 1997

**Judge, William Q.** The leader's shadow : exploring and developing executive character / William Q. Judge. Thousand Oaks, Calif. : Sage Publications, c1999. xx,

216 p. : ill. ; 24 cm. Includes bibliographical references (p. 197-207) and index. ISBN 0-7619-1538-9 (acid-free paper) ISBN 0-7619-1539-7 (pbk. : acid-free paper) DDC 658.4/092
*1. Leadership. 2. Executive ability. 3. Chief executive officers. I. Title.*
TC HD57.7 .J83 1999

**Judgment.**
Sweeney, Jim. 1937- Larchmont, NY : Eye on Education, c1997.
TC LB2806 .S88 1997

**JUDGMENT.**
Hammond, Kenneth R. Judgments under stress. New York : Oxford University Press, 2000.
TC BF441 .H27 2000

Judgment and decision making. 2nd ed. Cambridge, U.K. : New York, NY : Cambridge University Press, 2000.
TC BF441 .J79 2000

Judgment and decision making. Mahwah, N.J. : L. Erlbaum Associates, 1999.
TC BF448 .J83 1999

Rights and wrongs. San Francisco, [CA] : Jossey-Bass, c2000.
TC BF723.M54 L38 2000

Sweeney, Jim, 1937- Judgment. Larchmont, NY : Eye on Education, c1997.
TC LB2806 .S88 1997

**JUDGMENT (AESTHETICS).**
Scruton, Roger. Art and imagination. South Bend, Ind. : St. Augustine's Press, 1998.
TC BH301.J8 S37 1998

**Judgment and decision making :** an interdisciplinary reader / edited by Terry Connolly, Hal R. Arkes, Kenneth R. Hammond. 2nd ed. Cambridge, U.K. ; New York, NY : Cambridge University Press, 2000. xviii, 786 p. : ill. ; 23 cm. (Cambridge series on judgment and decision making) Includes bibliographical references and indexes. ISBN 0-521-62355-3 (hardcover) ISBN 0-521-62602-1 (pbk.) DDC 302.3
*1. Decision making. 2. Judgment. I. Connolly, Terry. II. Arkes, Hal R., 1945- III. Hammond, Kenneth R. IV. Series.*
TC BF441 .J79 2000

**Judgment and decision making :** neo-Brunswikian and process-tracing approaches / edited by Peter Juslin, Henry Montgomery. Mahwah, N.J. : L. Erlbaum Associates, 1999. viii, 344 p. : ill. ; 24 cm. Includes bibliographical references and indexes. ISBN 0-8058-3254-8 (hardcover : alk. paper) DDC 153.8/3
*1. Decision making. 2. Judgment. I. Juslin, Peter. II. Montgomery, Henry.*
TC BF448 .J83 1999

**Judgment day [videorecording].**
Africans in America [videorecording]. [Boston, Mass.] : WGBH Educational Foundation ; South Burlington, VT : WGBH Boston Video [distributor], c1998.
TC E441 .A47 1998

**JUDGMENT (LOGIC).** *See* REASONING.

**JUDGMENT - SEX DIFFERENCES - RESEARCH.**
Gender and the interpretation of emotion [videorecording]. Princeton, NJ : Films for the Humanities & Sciences, c1997.
TC BF592.F33 G4 1997

**JUDGMENTS BY PEERS.** *See* JURY.

**Judgments under stress.**
Hammond, Kenneth R. New York : Oxford University Press, 2000.
TC BF441 .H27 2000

**Juilliard.**
Olmstead, Andrea. Urbana : University of Illinois Press, c1999.
TC MT4.N5 J846 1999

**JUILLIARD SCHOOL.**
Olmstead, Andrea. Juilliard. Urbana : University of Illinois Press, c1999.
TC MT4.N5 J846 1999

**Julie of the wolves by Jean Craighead George.**
Beech, Linda Ward. New York : Scholastic, c1996.
TC LB1573 .B434 1996

**Julie Rrap.**
Alexander, George, 1949- [Sidney] : Piper Press, 1998.
TC TR654 .A44 1998

**JUMP ROPE.** *See* ROPE SKIPPING.

**Jumping the queue.**
Kelman, Mark. Cambridge, Mass. : Harvard University Press, 1997.
TC KF4215 .K45 1997

**Jung, C. G. (Carl Gustav), 1875-1961.**
Jung on film [videorecording]. [Chicago, Ill.?] : Public Media Video, c1990.
TC BF109.J8 J4 1990

Jung on film [videorecording]. [Chicago, Ill.?] : Public Media Video, c1990.
TC BF109.J8 J4 1990

**JUNG, C. G. (CARL GUSTAV), 1875-1961.**
Jungian thought in the modern world. London : New York : Free Association, 2000.
TC BF173.J85 J85 2000

Stevens, Anthony. On Jung. 2nd ed. Princeton, N.J. : Princeton University Press, 1999.
TC BF173 .S828 1999

**JUNG, C. G. (CARL GUSTAV), 1875-1961 - INTERVIEWS.**
Jung on film [videorecording]. [Chicago, Ill.?] : Public Media Video, c1990.
TC BF109.J8 J4 1990

Jung on film [videorecording]. [Chicago, Ill.?] : Public Media Video, c1990.
TC BF109.J8 J4 1990

**Jung on film** [videorecording] : Carl Gustav Jung interviewed in Zurich, Switzerland on August 5-8, 1957 / [presented by Stephen] Segaller Films ; [produced by KUHT Film Productions] ; filmed by John W. Meaney ; [directed and photographed by Dr. John W. Meaney]. [Chicago, Ill.?] : Public Media Video, c1990. 1 videocassette (VHS) (78 min.) : sd., b&w ; 1/2 in. (Biography) At head of title: Home Vision a Films Incorporated Company presents ... Series title on cassette label: Biography. VHS. Catalogued from credits and container. Interviewer, Richard I. Evans. Excerpts selected by Merrill Berger for Segaller Films ; editors: James L. Bauer, Arnold Bergene; sound recording: Patrick Coakley. Originally produced as documentary film in Switzerland in 1957. "A Public Media Incorporated Release"--Container. For students of psychology, psychoanalysis and psychiatry. SUMMARY: By arrangement with the University of Houston, Segaller presents a newly edited 78 min. version of the interview with C.G. Jung, originally recorded in Zürich on Aug. 5-8, 1957. Touches on all the major themes in Jung's psychological researches and analytical work. The pioneering analytical psychologist discusses his collaboration with Sigmund Freud, the insights he gained while listening to his patients' dreams, and reflects on the turns and directions his life took.
*1. Jung, C. G. - (Carl Gustav), - 1875-1961 - Interviews. 2. Psychoanalysts - Switzerland - Interviews. 3. Psychoanalysis. 4. Freud, Sigmund. - 1856-1939. I. Jung, C. G. (Carl Gustav), 1875-1961. II. Evans, Richard I. (Richard Isadore). 1922- III. Meaney, John W. IV. Segaller Films. V. KUHT Film Productions. VI. Films Incorporated. VII. Home Vision (Firm) VIII. Public Media Video (Firm) IX. Pubic Media Incorporated (Wilmette, Ill.) X. Title: Carl Gustav Jung interviewed in Zurich, Switzerland on August 5-8, 1957 [videorecording] XI. Title: Home Vision a Films Incorporated Company presents ... XII. Title: Biography XIII. Series: Biography (Public Media Video)*
TC BF109.J8 J4 1990

**Jung on film** [videorecording] : Carl Gustav Jung interviewed in Zurich, Switzerland on August 5-8, 1957 / [presented by Stephen] Segaller Films ; [produced by KUHT Film Productions] ; filmed by John W. Meaney ; [directed and photographed by Dr. John W. Meaney]. [Chicago, Ill.?] : Public Media Video, c1990. 1 videocassette (VHS) (78 min.) : sd., b&w ; 1/2 in. (Biography) At head of title: Home Vision a Films Incorporated Company presents ... Series title on cassette label: Biography. VHS. Catalogued from credits and container. Interviewer, Richard I. Evans. Excerpts selected by Merrill Berger for Segaller Films ; editors: James L. Bauer, Arnold Bergene; sound recording: Patrick Coakley. Originally produced as documentary film in Switzerland in 1957. "A Public Media Incorporated Release"--Container. For students of psychology, psychoanalysis and psychiatry. SUMMARY: By arrangement with the University of Houston, Segaller presents a newly edited 78 min. version of the interview with C.G. Jung, originally recorded in Zürich on Aug. 5-8, 1957. Touches on all the major themes in Jung's psychological researches and analytical work. The pioneering analytical psychologist discusses his collaboration with Sigmund Freud, the insights he gained while listening to his patients' dreams, and reflects on the turns and directions his life took.
*1. Jung, C. G. - (Carl Gustav), - 1875-1961 - Interviews. 2. Psychoanalysts - Switzerland - Interviews. 3. Psychoanalysis. 4. Freud, Sigmund. - 1856-1939. I. Jung, C. G. (Carl Gustav), 1875-1961. II. Evans, Richard I. (Richard Isadore), 1922- III. Meaney, John W. IV. Segaller Films. V. KUHT Film*

Productions. VI. Films Incorporated. VII. Home Vision (Firm) VIII. Public Media Video (Firm) IX. Pubic Media Incorporated (Wilmette, Ill.) X. Title: Carl Gustav Jung interviewed in Zurich, Switzerland on August 5-8, 1957 [videorecording] XI. Title: Home Vision a Films Incorporated Company presents ... XII. Title: Biography XIII. Series: Biography (Public Media Video)
*TC BF109.J8 J4 1990*

**JUNGIAN PSYCHOLOGY.**
Luke, Helen M., 1904- Such stuff as dreams are made on. New York : Parabola Books, c2000.
*TC BF1091 .L82 2000*

Pathways into the Jungian world. London ; New York : Routledge, 2000.
*TC BF175 .P29 2000*

Stevens, Anthony. The two million-year-old self. New York : Fromm International Publishing, 1997.
*TC BF175.5.A72 S75 1997*

**Jungian thought in the modern world** / edited by Elphis Christopher and Hester Solomon. London ; New York : Free Association, 2000. xxvi, 277 p.: ill. ; 24 cm. Includes bibliographical references and index. ISBN 1-85343-466-3 ISBN 1-85343-467-1 (pbk.) DDC 150.1954
*1. Jung, C. G. - (Carl Gustav), - 1875-1961. 2. Psychoanalysis. I. Solomon, Hester. II. Christopher, Elphis, 1936-*
*TC BF173.J85 J85 2000*

**Junion-Metz, Gail, 1947-** Creating a power web site : HTML, tables, imagemaps, frames, and forms / by Gail Junion-Metz and Brad Stephens. New York : Neal-Schuman, c1998. xviii, 199 p. : ill. ; 28 cm. + 1 computer laser optical disc (4 3/4 in.). Includes bibliographical references (p. [171]-176) and index. ISBN 1-55570-323-2 DDC 005.7/2
*1. Web sites - Design. 2. Library information networks. 3. Web sites - United States - Design. 4. Library information networks - United States. I. Stephens, Brad. II. Title.*
*TC Z674.75.W67 J86 1998*

**Junior college journal.**
Community and junior college journal. Washington, D.C. : American Association of Community and Junior Colleges, 1972-1985.

**Junior college journal.** Washington, D.C. [etc.] 42 v. ill. (incl. diagrs.) plates. 23-28 cm. Frequency: Monthly during the college year. v. 1-42, no.9; Oct. 1930-June/July 1972. Official journal of the American Association of Junior Colleges. Vols. 1-22 in microfilm edition. Vols. 1-8, Oct. 1930-May 1938, issued under the joint editorial auspices of the American Association of Junior Colleges and the School of Education of Stanford University, and published by the Stanford University Press, Stanford University, Calif. Continued by: Community and junior college journal ISSN: 0190-3160. ISSN 0022-653X DDC 378.05
*1. Junior colleges - Periodicals. I. American Association of Junior Colleges. II. Stanford University. School of Education. III. Title: Community and junior college journal*

**JUNIOR COLLEGES.** *See* **COMMUNITY COLLEGES.**

**JUNIOR COLLEGES - PERIODICALS.**
Community and junior college journal. Washington, D.C. : American Association of Community and Junior Colleges, 1972-1985.

Junior college journal. Washington, D.C. [etc.]

**JUNIOR COLLEGES - UNITED STATES - CASE STUDIES.**
Two-year colleges for women and minorities. New York : Falmer Press, 1999.
*TC LB2328.15.U6 T96 1999*

**Junior edition** [computer file] [Farmington Hills, Mi.] : The Gale Group, c1999. Computer data. Mode of access: World Wide Web. Subscription and registration are required for access. Text. System requirements: Internet connectivity, World Wide Web browser. Title from main search screen viewed September 18, 2000. Description based on content as of September, 2000. On menu screen: InfoTrac. Covers current year to date plus the three previous years. Updated daily. Audience: junior high and middle school students. Accessed through Infotrac web interface. SUMMARY: "A collection of full-text oriented toward junior high and middle school students. In addition to material from periodicals, the database also includes newspaper articles, an encyclopedia, and a variety of other reference material. Covered subjects include politics and current events; consumer electronics; arts and entertainment; automobiles; recreation and leisure; crime; personal finances; and food."-- Gale Group Collections help screen. URL: http://infotrac.galegroup.com/itweb/new30429?id=newlog&db=STOJ
*1. Periodicals - Indexes - Computer network resources. 2. Reference sources - Juvenile literature - Computer network resources. I. Gale Group. II. Title: InfoTrac.*

**The Junior high clearing house.** Lebanon, Pa., Junior High School Clearing House. 1 v. 25 cm. Frequency: Eight no. a year. v. 3; 1928-29. Additional holdings in microfilm. See Microfilm: 2092 Continues: Junior high school clearing house. Continued by: Junior-senior high school clearing house (DLC)sn 87021674 (OCoLC)2273285.
*1. Education, Secondary - Periodicals. 2. Education - Periodicals. 3. Junior high schools - Periodicals. I. Title: Junior high school clearing house II. Title: Junior-senior high school clearing house*

**Junior high school clearing house.**
The Junior high clearing house. Lebanon, Pa., Junior High School Clearing House.

**JUNIOR HIGH SCHOOL STUDENTS.**
Kinnamon, James C. A comparison of structural knowledge in eighth graders and college students. 1999.
*TC 085 K6194*

**JUNIOR HIGH SCHOOL STUDENTS - ATTITUDES.**
Darwiche, Chirine Hijazi. The Beacons. 1997.
*TC 06 no. 10761*

**JUNIOR HIGH SCHOOLS.** *See* **MIDDLE SCHOOLS.**

**JUNIOR HIGH SCHOOLS - NEW YORK (STATE) - NEW YORK - CASE STUDIES.**
Darwiche, Chirine Hijazi. The Beacons. 1997.
*TC 06 no. 10761*

**JUNIOR HIGH SCHOOLS - PERIODICALS.**
The Junior high clearing house. Lebanon, Pa., Junior High School Clearing House.

**JUNIOR HIGH SCHOOLS - STUDENTS.** *See* **JUNIOR HIGH SCHOOL STUDENTS.**

**Junior-senior high school clearing house.**
The Junior high clearing house. Lebanon, Pa., Junior High School Clearing House.

**JURATORS.** *See* **JURORS.**

**JURIES.** *See* **JURY.**

**JURISPRUDENCE.** *See* **LAW.**

**JURORS - UNITED STATES.**
Flaton, Robin Anne. Effect of deliberation on juror reasoning. 1999.
*TC 085 F612*

**JURY.** *See* **VERDICTS.**

**JURY MEMBERS.** *See* **JURORS.**

**JURY - UNITED STATES - DECISION MAKING.**
Flaton, Robin Anne. Effect of deliberation on juror reasoning. 1999.
*TC 085 F612*

**JURYMEN.** *See* **JURORS.**

**Juslin, Peter.**
Judgment and decision making. Mahwah, N.J. : L. Erlbaum Associates, 1999.
*TC BF448 .J83 1999*

**Just around the corner.**
Jacobs, Leland B. (Leland Blair), 1907- New York : H. Holt, 1993.
*TC PS3560.A2545 J87 1993*

**Just one more story.**
Steer, Dugald. New York : Dutton Children's Books, 1999.
*TC PZ7.S81534 Ju 1999*

**Just sex :** students rewrite the rules on sex, violence, activism, and equality / edited by Jodi Gold and Susan Villari. Lanham, MD : Rowman & Littlefield, 2000. xxvi, 323 p. ; 23 cm. Includes bibliographical references and index. ISBN 0-8476-9333-3 (cl. : alk. paper) ISBN 0-8476-9332-5 (pbk. : alk. paper) DDC 306.7
*1. Sex. 2. Sex customs. 3. Sex differences (Psychology) 4. Students - Sexual behavior. 5. Sex discrimination. I. Gold, Jodi. II. Villari, Susan, 1957-*
*TC HQ21 .J87 1999*

**JUSTICE.** *See* **SOCIAL JUSTICE.**

**JUSTICE, ADMINISTRATION OF.** *See* **CRIMINAL JUSTICE, ADMINISTRATION OF; DISPUTE RESOLUTION (LAW).**

**Justman, Stewart.** The psychological mystique / Stewart Justman. Evanston, Ill. : Northwestern University Press, 1998. 181 p. ; 24 cm. (Rethinking theory) Includes bibliographical references (p. 142-179) and index. ISBN 0-8101-1601-4 (alk. paper) DDC 150/.1
*1. Psychology - Philosophy. 2. Ethnopsychology. I. Title. II. Series.*
*TC BF38 .J87 1998*

**JUVENILE BOOKS.** *See* **CHILDREN'S BOOKS.**

**JUVENILE CORRECTIONS.** *See* **JUVENILE DELINQUENCY.**

**JUVENILE CORRECTIONS - OREGON.**
Teen killers [videorecording]. Princeton, NJ : Films for the Humanities and Sciences, c1998-1999.
*TC HV9067.H6 T4 1999*

**JUVENILE DELINQUENCY.** *See also* **JUVENILE CORRECTIONS; REFORMATORIES; SCHOOL VIOLENCE.**
Cullingford, Cedric. The causes of exclusion :. London : Kogan Page ; Sterling, VA : Stylus, 1999.
*TC HV6166 .C85 1999*

Rosen, Sidney M. Toward a gang solution. [Norman, Okla.?] NRC Youth Services, 1996.
*TC HV6439.U7 R67 1996*

**JUVENILE DELINQUENCY - GOVERNMENT POLICY - UNITED STATES.**
Zimring, Franklin E. American youth violence. New York : Oxford University Press, 1998.
*TC HV9104 .Z57 1998*

**JUVENILE DELINQUENCY - HAWAII - CASE STUDIES.**
Rosen, Sidney M. Toward a gang solution. [Norman, Okla.?] NRC Youth Services, 1996.
*TC HV6439.U7 R67 1996*

**JUVENILE DELINQUENCY - PERIODICALS.**
The Journal of delinquency. Whittier, Calif. : Whittier State School, Dept. of Research, 1916-c1928.

**JUVENILE DELINQUENCY - TEXAS - PREVENTION.**
Turk, William L. When juvenile crime comes to school. Lewiston, NY : E. Mellen Press, 1999.
*TC HV6250.4.S78 T87 1999*

**JUVENILE DELINQUENCY - UNITED STATES - PREVENTION.**
Bemak, Fred. Violent and aggressive youth. Thousand Oaks, Calif. ; London : Corwin Press, c2000.
*TC LB3013.3 .B45 2000*

Turk, William L. When juvenile crime comes to school. Lewiston, NY : E. Mellen Press, 1999.
*TC HV6250.4.S78 T87 1999*

**JUVENILE DELINQUENTS.** *See* **GANGS.**

**JUVENILE DISEASES.** *See* **CHILDREN - DISEASES.**

**JUVENILE DRAMA.** *See* **CHILDREN'S PLAYS.**

**JUVENILE FICTION.** *See* **CHILDREN'S STORIES.**

**JUVENILE FILMS.** *See* **MOTION PICTURES FOR CHILDREN.**

**JUVENILE HOMICIDE - UNITED STATES.**
Teen killers [videorecording]. Princeton, NJ : Films for the Humanities and Sciences, c1998-1999.
*TC HV9067.H6 T4 1999*

**JUVENILE JUSTICE, ADMINISTRATION OF.** *See also* **JUVENILE CORRECTIONS.**
Governing childhood. Aldershot, England ; Brookfield, Vt. : Dartmouth, c1997.
*TC HQ789 .G68 1997*

**JUVENILE JUSTICE, ADMINISTRATION OF - UNITED STATES.**
Zimring, Franklin E. American youth violence. New York : Oxford University Press, 1998.
*TC HV9104 .Z57 1998*

**JUVENILE LITERATURE.** *See* **CHILDREN'S LITERATURE.**

**JUVENILE MURDER.** *See* **JUVENILE HOMICIDE.**

**JUVENILE SERIES (PUBLICATIONS).** *See* **CHILDREN'S LITERATURE IN SERIES.**

**JUVENILE SEX OFFENDERS.** *See* **TEENAGE SEX OFFENDERS.**

**Juvenile sex offenders** [videorecording] : voices unheard / a presentation of Films for the Humanities & Sciences ; [presented by] B Productions ; a film by Beth B. : producer/director, Beth B. ; produced in co-production with the Banff Centre for the Arts. Princeton, N.J. : Films of the Humanities & Sciences, c1998. 1 videocassette (58 min.) : sd., col. ; 1/2 in. VHS. Catalogued from credits and container. Cinematographers, Phil Parmet, Tony Hettinger ; editor, Melody London ; music composer, Jim Filer Coleman; sound recordist, Daniel McIntosh, Jon Dunlap. For adolescents through adult. SUMMARY: This program goes to a lock-down and into the community to develop a profile of juvenile sex

offenders and to study the work of organizations attempting to reintegrate juvenile offenders into society. Visits Starr Commonwealth, an open facility, Plainfield Juvenile Correctional Facility, Wood Youth Center and others as offenders talk about their backgrounds and their crimes. As viewers we sit in on group therapy and listen. Clips throughout the film acquaint us with offenders who have been abused themselves as children and many of whom use sex like a drug. And we listen as therapists discuss trying to teach offenders internal controls and empathy with their victims and a Prevention Plan to prevent recidivism.
*1. Teenage sex offenders - United States - Psychology. 2. Teenage sex offenders - Rehabilitation - United States. 3. Teenage sex offenders - Mental health services - United States. 4. Incest - United States - Psychological aspects. 5. Community mental health services for teenagers - United States. 6. Sex offenders - United States - Psychology. 7. Sex offenders - Rehabilitation - United States. 8. Sex offenders - Mental health services - United States. I. B., Beth. II. Banff Centre for the Arts. III. Films for the Humanities (Firm) IV. Title: Voices unheard [videorecording]*
**TC HV9067.S48 J8 1998**

**JUVENILE SOFTWARE. See CHILDREN'S SOFTWARE.**

**K. D. Ushinsky.**
Ushinskiĭ, K. D. (Konstantin Dmitrievich), 1824-1870. [Selected works. English. 1975] Moscow : Progress, 1975.
**TC LB675 .U8213 1975**

**K-eight.** [Philadelphia, American Pub. Co.] v. ill. 28 cm. Frequency: 7 no. a year. Sept./Oct. 1971-Spring 1975. "Learning through media." Formed by the union of Educate and Modern media teacher. Sept./Oct. 1971-Apr./May 1974 also called v. 1-3, no. 7. DDC 371.33/05
*1. Audio-visual education - Periodicals. 2. Teaching - Aids and devices - Periodicals I. Title: Educate*

**K-THEORY - CONGRESSES.**
Algebra, K-theory, groups, and education. Providence, R.I. : American Mathematical Society, c1999.
**TC QA150 .A419 1999**

**The Kadelpian quarterly review** / Executive Council of the Kappa Delta Pi Fraternity. [S.l.] : The Council, 1926- 1 v. : ill. ; 25 cm. Frequency: Quarterly. Began publication with vol. 6, no. 1 in Nov. 1926 and ceased with vol. 6, no. 4 in June 1927? Continues: Kappa Delta Pi record (OCoLC)8324078. Continued by: Kadelpian review (OCoLC)7505013.
*1. Education - Periodicals. I. Kappa Delta Pi Fraternity. Executive Council. II. Title: Kappa Delta Pi record III. Title: Kadelpian review*

**Kadelpian review.**
The Kadelpian quarterly review . [S.l.] : The Council, 1926-

**Kadono, Eiko.** Grandpa's soup / written by Eiko Kadono ; illustrated by Satomi Ichikawa. Grand Rapids, MI : Eerdmans Books for Young Readers, 1999. 32 p. : col. ill. ; 25 cm. SUMMARY: After the death of his wife, an old man gradually realizes that making the soup she used to cook and sharing it with friends eases his loneliness. ISBN 0-8028-5195-9 (cloth : alk. paper) DDC [E]
*1. Soups - Fiction. 2. Loneliness - Fiction. 3. Grief - Fiction. 4. Sharing - Fiction. I. Ichikawa, Satomi, ill. II. Title.*
**TC PZ7.K1167 Gr 1999**

**Kaeppler, Adrienne Lois.**
Exhibiting dilemmas. Washington, D.C. : Smithsonian Insitution Press, c1997.
**TC AM151 .E96 1997**

**Kahn, Alfred J., 1919-** Big cities in the welfare transition / Alfred J. Kahn and Sheila B. Kamerman. New York City : Cross-National Studies Research Program, Columbia University School of Social Work, 1998. x, 263 p. ; 23 cm. Report of a roundtable working between 1995 and 1997 to draw conclusions of the programs reported in the series 'Confronting the new politics of child and family policy in the United States'. Includes bibliographical references.
*1. Public welfare - United States. 2. Human services - Government policy - United States. 3. Cities and towns - United States. 4. State-local relations - United States. 5. United States - Social policy - 1993- I. Kamerman, Sheila B. II. Columbia University. School of Social Work. Cross-National Studies Research Program. III. Title.*
**TC HV91 .K27 1998**

**Kahn, Herman, 1922-** The year 2000 : a framework for speculation on the next thirty-three years / by Herman Kahn and Anthony J. Wiener ; with contributions from other staff members of the Hudson Institute ; introduction by Daniel Bell. New York : Macmillan, c1967. xxviii, 431 p. : ill. ; 24 cm. Includes bibliographical references and indexes. DDC 301.2
*1. Twentieth century - Forecasts. I. Wiener, Anthony J. II. Hudson Institute. III. Title.*

**TC CB160 .K3 1967**

**Kahn, Jessica L.** Ideas and strategies for the one-computer classroom / Jessica Kahn. Eugene, OR : International Society for Technology in Education, c1998. x, 138 p. : ill. ; 29 cm. Cover title: Ideas & strategies for the one-computer classroom. Includes bibliographical references (p. 111) and index. ISBN 1-56484-132-4
*1. Computer-assisted instruction. 2. Education - Data processing. I. International Society for Technology in Education. II. Title. III. Title: One-computer classroom IV. Title: Ideas & strategies for the one-computer classroom*
**TC LB1028.5 .K25 1998**

**Kahn, Peter H.** The human relationship with nature : development and culture / Peter H. Kahn, Jr. Cambridge, Mass. : MIT Press, c1999. xiv, 281 p. ; 24 cm. Includes bibliographical references (p. [253]-275) and index. ISBN 0-262-11240-X (hardcover : alk. paper) DDC 155.9/1
*1. Nature - Psychological aspects. 2. Nature - Psychological aspects - Cross-cultural studies. 3. Environmental psychology. I. Title.*
**TC BF353.5.N37 K34 1999**

**Kainer, Rochelle G. K., 1936-** The collapse of the self and its therapeutic restoration / Rochelle G.K. Kainer. Hillsdale, NJ : London : Analytic Press, 1999. xiv, 206 p. ; 24 cm. (Relational perspectives book series ; v. 15) Includes bibliographical references (p. 185-193) and index. ISBN 0-88163-311-9 (paperback) ISBN 0-88163-317-8 (hardback) DDC 616.89/17
*1. Self. 2. Psychoanalysis. I. Title. II. Series.*
**TC RC489.S43 K35 1999**

**KAIULANI, PRINCESS OF HAWAII, 1875-1899 - JUVENILE LITERATURE.**
Linnea, Sharon. Princess Ka'iulani. Grand Rapids, Mich. : Eerdmans Books for Young Readers, 1999.
**TC DU627.17.K3 L56 1999**

**Kajikawa, Kimiko.** Sweet dreams : how animals sleep / Kimiko Kajikawa. 1st ed. New York : Henry Holt, c1999. [30 p.] : col. ill. ; 26 cm. SUMMARY: Rhyming verses followed by factual information briefly describe the sleep habits of a variety of animals. ISBN 0-8050-5890-7 (alk. paper) DDC 591.5/19
*1. Sleep behavior in animals - Juvenile literature. 2. Animals - Sleep behavior. 3. Sleep. I. Title.*
**TC QL755.3 .K36 1999**

**Kalantzis, Mary.**
Multiliteracies. London ; New York : Routledge, 2000.
**TC LC149 .M85 2000**

**Kale, Shelly.** My museum journal : a writing and sketching book / Shelly Kale and Lisa Vihos ; drawings by Otto Steininger. Los Angeles, CA : J. Paul Getty Museum, c2000. 44 p. : ill. (some col.) ; ports. ; 27 cm. SUMMARY: Encourages children create their own works of art to express their views and feelings about the world around them by using art works from the J. Paul Getty Museum as a starting point. ISBN 0-89236-570-6
*1. J. Paul Getty Museum - Juvenile literature. 2. J. Paul Getty Museum - Juvenile literature. 3. Art appreciation - Juvenile literature. 4. Art - Psychology - Juvenile literature. 5. Creation (Literary, artistic, etc.) - Juvenile literature. 6. Art appreciation - Juvenile literature. 7. Art - Psychology - Juvenile literature. I. Vihos, Lisa. II. Steininger, Otto. III. J. Paul Getty Museum. IV. Title.*
**TC N7440 .K35 2000**

**Kalfatovic, Martin R., 1961-** The New Deal fine arts projects : a bibliography, 1933-1992 / by Martin R. Kalfatovic. Metuchen, N.J. : Scarecrow Press, 1994. lxxii, 504 p. ; 22 cm. Includes indexes. ISBN 0-8108-2749-2 DDC 016.3530085/4
*1. Federal aid to the arts - United States - Bibliography. 2. Art - Conservation and restoration - United States - Bibliography. 3. New Deal, 1933-1939. I. Title.*
**TC Z5961.U5 K36 1994**

**Kalmanson, Dan.**
Autism--a world apart [videorecording]. Boston, MA : Fanlight Productions, [1989, c1988].
**TC RJ506 .A98 1988**

**Kaluza, Jens.**
Evans, Karen, 1949- Learning and work in the risk society. New York : St. Martin's Press, 2000.
**TC HD6278.G4 E93 2000**

**Kalverboer, Alex Fedde.**
Current issues in developmental psychology. Dordrecht ; Boston ; London : Kluwer Academic Publishers, c1999.
**TC RJ134 .C868 1999**

**Kalyanpur, Maya.** Culture in special education : building reciprocal family-professional relationships / by Maya Kalyanpur and Beth Harry. Baltimore, Md. :

P.H. Brookes Pub., c1999. xxii, 159 p. ; 23 cm. Includes bibliographical references (p. 133-150) and index. ISBN 1-55766-376-9 (alk. paper) DDC 371.9/04
*1. Special education - Social aspects - United States - Case studies. 2. Educational anthropology - United States - Case studies. 3. Special education - Parent participation - United States - Case studies. I. Harry, Beth. II. Title.*
**TC LC3969 .K35 1999**

Harry, Beth. Building cultural reciprocity with families. Baltimore, Md. : P.H. Brookes Pub. Co., c1999.
**TC LC3969 .H377 1999**

**Kameenui, Edward J.**
What reading research tells us about children with diverse learning needs. Mahwah, N.J. : Erlbaum, 1998.
**TC LB1050.5 .W47 1998**

**Kamerling, Leonard.**
Heart of the country [videorecording]. [New York, NY : First Run/Icarus Films, 1998].
**TC LB1565.H6 H3 1998**

**Kamerman, Sheila B.**
Kahn, Alfred J., 1919- Big cities in the welfare transition. New York City : Cross-National Studies Research Program, Columbia University School of Social Work, 1998.
**TC HV91 .K27 1998**

**Kamhi, Michelle Marder.**
Torres, Louis, 1938- What art is. Chicago, Ill. : Open Court, c2000.
**TC PS3535.A547 Z9 2000**

**Kamil, Michael L.**
Handbook of reading research. New York : Longman, c1984-<2000 >
**TC LB1050 .H278 2000**

**Kaminker, Laura.**
d-a-t-e rape [videorecording]. [Charleston, WV] : Cambridge Educational, c1994.
**TC RC560.R36 D3 1994**

**Kamler, Barbara.**
Constructing gender and difference. Cresskill, N.J. : Hampton Press, c1999.
**TC BF723.S42 C66 1999**

**Kampwirth, Thomas J.** Collaborative consultation in the schools : effective practices for students with learning and behavior problems / Thomas J. Kampwirth. Upper Saddle River, N.J. : Merrill, c1999. xvi, 335 p. ; 24 cm. Includes bibliographical references and index. ISBN 0-13-755901-1 DDC 371.9
*1. Educational counseling - United States. 2. Group work in education - United States. 3. Learning disabled children - Services for - United States. 4. Problem children - Services for - United States. 5. School management and organization - United States. I. Title.*
**TC LB1027.5 .K285 1999**

**Kamusikiri, Sandra, 1949-.**
Assessment of writing. New York : Modern Language Association of America, 1996.
**TC PE1404 .A88 1996**

**KANAYAMA ELEMENTARY SCHOOL.**
Heart of the country [videorecording]. [New York, NY : First Run/Icarus Films, 1998].
**TC LB1565.H6 H3 1998**

**Kane, Francis, 1944-** Neither beasts nor gods : civic life and the public good / by Francis Kane. Dallas : Southern Methodist University Press, 1998. 168 p. ; 24 cm. Includes bibliographical references (p. [143]-162) and index. ISBN 0-87074-422-4 (cloth) ISBN 0-87074-423-2 (paper) DDC 320/.01/1
*1. Common good. 2. Public interest. 3. Political participation. I. Title.*
**TC JC330.15 .K36 1998**

**Kane, Georgann.**
The climate puzzle [videorecording]. [New York, N.Y.?] : Unapix Entertainment, Inc. [distributor], c1996.
**TC QB631.2 .C5 1996**

The living machine [videorecording]. [New York, N.Y.?] : Unapix Entertainment, Inc. [distributor], c1996.
**TC QB631.2 .L5 1996**

The solar sea [videorecording]. [New York, N.Y.?] : Unapix Entertainment, Inc. [distributor], c1996.
**TC QB631.2 .S6 1996**

**Kane, Jeffrey, 1952-.**
Education, information, and transformation. Upper Saddle River, N.J. : Merrill, c1999.

**TC BF441 .E25 1999**

**Kane, Thomas J.** The price of admission : rethinking how Americans pay for college / Thomas J. Kane. Washington, D.C. : Brookings Institution Press ; New York : Russell Sage Foundation, c1999. ix, 164 p. : ill. ; 24 cm. Includes bibliographical references (p. 155-160) and index. ISBN 0-8157-5014-5 (cloth : alk. paper) ISBN 0-8157-5013-7 (pbk. : alk. paper) DDC 378.3/0973
*1. College costs - United States. 2. Student aid - United States. 3. Government aid to education - United States. 4. Parents - United States - Finance, Personal. I. Title.*
**TC LB2342 .K35 1999**

**KANGAROOS.**
Markle, Sandra. Outside and inside kangaroos. 1st ed. New York, N.Y. : Atheneum Books for Young Readers, c1999.
**TC QL737.M35 M272 1999**

**KANGAROOS - JUVENILE LITERATURE.**
Markle, Sandra. Outside and inside kangaroos. 1st ed. New York, N.Y. : Atheneum Books for Young Readers, c1999.
**TC QL737.M35 M272 1999**

**KANNER SYNDROME.** *See* **AUTISM IN CHILDREN.**

**KANNER'S SYNDROME.** *See* **AUTISM IN CHILDREN.**

**Kanpol, Barry.**
From nihilism to possibility. Cresskill, N.J. : Hampton Press, c1999.
**TC LC5141 .F76 1999**

**Kansanen, Pertti, 1940-.**
Teachers' pedagogical thinking. New York : P. Lang, 2000.
**TC LB1775 . T4179 2000**

**Kansas-National Education Association.**
The Kansas teacher. Topeka, Kansas-NEA.

**The Kansas teacher.** Topeka, Kansas-NEA. Ceased publication 1983. Cf. Letter from publisher. Frequency varies. Official publication of the Kansas-National Education Association. Continued by: Issues (Topeka, Kan.) (OCoLC)10766788. ISSN 0022-8834
*1. Kansas-National Education Association. II. Title: Issues (Topeka, Kan.)*

**Kaplan, Bernard.**
Development and the arts. Hillsdale, N.J. : L. Erlbaum Associates, 1994.
**TC N71 .D495 1994**

**Kaplan de Drimer, Alicia.** Los amigos del Hada Melina / Alicia K. de Drimer. Buenos Aires : Intercoop Editora Cooperativa, [1995?]-1998. v. <3-4 > : ill. ; 22 cm. (Serie Divulgación) PARTIAL CONTENTS: v. 1. Papá chingolo ; De regreso ; Una pareja despareja -- v. 2. Me han robado el nido! ; Los pingüinos también tienen frío ; Los osos viajeros -- v. 3. Tortuguitas ; Donde está el osito hormiguero? -- v. 4. El jaguar y el teruteru ; La perdíz y el colibrí ISBN 950-9012-56-4 (obra comp.) ISBN 950-9012-54-8 (t. 1) ISBN 950-9012-55-6 (t. 2) ISBN 950-9012-64-5 (t. 3) ISBN 950-9012-65-3 (t. 4)
*I. Title. II. Series: Serie Divulgación (INTERCOOP, Editora Cooperativa Ltda.)*
**TC PQ7798.21.A64 A65 1995**

**Kaplan, Tony.**
Hendriks, Jean Harris. When father kills mother. 2nd ed. London ; Philadelphia : Routledge, 2000.
**TC RJ506.U96 .B53 2000**

**Kappa Delta Pi Fraternity. Executive Council.**
The Kadelpian quarterly review . [S.l.] : The Council, 1926-

**Kappa Delta Pi (Honor society).**
Life cycle of the career teacher. [Indianapolis, Ind.] : Kappa Delta Pi ; Thousand Oaks, Calif. : Corwin Press, c2000.
**TC LB1775.2 .L54 2000**

**Kappa Delta Pi record.**
The Kadelpian quarterly review . [S.l.] : The Council, 1926-

**Karabel, Harry J.**
Exploring the English language [videorecording]. [Princeton, N.J.] : Video Tutor ; [Chesterton, Ind.? : Distributed by] Griffin Media Design, 1988, c1986.

**Karachi. Jamia Institute of Education.**
The Jamia educational quarterly. Malir City, Karachi : Jamia Millia Institute of Education, 1960-1972.

**Karas, G. Brian.** The windy day / G. Brian Karas. 1st ed. New York : Simon & Schuster Books for Young Readers, 1998. 1 v. (unpaged) : col. ill. ; 29 cm. SUMMARY: One day the wind blows into a tidy little town,

giving a tidy little boy named Bernard a hint of how wonderful and exciting the world is. ISBN 0-689-81449-6 DDC [E]
*1. Winds - Fiction. I. Title.*
**TC PZ7.K1296 Wi 1998**

**Kardiner, Abram, 1891-** The mark of oppression: a psychosocial study of the American Negro, by Abram Kardiner and Lionel Ovesey. [1st ed.]. New York, Norton [1951] xvii, 396 p. 25 cm. Includes index. DDC 325.260973
*1. Afro-Americans - Psychology. 2. Afro-Americans - Social conditions. I. Ovesey, Lionel, joint author. II. Title.*
**TC E185.625 .K3**

**Kareem, Jafar.**
Intercultural therapy. [2nd ed.]. Oxford ; Malden, MA : Blackwell Science, 2000.
**TC RC455.4.E8 I57 2000**

**Karim, Abul Bashr Mohammed Fazlul.**
Death. Amsterdam : VU University Press, 1998.
**TC R726.8 .D42 1998**

**Karlin, Marc.**
Photomontage today, Peter Kennard [videorecording]. [London] : Art Council of Great Britain ; Ho-Ho-Kus, N.J. : [distributed by] Anthony Roland Collection of Films on Art, c1982.
**TC TR685 .P45 1982**

**Karlins, Marvin.** Persuasion: how opinions and attitudes are changed [by] Marvin Karlins [and] Herbert I. Abelson. 2d ed. New York, Springer Pub. Co. [1970] xi, 179 p. 22 cm. First ed., 1959, by H. I. Abelson. Bibliography: p. 161-174. DDC 153.8/52
*1. Persuasion (Psychology) I. Abelson, Herbert Irving, 1926- joint author. II. Title.*
**TC BF637.P4 K27 1970**

**Karlsson, Jan, 1940-** Antioxidants and exercise / Jan Karlsson. Champaign, IL : Human Kinetics, c1997. x, 211 p. : ill. ; 24 cm. Includes bibliographical references (p. 183-201) and index. ISBN 0-87322-896-0 DDC 612/.044
*1. Antioxidants. 2. Exercise - Physiological aspects. 3. Free radicals (Chemistry) - Pathophysiology. 4. Sports medicine. 5. Exercise - physiology. 6. Antioxidants - metabolism. 7. Free Radicals - metabolism. I. Title.*
**TC RB170 .K37 1997**

**Karmel, Pepe.**
Varnedoe, Kirk, 1946- Jackson Pollock. New York : Museum of Modern Art : Distributed in the U.S. and Canada by Harry N. Abrams, c1998.
**TC ND237.P73 A4 1998**

**Karnataka State Education Federation.**
Journal of the Karnataka State Education Federation. [Bangalore, India] : The Federation, [1973?]-

**Karnes, Frances A.** Gifted children and legal issues : an update / Frances A. Karnes and Ronald G. Marquardt. Scottsdale, AZ : Gifted Psychology Press, 2000. x, 230 p. ; 23 cm. Includes bibliographical references and index. ISBN 0-910707-34-0 DDC 344.73/07915
*1. Gifted children - Education - Law and legislation - United States. 2. Gifted children - Legal status, laws, etc. - United States. I. Marquardt, Ronald G., 1939- II. Title.*
**TC KF4209.5 .K369 2000**

Gifted children and legal issues in education. Dayton, Ohio : Ohio Psychology Press, c1991.
**TC KF4209.5 .G54 1991**

Gifted children and the law : mediation, due process, and court cases / Frances A. Karnes and Ronald G. Marquardt. Dayton, Ohio : Ohio Psychology Press, c1991. xv, 206 p. : ill. ; 23 cm. Includes bibliographical references and index. ISBN 0-910707-15-4 DDC 344.73/07915; 347.3047915
*1. Gifted children - Education - Law and legislation - United States. 2. Gifted children - Legal status, laws, etc. - United States. I. Marquardt, Ronald G., 1939- II. Title.*
**TC KF4209.5 .K37 1991**

**Karol, Tom.**
Matisse, voyages [videorecording]. [Chicago, Ill.] : Home Vision ; [S.l.] : Distributed worldwide by RM Associates, c1989.
**TC ND553.M37 M37 1989**

**Karp, Karen, 1951-.**
Feisty females. Portsmouth, NH : Heinemann, c1998.
**TC QA11 .F44 1998**

**Kárpáti, Andrea.** Látni tanulunk : a műelemzés tanítása az általános iskolában / Kárpáti Andrea. Budapest : Akadémiai Kiadó, 1991. 214 p. : ill. ; 24 cm. (Közoktatási kutatások, 0238-6577) Includes bibliographical references (p. 189-196). ISBN 963-05-5919-6
*1. Art appreciation - Study and teaching. I. Title. II. Series.*
**TC N85 .K35 1991**

**Karr, Kathleen.** Man of the family / Kathleen Karr. 1st ed. New York : Farrar, Straus and Giroux, 1999. 178 p. ; 20 cm. SUMMARY: During the 1920s, life for Istvan, the eldest child of a Hungarian-American family, holds both joy and sadness. ISBN 0-374-34764-6 DDC [Fic]
*1. Hungarian Americans - Juvenile fiction. 2. Hungarian Americans - Fiction. 3. Fathers and sons - Fiction. 4. Family life - New Jersey - Fiction. 5. New Jersey - Fiction. I. Title.*
**TC PZ7.K149 Man 1999**

**Kaschak, Ellyn, 1943-.**
For love or money. New York : Haworth Press, c1999.
**TC RC489.F45 F67 1999**

**Kaser, Joyce S.**
Enhancing program quality in science and mathematics. Thousand Oaks, Calif. : Corwin Press, c1999.
**TC LB1585.3 .E55 1999**

**Kashima, Yoshihisa, 1957-.**
Social psychology and cultural context. Thousand Oaks, Calif. : Sage Publications, c1999.
**TC HM1033 .S64 1999**

**Kashiwagi, Hiroshi.**
Rabbit in the moon [videorecording]. San Francisco, Calif. : Wabi-Sabi Productions, 1999.
**TC D753.8 .R3 1999**

**Kasper, Loretta F. (Loretta Frances), 1951-** Content-based college ESL instruction / Loretta F. Kasper ; with Marcia Babbitt ... [et al.]. Mahwah, N.J. : Lawrence Erlbaum Associates, 2000. xiv, 227 p. : ill. ; 23 cm. Includes bibliographical references and indexes. ISBN 0-8058-3076-6 (alk. paper) DDC 428/.0071/173
*1. English language - Study and teaching (Higher) - Foreign speakers. 2. English language - Study and teaching (Higher) - United States. 3. Interdisciplinary approach in education. I. Title.*
**TC PE1128.A2 K376 2000**

**Kastenbaum, Robert.** Death, society, and human experience / Robert J. Kastenbaum. 6th ed. Boston : Allyn and Bacon, c1998. xvii, 441 p. : ill. ; 24 cm. Includes bibliographical references and index. ISBN 0-205-26477-8 (pbk.) DDC 306.9
*1. Death - Psychological aspects. 2. Death - Social aspects. I. Title.*
**TC BF789.D4 K36 1998**

**Kaszniak, Alfred W., 1949-.**
Toward a science of consciousness III. Cambridge, Mass. : MIT Press, c1999.
**TC BF311 .T67 1999**

**Kate Douglas Wiggin's Rebecca of Sunnybrook Farm.**
Wiggin, Kate Douglas Smith, 1856-1923. Rebecca of Sunnybrook Farm. Boston, New York [etc.] : Houghton, Mifflin Company, [c1903] (Cambridge, Mass. : Riverside Press)
**TC PZ7.W638 Re 1903**

**Katsikides, Savvas.** The societal impact of technology / Savvas A. Katsikides. Aldershot, Hants, England ; Brookfield, Vt. : Ashgate, c1998. xiii, 114 p. ; 23 cm. Includes bibliographical references. DDC 303.48/3
*1. Technology - Social aspects. I. Title.*
**TC T14.5 .K373 1998**

**KATSINA COLLEGE - HISTORY - 20TH CENTURY.**
Hubbard, James P. (James Patrick), 1945- Education under colonial rule. Lanham : University Press of America, 2000
**TC LG483.K78 H83 2000**

**Katz, Karen.** The colors of us / by Karen Katz. 1st ed. New York : Holt, 1999. 1v. (unpaged) : col. ill. ; 27 cm. SUMMARY: Seven-year-old Lena and her mother observe the variations in the color of their friends' skin, viewed in terms of foods and things found in nature. ISBN 0-8050-5864-8 (hardcover : alk. paper) DDC [Fic]
*1. Racially mixed people - Fiction. I. Title.*
**TC PZ7.K15745 Co 1999**

**Katz, Mitchell H.** Multivariable analysis : a practical guide for clinicians / Mitchell H. Katz. Cambridge, UK ; New York : Cambridge University Press, 1999. xv, 192 p. : ill. ; 24 cm. Includes bibliographical references and index. ISBN 0-521-59301-8 (hb) ISBN 0-521-59693-9 (pbk.) DDC 610/.7/27
*1. Medicine - Research - Statistical methods. 2. Multivariate analysis. 3. Biometry. 4. Medical statistics. I. Title.*
**TC R853.S7 K38 1999**

**Katz, Tal Y.** Self-construal as a moderator of the effects of task and reward interdependence of group performance / by Tal Y. Katz. 1999. xiv, 141 leaves ; 29 cm. Typescript ; issued also on microfilm. Thesis (Ph.D.)-- Columbia University, 1999. Includes bibliographical references

(l. 109-115)
*1. Work groups. 2. Group problem solving. 3. Character tests. 4. Self-perception. 5. Competition - Psychology. 6. Motivation (Psychology). 7. Goal (Psychology). I. Title.*
*TC 085 K1524*

**Katz, Yaacov Julian.**
Affective education. London : New York : Cassell, 1998.
*TC LB1072 .A38 1998*

**Kauchak, Donald P., 1946-.**
Eggen, Paul D., 1940- Strategies for teachers. 4th ed. Boston : Allyn and Bacon, 2001.
*TC LB1027.3 .E44 2001*

**Kaufer, David S.** Designing interactive worlds with words : principles of writing as representational composition / David S. Kaufer, Brian S. Butler. Mahwah, N.J. : Lawrence Erlbaum Associates, 2000. xxiv, 285 p. : ill. ; 24 cm. Includes bibliographical references (p. 279-280) and indexes. ISBN 0-8058-3423-0 ISBN 0-8058-3424-9 (pbk.) DDC 808/.042/07
*1. English language - Rhetoric - Study and teaching. 2. Report writing - Study and teaching. 3. Representation (Philosophy) 4. Authors and readers. I. Butler, Brian S. II. Title.*
*TC PE1404 .K38 2000*

**Kaufman, Alan S.** Essentials of WISC-III and WPPSI-R assessment / Alan S. Kaufman and Elizabeth O. Lichtenberger. New York ; Chichester [England] : Wiley, c2000. x, 292 p. : ill. ; 22 cm. (Essentials of psychological assessment series) Includes bibliographical references (p. 272-283) and index. ISBN 0-471-34501-6 (pbk. : alk. paper) DDC 155.4/1393
*1. Wechsler Intelligence Scale for Children. 2. Wechsler Preschool and Primary Scale of Intelligence. I. Lichtenberger, Elizabeth O. II. Title. III. Series.*
*TC BF432.5.W42 K36 2000*

**Kaufman, Jeff, ill.**
Jacobs, Leland B. (Leland Blair), 1907- Just around the corner. New York : H. Holt, 1993.
*TC PS3560.A2545 J87 1993*

**KAUFMAN, NICOLE.**
Kaufman, Sandra Z., 1928- Retarded isn't stupid, mom!. Rev. ed. Baltimore : P.H. Brookes Pub., 1999.
*TC HV894 .K383 1999*

**Kaufman, Paul, 1935-.**
Goleman, Daniel. The creative spirit. New York, N.Y., U.S.A. : Dutton, c1992.
*TC BF408 .G57 1992*

**Kaufman, Robert Jay, ill.**
Blumenthal, Nancy. Count-a-saurus. New York : Four Winds Press, c1989.
*TC QA113 .B57 1989*

**Kaufman, Sandra Z., 1928-** Retarded isn't stupid, mom! / by Sandra Z. Kaufman. Rev. ed. Baltimore : P.H. Brookes Pub., 1999. xxi, 242 p. : ill. ; 21 cm. Includes bibliographical references (p. 235-240). ISBN 1-55766-378-5 (paperback) DDC 362.3/092
*1. Kaufman, Nicole. 2. Mentally handicapped children - United States - Biography. I. Title.*
*TC HV894 .K383 1999*

**Kaul, Chandrika.**
Statistical handbook on consumption and wealth in the United States. Phoenix, Ariz. : Oryx Press, 1999.
*TC HC110.C6 S73 1999*

**Kaul, Inge.**
Global public goods. New York : Oxford University Press, 1999.
*TC HB846.5 .G55 1999*

**Kaupelis, Robert.** Learning to draw; a creative approach to expressive drawing; by Robert Kaupelis. New York, Watson-Guptill Publications [1966] 138, [6] p. bill. ; 27 cm. Bibliography: p. [142] DDC 741.4
*1. Drawing - Instruction. I. Title.*
*TC NC730 .K36*

**Kavanagh, Gaynor.** Dream spaces : memory and the museum / Gaynor Kavanagh. New York : Leicester University Press, 2000. v111, 200 p. : ill. ; 24 cm. Includes bibliographical references and index. ISBN 0-7185-0207-8 ISBN 0-7185-0228-0 (pbk.) DDC 069
*1. Museums - Philosophy. 2. Museums - Social aspects. 3. Museums - Educational aspects. 4. Memory (Philosophy) 5. Memory - Social aspects. 6. Learning, Psychology of. 7. Communication and culture. I. Title.*
*TC AM7 .K37 2000*

Making histories in museums. London ; New York : Leicester University Press, 1996.
*TC AM7 .M35 1996*

**Kawachi, Ichirō.**
The society and population health reader. Volume I. New York, N.Y. : The New Press, c1999.

*TC RA418 .S6726 1999*

**Kay, J. W. (Jim W.).**
Statistics and neural networks. Oxford : New York : Oxford University Press, 1999.
*TC QA276 .S78343 1999*

**Kay, Verla.** Gold fever / Verla Kay ; illustrations by S.D. Schindler. New York : Putnam's, c1999. 1 v. (unpaged) : col. ill. ; 21 x 26 cm. SUMMARY: In this brief rhyming story set during the gold rush, Jasper leaves his family and farm to pursue his dream of finding gold. ISBN 0-399-23027-0 DDC [E]
*1. Gold mines and mining - Fiction. 2. West (U.S.) - Fiction. 3. Stories in rhyme. I. Schindler, S. D., ill. II. Title.*
*TC PZ8.3.K225 Go 1999*

Iron horses / by Verla Kay ; illustrated by Michael McCurdy. New York : Putnam, c1999. 1 v. (unpaged) : col. lll. ; 21 x 27 cm. SUMMARY: Illustrations and simple rhyming text depict the race to construct railroads across the country during the second half of the nineteenth century. ISBN 0-399-23119-6 DDC [E]
*1. Railroads - Fiction. 2. Stories in rhyme. I. McCurdy, Michael, ill. II. Title.*
*TC PZ8.3.K225 Ir 1999*

**Kayser, Daniel.**
Modelling changes in understanding. Amsterdam ; New York : Pergamon, 1999.
*TC BF319 .M55 1999*

**KAZAKHS - CHINA - HISTORY - 20TH CENTURY.**
Benson, Linda. China's last Nomads. Armonk, N.Y. : M.E. Sharpe, c1998.
*TC DS731.K38 B46 1998*

**KAZAKS. See KAZAKHS.**

**Kazdin, Alan E.**
Encyclopedia of psychology. Washington, D.C. : American Psychological Association, 2000.
*TC BF31 .E52 2000*

**KDD (INFORMATION RETRIEVAL). See DATA MINING.**

**Kearns, David T.** A legacy of learning : your stake in standards and new kinds of public schools / David T. Kearns and James Harvey. Washington, D.C. : Brookings Institution Press, c2000. xii, 226 p. ; 24 cm. Includes bibliographical references and index. ISBN 0-8157-4894-9 (alk. paper) DDC 371.01/0973
*1. Educational change - United States. 2. Public schools - United States - Evaluation. 3. Education - Standards - United States. I. Harvey, James, 1944- II. Title.*
*TC LA217.2 .K43 2000*

**Keates, Anita.** Dyslexia and information and communications technology : a guide for teachers and parents / Anita Keates. London : D. Fulton Publishers, 2000. vii, 88 p. : ill. ; 30 cm. Includes bibliographical references (p. 86) and index. ISBN 1-85346-651-4
*1. Dyslexic children - Education. 2. Dyslexia. 3. Computer-assisted instruction. I. Title.*
*TC LC4708.5K43 2000*

**Keating, Tom, 1941-** Saturday school : how one town kept out "the Jewish", 1902-1932 / by Tom Keating. Bloomington, Ind. : Phi Delta Kappa Educational Foundation, c1999. 60 p. : ill. ; 23 cm. Includes bibliographical references (p. 57-58). ISBN 0-87367-813-3
*1. Discrimination in education - Georgia - Decatur - History - 20th century. 2. Jews - Georgia - Decatur - History - 20th century. 3. Decatur (GA.) - Ethnic relations - History - 20th century. I. Title.*
*TC LC212.23.D43 K42 1999*

**Keating, W. Dennis (William Dennis).**
Rebuilding urban neighborhoods. Thousand Oaks, Calif. : Sage Publications, c1999.
*TC HT175 .R425 1999*

**Keefe, James W.** Instruction and the learning environment / James W. Keefe, John M. Jenkins. Larchmont, NY : Eye On Education, c1997. xviii, 189 p. : ill. ; 24 cm. (The school leadership library) Includes bibliographical references (p. 175-189). ISBN 1-88300-128-5 DDC 371.2/01
*1. School supervision - United States. 2. Learning. 3. Teaching - United States. 4. Educational leadership - United States. I. Jenkins, John M. II. Title. III. Series.*
*TC LB2806.4 .K44 1997*

**Keefe, Laurence E.** The life of a photograph : archival processing, matting, framing, storage / Laurence E. Keefe, Dennis Inch. 2nd ed. Boston : Focal Press, c1990. xi, 384 p. : ill. ; 27 cm. Includes bibliographical references (p. 372-373) and index. ISBN 0-240-80024-9 DDC 771/.46
*1. Photographs - Conservation and restoration. 2.*

*Photographs - Trimming, mounting, etc. I. Inch, Dennis. II. Title.*
*TC TR465 .K44 1990*

**Keegan, Jane P.**
Third world peoples, a Gospel perspective. Maryknoll, NY : Maryknoll Fathers and Brothers, c1987.
*TC F1439.T54 1987*

**Keegan, Mark.** Scenario educational software : design and development of discovery learning / Mark Keegan. Englewood Cliffs, N.J. : Educational Technology Publications, c1995. xii, 354 p. : ill. ; 26 cm. Includes bibliographical references and indexes. ISBN 0-87778-282-2 DDC 371.3/9445
*1. Computer-assisted instruction - Authorship. 2. Computer-assisted instruction - Software. 3. Computer software - Development. 4. Instructional systems - Design. 5. Education - Simulation methods. I. Title.*
*TC LB1028.6 .K44 1995*

**Keeler, Patricia A., ill.**
Fleisher, Paul, 1951- Brain food. Tucson, AZ : Zephyr Press, c1997.
*TC GV1480 .F54 1997*

**KEELEY CURE. See ALCOHOLISM - TREATMENT.**

**Keen, Carl L.**
Nutrition and immunology. Totowa, N.J. : Humana Press, c2000.
*TC QP141 .N7767 2000*

**Keen, Ernest, 1937-** Chemicals for the mind : psychopharmacology and human consciousness / Ernest Keen. Westport, Conn. ; London : Praeger, 2000. xviii, 142 p. : ill. ; 25 cm. Includes bibliographical referrences (p. [131]-138) and index. ISBN 0-275-96775-1 (alk. paper) DDC 615/.78
*1. Psychopharmacology. 2. Consciousness. 3. Altered states of consciousness. I. Title.*
*TC RM315 .K44 2000*

**Keene, Thomas W.**
Gregory, Vicki L., 1950- Multicultural resources on the Internet. The United States and Canada. Englewood, Colo. : Libraries Unlimited, 1999.
*TC E184.A1 G874 1999*

**Keep American Beautiful, Inc.**
Get a grip [videorecording]. Racine, WI : S.C. Johnson and Son, Inc., 1999, c1998.
*TC TD170 .G4 1999*

**Keep talking that book!.**
Littlejohn, Carol. Worthington, Ohio : Linworth Pub., 2000.
*TC Z716.3 .L58 2000*

**Keeping score.**
Shannon, Ann. Washington, D.C. : National Academy Press, 1999.
*TC QA135.5 .S45 1999x*

**Keeves, John P.**
Australian education. Camberwell, Vic. : Australian Council for Educational Research, 1998.
*TC LA2102.7 .A87 1998*

Literacy and numeracy in Australian schools. Canberra : Australian Gov. Pub. Service, 1976-
*TC LA2102 .L57 1976*

**Keeves, John P., joint author.**
Bourke, S. F. The mastery of literacy and numeracy. Canberra : Australian Govt. Pub. Service, 1977.
*TC LA2102 .B68 1977*

**Kehoe, John W.** A handbook for enhancing the multicultural climate of the school / written by John W. Kehoe ; with contributions by Yvonne M. Hébert for Alternatives to Racism. [Vancouver, B.C.] : Western Education Development Group, Faculty of Education, University of British Colombia, c1984. v, 93 p. : ill. ; 28 cm. Includes bibliographical references. ISBN 0-88865-025-6
*1. Intercultural education - Canada - Handbooks, manuals, etc. 2. Intercultural education - Canada - Curricula - Handbooks, manuals, etc. 3. Canada - Race relations - Handbooks, manuals, etc. 4. Cultural relations - Handbooks, manuals, etc. I. Hébert, Yvonne M., 1942- II. Title.*
*TC LC1099 .K438 1984*

**Keil, Frank C., 1952-.**
Explanation and cognition. Cambridge, Mass. : MIT Press, c2000.
*TC BF311 .E886 2000*

**Keiser, Shelby.**
Accommodations in higher education under the Americans with Disabilities Act (ADA) :. DeWitt, NY : GSI Publications, 2000.

*TC RA1055.5 A28 2000*

**Keita, Gwendolyn Puryear.**
Work and well-being. Washington, DC : American
Psychological Association, c1992.
*TC RC967.5 .W67 1992*

**Keith-Spiegel, Patricia.** The complete guide to graduate
school admission : psychology, counseling, and
related professions / Patricia Keith-Spiegel, Michael
W. Wiederman. 2nd ed. Mahwah, N.J. : London : L.
Erlbaum Associates, 2000. xiii, 280 p. ; 27 cm. Includes
bibliographical references (p. 279-280). ISBN 0-8058-3120-7
(hbk. : alk. paper) ISBN 0-8058-3121-5 (pbk. : alk. paper)
DDC 150/.71/173
*1. Psychology - Study and teaching (Graduate) 2. Universities
and colleges - Admission. I. Wiederman, Michael W. II. Title.*
*TC BF77 .K35 2000*

**Kellar, William Henry, 1952-** Make haste slowly :
moderates, conservatives, and school desegregation in
Houston / William Henry Kellar. 1st ed. College
Station : Texas A&M University Press, c1999. xv, 226
p. : ill. ; 25 cm. (The centennial series of the Association of
Former Students, Texas A&M University ; no. 80) Includes
bibliographical references (p. [179]-211) and index. ISBN
0-89096-818-7 (alk. paper) DDC 379.2/63/097641411
*1. School integration - Texas - Houston - History. 2. Houston
Independent School District - History. 3. Afro-Americans -
Civil rights - Texas - Houston - History. I. Title. II. Series.*
*TC LC214.23.H68 K45 1999*

**Keller, Colleen, 1949-** Health promotion for the
elderly / Colleen Keller, Julie Fleury. Thousand Oaks,
Calif. ; London : Sage Publications, c2000. ix, 181 p. ;
22 cm. Includes bibliographical references (p. 134-174) and
index. ISBN 0-7619-1473-0 (hbk. : acid-free paper) ISBN
0-7619-1474-9 (pbk. : acid-free paper) DDC 613/.0438
*1. Aged - Health and hygiene. 2. Health promotion. I. Fleury,
Julie. II. Title.*
*TC RA564.8 .K438 2000*

**Keller, M. Jean.**
Caregiving--leisure and aging. New York : Haworth
Press, c1999.
*TC HV1451 .C327 1999*

**Kellie McGarrh's hangin' in tough.**
McGarrh, Kellie, d. 1995. New York : P. Lang, c2000.
*TC LA2317.D6185 M34 2000*

**Kellogg, Whit.**
Ballet class for beginners [videorecording]. W. Long
Branch, NJ : Kultur, c1981.
*TC GV1589 .B3 1981*

**Kellough, Richard D. (Richard Dean).**
Kim, Eugene C. A resource guide for secondary
school teaching. 5th ed. New York : Macmillan Pub.
Co., c1991.
*TC LB1737.A3 K56 1991 5th ed.*

**Kelly, Anne.**
From maestro to manager. Dublin : Oak Tree Press in
association with the Graduate School of Business,
University College Dublin, c1997.
*TC NX770.E85 F76 1997*

**Kelly, Anthony E.**
Handbook of research design in mathematics and
science education. Mahwah, N.J. : Lawrence Erlbaum,
1999.
*TC QA11 .H256 1999*

**Kelly, Catherine E.** In the New England fashion :
reshaping women's lives in the nineteenth century /
Catherine E. Kelly. Ithaca, N.Y. : Cornell University
Press, 1999. xii, 258 p. : ill. ; 25 cm. Includes bibliographical
references and index. ISBN 0-8014-3076-3 (cloth : alk. paper)
DDC 305.4/0974
*1. Women - New England - History. 2. Rural women - New
England - History. 3. Middle class - New England - History. I.
Title.*
*TC HQ1438.N35 K45 1999*

**Kelly, David H.**
Kelly, Gail Paradise. French colonial education. New
York : AMS Press, c2000.
*TC LA1186 .K45 2000*

**Kelly, Deirdre M.** Pregnant with meaning : teen
mothers and the politics of inclusive schooling /
Deirdre M. Kelly. New York : P. Lang, c2000. xi, 257
p. ; 24 cm. (Adolescent cultures, school, and society ; vol. 13)
Includes bibliographical references (p. [223]-248) and index.
ISBN 0-8204-4536-3 (pbk. : alk. paper) DDC 306.43
*1. Teenage mothers - Education - Social aspects - British
Columbia - Case studies. 2. Pregnant schoolgirls - Education -
Social aspects - British Columbia - Case studies. 3. Feminism
and education. I. Title. II. Series: Adolescent cultures,
school & society ; vol. 13.*
*TC LC4094.2.B8 K45 2000*

**Kelly, Donald P.**
The ethnographic eye. New York : Falmer Press,
2000.
*TC LB45 .E837 2000*

**Kelly, Evelyn B.** Legal basics : a handbook for
educators / by Evelyn B. Kelly. Bloomington, Ind. :
Phi Delta Kappa Educational Foundation, c1998. 114
p. 23 cm. ISBN 0-87367-806-0
*1. Educators - Legal status, etc. - United States - Popular
works. 2. Educational law and legislation - United States -
Popular works. I. Title.*
*TC KF390.E3 K45 1998*

**Kelly, Franklin.**
Cikovsky, Nicolai. Winslow Homer. Washington,
D.C. : National Gallery of Art, 1995.
*TC N6537.H58 A4 1995*

**Kelly, Gail Paradise.** French colonial education : essays
on Vietnam and West Africa / by Gail Paradise Kelly ;
edited by David H. Kelly. New York : AMS Press,
c2000. viii, 271 p. : 23 cm. Includes bibliographical
references and index. ISBN 0-404-61680-1 (alk. paper) DDC
370/.9597/0904
*1. Education - Vietnam - French influences. 2. Education -
Africa, French-speaking West - French influences. 3.
Education - Vietnam - History. 4. Education - Africa, French-
speaking West - History. 5. France - Colonies - Asia - History.
6. France - Colonies - Africa - History. I. Kelly, David H. II.
Title.*
*TC LA1186 .K45 2000*

**Kelly, Gerard, 1959-** Retrofuture : rediscovering our
roots, recharting our routes / Gerard Kelly. Downers
Grove, Ill. : InterVarsity Press, c1999. 237 p. ; 21 cm.
Includes bibliographical references (p. [223]-237). ISBN 0-
8308-2264-X (paper : alk. paper) DDC 306/.09/04
*1. Social history - 20th century. 2. Social change. 3.
Technology and civilization. 4. Religion and culture. I. Title.*
*TC HN17.5 .K439 1999*

**Kelly, Larry K., 1936-.**
Norton, M. Scott. Resource allocation. Larchmont,
N.Y. : Eye on Education, c1997.
*TC LB2805 .N73 1997*

**KELLY, MARY, 1941- - CRITICISM AND
INTERPRETATION.**
Olkowski, Dorothea. Gilles Deleuze and the ruin of
representation. Berkeley : University of California
Press, c1999.
*TC N6537.K42 O44 1999*

**Kelly, Maura.**
The Internet in action for math & science 7-12
[videorecording]. [New York] : Thirteen-WNET ;
[Alexandria, Va. : distributed by] PBS Video, c1997.
*TC LB1044.87 .I453 1997*

The Internet in action for math & science K-6
[videorecording]. [New York] : Thirteen-WNET ;
[Alexandria, Va. : distributed by] PBS Video, c1998.
*TC LB1044.87 .I45 1998*

**Kelly, Michael, 1946-.**
Pierre Bourdieu. Bern ; New York : P. Lang, c1999.
*TC HM621 .P54 1999*

**Kelly, Sean M., 1957-.**
Ken Wilber in dialogue. 1st Quest ed. Wheaton, Ill. :
Theosophical Pub. House, 1998.
*TC BF204.7 .K46 1998*

**Kelman, Mark.** Jumping the queue : an inquiry into the
legal treatment of students with learning disabilities /
Mark Kelman, Gillian Lester. Cambridge, Mass. :
Harvard University Press, 1997. x, 313 p. ; 25 cm.
Includes bibliographical references (p. [233]-307) and index.
ISBN 0-674-48909-8 (alk. paper) DDC 344.73/0791
*1. Learning disabled children - Legal status, laws, etc. - United
States. 2. Special education - law and legislation - United
States. I. Lester, Gillian. II. Title.*
*TC KF4215 .K45 1997*

**Kelsey, Ann L.**
Cohn, John M. Writing and updating technology
plans. New York : Neal-Schuman Publishers, 2000.
*TC Z678.9.A4 U623 2000*

**Kem byt'?.**
Mayakovsky, Vladimir, 1893-1930. [Moskva] :
Gosudarstvennoe izdatel'stvo, 1929.
*TC PN6110.O32 M39 1929 Rus*

**Kemerer, Frank R.**
School choice and social controversy. Washington,
D.C. : Brookings Institution Press, c1999.
*TC LB1027.9 .S352 1999*

**Ken Wilber in dialogue :** conversations with leading
transpersonal thinkers / edited by Donald Rothberg
and Sean Kelly. 1st Quest ed. Wheaton, Ill. :
Theosophical Pub. House, 1998. xiv, 413 p. : ill. ; 23 cm.

"Quest Books." Includes bibliographical references and index.
ISBN 0-8356-0766-6 (pbk.) DDC 150.19/8
*1. Transpersonal psychology. I. Rothberg, Donald Jay. II.
Kelly, Sean M., 1957-*
*TC BF204.7 .K46 1998*

**Kendall, John S.**
Marzano, Robert J. Essential knowledge. Aurora,
Colo. : McREL, 1999.
*TC LB3060.83 .M36 1999*

**Kendall, Marion D.** Dying to live : how our bodies fight
disease / Marion Kendall. Cambridge ; New York :
Cambridge University Press, c1998. xi, 196 p. : ill. ; 24
cm. Includes index. ISBN 0-521-58479-5 (hb) DDC 616.07/9
*1. Immune system - Popular works. I. Title.*
*TC QR181.7 .K46 1998*

**Kendall, Maurice G. (Maurice George), 1907-** The
advanced theory of statistics. 4th ed. London, C.
Griffin, 1948. 2 v. diagrs. 28 cm. Set made of various
editions. V.1--4th ed. V.2--2nd. ed.
*1. Statistics. I. Title.*
*TC QA276 .K4262 1948*

**Kendall, Maurice George.** The advanced theory of
statistics. 3d ed. New York, Hafner Pub. Co., 1951. 2
v. : diagrs. ; 28 cm. Bibliography: v.2, p. 442-503. Library has
v. 2
*1. Statistics. I. Title.*
*TC QA276 .K38 1951*

**Kendall, Philip C.**
Child and adolescent therapy. 2nd ed. New York :
Guilford Press, c2000.
*TC RJ505.C63 C45 2000*

**Kendall, Russ. ill.**
Waters, Kate. Mary Geddy's day :. 1st ed. New York :
Scholastic Press, 1999.
*TC PZ7.W26434 Mar 1999*

**Kendler, Howard H., 1919-** Amoral thoughts about
morality : the intersection of science, psychology, and
ethics / by Howard H. Kendler. Springfield, Ill. : C.C.
Thomas, c2000. xi, 198 p. ; 27 cm. Includes bibliographical
references (p. 175-184) and indexes. ISBN 0-398-07028-8
(hardcover) ISBN 0-398-07029-6 (pbk.) DDC 174/.915
*1. Psychology - Moral and ethical aspects. 2. Psychology,
Applied - Moral and ethical aspects. 3. Psychology - Social
aspects. 4. Psychology, Applied - Social aspects. I. Title.*
*TC BF76.4 .K47 2000*

**Kendrick, Laura.** Animating the letter : the figurative
embodiment of writing from late antiquity to the
Renaissance / Laura Kendrick. Columbus, Ohio :
Ohio State University Press, c1999. ix, 326 p., 8 p. of
plates : ill. (some col.) ; 25 cm. Includes bibliographical
references (p. 227-309) and indexes. ISBN 0-8142-0822-3
(cloth : alk. paper) DDC 302.2/244/0902
*1. Initials. 2. Illumination of books and manuscripts. Medieval.
I. Title.*
*TC NK3610 .K46 1999*

**Kenig, Sylvia.** Who plays? who pays? who cares? : a
case study in applied sociology, political economy,
and the community mental health centers movement /
Sylvia Kenig. Amityville, N.Y. : Baywood Pub. Co.,
c1992. xi, 221 p. ; 24 cm. (Political economy of health care
series) Includes bibliographical references and indexes. ISBN
0-89503-093-4 (cloth) ISBN 0-89503-092-6 (paper) DDC
362.2/2
*1. Community mental health services - Economic aspects -
United States. 2. Community mental health services - Political
aspects - United States. 3. Social psychiatry - United States. I.
Title. II. Series.*
*TC RA790.6 .K46 1992*

**Kennard, Peter.**
Photomontage today, Peter Kennard [videorecording].
[London] : Art Council of Great Britain ; Ho-Ho-Kus,
N.J. : [distributed by] Anthony Roland Collection of
Films on Art, c1982.
*TC TR685 .P45 1982*

**KENNARD, PETER.**
Photomontage today, Peter Kennard [videorecording].
[London] : Art Council of Great Britain ; Ho-Ho-Kus,
N.J. : [distributed by] Anthony Roland Collection of
Films on Art, c1982.
*TC TR685 .P45 1982*

**Kennedy, Barbara M.**
The cybercultures reader. London ; New York :
Routledge, 2000.
*TC T14.5 .C934 2000*

**Kennedy, Bruce P.**
The society and population health reader. Volume I.
New York, N.Y. : The New Press, c1999.
*TC RA418 .S6726 1999*

**Kennedy, Leonard M.** Guiding children's learning of mathematics / Leonard M. Kennedy, Steve Tipps. 9th ed. Belmont, CA : Wadsworth/Thomson Learning, c2000. xvii, 622 p. : ill. ; 28 cm. Includes bibliographical references and index. ISBN 0-534-54955-1 DDC 372.7
*1. Mathematics - Study and teaching (Elementary) I. Tipps, Steven. II. Title.*
**TC QA135.5 .K43 2000**

**Kennedy, Michael, 1926-** Richard Strauss : man, musician, enigma / Michael Kennedy. Cambridge, UK ; New York, NY, USA : Cambridge University Press, 1999. xvi, 451 p. : ill. ; 24 cm. Includes bibliographical references (p. 422-426) and index. ISBN 0-521-58173-7 (hardback) DDC 780/.92
*1. Strauss, Richard. - 1864-1949. 2. Composers - Germany - Biography. I. Title.*
**TC ML410.S93 K46 1999**

**Kennedy, Robert Loren. 1951-.** Time and learning :. Bloomington, IN : Phi Delta Kappa International, c1998.
**TC LB3032 .T562 1998**

**Kennedy, Rosa L., 1938-** A school for healing : alternative strategies for teaching at-risk students / Rosa L. Kennedy and Jerome A. Morton. New York : P. Lang, c1999. xii, 187 p. ; 23 cm. (Counterpoints ; vol. 105) Includes bibliographical references (p. [181]-182) and index. ISBN 0-8204-4263-1 (pbk. : alk. paper) DDC 371.04
*1. Alternative schools - United States - Case studies. 2. Socially handicapped youth - Education - United States - Case studies. 3. High school dropouts - Education - United States - Case studies. I. Morton, Jerome H., 1942- II. Title. III. Series: Counterpoints (New York, N.Y.) ; vol. 105.*
**TC LC46.4 .K46 1999**

**Kenney, Anne R., 1950-** Moving theory into practice : digital imaging for libraries and archives/ Anne R. Kenney, Oya Y. Rieger, editors and principal authors. Mountain View, CA : Research Libraries Group, 2000. x, 189 p. : ill. ; 28 cm. Includes bibliographical references and index. CONTENTS: 1. Introduction : moving theory into practice / Anne R. Kenney and Oya Y. Rieger -- 2. Selection for digital conversion / Paula De Stefano -- 3. Digital benchmarking for conversion and access / Anne R. Kenney -- 4. Establishing a quality control program / Oya Y. Rieger -- 5. Metadata : principles, practices, and challenges / Carl Lagoze and Sandra Payette -- 6. Enhancing access to digital image collections : system building and image processing / John Price-Wilkin -- 7. Image management systems and Web delivery / Peter B. Hirtle -- 8. Projects to programs: developing a digital preservation policy / Oya Y. Rieger -- 9. Projects to programs: mainstreaming digital imaging initiatives / Anne R. Kenney. ISBN 0-9700225-0-6
*1. Library materials - Digitization. 2. Archival materials - Digitization. 3. Image processing - Digital techniques. 4. Digital preservation. I. Rieger, Oya Y. II. Research Libraries Group III. Title. IV. Title: Digital imaging for libraries and archives*
**TC Z681.3.D53 K37**

**Kenny, Dianna T.** Stress and health. Amsterdam : Harwood Academic ; Abingdon : Marston, 2000.
**TC RA785 .S774 2000**

**Kenny, Máirín.** The routes of resistance : travellers and second-level schooling / Máirín Kenny. Aldershot, Hants, England : Brookfield, Vt. : Ashgate, c1997. xi, 313 p. ; 23 cm. Includes bibliographical references (p. 298-313). ISBN 1-85972-628-3
*1. Irish Travellers (Nomadic people) - Education (Secondary) - Ireland. I. Title.*
**TC LC3650.I74 K45 1997**

**Kent, Raymond D.** Singh, Sadanand. Illustrated dictionary of speech-language pathology. San Diego : Singular Pub. Group, c2000.
**TC RC423 .S533 2000**

Voice quality measurement. San Diego : Singular Pub. Group, c2000.
**TC RF510 .V67 2000**

**Kent, Richard Burt.** Beyond room 109 : developing independent study projects / Richard Kent. Portsmouth, NH : Heinemann, 2000. vii, 152 p. : ill., map ; 24 cm. Includes bibliographical references (p. 148-149) and index. ISBN 0-86709-492-3 DDC 371.39/43
*1. Independent study - United States. 2. Project method in teaching. I. Title. II. Title: Beyond room one hundred nine*
**TC LB1049 .K45 2000**

**Kentucky high school quarterly.** Lexington, Ky. : Department of Education, State University of Kentucky, 1915-1927. 13 v. : ill. ; 24-27 cm. Frequency: Quarterly. Vol. 1, no. 1 (Jan. 1915)-v. 13, no. 4 (Oct. 1927). Description based on: Vol. 1, no. 2 (Apr. 1915); title from cover. Editors: Jan. 1915-Oct. 1923, J. T. Cotton Noe.--Jan.

1924-Oct. 1927, W. S. Taylor. No more published. Imprint varies: 1915-19 , Dept. of Education, State University of Kentucky: 19 -1927, College of Education, University of Kentucky.
*1. Education - Periodicals. 2. High schools - Periodicals. 3. High schools - Kentucky - Periodicals. I. Cotton Noe, James Thomas, 1864- ed. II. Taylor, William Septimus, 1885, ed. III. University of Kentucky. Dept. of Education. IV. University of Kentucky. College of Education.*

**KENYA - COLONIAL INFLUENCE.**
Decolonization & independence in Kenya, 1940-93. London : J. Currey ; Athens : Ohio University Press, 1995.
**TC DT433.58 .D4 1995**

**Kenya education journal.** Nairobi. v. 1- May 1958- .
*1. Education - Kenya - Periodicals. I. Title.*

**KENYA - POLITICS AND GOVERNMENT - 1963-1978.**
Decolonization & independence in Kenya, 1940-93. London : J. Currey ; Athens : Ohio University Press, 1995.
**TC DT433.58 .D4 1995**

Mungazi, Dickson A. The last British liberals in Africa. Westport, Conn. : Praeger, 1999.
**TC DT2979.T63 M86 1999**

**KENYA - POLITICS AND GOVERNMENT - 1978-.**
Decolonization & independence in Kenya, 1940-93. London : J. Currey ; Athens : Ohio University Press, 1995.
**TC DT433.58 .D4 1995**

**KENYA - POLITICS AND GOVERNMENT - TO 1963.**
Decolonization & independence in Kenya, 1940-93. London : J. Currey ; Athens : Ohio University Press, 1995.
**TC DT433.58 .D4 1995**

Mungazi, Dickson A. The last British liberals in Africa. Westport, Conn. : Praeger, 1999.
**TC DT2979.T63 M86 1999**

**Kenyatta, Mary L., 1944-.** Critical ethnicity. Lanham, Md. : Rowman & Littlefield, c1999.
**TC LC212.2 .C75 1999**

**Kepner, Charles Higgins, 1922-** The new rational manager / Charles H. Kepner, Benjamin B. Tregoe. Princeton, N.J. (P.O. Box 704, Research Rd., Princeton 08540) : Princeton Research Press, c1981. 224 p. : ill. ; 26 cm. Includes index. DDC 658.4/03
*1. Management. 2. Problem solving. 3. Decision making. I. Tregoe, Benjamin B. II. Title.*
**TC HD31 .K456 1981**

**KERAMICS. See CERAMICS.**

**Kerber, Linda K.** Women's America. 5th ed. New York : Oxford University Press, 2000.
**TC HQ1426 .W663 2000**

**Kerlin, Robert Thomas, 1866-1950.** Negro poets and their poems / by Robert T. Kerlin. 3d ed., rev. and enl. Washington, D. C. : Associated Publishers, c1935. xxii, 354 p., [1] leaf of plates : ill., ports. ; 20 cm. "Index of authors, with biographical and bibliographical notes": p. 333-347.
*1. Afro-American authors - Biography. 2. American poetry - Afro-American authors. I. Title.*
**TC PS591.N4 K4 1935**

**Kern, Richard (Richard Geyman).** Network-based language teaching. Cambridge, U.K. ; New York : Cambridge University Press, 2000.
**TC P53.285 .N48 2000**

**Kernan, Alvin B.** In Plato's cave / Alvin Kernan. New Haven : Yale University Press, c1999. xix, 309 p. : ill. ; 24 cm. Includes index. ISBN 0-300-07589-8 (hardcover : alk. paper) DDC 378.73
*1. Education, Higher - Aims and objectives - United States. 2. Kernan, Alvin B. 3. Educators - United States - Biography. I. Title.*
**TC LA227.4 .K468 1999**

**KERNAN, ALVIN B.**
Kernan, Alvin B. In Plato's cave. New Haven : Yale University Press, c1999.
**TC LA227.4 .K468 1999**

**Kerns, Kathryn A., 1961-.** Family and peers. Westport, Conn. : Praeger, 2000.
**TC HQ755.85 .F365 2000**

**Keroes, Jo.** Tales out of school : gender, longing, and the teacher in fiction and film / Jo Keroes. Carbondale : Southern Illinois University Press, c1999. x, 164 p. ; 24 cm. Includes bibliographical references

(p. 149-155) and index. ISBN 0-8093-2238-2 DDC 813.008/0352372
*1. American fiction - History and criticism. 2. Teacher-student relationships in literature. 3. English fiction - History and criticism. 4. Gender identity in literature. 5. Teachers in motion pictures. 6. Education in literature. 7. Authority in literature. 8. Teachers in literature. 9. Schools in literature. 10. Desire in literature. I. Title.*
**TC PS374.T43 K47 1999**

**Kesner, Raymond P.** Neurobiology of learning and memory. San Diego : Academic Press, c1998.
**TC QP408 .N492 1998**

**Kessler, Rachael, 1946-** The soul of education : helping students find connection, compassion, and character at school / Rachael Kessler. Alexandria, Va. : Association for Supervision and Curriculum Development, c2000. xviii, 181 p. ; 23 cm. Includes bibliographical references and index. "ASCD stock no. 100045"--T.p. verso. CONTENTS: Honoring young voices -- Deep connection -- Silence and stillness -- Meaning and purpose -- Joy -- Creativity -- Transcendence -- Initiation -- Conclusion: from fear to dialogue, from standoff to collaboration. ISBN 0-87120-373-1 (pbk.)
*1. Affective education - United States. 2. Emotions - Study and teaching (Secondary) - United States. 3. Social skills - Study and teaching (Secondary) - United States. 4. Education, Secondary - Activity programs - United States. I. Title.*
**TC LB1072 .K48 2000**

**Kestenberg Amighi, Janet.** The meaning of movement. Amsterdam : Gordon and Breach, c1999.
**TC RC473.K47 M4 1999**

**KESTENBERG MOVEMENT PROFILE.**
The meaning of movement. Amsterdam : Gordon and Breach, c1999.
**TC RC473.K47 M4 1999**

**Ketcham, Sallie.** Bach's big adventure / by Sallie Ketcham ; illustrated by Timothy Bush. New York : Orchard Books, 1999. 1 v. (unpaged) : ill. ; 27 cm. SUMMARY: When young Sebastian Bach learns that old Adam Reinken of Hamburg is a better organist than himself, he sets out to meet his rival. ISBN 0-531-30140-0 (trade : alk. paper) ISBN 0-531-33140-7 (lib. bdg. : alk. paper) DDC [E]
*1. Bach, Johann Sebastian, - 1685-1750 - Juvenile fiction. 2. Bach, Johann Sebastian, - 1685-1750 - Fiction. 3. Organists - Fiction. I. Bush, Timothy, ill. II. Title.*
**TC PZ7.K488 Bac 1999**

**Keteyian, Steven J.** Foss, Merle L., 1936- Fox's physiological basis for exercise and sport. 6th ed. / Merle L. Foss, Steven J. Keteyian. Boston, Mass. : WCB/McGraw-Hill, c1998.
**TC RC1235 .F65 1998**

Muller, Susan. Student study guide to accompany Fox's physiological basis for exercise and sport. 6th ed. Boston, Mass. : WCB/McGraw-Hill, c1998.
**TC RC1235 .F65 1998 guide**

**KETOSIS PRONE DIABETES. See DIABETES.**

**Ketteman, Helen.** Shoeshine Whittaker / Helen Ketteman ; illustrations by Scott Goto. New York : Walker & Co., 1999. 1v. (unpaged) : col. ill. ; 29 cm. SUMMARY: Shoeshine Whittaker manages to meet the challenge of plying his trade in the aptly named town of Mudville. ISBN 0-8027-8714-2 ISBN 0-8027-8715-0 (reinforced) DDC [E]
*1. Shoe shiners - Fiction. 2. Tall tales. I. Goto, Scott, ill. II. Title.*
**TC PZ7.K494 Sh 1999**

**Ketteridge, Steve.** A handbook for teaching and learning in higher education. London : Kogan Page, 1999.
**TC LB2331 .H29 1999**

**Kevin Dawkins Productions.** ADHD [videorecording]. New York, NY : Guilford Publications, Inc., c1992.
**TC RJ506.H9 A3 1992**

Understanding the defiant child [videorecording]. New York : Guilford Publications, c1997.
**TC HQ755.7 .U63 1997**

**Key aspects of comfort :** management of pain, fatigue, and nausea / Sandra G. Funk ... [et al.], editors. New York : Springer Pub. Co., c1989. xvii, 341 p. : ill. ; 24 cm. (Disseminating nursing research) Research conducted by the Disseminating Nursing Research Project. Includes bibliographies and index. ISBN 0-8261-6760-8 DDC 616/.047
*1. Pain - Nursing. 2. Fatigue - Nursing. 3. Nausea - Nursing. 4. Human comfort. I. Funk, Sandra G. II. Disseminating Nursing Research Project. III. Series.*
**TC RT87.P35 K48 1989**

**Key, Daphne.** Literacy shutdown : stories of six American women / Daphne Key. Newark, Del. : International Reading Association ; Chicago, Ill. : National Reading Conference, c1998. xiii, 126 p. ; 23 cm. (Literacy studies series) Includes bibliographical references (p. 115-118) and indexes. DDC 302.2/244
  *1. Women - Education - Southern States - Case studies. 2. Literacy - Social aspects - Southern States - Case studies. 3. Women - Southern States - Social conditions - Case studies. I. International Reading Association. II. National Reading Conference (U.S.) III. Title. IV. Series.*
  *TC LC1752 .K49 1998*

**Key issues for primary schools.**
  Farrell, Michael. London ; New York : Routledge, 1999.
  *TC LA633 .F37 1999*

**Key readings in social psychology**
  The self in social psychology. Philadelphia ; Hove [England] : Psychology Press, c1999.
  *TC HM1033 .S45 1999*

**Key readings in testing** / Harley D. Christiansen, editor. 1st ed. Tucson, Ariz. : P. Juul Press, c1985. 96 p. ; 28 cm. Includes bibliographies. ISBN 0-915456-06-0 (pbk.) DDC 153.9/3
  *1. Psychological tests. 2. Psychological tests - Social aspects. 3. Counseling. I. Christiansen, Harley Duane.*
  *TC BF176 .K48 1985*

**Key texts (Bristol, England)**
  Collingwood, R. G. (Robin George), 1889-1943. Outlines of a philosophy of art. Bristol : Thoemmes, 1994, c1925.
  *TC N70 .C6 1994*

  MacIntyre, Alasdair C. The unconscious. Bristol, England : Thoemmes Press, 1997, c1958.
  *TC BF315 .M23 1997*

**Key themes in ancient history**
  Garnsey, Peter. Food and society in classical antiquity. Cambridge, U.K. ; New York : Cambridge University Press, 1999.
  *TC GT2853.G8 G37 1999*

**Key to teaching and learning on-line.**
  Salmon, Gilly. E-moderating. London : Kogan Page ; Sterling, VA : Stylus, 2000.
  *TC LB1044.87 .S25 2000*

**Key to teaching and learning online.**
  Salmon, Gilly. E-moderating. London : Kogan Page ; Sterling, VA : Stylus, 2000.
  *TC LB1044.87 .S25 2000*

**Key words in multicultural interventions** : a dictionary / edited by Jeffrey Scott Mio ... [et al.]. Westport, Conn. : Greenwood Press, 1999. x, 306 p. ; 25 cm. Includes bibliographical references (p. [279]-286) and index. ISBN 0-313-29547-6 (alk. paper) DDC 303.48/2/03
  *1. Cross-cultural counseling - Dictionaries. 2. Psychotherapy - Dictionaries. I. Mio, Jeffrey Scott.*
  *TC BF637.C6 K493 1999*

**KEYBOARD INSTRUMENT MUSIC.** *See* **PIANO MUSIC.**

**Keyboarding skills for children with disabilities.**
  Penso, Dorothy E. London ; Philadelphia, Pa. : Whurr, 1999.
  *TC LC4024 .P467 1999*

**Keyes, Maureen W.**
  Capper, Colleen A., 1960- Meeting the needs of students of all abilities. Thousand Oaks, Calif. : Corwin Press, c2000.
  *TC LC1201 .C36 2000*

**Keys, David Patrick, 1955-** Confronting the drug control establishment : Alfred Lindesmith as a public intellectual / David Patrick Keys and John F. Galliher. Albany, N.Y. : State University of New York Press, c2000. ix, 235 p. : ill., facsims. ; 24 cm. (SUNY series in deviance and social control) Includes bibliographical references (p. 213-218) and indexes. ISBN 0-7914-4393-0 (hbk. : alk. paper) ISBN 0-7914-4394-9 (pbk. : alk. paper) DDC 301/.092
  *1. Lindesmith, Alfred Ray, - 1905- 2. Social psychologists - United States - Biography. 3. Sociologists - United States - Biography. 4. Opium habit. 5. Drug legalization - United States. I. Galliher, John F. II. Title. III. Series.*
  *TC HM1031.L56 K49 2000*

**Keys, Susan.**
  Bemak, Fred. Violent and aggressive youth. Thousand Oaks, Calif. ; London : Corwin Press, c2000.
  *TC LB3013.3 .B45 2000*

**Keys to the classroom** : a teacher's guide to the first month of school / Carrol Moran ... [et al.]. 2nd ed. Thousand Oaks, Calif. : Corwin Press, c2000. x, 227 p. : ill. ; 30 cm. English and Spanish. Includes bibliographical

references (p. 224-225). ISBN 0-7619-7554-3 (cloth : alk. paper) ISBN 0-7619-7555-1 (pbk. : alk. paper) DDC 372.1102
  *1. Elementary school teaching - Handbooks, manuals, etc. 2. Education, Elementary - Curricula - Handbooks, manuals, etc. 3. First year teachers - Handbooks, manuals, etc. I. Moran, Carrol.*
  *TC LB1555 .K49 2000*

**Kezar, Adrianna J.**
  Moving beyond the gap between research and practice in higher education. San Francisco, Calif. : Jossey-Bass, c2000.
  *TC LA227.4 .M68 2000*

**Khalid, Adeeb, 1964-** The politics of Muslim cultural reform : jadidism in Central Asia / Adeeb Khalid. Berkeley : University of California Press, c1998. xx, 335 p. : maps ; 24 cm. (Comparative studies on Muslim societies ; 27) Includes bibliographical references (p. 303-326) and index. ISBN 0-520-21355-6 (alk. paper) ISBN 0-520-21356-4 (alk. paper) DDC 958/.04
  *1. Islam - Asia, Central. 2. Islam and politics - Asia, Central. 3. Islam and state - Asia, Central. 4. Islam - Social aspects - Asia, Central. 5. Asia, Central - Politics and government. I. Title. II. Series.*
  *TC BP63.A34 K54 1998*

**Khatena, Joe.** Developing creative talent in art : a guide for parents and teachers / by Joe Khatena and Nelly Khatena. Stamford, Conn. : Ablex Publ., c1999. xiv, 195 p., [8] p. of plates : ill. (some col.) ; 24 cm. (Publications in creativity research) Includes bibliographical references (p. 181-185) and indexes. ISBN 1-56750-407-8 (hbk.) ISBN 1-56750-408-6 (pbk.) DDC 155.4/1335
  *1. Child artists. 2. Creative ability in children - Testing. 3. Gifted children - Identification. 4. Creation (Literary, artistic, etc.) I. Khatena, Nelly. II. Title. III. Series.*
  *TC NX164.C47 K53 1999*

  Enhancing creativity of gifted children : a guide for parents and teachers / Joe Khatena. Cresskill, N.J. : Hampton Press, c2000. xvi, 248 p. : ill. ; 24 cm. (Perspectives on creativity) Includes bibliographical references (p. 229-239) and indexes. ISBN 1-57273-228-8 (cloth) ISBN 1-57273-229-6 (paper) DDC 371.95
  *1. Gifted children - Education. 2. Creative thinking in children. I. Title. II. Series.*
  *TC LC3993 .K56 2000*

**Khatena, Nelly.**
  Khatena, Joe. Developing creative talent in art. Stamford, Conn. : Ablex Publ., c1999.
  *TC NX164.C47 K53 1999*

**KIBBUTZIM.**
  The transformation of collective education in the kibbutz. Frankfurt am Main ; New York : P. Lang, 1999.
  *TC LC1027.I75 T73 1999*

**KIBEI NISEI.** *See* **JAPANESE AMERICANS.**

**Kidd, Pamela Stinson.**
  Family nurse practitioner certification review. St. Louis : Mosby, c1999.
  *TC RT120.F34 F353 1998*

**KIDNAPPING - ARIZONA - CLIFTON - HISTORY - 20TH CENTURY.**
  Gordon, Linda. The great Arizona orphan abduction. Cambridge, Mass. : Harvard University Press, 1999.
  *TC F819.C55 G67 1999*

**Kids edition** [computer file] [Farmington Hills, Mi.] : The Gale Group, c1999. Computer data. Mode of access: World Wide Web. Subscription and registration are required for access. Text. System requirements: Internet connectivity, World Wide Web browser. Title from main search screen viewed September 18, 2000. Description based on content as of September, 2000. On main screen: InfoTrac. Covers current year to date plus the three previous years. Updated daily. Audience: primary school students. Accessed through Infotrac web interface. SUMMARY: "A collection of full-text material oriented toward primary school students. In addition to material from periodicals, the database also includes newspaper articles, reference material and maps."-- Gale Group Collections help screen. URL: http://web5.infotrac.galegroup.com/itw/session/
  *1. Periodicals - Indexes - Computer network resources. 2. Reference sources - Juvenile literature - Computer network resources. I. Gale Group. II. Title: InfoTrac.*

**Kids killing kids.**
  Capozzoli, Thomas. Boca Raton, Fla. ; London : St. Lucie Press, c2000.
  *TC LB3013.3 .C37 2000*

**Kids' media culture** / edited by Marsha Kinder. Durham [N.C.] ; London : Duke University Press, 1999. viii, 338 p. : ill. ; 25 cm. (Console-ing passions) Includes bibliographical references (p. [317]-322) and index. ISBN 0-8223-2350-8 (hbk. : alk. paper) ISBN 0-8223-2371-0

(pbk. : alk. paper) DDC 302.23/083
  *1. Mass media and children - United States. 2. Child consumers - United States. I. Kinder, Marsha. II. Series.*
  *TC HQ784.M3 K54 1999*

**Kids on the Internet.**
  Morton, Jessica G. Kids on the 'Net. Portsmouth, NH : Heinemann, c1998.
  *TC LB1044.87 .M67 1998*

**Kids on the 'Net.**
  Morton, Jessica G. Portsmouth, NH : Heinemann, c1998.
  *TC LB1044.87 .M67 1998*

**Kids raised by the government.**
  Schwartz, Ira M. Westport, Conn. : Praeger, 1999.
  *TC HV741 .S367 1999*

**Kiefte, Kees de, ill.**
  Livingston, Myra Cohn. Cricket never does. New York : Margaret K. McElderry Books, c1997.
  *TC PS3562.I945 C75 1997*

**Kiernan, Michael.**
  Bacon, Francis, 1561-1626. The advancement of learning. Oxford : Clarendon, 2000.
  *TC B1191 .K545 2000*

**Kierner, Cynthia A., 1958-** Beyond the household : women's place in the early South, 1700-1835 / Cynthia A. Kierner. Ithaca, NY : Cornell University Press, 1998. xii, 292 p. : ill. ; 24 cm. Includes bibliographical references (p. 219-285) and index. ISBN 0-8014-3453-X (hardcover : alk. paper) ISBN 0-8014-8462-6 (pbk. : alk. paper) DDC 305.42/0975
  *1. Women in public life - Southern States - History. 2. Women - Southern States - History. I. Title.*
  *TC HQ1391.U5 K55 1998*

**Kiesler, Donald J.** Beyond the disease model of mental disorders / Donald J. Kiesler. Westport, Conn. : Praeger, c1999. xv, 226 p. ; 24 cm. References: p. [205]-218. Includes bibliographical references and indexes. ISBN 0-275-96570-8 (alk. paper) DDC 616.89/071
  *1. Mental illness - Etiology. I. Title.*
  *TC RC454.4 .K52 1999*

**Kiesler, Kate, ill.**
  George, Kristine O'Connell. Old Elm speaks. New York : Clarion Books, c1998.
  *TC PS3557.E488 O4 1998*

**Kiley, Richard.**
  The blue planet [videorecording]. [New York, N.Y.?] : Unapix Entertainment, Inc. [distributor], c1996.
  *TC QB631.2 .B5 1996*

  The climate puzzle [videorecording]. [New York, N.Y.?] : Unapix Entertainment, Inc. [distributor], c1996.
  *TC QB631.2 .C5 1996*

  The living machine [videorecording]. [New York, N.Y.?] : Unapix Entertainment, Inc. [distributor], c1996.
  *TC QB631.2 .L5 1996*

  Fate of the earth [videorecording]. [New York, N.Y.?] : Unapix Entertainment, Inc. [distributor], c1996.
  *TC QB631.2 .F3 1996*

  Gifts from the earth [videorecording]. [New York, N.Y.?] : Unapix Entertainment, Inc. [distributor], c1996.
  *TC QB631.2 .G5 1996*

  The solar sea [videorecording]. [New York, N.Y.?] : Unapix Entertainment, Inc. [distributor], c1996.
  *TC QB631.2 .S6 1996*

  Tales from other worlds [videorecording]. [New York, N.Y.?] : Unapix Entertainment, Inc. [distributor], c1996.
  *TC QB631.2 .T3 1996*

  Tales from other worlds [videorecording]. [New York, N.Y.?] : Unapix Entertainment, Inc. [distributor], c1996.
  *TC QB631.2 .T3 1996*

**KILLERS.** *See* **MURDERERS.**

**KILLING, MERCY.** *See* **EUTHANASIA.**

**KILLING ONESELF.** *See* **SUICIDE.**

**Kilmurray, Elaine.**
  Sargent, John Singer, 1856-1925. John Singer Sargent. Princeton : Princeton University Press, 1998.
  *TC ND237.S3 A4 1998a*

**KILNS.**
  Minogue, Coll. Wood-fired ceramics. London : A & C

Black : Philadelphia : University of Pennsylvania Press, 2000.
*TC TP841 .M57 2000*

**KILPATRICK, WILLIAM HEARD, 1871-1965.**
Beineke, John A. And there were giants in the land. New York : P. Lang, c1998.
*TC LB875.K54 B44 1998*

**Kilpatrick, William Heard, 1871-1965. ed.**
Frontiers of democracy. New York, Progressive Education Association, etc., 1934-

**Kim, Eugene C.** A resource guide for secondary school teaching : planning for competence / Eugene C. Kim, Richard D. Kellough. 5th ed. New York : Macmillan Pub. Co., c1991. xx, 499 p. : ill. ; 28 cm. Includes bibliographical references and index. ISBN 0-02-363860-5 DDC 373.19
*1. High school teaching. 2. Curriculum planning. I. Kellough, Richard D. (Richard Dean) II. Title.*
*TC LB1737.A3 K56 1991 5th ed.*

**Kim, Henny H. 1968-.**
Guns and violence. San Diego : Greenhaven Press, c1999.
*TC HV7436 .G8774 1999*

**Kim, Hesook Suzie.** The nature of theoretical thinking in nursing / Hesook Suzie Kim. 2nd ed. New York : Springer Pub. Co., c2000. xiii, 266 p. ; 24 cm. Includes bibliographical references and indexes. ISBN 0-8261-1306-0 DDC 610.73/01
*1. Nursing - Philosophy. 2. Models, Theoretical. 3. Nursing. 4. Philosophy, Nursing.*
*TC RT84.5 .K545 2000*

Nursing theories. New York : Springer Pub. Co., c1999.
*TC RT84.5 .N8795 1999*

**Kim, Jim Yong.**
Dying for growth. Monroe, Me. : Common Courage Press, c2000.
*TC RA418.5.P6 D95 2000*

**Kim, Jinyoung.** Effects of word type, context, and vocal assistance on children's pitch-matching abilities : an early childhood educator's view / by Jinyoung Kim. 1998. x, 182 leaves : ill., music ; 29 cm. Issued also on microfilm. Thesis (Ed.D.)--Teachers College, Columbia University, 1998. Includes bibliographical references (leaves 82-87). Includes tables.
*1. Early childhood education. 2. Musical pitch. 3. Child development. 4. Music - Instruction and study. 5. Music - Psychological aspects. I. Title.*
*TC 06 no. 10954*

**Kim, T'ae-ch'ang.**
The thirteenth labor. Amsterdam : Gordon and Breach Publishers, c1999.
*TC Q181.3 .T45 1999*

**Kimball, Roger, 1953-** Tenured radicals : how politics has corrupted our higher education / Roger Kimball. Rev. ed., with a new introd. by the author, 1st Elephant pbk. ed. Chicago : Elephant Paperbacks, 1998. xix, 246 p. ; 21 cm. Includes bibliographical references and index. ISBN 1-56663-195-5 (alk. paper) DDC 378/.012/0973
*1. Education, Humanistic - United States. 2. Education, Higher - United States. 3. Politics and education - United States. 4. Radicalism - United States. I. Title.*
*TC LC1023 .K56 1998*

**Kimmel, Stacey E.**
Interdisciplinary education. New York, NY : College Entrance Examination Board, 1999.
*TC LB2361 .I58 1999*

**Kimmelman, Michael.** Portraits : talking with artists at the Met, the Modern, the Louvre, and elsewhere / Michael Kimmelman. 1st ed. New York : Random House, c1998. xviii, 265 p. : ill. ; 25 cm. Published simultaneously in Canada by Random House of Canada Limited, Toronto. Includes index. ISBN 0-679-45219-2 (alk. paper) DDC 701/.15
*1. Artists - Interviews. 2. Artists - Psychology. 3. Artists and museums. 4. Art appreciation. I. Title.*
*TC N71 .K56 1998*

**Kinane, Vincent.**
Essays on the history of Trinity College Library, Dublin. Dublin : Four Courts, c2000.
*TC Z792.5.T75 E87 2000*

**Kincheloe, Joe L.** The stigma of genius : Einstein, consciousness, and education / Joe L. Kincheloe, Shirley R. Steinberg and Deborah J. Tippins. New York : Canterbury [England] : P. Lang, c1999. xxvi, 218 p. ; 23 cm. (Counterpoints ; vol. 111) Includes bibliographical references (p. [199]-210) and index. ISBN 0-8204-4431-6 (pbk) DDC 370/.1

*1. Einstein, Albert. - 1879-1955 - Views on education. 2. Education - Philosophy. 3. Teaching. 4. Critical pedagogy. 5. Genius. 6. Gifted children - Education. I. Steinberg, Shirley R., 1952- II. Tippins, Deborah J. III. Title. IV. Series: Counterpoints (New York, N.Y.) ; vol. 111.*
*TC LB875.E562 K56 1999*

What is indigenous knowledge? New York : Falmer Press, 1999.
*TC GN476 .W47 1999*

**Kinder, Marsha.**
Kids' media culture. Durham [N.C.] : London : Duke University Press, 1999.
*TC HQ784.M3 K54 1999*

**KINDERGARTEN. See FULL-DAY KINDERGARTEN; NURSERY SCHOOLS.**

**The Kindergarten and first grade.** Springfield, Mass. : Milton Bradley Co., 1916-[1924] 9 v. : ill. ; 31 cm. Frequency: Monthly (except July and Aug.). Vol. 1, no. 1 (Jan. 1916)-v. 9 (June 1924). Title from cover. "A magazine of practical help and suggestion for teachers of kindergarten and first primary grade." Editors: Jan. 1916-June 1924, May Murray; Sept. 1924- C.S. Bailey. Kindergarten review (OCoLC)1714629. Continued by: Kindergarten and first grade magazine (OCoLC)6204211.
*1. Kindergarten - Periodicals. 2. First grade (Education) - Periodicals. I. Bailey, Carolyn Sherwin, 1875-1961. II. Murray, May. III. Title: Kindergarten review IV. Title: Kindergarten and first grade magazine*

**Kindergarten and first grade magazine.**
The Kindergarten and first grade. Springfield, Mass. : Milton Bradley Co., 1916-[1924]

**KINDERGARTEN - COLORADO.**
Clay, Cheryl D., 1947- Schooling at-risk Native American children. New York : Garland Pub., 1998.
*TC E99.U8 C53 1998*

**Kindergarten for teacher and parents.**
Kindergarten primary magazine. Chicago [etc.], A. B. Stockham & Co., [etc.]

**KINDERGARTEN - HISTORY - CROSS-CULTURAL STUDIES.**
Kindergartens and cultures. New Haven [Conn.] ; London : Yale University Press, c2000.
*TC LB1199 .K58 2000*

**KINDERGARTEN - INTERACTIVE MULTIMEDIA.**
Dr. Seuss kindergarten [computer file] Windows / Macintosh CD-ROM ; v. 1.0. Novato, CA : Brøderbund, c1998.
*TC LB1195 .D77 1998*

**KINDERGARTEN - JUVENILE SOFTWARE.**
Dr. Seuss kindergarten [computer file] Windows / Macintosh CD-ROM ; v. 1.0. Novato, CA : Brøderbund, c1998.
*TC LB1195 .D77 1998*

**Kindergarten magazine Sept. 1891-June 1907.**
Kindergarten primary magazine. Chicago [etc.], A. B. Stockham & Co., [etc.]

**KINDERGARTEN - PERIODICALS.**
Child life. London, G. Philip & Son.

The Kindergarten and first grade. Springfield, Mass. : Milton Bradley Co., 1916-[1924]

Kindergarten primary magazine. Chicago [etc.], A. B. Stockham & Co., [etc.]

**Kindergarten primary magazine.** Chicago [etc.], A. B. Stockham & Co., [etc.] v. -45; Sept. 1891-June 1933. Title varies: Kindergarten magazine Sept. 1891-June 1907. Continues: Kindergarten for teacher and parents.
*1. Education - Periodicals. 2. Kindergarten - Periodicals. I. Title: Kindergarten magazine Sept. 1891-June 1907 II. Title: Kindergarten for teacher and parents*

**Kindergarten review.**
The Kindergarten and first grade. Springfield, Mass. : Milton Bradley Co., 1916-[1924]

**KINDERGARTEN - SOCIAL ASPECTS - NEW YORK (STATE) - CASE STUDIES.**
Schmidt, Patricia Ruggiano, 1944- Cultural conflict and struggle. New York : P. Lang, c1998.
*TC LB1181 .S36 1998*

**KINDERGARTEN - UNITED STATES.**
Paley, Vivian Gussin, 1929- White teacher. Cambridge, Mass. : Harvard University Press, 2000.
*TC LC2771 .P34 2000*

**KINDERGARTEN - UNITED STATES - CONGRESSES.**
The transition to kindergarten. Baltimore : P.H. Brookes Pub., c1999.

*TC LB1205 .T72 1999*

**Kindergartens & cultures.**
Kindergartens and cultures. New Haven [Conn.] ; London : Yale University Press, c2000.
*TC LB1199 .K58 2000*

**Kindergartens and cultures :** the global diffusion of an idea / edited by Roberta Wollons. New Haven [Conn.] ; London : Yale University Press, c2000. viii, 301 p. ; 25 cm. Other title: Kindergartens & cultures. Includes bibliographical references and index. ISBN 0-300-07788-2 (cloth : alk. paper) DDC 372.21/8/09
*1. Kindergarten - History - Cross-cultural studies. I. Wollons, Roberta Lyn, 1947- II. Title: Kindergartens & cultures*
*TC LB1199 .K58 2000*

**[Kindheit und Trauma. English.]** Childhood and trauma : separation, abuse, war / edited by Elisabeth Ullmann and Werner Hilweg. Aldershot, Hants, UK : Brookfield, Vt., USA : Ashgate, c1999. xvi, 227 p. : ill. ; 23 cm. Translation of: Kindheit und Trauma. Göttingen : Vandenhoeck & Ruprecht, 1997. Includes bibliographical references and index. ISBN 0-7546-1074-8 ISBN 0-7546-1259-7 (pbk.) DDC 362.7
*1. Psychic trauma in children. 2. Children and war. 3. Child psychology. 4. Children - Legal status, laws, etc. I. Ullmann, Elisabeth. 1966- II. Hilweg, Werner, 1950- III. Title.*
*TC RJ506.P66 K613 1999*

**KINDNESS - FICTION.**
Fuchshuber, Annegert. [Karlinchen. English] Carly. 1st ed. New York : The Feminist Press, c1997.
*TC PZ7.F94 Car 1997*

**Kinds of living things.**
DiscoveryWorks. Parsippany, NJ : Silver Burdett Ginn, c1996-
*TC LB1585 .D574 1996*

**Kindsvatter, Richard.**
**Dynamics of effective teaching.**
Dynamics of effective teaching. 4th ed. New York ; Harlow, England : Longman, c2000.
*TC LB1737.U6 K56 2000*

**KINESIOLOGY. See HUMAN LOCOMOTION; HUMAN MECHANICS; MOVEMENT EDUCATION.**

**King, Alison.**
Cognitive perspectives on peer learning. Mahwah, N.J. : L. Erlbaum, 1999.
*TC LB1031.5 .C65 1999*

**King, Cynthia R.**
Quality of life from nursing and patient perspectives. Sudbury, Mass. : London : Jones and Bartlett, c1998.
*TC RC262 .Q34 1998*

**King, Gail, 1949-** Counselling skills for teachers : talking matters / Gail King. Buckingham [England] : Philadelphia : Open University Press, 1999. x, 138 p. ; 23 cm. Includes bibliographical references (p. [129]-134) and index. ISBN 0-335-20001-X (hb) ISBN 0-335-20000-1 (pb) DDC 373.14/046
*1. Teacher participation in educational counseling - Great Britain. 2. Counseling in secondary education - Great Britain. 3. Pastoral counseling - Great Britain. I. Title.*
*TC LB1620.53.G7 K56 1999*

**King, Kenneth, 1940-.**
Changing international aid to education. Paris : Unesco Pub./NORRAG. 1999.
*TC LC2607 .C42 1999*

Learning from experience. The Hague : Centre for the Study of Education in Developing Countries, c1995.
*TC LC2610 .L43 1995*

**King, Matthew Jay.**
Partners in progress. San Francisco, Calif. : Jossey-Bass Inc., c1999.
*TC LC3981 .P27 1999*

**King, Patricia, 1942-.**
Violence in families. Washington, D.C. : National Academy Press, 1998.
*TC HV6626.2 .V56 1998*

**King, Thomas W.** Modern Morse code in rehabilitation and education : new applications in assistive technology / Thomas Wayne King. Boston : Allyn and Bacon, c2000. xii, 308 p. ; 23 cm. Includes bibliographical references (p. 163-191) and index. ISBN 0-205-28751-4 DDC 362.4/0483
*1. Self-help devices for the disabled. 2. Morse code. 3. Handicapped - Rehabilitation - Technological innovations. 4. Handicapped - Education - Technological innovations. I. Title.*
*TC HV1569.5 .K55 2000*

**King Tree.**
French, Fiona. London, Oxford University Press, 1973.

*TC PZ7.F8887 Ki3*

**King, Wayne E.** AGS United States history / by Wayne E. King and John L. Napp. Teacher's ed. Circle Pines, Minn. : AGS, American Guidance Service, c1998. T22, xx, 850 p. : col. ill. ; 29 cm. Includes index. ISBN 0-7854-1419-3 DDC 973/.071/273
*1. United States - History. 2. United States - History - Study and teaching (Secondary) I. Napp, John L. II. Title. III. Title: American Guidance Service United States history*
***TC E175.8 .K56 1998 Teacher's Ed.***

Napp, John L. AGS United States history. Circle Pines, Minn. : AGS, American Guidance Service, c1998.
***TC E178.1 .N36 1998***

Napp, John L. Our nation's history. Baltimore, Md. : Media Materials, c1989.
***TC E178.3 .N36 1998***

Napp, John L. Our nation's history. Baltimore, Md. : Media Materials, c1989.
***TC E178.3 .N36 1998***

Napp, John L. Our nation's history. Baltimore, Md. : Media Materials, c1989.
***TC E178.3 .N36 1998***

**Kingen, Sharon.** Teaching language arts in middle schools : connecting and communicating / by Sharon Kingen. Mahwah, NJ : Lawrence Erlbaum, 2000. xvi, 605 p. ; 28 cm. Includes bibliographical references (p.581-592) and index. ISBN 0-8058-3055-3 (pbk. : alk. paper) DDC 428/.0071/2
*1. Language arts (Middle school) - United States - Handbooks, manuals, etc. 2. Middle school teaching - United States - Handbooks, manuals, etc. I. Title.*
***TC LB1631 .K493 2000***

**Kingma, Johannes.**
Conceptual issues in research on intelligence. Stamford, Conn. : JAI Press , 1998.
***TC BF311 .A38 v. 5 1998***

**Kinjaram, Ramaiah.** Educational performance of scheduled castes / Ramaiah Kinjaram. New Delhi : APH Pub. Corp., [1998?] xvi, 163 p. ; 22 cm.
SUMMARY: Study based on the data from Andhra Pradesh, India Includes bibliographical references (p. [147]-156) and index. ISBN 81-7648-022-3
*1. Socially handicapped - Education - India. 2. Socially handicapped - Education - India - Statistics. 3. India - Scheduled tribes - Education. I. Title.*
***TC LC4097.I4 K55 1998***

**Kinloch, Graham Charles.** The comparative understanding of intergroup realtions [i.e. relations] : a worldwide analysis / Graham C. Kinloch. Boulder, CO : Westview Press, 1999. xii, 207 p. ; 24 cm. Includes bibliographical references (p. 179-195) and indexes. ISBN 0-8133-9025-7 (alk. paper) DDC 302.3/4
*1. Intergroup relations. 2. Social psychology. I. Title. II. Title: The comparative understanding of intergroup relations*
***TC HM131 .K495 1999***

**Kinnamon, James C.** A comparison of structural knowledge in eighth graders and college students : applications for information systems / by James C. Kinnamon. 1999. vi, 241 leaves ; 29 cm. Typescript; issued also on microfilm. Thesis (Ph.D.)--Columbia University, 1999. Includes bibliographical references (leaves 126-135).
*1. College students. 2. Junior high school students. 3. Thought and thinking. 4. Knowledge, Psychology of. 5. Human information processing. 6. Categorization (Psychology) 7. Mental representation. 8. Cognition - Age factors. I. Title.*
***TC 085 K6194***

**Kinnear, Karen L.** Single parents : a reference handbook / Karen L. Kinnear. Santa Barbara, Calif. : ABC-CLIO, c1999. xv, 263 p. : ill. ; 24 cm. (Contemporary world issues) Includes bibliographical references and index. ISBN 1-57607-033-6 (alk. paper) DDC 306.85/6
*1. Single parents - United States - Handbooks, manuals, etc. I. Title. II. Series.*
***TC HQ759.915 .K56 1999***

**Kinneavy, James L., 1920-.**
Ethical issues in college writing. New York ; Canterbury [England] : Peter Lang, c1999.
***TC PE1404 .E84 1999***

A Rhetoric of doing. Carbondale : Southern Illinois University Press, c1992.
***TC PE1404 .R496 1992***

**Kinney, Jean, 1943-** Loosening the grip : a handbook of alcohol information / Jean Kinney ; illustrations by Stuart Copans. 6th ed. Boston : McGraw-Hill, c2000. xviii, 558 p. : ill. ; 24 cm. Includes bibliographical references and index. ISBN 0-07-289106-8 (pbk. : alk. paper) DDC 362.292
*1. Alcoholism - United States - Handbooks, manuals, etc. 2. Alcoholism - Treatment - United States - Handbooks, manuals, etc. I. Title.*
***TC HV5292 .K53 2000***

**Kinsbruner, Jay.** Not of pure blood : the free people of color and racial prejudice in nineteenth-century Puerto Rico / Jay Kinsbruner. Durham : Duke University Press, 1996. xiv, 176 p. : ill., maps ; 23 cm. Includes bibliographical references (p. [157]-170) and index. ISBN 0-8223-1836-9 (alk. paper) ISBN 0-8223-1842-3 (pbk. : alk. paper) DDC 305.896/07295
*1. Blacks - Puerto Rico - Social conditions. 2. Puerto Rico - History - To 1898. 3. Racism - Puerto Rico - History - 19th century. 4. Prejudices - Puerto Rico - History - 19th century. 5. Puerto Rico - Race relations. I. Title.*
***TC F1983.B55 K56 1996***

**Kinsey, Alfred C. (Alfred Charles), 1894-1956.**
Sexual behavior in the human female. Bloomington, Ind. : Indiana University Press, [1998]
***TC HQ29 .S487 1998***

Sexual behavior in the human male / Alfred C. Kinsey, Wardell B. Pomeroy, Clyde E. Martin. Bloomington, Ind. : Indiana University Press, [1998]. xv, 804 p. : ill. ; 24 cm. Originally published: Philadelphia : W.B. Saunders Co., 1948. Includes bibliographical references and index. ISBN 0-253-33412-8 (cloth : alk. paper) DDC 306.7/081
*1. Men - Sexual behavior. I. Pomeroy, Wardell Baxter. II. Martin, Clyde E. (Clyde Eugene) III. Title.*
***TC HQ28 .K55 1998***

**Kinsey Institute for Research in Sex, Gender, and Reproduction.**
The Role of theory in sex research. Bloomington, IN : Indiana University Press, 2000.
***TC HQ60 .R65 2000***

**The Kinsey Institute series**
(v. 6) The Role of theory in sex research. Bloomington, IN : Indiana University Press, 2000.
***TC HQ60 .R65 2000***

**Kinsey, Joni.** Plain pictures : images of the American prairie / Joni L. Kinsey. Washington, : Published for the University of Iowa Museum of Art by the Smithsonian Institution Press, 1996. xx, 236 p. : ill. (some col.), col. map ; 25 x 26 cm. "The University of Iowa Museum of Art, August 17 to November 3, 1996; Amon Carter Museum, November 23, 1996 to February 25, 1997; Joslyn Museum of Art, April 19 to July 27, 1997"--T.p. verso. Includes bibliographical references (p. 225-232) and index. ISBN 1-56098-688-3 (alk. paper) ISBN 1-56098-630-1 (pbk. : alk. paper) DDC 760/.0443678
*1. Middle West in art. 2. Prairies in art. 3. Pastoral art - United States. I. University of Iowa. Museum of Art. II. Amon Carter Museum of Western Art. III. Joslyn Museum of Art. IV. Title.*
***TC N8214.5.U6 K56 1996***

**KINSHIP.** *See also* **FAMILY.**
Technologies of procreation. 2nd ed. New York : Routledge, 1999.
***TC HQ761 .T43 1999***

**Kirby, Anne.** Elementary school English / Anne Kirby, Craig B. Vittetoe, consultant. Teachers' ed. Palo Alto, Calif. : Addison-Wesley Publishing Company, 1967. v. : ill. ; 24 x 22 cm. Includes index.
*1. English language - Study and teaching (Elementary) 2. English language - Grammar - Problems, exercises, etc. 3. English language - Composition and exercises. I. Vittetoe, Craig B. II. Title.*
***TC PE1112 .K57 1967 Teachers' Ed.***

Elementary school English / Anne Kirby, Craig B. Vittetoe, consultant. Palo Alto, Calif. : Addison-Wesley Publishing Company, 1967. v. : ill. ; 24 cm.
*1. English language - Grammar - Problems, exercises, etc. 2. English language - Composition and exercises. I. Vittetoe, Craig B. II. Title.*
***TC PE1112 .K57 1967***

**Kirby, Peggy C.**
Blase, Joseph. Bringing out the best in teachers. 2nd ed. Thousand Oaks, Calif. : Corwin Press, c2000.
***TC LB2840 .B57 2000***

**Kirby, Sandy.** Sight lines : women's art and feminist perspectives in Australia / Sandy Kirby. Tortola, BVI : Craftsman House in association with Gordon and Breach ; New York : Distributed in the USA by STBS Ltd., 1992. 157 p. : ill. (some col.) ; 31 cm. Includes bibliographical references (p. 142-148) and index. ISBN 976-8097-26-4 (Craftsman) ISBN 2-88124-896-9 (Gordon and Breach) DDC 704/.042/099409045
*1. Feminism and art - Australia. 2. Art, Modern - 20th century - Australia. 3. Women artists - Australia - Biography - History and criticism. I. Title.*
***TC N72.F45 K57 1992***

**Kirby, Sheila Nataraj, 1946-** Staffing at-risk school districts in Texas : problems and prospects / Sheila Nataraj Kirby, Scott Naftel, Mark Berends. Santa Monica, CA : Rand, 1999. xix, 87 p. : ill. ; 23 cm. "Supported by the U.S. Department of Education." Includes bibliographical references (p. 79-87). ISBN 0-8330-2760-3 DDC 331.12/313711/009764
*1. Minority teachers - Supply and demand - Texas - Longitudinal studies. 2. Children of minorities - Education - Texas - Longitudinal studies. I. Naftel, Scott, 1952- II. Berends, Mark, 1962- III. Rand Corporation. IV. U.S. Dept. of Education. V. Title.*
***TC LB2833.3.T4 K57 1999***

**Kirch, Olaf.** Linux network administrator's guide / Olaf Kirch & Terry Dawson. 2nd ed. Cambridge, Mass. : O'Reilly, 2000. xxix, 474 p. : ill. ; 23 cm. Rev. ed. of: Linux system administration, 1999. ISBN 1-56592-400-2 DDC 005.4/469
*1. Linux. 2. Operating systems (Computers) I. Dawson, Terry. II. Kirch, Olaf. Linux system administration. III. Title.*
***TC QA76.76.O63 K566 2000***

**Linux system administration.**
Kirch, Olaf. Linux network administrator's guide. 2nd ed. Cambridge, Mass. : O'Reilly, 2000.
***TC QA76.76.O63 K566 2000***

**Kirchner, Glenn.** Children's games from around the world : a collection of time-honored traditional games plus new and cooperative games invented by children from 50 countries / Glenn Kirchner. 2nd ed. Boston : Allyn and Bacon, c2000. xii, 212 p. : ill. ; 28 cm. Includes bibliographical references (p.202) and index. ISBN 0-205-29627-0 DDC 796.1/4
*1. Games. I. Title.*
***TC GV1203 .K65 2000***

**KIRGHIZ-KAISSACKS.** *See* **KAZAKHS.**

**KIRGHIZ-KAZAKS.** *See* **KAZAKHS.**

**Kirk, Daniel.** Breakfast at the Liberty Diner / Daniel Kirk. 1st ed. New York : Hyperion Books for Children, c1997. 1 v. (unpaged) : col. ill. ; 29 cm.
SUMMARY: Bobby, his mother, and his baby brother are having breakfast at the Liberty Diner when President Franklin Roosevelt stops in for a visit. ISBN 0-7868-2243-0 (lib. bdg.) ISBN 0-7868-0303-7 (trade) DDC [E]
*1. Diners (Restaurants) - Fiction. 2. Roosevelt, Franklin D. - (Franklin Delano), - 1882-1945 - Fiction. 3. Physically handicapped - Fiction. I. Title.*
***TC PZ7.K6339 Br 1997***

**Kirk, David, 1958-** Schooling bodies : school practice and public discourse, 1880-1950 / David Kirk. London : Washington, D.C. : Leicester University Press, 1998. 148 p. ; 25 cm. Includes bibliographical references and index. ISBN 0-7185-0100-4 DDC 613.7/071/041
*1. Physical education and training - Australia - History - 19th century. 2. Physical education and training - Australia - History - 20th century. 3. Physical education and training - Great Britain - History - 19th century. 4. Physical education and training - Great Britain - History - 20th century. I. Title.*
***TC GV315 .K57 1998***

Senior physical education. Champaign, IL : Human Kinetics, c1999.
***TC GV315 .S434 1999***

**Kirk, Heidi.**
Fuchshuber, Annegert. [Karlinchen. English] Carly. 1st ed. New York : The Feminist Press, c1997.
***TC PZ7.F94 Car 1997***

**Kirk, Robert, 1933-** Relativism and reality : a contemporary introduction / Robert Kirk. London ; New York : Routledge, 1999. x, 192 p. ; 24 cm. Includes bibliographical references (p. 184-187) and index. ISBN 0-415-20817-3 (hbk : alk. paper) ISBN 0-415-20816-5 (pbk. : alk. paper) DDC 149/.2
*1. Realism. 2. Relativity. I. Title.*
***TC B835 .K57 1999***

**Kirk, Samuel Alexander, 1904-** 10 years of research at the Institute for Research on Exceptional Children, University of Illinois, 1952-1962 / compiled by Samuel A. Kirk and Barbara D. Bateman. [Urbana : s.n.], 1964. 52 p. ; 23 cm. Authors' names in reverse order in 1963 ed. Includes bibliographies.
*1. Illinois. - University. - Institute for Research on Exceptional Children. 2. Exceptional children. I. Bateman, Barbara D., joint author. II. Title.*
***TC HQ773.7 .I4 1964***

**Kirkpatrick, Jeane J.** The new Presidential elite : men and women in national politics / Jeane Kirkpatrick, with the assistance of Warren E. Miller ... [et al.]. New York : Russell Sage Foundation : [distributed by Basic Books], c1976. xix, 605 p. ; 24 cm. Includes bibliographical references and index. ISBN 0-87154-475-X

DDC 301.5/92/0973
*1. Political participation - United States. 2. Political conventions - United States. 3. Women in politics - United States. I. Miller. Warren E. (Warren Edward). 1924- joint author. II. Russell Sage Foundation. III. Title.*
**TC JK1764 .K57**

**Kirsch, Irving, 1943-.**
How expectancies shape experience. 1st ed.
Washington, DC : American Psychological
Association, c1999.
**TC BF323.E8 H69 1999**

**Kirwan, James, 1961-** Beauty / James Kirwan.
Manchester : Manchester University Press, 1999. x,
182 p. ; 22 cm. Includes bibliographical references and index.
ISBN 0-7190-5571-7 ISBN 0-7190-5572-5 (pbk.) DDC 111.85
*1. Aesthetics. I. Title.*
**TC BH39 .K57 1999**

**Kiss and tell.**
Ericksen, Julia A., 1941- Cambridge, Mass. : Harvard
University Press, 1999.
**TC HQ18.U5 E75 1999**

**Kitchener, Karen S.** Foundations of ethical practice,
research, and teaching in psychology / Karen Strohm
Kitchener. Mahwah, N.J. : L. Erlbaum, 2000. xiii, 318
p. : ill. ; 27 cm. Includes bibliographical references (p. 277-
302) and index. ISBN 0-8058-2309-3 (alk. paper) DDC 174/
.915
*1. Psychologists - Professional ethics. 2. Psychology - Moral
and ethical aspects. 3. Psychology - Research - Moral and
ethical aspects. 4. Psychology - Study and teaching - Moral
and ethical aspects. I. Title.*
**TC BF76.4 .K58 2000**

**Klaassen, R. G.** Effective lecturing behaviour in
English-medium instruction : a pilot study / R.G.
Klaassen, J. Snippe. Delft, Netherlands : Delft
University Press, 1999. 47 p. : ill. ; 24 cm. (WTM-series ;
[3]) Includes bibliographical references (p. 41-43). ISBN 90-
407-1882-2
*1. Lecture method in teaching. 2. College teaching -
Netherlands - Delft. 3. Effective teaching - Netherlands - Delft.
4. Language and education - Netherlands - Delft. 5. English
language - Netherlands - Delft. I. Snipt. J. (Joke) II. Title. III.
Series: WTM-series ; 3.*
**TC LB2393 .K53 1999**

**Klages, Mary.** Woeful afflictions : disability and
sentimentality in Victorian America / Mary Klages.
Philadelphia : University of Pennsylvania Press,
c1999. 250 p. : ill. ; 24 cm. Includes bibliographical
references (p. [233]-241) and index. ISBN 0-8122-3499-5
(acid-free paper) DDC 362.4/0973/09034
*1. Handicapped - United States - History - 19th century. 2.
Handicapped - United States - Public opinion. 3. Handicapped
in mass media - History. 4. Handicapped in literature - History
and criticism. 5. Public opinion - United States. I. Title.*
**TC HV1553 .K53 1999**

**Klahr, David.** Exploring science : the cognition and
development of discovery processes / David Klahr
with Kevin Dunbar ... [et al.] ; foreword by Herbert A.
Simon. Cambridge, Mass. : MIT Press, c2000. xvi, 239
p. : ill. ; 24 cm. "A Bradford book." Includes bibliographical
references and indexes. ISBN 0-262-11248-5 (hc. : alk. paper)
DDC 509
*1. Discoveries in science. I. Title.*
**TC Q180.55.D57 K55 2000**

**Klandt, Heinz.**
Educating entrepreneurs for wealth creation.
Aldershot, Hants, England : Brookfield, USA :
Ashgate, 1998.
**TC HF1106 .E378 1998**

**Klaus Lucka directing [videorecording].**
The filming of a television commercial
[videorecording]. Minneapolis, Minn. : Media Loft,
c1992.
**TC HF6146.T42 F5 1992**

**Kleban, Morton H.**
The many dimensions of aging. New York : Springer
Pub., c2000.
**TC HQ1061 .M337 2000**

**Kleeblatt, Norman L.** An expressionist in Paris : the
paintings of Chaim Soutine / Norman L. Kleeblatt and
Kenneth E. Silver ; with contributions by Romy
Golan ... [et al.]. Munich ; New York : Jewish
Museum, c1998. 207 p. : ill. (some col.) ; 31 cm. Published
in conjunction with the exhibition of the same name presented
at the Jewish Museum, New York, Apr. 23-Aug. 16, 1998, the
Los Angeles County Museum of Art, Sept. 27, 1998-Jan. 3,
1999, and the Cincinnati Art Museum, Feb. 14-May 2, 1999.
Includes bibliographical references (p. 203-205). ISBN 3-
7913-1932-9 DDC 759.4
*1. Soutine, Chaim, - 1893-1943 - Exhibitions. 2. Expressionism
(Art) - France - Paris - Exhibitions. I. Soutine, Chaim, 1893-*

*1943. II. Silver. Kenneth E. III. Golan, Romy. IV. Jewish
Museum (New York, N.Y.) V. Los Angeles County Museum of
Art. VI. Cincinnati Art Museum. VII. Title. VIII. Title:
Paintings of Chaim Soutine IX. Title: Chaim Soutine*
**TC ND553.S7 A4 1998**

**Klein, Harriet B.** Intervention planning for adults with
communication problems : a guide for clinical
practicum and profesional practice. Volume 2 /
Harriet B. Klein, Nelson Moses. Boston : Allyn and
Bacon, c1999. xv, 416 p. : ill. ; 24 cm. "Volume II"--Spine.
A companion to the first volume: Intervention planning for
children with communication disorders. Includes
bibliographical references and index. DDC 616.85/506
*1. Communicative disorders - Treatment. 2. Communicative
disorders - Patients - Rehabilitation. 3. Medical protocols. 4.
Language Disorders - therapy. 5. Speech Disorders - therapy.
I. Moses. Nelson. II. Title.*
**TC RC423 .K57 1999**

**Klein, Katherine J.**
Multilevel theory, research, and methods in
organizations. 1st ed. San Francisco : Jossey-Bass,
c2000.
**TC HF5548.8 .M815 2000**

**Klein, M. Diane.**
Cook, Ruth E. Adapting early childhood curricula for
children in inclusive settings. 5th ed. Englewood
Cliffs, N.J. : Merrill, c2000.
**TC LC4019.2 .C66 2000**

**KLEIN, MELANIE.**
Caper, Robert. Immaterial facts. London ; New York :
Routledge, 2000.
**TC BF173 .C35 2000**

**Klein, Raymond M.**
Converging methods for understanding reading and
dyslexia. Cambridge, Mass. ; London : MIT Press,
c1999.
**TC LB1050.5 .C662 1999**

**Klein, Reva** Defying disaffection : how schools are
winning the hearts and minds of reluctant students /
Reva Klein. Staffordshire, England : Trentham Books,
1999. xx, 161 p. ; 24 cm. Includes bibliographical references
and index. ISBN 1-85856-161-2 DDC 371.93
*1. Socially handicapped children - Education - United States.
2. Alienation (Social psychology) - United States. 3. School
environment - United States. 4. Socially handicapped children -
Education - Great Britain. 5. Alienation (Social psychology) -
Great Britain. 6. School environment - Great Britain. I. Title.*
**TC LC4091 .K53 1999**

**Klein, Robert H.**
Group psychotherapy for psychological trauma. New
York : Guilford Press, c2000.
**TC RC552.P67 G76 2000**

**Klein, Stephen B.**
Handbook of contemporary learning theories.
Mahwah, N.J. ; London : Lawrence Erlbaum
Associates, 2001.
**TC LB1060 .H3457 2001**

**Kleinbaum, David G.**
Applied regression analysis and other multivariable
methods. 3rd ed. / David G. Kleinbaum ... [et al.].
Pacific Grove : Duxbury Press, c1998.
**TC QA278 .A665 1998**

**Applied regression analysis and other
multivariable methods.**
Applied regression analysis and other multivariable
methods. 3rd ed. / David G. Kleinbaum ... [et al.].
Pacific Grove : Duxbury Press, c1998.
**TC QA278 .A665 1998**

**Klenow, Carol.**
Reforming the Electoral College [videorecording].
[Boulder, Colo.? : Social Science Education
Consortium?], c1996.
**TC H62.5.U5 R4 1996**

**Klerman, Gerald L., 1928-.**
Weissman, Myrna M. Comprehensive guide to
interpersonal psychotherapy. New York: Basic Books,
c2000.
**TC RC480.8 .W445 2000**

**Kliebard, Herbert M.**
Curriculum and consequence. New York : Teachers
College Press, c2000.
**TC LB1570 .C88379 2000**

**KLIEBARD, HERBERT M.**
Curriculum and consequence. New York : Teachers
College Press, c2000.
**TC LB1570 .C88379 2000**

**Klima, Edward S., 1931-.**
The signs of language revisited. Mahwah, N.J. :
L.Erlbaum, 2000.

**TC HV2474 .S573 2000**

**Kline, Michael V.**
Promoting health in multicultural populations.
Thousand Oaks. Calif. : Sage Publications, c1999.
**TC RA448.4 .P76 1999**

**Kline, Paul.** The handbook of psychological testing /
Paul Kline. 2nd ed. London : New York : Routledge,
2000. vii, 744 p. : ill. ; 25 cm. Includes bibliographical
references (p. [683]-721) and indexes. ISBN 0-415-21157-3
(hbk.) ISBN 0-415-21158-1 (pbk.) DDC 150/.28/7
*1. Psychological tests. 2. Psychometrics. I. Title.*
**TC BF176 .K575 2000**

**Klinkner, Philip A.** The unsteady march : the rise and
decline of racial equality in America / Philip A.
Klinkner with Rogers M. Smith. Chicago : University
of Chicago Press, c1999. vii, 417 p. ; 24 cm. Includes
bibliographical references (p. 353-406) and index. ISBN
0-226-44339-6 (alk. paper) DDC 305.896/073
*1. Afro-Americans - Civil rights - History. 2. United States -
Race relations. 3. Afro-Americans - Government policy -
History. I. Smith, Rogers M., 1953- II. Title.*
**TC E185 .K55 1999**

**KLONDIKE GOLD FIELDS.** *See* **KLONDIKE
RIVER VALLEY (YUKON) - GOLD
DISCOVERIES.**

**KLONDIKE RIVER VALLEY (YUKON) - GOLD
DISCOVERIES.**
Jones, Charlotte Foltz. Yukon gold. 1st ed. New
York : Holiday House, c1999.
**TC F1095.K5 J66 1999**

**KLONDIKE RIVER VALLEY (YUKON) - GOLD
DISCOVERIES - JUVENILE LITERATURE.**
Jones, Charlotte Foltz. Yukon gold. 1st ed. New
York : Holiday House, c1999.
**TC F1095.K5 J66 1999**

**KLONDIKE VALLEY (YUKON).** *See* **KLONDIKE
RIVER VALLEY (YUKON).**

**Klonsky, Michael.**
A simple justice. New York : Teachers College Press,
2000.
**TC LC213.2 .S56 2000**

**Klorer, P. Gussie.** Expressive therapy with troubled
children / by P. Gussie Klorer. Northvale, NJ : Jason
Aronson, 2000. xiv, 282 p. : ill. ; 24 cm. ISBN 0-7657-
0223-1 DDC 618.92/891656
*1. Art therapy for children. I. Title.*
**TC RJ505.A7 K56 2000**

**Klugman, Marie R.**
Freed, Jann E. A culture for academic excellence.
Washington, D.C. : Graduate School of Education and
Human Development, George Washington University,
1997.
**TC LB2341 .F688 1997**

**Klutch, Richard J.**
Bumby, Douglas R. Mathematics. 2nd ed. Columbus,
Ohio : C.E. Merrill, c1982-<1986.>
**TC QA154.2 .B8 1982**

**Klutch, Richard J., joint author.**
Bumby, Douglas R. Mathematics. Columbus, Ohio :
C.E. Merrill, c1978-1979.
**TC QA39.2 .B85 1980**

**Knaft, Kathleen Astin.**
Concept development in nursing. 2nd ed.
Philadelphia : Saunders, c2000.
**TC RT84.5 .C6624 2000**

**Knapp, Richard F., 1945-.**
Wadelington, Charles Weldon. Charlotte Hawkins
Brown & Palmer Memorial Institute. Chapel Hill ;
London : University of North Carolina Press, c1999.
**TC LA2317.B598 W33 1999**

**Knapp, Sara D.** The contemporary thesaurus of search
terms and synonyms : a guide for natural language
computer searching / Sara D. Knapp. 2nd ed. Phoenix,
Ariz. : Oryx Press, 2000. xxiii, 682 p. ; 29 cm. Includes
bibliographical references (p. [681]-682). ISBN 1-57356-107-
X (alk. paper) DDC 025.4/9
*1. Electronic information resource searching - English-
speaking countries. 2. English language - Terms and phrases.
3. Social sciences - English-speaking countries - Terminology.
I. Title.*
**TC ZA4060 .K58 2000**

**Knapper, Christopher.** Lifelong learning in higher
education / Christopher K. Knapper and Arthur J.
Cropley. 3rd ed. London : Kogan Page, 2000. xvii, 238
p. ; 24 cm. Previous ed.: 1991. Includes bibliographical
references (p. 211-232) and index. ISBN 0-7494-2794-9
*1. Continuing education. 2. Education, Higher. I. Cropley, A. J.
II. Title.*

*TC LC5215 .K593 2000*
Using consultants to improve teaching. San
Francisco : Jossey-Bass, c1999.
*TC LB2799.2 .U83 1999*

**Kneen, Maggie, ill.**
Preston, Tim. The lonely scarecrow. 1st American ed.
New York : Dutton Children's Books, 1999.
*TC PZ7.P9237 Lo 1999*

**Knight, Pamela, 1940-** The care and education of a deaf
child : a book for parents / Pamela Knight and Ruth
Swanwick. Clevedon [England] ; Buffalo [N.Y.] :
Multilingual Matters, c1999. xvi, 191 p. : ill. ; 22 cm.
(Parents' and teachers' guides ; no. 4) Includes bibliographical
references (p. 186-187) and index. ISBN 1-85359-459-8 (hbk. :
alk. paper) ISBN 1-85359-458-X (pbk. : alk. paper) DDC 649/
.1512
*1. Deaf children - Great Britain. 2. Deaf children -
Great Britain - Language. 3. Deaf children - Education - Great
Britain. I. Swanwick, Ruth, 1963- II. Title. III. Series.*
*TC HV2716 .K65 1999*

**Knight, Peter, 1947-.**
The politics of professionalism. London : Continuum,
2000.
*TC LB1779 .M33 2000*

**Knoblock, Peter, 1934-.**
Preparing humanistic teachers for troubled children.
Syracuse, N.Y. : Division of Special Education and
Rehabilitation, Syracuse University, [1974?]
*TC LC4801 .P73*

**Knottnerus, J. David.** The social worlds of male and
female children in the nineteenth century French
educational system : youth, rituals and elites / J.
David Knottnerus and Frédérique Van de Poel-
Knottnerus. Lewiston, N.Y. ; Lampeter, Wales :
Edwin Mellen Press, c1999. iv, 155 p. ; 24 cm. (Mellen
studies in education ; v. 46) Includes bibliographical references
(p. [137]-151) and index. ISBN 0-7734-7912-0 DDC 306.43/
2/094409034
*1. Education - Social aspects - France - History - 19th century.
2. Elite (Social sciences) - France - History - 19th century. 3.
Boarding schools - France - History - 19th century. 4. Sex
differences in education - Social aspects - France - History -
19th century. I. Van de Poel-Knottnerus, Frédérique. II. Title.
III. Series.*
*TC LC191.8.F8 K66 1999*

**Knowing and teaching elementary mathematics.**
Ma, Liping. Mahwah, N.J. : Lawrence Erlbaum
Associates, 1999.
*TC QA135.5 .M22 1999*

**Knowledge and power in higher education :** a reader /
edited by Richard Harvey Brown and J. Daniel
Schubert. New York ; London : Teachers College
Press, c2000. vi, 207 p. ; 24 cm. Includes bibliographical
references and index. ISBN 0-8077-3906-5 (hbk. : alk. paper)
ISBN 0-8077-3905-7 (pbk. : alk. paper) DDC 378
*1. Education, Higher - Political aspects. 2. Knowledge,
Sociology of. 3. Scientism - Political aspects. 4. Higher
education and state. I. Brown, Richard Harvey. II. Schubert, J.
Daniel.*
*TC LC171 .K62 2000*

**Knowledge and power in the global economy :** politics
and the rhetoric of school reform / edited by David A.
Gabbard. Mahwah, N.J. : L. Erlbaum Associates,
2000. xxiii, 430 p. ; 24 cm. (Sociocultural, political, and
historical studies in education) Includes bibliographical
references and indexes. ISBN 0-8058-2433-2 (hard : alk.
paper) ISBN 0-8058-2434-0 (pbk. : alk. paper) DDC 370.11/5
*1. Education - Economic aspects - United States. 2. Politics
and education - United States. 3. Educational change - United
States. 4. Curriculum change - United States. 5. Critical
pedagogy - United States. I. Gabbard, David. II. Series.*
*TC LC66 .K66 2000*

**KNOWLEDGE, ATTITUDES, PRACTICE.**
Baker, Susan Keane. Managing patient expectations.
San Francisco : Jossey Bass Publishers, 1998.
*TC R727.3 .B28 1998*

**KNOWLEDGE-BASED SYSTEMS (COMPUTER
SCIENCE).** *See* **EXPERT SYSTEMS
(COMPUTER SCIENCE).**

**KNOWLEDGE, BOOKS OF.** *See*
**ENCYCLOPEDIAS AND DICTIONARIES.**

**KNOWLEDGE, CLASSIFICATION OF.** *See*
**CLASSIFICATION.**

**KNOWLEDGE - CONGRESSES.**
Memory, brain, and belief. Cambridge, Mass. ;
London : Harvard University Press, 2000.
*TC QP406 .M44 2000*

**KNOWLEDGE DISCOVERY IN DATABASES.** *See*
**DATA MINING.**

**The knowledge factory.**
Aronowitz, Stanley. Boston : Beacon Press, c2000.
*TC LA227.4 .A76 2000*

**KNOWLEDGE MANAGEMENT.** *See also*
**INFORMATION TECHNOLOGY;
INTELLECTUAL CAPITAL;
ORGANIZATIONAL LEARNING.**
Centre for Educational Research and Innovation.
Knowledge management in the learning society.
Paris : Organisation for Economic Co-operation and
Development, 2000.
*TC HD30.2 .C462 2000*

**Knowledge management in the learning society.**
Centre for Educational Research and Innovation.
Paris : Organisation for Economic Co-operation and
Development, 2000.
*TC HD30.2 .C462 2000*

**KNOWLEDGE OF SELF, THEORY OF.** *See*
**SELF-KNOWLEDGE, THEORY OF.**

**KNOWLEDGE, PSYCHOLOGY OF.**
Kinnamon, James C. A comparison of structural
knowledge in eighth graders and college students.
1999.
*TC 085 K6194*

**KNOWLEDGE, REFLEXIVE.** *See* **SELF-
KNOWLEDGE, THEORY OF.**

**KNOWLEDGE, SOCIOLOGY OF.**
Knowledge and power in higher education. New
York ; London : Teachers College Press, c2000.
*TC LC171 .K62 2000*

Television and common knowledge. New York :
Routledge, 1999.
*TC PN1992.6 .T379 1999*

**KNOWLEDGE, THEORY OF.** *See also* **BELIEF
AND DOUBT; EXPERTISE; IDENTITY;
INQUIRY (THEORY OF KNOWLEDGE);
INTELLECT; INTUITION; OTHER MINDS
(THEORY OF KNOWLEDGE);
PERCEPTION; RATIONALISM;
SCIENTISM; SELF-KNOWLEDGE, THEORY
OF; SENSES AND SENSATION; VALUES.**
Bernstein, Basil B. Pedagogy, symbolic control, and
identity. Lanham, Md. : Rowman & Littlefield, 2000.
*TC LC191 .B456 2000*

Bruner, Jerome Seymour. On knowing. Cambridge,
Belknap Press of Harvard University Press, 1962.
*TC LB885 .B778*

Clancey, William J. Conceptual coordination.
Mahwah, N.J. : L. Erlbaum Associates, 1999.
*TC BF311 .C5395 1999*

Development of mental representation. Mahwah, NJ :
L. Erlbaum Associates, c1999.
*TC BF723.M43 T47 1999*

Education, information, and transformation. Upper
Saddle River, N.J. : Merrill, c1999.
*TC BF441 .E25 1999*

Locke, John, 1632-1704. [Some thoughts concerning
education] Some thoughts concerning education :
Indianapolis : Hackett Pub. Co., c1996.
*TC LB475.L6 L63 1996*

Meichenbaum, Donald. Nurturing independent
learners. Cambridge, Mass. : Brookline Books, c1998.
*TC LB1031.4 .M45 1998*

New perspectives on conceptual change. 1st ed.
Amsterdam ; New York ; Oxford : Pergamon, 1999.
*TC LB1062 .N49 1999*

Robbins, Carol Braswell. An examination of critical
feminist pedagogy in practice. 1999.
*TC 06 no. 11067*

The Robot in the garden. Cambridge, Mass. : MIT
Press, 2000.
*TC TJ211 .R537 2000*

Varela, Francisco J., 1945- [Know-how per l'etica.
English] Ethical know-how. Stanford, Calif. : Stanford
University Press, 1999.
*TC BJ1012 .V3813 1999*

**KNOWLEDGE, THEORY OF - CASE STUDIES.**
Mirochnik, Elijah, 1952- Teaching in the first person.
New York : P. Lang, c2000.
*TC LB1033 .M546 2000*

**KNOWLEDGE, THEORY OF - EARLY WORKS
TO 1800.**
Bacon, Francis, 1561-1626. The advancement of
learning. Oxford : Clarendon, 2000.

*TC B1191 .K545 2000*

**KNOWLEDGE, THEORY OF, IN LITERATURE.**
Barney, Richard A., 1955- Plots of enlightenment.
Stanford, Calif. : Stanford University Press, c1999.
*TC PR858.E38 B37 1999*

**KNOWLEDGE, THEORY OF - POLITICAL
ASPECTS.**
Beverley, John. Subalternity and representation.
Durham [N.C.] ; London : Duke University Press,
1999.
*TC HM1136 .B48 1999*

**KNOWLEDGE, THEORY OF (RELIGION).**
Martin, Robert K., 1959- The incarnate ground of
Christian faith. Lanham, Md. : University Press of
America, c1998.
*TC BV1464 .M37 1998*

**Knowlton, Jack.** Maps & globes / by Jack Knowlton ;
pictures by Harriett Barton. New York :
HarperCollins, c1985. 42 p. : col. ill. ; 26 cm. (Reading
rainbow book) SUMMARY: A brief history of mapmaking, a
simple explanation of how to read maps and globes, and an
introduction to the many different kinds of maps there are.
*1. Maps - Juvenile literature. 2. Globes - Juvenile literature. I.
Barton, Harriett, ill. II. Title. III. Title: Maps and globes. IV.
Series.*
*TC GA105.6 .K58 1985*

**Knox, Carolyn W.** AGS English for the world of work /
by Carolyn W. Knox. Circle Pines, Minn. : American
Guidance Service, c1997. vii, 285 p. : col. ill. ; 24 cm.
Includes index. ISBN 0785408592H
*1. English language - Business English. I. Title. II. Title:
American Guidance Service English for the world of work*
*TC PE1127.W65 K66 1997*

AGS English for the world of work / by Carolyn W.
Knox. Teacher's ed. Circle Pines, Minn. : American
Guidance Service, c1997. T16, viii, 303 p. : col. ill. ; 29
cm. "This textbook is intended for secondary students and
adults who are planning to enter the world of work soon after
the course."--T4. Includes index. ISBN 0-7854-0861-4
*1. English language - Study and teaching (Secondary) 2.
English language - Business English. I. Title. II. Title:
American Guidance Service English for the world of work*
*TC PE1127.W65 K66 1997 Teacher's Ed.*

**KOALICIJA "ZAJEDNO.".**
[Ajmo, ajde, svi u šetnju. English.] Protest in
Belgrade. Budapest, Hungary ; New York, NY, USA :
Central European University Press, 1999.
*TC DR2044 .A3913 1999*

**Koballa, Thomas R.**
Cases in middle and secondary science education.
Upper Saddle River, N.J. : Merrill, c2000.
*TC Q181 .C348 2000*

**Kobiecość i męskość jako kategorie społeczno-
kulturowe w studiach feministycznych.**
Gontarczyk, Ewa. Poznań : Eruditus, 1995.
*TC HQ1181.P7 G66 1995*

**Koblik, Steven.**
Distinctively American. New Brunswick [N.J.] :
Transaction Publishers, [2000]
*TC LA226 .D57 2000*

**Kochhar, Carol.**
**Handbook for successful inclusion.**
Kochhar, Carol. Successful inclusion. 2nd ed.
Upper Saddle River, NJ : Prentice Hall, c2000.
*TC LC1201 .K63 2000*

Successful inclusion : practical strategies for a shared
responsibility / Carol A. Kochhar, Lynda L. West,
Juliana Taymans. 2nd ed. Upper Saddle River, NJ :
Prentice Hall, c2000. xvi, 250 p. : ill. ; 28 cm. Rev. ed. of:
Handbook for successful inclusion. 1996. Includes
bibliographical references and index. ISBN 0-13-921172-1
DDC 371.9/046
*1. Inclusive education - United States - Handbooks, manuals,
etc. 2. Handicapped children - Education - United States -
Handbooks, manuals, etc. I. West, Lynda L. II. Taymans,
Juliana M. III. Kochhar, Carol. Handbook for successful
inclusion. IV. Title.*
*TC LC1201 .K63 2000*

**Kögler, Hans Herbert, 1960-.**
Empathy and agency. Boulder, Colo. ; Oxford :
Westview Press, 2000.
*TC BF64 .E67 2000*

**Kohl, Helen.**
DeFelice, Stephen L., 1936- The carnitine defense.
[Emmaus, Pa.] : Rodale Press ; [New York] :
Distributed to the book trade by St. Martin's Press,
c1999.
*TC RC685.C6 D4235 1999*

**Kohl, Kay Jordan, 1940-.**
Postbaccalaureate futures. Phoenix, AZ : Oryx Press, 2000.
*TC LB2371.4 .P68 2000*

**Kohlstedt, Sally Gregory, 1943-.**
History of women in the sciences. Chicago, Ill. : University of Chicago Press, c1999.
*TC Q130 .H58 1999*

**Kohn, Alfie.** Punished by rewards : the trouble with gold stars, incentive plans, A's, praise, and other bribes / Alfie Kohn ; with a new afterword by the author. Boston : Houghton Mifflin Co., 1999, c1993. xiv, 431 ; 24 cm. Includes bibliographical references (p. 377-411) and indexes. CONTENTS: Skinner-Boxed: The legacy of behaviorism -- Is it right to reward? -- Is it effective to reward? -- The trouble with carrots: Four reasons rewards fail -- Cutting the interest rate: The fifth reason rewards fail -- The praise problem -- Pay for performance: Why behaviorism doesn't work in the workplace -- Lures for learning: Why behaviorism doesn't work in the classroom -- Bribes for behaving: Why behaviorism doesn't help children become good people -- Thank God it's Monday: The roots of motivation in the workplace -- Hooked on learning: The roots of motivation in the classroom -- Good kids without goodies. ISBN 0-618-00181-6
*1. Reward (Psychology) 2. Motivation (Psychology) 3. Behaviorism (Psychology) I. Title.*
*TC BF505.R48 K65 1999*

What to look for in a classroom : and other essays / Alfie Kohn. 1st ed. San Francisco : Jossey-Bass, c1998. xiv, 289 p. ; 24 cm. Includes bibliographical references and index. CONTENTS: The limits of teaching skills -- The trouble with school uniforms -- Beyond discipline -- How not to teach values : a critical look at character education -- Resistance to cooperative learning : making sense of its deletion and dilution -- "A lot of fat kids who don't like to read" : the effects of Pizza Hut's Book it! program and other reading incentives -- Grading : the issue is not how but why -- Grade inflation and other red herrings -- Only for my kid : how privileged parents undermine school reform -- Suffer the restless children -- The truth about self-esteem -- Television and children : reviewing the evidence -- The five-hundred-pound gorilla -- The false premises of school choice plans -- Students don't "work" they learn -- The littlest customers : TQM goes to school -- Caring kids : the role of the schools -- Choices for children : why and how to let students decide -- What to look for in a classroom. ISBN 0-7879-4453-X (cloth) DDC 371.1
*1. Teachers. 2. Teaching. 3. Classroom management. 4. Learning. 5. Teacher-student relationships. 6. School management and organization. I. Title.*
*TC LB1775 .K643 1998*

**Kohn, Daniel B., 1963-** Practical pedagogy for the Jewish classroom : classroom management, instruction, and curriculum development / Daniel B. Kohn. Westport, Conn. : Greenwood Press, 1999. xiv, 202 p. ; 22 cm. (The Greenwood educators' reference collection, 1056-2192) Includes bibliography (p. [191]-196) and index. ISBN 0-313-30931-0 (alk. paper) DDC 296.6/8/0835
*1. Jewish religious education of teenagers. 2. Jewish religious education - Teaching methods. I. Title. II. Series.*
*TC BM108 .K65 1999*

**Kohn, Howard.** We had a dream : a tale of the struggles for integration in America / Howard Kohn. New York : Simon & Schuster, 1998. 366 p. ; 25 cm. Includes index. ISBN 0-684-80874-9 DDC 305.8/009752/51
*1. Prince George's County (Md.) - Race relations. 2. Prince George's County (Md.) - Biography. 3. Afro-Americans - Civil rights - Maryland - Prince George's County - History - 20th century. 4. Interracial dating - Maryland - Prince George's County. 5. Interracial marriage - Maryland - Prince George's County. 6. United States - Race relations - Case studies. I. Title.*
*TC F187.P9 K64 1998*

**Kohon, Gregorio** No lost certainties to be recovered. London : Karnac Books, 1999. xvi, 204 p. ; 23 cm. Includes bibliographical references and index. ISBN 1-85575-210-7 DDC 150.1
*1. Psychoanalysis*
*TC BF173 .K64 1999*

**KOHUT, HEINZ.**
Greif, Gary F. The tragedy of the self. Lanham, Md. ; Oxford : University Press of America, c2000.
*TC BF175.5.S44 G74 2000*

**Koide, Tan.** May we sleep here tonight? / Tan Koide ; illustrated by Yasuko Koide. New York : Atheneum, 1981. [32] p. : col. ill. ; 46 x 38 cm. SUMMARY: Several lost animals find a cozy house in the woods, settle down for the night, and are startled with the house's very big owner arrives. ISBN 0-02-109109-9
*1. Animals - Fiction. I. Koide, Yasuko, ill. II. Title.*

*TC PZ7.K8293 May 1981*

**Koide, Yasuko, ill.**
Koide, Tan. May we sleep here tonight? New York : Atheneum, 1981.
*TC PZ7.K8293 May 1981*

**Koivu-Rybicki, Victoria T.**
Madigan, Dan. The writing lives of children. York, ME : Stenhouse Publishers, 1997.
*TC LB1042 .M24 1997*

**Koja, Stephan.**
America. Munich, Germany ; London ; New York : Prestel, c1999.
*TC ND210 .A724 1999*

**Kokusai Kyōiku Jōhō Sentā.**
A Teacher's & textbook writers' handbook on Japan. 5th., rev. printing. Tokyo : International Society for Educational Information, c1993.
*TC DS806 .T34 1993*

**Kolander, Cheryl A.** Contemporary women's health : issues for today and the future / Cheryl A. Kolander, Danny J. Ballard, Cynthia K. Chandler. Boston, Mass. : WCB/McGraw-Hill, c1999. xvii, 462 p. : ill. (some col.) ; 26 cm. Includes bibliographical references and index. ISBN 0-8151-0626-2 DDC 613/.04244
*1. Women - Health and hygiene. I. Ballard, Danny J. II. Chandler, Cynthia K. III. Title.*
*TC RA778 .K7245 1999*

**Kolenberg, Hendrik.**
Art Gallery of New South Wales. Australian drawings from the gallery's collection. Sydney : Art Gallery of New South Wales, 1997.
*TC NC369 .A78 1997*

Art Gallery of New South Wales. Australian prints from the gallery's collection. Sydney : Art Gallery of New South Wales, c1998.
*TC NE789 .A77 1998*

Australian watercolours from the gallery's collection : 1880s to 1990s / Hendrik Kolenberg. Sydney, [Australia] : Art Gallery of New South Wales, 1995. 128 p. : col. ill. ; 31 cm. Published in conjunction with an exhibition held at the Art Gallery of New South Wales, 18 Nov. 1995 - 14 Jan. 1996. Includes bibliographical references (p. 126-127) and index. ISBN 0-7310-5068-1
*1. Watercolor painting, Australian - Exhibitions. 2. Watercolor painting - 19th century - Australia - Exhibitions. 3. Watercolor painting - 20th century - Australia - Exhibitions. 4. Art Gallery of New South Wales - Exhibitions. I. Art Gallery of New South Wales. II. Title.*
*TC ND2089 .K64 1995*

**Kolko, Beth E.**
Race in cyberspace. New York ; London : Routledge, 2000.
*TC HT1523 .R252 2000*

**Kollak, Ingrid.**
Nursing theories. New York : Springer Pub. Co., c1999.
*TC RT84.5 .N8795 1999*

**Komar, Vitaly.**
Painting by numbers. Berkeley : University of California Press, [1999]
*TC ND1140 .P26 1999*

**Komives, Susan R., 1946-** Exploring leadership : for college students who want to make a difference / Susan R. Komives, Nance Lucas, Timothy R. McMahon. 1st ed. San Francisco : Jossey-Bass Publishers, c1998. xix, 347 p. : ill. ; 23 cm. Includes bibliographical references (p. 315-328) and indexes. ISBN 0-7879-0929-7 (alk. paper) DDC 378.1/98
*1. Student activities - United States. 2. Leadership - Study and teaching (Higher) - United States. 3. Interpersonal relations - United States. I. Lucas, Nance, 1960- II. McMahon, Timothy R., 1951- III. Title.*
*TC LB3605 .K64 1998*

**Komm mit :** Holt German. Austin, Tex. : Holt, Rinehart and Winston, c1995-96. 3 v. : col. ill., map ; 27 cm. Includes indexes. ISBN 0-03-032519-6 (l. 1) ISBN 0-03-032552-8 (l. 2) ISBN 0-03-032557-9 (l. 3)
*1. German language - Textbooks for foreign speakers - English. 2. German language - Grammar. I. Title.*
*TC PF3111 .K65 1998*

**Komm mit :** Holt German. Teacher's ed. Austin, Tex. : Holt, Rinehart and Winston, 1995-96. 3 v. : col. ill., col. maps ; 27 cm. Includes indexes. ISBN 0-03-032522-6 (l. 1) ISBN 0-03-032553-6 (l. 2) ISBN 0-03-032558-7 (l. 1)
*1. German language - Textbooks for foreign speakers - English. 2. German language - Grammar. 3. German language - Study and teaching - Foreign speakers. I. Title.*

**Komm mit :** Holt German; Practice and activity book. Austin, Tex. : Holt, Rinehart and Winston, c1995. 3 v. : ill. ; 28 cm. ISBN 0-03-032524-2 (l. 1) ISBN 0-03-095061-9 (l. 2) ISBN 0-03-095075-9 (l. 3)
*1. German language - Textbooks for foreign speakers - English. 2. German language - Grammar. I. Title.*
*TC PF3111 .K653 1995*

**Konecny, Peter, 1963-** Builders and deserters : students, state, and community in Leningrad, 1917-1941 / Peter Konecny. Montreal : McGill-Queen's University Press, 1999. xiii, 358 p. ; 24 cm. Includes bibliographical references and index. ISBN 0-7735-1881-9 DDC 378.47/21/09041
*1. Education, Higher - Political aspects - Russia (Federation) - Saint Petersburg. 2. Higher education and state - Soviet Union - History. I. Title.*
*TC LA839.5.L45 K65 1999*

**Kontra, Miklós.**
Language, a right and a resource. Budapest, Hungary ; New York : Central European University Press, c1999.
*TC P119.3 .L277 1999*

**Koocher, Gerald P.**
Psychologists' desk reference. New York : Oxford University Press, 1998.
*TC RC467.2 .P78 1998*

**Koorey, Stefani, 1959-.**
Peterson, Carolyn Sue, 1938- Story programs. 2nd ed. Lanham, Md. : Scarecrow Press, 2000.
*TC LB1042 .P47 2000*

**Kooy, Mary.**
Fiction, literature and media. Amsterdam : Amsterdam University Press, c1999.
*TC LB1575.8 .F53 1999*

**Kopff, E. Christian.** The devil knows Latin : why America needs the classical tradition / E. Christian Kopff. Wilmington, Del. : ISI Books, 1999. xvii, 313 p. ; 22 cm. ISBN 1-88292-625-0 DDC 480/.071/073
*1. Classical philology - Study and teaching - United States. 2. Civilization, Classical - Study and teaching - United States. 3. United States - Civilization - Classical influences. 4. Classical education - United States. 5. Classicism - United States. I. Title.*
*TC PA78.U6 K67 1999*

**Kopp, Jaine.**
Gonsalves, Philip. Build it! festival. Berkeley, CA : Great Explorations in Math and Science (GEMS), Lawrence Hall of Science, University of California at Berkeley, c1995.
*TC QA462 .G66 1995*

**Kopta, Stephen M., 1951-.**
Stilwell, Barbara M. Right vs. wrong--. Bloomington : Indiana University Press, c2000.
*TC BJ1471 .S69 2000*

**Kordalewski, John.** Standards in the classroom : how teachers and students negotiate learning / John Kordalewski ; foreword by Catherine G. Krupnick. New York ; London : Teachers College Press, c2000. xi, 207 p. ; 24 cm. Includes bibliographical references (p. 199-201) and index. ISBN 0-8077-3947-2 (cloth : alk. paper) ISBN 0-8077-3946-4 (paper : alk. paper) DDC 371.27/1
*1. Education - Standards - United States. 2. Educational tests and measurements - United States. 3. Teaching - United States. I. Title.*
*TC LB3060.83 .K67 2000*

**The Korean Americans.**
Hurh, Won Moo. Westport, Conn. : Greenwood Press, c1998.
*TC E184.K6 H875 1998*

**KOREAN AMERICANS.**
Hurh, Won Moo. The Korean Americans. Westport, Conn. : Greenwood Press, c1998.
*TC E184.K6 H875 1998*

**KOREAN AMERICANS - FICTION.**
Pak, Soyung. Dear Juno. New York : Viking, 1999.
*TC PZ7.P173 De 1999*

**KOREAN AMERICANS - UNITED STATES.** *See* KOREAN AMERICANS.

**KOREANS - UNITED STATES.** *See* **KOREAN AMERICANS.**

**Koretz, Daniel M.**
National Research Council (U.S.). Committee on Embedding Common Test Items in State and District Assessments. Embedding questions. Washington, DC : National Academy Press, c1999.
*TC LB3051 .N319 1999*

**Korrespondenz-blatt** / Luzerner Staatspersonalverband, Beamtenverein der Stadt Luzern, Gemeindeschreiberverband des Kantons Luzern. Luzern : Luzerner Staatspersonalverband, 1947- 23 cm. Frequency: 6x jährl. Former frequency: 7x jährl. Jg. 33, Nr. 7 (Juli 1947)- . Name des Verbandes wechselt: 1986 'Staatspersonalverband des Kantons Luzern', 1947 'Verband der Beamten und Angestellten'. Neues Format ab 1997: 32 cm. Umschlagtitel ab 1997: Blatt. Continues: Korrespondenzblatt des Verbandes der Beamten und Angestellten und des Gemeindeschreiber-Vereins des Kts. Luzern.
*I. Luzerner Staatspersonalverband. II. Beamtenverein der Stadt Luzern. III. Gemeindeschreiberverband des Kantons Luzern. IV. Staatspersonalverband des Kantons Luzern. V. Verband der Beamten und Angestellten des Kantons Luzern. VI. Title: Blatt VII. Title: Korrespondenzblatt des Verbandes der Beamten und Angestellten und des Gemeindeschreiber-Vereins des Kts. Luzern*

**Korrespondenzblatt des Verbandes der Beamten und Angestellten und des Gemeindeschreiber-Vereins des Kts. Luzern.**
Korrespondenz-blatt. Luzern : Luzerner Staatspersonalverband, 1947-

**KORSAKOFF PSYCHOSIS.** *See* **KORSAKOFF'S SYNDROME.**

**KORSAKOFF SYNDROME.** *See* **KORSAKOFF'S SYNDROME.**

**KORSAKOFF'S SYNDROME - DIAGNOSIS.**
Disorders due to psychoactive substance abuse [videorecording]. Princeton, N.J. : Films for the Humanities & Sciences, 1998.
*TC RC564 .D5 1998*

**KORSAKOFF'S SYNDROME - PATIENTS.**
Disorders due to psychoactive substance abuse [videorecording]. Princeton, N.J. : Films for the Humanities & Sciences, 1998.
*TC RC564 .D5 1998*

**Korta, Kepa.**
Cognition, agency, and rationality. Boston : Kluwer Academic, 1999.
*TC BC177 .C45 1999*

**Koshewa, Allen.** Discipline and democracy : teachers on trial / Allen Koshewa ; foreword by Jerome C. Harste. Portsmouth, NH : Heinemann, c1999. xi, 228 p. ; 23 cm. Includes bibliographical references (p. 223-228). ISBN 0-325-00181-2 (acid-free paper) DDC 371.102/4
*1. School discipline. 2. Classroom management. I. Title.*
*TC LB3011 .K66 1999*

**Koshiyama, Mits.**
Rabbit in the moon [videorecording]. San Francisco, Calif. : Wabi-Sabi Productions, 1999.
*TC D753.8 .R3 1999*

**Koshy, Valsa, 1945-.**
Mathematics for primary teachers. London ; New York : Routledge, 2000.
*TC QA135.5 .K67 2000*

**Kosmer, Ellen Virginia, ill.**
Honan, Linda. Picture the Middle Ages. Amawalk, N.Y. : Golden Owl Pub. Co. : Higgins Armory Museum, c1994.
*TC CB351 .H58 1994*

**Kosmoski, Georgia J.** Managing difficult, frustrating, and hostile conversations : strategies for savvy administrators / by Georgia J. Kosmoski, Dennis R. Pollack. Thousand Oaks, Calif. : Sage Publications, c2000. xii, 108 p. ; 24 cm. Includes bibliographical references and index. CONTENTS: Calming the angry screamer -- Dealing with public embarrassment or humiliation -- Handling legitimate complaints -- Defusing situations that involve drugs or alcohol -- Refusing to be coerced -- Discouraging the dependent personality -- Serving as mediator when friction exists -- Disabling the back stabber -- Maintaining confidentiality -- Discussion : what works in all cases. ISBN 0-8039-6808-6 (alk. paper) ISBN 0-8039-6809-4 (pbk. : alk. paper) DDC 371.5
*1. Conflict management - United States. 2. School administrators - United States. 3. Aggressiveness - United States. 4. Mediation - United States. 5. Behavior modification - United States. I. Pollack, Dennis R. II. Title.*
*TC LB3011.5 .K67 2000*

**Koss-Chioino, Joan.** Working with Latino youth : culture, development, and context / Joan D. Koss-Chioino, Luis A. Vargas. 1st ed. San Francisco : Jossey-Bass, c1999. xx, 236 p. ; 23 cm. Includes bibliographical references and index. ISBN 0-7879-4325-8 (alk. paper) DDC 616.89/0089/68073
*1. Hispanic American youth - Mental health. 2. Hispanic American youth - Mental health services. I. Vargas, Luis A., 1951- II. Title.*

*TC RC451.5.H57 K67 1999*

**Kostick, Karla.**
Donnell Library Center. Video. New York : New York Public Library, 1990.
*TC PN1992.95 .D66*

**Kotinsky, Ruth, 1903- joint author.**
Thayer, Vivian Trow, 1886- Reorganizing secondary education; New York, Appleton-Century [c1939]
*TC LB1607 .T5*

**Kottak, Conrad Phillip.**
Strategies in teaching anthropology. Upper Saddle River, N.J. : Prentice Hall, c2000.
*TC GN43 .S77 2000*

**Kotter, John P., 1947-** John P. Kotter on what leaders really do / John P. Kotter. Boston : Harvard Business School Press, c1999. 184 p. ; 22 cm. (A Harvard business review book) Includes bibliographical references and index. ISBN 0-87584-897-4 (alk. paper) DDC 658.4/092
*1. Leadership. I. Title. II. Series: Harvard business review book series*
*TC HD57.7 .K665 1999*

**Kottler, Jeffrey A.** On being a teacher / by Jeffrey A. Kottler, Stanley J. Zehm. 2nd ed. Thousand Oaks, Calif. : Corwin Press, c2000. xiv, 151 p. ; 22 cm. Subtitle on cover : Human dimension. Includes bibliographical references (p. 141-148) and index. CONTENTS: On being a teacher -- On being a learner -- On struggling with the challenges of the profession -- On being a relationship specialist -- On being an effective communicator -- On being a helper -- On avoiding burnout and rustout -- On being reflective -- On being passionately committed. ISBN 0-7619-7695-7 (cloth : alk. paper) ISBN 0-7619-7696-5 (pbk. : alk. paper) DDC 371.102
*1. Teaching. 2. Motivation in education. 3. Teachers. I. Zehm, Stanley J. II. Title.*
*TC LB1025.3 .Z44 2000*

Powell, Richard R., 1951- Classrooms under the influence. Newbury Park, Calif. : Corwin Press, c1995.
*TC HV5824.Y68 P69 1995*

**Kouki, Rafa.** Telelearning via the Internet / Rafa Kouki, David Wright. Hershey, PA : Idea Group Pub., c1999. 197 p. : ill. ; 25 cm. Includes bibliographical references (p. 188-193) and index. ISBN 1-87828-953-5 DDC 378.1/7344678
*1. Distance education. 2. Teaching - Computer network resources. 3. Internet (Computer network) in education. 4. Education - Computer network resources. I. Wright, David, 1947- II. Title.*
*TC LC5800 .K68 1999*

**Kovacs, George.** Literal literacy II : what every American needs to know second / George Kovacs. Lewiston, NY : E. Mellen Press, c1993. 145 p. ; 24 cm. "Companion volume to Literal literacy : what every American needs to know first"--Pref. ISBN 0-7734-3044-X DDC 428/.00973
*1. English language - United States - Errors of usage. 2. English language - United States - Usage. 3. Literacy - United States. 4. Americanisms. I. Title.*
*TC PE2827 .K682 1993*

**Kövecses, Zoltán.** Metaphor and emotion : language, culture, and body in human feeling / Zoltán Kövecses. Cambridge ; New York : Cambridge University Press ; Paris : Editions de la Maison des Sciences de l'Homme, 2000. xvi, 223 p. : ill. ; 24 cm. (Studies in emotion and social interaction. Second series) Includes bibliographical references (p. 201-209) and index. ISBN 0-521-64163-2 DDC 152.4
*1. Language and emotions. 2. Emotions and cognition. 3. Emotions - Sociological aspects. I. Title. II. Series.*
*TC BF582 .K68 2000*

**Kovner, Christine Tassone.**
Finkler, Steven A. Financial management for nurse managers and executives. 2nd ed. Philadelphia ; London : W.B. Saunders, c2000.
*TC RT86.7 .F46 2000*

**Kowalski, Robin M.**
Behaving badly. 1st ed. Washington, D.C. : American Psychological Association, 2001.
*TC HM1106 .B45 2001*

**Kowalski, Theodore J.**
Public relations in schools. 2nd ed. Upper Saddle River, N.J. : Merrill, c2000.
*TC LB2847 .P82 2000*

**Kozleski, Elizabeth B.**
Sands, Deanna J. Inclusive education for the 21st century. Belmont, CA : Wadsworth/Thomson Learning, 2000.
*TC LC1201 .S27 2000*

**Kozlowski, Steve W. J.**
Multilevel theory, research, and methods in organizations. 1st ed. San Francisco : Jossey-Bass, c2000.
*TC HF5548.8 .M815 2000*

**Kozma, Robert B.**
Innovations in science and mathematics education. Mahwah, N.J. : L. Erlbaum, 2000.
*TC Q181 .I654 1999*

**Közoktatási kutatások**
Kárpáti, Andrea. Látni tanulunk. Budapest : Akadémiai Kiadó, 1991.
*TC N85 .K35 1991*

**Kozol, Jonathan.** Ordinary resurrections : children in the years of hope / Jonathan Kozol. 1st ed. New York : Crown Publishers, c2000. ix, 388 p. ; 25 cm. Includes bibliographical references (p. 343-366) and index. ISBN 0-517-70000-X DDC 305.23/0974/1
*1. Children - New York (State) - New York - Social conditions. 2. Socially handicapped children - New York (State) - New York. 3. Mott Haven (New York, N.Y.) - Social conditions. I. Title.*
*TC HQ792.U5 K69 2000*

Savage inequalities : children in America's schools / Jonathan Kozol. 1st Harper Perennial ed. New York : HarperPerennial, 1992. ix, 261 p. ; 21 cm. Reprint. Originally published: New York : Crown, 1991. Includes bibliographical references and index. ISBN 0-06-097499-0 DDC 371.96/7
*1. Socially handicapped children - Education - United States. 2. Children of minorities - Education - United States. 3. Education, Urban - Social aspects - United States. I. Title.*
*TC LC4091 .K69 1992*

**Kraft, Leland M.**
Ballet class for beginners [videorecording]. W. Long Branch, NJ : Kultur, c1981.
*TC GV1589 .B3 1981*

Tap dancing for beginners [videorecording]. W. Long Branch, NJ : Kultur, c1981.
*TC GV1794 .T3 1981*

**Kralovec, Etta.** The end of homework : how homework disrupts families, overburdens children, and limits learning / Etta Kralovec and John Buell. Boston, Mass. : Beacon Press, c2000. xi, 119 p. ; 23 cm. Includes bibliographical references (p. 103-111) and index. ISBN 0-8070-4218-8 (alk. paper) DDC 371.3/028/1
*1. Homework - Social aspects - United States. 2. Education - Parent participation - United States. 3. Home and school - United States. 4. Educational change - United States. I. Buell, John. II. Title.*
*TC LB1048 .K73 2000*

**Kramer, Elizabeth Jane.**
Immigrant women's health. 1st ed. San Francisco : Jossey-Bass, c1999.
*TC RA448.5.I44 I44 1999*

**Kramer, Selma.**
Brothers and sisters. Northvale, N.J. : J. Aronson, c1999.
*TC BF723.S43 B78 1999*

**Krass, Peter.**
The book of leadership wisdom. New York : Wiley, c1998.
*TC HD57.7 .B66 1998*

**Kratochwill, Thomas R.**
Behavioral assessment in schools. 2nd ed. New York : Guilford Press, c2000.
*TC LB1124 .B435 2000*

Conducting school-based assessments of child and adolescent behavior. New York : Guilford Press, c2000.
*TC LB1124 .C66 2000*

**Kratzke, Peter, 1960-.**
Short stories in the classroom. Urbana, Ill. : National Council of Teachers of English, c1999.
*TC PS374.S5 S48 1999*

**Kraus, Anne Marie.** Folktale themes and activities for children / Anne Marie Kraus ; calligraphy by Susan K. Bins. Englewood, Colo. : Teacher Ideas Press, c1998-1999. 2 v. : ill. ; 28 cm. (Learning through folklore series) Includes bibliographical references and index. CONTENTS: v. 1. Pourquoi tales -- v. 2. Trickster and transformation tales. ISBN 1-56308-521-6 (v. 1) ISBN 1-56308-608-5 (v. 2) DDC 372.64
*1. Tales - Study and teaching (Elementary) 2. Folklore and children. I. Bins, Susan K. II. Title. III. Series.*
*TC GR45 .K73 1998*

**Krauss, Rosalind E.** Bachelors / Rosalind E. Krauss. Cambridge, Mass. : MIT Press, c1999. 222 p. : ill. ; 24 cm. "October books." Includes bibliographical references (p.

[207]-218) and index. ISBN 0-262-11239-6 (hc : alk. paper) DDC 704/.042
*1. Feminism and the arts. 2. Originality in art. 3. Surrealism - Influence. 4. Women artists - Psychology. I. Title.*
**TC NX180.F4 K73 1999**

The optical unconscious / Rosalind E. Krauss. 1st MIT Press pbk. ed. Cambridge, Mass. : MIT Press, 1994. 353 p. : ill. ; 24 cm. "An October book." "Fourth printing, 1996"--T.p. verso. Includes bibliographical references (p. [331]-337) and index. ISBN 0-262-61105-8 DDC 701
*1. Visual perception. 2. Optical illusions. 3. Artists - Psychology. I. Title.*
**TC N7430.5 .K73 1994**

**Kraye, Jill.** Humanism and early modern philosophy. London ; New York : Routledge, 2000.
**TC B821 .H657 2000**

**Kress, Gunther R.** Early spelling : between convention to creativity / Gunther Kress. London ; New York : Routledge, 2000. xvii, 237 p. : ill. ; 25 cm. Includes bibliographical references (p. [233]-234) and index. ISBN 0-415-18065-1 (hbk.) ISBN 0-415-18066-X (pbk.) DDC 401/.93
*1. Language and languages - Orthography and spelling. 2. Children - Language. 3. Literacy. 4. Creativity (Linguistics) I. Title.*
**TC P240.2 .K74 2000**

**Kress, Jacqueline E.**
Fry, Edward Bernard, 1925- The reading teacher's book of lists. 3rd ed. Englewood Cliffs, NJ : Prentice Hall, c1993.
**TC LB1050.2 .F79 1993**

Fry, Edward Bernard, 1925- The reading teacher's book of lists. 4th ed. Paramus, N.J. : Prentice Hall, c2000.
**TC LB1050.2 .F79 2000**

**Krestan, Jo Ann.**
Bridges to recovery. New York ; London : Free Press, c2000.
**TC HV5199.5 .B75 2000**

**Krislov, Samuel, ed.**
Compliance and the law; Beverly Hills, Sage Publications [1972]
**TC K376 .C66**

**KRISTIANSUND, NORWAY. OFFENTLIGE HøGRE ALLMENNSKOLE.**
Husby, Egil, 1913- Den høgre skolen, 1864-1964. Kristiansund, 1966.

**Krol-Sinclair, Barbara.**
Paratore, Jeanne R. What should we expect of family literacy? Newark, Del. : International Reading Association ; Chicago , Ill. : National Reading Conference, c1999.
**TC LC151 .P37 1999**

**Kronenberger, William G.** Child clinician's handbook / William G. Kronenberger, Robert G. Meyer. 2nd ed. Boston : Allyn and Bacon, c2001. xvii, 557 p. ; 25 cm. Includes bibliographical references and index. ISBN 0-205-29621-1
*1. Mental Disorders - diagnosis - Child - Handbooks. 2. Mental Disorders - therapy - Child - Handbooks. I. Meyer, Robert G. II. Title.*
**TC RJ499.3 .K76 2001**

**Krop, Richard A., 1962-.**
Vernez, Georges. Closing the education gap. Santa Monica, CA : RAND, 1999.
**TC LC213.2 .V47 1999**

**Krueger, Richard A.** Focus groups : a practical guide for applied research / by Richard A. Krueger & Mary Anne Casey. 3rd ed. Thousand Oaks, Calif. : Sage Publications, c2000. xvi, 215 p. : . ill. ; 25 cm. Includes bibliographical references and index. ISBN 0-7619-2070-6 (acid-free paper) ISBN 0-7619-2071-4 (pbk. : acid-free paper) DDC 361.6/1/068
*1. Focused group interviewing. 2. Social sciences - Methodology. I. Casey, Mary Anne. II. Title.*
**TC H61.28 .K78 2000**

**Kruegler, Christopher.**
Ackerman, Peter. Strategic nonviolent conflict. Westport, Conn. : Praeger, 1994.
**TC JC328.3 .A28 1994**

Protest, power, and change. New York : Garland Pub., 1997.
**TC HM278 .P76 1997**

**Krulik, Stephen.** Teaching middle school mathematics : activities, materials, and problems / Stephen Krulik, Jesse A. Rudnick. Boston : Allyn and Bacon, c2000. v, 282 p. : ill. ; 28 cm. Includes index. ISBN 0-205-28628-3 (pbk.) DDC 510/.71/273

*1. Mathematics - Study and teaching (Middle school) I. Rudnick, Jesse A. II. Title.*
**TC QA11 .K818 2000**

**Krumgold, Joseph, 1908-** Onion John / by Joseph Krumgold ; illustrated by Symeon Shimin. New York, N.Y. : Thomas Y. Crowell Company, 1959. 248, [1] p. : ill. ; 21 cm. SUMMARY: His friendship with the town odd-jobs man, Onion John, causes a conflict between Andy and his father. ISBN 0-690-59957-9
*1. Fathers and sons - Juvenile fiction. 2. Friendship - Juvenile fiction. I. Shimin, Symeon, 1902- II. Title.*
**TC XFK942**

**Krumholz, Norman.**
Rebuilding urban neighborhoods. Thousand Oaks, Calif. : Sage Publications, c1999.
**TC HT175 .R425 1999**

**Kubiszyn, Tom.** Educational testing and measurement : classroom application and practice / Tom Kubiszyn, Gary Borich. 6th ed. New York : J. Wiley & Sons, c2000. xiv, 530 p. : ill. ; 25 cm. Includes bibliographical references (p. 509-520) and index. ISBN 0-471-36496-7 DDC 371.26/0973
*1. Educational tests and measurements - United States. I. Borich, Gary D. II. Title.*
**TC LB3051 .K8 2000**

**Kuhl, Patricia K. (Patricia Katherine), 1946-.**
Gopnik, Alison. The scientist in the crib. New York : William Morrow & Co., 1999.
**TC BF311 .G627 1999**

**Kuhn, Annette.** Family secrets : acts of memory and imagination / Annette Kuhn. London ; New York : Verso, 1995. viii, 128 p. : ill. ; 24 cm. Includes bibliographical references (p. 127-128). ISBN 0-86091-479-8 ISBN 0-86091-629-4 (pbk.) DDC 929/.2/0973
*1. Kuhn family. 2. Kuhn, Annette. 3. Autobiographical memory. 4. Photography of families. 5. Women - United States - Biography. I. Title.*
**TC CT274 .K84 1995**

**KUHN, ANNETTE.**
Kuhn, Annette. Family secrets. London ; New York : Verso, 1995.
**TC CT274 .K84 1995**

**KUHN FAMILY.**
Kuhn, Annette. Family secrets. London ; New York : Verso, 1995.
**TC CT274 .K84 1995**

**Kuhn, James C., 1966-.**
Academic freedom. Westport, Conn. : Greenwood Press, 2000.
**TC LC72.2 .A29 2000**

**KUHT Film Productions.**
Jung on film [videorecording]. [Chicago, Ill.?] : Public Media Video, c1990.
**TC BF109.J8 J4 1990**

Jung on film [videorecording]. [Chicago, Ill.?] : Public Media Video, c1990.
**TC BF109.J8 J4 1990**

**Kultur International Films.**
Ballet class for beginners [videorecording]. W. Long Branch, NJ : Kultur, c1981.
**TC GV1589 .B3 1981**

Ballet class [videorecording]. W. Long Branch, NJ : Kultur, c1984.
**TC GV1589 .B33 1984**

Ballroom dancing for beginners [videorecording]. W. Long Branch, N.J. Kultur, c1993.
**TC GV1753.7 .B3 1993**

Ballroom dancing for beginners [videorecording]. W. Long Branch, N.J. Kultur, c1993.
**TC GV1753.7 .B3 1993**

Jazz dance class [videorecording]. W. Long Branch, NJ : Kultur, [1992?]
**TC GV1784 .J3 1992**

Seurat [videorecording]. West Long Branch, NJ : Kultur, c1999.
**TC ND553.S5 S5 1999**

Tap dancing for beginners [videorecording]. W. Long Branch, NJ : Kultur, c1981.
**TC GV1794 .T3 1981**

**Kultura i społeczeństwo.** Warszawa [Państwowe Wydawn. Naukowe] v. tables. 24 cm. Frequency: Quarterly. t. 1- 1957- . Indexed selectively by: America, history and life 0002-7065 1957-. Indexed selectively by: Historical abstracts. Part A. Modern history abstracts 0363-2717 1957-. Indexed selectively by: Historical abstracts. Part B. Twentieth century abstracts 0363-2725 1957-. Indexed selectively by: Sociological abstracts 0038-0202. Indexed

selectively by: Social welfare, social planning/policy & social development 0195-7988. Issued by Zakład Socjologii i Historii Kultury of the Polska Akademia Nauk. ISSN 0023-5172
*I. Polska Akademia Nauk. Zakład Socjologii i Historii Kultury.*

**Kumar, David D.**
Science, technology, and society. New York : Kluwer Academic/Plenum, c2000.
**TC Q181 .S38225 1999**

**Kunitz, Stephen J.** Drinking, conduct disorder, and social change : Navajo experiences / Stephen J. Kunitz, Jerrold E. Levy with K. Ruben Gabriel ... [et al.]. Oxford ; New York : Oxford University Press, 2000. xiii, 262 p. : ill. ; 24 cm. Includes bibliographical references (p. 241-254) and index. ISBN 0-19-513615-2 (cloth : acid-free paper) DDC 362.292/089/972
*1. Navajo Indians - Alcohol use. 2. Navajo Indians - Social conditions. 3. Alcoholism - Psychological aspects. 4. Antisocial personality disorders. I. Levy, Jerrold E., 1930- II. Title.*
**TC E99.N3 K88 2000**

**Kunz, Linda Ann.** English modals in American talk shows / by Linda Ann Kunz. 1999. viii, 242 leaves : ill. ; 29 cm. Typescript; issued also on microfilm. Thesis (Ed.D.)--Teachers College, Columbia University, 1999. Includes bibliographical references (leaves 226-237).
*1. English language - Spoken English - United States. 2. English language - Spoken English - Modality. 3. Talk shows - United States. 4. Television programs - United States. 5. Language and culture. 6. Modality (Linguistics) 7. Linguistic change - Social aspects. I. Siegel, Eli, 1902- Aesthetics. II. Title.*
**TC 06 no. 11136**

**Kuper, Adam.** Among the anthropologists : history and context in anthropology / Adam Kuper. London ; New Brunswick, NJ : Athlone Press ; Somerset, N.J. : Distributed in the United States by Transaction Publishers, 1999. x, 214 p. ; 23 cm. Includes bibliographical references and index. ISBN 0-485-11536-0 (alk. paper) DDC 306/.0968
*1. Ethnology. 2. Ethnology - Africa, Southern. 3. Africa, Southern - Social life and customs. I. Title.*
**TC GN325 .K89 1999**

**Kurin, Richard, 1950-** Reflections of a culture broker : a view from the Smithsonian / Richard Kurin. Washington, D.C. : Smithsonian Institution Press, c1997. xv, 315 p. : ill. ; 24 cm. Includes bibliographical references (p. 287-307) and index. ISBN 1-56098-789-8 (alk. paper) ISBN 1-56098-757-X (pbk. : alk. paper) DDC 069/.09753
*1. Smithsonian Institution - Management. 2. Smithsonian Institution - Public relations. 3. Anthropological museums and collections - Washington (D.C.) - Management. 4. Museum exhibits - Political aspects - United States. 5. Museum techniques - United States. 6. Culture conflict - United States. 7. United States - Cultural policy. I. Title.*
**TC GN36.U62 D5775 1997**

**Kurlantzick, Lewis S. (Lewis Samuel), 1944-.**
Bard, Robert L. Copyright duration. San Fransisco : Austin & Winfield, 1999.
**TC KF3010 .B37 1999**

**Kurtis, Arlene Harris.** Puerto Ricans, from island to mainland / by Arlene Harris Kurtis. New York : J. Messner, c1969. 96 p. : ill., maps, ports. ; 22 cm. SUMMARY: Traces the history and development of Puerto Rico from about 50 B.C. to the present day, and discusses the problems and contributions of modern Puerto Ricans who move to the mainland. ISBN 0-671-32084-X DDC 972/.95
*1. Puerto Rico - History - Juvenile literature. 2. Puerto Ricans - United States - Juvenile literature. 3. Puerto Rico - History. 4. Puerto Ricans - United States. I. Title.*
**TC F1958.3 .K8**

**Kurtz, Jane.**
Buzzeo, Toni. Terrific connections with authors, illustrators, and storytellers. Englewood, Colo. : Libraries Unlimited, 1999.
**TC LB1575.5.U5 B87 1999**

Faraway home / Jane Kurtz ; illustrated by E.B. Lewis. San Diego : Harcourt, c2000. 1 v. (unpaged) : col. ill. ; 29 cm. "Gulliver books." SUMMARY: Desta's father, who needs to return briefly to his Ethiopian homeland, describes what it was like for him to grow up there. ISBN 0-15-200036-4 DDC [E]
*1. Ethiopia - Fiction. 2. Fathers and daughters - Fiction. 3. Afro-Americans - Fiction. I. Lewis, Earl B., ill. II. Title.*
**TC PZ7.K9626 Far 2000**

**Kushner, Saville.** Personalizing evaluation / Saville Kushner. London ; Thousand Oaks, Calif. : SAGE, 2000. xv, 223 p. ; 24 cm. Includes bibliographical references (p. [210]-216) and index. ISBN 0-7619-6361-8 ISBN 0-7619-6362-6 (pbk.)
*1. Educational evaluation - Great Britain - Case studies. I. Title.*

*TC LB2822.75 .K87 2000*

**Kutzer, M. Daphne.** Empire's children : empire and imperialism in classic British children's books / M. Daphne Kutzer. New York : Garland Pub., 2000. xxii, 157 p. ; 24 cm. (Garland reference library of the humanities ; v. 2005. Children's literature and culture ; v. 16) Includes bibliographical references (p. 143-149) and index. ISBN 0-8153-3491-5 (acid-free paper) ISBN 0-8153-3895-3 (pbk. : acid-free paper) DDC 823/.809358
*1. Children's stories, English - History and criticism. 2. Imperialism in literature. 3. Colonies in literature. I. Title. II. Series: Garland reference library of the humanities ; vol. 2005. III. Series: Garland reference library of the humanities. Children's literature and culture ; v. 16.*
*TC PR830.I54 K88 2000*

**KWAKIUTL INDIANS - WOOD-CARVING.** *See* **KWAKIUTL WOOD-CARVING.**

**KWAKIUTL WOOD-CARVING - JUVENILE LITERATURE.**
Sullivan, Missy. The Native American look book. New York : The New Press, 1996.
*TC E98.A7 S93 1996*

**Kwartalnik pedagogiczny.** [Warszawa] Państwowe Wydawn. Naukowe. v. ill. 24 cm. Began publication in 1956. Cf. Katalog prasy polskiej, 1957. ISSN 0023-5938
*1. Education - Periodicals. I. Suchodolski, Bogdan, ed.*

**Kwolek-Folland, Angel.** Incorporating women : a history of women and business in the United States / Angel Kwolek-Folland. New York : Twayne Publishers, 1998. xv, 275 p. ; 23 cm. (Twayne's evolution of modern business series) Includes bibliographical references and index. ISBN 0-8057-4519-X (alk. paper) DDC 331.4/0973
*1. Businesswomen - United States - History. 2. Women-owned business enterprises - United States - History. I. Title. II. Title: History of women and business in the United States III. Series.*
*TC HD6095 .K85 1998*

**L.**
Dombroski, Ann P. Administrative problem solving. 1999.
*TC 06 no. 11104*

**La Fontaine, Jean de, 1621-1695.**
[Fables. English. Selections]
Marc Chagall : the Fables of La Fontaine / Jean de La Fontaine ; illustrated by Marc Chagall ; [English translation by Elizur Wright, Jr.]. New York : New Press : Distributed by W.W. Norton, [1997] 141 p. : ill. (some col.) ; 25 cm. Originally published to accompany an exhibition held at the Musée d'art moderne, Céret, 28 Oct. 1995-8 Jan. 1996, and the Musée national message biblique Marc Chagall, Nice, 13 Jan.-25 Mar. 1996. Includes bibliographical references (p. 138-141). ISBN 1-56584-322-3
*1. Chagall, Marc, - 1887- - Exhibitions. 2. La Fontaine, Jean de, - 1621-1695. - Fables - Exhibitions. I. Chagall, Marc, 1887- II. Wright, Elizur, 1804-1885. III. Musée d'art moderne (Céret, France) IV. Musée national Message biblique Marc Chagall. V. Title. VI. Title: Fables of La Fontaine*
*TC PQ1811.E3 W6 1997*

**FABLES EXHIBITIONS.**
La Fontaine, Jean de, 1621-1695. [Fables. English. Selections] Marc Chagall. New York : New Press : Distributed by W.W. Norton, [1997]
*TC PQ1811.E3 W6 1997*

**La gestion décentralisée au niveau des écoles fre.**
Abu-Duhou, Ibtisam. School-based management. Paris : International Institute for Educational Planning (IIEP) ; Paris : Unesco, 1999.
*TC LB5 .F85 1999*

**La gestion stratégique des biens en capital des établissements d'enseignement supérieur fre.**
Programme on Educational Building. Strategic asset management for tertiary institutions. Paris : Organisation for Economic Co-operation and Development, c1999.
*TC LB3223 .P76 1999*

**LABOR.** *See* **WORK; WORKING CLASS.**

**LABOR AND CAPITAL.** *See* **INDUSTRIAL RELATIONS.**

**LABOR AND LABORING CLASSES.** *See* **LABOR; LABOR MOVEMENT; WORKING CLASS.**

**LABOR AND LABORING CLASSES IN MOTION PICTURES.** *See* **WORKING CLASS IN MOTION PICTURES.**

**Labor and social change**
Howes, Ruth (Ruth Hege) Their day in the sun. Philadelphia, PA : Temple University Press, 1999.
*TC QC773.3.U5 H68 1999*

**LABOR EXCHANGES.** *See* **EMPLOYMENT AGENCIES.**

**LABOR FORCE.** *See* **LABOR SUPPLY.**

**LABOR FORCE PARTICIPATION.** *See* **LABOR SUPPLY.**

**LABOR IN ART.**
Dabakis, Melissa. Visualizing labor in American sculpture. New York : Cambridge University Press, 1999.
*TC NB1952.L33 D24 1999*

**LABOR LAWS AND LEGISLATION.** *See* **LEAVE OF ABSENCE - LAW AND LEGISLATION; MATERNITY LEAVE - LAW AND LEGISLATION; PARENTAL LEAVE - LAW AND LEGISLATION; SEX DISCRIMINATION IN EMPLOYMENT - LAW AND LEGISLATION; SICK LEAVE - LAW AND LEGISLATION.**

**LABOR LAWS AND LEGISLATION, INTERNATIONAL.**
Action against child labour. Geneva : International Labour Office, c2000.
*TC HD6231 .A28 2000*

**LABOR LAWS AND LEGISLATION - UNITED STATES.**
Gold, Michael Evan. An introduction to labor law. 2nd ed. Ithaca : ILR Press, c1998.
*TC KF3319 .G62 1998*

**LABOR LEADERS.** *See* **WOMEN LABOR LEADERS.**

**LABOR-MANAGEMENT RELATIONS.** *See* **INDUSTRIAL RELATIONS.**

**LABOR MARKET.** *See* **LABOR SUPPLY.**

**LABOR MARKET - GOVERNMENT POLICY.** *See* **MANPOWER POLICY.**

**LABOR MARKET POLICY.** *See* **MANPOWER POLICY.**

**LABOR MARKET - UNITED STATES.**
Job creation. Washington, DC : Joint Center for Political and Economic Studies ; Lanham, Md. ; Oxford : University Press of America, c1998.
*TC HD8081.A65 J63 1998*

**LABOR MOBILITY.** *See* **LABOR SUPPLY.**

**LABOR MOBILITY - UNITED STATES.**
Stanback, Thomas M. Cities in transition. Totowa, N.J. : Allanheld, Osmun, 1982.
*TC HD5724 .S649 1982*

**LABOR MOVEMENT - CUBA - HISTORY - 19TH CENTURY.**
Casanovas, Joan. Bread, or bullets!. Pittsburgh : University of Pittsburgh Press, c1998.
*TC HD8206 .C33 1998*

**LABOR MOVEMENT - UNITED STATES - HISTORY.**
Cobb, William H. Radical education in the rural South. Detroit : Wayne State University Press, 2000.
*TC LD1276 .C63 2000*

**LABOR NEGOTIATIONS.** *See* **COLLECTIVE BARGAINING.**

**LABOR - NORTH AMERICA - HISTORY.**
Oldenziel, Ruth, 1958- Making technology masculine. Amsterdam : Amsterdam University Press, c1999.
*TC HD8072 .O57 1999*

**LABOR POLICY.** *See* **MANPOWER POLICY.**

**LABOR RELATIONS.** *See* **INDUSTRIAL RELATIONS.**

**LABOR STANDARDS (LABOR LAW).** *See* **LABOR LAWS AND LEGISLATION.**

**LABOR SUPPLY.** *See* **HARD-CORE UNEMPLOYED; HUMAN CAPITAL; JOB VACANCIES; LABOR MOBILITY; MANPOWER POLICY; UNEMPLOYMENT.**

**LABOR SUPPLY - EFFECT OF EDUCATION ON - GERMANY (EAST).**
Evans, Karen, 1949- Learning and work in the risk society. New York : St. Martin's Press, 2000.
*TC HD6278.G4 E93 2000*

**LABOR SUPPLY - UNITED STATES.**
Stanback, Thomas M. Cities in transition. Totowa, N.J. : Allanheld, Osmun, 1982.
*TC HD5724 .S649 1982*

**LABOR TURNOVER.** *See* **LABOR MOBILITY.**

**Labor union collection.**
The classroom teacher. Berkeley, Calif., Berkeley Federation of Teachers Local 1078.

**LABOR UNIONS - SOCIAL ASPECTS - UNITED STATES.**
Meeting human needs, toward a new public philosophy. Washington : American Enterprise Institute for Public Policy Research, c1982.
*TC HD60.5.U5 M427 1982*

**LABOR - UNITED STATES - HISTORY.**
Oldenziel, Ruth, 1958- Making technology masculine. Amsterdam : Amsterdam University Press, c1999.
*TC HD8072 .O57 1999*

**LABORATORIES.**
Biehle, James T. NSTA guide to school science facilities. Arlington, VA : National Science Teachers Association, c1999.
*TC Q183.3.A1 B54 1999*

**LABORATORIES, CURRICULUM.** *See* **INSTRUCTIONAL MATERIALS CENTERS.**

**LABORATORY SCHOOLS.** *See also* **DEMONSTRATION CENTERS IN EDUCATION.**
Lawrence, Alexandria Teresa. Cooperating teachers' perceptions of the nature and quality of professional development in a professional development school collaboration. 1999.
*TC 06 no. 11141*

Lawrence, Alexandria Teresa. Cooperating teachers' perceptions of the nature and quality of professional development in a professional development school collaboration. 1999.
*TC 06 no. 11141*

Lawrence, Alexandria Teresa. Cooperating teachers' perceptions of the nature and quality of professional development in a professional development school collaboration. 1999.
*TC 06 no. 11141*

**LABORATORY SCHOOLS - UNITED STATES.**
Collaborative reform and other improbable dreams. Albany, N.Y. : State University of New York Press, 2000.
*TC LB2154.A3 C65 2000*

Research on professional development schools. Thousand Oaks, Calif. : Corwin Press, c1999.
*TC LB2154.A3 R478 1999*

**LABORATORY SCHOOLS - UNITED STATES - CASE STUDIES.**
Campoy, Renee W. A professional development school partnership. Westport, Conn. : Bergin & Garvey, 2000.
*TC LB2154.A3 C36 2000*

**Laborde, Ilia M.** Rediscovering San Cristóbal Canyon : constructing better student ecological perspectives using technology and a model of global education in a central Puerto Rican secondary school pilot project / by Ilia M. Laborde. 1996. viii, 147 leaves : ill., maps, plans ; 29 cm.+ 2 videos + 3 Bulletins bd. in 2 v.(32 p. : ill. ; 28 cm.) each + 2 Poems (30 p. : ill. ; 22 cm.) each. Typescript; issued also on microfilm. Accompanying materials in Spanish. Thesis (Ed.D.)--Teachers College, Columbia University, 1996. Includes bibliographical references (leaves 125-135).
*1. Bonifacio Sánchez High School (Aibonito, P.R.) 2. San Cristóbal Canyon (P.R.) - Environmental conditions. 3. Ecology - Study and teaching (Secondary) - Puerto Rico. 4. Education, Secondary - Activity programs - Puerto Rico. 5. Educational technology - Puerto Rico. 6. Multimedia systems - Puerto Rico. 7. Interdisciplinary approach in education - Puerto Rico. 8. School field trips - Puerto Rico. I. Title.*
*TC 06 no. 10660*

Rediscovering San Cristóbal Canyon : constructing better student ecological perspectives using technology and a model of global education in a central Puerto Rican secondary school pilot project / by Ilia M. Laborde. 1996. viii, 147 leaves : ill., maps, plans ; 29 cm.+ 2 videos + 3 Bulletins bd. in 2 v.(32 p. : ill. ; 28 cm.) each + 2 Poems (30 p. : ill. ; 22 cm.) each. Typescript; issued also on microfilm. Accompanying materials in Spanish. Thesis (Ed.D.)--Teachers College, Columbia University, 1996. Includes bibliographical references (leaves 125-135).
*1. Bonifacio Sánchez High School (Aibonito, P.R.) 2. San Cristóbal Canyon (P.R.) - Environmental conditions. 3. Ecology - Study and teaching (Secondary) - Puerto Rico. 4. Education, Secondary - Activity programs - Puerto Rico. 5. Educational technology - Puerto Rico. 6. Multimedia systems - Puerto Rico. 7. Interdisciplinary approach in education - Puerto Rico. 8. School field trips - Puerto Rico. I. Title.*
*TC 06 no. 10660*

**LABORERS.** *See* **EMPLOYEES.**

**LABORING CLASS.** *See* **WORKING CLASS.**

**LaBuda, Everett.**
The filming of a television commercial [videorecording]. Minneapolis, Minn. : Media Loft, c1992.
*TC HF6146.T42 F5 1992*

**LABYRINTH (EAR).** *See* **COCHLEA.**

**Lacan and the matter of origins.**
Barzilai, Shuli. Stanford, Calif. : Stanford University Press, 1999.
*TC BF17 .B2145 1999*

**LACAN, JACQUES, 1901-.**
Barzilai, Shuli. Lacan and the matter of origins. Stanford, Calif. : Stanford University Press, 1999.
*TC BF17 .B2145 1999*

Forrester, John. The seductions of psychoanalysis. 1st pbk. ed. Cambridge ; New York : Cambridge University Press, 1991 (1992 printing)
*TC RC504 .F63 1991*

Mathelin, Catherine. [Raisins verts et dents agacées. English] Lacanian psychotherapy with children. New York : The Other Press, 1999.
*TC RJ504.2 .M3913 1999*

Safouan, Moustafa. [Jacques Lacan et la question de la formation des analystes. English] Jacques Lacan and the question of psychoanalytic training. New York : St. Martin's Press, 2000.
*TC BF173.L15 S2414 2000*

Seshadri-Crooks, Kalpana. Desiring whiteness. London ; New York : Routledge, 2000.
*TC BF175.4.R34 S47 2000*

**The Lacanian clinical field**
Mathelin, Catherine. [Raisins verts et dents agacées. English] Lacanian psychotherapy with children. New York : The Other Press, 1999.
*TC RJ504.2 .M3913 1999*

**Lacanian psychotherapy with children.**
Mathelin, Catherine. [Raisins verts et dents agacées. English] New York : The Other Press, 1999.
*TC RJ504.2 .M3913 1999*

**LaCapra, Dominick, 1939-** History and reading : Tocqueville, Foucault, French studies / Dominick LaCapra. Toronto : University of Toronto Press, c2000. 235 p. ; 22 cm. (Green College lecture series) Includes index. Includes bibliographical references. ISBN 0-8020-4394-1 (bound) ISBN 0-8020-8200-9 (pbk.) DDC 944/.007/2
*1. France - Study and teaching. 2. France - Historiography. 3. Literature and history. 4. History - Methodology. 5. Tocqueville, Alexis de, - 1805-1859. - Ancien régime et la révolution. 6. Foucault, Michel. - Folie et déraison. 7. France - Étude et enseignement. 8. France - Historiographie. 9. Littérature et histoire. 10. Histoire - Méthodologie. 11. Tocqueville, Alexis de, - 1805-1859. - Ancien régime et la révolution. 12. Foucault, Michel. - Folie et déraison. I. Title. II. Series.*
*TC DC36.9.L32 1999*

**Lacks, Patricia.** Bender Gestalt screening for brain dysfunction / Patricia Lacks. 2nd ed. New York : John Wiley & Sons, c1999. xviii, 264 p. : ill. ; 29 cm. Includes bibliographical references (p. 241-251) and index. ISBN 0-471-24257-8 (cloth) DDC 616.8/0475
*1. Bender-Gestalt Test. 2. Brain - Diseases - Diagnosis. 3. Bender-Gestalt Test. 4. Delirium, Dementia, Amnestic, Cognitive Disorders - diagnosis. I. Title.*
*TC RC386.6.B46 L3 1999*

**Lacy, Gary L.** Head start social services : how African American mothers use and perceive it / Gary L. Lacy. New York : Garland Pub., 1999. xix, 113 p. ; 23 cm. (Garland studies on children of poverty) Includes bibliographical references (p. 105-110) and index. ISBN 0-8153-3384-6 (alk. paper) DDC 362.83/928/08996073
*1. Afro-American single mothers - Services for. 2. Head Start Program (U.S.) 3. Head Start programs - United States. I. Title. II. Series: Children of poverty.*
*TC HV699 .L33 1999*

**Ladd, Everett Carll.** The Ladd report / Everett Carll Ladd. New York : Free Press, c1999. xiii, 210 p. : ill. ; 25 cm. Includes bibliographical references (p. 199-206) and index. Table of contents URL: http://lcweb.loc.gov/catdir/toc/98-31380.html ISBN 0-684-83735-8 DDC 361.3/7/0973
*1. Voluntarism - United States. I. Title.*
*TC HN90.V64 L33 1999*

**Ladd, Helen F.**
Fiske, Edward B. When schools compete. Washington, D.C. : Brookings Institution Press, c2000.

---

*TC LB2822.84.N45 F58 2000*
Making money matter. Washington, D.C. : National Academy Press, c1999.
*TC LB2825 .M27 1999*

**The Ladd report.**
Ladd, Everett Carll. New York : Free Press, c1999.
*TC HN90.V64 L33 1999*

**Ladd, Tony.** Muscular Christianity : evangelical Protestants and the development of American sport / Tony Ladd, James A. Mathisen. Grand Rapids, Mich. : Baker Books, c1999. 288 p. : ill. ; 23 cm. Includes bibliographical references (p. 247-281) and indexes. ISBN 0-8010-5847-3 (pbk.) DDC 796/.088/2044
*1. Sports - United States - Religious aspects - History. 2. Evangelicalism - United States - History. I. Mathisen. James A. II. Title.*
*TC GV706.42 .L34 1999*

**Lafferty, William, 1939-.**
Towards sustainable development. New York, N.Y. : St. Martin's Press, 1999.
*TC HD75.6 .T695 1999*

**LaFrance, David G. (David Gerald), 1948-.**
Thomson, Guy P. C., 1949- Patriotism, politics, and popular liberalism in nineteenth-century Mexico. Wilmington, De. : Scholarly Resources, 1999.
*TC F1326.L83 T5 1999*

**Lagemann, Ellen Condliffe, 1945-** An elusive science : the troubling history of education research / Ellen Condliffe Lagemann. Chicago : University of Chicago Press, 2000. xvii, 302 p. ; 24 cm. Includes bibliographical references (p. 247-282) and index. ISBN 0-226-46772-4 (alk. paper) DDC 370/.7/2
*1. Education - Research - United States - History. 2. Education - Research - Social aspects - United States. I. Title.*
*TC LB1028.25.U6 L33 2000*

The politics of knowledge : the Carnegie Corporation, philanthropy, and public policy / Ellen Condliffe Lagemann. 1st ed. Middletown, Conn. : Wesleyan University Press, c1989. xv, 347 p. ; 24 cm. Bibliography : p. 267-334. Includes index. ISBN 0-8195-5204-6 DDC 361.7/632/0973
*1. Carnegie Corporation of New York. 2. Endowments - United States. 3. United States - Social policy. I. Title.*
*TC HV97.C3 L34 1989*

**Lahelma, Elina.** Making spaces. New York : St. Martin's Press, 2000.
*TC LC208.4 .M35 2000*

**Lai, Kwok-Wing.** Net-working. Dunedin, N.Z. : University of Otago Press, 1999.
*TC LB1044.87 .N47 1999*

**LAING, R. D. (RONALD DAVID), 1927-.**
Burston, Daniel, 1954- The crucible of experience. Cambridge, Mass. : Harvard University Press, c2000.
*TC RC438.6.L34 B86 2000*

**Lajoie, Susanne.**
Reflections on statistics. Mahwah, N.J. : L. Erlbaum, 1998.
*TC QA276.18 .R44 1998*

**Lajoux, Jean-Dominiques.**
Tassili N'Ajjer [videorecording]. [S.l.] : Editions Cinégraphiques ; Northbrook, Ill. : [distributed by] the Roland Collection, c1968.
*TC N5310.5.A4 T3 1968*

**Lakin, Charlie K.**
Punishment and aversive stimulation in special education. Reston, Va. : Council for Exceptional Children, 1982.
*TC LC4169 .P8 1982*

**Lakota hoop dancer.**
Left Hand Bull, Jacqueline. 1st ed. New York : Dutton Children's Books, c1999.
*TC E99.T34 L43 1999*

**LAKOTA INDIANS.** *See* **TETON INDIANS.**

**Lalljee, Barbara.**
An Introduction to oracy. London : Cassell, 1998.
*TC P95.4.G7 I58 1998*

**Lam-Chan, Gladys Lan Tak.** Parenting in stepfamilies : social attitudes, parental perceptions and parental behaviours in Hong Kong / Gladys Lan Tak Lam-Chan. Aldershot ; Brookfield USA : Ashgate, c1999. ix, 289 p. ; 23 cm. (Social and political studies from Hong Kong) Includes bibliographical references (p. 273-289). ISBN 1-84014-969-8 DDC 306.874
*1. Parent and child - China - Hong Kong. 2. Stepchildren - China - Hong Kong - Family relationships. 3. Stepmothers - China - Hong Kong - Family relationships. 4. Hong Kong (China) - Social conditions. 5. Parenting - China - Hong Kong.*

---

*6. Stepparents - China - Hong Kong. 7. Stepfamilies - China - Hong Kong. I. Title. II. Series.*
*TC HQ759.92 .L34 1999*

**Lam, T. Y. (Tsit-Yuen), 1942-.**
Algebra, K-theory, groups, and education. Providence, R.I. : American Mathematical Society, c1999.
*TC QA150 .A419 1999*

**Lamb, Michael E., 1953-.**
The role of the father in child development. 3rd ed. New York : Wiley, c1997
*TC HQ756 .R64 1997*

**Lambert, H.L., ed.**
The Journal of Arkansas education. [Little Rock : Arkansas Educational Association, 1923-1975].

**Lambert, Leo M.**
Linking America's schools and colleges. Washington, D.C. : American Association for Higher Education, 1991.
*TC LB2331.53 .L56 1991*

**Lambert, Richard D.**
Language policy and pedagogy. Philadelphia : J. Benjamins, c2000.
*TC P53 .L364 2000*

**Laming, D. R. J. (Donald Richard John)** The measurement of sensation / Donald Laming. Oxford ; New York : Oxford University Press, 1997. xiii, 262 p. : ill. ; 24 cm. (Oxford psychology series ; no. 30) (Oxford science publications) Includes bibliographical references (p. [227]-245) and indexes. ISBN 0-19-852342-4 (hardbound) DDC 612.8/028/7
*1. Senses and sensation - Testing. 2. Psychology, Experimental. I. Title. II. Series. III. Series: Oxford science publications*
*TC QP435 .L34 1997*

**Lamm, Sharon Lea.** The connection between action reflection learning and transformative learning : an awakening of human qualities in leadership / by Sharon Lea Lamm. 2000. xiii, 363 leaves ; 29 cm. Issued also on microfilm. Thesis (Ed.D.)--Teachers College, Columbia University, 2000. Includes bibliographical references (leaves 278-290).
*1. Adult education. 2. Learning, Psychology of. 3. Experiential learning. 4. Leadership. 5. Adult education - Evaluation. 6. Creative thinking. 7. Total quality management. 8. Transfer of training. I. Title.*
*TC 06 no. 11230*

**Lamon, Susan J., 1949-** More : in-depth discussion of the reasoning activities in "Teaching fractions and ratios for understanding" / Susan J. Lamon. Mahwah, N.J. : L. Erlbaum Associates, 1999. viii, 189 p. : ill. ; 26 cm. ISBN 0-8058-3299-8 DDC 372.7/2
*1. Fractions - Study and teaching (Elementary) 2. Ratio and proportion - Study and teaching (Elementary) I. Lamon. Susan J., 1949- Teaching fractions and ratios for understanding. II. Title.*
*TC QA137 .L34 1999*

**Teaching fractions and ratios for understanding.**
Lamon, Susan J., 1949- More. Mahwah, N.J. : L. Erlbaum Associates, 1999.
*TC QA137 .L34 1999*

**Lamphere, Louise.**
Situated lives. New York : Routledge, 1997.
*TC GN479.65 .S57 1997*

**Lamping, Alwena.** NTC's Italian grammar / Alwena Lamping ; consultant, Denise De Rôme. Lincolnwood, Ill., U.S.A. : NTC Pub. Group, 1998. 192 p. ; 18 cm. English and Italian. Includes index. ISBN 0-8442-8080-1 (pbk.) DDC 458.2/421
*1. Italian language - Grammar - Handbooks, manuals, etc. I. De Rôme, Denise. II. National Textbook Company. III. Title. IV. Title: Italian grammar*
*TC PC1112 .L34 1998*

**Lancet (London, England).**
[Lancet (North American ed.)] The lancet. North American ed. Boston : Little, Brown and Co., c1966-

**[Lancet (North American ed.)]** The lancet. North American ed. Boston : Little, Brown and Co., c1966- v. : ill. ; 28 cm. Frequency: Weekly. No. 7453 (2 July 1966)- . Published: Baltimore, MD : Williams & Wilkins, c1990- ; New York, NY : The Lancet Ltd., <c1997-> Title from caption. LC set includes scattered issues from the London edition. Indexed by: Bibliography of agriculture 0006-1530 1996. Indexed in its entirety by: General science index 0363-5465 1992-. Indexed selectively by: Biological abstracts 0006-3169 1990-. Indexed by: Selected water resources abstracts 0037-136X. Indexed selectively by: Cumulative index to nursing & allied health literature 0146-5554. Indexed selectively by: Life sciences collection. Indexed selectively by: Population index 0032-4701. Vols. for 1966-1989 also number the Jan.-June issues as v. 1 and the July-Dec. issues as v. 2, each year; vols. for 1990- numbered as v. 335, no. 8680- Supplements

accompany some volumes. Also available via the World Wide Web; online version available to subscribers with a site license, <1996-> The editorial contents of this edition are identical to the London edition, which has been published since 1823 and from which it adopts its numbering. Selected articles from the London edition are also published at monthly intervals in Spanish, Italian, German, and French editions of the Lancet. Has supplement <1995-> issued each Dec. with title: Reviews (New York, N.Y.). Has supplement: Reviews (New York, N.Y.) <1995-> (DLC)sn 97033991 (OCoLC)35825104. Other editions available: Lancet (London, England) ISSN: 0140-6736 (OCoLC)1755507. ISSN 0099-5355 DDC 610/.5
*1. Medicine - Periodicals. 2. Medicine - periodicals. I. Title: Reviews (New York, N.Y.) <1995-> II. Title: Lancet (London, England)*

**LAND-GRANT COLLEGES.** *See* STATE UNIVERSITIES AND COLLEGES.

**LAND RUSH, OKLAHOMA, 1889.** *See* OKLAHOMA - HISTORY - LAND RUSH, 1889.

**Land, sea & sky :** poems to celebrate the earth / selected and illustrated with photographs by Catherine Paladino. 1st ed. Boston : Joy Street Books, c1993. 32 p. : col. ill. ; 28 cm. SUMMARY: A collection of poems celebrating nature, by such authors as Walt Whitman, Langston Hughes, and Myra Cohn Livingston. ISBN 0-316-68892-4 DDC 811.008/036
*1. Nature - Juvenile poetry. 2. Nature - Pictorial works. 3. Children's poetry, American. 4. Nature - Poetry. 5. American poetry - Collections. I. Paladino, Catherine. II. Title: Land, sea, and sky.*
*TC PS595.N22 L36 1993*

**Land, sea, and sky.** Land, sea & sky. 1st ed. Boston : Joy Street Books, c1993.
*TC PS595.N22 L36 1993*

**LAND TENURE.** *See* PEASANTRY.

**LAND USE - PLANNING.** *See* CITY PLANNING.

**LAND USE, RURAL.** *See* AGRICULTURE; AGRICULTURE - ECONOMIC ASPECTS.

**LAND USE, URBAN.** *See* URBAN RENEWAL.

**LAND USE, URBAN - MANAGEMENT.** *See* CITY PLANNING.

**LAND USE, URBAN - PLANNING.** *See* CITY PLANNING.

**Landau, Barbara, 1949-.** Perception, cognition, and language. Cambridge, Mass. : MIT, c2000.
*TC BF455 .P389 2000*

**Landels, John G. (John Gray), 1926-** Music in ancient Greece and Rome / John G. Landels. London ; New York : Routledge, 1999. xii, 296 p. : ill. ; 24 cm. Includes bibliographical references (p. 276-291) and index. ISBN 0-415-16776-0 (hb) DDC 780/.938
*1. Music, Greek and Roman - History and criticism. I. Title.*
*TC ML169 .L24 1999*

**LANDFORMS.** *See* ISLANDS; SEASHORE.

**Landmark law cases & American society** Ball, Howard. The Bakke case. Lawrence, Kan. : University Press of Kansas, 2000.
*TC KF228.B34 B35 2000*

**Landow, George P.**
**Hypertext.**
Landow, George P. Hypertext 2.0. Rev., amplified ed. Baltimore : Johns Hopkins University Press, 1997.
*TC PN81 .L28 1997*

Hypertext 2.0 / George P. Landow. Rev., amplified ed. Baltimore : Johns Hopkins University Press, 1997. x, 353 p. : ill. ; 24 cm. (Parallax) Rev. of: Hypertext. c1992. Includes bibliographical references (p. [321]-343) and index. ISBN 0-8018-5585-3 (alk. paper) ISBN 0-8018-5586-1 (pbk. : alk. paper) DDC 801/.95
*1. Criticism. 2. Literature and technology. 3. Hypertext systems. I. Landow, George P. Hypertext. II. Title. III. Title: Hypertext two point zero IV. Series: Parallax (Baltimore, Md.)*
*TC PN81 .L28 1997*

**Landrum, R. Eric.** Protecting human subjects. 1st ed. Washington, DC : American Psychological Association, c1999.
*TC BF181 .P65 1999*

**Landry, Bart.** Black working wives : pioneers of the American family revolution / Bart Landry. Berkeley : University of California Press, c2000. xiv, 260 p. : ill. ; 24 cm. (The George Gund Foundation imprint in African American studies) Includes bibliographical references and index. ISBN 0-520-21826-4 (cloth : alk. paper) DDC 306.85/

0973
*1. Dual-career families - United States - History. 2. Afro-American families - History. 3. Afro-American women - Employment - History. 4. Married women - Employment - United States - History. I. Title. II. Series.*
*TC HQ536 .L335 2000*

**LANDSCAPE ARCHITECTURE.** *See* LANDSCAPE DESIGN.

**LANDSCAPE DESIGN - UNITED STATES.** Dober, Richard P. Campus landscape. New York : Wiley, c2000.
*TC LB3223.3 .D65 2000*

**LANDSCAPE IN ART - EXHIBITIONS.** Modernstarts. New York : Museum of Modern Art : Distributed by Harry N. Abrams, c1999.
*TC N620.M9 M63 1999*

**LANDSCAPE PAINTERS.** *See* BARBIZON SCHOOL.

**LANDSCAPE PAINTING - 19TH CENTURY - FRANCE.** *See* BARBIZON SCHOOL.

**Landscapes and language.** Cutchin, Kay Lynch. Cambridge, UK ; New York, NY, USA : Cambridge University Press, 1999.
*TC PE1128 .C88 1999*

**Landscapes in early childhood education :** cross national perspectives on empowerment, a guide for the new millennium / edited by Jacqueline Hayden. New York : P. Lang, 2000. xv, 467 p. ; 23 cm. (Rethinking childhood ; vol. 4) Includes bibliographical references. ISBN 0-8204-3735-2 (alk. paper) DDC 372.21
*1. Early childhood education - Cross-cultural studies. I. Hayden, Jacqueline, 1952- II. Series.*
*TC LB1139.23 .L26 2000*

**Landscapes in my mind.** Sanguineti, Vincenzo R. Madison, Conn. : Psychosocial Press, c1999.
*TC BF697 .S2394 1999*

**Landscapes of betrayal, landscapes of joy.** Childress, Herb, 1958- Albany [N.Y.] : State University of New York Press, c2000.
*TC HQ796 .C458237 2000*

**Landy, Joanne M.**
**Complete Motor Skills Activities Program**
(bk. 1.) Landy, Joanne M. Ready-to-use fundamental motor skills & movement activities for young children. West Nyack, NY : Center for Applied Research in Education, c1999.
*TC GV452 .L355 1999*

Ready-to-use fundamental motor skills & movement activities for young children : teaching, assessment & remediation / Joanne M. Landy & Keith R. Burridge. West Nyack, NY : Center for Applied Research in Education, c1999. xxxi, 271 p. : ill. ; 28 cm. (Complete Motor Skills Activities Program ; bk. 1) Includes bibliographical references (p. 271). ISBN 0-13-013941-6 DDC 372.86
*1. Movement education. 2. Motor learning. 3. Education, Elementary - Activity programs. I. Burridge, Keith R. II. Title. III. Title: Fundamental motor skills & movement activities for young children IV. Series: Landy, Joanne M. Complete Motor Skills Activities Program ; bk. 1.*
*TC GV452 .L355 1999*

**Lane, Harlan L.** The signs of language revisited. Mahwah, N.J. : L.Erlbaum, 2000.
*TC HV2474 .S573 2000*

**Lane, Joan.** Italian painting before 1400 [videorecording]. [London] : The National Gallery, c1989.

Italian painting before 1400 [videorecording]. [London] : The National Gallery, c1989.
*TC ND1575 .I87 1989*

**Lane, Margaret, 1907-** The Beatrix Potter country cookery book / Margaret Lane. London : F. Warne, 1981. 120 p. : ill. (some col.) ; 19 cm. Includes index. ISBN 0-7232-2777-2 DDC 641.5941
*1. Cookery, British. I. Potter, Beatrix, 1866-1943. II. Title.*
*TC TX717 .L355 1981*

**Lane, Nancy D.** Techniques for student research : a comprehensive guide to using the library / Nancy Lane, Margaret Chisholm, and Carolyn Mateer. New York : Neal-Schuman Publishers, 2000. xv, 277 p. ; 23 cm. Includes index. ISBN 1-55570-367-4 (alk. paper) DDC 025.5/24
*1. Library research - United States. 2. Report writing - United States. I. Chisholm, Margaret E. II. Mateer, Carolyn. III. Title.*
*TC Z710 .L36 2000*

**Lang, Peter, 1935-.** Affective education. London ; New York : Cassell, 1998.
*TC LB1072 .A38 1998*

**Langan, Thomas.** Surviving the age of virtual reality / Thomas Langan. Columbia, Mo. ; London : University of Missouri Press, c2000. 184 p. ; 24 cm. Includes bibliographical references and index. ISBN 0-8262-1252-2 (alk. paper) DDC 909.82
*1. Meaning (Philosophy) 2. Civilization, Modern - 20th century. I. Title.*
*TC B105.M4 L355 2000*

**Lange, Dorothea.** Dorothea Lange--a visual life. Washington : Smithsonian Institution Press, c1994.
*TC TR140.L3 D67 1994*

**LANGE, DOROTHEA.** Dorothea Lange--a visual life. Washington : Smithsonian Institution Press, c1994.
*TC TR140.L3 D67 1994*

**Lange, Thomas, 1967-** Rethinking higher education / Thomas Lange. London : IEA Education and Training Unit, 1998, 59 p. : ill. ; 22 cm. (Studies in education ; no. 6) Includes bibliographical references. ISBN 0-255-36421-0 (pbk) DDC 378.41
*1. Education, Higher - Great Britain. 2. Higher education and state - Great Britain. I. Institute of Economic Affairs. Education and Training Unit. II. Title. III. Series.*
*TC LB2342.2.G7 L364 1998*

**Langella, Frank.** Stephen Hawking's universe [videorecording]. [Alexandria, Va.] : PBS Video; Burbank, CA : Distributed by Warner Home Video, c1997.
*TC QB982 .S7 1997*

**Langendorf, Trudi, 1955-.** Scheinfeld, Daniel, 1933- Strengthening refugee families. Chicago, Ill. : Lyceum Books, c1997.
*TC HV640.4.U54 S34 1997*

**Langer, Arthur Mark.** Faculty assessment of mentoring roles at SUNY Empire State College / by Arthur Mark Langer. 1999. xii, 208 leaves ; 29 cm. Typescript also on microfilm. Thesis (Ed.D.)--Teachers College, Columbia University, 1999. Includes bibliographical references (leaves 159-169).
*1. Empire State College - Faculty. 2. Mentoring in education - New York (State) 3. Minorities - Education (Higher) - New York (State) 4. Adult education - Evaluation - New York (State) 5. Counseling in higher education. I. Empire State College. II. Title.*
*TC 06 no. 11138*

**Langer, Freddy, 1957-.** Hine, Lewis Wickes, 1874-1940. The Empire State Building. Munich ; New York : Prestel, c1998.
*TC TR820.5 .H5634 1998*

**Langford, Janet.** Lee, Carol K. Learning about books & libraries. Fort Atkinson, Wis. : Alleyside Press, 2000.
*TC Z711.2 .L455 2000*

**Langford, Wendy, 1960-** Revolutions of the heart : gender, power and the delusions of love / Wendy Langford. London ; New York : Routledge, 1999. xiii, 168 p. ; 25 cm. Includes bibliographical references (p. 158-163) and index. ISBN 0-415-16297-1 (hardcover) ISBN 0-415-16298-X (pbk.) DDC 306.7
*1. Love. 2. Man-woman relationships. I. Title.*
*TC BF575.L8 L266 1999*

**Langhelle, Oluf.** Towards sustainable development. New York, N.Y. : St. Martin's Press, 1999.
*TC HD75.6 .T695 1999*

**Langhorne, Mary Jo.** Developing an information literacy program K-12. New York : Neal-Schuman, c1998.
*TC Z711.2 .D49 1998*

**Langsted, Ole.** Research on socialization of young children in the Nordic countries. Aarhus : Aarhus University Press, c1989.
*TC Z7164.S678 R47 1989*

**LANGUAGE.** The neurocognition of language. Oxford ; New York : Oxford University Press, 1999.
*TC QP399 .N483 1999*

**Language & social processes** Constructing gender and difference. Cresskill, N.J. : Hampton Press, c1999.
*TC BF723.S42 C66 1999*

**Language, a right and a resource :** approaching linguistic human rights / edited by Miklós Kontra ... [et al.]. Budapest, Hungary ; New York : Central European University Press, c1999. xi, 346 p. : ill., map ; 23 cm. Includes bibliographical references and index. ISBN 9639116637 ISBN 9639116645 (pbk.) DDC 306.44
*1. Language and languages - Political aspects. 2. Language and languages - Moral and ethical aspects. 3. Human rights. I. Kontra, Miklós.*
*TC P119.3 .L277 1999*

**LANGUAGE ACQUISITION.** *See also*
**INTERLANGUAGE (LANGUAGE LEARNING); LANGUAGE TRANSFER (LANGUAGE LEARNING); SECOND LANGUAGE ACQUISITION.**
Bloom, Paul, 1963- How children learn the meanings of words. Cambridge, MA : MIT Press, c2000.
*TC P118 .B623 2000*

Brown, H. Douglas, 1941- Principles of language learning and teaching. 2nd ed. Englewood Cliffs, N.J. : Prentice-Hall, c1987.
*TC P51 .B775 1987*

Cook, V. J. (Vivian James), 1940- Chomsky's universal grammar. 2nd [updated] ed. Oxford, OX, UK ; Cambridge, Mass., USA : Blackwell Publishers, 1996.
*TC P85.C47 C66 1996*

Fahey, Kathleen R. Language development, differences, and disorders. Austin, Tex. : PRO-ED, c2000.
*TC LB1139.L3 F35 2000*

Learning to read. Dordrecht : Boston : Kluwer Academic Publishers, 1999.
*TC LB1050.2 .L42 1999*

Nunan, David. Second language teaching & learning. Boston, Mass. : Heinle & Heinle Publishers, c1999.
*TC P118.2 .N86 1999*

Oller, D. Kimbrough. The emergence of the speech capacity. Mahwah, N.J. : Lawrence Erlbaum Associates, 2000.
*TC P118 .O43 2000*

Peccei, Jean Stilwell. Child language. 2nd ed. London ; New York : Routledge, 1999.
*TC P118 .P38 1999*

Perception, cognition, and language. Cambridge, Mass. : MIT, c2000.
*TC BF455 .P389 2000*

Plunkett, Kim. Preliminary approaches to language development. Aarhus, Denmark : Aarhus University Press, c1985.
*TC P118 .P6 1985*

Siraj-Blatchford, Iram. Supporting identity, diversity and language in the early years. Buckingham [England] ; Philadelphia : Open University Press, 2000.
*TC LB1139.3.G7 S57 2000*

Specific language impairment in children. Hillsdale, N.J. : Lawrence Erlbaum, 1998.
*TC RJ496.L35 S643 1998*

Tesar, Bruce. Learnability in optimality theory. Cambridge, Mass. : MIT Press, c2000.
*TC P158.42 .T47 2000*

**Language acquisition & language disorders**
(v. 5) Language transfer in language learning. Rev. ed. with corrections. Amsterdam ; Philadelphia : J. Benjamins Pub. Co., 1994.
*TC P118.25 .L36 1994*

**Language acquisition: a journal of developmental linguistics.**
Specific language impairment in children. Hillsdale, N.J. : Lawrence Erlbaum, 1998.
*TC RJ496.L35 S643 1998*

**LANGUAGE ACQUISITION - CASE STUDIES.**
Deuchar, M. (Margaret) Bilingual acquisition. Oxford ; New York : Oxford University Press, 2000.
*TC P118 .D439 2000*

**LANGUAGE ACQUISITION - CONGRESSES.**
Child Language Research Forum (29th : 1997 : Stanford University) The proceedings of the twenty-ninth Annual Child Language Research Forum. [Stanford] : Published for the Stanford Linguistics Association by the Center for the Study of Language and Information, c1998.
*TC P118 .C4558 1997*

Language acquisition. 1st ed. Amsterdam ; New York : North-Holland, 1999.

*TC P118 .L2539 1999*

New directions in language development and disorders. New York : Kluwer Academic/Plenum Publishers, c2000.
*TC P118 .N49 2000*

**Language acquisition :** knowledge representation and processing / Antonella Sorace, Caroline Heycock, Richard Shillcock, editors. 1st ed. Amsterdam ; New York : North-Holland, 1999, 263 p. : ill. ; 25 cm. Papers presented at a conference held in Edinburgh in April 1997. Includes bibliographical references and indexes. ISBN 0-08-043370-7 (hc) DDC 401/.93
*1. Language acquisition - Congresses. I. Sorace, Antonella. II. Heycock, Caroline B., 1960- III. Shillcock, Richard.*
*TC P118 .L2539 1999*

**LANGUAGE ACQUISITION - LONGITUDINAL STUDIES.**
Painter, Clare, 1947- Learning through language in early childhood. London ; New York : Cassell, 1999.
*TC LB1139.5.L35 P35 1999*

**LANGUAGE ACQUISITION - PARENT PARTICIPATION.**
Machado, Jeanne M. Early childhood experiences in language arts. 6th ed. Albany, N.Y. : Delmar Publishers, c1999.
*TC LB1139.5.L35 M335 1999*

**LANGUAGE ACQUISITION - RESEARCH - DATA PROCESSING.**
MacWhinney, Brian. The CHILDES project. 3rd ed. Mahwah, N.J. : Lawrence Erlbaum, 2000.
*TC LB1139.L3 M24 2000*

**LANGUAGE ACQUISITION - RESEARCH - METHODOLOGY.**
Methods for studying language production. Mahwah, N.J. : Lawrence Erlbaum Associates, 2000.
*TC P118 .M47 2000*

**LANGUAGE ACQUISTION.**
Goldsworthy, Candace L. Sourcebook of phonological awareness activities. San Diego : Singular Pub. Group, c1998.
*TC LB1050.5 .G66 1998*

**Language alive in the classroom** / edited by Rebecca S. Wheeler. Westport, Conn. : Praeger, 1999. xiv, 228 p. ; 24 cm. Includes bibliographical references and index. ISBN 0-275-96055-2 (alk. paper) ISBN 0-275-96056-0 (pbk. : alk. paper) DDC 410/.71
*1. Language and languages - Study and teaching. I. Wheeler, Rebecca S., 1952-*
*TC P51 .L338 1999*

**Language and automation.** Washington, Center for Applied Linguistics. 26 cm. no. 1- spring 1970- . Published under the auspices of the International Committee on Computational Linguistics. ISSN 0023-8287 DDC 016.029/94
*1. Computational linguistics - Bibliography - Periodicals. I. Center for Applied Linguistics. II. International Committee on Computational Linguistics.*

**Language and computers**
(no. 27) Lorenz, Gunter R. Adjective intensification--learners versus native speakers. Amsterdam ; Atlanta, GA : Rodopi, 1999.
*TC PE1074.5 .L67 1999*

**Language and conceptualization** / edited by Jan Nuyts and Eric Pederson. 1st paperback ed. Cambridge [England] ; New York : Cambridge University Press, 1999. viii, 281 p. : ill. ; 23 cm. (Language, culture, and cognition ; 1) Includes bibliographical references and indexes. ISBN 0-521-77481-0 (pbk.) ISBN 0-521-55303-2 (hbk.) DDC 401/.9
*1. Psycholinguistics. 2. Concepts. 3. Cognition. I. Nuyts, Jan. II. Pederson, Eric. III. Series.*
*TC P37 .L354 1999*

**LANGUAGE AND CULTURE.** *See also*
**SOCIOLINGUISTICS.**
Culturally speaking. London ; New York : Continuum ; [New York] : [Cassell], 2000.
*TC GN345.6 .C86 2000*

Gordon, Tatiana. Russian language directives. 1998.
*TC 06 no. 10940*

Kunz, Linda Ann. English modals in American talk shows. 1999.
*TC 06 no. 11136*

Lockwood, David G. Functional approaches to language, culture, and cognition. Amsterdam ; Philadelphia : J. Benjamins, c2000.
*TC P147 .L63 1998*

Ong, Walter J. Orality and literacy. London ; New York : Routledge, 1988.

*TC P35 .O5 1988*
Perkins, Revere D. (Revere Dale) Deixis, grammar, and culture. Amsterdam ; Philadelphia : J. Benjamins Pub. co., 1992.
*TC P35 .P47 1992*

Pierre Bourdieu. Bern ; New York : P. Lang, c1999.
*TC HM621 .P54 1999*

Skutnabb-Kangas, Tove. Linguistic genocide in education, or worldwide diversity and human rights? Mahwah, N.J. : L. Erlbaum Associates, 2000.
*TC P40.8 .S58 2000*

Stubbs, Michael, 1947- Text and corpus analysis. Oxford, OX, UK ; Cambridge, Mass., USA : Blackwell Publishers, c1996.
*TC P302 .S773 1996*

**LANGUAGE AND CULTURE - CHINA.**
Culture, literacy, and learning English. Portsmouth, NH : Boynton/Cook Publishers, c1998.
*TC PE1130.C4 C85 1998*

**LANGUAGE AND CULTURE - HANDBOOKS, MANUALS, ETC.**
Handbook of language & ethnic identity. New York : Oxford University Press, 1999.
*TC P35 .H34 1999*

**LANGUAGE AND CULTURE - MEXICO - YUCATÁN (STATE).**
Hanks, William F. Intertexts. Lanham : Rowman & Littlefield Publishers, Inc., c2000.
*TC P35.5.M6 H36 2000*

**LANGUAGE AND CULTURE - PAKISTAN.**
Rahman, Tariq. Language, education, and culture. Islamabad : Sustainable Development Policy Institute : Karachi : Oxford Uinversity Press, 1999.
*TC P119.32.P18 R35 1999*

**LANGUAGE AND CULTURE - STUDY AND TEACHING.**
Culture in second language teaching and learning. Cambridge, U.K. ; New York : Cambridge University Press, 1999.
*TC P53 .C77 1999*

Pathways to culture. Yarmouth, ME : Intercultural Press, c1997.
*TC P53 .P37 1997*

**LANGUAGE AND CULTURE - STUDY AND TEACHING - STANDARDS - UNITED STATES.**
Foreign language standards. Lincolnwood, Ill., U.S.A. : National Textbook Company in conjunction with the American Council on the Teaching of Foreign Languages, c1999.
*TC P53 .F674 1999*

**LANGUAGE AND CULTURE - UNITED STATES - AUDIO-VISUAL AIDS.**
Hidden messages. Yarmouth, Me. : Intercultural Press, c1998.
*TC LC1099.3 .H53 1998*

**LANGUAGE AND EDUCATION.** *See also*
**EDUCATION, BILINGUAL; LANGUAGE AND LANGUAGES - STUDY AND TEACHING; LANGUAGES, MODERN - STUDY AND TEACHING; NATIVE LANGUAGE AND EDUCATION; NATIVE LANGUAGE - STUDY AND TEACHING.**
Genre and institutions. London ; Washington : Cassell, 1997.
*TC P302.84 .G46 1997*

Pierre Bourdieu. Bern ; New York : P. Lang, c1999.
*TC HM621 .P54 1999*

Rights to language. Mahwah, N.J. : L. Erlbaum Associates, 2000.
*TC P119.3 .R54 2000*

Skutnabb-Kangas, Tove. Linguistic genocide in education, or worldwide diversity and human rights? Mahwah, N.J. : L. Erlbaum Associates, 2000.
*TC P40.8 .S58 2000*

Text in education and society. Singapore : Singapore University Press ; Singapore ; River Edge, N.J. : World Scientific, c1998.
*TC P40.8 .T48 1998*

**LANGUAGE AND EDUCATION - ENCYCLOPEDIAS.**
Concise encyclopedia of educational linguistics. Amsterdam ; New York : Elsevier, 1999.
*TC P40.8 .C66 1999*

**The language and education library**
(14) Rassool, Naz, 1949- Literacy for sustainable development in the age of information. Clevedon

[England] ; Philadelphia : Multilingual Matters,
c1999.
*TC LC149 .R37 1999*

(15) Ryan, James, 1952 Oct. 18- Race and ethnicity
in multi-ethnic schools. Clevedon [England] ;
Philadelphia : Multilingual Matters, c1999.
*TC LC3734 .R93 1999*

(16) Egbo, Benedicta, 1954- Gender, literacy, and
life chances in Sub-Saharan Africa. Clevedon ;
Buffalo : Multilingual Matters, c2000.
*TC LC2412 .E42 2000*

### LANGUAGE AND EDUCATION - NETHERLANDS - DELFT.
Klaassen, R. G. Effective lecturing behaviour in
English-medium instruction. Delft, Netherlands : Delft
University Press, 1999.
*TC LB2393 .K53 1999*

### LANGUAGE AND EDUCATION - PAKISTAN.
Rahman, Tariq. Language, education, and culture.
Islamabad : Sustainable Development Policy
Institute ; Karachi : Oxford Uinversity Press, 1999.
*TC P119.32.P18 R35 1999*

### LANGUAGE AND EDUCATION - PERIODICALS.
Working papers in educational linguistics.
[Philadelphia]: Language in Education Division,
Graduate School of Education, University of
Pennsylvania,
*TC P40.8 .W675*

### LANGUAGE AND EDUCATION - SOCIAL ASPECTS - UNITED STATES.
Bartolomé, Lilia I. The misteaching of academic
discourses. Boulder, Colo. : Westview Press, 1998.
*TC LB1033.5 .B37 1998*

### LANGUAGE AND EDUCATION - UNITED STATES.
Lopez, Marianne Exum, 1960- When discourses
collide. New York : P. Lang, c1999.
*TC HQ792.U5 L665 1999*

Toohey, Kelleen, 1950- Learning English at school.
Clevedon, [England] ; Buffalo : Multilingual Matters,
2000.
*TC PE1128.A2 T63 2000*

### LANGUAGE AND EMOTION.
Speaking of emotions. Berlin ; New York : Mouton de
Gruyter, 1998.
*TC BF591. S64 1998*

### LANGUAGE AND EMOTIONS.
Kövecses, Zoltán. Metaphor and emotion.
Cambridge ; New York : Cambridge University
Press ; Paris : Editions de la Maison des Sciences de
l'Homme, 2000.
*TC BF582 .K68 2000*

### LANGUAGE AND LANGUAGES. *See also*
**BILINGUALISM; CHILDREN - LANGUAGE;
LANGUAGE AND EDUCATION;
LINGUISTIC CHANGE; LINGUISTICS;
NATIVE LANGUAGE; RACISM IN
LANGUAGE; SEMANTICS; SEMANTICS
(PHILOSOPHY); SIGN LANGUAGE;
SOCIOLINGUISTICS; SPEECH; VOICE;
WRITING; WRITTEN COMMUNICATION.**
Learning, language, and invention. Aldershot,
Hampshire, Great Britain : Variorum ; Brookfield, Vt.,
USA : Ashgate Pub. Co. ; Paris, France : Société
internationale de l'Astrolabe, 1994.
*TC AC5 .L38 1994*

### LANGUAGE AND LANGUAGES - ABILITY TESTING.
Allison, Desmond. Language testing and evaluation.
Singapore : Singapore University Press ; Singapore ;
River Edge, N.J. : World Scientific, c1999.
*TC P53.4 .A45 1999*

Literacy assessment of second language learners.
Boston ; London : Allyn and Bacon, c2001.
*TC P53.4 .L58 2001*

North, Brian, 1950- The development of a common
framework scale of language proficiency. New York :
P. Lang, c2000.
*TC P53.4 .N67 2000*

Sasaki, Miyuki, 1959- Second language proficiency,
foreign language aptitude, and intelligence. New
York : P. Lang, c1999.
*TC P53.4 .S27 1999*

### LANGUAGE AND LANGUAGES - ABSTRACTS - DATABASES.
[LLBA (Online)] LLBA [computer file]. [Norwood,
MA] : SilverPlatter International, [1993- Computer
data and program.

[LLBA (Online)] LLBA [computer file]. [Norwood,
MA] : SilverPlatter International, [1993- Computer
data and program.

[LLBA (Online)] LLBA [computer file]. [Norwood,
MA] : SilverPlatter International, [1993- Computer
data and program.
*TC NETWORKED RESOURCE*

### LANGUAGE AND LANGUAGES - ACQUISITION.
*See* **LANGUAGE ACQUISITION.**

### LANGUAGE AND LANGUAGES - AUDIO-VISUAL AIDS - PERIODICALS.
Audio-visual language journal. London.

### LANGUAGE AND LANGUAGES - CODE WORDS.
USMARC code list for languages. 1996 ed.
Washington, D.C. : Cataloging Distribution Service,
Library of Congress, 1996.
*TC Z699.35.M28 U79 1997*

### LANGUAGE AND LANGUAGES - COMPUTER-ASSISTED INSTRUCTION.
Computer assisted language learning (CALL). Lisse
[Netherlands] ; Exton, PA : Swets & Zeitlinger, 1999.
*TC P53.28 .C6634 1999*

Worldcall. Lisse, Netherlands ; Abingdon [England] ;
Exton, PA : Swets & Zeitlinger, c1999.
*TC P53.28 .W67 1999*

### LANGUAGE AND LANGUAGES - DATA PROCESSING. *See* COMPUTATIONAL LINGUISTICS.

### LANGUAGE AND LANGUAGES - FICTION.
Brooke, William J. A is for aarrgh!. 1st ed. New
York : HarperCollinsPublishers, 1999.
*TC PZ7.B78977 Ig 1999*

### LANGUAGE AND LANGUAGES - GOVERNMENT POLICY. *See* LANGUAGE POLICY.

### LANGUAGE AND LANGUAGES - GRAMMAR, COMPARATIVE. *See* GRAMMAR, COMPARATIVE AND GENERAL.

### LANGUAGE AND LANGUAGES - MORAL AND ETHICAL ASPECTS.
Language, a right and a resource. Budapest, Hungary ;
New York : Central European University Press,
c1999.
*TC P119.3 .L277 1999*

### LANGUAGE AND LANGUAGES - ORIGIN.
Loritz, Donald, 1947- How the brain evolved
language. New York : Oxford University Press, 1999.
*TC P116 .L67 1999*

Oller, D. Kimbrough. The emergence of the speech
capacity. Mahwah, N.J. : Lawrence Erlbaum
Associates, 2000.
*TC P118 .O43 2000*

### LANGUAGE AND LANGUAGES - ORTHOGRAPHY AND SPELLING.
Kress, Gunther R. Early spelling. London ; New
York : Routledge, 2000.
*TC P240.2 .K74 2000*

### LANGUAGE AND LANGUAGES - PERIODICALS.
Foundations of language; Dordrecht, Holland, Reidel.

### LANGUAGE AND LANGUAGES - PHILOSOPHY.
*See also* **SPEECH ACTS (LINGUISTICS).**
Berthoff, Ann E. The mysterious barricades. Toronto ;
Buffalo : University of Toronto Press, c1999.
*TC P106 .B463 1999*

Devlin, Keith J. The math gene. [New York] : Basic
Books, 2000.
*TC QA141 .D48 2000*

### LANGUAGE AND LANGUAGES - POLITICAL ASPECTS. *See also* LINGUISTIC MINORITIES.
Language, a right and a resource. Budapest, Hungary ;
New York : Central European University Press,
c1999.
*TC P119.3 .L277 1999*

### LANGUAGE AND LANGUAGES - RHETORIC. *See* RHETORIC.

### LANGUAGE AND LANGUAGES - SEX DIFFERENCES - CONGRESSES.
Rethinking language and gender research. London ;
New York : Longman, 1996.
*TC P120.S48 R48 1996*

### LANGUAGE AND LANGUAGES - SOCIAL ASPECTS. *See* SOCIOLINGUISTICS.

### LANGUAGE AND LANGUAGES - SOCIOLOGICAL ASPECTS. *See* SOCIOLINGUISTICS.

### LANGUAGE AND LANGUAGES - STUDY AND TEACHING. *See also* **INTERLANGUAGE (LANGUAGE LEARNING); LANGUAGE TRANSFER (LANGUAGE LEARNING).**
Asher, James J. (James John), 1929- Learning another
language through actions. 4th ed. Los Gatos, Calif. :
Sky Oaks Productions, 1993.
*TC PB36 .A8 1993*

Blaz, Deborah. Teaching foreign languages in the
block. Larchmont, NY : Eye on Education, c1998.
*TC P51 .B545 1998*

Brown, H. Douglas, 1941- Principles of language
learning and teaching. 2nd ed. Englewood Cliffs,
N.J. : Prentice-Hall, c1987.
*TC P51 .B775 1987*

Cary, Stephen. Working with second language
learners. Portsmouth, NH : Heinemann, c2000.
*TC P53 .C286 2000*

Cava, Margaret T. Second language learner strategies
and the unsuccessful second language writer. 1999.
*TC 085 C295*

A challenge to change. New York : College Entrance
Examination Board, 1999.
*TC P51 .C427 1999*

Culture in second language teaching and learning.
Cambridge, U.K. ; New York : Cambridge University
Press, 1999.
*TC P53 .C77 1999*

Guillot, Marie-Noëlle, 1955- Fluency and its teaching.
Clevedon, England ; Philadelphia, Pa. : Multilingual
Matters, c1999.
*TC P53.6 .G85 1999*

Indigenous community-based education. Clevedon
[England] ; Philadelphia : Multilingual Matters,
c1999.
*TC LC1036 .I43 1999*

Language alive in the classroom. Westport, Conn. :
Praeger, 1999.
*TC P51 .L338 1999*

Language issues. White Plains, N.Y. : Longman
Publishers USA, c1995.
*TC P51 .L346 1995*

Language policy and pedagogy. Philadelphia : J.
Benjamins, c2000.
*TC P53 .L364 2000*

Learner autonomy in language learning. Frankfurt am
Main ; New York : Peter Lang, c1999.
*TC P53 .L378 1999*

The learning strategies handbook. White Plains, NY :
Longman, c1999.
*TC P51 .L43 1999*

McKay, Heather, 1950- Teaching adult second
language learners. Cambridge ; New York :
Cambridge University Press, 1999.
*TC P53 .M33 1999*

Nunan, David. Second language teaching & learning.
Boston, Mass. : Heinle & Heinle Publishers, c1999.
*TC P118.2 .N86 1999*

Nunan, David. Second language teaching & learning.
Boston, Mass. : Heinle & Heinle Publishers, c1999.
*TC P118.2 .N86 1999*

Pathways to culture. Yarmouth, ME : Intercultural
Press, c1997.
*TC P53 .P37 1997*

Reflections and connections. Cresskill, N.J. : Hampton
Press, c1999.
*TC P51 .R36 1999*

Richards, Jack C. The language teaching matrix.
Cambridge [England] ; New York : Cambridge
University Press, 1990.
*TC P51 .R48 1990*

Riggenbach, Heidi. Discourse analysis in the language
classroom. Ann Arbor : University of Michigan Press,
c1999-
*TC P53.2965 .R54 1999*

### LANGUAGE AND LANGUAGES - STUDY AND TEACHING - COMPUTER NETWORK RESOURCES.
Network-based language teaching. Cambridge, U.K. ;
New York : Cambridge University Press, 2000.
*TC P53.285 .N48 2000*

## LANGUAGE AND LANGUAGES - STUDY AND TEACHING - EVALUATION.
Allison, Desmond. Language testing and evaluation. Singapore : Singapore University Press ; Singapore ; River Edge, N.J. : World Scientific, c1999.
*TC P53.4 .A45 1999*

Managing evaluation and innovation in language teaching. New York : Longman, 1998.
*TC P53.63 .M36 1998*

## LANGUAGE AND LANGUAGES - STUDY AND TEACHING - HANDBOOKS, MANUALS, ETC.
Shrum, Judith L. Teacher's handbook. 2nd ed. Boston, Mass. : Heinle & Heinle, c2000.
*TC P51 .S48 2000*

## LANGUAGE AND LANGUAGES - STUDY AND TEACHING (HIGHER).
Schneider, Elke. Multisensory structured metacognitive instruction. Frankfurt am Main ; New York : P. Lang, c1999.
*TC P53.7 .S357 1999*

## LANGUAGE AND LANGUAGES - STUDY AND TEACHING (HIGHER) - UNITED STATES.
Preparing a nation's teachers. New York : Modern Language Association of America, 1999.
*TC PE68.U5 P74 1999*

## LANGUAGE AND LANGUAGES - STUDY AND TEACHING - PERIODICALS.
Audio-visual language journal. London.

Języki obce w szkole. Warszawa : Wydawn. Szkolne i Pedagogiczne,

Levende talen magazine. Amsterdam : Vereniging van Leraren in Levenden Talen, 2000-

Working papers in educational linguistics. [Philadelphia]: Language in Education Division, Graduate School of Education, University of Pennsylvania,
*TC P40.8 .W675*

## LANGUAGE AND LANGUAGES - STUDY AND TEACHING - PHYSIOLOGICAL ASPECTS.
The neurocognition of language. Oxford ; New York : Oxford University Press, 1999.
*TC QP399 .N483 1999*

## LANGUAGE AND LANGUAGES - STUDY AND TEACHING - PSYCHOLOGICAL ASPECTS.
Schneider, Elke. Multisensory structured metacognitive instruction. Frankfurt am Main ; New York : P. Lang, c1999.
*TC P53.7 .S357 1999*

## LANGUAGE AND LANGUAGES - STUDY AND TEACHING - RESEARCH.
Foreign language standards. Lincolnwood, Ill., U.S.A. : National Textbook Company in conjunction with the American Council on the Teaching of Foreign Languages, c1999.
*TC P53 .F674 1999*

## LANGUAGE AND LANGUAGES - STUDY AND TEACHING - STANDARDS - UNITED STATES.
Foreign language standards. Lincolnwood, Ill., U.S.A. : National Textbook Company in conjunction with the American Council on the Teaching of Foreign Languages, c1999.
*TC P53 .F674 1999*

## LANGUAGE AND LANGUAGES - STUDY AND TEACHING - TECHNOLOGICAL INNOVATIONS.
Worldcall. Lisse, Netherlands ; Abingdon [England] ; Exton, PA : Swets & Zeitlinger, c1999.
*TC P53.28 .W67 1999*

## LANGUAGE AND LANGUAGES - STUDY AND TEACHING - UNITED STATES.
Osborn, Terry A., 1966- Critical reflection and the foreign language classroom. Westport, Conn. ; London : Bergin & Garvey, 2000.
*TC P57.U7 O78 2000*

## LANGUAGE AND LANGUAGES - VARIATION.
*See also* SUBLANGUAGE.
Functional categories, argument structure and parametric variation. Edinburgh : Centre for Cognitive Study, University of Edinburgh, c1994.
*TC P151 .F86 1994*

Pupipat, Apisak. Scientific writing and publishing in English in Thailand. 1998.
*TC 06 no. 10981*

**Language and literacy development in children who are deaf.**

Schirmer, Barbara R. 2nd ed. Boston : Allyn and Bacon, 2000.
*TC HV2443 .S33 2000*

**Language and literacy series (New York, N.Y.)**
Handel, Ruth D. Building family literacy in an urban community. New York : Teachers College Press, c1999.
*TC LC152.N58 H36 1999*

Reading for meaning. New York ; London : Teachers College Press, c2000.
*TC LB1050.45 .R443 2000*

So much to say. New York : Teachers College Press, c1999.
*TC PE1128.A2 S599 1999*

**Language and mind.**
Chomsky, Noam. Enl. ed. New York : Harcourt Brace Jovanovich, [1972].
*TC P106 .C52 1972*

## LANGUAGE AND RACISM. *See* RACISM IN LANGUAGE.

**Language and reading success.**
Biemiller, Andrew, 1939- Cambridge, Mass. : Brookline Books, c1999.
*TC LB1139.L3 B48 1999*

## LANGUAGE AND SEX. *See* LANGUAGE AND LANGUAGES - SEX DIFFERENCES.

## LANGUAGE AND SOCIETY. *See* SOCIOLINGUISTICS.

## LANGUAGE AND STATE. *See* LANGUAGE POLICY.

## LANGUAGE ARTS. *See also* COMPOSITION (LANGUAGE ARTS); LANGUAGE ARTS (MIDDLE SCHOOL); READING.
The changing face of whole language. Newark, Del. : International Reading Association ; Victoria, Australia : Australian Literacy Educators' Association, c1997.
*TC LB1050.35 .C43 1997*

Fiction, literature and media. Amsterdam : Amsterdam University Press, c1999.
*TC LB1575.8 .F53 1999*

Horsman, Jenny. Too scared to learn. Mahwah, N.J. : L. Erlbaum Associates, Publishers, 2000.
*TC LC1481 . H67 2000*

Issues and trends in literacy education. 2nd ed. Boston : Allyn and Bacon, c2000.
*TC LB1576 .I87 2000*

Pinnell, Gay Su. Word matters. Portsmouth, NH : Heinemann, c1998.
*TC LB1573.3 .P55 1998*

Tchudi, Susan J. (Susan Jane), 1945- The English language arts handbook. 2nd ed. Portsmouth, NH : Boynton/Cook, c1999.
*TC LB1576 .T358 1999*

Ting, Yenren, 1948- Learning English text by heart in a Chinese university. [New York : Columbia University], 1999.
*TC 085 T438*

## LANGUAGE ARTS - ABILITY TESTING - UNITED STATES - CASE STUDIES.
Simmons, Jay, 1947- You never asked me to read. Boston : Allyn and Bacon, c2000.
*TC LB1050.46 .S535 2000*

**Language arts and environmental awareness.**
Roberts, Patricia, 1936- New Haven, Conn. : Linnet Professional Publications, 1998.
*TC Z5863.E55 R63 1998*

## LANGUAGE ARTS - COMPUTER-ASSISTED INSTRUCTION.
Jody, Marilyn, 1932- Using computers to teach literature. 2nd ed. Urbana, Ill. : National Council of Teachers of English, c1998.
*TC LB1050.37 J63 1998*

## LANGUAGE ARTS - CORRELATION WITH CONTENT SUBJECTS. *See also* CONTENT AREA READING.
Chatton, Barbara. Blurring the edges. Portsmouth, NH : Heinemann, c1999.
*TC LB1576 .C46 1999*

Echevarria, Jana, 1956- Making content comprehensible for English language learners. Boston, MA : Allyn and Bacon, 2000.
*TC PE1128.A2 E24 2000*

## LANGUAGE ARTS - CORRELATION WITH CONTENT SUBJECTS - UNITED STATES.
Allan, Karen Kuelthau. Literacy and learning. Boston : Houghton Mifflin, c2000.
*TC LB1631 .A37 2000*

Miller, Wilma H. Ready-to-use activities & materials for improving content reading skills. West Nyack, NY : Center For Applied Research in Education, c1999.
*TC LB1576 .M52 1999*

## LANGUAGE ARTS (EARLY CHILDHOOD).
Children achieving. Newark, Del. : International Reading Association, c1998.
*TC LB1139.5.R43 C55 1998*

Machado, Jeanne M. Early childhood experiences in language arts. 6th ed. Albany, N.Y. : Delmar Publishers, c1999.
*TC LB1139.5.L35 M335 1999*

McCarrier, Andrea. Interactive writing. Portsmouth, NH : Heinemann, c2000.
*TC LB1139.5.L35 M39 2000*

Miller, Wilma H. Strategies for developing emergent literacy. 1st ed. Boston : McGraw-Hill, c2000.
*TC LB1139.5.L35 M55 2000*

Mountain, Lee Harrison. Early 3 Rs. Mahwah, N.J. ; London : L. Erlbaum Associates, 2000.
*TC LB1139.23 .M68 2000*

Play and literacy in early childhood. Mahwah, N.J. : Lawrence Erlbaum Associates, Publishers, 2000.
*TC LB1140.35.P55 P557 2000*

Stirring the waters. Portsmouth, NH : Heinemann, c1999.
*TC LB1139.5.L35 S85 1999*

## LANGUAGE ARTS (EARLY CHILDHOOD) - COMPUTER-ASSISTED INSTRUCTION.
Casey, Jean Marie. Early literacy. Rev. ed. Englewood, Colo. : Libraries Unlimited, 2000.
*TC LB1139.5.L35 C37 2000*

## LANGUAGE ARTS (EARLY CHILDHOOD) - GREAT BRITAIN.
Whitehead, Marian R. Supporting language and literacy development in the early years. Buckingham [England] ; Philadelphia : Open University Press, 1999.
*TC LB1139.5.L35 W53 1999*

## LANGUAGE ARTS (EARLY CHILDHOOD) - LONGITUDINAL STUDIES.
Painter, Clare, 1947- Learning through language in early childhood. London ; New York : Cassell, 1999.
*TC LB1139.5.L35 P35 1999*

## LANGUAGE ARTS (EARLY CHILDHOOD) - STUDY AND TEACHING. *See* LANGUAGE ARTS (EARLY CHILDHOOD).

## LANGUAGE ARTS (EARLY CHILDHOOD) - UNITED STATES.
Dorn, Linda J. Apprenticeship in literacy. York, Me. : Stenhouse Publishers, c1998.
*TC LB1139.5.L35 D67 1998*

McGee, Lea M. Literacy's beginnings. 3rd ed. Boston ; London : Allyn and Bacon, c2000.
*TC LB1139.5.R43 M33 2000*

Paul, Dierdre Glenn, 1964- Raising Black children who love reading and writing. Westport, Conn. : Bergin & Garvey, 2000.
*TC LC2778.L34 P28 2000*

## LANGUAGE ARTS (ELEMENTARY).
Call it courage. New York : Macmillan/McGraw-Hill, c1997.
*TC LB1576 .S66 1997 Gr.6 l.12 u.6*

Coming home. New York : Macmillan/McGraw-Hill, c1997.
*TC LB1576 .S66 1997 Gr.6 l.12 u.5*

Cooper, J. David (James David), 1942- Discover : Grade 1, level 1.5, [Themes 9 and 10]. Boston : Houghton Mifflin, 1997.
*TC LB1575.8 .C6616 1997*

Dare to discover. New York : Macmillan/McGraw-Hill, c1997.
*TC LB1576 .S66 1997 Gr.6 l.12 u.2*

Ewart, Franzeska G. Let the shadows speak. Stoke on Trent, Staffordshire, England : Trentham Books, 1998.
*TC PN1979.S5 E8 1998*

Getting to know you. New York : Macmillan/McGraw-Hill, c1997.

*TC LB1576 .S66 1997 Gr.5 l.11 u.4*

Make a wish. New York : Macmillan/McGraw-Hill, c1997.
*TC LB1576 .S66 1997 Gr.4 l.10 u.1*

Making the grade. New York : Macmillan/McGraw-Hill, c1997.
*TC LB1576 .S66 1997 Gr.6 l.12 u.1*

Memories to keep. New York : Macmillan/McGraw-Hill, c1997.
*TC LB1576 .S66 1997 Gr.4 l.10 u.5*

Naturally. New York : Macmillan/McGraw-Hill, c1997.
*TC LB1576 .S66 1997 Gr.4 l.10 u.2*

Pitch in. New York : Macmillan/McGraw-Hill, c1997.
*TC LB1576 .S66 1997 Gr.4 l.10 u.4*

Ragno, Nancy N. World of language. [Teacher ed.]. Morristown, NJ : Silver Burdett & Ginn, c1990.

Ragno, Nancy N. World of language. [Teacher ed.]. Morristown, NJ : Silver Burdett & Ginn, c1990.

Ragno, Nancy N. World of language. [Teacher ed.]. Morristown, NJ : Silver Burdett & Ginn, c1990.

Ragno, Nancy Nickell. World of language. Needham, Ma. : Silver Burdett Ginn, c1996.
*TC LB1576 .S4471 1996*

Ragno, Nancy Nickell. World of language. Needham, Mass. : Silver Burdett Ginn, c1996.
*TC LB1576 .S4471 1996*

Ramírez de Mellor, Elva Fun with English. Pupil's ed. Mexico : McGraw-Hill c1987
*TC PE1129.S8 .R35 1987*

Ramírez de Mellor, Elva Fun with english. Mexico : McGraw-Hill c1987
*TC PE1129.S8 .R35 1987*

Reading and writing in elementary classrooms. 4th ed. New York : Longman, c2000.
*TC LB1573 .R279 2000*

Routman, Regie. Conversations. Portsmouth, NH : Heinemann, c2000.
*TC LB1576 .R757 1999*

Rubin, Dorothy. Teaching elementary language arts. 6th ed. Boston : Allyn and Bacon, c2000.
*TC LB1576 .R773 2000*

Scenes of wonder. New York : Macmillan/McGraw-Hill, c1997.
*TC LB1576 .S66 1997 Gr.5 l.11 u.1*

Take the high road. New York : Macmillan/McGraw-Hill, c1997.
*TC LB1576 .S66 1997 Gr.5 l.11 u.5*

That's what friends are for. New York : Macmillan/McGraw-Hill, c1997.
*TC LB1576 .S66 1997 Gr.4 l.10 u.3*

Time & time again. New York : Macmillan/McGraw-Hill, c1997.
*TC LB1576 .S66 1997 Gr.6 l.12 u.4*

Twice-told tales. New York : Macmillan/McGraw-Hill, c1997.
*TC LB1576 .S66 1997 Gr.4 l.10 u.6*

Unlikely heroes. New York : Macmillan/McGraw-Hill, c1997.
*TC LB1576 .S66 1997 Gr.6 l.12 u.3*

What is visual literacy? York, Maine : Stenhouse Pub., c1996.
*TC LB1068 .W45 1996*

Winning attitudes. New York : Macmillan/McGraw-Hill, c1997.
*TC LB1576 .S66 1997 Gr.5 l.11 u.3*

Wollman-Bonilla, Julie. Family message journals. Urbana, Ill. : National Council of Teachers of English, c2000.
*TC LB1576 .W644 2000*

World of language. Needham, Mass. : Silver Burdett Ginn, c1996.
*TC LB1576 .S4471 1996*

World of language. Teacher ed. Needham, Mass. : Silver Burdett Ginn, c1996.
*TC LB1576 .S4471 1996 Teacher Ed.*

Worlds of change. New York : Macmillan/McGraw-Hill, c1997.
*TC LB1576 .S66 1997 Gr.5 l.11 u.2*

Zoom in. New York : Macmillan/McGraw-Hill, c1997.

*TC LB1576 .S66 1997 Gr.5 l.11 u.6*

## LANGUAGE ARTS (ELEMENTARY) - ACTIVITY PROGRAMS - HANDBOOKS, MANUALS, ETC.
Walmsley, Bonnie Brown. Teaching with favorite Marc Brown books. New York : Scholastic Professional Books, c1998.
*TC LB1576 .W258 1998*

## LANGUAGE ARTS (ELEMENTARY) - BIBLIOGRAPHY.
Roberts, Patricia, 1936- Language arts and environmental awareness. New Haven, Conn. : Linnet Professional Publications, 1998.
*TC Z5863.E55 R63 1998*

## LANGUAGE ARTS (ELEMENTARY) - COMPUTER-ASSISTED INSTRUCTION.
Casey, Jean Marie. Creating the early literacy classroom. Englewood, Colo. : Libraries Unlimited, c2000.
*TC LB1576.7 .C38 2000*

Linking literacy and technology. Newark, Del. : International Reading Association, c2000.
*TC LB1576.7 .L56 2000*

## LANGUAGE ARTS (ELEMENTARY) - GREAT BRITAIN.
Drever, Mina. Teaching English in primary classrooms. Stoke on Trent, Staffordshire, England : Trentham Books, 1999.
*TC LB1576 .D749 1999*

## LANGUAGE ARTS (ELEMENTARY) - HANDBOOKS, MANUALS, ETC.
Promoting literacy in grades 4-9. Boston ; London : Allyn and Bacon, c2000.
*TC LB1576 .P76 2000*

## LANGUAGE ARTS (ELEMENTARY) - STUDY AND TEACHING. *See* LANGUAGE ARTS (ELEMENTARY).

## LANGUAGE ARTS (ELEMENTARY) - UNITED STATES.
Carr, Janine Chappell. A child went forth. Portsmouth, NH : Heinemann, 1999.
*TC LB1576 .C31714 1999*

Fraser, Jane. On their way. Portsmouth, NH : Heinemann, c1994.
*TC LB1576 .F72 1994*

Madigan, Dan. The writing lives of children. York, ME : Stenhouse Publishers, 1997.
*TC LB1042 .M24 1997*

Paul, Dierdre Glenn, 1964- Raising Black children who love reading and writing. Westport, Conn. : Bergin & Garvey, 2000.
*TC LC2778.L34 P28 2000*

## LANGUAGE ARTS (ELEMENTARY) - UNITED STATES - CASE STUDIES.
Richards, Janet C. Elementary literacy lessons. Mahwah, N.J. : L. Erlbaum Associates, 2000.
*TC LB1576 .R517 2000*

## LANGUAGE ARTS - HANDBOOKS, MANUALS, ETC.
Adams, Arlene. Handbook for literacy tutors. Springfield, Ill. : C.C. Thomas, Publisher, c1999.
*TC LB1576 .A3893 1999*

**Language arts in the early childhood classroom.**
Stewig, John W. Belmont [Calif.] : Wadsworth Pub. Co., c1995.
*TC LB1140.5.L3 S72 1995*

## LANGUAGE ARTS (MIDDLE SCHOOL) - HANDBOOKS, MANUALS, ETC.
Promoting literacy in grades 4-9. Boston ; London : Allyn and Bacon, c2000.
*TC LB1576 .P76 2000*

## LANGUAGE ARTS (MIDDLE SCHOOL) - STUDY AND TEACHING. *See* LANGUAGE ARTS (MIDDLE SCHOOL).

## LANGUAGE ARTS (MIDDLE SCHOOL) - UNITED STATES - HANDBOOKS, MANUALS, ETC.
Kingen, Sharon. Teaching language arts in middle schools. Mahwah, NJ : Lawrence Erlbaum, 2000.
*TC LB1631 .K493 2000*

## LANGUAGE ARTS - MIDDLE WEST - CASE STUDIES.
MacGregor-Mendoza, Patricia, 1963- Spanish and academic achievement among Midwest Mexican youth. New York ; London : Garland Pub., 1999.
*TC LC2686.4 .M33 1999*

## LANGUAGE ARTS (PRESCHOOL).
Jalongo, Mary Renck. Early childhood language arts. 2nd ed. Boston ; London : Allyn and Bacon, c2000.
*TC LB1140.5.L3 J35 2000*

Stewig, John W. Language arts in the early childhood classroom. Belmont [Calif.] : Wadsworth Pub. Co., c1995.
*TC LB1140.5.L3 S72 1995*

## LANGUAGE ARTS (PRESCHOOL) - GREAT BRITAIN.
Thompson, Linda, 1949- Young bilingual children in nursery school. Clevedon, UK ; Buffalo, NY : Multilingual Matters, c2000.
*TC LC3723 .T47 2000*

## LANGUAGE ARTS (PRESCHOOL) - STUDY AND TEACHING. *See* LANGUAGE ARTS (PRESCHOOL).

## LANGUAGE ARTS (PRESCHOOL) - UNITED STATES - CASE STUDIES.
Ballenger, Cynthia. Teaching other people's children. New York : Teachers College Press, c1999.
*TC LC3746 .B336 1999*

Meier, Daniel R. Scribble scrabble--teaching children to become successful readers and writers. New York : Teachers College Press, c2000.
*TC LB1140.5.L3 M45 2000*

Wilson, Catherine S. Telling a different story. New York ; London : Teachers College Press, c2000.
*TC LC5131 .W49 2000*

## LANGUAGE ARTS (PRIMARY).
Better together. New York : Macmillan/McGraw-Hill, c1997.
*TC LB1576 .S66 1997 Gr.2 l.6 u.3*

Community spirit. New York : Macmillan/McGraw-Hill, c1997.
*TC LB1576 .S66 1997 Gr.3 l.9 u.1*

Eureka. New York : Macmillan/McGraw-Hill, c1997.
*TC LB1576 .S66 1997 Gr.2 l.6 u.2*

Family album. New York : Macmillan/McGraw-Hill, c1997.
*TC LB1576 .S66 1997 Gr.3 l.8 u.3*

Family fun:. New York : Macmillan/McGraw-Hill, c1997.
*TC LB1576 .S66 1997 Gr.2 l.6 u.1*

Forces of nature. New York : Macmillan/McGraw-Hill, c1997.
*TC LB1576 .S66 1997 Gr.3 l.9 u.2*

Good thinking. New York : Macmillan/McGraw-Hill, c1997.
*TC LB1576 .S66 1997 Gr.3 l.8 u.1*

Hand in hand. New York : Macmillan/McGraw-Hill, c1997.
*TC LB1576 .S66 1997 Gr.2 l.7 u.2*

Let's pretend. New York : Macmillan/McGraw-Hill, c1997.
*TC LB1576 .S66 1997 Gr.1 l.5 u.1*

Opitz, Michael F. Rhymes & reasons. Portsmouth, NH : Heinemann, c2000.
*TC LB1528 .O65 2000*

Out and about. New York : Macmillan/McGraw-Hill, c1997.
*TC LB1576 .S66 1997 Gr.1 l.2*

Penpals. New York : Macmillan/McGraw-Hill, c1997.
*TC LB1576 .S66 1997 Gr.2 l.7 u.1*

Pocket chart kit [kit]. Chicago, Ill. : Open Court Publishing Company, c1995.
*TC LB1573.3 .P6 1995*

Read all about it. New York : Macmillan/McGraw-Hill, c1997.
*TC LB1576 .S66 1997 Gr.1 l.1*

See for yourself. New York : Macmillan/McGraw-Hill, c1997.
*TC LB1576 .S66 1997 Gr.3 l.8 u.2*

Something new. New York : Macmillan/McGraw-Hill, c1997.
*TC LB1576 .S66 1997 Gr.1 l.3*

Surprises along the way:. New York : Macmillan/McGraw-Hill, c1997.
*TC LB1576 .S66 1997 Gr.1 l.4 u.2*

Take a closer look. New York : Macmillan/McGraw-Hill, c1997.
*TC LB1576 .S66 1997 Gr.1 l.4 u.1*

Teamwork. New York : Macmillan/McGraw-Hill, c1997.

*TC LB1576 .S66 1997 Gr.3 l.9 u.3*

True-blue friends. New York : Macmillan/McGraw-Hill, c1997.
*TC LB1576 .S66 1997 Gr.1 l.5 u.2*

World of language. Morristown, N.J. : Silver Burdett Ginn, c1996.
*TC LB1576 .S4471 1996 Pict. Bks.*

## LANGUAGE ARTS (PRIMARY) - GREAT BRITAIN.
Into the enchanted forest. Stoke on Trent, Staffordshire : Trentham Books, 1999.
*TC LB1528 .I68 1999*

## LANGUAGE ARTS (PRIMARY) - STUDY AND TEACHING. *See* LANGUAGE ARTS (PRIMARY).

## LANGUAGE ARTS - REMEDIAL TEACHING.
Fahey, Kathleen R. Language development, differences, and disorders. Austin, Tex. : PRO-ED, c2000.
*TC LB1139.L3 F35 2000*

Miller, Wilma H. Strategies for developing emergent literacy. 1st ed. Boston : McGraw-Hill, c2000.
*TC LB1139.5.L35 M55 2000*

## LANGUAGE ARTS - REMEDIAL TEACHING - UNITED STATES.
Miller, Wilma H. Ready-to-use activities & materials for improving content reading skills. West Nyack, NY : Center For Applied Research in Education, c1999.
*TC LB1576 .M52 1999*

## LANGUAGE ARTS (SECONDARY) - EVALUATION.
Benjamin, Amy, 1951- English teacher's guide to performance tasks and rubrics, high school. Larchmont, N.Y. : Eye On Education, 2000.
*TC LB1631 .B383 2000*

## LANGUAGE ARTS (SECONDARY) - SOCIAL ASPECTS - UNITED STATES.
Reconceptualizing the literacies in adolescents' lives. Mahwah, N.J. : L. Erlbaum Associates, 1998.
*TC LB1631 .R296 1998*

## LANGUAGE ARTS (SECONDARY) - STUDY AND TEACHING. *See* LANGUAGE ARTS (SECONDARY).

## LANGUAGE ARTS (SECONDARY) - UNITED STATES.
Allan, Karen Kuelthau. Literacy and learning. Boston : Houghton Mifflin, c2000.
*TC LB1631 .A37 2000*

Brozo, William G. Readers, teachers, learners. 3rd ed. Upper Saddle River, N.J. : Merrill, c1999.
*TC LB1632 .B7 1999*

Christenbury, Leila. Making the journey. 2nd ed. Portsmouth, NH : Boynton/Cook Publishers, c2000.
*TC LB1631 .C4486 2000*

## LANGUAGE ARTS (SECONDARY) - UNITED STATES - CONGRESSES.
A middle mosaic. Urbana, Ill. : National Council of Teachers of English, c2000.
*TC LB1631 .A2 2000*

## LANGUAGE ARTS - SOCIAL ASPECTS - UNITED STATES.
The literacy connection. Cresskill, N.J. : Hampton Press, c1999.
*TC LC151 .L482 1999*

## LANGUAGE ARTS - STANDARDS - UNITED STATES.
Lockwood, Anne Turnbaugh. Standards. Thousand Oaks, Calif. : Corwin Press, c1998.
*TC LB3060.83 .L63 1998*

Standards-based K-12 language arts curriculum. Boston : Allyn and Bacon, c2000.
*TC LB1576 .S747 2000*

## LANGUAGE ARTS - STUDY AND TEACHING. *See* LANGUAGE ARTS.

## LANGUAGE ARTS - STUDY AND TEACHING (EARLY CHILDHOOD). *See* LANGUAGE ARTS (EARLY CHILDHOOD).

## LANGUAGE ARTS - STUDY AND TEACHING (ELEMENTARY). *See* LANGUAGE ARTS (ELEMENTARY).

## LANGUAGE ARTS - STUDY AND TEACHING (MIDDLE SCHOOL). *See* LANGUAGE ARTS (MIDDLE SCHOOL).

## LANGUAGE ARTS - STUDY AND TEACHING (PRESCHOOL). *See* LANGUAGE ARTS (PRESCHOOL).

## LANGUAGE ARTS - STUDY AND TEACHING (PRIMARY). *See* LANGUAGE ARTS (PRIMARY).

## LANGUAGE ARTS - STUDY AND TEACHING (SECONDARY). *See* LANGUAGE ARTS (SECONDARY).

## LANGUAGE ARTS TEACHERS - HANDBOOKS, MANUALS, ETC.
Adams, Arlene. Handbook for literacy tutors. Springfield, Ill. : C.C. Thomas, Publisher, c1999.
*TC LB1576 .A3893 1999*

## LANGUAGE ARTS - UNITED STATES.
Asian-American education. Westport, Conn. : Bergin & Garvey, 1999.
*TC LC2632 .A847 1999*

Harwayne, Shelley. Lifetime guarantees. Portsmouth, NH : Heinemann, c2000.
*TC LB1575 . H38 2000*

Standards-based K-12 language arts curriculum. Boston : Allyn and Bacon, c2000.
*TC LB1576 .S747 2000*

## LANGUAGE AWARENESS IN CHILDREN.
Blachman, Benita A. Road to the code. Baltimore : Paul H. Brookes, c2000.
*TC LB1139.L3 B53 2000*

## Language change.
Aitchison, Jean, 1938- 2nd ed. Cambridge [England] ; New York : Cambridge University Press, 1991.
*TC P142 .A37 1991*

## Language, culture, and cognition
(1) Language and conceptualization. 1st paperback ed. Cambridge [England] ; New York : Cambridge University Press, 1999.
*TC P37 .L354 1999*

## Language, culture, and curriculum.
Indigenous community-based education. Clevedon [England] ; Philadelphia : Multilingual Matters, c1999.
*TC LC1036 .I43 1999*

## LANGUAGE DATA PROCESSING. *See* COMPUTATIONAL LINGUISTICS.

## Language development and social interaction in blind children.
Pérez Pereira, Miguel. Hove, UK : Psychology Press, c1999.
*TC P118 .P37 1999*

## Language development, differences, and disorders.
Fahey, Kathleen R. Austin, Tex. : PRO-ED, c2000.
*TC LB1139.L3 F35 2000*

## LANGUAGE DEVELOPMENT DISORDERS - PHYSIOPATHOLOGY.
Love, Russell J. Childhood motor speech disability. 2nd ed. Boston ; London : Allyn and Bacon, c2000.
*TC RJ496.S7 L68 2000*

## LANGUAGE DEVELOPMENT IN CHILDREN. *See also* CHILDREN - LANGUAGE; LANGUAGE ACQUISITION.
Specific language impairment in children. Hillsdale, N.J. : Lawrence Erlbaum , 1998.
*TC RJ496.L35 S643 1998*

## Language, discourse, society.
Safouan, Moustafa. [Jacques Lacan et la question de la formation des analystes. English] Jacques Lacan and the question of psychoanalytic training. New York : St. Martin's Press, 2000.
*TC BF173.L15 S2414 2000*

## LANGUAGE DISORDERS. *See also* APHASIA; DYSLEXIA.
Augmentative and alternative communication. London : Whurr, 1999.
*TC RC429 .A94 1999*

Crystal, David, 1941- Introduction to language pathology. 4th ed. London : Whurr Publishers, c1998.
*TC RC423 .C76 1998*

## LANGUAGE DISORDERS.
Diagnosis in speech-language pathology. 2nd ed. San Diego : Singular, c2000.
*TC RC423 .D473 2000*

## LANGUAGE DISORDERS.
Vinson, Betsy Partin. Language disorders across the lifespan. San Diego : Singular Pub. Group, c1999.
*TC RC423 .V56 1999*

## Language disorders across the lifespan.
Vinson, Betsy Partin. San Diego : Singular Pub. Group, c1999.
*TC RC423 .V56 1999*

## LANGUAGE DISORDERS - CONGRESSES.
New directions in language development and disorders. New York : Kluwer Academic/Plenum Publishers, c2000.
*TC P118 .N49 2000*

## LANGUAGE DISORDERS - DICTIONARIES.
Singh, Sadanand. Illustrated dictionary of speech-language pathology. San Diego : Singular Pub. Group, c2000.
*TC RC423 .S533 2000*

## LANGUAGE DISORDERS - DICTIONARY - ENGLISH.
Singh, Sadanand. Illustrated dictionary of speech-language pathology. San Diego : Singular Pub. Group, c2000.
*TC RC423 .S533 2000*

## LANGUAGE DISORDERS IN ADOLESCENCE.
Nelson, Nickola. Childhood language disorders in context. 2nd ed. Boston : Allyn & Bacon, c1998.
*TC RJ496.L35 N46 1998*

Vinson, Betsy Partin. Language disorders across the lifespan. San Diego : Singular Pub. Group, c1999.
*TC RC423 .V56 1999*

## LANGUAGE DISORDERS IN CHILDREN.
Fahey, Kathleen R. Language development, differences, and disorders. Austin, Tex. : PRO-ED, c2000.
*TC LB1139.L3 F35 2000*

Nelson, Nickola. Childhood language disorders in context. 2nd ed. Boston : Allyn & Bacon, c1998.
*TC RJ496.L35 N46 1998*

Slingerland, Beth H. A multi-sensory approach to language arts for specific language disability children. Cambridge, Mass. : Educators Pub. Service, c1976-<c1981 >
*TC LC4704.85 .S59 1976*

Specific language impairment in children. Hillsdale, N.J. : Lawrence Erlbaum , 1998.
*TC RJ496.L35 S643 1998*

Vinson, Betsy Partin. Language disorders across the lifespan. San Diego : Singular Pub. Group, c1999.
*TC RC423 .V56 1999*

## LANGUAGE DISORDERS IN CHILDREN - CASE STUDIES.
Chiat, Shula. Understanding children with language problems. Oxford [England] ; New York : Cambridge University Press, 2000.
*TC RJ496.L35 C46 2000*

## LANGUAGE DISORDERS IN OLD AGE.
Vinson, Betsy Partin. Language disorders across the lifespan. San Diego : Singular Pub. Group, c1999.
*TC RC423 .V56 1999*

## LANGUAGE DISORDERS - RESEARCH - METHODOLOGY.
Methods for studying language production. Mahwah, N.J. : Lawrence Erlbaum Associates, 2000.
*TC P118 .M47 2000*

## LANGUAGE DISORDERS - THERAPY.
Klein, Harriet B. Intervention planning for adults with communication problems : Volume 2. Boston : Allyn and Bacon, c1999.
*TC RC423 .K57 1999*

Measuring outcomes in speech-language pathology. New York : Thieme, 1998.
*TC RC423 .M39 1997*

## Language, education, and culture.
Rahman, Tariq. Islamabad : Sustainable Development Policy Institute ; Karachi : Oxford Uinversity Press, 1999.
*TC P119.32.P18 R35 1999*

## LANGUAGE EXPERIENCE APPROACH IN EDUCATION. *See also* READING - LANGUAGE EXPERIENCE APPROACH.
The changing face of whole language. Newark, Del. : International Reading Association ; Victoria, Australia : Australian Literacy Educators' Association, c1997.
*TC LB1050.35 .C43 1997*

Making justice our project. Urbana, Ill. : National Council of Teachers of English, c1999
*TC LB1576 .M3613 1999*

Mikkelsen, Nina. Words and pictures. Boston : McGraw-Hill, c2000.

*TC LB1575 .M55 2000*

**LANGUAGE EXPERIENCE APPROACH IN EDUCATION - LONGITUDINAL STUDIES.**
Painter, Clare, 1947- Learning through language in early childhood. London ; New York : Cassell, 1999.
*TC LB1139.5.L35 P35 1999*

**LANGUAGE EXPERIENCE APPROACH IN EDUCATION - UNITED STATES.**
Fredericks, Anthony D. More social studies through children's literature. Englewood, Colo. : Teacher Ideas Press, 2000.
*TC LB1584 .F659 2000*

Rogovin, Paula. Classroom interviews. Portsmouth, NH : Heinemann, c1998.
*TC LB1537 .R58 1998*

**LANGUAGE FOR SPECIAL PURPOSES.** *See* **SUBLANGUAGE.**

**Language in society (Oxford, England)**
Chambers, J. K. Sociolinguistic theory. Oxford, UK ; Cambridge, Mass., USA : Blackwell, 1995.
*TC P40 .C455 1995*

(23.) Stubbs, Michael, 1947- Text and corpus analysis. Oxford, OX, UK ; Cambridge, Mass., USA : Blackwell Publishers, c1996.
*TC P302 .S773 1996*

**Language issues :** readings for teachers / [edited by] Diane Bennett Durkin. White Plains, N.Y. : Longman Publishers USA, c1995. xi, 484 p. : ill., maps ; 24 cm. Includes bibliographical references and index. ISBN 0-8013-0951-4 DDC 418
*1. Language and languages - Study and teaching. I. Durkin, Diane Bennett.*
*TC P51 .L346 1995*

**Language knowledge for primary teachers.**
Wilson, Angela. London : David Fulton, 1999.
*TC LB1576 .W557 1999*

**Language learning online :** theory and practice in the ESL and L2 computer classroom / edited by Janet Swaffar ... [et al.]. Austin : Labyrinth Publications, c1998. 200 p. : ill. ; 23 cm. Includes bibliographical references and index. ISBN 1-89143-011-4 (pbk.) ISBN 1-89143-012-2 (electronic format) DDC 428/.0078/5
*1. English language - Study and teaching - Foreign speakers - Data processing. 2. Second language acquisition - Computer-assisted instruction. 3. English language - Computer-assisted instruction. 4. Online data processing. I. Swaffar, Janet K.*
*TC PE1128.A2 L2955 1998*

**LANGUAGE PLANNING.** *See also* **LANGUAGE POLICY.**
Language policy and pedagogy. Philadelphia : J. Benjamins, c2000.
*TC P53 .L364 2000*

Rights to language. Mahwah, N.J. : L. Erlbaum Associates, 2000.
*TC P119.3 .R54 2000*

**LANGUAGE POLICY.**
Language policy and pedagogy. Philadelphia : J. Benjamins, c2000.
*TC P53 .L364 2000*

Rights to language. Mahwah, N.J. : L. Erlbaum Associates, 2000.
*TC P119.3 .R54 2000*

Skutnabb-Kangas, Tove. Linguistic genocide in education, or worldwide diversity and human rights? Mahwah, N.J. : L. Erlbaum Associates, 2000.
*TC P40.8 .S58 2000*

**Language policy and pedagogy :** essays in honor of A. Ronald Walton / edited by Richard D. Lambert, Elana Shohamy. Philadelphia : J. Benjamins, c2000. xii, 279 p. : ill. ; 23 cm. Includes bibliographical references and index. ISBN 1-55619-763-2 (alk. paper) DDC 418/.007
*1. Language and languages - Study and teaching. 2. Language policy. 3. Language planning. I. Lambert, Richard D. II. Shohamy, Elana Goldberg. III. Walton, A. Ronald.*
*TC P53 .L364 2000*

**LANGUAGE POLICY - ASIA - CONGRESSES.**
Bilingualism Through the Classroom : Strategies and Practices (1995 : Universiti Brunei Darussalam) Bilingualism through the classroom : strategies and practices. [Bandar Seri Begawan : Universiti Brunei Darussalam, 1995]
*TC P115 .B57 1995*

**LANGUAGE POLICY - CONGRESSES.**
Bilingualism Through the Classroom : Strategies and Practices (1995 : Universiti Brunei Darussalam) Bilingualism through the classroom : strategies and practices. [Bandar Seri Begawan : Universiti Brunei Darussalam, 1995]

*TC P115 .B57 1995*

**LANGUAGE POLICY - DEVELOPING COUNTRIES - CONGRESSES.**
Linguistic minorities and literacy. Berlin ; New York : Mouton Publishers, 1984.
*TC P119.315 .L56 1984*

**LANGUAGE POLICY - PAKISTAN.**
Rahman, Tariq. Language, education, and culture. Islamabad : Sustainable Development Policy Institute ; Karachi : Oxford Uinversity Press, 1999.
*TC P119.32.P18 R35 1999*

**Language, power, and pedagogy.**
Cummins, Jim, 1949- Clevedon [England] ; Buffalo [N.Y.] : Multilingual Matters, c2000.
*TC LC3719 .C86 2000*

**Language, power, and social process**
(1) Talk, work, and institutional order. Berlin ; New York : Mouton de Gruyter, 1999.
*TC P95 .T286 1999*

**LANGUAGE SCHOOLS.** *See* **LANGUAGE AND LANGUAGES - STUDY AND TEACHING; LANGUAGES, MODERN - STUDY AND TEACHING.**

**Language sciences.**
Language sciences. Bloomington, Indiana University Research Center for the Language Sciences.

**Language sciences.** Bloomington, Indiana University Research Center for the Language Sciences. 48 no. ill. 27 cm. Frequency: 5 no. a year. no. 1-48; May 1968-1977. Author index: No. 1-10, May 1968-Apr. 1970, in no. 11. Continued by: Language sciences. ISSN 0023-8341
*I. Indiana University. Research Center for the Language Sciences. II. Title: Language sciences*

**Language, speech, and communication.**
Converging methods for understanding reading and dyslexia. Cambridge, Mass. ; London : MIT Press, c1999.
*TC LB1050.5 .C662 1999*

The syntax of American Sign Language. Cambridge, Mass. : MIT Press, c2000.
*TC HV2474 .S994 2000*

**LANGUAGE TEACHERS.** *See* **ENGLISH TEACHERS.**

**LANGUAGE TEACHERS - TRAINING OF.**
Grenfell, Michael, 1953- Training teachers in practice. Clevedon, UK ; Philadelphia : Multilingual Matters, c1998.
*TC P53.85 .G74 1998*

On becoming a language educator. Mahwah, NJ : Lawrence Erlbaum, 1997.
*TC P53.85 .O5 1997*

**LANGUAGE TEACHERS - TRAINING OF - UNITED STATES.**
Preparing a nation's teachers. New York : Modern Language Association of America, 1999.
*TC PE68.U5 P74 1999*

**The language teaching matrix.**
Richards, Jack C. Cambridge [England] ; New York : Cambridge University Press, 1990.
*TC P51 .R48 1990*

**Language testing and evaluation.**
Allison, Desmond. Singapore : Singapore University Press ; Singapore ; River Edge, N.J. : World Scientific, c1999.
*TC P53.4 .A45 1999*

**Language transfer in language learning** / edited by Susan M. Gass, Larry Selinker. Rev. ed. with corrections. Amsterdam ; Philadelphia : J. Benjamins Pub. Co., 1994. 236 p. : ill. ; 23 cm. (Language acquisition & language disorders, 0925-0123 ; v. 5) Includes bibliographical references. ISBN 90-272-2469-2 (Eur.) ISBN 1-55619-241-X (Hb. : alk. paper) ISBN 90-272-2476-5 (Eur.) ISBN 1-55619-248-7 (pbk. : alk. paper)
*1. Language transfer (Language learning) 2. Interlanguage (Language learning) 3. Second language acquisition. I. Gass, Susan M. II. Selinker, Larry, 1937- III. Series.*
*TC P118.25 .L36 1994*

**LANGUAGE TRANSFER (LANGUAGE LEARNING).** *See also* **INTERFERENCE (LINGUISTICS).**
Language transfer in language learning. Rev. ed. with corrections. Amsterdam ; Philadelphia : J. Benjamins Pub. Co., 1994.
*TC P118.25 .L36 1994*

O'Riordan, Mary. Strategic use of transfer and explicit linguistic knowledge. 1998.

*TC 06 no. 10975*

**Language workbooks**
Peccei, Jean Stilwell. Child language. 2nd ed. London ; New York : Routledge, 1999.
*TC P118 .P38 1999*

**LANGUAGES.** *See* **LANGUAGE AND LANGUAGES.**

**LANGUAGES, FOREIGN.** *See* **LANGUAGES, MODERN.**

**LANGUAGES IN CONTACT.** *See* **BILINGUALISM.**

**LANGUAGES, LIVING.** *See* **LANGUAGES, MODERN.**

**LANGUAGES, MIXED.** *See* **INTERLANGUAGE (LANGUAGE LEARNING).**

**LANGUAGES, MODERN - STUDY AND TEACHING.**
Chambers, Gary N., 1956- Motivating language learners. Clevedon [U.K.] ; Buffalo : Multilingual Matters, c1999.
*TC PB35 .C517 1999*

Grenfell, Michael, 1953- Modern languages and learning strategies. London ; New York : Routledge, 1999.
*TC PB35 .G783 1999*

Roberts, J. T. (John T.) Two French language teaching reformers reassessed. Lewiston [N.Y.] : E. Mellen Press, c1999.
*TC PB35 .R447 1999*

Teaching modern foreign languages at advanced level. London ; New York : Routledge, 1999.
*TC PB35 .T42 1999*

Writing across languages. Stamford, Conn. : Ablex Pub., c2000.
*TC PB36 .W77 2000*

**LANGUAGES, MODERN - STUDY AND TEACHING - EUROPE.**
Introducing learner autonomy in teacher education. Strasbourg : Council of Europe Pub., c1999.
*TC PB38.E8 I567 1999*

Learner autonomy. Strasbourg : Council of Europe Pub., c1999.
*TC PB38.E8 L424 1999*

**LANGUAGES, NATIONAL.** *See* **LANGUAGE POLICY.**

**LANGUAGES, OFFICIAL.** *See* **LANGUAGE POLICY.**

**LANGUE D'OÏL.** *See* **FRENCH LANGUAGE.**

**Lanker, Brian.**
Sport photography today! [videorecording]. Minneapolis, Minn. : Media Loft, c1992.
*TC TR821 .S64 1992*

**Lanning, Greg.**
Our friends at the bank [videorecording]. New York, NY : First Run/Icarus Films, 1997.
*TC HG3881.5.W57 O87 1997*

**Lannon, Richard.**
Lewis, Thomas. A general theory of love. New York : Random House, 2000.
*TC BF575.L8 L49 2000*

**Lanterns.**
Edelman, Marian Wright. Boston : Beacon Press, c1999.
*TC E185.97.E33 A3 1999*

**Lanzer, Mona E.**
Basic English [videorecording]. [Roslyn Heights, N.Y.] : Video Aided Instruction, [c1995].
*TC PE1128 .B3 1995*

Intermediate English [videorecording]. [Roslyn Heights, N.Y.] : Video Aided Instruction, [c1995].
*TC PE1128 .I5 1995*

**Lanzer, Peter.**
Basic English [videorecording]. [Roslyn Heights, N.Y.] : Video Aided Instruction, [c1995].
*TC PE1128 .B3 1995*

Intermediate English [videorecording]. [Roslyn Heights, N.Y.] : Video Aided Instruction, [c1995].
*TC PE1128 .I5 1995*

**LaPidus, Jules B.**
Postbaccalaureate futures. Phoenix, AZ : Oryx Press, 2000.
*TC LB2371.4 .P68 2000*

**LARGE ANIMAL MEDICINE.** *See* **VETERINARY MEDICINE.**

**LARGE ANIMAL VETERINARIANS.** *See* **VETERINARIANS.**

**LARGE ANIMAL VETERINARY MEDICINE.** *See* **VETERINARY MEDICINE.**

**LARGE TYPE BOOKS.**
White, Gillian, 1945- The plague stone. Large print ed. Thorndike, Me., USA : G.K. Hall ; Bath, Avon, England : Chivers Press, 1996, c1990.
*TC PR6073.H4925 P58 1996*

**LARIDAE.** *See* **GULLS.**

**Larimore, Victoria.**
The Amish [videorecording]. Oak Forest, IL : MPI Home Video, 1988.

The Amish [videorecording]. Oak Forest, Ill. : MPI Home Video, c1988.
*TC BX8129.A5 A5 1988*

**LARINAE.** *See* **GULLS.**

**Larsen, Eric.**
Hill, Clifford. Children and reading tests. Stamford, Conn. : Ablex Pub. Corp., c2000.
*TC LB1050.46 .H55 2000*

**Larson, Edward J. (Edward John)** Summer for the gods : the Scopes trial and America's continuing debate over science and religion / Edward J. Larson. New York : BasicBooks, c1997. x, 318 p. : ill. ; 25 cm. Includes bibliographical references (p. 267-305) and index. ISBN 0-465-07509-6 DDC 345.73/0288
*1. Scopes, John Thomas - Trials, litigation, etc. 2. Evolution - Study and teaching - Law and legislation - United States. I. Title.*
*TC KF224.S3 L37 1997*

**Larson, Greg.**
Ballet class [videorecording]. W. Long Branch, NJ : Kultur, c1984.
*TC GV1589 .B33 1984*

**Larson, Reed W.**
Homeless and working youth around the world. San Francisco : Jossey-Bass, 1999.
*TC HV4493 .H655 1999*

**LARYNX.** *See also* **VOICE.**
The Artificial larynx handbook. New York : Grune & Stratton, c1978.
*TC RF538 .A77*

**LARYNX - DISEASES.** *See also* **VOICE DISORDERS.**
Boone, Daniel R. The voice and voice therapy. 6th ed. Boston : London : Allyn & Bacon, c2000.
*TC RF540 .B66 2000*

**LAS POSADAS (SOCIAL CUSTOM).** *See* **POSADAS (SOCIAL CUSTOM).**

**Lashley, Felissa R.**
**Clinical genetics in nursing practice.**
Lashley, Felissa R., 1941- Clinical genetics in nursing practice. 2nd ed. New York : Springer, c1998.
*TC RB155 .L37 1998*

**Lashley, Felissa R., 1941-** Clinical genetics in nursing practice / by Felissa R. (Cohen) Lashley. 2nd ed. New York : Springer, c1998. xvi, 543 p. : ill. ; 27 cm. Includes bibliographical references and index. ISBN 0-8261-1177-7 DDC 616/.042/024613
*1. Medical genetics. 2. Nursing. 3. Genetics, Medical - nurses' instruction. 4. Hereditary Diseases - nurses' instruction. I. Lashley, Felissa R. Clinical genetics in nursing practice. II. Title.*
*TC RB155 .L37 1998*

**Lashway, Larry.** Measuring leadership : a guide to assessment for development of school executives / Larry Lashway ; foreword by Kenneth Leithwood. Eugene, OR : ERIC Clearinghouse on Educational Management, University of Oregon, 1999. viii, 120 p. : ill. ; 23 cm. Includes bibliographical references (p. 117-119). ISBN 0-86552-140-9 DDC 371.2/00973
*1. Educational leadership - United States. 2. School management and organization - United States. I. Title.*
*TC LB2806 .L28 1999*

**Laskin, Emma.**
Gardner, Howard. Leading minds. New York, NY : BasicBooks, c1995.
*TC HM141 .G35 1995*

**Lasky, Kathryn.** Star split / Kathryn Lasky. 1st ed. New York : Hyperion Books for Children, 1999. 203 p. 22 cm. SUMMARY: In 3038, thirteen-year-old Darci uncovers an underground movement to save the human race from genetic enhancement technology. ISBN 0-7868-0459-9 (trade : alk.

paper) ISBN 0-7868-2401-8 (lib. : alk. paper) DDC [Fic]
*1. Genetic engineering - Fiction. 2. Cloning - fiction. 3. Science fiction. I. Title.*
*TC PZ7.L3274 St 1999*

**Lassen, Inger.**
Interactional perspectives on LSP. Aalborg Øst, Denmark : Centre for Languages and Intercultural Studies, Aalborg University, 1997.
*TC P120.S9 I58 1997*

**The last British liberals in Africa.**
Mungazi, Dickson A. Westport, Conn. : Praeger, 1999.
*TC DT2979.T63 M86 1999*

**The last choice.**
Prado, C. G. 2nd ed. Westport, Conn. : Greenwood Press, 1998.
*TC HV6545.2 .P7 1998*

**Latash, Mark L., 1953-** Neurophysiological basis of movement / Mark L. Latash. Champaign, IL : Human Kinetics, c1998. x, 269 p. : ill. ; 29 cm. Includes bibliographical references and index. ISBN 0-88011-756-7 DDC 612.7/6
*1. Locomotion. 2. Neurophysiology. 3. Motor ability. 4. Movement disorders. I. Title.*
*TC QP301 .L364 1998*

**Latchem, C. R. (Colin R.).**
Staff development in open and flexible learning. London ; New York : Routledge, 1998.
*TC LC5800 .S83 1998*

**LATERALITY.**
Aphasia in atypical populations. Mahwah, N.J. : Lawrence Erlbaum Associates, 1998.
*TC RC425 .A637 1998*

Myers, Penelope S. Right hemisphere damage. San Diego : Singular Pub., c1999.
*TC RC423 .M83 1999*

**Lathem, Edward Connery.**
Miraculously builded in our hearts. Hanover : Dartmouth University Press, 1999.
*TC LD1438 .M573 1999*

**Lathlean, Judith.**
Binnie, Alison. Freedom to practise. Oxford ; Boston : Butterworth-Heinemann, 1999.
*TC RT41 .B56 1999*

**Lathrop, Ann.** Student cheating and plagiarism in the Internet era : a wake-up call / Ann Lathrop and Kathleen Foss. Englewood, Colo. : Libraries Unlimited, 2000. xiv, 255 p. ; 24 cm. Includes bibliographical references (p. 227-238) and index. ISBN 1-56308-841-X (pbk.) DDC 371.5/8
*1. Cheating (Education) 2. Internet in education. I. Foss, Kathleen E. II. Title.*
*TC LB3609 .L28 2000*

**Latimer, Leah Y.** Higher ground : preparing African-American children for college / Leah Y. Latimer ; foreword by Johnnetta B. Cole. New York : Avon Books, c1999. xii, 308 p. ; 21 cm. Includes bibliographical references (p. 299-300) and index. ISBN 0-380-79919-7 (pbk.)
*1. Afro-Americans - Education (Higher) 2. Afro-Americans students. 3. Universities and colleges - United States - Admission. I. Title.*
*TC LC2781 .L27 1999*

**LATIN AMERICANS.** *See* **MESTIZOS.**

**LATIN AMERICANS - UNITED STATES.** *See* **HISPANIC AMERICANS.**

**Latin for Americans. First book.**
Ullman, B. L. (Berthold Louis), 1882-1965. 7th ed. Woodland Hills, Calif. : Glencoe, c1990.
*TC PA2087.5 .U339 1990*

Ullman, B. L. (Berthold Louis), 1882-1965. 7th ed. Woodland Hills, Calif. : Glencoe, c1990.
*TC PA2087.5 .U339 1990 First Book*

**Latin for Americans. Second book.**
Ullman, B. L. (Berthold Louis), 1882-1965. 7th ed. Mission Hills, Calif. : Glencoe, c1990.
*TC PA2087.5 .U339 1990 Teacher's Guide*

Ullman, B. L. (Berthold Louis), 1882-1965. 7th ed. Mission Hills, Calif. : Glencoe, c1990.
*TC PA2087.5 .U339 1990*

Ullman, B. L. (Berthold Louis), 1882-1965. 7th ed. Mission Hills, Calif. : Glencoe, c1990.
*TC PA2087.5 .U339 1990 Third Book*

Ullman, B. L. (Berthold Louis), 1882-1965. 7th ed. Mission Hills, Calif. : Glencoe, c1990.

*TC PA2087.5 .U339 1990 Second Book*

**Latin for Americans. Third book.**
Ullman, B. L. (Berthold Louis), 1882-1965. 7th ed. Mission Hills, Calif. : Glencoe, a division of Macmillan Pub. Co., c1990.
*TC PA2087.5 .U399 1990*

**LATIN LANGUAGE.** *See* **CLASSICAL PHILOLOGY.**

**LATIN LANGUAGE - GRAMMAR.**
Jenney, Charles. First year Latin workbook. Newton, Mass. : Allyn and Bacon, c1987.
*TC PA2087.5 .J46 1987*

Jenney, Charles. Fourth year Latin. Needham, Mass. : Prentice Hall, c1990.
*TC PA2087.5 .J463 1990*

Jenney, Charles. Jenney's first year Latin. Needham, Mass. : Prentice Hall, c1990.
*TC PA2087.5 .J46 1990*

Jenney, Charles. Jenney's second year Latin. Newton, Mass. : Allyn and Bacon, c1987.
*TC PA2087.5 .J461 1987*

Ullman, B. L. (Berthold Louis), 1882-1965. Latin for Americans. First book. 7th ed. Woodland Hills, Calif. : Glencoe, c1990.
*TC PA2087.5 .U339 1990*

Ullman, B. L. (Berthold Louis), 1882-1965. Latin for Americans. First book. 7th ed. Woodland Hills, Calif. : Glencoe, c1990.
*TC PA2087.5 .U339 1990 First Book*

Ullman, B. L. (Berthold Louis), 1882-1965. Latin for Americans. Second book. 7th ed. Mission Hills, Calif. : Glencoe, c1990.
*TC PA2087.5 .U339 1990 Teacher's Guide*

Ullman, B. L. (Berthold Louis), 1882-1965. Latin for Americans. Second book. 7th ed. Mission Hills, Calif. : Glencoe, c1990.
*TC PA2087.5 .U339 1990*

Ullman, B. L. (Berthold Louis), 1882-1965. Latin for Americans. Second book. 7th ed. Mission Hills, Calif. : Glencoe, c1990.
*TC PA2087.5 .U339 1990 Third Book*

Ullman, B. L. (Berthold Louis), 1882-1965. Latin for Americans. Second book. 7th ed. Mission Hills, Calif. : Glencoe, c1990.
*TC PA2087.5 .U339 1990 Second Book*

Ullman, B. L. (Berthold Louis), 1882-1965. Latin for Americans. Third book. 7th ed. Mission Hills, Calif. : Glencoe, a division of Macmillan Pub. Co., c1990.
*TC PA2087.5 .U399 1990*

**LATIN LANGUAGE - READERS.**
Jenney, Charles. Third year Latin. Newton, Mass. : Allyn and Bacon, c1987.
*TC PA2087.5 .J462 1987*

Ullman, B. L. (Berthold Louis), 1882-1965. Latin for Americans. First book. 7th ed. Woodland Hills, Calif. : Glencoe, c1990.
*TC PA2087.5 .U339 1990*

Ullman, B. L. (Berthold Louis), 1882-1965. Latin for Americans. First book. 7th ed. Woodland Hills, Calif. : Glencoe, c1990.
*TC PA2087.5 .U339 1990 First Book*

Ullman, B. L. (Berthold Louis), 1882-1965. Latin for Americans. Second book. 7th ed. Mission Hills, Calif. : Glencoe, c1990.
*TC PA2087.5 .U339 1990 Teacher's Guide*

Ullman, B. L. (Berthold Louis), 1882-1965. Latin for Americans. Second book. 7th ed. Mission Hills, Calif. : Glencoe, c1990.
*TC PA2087.5 .U339 1990*

Ullman, B. L. (Berthold Louis), 1882-1965. Latin for Americans. Second book. 7th ed. Mission Hills, Calif. : Glencoe, c1990.
*TC PA2087.5 .U339 1990 Third Book*

Ullman, B. L. (Berthold Louis), 1882-1965. Latin for Americans. Second book. 7th ed. Mission Hills, Calif. : Glencoe, c1990.
*TC PA2087.5 .U339 1990 Second Book*

Ullman, B. L. (Berthold Louis), 1882-1965. Latin for Americans. Third book. 7th ed. Mission Hills, Calif. : Glencoe, a division of Macmillan Pub. Co., c1990.
*TC PA2087.5 .U399 1990*

**LATIN LANGUAGE - STUDY AND TEACHING - PERIODICALS.**
Latin teaching. [Shrewsbury, Eng.? : Association for the Reform of Latin Teaching], -1986.

**LATIN LITERATURE.** _See_ **CLASSICAL PHILOLOGY.**

**LATIN PHILOLOGY.** _See_ **CLASSICAL PHILOLOGY; LATIN LANGUAGE.**

**Latin teaching.** [Shrewsbury, Eng.? : Association for the Reform of Latin Teaching],    -1986. v. ; 21 cm. Frequency: Annual, <1979>-1986. Began in 1913. Cf. Union list of serials. -v. 37 [i.e. v. 36], no. 6 (1986). Description based on: Vol. 35, no. 6 (1979); title from cover. ISSN 0023-8821 DDC 478/.07
_1. Latin language - Study and teaching - Periodicals. I. Association for the Reform of Latin Teaching._

**Latino communities**
MacGregor-Mendoza, Patricia, 1963- Spanish and academic achievement among Midwest Mexican youth. New York ; London : Garland Pub., 1999.
_TC LC2686.4 .M33 1999_

Trujillo, Armando L. Chicano empowerment and bilingual education. New York : Garland Pub., c1998.
_TC LC2688.C79 T78 1998_

**LATINOS (UNITED STATES).** _See_ **HISPANIC AMERICANS.**

**Látni tanulunk.**
Kárpáti, Andrea, Budapest : Akadémiai Kiadó, 1991.
_TC N85 .K35 1991_

**Lau, Linda, 1958-.**
Distance learning technologies. Hershey, PA ; London : Idea Group Pub., c2000.
_TC LC5803.C65 D57 2000_

**LAUGHTER - DATA PROCESSING.**
Jones, Carl Mounsey. The film-audience relationship. 1997.
_TC 06 no. 10769_

Jones, Carl Mounsey. The film-audience relationship. 1997.
_TC 06 no. 10769_

**LAUGHTER - FICTION.**
Stevenson, James, 1929- Don't make me laugh. 1st ed. New York : Farrar, Straus and Giroux, c1999.
_TC PZ7.S84748 Do 1999_

**LAUGHTER - PHYSIOLOGICAL ASPECTS.**
Davis, D. Diane (Debra Diane), 1963- Breaking up (at) totality. Carbondale : Southern Illinois University Press, c2000.
_TC PE1404 .D385 2000_

**LAUGHTER - PSYCHOLOGICAL ASPECTS.**
Davis, D. Diane (Debra Diane), 1963- Breaking up (at) totality. Carbondale : Southern Illinois University Press, c2000.
_TC PE1404 .D385 2000_

**LAUGHTER - SOCIAL ASPECTS.**
Davis, D. Diane (Debra Diane), 1963- Breaking up (at) totality. Carbondale : Southern Illinois University Press, c2000.
_TC PE1404 .D385 2000_

**Laupa, Marta.**
Rights and wrongs. San Francisco, [CA] : Jossey-Bass, c2000.
_TC BF723.M54 L38 2000_

**Laurence, David Ernst.**
Preparing a nation's teachers. New York : Modern Language Association of America, 1999.
_TC PE68.U5 P74 1999_

**Laurie, Donald L.** The real work of leaders : a report from the front lines of management / Donald L. Laurie. Cambridge, Mass. : Perseus Pub.. 2000. xiv. 203 p. ; 25 cm. Includes bibliographical references (p. 191-194) and index. CONTENTS: pt. 1. A leader's real time. 1. What should leaders do? -- 2. How should leaders do what they do? -- pt. 2. A leader's real role. 3. The seven essential acts of leadership -- 4. Stand back and see -- 5. Communicate what is real -- 6. Clarify competing values -- 7. Support change in values -- 8. Promote dialogue -- 9. Regulate distress -- 10. Make everyone collectively responsible -- 11. Questions and answers -- Epilogue : the value leaders add. ISBN 0-7382-0249-5
_1. Leadership. 2. Management. I. Title._
_TC HD57.7 .L387 2000_

**Lava, Valerie Forkin.** Early intervention : experiences of families and professionals / by Valery Forkin Lava. 1998. xii, 460 leaves ; 29 cm. Typescript; issued also on microfilm. Thesis (Ed.D.) -- Teachers College, Columbia University, 1998. Includes bibliographical references (leaves 425-442).
_1. Handicapped children - Services for - Case studies. 2. Handicapped children - Education (Early childhood). 3. Early childhood education - Parent participation - Case studies. 4._

_Social work with handicapped children. 5. Handicapped children - Family relationships - Case studies. I. Title._
_TC 06 no. 11140_

**Lavalette, Michael.**
Hobbs, Sandy. Child labor. Santa Barbara, Calif. : ABC-CLIO, 1999.
_TC HD6231 .H63 1999_

**Lavatelli, Celia Stendler, 1911-** Piaget's theory applied to an early childhood curriculum. [1st ed.]. Boston : American Science and Engineering, [c1970]. 163p. : ill. ; 23 cm. (Center for Media Development, inc. book.) Includes index. Bibliography: p.146-149.
_1. Piaget, Jean. - 1896- 2. Education, Preschool - 1965- - Curricula. 3. Nursery schools - Curricula. 4. Child development. I. Title._
_TC LB1140.2 .L3_

**LAW AND ART.** _See_ **ARTISTS' CONTRACTS; ARTISTS - LEGAL STATUS, LAWS, ETC.**

**LAW AND FACT.** _See_ **JURY.**

**LAW AND MENTAL ILLNESS.** _See_ **MENTAL HEALTH LAWS.**

**Law and public policy**
Levesque, Roger J. R. Adolescents, sex, and the law. 1st ed. Washington, DC : American Psychological Association, c2000.
_TC KF479 .L48 2000_

**Law and school reform :** six strategies for promoting educational equity / edited by Jay P. Heubert. New Haven [Conn.] : Yale University Press, c1999. xv, 423 p. ; 25 cm. Includes bibliographical references and index. ISBN 0-300-07595-2 (alk. paper)
_1. Educational equalization - United States. 2. Educational law and legislation - United States. 3. Education - United States - Finance. 4. Minorities - Education - United States. 5. Special education - United States. 6. Educational change - United States. I. Heubert, Jay Philip. II. Title: Six strategies for promoting educational equity._
_TC LC213.2. L38 1999_

**LAW AND SEX.** _See_ **SEX AND LAW.**

**Law, Andrew.**
Gender and the interpretation of emotion [videorecording]. Princeton, NJ : Films for the Humanities & Sciences, c1997.
_TC BF592.F33 G4 1997_

**LAW, ANGLO-AMERICAN.** _See_ **LAW - UNITED STATES.**

**LAW, ARAB.** _See_ **ISLAMIC LAW.**

**LAW - DICTIONARIES.**
Black, Henry Campbell, 1860-1927. Black's law dictionary. 7th ed. / Bryan A. Garner, editor in chief. St. Paul, MN : West Group, 1999.
_TC KF156 .B53 1999_

**Law dictionary.**
Black, Henry Campbell, 1860-1927. Black's law dictionary. 7th ed. / Bryan A. Garner, editor in chief. St. Paul, MN : West Group, 1999.
_TC KF156 .B53 1999_

**LAW, ECCLESIASTICAL.** _See_ **ECCLESIASTICAL LAW.**

**LAW, EDUCATIONAL.** _See_ **EDUCATIONAL LAW AND LEGISLATION.**

**LAW, EMIGRATION.** _See_ **EMIGRATION AND IMMIGRATION LAW.**

**LAW ENFORCEMENT.** _See_ **CRIMINAL INVESTIGATION.**

**LAW ENFORCEMENT OFFICERS.** _See_ **POLICE.**

**Law for galleries.**
DuBoff, Leonard D. The law (in plain English) for galleries. 2nd ed. New York : Allworth Press, c1999.
_TC KF2042.A76 D836 1999_

**LAW, IMMIGRATION.** _See_ **EMIGRATION AND IMMIGRATION LAW.**

**The law (in plain English) for galleries.**
DuBoff, Leonard D. 2nd ed. New York : Allworth Press, c1999.
_TC KF2042.A76 D836 1999_

**LAW IN THE KORAN.** _See_ **ISLAMIC LAW.**

**Law in the schools.**
Valente, William D. 4th ed. Upper Saddle River, N.J. : Merrill, c1998.
_TC KF4119 .V28 1998_

**LAW, INDUSTRIAL.** _See_ **LABOR LAWS AND LEGISLATION.**

**LAW, ISLAMIC.** _See_ **ISLAMIC LAW.**

**LAW, LABOR.** _See_ **LABOR LAWS AND LEGISLATION.**

**Law, meaning, and violence**
Ferguson, Ann Arnett, 1940- Bad boys. Ann Arbor : University of Michigan Press, c2000.
_TC LC2771 .F47 2000_

**LAW OF SUCCESSION.** _See_ **INHERITANCE AND SUCCESSION.**

**LAW, ORIENTAL.** _See_ **ISLAMIC LAW.**

**LAW - PERIODICALS.** _See_ **LAW REVIEWS.**

**LAW, POVERTY.** _See_ **PUBLIC WELFARE - LAW AND LEGISLATION.**

**LAW REVIEWS - NORTH CAROLINA.**
Wake Forest law review. [Winston-Salem, N.C., Wake Forest Law Review Association, etc.]
_TC K27 .A36_

**LAW REVIEWS - PERIODICALS.** _See_ **LAW REVIEWS.**

**LAW, SEMITIC.** _See_ **ISLAMIC LAW.**

**Law, Sue.** Educational leadership and learning : practice, policy, and research / Sue Law and Derek Glover. Buckingham [England] ; Philadelphia : Open University Press, 2000. xii, 305 p. ; 25 cm. Includes bibliographical references (p.265-290) and index. ISBN 0-335-19753-1 (hard) ISBN 0-335-19752-3 (pbk). DDC 371.2/00941
_1. Educational leadership - Great Britain. 2. School management and organization - Great Britain. 3. School administrators - Great Britain. I. Glover, Derek. II. Title._
_TC LB2900.5 .L39 1999_

**LAW - UNITED STATES - DICTIONARIES.**
Black, Henry Campbell, 1860-1927. Black's law dictionary. 7th ed. / Bryan A. Garner, editor in chief. St. Paul, MN : West Group, 1999.
_TC KF156 .B53 1999_

**Lawler, Edward E.**
Doing research that is useful for theory and practice. Lanham, Md. : Oxford : Lexington Books, c1999.
_TC HD58.7 .D65 1999_

Mohrman, Allan M. Designing performance appraisal systems. 1st ed. San Francisco : Jossey-Bass Publishers, 1989.
_TC HF5549.5.P35 M64 1989_

**Lawlor, Hugh.**
Field, Kit. Effective subject leadership. London ; New York : Routledge, 2000.
_TC LB2806.15 .F54 2000_

**LAWMAKERS.** _See_ **LEGISLATORS.**

**Lawn, Martin.**
Silences & images. New York : P. Lang, c1999.
_TC LA128 .S55 1999_

**Lawrence, Alexandria Teresa.** Cooperating teachers' perceptions of the nature and quality of professional development in a professional development school collaboration. 1999. 167 leaves ; 29 cm. Includes tables. Typescript; issued also on microfilm. Thesis (Ed.D.)--Teachers College, Columbia University, 1999. Includes bibliographical references (leaves 143-147).
_1. Teachers - Training of. 2. College-school cooperation. 3. Laboratory schools. 4. Student teaching. 5. Education - Aims and objectives. 6. Teachers - Recruiting. I. Holmes Group (U.S.) II. Title._
_TC 06 no. 11141_

Cooperating teachers' perceptions of the nature and quality of professional development in a professional development school collaboration. 1999. 167 leaves ; 29 cm. Includes tables. Typescript; issued also on microfilm. Thesis (Ed.D.)--Teachers College, Columbia University, 1999. Includes bibliographical references (leaves 143-147).
_1. Teachers - Training of. 2. College-school cooperation. 3. Laboratory schools. 4. Student teaching. 5. Education - Aims and objectives. 6. Teachers - Recruiting. 7. Holmes Group (U.S.) I. Title._
_TC 06 no. 11141_

Cooperating teachers' perceptions of the nature and quality of professional development in a professional development school collaboration. 1999. 167 leaves ; 29 cm. Includes tables. Typescript; issued also on microfilm. Thesis (Ed.D.)--Teachers College, Columbia University, 1999. Includes bibliographical references (leaves 143-147).
_1. Teachers - Training of. 2. College-school cooperation. 3. Laboratory schools. 4. Student teaching. 5. Education - Aims and objectives. 6. Teachers - Recruiting. 7. Holmes Group (U.S.) I. Title._

**TC 06 no. 11141**

**Lawrence, Brenda, 1954-.**
Murray, Louis, 1944- Practitioner-based enquiry.
London ; New York : Falmer Press, 2000.
*TC LB1028.24 .M87 2000*

**Lawrence Hall of Science.**
Goodman, Jan M. Group solutions : : [Teacher's guide]. Rev. Berkeley, Calif. : Lawrence Hall of Science, University of California, 1997, c1992.
*TC QA8.7 .G5 1997*

**Lawrence-Lightfoot, Sara, 1944-** The art and science of portraiture / Sara Lawrence-Lightfoot, Jessica Hoffmann Davis. 1st ed. San Francisco : Jossey-Bass, c1997. xvii, 293 p. : ill. ; 25 cm. Includes bibliographical references (p. 283-287) and index. ISBN 0-7879-1064-3 (cloth) DDC 300/.72
*1. Social sciences - Research. 2. Social sciences - Methodology. 3. Portraits - Social aspects. 4. Art and society. 5. Art and science. I. Davis, Jessica Hoffmann, 1943- II. Title.*
*TC H62 .L33 1997*

**LAWRENCE LIVERMORE NATIONAL LABORATORY - EMPLOYEES.**
Gusterson, Hugh. Nuclear rites. "First paperback printing 1998". Berkeley : University of California Press, 1998.
*TC U264.4.C2 G87 1998*

**Lawrence, Steven.**
Renz, Loren. Arts funding. 3rd ed. [New York, N.Y.] : Foundation Center, c1998.
*TC NX711.U5 R4 1998*

**Lawrence, W. Gordon.**
Social dreaming @ work. London : Karnac Books, 1998.
*TC BF1078 .S55 1998*

**Laws, D. Richard.**
Remaking relapse prevention with sex offenders. Thousand Oaks, Calif. : Sage Publications, c2000.
*TC RC560.S47 R46 2000*

**Lawson, David M.**
Casebook in family therapy. Belmont : Brooks/Cole, c1999.
*TC RC488.5 .C369 1999*

**Lawton, Barbara.**
Taking supervision forward. London : Sage, 2000.
*TC BF637.C6 T35 2000*

**Lawton, Denis.**
Gordon, Peter, 1927- Royal education. London ; Portland, OR : Frank Cass, 1999.
*TC LC4945.G72 G67 1999*

**Lawton, Denis, 1931-.**
Education for values. London : Sterling, VA : Kogan Page, 2000.
*TC LC268 .E38 2000*

**Lawton, M. Powell (Mortimer Powell), 1923-.**
The many dimensions of aging. New York : Springer Pub., c2000.
*TC HQ1061 .M337 2000*

**Lawyer-Brook, Dianna, 1949-** Shifting focus : a handbook for ITV educators / Dianna Lawyer-Brook, Vicki McVey ; illustrations by George Blevins. Lanham, Md. ; London : Scarecrow Press, 2000. v, 147 p. : ill. ; 23 cm. Includes bibliographical references (p. 141-142) and index. ISBN 0-8108-3756-0 (alk. paper) DDC 371.33/58
*1. Television in education - United States - Handbooks, manuals, etc. 2. Interactive television - United States - Handbooks, manuals, etc. 3. Teaching - United States - Aids and devices - Handbooks, manuals, etc. I. McVey, Vicki. II. Title.*
*TC LB1044.7 .L313 2000*

**LAY JUDGES.** *See* **JURY.**

**Lazarus, Richard S.** Stress and emotion : a new synthesis / Richard S. Lazarus. New York : Springer Pub. Co., c1999. xiv, 342 p. : ill. ; 23 cm. Includes bibliographical references (p. 287-327) and indexes. ISBN 0-8261-1250-1 (hardcover) DDC 155.9/042
*1. Stress (Psychology) 2. Emotions. I. Title.*
*TC BF575.S75 L315 1999*

**Lazear, David G.** Eight ways of knowing : teaching for multiple intelligences : a handbook of techniques for expanding intelligence / David Lazear ; with foreword by Howard Gardner ; [editor, Heidi Ray ; indexer, McVey & Associates, Inc.]. 3rd ed. Arlington Heights, Ill. : SkyLight Training and Pub., c1999. x, 260 p. : ill. ; 28 cm. Rev. ed. of: Seven ways of knowing. 2nd ed. c1991. Includes bibliographical references (p. 245-249) and index. "2333-V"--T.p. verso. "Item number 1669"--T.p. verso. ISBN 1-57517-118-X

*1. Learning. 2. Cognitive styles. 3. Multiple intelligences. 4. Teaching. I. Ray, Heidi. II. Lazear, David G. Seven ways of knowing. III. Title. IV. Title: Teaching for multiple intelligences*
*TC LB1060 .L39 1999*

**Seven ways of knowing.**
Lazear, David G. Eight ways of knowing. 3rd ed. Arlington Heights, Ill. : SkyLight Training and Pub., c1999.
*TC LB1060 .L39 1999*

**Lazić, Mladen.**
[Ajmo, ajde, svi u šetnju. English.] Protest in Belgrade. Budapest, Hungary ; New York, NY, USA : Central European University Press, 1999.
*TC DR2044 .A3913 1999*

**LD ADULTS.** *See* **LEARNING DISABLED.**

**LDC'S.** *See* **DEVELOPING COUNTRIES.**

**LDJ Productions Inc.**
Paris [videorecording]. New York, NY : V.I.E.W. Video, c1996.
*TC DC707 .P3 1996*

**Le Tang, Henry.4dnc.**
Tap dancing for beginners [videorecording]. W. Long Branch, NJ : Kultur, c1981.
*TC GV1794 .T3 1981*

**Lea, Mary R. (Mary Rosalind), 1950-.**
Student writing in higher education. Philadelphia, Pa. : Open University Press, c2000.
*TC PE1404 .S84 2000*

**The LEA series on special education and disability**
Contemporary special education research. Mahwah, N.J. : Lawrence Erlbaum, c2000.
*TC LC4019 .C575 2000*

What reading research tells us about children with diverse learning needs. Mahwah, N.J. : Erlbaum, 1998.
*TC LB1050.5 .W47 1998*

**Leach, Fiona E.**
Education, cultures, and economics. New York : Falmer Press, 1999.
*TC LC191.8.D44 E38 1999*

**Leach, John.**
Practical work in science education :. 1. ed. Frederiksberg, Denmark : Roskilde University Press ; Dordrecht, Holland : Kluwer Acdemic, 1999.
*TC Q181 .P73 1999*

**LEADERS, CIVIC.** *See* **CIVIC LEADERS.**

**Leaders, groups, and influence.**
Hollander, Edwin Paul, 1927- New York, Oxford University Press, 1964.
*TC HM141 .H58*

**Leaders in the crucible.**
Nelson, Stephen James, 1947- Westport, Conn. : Bergin & Garvey, 2000.
*TC LB2341 .N386 2000*

**LEADERS - RATING OF.**
Bazigos, Michael Nicholas. The relationship of upward feedback disparities to leader performance. 1999.
*TC 085 B33*

**The leader's shadow.**
Judge, William Q. Thousand Oaks, Calif. : Sage Publications, c1999.
*TC HD57.7 .J83 1999*

**LEADERSHIP.** *See also* **EDUCATIONAL LEADERSHIP; ELITE (SOCIAL SCIENCES); POLITICAL LEADERSHIP.**
Crow, Gary Monroe, 1947- Princeton, NJ : Eye on Education, c1996.
*TC LB2831.92 .C76 1996*

**LEADERSHIP.**
Allen, Kathleen E. Systemic leadership. Lanham, Md. : University Press of America, c2000.
*TC HD57.7 .A42 2000*

The book of leadership wisdom. New York : Wiley, c1998.
*TC HD57.7 .B66 1998*

Deming, W. Edwards (William Edwards), 1900- The new economics. 2nd ed. Cambridge, Mass. ; London : MIT Press, 2000.
*TC HD62.15 .D46 2000*

Dombroski, Ann P. Administrative problem solving. 1999.

**TC 06 no. 11104**
Dombroski, Ann P. Administrative problem solving. 1999.
*TC 06 no. 11104*

Fressola, Maria C. How nurse executives learned to become leaders. 1998.
*TC 06 no. 11115*

Fressola, Maria C. How nurse executives learned to become leaders. 1998.
*TC 06 no. 11115*

Gardner, Howard. Leading minds. New York, NY : BasicBooks, c1995.
*TC HM141 .G35 1995*

Gendering elites. Houndmills, Basingstoke, Hampshire : Macmillan Press ; New York : St. Martin's Press, 2000.
*TC HM1261 .G46 2000*

Grossman, Sheila. The new leadership challenge. Philadelphia : F.A. Davis, c2000.
*TC RT89 .G77 2000*

Grossman, Sheila. The new leadership challenge. Philadelphia : F.A. Davis, c2000.
*TC RT89 .G77 2000*

Handbook of gender & work. Thousand Oaks, CA : Sage Publications, Inc., c1999.
*TC HQ1233 .H33 1999*

Judge, William Q. The leader's shadow. Thousand Oaks, Calif. : Sage Publications, c1999.
*TC HD57.7 .J83 1999*

Kotter, John P., 1947- John P. Kotter on what leaders really do. Boston : Harvard Business School Press, c1999.
*TC HD57.7 .K665 1999*

Lamm, Sharon Lea. The connection between action reflection learning and transformative learning. 2000.
*TC 06 no. 11230*

Laurie, Donald L. The real work of leaders. Cambridge, Mass. : Perseus Pub., 2000.
*TC HD57.7 .L387 2000*

Leading beyond the walls. 1st ed. San Francisco : Jossey-Bass, c1999.
*TC HD57.7 .L4374 1999*

Managing the dream. Cambridge, Mass. : Perseus Pub., c2000.
*TC HD67.7.B4643 2000*

Marriner-Tomey, Ann, 1943- Guide to nursing management and leadership. 6th ed. St. Louis, Mo. : Mosby, 2000.
*TC RT89.3 M37 2000*

Marriner-Tomey, Ann, 1943- Guide to nursing management and leadership. 6th ed. St. Louis, Mo. : Mosby, 2000.
*TC RT89.3 M37 2000*

McGuffin, Jo A. The nurse's guide to successful management. St. Louis, Mo. : Mosby, c1999.
*TC RT89 .M436 1999*

Misumi, Jūji, 1924- Rīdashippu kōdō no kagaku =
*TC HM141 .M48 1978*

O'Toole, James. Leadership A to Z. 1st ed. San Francisco, CA : Jossey-Bass Publishers, c1999.
*TC HD57.7 .O87 1999*

Ray, R. Glenn. The facilitative leader. Upper Saddler River, NJ : Prentice Hall, c1999.
*TC HD66 .R3918 1999*

Rost, Joseph C. (Joseph Clarence), 1931- Leadership for the twenty-first century. New York : Praeger, 1991.
*TC HM141 .R685 1991*

Skyhooks for leadership. New York : AMACOM, American Management Association, c1999.
*TC HD58.8 .S577 1999*

Ulrich, David, 1953- Results-based leadership. Boston : Harvard Business School Press, 1999.
*TC HD57.7 .U45 1999*

Viney, John. Drive. 1st U.S. ed. New York, N.Y. : Bloomsbury, 1999.
*TC HD57.7 .V564 1999*

Wheatley, Margaret J. Leadership and the new science. 2nd ed. San Francisco : Berrett-Koehler Publishers, c1999.
*TC HD57.7 .W47 1999*

**Leadership A to Z.**
O'Toole, James. 1st ed. San Francisco, CA : Jossey-Bass Publishers, c1999.
*TC HD57.7 .O87 1999*

**LEADERSHIP - ADDRESSES, ESSAYS, LECTURES.**
Hollander, Edwin Paul, 1927- Leaders, groups, and influence New York, Oxford University Press, 1964.
*TC HM141 .H58*

**Leadership and management of programs for young children.**
Shoemaker, Cynthia. 2nd ed. Upper Saddle River, N.J. : Merrill, 2000.
*TC LB2822.6 .S567 2000*

**Leadership and nursing care management.**
Huber, Diane. 2nd ed. Philadelphia : W.B. Saunders, c2000.
*TC RT89 .H83 2000*

**Leadership and the new science.**
Wheatley, Margaret J. 2nd ed. San Francisco : Berrett-Koehler Publishers, c1999.
*TC HD57.7 .W47 1999*

**LEADERSHIP - CASE STUDIES.**
Gardner, Howard. Leading minds. New York, NY : BasicBooks, c1995.
*TC HM141 .G35 1995*

**Leadership development in women's civic organizations.**
Robinson, Anna Bess. 1999.
*TC 06 no. 11168*

**Leadership for the 21st century.**
Rost, Joseph C. (Joseph Clarence), 1931- Leadership for the twenty-first century. New York : Praeger, 1991.
*TC HM141 .R685 1991*

**Leadership for the twenty-first century.**
Rost, Joseph C. (Joseph Clarence), 1931- New York : Praeger, 1991.
*TC HM141 .R685 1991*

**Leadership in a democracy.**
National Institute of Social Sciences. Journal of the National Institute of Social Sciences. [New York]

**Leadership in early childhood.**
Rodd, Jillian. 2nd edition. New York : Teachers College Press, 1998.
*TC LB1776.4.A8 R63 1998*

**LEADERSHIP IN WOMEN.**
Handbook of gender & work. Thousand Oaks, CA : Sage Publications, Inc., c1999.
*TC HQ1233 .H33 1999*

**LEADERSHIP IN WOMEN - NEW YORK (STATE) - SUFFOLK COUNTY.**
Robinson, Anna Bess. Leadership development in women's civic organizations. 1999.
*TC 06 no. 11168*

**LEADERSHIP IN WOMEN - UNITED STATES - CASE STUDIES.**
Henderson, Katharine Rhodes. The public leadership of women of faith. 2000.
*TC 06 no. 11276*

**LEADERSHIP - MORAL AND ETHICAL ASPECTS - CASE STUDIES.**
Coles, Robert. Lives of moral leadership. 1st ed. New York : Random House, c2000.
*TC BJ1547.4 .C64 2000*

**LEADERSHIP - MORAL AND ETHICAL ASPECTS - CONGRESSES.**
Education, leadership, and business ethics. Boston, MA : Kluwer Academic Publishers, c1998.
*TC HF5387 .E346 1998*

**LEADERSHIP - NURSES' INSTRUCTION.**
Grant, Ann Boyle. Nursing leadership, management & research. Springhouse, Pa. : Springhouse Corp., c1999.
*TC RT89 .G727 1999*

**Leadership of schools.**
Thody, Angela. London ; Herndon, Va. : Cassell, 1997.
*TC LB2831.726.G7 T56 1997*

**Leadership orientations of school administrators.**
Durocher, Elizabeth Antoinette. 1995.
*TC 06 no. 10583a*

**LEADERSHIP - OUTLINE, SYLLABI, ETC.**
Grant, Ann Boyle. Nursing leadership, management & research. Springhouse, Pa. : Springhouse Corp., c1999.

*TC RT89 .G727 1999*

**LEADERSHIP - PSYCHOLOGICAL ASPECTS.**
Tobe, Dorothy Echols. The development of cognitive leadership frames among African American female college presidents. 1999.
*TC 06 no. 11187*

**LEADERSHIP - SOCIAL ASPECTS.**
Tobe, Dorothy Echols. The development of cognitive leadership frames among African American female college presidents. 1999.
*TC 06 no. 11187*

**LEADERSHIP - STUDY AND TEACHING (HIGHER) - UNITED STATES.**
Komives, Susan R., 1946- Exploring leadership. 1st ed. San Francisco : Jossey-Bass Publishers, c1998.
*TC LB3605 .K64 1998*

**LEADERSHIP - UNITED STATES - RELIGIOUS ASPECTS.**
Henderson, Katharine Rhodes. The public leadership of women of faith. 2000.
*TC 06 no. 11276*

**Leading academic change.**
Lucas, Ann F. 1st ed. San Francisco : Jossey-Bass, c2000.
*TC LB2341 .L82 2000*

**Leading beyond the walls** / Frances Hesselbein, Marshall Goldsmith, Iain Somerville, editors. 1st ed. San Francisco : Jossey-Bass, c1999. xii, 297 p. ; 24 cm. (Wisdom to action series) "The Peter F. Drucker Foundation for Nonprofit Management"--P. [iv]. Includes index.
CONTENTS: New strategies for a world without walls -- Transforming organizations for new realities -- The new requirements of leadership -- Leading the larger community.
ISBN 0-7879-4593-5 (perm. paper) DDC 658.4/092
*1. Leadership. 2. Organizational change. 3. Management. I. Hesselbein, Frances. II. Goldsmith, Marshall. III. Somerville, Iain. IV. Peter F. Drucker Foundation for Nonprofit Management. V. Series.*
*TC HD57.7 .L4374 1999*

**Leading minds.**
Gardner, Howard. New York, NY : BasicBooks, c1995.
*TC HM141 .G35 1995*

**Leading schools in times of change** / Christopher Day ... [et al.]. Buckingham [England] ; Philadelphia : Open University Press, 2000. xvi, 197 p. ; 23 cm. Includes bibliographical references (p. [179]-191) and index. ISBN 0-335-20583-6 (hb) ISBN 0-335-20582-8 (pb) DDC 371.2/00941
*1. Educational leadership - Great Britain. 2. School management and organization - Great Britain. 3. Educational change - Great Britain. I. Day, Christopher. ACP.*
*TC LB2900.5 .L45 2000*

**Leading the race.**
Moore, Jacqueline M., 1965- Charlottesville : University Press of Virginia, 1999.
*TC E185.93.D6 M66 1999*

**Leading without power.**
De Pree, Max. 1st ed. San Francisco, Calif. : Jossey-Bass, c1997.
*TC HN90.V64 D4 1997*

**Leading young children to music.**
Haines, B. Joan E. (Beatrice Joan Elizabeth), 1920- 6th ed. Upper Saddle River, NJ : Merrill, c2000.
*TC MT1 .H13 2000*

**League of Nations.** Bulletin de la coopération intellectuelle / Société des nations. Paris : Institut international de coopération intellectuelle, [1931?-1932?] 16 v. ; 23 cm. Frequency: Monthly. 1 (janv. 1931) - 16 (avril 1932). Title from cover. Some issues are combined. Continues: Coopération intellectuelle (Paris, France : 1929) (DLC)   30018705 (OCoLC)8818112. Continued by: League of Nations. Coopération intellectuelle (DLC)   32034024 (OCoLC)2259796.
*1. Intellectual cooperation - Periodicals. 2. Intellectual cooperation - Bibliography - Periodicals. I. International Institute of Intellectual Co-operation. II. Title. III. Title: Coopération intellectuelle (Paris, France : 1929) IV. Title: League of Nations. Coopération intellectuelle*

**League of Nations. Coopération intellectuelle.**
League of Nations. Bulletin de la coopération intellectuelle. Paris : Institut international de coopération intellectuelle, [1931?-1932?]

**Leahey, Thomas Hardy.** A history of psychology : main currents in psychological thought / Thomas Hardy Leahey. 5th ed. Upper Saddle River, N.J. : Prentice Hall, c2000. xxi, 570 p. : ill. ; 25 cm. Includes bibliographical references and index. ISBN 0-13-011286-0

DDC 150/.9
*1. Psychology - History. I. Title.*
*TC BF81 .L4 2000*

**Lean, Michael E. J.** Clinical handbook of weight management / Michael E. J. Lean. London : Martin Dunitz, Ltd. ; distributed in the USA, Canada and Brazil by Blackwell Science, Ltd., c1998. vi, 113 p. : col. ill. ; 21 cm. Includes bibliographical references (p. 105-107) and index. ISBN 1-85317-542-0
*1. Obesity - Prevention. 2. Weight loss - Management. 3. Obesity - prevention & control. 4. Obesity - therapy. I. Title.*
*TC RC628 .L436 1998*

**Learmonth, James, 1939-.**
Teaching and learning in cities. [S.l.] : Whitbread, 1993.
*TC LC5115 .T43 1993*

**LEARN AND SERVE AMERICA HIGHER EDUCATION (PROGRAM) - EVALUATION.**
Combining service and learning in higher education. Santa Monica, CA : RAND Education, 1999.
*TC LC220.5 .C646 1999*

**Learnability in optimality theory.**
Tesar, Bruce. Cambridge, Mass. : MIT Press, c2000.
*TC P158.42 .T47 2000*

**LEARNED INSTITUTIONS AND SOCIETIES.** *See* LEARNING AND SCHOLARSHIP.

**LEARNED WRITING.** *See* ACADEMIC WRITING.

**Learner autonomy in language learning :** defining the field and effecting change / Sara Cotterall, David Crabbe, editors. Frankfurt am Main ; New York : Peter Lang, c1999. ix, 184 p. : ill ; 21 cm. (Bayreuth contributions to glottodidactics = bayreuther Beiträge zur Glottodidaktik ; vol. 8) Includes bibliographical references. ISBN 0-8204-4337-9 DDC 418/.007
*1. Language and languages - Study and teaching. 2. Autonomy (Psychology) I. Cotterall, Sara. II. Crabbe, David. III. Symposium on Learner Autonomy (1996 : Juväskylä, Finland) IV. Series: Bayreuth contributions to glottodidactics ; vol. 8.*
*TC P53 .L378 1999*

**Learner autonomy :** the teachers' views / compiled and edited by G. Camilleri. Strasbourg : Council of Europe Pub., c1999. 81 p. ; ill. ; 24 cm. "European Centre for Modern Languages." Includes bibliographical references. ISBN 92-871-4078-2
*1. Languages, Modern - Study and teaching - Europe. I. Camilleri, George. II. European Centre for Modern Languages. III. Council of Europe.*
*TC PB38.E8 L424 1999*

**Learner-centered assessment on college campuses.**
Huba, Mary E. Boston ; London : Allyn and Bacon, c2000.
*TC LB2331 .H83 2000*

**Learner-directed assessment in ESL** / edited by Glayol Ekbatani, Herbert Pierson. Mahwah, N.J. : Lawrence Erlbaum Associates, 2000. xiv, 171 p. : ill. ; 23 cm. Includes bibliographical references (p. 153-164) and indexes. ISBN 0-8058-3067-7 (alk. paper) ISBN 0-8058-3068-5 (pbk. : alk. paper) DDC 428/.007
*1. English language - Study and teaching - Foreign speakers. 2. English language - Ability testing. I. Ekbatani, Glayol. II. Pierson, Herbert D. (Herbert DeLeon), 1941-*
*TC PE1128.A2 L359 2000*

**LEARNING.** *See also* ACTIVE LEARNING; ADULT LEARNING; COGNITIVE LEARNING; EXPERIENTIAL LEARNING; MASTERY LEARNING; OPEN LEARNING; ORGANIZATIONAL LEARNING; VISUAL LEARNING.
Jones, John Charles. New York, Harcourt, Brace & World [1967]
*TC LB1051 .J59 1967*

**LEARNING.**
Banner, James M., 1935- The elements of learning. New Haven, Conn. : Yale University Press, c1999.
*TC LB1060 .B36 1999*

Baxter Magolda, Marcia B., 1951- Creating contexts for learning and self-authorship. 1st ed. Nashville [Tenn.] : Vanderbilt University Press, 1999.
*TC LB1025.3 .B39 1999*

Biggs, John B. (John Burville). Teaching for quality learning at university :. Buckingham, UK ; Philadelphia : Society for Research into Higher Education : Open University Press, 1999.
*TC LB2331 .B526 1999*

Britzman, Deborah P., 1952- Lost subjects, contested objects. Albany : State University of New York Press, c1998.

TC LB1060 .B765 1998

Bruner, Jerome Seymour. On knowing; Cambridge, Belknap Press of Harvard University Press, 1962.
TC LB885 .B778

Bruning, Roger H. Cognitive psychology and instruction. 3rd ed. Upper Saddle River, N.J. : Merrill, c1999.
TC LB1060 .B786 1999

Champions of change. Washington, DC : Arts Education Partnership : President's Committee on the Arts and the Humanities, [1999]
TC NX304.A1 C53 1999

Chuska, Kenneth R. Improving classroom questions. Bloomington, Ind. : Phi Delta Kappa Educational Foundation, 1995.
TC LB1027.44 .C58 1995

Classroom issues. London ; New York : Falmer Press, 2000.
TC LC268 .C52 2000

Curriculum planning. 7th ed. Boston : Allyn and Bacon, c2000.
TC LB2806.15 .C868 2000

Davis, Brent. Engaging minds. Mahwah, N.J. : L. Erlbaum Associates, 2000.
TC LB1060 .D38 2000

Elliott, Geoffrey, Dr. Lifelong learning. London ; Philadelphia : Jessica Kingsley Publishers, c1999.
TC LB1060 .E447 1999

Everyone a teacher. Notre Dame, Ind. : University of Notre Dame Press, c2000.
TC LB1025.3 .E87 2000

Handbook of contemporary learning theories. Mahwah, N.J. ; London : Lawrence Erlbaum Associates, 2001.
TC LB1060 .H3457 2001

Handbook of self-regulation. San Diego : Academic, 2000.
TC BF632 .H254 2000

Johnson, Andrew P. Up and out :. Boston : Allyn and Bacon, c2000.
TC LB1590.3 .J64 2000

Jones, John Charles. Learning New York, Harcourt, Brace & World [1967]
TC LB1051 .J59 1967

Keefe, James W. Instruction and the learning environment. Larchmont, NY : Eye On Education, c1997.
TC LB2806.4 .K44 1997

Kohn, Alfie. What to look for in a classroom. 1st ed. San Francisco : Jossey-Bass, c1998.
TC LB1775 .K643 1998

Lazear, David G. Eight ways of knowing. 3rd ed. Arlington Heights, Ill. : SkyLight Training and Pub., c1999.
TC LB1060 .L39 1999

Learning, language, and invention. Aldershot, Hampshire, Great Britain : Variorum ; Brookfield, Vt., USA : Ashgate Pub. Co. ; Paris, France : Société internationale de l'Astrolabe, 1994.
TC AC5 .L38 1994

Learning. Berlin ; New York : Walter de Gruyter, 1999.
TC QP408 .L44 1999

Learning sites. 1st ed. Amsterdam ; New York : Pergamon, 1999.
TC LB1060 .L4245 1999

Mentkowski, Marcia. Learning that lasts. 1st ed. San Francisco : Jossey-Bass, c2000.
TC LB1060 .M464 2000

Newton, Douglas P. Teaching for understanding. London ; New York : Routledge/Falmer, 2000.
TC LB1025.3 .N495 1999

Rachlin, Howard, 1935- Behavior and learning. San Francisco : W. H. Freeman, c1976.
TC BF319 .R327

Researching school experience. London ; New York : Falmer Press, 1999.
TC LB1027 .R453 1999

School climate. London ; Philadelphia : Falmer Press, 1999.
TC LC210 .S35 1999

Schunk, Dale H. Learning theories. 3rd ed. Upper Saddle River, N.J. : Merrill, c2000.

TC LB1060 .S37 2000

Study to teach. London ; New York : Routledge, 2000.
TC LB1707 .S88 2000

Teaching and learning on the edge of the millennium :. San Francisco : Jossey-Bass, c1999.
TC LB2331 .T35 1999

Tileston, Donna Walker. Ten best teaching practices. Thousand Oaks, Calif. : Corwin Press, c2000.
TC LB1775.2 .T54 2000

Ulrich, Deborah L. Interactive group learning. New York : Springer, c1999.
TC RT76 .U46 1999

**Learning a second language through interaction.**
Ellis, Rod. Amsterdam ; Philadelphia : J. Benjamins, c1999.
TC P118.2 .E38 1999

**LEARNING ABILITY.** *See also* **LEARNING, PSYCHOLOGY OF.**
Tesar, Bruce. Learnability in optimality theory. Cambridge, Mass. : MIT Press, c2000.
TC P158.42 .T47 2000

**Learning about books & libraries.**
Lee, Carol K. Fort Atkinson, Wis. : Alleyside Press, 2000.
TC Z711.2 .L455 2000

**Learning about books and libraries.**
Lee, Carol K. Learning about books & libraries. Fort Atkinson, Wis. : Alleyside Press, 2000.
TC Z711.2 .L455 2000

**Learning activity and development** / edited by Mariane Hedegaard and Joachim Lompscher. Aarhus : Aarhus Universit #, 1999. 332 p. : ill. ; 25 cm. ISBN 87-7288-815-6
*1. Learning - Addresses, essays, lectures. 2. Learning, Psychology of. 3. Educational psychology. 4. Teaching - Addresses. essays, lectures. 5. Developmental psychology. I. Hedegaard, Mariane. II. Lompscher, Joachim.*
TC LB1060 .L43 1999

**LEARNING - ADDRESSES, ESSAYS, LECTURES.**
Learning activity and development. Aarhus : Aarhus Universit #, 1999.
TC LB1060 .L43 1999

**LEARNING AND SCHOLARSHIP.** *See* **CULTURE; EDUCATION; HUMANISM; HUMANITIES; RESEARCH.**

**LEARNING AND SCHOLARSHIP - HISTORY.**
Barzun, Jacques, 1907- From dawn to decadence. 1st ed. New York : HarperCollins, c2000.
TC CB245 .B365 2000

Proctor, Robert E., 1945- Defining the humanities. 2nd ed. Bloomington : Indiana University Press, c1998.
TC AZ221 .P75 1998

**LEARNING AND SCHOLARSHIP - HISTORY - MEDIEVAL, 500-1500.** *See* **EDUCATION, MEDIEVAL.**

**LEARNING AND SCHOLARSHIP - NETHERLANDS - PERIODICALS.**
Higher education and research in the Netherlands. The Hague, Netherlands Foundation for International Cooperation.

**LEARNING AND SCHOLARSHIP - POLITICAL ASPECTS.**
Beverley, John. Subalternity and representation. Durham [N.C.] ; London : Duke University Press, 1999.
TC HM1136 .B48 1999

**LEARNING AND SCHOLARSHIP - TECHNOLOGICAL INNOVATIONS.**
Information technology and scholarship. Oxford : Oxford University Press for the British Academy, c1999.
TC AZ186 .I556 1999

Information technology and scholarship. Oxford : Oxford University Press for the British Academy, c1999.
TC AZ186 .I556 1999

**LEARNING AND SCHOLARSHIP - UNITED STATES.**
Berlinerblau, Jacques. Heresy in the University. New Brunswick, N.J. : Rutgers University Press, c1999.
TC DF78.B3983 B47 1999

**LEARNING AND SCHOLARSHIP - UNITED STATES - HISTORY.**
Gilman, Sander L. The fortunes of the humanities: Stanford, Calif. : Stanford University Press, c2000.

TC AZ183.U5 G55 2000

**Learning and studying.**
Hartley, James, Ph. D. London ; New York : Routledge, 1998.
TC BF318 .H365 1998

**Learning and teaching about the history of Europe in the 20th century.**
The challenges of the information and communication technologies facing history teaching. Strasbourg : Council of Europe Pub., c1999.
TC D424 .C425 1999

Towards a pluralist and tolerant approach to teaching history. Strasbourg : Council of Europe Pub., c1999.
TC D424 .T665 1999

**Learning and teaching in a complex world.**
Davis, Brent. Engaging minds. Mahwah, N.J. : L. Erlbaum Associates, 2000.
TC LB1060 .D38 2000

**Learning and teaching in physical education** / edited by Colin A. Hardy and Mick Mawer. London ; Philadelphia, PA : Falmer Press, 1999. vii, 240 p. ; 24 cm. Includes bibliographical references and index. ISBN 0-7507-0875-1 (cased) ISBN 0-7507-0874-3 (paper)
*1. Physical education and training - Study and teaching - Great Britain. 2. Physical education teachers - Great Britain. I. Hardy, Colin A. II. Mawer, Michael.*
TC GV361 .L42 1999

**Learning and work in the risk society.**
Evans, Karen, 1949- New York : St. Martin's Press, 2000.
TC HD6278.G4 E93 2000

**Learning another language through actions.**
Asher, James J. (James John), 1929- 4th ed. Los Gatos, Calif. : Sky Oaks Productions, 1993.
TC PB36 .A8 1993

**LEARNING, ART OF.** *See* **STUDY SKILLS.**

**Learning circles** : creating conditions for professional development / Michelle Collay ... [et al.]. Thousand Oaks, Calif. : Corwin Press, c1998. xxiv, 141 p. ; 24 cm. Includes bibliographical references (p. 133-136) and index. CONTENTS: Creating conditions. What are learning circles? Background of our thinking. The six essential conditions -- Building community. What is community? Initiating community. Maintaining community. Sustaining community. Transforming community. Building community together -- Constructing knowledge. Knowing naturally. Relating whole and parts. Designing learning. Folding paper. Playing baby. Reinventing kindergarten. Ways of knowing -- Supporting learners. Learning about group processes. Learning in small groups. Supporting preservice teachers. Supporting professional development. Supporting teacher research -- Documenting reflection. Complex systems. A letter to myself. Reflection on stepping-stones. Metaphor as reflection. Journaling. Reflecting with colleagues. Structured reflection. Reflection for program evaluation. Reflection within learning circles -- Assessing expectations. Beliefs about assessment. Appropriate assessment. Approaches to assessment. Self-assessment. Peer assessment. Portfolio assessment. Changing the culture of assessment -- Changing cultures. Interdependent networks and cultures. Understanding culture. Making sense of culture in learning circles. Learning about cultures through artifacts. Learning about cultures through dance. Learning about cultures through acting. Mentoring others about culture. Cultural assumptions about leaders. Teaching as leading -- Re-creating conditions. Reconstructing learning CONTENTS: circles. Practical considerations. Variations on a theme. Re-creating conditions in classrooms. Re-creating conditions in schools or districts. Where from here? Conclusion. ISBN 0-8039-6675-X (cloth : acid-free paper) ISBN 0-8039-6676-8 (pbk. : acid-free paper) DDC 370/.71/1
*1. Group work in education - United States. 2. Cooperativeness - United States. 3. Teachers - In-service training - United States. 4. Teaching - United States. I. Collay, Michelle.*
TC LB1032 .L355 1998

**Learning communities in education** : issues, strategies and contexts / edited by John Retallick, Barry Cocklin, and Kennece Coombe. London ; New York : Routledge, 1999. xi, 297 p. : ill. ; 24 cm. (Routledge research in education ; 1) Includes bibliographical references and index. ISBN 0-415-19760-0 DDC 370.11
*1. Education - Aims and objectives. 2. Educational sociology. 3. School environment. 4. Educational change. I. Retallick, John, 1945- II. Cocklin, Barry, 1946- III. Coombe, Kennece, 1954- IV. Series.*
TC LB14.7 .L43 1999

**Learning community.**
Calderwood, Patricia E., 1954- New York : Teachers College Press, c2000.
TC LB1032 .C34 2000

**Learning computers, speaking English.**
Quann, Steve. Ann Arbor : University of Michigan Press, c2000.
*TC PE1128.A2 .Q83 2000*

**Learning, development, and conceptual change**
Newcombe, Nora S. Making space. Cambridge, Mass. : MIT Press, 2000.
*TC BF723.S63 N49 2000*

**LEARNING DISABILITIES.**
Hardman, Michael L. Human exceptionality. 6th ed. Boston : Allyn and Bacon, c1999.
*TC HV1568 .H37 1999*

Orenstein, Myrna. Smart but stuck. New York : Haworth Press, c2000.
*TC RC394.L37 O74 2000*

Schneider, Elke. Multisensory structured metacognitive instruction. Frankfurt am Main ; New York : P. Lang, c1999.
*TC P53.7 .S357 1999*

Slingerland, Beth H. A multi-sensory approach to language arts for specific language disability children. Cambridge, Mass. : Educators Pub. Service, c1976- <c1981 >
*TC LC4704.85 .S59 1976*

**Learning disabilities and life stories** / edited by Pano Rodis, Andrew Garrod, Mary Lynn Boscardin. Boston : Allyn and Bacon, c2001. xxii, 247 p. : ill. ; 24 cm. Includes bibliographical references (p.235-239) and index. ISBN 0-205-32010-4 DDC 362.4
*1. Learning disabled - Education (Higher) - United States - Case studies. 2. Learning disabilities - United States - Case studies. 3. Learning disabled - United States - Biography. I. Rodis, Pano. II. Garrod, Andrew, 1937- III. Boscardin, Mary Lynn.*
*TC LC4818.38 .L42 2001*

**LEARNING DISABILITIES - TREATMENT - MISCELLANEA.**
Jackson, Eve, 1949- Learning disability in focus. London ; Philadelphia : Jessica Kingsley, c1999.
*TC RC489.P56 J33 1999*

**LEARNING DISABILITIES - UNITED STATES.**
McGregor, Gail Inclusive schooling practices. [S.l.] : Allegheny University of Health Sciences ; Balitmore : Distributed exclusively by Paul H. Brookes Publishing, c1998.
*TC LC4031 .M394 1998*

**LEARNING DISABILITIES - UNITED STATES - CASE STUDIES.**
Learning disabilities and life stories. Boston : Allyn and Bacon, c2001.
*TC LC4818.38 .L42 2001*

**Learning disability in focus.**
Jackson, Eve, 1949- London ; Philadelphia : Jessica Kingsley, c1999.
*TC RC489.P56 J33 1999*

**LEARNING DISABLED ADULTS.** See **LEARNING DISABLED.**

**LEARNING DISABLED - BIOGRAPHY.**
Gray, Barry, 1944- Lifemaps of people with learning difficulties. London ; Philadelphia : Jessica Kingsley, 1999.
*TC HV3004 .G73 1999*

**LEARNING DISABLED CHILDREN - COMPUTER-ASSISTED EDUCATION - CONGRESSES.**
Penso, Dorothy E. Keyboarding skills for children with disabilities. London ; Philadelphia, Pa. : Whurr, 1999.
*TC LC4024 .P467 1999*

**LEARNING DISABLED CHILDREN - EDUCATION - LANGUAGE ARTS.**
Slingerland, Beth H. A multi-sensory approach to language arts for specific language disability children. Cambridge, Mass. : Educators Pub. Service, c1976- <c1981 >
*TC LC4704.85 .S59 1976*

**LEARNING DISABLED CHILDREN - EDUCATION - SOCIAL ASPECTS - GREAT BRITAIN.**
Mittler, Peter J. Working towards inclusive education. London : D. Fulton Publishers, 2000.
*TC LC1203.G7 M58 2000*

**LEARNING DISABLED CHILDREN - EDUCATION - UNITED STATES.**
Behavioral assessment in schools. 2nd ed. New York : Guilford Press, c2000.
*TC LB1124 .B435 2000*

Eisenberger, Joanne, 1942- Self efficacy. Larchmont, N.Y. : Eye On Education, c2000.
*TC LC4705 .C67 2000*

Jones, Carroll J. Curriculum-based assessment. Springfield, Ill. : C.C. Thomas, Publisher, c1998.
*TC LB3060.32.C74 J66 1998*

Vallecorsa, Ada, 1948- Students with mild disabilities in general education settings. Upper Saddle River, N.J. : Merrill, c2000.
*TC LC4705 .V35 2000*

Vaughn, Sharon, 1952- Teaching exceptional, diverse, and at-risk students in the general education classroom. 2nd ed. Boston : Allyn and Bacon, 2000.
*TC LC3981 .V28 2000*

**LEARNING DISABLED CHILDREN - GREAT BRITAIN - BIOGRAPHY.**
Gregory, Jane, 1960- Bringing up a challenging child at home. London ; Philadelphia : Jessica Kingsley Publishers, 2000.
*TC HQ759.913 .G74 2000*

**LEARNING DISABLED CHILDREN - LEGAL STATUS, LAWS, ETC. - UNITED STATES.**
Kelman, Mark. Jumping the queue. Cambridge, Mass. : Harvard University Press, 1997.
*TC KF4215 .K45 1997*

**LEARNING DISABLED CHILDREN - SERVICES FOR - UNITED STATES.**
Kampwirth, Thomas J. Collaborative consultation in the schools. Upper Saddle River, N.J. : Merrill, c1999.
*TC LB1027.5 .K285 1999*

**LEARNING DISABLED CHILDREN - UNITED STATES - CASE STUDIES.**
Simmons, Jay, 1947- You never asked me to read. Boston : Allyn and Bacon, c2000.
*TC LB1050.46 .S535 2000*

**LEARNING DISABLED - COUNSELING OF.**
Wren, Carol T. Hanging by a twig. 1st ed. New York ; London : Norton, c2000.
*TC RC394.L37 W74 2000*

**LEARNING DISABLED - EDUCATION (HIGHER) - UNITED STATES - CASE STUDIES.**
Learning disabilities and life stories. Boston : Allyn and Bacon, c2001.
*TC LC4818.38 .L42 2001*

**LEARNING DISABLED - INTELLIGENCE LEVELS.**
Orenstein, Myrna. Smart but stuck. New York : Haworth Press, c2000.
*TC RC394.L37 O74 2000*

**LEARNING DISABLED - MENTAL HEALTH.**
Orenstein, Myrna. Smart but stuck. New York : Haworth Press, c2000.
*TC RC394.L37 O74 2000*

Wren, Carol T. Hanging by a twig. 1st ed. New York ; London : Norton, c2000.
*TC RC394.L37 W74 2000*

**LEARNING DISABLED - PSYCHOLOGY.**
Gray, Barry, 1944- Lifemaps of people with learning difficulties. London ; Philadelphia : Jessica Kingsley, 1999.
*TC HV3004 .G73 1999*

Orenstein, Myrna. Smart but stuck. New York : Haworth Press, c2000.
*TC RC394.L37 O74 2000*

**LEARNING DISABLED - UNITED STATES - BIOGRAPHY.**
Learning disabilities and life stories. Boston : Allyn and Bacon, c2001.
*TC LC4818.38 .L42 2001*

**LEARNING DISABLED - VOCATIONAL GUIDANCE.**
Janus, Raizi Abby. Mapping careers with LD and ADD clients. New York : Columbia University Press, c1999.
*TC HV1568.5 .J36 1999*

Janus, Raizi Abby. Mapping careers with LD and ADD clients. New York : Columbia University Press, c1999.
*TC HV1568.5 .J36 1999*

**LEARNING DISORDERS.** See **LEARNING DISABILITIES.**

**Learning English at school.**
Toohey, Kelleen, 1950- Clevedon, [England] ; Buffalo : Multilingual Matters, 2000.
*TC PE1128.A2 T63 2000*

**Learning English text by heart in a Chinese university.**
Ting, Yenren, 1948- [New York : Columbia University], 1999.
*TC 085 T438*

**LEARNING - EVALUATION.**
Huba, Mary E. Learner-centered assessment on college campuses. Boston ; London : Allyn and Bacon, c2000.
*TC LB2331 .H83 2000*

**LEARNING, EXPERIENTIAL.** See **EXPERIENTIAL LEARNING.**

**Learning for living.**
Learning for living series. [Toronto]

**Learning for living series.** [Toronto] v. ill. Learning for living. Published by the Canadian Association for Adult Education for the Fun d for Adult Education.
*I. Canadian Association for Adult Education. II. Fund for Adult Education (U.S.). III. Title: Learning for living*

**LEARNING FOR MASTERY.** See **MASTERY LEARNING.**

**Learning from experience :** policy and practice in aid to higher education / editors, Lene Buchert, Kenneth King. The Hague : Centre for the Study of Education in Developing Countries, c1995. 261 p. : ill. ; 24 cm. (CESO paperback ; no. 24) Includes bibliographical references. ISBN 90-6443-170-1 DDC 379.1/54/091724
*1. Education, Higher - Developing countries - Finance. 2. Educational assistance. 3. World Bank. I. Buchert, Lene. II. King, Kenneth, 1940- III. Series.*
*TC LC2610 .L43 1995*

**Learning from others :** international comparisons in education / edited by Diane Shorrocks-Taylor and Edgar W. Jenkins. Dordrecht [Netherlands] ; Boston : Kluwer Academic Publishers, c2000. iv, 322 p. : ill. ; 25 cm. (Science & technology education library ; v. 8) Includes bibliographical references (p. 303-313) and indexes. ISBN 0-7923-6343-4 (alk. paper) DDC 370/.9
*1. Comparative education. 2. Academic achievement - Cross-cultural studies. 3. Educational evaluation - Cross-cultural studies. I. Shorrocks-Taylor, Diane. II. Jenkins, E. W. (Edgar William) III. Angell, Carl. IV. Series.*
*TC LB43 .L42 2000*

**Learning from our lives.**
Dominicé, Pierre. 1st ed. San Francisco : Jossey-Bass, c2000.
*TC LB1029.B55 D64 2000*

**Learning from our mistakes :** difficulties and failures in feminist therapy / Marcia Hill, Esther D. Rothblum, editors. New York : Haworth Press, c1998. 126 p. ; 22 cm. "Learning from our mistakes: difficulties and failures in feminist therapy has been co-published simultaneously as Women & therapy, Volume 21, Number 3, 1998." Includes bibliographical references and index. ISBN 0-7890-0670-7 (pbk. : acid-free paper) DDC 616.89/14/082
*1. Feminist therapy. 2. Women and psychoanalysis. I. Hill, Marcia. II. Rothblum, Esther D.*
*TC RC489.F45 L43 1998*

**Learning in a changing environment.**
Educational innovation in economics and business. IV, Learning in a changing environment. Boston, MA : Kluwer Academic Publishers, c1999.
*TC HB74.5 .E3333 1999*

**Learning in action.**
Garvin, David A. Boston, Mass. : Harvard Business School Press, 2000.
*TC HD58.82 .G37 2000*

**Learning in doing**
The Computer as medium. Cambridge [England] ; New York : Cambridge University Press, 1993.
*TC QA76.5 .C612554 1993*

Vygotskian perspectives on literacy research. Cambridge, U.K. ; New York : Cambridge University Press, 2000.
*TC LB1060 .V95 2000*

**LEARNING - IN INFANCY & CHILDHOOD.**
Shore, Rima. Rethinking the brain. New York : Families and Work Institute, c1997.
*TC RJ486.5 .S475 1997*

**Learning in New York (Albany, N.Y.).**
[Inside education (Albany, N.Y.)] Inside education. Albany : New York State Education Dept., 1968-1983.

**Learning institutionalized :** teaching in the medieval university / edited by John Van Engen. Notre Dame, Ind. : University of Notre Dame Press, c2000. viii, 277 p. ; 24 cm. (Notre Dame conferences in medieval studies ; no. 9) "Papers first delivered at a conference held in September

1992"--Pref. Includes bibliographical references. ISBN
0-268-01328-4 (cloth : alk. paper) DDC 378.1/2/094
*1. Universities and colleges - Europe - Congresses. 2.
Education. Medieval - Europe - Congresses. 3. College
teaching - Europe - Congresses. I. Van Engen, John H. II.
Series: Notre Dame conferences in medieval studies ; 9.*
**TC LA177 .L43 2000**

**Learning journals.**
Moon, Jennifer A. London : Kogan Page, 1999.
**TC PE1408 .M66 1999**

**Learning, language, and invention :** essays presented
to Francis Maddison / edited by W.D. Hackmann &
A.J. Turner. Aldershot, Hampshire, Great Britain :
Variorum ; Brookfield, Vt., USA : Ashgate Pub. Co. ;
Paris, France : Société internationale de l'Astrolabe,
1994. xv, 333 p. : ill. ; 24 cm. (Astrolabica ; no. 6) Includes
bibliographical references and index. ISBN 0-86078-467-3
DDC 081
*1. Learning. 2. Language and languages. 3. Inventions. 4.
Material culture. I. Maddison, Francis Romeril. II. Hackmann,
Willem Dirk. III. Turner, Anthony John. IV. Series.*
**TC AC5 .L38 1994**

**Learning literature in an era of change :** innovations
in teaching / edited by Dona J. Hickey and Donna
Reiss ; foreword by Kenneth Bruffee. Sterling, Va. :
Stylus Pub., c2000. xxvi, 211 p. : ill. ; 23 cm. Includes
bibliographical references and indexes. ISBN 1-57922-017-7
(cl : alk. paper ISBN 1-57922-018-5 (pb : alk. paper) DDC
807/.1/1
*1. Literature - Study and teaching (Higher) 2. Literature -
Study and teaching (Higher) - Technological innovations. I.
Hickey, Dona J. II. Reiss, Donna, 1944-*
**TC PN59 .L39 2000**

**LEARNING, MACHINE.** *See* **MACHINE
LEARNING.**

**Learning Matters, Inc.**
Education's big gamble [videorecording]. New York,
NY : Merrow Report, c1997.
**TC LB2806.36 .E3 1997**

**LEARNING ORGANIZATIONS.** *See*
**ORGANIZATIONAL LEARNING.**

**LEARNING - PHILOSOPHY - EARLY WORKS
TO 1800.**
Bacon, Francis, 1561-1626. The advancement of
learning. Oxford : Clarendon, 2000.
**TC B1191 .K545 2000**

**LEARNING - PHYSIOLOGICAL ASPECTS.**
Baker, Justine C. A neural network guide to teaching.
Bloomington, Ind. : Phi Delta Kappa Educational
Foundation, c1998.
**TC LB1057 .B35 1998**

Neurobiology of learning and memory. San Diego :
Academic Press, c1998.
**TC QP408 .N492 1998**

Sylwester, Robert. A biological brain in a cultural
classroom. Thousand Oaks, Calif. : Corwin Press,
c2000.
**TC LB3011.5 .S95 2000**

**LEARNING - PHYSIOLOGY.**
Neurobiology of learning and memory. San Diego :
Academic Press, c1998.
**TC QP408 .N492 1998**

**Learning policy.**
Ainley, Patrick. Basingstoke, Hampshire : Macmillan
Press ; New York : St. Martin's Press, 1999.
**TC LC93.G7 A76 1999**

**LEARNING PROCESS.** *See* **LEARNING.**

**LEARNING - PSYCHOLOGICAL ASPECTS.** *See*
**LEARNING, PSYCHOLOGY OF.**

**LEARNING, PSYCHOLOGY OF.** *See also*
**BEHAVIOR MODIFICATION;
COMPREHENSION; FEEDBACK
(PSYCHOLOGY); MOTIVATION IN
EDUCATION; PROGRAMMED
INSTRUCTION; VERBAL LEARNING.**
Asher, James J. (James John), 1929- Learning another
language through actions. 4th ed. Los Gatos, Calif. :
Sky Oaks Productions, 1993.
**TC PB36 .A8 1993**

Banner, James M., 1935- The elements of learning.
New Haven, Conn. : Yale University Press, c1999.
**TC LB1060 .B36 1999**

Baynes, Joyce Frisby. The development of a van
Hiele-based summer geometry program and its impact
on student van Hiele level and achievement in high
school geometry. 1998.

**TC 06 no. 10915**
Berel, Marianne. Musical play sessions. [S.l. : s.n.],
1994.
**TC ML3920 .B45 1994**

Bruer, John T., 1949- The myth of the first three
years. New York : Free Press, c1999.
**TC BF318 .B79 1999**

Claxton, Guy. Wise up. 1st U.S. ed. New York, N.Y. :
Bloomsbury : Distributed to the trade by St. Martin's
Press, 1999.
**TC BF318 .C55 1999**

DiSessa, Andrea A. Changing minds. Cambridge,
MA : MIT Press, c2000.
**TC LB1028.43 .D57 2000**

Driscoll, Marcy Perkins. Psychology of learning for
instruction. 2nd ed. Boston ; London : Allyn and
Bacon, c2000.
**TC LB1060 .D75 2000**

Eddy, Jennifer B.K. Multiple intelligences, styles, and
proficiency. 1999.
**TC 085 E10**

Education, information, and transformation. Upper
Saddle River, N.J. : Merrill, c1999.
**TC BF441 .E25 1999**

Eggen, Paul D., 1940- Strategies for teachers. 4th ed.
Boston : Allyn and Bacon, 2001.
**TC LB1027.3 .E44 2001**

Finkel, Donald L., 1943- Teaching with your mouth
shut. Portsmouth, NH Boynton/Cook Publishers,
c2000.
**TC LB1026 .F49 2000**

Gopnik, Alison. The scientist in the crib. New York :
William Morrow & Co., 1999.
**TC BF311 .G627 1999**

Handbook of contemporary learning theories.
Mahwah, N.J. ; London : Lawrence Erlbaum
Associates, 2001.
**TC LB1060 .H3457 2001**

Hart, Susan. Thinking through teaching. London :
David Fulton, 2000.
**TC LB1025.3 .H37 2000**

Hartley, James, Ph. D. Learning and studying.
London ; New York : Routledge, 1998.
**TC BF318 .H365 1998**

Hashway, Robert M. Developmental cognitive styles.
San Francisco : Austin & Winfield Publishers, 1998.
**TC LB1060 .H373 1998**

How people learn. Expanded ed. Washington, D.C. :
National Academy Press, c2000.
**TC LB1060 .H672 2000**

Human cognition and social agent technology.
Amsterdam ; Philadelphia : John Benjamins, c2000.
**TC BF311 .H766 2000**

Johnston, Jane, 1954- Enriching early scientific
learning. Philadelphia : Open University Press, 1999.
**TC Q181 .J58 1999**

Kavanagh, Gaynor. Dream spaces. New York :
Leicester University Press, 2000.
**TC AM7 .K37 2000**

Lamm, Sharon Lea. The connection between action
reflection learning and transformative learning. 2000.
**TC 06 no. 11230**

Learning activity and development. Aarhus : Aarhus
Universit #. 1999.
**TC LB1060 .L43 1999**

Martinez, Michael E. Education as the cultivation of
intelligence. Mahwah, N.J. ; London : Lawrence
Erlbaum Associates, 2000.
**TC LB1060 .M337 2000**

Milner, Peter M. The autonomous brain. Mahwah,
N.J. : L. Erlbaum Associates, 1999.
**TC BF161 .M5 1999**

Modelling changes in understanding. Amsterdam ;
New York : Pergamon, 1999.
**TC BF319 .M55 1999**

Murphy, Lois Barclay, 1902- The individual child.
Washington : Department of Health Education, and
Welfare : for sale by the Supt. of Docs., U. S. Govt.
Print. Off., 1973.

New perspectives on conceptual change. 1st ed.
Amsterdam ; New York ; Oxford : Pergamon, 1999.

**TC LB1062 .N49 1999**
Nord, Michael B. Music in the classroom (MITC).
1998.
**TC 06 no. 10974**

Oldfather, Penny. Learning through children's eyes.
1st ed. Washington, DC : American Psychological
Association, c1999.
**TC LB1060 .O43 1999**

Pierce, W. David. Behavior analysis and learning. 2nd
ed. Upper Saddle River, N.J. : Prentice Hall, c1999.
**TC BF199 .P54 1999**

Race, Phil. 500 tips on group learning. London :
Kogan Page, 2000.
**TC LB1032 .A15 2000**

Ryan, Sharon Kaye. Freedom to choice. 1998.
**TC 06 no. 11034**

Schank, Roger C., 1946- Dynamic memory revisited.
[2nd ed.]. Cambridge ; New York : Cambridge
University Press, 1999.
**TC BF371 .S365 1999**

Schunk, Dale H. Learning theories. 3rd ed. Upper
Saddle River, N.J. : Merrill, c2000.
**TC LB1060 .S37 2000**

Seo, Kyoung-Hye. Children's construction of personal
meanings of mathematical symbolism in a reform-
oriented classroom. 2000.
**TC 06 no. 11310**

Taylor, Kathleen, 1943- Developing adult learners. 1st
ed. San Francisco : Jossey-Bass, c2000.
**TC LC5225.L42 T39 2000**

Teaching and learning thinking skills. Lisse
[Netherlands] ; Exton, PA : Swets & Zeitlinger,
c1999.
**TC LB1590.3 .T36 1999**

Teaching to promote intellectual and personal
maturity :. San Francisco : Jossey-Bass, c2000.
**TC LB1060 .T43 2000**

Ting, Yenren, 1948- Learning English text by heart in
a Chinese university. [New York : Columbia
University], 1999.
**TC 085 T438**

Tsai, Chin-Chung. The interrelationships between
junior high school students' scientific epistemologicl
beliefs, learning environment preferences and their
cognitive structure outcomes. 1996.
**TC 06 no. 10713**

Zachary, Lois J. The mentor's guide. 1st ed. San
Francisco : Jossey-Bass Publishers, c2000.
**TC LB1731.4 .Z23 2000**

**LEARNING, PSYCHOLOGY OF - CONGRESSES.**
Cognitive perspectives on peer learning. Mahwah,
N.J. : L. Erlbaum, 1999.
**TC LB1031.5 .C65 1999**

Vygotskian perspectives on literacy research.
Cambridge, U.K. ; New York : Cambridge University
Press, 2000.
**TC LB1060 .V95 2000**

**LEARNING, PSYCHOLOGY OF, IN OLD AGE.**
Glendenning, Frank. Teaching and learning in later
life. Aldershot, Hants, Eng. ; Burlington, Vt. :
Ashgate / Arena, c2000.
**TC LC5457 .G54 2000**

**LEARNING - RESEARCH.**
Problem-based learning. Mahwah, N.J. : L. Erlbaum
Associates, 2000.
**TC LB1027.42 .P78 2000**

**LEARNING RESOURCE CENTERS.** *See*
**INSTRUCTIONAL MATERIALS CENTERS.**

**Learning resources.**
Audiovisual instruction. Washington, D.C : Dept. of
Audiovisual Instruction, NEA, 1956-1978.

**Learning resources.** [Washington, Association for
Educational Communications and Technology] 2 v. ill.
29 cm. Frequency: 5 no. a year. v. 1-2, no. 3; Dec. 1974-May
1975. Vol. 1 complete in one no. Previously issued as a
supplement to: Audiovisual instruction, ISSN 0004-7635.
Supplement to: Audiovisual instruction ISSN: 0004-7635
(OCoLC)5053653 (DLC)   5930807. ISSN 0190-1974
*I. Association for Educational Communications and
Technology. II. Title: Audiovisual instruction. III. Title:
Audiovisual instruction*

**Learning :** rule extraction and representation / editors,
Angela D. Friederici, Randolf Menzel. Berlin ; New
York : Walter de Gruyter, 1999. xiv, 290 p. : ill. ; 25 cm.
Includes bibliographical references and index. ISBN

3-11-016133-8 (cloth : alk. paper) DDC 612.8/2
1. Learning. 2. Neuropsychology. 3. Cognitive neuroscience. 4.
Evoked potentials (Electrophysiology) I. Friederici, Angela D.
II. Menzel, Randolf, 1940-
TC QP408 .L44 1999

**Learning schools, learning systems.**
Clarke, Paul, 1961- London ; New York : Continuum,
2000.
TC LB1027 .C468 2000

**Learning sites** : social and technological resources for
learning / edited by Joan Bliss, Roger Säljö, and Paul
Light. 1st ed. Amsterdam ; New York : Pergamon,
1999. xiv, 312 p. : ill. ; 25 cm. (Advances in learning and
instruction series) "Earli." Includes bibliographical references
(p. 259-292) and indexes. ISBN 0-08-043350-2 (hc : alk.
paper) DDC 370.15/23
1. Learning. 2. Context effects (Psychology) 3. Cognition -
Social aspects. 4. Machine learning. 5. Educational
technology. I. Bliss, Joan. II. Säljö, Roger, 1948- III. Light,
Paul. IV. European Association for Research on Learning and
Instruction. V. Series.
TC LB1060 .L4245 1999

**LEARNING - SOCIAL ASPECTS.**
Flecha, Ramón. [Compartiendo palabras. English]
Sharing words. Lanham, Md. ; Oxford : Rowman &
Littlefield Publishers, c2000.
TC LB1060 .F5913 2000

How people learn. Expanded ed. Washington, D.C. :
National Academy Press, c2000.
TC LB1060 .H672 2000

Light, Paul. Social processes in children's learning.
Cambridge, U.K. ; New York : Cambridge University
Press, 1999.
TC LB1060 .L533 1999

**LEARNING STRATEGIES.**
Individualisation. Oxford : Modern English
Publications, 1982.
TC LC32 .I53 1982

Sosin, Adrienne. Achieving styles preferences of
students in an urban graduate teacher education
program. 1996.
TC 06 no. 10701

Vella, Jane Kathryn, 1931- Taking learning to task.
San Francisco, Calif. : Jossey-Bass, c2000.
TC LC5225.L42 V43 2000

**The learning strategies handbook** / Anna Uhl
Chamot ... [et al.]. White Plains, NY : Longman,
c1999. vi, 249 p. : ill. ; 28 cm. Includes bibliographical
references (p. 239-246) and index. ISBN 0-201-38548-1 DDC
418/.007
1. Language and languages - Study and teaching. I. Chamot,
Anna Uhl.
TC P51 .L43 1999

**LEARNING - STUDY AND TEACHING.**
Bligh, Donald A. What's the point in discussion?
Exeter, Eng. ; Portland, OR : Intellect, 2000.
TC LC6519 .B555 2000

**LEARNING SYSTEMS.** See **INSTRUCTIONAL
SYSTEMS.**

**LEARNING TEAMS.** See **TEAM LEARNING
APPROACH IN EDUCATION.**

**Learning that lasts.**
Mentkowski, Marcia. 1st ed. San Francisco : Jossey-
Bass, c2000.
TC LB1060 .M464 2000

**Learning the language of addiction counseling.**
Miller, Geraldine A., 1955- Boston : Allyn and Bacon,
c1999.
TC RC564 .M536 1999

**Learning theories.**
Schunk, Dale H. 3rd ed. Upper Saddle River, N.J. :
Merrill, c2000.
TC LB1060 .S37 2000

**Learning through children's eyes.**
Oldfather, Penny. 1st ed. Washington, DC : American
Psychological Association, c1999.
TC LB1060 .O43 1999

**Learning through folklore series**
Kraus, Anne Marie. Folktale themes and activities for
children. Englewood, Colo. : Teacher Ideas Press,
c1998-1999.
TC GR45 .K73 1998

**Learning through language in early childhood.**
Painter, Clare, 1947- London ; New York : Cassell,
1999.
TC LB1139.5.L35 P35 1999

**Learning through problems.**
Trafton, Paul R. Portsmouth, NH : Heinemann, c1999.
TC QA135.5 .T685 1999

**Learning to be adolescent.**
LeTendre, Gerald K. New Haven [Conn.] ; London :
Yale University Press, c2000.
TC LB1135 .L47 2000

**Learning to draw.**
Kaupelis, Robert. New York, Watson-Guptill
Publications [1966]
TC NC730 .K36

**Learning to lead in higher education.**
Ramsden, Paul. London ; New York : Routledge,
1998.
TC LB2341 .R32 1998

**Learning to love.**
Wilson, John, 1928- Houndmills [England] :
Macmillan Press ; New York : St. Martin's Press,
2000.
TC BF575.L8 .W555 2000

**Learning to read** : an integrated view from research
and practice / edited by Terezinha Nunes. Dordrecht ;
Boston : Kluwer Academic Publishers, 1999. xii, 391
p. : ill. ; 25 cm. (Neuropsychology and cognition ; 17) Includes
bibliographical references. ISBN 0-7923-5513-X (hc. : alk.
paper) DDC 428/.4
1. Reading. 2. Reading, Psychology of. 3. Reading disability. 4.
Reading - Remedial teaching. 5. Language acquisition. 6.
Literacy. I. Nunes, Terezinha. II. Series.
TC LB1050.2 .L42 1999

**Learning to read in China.**
Ingulsrud, John E. Lewiston, N.Y. ; Lampeter, Wales :
Mellen, c1999.
TC LB1577.C48 I54 1999

**Learning to rival.**
Flower, Linda. Mahwah, New Jersey : Lawrence
Erlbaum Associates, c2000.
TC PE1404 .F59 2000

**Learning to teach.**
Nicholls, Gill. London : Kogan Page, 1999.
TC LB1727.G7 N53 1999

**Learning to teach history in the secondary school.**
Haydn, Terry, 1951- London ; New York : Routledge,
1997.
TC D16.25 .H38 1997

**Learning to teach in the secondary school** : a
companion to school experience / [edited by] Susan
Capel, Marilyn Leask, and Tony Turner. 2nd ed.
London ; New York : Routledge, 1999. xviii, 482 p. :
ill. ; 25 cm. Includes bibliographical references (p. ) and index.
ISBN 0-415-19937-9 DDC 373.1102
1. High school teaching - Handbooks, manuals, etc. 2.
Classroom management - Handbooks, manuals, etc. I. Capel,
Susan Anne, 1953- II. Leask, Marilyn, 1950- III. Turner, Tony,
1935-
TC LB1737.A3 L43 1999

**Learning to teach mathematics in the secondary
school** : a companion to school experience / edited by
Sue Johnston-Wilder ... [et al.]. New York :
Routledge, 1999. xix, 267 p. : ill. ; 25 cm. Includes
bibliographical references (p. [249]-258) and indexes. ISBN
0-415-16280-7 DDC 510/.71/2
1. Mathematics - Study and teaching (Secondary) - United
States I. Johnston-Wilder, Sue.
TC QA13 .L4 1999

**Learning to teach religious education in the
secondary school.**
Wright, Andrew, 1958- London ; New York :
Routledge, 2000.
TC LC410.G7 W75 2000

**Learning to teach subjects in the secondary school
series**
Haydn, Terry, 1951- Learning to teach history in the
secondary school. London ; New York : Routledge,
1997.
TC D16.25 .H38 1997

Wright, Andrew, 1958- Learning to teach religious
education in the secondary school. London ; New
York : Routledge, 2000.
TC LC410.G7 W75 2000

**Learning to teach using ICT in the secondary school** /
edited by Marilyn Leask and Norbert Pachler.
London ; New York : Routledge, 1999. xix, 273 p. : ill. ;
25 cm. Includes bibliographical references and indexes. ISBN
0-415-19432-6 (pbk. : alk. paper)
1. Computer-assisted instruction - Great Britain - Case studies.
2. Information technology - Great Britain - Case studies. 3.
Education, Secondary - Great Britain - Data processing - Case
studies. 4. Education - Great Britain - Computer network

resources - Case studies. I. Leask, Marilyn, 1950- II. Pachler,
Norbert.
TC LB1028.5 .L3884 1999

**Learning today.**
Library-college journal. [Norman, Okla., etc.],
Library-College Associates]

**Learning together with clients.**
Petkoski, Djordjija B. Washington, D.C. : World
Bank, c1997.
TC HQ4420.8.P48 1997

**LEARNING, VERBAL.** See **VERBAL LEARNING.**

**LEARNING, VISUAL.** See **VISUAL LEARNING.**

**Leary, Timothy.** Politics of self-determination /
Timothy Leary. Berkeley, Ca. ; Ronin Pub., c2000. 96
p. : ill. ; 22 cm. ISBN 1-57951-015-9
1. Personality development. 2. Personality assessment. I. Title.
TC BF723.P4 L43 2000

**LEA's communication series**
Balancing the secrets of private disclosures. Mahwah,
N.J. : Lawrence Erlbaum Associates, Publishers,
2000.
TC BF697.5.S427 B35 2000

Communication and aging. 2nd ed. Mahwah, NJ ;
London : L. Erlbaum, 2000.
TC HQ1064.U5 C5364 2000

Penman, Robyn. Reconstructing communicating.
Mahwah, N.J. ; London : Lawrence Erlbaum
Associates, 2000.
TC BF637.C45 P435 2000

**Lea's communication series**
Power in the blood. Mahwah, N.J. : Erlbaum, 1999.
TC RA644.A25 P69 1999

**LEA's personal relationships series.**
Adolescent relationships and drug use. Mahwah, N.J. ;
London : Lawrence Erlbaum Associates, 2000.
TC HV5824.Y68 A315 2000

**LEA's series on personal relationships**
Bennett, Joel B. Time and intimacy. Mahwah, N.J. ;
London : Lawrence Erlbaum Associates, 2000.
TC BF575.I5 B45 2000

Honeycutt, James M. Cognition, communication, and
romantic relationships. Mahwah, N.J. ; London : L.
Erlbaum Associates, 2001.
TC BF575.I5 H66 2001

**Leashore, Bogart R.**
The challenge of permanency planning in a
multicultural society. New York : Haworth Press,
c1997.
TC HV741 .C378 1997

**Leask, Marilyn, 1950-.**
Learning to teach in the secondary school. 2nd ed.
London ; New York : Routledge, 1999.
TC LB1737.A3 L43 1999

Learning to teach using ICT in the secondary school.
London ; New York : Routledge, 1999.
TC LB1028.5 .L3884 1999

**LEAST DEVELOPED COUNTRIES.** See
**DEVELOPING COUNTRIES.**

**LEAST SQUARES.** See **PROBABILITIES.**

**LEATHER - CONSERVATION AND
RESTORATION.**
Sturge, Theodore. The conservation of leather
artefacts. London : The Leather Conservation Centre,
2000.
TC N8555 .S8 2000

**Leather Conservation Centre.**
Sturge, Theodore. The conservation of leather
artefacts. London : The Leather Conservation Centre,
2000.
TC N8555 .S8 2000

**LEATHER WORK - CONSERVATION AND
RESTORATION.**
Sturge, Theodore. The conservation of leather
artefacts. London : The Leather Conservation Centre,
2000.
TC N8555 .S8 2000

**Leathers, Howard D.**
Foster, Phillips, 1931- The world food problem. 2nd
ed. Boulder : Lynne Rienner Publishers, 1999.
TC HD9018.D44 F68 1999

**LEATHERWORK, MANDINGO.**
Frank, Barbara E. Mande potters & leatherworkers.
Washington, D.C. : Smithsonian Institution Press,
1998.

*TC DT474.6.M36 F73 1998*

**LEAVE FOR PARENTING.** *See* **PARENTAL LEAVE.**

**LEAVE OF ABSENCE.** *See* **PARENTAL LEAVE; SICK LEAVE.**

**LEAVE OF ABSENCE - LAW AND LEGISLATION - UNITED STATES.**
Commission on Family and Medical Leave (U.S.) A Workable balance. Washington, DC : Commission on Leave : Women's Bureau, U.S. Dept. of Labor, [1996]
*TC HD5115.6.U5 C66 1996*

**LEAVE OF ABSENCE - UNITED STATES.**
Commission on Family and Medical Leave (U.S.) A Workable balance. Washington, DC : Commission on Leave : Women's Bureau, U.S. Dept. of Labor, [1996]
*TC HD5115.6.U5 C66 1996*

**Leavell, Alexandra G.**
Hinely, Reg. Education in Edge City. 2nd ed. Mahwah, N.J. : L. Erlbaum Associates, 2000.
*TC LB1029.C37 H45 2000*

**Leavitt, Harold J.**
Lipman-Blumen, Jean. Hot groups. New York : Oxford University Press, 1999.
*TC HD58.9 .L56 1999*

**Leblanc, Hugues, 1924-.**
Roeper, Peter. Probability theory and probability logic. Toronto : Buffalo : University of Toronto Press, c1999.
*TC BC141 .R64 1999*

**Lebon, Rachel L., 1951-** The professional vocalist : a handbook for commercial singers and teachers / Rachel L. Lebon. Lanham, Md. : Scarecrow Press, 1999. xiv, 146 p. : ill. ; 23 cm. Includes bibliographical references (p. 137-139) and index. ISBN 0-8108-3565-7 (alk. paper) ISBN 0-8108-3566-5 (pbk. : alk. paper) DDC 783
*1. Singing - Instruction and study. 2. Singing - Vocational guidance. I. Title.*
*TC MT855 .L43 1999*

**Lebow, Eileen F.** The bright boys : a history of Townsend Harris High School / Eileen F. Lebow. Westport, Conn. : Greenwood Press, c2000. viii, 227 p. :bill. ; 24 cm. (Contributions to the study of education, 0196-707X ; no. 80) Includes bibliographical references and index. ISBN 0-313-31479-9 (alk. paper) DDC 373.747/1
*1. Townsend Harris High School (Manhattan, New York, N.Y.) - History. I. Title. II. Series.*
*TC LD7501.N5 T692 2000*

**Lebredo, Raquel.**
Jarvis, Ana C. Getting along in Spanish. Lexington, Mass. : D.C. Heath, c1984.
*TC PC4121 .J37 1984*

**Lebrun, Yvan.**
Aphasia in atypical populations. Mahwah, N.J. : Lawrence Erlbaum Associates, 1998.
*TC RC425 .A637 1998*

**Lectura para maestros.**
Pan American Union. Division of Intellectual Cooperation. Washington, D.C., Oficina de Cooperación Intelectual, Unión Panamericana, 193 -

**LECTURE METHOD IN TEACHING.**
Carbone, Elisa Lynn. Teaching large classes. Thousand Oaks, Calif. : Sage Publications, c1998.
*TC LB2331 .C336 1998*

A handbook for teaching and learning in higher education. London : Kogan Page, 1999.
*TC LB2331 .H29 1999*

Klaassen, R. G. Effective lecturing behaviour in English-medium instruction. Delft, Netherlands : Delft University Press, 1999.
*TC LB2393 .K53 1999*

**Lecture notes in computer science**
(1696) ECDL '99 (3rd : 1999 : Paris, France) Research and advanced technology for digital libraries. Berlin ; New York : Springer, c1999.
*TC ZA4080 .E28 1999*

(1715.) MLDM'99 (1999 : Leipzig, Germany) Machine learning and data mining in pattern recognition. Berlin ; New York : Springer, c1999.
*TC Q327 .M56 1999*

**Lecture notes in computer science. Lecture notes in artificial intelligence.**
MLDM'99 (1999 : Leipzig, Germany) Machine learning and data mining in pattern recognition. Berlin ; New York : Springer, c1999.
*TC Q327 .M56 1999*

**Lederer, Jane.** Participation in active euthanasia and assisted suicide and attitudes and interpersonal values of physicians and nurses / by Jane Lederer. 1996. xi, 184 leaves ; 29 cm. Typescript; issued also on microfilm. Thesis (Ed.D.)--Teachers College, Columbia University, 1996. Includes bibliographical references (leaves 145-150).
*1. Euthanasia - Moral and ethical aspects. 2. Assisted suicide - United States - Moral and ethical aspects. 3. Terminally ill - United States - Psychology. 4. Physicians - United States - Professional ethics. 5. Nursing ethics - United States. 6. Right to die - Moral and ethical aspects. I. Title.*
*TC 06 no. 10849*

**Lederer, William J., 1912-** The ugly American / by William J. Lederer and Eugene Burdick. 1st ed. New York : Norton, 1958. 285 p. ; 22 cm.
*1. International relations - Fiction. 2. National characteristics, American - Fiction. 3. United States - Relations - Asia - Fiction. 4. United States - Relations - Foreign countries - Fiction. I. Burdick, Eugene. II. Title.*
*TC PS3523 .E27U35 1958*

**Lederman, Norman G.**
Examining pedagogical content knowledge. Dordrecht ; London : Kluwer Academic, c1999.
*TC Q181 .E93 1999*

**Lee, Anthony W., 1960-** Painting on the left : Diego Rivera, radical politics, and San Francisco's public murals / Anthony W. Lee. Berkeley : University of California Press, c1999. xx, 264 p. : ill. (some col.) ; 26 cm. Includes bibliographical references (p. 225-254) and index. ISBN 0-520-21133-2 (alk. paper) DDC 759.972
*1. Rivera, Diego. - 1886-1957 - Political and social views. 2. Mural painting and decoration - 20th century - California - San Francisco - Themes, motives. 3. Street art - California - San Francisco. I. Title.*
*TC ND259.R5 L44 1999*

**Lee, Carol D.**
Vygotskian perspectives on literacy research. Cambridge, U.K. ; New York : Cambridge University Press, 2000.
*TC LB1060 .V95 2000*

**Lee, Carol K.** Learning about books & libraries : a goldmine of games / Carol K. Lee and Janet Langford. Fort Atkinson, Wis. : Alleyside Press, 2000. 95 p. : ill. ; 28 cm. (Library & information skills) Includes bibliographical references and index. ISBN 1-57950-051-X (soft : alk. paper) DDC 027.62/5
*1. Library orientation for school children - United States. 2. Elementary school libraries - United States - Problems, exercises, etc. 3. Educational games - United States. 4. Library orientation for school children. 5. Elementary school libraries - Problems, exercises, etc. 6. Educational games. I. Langford, Janet. II. Title. III. Title: Learning about books and libraries IV. Series.*
*TC Z711.2 .L455 2000*

**Lee, Christina.** Women's health : psychological and social perspectives / Christina Lee. London ; Thousand Oaks, Calif. : Sage, 1998. viii, 238 p. ; 24 cm. (Behaviour and health) Includes bibliographical references (p. [183]-233) and index. ISBN 0-7619-5728-6 (hbk.) ISBN 0-7619-5729-4 (pbk.)
*1. Women - Health and hygiene - Psychological aspects. 2. Women - Health and hygiene - Social aspects. 3. Women - Psychology. I. Title. II. Series.*
*TC RA564.85 .L443 1998*

**Lee, J. Scott, 1948-.**
Core texts in conversation . Lanham, MD : University Press of America, 2000.
*TC LB2361.5 .C68 2000*

**Lee, Jeanne M.** I once was a monkey : stories Buddha told / Jeanne M. Lee. 1st ed. New York : Farrar, Straus and Giroux, 1999. 1 v. (unpaged) : ill. (some col.) ; 28 cm. SUMMARY: A retelling of six Jatakas, or birth stories, which illustrate some of the central tenets of Buddha's teachings, such as compassion, honesty, and thinking clearly before acting. ISBN 0-374-33548-6 DDC 294.3/82325
*1. Tipitaka. - Suttapiṭaka. - Khuddakanikāya. - Jātaka - Paraphrases. English. 2. Jataka stories. English. 3. Jataka stories. I. Title.*
*TC BQ1462.E5 L44 1999*

**Lee, John, 1944-.**
Improving teaching and learning in the core curriculum. London : New York : Falmer Press, 2000.
*TC LB1564.G7 I475 2000*

**Lee, Kang.**
Childhood cognitive development. Malden, Mass. : Blackwell, 2000.
*TC BF723.C5 C487 2000*

**Lee, Yoonmi.** Modern education, textbooks and the image of the nation : politics of modernization and nationalism in Korean education, 1880-1910 / Yoonmi Lee. New York ; London : Garland Pub., 2000. x, 157 p. ; 24 cm. (East Asia: history, politics, sociology, culture) Includes bibliographical references (p. 137-154) and index. ISBN 0-8153-3874-0 (alk. paper) DDC 370/.9519
*1. Textbooks - Korea - History. 2. Textbooks - Social aspects - Korea. 3. Nationalism and education - Korea. I. Title. II. Series: East Asia (New York. N.Y.)*
*TC LB3048.K6 L44 2000*

**Leeper, Ethel M.**
Murphy, Lois Barclay, 1902- The individual child. Washington : Department of Health Education, and Welfare : for sale by the Supt. of Docs., U. S. Govt. Print. Off., 1973.

**Lees, John, 1951-.**
Clinical counselling in context. London ; New York : Routledge, 1999.
*TC RC466 .C55 1999*

**Leff, Gordon.**
The medieval church. Woodbridge, Suffolk ; Rochester, NY : Published for the Ecclesiastical History Society by the Boydell Press, 1999.
*TC BR270 .M43 1999*

**Leffert, Nancy, 1949-.**
Scales, Peter, 1949- Developmental assets. Minneapolis : Search Institute, c1999.
*TC BF724 .S327 1999*

**Left back.**
Ravitch, Diane. New York : Simon & Schuster, c2000.
*TC LA216 .R28 2000*

**Left Hand Bull, Jacqueline.** Lakota hoop dancer / text by Jacqueline Left Hand Bull and Suzanne Haldane ; with photographs by Suzanne Haldane. 1st ed. New York : Dutton Children's Books, c1999. [32] p. : col. ill. ; 25 x 26 cm. Includes bibliographical references (p. [32]). SUMMARY: Follows the activities of Kevin Locke, a Hunkpapa Indian, as he prepares for and performs the traditional Lakota hoop dance. ISBN 0-525-45413-6 (hc) DDC 793.3/19783/0899752
*1. Teton Indians - Juvenile literature. 2. Hoop dance - South Dakota - Juvenile literature. 3. Hoop dance. 4. Teton Indians. 5. Indians of North America - South Dakota. I. Haldane, Suzanne, ill. II. Title.*
*TC E99.T34 L43 1999*

**Legacy of hate.**
Perlmutter, Philip. Armonk, N.Y. ; London : M.E. Sharpe, c1999.
*TC BF575.H3 P47 1999*

**A legacy of learning.**
Kearns, David T. Washington, D.C. : Brookings Institution Press, c2000.
*TC LA217.2 .K43 2000*

**Legal basics.**
Kelly, Evelyn B. Bloomington, Ind. : Phi Delta Kappa Educational Foundation, c1998.
*TC KF390.E3 K45 1998*

**LEGAL BIBLIOGRAPHY.** *See* **LEGAL RESEARCH.**

**LEGAL DOCUMENTS.** *See* **FALSE CERTIFICATION.**

**Legal guide for the visual artist.**
Crawford, Tad, 1946- 3rd ed. New York : Allworth Press : Copublished with the American Council for the Arts ; Cincinnati, Ohio : Distributor to the trade in the United States and Canada, North Light Books, c1995.
*TC KF390.A7 C73 1995*

**LEGAL HOLIDAYS.** *See* **HOLIDAYS.**

**Legal problems of religious and private schools.**
Mawdsley, Ralph D. 4th ed. Dayton, OH : Education Law Association, c2000.
*TC KF4124.5 .M38 2000*

**Legal research.**
Pauwels, Colleen Kristl, 1946- Bloomington, Ind. : Phi Delta Kappa Educational Foundation, c1999.
*TC KF240 .P38 1999*

**LEGAL RESEARCH - UNITED STATES.**
Pauwels, Colleen Kristl, 1946- Legal research. Bloomington, Ind. : Phi Delta Kappa Educational Foundation, c1999.
*TC KF240 .P38 1999*

**LEGALIZATION OF ILLEGAL DRUGS.** *See* **DRUG LEGALIZATION.**

**The legend of Freud.**
Weber, Samuel M. [Freud-Legende. English] Expanded ed. Stanford, Calif. : Stanford University Press, 2000, c1982.

TC BF173.F85 W2813 2000

LEGENDS. *See* MYTHOLOGY.

**LEGENDS - BIBLIOGRAPHY.**
Perry, Phyllis Jean. Myths, legends & tales. Ft.
Atkinson, Wis. : Alleyside Press, c1999.
*TC Z7836 .P47 1999*

**LEGENDS - BRITISH COLUMBIA - PACIFIC
    COAST.**
Wyatt, Gary, 1958- Mythic beings. Vancouver :
Douglas & McIntyre ; Seattle : University of
Washington Press, c1999.
*TC E78.B9 W93 1999*

**LEGENDS - STUDY AND TEACHING
    (ELEMENTARY).**
Perry, Phyllis Jean. Myths, legends & tales. Ft.
Atkinson, Wis. : Alleyside Press, c1999.
*TC Z7836 .P47 1999*

**Léger, Fernand, 1881-1955.**
    [Fonctions de la peinture. English]
    Functions of painting, by Fernand Léger. Translated
    by Alexandra Anderson. Edited and introduced by
    Edward F. Fry. With a pref. by George L. K.
    Morris. New York, Viking Press [1973] xxxiv, 221
    p. : ill. ; 22 cm. (The Documents of 20th-century art)
    Translation of Fonctions de la peinture. Bibliography: p.
    [193]-215. ISBN 0-670-33221-6 ISBN 0-670-01945-3 (pbk)
    DDC 701
    *1. Art - Philosophy. 2. Aesthetics. 3. Art and society. I. Title. II.
    Series.*
    *TC N70 .L45213 1973*

**Leggo, Carleton Derek, 1953-** Teaching to wonder :
    responding to poetry in the secondary classroom / Carl
    Leggo. Vancouver : Pacific Educational Press, c1997.
    144 p. ; 23 cm. Includes bibliographical references and index.
    ISBN 1-89576-631-1 DDC 808.1/071/2
    *1. Poetry - Study and teaching (Secondary) 2. Poésie - Étude et
    enseignement (Secondaire) I. Title.*
    *TC PN1101 .L43 1997*

**Legislating for higher education in Europe**
    (v. 2) Groof, Jan de. Democracy and governance in
    higher education. The Hague ; Boston : Kluwer
    Law International, 1998.
    *TC LB2341.8.E85 G76 1998*

**LEGISLATION.** *See* LAW.

**LEGISLATION, NURSING - UNITED STATES.**
Nurse's legal handbook. 4th ed. Springhouse, Pa. :
Springhouse Corp., c2000.
*TC RT86.7 .N88 2000*

**LEGISLATIVE BODIES - COMMITTEES.** *See*
    LEGISLATIVE HEARINGS.

**LEGISLATIVE BODIES - UNITED STATES -
    STATES - COMMITTEES - DIRECTORIES.**
CSG state directory. Directory II, Legislative
leadership, committees & staff. Lexington, Ky. :
Council of State Governments, c1998-
*TC JK2495 .S688*

**LEGISLATIVE BODIES - UNITED STATES -
    STATES - OFFICIALS AND EMPLOYEES -
    DIRECTORIES.**
CSG state directory. Directory II, Legislative
leadership, committees & staff. Lexington, Ky. :
Council of State Governments, c1998-
*TC JK2495 .S688*

**LEGISLATIVE DOCUMENTS.** *See*
    LEGISLATIVE HEARINGS.

**LEGISLATIVE HEARINGS - UNITED STATES -
    STUDY AND TEACHING - SIMULATION
    METHODS.**
We the people simulated congressional hearing
[videorecording]. [Boulder, Colo.] : Social Science
Education Consortium, c1997.
*TC KF4208.5.L3 W4 1997*

**LEGISLATIVE HISTORIES.** *See* LEGISLATIVE
    HEARINGS.

**Legislative leadership, committees & staff.**
CSG state directory. Directory II, Legislative
leadership, committees & staff. Lexington, Ky. :
Council of State Governments, c1998-
*TC JK2495 .S688*

**Legislative leadership, committees and staff.**
CSG state directory. Directory II, Legislative
leadership, committees & staff. Lexington, Ky. :
Council of State Governments, c1998-
*TC JK2495 .S688*

**LEGISLATIVE POWER.** *See* LEGISLATIVE
    BODIES; STATE GOVERNMENTS.

**LEGISLATORS - UNITED STATES - STATES -
    DIRECTORIES.**
CSG state directory. Directory I, Elective officials.
Lexington, Ky. : The Council, c1998-
*TC JK2403 .S69*

**LEGISLATURES.** *See* LEGISLATIVE BODIES.

**Lehning, James R., 1947-** Peasant and French : cultural
    contact in rural France during the nineteenth century /
    James R. Lehning. Cambridge [England] ; New York :
    Cambridge University Press, 1995. xii, 239 p. : maps ; 24
    cm. Includes bibliographical references (p. 211-234) and index.
    ISBN 0-521-46210-X ISBN 0-521-46770-5 (pbk.) DDC
    944.06
    *1. National characteristics, French. 2. Nationalism - France -
    History - 19th century. 3. Peasantry - France - Political
    activity. 4. France - Cultural policy - History - 19th century. I.
    Title.*
    *TC DC34 .L5 1995*

**Lehrer, Richard.**
    Designing learning environments for developing
    understanding of geometry and space. Mahwah, N.J. :
    Lawrence Erlbaum, c1998.
    *TC QA461 .L45 1998*

**Lehrproben und lehrgänge aus der praxis der
    höheren lehranstalten.**
Lehrproben und lehrgänge aus der praxis der höheren
lehranstalten. Halle a.S., Buchhandlung des
Waisenhauses.

**Lehrproben und lehrgänge aus der praxis der
    höheren lehranstalten.** Zur förderung der zwecke des
    erziehenden unterrichts, von Otto Frick und Gustav
    Richter begründet und unter mitwirkung bewährter
    schulmänner hrsg. ... Halle a.S., Buchhandlung des
    Waisenhauses. v. 24 cm. Frequency: Quarterly. Title varies
    slightly. Editors: W. Fries (with H. Meier, 1895; R. Menge,
    1896-1912)
    *1. Title: Lehrproben und lehrgänge aus der praxis der höheren
    lehranstalten*

**Leibold, Cheryl.**
    Pennsylvania Academy of the Fine Arts. Eakins and
    the photograph. Washington : Published for the
    Pennsylvania Academy of the Fine Arts by the
    Smithsonian Institution Press, c1994.
    *TC TR652 .P46 1994*

**Leibs, Andrew.** A field guide for the sight-impaired
    reader : a comprehensive resource for students,
    teachers, and librarians / Andrew Leibs ; foreword by
    Richard Scribner. Westport, Conn. : London :
    Greenwood Press, 1999. xxv, 247 p. ; 24 cm. Includes
    bibliographical references (p. [243]-244) and index. ISBN
    0-313-30969-8 (alk. paper) DDC 011.63
    *1. Blind - United States - Books and reading. 2. Visually
    handicapped - United States - Books and reading. I. Title.*
    *TC HV1731 .L45 1999*

**Leicester, Mal.**
    Classroom issues. London ; New York : Falmer Press,
    2000.
    *TC LC268 .C52 2000*

    Institutional issues. London ; New York : Falmer
    Press, 2000.
    *TC LC191 .I495 2000*

    Moral education and pluralism. London ; New York :
    Falmer Press, 2000.
    *TC LC268 .M683 2000*

    Politics, education and citizenship. London ; New
    York : Falmer Press, 2000.
    *TC LC1091 .P54 2000*

    Spiritual and religious education. London ; New
    York : Falmer Press, 2000.
    *TC BL42 .S68 2000*

    Systems of education. London ; New York : Falmer
    Press, 2000.
    *TC LC191 .S98 2000*

**Leicester museum studies series.**
    Godly things. New York : Leicester University Press,
    2000.
    *TC BL45 .G63 2000*

**Leicester Museum Studies Series**
    Pearce, Susan M. Archaeological curatorship.
    Washington, D.C. : Smithsonian Institution Press,
    1996.
    *TC AM7 .P43 1996*

**Leichter, Howard M.**
    Health policy reform in America. 2nd ed. Armonk,
    N.Y. : M.E. Sharpe, c1997.
    *TC RA395.A3 H42564 1997*

**Leigh, Wilhelmina.**
    Job creation. Washington, DC : Joint Center for
    Political and Economic Studies ; Lanham, Md. ;
    Oxford : University Press of America, c1998.
    *TC HD8081.A65 J63 1998*

**LEISURE.** *See also* RECREATION.
    Caregiving--leisure and aging. New York : Haworth
    Press, c1999.
    *TC HV1451 .C327 1999*

**Leisure and culture.**
    Rojek, Chris. Houndmills [England] : Macmillan
    Press ; New York : St. Martin's Press, 2000.
    *TC GV14.45 .R657 2000*

**LEISURE - RESEARCH.**
    Riddick, Carol Cutler. Evaluative research in
    recreation, park, and sport settings. [Champaign, Ill.? :
    Sagamore Publishing], c1999.
    *TC GV181.46 .R533 1999*

**LEISURE - SOCIOLOGICAL ASPECTS.**
    Rojek, Chris. Leisure and culture. Houndmills
    [England] : Macmillan Press ; New York : St.
    Martin's Press, 2000.
    *TC GV14.45 .R657 2000*

**LEISURE TIME.** *See* LEISURE.

**Leithwood, Kenneth A.** Changing leadership for
    changing times / Kenneth Leithwood, Doris Jantzi,
    and Rosanne Steinbach. Buckingham ; Philadelphia :
    Open University Press, 1999. viii, 254 p. ; 24 cm.
    (Changing education series) Includes bibliographical
    references (p. [224]-245) and index. ISBN 0-335-19523-7
    (hardbound) ISBN 0-335-19522-9 (pbk.) DDC 371.2
    *1. Educational leadership. 2. School management and
    organization. 3. School improvement programs. I. Jantzi,
    Doris. II. Steinbach, Rosanne, 1942- III. Title. IV. Series:
    Changing education.*
    *TC LB2805 .L358 1999*

    Educational accountability : the state of the art /
    International Network for Innovative School Systems
    (INIS) ; Kenneth Leithwood, Karen Edge, Doris
    Jantzi. Gütersloh : Bertelsmann Foundation
    Publishers, 1999. 199 p. ; 21 cm. Includes bibliographical
    references (p. 189-197). CONTENTS: Acknowledgements --
    Section A. A framework for understanding educational
    accountability -- Section B. The accountability toolbox --
    Section C. Accountability policies and practices in selected
    countries -- Summary -- References -- The authors. ISBN 3-
    89204-435-X
    *1. Educational accountability. I. Edge, Karen. II. Jantzi, Doris.
    III. International Network for Innovative School Systems. IV.
    Title.*
    *TC LB2806.22 .L45 1999*

**Lelwica, Michelle Mary.** Starving for salvation : the
    spiritual dimensions of eating problems among
    American girls and women / Michelle Mary Lelwica.
    New York : Oxford University Press, 1999. x, 210 p. ;
    24 cm. Includes bibliographical references (p. 191-200) and
    index. ISBN 0-19-512743-9 (cloth : acid-free paper) DDC
    616.85/26/0082
    *1. Eating disorders - Patients - Religious life. 2. Women -
    Health and hygiene - Religious aspects. I. Title.*
    *TC RC552.E18 L44 1999*

**Lemaire, Donald.**
    Building effective evaluation capacity. New
    Brunswick, N.J. : Transaction Publishers, c1999.
    *TC JF1351 .B83 1999*

**Lemann, Nicholas.** The big test : : the secret history of
    the American meritocracy / Nicholas Lemann. 1st ed.
    New York : Farrar, Straus and Giroux, 1999. viii, 406
    p. ; 24 cm. Includes bibliographical references (p. [351]-389)
    and index. ISBN 0-374-29984-6 (alk. paper)
    *1. Chauncey, Henry, - 1905- 2. Educational Testing Service -
    History. 3. Educational tests and measurements - United
    States - History - 20th century. 4. Ability - United States -
    Testing - History - 20th century. 5. Intelligence tests - United
    States - History - 20th century. 6. Elite (Social sciences) -
    United States. I. Title.*
    *TC LB3051 .L44 1999*

**Lemasson, Jean-Pierre.**
    A new world of knowledge. Ottawa : International
    Development Research Centre, c1999.
    *TC LC1090 N38 1999*

**Lendon, Nigel.**
    The painters of the Wagilag sisters story 1937-1997.
    Canberra, ACT : The National Gallery of Australia,
    1997.
    *TC ND1101 .P395 1997*

**L'ENGLE, MADELEINE.**
    **WRINKLE IN TIME.**
    Beech, Linda Ward. A wrinkle in time by
    Madeleine L'Engle. New York : Scholastic, c1997.

**TC LB1573 .B435 1997**

**Length and area.**
Radó, Tibor, 1895-1965. New York, American Mathematical Society, 1948.
**TC QA611 .R3**

**LENGTH OF SCHOOL DAY.** *See* **SCHOOL DAY.**

**Lenington, Robert L.** Managing higher education as a business / by Robert L. Lenington. Phoenix, Ariz. : Oryx Press, 1996. x, 190 p. : ill. ; 24 cm. (American Council on Education/Oryx Press series on higher education) Includes bibliographical references (p. [171]-175) and index. ISBN 1-57356-023-5 (alk. paper) DDC 378/.1/0973
*1. Education, Higher - United States - Administration. 2. Education, Higher - United States - Business management. I. Title. II. Series.*
**TC LB2341 .L426 1996**

**Lensch, Carol R., 1949-** Making sense of attention deficit/hyperactivity disorder / Carol R. Lensch. Westport, Conn. ; London : Bergin & Garvey, 2000. xvi, 140 p. ; 25 cm. Includes bibliographical references and index. ISBN 0-89789-700-5 (alk. paper) DDC 616.85/89
*1. Attention-deficit hyperactivity disorder. I. Title.*
**TC RJ506.H9 L46 2000**

**L'Enseignement Mathematique.** Paris [etc.]. Vol.1-40, 1899-1954, in v.40. ISSN 0013-8584

**L'Enseignement Mathematique.** Paris [etc.]. Vol.1-40, 1899-1954, in v.40. ISSN 0013-8584

**L'Enseignement Public** Title varies: Revue Pedagogique. Volume Numbering Irregular Beginning 1929

**Lensmire, Timothy J., 1961-** Powerful writing/ responsible teaching / Timothy J. Lensmire. New York : Teachers College Press, c2000. ix, 134 p. ; 24 cm. (Critical issues in educational leadership series) Includes bibliographical references (p. 123-129) and index. ISBN 0-8077-3956-1 (pbk. : alk. paper) ISBN 0-8077-3957-X (cloth : alk. paper) DDC 808/.042/071173
*1. English language - Composition and exercises - Study and teaching. 2. Critical pedagogy. I. Title. II. Series.*
**TC LB1576 .L42 2000**

**Lent, Robert W. (Robert William), 1953-.**
Handbook of counseling psychology. 3rd ed. New York : J. Wiley, c2000.
**TC BF637.C6 H315 2000**

**LENTIVIRUS INFECTIONS.** *See* **HIV INFECTIONS.**

**Lenzenweger, Mark F.**
Frontiers of developmental psychopathology. New York : Oxford University Press, 1996.
**TC RC454.4 .F76 1996**

Origins and development of schizophrenia. Washington, DC : American Psychological Association, c1998.
**TC RC514 .O75 1998**

**Leo-Rhynie, Elsa.** Gender mainstreaming in education : a reference manual for governments and other stakeholders / Elsa Leo-Rhynie and the Institute of Development and Labour Law, University of Cape Town, South Africa. London : Commonwealth Secretariat, c1999. 70 p. ; 30 cm. (Gender management system series) Includes bibliographical references (p. 43-44). ISBN 0-85092-598-3
*1. Women - Education - Commonwealth countries. 2. Women - Education - Developing countries. 3. Sex discrimination in education - Commonwealth countries. I. Commonwealth Secretariat. II. University of Cape Town. Institute of Development and Labour Law. III. Title. IV. Series: Gender management system series*
**TC LC2572 .L46 1999**

**Leonard-Barton, Dorothy.** When sparks fly : igniting creativity in groups / Dorothy A. Leonard, Walter C. Swap. Boston, Mass. : Harvard Business School Press, 1999. x, 242 p. : ill. ; 24 cm. Includes bibliographical references (p. [221]-228) and index. ISBN 0-87584-865-6 (alk. paper) DDC 658.4/036
*1. Creative ability in business. 2. Teams in the workplace. 3. Social groups. I. Swap, Walter C. II. Title.*
**TC HD53 .L46 1999**

**Leonard, J. S. (James S.).**
Making Mark Twain work in the classroom. Durham [N.C.] : Duke University Press, 1999.
**TC PS1338 .M23 1999**

**Leonard, John, 1938-.**
Pai, Hang Young. Chisanbop finger calculation method. New York : McCormick-Mathers Pub. Co., 1981.
**TC QA115 .P23 1981**

Pai, Hang Young. Chisanbop. Teacher's annotated ed. New York : American Book Co., 1980.

**TC QA115 .P23 1980 Teacher's Ed.**

Pai, Hang Young. Chisanbop. New York : American Book Co., 1980.
**TC QA115 .P23 1980**

Pai, Hang Young. Chisanbop. New York : American Book Co., 1980.
**TC QA115 .P231 1980**

Pai, Hang Young. Chisanbop. Teacher's annotated ed. New York : American Book Co., 1980.
**TC QA115 .P231 1980 Teacher's Ed.**

**Leonard, Kenneth E.**
Psychological theories of drinking and alcoholism. 2nd ed. New York : Guilford Press, c1999.
**TC HV5045 .P74 1999**

**Leonard, Pauline E.**
The values of educational administration. London : Falmer, 1999.
**TC LB2806 .V255 1999**

**Leonard, Thomas, 1948-** Bayesian methods : an analysis for statisticians and interdisciplinary researchers / Thomas Leonard, John S.J. Hsu. Cambridge, U.K. ; New York : Cambridge University Press, 1999. xiv, 333 p. : ill. ; 26 cm. (Cambridge series in statistical and probabilistic mathematics) Includes bibliographical references (p. 303-319) and indexes. ISBN 0-521-59417-0 (hardback) DDC 519.5/42
*1. Bayesian statistical decision theory. I. Hsu, John S. J., 1955- II. Title. III. Series: Cambridge series on statistical and probabilistic mathematics.*
**TC QA279.5 .L45 1999**

**Leonard, Thomas, 1955- ill.**
Dunphy, Madeleine. Here is the African savanna. 1st ed. New York : Hyperion Books for Children, c1999.
**TC QH194 .D86 1999**

**Leonardo (Series) (Cambridge, Mass.)**
The Robot in the garden. Cambridge, Mass. : MIT Press, 2000.
**TC TJ211 .R537 2000**

**Leonardo, Zeus, 1968-.**
Charting terrains of Chicana(o)/Latina(o) education. Cresskill, N.J. : Hampton Press, c2000.
**TC LC2669 .C42 2000**

**Leone, Bruno, 1939-.**
Poverty. San Diego, CA : Greenhaven Press, c1994.
**TC HC110.P6 P63 1994**

**Lephart, Scott M., 1961-.**
Proprioception and neuromuscular control in joint stability. [Champaign, IL] : Human Kinetics, c2000.
**TC QP454 .P77 2000**

**LePore, Ernest, 1950-.**
What is cognitive science? Malden, Mass. : Blackwell, 1999.
**TC BF311 .W48 1999**

**LEPORIDAE.** *See* **RABBITS.**

**LEPUS.** *See* **HARES.**

**Lerner, Neal.**
Gillespie, Paula. The Allyn and Bacon guide to peer tutoring. Boston : Allyn & Bacon, c2000.
**TC LB1031.5 .G55 2000**

**Lerner, Richard M.**
Adolescents and their families. New York : Garland Pub., 1999.
**TC HQ796 .A33533 1999**

Family diversity and family policy : strengthening families for America's children / Richard M. Lerner, Elizabeth E. Sparks and Laurie D. McCubbin. Boston ; London : Kluwer Academic, c1999. xi, 168 p. : ill. ; 25 cm. (Outreach scholarship ; 2) Includes bibliographical references (p. [141]-156) and indexes. ISBN 0-7923-8612-4 (alk. paper) DDC 306.85/0973
*1. Family - United States. 2. Family policy - United States. 3. Pluralism (Social sciences) - United States. I. Sparks, Elizabeth E. II. McCubbin, Laurie D. III. Title. IV. Series.*
**TC HQ535 .L39 1999**

Scales, Peter, 1949- Developmental assets. Minneapolis : Search Institute, c1999.
**TC HQ724 .S327 1999**

**LESBIAN AND GAY STUDIES.** *See also* **GAY AND LESBIAN STUDIES.**
Reader's guide to lesbian and gay studies. Chicago : Fitzroy Dearborn Publishers, 2000.
**TC HQ75.15 .R43 2000**

**Lesbian and gay studies and the teaching of English :** positions, pedagogies, and cultural politics / edited by William J. Spurlin. Urbana, Ill. : National Council of Teachers of English, 2000. xxxiii, 326 p. ; 23 cm. Includes bibliographical references and index. ISBN 0-8141-2794-0 (pbk.) DDC 420/.71
*1. English philology - Study and teaching. 2. English philology - Study and teaching - Political aspects. 3. Homosexuality and literature - Study and teaching. 4. Gays' writings - Study and teaching. 5. Homosexuality - Study and teaching. 6. Gay and lesbian studies. 7. Lesbians in literature. 8. Gay men in literature. I. Spurlin, William J., 1954-*
**TC PE66 .L45 2000**

**LESBIAN COLLEGE STUDENTS - UNITED STATES - BIOGRAPHY.**
Out & about campus. 1st ed. Los Angeles : Alyson Books, 2000.
**TC LC2574.6 .O87 2000**

**LESBIAN STUDENTS - UNITED STATES.**
School experiences of gay and lesbian youth. New York : Harrington Park Press, c1997.
**TC LC2575 .S36 1997**

**LESBIAN STUDIES.** *See* **GAY AND LESBIAN STUDIES.**

**LESBIAN TEACHERS - FLORIDA - INTERVIEWS.**
Sanlo, Ronni L., 1947- Unheard voices. Westport, Conn. ; London : Bergin & Garvey, 1999.
**TC LB2844.1.G39 S36 1999**

**LESBIANISM IN THE WORKPLACE.** *See* **HOMOSEXUALITY IN THE WORKPLACE.**

**LESBIANISM - STUDY AND TEACHING.** *See* **GAY AND LESBIAN STUDIES.**

**LESBIANS - COUNSELING OF.**
Handbook of counseling and psychotherapy with lesbian, gay, and bisexual clients. 1st ed. Washington, DC ; London : American Psychological Association, c2000.
**TC BF637.C6 H3125 2000**

**LESBIANS - IDENTITY.**
Thinking queer. New York : Peter Lang, c2000.
**TC LC192.6 .T55 2000**

**LESBIANS IN LITERATURE.**
Lesbian and gay studies and the teaching of English. Urbana, Ill. : National Council of Teachers of English, 2000.
**TC PE66 .L45 2000**

**LESBIANS - STUDY AND TEACHING.** *See* **GAY AND LESBIAN STUDIES.**

**Leseman, Paul.**
Effective early education. New York : Falmer Press, 1999.
**TC LB1139.23 .E44 1999**

**Lesh, Richard A.**
Handbook of research design in mathematics and science education. Mahwah, N.J. : Lawrence Erlbaum, 1999.
**TC QA11 .H256 1999**

**Lesko, Nancy.**
Masculinities at school. Thousand Oaks, Calif. : SAGE, c2000.
**TC LC1390 .M37 2000**

**Leslie, Julian C.** Behavior analysis : foundations and applications to psychology / Julian C. Leslie, Mark F. O'Reilly. Amsterdam, Netherlands : Harwood Academic Publishers, c1999. xxvi, 361 p. : ill. ; 24 cm. Includes bibliographical references (p. 335-350) and indexes. ISBN 90-5702-485-3
*1. Behaviorism (Psychology) 2. Conditioned response. 3. Psychology. I. O'Reilly, Mark F. II. Title.*
**TC BF199 .L47 1999**

**Leslie, Larry L.**
ASHE reader on finance in higher education. Needham Heights, MA : Ginn Press, c1986.
**TC LB2342 .A76 1990**

**LESS DEVELOPED COUNTRIES.** *See* **DEVELOPING COUNTRIES.**

**Lessac, Frané, ill.**
Pomerantz, Charlotte. The chalk doll. New York : Lippincott, c1989.
**TC PZ7.P77 Ch 1989**

**Lessem, Don.** Dinosaurs to dodos : an encyclopedia of extinct animals / by Don Lessem ; illustrated by Jan Sovak. 1st ed. New York : Scholastic Reference, 1999. 112 p. : col. ill. ; 29 cm. Includes bibliographical references (p. 112) and index. SUMMARY: Presents the names, physical characteristics, and places of origin of a variety of extinct animals, arranged chronologically into eras, periods, and epochs, and discusses times of mass extinction. ISBN 0-590-31684-2 (hardcover) DDC 560
*1. Vertebrates, Fossil - Encyclopedias, Juvenile. 2. Extinct*

animals - Encyclopedias. Juvenile. 3. Prehistoric animals. 4. Vertebrates, Fossil. 5. Extinct animals. 6. Extinction (Biology) I. Sovak, Jan, 1953- ill. II. Title.
**TC QE842 .L47 1999**

**Lesser, Carolyn.** Spots : counting creatures from sky to sea / Carolyn Lesser ; illustrated by Laura Regan. 1st ed. San Diego : Harcourt Brace, c1999. 1 v. (unpaged) : col. ill. ; 25 x 27 cm. SUMMARY: Spotted animals from around the world, including a leopard ray, ringed seals, reticulated giraffes, and tundra butterflies, introduce the numbers from one to ten. ISBN 0-15-200666-4 DDC 513.2/11 1. Counting - Juvenile literature. 2. Animals - Juvenile literature. 3. Animals. 4. Counting. I. Regan, Laura, ill. II. Title.
**TC QA113 .L47 1999**

**Lesson in life [videorecording].**
Sean's story [videorecording]. Princeton, N.J. : Films for the Humanities & Sciences ; [S.l. : distributed by] ABC Multimedia : Capital Cities/ABC, c1994.
**TC LC1203.M3 .S39 1994**

**LESSON PLANNING.**
Ball, Wanda H., 1953- Socratic seminars in the block. Larchmont, N.Y. : Eye On Education, 2000.
**TC LB1027.44 .B35 2000**

Robbins, Pamela. Thinking inside the block schedule. Thousand Oaks, Calif. : Corwin Press, c2000.
**TC LB3032.2 .R63 2000**

V'elez Arias, Hiram Oscar. A multi-case study of physical education teachers and working conditions in inner-city schools /by Hiram Oscar V'elez Arias. 1998.
**TC 06 no. 11001**

**LESSON PLANNING - UNITED STATES.**
Borich, Gary D. Effective teaching methods. 4th ed. Upper Saddle River, N.J. : Merrill, c2000.
**TC LB1025.3 .B67 2000**

**LESSON PLANNING - UNITED STATES - HANDBOOKS, MANUALS, ETC.**
Conroy, Mary Ann. 101 ways to integrate personal development into core curriculum. Lanham : University Press of America, c2000.
**TC LC311 .C65 2000**

**Lessons from library power.**
Zweizig, Douglas. Englewood, Colo. : Libraries Unlimited, 1999.
**TC Z675.S3 Z94 1999**

**Lessons from Mount Kilimanjaro.**
Stambach, Amy, 1966- New York : Routledge, 2000.
**TC LA1844.K54 S72 2000**

**Lester, Gillian.**
Kelman, Mark. Jumping the queue. Cambridge, Mass. : Harvard University Press, 1997.
**TC KF4215 .K45 1997**

**Let the shadows speak.**
Ewart, Franzeska G. Stoke on Trent, Staffordshire, England : Trentham Books, 1998.
**TC PN1979.S5 E8 1998**

**LeTendre, Gerald K.**
Competitor or ally? New York : Falmer Press, 1999.
**TC LA1312 .C667 1999**

Learning to be adolescent : growing up in U.S. and Japanese middle schools / Gerald K. LeTendre ; foreword by Thomas P. Rohlen. New Haven [Conn.] ; London : Yale University Press, c2000. xxii, 234 p. : ill. ; 25 cm. Includes bibliographical references (p. 197-227) and index. CONTENTS: Foreword / Thomas P. Rohlen -- 1. What Is Adolescence? -- 2. Oak Grove and Kotani -- 3. The Common Problem of Responsibility -- 4. Puberty and Sexuality - Hormones, Energy, and Rebellion -- 5. Toward Maturity: Self-Control and Academic Goals -- 6. Managing Crises -- 7. The Disruptive Adolescent, Defiance, Delinquency and the Family -- 8. Creativity and Self-Expression -- 9. How Adolescence Gets Institutionalized -- Conclusion: Adolescence, Self, and Life Course -- App. 2. Glossary of Japanese Terms. ISBN 0-300-08438-2 (alk. paper) DDC 373.18 DDC 373.18 1. Adolescence - United States - Case studies. 2. Adolescence - Japan - Case studies. 3. Middle school students - United States - Conduct of life - Case studies. 4. Middle school students - Japan - Conduct of life - Case studies. 5. Adolescent psychology - Cross-cultural studies. I. Title.
**TC LB1135 .L47 2000**

**Let's eat!.**
Zamorano, Ana. New York : Scholastic Press, 1997.
**TC PZ7.Z25455 Le 1997**

**Let's face it.**
Ross, Peter. Sydney, Australia : Art Gallery of New South Wales, 1999.

**TC ND1327.A86 R67 1999**

**Let's pretend :** teacher's planning guide. New York : Macmillan/McGraw-Hill, c1997. 1 v. (various pagings) : col. ill. ; 31 cm. (Spotlight on literacy ; Gr.1 l.5 u.1) (The road to independent reading) Includes index. ISBN 0-02-181155-5 1. Language arts (Primary) 2. Reading (Primary) I. Series. II. Series: The road to independent reading
**TC LB1576 .S66 1997 Gr.1 L5 u.1**

**Let's put kids first, finally.**
Achilles, Charles M. Thousand Oaks, Calif. : Corwin Press, c1999.
**TC LB3013.2 .A34 1999**

**Let's read!.**
Stull, Elizabeth Crosby. West Nyack, NY : Center for Applied Research in Education, c2000.
**TC LB1573 .S896 2000**

**Let's-read-and-find-out science book**
Berger, Melvin. Germs make me sick!. 1st ed. New York : Crowell, c1985.
**TC QR57 .B47 1985**

**Let's-read-and-find-out science. Stage 1**
Fraser, Mary Ann. Where are the night animals? 1st ed. New York : HarperCollins Publishers, c1999.
**TC QL755.5 .F735 1999**

Goldin, Augusta R. Ducks don't get wet. Newly illustrated ed. New York : HarperCollinsPublishers, c1999.
**TC QL696.A52 G64 1999**

**LETTER-SOUND ASSOCIATION. See READING - PHONETIC METHOD.**

**LETTER WRITING. See LETTERS.**

**LETTERS - FICTION.**
Collins, Pat Lowery. Signs and wonders. Boston : Houghton Mifflin, 1999.
**TC PZ7.C69675 Si 1999**

Pak, Soyung. Dear Juno. New York : Viking, 1999.
**TC PZ7.P173 De 1999**

Sappey, Maureen Stack, 1952- Letters from Vinnie. Asheville, NC : Front Street, 1999.
**TC PZ7.S2388 Le 1999**

**Letters from Vinnie.**
Sappey, Maureen Stack, 1952- Asheville, NC : Front Street, 1999.
**TC PZ7.S2388 Le 1999**

**LETTERS OF THE ALPHABET. See ALPHABET.**

**Letts, William J., 1965-.**
Queering elementary education. Lanham, Md. : Oxford : Rowman & Littlefield, c1999.
**TC LC192.6 .Q85 1999**

**Leutholtz, Brian C.** Exercise and disease management / Brian C. Leutholtz, Ignacio Ripoll. Boca Raton : CRC Press, c1999. xx, 220 p. ; 26 cm. 1 computer optical disc(43/4 in.). (CRC series in exercise physiology) Includes bibliographical references and index. ISBN 0-8493-8713-2 (alk. paper) DDC 615.8/2 1. Exercise therapy. 2. Exercise - Health aspects. 3. Medicine, Preventive. 4. Exercise Therapy. 5. Exercise. 6. Primary Prevention. I. Ripoll, Ignacio. II. Title. III. Series.
**TC RM725 .L45 1999**

**LEVANT. See MIDDLE EAST.**

**LEVEL OF ASPIRATION. See STUDENT ASPIRATIONS.**

**Levende talen.**
Levende talen magazine. Amsterdam : Vereniging van Leraren in Levenden Talen, 2000-

**Levende talen magazine.** Amsterdam : Vereniging van Leraren in Levenden Talen. v. : ill. ; 27 cm. Frequency: Eight issues yearly. Jaarg. 87, nr. 1 (jan. 2000)- . Title from cover. Continues: Levende talen ISSN: 0024-1539 (DLC)   63047559 (OCoLC)7938860. ISSN 1566-2705 1. Philology, Modern - Periodicals. 2. Literature, Modern - Periodicals. 3. Language and languages - Study and teaching - Periodicals. I. Vereniging van Leraren in Levende Talen. II. Title: Levende talen

**Leventhal, Tama.** Poverty and turbulence : familial and neighborhood influences on children's achievement / Tama Leventhal. 1999. xi, 198 leaves ; 29 cm. Issued also on microfilm. Thesis (Ph.D.)--Columbia University, 1999. Includes tables. Includes bibliographical references (leaves 155-179). 1. Infants - United States - Intelligence testing - Longitudinal studies. 2. Children - United States - Intelligence testing - Longitudinal studies. 3. Child development. 4. Neighborhood - United States - Economic aspects. 5. Family life surveys - United States - Longitudinal studies. 6. Mother and child - United States - Psychological aspects. I. Title. II. Title:

Familial and neighborhood influences on children's achievement
**TC 085 L5515**

**Levesque, Karen.**
Vocational education in the United States. Washington, DC : U.S. Dept. of Education, Office of Educational Research and Improvement : For sale by the U.S. G.P.O., Supt. of Docs., [2000]
**TC LC1045 .V5874 2000**

**Levesque, Roger J. R.** Adolescents, sex, and the law : preparing adolescents for responsible citizenship / Roger J.R. Levesque. 1st ed. Washington, DC : American Psychological Association, c2000. x, 392 p. ; 26 cm. (Law and public policy) Includes bibliographical references and indexes. ISBN 1-55798-609-6 (alk. paper) DDC 346.7301/35 1. Teenagers - Legal status, laws, etc. - United States. 2. Sex and law - United States. I. Title. II. Series.
**TC KF479 .L48 2000**

**Levin, Barbara B.**
Who learns what from cases and how? Mahwah, N.J. : L. Erlbaum Associates, 1999.
**TC LB1029.C37 W56 1999**

**Levin, Diane E.** Remote control childhood? : combating the hazards of media culture / Diane E. Levin. Washington, D.C. : National Association for the Education of Young Children, c1998. viii, 184 p. : ill. ; 28 cm. (NAEYC ; #326) Includes bibliographical references (p. 164-166). ISBN 0-935989-84-6 DDC 305.23 1. Mass media and children. 2. Violence in mass media. 3. Parenting. I. Title. II. Series: NAEYC (Series) ; #326.
**TC P94.5.C55 L48 1998**

**Levin, James, 1946-** Principles of classroom management : a professional decision-making model / James Levin, James F. Nolan. 3rd ed. Boston : Allyn and Bacon, c2000. xxiii, 246 p. : ill. ; 23 cm. Includes bibliographical references and index. ISBN 0-205-28862-6 DDC 371.102/4 1. Classroom management - United States - Problems, exercises, etc. 2. Teaching - United States - Problems, exercises, etc. I. Nolan, James F., 1950- II. Title.
**TC LB3013 .L475 2000**

**Levin, Marc, 1951-.**
The politics of addiction [videorecording]. Princeton, NJ : Films for the Humanities & Sciences, c1998.
**TC RC564 .P59 1998**

**Levine, Gail Carson.** Princess Sonora and the long sleep / Gail Carson Levine ; illustrated by Mark Elliott. 1st ed. New York : HarperCollins Publishers, c1999. 107 p. : ill. ; 19 cm. "The princess tales." SUMMARY: In this retelling of the fairy tale Sleeping Beauty, Princess Sonora, who is ten times smarter than anyone else, vows to choose for herself the best time to be pricked by the spindle. ISBN 0-06-028064-6 ISBN 0-06-028065-4 (lib. bdg.) DDC 398.2/0973/02 1. Fairy tales. 2. Folklore. I. Elliott, Mark, ill. II. Title. III. Title: Sleeping Beauty. English.
**TC PZ8.L4793 Pq 1999**

**Levine, James A.** Working fathers : new strategies for balancing work and family / James A. Levine and Todd L. Pittinsky. Reading, Mass. : Addison-Wesley, c1997. xiii, 274 p. ; 24 cm. Includes bibliographical references (p. 233-257) and index. ISBN 0-201-14938-9 (alk. paper) DDC 306.874/2 1. Fathers - United States - Psychology. 2. Fathers - United States - Employment. 3. Work and family - United States - Psychological aspects. I. Pittinsky, Todd L. II. Title.
**TC HQ756 .L474 1997**

**Levine, Martin G.**
Sharp, Richard M. The best Web sites for teachers. 3rd ed. Eugene, OR : International Society for Technology in Education, 2000.
**TC LB1044.87 .S52 2000**

**Levine, Michael P.**
Preventing eating disorders. Philadelphia, PA : Brunner/Mazel, c1999.
**TC RC552.E18 P744 1999**

**Levine, Michael P. (Michael Philip).**
The analytic Freud. London ; New York : Routledge, 2000.
**TC BF109.F74 A84 2000**

**Levine, Richard.**
Paris [videorecording]. New York, NY : V.I.E.W. Video, c1996.
**TC DC707 .P3 1996**

**Levine, Samuel, 1927-** A programmed introduction to research [by] Samuel Levine [and] Freeman F. Elzey. Belmont, Calif. : Wadsworth Pub. Co. [1968] viii, 236 p. 26 cm. DDC 150/.1/8

1. *Psychology - Research - Programmed instruction. I. Elzey, Freeman F., joint author. II. Title.*
**TC BF76.5 .L44**

**Levinson, David, 1947-.**
Encyclopedia of human emotions. New York : Macmillan Reference USA, c1999.
**TC BF531 .E55 1999**

**Levinson, Meira.** The demands of liberal education / Meira Levinson. Oxford ; New York : Oxford University Press, 1999. ix, 237 p. ; 25 cm. Includes bibliographical references (p. [171]-228) and index. ISBN 0-19-829544-8 DDC 370.11/2
1. *Citizenship - Study and teaching. 2. Liberalism. 3. Autonomy (Psychology) 4. Education - Aims and objectives. 5. Education and state. I. Title.*
**TC LC1091 .L38 1999**

**Levinson, Nick.**
On pictures and paintings [videorecording]. Peasmarsh, East Sussex, Eng. ; Ho-Ho-kus, NJ : Roland Collection, 1992.
**TC ND195.O45 1992**

**Levitt, Mairi.** Nice when they are young : contemporary Christianity in families and schools / Mairi Levitt. Aldershot, Hants, England ; Brookfield, Vt. : Avebury, c1996. viii, 171 p. ; ill. ; 23 cm. Includes bibliographical references (p. 163-171). ISBN 1-85972-388-8
1. *Christian education - England. 2. Christian education - England (County) - Case studies. 3. Religious education - England. I. Title.*
**TC BV1475.2 .L45 1996**

**Levy, Alan Howard.** Government and the arts : debates over federal support of the arts in America from George Washington to Jesse Helms / Alan Howard Levy. Lanham, Md. : University Press of America, c1997. xi, 147 p. ; 23 cm. Includes bibliographical references (p. [139]-142) and index. ISBN 0-7618-0674-1 (cloth : alk. paper) DDC 700/.973
1. *Federal aid to the arts - United States. 2. Art patronage - United States. I. Title.*
**TC NX735 .L48 1997**

**Levy, Daniel.**
Myth, reality, and reform. Washington, D.C. : Inter-American Development Bank, 2000.
**TC LA543 .M46 2000**

**Levy, Jerrold E., 1930-.**
Kunitz, Stephen J. Drinking, conduct disorder, and social change. Oxford ; New York : Oxford University Press, 2000.
**TC E99.N3 K88 2000**

**Levy, Mike.**
Worldcall. Lisse, Netherlands ; Abingdon [England] ; Exton, PA : Swets & Zeitlinger, c1999.
**TC P53.28 .W67 1999**

**Levy, Steven T.**
The therapeutic alliance. Madison, Conn. : International Universities Press, c2000.
**TC RC489.T66 T468 2000**

**Levy, Terry M.** Handbook of attachment interventions / edited by Terry M. Levy. San Diego, Calif. : Academic, c2000. xiv, 289 p. ; ill. ; 23 cm. Includes bibliographical references and index. ISBN 0-12-445860-2
1. *Attachment behavior in children. I. Title.*
**TC RJ507.A77 L47 2000**

**Lewin, Betsy, ill.**
Prigger, Mary Skillings. Aunt Minnie McGranahan. New York : Clarion Books, c1999.
**TC PZ7.P93534 Au 1999**

**Lewin, Ted, ill.**
Borden, Louise. A. Lincoln and me. New York : Scholastic, 1999.
**TC PZ7.B64827 An 1999**

High, Linda Oatman. Barn savers. 1st ed. Honesdale, Pa. : Caroline House/Boyds Mills Press, 1999.
**TC PZ7.H543698 Bar 1999**

**Lewis, Ann, 1950-** Researching children's perspectives / edited by Ann Lewis and Geoff Lindsay. Buckingham ; Philadelphia : Open University Press, 2000. xv, 239 p. ; ill. ; 23 cm. Includes bibliographical references (p. [219]-234) and index. ISBN 0-335-20280-2 (hb) ISBN 0-335-20279-9 (pb) DDC 305.23/07
1. *Children - Research - Methodology. 2. Children - Attitudes. I. Lindsay, Geoff II. Title.*
**TC HQ767.85 .L49 2000**

**LEWIS, C. S. (CLIVE STAPLES), 1898-1963. THE LION, THE WITCH AND THE WARDROBE.**
Rawlings, Carol Miller. The lion, the witch and the wardrobe by C. S. Lewis. New York : Scholastic, c1997.

**TC LB1573 .R38 1997**

**Lewis, Carol M.**
The process of group psychotherapy. Washington, DC : American Psychological Association, c2000.
**TC RC488 .P75 2000**

**Lewis, Cindy.**
Loud, proud & passionate. 1st ed. Eugene, OR : Mobility International USA, 1997.
**TC HV1569.3.W65 L68 1997**

**Lewis' dictionary of occupational and environmental safety and health** / [edited by] Jeffrey W. Vincoli. Boca Raton : Lewis Publishers, c2000. 1093 p. : ill. ; 29 cm. Dictionary of occupational and environmental safety and health. ISBN 1-56670-399-9 (alk. paper) DDC 363.11/03
1. *Industrial safety - Dictionaries. 2. Environmental health - Dictionaries. I. Vincoli, Jeffrey W.*
**TC T55 .L468 2000**

**Lewis, Earl B., ill.**
Kurtz, Jane. Faraway home. San Diego : Harcourt, c2000.
**TC PZ7.K9626 Far 2000**

**Lewis, Edith Anne.**
Empowering women of color. New York : Columbia University Press, c1999.
**TC HV1445 .E45 1999**

**Lewis, Frances Marcus.**
Health behavior and health education. 2nd ed. San Francisco : Jossey-Bass, 1997.
**TC RA776.9 .H434 1997**

**Lewis, Lionel S. (Lionel Stanley)** When power corrupts : academic governing boards in the shadow of the Adelphi case / Lionel S. Lewis. New Brunswick, NJ : Transaction Publishers, c2000. x, 195 p. ; 25 cm. Includes bibliographical references and index. ISBN 0-7658-0031-4 DDC 378.747/245
1. *Adelphi University - Administration - Case studies. 2. Adelphi University - Faculty - Case studies. 3. Teacher-administrator relationships - New York (State) - Garden City - Case studies. 4. Diamandopoulos, Peter. I. Title.*
**TC LD25.8 .L49 2000**

**Lewis, Maureen.**
Literacy in the secondary school. London : David Fulton, 2000.
**TC LB1632 .L587 2000**

**Lewis, Michael, 1937 Jan. 10-.**
Handbook of emotions. 2nd ed. New York : Guilford Press, c2000.
**TC BF561 .H35 2000**

**Lewis, Nancy Breslau.**
Greenspan, Stanley I. Building healthy minds. Cambridge, MA : Perseus, 1999.
**TC HQ772 .G672 1999**

**Lewis, Rena B.** Teaching special students in general education classrooms / Rena B. Lewis, Donald H. Doorlag. 5th ed. Upper Saddle River, N.J. : Merrill, c1999. xvi, 519 p. : col. ill. ; 26 cm. Rev. ed. of: Teaching special students in the mainstream. 4th ed. c1995. Includes bibliographical references (p. 481-501) and indexes. ISBN 0-13-095307-5 DDC 371.9
1. *Inclusive education - United States. 2. Special education - United States. 3. Mainstreaming in education - United States. I. Lewis, Rena B. Teaching special students in the mainstream. II. Doorlag, Donald H. III. Title.*
**TC LC1201 .L48 1999**

**Teaching special students in the mainstream.**
Lewis, Rena B. Teaching special students in general education classrooms. 5th ed. Upper Saddle River, N.J. : Merrill, c1999.
**TC LC1201 .L48 1999**

**Lewis, Sydney, 1952-** A totally alien life-form : teenagers / Sydney Lewis. New York : New Press : Distributed by W.W. Norton, c1996. 363 p. ; 25 cm. ISBN 1-56584-282-0 (hardcover) DDC 305.23/5/0973
1. *Teenagers - United States - Interviews. 2. Teenagers - United States - Social conditions. I. Title.*
**TC HQ796 .L3995 1996**

**Lewis, Thomas.** A general theory of love / Thomas Lewis, Fari Amini, Richard Lannon. New York : Random House, 2000. viii, 274 p. ; ill. ; 22 cm. Includes bibliographical references (p. [241]-254) and index. ISBN 0-375-50389-7 (hc)
1. *Love. 2. Love - Physiological aspects. I. Amini, Fari. II. Lannon, Richard. III. Title.*
**TC BF575.L8 L49 2000**

**Lewis, Tuni.**
Jazz dance class [videorecording]. W. Long Branch, NJ : Kultur, [1992?]
**TC GV1784 .J3 1992**

**LEXICOGRAPHERS - UNITED STATES - BIOGRAPHY.**
Micklethwait, David. Noah Webster and the American dictionary. Jefferson, N.C. : McFarland, c2000.
**TC PE65.W5 M53 2000**

**LEXICOGRAPHY.**
Pearson, Jennifer. Terms in context. Amsterdam ; Philadelphia : J. Benjamins, c1998.
**TC P305.18.D38 P4 1998**

**LEXICOLOGY.** *See* **SEMANTICS; VOCABULARY.**

**Li, Duan-Duan.** Expressing needs and wants in a second language : an ethnographic study of Chinese immigrant women's requesting behavior / by Duan-Duan Li. ix, 320 leaves : ill. ; 29 cm. Typescript; issued also on microfilm. Thesis (Ed.D.)--Teachers College, Columbia University, 1998. Includes bibliographical references (leaves 298-316).
1. *Chinese American women - Language. 2. English language - Foreign speakers. 3. Second language acquisition. 4. Interlanguage (Language learning) 5. Sociolinguistics. 6. Communication and culture. 7. Communication - Social aspects. 8. Speech acts (Linguistics) 9. Pragmatics. I. Title. II. Title: Ethnographic study of Chinese immigrant women's requesting behavior*
**TC 06 no. 10958**

**Li, Tze-chung, 1927-** Social science reference sources : a practical guide / Tze-chung Li. 3rd ed. Westport, Conn. : Greenwood Press, 2000. xxvii, 495 p. ; 25 cm. Includes bibliographical references and indexes. ISBN 0-313-30483-1 (alk. paper)
1. *Social sciences - Bibliography. 2. Social sciences - Bibliography of bibliographies. 3. Social sciences - Reference books - Bibliography. I. Title.*
**TC Z7161.A1 L5 2000**

**LIABILITY (LAW).** *See* **MALPRACTICE.**

**LIABILITY, LEGAL - MISCELLANEA - HANDBOOKS, MANUALS, ETC.**
Nursing documentation. Thousand Oaks, Calif. : Sage Publications, c1999.
**TC RT50 .N87 1999**

**LIABILITY, LEGAL - UNITED STATES.**
Nursing documentation. Thousand Oaks, Calif. : Sage Publications, c1999.
**TC RT50 .N87 1999**

**LIABILITY, PROFESSIONAL.** *See* **MALPRACTICE.**

**Libby, Wendy M. L.** Using art to make art creative activities using masterpieces/ Wendy M. L. Libby. Albany, N.Y. : Delmar Publishers, 2000. xiv, 250 p. : ill. ; 28 cm. Includes bibliographical references and index. ISBN 0-7668-1505-6 DDC 372.5/044
1. *Art - Study and teaching (Elementary) - United States. I. Title.*
**TC N362 .L49 2000**

**LIBEL AND SLANDER.** *See* **HATE SPEECH; PRIVACY, RIGHT OF.**

**The liberal arts advantage.**
Giangrande, Gregory. New York : Avon Books, c1998.
**TC HF5382.7 .G53 1998**

**LIBERAL ARTS EDUCATION.** *See* **EDUCATION, HUMANISTIC.**

**LIBERAL EDUCATION.** *See* **EDUCATION, HUMANISTIC.**

**LIBERALISM.**
Levinson, Meira. The demands of liberal education. Oxford ; New York : Oxford University Press, 1999.
**TC LC1091 .L38 1999**

**LIBERALISM - AFRICA, SUB-SAHARAN - HISTORY - 20TH CENTURY.**
Mungazi, Dickson A. The last British liberals in Africa. Westport, Conn. : Praeger, 1999.
**TC DT2979.T63 M86 1999**

**LIBERALISM - GERMANY - FRANKFURT AM MAIN - HISTORY - 19TH CENTURY.**
Palmowski, Jan. Urban liberalism in imperial Germany. Oxford ; New York : Oxford University Press, 1999.
**TC DD901.F78 P35 1999**

**LIBERALISM - GREAT BRITAIN - HISTORY - 20TH CENTURY.**
Mungazi, Dickson A. The last British liberals in Africa. Westport, Conn. : Praeger, 1999.
**TC DT2979.T63 M86 1999**

**LIBERALISM - UNITED STATES.**
Abowitz, Kathleen Knight. Making meaning of community in an American high school. Cresskill, N.J. : Hampton Press, c2000.
*TC LC311 .A36 2000*

Gordon, Mordechai. Toward an integrative conception of authority in education. 1997.
*TC 085 G656*

Macedo, Stephen, 1957- Diversity and distrust. Cambridge, Mass. ; London : Harvard University Press, 2000.
*TC LA217.2 .M33 2000*

**LIBERALISM - UNITED STATES - HISTORY - 20TH CENTURY.**
Cochran, David Carroll. The color of freedom. Albany : State University of New York Press, c1999.
*TC E185.615 .C634 1999*

Without justice for all. Boulder, Colo. : Westview Press, 1999.
*TC E185.615 .W57 1999*

**Liberating method.**
DeVault, Marjorie L., 1950- Philadelphia : Temple University Press, 1999.
*TC HQ1180 .D48 1999*

**LIBERATION.** *See* **LIBERTY.**

**LIBERATION MOVEMENTS (CIVIL RIGHTS).** *See* **CIVIL RIGHTS MOVEMENTS.**

**LIBERTARIANISM.** *See* **ANARCHISM; LIBERTY.**

**LIBERTY.** *See also* **ACADEMIC FREEDOM; EQUALITY; LIBERALISM.**
Tarcov, Nathan. Locke's education for liberty. Lanham, Md. : Lexington Books, c1999.
*TC LB475.L72 T27 1999*

**LIBERTY - CONGRESSES.**
Freedom, equality, and social change. Lewiston : E. Mellen Press, c1989.
*TC HM216 .F83 1989*

**LIBERTY ENLIGHTENING THE WORLD (STATUE).** *See* **STATUE OF LIBERTY (NEW YORK, N.Y.).**

**LIBERTY OF CONSCIENCE.** *See* **PUBLIC OPINION.**

**LIBERTY OF INFORMATION.** *See* **FREEDOM OF INFORMATION.**

**LIBERTY OF SPEECH.** *See* **FREEDOM OF SPEECH.**

**Libeskind, Shlomo.**
Billstein, Rick. A problem solving approach to mathematics for elementary school teachers. 5th ed. Reading, Mass. : Addison-Wesley, c1993.
*TC QA135.5 .B49 1993*

**LIBRARIANS.** *See* **COLLEGE LIBRARIANS; LIBRARIES.**

**Librarians as learners, librarians as teachers** : the diffusion of Internet expertise in the academic library / edited by Patricia O'Brien Libutti. Chicago : Association of College and Research Libraries, 1999.
xii, 296 p. : ill. ; 23 cm. Includes bibliographical references. ISBN 0-8389-8003-1 DDC 027.7
*1. Academic libraries - United States. 2. Internet (Computer network) literacy - United States. 3. Computer literacy - United States. 4. College librarians - United States. 5. Library information networks - United States. I. Libutti. Patricia O'Brien.*
*TC Z675.U5 L415 1999*

**LIBRARIANS - CERTIFICATION - UNITED STATES - PERIODICALS.**
Requirements for certification of teachers, counselors, librarians, administrators for elementary and secondary schools. Chicago : University of Chicago Press, 1989-
*TC LB1171 .W6*

**LIBRARIES.** *See* **ACADEMIC LIBRARIES; DIGITAL LIBRARIES; LIBRARIANS; PUBLIC LIBRARIES; RESEARCH LIBRARIES; SCHOOL LIBRARIES; SMALL LIBRARIES.**

**LIBRARIES AND EDUCATION - EXPERIMENTAL METHODS - PERIODICALS.**
The Library-college experimenter: a clearinghouse. Norman, Okla., Library-College Associates, Inc.

**LIBRARIES AND FAMILIES.** *See* **LIBRARIES - SERVICES TO FAMILIES.**

**LIBRARIES AND HANDICAPPED CHILDREN.** *See* **CHILDREN'S LIBRARIES.**

**LIBRARIES AND HANDICAPPED CHILDREN - UNITED STATES.**
Including families of children with special needs. New York : Neal Schuman Publishers, c1999.
*TC Z711.92.H3 16 1999*

**LIBRARIES AND NEW LITERATES - UNITED STATES.**
Talan, Carole. Founding and funding family literacy programs. New York : Neal-Schuman, c1999.
*TC Z716.45 .T35 1999*

**LIBRARIES AND PUPPETS - UNITED STATES.**
Druce, Arden. Paper bag puppets. Lanham, MD : Scarecrow Press, 1999.
*TC Z718.3 .D78 1999*

**LIBRARIES AND READERS - PROGRAMMED INSTRUCTION.** *See* **LIBRARY ORIENTATION.**

**LIBRARIES AND READERS - UNITED STATES.**
People come first. Chicago : Association of College and Research Libraries, 1999.
*TC Z674 .A75*

**LIBRARIES AND SCHOOLS.** *See* **CHILDREN'S LIBRARIES; SCHOOL LIBRARIES.**

**LIBRARIES AND STUDENTS.** *See* **LIBRARY ORIENTATION FOR HIGH SCHOOL STUDENTS; LIBRARY ORIENTATION FOR SCHOOL CHILDREN.**

**LIBRARIES AND THE BLIND - UNITED STATES.**
Mates, Barbara T. Adaptive technology for the Internet. Chicago, Ill. : American Library Association, 1999.
*TC Z675.B M38 1999*

**LIBRARIES AND THE HANDICAPPED - UNITED STATES.**
Mates, Barbara T. Adaptive technology for the Internet. Chicago, Ill. : American Library Association, 1999.
*TC Z675.B M38 1999*

**LIBRARIES AND THE HANDICAPPED - UNITED STATES - CASE STUDIES.**
DeCandido, GraceAnne A. Transforming libraries. Washington, D.C. : Association of Research Libraries, Office of Leadership and Management Services, c1999.
*TC Z711.92.H3 D43 1999*

**LIBRARIES - ARRANGEMENT OF BOOKS ON SHELVES.** *See* **CLASSIFICATION - BOOKS.**

**LIBRARIES - CANADA.**
Library storage facilities, management, and services. Washington, DC : Association of Research Libraries, Office of Leadership and Management Services, 1999.
*TC Z675.S75 L697 1999*

**LIBRARIES, CHILDREN'S.** *See* **CHILDREN'S LIBRARIES.**

**LIBRARIES - CHILDREN'S ROOMS.** *See* **CHILDREN'S LIBRARIES.**

**LIBRARIES - CLASSIFICATION.** *See* **CLASSIFICATION - BOOKS.**

**LIBRARIES - COMPUTER NETWORKS.** *See* **LIBRARY INFORMATION NETWORKS.**

**LIBRARIES, COUNTY.** *See* **PUBLIC LIBRARIES.**

**LIBRARIES, DEPOSIT.** *See* **LIBRARIES, STORAGE.**

**LIBRARIES, ELEMENTARY SCHOOL.** *See* **ELEMENTARY SCHOOL LIBRARIES.**

**LIBRARIES - EXHIBITIONS.** *See* **LIBRARY EXHIBITS.**

**LIBRARIES FOR THE BLIND.** *See* **LIBRARIES AND THE BLIND.**

**LIBRARIES - GERMANY.**
Schurer, Heinz. GER Bulletin [London, German educational reconstruction, 1946]

**LIBRARIES, HIGH SCHOOL.** *See* **HIGH SCHOOL LIBRARIES.**

**LIBRARIES - INFORMATION NETWORKS.** *See* **LIBRARY INFORMATION NETWORKS.**

**LIBRARIES - PROGRAMMED INSTRUCTION.** *See* **LIBRARY ORIENTATION.**

**LIBRARIES, PUBLIC.** *See* **PUBLIC LIBRARIES.**

**LIBRARIES - PUBLIC RELATIONS.**
Marketing and public relations activities in ARL Libraries. Washington, DC : Association of Research Libraries, Office of Leadership and Management Services, c1999.
*TC Z176.3 .M2875 1999*

**LIBRARIES, REPOSITORY.** *See* **LIBRARIES, STORAGE.**

**LIBRARIES, RESEARCH.** *See* **RESEARCH LIBRARIES.**

**LIBRARIES - SECURITY MEASURES.**
Management of library security. Washington, DC : Systems and Procedures Exchange Center, Office of Leadership and Management Services, Association of Research Libraries, c1999.
*TC Z679.6 .M26 1999*

**LIBRARIES - SERVICE - MARKETING.**
Marketing and public relations activities in ARL Libraries. Washington, DC : Association of Research Libraries, Office of Leadership and Management Services, c1999.
*TC Z176.3 .M2875 1999*

**LIBRARIES - SERVICES TO FAMILIES - UNITED STATES.**
Including families of children with special needs. New York : Neal Schuman Publishers, c1999.
*TC Z711.92.H3 16 1999*

**LIBRARIES - SERVICES TO PRESCHOOL CHILDREN - UNITED STATES.**
Including families of children with special needs. New York : Neal Schuman Publishers, c1999.
*TC Z711.92.H3 16 1999*

**LIBRARIES, SMALL.** *See* **SMALL LIBRARIES.**

**LIBRARIES - SPECIAL COLLECTIONS - ELECTRONIC INFORMATION RESOURCES.**
Borgman, Christine L., 1951- From Gutenberg to the global information infrastructure. Cambridge, Mass. : MIT Press, 2000.
*TC ZA3225 .B67 2000*

**LIBRARIES, STORAGE - CANADA.**
Library storage facilities, management, and services. Washington, DC : Association of Research Libraries, Office of Leadership and Management Services, 1999.
*TC Z675.S75 L697 1999*

**LIBRARIES, STORAGE - UNITED STATES.**
Library storage facilities, management, and services. Washington, DC : Association of Research Libraries, Office of Leadership and Management Services, 1999.
*TC Z675.S75 L697 1999*

**LIBRARIES - UNITED STATES.**
Library storage facilities, management, and services. Washington, DC : Association of Research Libraries, Office of Leadership and Management Services, 1999.
*TC Z675.S75 L697 1999*

**LIBRARIES - UNITED STATES - DATA PROCESSING - PLANNING.**
Cohn, John M. Writing and updating technology plans. New York : Neal-Schuman Publishers, 2000.
*TC Z678.9.A4 U623 2000*

**LIBRARIES - UNITED STATES - GIFTS, LEGACIES.**
Zweizig, Douglas. Lessons from library power. Englewood, Colo. : Libraries Unlimited, 1999.
*TC Z675.S3 Z94 1999*

**LIBRARIES - UNITED STATES - SPECIAL COLLECTIONS - COMPUTER NETWORK RESOURCES.**
Mates, Barbara T. Adaptive technology for the Internet. Chicago, Ill. : American Library Association, 1999.
*TC Z675.B M38 1999*

**LIBRARIES - UNITED STATES - SPECIAL COLLECTIONS - ELECTRONIC INFORMATION RESOURCES.**
Borgman, Christine L., 1951- From Gutenberg to the global information infrastructure. Cambridge, Mass. : MIT Press, 2000.
*TC ZA3225 .B67 2000*

**LIBRARIES - UNITED STATES - SPECIAL COLLECTIONS - ELECTRONIC INFORMATION RESOURCES - CONGRESSES.**
Technology and scholarly communication. Berkeley, Calif. : University of California Press ; [Pittsburgh?] : Published in association with the Andrew K. Mellon Foundation, c1999.

*TC Z479 .T43 1999*

**LIBRARIES - UNITED STATES - SPECIAL COLLECTIONS - SCIENCE.**
Exploring science in the library. Chicago : American Library Association, 2000.
*TC Z675.S3 E97 2000*

**LIBRARIES, UNIVERSITY AND COLLEGE.** *See* **ACADEMIC LIBRARIES.**

**Library & information skills**
Lee, Carol K. Learning about books & libraries. Fort Atkinson, Wis. : Alleyside Press, 2000.
*TC Z711.2 .L455 2000*

**LIBRARY ADMINISTRATION - CANADA.**
Library storage facilities, management, and services. Washington, DC : Association of Research Libraries, Office of Leadership and Management Services, 1999.
*TC Z675.S75 L697 1999*

**LIBRARY ADMINISTRATION - UNITED STATES.**
Library storage facilities, management, and services. Washington, DC : Association of Research Libraries, Office of Leadership and Management Services, 1999.
*TC Z675.S75 L697 1999*

**Library and information problem-solving skills series**
Doggett, Sandra L. Beyond the book. Englewood, Colo. : Libraries Unlimited, 2000.
*TC ZA4065 .D64 2000*

**LIBRARY ARCHITECTURE - UNITED STATES - HISTORY - 19TH CENTURY.**
Breisch, Kenneth A. Henry Hobson Richardson and the small public library in America. Cambridge, Mass. : MIT Press, c1997.
*TC Z679.2.U54 B74 1997*

**LIBRARY BUILDINGS.** *See* **LIBRARIES, STORAGE; READING ROOMS.**

**LIBRARY CATALOGS.** *See* **CATALOGING.**

**LIBRARY CLASSIFICATION.** *See* **CLASSIFICATION - BOOKS.**

**Library-College Associates.**
The Library-college experimenter: a clearinghouse. Norman, Okla., Library-College Associates, Inc.

Library-college journal. [Norman, Okla., etc., Library-College Associates]

**The Library-college experimenter: a clearinghouse.**
Norman, Okla., Library-College Associates, Inc. 5 v. v. 1-[v. 5, no. 3]; Feb. 1975-Nov. 1979.
*1. Education - Experimental methods - Periodicals. 2. Libraries and education - Experimental methods - Periodicals. I. Library-College Associates.*

**Library-college journal.** [Norman, Okla., etc., Library-College Associates] 4 v. ill. v. 1-4, no. 3; winter 1968-summer 1971. "A magazine of educational innovation." Continued by: Library today ISSN: 0091-7281 (DLC) 73641566. ISSN 0024-225X
*I. Library-College Associates. II. Title: Learning today*

**LIBRARY COOPERATION.** *See* **INTELLECTUAL COOPERATION; LIBRARIES, STORAGE; LIBRARY INFORMATION NETWORKS.**

**LIBRARY DISPLAYS.** *See* **LIBRARY EXHIBITS.**

**LIBRARY EMPLOYEES.** *See* **LIBRARIANS.**

**LIBRARY EXHIBITS - UNITED STATES.**
Skaggs, Gayle, 1952- On display. Jefferson, NC : McFarland, c1999.
*TC Z675.S3 S5975 1999*

**LIBRARY INFORMATION NETWORKS.**
Junion-Metz, Gail, 1947- Creating a power web site. New York : Neal-Schuman, c1998.
*TC Z674.75.W67 J86 1998*

The library Web. Medford, NJ : Information Today, 1997.
*TC Z674.75.W67 L53 1997*

**LIBRARY INFORMATION NETWORKS - UNITED STATES.**
Junion-Metz, Gail, 1947- Creating a power web site. New York : Neal-Schuman, c1998.
*TC Z674.75.W67 J86 1998*

Librarians as learners, librarians as teachers. Chicago : Association of College and Research Libraries, 1999.
*TC Z675.U5 L415 1999*

The library Web. Medford, NJ : Information Today, 1997.
*TC Z674.75.W67 L53 1997*

**LIBRARY INSTRUCTION.** *See* **LIBRARY ORIENTATION.**

**LIBRARY MATERIALS.** *See* **BOOKS; PERIODICALS.**

**LIBRARY MATERIALS - DIGITIZATION.**
Kenney, Anne R., 1950- Moving theory into practice. Mountain View, CA : Research Libraries Group, 2000.
*TC Z681.3.D53 K37*

**LIBRARY NETWORKS.** *See* **LIBRARY INFORMATION NETWORKS.**

**Library of Congress. Network Development and MARC Standards Office.**
USMARC code list for countries. 1993 ed. Washington, D.C. : Cataloging Distribution Service, Library of Congress, 1993.
*TC Z699.35.M28 U78 1993*

USMARC code list for geographic areas. 1998 ed. Washington, D.C. : Cataloging Distribution Service, Library of Congress, 1998.
*TC Z695.1.G4 U83 1998*

USMARC code list for languages. 1996 ed. Washington, D.C. : Cataloging Distribution Service, Library of Congress, 1996.
*TC Z699.35.M28 U79 1997*

USMARC code list for relators, sources, description conventions. 1997 ed. Washington, DC : Cataloging Distribution Service, Library of Congress, 1997.
*TC Z699.35.M28 U795 1997*

**Library of music and musicians**
Jean-Aubry, G. (Georges), 1882-1950. [Musique française d'aujourd'hui. English] French music of to-day. 4th ed. London, K. Paul, Trench, Trubner, 1926.
*TC ML60.A82 E8 1926*

**The library of object relations**
McCormack, Charles C. Treating borderline states in marriage. Northvale, NJ : Jason Aronson, 2000.
*TC RC488.5 .M392 2000*

**Library of substance abuse and addiction treatment**
Twerski, Abraham J. Substance-abusing high achievers. Northvale, N.J. : Aronson, 1998.
*TC RC564.5.S83 T94 1998*

**LIBRARY ORIENTATION FOR HIGH SCHOOL STUDENTS - UNITED STATES.**
Developing an information literacy program K-12. New York : Neal-Schuman, c1998.
*TC Z711.2 .D49 1998*

Stanley, Deborah B. Practical steps to the research process for high school. Englewood, Colo. : Libraries Unlimited, 1999.
*TC Z711.2 .S72 1999*

**LIBRARY ORIENTATION FOR SCHOOL CHILDREN.**
Lee, Carol K. Learning about books & libraries. Fort Atkinson, Wis. : Alleyside Press, 2000.
*TC Z711.2 .L455 2000*

**LIBRARY ORIENTATION FOR SCHOOL CHILDREN - UNITED STATES.**
Developing an information literacy program K-12. New York : Neal-Schuman, c1998.
*TC Z711.2 .D49 1998*

Duncan, Donna. I-Search, you search, we all to learn to research. New York : Neal-Schuman Publishers, 2000.
*TC Z711.2 .D86 2000*

Lee, Carol K. Learning about books & libraries. Fort Atkinson, Wis. : Alleyside Press, 2000.
*TC Z711.2 .L455 2000*

**LIBRARY ORIENTATION - JUVENILE FILMS.**
Exploring the English language [videorecording]. [Princeton, N.J.] : Video Tutor ; [Chesterton, Ind.? : Distributed by] Griffin Media Design, 1988, c1986.

**LIBRARY PLANNING.**
Marketing and public relations activities in ARL Libraries. Washington, DC : Association of Research Libraries, Office of Leadership and Management Services, c1999.
*TC Z176.3 .M2875 1999*

**LIBRARY POWER (PROGRAM).**
Zweizig, Douglas. Lessons from library power. Englewood, Colo. : Libraries Unlimited, 1999.
*TC Z675.S3 Z94 1999*

**LIBRARY RESEARCH - STUDY AND TEACHING.** *See* **LIBRARY ORIENTATION.**

**LIBRARY RESEARCH - UNITED STATES.**
Lane, Nancy D. Techniques for student research. New York : Neal-Schuman Publishers, 2000.
*TC Z710 .L36 2000*

**LIBRARY RESOURCES.** *See* **LIBRARIES - SPECIAL COLLECTIONS.**

**Library science text series**
Woolls, Blanche. The school library media manager. 2nd ed. Englewood, CO : Libraries Unlimited, 1999.
*TC Z675.S3 W8735 1999*

**LIBRARY SERVICES - CANADA.**
Library storage facilities, management, and services. Washington, DC : Association of Research Libraries, Office of Leadership and Management Services, 1999.
*TC Z675.S75 L697 1999*

**LIBRARY SERVICES TO HANDICAPPED CHILDREN.** *See* **LIBRARIES AND HANDICAPPED CHILDREN.**

**LIBRARY SERVICES TO READERS.** *See* **LIBRARIES AND READERS.**

**LIBRARY SERVICES TO THE BLIND.** *See* **LIBRARIES AND THE BLIND.**

**LIBRARY SERVICES TO THE HANDICAPPED.** *See* **LIBRARIES AND THE HANDICAPPED.**

**LIBRARY SERVICES - UNITED STATES.**
Library storage facilities, management, and services. Washington, DC : Association of Research Libraries, Office of Leadership and Management Services, 1999.
*TC Z675.S75 L697 1999*

**LIBRARY SPECIAL COLLECTIONS.** *See* **LIBRARIES - SPECIAL COLLECTIONS.**

**Library storage facilities, management, and services :**
a SPEC kit / compiled by Jan Merrill-Oldham, Jutta Reed-Scott. Washington, DC : Association of Research Libraries, Office of Leadership and Management Services, 1999. 193 p. : ill. ; 28 cm. (SPEC kit ; 242) (SPEC flyer ; 242) "May 1999." Includes SPEC flyer 242.
*1. Libraries. Storage - United States. 2. Libraries. Storage - Canada. 3. Libraries - United States. 4. Libraries - Canada 5. Library Administration - United States. 6. Library Administration - Canada 7. Library Services - Canada 8. Library Services - United States 9. Universities - United States 10. Universities - Canada I. Merrill-Oldham, Jan. 1947- II. Reed-Scott, Jutta. 1936- III. Association of Research Libraries. Office of Leadership and Management Services IV. Series. V. Series: SPEC flyer ; 242*
*TC Z675.S75 L697 1999*

**LIBRARY USER ORIENTATION.** *See* **LIBRARY ORIENTATION.**

**The library Web** / Julie M. Still, editor. Medford, NJ : Information Today, 1997. vii, 221 p. ; 24 cm. Includes bibliographical references and index. ISBN 1-57387-034-X DDC 025.04
*1. Library information networks. 2. World Wide Web. 3. Library information networks - United States. 4. Web sites - Design. 5. Web sites - United States - Design. I. Still, Julie.*
*TC Z674.75.W67 L53 1997*

**Libster, Martha.** Demonstrating care : the art of integrative nursing / Martha Libster. Albany, NY : Delmar Thomson Learning, 2000. xvi, 288 p. : ill. ; 24 cm. Includes bibliographical references and index. ISBN 0-7668-1766-0
*1. Nursing - Psychological aspects. 2. Nursing - Philosophy. 3. Nurse and patient. 4. Nursing Care - methods. 5. Alternative Medicine. 6. Nurse-Patient Relations. 7. Nursing Theory. I. Title.*
*TC RT86 .L535 2000*

**Libutti, Patricia O'Brien.**
Librarians as learners, librarians as teachers. Chicago : Association of College and Research Libraries, 1999.
*TC Z675.U5 L415 1999*

**LICENSE AGREEMENTS.** *See* **MERCHANDISE LICENSING.**

**LICENSING, MERCHANDISE.** *See* **MERCHANDISE LICENSING.**

**Lichtenberg, James W.**
Scientist-practitioner perspectives on test interpretation. Boston, Mass. : Allyn and Bacon, c1999.
*TC BF176 .S37 1999*

**Lichtenberg, Peter A.**
Handbook of assessment in clinical gerontology. New York : Wiley, 1999.
*TC RC451.4.A5 H358 1999*

**Lichtenberger, Elizabeth O.**
Kaufman, Alan S. Essentials of WISC-III and WPPSI-R assessment. New York ; Chichester [England] : Wiley, c2000.
*TC BF432.5.W42 K36 2000*

**Lichtenstein, Roy, 1923-.**
Roy Lichtenstein [videorecording]. [Chicago, IL] : Home Vision : [S.l.] : distributed worldwide by RM Asssociates, c1991.
*TC ND237.L627 R6 1991*

**LICHTENSTEIN, ROY, 1923-.**
Roy Lichtenstein [videorecording]. [Chicago, IL] : Home Vision : [S.l.] : distributed worldwide by RM Asssociates, c1991.
*TC ND237.L627 R6 1991*

**Lichtman, Brenda, 1948-** More innovative games / Brenda Lichtman. Champaign, IL : Human Kinetics, c1999. xi, 187 p. : ill. ; 23 cm. Includes bibliographical references (p. 181-182) and index. ISBN 0-88011-712-5 DDC 372.86
*1. Physical education for children. 2. Games. I. Title.*
*TC GV443 .L516 1999*

**Lick, Dale W.**
New directions in mentoring. London ; New York : Falmer, 1999.
*TC LB1731.4 .N49 1999*

**Liddell, Debora L.**
Powerful programming for student learning. San Francisco : Jossey-Bass, c2000.
*TC LB2343 .P643 2000*

**Lie, Henry.**
Thornes, Robin. Introduction to Object ID. [Los Angeles] : Getty Information Institute, c1999.
*TC N3998 .T457 1999*

**Lieberman, Ann.** Teachers--transforming their world and their work / Ann Lieberman and Lynne Miller. New York : Teachers College Press ; Alexandria, Va. : Association for Supervision and Curriculum Development, c1999. xiii, 104 p. : ill. ; 23 cm. (The series on school reform) Includes bibliographical references (p. 93-97) and index. ISBN 0-8077-3858-1 (paper : alk. paper) DDC 371.102/0973
*1. Teaching - United States. 2. Public schools - United States. 3. Teacher effectiveness - United States. 4. Educational change - United States. I. Miller, Lynne, 1945- II. Title. III. Series.*
*TC LB1025.3 .L547 1999*

**Lieberman, Carl, 1941-** Educational expenditures and economic growth in the American States / Carl Lieberman. Akron, Ohio : Midwest Press Incorporated, 1998. vi, 122 p. ; 23 cm. ISBN 0-9646524-4-7
*1. Education - Economic aspects - United States - States - Statistics. 2. Education - United States - Finance - Statistics. 3. Economic development - Effect of education on - Statistics. I. Title.*
*TC LC66 .L45 1998*

**Lieberman, Myron, 1919-** Understanding the teacher union contract : a citizen's handbook / Myron Lieberman. New Brunswick, N.J. : Social Philosophy and Policy Foundation : Transaction Publishers, 2000. xiv, 219 p. ; 24 cm. (New studies in social policy ; no. 1) Series statement on jacket. Includes bibliographical references (p. 209-210) and index. ISBN 0-7658-0014-4 (cloth) ISBN 0-7658-0681-9 (pbk). DDC 344.73/078
*1. Teachers' contracts - United States. I. Title. II. Series: [New studies in social policy] ; 1.*
*TC KF3409.T4 L54 2000*

**Liebert, Wolf-Andreas, 1959-.**
Discourse and perspective in cognitive linguistics. Amsterdam ; Philadelphia : J. Benjamins, c1997.
*TC P165 .D57 1997*

**Lied von der Erde.**
Hefling, Stephen E. Mahler, Das Lied von der Erde = Cambridge, UK ; New York : Cambridge University Press, c2000.
*TC MT121.M34 H44 2000*

**LIEDER.** *See* SONGS.

**Liefer, Neil.**
Sport photography today! [videorecording]. Minneapolis, Minn. : Media Loft, c1992.
*TC TR821 .S64 1992*

**Lienau, C. C.**
Richardson, Lewis Fry, 1881-1953. Statistics of deadly quarrels. Pacific Grove, Ca. Boxwood Press [1960]
*TC U21.7 .R5 1960*

**Lienhard, John H., 1930-** The engines of our ingenuity : an engineer looks at technology and culture / John H. Lienhard. Oxford ; New York : Oxford University Press, 2000. viii, 262 p. : ill. ; 25 cm. Includes bibliographical references (p. 243-253) and index. ISBN 0-19-513583-0 DDC 303.48/3
*1. Technology - Social aspects. 2. Creative ability in technology. I. Title.*
*TC T14.5 .L52 2000*

**Lies across America.**
Loewen, James W. New York : New Press : Distributed by W.W. Norton, c1999.
*TC E159 .L64 1999*

**Lieshout, C. F. M. van.**
Developing talent across the lifespan. Hove [U.K.] : Psychology Press ; Philadelphia : Taylor & Francis, 2000.
*TC BF713 .D48 2000*

**LIFE.** *See* DEATH; QUALITY OF LIFE.

**Life & loss.**
Goldman, Linda, 1946- 2nd ed. Philadelphia : Accelerated Development, c2000.
*TC BF723.G75 G65 2000*

**Life and death aboard the U.S.S. Essex.**
Streb, Richard W. Pittsburgh, Pa. : Dorrance Pub. Co., c1999.
*TC D774.E7 S77 1999*

**The life and letters of Walter H. Page.**
Hendrick, Burton Jesse, 1870-1949. Garden City, N.Y. : Doubleday, Page & Co., 1925.
*TC E664.P15 H45 1925*

**Life and loss.**
Goldman, Linda, 1946- Life & loss. 2nd ed. Philadelphia : Accelerated Development, c2000.
*TC BF723.G75 G65 2000*

**LIFE (BIOLOGY).** *See* BIOLOGY.

**LIFE CARE COMMUNITIES - UNITED STATES - MANAGEMENT.**
Pearce, Benjamin W. Senior living communities. Baltimore : Johns Hopkins University Press, 1998.
*TC HD7287.92.U54 P4 1998*

**LIFE CHANGE EVENTS.** *See also* STRESS (PSYCHOLOGY).
Loss and trauma. Philadelphia, PA : Brunner-Routledge, c2000.
*TC BF575.D35 L67 2000*

**LIFE CHANGE EVENTS - CONGRESSES.**
Developmental perspectives on trauma. Rochester, N.Y., USA : University of Rochester Press, 1997.
*TC RJ499 .D4825 1997*

**LIFE CHANGE EVENTS - PSYCHOLOGICAL ASPECTS.**
Nemeroff, Robin. Stress, social support, and psychological distress in late life. 1999.
*TC 085 N341*

**LIFE CYCLE, HUMAN.** *See also* ADULTHOOD; CHILDREN; DEVELOPMENTAL PSYCHOLOGY; YOUTH.
Settersten, Richard A. Lives in time and place. Amityville, N.Y. : Baywood Pub., c1999.
*TC BF713 .S48 1999*

Stress, coping, and health in families. Thousand Oaks, Calif. : Sage Publications, c1998.
*TC RC455.4.F3 S79 1998*

**Life cycle of the career teacher** / edited by Betty E. Steffy ... [et al.]. [Indianapolis, Ind.] : Kappa Delta Pi ; Thousand Oaks, Calif. : Corwin Press, c2000. xiv, 128 p. : ill. ; 24 cm. Includes bibliographical references and index. ISBN 0-7619-7539-X (cloth) ISBN 0-7619-7540-3 (paper) DDC 371.1/00973
*1. Teachers - United States - Case studies. 2. Teachers - Training of - United States - Case studies. 3. Teachers - In-service training - United States - Case studies. I. Steffy, Betty E. II. Kappa Delta Pi (Honor society)*
*TC LB1775.2 .L54 2000*

**LIFE EVENTS, STRESSFUL.** *See* LIFE CHANGE EVENTS.

**LIFE EXPERIENCES, STRESSFUL.** *See* LIFE CHANGE EVENTS.

**LIFE HISTORIES.** *See* BIOGRAPHY.

**Life in the camps [picture].**
[Japanese-American internment picture. Amawalk, NY : Jackdaw Publications, c1999.
*TC TR820.5 .J3 1999*

**A life is more than a moment.**
Counts, I. Wilmer (Ira Wilmer), 1931- Bloomington, IN : Indiana University Press, c1999.
*TC LC214.23.L56 C68 1999*

**The life of a photograph.**
Keefe, Laurence E. 2nd ed. Boston : Focal Press, c1990.
*TC TR465 .K44 1990*

**Life of William Heard Kilpatrick.**
Beineke, John A. And there were giants in the land. New York : P. Lang, c1998.
*TC LB875.K54 B44 1998*

**LIFE ON OTHER PLANETS.** *See also* HUMAN-ALIEN ENCOUNTERS.
Stephen Hawking's universe [videorecording]. [Alexandria, Va.] : PBS Video; Burbank, CA : Distributed by Warner Home Video, c1997.
*TC QB982 .S7 1997*

**LIFE, QUALITY OF.** *See* QUALITY OF LIFE.

**Life science.**
LifeScience. Wien ; New York : Springer, 1999.
*TC T14.5 L54 1999*

**LIFE SCIENCES.** *See* AGRICULTURE; BIOLOGY; MEDICINE.

**LIFE SCIENCES - SOCIAL ASPECTS.**
LifeScience. Wien ; New York : Springer, 1999.
*TC T14.5 L54 1999*

**LIFE SCIENCES - STUDY AND TEACHING - UNITED STATES.**
Rhoton, Jack Issues in science education. Arlington, Va. National Science Teachers Association: National Science Education Leadership Association, c1997.
*TC Q181 .R56 1996*

**LIFE SCIENCES - VOCATIONAL GUIDANCE - UNITED STATES.**
Trends in the early careers of life scientists. Washington, DC : National Academy Press, 1998.
*TC QH314 .T74 1998*

**LIFE SCIENTISTS - EMPLOYMENT - UNITED STATES.**
Trends in the early careers of life scientists. Washington, DC : National Academy Press, 1998.
*TC QH314 .T74 1998*

**LIFE SCIENTISTS - TRAINING OF - UNITED STATES.**
Trends in the early careers of life scientists. Washington, DC : National Academy Press, 1998.
*TC QH314 .T74 1998*

**LIFE SKILLS.** *See* CONDUCT OF LIFE; FUNCTIONAL LITERACY; SOCIAL SKILLS; STUDY SKILLS.

**LIFE, SPIRITUAL.** *See* SPIRITUAL LIFE.

**LIFE STYLE.** *See* LIFESTYLES.

**LIFE STYLES.** *See* LIFESTYLES.

**Life-threatening behavior.** [New York, Behavioral Publications, inc.] v. 23 cm. Frequency: Quarterly. v. 1-4; spring 1971-winter 1974. Official publication of the American Association of Suicidology. Indexed by: Index medicus 0019-3879. Indexed by: Abstracts on criminology and penology. Indexed by: Social sciences citation index. Indexed by: Current contents. Continued by: Suicide ISSN: 0360-1390 (DLC) 75646988. ISSN 0047-4592 DDC 616.85/8445/005
*1. Suicide - Periodicals. 2. Suicide - Prevention - Periodicals. 3. Behavior - periodicals. 4. Suicide - periodicals. I. American Association of Suicidology. II. Title: Suicide*

**Life would be easy if it weren't for other people.**
Podesta, Connie. Thousand Oaks, Calif. : Corwin Press, c1999.
*TC BF637.I48 P63 1999*

**LIFECARE COMMUNITIES.** *See* LIFE CARE COMMUNITIES.

**Lifelong and continuing education : :** what is a learning society? / edited by Paul Oliver. Aldershot, Hants, England ; Brookfield, Vt. : Ashgate, 1999. xi, 242 p. ; 23 cm. (Monitoring change in education.) Includes bibliographical references. ISBN 1-84014-905-1 ISBN 1-84014-905-1
*1. Continuing education. 2. Continuing education - Philosophy. I. Oliver, Paul. II. Series.*
*TC LC5215 L464 1999*

**LIFELONG EDUCATION.** *See* CONTINUING EDUCATION.

**Lifelong learning.**
Elliott, Geoffrey, Dr. London ; Philadelphia : Jessica Kingsley Publishers, c1999.

*TC LB1060 .E447 1999*

**Lifelong learning in higher education.**
Knapper, Christopher. 3rd ed. London : Kogan Page, 2000.
*TC LC5215 .K593 2000*

**Lifemaps of people with learning difficulties.**
Gray, Barry, 1944- London ; Philadelphia : Jessica Kingsley, 1999.
*TC HV3004 .G73 1999*

**Lifemaps of people with learning disabilities.**
Gray, Barry, 1944- Lifemaps of people with learning difficulties. London ; Philadelphia : Jessica Kingsley, 1999.
*TC HV3004 .G73 1999*

**LifeScience** / herausgegeben von Gerfried Stocker und Christine Schöpf. Wien ; New York : Springer, 1999. 447 p. : ill. (some col.) ; 24 cm. Added title page title: Ars Electronica 99. "Ars electronica : Festival für Kunst, Technologie und Gesellschaft = Ars electronica : Festival of Art, Technology and Society." Includes bibliographical references. English and German. ISBN 3-211-83368-4
*1. Life sciences - Social aspects. 2. Art and technology. 3. Technology and the arts. 4. Computer art. I. Stocker, Gerfried. II. Schöpf, Christine. III. Ars Electronica. (1999 : Linz, Austria). IV. Title: Life science. V. Title: Ars Electronica 99.*
*TC T14.5 L54 1999*

**LIFESTYLES.**
Miles, Steven. Youth lifestyles in a changing world. Buckingham ; Philadelphia : Open University Press, 2000.
*TC HQ796 .M4783 2000*

**LIFESTYLES - PSYCHOLOGICAL ASPECTS.**
Walters, Glenn D. Beyond behavior. Westport, Conn. ; London : Praeger, 2000.
*TC BF353 .W356 2000*

Walters, Glenn D. The self-altering process. Westport, Conn. : Praeger, 2000.
*TC BF637.C4 W35 2000*

**Lifetime guarantees.**
Harwayne, Shelley. Portsmouth, NH : Heinemann, c2000.
*TC LB1575 . H38 2000*

**LIGHT.** *See* **COLOR.**

**Light, Andrew, 1966-.**
Technology and the good life? Chicago ; London : University of Chicago Press, 2000.
*TC T14 .T386 2000*

**LIGHT IN ART.**
Miller, Jonathan, 1934- On reflection. London : National Gallery Publications ; [New Haven, Conn.] : Distributed by Yale University Press, c1998.
*TC N8224.M6 M54 1998*

**Light, Paul.**
Learning sites. 1st ed. Amsterdam ; New York : Pergamon, 1999.
*TC LB1060 .L4245 1999*

Social processes in children's learning / Paul Light and Karen Littleton. Cambridge, U.K. ; New York : Cambridge University Press, 1999. xviii, 119 p. : ill. ; 24 cm. (Cambridge studies in cognitive and perceptual development) Includes bibliographical references (p. 101-115) and index. ISBN 0-521-59308-5 (hbk.) ISBN 0-521-59691-2 (pbk.) DDC 370.15/23
*1. Learning - Social aspects. 2. Social interaction in children. 3. Group work in education. I. Littleton, Karen. II. Title. III. Series.*
*TC LB1060 .L533 1999*

**The Lighthouse handbook on vision impairment and vision rehabilitation** / editors, Barbara Silverstone ... [et al.]. New York, N.Y. : Oxford University Press, 2000. 2 v. : ill. ; 29 cm. "Published under the auspices of Lighthouse International." Includes bibliographical references and index. CONTENTS: v. 1. Vision impairment -- v. 2. Vision rehabilitation. ISBN 0-19-509489-1 (2 v. set) ISBN 0-19-509516-2 (v. 1) ISBN 0-19-509517-0 (v. 2)
*1. Vision disorders. 2. Visually handicapped - Rehabilitation. I. Silverstone, Barbara, 1931- II. Lighthouse International. III. Title: Vision impairment and vision rehabilitation*
*TC RE91 .L54 2000*

**Lighthouse International.**
The Lighthouse handbook on vision impairment and vision rehabilitation. New York, N.Y. : Oxford University Press, 2000.
*TC RE91 .L54 2000*

**Like letters in running water.**
Doll, Mary Aswell. Mahwah, N.J. ; London : L. Erlbaum Publishers, 2000.

*TC LB1575 .D64 2000*

**LIKERT SCALE.**
Foye, Stephanie Diane. Using item response theory methods to explore the effect of item wording on Likert data. 1997.
*TC 085 F82*

**Lillo-Martin, Diane C. (Diane Carolyn), 1959-**
Universal grammar and American sign language : setting the null argument parameters / Diane C. Lillo-Martin. Dordrecht ; Boston : Kluwer Academic Publishers, c1991. xvi, 244 p. : ill. ; 23 cm. (Studies in theoretical psycholinguistics ; v. 13) Revision of the author's thesis (Ph. D.--University of California, San Diego, 1986). Includes bibliographical references (p. 218-234) and indexes. ISBN 0-7923-1419-0 (HB : acid-free paper) DDC 419
*1. American Sign Language - Grammar. 2. Grammar, Comparative and general. I. Title. II. Series.*
*TC HV2474 .L55 1991*

**Lim, Shirley.**
Power, race, and gender in academe. New York : Modern Language Association, 2000.
*TC LC3727 .P69 2000*

**Limerick, Patricia Nelson, 1951-.**
White, Richard, 1947- The frontier in American culture. Chicago : The Library ; Berkeley : University of California Press, c1994.
*TC F596 .W562 1994*

**LIMERICKS, JUVENILE.**
Hubbell, Patricia. Boo!. 1st ed. New York : Marshall Cavendish, 1998.
*TC PS3558.U22 B66 1998*

**LIMITATIONS, CONSTITUTIONAL.** *See* **CONSTITUTIONAL LAW.**

**LIMITED COMPANIES.** *See* **CORPORATIONS.**

**LIMITS (MATHEMATICS).** *See* **CALCULUS.**

**Limón, José.** José Limón : an unfinished memoir / edited by Lynn Garafola ; introduction by Deborah Jowitt ; foreword by Carla Maxwell ; afterword by Norton Owen. Hanover, NH : University Press of New England, [1998?] xx, 207 p. : ill. ; 26 cm. (Studies in dance history) Includes bibliographical references (p. 173-194) and index. ISBN 0-8195-6374-9 (alk. paper) DDC 792.8/028/092
*1. Limón, José. 2. Dancers - United States - Biography. 3. Choreographers - United States - Biography. I. Garafola, Lynn. II. Title. III. Series: Studies in dance history (Unnumbered)*
*TC GV1785.L515 A3 1998*

**LIMÓN, JOSÉ.**
Limón, José. José Limón. Hanover, NH : University Press of New England, [1998?]
*TC GV1785.L515 A3 1998*

**Lin, Catharine.**
Milbank Memorial Library story hour [videorecording]. [New York : Milbank Memorial Library, 1999]
*TC Z718.3 .M5 1999 Series 3 Prog. 6*

**LINCOLN, ABRAHAM, 1809-1865 - FICTION.**
Borden, Louise. A. Lincoln and me. New York : Scholastic, 1999.
*TC PZ7.B64827 An 1999*

Sappey, Maureen Stack, 1952- Letters from Vinnie. Asheville, NC : Front Street, 1999.
*TC PZ7.S2388 Le 1999*

**LINCOLN, ABRAHAM, 1809-1865 - JUVENILE FICTION.**
Borden, Louise. A. Lincoln and me. New York : Scholastic, 1999.
*TC PZ7.B64827 An 1999*

**Lincoln, Paul.**
Supporting improving primary schools. London ; New York : Falmer Press, 2000.
*TC LB2822.84.E64 S86 1999*

**Lincoln, Yvonna S.**
Handbook of qualitative research. 2nd ed. Thousand Oaks, Calif. : Sage Publications, c2000.
*TC H62 .H2455 2000*

**Lind, Karen.**
Charlesworth, Rosalind. Math and science for young children. 3rd ed. Albany, NY : Delmar Publishers, c1999.
*TC QA135.5 .C463 1999*

Exploring science in early childhood : a developmental approach / Karen K. Lind. 3rd ed. Albany, NY ; London : Delmar/Thomson Learning, c2000. x, 358 p., [8] p. of plates : ill., forms ; 23 cm. Cover title: Exploring science in early childhood education. Includes

bibliographical references and index. CONTENTS: Sect. I. Concept Development in Science. Unit 1. How Concepts Develop. Unit 2. How Concepts Are Acquired. Unit 3. Promoting Young Children's Concept Development Through Problem Solving. Unit 4. Assessing the Child's Developmental Level. Unit 5. The Basics of Science. Unit 6. How Young Scientists Use Concepts. Unit 7. Planning for Science Investigations -- Sect. II. Fundamental Concepts, Skills, and Activities. Unit 8. Fundamental Concepts in Science. Unit 9. Language and Concept Formation. Unit 10. Applications of Fundamental Concepts in Preprimary Science. Unit 11. Integrating the Curriculum Through Dramatic Play and Thematic Units and Projects. Unit 12. Higher-Level Activities Used in Science Units and Activities -- Sect. III. Using Skills, Concepts, and Attitudes for Scientific Investigations in the Primary Grades. Unit 13. Overview of Primary Science. Unit 14. Life Science. Unit 15. Physical Science. Unit 16. Earth and Space Science and the Environment. Unit 17. Health and Nutrition -- Sect. IV. The Science Environment. Unit 18. Materials and Resources for Science. Unit 19. Science in Action. Unit 20. Science in the Home. App. A. Developmental Assessment Tasks -- App. B. Children's Books with Science Concepts -- App. C. Code of Practice on Use of Animals in Schools. ISBN 0-7668-0231-0 DDC 372.3/5 DDC 372.3/5
*1. Science - Study and teaching (Primary) 2. Science - Study and teaching (Early childhood) I. Title. II. Title: Exploring science in early childhood education*
*TC LB1532 .L47 2000*

**Lindberg, Gary.**
Sport photography today! [videorecording]. Minneapolis, Minn. : Media Loft, c1992.
*TC TR821 .S64 1992*

**LINDBERGH, CHARLES A. (CHARLES AUGUSTUS), 1902-1974.**
Burleigh, Robert. Flight. New York : Philomel Books, c1991.
*TC TL540.L5 B83 1991*

**LINDBERGH, CHARLES A. (CHARLES AUGUSTUS), 1902-1974 - JUVENILE LITERATURE.**
Burleigh, Robert. Flight. New York : Philomel Books, c1991.
*TC TL540.L5 B83 1991*

**Linden, Wim J. van der.**
Computerized adaptive testing. Dordrecht ; Boston : Kluwer Academic, c2000.
*TC LB3060.32.C65 C66 2000*

**LINDESMITH, ALFRED RAY, 1905-.**
Keys, David Patrick, 1955- Confronting the drug control establishment. Albany, N.Y. : State University of New York Press, c2000.
*TC HM1031.L56 K49 2000*

**Lindholm, Charles, 1946-.**
Hall, John A., 1949- Is America breaking apart? Princeton, NJ : Princeton University Press, c1999.
*TC HN59.2 .H34 1999*

**Lindley, Thomas, ill.**
Steiner, Joan (Joan Catherine) Look-alikes, jr.. 1st ed. Boston : Little, Brown, c1999.
*TC GV1507.P47 S747 1999*

**Lindsay, Arturo.**
Santería aesthetics in contemporary Latin American art. Washington : Smithsonian Institution Press, c1996.
*TC N72.R4 S26 1996*

**Lindsay, Geoff.**
Lewis, Ann, 1950- Researching children's perspectives. Buckingham ; Philadelphia : Open University Press, 2000.
*TC HQ767.85 .L49 2000*

**Lines of activity.**
Jackson, Shannon, 1967- Ann Arbor : University of Michigan Press, c2000.
*TC HV4196.C4 J33 2000*

**LINES, RAILROAD.** *See* **RAILROADS.**

**Ling, Peter.**
Inglis, Alistair. Delivering digitally. London : Kogan Page, c1999.
*TC LB1044.87 .I545 1999*

**Lingua ex machina.**
Calvin, William H., 1939- Cambridge, Mass. ; London : MIT Press, c2000.
*TC QP399 .C35 2000*

**LINGUISTIC ANALYSIS (LINGUISTICS).** *See* **COMPONENTIAL ANALYSIS (LINGUISTICS).**

**A linguistic approach to reading and writing.**
Scholes, Robert J. Lewiston, N.Y. : E. Mellen Press, c1999.
*TC P211 .S383 1999*

**LINGUISTIC CHANGE.**
Aitchison, Jean, 1938- Language change. 2nd ed. Cambridge [England] ; New York : Cambridge University Press, 1991.
*TC P142 .A37 1991*

Fischer, Steven R. A history of language. London : Reaktion Books, 1999.
*TC P140 .F57 1999*

Perkins, Revere D. (Revere Dale) Deixis, grammar, and culture. Amsterdam ; Philadelphia : J. Benjamins Pub. co., 1992.
*TC P35 .P47 1992*

**LINGUISTIC CHANGE - SOCIAL ASPECTS.**
Fischer, Steven R. A history of language. London : Reaktion Books, 1999.
*TC P140 .F57 1999*

Kunz, Linda Ann. English modals in American talk shows. 1999.
*TC 06 no. 11136*

**LINGUISTIC CREATIVITY.** *See* **CREATIVITY (LINGUISTICS).**

**Linguistic genocide in education, or worldwide diversity and human rights?.**
Skutnabb-Kangas, Tove. Mahwah, N.J. : L. Erlbaum Associates, 2000.
*TC P40.8 .S58 2000*

**LINGUISTIC INTERFERENCE.** *See* **INTERFERENCE (LINGUISTICS).**

**Linguistic minorities and literacy :** language policy issues in developing countries / edited by Florian Coulmas. Berlin ; New York : Mouton Publishers, 1984. x, 133 p. : ill. ; 23 cm. (Trends in linguistics. Studies and monographs ; 26) Most of the papers are based on presentations given at a workshop held under the auspices of the United Nations University in Tokyo, Sept. 4-5, 1982. Includes bibliographies and index. ISBN 3-11-009867-9 DDC 409/.172/4
*1. Linguistic minorities - Developing countries - Congresses. 2. Literacy - Developing countries - Congresses. 3. Language policy - Developing countries - Congresses. I. Coulmas, Florian. II. United Nations University. III. Series.*
*TC P119.315 .L56 1984*

**LINGUISTIC MINORITIES - DEVELOPING COUNTRIES - CONGRESSES.**
Linguistic minorities and literacy. Berlin ; New York : Mouton Publishers, 1984.
*TC P119.315 .L56 1984*

**LINGUISTIC MINORITIES - EDUCATION - EUROPE.**
Teaching the mother tongue in a multilingual Europe. London : Cassell, 1998.
*TC P53.5 .T43 1998*

**LINGUISTIC MINORITIES - EDUCATION - SOCIAL ASPECTS - UNITED STATES - CASE STUDIES.**
Freeman, Rebecca D. (Rebecca Diane), 1960- Bilingual education and social change. Clevedon [England] ; Philadelphia : Multilingual Matters, c1998.
*TC LC3731 .F72 1998*

**LINGUISTIC MINORITIES - EDUCATION - UNITED STATES.**
Literacy instruction for culturally and linguistically diverse students. Newark, Del. : International Reading Association, c1998.
*TC LC3731 .L566 1998*

**LINGUISTIC MINORITIES - EDUCATION - UNITED STATES - EVALUATION.**
Educating language-minority children. New Brunswick (U.S.A.) : Transaction Publishers, c2000.
*TC LC3731 .E374 2000*

**LINGUISTIC MINORITIES - NEW YORK (STATE) - NEW YORK.**
The multilingual Apple. Berlin ; New York : Mouton de Gruyter, 1997.
*TC P40.5.L56 M8 1997*

**LINGUISTIC SCIENCE.** *See* **LINGUISTICS.**

**LINGUISTICS.** *See also* **AREAL LINGUISTICS; COMPONENTIAL ANALYSIS (LINGUISTICS); CREATIVITY (LINGUISTICS); FUNCTIONALISM (LINGUISTICS); GOVERNMENT-BINDING THEORY (LINGUISTICS); GRAMMAR, COMPARATIVE AND GENERAL;**

**MODALITY (LINGUISTICS); PHONETICS; SOCIOLINGUISTICS; SPEECH ACTS (LINGUISTICS).**
Linguistics. Cambridge, UK ; New York, NY : Cambridge University Press, 1999.
*TC P121 .L528 1999*

**Linguistics & language behavior abstracts.**
[LLBA (Online)] LLBA [computer file]. [Norwood, MA] : SilverPlatter International, [1993- Computer data and program.

[LLBA (Online)] LLBA [computer file]. [Norwood, MA] : SilverPlatter International, [1993- Computer data and program.

[LLBA (Online)] LLBA [computer file]. [Norwood, MA] : SilverPlatter International, [1993- Computer data and program.
*TC NETWORKED RESOURCE*

**LINGUISTICS - ABSTRACTS - DATABASES.**
[LLBA (Online)] LLBA [computer file]. [Norwood, MA] : SilverPlatter International, [1993- Computer data and program.

[LLBA (Online)] LLBA [computer file]. [Norwood, MA] : SilverPlatter International, [1993- Computer data and program.

[LLBA (Online)] LLBA [computer file]. [Norwood, MA] : SilverPlatter International, [1993- Computer data and program.
*TC NETWORKED RESOURCE*

**Linguistics :** an introduction / Andrew Radford ... [et al.]. Cambridge, UK ; New York, NY : Cambridge University Press, 1999. xvi, 438 p. ; 24 cm. Includes bibliographical references (p. 424-428) and index. ISBN 0-521-47261-X (hc.) ISBN 0-521-47854-5 (pbk.) DDC 410
*1. Linguistics. I. Radford, Andrew.*
*TC P121 .L528 1999*

**Linguistics and language behavior abstracts.**
[LLBA (Online)] LLBA [computer file]. [Norwood, MA] : SilverPlatter International, [1993- Computer data and program.

[LLBA (Online)] LLBA [computer file]. [Norwood, MA] : SilverPlatter International, [1993- Computer data and program.

[LLBA (Online)] LLBA [computer file]. [Norwood, MA] : SilverPlatter International, [1993- Computer data and program.
*TC NETWORKED RESOURCE*

**LINGUISTICS - DATA PROCESSING.** *See* **COMPUTATIONAL LINGUISTICS.**

**LINGUISTICS - RESEARCH.**
Researching language in schools and communities. London ; Washington [D.C.] : Cassell, 2000.
*TC P53 .R463 2000*

**LINGUISTS.** *See* **LEXICOGRAPHERS.**

**Link, Martin A., joint author.**
Blood, Charles L., 1929- The goat in the rug. New York : Four Winds Press, 1976.
*TC PZ7.B6227 Go 1976*

**Linking America's schools and colleges :** guide to partnerships & national directory / by Franklin P. Wilbur, Leo M. Lambert [editors]. Washington, D.C. : American Association for Higher Education, 1991. ix, 307 p. ; 28 cm. "Endorsed by National Association of Secondary School Principals, American Association of Community and Junior Colleges, American Association for Higher Education." Includes index. ISBN 1-56377-000-8 DDC 378.1/03
*1. College-school cooperation - United States - Directories. I. Wilbur, Franklin P. II. Lambert, Leo M.*
*TC LB2331.53 .L56 1991*

**Linking literacy and technology :** a guide for K-8 classrooms / Shelley B. Wepner, William J. Valmont, Richard Thurlow, editors. Newark, Del. : International Reading Association, c2000. xiv, 252 p. : ill. ; 23 cm. Includes bibliographical references and indexes. ISBN 0-87207-258-4 DDC 372.133/4
*1. Language arts (Elementary) - Computer-assisted instruction. 2. Computers and literacy. 3. Educational technology. I. Wepner, Shelley B., 1951- II. Valmont, William J. III. Thurlow, Richard.*
*TC LB1576.7 .L56 2000*

**Linking theory to practice :** case studies for working with college students / edited by Frances K. Stage, Michael Dannells. 2nd ed. Philadelphia, Pa. : Taylor and Francis, 2000. xviii, 228 p. ; 24 cm. Stage's name appears as principal author on the earlier edition. Includes bibliographical references. ISBN 1-56032-865-7 (alk. paper) DDC 378.9/946
*1. Student affairs services - United States - Case studies. 2.*

College student personnel administrators - Training of - United States. I. Stage, Frances K. II. Dannells, Michael.
*TC LB2342.9 .L56 2000*

**Linn, Marcia C.** Computers, teachers, peers : science learning partners / Marcia C. Linn, Sherry Hsi. Mahwah, N.J. : L. Erlbaum Associates, 2000. xxxv, 460 p. : ill. ; 23 cm. + 1 computer laser optical disc (4 3/4 in.). Includes bibliographical references (p. 369-380) and index. ISBN 0-8058-3343-9 (pbk. : alk. paper) DDC 507/.1/2
*1. Science - Study and teaching (Middle school) - United States - Case studies. 2. Science - Study and teaching (Secondary) - United States - Case studies. 3. Computer-assisted instruction - United States - Case studies. 4. Group work in education - United States - Case studies. I. Hsi, Sherry. II. Title.*
*TC LB1585.3 .L56 2000*

**Linn, Robert L.** Measurement and assessment in teaching / Robert L. Linn, Norman E. Gronlund ; [editor, Kevin M. Davis ; illustrations, Carlisle Communications, Inc.]. 8th ed. Upper Saddle River, N.J. : Merrill, c2000. xvi, 574 p. : ill. ; 25 cm. Includes bibliographical references and indexes. ISBN 0-13-878356-X DDC 371.26
*1. Educational tests and measurements. I. Gronlund, Norman Edward, 1920- II. Davis, Kevin M. III. Title.*
*TC LB3051 .L545 2000*

**Linnea, Sharon.** Princess Ka'iulani : hope of a nation, heart of a people / Sharon Linnéa. Grand Rapids, Mich. : Eerdmans Books for Young Readers, 1999. xviii, 234 p. : ill., 1 map ; 23 cm. Includes bibliographical references (p. 223-225) and index. ISBN 0-8028-5088-X (pbk. : alk. paper) ISBN 0-8028-5145-2 (cloth :alk. paper) DDC 996.9/02/092
*1. Kaiulani, - Princess of Hawaii, - 1875-1899 - Juvenile literature. 2. Princesses - Hawaii - Biography - Juvenile literature. 3. Hawaii - History - Juvenile literature. I. Title.*
*TC DU627.17.K3 L56 1999*

**LINOLEUM BLOCK-PRINTING, AUSTRALIAN - EXHIBITIONS.**
National Gallery of Victoria. In relief. Melbourne : National Gallery of Victoria, c1997.
*TC NE1190.25 .G72 1997*

**Linton, Jonathan, ill.**
Evans, Richard Paul. The dance. 1st ed. New York : Simon & Schuster Books for Young Readers, c1999.
*TC PZ7.E89227 Dan 1999*

**Linux.**
Maximum Linux security. Indianapolis, Ind. : Sams, c2000.
*TC QA76.9.A25 M385 2000*

Carling, M. Linux system administration. Indianapolis, IN : New Riders, c2000.
*TC QA76.76.O63 C3755 2000*

Kirch, Olaf. Linux network administrator's guide. 2nd ed. Cambridge, Mass. : O'Reilly, 2000.
*TC QA76.76.O63 K566 2000*

Maximum Linux security. Indianapolis, Ind. : Sams, c2000.
*TC QA76.9.A25 M385 2000*

Maxwell, Steven. Red hat linux network management tools. New York : McGraw Hill, c2000.
*TC QA76.76.O63 M373339 2000*

Pfaffenberger, Bryan, 1949- Mastering GNOME. San Francisco, CA : Sybex, Inc., 1999.
*TC QA76.9.U83 P453 1999*

Pitts, David. Red Hat Linux 6 unleashed. [Indianapolis, Ind.] : SAMS, c1999.
*TC QA76.76.O63 P56148 1999*

**LINUX (COMPUTER FILE).**
Red Hat Linux :. Indianapolis, Ind. : Que : Macmillan USA, c2000.
*TC QA76.76.O63 R43 2000*

**Linux network administrator's guide.**
Kirch, Olaf. 2nd ed. Cambridge, Mass. : O'Reilly, 2000.
*TC QA76.76.O63 K566 2000*

**Linux security.**
Maximum Linux security. Indianapolis, Ind. : Sams, c2000.
*TC QA76.9.A25 M385 2000*

**Linux system administration.**
Carling, M. Indianapolis, IN : New Riders, c2000.
*TC QA76.76.O63 C3755 2000*

**L'investissement dans le capital humain : une comparaison internationale.**
Human capital investment. Paris : Organisation for Economic Co-operation and Development, c1998.

### TC HD4904.7 .H843 1998

**Lion and the unicorn.**
[Lion and the unicorn (Baltimore, Md. : Online)] The lion and the unicorn [computer file]. Baltimore, MD : Johns Hopkins University Press, c1995-
*TC EJOURNALS*

**[Lion and the unicorn (Baltimore, Md. : Online)]** The lion and the unicorn [computer file]. Baltimore, MD : Johns Hopkins University Press, c1995- Frequency: Semiannual. 19.1 (June 1995)- . Title from title screen. Text (electronic journal) Also available in a print ed. Mode of access: Internet via World Wide Web. Digitized and made available by: Project Muse. URL: http://muse.jhu.edu/journals/lion%5Fand%5Fthe%5Funicorn/ Available in other form: Lion and the unicorn ISSN: 0147-2593 (DLC) 77646850 (OCoLC)3134351. ISSN 1080-6563 DDC 809
*1. Children's literature - History and criticism - Periodicals. I. Project Muse. II. Title: Lion and the unicorn*
*TC EJOURNALS*

**The lion, the witch and the wardrobe by C. S. Lewis.**
Rawlings, Carol Miller. New York : Scholastic, c1997.
*TC LB1573 .R38 1997*

**LIPIDES.** *See* **LIPIDS.**

**LIPIDS.**
Lipids in health and nutrition. Cambridge : Royal Society of Chemistry, c1999.
*TC QP751 .L57 1999*

Lipids in health and nutrition. Cambridge : Royal Society of Chemistry, c1999.
*TC QP751 .L57 1999*

**Lipids in health and nutrition** / edited by J.H.P. Tyman. Cambridge : Royal Society of Chemistry, c1999. xi, 156 p. : ill. ; 24 cm. (Special publication ; no. 244) Includes bibliographical references and index. "Based on the proceedings of a two-day symposium of the Lipid Group of the RSC Perkin Division on Lipids in Health and Nutrition held on 9-10 September 1996 at Sheffield Hallam University, UK"-- T.p. verso. ISBN 0-85404-798-0 DDC 572.57
*1. Lipids. 2. Lipids - Metabolism. 3. Lipids in human nutrition. 4. Lipids in human nutrition. 5. Lipids - Metabolism. 6. Lipids. I. Tyman, J. H. P. (John H P) II. Series: Special publication (Royal Society of Chemistry (Great Britain)) ; no. 244.*
*TC QP751 .L57 1999*

**LIPIDS IN HUMAN NUTRITION.**
Lipids in health and nutrition. Cambridge : Royal Society of Chemistry, c1999.
*TC QP751 .L57 1999*

Lipids in health and nutrition. Cambridge : Royal Society of Chemistry, c1999.
*TC QP751 .L57 1999*

Sims, Laura S., 1943- The politics of fat. Armonk, N.Y. : M.E. Sharpe, c1998.
*TC TX360.U6 S58 1998*

**LIPIDS - METABOLISM.**
Lipids in health and nutrition. Cambridge : Royal Society of Chemistry, c1999.
*TC QP751 .L57 1999*

Lipids in health and nutrition. Cambridge : Royal Society of Chemistry, c1999.
*TC QP751 .L57 1999*

**LIPINS.** *See* **LIPIDS.**

**Lipkin, Lisa.** Bringing the story home : the complete guide to storytelling for parents / by Lisa Lipkin. New York : W.W. Norton & Co., c2000. 220 p. ; 22 cm. Includes bibliographical references. ISBN 0-393-04775-X DDC 649/.58
*1. Storytelling. 2. Family recreation. I. Title. II. Title: Complete guide to storytelling for parents*
*TC LB1042 .L515 2000*

**Lipman-Blumen, Jean.** Hot groups : seeding them, feeding them, and using them to ignite your organization / Jean Lipman-Blumen, Harold J. Leavitt. New York : Oxford University Press, 1999. xvi, 299 p. ; 24 cm. Includes bibliographical references (p. [283]-290) and index. ISBN 0-19-512686-6 (alk. paper) DDC 658.4/036
*1. Organizational effectiveness. 2. Group decision making. 3. Industrial efficiency. I. Leavitt, Harold J. II. Title.*
*TC HD58.9 .L56 1999*

**LIPOIDS.** *See* **LIPIDS.**

**Lippard, Lucy R.**
Partial recall. 1st ed. New York : New Press : Distributed by W.W. Norton & Co., Inc., 1992.
*TC E89 .P33 1992*

**Lippe, Anna Louise von der.**
Personality development in adolescence. London ; New York : Routledge, c1998.
*TC BF724.3.P4 P47 1998*

**Lippert, Rick Allen.**
Ballroom dancing for beginners [videorecording]. W. Long Branch, N.J. : Kultur, c1993.
*TC GV1753.7 .B3 1993*

Ballroom dancing for beginners [videorecording]. W. Long Branch, N.J. : Kultur, c1993.
*TC GV1753.7 .B3 1993*

**Lippert, Robin Alissa.** Conflating the self with the body : the influence of depression, gender role, perfectionism, and self-silencing on body esteem / Robin Alissa Lippert. 1999. vii, 135 leaves ; 29 cm. Thesis (Ph.D.)--Columbia University, 1999. Includes also on microfilm. Thesis (Ph.D.)--Columbia University, 1999. Includes bibliographical references (leaves 100-108).
*1. Men - Psychology. 2. Women - Psychology. 3. Self-actualization (Psychology) - Social aspects. 4. Body image - Social aspects. 5. Self-esteem - Sex differences. 6. Perfectionism (Personality trait). 7. Depression, Mental - Social aspects. 8. Mental health. 9. Stigma (Social psychology). 10. Self-acceptance. I. Title. II. Title: Influence of depression, gender, gender role, perfectionism, and self-silencing on body esteem*
*TC 085 L655*

**Lipschutz, Peggy.**
Berel, Marianne. Musical play sessions. [S.l. : s.n.], 1994.
*TC ML3920 .B45 1994*

**Lipsey, Mark W.**
Rossi, Peter Henry, 1921- Evaluation. 6th ed. Thousand Oaks, Calif. : Sage Publications, c1999.
*TC H62 .R666 1999*

**Liquid pleasures.**
Burnett, John, 1925- London ; New York : Routledge, 1999.
*TC TX815 .B87 1999*

**LIQUIDS.** *See* **BEVERAGES.**

**LIQUOR PROBLEM.** *See* **ALCOHOLISM; DRINKING OF ALCOHOLIC BEVERAGES.**

**LIQUOR TRAFFIC.** *See* **ALCOHOLIC BEVERAGE INDUSTRY.**

**The listener.**
Wheelis, Allen, 1915- New York : W.W. Norton, 1999.
*TC BF109.W44 A3 1999*

**LISTENING.** *See also* **HEARING.**
Merker, Hannah. 1st Southern Methodist Univ. Press ed. Dallas, Tex. : Southern Methodist University Press, 2000.
*TC BF323.L5 M37 2000*

**LISTENING.**
McCaslin, Mary M. Listening in classrooms. 1st ed. New York : HarperCollins College Publishers, c1996.
*TC LB1033 .M34 1996*

Merker, Hannah. Listening. 1st Southern Methodist Univ. Press ed. Dallas, Tex. : Southern Methodist University Press, 2000.
*TC BF323.L5 M37 2000*

**LISTENING - FICTION.**
Conrad, Pam. Blue willow. New York : Philomel Books, c1999.
*TC PZ7.C76476 Bl 1999*

**Listening in classrooms.**
McCaslin, Mary M. 1st ed. New York : HarperCollins College Publishers, c1996.
*TC LB1033 .M34 1996*

**Listening to patients.**
Druss, Richard G., 1933- Oxford ; New York : Oxford University Press, 2000.
*TC RC480.8 .D78 2000*

**Literacies**
Global literacies and the World-Wide Web. London ; New York : Routledge, 2000.
*TC P94.6 .G58 2000*

Multiliteracies. London ; New York : Routledge, 2000.
*TC LC149 .M85 2000*

Situated literacies. London ; New York : Routledge, 2000.
*TC LC149 .S52 2000*

**Literacies** : reading, writing, interpretation / Terence Brunk ... [et al.]. 2nd ed. New York : W.W. Norton, c2000. xlv, 813 p. : ill. ; 23 cm. ISBN 0-393-97537-1 (pbk.) DDC 808/.0427

*1. College readers. 2. Report writing - Problems, exercises, etc. 3. English language - Rhetoric - Problems, exercises, etc. I. Brunk, Terence.*
*TC PE1417 .L62 2000*

**LITERACY.** *See also* **COMPUTERS AND LITERACY; FUNCTIONAL LITERACY; LIBRARIES AND NEW LITERATES.**
Cooper, J. David (James David), 1942- 4th ed. Boston : Houghton Mifflin Co., c2000.
*TC LB1050.45 .C76 2000*

**LITERACY.**
Brown, Stephen Gilbert. Words in the wilderness. Albany : State University of New York Press, c2000.
*TC E99.A86 B76 2000*

Children achieving. Newark, Del. : International Reading Association, c1998.
*TC LB1139.5.R43 C55 1998*

Cooper, J. David (James David), 1942- Literacy. 4th ed. Boston : Houghton Mifflin Co., c2000.
*TC LB1050.45 .C76 2000*

DiSessa, Andrea A. Changing minds. Cambridge, MA : MIT Press, c2000.
*TC LB1028.43 .D57 2000*

Dugan, JoAnn R. Advancing the world of literacy. Carrollton, Ga. : College Reading Association, 1999.
*TC LB2395 .C62 1999*

Educational computing in the schools. New York : Haworth Press, 1999.
*TC LB1028.3 .E332 1999*

The future of literacy in a changing world. Rev. ed. Cresskill, N.J. : Hampton Press, c1998.
*TC LC149 .F87 1998*

Issues and trends in literacy education. 2nd ed. Boston : Allyn and Bacon, c2000.
*TC LB1576 .I87 2000*

Kress, Gunther R. Early spelling. London : New York : Routledge, 2000.
*TC P240.2 .K74 2000*

Learning to read. Dordrecht ; Boston : Kluwer Academic Publishers, 1999.
*TC LB1050.2 .L42 1999*

Literacy in the secondary school. London : David Fulton, 2000.
*TC LB1632 .L587 2000*

Machado, Jeanne M. Early childhood experiences in language arts. 6th ed. Albany, N.Y. : Delmar Publishers, c1999.
*TC LB1139.5.L35 M335 1999*

Miller, Wilma H. Strategies for developing emergent literacy. 1st ed. Boston : McGraw-Hill, c2000.
*TC LB1139.5.L35 M55 2000*

Multiliteracies. London ; New York : Routledge, 2000.
*TC LC149 .M85 2000*

Reconceptualizing literacy in the media age. Stamford, Conn. : Jai Press, c2000.
*TC LB1050 .A38 v.7*

Scholes, Robert J. A linguistic approach to reading and writing. Lewiston, N.Y. : E. Mellen Press, c1999.
*TC P211 .S383 1999*

Taylor, Denny, 1947- Family literacy. Portsmouth, NH : Heinemann, c1998.
*TC LC149 .T37 1998*

The welfare-to-work challenge for adult literacy educators. San Francisco, CA : Jossey-Bass Publishers, 1999.
*TC LC149.7 .W43 1999*

**LITERACY - ABILITY TESTING.**
Literacy assessment of second language learners. Boston ; London : Allyn and Bacon, c2001.
*TC P53.4 .L58 2001*

**LITERACY - AFRICA, SUB-SAHARAN.**
Egbo, Benedicta, 1954- Gender, literacy, and life chances in Sub-Saharan Africa. Clevedon ; Buffalo : Multilingual Matters, c2000.
*TC LC2412 .E42 2000*

**Literacy and bilingualism.**
Brisk, Maria. Mahwah, N.J. : L. Erlbaum Associates, c2000.
*TC LC3731 .B684 2000*

**LITERACY AND COMPUTERS.** *See* **COMPUTERS AND LITERACY.**

**Literacy and learning.**
Allan, Karen Kuelthau. Boston : Houghton Mifflin, c2000.
*TC LB1631 .A37 2000*

**Literacy and numeracy in Australian schools** / J. P. Keeves [et al.]. Canberra : Australian Gov. Pub. Service, 1976- v. : ill. ; 25 cm. (ERDC report ; no. 8-) (Australian studies in school performance ; v. 1-) "The Australian Council for Educational Research was commissioned to prepare this research study by the Education Research and Development Committee." Bibliography: v. 1, p. 113-114. PARTIAL CONTENTS: v. 1. Keeves, J. P. et al. A first report.--v. 2. Bourke, S. F. and Lewis, R. Item report. DDC 379/.151/0994
*1. Education - Australia - Evaluation. 2. Educational surveys - Australia. 3. Educational tests and measurements - Australia. 4. Numeracy - Australia. I. Keeves, John P. II. Australian Council for Educational Research. III. Australia. Education Research and Development Committee. IV. Series. V. Series: E.R.D.C. report ; no. 8-.*
*TC LA2102 .L57 1976*

**Literacy as a moral imperative.**
Powell, Rebecca, 1949- Lanham, Md. : Rowman & Littlefield Publishers, c1999.
*TC LC151 .P69 1999*

**Literacy assessment of second language learners** / [edited by] Sandra Rollins Hurley, Josefina Villamil Tinajero. Boston ; London : Allyn and Bacon, c2001. xvi, 190 p. : ill. ; 24 cm. Includes bibliographical references and index. ISBN 0-205-27443-9 (pbk.) DDC 418/.0076
*1. Language and languages - Ability testing. 2. Literacy - Ability testing. 3. Education, Bilingual. I. Hurley, Sandra Rollins. II. Villamil Tinajero, Josefina.*
*TC P53.4 .L58 2001*

**LITERACY - BIBLIOGRAPHIES.**
Finlay, Ann, 1944- The National Literacy Trust's international annotated bibliography of books on literacy. Stoke-on-Trent : Trentham Books, 1999.
*TC LC149 .F565 1999*

**LITERACY - CALIFORNIA - EVALUATION - HANDBOOKS, MANUALS, ETC.**
Barr, Mary A. (Mary Anderson) Assessing literacy with the Learning Record. Portsmouth, NH : Heinemann, c1999.
*TC LB1029.P67 B37 1999*

**LITERACY - CALIFORNIA - HANDBOOKS, MANUALS, ETC.**
Assessing literacy with the Learning Record. Portsmouth, NH : Heinemann, c1999.
*TC LB1029.P67 B37 1999b*

**Literacy campaign in NEP-Era Russia.**
Clark, Charles E., 1960- Uprooting otherness. Selinsgrove [Pa.] : Susquehanna University Press ; London : Associated University Presses, c2000.
*TC LC156.S65 C56 2000*

**LITERACY CAMPAIGNS.** *See* **LITERACY PROGRAMS.**

**LITERACY - CANADA - CASE STUDIES.**
Henry, Annette, 1955- Taking back control. Albany : State University of New York Press, c1998.
*TC LB1775.4.C2 H45 1998*

**LITERACY - CHINA.**
Culture, literacy, and learning English. Portsmouth, NH : Boynton/Cook Publishers, c1998.
*TC PE1130.C4 C85 1998*

**LITERACY, COMPUTER.** *See* **COMPUTER LITERACY.**

**The literacy connection** / edited by Ronald A. Sudol, Alice S. Horning. Cresskill, N.J. : Hampton Press, c1999. xv, 255 p. ; 24 cm. Includes bibliographical references and indexes. ISBN 1-57273-216-4 (hbk.) ISBN 1-57273-217-2 (pbk.) DDC 302.2/244
*1. Literacy - Social aspects - United States. 2. Language arts - Social aspects - United States. 3. Critical pedagogy - United States. I. Sudol, Ronald A., 1943- II. Horning, Alice S.*
*TC LC151 .L482 1999*

**LITERACY - DEVELOPING COUNTRIES - CONGRESSES.**
Linguistic minorities and literacy. Berlin ; New York : Mouton Publishers, 1984.
*TC P119.315 .L56 1984*

**LITERACY - ECONOMIC ASPECTS - STATISTICS.**
International Adult Literacy Survey. Literacy in the information age. Paris : Organisation for Economic Co-operation and Development; Ottawa : Statistics Canada, 2000.
*TC LC149 .L59 2000*

**Literacy for sustainable development in the age of information.**
Rassool, Naz, 1949- Clevedon [England] ; Philadelphia : Multilingual Matters, c1999.
*TC LC149 .R37 1999*

**Literacy from home to school.**
Campbell, Robin, 1937- Stoke on Trent, Staffordshire, Eng. : Trentham Books, 1999.
*TC LB1140.2 .C35 1999*

**LITERACY - GOVERNMENT POLICY.** *See* **LITERACY PROGRAMS.**

**LITERACY - GOVERNMENT POLICY - STATISTICS.**
International Adult Literacy Survey. Literacy in the information age. Paris : Organisation for Economic Co-operation and Development; Ottawa : Statistics Canada, 2000.
*TC LC149 .L59 2000*

**LITERACY - GREAT BRITAIN.**
Improving literacy in the primary school. London ; New York : Routledge, 1998.
*TC LB1573 .I56 1998*

Teaching through texts. London ; New York : Routledge, 1999.
*TC LB1573 .T39 1999*

Winston, Joe. Drama, literacy and moral education 5-11. London : David Fulton, 2000.
*TC LC268 .W667 2000*

**LITERACY - GREAT BRITAIN - HISTORY - 17TH CENTURY.**
Wheale, Nigel. Writing and society. London ; New York : Routledge, 1999.
*TC PR438.P65 W75 1999*

**LITERACY - ILLINOIS - CHICAGO - CASE STUDIES.**
Barone, Diane M. Resilient children. Newark, Del. : International Reading Association ; Chicago : National Reading Conference, c1999.
*TC LC4806.4 .B37 1999*

**Literacy in the secondary school** / edited by Maureen Lewis and David Wray. London : David Fulton, 2000. x, 182 p. : ill. ; 25 cm. Includes bibliographical references and index. ISBN 1-85346-655-7
*1. Literacy. 2. Reading (Secondary) - Great Britain. 3. English language - Great Britain - Composition and exercises. 4. English language - Study and teaching (Secondary) - Great Britain. I. Lewis, Maureen. II. Wray, David. 1950-*
*TC LB1632 .L587 2000*

**Literacy instruction for culturally and linguistically diverse students** : a collection of articles and commentaries / Michael F. Opitz, editor. Newark, Del. : International Reading Association, c1998. viii, 329 p. : ill. ; 26 cm. Includes bibliographical references and index. ISBN 0-87207-194-4 (alk. paper) DDC 370.117
*1. Linguistic minorities - Education - United States. 2. Children of minorities - Education - United States. 3. Reading - United States. 4. Literacy - United States. 5. Multicultural education - United States. I. Opitz, Michael F. II. International Reading Association.*
*TC LC3731 .L566 1998*

**Literacy instruction in half- and whole-day kindergarten.**
Morrow, Lesley Mandel. Newark, Del. : International Reading Association ; Chicago, Ill. : National Reading Conference, c1998.
*TC LB1181.2 .M67 1998*

**LITERACY PROGRAMS.** *See* **FAMILY LITERACY PROGRAMS.**

**LITERACY PROGRAMS - CALIFORNIA - CASE STUDIES.**
Samway, Katharine Davies. Buddy reading. Portsmouth, NH : Heinemann, c1995.
*TC LB1031.5 .S36 1995*

**LITERACY PROGRAMS - EL SALVADOR - CASE STUDIES.**
Purcell-Gates, Victoria. Now we read, we see, we speak. Mahwah, N.J. : L. Erlbaum Associates, Publishers, 2000.
*TC LC155.S22 P87 2000*

**LITERACY PROGRAMS - SOVIET UNION - HISTORY - 20TH CENTURY.**
Clark, Charles E., 1960- Uprooting otherness. Selinsgrove [Pa.] : Susquehanna University Press ; London : Associated University Presses, c2000.
*TC LC156.S65 C56 2000*

**LITERACY PROGRAMS - UNITED STATES.**
Promoting literacy in grades 4-9. Boston ; London : Allyn and Bacon, c2000.

*TC LB1576 .P76 2000*

**Literacy shutdown.**
Key, Daphne. Newark, Del. : International Reading Association ; Chicago, Ill. : National Reading Conference, c1998.
*TC LC1752 .K49 1998*

**LITERACY - SOCIAL ASPECTS.**
The explicit teaching of reading. Newark, Del. : International Reading Association, c1999.
*TC LB1573 .E96 1999*

Horsman, Jenny. Too scared to learn. Mahwah, N.J. : L. Erlbaum Associates, Publishers, 2000.
*TC LC1481 . H67 2000*

Rassool, Naz, 1949- Literacy for sustainable development in the age of information. Clevedon [England] ; Philadelphia : Multilingual Matters, c1999.
*TC LC149 .R37 1999*

Situated literacies. London ; New York : Routledge, 2000.
*TC LC149 .S52 2000*

**LITERACY - SOCIAL ASPECTS - CONGRESSES.**
Vygotskian perspectives on literacy research. Cambridge, U.K. ; New York : Cambridge University Press, 2000.
*TC LB1060 .V95 2000*

**LITERACY - SOCIAL ASPECTS - SOUTHERN STATES - CASE STUDIES.**
Key, Daphne. Literacy shutdown. Newark, Del. : International Reading Association ; Chicago, Ill. : National Reading Conference, c1998.
*TC LC1752 .K49 1998*

**LITERACY - SOCIAL ASPECTS - UNITED STATES.**
The literacy connection. Cresskill, N.J. : Hampton Press, c1999.
*TC LC151 .L482 1999*

Powell, Rebecca, 1949- Literacy as a moral imperative. Lanham, Md. : Rowman & Littlefield Publishers, c1999.
*TC LC151 .P69 1999*

Reconceptualizing the literacies in adolescents' lives. Mahwah, N.J. : L. Erlbaum Associates, 1998.
*TC LB1631 .R296 1998*

Selfe, Cynthia L., 1951- Technology and literacy in the twenty-first century. Carbondale : Southern Illinois University Press, c1999.
*TC LC149.5 .S45 1999*

**LITERACY - SOVIET UNION - HISTORY - 20TH CENTURY.**
Clark, Charles E., 1960- Uprooting otherness. Selinsgrove [Pa.] : Susquehanna University Press ; London : Associated University Presses, c2000.
*TC LC156.S65 C56 2000*

**LITERACY - STATISTICS.**
International Adult Literacy Survey. Literacy in the information age. Paris : Organisation for Economic Co-operation and Development; Ottawa : Statistics Canada, 2000.
*TC LC149 .L59 2000*

**LITERACY - STATISTICS - PERIODICALS.**
[Statistical yearbook (Unesco)] Statistical yearbook = [Paris : Unesco], 1987-
*TC AZ361 .U45*

**Literacy studies series**
Alvermann, Donna E. Popular culture in the classroom. Newark, Del. : International Reading Association ; Chicago, Ill. : National Reading Conference, c1999.
*TC P91.3 .A485 1999*

Barone, Diane M. Resilient children. Newark, Del. : International Reading Association ; Chicago : National Reading Conference, c1999.
*TC LC4806.4 .B37 1999*

Key, Daphne. Literacy shutdown. Newark, Del. : International Reading Association ; Chicago, Ill. : National Reading Conference, c1998.
*TC LC1752 .K49 1998*

Morrow, Lesley Mandel. Literacy instruction in half- and whole-day kindergarten. Newark, Del. : International Reading Association ; Chicago, Ill. : National Reading Conference, c1998.
*TC LB1181.2 .M67 1998*

Paratore, Jeanne R. What should we expect of family literacy? Newark, Del. : International Reading Association ; Chicago , Ill. : National Reading Conference, c1999.

TC LC151 .P37 1999

**LITERACY - STUDY AND TEACHING.**
Geekie, Peter. Understanding literacy development.
Stoke on Trent, England : Trentham Books, 1999.
*TC LC149 .G44 1999*

**LITERACY - STUDY AND TEACHING - AUDIO-VISUAL AIDS.**
Welch, Kathleen E. Electric rhetoric. Cambridge,
Mass. : MIT Press, c1999.
*TC P301.5.D37 W45 1999*

**LITERACY - STUDY AND TEACHING (EARLY CHILDHOOD).**
Campbell, Robin, 1937- Literacy from home to
school :. Stoke on Trent, Staffordshire, Eng. :
Trentham Books, 1999.
*TC LB1140.2 .C35 1999*

**LITERACY - STUDY AND TEACHING - GREAT BRITAIN.**
Unlocking literacy. London : David Fulton, 2000.
*TC LC149 .U485 2000*

**LITERACY, TECHNOLOGICAL.** *See*
**TECHNOLOGICAL LITERACY.**

**LITERACY - TECHNOLOGICAL INNOVATIONS - UNITED STATES - HISTORY.**
Gitelman, Lisa. Scripts, grooves, and writing
machines. Stanford, Calif. : Stanford University Press,
c1999.
*TC P96.T422 U6343*

**LITERACY TESTING.** *See* **READING - ABILITY TESTING.**

**LITERACY - UNITED STATES.**
Bertman, Stephen. Cultural amnesia. Westport,
Conn. ; London : Praeger, 2000.
*TC HN59.2 .B474 2000*

Brisk, Maria. Literacy and bilingualism. Mahwah,
N.J. : L. Erlbaum Associates, c2000.
*TC LC3731 .B684 2000*

Bybee, Rodger W. Achieving scientific literacy.
Portsmouth, NH : Heinemann, c1997.
*TC Q183.3.A1 B92 1997*

Harwayne, Shelley. Lifetime guarantees. Portsmouth,
NH : Heinemann, c2000.
*TC LB1575 . H38 2000*

Kovacs, George. Literal literacy II. Lewiston, NY : E.
Mellen Press, c1993.
*TC PE2827 .K682 1993*

Literacy instruction for culturally and linguistically
diverse students. Newark, Del. : International Reading
Association, c1998.
*TC LC3731 .L566 1998*

McGee, Lea M. Literacy's beginnings. 3rd ed.
Boston : London : Allyn and Bacon, c2000.
*TC LB1139.5.R43 M33 2000*

Morrow, Lesley Mandel. Literacy instruction in half-
and whole-day kindergarten. Newark, Del. :
International Reading Association ; Chicago, Ill. :
National Reading Conference, c1998.
*TC LB1181.2 .M67 1998*

**LITERACY - UNITED STATES - CASE STUDIES.**
Meier, Daniel R. Scribble scrabble--teaching children
to become successful readers and writers. New York :
Teachers College Press, c2000.
*TC LB1140.5.L3 M45 2000*

Literacy's beginnings.
McGee, Lea M. 3rd ed. Boston ; London : Allyn and
Bacon, c2000.
*TC LB1139.5.R43 M33 2000*

Literal literacy II.
Kovacs, George. Lewiston, NY : E. Mellen Press,
c1993.
*TC PE2827 .K682 1993*

**LITERARY COOKBOOKS.**
Cotler, Amy. The secret garden cookbook. 1st ed.
New York : HarperCollins Publishers, c1999.
*TC TX717 .C588 1999*

**LITERARY CRITICISM.** *See* **CRITICISM.**

**LITERARY FORM.** *See also* **FICTION GENRES.**
Romano, Tom. Blending genre, altering style.
Portsmouth, NH : Boynton/Cook ; Heinemann, c2000.
*TC PE1404 .R635 2000*

**LITERARY MOVEMENTS.** *See*
**POSTMODERNISM (LITERATURE);**
**ROMANTICISM.**

**Literary pedagogics after deconstruction :** scenarios
and perspectives in the teaching of English literature /
edited by Per Serritslev Petersen. Aarhus, Denmark :
Aarhus University Press, 1992. 110 p. ; 22 cm. (Dolphin ;
22) Includes bibliographical references (p. 106-110). ISBN
87-7288-372-3
*1. English literature - Study and teaching. I. Petersen, Per
Serritslev. II. Series: Dolphin (Arhus, Denmark) ; no. 22.*
*TC PR33 .L58 1992*

**LITERARY PROPERTY.** *See* **COPYRIGHT.**

**LITERATURE.** *See also* **APOCALYPTIC**
**LITERATURE; ART AND LITERATURE;**
**AUTHORS; AUTHORSHIP; CHILDREN'S**
**LITERATURE; CLASSICISM; CREATION**
**(LITERARY, ARTISTIC, ETC.); CRITICISM;**
**DIARIES; DRAMA; FICTION; FOLK**
**LITERATURE; GAYS' WRITINGS;**
**LEGENDS; LETTERS; POETRY; WIT AND**
**HUMOR; WOMEN AND LITERATURE;**
**YOUNG ADULT LITERATURE.**
Woodring, Carl, 1919- New York : Columbia
University Press, 1999.
*TC PN70 .W66 1999*

**LITERATURE.**
Goldsworthy, Candace L. Sourcebook of phonological
awareness activities. San Diego : Singular Pub.
Group, c1998.
*TC LB1050.5 .G66 1998*

**LITERATURE AND ART.** *See* **ART AND**
**LITERATURE.**

**LITERATURE AND HISTORY.**
LaCapra, Dominick, 1939- History and reading.
Toronto : University of Toronto Press, c2000.
*TC DC36.9.L32 1999*

**LITERATURE AND HOMOSEXUALITY.** *See*
**HOMOSEXUALITY AND LITERATURE.**

**LITERATURE AND MORALS.** *See* **CENSORSHIP.**

**LITERATURE AND PAINTING.** *See* **ART AND**
**LITERATURE.**

**LITERATURE AND POLITICS.** *See* **POLITICS**
**AND LITERATURE.**

**LITERATURE AND SCULPTURE.** *See* **ART AND**
**LITERATURE.**

**LITERATURE AND SOCIETY - ENGLAND -**
**LONDON - HISTORY - 19TH CENTURY.**
Black, Barbara J., 1962- On exhibit. Charlottesville ;
London : University Press of Virginia, 2000.
*TC AM43.L6 B53 2000*

**LITERATURE AND SOCIETY - GREAT**
**BRITAIN - HISTORY - 17TH CENTURY.**
Wheale, Nigel. Writing and society. London ; New
York : Routledge, 1999.
*TC PR438.P65 W75 1999*

**LITERATURE AND SOCIETY - UNITED**
**STATES - HISTORY.**
True, Michael. An energy field more intense than war.
1st ed. Syracuse, N.Y. : Syracuse University Press,
1995.
*TC PS169.N65 T78 1995*

**LITERATURE AND SOCIETY - UNITED**
**STATES - HISTORY - 19TH CENTURY.**
Mensh, Elaine, 1924- Black, white, and Huckleberry
Finn. Tuscaloosa : University of Alabama Press,
c2000.
*TC PS1305 .M46 2000*

**LITERATURE AND SOCIETY - UNITED**
**STATES - HISTORY - 19TH CENTURY -**
**STUDY AND TEACHING.**
Making Mark Twain work in the classroom. Durham
[N.C.] : Duke University Press, 1999.
*TC PS1338 .M23 1999*

**LITERATURE AND SOCIOLOGY.** *See*
**LITERATURE AND SOCIETY.**

**LITERATURE AND STATE.** *See* **POLITICS AND**
**LITERATURE.**

**LITERATURE AND TECHNOLOGY.**
Landow, George P. Hypertext 2.0. Rev., amplified ed.
Baltimore : Johns Hopkins University Press, 1997.
*TC PN81 .L28 1997*

**Literature and the child :** romantic continuations,
postmodern contestations / edited by James Holt
McGavran. Iowa City : University of Iowa Press,
c1999. 269 p. : ill. ; 25 cm. Includes bibliographical
references and index. ISBN 0-87745-690-9 (alk. paper) DDC
820.9/9282
*1. Children's literature, English - History and criticism. 2.
Children's literature, American - History and criticism. 3.*

*Children - Books and reading. 4. Postmodernism (Literature)*
*5. Romanticism. I. McGavran, James Holt.*
*TC PR990 .L58 1999*

**LITERATURE, APOCALYPTIC.** *See*
**APOCALYPTIC LITERATURE.**

**LITERATURE - APPRECIATION - GREAT**
**BRITAIN - HISTORY.**
Pearson, Jacqueline, 1949- Women's reading in
Britain, 1750-1835. Cambridge, UK ; New York :
Cambridge University Press, 1999.
*TC PR756.W65 P43 1999*

**LITERATURE - CENSORSHIP.** *See*
**CENSORSHIP.**

**LITERATURE - EVALUATION.** *See* **BOOKS AND**
**READING; CRITICISM; LITERATURE -**
**HISTORY AND CRITICISM.**

**LITERATURE, EXPERIMENTAL - STUDY AND**
**TEACHING (SECONDARY) - CASE**
**STUDIES.**
Harper, Helen J., 1957- Wild words-dangerous
desires. New York : Peter Lang, c2000.
*TC LB1631 .H267 2000*

**Literature for young children.**
Glazer, Joan I. 4th ed. Upper Saddle River, N.J. :
Merrill, 2000.
*TC Z1037.A1 G573 2000*

**LITERATURE - HISTORY AND CRITICISM -**
**THEORY, ETC.**
Barone, Tom. Aesthetics, politics, and educational
inquiry. New York : P. Lang, 2000.
*TC LB1028 .B345 2000*

Shattuck, Roger. Candor and perversion. 1st ed. New
York : W.W. Norton, c1999.
*TC PN52 .S53 1999*

**Literature in English subject test.**
Cracking the GRE literature in English subject test.
New York : Random House, 1996-
*TC LB2367.4 .L58*

**LITERATURE IN MATHEMATICS EDUCATION.**
Borasi, Raffaella. Reading counts. New York ;
London : Teachers College Press, c2000.
*TC QA11 .B6384 2000*

Feisty females. Portsmouth, NH : Heinemann, c1998.
*TC QA11 .F44 1998*

**Literature links for nutrition and health.**
Ubbes, Valerie A. Boston : Allyn and Bacon, c2000.
*TC TX364 .U253 2000*

**LITERATURE, MODERN - 20TH CENTURY.** *See*
**POSTMODERNISM (LITERATURE).**

**LITERATURE, MODERN - 20TH CENTURY -**
**HISTORY AND CRITICISM.**
Guevara-Vázquez, Fabián. El indigena en la novela de
la Revolucion Mexicana. 1999.
*TC 085 G934*

**LITERATURE, MODERN - PERIODICALS.**
Levende talen magazine. Amsterdam : Vereniging van
Leraren in Levenden Talen, 2000-

**LITERATURE - POLITICAL ASPECTS.** *See*
**POLITICS AND LITERATURE.**

**LITERATURE, POPULAR.** *See* **POPULAR**
**LITERATURE.**

**LITERATURE - PSYCHOLOGY.** *See*
**AESTHETICS.**

**LITERATURE - SOCIAL ASPECTS.** *See*
**LITERATURE AND SOCIETY.**

**LITERATURE - STUDY AND TEACHING.**
Cornett, Claudia E. The arts as meaning makers.
Upper Saddle River, N.J. : Merrill, 1999.
*TC LB1591 .C67 1999*

Doll, Mary Aswell. Like letters in running water.
Mahwah, N.J. ; London : L. Erlbaum Publishers,
2000.
*TC LB1575 .D64 2000*

Fiction, literature and media. Amsterdam :
Amsterdam University Press, c1999.
*TC LB1575.8 .F53 1999*

**LITERATURE - STUDY AND TEACHING**
**(ELEMENTARY).**
Cooper, J. David (James David), 1942- Discover :
Grade 1, level 1.5, [Themes 9 and 10]. Boston :
Houghton Mifflin, 1997.
*TC LB1575.8 .C6616 1997*

**LITERATURE - STUDY AND TEACHING (ELEMENTARY) - UNITED STATES.**
Children's literature in the elementary school. 7th ed. Dubuque, IA : McGraw-Hill, c2001.
*TC LB1575.5.U5 H79 2001*

Polette, Nancy. Gifted books, gifted readers. Englewood, Colo. : Libraries Unlimited, 2000.
*TC LB1575.5.U5 P64 2000*

**LITERATURE - STUDY AND TEACHING (HIGHER).**
Learning literature in an era of change. Sterling, Va. : Stylus Pub., c2000.
*TC PN59 .L39 2000*

**LITERATURE - STUDY AND TEACHING (HIGHER) - TECHNOLOGICAL INNOVATIONS.**
Learning literature in an era of change. Sterling, Va. : Stylus Pub., c2000.
*TC PN59 .L39 2000*

**LITERATURE - STUDY AND TEACHING (HIGHER) - UNITED STATES.**
Caughie, Pamela L., 1953- Passing and pedagogy. Urbana : University of Illinois Press, c1999.
*TC PN61 .C38 1999*

Woodring, Carl, 1919- Literature. New York : Columbia University Press, 1999.
*TC PN70 .W66 1999*

**LITERATURE - WOMEN AUTHORS.**
Crossing boundaries. Champaign, IL : Human Kinetics, c1999.
*TC PN6071.S62 C76 1999*

**LITERATURES OF AMERICA.** *See* **AMERICA - LITERATURES.**

**LITHOGRAPHS.** *See* **LITHOGRAPHY.**

**LITHOGRAPHY - METAL PLATE PROCESSES - TECHNIQUE.**
Etching [videorecording]. Northbrook, Ill. : Peasmarsh, East Sussex, Eng. : Roland Collection of Films on Art, c1990.
*TC NE2043 .E87 1990*

**LITTERATEURS.** *See* **AUTHORS.**

**LITTÉRATURE ET HISTOIRE.**
LaCapra, Dominick, 1939- History and reading. Toronto : University of Toronto Press, c2000.
*TC DC36.9.L32 1999*

**Little, Angela.**
Education, cultures, and economics. New York : Falmer Press, 1999.
*TC LC191.8.D44 E38 1999*

**The little ballerina.**
Grindley, Sally. 1st American ed. New York : DK Pub., 1999.
*TC GV1787.5 .G75 1999*

**The little band.**
Sage, James. 1st ed. New York : M.K. McElderry Books ; Toronto : Collier Macmillan Canada ; New York : Maxwell Macmillan International Pub. Group, c1991.
*TC PZ7.S1304 Li 1991*

**Little bunny on the move.**
McCarty, Peter. 1st ed. New York : Holt, 1999.
*TC PZ7.M47841327 Li 1999*

**Little, Carl.** The watercolors of John Singer Sargent / Carl Little ; picture editor & designer, Arnold Skolnick. Berkeley : University of California Press, c1998. 160 p. : col. ill. ; 28 cm. "A Chameleon book"--T.p. verso. Includes bibliographical references (p. 19) and index. ISBN 0-520-21969-4 (alk. paper) ISBN 0-520-21970-8 (alk. paper) DDC 759.13
*1. Sargent, John Singer, - 1856-1925 - Criticism and interpretation. I. Sargent, John Singer, 1856-1925 II. Title.*
*TC ND1839.S32 L58 1998*

**Little factory.**
Weeks, Sarah. 1st ed. [New York] : Laura Geringer book, c1998.
*TC PZ7.W4125 Li 1998*

**LITTLE HUNTING CREEK PLANTATION (VA.).** *See* **MOUNT VERNON (VA. : ESTATE).**

**Little Polar Bear and the brave little hare.**
De Beer, Hans. [Kleine Eisbär und der Angsthase. English] New York : North-South Books, 1998.
*TC PZ7.D353 Liv 1998*

**Littlejohn, Carol.** Keep talking that book! / Carol Littlejohn. Worthington, Ohio : Linworth Pub., 2000. xi, 170 p. : ill. ; 28 cm. (Professional growth series) "Booktalks to promote reading, volume two." "This book is a companion

to: Talk that book : booktalks to promote reading"--Introd. Includes indexes. ISBN 0-938865-92-7 DDC 028/.9
*1. Book talks. 2. Best books. I. Title. II. Series.*
*TC Z716.3 .L58 2000*

Talk that book! booktalks to promote reading / by Carol Littlejohn. Worthington, Ohio : Linworth Publishing, 1999. xi, 166 p. ; 28 cm. (Professional growth series) "A publication of The Book Report & Library Talk, Professional Growth Series"--T.p. Includes bibliographical references and indexes. ISBN 0-938865-75-7
*1. Book talks. 2. Children - Books and reading - United States. 3. Children's literature - Bibliography. 4. Young adults - Books and reading - United States. I. Title. II. Title: Booktalks to promotion reading III. Series.*
*TC Z1037.A2 L58 1999*

**LITTLE'S DISEASE.** *See* **CEREBRAL PALSY.**

**Littlesugar, Amy.** Tree of hope / Amy Littlesugar ; [illustrated by] Floyd Cooper. New York : Philomel Books, 1999. 1 v. (unpaged) : col. ill. ; 28 cm. SUMMARY: Florrie's daddy used to be a stage actor in Harlem before the Depression forced the Lafayette Theater to close, but he gets a chance to act again when Orson Welles reopens the theater to stage an all-black version of Macbeth. ISBN 0-399-23300-8 DDC [E]
*1. Afro-Americans - Juvenile fiction. 2. Afro-Americans - Fiction. 3. Actors and actresses - Fiction. 4. Depressions - 1929 - Fiction. 5. Harlem (New York, N.Y.) - Fiction. I. Cooper, Floyd, ill. II. Title.*
*TC PZ7.L7362 Tr 1999*

**Littleton, Karen.**
Light, Paul. Social processes in children's learning. Cambridge, U.K. ; New York : Cambridge University Press, 1999.
*TC LB1060 .L533 1999*

Making sense of social development. London ; New York : Routledge in association with the Open University, 1999.
*TC HQ783 .L57 1999*

**Littlewood, Roland.**
Intercultural therapy. [2nd ed.]. Oxford ; Malden, MA : Blackwell Science, 2000.
*TC RC455.4.E8 I57 2000*

**Littrell, John M., 1944-** Brief counseling in action / John M. Littrell. 1st ed. New York : W. W. Norton, c1998. xvii, 246 p. : ill. ; 24 cm. "A Norton professional book." Includes bibliographical references (p. [229]-236) and index. ISBN 0-393-70265-0 DDC 616.89/14
*1. Brief psychotherapy. 2. Solution-focused brief therapy. I. Title.*
*TC RC480.55 .L58 1998*

**Liu, Judith, 1950-.**
The ethnographic eye. New York : Falmer Press, 2000.
*TC LB45 .E837 2000*

**Liu, Leping.**
Information technology in educational research and statistics. New York : Haworth Press, 1999.
*TC LB1028.3 .I51945 1999*

**Lives and legacies**
Philosophers and religious leaders. Phoenix, Ariz. : Oryx Press, 1999.
*TC B104 .P48 1999*

**Lives in context**
Weisfeld, Glenn, 1943- Evolutionary principles of human adolescence. New York, NY : Basic Books, 1999.
*TC BF724 .W35 1999*

**Lives in progress.**
McWilliam, P. J. Baltimore : P.H. Brookes, c2000.
*TC HV741 .M3128 2000*

**Lives in time and place.**
Settersten, Richard A. Amityville, N.Y. : Baywood Pub., c1999.
*TC BF713 .S48 1999*

**Lives of moral leadership.**
Coles, Robert. 1st ed. New York : Random House, c2000.
*TC BJ1547.4 .C64 2000*

**LIVESTOCK.** *See* **HORSES; SHEEP.**

**LIVESTOCK BREEDS.** *See* **HORSE BREEDS.**

**LIVESTOCK - DISEASES.** *See* **VETERINARY MEDICINE.**

**LIVESTOCK - LOSSES.** *See* **VETERINARY MEDICINE.**

**LIVESTOCK MEDICINE.** *See* **VETERINARY MEDICINE.**

**Living in contradiction.**
Fleischer, Lee. 1998.
*TC 06 no. 11021*

**LIVING LANGUAGES.** *See* **LANGUAGES, MODERN.**

**The living machine** [videorecording] / a production of WQED Pittsburgh in association with the National Academy of Sciences ; series producer, Gregory Andorfer ; written by Gregory Andorfer, Georgann Kane. [New York, N.Y.?] : Unapix Entertainment, Inc. [distributor], c1996. 1 videocassette (60 min.) : sd., col. with b&w sequences ; 1/2 in. (Planet Earth ; 1) At head of title: Unapix Consumer Products feature presentation [videorecording]. VHS. Catalogued from credits and container. Narrator, Richard Kiley. Sound, Roger Phenix; photography by Norris Brock; music by Jack Tillar. "Major funding by the Annenberg/CPB Project"--Container. For adolescent through adult. SUMMARY: Plate tectonics, one of the most important discoveries of the 20th century, is explored with world-renowned scientists on location. They are at Kilauea Volcano during a dramatic eruption, aboard the submersible craft Alvin as it dives to the bottom of the Atlantic, and in pursuit of the cause of the worst earthquakes in American history.
*1. Earthquakes. 2. Volcanoes. 3. Plate tectonics. 4. Geophysics. 5. Documentary television programs. I. Andorfer, Gregory. II. Kane, Georgann. III. Kiley, Richard. IV. WQED (Television station : Pittsburgh, Pa.) V. National Academy of Sciences (U.S.) VI. Annenberg/CPB Project. VII. Unapix Entertainment, Inc. VIII. Unapix Consumer Products. IX. Title: Unapix Consumer Products feature presentation [videorecording] X. Series.*
*TC QB631.2 .L5 1996*

**LIVING TOGETHER.** *See* **UNMARRIED COUPLES.**

**Living well is the best revenge.**
Tomkins, Calvin, 1925- 1998 Modern Library ed. New York : Modern Library, c1998.
*TC ND237.M895 T66 1998*

**Living with the earth.**
Moore, Gary S. Boca Raton, Fla. : Lewis Publishers, c1999.
*TC RA565 .M665 1999*

**Livingston, Jane.** The art of Richard Diebenkorn / Jane Livingston ; with essays by John Elderfield, Ruth Fine, and Jane Livingston. New York : Whitney Museum of American Art ; Berkeley : University of California Press, c1997. 276 p. : ill. (chiefly col.) ; 32 cm. Exhibition held at the Whitney Museum of American Art on Oct. 9, 1997-Jan.11, 1998, and others. Includes bibliographical references (p. 267-270). ISBN 0-520-21257-6 (University of California : cloth) ISBN 0-520-21258-4 (Univeristy of California : pbk.) ISBN 0-87427-107-X (Whitney Museum of American Art : alk. paper) DDC 759.13
*1. Diebenkorn, Richard. - 1922- - Exhibitions. 2. Diebenkorn, Richard, - 1922- - Criticism and interpretation. I. Diebenkorn, Richard, 1922- II. Elderfield, John. III. Whitney Museum of American Art. IV. Title.*
*TC N6537.D447 A4 1997*

**Livingston, Myra Cohn.** Celebrations / Myra Cohn Livingston, poet ; Leonard Everett Fisher, painter. 1st ed. New York : Holiday House, c1985. 32 p. : col. ill. ; 29 cm. SUMMARY: A collection of poems on the holidays of the year, from New Year's Day through Martin Luther King Day, Passover, Labor Day, Halloween, and others, to Christmas Eve. ISBN 0-8234-0550-8 (lib. bdg.) ISBN 0-8234-0550-8 DDC 811/.54
*1. Holidays - Juvenile poetry. 2. Children's poetry, American. 3. Holidays - Poetry. I. Fisher, Leonard Everett, ill. II. Title.*
*TC PS3562.I945 C4 1985*

Cricket never does : a collection of haiku and tanka / Myra Cohn Livingston ; illustrated by Kees de Kiefte. New York : Margaret K. McElderry Books, c1997. 42 p. : ill. ; 22 cm. Includes index. SUMMARY: A collection of more than fifty original haiku and tanka verses about the four seasons. ISBN 0-689-81123-3 DDC 811/.54
*1. Seasons - Juvenile poetry. 2. Children's poetry, American. 3. Haiku, American. 4. Waka, American. 5. Seasons - Poetry. 6. Haiku. 7. Waka. 8. American poetry. I. Kiefte, Kees de, ill. II. Title.*
*TC PS3562.I945 C75 1997*

Earth songs / Myra Cohn Livingston, poet ; illustrated by Leonard Everett Fisher, painter. 1st ed. New York : Holiday House, c1986. [27] p. : col. ill. ; 29 cm. SUMMARY: A poetic tribute to that little O, the earth, its continents, clay, hills, forests, and seas. ISBN 0-8234-0615-6 (lib. bdg) DDC 811/.54
*1. Earth - Juvenile poetry. 2. Children's poetry, American. 3. Earth - Poetry. 4. American poetry. I. Fisher, Leonard Everett, ill. II. Title.*

*TC PS3562.I945 E3 1986*

Flights of fancy and other poems / Myra Cohn Livingston. 1st ed. New York : M.K. McElderry Books ; Toronto : Maxwell Macmillan Canada ; New York : Maxwell Macmillan International, c1994. 40 p. ; 22 cm. ISBN 0-689-50613-9 DDC 811.54
*1. Children's poetry, American. I. Title.*
***TC PS3562.I945 F58 1994***

If the owl calls again. 1st ed. New York : M.K. McElderry Books ; Toronto : Collier Macmillan ; New York : Maxwell Macmillan, c1990.
***TC PN6109.97 .I3 1990***

No way of knowing : Dallas poems / Myra Cohn Livingston. 1st ed. New York : Atheneum, 1980. 45 p. ; 22 cm. "A Margaret K. McElderry book." SUMMARY: Poems based on the author's experiences in the black community of Dallas, Texas, from 1952 to 1964. ISBN 0-689-50179-X DDC 811/.54
*1. Afro-Americans - Texas - Dallas - Juvenile poetry. 2. Children's poetry, American. 3. Afro-Americans - Texas - Dallas - Poetry. 4. American poetry. I. Title.*
***TC PS3562.I945 N6 1980***

Poems for fathers. 1st ed. New York : Holiday House, c1989.
***TC PS595.F39 P64 1989***

Riddle-me rhymes. 1st ed. New York : M.K. McElderry Books ; Toronto : Maxwell Macmillan Canada ; New York : Maxwell Macmillan International, c1994.
***TC PN6371.5 .R53 1994***

Sea songs / Myra Cohn Livingston, poet Leonard Everett Fisher, painter. 1st ed. New York : Holiday House, c1986. [32] p. : col. ill. ; 29 cm. SUMMARY: Poetic images of cresting waves, mermaids, sunken ships, and other aspects of the sea. ISBN 0-8234-0591-5 DDC 811/.54
*1. Sea poetry, American. 2. Children's poetry, American. 3. Sea poetry. 4. American poetry. I. Fisher, Leonard Everett, ill. II. Title.*
***TC PS3562.I945 S4 1986***

Sky songs / Myra Cohn Livingston, poet ; Leonard Everett Fisher, painter. 1st ed. New York : Holiday House, c1984. 31 p. : col. ill. ; 29 cm. SUMMARY: Fourteen poems about the various aspects of the sky such as the moon, clouds, stars, storms, and sunsets. ISBN 0-8234-0502-8 DDC 811/.54
*1. Sky - Juvenile poetry. 2. Children's poetry, American. 3. Sky - Poetry. 4. American poetry. I. Fisher, Leonard Everett, ill. II. Title.*
***TC PS3562.I945 S5 1984***

Up in the air / Myra Cohn Livingston ; illustrated by Leonard Everett Fisher. 1st ed. New York : Holiday House, c1989. [32] p. : col. ill. ; 29 cm. SUMMARY: A poem describing the sights and sensations of flying in an airplane. ISBN 0-8234-0736-5 (lib. bdg.) DDC 811/.54
*1. Flight - Juvenile poetry. 2. Airplanes - Juvenile poetry. 3. Children's poetry, American. 4. Flight - Poetry. 5. Airplanes - Poetry. 6. American poetry. I. Fisher, Leonard Everett, ill. II. Title.*
***TC PS3562.I945 U6 1989***

The way things are, and other poems. Illustrated by Jenni Oliver. [1st ed.]. New York, Atheneum, 1974. 40 p. illus. 21 cm. "A Margaret K. McElderry book." SUMMARY: A collection of poems describing different feelings, places, and things. ISBN 0-689-50008-4 DDC 811/.5/4
*1. American poetry. I. Title.*
***TC PZ8.3.L75 Way***

**Livingstone, D. W.** Public attitudes towards education in Ontario, 1996 : the eleventh OISE/UT Survey / D.W. Livingstone, D. Hart, L.E. Davie. Toronto : OISE/UT in association with University of Toronto Press, 1997. x, 116 p. ; 23 cm. Includes bibliographical references (p. [107]-116). ISBN 0-8020-8039-1
*1. Education - Ontario - Public opinion. 2. Public opinion - Ontario. I. Hart, D. J., 1948- II. Davie, Lynn. III. Ontario Institute for Studies in Education. IV. Title.*
***TC LA418.06 L58 1997***

**Livingstone, Marco.** Jim Dine : the alchemy of images / Marco Livingstone ; with commentary by Jim Dine. New York : Monacelli Press, 1998. 352 p. : ill. (some col.) ; 32 cm. Includes bibliographical references (p. 340-343) and index. ISBN 1-88525-479-2 DDC 709/.2
*1. Dine, Jim, - 1935- - Themes, motives. 2. Dine, Jim, - 1935- - Criticism and interpretation. I. Dine, Jim, 1935- II. Title. III. Title: Alchemy of images*
***TC N6537.D5 A4 1998***

**Livo, Norma J., 1929-** Celebrating the earth : stories, experiences, and activities / Norma J. Livo. Englewood, Colo. : Teacher Ideas Press, 2000. xvii, 174 p. : ill. ; 28 cm. Includes bibliographical references (p. 165-168) and index. ISBN 1-56308-776-6 (paper) DDC 372.3/57
*1. Animals. 2. Animals - Folklore. 3. Animals - Study and teaching - Activity programs. I. Title.*
***TC QL50 .L57 2000***

**LIZARDS.** *See* **IGUANAS.**

**LLBA disc.**
[LLBA (Online)] LLBA [computer file]. [Norwood, MA] : SilverPlatter International, [1993- Computer data and program.

[LLBA (Online)] LLBA [computer file]. [Norwood, MA] : SilverPlatter International, [1993- Computer data and program.

[LLBA (Online)] LLBA [computer file]. [Norwood, MA] : SilverPlatter International, [1993- Computer data and program.
***TC NETWORKED RESOURCE***

**[LLBA (Online)]** LLBA [computer file]. [Norwood, MA] : SilverPlatter International, [1993- Computer data and program. Title in publisher's catalog: Linguistics and language behavior abstracts. Formerly entitled: LLBA disc. Other title: Linguistics & language behavior abstracts. Title from search screen (viewed Aug. 10, 1999). Coverage: 1973- Search software: WebSPIRS. Subscription and registration required for access. Text (bibliographic citations and abstracts) SUMMARY: A database of abstracts covering three areas: research in linguistics, research in language, and research in speech, language and hearing pathology. The database consists of bibliographic records with abstracts citing journal articles, books, book chapters, dissertations, and reviews of books and other media. Over 2,600 journals from 50 countries are scanned for inclusion and approximately 17,000 new records are added annually. Electronic version of the print title: LLBA, Linguistics and language behavior abstracts. Mode of access: Internet via World Wide Web. System requirements: World Wide Web browser. Data from Sociological Abstracts, Inc. Electronic database URL: http://www/perl/dcis/ej-access?spirs
*1. Linguistics - Abstracts - Databases. 2. Language and languages - Abstracts - Databases. I. SilverPlatter Information, Inc. II. Sociological Abstracts, Inc. III. Title: Linguistics and language behavior abstracts IV. Title: LLBA disc V. Title: Linguistics & language behavior abstracts*

**[LLBA (Online)]** LLBA [computer file]. [Norwood, MA] : SilverPlatter International, [1993- Computer data and program. Title in publisher's catalog: Linguistics and language behavior abstracts. Formerly entitled: LLBA disc. Other title: Linguistics & language behavior abstracts. Title from search screen (viewed Aug. 10, 1999). Coverage: 1973- Search software: WebSPIRS. Subscription and registration required for access. Text (bibliographic citations and abstracts) SUMMARY: A database of abstracts covering three areas: research in linguistics, research in language, and research in speech, language and hearing pathology. The database consists of bibliographic records with abstracts citing journal articles, books, book chapters, dissertations, and reviews of books and other media. Over 2,600 journals from 50 countries are scanned for inclusion and approximately 17,000 new records are added annually. Electronic version of the print title: LLBA, Linguistics and language behavior abstracts. Mode of access: Internet via World Wide Web. System requirements: World Wide Web browser. Data from Sociological Abstracts, Inc. Electronic database URL: http://www/perl/dcis/ej-access?spirs
*1. Linguistics - Abstracts - Databases. 2. Language and languages - Abstracts - Databases. I. SilverPlatter Information, Inc. II. Sociological Abstracts, Inc. III. Title: Linguistics and language behavior abstracts IV. Title: LLBA disc V. Title: Linguistics & language behavior abstracts*

**[LLBA (Online)]** LLBA [computer file]. [Norwood, MA] : SilverPlatter International, [1993- Computer data and program. Title in publisher's catalog: Linguistics and language behavior abstracts. Formerly entitled: LLBA disc. Other title: Linguistics & language behavior abstracts. Title from search screen (viewed Aug. 10, 1999). Coverage: 1973- Search software: WebSPIRS. Subscription and registration required for access. Text (bibliographic citations and abstracts) SUMMARY: A database of abstracts covering three areas: research in linguistics, research in language, and research in speech, language and hearing pathology. The database consists of bibliographic records with abstracts citing journal articles, books, book chapters, dissertations, and reviews of books and other media. Over 2,600 journals from 50 countries are scanned for inclusion and approximately 17,000 new records are added annually. Electronic version of the print title: LLBA, Linguistics and language behavior abstracts; also available on CD-ROM. Mode of access: Internet via World Wide Web. System requirements: World Wide Web browser. Data from Sociological Abstracts, Inc. Electronic database URL: http://webspirs3.silverplatter.com/cgi-bin/waldo.cgi/LL
*1. Linguistics - Abstracts - Databases. 2. Language and languages - Abstracts - Databases. I. SilverPlatter Information, Inc. II. Sociological Abstracts, Inc. III. Title: Linguistics and language behavior abstracts IV. Title: LLBA disc V. Title: Linguistics & language behavior abstracts*
***TC NETWORKED RESOURCE***

**Llinás Alvarez, Edgar.** Vida y obra de Ramón Beteta / Edgar Llinás Alvarez. 1. ed. México : [s.n.], 1996 (México, D.F. : Impresora Galve) xxv, 215 p. : ill. ; 23 cm. + 1 pamphlet (138 p. ; 23 cm.). Includes pamphlet:el ideario revolucionario de Ram@oon Beteta Includes bibliographical references.
*1. Beteta, Ramón. - 1901-1965. 2. Mexico - Politics and government - 1910-1946. 3. Mexico - Politics and government - 1946-1970. 4. Mexico - Economic policy. 5. Politicians - Mexico - Biography. 6. Ambassadors - Mexico - Biography. I. Llin@oas Alvarez, Edgar. Ideario revolucionario de Ram@oon Beteta II. Title.*
***TC F1234.B56 L5 1996***

**Llin@oas Alvarez, Edgar.**
**Ideario revolucionario de Ramoon Beteta**
Llinás Alvarez, Edgar. Vida y obra de Ramón Beteta. 1. ed. México : [s.n.], 1996 (México, D.F. : Impresora Galve)
***TC F1234.B56 L5 1996***

**Lloyd, Megan, ill.**
Otto, Carolyn. Pioneer church. 1st ed. New York : Henry Holt, 1999
***TC PZ7.O8794 Pi 1999***

**LNAGUAGE ARTS (PRIMARY).**
Teacher toolbox [kit]. Chicago, Ill. : Open Court Pub. Co., c1995.
***TC LB1573.3 .T4 1995***

**Loader, Brian, 1958-.**
Digital democracy. London ; New York : Routledge, 1999.
***TC JF1525.A8 D54 1999***

**LOANS.** *See* **STUDENT AID.**

**Loase, John Frederick, 1947-** Sigfluence III : the key to "It's a wonderful life" / John F. Loase. Lanham, Md. : University Press of America, c1996. 103 p. ; 23 cm. Includes bibliographical references (p. [100]-103) and index. ISBN 0-7618-0207-X (cloth : alk. paper) DDC 155.9/2
*1. Influence (Psychology) 2. Example - Psychological aspects. 3. Social influence. 4. Success - Psychological aspects. 5. It's a wonderful life (Motion picture) I. Title. II. Title: Sigfluence three*
***TC BF774 .L63 1996***

**Lobato, Joanne (Joanne Elizabeth).**
Future basics. Golden, Colo. : National Council of Supervisors of Mathematics, c1998.
***TC QA141 .C43 1998***

**LOCAL FINANCE.** *See* **GRANTS-IN-AID.**

**LOCAL GOVERNMENT.** *See* **LOCAL OFFICIALS AND EMPLOYEES; PUBLIC ADMINISTRATION; STATE-LOCAL RELATIONS.**

**LOCAL JUNIOR COLLEGES.** *See* **COMMUNITY COLLEGES.**

**Local knowledge and wisdom in higher education** / edited by G.R. (Bob) Teasdale and Zane Ma Rhea. 1st ed. Oxford : Published for the IAU Press [by] Pergamon, 2000. xxxi, 264 p. : ill. ; 24 cm. (Issues in higher education) "UNESCO." Includes bibliographical references (p. 237-255) and index. ISBN 0-08-043453-3 (HC) DDC 378
*1. Indigenous peoples - Education (Higher) 2. Education, Higher - Cross-cultural studies. I. Teasdale, G. R. (G. Robert) II. Ma Rhea, Zane. III. Unesco. IV. Series: Issues in higher education (Oxford, England)*
***TC GN380 .L63 2000***

**LOCAL OFFICIALS AND EMPLOYEES - UNITED STATES.**
Conyers, James E., 1932- Black elected officials. New York : Russell Sage Foundation, c1976.
***TC JK1924 .C65***

**LOCAL-STATE RELATIONS.** *See* **STATE-LOCAL RELATIONS.**

**Locating and correcting reading difficulties.**
Shanker, James L. 7th ed. Upper Saddle River, N.J. : Merrill, c1998.
***TC LB1050.5 .E38 1998***

**Lochhead, Jack, 1944-.**
Whimbey, Arthur. Problem solving and comprehension. 6th ed. Mahwah, N.J. : Lawrence Erlbaum Associates, 1999.
***TC BF449 .W45 1999***

**Lock, Corey.**
International narratives on becoming a teacher educator. Lewiston, N.Y. ; Lampeter,Wales : E. Mellen Press, c2000.

*TC LB1737.5 .I58 2000*

**Locke, Edwin A.**
Industrial and organizational psychology. Oxford,
UK : Malden, Mass. : Blackwell Business, 2000.
*TC HF5548.8 .I5233 2000*

**Locke, John, 1632-1704.**
**Of the conduct of the understanding.**
Locke, John, 1632-1704. [Some thoughts
concerning education] Some thoughts concerning
education ; Indianapolis : Hackett Pub. Co., c1996.
*TC LB475.L6 L63 1996*

**[Some thoughts concerning education]**
Some thoughts concerning education ; and, Of the
conduct of the understanding / John Locke ; edited,
with introduction and notes, by Ruth W. Grant and
Nathan Tarcov. Indianapolis : Hackett Pub. Co.,
c1996. xxv, 227 p. ; 22 cm. Includes bibliographical
references (p. xxi-xxiii). ISBN 0-87220-335-2 (cloth : alk.
paper) ISBN 0-87220-334-4 (paper : alk. paper) DDC 370/
.1
*1. Education - Philosophy. 2. Knowledge, Theory of. 3.
Intellect. 4. Reasoning. I. Grant, Ruth Weissbourd, 1951- II.
Tarcov, Nathan. III. Locke, John, 1632-1704. Of the conduct of
the understanding. IV. Title. V. Title: Of the conduct of the
understanding. VI. Title: Some thoughts concerning
education ; and, Of the conduct of the understanding*
*TC LB475.L6 L63 1996*

**LOCKE, JOHN, 1632-1704.**
Tarcov, Nathan. Locke's education for liberty.
Lanham, Md. : Lexington Books, c1999.
*TC LB475.L72 T27 1999*

**Locke, Virginia O.**
Hetherington, E. Mavis (Eileen Mavis), 1926- Child
psychology. 5th ed. Boston : McGraw-Hill College,
c1999.
*TC BF721 .H418 1999*

**Locke's education for liberty.**
Tarcov, Nathan. Lanham, Md. : Lexington Books,
c1999.
*TC LB475.L72 T27 1999*

**Lockhart, Laura.**
Duncan, Donna. I-Search, you search, we all to learn
to research. New York : Neal-Schuman Publishers,
2000.
*TC Z711.2 .D86 2000*

**Lockley, Paul.** Counselling women in violent
relationships / Paul Lockley. London ; New York :
Free Association Books, 1999. 259 p. ; 24 cm. Includes
bibliographical references (p. [218]-246) and index. ISBN 1-
85343-451-5 ISBN 1-85343-452-3 (pbk)
*1. Abused women - Services for - Great Britain. 2. Abused
wives - Services for - Great Britain. 3. Family violence - Great
Britain. I. Title.*
*TC HV6626.23.G7 L624 1999*

**Lockwood, Anne Turnbaugh.** Standards : from policy
to practice / Anne Turnbaugh Lockwood. Thousand
Oaks, Calif. : Corwin Press, c1998. vii, 62 p. ; 23 cm.
(Controversial issues in education) Includes bibliographical
references (p. 60-62). CONTENTS: Standards in the context of
democracy / Thomas A. Romberg -- Standards-based
mathematics reform in practice / Diane J. Briars -- Equity in
the standards movement / Walter G. Secada -- Standards for
English language learners / Deborah J. Short -- ESL standards
enacted / Maria Helena Malagón. ISBN 0-8039-6622-9 (cloth :
acid-free paper) ISBN 0-8039-6270-3 (pbk. : acid-free paper)
DDC 379.1/58/0973
*1. Education - Standards - United States. 2. Mathematics -
Study and teaching - Standards - United States. 3. Language
arts - Standards - United States. I. Title. II. Series.*
*TC LB3060.83 .L63 1998*

**Lockwood, David G.** Functional approaches to
language, culture, and cognition : papers in honor of
Sydney M. Lamb / David G. Lockwood, Peter H.
Fries, James E. Copeland. Amsterdam ; Philadelphia :
J. Benjamins, c2000. xxxiv, 656 p.: ill. ; 23 cm.
(Amsterdam studies in the theory and history of linguistic
science. Series IV, Current issues in linguistic theory, 0304-
0763 ; v. 163) Includes bibliographical references and index.
ISBN 1-55619-879-5 (alk. paper) DDC 410/.1/8
*1. Functionalism (Linguistics) 2. Cognitive grammar. 3.
Historical linguistics. 4. Language and culture. I. Fries, Peter
Howard. II. Copeland, James E. III. Title. IV. Series.*
*TC P147 .L63 1998*

**Lockwood, Fred.**
Staff development in open and flexible learning.
London ; New York : Routledge, 1998.
*TC LC5800 .S83 1998*

**LOCOMOTION.** *See also* **FLIGHT;**
**HORSEMANSHIP; HUMAN LOCOMOTION.**

Latash, Mark L., 1953- Neurophysiological basis of
movement. Champaign, IL : Human Kinetics, c1998.
*TC QP301 .L364 1998*

**LOCOMOTION - REGULATION.**
Orlovsky, G. N. (Grigoriĭ Nikolaevich) Neuronal
control of locomotion. Oxford ; New York : Oxford
University Press, 1999.
*TC QP303 .O75 1999*

**LOCOMOTIVE ENGINEERS - FICTION.**
Moss, Marissa. True heart. 1st ed. San Diego : Silver
Whistle, c1999.
*TC PZ7.M8535 Tr 1999*

**LOCOMOTIVES - FICTION.**
Ó Flatharta, Antoine. The prairie train. New York :
Crown Publishers, 1997.
*TC PZ7.O331275 Pr 1997*

**Locust, Jimmy.**
Jazz dance class [videorecording]. W. Long Branch,
NJ : Kultur, [1992?]
*TC GV1784 .J3 1992*

**Loeb, Paul Rogat, 1952-** Soul of a citizen : living with
conviction in a cynical time / Paul Rogat Loeb. 1st St.
Martin's Griffin ed. New York : St. Martin's Griffin,
1999. 362 p. ; 21 cm. Includes bibliographical references (p.
[350]-357). ISBN 0-312-20435-3 DDC 361.2/0973
*1. Social action - United States. 2. Social participation - United
States. 3. Community organization - United States. I. Title.*
*TC HN65 .L58 1999*

**Loewen, James W.** Lies across America : what our
historic sites get wrong / James W. Loewen. New
York : New Press : Distributed by W.W. Norton,
c1999. 480 p. : ill. ; 24 cm. Includes bibliographical
references and index. ISBN 1-56584-344-4 DDC 973
*1. Historic sites - United States. 2. Monuments - United States.
3. United States - History - Errors, inventions, etc. I. Title.*
*TC E159 .L64 1999*

**LOGIC.** *See also* **IDENTITY; REASONING;**
**THOUGHT AND THINKING.**
Roeper, Peter. Probability theory and probability
logic. Toronto ; Buffalo : University of Toronto Press,
c1999.
*TC BC141 .R64 1999*

**LOGIC, DEDUCTIVE.** *See* **LOGIC.**

**LOGIC - EARLY WORKS TO 1800.**
Bacon, Francis, 1561-1626. The advancement of
learning. Oxford : Clarendon, 2000.
*TC B1191 .K545 2000*

**LOGIC MACHINES.** *See* **ARTIFICIAL**
**INTELLIGENCE.**

**LOGIC, SYMBOLIC AND MATHEMATICAL.** *See*
**SCIENCE - METHODOLOGY; SEMANTICS**
**(PHILOSOPHY).**

**LOGICAL POSITIVISM.** *See* **SEMANTICS**
**(PHILOSOPHY).**

**LOGICAL SEMANTICS.** *See* **SEMANTICS**
**(PHILOSOPHY).**

**Lohstoeter, Lori, ill.**
Garne, S. T. By a blazing blue sea. San Diego :
Harcourt Brace & Co., 1999.
*TC PZ8.3.G1866 By 1999*

**Lomax, Richard G.**
Schumacker, Randall E. A beginner's guide to
structural equation modeling. Mahwah, N.J. : L.
Erlbaum Associates, 1996.
*TC QA278 .S36 1996*

**Lompscher, Joachim.**
Learning activity and development. Aarhus : Aarhus
Universit #, 1999.
*TC LB1060 .L43 1999*

**Loncke, Filip.**
Augmentative and alternative communication.
London : Whurr, 1999.
*TC RC429 .A94 1999*

**LONDON (ENGLAND) - CIVILIZATION - 19TH**
**CENTURY.**
Black, Barbara J., 1962- On exhibit. Charlottesville ;
London : University Press of Virginia, 2000.
*TC AM43.L6 B53 2000*

**LONDON (ENGLAND) - INTELLECTUAL LIFE -**
**19TH CENTURY.**
Black, Barbara J., 1962- On exhibit. Charlottesville ;
London : University Press of Virginia, 2000.
*TC AM43.L6 B53 2000*

**LONDON (ENGLAND) - INTELLECTUAL LIFE -**
**20TH CENTURY.**

Women in the milieu of Leonard and Virginia Woolf.
New York : Pace University Press, 1998.
*TC PR6045.O72 Z925 1998*

**LONDON (ENGLAND) - POLITICS AND**
**GOVERNMENT.**
Gatter, Philip. Identity and sexuality. New York :
Cassell, 1999.
*TC HQ1075.5.G7 G37 1999*

**LONDON (ENGLAND) - SOCIAL CONDITIONS.**
Gatter, Philip. Identity and sexuality. New York :
Cassell, 1999.
*TC HQ1075.5.G7 G37 1999*

**London studies in the history of philosophy**
Humanism and early modern philosophy. London ;
New York : Routledge, 2000.
*TC B821 .H657 2000*

**London studies on South Asia**
(no. 18) The Great Indian education debate.
Richmond : Curzon, 1999.
*TC LA1151 .G743 1999*

**London Weekend Television, ltd.**
Andy Warhol [videorecording]. [Chicago, IL] : Home
Vision [distributor],cc1987.
*TC N6537.W28 A45 1987*

Andy Warhol [videorecording]. [Chicago, IL] : Home
Vision [distributor],cc1987.
*TC N6537.W28 A45 1987*

Jackson Pollock [videorecording]. [Chicago, Ill.] :
Home Vision : [S.l.] : Distributed Worldwide by RM
Associates, c1987.
*TC ND237.P73 J3 1987*

Marc Chagall [videorecording]. [Chicago, Ill.] : Home
Vision [distributor], c1985.
*TC ND699.C5 C5 1985*

Roy Lichtenstein [videorecording]. [Chicago, IL] :
Home Vision : [S.l.] : distributed worldwide by RM
Asssociates, c1991.
*TC ND237.L627 R6 1991*

**LONELINESS - FICTION.**
Kadono, Eiko. Grandpa's soup. Grand Rapids, MI :
Eerdmans Books for Young Readers, 1999.
*TC PZ7.K1167 Gr 1999*

Preston, Tim. The lonely scarecrow. 1st American ed.
New York : Dutton Children's Books, 1999.
*TC PZ7.P9237 Lo 1999*

**LONELINESS IN ADOLESCENCE.**
Lonliness in childhood and adolescence. New York :
Cambridge University Press, 1999.
*TC BF723.L64 L64 1999*

**LONELINESS IN CHILDREN.**
Lonliness in childhood and adolescence. New York :
Cambridge University Press, 1999.
*TC BF723.L64 L64 1999*

**The lonely scarecrow.**
Preston, Tim. 1st American ed. New York : Dutton
Children's Books, 1999.
*TC PZ7.P9237 Lo 1999*

**Long, Elenore.**
Flower, Linda. Learning to rival. Mahwah, New
Jersey : Lawrence Erlbaum Associates, c2000.
*TC PE1404 .F59 2000*

**Long road back [videorecording].**
Starting over [videorecording]. [Charleston, W.V.] :
Cambridge Educational, c1994.
*TC HV1435.C3 S7 1994*

**LONG-TERM CARE INSURANCE.** *See*
**INSURANCE, LONG-TERM CARE.**

**LONG-TERM CARE OF THE SICK -**
**GOVERNMENT POLICY - UNITED STATES.**
Public and private responsibilities in long-term care.
Baltimore : Johns Hopkins University Press, 1998.
*TC RA644.6 .P8 1998*

**LONG-TERM CARE OF THE SICK - UNITED**
**STATES - FINANCE.**
Public and private responsibilities in long-term care.
Baltimore : Johns Hopkins University Press, 1998.
*TC RA644.6 .P8 1998*

**LONGEVITY.** *See* **AGING; OLD AGE.**

**A longitudinal case study of the musical/aesthetic**
**experience of adolescent choral musicians.**
Gangi, Robyn Joseph. 1998.
*TC 06 no. 10932*

**LONGITUDINAL STUDIES - IN INFANCY &**
**CHILDHOOD.**
In the long run--longitudinal studies of

psychopathology in children. Washington, DC : American Psychiatric Press, c1999.
*TC RC321 .G7 no. 143*

**Longman bibliography of composition and rhetoric.**
CCCC bibliography of composition and rhetoric. Carbondale : Southern Illinois University Press, c1990-
*TC Z5818.E5 L66*

**Longman keys to language teaching**
Edge, Julian, 1948- Mistakes and correction. London ; New York : Longman, 1989.
*TC PE1128.A2 E28 1989*

**Longworth, Norman.** Making lifelong learning work : learning cities for a learning century / Norman Longworth. London : Kogan Page, 1999. xi, 227 p. ; 24 cm. Includes bibliographical references and index. ISBN 0-7494-2727-2
*1. Adult education. 2. Continuing education. I. Title.*
*TC LC5225.L42 L66 1999*

**Lonliness in childhood and adolescence** / edited by Ken J. Rotenberg, Shelley Hymel. New York : Cambridge University Press, 1999. viii, 404 p. : ill. ; 24 cm. ISBN 0-521-56135-3 (hardcover) DDC 155.4/18
*1. Loneliness in children. 2. Loneliness in adolescence. I. Rotenberg, Ken J. II. Hymel, Shelley.*
*TC BF723.L64 L64 1999*

**Look-alikes, jr.**
Steiner, Joan (Joan Catherine) 1st ed. Boston : Little, Brown, c1999.
*TC GV1507.P47 S747 1999*

**Look-alikes, junior.**
Steiner, Joan (Joan Catherine) Look-alikes, jr.. 1st ed. Boston : Little, Brown, c1999.
*TC GV1507.P47 S747 1999*

**Look around.**
Fisher, Leonard Everett. New York, N.Y., U.S.A. : Viking Kestrel, 1987.
*TC QA447 .F5 1987*

**A look backward and forward at American professional women and their families** / edited by Rita J. Simon. Lanham : University Press of America, 1999. viii, 166 p. ; 23 cm. ISBN 0-7618-1581-3 (cloth : alk. paper) ISBN 0-7618-1582-1 (pbk. : alk. paper) DDC 305.4
*1. Working mothers - United States - Congresses. 2. Work and family - United States - Congresses. 3. Women in the professions - United States - Congresses. 4. Businesswomen - United States - Congresses. 5. Women soldiers - United States - Congresses. I. Simon, Rita James.*
*TC HQ759.48 .L66 1999*

**Look what I did with a shell!.**
Sohi, Morteza E. New York : Walker & Co., 2000.
*TC TT862 .S64 2000*

**Looking afresh at the primary curriculum series**
Improving teaching and learning in the core curriculum. London ; New York : Falmer Press, 2000.
*TC LB1564.G7 I475 2000*

Improving teaching and learning in the humanities. London : Falmer ; New York : Published in the USA and Canada by Garland, 1999.
*TC LB1564.G7 I47 1999*

**Looking at looking :** an introduction to the intelligence of vision / editor, Theodore E. Parks ; with contributions by Irvin Rock ... [et al.]. Thousand Oaks, Calif. ; London : Sage Publications, c2001. xviii, 125 p. : ill. (some col.) ; 22 cm. Includes bibliographical references (p. 119-120) and index. ISBN 0-7619-2204-0 (pbk. : alk. paper) DDC 152.14
*1. Visual perception. 2. Visual communication. 3. Human information processing. 4. Image processing. I. Parks, Theodore E. II. Rock, Irvin.*
*TC BF241 .L64 2001*

**Looking closer 2 :** critical writings on graphic design / edited by Michael Bierut ... [et al.] ; introduction by Steven Heller. New York : Allworth Press : American Institute of Graphic Arts, c1997. xiii, 273 p. ; 25 cm. Includes bibliographical references and index. ISBN 1-88055-956-0
*1. Commercial art. 2. Graphic arts. I. Bierut, Michael. II. American Institute of Graphic Arts. III. Title: Looking closer two IV. Title: Critical writings on graphic design*
*TC NC997 .L632 1997*

**Looking closer :** critical writings on graphic design / edited by Michael Bierut ... [et al.] ; introduction by Steven Heller ; associate editors, Elinor Pettit, Theodore Gachot. New York : Allworth Press ; American Institute of Graphic Arts ; Saint Paul, MN : Distributor, Consortium Book Sales & Distribution, c1994. 245 p. ; 25 cm. Includes bibliographical references (p. [233]-235) and index. ISBN 1-88055-915-3

*1. Commercial art. 2. Graphic arts. I. Bierut, Michael. II. American Institute of Graphic Arts.*
*TC NC997 .L63 1994*

**Looking closer two.**
Looking closer 2. New York : Allworth Press ; American Institute of Graphic Arts, c1997.
*TC NC997 .L632 1997*

**Looking out. Climbing up. Going far.** Teacher's ed. New York, N.Y. : American Book Cpmpany, c1980. xiv, 412 p. : ill. (some col.) ; 28 cm. (American readers ; PP1-2-3) Includes index. ISBN 0-278-45838-6
*1. Readers (Primary) 2. Reading (Primary) I. Series.*
*TC PE1119 .L66 1980 Teacher's Ed.*

**Looking out. Climbing up. Going far.** Teacher's ed. Lexington, Mass. : D.C. Heath and Cpmpany, c1986. T30, 505 p. : ill. (some col.) ; 28 cm. (Heath American readers ; PP1-2-3) Includes index. ISBN 0-669-08046-2
*1. Readers (Primary) 2. Reading (Primary) I. Series.*
*TC PE1119 .L66 1986 Teacher's Ed.*

**Looking out. Climbing up. Going far :** workbook. Teacher's ed. New York, N.Y. : American Book Company, c1980. 160 p. : ill. ; 28 cm. (American readers ; PP1-2-3) Includes index. ISBN 0-278-45922-6
*1. Readers (Primary) 2. Reading (Primary) I. Series.*
*TC PE1119 .L66 1980 Teacher's Ed. Workbook*

**Looking out. Climbing up. Going far :** workbook. Teacher's ed. Lexington, Mass. : D.C. Heath and Cpmpany, c1983. 160 p. : ill. ; 28 cm. (American readers ; PP1-2-3) Includes index. ISBN 0-669-04969-7
*1. Readers (Primary) 2. Reading (Primary) I. Series.*
*TC PE1119 .L66 1983 Teacher's Ed. Workbook*

**Loomis, John A., 1951-** Revolution of forms : Cuba's forgotten art schools / John A. Loomis ; foreword by Gerardo Mosquera. New York : Princeton Architectural Press, c1999. xxxiii, 186 p. : ill. (some col.) ; 28 cm. Includes bibliographical references (p. 183-186). ISBN 1-56898-157-0 (pbk. : alk. paper) DDC 727/.47/09729124
*1. Art schools - Cuba - Havana. 2. Organic architecture - Cuba - Havana. 3. Communism and architecture - Cuba - Havana. 4. Architecture - Political aspects - Cuba - Havana. 5. Architecture, Modern - 20th century - Cuba. 6. Cubanacán (Havana, Cuba) - Buildings, structures, etc. 7. Porro, Ricardo. - 1925- 8. Garatti, Vittorio, - 1927- 9. Gottardi, Roberto, - 1927- I. Title.*
*TC NA6602.A76 L66 1999*

**Looper, Sandra.**
Wyatt, Robert Lee, 1940- So you have to have a portfolio. Thousand Oaks, Calif. : Corwin Press, c1999.
*TC LB1728 .W93 1999*

**Loosening the grip.**
Kinney, Jean, 1943- 6th ed. Boston : McGraw-Hill, c2000.
*TC HV5292 .K53 2000*

**Lopez-Bote, Clemente J.**
Antioxidants in muscle foods. New York ; Chichester [England] : John Wiley, c2000.
*TC TX556.M4 A57 2000*

**Lopez, Marianne Exum, 1960-** When discourses collide : an ethnography of migrant children at home and in school / Marianne Exum Lopez. New York : P. Lang, c1999. xii, 211 p. ; 23 cm. (Rethinking childhood ; vol. 11) Includes bibliographical references (p. [203]-208) and index. ISBN 0-8204-4165-1 (alk. paper) DDC 305.23
*1. Children of migrant laborers - United States. 2. Children of migrant laborers - Education - United States. 3. Children of migrant laborers - Services for - United States. 4. Language and education - United States. 5. Discourse analysis. 6. Home and school - United States. I. Title. II. Series.*
*TC HQ792.U5 L665 1999*

**Lopez, Richard.**
Conducting drug abuse research with minority populations. New York : Haworth Press, c1999.
*TC HV5824.E85 C66 1999*

**LÓPEZ Y FUENTES, GREGORIO, 1897-1966. INDIO.**
Guevara-Vázquez, Fabián. El indigena en la novela de la Revolucion Mexicana. 1999.
*TC 085 G934*

**Lorbeer, George C.**
**Science activities for children.**
Lorbeer, George C. Science activities for elementary students. 11th ed. Boston : McGraw-Hill, c2000.
*TC LB1585.3 .L67 2000*

Science activities for elementary students / George C. Lorbeer. 11th ed. Boston : McGraw-Hill, c2000. xiv, 415 p. : ill. ; 28 cm. Rev. ed. of: Science activities for children. 10th ed. 1996. Includes index. ISBN 0-697-37789-X DDC

372.3/5044
*1. Science - Study and teaching (Elementary) - United States - Handbooks, manuals, etc. 2. Teaching - Aids and devices - Handbooks, manuals, etc. 3. Science - Study and teaching - Activity programs - United States - Handbooks, manuals, etc. I. Lorbeer, George C. Science activities for children. II. Title.*
*TC LB1585.3 .L67 2000*

**Lord Byron at Harrow School.**
Elledge, Paul. Baltimore : Johns Hopkins University Press, c2000.
*TC PR4382 .E36 2000*

**LORD BYRON HIGH SCHOOL.**
Fink, Dean, 1936- Good schools/real schools. New York : Teachers College Press, c2000.
*TC LB2822.84.C2 F56 2000*

**Lordahl, Jo Ann.** Reflections for busy educators : 180 affirmations to help you through the school year / Jo Ann Lordahl. Thousand Oaks, Calif. : Corwin Press, c1995. vii, 103 p. ; 24 cm. Includes bibliographical references (p. 99-103). ISBN 0-8039-6376-9 (alk. paper) ISBN 0-8039-6320-3 (pbk. : alk. paper) DDC 370
*1. Education - Quotations, maxims, etc. 2. Quotations, English. I. Title.*
*TC PN6084.E38 L67 1995*

**Lorenz, Gunter R.** Adjective intensification--learners versus native speakers : a corpus study of argumentative writing / Gunter R. Lorenz. Amsterdam ; Atlanta, GA : Rodopi, 1999. 321 p. ; 23 cm. (Language and computers ; no. 27) Revision of the author's thesis (doctoral)--University of Augsburg, 1996. Includes bibliographical references (p. [219]-245). ISBN 90-420-0528-9
*1. English language - Discourse analysis - Data processing. 2. English language - Research - Data processing. 3. Semantics - Data processing. 4. Computational linguistics. I. Title. II. Series: Language and computers ; no. 27*
*TC PE1074.5 .L67 1999*

**Lorini, Alessandra, 1949-** Rituals of race : American public culture and the search for racial democracy / Alessandra Lorini. Charlottesville : University Press of Virginia, 1999. xix, 305 p. : ill., ; 24 cm. (Carter G. Woodson Institute series in Black studies) Includes bibliographical references (p. [257]-287) and index. ISBN 0-8139-1870-7 (cloth : alk. paper) ISBN 0-8139-1871-5 (pbk. : alk. paper) DDC 305.8/00973
*1. United States - Race relations - Political aspects. 2. United States - Social life and customs - 1865-1918. 3. Festivals - Political aspects - United States - History. 4. Pageants - Political aspects - United States - History. 5. Exhibitions - Political aspects - United States - History. 6. Popular culture - Political aspects - United States - History. 7. Afro-Americans - Civil rights - History - 19th century. 8. Afro-Americans - Civil rights - History - 20th century. 9. Democracy - United States - History. I. Title. II. Series.*
*TC E185.61 .L675 1999*

**Loritz, Donald, 1947-** How the brain evolved language / Donald Loritz. New York : Oxford University Press, 1999. 227 p. ; 24 cm. Includes bibliographical references (p. 195-217) and index. ISBN 0-19-511874-X (hardcover : alk. paper) DDC 401
*1. Language and languages - Origin. 2. Biolinguistics. 3. Grammar, Comparative and general. 4. Human evolution. I. Title.*
*TC P116 .L67 1999*

**Lorre, Arlene.**
Step on a crack [videorecording]. Boston, MA : Fanlight Productions, 1996.
*TC RC533 .S7 1996*

**LORRIES (MOTOR VEHICLES).** *See* **TRUCKS.**

**LOS ANGELES (CALIF.) - BUILDINGS, STRUCTURES, ETC. - JUVENILE LITERATURE.**
Seibold, J.otto. Going to the Getty. Los Angeles : J. Paul Getty Museum, c1997.
*TC NA6813.U6 L678 1997*

**LOS ANGELES (CALIF.) - HISTORY.**
Abu-Lughod, Janet L. New York, Chicago, Los Angeles. Minneapolis : University of Minnesota Press, c1999.
*TC HT123 .A613 1999*

**Los Angeles County Museum of Art.**
Exiles + emigrés. Los Angeles, Calif. : Los Angeles County Museum of Art ; New York : H.N. Abrams, c1997.
*TC N6512 .E887 1997*

Kleeblatt, Norman L. An expressionist in Paris. Munich ; New York : Jewish Museum, c1998.
*TC ND553.S7 A4 1998*

**Losco, Joseph.**
Higher education in transition. Westport, Conn. ;
London : Bergin & Garvey, 2000.
*TC LA227.4 .H53 2000*

**Losing Louisa.**
Caseley, Judith. 1st ed. New York : Farrar, Straus and
Giroux, c1999.
*TC PZ7.C2677 Lo 1999*

**Losing the race.**
McWhorter, John H. New York : Free Press, c2000.
*TC E185.625 .M38 2000*

**LOSING WEIGHT.** *See* **WEIGHT LOSS.**

**Loss and trauma :** general and close relationship
perspectives / edited by John H. Harvey, Eric D.
Miller. Philadelphia, PA : Brunner-Routledge, c2000.
xxv, 415 p. ; 24 cm. Includes bibliographical references and
index. ISBN 1-58391-012-3 (case : alk. paper) ISBN
1-58391-013-1 (pbk. : alk. paper) DDC 155.9/3
*1. Loss (Psychology) 2. Grief. 3. Adjustment (Psychology) 4.
Life change events. 5. Bereavement - Psychological aspects. I.
Harvey, John H., 1943- II. Miller, Eric D., 1972-*
*TC BF575.D35 L67 2000*

**LOSS OF LOVED ONES BY DEATH.** *See*
**BEREAVEMENT.**

**LOSS OF WEIGHT.** *See* **WEIGHT LOSS.**

**LOSS (PSYCHOLOGY).** *See also*
**BEREAVEMENT; GRIEF.**
Archer, John, 1944- The nature of grief. London ;
New York : Routledge, 1999.
*TC BF575.G7 A73 1999*

Boss, Pauline. Ambiguous loss. Cambridge, Mass. :
Harvard University Press, 1999.
*TC BF575.D35 B67 1999*

Davidman, Lynn, 1955- Motherloss. Berkeley, Calif. :
University of California ·Press, c2000.
*TC BF575.G7 D37 2000*

Loss and trauma. Philadelphia, PA : Brunner-
Routledge, c2000.
*TC BF575.D35 L67 2000*

Rosenblatt, Paul C. Parent grief. Philadelphia ; Hove
[England] : Brunner/Mazel, c2000.
*TC BF575.G7 R673 2000*

**LOSS (PSYCHOLOGY) IN CHILDREN.**
Goldman, Linda, 1946- Life & loss. 2nd ed.
Philadelphia : Accelerated Development, c2000.
*TC BF723.G75 G65 2000*

**LOST AND FOUND POSSESSIONS - FICTION.**
Baker, Leslie A. Paris cat. 1st ed. Boston, Mass. :
Little, Brown, c1999.
*TC PZ7.B1744 Par 1999*

Jonas, Ann. Where can it be? 1st ed. New York :
Greenwillow Books, c1986.
*TC PZ7.J664 Wi 1986*

Willard, Nancy. The tale I told Sasha. 1st ed. Boston :
Little, Brown, c1999.
*TC PZ8.3.W668 Tal 1999*

**Lost boys.**
Garbarino, James. New York : Free Press, c1999.
*TC HQ799.2.V56 G37 1999*

**The lost daughters of China.**
Evans, Karin. New York : J.P. Tarcher/Putnam,
c2000.
*TC HV1317 .E93 2000*

**Lost soul of modern education.**
Grote, John E. Paideia agonistes. Lanham, Md. :
University Press of America, c2000.
*TC LC1011 .G76 2000*

**Lost subjects, contested objects.**
Britzman, Deborah P., 1952- Albany : State
University of New York Press, c1998.
*TC LB1060 .B765 1998*

**Lost words.**
Jacyna, L. S. Princeton, N.J. ; Oxford : Princeton
University Press, c2000.
*TC RC425 .J33 2000*

**Lott, Johnny W., 1944-.**
Billstein, Rick. A problem solving approach to
mathematics for elementary school teachers. 5th ed.
Reading, Mass. : Addison-Wesley, c1993.
*TC QA135.5 .B49 1993*

**Loud, proud & passionate :** including women with
disabilities in international development programs /
Edited by Cindy Lewis and Susan Sygall. 1st ed.
Eugene, OR : Mobility International USA, 1997. xxiii,
267 p. ports. ; 18 x 22 cm. "Resource materials": p. 136-202.

*1. Handicapped women x International cooperation. 2.
Women's rights - International cooperation. 3. Women in
development. 4. Women in community development. I. Lewis.
Cindy. II. Sygall. Susan. III. Mobility International USA
(Organization) IV. Title: Loud, proud and passionate*
*TC HV1569.3.W65 L68 1997*

**Loud, proud and passionate.**
Loud, proud & passionate. 1st ed. Eugene, OR :
Mobility International USA, 1997.
*TC HV1569.3.W65 L68 1997*

**Louden, William.** Understanding teaching : continuity
and change in teachers' knowledge / William Louden.
New York : Cassell : Teachers College Press,
Teachers College. Columbia University, 1991. xvii,
206 p. ; 22 cm. (Teacher development) Includes bibliographical
references (p. 198-203) and index. ISBN 0-8077-3101-3 (pbk. :
Teachers College Press) ISBN 0-8077-3102-1 (hardback :
Teachers College Press) DDC 371.1/02
*1. Teaching - Case studies. 2. Teachers - Canada - Case
studies. 3. Education, Secondary - Canada - Case studies. I.
Title. II. Series.*
*TC LB1025.3 .L68 1991*

**LOUDNESS PERCEPTION.**
Venema, Ted. Compression for clinicians. San Diego,
Calif. : Singular Pub. Group, c1998.
*TC RF300 .V46 1998*

**Loue, Sana.** Gender, ethnicity, and health research /
Sana Loue. New York : Kluwer Academic/Plenum
Publishers, c1999. xiii, 195 p. : ill. ; 26 cm. Includes
bibliographical references and index. ISBN 0-306-46172-2
DDC 362.1/089
*1. Minorities - Medical care. 2. Health - Research - Cross-
cultural studies. 3. Social medicine. I. Title.*
*TC RA448.4 .L68 1999*

**Louis, Linda L.**
**In the paint.**
Milbank Memorial Library story hour
[videorecording]. [New York : Milbank Memorial
Library, 1999]
*TC Z718.3 .M5 1999 Series 3 Prog. 6*

Milbank Memorial Library story hour
[videorecording]. [New York : Milbank Memorial
Library, 1999]
*TC Z718.3 .M5 1999 Series 3 Prog. 6*

**Louisiana Purchase Exposition (1904 : Saint Louis,
Mo.).**
Portraits of native Americans. New York : New
Press : Distributed by W.W. Norton, c1994.
*TC TR140.C388 C48*

**Louisiana schools.**
Journal of the Louisiana Teachers' Association.
[Baton Rouge] : The Association, [1923-1932],
(Baton Rouge, La. : Gladney's Print Shop)

**Louisiana Teachers' Association.**
Journal of the Louisiana Teachers' Association.
[Baton Rouge] : The Association, [1923-1932],
(Baton Rouge, La. : Gladney's Print Shop)

**Lourie, Peter.** Rio Grande : : from the Rocky
Mountains to the Gulf of Mexico / Peter Lourie. 1st
ed. Honesdale, Pa. : Boyds Mills Press, 1999. 46 p. : ill.
(some col.), col. map ; 21 x 27 cm. ISBN 1-56397-706-0
*1. Rio Grande Valley - Juvenile literature. 2. Rio Grande -
Juvenile literature. 3. Rio Grande. <Juvenile subject
heading>. 4. Rio Grande Valley. <Juvenile subject heading>.
I. Title.*
*TC F392.R5 L68 1999*

**LOVE.** *See also* **FRIENDSHIP; INTIMACY
(PSYCHOLOGY); MARRIAGE.**
Brown, Norman M., 1942- Love and intimate
relationships. Philadelphia ; Hove [England] :
Brunner/Mazel, c2000.
*TC BF575.L8 B75 2000*

Burch, Kerry T., 1957- Eros as the educational
principle of democracy. New York : P. Lang, c2000.
*TC LC196 .B75 2000*

Close relationships. Thousand Oaks, Calif. : Sage
Publications, c2000.
*TC HM1106 .C55 2000*

Honeycutt, James M. Cognition, communication, and
romantic relationships. Mahwah, N.J. ; London : L.
Erlbaum Associates, 2001.
*TC BF575.I5 H66 2001*

Janov, Arthur. The biology of love. Amherst, N.Y. :
Prometheus Books, 2000.
*TC BF720.E45 .J36 2000*

Langford, Wendy, 1960- Revolutions of the heart.
London ; New York : Routledge, 1999.

**TC BF575.L8 L266 1999**

Lewis, Thomas. A general theory of love. New York :
Random House, 2000.
*TC BF575.L8 L49 2000*

Magno, Joseph. Self-love. Lanham, Md. ; Oxford :
University Press of America, c2000.
*TC BF575.L8 M29 2000*

Odent, Michel, 1930- The scientification of love.
London ; New York : Free Association Books, 1999.
*TC BF575.L8 O33 1999*

Wilson, John, 1928- Learning to love. Houndmills
[England] : Macmillan Press ; New York : St.
Martin's Press, 2000.
*TC BF575.L8 .W555 2000*

**Love and intimate relationships.**
Brown, Norman M., 1942- Philadelphia ; Hove
[England] : Brunner/Mazel, c2000.
*TC BF575.L8 B75 2000*

**LOVE IN ADOLESCENCE.**
The development of romantic relationships in
adolescence. Cambridge, U.K. ; New York :
Cambridge University Press, 1999.
*TC BF724.3.L68 D48 1999*

**Love, Patrick G.** Understanding and applying cognitive
development theory / Patrick G. Love, Victoria L.
Guthrie, authors. San Francisco : Jossey-Bass, c1999.
107 p. : ill. ; 23 cm. (New directions for student services,
0164-7970 ; no. 88) "Winter 1999." Includes bibliographical
references (p. 95-99) and index. ISBN 0-7879-4870-5 DDC
378.194 DDC LOVE
*1. Counseling in higher education. 2. College student
development programs. I. Guthrie, Victoria L. II. Title. III.
Series: New directions for student services ; no. 88*
*TC LB2343 .L65 1999*

**LOVE - PHYSIOLOGICAL ASPECTS.**
Janov, Arthur. The biology of love. Amherst, N.Y. :
Prometheus Books, 2000.
*TC BF720.E45 .J36 2000*

Lewis, Thomas. A general theory of love. New York :
Random House, 2000.
*TC BF575.L8 L49 2000*

Odent, Michel, 1930- The scientification of love.
London ; New York : Free Association Books, 1999.
*TC BF575.L8 O33 1999*

**Love, Russell J.** Childhood motor speech disability /
Russell J. Love. 2nd ed. Boston ; London : Allyn and
Bacon, c2000. vi, 202 p. : ill. ; 23 cm. Includes
bibliographical references and index. ISBN 0-205-29781-1
(pbk.) DDC 618.92/855
*1. Speech disorders in children. 2. Cerebral palsied children.
3. Dysarthria - Child. 4. Language Development Disorders -
physiopathology. 5. Motor Skills - physiology. 6. Speech
Disorders - Child. I. Title.*
*TC RJ496.S7 L68 2000*

**Loveless, Tom, 1954-.**
Conflicting missions? Washington, D.C. : Brookings
Institution Press, c2000.
*TC LB2844.53.U62 C66 2000*

**Lovell, Jonathan H.**
The portfolio standard. Portsmouth, NH : Heinemann,
c2000.
*TC LB1029.P67 P69 2000*

**The lovemap guidebook.**
Money, John, 1921- New York : Continuum, c1999.
*TC BF692 .M57 1999*

**Lovitt, Thomas C.** Preventing school failure : tactics for
teaching adolescents / Thomas C. Lovitt. 2nd ed.
Austin, Tex. : Pro-Ed. : c2000. xiv, 389 p. : ill. ; 26 cm.
Includes bibliographical references and indexes. ISBN
0-89079-824-9 (pbk. : alk. paper) DDC 371.2/1973
*1. Dropouts - United States - Prevention. 2. Handicapped
youth - Education - United States. 3. Special education -
United States. I. Title.*
*TC LC146.6 .L68 2000*

**The low-down laundry line blues.**
Millen, C. M. Boston : Houghton Mifflin, 1999.
*TC PZ7.M6035 Lo 1999*

**LOW-INCOME PEOPLE.** *See* **POOR.**

**Lowe, Lara.**
Seurat [videorecording]. West Long Branch, NJ :
Kultur, c1999.
*TC ND553.S5 S5 1999*

**Lowenfeld, Viktor.** Creative and mental growth. Rev.
ed. New York, Macmillan [1952] 408 p. : ill. ; 25 cm.
Includes bibliographical references and index.
*1. Art - Study and teaching. 2. Creation (Literary, artistic, etc.)
3. Children as artists. 4. Art - Psychology. I. Title.*

*TC N350 .L62 1952*

**LOWER RIO GRANDE VALLEY (TEX.) -
EMIGRATION AND IMMIGRATION -
PICTORIAL WORKS.**
Anastos, Phillip. Illegal. New York : Rizzoli, 1991.
*TC F392.R5 A53 1991*

**Lowman, Kathleen D., 1948-.**
Activities handbook for the teaching of psychology.
Washington, D.C. : American Psychological
Association, c1981-<c1999 >
*TC BF78 .A28*

**Lowther, Deborah L.**
Morrison, Gary R. Integrating computer technology
into the classroom. Upper Saddle River, N.J. : Merrill,
c1999.
*TC LB1028.5 .M6373 1999*

**LOYALTY OATHS - UNITED STATES.**
Rabbit in the moon [videorecording]. San Francisco,
Calif. : Wabi-Sabi Productions, 1999.
*TC D753.8 .R3 1999*

**LOYALTY TESTS. See LOYALTY OATHS.**

**Loyrette, Henri.**
Tinterow, Gary. Origins of impressionism. New
York : Metropolitan Museum of Art : Distributed by
H.N. Abrams, c1994.
*TC ND547.5.I4 L6913 1994*

**Lu, Min-Zhan, 1946-.**
Comp tales. New York : Longman, c2000.
*TC PE1404 .C617 2000*

**Lucas, Ann F.** Leading academic change : essential
roles for department chairs / Ann F. Lucas and
associates ; foreword by R. Eugene Rice. 1st ed. San
Francisco : Jossey-Bass, c2000. xxxi, 310 p. ; 23 cm.
(The Jossey-Bass higher and adult education series) Includes
bibliographical references and index. ISBN 0-7879-4682-6
(alk. paper) DDC 378.1/11
*1. Departmental chairmen (Universities) 2. Educational
change. I. Title. II. Series.*
*TC LB2341 .L82 2000*

**LUCAS, JUAN FRANCISCO.**
Thomson, Guy P. C., 1949- Patriotism, politics, and
popular liberalism in nineteenth-century Mexico.
Wilmington, De. : Scholarly Resources, 1999.
*TC F1326.L83 T5 1999*

**LUCAS, JUAN FRANCISCO - MILITARY
LEADERSHIP.**
Thomson, Guy P. C., 1949- Patriotism, politics, and
popular liberalism in nineteenth-century Mexico.
Wilmington, De. : Scholarly Resources, 1999.
*TC F1326.L83 T5 1999*

**Lucas, Nance, 1960-.**
Komives, Susan R., 1946- Exploring leadership. 1st
ed. San Francisco : Jossey-Bass Publishers, c1998.
*TC LB3605 .K64 1998*

**Lucciani, Leslie.**
Making the most of early communication
[videorecording]. New York, NY : Distributed by
AFB Press, c1997.
*TC HV1597.2 .M3 1997*

**Luce-Kapler, Rebecca.**
Davis, Brent. Engaging minds. Mahwah, N.J. : L.
Erlbaum Associates, 2000.
*TC LB1060 .D38 2000*

**LUCIA ZENTENO (LEGENDARY CHARACTER).
See ZENTENO, LUCIA (LEGENDARY
CHARACTER).**

**Luciana, James.** The art of enhanced photography : :
beyond the photographic image / James Luciana,
Judith Watts. Gloucester, Mass. : Rockport Publishers,
c1999. 144 p. : ill. (some col.) ; 29 cm. Enhanced
photography. Includes index. ISBN 1-56496-379-9
*1. Art and photography. 2. Photography - Technique. I. Watts,
Judith. II. Title. III. Title: Enhanced photography.*
*TC TR654 .L83 1999*

**Lucka, Klaus.**
The filming of a television commercial
[videorecording]. Minneapolis, Minn. : Media Loft,
c1992.
*TC HF6146.T42 F5 1992*

**LUCKA, KLAUS.**
The filming of a television commercial
[videorecording]. Minneapolis, Minn. : Media Loft,
c1992.
*TC HF6146.T42 F5 1992*

**LuckaFilm (Firm).**
The filming of a television commercial

[videorecording]. Minneapolis, Minn. : Media Loft.
c1992.
*TC HF6146.T42 F5 1992*

**Lucy's legacy.**
Jolly, Alison. Cambridge, Mass. ; London : Harvard
University Press, 1999.
*TC GN281 .J6 1999*

**LUDICROUS, THE. See WIT AND HUMOR.**

**Ludmerer, Kenneth M.** Time to heal : American
medical education from the turn of the century to the
era of managed care / Kenneth M. Ludmerer. Oxford ;
New York : Oxford University Press, 1999. xxvi, 514
p. : ill. ; 24 cm. Includes bibliographical references (p. 401-
494) and index. ISBN 0-19-511837-5 (acid-free paper) DDC
610/.71/1730904
*1. Medical education - United States - History - 20th century.
2. Education, Medical - history - United States. 3. History of
Medicine. 20th Cent. - United States. I. Title. II. Title:
American medical education in the 20th century*
*TC R745 .L843 1999*

**Luit, J. E. H. van, 1953-.**
Teaching and learning thinking skills. Lisse
[Netherlands] ; Exton, PA : Swets & Zeitlinger,
c1999.
*TC LB1590.3 .T36 1999*

**Luke, Helen M., 1904-** Such stuff as dreams are made
on : the autobiography and journals of Helen M.
Luke / introduction by Charles H. Taylor ; journals
edited by Barbara Mowat. New York : Parabola
Books, c2000. xiv, 267 p., [8] p. of plates : ill. ; 25 cm.
ISBN 0-930407-47-4 DDC 150.19/54/092
*1. Dreams. 2. Dream interpretation. 3. Spiritual life. 4. Jungian
psychology. 5. Luke, Helen M. - 1904- I. Mowat, Barbara A.
II. Title.*
*TC BF1091 .L82 2000*

**LUKE, HELEN M., 1904-.**
Luke, Helen M., 1904- Such stuff as dreams are made
on. New York : Parabola Books, c2000.
*TC BF1091 .L82 2000*

**Luker, Mark A., 1947-.**
Preparing your campus for a networked future. 1st ed.
San Francisco : Jossey-Bass, c2000.
*TC LB2395.7 .P74 2000*

**LULLABIES.**
All the pretty little horses. New York : Clarion Books,
c1999.
*TC PZ8.3 .A4165 1999*

**LULLABIES - TEXTS.**
All the pretty little horses. New York : Clarion Books,
c1999.
*TC PZ8.3 .A4165 1999*

**Lulofs, Roxane Salyer.** Conflict : from theory to action /
Roxane S. Lulofs, Dudley D. Cahn. 2nd ed. Boston :
Allyn and Bacon, c2000. xv, 384 p. : ill. ; 24 cm. Includes
bibliographical references (p. 364-380) and index. ISBN
0-205-29030-2 (alk. paper) DDC 303.6
*1. Conflict (Psychology) 2. Interpersonal conflict. 3. Conflict
management. I. Cahn, Dudley D. II. Title.*
*TC BF637.I48 L85 2000*

**Lulu's busy day.**
Uff, Caroline. New York : Walker, 2000.
*TC PZ7.U285 Lu 2000*

**Lumpa, Dale, 1961-.**
Whitaker, Todd, 1959- Motivating and inspiring
teachers. Larchmont, N.Y. : Eye on Education, c2000.
*TC LB2840 .W45 2000*

**Lund, Jon P.**
Powerful programming for student learning. San
Francisco : Jossey-Bass, c2000.
*TC LB2343 .P643 2000*

**LUNDA. See PUFFINS.**

**Lundberg, Ante.**
The environment and mental health. Mahwah, N.J. :
Lawrence Erlbaum Associates, c1998.
*TC RC455.4.E58 E528 1998*

**Lundberg, Ingvar.**
Dyslexia. Dordrecht ; Boston, Mass : Kluwer
Academic, 1999.
*TC RC394 .D9525 1999*

**Lundeberg, Mary A.**
Who learns what from cases and how? Mahwah, N.J. :
L. Erlbaum Associates, 1999.
*TC LB1029.C37 W56 1999*

**Lune rebelle.**
Horn, Rebecca, 1944- Rebecca Horn. [Stuttgart] :
Edition Cantz, 1993.

*TC NB573.H78 H785 1993*

**Lunenfeld, Peter.** Snap to grid : a user's guide to digital
arts, media, and cultures / Peter Lunenfeld.
Cambridge, MA : MIT, 2000. xxv, 226 p. : ill. ; 24 cm.
Includes bibliographical references and index. ISBN 0-262-
12226-X (hc : alk. paper) DDC 006.7
*1. Computers and civilization. 2. Art, Modern--20th century. 3.
Digital media. 4. Multimedia systems.*
*TC QA76.9.C66 L86 2000*

**Lupton, Deborah.**
Risk and sociocultural theory. Cambridge, U.K. ; New
York : Cambridge University Press, 1999.
*TC HM1101 .R57 1999*

**Lusaka, Jane.**
Visual journal. Washington, DC : Smithsonian
Institution Press, c1996.
*TC TR820.5 .V57 1996*

**Luthar, Suniya S.** Poverty and children's adjustment /
Suniya S. Luthar. Thousand Oaks, Calif. : Sage
Publications, c1999. xii, 131 p. ; 22 cm. (Developmental
clinical psychology and psychiatry series ; v. 41) Includes
bibliographical references (p. 95-114) and indexes. ISBN
0-7619-0518-9 (cloth : acid-free paper) ISBN 0-7619-0519-7
(pbk. : acid-free paper) DDC 362.7/086/9420973
*1. Poor children - United States - Psychology. 2. Socially
handicapped children - United States - Psychology. 3.
Poverty - United States - Psychological aspects. 4. Adjustment
(Psychology) in children - United States. 5. Child
psychopathology - United States. I. Title. II. Series:
Developmental clinical psychology and psychiatry ; v. 41.*
*TC HV741 .L88 1999*

**LUTHERAN CHURCH - TEXAS - CLERGY.**
Zersen, David John. Independent learning among
clergy. 1998.
*TC 06 no. 11008*

**Lutjens, Louette R. Johnson.**
Tiffany, Constance Rimmer. Planned change theories
for nursing. Thousand Oaks : Sage Publications,
c1998.
*TC RT89 .T54 1998*

**Lutkehaus, Nancy.**
Gendered missions. Ann Arbor : University of
Michigan Press, c1999.
*TC BV2610 .G46 1999*

**Luttinger, Nina.**
Dicum, Gregory. The coffee book. New York : New
Press : Distributed by W.W. Norton, c1999.
*TC HD9199.A2 D53 1999*

**Lutz, Catherine.** Reading National geographic /
Catherine A. Lutz and Jane L. Collins. Chicago :
University of Chicago Press, 1993. xvii, 309 p. : ill. ; 24
cm. Includes bibliographical references (p. 289-300) and index.
ISBN 0-226-49723-2 ISBN 0-226-49724-0 (pbk.) DDC 910/.5
*1. National geographic. 2. American periodicals - History -
20th century. 3. Books and reading - United States - History -
20th century. I. Collins, Jane Lou, 1954- II. Title.*
*TC G1.N275 L88 1993*

**Lutz, Tom.** Crying : the natural and cultural history of
tears / Tom Lutz. 1st ed. New York ; London : W.W.
Norton, c1999. 352 p. : ill. ; 25 cm. Includes bibliographical
references (p. [305]-337) and index. ISBN 0-393-04756-3
DDC 152.4
*1. Crying. 2. Crying - History. I. Title.*
*TC BF575.C88 L87 1999*

**Lutz, William.**
Assessment of writing. New York : Modern Language
Association of America, 1996.
*TC PE1404 .A88 1996*

**Luzadder, Patrick K.**
Marsh, Valerie. True tales of heroes & heroines. Fort
Atkinson, Wis. : Alleyside Press, c1999.
*TC CT85 .M37 1999*

**Luzerner Staatspersonalverband.**
Korrespondenz-blatt. Luzern : Luzerner
Staatspersonalverband, 1947-

**Luzzo, Darrell Anthony.**
Career counseling of college students. Washington,
DC : American Psychological Association, c2000.
*TC LB2343 .C3273 2000*

**Lycan, William G.**
Mind and cognition. 2nd ed. Malden, Mass. :
Blackwell Publishers, 1999.
*TC BF171 .M55 1999*

**Lyke, James.** Creative piano teaching / James Lyke,
Yvonne Enoch, Geoffrey Haydon. 3rd ed. Champaign,
Ill. : Stipes Pub. Co., c1996. vii, 505 p. : ill., music ; 23
cm. Includes bibliographical references. ISBN 0-87563-640-3

*1. Piano - Instruction and study. I. Enoch, Yvonne. II. Haydon, Geoffrey. III. Title.*
**TC MT220 .L95 1996**

**Lyman, Linda L.** How do they know you care? : the principal's challenge / Linda L. Lyman ; foreword by Roland S. Barth. New York : Teachers College Press, c2000. xv, 175 p. : ill. ; 23 cm. Includes bibliographical references (p. 161-166) and index. ISBN 0-8077-3930-8 (cloth : alk. paper) ISBN 0-8077-3929-4 (pbk. : alk. paper) DDC 371.2/012
*1. Principals - Illinois - Case studies. 2. Educational leadership - Illinois - Case studies. 3. Caring. 4. Hinton, Kenneth H. I. Title.*
**TC LB2831.924.13 L96 2000**

**Lynaugh, Joan E.**
Fairman, Julie. Critical care nursing. Philadelphia : University of Pennsylvania Press, c1998.
**TC RT120.I5 F34 1998**

**Lynch, David.**
Macromedia Dreamweaver 3 [computer file]. Version 3.0 ; Windows 95, Windows 98, Windows NT ; Education version. San Francisco, CA : Macromedia, c1999. Computer program.
**TC TK5105.8883 .M33 1999**

**Lynch, Sharon J.** Equity and science education reform / Sharon J. Lynch. Mahwah, N.J. ; London : L. Erlbaum Associates, 2000. xvi, 300 p. : ill. ; 24 cm. Includes bibliographical references (p. 273-289) and indexes. ISBN 0-8058-3248-3 (hbk. : alk. paper) ISBN 0-8058-3249-1 (pbk. : alk. paper) DDC 507.1
*1. Science - Study and teaching - United States. 2. Educational equalization - United States. I. Title.*
**TC LB1585.3 .L96 2000**

**Lynn, Richard.** Personality and national character [by] R. Lynn. [1st ed.]. Oxford, New York, Pergamon Press [1971] xiv, 201 p. : ill. ; 22 cm. (International series of monographs in experimental psychology, v. 12) Includes index. Bibliography: p. 182-193. ISBN 0-08-016516-8 DDC 155.8/9
*1. Personality and culture. 2. National characteristics. I. Title.*
**TC BF698.9.C8 L9 1971**

**Lyon, Gabrielle.**
A simple justice. New York : Teachers College Press, 2000.
**TC LC213.2 .S56 2000**

**Lyon Video Inc.**
Grounded for life [videorecording]. Charleston, WV : Cambridge Research Group, Ltd., 1988.
**TC HQ759.4 .G7 1988**

**LYOTARD, JEAN FRANÇOIS.**
Gordon, Mordechai. Toward an integrative conception of authority in education. 1997.
**TC 085 G656**

**LYRIC POETRY.** *See* **SONGS.**

**M Magna System, Inc. presents... [videorecording].**
Diversity [videorecording]. Barrington, IL : Magna Systems, Inc., 1996.
**TC LB1139.25 .D5 1996**

**M. Margaret Michael, Sister, O.P.** This is our land / by Sister M. Margaret Michael, O.P. and Mary Synon. New ed. Boston, Mass. : Ginn and Company, 1955. 399 p. : ill. (some col.) ; 23 cm. (Faith and freedom) On spine: IV. "Published for the Catholic university of America press, Washington, D.C." For grade K-4.
*1. Readers (Elementary) I. Synon, Mary. II. Title.*
**TC PE1121 .M52 1955**

**Ma, Liping.** Knowing and teaching elementary mathematics : teachers' understanding of fundamental mathematics in China and the United States / Liping Ma. Mahwah, N.J. : Lawrence Erlbaum Associates, 1999. xxv, 166 p. : ill. ; 24 cm. (Studies in mathematical thinking and learning series) Includes bibliographical references (p. 156-160) and indexes. ISBN 0-8058-2908-3 (cloth : alk. paper) ISBN 0-8058-2909-1 (pbk. : alk. paper) DDC 372.7/0973
*1. Mathematics - Study and teaching (Elementary) - United States. 2. Mathematics - Study and teaching (Elementary) - China. 3. Comparative education. I. Title. II. Series: Studies in mathematical thinking and learning.*
**TC QA135.5 .M22 1999**

**Ma Rhea, Zane.**
Local knowledge and wisdom in higher education. 1st ed. Oxford : Published for the IAU Press [by] Pergamon, 2000.
**TC GN380 .L63 2000**

**Maass, Vera Sonja.** Counseling single parents : a cognitive-behavioral approach / Vera Sonja Maass, Margery A. Neely. New York : Springer Pub. Co., c2000. xiii, 375 p. : ill. ; 24 cm. Includes bibliographical

references (p. 351-363) and indexes. CONTENTS: Ch. 1. Background for Counseling and Therapy -- Ch. 2. Practical Theory-Building -- Ch. 3. Systematic Counseling Phases -- Ch. 4. Designating the Problem Area(s) -- Ch. 5. Identifying What Does Not Work -- Ch. 6. Introducing the Idea of Choices -- Ch. 7. Starting and Proceeding Along the Chosen Path -- Ch. 8. Reevaluating Progress -- Ch. 9. Generalizing Learning onto Other Situations -- Ch. 10. Reconceptualizing the Self -- Ch. 11. Coordinating and Balancing the Worlds We Live In -- Ch. 12. Where We Have Been - Where Are We Going? ISBN 0-8261-1313-3 (hc) DDC 306.85/6 DDC 306.85/6
*1. Single parents - Counseling of. 2. Cognitive therapy. 3. Single-parent families. I. Neely, Margery A. II. Title.*
**TC HQ759.915 .M23 2000**

**Maassen, Peter A. M.**
From the eye of the storm. Dordrecht ; Boston ; London: Kluwer Academic Publishers, c1999.
**TC LB2341.8.E85 F76 1999**

**Maben, Adrian.**
Monsieur René Magritte [videorecording]. [Chicago, Ill.] : Home Vision [distributor], c1978.
**TC ND673.M35 M6 1978**

**Mabry, Linda.** Portfolios plus : a critical guide to alternative assessment / Linda Mabry. Thousand Oaks, Calif. : Corwin Press, c1999. ix, 195 p. : ill. ; 30 cm. Includes bibliographical references (p. 177-189) and index. ISBN 0-8039-6610-5 (cloth : acid-free paper) ISBN 0-8039-6611-3 (pbk : acid-free paper) DDC 371.27
*1. Educational tests and measurements - United States. 2. Examinations - United States - Scoring. 3. Examinations - Validity - United States. 4. Portfolios in education - United States. I. Title.*
**TC LB3051 .M4243 1999**

**MACARONI PRODUCTS.** *See* **PASTA PRODUCTS.**

**MacCann, Donnarae.** White supremacy in children's literature : characterizations of African Americans, 1830-1900 / Donnarae MacCann. New York : Garland Pub., 1998. xxxiv, 274 p. ; 23 cm. (Garland reference library of social science ; vol. 1043. Children's literature and culture ; vol. 4) Includes bibliographical references (p. [243]-260) and indexes. ISBN 0-8153-2056-6 (acid-free paper) DDC 810.9/3520396073/09034
*1. American literature - 19th century - History and criticism. 2. Afro-Americans in literature. 3. White supremacy movements - United States - History - 19th century. 4. American literature - White authors - History and criticism. 5. Children's literature, American - History and criticism. 6. Characters and characteristics in literature. 7. Racism in literature. I. Title. II. Series: Garland reference library of social science ; v. 1043. III. Series: Garland reference library of social science. Children's literature and culture series ; v. 4.*
**TC PS173.N4 M33 1998**

**Macciomei, Nancy R.**
Behavioral management in the public schools. Westport, Conn. ; London : Praeger, 1999.
**TC LB1060.2 .B44 1999**

**MacCurdy, Marian M.**
Writing and healing. Urbana, Ill. : National Council of Teachers of English, c2000.
**TC RC489.W75 W756 2000**

**MacCuspie, P. Ann (Patricia Ann), 1950-** Promoting acceptance of children with disabilities : from tolerance to inclusion / by P. Ann MacCuspie. Halifax, N.S. : Atlantic Provinces Special Education Authority, c1996. xi, 235 p. ; 23 cm. Includes bibliographical references. ISBN 0-9680388-0-8 (pbk.) DDC 371.91
*1. Handicapped students - Education - United States. 2. Handicapped children - Education - United States. I. Atlantic Provinces Special Education Authority (Canada) II. Title.*
**TC LC4301 .M33 1996**

**MacDonald, Margaret Read, 1940-.**
Traditional storytelling today. Chicago : Fitzroy Dearborn Publishers, 1999.
**TC GR72 .T73 1999**

**Mace, Nancy L.** The 36-hour day : a family guide to caring for persons with Alzheimer disease, related dementing illnesses, and memory loss in later life / Nancy L. Mace, Peter V. Rabins. 3rd ed. Baltimore : Johns Hopkins University Press, 1999. xx, 339 p. ; 24 cm. (A Johns Hopkins Press health book) Includes bibliographical references (p. [313]-316) and index. ISBN 0-8018-6148-9 (alk. paper) ISBN 0-8018-6149-7 (pbk. : alk. paper)
*1. Alzheimer's disease - Patients - Home care. 2. Senile dementia - Patients - Home care. 3. Dementia. 4. Alzheimer Disease. 5. Home Nursing. 6. Caregivers. I. Rabins, Peter V. II. Title. III. Title: Thirty-six hour day IV. Series.*
**TC RC523 .M33 1999**

**Macedo, Donaldo P. (Donaldo Pereira), 1950-.**
Chomsky, Noam. Chomsky on miseducation. Lanham, Md. ; Oxford : Rowman & Littlefield Publishers, c2000.
**TC LB885.C522 A3 2000**

Dancing with bigotry : beyond the politics of tolerance / by Donaldo Macedo and Lilia I. Bartolomé. New York : St. Martin's Press, 1999. xv, 175 p. ; 22 cm. Includes bibliographical references (p. 162-170) and index. ISBN 0-312-21608-4 DDC 370.11/5
*1. Critical pedagogy - United States. 2. Multicultural education - United States. I. Bartolomé, Lilia I. II. Title.*
**TC LC196.5.U6 D26 1999**

**Macedo, Stephen, 1957-** Diversity and distrust : civic education in a multicultural democracy / Stephen Macedo. Cambridge, Mass. : Harvard University Press, 2000. xvi, 343 p. ; 25 cm. Includes bibliographical references (p. [281]-336) and index. ISBN 0-674-21311-4 (alk. paper) DDC 371.01/0973
*1. Public schools - United States. 2. Moral education - United States. 3. Citizenship - Study and teaching - United States. 4. Liberalism - United States. 5. Multiculturalism - United States. I. Title.*
**TC LA217.2 .M33 2000**

**Macfadyen, Tony.**
Bailey, Richard. Teaching physical education 5-11. New York : Continuum, 2000.
**TC GV443 .B34 2000**

**MacGregor, Jean.**
Strategies for energizing large classes : from small groups to learning communities. San Francisco, Calif. : Jossey-Bass, 2000.
**TC LB2361.5 .S77 2000**

**MacGregor-Mendoza, Patricia, 1963-** Spanish and academic achievement among Midwest Mexican youth : the myth of the barrier / Patricia MacGregor-Mendoza. New York ; London : Garland Pub., 1999. xvi, 178 p. ; 23 cm. (Latino communities) Includes bibliographical references (p. 163-174) and index. CONTENTS: Ch. 1. Language and Academic Achievement -- Ch. 2. Statement of the Problem -- Ch. 3. Methodology -- Ch. 4. Variables Related to Academic Achievement -- Ch. 5. Mexicans, Spanish and Academic Success. ISBN 0-8153-3345-5 (alk. paper) DDC 371.82968/7/073 DDC 371.82968/7/073
*1. Mexican American youth - Education - Middle West - Case studies. 2. Language arts - Middle West - Case studies. 3. Spanish language - Study and teaching - Middle West - Case studies. 4. Academic achievement - Middle West - Case studies. I. Title. II. Series.*
**TC LC2686.4 .M33 1999**

**Machado, Jeanne M.** Early childhood experiences in language arts : emerging literacy / Jeanne M. Machado. 6th ed. Albany, N.Y. : Delmar Publishers, c1999. xi, 580 p. : ill. (some col.) ; 24 cm. Includes bibliographical references (p. 557-570) and index. ISBN 0-8273-8361-4 DDC 372.6
*1. Language arts (Early childhood) 2. Language acquisition - Parent participation. 3. Literacy. I. Title.*
**TC LB1139.5.L35 M335 1999**

**MACHINE DATA STORAGE AND RETRIEVAL.** *See* **INFORMATION STORAGE AND RETRIEVAL SYSTEMS.**

**MACHINE INTELLIGENCE.** *See* **ARTIFICIAL INTELLIGENCE.**

**MACHINE LEARNING.**
Learning. 1st ed. Amsterdam ; New York : Pergamon, 1999.
**TC LB1060 .L4245 1999**

Modelling changes in understanding. Amsterdam ; New York : Pergamon, 1999.
**TC BF319 .M55 1999**

Thornton, Christopher James. Truth from trash. Cambridge, Mass. ; London : MIT Press, c2000.
**TC Q325.4 .T47 2000**

**Machine learning and data mining in pattern recognition.**
MLDM'99 (1999 : Leipzig, Germany) Berlin ; New York : Springer, c1999.
**TC Q327 .M56 1999**

**MACHINE LEARNING - CONGRESSES.**
MLDM'99 (1999 : Leipzig, Germany) Machine learning and data mining in pattern recognition. Berlin ; New York : Springer, c1999.
**TC Q327 .M56 1999**

**MACHINE-READABLE BIBLIOGRAPHIC DATA FORMATS.** *See* **MARC FORMATS.**

**MACHINE-READABLE CATALOGING FORMATS.** *See* MARC FORMATS.

**MACHINE THEORY.** *See* ARTIFICIAL INTELLIGENCE; COMPUTERS; MACHINE LEARNING.

**MACHINERY.** *See* LOCOMOTIVES; TEXTILE MACHINERY.

**MacIntyre, Alasdair C.** The unconscious : a conceptual analysis / Alaisdair C. MacIntyre. Bristol, England : Thoemmes Press, 1997, c1958. ix, 100 p. ; 22 cm. (Key texts (Bristol, England)) Reprint. Originally published: [S.l.] : Humanities Press, 1958. Includes bibliographical references (p. vii-ix) and index. ISBN 1-85506-520-7 (pbk.)
*1. Subconsciousness. 2. Freud, Sigmund, - 1856-1939. I. Title. II. Series.*
*TC BF315 .M23 1997*

**Mack, Kibibi Voloria C.** Parlor ladies and ebony drudges : African American women, class, and work in a South Carolina community / Kibibi Voloria C. Mack ; with a foreword by Elizabeth Fox-Genovese. 1st ed. Knoxville : University of Tennessee Press, c1999. xxvii, 233 p. : ill. ; 24 cm. Includes bibliographical references (p. [215]-227) and index. CONTENTS: Upper-class African Americans -- Upper-class women's work outside the home -- Upper-class women's work inside the home -- Middle-class African Americans -- Middle-class women's work outside the home -- Middle-class women's work inside the home -- Working-class African Americans -- Working-class women's work outside the home -- Working-class women's work inside the home. ISBN 1-57233-030-9 (cloth : alk. paper) DDC 305.48/896/075779
*1. Afro-American women - South Carolina - Orangeburg - Social conditions. 2. Social classes - South Carolina - Orangeburg - History. 3. Orangeburg (S.C.) - Social conditions. I. Title. II. Title: And ebony drudges*
*TC F279.O6 M33 1999*

**MacKenzie, Donald A.** The social shaping of technology. 2nd ed. Buckingham [England] ; Philadelphia : Open University Press, c1999.
*TC T14.5 .S6383 1999*

**Mackinnon, Laurel T., 1953-** Advances in exercise immunology / Laurel T. Mackinnon. Champaign, IL : Human Kinetics, c1999. xii, 363 p. : ill. ; 24 cm. Includes bibliographical references (p. 327-351) and index. ISBN 0-88011-562-9 DDC 616.07/9
*1. Exercise - Immunological aspects. 2. Exercise - physiology. 3. Immunity. I. Title. II. Title: Exercise immunology*
*TC QP301 .M159 1999*

**Macklin, M. Carole.** Advertising to children. Thousand Oaks, Calif. : Sage Publications, c1999.
*TC HQ784.T4 A29 1999*

**MACLACHLAN, PATRICIA. SARAH, PLAIN AND TALL.**
Beech, Linda Ward. Sarah, plain and tall by Patricia MacLachlan. New York : Scholastic, c1996.
*TC LB1573 .B436 1996*

**MacLeod-Brudenell, Iain.**
Siraj-Blatchford, John, 1952- Supporting science, design and technology in the early years. Philadelphia, Pa. : Open University Press, 1999.
*TC T65.3 .S55 1999*

**Macmillan/McGraw-Hill math anthology.**
Math anthology. New York : Macmillan/McGraw-Hill Pub. Co., c1993.
*TC QA141.3 .M37 1993*

Math anthology. New York : Macmillan/McGraw-Hill Pub. Co., c1993.
*TC QA141.3 .M37 1993*

**Macmillan predictable big books.**
Arnold, Virginia A. New York : Macmillan Publishing Co., 1990,
*TC LB1181.2 .A76 1990*

**Macnamara, John.** Through the rearview mirror : historical reflections on pschology / John Macnamara. Cambridge, Mass. : MIT Press, 1999. xix, 291 p. ; 24 cm. "A Bardford book." Includes bibliographical references and index. ISBN 0-262-13352-0 (hc : alk. paper) DDC 150/.9
*1. Psychology - History. 2. Psychology and philosophy. I. Title.*
*TC BF105 .M33 1999*

**MacPhail-Wilcox, Bettye.**
Ward, Michael E., 1953- Delegation and empowerment. Larchmont, NY : Eye on Education, c1999.
*TC LB2831.92 .W37 1999*

**Macrae, C. Neil.**
Stereotype activation and inhibition. Mahwah, N.J. : L. Erlbaum Associates, 1998.

*TC BF323.S63 S75 1998*

**Macromedia Dream weaver [computer file].**
Macromedia Dreamweaver 3 [computer file]. Version 3.0 ; Windows 95, Windows 98, Windows NT ; Education version. San Francisco, CA : Macromedia, c1999. Computer program.
*TC TK5105.8883 .M33 1999*

**Macromedia Dreamweaver 3** [computer file] : the solution for professional web site design and production / Macromedia ; directed by Kevin Lynch, Paul Madar. Version 3.0 ; Windows 95, Windows 98, Windows NT ; Education version. San Francisco, CA : Macromedia, c1999. Computer program. 1 computer optical disc ; 4 3/4 in. + 1 user guide (440 p. : ill. ; 23 cm.). System requirements for Windows: 120+MHz Pentium PC; 32MB RAM; Windows 95, 98 or NT 4.0 or later; 20MB available hard disk space; 256-color monitor capable of 800 x 600 pixel resolution; CD-ROM drive. Title from title screen ; edition statements from title screen, disc surface, and box. SUMMARY: Authoring tool for creating and managing Web sites and pages. You can create and edit cross-platform, cross browser pages. Provides advanced design and layout tools, easy to use Dynamic HTML features such as animated layers and behaviors without writing a line of code. Imports HTML documents without reformatting code. Issued in box.
*1. Dreamweaver (Computer file) 2. Web sites - Authoring programs. 3. Web sites - Design - Software. 4. Web publishing - Software. I. Lynch, David. II. Madar, Paul. III. Macromedia (Firm) IV. Title: Dreamweaver [computer file] V. Title: Macromedia Dream weaver [computer file]*
*TC TK5105.8883 .M33 1999*

**Macromedia (Firm).**
Macromedia Dreamweaver 3 [computer file]. Version 3.0 ; Windows 95, Windows 98, Windows NT ; Education version. San Francisco, CA : Macromedia, c1999. Computer program.
*TC TK5105.8883 .M33 1999*

**Macronutrients.**
The nutty, nougat-filled world of human nutrition [videorecording]. [Arlington, Va.] : Cerebellum Corp., c1998.
*TC QP141 .N8 1998*

**MACROPODIDAE.** *See* KANGAROOS.

**MACUA INDIANS.** *See* MACUNA INDIANS.

**MACUNA INDIANS - RELIGION.**
Arhem, Kaj. Makuna. Washington : Smithsonian Institution Press, c1998.
*TC F2270.2.M33 A68 1998*

**MACUNA INDIANS - RITES AND CEREMONIES.**
Arhem, Kaj. Makuna. Washington : Smithsonian Institution Press, c1998.
*TC F2270.2.M33 A68 1998*

**MACUNA PHILOSOPHY.**
Arhem, Kaj. Makuna. Washington : Smithsonian Institution Press, c1998.
*TC F2270.2.M33 A68 1998*

**MacWhinney, Brian.** The CHILDES project : tools for analyzing talk / Brian MacWhinney. 3rd ed. Mahwah, N.J. : Lawrence Erlbaum, 2000. 2 v. : ill. ; 27 cm. + 1 computer optical disc (4 3/4 in.). Includes bibliographical references and indexes. System requirements: Windows or Macintosh. CONTENTS: v. 1. Transcription format and programs -- v. 2. The database. ISBN 0-8058-2995-4 (v. 1 : alk. paper) ISBN 0-8058-3572-5 (v. 2 : alk. paper) DDC 155.4/136/0285
*1. Children - Language - Data processing. 2. Language acquisition - Research - Data processing. I. Title. II. Title: Child Language Data Exchange System project*
*TC LB1139.L3 M24 2000*

**Mad summer night's dream.**
Brown, Ruth. 1st American ed. New York : Dutton Children's Books, 1999.
*TC PZ8.3.B8155 Mad 1999*

**Mad travelers.**
Hacking, Ian. Charlottesville, Va. : University Press of Virginia, 1998.
*TC RC553.F83 H33 1998*

**Madar, Paul.**
Macromedia Dreamweaver 3 [computer file]. Version 3.0 ; Windows 95, Windows 98, Windows NT ; Education version. San Francisco, CA : Macromedia, c1999. Computer program.
*TC TK5105.8883 .M33 1999*

**Madden, Steven J.**
Service learning across the curriculum. Lanham, Md. : University Press of America, c2000.
*TC LC221 .S47 2000*

**Maddison, Francis Romeril.**
Learning, language, and invention. Aldershot, Hampshire, Great Britain : Brookfield, Vt., USA : Ashgate Pub. Co. ; Paris, France : Société internationale de l'Astrolabe, 1994.
*TC AC5 .L38 1994*

**Maddock, Su.** Challenging women : gender, culture, and organization / Su Maddock. London ; Thousand Oaks, Calif. : Sage, 1999. 258 p. ; 24 cm. Includes bibliographical references (p. [228]-249) and index. ISBN 0-7619-5150-4 ISBN 0-7619-5151-2 (pbk.).
*1. Women in politics. 2. Women in the civil service. 3. Women public officers. 4. Women executives. 5. Organizational change. 6. Sex role in the work environment. I. Title.*
*TC HQ1236 .M342 1999*

**Maddux, Cleborne D., 1942-.**
Information technology in educational research and statistics. New York : Haworth Press, 1999.
*TC LB1028.3 .I51945 1999*

**Madigan, Dan.** The writing lives of children / Dan Madigan, Victoria T. Koivu-Rybicki. York, ME : Stenhouse Publishers, 1997. viii, 120 p. ; 23 cm. Includes bibliographical references (p.119-120). ISBN 1-57110-011-3 (alk. paper) DDC 372.67/7
*1. Storytelling - United States. 2. Children - United States - Diaries 3. Language arts (Elementary) - United States. I. Koivu-Rybicki, Victoria T. II. Title.*
*TC LB1042 .M24 1997*

**Madjar, Irena.**
Nursing and the experience of illness. London ; New York : Routledge, 1999.
*TC RT86 .N886 1999*

**MADNESS.** *See* ANGER; MENTAL ILLNESS.

**Madness and democracy.**
Gauchet, Marcel. [La pratique de l'esprit humain. English] Princeton, N.J. : Princeton University Press, c1999.
*TC RC439 .G2813 1999*

**Madrigal, Antonio Hernandez.** Erandi's braids / written by Antonio Hernandez Madrigal ; illustrated by Tomie dePaola. New York : Putnam's, c1999. 1 v. (unpaged) : col. ill. ; 26 cm. SUMMARY: In a poor Mexican village, Erandi surprises her mother by offering to sell her long, beautiful hair in order to raise enough money to buy a new fishing net. ISBN 0-399-23212-5 DDC [E]
*1. Hair - Fiction. 2. Mothers and daughters - Fiction. 3. Mexico - Fiction. I. De Paola, Tomie, ill. II. Title.*
*TC PZ7.M26575 Er 1999*

**Madsen, Benedicte, 1943-** Survival in the organization : Gunnar Hjelholt looks back at the concentration camp from an organizational perspective / by Benedicte Madsen and Søren Willert ; [translated by Edith Matteson]. Aarhus [Denmark] ; Oakville, Conn. : Aarhus University Press, c1996. 96 p. : ill. ; 22 cm. "Gunnar Hjelholt's publications": p. [89]-91. Includes bibliographical references and indexes. ISBN 87-7288-539-4 (alk. paper) DDC 940.54/7243
*1. Hjelholt, Gunnar. 2. World War, 1939-1945 - Prisoners and prisons, German. 3. Porta Westfalica (Concentration camp) 4. Prisoners of war - Germany - Biography. 5. Prisoners of war - Denmark - Biography. 6. Concentration camps - Psychological aspects. I. Willert, Søren. II. Title.*
*TC D805.G3 M24 1996*

**MAECENATISM.** *See* ART PATRONAGE.

**Maestro, Betsy.** The story of the Statue of Liberty / by Betsy Maestro ; illustrated by Giulio Maestro. New York : Lothrop, Lee & Shepard Books, 1986. 39 p. : ill. ; 29 cm. SUMMARY: Describes the creation of the huge statue given by France to the United States and its erection in New York Harbor as a symbol of liberty. ISBN 0-688-05773-X ISBN 0-688-05774-8 (lib. bdg.) DDC 730/.92/4
*1. Statue of Liberty (New York, N.Y.) - Juvenile literature. 2. Bartholdi, Frédéric Auguste, - 1834-1904 - Juvenile literature. 3. New York (N.Y.) - Buildings, structures, etc. - Juvenile literature. 4. Statue of Liberty (New York, N.Y.) 5. National monuments. 6. Statues. 7. Statue of Liberty (New York, N.Y.) 8. Bartholdi, Fr ed-eric Auguste, - 1834-1904. I. Maestro, Giulio, ill. II. Title.*
*TC NB553.B3 A75 1986*

**Maestro, Giulio, ill.**
Maestro, Betsy. The story of the Statue of Liberty. New York : Lothrop, Lee & Shepard Books, 1986.
*TC NB553.B3 A75 1986*

**Maestro music instrument instructional video ... for**
The cello [videorecording]. Van Nuys, CA : Backstage Pass Productions ; Canoga Park, Calif. : [Distributed by] MVP, c1995.
*TC MT305 .C4 1995*

The drums [videorecording]. Van Nuys, CA : Backstage Pass Productions ; Canoga Park, Calif. : [Distributed by] MVP Home Entertainment, c1998.
*TC MT662.3 .S6 1998*

The flute [videorecording]. Van Nuys, CA : Backstage Pass Productions ; Canoga Park, Calif. : [Distributed by] MVP, c1995.
*TC MT345 .F6 1995*

The trombone [videorecording]. Van Nuys, CA : Backstage Pass Productions ; Canoga Park, Calif. : [Distributed by] MVP, c1998.
*TC MT465 .T7 1998*

The viola [videorecording]. Van Nuys, CA : Backstage Pass Productions ; Canoga Park, Calif. : [Distributed by] MVP Home Entertainment, c1991.
*TC MT285 .V5 1991*

The viola [videorecording]. Van Nuys, CA : Backstage Pass Productions ; Canoga Park, Calif. : [Distributed by] MVP Home Entertainment, c1995.
*TC MT285 .V5 1995*

The violin [videorecording]. Van Nuys, CA : Backstage Pass Productions ; Canoga Park, Calif. : [Distributed by] MVP, c1998.
*TC MT265 .V5 1998*

**Maffit, Rocky, 1952-** Rhythm & beauty : : the art of percussion / Rocky Maffit ; foreword by Evelyn Glennie ; photography by Chris Brown. New York : Watson-Guptill Publications, c1999. 135 p. : ill. ; 28 cm. 1 compact digital sound disc (4 4/3 in.). Includes discography (p. 124-125), bibliographical references (p. 122-123), videography (p. 123), and index (p.134-135). SUMMARY: Presents a sample of percussion instruments from around the world; and the accompanying compact disk was "produced as a companion CD for the book 'Rhythm & Beauty: The Art of Percussion'" which contains songs featuring sounds of the instruments discussed in the book. ISBN 0-8230-8406-X (hardcover)
*1. Percussion instruments. I. Title.*
*TC ML1030 .M34 1999*

**MAGAZINES.** *See* **PERIODICALS.**

**MAGDALENO, MAURICIO, 1906-.**
Guevara-Vázquez, Fabián. El indigena en la novela de la Revolucion Mexicana. 1999.
*TC 085 G934*

**Magg, Rebecca.**
The flute [videorecording]. Van Nuys, CA : Backstage Pass Productions ; Canoga Park, Calif. : [Distributed by] MVP, c1995.
*TC MT345 .F6 1995*

**MAGIC - FICTION.**
Rowling, J. K. Harry Potter and the Chamber of Secrets. New York : Arthur A. Levine Books, 1999.
*TC PZ7.R7968 Har 1999*

Rowling, J. K. Harry Potter and the prisoner of Azkaban. New York : Arthur A. Levine Books, 1999.
*TC PZ7.R79835 Ham 1999*

**The magic of Matsumoto.**
Barrett, Carolyn M., 1941- Palm Springs, CA : ETC Publications, c1995.
*TC MT1 .B325 1995*

**MAGICIANS.** *See* **WIZARDS.**

**Magid, Andy R.**
Algebra, K-theory, groups, and education. Providence, R.I. : American Mathematical Society, c1999.
*TC QA150 .A419 1999*

**Magie, Dian.**
Building America's communities H. Washington, D.C. : Americans for the Arts (Organization) ; Institute for Community Development and the Arts, 1997.
*TC NX180.A77 B95 1997*

Resource development handbook. [Washington, D.C.] : National Assembly of Local Arts Agencies, Institute for Community Development and the Arts, 1995.
*TC NX110 .R47 1995*

**Magill bibliographies**
Peck, David R. American ethnic literatures. Pasadena, Calif. : Salem Press, c1992.
*TC Z1229.E87 P43 1992*

**Magna Systems.**
Diversity [videorecording]. Barrington, IL : Magna Systems, Inc., 1996.
*TC LB1139.25 .D5 1996*

**MAGNANIMITY.** *See* **GENEROSITY.**

**Magnavita, Jeffrey J.** Relational therapy for personality disorders / Jeffrey J. Magnavita. New York : Wiley, c2000. xviii, 291 p. : ill. ; 25 cm. (Wiley series in couples and family dynamics and treatment) Includes bibliographical references (p. 249-267) and indexes. ISBN 0-471-29566-3 (alk. paper) DDC 616.89/14
*1. Brief psychotherapy. 2. Psychodynamic psychotherapy. 3. Personality disorders - Treatment. I. Title. II. Series: Wiley series in couples and family dynamics and treatment*
*TC RC554 .M228 2000*

**MAGNET SCHOOLS.** *See* **SCHOOL INTEGRATION.**

**MAGNETISM.** *See* **ELECTRICITY.**

**Magno, Joseph.** Self-love : the heart of healing / Joseph A. Magno. Lanham, Md. ; Oxford : University Press of America, c2000. xx, 196 p. ; 24 cm. Includes bibliographical references and index. ISBN 0-7618-1573-2 (hbk. : alk. paper) ISBN 0-7618-1574-0 (pbk. : alk. paper) DDC 158.1
*1. Love. 2. Self-acceptance. I. Title.*
*TC BF575.L8 M29 2000*

**Magnuson, Douglas.**
Residential education as an option for at-risk youth. New York : Haworth Press, c1996.
*TC HV862 .R473 1996*

**Magritte, René, 1898-1967.**
Monsieur René Magritte [videorecording]. [Chicago, Ill.] : Home Vision [distributor], c1978.
*TC ND673.M35 M6 1978*

**MAGRITTE, RENÉ, 1898-1967.**
Monsieur René Magritte [videorecording]. [Chicago, Ill.] : Home Vision [distributor], c1978.
*TC ND673.M35 M6 1978*

**Magritte [videorecording].**
Monsieur René Magritte [videorecording]. [Chicago, Ill.] : Home Vision [distributor], c1978.
*TC ND673.M35 M6 1978*

**Maguire, Gregory.** The good liar / Gregory Maguire. New York : Clarion Books, c1999. 129 p. ; 21 cm. "First published in 1995 by The O'Brien Press Ltd., Dublin, Ireland." SUMMARY: Now an old man living in the United States, Marcel recalls his childhood in German-occupied France, especially the summer that he and his older brother Rene befriended a young German soldier. ISBN 0-395-90697-0 DDC [Fic]
*1. World War. 1939-1945 - France - Juvenile fiction. 2. World War, 1939-1945 - France - Fiction. 3. France - History - German occupation, 1940-1945 - Fiction. I. Title.*
*TC PZ7.M2762 Go 1999*

**Mahalingam, Ram.**
Multicultural curriculum. New York : Routledge, 2000.
*TC LC1099 .M816 2000*

**Mahammad, Hasna.** Multicultural education : what was expected of teachers in a district-wide implementation process / by Hasna Mahammad. 1998. xii, 209 leaves ; 29 cm. Typescript; issued also on microfilm. Thesis (Ed.D.)-- Teachers College, Columbia University, 1998. Includes bibliographical references (leaves 167-172).
*1. Multicultural education - New York (State) 2. Middle school teachers - New York (State) - Attitudes. 3. Stereotype (Psychology) 4. Middle school teachers - In-service training - New York (State) 5. Minorities - Education (Middle school) - New York (State) 6. Middle school education - New York (State) - Curricula. 7. School improvement programs - New York (State) 8. Educational equalization - New York (State) I. Title.*
*TC 06 no. 11033*

**Mahlase, Shirley Motleke.** The careers of women teachers under apartheid / Shirley Motleke Mahlase. Harare : SAPES Books, c1997. v, 207 p. : ill. ; 21 cm. (Southern Africa specialised studies series) Spine title: Women teachers under apartheid. "SAPES Trust"--P. [4] of cover. "Southern African Regional Institute for Policy Studies ..."-- Ser. t.p. Based on author's thesis (doctoral)--University of Cambridge, U.K. Includes bibliographical references (p. [189]-202) and indexes. ISBN 1-77905-061-5 ISBN 1-77905-060-7 (cover)
*1. Women teachers - South Africa. 2. Apartheid - South Africa. I. SAPES Trust. II. Southern Africa Regional Institute for Policy Studies. III. Title. IV. Title: Women teachers under apartheid V. Series.*
*TC LB2832.4.S6 M35 1997*

**Mahler, Das Lied von der Erde.**
Hefling, Stephen E. Cambridge, UK ; New York : Cambridge University Press, c2000.
*TC MT121.M34 H44 2000*

**MAHLER, GUSTAV, 1860-1911.**
**LIED VON DER ERDE.**
Hefling, Stephen E. Mahler, Das Lied von der

Erde = Cambridge, UK ; New York : Cambridge University Press, c2000.
*TC MT121.M34 H44 2000*

**SYMPHONIES, NO. 4, G MAJOR**
Zychowicz, James L. Mahler's Fourth symphony. New York : Oxford University Press, 2000.
*TC MT130.M25 Z93 2000*

**Mahler's Fourth symphony.**
Zychowicz, James L. New York : Oxford University Press, 2000.
*TC MT130.M25 Z93 2000*

**MAHORKA.** *See* **TOBACCO.**

**Maidment, Lauren.**
Teaching and learning in cities. [S.l.] : Whitbread, 1993.
*TC LC5115 .T43 1993*

**The mainstreaming handbook.**
Coughlin, Debbie. Portsmouth, NH : Heinemann, c2000.
*TC LC1201 .C68 2000*

**MAINSTREAMING IN EDUCATION.** *See also* **INCLUSIVE EDUCATION.**
Block, Martin E., 1958- A teacher's guide to including students with disabilities in general physical education. 2nd ed. Baltimore, Md. : Paul H. Brookes Pub. Co., c2000.
*TC GV445 .B56 2000*

Cook, Ruth E. Adapting early childhood curricula for children in inclusive settings. 5th ed. Englewood Cliffs, N.J. : Merrill, c2000.
*TC LC4019.2 .C66 2000*

**MAINSTREAMING IN EDUCATION - CASE STUDIES.**
Inclusive education at work. Paris : Organisation for Economic Co-operation and Development, 1999.
*TC LC4015 .I525 1999*

**MAINSTREAMING IN EDUCATION - COLORADO.**
Clay, Cheryl D., 1947- Schooling at-risk Native American children. New York : Garland Pub., 1998.
*TC E99.U8 C53 1998*

**MAINSTREAMING IN EDUCATION - CROSS-CULTURAL STUDIES.**
Inclusive education. London ; Philadelphia : Falmer Press, 1999.
*TC LC1200 .I53 1999*

**MAINSTREAMING IN EDUCATION - ENGLAND - LEICESTER.**
Croll, Paul. Special needs in the primary school. London : Cassell, 2000.
*TC LC4036.G6 C763 2000*

**MAINSTREAMING IN EDUCATION - GREAT BRITAIN.**
Beveridge, Sally. Special educational needs in schools. 2nd ed. London ; New York : Routledge, 1999.
*TC LC3986.G7 B48 1999*

Watson, Linda R., 1950- Deaf and hearing impaired pupils in mainstream schools. London : David Fulton, c1999.
*TC LC1203.G7 W387 1999*

**MAINSTREAMING IN EDUCATION - MARYLAND.**
Sean's story [videorecording]. Princeton, N.J. : Films for the Humanities & Sciences ; [S.l. : distributed by] ABC Multimedia : Capital Cities/ABC, c1994.
*TC LC1203.M3 .S39 1994*

**MAINSTREAMING IN EDUCATION - UNITED STATES.**
Idol, Lorna. Collaborative consultation. 3rd ed. Austin, Tex. : PRO-ED, c2000.
*TC LC4019 .I35 2000*

Inclusion practices with special needs students. New York : Haworth Press, c1999.
*TC LC1201 .I538 1999*

Lewis, Rena B. Teaching special students in general education classrooms. 5th ed. Upper Saddle River, N.J. : Merrill, c1999.
*TC LC1201 .L48 1999*

McGregor, Gail Inclusive schooling practices. [S.l.] : Allegheny University of Health Sciences ; Balitmore : Distributed exclusively by Paul H. Brookes Publishing, c1998.
*TC LC4031 .M394 1998*

Vallecorsa, Ada, 1948- Students with mild disabilities in general education settings. Upper Saddle River, N.J. : Merrill, c2000.

## Mainstreaming in education - United States.

**TC LC4705 .V35 2000**

Vaughn, Sharon, 1952- Teaching exceptional, diverse, and at-risk students in the general education classroom. 2nd ed. Boston : Allyn and Bacon, 2000.
**TC LC3981 .V28 2000**

### MAINSTREAMING IN EDUCATION - UNITED STATES - CASE STUDIES.
Coughlin, Debbie. The mainstreaming handbook. Portsmouth, NH : Heinemann, c2000.
**TC LC1201 .C68 2000**

**Maintaining children in school.**
Vernon, Jeni. London : National Children's Bureau Enterprises, c1998.
**TC LB3081 .V47 1998**

**Maintaining the momentum.**
McKellin, Karen, 1950- Victoria, B.C. : British Columbia Centre for International Education, c1998.
**TC LC1090 .M24 1998**

**Majallat al-tarbiyah al-ḥadīthah.** al-Qāhirah : al-Jāmiʻah al-Amrīkīyah bi-al-Qāhirah, 1928- . v. ; 25 cm. Frequency: Four no. per academic year. al-Sanah 1. al-ʻAdad 1. (Jan. 1928)- . Cover title: Journal of modern education. Editor: 1928-Apr. 1966: Amīr Buqṭur. Arabic or English. Vol. -31 issued by the University's Kullīyat al-Muʻallimīn; vol. 32-34 by its Kullīyat al-Tarbiyah. Vols. 21-30, 1948-57, with v. 30.
*1. Education - Periodicals. I. Buqṭur, Amīr, 1896-1966. II. American University at Cairo. III. American University at Cairo. Kullīyat al-Muʻallimīn. IV. American University at Cairo. Kullīyat al-Tarbiyah. V. American University at Cairo. Journal of modern education. VI. Title: Journal of modern education*

**Majasan, James.** Qualitative education and development / J.A. Majasan. Ibadan : Spectrum Books Limited ; Channel Islands, UK : In association with Safari Books (Export) ; Oxford, UK : African Books Collective Ltd. (Distributor), 1998. ix, 118 p. : maps ; 21 cm. Includes bibliographical references (p. [109]-111) and index. ISBN 9780290575 DDC 370.11
*1. Education - Aims and objectives - Developing countries. 2. Economic development - Effect of education on. 3. Education - Economic aspects. I. Title.*
**TC LC2605 .M32 1998**

**Major, Cherie.**
Teaching to teach. Washington, DC : National Education Association, 1999.
**TC LB1715 .T436 1999**

**Major health care policies.**
Health Policy Tracking Service. 8th ed. Washington, D.C. : Health Policy Tracking Service, 2000.
**TC KF3821 .H4 2000**

**Major state health care policies.**
Health Policy Tracking Service. Major health care policies. 8th ed. Washington, D.C. : Health Policy Tracking Service, 2000.
**TC KF3821 .H4 2000**

**Majorek, Czesław.**
Education in a global society. Boston : Allyn and Bacon, c2000.
**TC LB43 .E385 2000**

**Majoring in the rest of your life.**
Carter, Carol. Upper Saddle River, NJ : Prentice Hall, c2000.
**TC HF5382.5.U5 C373 2000**

**MAJORITIES.** *See* MINORITIES.

### MAKANYA, KATIE, 1873-1955.
McCord, Margaret (McCord Nixon) The calling of Katie Makanya. New York : J. Wiley, 1995.
**TC CT1929.M34 M38 1995**

**Make a wish :** teacher's planning guide. New York : Macmillan/McGraw-Hill, c1997. 1 v. (various pagings) : col. ill. ; 31 cm. (Spotlight on literacy ; Gr.4 l.10 u.1) (The road to independent reading) Includes index. ISBN 0-02-181172-5
*1. Language arts (Elementary) 2. Reading (Elementary) I. Series. II. Series: The road to independent reading*
**TC LB1576 .S66 1997 Gr.4 l.10 u.1**

**Make haste slowly.**
Kellar, William Henry, 1952- 1st ed. College Station : Texas A&M University Press, c1999.
**TC LC214.23.H68 K45 1999**

**Make me a peanut butter sandwich and a glass of milk.**
Robbins, Ken. New York : Scholastic, c1992.
**TC TX814.5.P38 R63 1992**

**Make money performing in schools.**
Heflick, David. How to make money performing in schools. Orient, Wash. : Silcox Productions, c1996.

**TC LB3015 .H428 1996**

**Make way for Dumb Bunnies.**
Denim, Sue, 1966- New York : Blue Sky Press, c1996.
**TC PZ7.D4149 Mak 1996**

**MAKHORKA.** *See* TOBACCO.

**Making a difference.**
Fiedler, Craig R. Boston : London : Allyn and Bacon, c2000.
**TC LC4031 .F52 2000**

Weinstein, Miriam (Miriam H.) Rev. & exp. 2nd ed. Gabriola Island, BC, Can. : New Society Publishers, 2000.
**TC LB2338 W45 2000**

**Making a place for kids with disabilities.**
Fink, Dale Borman, 1949- Westport, Conn. : Praeger, 2000.
**TC GV183.6 .F56 2000**

**The making and unmaking of a university museum.**
Young, Brian, 1940- Montreal : McGill-Queen's University Press, c2000.
**TC FC21 .Y68 2000**

**Making art safely.**
Spandorfer, Merle, 1934- New York : Van Nostrand Reinhold, c1993.
**TC RC963.6.A78 S62 1993**

**Making assessment elementary.**
Strickland, Kathleen. Portsmouth, NH : Heinemann, 2000.
**TC LB3051 .S873 1999**

**Making choices.** Teacher's ed. New York, N.Y. : American Book Company, c1993. xvi, 539 p. : ill. (some col.) ; 28 cm. (American readers ; 6) Includes index. C.2 has different paging: "Scope and sequence chart for Changing Views" on p. 536-537, "Index" on p. 538-540, "Acknowledgements" on p. 541, "Introduction to end of unit tests" on p. 542, "Answer key - end of unit tests" on p. 543-544. ISBN 0-278-45861-0
*1. Readers (Elementary) 2. Reading (Elementary) I. Series.*
**TC PE1121 .M34 1980 Teacher's Ed.**

**Making choices.** New York, N.Y. : American Book Company, c1980. 480 p. : ill. (some col.) ; 24 cm. (American readers ; 6) ISBN 0-278-45830-0
*1. Readers (Elementary) I. Series.*
**TC PE1121 .M34 1980**

**Making choices.** Teacher's ed. Lexington, Mass. : D.C. Heath & co., c1986. T30, 726 p. : ill. (some col.) ; 28 cm. (Heath American readers ; 6) Includes index. ISBN 0-669-08056-x
*1. Readers (Elementary) 2. Reading (Elementary) I. Series.*
**TC PE1121 .M34 1986 Teacher's Ed.**

**Making choices.** Lexington, Mass. : D.C. Heath & co., c1986. 623 p. : ill. (some col.) ; 24 cm. (Heath American readers) ISBN 0-669-08039-x
*1. Readers (Elementary) I. Series.*
**TC PE1121 .M34 1986**

**Making choices :** parent-child activity pad / Lexington, Mass. : D.C. Heath & co., c1986. 115 p. : ill. ; 28x22 cm. (Heath American readers) Includes index. Title from cover. ISBN 0-669-08633-9
*1. Readers (Elementary) 2. Reading (Elementary) - Problems, exercises, etc. I. Title: Parent-child activity pad II. Series.*
**TC PE1121 .M34 1986 Activity Pad**

**Making choices :** skills master. Lexington, Mass. : D.C. Heath & Co., c1986. 1 v. (various pagings) : ill. ; 28x22 cm. (Heath American readers) Includes index. ISBN 0-669-09103-0
*1. Readers (Elementary) 2. Reading (Elementary) - Problems, exercises, etc. I. Series.*
**TC PE1121 .M34 1986 Skills Pad**

**Making choices :** time saver resource binder. Lexington, Mass. : D.C. Heath & co., c1986. 1 v. (various pagings) : ill. ; 28 cm. (Heath American readers) Includes index. ISBN 0-669-10374-8
*1. Readers (Elementary) 2. Reading (Elementary) I. Title: Time saver resource binder II. Series.*
**TC PE1121 .M34 1986 Resource Binder**

**Making choices :** workbook. Teacher's ed. New York, N.Y. : American Book Company, c1980. 126 p. : ill. (some col.) ; 28 cm. (American readers ; 6) Includes index. ISBN 0-278-45942-0
*1. Readers (Elementary) 2. Reading (Elementary) I. Title: Workbook for making choices. II. Series.*
**TC PE1121 .M34 1980 Teacher's Ed. Workbook**

**Making choices :** workbook. Teacher's ed. Lexington, Mass. : D.C. Heath & co., c1986. 158 p. : ill. (some col.) ; 28 cm. (Heath American readers) Includes index. ISBN 0-

669-08116-7
*1. Readers (Elementary) 2. Reading (Elementary) I. Series.*
**TC PE1121 .M34 1986 Teacher's Ed. Workbook**

**Making citizen-soldiers.**
Neiberg, Michael S. Cambridge, Mass. ; London : Harvard University Press, 2000.
**TC U428.5 .N45 2000**

**Making content comprehensible for English language learners.**
Echevarria, Jana, 1956- Boston, MA : Allyn and Bacon, 2000.
**TC PE1128.A2 E24 2000**

**Making histories in museums.**
Making histories in museums. London ; New York : Leicester University Press, 1996.
**TC AM7 .M35 1996**

**Making histories in museums** / edited by Gaynor Kavanagh. London ; New York : Leicester University Press, 1996. xv, 285 p. : ill. ; 24 cm. (Making histories in museums). Includes bibliographical references and index. ISBN 0-7185-0007-5 (hardcover)
*1. Museums - History. 2. Historical museums - History. 3. Museum techniques - History. 4. Historiography - History. 5. History - Methodology. I. Kavanagh, Gaynor. II. Series*
**TC AM7 .M35 1996**

**Making justice our project :** teachers working toward critical whole language practice / edited by Carole Edelsky. Urbana, Ill. : National Council of Teachers of English, c1999 xii, 369 p. ; 23 cm. Includes bibliographical references and index. "NCTE stock number 30445-3050"--T.p. verso. ISBN 0-8141-3044-5 (paper) DDC 370.11/5
*1. Language experience approach in education. 2. Critical pedagogy. I. Edelsky, Carole.*
**TC LB1576 .M3613 1999**

**Making learning happen.**
Golub, Jeffrey N., 1944- Portsmouth, NH : Boynton/Cook Publishers, c2000.
**TC LB1631 .G623 2000**

**Making lifelong learning work.**
Longworth, Norman. London : Kogan Page, 1999.
**TC LC5225.L42 L66 1999**

**Making Mark Twain work in the classroom** / edited by James S. Leonard. Durham [N.C.] : Duke University Press, 1999. viii, 348 p. : ill. ; 24 cm. Includes bibliographical references and index. ISBN 0-8223-2278-1 (cloth : alk. paper) ISBN 0-8223-2297-8 (paper : alk. paper) DDC 818/.409
*1. Twain, Mark, - 1835-1910 - Study and teaching. 2. Twain, Mark, - 1835-1910. - Adventures of Huckleberry Finn. 3. Literature and society - United States - History - 19th century - Study and teaching. 4. Social classes in literature - Study and teaching. 5. Adventure stories. American - Study and teaching. 6. Sex role in literature - Study and teaching. 7. Race in literature - Study and teaching. I. Leonard, J. S. (James S.)*
**TC PS1338 .M23 1999**

**Making meaning of community in an American high school.**
Abowitz, Kathleen Knight. Cresskill, N.J. : Hampton Press, c2000.
**TC LC311 .A36 2000**

**Making money matter :** financing America's schools / Helen F. Ladd and Janet S. Hansen, editors ; Committee on Education Finance, Commission on Behavioral and Social Sciences and Education, National Research Council. Washington, D.C. : National Academy Press, c1999. xiii, 352 p. ; 24 cm. Includes bibliographical references (p. 276-313) and index. ISBN 0-309-06528-3
*1. Education - Finance - United States. 2. Educational productivity - United States. 3. Educational equalization - United States. 4. Educational change - United States. I. Ladd, Helen F. II. Hansen, Janet S. III. National Research Council (U.S.). Committee on Education Finance. IV. Title. V. Title: Financing America's schools*
**TC LB2825 .M27 1999**

**The making of citizens.**
Buckingham, David, 1954- London ; New York : Routledge, 2000.
**TC HQ784.T4 .B847 2000**

**Making sense of academic life.**
Taylor, Peter G., 1951- Philadelphia, PA : Open University Press, 1999.
**TC LB1778 .T39 1999**

**Making sense of attention deficit/hyperactivity disorder.**
Lensch, Carol R., 1949- Westport, Conn. ; London : Bergin & Garvey, 2000.
**TC RJ506.H9 L46 2000**

**Making sense of social development** / edited by Martin Woodhead, Dorothy Faulkner, and Karen Littleton. London ; New York : Routledge in association with the Open University, 1999. vi, 278 p. : ill. ; 23 cm. Includes bibliographical references and index. ISBN 0-415-17374-4 (pbk. : alk. paper) DDC 305.231
*1. Child development. I. Woodhead, Martin. II. Faulkner, Dorothy. III. Littleton, Karen. IV. Open University.*
*TC HQ783 .L57 1999*

**Making space.**
Newcombe, Nora S. Cambridge, Mass. : MIT Press, 2000.
*TC BF723.S63 N49 2000*

**Making spaces :** citizenship and difference in schools / Tuula Gordon, Janet Holland, and Elina Lahelma. New York : St. Martin's Press, 2000. vii, 235 p. : ill. ; 22 cm. Includes bibliographical references and index. ISBN 0-312-22619-5 (cloth) DDC 306.43
*1. High school students - England - London - Social conditions - Cross-cultural studies. 2. High school students - Finland - Helsinki - Social conditions - Cross-cultural studies. 3. Education, Secondary - England - London - Cross-cultural studies. 4. Education, Secondary - Finland - Helsinki - Cross-cultural studies. 5. Sex differences in education - England - London - Cross-cultural studies. 6. Sex differences in education - Finland - Helsinki - Cross-cultural studies. I. Gordon, Tuula. II. Holland, Janet. III. Lahelma, Elina.*
*TC LC208.4 .M35 2000*

**Making technology masculine.**
Oldenziel, Ruth, 1958- Amsterdam : Amsterdam University Press, c1999.
*TC HD8072 .O57 1999*

**Making textile studies matter.**
Peterat, Linda, 1946- Vancouver : Pacific Educational Press, 1999.
*TC TX340 .P47 1999*

**Making the grade :** teacher's planning guide. New York : Macmillan/McGraw-Hill, c1997. 1 v. (various pagings) : col. ill. ; 31 cm. (Spotlight on literacy ; Gr.6 l.12 u.1) (The road to independent reading) Includes index. ISBN 0-02-183194-7
*1. Language arts (Elementary) 2. Reading (Elementary) I. Series. II. Series: The road to independent reading*
*TC LB1576 .S66 1997 Gr.6 l.12 u.1*

**Making the journey.**
Christenbury, Leila. 2nd ed. Portsmouth, NH : Boynton/Cook Publishers, c2000.
*TC LB1631 .C4486 2000*

**Making the most of early communication**
[videorecording] / California State University, Northridge ; project director, Deborah Chen ; project coordinator, Pam Schachter ; produced by Janice Reynolds ; director, Kim Schneider ; script by Deborah Chen, Pam Schachter, Jack Jones. New York, NY : Distributed by AFB Press, c1997. 1 videocassette (34 min.) : sd., col. ; 1/2 in. + 1 discussion guide (28 p. ; 22 cm.). VHS. Cataloged from credits and container and accompanying material. Closed captioned. Narrator: Leslie Lucciani. Edited by Kim Schneider ; camera, Dave Butterfeld ; audio, Ben Attridge. Cassette label in typeface and braille. For those who work with visually impaired, hearing impaired and multiply disabled children. SUMMARY: An instructive film for those working towards establishing communication with the visually impaired, the hearing impaired, and those with multiple handicaps-- for parents, teachers, administrators, counselors, special education students, etc. It features many partially deaf-blind children, their families and teachers. The points emphasized are: make the most of a child's available senses, use enjoyable games, repetition and routines, and provide systematic and direct instruction. ISBN 0-89128-296-3 (video) ISBN 0-89128-302-1 (guide)
*1. Vision disorders in children. 2. Hearing disorders in children. 3. Visually handicapped children - Education (Early childhood) 4. Visually handicapped children - Rehabilitation. 5. Visually handicapped children - Psychology. 6. Visually handicapped children - Language. 7. Hearing impaired children - Education (Early childhood) 8. Hearing impaired children - Rehabilitation. 9. Hearing impaired children - Psychology. 10. Hearing impaired children - Language. 11. Blind-deaf children - Means of communication. 12. Blind-deaf children - Education (Early childhood) 13. Blind-deaf children - Rehabilitation. 14. Blind-deaf children - Psychology. 15. Blind-deaf children - Language. 16. Children, Blind - Education (Early childhood) 17. Children, Blind - Rehabilitation. 18. Children, Blind - Psychology. 19. Children, Blind - Language. 20. Children, Deaf - Education (Early childhood) 21. Children, Deaf - Rehabilitation. 22. Children, Deaf - Psychology. 23. Children, Deaf - Language. 24. Handicapped children - Education (Early childhood) 25. Handicapped children - Rehabilitation. 26. Handicapped children - Psychology. 27. Handicapped children - Language. 28. Special education. 29. Special education - Parent participation. 30. Video recordings for the hearing impaired. I.*

*Lucciani. Leslie. II. Chen, Deborah. III. Schachter. Pam Brown, 1952- IV. Reynolds. Janice. V. Schneider, Kim. VI. Jones. Jack. VII. California State University, Northridge. VIII. AFB Press.*
*TC HV1597.2 .M3 1997*

**Making the right calls.**
Sweeney, Jim, 1937- Judgment. Larchmont, NY : Eye on Education, c1997.
*TC LB2806 .S88 1997*

**Making vocational choices.**
Holland, John L. 3rd ed. Odessa, Fla. : Psychological Assessment Resources, c1997.
*TC HF5381 .H5668 1997*

**Makosana, I. Nokuzola Zola.** Social factors in the positioning of black women in South African universities / by I. Nokuzola Zola Makosana. 1997. ix, 293 ; 29 cm. Typescript; issued also on microfilm. Thesis (Ed.D.)--Teachers College, Columbia University, 1997. Includes bibliographical references (leaves 274-293).
*1. Women, Black - Education (Higher) - South Africa - Case studies. 2. Women, Black - Education (Higher) - South Africa - History - 20th century. 3. Women college teachers, Black - South Africa - Case studies. 4. Women college teachers, Black - Employment - South Africa - Case studies. 5. Sex discrimination in higher education - South Africa. 6. Marginality, Social - South Africa - History. I. Title. II. Title: Black women in South African universities*
*TC 06 no. 10825*

**Makosky, Vivian Parker.**
Activities handbook for the teaching of psychology. Washington, D.C. : American Psychological Association, c1981-<c1999 >
*TC BF78 .A28*

**Makuna.**
Arhem, Kaj. Washington : Smithsonian Institution Press, c1998.
*TC F2270.2.M33 A68 1998*

**MAKUNA INDIANS.** *See* **MACUNA INDIANS.**

**MALADJUSTED CHILDREN.** *See* **PROBLEM CHILDREN.**

**MALADJUSTED YOUTH.** *See* **PROBLEM YOUTH.**

**MALADJUSTMENT (PSYCHOLOGY).** *See* **ADJUSTMENT (PSYCHOLOGY).**

**Malana, D.**
Critical technologies and competitiveness. Huntington, New York : Nova Science Publishers, c2000.
*TC HC110.T4 C74 2000*

**Malaro, Marie C.** Museum governance : mission, ethics, policy / Marie C. Malaro. Washington : Smithsonian Institution Press, c1994. viii, 183 p. ; 23 cm. Includes bibliographical references (p. 163-183). ISBN 1-56098-363-9 DDC 069.5
*1. Museums - Management. 2. Nonprofit organizations - Management. 3. Museums - Public relations. 4. Cultural property, Protection of. 5. Ethics. 6. Museum techniques. I. Title.*
*TC AM121 .M35 1994*

**Male and female.**
Mead, Margaret, 1901-1978. London : Victor Gollancz, c1949.
*TC HQ21 .M464 1949*

Mead, Margaret, 1901-1978. London : Victor Gollancz, c1949.
*TC HQ21 .M464 1949*

**Male and female in today's world.**
Tumin, Melvin Marvin, 1919- New York : Harcourt Brace Jovanovich, c1980.
*TC GN479.65 .T95 1980*

**MALE-FEMALE RELATIONSHIPS.** *See* **MAN-WOMAN RELATIONSHIPS.**

**Male/female roles :** opposing viewpoints / Laura K. Egendorf, book editor. San Diego, Calif. : Greenhaven Press, c2000. 186 p. : ill. ; 23 cm. (Opposing viewpoints series) Includes bibliographical references and index. ISBN 0-7377-0130-7 (pbk.: alk. paper) ISBN 0-7377-0131-5 (lib. : alk. paper) DDC 305.3
*1. Sex role. 2. Sex role - United States. I. Egendorf, Laura K., 1973- II. Series. III. Series: Opposing viewpoints series (Unnumbered)*
*TC HQ1075 .M353 2000*

**MALE GAYS.** *See* **GAY MEN.**

**MALE NUDE IN ART.**
Cooper, Emmanuel. Fully exposed. 2nd ed. London ; New York : Routledge, c1995.

*TC TR674 .C66 1995*

Solomon-Godeau, Abligail. Male trouble :. London : Thames and Hudson, c1997.
*TC N6847.5.N35 S64 1997*

**Male nude in photography.**
Cooper, Emmanuel. Fully exposed. 2nd ed. London ; New York : Routledge, c1995.
*TC TR674 .C66 1995*

**MALE PHOTOGRAPHY.** *See* **PHOTOGRAPHY OF MEN.**

**MALE RAPE VICTIMS - PSYCHOLOGY.**
d·a·t·e rape [videorecording]. [Charleston, WV] : Cambridge Educational, c1994.
*TC RC560.R36 D3 1994*

**MALE SEXUAL ABUSE VICTIMS.**
Gartner, Richard B. Betrayed as boys. New York : Guilford Press, c1999.
*TC RC569.5.A28 G37 1999*

**Male trouble.**
Solomon-Godeau, Abligail. London : Thames and Hudson, c1997.
*TC N6847.5.N35 S64 1997*

**Malen, Betty.**
Balancing local control and state responsibility for K-12 education. Larchmont, NY : Eye on Education, 2000.
*TC LC89 .B35 2000*

**MALIGNANT TUMORS.** *See* **CANCER.**

**Malik, Ahmed Nawaz.**
Rugh, Andrea B. Teaching practices to increase student achievement. Cambridge, Mass. : B.R.I.D.G.E.S. Basic Research and Implementation in Developing Education Systems, [1991].
*TC LB1025.2 .R83 1991*

**Malik, Jamal.** Colonization of Islam : dissolution of traditional insitutions in Pakistan / Jamal Malik. New Delhi : Manohar, 1996. xiv, 350 p. ; 23 cm. Includes bibliographical references and index. ISBN 81-7304-148-2
*1. Islam - Pakistan. 2. Islam - Social aspects - Pakistan. 3. Islam and politics - Pakistan. 4. Islamic law - Pakistan. I. Title.*
*TC BP173.25 .M34 1996*

**Malin, Nigel.**
Professionalism, boundaries, and the workplace. New York : Routledge, 2000.
*TC HV10.5 .P74 2000*

**MALINKE (AFRICAN PEOPLE).** *See* **MANDINGO (AFRICAN PEOPLE).**

**Mallat, Kathy.** Brave bear / Kathy Mallat. New York : Walker, 1999. 1 vol. (unpaged) : col. ill. ; 29 cm. SUMMARY: A bear bravely goes out on a limb to help a baby bird get back to its nest. ISBN 0-8027-8704-5 (hardcover) ISBN 0-8027-8705-3 (reinforced) DDC [E]
*1. Bears - Fiction. 2. Birds - Fiction. 3. Courage - Fiction. I. Title.*
*TC PZ7.M29455 Br 1999*

**MALLEABILITY (PSYCHOLOGY).** *See* **ADAPTABILITY (PSYCHOLOGY).**

**Mallery, Anne L.** Creating a catalyst for thinking : the integrated curriculum / Anne L. Mallery. Boston : Allyn and Bacon, c2000. xvii, 184 p. : ill. ; 29 cm. Includes bibliographical references and index. ISBN 0-205-28671-2 (alk. paper) DDC 375/.001
*1. Curriculum planning - United States. 2. Interdisciplinary approach in education - United States. 3. Student participation in curriculum planning - United States. I. Title.*
*TC LB2806.15 .M34 2000*

**MALLET INSTRUMENTS.** *See* **PERCUSSION INSTRUMENTS.**

**MALLET PERCUSSION.** *See* **PERCUSSION INSTRUMENTS.**

**MALLET PERCUSSIONS.** *See* **PERCUSSION INSTRUMENTS.**

**MALLETT, MARGARET.** Young researchers : informational reading and writing in the early and primary years / Margaret Mallett. London ; New York : Routledge, 1999. xv, 196 p. : ill. ; 24 cm. Includes bibliographical references (p. [187]-191) and indexes. ISBN 0-415-21657-5 (alk. paper) ISBN 0-415-17951-3 (pbk : alk. paper) DDC 372.6
*1. Reading (Elementary) - Great Britain. 2. Reading (Early childhood) - Great Britain. 3. English language - Composition and exercises - Study and teaching (Elementary) - Great Britain. 4. English language - Composition and exercises - Study and teaching (Early childhood) - Great Britain. I. Title.*
*TC LB1576 .M3627 1999*

**Mallinson, George G.** Silver Burdett science / George G. Mallinson ... [et al.] Morristown, N.J. : Silver Burdett, c1987. 6 v. : ill. ; 23 cm. Includes index. Each volume designed for a specific grade, from 1-6. "The Silver Burdette elementary science program"--verso T.p. ISBN 0-382-13435-4 (gr.1) ISBN 0-382-13436-2 (gr.2) ISBN 0-382-13437-0 (gr.3) ISBN 0-382-13438-9 (gr.4) ISBN 0-382-13439-7 (gr.5) ISBN 0-382-13440-0 (gr.6)
*1. Science. I. Silver Burdett Company.*
*TC Q161 .M34 1987*

Silver Burdett science [grade 6]. Centennial ed. Morristown, NJ : Silver Burdett, c1985.
*TC lb*

Silver Burdett science [grade 6]. Centennial ed. Morristown, NJ : Silver Burdett, c1985.
*TC lb*

**Malloy, Edward A.**
Colleges and universities as citizens. Boston : Allyn and Bacon, c1999.
*TC LC220.5 .C644 1999*

**MALNUTRITION.** *See* **NUTRITION.**

**MALNUTRITION - DEVELOPING COUNTRIES.**
Foster, Phillips, 1931- The world food problem. 2nd ed. Boulder : Lynne Rienner Publishers, 1999.
*TC HD9018.D44 F68 1999*

**Malone, David.**
Teen violence [videorecording]. Princeton, NJ : Films for the Humanities & Sciences, c1998.
*TC RJ506.V56 T44 1998*

**Maloney, Karen E.**
Women's philosophies of education. Upper Saddle River, N.J. : Merrill, c1999.
*TC LC1752 .T46 1999*

**Malouff, John M.**
Schutte, Nicola S. (Nicola Susanne) Measuring emotional intelligence and related constructs. Lewiston, N.Y. ; Lampeter, Wales : E. Mellen Press, c1999.
*TC BF576.3 .S38 1999*

**Malpa, Alfred P.**
Fenn, Patricia. Rewards of merit. [Schoharie, N.Y.] : Ephemera Society of America ; Charlottesville [Va.] : Distributed by Howell Press, Inc., c1994.
*TC LA230 .F46 1994*

**MALPRACTICE - LAW AND LEGISLATION.** *See* **MALPRACTICE.**

**MALPRACTICE - UNITED STATES - LEGISLATION.**
Nurse's legal handbook. 4th ed. Springhouse, Pa. : Springhouse Corp., c2000.
*TC RT86.7 .N88 2000*

**MALPRACTICE - UNITED STATES - NURSES' INSTRUCTION.**
Nurse's legal handbook. 4th ed. Springhouse, Pa. : Springhouse Corp., c2000.
*TC RT86.7 .N88 2000*

**MALTHUSIANISM.** *See* **POPULATION.**

**MALTREATED CHILDREN.** *See* **ABUSED CHILDREN.**

**MALTREATMENT OF CHILDREN.** *See* **CHILD ABUSE.**

**Mambo :** art irritates life. Sidney : Mambo Graphics, c1994. 118 p. : col. ill. ; 24 cm. Cover title. Includes bibliographical references. ISBN 0-646-18798-8
*1. Mambo Graphics (Surry Hills, N.S.W.) 2. Australian wit and humor, Pictorial. I. Mambo Graphics (Surry Hills, N.S.W.)*
*TC NC1761.M36 A4 1994*

**Mambo Graphics (Surry Hills, N.S.W.).**
Mambo. Sidney : Mambo Graphics, c1994.
*TC NC1761.M36 A4 1994*

**MAMBO GRAPHICS (SURRY HILLS, N.S.W.).**
Mambo. Sidney : Mambo Graphics, c1994.
*TC NC1761.M36 A4 1994*

**MAMMARY GLANDS.** *See* **BREAST.**

**Mammen, Jens.**
Essays in general psychology. Aarhus : Aarhus University Press, c1989.
*TC BF38 .E78 1989*

**MAN.** *See* **HUMAN BEINGS.**

**Man alive... aging and saging [videorecording].**
Aging and saging [videorecording]. Princeton, NJ : Films for the Humanities & Sciences : Distributed by Canadian Broadcasting Corporation, 1998.
*TC BF724.55.A35 A35 1998*

**Man alive (Television program).**
Aging and saging [videorecording]. Princeton, NJ : Films for the Humanities & Sciences : Distributed by Canadian Broadcasting Corporation, 1998.
*TC BF724.55.A35 A35 1998*

**MAN-ANIMAL RELATIONSHIPS.** *See* **HUMAN-ANIMAL RELATIONSHIPS.**

**Man (London, England : 1901 : Online).**
[Journal of the Royal Anthropological Institute of Great Britain and Ireland (Online)] The journal of the Royal Anthropological Institute of Great Britain and Ireland [computer file]. London [England] : The Institute, 1907-1965.
*TC EJOURNALS*

**MAN-MACHINE CONTROL SYSTEMS.** *See* **HUMAN-MACHINE SYSTEMS.**

**MAN-MACHINE SYSTEMS.** *See* **HUMAN-MACHINE SYSTEMS.**

**Man of the family.**
Karr, Kathleen. 1st ed. New York : Farrar, Straus and Giroux, 1999.
*TC PZ7.K149 Man 1999*

**MAN, PREHISTORIC.** *See* **PREHISTORIC PEOPLES.**

**MAN-WOMAN RELATIONSHIPS.**
Dryden, Caroline. Being married, doing gender. London ; New York : Routledge, 1999.
*TC HQ734 .D848 1999*

Langford, Wendy, 1960- Revolutions of the heart. London ; New York : Routledge, 1999.
*TC BF575.L8 L266 1999*

**MAN-WOMAN RELATIONSHIPS - CÔTE D'IVOIRE.**
Ravenhill, Philip L. Dreams and reverie. Washington : Smithsonian Institution Press, c1996.
*TC NB1255.C85 R38 1996*

**MANAGED BEHAVIORAL HEALTH CARE.** *See* **MANAGED MENTAL HEALTH CARE.**

**Managed care and the inner city.**
Andrulis, Dennis P. San Francisco : Jossey-Bass, 1999.
*TC RA413.5.U5 A57 1999*

**Managed care in the inner city.**
Andrulis, Dennis P. Managed care and the inner city. San Francisco : Jossey-Bass, 1999.
*TC RA413.5.U5 A57 1999*

**MANAGED CARE PLANS (MEDICAL CARE).** *See also* **MANAGED MENTAL HEALTH CARE.**
Couples therapy in managed care. New York : Haworth Press, c1999.
*TC RC488.5 .C64385 1999*

**MANAGED CARE PLANS (MEDICAL CARE) - UNITED STATES.**
Andrulis, Dennis P. Managed care and the inner city. San Francisco : Jossey-Bass, 1999.
*TC RA413.5.U5 A57 1999*

**MANAGED CARE PROGRAMS (MEDICAL CARE).** *See* **MANAGED CARE PLANS (MEDICAL CARE).**

**MANAGED CARE PROGRAMS - UNITED STATES.**
Andrulis, Dennis P. Managed care and the inner city. San Francisco : Jossey-Bass, 1999.
*TC RA413.5.U5 A57 1999*

**MANAGED CARE SYSTEMS (MEDICAL CARE).** *See* **MANAGED CARE PLANS (MEDICAL CARE).**

**MANAGED HEALTH CARE.** *See* **MANAGED CARE PLANS (MEDICAL CARE).**

**MANAGED MENTAL HEALTH CARE.**
Johnson, Lynn D. Psychotherapy in the age of accountability. 1st ed. New York : W.W. Norton & Co., c1995.
*TC RC480.55 .J64 1995*

**MANAGED MENTAL HEALTH CARE - UNITED STATES.**
Cummings, Nicholas A. The value of psychological treatment. Phoenix, AZ : Zeig, Tucker & Co., 1999.
*TC RA790.6 .C85 1999*

**MANAGED MENTAL HEALTH SERVICES.** *See* **MANAGED MENTAL HEALTH CARE.**

**Managed professionals.**
Rhoades, Gary. Albany : State University of New York Press, c1998.

*TC LB2331.72 .R56 1998*

**MANAGEMENT.** *See also* **CONFLICT MANAGEMENT; EMERGENCY MANAGEMENT; EXECUTIVES; INDUSTRIAL MANAGEMENT; INDUSTRIAL RELATIONS; INFORMATION RESOURCES MANAGEMENT; ORGANIZATION; ORGANIZATIONAL BEHAVIOR; ORGANIZATIONAL CHANGE; ORGANIZATIONAL EFFECTIVENESS; PERSONNEL MANAGEMENT; SCHOOL MANAGEMENT AND ORGANIZATION; TIME MANAGEMENT; TOTAL QUALITY MANAGEMENT.**
Kepner, Charles Higgins, 1922- The new rational manager. Princeton, N.J. (P.O. Box 704, Research Rd., Princeton 08540) : Princeton Research Press, c1981.
*TC HD31 .K456 1981*

Laurie, Donald L. The real work of leaders. Cambridge, Mass. : Perseus Pub., 2000.
*TC HD57.7 .L387 2000*

Leading beyond the walls. 1st ed. San Francisco : Jossey-Bass, c1999.
*TC HD57.7 .L4374 1999*

Misumi, Jūji, 1924- Rīdạshippu kōdō no kagaku =
*TC HM141 .M48 1978*

O'Toole, James. Leadership A to Z. 1st ed. San Francisco, CA : Jossey-Bass Publishers, c1999.
*TC HD57.7 .O87 1999*

Viney, John. Drive. 1st U.S. ed. New York, N.Y. : Bloomsbury, 1999.
*TC HD57.7 .V564 1999*

**Management and administration skills for the mental health professional** / edited by William O'Donohue, Jane E. Fisher. San Diego, Calif. London : Academic, c1999. xv, 357 p. : ill. ; 23 cm. (Practical resources for the mental health professional.) Includes bibliographical references and indexes. ISBN 0-12-524195-X
*1. Mental health services - Management. I. O'Donohue, William. II. Fisher, Jane E. (Jane Ellen) 1957- III. Series.*
*TC RA790 .M325 1999*

**Management and leadership in education series (Cassell Ltd.)**
Thody, Angela. Leadership of schools. London ; Herndon, Va. : Cassell, 1997.
*TC LB2831.726.G7 T56 1997*

**Management challenges for the 21st century.**
Drucker, Peter Ferdinand, 1909- 1st ed. New York : HarperBusiness, c1999.
*TC HD30.27 .D78 1999*

**Management challenges for the twenty-first century.**
Drucker, Peter Ferdinand, 1909- Management challenges for the 21st century. 1st ed. New York : HarperBusiness, c1999.
*TC HD30.27 .D78 1999*

**MANAGEMENT DEVELOPMENT.** *See* **EXECUTIVES - TRAINING OF.**

**Management education and development.**
Management learning. London ; Thousand Oaks, CA : Sage Publications, c1994-

**MANAGEMENT - EMPLOYEE PARTICIPATION.**
Ostroff, Frank. The horizontal organization. New York : Oxford University Press, 1999.
*TC HD66 .O68 1999*

**MANAGEMENT - EVALUATION.**
Boulmetis, John. The ABCs of evaluation. 1st ed. San Francisco, Calif. : Jossey-Bass, c2000.
*TC HD31 .B633 2000*

**Management fads in higher education.**
Birnbaum, Robert. San Francisco : Jossey-Bass, 2000.
*TC LB2341 .B49 2000*

**MANAGEMENT - FORECASTING.**
Drucker, Peter Ferdinand, 1909- Management challenges for the 21st century. 1st ed. New York : HarperBusiness, c1999.
*TC HD30.27 .D78 1999*

**MANAGEMENT, INDUSTRIAL.** *See* **INDUSTRIAL MANAGEMENT.**

**MANAGEMENT INFORMATION SYSTEMS.** *See also* **INFORMATION RESOURCES MANAGEMENT.**
Walton, Richard E. Up and running. Boston, Mass. : Harvard Business School Press, c1989.
*TC T58.6 .W345 1989*

**MANAGEMENT - JAPAN.**
Misumi, Jūji, 1924- Rīdashippu kōdō no kagaku =
*TC HM141 .M48 1978*

**Management learning.** London ; Thousand Oaks, CA : Sage Publications, c1994- v. : ill. ; 25 cm. Frequency: Quarterly. Vol. 25, no. 1- . Title from cover. SUMMARY: "The international journal for managerial and organizational learning and development." Also available via World Wide Web; OCLC FirstSearch Electronic Collections Online; Subscription required for access to abstracts and full text. URL: http://firstsearch.oclc.org URL: http:// firstsearch.oclc.org/journal=1350-5076;screen=info;ECOIP Available in other form: Management learning (Online) (OCoLC)41552077. Continues: Management education and development ISSN: 0047-5688 (DLC)  73646438 (OCoLC)1788812. ISSN 1350-5076 DDC 658.4/007/1042
*1. Industrial management - Study and teaching - Periodicals. 2. Business education - Periodicals. 3. Executives - Training of - Periodicals. I. Title: Management learning (Online) II. Title: Management education and development*

**Management learning (Online).**
Management learning. London ; Thousand Oaks, CA : Sage Publications, c1994-

**MANAGEMENT - MORAL AND ETHICAL ASPECTS.**
Managerial ethics. Mahwah, N.J. : Lawrence Erlbaum Assocs., 1998.
*TC HF5387 .M3345 1998*

**MANAGEMENT OF CONFLICT.** *See* **CONFLICT MANAGEMENT.**

**The management of eating disorders and obesity /** edited by David J. Goldstein ; foreword by Albert J. Stunkard. Totowa, N.J. : Humana Press, c1999. xvi, 367 p. : ill. ; 26 cm. (Nutrition and health) Includes bibliographical references and index. ISBN 0-89603-407-0 (alk. paper) DDC 616.85/2606
*1. Eating disorders - Prevention. 2. Obesity - Prevention. 3. Anorexia nervosa. 4. Bulimia. 5. Eating Disorders - therapy. 6. Obesity - therapy. I. Goldstein, David J. (David Joel), 1947- II. Series: Nutrition and health (Totowa, N.J.)*
*TC RC552.E18 M364 1999*

**Management of failing Diploma in Social Work students.**
Sharp, Mavis, 1945- The management of failing DipSW students. Aldershot ; Brookfield, Vt. : Ashgate, c1999.
*TC HV11.8.G7 S53 1999*

**The management of failing DipSW students.**
Sharp, Mavis, 1945- Aldershot ; Brookfield, Vt. : Ashgate, c1999.
*TC HV11.8.G7 S53 1999*

**Management of library security :** a SPEC kit / compiled by George J. Soete, with the assistance of Glen Zimmerman. Washington, DC : Systems and Procedures Exchange Center, Office of Leadership and Management Services, Association of Research Libraries, c1999. 101 p. : ill. ; 28 cm. (SPEC kit, 0160-3582 ; 247) (SPEC flyer, 0160-3574 ; 247) "July 1999." Includes SPEC flyer, 247. Includes bibliographical references (p. 101).
*1. Libraries - Security measures. I. Soete, George J. II. Zimmerman, Glen. III. Title. IV. Series. V. Series: SPEC flyer, 0160-3574 ; 247*
*TC Z679.6 .M26 1999*

**MANAGEMENT OF SELF.** *See* **SELF-MANAGEMENT (PSYCHOLOGY).**

**Management practice in dietetics.**
Hudson, Nancy R. Australia ; Belmont, Calif. : Wadsworth, c2000.
*TC TX911.3.M27 H83 2000*

**Management research.**
The Bi-monthly review of management research. [Dolton, Ill. : A. Thomas Beales 1972-1974].

**Management research(Amherst, Mass.).**
The Bi-monthly review of management research. [Dolton, Ill. : A. Thomas Beales 1972-1974].

**Management research (Dolton, Ill. : 1971).**
The Bi-monthly review of management research. [Dolton, Ill. : A. Thomas Beales 1972-1974].

**MANAGEMENT, SELF (PSYCHOLOGY).** *See* **SELF-MANAGEMENT (PSYCHOLOGY).**

**MANAGEMENT, STRESS.** *See* **STRESS MANAGEMENT.**

**MANAGEMENT TEAMS IN SCHOOLS.** *See* **SCHOOL MANAGEMENT TEAMS.**

**MANAGEMENT TRAINING.** *See* **EXECUTIVES - TRAINING OF.**

**Managerial ethics :** moral management of people and processes / edited by Marshall Schminke. Mahwah, N.J. : Lawrence Erlbaum Assocs., 1998. x, 233 p. : ill. ; 23 cm. Includes bibliographical references and indexes. ISBN 0-8058-2492-8 (pbk. : alk. paper) DDC 174/.4
*1. Management - Moral and ethical aspects. 2. Business ethics. I. Schminke, Marshall.*
*TC HF5387 .M3345 1998*

**Managerialism and nursing.**
Traynor, Michael, 1956- London ; New York : Routledge, 1999.
*TC RT86.45 .T73 1999*

**MANAGERS.** *See* **EXECUTIVES.**

**MANAGERS - PSYCHOLOGY.**
Bazigos, Michael Nicholas. The relationship of upward feedback disparities to leader performance. 1999.
*TC 085 B33*

**Managing academic affairs.**
Dimensions of managing academic affairs in the community college. San Francisco : Jossey-Bass, 2000.
*TC LB2341 .D56 2000*

**Managing change.**
Anstey, Mark. 2nd ed. Kenwyn : Juta, 1999.
*TC HD42 .A57 1999*

**Managing chronic illness in the classroom.**
Wishnietsky, Dorothy Botsch. Bloomington, Ind. : Phi Delta Kappa Educational Foundation, c1996.
*TC LC4561 .W57 1996*

**Managing colleges and universities**
Gledhill, John M., 1948- Managing students. Buckingham ; Philadelphia : Open University Press, 1999.
*TC LB2341.8.G7 G54 1996*

Humfrey, Christine, 1947- Managing international students. Philadelphia, Penn : Society for Research into Higher Education & Open University Press, 1999.
*TC LB2376.6.G7 H86 1999*

**Managing colleges and universities :** issues for leadership / edited by Allan M. Hoffman, Randal W. Summers ; foreword by Dean L.  Hubbard. Westport, Conn. : Bergin & Garvey, 2000. xii, 221 p. : ill. ; 25 cm. Includes bibliographical references and index. ISBN 0-89789-645-9 (alk. paper) DDC 378.73
*1. Universities and colleges - United States - Administration. 2. Educational leadership - United States. I. Hoffman, Allan M. (Allan Michael) II. Summers, Randal W., 1946-*
*TC LB2341 .M2779 2000*

**Managing colleges effectively series**
(4) Ruddiman, Ken. Strategic management of college premises. London : Falmer, 1999.
*TC LB3223.5.G7 R84 1999*

**MANAGING CONFLICT.** *See* **CONFLICT MANAGEMENT.**

**Managing difficult, frustrating, and hostile conversations.**
Kosmoski, Georgia J. Thousand Oaks, Calif. : Sage Publications, c2000.
*TC LB3011.5 .K67 2000*

**Managing equal opportunities in higher education.**
Woodward, Diana, 1948- Buckingham [England] ; Philadelphia : Society for Research into Higher Education : Open University Press, 2000.
*TC LC213.3.G7 W66 2000*

**Managing evaluation and innovation in language teaching :** building bridges / edited by Pauline Rea-Dickins and Kevin P. Germaine. New York : Longman, 1998. xxi, 294 p. ; 21 cm. (Applied linguistics and language study) Includes bibliographical references (p.269-290) and index. ISBN 0-582-30373-7 (pbk.) DDC 407
*1. Language and languages - Study and teaching - Evaluation. 2. Educational innovations. I. Rea-Dickins, Pauline. II. Germaine, Kevin P., 1953- III. Series.*
*TC P53.63 .M36 1998*

**Managing higher education as a business.**
Lenington, Robert L. Phoenix, Ariz. : Oryx Press, 1996.
*TC LB2341 .L426 1996*

**Managing international students.**
Humfrey, Christine, 1947- Philadelphia, Penn : Society for Research into Higher Education & Open University Press, 1999.
*TC LB2376.6.G7 H86 1999*

**Managing patient expectations.**
Baker, Susan Keane. San Francisco : Jossey Bass Publishers, 1998.

*TC R727.3 .B28 1998*

**Managing professional development in schools.**
Blandford, Sonia. London ; New York : Routledge, 2000.
*TC LB1731 .B57 2000*

**Managing quality fads.**
Cole, Robert E. New York : Oxford University Press, 1999.
*TC HD66 .C539 1999*

**Managing quality in young children's programs :** the leader's role / Mary L. Culkin, editor ; foreword by Sharon Lynn Kagan. New York : Teachers College Press, c2000. xi, 243 p. : ill. ; 23 cm. (Early childhood education series) Includes bibliographical references and index. ISBN 0-8077-3916-2 (pbk. : alk. paper) DDC 372.12
*1. Early childhood education - United States - Administration. 2. Educational leadership - United States. I. Culkin, Mary L. II. Series: Early childhood education series (Teachers College Press)*
*TC LB2822.6 .M36 2000*

**Managing strategy.**
Watson, David, 1949- Buckingham [England] ; Philadelphia : Open University Press, 2000.
*TC LB2341.8.G7 W28 2000*

**Managing stress.**
Edworthy, Ann, 1952- Buckingham [England] ; Philadelphia : Open University Press, 2000.
*TC LB2333.3 .E39 2000*

**Managing students.**
Gledhill, John M., 1948- Buckingham ; Philadelphia : Open University Press, 1999.
*TC LB2341.8.G7 G54 1996*

**Managing technology in the early childhood classroom.**
Campbell, Hope. Westminster, CA : Teacher Created Materials, c1999.
*TC LB1139.35.C64 C36 1999*

**Managing technology in the middle school classroom.**
Gardner, Paul (Paul Henry) Huntington Beach, CA : Teacher Created Materials, c1996.
*TC LB1028.5 .C353 1996*

**Managing the academic unit.**
Bolton, Allan. Buckingham [England] ; Philadelphia : Open University Press, c2000.
*TC LB2341 .B583 2000*

**Managing the defiant child : a guide to parent training [videorecording].**
Understanding the defiant child [videorecording]. New York : Guilford Publications, c1997.
*TC HQ755.7 .U63 1997*

**Managing the dream :** reflections on leadership and change / Warren Bennis ; foreword by Tom Peters. Cambridge, Mass. : Perseus Pub., c2000. xxviii, 317 p. : ill. ; 21 cm. Includes index. ISBN 0-7382-0332-7
*1. Leadership.*
*TC HD67.7.B4643 2000*

**Managing the licensing of electronic products :** a SPEC kit / compiled by George J. Soete, with the assistance of Trisha Davis. Washington, DC : Systems and Procedures Exchange Center, Office of Leadership and Management Service, Association of Research Libraries, c1999. 68 p. ; 28 cm. (SPEC flyer ; 248) (Spec kit, 0160-3582 ; 248) Includes bibliographical references (65-68).
*1. Merchandise licensing - United States. 2. Electronic publications - Licenses - United States. I. Soete, George J. II. Davis, Trisha. III. Association of Research Libraries. Office of Leadership and Management Services. IV. Series. V. Series: Spec flyer ; no. 248.*

**Managing the licensing of electronic products :** a SPEC kit / compiled by George J. Soete, with the assistance of Trisha Davis. Washington, DC : Systems and Procedures Exchange Center, Office of Leadership and Management Service, Association of Research Libraries, c1999. 68 p. ; 28 cm. (SPEC flyer ; 248) (Spec kit, 0160-3582 ; 248) Includes bibliographical references (65-68).
*1. Merchandise licensing - United States. 2. Electronic publications - Licenses - United States. I. Soete, George J. II. Davis, Trisha. III. Association of Research Libraries. Office of Leadership and Management Services. IV. Series. V. Series: Spec flyer ; no. 248.*

**Managing the licensing of electronic products :** a SPEC kit / compiled by George J. Soete, witht he assistance of Trisha Davis. Washington, DC : Systems and Procedures Exchange Center, Office of Leadership and Management Service, Association of Research Libraries, c1999. 68 p. ; 28 cm. (SPEC kit, 0160-3582 ; 248) (SPEC flyer, 0160-3574; 248) "August

1999." Includes SPEC flyer, 248. Includes bibliographic references (65-68).
*1. Merchandise licensing - United States. 2. Electronic publications - Licenses - United States. I. Soete, George J. II. Davis, Trisha. III. Association of Research Libraries. Office of Leadership and Management Services. IV. Series. V. Series: SPEC flyer, 0160-3574; 248*
*TC HF5429.255 .M26 1999*

**Managing universities and colleges**
Bolton, Allan. Managing the academic unit. Buckingham [England] ; Philadelphia : Open University Press, c2000.
*TC LB2341 .B583 2000*

Edworthy, Ann, 1952- Managing stress. Buckingham [England] ; Philadelphia : Open University Press, 2000.
*TC LB2333.3 .E39 2000*

Watson, David, 1949- Managing strategy. Buckingham [England] ; Philadelphia : Open University Press, 2000.
*TC LB2341.8.G7 W28 2000*

**Managing unmanageable students.**
McEwan, Elaine K., 1941- Thousand Oaks, Calif. : Corwin Press, c2000.
*TC LC4801.5 .M39 2000*

**Managing your academic career.**
Sadler, D. Royce (David Royce) St Leonards, N.S.W., Australia : Allen & Unwin, 1999.
*TC LB1778 .S23 1999*

**MANCHESTER (ENGLAND) - POLITICS AND GOVERNMENT.**
Hewitt, Martin. The emergence of stability in the industrial city. Aldershot, England : Scolar Press ; Brookfield, Vt., USA : Ashgate Pub. Co., c1996.
*TC HN398.M27 H48 1996*

**MANCHESTER (ENGLAND) - SOCIAL CONDITIONS.**
Hewitt, Martin. The emergence of stability in the industrial city. Aldershot, England : Scolar Press ; Brookfield, Vt., USA : Ashgate Pub. Co., c1996.
*TC HN398.M27 H48 1996*

**MANCHESTER (GREATER MANCHESTER).** See MANCHESTER (ENGLAND).

**MANCHESTER REGION (IOWA) - BIOGRAPHY - JUVENILE LITERATURE.**
Gillespie, Sarah (Sarah L.) A pioneer farm girl. Mankato, Minn. : Blue Earth Books, c2000.
*TC F629.M28 G55 2000*

**MANCHESTER REGION (IOWA) - SOCIAL LIFE AND CUSTOMS - JUVENILE LITERATURE.**
Gillespie, Sarah (Sarah L.) A pioneer farm girl. Mankato, Minn. : Blue Earth Books, c2000.
*TC F629.M28 G55 2000*

**MANDÉ (AFRICAN PEOPLE).** See MANDINGO (AFRICAN PEOPLE).

**Mande potters & leatherworkers.**
Frank, Barbara E. Washington, D.C. : Smithsonian Institution Press, 1998.
*TC DT474.6.M36 F73 1998*

**Mande potters and leatherworkers.**
Frank, Barbara E. Mande potters & leatherworkers. Washington, D.C. : Smithsonian Institution Press, 1998.
*TC DT474.6.M36 F73 1998*

**MANDING (AFRICAN PEOPLE).** See MANDINGO (AFRICAN PEOPLE).

**MANDINGO (AFRICAN PEOPLE) - INDUSTRIES.**
Frank, Barbara E. Mande potters & leatherworkers. Washington, D.C. : Smithsonian Institution Press, 1998.
*TC DT474.6.M36 F73 1998*

**MANDINGUE (AFRICAN PEOPLE).** See MANDINGO (AFRICAN PEOPLE).

**MANDINKA (AFRICAN PEOPLE).** See MANDINGO (AFRICAN PEOPLE).

**MANDINO (AFRICAN PEOPLE).** See MANDINGO (AFRICAN PEOPLE).

**Mandle, Joan D.** Can we wear our pearls and still be feminists? : memoirs of a campus struggle / Joan D. Mandle. Columbia : University of Missouri Press, c2000. x, 210 p. ; 23 cm. Includes bibliographical references. ISBN 0-8262-1289-1 (alk. paper) DDC 305.42/07
*1. Women's studies - New York (State) 2. Colgate University. I. Title.*
*TC HQ1181.U5 M37 2000*

**Manegold, Catherine S.** In glory's shadow : Shannon Faulkner, the Citadel, and a changing America / Catherine S. Manegold. 1st ed. New York : Alfred A. Knopf, 1999. x, 330 p., [16] p. of plates : ill. ; 24 cm. Includes index. ISBN 0-679-44635-4 (alk. paper) DDC 344.73/0798
*1. Citadel, the Military College of South Carolina - Trials, litigation, etc. 2. Faulkner, Shannon - Trials, litigation, etc. 3. Sex discrimination in higher education - Law and legislation - United States. 4. Sex discrimination against women - Law and legislation - United States. 5. Sex discrimination in higher education - South Carolina - Charleston. I. Title.*
*TC KF228.C53 M36 1999*

**MANHATTAN NEW SCHOOL (NEW YORK, N.Y.).**
Harwayne, Shelley. Going public. Portsmouth, NH : Heinemann, c1999.
*TC LB2822.5 .H37 1999*

Harwayne, Shelley. Lifetime guarantees. Portsmouth, NH : Heinemann, c2000.
*TC LB1575 . H38 2000*

**MANHATTAN PROJECT (U.S.) - HISTORY.**
Howes, Ruth (Ruth Hege) Their day in the sun. Philadelphia, PA : Temple University Press, 1999.
*TC QC773.3.U5 H68 1999*

**Manheimer's cataloging and classification.**
Saye, Jerry D. 4th ed., rev. and expanded. New York : Marcel Dekker, c2000.
*TC Z693 .S28 2000*

**MANIA.** See HYPOMANIA; MANIC-DEPRESSIVE ILLNESS.

**MANIA - DIAGNOSIS.**
Mood disorders [videorecording]. Princeton, N.J. : Films for the Humanities & Sciences, 1998.
*TC RC537 .M6 1998*

**MANIA - PATIENTS.**
Mood disorders [videorecording]. Princeton, N.J. : Films for the Humanities & Sciences, 1998.
*TC RC537 .M6 1998*

**Maniac Magee by Jerry Spinelli.**
Beech, Linda Ward. New York : Scholastic, c1997.
*TC LB1573 .B4311 1997*

**MANIC DEPRESSION.** See MANIC-DEPRESSIVE ILLNESS.

**MANIC-DEPRESSION.**
First break [videorecording]. Boston, MA : Fanlight Productions, c1997.
*TC RC465 .F5 1997*

First break [videorecording]. Boston, MA : Fanlight Productions, c1997.
*TC RC465 .F5 1997*

**MANIC-DEPRESSIVE ILLNESS.** *See also* DEPRESSION, MENTAL; MANIA.
Depression and manic depression [videorecording]. Boston, MA : Fanlight Productions, c1996.
*TC RC537 .D46 1996*

When the brain goes wrong [videorecording]. Short version. Boston, MA : Fanlight Productions [dist.], c1992.
*TC RC386 .W54 1992*

**MANIC-DEPRESSIVE ILLNESS - DIAGNOSIS.**
Mood disorders [videorecording]. Princeton, N.J. : Films for the Humanities & Sciences, 1998.
*TC RC537 .M6 1998*

**MANIC-DEPRESSIVE ILLNESS - PATIENTS.** See MANIC-DEPRESSIVE PERSONS.

**MANIC-DEPRESSIVE PERSONS.**
Mood disorders [videorecording]. Princeton, N.J. : Films for the Humanities & Sciences, 1998.
*TC RC537 .M6 1998*

**MANIC-DEPRESSIVE PERSONS - CASE STUDIES.**
First break [videorecording]. Boston, MA : Fanlight Productions, c1997.
*TC RC465 .F5 1997*

First break [videorecording]. Boston, MA : Fanlight Productions, c1997.
*TC RC465 .F5 1997*

**MANIC-DEPRESSIVE PERSONS - FAMILY RELATIONSHIPS.**
First break [videorecording]. Boston, MA : Fanlight Productions, c1997.
*TC RC465 .F5 1997*

First break [videorecording]. Boston, MA : Fanlight Productions, c1997.

*TC RC465 .F5 1997*

**MANIC-DEPRESSIVE PERSONS - INTERVIEWS.**
First break [videorecording]. Boston, MA : Fanlight Productions, c1997.
*TC RC465 .F5 1997*

First break [videorecording]. Boston, MA : Fanlight Productions, c1997.
*TC RC465 .F5 1997*

**MANIC-DEPRESSIVE PSYCHOSES.** See MANIC-DEPRESSIVE ILLNESS.

**MANIC-DEPRESSIVE PSYCHOSIS.** See MANIC-DEPRESSIVE ILLNESS.

**MANIC-DEPRESSIVES.** See MANIC-DEPRESSIVE PERSONS.

**MANIC DISORDER.** See MANIA.

**MANIC STATE.** See MANIA.

**Manifest rationality.**
Johnson, Ralph H. Mahwah, N.J. ; London : Lawrence Erlbaum Associates, 2000.
*TC BC177 .J54 2000*

**MANINKAALU (AFRICAN PEOPLE).** See MANDINGO (AFRICAN PEOPLE).

**MANIPULATIVE BEHAVIOR.**
Gass, Robert H. Persuasion, social influence, and compliance gaining. Boston : Allyn and Bacon, c1999.
*TC BF637.P4 G34 1999*

**MANIPULATIVE BOOKS.** See TOY AND MOVABLE BOOKS.

**MANIPULATORS (MECHANISM).** See ROBOTS.

**MANKIND.** *See* HUMAN BEINGS.

**Manley, Geoffrey A.**
Auditory worlds. Weinheim [Germany] : Wiley-VCH, c2000.
*TC QP461 .A93 2000*

**MANNERS AND CUSTOMS.** *See also* CLOTHING AND DRESS; COSTUME; COUNTRY LIFE; DRINKING CUSTOMS; FADS; FESTIVALS; FOLKLORE; FOOD HABITS; FRONTIER AND PIONEER LIFE; GIFTS; HALLOWEEN; HOLIDAYS; LIFESTYLES; RECREATION; RITES AND CEREMONIES; SEAFARING LIFE; SEX CUSTOMS.
Barer-Stein, Thelma. You eat what you are. 2nd ed. Toronto : Firefly Books, 1999.
*TC GT2850 .B37 1999*

**Manning, Kathleen, 1954-** Ritual, ceremonies, and cultural meaning in higher education / Kathleen Manning. Westport, Conn. : Bergin & Garvey, 2000. x, 169 p. ; 24 cm. (Critical studies in education and culture series, 1064-8615) Includes bibliographical references (p. [153]-159) and index. ISBN 0-89789-504-5 (alk. paper) DDC 306.43
*1. Education, Higher - Social aspects - United States. 2. Educational anthropology - United States. I. Title. II. Series.*
*TC LC191.9 .M26 2000*

**Manning, M. Lee.** Multicultural education of children and adolescents / M. Lee Manning, Leroy G. Baruth. 3rd ed. Boston : Allyn and Bacon, c2000. xviii, 382 p. : ill. ; 24 cm. Includes bibliographical references (p. 358-369) and indexes. ISBN 0-205-29760-9 DDC 370.117
*1. Multicultural education - United States. 2. Indians of North America - Education. 3. Afro-American children - Education. 4. Asian American children - Education. 5. Hispanic American children - Education. I. Baruth, Leroy G. II. Title.*
*TC LC1099.3 .M36 2000*

**Manno, Bruno V.**
Finn, Chester E., 1944- Charter schools in action. Princeton, N.J. : Princeton University Press, c2000.
*TC LB2806.36 .F527 2000*

**Mannoia, V. James.** Christian liberal arts : an education that goes beyond / V. James Mannoia, Jr. Lanham, Md. : Rowman & Littlefield, c2000. xi, 241 p. ; 23 cm. Includes bibliographical references (p. 227-229) and index. ISBN 0-8476-9958-7 (alk. paper) ISBN 0-8476-9959-5 (pbk. : alk. paper) DDC 371.07
*1. Church colleges - United States. 2. Education, Humanistic - United States. I. Title.*
*TC LC427 .M26 2000*

**MANPOWER.** See LABOR; LABOR SUPPLY.

**MANPOWER DEVELOPMENT AND TRAINING.** *See* OCCUPATIONAL TRAINING.

**MANPOWER PLANNING.** *See* ORGANIZATIONAL CHANGE.

**MANPOWER POLICY.** *See also* **LABOR SUPPLY; UNEMPLOYMENT.**
Gilley, Jerry W. Organizational learning, performance, and change. Cambridge, Mass. : Perseus, c2000.
*TC HF5549.5.M3 G555 2000*

**MANPOWER POLICY - UNITED STATES - HISTORY - 20TH CENTURY - ADDRESSES, ESSAYS, LECTURES.**
Employing the unemployed. New York : Basic Books, inc., c1980.
*TC HD5724 .E43 1980*

**MANPOWER TRAINING PROGRAMS.** *See* **OCCUPATIONAL TRAINING.**

**MANPOWER UTILIZATION.** *See* **MANPOWER POLICY; PERSONNEL MANAGEMENT.**

**Mansfield, Janet.** Contemporary ceramic art in Australia and New Zealand / Janet Mansfield. Roseville East, NSW : Craftsman House, 1995. 168 p. : col. ill. ; 32 cm. Includes bibliographical references (p. 168) and index. ISBN 976-8097-32-9 DDC 730/.0994/09045
*1. Pottery, Australian. 2. Pottery - 20th century - Australia. 3. Pottery, New Zealand. 4. Pottery - 20th century - New Zealand. I. Title.*
*TC NK4179 .M36 1995*

**MANSLAUGHTER.** *See* **HOMICIDE; MURDER.**

**Manson, Dave.**
Seurat [videorecording]. West Long Branch, NJ : Kultur, c1999.
*TC ND553.S5 S5 1999*

**Manson, Janet M.**
Women in the milieu of Leonard and Virginia Woolf. New York : Pace University Press, 1998.
*TC PR6045.O72 Z925 1998*

**Manson, Tony.**
Preparation, collaboration, and emphasis on the family in school counseling for the new millennium. Lewiston : E. Mellen Press, c2000.
*TC LB1027.5 .P6525 2000*

**Manton, Catherine, 1942-** Fed up : women and food in America / Catherine Manton. Westport, Conn. : Bergin & Garvey, 1999. xiv, 170 p. ; 24 cm. Includes bibliographical references (p. [159]-164) and index. ISBN 0-89789-629-7 (pbk. : alk. paper) ISBN 0-89789-448-0 (alk. paper) DDC 305.4/0973
*1. Women - United States - Social conditions. 2. Women - United States - Psychology. 3. Food - Social aspects - United States. 4. Food habits - United States. I. Title.*
*TC HQ1410 .M355 1999*

**A manual of European languages for librarians.**
Allen, C. G. (Charles Geoffry) 2nd ed. New Providence, NJ : Bowker-Saur, c1999.
*TC P380 .A4 1999*

**MANUAL TRAINING.** *See* **DESIGN; DRAWING; HANDICRAFT.**

**Manual training and vocational eduation Sept. 1914-June 1916.**
Industrial education magazine. Chicago, Ill. : The University of Chicago Press, 1899-1939.

**Manual training magazine Oct. 1899-June 1914, Sept. 1916-June 1922.**
Industrial education magazine. Chicago, Ill. : The University of Chicago Press, 1899-1939.

**MANUAL TRAINING - PERIODICALS.**
Industrial arts magazine. Milwaukee [etc.] Bruce Publishing Co.

Industrial education. Greenwich, Conn., Macmillan Professional Magazines.

Industrial education magazine. Chicago, Ill. : The University of Chicago Press, 1899-1939.

**Manuel, Denis.**
Monsieur René Magritte [videorecording]. [Chicago, Ill.] : Home Vision [distributor], c1978.
*TC ND673.M35 M6 1978*

**MANUFACTURING INDUSTRIES.** *See* **BOOK INDUSTRIES AND TRADE; TEXTILE INDUSTRY.**

**MANUSCRIPTS.** *See* **ARCHIVAL MATERIALS; SCROLLS.**

**The many dimensions of aging** / Robert L. Rubinstein, Miriam Moss, Morton H. Kleban, editors. New York : Springer Pub., c2000. xxvi, 289 p. ; 24 cm. "Dedicated to M. Powell Lawton"--Prel. p. Includes bibliographical references and index. ISBN 0-8261-1247-1 DDC 305.26
*1. Aged - Psychology. 2. Aged - Health and hygiene. 3. Aged - Social conditions. 4. Quality of life. 5. Gerontology. I.*
*Rubinstein, Robert L. II. Moss, Miriam. III. Kleban, Morton H. IV. Lawton, M. Powell (Mortimer Powell), 1923-*
*TC HQ1061 .M337 2000*

**The many faces of giftedness** : lifting the masks / [edited by] Alexinia Young Baldwin, Wilma Vialle. Belmont, CA : Wadsworth Pub. Co., c1999. xxiii. 296 p. : ill. ; 23 cm. Includes bibliographical references and index. ISBN 0-7668-0006-7 (pbk.) DDC 371.95
*1. Gifted children - Psychology - United States. 2. Gifted children - Psychology - Australia. 3. Gifted children - Psychology - Case studies. I. Baldwin, Alexinia Y. II. Vialle, Wilma.*
*TC BF723.G5 M36 1999*

**Many, Paul.** My life, take two / Paul Many. New York : Walker & Co., 2000. 188 p. ; 22 cm. SUMMARY: During the summer before his senior year, Neal, to prove he can be responsible, tries to figure out a way to keep from losing the memories of his dead father while completing a documentary film for class and to decide what he wants to do with his life. ISBN 0-8027-8708-8 DDC [Fic]
*1. Self-perception - Fiction. 2. Fathers and sons - Fiction. 3. Motion pictures - Production and direction - Fiction. I. Title.*
*TC PZ7.M3212 My 2000*

**MANZANAR WAR RELOCATION CENTER.**
Rabbit in the moon [videorecording]. San Francisco, Calif. : Wabi-Sabi Productions, 1999.
*TC D753.8 .R3 1999*

**Manzo, Rita, 1955-.**
McDiarmid, Tami, 1960- Critical challenges for primary students. Burnaby, B.C. : Field Relations and Teacher In-Service Education, Faculty of Education, Simon Fraser University, c1996.
*TC LB1590.3 .M36 1996*

**MAORI (NEW ZEALAND PEOPLE) - ETHNIC IDENTITY.**
Thomas, Nicholas. Possessions. New York, N.Y. : Thames and Hudson, c1999.
*TC N5313 .T46 1999*

**MAORIS.** *See* **MAORI (NEW ZEALAND PEOPLE).**

**Mapping careers with LD and ADD clients.**
Janus, Raizi Abby. New York : Columbia University Press, c1999.
*TC HV1568.5 .J36 1999*

**MAPPING OF THE BRAIN.** *See* **BRAIN MAPPING.**

**Maps & globes.**
Knowlton, Jack. New York : HarperCollins, c1985.
*TC GA105.6 .K58 1985*

**Maps and globes.**
Knowlton, Jack. Maps & globes. New York : HarperCollins, c1985.
*TC GA105.6 .K58 1985*

**MAPS - JUVENILE LITERATURE.**
Knowlton, Jack. Maps & globes. New York : HarperCollins, c1985.
*TC GA105.6 .K58 1985*

**Maps of meaning.**
Peterson, Jordan B. New York : Routledge, 1999.
*TC BF175.5.A72 P48 1999*

**Marc, Alexandre, 1956-.**
World Bank. African art. Washington, D.C. : World Bank, c1998.
*TC N7391.65 .W67 1998*

**Marc Chagall.**
La Fontaine, Jean de, 1621-1695. [Fables. English. Selections] New York : New Press : Distributed by W.W. Norton, [1997]
*TC PQ1811.E3 W6 1997*

**Marc Chagall** [videorecording] / produced and directed by Kim Evans ; edited and presented by Melvyn Bragg. [Chicago, Ill.] : Home Vision [distributor], c1985. 1 videocassette (VHS) (55 min.) : sd., col. with b&w sequences ; 1/2 in. (Portrait of an artist ; v. 13) Title on cassette: Chagall. At head of title: Home Vision ... presents an RM Arts production... [videorecording]. VHS. Catalogued from credits and container. Film camera, Paul Bond ; film editor, Gary Keating ; film sound, Trevor Carless. "A London Weekend Television co-production with RM Arts."--Container. Produced by London Weekend Television, ltd. in 1984. For adolescents through adult. SUMMARY: Explores the life and work of Marc Chagall.
*1. Chagall, Marc, - 1887- 2. Painters - Russian S.F.S.R. - Biography. 3. Painters - France - Biography. I. Chagall, Marc, 1887- II. Evans, Kim. III. Bragg, Melvyn, 1939- IV. Home Vision (Firm) V. RM Arts (Firm) VI. London Weekend Television, ltd. VII. Title. VIII. Title: Chagall IX. Title: Home Vision ... presents an RM Arts production... [videorecording] X. Series.*

*TC ND699.C5 C5 1985*

**MARC FORMATS - UNITED STATES.**
USMARC code list for countries. 1993 ed. Washington, D.C. : Cataloging Distribution Service, Library of Congress, 1993.
*TC Z699.35.M28 U78 1993*

USMARC code list for geographic areas. 1998 ed. Washington, D.C. : Cataloging Distribution Service, Library of Congress, 1998.
*TC Z695.1.G4 U83 1998*

USMARC code list for languages. 1996 ed. Washington, D.C. : Cataloging Distribution Service, Library of Congress, 1996.
*TC Z699.35.M28 U79 1997*

USMARC code list for relators, sources, description conventions. 1997 ed. Washington, DC : Cataloging Distribution Service, Library of Congress, 1997.
*TC Z699.35.M28 U795 1997*

**MARC SYSTEM.** *See* **MARC FORMATS.**

**MARCEL, CLAUDE, 19TH CENT.**
Roberts, J. T. (John T.) Two French language teaching reformers reassessed. Lewiston [N.Y.] : E. Mellen Press, c1999.
*TC PB35 .R447 1999*

**Marching along.** Teacher's ed. New York, N.Y. : American Book Company, c1980. xvi, 412 p. : col. ill. ; 28 cm. (American readers ; 2-1) Includes index. C.2 has "Answer key - end of unit tests" on p. 413-414. ISBN 0-278-45848-3
*1. Readers (Primary) 2. Reading (Primary) I. Series.*
*TC PE1119 .M37 1980 Teacher's Ed.*

**Marching along.** New York, N.Y. : American Book Company, c1980. 256 p. : col. ill. ; 24 cm. (American readers ; 2-1) ISBN 0-278-45815-7
*1. Readers (Primary) I. Series.*
*TC PE1119 .M37 1980*

**Marching along.** Teacher's ed. Lexington, Mass. : D.C. Heath and Company, c1983. xxxii, 424 p. : col. ill. ; 28 cm. (American readers ; 2-1) Includes index. ISBN 0-669-04985-9
*1. Readers (Primary) 2. Reading (Primary) I. Series.*
*TC PE1119 .M37 1983 Teacher's Ed.*

**Marching along.** Lexington, Mass. : D.C. Heath and Company, c1983. 272 p. : col. ill. ; 24 cm. (American readers ; 2-1) ISBN 0-669-04984-0
*1. Readers (Primary) I. Series.*
*TC PE1119 .M37 1983*

**Marching along.** Teacher's ed. Lexington, Mass. : D.C. Heath and Company, c1986. T32, 489 p. : col. ill. ; 28 cm. (Heath American readers ; 2-1) Includes index. ISBN 0-669-08049-7
*1. Readers (Primary) 2. Reading (Primary) I. Series.*
*TC PE1119 .M37 1986 Teacher's Ed.*

**Marching along** : workbook. Teacher's ed. New York, N.Y. : D.C. Heath and Company, c1983. 128 p. : col. ill. ; 28 cm. (American readers ; 2-1) Includes index. ISBN 0-278-45928-5
*1. Readers (Primary) 2. Reading (Primary) I. Series.*
*TC PE1119 .M37 1980 Teacher's Ed. Workbook*

**Marching along** : workbook. Teacher's ed. Lexington, Mass. : D.C. Heath and Company, c1983. 128 p. : col. ill. ; 28 cm. (American readers ; 2-1) Includes index. ISBN 0-669-04992-1
*1. Readers (Primary) 2. Reading (Primary) I. Series.*
*TC PE1119 .M37 1983 Teacher's Ed. Workbook*

**MARCUSE, HERBERT, 1898 - -AESTHETICS.**
Reitz, Charles. Art, alienation, and the humanities. Albany : State University of New York Press, c2000.
*TC B945.M2984 R45 2000*

**Mardell, Ben.** From basketball to the Beatles : in search of compelling early childhood curriculum / Ben Mardell ; foreword by Eleanor Duckworth. Portsmouth, NH : Heinemann, 1999. xviii, 171 p. : ill. ; 24 cm. Includes bibliographical references (p.171). DDC 372.19
*1. Early childhood education - United States - Curricula. 2. Education, Preschool - United States - Curricula. I. Title.*
*TC LB1139.4 .M27 1999*

**Marek, Ann M.**
Reflections and connections. Cresskill, N.J. : Hampton Press, c1999.
*TC P51 .R36 1999*

**Marek, Tadeusz.**
Professional burnout. Washington, DC : Taylor & Francis, c1993.
*TC BF481 .P77 1993*

**Margaret S. Mahler Symposium on Child Development (29th : 1998 : Philadelphia, Pa.).**
Brothers and sisters. Northvale, N.J. : J. Aronson, c1999.
*TC BF723.S43 B78 1999*

**MARGINAL PEOPLES.** *See* **MARGINALITY, SOCIAL.**

**MARGINALITY, SOCIAL.** *See also* **SOCIALLY HANDICAPPED.**
Beverley, John. Subalternity and representation. Durham [N.C.] ; London : Duke University Press, 1999.
*TC HM1136 .B48 1999*

Comparative anomie research. Aldershot, Hants, England ; Brookfield, Vt., USA : Ashgate, c1999.
*TC HM816 .C65 1999*

Middleton, Laura. Disabled children. Malden, Mass. : Blackwell Sciences, 1999.
*TC HV888 .M53 1999*

**MARGINALITY, SOCIAL - GREAT BRITAIN.**
Preece, Julia. Combating social exclusion in university adult education. Aldershot ; Brookfield, Vt. : Ashgate, c1999.
*TC LC5256.G7 P84 1999*

**MARGINALITY, SOCIAL - POLITICAL ASPECTS - LATIN AMERICA.**
Beverley, John. Subalternity and representation. Durham [N.C.] ; London : Duke University Press, 1999.
*TC HM1136 .B48 1999*

**MARGINALITY, SOCIAL - SOUTH AFRICA - HISTORY.**
Makosana, I. Nokuzola Zola. Social factors in the positioning of black women in South African universities. 1997.
*TC 06 no. 10825*

**Margins, center, and the spaces in-between.**
Asher, Nina. 1999.
*TC 06 no. 11080*

**Marienau, Catherine.**
Taylor, Kathleen, 1943- Developing adult learners. 1st ed. San Francisco : Jossey-Bass, c2000.
*TC LC5225.L42 T39 2000*

**Marin, Oscar.**
International Symposium on Attention and Performance (11th : 1984 : Eugene, Or.) Attention and performance XI. Hillsdale, N.J. : L. Erlbaum Associates, 1985.
*TC BF321 .A82 1985*

**MARINE ACCIDENTS.** *See* **SHIPWRECKS.**

**MARINE DISASTERS.** *See* **SHIPWRECKS.**

**MARINE ECOLOGY.**
Markle, Sandra. Down, down, down in the ocean. New York : Walker, 1999.
*TC QH541.5.S3 M2856 1999*

**MARINE ECOLOGY - JUVENILE LITERATURE.**
Markle, Sandra. Down, down, down in the ocean. New York : Walker, 1999.
*TC QH541.5.S3 M2856 1999*

**MARINERS.** *See* **SAILORS.**

**MARITAL COMMUNICATION.** *See* **COMMUNICATION IN MARRIAGE.**

**MARITAL COUNSELING.** *See* **MARRIAGE COUNSELING.**

**MARITAL PSYCHOTHERAPY.** *See also* **MARRIAGE COUNSELING.**
Couples on the fault line. New York, NY : Guilford Press, 2000.
*TC RC488.5 .C6435 2000*

Couples therapy in managed care. New York : Haworth Press, c1999.
*TC RC488.5 .C64385 1999*

McCormack, Charles C. Treating borderline states in marriage. Northvale, NJ : Jason Aronson, 2000.
*TC RC488.5 .M392 2000*

Shaddock, David. Contexts and connections. New York : Basic Books, 2000.
*TC RC488.5 .S483 2000*

**MARITAL PSYCHOTHERAPY - HANDBOOKS, MANUALS, ETC.**
Preventive approaches in couples therapy. Philadelphia : Brunner/Mazel, 1999.
*TC RC488.5 .P74 1999*

**MARITAL STATUS.** *See* **MARRIED PEOPLE.**

**MARITAL THERAPY.** *See* **MARITAL PSYCHOTHERAPY.**

**MARITAL THERAPY.**
Nichols, William C. Systemic family therapy. New York : Guilford Press, c1986.
*TC RC488.5 .N535 1986*

**Marjoribanks, Kevin.**
Australian education. Camberwell, Vic. : Australian Council for Educational Research, 1998.
*TC LA2102.7 .A87 1998*

**Mark, Jan.** The Midas touch / Jan Mark ; illustrated by Juan Wijngaard. 1st U.S. ed. Cambridge, MA : Candlewick Press, 1999. 1 v. (unpaged) : col. ill. ; 29 cm. SUMMARY: A retelling of the classic story of King Midas, who foolishly wishes that everything he touch be turned to gold, and only then realizes his horrible mistake. ISBN 0-7636-0488-7 (alk. paper) DDC 398.2/0938/02
*1. Midas (Legendary character) - Juvenile literature. 2. Midas (Legendary character) 3. Mythology, Greek. I. Wijngaard, Juan, ill. II. Title.*
*TC BL820.M55 M33 1999*

**The mark of oppression.**
Kardiner, Abram, 1891- [1st ed.]. New York, Norton [1951]
*TC E185.625 .K3*

**Mark Rothko.**
Rothko, Mark, 1903-1970. New Haven : Yale University Press ; Washington, D.C. : National Gallery of Art, c1998.
*TC ND237.R725 A4 1998*

Weiss, Jeffrey. Washington : National Gallery of Art ; New Haven, Conn. : Yale University Press, c1998.
*TC N6537.R63 A4 1998*

**Markee, Numa.** Conversation analysis / Numa Markee. Mahwah, N.J. : L. Erlbaum Associates, c2000. xv, 216 p. : ill. ; 24 cm. (Second language acquisition research) Includes bibliographical references (p. 183-202) and indexes. ISBN 0-8058-1999-1 (cloth : acid-free paper) ISBN 0-8058-2000-0 (pbk. : acid-free paper) DDC 302.3/46
*1. Conversation analysis. 2. Second language acquisition. I. Title. II. Series.*
*TC P95.45 .M35 2000*

**The market approach to education.**
Witte, John F. Princeton, N.J. : Princeton University Press, c2000.
*TC LB2828.85.W6 W58 2000*

**Market Data Retrieval (Firm).**
MDR's school directory. Connecticut. Shelton, CT : Market Data Retrieval, c1995-
*TC L903.C8 M37*

MDR's school directory. New Jersey. Shelton, CT : Market Data Retrieval, c1995-
*TC L903.N5 M37*

MDR's school directory. New York. Shelton, CT : Market Data Retrieval, c1995-
*TC L903.N7 M37*

MDR's school directory. Pennsylvania. Shelton, CT : Market Data Retrieval, 1995-
*TC L903.P4 M37*

**Market Data Retrieval's CIC school directory. Connecticut.**
MDR's school directory. Connecticut. Shelton, CT : Market Data Retrieval, c1995-
*TC L903.C8 M37*

**Market Data Retrieval's CIC school directory. New Jersey.**
MDR's school directory. New Jersey. Shelton, CT : Market Data Retrieval, c1995-
*TC L903.N5 M37*

**Market Data Retrieval's CIC school directory. New York.**
MDR's school directory. New York. Shelton, CT : Market Data Retrieval, c1995-
*TC L903.N7 M37*

**Market Data Retrieval's CIC school directory. Pennsylvania.**
MDR's school directory. Pennsylvania. Shelton, CT : Market Data Retrieval, 1995-
*TC L903.P4 M37*

**Market Data Retrieval's school directory. Connecticut.**
MDR's school directory. Connecticut. Shelton, CT : Market Data Retrieval, c1995-
*TC L903.C8 M37*

**Market Data Retrieval's school directory. New Jersey.**
MDR's school directory. New Jersey. Shelton, CT : Market Data Retrieval, c1995-
*TC L903.N5 M37*

**Market Data Retrieval's school directory. New York.**
MDR's school directory. New York. Shelton, CT : Market Data Retrieval, c1995-
*TC L903.N7 M37*

**Market Data Retrieval's school directory. Pennsylvania.**
MDR's school directory. Pennsylvania. Shelton, CT : Market Data Retrieval, 1995-
*TC L903.P4 M37*

**MARKET ECONOMY.** *See* **CAPITALISM.**

**MARKET, LABOR.** *See* **LABOR MARKET.**

**Market values in American higher education.**
Smith, Charles W., 1938- Lanham, Md. : Oxford : Rowman & Littlefield, 2000.
*TC LB2342 .S55 2000*

**MARKETING.** *See also* **RETAIL TRADE.**
Nelson, Carol, 1953- Women's market handbook. Detroit : Gale Research, c1994.
*TC HF5415 .N3495 1994*

**Marketing and public relations activities in ARL Libraries** : a SPEC kit / compiled by Evelyn Ortiz Smykla ... [et al.]. Washington, DC : Association of Research Libraries, Office of Leadership and Management Services, c1999. 109 p. ; 28 cm. (Spec kit, 0160-3582 ; 240) (Spec flyer, 0160-3574 ; 240) "April 1999." At head of title : SPEC, Systems and Procedures Exchange Center. Includes SPEC flyer 240. Includes bibliographical references (p. 107-109).
*1. Libraries - Public relations. 2. Libraries - Service - Marketing. 3. Library planning. 4. Association of Research Libraries. I. Association of Research Libraries. Office of Leadership and Management Services. II. Association of Research Libraries. Systems and Procedures Exchange Center. III. Title. IV. Series. V. Series: Spec flyer, 0160-3574 ; 240*
*TC Z176.3 .M2875 1999*

**MARKETING RESEARCH.**
Chandler, Tomasita M. Children and adolescents in the market place. Ann Arbor, Mich. : Pierian Press, 1999.
*TC HF5822 .C43 1999*

**MARKETS.** *See* **LABOR MARKET.**

**MARKING (STUDENTS).** *See* **GRADING AND MARKING (STUDENTS).**

**Markle, Sandra.** Down, down, down in the ocean / Sandra Markle ; illustrations by Bob Marstall. New York : Walker, 1999. 32 p. : col. ill. ; 23 x 29 cm. SUMMARY: Describes a number of creatures that comprise a Pacific Ocean ecosystem, as found off the coast of California at three different depths--0 to 200 meters, 200 to 1000 meters, and the seafloor. ISBN 0-8027-8654-5 (hc) ISBN 0-8027-8655-3 (rein.) DDC 577.7
*1. Marine ecology - Juvenile literature. 2. Ocean. 3. Marine ecology. 4. Ecology. I. Marstall, Bob, ill. II. Title.*
*TC QH541.5.S3 M2856 1999*

Outside and inside kangaroos / by Sandra Markle. 1st ed. New York, N.Y. : Atheneum Books for Young Readers, c1999. 40 p. : col. ill. ; 24 x 26 cm. SUMMARY: Describes the inner and outer workings of kangaroos, including their diet, anatomy, and life cycle. ISBN 0-689-81456-9 DDC 599.2/2
*1. Kangaroos - Juvenile literature. 2. Kangaroos. I. Title.*
*TC QL737.M35 M272 1999*

**Markman, Arthur B.**
Cognitive dynamics. Mahwah, N.J. ; London : L. Erlbaum, 2000.
*TC BF316.6 .C64 2000*

**Markos, Nancy J. Egner, 1949-.**
Colvin, A. Vonnie, 1951- Teaching the nuts and bolts of physical education. Champaign, IL : Human Kinetics, c2000.
*TC GV443 .C59 2000*

**Markowitsch, Hans J., 1949-.**
Cognitive neuroscience of memory. Seattle ; Toronto : Hogrefe & Huber, c1999.
*TC QP406 .C63 1999*

**Markowitz, John C., 1954-.**
Weissman, Myrna M. Comprehensive guide to interpersonal psychotherapy. New York: Basic Books, c2000.
*TC RC480.8 .W445 2000*

**Marks, Carole.** The power of pride : stylemakers and rulebreakers of the Harlem Renaissance / Carole Marks and Diana Edkins. 1st ed. New York : Crown

Publishers, c1999. 272 p. : ill. ; 26 cm. Includes index.
ISBN 0-609-60096-6
*1. Afro-Americans - Intellectual life - 20th century - Sources. 2.
Harlem Renaissance. 3. Afro-American arts - History - 20th
century - Sources. 4. Afro-American intellectuals - Biography.
5. Afro-American artists - Biography. 6. Afro-American
authors - Biography. 7. Harlem (New York, N.Y.) - Intellectual
life - Sources. 8. New York (N.Y.) - Intellectual life - Sources. I.
Edkins, Diana. II. Title.*
**TC E185.6 .M35 1999**

**Marks, Deborah, 1964-** Disability : controversial
debates and psychosocial perspectives / Deborah
Marks. London ; New York : Routledge, 1999. xiv, 217
p. ; 22 cm. Includes bibliographical references (p. [193]-209)
and index. ISBN 0-415-16202-5 (hbk) ISBN 0-415-16203-3
(pbk) DDC 362.4
*1. Disability studies. 2. Sociology of disability. 3.
Handicapped. I. Title.*
**TC HV1568.2 .M37 1999**

**Marks, Edward S.** Entry strategies for school
consultation / Edward S. Marks. New York : Guilford
Press, c1995. xv, 287 p. : ill. ; 24 cm. (The Guilford school
practitioner series) Includes bibliographical references (p.
261-278) and index. ISBN 0-89862-368-5 (alk. paper) DDC
371.7/13
*1. Educational consultants - United States. 2. Educational
counseling - United States. 3. School children - Mental health
services - United States. I. Title. II. Series.*
**TC LB2799.2 .M36 1995**

**Marples, Richard.**
The aims of education. London ; New York :
Routledge, 1999.
**TC LB41 .A36353 1999**

**Marquardt, Michael J.**
Schwandt, David R. Organizational learning. Boca
Raton, Fla. : St. Lucie Press, c2000.
**TC HD58.82 .S39 2000**

**Marquardt, Ronald G., 1939-.**
Gifted children and legal issues in education. Dayton,
Ohio : Ohio Psychology Press, c1991.
**TC KF4209.5 .G54 1991**

Karnes, Frances A. Gifted children and legal issues.
Scottsdale, AZ : Gifted Psychology Press, 2000.
**TC KF4209.5 .K369 2000**

Karnes, Frances A. Gifted children and the law.
Dayton, Ohio : Ohio Psychology Press, c1991.
**TC KF4209.5 .K37 1991**

**Marquardt, Thomas P.**
Communication sciences and disorders. San Diego :
Singular Pub. Group/Thomson Learning, c2000.
**TC RC423 .C647 2000**

**Marr, Lisa.** Sexually transmitted diseases : a physician
tells you what you need to know / Lisa Marr.
Baltimore, Md : The Johns Hopkins University Press,
1998. xiii, 341 p. : ill. ; 24 cm. (A Johns Hopkins Press health
book) Includes bibliographical references (p. 307-324) and
index. ISBN 0-8018-6042-3 (alk. paper) ISBN 0-8018-6043-1
(pbk. : alk. paper) DDC 616.95/1
*1. Sexually transmitted diseases - Popular works. I. Title. II.
Series.*
**TC RC200.2 .M27 1998**

**MARRIAGE. See also COMMUNICATION IN
MARRIAGE; DIVORCE; FAMILY; HOME;
INTERMARRIAGE; REMARRIAGE;
WEDDINGS.**
Cavan, Ruth (Shonle) 1896- ed. Marriage and family
in the modern world, 2d ed. New York, Crowell
[1965]
**TC HQ734 .C382 1965**

**Marriage and family in the modern world.**
Cavan, Ruth (Shonle) 1896- ed. 2d ed. New York,
Crowell [1965]
**TC HQ734 .C382 1965**

**MARRIAGE COUNSELING. See FAMILY
PSYCHOTHERAPY; MARITAL
PSYCHOTHERAPY; SEX COUNSELING.**

**MARRIAGE COUNSELING - HANDBOOKS,
MANUALS, ETC.**
Preventive approaches in couples therapy.
Philadelphia : Brunner/Mazel, 1999.
**TC RC488.5 .P74 1999**

**MARRIAGE GUIDANCE. See MARRIAGE
COUNSELING.**

**MARRIAGE - INDIA.**
Derné, Steve, 1960- Culture in action. Albany : State
University of New York Press, c1995.
**TC HQ670 .D46 1995**

**MARRIAGE, INTERRACIAL. See INTERRACIAL
MARRIAGE.**

**MARRIAGE MENTORING. See MARRIAGE
COUNSELING.**

**MARRIAGE, MIXED. See INTERMARRIAGE.**

**MARRIAGE - PERIODICALS.**
Familyculture. Boston, Mass. : [s.n.],

**MARRIAGE - PSYCHOLOGICAL ASPECTS.**
Dryden, Caroline. Being married, doing gender.
London ; New York : Routledge, 1999.
**TC HQ734 .D848 1999**

**MARRIAGE PSYCHOTHERAPY. See MARITAL
PSYCHOTHERAPY.**

**MARRIAGE - RELIGIOUS ASPECTS -
HINDUISM.**
Derné, Steve, 1960- Culture in action. Albany : State
University of New York Press, c1995.
**TC HQ670 .D46 1995**

**MARRIAGE - UGANDA.**
Gitta, Cosmas. International human rights. 1998.
**TC 085 G4398**

**MARRIAGE - UNITED STATES.**
Gottman, John Mordechai. Why marriages succeed or
fail :. 1st Fireside ed. New York : Fireside, 1995.
**TC HQ536 .G68 1994**

**MARRIAGE - UNITED STATES - PERIODICALS.**
The Family coordinator. Minneapolis, Minn. :
National Council on Family Relations, c1968-

**MARRIED LIFE. See MARRIAGE.**

**MARRIED PEOPLE. See MARRIED WOMEN.**

**MARRIED PEOPLE - COUNSELING OF. See
MARRIAGE COUNSELING.**

**MARRIED PEOPLE - EMPLOYMENT. See
MOTHERS - EMPLOYMENT.**

**MARRIED PEOPLE - FICTION.**
Stegner, Wallace Earle, 1909- Angle of repose. New
York : Modern Library, 2000.
**TC PS3537.T316 A8 2000**

**MARRIED PEOPLE - HEALTH AND HYGIENE.**
The psychology of couples and illness. 1st ed.
Washington, D.C. : American Psychological
Association, c2000.
**TC R726.5 .P785 2000**

**MARRIED PERSONS. See MARRIED PEOPLE.**

**MARRIED WOMEN - EMPLOYMENT - UNITED
STATES - HISTORY.**
Landry, Bart. Black working wives. Berkeley :
University of California Press, c2000.
**TC HQ536 .L335 2000**

**Marriner-Tomey, Ann, 1943-** Guide to nursing
management and leadership / Ann Marriner-Tomey.
6th ed. St. Louis, Mo. : Mosby, 2000. xvii, 525 p. : ill. ;
24 cm. Includes bibliographical references and index. ISBN 0-
323-01066-0 DDC 362.1/73/068
*1. Nursing services - Administration. 2. Leadership. 3.
Nursing, Supervisory. 4. Leadership. I. Title.*
**TC RT89.3 M37 2000**

**Marschall, Melissa, 1968-.**
Schneider, Mark, 1946- Choosing schools. Princeton,
N.J. ; Oxford : Princeton University Press, c2000.
**TC LB1027.9 .S32 2000**

**Marschark, Marc.**
The deaf child in the family and at school. Mahwah,
N.J. : Lawrence Erlbaum Associates, 2000.
**TC HV2392.2 .D43 2000**

**Marsden, Michael T.**
Pioneers in popular culture studies. Bowling Green,
OH : Bowling Green State University Popular Press,
c1999.
**TC E169.04 .P563 1999**

**Marsh, Colin J.** Curriculum : alternative approaches,
ongoing issues / Colin J. Marsh, George Willis. 2nd.
ed. Upper Saddle River, N.J. : Merrill, c1999. xvii, 363
p. : ill. ; 25 cm. Includes bibliographical references and
indexes. ISBN 0-13-757071-6 DDC 375/.000973
*1. Education - United States - Curricula. 2. Curriculum
planning - United States. 3. Curriculum evaluation - United
States. 4. Curriculum change - United States. I. Willis, George,
1941- II. Title.*
**TC LB1570 .M3667 1999**

**Marsh, David D.**
The new American high school. Thousand Oaks,
Calif. : Corwin Press, c1999.
**TC LA222 .N49 1999**

**Marsh, Robert Mortimer.** The great transformation :
social change in Taipei, Taiwan since the 1960s /
Robert M. Marsh. Armonk, N.Y. : M.E. Sharpe,
c1996. vii, 409 p. : ill., map ; 24 cm. (Taiwan in the modern
world) "An East Gate book." Includes bibliographical
references (p. 389-398) and index. ISBN 1-56324-787-9
(hardcover : alk. paper) ISBN 1-56324-788-7 (pbk. : alk.
paper) DDC 303.4/095124/9
*1. Taipei (Taiwan) - Social conditions. 2. Social change -
Taiwan - Taipei. I. Title. II. Series.*
**TC HN749.T35 M37 1996**

**Marsh, Valerie.** Storytelling with shapes & numbers /
by Valerie Marsh ; illustrated by Patrick K. Luzadder.
Ft. Atkinson, Wis. : Alleyside Press, c1999. 84 p. ill. ;
28 cm. ISBN 1-57950-024-2 (alk. paper) DDC 372.67/7
*1. Storytelling. 2. Paper work. 3. Shapes. 4. Numerals. I. Title.
II. Title: Storytelling with shapes and numbers*
**TC LB1042 .M2874 1999**

True tales of heroes & heroines / Valerie Marsh ;
illustrated by Patrick K. Luzadder. Fort Atkinson,
Wis. : Alleyside Press, c1999. 93 p. : ill. ; 28 cm. Includes
bibliographical references. ISBN 0-917846-93-1 (pbk. : alk.
paper) DDC 920.02
*1. Biography - Study and teaching. 2. Storytelling - United
States. 3. United States - Biography - Study and teaching. I.
Luzadder, Patrick K. II. Title. III. Title: True tales of heroes
and heroines*
**TC CT85 .M37 1999**

**Marshak, Laura E.** Disability and the family life
cycle : [recognizing and treating developmental
challenges] / Laura E. Marshak, Milton Seligman and
Fran Prezant. New York : Basic Books, c1999. xiii, 318
p. ; 24 cm. Includes bibliographical
references (p. 281-308) and index. ISBN 0-465-01632-4
(cloth) DDC 362.4
*1. Handicapped - Home care. 2. Handicapped - Family
relationships. I. Seligman, Milton, 1937- II. Prezant, Fran. III.
Title.*
**TC HV1568 .M277 1999**

**Marshall, Catherine.** Designing qualitative research /
Catherine Marshall, Gretchen B. Rossman. 3rd ed.
Thousand Oaks, Calif. : Sage Publications, c1999. xvi,
224 p. : ill. ; 24 cm. Includes bibliographical references and
index. ISBN 0-7619-1339-4 ISBN 0-7619-1340-8 (pbk.) DDC
300/.72
*1. Social sciences - Research - Methodology. I. Rossman,
Gretchen B. II. Title.*
**TC H62 .M277 1999**

**Marshall, J. Dan.** Turning points in curriculum : a
contemporary American memoir / J. Dan Marshall,
James T. Sears, William H. Schubert ; [editor, Debra
A. Stollenwerk]. Upper Saddle River, N.J. : Merrill,
c2000. xxvi, 292 p. ; 23 cm. Includes bibliographical
references (p. 249-278) and index. ISBN 0-02-376451-1 DDC
375/.001/0973
*1. Education - United States - Curricula - History - 20th
century. 2. Curriculum planning - United States. I. Sears,
James T. (James Thomas), 1951- II. Schubert, William Henry.
III. Stollenwerk, Debra A. IV. Title.*
**TC LB1570 .M36675 2000**

**Marshall, James, 1942-** Swine lake / James Marshall ;
[pictures] Maurice Sendak. 1st ed. [New York] :
Harper Collins Publishers, 1999. [40] p. : col. ill. ; 24 cm.
"Michael Di Capua books." SUMMARY: A hungry wolf
attends a performance of Swine Lake, performed by the
Boarshoi Ballet, intending to eat the performers, but he is so
entranced by the story unfolding on the stage that he forgets
about his meal. ISBN 0-06-205171-7 DDC [E]
*1. Ballet - Fiction. 2. Pigs - Fiction. 3. Wolves - Fiction. I.
Sendak, Maurice, ill. II. Title.*
**TC PZ7 .M35672 Sw 1999**

**Marshall, James (James D.).**
Education policy. Cheltenham, UK : Northampton,
MA : Edward Elgar Pub., c1999.
**TC LC71 .E32 1999**

Peters, Michael (Michael A.), 1948- Wittgenstein.
Westport, Conn. : Bergin & Garvey, 1999.
**TC B3376.W564 P388 1999**

**Marshall, Kit.**
Burz, Helen L. Performance-based curriculum for
music and the visual arts. Thousand Oaks, Calif. :
Corwin Press, c1999.
**TC LB1591 .B84 1999**

**Marshall, Robert H.** AGS earth science / by Robert H.
Marshall, Allen Rosskopf. Circle Pines, Minn. : AGS,
American Guidance Service, c1997. x, 310 p. : col. ill. ;
25 cm. Includes index. ISBN 0-7854-0995-5
*1. Earth sciences. I. Rosskopf, Allen. II. Title. III. Title:
American Guidance Service earth science*
**TC QE28 .M37 1997**

AGS earth science : teacher's guide / by Robert H. Marshall, Allen Rosskopf. Teacher's ed. Circle Pines, Minn. : AGS, American Guidance Service, c1997. xii, 188 p. : ill. ; 28 cm. Includes index. ISBN 0-7854-0996-3
1. Earth sciences. 2. Earth sciences - Study and teaching (Elementary) I. Rosskopf, Allen. II. Title. III. Title: American Guidance Service earth science
TC QE28 .M37 1997 Teacher's Ed.

AGS physical science / by Robert H. Marshall, Donald H. Jacobs. Circle Pines, Minn. : AGS, American Guidance Service, c1997. xi, 341 p. : col. ill. ; 25 cm. Includes index. ISBN 0-7854-1017-1
1. Physical sciences. I. Jacobs, Donald H. II. Title. III. Title: American Guidance Service physical science
TC QC23 .M37 1997

AGS physical science : teacher's guide / by Robert H. Marshall, Donald H. Jacobs. Teacher's ed. Circle Pines, Minn. : AGS, American Guidance Service, c1997. xii, 180 p. : ill. ; 28 cm. ISBN 0-7854-1018-x
1. Physical sciences. 2. Physical sciences - Study and teaching (Elementary) I. Jacobs, Donald H. II. Title. III. Title: American Guidance Service physical science
TC QC23 .M37 1997 Teacher's Ed.

Marshall, Stephanie.
A handbook for teaching and learning in higher education. London : Kogan Page, 1999.
TC LB2331 .H29 1999

Marshall, Victor W.
The self and society in aging processes. New York : Springer Pub., c1999.
TC HQ1061 .S438 1999

Marstall, Bob, ill.
Markle, Sandra. Down, down, down in the ocean. New York : Walker, 1999.
TC QH541.5.S3 M2856 1999

MARSUPIALIA. See KANGAROOS.

Martell, Hazel. Food & feasts with the Vikings / Hazel Mary Martell. Parsippany, N.J. : New Discovery Books, c1995. 32 p. : ill. (some col.), col. maps ; 28 cm. (Food & feasts) "A Zoë book"--T.p verso. Includes bibliographical references (p. 31) and index. ISBN 0-02-726317-7 DDC 394.1/2/0948
1. Vikings - Food - Juvenile literature. 2. Vikings - Social life and customs - Juvenile literature. 3. Social history - Medieval, 500-1500 - Juvenile literature. 4. Food habits - History - To 1500 - Juvenile literature. 5. Cookery, Viking - Juvenile literature. 6. Northmen - Food - Juvenile literature. 7. Northmen - Social life and customs - Juvenile literature. 8. Cookery, Medieval - Juvenile literature. 9. Food habits - Scandinavia. 10. Vikings - Social life and customs. 11. Cookery, Scandinavian. I. Title. II. Title: Food and feasts with the Vikings. III. Series.
TC DL65 .M359 1995

Martha Holden Jennings Foundation.
[Journal (Martha Holden Jennings Foundation)] Journal. [Cleveland : The Foundation, 1974-

Martha Holden Jennings journal.
[Journal (Martha Holden Jennings Foundation)] Journal. [Cleveland : The Foundation, 1974-

Martin, Bill, 1916- Brown bear, brown bear, what do you see? / by Bill Martin, Jr. ; pictures by Eric Carle. New York : H. Holt, 1992. 1 v. (unpaged) : col. ill. ; 27 cm. Originally published: New York : Holt, Rinehart, and Winston, 1967. SUMMARY: Children see a variety of animals, each one a different color, and a teacher looking at them. ISBN 0-8050-1744-5 (acid-free paper) DDC [E]
1. Color - Fiction. 2. Animals - Fiction. 3. Stories in rhyme. I. Carle, Eric, ill. II. Title.
TC PZ8.3.M418 Br 1992

Martin, Clyde E. (Clyde Eugene).
Kinsey, Alfred C. (Alfred Charles), 1894-1956. Sexual behavior in the human male. Bloomington, Ind. : Indiana University Press, [1998].
TC HQ28 .K55 1998

Martin, Danny Bernard. Mathematics success and failure among African-American youth : the roles of sociohistorical context, community forces, school influence, and individual agency / Danny Bernard Martin. Mahwah, N.J. : Lawrence Erlbaum, 2000. xii, 202 p. : ill. ; 24 cm. (Studies in mathematical thinking and learning) Includes bibliographical references (p. 190-195) and indexes. ISBN 0-8058-3042-1 (cloth : alk. paper) DDC 510/.71/0973
1. Mathematics - Study and teaching - United States. 2. Afro-American students - Education. I. Title. II. Series.
TC QA13 .M145 2000

Martin, David Jerner. Elementary science methods : a constructivist approach / David Jerner Martin. 2nd ed. Belmont, CA : Wadsworth, c2000. xx, 556 p. : ill. ; 23 cm. Includes bibliographical references and indexes. ISBN 0-534-55630-2 DDC 372.3/5044

1. Science - Study and teaching (Elementary) - United States. 2. Constructivism (Education) - United States. 3. Science - Study and teaching (Preschool) - United States. I. Title.
TC LB1585.3 .M37 2000

Martin, Debra Bayles.
Bridge.
Borich, Gary D. Effective teaching methods. 4th ed. Upper Saddle River, N.J. : Merrill, c2000.
TC LB1025.3 .B67 2000

Martin, Elaine, 1948- Changing academic work : developing the learning university / Elaine Martin. Buckingham ; Philadelphia : Society for Research into Higher Education : Open University Press, 1999. x, 166 p. ; 23 cm. Includes bibliographical references and index. ISBN 0-335-19884-8 (hb) ISBN 0-335-19883-X (pb) DDC 378
1. Education, Higher. 2. College teaching. 3. College teachers - Job stress. 4. Educational change. I. Title.
TC LA184 .M37 1999

Martin, F. X. (Francis X.).
A new history of Ireland. Oxford [England] : Clarendon Press ; New York : Oxford University Press, <1976-1986 >
TC DA912 .N48

Martin, Francis G.
Baker, Justine C. A neural network guide to teaching. Bloomington, Ind. : Phi Delta Kappa Educational Foundation, c1998.
TC LB1057 .B35 1998

Martin, Frederick N.
Communication sciences and disorders. San Diego : Singular Pub. Group/Thomson Learning, c2000.
TC RC423 .C647 2000

Martin, J. R.
Genre and institutions. London ; Washington : Cassell, 1997.
TC P302.84 .G46 1997

Martin, Jane Roland, 1929- Coming of age in academe : rekindling women's hopes and reforming the academy / Jane Roland Martin ; with a foreword by Gloria Steinem. New York ; London : Routledge, 2000. xxv, 266 p. ; 24 cm. Includes bibliographical references (p. 183-202) and index. ISBN 0-415-92487-1 (hbk.) ISBN 0-415-92488-X (pbk.) DDC 378.1/982
1. Feminism and education - United States. 2. Women - Education (Higher) - United States. 3. Universities and colleges - United States - Sociological aspects. 4. Educational change - United States. I. Title.
TC LC197 .M37 2000

Martin, Larry G.
The welfare-to-work challenge for adult literacy educators. San Francisco, CA : Jossey-Bass Publishers, 1999.
TC LC149.7 .W43 1999

Martin, Michael, OBE. Dictionary of hearing / Michael C. Martin, Ian R. Summers. London : Whurr, 1999. 108 p. : ill. ; 23 cm. Includes bibliographical references (p. 108). ISBN 1-86156-132-6 DDC 573.8903
1. Hearing - Dictionaries. 2. Audiology - Dictionaries. 3. Hearing - Dictionaries. 4. Audiology - Dictionaries. I. Summers, Ian R. II. Title.
TC QP461 .M375 1999

Martin, Paul R., 1951-.
Bateson, P. P. G. (Paul Patrick Gordon), 1938- Design for a life. New York ; London : Simon & Schuster c2000.
TC BF341 .B37 2000

Martin, Philip, 1938-.
Stephen Hawking's universe [videorecording]. [Alexandria, Va.] : PBS Video; Burbank, CA : Distributed by Warner Home Video, c1997.
TC QB982 .S7 1997

Martin, Robert J. A study of the reflective practices of physical education student teachers / by Robert J. Martin. 1998. viii, 180 leaves ; 29 cm. Issued also on microfilm. Thesis (Ed.D.)--Teachers College, Columbia University, 1998. Includes bibliographical references (leaves 139-147).
1. Physical education teachers - In-service training. 2. Student teachers. 3. Interaction analysis in education. 4. Self-evaluation. 5. Physical education and training - Study and teaching. 6. Self-evaluation. 7. Experiential learning. 8. Self-knowledge, Theory of. I. Title.
TC 06 no. 11031

Martin, Robert K., 1959- The incarnate ground of Christian faith : towards a Christian theological epistemology for the educational ministry of the church / Robert K. Martin. Lanham, Md. : University Press of America, c1998. viii, 365 p. ; 23 cm. Includes bibliographical references (p. [353]-359) and index. ISBN

0-7618-1255-5 (alk. paper) DDC 268/.01
1. Christian education - Philosophy. 2. Knowledge, Theory of (Religion) I. Title.
TC BV1464 .M37 1998

Martinello, Marian L. Interdisciplinary inquiry in teaching and learning / Marian L. Martinello, Gillian E. Cook. 2nd. ed. Upper Saddle River, N.J. : Merrill, c2000. x, 214 p. : ill. ; 24 cm. Includes bibliographical references (p. 201-2080 and index. ISBN 0-13-923954-5 DDC 375/.000973
1. Interdisciplinary approach in education - United States. 2. Interdisciplinary approach to knowledge. 3. Education - United States - Curricula. I. Cook, Gillian Elizabeth, 1934- II. Title.
TC LB1570 .M3675 2000

Martínez, Corinne, 1965-.
Charting terrains of Chicana(o)/Latina(o) education. Cresskill, N.J. : Hampton Press, c2000.
TC LC2669 .C42 2000

Martinez, Joe L.
Neurobiology of learning and memory. San Diego : Academic Press, c1998.
TC QP408 .N492 1998

Martinez, Michael E. Education as the cultivation of intelligence / Michael E. Martinez. Mahwah, N.J. ; London : Lawrence Erlbaum Associates, 2000. x, 227 p. : ill. ; 24 cm. (The educational psychology series) Includes bibliographical references (p. 193-214) and indexes. ISBN 0-8058-3251-3 (cloth : alk. paper) DDC 370.15/23
1. Learning, Psychology of. 2. Intelligence. 3. Education - Aims and objectives. I. Title. II. Series.
TC LB1060 .M337 2000

Martino, Massimo.
Farr, Dennis, 1929- Francis Bacon. New York : Harry N. Abrams in association with the Trust for Museum Exhibitions, 1999.
TC ND497.B16 A4 1999

Martinot, Claude, ill.
German picture dictionary. Princeton, NJ : Berlitz Pub. Co., 1997.
TC PF3629 .G47 1997

Martohardjono, Gita, 1956-.
The generative study of second language acquisition. Mahwah, N.J. : L. Erlbaum, 1998.
TC P118.2 .G46 1998

Marty, Martin E., 1928- The glory and the power : the fundamentalist challenge to the modern world / Martin E. Marty and R. Scott Appleby. Boston : Beacon Press, c1992. viii, 225 p. : ill. ; 23 cm. "Companion to ... a series of film and radio documentaries that aired on the Public Broadcasting System (PBS) and National Public Radio (NPR) in 1992"--Acknowledgments. Includes bibliographical references (p. [203]-216) and index. ISBN 0-8070-1216-5 ISBN 0-8070-1217-3 (pbk.) DDC 291/.09/04
1. Religious fundamentalism - Comparative studies. I. Appleby, R. Scott, 1956- II. Title. III. Title: Glory and the power (Radio program) IV. Title: Glory and the power (Television program)
TC BL238 .M37 1992

Maruish, Mark E. (Mark Edward).
Handbook of psychological assessment in primary care settings. Mahwah, NJ : Lawrence Erlbaum Associates, Publishers, 2000.
TC RC469 .H374 2000

The use of psychological testing for treatment planning and outcome assessment. 2nd ed. Mahwah, N.J. : Lawrence Erlbaum Associates, c1999.
TC RC473.P79 U83 1999

MARXIAN SCHOOL OF SOCIOLOGY. See FRANKFURT SCHOOL OF SOCIOLOGY.

MARXISM. See SOCIALISM.

Marxism for our times.
James, C. L. R. (Cyril Lionel Robert), 1901- Jackson, Miss.: University Press of Mississippi, c1999.
TC HX44 .J25 1999

The Mary and Tim Gray series for the study of Catholic higher education
Burns, Robert E., 1927- Being Catholic, being American. Notre Dame, Ind. : University of Notre Dame Press, c1999.
TC LD4113 .B87 1999

MARY, BLESSED VIRGIN, SAINT - FICTION.
De Paola, Tomie. The night of Las Posadas. New York : Putnam's, 1999.
TC PZ7.D439 Ni 1999

Mary Cassatt, modern woman.
Cassatt, Mary, 1844-1926. 1st ed. New York : Art Institute of Chicago in association with H.N. Abrams, c1998.

**TC N6537.C35 A4 1998**

**Mary Cassatt** [videorecording] : Impressionist from
Philadelphia / a production of WNET/13 ; produced
and directed by Perry Miller Adato ; writer, Dorothy
Monet. [Chicago, Ill.]: Home Vision, c1977. 1
videocassette (VHS) (30 min.) : sd., col. with b&w sequences ;
1/2 in. (Portrait of an artist) (Women in art) Title on container:
Cassatt [videorecording]. VHS. Catalogued from credits on
container. Camera, Tom Spain, Jean Monsigny, Chuck
Clifton ; sound, Richard Blofson, Bernard Ortion ; film editor,
Nina Schulman. "A Public Media Incorporated Release"--
Container. "CAS 010"--Container. Produced by Educational
Broadcasting Corporation in 1975. Produced by WNET/
Thirteen for Women in Art. For adolescent through adult.
SUMMARY: Focuses on the life and work of the American
Impressionist painter Mary Cassatt. ISBN 0-7800-0119-2
*1. Cassatt, Mary, - 1844-1926. 2. Painters - United States -
Biography. 3. Impressionism (Art) - United States. 4. Women in
art. 5. Documentary films. 6. Biographical films. I. Cassatt,
Mary, 1844-1926. II. Adato, Perry Miller. III. Monet, Dorothy.
IV. WNET (Television station : New York, N.Y.) V. Home
Vision (Firm) VI. Public Media Incorporated (Wilmette, Ill.)
VII. Educational Broadcasting Corporation. VIII. Title:
Impressionist from Philadelphia [videorecording] IX. Title:
Cassatt [videorecording] X. Series. XI. Series: Women in art*
**TC ND237.C3 M37 1977**

**Mary Geddy's day.**
Waters, Kate. 1st ed. New York : Scholastic Press,
1999.
**TC PZ7.W26434 Mar 1999**

**Mary McLeod Bethune.**
Bethune, Mary McLeod, 1875-1955. [Selections.
1999] Bloomington : Indiana University Press, c1999.
**TC E185.97.B34 A25 1999**

**MARYLAND - HISTORY - COLONIAL PERIOD,
CA. 1600-1775 - FICTION.**
McGill, Alice. Molly Bannaky. Boston, Mass. :
Houghton Mifflin, 1999.
**TC PZ7.M478468 Mol 1999**

**MARYLAND - RACE RELATIONS.**
Fuke, Richard Paul, 1940- Imperfect equality. New
York : Fordham University Press, 1999.
**TC E185.93.M2 F85 1999**

**Marzano, Robert J.** Essential knowledge : the debate
over what American students should know / Robert J.
Marzano and John S. Kendall with Barbara B. Gaddy.
Aurora, Colo. : McREL, 1999. xiii, 450 p. ; 26 cm.
Includes bibliographical references (p.421-434) and index.
ISBN 1-89347-600-6 (alk. paper) DDC 379.1/58
*1. Education - Standards - United States. 2. Curriculum
planning - United States. 3. Education - United States -
Curricula. 4. Education - Aims and objectives - United States.
I. Kendall, John S. II. Gaddy, Barbara B., 1953- III. Title.*
**TC LB3060.83 .M36 1999**

**Marzollo, Jean.**
Wick, Walter. I spy treasure hunt. New York :
Scholastic, c1999.
**TC GV1507.P47 W5296 1999**

**Mas, Dorinda.**
Gardner, Paul (Paul Henry) Managing technology in
the middle school classroom. Huntington Beach, CA :
Teacher Created Materials, c1996.
**TC LB1028.5 .C353 1996**

**MASA INDIANS. See MACUNA INDIANS.**

**Masculinities at school** / edited by Nancy Lesko.
Thousand Oaks, Calif. : SAGE, c2000. xxx, 360 p. : 1
ill. ; 22 cm. (Research on men and masculinities series ; 11)
Includes bibliographical references and index. ISBN 0-7619-
1493-5 ISBN 0-7619-1494-3 (pbk). DDC 371.8019
*1. Boys - Education - Social aspects. 2. Masculinity. 3. Sex
differences in education - Social aspects. 4. Gender identity. 5.
Masculinity. 6. School environment. 7. Students - Psychology.
I. Lesko, Nancy. II. Series.*
**TC LC1390 .M37 2000**

**MASCULINITY.**
Ferguson, Ann Arnett, 1940- Bad boys. Ann Arbor :
University of Michigan Press, c2000.
**TC LC2771 .F47 2000**

Masculinities at school. Thousand Oaks, Calif. :
SAGE, c2000.
**TC LC1390 .M37 2000**

Masculinities at school. Thousand Oaks, Calif. :
SAGE, c2000.
**TC LC1390 .M37 2000**

**MASCULINITY (PSYCHOLOGY). See also
MASCULINITY.**
Burstyn, Varda. The rites of men. Toronto ; Buffalo :
University of Toronto Press, 1999.

**TC GV706.5 .B87 1999**

**MASCULINITY (PSYCHOLOGY) IN ART.**
Solomon-Godeau, Abligail. Male trouble :. London :
Thames and Hudson, c1997.
**TC N6847.5.N35 S64 1997**

**MASCULINITY - UNITED STATES.**
Canada, Geoffrey. Reaching up for manhood. Boston :
Beacon Press, c1998.
**TC HQ775 .C35 1998**

**Mash, Eric J.**
Banff International Conference on Behavior
Modification, 4th, 1972. Behavior change.
Champaign, Ill. : Research Press, 1974, c1973.
**TC BF637.B4 B354 1972**

**Maslach, Christina.**
Professional burnout. Washington, DC : Taylor &
Francis, c1993.
**TC BF481 .P77 1993**

**Masling, Joseph M.**
Empirical perspectives on object relations theory. 1st
ed. Washington, DC : American Psychological
Association, c1994.
**TC BF175.5.O24 E85 1994**

**MASOCHISM. See SUFFERING.**

**Mason, Mary Ann.**
Childhood in America. New York : New York
University Press, c2000.
**TC HQ792.U5 C4199 1999**

**Mason, Teresa.**
Ballroom dancing for beginners [videorecording]. W.
Long Branch, N.J. Kultur, c1993.
**TC GV1753.7 .B3 1993**

Ballroom dancing for beginners [videorecording]. W.
Long Branch, N.J. Kultur, c1993.
**TC GV1753.7 .B3 1993**

**Masotti, Louis H.** Riots and rebellion; civil violence in
the urban community. Edited, with an introd., by
Louis H. Masotti [and] Don R. Bowen. Beverly Hills,
Calif., Sage Publications [1968] 459 p. 24 cm.
Bibliography: p. [441]-451. DDC 364.14/3/0973
*1. Riots - U.S. I. Bowen, Don R., joint author. II. Title.*
**TC HV6477 .M37**

**MASS COMMUNICATION. See
COMMUNICATION;
TELECOMMUNICATION.**

**MASS CULTURE. See POPULAR CULTURE.**

**MASS MEDIA. See also MOTION PICTURES;
RADIO BROADCASTING; TELEVISION
BROADCASTING.**
The Computer as medium. Cambridge [England] ;
New York : Cambridge University Press, 1993.
**TC QA76.5 .C612554 1993**

**MASS MEDIA AND CHILDREN.**
Buckingham, David, 1954- After the death of
childhood. Malden, MA : Polity Press, 2000.
**TC HQ784.M3 B83 2000**

Levin, Diane E. Remote control childhood?
Washington, D.C. : National Association for the
Education of Young Children, c1998.
**TC P94.5.C55 L48 1998**

Tobin, Joseph Jay. "Good guys don't wear hats". New
York : Teachers College Press, c2000.
**TC HQ784.M3 T63 2000**

**MASS MEDIA AND CHILDREN - UNITED
STATES.**
Calvert, Sandra L. Children's journeys through the
information age. 1st ed. Boston : McGraw-Hill
College, c1999.
**TC HQ784.T4 C24 1999**

Kids' media culture. Durham [N.C.] ; London : Duke
University Press, 1999.
**TC HQ784.M3 K54 1999**

**MASS MEDIA AND CULTURE - UNITED
STATES.**
Seabrook, John. Nobrow. 1st ed. New York : A.A.
Knopf ; Distributed by Random House, 2000.
**TC P94.65.U6 S4 2000**

**MASS MEDIA AND EDUCATION.**
Cortés, Carlos E. The children are watching. New
York : Teachers College Press, c2000.
**TC P96.M83 C67 2000**

**MASS MEDIA AND MINORITIES - UNITED
STATES.**
Investing in diversity. Washington, D.C. : Aspen
Institute, Communications and Society Program,
c1998.

**TC P94.5.M552 U647 1997**

**MASS MEDIA AND RACE PROBLEMS. See
MASS MEDIA AND RACE RELATIONS.**

**MASS MEDIA AND RACE RELATIONS - UNITED
STATES.**
Holtzman, Linda, 1949- Media messages. Armonk,
NY : M.E. Sharpe, 2000.
**TC P94.5.M552 U646 2000**

**MASS MEDIA AND SEX - UNITED STATES.**
Holtzman, Linda, 1949- Media messages. Armonk.
NY : M.E. Sharpe, 2000.
**TC P94.5.M552 U646 2000**

**MASS MEDIA AND THE AGED - UNITED
STATES.**
Riggs, Karen E. Mature audiences. New Brunswick,
N.J. : Rutgers University Press, c1998.
**TC HQ1064.U5 R546 1998**

**MASS MEDIA AND THE ARTS.**
Carroll, Noël (Noël E.) A philosophy of mass art.
Oxford : Clarendon Press ; New York : Oxford
University Press, 1998.
**TC NX180.M3 C37 1998**

**MASS MEDIA - AUDIENCES. See also
TELEVISION VIEWERS.**
Jones, Carl Mounsey. The film-audience relationship.
1997.
**TC 06 no. 10769**

Jones, Carl Mounsey. The film-audience relationship.
1997.
**TC 06 no. 10769**

Owen, Bruce M. The Internet challenge to television.
Cambridge, Mass. : Harvard University Press, 1999.
**TC HE8700.8 .O826 1999**

**MASS MEDIA IN EDUCATION - UNITED
STATES.**
Glander, Timothy Richard, 1960- Origins of mass
communications research during the American Cold
War. Mahwah, N.J. ; London : L. Erlbaum, 2000.
**TC P91.5.U5 G57 2000**

**MASS MEDIA LITERACY. See MEDIA
LITERACY.**

**MASS MEDIA - POLITICAL ASPECTS.**
Gender, politics and communication. Cresskill, N.J. :
Hampton Press, c2000.
**TC P94.5.W65 G46 2000**

**MASS MEDIA - RESEARCH - UNITED STATES -
HISTORY.**
Glander, Timothy Richard, 1960- Origins of mass
communications research during the American Cold
War. Mahwah, N.J. ; London : L. Erlbaum, 2000.
**TC P91.5.U5 G57 2000**

**MASS MEDIA - SOCIAL ASPECTS - HISTORY.**
DeFleur, Melvin L. (Melvin Lawrence), 1923-
Theories of mass communication. New York : D.
McKay, c1966.
**TC HM258 .D35 1966**

**MASS MEDIA - SOCIAL ASPECTS - UNITED
STATES.**
Giroux, Henry A. Channel surfing. 1st ed. New York :
St. Martin's Press, 1997.
**TC HQ799.7 .G57 1997**

Holtzman, Linda, 1949- Media messages. Armonk,
NY : M.E. Sharpe, 2000. .
**TC P94.5.M552 U646 2000**

**MASS MEDIA - SOCIAL ASPECTS - UNITED
STATES - HISTORY.**
DeFleur, Melvin L. (Melvin Lawrence), 1923-
Theories of mass communication. New York : D.
McKay, c1966.
**TC HM258 .D35 1966**

**MASS MEDIA - TECHNOLOGICAL
INNOVATIONS.**
Bolter, J. David, 1951- Remediation. Cambridge,
Mass. : MIT Press, c1999.
**TC P96.T42 B59 1998**

**MASS POLITICAL BEHAVIOR. See POLITICAL
PARTICIPATION.**

**MASS PSYCHOLOGY. See SOCIAL
PSYCHOLOGY.**

**MASS SCREENING.**
HIV and AIDS. Oxford ; New York ; Oxford
University Press, 1999.
**TC RA644.A25 H57855 1999**

**MASS SOCIETY. See POPULAR CULTURE.**

**MASSACHUSETTS - RACE RELATIONS.**
Forten, Charlotte L. A free Black girl before the Civil
War. Mankato, Minn. : Blue Earth Books, c2000.
*TC F74.S1 F67 2000*

**MASSACHUSETTS - SOCIAL LIFE AND
CUSTOMS.**
Forten, Charlotte L. A free Black girl before the Civil
War. Mankato, Minn. : Blue Earth Books, c2000.
*TC F74.S1 F67 2000*

**Massey, Gerald J.**
Science at century's end. Pittsburgh, Pa. : University
of Pittsburgh Press, c2000.
*TC Q175 .S4193 2000*

**Massey, Veta H.**
Grant, Ann Boyle. Nursing leadership, management &
research. Springhouse, Pa. : Springhouse Corp.,
c1999.
*TC RT89 .G727 1999*

**Master classes in education series**
Black, P. J. (Paul Joseph), 1930- Testing, friend or
foe? London ; Washington : Falmer Press, 1998.
*TC LB3056.E54 B53 1998*

Ross, Alistair, 1946- Curriculum. London ; New
York : Falmer Press, 2000.
*TC LB1564.G7 R66 2000*

**MASTER OF BUSINESS ADMINISTRATION
DEGREE.**
Crainer, Stuart. Gravy training. 1st ed. San Francisco :
Jossey-Bass Publishers, c1999.
*TC HF1111 .C7 1999*

**MASTER TEACHERS - GREAT BRITAIN.**
Bell, Derek, 1950- Towards effective subject
leadership in the primary school. Buckingham
[England] ; Philadelphia : Open University Press,
c1999.
*TC LB2832.4.G7 B45 1999*

**Mastering Access 97 development.**
Balter, Alison. [Mastering Access 97 development]
Alison Balter's Mastering Access 97 development.
2nd ed. Indianapolis, Ind. : Sams Pub., [c1997]
*TC QA76.9.D3 B32 1997*

**Mastering GNOME.**
Pfaffenberger, Bryan, 1949- San Francisco, CA :
Sybex, Inc., 1999.
*TC QA76.9.U83 P453 1999*

**Mastering piano technique.**
Fink, Seymour. Portland, Or.: Amadeus Press, c1992.
*TC MT220 .F44 1992*

**Mastering research.**
Chen, Sheying. Chicago : Nelson-Hall, c1998.
*TC BF76.5 .C44 1998*

**Masterpasqua, Frank.**
The Psychological meaning of chaos. 1st ed.
Washington, D.C. : American Psychological
Association, c1997.
*TC RC437.5 .P762 1997*

**Master's degree studies from the Institute of
International Education**
(no 1) Tuijnman, Albert. Recurrent education and
socioeconomic success. [Stockholm] : Institute of
International Education, University of Stockholm,
c1986.
*TC LC5215 .T84 1986*

**Masters of color and light.**
Ferber, Linda S. Washington : Brooklyn Museum of
Art in Association with Smithsonian Institution Press,
c1998.
*TC ND1807 .F47 1998*

**MASTERY LEARNING.** *See* **INDIVIDUALIZED
INSTRUCTION.**

**MASTERY LEARNING - UNITED STATES.**
Meichenbaum, Donald. Nurturing independent
learners. Cambridge, Mass. : Brookline Books, c1998.
*TC LB1031.4 .M45 1998*

**The mastery of literacy and numeracy.**
Bourke, S. F. Canberra : Australian Govt. Pub.
Service, 1977.
*TC LA2102 .B68 1977*

**Mátai, Mária D.**
Gegő, Elek, 1805-1844. Népoktató. Budapest :
Országos Pedagógiai Könyvtár és Múzeum, [1997]
*TC LC227 .G44 1997*

**Matching books to readers.**
Fountas, Irene C. Portsmouth, NH : Heinemann,
c1999.
*TC LB1573 .F68*

**Maté, Gabor.** Scattered : how attention deficit disorder
originates and what you can do about it / Gabor Maté.
1st American ed. New York, N.Y., U.S.A. : Dutton,
1999. xix, 348 p. : ill. ; 24 cm. Includes bibliographical
references and index. ISBN 0-525-94412-5 (alk. paper) DDC
616.85/89
*1. Attention-deficit hyperactivity disorder - Psychological
aspects. 2. Attention-deficit hyperactivity disorder -
Environmental aspects. I. Title.*
*TC RJ506.H9 M42326 1999*

**MATE SELECTION.** *See* **MAN-WOMAN
RELATIONSHIPS.**

**Mateer, Carolyn.**
Lane, Nancy D. Techniques for student research. New
York : Neal-Schuman Publishers, 2000.
*TC Z710 .L36 2000*

**MATERIA MEDICA.** *See* **DRUGS.**

**MATERIAL CULTURE.** *See also* **ANTIQUITIES;
FOLKLORE; TECHNOLOGY.**
Glassie, Henry H. Bloomington : Indiana University
Press, 1999.
*TC GN406 .G53 1999*

**MATERIAL CULTURE.**
Glassie, Henry H. Material culture. Bloomington :
Indiana University Press, 1999.
*TC GN406 .G53 1999*

Learning, language, and invention. Aldershot,
Hampshire, Great Britain : Variorum ; Brookfield, Vt.,
USA : Ashgate Pub. Co. : Paris, France : Société
internationale de l'Astrolabe, 1994.
*TC AC5 .L38 1994*

**Material culture (Indiana University, Bloomington)**
(1.) Glassie, Henry H. The potter's art.
Philadelphia : Material Culture ; Bloomington :
Indiana University Press, 1999.
*TC NK4235 .G54 1999*

**MATERIALISM.** *See* **DUALISM.**

**MATERIALS, ARCHIVAL.** *See* **ARCHIVAL
MATERIALS.**

**MATERIALS HANDLING.** *See* **TRUCKS.**

**MATERIALS, LIBRARY.** *See* **LIBRARY
MATERIALS.**

**MATERNAL BEHAVIOR IN ANIMALS.** *See*
**PARENTAL BEHAVIOR IN ANIMALS.**

**Maternal, child & adolescent health profile 1993.**
Maternal, child and adolescent health profile. Albany,
N.Y. : New York State Dept. of Health, 1996.
*TC HV742.N7 B83 1996*

**Maternal, child and adolescent health profile :** New
York State 1993. Albany, N.Y. : New York State
Dept. of Health, 1996. xiv, 67 p. : maps ; 22 x 28 cm.
Cover title: Maternal, child & adolescent health profile 1993.
"December 1996." Includes bibliographical references (p. 60-
61).
*1. Health surveys - New York (State) 2. Family Health - New
York - statistics. 3. Public health - New York (State) - Statistics.
4. Children - Health and hygiene - New York (State) -
Statistics. 5. Teenagers - Health and hygiene - New York
(State) - Statistic. 6. Mothers - New York (State) - Health and
hygiene - Statistics. I. New York (State). Dept. of Health. II.
Title. III. Title: Maternal, child & adolescent health profile
1993 IV. Title: MCAHP*
*TC HV742.N7 B83 1996*

**MATERNAL-FETAL MEDICINE.** *See*
**OBSTETRICS.**

**MATERNITY.** *See* **MOTHERHOOD.**

**MATERNITY LEAVE - LAW AND
LEGISLATION - UNITED STATES.**
Commission on Family and Medical Leave (U.S.) A
Workable balance. Washington, DC : Commission on
Leave ; Women's Bureau, U.S. Dept. of Labor, [1996]
*TC HD5115.6.U5 C66 1996*

**MATERNITY LEAVE - UNITED STATES.**
Commission on Family and Medical Leave (U.S.) A
Workable balance. Washington, DC : Commission on
Leave ; Women's Bureau, U.S. Dept. of Labor, [1996]
*TC HD5115.6.U5 C66 1996*

**Mates, Barbara T.** Adaptive technology for the
Internet : making electronic resources accessible /
Barbara T. Mates ; with contributions by Doug
Wakefield and Judith Dixon. Chicago, Ill. : American
Library Association, 1999. xi, 192 p. ; 26 cm. Includes
index. Includes bibliographical references. ISBN 0-8389-
0752-0 DDC 027.6/63
*1. Libraries and the blind - United States. 2. Libraries and the
handicapped - United States. 3. Libraries - United States -
Special collections - Computer network resources. 4. Blind,*

*Apparatus for the - United States. 5. Adaptive computing -
United States. I. Wakefield, Doug. II. Dixon, Judith M. III.
Title.*
*TC Z675.B M38 1999*

**MATH.** *See* **MATHEMATICS.**

**Math and science for young children.**
Charlesworth, Rosalind. 3rd ed. Albany, NY : Delmar
Publishers, c1999.
*TC QA135.5 .C463 1999*

**Math anthology :** stories, poems, and songs : I can!
Math activity program. New York : Macmillan/
McGraw-Hill Pub. Co., c1993. xvii, 220 p. : ill., music ;
28 cm. (Mathematics in action.) Includes indexes.
"Macmillan/McGraw-Hill". "Grades kindergarten, 1 and 2"--
Cover. ISBN 0-02-109095-5
*1. Mathematics - Study and teaching (Primary) 2.
Mathematics - Juvenile literature I. Title: Macmillan/
McGraw-Hill math anthology II. Title: I can! Math activity
program III. Series.*
*TC QA141.3 .M37 1993*

**Math anthology :** stories, poems, and songs : I can!
Math activity program. New York : Macmillan/
McGraw-Hill Pub. Co., c1993. xvii, 220 p. : ill., music ;
28 cm. (Mathematics in action.) Includes indexes.
"Macmillan/McGraw-Hill". "Grades kindergarten, 1 and 2"--
Cover. ISBN 0-02-109095-5
*1. Mathematics - Study and teaching (Primary) 2.
Mathematics - Juvenile literature I. Title: Macmillan/
McGraw-Hill math anthology II. Title: I can! Math activity
program III. Series.*
*TC QA141.3 .M37 1993*

**Math around the world :** teacher's guide / Beverly
Braxton. Berkeley, CA : Lawrence Hall of Science,
University of California at Berkeley, c1995. x, 190 p. :
ill. ; 28 cm. "LHS GEMS." "Grades 5-8." Includes
bibliographical references. ISBN 0-912511-94-x
*1. Games in mathematics education. 2. Mathematics - Study
and teaching (Elementary). 3. Interdisciplinary approach in
education. 4. Intercultural education. I. Braxton, Beverly. II.
GEMS (Project).*
*TC QA20.G35 M384 1995*

**Math detective [computer file].**
Carmen Sandiego [computer file]. Novato, Calif. :
Brøderbund Software, 1998. Computer data and
program.
*TC QA115 .C37 1998*

**The math gene.**
Devlin, Keith J. [New York] : Basic Books, 2000.
*TC QA141 .D48 2000*

**Math gene.**
Devlin, Keith J. The math gene. [New York] : Basic
Books, 2000.
*TC QA141 .D48 2000*

**Math is language too.**
Whitin, Phyllis. Urbana, Ill. : National Council of
Teachers of English, c2000.
*TC QA8.7 .W48 2000*

**Mathelin, Catherine.**
[Raisins verts et dents agacées. English]
Lacanian psychotherapy with children : the broken
piano / Catherine Mathelin ; translated by Susan
Fairfield ; noted by Judith Feher Gurewich. New
York : The Other Press, 1999. xxiv, 194 p. : ill ; 21 cm.
(The Lacanian clinical field) Includes bibliographical
references and index. ISBN 1-89274-601-8 (softcover : alk.
paper) DDC 618.92/8917
*1. Child analysis - Case studies. 2. Lacan, Jacques, - 1901-1.
Title. II. Series.*
*TC RJ504.2 .M3913 1999*

**MATHEMATICA (COMPUTER FILE).**
Torrence, Bruce F. (Bruce Follett), 1963- The
student's introduction to Mathematica. Cambridge ;
New York : Cambridge University Press, 1999.
*TC QA76.95 .T67 1999*

**MATHEMATICAL ABILITY.** *See also*
**NUMERACY.**
Devlin, Keith J. The math gene. [New York] : Basic
Books, 2000.
*TC QA141 .D48 2000*

Tokar, Inna. Schools for the mathematically talented
in the former Soviet Union. 1999.
*TC 085 T572*

**MATHEMATICAL ABILITY - SEX
DIFFERENCES.**
Cooper, Barry, 1950- Assessing children's
mathematical knowledge. Buckingham ;
Philadelphia : Open University Press, 2000.
*TC QA135.5 .C5955 2000*

Feisty females. Portsmouth, NH : Heinemann, c1998.
*TC QA11 .F44 1998*

**MATHEMATICAL ABILITY - TESTING.**
Feldberg, Suzanne. A comparison of different types of mathematical problem-solving hints selected by concrete and formal operational subjects in a hypercard environment. 1998.
*TC 085 F316*

**MATHEMATICAL ANALYSIS.** *See also*
    **ALGEBRA; CALCULUS.**
Stahl, Saul. Real analysis. New York : J. Wiley, c1999.
*TC QA300 .S882 1999*

**MATHEMATICAL LINGUISTICS.** *See*
    **COMPUTATIONAL LINGUISTICS.**

**MATHEMATICAL MODELS.**
Snijders, Tom A. B. Multilevel analysis. Thousand Oaks, Calif. ; London : SAGE, 1999.
*TC QA278 .S645 1999*

**MATHEMATICAL NOTATION.**
Seo, Kyoung-Hye. Children's construction of personal meanings of mathematical symbolism in a reform-oriented classroom. 2000.
*TC 06 no. 11310*

Symbolizing and communicating in mathematics classrooms. Mahwah, N.J. : Lawrence Erlbaum Associates, 2000.
*TC QA11 .S873 2000*

**MATHEMATICAL PHYSICS.** *See* **ELECTRICITY.**

**MATHEMATICAL STATISTICS.** *See also*
    **ANALYSIS OF VARIANCE;**
    **PROBABILITIES; SAMPLING**
    **(STATISTICS).**
Bottenberg, Robert Alan. Applied multiple linear regression. Lackland Air Force Base, Texas, 6570th Personnel Research Laboratory Aerospace Medical Division, Air Force Systems Command, 1963
*TC QA276 .B67 1963*

Du, Zuru. Modeling conditional item dependencies with a three-parameter logistic testlet model. 1998.
*TC 085 D84*

Everitt, Brian. Chance rules. New York : Copernicus, c1999.
*TC QA273 .E84 1999*

Statistics and neural networks. Oxford ; New York : Oxford University Press, 1999.
*TC QA276 .S78343 1999*

**MATHEMATICAL STATISTICS - HISTORY.**
Stigler, Stephen M. Statistics on the table. Cambridge, Mass. : Harvard University Press, 1999.
*TC QA276.15 .S755 1999*

**MATHEMATICAL STATISTICS - STUDY AND**
    **TEACHING.**
Reflections on statistics. Mahwah, N.J. : L. Erlbaum, 1998.
*TC QA276.18 .R44 1998*

**MATHEMATICAL STATISTICS - STUDY AND**
    **TEACHING (ELEMENTARY).**
Cuomo, Celia, 1956- In all probability. Berkeley, CA : Lawrence Hall of Science, University of California, Berkeley, c1998.
*TC QA276.18 .C866 1998*

**MATHEMATICIANS - ENGLAND - OXFORD -**
    **INTELLECTUAL LIFE.**
Oxford figures. Oxford ; New York : Oxford University Press, 2000.
*TC QA14.G73 O947 2000*

**MATHEMATICIANS - ENGLAND - OXFORD -**
    **SOCIAL LIFE AND CUSTOMS.**
Oxford figures. Oxford ; New York : Oxford University Press, 2000.
*TC QA14.G73 O947 2000*

**MATHEMATICS.** *See also* **ALGEBRA;**
    **ARITHMETIC; FRACTIONS; GEOMETRY;**
    **NUMERACY; PROBABILITIES.**
Bumby, Douglas R. 2nd ed. Columbus, Ohio : C.E. Merrill, c1982-<1986.>
*TC QA154.2 .B8 1982*

Bumby, Douglas R. Columbus, Ohio : C.E. Merrill, c1978-1979.
*TC QA39.2 .B85 1980*

**MATHEMATICS.**
Bumby, Douglas R. Mathematics. Columbus, Ohio : C.E. Merrill, c1978-1979.
*TC QA39.2 .B85 1980*

Elementary mathematics. New York : Holt, Rinehart and Winson, 1966.
*TC QA107 .E53 1966*

Farmer, Lesley S. J. Go figure!. Englewood, Colo. : Teacher Ideas Press, 1999.
*TC QA39.2 .F373 1999*

Haenisch, Siegfried AGS pre-algebra. Circle Pines, Minn. : AGS, American Guidance Service, c1998.
*TC QA107 .H33 1998*

Haenisch, Siegfried AGS pre-algebra. Teacher's ed. Circle Pines, Minn. : AGS, American Guidance Service, c1998.
*TC QA107 .H33 1998 Teacher's Ed.*

Haenisch, Siegfried AGS pre-algebra. Teacher's ed. Circle Pines, Minn. : AGS, American Guidance Service, c1998.
*TC QA107 .H33 1998 Teacher's Ed.*

Haenisch, Siegfried AGS pre-algebra. Teacher's ed. Circle Pines, Minn. : AGS, American Guidance Service, c1998.
*TC QA107 .H33 1998 Teacher's Ed.*

I can do it. New York : Macmillan/McGraw-Hill School Publishing Co., 1994.
*TC QA139 .M37 1994*

Mathematics for mastery. Teacher's ed. Morristown, N. J. : Silver Burdett, 1981.
*TC QA107 .M375 1981 Teacher's Ed.*

Treff, August V. AGS basic math skills. Circle Pines, Minn. : AGS, American Guidance Service, c1997.
*TC QA107 .T73 1997*

Treff, August V. AGS basic math skills. Teacher's ed. Circle Pines, Minn. : AGS, American Guidance Service, c1997.
*TC QA107 .T73 1997 Teacher's Ed.*

Vogeli, Bruce R. Mathematics for mastery. Teacher's ed. Morristown, N. J. : Silver Burdett, 1978.
*TC QA107 .M375 1978 Teacher's Ed.*

**Mathematics and distance education on the internet.**
Anderson, Dennis S. 1999.
*TC 085 An2317*

**MATHEMATICS - COMPETITIONS - SOVIET**
    **UNION.**
Tokar, Inna. Schools for the mathematically talented in the former Soviet Union. 1999.
*TC 085 T572*

**MATHEMATICS - COMPUTER SIMULATION.**
Modeling and simulation in science and mathematics education. New York : Springer, c1999.
*TC Q181 .M62 1999*

**MATHEMATICS - CONGRESSES.**
International Congress of Mathematicians (new series) (7th : 1954 : Amsterdam) Proceedings of the International Congress of Mathematicians, 1954, Groningen, E. P. Noordhoff, 1954-1957.
*TC QA2 .I612 1954*

**MATHEMATICS - DATA PROCESSING.**
Torrence, Bruce F. (Bruce Follett), 1963- The student's introduction to Mathematica. Cambridge ; New York : Cambridge University Press, 1999.
*TC QA76.95 .T67 1999*

**MATHEMATICS - ENGLAND - OXFORD -**
    **HISTORY.**
Oxford figures. Oxford ; New York : Oxford University Press, 2000.
*TC QA14.G73 O947 2000*

**MATHEMATICS - EXAMINATIONS,**
    **EXERCISES, ETC.**
Mathematics for mastery. Morristown, N. J. : Silver Burdett, 1981.
*TC QA107 .M375 1981 Tests*

**Mathematics for elementary school teachers.**
Billstein, Rick. A problem solving approach to mathematics for elementary school teachers. 5th ed. Reading, Mass. : Addison-Wesley, c1993.
*TC QA135.5 .B49 1993*

**Mathematics for mastery.**
McKillip, William D. Teacher's ed. Morristown, N.J. : Silver Burdett, 1981.
*TC QA107 .M375 1981 Teacher's ed. K*

McKillip, William D. Teacher's ed. Morristown, N.J. : Silver Burdett, 1981.
*TC QA107 .M375 1981 Teacher's ed. K*

McKillip, William D. Teacher's ed. Morristown, N.J. : Silver Burdett, 1981.

*TC QA107 .M375 1981 Teacher's ed. K*

**Mathematics for mastery.** Teacher's ed. Morristown, N. J. : Silver Burdett, 1981. v. : col. ill. ; 24 cm. Includes index. ISBN 0-382-01607-6 (v. 1) ISBN 0-382-01609-2 (v. 3) ISBN 0-382-01613-0 (v. 7) ISBN 0-382-01614-9 (v. 8) ISBN 0-382-01606-8 (K)
*1. Mathematics. 2. Mathematics - Study and teaching (Elementary). I. Title.*
*TC QA107 .M375 1981 Teacher's Ed.*

**Mathematics for mastery :** tests. Morristown, N. J. : Silver Burdett, 1981. 6-44 p. : ill. ; 24 cm. ISBN 0-382-01640-8
*1. Mathematics - Examinations, exercises, etc.*
*TC QA107 .M375 1981 Tests*

**Mathematics for primary teachers** / edited by Valsa Koshy, Paul Ernest, and Ron Casey. London ; New York : Routledge, 2000. xiii, 225 p. : ill. ; 25 cm. Includes bibliographical references and index. ISBN 0-415-20090-3 pb DDC 372.7/044
*1. Mathematics - Study and teaching (Primary) I. Koshy, Valsa, 1945- II. Ernest, Paul. III. Casey, Ron.*
*TC QA135.5 .K67 2000*

**MATHEMATICS, GREEK.**
Stein, Sherman K. Archimedes. Washington, D.C. : Mathematical Association of America, c1999.
*TC QA31 .S84 1999*

**MATHEMATICS - HISTORY.**
Grattan-Guinness, I. [Fontana history of the mathematical sciences] The Norton history of the mathematical sciences. 1st American ed. New York : W.W. Norton, 1998.
*TC QA21 .G695 1998*

Johnson, Art, 1946- Famous problems and their mathematicians. Englewood, Colo. : Teacher Ideas Press, 1999.
*TC QA43 .J56 1999*

**Mathematics in action.**
Hoffer, Alan R. I can! : Teacher's guide. New York : Macmillan/McGraw-Hill School Publishing Co., 1996.
*TC QA139 .H63 1996*

Hoffer, Alan R. I can! : Teacher's guide. New York : Macmillan/McGraw-Hill School Publishing Co., 1996.
*TC QA139 .H63 1996*

I can do it. Teacher's ed. New York : Macmillan/ McGraw-Hill School Publishing Co., 1994.
*TC QA139 .H63 1994 Teacher's Ed.*

I can do it. New York : Macmillan/McGraw-Hill School Publishing Co., 1994.
*TC QA139 .M37 1994*

Math anthology. New York : Macmillan/McGraw-Hill Pub. Co., c1993.
*TC QA141.3 .M37 1993*

Math anthology. New York : Macmillan/McGraw-Hill Pub. Co., c1993.
*TC QA141.3 .M37 1993*

**Mathematics in the primary school :** a sense of progression / edited by Christine Hopkins, Sue Gifford, and Sandy Pepperell. 2nd ed. London : D. Fulton, 2000. viii, 180 p. : ill. ; 25 cm. "Written by the team of tutors at the Centre for Mathematics Education, Roehampton Institute London." "Published in association with Roehampton Institute London." Includes bibliographical references (p. [192]-194) and index. ISBN 1-85346-592-5 DDC 372.7/044
*1. Mathematics - Study and teaching (Primary) I. Hopkins, Christine. II. Gifford, Susan. III. Pepperell, Sandy. IV. Roehampton Institute. Centre for Mathematics Education.*
*TC QA135.5 .M36934 1999*

**MATHEMATICS - JUVENILE LITERATURE.**
Math anthology. New York : Macmillan/McGraw-Hill Pub. Co., c1993.
*TC QA141.3 .M37 1993*

Math anthology. New York : Macmillan/McGraw-Hill Pub. Co., c1993.
*TC QA141.3 .M37 1993*

**Mathematics, learning, and cognition**
Speiser, R. (Robert) Five women build a number system. Stamford, Conn. : Ablex Pub., c2000.
*TC QA135.5 .S5785 2000*

**Mathematics on the Internet.**
Ameis, Jerry A. Upper Saddle River, N.J. : Merrill, 2000.
*TC QA41.6 .A64 2000*

**MATHEMATICS - PERIODICALS.**
Archimedes; Regensburg, Josef Habbel.

Bulletin (new series) of the American Mathematical Society. Providence, R.I. : The Society, 1979-

The Fibonacci quarterly. [St. Mary's College, Calif., Fibonacci Association]

Journal de mathématiques élémentaires. [Paris : s.n.,

## MATHEMATICS - PHILOSOPHY.
Devlin, Keith J. The math gene. [New York] : Basic Books, 2000.
*TC QA141 .D48 2000*

## MATHEMATICS - PROBLEMS, EXERCISES, ETC.
Johnson, Art, 1946- Famous problems and their mathematicians. Englewood, Colo. : Teacher Ideas Press, 1999.
*TC QA43 .J56 1999*

Maylone, Nelson John. That can't be right!. Lancaster, PA : Technomic Pub. Co., c1999.
*TC QA43 .M367 1999*

**A mathematics series**
Decimals [videorecording]. Princeton, N.J. : Video Tutor, 1988.
*TC QA117 .D4 1988*

Fractions [videorecording]. Princeton, N.J. : Video Tutor, 1988.
*TC QA117 .F7 1988*

The high school proficiency test [videorecording]. Princeton, N.J. : Video Tutor, 1988.
*TC QA445 .H5 1988*

Number concepts [videorecording]. Princeton, N.J. : Video Tutor, 1988.
*TC QA117 .N8 1988*

Number concepts [videorecording]. Princeton, N.J. : Video Tutor, 1988.
*TC QA117 .N8 1988*

Percents [videorecording]. Princeton, N.J. : Video Tutor, 1988.

Percents [videorecording]. Princeton, N.J. : Video Tutor, 1988.
*TC QA117 .P4 1988*

Pre-algebra [videorecording]. Princeton, N.J. : Video Tutor, 1988.
*TC QA152.2 .P6 1988*

Word problems [videorecording]. Princeton, N.J. : Video Tutor, 1988.
*TC QA139 .W6 1988*

## MATHEMATICS - SOVIET UNION - TEXTBOOKS.
Moro, M. I. Russian grade 1 mathematics. Chicago : University of Chicago School of Mathematics Project, 1992.
*TC QA14.R9 R8611 1992*

Moro, M. I. Russian grade 2 mathematics. Chicago : University of Chicago School of Mathematics Project, 1992.
*TC QA14.R9 R8711 1992*

Russian grade 3 mathematics. Chicago : University of Chicago School of Mathematics Project, 1992.
*TC QA14.R9 R8811 1992*

## MATHEMATICS - STATISTICAL METHODS. See MATHEMATICAL STATISTICS.

## MATHEMATICS - STUDY AND TEACHING.
Borasi, Raffaella. Reading counts. New York ; London : Teachers College Press, c2000.
*TC QA11 .B6384 2000*

Creativity in the classroom. Burbank, CA : Disney Learning Partnership, c1999.
*TC LB1062 .C7 1999*

Curriculum frameworks for mathematics and science. Vancouver, Canada : Pacific Educational Press, c1993.
*TC QA11 .C87 1993*

Feisty females. Portsmouth, NH : Heinemann, c1998.
*TC QA11 .F44 1998*

Future basics. Golden, Colo. : National Council of Supervisors of Mathematics, c1998.
*TC QA141 .C43 1998*

Herriot, Sarah T. The Slow learner project: [Stanford, Calif.: Leland Stanford Junior University; 1967]
*TC QA11 .S25 no.5*

National contexts for mathematics & science education. Vancouver : Pacific Educational Press, 1997.

*TC Q181 N37 1997*

Symbolizing and communicating in mathematics classrooms. Mahwah, N.J. : Lawrence Erlbaum Associates, 2000.
*TC QA11 .S873 2000*

Whitin, Phyllis. Math is language too. Urbana, Ill. : National Council of Teachers of English, c2000.
*TC QA8.7 .W48 2000*

## MATHEMATICS - STUDY AND TEACHING - ACTIVITY PROGRAMS.
Hoffer, Alan R. I can! : Teacher's guide. New York : Macmillan/McGraw-Hill School Publishing Co., 1996.
*TC QA139 .H63 1996*

Hoffer, Alan R. I can! : Teacher's guide. New York : Macmillan/McGraw-Hill School Publishing Co., 1996.
*TC QA139 .H63 1996*

I can do it. Teacher's ed. New York : Macmillan/McGraw-Hill School Publishing Co., 1994.
*TC QA139 .H63 1994 Teacher's Ed.*

## MATHEMATICS - STUDY AND TEACHING - AUDIO-VISUAL AIDS.
Anderson, Dennis S. Mathematics and distance education on the internet. 1999.
*TC 085 An2317*

## MATHEMATICS - STUDY AND TEACHING - COMPUTER-ASSISTED INSTRUCTION.
FOX, BOB. Using ICT in primary mathematics. London : D. Fulton, 2000.
*TC QA20.C65 F69 2000*

## MATHEMATICS - STUDY AND TEACHING - COMPUTER NETWORK RESOURCES.
Ameis, Jerry A. Mathematics on the Internet. Upper Saddle River, N.J. : Merrill, 2000.
*TC QA41.6 .A64 2000*

## MATHEMATICS - STUDY AND TEACHING - CONGRESSES.
Algebra, K-theory, groups, and education. Providence, R.I. : American Mathematical Society, c1999.
*TC QA150 .A419 1999*

Discrete mathematics in the schools. Providence, R.I. : American Mathematical Society, National Council of Teachers of Mathematics, c1997.
*TC QA11.A1 D57 1997*

## MATHEMATICS - STUDY AND TEACHING (EARLY CHILDHOOD) - UNITED STATES.
Dialogue on early childhood science, mathematics, and technology education. Washington, DC : American Association for the Advancement of Science/Project 2061, 1999.
*TC LB1139.5.S35 D53 1999*

## MATHEMATICS - STUDY AND TEACHING (ELEMENTARY).
Baroody, Arthur J., 1947- Fostering children's mathematical power. Mahwah, N.J. : Lawrence Erlbaum Associates, 1998.
*TC QA135.5 .B2847 1998*

Billstein, Rick. A problem solving approach to mathematics for elementary school teachers. 5th ed. Reading, Mass. : Addison-Wesley, c1993.
*TC QA135.5 .B49 1993*

Brandy, Tim. So what? Portsmouth, NH : Heinemann, c1999.
*TC QA135.5 .B6785 1999*

Elementary mathematics, patterns and structure; accelerated sequence. Teacher's ed. New York, Holt, Rinehart and Winston [c1966]

Environmental justice. Menlo Park, Calif. : Institute for Research on Learning, c1998.
*TC QA135.5 .E68 1998*

Feldberg, Suzanne. A comparison of different types of mathematical problem-solving hints selected by concrete and formal operational subjects in a hypercard environment. 1998.
*TC 085 F316*

Guppies. Menlo Park, Calif. : Institute for Research on Learning, c1997.
*TC QA135.5 .G86 1997*

Kennedy, Leonard M. Guiding children's learning of mathematics. 9th ed. Belmont, CA : Wadsworth/Thomson Learning, c2000.
*TC QA135.5 .K43 2000*

Math around the world. Berkeley, CA : Lawrence Hall of Science, University of California at Berkeley, c1995.

*TC QA20.G35 M384 1995*

Mathematics for mastery. Teacher's ed. Morristown, N. J. : Silver Burdett, 1981.
*TC QA107 .M375 1981 Teacher's Ed.*

ROBBINS, BRIAN. Inclusive mathematics 5-11. London ; New York : Continuum, 2000.
*TC QA135.5 .R63 2000*

Schwieger, Ruben D. Teaching elementary school mathematics. Belmont, CA : Wadsworth Pub., 1999.
*TC QA135.5 .S329 1999*

Sheffield, Linda Jensen, 1949- Teaching and learning elementary and middle school mathematics. 4th ed. New York : Wiley, c2000.
*TC QA135.5 .S48 2000*

Speiser, R. (Robert) Five women build a number system. Stamford, Conn. : Ablex Pub., c2000.
*TC QA135.5 .S5785 2000*

Teaching and learning thinking skills. Lisse [Netherlands] ; Exton, PA : Swets & Zeitlinger, c1999.
*TC LB1590.3 .T36 1999*

Vogeli, Bruce R. Mathematics for mastery. Teacher's ed. Morristown, N. J. : Silver Burdett, 1978.
*TC QA107 .M375 1978 Teacher's Ed.*

Whitin, David Jackman, 1947- It's the story that counts. Portsmouth, NH : Heinemann, c1995.
*TC QA135.5 .W465 1995*

Wolves and caribou unit. Menlo Park, Calif. : Institute for Research on Learning, 1998, c1995.
*TC QA135.5 .W64 1995*

## MATHEMATICS - STUDY AND TEACHING (ELEMENTARY) - CASE STUDIES.
Seo, Kyoung-Hye. Children's construction of personal meanings of mathematical symbolism in a reform-oriented classroom. 2000.
*TC 06 no. 11310*

## MATHEMATICS - STUDY AND TEACHING (ELEMENTARY) - CHINA.
Ma, Liping. Knowing and teaching elementary mathematics. Mahwah, N.J. : Lawrence Erlbaum Associates, 1999.
*TC QA135.5 .M22 1999*

## MATHEMATICS - STUDY AND TEACHING (ELEMENTARY) - COMPUTER NETWORK RESOURCES.
The Internet in action for math & science K-6 [videorecording]. [New York] : Thirteen-WNET ; [Alexandria, Va. : distributed by] PBS Video, c1998.
*TC LB1044.87 .I45 1998*

## MATHEMATICS - STUDY AND TEACHING (ELEMENTARY) - ENGLAND - EVALUATION.
Cooper, Barry, 1950- Assessing children's mathematical knowledge. Buckingham ; Philadelphia : Open University Press, 2000.
*TC QA135.5 .C5955 2000*

## MATHEMATICS - STUDY AND TEACHING (ELEMENTARY) - ENGLAND - SOCIAL ASPECTS.
Cooper, Barry, 1950- Assessing children's mathematical knowledge. Buckingham ; Philadelphia : Open University Press, 2000.
*TC QA135.5 .C5955 2000*

## MATHEMATICS - STUDY AND TEACHING (ELEMENTARY) - GREAT BRITAIN - CASE STUDIES.
Sawyer, Ann Elisabeth. Developments in elementary mathematics teaching. Portsmouth, NH : Heinemann, c1995.
*TC QA135.5 .S278 1995*

## MATHEMATICS - STUDY AND TEACHING (ELEMENTARY) - SOVIET UNION.
Moro, M. I. Russian grade 1 mathematics. Chicago : University of Chicago School of Mathematics Project, 1992.
*TC QA14.R9 R8611 1992*

Moro, M. I. Russian grade 2 mathematics. Chicago : University of Chicago School of Mathematics Project, 1992.
*TC QA14.R9 R8711 1992*

Russian grade 3 mathematics. Chicago : University of Chicago School of Mathematics Project, 1992.
*TC QA14.R9 R8811 1992*

## MATHEMATICS - STUDY AND TEACHING (ELEMENTARY) - UNITED STATES.
Ma, Liping. Knowing and teaching elementary

mathematics. Mahwah, N.J. : Lawrence Erlbaum
Associates, 1999.
*TC QA135.5 .M22 1999*

Reflecting on practice in elementary school
mathematics. Reston, Va. : National Council of
Teachers of Mathematics, c1999.
*TC QA135.5 .R426 1999*

**MATHEMATICS - STUDY AND TEACHING
(HIGHER) - ENGLAND - OXFORD -
HISTORY.**
Oxford figures. Oxford ; New York : Oxford
University Press, 2000.
*TC QA14.G73 O947 2000*

**MATHEMATICS - STUDY AND TEACHING
(HIGHER) - UNITED STATES.**
Transforming undergraduate education in science,
mathematics, engineering, and technology.
Washington, DC : National Academy Press, 1999.
*TC Q183.3.A1 T73 1999*

**MATHEMATICS - STUDY AND TEACHING
(MIDDLE SCHOOL).**
Brahier, Daniel J. Teaching secondary and middle
school mathematics. Boston : Allyn and Bacon, 2000.
*TC QA11 .B6999 2000*

Krulik, Stephen. Teaching middle school
mathematics. Boston : Allyn and Bacon, c2000.
*TC QA11 .K818 2000*

Sheffield, Linda Jensen, 1949- Teaching and learning
elementary and middle school mathematics. 4th ed.
New York : Wiley, c2000.
*TC QA135.5 .S48 2000*

**MATHEMATICS - STUDY AND TEACHING
(MIDDLE SCHOOL) - CASE STUDIES.**
Implementing standards-based mathematics
instruction. New York : Teachers College Press,
c2000.
*TC QA135.5 .I525 2000*

**MATHEMATICS - STUDY AND TEACHING
(MIDDLE SCHOOL) - COMPUTER
NETWORK RESOURCES.**
The Internet in action for math & science 7-12
[videorecording]. [New York] : Thirteen-WNET ;
[Alexandria, Va. : distributed by] PBS Video, c1997.
*TC LB1044.87 .I453 1997*

The Internet in action for math & science K-6
[videorecording]. [New York] : Thirteen-WNET ;
[Alexandria, Va. : distributed by] PBS Video, c1998.
*TC LB1044.87 .I45 1998*

**MATHEMATICS - STUDY AND TEACHING
(PRIMARY).**
Charlesworth, Rosalind. Math and science for young
children. 3rd ed. Albany, NY : Delmar Publishers,
c1999.
*TC QA135.5 .C463 1999*

Hoffer, Alan R. I can! : Teacher's guide. New York :
Macmillan/McGraw-Hill School Publishing Co.,
1996.
*TC QA139 .H63 1996*

Hoffer, Alan R. I can! : Teacher's guide. New York :
Macmillan/McGraw-Hill School Publishing Co.,
1996.
*TC QA139 .H63 1996*

I can do it. Teacher's ed. New York : Macmillan/
McGraw-Hill School Publishing Co., 1994.
*TC QA139 .H63 1994 Teacher's Ed.*

Math anthology. New York : Macmillan/McGraw-Hill
Pub. Co., c1993.
*TC QA141.3 .M37 1993*

Math anthology. New York : Macmillan/McGraw-Hill
Pub. Co., c1993.
*TC QA141.3 .M37 1993*

Mathematics for primary teachers. London ; New
York : Routledge, 2000.
*TC QA135.5 .K67 2000*

Mathematics in the primary school. 2nd ed. London :
D. Fulton, 1999.
*TC QA135.5 .M36934 1999*

Trafton, Paul R. Learning through problems.
Portsmouth, NH : Heinemann, c1999.
*TC QA135.5 .T685 1999*

**MATHEMATICS - STUDY AND TEACHING
(PRIMARY) - EVALUATION.**
Danielson, Charlotte. A collection of performance
tasks and rubrics. Larchmont, NY : Eye On
Education, c1999.
*TC QA135.5 .D244 1999*

**MATHEMATICS - STUDY AND TEACHING
(PRIMARY) - GREAT BRITAIN.**
Hughes, Martin, 1949 May 15- Numeracy and
beyond. Buckingham [England] ; Philadelphia : Open
University Press, 2000.
*TC QA135.5 .H844 2000*

**MATHEMATICS - STUDY AND TEACHING
(PRIMARY) - JAPAN.**
Hughes, Martin, 1949 May 15- Numeracy and
beyond. Buckingham [England] ; Philadelphia : Open
University Press, 2000.
*TC QA135.5 .H844 2000*

**MATHEMATICS - STUDY AND TEACHING
(PRIMARY) - UNITED STATES.**
Issues in teaching numeracy in primary schools.
Buckingham [England] ; Philadelphia : Open
University Press, 1999.
*TC QA135.5 .I77 1999*

**MATHEMATICS - STUDY AND TEACHING -
RESEARCH.**
Handbook of research design in mathematics and
science education. Mahwah, N.J. : Lawrence Erlbaum,
1999.
*TC QA11 .H256 1999*

Nickson, Marilyn. Teaching and learning
mathematics. London ; New York : Cassell, 2000.
*TC QA11 .N524 2000*

**MATHEMATICS - STUDY AND TEACHING
(SECONDARY).**
Brahier, Daniel J. Teaching secondary and middle
school mathematics. Boston : Allyn and Bacon, 2000.
*TC QA11 .B6999 2000*

Bumby, Douglas R. Mathematics. 2nd ed. Columbus,
Ohio : C.E. Merrill, c1982-<1986.>
*TC QA154.2 .B8 1982*

Connecting mathematics and science to workplace
contexts. Thousand Oaks, Calif. : Corwin Press,
c1999.
*TC QA11 .C655 1999*

Elementary mathematics, patterns and structure;
accelerated sequence. Teacher's ed. New York, Holt,
Rinehart and Winston [c1966]

Modeling and simulation in science and mathematics
education. New York : Springer, c1999.
*TC Q181 .M62 1999*

Teaching secondary mathematics. Mahwah, N.J. : L.
Erlbaum Associates, 1997.
*TC QA11 .T357 1997*

**MATHEMATICS - STUDY AND TEACHING
(SECONDARY) - CASE STUDIES.**
Wiltshire, Michael A. Integrating mathematics and
science for below average ninth grade students. 1997.
*TC 06 no. 10847*

**MATHEMATICS - STUDY AND TEACHING
(SECONDARY) - COMPUTER NETWORK
RESOURCES.**
The Internet in action for math & science 7-12
[videorecording]. [New York] : Thirteen-WNET ;
[Alexandria, Va. : distributed by] PBS Video, c1997.
*TC LB1044.87 .I453 1997*

**MATHEMATICS - STUDY AND TEACHING
(SECONDARY) - UNITED STATES.**
Learning to teach mathematics in the secondary
school. New York : Routledge, 1999.
*TC QA13 .L4 1999*

**MATHEMATICS - STUDY AND TEACHING -
STANDARDS - UNITED STATES.**
Lockwood, Anne Turnbaugh. Standards. Thousand
Oaks, Calif. : Corwin Press, c1998.
*TC LB3060.83 .L63 1998*

**MATHEMATICS - STUDY AND TEACHING -
TECHNOLOGICAL INNOVATIONS.**
Innovations in science and mathematics education.
Mahwah, N.J. : L. Erlbaum, 2000.
*TC Q181 .I654 1999*

**MATHEMATICS - STUDY AND TEACHING -
UNITED STATES.**
Designing mathematics or science curriculum
programs. Washington, D.C. : National Academy
Press, 1999.
*TC Q183.3.A1 D46 1999*

Enhancing program quality in science and
mathematics. Thousand Oaks, Calif. : Corwin Press,
c1999.
*TC LB1585.3 .E55 1999*

Facing the consequences. Dordrecht ; Boston : Kluwer
Academic Publishers, c1999.

*TC QA13 .F33 1999*

Global perspectives for local action. Washington,
D.C. : National Academy Press, 1999.
*TC LB1583.3 .G56 1999*

Martin, Danny Bernard. Mathematics success and
failure among African-American youth. Mahwah,
N.J. : Lawrence Erlbaum, 2000.
*TC QA13 .M145 2000*

Shannon, Ann. Keeping score. Washington, D.C. :
National Academy Press, 1999.
*TC QA135.5 .S45 1999x*

**MATHEMATICS - STUDY AND TEACHING -
UNITED STATES - STANDARDS.**
Principles and standards for school mathematics.
Reston, VA : National Council of Teachers of
Mathematics, c2000.
*TC QA13 .P735 2000*

**Mathematics success and failure among African-
American youth.**
Martin, Danny Bernard. Mahwah, N.J. : Lawrence
Erlbaum, 2000.
*TC QA13 .M145 2000*

**MATHEMATICS TEACHERS - IN-SERVICE
TRAINING - UNITED STATES.**
Enhancing program quality in science and
mathematics. Thousand Oaks, Calif. : Corwin Press,
c1999.
*TC LB1585.3 .E55 1999*

**Mathers, Petra, ill.**
Purdy, Carol. Mrs. Merriwether's musical cat. New
York : Putnam, c1994.
*TC PZ7.P9745 Mr 1994*

**Matheson, David.**
An introduction to the study of education. London :
David Fulton, 1999.
*TC LA632 .I58 1999*

**Mathew Brady and the image of history.**
Panzer, Mary. Washington, D.C. : Smithsonian
Institution Press for the National Portrait Gallery,
c1997.
*TC TR140.B7 P36 1997*

**Mathews, Judith R.**
Hawkins, Robert P., 1931- Measuring behavioral
health outcomes. New York : Kluwer Academic/
Plenum Publishers, c1999.
*TC RJ503.5 .H39 1999*

**Mathews, Samuel R.**
Gillet, Jean Wallace. Understanding reading
problems. 5th ed. New York ; Harlow, England :
Longman, c2000.
*TC LB1050.46 .G55 2000*

**Mathis, Melissa Bay.** Animal house / Melissa Bay
Mathis. 1st ed. New York : Simon & Schuster Books
for Young Readers, 1999. 1 v. (unpaged) col. ill. 29 cm.
SUMMARY: Various animals offer suggestions to make a
children's treehouse a fun place to play. ISBN 0-689-81594-8
DDC [E]
*1. Tree houses - Fiction. 2. Animals - Fiction. 3. Stories in
rhyme. I. Title.*
*TC PZ8.3.M4265 Ap 1999*

**Mathis, Nancy.**
Annual State of American Education Address (7th :
February 22, 2000 : Durham, N.C.) The seventh
annual state of American education address
[videorecording]. [Washington, D.C. : U.S. Dept. of
Education], 2000.

Powerful middle schools : teaching and learning for
young adolescents (2000) Powerful middle schools
[videorecording]. [Washington, D.C.?] : U.S. Dept. of
Education, [2000].
*TC LB1623 .P6 2000*

**Mathis, Nancya.**
Modernizing schools : technology and buildings for a
new century (September 19, 2000 : Washington, D.C.)
Modernizing schools [videorecording]. [Washington,
D.C.] : U.S. Dept. of Education, [2000].
*TC LB3205 .M64 2000*

Modernizing schools : technology and buildings for a
new century (September 19, 2000 : Washington, D.C.)
Modernizing schools [videorecording]. [Washington,
D.C.] : U.S. Dept. of Education, [2000].
*TC LB3205 .M64 2000*

**Mathisen, James A.**
Ladd, Tony. Muscular Christianity. Grand Rapids,
Mich. : Baker Books, c1999.
*TC GV706.42 .L34 1999*

**Matisse, Henri, 1869-1954.**
Matisse, voyages [videorecording]. [Chicago, Ill.] :
Home Vision ; [S.l.] : Distributed worldwide by RM
Associates, c1989.
*TC ND553.M37 M37 1989*

**MATISSE, HENRI, 1869-1954.**
Matisse, voyages [videorecording]. [Chicago, Ill.] :
Home Vision ; [S.l.] : Distributed worldwide by RM
Associates, c1989.
*TC ND553.M37 M37 1989*

**Matisse [videorecording].**
Matisse, voyages [videorecording]. [Chicago, Ill.] :
Home Vision ; [S.l.] : Distributed worldwide by RM
Associates, c1989.
*TC ND553.M37 M37 1989*

**Matisse, voyages** [videorecording] / an RM Arts, Le
Centre Georges Pompidou, LA SEPT coproduction ;
written and directed by Didier Baussy ; production
company, D.B. Arts Films ; English version by
Mechthild Offermanns ; adapted by Waldemar
Januszczak. [Chicago, Ill.] : Home Vision ; [S.l.] :
Distributed worldwide by RM Associates, c1989. 1
videocassette (58 min.) : sd., col. with b&w sequences ; 1/2 in.
(Portrait of an artist) Container title : Matisse [videorecording].
Series title on container: Henri Matisse [videorecording]. At
head of title : Home Vision... presents an RM ARTS
Production... [videorecording]. VHS. Catalogued from credits,
container and cassette label. Narrators: James Greene, Tom
Karol. Camera, Eric Amblard, Komal Kotowski, Frédéric
Varist; editors, Delphine Desfons, Dominique Paley ; music,
Bertrand Lenclos, Didier Baussy. "MAT 02"--Container.
Produced by RM Arts, Centre Pompidou, La SEPT in 1987.
General. SUMMARY: Highlights the development of
Matisse's works from his early canvases through his
involvement with the Fauvist movement to his later works.
Also explores the inspiration and renewed vigor he found in
travelling the world.
*1. Matisse, Henri - 1869-1954. 2. Painters - France -
Biography. 3. Documentary television programs. I. Matisse,
Henri, 1869-1954. II. Baussy, Didier. III. Greene, James. IV.
Karol, Tom. V. RM Arts (Firm) VI. Centre Georges Pompidou.
VII. SEPT (Television station : France) VIII. Home Vision
(Firm) IX. D.B. Arts Films. X. Title: Matisse [videorecording]
XI. Title: Henri Matisse [videorecording] XII. Title: Home
Vision... presents an RM ARTS Production... [videorecording]
XIII. Series.*
*TC ND553.M37 M37 1989*

**Matos Rodríguez, Félix V., 1962-** Women and urban
change in San Juan, Puerto Rico, 1820-1868 / Félix V.
Matos Rodríguez. Gainesville, Fla. : University Press
of Florida, c1999. xi, 180 p. ; 24 cm. Includes
bibliographical references (p. [159]-176) and index. ISBN
0-8130-1676-2 (cloth : alk. paper) DDC 305.4/097295/1
*1. Women - Puerto Rico - San Juan - History. 2. Working class
women - Puerto Rico - San Juan - Social conditions. 3.
Women - Puerto Rico - San Juan - Economic conditions. 4.
City and town life - Puerto Rico - San Juan - History. I. Title.*
*TC HQ1522 .M38 1999*

**MATRIARCHY.** *See* **FAMILY.**

**MATRIMONY.** *See* **MARRIAGE.**

**Matrona docta.**
Hemelrijk, Emily Ann, 1953- London ; New York :
Routledge, 1999.
*TC HQ1136 .H45 1999*

**Mattelart, Armand.**
**[Mondialisation de la communication. English]**
Networking the world, 1794-2000 / Armand
Mattelart ; translated by Liz Carey-Libbrecht and
James A. Cohen. Minneapolis, MN ; London :
University of Minnesota Press, c2000. viii, 129 p. ; 23
cm. Includes bibliographical references (p. 125-129). ISBN
0-8166-3287-1 (hbk.) ISBN 0-8166-3288-X (pbk.) DDC
384/.09
*1. Telecommunication - History. 2. Technological innovations -
History. I. Title.*
*TC HE7631 .M37513 2000*

**MATTER.** *See also* **DARK MATTER
(ASTRONOMY).**
Brandwein, Paul F. (Paul Franz), 1912- Curie ed. New
York : Harcourt Brace Jovanovich, 1980.
*TC Q161.2 .C66 1980*

**MATTER.**
Stephen Hawking's universe [videorecording].
[Alexandria, Va.] : PBS Video; Burbank, CA :
Distributed by Warner Home Video, c1997.
*TC QB982 .S7 1997*

**MATTER - CONSTITUTION.**
Stephen Hawking's universe [videorecording].
[Alexandria, Va.] : PBS Video; Burbank, CA :
Distributed by Warner Home Video, c1997.

*TC QB982 .S7 1997*

**MATTER, DARK (ASTRONOMY).** *See* **DARK
MATTER (ASTRONOMY).**

**MATTER, NONLUMINOUS (ASTRONOMY).** *See*
**DARK MATTER (ASTRONOMY).**

**MATTER, UNOBSERVED (ASTRONOMY).** *See*
**DARK MATTER (ASTRONOMY).**

**MATTER, UNSEEN (ASTRONOMY).** *See* **DARK
MATTER (ASTRONOMY).**

**Matthews, Becky.**
Snell, Alma Hogan. Grandmother's grandchild.
Lincoln : University of Nebraska Press, c2000.
*TC E99.C92 S656 2000*

**Matthews, Ian, PhD.**
Vetter, Norman. Epidemiology and public health
medicine. Edinburgh ; New York : Churchill
Livingstone, 1999.
*TC RA427 .V48 1999*

**Matthews, L. Joseph, 1950-.**
Crow, Gary Monroe, 1947- Leadership. Princeton,
NJ : Eye on Education, c1996.
*TC LB2831.92 .C76 1996*

**Matthews, Michael R.**
Constructivism in science education. Dordrecht ;
Boston : Kluwer Academic, c1998.
*TC Q181 .C612 1998*

**Matthews, Sandra.** Pregnant pictures / Sandra
Matthews and Laura Wexler. New York : Routledge,
2000. xvii, 263 p. : ill. ; 24 cm. Includes index. Notes: p. 241-
257. ISBN 0-415-90449-8 (acid-free paper) DDC 779/.24
*1. Pregnant women - Portraits. 2. Portrait photography. I.
Wexler, Laura. II. Title.*
*TC TR681.P67 M38 2000*

**Matthews, Tom, 1949-** Always inventing : a
photobiography of Alexander Graham Bell / by Tom
L. Matthews. Washington, D.C. : National Geographic
Society, c1999. 64 p. : ill., maps ; 29 cm. Includes
bibliographical references (p. 62-63) and index. SUMMARY:
A biography, with photographs and quotes from Bell himself,
which follows this well known inventor from his childhood in
Scotland through his life-long efforts to come up with ideas
that would improve people's lives. ISBN 0-7922-7391-5 DDC
621.385/092
*1. Bell, Alexander Graham, - 1847-1922 - Juvenile literature.
2. Bell, Alexander Graham, - 1847-1922 - Portraits - Juvenile
literature. 3. Inventors - United States - Biography - Juvenile
literature. I. Title.*
*TC TK6143.B4 M37 1999*

**Mattingly, Christopher.**
The salsa-riffic world of Spanish [videorecording].
[Arlington, Va.] : Cerebellum Corp., c1998.
*TC PC4112.7 .S25 1998*

**Matula, Kathleen.**
Black, Maureen M. Essentials of Bayley scales of
infant development--II assessment. New York :
Wiley, c2000.
*TC RJ151.D48 B52 2000*

**Matulka, Denise I.** Picture this : picture books for
young adults : a curriculum-related annotated
bibliography / Denise I. Matulka. Westport, Conn. :
Greenwood Press, 1997. xx, 267 p. : ill. ; 24 cm. Includes
bibliographical references and indexes. ISBN 0-313-30182-4
(alk. paper) DDC 016.0285/5
*1. Picture books - Bibliography. 2. Teenagers - United States -
Books and reading. 3. Young adult literature - Bibliography. I.
Title.*
*TC Z1033.P52 M37 1997*

**MATURATION (PSYCHOLOGY).**
Beyond heredity and environment. Boulder :
Westview Press, 1995.
*TC BF341 .B48 1995*

Creativity, spirituality, and transcendence. Stamford,
Conn. : Ablex, c2000.
*TC BF411 .C76 2000*

**MATURATION (PSYCHOLOGY) -
CONGRESSES.**
Spirituality, ethics, and relationship in adulthood.
Madison, Conn. : Psychosocial Press, c2000.
*TC BF724.5 .S68 2000*

**MATURATION (PSYCHOLOGY) IN
LITERATURE.**
Barney, Richard A., 1955- Plots of enlightenment.
Stanford, Calif. : Stanford University Press, c1999.
*TC PR858.E38 B37 1999*

**Mature audiences.**
Riggs, Karen E. New Brunswick, N.J. : Rutgers
University Press, c1998.

**Maudsley monographs**
(no. 42) Mental health in our future cities. Hove,
England : Psychology Press, c1998.
*TC RA790.5 .M4196 1998*

**Maughan, Ron J.**
Nutrition in sport. Osney Mead, Oxford ; Malden,
MA : Blackwell Science, 2000.
*TC QP141 .N793 2000*

**Maurer, Donna, 1961-.**
Interpreting weight. New York : Aldine de Gruyter,
c1999.
*TC RA645.O23 I55 1999*

Weighty issues. Hawthorne, N.Y. : Aldine de Gruyter,
c1999.
*TC RA645.O23 W45 1999*

**Maurer, Konrad, 1943-.**
Concepts of Alzheimer disease. Baltimore, Md. :
London : Johns Hopkins University Press, 2000.
*TC RC523 .C657 2000*

**Mawdsley, Ralph D.** Legal problems of religious and
private schools / Ralph D. Mawdsley. 4th ed. Dayton,
OH : Education Law Association, c2000. 290 p. ; 24 cm.
(Monograph series ; no. 65.) Includes bibliographical
references and index. ISBN 1-56534-101-5
*1. Church schools - Law and legislation - United States. 2.
Private schools - Law and legislation - United States. I.
Education Law Association (U.S.) II. Title. III. Series:
Monograph series (Education Law Association (U.S.)) ; no. 65.*
*TC KF4124.5 .M38 2000*

**Mawer, Michael.**
Learning and teaching in physical education. London ;
Philadelphia, PA : Falmer Press, 1999.
*TC GV361 .L42 1999*

**Maximum Linux security** : a hacker's guide to
protecting your Linux server and workstation /
Anonymous. Indianapolis, Ind. : Sams, c2000. xvii, 743
p. : ill. ; 23 cm. + 1 computer laser optical disc (4 3/4 in.).
Includes index. ISBN 0-672-31670-6 (pbk.)
*1. Computer security 2. Linux. 3. Operating systems
(Computers) I. Title: Linux security II. Title: Linux*
*TC QA76.9.A25 M385 2000*

**MAXWELL, ANNA CAROLINE - BIOGRAPHY.**
Smalls, Sadie Marian. Anna Caroline Maxwell's
contributions to nursing. 1996.
*TC 06 no. 10698*

**MAXWELL, ANNA CAROLINE -
CONTRIBUTIONS IN NURSING SERVICES.**
Smalls, Sadie Marian. Anna Caroline Maxwell's
contributions to nursing. 1996.
*TC 06 no. 10698*

**Maxwell, Kenneth, 1941-** Pombal, paradox of the
Enlightenment / Kenneth Maxwell. Cambridge
[England] ; New York, NY : Cambridge University
Press, 1995. xvii, 200 p., [8] p. of plates : ill. (some col.) ; 26
cm. Includes bibliographical references (p. 175-185) and index.
ISBN 0-521-45044-6 DDC 946.9/03/092
*1. Pombal, Sebastião José de Carvalho e Melo, - Marquês de, -
1699-1782. 2. Portugal - Politics and government - 1750-1777.
3. Enlightenment. 4. Statesmen - Portugal - Biography. I. Title.*
*TC DP641 .M39 1995*

**Maxwell, Steven.** Red hat linux network management
tools / Steve Maxwell. New York : McGraw Hill,
c2000. xxviii, 683 p. : ill. ; 23 cm. + 2 computer laser optical
discs (4 3/4 in.). Includes index. ISBN 0-07-212260-9 (alk.
paper) ISBN 0-07-212261-7 (CD-ROM) ISBN 0-07-212602-7
(CD-ROM) ISBN 0-07-212262-5 (set) DDC 005.4/4769
*1. Linux. 2. Operating systems (Computers) 3. Computer
networks - Management. I. Title.*
*TC QA76.76.O63 M373339 2000*

**MAY DAY - FICTION.**
Mora, Pat. The rainbow tulip. New York : Viking,
1999.
*TC PZ7.M78819 Rai 1999*

**May, Frank B.** Unraveling the seven myths of reading :
assessment and intervention practice for counteracting
their effect / Frank B. May. Boston : Allyn and Bacon,
c2001. vi, 218 p. : ill. ; 24 cm. ISBN 0-205-30914-3 DDC
428.4
*1. Reading. 2. Reading comprehension. 3. Reading disability. I.
Title.*
*TC LB1050.2 .M364 2001*

**MAY (MONTH) - FOLKLORE.** *See* **MAY DAY.**

**May, Stephen, 1962-.**
Indigenous community-based education. Clevedon
[England] ; Philadelphia : Multilingual Matters,
c1999.

*TC LC1036 .I43 1999*

**May we sleep here tonight?.**
Koide, Tan. New York : Atheneum, 1981.
***TC PZ7.K8293 May 1981***

**MAYA LANGUAGE - SOCIAL ASPECTS.**
Hanks, William F. Intertexts. Lanham : Rowman & Littlefield Publishers, Inc., c2000.
***TC P35.5.M6 H36 2000***

**Mayakovsky, Vladimir, 1893-1930.** Kem byt'? / V. Maiakovskiĭ ; ris. N. Shifrin. [Moskva] : Gosudarstvennoe izdatel'stvo, 1929. [12] leaves : col. ill. ; 23 x 19 cm. Cover title.
*1. Children's poetry, Russian - 20th century. 2. Occupations - Soviet Union - Juvenile poetry. I. Shifrin, Nisson Abramovich, 1892- II. Title.*
***TC PN6110.O32 M39 1929 Rus***

**MAYAN LANGUAGES.** *See* **MAYA LANGUAGE.**

**Maybury, Mark T.**
Intelligent multimedia information retrieval. Menlo Park, Calif. : AAAI Press ; Cambridge, Mass. : MIT Press, c1997.
***TC QA76.575 .I577 1997***

**Maycunich, Ann.**
Gilley, Jerry W. Organizational learning, performance, and change. Cambridge, Mass. : Perseus, c2000.
***TC HF5549.5.M3 G555 2000***

**Mayer, Bernard S., 1946-** The dynamics of conflict resolution : a practitioner's guide / Bernard S. Mayer. 1st ed. San Francisco : Jossey-Bass Publishers, c2000. xvi, 263 p. : ill. ; 24 cm. Includes bibliographical references (p. 251-254) and index. ISBN 0-7879-5019-X (hard : alk. paper) DDC 303.6/9
*1. Interpersonal conflict. 2. Conflict (Psychology) 3. Conflict management. 4. Negotiation. 5. Problem solving. I. Title.*
***TC BF637.I48 M39 2000***

**Mayer, Marianna.** Iron John / as told by Marianna Mayer ; illustrated by Winslow Pels. New York : Morrow Junior Books, 1998. 1v. (unpaged) : col. ill. ; 31 cm. SUMMARY: With the help of Iron John, also known as the wild man of the forest, a young prince makes his way in the world and finds his true love. ISBN 0-688-11554-3 (tr) ISBN 0-688-11555-1 (le) DDC 398.2/0943/02; E
*1. Fairy tales. 2. Folklore - Germany. I. Pels, Winslow, 1947- ill. II. Title.*
***TC PZ8.M4514 Ir 1998***

Women warriors : myths and legends of heroic women / Marianna Mayer ; illustrated by Julek Heller. New York : Morrow Junior Books, 1999. 1v. (unpaged) : col. ill. ; 29 cm. SUMMARY: A collection of twelve traditional tales about female military leaders, war goddesses, women warriors, and heroines from around the world, including such countries as Japan, Ireland, and Zimbabwe. ISBN 0-688-15522-7 (rte.) DDC 398/.082
*1. Women heroes - Folklore. 2. Tales. 3. Heroes - Folklore. 4. Women - Folklore. 5. Folklore. I. Heller, Julek, ill. II. Title.*
***TC PZ8.1.M46 Wo 1999***

**Mayers, R. Stewart, 1959-.**
Zepeda, Sally J., 1956- Supervision and staff development in the block. Larchmont, N.Y. : Eye On Education, c2000.
***TC LB3032.2 .Z46 2000***

**Maylone, Nelson John.** That can't be right! : using counterintuitive math problems / Nelson John Maylone. Lancaster, PA : Technomic Pub. Co., c1999. 131 p. ; 23 cm. Includes bibliographical references (p. 19) and index. ISBN 1-56676-676-1 DDC 510/.76
*1. Mathematics - Problems, exercises, etc. I. Title.*
***TC QA43 .M367 1999***

**Maylor, Elizabeth A.**
Models of cognitive aging. Oxford ; New York : Oxford University Press, 2000.
***TC BF724.55.C63 M63 2000***

**Mazo, Joseph H.** Prime movers : the makers of modern dance in America / Joseph H. Mazo. 2nd revised edition. Princeton, NJ. : Princeton Book Co. Pub., c2000. 384 p. : ill., ports. ; 23 cm. Bibliography: p. [301]-311. Includes index. CONTENTS: Loie Fuller -- Isadora Duncan -- Ruth St. Denis -- Ted Shawn -- Doris Humphrey -- Martha Graham -- Merce Cunningham -- Nikolais, Ailey, Taylor -- Twyla Tharp. ISBN 0-87127-211-3
*1. Modern dance - History. 2. Dancing - United States - History. 3. Dancers - Biography. 4. Choreographers - Biography. I. Title.*
***TC GV1783 .M347 2000***

**Mazurek, Kas.**
Education in a global society. Boston : Allyn and Bacon, c2000.
***TC LB43 .E385 2000***

**Mazzarella, Sharon R.**
Growing up girls. New York : P. Lang, c1999.
***TC HQ798 .G76 1999***

**McAdams, Donald R.** Fighting to save our urban schools-- and winning! : lessons from Houston / Donald R. McAdams. New York : Teachers College Press, c2000. xvii, 293 p. ; 24 cm. Includes bibliographical references (p. 273-281) and index. ISBN 0-8077-3884-0 (alk. paper) ISBN 0-8077-3885-9 (alk. paper) DDC 370/.9173/2
*1. Education, Urban - Texas - Houston - Case studies. 2. Educational change - Texas - Houston - Case studies. I. Title.*
***TC LC5133.H8 M32 2000***

**McAdoo, Harriette Pipes.**
Family ethnicity. 2nd ed. Thousand Oaks, Calif. : Sage Publications, c1999.
***TC E184.A1 F33 1999***

**MCAHP.**
Maternal, child and adolescent health profile. Albany, N.Y. : New York State Dept. of Health, 1996.
***TC HV742.N7 B83 1996***

**McAllister, Carol H.**
Callison, William. Elementary school principal's handbook. Lancaster, Pa. : Technomic, c1999.
***TC LB2822.5 .C34 1999***

**McAuliffe, Chris.** Art and suburbia : a world art book / by Chris McAuliffe. Roseville East, NSW : Craftsman House, c1996. 136 p. : ill. (some col.) ; 27 cm. Includes bibliographical references (p. 129-131) and index. ISBN 976-641-029-1
*1. Art, Modern - 20th century - Australia. 2. Art, Australian. 3. Suburbs - Australia - History. 4. Suburban life in art. I. Title.*
***TC N7400.2 .M32 1996***

**McBain, Lesley.**
The adult student's guide. Berkley trade pbk. ed. New York, N.Y. : Berkley Books, 1999.
***TC L901 .A494 1999***

**McBratney, Sam.** The dark at the top of the stairs / Sam McBratney ; illustrated by Ivan Bates. 1st U.S. ed. Cambridge, Mass. : Candlewick Press, c1996. 1 v. (unpaged) : col. ill. ; 31 cm. SUMMARY: Knowing that he must satisfy their curiosity, an old mouse agrees to show three young mice the "monster" at the top of the stairs. ISBN 1-56402-640-X DDC [E]
*1. Mice - Fiction. 2. Curiosity - Fiction. I. Bates, Ivan, ill. II. Title.*
***TC PZ7.M47826 DAr 1996***

**McBride, Michael B.** Meeting the national standards with handbells and handchimes / Michael B. McBride and Marva Baldwin. Lanham, MD : Scarecrow Press, 2000. v. 76 p. : ill. ;c28 cm. Includes bibliographical references. ISBN 0-8108-3740-4 (p : alk. paper) DDC 786.8/8485193/071073
*1. Handbell ringing - Standards. 2. Handbells - Instruction and study. 3. Handchimes - Instruction and study. I. Baldwin, Marva. II. Title.*
***TC MT711 .M35 2000***

**McBrien, J. Lynn.**
Ottenburg, Susan D. Education today. 2nd. ed. Boston : Educational Publishing Group, Education Today, c1996.
***TC LC225.3 .O88 1996***

**McCabe, Edward R. B.**
McCabe, Linda. How to succeed in academics. San Diego, Calif. : Academic, c2000.
***TC LB2331.7 .M34 2000***

**McCabe, Linda.** How to succeed in academics / Linda L. McCabe, Edward R.B. McCabe. San Diego, Calif. : Academic, c2000. xvii, 152 p. ; 23 cm. Includes index. CONTENTS: Preface -- 1. Introductory overview: establishing personal goals and tracking your career -- 2. Selecting a training environment: choosing a training program, training institution, and mentor -- 3. Selecting a position in academia: choosing a department, institution, and mentor -- 4. Selecting grant opportunities: understanding the organization of the NIH, other governmental entities, and private foundations -- 5. Writing a grant: selecting the specific aims, preparing the budget, and developing the research proposal -- 6. Grant review: how review groups work, responding to the reviewers' feedback, and preparing the revised application -- 7. Preparation of abstracts for scientific meetings -- 8. Presentations at scientific meetings: preparation of effective slides and posters -- 9. The 10-minute talk -- 10. The 1-hour talk, including the job application seminar -- 11. Selecting a journal: instructions for authors, recommending reviewers, and submitting the manuscript -- 12. How to write research papers -- 13. How to write review articles and chapters -- 14. Manuscript review -- 15. Ethical behavior -- 16. Leadership -- 17. Preparing a curriculum vitae -- 18. Summary: gauging success -- Index. ISBN 0-12-481833-1
*1. Universities and colleges - Faculty - Vocational guidance. 2. Career development. I. McCabe, Edward R. B. II. Title.*
***TC LB2331.7 .M34 2000***

**McCaffrey, Robert J.**
Practitioner's guide to evaluating change with neuropsychological assessment instruments. New York : Kluwer Academic/Plenum Publishers, c2000.
***TC RC386.6.N48 P73 2000***

**McCall, George J.** Social psychology, a sociological approach / George J. McCall, J.L. Simmons ; with glossary prepared by Nola Simmons. New York : Free Press, c1982. xxi, 502 p. : ill. ; 25 cm. Includes bibliographical references (p.457-481) and indexes. ISBN 0-02-920640-5 DDC 302
*1. Social psychology. I. Simmons, J. L. (Jerry Laird), 1933- II. Title.*
***TC HM251 .M38 1982***

**McCallum, Robyn.** Ideologies of identity in adolescent fiction : the dialogic construction of subjectivity / Robyn McCallum. New York : Garland Pub., 1999. viii, 285 p. ; 22 cm. (Garland reference library of social science ; v. 1094. Children's literature and culture ; v. 8) Includes bibliographical references and index. ISBN 0-8153-2290-9 (alk. paper) DDC 809.3/00835
*1. Young adult fiction - History and criticism. 2. Children's stories - History and criticism. 3. Subjectivity in literature. 4. Self in literature. 5. Identity (Psychology) in literature. 6. Social interaction in literature. 7. Fiction - Technique. 8. Narration (Rhetoric) I. Title. II. Series: Garland reference library of social science ; v. 1094. III. Series: Garland reference library of social science. Children's literature and culture series ; v. 8.*
***TC PN3443 .M38 1999***

Stephens, John, 1944- Retelling stories, framing culture. New York : Garland Pub., 1998.
***TC PN1009.A1 S83 1998***

**McCandless, Amy Thompson, 1946-** The past in the present : women's higher education in the twentieth-century American South / Amy Thompson McCandless. Tuscaloosa : University of Alabama Press, c1999. x, 389 p. : ill. ; 24 cm. Includes bibliographical references (p. 347-371) and index. ISBN 0-8173-0945-4 (alk. paper) ISBN 0-8173-0994-2 (pbk. : alk. paper) DDC 378.1/9822
*1. Women - Education (Higher) - Southern States - History - 20th century. 2. Women college students - Southern States - Conduct of life - History - 20th century. 3. Universities and colleges - Southern States - Sociological aspects - History - 20th century. I. Title.*
***TC LC1756 .M24 1999***

**McCann, Damian.**
The practice of counselling in primary care. London ; Thousand Oaks, Calif. : SAGE Publications, 1999.
***TC R727.4 .P733 1999***

**McCann, Michael, 1943-** Artist beware / by Michael McCann. [2nd ed.]. New York, NY : Lyons & Burford, c1992. xii, 564 p. : ill. ; 23 cm. Includes bibliographical references (p. 549-555) and index. ISBN 1-55821-175-6 DDC 702/.8/9
*1. Artists - Diseases. 2. Artisans - Diseases. 3. Artists' materials - Toxicology. I. Title.*
***TC RC963.6.A78 M32 1992***

Health hazards manual for artists / Michael McCann. 4th rev. and augm. ed. New York, NY : Lyons & Burford, c1994. xi, 132 p. : ill. ; 23 cm. Includes bibliographical references (p. 120-129) and index. ISBN 1-55821-306-6 DDC 700/.28/9
*1. Artists - Health and hygiene - Handbooks, manuals, etc. 2. Artisans - Health and hygiene - Handbooks, manuals, etc. I. Title.*
***TC RC963.6.A78 M324 1994***

**McCarrier, Andrea.** Interactive writing : how language and literacy come together, K-2 / Andrea McCarrier, Gay Su Pinnell, Irene C. Fountas. Portsmouth, NH : Heinemann, c2000. xx, 297 p. : ill. ; 28 cm. Title from cip: Interactive writing : language and literacy and how it all comes together. Includes bibliographical references (p. 285-288) and index. ISBN 0-325-00209-6 (acid-free paper) DDC 372.62/3
*1. English language - Composition and exercises - Study and teaching (Early childhood) 2. Language arts (Early childhood) I. Fountas, Irene C. II. Pinnell, Gay Su. III. Title. IV. Title: How language and literacy come togethe, k-2 V. Title: Interactive writing : language and literacy and how it all comes together.*
***TC LB1139.5.L35 M39 2000***

**McCarthy, Cameron.**
Multicultural curriculum. New York : Routledge, 2000.
***TC LC1099 .M816 2000***

**McCarthy, Lucille Parkinson, 1944-.**
Fishman, Stephen M. Unplayed tapes. Urbana, Ill. : National Council of Teachers of English : New York : Teachers College Press, c2000.
*TC LB1028.24 .F52 2000*

**McCarthy, Patricia A.**
Rehabilitative audiology. 3rd ed. Philadelphia, PA : Lippincott Williams & Wilkins, c2000.
*TC RF297 .R44 2000*

**McCarthy, Ronald M.**
Protest, power, and change. New York : Garland Pub., 1997.
*TC HM278 .P76 1997*

**McCarthy, Tara.** My brother Sam is dead by James Lincoln Collier and Christopher Collier / written by Tara McCarthy. New York : Scholastic, c1997. 16 p. : ill. ; 28 cm. (Scholastic literature guide. Grades 4-8.) "Author biographies, chapter summaries, discussion questions, vocabulary builders, assessment strategies, reproducibles, cross-curricular activities for students of all learning styles."-- Cover. ISBN 0-590-37362-5 (pbk.)
*1. Collier, James Lincoln. - 1928- / - My brother Sam is dead. 2. Collier, Christopher. - 1930- / - My brother Sam is dead. 3. Children's literature - Study and teaching. 4. Reading (Elementary) I. Title. II. Series.*
*TC LB1573 .M32 1997*

**McCarthy, William H.** Reducing urban unemployment : what works at the local level / William H. McCarthy with David R. Jones, R. Leo Penne, Lucy R. Watkins. Washington, D.C. : National League of Cities, c1985. ix, 109 p. : ill. ; 23 cm. "October 1985." Bibliography: p. 16. ISBN 0-933729-06-5 (pbk.) DDC 331.13/77/0973
*1. Unemployment - United States. 2. Structural unemployment - United States. 3. Youth - Employment - United States. I. National League of Cities. II. Title.*
*TC HD5724 .M34 1985*

**McCartney, Elspeth.** Speech/language therapists and teachers working together : a systems approach to collaboration / edited by Elspeth McCartney. London : Whurr, 1999. x, 188 p. ; 24 cm. Includes bibliographical references and index. ISBN 1-86156-124-5 DDC 371.9142
*1. Teachers - Great Britain. 2. Speech therapy - Great Britain. 3. Speech therapists - Great Britain. I. Title.*
*TC LB3454 .M32 1999*

**McCarty, Peter.** Little bunny on the move / written and illustrated by Peter McCarty. 1st ed. New York : Holt, 1999. 1 v. (unpaged) : col. ill. ; 24 cm. SUMMARY: A little bunny rabbit hurries past five fat sheep, over train tracks, and across an open field on his way to a special destination. ISBN 0-8050-4620-8 (alk. paper) DDC [E]
*1. Rabbits - Fiction. 2. Home - Fiction. I. Title.*
*TC PZ7.M47841327 Li 1999*

**McCaslin, Mary M.** Listening in classrooms / Mary M. McCaslin, Thomas L. Good. 1st ed. New York : HarperCollins College Publishers, c1996. xvii, 232 p. : ill. ; 24 cm. Includes bibliographical references and indexes. ISBN 0-673-46881-X DDC 371.1/023
*1. Teacher-student relationships. 2. Communication in education. 3. Listening. 4. Group work in education. 5. Students - Interviews. 6. Home and school. I. Good, Thomas L., 1943- II. Title.*
*TC LB1033 .M34 1996*

**McClafferty, Karen A.**
Challenges of urban education. Albany : State Unviersity of New York Press, c2000.
*TC LC5131 .C38 2000*

**McClain, Kay.**
Symbolizing and communicating in mathematics classrooms. Mahwah, N.J. : Lawrence Erlbaum Associates, 2000.
*TC QA11 .S873 2000*

**McCleary, Lloyd E. (Lloyd Everald), 1924-.**
Crow, Gary Monroe, 1947- Leadership. Princeton, NJ : Eye on Education, c1996.
*TC LB2831.92 .C76 1996*

**McCloskey, Deirdre N.** Crossing : a memoir / Deirdre McCloskey. Chicago, Ill. : University of Chicago Press, 1999. xvi, 266 p. : ill. ; 24 cm. ISBN 0-226-55668-9 (alk. paper) DDC 305.9/066
*1. McCloskey, Deirdre N. 2. Transsexuals - United States - Biography. 3. Transsexuals - United States - Psychology. 4. Gender identity - United States - Psychological aspects. I. Title.*
*TC HQ77.8.M39 A3 1999*

**MCCLOSKEY, DEIRDRE N.**
McCloskey, Deirdre N. Crossing. Chicago, Ill. : University of Chicago Press, 1999.
*TC HQ77.8.M39 A3 1999*

**McCluskey, Audrey T.**
Bethune, Mary McLeod, 1875-1955. [Selections. 1999] Mary McLeod Bethune. Bloomington : Indiana University Press, c1999.
*TC E185.97.B34 A25 1999*

**McConkey, Edwin H.** Human genetics : the molecular revolution / Edwin H. McConkey. Boston : Jones and Bartlett Publishers, c1993. xiii, 322 p. : ill. (some col.) ; 29 cm. (The Jones and Bartlett series in biology) Includes bibliographical references and index. ISBN 0-86720-854-6 DDC 616/.042
*1. Human genetics. 2. Human molecular genetics. 3. Genetics, Medical. I. Title. II. Series.*
*TC QH431 .M3298 1993*

**McConnell, David, 1951-** Implementing computer supported cooperative learning. / David McConnell. 2nd ed. London : Kogan Page, 2000. vi, 265 p. : ill. ; 24 cm. Previous ed.: 1994. Includes bibliographical references and index. ISBN 0-7494-3135-0
*1. Group work in education. 2. Education - Data processing. 3. Open learning. 4. Distance education. 5. Computer conferencing in education. 6. Internet (Computer network) in education. I. Title.*
*TC LB1032 .M38 2000*

**McConnell, David L., 1959-** Importing diversity : inside Japan's JET Program / David L. McConnell. Berkeley : University of California Press, c2000. xviii, 328 p. : ill. ; 23 cm. Includes bibliographical references (p. 309-316) and index. ISBN 0-520-21635-0 (alk. paper) ISBN 0-520-21636-9 (alk. paper) DDC 370.117/0952
*1. JET Puroguramu. 2. Educational exchanges - Social aspects - Japan. 3. Multicultural education - Japan. I. Title.*
*TC LB2285.J3 M33 2000*

**McCord, Joan.**
Violence and childhood in the inner city. Cambridge, UK ; New York : Cambridge University Press, 1997.
*TC HN90.V5 V532 1997*

**McCord, Margaret (McCord Nixon)** The calling of Katie Makanya : a memoir of South Africa / Margaret McCord. New York : J. Wiley, 1995. ix, 252 p., [8] p. of plates : ill. ; 25 cm. ISBN 0-471-17890-X (alk. paper) DDC 968.05/092
*1. Makanya, Katie. - 1873-1955. 2. Women, Black - South Africa - Biography. 3. Women, Black - South Africa - Social life and customs. 4. South Africa - Biography. I. Title.*
*TC CT1929.M34 M38 1995*

**MCCORD MUSEUM OF CANADIAN HISTORY - HISTORY.**
Young, Brian, 1940- The making and unmaking of a university museum. Montreal : McGill-Queen's University Press, c2000.
*TC FC21 .Y68 2000*

**McCord, Robert S.**
Counts, I. Wilmer (Ira Wilmer), 1931- A life is more than a moment. Bloomington, IN : Indiana University Press, c1999.
*TC LC214.23.L56 C68 1999*

**McCormack, Charles C.** Treating borderline states in marriage : dealing with oppositionalism, ruthless aggression, and severe resistance / Charles C. McCormack. Northvale, NJ : Jason Aronson, 2000. xvi, 359 p. ; 24 cm. (The library of object relations) Includes bibliographical references (p. 349-353) and index. ISBN 0-7657-0190-1 DDC 616.89/156
*1. Marital psychotherapy. 2. Borderline personality disorder. I. Title. II. Series.*
*TC RC488.5 .M392 2000*

**McCormick, Kevin, 1944-** Engineers in Japan and Britain : education, training and employment / Kevin McCormick. London ; New York : Routledge, 2000. xxii, 302 p. ; 24 cm. (Nissan Institute/Routledge Japanese studies series) Includes bibliographical references (p. [276]-296) and index. ISBN 0-415-16181-9 (alk. paper) DDC 620/.0071/052
*1. Engineering - Study and teaching - Japan. 2. Engineering - Study and teaching - Great Britain. 3. Engineers - Training of - Japan. 4. Engineers - Training of - Great Britain. I. Title. II. Series.*
*TC T155 .M37 2000*

**McCubbin, Hamilton I.**
Stress, coping, and health in families. Thousand Oaks, Calif. : Sage Publications, c1998.
*TC RC455.4.F3 S79 1998*

**McCubbin, Laurie D.**
Lerner, Richard M. Family diversity and family policy. Boston ; London : Kluwer Academic, c1999.
*TC HQ535 .L39 1999*

**McCullough, Frances Monson, 1939-.**
Earth, air, fire & water. Rev. ed. New York, N.Y. : Harper & Row, c1989.

*TC PN6101 .E37 1989*

**McCullough, Leigh.**
Reconciling empirical knowledge and clinical experience. 1st ed. Washington, DC : American Psychological Association, c1999.
*TC RC480 .R395 1999*

**McCullough, Michael E.**
Forgiveness. New York : Guilford Press, c1999.
*TC BF637.F67 F67 1999*

**McCully, Emily Arnold.** Mouse practice / story and pictures by Emily Arnold McCully. 1st ed. New York : Arthur A. Levine Books/Scholastic Press, 1999. 1 v. (unpaged). col. ill. 22 x 26 cm. SUMMARY: Monk the little mouse learns from his parents that practice is the way to succeed--whether it is in playing baseball or in playing music. ISBN 0-590-68220-2 (hc.) ISBN 0-590-68267-9 (pbk.) DDC [E]
*1. Mice - Fiction. 2. Baseball - Fiction. I. Title.*
*TC PZ7.M13913 Mo 1999*

**McCurdy, David W.**
Strategies in teaching anthropology. Upper Saddle River, N.J. : Prentice Hall, c2000.
*TC GN43 .S77 2000*

**McCurdy, Michael, ill.**
Kay, Verla. Iron horses. New York : Putnam, c1999.
*TC PZ8.3.K225 Ir 1999*

**McCutcheon, Marc.**
The Facts on File student's thesaurus. 2nd ed. New York : Facts on File, 2000.
*TC PE1591 .H45 2000*

**McDermott, Kathryn A., 1969-** Controlling public education : localism versus equity / Kathryn A. McDermott. Lawrence : University Press of Kansas, c1999. xiv, 205 p. ; 24 cm. (Studies in government and public policy) Includes bibliographical references (p. 179-196) and index. ISBN 0-7006-0971-7 (cloth : alk. paper) ISBN 0-7006-0972-5 (paper : alk. paper) DDC 379.746/8
*1. Educational equalization - Connecticut - New Haven Metropolitan Area - Case studies. 2. Schools - Decentralization - Social aspects - Connecticut - New Haven Metropolitan Area - Case studies. 3. Education and state - Connecticut - New Haven Metropolitan Area - Case studies. I. Title. II. Series.*
*TC LC213.23.N39 M34 1999*

**McDiarmid, Tami, 1960-** Critical challenges for primary students / Tami McDiarmid, Rita Manzo, Trish Musselle. Burnaby, B.C. : Field Relations and Teacher In-Service Education, Faculty of Education, Simon Fraser University, c1996. xvii, 66 p. : ill. ; 28 cm. (Critical challenges across the curriculum series, 1205-9730 ; 2) Includes bibliographical references. On Cover: TC², the Critical Thinking Cooperative. ISBN 0-86491-147-5 DDC 372.13
*1. Critical thinking - Study and teaching (Primary) 2. Pensée critique - Étude et enseignement (Primaire) I. Manzo, Rita, 1955- II. Musselle, Trish, 1968- III. Critical Thinking Cooperative. IV. Simon Fraser University. Faculty of Education. Field Relations and Teacher In-Service Education. V. Title. VI. Series.*
*TC LB1590.3 .M36 1996*

**McDonald, James C.**
The Allyn & Bacon sourcebook for college writing teachers. Boston ; London : Allyn and Bacon, 2000.
*TC PE1404 .A45 2000*

**McDonald, Libby.**
New school order [videorecording]. New York : First Run/Icarus Films, 1996.
*TC LB2831.583.P4 N4 1996*

**McDonald, Megan.** The night Iguana left home / by Megan McDonald ; pictures by Ponder Goembel. 1st ed. New York : DK Ink, 1999. 1 v. (unpaged) : col. ill. ; 29 cm. "A Richard Jackson book"--P. preceding t.p. SUMMARY: Although her friend Alison Frogley treats her very well, Iguana feels that something is missing in her life. ISBN 0-7894-2581-5 DDC [E]
*1. Iguanas - Fiction. 2. Friendship - Fiction. 3. Contentment - Fiction. I. Goembel, Ponder, ill. II. Title.*
*TC PZ7.M478419 Ni 1999*

**McDonald, Roderick P.** Test theory : a unified treatment / Roderick P. McDonald. Mahwah, N.J. ; London : L. Erlbaum Associates, 1999. xi, 485 p. : ill. ; 24 cm. Includes bibliographical references (p. 469-475) and indexes. ISBN 0-8058-3075-8 (cloth : alk. paper) DDC 150/.28/7
*1. Psychology - Statistical methods. 2. Psychometrics. 3. Social sciences - Statistical methods. I. Title.*
*TC BF39 .M175 1999*

**McDonald, Skye.**
Communication disorders following traumatic brain

injury. Hove, East Sussex, UK : Psychology Press, c1999.
**TC RD594 .C648 1999**

**McDonnell, Lorraine, 1947-.**
Rediscovering the democratic purposes of education. Lawrence : University Press of Kansas, c2000.
**TC LC89 .R43 2000**

**McDowell, John Holmes, 1946-.**
Traditional storytelling today. Chicago : Fitzroy Dearborn Publishers, 1999.
**TC GR72 .T73 1999**

**McDowell, Steve.**
Race, Philip. 500 computing tips for teachers and lecturers. 2nd ed. London : Kogan Page ; Sterling, VA : Stylus Pub., 1999.
**TC LB1028.43 .R33 1999**

**McElmeel, Sharron L.** 100 most popular children's authors : biographical sketches and bibliographies / Sharron L. McElmeel. Englewood, Colo. : Libraries Unlimited, 1999. xxxi, 495 p. : ill. ; 26 cm. (Popular authors series) Includes bibliographical references and index. ISBN 1-56308-646-8 (cloth) DDC 810.9/9282
*1. Children's literature, American - Bio-bibliography - Dictionaries. 2. Children's literature, English - Bio-bibliography - Dictionaries. 3. Authors, American - Biography - Dictionaries. 4. Authors, English - Biography - Dictionaries. I. Title. II. Title: One hundred most popular children's authors III. Series.*
**TC PS490 .M39 1999**

**McElroy, Lorie Jenkins.**
Women's voices. Detroit : UXL, 1997.
**TC HQ1410 .W688 1997**

**McEwan, Barbara, 1946-** The art of classroom management : effective practices for building equitable learning communities / Barbara McEwan ; [editor by Debra A. Stollenwerk]. Upper Saddle River, N.J. : Merrill, c2000. xviii, 233 p. : ill. 24 cm. Includes bibliographical references (p. [227]-230) and index. ISBN 0-13-079975-0 DDC 371.102/4
*1. Classroom management - Social aspects - United States. 2. Multicultural education - United States. 3. Educational equalization - United States. I. Stollenwerk, Debra A. II. Title.*
**TC LB3013 .M383 2000**

**McEwan, Elaine K., 1941-** Managing unmanageable students : practical solutions for administrators / Elaine K. McEwan, Mary Damer. Thousand Oaks, Calif. : Corwin Press, c2000. xiv, 177 p. : ill. ; 29 cm. Includes bibliographical references (p. 168-177). ISBN 0-8039-6786-1 (cloth : alk. paper) ISBN 0-8039-6787-X (pbk. : alk. paper) DDC 371.5/8
*1. Problem children - Education - United States. 2. Behavior modification - United States. 3. Teacher-student relationships - United States. 4. Educational change - United States. I. Damer, Mary. II. Title.*
**TC LC4801.5 .M39 2000**

**McEwen, Katharine, ill.**
Rowan, Kate. I know how we fight germs. Cambridge, Mass. : Candlewick Press, 1999.
**TC QR57 .R69 1999**

**McFarlane, Stephen C.**
Boone, Daniel R. The voice and voice therapy. 6th ed. Boston : London : Allyn & Bacon, c2000.
**TC RF540 .B66 2000**

**McFayden, Carol.**
Italian painting before 1400 [videorecording]. [London] : The National Gallery, c1989.

Italian painting before 1400 [videorecording]. [London] : The National Gallery, c1989.
**TC ND1575 .I87 1989**

**McGarrh, Kellie, d. 1995.** Kellie McGarrh's hangin' in tough : Mildred E. Doyle, school superintendent / edited by Clinton B. Allison. New York : P. Lang, c2000. xv, 140 p. ; 23 cm. (History of schools and schooling ; vol. 3) Author's doctoral dissertation, revised and edited after her death. Includes bibliographical references (p. [131]-135) and index. ISBN 0-8204-3744-1 (pbk : alk. paper) DDC 371.2/011
*1. Doyle, Mildred E. - (Mildred Eloise), - 1904-1989. 2. School superintendents - Tennessee - Biography. 3. Women school superintendents - Tennessee - Biography. 4. Feminism and education. I. Allison, Clinton B. II. Title. III. Title: Hangin' in tough IV. Series: History of schools and schooling ; v. 3.*
**TC LA2317.D6185 M34 2000**

**McGarty, Craig.** Categorization in social psychology / Craig McGarty. London ; Thousand Oaks, Calif. : SAGE Publications, 1999. xiv, 293 p. : ill. ; 25 cm. Includes bibliographical references (p. [264]285) and indexes. ISBN 0-7619-5953-X ISBN 0-7619-5954-8 (pbk) DDC 302/.1
*1. Categorization (Psychology) 2. Social perception. I. Title.*

**TC BF445 .M34 1999**

**McGavran, James Holt.**
Literature and the child. Iowa City : University of Iowa Press, c1999.
**TC PR990 .L58 1999**

**McGee, Hannah M., 1959-.**
Individual quality of life. Amsterdam : Harwood Academic, c1999.
**TC RA407 .I54 1999**

**McGee, Lea M.** Literacy's beginnings : supporting young readers and writers / Lea M. McGee, Donald J. Richgels. 3rd ed. Boston ; London : Allyn and Bacon, c2000. xvii, 396 p. : ill. ; 24 cm. Includes bibliographical references and indexes. ISBN 0-205-29931-8 (alk. paper) DDC 372.6/0973
*1. Reading (Early childhood) - United States. 2. Language arts (Early childhood) - United States. 3. Literacy - United States. I. Richgels, Donald J., 1949- II. Title.*
**TC LB1139.5.R43 M33 2000**

**McGettigan, Timothy.** Utopia on wheels : blundering down the road to reality / Timothy McGettigan. Lanham, MD : University Press of America, c1999. viii, 141 p. ; 23 cm. Includes bibliographical references (p. [127]-135) and index. ISBN 0-7618-1465-5 (pbk. : alk. paper) DDC 303.3
*1. Power (Social sciences) 2. McGettigan, Timothy - Journeys. I. Title.*
**TC HM1256 .M34 1999**

**MCGETTIGAN, TIMOTHY - JOURNEYS.**
McGettigan, Timothy. Utopia on wheels. Lanham, MD : University Press of America, c1999.
**TC HM1256 .M34 1999**

**McGill, Alice.** Molly Bannaky / written by Alice McGill ; pictures by Chris Soentpiet. Boston, Mass. : Houghton Mifflin, 1999. 1 v. (unpaged) : col. ill. ; 33 cm. SUMMARY: Relates how Benjamin Banneker's grandmother journeyed from England to Maryland in the late seventeenth century, worked as an indentured servant, began a farm of her own, and married a freed slave. ISBN 0-395-72287-X DDC [E]
*1. Bannaky, Molly, - b. ca. 1666 - Juvenile fiction. 2. Banneker, Benjamin, - 1731-1806 - Family - Juvenile fiction. 3. Bannaky, Molly, - b. ca. 1666 - Fiction. 4. Banneker, Benjamin, - 1731-1806 - Family - Fiction. 5. Maryland - History - Colonial period, ca. 1600-1775 - Fiction. 6. Interracial marriage - Fiction. 7. Slavery - Fiction. 8. Afro-Americans - Fiction. I. Soentpiet, Chris K., ill. II. Title.*
**TC PZ7.M478468 Mol 1999**

**McGillis, Roderick.** Voices of the other : children's literature and the postcolonial context / Roderick McGillis. New York : Garland Publishing,, Inc., c2000. xxxii, 280 p. ; 23 cm. (Children's literature and culture ; v. 10) (Garland reference library of the humanities ; v. 2126) ISBN 0-8153-3284-X
*1. Children's literature - History and criticism. I. Title. II. Series: Children's literature and culture ; v. 10 III. Series: Garland reference library of the humanities ; v. 2126*
**TC PN344 .M35 2000**

**McGillivray, Anne.**
Governing childhood. Aldershot, England ; Brookfield, Vt. : Dartmouth, c1997.
**TC HQ789 .G68 1997**

**McGinn, Noel F., 1934-.**
Welsh, Thomas. Decentralization of education. Paris : International Institute for Educational Planning (IIEP) ; Paris : UNESCO, 1999.
**TC LB5 .F85 v.64**

**McGoldrick, Monica.** Genograms : assessment and intervention / Monica McGoldrick, Randy Gerson, Sylvia Shellenberger. 2nd ed. New York : W.W. Norton, 1999. xvi, 234 p. : ill. ; 24 cm. "A Norton professional book." Prev. ed. cataloged with title: Genograms in family assessment. Includes bibliographical references (p. 199-226) and index. ISBN 0-393-70283-9 ISBN 0-393-70294-4 (pbk.) DDC 616.89/156
*1. Family psychotherapy - Technique. 2. Behavioral assessment - Charts, diagrams, etc. I. McGoldrick, Monica. Genograms in family assessment. II. Gerson, Randy. III. Shellenberger, Sylvia. IV. Title.*
**TC RC488.5 .M395 1999**

**Genograms in family assessment.**
McGoldrick, Monica. Genograms. 2nd ed. New York : W.W. Norton, 1999.
**TC RC488.5 .M395 1999**

**McGrane, Bernard.**
Bell, Inge. This book is not required. Rev. ed., new ed. / by Team Bell, Lynette Albovias ... [et al.]. Thousand Oaks, Calif. : Pine Forge Press, c1999.
**TC LA229 .B386 1999**

**McGraw-Hill, inc.**
Connect with English [videorecording]. S. Burlington, Vt. : The Annenberg/CPB Collection, c1997.
**TC PE1128 .C66 1997**

**McGraw-Hill series in developmental psychology**
Calvert, Sandra L. Children's journeys through the information age. 1st ed. Boston : McGraw-Hill College, c1999.
**TC HQ784.T4 C24 1999**

**MCGRAW, MYRTLE B. (MYRTLE BYRAM), 1899- -CONTRIBUTIONS IN CHILD DEVELOPMENT.**
Beyond heredity and environment. Boulder : Westview Press, 1995.
**TC BF341 .B48 1995**

**McGreal, Thomas L.**
Danielson, Charlotte. Teacher evaluation to enhance professional practice. Alexandria, Va. : Association for Supervision and Curriculum Development, c2000.
**TC LB2838 .D26 2000**

**McGregor, Gail** Inclusive schooling practices : pedagogical and research foundations : a synthesis of the literature that informs best practices about inclusive schooling / Gail McGregor, R. Timm Vogelsberg. [S.l.] : Allegheny University of Health Sciences ; Balitmore : Distributed exclusively by Paul H. Brookes Publishing, c1998. 97, 2, 45 p. : ill. ; 28 cm. Includes bibliographical references (p. 74-97). ISBN 1-55766-395-5
*1. Inclusive education - United States. 2. Mainstreaming in education - United States. 3. Learning disabilities - United States. 4. Special education - United States. I. Vogelsberg, R. Timm. II. Title.*
**TC LC4031 .M394 1998**

**McGrew, Kevin S.**
Flanagan, Dawn P. The Wechsler intelligence scales and Gf-Gc theory. Boston ; London : Allyn and Bacon, c2000.
**TC BF432.5.W4 F53 2000**

**McGuffin, Jo A.** The nurse's guide to successful management : a desk reference / Jo McGuffin. St. Louis, Mo. : Mosby, c1999. xvii, 332 p. ; 22 cm. Includes bibliographical references and index. ISBN 0-323-00388-5 DDC 362.1/73/068
*1. Nursing services - Administration. 2. Nursing, Supervisory - organization & administration. 3. Nurse Administrators - organization & administration. 4. Leadership. 5. Personnel Administration. Hospital - methods. 6. Nursing Staff - organization & administration.*
**TC RT89 .M436 1999**

**MCGUIGAN, DOROTHY GIES. DANGEROUS EXPERIMENT.**
Bordin, Ruth Birgitta Anderson, 1917- Women at Michigan. Ann Arbor : University of Michigan Press, c1999.
**TC LD3280 .B67 1999**

**McGuiness, John.** Counselling in schools : new perspectives / John McGuiness. London ; New York : Cassell, 1998. xi, 128 p. : ill. ; 25 cm. (Cassell studies in pastoral care and personal and social education) Includes bibliographical references (p. [120]-125) and index. ISBN 0-304-33354-9 (hardcover) ISBN 0-304-33356-5 (pbk.) DDC 371.4
*1. Educational counseling - Great Britain. I. Title. II. Series.*
**TC LB1027.5 .M367 1998**

**McHenry, Henry Davis.** From cognition to being : prolegomena for teachers / Henry Davis McHenry, Jr. Ottawa : University of Ottawa Press, c1999. xviii, 189 p. : ill. ; 23 cm. (Mentor series ; no. 2) Includes bibliographical references (p. [179]-181) and index. ISBN 0-7766-0455-4 DDC 371.102/01
*1. Teaching - Philosophy. I. Title. II. Series.*
**TC LB1025.3 .M36 1999**

**McHenry, Robert.**
Her heritage [computer file]. Cambridge, MA : Pilgrim New Media, c1994. Interactive multimedia.
**TC HQ1412 .A43 1994**

**McIlvane, William J.**
Perspectives on fundamental processes in intellectual functioning. Stamford, Conn. : Ablex Pub. Corp., c1998-
**TC BF444 .P42 1998**

**McIntyre, D. John.**
Educators healing racism. Reston, VA : Association of Teacher Educators ; Olney, MD : Association for Childhood Education International, c1999.
**TC LC212.2 .E38 1999**

Research on effective models for teacher education. Thousand Oaks, Calif. : Corwin Press, Inc., c2000.

**TC LB1715 .R42 2000**
Research on professional development schools.
Thousand Oaks, Calif. : Corwin Press, c1999.
**TC LB2154.A3 R478 1999**

**McKay, Alexander, 1962-** Sexual ideology and
schooling : towards democratic sexuality education /
Alexander McKay. London, Ont. : Althouse Press,
1998, ii, 214 p. ; 24 cm. Includes bibliographical references
and index. ISBN 0-920354-43-2 (pbk.) DDC 613.9/071
*1. Sex instruction. 2. Éducation sexuelle. I. Title.*
**TC HQ57.3 .M34 1998**

**McKay, Heather, 1950-** Teaching adult second
language learners / Heather McKay, Abigail H. Tom.
Cambridge ; New York : Cambridge University Press,
1999, viii, 234 p. ; 23 cm. (Cambridge handbooks for
language teachers) ISBN 0-521-64990-0 (pbk.) DDC 418/
.0071/5
*1. Language and languages - Study and teaching. 2. Second
language acquisition. 3. Adult education. I. Tom, Abigail,
1941- II. Title. III. Series.*
**TC P53 .M33 1999**

**McKay, Nellie Y.**
The Norton anthology of African American literature.
1st ed. New York : W.W. Norton & Co., c1997.
**TC PS508.N3 N67 1996**

**McKay, Sandra.**
New immigrants in the United States. Cambridge,
U.K. ; New York : Cambridge University Press, 2000.
**TC PE1128 .N384 1999**

**McKay social science series**
DeFleur, Melvin L. (Melvin Lawrence), 1923-
Theories of mass communication. New York : D.
McKay, c1966.
**TC HM258 .D35 1966**

**McKearnan, Sarah.**
The consensus building handbook. Thousand Oaks,
Calif. : Sage Publications, c1999.
**TC HM746 .C66 1999**

**McKechnie, Jim.**
Hobbs, Sandy. Child labor. Santa Barbara, Calif. :
ABC-CLIO, 1999.
**TC HD6231 .H63 1999**

**McKee, David.** Hide-and-seek Elmer / David McKee.
1st U.S. ed. New York : Lothrop, Lee & Shepard
Books, c1998. 1 v. (unpaged) : col. ill. ; 22 cm. Cover title.
"First published 1998 in Great Britain by Andersen Press Ltd.".
ISBN 0-688-16127-8
*1. Elephants - Fiction. <Juvenile subject heading>. I. Title.*
**TC PZ7.M19448 Hi 1998**

**McKellin, Karen, 1950-** Maintaining the momentum :
the internationalization of British Columbia's post
secondary institutions / [Karen McKellin]. Victoria,
B.C. : British Columbia Centre for International
Education, c1998. iv, 93 p. : ill. ; 28 cm. Includes
bibliographical references. Cover title. ISBN 0-9697201-4-9
(pbk.) DDC 378/.016/09711
*1. International education - British Columbia. 2. Education,
Higher$\pm$British Columbia. 3. Universities and colleges -
British Columbia - Curricula. 4. Éducation internationale -
Colombie-Britannique. 5. Enseignement supérieur -
Colombie-Britannique. 6. Enseignement universitaire -
Colombie-Britannique - Programmes d'études. I. British
Columbia Centre for International Education. II. Title.*
**TC LC1090 .M24 1998**

**McKenna, Michael C.**
Issues and trends in literacy education. 2nd ed.
Boston : Allyn and Bacon, c2000.
**TC LB1576 .I87 2000**

**McKillip, William D.** Mathematics for mastery :
teacher's edition K / by William D. McKillip.
Teacher's ed. Morristown, N.J. : Silver Burdett, 1981.
xi, 112T v. : ill. (some col.) : 28 cm. ISBN 0-382-01606-8
*1. Arithmatics - Problems, exercises, etc. 2. Arithmatics - Study
and teaching (Early childhood) I. Title.*
**TC QA107 .M375 1981 Teacher's ed. K**

Mathematics for mastery : teacher's edition K / by
William D. McKillip. Teacher's ed. Morristown,
N.J. : Silver Burdett, 1981. xi, 112T v. : ill. (some col.) :
28 cm. ISBN 0-382-01606-8
*1. Arithmatics - Problems, exercises. etc. 2. Arithmatics - Study
and teaching (Early childhood) I. Title.*
**TC QA107 .M375 1981 Teacher's ed. K**

Mathematics for mastery : teacher's edition K / by
William D. McKillip. Teacher's ed. Morristown,
N.J. : Silver Burdett, 1981. xi, 112T v. : ill. (some col.) :
28 cm. ISBN 0-382-01606-8
*1. Arithmetic - Problems, exercises, etc. 2. Arithmetic - Study
and teaching (Early childhood) I. Title.*
**TC QA107 .M375 1981 Teacher's ed. K**

**McKittrick, Anne.**
Assessing literacy with the Learning Record.
Portsmouth, NH : Heinemann, c1999.
**TC LB1029.P67 B37 1999b**

Barr, Mary A. (Mary Anderson) Assessing literacy
with the Learning Record. Portsmouth, NH :
Heinemann, c1999.
**TC LB1029.P67 B37 1999**

**McLain, Tim, 1970-** How to create successful Internet
projects / Timothy McLain. El Segundo, Calif. :
Classroom Connect, c1999. x, 101 p. : ill. ; 26 cm. ISBN
0-932577-73-3
*1. Internet (Computer network) - Study and teaching. 2.
Computer network resources - Study and teaching. 3.
Education, Elementary - Computer network resources. 4.
Education, Secondary - Computer network resources. I.
Classroom Connect. II. Title.*
**TC LB1044.87 .M35 1999**

**McLaren, Peter, 1948-** Che Guevara, Paulo Freire, and
the pedagogy of revolution / Peter McLaren ;
foreword by Ana Maria Araújo Freire. Lanham
[Md.] : Rowman & Littlefield Publishers, c2000. xxx,
220 p. : ill. ; 23 cm. (Culture and education series) Includes
bibliographical references and index. ISBN 0-8476-9532-8
(cloth : alk. paper) ISBN 0-8476-9533-6 (paper : alk. paper)
DDC 370.11/5
*1. Guevara, Ernesto, - 1928-1967. 2. Freire, Paulo, - 1921- 3.
Critical pedagogy. I. Title. II. Series.*
**TC LC196 .M29 2000**

The politics of multiculturalism and bilingual
education. Boston : McGraw-Hill, c2000.
**TC LC1099.3 .P64 2000**

Schooling as a ritual performance : toward a political
economy of educational symbols and gestures / Peter
McLaren. 3rd ed. Lanham, Md. : Rowman &
Littlefield, c1999. lxxiii, 354 p. : ill. ; 22 cm. (Culture and
education series) Includes bibliographical references and
indexes. ISBN 0-8476-9195-0 (cloth : alk. paper) ISBN
0-8476-9196-9 (pbk. : alk. paper) DDC 370.11/5
*1. Catholic schools - Ontario - Toronto - Case studies. 2.
Education - Aims and objectives. 3. Education - Social
aspects - Ontario - Toronto - Case studies. 4. Educational
anthropology - Ontario - Toronto - Case studies. I. Title. II.
Series.*
**TC LC504.3.T67 M35 1999**

**McLaughlin, Margaret J.**
Special education and school reform in the United
States and Britain. London ; New York : Routledge,
2000.
**TC LC3986.G7 S64 2000**

**McLean, Ian, Dr.** The art of Gordon Bennett / Ian
McLean, Gordon Bennett. Roseville East, NSW :
Craftsman House, 1996. 140 p. : ill. (some col.) ; 30 cm.
Includes bibliographical references (p. 133-136). ISBN 90-
5703-221-X
*1. Bennett, Gordon. - 1955- - Criticism and interpretation. I.
Bennett, Gordon, 1955- II. Title.*
**TC N7405.B46 M39 1996**

**McLeish, Elizabeth A.**
Processes of transition in education systems.
Wallingford : Symposium, 1998.
**TC LC71 .P7 1998**

**McLeod, Ellen Mary Easton, 1945-** In good hands : the
women of the Canadian Handicrafts Guild / Ellen
Easton McLeod. Montreal ; Ithaca : Published for
Carleton University by McGill-Queen's University
Press, c1999. xiii, 361 p. : ill., ports. ; 24 cm. (Women's
experience series ; 10) Includes bibliographical references and
index. ISBN 0-88629-356-1
*1. Peck, Alice, - 1855-1943. 2. Phillips, May. - 1856-1937. 3.
Canadian Handicrafts Guild - History. I. Title. II. Series:
Women's experience series ; 10*
**TC NK841 .M38 1999**

**McLeod, John, 1951-** An introduction to counselling /
John McLeod. 2nd ed. Buckingham [England] ;
Philadelphia, PA : Open University Press, 1998. xv,
446 p. ; 26 cm. Includes bibliographical references (p. [387]-
429) and index. ISBN 0-335-19710-8 (hbk.) ISBN
0-335-19709-4 (pbk.) DDC 361/.06
*1. Counseling. I. Title.*
**TC BF637.C6 M379 1998**

**McMahon, Anthony.** Damned if you do, damned if you
don't : working in child welfare / Anthony McMahon.
Aldershot, England ; Brookfield, USA : Ashgate,
1998. vii, 129 p. ; 23 cm. Includes bibliographical references
(p. 119-129). ISBN 1-85972-616-X DDC 362.76/532
*1. Social work with children - Illinois - Chicago. 2. Social work
with minorities - Illinois - Chicago. 3. Social workers -
Illinois - Chicago. 4. Child welfare - Illinois - Chicago. I. Title.*

**TC HV743.C5 M35 1998**

**McMahon, Timothy R., 1951-.**
Komives, Susan R., 1946- Exploring leadership. 1st
ed. San Francisco : Jossey-Bass Publishers, c1998.
**TC LB3605 .K64 1998**

**MCMASTER UNIVERSITY - STUDENTS -
RELIGIOUS LIFE.**
Bramadat, Paul A. The church on the world's turf.
Oxford ; New York : Oxford University Press, 2000.
**TC BV970.16 B73 2000**

**McMeen, George H.**
Upton, Clifford Brewster. 1877- American
Arithmetic. 2nd ed. New York, N.Y. : American Book
Company, 1963.
**TC QA103 .U67 1963**

**McMillan, Bruce.** Nights of the pufflings / written and
photo-illustrated by Bruce McMillan. Boston :
Houghton Mifflin Co., 1995. 32 p. : col. ill. ; 27 cm.
Includes bibliographical references (p. 32). ISBN 0-395-
70810-9 DDC 598.3/3
*1. Puffins - Iceland - Juvenile literature. 2. Puffins. 3. Zoology -
Iceland. I. Title.*
**TC QL696.C42 M39 1995**

**McMillan, James H.** Educational research :
fundamentals for the consumer / James H. McMillan.
3rd ed. New York ; Harlow, England : Longman,
c2000. xvii, 377 p. : ill. ; 24 cm. Includes bibliographical
references (p. 368-372) and index. ISBN 0-321-02337-4 (pbk.)
DDC 370/.7/2
*1. Education - Research. I. Title.*
**TC LB1028 .M364 2000**

**McMullen, Patricia A.**
Converging methods for understanding reading and
dyslexia. Cambridge, Mass. ; London : MIT Press,
c1999.
**TC LB1050.5 .C662 1999**

**McMurray, Robert G.** Concepts in fitness
programming / Robert G. McMurray. Boca Raton :
CRC Press, c1999. 301 p. : ill. ; 24 cm. (CRC series in
exercise physiology) Includes bibliographical references and
index. ISBN 0-8493-8714-0 (alk. paper) DDC 613.7/1
*1. Exercise. 2. Physical fitness. 3. Nutrition. I. Title. II. Series.*
**TC QP301 .M3754 1999**

**McNamara, Eddie.** Positive pupil management and
motivation : : a secondary teacher's guide / Eddie
McNamara. London : David Fulton, 1999. 170 p. : ill. ;
25 cm. Includes bibliographical references and index. ISBN 1-
85346-634-4
*1. Classroom management - Great Britain. 2. High school
teaching - Great Britain. 3. Motivation in education - Great
Britain. I. Title.*
**TC LB3013 .M336 1999**

**McNamara, Patrick, 1956-** Mind and variability :
mental Darwinism, memory, and self / Patrick
McNamara. Westport, Conn. : Praeger, 1999. xiii, 163
p. ; 25 cm. (Human evolution, behavior, and intelligence,
1063-2158) Includes bibliographical references (p. [151]-160)
and index. ISBN 0-275-96383-7 (alk. paper) DDC 153.1/2
*1. Memory. 2. Brain - Evolution. 3. Identity (Psychology) 4.
Genetic psychology. I. Title. II. Series.*
**TC BF371 .M385 1999**

**McNay, Ian.**
Bligh, Donald, 1936- Understanding higher education.
Oxford : Intellect, 1999.
**TC LA637 .B55 1999**

**McNeil, Elton B., ed.** The nature of human conflict.
Edited by Elton B. McNeil. Englewood Cliffs, N.J. :
Prentice-Hall [1965] xvi, 315 p. illus. 24 cm. "A publication
from the Center for Research on Conflict Resolution, the
University of Michigan." Includes bibliographies. DDC 301.23
*1. War and society. I. University of Michigan. Center for
Research on Conflict Resolution. II. Title.*
**TC HM36.5 .M25**

**McNeil, Linda M.** Contradictions of school reform :
educational costs of standardized testing / Linda M.
McNeil. New York : Routledge, 2000. xxxii, 304 p. ; 24
cm. (Critical social thought) Spine title: Contradictions of
reform. Includes bibliographical references (p. 285-295) and
index. ISBN 0-415-92073-6 (hard) ISBN 0-415-92074-4 (pbk.)
DDC 379.1/58/0973
*1. Education - Standards - United States. 2. School
improvement programs - United States. I. Title. II. Title:
Contradictions of reform III. Series.*
**TC LB3060.83 .M38 2000**

**McNeill, Patricia, 1941-.**
Geever, Jane C. The Foundation Center's guide to
proposal writing. Rev. ed. New York : Foundation
Center, c1997.
**TC HG177.5.U6 G44 1997**

**McNeilly, Robert B.** Healing the whole person : a solution-focused approach to using empowering language, emotions, and actions in therapy / Robert B. McNeilly ; foreword by Bill O'Hanlon. New York ; Chichester [England] : John Wiley & Sons, c2000. xviii, 190 p. ; 24 cm. Includes bibliographical references (p. 183-184) and index. CONTENTS: 1. General Principles -- 2. Language in Counseling -- 3. Emotions and the Body in Counseling -- 4. Emotional and Body Interventions -- 5. Strategies in Action -- 6. Declarations as Pathways to Solutions -- 7. Ethics: An Evolution. ISBN 0-471-38274-4 (cloth : alk. paper) DDC 616.89/14 DDC 616.89/14
*1. Solution-focused brief therapy. 2. Brief psychotherapy. I. Title.*
***TC RC489.S65 M38 2000***

**McNergney, Robert F.** Foundations of education : the challenge of professional practice / Robert F. McNergney, Joanne M. Herbert. 3rd ed. Boston ; London : Allyn and Bacon, c2001. xxi, 599 p. : col. ill. ; 27 cm. Includes bibliographical references (p. 557-573) and indexes. ISBN 0-205-31691-3 DDC 370/.973
*1. Teaching - Vocational guidance - United States. 2. Education - United States. I. Herbert, Joanne M. II. Title.*
***TC LB1775.2 .M32 2001***

**McNiff, Jean.**
Rethinking pastoral care. London ; New York : Routledge, 1999.
***TC LB1620.53.I73 R48 1999***

**McNulty, John L.**
Graham, John R. (John Robert), 1940- MMPI-2 correlates for outpatient community mental health settings. Minneapolis : University of Minnesota Press, c1999.
***TC RC473.M5 G733 1999***

**McPherson, Marion White.**
Popplestone, John A. An illustrated history of American psychology. 2nd ed. Akron, Ohio : The University of Akron Press, c1999.
***TC BF108.U5 P67 1999***

**McVey, R. Steve.**
Capozzoli, Thomas. Kids killing kids. Boca Raton, Fla. : London : St. Lucie Press, c2000.
***TC LB3013.3 .C37 2000***

**McVey, Vicki.**
Lawyer-Brook, Dianna, 1949- Shifting focus. Lanham, Md. ; London : Scarecrow Press, 2000.
***TC LB1044.7 .L313 2000***

**McWhorter, John H.** Losing the race : self-sabotage in Black America / John H. McWhorter. New York : Free Press, c2000. xv, 285 p. ; 25 cm. Includes bibliographical references (p. 263-269) and index. ISBN 0-684-83669-6 DDC 305.896/073
*1. Afro-Americans - Psychology. 2. Afro-Americans - Social conditions - 1975- 3. Afro-Americans - Education. 4. Success - Psychological aspects. 5. Self-defeating behavior. I. Title.*
***TC E185.625 .M38 2000***

**McWilliam, Erica.** Pedagogical pleasures / Erica McWilliam. New York ; Canterbury [England] : P. Lang, c1999. xii, 197 p. ; 23 cm. (Eruptions ; vol. 1) Includes bibliographical references (p. [187]-197). ISBN 0-8204-3800-6 (pbk.) DDC 371.1/1
*1. Teachers - Attitudes. 2. Pleasure. 3. Teaching. 4. Feminism and education. I. Title. II. Series.*
***TC LB1775 .M319 1999***

**McWilliam, P. J.** Lives in progress : case stories in early intervention / by P.J. McWilliam, with invited contributors. Baltimore : P.H. Brookes, c2000. xix, 245 p. ; 23 cm. Includes bibliographical references (p. 237-245). ISBN 1-55766-365-3 DDC 362.7/0973
*1. Social work with children - United States - Case studies. 2. Social case work - United States - Case studies. I. McWilliam, P. J., 1953- II. Title. III. Title: Case stories in early intervention*
***TC HV741 .M3128 2000***

**McWilliam, P. J., 1953-.**
McWilliam, P. J. Lives in progress. Baltimore : P.H. Brookes, c2000.
***TC HV741 .M3128 2000***

**MDR's sales manager's guide to the U.S. school market.**
MDR's school directory. Connecticut. Shelton, CT : Market Data Retrieval, c1995-
***TC L903.C8 M37***

MDR's school directory. New Jersey. Shelton, CT : Market Data Retrieval, c1995-
***TC L903.N5 M37***

MDR's school directory. New York. Shelton, CT : Market Data Retrieval, c1995-
***TC L903.N7 M37***

MDR's school directory. Pennsylvania. Shelton, CT : Market Data Retrieval, 1995-
***TC L903.P4 M37***

**MDR's school directory.** Connecticut. Shelton, CT : Market Data Retrieval, c1995- v. : ill. ; 28 cm. Frequency: Annual. 1994/95- . Market Data Retrieval's school directory. Connecticut. School directory. Connecticut. Running title: Connecticut school directory. Complemented by: MDR's sales manager's guide to the U.S. school market. Continues: Market Data Retrieval's CIC school directory. Connecticut ISSN: 1067-6481 (DLC) 93664030 (OCoLC)25334934. MDR's sales manager's guide to the U.S. school market ISSN: 1071-7471 (DLC) 95664063 (OCoLC)31459213. ISSN 1077-7458 DDC 371/.0025746
*1. Schools - Connecticut - Directories. 2. School districts - Connecticut - Directories. 3. School enrollment - Connecticut - Statistics - Periodicals. I. Market Data Retrieval (Firm) II. Title: Market Data Retrieval's school directory. Connecticut III. Title: School directory. Connecticut IV. Title: Connecticut school directory V. Title: Market Data Retrieval's CIC school directory. Connecticut VI. Title: MDR's sales manager's guide to the U.S. school market*
***TC L903.C8 M37***

**MDR's school directory.** New Jersey. Shelton, CT : Market Data Retrieval, c1995- v. : ill. ; 28 cm. Frequency: Annual. 1994/95- . Market Data Retrieval's school directory. New Jersey. School directory. New Jersey. Running title: New Jersey school directory. Complemented by: MDR's sales manager's guide to the U.S. school market. Continues: Market Data Retrieval's CIC school directory. New Jersey ISSN: 1067-6716 (DLC) 93664055 (OCoLC)25335156. MDR's sales manager's guide to the U.S. school market ISSN: 1071-7471 (DLC) 95664063 (OCoLC)31459213. ISSN 1077-7695 DDC 371/.0025749
*1. Schools - New Jersey - Directories. 2. School districts - New Jersey - Directories. 3. School enrollment - New Jersey - Statistics - Periodicals. I. Market Data Retrieval (Firm) II. Title: Market Data Retrieval's school directory. New Jersey III. Title: School directory. New Jersey IV. Title: New Jersey school directory V. Title: Market Data Retrieval's CIC school directory. New Jersey VI. Title: MDR's sales manager's guide to the U.S. school market*
***TC L903.N5 M37***

**MDR's school directory.** New York. Shelton, CT : Market Data Retrieval, c1995- v. : ill. ; 28 cm. Frequency: Annual. 1994/95- . Market Data Retrieval's school directory. New York. School directory. New York. Running title: New York school directory. Complemented by: MDR's sales manager's guide to the U.S. school market. Continues: Market Data Retrieval's CIC school directory. New York ISSN: 1067-6732. MDR's sales manager's guide to the U.S. school market ISSN: 1071-7471. ISSN 1077-7717 DDC 371/.0025747
*1. Schools - New York - Directories. 2. School districts - New York - Directories. 3. School enrollment - New York - Statistics - Periodicals. I. Market Data Retrieval (Firm) II. Title: Market Data Retrieval's school directory. New York III. Title: School directory. New York IV. Title: New York school directory V. Title: Market Data Retrieval's CIC school directory. New York VI. Title: MDR's sales manager's guide to the U.S. school market*
***TC L903.N7 M37***

**MDR's school directory.** Pennsylvania. Shelton, CT : Market Data Retrieval, 1995- v. : ill. ; 28 cm. Frequency: Annual. 1994/95- . Market Data Retrieval's school directory. Pennsylvania. School directory. Pennsylvania. Running title: Pennsylvania school directory. Complemented by: MDR's sales manager's guide to the U.S. school market. Continues: Market Data Retrieval's CIC school directory. Pennsylvania ISSN: 1067-6791 (DLC) 93664039 (OCoLC)25335232. MDR's sales manager's guide to the U.S. school market ISSN: 1071-7471 (DLC) 95664063 (OCoLC)31459213. ISSN 1077-7776 DDC 371/.0025748
*1. Schools - Pennsylvania - Directories. 2. School districts - Pennsylvania - Directories. 3. School enrollment - Pennsylvania - Statistics - Periodicals. I. Market Data Retrieval (Firm) II. Title: Market Data Retrieval's school directory. Pennsylvania III. Title: School directory. Pennsylvania IV. Title: Pennsylvania school directory V. Title: Market Data Retrieval's CIC school directory. Pennsylvania VI. Title: MDR's sales manager's guide to the U.S. school market*
***TC L903.P4 M37***

**MDS.** *See* **PHYSICIANS.**

**Mead, George Herbert, 1863-1931.** Play, school, and society / George Herbert Mead ; edited and introduced by Mary Jo Deegan. New York : Peter Lang, c1999. cxii, 157 p. : ill. ; 24 cm. (American university studies. Series XI, Anthropology and sociology ; vol. 71) Selections from Mead's published work, as well as some archival material. Includes bibliographical references (p. [125]-150) and indexes. ISBN 0-8204-3823-5 DDC 306.4/81
*1. Play - Social aspects. 2. Socialization. 3. Education. I. Deegan, Mary Jo. 1946- II. Title. III. Series: American university studies. Series XI. Anthropology/sociology ; vol. 71.*
***TC HQ782 .M43 1999***

**Mead, Margaret, 1901-1978.** Male and female : a study of the sexes in a changing world / by Margaret Mead. London : Victor Gollancz, c1949. xii, 477 p. ; 23 cm. "The substance of this book was given as The Jacob Gimbel Lectures in Sex Psychology under the auspices of Stanford University and the University of California, San Francisco, California, November, 1946" -- T.p. verso. Includes bibliographical referenceses and indexes.
*1. Sex. 2. Women. 3. Men. 4. Human beings. I. Title. II. Title: Study of the sexes in a changing world*
***TC HQ21 .M464 1949***

Male and female : a study of the sexes in a changing world / by Margaret Mead. London : Victor Gollancz, c1949. xii, 477 p. ; 23 cm. "The substance of this book was given as The Jacob Gimbel Lectures in Sex Psychology under the auspices of Stanford University and the University of California, San Francisco, California, November, 1946" -- T.p. verso. Includes bibliographical references and indexes.
*1. Sex. 2. Women. 3. Men. 4. Human beings. I. Title. II. Title: Study of the sexes in a changing world*
***TC HQ21 .M464 1949***

**MEAD, MARGARET, 1901-1978 - PHOTOGRAPH COLLECTIONS.**
Sullivan, Gerald. Margaret Mead, Gregory Bateson, and Highland Bali. Chicago, IL : University of Chicago Press, 1999.
***TC GN635.I65 S948 1999***

**Meadow-Orlans, Kathryn P.**
The deaf child in the family and at school. Mahwah, N.J. : Lawrence Erlbaum Associates, 2000.
***TC HV2392.2 .D43 2000***

**Meaney, John W.**
Jung on film [videorecording]. [Chicago, Ill.?] : Public Media Video, c1990.
***TC BF109.J8 J4 1990***

Jung on film [videorecording]. [Chicago, Ill.?] : Public Media Video, c1990.
***TC BF109.J8 J4 1990***

**Meaning in technology.**
Pacey, Arnold. Cambridge, Mass. : MIT Press, c1999.
***TC T14 .P28 1999***

**Meaning-making frameworks for psychotherapy.**
Constructions of disorder. 1st ed. Washington, DC : American Psychological Association, c2000.
***TC RC437.5 .C647 2000***

**The meaning of movement :** developmental and clinical perspectives of the Kestenberg Movement Profile / Janet Kestenberg Amighi ... [et al.]. Amsterdam : Gordon and Breach, c1999. xiv, 369 p. : ill. ; 26 cm. Includes bibliographical references and indexes. ISBN 90-5700-528-X
*1. Kestenberg Movement Profile. 2. Movement, Psychology of. 3. Movement therapy. 4. Mind and body therapies. I. Kestenberg Amighi, Janet. II. Title: Developmental and clinical perspectives of the Kestenberg Movement Profile*
***TC RC473.K47 M4 1999***

**MEANING (PHILOSOPHY).**
Langan, Thomas. Surviving the age of virtual reality. Columbia, Mo. ; London : University of Missouri Press, c2000.
***TC B105.M4 L355 2000***

**MEANING (PSYCHOLOGY).** *See also* **LANGUAGE AND LANGUAGES; SEMANTICS; SEMANTICS (PHILOSOPHY).**
Gibbs, Raymond W. Intentions in the experience of meaning. New York : Cambridge University Press, 1999.
***TC BF463.M4 G53 1999***

Peterson, Jordan B. Maps of meaning. New York : Routledge, 1999.
***TC BF175.5.A72 P48 1999***

An update on adult development theory :. San Francisco, CA : Jossey-Bass Publishers, 1999.
***TC LC5225.L42 U63 1999***

**Meaningful care :** a multidisciplinary approach to the meaning of care for people with mental retardation / edited by Joop Stolk, Theo A. Boer and Ruth Seldenrijk. Dordrecht ; Boston ; London : Kluwer Academic Publishers, c2000. xv, 189 p. ; 25 cm. Includes bibliographical references and index. ISBN 0-7923-6291-8 (alk. paper) DDC 362.3/8
*1. Mentally handicapped - Care - Moral and ethical aspects. 2. Mental retardation - Religious aspects. I. Stolk, Joop. II. Boer, Theodoor Adriaan, 1960- III. Seldenrijk, R.*
***TC HV3004 .M34 2000***

**Measham, D. C.** English now and then, by D.C.
Measham. Cambridge [Eng.] University Press, 1965.
viii, 137, [1] p. : ill. ; 23 cm. Bibliography: p. 137-[138].
*1. English language - History. 2. English language - Rhetoric.*
*3. English language - Grammar. I. Title.*
**TC PE1112 .M4**

**Measurement and analysis in psychosocial research.**
Chen, Sheying. Aldershot, Hants, UK : Brookfield
USA : Avebury, c1997.
**TC RC473.P79 C46 1997**

**Measurement and assessment in teaching.**
Linn, Robert L. 8th ed. Upper Saddle River, N.J. :
Merrill, c2000.
**TC LB3051 .L545 2000**

**MEASUREMENT, MENTAL.** *See*
**PSYCHOMETRICS.**

**The measurement of sensation.**
Laming, D. R. J. (Donald Richard John) Oxford ; New
York : Oxford University Press, 1997.
**TC QP435 .L34 1997**

**MEASUREMENT, PSYCHOLOGICAL.** *See*
**PSYCHOMETRICS.**

**Measures for clinical practice.**
Corcoran, Kevin (Kevin J.) 3rd ed. New York :
London : Free Press, c2000.
**TC BF176 .C66 2000**

**Measuring and evaluating school learning.**
Carey, Lou. 2nd ed. Boston : Allyn and Bacon, c1994.
**TC LB3051 .C36 1994**

Carey, Lou. 3rd ed. Boston ; London : Allyn and
Bacon, c2001.
**TC LB3051 .C36 2001**

**Measuring and improving patient satisfaction.**
Shelton, Patrick J. Gaithersburg, Md. : Aspen
Publishers, 2000.
**TC RA399.A1 S47 2000**

**Measuring behavioral health outcomes.**
Hawkins, Robert P., 1931- New York : Kluwer
Academic/Plenum Publishers, c1999.
**TC RJ503.5 .H39 1999**

**Measuring emotional intelligence and related**
**constructs.**
Schutte, Nicola S. (Nicola Susanne) Lewiston, N.Y. ;
Lampeter, Wales : E. Mellen Press, c1999.
**TC BF576.3 .S38 1999**

**Measuring leadership.**
Lashway, Larry. Eugene, OR : ERIC Clearinghouse
on Educational Management, University of Oregon,
1999.
**TC LB2806 .L28 1999**

**Measuring outcomes in speech-language pathology /**
edited by Carol M. Frattali. New York : Thieme,
1998. xviii, 588 p. : ill. ; 26 cm. Includes bibliographical
references and index. ISBN 0-86577-718-7 (TMP) ISBN
3-13-109731-0 (GTV) DDC 616.85/506
*1. Speech therapy - Evaluation. 2. Outcome assessment*
*(Medical care) 3. Speech Disorders - therapy. 4. Treatment*
*Outcome. 5. Language Disorders - therapy. 6. Speech-*
*Language Pathology. I. Frattali, Carol.*
**TC RC423 .M39 1997**

**Measuring student knowledge and skills.**
Organisation for Economic Co-operation and
Development (Paris) Paris : Organisation for
Economic Co-operation and Development, 2000.
**TC LB3051 .M44 2000**

**Measuring student knowledge and skills :** a new
framework for assessment. Paris : Organisation for
Economic Co-operation and Development, c1999. 81
p. : ill. ; 28 cm. "Sets out the conceptual framework underlying
the OECD/PISA [Programme for International Student
Assessment] assessments"--foreword. Includes bibliographical
references (p. 73-75). ISBN 92-64-17053-7 (pbk.) DDC 370
*1. Programme for International Student Assessment. 2.*
*Educational tests and measurements - OECD countries. 3.*
*Competency based education - OECD countries. 4.*
*Educational evaluation. 5. Academic achievement - Evaluation.*
*I. Schleicher, Andreas. II. Organisation for Economic Co-*
*operation and Development. III. Organisation for Economic*
*Co-operation and Development. Directorate for Education,*
*Employment, Labour, and Social Affairs. Statistics and*
*Indicators Division.*
**TC LB3051 .M43 1999**

**Measuring up :** challenges minorities face in
educational assessment / edited by Arie L. Nettles,
Michael T. Nettles. Boston : Kluwer Academic
Publishers, c1999. xvi, 266 p. : ill. ; 25 cm. (Evaluation in
education and human services) Includes bibliographical
references and index. ISBN 0-7923-8401-6 (alk. paper) DDC
371.26/01/3
*1. Educational tests and measurements - Social aspects -*
*United States. 2. Minority students - Rating of - United States.*
*3. Test bias - United States. 4. Educational equalization -*
*United States. I. Nettles, Arie L. II. Nettles, Michael T., 1955-*
*III. Series.*
**TC LB3051 .M4627 1999**

**MEAT - QUALITY.**
Antioxidants in muscle foods. New York ; Chichester
[England] : John Wiley, c2000.
**TC TX556.M4 A57 2000**

**MEATS.** *See* **MEAT.**

**MECHANIC ARTS.** *See* **INDUSTRIAL ARTS.**

**MECHANICAL VENTILATORS (MEDICAL**
**EQUIPMENT).** *See* **RESPIRATORS**
**(MEDICAL EQUIPMENT).**

**The mechanism of evolution.**
Dowdeswell, W. H. (Wilfrid Hogarth) 3d ed. London,
Heinemann, 1963
**TC QH366 .D68 1963**

**MECHANIZED INFORMATION STORAGE AND**
**RETRIEVAL SYSTEMS.** *See* **INFORMATION**
**STORAGE AND RETRIEVAL SYSTEMS.**

**Meddaugh, Susan, ill.**
Dee, Ruby. Two ways to count to ten. New York : H.
Holt, c1988.
**TC PZ8.1.D378 Tw 1988**

Dee, Ruby. Two ways to count to ten. New York : H.
Holt, c1988.
**TC PZ8.1.D378 Tw 1988a**

Dee, Ruby. Two ways to count to ten. 1st ed. New
York : H. Holt, c1988.
**TC PZ8.1.D378 Tw 1988**

**Medeiros, Denis M.**
Wildman, Robert E. C., 1964- Advanced human
nutrition. Boca Raton : CRC Press, c2000.
**TC QP141 .W512 2000**

**Media & cultural studies**
(1) Interactive television. Aalborg, Denmark :
Aalborg University Press, 1999.
**TC HE8700.95 .I57 1999**

**Media and literacy.**
Adams, Dennis M. 2nd ed. Springfield, Ill. : C.C.
Thomas, c2000.
**TC LB1043 .A33 2000**

**MEDIA CENTERS (EDUCATION).** *See*
**INSTRUCTIONAL MATERIALS CENTERS.**

**Media, education and culture**
Buckingham, David, 1954- The making of citizens.
London ; New York : Routledge, 2000.
**TC HQ784.T4 .B847 2000**

**Media, education, culture.**
Digital diversions. London : UCL Press, 1998.
**TC QA76.575 .D536 1998**

**MEDIA LITERACY - HANDBOOKS, MANUALS,**
**ETC.**
Brunner, Cornelia, Dr. The new media literacy
handbook. New York : Anchor Books, 1999.
**TC LB1028.3 .B77 1999**

**MEDIA LITERACY - STUDY AND TEACHING.**
Alvermann, Donna E. Popular culture in the
classroom. Newark, Del. : International Reading
Association ; Chicago, Ill. : National Reading
Conference, c1999.
**TC P91.3 .A485 1999**

**Media Loft (Firm).**
The filming of a television commercial
[videorecording]. Minneapolis, Minn. : Media Loft,
c1992.
**TC HF6146.T42 F5 1992**

The power of idea : [videorecording]. Minneapolis,
Minn. : Media Loft, c1992.
**TC TR690 .P5 1992**

Sport photography today! [videorecording].
Minneapolis, Minn. : Media Loft, c1992.
**TC TR821 .S64 1992**

The sight and insight of Ernst Haas [videorecording].
Minneapolis, Minn. : Media Loft, 1992.
**TC TR647.H3 S5 1992**

**Media messages.**
Holtzman, Linda, 1949- Armonk, NY : M.E. Sharpe,
2000.
**TC P94.5.M552 U646 2000**

**MEDIA PROGRAMS (EDUCATION).** *See*
**TEACHING - AIDS AND DEVICES.**

**MEDIA PROGRAMS (EDUCATION) - UNITED**
**STATES.**
Bucher, Katherine Toth, 1947- Information
technology for schools. 2nd ed. Worthington, Ohio :
Linworth Pub., c1998.
**TC Z675.S3 B773 1998**

**MEDIA PROGRAMS (EDUCATION) - UNITED**
**STATES - ADMINISTRATION.**
Woolls, Blanche. The school library media manager.
2nd ed. Englewood, CO : Libraries Unlimited, 1999.
**TC Z675.S3 W8735 1999**

**MEDIATION.** *See also* **DISPUTE RESOLUTION**
**(LAW).**
Gilhooley, James. Using peer mediation in classrooms
and schools. Thousand Oaks, Calif. : Corwin Press,
c2000.
**TC LB1027.5 .G48 2000**

Tillett, Gregory, Ph. D. Resolving conflict :. 2nd ed.
Oxford ; New York : Oxford University Press, 1999.
**TC HM132 .T55 1999**

**MEDIATION - UNITED STATES.**
Kosmoski, Georgia J. Managing difficult, frustrating,
and hostile conversations. Thousand Oaks, Calif. :
Sage Publications, c2000.
**TC LB3011.5 .K67 2000**

**MEDICAL AND HEALTH CARE INDUSTRY.** *See*
**MEDICAL CARE.**

**MEDICAL BACTERIOLOGY.** *See* **BACTERIAL**
**DISEASES.**

**MEDICAL CARE.** *See* **DISCRIMINATION IN**
**MEDICAL CARE; HEALTH FACILITIES;**
**HOSPITAL CARE; LONG-TERM CARE OF**
**THE SICK; MANAGED CARE PLANS**
**(MEDICAL CARE); MENTAL HEALTH**
**SERVICES; NURSING SERVICES;**
**PREVENTIVE HEALTH SERVICES;**
**PRIMARY CARE (MEDICINE); SCHOOL**
**HEALTH SERVICES; TRANSCULTURAL**
**MEDICAL CARE.**

**MEDICAL CARE - ADMINISTRATION.** *See*
**HEALTH SERVICES ADMINISTRATION.**

**MEDICAL CARE - CANADA.**
Armstrong, Pat, 1945- Universal health care. New
York : New Press : Distributed by W.W. Norton,
c1998.
**TC RA412.5.C3 A76 1998**

**MEDICAL CARE - DECISION MAKING -**
**PHILOSOPHY.**
Chapman, Gretchen B., 1965- Decision making in
health care. New York : Cambridge University Press,
2000.
**TC R723.5 .C48 2000**

**MEDICAL CARE - DECISION MAKING -**
**PSYCHOLOGICAL ASPECTS.**
Chapman, Gretchen B., 1965- Decision making in
health care. New York : Cambridge University Press,
2000.
**TC R723.5 .C48 2000**

**MEDICAL CARE - ECONOMIC ASPECTS.** *See*
**MEDICAL ECONOMICS.**

**MEDICAL CARE - EVALUATION.** *See also*
**OUTCOME ASSESSMENT (MEDICAL**
**CARE); PATIENT SATISFACTION.**
Gill, Kenneth Joseph. Social psychological artifacts in
the measurement of consumer satisfaction with health
care. 1996.
**TC 085 G396**

**MEDICAL CARE FACILITIES.** *See* **HEALTH**
**FACILITIES.**

**MEDICAL CARE FOR THE AGED.** *See* **AGED -**
**MEDICAL CARE.**

**MEDICAL CARE - GOVERNMENT POLICY.** *See*
**MEDICAL POLICY.**

**MEDICAL CARE INSTITUTIONS.** *See* **HEALTH**
**FACILITIES.**

**MEDICAL CARE - MANAGEMENT.** *See*
**HEALTH SERVICES ADMINISTRATION.**

**MEDICAL CARE - MORAL AND ETHICAL**
**ASPECTS.** *See* **MEDICAL ETHICS.**

**MEDICAL CARE - NEEDS ASSESSMENT -**
**CONGRESSES.**
Unmet need in psychiatry. Cambridge, U.K. ; New
York, NY : Cambridge University Press, 2000.

*TC RA790.5 .U565 2000*

**MEDICAL CARE - PLANNING.** *See* **HEALTH PLANNING.**

**MEDICAL CARE PLANNING.** *See* **HEALTH PLANNING.**

**MEDICAL CARE - POLITICAL ASPECTS - UNITED STATES.**
Rovner, Julie. Health care policy and politics A to Z. Washington, DC : CQ Press, 2000.
*TC RA395.A3 R685 1999*

**MEDICAL CARE REFORM.** *See* **HEALTH CARE REFORM.**

**MEDICAL CARE - SOCIAL ASPECTS.** *See* **SOCIAL MEDICINE.**

**MEDICAL CARE - STANDARDS - UNITED STATES.**
Sherman, V. Clayton. Raising standards in American health care. 1st ed. San Francisco : Jossey-Bass, c1999.
*TC RA395.A3 S483 1999*

**MEDICAL CARE - UNITED STATES.**
Fressola, Maria C. How nurse executives learned to become leaders. 1998.
*TC 06 no. 11115*

Fressola, Maria C. How nurse executives learned to become leaders. 1998.
*TC 06 no. 11115*

Health care and its costs. 1st ed. New York : Norton, c1987.
*TC RA395.A3 H392 1987*

O'Brien, Lawrence J. Bad medicine. Amherst, N.Y. : Prometheus Books, c1999.
*TC RA395.A3 O28 1999*

Remaking health care in America. 1st ed. San Francisco : Jossey-Bass Publishers, c1996.
*TC RA395.A3 R46 1996*

**MEDICAL CARE - UNITED STATES - FINANCE.**
Health care and its costs. 1st ed. New York : Norton, c1987.
*TC RA395.A3 H392 1987*

**MEDICAL CARE - UNITED STATES - FORECASTING.**
Morrison, J. Ian, 1952- Health care in the new millennium. 1st ed. San Francisco : Jossey-Bass Publishers, c2000.
*TC RA395.A3 M675 2000*

**MEDICAL CARE USE.** *See* **MEDICAL CARE - UTILIZATION.**

**MEDICAL CARE - UTILIZATION - SEX DIFFERENCES.**
Gender inequalities in health. Buckingham [England] ; Philadelphia : Open University Press, 2000.
*TC RA564.85 .G4653 2000*

**MEDICAL CENTERS.** *See* **HOSPITALS.**

**MEDICAL COLLEGES - CALIFORNIA - ADMISSION.**
Ball, Howard. The Bakke case. Lawrence, Kan. : University Press of Kansas, 2000.
*TC KF228.B34 B35 2000*

**MEDICAL COLLEGES - MICHIGAN - ANN ARBOR - HISTORY.**
Davenport, Horace Willard, 1912- Not just any medical school. Ann Arbor : University of Michigan Press, c1999.
*TC R747.U6834 D38 1999*

**MEDICAL COOPERATION.** *See* **HEALTH FACILITIES - AFFILIATIONS.**

**MEDICAL DISCLOSURE.** *See* **INFORMED CONSENT (MEDICAL LAW).**

**MEDICAL DOCTORS.** *See* **PHYSICIANS.**

**MEDICAL ECONOMICS - MORAL AND ETHICAL ASPECTS.**
The global challenge of health care rationing. Buckingham [England] ; Philadelphia : Open University Press, 2000.
*TC RA394.9 .G56 2000*

**MEDICAL ECONOMICS - UNITED STATES.**
O'Brien, Lawrence J. Bad medicine. Amherst, N.Y. : Prometheus Books, c1999.
*TC RA395.A3 O28 1999*

**MEDICAL EDUCATION.** *See* **DISCRIMINATION IN MEDICAL EDUCATION.**

**MEDICAL EDUCATION - FINANCE.** *See* **MEDICINE - SCHOLARSHIPS, FELLOWSHIPS, ETC.**

**MEDICAL EDUCATION - UNITED STATES - HISTORY - 20TH CENTURY.**
Ludmerer, Kenneth M. Time to heal. Oxford ; New York : Oxford University Press, 1999.
*TC R745 .L843 1999*

**MEDICAL ETHICS.** *See also* **EUTHANASIA; INFORMED CONSENT (MEDICAL LAW); NURSING ETHICS; SOCIAL MEDICINE.**
Radest, Howard B., 1928- From clinic to classroom. Westport, Conn. : London : Praeger, 2000.
*TC R725.5 .R33 2000*

**MEDICAL ETHICS - SOCIAL ASPECTS.**
Ethics and community in the health care professions. London : New York : Routledge, 1999.
*TC R725.5 .E87 1999*

**MEDICAL FACILITIES.** *See* **HEALTH FACILITIES.**

**MEDICAL FELLOWSHIPS.** *See* **MEDICINE - SCHOLARSHIPS, FELLOWSHIPS, ETC.**

**MEDICAL GENETICS.**
Lashley, Felissa R., 1941- Clinical genetics in nursing practice. 2nd ed. New York : Springer, c1998.
*TC RB155 .L37 1998*

**MEDICAL LAWS AND LEGISLATION.** *See* **ASSISTED SUICIDE - LAW AND LEGISLATION; HEALTH FACILITIES - LAW AND LEGISLATION; PUBLIC HEALTH LAWS; STERILIZATION, EUGENIC - LAW AND LEGISLATION.**

**MEDICAL MANPOWER.** *See* **MEDICAL PERSONNEL.**

**MEDICAL MICROBIOLOGY.** *See* **INFECTION.**

**Medical Officers of Schools Association.** Handbook of school health / The Medical Officers of Schools Association. 18th ed. Stoke-on-Trent : Trentham, 1998. xviii, 316 p. ; 23 cm. Previous ed.: 1992. Includes bibliographical references and index. ISBN 1-85856-081-0 (pbk) DDC 371.710941
*1. School health services - Great Britain - Handbooks, manuals, etc. 2. School children - Health and hygiene - Great Britain - Handbooks, manuals, etc. 1. Title.*
*TC LB3409.G7 H36 1998*

**MEDICAL PERSONNEL.** *See* **MENTAL HEALTH PERSONNEL; NURSES; PHYSICIANS.**

**MEDICAL PERSONNEL AND PATIENT.** *See also* **PATIENT SATISFACTION.**
Bohmer, Carol. The wages of seeking help. Westport, Conn. : London : Praeger, 2000.
*TC RC560.S44 B67 2000*

Gill, Kenneth Joseph. Social psychological artifacts in the measurement of consumer satisfaction with health care. 1996.
*TC 085 G396*

**MEDICAL PERSONNEL AND PATIENT - PSYCHOLOGICAL ASPECTS.**
Fenichel, Ann. The relationship between health care clinicians' relational abilities and psychosocial orientation to patient care, and patient adherence with medical treatment. 1998.
*TC 085 F352*

**MEDICAL PERSONNEL - EDUCATION.** *See* **MEDICAL EDUCATION.**

**MEDICAL PERSONNEL - MALPRACTICE.** *See* **INFORMED CONSENT (MEDICAL LAW).**

**MEDICAL PERSONNEL - MORAL AND ETHICAL ASPECTS.**
Ethics and community in the health care professions. London ; New York : Routledge, 1999.
*TC R725.5 .E87 1999*

**MEDICAL PERSONNEL - PROFESSIONAL ETHICS - GREAT BRITAIN.**
Professionalism, boundaries, and the workplace. New York : Routledge, 2000.
*TC HV10.5 .P74 2000*

**MEDICAL PERSONNEL - PSYCHOLOGY.**
Burnard, Philip. Counselling skills for health professionals. 3rd ed. Cheltenham, U.K. : Stanley Thornes, 1999.
*TC BF637.C6 B82 1999*

**MEDICAL PERSONNEL - SEXUAL BEHAVIOR.**
Bohmer, Carol. The wages of seeking help. Westport, Conn. ; London : Praeger, 2000.

*TC RC560.S44 B67 2000*

**MEDICAL POLICY.** *See also* **HEALTH CARE REFORM; HEALTH PLANNING.**
Nelson, Joan M. Reforming health and education. Washington, DC : Overseas Development Council ; Baltimore, MD : Distributed by the Johns Hopkins University Press, c1999.
*TC HG3881.5.W57 N447 1999*

Tulchinsky, Theodore H. The new public health. San Diego, Calif. : London : Academic Press, c2000.
*TC RA425 .T85 2000*

Tulchinsky, Theodore H. The new public health. San Diego, Calif. : London : Academic Press, c2000.
*TC RA425 .T85 2000*

**MEDICAL POLICY - ASIA, SOUTHEASTERN - CASE STUDIES.**
Ramesh, M., 1960- Welfare capitalism in southeast Asia. New York : St. Martin's Press, c2000.
*TC HN690.8.A8 R35 2000*

**MEDICAL POLICY - UNITED STATES.**
Health policy reform in America. 2nd ed. Armonk, N.Y. : M.E. Sharpe, c1997.
*TC RA395.A3 H42564 1997*

Rovner, Julie. Health care policy and politics A to Z. Washington, DC : CQ Press, 2000.
*TC RA395.A3 R685 1999*

**MEDICAL POLICY - UNITED STATES - FORECASTING.**
Morrison, J. Ian, 1952- Health care in the new millennium. 1st ed. San Francisco : Jossey-Bass Publishers, c2000.
*TC RA395.A3 M675 2000*

**MEDICAL POLICY - UNITED STATES - STATES.**
Health policy reform in America. 2nd ed. Armonk, N.Y. : M.E. Sharpe, c1997.
*TC RA395.A3 H42564 1997*

Health Policy Tracking Service. Major health care policies. 8th ed. Washington, D.C. : Health Policy Tracking Service, 2000.
*TC KF3821 .H4 2000*

**Medical prescription of narcotics**
(vol. 2) Cost benefit analysis of heroin maintenance treatment. Basel ; New York : Karger, c2000.
*TC RC568.H4 C67 2000*

**MEDICAL PROFESSION.** *See* **MEDICINE; PHYSICIANS.**

**MEDICAL PROTOCOLS.**
Klein, Harriet B. Intervention planning for adults with communication problems : Volume 2. Boston : Allyn and Bacon, c1999.
*TC RC423 .K57 1999*

**MEDICAL RECORDS.** *See* **NURSING RECORDS.**

**MEDICAL REFORMERS.** *See* **HEALTH REFORMERS.**

**MEDICAL REHABILITATION.** *See* **OCCUPATIONAL THERAPY.**

**MEDICAL REHABILITATION - PSYCHOLOGICAL ASPECTS - HANDBOOKS, MANUALS, ETC.**
Handbook of rehabilitation psychology. 1st ed. Washington, DC : American Psychological Association c2000.
*TC R726.7 .H366 2000*

**MEDICAL RESEARCH.** *See* **MEDICINE - RESEARCH.**

**MEDICAL SCHOLARSHIPS.** *See* **MEDICINE - SCHOLARSHIPS, FELLOWSHIPS, ETC.**

**MEDICAL SCHOOLS.** *See* **MEDICAL COLLEGES.**

**MEDICAL SCIENCES.** *See also* **HUMAN ANATOMY; MEDICINE; NEUROSCIENCES.**
Vital signs. Edinburgh : Edinburgh University Press, c1998.
*TC HQ1190 .V56 1998*

Vital signs. Edinburgh : Edinburgh University Press, c1998.
*TC HQ1190 .V56 1998*

**MEDICAL SERVICES.** *See* **MEDICAL CARE.**

**MEDICAL SOCIAL WORK - UNITED STATES.**
Social work in pediatrics. New York : Haworth Press, c1995.
*TC HV688.U5 S63 1995*

**MEDICAL SOCIOLOGY.** *See* **SOCIAL MEDICINE.**

**MEDICAL STATISTICS.** *See also* **HEALTH STATUS INDICATORS.**
Katz, Mitchell H. Multivariable analysis. Cambridge, UK ; New York : Cambridge University Press, 1999.
*TC R853.S7 K38 1999*

**MEDICAL SUPPLIES.** *See* **DRUGS.**

**MEDICAL VIROLOGY.** *See* **VIRUS DISEASES.**

**Medications for school-age children.**
Brown, Ronald T. New York : Guilford Press, c1998.
*TC RJ560 .B76 1998*

**MEDICINE.** *See also* **ALTERNATIVE MEDICINE; CLINICAL MEDICINE; DISEASES; GERIATRICS; GYNECOLOGY; HEALTH; NEUROLOGY; NURSING; OBSTETRICS; PEDIATRICS; PHYSICIANS; SPORTS MEDICINE; VETERINARY MEDICINE.**
GrantFinder : Medicine. New York, NY : St. Martin's Press,
*TC LB2337.2 .G73*

**MEDICINE, ALTERNATIVE.** *See* **ALTERNATIVE MEDICINE.**

**MEDICINE AND PSYCHOLOGY.** *See also* **CLINICAL HEALTH PSYCHOLOGY; HEALTH BEHAVIOR; PSYCHIATRY.**
Chiozza, Luis A. Why do we fall ill? Madison, Conn. : Psychosocial Press, c1999.
*TC R726.7 .C48 1999*

Reframing health behavior change with behavioral economics. Mahwah, N.J. ; London : Lawrence Erlbaum, 2000.
*TC RA776.9 .R433 2000*

**Medicine and science in sports.** Madison, Wisc. 11 v. v. 1-11 ; Mar. 1969 - 1979. Other title: Journal of medicine and science in sports. Published by the American College of Sports Medicine. Continued by: Medicine and science in sports and exercise.
*1. Sports medicine - Periodicals. 2. Physical education and training - Periodicals. I. American College of Sports Medicine. II. Title: Medicine and science in sports and exercise.*

**Medicine and science in sports and exercise.**
Medicine and science in sports. Madison, Wisc.

**MEDICINE AND SPORTS.** *See* **SPORTS MEDICINE.**

**MEDICINE AND STATE.** *See* **MEDICAL POLICY.**

**MEDICINE, CLINICAL.** *See* **CLINICAL MEDICINE.**

**MEDICINE, COMPARATIVE.** *See* **PHYSIOLOGY, COMPARATIVE.**

**MEDICINE, CROSS-CULTURAL.** *See* **TRANSCULTURAL MEDICAL CARE.**

**MEDICINE - ECONOMIC ASPECTS.** *See* **MEDICAL ECONOMICS.**

**MEDICINE - ENGLAND - CAMBRIDGE - HISTORY - 19TH CENTURY.**
Weatherall, Mark. Gentlemen, scientists, and doctors. Woodbridge, Suffolk ; Rochester, N.Y. : Boydell Press : Cambridge University Library, 2000.
*TC R487 .W43 2000*

**MEDICINE - ENGLAND - CAMBRIDGE - HISTORY - 20TH CENTURY.**
Weatherall, Mark. Gentlemen, scientists, and doctors. Woodbridge, Suffolk ; Rochester, N.Y. : Boydell Press : Cambridge University Library, 2000.
*TC R487 .W43 2000*

**MEDICINE - FELLOWSHIPS.** *See* **MEDICINE - SCHOLARSHIPS, FELLOWSHIPS, ETC.**

**MEDICINE - HISTORY.**
Harding, Anne S. Milestones in health and medicine. Phoenix : Oryx Press, 2000.
*TC R133 .H36 2000*

**Medicine in colonial America.**
Reiss, Oscar, 1925- Lanham : University Press of America, 2000.
*TC RC151 .R44 2000*

**MEDICINE, INDUSTRIAL.** *See also* **INDUSTRIAL NURSING; INDUSTRIAL PSYCHIATRY.**
Moore, Gary S. Living with the earth. Boca Raton, Fla. : Lewis Publishers, c1999.
*TC RA565 .M665 1999*

**MEDICINE, MILITARY.** *See* **MILITARY NURSING.**

**MEDICINE - MORAL AND ETHICAL ASPECTS.** *See* **MEDICAL ETHICS.**

**MEDICINE - PERIODICALS.**
[Lancet (North American ed.)] The lancet. North American ed. Boston : Little, Brown and Co., c1966-

**MEDICINE - PERIODICALS.**
[Lancet (North American ed.)] The lancet. North American ed. Boston : Little, Brown and Co., c1966-

**MEDICINE - PHILOSOPHY.**
Galland, Leo. The four pillars of healing. 1st ed. New York : Random House, c1997.
*TC R733 .G35 1997*

**MEDICINE, PHYSICAL.** *See* **MEDICAL REHABILITATION.**

**MEDICINE, POPULAR - ENCYCLOPEDIAS.**
Sharma, R. (Rajendra), 1959- The family encyclopedia of health. Boston : Element Books, 1999.
*TC RC81.A2 S53 1999*

**MEDICINE - POPULAR WORKS.** *See* **MEDICINE, POPULAR.**

**MEDICINE, PREVENTIVE.** *See also* **HYGIENE; PREVENTIVE HEALTH SERVICES; PUBLIC HEALTH.**
Jonas, Steven. Talking about health and wellness with patients. New York : Springer, c2000.
*TC RA427.8 .J66 2000*

Leutholtz, Brian C. Exercise and disease management. Boca Raton : CRC Press, c1999.
*TC RM725 .L45 1999*

**MEDICINE, PREVENTIVE - HANDBOOKS, MANUALS, ETC.**
Handbook of health promotion and disease prevention. New York : Kluwer Academic/Plenum Publishers, c1999.
*TC RA427.8 .H36 1999*

**MEDICINE, PSYCHOSOMATIC.**
How expectancies shape experience. 1st ed. Washington, DC : American Psychological Association, c1999.
*TC BF323.E8 H69 1999*

**MEDICINE, REHABILITATION.** *See* **MEDICAL REHABILITATION.**

**MEDICINE - RESEARCH.**
The Horizons of health. Cambridge, Mass. : Harvard University Press, 1977.
*TC R850 .H67*

**MEDICINE - RESEARCH GRANTS - DIRECTORIES.**
GrantFinder : Medicine. New York, NY : St. Martin's Press,
*TC LB2337.2 .G73*

**MEDICINE - RESEARCH - STATISTICAL METHODS.**
Katz, Mitchell H. Multivariable analysis. Cambridge, UK : New York : Cambridge University Press, 1999.
*TC R853.S7 K38 1999*

**MEDICINE - RESEARCH - UNITED STATES.**
The Horizons of health. Cambridge, Mass. : Harvard University Press, 1977.
*TC R850 .H67*

**MEDICINE - SCHOLARSHIPS, FELLOWSHIPS, ETC. - DIRECTORIES.**
GrantFinder : Medicine. New York, NY : St. Martin's Press,
*TC LB2337.2 .G73*

**MEDICINE, SOCIAL.** *See* **SOCIAL MEDICINE.**

**MEDICINE - SOCIAL ASPECTS.** *See* **SOCIAL MEDICINE.**

**MEDICINE, STATE.** *See* **MEDICINE, PREVENTIVE; PUBLIC HEALTH.**

**MEDICINE - TERMINOLOGY.**
Golper, Lee Ann C., 1948- Sourcebook for medical speech pathology. 2nd ed. San Diego, Calif. : Singular Pub. Group, c1998.
*TC RC423 .G64 1998*

**MEDICINE, TRANSCULTURAL.** *See* **TRANSCULTURAL MEDICAL CARE.**

**MEDICINE, VETERINARY.** *See* **VETERINARY MEDICINE.**

**The medieval church :** universities, heresy, and the religious life : essays in honour of Gordon Leff / edited by Peter Biller and Barrie Dobson. Woodbridge, Suffolk ; Rochester, NY : Published for the Ecclesiastical History Society by the Boydell Press, 1999. xvii, 362 p. ; 23 cm. (Studies in church history. Subsidia ; 11) Includes bibliographical references and index. ISBN 0-9529733-3-2 (alk. paper) DDC 270.3
*1. Church history - Middle Ages, 600-1500. 2. Heresies, Christian - History - Middle Ages, 600-1500. 3. Monastic and religious life - History - Middle Ages, 600-1500. 4. Universities and colleges - Europe - History. 5. Education, Medieval. I. Leff, Gordon. II. Biller, Peter. III. Dobson, R. B. (Richard Barrie) IV. Series.*
*TC BR270 .M43 1999*

**MEDIEVAL CIVILIZATION.** *See* **CIVILIZATION, MEDIEVAL.**

**MEDIEVAL COOKERY.** *See* **COOKERY, MEDIEVAL.**

**MEDIEVAL EDUCATION.** *See* **EDUCATION, MEDIEVAL.**

**MEDIEVAL HISTORY.** *See* **MIDDLE AGES - HISTORY.**

**MEDIEVAL PANEL PAINTING.** *See* **PANEL PAINTING, MEDIEVAL.**

**MEDIEVAL PERIOD.** *See* **MIDDLE AGES.**

**MEDIEVALISM.** *See* **MIDDLE AGES.**

**MEDIEVALISM IN LITERATURE.**
Barnhouse, Rebecca. Recasting the past. Portsmouth, NH : Boynton/Cook Publishers, c2000.
*TC PN3443 .B37 2000*

**MEDITERRANEAN REGION, EASTERN.** *See* **MIDDLE EAST.**

**MEDIUM-SIZED BUSINESS.** *See* **SMALL BUSINESS.**

**Medvic, Emily Fisher.**
Fisher, Bobbi. Perspectives on shared reading. Portsmouth, NH : Heinemann, c2000.
*TC LB1573 .F528 2000*

**Meeks Heit Publishing Company.**
Meeks, Linda Brower. Comprehensive school health education. 2nd edition. Blacklick, OH : Meeks Heit Pub. Co., c1996.
*TC RA440.3.U5 M445 1996*

**Meeks, Linda Brower.** Comprehensive school health education / Linda B. Meeks, Philip Heit, Randy Page. 2nd edition. Blacklick, OH : Meeks Heit Pub. Co., c1996. xxvi, 835 p. : ill. ; 28 cm. Includes index. ISBN 1-88669-309-9
*1. Health education - United States. I. Heit, Philip. II. Page, Randy M. III. Meeks Heit Publishing Company. IV. Title.*
*TC RA440.3.U5 M445 1996*

**Meese, Ruth Lyn.** Teaching learners with mild disabilities : integrating research and practice / Ruth Lyn Meese. 2nd ed. Belmont, CA : Wadsworth/ Thomson Learning, c2001. xvii, 629 p. : ill. ; 24 cm. Includes bibliographical references (p. 561-611) and index. ISBN 0-534-57852-7 (acid-free paper) DDC 371.9/071/073
*1. Handicapped children - Education - United States - Case studies. 2. Special education - Study and teaching - United States. I. Title.*
*TC LC4031 .M44 2001*

**Meeting challenges.**
Nelson, Joan Lexington, Mass. : D. C. Heath and Company, c1983.
*TC PE1121 .M43 1983*

**Meeting challenges.** Teacher's ed. New York, N.Y. : American Book Co., c1980. xviii, 328 p. : ill. (some col.) ; 28 cm. (American readers ; 8) ISBN 0-278-45763-0
*1. Readers (Elementary) 2. Reading (Elementary) I. Series.*
*TC PE1121 .M43 1980 Teacher's Ed.*

**Meeting challenges** / Lexington, Mass. : D. C. Heath and Company, c1983. 512 p. : ill. (some col.) ; 24 cm. (American readers ; 8) ISBN 0-669-05093-8
*1. Readers (Elementary) I. Title.*
*TC PE1121 .M43 1983*

**Meeting challenges.** Teacher's ed. Lexington, Mass. : D.C. Heath and Company, c1983. xxxiv, 419 p. : ill. (some col.) ; 28 cm. (American readers ; 8) Includes index. ISBN 0-669-05094-6
*1. Readers (Elementary) 2. Reading (Elementary) I. Series.*
*TC PE1121 .M43 1983 Teacher's Ed.*

**Meeting challenges.** Lexington, Mass. : D.C. Heath and Company, c1983. 512 p. : ill. (some col.) ; 24 cm. (American readers ; 8) ISBN 0-669-05093-8
*1. Readers (Elementary) I. Series.*
*TC PE1121 .M43 1983*

**Meeting challenges.** Teacher's ed. Lexington, Mass. : D.C. Heath and Company, c1986. T32, 480 p. : col. ill. ; 28 cm. (Heath American readers ; 8) Includes index. ISBN 0-

669-08058-6
*1. Readers (Elementary) 2. Reading (Elementary) I. Series.*
***TC PE1121 .M43 1986 Teacher's Ed.***

**Meeting challenges.** Lexington, Mass. : D.C. Heath and Company, c1986. 512 p. : col. ill. ; 24 cm. (Heath American readers ; 8) ISBN 0-669-08041-1
*1. Readers (Elementary) I. Series.*
***TC PE1121 .M43 1986***

**Meeting challenges :** skills pad. Lexington, Mass. : D. C. Heath and Company, c1986. 1 v. (various pagings) : ill. ; 28x21 cm. (Heath American Readers ; 8) ISBN 0-669-09105-7
*1. Readers (Elementary) 2. Reading (Elementary) I. Series.*
***TC PE1121 .M43 1986 Skills Pad***

**Meeting challenges :** workbook. Teacher's ed. Lexington, Mass. : D. C. Heath and Company, c1983. 96 p. : ill. ; 28 cm. (American readers ; 8) Includes index. ISBN 0-669-05096-2
*1. Readers (Elementary) 2. Reading (Elementary) I. Series.*
***TC PE1121 .M43 1983 Teacher's Ed. Workbook***

**Meeting challenges :** workbook. Teacher's ed. Lexington, Mass. : D.C. Heath and Company, c1986. 96 p. : ill. ; 28 cm. (Heath American readers ; 8) Includes index. ISBN 0-669-08118-3
*1. Readers (Elementary) 2. Reading (Elementary) I. Series.*
***TC PE1121 .M43 1986 Teacher's Ed. Workbook***

**Meeting human needs, toward a new public philosophy** / Jack A. Meyer, editor. Washington : American Enterprise Institute for Public Policy Research, c1982. 469 p. : ill. ; 23 cm. Includes bibliographical references. ISBN 0-8447-1358-9 (pbk.) ISBN 0-8447-1359-7 (hard) DDC 361.7/0973
*1. Industries - Social aspects - United States. 2. Labor unions - Social aspects - United States. 3. Associations, institutions, etc. - United States. I. Meyer, Jack A., 1944- II. American Enterprise Institute for Public Policy Research.*
***TC HD60.5.U5 M427 1982***

**Meeting the national standards with handbells and handchimes.**
McBride, Michael B. Lanham, MD : Scarecrow Press, 2000.
***TC MT711 .M35 2000***

**Meeting the needs of students of all abilities.**
Capper, Colleen A., 1960- Thousand Oaks, Calif. : Corwin Press, c2000.
***TC LC1201 .C36 2000***

**MEETINGS.** *See* **FORUMS (DISCUSSION AND DEBATE).**

**Megagifts.**
Panas, Jerold. Chicago, Ill. : Pluribus Press, c1984.
***TC HV41 .P34 1984***

**Meichenbaum, Donald.** Nurturing independent learners : helping students take charge of their learning / Donald Meichenbaum & Andrew Biemiller. Cambridge, Mass. : Brookline Books, c1998. xiv, 287 p. : ill., forms ; 26 cm. Includes bibliographical references (p. [267]-278) and index. ISBN 1-57129-047-8 DDC 370.15/23
*1. Mastery learning - United States. 2. Academic achievement - United States. 3. Knowledge, Theory of. I. Biemiller, Andrew, 1939- II. Title.*
***TC LB1031.4 .M45 1998***

**Meier, Daniel R.** Scribble scrabble--teaching children to become successful readers and writers / Daniel R. Meier. New York : Teachers College Press, c2000. x, 153 p. : col. ill. ; 23 cm. Includes bibliographical references and index. ISBN 0-8077-3883-2 (cloth : alk. paper) ISBN 0-8077-3882-4 (pbk. : alk. paper) DDC 372.6
*1. Language arts (Preschool) - United States - Case studies. 2. City children - Education (Preschool) - United States - Case studies. 3. Literacy - United States - Case studies. I. Title. II. Title: Teaching children to become successful readers and writers*
***TC LB1140.5.L3 M45 2000***

**Meier, Dave.** The accelerated learning handbook : a creative guide to designing and delivering faster, more effective training programs / by Dave Meier. New York : McGraw Hill, c2000. xxix, 274 p. : ill. ; 25 cm. Includes bibliographical references (p. 249-256) and index. ISBN 0-07-135547-2 (alk. paper) DDC 153.1/52
*1. Educational acceleration - United States - Handbooks, manuals, etc. I. Title. II. Title: Creative guide to designing and delivering faster, more effective training programs*
***TC LB1029.A22 M45 2000***

**Meier, Deborah.**
Will standards save public education? Boston : Beacon Press, c2000.
***TC LB3060.83 .W55 2000***

**Meignant, Michel, 1936-.**
Tassili N'Ajjer [videorecording]. [S.l.] : Editions Cinégraphiques ; Northbrook, Ill. : [distributed by] the Roland Collection, c1968.
***TC N5310.5.A4 T3 1968***

**Meiner, Sue.**
Nursing documentation. Thousand Oaks, Calif. : Sage Publications, c1999.
***TC RT50 .N87 1999***

**Meister, Denise G., 1951-.**
Nolan, James F., 1950- Teachers and educational change. Albany : State University of New York Press, c2000.
***TC LB1777.2 .N64 2000***

**Melamid, Aleksandr.**
Painting by numbers. Berkeley : University of California Press, [1999]
***TC ND1140 .P26 1999***

**MELANCHOLIA.** *See* **DEPRESSION, MENTAL; MANIC-DEPRESSIVE ILLNESS.**

**MELANCHOLY.** *See also* **DEPRESSION, MENTAL.**
Smith, Jeffery, 1961- Where the roots reach for water. New York : North Point Press, 1999.
***TC BF575.M44 S55 1999***

**MELANCHOLY - HISTORY.**
Smith, Jeffery, 1961- Where the roots reach for water. New York : North Point Press, 1999.
***TC BF575.M44 S55 1999***

**Melbourne University history monographs**
(17) Dunt, Lesley, 1944- Speaking worlds. Parkville, Vic. : History Department, The University of Melbourne, c1993.
***TC LA2101 .D96 1993***

**Mellen studies in education**
(v. 18) DeBoer, Peter P. Origins of teacher education at Calvin College, 1900-1930. Lewiston : E. Mellen Press, c1991.
***TC LD785 .D43 1991***

(v. 3) Nemeth, Charles P., 1951- A status report on contemporary criminal justice education. Lewiston, NY, USA : E. Mellen Press, c1989.
***TC HV7419.5 .N45 1989***

(v. 32) Watersheds in higher education. Lewiston, N.Y. : E. Mellen Press, c1997.
***TC LA228 .W28 1997***

(v. 44) Challenges and opportunities for education in the 21st century. Lewiston, NY : Edwin Mellen Press, c1999.
***TC LA209.2 .C45 1999***

(v. 45) Birnbaum, Barry W. Connecting special education and technology for the 21st century. Lewiston, N.Y. : Lampeter, Wales : E. Mellen Press, c1999.
***TC LC3969.5 .B57 1999***

(v. 46) Knottnerus, J. David. The social worlds of male and female children in the nineteenth century French educational system. Lewiston, N.Y. ; Lampeter, Wales : Edwin Mellen Press, c1999.
***TC LC191.8.F8 K66 1999***

(v. 48) Preparation, collaboration, and emphasis on the family in school counseling for the new millennium. Lewiston : E. Mellen Press, c2000.
***TC LB1027.5 .P6525 2000***

**Mellen Studies in education**
(v.42) International narratives on becoming a teacher educator. Lewiston, N.Y. : Lampeter,Wales : E. Mellen Press, c2000.
***TC LB1737.5 .I58 2000***

**Mellgren, Lars.** New horizons in English, [workbooks] / Lars Mellgren, Michael Walker ; consulting editor, John A. Upshur. Reading, Mass. : Addison-Wesley Pub. Co., 1973-c1978. (v.1,3). : ill. ; 29 cm.
*1. English language - Study and teaching. 2. Reading (Adult education) I. Title.*
***TC PE1128 .M38***

**Mellins, Thomas.**
Stern, Robert A. M. New York 1880. New York, N.Y. : Monacelli Press, 1999.
***TC NA735.N5 S727 1999***

**Mellon, Susan.**
Crawford, Tad, 1946- The artist-gallery partnership. [2nd ed.]. New York : Allworth Press, c1998.
***TC KF947 .C7 1998***

**Meltzer, Milton, 1915-** The amazing potato : a story in which the Incas, Conquistadors, Marie Antoinette, Thomas Jefferson, wars, famines, immigrants, and french fries all play a part / Milton Meltzer. 1st ed. New York, NY : HarperCollins, c1992. 116 p. : ill. ; 22 cm. Includes bibliographical references (p. 101-103) and index. SUMMARY: Introduces the history, effects, and current uses of the potato in the world marketplace. ISBN 0-06-020806-6 ISBN 0-06-020807-4 (lib bdg.) DDC 635/.21
*1. Potatoes - History - Juvenile literature. 2. Potatoes - Social aspects - Juvenile literature. 3. Potatoes - Juvenile literature. 4. Potatoes. I. Title.*
***TC SB211.P8 M53 1992***

**Meltzoff, Andrew N.**
Gopnik, Alison. The scientist in the crib. New York : William Morrow & Co., 1999.
***TC BF311 .G627 1999***

**Melville, Tom.** The tented field : a history of cricket in America / Tom Melville. Bowling Green, OH : Bowling Green State University Popular Press, c1998. vii, 280 p. : ill. ; 24 cm. Includes bibliographical references (p. 163-207) and index. ISBN 0-87972-769-1 (cloth) ISBN 0-87972-770-5 (pbk.) DDC 796.358/0973
*1. Cricket - United States - History. I. Title.*
***TC GV928.U6 M45 1998***

**Melzer, Arthur M.**
Democracy & the arts. Ithaca : Cornell University Press, c1999.
***TC NX180.S6 D447 1999***

**Melzi, Gigliana.**
Paratore, Jeanne R. What should we expect of family literacy? Newark, Del. : International Reading Association ; Chicago , Ill. : National Reading Conference, c1999.
***TC LC151 .P37 1999***

**MEMBERS OF CONGRESS (UNITED STATES).** *See* **LEGISLATORS - UNITED STATES.**

**MEMBERS OF CONGRESS (UNITED STATES HOUSE OF REPRESENTATIVES).** *See* **LEGISLATORS - UNITED STATES.**

**MEMBERS OF CONGRESS (UNITED STATES SENATE).** *See* **LEGISLATORS - UNITED STATES.**

**MEMBERS OF JURIES.** *See* **JURORS.**

**MEMBERS OF PARLIAMENT.** *See* **LEGISLATORS.**

**Memoir of James Jackson.**
Paul, Susan, fl. 1837. Memoir of James Jackson, the attentive and obedient scholar, who died in Boston, October 31, 1833, aged six years and eleven months. Cambridge, MA : Harvard University Press, 2000.
***TC F73.9.N4 P38 2000***

**Memoir of James Jackson, the attentive and obedient scholar, who died in Boston, October 31, 1833, aged six years and eleven months.**
Paul, Susan, fl. 1837. Cambridge, MA : Harvard University Press, 2000.
***TC F73.9.N4 P38 2000***

**MÉMOIRE - CONGRÈS.**
Cognitive neuroscience of memory. Seattle ; Toronto : Hogrefe & Huber, c1999.
***TC QP406 .C63 1999***

**MEMOIRS.** *See* **AUTOBIOGRAPHY; BIOGRAPHY.**

**MEMORIALS.** *See* **HOLIDAYS; MONUMENTS; WAR MEMORIALS.**

**MEMORIES, FALSE.** *See* **FALSE MEMORY SYNDROME.**

**Memories to keep :** teacher's planning guide. New York : Macmillan/McGraw-Hill, c1997. 1 v. (various pagings) : col. ill. ; 31 cm. (Spotlight on literacy ; Gr.4 l.10 u.5) (The road to independent reading) Includes index. ISBN 0-02-181176-8
*1. Language arts (Elementary) 2. Reading (Elementary) I. Series. II. Series: The road to independent reading*
***TC LB1576 .S66 1997 Gr.4 l.10 u.5***

**MEMORY.** *See also* **ATTENTION; AUTOBIOGRAPHICAL MEMORY; COMPREHENSION; LEARNING, PSYCHOLOGY OF; RECOLLECTION (PSYCHOLOGY).**
Samuel, David. New York : New York University Press, c1999.
***TC QP406 .S26 1999***

**MEMORY.**
Ableman, Paul. The secret of consciousness. London ; New York : Marion Boyars, 1999.

*TC BF311 .A195 1999*

Engelkamp, Johannes. [Erinnern eigener Handlungen. English] Memory for actions. Hove, East Sussex, UK : Psychology Press, c1998.
*TC BF371 .E5413 1998*

Jones, Janet L. The psychotherapist's guide to human memory. New York : Basic Books, c1999.
*TC BF371 .J66 1999*

McNamara, Patrick, 1956- Mind and variability. Westport, Conn. : Praeger, 1999.
*TC BF371 .M385 1999*

Memory observed. 2nd ed. New York : Worth Publishers, c2000.
*TC BF371 .M455 2000*

Parkin, Alan J. Memory, a guide for professionals. Chichester, England ; New York : J. Wiley, c1999.
*TC BF371 .P275 1999*

Prager, Jeffrey, 1948- Presenting the past. Cambridge, Mass. : Harvard University Press, 1998.
*TC BF175.4.C84 P73 1998*

Schank, Roger C., 1946- Dynamic memory revisited. [2nd ed.]. Cambridge ; New York : Cambridge University Press, 1999.
*TC BF371 .S365 1999*

Stratification in cognition and consciousness. Amsterdam ; Philadelphia : J. Benjamins, c1999.
*TC BF444 .S73 1999*

The treasure chests of mnemosyne. Dresden : Verlag der Kunst, 1998.
*TC BF371 .T7413 1998*

**Memory, a guide for professionals.**
Parkin, Alan J. Chichester, England ; New York : J. Wiley, c1999.
*TC BF371 .P275 1999*

**MEMORY - AGE FACTORS - RESEARCH.**
Embiricos, Anne-Marie T. The effects of content knowledge and strategies on memory development among 4- and 6-year-old children. 1998.
*TC 085 Em22*

Embiricos, Anne-Marie T. The effects of content knowledge and strategies on memory development among 4- and 6-year-old children. 1998.
*TC 085 Em22*

**Memory and methodology** / edited by Susannah Radstone. Oxford ; New York : Berg, 2000. x, 228 p. ; 23 cm. Includes bibliographical references and index. ISBN 1-85973-296-8 ISBN 1-85973-202-X (pbk.) DDC 306.42
*1. Memory (Philosophy) 2. History - Methodology. 3. Social sciences - Methodology. 4. Memory (Philosophy) 5. History - Methodology. 6. Social sciences - Methodology. I. Radstone, Susannah.*
*TC BD181.7 .M46 2000*

**MEMORY, AUTOBIOGRAPHICAL. See AUTOBIOGRAPHICAL MEMORY.**

**Memory, brain, and belief** / edited by Daniel L. Schacter, Elaine Scarry. Cambridge, Mass. ; London : Harvard University Press, 2000. viii, 348 p. : ill. ; 25 cm. Includes bibliographical references and index. ISBN 0-674-00061-7 (alk. paper) DDC 612.8/2
*1. Memory - Congresses. 2. Belief and doubt - Congresses. 3. Cognitive neuroscience - Congresses. 4. Memory Disorders - physiopathology - Congresses. 5. Brain - Congresses. 6. Delusions - Congresses. 7. Knowledge - Congresses. 8. Memory - physiology - Congresses. 9. Self Concept - Congresses. I. Schacter, Daniel L. II. Scarry, Elaine.*
*TC QP406 .M44 2000*

**MEMORY - CASE STUDIES.**
Prager, Jeffrey, 1948- Presenting the past. Cambridge, Mass. : Harvard University Press, 1998.
*TC BF175.4.C84 P73 1998*

**MEMORY - CONGRESSES.**
Cognitive neuroscience of memory. Seattle ; Toronto : Hogrefe & Huber, c1999.
*TC QP406 .C63 1999*

Memory, brain, and belief. Cambridge, Mass. ; London : Harvard University Press, 2000.
*TC QP406 .M44 2000*

Memory, consciousness, and the brain. Philadelphia ; London : Psychology Press, c2000.
*TC BF371 .M4483 2000*

**Memory, consciousness, and the brain** : the Tallinn Conference / edited by Endel Tulving. Philadelphia ; London : Psychology Press, c2000. xviii, 397 p. : ill. ; 25 cm. Includes bibliographical references and indexes. ISBN 1-84169-015-5 (hardcover : alk. paper) DDC 153.1/2

*1. Memory - Congresses. 2. Consciousness - Congresses. I. Tulving, Endel.*
*TC BF371 .M4483 2000*

**MEMORY DISORDERS. See FUGUE (PSYCHOLOGY).**

**MEMORY DISORDERS - PHYSIOPATHOLOGY - CONGRESSES.**
Memory, brain, and belief. Cambridge, Mass. : London : Harvard University Press, 2000.
*TC QP406 .M44 2000*

**MEMORY, FALSE. See FALSE MEMORY SYNDROME.**

**MEMORY - FICTION.**
Nikly, Michelle. [Royaume des parfums. English] The perfume of memory. 1st American ed. New York : A.A. Levine Books, 1998.
*TC PZ7.N585 Pe 1998*

**Memory for actions.**
Engelkamp, Johannes. [Erinnern eigener Handlungen. English] Hove, East Sussex, UK : Psychology Press, c1998.
*TC BF371 .E5413 1998*

**MEMORY - HANDBOOKS, MANUALS, ETC.**
The Oxford handbook of memory. Oxford ; New York : Oxford University Press, 2000.
*TC BF371 .O84 2000*

**MEMORY IN CHILDREN.**
Children's source monitoring. Mahwah, N.J. ; London : Lawrence Erlbaum Associates, 2000.
*TC BF723.M4 C45 2000*

Howe, Mark L. The fate of early memories. Washington, DC : American Psychological Association, c2000.
*TC BF378.E17 H69 2000*

**MEMORY IN CHILDREN - RESEARCH.**
Embiricos, Anne-Marie T. The effects of content knowledge and strategies on memory development among 4- and 6-year-old children. 1998.
*TC 085 Em22*

Embiricos, Anne-Marie T. The effects of content knowledge and strategies on memory development among 4- and 6-year-old children. 1998.
*TC 085 Em22*

**Memory observed** : remembering in natural contexts / selections and commentary by Ulric Neisser, Ira E. Hyman, Jr. 2nd ed. New York : Worth Publishers, c2000. xiv, 529 p. : ill. ; 24 cm. Includes bibliographical references and indexes. ISBN 0-7167-3319-6 DDC 153.1/2
*1. Memory. 2. Memory - Research - Field work. I. Neisser, Ulric. II. Hyman, Ira E.*
*TC BF371 .M455 2000*

**MEMORY (PHILOSOPHY).**
Kavanagh, Gaynor. Dream spaces. New York : Leicester University Press, 2000.
*TC AM7 .K37 2000*

Memory and methodology. Oxford ; New York : Berg, 2000.
*TC BD181.7 .M46 2000*

Memory and methodology. Oxford ; New York : Berg, 2000.
*TC BD181.7 .M46 2000*

Museums and memory. Stanford, Calif. : Stanford University Press, c2000.
*TC AM7 .M8815 2000*

**MEMORY - PHYSIOLOGICAL ASPECTS.**
Neurobiology of learning and memory. San Diego : Academic Press, c1998.
*TC QP408 .N492 1998*

Samuel, David. Memory. New York : New York University Press, c1999.
*TC QP406 .S26 1999*

**MEMORY - PHYSIOLOGY.**
Neurobiology of learning and memory. San Diego : Academic Press, c1998.
*TC QP408 .N492 1998*

**MEMORY - PHYSIOLOGY - CONGRESSES.**
Memory, brain, and belief. Cambridge, Mass. ; London : Harvard University Press, 2000.
*TC QP406 .M44 2000*

**MEMORY - RESEARCH - FIELD WORK.**
Memory observed. 2nd ed. New York : Worth Publishers, c2000.
*TC BF371 .M455 2000*

**MEMORY - RESEARCH - UNITED STATES.**
Buse, William Joseph. The alternate session. 1999.

*TC 085 B9603*

**MEMORY - SOCIAL ASPECTS.**
Kavanagh, Gaynor. Dream spaces. New York : Leicester University Press, 2000.
*TC AM7 .K37 2000*

**MEMORY - SOCIAL ASPECTS - UNITED STATES.**
Bertman, Stephen. Cultural amnesia. Westport, Conn. ; London : Praeger, 2000.
*TC HN59.2 .B474 2000*

Rosenzweig, Roy. The presence of the past. New York : Columbia University Press, c1998.
*TC E179.5 .R67 1998*

**Memphis Brooks Museum of Art.**
Myth, magic and mystery. Boulder, Colo. : Roberts Rinehart Publishers ; [Norfolk, Va.] : in cooperation with the Chrysler Museum of Art, c1996.
*TC NC975 .M98 1996*

**MEN. See also AGED MEN; BROTHERS; FATHERS; GAY MEN; MASCULINITY; PHOTOGRAPHY OF MEN; UNCLES.**
Mead, Margaret, 1901-1978. Male and female. London : Victor Gollancz, c1949.
*TC HQ21 .M464 1949*

Mead, Margaret, 1901-1978. Male and female. London : Victor Gollancz, c1949.
*TC HQ21 .M464 1949*

**MEN, AFRO-AMERICAN. See AFRO-AMERICAN MEN.**

**MEN IN BLACK (UFO PHENOMENON). See UNIDENTIFIED FLYING OBJECTS - SIGHTINGS AND ENCOUNTERS.**

**MEN - PSYCHOLOGY.**
Gartner, Richard B. Betrayed as boys. New York : Guilford Press, c1999.
*TC RC569.5.A28 G37 1999*

**MEN - PSYCHOLOGY.**
Lippert, Robin Alissa. Conflating the self with the body. 1999.
*TC 085 L655*

**MEN RAPE VICTIMS. See MALE RAPE VICTIMS.**

**MEN - RELATIONS WITH WOMEN. See MAN-WOMAN RELATIONSHIPS.**

**MEN - RESEARCH - UNITED STATES.**
Gender, culture, and ethnicity. Mountain View, Calif. : Mayfield Pub. Co., c1999.
*TC HQ1181.U5 G45 1999*

**MEN - SEXUAL BEHAVIOR.**
Kinsey, Alfred C. (Alfred Charles), 1894-1956. Sexual behavior in the human male. Bloomington, Ind. : Indiana University Press, [1998].
*TC HQ28 .K55 1998*

**MEN - UNITED STATES. See AFRO-AMERICAN MEN.**

**MEN - UNITED STATES - SEXUAL BEHAVIOR.**
Hite, Shere. The Hite report on male sexuality. 1st Ballantine Book ed. New York : Ballantine Books, 1982.
*TC HQ28 .H57 1982*

**MEN-WOMEN RELATIONSHIPS. See MAN-WOMAN RELATIONSHIPS.**

**MENC's strategies for teaching series.**
Hall, Louis O. Strategies for teaching. Reston, VA : Music Educators National Conference, c1997.
*TC MT1.H136 S77 1997*

**Mendel, Lisa Lucks.**
**Singular's illustrated dictionary of audiology.**
Mendel, Lisa Lucks. Singular's pocket dictionary of audiology. San Diego : Singular Pub. Group, c1999.
*TC RF290 .M4642 1999*

Singular's pocket dictionary of audiology / Lisa Lucks Mendel, Jeffrey L. Danhauer, Sadanand Singh ; with contributions from Jennifer Mead and Jennifer Stewart. San Diego : Singular Pub. Group, c1999. ix, 431 p. ; 18 cm. This ed. lacks the illustrations of Singular's illustrated dictionary of audiology. Includes bibliographical references (p. 428-431). ISBN 0-7693-0042-1 (softcover : alk. paper) DDC 617.8/003
*1. Audiology - Dictionaries. I. Mendel, Lisa Lucks. Singular's illustrated dictionary of audiology. II. Danhauer, Jeffrey L. III. Singh, Sadanand. IV. Title. V. Title: Pocket dictionary of audiology*
*TC RF290 .M4642 1999*

**Mendelssohn-Bartholdy, Felix, 1809-1847.**
[Paulus. Vocal score. English]
Saint Paul; an oratorio, for full chorus of mixed voices, soprano, alto, tenor and bass soli with piano accompaniment / by Felix Mendelssohn. New York, G. Schirmer [19--] vocal score (207 p.) 26 cm. (G. Schirmer's editions of oratorios and cantatas) Text from the Bible.
*1. Oratorios - Vocal scores with piano. I. Title. II. Title: St. Paul. III. Series.*
*TC M2003.M53 S35*

**Mendes, Valerie D.**
Miller, Jonathan, 1934- On reflection. London : National Gallery Publications : [New Haven, Conn.] : Distributed by Yale University Press, c1998.
*TC N8224.M6 M54 1998*

**Mendlewicz, J. (Julien).**
New therapeutic indications of antidepressants. Basel ; New York : Karger, c1997.
*TC RM332 .N475 1997*

**Mendoza, Maria Adalia.** A study to compare inner city Black men and women completers and non-attenders of diabetes self-care classes / by Maria Adalia Mendoza. 1999. x, 166 leaves ; 29 cm. Issued also on microfilm. Thesis (Ed.D.)--Teachers College, Columbia University, 1999. Includes bibliographical references (leaves 139-147).
*1. Diabetes - Patients - Education - New York (State) - New York. 2. Diabetics - New York (State) - New York - Attitudes. 3. African Americans - Health and hygiene - New York (State) - New York. 4. Health behavior - Social aspects. 5. Health behavior - Psychological aspects. 6. Self-care, Health. 7. Self-help groups. 8. Bronx (New York, N.Y.) I. Title.*
*TC 06 no. 11206*

**MENÉNDEZ, MIGUEL ANGEL.**
Guevara-Vázquez, Fabián. El indigena en la novela de la Revolucion Mexicana. 1999.
*TC 085 G934*

**Menezes, Isabel.**
Affective education. London ; New York : Cassell, 1998.
*TC LB1072 .A38 1998*

**Menn, Lise.**
Methods for studying language production. Mahwah, N.J. : Lawrence Erlbaum Associates, 2000.
*TC P118 .M47 2000*

**MENNONITES.** *See also* **AMISH.**
The Amish [videorecording]. Oak Forest, IL : MPI Home Video, 1988.

**MENNONITES - SOCIAL LIFE AND CUSTOMS.**
The Amish [videorecording]. Oak Forest, IL : MPI Home Video, 1988.

**Mensh, Elaine, 1924-** Black, white, and Huckleberry Finn : re-imagining the American dream / Elaine Mensh and Harry Mensh. Tuscaloosa : University of Alabama Press, c2000. 167 p. ; 24 cm. Includes bibliographical references (p. [149]-159) and index. ISBN 0-8173-0995-0 (alk. paper) DDC 813/.4
*1. Twain, Mark, - 1835-1910. - Adventures of Huckleberry Finn. 2. Literature and society - United States - History - 19th century. 3. Twain, Mark, - 1835-1910 - Political and social views. 4. Adventure stories, American - History and criticism. 5. National characteristics, American, in literature. 6. Fugitive slaves in literature. 7. Race relations in literature. 8. Afro-Americans in literature. 9. Whites in literature. I. Mensh, Harry, 1911- II. Title.*
*TC PS1305 .M46 2000*

**Mensh, Harry, 1911-.**
Mensh, Elaine, 1924- Black, white, and Huckleberry Finn. Tuscaloosa : University of Alabama Press, c2000.
*TC PS1305 .M46 2000*

**MENTAL DEFICIENCY.** *See* **MENTAL RETARDATION.**

**MENTAL DEPRESSION.** *See* **DEPRESSION, MENTAL.**

**MENTAL DISCIPLINE.** *See* **EDUCATION; MEMORY.**

**MENTAL DISEASES.** *See* **MENTAL ILLNESS; PSYCHOLOGY, PATHOLOGICAL.**

**MENTAL DISORDERS.** *See* **MENTAL ILLNESS; PSYCHOLOGY, PATHOLOGICAL.**

**MENTAL DISORDERS.**
Frontiers of developmental psychopathology. New York : Oxford University Press, 1996.
*TC RC454.4 .F76 1996*

Gender and its effects on psychopathology. Washington, DC : American Psychiatric Press, c2000.

*TC RC455.4.S45 G465 2000*
Psychiatric and behavioural disorders in developmental disabilities and mental retardation. Cambridge, UK ; New York, NY, USA : Cambridge University Press, 1999.
*TC RC451.4.M47 P77 1999*

**MENTAL DISORDERS - ADOLESCENCE.**
Canino, Ian A. Culturally diverse children and adolescents. 2nd ed. New York : Guilford Press, c2000.
*TC RJ507.M54 C36 2000*

**MENTAL DISORDERS - CHILD.**
Canino, Ian A. Culturally diverse children and adolescents. 2nd ed. New York : Guilford Press, c2000.
*TC RJ507.M54 C36 2000*

Play diagnosis and assessment. 2nd ed. New York : John Wiley & Sons, c2000.
*TC RJ505.P6 P524 1999*

**MENTAL DISORDERS - DIAGNOSIS.**
Gardner, Richard A. Developmental conflicts and diagnostic evaluation in adolescent psychotherapy. Northvale, N.J. : J. Aronson, c1999.
*TC RJ503 .G376 1999*

Play diagnosis and assessment. 2nd ed. New York : John Wiley & Sons, c2000.
*TC RJ505.P6 P524 1999*

**MENTAL DISORDERS - DIAGNOSIS - CHILD - HANDBOOKS.**
Kronenberger, William G. Child clinician's handbook. 2nd ed. Boston : Allyn and Bacon, c2001.
*TC RJ499.3 .K76 2001*

**MENTAL DISORDERS - DIAGNOSIS - CONGRESSES.**
Basic and clinical science of mental and addictive disorders. Basel ; New York : Karger, c1997.
*TC RC327 .B37 1997*

**MENTAL DISORDERS - ENCYCLOPEDIAS.**
Encyclopedia of mental health. San Diego : Academic Press, c1998.
*TC RA790.5 .E53 1998*

**MENTAL DISORDERS - ETIOLOGY.**
The environment and mental health. Mahwah, N.J. : Lawrence Erlbaum Associates, c1998.
*TC RC455.4.E58 E528 1998*

**MENTAL DISORDERS - IN ADOLESCENCE.**
Gardner, Richard A. Developmental conflicts and diagnostic evaluation in adolescent psychotherapy. Northvale, N.J. : J. Aronson, c1999.
*TC RJ503 .G376 1999*

**MENTAL DISORDERS - IN INFANCY & CHILDHOOD.**
In the long run--longitudinal studies of psychopathology in children. Washington, DC : American Psychiatric Press, c1999.
*TC RC321 .G7 no. 143*

**MENTAL DISORDERS - IN OLD AGE.**
Assessment in geriatric psychopharmacology. New Canaan, Conn. : Mark Powley Associates, 1983.
*TC WT150 .A846 1983*

**MENTAL DISORDERS - INFANT.**
Play diagnosis and assessment. 2nd ed. New York : John Wiley & Sons, c2000.
*TC RJ505.P6 P524 1999*

**MENTAL DISORDERS - THERAPY.**
Gauchet, Marcel. [La pratique de l'esprit humain. English] Madness and democracy. Princeton, N.J. : Princeton University Press, c1999.
*TC RC439 .G2813 1999*

Psychiatry and religion. 1st ed. Washington, DC : American Psychiatric Press, c2000.
*TC RC455.4.R4 P755 2000*

**MENTAL DISORDERS - THERAPY - CHILD - HANDBOOKS.**
Kronenberger, William G. Child clinician's handbook. 2nd ed. Boston : Allyn and Bacon, c2001.
*TC RJ499.3 .K76 2001*

**MENTAL DISORDERS - THERAPY - CONGRESSES.**
Basic and clinical science of mental and addictive disorders. Basel ; New York : Karger, c1997.
*TC RC327 .B37 1997*

**MENTAL DISORDERS - THERAPY - CONGRESSES.**
Unmet need in psychiatry. Cambridge, U.K. ; New York, NY : Cambridge University Press, 2000.

*TC RA790.5 .U565 2000*

**MENTAL HEALING.** *See also* **MIND AND BODY; NEW THOUGHT.**
Druss, Richard G., 1933- Listening to patients :. Oxford ; New York : Oxford University Press, 2000.
*TC RC480.8 .D78 2000*

**MENTAL HEALING - HISTORY.**
Bromberg, Walter, 1900- The mind of man. 4th ed. New York : Harper & Brothers, 1937.
*TC RC480 .B7*

**MENTAL HEALTH.** *See also* **CHILD MENTAL HEALTH; MENTAL ILLNESS; PERSONALITY; PSYCHIATRY; PSYCHOLOGY; PSYCHOLOGY, PATHOLOGICAL; SELF-ACTUALIZATION (PSYCHOLOGY); SOCIAL PSYCHIATRY; STRESS (PSYCHOLOGY).**
Gutin, Nina J. Differential object representations in inpatients with narcissistic and borderline personality disorders and normal controls. 1997.
*TC 085 G975*

Lippert, Robin Alissa. Conflating the self with the body. 1999.
*TC 085 L655*

Morgan, Brian L. G. Brainfood. Tucson, Ariz. : Body Press, c1987.
*TC QP376 .M62 1987*

**MENTAL HEALTH CARE.** *See* **MENTAL HEALTH SERVICES.**

**MENTAL HEALTH CLINICS.** *See* **COMMUNITY MENTAL HEALTH SERVICES.**

**MENTAL HEALTH CONSULTATION.**
Donahue, Paul J. Mental health consultation in early childhood. Baltimore, MD : Paul H. Brookes Publishing, 2000.
*TC RJ499 .D595 2000*

**Mental health consultation in early childhood.**
Donahue, Paul J. Baltimore, MD : Paul H. Brookes Publishing, 2000.
*TC RJ499 .D595 2000*

**MENTAL HEALTH COUNSELING.** *See also* **PSYCHOTHERAPY.**
Clinical counselling in context. London ; New York : Routledge, 1999.
*TC RC466 .C55 1999*

**MENTAL HEALTH - DICTIONARIES.**
Encyclopedia of mental health. San Diego : Academic Press, c1998.
*TC RA790.5 .E53 1998*

**MENTAL HEALTH EDUCATION.**
Mio, Jeffrey Scott. Resistance to multiculturalism :. Philadelphia, PA : Brunner/Mazel, c2000.
*TC HM1271 .M56 2000*

**MENTAL HEALTH - ENCYCLOPEDIAS.**
Encyclopedia of mental health. San Diego : Academic Press, c1998.
*TC RA790.5 .E53 1998*

**MENTAL HEALTH - ENVIRONMENTAL ASPECTS.**
The environment and mental health. Mahwah, N.J. : Lawrence Erlbaum Associates, c1998.
*TC RC455.4.E58 E528 1998*

**Mental health in our future cities** / edited by David Goldberg and Graham Thornicroft. Hove, England : Psychology Press, c1998. xii, 290 p. : ill. ; 24 cm. (Maudsley monographs ; no. 42) Includes bibliographical references and index. ISBN 0-86377-546-2 DDC 362.2/2
*1. Community mental health services. 2. Cities and towns. I. Goldberg, David P. II. Thornicroft, Graham. III. Series.*
*TC RA790.5 .M4196 1998*

**MENTAL HEALTH LAWS - UNITED STATES - POPULAR WORKS.**
Bernstein, Barton E. The portable lawyer for mental health professionals. New York : J. Wiley, c1998.
*TC KF3828.Z9 B47 1998*

**MENTAL HEALTH NURSING.** *See* **PSYCHIATRIC NURSING.**

**MENTAL HEALTH PERSONNEL.** *See* **PSYCHIATRIC NURSING; PSYCHOTHERAPISTS.**

**MENTAL HEALTH PERSONNEL - LEGAL STATUS, LAWS, ETC. - UNITED STATES - POPULAR WORKS.**
Bernstein, Barton E. The portable lawyer for mental health professionals. New York : J. Wiley, c1998.
*TC KF3828.Z9 B47 1998*

**MENTAL HEALTH POLICY.**
Prior, Pauline. Gender and mental health. New York :
New York University Press, 1999.
*TC RC455.4.S45 P75 1999*

**MENTAL HEALTH PROMOTION.**
Hays, Kate F. Working it out. 1st ed. Washington,
DC : American Psychological Association, c1999.
*TC RC489.E9 H39 1999*

Page, Randy M. Fostering emotional well-being in the
classroom. 2nd ed. Sudbury, Mass. ; London : Jones
and Bartlett Publishers, c2000.
*TC LB3430 .P34 2000*

**MENTAL HEALTH - RESEARCH.** *See*
**PSYCHIATRY - RESEARCH.**

**MENTAL HEALTH - RESEARCH -
METHODOLOGY.**
Chen, Sheying. Measurement and analysis in
psychosocial research. Aldershot, Hants, UK :
Brookfield USA : Avebury, c1997.
*TC RC473.P79 C46 1997*

**MENTAL HEALTH SERVICES.** *See* **CHILD
MENTAL HEALTH SERVICES;
COMMUNITY MENTAL HEALTH
SERVICES; MANAGED MENTAL HEALTH
CARE.**

**MENTAL HEALTH SERVICES FOR CHILDREN.**
*See* **CHILD MENTAL HEALTH SERVICES.**

**MENTAL HEALTH SERVICES - MANAGEMENT.**
Management and administration skills for the mental
health professional. San Diego, Calif. London :
Academic, c1999.
*TC RA790 .M325 1999*

**MENTAL HEALTH SERVICES - PERIODICALS.**
Family and child mental health journal. New York,
NY : Human Sciences Press, [c1980-c1982]

Issues in child mental health. [New York, Human
Sciences Press]

**MENTAL HEALTH SERVICES - UNITED
STATES.**
Cummings, Nicholas A. The value of psychological
treatment. Phoenix, AZ : Zeig, Tucker & Co., 1999.
*TC RA790.6 .C85 1999*

**MENTAL HEALTH SERVICES - UTILIZATION -
CONGRESSES.**
Unmet need in psychiatry. Cambridge, U.K. ; New
York, NY : Cambridge University Press, 2000.
*TC RA790.5 .U565 2000*

**MENTAL HEALTH SERVICES - UTILIZATION -
UNITED STATES.**
Cummings, Nicholas A. The value of psychological
treatment. Phoenix, AZ : Zeig, Tucker & Co., 1999.
*TC RA790.6 .C85 1999*

**MENTAL HEALTH - UNITED STATES -
LONGITUDINAL STUDIES.**
Srole, Leo. Personal history & health. New
Brunswick, N.J. : Transaction Publishers, c1998.
*TC RA790.6 .S7 1998*

**MENTAL HYGIENE.** *See* **MENTAL HEALTH.**

**MENTAL ILLNESS.** *See also* **MENTAL HEALTH.**
First break [videorecording]. Boston, MA : Fanlight
Productions, c1997.
*TC RC465 .F5 1997*

First break [videorecording]. Boston, MA : Fanlight
Productions, c1997.
*TC RC465 .F5 1997*

First break [videorecording]. Boston, MA : Fanlight
Productions, c1997.
*TC RC465 .F5 1997*

Pathology and the postmodern. London ; Thousand
Oaks : SAGE, 2000.
*TC BF636 .P38 2000*

Tessler, Richard C. Family experiences with mental
illness. Westport, Conn. ; London : Auburn House,
2000.
*TC RC455.4.F3 T46 2000*

**MENTAL ILLNESS AND LAW.** *See* **MENTAL
HEALTH LAWS.**

**MENTAL ILLNESS - CHEMOTHERAPY.**
Tasman, Allan, 1947- The doctor-patient relationship
in pharmacotherapy. New York : Guilford Press,
c2000.
*TC RC483.3 .T375 2000*

**MENTAL ILLNESS - DIAGNOSIS.**
Challenge cases [videorecording]. Princeton, N.J. :
Films for the Humanities & Sciences, 1998.

*TC RC455.2.C4 C4 1998*
House. Alvin E. DSM-IV diagnosis in the schools.
New York : Guilford Press, c1999
*TC RJ503.5 .H68 1999*

The use of psychological testing for treatment
planning and outcome assessment. 2nd ed. Mahwah,
N.J. : Lawrence Erlbaum Associates, c1999.
*TC RC473.P79 U83 1999*

**MENTAL ILLNESS - DICTIONARIES.**
Encyclopedia of mental health. San Diego : Academic
Press, c1998.
*TC RA790.5 .E53 1998*

**MENTAL ILLNESS - ENVIRONMENTAL
ASPECTS.**
The environment and mental health. Mahwah, N.J. :
Lawrence Erlbaum Associates, c1998.
*TC RC455.4.E58 E528 1998*

**MENTAL ILLNESS - ETIOLOGY.**
Adversity, stress, and psychopathology. New York :
Oxford University Press, 1998.
*TC RC455.4.S87 A39 1998*

Frontiers of developmental psychopathology. New
York : Oxford University Press, 1996.
*TC RC454.4 .F76 1996*

Kiesler, Donald J. Beyond the disease model of
mental disorders. Westport, Conn. : Praeger, c1999.
*TC RC454.4 .K52 1999*

**MENTAL ILLNESS - FORECASTING -
LONGITUDINAL STUDIES.**
Srole, Leo. Personal history & health. New
Brunswick, N.J. : Transaction Publishers, c1998.
*TC RA790.6 .S7 1998*

**MENTAL ILLNESS - GERMANY - HISTORY -
16TH CENTURY.**
Midelfort, H. C. Erik A history of madness in
sixteenth-century Germany. Stanford, Calif. : Stanford
University Press, c1999.
*TC RC450.G3 M528 1999*

**MENTAL ILLNESS IN CHILDREN.** *See* **CHILD
PSYCHOPATHOLOGY.**

**MENTAL ILLNESS - LAW AND LEGISLATION.**
*See* **MENTAL HEALTH LAWS.**

**MENTAL ILLNESS - NURSING.** *See*
**PSYCHIATRIC NURSING.**

**MENTAL ILLNESS - PATIENTS.** *See*
**MENTALLY ILL.**

**MENTAL ILLNESS - PHILOSOPHY.**
Grant, Brian W., 1939- The condition of madness.
Lanham, Md : University Press of America, 1999.
*TC RC437.5 .G73 1999*

**MENTAL ILLNESS - POPULAR WORKS.**
Nathan, Peter E. Treating mental disorders. New
York : Oxford University Press, 1999.
*TC RC480.515 .N38 1999*

**MENTAL ILLNESS - PUBLIC OPINION.**
Wahl, Otto F. Telling is risky business. New
Brunswick, N.J. ; London : Rutgers University Press,
c1999.
*TC RC454.4 .W327 1999*

**MENTAL ILLNESS - RESEARCH.** *See*
**PSYCHIATRY - RESEARCH.**

**MENTAL ILLNESS - SEX FACTORS.**
Gender and its effects on psychopathology.
Washington, DC : American Psychiatric Press, c2000.
*TC RC455.4.S45 G465 2000*

Prior, Pauline. Gender and mental health. New York :
New York University Press, 1999.
*TC RC455.4.S45 P75 1999*

Prior, Pauline. Gender and mental health. New York :
New York University Press, 1999.
*TC RC455.4.S45 P75 1999*

**MENTAL ILLNESS - SOCIAL ASPECTS.**
Gauchet, Marcel. [La pratique de l'esprit humain.
English] Madness and democracy. Princeton, N.J. :
Princeton University Press, c1999.
*TC RC439 .G2813 1999*

Handbook of the sociology of mental health. New
York : Kluwer Academic/Plenum Publishers, c1999.
*TC RC455 .H2874 1999*

**MENTAL ILLNESS - TREATMENT -
EVALUATION.** *See also* **PSYCHIATRIC
RATING SCALES.**
The use of psychological testing for treatment
planning and outcome assessment. 2nd ed. Mahwah,
N.J. : Lawrence Erlbaum Associates, c1999.

*TC RC473.P79 U83 1999*

**MENTAL ILLNESS - TREATMENT -
EVALUATION - MISCELLANEA.**
Nathan, Peter E. Treating mental disorders. New
York : Oxford University Press, 1999.
*TC RC480.515 .N38 1999*

**MENTAL ILLNESS - UNITED STATES -
LONGITUDINAL STUDIES.**
Srole, Leo. Personal history & health. New
Brunswick, N.J. : Transaction Publishers, c1998.
*TC RA790.6 .S7 1998*

**MENTAL ILLNESSS - EPIDEMIOLOGY -
CONGRESSES.**
Unmet need in psychiatry. Cambridge, U.K. ; New
York, NY : Cambridge University Press, 2000.
*TC RA790.5 .U565 2000*

**MENTAL IMAGERY.** *See* **IMAGERY
(PSYCHOLOGY); IMAGINATION.**

**MENTAL IMAGES.** *See* **IMAGERY
(PSYCHOLOGY); IMAGINATION.**

**MENTAL PATIENTS.** *See* **MENTALLY ILL.**

**MENTAL PHILOSOPHY.** *See* **PHILOSOPHY;
PSYCHOLOGY.**

**MENTAL PROCESSES - PHYSIOLOGY.**
Grigsby, Jim. Neurodynamics of personality. New
York : Guilford Press, 2000.
*TC BF698.9.B5 G741 2000*

**MENTAL REPRESENTATION.**
Cognitive dynamics. Mahwah, N.J. ; London : L.
Erlbaum, 2000.
*TC BF316.6 .C64 2000*

Kinnamon, James C. A comparison of structural
knowledge in eighth graders and college students.
1999.
*TC 085 K6194*

Touch, representation, and blindness. Oxford ; New
York : Oxford University Press, 2000.
*TC BF275 .T68 2000*

**MENTAL REPRESENTATION - CONGRESSES.**
Metarepresentations. Oxford ; New York : Oxford
University Press, c2000.
*TC BF316.6 .M48 2000*

Understanding representation in the cognitive
sciences. New York : Kluwer Academic/Plenum
Publishers, c1999.
*TC BF316.6 U63 1999*

**MENTAL REPRESENTATION IN CHILDREN.**
Development of mental representation. Mahwah, NJ :
L. Erlbaum Associates, c1999.
*TC BF723.M43 T47 1999*

**MENTAL RETARDATION.** *See also* **DOWN
SYNDROME; INTELLECT; MENTALLY
HANDICAPPED.**
Baroff, George S. 3rd ed. Philadelphia, Pa. : Brunner/
Mazel, c1999.
*TC RC570 .B27 1999*

**MENTAL RETARDATION.**
Baroff, George S. Mental retardation. 3rd ed.
Philadelphia, Pa. : Brunner/Mazel, c1999.
*TC RC570 .B27 1999*

Baroff, George S. Mental retardation. 3rd ed.
Philadelphia, Pa. : Brunner/Mazel, c1999.
*TC RC570 .B27 1999*

**MENTAL RETARDATION.**
Baroff, George S. Mental retardation. 3rd ed.
Philadelphia, Pa. : Brunner/Mazel, c1999.
*TC RC570 .B27 1999*

Psychiatric and behavioural disorders in
developmental disabilities and mental retardation.
Cambridge, UK ; New York, NY, USA : Cambridge
University Press, 1999.
*TC RC451.4.M47 P77 1999*

**MENTAL RETARDATION - MORAL AND
ETHICAL ASPECTS.**
Byrne, Peter, 1950- Philosophical and ethical
problems in mental handicap / Peter Byrne. New
York : St. Martin's Press , 2000.
*TC HV3004 .B95 2000*

**MENTAL RETARDATION - RELIGIOUS
ASPECTS.**
Meaningful care. Dordrecht ; Boston ; London :
Kluwer Academic Publishers, c2000.
*TC HV3004 .M34 2000*

**MENTAL RETARDATION - UNITED STATES.**
Angrosino, Michael V. Opportunity house. Walnut Creek, CA : AltaMira Press, c1998.
*TC HV3006.A4 A48 1998*

**MENTAL STATUS EXAMINATION.**
Insight and psychosis. New York : Oxford University Press, 1998.
*TC RC512 .I49 1998*

**MENTAL STEREOTYPE.** *See* STEREOTYPE (PSYCHOLOGY).

**MENTAL STRESS.** *See* STRESS (PSYCHOLOGY).

**MENTAL TESTS.** *See* EDUCATIONAL TESTS AND MEASUREMENTS; INTELLIGENCE TESTS; PSYCHOLOGICAL TESTS.

**MENTAL TYPES.** *See* TYPOLOGY (PSYCHOLOGY).

**MENTALLY DEFICIENT.** *See* MENTALLY HANDICAPPED.

**MENTALLY DEPRESSED PEOPLE.** *See* DEPRESSED PERSONS.

**MENTALLY DEPRESSED PERSONS.** *See* DEPRESSED PERSONS.

**MENTALLY HANDICAPPED.** *See also* LEARNING DISABLED; MENTAL RETARDATION; MENTALLY ILL; SOCIAL WORK WITH THE MENTALLY HANDICAPPED.
Byrne, Peter, 1950- Philosophical and ethical problems in mental handicap / Peter Byrne. New York : St. Martin's Press , 2000.
*TC HV3004 .B95 2000*

**MENTALLY HANDICAPPED AGED - SERVICES FOR - NEW JERSEY.**
Smith, Irmhild Wrede. The effect of structured exercise and structured reminiscing on agitation and aggression in geriatric psychiatric patients. 1996.
*TC 06 no. 10700*

**MENTALLY HANDICAPPED - BEHAVIOR MODIFICATION.**
Challenging behaviour. London : D. Fulton, 1998.
*TC RC451.4.M47 C492 1998*

**MENTALLY HANDICAPPED - BEHAVIOR MODIFICATION - GREAT BRITAIN - CASE STUDIES.**
Challenging behaviour. London : D. Fulton, 1998.
*TC RC451.4.M47 C492 1998*

**MENTALLY HANDICAPPED - BIOGRAPHY.**
Gray, Barry, 1944- Lifemaps of people with learning difficulties. London ; Philadelphia : Jessica Kingsley, 1999.
*TC HV3004 .G73 1999*

**MENTALLY HANDICAPPED - CARE.**
Baroff, George S. Mental retardation. 3rd ed. Philadelphia, Pa. : Brunner/Mazel, c1999.
*TC RC570 .B27 1999*

**MENTALLY HANDICAPPED - CARE AND TREATMENT.** *See* MENTALLY HANDICAPPED - CARE.

**MENTALLY HANDICAPPED - CARE - MORAL AND ETHICAL ASPECTS.**
Meaningful care. Dordrecht ; Boston ; London : Kluwer Academic Publishers, c2000.
*TC HV3004 .M34 2000*

**MENTALLY HANDICAPPED CHILDREN.** *See* LEARNING DISABLED CHILDREN; MENTALLY ILL CHILDREN.

**MENTALLY HANDICAPPED CHILDREN - .**
Democratic dialogue with special needs students. [Boulder, Colo.] : Social Science Education Consortium, c1997.
*TC LC4069.3 .D4 1997*

**MENTALLY HANDICAPPED CHILDREN - EDUCATION.**
Furneaux, Barbara. The special child. Harmondsworth : Penguin, 1969.
*TC LC4661 .F87*

**MENTALLY HANDICAPPED CHILDREN - EDUCATION - AIMS AND OBJECTIVES - UNITED STATES.**
Democratic dialogue with special needs students. [Boulder, Colo.] : Social Science Education Consortium, c1997.
*TC LC4069.3 .D4 1997*

**MENTALLY HANDICAPPED CHILDREN - EDUCATION (ELEMENTARY) - MARYLAND.**

Sean's story [videorecording]. Princeton, N.J. : Films for the Humanities & Sciences ; [S.l. : distributed by] ABC Multimedia : Capital Cities/ABC, c1994.
*TC LC1203.M3 .S39 1994*

**MENTALLY HANDICAPPED CHILDREN - EDUCATION - PERIODICALS.**
Forward trends. London, National Council for Special Education [etc.]

**MENTALLY HANDICAPPED CHILDREN - UNITED STATES - BIOGRAPHY.**
Kaufman, Sandra Z., 1928- Retarded isn't stupid, mom!. Rev. ed. Baltimore : P.H. Brookes Pub., 1999.
*TC HV894 .K383 1999*

**MENTALLY HANDICAPPED - EDUCATION - UNITED STATES - PERIODICALS.**
Journal of psycho-asthenics. Faribault, Minn. : Association of American Institutions for Feeble-Minded, [1896-1918]

**MENTALLY HANDICAPPED - EMPLOYMENT - UNITED STATES.**
Human Resources Center (N.Y.) Employment of the mentally retarded in a competitive industrial setting, March 1, 1962 - February 28, 1967. Albertson, N.Y. [1967?]
*TC HV3005 .H85*

**MENTALLY HANDICAPPED - IOWA - BIOGRAPHY.**
Walz, Thomas, 1933- The unlikely celebrity. Carbondale : Southern Illinois University Press, c1998.
*TC HV3006.S33 W35 1998*

**MENTALLY HANDICAPPED - LEGAL STATUS, LAWS, ETC.** *See* MENTAL HEALTH LAWS.

**MENTALLY HANDICAPPED - MENTAL HEALTH.**
Psychiatric and behavioural disorders in developmental disabilities and mental retardation. Cambridge, UK ; New York, NY, USA : Cambridge University Press, 1999.
*TC RC451.4.M47 P77 1999*

**MENTALLY HANDICAPPED - MENTAL HEALTH SERVICES.**
Psychiatric and behavioural disorders in developmental disabilities and mental retardation. Cambridge, UK ; New York, NY, USA : Cambridge University Press, 1999.
*TC RC451.4.M47 P77 1999*

**MENTALLY HANDICAPPED - PERIODICALS.**
Journal of psycho-asthenics. Faribault, Minn. : Association of American Institutions for Feeble-Minded, [1896-1918]

**MENTALLY HANDICAPPED - PSYCHOLOGICAL TESTING.**
Yamusah, Salifu. An investigation of the relative effectiveness of the composite approach and the phenomenological method for enhancing self-esteem in adults with mental retardation. 1998.
*TC 085 Y146*

**MENTALLY HANDICAPPED - PSYCHOLOGY.**
Gray, Barry, 1944- Lifemaps of people with learning difficulties. London ; Philadelphia : Jessica Kingsley, 1999.
*TC HV3004 .G73 1999*

**MENTALLY HANDICAPPED - REHABILITATION - GREAT BRITAIN.**
Therapy and learning difficulties. Boston, Mass : Butterworth-Heinemann, 1999.
*TC HV3008.G7 T48 1999*

**MENTALLY HANDICAPPED - REHABILITATION - UNITED STATES.**
Human Resources Center (N.Y.) Employment of the mentally retarded in a competitive industrial setting, March 1, 1962 - February 28, 1967. Albertson, N.Y. [1967?]
*TC HV3005 .H85*

**MENTALLY HANDICAPPED - SERVICES FOR.**
Jackson, Eve, 1949- Learning disability in focus. London : Philadelphia : Jessica Kingsley, c1999.
*TC RC489.P56 J33 1999*

**MENTALLY HANDICAPPED - SERVICES FOR - GREAT BRITAIN.**
Therapy and learning difficulties. Boston, Mass : Butterworth-Heinemann, 1999.
*TC HV3008.G7 T48 1999*

**MENTALLY HANDICAPPED TEENAGERS - LONGITUDINAL STUDIES.**
Smith, Mieko Kotake. Adolescents with emotional

and behavioral disabilities. Lewiston, NY : E. Mellen Press, c1998.
*TC RJ503 .S63 1998*

**MENTALLY HANDICAPPED WOMEN.**
Women with intellectual disabilities. London ; Philadelphia : Jessica Kingsley Publishers, 2000.
*TC HV3009.5.W65 W66 2000*

**MENTALLY ILL.** *See* DEPRESSED PERSONS; MANIC-DEPRESSIVE PERSONS; PSYCHIATRIC HOSPITAL PATIENTS; SCHIZOPHRENICS.

**MENTALLY ILL - CARE.**
Bromberg, Walter, 1900- The mind of man. Harper colophon ed. New York : Harper & Row, 1963.
*TC RC480 .B7 1963*

Bromberg, Walter, 1900- The mind of man. 4th ed. New York : Harper & Brothers, 1937.
*TC RC480 .B7*

**MENTALLY ILL - CASE STUDIES.**
First break [videorecording]. Boston, MA : Fanlight Productions, c1997.
*TC RC465 .F5 1997*

First break [videorecording]. Boston, MA : Fanlight Productions, c1997.
*TC RC465 .F5 1997*

First break [videorecording]. Boston, MA : Fanlight Productions, c1997.
*TC RC465 .F5 1997*

**MENTALLY ILL CHILDREN.** *See* AUTISTIC CHILDREN.

**MENTALLY ILL CHILDREN - EDUCATION.**
Collins, Christopher G. Teaching the emotionally handicapped child. Danville, Ill. : Interstate Printers & Publishers, c1983.
*TC LC4165 .C62 1983*

**MENTALLY ILL CHILDREN - EDUCATION - ADDRESSES, ESSAYS, LECTURES.**
Punishment and aversive stimulation in special education. Reston, Va. : Council for Exceptional Children, 1982.
*TC LC4169 .P8 1982*

**MENTALLY ILL CHILDREN - LONGITUDINAL STUDIES.**
In the long run--longitudinal studies of psychopathology in children. Washington, DC : American Psychiatric Press, c1999.
*TC RC321 .G7 no. 143*

**MENTALLY ILL - FAMILY RELATIONSHIPS.** *See also* FAMILY PSYCHOTHERAPY.
First break [videorecording]. Boston, MA : Fanlight Productions, c1997.
*TC RC465 .F5 1997*

First break [videorecording]. Boston, MA : Fanlight Productions, c1997.
*TC RC465 .F5 1997*

First break [videorecording]. Boston, MA : Fanlight Productions, c1997.
*TC RC465 .F5 1997*

Tessler, Richard C. Family experiences with mental illness. Westport, Conn. ; London : Auburn House, 2000.
*TC RC455.4.F3 T46 2000*

**MENTALLY ILL - INTERVIEWS.**
First break [videorecording]. Boston, MA : Fanlight Productions, c1997.
*TC RC465 .F5 1997*

First break [videorecording]. Boston, MA : Fanlight Productions, c1997.
*TC RC465 .F5 1997*

First break [videorecording]. Boston, MA : Fanlight Productions, c1997.
*TC RC465 .F5 1997*

**MENTALLY ILL - LEGAL STATUS, LAWS, ETC.** *See* MENTAL HEALTH LAWS.

**MENTALLY ILL - REHABILITATION.**
Rowan, Tim, 1952- Solution-oriented therapy for chronic and severe mental illness. New York : Wiley, c1999.
*TC RC480.53 .R69 1999*

**MENTALLY ILL - SERVICES FOR.**
Prior, Pauline. Gender and mental health. New York : New York University Press, 1999.
*TC RC455.4.S45 P75 1999*

**MENTALLY ILL WOMEN - SERVICES FOR.**
Prior, Pauline. Gender and mental health.
New York : New York University Press, 1999.
*TC RC455.4.S45 P75 1999*

**MENTALLY RETARDED.** *See* **MENTALLY HANDICAPPED.**

**MENTALLY RETARDED CHILDREN.** *See* **MENTALLY HANDICAPPED CHILDREN.**

**Mentkowski, Marcia.** Learning that lasts : integrating learning, development, and performance in college and beyond / Marcia Mentkowski and associates. 1st ed. San Francisco : Jossey-Bass, c2000. xxxi, 536 p. ; 23 cm. (The Jossey-Bass higher and adult education series) Includes bibliographical references and indexes. CONTENTS: Themes and purposes -- Educators' ways of knowing about learning -- Student as learner -- Learner as developing person -- Graduate as performer and contributor -- Integrating domains of growth through transformative learning -- Creating the learning-to-teaching connection -- Integrating theory, research, and practice -- Thinking through a curriculum for learning that lasts -- Rethinking inquiry that improves teaching and learning -- Transforming the college culture toward learning that lasts -- Looking ahead. ISBN 0-7879-4482-3 (hard : acid-free paper) DDC 370.15/23
*1. Learning. 2. College teaching - United States. 3. Education, Higher - United States - Curricula. 4. Critical thinking - Study and teaching (Higher) - United States. I. Title. II. Series.*
*TC LB1060 .M464 2000*

**Mentor series**
(no. 2) McHenry, Henry Davis. From cognition to being. Ottawa : University of Ottawa Press, c1999.
*TC LB1025.3 .M36 1999*

**MENTOR TEACHERS.** *See* **MASTER TEACHERS.**

**MENTORING IN EDUCATION.**
Arias, Rafael. Analysis of discourse in an ESL peer-mentoring teacher group. 1999.
*TC 06 no. 10791*

New directions in mentoring. London ; New York : Falmer, 1999.
*TC LB1731.4 .N49 1999*

Zachary, Lois J. The mentor's guide. 1st ed. San Francisco : Jossey-Bass Publishers, c2000.
*TC LB1731.4 .Z23 2000*

**MENTORING IN EDUCATION - GREAT BRITAIN.**
Bell, Derek, 1950- Towards effective subject leadership in the primary school. Buckingham [England] ; Philadelphia : Open University Press, c1999.
*TC LB2832.4.G7 B45 1999*

Bleach, Kevan. The induction and mentoring of newly qualified teachers :. London : David Fulton, 1999.
*TC LB1729 .B584 1999*

**MENTORING IN EDUCATION - NEW YORK (STATE).**
Langer, Arthur Mark. Faculty assessment of mentoring roles at SUNY Empire State College. 1999.
*TC 06 no. 11138*

**MENTORING IN EDUCATION - TURKEY - ANKARA.**
Seferoglu, Süleyman Sadi. Elementary school teacher development. 1996.
*TC 06 no. 10693*

**MENTORING IN EDUCATION - UNITED STATES.**
A better beginning. Alexandria, Va. : Association for Supervision and Curriculum Development, c1999.
*TC LB2844.1.N4 B48 1999*

Caring as tenacity. Cresskill, N.J. : Hampton Press, c2000.
*TC LC5131 .C35 2000*

Gottesman, Barbara Little. Peer coaching for educators. 2nd ed. Lanham, Md. : Scarecrow Press, 2000.
*TC LB1029.T4 G68 2000*

Guiding teacher learning. Washington. DC : AACTE, c1997.
*TC LB1731 .G85 1997*

Podsen, India, 1945- Coaching & mentoring first-year and student teachers. Larchmont, NY : Eye On Education, c2000.
*TC LB1731.4 .P63 2000*

**MENTORING IN EDUCATION - UNITED STATES - CASE STUDIES.**
Gardiner, Mary E., 1953- Coloring outside the lines. Albany : State University of New York Press, c2000.

*TC LB2831.82 .G37 2000*

**MENTORING IN THE PROFESSIONS.**
Arias, Rafael. Analysis of discourse in an ESL peer-mentoring teacher group. 1999.
*TC 06 no. 10791*

Enhancing the postdoctoral experience for scientists and engineers. Washington, DC : National Academy Press, 2000.
*TC Q147 .E53 2000*

**MENTORING - UNITED STATES.**
Edelman, Marian Wright. Lanterns. Boston : Beacon Press, c1999.
*TC E185.97.E33 A3 1999*

**The mentor's guide.**
Zachary, Lois J. 1st ed. San Francisco : Jossey-Bass Publishers, c2000.
*TC LB1731.4 .Z23 2000*

**MENTORS IN EDUCATION.** *See also* **MENTORING IN EDUCATION.**
Flaxman, Erwin. Youth mentoring: New York, N.Y. : ERIC Clearinghouse on Urban Education, 1988.
*TC LC4065 .F53 1988*

**MENTORSHIP.** *See* **MENTORING.**

**MENUS.** *See* **DINNERS AND DINING.**

**Menzel, Randolf, 1940-.**
Learning. Berlin ; New York : Walter de Gruyter, 1999.
*TC QP408 .L44 1999*

**MERCADO COMÚN CENTROAMERICANO COUNTRIES.** *See* **CENTRAL AMERICA.**

**Merce Cunningham.**
Vaughan, David, 1924- 1st ed. New York, NY : Aperture, c1997.
*TC GV1785.C85 V38 1997*

**Mercer, G. (Geoffrey).**
Barnes, Colin, 1946- Exploring disability. Cambridge, UK : Polity Press ; Malden, MA : Blackwell Publishers, 1999.
*TC HV1568 .B35 1999*

**MERCHANDISE LICENSING - UNITED STATES.**
Managing the licensing of electronic products. Washington, DC : Systems and Procedures Exchange Center, Office of Leadership and Management Service, Association of Research Libraries, c1999.

Managing the licensing of electronic products. Washington, DC : Systems and Procedures Exchange Center, Office of Leadership and Management Service, Association of Research Libraries, c1999.

Managing the licensing of electronic products. Washington, DC : Systems and Procedures Exchange Center, Office of Leadership and Management Service, Association of Research Libraries, c1999.
*TC HF5429.255 .M26 1999*

**MERCHANDISING.** *See* **MERCHANDISE LICENSING.**

**Merchant, Betty M.**
Multiple and intersecting identities in qualitative research. Mahwah, N.J. ; London : L. Erlbaum Associates, 2001.
*TC LB1028.25.U6 M85 2001*

**Mercuri, Eugenio.**
Dubowitz, Lilly M. S. The neurological assessment of the preterm and full-term newborn infant. 2nd ed. London : Mac Keith, 1999.
*TC RJ486 .D85 1999*

**MERCY DEATH.** *See* **EUTHANASIA.**

**Merecki, Victoria.**
Griss, Susan. Minds in motion. Portsmouth, NH : Heinemann, c1998.
*TC LB1592 .G75 1998*

**Merena, Elizabeth.**
Donnell Library Center. Video. New York : New York Public Library, 1990.
*TC PN1992.95 .D66*

**MERIDEN (CONN.) - BIOGRAPHY - JUVENILE LITERATURE.**
De Paola, Tomie. 26 Fairmount Avenue. New York : G.P. Putnam's Sons, c1999.
*TC PS3554.E11474 Z473 1999*

**Merker, Hannah.** Listening : ways of hearing in a silent world / Hannah Merker ; with a new foreword by Henry Kisor and new author's notes. 1st Southern Methodist Univ. Press ed. Dallas, Tex. : Southern Methodist University Press, 2000. xi, 209 p. : ill. ; 23 cm. "Portions published in 1992 in No walls of stone by Gallaudet

University." Originally published: New York : HarperCollins Publishers, 1994. ISBN 0-87074-448-8 (paper: acid-free paper) DDC 153.6/8
*1. Listening. 2. Hearing impaired - Biography. 3. Merker, Hannah. I. Title.*
*TC BF323.L5 M37 2000*

**MERKER, HANNAH.**
Merker, Hannah. Listening. 1st Southern Methodist Univ. Press ed. Dallas, Tex. : Southern Methodist University Press, 2000.
*TC BF323.L5 M37 2000*

**Merleau-Ponty, Maurice, 1908-1961.**
**[Phénoménologie de la perception. English]**
Phenomenology of perception / by M. Merleau-Ponty ; translated from the French by Colin Smith. London ; New York : Routledge, 1962. xxi, 466 p. : ill. ; 22 cm. Includes bibliographical references (p. 457-462) and index. ISBN 0-415-04556-8
*1. Phenomenology. 2. Perception (Philosophy) I. Title.*
*TC B829.5 .M413 1962*

Phenomenology of perception / by M. Merleau-Ponty ; translated from the French by Colin Smith. London : Routledge & K. Paul ; New Jersey : Humanities Press, 1986, c1962. xxi, 466 p. ; 22 cm. Translation of Phénoménologie de la perception. Bibliography: p. 457-462. Includes index. ISBN 0-391-02551-1
*1. Phenomenology. I. Title.*
*TC B829.5 .M413 1986*

The primacy of perception, and other essays on phenomenological psychology, the philosophy of art, history, and politics / Edited, with an introd. by James M. Edie. [Evanston, Ill.] : Northwestern University Press, 1964. xix,228p. ; 24cm. (Northwestern University studies in phenomenology & existential philosophy.) Bibliographical footnotes. ISBN 0-8101-0165-3 (cloth) ISBN 0-8101-0164-5 (pbk.)
*1. Phenomenology. I. Title. II. Series.*
*TC B2430.M378 E5 1964*

**[Sens et non-sens. English]**
Sense and non-sense. Translated, with a pref. by Hubert L. Dreyfus & Patricia Allen Dreyfus. [Evanston, Ill.] Northwestern University Press, 1964. xxvii, 193 p. ; 24 cm. (Northwestern University studies in phenomenology & existential philosophy) Includes index. Bibliography: p. 189. Bibliographical footnotes. "This translation...is based on the third edition, issued by Nagel in 1961." Translation of: Sens et non-sens.
*1. Phenomenology. I. Title. II. Series: Northwestern University studies in phenomenology & existential philosophy*
*TC B2430.M379 S43 1964*

**Merriam, Sharan B.**
**Case study research in education.**
Merriam, Sharan B. Qualitative research and case study applications in education. 2nd ed. San Francisco : Jossey-Bass Publishers, c1998.
*TC LB1028 .M396 1998*

Qualitative research and case study applications in education / Sharan B. Merriam. 2nd ed. San Francisco : Jossey-Bass Publishers, c1998. xviii, 275 p. : ill. ; 24 cm. (A joint publication of the Jossey-Bass education series and the Jossey-Bass higher and adult education series) Rev. and expanded ed. of: Case study research in education. 1st ed. 1988. Includes bibliographical references (p. 247-265) and indexes. ISBN 0-7879-1009-0 (acid-free paper) DDC 370/.7/2
*1. Education - Research - Methodology. 2. Education - Research - Case studies. 3. Case method. I. Merriam, Sharan B. Case study research in education. II. Title. III. Series: Jossey-Bass education series. IV. Series: Jossey-Bass higher and adult education series.*
*TC LB1028 .M396 1998*

**Merriam-Webster, Inc.**
Her heritage [computer file]. Cambridge, MA : Pilgrim New Media, c1994. Interactive multimedia.
*TC HQ1412 .A43 1994*

**Merrien, François-Xavier.**
Towards a new model of governance for universities? London ; Philadelphia : Jessica Kingsley, c1999.
*TC LC171 .T683 1999*

**Merrill, Barbara.** Gender, change and identity : : mature women students in universities / Barbara Merrill. Aldershot, Hants, England : Brookfield, Vt. : Ashgate, c1999, viii, 227 p. ; 23 cm. Includes bibliographical references (p. 211-224) and index. ISBN 1-84014-993-0
*1. Women - Education (Higher) - Great Britain. 2. Adult education of women - Great Britain. 3. Adult education of women - Social aspects - Great Britain. I. Title.*
*TC LC2046 .M477 1999*

**Merrill-Oldham, Jan, 1947-.**
Library storage facilities, management, and services. Washington, DC : Association of Research Libraries, Office of Leadership and Management Services, 1999.
*TC Z675.S75 L697 1999*

**Merriman, Scott A., 1968-.**
History.edu. Armonk, N.Y. ; London : M.E. Sharpe, c2001.
*TC D16.3 .H53 2001*

**Merrow report**
Education's big gamble [videorecording]. New York, NY : Merrow Report, c1997.
*TC LB2806.36 .E3 1997*

**Merton, Elda L.**
Brueckner, Leo J. Moving ahead in arithmetic. New York, N.Y. : Holt, Rinehart and Winston, 1963.
*TC QA107 .B78 1963*

Brueckner, Leo J. Moving ahead in arithmetic. New York, N.Y. : Holt, Rinehart and Winston, 1963.
*TC QA107 .B78 1963*

Brueckner, Leo J. Moving ahead in arithmetic. New York : Holt, Rinehart and Winston, 1963.
*TC QA107 .B78 1963*

Brueckner, Leo J. Moving ahead in arithmetic. New York : Holt, Rinehart and Winston, 1963.
*TC QA107 .B78 1963*

**MESMERISM.** *See* **HYPNOTISM.**

**MESO-AMERICA.** *See* **INDIANS OF MEXICO.**

**MESO-AMERICAN INDIANS.** *See* **INDIANS OF MEXICO.**

**MESOAMERICA.** *See* **INDIANS OF MEXICO.**

**MESOAMERICAN INDIANS.** *See* **INDIANS OF MEXICO.**

**The message within :** the role of subjective experience in social cognition and behavior / edited by Herbert Bless, Joseph P. Forgas. Philadelphia, Pa. : Psychology Press, 2000. xvi, 402 p. : ill. ; 24 cm. Includes bibliographical references and indexes. ISBN 1-84169-020-1 (case : alk. paper) ISBN 0-86377-690-6 (pbk. : alk. paper) DDC 153
*1. Subjectivity. 2. Cognition - Social aspects. 3. Social psychology. I. Bless, Herbert. II. Forgas, Joseph P.*
*TC BF697 .M457 2000*

**Messing, Lynn S.**
Gesture, speech, and sign. Oxford [England] ; New York : Oxford University Press, c1999.
*TC P117 .G469 1999*

**MESTIÇOS.** *See* **MESTIZOS.**

**MESTIZOS - BIOGRAPHY.**
Nash, Gary B. Forbidden love. 1st ed. New York : H. Holt, 1999.
*TC E184.M47 N47 1999*

**MESTIZOS - UNITED STATES - BIOGRAPHY.**
Nash, Gary B. Forbidden love. 1st ed. New York : H. Holt, 1999.
*TC E184.M47 N47 1999*

**MESTIZOS - UNITED STATES - HISTORY.**
Nash, Gary B. Forbidden love. 1st ed. New York : H. Holt, 1999.
*TC E184.M47 N47 1999*

**META-ANALYSIS.**
Contemporary special education research. Mahwah, N.J. : Lawrence Erlbaum, c2000.
*TC LC4019 .C575 2000*

**METABOLISM.**
Biochemical and physiological aspects of human nutrition. Philadelphia : W.B. Saunders, c1999.
*TC QP141 .B57 1999*

Exercise metabolism. Champaign, IL : Human Kinetics, c1995.
*TC QP301 .E967 1995*

Groff, James L. Advanced nutrition and human metabolism. 3rd ed. Belmont, CA : West/Wadsworth, c2000.
*TC QP141 .G76 2000*

The nutty, nougat-filled world of human nutrition [videorecording]. [Arlington, Va.] : Cerebellum Corp., c1998.
*TC QP141 .N8 1998*

Wildman, Robert E. C., 1964- Advanced human nutrition. Boca Raton : CRC Press, c2000.
*TC QP141 .W512 2000*

**METABOLISM - DISORDERS.** *See* **OBESITY.**

**METACOGNITION.**
Cava, Margaret T. Second language learner strategies and the unsuccessful second language writer. 1999.
*TC 085 C295*

Eddy, Jennifer B.K. Multiple intelligences, styles, and proficiency. 1999.
*TC 085 E10*

Felton, Mark Kenji. Metacognitive reflection and strategy development in argumentive discourse. 1999.
*TC 085 F34*

Schneider, Elke. Multisensory structured metacognitive instruction. Frankfurt am Main ; New York : P. Lang, c1999.
*TC P53.7 .S357 1999*

**Metacognitive reflection and strategy development in argumentive discourse.**
Felton, Mark Kenji. 1999.
*TC 085 F34*

**METAFICTION.** *See* **FICTION.**

**METAL PLATE PROCESSES (LITHOGRAPHY).** *See* **LITHOGRAPHY - METAL PLATE PROCESSES.**

**Metalinguistic activity in learning to write.**
Amsterdam : Amsterdam University Press, c2000. 228 p. ; 24 cm. (Studies in writing) Includes bibliographical references and indexes. ISBN 90-5356-341-5
*1. Composition (Language arts) - Study and teaching. I. CAMPS, ANNA.*
*TC PN181 .M48 2000*

**METAPHOR.**
Discourse and perspective in cognitive linguistics. Amsterdam ; Philadelphia : J. Benjamins, c1997.
*TC P165 .D57 1997*

Stepansky, Paul E. Freud, surgery, and the surgeons. Hillsdale, NJ : Analytic Press, 1999.
*TC RC506 .S733 1999*

Stepansky, Paul E. Freud, surgery, and the surgeons. Hillsdale, NJ : Analytic Press, 1999.
*TC RC506 .S733 1999*

**Metaphor and emotion.**
Kövecses, Zoltán. Cambridge ; New York : Cambridge University Press ; Paris : Editions de la Maison des Sciences de l'Homme, 2000.
*TC BF582 .K68 2000*

**METAPHYSICS.** *See* **COSMOLOGY; GOD; KNOWLEDGE, THEORY OF; PHILOSOPHY OF MIND; VALUES.**

**Metarepresentations :** a multidisciplinary perspective / edited by Dan Sperber. Oxford ; New York : Oxford University Press, c2000. 448 p. : ill. ; 24 cm. (Vancouver studies in cognitive science ; v. 10) Includes bibliographical references. ISBN 0-19-514114-8 ISBN 0-19-514115-6 (pbk.)
*1. Mental representation - Congresses. 2. Thought and thinking - Congresses. 3. Cognitive science - Congresses. I. Sperber, Dan. II. Series.*
*TC BF316.6 .M48 2000*

**Metcalfe, Jean D. LeDrew.**
Jocelin, Elizabeth, 1596-1622. The mothers legacy to her vnborn [i.e. unborn] childe [i.e. child]. Toronto : University of Toronto Press, 2000.
*TC BV4570 .J62 2000*

**METEOROLOGY.** *See* **CLOUDS; SEASONS.**

**METHOD OF STUDY.** *See* **STUDY SKILLS.**

**METHOD OF WORK.** *See* **WORK.**

**Methoden der empirischen Sozialforschung.**
Atteslander, Peter M., 1926- Berlin : De Gruyter, 1969.
*TC H62 .A8*

**METHODIST CHURCH - ZIMBABWE - HISTORY.**
Ranger, T. O. (Terence O.) Are we not also men? Harare : Baobab ; Portsmouth, NH : Heinemann, 1995.
*TC DT2974 .R36 1995*

**METHODOLOGY.** *See* **PROBLEM SOLVING; RESEARCH.**

**Methods for studying language production** / edited by Lise Menn, Nan Bernstein Ratner. Mahwah, N.J. : Lawrence Erlbaum Associates, 2000. vi, 438 p. : ill. ; 23 cm. Includes bibliographical references and index. ISBN 0-8058-3033-2 (c : alk. paper) ISBN 0-8058-3034-0 (p : alk. paper) DDC 401/.43/072
*1. Language acquisition - Research - Methodology. 2.*

*Language disorders - Research - Methodology. I. Menn, Lise. II. Ratner, Nan Bernstein.*
*TC P118 .M47 2000*

**Methods in nursing research**
(v. 1) Roper, Janice M. Ethnography in nursing research. Thousand Oaks, Calif. : Sage Publications, c2000.
*TC RT81.5 .R66 2000*

**Methods that matter.**
Daniels, Harvey, 1947- York, Me. : Stenhouse Publishers, c1998.
*TC LB1027 .D24 1998*

**The metrics of science and technology.**
Geisler, Eliezer, 1942- Westport, Conn. : Quorum Books, 2000.
*TC Q175.5 .G43 2000*

**METROPOLITAN AREAS.** *See* **SUBURBS; URBAN RENEWAL.**

**METROPOLITAN AREAS - UNITED STATES.**
Stanback, Thomas M. Cities in transition. Totowa, N.J. : Allanheld, Osmun, 1982.
*TC HD5724 .S649 1982*

**METROPOLITAN AREAS - UNITED STATES - HISTORY - CASE STUDIES.**
Abu-Lughod, Janet L. New York, Chicago, Los Angeles. Minneapolis : University of Minnesota Press, c1999.
*TC HT123 .A613 1999*

**METROPOLITAN GOVERNMENT.** *See* **STATE-LOCAL RELATIONS.**

**Metropolitan Museum of Art (New York, N.Y.).**
Cikovsky, Nicolai. Winslow Homer. Washington, D.C. : National Gallery of Art, 1995.
*TC N6537.H58 A4 1995*

Ingres, Jean-Auguste-Dominique, 1780-1867. Portraits by Ingres. New York : Metropolitan Museum of Art : Distributed by Harry N. Abrams, c1999.
*TC ND1329.I53 A4 1999*

Tinterow, Gary. Origins of impressionism. New York : Metropolitan Museum of Art : Distributed by H.N. Abrams, c1994.
*TC ND547.5.I4 L6913 1994*

**Metz, Nancy Davis.**
Student development in college unions and student activities. Bloomington, Ind. : Association of College Unions-International, c1996.
*TC LB2343.4 .S84 1996*

**Metzger, Jan.**
Brownell, Gregg. A PC for the teacher. Belmont, CA : Wadsworth Pub. Co., c1999.
*TC LB1028.43 .B755 1999*

**Metzler, Michael W., 1952-** Instructional models for physical education / Michael W. Metzler. Boston : Allyn and Bacon, c2000. xxviii, 388 p. : ill. ; 24 cm. Includes bibliographical references and index. ISBN 0-205-26418-2 DDC 613.7/071/073
*1. Physical education and training - Study and teaching - United States. 2. Physical education teachers - Training of - United States. I. Title.*
*TC GV363 .M425 2000*

**Metzner, Ralph.** Green psychology : transforming our relationship to the earth / Ralph Metzner. Rochester, Vt. : Park Street Press, c1999. x, 229 p. : ill. ; 23 cm. Includes bibliographical references (p. 214-221) and index. ISBN 0-89281-798-4 (alk. paper) DDC 155.9/1
*1. Nature - Psychological aspects. 2. Environmental psychology. 3. Environmentalism - Psychological aspects. 4. Human ecology - Religious aspects. 5. Psychology and religion. I. Title.*
*TC BF353.5.N37 M47 1999*

**MEXICAN AMERICAN YOUTH - EDUCATION - MIDDLE WEST - CASE STUDIES.**
MacGregor-Mendoza, Patricia, 1963- Spanish and academic achievement among Midwest Mexican youth. New York ; London : Garland Pub., 1999.
*TC LC2686.4 .M33 1999*

**MEXICAN AMERICAN YOUTH - SOCIAL CONDITIONS - TEXAS - CASE STUDIES.**
Valenzuela, Angela. Subtractive schooling. Albany : State University of New York Press, c1999.
*TC LC2683.4 .V35 1999*

**MEXICAN AMERICANS - ARIZONA - CLIFTON - HISTORY - 20TH CENTURY.**
Gordon, Linda. The great Arizona orphan abduction. Cambridge, Mass. : Harvard University Press, 1999.
*TC F819.C55 G67 1999*

**MEXICAN AMERICANS - EDUCATION (SECONDARY) - TEXAS - CASE STUDIES.**
Valenzuela, Angela. Subtractive schooling. Albany : State University of New York Press, c1999.
*TC LC2683.4 .V35 1999*

**MEXICAN AMERICANS - EDUCATION - TEXAS - CRYSTAL CITY.**
Trujillo, Armando L. Chicano empowerment and bilingual education. New York : Garland Pub., c1998.
*TC LC2688.C79 T78 1998*

**MEXICAN AMERICANS - FICTION.**
Mora, Pat. The rainbow tulip. New York : Viking, 1999.
*TC PZ7.M78819 Rai 1999*

**MEXICAN AMERICANS - JUVENILE FICTION.**
Mora, Pat. The rainbow tulip. New York : Viking, 1999.
*TC PZ7.M78819 Rai 1999*

**MEXICAN AMERICANS - TEXAS - CRYSTAL CITY - POLITICS AND GOVERNMENT.**
Trujillo, Armando L. Chicano empowerment and bilingual education. New York : Garland Pub., c1998.
*TC LC2688.C79 T78 1998*

**MEXICAN AMERICANS - UNITED STATES.** *See* MEXICAN AMERICANS.

**MEXICAN-STYLE RIDERS.** *See* CHARROS.

**MEXICO - ECONOMIC POLICY.**
Llinás Alvarez, Edgar. Vida y obra de Ramón Beteta. 1. ed. México : [s.n.], 1996 (México, D.F. : Impresora Galve)
*TC F1234.B56 L5 1996*

**MEXICO - FICTION.**
Madrigal, Antonio Hernández. Erandi's braids. New York : Putnam's, c1999.
*TC PZ7.M26575 Er 1999*

**MEXICO - HISTORY - 19TH CENTURY.**
Thomson, Guy P. C., 1949- Patriotism, politics, and popular liberalism in nineteenth-century Mexico. Wilmington, De. : Scholarly Resources, 1999.
*TC F1326.L83 T5 1999*

**MEXICO - HISTORY - REVOLUTION, 1910-1920 - FICTION.**
Guevara-Vázquez, Fabián. El indigena en la novela de la Revolucion Mexicana. 1999.
*TC 085 G934*

**MEXICO - LANGUAGES.** *See* MAYA LANGUAGE.

**MEXICO - LITERATURES.**
Guevara-Vázquez, Fabián. El indigena en la novela de la Revolucion Mexicana. 1999.
*TC 085 G934*

**MEXICO - POLITICS AND GOVERNMENT - 1910-1946.**
Llinás Alvarez, Edgar. Vida y obra de Ramón Beteta. 1. ed. México : [s.n.], 1996 (México, D.F. : Impresora Galve)
*TC F1234.B56 L5 1996*

**MEXICO - POLITICS AND GOVERNMENT - 1946-1970.**
Llinás Alvarez, Edgar. Vida y obra de Ramón Beteta. 1. ed. México : [s.n.], 1996 (México, D.F. : Impresora Galve)
*TC F1234.B56 L5 1996*

**MEXICO - SOCIAL LIFE AND CUSTOMS.**
Ancona, George. Charro. 1st ed. San Diego : Harcourt Brace, c1999.
*TC F1210 .A747 1999*

Diamant, Gertrude, 1901- The days of Ofelia. Boston, Houghton Mifflin company, 1942.
*TC F1210 .D5*

**MEXICO - SOCIAL LIFE AND CUSTOMS - JUVENILE LITERATURE.**
Ancona, George. Charro. 1st ed. San Diego : Harcourt Brace, c1999.
*TC F1210 .A747 1999*

**MEXQUITIC (MEXICO) - RURAL CONDITIONS.**
Behar, Ruth, 1956- Translated woman. Boston : Beacon Press, c1993.
*TC HQ1465.M63 B44 1993*

**Meyen, Edward L.**
Special education & student disability. 4th ed. Denver, Colo. : Love Pub. Co., c1995.
*TC LC3965 .E87 1995*

**Meyer, Aleta Lynn.**
Promoting nonviolence in early adolescence. New York : Kluwer Academic/Plenum Publishers, c2000.

*TC HM1126 .P76 2000*

**Meyer, Jack A., 1944-.**
Meeting human needs, toward a new public philosophy. Washington : American Enterprise Institute for Public Policy Research, c1982.
*TC HD60.5.U5 M427 1982*

**Meyer, Karl Ernest.** The art museum : power, money, ethics : a Twentieth Century Fund report / by Karl E. Meyer. 1st ed. New York : Morrow, 1979. 352 p. : ill. ; 24 cm. Includes bibliographical references ([334-344) and index. ISBN 0-688-03390-3 DDC 069/.9/7
*1. Art museums - United States. I. Twentieth Century Fund. II. Title.*
*TC N510 .M47*

**Meyer, Luanna H.**
Behavioral intervention. Baltimore, Md. : Paul H. Brookes Pub., c1999.
*TC BF637.B4 B452 1999*

**Meyer, Robert G.**
Kronenberger, William G. Child clinician's handbook. 2nd ed. Boston : Allyn and Bacon, c2001.
*TC RJ499.3 .K76 2001*

**Mfantsipim and the making of Ghana.**
Boahen, A. Adu. Accra, Ghana : Sankofa Educational Publishers, c1996.
*TC LG497.M42 B62 1996*

**MFANTSIPIM SCHOOL - HISTORY.**
Boahen, A. Adu. Mfantsipim and the making of Ghana. Accra, Ghana : Sankofa Educational Publishers, c1996.
*TC LG497.M42 B62 1996*

**M.H. DE YOUNG MEMORIAL MUSEUM - HISTORY - JUVENILE FICTION.**
Frank, Phil. The ghost of the de Young Museum. [San Francisco : Fine Arts Museums of San Francisco, 1995]
*TC N739.5 .F72 1995*

**M.H. DE YOUNG MEMORIAL MUSEUM - JUVENILE FICTION.**
Frank, Phil. The ghost of the de Young Museum. [San Francisco : Fine Arts Museums of San Francisco, 1995]
*TC N739.5 .F72 1995*

**Miall, Hugh.** Contemporary conflict resolution : the prevention, management and transformation of deadly conflicts / Hugh Miall, Oliver Ramsbotham, Tom Woodhouse. Cambridge, UK : Polity Press ; Malden, MA : Blackwell, 1999. xviii, 270 p. : ill. ; maps ; 24 cm. Includes bibliographical references (p. [226]-263) and index. ISBN 0-7456-2034-5 (hb) ISBN 0-7456-2035-3 (pb) DDC 327.1/7
*1. Pacific settlement of international disputes. 2. Conflict management. 3. Peace. I. Ramsbotham, Oliver. II. Woodhouse, Tom. III. Title.*
*TC JZ6010 .M53 1999*

**MICE - FICTION.**
Brooks, Nigel. Town mouse house. New York : Walker & Co., c2000.
*TC PZ7.B7977 To 2000*

McBratney, Sam. The dark at the top of the stairs. 1st U.S. ed. Cambridge, Mass. : Candlewick Press, c1996.
*TC PZ7.M47826 DAr 1996*

McCully, Emily Arnold. Mouse practice. 1st ed. New York : Arthur A. Levine Books/Scholastic Press, 1999.
*TC PZ7.M13913 Mo 1999*

Sathre, Vivian. Three kind mice. 1st ed. San Diego : Harcourt Brace, c1997.
*TC PZ8.3.S238 Th 1997*

Vincent, Gabrielle. [Ernest et Célestine chez le photographe. English] Smile, Ernest and Celestine. 1st American ed. New York : Greenwillow Books, c1982.
*TC PZ7.V744 Sm 1982*

Yolen, Jane. Mouse's birthday. New York : Putnam's, c1993.
*TC PZ8.3.Y76 Mo 1993*

**Michael Camerini, Inc.**
The frescoes of Diego Rivera [videorecording]. [Detroit, Mich.] : Founders Society, Detroit Institute of Arts ; [Chicago, Ill.?] : Home Vision [distributor], c1986.
*TC ND259.R5 F6 1986*

**Michel, Patrick.** Using action research for school restructuring and organizational change / by Patrick Michel. 2000. vi, 164 leaves : ill. ; 29 cm. Includes tables. Issued also on microfilm. Thesis (Ed.D.) -- Teachers College, Columbia University, 2000. Includes bibliographical references

(leaves 148-161).
*1. Information technology - Social aspects. 2. Educational innovations - United States. 3. Action research in education. 4. School improvement programs - United States. 5. School management and organization - United States. 6. Educational change - United States. 7. Organizational change. 8. Public schools - United States - History. 9. Education - United States. 10. Information society. I. Title.*
*TC 06 no. 11295*

Using action research for school restructuring and organizational change / by Patrick Michel. 2000. vi, 164 leaves : ill. ; 29 cm. Includes tables. Issued also on microfilm. Thesis (Ed.D.) -- Teachers College, Columbia University, 2000. Includes bibliographical references (leaves 148-161)
*1. Information technology - Social aspects. 2. Action research in education. 3. School management and organization. 4. Educational change - United States. 5. Organizational change. 6. Public schools - NBusiness management. I. Title.*
*TC 06 no. 11295*

**Michel, Sonya, 1942-** Children's interests/mothers' rights : the shaping of America's child care policy / Sonya Michel. New Haven, CT : Yale University Press, c1999. xii, 410 p. : ill. ; 24 cm. Includes bibliographical references and index. ISBN 0-300-05951-5 (alk. paper) DDC 362.71/2/0973
*1. Child care - Government policy - United States - History. 2. Child care services - United States - History. I. Title.*
*TC HQ778.63 .M52 1999*

**Michelson, Richard.** A book of flies / by Richard Michelson ; illustrated by Leonard Baskin. New York : Cavendish Children's Books, 1999. 1v. (unpaged) : col. ill. ; 22 cm. SUMMARY: Humorous poems about different kinds of flies are accompanied by factual information about these creatures. ISBN 0-7614-5050-5 DDC 811/.54
*1. Flies - Juvenile poetry. 2. Children's poetry, American. 3. Flies - Poetry. 4. American poetry. I. Baskin, Leonard, 1922- ill. II. Title.*
*TC PS3563.I34 B66 1999*

Grandpa's gamble / Richard Michelson. New York : Marshall Cavendish, 1999. 1v. (unpaged) : col. ill. ; 26 cm. SUMMARY: When Grandpa tells a boy and his sister why he prays so much they stop thinking that he is just a boring old man. ISBN 0-7614-5034-3 DDC [Fic]
*1. Grandfathers - Fiction. 2. Jews - United States - Fiction. 3. Immigrants - Fiction. 4. Prayer - Fiction. I. Title.*
*TC PZ7.M581915 Gr 1999*

**Michigan Social Studies Education Project.**
Reforming the Electoral College [videorecording]. [Boulder, Colo.? : Social Science Education Consortium?], c1996.
*TC H62.5.U5 R4 1996*

**Mickelson, Roslyn Arlin, 1948-.**
Children on the streets of the Americas. London ; New York : Routledge, 2000.
*TC HV887.B8 C475 2000*

**Micklethwait, David.** Noah Webster and the American dictionary / David Micklethwait. Jefferson, N.C. : McFarland, c2000. vii, 350 p. : ill. ; 26 cm. Includes bibliographical references (p. 309-314) and index. ISBN 0-7864-0640-2 (library binding : alk. paper) DDC 423/.092
*1. Webster, Noah - 1758-1843. 2. Webster, Noah, - 1758-1843. - American dictionary of the English language. 3. Encyclopedias and dictionaries - History and criticism. 4. English language - United States - Lexicography - History. 5. English language - Lexicography - History. 6. Lexicographers - United States - Biography. 7. Educators - United States - Biography. I. Title.*
*TC PE65.W5 M53 2000*

**Micklethwait, Lucy.** A child's book of art : discover great paintings / Lucy Micklethwait. 1st American ed. New York : DK Pub., c1999. 31 p. : ill. ; 33 cm. Originally published: London ; New York : Dorling Kindersley, 1993. Includes index. SUMMARY: Invites the reader to take a closer look at paintings by such artists as Botticelli, Bruegel, Velasquez, Copley, and Van Gogh, providing information about the artist, subject, and medium of each work of art. ISBN 0-7894-4283-3 DDC 701/.1
*1. Art appreciation - Juvenile literature. 2. Art appreciation. I. Title.*
*TC N7477 .M53 1999*

**MICRO COMPUTERS.** *See* MICROCOMPUTERS.

**MICROBES.** *See* BACTERIA.

**Microcomputer abstracts.**
Internet & personal computing abstracts. Medford, N.J. : Information Today, Inc., c2000-
*TC QA75.5 .M5*

**MICROCOMPUTER-AIDED INSTRUCTION.** *See*
  **COMPUTER-ASSISTED INSTRUCTION.**

**MICROCOMPUTER-ASSISTED INSTRUCTION.**
  *See* **COMPUTER-ASSISTED INSTRUCTION.**

**MICROCOMPUTER-ASSISTED LEARNING.** *See*
  **COMPUTER-ASSISTED INSTRUCTION.**

**MICROCOMPUTER-BASED INSTRUCTION.** *See*
  **COMPUTER-ASSISTED INSTRUCTION.**

**MICROCOMPUTER USES IN EDUCATION.** *See*
  **EDUCATION - DATA PROCESSING.**

**MICROCOMPUTERS.**
  Barnicle, Katherine Ann. Evaluation of the interaction
  between users of screen reading technology and
  graphical user interface elements. 1999.
  *TC 085 B265*

  Brownell, Gregg. A PC for the teacher. Belmont, CA :
  Wadsworth Pub. Co., c1999.
  *TC LB1028.43 .B755 1999*

**MICROCOMPUTERS - ABSTRACTS -**
  **PERIODICALS.**
  Internet & personal computing abstracts. Medford,
  N.J. : Information Today, Inc., c2000-
  *TC QA75.5 .M5*

**MICROCOMPUTERS IN EDUCATION.** *See*
  **EDUCATION - DATA PROCESSING.**

**MICROCOMPUTERS - INDEXES -**
  **PERIODICALS.**
  Internet & personal computing abstracts. Medford,
  N.J. : Information Today, Inc., c2000-
  *TC QA75.5 .M5*

**MICROCOMPUTERS - STUDY AND TEACHING.**
  Geisert, Paul. Teachers, computers, and curriculum.
  3rd ed. Boston : Allyn and Bacon, c2000.
  *TC LB1028.5 .G42 2000*

**MICROENTERPRISES.** *See* **SMALL BUSINESS.**

**A microgenetic study of science reasoning in social
  context.**
  Andersen, Christopher Lawrence. 1998.
  *TC 085 An2305*

**MICROHABITAT.** *See* **NICHE (ECOLOGY).**

**Micronutrients.**
  The nutty, nougat-filled world of human nutrition
  [videorecording]. [Arlington, Va.] : Cerebellum Corp.,
  c1998.
  *TC QP141 .N8 1998*

**MICROORGANISMS.** *See* **VIRUSES.**

**MICROS (MICROCOMPUTERS).** *See*
  **MICROCOMPUTERS.**

**MICROSOFT ACCESS.**
  Balter, Alison. [Mastering Access 97 development]
  Alison Balter's Mastering Access 97 development.
  2nd ed. Indianapolis, Ind. : Sams Pub., [c1997]
  *TC QA76.9.D3 B32 1997*

**Microsoft Corporation.**
  Microsoft encarta Africana [computer file]. Redmond,
  WA : Microsoft Corp., c1999. Computer data and
  programs.
  *TC DT14 .M527 1999*

  Microsoft encarta Africana [computer file]. Redmond,
  WA : Microsoft Corp., c1999. Computer data and
  programs.
  *TC DT3 .M53 1999x*

**Microsoft encarta Africana** [computer file] / edited by
  Kwame Anthony Appiah and Henry Louis Gates, Jr.
  Redmond, WA : Microsoft Corp., c1999. Computer
  data and programs. 2 computer optical discs : sd., col. ; 4 3/
  4 in. + guide (4 p.). System requirements: Multimedia PC
  with a 486DX/66 MHz or higher microprocessor (Pentium
  recommended) ; Microsoft Windows 95, 98, or NT version 4.0
  or later ; 16 MB of RAM for Windows 95, 24 MB of RAM for
  Windows 98 or NT ; 30 MB of available hard-disk space ; 2X
  speed or faster CD-ROM drive ; super VGA, 256 or higher-
  color monitor supporting 640x480 or higher resolution ; local
  bus video with 1 MB or more of VRAM ; sound card with
  speakers or headphones. SUMMARY: A multimedia
  encyclopedia with more than 3000 articles, 2500 videos, audio
  clips, maps and photographs, and an interactive timeline of
  Africans and people of African descent. "Comprehensive
  encyclopedia of Black history and culture"--Disc label. Source
  of title: title screen. [Copyright] "Brooklyn Museum of Art,
  1999." On title screen "[copyright]" appears as the copyright
  symbol. Accompanying guide contains installation instructions.
  Issued in box. "0998 part no. X03-88553"--Container. ISBN
  0-7356-0057-0
  *1. Africa - Civilization - Encyclopedias. 2. Afro-Americans -
  Encyclopedias. 3. Civilization, Western - African influences -*

**Encyclopedias.** *I. Appiah, Anthony. II. Gates, Henry Louis. III.
  Brooklyn Museum of Art. IV. Microsoft Corporation. V. Title:
  Encarta Africana*
  *TC DT14 .M527 1999*

**Microsoft encarta Africana** [computer file] / edited by
  Kwame Anthony Appiah and Henry Louis Gates, Jr.
  Redmond, WA : Microsoft Corp., c1999. Computer
  data and programs. 2 computer optical discs : sd., col. ; 4 3/
  4 in. + guide (4 p.). System requirements: Multimedia PC with
  a 486DX/66 MHz or higher microprocessor (Pentium
  recommended) ; Microsoft Windows 95, 98, or NT version 4.0
  or later ; 16 MB of RAM for Windows 95, 24 MB of RAM for
  Windows 98 or NT ; 30 MB of available hard-disk space ; 2X
  speed or faster CD-ROM drive ; super VGA, 256 or higher-
  color monitor supporting 640x480 or higher resolution ; local
  bus video with 1 MB or more of VRAM ; sound card with
  speakers or headphones. SUMMARY: A multimedia
  encyclopedia with more than 3000 articles, 2500 videos, audio
  clips, maps and photographs, and an interactive timeline of
  Africans and people of African descent. "Comprehensive
  encyclopedia of Black history and culture"--Disc label. Source
  of title: title screen. [Copyright] "Brooklyn Museum of Art,
  1999." On title screen "[copyright]" appears as the copyright
  symbol. Accompanying guide contains installation instructions.
  Issued in box. "0998 part no. X03-88553"--Container. ISBN
  0-7356-0057-0
  *1. Africa - Civilization - Encyclopedias. 2. Afro-Americans -
  Encyclopedias. 3. Civilization, Western - African influences -
  Encyclopedias. I. Appiah, Anthony. II. Gates, Henry Louis. III.
  Brooklyn Museum of Art. IV. Microsoft Corporation. V. Title:
  Encarta Africana*
  *TC DT3 .M53 1999x*

**MICROSOFT POWERPOINT (COMPUTER
  FILE).**
  Idzal, June M. Multimedia authoring tools and teacher
  training. 1997.
  *TC 06 no. 10816*

**Microsoft Project 2000 120-day trial edition /.**
  MORRISON, GARY R. Designing effective
  instruction. 3rd ed. New York : John Wiley, c2001.
  *TC LB1028.38 .K46 2001*

**MICROSOFT WINDOWS (COMPUTER FILE).**
  Balter, Alison. [Mastering Access 97 development]
  Alison Balter's Mastering Access 97 development.
  2nd ed. Indianapolis, Ind. : Sams Pub., [c1997]
  *TC QA76.9.D3 B32 1997*

  Unix and Windows 2000 handbook. Upper Saddle
  River, NJ : Prentice Hall, 2000.
  *TC QA76.76.O63 U58 2000*

**Miczek, Klaus A.**
  Understanding and preventing violence. Washington,
  D.C. : National Academy Press, 1993-1994.
  *TC HN90.V5 U53 1993*

**MID-CAREER CHANGES.** *See* **CAREER
  CHANGES.**

**MID-LIFE CAREER CHANGES.** *See* **CAREER
  CHANGES.**

**Mid Term Conference of Heads of Universities (4th :
  1997 : Chulalongkorn University).**
  The universities' responsibilities to society. 1st ed.
  New York : Pergamon, published for the IAU Press,
  2000.
  *TC LC191.9 .U55 2000*

**MIDAS (LEGENDARY CHARACTER).**
  Mark, Jan. The Midas touch. 1st U.S. ed. Cambridge,
  MA : Candlewick Press, 1999.
  *TC BL820.M55 M33 1999*

**MIDAS (LEGENDARY CHARACTER) -
  JUVENILE LITERATURE.**
  Mark, Jan. The Midas touch. 1st U.S. ed. Cambridge,
  MA : Candlewick Press, 1999.
  *TC BL820.M55 M33 1999*

**The Midas touch.**
  Mark, Jan. 1st U.S. ed. Cambridge, MA : Candlewick
  Press, 1999.
  *TC BL820.M55 M33 1999*

**Middaugh, Michael F., 1945-.**
  Analyzing costs in higher education. San Francisco,
  Calif. : Jossey-Bass Publishers, c2000.
  *TC LB2342 .A68 2000*

**MIDDLE AGE.** *See* **AGING.**

**MIDDLE AGE - UNITED STATES.**
  Wise women. New York ; London : Routledge, 2000.
  *TC LB2837 .W58 2000*

**MIDDLE AGES.** *See* **CIVILIZATION,
  MEDIEVAL.**

**MIDDLE AGES - CIVILIZATION.** *See*
  **CIVILIZATION, MEDIEVAL.**

**MIDDLE AGES - HISTORY - JUVENILE
  LITERATURE.**
  Honan, Linda. Picture the Middle Ages. Amawalk,
  N.Y. : Golden Owl Pub. Co. : Higgins Armory
  Museum, c1994.
  *TC CB351 .H58 1994*

**MIDDLE AGES IN LITERATURE.**
  Barnhouse, Rebecca. Recasting the past. Portsmouth,
  NH : Boynton/Cook Publishers, c2000.
  *TC PN3443 .B37 2000*

**MIDDLE AGES IN LITERATURE - STUDY AND
  TEACHING.**
  Barnhouse, Rebecca. Recasting the past. Portsmouth,
  NH : Boynton/Cook Publishers, c2000.
  *TC PN3443 .B37 2000*

**MIDDLE AGES - STUDY AND TEACHING
  (ELEMENTARY).**
  Honan, Linda. Picture the Middle Ages. Amawalk,
  N.Y. : Golden Owl Pub. Co. : Higgins Armory
  Museum, c1994.
  *TC CB351 .H58 1994*

**MIDDLE CLASS - ALABAMA - BIRMINGHAM -
  HISTORY.**
  Feldman, Lynne B. A sense of place. Tuscaloosa,
  Ala. ; London : University of Alabama Press, c1999.
  *TC F334.B69 N437 1999*

**MIDDLE CLASS - GERMANY - FRANKFURT AM
  MAIN - HISTORY - 19TH CENTURY.**
  Palmowski, Jan. Urban liberalism in imperial
  Germany. Oxford ; New York : Oxford University
  Press, 1999.
  *TC DD901.F78 P35 1999*

**MIDDLE CLASS - NEW ENGLAND - HISTORY.**
  Kelly, Catherine E. In the New England fashion.
  Ithaca, N.Y. : Cornell University Press, 1999.
  *TC HQ1438.N35 K45 1999*

**MIDDLE CLASS - SOCIAL CONDITIONS.** *See*
  **MIDDLE CLASS.**

**MIDDLE CLASS WOMEN - EDUCATION
  (SECONDARY) - UNITED STATES.**
  Proweller, Amira. Constructing female identities.
  Albany : State University of New York Press, c1998.
  *TC LC1755 .P76 1998*

**MIDDLE CLASSES.** *See* **MIDDLE CLASS.**

**MIDDLE EAST - SOCIAL POLICY.**
  Shukri, Shirin J. A. Social changes and women in the
  Middle East. Aldershot ; Brookfield, Vt. : Ashgate,
  c1999.
  *TC HQ1726.5 .S58 1999*

**MIDDLE MANAGERS.**
  Understanding the work and career paths of midlevel
  administrators. San Francisco : Jossey-Bass, 2000.
  *TC LB2341 .N5111 2000*

**A middle mosaic :** a celebration of reading, writing, and
  reflective practice at the middle level / edited by
  Elizabeth Close, Katherine D. Ramsey. Urbana, Ill. :
  National Council of Teachers of English, c2000. viii,
  130 p. : ill. ; 27 cm. "NCTE stock number: 00341-3050"--T.p.
  verso. Includes bibliographical references. ISBN 0-8141-
  0034-1 DDC 428/.0071/2
  *1. Language arts (Secondary) - United States - Congresses. 2.
  English language - Study and teaching (Secondary) - United
  States - Congresses. 3. English language - United States -
  Composition and exercises - Congresses. 4. Reflection
  (Philosophy) - Congresses. I. Close, Elizabeth, 1941- II.
  Ramsey, Katherine D., 1944- III. Title: Celebration of reading,
  writing, and reflective practice at the middle level*
  *TC LB1631 .A2 2000*

**MIDDLE SCHOOL EDUCATION - NEW YORK
  (STATE) - CURRICULA.**
  Mahammad, Hasna. Multicultural education. 1998.
  *TC 06 no. 11033*

**MIDDLE SCHOOL EDUCATION - UNITED
  STATES.**
  Snodgrass, Dawn M., 1955- Collaborative learning in
  middle and secondary schools. Larchmont, N.Y. : Eye
  On Education, 2000.
  *TC LB1032 .S62 2000*

**MIDDLE SCHOOL EDUCATION - UNITED
  STATES - CURRICULA.**
  Art works!. Portsmouth, NH : Heinemann, c1999.
  *TC LB1628.5 .A78 1999*

  Queen, J. Allen. Curriculum practice in the
  elementary and middle school. Upper Saddle River,
  N.J. : Merrill, c1999.

*TC LB1570 .Q45 1999*

Rasool, Joan. Multicultural education in middle and secondary classrooms. Belmont, CA : Wadsworth, c2000.
*TC LC1099.3 .R38 2000*

**Middle-school Mathematics through Applications Project.**
Environmental justice. Menlo Park, Calif. : Institute for Research on Learning, c1998.
*TC QA135.5 .E68 1998*

Guppies. Menlo Park, Calif. : Institute for Research on Learning, c1997.
*TC QA135.5 .G86 1997*

Wolves and caribou unit. Menlo Park, Calif. : Institute for Research on Learning, 1998, c1995.
*TC QA135.5 .W64 1995*

**MIDDLE SCHOOL PRINCIPALS - UNITED STATES.**
Powerful middle schools : teaching and learning for young adolescents (2000) Powerful middle schools [videorecording]. [Washington, D.C.?] : U.S. Dept. of Education, [2000].
*TC LB1623 .P6 2000*

**MIDDLE SCHOOL STUDENTS - COUNSELING OF.** *See* **COUNSELING IN MIDDLE SCHOOL EDUCATION.**

**MIDDLE SCHOOL STUDENTS - JAPAN - CONDUCT OF LIFE - CASE STUDIES.**
LeTendre, Gerald K. Learning to be adolescent. New Haven [Conn.] ; London : Yale University Press, c2000.
*TC LB1135 .L47 2000*

**MIDDLE SCHOOL STUDENTS - NEW YORK (STATE) - NEW YORK - ATTITUDES.**
Tsamasiros, Katherine V. Using interactive multimedia software to improve cognition of complex imagery in adolescents. 1998.
*TC 06 no. 10905*

**MIDDLE SCHOOL STUDENTS - NEW YORK (STATE) - SOCIAL ASPECTS.**
Schlanger, Dean J. An exploration of school belongingness. 1998.
*TC 06 no. 10993*

**MIDDLE SCHOOL STUDENTS - UNITED STATES.**
Powerful middle schools : teaching and learning for young adolescents (2000) Powerful middle schools [videorecording]. [Washington, D.C.?] : U.S. Dept. of Education, [2000].
*TC LB1623 .P6 2000*

**MIDDLE SCHOOL STUDENTS - UNITED STATES - CONDUCT OF LIFE - CASE STUDIES.**
LeTendre, Gerald K. Learning to be adolescent. New Haven [Conn.] ; London : Yale University Press, c2000.
*TC LB1135 .L47 2000*

**MIDDLE SCHOOL TEACHERS - ATTITUDES.**
Rutter, Alison Lee. Professional growth of two multidisciplinary teams within a professional development school. 1999.
*TC 06 no. 11171*

**MIDDLE SCHOOL TEACHERS - IN-SERVICE TRAINING.**
Rutter, Alison Lee. Professional growth of two multidisciplinary teams within a professional development school. 1999.
*TC 06 no. 11171*

**MIDDLE SCHOOL TEACHERS - IN-SERVICE TRAINING - NEW YORK (STATE).**
Mahammad, Hasna. Multicultural education. 1998.
*TC 06 no. 11033*

**MIDDLE SCHOOL TEACHERS - NEW YORK (STATE) - ATTITUDES.**
Mahammad, Hasna. Multicultural education. 1998.
*TC 06 no. 11033*

**MIDDLE SCHOOL TEACHERS - TRAINING OF - UNITED STATES.**
Practicing what we preach. New York : Falmer Press, 1999.
*TC LB1735.5 .P73 1999*

**MIDDLE SCHOOL TEACHERS - UNITED STATES.**
Powerful middle schools : teaching and learning for young adolescents (2000) Powerful middle schools [videorecording]. [Washington, D.C.?] : U.S. Dept. of Education, [2000].

*TC LB1623 .P6 2000*

**MIDDLE SCHOOL TEACHERS - UNITED STATES - CASE STUDIES.**
Siskind, Theresa Gayle, 1951- Cases for middle school educators. Lanham, Md. ; London : Scarecrow Press, 2000.
*TC LB1623.5 .S57 2000*

**MIDDLE SCHOOL TEACHING.**
Clark, Leonard H. Secondary and middle school teaching methods. 7th ed. Englewood Cliffs, N.J. : Merrill, c1996.
*TC LB1737.A3 C53 1996*

**MIDDLE SCHOOL TEACHING - UNITED STATES - HANDBOOKS, MANUALS, ETC.**
Kingen, Sharon. Teaching language arts in middle schools. Mahwah, NJ : Lawrence Erlbaum, 2000.
*TC LB1631 .K493 2000*

**MIDDLE SCHOOLS.** *See* **COUNSELING IN MIDDLE SCHOOL EDUCATION; ELEMENTARY SCHOOLS; JUNIOR HIGH SCHOOLS.**

**MIDDLE SCHOOLS - DATA PROCESSING - HANDBOOKS, MANUALS, ETC.**
Gardner, Paul (Paul Henry) Managing technology in the middle school classroom. Huntington Beach, CA : Teacher Created Materials, c1996.
*TC LB1028.5 .C353 1996*

**MIDDLE SCHOOLS - JAPAN - CASE STUDIES.**
Whitman, Nancy C. A case study of Japanese middle schools, 1983-1998. Lanham, Md. ; Oxford : University Press of America, c2000.
*TC LA1316 .W45 2000*

**MIDDLE SCHOOLS - NEW YORK (STATE) - CURRICULA - CASE STUDIES.**
Carr, Richard John. The application of multimedia in arts-integrated curricula. 1998.
*TC 06 no. 10919*

**MIDDLE SCHOOLS - UNITED STATES.**
Powerful middle schools : teaching and learning for young adolescents (2000) Powerful middle schools [videorecording]. [Washington, D.C.?] : U.S. Dept. of Education, [2000].
*TC LB1623 .P6 2000*

Rettig, Michael D., 1950- Scheduling strategies for middle schools. Larchmont, NY : Eye On Education, 2000.
*TC LB3032.2 .R48 2000*

Talking across boundaries. [New York] : [Bruner Foundation], 1996.
*TC LB1623.5 .T35 1996*

**MIDDLE SCHOOLS - UNITED STATES - CASE STUDIES.**
Siskind, Theresa Gayle, 1951- Cases for middle school educators. Lanham, Md. ; London : Scarecrow Press, 2000.
*TC LB1623.5 .S57 2000*

**MIDDLE WEST IN ART.**
Kinsey, Joni. Plain pictures. Washington, : Published for the University of Iowa Museum of Art by the Smithsonian Institution Press, 1996.
*TC N8214.5.U6 K56 1996*

**Middlemarch Films.**
Summerhill at 70 [videorecording]. Princeton, N.J. : Films for the Humanities, c1992.
*TC LF795.L692953 S9 1992*

**Middleton, Bernard C., 1924-** Recollections : an autobiography of Bernard C. Middleton. New Castle, Del. : Oak Knoll Press, 2000. xii, 126 p. 8 p. of plates : ill. (some) ; 26 cm. Includes bibliographical references and index. ISBN 1-58456-016-9 DDC 686.3/0092
*1. Middleton, Bernard C., - 1924- 2. Bookbinders - Great Britain - Biography. 3. Books - Conservation and restoration - Great Britain - History - 20th century. I. Title.*
*TC Z269.2.M53 A3 2000*

**MIDDLETON, BERNARD C., 1924-.**
Middleton, Bernard C., 1924- Recollections. New Castle, Del. : Oak Knoll Press, 2000.
*TC Z269.2.M53 A3 2000*

**Middleton, Laura.** Disabled children : challenging social exclusion / Laura Middleton. Malden, Mass. : Blackwell Sciences, 1999. xi, 164 p. ; 24 cm. (Working together for children, young people, and their families) Includes bibliographical references and index. ISBN 0-632-05055-1 (pbk) DDC 362.4/048/083
*1. Handicapped children - Services for. 2. Handicapped children - Social conditions. 3. Social work with handicapped children. 4. Marginality, Social. I. Title. II. Series.*

*TC HV888 .M53 1999*

**MIDEAST.** *See* **MIDDLE EAST.**

**Midelfort, H. C. Erik** A history of madness in sixteenth-century Germany / H.C. Erik Midelfort. Stanford, Calif. : Stanford University Press, c1999. xvi, 438 p. : ill., maps ; 25 cm. Includes bibliographical references (p. [391]-425) and index. ISBN 0-8047-3334-1 (cloth : acid-free paper) DDC 618.89/00943/09031
*1. Mental illness - Germany - History - 16th century. 2. Social psychiatry - Germany - History - 16th century. I. Title.*
*TC RC450.G3 M528 1999*

**Midgley, David.** New directions in transactional analysis counselling : an explorers handbook / David Midgley. London ; New York : Free Association Books, 1999. xi, 153 p. : ill. ; 23 cm. Includes bibliographical references (p. [145]-147) and index. ISBN 1-85343-430-2 ISBN 1-85343-429-9 (pbk)
*1. Transactional analysis. I. Title.*
*TC RC489.T7M535 1999*

**MIDLIFE.** *See* **MIDDLE AGE.**

**MIGRANT LABOR.** *See* **CHILDREN OF MIGRANT LABORERS.**

**MIGRANT LABORERS' CHILDREN.** *See* **CHILDREN OF MIGRANT LABORERS.**

**MIGRATION, INTERNAL.** *See* **LABOR MOBILITY.**

**MIGRATION, INTERNATIONAL.** *See* **EMIGRATION AND IMMIGRATION.**

**MIGRATION OF ANIMALS.** *See* **ANIMAL MIGRATION.**

**Mikkelsen, Nina.** Words and pictures : lessons in children's literature and literacies / Nina Mikkelsen. Boston : McGraw-Hill, c2000. xxvii, 481 p. : ill. ; 24 cm. Includes bibliographical references (p. 462-471) and index. ISBN 0-697-39357-7 (alk. paper) DDC 372.64
*1. Children's literature - Study and teaching (Elementary) 2. Children - Books and reading. 3. Language experience approach in education. I. Title.*
*TC LB1575 .M55 2000*

**Mil palabras en inglés.**
1,000 palabras en inglés. Princeton : Berlitz Kids, c1998.
*TC PC4680 .A12 1998*

1,000 Spanish words. Princeton, N.J. : Berlitz Kids, c1998.
*TC PC4680 .A13 1998*

**Milbank Memorial Library.**
Milbank Memorial Library story hour [videorecording]. [New York : Milbank Memorial Library, 1999].
*TC Z718.3 .M5 1999 Series 3 Prog. 11*

Milbank Memorial Library story hour [videorecording]. [New York : Milbank Memorial Library, 1999]
*TC Z718.3 .M5 1999 Series 3 Prog. 6*

**MILBANK MEMORIAL LIBRARY - PICTORIAL WORKS.**
[Teachers College Library. [picture] 1940.
*TC TCX/H5*

**Milbank Memorial Library. Resource Center.**
Milbank Memorial Library story hour [videorecording]. [New York : Milbank Memorial Library, 1999].
*TC Z718.3 .M5 1999 Series 3 Prog. 11*

**Milbank Memorial Library Special Collections.**
[Teachers College Library. [picture] 1940.
*TC TCX/H5*

**Milbank Memorial Library story hour**
[videorecording] : December 22, 1999 / [lighting and taping by Angelo Miranda ; written by Jennifer Govan ; produced by the Resource Center, Teachers College, Columbia University]. [New York : Milbank Memorial Library, 1999]. 1 videocassette (60 min.) : sd., col. ; 1/2 in. + 1 script ([7] leaves ; 28 cm.) + 1 program ([4] p. ; 22 cm.). (Milbank Memorial Library's story hour program. Series 3 ; prog. 11) VHS and SVHS. Narrator: Cécile Hastie; puppeteers: Maria del Pilar Pastor, Jennifer Govan; Santa's helper, Laura Moran. Conducted by Cécile Hastie. Filmed on December 22, 1999, 10-11 A.M., in the Resource Center of Milbank Memorial Library. For primary grades. SUMMARY: A Sing Along Christmas, a puppet show in one act, written by Jennifer Govan, Assistant Director of Milbank Memorial Library, is performed by puppeteers, Jennifer Govan and Maria del Pilar Pastor, Collection and Curriculum Bibliographer of the Resource Center, with singing conducted by Cécile Hastie, Reference Librarian. The show was performed for kindergartners and first graders from Corpus Christi School in

the Resource Center of Milbank Memorial Library, Teachers College, Columbia University. Library has an added xerox copy of the accompanying program. Copy 2 of the tape is SVHS.

*1. Puppet plays, American - New York (State) - New York. 2. Christmas plays, American - New York (State) - New York. 3. Storytelling - New York (State) - New York. 4. Video recordings for children. I. Miranda, Angelo L.. Jr. II. Hastie, Cécile A. III. Govan. Jennifer Lee. Sing Along Christmas. IV. Govan. Jennifer Lee. V. Pastor, Maria del Pilar. VI. Moran, Laura. VII. Milbank Memorial Library. Resource Center. VIII. Milbank Memorial Library. IX. Series.*
**TC Z718.3 .M5 1999 Series 3 Prog. 11**

**Milbank Memorial Library story hour**
[videorecording] : November 12, 1999 / [filming by Angelo Miranda and/or Catharine Lin]. [New York : Milbank Memorial Library, 1999] 1 videocassette (60 min.) : sd., col. ; 1/2 in. (Milbank Memorial Library's story hour program. Series 3 ; prog. 6) VHS. Cast: Reader: Linda Louis, author of In the Paint. Filmed on November 12, 1999 in the Resource Center of Milbank Memorial Library. For primary grades. SUMMARY: In the Paint by Linda Louis and Patrick Ewing is read by author, Linda Louis, to 6-8 year olds from the Grant Day Care, After-School center, on November 12, 1999, in the Milbank Memorial Library Resource Center, Teachers College, Columbia University.
*1. Storytelling - New York (State) - New York. 2. Video recordings for children. I. Miranda, Angelo L.. Jr. II. Lin, Catharine. III. Louis, Linda L. IV. Louis, Linda L. In the paint. V. Ewing, Patrick Aloysius, 1962- VI. Milbank Memorial Library. VII. Series.*
**TC Z718.3 .M5 1999 Series 3 Prog. 6**

**Milbank Memorial Library's story hour program. Series 3**
(prog. 11) Milbank Memorial Library story hour [videorecording]. [New York : Milbank Memorial Library, 1999].
**TC Z718.3 .M5 1999 Series 3 Prog. 11**

(prog. 6) Milbank Memorial Library story hour [videorecording]. [New York : Milbank Memorial Library, 1999]
**TC Z718.3 .M5 1999 Series 3 Prog. 6**

**Mildenstein, Jeffrey, 1957-1989.**
Jazz dance class [videorecording]. W. Long Branch, NJ : Kultur, [1992?]
**TC GV1784 .J3 1992**

**Miles, Elaine.**
Miles, T. R. (Thomas Richard) Dyslexia. 2nd ed. Philadelphia ; Buckingham : Open University Press, 1999.
**TC RC394.W6 M55 1998**

**Miles, Steven.** Youth lifestyles in a changing world / Steven Miles. Buckingham ; Philadelphia : Open University Press, 2000. x, 177 p. ; 24 cm. Includes bibliographical references (p. [162]-171) and index. ISBN 0-335-20099-0 (hb) ISBN 0-335-20098-2 (pbk.) DDC 305.235
*1. Youth - Social conditions. 2. Young consumers 3. Lifestyles 4. Social change I. Title.*
**TC HQ796 .M4783 2000**

**Miles, T. R. (Thomas Richard)** Dyslexia : a hundred years on / T.R. Miles and Elaine Miles. 2nd ed. Philadelphia ; Buckingham : Open University Press, 1999, vii, 198 p. ; 23 cm. Includes bibliographical references and index. ISBN 0-335-20034-6 (pbk.) DDC 616.85/53
*1. Dyslexia. 2. Dyslexia I. Miles, Elaine. II. Title.*
**TC RC394.W6 M55 1998**

**Milestones in health and medicine.**
Harding, Anne S. Phoenix : Oryx Press, 2000.
**TC R133 .H36 2000**

**Milgram, Roberta M.**
Hong, Eunsook. Homework. Westport, Conn. : Bergin & Garvey, 2000.
**TC LB1048 .H69 2000**

**MILGRAM, STANLEY. OBEDIENCE TO AUTHORITY.**
Obedience to authority. Mahwah, N.J. ; London : Lawrence Erlbaum Associates, 2000.
**TC HM1251 .O24 2000**

**Milgrim, David, ill.**
Carrick, Carol. Patrick's dinosaurs on the Internet. New York : Clarion Books, 1999.
**TC PZ7.C2344 Patf 1999**

**MILITARISM. See IMPERIALISM.**

**MILITARISM - GREAT BRITAIN - HISTORY.**
Penn, Alan, 1926- Targeting schools. London ; Portland, OR : Woburn Press, 1999.
**TC GV443 .P388 1999**

**MILITARY AND CIVILIAN POWER.** *See* **CIVIL-MILITARY RELATIONS.**

**MILITARY ART AND SCIENCE.** *See* **WAR.**

**MILITARY BASES - UNITED STATES.**
Foreman, Grant, 1869-1953. Advancing the frontier, 1830-1860. Norman : University of Oklahoma Press, 1968 printing, c1933.
**TC E93 .F67 1968**

**MILITARY CAMPS.** *See* **CONCENTRATION CAMPS.**

**MILITARY-CIVIL RELATIONS.** *See* **CIVIL-MILITARY RELATIONS.**

**MILITARY COMBAT.** *See* **COMBAT.**

**MILITARY DRILL.** *See* **DRILL AND MINOR TACTICS.**

**MILITARY FACILITIES.** *See* **MILITARY BASES.**

**MILITARY GOVERNMENT.** *See* **CIVIL-MILITARY RELATIONS.**

**MILITARY HISTORIOGRAPHY.** *See* **MILITARY HISTORY.**

**MILITARY HISTORY - HISTORIOGRAPHY.** *See* **MILITARY HISTORY.**

**MILITARY HISTORY - STATISTICS.**
Richardson, Lewis Fry, 1881-1953. Statistics of deadly quarrels. Pacific Grove, Ca. Boxwood Press [1960]
**TC U21.7 .R5 1960**

**MILITARY INSTALLATIONS.** *See* **MILITARY BASES.**

**MILITARY NURSING - UNITED STATES - HISTORY.**
Sarnecky, Mary T. A history of the U.S. Army Nurse Corps. Philadelphia : University of Pennsylvania Press, c1999.
**TC UH493 .S27 1999**

**MILITARY PARKS.** *See* **WAR MEMORIALS.**

**MILITARY POLICY.** *See* **MILITARISM.**

**MILITARY POSTS.** *See* **MILITARY BASES.**

**MILITARY SOCIOLOGY.** *See* **SOCIOLOGY, MILITARY.**

**MILITARY STATIONS.** *See* **MILITARY BASES.**

**MILITIA MOVEMENTS - FICTION.**
Naylor, Phyllis Reynolds. Walker's Crossing. New York : Atheneum Books for Young Readers, c1999.
**TC PZ7.N24 Wai 1999**

**MILK.**
Robbins, Ken. Make me a peanut butter sandwich and a glass of milk. New York : Scholastic, c1992.
**TC TX814.5.P38 R63 1992**

**MILK - COMPOSITION.**
Milk quality. 1st ed. London ; New York : Blackie, 1995.
**TC SF251 .M65 1995**

**MILK - JUVENILE LITERATURE.**
Robbins, Ken. Make me a peanut butter sandwich and a glass of milk. New York : Scholastic, c1992.
**TC TX814.5.P38 R63 1992**

**MILK - QUALITY.**
Milk quality. 1st ed. London ; New York : Blackie, 1995.
**TC SF251 .M65 1995**

**Milk quality** / edited by F. Harding. 1st ed. London ; New York : Blackie, 1995. xiii, 166 p. ; 24 cm. Includes bibliographical references and index. ISBN 0-7514-0354-7
*1. Milk - Quality. 2. Milk - Composition. I. Harding, F.*
**TC SF251 .M65 1995**

**Millard, A. R. (Alan Ralph)** Reading and writing in the time of Jesus / Alan Millard. New York : New York University Press, 2000. 288 p. : ill. ; 24 cm. Includes bibliographical references (p. [230]-253) and indexes. ISBN 0-8147-5637-9 (cloth : alk. paper) DDC 225.9/5
*1. Bible - N.T. - Gospels - History of contemporary events. 2. Written communication - Mediterranean Region - History. 3. Books and reading - Mediterranean Region - History. I. Title.*
**TC BS2555.5 .M55 2000**

**Millard, Elaine.**
Gender in the secondary curriculum. London ; New York : Routledge, 1998.
**TC LC212.93.G7 G46 1998**

**Millbower, Lenn, 1951-** Training with a beat : the teaching power of music / Lenn Millbower ; foreword by Margaret Parkin. 1st ed. Sterling, Va. : Stylus,

c2000. xviii, 205 p. ; 24 cm. Includes bibliographical references and index. ISBN 1-57922-000-2 (cloth : alk. paper) DDC 781/.071
*1. Music - Psychological aspects. 2. Music. Influence of. 3. Music in education. I. Title.*
**TC ML3830 .M73 2000**

**Millen, C. M.** The low-down laundry line blues / C.M. Millen ; illustrated by Christine Davenier. Boston : Houghton Mifflin, 1999. 1 v. (unpaged) : col. ill. ; 26 cm. SUMMARY: While one sister sits around moping, the other tries to find a way to cheer her up. ISBN 0-395-87497-1 DDC [E]
*1. Sisters - Fiction. 2. Mood (Psychology) - Fiction. 3. Rope skipping - Fiction. I. Davenier, Christine, ill. II. Title.*
**TC PZ7.M6035 Lo 1999**

**MILLENNIALISM IN LITERATURE.**
Williams, John Tyerman. Pooh and the millennium. 1st American ed. New York : Dutton Books, 1999.
**TC PR6025.I65 Z975 1999**

**Miller, Arthur I.** Insights of genius : imagery and creativity in science and art / Arthur I. Miller. 1st MIT Press pbk. ed. Cambridge, Mass. : MIT Press, 2000. xxiii, 482 p. ;c23 cm. Originally published: New York : Copernicus, c1996. Includes bibliographical references and index. ISBN 0-262-63199-7 (pb : alk. paper) DDC 530/.01
*1. Physics - Methodology. 2. Science - Methodology. 3. Creative ability in science. I. Title.*
**TC QC6 .M44 2000**

**Miller-Bernal, Leslie, 1946-** Separate by degree : women students' experiences in single-sex and coeducational colleges / Leslie Miller-Bernal. New York : P. Lang, c2000. xxi, 375 p. : ill. ; 24 cm. (History of schools and schooling ; v. 9) Includes bibliographical references and index. ISBN 0-8204-4412-X (pbk. : alk. paper) DDC 378.1/9822
*1. Women college students - Northeastern States - Longitudinal studies. 2. Coeducation - United States - Longitudinal studies. 3. Small colleges - Northeastern States - History - Case studies. I. Title. II. Series.*
**TC LC1601 .M55 2000**

**Miller, Carrol T.**
Ottenburg, Susan D. Education today. 2nd. ed. Boston : Educational Publishing Group, Education Today, c1996.
**TC LC225.3 .O88 1996**

**Miller, Denise (Denise J.).**
Museum of Contemporary Photography (Columbia College (Chicago, Ill.)) Photography's multiple roles. Chicago : Museum of Contemporary Photography, Columbia College ; New York : Dap, Inc., c1998.
**TC TR187 .M87 1998**

**Miller, Eric D., 1972-.**
Loss and trauma. Philadelphia, PA : Brunner-Routledge, c2000.
**TC BF575.D35 L67 2000**

**Miller, Estelle L.** Fears expressed by female reentry students at an urban community college : qualitative study / by Estelle L. Miller. 1997. viii, 220 leaves ; 29 cm. Typescript; issued also on microfilm. Thesis (Ed.D.) -- Teachers College, Columbia University, 1997. Includes bibliographical references (leaves 187-194).
*1. Community college students. 2. Women college students - Attitudes. 3. Fear of failure. 4. Self-perception in women. 5. Motivation in education. 6. Continuing education. I. Title.*
**TC 06 no. 10864**

**Miller, Geraldine A., 1955-** Learning the language of addiction counseling / Geraldine A. Miller. Boston : Allyn and Bacon, c1999. xi, 243 p. : ill. ; 23 cm. Includes bibliographical references and index. ISBN 0-205-26318-6 (pbk.) DDC 616.86/06
*1. Drug abuse counseling. 2. Substance abuse - Patients - Counseling of. 3. Narcotic addicts - Patients - Counseling of. I. Title. II. Title: Addiction counseling*
**TC RC564 .M536 1999**

**Miller, John P., 1943-** Education and the soul : toward a spiritual curriculum / John P. Miller ; with a foreword by Thomas Moore. Albany : State University of New York Press, c2000. ix, 168 p. ; 23 cm. Includes bibliographical references (p. 153-159) and index. ISBN 0-7914-4341-8 (hc : alk. paper) ISBN 0-7914-4342-6 (pbk. : alk. paper) DDC 370.11/4
*1. Moral education. 2. Spiritual formation. 3. Education - Curricula. 4. Soul. I. Title.*
**TC LC268 .M52 2000**

**Miller, Jonathan, 1934-** On reflection / Jonathan Miller ; [editor, Valerie Mendes]. London : National Gallery Publications ; [New Haven, Conn.] : Distributed by Yale University Press, c1998. 224 p. : ill. (some col.) ; 29 cm. "Published to accompany an exhibition entitled Mirror image: Jonathan Miller on reflection, at the National Gallery, London, 16 September-13 December

1998"--T.p. verso. Illustrated lining papers. Includes
bibliographical references (p. 214-215) and index. ISBN
1-85709-236-8 (hardback) ISBN 1-85709-237-6 (pbk.) ISBN
0-300-07713-0 DDC 701/.8
*1. Mirrors in art. 2. Reflections. 3. Reflection (Optics) in art. 4.
Light in art. 5. Art - Philosophy. I. Mendes, Valerie D. II.
National Gallery (Great Britain) III. Title.*
*TC N8224.M6 M54 1998*

**Miller, Lynne, 1945-.**
Lieberman, Ann. Teachers--transforming their world
and their work. New York : Teachers College Press ;
Alexandria, Va. : Association for Supervision and
Curriculum Development, c1999.
*TC LB1025.3 .L547 1999*

**Miller, Margary Staman.**
Allan, Karen Kuelthau. Literacy and learning.
Boston : Houghton Mifflin, c2000.
*TC LB1631 .A37 2000*

**Miller, Melvin E.**
Creativity, spirituality, and transcendence. Stamford,
Conn. : Ablex, c2000.
*TC BF411 .C76 2000*

Spirituality, ethics, and relationship in adulthood.
Madison, Conn. : Psychosocial Press, c2000.
*TC BF724.5 .S68 2000*

**Miller, Michelle A., 1960-.**
Adolescent relationships and drug use. Mahwah, N.J. ;
London : Lawrence Erlbaum Associates, 2000.
*TC HV5824.Y68 A315 2000*

**Miller, Patricia H.**
Toward a feminist developmental psychology. New
York : Routledge, 2000.
*TC BF713 .T66 2000*

**Miller, Richard I.** Evaluating, improving, and judging
faculty performance in two-year colleges / Richard I.
Miller, Charles Finley, Candace Shedd Vancko.
Westport, Conn. ; London : Bergin & Garvey, 2000.
xiv, 188 p. : ill., forms ; 25 cm. Includes bibliographical
references (p. [171]-181) and index. ISBN 0-89789-692-0 (alk.
paper) DDC 378.1/224
*1. Community college teachers - Rating of - United States. 2.
Community college teachers - In-service training - United
States. I. Finley, Charles. II. Vancko, Candace Shedd. III. Title.*
*TC LB2333 .M49 2000*

**Miller, Tracie L.**
Nutritional aspects of HIV infection. London ; New
York : Arnold : Co-published in the United States by
Oxford University Press, 1999.
*TC RC607.A26 N895 1998*

**Miller, Warren E. (Warren Edward), 1924- joint
author.**
Kirkpatrick, Jeane J. The new Presidential elite. New
York : Russell Sage Foundation : [distributed by Basic
Books], c1976.
*TC JK1764 .K57*

**Miller, Wayne C.**
The nutty, nougat-filled world of human nutrition
[videorecording]. [Arlington, Va.] : Cerebellum Corp.,
c1998.
*TC QP141 .N8 1998*

**Miller, William L. (William Lloyd), 1949-.**
Doing qualitative research. 2nd ed. Thousand Oaks,
Calif. : Sage Publications, c1999
*TC R853.S64 D65 1999*

**Miller, William R.**
Integrating spirituality into treatment. 1st ed.
Washington, DC : American Psychological
Association, c1999.
*TC RC489.R46 I58 1999*

**Miller, Wilma H.**
**Reading & writing remediation kit.**
Miller, Wilma H. Ready-to-use activities &
materials for improving content reading skills. West
Nyack, NY : Center For Applied Research in
Education, c1999.
*TC LB1576 .M52 1999*

Ready-to-use activities & materials for improving
content reading skills / Wilma H. Miller : illustrations
by Eileen Ciavarella. West Nyack, NY : Center For
Applied Research in Education, c1999, xxi, 499 p. : ill. ;
28 cm. Rev. ed. of: Reading & writing remediation kit. c1997.
Includes bibliographical references. ISBN 0-13-007815-8 DDC
372.6
*1. Language arts - Correlation with content subjects - United
States. 2. Content area reading - United States. 3. English
language - Composition and exercises - Study and teaching -
United States. 4. Language arts - Remedial teaching - United
States. 5. Teaching - United States - Aids and devices. I. Miller,
Wilma H. Reading & writing remediation kit. II. Title. III.*

*Title: Ready-to-use activities and materials for improving
content reading skills*
*TC LB1576 .M52 1999*

Strategies for developing emergent literacy / by
Wilma H. Miller. 1st ed. Boston : McGraw-Hill,
c2000. x, 310 p. : ill. ; 28 cm. Includes bibliographical
references and indexes. ISBN 0-07-289372-9 DDC 372.6
*1. Language arts (Early childhood) 2. Language arts -
Remedial teaching. 3. Literacy. I. Title.*
*TC LB1139.5.L35 M55 2000*

**Millhorn, Jim, 1953-** Student's companion to the World
Wide Web : social sciences and humanities
resources / Jim Millhorn. Lanham, Md. ; London :
Scarecrow Press, 1999. v, 101 p. : ill., maps ; 28 cm. ISBN
0-8108-3680-7 (pbk.) DDC 025.06/3
*1. Social sciences - Computer network resources - Directories.
2. Humanities - Computer network resources - Directories. 3.
World Wide Web (Information retrieval system) I. Title.*
*TC H61.95 .M55 1999*

**Millman, Ernest Joel.**
Srole, Leo. Personal history & health. New
Brunswick, N.J. : Transaction Publishers, c1998.
*TC RA790.6 .S7 1998*

**Millon, Theodore.** Personality disorders in modern life /
Theodore Millon and Roger Davis ; with Carrie
Millon, Luis Escovar, and Sarah Meagher. New
York ; Chichester [England] : John Wiley & Sons,
c2000. xvii, 581 p. : ill. ; 26 cm. Includes bibliographical
references (p. 531-549) and indexes. CONTENTS: Ch. 1.
Personality Disorders: Current Concepts and Classical
Foundations -- Ch. 2. Contemporary Perspectives -- Ch. 3.
Assessment and Therapy of the Personality Disorders -- Ch. 4.
The Antisocial Personality -- Ch. 5. The Avoidant
Personality -- Ch. 6. The Obsessive-Compulsive Personality --
Ch. 7. The Dependent Personality -- Ch. 8. The Histrionic
Personality -- Ch. 9. The Narcissistic Personality -- Ch. 10. The
Schizoid Personality -- Ch. 11. The Schizotypal Personality --
Ch. 12. The Paranoid Personality -- Ch. 13. The Borderline
Personality -- Ch. 14. Personality Disorders from the
Appendix of DSM-IV -- Ch. 15. Personality Disorders from
the Appendix of DSM-III-R. ISBN 0-471-32355-1 (cloth : alk.
paper) DDC 616.89 DDC 616.89
*1. Personality disorders. 2. Personality Disorders. I. Davis,
Roger Dale. II. Title.*
*TC RC554 .M537 2000*

Personality-guided psychotherapy / Theodore Millon ;
with contributing associates, Seth Grossman ... [ et
al.] ; foreword by Roger D. Davis. New York : J.
Wiley c1999. xvi, 776 p. : ill. ; 26 cm. Includes
bibliographical references (p. 715-733) and indexes. ISBN
0-471-52807-2 (alk. paper) DDC 616.89/14
*1. Psychotherapy - Handbooks, manuals, etc. 2. Personality
disorders - Treatment - Handbooks, manuals, etc. 3.
Psychotherapy - methods. 4. Personality Disorders. I.
Grossman, Seth. II. Title.*
*TC RC480.5 .M54 1999*

**MILLS AND MILL-WORK. See FACTORIES.**

**MILLS (BUILDINGS). See FACTORIES.**

**Mills, Claudia.** You're a brave man, Julius
Zimmerman / Claudia Mills. 1st ed. New York :
Farrar Straus Giroux, c1999. 152 p. ; 22 cm. Sequel to:
Losers, Inc. SUMMARY: Twelve-year-old Julius has his hands
full over the summer when his mother attempts to improve his
grades and teach him responsibility by signing him up for a
French class and getting him a job babysitting. ISBN 0-374-
38708-7 DDC [Fic]
*1. Identity - Fiction. 2. Self-acceptance - Fiction. 3. Mothers
and sons - Fiction. 4. Schools - Fiction. 5. Babysitting -
Fiction. I. Title.*
*TC PZ7.M63963 Yo 1999*

**Mills, Jean, 1947-.**
Childhood studies. London ; New York : Routledge,
2000.
*TC HQ767.85 .C483 2000*

**Mills** [picture] : early textile workers. Amawalk, NY :
Jackdaw Publications, c1999. 12 posters : b&w ; 43 x 56
cm. + 1 leaflet ([6] p. : ill. ; 28 cm.). (Jackdaw photo
collections : PC 107) Compiled by Bill Eames ; edited by Jan
Morrissey. SUMMARY: 12 historical photo-posters depicting
the mills and early textile workers. CONTENTS: 1. Crowded
spinning room in textile mill -- 2. Spinning room -- 3. Beaming
and yarn inspection -- 4. Fine roving frames -- 5. Mill "Doffer
boys" and sweeper -- 6. Small youngsters and large
machines -- 7. "Doffer girl" -- 8. Cloth inspection -- 9. Cotton
mill baseball team -- 10. Men and women operate knitting
machines -- 11. Field to fabric -- 12. Modernized textile mill.
ISBN 1-56696-164-5
*1. Textile workers - United States - History - Pictorial works.
2. Textile machinery - United States - History - Pictorial
works. 3. Documentary photography - United States. I. Eames,*

*Bill. II. Morrissey, Jan. III. Jackdaw Publications. IV. Title:
Early textile workers [picture] V. Series.*
*TC TR820.5 .M5 1999*

**Mills, Richard W.**
Childhood studies. London ; New York : Routledge,
2000.
*TC HQ767.85 .C483 2000*

**Mills, Rosemary S.L.** The developmental psychology of
personal relationships / edited by Rosemary S.L. Mills
and Steve Duck. Chichester ; New York : John Wiley,
c2000. xv, 287 p. : ill. ; 25 cm. Includes bibliographical
references (p. [219]-271) and indexes. ISBN 0-471-99880-X
(pbk.) DDC 155.4/18
*1. Interpersonal relations in children. I. Duck, Steve. II. Title.*
*TC BF723.I646 M55 2000*

**Millward, Alan.**
Theorising special education. London ; New York :
Routledge, 1998.
*TC LC3986.G7 T54 1998*

**MILNE, A. A. (ALAN ALEXANDER), 1882-1956 -
CHARACTERS - WINNIE-THE-POOH.**
Williams, John Tyerman. Pooh and the millennium.
1st American ed. New York : Dutton Books, 1999.
*TC PR6025.I65 Z975 1999*

**Milner, Peter M.** The autonomous brain : a neural
theory of attention and learning / Peter M. Milner.
Mahwah, N.J. : L. Erlbaum Associates, 1999. x, 155
p. : ill. ; 23 cm. Includes bibliographical references (p. [126]-
140) and indexes. ISBN 0-8058-3211-4 (hardcover : alk.
paper) DDC 153.1
*1. Mind and body. 2. Brain - Psychophysiology. 3. Attention. 4.
Learning, Psychology of. I. Title.*
*TC BF161 .M5 1999*

**Milroy, James.** Authority in language : investigating
standard English / James Milroy and Lesley Milroy.
3rd ed. London [England] ; New York : Routledge,
1999. xi, 173 p. ; 25 cm. Includes bibliographical references
(p. 161-170) and index. ISBN 0-415-17412-0 (hbk) ISBN
0-415-17413-9 (pbk) DDC 428
*1. Standard language. 2. English language - Standardization.
3. English language - Variation. I. Milroy, Lesley. II. Title.*
*TC P368 .M54 1999*

**Milroy, Lesley.**
Milroy, James. Authority in language. 3rd ed. London
[England] ; New York : Routledge, 1999.
*TC P368 .M54 1999*

**MIND.** *See* **BRAIN; INTELLECT; KNOWLEDGE,
THEORY OF; MIND AND BODY;
PSYCHOLOGY; THOUGHT AND
THINKING.**

**MIND AND BODY.** *See also* **BODY IMAGE;
BODY, HUMAN; BODY, HUMAN
(PHILOSOPHY); CONSCIOUSNESS;
INTENTIONALITY (PHILOSOPHY);
MENTAL HEALING; OTHER MINDS
(THEORY OF KNOWLEDGE); SELF.
PSYCHOPHYSIOLOGY; SELF.**
Chiozza, Luis A. Why do we fall ill? Madison,
Conn. : Psychosocial Press, c1999.
*TC R726.7 .C48 1999*

Milner, Peter M. The autonomous brain. Mahwah,
N.J. : L. Erlbaum Associates, 1999.
*TC BF161 .M5 1999*

Mind and cognition. 2nd ed. Malden, Mass. :
Blackwell Publishers, 1999.
*TC BF171 .M55 1999*

Mind myths. Chichester, England ; New York : J.
Wiley & Sons, c1999.
*TC BF161 .M556 1999*

Mind myths. Chichester, England ; New York : J.
Wiley & Sons, c1999.
*TC BF161 .M556 1999*

Nursing and the experience of illness. London ; New
York : Routledge, 1999.
*TC RT86 .N886 1999*

Rowlands, Mark. The body in mind. Cambridge,
U.K. ; New York : Cambridge University Press, 1999.
*TC BD418.3 .R78 1999*

Wilton, Richard. Consciousness, free will, and the
explanation of human behavior. Lewiston, N.Y. : E.
Mellen Press, c2000.
*TC BF161 .W495 2000*

**MIND AND BODY - HISTORY.**
Ostenfeld, Erik Nis. Ancient Greek psychology and
the modern mind-body debate. Aarhus, Denmark :
Aarhus University Press, 1987.
*TC BF161 .O88 1987*

**MIND AND BODY THERAPIES.**
Beyond talk therapy. 1st ed. Washington, DC : American Psychological Association, c1999.
*TC RC489.A72 B49 1999*

The meaning of movement. Amsterdam : Gordon and Breach, c1999.
*TC RC473.K47 M4 1999*

**Mind and cognition :** an anthology / edited by William G. Lycan. 2nd ed. Malden, Mass. : Blackwell Publishers, 1999. xii, 540 p. : ill ; 26 cm. (Blackwell philosophy anthologies ; 8) Includes bibliographical references and indexes. ISBN 0-631-21204-3 (hardcover : alk. paper) ISBN 0-631-20545-4 (pbk. : alk. paper) DDC 128/.2
*1. Mind and body. 2. Thought and thinking. 3. Cognitive science. I. Lycan, William G. II. Series: Blackwell philosophy anthologies ; 8*
*TC BF171 .M55 1999*

**The mind and its discontents.**
Gillett, Grant, 1950- Oxford ; New York : Oxford University Press, c1999.
*TC BD418.3 .G555 1999*

**Mind and variability.**
McNamara, Patrick, 1956- Westport, Conn. : Praeger, 1999.
*TC BF371 .M385 1999*

**MIND-BODY RELATIONS (METAPHYSICS).**
Nursing and the experience of illness. London ; New York : Routledge, 1999.
*TC RT86 .N886 1999*

**MIND-CURE.** *See* **CHRISTIAN SCIENCE; MENTAL HEALING; MIND AND BODY.**

**Mind myths :** exploring popular assumptions about the mind and brain / edited by Sergio Della Sala. Chichester, England ; New York : J. Wiley & Sons, c1999. xvi, 291 p. : ill. ; 25 cm. Includes bibliographical references (p. [255]-285) and index. ISBN 0-471-98303-9 (alk. paper) DDC 153
*1. Mind and body. 2. Brain. 3. Intellect. 4. Brain. 5. Intellect. 6. Mind and body. I. Della Sala, Sergio.*
*TC BF161 .M556 1999*

**The mind of man.**
Bromberg, Walter, 1900- Harper colophon ed. New York : Harper & Row, 1963.
*TC RC480 .B7 1963*

Bromberg, Walter, 1900- 4th ed. New York : Harper & Brothers, 1937.
*TC RC480 .B7*

**MIND, PHILOSOPHY OF.** *See* **PHILOSOPHY OF MIND.**

**MIND, THEORY OF.** *See* **PHILOSOPHY OF MIND.**

**Mindess, Anna.** Reading between the signs : intercultural communication for sign language interpreters / Anna Mindess with Thomas K. Holcomb, Daniel Langholtz, and Priscilla Poynor Moyers ; foreword by Sharon Neumann Solow. Yarmouth, Me. : Intercultural Press, c1999. xiii, 259 p. ; 23 cm. Includes bibliographical references (p. 235-241) and index. ISBN 1-87786-473-0 DDC 419
*1. Interpreters for the deaf - United States. 2. Communication and culture - United States. 3. Intercultural communication - United States. 4. Deaf - Means of communication - United States. 5. American Sign Language. I. Title.*
*TC HV2402 .M56 1999*

**Minds behind the brain.**
Finger, Stanley. Oxford ; New York : Oxford University Press, 2000.
*TC QP353 .F549 2000*

**Minds in motion.**
Griss, Susan. Portsmouth, NH : Heinemann, c1998.
*TC LB1592 .G75 1998*

**Minds in the making :** essays in honor of David R. Olson / edited by Janet Wilde Astington. Oxford ; Malden, Mass. : Blackwell, 2000. xx, 299 p. : ill. ; 26 cm. Includes bibliographical references and indexes. ISBN 0-631-21805-X (alk. paper) ISBN 0-631-21806-8 (alk. paper) DDC 153
*1. Cognition in children. 2. Philosophy of mind in children. 3. Children - Language. I. Olson, David R., 1935- II. Astington, Janet W.*
*TC BF723.C5 M56 2000*

**MINDS OF OTHERS (THEORY OF KNOWLEDGE).** *See* **OTHER MINDS (THEORY OF KNOWLEDGE).**

**MINERAL RESOURCES CONSERVATION - ANTARCTICA - FICTION.**
Robinson, Kim Stanley. Antarctica. New York : Bantam Books, c1998.

*TC PS3568.O2893 A82 1998*

**MINERVA (ROMAN DEITY).** *See* **ATHENA (GREEK DEITY).**

**MINES AND MINERAL RESOURCES.** *See* **GOLD MINES AND MINING.**

**MINIATURE OBJECTS.** *See* **TOYS.**

**MINICOMPUTERS.** *See* **MICROCOMPUTERS.**

**MINIMAL BRAIN DYSFUNCTION IN CHILDREN.** *See* **ATTENTION-DEFICIT HYPERACTIVITY DISORDER; LEARNING DISABILITIES.**

**MINIMAL COMPETENCY TESTS.** *See* **COMPETENCY BASED EDUCATIONAL TESTS.**

**MINIMALIST THEORY (LINGUISTICS).**
Cook, V. J. (Vivian James), 1940- Chomsky's universal grammar. 2nd [updated] ed. Oxford, OX, UK ; Cambridge, Mass., USA : Blackwell Publishers, 1996.
*TC P85.C47 C66 1996*

**MINISTERS (DIPLOMATIC AGENTS).** *See* **AMBASSADORS.**

**MINISTRIES, GOVERNMENT.** *See* **EXECUTIVE DEPARTMENTS.**

**MINISTRIES, STATE.** *See* **EXECUTIVE DEPARTMENTS.**

**Ministry of Education Government of India.**
Indian Journal of Educational Administration and Research. New Delhi

**MINNESOTA - HISTORY - CIVIL WAR, 1861-1865 - PERSONAL NARRATIVES - JUVENILE LITERATURE.**
Bircher, William, 1845-1917. A Civil War drummer boy. Mankato, Minn. : Blue Earth Books, c2000.
*TC E601 .B605 2000*

**MINNESOTA MULTIPHASIC PERSONALITY INVENTORY.**
Butcher, James Neal, 1933- A beginner's guide to the MMPI-2. 1st ed. Washington, DC : American Psychological Association, c1999.
*TC BF698.8.M5 B86 1999*

Graham, John R. (John Robert), 1940- MMPI-2. 3rd ed. New York : Oxford University Press, 1999.
*TC RC473.M5 G73 1999*

Graham, John R. (John Robert), 1940- MMPI-2 correlates for outpatient community mental health settings. Minneapolis : University of Minnesota Press, c1999.
*TC RC473.M5 G733 1999*

Greene, Roger L. The MMPI-2. 2nd ed. Boston : Allyn and Bacon, c2000.
*TC BF698.8.M5 G74 2000*

Pope, Kenneth S. The MMPI, MMPI-2, & MMPI-A in court. 2nd ed. Washington, DC : American Psychological Association, 2000.
*TC KF8965 .P66 1999*

**MINNESOTA MULTIPHASIC PERSONALITY INVENTORY - VALIDITY.**
Graham, John R. (John Robert), 1940- MMPI-2 correlates for outpatient community mental health settings. Minneapolis : University of Minnesota Press, c1999.
*TC RC473.M5 G733 1999*

**MINNESOTA NEW COUNTRY SCHOOL (LESUEUR, MINN.).**
Education's big gamble [videorecording]. New York, NY : Merrow Report, c1997.
*TC LB2806.36 .E3 1997*

**MINNESOTA PERSONALITY SCALE.** *See* **MINNESOTA MULTIPHASIC PERSONALITY INVENTORY.**

**Minnesota symposia on child psychology (Series)**
(v. 31.) The effects of early adversity on neurobehavioral development. Mahwah, N.J. : L. Erlbaum Associates, 2000.
*TC RJ499 .E34 2000*

**Minogue, Coll.** Wood-fired ceramics : contemporary practices / Coll Minogue and Robert Sanderson. London : A & C Black ; Philadelphia : University of Pennsylvania Press, 2000. 160 p. : col. ill. ; 29 cm. Includes bibliographical references (p. 158-159) and index. ISBN 0-7136-4621-7 (A & C Black : alk. paper) ISBN 0-8122-3514-2 (Univ. of Penn. : alk. paper) DDC 738.1/43
*1. Kilns. 2. Ceramics. I. Sanderson, Robert. II. Title.*

*TC TP841 .M57 2000*

**MINOR ARTS.** *See* **DECORATIVE ARTS.**

**MINOR TACTICS.** *See* **DRILL AND MINOR TACTICS.**

**Minor, Wendell, ill.**
George, Jean Craighead, 1919- Snow Bear. 1st ed. New York : Hyperion Books for Children, 1999.
*TC PZ7.G2933 Sn 1999*

**MINORITIES.** *See* **ASSIMILATION (SOCIOLOGY); CHILDREN OF MINORITIES; DISCRIMINATION; ETHNIC ATTITUDES; ETHNIC RELATIONS; LINGUISTIC MINORITIES; MASS MEDIA AND MINORITIES; MINORITY STUDENTS; RACE RELATIONS; SOCIAL WORK WITH MINORITIES.**

**MINORITIES - ALCOHOL USE - UNITED STATES - PREVENTION.**
Bridges to recovery. New York ; London : Free Press, c2000.
*TC HV5199.5 .B75 2000*

**MINORITIES AS A THEME IN LITERATURE.** *See* **MINORITIES IN LITERATURE.**

**MINORITIES - CANADA - COMPUTER NETWORK RESOURCES - DIRECTORIES.**
Gregory, Vicki L., 1950- Multicultural resources on the Internet. The United States and Canada. Englewood, Colo. : Libraries Unlimited, 1999.
*TC E184.A1 G874 1999*

**MINORITIES - COUNSELING OF - GREAT BRITAIN.**
Banks, Nick. White counsellors--Black clients. Aldershot, Hants, England ; Brookfield, Vt. : Ashgate, c1999.
*TC HV3177.G7 B36 1999*

**MINORITIES - EDUCATION.** *See also* **EDUCATION, BILINGUAL.**
Bowe, Frank. Universal design in education. Westport, Conn. ; London : Bergin & Garvey, 2000.
*TC LB1028.38 .B69 2000*

Enhancing education in heterogeneous schools. Ramat-Gan : Bar-Ilan University Press, [1997]
*TC LC214 .E54 1997*

Ford, Terry. Becoming multicultural :. New York : Falmer Press, 1999.
*TC LC1099 .F674 1999*

**MINORITIES - EDUCATION - AUSTRALIA - ADDRESSES, ESSAYS, LECTURES.**
Bourke, S. F. The mastery of literacy and numeracy. Canberra : Australian Govt. Pub. Service, 1977.
*TC LA2102 .B68 1977*

**MINORITIES - EDUCATION - CANADA.**
Garcia, Ricardo L. Teaching for diversity. Bloomington, Ind. : Phi Delta Kappa Educational Foundation, 1998.
*TC LC1099.3 .G367 1998*

**MINORITIES - EDUCATION - ECONOMIC ASPECTS - UNITED STATES.**
Vernez, Georges. Closing the education gap. Santa Monica, CA : RAND, 1999.
*TC LC213.2 .V47 1999*

**MINORITIES - EDUCATION (ELEMENTARY) - NEW YORK (STATE) - NEW YORK.**
Thompson, Melvin R. The implementation of multicultural curricula in the New York City public elementary schools. 1999.
*TC 06 no. 11186*

**MINORITIES - EDUCATION (GRADUATE) - NEW YORK (STATE).**
Sosin, Adrienne. Achieving styles preferences of students in an urban graduate teacher education program. 1996.
*TC 06 no. 10701*

**MINORITIES - EDUCATION - GREAT BRITAIN.**
Richardson, Robin. Inclusive schools, inclusive society. Stoke on Trent, Staffordshire, England : Trentham Books, 1999.
*TC LC212.3.G7 R523 1999*

**MINORITIES - EDUCATION - GREAT BRITAIN - CASE STUDIES.**
Moore, Alex, 1947- Teaching multicultured students. London ; New York : Falmer Press, 1999.
*TC LC3736.G6 M66 1999*

**MINORITIES - EDUCATION (HIGHER) - GREAT BRITAIN.**
Woodward, Diana, 1948- Managing equal opportunities in higher education. Buckingham

[England] ; Philadelphia : Society for Research into Higher Education : Open University Press, 2000.
*TC LC213.3.G7 W66 2000*

**MINORITIES - EDUCATION (HIGHER) - NEW YORK (STATE).**
Langer, Arthur Mark. Faculty assessment of mentoring roles at SUNY Empire State College. 1999.
*TC 06 no. 11138*

**MINORITIES - EDUCATION (HIGHER) - UNITED STATES.**
Capeheart-Meningall, Jennifer. Quality of students of color efort on a predominantly white college and the internal environmental elements that influence involvement. 1998.
*TC 06 no. 10874*

**MINORITIES - EDUCATION (HIGHER) - UNITED STATES - CASE STUDIES.**
Two-year colleges for women and minorities. New York : Falmer Press, 1999.
*TC LB2328.15.U6 T96 1999*

**MINORITIES - EDUCATION (MIDDLE SCHOOL) - NEW YORK (STATE).**
Mahammad, Hasna. Multicultural education. 1998.
*TC 06 no. 11033*

**MINORITIES - EDUCATION (PRESCHOOL) - CANADA.**
Chud, Gyda. Early childhood education for a multicultural society. [Vancouver] : Western Education Development Group, Faculty of Education, The University of British Columbia, c1985.
*TC LC1099 .C494 1985*

**MINORITIES - EDUCATION (SECONDARY) - CANADA - CASE STUDIES.**
Ryan, James, 1952 Oct. 18- Race and ethnicity in multi-ethnic schools. Clevedon [England] ; Philadelphia : Multilingual Matters, c1999.
*TC LC3734 .R93 1999*

**MINORITIES - EDUCATION - SOCIAL ASPECTS.**
Cummins, Jim, 1949- Language, power, and pedagogy. Clevedon [England] ; Buffalo [N.Y.] : Multilingual Matters, c2000.
*TC LC3719 .C86 2000*

**MINORITIES - EDUCATION - SOCIAL ASPECTS - UNITED STATES.**
Gordon, June A., 1950- The color of teaching. London ; New York : RoutledgeFalmer, c2000.
*TC LB2835.25 .G67 2000*

**MINORITIES - EDUCATION - UNITED STATES.**
Banks, James A. Cultural diversity and education. 4th ed. Boston ; London : Allyn & Bacon, c2001.
*TC LC3731 .B365 2001*

Critical ethnicity. Lanham, Md. : Rowman & Littlefield, c1999.
*TC LC212.2 .C75 1999*

Garcia, Ricardo L. Teaching for diversity. Bloomington, Ind. : Phi Delta Kappa Educational Foundation, c1998.
*TC LC1099.3 .G367 1998*

Gill, Walter. A common sense guide to non-traditional urban education. Nashville, Tenn. : James C. Winston Publishing Co., Inc., c1998.
*TC LC5115 .G55 1998*

Law and school reform. New Haven [Conn.] : Yale University Press, c1999.
*TC LC213.2. L38 1999*

Race is-- race isn't. Boulder, CO : Westview Press, c1999.
*TC LC3731 .R27 1999*

**MINORITIES - EDUCATION - UNITED STATES - HISTORY.**
Spring, Joel H. Deculturalization and the struggle for equality. 3rd ed. Boston : McGraw-Hill, c2001.
*TC LC3731 .S68 2001*

**MINORITIES - EMPLOYMENT.** *See* **AFFIRMATIVE ACTION PROGRAMS.**

**MINORITIES - HEALTH AND HYGIENE.** *See* **MINORITIES - MEDICAL CARE.**

**MINORITIES - HEALTH AND HYGIENE - UNITED STATES.**
Minority health in America. Baltimore, Md. : Johns Hopkins University Press, 2000.
*TC RA448.4 .M566 2000*

United States. Dept. of Health and Human Services. Task Force on Black and Minority Health. Report of the Secretary's Task Force on Black & Minority Health. Washington, D.C. : U.S. Dept. of Health and Human Services, [1985-<1986 >

*TC RA448.5.N4 U55 1985*

**MINORITIES - HEALTH AND HYGIENE - UNITED STATES - STATISTICS.**
United States. Dept. of Health and Human Services. Task Force on Black and Minority Health. Report of the Secretary's Task Force on Black & Minority Health. Washington, D.C. : U.S. Dept. of Health and Human Services, [1985-<1986 >
*TC RA448.5.N4 U55 1985*

**MINORITIES IN LITERATURE - STUDY AND TEACHING.**
Teaching the literatures of early America. New York : Modern Language Association of America, 1999.
*TC PS186 .T43 1999*

**MINORITIES IN MASS MEDIA - UNITED STATES.**
Investing in diversity. Washington, D.C. : Aspen Institute, Communications and Society Program, c1998.
*TC P94.5.M552 U647 1997*

**MINORITIES IN TECHNOLOGY.**
Diversity in technology education. New York : Glencoe, c1998.
*TC T61 .A56 47th 1998*

Diversity in technology education. New York : Glencoe, c1998.
*TC T61 .A56 47th 1998*

**MINORITIES - MEDICAL CARE.** *See also* **MINORITIES - HEALTH AND HYGIENE.**
Loue, Sana. Gender, ethnicity, and health research. New York : Kluwer Academic/Plenum Publishers, c1999.
*TC RA448.4 .L68 1999*

**MINORITIES - MEDICAL CARE - UNITED STATES.**
Promoting health in multicultural populations. Thousand Oaks, Calif. : Sage Publications, c1999.
*TC RA448.4 .P76 1999*

**MINORITIES - PSYCHOLOGICAL TESTING.**
Handbook of cross-cultural and multicultural personality assessment. Mahwah, N.J. ; London : Lawrence Erlbaum Associates, 2000.
*TC RC473.P79 H36 2000*

**MINORITIES - PSYCHOLOGICAL TESTING - UNITED STATES.**
Valencia, Richard R. Intelligence testing and minority students. Thousand Oaks, Calif. : Sage Publications, [2000]
*TC BF431.5.U6 V35 2000*

**MINORITIES - SOCIAL CONDITIONS.**
Fenton, Steve, 1942- Ethnicity. Lanham, Md. : Rowman & Littlefield, c1999.
*TC GN495.6 .F46 1999x*

**MINORITIES - SUBSTANCE USE - UNITED STATES - PREVENTION.**
Bridges to recovery. New York ; London : Free Press, c2000.
*TC HV5199.5 .B75 2000*

**MINORITIES - UNITED STATES.**
Family ethnicity. 2nd ed. Thousand Oaks, Calif. : Sage Publications, c1999.
*TC E184.A1 F33 1999*

**MINORITIES - UNITED STATES - COMPUTER NETWORK RESOURCES - DIRECTORIES.**
Gregory, Vicki L., 1950- Multicultural resources on the Internet. The United States and Canada. Englewood, Colo. : Libraries Unlimited, 1999.
*TC E184.A1 G874 1999*

**MINORITIES - UNITED STATES - DRUG USE - RESEARCH.**
Conducting drug abuse research with minority populations. New York : Haworth Press, c1999.
*TC HV5824.E85 C66 1999*

**MINORITIES - UNITED STATES - SOCIAL CONDITIONS.**
Addressing cultural issues in organizations. Thousand Oaks, Calif. : Sage Publications, 2000.
*TC E184.A1 A337 2000*

**MINORITY CHILDREN.** *See* **CHILDREN OF MINORITIES.**

**MINORITY COLLEGE ADMINISTRATORS - EMPLOYMENT - UNITED STATES.**
Rai, Kul B. Affirmative action and the university. Lincoln : University of Nebraska Press, 2000.
*TC LC212.42 .R35 2000*

**MINORITY COLLEGE STUDENTS.**
Flower, Linda. Learning to rival. Mahwah, New Jersey : Lawrence Erlbaum Associates, c2000.
*TC PE1404 .F59 2000*

**MINORITY COLLEGE TEACHERS - EMPLOYMENT - UNITED STATES.**
Rai, Kul B. Affirmative action and the university. Lincoln : University of Nebraska Press, 2000.
*TC LC212.42 .R35 2000*

**MINORITY COLLEGE TEACHERS - SELECTION AND APPOINTMENT - UNITED STATES.**
Power, race, and gender in academe. New York : Modern Language Association, 2000.
*TC LC3727 .P69 2000*

Turner, Caroline Sotello Viernes. Faculty of color in academe. Boston : Allyn and Bacon, c2000.
*TC LB2332.72 .T87 2000*

**MINORITY COLLEGE TEACHERS - UNITED STATES.**
Aguirre, Adalberto. Women and minority faculty in the academic workplace. San Francisco, Calif. : Jossey-Bass c2000.
*TC LB2332.3 .A35 2000*

Power, race, and gender in academe. New York : Modern Language Association, 2000.
*TC LC3727 .P69 2000*

**MINORITY COLLEGE TEACHERS - UNITED STATES - CASE STUDIES.**
Succeeding in an academic career. Westport, Conn. : Greenwood Press, 2000.
*TC LB2331.72 .S83 2000*

**MINORITY EXECUTIVES.** *See* **MINORITY COLLEGE ADMINISTRATORS.**

**MINORITY GROUP CHILDREN.** *See* **CHILDREN OF MINORITIES.**

**MINORITY GROUPS.** *See* **MINORITIES.**

**MINORITY HANDICAPPED - EDUCATION - UNITED STATES - CASE STUDIES.**
Harry, Beth. Building cultural reciprocity with families. Baltimore, Md. : P.H. Brookes Pub. Co., c1999.
*TC LC3969 .H377 1999*

**Minority health in America :** findings and policy implications from the Commonwealth Fund minority health survey / edited by Carol J.R. Hogue, Martha A. Hargraves, Karen Scott Collins. Baltimore, Md. : Johns Hopkins University Press, 2000. xviii, 326 p. : ill. ; 24 cm. Includes bibliographical references and indexes. ISBN 0-8018-6298-1 (alk. paper) ISBN 0-8018-6299-X (pbk. : alk. paper) DDC 362.1/089/00973
*1. Minorities - Health and hygiene - United States. 2. Health surveys - United States. I. Hogue, Carol J. R. II. Hargraves, Martha A. III. Collins, Karen Scott. IV. Commonwealth Fund.*
*TC RA448.4 .M566 2000*

**MINORITY LANGUAGES.** *See* **LINGUISTIC MINORITIES.**

**MINORITY LITERATURE (AMERICAN).** *See* **AMERICAN LITERATURE - MINORITY AUTHORS.**

**MINORITY STUDENTS - NEW YORK (STATE) - ATTITUDES - CASE STUDIES.**
Schlanger, Dean J. An exploration of school belongingness. 1998.
*TC 06 no. 10993*

**MINORITY STUDENTS - RATING OF - UNITED STATES.**
Measuring up. Boston : Kluwer Academic Publishers, c1999.
*TC LB3051 .M4627 1999*

**MINORITY TEACHERS - RECRUITING - UNITED STATES.**
Gordon, June A., 1950- The color of teaching. London ; New York : RoutledgeFalmer, c2000.
*TC LB2835.25 .G67 2000*

**MINORITY TEACHERS - SUPPLY AND DEMAND - TEXAS - LONGITUDINAL STUDIES.**
Kirby, Sheila Nataraj, 1946- Staffing at-risk school districts in Texas. Santa Monica, CA : Rand, 1999.
*TC LB2833.3.T4 K57 1999*

**MINORITY TEACHERS - UNITED STATE - RECRUITING.**
Orsini, Alfonso J. The color of excellence. 1999.
*TC 06 no. 11209*

**MINORITY TEACHERS - UNITED STATES - SELECTION AND APPOINTMENT.**
Orsini, Alfonso J. The color of excellence. 1999.
*TC 06 no. 11209*

**MINORITY TEENAGERS - CHINA - HONG KONG.**
Chinese adolescents in Britain and Hong Kong. Aldershot ; Brookfield, USA : Ashgate, c1999.
*TC DA125.C5 C47 1999*

**MINORITY TEENAGERS - GREAT BRITAIN.**
Chinese adolescents in Britain and Hong Kong. Aldershot ; Brookfield, USA : Ashgate, c1999.
*TC DA125.C5 C47 1999*

**MINORITY TEENAGERS - MENTAL HEALTH.**
Canino, Ian A. Culturally diverse children and adolescents. 2nd ed. New York : Guilford Press, c2000.
*TC RJ507.M54 C36 2000*

**MINORITY TEENAGERS - UNITED STATES.**
Adolescents and their families. New York : Garland Pub., 1999.
*TC HQ796 .A33533 1999*

**MINORITY WOMEN - SERVICES FOR - UNITED STATES.**
Empowering women of color. New York : Columbia University Press, c1999.
*TC HV1445 .E45 1999*

**MINORITY WOMEN - UNITED STATES - PSYCHOLOGY.**
Empowering women of color. New York : Columbia University Press, c1999.
*TC HV1445 .E45 1999*

**Mintrom, Michael, 1963-** Policy entrepreneurs and school choice / Michael Mintrom. Washington, DC : Georgetown University Press, c2000. xi, 324 p. ; 23 cm. (American governance and public policy series) Includes bibliographical references (p. [301]-315) and index. ISBN 0-87840-771-5 (pbk. : alk. paper) ISBN 0-87840-770-7 (cloth : alk. paper) DDC 379.1/11/0973
*1. School choice - United States. 2. Education and state - United States. 3. Policy sciences. I. Title. II. Series: American governance and public policy.*
*TC LB1027.9 .M57 2000*

**Mintzes, Joel J.**
Assessing science understanding :. San Diego, Calif. London : Academic, 2000.
*TC Q181 .A87 2000*

**Mio, Jeffrey Scott.**
Key words in multicultural interventions. Westport, Conn. : Greenwood Press, 1999.
*TC BF637.C6 K493 1999*

Resistance to multiculturalism : : issues and interventions / Jeffery Scott Mio, Gene I. Awakuni. Philadelphia, PA : Brunner/Mazel, c2000. xvii, 177 p. ; 24 cm. Includes bibliographical references and index. ISBN 0-87630-954-6 (case : alk. paper) ISBN 0-87630-955-4 (pa. : alk. paper)
*1. Multiculturalism. 2. Multicultural education. 3. Mental health education. 4. Racism. 5. Stereotype (Psychology). 6. Avoidance (Psychology). I. Awakuni, Gene I. II. Title.*
*TC HM1271 .M56 2000*

**MIRACLES.**
Schick, Theodore. How to think about weird things. 2nd ed. Mountain View, Calif. : Mayfield Pub., c1999.
*TC BC177 .S32 1999*

**Miraculously builded in our hearts :** a Dartmouth reader / edited by Edward Connery Lathem and David M. Shribman. Hanover : Dartmouth University Press, 1999. xiv, 408 p. ; 24 cm. Includes bibliographical references. ISBN 1-58465-054-0
*1. Dartmouth College. I. Lathem, Edward Connery. II. Shribman, David M.*
*TC LD1438 .M573 1999*

**Miranda, Angelo L., Jr.**
Milbank Memorial Library story hour [videorecording]. [New York : Milbank Memorial Library, 1999].
*TC Z718.3 .M5 1999 Series 3 Prog. 11*

Milbank Memorial Library story hour [videorecording]. [New York : Milbank Memorial Library, 1999]
*TC Z718.3 .M5 1999 Series 3 Prog. 6*

**Miranne, Kristine B.**
Gendering the city. Lanham [Md.] : Rowman & Littlefield, c2000.
*TC HT166 .G4614 2000*

**Miringoff, Marc L.** The social health of the nation : how America is really doing / Marc Miringoff, Marque-Luisa Miringoff ; contributing author Sandra Opdycke. New York : Oxford University Press, 1999. xiv, 245 p. : ill. ; 25 cm. Includes bibliographical references and index. ISBN 0-19-513348-X (cloth) ISBN 0-19-513349-8 (paper)
*1. United States - Social conditions - 1971- 2. Social indicators - United States. I. Miringoff, Marque-Luisa, 1947- II. Opdycke, Sandra. III. Title.*
*TC HN59.2 .M57 1999*

**Miringoff, Marque-Luisa, 1947-.**
Miringoff, Marc L. The social health of the nation. New York : Oxford University Press, 1999.
*TC HN59.2 .M57 1999*

**Mirochnik, Elijah, 1952-** Teaching in the first person : understanding voice and vocabulary in learning relationships / Elijah Mirochnik. New York : P. Lang, c2000. x, 145 p. : port. ; 23 cm. (Counterpoints, 1058-1634 ; v. 99) Includes bibliographical references (p. [133]-140) and index. ISBN 0-8204-4157-0 (alk. paper) DDC 371.102/3
*1. Teacher-student relationships - United States - Case studies. 2. Knowledge, Theory of - Case studies. 3. Interaction analysis in education - Case studies. I. Title. II. Series: Counterpoints (New York, N.Y.) ; vol. 99.*
*TC LB1033 .M546 2000*

**Mirrored images.**
Trencher, Susan R. Westport, CT : Bergin & Garvey, 2000.
*TC GN17.3.U6 T74 2000*

**MIRRORS IN ART.**
Miller, Jonathan, 1934- On reflection. London : National Gallery Publications ; [New Haven, Conn.] : Distributed by Yale University Press, c1998.
*TC N8224.M6 M54 1998*

**MISCELLANEOUS FACTS. *See* HANDBOOKS, VADE-MECUMS, ETC.; QUESTIONS AND ANSWERS.**

**MISCOMMUNICATION.**
Young, Robert L. (Robert Louis), 1949- Understanding misunderstandings. 1st ed. Austin : University of Texas Press, 1999.
*TC BF637.C45 Y69 1999*

**MISCONDUCT IN OFFICE. *See* FALSE CERTIFICATION.**

**MISCUE ANALYSIS.**
Wilde, Sandra. Miscue analysis made easy. Portsmouth, NH : Heinemann, c2000.
*TC LB1050.33 .W54 2000*

**Miscue analysis made easy.**
Wilde, Sandra. Portsmouth, NH : Heinemann, c2000.
*TC LB1050.33 .W54 2000*

**MISDEMEANORS. *See* CRIME.**

**The mismeasure of desire.**
Stein, Edward, 1965- Oxford ; New York : Oxford University Press, 1999.
*TC HQ76.25 .S69 1999*

**Misreading reading.**
Coles, Gerald. Portsmouth, NH : Heinemann, c2000.
*TC LB1050.6 .C65 2000*

**Misrepresentation in the marketplace and beyond :** ethics under siege / [edited by Peggy C. Askins] ; prepared by the Task Force on Credential Fraud. Washington, DC : American Association of Collegiate Registrars and Admissions Officers, 1996. viii, 56 p. : ill. ; 23 cm. Includes bibliographical references (p. 53-55) and index. ISBN 0-929851-69-2 DDC 379.1/58/0973
*1. Universities and colleges - Accreditation - United States. 2. False certification - United States. 3. Diploma mills - United States. I. Askins, Peggy C. (Peggy Corley) II. AACRAO Task Force on Credential Fraud. III. American Association of Collegiate Registrars and Admissions Officers. IV. Title: Ethics under siege*
*TC LB2331.615.U6 M57 1996*

**Missed connections.**
Stenross, Barbara, 1946- Philadelphia : Temple University Press, 1999.
*TC RF291 .S74 1999*

**MISSION INDIANS OF CALIFORNIA. *See* INDIANS OF NORTH AMERICA - CALIFORNIA.**

**The mission of art.**
Grey, Alex. 1st ed. Boston : Shambhala, 1998.
*TC N6537.G718 A4 1998*

**MISSIONARIES. *See* WOMEN MISSIONARIES.**

**MISSIONARIES, WOMEN. *See* WOMEN MISSIONARIES.**

**MISSIONS. *See* WOMEN IN MISSIONARY WORK.**

**MISSIONS - EDUCATIONAL WORK.**
Murphy, Daniel. A history of Irish emigrant and missionary education. Dublin, Ireland ; Portland, Ore. : Four Courts Pres, c2000.
*TC BV2630.M87 2000*

**MISSIONS, FOREIGN. *See* MISSIONS.**

**MISSIONS - HISTORY.**
Gendered missions. Ann Arbor : University of Michigan Press, c1999.
*TC BV2610 .G46 1999*

**MISSIONS, IRISH.**
Murphy, Daniel. A history of Irish emigrant and missionary education. Dublin, Ireland ; Portland, Ore. : Four Courts Pres, c2000.
*TC BV2630.M87 2000*

**Mistakes and correction.**
Edge, Julian, 1948- London ; New York : Longman, 1989.
*TC PE1128.A2 E28 1989*

**The misteaching of academic discourses.**
Bartolomé, Lilia I. Boulder, Colo. : Westview Press, 1998.
*TC LB1033.5 .B37 1998*

**Misumi, Jūji, 1924-** Rīdāshippu kōdō no kagaku = The behavioral science of leadership / Misumi Jyūji. Behavioral science of leadership. Includes bibliographical references.
*1. Leadership. 2. Social groups. 3. Management. 4. Management - Japan. I. Title. II. Title: Behavioral science of leadership*
*TC HM141 .M48 1978*

**MITC, site prototypes.**
Nord, Michael B. Music in the classroom (MITC). 1998.
*TC 06 no. 10974*

**Mitchell, B. R. (Brian R.).**
**European historical statistics, 1750 1975.**
Mitchell, B. R. (Brian R.) International historical statistics. 4th ed. London : Macmillan Reference ; New York, N.Y. : Grove's dictionaries [division of Stockton Press], 1998.
*TC HA1107 .M53 1998*

International historical statistics, Africa, Asia & Oceania, 1750-1993 / B.R. Mitchell. 3rd ed. London : Macmillan Reference ; New York : Ggrove's Dictionaries[division of Stockton Press], 1998. xix, 1113 p. ; 29 cm. Includes bibliographical references. ISBN 0-333-72691-X (UK) ISBN 1-56159-234-X (US) ISBN 1-56159-233-1 (set)
*1. Africa - Statistics - History. 2. Asia - Statistics - History. 3. Oceania - Statistics - History. I. Title.*
*TC HA1107 .M54 1998*

International historical statistics : Europe, 1750-1993 / B.R. Mitchell. 4th ed. London : Macmillan Reference ; New York, N.Y. : Grove's dictionaries [division of Stockton Press], 1998. xvii, 959 p. ; 29 cm. Rev. ed. of: European historical statistics, 1750-1975. 2nd rev. ed. 1980. Includes bibliographical references. ISBN 0-333-72690-1 ISBN 1-56159-236-6
*1. Europe - Statistics - History. I. Mitchell, B. R. (Brian R.) European historical statistics, 1750-1975. II. Title.*
*TC HA1107 .M53 1998*

International historical statistics : the Americas, 1750-1993 / B.R. Mitchell. 4th ed. London : Macmillan Reference ; New YorkGrove Dictionaries[division of : Stockton Press], 1998. xv, 830 p. ; 29 cm. Includes bibliographical references. ISBN 0-333-72689-8 (UK) ISBN 1-56159-235-8 (US)
*1. Statistics - History. 2. America - Statistics - History. I. Title.*
*TC HA1107 .M55 1998*

**Mitchell, Bruce M.** Encyclopedia of multicultural education / Bruce M. Mitchell and Robert E. Salsbury. Westport, Conn. : Greenwood Press, 1999. viii, 304 p. ; 25 cm. Includes bibliographical references (p.293- 298) and index. ISBN 0-313-30029-1 (alk. paper) DDC 370.117/0973
*1. Multicultural education - United States - Encyclopedias. 2. Multicultural education - Encyclopedias. I. Salsbury, Robert E. II. Title.*
*TC LC1099.3 .M58 1999*

Multicultural education in the U.S. : a guide to policies and programs in the 50 states / Bruce M. Mitchell and Robert E. Salsbury. Westport, Conn. ; London : Greenwood Press, 2000. viii, 281 p. ; 25 cm. Includes bibliographical references (p. [275]-276) and index. ISBN 0-313-30859-4 (alk. paper) DDC 370.117/0973

*1. Multicultural education - United States - States. 2. Education and state - United States - States. I. Salsbury, Robert E. II. Title. III. Title: Multicultural education in the US*
**TC LC1099.3 .M59 2000**

**Mitchell, Christine.**
Hughes, Martin, 1949 May 15- Numeracy and beyond. Buckingham [England] ; Philadelphia : Open University Press, 2000.
**TC QA135.5 .H844 2000**

**Mitchell, Claudia.**
Weber, Sandra. That's funny, you don't look like a teacher!. London ; Washington, D.C. : Falmer Press, 1995.
**TC LB1775.4.G7 W43 1995**

**Mitchell, Lucy (Sprague) 1878-** Two lives; the story of Wesley Clair Mitchell and myself. New York, Simon and Schuster, 1953. 575 p. : ill. ; 22 cm. Includes bibliographical references. DDC 923.373
*1. Mitchell, Wesley Clair, - 1874-1948. I. Title.*
**TC HB119.M5 M52**

**Mitchell, Peter, 1959-.**
Children's reasoning and the mind. Hove : Psychology, c2000.
**TC BF723.R4 C555 2000**

**Mitchell, Theodore R.**
Challenges of urban education. Albany : State Unviersity of New York Press, c2000.
**TC LC5131 .C38 2000**

**Mitchell, Tracy, ill.**
Dodds, Dayle Ann. The Great Divide. 1st ed. Cambridge, MA : Candlewick Press, 1999.
**TC PZ8.3.D645 Gr 1999**

**MITCHELL, WESLEY CLAIR, 1874-1948.**
Mitchell, Lucy (Sprague) 1878- Two lives; New York, Simon and Schuster, 1953.
**TC HB119.M5 M52**

**Mitchell, William J. (William John), 1944-** E-topia : "urban life, Jim--but not as we know it" / William J. Mitchell. Cambridge, Mass. : MIT Press, 1999. 184 p. ; 24 cm. Includes bibliographical references and index. ISBN 0-262-13355-5 (hc : alk. paper) DDC 303.48/33
*1. Telecommunication - Social aspects. 2. Computer networks - Social aspects. 3. Information superhighway - Social aspects. 4. Cities and towns. I. Title.*
**TC HE7631 .M58 1999**

**Mittler, Peter J.** Working towards inclusive education : social contexts / Peter Mittler. London : D. Fulton Publishers, 2000. xi, 212 p. ; 25 cm. Includes bibliographical references (p. [193]-204) and index. ISBN 1-85346-698-0 DDC 371.90460941
*1. Inclusive education - Social aspects - Great Britain. 2. Handicapped children - Education - Social aspects - Great Britain. 3. Learning disabled children - Education - Social aspects - Great Britain. I. Title.*
**TC LC1203.G7 M58 2000**

**Mixed bag.**
Hutchinson, Helene D. [Glenview, Ill.] Scott, Foresman [1970]
**TC PE1122 .H85**

**MIXED ECONOMY - CHINA - GUANGZHOU.**
Ikels, Charlotte. The return of the god of wealth. Stanford, Calif. : Stanford University Press, c1996.
**TC HC428.C34 I38 1996**

**MIXED MARRIAGE. See INTERMARRIAGE.**

**MIXED MEDIA PAINTING.**
Alexander, George, 1949- Julie Rrap. [Sidney] : Piper Press, 1998.
**TC TR654 .A44 1998**

**MIXED SCHIZOPHRENIC AND AFFECTIVE PSYCHOSIS. See SCHIZOAFFECTIVE DISORDERS.**

**Mixer, Joseph R., 1923-** Principles of professional fundraising : useful foundations for successful practice / Joseph R. Mixer. 1st ed. San Francisco : Jossey-Bass, c1993. xx, 277 p. ; 24 cm. (The Jossey-Bass nonprofit sector series) Includes bibliographical references (p. 253-268) and index. ISBN 1-55542-590-9 (acid-free paper) DDC 361.7/068/1
*1. Fund raising - United States. 2. Nonprofit organizations - United States. I. Title. II. Series.*
**TC HV41.9.U5 M58 1993**

**Miyamoto, Frank.**
Rabbit in the moon [videorecording]. San Francisco, Calif. : Wabi-Sabi Productions, 1999.
**TC D753.8 .R3 1999**

**Mizumura, Kazue.**
Zolotow, Charlotte, 1915- River winding. 1st ed. New York : Crowell, [1978]

**TC PZ8.3.Z6 Ri 1978**

**The MLA style manual.**
Gibaldi, Joseph, 1942- New York : Modern Language Association of America, 1985.
**TC PN147 .G53 1998**

**MLDM'99 (1999 : Leipzig, Germany)** Machine learning and data mining in pattern recognition : First International Workshop, MLDM'99, Leipzig, Germany, September 16-18, 1999 : proceedings / Petra Perner, Maria Petrou (eds.). Berlin : New York : Springer, c1999. viii, 215 p. : ill. ; 24 cm. (Lecture notes in computer science ; 1715. Lecture notes in artificial intelligence) Includes bibliographical references and index. ISBN 3-540-66596-X (softcover)
*1. Pattern perception - Congresses. 2. Machine learning - Congresses. 3. Data mining - Congresses. 4. Image processing - Congresses. I. Perner, Petra. II. Petrou, Maria. III. Title. IV. Series: Lecture notes in computer science ; 1715. V. Series: Lecture notes in computer science. Lecture notes in artificial intelligence.*
**TC Q327 .M56 1999**

**MMPI.**
Graham, John R. (John Robert), 1940- MMPI-2 correlates for outpatient community mental health settings. Minneapolis : University of Minnesota Press, c1999.
**TC RC473.M5 G733 1999**

**MMPI-2.**
Graham, John R. (John Robert), 1940- 3rd ed. New York : Oxford University Press, 1999.
**TC RC473.M5 G73 1999**

**The MMPI-2.**
Greene, Roger L. 2nd ed. Boston : Allyn and Bacon, c2000.
**TC BF698.8.M5 G74 2000**

**MMPI-2 correlates for outpatient community mental health settings.**
Graham, John R. (John Robert), 1940- Minneapolis : University of Minnesota Press, c1999.
**TC RC473.M5 G733 1999**

**The MMPI, MMPI-2, & MMPI-A in court.**
Pope, Kenneth S. 2nd ed. Washington, DC : American Psychological Association, 2000.
**TC KF8965 .P66 1999**

**MMPI, MMPI-2, and MMPI-A in court.**
Pope, Kenneth S. The MMPI, MMPI-2, & MMPI-A in court. 2nd ed. Washington, DC : American Psychological Association, 2000.
**TC KF8965 .P66 1999**

**MMPI (PERSONALITY TEST). See MINNESOTA MULTIPHASIC PERSONALITY INVENTORY.**

**MNEMONICS. See also MEMORY.**
Embiricos, Anne-Marie T. The effects of content knowledge and strategies on memory development among 4- and 6-year-old children. 1998.
**TC 085 Em22**

Embiricos, Anne-Marie T. The effects of content knowledge and strategies on memory development among 4- and 6-year-old children. 1998.
**TC 085 Em22**

**MNES (INTERNATIONAL BUSINESS ENTERPRISES). See INTERNATIONAL BUSINESS ENTERPRISES.**

**MOBILE GENETIC ELEMENTS. See VIRUSES.**

**MOBILE RADIO STATIONS. See CITIZENS BAND RADIO.**

**Mobility International USA (Organization).**
Loud, proud & passionate. 1st ed. Eugene, OR : Mobility International USA, 1997.
**TC HV1569.3.W65 L68 1997**

**MOBILITY, LABOR. See LABOR MOBILITY.**

**MOBILITY, OCCUPATIONAL. See OCCUPATIONAL MOBILITY.**

**MOBS. See RIOTS.**

**Democratic dialogue with special needs students :** Mike Pezone & Alan Singer / produced by the Social Science Education Consortium. [Boulder, Colo.] : Social Science Education Consortium, c1997. 1 videocassette (25 min.) : sd., col. ; 1/2 in. VHS. Catalogued from credits and cassette label. Title from cassette label. Edited by Vicki Murray-Kurzban. For educators, especially teachers of "at-risk" students. SUMMARY: Mike Pezone, teacher at Russell Sage Junior High, discusses how he teaches "at-risk" kids, the "kids that no one invests in", kids with ADD, learning disabilities, hearing challenges, etc. He stresses learning self-worth and validation as human beings, over content,

emphasizing his students' need to listen to each other, their need to speak and the importance of everyone's voice being heard. In this class the students evaluate themselves. We view his students in action during a democratic dialogue and later in a Social Studies discussion. CONTENTS: Russell Sage Junior High : democratic dialogue with special needs students -- Mike Pezone's "8B7" class with Alan Singer from Hofstra University -- Who are the 8B7? -- Outcomes/Rationale -- Set up for Project -- Practice/rehearsal for performance -- The dialogue -- Debriefing -- Effort or result : how should teachers grade? -- Russell Sage Junior High : Mike Pezone's 9-C Social Studies class discussion.
*1. Civics - Study and teaching (Middle school) - United States. 2. Citizenship - Study and teaching (Middle school) - United States. 3. Education - Standards - United States. I. Social Science Education Consortium.*

**MODALITY (LINGUISTICS).**
Discourse and perspective in cognitive linguistics. Amsterdam ; Philadelphia : J. Benjamins, c1997.
**TC P165 .D57 1997**

Kunz, Linda Ann. English modals in American talk shows. 1999.
**TC 06 no. 11136**

**MODEL. See EXAMPLE.**

**MODEL CITIES. See CITY PLANNING; URBAN RENEWAL.**

**MODEL SCHOOL NO. 25 (MOSCOW, RUSSIA) - HISTORY.**
Holmes, Larry E. (Larry Eugene), 1942- Stalin's school. Pittsburgh, Pa. : University of Pittsburgh Press, c1999.
**TC LF4435.M657 H65 1999**

**MODEL SCHOOLS. See LABORATORY SCHOOLS.**

**Modeling and simulation in science and mathematics education** / Wallace Feurzeig, Nancy Roberts, editors. New York : Springer, c1999. xviii, 334 p. : ill. ; 24 cm. + 1 computer optical disc (4 3/4 in.). (Modeling dynamic systems) Includes bibliographical references and index. ISBN 0-387-98316-3 (hc : alk. paper) DDC 501/.13
*1. Science - Study and teaching (Secondary) 2. Science - Computer simulation. 3. Mathematics - Study and teaching (Secondary) 4. Mathematics - Computer simulation. 5. Computer-assisted instruction. I. Feurzeig, W. II. Roberts, Nancy, 1938- III. Series.*
**TC Q181 .M62 1999**

**Modeling changes in understanding.**
Modelling changes in understanding. Amsterdam ; New York : Pergamon, 1999.
**TC BF319 .M55 1999**

**Modeling conditional item dependencies with a three-parameter logistic testlet model.**
Du, Zuru. 1998.
**TC 085 D84**

**Modeling dynamic systems**
Modeling and simulation in science and mathematics education. New York : Springer, c1999.
**TC Q181 .M62 1999**

**Modelling changes in understanding :** case studies in physical reasoning / edited by Daniel Kayser and Stella Vosniadou. Amsterdam ; New York : Pergamon, 1999. xi, 302 p. : ill. ; 25 cm. (Advances in learning and instruction series) Includes bibliographical references (p. 280-295) and index. ISBN 0-08-043454-1 DDC 153.1
*1. Learning, Psychology of. 2. Change (Psychology) 3. Concepts. 4. Machine learning. I. Kayser, Daniel. II. Vosniadou, Stella. III. Title: Modeling changes in understanding IV. Series.*
**TC BF319 .M55 1999**

**Models in the policy process.**
Greenberger, Martin, 1931- New York : Russell Sage Foundation : [distributed by Basic Books], c1976.
**TC H61 .G667**

**MODELS, NURSING.**
Nursing theories. New York : Springer Pub. Co., c1999.
**TC RT84.5 .N8795 1999**

**Models of cognitive aging** / edited by Timothy J. Perfect and Elizabeth A. Maylor. Oxford ; New York : Oxford University Press, 2000. x, 310 p. : ill. ; 24 cm. (Debates in psychology) Includes bibliographical references and index. ISBN 0-19-852433-2 (hbk. : alk. paper) ISBN 0-19-852437-4 (pbk. : alk. paper) DDC 155.67/13
*1. Cognition - Age factors. 2. Aging - Psychological aspects. I. Perfect, Timothy J. II. Maylor, Elizabeth A. III. Series.*
**TC BF724.55.C63 M63 2000**

**MODELS, PSYCHOLOGICAL.**
Frontiers of developmental psychopathology. New
York : Oxford University Press, 1996.
*TC RC454.4 .F76 1996*

**MODELS, THEORETICAL.**
Kim, Hesook Suzie. The nature of theoretical thinking
in nursing. 2nd ed. New York : Springer Pub. Co.,
c2000.
*TC RT84.5 .K545 2000*

**MODERN AESTHETICS.** *See* **AESTHETICS,
MODERN.**

**MODERN ARCHITECTURE.** *See*
**ARCHITECTURE, MODERN.**

**MODERN ART.** *See* **ART, MODERN;
MODERNISM (ART).**

**Modern art and the Romantic vision.**
Tekiner, Deniz. Lanham, Md. : University Press of
America, c2000.
*TC N6465.R6 T43 2000*

**Modern art, practices & debates (Television
program)**
On pictures and paintings [videorecording].
Peasmarsh, East Sussex, Eng. ; Ho-Ho-kus, NJ :
Roland Collection, 1992.
*TC ND195.045 1992*

**MODERN ARTS.** *See* **ARTS, MODERN.**

**MODERN CIVILIZATION.** *See* **CIVILIZATION,
MODERN.**

**MODERN DANCE.**
Fleming, Bruce. Sex, art, and audience. New York :
Canterbury [England] : P. Lang, c2000.
*TC GV1588.3 .F54 2000*

**MODERN DANCE - HISTORY.**
Mazo, Joseph H. Prime movers. 2nd revised edition.
Princeton, NJ. : Princeton Book Co. Pub., c2000.
*TC GV1783 .M347 2000*

**MODERN DANCE - SOCIAL ASPECTS - UNITED
STATES - HISTORY.**
Thomas, Helen, 1947- Dance, modernity, and culture.
London ; New York : Routledge, 1995.
*TC GV1588.6 .T46 1995*

**MODERN DANCING.** *See* **MODERN DANCE.**

**Modern education, textbooks and the image of the
nation.**
Lee, Yoonmi. New York ; London : Garland Pub.,
2000.
*TC LB3048.K6 L44 2000*

**Modern educational measurement.**
Popham, W. James. 3rd ed. Boston : Allyn and Bacon,
c2000.
*TC LB3051 .P6143 2000*

**Modern English in action.**
Christ, Henry I. (Henry Irving), 1915- Lexington,
Mass. : D. C. Heath, 1978
*TC PE1112 .C47 1978*

Christ, Henry I. (Henry Irving), 1915- Lexington,
Mass. : D. C. Heath, 1975
*TC PE1112 .C47 1975*

Christ, Henry I. (Henry Irving), 1915- Teacher's ed.
Lexington, Mass. : D. C. Heath, 1975
*TC PE1112 .C47 1975 Teacher's Ed.*

Christ, Henry I. (Henry Irving), 1915- Teacher's ed.
Lexington, Mass. : D. C. Heath, 1978
*TC PE1112 .C47 1978 Teacher's ed.*

Christ, Henry I. (Henry Irving), 1915- Teacher's ed.
Lexington, Mass. : D. C. Heath, 1978
*TC PE1112 .C47 1978 Teacher's Ed.*

Christ, Henry I. (Henry Irving), 1915- Teacher's ed.
Lexington, Mass. : D. C. Heath, 1978
*TC PE1112 .C47 1978 Teacher's Ed.*

**MODERN HISTORY.** *See* **HISTORY, MODERN.**

**Modern Language Association of America.**
Gibaldi, Joseph, 1942- The MLA style manual. New
York : Modern Language Association of America,
1985.
*TC PN147 .G53 1998*

**MODERN LANGUAGES.** *See* **LANGUAGES,
MODERN.**

**Modern languages and learning strategies.**
Grenfell, Michael, 1953- London ; New York :
Routledge, 1999.
*TC PB35 .G783 1999*

**Modern languages in practice**
(9) Grenfell, Michael, 1953- Training teachers in
practice. Clevedon, UK : Philadelphia :
Multilingual Matters, c1998.
*TC P53.85 .G74 1998*

(11) Guillot, Marie-Noëlle, 1955- Fluency and its
teaching. Clevedon, England ; Philadelphia, Pa. :
Multilingual Matters, c1999.
*TC P53.6 .G85 1999*

(12) Chambers, Gary N., 1956- Motivating
language learners. Clevedon [U.K.] ; Buffalo :
Multilingual Matters, c1999.
*TC PB35 .C517 1999*

**MODERN LITERATURE.** *See* **LITERATURE,
MODERN.**

**Modern Morse code in rehabilitation and education.**
King, Thomas W. Boston : Allyn and Bacon, c2000.
*TC HV1569.5 .K55 2000*

**Modern nutrition (Boca Raton, Fla.)**
Wildman, Robert E. C., 1964- Advanced human
nutrition. Boca Raton : CRC Press, c2000.
*TC QP141 .W512 2000*

**MODERN PAINTING.** *See* **PAINTING, MODERN.**

**MODERN PHILOSOPHY.** *See* **PHILOSOPHY,
MODERN.**

**Modern problems of pharmacopsychiatry**
(vol. 25) Mood disorders. Basel ; New York :
Karger, c1997.
*TC RC483 .M6 1997*

**MODERN SCULPTURE.** *See* **SCULPTURE,
MODERN.**

**Modern starts.**
Modernstarts. New York : Museum of Modern Art :
Distributed by Harry N. Abrams, c1999.
*TC N620.M9 M63 1999*

**Modern works, modern problems?.**
Institute of Paper Conservation. [England] : Institute
of Paper Conservation, c1994.
*TC N8560 .I59 1994*

**MODERNISM (AESTHETICS).**
On pictures and paintings [videorecording].
Peasmarsh, East Sussex, Eng. ; Ho-Ho-kus, NJ :
Roland Collection, 1992.
*TC ND195.045 1992*

**MODERNISM (ART).** *See also* **ART, MODERN -
20TH CENTURY; EXPRESSIONISM (ART);
IMPRESSIONISM (ART);
POSTMODERNISM.**
On pictures and paintings [videorecording].
Peasmarsh, East Sussex, Eng. ; Ho-Ho-kus, NJ :
Roland Collection, 1992.
*TC ND195.045 1992*

Smith, Bernard, 1916- Modernism's history. New
Haven : Yale University Press, 1998.
*TC N6494.M64 S65 1998*

**MODERNISM IN ART.** *See* **MODERNISM (ART).**

**MODERNISM (LITERATURE).** *See*
**LITERATURE, EXPERIMENTAL;
POSTMODERNISM (LITERATURE).**

**Modernism's history.**
Smith, Bernard, 1916- New Haven : Yale University
Press, 1998.
*TC N6494.M64 S65 1998*

**MODERNIST ART.** *See* **MODERNISM (ART).**

**MODERNIST-FUNDAMENTALIST
CONTROVERSY.** *See* **FUNDAMENTALISM.**

**Modernity's wager.**
Seligman, A. Princeton, NJ : Princeton University
Press, 2000.
*TC HM1251 .S45 2000*

**Modernizing schools : technology and buildings for a
new century (September 19, 2000 : Washington,
D.C.)** Modernizing schools [videorecording] :
technology and buildings for a new century /
[presented by the] U.S. Department of Education in
partnership with the National Alliance of Business
with the U.S. Chamber of Commerce and the
Committee for Economic Development. [Washington,
D.C.] : U.S. Dept. of Education, [2000]. 1 videocassette
(ca. 60 min.) : sd., col. ; 1/2 in. (Satellite town meeting ; 72)
VHS. Catalogued from credits and data sheet. Closed
captioned. Host, U.S. Secretary of Education, Richard Riley;
moderator, Nancy Mathis. A call-in and web-cast Satellite
Town meeting held in Washington, D.C., Tuesday, September
19, 2000, 8:00-9:00 P.M. (ET). For educators, parents and
students. SUMMARY: Moderated by Nancy Mathis and hosted

by Secretary of Education, Richard Riley, the panel discusses
creating schools for the 21rst century, meeting the challenges
of increased student populations and outfitting worn-out
structures with new facilities to accomodate teaching and
learning in the new century. Questions such as: what schools
for the 21rst century should look like, how they can be centers
of their communities, how they can help students to connect to
the community and the real world, and many others, are
addressed.
*1. School facitilius - United States - Design and construction.
2. School buildings - United States - Maintenance and repair.
3. Educational technology - United States. 4. Video recordings
for the hearing impaired. I. Mathis, Nancya. II. Riley, Richard
W. (Richard Wilson) III. United States. Dept. of Education. IV.
Committee for Economic Development. V. National Alliance of
Business. VI. Chamber of Commerce of the United States of
America. VII. Title. VIII. Title: Technology and buildings for a
new century [videorecording] IX. Series: OIIA satellite town
meeting ; 72.*
*TC LB3205 .M64 2000*

Modernizing schools [videorecording] : technology
and buildings for a new century / [presented by the]
U.S. Department of Education in partnership with the
National Alliance of Business with the U.S. Chamber
of Commerce and the Committee for Economic
Development. [Washington, D.C.] : U.S. Dept. of
Education, [2000]. 1 videocassette (ca. 60 min.) : sd., col. ;
1/2 in. (Satellite town meeting ; 72) VHS. Catalogued from
credits and data sheet. Closed captioned. Host, U.S. Secretary
of Education, Richard Riley; moderator, Nancy Mathis. A
call-in and web-cast Satellite town meeting held in
Washington, D.C., Tuesday, September 19, 2000, 8:00-9:00
P.M. (ET). For educators, parents and students. SUMMARY:
Moderated by Nancy Mathis and hosted by Secretary of
Education, Richard Riley, the panel discusses creating schools
for the 21rst century, meeting the challenges of increased
student populations and outfitting worn-out structures with new
facilities to accomodate teaching and learning in the new
century. Questions such as: what schools for the 21rst century
should look like, how they can be centers of their communities,
how they can help students to connect to the community and
the real world, and many others, are addressed.
*1. School facitilius - United States - Design and construction.
2. School buildings - United States - Maintenance and repair.
3. Educational technology - United States. 4. Video recordings
for the hearing impaired. I. Mathis, Nancya. II. Riley, Richard
W. (Richard Wilson) III. United States. Dept. of Education. IV.
Committee for Economic Development. V. National Alliance of
Business. VI. Chamber of Commerce of the United States of
America. VII. Title. VIII. Title: Technology and buildings for a
new century [videorecording] IX. Series: OIIA satellite town
meeting ; 72.*
*TC LB3205 .M64 2000*

**Modernizing schools [videorecording].**
Modernizing schools : technology and buildings for a
new century (September 19, 2000 : Washington, D.C.)
[Washington, D.C.] : U.S. Dept. of Education, [2000].
*TC LB3205 .M64 2000*

Modernizing schools : technology and buildings for a
new century (September 19, 2000 : Washington, D.C.)
[Washington, D.C.] : U.S. Dept. of Education, [2000].
*TC LB3205 .M64 2000*

**Modernstarts : people, places, things** / edited by John
Elderfield, Peter Reed, Mary Chan, Maria del Carmen
González. New York : Museum of Modern Art :
Distributed by Harry N. Abrams, c1999. 360 p. : ill.
(some col.), ports. ; 31 cm. Catalog of an exhibition held Oct.
7, 1999-March 14, 2000. "ModernStarts is the first of three
cycles of exhibitions organized by the Museum...under the
banner MoMA2000 to mark the millennium"--p. 8. "This book
is an illustrated guide to the visual arts of the period 1880
through 1920 as represented in the collection of The Museum
of Modern Art"--p. 17. Includes bibliographical references (p.
350-355) and index of illustrations. ISBN 0-8109-6203-9
(Abrams) ISBN 0-87070-025-1 (MoMA/Thames & Hudson :
cloth) ISBN 0-87070-024-3 (MoMA/Thames & Hudson : pbk.)
*1. Museum of Modern Art (New York, N.Y.) - Exhibitions. 2.
Art, Modern - 20th century - Exhibitions. 3. Art, Modern - 19th
century - Exhibitions. 4. Human beings in art - Exhibitions. 5.
Landscape in art - Exhibitions. 6. Object (Aesthetics) -
Exhibitions. I. Elderfield, John. II. Reed, Peter. III. Chan,
Mary, 1965- IV. González, Maria del Carmen. V. Museum of
Modern Art (New York, N.Y.) VI. Title: Modern starts VII.
Title: MoMA2000 VIII. Title: MoMA 2000 IX. Title: People,
places, things*
*TC N620.M9 M63 1999*

**Modgil, Celia.**
Classroom issues. London ; New York : Falmer Press,
2000.
*TC LC268 .C52 2000*

Institutional issues. London ; New York : Falmer
Press, 2000.

*TC LC191 .I495 2000*

Moral education and pluralism. London ; New York : Falmer Press, 2000.
*TC LC268 .M683 2000*

Politics, education and citizenship. London ; New York : Falmer Press, 2000.
*TC LC1091 .P54 2000*

Spiritual and religious education. London ; New York : Falmer Press, 2000.
*TC BL42 .S68 2000*

Systems of education. London ; New York : Falmer Press, 2000.
*TC LC191 .S98 2000*

**Modgil, Sohan.**
Classroom issues. London ; New York : Falmer Press, 2000.
*TC LC268 .C52 2000*

Institutional issues. London ; New York : Falmer Press, 2000.
*TC LC191 .I495 2000*

Moral education and pluralism. London ; New York : Falmer Press, 2000.
*TC LC268 .M683 2000*

Politics, education and citizenship. London ; New York : Falmer Press, 2000.
*TC LC1091 .P54 2000*

Spiritual and religious education. London ; New York : Falmer Press, 2000.
*TC BL42 .S68 2000*

Systems of education. London ; New York : Falmer Press, 2000.
*TC LC191 .S98 2000*

**Modifying schoolwork.**
Janney, Rachel. Baltimore, Md. : Paul H. Brookes Pub., c2000.
*TC LC1201 .J26 2000*

**Modra, Ron.**
Sport photography today! [videorecording]. Minneapolis, Minn. : Media Loft, c1992.
*TC TR821 .S64 1992*

**MODULAR APPROACH IN EDUCATION.** *See* **INDEPENDENT STUDY.**

**Moemeka, Andrew A. (Andrew Azukaego)**
Development communication in action : building understanding and creating participation / Andrew A. Moemeka. Lanham, Md. : University Press of America, c2000. xvi, 325 p. : ill. ; 24 cm. Includes bibliographical references (p. [285]-313) and indexes. ISBN 0-7618-1571-6 (alk. paper) ISBN 0-7618-1572-4 (pbk. : alk. paper) DDC 384
*1. Communication in economic development. 2. Communication in community development. I. Title.*
*TC HD76 .M644 2000*

**Moessinger, Pierre.**
[Irrationalité individuelle et ordre social. English]
The paradox of social order : linking psychology and sociology / Pierre Moessinger ; translated by Stephen Scher, Francesca Worrall. New York : Aldine de Gruyter, c2000. xi, 152 p. ; 23 cm. (Sociological imagination and structural change) Includes bibliographical references (p. [135]-147) and indexes. ISBN 0-202-30575-9 (cloth : alk. paper) ISBN 0-202-30576-7 (pbk. : alk. paper) DDC 302.5/4
*1. Individualism. 2. Social psychology. 3. Social values. I. Title. II. Series.*
*TC HM1276 .M6413 2000*

**Moeyaert, Bart.**
[Blote handen. English]
Bare hands / Bart Moeyaert ; translated by David Colmer. 1st ed. Asheville, N.C. : Front Street, 1998. 111 p. ; 22 cm. SUMMARY: A boy confronts his mother's suitor on New Year's Eve when the boy kills the man's duck and, in a fit of anger, the man kills the boy's dog. ISBN 1-88691-032-4 (alk. paper) DDC [Fic]
*1. Revenge - Fiction. 2. Dogs - Fiction. 3. Family problems - Fiction. 4. New Year - Fiction. 5. Fireworks - Fiction. 6. Belgium - Fiction. I. Colmer, David, 1964- II. Title.*
*TC PZ7.M7227 Bar 1998*

**Moffatt, Courtney W.** How to get a teaching job / Courtney W. Moffatt, Thomas L. Moffatt. Boston ; London : Allyn and Bacon, c2000. xiii, 174 p. : ill. ; 24 cm. Includes bibliographical references (p. 169) and index. ISBN 0-205-29924-5 DDC 370/.23/73
*1. Teachers - Employment - United States - Handbooks, manuals, etc. 2. Teaching - Vocational guidance - United States - Handbooks, manuals, etc. I. Moffatt, Thomas L. II. Title.*

*TC LB1780 .M64 2000*

**Moffatt, Thomas L.**
Moffatt, Courtney W. How to get a teaching job. Boston ; London : Allyn and Bacon, c2000.
*TC LB1780 .M64 2000*

**Moffatt, Tracey.** Tracey Moffatt : fever pitch / text by Gael Newton and Tracey Moffatt. Annandale, N.S.W., Australia : Piper Press, c1995. 119 p. : ill. (some col.) ; 27 cm. Includes bibliographical references (p. 23-24). ISBN 0-9587984-5-1
*1. Moffatt, Tracey. I. Newton, Gael. II. Title. III. Title: Fever pitch.*
*TC TR647 .M843 1995*

**MOFFATT, TRACEY.**
Moffatt, Tracey. Tracey Moffatt. Annandale, N.S.W., Australia : Piper Press, c1995.
*TC TR647 .M843 1995*

**Moffitt, Robert.**
Welfare, the family, and reproductive behavior. Washington, D.C. : National Academy Press, 1998.
*TC HV91 .W478 1998*

**MOHAMMEDANISM.** *See* **ISLAM.**

**Mohrman, Allan M.** Designing performance appraisal systems : aligning appraisals and organizational realities / Allan M. Mohrman, Jr., Susan M. Resnick-West, Edward E. Lawler III, in collaboration with Michael J. Driver, Mary Ann Von Glinow, J. Bruce Prince. 1st ed. San Francisco : Jossey-Bass Publishers, 1989. xix, 227 p. : ill. ; 24 cm. (The Jossey-Bass management series) Includes bibliographical references. ISBN 1-55542-149-0 (alk. paper) DDC 658.3/125
*1. Performance standards. 2. Employees, Rating of. I. Resnick-West, Susan M., 1951- II. Lawler, Edward E. III. Title. IV. Series.*
*TC HF5549.5.P35 M64 1989*

**Moi, Toril.** What is a woman? : and other essays / Toril Moi. Oxford ; New York : Oxford University Press, 1999. xxiv, 517 p. ; 24 cm. Includes bibliographical references (p. [477]-497) and index. ISBN 0-19-812242-X DDC 305.42/01
*1. Feminist theory. 2. Feminism and literature. 3. Women and literature. I. Title.*
*TC HQ1190 .M64 1999*

**Moir, Martin.**
The Great Indian education debate. Richmond : Curzon, 1999.
*TC LA1151 .G743 1999*

**MOLESTING OF CHILDREN.** *See* **CHILD SEXUAL ABUSE.**

**Molfese, Dennis L.**
Temperament and personality development across the life span. Mahwah, NJ : L. Erlbaum Associates, 2000.
*TC BF798 .T46 2000*

**Moline, Steve.**
What is visual literacy? York, Maine : Stenhouse Pub., c1996.
*TC LB1068 .W45 1996*

**Møller, Aage R.** Hearing, its physiology and pathophysiology / Aage R. Møller. San Diego : Academic Press, c2000. xvi, 515 p. : ill. ; 24 cm. Includes bibliographical references (p. [485]-493) and index. ISBN 0-12-504255-8
*1. Ear - Physiology. 2. Ear - Pathophysiology. 3. Hearing. I. Title.*
*TC QP461 .M65 2000*

**Molly Bannaky.**
McGill, Alice. Boston, Mass. : Houghton Mifflin, 1999.
*TC PZ7.M478468 Mol 1999*

**MoMA 2000.**
Modernstarts. New York : Museum of Modern Art : Distributed by Harry N. Abrams, c1999.
*TC N620.M9 M63 1999*

**MoMA2000.**
Modernstarts. New York : Museum of Modern Art : Distributed by Harry N. Abrams, c1999.
*TC N620.M9 M63 1999*

**MOMS.** *See* **MOTHERS.**

**MONARCHY - IRAN - HISTORY - 19TH CENTURY.**
Amanat, Abbas. Pivot of the universe. Berkeley : University of California Press, c1997.
*TC DS307.N38 A63 1997*

**MONASTIC AND RELIGIOUS LIFE - HISTORY - MIDDLE AGES, 600-1500.**
The medieval church. Woodbridge, Suffolk ;

Rochester, NY : Published for the Ecclesiastical History Society by the Boydell Press, 1999.
*TC BR270 .M43 1999*

**MONASTIC LIFE.** *See* **MONASTIC AND RELIGIOUS LIFE.**

**MONASTICISM AND RELIGIOUS ORDERS.** *See* **MONASTIC AND RELIGIOUS LIFE.**

**Mondrian, Piet, 1872-1944.**
Piet Mondrian, 1872-1944. Milan : Leonardo Arte, 1994.
*TC N6953.M64 A4 1994*

**MONDRIAN, PIET, 1872-1944.**
Piet Mondrian, 1872-1944. Milan : Leonardo Arte, 1994.
*TC N6953.M64 A4 1994*

**MONET, CLAUDE, 1840-1926.**
Impressionism [videorecording]. [London] : The National Gallery : Tillingham, Peasmarsh, East Sussex, England : Ho-Ho-Kus, NJ : Distributed by The Roland Collection, c1990.
*TC ND547.5.I4 A7 1990*

**Monet, Dorothy.**
Mary Cassatt [videorecording]. [Chicago, Ill.]: Home Vision, c1977.
*TC ND237.C3 M37 1977*

**Monet, Gaby.**
Norman Rockwell's world -- an American dream [videorecording]. [Chicago, Ill] : Home Vision, 1987, c1972.
*TC ND237.R68 N6 1987*

**MONEY.** *See* **BANKS AND BANKING; WEALTH.**

**Money, John, 1921-** The lovemap guidebook : a definitive statement / John Money. New York : Continuum, c1999. 284 p. ; 24 cm. Includes bibliographical references (p. [247]-262) and indexes. ISBN 0-8264-1203-3 (hc. : alk. paper) DDC 306.7
*1. Sexual attraction. 2. Sexology. I. Title.*
*TC BF692 .M57 1999*

**MONEY RAISING.** *See* **FUND RAISING.**

**MONGOLISM.** *See* **DOWN SYNDROME.**

**MONGOLISM (DISEASE).** *See* **DOWN SYNDROME.**

**MONISM.** *See* **DUALISM.**

**Monitoring change in education.**
Lifelong and continuing education :. Aldershot, Hants, England ; Brookfield, Vt. : Ashgate, c1999.
*TC LC5215 L464 1999*

**Monk, Gerald, 1954-.**
Winslade, John. Narrative counseling in schools. Thousand Oaks, Calif. : Corwin Press, c1999.
*TC LB1027.5 .W535 1999*

**MONKEY NUTS.** *See* **PEANUTS.**

**MONKEYS - FICTION.**
Wiesmüller, Dieter. [Pin Kaiser und Fip Husar English] The adventures of Marco and Polo. New York : Walker & Co., 2000.
*TC PZ7.W6366 Ad 2000*

**Monograph in behavioral disorders.** Severe behavior disorders of children and youth / Arizona State University Teacher Educators for Children with Behavioral Disorders, and Council for Children with Behavioral Disorders. Reston, Va. : Council for Children with Behavioral Disorders, c1978-1986. 8 v. : ill. ; 23 cm. Summer 1978 - 1985. Severe behavior disorders of children and youth. Issues for 1984-1985 also called v. 7-v.8. Supplement to: Behavioral disorders.
*1. Problem children - Education. 2. Behaviorism (Psychology). 3. Educational psychology. I. Council for Children with Behavioral Disorders. II. Teacher Educators for Children with Behavior Disorders. III. Title: Severe behavior disorders of children and youth. IV. Title: Behavioral disorders.*
*TC BF721 .M65*

**Monograph of the National Council of Supervisors of Mathematics**
Future basics. Golden, Colo. : National Council of Supervisors of Mathematics, c1998.
*TC QA141 .C43 1998*

**Monograph series (Education Law Association (U.S.))**
(no. 65.) Mawdsley, Ralph D. Legal problems of religious and private schools. 4th ed. Dayton, OH : Education Law Association, c2000.
*TC KF4124.5 .M38 2000*

**Monographs in International Education**
Porter, James. Reschooling and the global future. Wallingford, U.K. : Symposium Books ; c1999.

**TC LB1029.G55 P67 1999**

**Monographs (National Assembly of Local Arts Agencies)**
(vol. 5, no. 2) Nagy, Martin. Rural America in transition. Washington, DC : NALAA, 1996.
*TC NX798 .N3 1996*

**Monographs of the Society for Research in Child Development**
(64, no. 4.) Adolescent siblings in stepfamilies. Chicago, Ill. : University of Chicago Press, 1999.
*TC LB1103.S6 v.64 no. 4*

(v. 65, no. 2.) Chen, Zhe, 1964- Across the great divide. Oxford : Blackwell, 2000.
*TC LB1103 .S6 v.65 no. 2*

**MONOPOLIES. See COMPETITION.**

**MONOTHEISM. See GOD.**

**MONOTYPE (ENGRAVING), AMERICAN.**
Moser, Joann. Singular impressions. Washington : Published for the National Museum of American Art by Smithsonian Institution Press, c1997.
*TC NE2245.U54 M67 1997*

**Monsieur René Magritte** [videorecording] / RM Productions, Antenne 2, WDR présentent... ; producteurs délégués, Michèle Arnaud, Reiner Moritz ; un film réalisé par Adrian Maben ; commentaires, Adrien Maben. [Chicago, Ill.] : Home Vision [distributor], c1978. 1 videocassette (60 min.) : sd., col. with b&w sequences ; 1/2 in. (Portrait of an artist ; v. 11) At head of title: Home Vision... presents... [videorecording]. Title on container: Magritte [videorecording]. VHS, Stereo, Hi-Fi. Catalogued from credits and container. Dits par Denis Manuel, Gérard Chevalier. Camera, Jacques Thomas-Gérard ; graphics, Marcel Combes, Jaques Puccio, Alain Garner ; music, Bela Bartok, Roger Waters ; research, Hélène de Chavagnac. Narration in English; credits in French. For adolescents through adult. SUMMARY: Belgian artist, René Magritte's surrealist paintings portray familiar objects and scenes as new and strange. This documentary highlights the artist's home and studio with archival film of interviews with the artiston his views as it documents his quiet life.
*1. Magritte, René, - 1898-1967. 2. Painters - Belgium - Biography. I. Magritte, René, 1898-1967. II. Maben, Adrian. III. Arnaud, Michèle. IV. Moritz, Reiner. V. Manuel, Denis. VI. Chevalier, Gérard. VII. R.M. Productions. VIII. Societe nationale de television en couleur "Antenne 2". IX. Westdeutscher Rundfunk. X. Home Vision (Firm) XI. Title: Home Vision... presents... [videorecording] XII. Title: Magritte [videorecording] XIII. Series.*
*TC ND673.M35 M6 1978*

**MONSTERS. See DRAGONS.**

**Montagu, Ashley, 1905-** The natural superiority of women / Ashley Montagu. 5th ed. Walnut Creek, Calif. : AltaMira Press, c1999. 335 p. ; 24 cm. Includes bibliographical references (p. 303-323) and index. CONTENTS: The natural superiority of women -- The subjection of women -- The social determinants of biological "facts" and social consequences -- Who said, "the inferior sex"? -- When "X" doesn't equal "Y" -- The sexual superiority of the female -- Are women more emotional than men? -- Was it true about women? -- The intelligence of the sexes -- Women and creativity -- The genius of woman as the genius of humanity -- Mutual aid -- Changing traditions -- Woman's task. ISBN 0-7619-8981-1 (cloth) ISBN 0-7619-8982-X (pbk.) DDC 305.4
*1. Women - Psychology. 2. Feminism - Psychological aspects. 3. Sex role. I. Title.*
*TC HQ1206 .M65 1999*

**Montalvo, Braulio.**
Isaacs, Marla Beth. [Difficult divorce] Therapy of the difficult divorce. Northvale, N.J. ; London : J. Aronson, c2000.
*TC RC488.6 .I83 2000*

**Montanelli, Dale S.**
People come first. Chicago : Association of College and Research Libraries, 1999.
*TC Z674 .A75*

**Montclair Art Museum.**
Paris 1900. New Brunswick, N.J. : Rutgers University Press ; Montclair, N.J. : Montclair Art Museum, c1999.
*TC N6510 .P28 1999*

**Montessori for the millennium.**
Wentworth, Roland A. Lubienski. Mahwah, N.J. : L. Erlbaum Associates, 1999.
*TC LB1029.M75 W46 1998*

**MONTESSORI METHOD OF EDUCATION.**
Wentworth, Roland A. Lubienski. Montessori for the millennium. Mahwah, N.J. : L. Erlbaum Associates, 1999.

**TC LB1029.M75 W46 1998**

**Montgomery, Henry.**
Judgment and decision making. Mahwah, N.J. : L. Erlbaum Associates, 1999.
*TC BF448 .J83 1999*

**Montgomery, Paula Kay.**
Doggett, Sandra L. Beyond the book. Englewood, Colo. : Libraries Unlimited, 2000.
*TC ZA4065 .D64 2000*

**Montgomery, Susan J., 1947-** Phillips Academy / Susan J. Montgomery and Roger G. Reed ; color photographs by Walter Smalling, Jr. New York : Princeton Architectural Press, 2000. x, 132 p. : ill. (some col.), plans, ports. ; 26 cm. (The campus guide) Front cover extends to form additional leaf. Includes bibliographical references (p. [124]-125) and index. DDC 727/.2/097445
*1. Phillips Academy - Buildings - Guidebooks. 2. Phillips Academy - Buildings - Pictorial works. 3. College buildings - Massachusetts - Andover. 4. Historic buildings - Massachusetts - Andover. 5. Andover (Mass.) - Buildings, structures, etc. 6. v - Guidebooks. I. Reed, Roger G., 1950- II. Smalling, Walter. III. Title. IV. Series: Campus guide (New York, N.Y.)*
*TC LD7501.A5 M65 2000*

**MONTHS - JUVENILE POETRY.**
Updike, John. A child's calendar. <Rev. ed.>. New York : Holiday House, 1999.
*TC PS3571.P4 C49 1999*

**MONTHS - POETRY.**
Updike, John. A child's calendar. <Rev. ed.>. New York : Holiday House, 1999.
*TC PS3571.P4 C49 1999*

**MONTICELLO (VA.).**
West, Patricia, 1958- Domesticating history. Washington [D.C.] : Smithsonian Institution Press, c1999.
*TC E159 .W445 1999*

**Montreal Museum of Fine Arts.**
Exiles + emigrés. Los Angeles, Calif. : Los Angeles County Museum of Art ; New York : H.N. Abrams, c1997.
*TC N6512 .E887 1997*

**MONUMENTS. See HISTORIC BUILDINGS; HISTORIC SITES; PUBLIC SCULPTURE; WAR MEMORIALS.**

**MONUMENTS - UNITED STATES.**
Loewen, James W. Lies across America. New York : New Press : Distributed by W.W. Norton, c1999.
*TC E159 .L64 1999*

**Moo, G. Gregory.** Power grab : the National Education Association's betrayal of our children / G. Gregory Moo. Washington, D.C. : Regnery Pub. ; Lanham, MD : Distributed to the trade by National Book Network, c1999. xxv, 335 p. : ill ; 24 cm. Includes bibliographical references and index. ISBN 0-89526-315-7 (alk. paper) DDC 370/.6/073
*1. National Education Association of the United States - History. 2. National Education Association of the United States - Political activity. 3. Public schools - United States - History. I. Title.*
*TC LB2844.53.U6 M66 1999*

**Mood and temperament.**
Watson, David. New York ; London : Guilford Press, c2000.
*TC BF698.9.E45 W38 2000*

**MOOD DISORDERS. See AFFECTIVE DISORDERS.**

**Mood disorders :** systematic medication management / volume editor, A. John Rush. Basel ; New York : Karger, c1997. viii, 262 p. ; 25 cm. (Modern problems of pharmacopsychiatry ; vol. 25) Includes bibliographical references and indexes. ISBN 3-8055-6223-3 (hardcover : alk. paper) DDC 616.89/5061
*1. Affective disorders - Chemotherapy. 2. Antidepressants - Effectiveness. 3. Psychotropic drugs - Effectiveness. 4. Electroconvulsive therapy. 5. Affective Disorders, Psychotic - drug therapy. 6. Psychotropic Drugs - therapeutic use. I. Rush, A. John. II. Series.*
*TC RC483 .M6 1997*

**Mood disorders** [videorecording] / a presentation of Films for the Humanities & Sciences ; University of Sheffield ; produced and directed by Steve Collier ; written by Dr. Steve Peters. Princeton, N.J. : Films for the Humanities & Sciences, 1998. 1 videocassette (39 min.) : sd., col. ; 1/2 in. (Differential diagnosis in psychiatry) Series subtitle: Visual aid based on ICD 10. VHS. Catalogued from credits and container. Commentary: John Graham Davies. Sound: Ken Hardy; cameras: Jackie Jones, Mark Parkin, Gary Wraith; graphics: Sean Purcell. Originally produced 1995-1997

at the University of Sheffield. "Clinical features of myotonic dystrophy and Huntington's disease" included in list of complete series on container no longer part of series. For students of psychiatry, clinical psychology and social work, and counselling. SUMMARY: "Mood disorders, or affective disorders, are discussed in this program together with their symptoms and differential diagnoses. Classifications are based upon the course and severity of the symptoms. The two main classifications of mood disorders-- manic and depressive-- are clearly defined and differentiated according to symptoms. The peristent mood disorders cyclothymia and dysthymia are discussed, along with medical causes of mood disorders, such as hypothalamic tumor. All symptoms are clearly illustrated in interviews with patients suffering from degrees of the various disorders."--Container.
*1. Affective disorders - Diagnosis. 2. Affective disorders - Patients. 3. Hypomania - Diagnosis. 4. Hypomania - Patients. 5. Depression, Mental - Diagnosis. 6. Depression, Mental - Patients. 7. Mania - Diagnosis. 8. Mania - Patients. 9. Manic-depressive illness - Diagnosis. 10. Manic-depressive persons. 11. Diagnosis, Differential. I. Peters, Steve, Dr. II. Collier, Steve. III. Davies, John Graham. IV. University of Sheffield. V. Films for the Humanities (Firm) VI. Title: Visual aid based on ICD 10 VII. Series.*
*TC RC537 .M6 1998*

**MOOD (PSYCHOLOGY).**
Ben-Ze'ev, Aharon. The subtlety of emotions. Cambridge, Mass. ; London : MIT Press, c2000.
*TC BF531 .B43 2000*

Emotion and social judgments. 1st ed. Oxford ; New York : Pergamon Press, 1991.
*TC BF531 .E4834 1991*

Feeling and thinking. Cambridge, U.K. ; New York : Cambridge University Press ; Paris : Editions de la Maison des Sciences de l'Homme, 2000.
*TC BF531 .F44 2000*

**MOOD (PSYCHOLOGY) - ENCYCLOPEDIAS.**
Encyclopedia of human emotions. New York : Macmillan Reference USA, c1999.
*TC BF531 .E55 1999*

**MOOD (PSYCHOLOGY) - FICTION.**
Millen, C. M. The low-down laundry line blues. Boston : Houghton Mifflin, 1999.
*TC PZ7.M6035 Lo 1999*

**Moody, Kate.** The children of Telstar : early experiments in school television production / Kate Moody. 1st ed. New York : Center for Understanding Media : Vantage Press, c1999. xv, 174 p. : ill. ; 24 cm. Includes bibliographical references (p. 153-161) and index. ISBN 0-533-12735-1 DDC 371.33/58
*1. Television in education - United States - History. 2. Television - Production and direction - History. I. Title.*
*TC LB1044.7 .M616 1999*

**Moody, T. W. (Theodore William), 1907-.**
A new history of Ireland. Oxford [England] : Clarendon Press ; New York : Oxford University Press, <1976-1986 >
*TC DA912 .N48*

**Moody, Wendell F.**
Jazz dance class [videorecording]. W. Long Branch, NJ : Kultur, [1992?]
*TC GV1784 .J3 1992*

**Moon, Bob, 1945-.**
Routledge international companion to education. London ; New York : Routledge, 2000.
*TC LB7 .R688 2000*

**MOON - FICTION.**
Jones, Joy. Tambourine moon. New York : Simon & Schuster, 1999.
*TC PZ7.J72025 Tam 1999*

Wynne-Jones, Tim. Builder of the moon. New York M.K. McElderry Books, c1988.
*TC PZ7.W993 Bu 1988*

**Moon, Jennifer A.** Learning journals : a handbook for academics, students and professional development / Jennifer A. Moon. London : Kogan Page, 1999. vii, 145 p. ; 24 cm. Includes bibliographical references and index. ISBN 0-7494-3045-1
*1. Academic writing. 2. Diaries - Authoship. 3. English language - Rhetoric. 4. Cognition and culture. I. Title.*
*TC PE1408 .M66 1999*

**Moon, Jennifer S.**
Alvermann, Donna E. Popular culture in the classroom. Newark, Del. : International Reading Association ; Chicago, Ill. : National Reading Conference, c1999.
*TC P91.3 .A485 1999*

**MOON, VOYAGES TO.** *See* **INTERPLANETARY VOYAGES.**

**Mooney, Jean F.**
Collaborative practice. Westport, Conn. ; London : Praeger, 1999.
*TC HV741 .C5424 1999*

**Moore, Alex, 1947-** Teaching multicultured students : culturism and anti-culturism in school classrooms / Alex Moore. London ; New York : Falmer Press, 1999. xii, 203 p. : ill. ; 25 cm. (Studies in inclusive education series) Includes bibliographical references (p. 186-195) and index. ISBN 0-7507-0826-3 ISBN 0-7507-0825-5 (pbk. : alk. paper) DDC 370.117/0941
*1. Education, Bilingual - Great Britain - Case studies. 2. Minorities - Education - Great Britain - Case studies. 3. Inclusive education - Great Britain - Case studies. I. Title. II. Series.*
*TC LC3736.G6 M66 1999*

**Moore, Gary S.** Living with the earth : concepts in environmental health s cience / Gary S. Moore. Boca Raton, Fla. : Lewis Publishers, c1999. 1 v. (various pagings) : ill. ; 25 cm. Includes bibliographical references and index. "A web-enhanced book"--Cover. ISBN 1-56670-357-3 (alk. paper) DDC 615.9/02
*1. Environmental health. 2. Medicine, Industrial. 3. Industrial hygiene. 4. Industrial safety. 5. Environmental health - Computer-assisted instruction. I. Title.*
*TC RA565 .M665 1999*

**Moore, Gwen, 1944-.**
Gendering elites. Houndmills, Basingstoke, Hampshire : Macmillan Press ; New York : St. Martin's Press, 2000.
*TC HM1261 .G46 2000*

**Moore, Jacqueline M., 1965-** Leading the race : the transformation of the Black elite in the nation's capital, 1880-1920 / Jacqueline M. Moore. Charlottesville : University Press of Virginia, 1999. xiii, 257 p. : ill. ; 25 cm. Includes bibliographical references (p. 241-248) and index. ISBN 0-8139-1903-7 (cloth : alk. paper) DDC 305.8960753
*1. Afro-Americans - Washington (D.C.) - Social conditions - 19th century. 2. Afro-Americans - Washington (D.C.) - Social conditions - 20th century. 3. Elite (Social sciences) - Washington (D.C.) - History - 19th century. 4. Elite (Social sciences) - Washington (D.C.) - History - 20th century. 5. Washington (D.C.) - Race relations. 6. Washington (D.C.) - Social conditions - 19th century. 7. Washington (D.C.) - Social conditions - 20th century. I. Title.*
*TC E185.93.D6 M66 1999*

**Moore, Jeanne L., joint author.**
Craddock, George W. Social disadvantagement and dependency. Lexington, Mass., Heath Lexington Books [1970]
*TC HD7256.U6 C438*

**Moore, John H., 1938-.**
Special education. San Francisco : EMText, c1992.
*TC LC3981 .S63 1992*

**Moore, Kevin, 1960-** Museums and popular culture / Kevin Moore. London ; New York : Leicester University Press, 1997. ix, 182 p. ; 25 cm. (Contemporary issues in museum culture) Includes bibliographical references and index. ISBN 0-7185-1435-1 (hc) DDC 069/.0941
*1. Museums - Great Britain - Philosophy. 2. Popular culture - Museums - Great Britain. 3. Museum techniques - Great Britain. 4. Museum exhibits - Great Britain. I. Title. II. Series.*
*TC AM41 .M66 1997*

**MOORE, MICHAEL G.**
Anderson, Dennis S. Mathematics and distance education on the internet. 1999.
*TC 085 An2317*

**Moorjani, Angela B.** Beyond fetishism and other excursions in psychopragmatics / Angela Moorjani. New York : St. Martin's Press, 2000. xiv, 178 p. : ill., ports. ; 22 cm. Includes bibliographical references and index. ISBN 0-312-22625-X DDC 150.19/5
*1. Psychoanalysis and culture. 2. Symbolism (Psychology) 3. Semiotics. 4. Peirce, Charles S. - (Charles Sanders), - 1839-1914. 5. Freud, Sigmund, - 1856-1939. I. Title.*
*TC BF175.4.C84 M663 2000*

**Moorton, Richard F.**
The eye expanded. Berkeley : University of California Press, c1999.
*TC DE59 .E93 1999*

**Mora, Pat.** The rainbow tulip / by Pat Mora ; illustrated by Elizabeth Sayles. New York : Viking, 1999. 1 v. (unpaged) col. ill. ; 26 cm. SUMMARY: A Mexican-American first-grader experiences the difficulties and pleasures of being different when she wears a tulip costume with all the colors of the rainbow for the school May Day parade. ISBN 0-670-87291-1 (hc). DDC [E]

*1. Mexican Americans - Juvenile fiction. 2. Mexican Americans - Fiction. 3. May Day - Fiction. 4. Schools - Fiction. I. Sayles, Elizabeth, ill. II. Title.*
*TC PZ7.M78819 Rai 1999*

**The moral animal.**
Wright, Robert, 1957- 1st Vintage books ed. New York : Vintage Books, 1995, c1994.
*TC GN365.9 .W75 1995*

**MORAL CONDITIONS.** *See* **SEX CUSTOMS.**

**MORAL DEVELOPMENT.**
Hoffman, Martin L. Empathy and moral development. Cambridge, U.K. ; New York : Cambridge University Press, 2000.
*TC BF723.M54 H64 2000*

Moral sensibilities and education. Bemmel : Concorde Pub. House, 1999-
*TC BF723.M54 M684 1999*

Rights and wrongs. San Francisco, [CA] : Jossey-Bass, c2000.
*TC BF723.M54 L38 2000*

Stewart, Therese Marie Klein. The challenges to sustaining Unification faith and the spiritual quest after seminary. 1996.
*TC 06 no. 10751*

Stilwell, Barbara M. Right vs. wrong--. Bloomington : Indiana University Press, c2000.
*TC BJ1471 .S69 2000*

**MORAL EDUCATION.** *See also* **JEWISH RELIGIOUS EDUCATION; MORAL EDUCATION (ELEMENTARY); MORAL EDUCATION (SECONDARY); RELIGIOUS EDUCATION.**
Carr, David, 1944- Professionalism and ethics in teaching. London ; New York : Routledge, 2000.
*TC LB1779 .C37 2000*

Carr, David, 1944- Professionalism and ethics in teaching. London ; New York : Routledge, 2000.
*TC LB1779 .C37 2000*

Classroom issues. London ; New York : Falmer Press, 2000.
*TC LC268 .C52 2000*

Education for spiritual, moral, social and cultural development. London ; New York : Continuum, 2000.
*TC LC268 .E384 2000*

Education for values. London ; Sterling, VA : Kogan Page, 2000.
*TC LC268 .E38 2000*

Green, Thomas F. Voices. Notre Dame, Ind. : University of Notre Dame Press, c1999.
*TC LC268 .G667 1999*

Haydon, Graham. Values, virtues and violence. Oxford ; Malden, MA : Blackwell Publishers, 1999.
*TC LC268 .H294 1999*

Hutcheon, Pat Duffy. Building character and culture. Westport, Conn. : Praeger, 1999.
*TC HQ783 .H88 1999*

Miller, John P., 1943- Education and the soul. Albany : State University of New York Press, c2000.
*TC LC268 .M52 2000*

Moral education and pluralism. London ; New York : Falmer Press, 2000.
*TC LC268 .M683 2000*

Moral sensibilities and education. Bemmel : Concorde Pub. House, 1999-
*TC BF723.M54 M684 1999*

Radest, Howard B., 1928- From clinic to classroom. Westport, Conn. : London : Praeger, 2000.
*TC R725.5 .R33 2000*

**Moral education and pluralism** / edited by Mal Leicester, Celia Modgil and Sohan Modgil. London ; New York : Falmer Press, 2000. vii, 249 p. ; 29 cm. (Education, culture, and values ; v. 4) Includes bibliographical references and index. ISBN 0-7507-1005-5 DDC 370.11/4
*1. Moral education. 2. Multicultural education - Moral and ethical aspects. I. Leicester, Mal. II. Modgil, Celia. III. Modgil, Sohan. IV. Series.*
*TC LC268 .M683 2000*

**MORAL EDUCATION (ELEMENTARY).**
Stilwell, Barbara M. Right vs. wrong--. Bloomington : Indiana University Press, c2000.
*TC BJ1471 .S69 2000*

**MORAL EDUCATION (ELEMENTARY) - GREAT BRITAIN.**
Improving teaching and learning in the humanities.

London : Falmer ; New York : Published in the USA and Canada by Garland, 1999.
*TC LB1564.G7 I47 1999*

Winston, Joe. Drama, literacy and moral education 5-11. London : David Fulton, 2000.
*TC LC268 .W667 2000*

**MORAL EDUCATION (ELEMENTARY) - POLAND.**
Gaweł-Luty, Elżbieta. Przetwarzanie informacji społecznych dla ocen moralnych u uczniów klas młodzoszkolnych. Słupsk : Wyższa Szkoła Pedagogiczna w Słupsku, 1996.
*TC LC314.P7 G37 1996*

**MORAL EDUCATION (SECONDARY).**
Stilwell, Barbara M. Right vs. wrong--. Bloomington : Indiana University Press, c2000.
*TC BJ1471 .S69 2000*

**MORAL EDUCATION (SECONDARY) - UNITED STATES.**
Abowitz, Kathleen Knight. Making meaning of community in an American high school. Cresskill, N.J. : Hampton Press, c2000.
*TC LC311 .A36 2000*

**MORAL EDUCATION - UNITED STATES.**
Annual State of American Education Address (7th : February 22, 2000 : Durham, N.C.) The seventh annual state of American education address [videorecording]. [Washington, D.C. : U.S. Dept. of Education], 2000.

Heath, Douglas H. Morale, culture, and character. 1st ed. Bryn Mawr, PA : Conrow Pub. House, c1999.
*TC LC311 .H43 1999*

Hutchinson, Jaylynne N., 1954- Students on the margins. Albany : State University of New York Press, c1999.
*TC LA210 .H88 1999*

Macedo, Stephen, 1957- Diversity and distrust. Cambridge, Mass. ; London : Harvard University Press, 2000.
*TC LA217.2 .M33 2000*

Powell, Rebecca, 1949- Literacy as a moral imperative. Lanham, Md. : Rowman & Littlefield Publishers, c1999.
*TC LC151 .P69 1999*

**MORAL EDUCATION - UNITED STATES - CURRICULA.**
Conroy, Mary Ann. 101 ways to integrate personal development into core curriculum. Lanham : University Press of America, c2000.
*TC LC311 .C65 2000*

**MORAL EDUCATION - UNITED STATES - HANDBOOKS, MANUALS, ETC.**
Conroy, Mary Ann. 101 ways to integrate personal development into core curriculum. Lanham : University Press of America, c2000.
*TC LC311 .C65 2000*

**Moral intuitions.**
Wilson, James Q. New Brunswick, N.J. : Transaction Publishers, c2000.
*TC BJ1472 .W55 2000*

**MORAL PHILOSOPHY.** *See* **ETHICS.**

**Moral sensibilities and education** / Wouter van Haaften, Thomas Wren, Agnes Tellings, eds. Bemmel : Concorde Pub. House, 1999- v. : ill. ; 21 cm. (Philosophy of moral education series ; 1) Includes bibliographical references. PARTIAL CONTENTS: I. The preschool child ISBN 90-76230-04-8
*1. Moral development. 2. Moral education. I. Haaften, A. W. van (A. Wouter), 1941- II. Wren, Thomas E. III. Tellings, Agnes. IV. Series: Philosophy of moral education series ; 1.*
*TC BF723.M54 M684 1999*

**Moral voice of college presidents.**
Nelson, Stephen James, 1947- Leaders in the crucible. Westport, Conn. : Bergin & Garvey, 2000.
*TC LB2341 .N386 2000*

**Morale, culture, and character.**
Heath, Douglas H. 1st ed. Bryn Mawr, PA : Conrow Pub. House, c1999.
*TC LC311 .H43 1999*

**MORALITY.** *See* **ETHICS.**

**MORALS.** *See* **CONDUCT OF LIFE; ETHICS.**

**Moran, Carrol.**
Keys to the classroom. 2nd ed. Thousand Oaks, Calif. : Corwin Press, c2000.
*TC LB1555 .K49 2000*

**Moran, Jeffrey P.** Teaching sex : the shaping of adolescence in the 20th century / Jeffrey P. Moran. Cambridge, Mass. : Harvard University Press, 2000. x, 281 p. : ill. ; 24 cm. Includes bibliographical references (p. 237-274) and index. DDC 613.9/071
*1. Sex instruction - United States - History. 2. Sex instruction for teenagers - United States - History. 3. Sexual ethics for teenagers - United States - History. 4. Teenagers - Sexual behavior - United States - History. 5. Adolescence - United States - History. I. Title.*
**TC HQ57.5.A3 M66 2000**

**Moran, Laura.** Milbank Memorial Library story hour [videorecording]. [New York : Milbank Memorial Library, 1999].
**TC Z718.3 .M5 1999 Series 3 Prog. 11**

**MORAVIANS - NORTH CAROLINA - WINSTON-SALEM - ANTIQUITIES.** South, Stanley A. Historical archaeology in Wachovia. New York : Kluwer Academic/Plenum Publishers, c1999.
**TC F264.W8 S66 1999**

**MORAVIANS - NORTH CAROLINA - WINSTON-SALEM - HISTORY - 18TH CENTURY.** South, Stanley A. Historical archaeology in Wachovia. New York : Kluwer Academic/Plenum Publishers, c1999.
**TC F264.W8 S66 1999**

**MORBIDITY. See DISEASES.**

**More!.** Chichester Clark, Emma. 1st American ed. New York : Doubleday Books for Young Readers/Bantam Doubleday Dell Pub., 1999.
**TC PZ7.C4335 Mo 1999**

**More.** Lamon, Susan J., 1949- Mahwah, N.J. : L. Erlbaum Associates, 1999.
**TC QA137 .L34 1999**

**More innovative games.** Lichtman, Brenda, 1948- Champaign, IL : Human Kinetics, c1999.
**TC GV443 .L516 1999**

**More social studies through children's literature.** Fredericks, Anthony D. Englewood, Colo. : Teacher Ideas Press, 2000.
**TC LB1584 .F659 2000**

**Morgan, Brian L. G.** Brainfood : nutrition and your brain / Brian L.G. Morgan and Roberta Morgan. Tucson, Ariz. : Body Press, c1987. xii, 202 p. : ill. ; 24 cm. Bibliography: p. 189-192. Includes index. ISBN 0-89586-565-3 ISBN 0-89586-558-0 (pbk.) DDC 612/.82
*1. Brain. 2. Nutrition. 3. Mental health. I. Morgan, Roberta, 1953- II. Title.*
**TC QP376 .M62 1987**

**Morgan, Chris.** Assessing open and distance learners / Chris Morgan and Meg O'Reilly. London : Kogan Page ; Sterling, VA : Stylus Pub., 1999. x, 229 p. ; 25 cm. (Open and distance learning series.) "The Open University." Includes bibliographical references (p. 224-227) and index. ISBN 0-7494-2875-9 ISBN 0-7494-2878-3 (pbk.)
*1. Distance education. 2. Open learning. I. O'Reilly, Meg. II. Open University. III. Title. IV. Series.*
**TC LC5800 .M67 1999**

**Morgan, David L.** Focus groups as qualitative research / David L. Morgan. 2nd ed. Thousand Oaks, Calif. : Sage Publications, c1997. viii, 80 p. ; 22 cm. (Qualitative research methods series ; v. 16) Includes bibliographical references (p. 75-79). ISBN 0-7619-0342-9 (alk. paper) ISBN 0-7619-0343-7 (pbk. : alk. paper) DDC 300/.723
*1. Focused group interviewing. 2. Social sciences - Research - Methodology. I. Title. II. Series: Qualitative research methods ; v. 16.*
**TC H61.28 .M67 1997**

**Morgan, George A. (George Arthur), 1936-.** Gliner, Jeffrey A. Research methods in applied settings. Mahwah, N.J. : Lawrence Erlbaum, 2000.
**TC H62 .G523 2000**

**Morgan, Michael.** Shanahan, James. Television and its viewers. Cambridge ; New York : Cambridge University Press, 1999.
**TC PN1992.6 .S417 1999**

**Morgan, Roberta, 1953-.** Morgan, Brian L. G. Brainfood. Tucson, Ariz. : Body Press, c1987.
**TC QP376 .M62 1987**

**Morgan, Sally, 1951-** The art of Sally Morgan / with an introduction by Jill Milroy. Ringwood, Vic., Australia ; New York : Viking, 1996. 170 p. : chiefly col. ill. ; 34 cm. ISBN 0-670-90354-X
*1. Morgan, Sally, - 1951- - Catalogs. 2. Art, Australian aboriginal - Catalogs. I. Title.*
**TC N7405.M68 A4 1996**

Care about education : a joint training curriculum for supporting children in public care / Sally Morgan. London : DfEE, 1999. v, 105 p ; 30 cm. Includes bibliographical references and index. ISBN 1-900990-46-6
*1. Institutional care - Great Britain. 2. Child care - Great Britain. 3. Socially handicapped children - Education - Great Britain. I. Great Britain. Department for Education and Employment. II. Great Britain. Department of Health. III. National Children's Bureau IV. Title.*
**TC HV59 .M67 1999**

**MORGAN, SALLY, 1951- - CATALOGS.** Morgan, Sally, 1951- The art of Sally Morgan. Ringwood, Vic., Australia ; New York : Viking, 1996.
**TC N7405.M68 A4 1996**

**Mori, Junko.** Negotiating agreement and disagreement in Japanese : connective expressions and turn construction / Junko Mori. Amsterdam ; Philadelphia, Pa. : J. Benjamins Pub. Co., c1999. xii, 240 p. : ill. ; 23 cm. (Studies in discourse and grammar, 0928-8929 ; v. 8) Includes bibliographical references (p. [219]-235) and index. ISBN 1-55619-374-2 (alk. paper) DDC 495.6/5
*1. Japanese language - Connectives. 2. Japanese language - Discourse analysis. I. Title. II. Series.*
**TC PL611.C6 M67 1999**

**Moriarity, Michael.** The frescoes of Diego Rivera [videorecording]. [Detroit, Mich.] : Founders Society, Detroit Institute of Arts ; [Chicago, Ill.?] : Home Vision [distributor], c1986.
**TC ND259.R5 F6 1986**

**Moriarty, William.** The sight and insight of Ernst Haas [videorecording]. Minneapolis, Minn. : Media Loft, 1992.
**TC TR647.H3 S5 1992**

**Morison, William James, 1943-.** Cox, Dwayne, 1950- The University of Louisville. [Lexington] : University Press of Kentucky, c2000.
**TC LD3131.L42 C69 2000**

**Moritz, Reiner.** Monsieur René Magritte [videorecording]. [Chicago, Ill.] : Home Vision [distributor], c1978.
**TC ND673.M35 M6 1978**

**Morken, Hubert.** The politics of school choice / Hubert Morken and Jo Renee Formicola. Lanham, Md. : Rowman & Littlefield Publishers, c1999. vii, 337 p. 24 cm. Includes bibliographical references (p. 315-324) and index. ISBN 0-8476-9720-7 (alk. paper) ISBN 0-8476-9721-5 (pbk. : alk. paper) DDC 379.1/11/0973
*1. School choice - United States. 2. School choice - Political aspects - United States. 3. Education and state - United States. I. Formicola, Jo Renee, 1941- II. Title.*
**TC LB1027.9 .M68 1999**

**Morley, Louise, 1954-** Organising feminisms : the micropolitics of the academy / Louise Morley. New York : St. Martin's Press, 1999. viii, 215 p. ; 22 cm. Includes bibliographical references and index. ISBN 0-312-21676-9 (cloth) ISBN 0-312-21678-5 (pbk.) DDC 378.1/9822
*1. Feminism and education. 2. Women - Education (Higher) 3. Education, Higher - Political aspects. 4. Educational equalization. I. Title.*
**TC LC197 .M67 1999**

**Morley, Patricia A.** The mountain is moving : Japanese women's lives / Patricia Morley. Washington Square, N.Y. : New York University Press, 1999. xiii, 226 p. : ill. ; 24 cm. Includes bibliographical references (p. 189-219) and index. ISBN 0-8147-5626-3 (cloth : alk. paper) DDC 305.42/0952
*1. Women - Japan - Social conditions. 2. Japan - Social conditions - 1945- I. Title.*
**TC HQ1762 .M64 1999**

**Moro, M. I.** Russian grade 1 mathematics / M.I. Moro, M.A. Bantova, and G.V. Beltyukova ; translator, Robert H. Silverman ; translation editor, Steven R. Young. Chicago : University of Chicago School of Mathematics Project, 1992. x, 205 p. : ill. ; 26 cm. (UCSMP Textbook Translations) ISBN 0-936745-50-9
*1. Mathematics - Study and teaching (Elementary) - Soviet Union. 2. Mathematics - Soviet Union - Textbooks. I. Bantova, M. A. II. Beltyukova, G. V. III. Silverman, Robert H. IV. Young, Steven R. V. Series.*
**TC QA14.R9 R8611 1992**

Russian grade 2 mathematics / M.I. Moro, and M.A. Bantova ; translator Robert H. Silverman : translation editor Steven R. Young. Chicago : University of Chicago School of Mathematics Project, 1992. xii, 292 p. : ill. ; 26 cm. (UCSMP Textbook Translations) ISBN 0-936745-51-7
*1. Mathematics - Study and teaching (Elementary) - Soviet Union. 2. Mathematics - Soviet Union - Textbooks. I. Bantova, M. A. II. Beltyukova, G. V. III. Silverman, Robert H. IV. Young, Steven R. V. Series.*
**TC QA14.R9 R8711 1992**

Russian grade 3 mathematics. Chicago : University of Chicago School of Mathematics Project, 1992.
**TC QA14.R9 R8811 1992**

**MORONS. See MENTALLY HANDICAPPED.**

**MORPHOLOGY (ANIMALS). See GROWTH.**

**Morphy, Howard.** Aboriginal art / Howard Morphy. London [England] : Phaidon, 1998. 447 p. : ill. (some col.), maps ; 22 cm. (Art & ideas) Includes bibliographical references (p. 434-439) and index. ISBN 0-7148-3752-0
*1. Art, Australian aboriginal. I. Title. II. Series.*
**TC N7400 .M67 1998**

**Morris and the kingdom of Knoll.** Hill, T. L. Malibu, Calif. : J. Paul Getty Museum and Children's Library Press, c1996.
**TC PZ7.H55744 Mo 1996**

**Morris, Bob.** The Internet in action for math & science 7-12 [videorecording]. [New York] : Thirteen-WNET ; [Alexandria, Va. : distributed by] PBS Video, c1997.
**TC LB1044.87 .I453 1997**

**Morris, Curtis L., 1940-.** Morris, Vivian Gunn, 1941- Creating caring and nurturing educational environments for African American children. Westport, Conn. ; London : Bergin & Garvey, 2000.
**TC LC2802.A2 M67 2000**

**Morris, Hughlett L.** Diagnosis in speech-language pathology. 2nd ed. San Diego : Singular, c2000.
**TC RC423 .D473 2000**

**Morris, Paul, 1951-.** Teacher education in the Asia-Pacific region. New York : Falmer Press, c2000.
**TC LB1727.A69 T42 2000**

**Morris, Timothy, 1959-** You're only young twice : children's literature and film / Tim Morris. Urbana : University of Illinois Press, c2000. xii, 186 p. ; 24 cm. Includes bibliographical references (p. [175]-182) and index. CONTENTS: Acknowledgments -- You're only young twice: adults, children, power, culture -- Beauties: coming to Black Beauty -- Beasts: dog stories and kids -- Goosebumps: what was series fiction doing in the 1990s? -- Impossibilities: The secret garden and Peter Pan -- Panic attacks: children as adults, adults as children in the movies -- Ambiguities: picture ISBN 0-252-02532-6 (alk. paper) DDC 820.9/8982
*1. Children's literature, English - History and criticism. 2. Children's literature, American - History and criticism. 3. Children's literature - Film and video adaptations. 4. Motion pictures and literature. 5. Children - Books and reading. I. Title.*
**TC PR990 .M67 2000**

**Morris, Vivian Gunn, 1941-** Creating caring and nurturing educational environments for African American children / Vivian Gunn Morris, Curtis L. Morris. Westport, Conn. ; London : Bergin & Garvey, 2000. xi, 216 p., [5] p. of plates : ill. ; 24 cm. Includes bibliographical references and index. ISBN 0-89789-689-0 (alk. paper) DDC 372.182996/073/761
*1. Afro-American children - Education - Alabama. 2. Afro-Americans - Education (Elementary) - Alabama. I. Morris, Curtis L., 1940- II. Title.*
**TC LC2802.A2 M67 2000**

**Morrison, Deanna.** Public issues discussion [videorecording] : Diana Hess at Denver High School 1997. [Boulder, Colo.] : Social Science Education Consortium, c1997.
**TC H62.3 .P4 1997**

Socratic seminar [videorecording]. [Boulder, Colo.] : Social Science Education Consortium, c1997.

**MORRISON, GARY R.** Designing effective instruction / Gary R. Morrison, Steven M. Ross, Jerrold E. Kemp. 3rd ed. New York : John Wiley, c2001. xxiii, 369 p. ; 24 cm. + 1 computer optical disk (4 3/4 in.). Other title: Microsoft Project 2000 120-day trial edition /. Includes bibliographical references and index. System requirements: 75 MHz Pentium PC running Windows 95 or NT4.0, 32 MB RAM, 30 MB hard disk space, VGA monitor, pointing device. ISBN 0-471-38795-9 ISBN 0-555-11880-0

DDC 371.3
1. *Instructional systems - Design I. Title: Microsoft Project 2000 120-day trial edition /*
**TC LB1028.38 .K46 2001**

**Morrison, Gary R.** Integrating computer technology into the classroom / Gary R. Morrison, Deborah L. Lowther, Lisa DeMeulle ; [editor, Debra A. Stollenwerk]. Upper Saddle River, N.J. : Merrill, c1999. xx, 379 p. : ill. ; 24 cm. Includes bibliographical references and index. DDC 371.33/4
1. *Computer-assisted instruction. 2. Computer managed instruction. 3. Computers - Study and teaching. 4. Instructional systems - Design. I. Lowther, Deborah L. II. DeMeulle, Lisa. III. Stollenwerk, Debra A. IV. Title.*
**TC LB1028.5 .M6373 1999**

**Morrison, George S.** Fundamentals of early childhood education / George S. Morrison. 2nd ed. Upper Saddle River, N.J. : Merrill, c2000. xi, 400 p. : ill. ; 24 cm. Includes bibliographical references and index. ISBN 0-13-012095-2 DDC 372.21
1. *Early childhood education - United States. I. Title.*
**TC LB1139.25 .M67 2000**

**Morrison, J. Ian, 1952-** Health care in the new millennium : vision, values, and leadership / Ian Morrison. 1st ed. San Francisco : Jossey-Bass Publishers, c2000. xix, 260 p. ; 24 cm. (The Jossey-Bass health care series) Includes bibliographical references and index. ISBN 0-7879-5115-3 (alk. paper)
1. *Medical care - United States - Forecasting. 2. Medical policy - United States - Forecasting. I. Title. II. Series: Jossey-Bass health care series*
**TC RA395.A3 M675 2000**

**Morrison, Taylor.** Civil War artist / Taylor Morrison. Boston : Houghton Mifflin, 1999. 32 p. : col. ill. ; 29 cm. "Walter Lorraine books." SUMMARY: Traces an illustrator's sketch of a Civil War battle from the time it leaves his hands, through the engraving and printing processes, and to its final publication in a newspaper. ISBN 0-395-91426-4 DDC 070.4/499737
1. *United States - History - Civil War, 1861-1865 - Press coverage - Juvenile literature. 2. United States - History - Civil War, 1861-1865 - Journalists - Juvenile literature. 3. Illustrators - United States - History - 19th century - Juvenile literature. 4. United States - History - Civil War, 1861-1865 - Press coverage. 5. Journalism. 6. Illustrators. I. Title.*
**TC E468.9 .M86 1999**

**Morrissey, Jan.**
Mills [picture]. Amawalk, NY : Jackdaw Publications, c1999.
**TC TR820.5 .M5 1999**

World War II [picture]. Amawalk, NY : Jackdaw Publications, c1999.
**TC TR820.5 .W6 1999**

**Morrow, Lesley Mandel.** Literacy instruction in half- and whole-day kindergarten : research to practice / Lesley Mandel Morrow, Dorothy S. Strickland, Deborah Gee Woo. Newark, Del. : International Reading Association ; Chicago, Ill. : National Reading Conference, c1998. xi, 203 p. : ill. ; 23 cm. (Literacy studies series) Includes bibliographical references (p. 180-187) and indexes. ISBN 0-87207-188-X (pbk.) DDC 372.4
1. *Reading (Kindergarten) - United States. 2. Literacy - United States. 3. Curriculum planning - United States. 4. School day - United States. 5. Full-day kindergarten - United States. I. Strickland, Dorothy S. II. Woo, Deborah Gee. III. Title. IV. Series.*
**TC LB1181.2 .M67 1998**

Tips for the reading team. Newark, Del. : International Reading Association, c1998.
**TC LB1573 .T57 1998**

**MORSE CODE.**
King, Thomas W. Modern Morse code in rehabilitation and education. Boston : Allyn and Bacon, c2000.
**TC HV1569.5 .K55 2000**

**Mortality immortality?** : the legacy of 20th-century art / edited by Miguel Angel Corzo. Los Angeles : Getty Conservation Institute, c1999. xx, 192 p. : col. ill. ; 28 cm. Based on a conference held at the Getty Center, Los Angeles, Mar. 25-27, 1998. Includes bibliographical references and index. ISBN 0-89236-528-5 (alk. paper) DDC 709/.04/00288
1. *Art, Modern - 20th century - Conservation and restoration - Congresses. I. Corzo, Miguel Angel. II. Getty Conservation Institute.*
**TC N6485 .M67 1999**

**MORTALITY, LAW OF.** See **MORTALITY.**

**MORTALITY - UNITED STATES - STATISTICS.**
United States. Dept. of Health and Human Services. Task Force on Black and Minority Health. Report of the Secretary's Task Force on Black & Minority Health. Washington, D.C. : U.S. Dept. of Health and Human Services, [1985-<1986 >
**TC RA448.5.N4 U55 1985**

**Morton, Jerome H., 1942-.**
Kennedy, Rosa L., 1938- A school for healing. New York : P. Lang, c1999.
**TC LC46.4 .K46 1999**

**Morton, Jessica G.** Kids on the 'Net : conducting Internet research in K-5 classrooms / Jessica G. Morton ; [editor, Amy L. Cohn]. Portsmouth, NH : Heinemann, c1998. xi, 84 p. : ill. ; 23 cm. "Beeline books." Includes bibliographical references (p. 81-84). ISBN 0-325-00021-2 DDC 371.33/467/8
1. *Internet (Computer network) in education. 2. Electronic mail systems. I. Cohn, Amy L. II. Title. III. Title: Kids on the Internet*
**TC LB1044.87 .M67 1998**

**Mosby, Tom, 1969-.**
Ilan pasin = Queensland : Cairns Regional Gallery, [1998?].
**TC DU125.T67 I53 1998**

**Moschovitis, Christos J. P.**
History of the Internet. Santa Barbara, Calif. : ABC-CLIO, c1999.
**TC TK5105.875.I57 H58 1999**

**Moseng, Elisabeth, ill.**
Steer, Dugald. Just one more story. New York : Dutton Children's Books, 1999.
**TC PZ7.S81534 Ju 1999**

**Mosenthal, Peter.**
Reconceptualizing literacy in the media age. Stamford, Conn. : Jai Press, c2000.
**TC LB1050 .A38 v.7**

**Moser, Joann.** Singular impressions : the monotype in America / Joann Moser. Washington : Published for the National Museum of American Art by Smithsonian Institution Press, c1997. x, 212 p. : ill. (some col.) ; 32 cm. Published on the occasion of the exhibition of the same name, organized by the National Museum of American Art, Smithsonian Institution, and presented from April 4 to August 3, 1997. Includes bibliographical references (p. 205-209) and index. ISBN 1-56098-737-5 (alk. paper) DDC 769.973
1. *Monotype (Engraving), American. I. National Museum of American Art (U.S.) II. Title.*
**TC NE2245.U54 M67 1997**

**Moses and the angels.**
Sobel, Ileene Smith. New York : Delacorte Press, c1999.
**TC BM580 .S55 1999**

**MOSES (BIBLICAL LEADER).**
Sobel, Ileene Smith. Moses and the angels. New York : Delacorte Press, c1999.
**TC BM580 .S55 1999**

**MOSES (BIBLICAL LEADER) IN RABBINICAL LITERATURE - JUVENILE LITERATURE.**
Sobel, Ileene Smith. Moses and the angels. New York : Delacorte Press, c1999.
**TC BM580 .S55 1999**

**MOSES (BIBLICAL LEADER) - JUVENILE LITERATURE.**
Sobel, Ileene Smith. Moses and the angels. New York : Delacorte Press, c1999.
**TC BM580 .S55 1999**

**Moses, Diana.**
Croll, Paul. Special needs in the primary school. London : Cassell, 2000.
**TC LC4036.G6 C763 2000**

**Moses, Nelson.**
Klein, Harriet B. Intervention planning for adults with communication problems : Volume 2. Boston : Allyn and Bacon, c1999.
**TC RC423 .K57 1999**

**Moses, Yolanda T.**
Strategies in teaching anthropology. Upper Saddle River, N.J. : Prentice Hall, c2000.
**TC GN43 .S77 2000**

**Mosha, R. Sambuli.** The heartbeat of indigenous Africa : a study of the Chagga educational system / R. Sambuli Mosha. New York ; London : Garland Publishing : [Falmer Press], 2000. xxv, 251 p. : maps ; 23 cm. (Garland reference library of social science ; v. 1442. Indigenous knowledge and schooling ; v. 3) Includes bibliographical references (p. 243-248) and index. ISBN 0-8153-3464-8 (hbk. : alk. paper) ISBN 0-8153-3618-7 (pbk. : alk. paper) DDC 306.43/096
1. *Educational sociology - Tanzania. 2. Chaga (African people) - Education. 3. Educational sociology - Africa. I. Title.*

II. *Series: Garland reference library of social science ; v. 1442. III. Series: Garland reference library of social science. Indigenous knowledge and schooling ; v. 3.*
**TC LC191.8.T29 M67 2000**

**Mosley, Jenny.** Quality circle time in the secondary school : : a handbook of good practice / Jenny Mosley and Marilyn Tew. London : David Fulton, 1999. x, 150 p. : ill. ; 30 cm. Includes bibliography and index. ISBN 1-85346-616-6
1. *Education, Secondary. 2. Self-esteem in adolescence. 3. Social interaction in adolescence. I. Tew, Marilyn. II. Title.*
**TC LB1032 .M67 1999**

**Moss, Alfred A., 1943-.**
Anderson, Eric, 1949- Dangerous donations. Columbia, Mo. : University of Missouri Press, c1999.
**TC LC2707 .A53 1999**

**Moss, John, 1957-.**
Issues in English teaching. London ; New York : Routledge, 2000.
**TC LB1576 .I89 2000**

**Moss, Marissa.** True heart / Marissa Moss ; illustrated by C. F. Payne. 1st ed. San Diego : Silver Whistle, c1999. 1 v. (unpaged) : col. ill. ; 29 cm. SUMMARY: At the turn of the century, a young woman who works on the railroad accomplishes her yearning ambition to become an engineer when a male engineer is injured and can't drive his train. ISBN 0-15-201344-X DDC [Fic]
1. *Locomotive engineers - Fiction. 2. Sex role - Fiction. 3. West (U.S.) - Fiction. I. Payne, C. F., ill. II. Title.*
**TC PZ7.M8535 Tr 1999**

**Moss, Miriam.**
The many dimensions of aging. New York : Springer Pub., c2000.
**TC HQ1061 .M337 2000**

**MOTHER AND CHILD. See also MOTHERS AND DAUGHTERS; MOTHERS AND SONS.**
Fivaz-Depeursinge, Elisabeth. The primary triangle :. New York : Basic Books, c1999.
**TC HQ755.85 .F583 1999**

Hrdy, Sarah Blaffer, 1946- Mother nature. 1st ed. New York : Pantheon Books, c1999.
**TC HQ759 .H784 1999**

**MOTHER AND CHILD - FICTION.**
Chwast, Seymour. Traffic jam. Boston : Houghton Mifflin, 1999.
**TC PZ7.C4893 Tr 1999**

Jewell, Nancy. Sailor Song. New York : Clarion Books, c1999.
**TC PZ7.J55325 Sai 1999**

**MOTHER AND CHILD - JAPAN - HISTORY - 20TH CENTURY.**
Uno, Kathleen S., 1951- Passages to modernity. Honolulu : University of Hawai'i Press, c1999.
**TC HQ778.7.J3 U56 1999**

**MOTHER AND CHILD - UNITED STATES - PSYCHOLOGICAL ASPECTS.**
Leventhal, Tama. Poverty and turbulence. 1999.
**TC 085 L5515**

**MOTHER-CHILD RELATIONSHIP. See MOTHER AND CHILD.**

**Mother nature.**
Hrdy, Sarah Blaffer, 1946- 1st ed. New York : Pantheon Books, c1999.
**TC HQ759 .H784 1999**

**MOTHER TONGUE. See NATIVE LANGUAGE.**

**MOTHERHOOD. See MOTHERS.**

**MOTHERHOOD - PSYCHOLOGICAL ASPECTS.**
Hrdy, Sarah Blaffer, 1946- Mother nature. 1st ed. New York : Pantheon Books, c1999.
**TC HQ759 .H784 1999**

**Mothering inner-city children.**
Rosier, Katherine Brown. New Brunswick, NJ : Rutgers University Press, 2000.
**TC HV1447.I53 R67 2000**

**Motherloss.**
Davidman, Lynn, 1955- Berkeley, Calif. : University of California Press, c2000.
**TC BF575.G7 D37 2000**

**MOTHERS. See HOUSEWIVES; MOTHERHOOD; PREGNANT WOMEN; STEPMOTHERS; TEENAGE MOTHERS; WORKING MOTHERS.**

**MOTHERS AND DAUGHTERS - FICTION.**
Madrigal, Antonio Hernandez. Erandi's braids. New York : Putnam's, c1999.

*TC PZ7.M26575 Er 1999*

Pomerantz, Charlotte. The chalk doll. New York : Lippincott, c1989.
*TC PZ7.P77 Ch 1989*

Rodowsky, Colby F. The Turnabout Shop. 1st ed. New York : Farrar, Straus and Giroux, c1998.
*TC PZ7.R6185 Tu 1998*

Vail, Rachel. Please, please, please. New York : Scholastic, c1998.
*TC PZ7.V1916 Pl 1998*

**Mothers and illicit drugs.**
Boyd, Susan C., 1953- Toronto ; Buffalo, NY : University of Toronto Press, 1999.
*TC HV5824.W6 B69 1999*

**MOTHERS AND SONS - FICTION.**
Chichester Clark, Emma. More!. 1st American ed. New York : Doubleday Books for Young Readers/ Bantam Doubleday Dell Pub., 1999.
*TC PZ7.C4335 Mo 1999*

Jones, Jennifer B. Dear Mrs. Ryan, you're ruining my life. New York : Walker & Co., 2000.
*TC PZ7.J7203 De 2000*

Mills, Claudia. You're a brave man, Julius Zimmerman. 1st ed. New York : Farrar Straus Giroux, c1999.
*TC PZ7.M63963 Yo 1999*

**MOTHERS AND SONS - UNITED STATES.**
Black sons to mothers. New York ; Canterbury [England] : P. Lang, c2000.
*TC LC2731 .B53 2000*

**Mothers at work.**
Hoffman, Lois Norma Wladis, 1929- Cambridge ; New York : Cambridge University Press, 1999.
*TC HQ759.48 .H63 1999*

**MOTHERS - DEATH - PSYCHOLOGICAL ASPECTS.**
Davidman, Lynn, 1955- Motherloss. Berkeley, Calif. : University of California Press, c2000.
*TC BF575.G7 D37 2000*

**MOTHERS - DRUG USE - CANADA.**
Boyd, Susan C., 1953- Mothers and illicit drugs. Toronto ; Buffalo, NY : University of Toronto Press, 1999.
*TC HV5824.W6 B69 1999*

**MOTHERS - DRUG USE - UNITED STATES.**
Boyd, Susan C., 1953- Mothers and illicit drugs. Toronto ; Buffalo, NY : University of Toronto Press, 1999.
*TC HV5824.W6 B69 1999*

**MOTHERS, EMPLOYED.** *See* **WORKING MOTHERS.**

**MOTHERS - EMPLOYMENT - UNITED STATES.**
Williams, Joan, 1952- Unbending gender. Oxford ; New York : Oxford University Press, c2000.
*TC HD4904.25 .W55 2000*

**MOTHERS - EMPLOYMENT - UNITED STATES - CASE STUDIES.**
Garey, Anita Ilta, 1947- Weaving work and motherhood. Philadelphia, PA : Temple University Press, 1999.
*TC HQ759.48 .G37 1999*

**The mothers legacy to her vnborn [i.e. unborn] childe [i.e. child].**
Jocelin, Elizabeth, 1596-1622. Toronto : University of Toronto Press, 2000.
*TC BV4570 .J62 2000*

**MOTHERS - NEW YORK (STATE) - HEALTH AND HYGIENE - STATISTICS.**
Maternal, child and adolescent health profile. Albany, N.Y. : New York State Dept. of Health, 1996.
*TC HV742.N7 B83 1996*

**MOTHERS - UNITED STATES - PUBLIC OPINION - HISTORY.**
Irving, Katrina. Immigrant mothers. Urbana : University of Illinois Press, c2000.
*TC HQ1419 .I75 2000*

**MOTHERS, WORKING.** *See* **WORKING MOTHERS.**

**MOTION.** *See* **MOVEMENT, PSYCHOLOGY OF.**

**MOTION PERCEPTION (VISION).**
Berthoz, A. [Sens du Mouvement. English] The brain's sense of movement. Cambridge, Mass. : Harvard University Press, 2000.
*TC QP493 .B47 2000*

**MOTION PICTURE DIRECTION.** *See* **MOTION PICTURES - PRODUCTION AND DIRECTION.**

**MOTION PICTURE DIRECTORS.** *See* **MOTION PICTURE PRODUCERS AND DIRECTORS.**

**MOTION PICTURE JOURNALISM - UNITED STATES.**
Headline stories of the century [videorecording]. Chicago, IL. : Distributed by Questar Video, Inc., c1992.
*TC D743 .H42 1992*

**MOTION PICTURE PLAYS - PRODUCTION AND DIRECTION.** *See* **MOTION PICTURES - PRODUCTION AND DIRECTION.**

**MOTION PICTURE PRODUCERS AND DIRECTORS - UNITED STATES - BIOGRAPHY.**
Andy Warhol [videorecording]. [Chicago, IL] : Home Vision [distributor],cc1987.
*TC N6537.W28 A45 1987*

Andy Warhol [videorecording]. [Chicago, IL] : Home Vision [distributor],cc1987.
*TC N6537.W28 A45 1987*

**MOTION PICTURE PRODUCTION.** *See* **MOTION PICTURES - PRODUCTION AND DIRECTION.**

**MOTION PICTURES.** *See* **CHILDREN IN MOTION PICTURES; CHILDREN'S FILMS; DANCE IN MOTION PICTURES, TELEVISION, ETC.; DOCUMENTARY FILMS; WORKING CLASS IN MOTION PICTURES; YOUNG ADULT FILMS.**

**MOTION PICTURES AND LITERATURE.**
Morris, Timothy, 1959- You're only young twice. Urbana : University of Illinois Press, c2000.
*TC PR990 .M67 2000*

**MOTION PICTURES - CATALOGS.**
Hulse, John. Teachable movies for elementary and middle school classrooms. Bloomington, Ind. : Phi Delta Kappa Educational Foundation, c1998.
*TC PN1998 .H76 1998*

**MOTION PICTURES - COSTUME.** *See* **COSTUME.**

**MOTION PICTURES - DIRECTION.** *See* **MOTION PICTURES - PRODUCTION AND DIRECTION.**

**MOTION PICTURES FOR CHILDREN - CATALOGS.**
Culturally diverse videos, audios, and CD-ROMS for children and young adults. New York : Neal-Schuman Publishers, 1999.
*TC PN1998 .M85 1999*

**MOTION PICTURES FOR YOUNG ADULTS.** *See* **YOUNG ADULT FILMS.**

**MOTION PICTURES - HISTORY.**
Robson, Emanuel W., 1897- The film answers back. London : John Lane, [1947]
*TC PN1993.5.A1 R6 1947*

**MOTION PICTURES IN EDUCATION.**
Hulse, John. Teachable movies for elementary and middle school classrooms. Bloomington, Ind. : Phi Delta Kappa Educational Foundation, c1998.
*TC PN1998 .H76 1998*

**MOTION PICTURES IN EDUCATION - PERIODICALS.**
Film forum review. [New York, N.Y.] : The Institute, 1946-

**MOTION PICTURES IN SEX INSTRUCTION - UNITED STATES - HISTORY.**
Eberwein, Robert T., 1940- Sex ed. New Brunswick, N.J. : Rutgers University Press, 1999.
*TC HQ56 .E19 1999*

**MOTION PICTURES - MORAL AND ETHICAL ASPECTS.**
Hulse, John. Teachable movies for elementary and middle school classrooms. Bloomington, Ind. : Phi Delta Kappa Educational Foundation, c1998.
*TC PN1998 .H76 1998*

**MOTION PICTURES - PERIODICALS.**
Film heritage. Dayton, Ohio, University of Dayton.

[Wide angle (Online)] Wide angle [computer file]. Baltimore, Md. : John Hopkins University Press, c1996-
*TC EJOURNALS*

**MOTION PICTURES - PRODUCTION AND DIRECTION.**
Cottringer, Anne. Movie magic. 1st American ed. New York : DK Pub., c1999.
*TC PN1995.9.P7 C66 1999*

**MOTION PICTURES - PRODUCTION AND DIRECTION - FICTION.**
Many, Paul. My life, take two. New York : Walker & Co., 2000.
*TC PZ7.M3212 My 2000*

**MOTION PICTURES - PRODUCTION AND DIRECTION - JUVENILE LITERATURE.**
Cottringer, Anne. Movie magic. 1st American ed. New York : DK Pub., c1999.
*TC PN1995.9.P7 C66 1999*

**MOTION PICTURES - SEMIOTICS.**
Drummond, Lee, 1944- American dreamtime. Lanham, Md. : Littlefield Adams Books, 1996.
*TC PN1995.9.M96 D78 1996*

**MOTION STUDY.** *See* **MOVEMENT, PSYCHOLOGY OF.**

**Motivating & inspiring teachers.**
Whitaker, Todd, 1959- Motivating and inspiring teachers. Larchmont, N.Y. : Eye on Education, c2000.
*TC LB2840 .W45 2000*

**Motivating and inspiring teachers.**
Whitaker, Todd, 1959- Larchmont, N.Y. : Eye on Education, c2000.
*TC LB2840 .W45 2000*

**Motivating language learners.**
Chambers, Gary N., 1956- Clevedon [U.K.] : Buffalo : Multilingual Matters, c1999.
*TC PB35 .C517 1999*

**Motivating others.**
Thompson, David P., 1959- Princeton, NJ : Eye On Education, c1996.
*TC LB2831.58 .T56 1996*

**Motivating students for lifelong learning** / Centre for Educational Research and Innovation. Paris : Organisation for Economic Co-operation and Development, c2000. 198 p. : maps ; 23 cm. (Education and skills) (What works in innovation in education) French title: Motiver les élèves: l'enjeu de l'apprentissage à vie. Includes bibliographical references (p. 193-198). ISBN 92-64-17193-2 *1. Motivation in education - OECD countries - Case studies. 2. School improvement programs - OECD countries - Case studies. 3. Continuing education - OECD countries - Case studies. 4. Educational change - OECD countries - Case studies. I. Centre for Educational Research and Innovation. II. Title: Motiver les élèves: l'enjeu de l'apprentissage à vie III. Series. IV. Series: What works in innovation in education*
*TC LB1065 .M669 2000*

**Motivation & emotion.**
Edwards, David C. Thousand Oaks, Calif. : Sage, c1999.
*TC BF503 .E38 1999*

**Motivation and emotion.**
Edwards, David C. Motivation & emotion. Thousand Oaks, Calif. : Sage, c1999.
*TC BF503 .E38 1999*

**MOTIVATION IN EDUCATION.**
Babbage, Keen J. High-impact teaching. Lancaster, Pa. : Technomic Pub. Co., c1998.
*TC LB1065 .B23 1998*

Campbell, Jack, Ed. D. Student discipline and classroom management. Springfield, Ill. : C.C. Thomas, c1999.
*TC LB3012 .C34 1999*

Chuska, Kenneth R. Improving classroom questions. Bloomington, Ind. : Phi Delta Kappa Educational Foundation, 1995.
*TC LB1027.44 .C58 1995*

Hong, Eunsook. Homework. Westport, Conn. : Bergin & Garvey, 2000.
*TC LB1048 .H69 2000*

Jones, Vernon F., 1945- Comprehensive classroom management. 6th ed. Boston : Allyn and Bacon, c2001.
*TC LB3013 .J66 2001*

Kottler, Jeffrey A. On being a teacher. 2nd ed. Thousand Oaks, Calif. : Corwin Press, c2000.
*TC LB1025.3 .Z44 2000*

Miller, Estelle L. Fears expressed by female reentry students at an urban community college : qualitative study. 1997.

*TC 06 no. 10864*

Oldfather, Penny. Learning through children's eyes.
1st ed. Washington, DC : American Psychological
Association, c1999.
*TC LB1060 .O43 1999*

Purkey, William Watson. What students say to
themselves. Thousand Oaks, Calif. : Corwin Press,
c2000.
*TC LB1062.6 .P87 2000*

Scheidecker, David, 1950- Bringing out the best in
students. Thousand Oaks, Calif. : Corwin Press,
c1999.
*TC LB1065 .S344 1999*

Small, Ruth V. Turning kids on to research.
Englewood, Colo. : Libraries Unlimited, 2000.
*TC LB1065 .S57 2000*

Whitaker, Todd, 1959- Motivating and inspiring
teachers. Larchmont, N.Y. : Eye on Education, c2000.
*TC LB2840 .W45 2000*

**MOTIVATION IN EDUCATION - CASE STUDIES.**
Inspiring students :. London : Kogan Page, 1999.
*TC LB1065 .I57 1999*

**MOTIVATION IN EDUCATION - GREAT
BRITAIN.**
McNamara, Eddie. Positive pupil management and
motivation :. London : David Fulton, 1999.
*TC LB3013 .M336 1999*

**MOTIVATION IN EDUCATION - OECD
COUNTRIES - CASE STUDIES.**
Motivating students for lifelong learning. Paris :
Organisation for Economic Co-operation and
Development, c2000.
*TC LB1065 .M669 2000*

**MOTIVATION IN EDUCATION - UNITED
STATES.**
Dynamics of effective teaching. 4th ed. New York ;
Harlow, England : Longman, c2000.
*TC LB1737.U6 K56 2000*

Engaging young readers. New York : Guilford Press,
c2000.
*TC LB1573 .E655 2000*

Thompson, David P., 1959- Motivating others.
Princeton, NJ : Eye On Education, c1996.
*TC LB2831.58 .T56 1996*

**MOTIVATION (PSYCHOLOGY).** *See also*
**ACHIEVEMENT MOTIVATION; BURN OUT
(PSYCHOLOGY); CONFLICT
(PSYCHOLOGY); EXPECTATION
(PSYCHOLOGY); GOAL (PSYCHOLOGY);
MOTIVATION IN EDUCATION; REWARD
(PSYCHOLOGY); SELF-ACTUALIZATION
(PSYCHOLOGY); SOCIAL DESIRABILITY;
WISHES.**
Cavalier, Robert P., 1933- Personal motivation.
Westport, Conn. ; London : Praeger, 2000.
*TC BF503 .C39 2000*

Edwards, David C. Motivation & emotion. Thousand
Oaks, Calif. : Sage, c1999.
*TC BF503 .E38 1999*

Emmons, Robert A. The psychology of ultimate
concerns. New York : Guilford Press, c1999.
*TC BF505.G6 E58 1999*

Katz, Tal Y. Self-construal as a moderator of the
effects of task and reward interdependence of group
performance. 1999.
*TC 085 K1524*

Kohn, Alfie. Punished by rewards. Boston : Houghton
Mifflin Co., 1999, c1993.
*TC BF505.R48 K65 1999*

Wilton, Richard. Consciousness, free will, and the
explanation of human behavior. Lewiston, N.Y. : E.
Mellen Press, c2000.
*TC BF161 .W495 2000*

**Motiver les élèves: l'enjeu de l'apprentissage à vie.**
Motivating students for lifelong learning. Paris :
Organisation for Economic Co-operation and
Development, c2000.
*TC LB1065 .M669 2000*

**MOTOR ABILITY.**
Latash, Mark L., 1953- Neurophysiological basis of
movement. Champaign, IL : Human Kinetics, c1998.
*TC QP301 .L364 1998*

Proprioception and neuromuscular control in joint
stability. [Champaign, IL] : Human Kinetics, c2000.

*TC QP454 .P77 2000*

**MOTOR ABILITY IN CHILDREN.** *See*
**PHYSICAL EDUCATION FOR CHILDREN.**

**Motor characteristics of the mentally retarded.**
Francis, Robert Jay. [Washington] U.S. Dept. of
Health, Education, and Welfare, Office of Education
[1960]
*TC RJ499 .F7 1960*

**MOTOR LEARNING.** *See also* **MOVEMENT
EDUCATION.**
Landy, Joanne M. Ready-to-use fundamental motor
skills & movement activities for young children. West
Nyack, NY : Center for Applied Research in
Education, c1999.
*TC GV452 .L355 1999*

**MOTOR NERVOUS SYSTEM.** *See* **EFFERENT
PATHWAYS.**

**MOTOR PATHWAYS.** *See* **EFFERENT
PATHWAYS.**

**MOTOR PSYCHOLOGY.** *See* **MOVEMENT,
PSYCHOLOGY OF.**

**MOTOR SKILLS - PHYSIOLOGY.**
Love, Russell J. Childhood motor speech disability.
2nd ed. Boston : London : Allyn and Bacon, c2000.
*TC RJ496.S7 L68 2000*

**MOTOR TRACTS.** *See* **EFFERENT PATHWAYS.**

**MOTOR-TRUCK DRIVERS.** *See* **TRUCK
DRIVERS.**

**MOTOR-TRUCKS.** *See* **TRUCKS.**

**MOTOR VEHICLE DRIVERS.** *See* **TRUCK
DRIVERS.**

**MOTOR VEHICLES.** *See* **TRUCKS.**

**MOTT HALL SCHOOL (NEW YORK, N.Y.).**
Graham, Sheila L. Urban minority gifted students.
1999.
*TC 06 no. 11119*

**MOTT HALL SCHOOL (NEW YORK, N.Y.) -
STUDENTS - ATTITUDES.**
Graham, Sheila L. Urban minority gifted students.
1999.
*TC 06 no. 11119*

**MOTT HAVEN (NEW YORK, N.Y.) - SOCIAL
CONDITIONS.**
Kozol, Jonathan. Ordinary resurrections. 1st ed. New
York : Crown Publishers, c2000.
*TC HQ792.U5 K69 2000*

**Mott, Vivian W.**
Charting a course for continuing professional
education :. San Francisco : Jossey-Bass, c2000.
*TC LC1072.C56 C55 2000*

**Motz, LaMoine L.**
Biehle, James T. NSTA guide to school science
facilities. Arlington, VA : National Science Teachers
Association, c1999.
*TC Q183.3.A1 B54 1999*

**Moule, Susan.**
Drever, Mina. Teaching English in primary
classrooms. Stoke on Trent, Staffordshire, England :
Trentham Books, 1999.
*TC LB1576 .D749 1999*

**Mount Kilimanjaro.**
Stambach, Amy, 1966- Lessons from Mount
Kilimanjaro. New York : Routledge, 2000.
*TC LA1844.K54 S72 2000*

**MOUNT VERNON (VA. : ESTATE).**
West, Patricia, 1958- Domesticating history.
Washington [D.C.] : Smithsonian Institution Press,
c1999.
*TC E159 .W445 1999*

**The mountain is moving.**
Morley, Patricia A. Washington Square, N.Y. : New
York University Press, 1999.
*TC HQ1762 .M64 1999*

**Mountain, Lee Harrison.** Early 3 Rs : how to lead
beginners into reading, writing, and arithme-talk / Lee
Mountain. Mahwah, N.J. ; London : L. Erlbaum
Associates, 2000. xiii, 163 p. ; 23 cm. Includes
bibliographical references (p. 159-160) and index. ISBN
0-8058-3400-1 (pbk. : alk. paper) DDC 372.21
*1. Early childhood education. 2. Language arts (Early
childhood) I. Title. II. Title: Early three Rs*
*TC LB1139.23 .M68 2000*

**MOURNING.** *See* **GRIEF.**

**MOUSE.** *See* **MICE.**

**Mouse practice.**
McCully, Emily Arnold. 1st ed. New York : Arthur A.
Levine Books/Scholastic Press, 1999.
*TC PZ7.M13913 Mo 1999*

**Mouse's birthday.**
Yolen, Jane. New York : Putnam's, c1993.
*TC PZ8.3.Y76 Mo 1993*

**Moustafa, Margaret.**
Dombey, Henrietta. Whole to part phonics. London :
Centre for Language in Primary Education : Language
Matters, c1998.
*TC LB1573.3 .D66 1998*

**MOUTH.** *See* **TEETH.**

**MOVABLE BOOKS.** *See* **TOY AND MOVABLE
BOOKS.**

**MOVEABLE BOOKS.** *See* **TOY AND MOVABLE
BOOKS.**

**MOVEMENT, AESTHETICS OF.**
Fleming, Bruce. Sex, art, and audience. New York ;
Canterbury [England] : P. Lang, c2000.
*TC GV1588.3 .F54 2000*

**MOVEMENT - CASE REPORT.**
Beyond talk therapy. 1st ed. Washington, DC :
American Psychological Association, c1999.
*TC RC489.A72 B49 1999*

**MOVEMENT DISORDERS.**
Latash, Mark L., 1953- Neurophysiological basis of
movement. Champaign, IL : Human Kinetics, c1998.
*TC QP301 .L364 1998*

**MOVEMENT EDUCATION.** *See also*
**MOVEMENT, PSYCHOLOGY OF.**
Colvin, A. Vonnie, 1951- Teaching the nuts and bolts
of physical education. Champaign, IL : Human
Kinetics, c2000.
*TC GV443 .C59 2000*

Landy, Joanne M. Ready-to-use fundamental motor
skills & movement activities for young children. West
Nyack, NY : Center for Applied Research in
Education, c1999.
*TC GV452 .L355 1999*

**MOVEMENT EDUCATION - UNITED STATES.**
Griss, Susan. Minds in motion. Portsmouth, NH :
Heinemann, c1998.
*TC LB1592 .G75 1998*

**The movement for community control of New York
City's schools, 1966-1970.**
Edgell, Derek. Lewiston, N.Y. : E. Mellen Press,
c1998.
*TC LB2862 .E35 1998*

**MOVEMENT PERCEPTION (VISION).** *See*
**MOTION PERCEPTION (VISION).**

**MOVEMENT, PSYCHOLOGY OF.** *See also*
**MOTION PERCEPTION (VISION);
MOVEMENT EDUCATION; PERCEPTUAL-
MOTOR PROCESSES.**
Francis, Robert Jay. Motor characteristics of the
mentally retarded. [Washington] U.S. Dept. of Health,
Education, and Welfare, Office of Education [1960]
*TC RJ499 .F7 1960*

The meaning of movement. Amsterdam : Gordon and
Breach, c1999.
*TC RC473.K47 M4 1999*

**MOVEMENT THERAPY.**
The meaning of movement. Amsterdam : Gordon and
Breach, c1999.
*TC RC473.K47 M4 1999*

**MOVEMENTS, HUMAN.** *See* **HUMAN
MECHANICS.**

**Movie magic.**
Cottringer, Anne. 1st American ed. New York : DK
Pub., c1999.
*TC PN1995.9.P7 C66 1999*

**MOVIES.** *See* **MOTION PICTURES.**

**Movies for elementary and middle school classrooms.**
Hulse, John. Teachable movies for elementary and
middle school classrooms. Bloomington, Ind. : Phi
Delta Kappa Educational Foundation, c1998.
*TC PN1998 .H76 1998*

**Moving ahead in arithmetic.**
Brueckner, Leo J. New York, N.Y. : Holt, Rinehart
and Winston, 1963.
*TC QA107 .B78 1963*

Brueckner, Leo J. New York, N.Y. : Holt, Rinehart
and Winston, 1963.

*TC QA107 .B78 1963*

Brueckner, Leo J. New York : Holt, Rinehart and Winston, 1963.
*TC QA107 .B78 1963*

Brueckner, Leo J. New York : Holt, Rinehart and Winston, 1963.
*TC QA107 .B78 1963*

**Moving beyond the gap between research and practice in higher education** / Adrianna J. Kezar, Peter Eckel, editors. San Francisco, Calif. : Jossey-Bass, c2000. 120 p. ; 23 cm. (New directions for higher education, no. 110.) Includes bibliographical references and index. CONTENTS: Understanding the research-to-practice gap : a national study of researchers' and practitioners' perspectives / Adrianna Kezar -- The tyranny of success : the research-practice tension / Marvin w. Peterson -- Reshaping the forces that perpetuate the research-practice gap : focus on new faculty / Carol L. Colbeck -- To be more useful : embracing interdisciplinary scholarship and dialogue / Clifton F. Conrad, Ramona Gunter -- The educational role of researchers / K. Patricia Cross -- Change as a scholarly act : higher education research transfer to practice / Judith A. Ramaley -- Toward better-informed decisions : reading groups as a campus tool / Peter Eckel, Adrianna Kezar, Devorah Lieberman -- Practitioners as researchers : bridging theory and practice / Deborah Hirsch -- Bridging the gap : multiple players, multiple approaches / Madeleine F. Green. ISBN 0-7879-5434-9 (pbk.) *1. Education, Higher - Aims and objectives - United States. I. Kezar, Adrianna J. II. Eckel, Peter J. III. Series.*
*TC LA227.4 .M68 2000*

**Moving into the 21st century.**
Dugan, JoAnn R. Advancing the world of literacy. Carrollton, Ga. : College Reading Association, 1999.
*TC LB2395 .C62 1999*

**Moving middle schools**
Art works!. Portsmouth, NH : Heinemann, c1999.
*TC LB1628.5 .A78 1999*

**Moving on.** Lexington, Mass. : D.C. Heath, c1983. T32, 457 p. : col. ill. ; 28 cm. (Heath American readers) Teacher's ed. Includes index. ISBN 0-669-08048-9
*1. Reading (Primary) 2. Readers (Primary) I. Series.*
*TC PE1119 .M68 1986 Teacher's Ed.*

**Moving on in your career.**
Ali, Lynda, 1946- London ; New York : RoutledgeFalmer, 2000.
*TC LB1778.4.G7 A45 2000*

**Moving on** / Mildred Bailey, consultant ... [et al.]. Lexington, Mass. : D.C. Heath, c1983. [2 v.] : ill. (some col.) ; 24-28 cm. (American readers ; 1) Teacher's ed. includes index. ISBN 0-669-04950-6 (reader) ISBN 0-669-04951-4 (teacher's ed.)
*1. Reading (Elementary) 2. Readers (Elementary) I. Bailey, Mildred. II. Series.*
*TC PE1117 .M68 1983*

**Moving on** / Mildred Bailey, consultant ... [et al.]. Lexington, Mass. : D.C. Heath, c1983. [2 v.] : ill. (some col.) ; 24-28 cm. (American readers ; 1) Teacher's ed. includes index. ISBN 0-669-04950-6 (reader) ISBN 0-669-04951-4 (teacher's ed.)
*1. Reading (Elementary) 2. Readers (Elementary) I. Bailey, Mildred. II. Series.*
*TC PE1117 .M68 1983*

**Moving on : workbook.** Lexington, Mass. : D.C. Heath, c1983. 128 p. : col. ill. ; 28 cm. (American readers ; 1) Teacher's ed. Includes index. ISBN 0-669-04957-3
*1. Reading (Primary) 2. Readers (Primary) I. Series.*
*TC PE1119 .M68 1983 Teacher's Ed. Workbook*

**MOVING-PICTURE AUTHORSHIP.**
Edmonds, Robert. Scriptwriting for the audio-visual media. New York : Teachers College Press, c1978.
*TC PN1991.7 .E3*

**MOVING-PICTURE JOURNALISM.** *See* MOTION PICTURE JOURNALISM.

**MOVING-PICTURE PRODUCERS AND DIRECTORS.** *See* MOTION PICTURE PRODUCERS AND DIRECTORS.

**MOVING-PICTURES.** *See* MOTION PICTURES.

**MOVING-PICTURES, DOCUMENTARY.** *See* DOCUMENTARY FILMS.

**MOVING-PICTURES FOR CHILDREN.** *See* MOTION PICTURES FOR CHILDREN.

**MOVING-PICTURES IN EDUCATION.** *See also* MOTION PICTURES IN EDUCATION.
Intercine. Rome.

**MOVING-PICTURES - PERIODICALS.**
Intercine. Rome.

**MOVING-PICTURES - REVIEWS.**
Simon, John Ivan. Private screenings New York, Macmillan [1967]
*TC PN1995 .S495*

**Moving theory into practice.**
Kenney, Anne R., 1950- Mountain View, CA : Research Libraries Group, 2000.
*TC Z681.3.D53 K37*

**Mowat, Barbara A.**
Luke, Helen M., 1904- Such stuff as dreams are made on. New York : Parabola Books, c2000.
*TC BF1091 .L82 2000*

**Mowrer, Robert R., 1956-.**
Handbook of contemporary learning theories. Mahwah, N.J. ; London : Lawrence Erlbaum Associates, 2001.
*TC LB1060 .H3457 2001*

**Moyers, Bill D.**
Changing lives [videorecording]. Princeton, NJ : Films for the Humanities & Sciences, c1998.
*TC RC564 .C54 1998*

The hijacked brain [videorecording]. Princeton, NJ : Films for the Humanities & Sciences, c1998.
*TC RC564 .H5 1998*

The next generation [videorecording]. Princeton, NJ : Films for the Humanities & Sciences, c1998.
*TC RC564 .N4 1998*

The politics of addiction [videorecording]. Princeton, NJ : Films for the Humanities & Sciences, c1998.
*TC RC564 .P59 1998*

Portrait of addiction [videorecording]. Princeton, NJ : Films for the Humanities & Sciences, c1998.
*TC HV5801 .P6 1998*

Portrait of addiction [videorecording]. Princeton, NJ : Films for the Humanities & Sciences, c1998.
*TC RC564 .P6 1998*

**The Moyers collection**
Changing lives [videorecording]. Princeton, NJ : Films for the Humanities & Sciences, c1998.
*TC RC564 .C54 1998*

The hijacked brain [videorecording]. Princeton, NJ : Films for the Humanities & Sciences, c1998.
*TC RC564 .H5 1998*

The next generation [videorecording]. Princeton, NJ : Films for the Humanities & Sciences, c1998.
*TC RC564 .N4 1998*

The politics of addiction [videorecording]. Princeton, NJ : Films for the Humanities & Sciences, c1998.
*TC RC564 .P59 1998*

Portrait of addiction [videorecording]. Princeton, NJ : Films for the Humanities & Sciences, c1998.
*TC HV5801 .P6 1998*

Portrait of addiction [videorecording]. Princeton, NJ : Films for the Humanities & Sciences, c1998.
*TC RC564 .P6 1998*

**Moyles, Janet R.**
The primary curriculum. New York : London : Routledge, 1998.
*TC LB1570 .P678 1998*

**MPD (PERSONALITY DISORDER).** *See* MULTIPLE PERSONALITY.

**MPI Home Video.**
The Amish [videorecording]. Oak Forest, IL : MPI Home Video, 1988.

**MPI Home Video (Firm).**
The Amish [videorecording]. Oak Forest, Ill. : MPI Home Video, c1988.
*TC BX8129.A5 A5 1988*

**Mrs. Merriwether's musical cat.**
Purdy, Carol. New York : Putnam, c1994.
*TC PZ7.P9745 Mr 1994*

**MT. VERNON (VA. : ESTATE).** *See* MOUNT VERNON (VA. : ESTATE).

**MUHAMMADANISM.** *See* ISLAM.

**MUI TSAI.** *See* SLAVERY.

**Mujer que brillaba aún más que el sol.**
Cruz Martinez, Alejandro, d. 1987. [Mujer que brillaba aún más que el sol. English & Spanish] The woman who outshone the sun. San Francisco, Calif. : Children's Book Press, c1991.
*TC F1221.Z3 C78 1991*

**Mulford, Carla, 1955-.**
Teaching the literatures of early America. New York : Modern Language Association of America, 1999.

*TC PS186 .T43 1999*

**Mullen, Carol A.**
New directions in mentoring. London ; New York : Falmer, 1999.
*TC LB1731.4 .N49 1999*

The postmodern educator. New York : P. Lang, c1999.
*TC LB1707 .P67 1999*

**Muller, Gilbert H.**
Gateways to democracy. San Francisco : Jossey-Bass, 1999.
*TC LB2328.N53 1999*

**Muller, Susan.** Student study guide to accompany Fox's physiological basis for exercise and sport / prepared by Susan Muller. 6th ed. Boston, Mass. : WCB/ McGraw-Hill, c1998. 151 p. : ill. ; 28 cm. ISBN 0-697-37618-4
*1. Sports - Physiological aspects. 2. Exercise - Physiological aspects. I. Keteyian, Steven J. II. Fox, Edward L. Physiological basis for exercise and sport. III. Fox, Edward L. Physiological basis of physical education and athletics. IV. Foss, Merle L. 1936- V. Title. VI. Title: Physiological basis for exercise and sport.*
*TC RC1235 .F65 1998 guide*

**MULTI-AGE GROUPING.** *See* NONGRADED SCHOOLS.

**A multi-case study of physical education teachers and working conditions in inner-city schools** /by Hiram Oscar V'elez Arias.
V'elez Arias, Hiram Oscar. 1998.
*TC 06 no. 11001*

**MULTI-HOSPITAL SYSTEMS.** *See* MULTIHOSPITAL SYSTEMS.

**MULTI-INSTITUTIONAL HOSPITAL SYSTEMS.** *See* MULTIHOSPITAL SYSTEMS.

**MULTI-INSTITUTIONAL SYSTEMS, HOSPITAL.** *See* MULTIHOSPITAL SYSTEMS.

**MULTI MEDIA PROGRAMS.** *See* MEDIA PROGRAMS (EDUCATION).

**A multi-sensory approach to language arts for specific language disability children.**
Slingerland, Beth H. Cambridge, Mass. : Educators Pub. Service, c1976-<c1981 >
*TC LC4704.85 .S59 1976*

**The multiage handbook :** a comprehensive resource for multiage practices / compiled by Jim Grant and Irv Richardson ; edited by Aldene Fredenburg. Peterborough, NH : Society for Developmental Education, c1996. 287 p. : ill. ; 28 cm. Includes bibliographical references (p.276-283) and index. Includes index. ISBN 1-88454-805-9 DDC 371.2/55
*1. Nongraded schools - Handbooks, manuals, etc. I. Grant, Jim, 1942- II. Richardson, Irv, 1956- III. Fredenburg, Aldene.*
*TC LB1029.N6 M754 1996*

**Multicultural aspects of counseling series**
(v. 13.) Fukuyama, Mary A. Integrating spirituality into multicultural counseling. Thousand Oaks, Calif. : Sage Publications, c1999.
*TC BF637.C6 F795 1999*

**Multicultural children in the early years.**
Woods, Peter, 1934- Clevedon ; Philadelphia : Multilingual Matters Ltd, c1999.
*TC LC3736.G6 W66 1999*

**Multicultural cookbook of life-cycle celebrations.**
Webb, Lois Sinaiko. Phoenix, AZ : Oryx Press, 2000.
*TC TX725.A1 W43 2000*

**MULTICULTURAL COUNSELING.** *See* CROSS-CULTURAL COUNSELING.

**Multicultural curriculum :** new directions for social theory, practice and policy / edited by Ram Mahalingam and Cameron McCarthy. New York : Routledge, 2000. ix, 310 p. : ill. ; 23 cm. Includes index. ISBN 0-415-92013-2 ISBN 0-415-92014-0 (pbk.) DDC 370.117
*1. Multicultural education - Curricula. 2. Multiculturalism. 3. Critical pedagogy. I. Mahalingam, Ram. II. McCarthy, Cameron.*
*TC LC1099 .M816 2000*

**MULTICULTURAL DIVERSITY IN THE WORKPLACE.** *See* DIVERSITY IN THE WORKPLACE.

**MULTICULTURAL EDUCATION.** *See also* EDUCATION, BILINGUAL.
Mahammad, Hasna. 1998.

*TC 06 no. 11033*

**MULTICULTURAL EDUCATION.**
Barchers, Suzanne I. Multicultural folktales.
Englewood, Colo. : Teacher Ideas Press, 2000.
*TC GR43.C4 B39 2000*

Classroom issues. London ; New York : Falmer Press,
2000.
*TC LC268 .C52 2000*

Cortés, Carlos E. The children are watching. New
York : Teachers College Press, c2000.
*TC P96.M83 C67 2000*

Diversity [videorecording]. Barrington, IL : Magna
Systems, Inc., 1996.
*TC LB1139.25 .D5 1996*

Education and racism :. Aldershot ; Brookfield, Vt. :
Ashgate, c1999.
*TC LC212.3.G7E48 1999*

Enhancing education in heterogeneous schools.
Ramat-Gan : Bar-Ilan University Press, [1997]
*TC LC214 .E54 1997*

Ford, Terry. Becoming multicultural :. New York :
Falmer Press, 1999.
*TC LC1099 .F674 1999*

Hicks, D. Emily. Ninety-five languages and seven
forms of intelligence. New York : P. Lang, c1999.
*TC LC196 .H53 1999*

Mio, Jeffrey Scott. Resistance to multiculturalism :.
Philadelphia, PA : Brunner/Mazel, c2000.
*TC HM1271 .M56 2000*

Paradigm debates in curriculum and supervision.
Westport, Conn. ; London : Bergin & Garvey, 2000.
*TC LB2806.4 .P37 2000*

Schlanger, Dean J. An exploration of school
belongingness. 1998.
*TC 06 no. 10993*

Trawick-Smith, Jeffrey W. Early childhood
development. 2nd ed. Upper Saddle River, N.J. :
Merrill, c2000.
*TC LB1115 .T73 2000*

**MULTICULTURAL EDUCATION - CANADA.**
Garcia, Ricardo L. Teaching for diversity.
Bloomington, Ind. : Phi Delta Kappa Educational
Foundation, 1998.
*TC LC1099.3 .G367 1998*

Racism and education. Ottawa : Canadian Teachers'
Federation, 1992.
*TC LC212.3.C3 R32 1992*

**MULTICULTURAL EDUCATION - CANADA -
CASE STUDIES.**
Ryan, James, 1952 Oct. 18- Race and ethnicity in
multi-ethnic schools. Clevedon [England] ;
Philadelphia : Multilingual Matters, c1999.
*TC LC3734 .R93 1999*

**MULTICULTURAL EDUCATION - CURRICULA.**
Multicultural curriculum. New York : Routledge,
2000.
*TC LC1099 .M816 2000*

**MULTICULTURAL EDUCATION -
ENCYCLOPEDIAS.**
Mitchell, Bruce M. Encyclopedia of multicultural
education. Westport, Conn. : Greenwood Press, 1999.
*TC LC1099.3 .M58 1999*

**Multicultural education for the 21st century** / Carlos
F. Díaz, editor. 1st ed. New York : Longman, 2001. ix,
243 p. ; 24 cm. Cover title: Multicultural education in the 21st
century. Includes bibliographical references and index. ISBN
0-321-05417-2 (pbk.) DDC 370.117/0973
*1. Multicultural education - United States. 2. Effective
teaching - United States. I. Díaz, Carlos (Carlos F.) II. Title:
Multicultural education in the 21st century. III. Title:
Multicultural education for the twenty-first century*
*TC LC1099.3 .M8163 2001*

**Multicultural education for the twenty-first century.**
Multicultural education for the 21st century. 1st ed.
New York : Longman, 2001.
*TC LC1099.3 .M8163 2001*

**MULTICULTURAL EDUCATION - GREAT
BRITAIN.**
Siraj-Blatchford, Iram. Supporting identity, diversity
and language in the early years. Buckingham
[England] ; Philadelphia : Open University Press,
2000.
*TC LB1139.3.G7 S57 2000*

**Multicultural education in middle and secondary
classrooms.**
Rasool, Joan. Belmont, CA : Wadsworth, c2000.

*TC LC1099.3 .R38 2000*

**Multicultural education in the 21st century.**
Multicultural education for the 21st century. 1st ed.
New York : Longman, 2001.
*TC LC1099.3 .M8163 2001*

**Multicultural education in the U.S.**
Mitchell, Bruce M. Westport, Conn. ; London :
Greenwood Press, 2000.
*TC LC1099.3 .M59 2000*

Mitchell, Bruce M. Multicultural education in the
U.S.. Westport, Conn. ; London : Greenwood Press,
2000.
*TC LC1099.3 .M59 2000*

**MULTICULTURAL EDUCATION - JAPAN.**
McConnell, David L., 1959- Importing diversity.
Berkeley : University of California Press, c2000.
*TC LB2285.J3 M33 2000*

**MULTICULTURAL EDUCATION - MORAL AND
ETHICAL ASPECTS.**
Moral education and pluralism. London ; New York :
Falmer Press, 2000.
*TC LC268 .M683 2000*

**MULTICULTURAL EDUCATION - NEW YORK
(STATE).**
Mahammad, Hasna. Multicultural education. 1998.
*TC 06 no. 11033*

**MULTICULTURAL EDUCATION - NEW YORK
(STATE) - CASE STUDIES.**
Schmidt, Patricia Ruggiano, 1944- Cultural conflict
and struggle. New York : P. Lang, c1998.
*TC LB1181 .S36 1998*

**MULTICULTURAL EDUCATION - NEW YORK
(STATE) - NEW YORK - CURRICULA.**
Thompson, Melvin R. The implementation of
multicultural curricula in the New York City public
elementary schools. 1999.
*TC 06 no. 11186*

**Multicultural education of children and adolescents.**
Manning, M. Lee. 3rd ed. Boston : Allyn and Bacon,
c2000.
*TC LC1099.3 .M36 2000*

**MULTICULTURAL EDUCATION - OKLAHOMA.**
Damm, Robert J., 1964- Repertoire, authenticity, and
instruction. New York ; London : Garland Pub., 2000.
*TC MT3.U6 O53 2000*

**MULTICULTURAL EDUCATION -
PERIODICALS.**
Intercultural education. New York, International
Council for Educational Development.

**Multicultural education series (New York, N.Y.)**
Cortés, Carlos E. The children are watching. New
York : Teachers College Press, c2000.
*TC P96.M83 C67 2000*

Gay, Geneva. Culturally responsive teaching. New
York : Teachers College Press, c2000.
*TC LC1099.3 . G393 2000*

**MULTICULTURAL EDUCATION - UNITED
STATES.**
Banks, James A. Cultural diversity and education. 4th
ed. Boston ; London : Allyn & Bacon, c2001.
*TC LC3731 .B365 2001*

Barnes, Barbara. Schools transformed for the 21st
century. Torrance, Calif. : Griffin Pub. Group, c1999.
*TC LA217.2 .B39 1999*

Campbell, Duane E. Choosing democracy. 2nd ed.
Upper Saddle River, N.J. : Merrill, c2000.
*TC LC1099.3 .C36 2000*

Critical ethnicity. Lanham, Md. : Rowman &
Littlefield, c1999.
*TC LC212.2 .C75 1999*

Critical knowledge for diverse teachers & learners.
Washington, DC : AACTE : ERIC, c1997.
*TC LB1715 .C732 1997*

The developmental process of positive attitudes and
mutual respect. Lewiston, N.Y. : E. Mellen Press,
c1999.
*TC LB2822.82 .D49 1999*

Education is politics. Portsmouth, NH : Boynton/
Cook, c1999.
*TC LC196.5.U6 E36 1999*

Foundational perpectives in multiculural education.
New York : Longman, c2000.
*TC LC1099.3 .F68 2000*

Garcia, Ricardo L. Teaching for diversity.
Bloomington, Ind. : Phi Delta Kappa Educational
Foundation, 1998.
*TC LC1099.3 .G367 1998*

Gay, Geneva. Culturally responsive teaching. New
York : Teachers College Press, c2000.
*TC LC1099.3 . G393 2000*

Literacy instruction for culturally and linguistically
diverse students. Newark, Del. : International Reading
Association, c1998.
*TC LC3731 .L566 1998*

Macedo, Donaldo P. (Donaldo Pereira), 1950-
Dancing with bigotry. New York : St. Martin's Press,
1999.
*TC LC196.5.U6 D26 1999*

Manning, M. Lee. Multicultural education of children
and adolescents. 3rd ed. Boston : Allyn and Bacon,
c2000.
*TC LC1099.3 .M36 2000*

McEwan, Barbara, 1946- The art of classroom
management. Upper Saddle River, N.J. : Merrill,
c2000.
*TC LB3013 .M383 2000*

Multicultural education for the 21st century. 1st ed.
New York : Longman, 2001.
*TC LC1099.3 .M8163 2001*

Multiple and intersecting identities in qualitative
research. Mahwah, N.J. ; London : L. Erlbaum
Associates, 2001.
*TC LC1028.25.U6 M85 2001*

Orsini, Alfonso J. The color of excellence. 1999.
*TC 06 no. 11209*

The politics of multiculturalism and bilingual
education. Boston : McGraw-Hill, c2000.
*TC LC1099.3 .P64 2000*

Professional development guide for educators.
Washington, D.C. : National Education Association of
the United States, 2000.
*TC LC1099.3 .P755 1999*

Robbins, Carol Braswell. An examination of critical
feminist pedagogy in practice. 1999.
*TC 06 no. 11067*

Teaching for a tolerant world, grades K-6. Urbana,
Ill. : National Council of Teachers of English, c1999.
*TC HM1271 .T43 1999*

Zarrillo, James. Teaching elementary social studies.
Upper Saddle River, N.J. : Merrill, c2000.
*TC LB1584 .Z27 2000*

**MULTICULTURAL EDUCATION - UNITED
STATES - ACTIVITY PROGRAMS.**
Experiential activities for intercultural learning.
Yarmouth, Me., USA : Intercultural Press, c1996-
*TC LC1099.3 .E97 1996*

**MULTICULTURAL EDUCATION - UNITED
STATES - AUDIO-VISUAL AIDS.**
Hidden messages. Yarmouth, Me. : Intercultural
Press, c1998.
*TC LC1099.3 .H53 1998*

**MULTICULTURAL EDUCATION - UNITED
STATES - CASE STUDIES.**
Educators healing racism. Reston, VA : Association
of Teacher Educators ; Olney, MD : Association for
Childhood Education International, c1999.
*TC LC212.2 .E38 1999*

**MULTICULTURAL EDUCATION - UNITED
STATES - CURRICULA.**
Hidden messages. Yarmouth, Me. : Intercultural
Press, c1998.
*TC LC1099.3 .H53 1998*

Rasool, Joan. Multicultural education in middle and
secondary classrooms. Belmont, CA : Wadsworth,
c2000.
*TC LC1099.3 .R38 2000*

**MULTICULTURAL EDUCATION - UNITED
STATES - ENCYCLOPEDIAS.**
Mitchell, Bruce M. Encyclopedia of multicultural
education. Westport, Conn. : Greenwood Press, 1999.
*TC LC1099.3 .M58 1999*

**MULTICULTURAL EDUCATION - UNITED
STATES - HISTORY.**
Spring, Joel H. Deculturalization and the struggle for
equality. 3rd ed. Boston : McGraw-Hill, c2001.
*TC LC3731 .S68 2001*

**MULTICULTURAL EDUCATION - UNITED
STATES - STATES.**
Mitchell, Bruce M. Multicultural education in the

EDUCATION: 2000

U.S.. Westport, Conn. : London : Greenwood Press, 2000.
*TC LC1099.3 .M59 2000*

**Multicultural folktales.**
Barchers, Suzanne I. Englewood, Colo. : Teacher Ideas Press, 2000.
*TC GR43.C4 B39 2000*

**Multicultural mental health.**
Handbook of multicultural mental health :. San Diego : Academic Press, c2000.
*TC RC455.4 .H36 2000*

**The multicultural resource series**
(v. 1) Professional development guide for educators. Washington, D.C. : National Education Association of the United States, 2000.
*TC LC1099.3 .P755 1999*

**Multicultural resources on the Internet. The United States and Canada.**
Gregory, Vicki L., 1950- Englewood, Colo. : Libraries Unlimited, 1999.
*TC E184.A1 G874 1999*

**MULTICULTURAL WORKFORCE.** *See* **DIVERSITY IN THE WORKPLACE.**

**MULTICULTURALISM.** *See also* **DIVERSITY IN THE WORKPLACE; ETHNICITY; MUSIC - EFFECT OF MULTICULTURALISM ON; PLURALISM (SOCIAL SCIENCES).**
The challenge of diversity. Aldershot, England ; Brookfield, Vt. : Avebury, 1996.
*TC JV225 .C530 1996*

Institutional issues. London ; New York : Falmer Press, 2000.
*TC LC191 .I495 2000*

Mio, Jeffrey Scott. Resistance to multiculturalism :. Philadelphia, PA : Brunner/Mazel, c2000.
*TC HM1271 .M56 2000*

Multicultural curriculum. New York : Routledge, 2000.
*TC LC1099 .M816 2000*

Multiliteracies. London ; New York : Routledge, 2000.
*TC LC149 .M85 2000*

Systems of education. London ; New York : Falmer Press, 2000.
*TC LC191 .S98 2000*

**MULTICULTURALISM - GOVERNMENT POLICY.** *See* **MULTICULTURALISM.**

**MULTICULTURALISM IN ART.**
Talking visions. New York, N.Y. : New Museum of Contemporary Art ; Cambridge, Mass. : MIT Press, c1998.
*TC NX180.F4 T36 1998*

**MULTICULTURALISM IN MASS MEDIA.**
Cortés, Carlos E. The children are watching. New York : Teachers College Press, c2000.
*TC P96.M83 C67 2000*

**MULTICULTURALISM - STUDY AND TEACHING (EARLY CHILDHOOD) - GREAT BRITAIN - CASE STUDIES.**
Woods, Peter, 1934- Multicultural children in the early years. Clevedon ; Philadelphia : Multilingual Matters Ltd, c1999.
*TC LC3736.G6 W66 1999*

**MULTICULTURALISM - STUDY AND TEACHING (HIGHER) - ACTIVITY PROGRAMS.**
Teaching about culture, ethnicity & diversity. Thousand Oaks : Sage Publications, c1998.
*TC HM101 .T38 1998*

**MULTICULTURALISM - UNITED STATES.**
Bartolomé, Lilia I. The misteaching of academic discourses. Boulder, Colo. : Westview Press, 1998.
*TC LB1033.5 .B37 1998*

Macedo, Stephen, 1957- Diversity and distrust. Cambridge, Mass. ; London : Harvard University Press, 2000.
*TC LA217.2 .M33 2000*

**MULTICULTURISM.**
Skutnabb-Kangas, Tove. Linguistic genocide in education, or worldwide diversity and human rights? Mahwah, N.J. : L. Erlbaum Associates, 2000.
*TC P40.8 .S58 2000*

**MULTIHOSPITAL SYSTEMS - NEW YORK (STATE) - NEW YORK - HISTORY - 20TH CENTURY.**

Opdycke, Sandra. No one was turned away. New York : Oxford University Press, 1999.
*TC RA982.N49 O63 1999*

**Multilevel analysis.**
Snijders, Tom A. B. Thousand Oaks, Calif. ; London : SAGE, 1999.
*TC QA278 .S645 1999*

**Multilevel theory, research, and methods in organizations :** foundations, extensions, and new directions / Katherine J. Klein, Steve W.J. Kozlowski, editors ; foreword by Sheldon Zedeck. 1st ed. San Francisco : Jossey-Bass, c2000. xxix, 605 p. : ill. ; 24 cm. (Jossey-Bass social & behavioral sciences series) (Jossey-Bass business & management series) (Frontiers of industrial and organizational psychology) Includes bibliographical references and indexes. ISBN 0-7879-5228-1 DDC 158.7
*1. Psychology, Industrial. 2. Complex organizations. I. Klein, Katherine J. II. Kozlowski, Steve W. J. III. Series. IV. Series: Frontiers of industrial and organizational psychology V. Series: Jossey-Bass social and behavioral science series.*
*TC HF5548.8 .M815 2000*

**The multilingual Apple :** languages in New York City / edited by Ofelia García, Joshua A. Fishman. Berlin ; New York : Mouton de Gruyter, 1997. xiv, 373 p. : map ; 24 cm. (Contributions to the sociology of language ; 77) Includes bibliographical references and index. ISBN 3-11-015089-1 (acid-free paper) DDC 306.44/09747/1
*1. Linguistic minorities - New York (State) - New York. 2. Sociolinguistics - New York (State) - New York. 3. New York (N.Y.) - Languages. I. García, Ofelia. II. Fishman, Joshua A. III. Series.*
*TC P40.5.L56 M8 1997*

**MULTILINGUALISM.** *See* **BILINGUALISM.**

**Multiliteracies :** literacy learning and the design of social futures / edited by Bill Cope and Mary Kalantzis for the New London Group. London ; New York : Routledge, 2000. xi, 350 p. : ill. ; 24 cm. (Literacies) Includes bibliographical references (p. 333-348) and index. ISBN 0-415-21420-3 (hbk) ISBN 0-415-21421-1 (pbk) DDC 302.2/244
*1. Literacy. 2. Multiculturalism. 3. English language - Study and teaching. I. Cope, Bill. II. Kalantzis, Mary. III. New London Group. IV. Series.*
*TC LC149 .M85 2000*

**Multimedia authoring tools and teacher training.**
Idzal, June M. 1997.
*TC 06 no. 10816*

**MULTIMEDIA COMPUTING.** *See* **MULTIMEDIA SYSTEMS.**

**MULTIMEDIA INFORMATION SYSTEMS.** *See* **MULTIMEDIA SYSTEMS.**

**MULTIMEDIA KNOWLEDGE SYSTEMS.** *See* **MULTIMEDIA SYSTEMS.**

**MULTIMEDIA SYSTEMS.** *See also* **WORLD WIDE WEB (INFORMATION RETRIEVAL SYSTEM).**
Idzal, June M. Multimedia authoring tools and teacher training. 1997.
*TC 06 no. 10816*

Intelligent multimedia information retrieval. Menlo Park, Calif. : AAAI Press ; Cambridge, Mass. : MIT Press, c1997.
*TC QA76.575 .I577 1997*

Lunenfeld, Peter. Snap to grid. Cambridge, MA : MIT, 2000.
*TC QA76.9.C66 L86 2000*

**MULTIMEDIA SYSTEMS - PUERTO RICO.**
Laborde, Ilia M. Rediscovering San Cristóbal Canyon. 1996.
*TC 06 no. 10660*

Laborde, Ilia M. Rediscovering San Cristóbal Canyon. 1996.
*TC 06 no. 10660*

**MULTIMEDIA SYSTEMS - SOCIAL ASPECTS.**
Digital diversions. London : UCL Press, 1998.
*TC QA76.575 .D536 1998*

**MULTINATIONAL CORPORATIONS.** *See* **INTERNATIONAL BUSINESS ENTERPRISES.**

**MULTINATIONAL ENTERPRISES.** *See* **INTERNATIONAL BUSINESS ENTERPRISES.**

**Multiple and intersecting identities in qualitative research** / edited by Betty M. Merchant, Arlette Ingram Willis. Mahwah, N.J. ; London : L. Erlbaum Associates, 2001. xvi, 146 p. ; 24 cm. Includes bibliographical references and indexes. ISBN 0-8058-2874-5

(cloth : alk. paper) ISBN 0-8058-2875-3 (paper : alk. paper) DDC 370/.7/2
*1. Education - Research - Social aspects - United States. 2. Qualitative research - United States. 3. Women in education - United States. 4. Multicultural education - United States. 5. Educational anthropology - United States. I. Merchant, Betty M. II. Willis, Arlette Ingram.*
*TC LB1028.25.U6 M85 2001*

**MULTIPLE BIRTH.** *See* **TRIPLETS; TWINS.**

**Multiple case study in three organizations in Spain.**
Sauquet, Alfonso. Conflict and team learning:. 2000.
*TC 06 no. 11308*

**MULTIPLE CONSCIOUSNESS.** *See* **MULTIPLE PERSONALITY.**

**MULTIPLE HOSPITAL SYSTEMS.** *See* **MULTIHOSPITAL SYSTEMS.**

**MULTIPLE INTELLIGENCES.**
Eddy, Jennifer B.K. Multiple intelligences, styles, and proficiency. 1999.
*TC 085 E10*

Lazear, David G. Eight ways of knowing. 3rd ed. Arlington Heights, Ill. : SkyLight Training and Pub., c1999.
*TC LB1060 .L39 1999*

**Multiple intelligences, styles, and proficiency.**
Eddy, Jennifer B.K. 1999.
*TC 085 E10*

**Multiple measures.**
Ardovino, Joan. Thousand Oaks, Calif. : Corwin Press, c2000.
*TC LB3051 .A745 2000*

**MULTIPLE PERSONALITIES.** *See* **MULTIPLE PERSONALITY.**

**MULTIPLE PERSONALITY.**
Acocella, Joan Ross. Creating hysteria. 1st ed. San Francisco : Jossey-Bass Publishers, c1999.
*TC RC569.5.M8 A28 1999*

**MULTIPLE PERSONALITY - CASE STUDIES.**
Goldberg, Arnold, 1929- Being of two minds. Hillsdale, NJ : Analytic Press, 1999.
*TC RC569.5.M8 G65 1999*

**MULTIPLE PERSONALITY DISORDER.** *See* **MULTIPLE PERSONALITY.**

**Multisensory environments.**
Pagliano, Paul. London : David Fulton, 1999.
*TC LC3965 .P345 1999*

**Multisensory guide for the blind and visually impaired.**
European modernism. New York, N.Y. : OpticalTouch Systems ; Louisville, Ky. : American Printing House for the Blind, c1998-1999.
*TC N6758 .A7 1999*

**Multisensory structured metacognitive instruction.**
Schneider, Elke. Frankfurt am Main ; New York : P. Lang, c1999.
*TC P53.7 .S357 1999*

**Multivariable analysis.**
Katz, Mitchell H. Cambridge, UK ; New York : Cambridge University Press, 1999.
*TC R853.S7 K38 1999*

**MULTIVARIATE ANALYSIS.** *See also* **CLUSTER ANALYSIS.**
Applied regression analysis and other multivariable methods. 3rd ed. / David G. Kleinbaum ... [et al.]. Pacific Grove : Duxbury Press, c1998.
*TC QA278 .A665 1998*

Bilodeau, Martin, 1961- Theory of multivariate statistics. New York : Springer, c1999.
*TC QA278 .B55 1999*

Byrne, Barbara M. Structural equation modeling with LISREL, PRELIS, and SIMPLIS. Mahwah, N.J. : L. Erlbaum Associates, 1998.
*TC QA278 .B97 1998*

Katz, Mitchell H. Multivariable analysis. Cambridge, UK ; New York : Cambridge University Press, 1999.
*TC R853.S7 K38 1999*

Multivariate applications in substance use research. Mahwah, N.J. : Lawrence Erlbaum Associates, 2000.
*TC HV5809 .M84 2000*

Schumacker, Randall E. A beginner's guide to structural equation modeling. Mahwah, N.J. : L. Erlbaum Associates, 1996.
*TC QA278 .S36 1996*

Snijders, Tom A. B. Multilevel analysis. Thousand Oaks, Calif. ; London : SAGE, 1999.

**TC QA278 .S645 1999**

**Multivariate applications book series**
Byrne, Barbara M. Structural equation modeling with LISREL, PRELIS, and SIMPLIS. Mahwah, N.J. : L. Erlbaum Associates, 1998.
**TC QA278 .B97 1998**

Embretson, Susan E. Item response theory for psychologists. Mahwah, N.J. : Lawrence Erlbaum Associates, Publishers, 2000.
**TC BF39 .E495 2000**

**Multivariate applications in substance use research :** new methods for new questions / edited by Jennifer S. Rose ... [et al.]. Mahwah, N.J. : Lawrence Erlbaum Associates, 2000. xiv, 339 p. : ill. ; 24 cm. Includes bibliographical references and indexes. ISBN 0-8058-2942-3 (cloth : alk. paper) DDC 362.29/01/519535
*1. Substance abuse - Research. 2. Multivariate analysis. 3. Substance abuse - Longitudinal studies - Statistical methods. I. Rose, Jennifer S.*
**TC HV5809 .M84 2000**

**MUNCHAUSEN SYNDROME BY PROXY.**
Allison, David B. Disordered mother or disordered diagnosis? :. Hillsdale, NJ : Analytic Press, 1998.
**TC RC569.5.M83 A38 1998**

**Mundry, Susan.**
Designing successful professional meetings and conferences in education. Thousand Oaks, Calif. : Corwin Press, c2000.
**TC LC6519 .D48 2000**

**Munene, Macharia.**
American studies in eastern Africa. Nairobi : Nairobi University Press, 1993.
**TC E172.9 .A47 1993**

**Mungazi, Dickson A.** The last British liberals in Africa : Michael Blundell and Garfield Todd / Dickson A. Mungazi. Westport, Conn. : Praeger, 1999. xvi, 285 p. : ill. ; 25 cm. Includes bibliographical references (p. [255]-276) and index. ISBN 0-275-96283-0 (alk. paper) DDC 325/.341/09226762
*1. Todd, Garfield. - 1908- 2. Zimbabwe - Politics and government - 1890-1965. 3. Zimbabwe - Politics and government - 1965-1979. 4. Blundell, Michael, - Sir, - 1907- 5. Kenya - Politics and government - To 1963. 6. Kenya - Politics and government - 1963-1978. 7. Great Britain - Colonies - Africa - Administration. 8. Liberalism - Great Britain - History - 20th century. 9. Liberalism - Africa, Sub-Saharan - History - 20th century. I. Title.*
**TC DT2979.T63 M86 1999**

**Munhall, Patricia L.**
The emergence of family into the 21st century. Boston : Jones and Bartlett Publishers ; [New York] : NLN Press, c2001.
**TC HQ535 .E44 2001**

Qualitative research proposals and reports : a guide / Patricia L. Munhall. Sudbury, MA : Jones and Bartlett, 2000. xi, 51 p. ; 22 cm. Includes bibliographical references. ISBN 0-7637-1171-3 (pbk.) DDC 610.73/07/2
*1. Nursing - Research - Methodology. 2. Qualitative research. I. Title.*
**TC RT81.5 .M854 2000**

**MUNICIPAL BONDS.** *See* **SCHOOL BONDS.**

**MUNICIPAL GOVERNMENT.** *See* **STATE-LOCAL RELATIONS.**

**MUNICIPAL JUNIOR COLLEGE TEACHERS.** *See* **COMMUNITY COLLEGE TEACHERS.**

**MUNICIPAL JUNIOR COLLEGES.** *See* **COMMUNITY COLLEGES.**

**MUNICIPALITIES.** *See* **CITIES AND TOWNS.**

**Munns, Evangeline.**
Theraplay. Northvale, N.J. : J. Aronson, c2000.
**TC RJ505.P6 T485 2000**

**Muñoz-Plaza, César A.**
Turk, Laurel Herbert, 1903- El español al día. Revised ed. Lexington, Mass. : D.C. Heath, c1974.
**TC PC4111 .T87 1974**

**Munsch, Robert N., 1945-** Ribbon rescue / Robert Munsch ; illustrated by Eugenie Fernandes. New York : Scholastic, 1999. 26 p. : col. ill, ; 26 cm. "Cartwheel books." SUMMARY: A young girl unselfishly gives away the ribbons from her new dress to help various people on their way to a wedding. ISBN 0-590-89012-3 DDC [E]
*1. Ribbons - Fiction. 2. Weddings - Fiction. 3. Generosity - Fiction. I. Eugenie, ill. II. Title.*
**TC PZ7.M927 Ri 1999**

**Munsterberg, Hugo, 1916-** World ceramics : from prehistoric to modern times / Hugo and Marjorie Munsterberg. New York : Penguin Studio Books,
c1998. 191 p. : col. ill. ; 29 cm. Includes index. DDC 738/.09
*1. Pottery - History. 2. Porcelain - History. I. Munsterberg, Marjorie. II. Title.*
**TC NK3780 .M86 1998**

**Munsterberg, Marjorie.**
Munsterberg, Hugo, 1916- World ceramics. New York : Penguin Studio Books, c1998.
**TC NK3780 .M86 1998**

**Munter, Agnes de.**
Snick, Anne. Women in educational [sic] policy-making. Leuven, Belgium : Leuven University Press, 1999.
**TC LC93.A2 S56 1999**

**MURAL PAINTING AND DECORATION.** *See* **CAVE PAINTINGS.**

**MURAL PAINTING AND DECORATION - 20TH CENTURY.** *See* **STREET ART.**

**MURAL PAINTING AND DECORATION - 20TH CENTURY - CALIFORNIA - SAN FRANCISCO - THEMES, MOTIVES.**
Lee, Anthony W., 1960- Painting on the left. Berkeley : University of California Press, c1999.
**TC ND259.R5 L44 1999**

**MURAL PAINTING AND DECORATION, MEXICAN.**
Folgarait, Leonard. Mural painting and social revolution in Mexico, 1920-1940. Cambridge ; New York, NY : Cambridge University Press, 1998.
**TC ND2644 .F63 1998**

The frescoes of Diego Rivera [videorecording]. [Detroit, Mich.] : Founders Society, Detroit Institute of Arts ; [Chicago, Ill.?] : Home Vision [distributor], c1986.
**TC ND259.R5 F6 1986**

**MURAL PAINTING AND DECORATION - MEXICO - HISTORY - 20TH CENTURY.**
Folgarait, Leonard. Mural painting and social revolution in Mexico, 1920-1940. Cambridge ; New York, NY : Cambridge University Press, 1998.
**TC ND2644 .F63 1998**

**Mural painting and social revolution in Mexico, 1920-1940.**
Folgarait, Leonard. Cambridge ; New York, NY : Cambridge University Press, 1998.
**TC ND2644 .F63 1998**

**MURALS.** *See* **MURAL PAINTING AND DECORATION.**

**MURDER.** *See* **HOMICIDE.**

**MURDER OFFENDERS.** *See* **MURDERERS.**

**MURDER - UNITED STATES.**
Teen killers [videorecording]. Princeton, NJ : Films for the Humanities and Sciences, c1998-1999.
**TC HV9067.H6 T4 1999**

**MURDERERS - UNITED STATES.**
Teen killers [videorecording]. Princeton, NJ : Films for the Humanities and Sciences, c1998-1999.
**TC HV9067.H6 T4 1999**

**Murdin, Lesley.** How much is enough? : endings in psychotherapy and counselling / Lesley Murdin. London ; New York : Routledge, 2000. viii, 176 p. ; 22 cm. Includes bibliographical references and index. ISBN 0-415-18892-X (hbk) ISBN 0-415-18893-8 (pbk.) DDC 616.89/14
*1. Psychotherapy - Termination. I. Title.*
**TC RC489.T45 M87 2000**

**Murphy, Daniel.** A history of Irish emigrant and missionary education / Daniel Murphy. Dublin, Ireland ; Portland, Ore. : Four Courts Pres, c2000. xx, 574 p. ; 24 cm. Includes bibliographical references (p. 531-542) and index. ISBN 1-85182-522-3
*1. Missions, Irish. 2. Missions - Educational work. I. Title.*
**TC BV2630.M87 2000**

**MURPHY, GERALD, 1888-1964.**
Tomkins, Calvin, 1925- Living well is the best revenge. 1998 Modern Library ed. New York : Modern Library, c1998.
**TC ND237.M895 T66 1998**

**MURPHY, JIM, 1947- /.**
**THE GREAT FIRE.**
Beech, Linda Ward. The great fire by Jim Murphy. New York : Scholastic, c1996.
**TC LB11573 .B437 1996**

Beech, Linda Ward. The great fire by Jim Murphy. New York : Scholastic, c1996.

**TC LB1573 .B437 1996**

**Murphy, John J. (John Joseph), 1955-** Brief intervention for school problems : collaborating for practical solutions / John J. Murphy, Barry L. Duncan. New York : Guilford Press, c1997. xii, 175 p. : ill. ; 24 cm. (The Guilford school practitioner series) Includes bibliographical references (p. 163-167) and index. ISBN 1-57230-174-0 (acid-free paper) DDC 371.93
*1. Problem children - Education - United States - Case studies. 2. Educational counseling - United States - Case studies. 3. Student assistance programs - United States - Case studies. 4. Problem children - Services for - United States - Case studies. I. Duncan, Barry L. II. Title. III. Series.*
**TC LC4802 .M87 1997**

**Murphy, Kevin R., 1952-.**
Cleveland, Jeanette. Women and men in organizations. Mahwah, N.J. ; London : Lawrence Erlbaum Associates, 2000.
**TC HD6060.65.U5 C58 2000**

**Murphy, Lois Barclay, 1902-** The individual child / Lois B. Murphy [and] Ethel M. Leeper. Washington : Department of Health Education, and Welfare : for sale by the Supt. of Docs., U. S. Govt. Print. Off., 1973. 24 p. ; ill. ; 26 cm. (DHEW publication no.(OCD) 74-1032.) (Caring for children ; no.7.)
*1. Education, Preschool. 2. Learning, Psychology of. 3. Personality. I. Leeper, Ethel M. II. Title. III. Series.*
**MURPHY, SARA.**
Tomkins, Calvin, 1925- Living well is the best revenge. 1998 Modern Library ed. New York : Modern Library, c1998.
**TC ND237.M895 T66 1998**

**Murphy, Sharon, 1955-.**
Albers, Peggy. Telling pieces. Mahwah, N.J. : L. Erlbaum Associates, 2000.
**TC N362.5 .A43 2000**

**Murphy, Shirley Rousseau.** Wind child / by Shirley Rousseau Murphy ; illustrated by the Dillons. New York, NY : HarperCollins, c1999. 1 v. (unpaged) : col. ill. ; 23 x 29 cm. Illustrators, Leo and Diane Dillon. SUMMARY: Unaware of her unusual parentage, Resshie grows up restless and longing to know the secrets of the wind and she uses her extraordinary ability as a weaver to help her achieve her dream. ISBN 0-06-024903-X ISBN 0-06-024904-8 (lib. bdg.) DDC [E]
*1. Fairy tales. 2. Winds - Fiction. 3. Weaving - Fiction. I. Dillon, Leo, ill. II. Dillon, Diane, ill. III. Title.*
**TC PZ8.M957 Wi 1999**

**Murphy, Stanley D.**
Eddy, John, 1932- International higher education systems. New ed. Lanham, Md. ; Oxford : University Press of America, c2000.
**TC LB2322.2 .E33 2000**

**Murphy, Timothy F., 1955-.**
Reader's guide to lesbian and gay studies. Chicago : Fitzroy Dearborn Publishers, 2000.
**TC HQ75.15 .R43 2000**

**Murray, Anne, 1952-.**
Ayers, Harry. Perspectives on behaviour. 2nd ed. London : David Fulton, 2000.
**TC LC4801 .A94 2000**

**Murray, Louis, 1944-** Practitioner-based enquiry : principles for postgraduate research / Louis Murray and Brenda Lawrence. London ; New York : Falmer Press, 2000. xiv, 241 p. ; 24 cm. (Social research and educational studies series ; 20) Includes bibliographical references (p. 230-235) and index. ISBN 0-7507-0772-0 (hbk. : alk. paper) ISBN 0-7507-0771-2 (pbk. : alk. paper) DDC 370/.7/2
*1. Action research in education - Great Britain. 2. Education - Research - Great Britain - Methodology. I. Lawrence, Brenda, 1954- II. Title. III. Series.*
**TC LB1028.24 .M87 2000**

**Murray, May.**
The Kindergarten and first grade. Springfield, Mass. : Milton Bradley Co., 1916-[1924]

**MUS MUSCULUS.** *See* **MICE.**

**MUSCLE.** *See* **MUSCLES.**

**MUSCLE, SKELETAL - METABOLISM.**
Exercise metabolism. Champaign, IL : Human Kinetics, c1995.
**TC QP301 .E967 1995**

**MUSCLES - PATHOPHYSIOLOGY - CONGRESSES.**
The physiology and pathophysiology of exercise tolerance. New York : Plenum Press, c1996.
**TC QP301 .P576 1996**

**MUSCLES - PHYSIOLOGY - CONGRESSES.**
The physiology and pathophysiology of exercise tolerance. New York : Plenum Press, c1996.
*TC QP301 .P576 1996*

**Muscular Christianity.**
Ladd, Tony. Grand Rapids, Mich. : Baker Books, c1999.
*TC GV706.42 .L34 1999*

**MUSCULAR SENSE.** *See* **MOVEMENT, PSYCHOLOGY OF.**

**MUSCULATURE.** *See* **MUSCLES.**

**MUSCULOSKELETAL SYSTEM.** *See* **JOINTS; MUSCLES.**

**Muse, Ivan.** Oral and nonverbal expression / Ivan Muse. Princeton, NJ : Eye On Education, c1996. xvi, 142 p. : ill. ; 24 cm. (The school leadership library) Includes bibliographical references. ISBN 1-88300-127-7 DDC 302.2/264
*1. Oral communication. 2. Communication in education. I. Title. II. Series.*
*TC P95 .M86 1996*

**Musée d'art et d'essai (Paris, France).**
Picasso [videorecording]. Chicago, IL : Home Vision, c1986.
*TC N6853.P5 P52 1986*

**Musée d'art moderne (Céret, France).**
La Fontaine, Jean de, 1621-1695. [Fables. English. Selections] Marc Chagall. New York : New Press : Distributed by W.W. Norton, [1997]
*TC PQ1811.E3 W6 1997*

**Musée d'art moderne de la ville de Paris.**
Weiss, Jeffrey. Mark Rothko. Washington : National Gallery of Art ; New Haven, Conn. : Yale University Press, c1998.
*TC N6537.R63 A4 1998*

**MUSÉE MCCORD D'HISTOIRE CANADIENNE - HISTOIRE.**
Young, Brian, 1940- The making and unmaking of a university museum. Montreal : McGill-Queen's University Press, c2000.
*TC FC21 .Y68 2000*

**Musée national Message biblique Marc Chagall.**
La Fontaine, Jean de, 1621-1695. [Fables. English. Selections] Marc Chagall. New York : New Press : Distributed by W.W. Norton, [1997]
*TC PQ1811.E3 W6 1997*

**Musée Picasso (Paris, France).**
Picasso [videorecording]. Chicago, IL : Home Vision, c1986.
*TC N6853.P5 P52 1986*

**MUSEOLOGY.** *See* **MUSEUM TECHNIQUES.**

**MUSEUM ARCHITECTURE - HISTORY - 19TH CENTURY.**
Yanni, Carla. Nature's museums. Baltimore, Md : Johns Hopkins University Press, 2000.
*TC QH70.A1 Y25 2000*

**Museum city video**
Paris [videorecording]. New York, NY : V.I.E.W. Video, c1996.
*TC DC707 .P3 1996*

**MUSEUM CONSERVATION METHODS.**
Schlichting, Carl. Working with polyethylene foam and fluted plastic sheet. Ottawa, Ontario, Canada : Canadian Conservation Institute, Dept. of Canadian Heritage, 1994.
*TC N8554 T25 no.14*

Strang, Thomas J. K. Controlling museum fungal problems. Ottawa : Canadian Conservation Institute, Department of Communications, [1991]
*TC TH9031 .S75 1991*

**MUSEUM CURATORS.**
Tropea, Judith. A day in the life of a museum curator. Mahwah, N.J. : Troll Associates, c1991.
*TC QE22.E53 T76 1991*

**MUSEUM CURATORS - UNITED STATES - BIOGRAPHY.**
Alexander, Edward P. (Edward Porter), 1907- The museum in America. Walnut Creek : AltaMira Press, c1997.
*TC AM11 .A55 1997*

**MUSEUM CURATORS - UNITED STATES - BIOGRAPHY - JUVENILE LITERATURE.**
Tropea, Judith. A day in the life of a museum curator. Mahwah, N.J. : Troll Associates, c1991.
*TC QE22.E53 T76 1991*

**MUSEUM DIRECTORS - UNITED STATES - BIOGRAPHY.**
Alexander, Edward P. (Edward Porter), 1907- The museum in America. Walnut Creek : AltaMira Press, c1997.
*TC AM11 .A55 1997*

**MUSEUM DISPLAYS.** *See* **MUSEUM EXHIBITS.**

**MUSEUM EDUCATIONAL SITE LICENSING PROJECT.**
Delivering digital images. Los Angeles, Calif. : Getty Information Institute, 1998.
*TC N59 .D45 1998*

**MUSEUM EXHIBITS - GREAT BRITAIN.**
Moore, Kevin, 1960- Museums and popular culture. London ; New York : Leicester University Press, 1997.
*TC AM41 .M66 1997*

**MUSEUM EXHIBITS - HISTORIOGRAPHY.**
Museums and memory. Stanford, Calif. : Stanford University Press, c2000.
*TC AM7 .M8815 2000*

**MUSEUM EXHIBITS - POLITICAL ASPECTS - UNITED STATES.**
Kurin, Richard, 1950- Reflections of a culture broker. Washington, D.C. : Smithsonian Institution Press, c1997.
*TC GN36.U62 D5775 1997*

**Museum governance.**
Malaro, Marie C. Washington : Smithsonian Institution Press, c1994.
*TC AM121 .M35 1994*

**The museum in America.**
Alexander, Edward P. (Edward Porter), 1907- Walnut Creek : AltaMira Press, c1997.
*TC AM11 .A55 1997*

**Museum looks at itself.**
De Salvo, Donna M. Past imperfect. Southampton, N.Y. : Parrish Art Museum, in association with the New Press, New York, N.Y., c1993.
*TC N750 .D4*

**Museum of Contemporary Photography (Columbia College (Chicago, Ill.))** Photography's multiple roles : art, document, market, science / Denise Miller ... [et al.]. Chicago : Museum of Contemporary Photography, Columbia College ; New York : Dap, Inc., c1998. 254 p. : ill. (some col.) ; 29 cm. Includes bibliographical references and index. ISBN 0-9658887-1-1 (hardcover : alk. paper) ISBN 0-9658887-2-X (pbk. : alk. paper) DDC 770/.1
*1. Photographic criticism. 2. Photography - United States. 3. Museum of Contemporary Photography (Columbia College (Chicago, Ill.)) - Photograph collections - Catalogs. 4. Photograph collections - Illinois - Chicago - Catalogs. I. Miller, Denise (Denise J.) II. Title.*
*TC TR187 .M87 1998*

**MUSEUM OF CONTEMPORARY PHOTOGRAPHY (COLUMBIA COLLEGE (CHICAGO, ILL.)) - PHOTOGRAPH COLLECTIONS - CATALOGS.**
Museum of Contemporary Photography (Columbia College (Chicago, Ill.)) Photography's multiple roles. Chicago : Museum of Contemporary Photography, Columbia College ; New York : Dap, Inc., c1998.
*TC TR187 .M87 1998*

**Museum of Fine Arts, Boston.**
Cikovsky, Nicolai. Winslow Homer. Washington, D.C. : National Gallery of Art, 1995.
*TC N6537.H58 A4 1995*

Sargent, John Singer, 1856-1925. John Singer Sargent. Princeton : Princeton University Press, 1998.
*TC ND237.S3 A4 1998a*

**Museum of Modern Art (New York, N.Y.).**
Modernstarts. New York : Museum of Modern Art : Distributed by Harry N. Abrams, c1999.
*TC N620.M9 M63 1999*

Piet Mondrian, 1872-1944. Milan : Leonardo Arte, 1994.
*TC N6953.M64 A4 1994*

Varnedoe, Kirk, 1946- Jackson Pollock. New York : Museum of Modern Art ; Distributed in the U.S. and Canada by Harry N. Abrams, c1998.
*TC ND237.P73 A4 1998*

Varnedoe, Kirk, 1946- Jasper Johns. New York : Museum of Modern Art : Distributed by Harry N. Abrams, c1996.
*TC N6537.J6 A4 1996*

Whitfield, Sarah, 1942- Bonnard. New York, N.Y. : Harry N. Abrams, 1998.
*TC ND553.B65 W45 1998*

**MUSEUM OF MODERN ART (NEW YORK, N.Y.) - EXHIBITIONS.**
Modernstarts. New York : Museum of Modern Art : Distributed by Harry N. Abrams, c1999.
*TC N620.M9 M63 1999*

**MUSEUM TECHNIQUES.** *See also* **MUSEUM EXHIBITS.**
Malaro, Marie C. Museum governance. Washington : Smithsonian Institution Press, c1994.
*TC AM121 .M35 1994*

Pearce, Susan M. Archaeological curatorship. Washington, D.C. : Smithsonian Institution Press, 1996.
*TC AM7 .P43 1996*

**MUSEUM TECHNIQUES - GREAT BRITAIN.**
Moore, Kevin, 1960- Museums and popular culture. London ; New York : Leicester University Press, 1997.
*TC AM41 .M66 1997*

**MUSEUM TECHNIQUES - HISTORY.**
Making histories in museums. London ; New York : Leicester University Press, 1996.
*TC AM7 .M35 1996*

**MUSEUM TECHNIQUES - UNITED STATES.**
Kurin, Richard, 1950- Reflections of a culture broker. Washington, D.C. : Smithsonian Institution Press, c1997.
*TC GN36.U62 D5775 1997*

**MUSEUM TECHNIQUES - VOCATIONAL GUIDANCE - JUVENILE LITERATURE.**
Tropea, Judith. A day in the life of a museum curator. Mahwah, N.J. : Troll Associates, c1991.
*TC QE22.E53 T76 1991*

**MUSEUM TRUSTEES - HANDBOOKS, MANUALS, ETC.**
Ullberg, Alan D. Museum trusteeship. Washington : American Association of Museums, 1981.
*TC AM121 .U44*

**Museum trusteeship.**
Ullberg, Alan D. Washington : American Association of Museums, 1981.
*TC AM121 .U44*

**MUSEUMS.** *See* **ANTHROPOLOGICAL MUSEUMS AND COLLECTIONS; ARCHAEOLOGICAL MUSEUMS AND COLLECTIONS; ART MUSEUMS; HISTORICAL MUSEUMS.**

**Museums & archaeology in West Africa** / edited by Claude Daniel Ardouin. Washington : Smithsonian Institution Press ; Oxford : J. Currey, c1997. xiv, 178 p. : ill., map ; 21 cm. "Published on behalf of the West African Museums Programme in association with the International African Institute." Includes bibliographical references and index. ISBN 1-56098-785-5 (Smithsonian Institution Press) ISBN 0-85255-237-8 (J. Currey) DDC 069/.096
*1. Museums - Africa, West. 2. Africa, West - Antiquities. I. Ardouin, Claude Daniel. II. West African Museums Programme. III. International African Institute. IV. Title: Museums and archaeology in West Africa*
*TC AM91.A358 M85 1997*

**MUSEUMS - ADMINISTRATION.**
Pearce, Susan M. Archaeological curatorship. Washington, D.C. : Smithsonian Institution Press, 1996.
*TC AM7 .P43 1996*

**MUSEUMS - AFRICA, WEST.**
Museums & archaeology in West Africa. Washington : Smithsonian Institution Press ; Oxford : J. Currey, c1997.
*TC AM91.A358 M85 1997*

**Museums and archaeology in West Africa.**
Museums & archaeology in West Africa. Washington : Smithsonian Institution Press ; Oxford : J. Currey, c1997.
*TC AM91.A358 M85 1997*

**Museums and memory** / edited by Susan A. Crane. Stanford, Calif. : Stanford University Press, c2000. x, 257 p. : ill. ; 24 cm. (Cultural sitings) Includes bibliographical references and index. ISBN 0-8047-3564-6 (cloth : alk. paper) ISBN 0-8047-3565-4 (pbk. : alk. paper) DDC 069
*1. Museums - Philosophy. 2. Museums - Historiography. 3. Museum exhibits - Historiography. 4. Memory (Philosophy) 5. Culture - Historiography. 6. History - Philosophy. I. Crane, Susan A. II. Series.*
*TC AM7 .M8815 2000*

**Museums and popular culture.**
Moore, Kevin. 1960- London ; New York : Leicester University Press, 1997.
*TC AM41 .M66 1997*

**MUSEUMS - EDUCATIONAL ASPECTS.**
Belcher, Michael. Exhibitions in museums. Washington, D.C. : Smithsonian Institution Press, c1991.
*TC AM7 .B3 1991*

Kavanagh, Gaynor. Dream spaces. New York : Leicester University Press, 2000.
*TC AM7 .K37 2000*

Readings in discipline-based art education. Reston, Va. : National Art Education Assoc., c2000.
*TC N87 .R43 2000*

**MUSEUMS - EMPLOYEES.** *See* MUSEUM CURATORS; MUSEUM DIRECTORS.

**MUSEUMS - ENGLAND - LONDON - HISTORY - 19TH CENTURY.**
Black, Barbara J., 1962- On exhibit. Charlottesville ; London : University Press of Virginia, 2000.
*TC AM43.L6 B53 2000*

**MUSEUMS - ENVIRONMENTAL ASPECTS.**
Strang, Thomas J. K. Controlling museum fungal problems. Ottawa : Canadian Conservation Institute, Department of Communications, [1991]
*TC TH9031 .S75 1991*

**MUSEUMS - EXHIBITIONS.**
Belcher, Michael. Exhibitions in museums. Washington, D.C. : Smithsonian Institution Press, c1991.
*TC AM7 .B3 1991*

**MUSEUMS - FICTION.**
Clement, Rod. Frank's great museum adventure. 1st American ed. [New York] : HarperCollinsPublishers, 1999.
*TC PZ7.C59114 Fr 1999*

**MUSEUMS - FURNITURE, EQUIPMENT, ETC.**
Schlichting, Carl. Working with polyethylene foam and fluted plastic sheet. Ottawa, Ontario, Canada : Canadian Conservation Institute, Dept. of Canadian Heritage, 1994.
*TC N8554 T25 no.14*

**MUSEUMS - GREAT BRITAIN - PHILOSOPHY.**
Moore, Kevin, 1960- Museums and popular culture. London ; New York : Leicester University Press, 1997.
*TC AM41 .M66 1997*

**MUSEUMS - HISTORIOGRAPHY.**
Museums and memory. Stanford, Calif. : Stanford University Press, c2000.
*TC AM7 .M8815 2000*

**MUSEUMS - HISTORY.**
Making histories in museums. London ; New York : Leicester University Press, 1996.
*TC AM7 .M35 1996*

**MUSEUMS - MANAGEMENT.**
Malaro, Marie C. Museum governance. Washington : Smithsonian Institution Press, c1994.
*TC AM121 .M35 1994*

**MUSEUMS - MANAGEMENT - PLANNING - HANDBOOKS, MANUALS, ETC.**
Building an emergency plan. Los Angeles, Calif. : Getty Conservation Institute, c1999.
*TC AM121 .B85 1999*

**MUSEUMS - PHILOSOPHY.**
Kavanagh, Gaynor. Dream spaces. New York : Leicester University Press, 2000.
*TC AM7 .K37 2000*

Museums and memory. Stanford, Calif. : Stanford University Press, c2000.
*TC AM7 .M8815 2000*

**MUSEUMS - PUBLIC RELATIONS.**
Malaro, Marie C. Museum governance. Washington : Smithsonian Institution Press, c1994.
*TC AM121 .M35 1994*

**MUSEUMS - SOCIAL ASPECTS.**
Kavanagh, Gaynor. Dream spaces. New York : Leicester University Press, 2000.
*TC AM7 .K37 2000*

**MUSEUMS - TECHNIQUE.** *See* MUSEUM TECHNIQUES.

**MUSEUMS - TRUSTEES.** *See* MUSEUM TRUSTEES.

**MUSEUMS - UNITED STATES - HISTORY.**
Alexander, Edward P. (Edward Porter), 1907- The museum in America. Walnut Creek : AltaMira Press, c1997.
*TC AM11 .A55 1997*

**MUSEVENI, YOWERI, 1944-.**
Our friends at the bank [videorecording]. New York, NY : First Run/Icarus Films, 1997.
*TC HG3881.5.W57 O87 1997*

**Mushroom in the rain.**
Ginsburg, Mirra. New York : Macmillan/McGraw-Hill, 1974.
*TC PZ10.3 .G455Mu 1974*

**MUSHROOMS - FICTION.**
Ginsburg, Mirra. Mushroom in the rain. New York : Macmillan/McGraw-Hill, 1974.
*TC PZ10.3 .G455Mu 1974*

**MUSIC.** *See* CHORAL MUSIC; CONSERVATORIES OF MUSIC; FOLK MUSIC; JAZZ; SCHOOL MUSIC; SINGING; VOICE.

**Music and child development :** the biology of music making : proceedings of the 1987 Denver conference / edited by Frank R. Wilson, Franz L. Roehmann. St. Louis, Mo. : MMB Music, c1990. xviii, 419 p. : ill. ; 26 cm. The second of a series of Biology of Music Making conferences. Includes bibliographical references. ISBN 0-918812-58-5 DDC 780/.83
*1. Music - Psychological aspects - Congresses. 2. Child musicians - Congresses. 3. Music - Instruction and study - Congresses. I. Biology of Music Making Conference (2nd : 1987 : Denver, Colo.) II. Roehmann, Franz L. III. Wilson, Frank R. IV. Title: Biology of music making.*
*TC ML3820 .M87 1990*

**MUSIC, CHORAL.** *See* CHORAL MUSIC.

**MUSIC, CLASSICAL.** *See* MUSIC.

**MUSIC - CONSERVATORIES.** *See* CONSERVATORIES OF MUSIC.

**MUSIC CONSERVATORIES.** *See* CONSERVATORIES OF MUSIC.

**Music, culture, & experience.**
Blacking, John. Chicago : University of Chicago Press, c1995.
*TC ML60 .B63 1995*

**Music, culture, and experience.**
Blacking, John. Music, culture, & experience. Chicago : University of Chicago Press, c1995.
*TC ML60 .B63 1995*

**MUSIC EDUCATION.** *See* MUSIC - INSTRUCTION AND STUDY.

**Music Educators National Conference (U.S.).**
Hall, Louis O. Strategies for teaching. Reston, VA : Music Educators National Conference, c1997.
*TC MT1.H136 S77 1997*

**MUSIC - EFFECT OF MULTICULTURALISM ON - FRANCE.**
Gingerich, Carol Joy. The French piano style of Fauré and Debussy. 1996.
*TC 06 no. 10644*

**MUSIC - FICTION.**
Gray, Libba Moore. When Uncle took the fiddle. New York : Orchard Books, 1999.
*TC PZ7.G7793 Wh 1999*

**Music for the piano.**
Friskin, James, 1886-1967. New York, Dover Publications [1973]
*TC ML128.P3 F7 1973*

**Music for young children.**
Andress, Barbara. Fort Worth, TX : Harcourt Brace College Publishers, c1998.
*TC MT810 .A6 1998*

**MUSIC - FRANCE - 20TH CENTURY.**
Gingerich, Carol Joy. The French piano style of Fauré and Debussy. 1996.
*TC 06 no. 10644*

**MUSIC - FRANCE - HISTORY AND CRITICISM.**
Jean-Aubry, G. (Georges), 1882-1950. [Musique française d'aujourd'hui. English] French music of to-day. 4th ed. London, K. Paul, Trench, Trubner, 1926.
*TC ML60.A82 E8 1926*

**MUSIC - FRANCE - PHILOSOPHY AND AESTHETICS.**
Gingerich, Carol Joy. The French piano style of Fauré and Debussy. 1996.
*TC 06 no. 10644*

**Music fundamentals, methods, and materials for the elementary classroom teacher.**
Rozmajzl, Michon. 3rd ed. New York ; Harlow, England : Longman, c2000.
*TC MT1 .R85 2000*

**MUSIC, GREEK (ANCIENT).** *See* MUSIC, GREEK AND ROMAN.

**MUSIC, GREEK AND ROMAN - HISTORY AND CRITICISM.**
Landels, John G. (John Gray), 1926- Music in ancient Greece and Rome. London ; New York : Routledge, 1999.
*TC ML169 .L24 1999*

**MUSIC-HALLS (VARIETY-THEATERS, CABARETS, ETC.).** *See* VAUDEVILLE.

**Music in American life**
Olmstead, Andrea. Juilliard. Urbana : University of Illinois Press, c1999.
*TC MT4.N5 J846 1999*

**Music in ancient Greece and Rome.**
Landels, John G. (John Gray), 1926- London ; New York : Routledge, 1999.
*TC ML169 .L24 1999*

**MUSIC IN ART.**
Cassidy, Donna. Painting the musical city. Washington, DC : Smithsonian Institution Press, c1997.
*TC ML85 .C37 1997*

Wade, Bonnie C. Imaging sound. Chicago : University of Chicago Press, c1998.
*TC ML338 .W318 1998*

**MUSIC IN EDUCATION.**
Millbower, Lenn, 1951- Training with a beat. 1st ed. Sterling, Va. : Stylus, c2000.
*TC ML3830 .M73 2000*

**Music in Latin American culture :** regional traditions / John M. Schechter, general editor ; contributors, Gage Averill ... [et al.]. New York : Schirmer Books, c1999. xvi, 496 p. : ill. ; 24 cm. Includes bibliographical references, discographies, filmographies, and index. ISBN 0-02-864750-5 (alk. paper) DDC 780/.98
*1. Music - Latin America - History and criticism. I. Schechter, John Mendell.*
*TC ML199 .M86 1999*

**Music in the classroom (MITC).**
Nord, Michael B. 1998.
*TC 06 no. 10974*

**MUSIC - INDIA - HISTORY AND CRITICISM.**
Wade, Bonnie C. Imaging sound. Chicago : University of Chicago Press, c1998.
*TC ML338 .W318 1998*

**MUSIC, INFLUENCE OF.**
Millbower, Lenn, 1951- Training with a beat. 1st ed. Sterling, Va. : Stylus, c2000.
*TC ML3830 .M73 2000*

**MUSIC - INSTRUCTION AND STUDY.** *See also* CONSERVATORIES OF MUSIC.
Blackburn, Lois. Whole music. Portsmouth, N.H. : Heinemann, c1998.
*TC MT1 .B643 1998*

Burz, Helen L. Performance-based curriculum for music and the visual arts. Thousand Oaks, Calif. : Corwin Press, c1999.
*TC LB1591 .B84 1999*

Kim, Jinyoung. Effects of word type, context, and vocal assistance on children's pitch-matching abilities. 1998.
*TC 06 no. 10954*

Page, Nick. Music as a way of knowing. York, Me. : Stenhouse Publishers ; Los Angeles, Calif. : Galef Institute, c1995.
*TC MT1 .P234 1995*

Swanwick, Keith. Teaching music musically. London ; New York : Routledge, 1999.
*TC MT1 .S946 1999*

**MUSIC - INSTRUCTION AND STUDY - CONGRESSES.**
Music and child development. St. Louis, Mo. : MMB Music, c1990.
*TC ML3820 .M87 1990*

**MUSIC - INSTRUCTION AND STUDY - JUVENILE.**
Andress, Barbara. Music for young children. Fort Worth, TX : Harcourt Brace College Publishers, c1998.
*TC MT810 .A6 1998*

Barrett, Carolyn M., 1941- The magic of Matsumoto. Palm Springs, CA : ETC Publications, c1995.
*TC MT1 .B325 1995*

**MUSIC - JUVENILE.** *See* **CHILDREN'S SONGS.**

**MUSIC - LATIN AMERICA - HISTORY AND CRITICISM.**
Music in Latin American culture. New York : Schirmer Books, c1999.
*TC ML199 .M86 1999*

**MUSIC, LATIN-AMERICAN.** *See* **MUSIC - LATIN AMERICA.**

**MUSIC - MOGUL EMPIRE - HISTORY AND CRITICISM.**
Wade, Bonnie C. Imaging sound. Chicago : University of Chicago Press, c1998.
*TC ML338 .W318 1998*

**MUSIC - PERFORMANCE.** *See also* **PERFORMANCE PRACTICE (MUSIC); SINGING.**
Schenker, Heinrich, 1868-1935. [Kunst des Vortrags. English] The art of performance. New York : Oxford University Press, 2000.
*TC MT220 .S24513 2000*

**MUSIC - PHILOSOPHY AND AESTHETICS.**
Gangi, Robyn Joseph. A longitudinal case study of the musical/aesthetic experience of adolescent choral musicians. 1998.
*TC 06 no. 10932*

**MUSIC - PHYSIOLOGICAL ASPECTS.** *See also* **VOICE.**
Singing development. London : Roehampton Institute, Centre for Advanced Studies in Music Education, Faculty of Education, [1997?]
*TC MT898 .S55 1997*

**MUSIC - PSYCHOLOGICAL ASPECTS.**
Kim, Jinyoung. Effects of word type, context, and vocal assistance on children's pitch-matching abilities. 1998.
*TC 06 no. 10954*

Millbower, Lenn, 1951- Training with a beat. 1st ed. Sterling, Va. : Stylus, c2000.
*TC ML3830 .M73 2000*

**MUSIC - PSYCHOLOGICAL ASPECTS - CONGRESSES.**
Music and child development. St. Louis, Mo. : MMB Music, c1990.
*TC ML3820 .M87 1990*

**MUSIC, ROMAN.** *See* **MUSIC, GREEK AND ROMAN.**

**MUSIC SCHOOLS.** *See* **CONSERVATORIES OF MUSIC.**

**MUSIC - SOCIAL ASPECTS.**
Blacking, John. Music, culture, & experience. Chicago : University of Chicago Press, c1995.
*TC ML60 .B63 1995*

**MUSIC - SOCIAL ASPECTS - UNITED STATES.**
Tawa, Nicholas E. High-minded and low-down. Boston : Northeastern University Press, c2000.
*TC ML3917.U6 T39 2000*

**MUSIC - STUDY AND TEACHING.** *See* **MUSIC - INSTRUCTION AND STUDY.**

**MUSIC TEACHERS.** *See* **VIOLIN TEACHERS.**

**MUSIC THERAPY.**
Berel, Marianne. Musical play sessions. [S.l. : s.n.], 1994.
*TC ML3920 .B45 1994*

**MUSIC THERAPY - CASE REPORT.**
Beyond talk therapy. 1st ed. Washington, DC : American Psychological Association, c1999.
*TC RC489.A72 B49 1999*

**MUSIC - TO 500.** *See* **MUSIC, GREEK AND ROMAN.**

**MUSIC - UNITED STATES.**
The Rice Institute pamphlet. Houston, Tex. : The Institute, 1915-1961.
*TC AS36 .W65*

**MUSIC - UNITED STATES - 19TH CENTURY - HISTORY AND CRITICISM.**
Tawa, Nicholas E. High-minded and low-down. Boston : Northeastern University Press, c2000.
*TC ML3917.U6 T39 2000*

**MUSIC - UNITED STATES - HISTORY AND CRITICISM.**
The Cambridge history of American music.

Cambridge, UK ; New York, NY : Cambridge University Press, 1998.
*TC ML200 .C36 1998*

**Musical/aesthetic experience of adolescent choral musicians.**
Gangi, Robyn Joseph. A longitudinal case study of the musical/aesthetic experience of adolescent choral musicians. 1998.
*TC 06 no. 10932*

**MUSICAL COMEDIES.** *See* **MUSICALS.**

**MUSICAL COMPOSITIONS.** *See* **MUSIC.**

**MUSICAL EDUCATION.** *See* **MUSIC - INSTRUCTION AND STUDY.**

**MUSICAL GROUPS.** *See* **BANDS (MUSIC).**

**MUSICAL INSTRUCTION.** *See* **MUSIC - INSTRUCTION AND STUDY.**

**MUSICAL INSTRUMENTS.** *See* **PERCUSSION INSTRUMENTS.**

**MUSICAL PITCH.**
Kim, Jinyoung. Effects of word type, context, and vocal assistance on children's pitch-matching abilities. 1998.
*TC 06 no. 10954*

**Musical play sessions.**
Berel, Marianne. [S.l. : s.n.], 1994.
*TC ML3920 .B45 1994*

**MUSICAL PLAYS.** *See* **MUSICALS.**

**MUSICAL REVUES, COMEDIES, ETC.** *See* **MUSICALS.**

**MUSICAL SHOWS.** *See* **MUSICALS.**

**MUSICAL THEATER.** *See* **MUSICALS.**

**MUSICAL WORKS.** *See* **MUSIC.**

**MUSICALS - UNITED STATES - HISTORY AND CRITICISM.**
Gilbert, Douglas, 1889-1948. American vaudeville, its life and times. New York, Dover Publications [c1940, c1968]
*TC PN1967 .G5 1968*

**MUSICIANS.** *See* **CHILD MUSICIANS; COMPOSERS.**

**MUSICIANS - FRANCE - BIOGRAPHY.**
Jean-Aubry, G. (Georges), 1882-1950. [Musique française d'aujourd'hui. English] French music of to-day. 4th ed. London, K. Paul, Trench, Trubner, 1926.
*TC ML60.A82 E8 1926*

**MUSICO-CALLISTHENICS.**
James, Phoebe L. Accompaniments for rhythmic expressions. [Los Angeles? : s.n.], c1946.
*TC M1993.J18 A3*

**Musiek, Frank E.** Contemporary perspectives in hearing assessment / Frank E. Musiek, William F. Rintelmann. Boston : Allyn and Bacon, 1999. x, 518 p. : ill. ; 29 cm. + 1 computer optical disc (4 3/4 in.). Includes bibliographical references and index. System requirements for the accompanying computer disc: Windows 95 or Windows 98, IBM-compatible PC, minimum 16MB, and CD-ROM drive. ISBN 0-205-27457-9 DDC 617.8/075
1. Audiometry. I. Rintelmann. William F. II. Title.
*TC RF294 .M87 1999*

**Musio, Carlo.**
International School of Biocybernetics (1997 : Naples, Italy) Neuronal bases and psychological aspects of consiousness. Singapore ; River Edge, N.J : World Scientific, c1999.
*TC QP411 .I56 1997*

**MUSLIM TEXTILE FABRICS.** *See* **TEXTILE FABRICS, ISLAMIC.**

**MUSLIM WOMEN - EGYPT - HISTORY.**
Badran, Margot. Feminists, Islam, and nation. Princeton, N.J. : Princeton University Press, c1995.
*TC HQ1793 .B33 1995*

**MUSLIM WOMEN - MIDDLE EAST - SOCIAL CONDITIONS.**
Shukri, Shirin J. A. Social changes and women in the Middle East. Aldershot ; Brookfield, Vt. : Ashgate, c1999.
*TC HQ1726.5 .S58 1999*

**MUSLIMISM.** *See* **ISLAM.**

**MUSLIMS IN INDIA.** *See* **MUSLIMS - INDIA.**

**MUSLIMS - INDIA - POLITICS AND GOVERNMENT.**
Hasan, Mushirul. Legacy of a Divided Nation. Boulder, Colo. : WestviewPress, c1997.

*TC DS479 .L36 1997*

**Musselle, Trish, 1968-.**
McDiarmid, Tami, 1960- Critical challenges for primary students. Burnaby, B.C. : Field Relations and Teacher In-Service Education, Faculty of Education, Simon Fraser University, c1996.
*TC LB1590.3 .M36 1996*

**MUSSULMANISM.** *See* **ISLAM.**

**MUSTELIDAE.** *See* **WEASELS.**

**Muth, Jon J. ill.**
Jennings, Patrick. Putnam and Pennyroyal. 1st ed. New York : Scholastic Press, 1999.
*TC PZ7.J4298715 Co 1999*

**Mutoro, Henry.**
American studies in eastern Africa. Nairobi : Nairobi University Press, 1993.
*TC E172.9 .A47 1993*

**Muuss, Rolf Eduard Helmut, 1924-.**
Adolescent behavior and society. 5th ed. Boston : McGraw-Hill, c1998.
*TC HQ796 .A3338 1998*

**MVP Home Entertainment (Firm).**
The cello [videorecording]. Van Nuys, CA : Backstage Pass Productions ; Canoga Park, Calif. : [Distributed by] MVP, c1995.
*TC MT305 .C4 1995*

The drums [videorecording]. Van Nuys, CA : Backstage Pass Productions ; Canoga Park, Calif. : [Distributed by] MVP Home Entertainment, c1998.
*TC MT662.3 .S6 1998*

The flute [videorecording]. Van Nuys, CA : Backstage Pass Productions ; Canoga Park, Calif. : [Distributed by] MVP, c1995.
*TC MT345 .F6 1995*

The trombone [videorecording]. Van Nuys, CA : Backstage Pass Productions ; Canoga Park, Calif. : [Distributed by] MVP, c1998.
*TC MT465 .T7 1998*

The viola [videorecording]. Van Nuys, CA : Backstage Pass Productions ; Canoga Park, Calif. : [Distributed by] MVP Home Entertainment, c1991.
*TC MT285 .V5 1991*

The viola [videorecording]. Van Nuys, CA : Backstage Pass Productions ; Canoga Park, Calif. : [Distributed by] MVP Home Entertainment, c1995.
*TC MT285 .V5 1995*

The violin [videorecording]. Van Nuys, CA : Backstage Pass Productions ; Canoga Park, Calif. : [Distributed by] MVP, c1998.
*TC MT265 .V5 1998*

**My brother Sam is dead by James Lincoln Collier and Christopher Collier.**
McCarthy, Tara. New York : Scholastic, c1997.
*TC LB1573 .M32 1997*

**My cat Jack.**
Casey, Patricia. 1st U.S. ed. Cambridge, Mass. : Candlewick Press, c1994.
*TC PZ7.C2679 My 1994*

**My father's dragon.**
Gannett, Ruth Stiles. New York : Random House, 1948.
*TC PZ7.G15 My 1948*

**My goose Betsy.**
Braun, Trudi. 1st U.S. ed. Cambridge, MA : Candlewick Press, 1999.
*TC PZ10.3.B745 My 1998*

**My life, take two.**
Many, Paul. New York : Walker & Co., 2000.
*TC PZ7.M3212 My 2000*

**My mane catches the wind :** poems about horses / selected by Lee Bennett Hopkins ; illustrated by Sam Savitt. 1st ed. New York: Harcourt Brace Jovanovich, c1979. 42 p. : ill. ; 26 cm. Includes index. SUMMARY: A collection of 22 poems about horses. ISBN 0-15-256343-1 DDC 808.81/9/36
1. Horses - Juvenile poetry. 2. Children's poetry. 3. Horses - Poetry. 4. Poetry - Collections. I. Hopkins, Lee Bennett. II. Savitt. Sam.
*TC PN6110.H7 M9*

**My museum journal.**
Kale, Shelly. Los Angeles, CA : J. Paul Getty Museum, c2000.
*TC N7440 .K35 2000*

**My sense of silence.**
Davis, Lennard J., 1949- Urbana : University of Illinois Press, c2000.

*TC HQ759.912 .D38 2000*

**My spiritual alphabet book.**
Bea, Holly, 1956- Tiburon, Calif. : H.J. Kramer,
c2000.
*TC BL625.5 .B43 1999*

**MYCOLOGY. See FUNGI.**

**Myers, Barbara.**
Etching [videorecording]. Northbrook, Ill. :
Peasmarsh, East Sussex, Eng. : Roland Collection of
Films on Art, c1990.
*TC NE2043 .E87 1990*

Screen printing [videorecording]. [Northbrook?], Ill. ;
Peasmarsh, East Sussex, Eng. : Roland Collection of
Films on Art, c1992.
*TC NE2238.G7 S4 1992*

**MYERS-BRIGGS TYPE INDICATOR.**
Quenk, Naomi L., 1936- Essentials of Myers-Briggs
type indicator assessment. New York : J. Wiley &
Sons, 2000.
*TC BF698.8.M94 Q45 1999*

**Myers, Kate.**
Whatever happened to equal opportunities in schools?
Buckingham [England] ; Philadelphia : Open
University Press, 2000.
*TC LC213.3.G7 W53 2000*

**Myers, Nancy.**
The writing teacher's sourcebook. 4th ed. New York :
Oxford University Press, 2000.
*TC PE1404 .W74 2000*

**Myers, Penelope S.** Right hemisphere damage :
disorders of communication and cognition / Penelope
S. Myers. San Diego : Singular Pub., c1999, xii, 280 p. :
ill. ; 26 cm. Includes bibliographical references (p. 247-269)
and index. ISBN 1-56593-224-2 DDC 616.85/5
*1. Communicative disorders. 2. Cognition disorders. 3. Brain
damage. 4. Cerebral hemispheres. 5. Brain Damage, Chronic -
complications. 6. Laterality. 7. Communication Disorders -
complications. 8. Cognition disorders - complications. I. Title.*
*TC RC423 .M83 1999*

**Myers, Samuel L.**
Turner, Caroline Sotello Viernes. Faculty of color in
academe. Boston : Allyn and Bacon, c2000.
*TC LB2332.72 .T87 2000*

**MYOCARDIAL ISCHEMIA. See CORONARY
HEART DISEASE.**

**MYODYNAMICS. See MUSCLES.**

**MYOLOGY. See MUSCLES.**

**The mysteries of the alphabet.**
Oauknin, Marc-Alain. [Mystères de l'alphabet.
English] 1st ed. New York : Abbeville Press, c1999.
*TC P211 .O913 1999*

**MYSTERIES, RELIGIOUS. See RITES AND
CEREMONIES.**

**The mysterious barricades.**
Berthoff, Ann E. Toronto ; Buffalo : University of
Toronto Press, c1999.
*TC P106 .B463 1999*

**MYSTERY AND DETECTIVE STORIES.**
Yep, Laurence. The case of the firecrackers. 1st ed.
New York : HarperCollins, c1999.
*TC PZ7.Y44 Cag 1999*

**Mystery of mysteries.**
Ruse, Michael. Cambridge, Mass. : Harvard
University Press, 1999.
*TC QH360.5 .R874 1999*

**MYSTICISM.**
Schick, Theodore. How to think about weird things.
2nd ed. Mountain View, Calif. : Mayfield Pub., c1999.
*TC BC177 .S32 1999*

**MYTH. See MYTHOLOGY.**

**MYTH IN LITERATURE.**
Doll, Mary Aswell. Like letters in running water.
Mahwah, N.J. ; London : L. Erlbaum Publishers,
2000.
*TC LB1575 .D64 2000*

**MYTH IN MOTION PICTURES.**
Drummond, Lee, 1944- American dreamtime.
Lanham, Md. : Littlefield Adams Books, 1996.
*TC PN1995.9.M96 D78 1996*

**Myth, magic and mystery :** one hundred years of
American children's book illustration / introductory
essay by Michael Patrick Hearn ; essays by Trinkett
Clark and H. Nichols B. Clark. Boulder, Colo. :
Roberts Rinehart Publishers ; [Norfolk, Va.] : in
cooperation with the Chrysler Museum of Art, c1996.

xii, 242 p. : ill. (some col.) ; 29 cm. Catalog of an exhibition
held at the Chrysler Museum of Art from  June 2-Sept.8, 1996,
at the Memphis Brooks Museum of Art from Nov. 3, 1996-Jan.
6, 1997 and at the Delaware Art Museum from Feb. 7-April 6,
1997. Includes bibliographical references (p. 207-235).
Includes index. ISBN 1-57098-079-9 (pbk.) ISBN
1-57098-080-2 (cloth)
*1. Illustrated children's books - United States - Exhibitions. 2.
Children's literature, American - Illustrations - Exhibitions. 3.
Illustration of books - 20th century - United States -
    Exhibitions. I. Hearn, Michael Patrick. II. Clark,
Trinkett. III. Clark, Henry Nichols Blake. IV. Chrysler
Museum. V. Memphis Brooks Museum of Art. VI. Delaware Art
Museum.*
*TC NC975 .M98 1996*

**The myth of the first three years.**
Bruer, John T., 1949- New York : Free Press, c1999.
*TC BF318 .B79 1999*

**Myth, reality, and reform :** Higher education policy in
Latin America / edited by Claudio de Moura Castro
and Daniel Levy. Washington, D.C. : Inter-American
Development Bank, 2000. 116 p. : ill. ; 23 cm. ISBN 1-
88693-860-1 DDC 378.8
*1. Education, Higher - Latin America. 2. Educational change -
Latin America. I. Levy, Daniel.*
*TC LA543 .M46 2000*

**Mythic beings.**
Wyatt, Gary, 1958- Vancouver : Douglas &
McIntyre ; Seattle : University of Washington Press,
c1999.
*TC E78.B9 W93 1999*

**MYTHOLOGY. See FOLKLORE; INDIAN
MYTHOLOGY.**

**MYTHOLOGY - DICTIONARIES.**
Pickering, David, 1958- A dictionary of folklore. New
York, N.Y. : Facts on File, 1999.
*TC GR35 .P53 1999*

**MYTHOLOGY, GREEK. See also MIDAS
(LEGENDARY CHARACTER).**
Mark, Jan. The Midas touch. 1st U.S. ed. Cambridge,
MA : Candlewick Press, 1999.
*TC BL820.M55 M33 1999*

Woff, Richard, 1953- Bright-eyed Athena. Los
Angeles, CA : J. Paul Getty Museum, 1999.
*TC BL820.M6 W64 1999*

**MYTHOLOGY, GREEK, IN ART.**
Barber, Antonia, 1932- Apollo & Daphne. Los
Angeles : J. Paul Getty Museum, 1998.
*TC ND1420 .B37 1998*

**MYTHOLOGY, INDIAN. See INDIAN
MYTHOLOGY.**

**MYTHOLOGY - JUVENILE LITERATURE -
BIBLIOGRAPHY.**
Perry, Phyllis Jean. Myths, legends & tales. Ft.
Atkinson, Wis. : Alleyside Press, c1999.
*TC Z7836 .P47 1999*

**MYTHOLOGY - MISCELLANEA.**
January, Brendan, 1972- The New York Public
Library amazing mythology. New York : Wiley, 2000.
*TC BL311 .J36 2000*

**MYTHOLOGY - MISCELLANEA - JUVENILE
LITERATURE.**
January, Brendan, 1972- The New York Public
Library amazing mythology. New York : Wiley, 2000.
*TC BL311 .J36 2000*

**MYTHOLOGY - STUDY AND TEACHING
(ELEMENTARY).**
Perry, Phyllis Jean. Myths, legends & tales. Ft.
Atkinson, Wis. : Alleyside Press, c1999.
*TC Z7836 .P47 1999*

**MYTHS. See MYTHOLOGY.**

**Myths, legends & tales.**
Perry, Phyllis Jean. Ft. Atkinson, Wis. : Alleyside
Press, c1999.
*TC Z7836 .P47 1999*

**Myths, legends, and tales.**
Perry, Phyllis Jean. Myths, legends & tales. Ft.
Atkinson, Wis. : Alleyside Press, c1999.
*TC Z7836 .P47 1999*

**Myths of childhood.**
Paris, Joel, 1940- Philadelphia, PA : Brunner/Mazel,
c2000.
*TC BF713 .P37 2000*

**Women in art**
Nevelson in process [videorecording]. Chicago, IL :
Public Media Inc., 1977.

*TC NB237.N43 N43 1977*

**Nadel, Lynn.**
Down syndrome. London : Whurr, 1999.
*TC RC571 .D675 1999*

**Naden, Corinne J.**
Gillespie, John Thomas, 1928- Characters in young
adult literature. Detroit : Gale Research, c1997.
*TC Z1037.A1 G47 1997*

**Nadezna, Julie.**
Building America's communities II. Washington,
D.C. : Americans for the Arts (Organization) ;
Institute for Community Development and the Arts,
1997.
*TC NX180.A77 B95 1997*

**Nadia's hands.**
English, Karen. 1st ed. Honesdale, PA : Boyds Mills
Press, 1999.
*TC PZ7.E7232 Na 1999*

**Naef, Hans, 1920-.**
Ingres, Jean-Auguste-Dominique, 1780-1867.
Portraits by Ingres. New York : Metropolitan Museum
of Art ; Distributed by Harry N. Abrams, c1999.
*TC ND1329.I53 A4 1999*

**NAEYC (Series)**
(#140.) Quality in child care. Washington, D.C. :
National Association for the Education of Young
Children, c1987.
*TC HQ778.7.U6 Q35 1987*

(#225, 227.) Reaching potentials. Washington, DC :
National Association for the Education of Young
Children, c1992-<1995>
*TC LB1140.23 .R36 1992*

(#326.) Levin, Diane E. Remote control childhood?
Washington, D.C. : National Association for the
Education of Young Children, c1998.
*TC P94.5.C55 L48 1998*

**Naftel, Scott, 1952-.**
Kirby, Sheila Nataraj, 1946- Staffing at-risk school
districts in Texas. Santa Monica, CA : Rand, 1999.
*TC LB2833.3.T4 K57 1999*

**Nagel, Stuart S., 1934-.**
Creativity. Huntington, NY : Nova Science
Publishers, c2000.
*TC BF408 .C7547 2000*

Teaching public administration and public policy.
Huntington, N.Y. : Nova Science Publishers, c1999.
*TC JF1338.A3 U59 1999*

**Nager, Nancy, 1951-.**
Revisiting a progressive pedagogy. Albany : State
University of New York Press, c2000.
*TC LB1117 .R44 2000*

**Nagy, Martin.** Rural America in transition : innovative
responses / by Martin Nagy. Washington, DC :
NALAA, 1996. 11 p. : 29 cm. (Monographs / National
Assembly of Local Arts Agencies ; vol. 5, no. 2) ISSN 1084-
645X
*1. Rural development - United States. 2. Arts - United States -
Societies, etc. 3. Art centers - United States. 4. Arts and
society - United States. 5. Arts - Economic aspects - United
States. 6. Arts - Environmental aspects - United States. 7. Arts
and youth - United States. I. National Assembly of Local Arts
Agencies. II. Title. III. Series: Monographs (National Assembly
of Local Arts Agencies) ; vol. 5, no. 2*
*TC NX798 .N3 1996*

**Nagy, Thomas F.** Ethics in plain English : an illustrative
casebook for psychologists / Thomas F. Nagy. 1st ed.
Washington, DC ; London : American Psychological
Association, c2000. x, 261 p. : ill. ; 26 cm. Includes
bibliographical references (p. 251-252) and index. ISBN
1-55798-604-5 (pbk. : alk. paper) DDC 174/.915
*1. Psychologists - Professional ethics. 2. Psychology - Moral
and ethical aspects. I. Title.*
*TC BF76.4 .N34 2000*

**NAIROBI (KENYA) - SOCIAL CONDITIONS -
PICTORIAL WORKS.**
Shootback. London : Booth-Clibborn, 1999.
*TC HV4160.5.N34 S45 1999*

**Nakadate, Neil.**
A Rhetoric of doing. Carbondale : Southern Illinois
University Press, c1992.
*TC PE1404 .R496 1992*

**Nakamura, Lisa.**
Race in cyberspace. New York ; London : Routledge,
2000.
*TC HT1523 .R252 2000*

**Nakanishi, Akira, 1928-**
[Sekai no moji. English]
Writing systems of the world : alphabets, syllabaries, pictograms / by Akira Nakanishi. 1st pbk. ed. Rutland, Vt. : C.E. Tuttle Co., 1990, c1980. 122 p., [1] folded leaf of plates : ill., col. map ; 26 cm. Translation of: Sekai no moji. 1975. Bibliography: p. 117-118. Includes index. ISBN 0-8048-1654-9 (pbk.)
*1. Writing. I. Title.*
**TC Z40 .N2613 1990**

**NAKED SINGULARITIES (COSMOLOGY).**
Stephen Hawking's universe [videorecording]. [Alexandria, Va.] : PBS Video; Burbank, CA : Distributed by Warner Home Video, c1997.
**TC QB982 .S7 1997**

**NAMBE PUEBLO (N.M.).**
Hazen-Hammond, Susan. Thunder Bear and Ko. 1st ed. New York : Dutton Children's Books, 1999.
**TC E99.T35 H36 1999**

**NAMBE PUEBLO (N.M.) - JUVENILE LITERATURE.**
Hazen-Hammond, Susan. Thunder Bear and Ko. 1st ed. New York : Dutton Children's Books, 1999.
**TC E99.T35 H36 1999**

**NAMES.** *See* **TERMS AND PHRASES.**

**NAMES, GEOGRAPHICAL - CATALOGING.** *See* **NAMES, GEOGRAPHICAL (CATALOGING).**

**NAMES, GEOGRAPHICAL (CATALOGING) - CODE WORDS.**
USMARC code list for countries. 1993 ed. Washington, D.C. : Cataloging Distribution Service, Library of Congress, 1993.
**TC Z699.35.M28 U78 1993**

USMARC code list for geographic areas. 1998 ed. Washington, D.C. : Cataloging Distribution Service, Library of Congress, 1998.
**TC Z695.1.G4 U83 1998**

**NAMES OF ANIMALS, COMMON.** *See* **ZOOLOGY - NOMENCLATURE (POPULAR).**

**Nancy Hanks lecture on arts and public policy.** [New York, NY] : American Council for the Arts, <1988-> v.1: ill. ; 28 cm. 1st- . (1988-1989: Series paper ; no. 2-3)
*1. Art and state - United States. 2. Federal aid to the arts - United States. I. American Council for the Arts. II. Series: Series paper (Gannett Foundation)*
**TC NX730 .N25**

**Napp, John L.** AGS United States history / by John Napp, Wayne King. Circle Pines, Minn. : AGS, American Guidance Service, c1998, xx, 792 p. : col. ill., maps ; 25 cm. Includes index. ISBN 0-7854-1418-5
*1. United States - History. I. King, Wayne E. II. Title. III. Title: American Guidance Service United States history*
**TC E178.1 .N36 1998**

King, Wayne E. AGS United States history. Teacher's ed. Circle Pines, Minn. : AGS, American Guidance Service, c1998.
**TC E175.8 .K56 1998 Teacher's Ed.**

Our nation's history / John Napp, Wayne King. Baltimore, Md. : Media Materials, c1989. xv, 714 p. : ill., maps ; 24 cm. Includes index. ISBN 0-7854-1418-5
*1. United States - History - Juvenile literature. I. King, Wayne E. II. Title.*
**TC E178.3 .N36 1998**

Our nation's history / John Napp, Wayne King. Baltimore, Md. : Media Materials, c1989. xv, 714 p. : ill., maps ; 24 cm. Includes index. ISBN 0-7854-1418-5
*1. United States - History - Juvenile literature. I. King, Wayne E. II. Title.*
**TC E178.3 .N36 1998**

Our nation's history / John Napp, Wayne King. Baltimore, Md. : Media Materials, c1989. xv, 714 p. : ill., maps ; 24 cm. Includes index. ISBN 0-7854-1418-5
*1. United States - History - Juvenile literature. I. King, Wayne E. II. Title.*
**TC E178.3 .N36 1998**

**Narahashi, Keiko, ill.**
Sage, James. The little band. 1st ed. New York : M.K. McElderry Books : Toronto : Collier Macmillan Canada ; New York : Maxwell Macmillan International Pub. Group, c1991.
**TC PZ7.S1304 Li 1991**

Serfozo, Mary. What's what? a guessing game/ 1st ed. New York, NY : Margaret K. McElderry Books, c1996.
**TC PZ7.S482 Wg 1996**

**NARCISSISM.**
Gutin, Nina J. Differential object representations in

inpatients with narcissistic and borderline personality disorders and normal controls. 1997.
**TC 085 G975**

**NARCISSISTIC INJURIES.** *See* **SELF-ESTEEM.**

**NARCOTIC ADDICTION.** *See* **NARCOTIC HABIT.**

**NARCOTIC ADDICTS.**
Goldberg, Ted. Demystifying drugs. New York : St. Martin's Press, 1999.
**TC HV5801 .G633 1999**

**NARCOTIC ADDICTS - INTERVIEWS.**
Changing lives [videorecording]. Princeton, NJ : Films for the Humanities & Sciences, c1998.
**TC RC564 .C54 1998**

The hijacked brain [videorecording]. Princeton, NJ : Films for the Humanities & Sciences, c1998.
**TC RC564 .H5 1998**

Portrait of addiction [videorecording]. Princeton, NJ : Films for the Humanities & Sciences, c1998.
**TC HV5801 .P6 1998**

Portrait of addiction [videorecording]. Princeton, NJ : Films for the Humanities & Sciences, c1998.
**TC RC564 .P6 1998**

**NARCOTIC ADDICTS - PATIENTS - COUNSELING OF.**
Miller, Geraldine A., 1955- Learning the language of addiction counseling. Boston : Allyn and Bacon, c1999.
**TC RC564 .M536 1999**

**NARCOTIC ADDICTS - REHABILITATION.**
Changing lives [videorecording]. Princeton, NJ : Films for the Humanities & Sciences, c1998.
**TC RC564 .C54 1998**

Granfield, Robert, 1955- Coming clean. New York ; London : New York University Press, c1999.
**TC HV4998 .G73 1999**

The politics of addiction [videorecording]. Princeton, NJ : Films for the Humanities & Sciences, c1998.
**TC RC564 .P59 1998**

Portrait of addiction [videorecording]. Princeton, NJ : Films for the Humanities & Sciences, c1998.
**TC HV5801 .P6 1998**

Portrait of addiction [videorecording]. Princeton, NJ : Films for the Humanities & Sciences, c1998.
**TC RC564 .P6 1998**

**NARCOTIC HABIT.** *See* **COCAINE HABIT; HEROIN HABIT.**

**NARCOTIC HABIT - COMPICATIONS - FLORIDA - ORLANDO.**
Heroin [videorecording]. [Princeton, N.J.] : Films for the Humanities & Sciences, c1998.
**TC HV5822.H4 H4 1998**

**NARCOTIC HABIT - FLORIDA - ORLANDO.**
Heroin [videorecording]. [Princeton, N.J.] : Films for the Humanities & Sciences, c1998.
**TC HV5822.H4 H4 1998**

**NARCOTIC HABIT - PHYSIOLOGICAL ASPECTS - RESEARCH.**
The hijacked brain [videorecording]. Princeton, NJ : Films for the Humanities & Sciences, c1998.
**TC RC564 .H5 1998**

**NARCOTIC HABIT - PHYSIOLOGICAL EFFECT - RESEARCH.**
The hijacked brain [videorecording]. Princeton, NJ : Films for the Humanities & Sciences, c1998.
**TC RC564 .H5 1998**

**NARCOTIC HABIT - PSYCHOLOGICAL ASPECTS.**
Portrait of addiction [videorecording]. Princeton, NJ : Films for the Humanities & Sciences, c1998.
**TC HV5801 .P6 1998**

Portrait of addiction [videorecording]. Princeton, NJ : Films for the Humanities & Sciences, c1998.
**TC RC564 .P6 1998**

**NARCOTIC HABIT - TREATMENT.**
Gewirtz, Abigail Hadassah. Coping strategies and stage of change among Vietnam combat veterans diagnosed with posttraumatic stress disorder and comorbid substance use disorders. 1997.
**TC 085 G338**

**NARCOTIC LAWS.** *See* **DRUG LEGALIZATION.**

**NARCOTICS, CONTROL OF.** *See also* **NARCOTIC HABIT.**
Goldberg, Ted. Demystifying drugs. New York : St. Martin's Press, 1999.

**TC HV5801 .G633 1999**

**NARRATION (RHETORIC).**
Clandinin, D. Jean. Narrative inquiry. 1st ed. San Francisco : Jossey-Bass Inc., c2000.
**TC LB1028 .C55 2000**

McCallum, Robyn. Ideologies of identity in adolescent fiction. New York : Garland Pub., 1999.
**TC PN3443 .M38 1999**

Quigley, Jean. The grammar of autobiography. Mahwah, N.J. : Lawrence Erlbaum Associates, c2000.
**TC PE1315.M6 Q54 2000**

**Narrative counseling in schools.**
Winslade, John. Thousand Oaks, Calif. : Corwin Press, c1999.
**TC LB1027.5 .W535 1999**

**Narrative inquiry.**
Clandinin, D. Jean. 1st ed. San Francisco : Jossey-Bass Inc., c2000.
**TC LB1028 .C55 2000**

**NARRATIVE WRITING.** *See* **NARRATION (RHETORIC).**

**Nash, Gary B.** Forbidden love : the secret history of mixed-race America / Gary B. Nash. 1st ed. New York : H. Holt, 1999. ix, 214 p. : ill. ; 24 cm. (Edge books) Includes bibliographical references (p. 187-204) and index. SUMMARY: Presents accounts of how mainly anonymous Americans have defied the official racial ideology and points out how guardians of the past have written that side of our history out of the record. ISBN 0-8050-4953-3 (acid-free paper) DDC 305.868/72073
*1. Mestizos - United States - History. 2. Mestizos - United States - Biography. 3. United States - Race relations. 4. Mestizos - Biography. 5. Racially mixed people - Biography. 6. United States - Race relations. I. Title. II. Series.*
**TC E184.M47 N47 1999**

**Nash, Renea D.** Everything you need to know about being a biracial/biethnic teen / Renea D. Nash. 1st ed. New York : Rosen Pub. Group, 1995. 64 p. : ill. (some col.) ; 25 cm. (The need to know library) Includes bibliographical references (p. 62) and index. ISBN 0-8239-1871-8 DDC 306.84/6
*1. Racially mixed children - United States - Juvenile literature. 2. Teenagers - United States - Life skills guides - Juvenile literature. 3. Ethnicity in children - United States - Juvenile literature. I. Title. II. Title: Being a biracial/biethnic teen III. Series.*
**TC HQ77.9 .N39 1995**

**Nash, Walter.** Creating texts : an introduction to the study of composition / Walter Nash and David Stacey. London ; New York : Longman, 1997. viii, 242 p. : ill. ; 22 cm. (English language series ; 20) Includes bibliographical references (p. [226]-233) and indexes. ISBN 0-582-24486-2 DDC 808/.042
*1. English language - Rhetoric. I. Stacey, David, 1955- II. Title. III. Series.*
**TC PE1408 .N22 1997**

**NĀṢIR AL-DĪN SHĀH, SHAH OF IRAN, 1831-1896.**
Amanat, Abbas. Pivot of the universe. Berkeley : University of California Press, c1997.
**TC DS307.N38 A63 1997**

**NASPA monograph series**
(v. 3) Deegan, William L. Translating theory into practice. 1st ed. [Columbus, Ohio] : National Association of Student Personnel Administrators, c1985.
**TC LB2343 .D356 1985**

**Natale, Samuel M.**
Business education and training. Lanham, Md. : University Press of America, c1997-<c2000 >
**TC LC1059 .B87**

**NATALITY.** *See* **FERTILITY, HUMAN.**

**Nathan Cummings Foundation.**
Race, ethnicity and culture in the visual arts. New York : American Council for the Arts, c1993.
**TC N70 .R32 1993**

**Nathan, Peter E.** Treating mental disorders : a guide to what works / Peter E. Nathan, Jack M. Gorman, Neil J. Salkind. New York : Oxford University Press, 1999. xxvii, 208 p. ; 25 cm. Includes index. ISBN 0-19-510228-2 (alk. paper) DDC 616.89
*1. Mental illness - Popular works. 2. Mental illness - Treatment - Evaluation - Miscellanea. 3. Consumer education. I. Gorman, Jack M. II. Salkind, Neil J. III. Title.*
**TC RC480.515 .N38 1999**

**Nation, Daryl.**
Changing university teaching :. London : Kogan Page ; Sterling, VA : Stylus Pub., 2000.

*TC LB2331 .C53 2000*

**National Academy of Sciences (U.S.).**
The blue planet [videorecording]. [New York, N.Y.?] : Unapix Entertainment, Inc. [distributor], c1996.
*TC QB631.2 .B5 1996*

The climate puzzle [videorecording]. [New York, N.Y.?] : Unapix Entertainment, Inc. [distributor], c1996.
*TC QB631.2 .C5 1996*

The living machine [videorecording]. [New York, N.Y.?] : Unapix Entertainment, Inc. [distributor], c1996.
*TC QB631.2 .L5 1996*

Fate of the earth [videorecording]. [New York, N.Y.?] : Unapix Entertainment, Inc. [distributor], c1996.
*TC QB631.2 .F3 1996*

Gifts from the earth [videorecording]. [New York, N.Y.?] : Unapix Entertainment, Inc. [distributor], c1996.
*TC QB631.2 .G5 1996*

The solar sea [videorecording]. [New York, N.Y.?] : Unapix Entertainment, Inc. [distributor], c1996.
*TC QB631.2 .S6 1996*

Tales from other worlds [videorecording]. [New York, N.Y.?] : Unapix Entertainment, Inc. [distributor], c1996.
*TC QB631.2 .T3 1996*

Tales from other worlds [videorecording]. [New York, N.Y.?] : Unapix Entertainment, Inc. [distributor], c1996.
*TC QB631.2 .T3 1996*

**National Alliance of Business.**
Annual State of American Education Address (7th : February 22, 2000 : Durham, N.C.) The seventh annual state of American education address [videorecording]. [Washington, D.C. : U.S. Dept. of Education], 2000.

Modernizing schools : technology and buildings for a new century (September 19, 2000 : Washington, D.C.) Modernizing schools [videorecording]. [Washington, D.C.] : U.S. Dept. of Education, [2000].
*TC LB3205 .M64 2000*

Modernizing schools : technology and buildings for a new century (September 19, 2000 : Washington, D.C.) Modernizing schools [videorecording]. [Washington, D.C.] : U.S. Dept. of Education, [2000].
*TC LB3205 .M64 2000*

Powerful middle schools : teaching and learning for young adolescents (2000) Powerful middle schools [videorecording]. [Washington, D.C.?] : U.S. Dept. of Education, [2000].
*TC LB1623 .P6 2000*

**National Art Education Association.**
Readings in discipline-based art education. Reston, Va. : National Art Education Assoc., c2000.
*TC N87 .R43 2000*

**National Assembly for Local Arts Agencies.**
Resource development handbook. [Washington, D.C.] : National Assembly of Local Arts Agencies, Institute for Community Development and the Arts, 1995.
*TC NX110 .R47 1995*

**National Assembly of Local Arts Agencies.**
Nagy, Martin. Rural America in transition. Washington, DC : NALAA, 1996.
*TC NX798 .N3 1996*

**The national assessment approach to exercise development.**
Finley, Carmen J. [Ann Arbor, Mich.] National Assessment of Educational Progress [1970]
*TC LB3051 .F53*

**National Association for the Education of Young Children.**
Developmentally appropriate practice in early childhood programs. Rev. ed. Washington, D.C. : National Association for the Education of Young Children, 1997.
*TC LB1139.25 .D48 1997*

Quality in child care. Washington, D.C. : National Association for the Education of Young Children, c1987.
*TC HQ778.7.U6 Q35 1987*

**National Association for Women Deans, Administrators & Counselors.** Journal.
[Washington, D.C. : National Association for Women

Deans, Administrators, & Counselors] 15 v. ; 23 cm.
Frequency: Quarterly. Vol. 37, no. 1 (fall 1973)-v. 51, no. 1 (fall 1987). Indexed in its entirety by: Education index 0013-1385. Continues: National Association of Women Deans and Counselors. Journal of the National Association of Women Deans and Counselors ISSN: 0027-870X (OCoLC)4629275. Continued by: Initiatives (Washington, D.C.) ISSN: 1042-413X. ISSN 0094-3460 DDC 378.1/94/05
*1. Women - Education. 2. Personnel service in education. I. Title: National Association of Women Deans and Counselors. Journal of the National Association of Women Deans and Counselors II. Title: Initiatives (Washington, D.C.)*

**National Association of Biblical Instructors. Journal of the National Association of Biblical Instructors.**
[Christian education (Chicago, Ill.)] Christian education. Chicago : [Council of Church Boards of Education in the United States of America,  -1952]

**National Association of Deans of Women (U.S.).**
Journal of the National Association of Deans of Women. Washington, D.C. : The Association, the Dept. of Deans of the National Education Association of the United States of America, [1938-1956]

**National Association of Deans of Women (U.S.). Bulletin.**
Journal of the National Association of Deans of Women. Washington, D.C. : The Association, the Dept. of Deans of the National Education Association of the United States of America, [1938-1956]

**National Association of Deans of Women (U.S.). Meeting. Proceedings of the ... Annual Meeting of the National Association of Deans of Women, Department of Superintendence, National Education Association.**
Journal of the National Association of Deans of Women. Washington, D.C. : The Association, the Dept. of Deans of the National Education Association of the United States of America, [1938-1956]

**National Association of Elementary School Principals (U.S.).**
An educators' guide to schoolwide reform. Arlington, Va. : Educational Research Service, c1999.
*TC LB2806.35 .E38 1999*

**National Association of Human Rights Workers.**
[Journal of intergroup relations (1970)] Journal of intergroup relations. Louisville, KY : National Association of Human Rights Workers,

**National Association of Independent Schools.**
Orsini, Alfonso J. The color of excellence. 1999.
*TC 06 no. 11209*

**National Association of Intergroup Relations Officials.**
[Journal of intergroup relations (1970)] Journal of intergroup relations. Louisville, KY : National Association of Human Rights Workers,

**National Association of Secondary School Principals (U.S.).**
An educators' guide to schoolwide reform. Arlington, Va. : Educational Research Service, c1999.
*TC LB2806.35 .E38 1999*

**National Association of Women Deans and Counselors.**
Journal of the National Association of Women Deans and Counselors. Washington, D.C. : The Association, 1956-1973.

**National Association of Women Deans and Counselors. Journal of the National Association of Women Deans and Counselors.**
National Association for Women Deans, Administrators & Counselors. Journal. [Washington, D.C. : National Association for Women Deans, Administrators, & Counselors]

**National Board for Historical Service.**
Historical outlook. Philadelphia, Pa. : McKinley Pub. Co., c1918-c1933.

**National Business Education Association.**
Business education forum. Reston, Va., National Business Education Association.

**National business education quarterly v.25, no. 1, Oct. 1970.**
Business education forum. Reston, Va., National Business Education Association.

**National Catholic Educational Association.** Bulletin - National Catholic Educational Association. [Washington] National Catholic Educational Association. v. 23 cm. v.  -63, no. 2;  -Nov. 1966.
SUMMARY: August issue includes Proceedings of the annual meeting. Vols. 57-61, 1960/61-1964/65, 1 v. Continues: Catholic Educational Association. Bulletin. Continued by: National Catholic Educational Association. NCEA bulletin

(OCLC) 1759102.
*1. Catholic Church - Education - United States - Periodicals. 2. Catholic schools - Periodicals. I. Title. II. Title: Catholic Educational Association. Bulletin III. Title: National Catholic Educational Association. NCEA bulletin*

Who are my sisters and brothers? Washington, D.C. : The Conference, c1996.
*TC BX1795.E44 W46 1996*

**National Catholic Educational Association. NCEA bulletin.**
National Catholic Educational Association. Bulletin - National Catholic Educational Association. [Washington] National Catholic Educational Association.

**National Center for Early Development & Learning (U.S.).**
The transition to kindergarten. Baltimore : P.H. Brookes Pub., c1999.
*TC LB1205 .T72 1999*

**National Center for Education Information (Washington, D.C.).**
Feistritzer, C. Emily. Alternative teacher certification. Washington, D.C. : National Center for Education Information, c2000.
*TC LB1771 .A47 2000*

**National Center for Education Statistics.**
Baker, Bruce D. A comparison of statistical and neural network models for forecasting educational spending. 1997.
*TC 06 no. 10792*

Vocational education in the United States. Washington, DC : U.S. Dept. of Education, Office of Educational Research and Improvement : For sale by the U.S. G.P.O., Supt. of Docs., [2000]
*TC LC1045 .V5874 2000*

**NATIONAL CHARACTERISTICS.** *See also* **ETHNOPSYCHOLOGY.**
Bar-Tal, Daniel. Shared beliefs in a society. Thousand Oaks, Calif. : Sage Publications, c2000.
*TC HM1041 .B37 2000*

Lynn, Richard. Personality and national character [1st ed.]. Oxford, New York, Pergamon Press [1971]
*TC BF698.9.C8 L9 1971*

**NATIONAL CHARACTERISTICS, AMERICAN.**
Hall, John A., 1949- Is America breaking apart? Princeton, NJ : Princeton University Press, c1999.
*TC HN59.2 .H34 1999*

Rosenzweig, Roy. The presence of the past. New York : Columbia University Press, c1998.
*TC E179.5 .R67 1998*

**NATIONAL CHARACTERISTICS, AMERICAN - FICTION.**
Lederer, William J., 1912- The ugly American. 1st ed. New York : Norton, 1958.
*TC PS3523 .E27U35 1958*

**NATIONAL CHARACTERISTICS, AMERICAN, IN LITERATURE.**
Mensh, Elaine, 1924- Black, white, and Huckleberry Finn. Tuscaloosa : University of Alabama Press, c2000.
*TC PS1305 .M46 2000*

**NATIONAL CHARACTERISTICS, FRENCH.**
Lehning, James R., 1947- Peasant and French. Cambridge [England] ; New York : Cambridge University Press, 1995.
*TC DC34 .L5 1995*

**NATIONAL CHARACTERISTICS, MEXICAN.**
Diamant, Gertrude, 1901- The days of Ofelia, Boston, Houghton Mifflin company, 1942.
*TC F1210 .D5*

**National Children's Bureau.**
Morgan, Sally, 1951- Care about education. London : DfEE, 1999.
*TC HV59 .M67 1999*

Vernon, Jeni. Maintaining children in school. London : National Children's Bureau Enterprises, c1998.
*TC LB3081 .V47 1998*

**National Committee on Film Forums.**
Film forum review. [New York, N.Y.] : The Institute, 1946-

**National Conference of State Legislatures.**
Health Policy Tracking Service. Major health care policies. 8th ed. Washington, D.C. : Health Policy Tracking Service, 2000.
*TC KF3821 .H4 2000*

**National Conference on Examination Malpractice in Nigerian Institutions of Learning. (1995 : Ondo State College of Education).**
Issues on examination malpractices in Nigeria :.
Ikere-Ekiti [Nigeria] : Ondo State College of Education, c1998.
*TC LB3058.N6 1848 1998*

**NATIONAL CONFERENCE ON TEACHER EDUCATION (1986 : UNIVERSITY OF CAPE COAST) - EVALUATION.**
Tamakloe, E. K. An evaluation of the National Conference on Teacher Education 1986. Accra : Ghana Universities Press, 1997.
*TC LB1727.G5 T36 1997*

**National Congress of Parents and Teachers. Georgia Branch.**
Home, school, and community. Atlanta, Ga. : Georgia Council of Social Agencies, 1923-1926.

**NATIONAL CONSCIOUSNESS.** *See* NATIONALISM.

**National contexts for mathematics & science education :** an encyclopedia of the educational systems participating in TIMSS / edited by David F. Robitaille. Vancouver : Pacific Educational Press, 1997. xi, 423 p. : ill. ; 29 cm. Includes bibliographical references. ISBN 1-89576-625-7 DDC 507/.1
*1. Third International Mathematics and Science Study. 2. Mathematics - Study and teaching. 3. Science - Study and teaching. 4. Curriculum evaluation. I. Robitaille, David F.*
*TC Q181 N37 1997*

**National Council for Educational Technology.**
British journal of educational technology. London, Councils and Education Press.

**National Council for Special Education.**
Forward trends. London, National Council for Special Education [etc.]

**National Council for the Social Studies.**
Historical outlook. Philadelphia, Pa. : McKinley Pub. Co., c1918-c1933.

**National Council of Educational Research and Training (India).**
Fifth survey of educational research, 1988-92. New Delhi : National Council of Educational Research and Training, 1997-
*TC LB1028 .F44 1997*

**National Council of Teachers of English.**
Passions, pedagogies, and 21st century technologies. Logan : Utah State University Press ; Urbana, Ill. : National Council of Teachers of English, c1999.
*TC PE1404 .P38 1999*

Trends & issues in postsecondary English studies. Urbana, Ill. : National Council of Teachers of English, c1999-
*TC PE65 .T75*

UpDrafts. Urbana, Ill. : National Council of Teachers of English, c2000.
*TC LB1775.2 .U63 2000*

**National Council of Teachers of English. Committee on Teaching about Genocide and Intolerance.**
Teaching for a tolerant world, grades K-6. Urbana, Ill. : National Council of Teachers of English, c1999.
*TC HM1271 .T43 1999*

**National Council of Teachers of Mathematics.**
Principles and standards for school mathematics. Reston, VA : National Council of Teachers of Mathematics, c2000.
*TC QA13 .P735 2000*

**National Council of the Churches of Chirst in the United States of America.**
The christian scholar. [Somerville, N.J., etc.]

**National Council of the Churches of Christ in the United States of America. Commission on Christian Higher Education.**
[Christian education (Chicago, Ill.)] Christian education. Chicago : [Council of Church Boards of Education in the United States of America, -1952]

**National Council on Family Relations.**
The Family coordinator. Minneapolis, Minn. : National Council on Family Relations, c1968-

**National Education Association. Department of Adult Education.**
Adult education quarterly. [s.l.] : The Dept., 1932-

**National Education Association of the United States.**
DiVincenzo, Joe. Group decision making. [S.l.] : NEA Professional Library : NEA Affiliate Capacity Building, c1999.

*TC LB2806 .D58 1999*

An educators' guide to schoolwide reform. Arlington, Va. : Educational Research Service, c1999.
*TC LB2806.35 .E38 1999*

Professional development guide for educators. Washington, D.C. : National Education Association of the United States, 2000.
*TC LC1099.3 .P755 1999*

Teaching to teach. Washington, DC : National Education Association, 1999.
*TC LB1715 .T436 1999*

Teaching with technology. Washington, D.C. : National Education Association of the United States, 1999.
*TC LB1044.88 .T44 1999*

**National Education Association of the United States. Dept. of Audiovisual Instruction.**
Audiovisual instruction. Washington, D.C : Dept. of Audiovisual Instruction, NEA, 1956-1978.

Instructional materials. [Washington, D.C.] : Dept. of Audio Visual Instruction, NEA, 1956.

**National Education Association of the United States. Dept. of Supervision and Curriculum Development.**
Building America. [New York : Published for the Dept. of Supervision and Curriculum Development by the Society for Curriculum Study, Inc. ; distributed by Americana Corporation, 1935-

**NATIONAL EDUCATION ASSOCIATION OF THE UNITED STATES - HISTORY.**
Moo, G. Gregory. Power grab. Washington, D.C. : Regnery Pub. ; Lanham, MD : Distributed to the trade by National Book Network, c1999.
*TC LB2844.53.U6 M66 1999*

**NATIONAL EDUCATION ASSOCIATION OF THE UNITED STATES - HISTORY - 1945-1953.**
Foster, Stuart J., 1960- Red alert!. New York ; Canterbury [England] : P. Lang, c2000.
*TC LC72.2 .F67 2000*

**NATIONAL EDUCATION ASSOCIATION OF THE UNITED STATES - POLITICAL ACTIVITY.**
Moo, G. Gregory. Power grab. Washington, D.C. : Regnery Pub. ; Lanham, MD : Distributed to the trade by National Book Network, c1999.
*TC LB2844.53.U6 M66 1999*

**NATIONAL EDUCATION ASSOCIATION'S TEACHER EDUCATION INITIATIVE.**
Teaching to teach. Washington, DC : National Education Association, 1999.
*TC LB1715 .T436 1999*

**National educational technology standards for students.**
International Society for Technology in Education. Eugene, OR : The Society, c1998.
*TC LB1028.3 .I569 1998*

**National Federation of Aboriginal Education Consultative Groups (Australia).**
Teaching Aboriginal studies. St Leonards, N.S.W. : Allen & Unwin, 1999.
*TC GN666 .T43 1999*

**National Federation of Licensed Practical Nurses, Inc.**
Bedside nurse. New York, National Federation of Licensed Practical Nurses, Inc., 1968-72.

**National Film Board of Canada.**
First break [videorecording]. Boston, MA : Fanlight Productions, c1997.
*TC RC465 .F5 1997*

First break [videorecording]. Boston, MA : Fanlight Productions, c1997.
*TC RC465 .F5 1997*

First break [videorecording]. Boston, MA : Fanlight Productions, c1997.
*TC RC465 .F5 1997*

**National forum on science and technology goals**
Harnessing science and technology for America's economic future. Washington, D.C. : National Academy Press, c1999.
*TC Q127.U5 H37 1999*

**National Gallery (Great Britain).**
Art in the making, Impressionism. London : National Gallery, in association with Yale University Press, c1991.
*TC ND547.5.I4 I4472 1991*

Impressionism [videorecording]. [London] : The National Gallery : Tillingham, Peasmarsh, East Sussex, England : Ho-Ho-Kus, NJ : Distributed by The Roland Collection, c1990.
*TC ND547.5.I4 A7 1990*

Ingres, Jean-Auguste-Dominique, 1780-1867. Portraits by Ingres. New York : Metropolitan Museum of Art : Distributed by Harry N. Abrams, c1999.
*TC ND1329.I53 A4 1999*

Italian painting before 1400 [videorecording]. [London] : The National Gallery, c1989.

Italian painting before 1400 [videorecording]. [London] : The National Gallery, c1989.
*TC ND1575 .I87 1989*

Miller, Jonathan, 1934- On reflection. London : National Gallery Publications ; [New Haven, Conn.] : Distributed by Yale University Press, c1998.
*TC N8224.M6 M54 1998*

**NATIONAL GALLERY (GREAT BRITAIN) - EXHIBITIONS.**
Art in the making, Impressionism. London : National Gallery, in association with Yale University Press, c1991.
*TC ND547.5.I4 I4472 1991*

**NATIONAL GALLERY (GREAT BRITAIN) - GUIDEBOOKS.**
Bomford, David. Colour. London : National Gallery Company ; [New Haven, Conn.] : Distributed by Yale Universtiy Press, 2000.
*TC ND1489 B66 2000*

**National Gallery of Art (U.S.).**
Cikovsky, Nicolai. Winslow Homer. Washington, D.C. : National Gallery of Art, 1995.
*TC N6537.H58 A4 1995*

Ingres, Jean-Auguste-Dominique, 1780-1867. Portraits by Ingres. New York : Metropolitan Museum of Art : Distributed by Harry N. Abrams, c1999.
*TC ND1329.I53 A4 1999*

Piet Mondrian, 1872-1944. Milan : Leonardo Arte, 1994.
*TC N6953.M64 A4 1994*

Sargent, John Singer, 1856-1925. John Singer Sargent. Princeton : Princeton University Press, 1998.
*TC ND237.S3 A4 1998a*

Weiss, Jeffrey. Mark Rothko. Washington : National Gallery of Art ; New Haven, Conn. : Yale University Press, c1998.
*TC N6537.R63 A4 1998*

**National Gallery of Australia.**
Butler, Roger. Poster art in Australia. Canberra : National Gallery of Australia, 1993.
*TC NC1807.A78 B88 1993*

The painters of the Wagilag sisters story 1937-1997. Canberra, ACT : The National Gallery of Australia, 1997.
*TC ND1101 .P395 1997*

**NATIONAL GALLERY OF AUSTRALIA - EXHIBITIONS.**
Butler, Roger. Poster art in Australia. Canberra : National Gallery of Australia, 1993.
*TC NC1807.A78 B88 1993*

**National Gallery of Victoria.** In relief : Australian wood engravings, woodcuts and linocuts / Kirsty Grant ; with contributions by Jason Smith. Melbourne : National Gallery of Victoria, c1997. 72 p. : ill. (some col.) ; 29 cm. Includes bibliographical references (p. 71-72). "This exhibition is drawn almost entirely from the permanent collection of the National Gallery of Victoria"--P. 6. ISBN 0-7241-0191-8
*1. Wood-engraving, Australian - Exhibitions. 2. Linoleum block-printing, Australian - Exhibitions. 3. National Gallery of Victoria - Exhibitions. I. Grant, Kirsty. II. Smith, Jason. III. Title. IV. Title: Australian wood engravings, woodcuts and linocuts.*
*TC NE1190.25 .G72 1997*

**NATIONAL GALLERY OF VICTORIA - EXHIBITIONS.**
National Gallery of Victoria. In relief. Melbourne : National Gallery of Victoria, c1997.
*TC NE1190.25 .G72 1997*

**NATIONAL GEOGRAPHIC.**
Lutz, Catherine. Reading National geographic. Chicago : University of Chicago Press, 1993.
*TC G1.N275 L88 1993*

**National Governors' Association. Committee on International Trade and Foreign Relations.**

Educating Americans for tomorrow's world. [Washington D.C.] : NGA, [1987]
*TC LC1099 .E225 1987*

**NATIONAL HEALTH INSURANCE - CANADA.**
Armstrong, Pat, 1945- Universal health care. New York : New Press : Distributed by W.W. Norton, c1998.
*TC RA412.5.C3 A76 1998*

**NATIONAL HERITAGE.** *See* **CULTURAL PROPERTY.**

**National High School Inspectors' Association.**
The High school quarterly. Athens, Ga. : University of Georgia, 1912-[1936]

**NATIONAL HOLIDAYS.** *See* **HOLIDAYS.**

**NATIONAL HOSPITALS.** *See* **PUBLIC HOSPITALS.**

**NATIONAL IDENTITY.** *See* **NATIONALISM.**

**NATIONAL INFORMATION INFRASTRUCTURE.** *See* **INFORMATION SUPERHIGHWAY.**

**National Institute for Occupational Safety and Health.**
Work and well-being. Washington, DC : American Psychological Association, c1992.
*TC RC967.5 .W67 1992*

**National Institute for Science Education (U.S.).**
Designing successful professional meetings and conferences in education. Thousand Oaks, Calif. : Corwin Press, c2000.
*TC LC6519 .D48 2000*

**National Institute of Child Health and Human Development (U.S.).**
National Reading Panel (U.S.) Report of the National Reading Panel : teaching children to read. [Washington, D.C.?] : National Institute of Child Health and Human Development, National Institutes of Health, [2000]
*TC LB1050 .N335 2000*

Symposium on Issues in Human Development (1967 : Philadelphia) Issues in human development; Washington, For sale by the Supt. of Docs., U. S. Govt. Print. Off. [1970?]
*TC RJ131.A1 S93 1967*

**National Institute of Social Sciences.** Journal of the National Institute of Social Sciences. [New York] v. ill. 24 cm. v. 1-  1915- . Distinctive title: Reconstruction after the war. Distinctive title: Government versus private railroads. Distinctive title: Leadership in a democracy. Distinctive title: International obligations. Distinctive title: International questions. Distinctive title: Goodwill towards peoples in the development of international relations. Vols. 1-11 also represents no. 47-57 of the Journal of the American Social Science Association. vols. 16-19 issued combined. SUMMARY: List of members in v. 2-4, 6-7, 9. Journal of the American Social Science Association.
*1. Social sciences - Periodicals. I. French, Lillie Hamilton, 1854- ed. II. Title: Reconstruction after the war III. Title: Government versus private railroads IV. Title: Leadership in a democracy V. Title: International obligations VI. Title: International questions VII. Title: Goodwill towards peoples in the development of international relations VIII. Title: Journal of the American Social Science Association*

**NATIONAL LANGUAGES.** *See* **LANGUAGE POLICY.**

**National League for Nursing.**
Annual guide to graduate nursing education programs. New York, N.Y. : National League for Nursing Press, c1995-
*TC RT75 .A5*

**National League for Nursing. Council of Associate Degree Nursing. Competencies Task Force.**
Educational competencies for graduates of associate degree nursing programs. [Rev.]. Sudbury, Mass. : Jones and Bartlett, 2000.
*TC RT74.5 .E38 2000*

**National League for Nursing. Research and Evaluation Division.**
Official guide to undergraduate nursing schools. Sudbury, Mass. : Jones and Bartlett Publishers, c2000.
*TC RT75.4 .O4 2000*

**National League of Cities.**
McCarthy, William H. Reducing urban unemployment. Washington, D.C. : National League of Cities, c1985.
*TC HD5724 .M34 1985*

**National Legal Conference on Immigration and Refugee Policy (6th : 1983 : Washington, D.C.)**
Immigration and refugee policy : proceedings of the 1983 Annual National Legal Conference on Immigration and Refugee Policy, April 21 and 22, 1983 / edited by Lydio F. Tomasi. 1st ed. New York : Center for Migration Studies, [1985] xi, 256 p. ; 24 cm. (In defense of the alien ; v. 6) Includes bibliographical references and index. ISBN 0-913256-65-X DDC 342.73/082; 347.30282
*1. Emigration and immigration law - United States - Congresses. 2. Refugees - Legal status. laws. etc. - United States - Congresses. I. Tomasi. Lydio F. II. Center for Migration Studies (U.S.) III. Title. IV. Series: In defense of the alien ; v. 6.*
*TC KF4819.A2 N375 1983*

**NATIONAL LITERACY CAMPAIGNS.** *See* **LITERACY PROGRAMS.**

**NATIONAL LITERACY PROGRAMS.** *See* **LITERACY PROGRAMS.**

**National Literacy Trust (Great Britain).**
Finlay, Ann, 1944- The National Literacy Trust's international annotated bibliography of books on literacy. Stoke-on-Trent : Trentham Books, 1999.
*TC LC149 .F565 1999*

**The National Literacy Trust's international annotated bibliography of books on literacy.**
Finlay, Ann, 1944- Stoke-on-Trent : Trentham Books, 1999.
*TC LC149 .F565 1999*

**NATIONAL MONUMENTS.**
Maestro, Betsy. The story of the Statue of Liberty. New York : Lothrop, Lee & Shepard Books, 1986.
*TC NB553.B3 A75 1986*

**National Museum of African Art (U.S.).**
Sieber, Roy, 1923- African art in the cycle of life. Washington, D.C. : Published for the National Museum of African Art by the Smithsonian Press, c1987.
*TC NB1091.65 .S54 1987*

**National Museum of American Art (U.S.)** American photographs : the first century from the Isaacs collection in the National Museum of American Art / Merry A. Foresta. Washington, D.C. : National Museum of American Art, Smithsonian Institution : Smithsonian Institution Press, c1996. 171 p. : col. ill. ; 29 cm. Catalog of an exhibition held at the National Museum of American Art, Smithsonian Institution, from Nov. 22, 1996-Apr. 20, 1997. Includes bibliographical references (p. 169-171). ISBN 1-56098-719-7 (pbk.) ISBN 1-56098-718-9 (cloth) DDC 779/.0973/074753
*1. Photography, Artistic - Exhibitions. 2. Photography - United States - History - 19th century - Exhibitions. 3. National Museum of American Art (U.S.) - Exhibitions. I. Foresta, Merry A. II. Title.*
*TC TR645.W18 N37 1996*

Moser, Joann. Singular impressions. Washington : Published for the National Museum of American Art by Smithsonian Institution Press, c1997.
*TC NE2245.U54 M67 1997*

**NATIONAL MUSEUM OF AMERICAN ART (U.S.) - EXHIBITIONS.**
National Museum of American Art (U.S.) American photographs. Washington, D.C. : National Museum of American Art, Smithsonian Institution : Smithsonian Institution Press, c1996.
*TC TR645.W18 N37 1996*

**National Museum of the American Indian (U.S.).**
Spirit capture. Washington : Smithsonian Institution Press in association with the National Museum of the American Indian, Smithsonian Institution, c1998.
*TC E77.5 .S65 1998*

When the rain sings. New York : Simon & Schuster Books for Young Readers, 1999.
*TC PS591.I55 W48 1999*

Woven by the grandmothers. Washington : Smithsonian Institution Press in association with the National Museum of the American Indian, Smithsonian Institution, c1996.
*TC E99.N3 W79 1996*

**NATIONAL MUSEUM OF THE AMERICAN INDIAN (U.S.).**
Spirit capture. Washington : Smithsonian Institution Press in association with the National Museum of the American Indian, Smithsonian Institution, c1998.
*TC E77.5 .S65 1998*

**NATIONAL MUSEUM OF THE AMERICAN INDIAN (U.S.) - EXHIBITIONS.**
Woven by the grandmothers. Washington :

Smithsonian Institution Press in association with the National Museum of the American Indian, Smithsonian Institution, c1996.
*TC E99.N3 W79 1996*

**NATIONAL MUSIC.** *See* **FOLK MUSIC; FOLK SONGS.**

**NATIONAL PATRIMONY.** *See* **CULTURAL PROPERTY.**

**NATIONAL PLANNING.** *See* **ECONOMIC POLICY.**

**National Portrait Gallery (Smithsonian Institution).**
Beaux, Cecilia, 1855-1942. Cecilia Beaux and the art of portraiture. Washington, DC : Published for the National Portrait Gallery by the Smithsonian Institution Press, 1995.
*TC ND1329.B39 A4 1995*

Panzer, Mary. Mathew Brady and the image of history. Washington, D.C. : Smithsonian Institution Press for the National Portrait Gallery, c1997.
*TC TR140.B7 P36 1997*

**National Protestant Council on Higher Education.**
The christian scholar. [Somerville, N.J., etc.]

**National Protestant Council on Higher Education (U.S.).**
[Christian education (Chicago, Ill.)] Christian education. Chicago : [Council of Church Boards of Education in the United States of America,  -1952]

**NATIONAL PSYCHOLOGY.** *See* **ETHNOPSYCHOLOGY.**

**National Public Health and Hospital Institute.**
Andrulis, Dennis P. Managed care and the inner city. San Francisco : Jossey-Bass, 1999.
*TC RA413.5.U5 A57 1999*

**National Reading Conference (U.S.).**
Key, Daphne. Literacy shutdown. Newark, Del. : International Reading Association ; Chicago, Ill. : National Reading Conference, c1998.
*TC LC1752 .K49 1998*

**National Reading Panel (U.S.)** Report of the National Reading Panel : teaching children to read : an evidence-based assessment of the scientific research literature on reading and its implications for reading instruction. [Washington, D.C.?] : National Institute of Child Health and Human Development, National Institutes of Health, [2000] 2 v. ; 28 cm. + 1 videocassette (sd., col. ; 1/2 in.). (NIH pub. ; no. 00-4769) Cover title. Shipping list no.: 2000-0247-P. "April 2000"--p. [4] of cover. Includes bibliographical references. CONTENTS: [v. 1. Report] -- [v. 2]. Reports of the subgroups. DDC 428.4/071/073
*1. Reading - United States. 2. Reading (Elementary) - Research - United States. I. National Institute of Child Health and Human Development (U.S.) II. Title. III. Title: Teaching children to read : an evidence-based assessment of the scientific research literature on reading and its implications for reading instruction IV. Title: Evidence-based assessment of the scientific research literature on reading and its implications for reading instruction V. Series: NIH publication ; no. 00-4769.*
*TC LB1050 .N335 2000*

**National Research Council (U.S.). Committee on Embedding Common Test Items in State and District Assessments.** Embedding questions : the pursuit of a common measure in uncommon tests / Committee on Embedding Common Test Items in State and District Assessments, Board on Testing and Assessment, Commission on Behavioral and Social Sciences and Education, National Research Council ; Daniel M. Koretz, Meryl W. Benthenal, Bert F. Green, editors. Washington, DC : National Academy Press, c1999. xiv, 82 p. : ill. ; 23 cm. Includes bibliographical references (p. 67-72). ISBN 0-309-06789-8 DDC 371.26
*1. Educational tests and measurements - United States. 2. Education and state - United States. I. Koretz, Daniel M. II. Bertenthal, Meryl W. III. Green, Bert F. IV. Title.*
*TC LB3051 .N319 1999*

**National Research Council (U.S.). Board on Biology.**
Forum on Biodiversity (1997 : National Academy of Sciences) Nature and human society. Washington, D.C. : National Academy Press, 2000.
*TC QH541.15.B56 F685 1997*

**National Research Council (U.S.). Commission on Behavioral and Social Sciences and Education.**
Critical perspectives on schooling and fertility in the developing world. Washington, D.C. : National Academy Press, 1999.
*TC LC2572 .C75 1998*

**National Research Council (U.S.). Commission on Physical Sciences, Mathematics, and Applications.**
The digital dilemma. Washington, D.C. : National Academy Press, c2000.
*TC KF2979 .D53 2000*

**National Research Council (U.S.). Committee on a Feasibility Study for a Strategic Education Research Program.**
Improving student learning. Washington, D.C. : National Academy Press, c1999.
*TC LB1028.25.U6 166 1999*

**National Research Council (U.S.). Committee on Developments in the Science of Learning.**
How people learn. Expanded ed. Washington, D.C. : National Academy Press, c2000.
*TC LB1060 .H672 2000*

**National Research Council (U.S.). Committee on Dimensions, Causes, and Implications of Recent Trends in the Careers of Life Scientists.**
Trends in the early careers of life scientists. Washington, DC : National Academy Press, 1998.
*TC QH314 .T74 1998*

**National Research Council (U.S.). Committee on Education Finance.**
Making money matter. Washington, D.C. : National Academy Press, c1999.
*TC LB2825 .M27 1999*

**National Research Council (U.S.). Committee on Future Directions for Cognitive Research on Aging.**
The aging mind: opportunities in cognitive research. Washington, D.C. : National Academy Press, c2000.
*TC BF724.55. C63 A48 2000*

**National Research Council (U.S.). Committee on Intellectual Property Rights and the Emerging Information Infrastructure.**
The digital dilemma. Washington, D.C. : National Academy Press, c2000.
*TC KF2979 .D53 2000*

**National Research Council (U.S.). Committee on Learning Research and Educational Practice.**
How people learn. Expanded ed. Washington, D.C. : National Academy Press, c2000.
*TC LB1060 .H672 2000*

**National Research Council (U.S.). Committee on Population.**
Critical perspectives on schooling and fertility in the developing world. Washington, D.C. : National Academy Press, 1999.
*TC LC2572 .C75 1998*

**National Research Council (U.S.). Committee on Science Education K-12.**
Designing mathematics or science curriculum programs. Washington, D.C. : National Academy Press, 1999.
*TC Q183.3.A1 D46 1999*

Global perspectives for local action. Washington, D.C. : National Academy Press, 1999.
*TC LB1583.3 .G56 1999*

**National Research Council (U.S.). Committee on Title I Testing and Assessment.**
Testing, teaching, and learning. Washington, D.C. : National Academy Press, c1999.
*TC LC3981 .T4 1999*

**National Research Council (U.S.). Computer Science and Telecommunications Board.**
The digital dilemma. Washington, D.C. : National Academy Press, c2000.
*TC KF2979 .D53 2000*

**National Research Council (U.S.). Mathematical Sciences Education Board.**
Designing mathematics or science curriculum programs. Washington, D.C. : National Academy Press, 1999.
*TC Q183.3.A1 D46 1999*

Global perspectives for local action. Washington, D.C. : National Academy Press, 1999.
*TC LB1583.3 .G56 1999*

Shannon, Ann. Keeping score. Washington, D.C. : National Academy Press, 1999.
*TC QA135.5 .S45 1999x*

**National Research Council (U.S.). Office of Special Projects.**
Harnessing science and technology for America's economic future. Washington, D.C. : National Academy Press, 1999.
*TC Q127.U5 H37 1999*

**National Research Council (U.S.). Panel on the Understanding and Control of Violent Behavior.**
Understanding and preventing violence. Washington, D.C. : National Academy Press, 1993-1994.
*TC HN90.V5 U53 1993*

**National school law reporter.**
The bi-weekly school law letter. Laramie, Wyo. : Published by R.R. Hamilton, 1951-1955.

**National Science Foundation (U.S.).**
Network science, a decade later. Mahwah, N.J. : Lawrence Erlbaum, 2000.
*TC LB1583.3 .N48 2000*

**National Science Teachers Association.**
Biehle, James T. NSTA guide to school science facilities. Arlington, VA : National Science Teachers Association, c1999.
*TC Q183.3.A1 B54 1999*

NSTA handbook / National Science Teachers Association. Washington, D.C. : The Association, v. ; 22 cm. Frequency: Annual. Title from cover. Description based on: 1982/83.
*1. National Science Teachers Association - Directories. 2. National Science Teachers Association - Handbooks, manuals, etc. I. Title.*
*TC Q145 .N38 1999*

**NATIONAL SCIENCE TEACHERS ASSOCIATION - DIRECTORIES.**
National Science Teachers Association. NSTA handbook. Washington, D.C. : The Association,
*TC Q145 .N38 1999*

**NATIONAL SCIENCE TEACHERS ASSOCIATION - HANDBOOKS, MANUALS, ETC.**
National Science Teachers Association. NSTA handbook. Washington, D.C. : The Association,
*TC Q145 .N38 1999*

**NATIONAL SECURITY.** *See* **ECONOMIC POLICY; INTERNATIONAL RELATIONS.**

**NATIONAL SERVICE.** *See* **ECONOMIC ASSISTANCE, DOMESTIC; VOLUNTARISM.**

**National Social Security Conference. Proceedings.**
American economic security. Washington, Chamber of Commerce of the United States of America.

**National Society for Crippled Children and Adults.**
The Crippled child. Chicago [etc.] National Society for Crippled Children and Adults [etc.]

**National Society for Performance and Instruction.**
Improving human performance. Washington, National Society for Performance and Instruction [etc.]

**National Society for Programmed Instruction.**
Improving human performance. Washington, National Society for Performance and Instruction [etc.]

**National Society for Programmed Instruction. NSPI journal.**
Improving human performance. Washington, National Society for Performance and Instruction [etc.]

**National Society for the Study of Education.**
American education. Chicago, Ill. : NSSE : Distributed by the University of Chicago Press, 2000.
*TC LB5 .N25 99th pt. 2*

Constructivism in education. Chicago, Ill. : NSSE : Distributed by the University of Chicago Press, 2000.
*TC LB5 .N25 99th pt. 1*

**NATIONAL SONGS.** *See* **FOLK SONGS.**

**NATIONAL STORYTELLING FESTIVAL.**
Sobol, Joseph Daniel. The storytellers' journey. Urbana : University of Illinois Press, c1999.
*TC GR72.3 .S62 1999*

**National Teacher Training Institute.**
The Internet in action for math & science 7-12 [videorecording]. [New York] : Thirteen-WNET ; [Alexandria, Va. : distributed by] PBS Video, c1997.
*TC LB1044.87 .I453 1997*

The Internet in action for math & science K-6 [videorecording]. [New York] : Thirteen-WNET ; [Alexandria, Va. : distributed by] PBS Video, c1998.
*TC LB1044.87 .I45 1998*

**National Textbook Company.**
Lamping, Alwena. NTC's Italian grammar. Lincolnwood, Ill., U.S.A. : NTC Pub. Group, 1998.
*TC PC1112 .L34 1998*

**National Textbook Company's beginner's Italian and English dictionary.**
NTC's beginner's Italian and English dictionary. Lincolnwood, Ill. : NTC Pub. Group, c1995.
*TC PC1640 .N83 1995*

**National Textbook language dictionaries.**
NTC's beginner's Italian and English dictionary. Lincolnwood, Ill. : NTC Pub. Group, c1995.
*TC PC1640 .N83 1995*

**NATIONAL TREASURE.** *See* **CULTURAL PROPERTY.**

**National variations in Jewish identity :** implications for Jewish education / edited by Steven M. Cohen and Gabriel Horenczyk. Albany, N.Y. : State University of New York Press, 1999. vi, 325 p. : ill. ; 23 cm. Includes bibliographical references and index. ISBN 0-7914-4371-X ISBN 0-7914-4372-8 (pbk. : alk. paper) DDC 305.892/4
*1. Jews - Identity - Congresses. 2. Jews - United States - Identity - Congresses. 3. Jews - Israel - Identity - Congresses. I. Cohen, Steven Martin. II. Horenczyk, Gabriel, 1954-*
*TC DS143 .N27 1999*

**NATIONAL VOCATIONAL QUALIFICATIONS (GREAT BRITAIN).**
Raggatt, Peter C. M. Government, markets and vocational qualifications. London ; New York : Falmer Press, 1999.
*TC HF5381.6 .R34 1999*

**NATIONALISM AND EDUCATION - ENGLAND - HISTORY.**
Heathorn, Stephen J., 1965- For home, country, and race. Toronto : University of Toronto Press, 1999.
*TC LC93.E5 H42 1999*

**NATIONALISM AND EDUCATION - GHANA.**
Quist, Hubert Oswald. Secondary education and nation-building. 1999.
*TC O85 Q52*

**NATIONALISM AND EDUCATION - KOREA.**
Lee, Yoonmi. Modern education, textbooks and the image of the nation. New York ; London : Garland Pub., 2000.
*TC LB3048.K6 L44 2000*

**NATIONALISM AND EDUCATION - SOUTH AFRICA.**
Cross, Michael. Imagery of identity in South African education, 1880-1990. Durham, N.C. : Carolina Academic Press, c1999.
*TC LA1539 .C76 1999*

**NATIONALISM - CUBA - HISTORY.**
Pérez, Louis A., 1943- On becoming Cuban. Chapel Hill : University of North Carolina Press, c1999.
*TC F1760 .P47 1999*

**NATIONALISM - FRANCE - HISTORY - 19TH CENTURY.**
Lehning, James R., 1947- Peasant and French. Cambridge [England] ; New York : Cambridge University Press, 1995.
*TC DC34 .L5 1995*

**NATIONALISM IN ART - EXHIBITIONS.**
Cikovsky, Nicolai. Winslow Homer. Washington, D.C. : National Gallery of Art, 1995.
*TC N6537.H58 A4 1995*

**NATIONALISM IN EDUCATION.** *See* **NATIONALISM AND EDUCATION.**

**NATIONALISM - MEXICO - PUEBLA (STATE) - HISTORY - 19TH CENTURY.**
Thomson, Guy P. C., 1949- Patriotism, politics, and popular liberalism in nineteenth-century Mexico. Wilmington, De. : Scholarly Resources, 1999.
*TC F1326.L83 T5 1999*

**NATIONALISM - STUDY AND TEACHING (ELEMENTARY) - ENGLAND - HISTORY.**
Heathorn, Stephen J., 1965- For home, country, and race. Toronto : University of Toronto Press, 1999.
*TC LC93.E5 H42 1999*

**NATIONALISME ET ÉDUCATION - ANGLETERRE - HISTOIRE.**
Heathorn, Stephen J., 1965- For home, country, and race. Toronto : University of Toronto Press, 1999.
*TC LC93.E5 H42 1999*

**NATIONALISME - ÉTUDE ET ENSEIGNEMENT (PRIMAIRE) - ANGLETERRE - HISTOIRE.**
Heathorn, Stephen J., 1965- For home, country, and race. Toronto : University of Toronto Press, 1999.
*TC LC93.E5 H42 1999*

**NATIONALITY (CITIZENSHIP).** *See* **CITIZENSHIP.**

**Native American art in the twentieth century :**
makers, meanings, histories / edited by W. Jackson
Rushing III. London ; New York : Routledge, 1999.
xxi, 214 p. : ill. (some col.) ; 26 cm. Includes bibliographic
references and index. ISBN 0-415-13747-0 (hc. : alk. paper)
ISBN 0-415-13748-9 (pbk. : alk. paper) DDC 704.03/97/00904
*1. Indian art - North America - History - 20th century. 2.*
*Indian art - Collectors and collecting - North America -*
*History - 20th century. 3. Indian art - North America - Themes.*
*motives. I. Rushing, W. Jackson.*
*TC E98.A7 R89 1999*

**The Native American look book.**
Sullivan, Missy. New York : The New Press, 1996.
*TC E98.A7 S93 1996*

**NATIVE AMERICANS.** *See* **INDIANS OF NORTH**
**AMERICA.**

**Native Americans (Garland Publishing, Inc.)**
Clay, Cheryl D., 1947- Schooling at-risk Native
American children. New York : Garland Pub., 1998.
*TC E99.U8 C53 1998*

Damm, Robert J., 1964- Repertoire, authenticity, and
instruction. New York ; London : Garland Pub., 2000.
*TC MT3.U6 O53 2000*

**NATIVE LANGUAGE AND EDUCATION.**
Fiction, literature and media. Amsterdam :
Amsterdam University Press, c1999.
*TC LB1575.8 .F53 1999*

Fiction, literature and media. Amsterdam :
Amsterdam University Press, c1999.
*TC LB1575.8 .F53 1999*

**NATIVE LANGUAGE AND EDUCATION - CASE**
**STUDIES.**
Indigenous educational models for contemporary
practice. Mahwah, N.J. : L. Erlbaum Associates, 2000.
*TC LC3719 .I53 2000*

**NATIVE LANGUAGE - STUDY AND TEACHING -**
**EUROPE.**
Teaching the mother tongue in a multilingual Europe.
London : Cassell, 1998.
*TC P53.5 .T43 1998*

**NATIVE LANGUAGE - USE IN SCHOOLS.** *See*
**NATIVE LANGUAGE AND EDUCATION.**

**NATIVE PEOPLES.** *See* **INDIGENOUS PEOPLES.**

**NATIVE RACES.** *See* **INDIGENOUS PEOPLES.**

**NATO/CCMS International Technical Meeting on**
**Air Pollution Modeling and its Application (22nd :**
**1996 : Clemont-Ferrand, France).**
Air pollution modeling and its application XII. New
York : Plenum Press, c1998.
*TC TD881 .A47523 1998*

**NATO challenges of modern society**
(v. 22.) Air pollution modeling and its application
XII. New York : Plenum Press, c1998.
*TC TD881 .A47523 1998*

**NATURAL HISTORY.** *See also* **BIOLOGY;**
**GEOLOGY; ZOOLOGY.**
Barnes-Svarney, Patricia L. The Oryx guide to natural
history. Phoenix, Ariz. : Oryx Press, 1999.
*TC QH45.2 .B37 1999*

**NATURAL HISTORY - MUSEUMS.** *See*
**NATURAL HISTORY MUSEUMS.**

**NATURAL HISTORY MUSEUMS - HISTORY -**
**19TH CENTURY.**
Yanni, Carla. Nature's museums. Baltimore, Md :
Johns Hopkins University Press, 2000.
*TC QH70.A1 Y25 2000*

**NATURAL HISTORY - STUDY AND TEACHING.**
*See* **NATURE STUDY.**

**NATURAL HISTORY - STUDY AND TEACHING**
**(ELEMENTARY).**
Taking inquiry outdoors. York, Me. : Stenhouse
Publishers, c2000.
*TC QH51 .T35 2000*

**NATURAL HISTORY - STUDY AND TEACHING**
**(ELEMENTARY) - ANECDOTES.**
Taking inquiry outdoors. York, Me. : Stenhouse
Publishers, c2000.
*TC QH51 .T35 2000*

**NATURAL LANGUAGE PROCESSING**
**(LINGUISTICS).** *See* **COMPUTATIONAL**
**LINGUISTICS.**

**NATURAL LAW.** *See* **LIBERTY.**

**NATURAL PHILOSOPHY.** *See* **PHYSICS.**

**NATURAL RESOURCES.**
Gifts from the earth [videorecording]. [New York,
N.Y.?] : Unapix Entertainment, Inc. [distributor],
c1996.
*TC QB631.2 .G5 1996*

**NATURAL SCIENCE.** *See* **NATURAL HISTORY;**
**SCIENCE.**

**NATURAL SELECTION.** *See also* **EVOLUTION**
**(BIOLOGY).**
Hrdy, Sarah Blaffer, 1946- Mother nature. 1st ed.
New York : Pantheon Books, c1999.
*TC HQ759 .H784 1999*

**The natural superiority of women.**
Montagu, Ashley, 1905- 5th ed. Walnut Creek, Calif. :
AltaMira Press, c1999.
*TC HQ1206 .M65 1999*

**NATURAL THEOLOGY.** *See* **CREATION.**

**A naturalistic inquiry of the relationship between**
**organizational change and informal learning in the**
**workplace.**
Skiba, Michaeline. 1999.
*TC 06 no. 11180*

**Naturalizing phenomenology :** issues in contemporary
phenomenology and cognitive science / edited by Jean
Petitot ... [et al.]. Stanford, Calif. : Stanford University
Press, c1999. xxi, 641 p. : ill. ; 24 cm. (Writing science)
Includes bibliographical references (p. 597-629) and indexes.
ISBN 0-8047-3322-8 (cloth : alk. paper) ISBN 0-8047-3610-3
(pbk. : alk. paper) DDC 142/.7
*1. Phenomenology. 2. Cognitive science. I. Petitot, Jean, 1944-*
*II. Series.*
*TC B829.5 .N38 1999*

**Naturally :** teacher's planning guide. New York :
Macmillan/McGraw-Hill, c1997. 1 v. (various pagings) :
col. ill. ; 31 cm. (Spotlight on literacy ; Gr.4 l.10 u.2)
(The road to independent reading) Includes index. ISBN 0-02-181173-3
*1. Language arts (Elementary) 2. Reading (Elementary) I.*
*Series. II. Series: The road to independent reading*
*TC LB1576 .S66 1997 Gr.4 l.10 u.2*

**Nature and human society.**
Forum on Biodiversity (1997 : National Academy of
Sciences) Washington, D.C. : National Academy
Press, 2000.
*TC QH541.15.B56 F685 1997*

**NATURE AND NURTURE.**
Bateson, P. P. G. (Paul Patrick Gordon), 1938- Design
for a life. New York ; London : Simon & Schuster
c2000.
*TC BF341 .B37 2000*

Beyond heredity and environment. Boulder :
Westview Press, 1995.
*TC BF341 .B48 1995*

Genius and eminence. 2nd ed. Oxford ; New York :
Pergamon Press, 1992.
*TC BF412 .G43 1992*

Howe, Michael J. A., 1940- The psychology of high
abilities. New York : New York University Press,
1999.
*TC BF723.A25 H69 1999*

The nature-nurture debate. Oxford ; Malden, Mass. :
Blackwell, 1999.
*TC BF341 .N39 1999*

Paris, Joel, 1940- Myths of childhood. Philadelphia,
PA : Brunner/Mazel, c2000.
*TC BF713 .P37 2000*

**NATURE - EFFECT OF HUMAN BEINGS ON.** *See*
*also* **HUMAN ECOLOGY.**
Fate of the earth [videorecording]. [New York,
N.Y.?] : Unapix Entertainment, Inc. [distributor],
c1996.
*TC QB631.2 .F3 1996*

**NATURE - EFFECT OF HUMAN BEINGS ON -**
**CONGRESSES.**
Forum on Biodiversity (1997 : National Academy of
Sciences) Nature and human society. Washington,
D.C. : National Academy Press, 2000.
*TC QH541.15.B56 F685 1997*

**NATURE - EFFECT OF HUMAN BEINGS ON -**
**FORECASTING.**
Brown, Lester Russell, 1934- Vital signs 2000 :. New
York : Norton, c2000.
*TC HD75.6 .B768 2000*

**NATURE - JUVENILE POETRY.**
Land, sea & sky. 1st ed. Boston : Joy Street Books,
c1993.
*TC PS595.N22 L36 1993*

**The nature-nurture debate :** the essential readings /
edited by Stephen J. Ceci and Wendy M. Williams.
Oxford ; Malden, Mass. : Blackwell, 1999. xi, 294 p. :
ill. ; 24 cm. (Essential readings in developmental psychology)
Includes bibliographical references and index. ISBN 0-631-
21738-X (alk. paper) ISBN 0-631-21739-8 (pbk. : alk.
paper) DDC 155.7
*1. Nature and nurture. I. Ceci, Stephen J. II. Williams, Wendy*
*M. (Wendy Melissa), 1960- III. Series.*
*TC BF341 .N39 1999*

**The nature of grief.**
Archer, John, 1944- London ; New York : Routledge,
1999.
*TC BF575.G7 A73 1999*

**The nature of human conflict.**
McNeil, Elton B., ed. Englewood Cliffs, N.J.,
Prentice-Hall [1965]
*TC HM36.5 .M25*

**NATURE - PICTORIAL WORKS.**
Land, sea & sky. 1st ed. Boston : Joy Street Books,
c1993.
*TC PS595.N22 L36 1993*

**NATURE - POETRY.**
Land, sea & sky. 1st ed. Boston : Joy Street Books,
c1993.
*TC PS595.N22 L36 1993*

**NATURE - PSYCHOLOGICAL ASPECTS.**
Kahn, Peter H. The human relationship with nature.
Cambridge, Mass. : MIT Press, c1999.
*TC BF353.5.N37 K34 1999*

Metzner, Ralph. Green psychology. Rochester, Vt. :
Park Street Press, c1999.
*TC BF353.5.N37 M47 1999*

**NATURE - PSYCHOLOGICAL ASPECTS -**
**CROSS-CULTURAL STUDIES.**
Kahn, Peter H. The human relationship with nature.
Cambridge, Mass. : MIT Press, c1999.
*TC BF353.5.N37 K34 1999*

**NATURE STUDY.** *See also* **ZOOLOGY.**
Olien, Rebecca. Walk this way!. Portsmouth, NH :
Heinemann, c1998.
*TC LB1047 .O55 1998*

**[Nature study class, P.S. 165]** [picture] 1935. 1 digital
image (black and white). 1 photograph ; original print, 8 x 10,
black and white. New York City Board of Education archives.
Special Collections archives, Milbank Memorial Library.
*1. Public school 165 (New York, N.Y.) - Pictorial works. 2.*
*Nature study - Pictorial works. 3. Owls - Pictorial works. 4.*
*Birds - Pictorial works. 5. Classrooms - Pictorial works.*
*New York (N.Y.) Board of Education*
*TC BE5564*

**[Nature study class, P.S. 165]** [picture] 1935. 1 digital
image (black and white). 1 photograph ; original print, 8 x 10,
black and white. New York City Board of Education archives.
Special Collections archives, Milbank Memorial Library.
repass
*1. Public school 165 (New York, N.Y.) - Pictorial works. 2.*
*Nature study - Pictorial works. 3. Owls - Pictorial works. 4.*
*Birds - Pictorial works. 5. Classrooms - Pictorial works. 1.*
*New York (N.Y.) Board of Education*
*TC BE5564*

**[Nature study class, P.S. 165]** [picture] 1935. 1 digital
image (black and white). 1 photograph ; original print, 8 x 10,
black and white. New York City Board of Education archives.
Special Collections Archives, Milbank Memorial Library.
repass
*1. Nature study - Pictorial works. 2. Owls - Pictorial works. 3.*
*Birds - Pictorial works. 4. Classrooms - Pictorial works. I.*
*Public school 165 (New York, N.Y.) ISSN: Pictorial works. II.*
*New York (N.Y.) Board of Education*
*TC BE5564*

**NATURE STUDY - PICTORIAL WORKS.**
[Nature study class, P.S. 165] [picture] 1935.
*TC BE5564*

[Nature study class, P.S. 165] [picture] 1935.
*TC BE5564*

[Nature study class, P.S. 165] [picture] 1935.
*TC BE5564*

**NatureCraft series**
Sohi, Morteza E. Look what I did with a shell!. New
York : Walker & Co., 2000.
*TC TT862 .S64 2000*

**Nature's museums.**
Yanni, Carla. Baltimore, Md : Johns Hopkins
University Press, 2000.
*TC QH70.A1 Y25 2000*

**Naumes, Margaret J.**
Naumes, William. The art & craft of case writing.
Thousand Oaks, Calif. : Sage Publications, c1999.
*TC LB1029.C37 N38 1999*

**Naumes, William.** The art & craft of case writing /
William Naumes, Margaret J. Naumes. Thousand
Oaks, Calif. : Sage Publications, c1999. xiii, 234 p. ; 24
cm. Includes bibliographical references (p. 211-220) and
indexes. ISBN 0-7619-1724-1 (cloth) ISBN 0-7619-1725-X
(pbk.) DDC 371.39
*1. Case method. 2. Textbooks - Authorship. I. Naumes,
Margaret J. II. Title. III. Title: Art and craft of case writing*
*TC LB1029.C37 N38 1999*

**NAUSEA - NURSING.**
Key aspects of comfort. New York : Springer Pub.
Co., c1989.
*TC RT87.P35 K48 1989*

**Nauta, Lodi.**
Between demonstration and imagination. Leiden,
Netherlands ; Boston : Brill, 1999.
*TC QB15 .B56 1999*

**NAUTICAL ASTRONOMY.** *See* TIME.

**NAVAHO INDIANS.** *See* NAVAJO INDIANS.

**NAVAJO INDIANS - ALCOHOL USE.**
Kunitz, Stephen J. Drinking, conduct disorder, and
social change. Oxford ; New York : Oxford University
Press, 2000.
*TC E99.N3 K88 2000*

**NAVAJO INDIANS - PHILOSOPHY.** *See* NAVAJO
PHILOSOPHY.

**NAVAJO INDIANS - SOCIAL CONDITIONS.**
Kunitz, Stephen J. Drinking, conduct disorder, and
social change. Oxford ; New York : Oxford University
Press, 2000.
*TC E99.N3 K88 2000*

**NAVAJO INDIANS - SOCIAL LIFE AND
CUSTOMS - EXHIBITIONS.**
Woven by the grandmothers. Washington :
Smithsonian Institution Press in association with the
National Museum of the American Indian,
Smithsonian Institution, c1996.
*TC E99.N3 W79 1996*

**NAVAJO INDIANS - TEXTILE INDUSTRY AND
FABRICS.** *See* NAVAJO TEXTILE FABRICS.

**NAVAJO PHILOSOPHY - EXHIBITIONS.**
Woven by the grandmothers. Washington :
Smithsonian Institution Press in association with the
National Museum of the American Indian,
Smithsonian Institution, c1996.
*TC E99.N3 W79 1996*

**NAVAJO TEXTILE FABRICS - EXHIBITIONS.**
Woven by the grandmothers. Washington :
Smithsonian Institution Press in association with the
National Museum of the American Indian,
Smithsonian Institution, c1996.
*TC E99.N3 W79 1996*

**NAVAJO TEXTILE FABRICS - FICTION.**
Blood, Charles L., 1929- The goat in the rug. New
York : Four Winds Press, 1976.
*TC PZ7.B6227 Go 1976*

**NAVAJO TEXTILE FABRICS - JUVENILE
FICTION.**
Blood, Charles L., 1929- The goat in the rug. New
York : Four Winds Press, 1976.
*TC PZ7.B6227 Go 1976*

**NAVAL HISTORY.** *See* MILITARY HISTORY.

**NAVAL PERSONNEL.** *See* SAILORS.

**Navarrete, Louis.**
Ballet class [videorecording]. W. Long Branch, NJ :
Kultur, c1984.
*TC GV1589 .B33 1984*

**Navigators.**
Jenoure, Terry. Albany, NY : State University of New
York Press, c2000.
*TC NX396.5 .J45 2000*

**Naylor, Larry L.**
Problems and issues of diversity in the United States.
Westport, Conn. : Bergin & Garvey, 1999.
*TC E184.A1 P76 1999*

**Naylor, Phyllis Reynolds.** A traitor among the boys /
Phyllis Reynolds Naylor. New York : Delacorte Press,
1999. 118 p. ; 22 cm. Sequel to: The girls' revenge.
SUMMARY: Despite a New Year's resolution to be nice to
their neighbors the Malloy girls, the Hatford boys find
themselves continuing their rivalry and war of practical jokes.
ISBN 0-385-32335-2 DDC [Fic]

*1. Practical jokes - Fiction. 2. Brothers - Fiction. 3. Sisters -
Fiction. I. Title.*
*TC PZ7.N24 Tpr 1999*

Walker's Crossing / Phyllis Reynolds Naylor. New
York : Atheneum Books for Young Readers, c1999.
232 p. ; 22 cm. "A Jean Karl book." SUMMARY: While living
on his family's ranch in Wyoming where he hopes to someday
be a cowboy, Ryan faces conflicts with his older brother who
becomes involved in a militia movement. ISBN 0-689-82939-6
DDC [Fic]
*1. Ranch life - Wyoming - Fiction. 2. Cowboys - Fiction 3.
Brothers - Fiction. 4. Prejudices - Fiction. 5. Militia
movements - Fiction. 6. Wyoming - Fiction. I. Title.*
*TC PZ7.N24 Wai 1999*

**NEA Professional Library (Association).**
DiVincenzo, Joe. Group decision making. [S.l.] : NEA
Professional Library : NEA Affiliate Capacity
Building, c1999.
*TC LB2806 .D58 1999*

**Neal-Barnett, Angela M., 1960-.**
Family and peers. Westport, Conn. : Praeger, 2000.
*TC HQ755.85 .F365 2000*

**Neal, Charles, 1948-.**
Therapeutic perspectives on working with lesbian, gay
and bisexual clients. Buckingham [England] ;
Philadelphia : Open University Press, 2000.
*TC RC451.4.G39 T476 2000*

**Neal-Schuman authoritative guide to evaluating
information on the Internet.**
Cooke, Alison. New York : Neal-Schuman Publishers,
c1999.
*TC ZA4201 .C66 1999*

**Neal-Schuman Internet policy handbook for
libraries.**
Smith, Mark, 1956- New York : Neal-Schuman,
c1999.
*TC Z692.C65 S66 1999*

**Neal-Schuman net-guide series.**
Cooke, Alison. Neal-Schuman authoritative guide to
evaluating information on the Internet. New York :
Neal-Schuman Publishers, c1999.
*TC ZA4201 .C66 1999*

Hollands, William D. Teaching the Internet to library
staff and users. New York : Neal-Schuman, c1999.
*TC ZA4201 .H65 1999*

Smith, Mark, 1956- Neal-Schuman Internet policy
handbook for libraries. New York : Neal-Schuman,
c1999.
*TC Z692.C65 S66 1999*

**Neale, Margo.**
Art Gallery of New South Wales. Yiribana. 2nd ed.
Sydney, Australia : The Gallery, 1998.
*TC N7401 .A765 1998*

**NEAR EAST.** *See* MIDDLE EAST.

**Neatby, Nicole, 1962-** Carabins ou activistes? :
l'idéalisme et la radicalisation de la pensée étudiante à
l'Université de Montréal au temps du duplessisme /
Nicole Neatby. Montréal ; Ithaca : McGill-Queen's
University Press, [1999?] c1997. 264 p. ; 23 cm. (Studies
on the history of Quebec = Etudes d'histoire du Québec, 1183-
4390) Includes bibliographical references (p. [243]-251) and
index. ISBN 0-7735-1834-7 (rel.) ISBN 0-7735-1835-5 (br.)
DDC 378.1/981/0971428
*1. Université de Montréal - Students - Political activity -
History. 2. Student movements - Québec (Province) -
Montréal - History. 3. Students - Québec (Province) -
Montréal - Political activity - History. 4. Québec (Province) -
History. I. Title. II. Series: Studies on the history of Quebec.*
*TC LA418.Q8 N42 1999*

**NEATNESS.** *See* ORDERLINESS.

**Neave, Guy R.**
From the eye of the storm. Dordrecht ; Boston ;
London: Kluwer Academic Publishers, c1999.
*TC LB2341.8.E85 F76 1999*

Groof, Jan de. Democracy and governance in higher
education. The Hague ; Boston : Kluwer Law
International, 1998.
*TC LB2341.8.E85 G76 1998*

The universities' responsibilities to society. 1st ed.
New York : Pergamon, published for the IAU Press,
2000.
*TC LC191.9 .U55 2000*

**Necessary but not sufficient.**
Wachs, Theodore D., 1941- 1st ed. Washington, DC :
American Psychological Association, c2000.
*TC BF713 .W33 2000*

**NECROMANCY.** *See* MAGIC.

**Nee-Benham, Maenette K. P.**
Case studies for school administrators. 1st ed.
Lancaster, PA : Technomic Pub. Co., c1999.
*TC LB2806 .C316 1999*

Indigenous educational models for contemporary
practice. Mahwah, N.J. : L. Erlbaum Associates, 2000.
*TC LC3719 .I53 2000*

**The need to know library**
Nash, Renea D. Everything you need to know about
being a biracial/biethnic teen. 1st ed. New York :
Rosen Pub. Group, 1995.
*TC HQ77.9 .N39 1995*

**NEEDLEWORK.** *See* WHITE WORK
EMBROIDERY.

**NEEDS ASSESSMENT.** *See* MEDICAL CARE -
NEEDS ASSESSMENT.

**NEEDS, TRAINING.** *See* TRAINING NEEDS.

**Neely, Margery A.**
Maass, Vera Sonja. Counseling single parents. New
York : Springer Pub. Co., c2000.
*TC HQ759.915 .M23 2000*

**NEGLECT (NEUROLOGY).** *See*
CEREBROVASCULAR DISEASE.

**NEGLIGENCE.** *See* MALPRACTICE.

**NEGOTIATING.** *See* NEGOTIATION.

**Negotiating adolescence in times of social change** /
edited by Lisa J. Crockett, Rainer K. Silbereisen.
Cambridge, U.K. ; New York : Cambridge University
Press, 2000. x, 309 p. : ill. ; 25 cm. Includes bibliographical
references (p. 299-302) and indexes. ISBN 0-521-62389-8
(hc.) DDC 305.235
*1. Adolescence. 2. Adolescent psychology. 3. Social change. I.
Crockett, Lisa J. II. Silbereisen, R. K. (Rainer K.), 1944-*
*TC HQ796 .N415 2000*

**Negotiating agreement and disagreement in
Japanese.**
Mori, Junko. Amsterdam : Philadelphia, Pa. : J.
Benjamins Pub. Co., c1999.
*TC PL611.C6 M67 1999*

**Negotiating identity.**
Gallin, Alice. Notre Dame, Ind. : University of Notre
Dame Press, c2000.
*TC LC501 .G36 2000*

**NEGOTIATION.** *See also* CONFLICT
MANAGEMENT.
Mayer, Bernard S., 1946- The dynamics of conflict
resolution. 1st ed. San Francisco : Jossey-Bass
Publishers, c2000.
*TC BF637.I48 M39 2000*

Shell, G. Richard, 1949- Bargaining for advantage.
New York : Viking, 1999.
*TC BF637.N4 S44 1999*

**NEGOTIATION IN BUSINESS.** *See* COLLECTIVE
BARGAINING.

**NEGOTIATION - UNITED STATES.**
Tomal, Daniel R. Discipline by negotiation. 1st ed.
Lancaster, Pa. : Technomic Pub. Co., c1999.
*TC LB3011.5 .T66 1999*

**NEGOTIATIONS.** *See* NEGOTIATION.

**NEGRITUDE.** *See* BLACKS - RACE IDENTITY.

**NEGRO ART.** *See* AFRO-AMERICAN ART; ART,
BLACK.

**NEGRO ARTISTS.** *See* AFRO-AMERICAN
ARTISTS.

**NEGRO ARTS.** *See* AFRO-AMERICAN ARTS.

**NEGRO AUTHORS.** *See* AFRO-AMERICAN
AUTHORS; AUTHORS, BLACK.

**NEGRO CHILDREN.** *See* AFRO-AMERICAN
CHILDREN; CHILDREN, BLACK.

**NEGRO CHURCHES.** *See* AFRO-AMERICAN
CHURCHES.

**NEGRO COLLEGE TEACHERS.** *See* AFRO-
AMERICAN COLLEGE TEACHERS.

**NEGRO-ENGLISH DIALECTS.** *See* BLACK
ENGLISH.

**NEGRO FAMILIES.** *See* AFRO-AMERICAN
FAMILIES.

**NEGRO LITERATURE.** *See* AMERICAN
LITERATURE - AFRO-AMERICAN
AUTHORS.

**NEGRO MUSIC.** *See* **AFRO-AMERICANS - MUSIC.**

**Negro poets and their poems.**
Kerlin, Robert Thomas, 1866-1950. 3d ed., rev. and enl. Washington, D. C. : Associated Publishers, c1935.
*TC PS591.N4 K4 1935*

**Negro slave songs in the United States.**
Fisher, Miles Mark, 1899- Secaucus, N.J. : Citadel Press, c1953.
*TC ML3556 .F58 1953*

**NEGRO SOLDIERS.** *See* **AFRO-AMERICAN SOLDIERS.**

**NEGRO SONGS.** *See* **AFRO-AMERICANS - MUSIC.**

**NEGRO STUDENTS.** *See* **AFRO-AMERICAN STUDENTS; STUDENTS, BLACK.**

**NEGRO UNIVERSITIES AND COLLEGES.** *See* **AFRO-AMERICAN UNIVERSITIES AND COLLEGES.**

**NEGRO YOUTH.** *See* **AFRO-AMERICAN YOUTH.**

**NEGROES.** *See* **AFRO-AMERICANS; BLACKS.**

**NEGROES AS SOLDIERS.** *See* **AFRO-AMERICAN SOLDIERS.**

**NEGROES IN BRAZIL.** *See* **BLACKS - BRAZIL.**

**NEGROES IN LITERATURE.** *See* **AFRO-AMERICANS IN LITERATURE.**

**Nehlig, Astrid.**
Childhood epilepsies and brain development. London : John Libbey, c1999.
*TC RJ496.E6 C45 1999*

**Neiberg, Michael S.** Making citizen-soldiers : ROTC and the ideology of American military service / Michael S. Neiberg. Cambridge, Mass. ; London : Harvard University Press, 2000. viii, 264 p. ; 25 cm. Includes bibliographical references (p. 207-250) and index. ISBN 0-674-54312-2 (alk. paper) DDC 355.2/232/071173
*1. United States. - Army. - Reserve Officers' Training Corps. 2. United States. - Air Force ROTC. 3. United States. - Naval Reserve Officers Training Corps. 4. United States - Armed Forces - Officers - Training of. I. Title.*
*TC U428.5 .N45 2000*

**Neiderhiser, Jenae M.**
Reiss, David, 1937- The relationship code. Cambridge, Mass. ; London : Harvard University Press, c2000.
*TC BF724 .R39 2000*

**Neidle, Carol Jan.**
The syntax of American Sign Language. Cambridge, Mass. : MIT Press, c2000.
*TC HV2474 .S994 2000*

**NEIGHBORHOOD.** *See* **GATED COMMUNITIES.**

**NEIGHBORHOOD ART PROJECTS.** *See* **COMMUNITY ART PROJECTS.**

**NEIGHBORHOOD CENTERS.** *See* **SOCIAL SETTLEMENTS.**

**NEIGHBORHOOD HEALTH CENTERS.** *See* **COMMUNITY HEALTH SERVICES.**

**NEIGHBORHOOD JUSTICE CENTERS.** *See* **DISPUTE RESOLUTION (LAW).**

**NEIGHBORHOOD - UNITED STATES - ECONOMIC ASPECTS.**
Leventhal, Tama. Poverty and turbulence. 1999.
*TC 085 L5515*

**NEIGHBORHOODS.** *See* **NEIGHBORHOOD.**

**NEIGHBORS - FICTION.**
Rosen, Michael, 1946- A Thanksgiving wish. New York : Blue Sky Press, c1999.
*TC PZ7.R71867 Tf 1999*

**Neilan, Brendan.**
Screen printing [videorecording]. [Northbrook?], Ill. ; Peasmarsh, East Sussex, Eng. : Roland Collection of Films on Art, c1992.
*TC NE2238.G7 S4 1992*

**NEILL, ALEXANDER SUTHERLAND, 1883-1973.**
Summerhill at 70 [videorecording]. Princeton, N.J. : Films for the Humanities, c1992.
*TC LF795.L692953 S9 1992*

**Neisser, Ulric.**
Memory observed. 2nd ed. New York : Worth Publishers, c2000.

*TC BF371 .M455 2000*

**Neither beasts nor gods.**
Kane, Francis, 1944- Dallas : Southern Methodist University Press, 1998.
*TC JC330.15 .K36 1998*

**Nekuee, Shervin.**
Education and racism :. Aldershot ; Brookfield, Vt. : Ashgate, c1999.
*TC LC212.3.G7E48 1999*

**Nell Blaine.**
Sawin, Martica. 1st ed. New York : Hudson Hills Press ; [Lanham, MD] : Distributed in the USA, its territories and possessions, and Canada by National Book Network, c1998.
*TC ND237.B597 S28 1998*

**Nellist, John G.** Understanding modern telecommunications and the information superhighway / John G. Nellist, Elliot M. Gilbert. Boston, Mass. : Artech House, 1999. xviii, 285 p.: ill., maps ; 24 cm. (Artech House telecommunications library) Includes bibliographical references and index. ISBN 0-89006-322-2 (alk. paper) DDC 384
*1. Computer networks. 2. Information superhighway. I. Gilbert, Elliot M. II. Title. III. Series.*
*TC TK5105.5 .N45 1999*

**Nelsen, Marjorie R.** Peak with books : an early childhood resource for balanced literacy / Marjorie R. Nelsen, Jan Nelsen-Parish ; [foreword by Jim Trelease]. 3rd ed. Thousand Oaks, Calif. : Corwin Press, c1999. xiii, 274 p. : ill. (some col.) ; 28 cm. Includes bibliographical references (p. [265]-270) and index. ISBN 0-8039-6796-9 (pbk. : alk. paper) DDC 011.62
*1. Children - Books and reading - United States. 2. Children's stories - Study and teaching - United States. 3. Reading - Parent participation - United States. I. Nelsen-Parish, Jan. II. Title.*
*TC Z1037.A1 N347 1999*

**Nelsen-Parish, Jan.**
Nelsen, Marjorie R. Peak with books. 3rd ed. Thousand Oaks, Calif. : Corwin Press, c1999.
*TC Z1037.A1 N347 1999*

**Nelson, Carol, 1953-** Women's market handbook : understanding and reaching today's most powerful consumer group / Carol Nelson ; guest foreword by Frances Lear. Detroit : Gale Research, c1994. xvi, 366 p. : ill. ; 25 cm. Gale professional library"--Spine. Includes bibliographical references (p. [353]-355) and index. ISBN 0-8103-9139-2 (alk. paper) DDC 658.8/348
*1. Marketing. 2. Advertising. 3. Women consumers. I. Title.*
*TC HF5415 .N3495 1994*

**Nelson, Charles A. (Charles Alexander).**
The effects of early adversity on neurobehavioral development. Mahwah, N.J. : L. Erlbaum Associates, 2000.
*TC RJ499 .E34 2000*

**Nelson, Dawn D.**
Vocational education in the United States. Washington, DC : U.S. Dept. of Education, Office of Educational Research and Improvement : For sale by the U.S. G.P.O., Supt. of Docs., [2000]
*TC LC1045 .V5874 2000*

**Nelson, Emmanuel S. (Emmanuel Sampath), 1954-.**
African American authors, 1745-1945. Westport, Conn. : Greenwood Press, 2000.
*TC PS153.N5 A32 2000*

**Nelson, Joan** Meeting challenges / author, Joan Nelson; senior consultant, Harold L. Herber ... [et al.]. Lexington, Mass. : D. C. Heath and Company, c1983. 512 p. : ill. (some col.) ; 24 cm. (American readers ; 8) ISBN 0-669-05093-8
*1. Readers (Elementary) I. Herber, Harold L. II. Title.*
*TC PE1121 .M43 1983*

**Nelson, Joan M.** Reforming health and education : the World Bank, the IDB, and complex institutional change / Joan M. Nelson. Washington, DC : Overseas Development Council ; Baltimore, MD : Distributed by the Johns Hopkins University Press, c1999. xviii, 103 p. ; 23 cm. (Policy essay ; no. 26) Includes bibliographical references. ISBN 1-56517-030-X (pbk.) DDC 362.1/0425
*1. World Bank. 2. Inter-American Development Bank. 3. Medical policy. 4. Education and state. I. Title. II. Series.*
*TC HG3881.5.W57 N447 1999*

**Nelson, Michael, 1949-** Alive at the core : exemplary approaches to general education in the humanities / Michael Nelson and associates. 1st ed. San Francisco : Jossey-Bass, c2000. xxxi, 375 p. ; 24 cm. (Jossey-Bass higher and adult education series) Includes bibliographical references and index. ISBN 0-7879-4760-1
*1. Humanities - Study and teaching (Higher) - United States. 2.*

*Education, Humanistic. 3. Universities and colleges - Curricula. I. Title. II. Series.*
*TC AZ183.U5 N45 2000*

**Nelson, Nickola.** Childhood language disorders in context : infancy through adolescence / Nickola Wolf Nelson. 2nd ed. Boston : Allyn & Bacon, c1998. xii, 628 p. : ill. ; 25 cm. Includes bibliographical references (p. 545-606) and indexes. ISBN 0-205-19787-6 DDC 618.92/855
*1. Language disorders in children. 2. Language disorders in adolescence. I. Title.*
*TC RJ496.L35 N46 1998*

**Nelson, Stephen James, 1947-** Leaders in the crucible : the moral voice of college presidents / Stephen James Nelson. Westport, Conn. : Bergin & Garvey, 2000. xix, 208 p. ; 25 cm. Includes bibliographical references (p. [197]-204) and index. ISBN 0-89789-742-0 (alk. paper) DDC 378.1/11
*1. Educational leadership - Moral and ethical aspects - United States. 2. College presidents - Professional ethics - United States. I. Title. II. Title: Moral voice of college presidents*
*TC LB2341 .N386 2000*

**Nemeroff, Charles B.**
The Corsini encyclopedia of psychology and behavioral science. 3rd ed. New York : Wiley, 2000.
*TC BF31 .E52 2000*

**Nemeroff, Robin.** Stress, social support, and psychological distress in late life : the moderating effects of perceived control and attachment / by Robin Nemeroff. 1999. vi, 89 leaves ; 29 cm. Typescript; issued also on microfilm. Thesis (Ph.D.)--Columbia University, 1999. Includes bibliographical references (leaves 66-75).
*1. Adjustment (Psychology) in old age. 2. Stress in old age. 3. Attachment behavior. 4. Life change events - Psychological aspects. 5. Aged - Counseling of. 6. Social work with the aged. I. Title.*
*TC 085 N341*

**Nemeth, Charles P., 1951-** A status report on contemporary criminal justice education : a definition of the discipline and an assessment of its curricula, faculty, and program characteristics / Charles P. Nemeth. Lewiston, NY, USA : E. Mellen Press, c1989. v, 160 p. ; 24 cm. (Mellen studies in education ; v. 3) Bibliography: p. 125-137. Includes index. ISBN 0-88946-938-5 DDC 364/.07/1173
*1. Criminal justice, Administration of - Study and teaching (Higher) - United States. I. Title. II. Series.*
*TC HV7419.5 .N45 1989*

**NEO-CONSERVATISM.** *See* **CONSERVATISM.**

**NEO-DADAISM.** *See* **POP ART.**

**NEO FIVE-FACTOR INVENTORY.**
Piedmont, Ralph L., 1958- The revised NEO Personality Inventory. New York : Plenum Press, c1998.
*TC BF698.8.N46 P54 1998*

**NEO PERSONALITY INVENTORY.**
Piedmont, Ralph L., 1958- The revised NEO Personality Inventory. New York : Plenum Press, c1998.
*TC BF698.8.N46 P54 1998*

**NEO-SCHOLASTICISM.**
Henle, R. J. (Robert John), 1909- The American Thomistic revival in the philosophical papers of R.J. Henle, S.J.. St. Louis, Mo. : Saint Louis University Press, c1999.
*TC B839 .H46 1999*

**NEOCLASSICISM (ART) - FRANCE - THEMES, MOTIVES.**
Solomon-Godeau, Abigail. Male trouble :. London : Thames and Hudson, c1997.
*TC N6847.5.N35 S64 1997*

**NEOCOLONIALISM.** *See* **COLONIES; IMPERIALISM.**

**NEONATES.** *See* **INFANTS (NEWBORN).**

**NEONATOLOGY.** *See* **INFANTS (NEWBORN).**

**NEOPLASMS - NURSING.**
Quality of life from nursing and patient perspectives. Sudbury, Mass. ; London : Jones and Bartlett, c1998.
*TC RC262 .Q34 1998*

**Népoktató.**
Gegő, Elek, 1805-1844. Budapest : Országos Pedagógiai Könyvtár és Múzeum, [1997]
*TC LC227 .G44 1997*

**Nering, Michael L.**
Yi, Qing. Simulating nonmodel-fitting responses in a CAT environment. Iowa City, Iowa : ACT, 1998.
*TC LB3051 .A3 no. 98-10*

**NERVOUS SYSTEM.** *See* **NEUROLOGIC EXAMINATION; NEUROSCIENCES.**

**NERVOUS SYSTEM - DISEASES.** *See* **COMMUNICATIVE DISORDERS; NEUROLOGY; PEDIATRIC NEUROLOGY.**

**NERVOUS SYSTEM DISEASES.**
Dubowitz, Lilly M. S. The neurological assessment of the preterm and full-term newborn infant. 2nd ed. London : Mac Keith, 1999.
*TC RJ486 .D85 1999*

**NERVOUS SYSTEM - DISEASES - DIAGNOSIS.** *See* **PSYCHODIAGNOSTICS.**

**NERVOUS SYSTEM DISEASES - DIAGNOSIS.**
Practitioner's guide to evaluating change with neuropsychological assessment instruments. New York : Kluwer Academic/Plenum Publishers, c2000.
*TC RC386.6.N48 P73 2000*

**Nesthus, Marie.**
Donnell Library Center. Video. New York : New York Public Library, 1990.
*TC PN1992.95 .D66*

**Net curriculum.**
Joseph, Linda C., 1949- Medford, N.J. : CyberAge Books, c1999.
*TC LB1044.87 .J67 1999*

**Net-working :** teaching, learning & professional development with the Internet / edited by Kwok-Wing Lai. Dunedin, N.Z. : University of Otago Press, 1999. 221 p. : ill. ; 25 cm. Includes bibliographical references and index. ISBN 1-87713-368-X (pbk.)
*1. Internet in education. 2. Education - Computer network resources. 3. Computer-assisted instruction. I. Lai, Kwok-Wing. II. Title: Teaching, learning & professional development with the Internet III. Title: Networking*
*TC LB1044.87 .N47 1999*

**NETHERLANDS - CHURCH HISTORY - 16TH CENTURY.**
Anglo-Dutch Historical Conference (13th : 1997) The education of a Christian society. Aldershot, Hants, England ; Brookfield, Vt. : Ashgate, c1999.
*TC BR377 .E38 1999*

**NETS, NEURAL (COMPUTER SCIENCE).** *See* **NEURAL NETWORKS (COMPUTER SCIENCE).**

**NETS, NEURAL (NEUROBIOLOGY).** *See* **NEURAL NETWORKS (NEUROBIOLOGY).**

**Nettl, Bruno, 1930-.**
Blacking, John. Music, culture, & experience. Chicago : University of Chicago Press, c1995.
*TC ML60 .B63 1995*

**Nettles, Arie L.**
Measuring up. Boston : Kluwer Academic Publishers, c1999.
*TC LB3051 .M4627 1999*

**Nettles, Michael T., 1955-.**
Measuring up. Boston : Kluwer Academic Publishers, c1999.
*TC LB3051 .M4627 1999*

**Nettleton, Gavin.**
Etching [videorecording]. Northbrook, Ill. : Peasmarsh, East Sussex, Eng. : Roland Collection of Films on Art, c1990.
*TC NE2043 .E87 1990*

**Nettleton, Gavin. rt.**
Screen printing [videorecording]. [Northbrook?], Ill. : Peasmarsh, East Sussex, Eng. : Roland Collection of Films on Art, c1992.
*TC NE2238.G7 S4 1992*

**Network-based language teaching :** concepts and practice / edited by Mark Warschauer and Richard Kern. Cambridge, U.K. ; New York : Cambridge University Press, 2000. xii, 240 p. : ill. ; 23 cm. (The Cambridge applied linguistics series) Includes bibliographical references and indexes. ISBN 0-521-66136-6 (hb) ISBN 0-521-66742-9 (pb) DDC 418/.00285
*1. Language and languages - Study and teaching - Computer network resources. I. Warschauer, Mark. II. Kern, Richard (Richard Geyman) III. Series: Cambridge applied linguistics series*
*TC P53.285 .N48 2000*

**NETWORK COMPUTERS.** *See* **COMPUTER NETWORKS.**

**Network science, a decade later :** the Internet and classroom learning / Alan Feldman ... [et al.] ; foreword by Barbara Means. Mahwah, N.J. : Lawrence Erlbaum, 2000. xxiv, 186 p. : ill. ; 23 cm. "This project was undertaken by TERC, Inc. ... Funded in part by a grant from the National Science Foundation." Includes bibliographical references (p. 171-175) and indexes. ISBN 0-8058-3425-7 (alk. paper) ISBN 0-8058-3426-5 (pbk. : alk. paper) DDC 507.8/5
*1. Science - United States - Computer-assisted instruction. 2. Internet (Computer network) in education - United States. I. Feldman, Alan, 1947- II. Technical Education Research Centers (U.S.) III. National Science Foundation (U.S.)*
*TC LB1583.3 .N48 2000*

**Networking.**
Net-working. Dunedin, N.Z. : University of Otago Press, 1999.
*TC LB1044.87 .N47 1999*

**NETWORKING, BUSINESS.** *See* **BUSINESS NETWORKS.**

**Networking the world, 1794-2000.**
Mattelart, Armand. [Mondialisation de la communication. English] Minneapolis, MN ; London : University of Minnesota Press, c2000.
*TC HE7631 .M37513 2000*

**NETWORKS (ASSOCIATIONS, INSTITUTIONS, ETC.).** *See* **ASSOCIATIONS, INSTITUTIONS, ETC.**

**NETWORKS, BUSINESS.** *See* **BUSINESS NETWORKS.**

**NETWORKS, COMPUTER.** *See* **COMPUTER NETWORKS.**

**NETWORKS, NEURAL (COMPUTER SCIENCE).** *See* **NEURAL NETWORKS (COMPUTER SCIENCE).**

**NETWORKS, NEURAL (NEUROBIOLOGY).** *See* **NEURAL NETWORKS (NEUROBIOLOGY).**

**NETWORKS OF LIBRARIES.** *See* **LIBRARY INFORMATION NETWORKS.**

**NETWORKS, SELF-HELP.** *See* **SELF-HELP GROUPS.**

**Neuberger Museum of Art.**
Catlett, Elizabeth, 1915- Elizabeth Catlett sculpture. [Purchase, N.Y.] : Neuberger Museum of Art, Purchase College, State University of New York ; Seattle : Distributed by University of Washington Press, c1998.
*TC NB259.C384 A4 1998*

**Neue Nationalgalerie (Germany).**
Exiles + emigrés. Los Angeles, Calif. : Los Angeles County Museum of Art ; New York : H.N. Abrams, c1997.
*TC N6512 .E887 1997*

**Neufeld, Jamie.**
Rationales for teaching young adult literature. Portland, Me. : Calendar Islands Publishers, 1999.
*TC PN59 .R33 1999*

**Neuman, David J.**
Joncas, Richard, 1953- Stanford University. 1st ed. New York : Princeton Architectural Press, 1999.
*TC LD3031 .J65 1999*

**Neuman, Susan B.**
Children achieving. Newark, Del. : International Reading Association, c1998.
*TC LB1139.5.R43 C55 1998*

**Neuner, John.** Teacher/swimmer : : "the mind-body connection" addressing the needs of the fearful swimmer / by John Neuner. New York : Jay Street, c1998. 140 p. : ill. ; 22 cm. ISBN 1-88593-422-6
*1. Swimming - Study and teaching. I. Title.*
*TC GV837 .N48 1998*

**NEURAL CIRCUITRY.** *See* **NEURAL NETWORKS (NEUROBIOLOGY).**

**NEURAL COMPUTERS.** *See also* **ARTIFICIAL INTELLIGENCE.**
Statistics and neural networks. Oxford ; New York : Oxford University Press, 1999.
*TC QA276 .S78343 1999*

**NEURAL NETS (COMPUTER SCIENCE).** *See* **NEURAL NETWORKS (COMPUTER SCIENCE).**

**NEURAL NETS (NEUROBIOLOGY).** *See* **NEURAL NETWORKS (NEUROBIOLOGY).**

**A neural network guide to teaching.**
Baker, Justine C. Bloomington, Ind. : Phi Delta Kappa Educational Foundation, c1998.
*TC LB1057 .B35 1998*

**Neural network learning.**
Anthony, Martin. Cambridge, U.K. ; New York : Cambridge University Press, 1999.
*TC QA76.87 .A58 1999*

**NEURAL NETWORKS (COMPUTER) - CONGRESSES.**
International School of Biocybernetics (1997 : Naples, Italy) Neuronal bases and psychological aspects of consiousness. Singapore ; River Edge, N.J : World Scientific, c1999.
*TC QP411 .I56 1997*

**NEURAL NETWORKS (COMPUTER SCIENCE).**
Anthony, Martin. Neural network learning. Cambridge, U.K. ; New York : Cambridge University Press, 1999.
*TC QA76.87 .A58 1999*

Baker, Bruce D. A comparison of statistical and neural network models for forecasting educational spending. 1997.
*TC 06 no. 10792*

Information theory and the brain. Cambridge [England] ; New York : Cambridge University Press, 2000.
*TC QP363.3 .I54 2000*

Statistics and neural networks. Oxford ; New York : Oxford University Press, 1999.
*TC QA276 .S78343 1999*

**NEURAL NETWORKS (NEUROBIOLOGY).**
Baker, Justine C. A neural network guide to teaching. Bloomington, Ind. : Phi Delta Kappa Educational Foundation, c1998.
*TC LB1057 .B35 1998*

Information theory and the brain. Cambridge [England] ; New York : Cambridge University Press, 2000.
*TC QP363.3 .I54 2000*

**NEURAL NETWORKS (NEUROBIOLOGY) - CONGRESSES.**
Peripheral and spinal mechanisms in the neural control of movement. Amsterdam ; Oxford : Elsevier, 1999.
*TC QP376.A1 P7 1999*

**NEURAL SCIENCES.** *See* **NEUROSCIENCES.**

**NEURASTHENIA.** *See* **DEPRESSION, MENTAL.**

**NEUROBEHAVIORAL DISORDERS.** *See* **DEMENTIA.**

**NEUROBIOLOGY.** *See also* **NEURAL NETWORKS (NEUROBIOLOGY).**
Neurobiology of learning and memory. San Diego : Academic Press, c1998.
*TC QP408 .N492 1998*

Neurobiology of learning and memory. San Diego : Academic Press, c1998.
*TC QP408 .N492 1998*

**Neurobiology of learning and memory** / edited by Joe L. Martinez, Jr., Raymond P. Kesner. San Diego : Academic Press, c1998. xvi, 456 p. : ill. ; 23 cm. Includes bibliographical references and index. ISBN 0-12-475655-7 DDC 573.8
*1. Learning - Physiological aspects. 2. Memory - Physiological aspects. 3. Neurobiology. 4. Learning - physiology. 5. Memory - physiology. 6. Neurobiology. I. Martinez, Joe L. II. Kesner, Raymond P.*
*TC QP408 .N492 1998*

**The neurocognition of language** / edited by Colin M. Brown and Peter Hagoort. Oxford ; New York : Oxford University Press, 1999. xiv, 409 p. : ill. ; 25 cm. ISBN 0-19-852448-X DDC 612.7/8
*1. Neurolinguistics. 2. Cognitive neuroscience. 3. Cognitive psychology. 4. Language and languages - Study and teaching - Physiological aspects. 5. Language. 6. Speech. 7. Neurophysiology. I. Brown, Colin M. II. Hagoort, Peter.*
*TC QP399 .N483 1999*

**Neurodynamics of personality.**
Grigsby, Jim. New York : Guilford Press, 2000.
*TC BF698.9.B5 G741 2000*

**Neurogenic communication disorders :** a functional approach / edited by Linda E. Worrall and Carol M. Frattali. New York : Thieme, 2000. xvi, 358 p. ; 26 cm. Includes bibliographical references and index. ISBN 0-86577-868-X
*1. Communicative disorders - Rehabilitation. 2. Deglutition disorders - Rehabilitation. 3. Communication Disorders - rehabilitation. 4. Deglutition Disorders - rehabilitation. I. Worrall, Linda. II. Frattali, Carol.*
*TC RC423 .N48 2000*

**NEUROLINGUISTIC PROGRAMMING.**
Goldberg, Marilee C. The art of the question. New York : Wiley, c1998.

*TC RC489.N47 G65 1998*

**NEUROLINGUISTICS.**
Calvin, William H., 1939- Lingua ex machina.
Cambridge, Mass. ; London : MIT Press, c2000.
*TC QP399 .C35 2000*

The neurocognition of language. Oxford ; New York :
Oxford University Press, 1999.
*TC QP399 .N483 1999*

Webster, Douglas B., 1934- Neuroscience of
communication. 2nd ed. San Diego : Singular
Publishing Group, c1999.
*TC QP355.2 .W43 1999*

**NEUROLOGIC EXAMINATION.**
Dubowitz, Lilly M. S. The neurological assessment of
the preterm and full-term newborn infant. 2nd ed.
London : Mac Keith, 1999.
*TC RJ486 .D85 1999*

**NEUROLOGIC EXAMINATION.**
Green, Joanne. Neuropsychological evaluation of the
older adult. San Diego : Academic Press, c2000.
*TC RC348 .G74 2000*

**NEUROLOGIC EXAMINATION.**
Green, Joanne. Neuropsychological evaluation of the
older adult. San Diego : Academic Press, c2000.
*TC RC348 .G74 2000*

**NEUROLOGIC MANIFESTATIONS OF
GENERAL DISEASES.** *See* **DELIRIUM.**

**The neurological assessment of the preterm and full-
term newborn infant.**
Dubowitz, Lilly M. S. 2nd ed. London : Mac Keith,
1999.
*TC RJ486 .D85 1999*

**NEUROLOGICAL SCIENCES.** *See*
**NEUROSCIENCES.**

**NEUROLOGY.** *See* **PEDIATRIC NEUROLOGY;
PSYCHOLOGY, PATHOLOGICAL.**

**NEUROLOGY, BEHAVIORAL.** *See* **CLINICAL
NEUROPSYCHOLOGY.**

**NEUROLOGY - POPULAR WORKS.**
Ramachandran, V. S. Phantoms in the brain. 1st ed.
New York : William Morrow, c1998.
*TC RC351 .R24 1998*

**Neuronal bases and psychological aspects of
consciousness.**
International School of Biocybernetics (1997 : Naples,
Italy) Singapore ; River Edge, N.J : World Scientific,
c1999.
*TC QP411 .I56 1997*

**Neuronal control of locomotion.**
Orlovsky, G. N. (Grigoriĭ Nikolaevich) Oxford ; New
York : Oxford University Press, 1999.
*TC QP303 .O75 1999*

**Neurophysiological basis of movement.**
Latash, Mark L., 1953- Champaign, IL : Human
Kinetics, c1998.
*TC QP301 .L364 1998*

**NEUROPHYSIOLOGY.** *See also*
**DEVELOPMENTAL NEUROPHYSIOLOGY;
SENSES AND SENSATION.**
Latash, Mark L., 1953- Neurophysiological basis of
movement. Champaign, IL : Human Kinetics, c1998.
*TC QP301 .L364 1998*

The neurocognition of language. Oxford ; New York :
Oxford University Press, 1999.
*TC QP399 .N483 1999*

Webster, Douglas B., 1934- Neuroscience of
communication. 2nd ed. San Diego : Singular
Publishing Group, c1999.
*TC QP355.2 .W43 1999*

**NEUROPSYCHIATRY.** *See* **NEUROLOGY.**

**Neuropsychological assessment in clinical practice :** a
guide to test interpretation and integration / [edited by]
Gary Groth-Marnat. New York : Wiley, c2000. xvi,
653 p. ; 26 cm. Includes bibliographical references and index.
ISBN 0-471-19325-9 (cloth : alk. paper) DDC 616.8/0475
*1. Neuropsychological Tests. 2. Neuropsychological tests. I.
Groth-Marnat, Gary.*
*TC RC386.6.N48 N474 2000*

**NEUROPSYCHOLOGICAL TESTS.**
Bell, Lisa M. Frontal lobe dysfunction in first episode
Schizophrenia. 1998.
*TC O85 B3995*

Clinician's guide to neuropsychological assessment.
2nd ed. Mahwah, N.J. : Lawrence Erlbaum
Associates, c2000.

*TC RC386.6.N48 G85 2000*

**NEUROPSYCHOLOGICAL TESTS.**
Clinician's guide to neuropsychological assessment.
2nd ed. Mahwah, N.J. : Lawrence Erlbaum
Associates, c2000.
*TC RC386.6.N48 G85 2000*

International handbook of neuropsychological
rehabilitation. New York : Kluwer Academic/Plenum
Publishers, c2000.
*TC RC387.5 .I478 2000*

Neuropsychological assessment in clinical practice.
New York : Wiley, c2000.
*TC RC386.6.N48 N474 2000*

**NEUROPSYCHOLOGICAL TESTS.**
Neuropsychological assessment in clinical practice.
New York : Wiley, c2000.
*TC RC386.6.N48 N474 2000*

Practitioner's guide to evaluating change with
neuropsychological assessment instruments. New
York : Kluwer Academic/Plenum Publishers, c2000.
*TC RC386.6.N48 P73 2000*

**NEUROPSYCHOLOGICAL TESTS.**
Practitioner's guide to evaluating change with
neuropsychological assessment instruments. New
York : Kluwer Academic/Plenum Publishers, c2000.
*TC RC386.6.N48 P73 2000*

**NEUROPSYCHOLOGY.** *See also* **CLINICAL
NEUROPSYCHOLOGY; COGNITIVE
NEUROSCIENCE.**
Berthoz, A. [Sens du Mouvement. English] The
brain's sense of movement. Cambridge, Mass. :
Harvard University Press, 2000.
*TC QP493 .B47 2000*

Case studies in the neuropsychology of reading. Hove,
East Sussex : Psychology Press, c2000.
*TC RC394.W6 .C37 2000*

Glynn, Ian. An anatomy of thought. Oxford ; New
York : Oxford University Press, [1999].
*TC QP360 .G595 1999*

Grigsby, Jim. Neurodynamics of personality. New
York : Guilford Press, 2000.
*TC BF698.9.B5 G741 2000*

Grigsby, Jim. Neurodynamics of personality. New
York : Guilford Press, 2000.
*TC BF698.9.B5 G741 2000*

Hobson, J. Allan, 1933- [Chemistry of conscious
states] Dreaming as delirium. 1st MIT Press ed.
Cambridge, Mass. : MIT Press, 1999.
*TC QP426 .H629 1999*

Learning. Berlin ; New York : Walter de Gruyter,
1999.
*TC QP408 .L44 1999*

Shore, Rima. Rethinking the brain. New York :
Families and Work Institute, c1997.
*TC RJ486.5 .S475 1997*

**Neuropsychology and cognition**
(16) Dyslexia. Dordrecht ; Boston, Mass : Kluwer
Academic, 1999.
*TC RC394 .D9525 1999*

(17) Learning to read. Dordrecht ; Boston : Kluwer
Academic Publishers, 1999.
*TC LB1050.2 .L42 1999*

**NEUROPSYCHOLOGY - CONGRESSES.**
International School of Biocybernetics (1997 : Naples,
Italy) Neuronal bases and psychological aspects of
consiousness. Singapore ; River Edge, N.J : World
Scientific, c1999.
*TC QP411 .I56 1997*

**NEUROPSYCHOLOGY - METHODS.**
Clinician's guide to neuropsychological assessment.
2nd ed. Mahwah, N.J. : Lawrence Erlbaum
Associates, c2000.
*TC RC386.6.N48 G85 2000*

Practitioner's guide to evaluating change with
neuropsychological assessment instruments. New
York : Kluwer Academic/Plenum Publishers, c2000.
*TC RC386.6.N48 P73 2000*

**NEUROSCIENCE.** *See* **NEUROSCIENCES.**

**NEUROSCIENCE - HISTORY.**
Concepts of Alzheimer disease. Baltimore, Md. ;
London : Johns Hopkins University Press, 2000.
*TC RC523 .C657 2000*

**Neuroscience of communication.**
Webster, Douglas B., 1934- 2nd ed. San Diego :
Singular Publishing Group, c1999.

*TC QP355.2 .W43 1999*

**NEUROSCIENCES.**
Dowling, John E. Creating mind. 1st ed. New York :
W.W. Norton, c1998.
*TC QP376 .D695 1998*

Webster, Douglas B., 1934- Neuroscience of
communication. 2nd ed. San Diego : Singular
Publishing Group, c1999.
*TC QP355.2 .W43 1999*

**NEUROSCIENCES COGNITIVES - CONGRÈS.**
Cognitive neuroscience of memory. Seattle ; Toronto :
Hogrefe & Huber, c1999.
*TC QP406 .C63 1999*

**NEUROSCIENCES - HISTORY.**
Finger, Stanley. Minds behind the brain. Oxford ;
New York : Oxford University Press, 2000.
*TC QP353 .F549 2000*

**NEUROSCIENCES - POPULAR WORKS.**
Horgan, John, 1953- The undiscovered mind. New
York : Free Press, c1999.
*TC RC343 .H636 1999*

Ramachandran, V. S. Phantoms in the brain. 1st ed.
New York : William Morrow, c1998.
*TC RC351 .R24 1998*

**NEUROSES.** *See also* **ANXIETY; DEPRESSION,
MENTAL; OBSESSIVE-COMPULSIVE
DISORDER; PHOBIAS.**
Wexberg, Erwin, 1889- Individual psychology, New
York, Cosmopolitan Book Corporation, 1929.
*TC BF175 .W48*

**NEUROSES - DIAGNOSIS.** *See also*
**PERSONALITY TESTS.**
Neurotic, stress-related, and somatoform disorders
[videorecording]. Princeton, N.J. : Films for the
Humanities & Sciences, 1998.
*TC RC530 .N4 1998*

**NEUROSES - PATIENTS.**
Neurotic, stress-related, and somatoform disorders
[videorecording]. Princeton, N.J. : Films for the
Humanities & Sciences, 1998.
*TC RC530 .N4 1998*

**NEUROSES - TREATMENT.**
Wurmser, Leon. [Flucht vor dem Gewissen. English]
The power of the inner judge. Northvale, N.J. : Jason
Aronson Inc., c2000.
*TC RC530 .W8713 2000*

**NEUROSIS.** *See* **NEUROSES.**

**NEUROSURGERY - IN INFANCY &
CHILDHOOD - PERIODICALS.**
Child's brain. Basel, New York, Karger.

**NEUROTIC DISORDERS.** *See* **NEUROSES.**

**NEUROTIC DISORDERS - THERAPY.**
Wurmser, Leon. [Flucht vor dem Gewissen. English]
The power of the inner judge. Northvale, N.J. : Jason
Aronson Inc., c2000.
*TC RC530 .W8713 2000*

**Neurotic, stress-related, and somatoform disorders**
[videorecording] / a presentation of Films for the
Humanities & Sciences ; University of Sheffield ;
produced and directed by Steve Collier ; written by
Dr. Steve Peters : Sheffield University Television.
Princeton, N.J. : Films for the Humanities & Sciences,
1998. 1 videocassette (46 min.) : sd., col. ; 1/2 in. (Differential
diagnosis in psychiatry) VHS. Catalogued from credits and
container. Commentary: John Graham Davies. Sound: Ken
Hardy; cameras: Jackie Jones, Mark Parkin, Gary Wraith;
graphics: Sean Purcell. Series subtitle: A visual aid based on
ICD 10. Originally produced 1995-1997 at the University of
Sheffield. "Clinical features of myotonic dystrophy and
Huntington's disease" included in list of complete series on
container no longer part of series. For students of psychiatry,
clinical psychology and social work, and counselling.
SUMMARY: "This program discusses the following disorders
and their differential diagnoses: phobic anxiety; anxiety;
obsessive-compulsive disorder, from minor to acute; stress
reactions and adjustment; and dissociative disorders. Sub-
disorders discussed include Korsakov's syndrome; agoraphobia
and social phobia; generalized anxiety and mixed-anxiety-and-
depressive disorder; panic disorder; and post-traumatic stress
syndrome. Patients suffering from each disorder exhibit the
various symptoms in interviews conducted by psychiatrists."--
Container.
*1. Phobias - Diagnosis. 2. Agoraphobia - Diagnosis. 3.
Agoraphobia - Patients. 4. Post-traumatic stress disorder -
Diagnosis. 5. Post-traumatic stress disorder - Patients. 6.
Obsessive-compulsive disorder - Diagnosis. 7. Obsessive-
compulsive disorder - Patients. 8. Panic disorders - Diagnosis.
9. Panic disorders - Patients. 10. Dissociative disorders -
Patients. 11. Dissociative disorders - Diagnosis. 12.*

*Somataform disorder - Diagnosis.* 13. *Somataform disorder - Patients.* 14. *Anxiety.* 15. *Neuroses - Diagnosis.* 16. *Neuroses - Patients.* 17. *Diagnosis, Differential.* I. *Peters, Steve, Dr.* II. *Collier, Steve.* III. *Davies, John Graham.* IV. *University of Sheffield.* V. *Films for the Humanities (Firm)* VI. *Series.*
*TC RC530 .N4 1998*

**NEUROTRANSMITTERS.** *See* **DOPAMINE.**

**Neusner, Jacob, 1932-** Reaffirming higher education / Jacob Neusner & Noam M.M. Neusner ; with an epilogue by William Scott Green. New Brunswick, U.S.A. : Transaction Publishers, c2000. xii, 209 p. ; 24 cm. Includes bibliographical references (p. 201-205) and index. ISBN 1-56000-425-8 (alk. paper) DDC 378.73
1. *Education, Higher - Aims and objectives - United States.* 2. *Universities and colleges - United States.* I. *Neusner, Noam M. M. (Noam Mordecai Menahem)* II. *Title.*
*TC LA227.4 .N47 2000*

**Neusner, Noam M. M. (Noam Mordecai Menahem).** Neusner, Jacob, 1932- Reaffirming higher education. New Brunswick, U.S.A. : Transaction Publishers, c2000.
*TC LA227.4 .N47 2000*

**Nevas, Debra Baron.** Factors affecting parental attitudes toward a child's therapist and therapy / Debra Baron Nevas. 1997. ix, 214 leaves ; 29 cm. Issued also on microfilm. Thesis (Ph.D.)--Columbia University, 1997. Includes bibliographical references (leaves 172-177).
1. *Child psychotherapy.* 2. *Child psychotherapy - Parent participation.* 3. *Parent and child.* 4. *Parents - Attitudes.* 5. *Psychotherapists - Attitudes.* 6. *Interpersonal relations.* I. *Title.*
*TC 085 N401*

**Nevelson in process** [videorecording] / a film by Susan Fanshel and Jill Godmilow ; a production of WNET/ 13 ; [directed by Susan Fanshel and Jill Godmilow]. Chicago, IL : Public Media Inc., 1977. 1 videocassette (VHS) (30 min.) : sd., col. with b&w sequences, 1/2 in. (Portrait of an artist) (Women in art) Title on container: Nevelson [videoreocording]. At head of title: Home Vision... presents... [videorecording]. VHS. Catalogued from credits and container and cassette label. Photographer, Jeri Sopanen; music by Robert Dennis ; sound by Phil Gleason ; edited by Jill Godmilow and Susan Fanshel. "NEV 010"--Container. "A Public Media Incorporated Release."--Container. For high school through adult. SUMMARY: Contrasts sculptor Louise Nevelson's public and private lives, demonstrates her technique of creating pieces out of discarded wood, and offers her thoughts on her work. Nevelson creates her special environmental art on camera. ISBN 0-7800-1337-9
1. *Nevelson, Louise, - 1899-1988.* 2. *Women sculptors - United States - Biography.* 3. *Sculptors - United States - Biography.* 4. *Sculpture, Modern - 20th century - United States.* 5. *Art, Modern - 20th century - United States.* 6. *Documentary films.* 7. *Biographical films.* I. *Nevelson, Louise, 1899-1988.* II. *Fanshel, Susan.* III. *Godmillow, Jill.* IV. *WNET (Television station : New York, N.Y.)* V. *Public Media Incorporated (Wilmette, Ill.)* VI. *Home Vision (Firm)* VII. *Title: Nevelson [videoreocording]* VIII. *Title: Home Vision... presents... [videorecording]* IX. *Series.* X. *Series: Women in art*
*TC NB237.N43 N43 1977*

**Nevelson, Louise, 1899-1988.** Nevelson in process [videorecording]. Chicago, IL : Public Media Inc., 1977.
*TC NB237.N43 N43 1977*

**NEVELSON, LOUISE, 1899-1988.** Nevelson in process [videorecording]. Chicago, IL : Public Media Inc., 1977.
*TC NB237.N43 N43 1977*

**Nevelson [videoreocording].** Nevelson in process [videorecording]. Chicago, IL : Public Media Inc., 1977.
*TC NB237.N43 N43 1977*

**Never too young to know.** Silverman, Phyllis R. New York : Oxford University Press, 2000.
*TC BF723.D3 S58 2000*

**Nevin, Ann.** Idol, Lorna. Collaborative consultation. 3rd ed. Austin, Tex. : PRO-ED, c2000.
*TC LC4019 .I35 2000*

**New accents (Routledge (Firm))** Ong, Walter J. Orality and literacy. London ; New York : Routledge, 1988.
*TC P35 .O5 1988*

**New Age Video (Firm).** Ballet class [videorecording]. W. Long Branch, NJ : Kultur, c1984.
*TC GV1589 .B33 1984*

**The new American high school** / David D. Marsh, Judy B. Codding and Associates. Thousand Oaks, Calif. : Corwin Press, c1999. xxi, 218 p. : ill. ; 24 cm. Includes

bibliographical references (p. 201-209) and index. CONTENTS: Just passing through : the life of an American high school / Judy B. Codding and Robert Rothman -- How did we get here, and where should we be going? / Marc S. Tucker -- Standards and assessment : the foundation of high school achievement / Robert Rothman -- Rethinking curriculum and instruction in the new American high school / David D. Marsh and Phillip Daro -- Standards-based classrooms in high schools : an illustration / Sally Hampton -- Beyond the CIM : pathways to the future / Jacqueline Kraemer, John Porter, and Marc S. Tucker -- A new high school design focused on student performance / Judy B. Codding and Marc S Tucker -- District redesign : direction, support, and accountality for standards-based high schools / David D. Marsh and Michael Strembitsky -- Some tough choices ahead / David D. Marsh. ISBN 0-8039-6225-8 (cloth : acid-free paper) ISBN 0-8039-6226-6 (pbk. : acid-free paper) DDC 373.73
1. *High schools - United States.* 2. *Educational change - United States.* 3. *Education, Secondary - United States - Administration.* 4. *Education, Secondary - United States - Curricula.* I. *Marsh, David D.* II. *Codding, Judy B., 1944-*
*TC LA222 .N49 1999*

**NEW AMERICAN SCHOOLS (ORGANIZATION).** Berends, Mark, 1962- Assessing the progress of New American Schools. Santa Monica, CA : RAND, 1999.
*TC LB2822.82 .B45 1999*

**New Americans (Westport, Conn.)** Gonzalez-Pando, Miguel. The Cuban Americans. Westport, Conn. : Greenwood Press, 1998.
*TC E184.C97 G64 1998*

Hurh, Won Moo. The Korean Americans. Westport, Conn. : Greenwood Press, c1998.
*TC E184.K6 H875 1998*

Ng, Franklin, 1947- The Taiwanese Americans. Westport, Conn. : Greenwood Press, 1998.
*TC E184.T35 N45 1998*

Torres-Saillant, Silvio. The Dominican Americans. Westport, Conn. : Greenwood Press, 1998.
*TC E184.D6 T67 1998*

**New choices in public education [videorecording].** Public charter schools : new choices in public education (May 3, 2000 : Washington, D.C.) Public charter schools [videorecording]. [Washington, D.C.] : U.S. Dept. of Education, [2000].
*TC LB2806.36 .P9 2000*

**The new class society.** Perrucci, Robert. Lanham, Md. : Rowman & Littlefield, 1999.
*TC HN90.S6 P47 1999*

**The new complete book of food.** Rinzler, Carol Ann. New York : Facts on File, c1999.
*TC TX353 .R525 1999*

**NEW CRITICISM.** Young, R. V., 1947- At war with the word. Wilmington, Del. : ISI Books, 1999.
*TC PN94 .Y68 1999*

**New Day Films.** The Choice of a lifetime [videorecording]. Hohokus, NJ : New Day Films, c1996.
*TC RC569 .C45 1996*

**NEW DEAL, 1933-1939.** Kalfatovic, Martin R., 1961- The New Deal fine arts projects. Metuchen, N.J. : Scarecrow Press, 1994.
*TC Z5961.U5 K36 1994*

**The New Deal fine arts projects.** Kalfatovic, Martin R., 1961- Metuchen, N.J. : Scarecrow Press, 1994.
*TC Z5961.U5 K36 1994*

**New democracy forum.** Will standards save public education? Boston : Beacon Press, c2000.
*TC LB3060.83 .W55 2000*

**New directions for adult and continuing education** (. no. 85) Addressing the spiritual dimensions of adult learning :. San Francisco : Jossey Bass, 2000.
*TC LC5219 .A25 2000*

(no. 82) Providing culturally relevant adult education. San Francisco : Jossey Bass, c1999.
*TC LC5219 .P76 1999*

(no. 83) The welfare-to-work challenge for adult literacy educators. San Francisco, CA : Jossey-Bass Publishers, 1999.
*TC LC149.7 .W43 1999*

(no.86) Charting a course for continuing professional education :. San Francisco : Jossey-Bass, c2000.

*TC LC1072.C56 C55 2000*

**New directions for adult continuing education** (no.84) An update on adult development theory :. San Francisco, CA : Jossey-Bass Publishers, 1999.
*TC LC5225.L42 U63 1999*

**New directions for child and adolescent development** (no. 87) Variability in the social construction of the child. San Francisco : Jossey-Bass, 2000.
*TC BF723.S62 .V37 2000*

(no. 88) Recent advances in the measurement of acceptance and rejection in the peer system. San Francisco : Jossey-Bass Publishers, c2000.
*TC BF723.165 R4 2000*

(no. 89) Rights and wrongs. San Francisco, [CA] : Jossey-Bass, c2000.
*TC BF723.M54 L38 2000*

(no.85) Homeless and working youth around the world. San Francisco : Jossey-Bass, 1999.
*TC HV4493 .H655 1999*

**New directions for community colleges** (no. 108.) Trends in community college curriculum. San Francisco : Jossey-Bass, c1999.
*TC LB2328.15.U6 T75 1999*

(no. 109.) Dimensions of managing academic affairs in the community college. San Francisco : Jossey-Bass, 2000.
*TC LB2341 .D56 2000*

(no.107) Gateways to democracy. San Francisco : Jossey-Bass, 1999.
*TC LB2328.N53 1999*

**New directions for education** (no. 86) How and why language matters in evaluation. San Francisco, CA : Jossey-Bass, c2000.
*TC H62 .H67 2000*

**New directions for evaluation** (no. 84.) Information technologies in evaluation. San Francisco, Calif. : Jossey-Bass, 1999.
*TC H62 .I54 1999*

(no.85) Evaluation as a democratic process. San Francisco, CA : Jossey-Bass, c2000.
*TC LB2806 .E79 2000*

**New directions for higher and adult education series.** How technology is changing institutional research. San Francisco, Calif. : Jossey-Bass Publishers, c1999.
*TC LB2326.3 .H69 1999*

**New directions for higher education** (no. 108.) Promising practices in recruitment, remediation, and retention. San Francisco, Calif. : Jossey-Bass, c1999.
*TC LB2331.72 .N48 1999*

(no. 109.) Involving commuter students in learning. San Francisco, Calif. : Jossey-Bass, 2000.
*TC LB2343.6 .I68 2000*

(no. 110.) Moving beyond the gap between research and practice in higher education. San Francisco, Calif. : Jossey-Bass, c2000.
*TC LA227.4 .M68 2000*

(no. 111) Understanding the work and career paths of midlevel administrators. San Francisco : Jossey-Bass, 2000.
*TC LB2341 .N5111 2000*

**New directions for institutional research** (no. 104.) What is institutional research all about ? San Francisco, Calif. : Jossey-Bass Publishers, c1999.
*TC LB2326.3 .W43 1999*

(no. 105) What contributes to job satisfaction among faculty and staff. San Francisco, Calif. : Jossey-Bass Publishers, c2000.
*TC LB2331.7 .W45 2000*

(v.103.) How technology is changing institutional research. San Francisco, Calif. : Jossey-Bass Publishers, c1999.
*TC LB2326.3 .H69 1999*

**New directions for program evaluation** (no. 5) Utilization of evaluative information. San Francisco : Jossey-Bass, 1980.
*TC H62.5.U5 U86*

**New directions for school leadership** (no. 11.) Reflections of first-year teachers on school culture. San Francisco : Jossey-Bass Inc., 1999.
*TC LB2844.1.N4 R44 1999*

(no. 12) Partners in progress. San Francisco, Calif. : Jossey-Bass Inc., c1999.

*TC LC3981 .P27 1999*

**New directions for student services**
(no. 87.) Creating successful partnerships between academic and student affairs. San Francisco : Jossey-Bass Publishers, 1999.
*TC LB2342.9 .C75 1999*

(no. 88) Love, Patrick G. Understanding and applying cognitive development theory. San Francisco : Jossey-Bass, c1999.
*TC LB2343 .L65 1999*

(no. 89.) The role student aid plays in enrollment management. San Francisco : Jossey-Bass Publishers, 2000.
*TC LB2337.4 .R655 2000*

(no. 90) Powerful programming for student learning. San Francisco : Jossey-Bass, c2000.
*TC LB2343 .P643 2000*

**New directions for teaching and learning**
(. no. 81) Strategies for energizing large classes : from small groups to learning communities. San Francisco, Calif. : Jossey-Bass, 2000.
*TC LB2361.5 .S77 2000*

(no. 79.) Using consultants to improve teaching. San Francisco : Jossey-Bass, c1999.
*TC LB2799.2 .U83 1999*

(no. 81) Strategies for energizing large classes : from small groups to learning communities. San Francisco, Calif. : Jossey-Bass, 2000.
*TC LB2361.5 .S77 2000*

**New directions for teaching and learning**
(no. 82) Teaching to promote intellectual and personal maturity :. San Francisco : Jossey-Bass, c2000.
*TC LB1060 .T43 2000*

**New directions for teaching and learning**
(no.80) Teaching and learning on the edge of the millennium :. San Francisco : Jossey-Bass, c1999.
*TC LB2331 .T35 1999*

**New directions in computers and composition studies**
Coogan, David. Electronic writing centers. Stamford, Conn. : Ablex Pub. Corp., c1999.
*TC PE1404 .C6347 1999*

**New Directions in computers and composition studies.**
Feminist cyberscapes. Stamford, Conn. : Ablex Pub., c1999.
*TC PE1404 .F39 1999*

**New directions in computers and composition studies.**
Transitions. Greenwich, Conn. : Ablex Pub. Corp., c1998.
*TC PE1404 .T74 1998*

**New directions in language development and disorders** / edited by Michael Perkins and Sara Howard. New York : Kluwer Academic/Plenum Publishers, c2000. xi, 303 p. : ill. ; 26 cm. Collection of selected papers presented at the 1998 Child Language Seminar held at the University of Sheffield. Cf. Pref. Includes bibliographical references and index. ISBN 0-306-46284-2 DDC 401/.93
*1. Language acquisition - Congresses. 2. Language disorders - Congresses. I. Perkins, Michael. II. Howard, Sara. III. Child Language Seminar (1998 : University of Sheffield)*
*TC P118 .N49 2000*

**New directions in mentoring :** creating a culture of synergy / edited by Carol A. Mullen and Dale W. Lick. London ; New York : Falmer, 1999. xv, 271 p. ; 24 cm. Includes bibliographical references and index. ISBN 0-7507-1010-1 ISBN 0-7507-1011-X (pbk) DDC 371.102
*1. Mentoring in education. I. Lick, Dale W. II. Mullen, Carol A.*
*TC LB1731.4 .N49 1999*

**New directions in transactional analysis counselling.**
Midgley, David. London ; New York : Free Association Books, 1999.
*TC RC489.T7M535 1999*

**New directions institutional research**
(no. 106) Analyzing costs in higher education. San Francisco, Calif. : Jossey-Bass, c2000.
*TC LB2342 .A68 2000*

**The new economics.**
Deming, W. Edwards (William Edwards), 1900- 2nd ed. Cambridge, Mass. ; London : MIT Press, 2000.
*TC HD62.15 .D46 2000*

**NEW ENGLAND - FICTION.**
Wiggin, Kate Douglas Smith, 1856-1923. Rebecca of Sunnybrook Farm. Boston, New York [etc.] :

Houghton, Mifflin Company, [c1903] (Cambridge, Mass. : Riverside Press)
*TC PZ7.W638 Re 1903*

**New feminist perspectives series**
Embodying bioethics. Lanham : Rowman & Littlefield Publishers, c1999.
*TC QH332 .E43 1999*

**New forum books**
Glenn, Charles Leslie, 1938- The ambiguous embrace. Princeton, N.J. : Princeton University Press, c2000.
*TC HV95 .G54 2000*

Novak, David, 1941- Covenantal rights. Princeton, N.J. : Princeton University Press, 2000.
*TC KC3 .N68 2000*

**New French thought**
Gauchet, Marcel. [La pratique de l'esprit humain. English] Madness and democracy. Princeton, N.J. : Princeton University Press, c1999.
*TC RC439 .G2813 1999*

**New Hampshire educator.**
The Bulletin of the New Hampshire State Teachers' Association. [Manchester, N.H.] : The Association, [1946]

**New Hampshire State Teachers' Association.**
The Bulletin of the New Hampshire State Teachers' Association. [Manchester, N.H.] : The Association, [1946]

**New high school high [videorecording].**
Heroin [videorecording]. [Princeton, N.J.] : Films for the Humanities & Sciences, c1998.
*TC HV5822.H4 H4 1998*

**A new history of Ireland** / edited by T.W. Moody, F.X. Martin, F.J. Byrne. Oxford [England] : Clarendon Press ; New York : Oxford University Press, <1976-1986 > v. <6,> : ill. ; 24 cm. Vol. 2 edited by Art Cosgrove; v. 5-6 by W.E. Vaughan. Includes bibliographies and indexes. PARTIAL CONTENTS: -- v. 2. Ireland under the Union, II, 1870-1921 ISBN 0-19-821739-0 (v. 3) ISBN 0-19-821751-X (v. 6 : acid-free paper) DDC 941.5
*1. Ireland - History. I. Moody, T. W. (Theodore William), 1907- II. Martin, F.X. (Francis X.) III. Byrne, F. J. (Francis John), 1934- IV. Cosgrove, Art.*
*TC DA912 .N48*

**New horizons in English, [workbooks].**
Mellgren, Lars. Reading, Mass. : Addison-Wesley Pub. Co., 1973-c1978.
*TC PE1128 .M38*

**New horizons in the economics of innovation**
Geuna, Aldo, 1965- The economics of knowledge production. Cheltenham, UK ; Northampton, MA : E. Elgar, c1999.
*TC Q180.E9 G48 1999*

**The new idea factory.**
Gross, Clifford M. Columbus, OH : Battelle Press, c2000.
*TC HD53 .G75 2000*

**New immigrants in the United States :** readings for second language education / [compiled by] Sandra Lee McKay, Sau-ling Cynthia Wong. Cambridge, U.K. : New York : Cambridge University Press, 2000. x, 461 p. ; 23 cm. (Cambridge language teaching library) ISBN 0-521-66087-4 ISBN 0-521-66798-4 (pbk.) DDC 428/.007
*1. English language - Textbooks for foreign speakers. 2. United States - Emigration and immigration - Problems, exercises, etc. 3. Immigrants - United States - Problems, exercises, etc. 4. Readers - Emigration and immigration. 5. Readers - Immigrants. I. McKay, Sandra. II. Wong, Sau-ling Cynthia. III. Series.*
*TC PE1128 .N384 1999*

**NEW INTERNATIONAL ECONOMIC ORDER.** *See* **INTERNATIONAL ECONOMIC RELATIONS.**

**NEW JERSEY - FICTION.**
Karr, Kathleen. Man of the family. 1st ed. New York : Farrar, Straus and Giroux, 1999.
*TC PZ7.K149 Man 1999*

**New Jersey school directory.**
MDR's school directory. New Jersey. Shelton, CT : Market Data Retrieval, c1995-
*TC L903.N5 M37*

**New labour's policies for schools :** raising the standard? London : David Fulton Publishers, c2000. xiii, 210 p. ; 25 cm. ISBN 1-85346-611-5 DDC 379.4
*1. Education and state - England. I. Docking, Jim.*
*TC LC93.G7 N59 2000*

**The new leadership challenge.**
Grossman, Sheila. Philadelphia : F.A. Davis, c2000.

*TC RT89 .G77 2000*

**New library of psychoanalysis**
(12) Segal, Hanna. Dream, phantasy, and art. London ; New York : Tavistock/Routledge, 1991.
*TC BF1078 .S375 1991*

**NEW LITERATES AND LIBRARIES.** *See* **LIBRARIES AND NEW LITERATES.**

**New London Group.**
Multiliteracies. London ; New York : Routledge, 2000.
*TC LC149 .M85 2000*

**The new media literacy handbook.**
Brunner, Cornelia, Dr. New York : Anchor Books, 1999.
*TC LB1028.3 .B77 1999*

**New millennium series**
Special education re-formed. London ; New York : Falmer Press, 2000.
*TC LC1203.G7 S72 1999*

**The new Oxford book of food plants.**
Vaughan, J. G. (John Griffith) Oxford ; New York : Oxford University Press, 1997.
*TC SB175 .V38 1997*

**The New painting :** impressionism 1874-1886 : documentation / [edited by] Ruth Berson. San Francisco, CA : Fine Arts Museums of San Francisco, c1996. 2 v. : ill. ; 29 cm. English and French. The exhibition catalogue "The New Painting: Impressionism, 1874-1886" published in 1986. CONTENTS: v. 1. Reviews -- v. 2. Exhibited works. ISBN 0-295-96704-8 DDC 759.4/074/44361
*1. Impressionism (Art) - France - Exhibitions. 2. Painting, French - Exhibitions. 3. Painting, Modern - 19th century - France - Exhibitions. 4. Art criticism - France - History - 19th century. I. Berson, Ruth. II. Fine Arts Museums of San Francisco.*
*TC ND547.5.I4 N38 1996*

**New perspectives on conceptual change** / edited by Wolfgang Schnotz, Stella Vosniadou and Mario Carretero. 1st ed. Amsterdam ; New York : Oxford : Pergamon, 1999. xxiv, 322 p. : ill. ; 25 cm. (Advances in learning and instruction series) "Earli." Includes bibliographical references (p. 283-314) and indexes. ISBN 0-08-043455-X DDC 370.15/23
*1. Concept learning. 2. Learning, Psychology of. 3. Knowledge, Theory of. I. Schnotz, Wolfgang, 1946- II. Vosniadou, Stella. III. Carretero, Mario. IV. European Association for Research on Learning and Instruction. V. Series.*
*TC LB1062 .N49 1999*

**The new Presidential elite.**
Kirkpatrick, Jeane J. New York : Russell Sage Foundation : [distributed by Basic Books], c1976.
*TC JK1764 .K57*

**The new public health.**
Tulchinsky, Theodore H. San Diego, Calif. ; London : Academic Press, c2000.
*TC RA425 .T85 2000*

**The new rational manager.**
Kepner, Charles Higgins, 1922- Princeton, N.J. (P.O. Box 704, Research Rd., Princeton 08540) : Princeton Research Press, c1981.
*TC HD31 .K456 1981*

**NEW RIGHT.** *See* **CONSERVATISM.**

**New school order** [videorecording] / produced & directed by Gini Reticker ; associate producer/writer, Libby McDonald. New York : First Run/Icarus Films, 1996. 1 videocassette (56 min.) : sd., col. ; 1/2 in. VHS. Cataloged from credits and container. Closed captioned. "A Constant Communications production." Editor, Kristen Huntley; photography, Joseph Friedman; sound editor, Margaret Crimmins, Paul Hsu; sound, Jeffrey Livesey, David Gladstone. For educators, parents of school children, and those interested in school boards and their political aspects. SUMMARY: Captures the dilemma of young families moving to suburban communities facing hostile confrontations with fiscally and socially conservative school boards in the battle over who should control schools and children's education. Documents the nine-month ordeal in the North Penn School District near Philadelphia, Pennsylvania, in which the Taxpayer's Association and Christian conservatives joined to create a powerful voting block, pitting conservatives against liberals and religious leaders against one another.
*1. School boards - Political aspects - United States. 2. Education - Social aspects - United States. 3. Education - Political aspects - United States. 4. Education - Finance - Law and legislation - United States. 5. Education and state - United States. 6. Church and education - United States. 7. Christianity and politics - United States. 8. Fundamentalism - Political aspects - United States. 9. Suburban schools - United States. 10. Video recordings for the hearing impaired. I. Reticker,*

Gini. II. McDonald, Libby. III. *Constant Communications Productions.* IV. *First Run/Icarus Films.*
*TC LB2831.583.P4 N4 1996*

**The new structure of school improvement.**
Joyce, Bruce R. Buckingham [England] ;
Philadelphia : Open University Press, 1999.
*TC LB2822.84.G7 J69 1999*

**New studies in aesthetics**
(vol. 30) Fleming, Bruce. Sex, art, and audience.
New York ; Canterbury [England] : P. Lang, c2000.
*TC GV1588.3 .F54 2000*

**[New studies in social policy]**
(1.) Lieberman, Myron, 1919- Understanding the
teacher union contract. New Brunswick, N.J. :
Social Philosophy and Policy Foundation :
Transaction Publishers, 2000.
*TC KF3409.T4 L54 2000*

**NEW SUPER-REALISM.** *See* **POP ART.**

**NEW TEACHERS.** *See* **FIRST YEAR TEACHERS.**

**New technologies for social research**
Popping, Roel. Computer-assisted text analysis.
Thousand Oaks, Calif. ; London : SAGE, c2000.
*TC P302 .P636 2000*

**New therapeutic indications of antidepressants /**
volume editors, J. Mendlewicz, N. Brunello, L.L.
Judd. Basel ; New York : Karger, c1997. vi, 138 p. : ill. ;
25 cm. (International Academy for Biomedical and Drug
Research ; vol. 12) Includes bibliographical references and
indexes. ISBN 3-8055-6436-8 (hardcover : acid-free paper)
DDC 616.85/27061
*1. Antidepressants. 2. Antidepressive Agents - therapeutic use.
3. Antidepressive Agents - pharmacology. I. Mendlewicz, J.
(Julien) II. Brunello, Nicoletta. III. Judd, Lewis L. IV. Series:
International Academy for Biomedical and Drug Research
(Series) ; vol. 12.*
*TC RM332 .N475 1997*

**NEW THOUGHT - HISTORY.**
Satter, Beryl, 1959- Each mind a kingdom. Berkeley :
University of California Press, c1999.
*TC BF639 .S124 1999*

**New traditions from Nigeria.**
Ottenberg, Simon. Washington, DC : Smithsonian
Institution Press, c1997.
*TC N7399.N52 N786 1997*

**New trends & issues in teaching Japanese**
**language & culture** / edited by Haruko M. Cook,
Kyoko Hijirida, Mildred Tahara. Honolulu ; Second
Language Teaching and Curriculum, University of
Hawai'i at Manoa, 1997. vii, 164 p. : ill. ; 25 cm.
(Technical Report ; #15) New trends and issues in teaching
Japanese language and culture. Includes bibliographical
references. CONTENTS: Beyond stereotype : teaching
Japanese culture through literature / Nobuko Miyama
Ochner -- A new look : the influence of vision technology on
narrative in Taishō / Elaine Gerbert -- Electronic networking
activities in Japanese language classrooms / Yukie Aida --
Psycholinguistic research on word identification in Japanese
Kanji : implications for JFL pedagogy / Hideko Shimizu --
Students' beliefs about learning Japanese orthography : beyond
the textbooks / Yoko Okita. CONTENTS: (Cont.) SPOT as a
placement test / Yukiko Abe Hatasa, Yasu-Hiko Tohsaku --
Cloze test performance of JSL learners and native first
graders / Sayoko Yamashita -- Situation-driven or structure-
driven? : teaching Japanese at the college level in the United
States / Naoya Fujita -- Developing pragmatic ability : insights
from the accelerated study of Japanese / Andrew D. Cohen.
ISBN 0-8248-2067-3
*1. Japanese language - Study and teaching (Higher) - United
States - English speakers. 2. Japanese literature - Study and
teaching (Higher) - United States. I. Cook, Haruko M. II.
Hijirida, Kyoko, 1937- III. Tahara, Mildred M., 1941- IV.
Title: New trends and issues in teaching Japanese language
and culture V. Series: Technical report (University of Hawaii
at Manoa. Second Language Teaching & Curriculum Center) ;
#15.*
*TC PL519 .N45 1997*

**New trends and issues in teaching Japanese language**
**and culture.**
New trends & issues in teaching Japanese language &
culture. Honolulu ; Second Language Teaching and
Curriculum, University of Hawai'i at Manoa, 1997.
*TC PL519 .N45 1997*

**New Video Group.**
The Irish in America [videorecording]. [New York,
N.Y.] : A&E Home Video ; New York, N.Y. :
Distributed by the New Video Group, 1997.
*TC E184.I6 I6 1997*

**New visions, new perspectives.**
Voigt, Anna. Roseville East, NSW : Craftsman
House, 1996.

*TC N7400.2 .V65 1996*

**New ways of thinking about the life course.**
An update on adult development theory :. San
Francisco, CA : Jossey-Bass Publishers, 1999.
*TC LC5225.L42 U63 1999*

**A new world of knowledge :** Canadian universities and
globalization / edited by Sheryl Bond and Jean-Pierre
Lemasson, Ottawa : International Development
Research Centre, c1999. xii, 294 p. : ill. ; 23 cm. Includes
bibliographical references: p. 283-294. Issued also in French
under title: Un nouveau monde du savoir. ISBN 0-88936-893-7
DDC 378/.016/0971
*1. International education - Canada. 2. Education, Higher -
Aims and objectives - Canada. 3. Universities and colleges -
Canada - International cooperation. 4. Éducation
internationale - Canada. 5. Enseignement supérieur -
Finalités - Canada. 6. Universités - Canada - Coopération
internationale. I. Bond, Sheryl. II. Lemasson, Jean-Pierre. III.
International Development Research Centre (Canada) IV.
Title: Canadian universities and globalization*
*TC LC1090 N38 1999*

**NEW YEAR - FICTION.**
Moeyaert, Bart. [Blote handen. English] Bare hands.
1st ed. Asheville, N.C. : Front Street, 1998.
*TC PZ7.M7227 Bar 1998*

**NEW YEAR'S DAY.** *See* **NEW YEAR.**

**New York 1880.**
Stern, Robert A. M. New York, N.Y. : Monacelli
Press, 1999.
*TC NA735.N5 S727 1999*

**New York before Chinatown.**
Tchen, John Kuo Wei. Baltimore : Johns Hopkins
University Press, 1999.
*TC DS706 .T4 1999*

**New York, Chicago, Los Angeles.**
Abu-Lughod, Janet L. Minneapolis : University of
Minnesota Press, c1999.
*TC HT123 .A613 1999*

**New York (N.Y.) Board of Education.**
High points in the work of the high schools of New
York City. New York City : Board of Education,
1931-1966.

[Nature study class, P.S. 165] [picture] 1935.
*TC BE5564*

[Nature study class, P.S. 165] [picture] 1935.
*TC BE5564*

[Nature study class, P.S. 165] [picture] 1935.
*TC BE5564*

**New York (N,Y.). Board of Education.**
Thompson, Melvin R. The implementation of
multicultural curricula in the New York City public
elementary schools. 1999.
*TC 06 no. 11186*

**NEW YORK (N.Y.) - BUILDINGS, STRUCTURES,**
**ETC.**
Stern, Robert A. M. New York 1880. New York,
N.Y. : Monacelli Press, 1999.
*TC NA735.N5 S727 1999*

**NEW YORK (N.Y.) - BUILDINGS, STRUCTURES,**
**ETC. - JUVENILE LITERATURE.**
Maestro, Betsy. The story of the Statue of Liberty.
New York : Lothrop, Lee & Shepard Books, 1986.
*TC NB553.B3 A75 1986*

**NEW YORK (N.Y.) - DIRECTORIES.**
The CARES directory in electronic form [computer
file] Maywood, NJ : ACIT,
*TC HV99.N59 S58*

**NEW YORK (N.Y.) - HISTORY.**
Abu-Lughod, Janet L. New York, Chicago, Los
Angeles. Minneapolis : University of Minnesota
Press, c1999.
*TC HT123 .A613 1999*

Harlem on my mind : cultural capital of Black
America, 1900-1968. New York : New Press :
Distributed by W.W. Norton & Co., c1995.
*TC F128.68.H3 S3 1995*

**NEW YORK (N.Y.) - HISTORY - 1775-1865.**
Tchen, John Kuo Wei. New York before Chinatown.
Baltimore : Johns Hopkins University Press, 1999.
*TC DS706 .T4 1999*

**NEW YORK (N.Y.) - HISTORY - 1865-1898.**
Tchen, John Kuo Wei. New York before Chinatown.
Baltimore : Johns Hopkins University Press, 1999.
*TC DS706 .T4 1999*

**New York (N.Y.). Human Resources Administration.**
The CARES directory in electronic form [computer
file] Maywood, NJ : ACIT,
*TC HV99.N59 S58*

**NEW YORK (N.Y.) - INTELLECTUAL LIFE -**
**SOURCES.**
Marks, Carole. The power of pride. 1st ed. New
York : Crown Publishers, c1999.
*TC E185.6 .M35 1999*

**NEW YORK (N.Y.) - LANGUAGES.**
The multilingual Apple. Berlin ; New York : Mouton
de Gruyter, 1997.
*TC P40.5.L56 M8 1997*

**NEW YORK (N.Y.) - PICTORIAL WORKS.**
Bernhardt, Debra E. Ordinary people, extraordinary
lives. New York : New York University Press, c2000.
*TC HD8085.N53 B47 2000*

**NEW YORK (N.Y.) - RACE RELATIONS -**
**HISTORY - 20TH CENTURY.**
Edgell, Derek. The movement for community control
of New York City's schools, 1966-1970. Lewiston,
N.Y. : E. Mellen Press, c1998.
*TC LB2862 .E35 1998*

**New York Public Library.**
The New York Public Library African American Desk
Reference. New york : Wiley, c1999.
*TC E185 .N487 1999*

**The New York Public Library African American**
**Desk Reference.** New york : Wiley, c1999. xiii, 606
p. : ill. ; 24 cm. At head of title: Schomburg Center for
Research in Black Culture "A Stonesong Press book." Includes
bibliographical references and index. ISBN 0-471-23924-0
*1. Afro-Americans - Encyclopedias. 2. Afro-Americans -
History - Encyclopedias. I. New York Public Library. II.
Schomburg Center for Research in Black Culture. III. Title:
Schomburg Center for Research in Black Culture.*
*TC E185 .N487 1999*

**The New York Public Library amazing mythology.**
January, Brendan, 1972- New York : Wiley, 2000.
*TC BL311 .J36 2000*

**New York public school administrators' business**
**directory.** Hackettstown, NJ : Kinsley Publications.
v. ; 22 cm. Frequency: Annual. 1972- .
*1. Schools - New York (State) - Directories. 2. Schools -
Furniture, equipment, etc. - Directories.*
*TC LB3280 .N4*

**New York school directory.**
MDR's school directory. New York. Shelton, CT :
Market Data Retrieval, c1995-
*TC L903.N7 M37*

**New York Society for the Experimental Study of**
**Education.**
Bulletin of the New York Society for the
Experimental Study of Education. [New York : The
Society,

**New York (State). Dept. of Health.**
[Health news (Albany, N.Y. : 1916)] Health news.
Albany, N.Y. : The Dept., 1916-1916.

Maternal, child and adolescent health profile. Albany,
N.Y. : New York State Dept. of Health, 1996.
*TC HV742.N7 B83 1996*

**NEW YORK (STATE) - SOCIAL LIFE AND**
**CUSTOMS.**
Richards, Caroline Cowles, 1842-1913. A nineteenth-
century schoolgirl. Mankato, Minn. : Blue Earth
Books, c2000.
*TC F129.C2 R53 2000*

**New York times.**
Current history and Forum. New York [C-H
Publishing Corporation; etc., etc., 1914-41]

[Current history (New York, N.Y. : 1916)] Current
history. [New York : New York Times Co., 1916-
1940]

**New York times current history.**
[Current history (New York, N.Y. : 1916)] Current
history. [New York : New York Times Co., 1916-
1940]

**Newberry Library.**
White, Richard, 1947- The frontier in American
culture. Chicago : The Library ; Berkeley : University
of California Press, c1994.
*TC F596 .W562 1994*

**NEWBORN INFANTS.** *See* **INFANTS**
**(NEWBORN).**

**Newbury House teacher development**
Campbell, Cherry. Teaching second-language writing.
Pacific Grove : Heinle & Heinle, c1998.

*TC PE1128.A2 C325 1998*

**Newby, Timothy J.**
Instructional technology for teaching and learning.
2nd ed. Upper Saddle River, N.J. : Merrill, c2000.
*TC LB1028.38 .I587 2000*

**Newcombe, Nora S.** Making space : the development of
spatial representation and reasoning / Nora S.
Newcombe and Janellen Huttenlocher. Cambridge,
Mass. : MIT Press, 2000. xii, 262 p. : ill. ; 24 cm.
(Learning, development, and conceptual change) "A Bradford
book." Includes bibliographical references (p. [227]-251) and
indexes. ISBN 0-262-14069-1 (alk. paper) DDC 155.4/13752
*1. Space perception in children. I. Huttenlocher, Janellen. II.
Title. III. Series.*
*TC BF723.S63 N49 2000*

**Newcomer, Susan.**
Haines, Dawn Denham. Writing together. 1st ed. New
York : Berkley Pub. Group, 1997.
*TC PN145 .H28 1997*

**Newham, Paul, 1962-** Using voice and theatre in
therapy : the practical application of voice movement
therapy / Paul Newham. London ; Philadelphia, Pa. :
Jessica Kingsley Publishers, 1999. 208 p. : ill. ; 24 cm.
Includes bibliographical references (p. 199) and index. ISBN
1-85302-591-7 (pbk. : alk. paper) DDC 616.89/1523
*1. Voice - Therapeutic use. 2. Psychodrama. I. Title.*
*TC RZ999 .N437 1999*

**Newhouse, Victoria.** Towards a new museum / Victoria
Newhouse. New York : Monacelli Press, 1998. 288 p. :
ill. (some col.) ; 27 cm. Includes bibliographical references (p.
272-281) and index. ISBN 1-88525-460-1 DDC 727/.7/09045
*1. Art museum architecture. 2. Architecture, Modern - 20th
century. I. Title.*
*TC NA6695 .N49 1998*

**NEWLY INDUSTRIALIZED COUNTRIES.** *See*
**DEVELOPING COUNTRIES.**

**NEWLY INDUSTRIALIZING COUNTRIES.** *See*
**DEVELOPING COUNTRIES.**

**Newman, Isadore.**
Theses and dissertations. Lanham, Md. : University
Press of America, 1997.
*TC LB2369 .T44 1997*

**Newman, Judith, 1943-** Tensions of teaching : beyond
tips to critical reflection / Judith M. Newman with Jim
Albright ... [et al.]. New York ; London : Teachers
College Press, c1998. xix, 210 p. ; 23 cm. (The practitioner
inquiry series) Includes bibliographical references. ISBN 0-
8077-3736-4 DDC 371.102/0973
*1. Teaching - United States. 2. Educational change - United
States. 3. Action research in education - United States. I. Title.
II. Series.*
*TC LB1025.3 .N49 1998*

**Newman, Marilyn Stephanie Mercedes, 1954-** Duet
literature for female voices with piano, organ or
unaccompanied : a comprehensive catalogue of vocal
chamber duets composed between 1820-1995 /
Marilyn Stephanie Mercedes Newman. 1998. 2 v. (x,
679 leaves) ; 29 cm. Typescript; issued also on microfilm.
Thesis (Ed.D.)--Teachers College, Columbia University, 1998.
Includes bibliographical references (leaves 570-575) and
indexes.
*1. Vocal duets with keyboard instrument - 19th century -
Bibliography. 2. Vocal duets with keyboard instrument - 20th
century - Bibliography. 3. Vocal duets. Unaccompanied -
Bibliography. I. Title. II. Title: Comprehensive catalogue of
vocal chamber duets*
*TC 06 no. 10897*

**Newman, Rebecca.** Educating homeless children :
witness to a cataclysm / Rebecca Newman. New
York ; London : Garland, 1999. ix, 355 p. ; 23 cm.
(Children of poverty) "A Garland series." Includes
bibliographical references (p. 313-333) and index.
CONTENTS: Ch. I. In Search of the Stories of Homeless
Schoolchildren -- Ch. II. Homeless Families and Students in
the Literature. The Extent and Nature of Family Homelessness.
Problematic Characteristics of Homeless Families. The
Education of Homeless Children -- Ch. III. An Ecological
Approach to Research. The Ecological Approach to Studying
Homelessness. Site and Sample. Data Collection -- Ch. IV. Six
Families, Beginnings and Endings. The Allen Family. The
Castro-Sanchez Family. The Enriquez Family. The Hall-
Ricks-Cardin Family. The Lechter-Lawrence Family. The
Mellon-Thompson Family -- Ch. V. Kara Mellon, A Case
Study. Prologue: English Reading. Kara's Family Background
and Daily Life. Kara's History of Academic and Behavior
Problems. Kara's Behavior and Academic Performance During
Her Time at the Chalet. Year's End: Kara Is Assigned to Full-
Time Special Education -- Ch. VI. Jeffrey Ricks, A Case
Study. Prologue: Matters at School Come to a Head. Jeffrey's
Family Background and Daily Life. Academic History.
Behavior and Academic Performance at Jefferson. From

Failure to Limited Success. Year's End: What of the Future? --
Ch. VII. Understanding How School and Family Contexts
Constrain Student Outcomes. Homelessness: Cause, Result,
Potentiator, and Opportunity. Factors Affecting School
Success. Understanding Outcomes: The Thompson-Mellon
Children. CONTENTS: Understanding Outcomes: The
Cardin-Ricks-Hall Children. Understanding Outcomes:
Amanda and Tim; Ricardo; Melanie -- Ch. VIII. Modest
Suggestions in the Face of Extensive Need. Homeless
Students: The Visibly At-Risk. Implications for Research,
Policy, and Practice Beyond the Domain of Schooling.
Suggestions for Educational Research. Suggestions for
Educational Policy. Suggestions for Educational Practice -- Ch.
IX. Witness to a Cataclysm -- App. A. The Families and
Children: Summary Tables -- App. B. Interview Guides -- App.
C. Extension of the Literature Review -- App. D. Empirical
Studies Consulted: An Annotated Guide to the Literature.
ISBN 0-8153-3475-3 (alk. paper) DDC 371.826/942 DDC
371.826/942
*1. Homeless children - Education - California - Case studies. I.
Title. II. Series.*
*TC LC5144.22.C2 N49 1999*

**Newman, Richard, 1930-.**
African American quotations. Phoenix, Ariz. : Oryx
Press, c1998.
*TC PN6081.3 .A36 1998*

**Newman, Stephanie.** Self-silencing, depression, gender
role, and gender role conflict in women and men /
Stephanie G. Newman. 1997. vii, 119 leaves ; 29 cm.
Typescript; issued also on microfilm. Thesis (Ph.D.)--
Columbia University, 1997. Includes bibliographical references
(leaves 103-111).
*1. Gender identity. 2. Role conflict. 3. Communication - United
States - Sex differences. 4. Depression, Mental - Social aspects.
5. Depression, Mental - Psychological aspects. 6. Adjustment
disorders. 7. Emotions - Health aspects. 8. Depression in
women. I. Title.*
*TC 085 N47*

**News bulletin <Feb. 1952>-Mar. 1953, June 1953-
Dec. 1953.**
The classroom teacher. Berkeley, Calif., Berkeley
Federation of Teachers Local 1078.

**NEWS PHOTOGRAPHY.** *See*
**PHOTOJOURNALISM.**

**Newsletter (College Reading Association).**
The Journal of the reading specialist. Bethlehem, Pa. :
The Association, c1962-

**Newsletter/faits nouveaux.**
[Education newsletter (Strasbourg, France)] Education
newsletter = Strasbourg [France] : Council of Europe,
1990-1995.
*TC LA620 .D6 1994*

**Newsome, Regina.**
d·a·t·e rape [videorecording]. [Charleston, WV] :
Cambridge Educational, c1994.
*TC RC560.R36 D3 1994*

**Newson, Mark.**
Cook, V. J. (Vivian James), 1940- Chomsky's
universal grammar. 2nd [updated] ed. Oxford, OX,
UK ; Cambridge, Mass., USA : Blackwell Publishers,
1996.
*TC P85.C47 C66 1996*

**NEWSPAPERS.** *See* **PERIODICALS.**

**NEWSREEL.** *See* **MOTION PICTURE
JOURNALISM.**

**Newsreel library of World War II.**
Headline stories of the century [videorecording].
Chicago, IL. : Distributed by Questar Video, Inc.,
c1992.
*TC D743 .H42 1992*

**NEWSREELS.** *See also* **MOTION PICTURE
JOURNALISM.**
Headline stories of the century [videorecording].
Chicago, IL. : Distributed by Questar Video, Inc.,
c1992.
*TC D743 .H42 1992*

**Newton, Douglas P.** Teaching for understanding : what
it is and how to do it / Douglas P. Newton. London ;
New York : Routledge/Falmer, 2000. x, 198 p. : ill. ; 25
cm. Includes bibliographical references and index. ISBN
0-415-22790-9 (hb) ISBN 0-415-22791-7 (pb) DDC 371.102
*1. Teaching. 2. Effective teaching. 3. Learning. I. Title.*
*TC LB1025.3 .N495 2000*

**Newton, Fred B.**
Ender, Steven C. Students helping students. 1st ed.
San Francisco : Jossey-Bass Publishers, c2000.
*TC LB1027.5 .E52 2000*

**Newton, Gael.**
Moffatt, Tracey. Tracey Moffatt. Annandale, N.S.W.,
Australia : Piper Press, c1995.
*TC TR647 .M843 1995*

**NEWTON, ISAAC, SIR, 1642-1727.**
Stephen Hawking's universe [videorecording].
[Alexandria, Va.] : PBS Video; Burbank, CA :
Distributed by Warner Home Video, c1997.
*TC QB982 .S7 1997*

**The next generation** [videorecording] / a presentation
of Films for the Humanities & Sciences ; a production
of Public Affairs Television, Inc. ; a presentation of
Thirteen/WNET New York ; produced and directed by
Kathleen Hughes, Tom Casciato. Princeton, NJ :
Films for the Humanities & Sciences, c1998. 1
videocassette (57 min.) : sd., col. ; 1/2 in. (The Moyers
collection) (Close to home. Moyers on addiction) Title on
cassette label: Close to home, the next generation
[videorecording]. VHS. Catalogued from credits and cassette
label and container. Host, Bill Moyers. Editor, Kris Kral ;
camera, Warren Jones, Bob Elfstrom, Kevin Graf ; music,
Richard Fiocca ; sound, Michael Stewart, Charlie Tomaras. For
adolescents through adult. SUMMARY: Experts are
increasingly focusing on prevention efforts based on
community and family. This documentary looks at two of
these efforts. One, Focus on Families, in Seattle, works with
parents addicted to heroin by teaching them how to repair the
damage to family wrought by drug abuse, and in spite of it,
how to raise strong, resilient children. In a second program,
Trust, in Miami, vigilant counselors in Dade County schools
watch for kids at risk of becoming drug addicts, and offer
immediate counseling for those who are already involved with
drugs. Nicotine addiction is addressed by a program that
provides classes designed to prevent students from smoking,
and another that helps them stop if they've already begun to
smoke. School officials, counselors, and students are
interviewed.
*1. Drug abuse - Prevention. 2. Youth - Drug use - Prevention.
3. Drug abuse - United States. 4. Youth - Tobacco use -
Prevention. 5. Teenagers - Drug use - Prevention. 6.
Teenagers - Tobacco use - Prevention. 7. Youth - Substance
use - Prevention. 8. Teenagers - Substance use - Prevention. 9.
Substance abuse - United States. 10. Tobacco habit - United
States. 11. Tobacco habit - Prevention. 12. Smoking -
Prevention. 13. Focus on Families (Program) 14. Trust
(Program) 15. Documentary television programs. I. Moyers,
Bill D. II. Hughes, Kathleen. III. Casciato, Tom. IV. Public
Affairs Television (Firm) V. WNET (Television station : New
York, N.Y.) VI. Films for the Humanities (Firm) VII. Title:
Close to home, the next generation [videorecording] VIII.
Series. IX. Series: Close to home (Series)*
*TC RC564 .N4 1998*

**NFB ONF... The National Film Board of Canada
presents...**
First break [videorecording]. Boston, MA : Fanlight
Productions, c1997.
*TC RC465 .F5 1997*

First break [videorecording]. Boston, MA : Fanlight
Productions, c1997.
*TC RC465 .F5 1997*

First break [videorecording]. Boston, MA : Fanlight
Productions, c1997.
*TC RC465 .F5 1997*

**Ng, Franklin, 1947-** The Taiwanese Americans /
Franklin Ng. Westport, Conn. : Greenwood Press,
1998. x, 163 p. : ill. ; 24 cm. (The new Americans, 1092-
6364) Includes bibliographical references (p. [151]-155) and
index. ISBN 0-313-29762-2 (alk. paper) DDC 305.895/1073
*1. Taiwanese Americans. I. Title. II. Series: New Americans
(Westport, Conn.)*
*TC E184.T35 N45 1998*

**Ng, Kit S.**
Counseling Asian families from a systems
perspective. Alexandria, Va. : American Counseling
Ass., c1999.
*TC RC451.5.A75 C68 1999*

**N.H.S.T.A. bulletin.**
The Bulletin of the New Hampshire State Teachers'
Association. [Manchester, N.H.] : The Association,
[1946]

**Nias, Jennifer.**
Researching school experience. London ; New York :
Falmer Press, 1999.
*TC LB1027 .R453 1999*

**Nice when they are young.**
Levitt, Mairi. Aldershot, Hants, England ; Brookfield,
Vt. : Avebury, c1996.
*TC BV1475.2 .L45 1996*

**NICHE (ECOLOGY).**
Hacking, Ian. Mad travelers. Charlottesville, Va. :
University Press of Virginia, 1998.

**TC RC553.F83 H33 1998**

**Nicholls, David, 1955-.**
The Cambridge history of American music.
Cambridge, UK ; New York, NY : Cambridge
University Press, 1998.
*TC ML200 .C36 1998*

**Nicholls, Gill.** Learning to teach : a handbook for
primary and secondary school teachers / Gill Nicholls.
London : Kogan Page, 1999. 224 p. : ill. ; 24 cm. Includes
bibliogrphical references and index. ISBN 0-7494-2865-1
DDC 370.71
*1. Teachers - Training of - Great Britain. I. Title.*
*TC LB1727.G7 N53 1999*

**Nichols, Eugene Douglas, 1923-.**
Elementary mathematics, patterns and structure;
accelerated sequence. Teacher's ed. New York, Holt,
Rinehart and Winston [c1966]

**Nichols, Janet.**
Bankhead, Elizabeth. Write it!. 2nd ed./MLA version.
Englewood, Colo. : Libraries Unlimited, c1999.
*TC LB1047.3 .W75 1999*

**Nichols, William C.**
Handbook of family development and intervention.
New York : Wiley, c2000.
*TC RC489.F33 .H36 2000*

Systemic family therapy : an integrative approach /
William C. Nichols and Craig A. Everett. New York :
Guilford Press, c1986. xv, 442 p. : ill. ; 24 cm. (The
Guilford family therapy series) Bibliography: p. 407-429.
Includes index. ISBN 0-89862-066-X DDC 616.89/156
*1. Family psychotherapy. 2. Family. 3. Family Therapy. 4.*
*Marital Therapy. I. Everett, Craig A. II. Title. III. Series.*
*TC RC488.5 .N535 1986*

**Nicholson, Barbara.**
**Oxford book of food plants.**
Vaughan, J. G. (John Griffith) The new Oxford
book of food plants. Oxford ; New York : Oxford
University Press, 1997.
*TC SB175 .V38 1997*

Vaughan, J. G. (John Griffith) The new Oxford book
of food plants. Oxford ; New York : Oxford
University Press, 1997.
*TC SB175 .V38 1997*

**Nichter, Mimi.** Fat talk : what girls and their parents say
about dieting / Mimi Nichter. Cambridge, Mass. :
Harvard University Press, 2000. 263 p. ; 24 cm.
Includes bibliographical references and index. ISBN
0-674-00229-6 (alk. paper) DDC 613.2/5/08352
*1. Teenage girls - Nutrition. 2. Reducing diets. 3. Obesity in*
*adolescence. 4. Body image in adolescence. I. Title.*
*TC RJ399.C6 N53 2000*

**Nicklaus, Janice, 1949-.**
Crawford, George. 1937- Philosophical & cultural
values. Larchmont, NY : Eye On Education, c2000.
*TC LB2831.92 .C72 2000*

**Nickson, Marilyn.** Teaching and learning mathematics :
a teacher's guide to recent research / Marilyn
Nickson. London ; New York : Cassell, 2000. xiii, 208
p. : ill. ; 24 cm. (Cassell education) Includes bibliographical
references (p. [181]-200) and index. ISBN 0-304-70618-3
*1. Mathematics - Study and teaching - Research. I. Title. II.*
*Series.*
*TC QA11 .N524 2000*

**Nicol, Adelheid A. M.** Presenting your findings : a
practical guide for creating tables / Adelheid A.M.
Nicol & Penny M. Pexman. 1st ed. Washington, DC :
American Psychological Association, c1999. vii, 157
p. : ill.; 25 cm. Includes bibliographical references and index.
ISBN 1-55798-593-6 DDC 001.4/22
*1. Statistics - Charts, diagrams, etc. I. Pexman, Penny M. II.*
*American Psychological Association. III. Title.*
*TC HA31 .N53 1999*

**NICOTIANA.** *See* **TOBACCO.**

**NICOTIANA TABACUM.** *See* **TOBACCO.**

**NICS (NEWLY INDUSTRIALIZED COUNTRIES).**
*See* **DEVELOPING COUNTRIES.**

**Nida, Eugène Albert, 1914-** Componential analysis of
meaning : an introduction to semantic structures / by
Eugene A. Nida. The Hague : Mouton, 1975. 272 p. :
ill. ; 25 cm. (Approaches to semiotics ; 57) Bibliography: p.
[234]-269. Includes index. DDC 412
*1. Semantics. 2. Componential analysis (Linguistics) 3.*
*Generative grammar. I. Title. II. Series.*
*TC P325 .N5*

**Nidiffer, Jana, 1957-** Pioneering deans of women :
more than wise and pious matrons / Jana Nidiffer ;
foreword by Mary Ann Dzuback. New York ;
London : Teachers College Press, c2000. xiv, 184 p. :

ill. ; 24 cm. (Athene series) Includes bibliographical references
(p. 157-174) and index. ISBN 0-8077-3915-4 (cloth : alk.
paper) ISBN 0-8077-3914-6 (paper : alk. paper) DDC 378.1/12
*1. Deans of women - United States - Biography. 2. Women*
*deans (Education) - United States - Biography. I. Title. II.*
*Series.*
*TC LC1620 .N53 2000*

**Niebrand, Chris.** The pocket mentor : a handbook for
teachers / Chris A. Niebrand, Elizabeth L. Horn,
Robina F. Holmes. Boston, Mass. : Allyn and Bacon,
2000. xix, 268 p. ; 23 cm. Includes bibliographical
references and index. ISBN 0-205-29693-9 (alk. paper) DDC
371.102
*1. Teachers - United States - Handbooks, manuals, etc. 2.*
*Teaching - United States - Handbooks, manuals, etc. 3.*
*Classroom management - United States - Handbooks, manuals,*
*etc. I. Horn, Elizabeth. II. Holmes, Robina F. III. Title.*
*TC LB1775.2 .N54 2000*

**Niehof, Anke. 1948-.**
Pennartz, Paul. The domestic domain :. Aldershot,
Hants, England ; Brookfield, Vt. : Ashgate, c1999.
*TC HQ728 .P46 1999*

**Nielsen, H. Dean.** The cost-effectiveness of distance
education for teacher training / H. Dean Nielsen,
Maria Teresa Tatto ; with Aria Djalil, N. Kularatne.
Cambridge, Mass. : B.R.I.D.G.E.S. Basic Research
and Implementation in Developing Educational
Systems, [1991]. iii, 32 p. : ill. ; 28 cm. (BRIDGES research
report series, no. 9.) "A project of the Harvard Institute for
International Development, the Harvard Graduate School of
Education, and the Office of Education, Bureau for Science and
Technology, United States Agency for International
Development"--Cover. "April 1991." Includes bibliographical
references (p. 31-32).
*1. Teachers - In-service training. 2. Distance education. I.*
*Tatto, Maria Teresa. II. Title. III. Series.*
*TC LB1731 .N43 1991*

**Nieman, David C., 1950-.**
Nutrition and exercise immunology. Boca Raton,
Fla. ; London : CRC Press, c2000.
*TC QP301 .N875 2000*

**Niemeyer, Robert A., 1954-.**
Constructions of disorder. 1st ed. Washington, DC :
American Psychological Association, c2000.
*TC RC437.5 .C647 2000*

**Nierop, Henk F. K. van.**
Anglo-Dutch Historical Conference (13th : 1997) The
education of a Christian society. Aldershot, Hants,
England ; Brookfield, Vt. : Ashgate, c1999.
*TC BR377 .E38 1999*

**Nieto, Sonia.**
Puerto Rican students in U.S. schools. Mahwah, NJ :
Lawrence Erlbaum Associates, 2000.
*TC LC2692 .P82 2000*

**Nietzsche, aesthetics, and modernity.**
Rampley, Matthew. Cambridge, U.K. ; New York :
Cambridge University Press, 2000.
*TC B3318.A4 R36 2000*

**NIETZSCHE, FRIEDRICH WILHELM, 1844-1900.**
Buse, William Joseph. The alternate session. 1999.
*TC 085 B9603*

**NIETZSCHE, FRIEDRICH WILHELM, 1844-1900 -**
**AESTHETICS.**
Rampley, Matthew. Nietzsche, aesthetics, and
modernity. Cambridge, U.K. ; New York : Cambridge
University Press, 2000.
*TC B3318.A4 R36 2000*

**NIGERIAN ART.** *See* **ART, NIGERIAN.**

**Night falls fast.**
Jamison, Kay R. 1st ed. New York : Knopf :
Distributed by Random House, 1999.
*TC RC569 .J36 1999*

**NIGHT - FICTION.**
Jones, Joy. Tambourine moon. New York : Simon &
Schuster, 1999.
*TC PZ7.J72025 Tam 1999*

**The night Iguana left home.**
McDonald, Megan. 1st ed. New York : DK Ink, 1999.
*TC PZ7.M478419 Ni 1999*

**The night of Las Posadas.**
De Paola, Tomie. New York : Putnam's, 1999.
*TC PZ7.D439 Ni 1999*

**NIGHT-SCHOOLS.** *See* **EVENING AND**
**CONTINUATION SCHOOLS.**

**NIGHTINGALE, FLORENCE, 1820-1910.**
Dossey, Barbara Montgomery. Florence Nightingale.
Springhouse, PA : Springhouse Corp., c2000.

**TC RT37.N5 D67 2000**

**Nights of the pufflings.**
McMillan, Bruce. Boston : Houghton Mifflin Co.,
1995.
*TC QL696.C42 M39 1995*

**NIH publication**
(no. 00-4769.) National Reading Panel (U.S.)
Report of the National Reading Panel : teaching
children to read. [Washington, D.C.?] : National
Institute of Child Health and Human Development,
National Institutes of Health, [2000]
*TC LB1050 .N335 2000*

**NIHILISM.** *See* **ANARCHISM.**

**Nihimásáni deiztł'ó.**
Woven by the grandmothers. Washington :
Smithsonian Institution Press in association with the
National Museum of the American Indian,
Smithsonian Institution, c1996.
*TC E99.N3 W79 1996*

**Nihon Kyōshokuin Kumiai.** Educational reform on
people's own initiative : how should education in
Japan be reformed now? / Japan Teachers Union.
[Tokyo? ] : Japan Teachers Union, 1984. 22 p. ; 26 cm.
(Educational reform series ; no. 1) Title from front cover. "The
first draft of people's educational reform plan" --cover. "April,
1984"--cover
*1. Education - Japan - Aims and objectives. 2. Educational*
*change - Japan - 1945- I. Title. II. Title: How should education*
*in Japan be reformed now III. Series.*
*TC LC210.8.N54 1984*

**Nijhof, Wim J., 1941-.**
Bridging the skills gap between work and education.
Dordrecht ; Boston : Kluwer Academic Publishers,
c1999.
*TC LC5056.A2 B75 1999*

**Nikly, Michelle.**
**[Royaume des parfums. English]**
The perfume of memory / by Michelle Nikly ;
illustrated by Jean Claverie 1st American ed. New
York : A.A. Levine Books, 1998. 1 v. (unpaged) : col.
ill. ; 32 cm. SUMMARY: When a disgruntled Grand Vizier
causes the queen and her subjects to lose their memories, a
perfume-maker named Rose helps them remember with the
evocative scents she creates. ISBN 0-439-08206-4 DDC
[Fic]
*1. Perfumes - Fiction. 2. Odors - Fiction. 3. Memory - Fiction.*
*I. Claverie, Jean, 1946- ill. II. Title.*
*TC PZ7.N585 Pe 1998*

**Nikolajeva, Maria.** From mythic to linear : time in
children's literature / Maria Nikolajeva. Lanham,
Md. : Children's Literature Association ; Scarecrow
Press, 2000. viii, 305 p. ; 23 cm. Includes bibliographical
references (p. [267]-293) and indexes. ISBN 0-8108-3713-7
(alk. paper) DDC 809/.89282
*1. Children's literature - History and criticism. 2. Time in*
*literature. I. Title.*
*TC PN1009.5.T55 N55 2000*

**Niles, Olive S.**
Phillips, James B. Accent. Glenview, Ill. : Scott,
Foresman, 1972.
*TC PE1121 .P54 1972*

**Nilsson, Lars-Göran, 1944-.**
Cognitive neuroscience of memory. Seattle ; Toronto :
Hogrefe & Huber, c1999.
*TC QP406 .C63 1999*

**NINETEEN HUNDREDS (CENTURY).** *See*
**TWENTIETH CENTURY.**

**NINETEEN TWENTIES - ECONOMIC ASPECTS -**
**PICTORIAL WORKS.**
Roaring twenties [picture]. Amawalk, NY : Jackdaw
Publications, c1997.
*TC E784 .R6 1997*

**NINETEEN TWENTIES - POLITICAL ASPECTS -**
**PICTORIAL WORKS.**
Roaring twenties [picture]. Amawalk, NY : Jackdaw
Publications, c1997.
*TC E784 .R6 1997*

**NINETEEN TWENTIES - SOCIAL ASPECTS -**
**PICTORIAL WORKS.**
Roaring twenties [picture]. Amawalk, NY : Jackdaw
Publications, c1997.
*TC E784 .R6 1997*

**A nineteenth-century schoolgirl.**
Richards, Caroline Cowles, 1842-1913. Mankato,
Minn. : Blue Earth Books, c2000.
*TC F129.C2 R53 2000*

**Ninety-five languages and seven forms of intelligence.**
Hicks, D. Emily. New York : P. Lang, c1999.
*TC LC196 .H53 1999*

**NINTH GRADE (EDUCATION) - CURRICULA.**
Wiltshire, Michael A. Integrating mathematics and science for below average ninth grade students. 1997.
*TC 06 no. 10847*

**Niparko, John K.**
Cochlear implants. Philadelphia : Lippincott Williams & Wilkins, c2000.
*TC RF305 .C6295 2000*

**NISEI. See JAPANESE AMERICANS.**

**Nissan Institute/Routledge Japanese studies series**
McCormick, Kevin, 1944- Engineers in Japan and Britain. London : New York : Routledge, 2000.
*TC T155 .M37 2000*

**NITROGEN FERTILIZERS.**
Huang, Wen-Yuan. The economic and environmental consequences of nutrient management in agriculture. Commack, N.Y. : Nova Science, c1999.
*TC S651 .H826 1999*

**NITROGEN FERTILIZERS - ENVIRONMENTAL ASPECTS.**
Huang, Wen-Yuan. The economic and environmental consequences of nutrient management in agriculture. Commack, N.Y. : Nova Science, c1999.
*TC S651 .H826 1999*

**NITROGEN IN AGRICULTURE. See NITROGEN FERTILIZERS.**

**Nixon, Howard L., 1944-** A sociology of sport / Howard L. Nixon II, James H. Frey. Belmont : Wadsworth Pub. Co., c1996. xix, 363 p. : ill. ; 24 cm. Includes bibliographical references (p. 316-344) and index. ISBN 0-534-24762-8 (acid-free paper) DDC 306.4/83
*1. Sports - Sociological aspects. I. Frey, James H. II. Title.*
*TC GV706.5 .N58 1996*

**NKRUMAH, KWAME, 1909-1972.**
Quist, Hubert Oswald. Secondary education and nation-building. 1999.
*TC 085 Q52*

**N'Namdi, George R.**
Edward Clark. Belleville Lake, Mich. : Belleville Lake Press, c1997.
*TC ND237.C524 E393 1997*

**No equal justice.**
Cole, David. New York : The New Press : Distributed by W. W. Norton, c1999.
*TC HV9950 .C65 1999*

**NO FIRST USE (NUCLEAR STRATEGY). See NUCLEAR WEAPONS.**

**No more prisons.**
Wimsatt, William Upski. [New York] : Soft Skull Press, [2000?]
*TC HV9276.5 .W567x 2000*

**No one was turned away.**
Opdycke, Sandra. New York : Oxford University Press, 1999.
*TC RA982.N49 O63 1999*

**No ordinary academics.**
Spafford, Shirley. Toronto : University of Toronto Press, 1999.
*TC HB74.9.C3 S62 1999*

**No way of knowing.**
Livingston, Myra Cohn. 1st ed. New York : Atheneum, 1980.
*TC PS3562.I945 N6 1980*

**Noah and the great flood.**
Gerstein, Mordicai. 1st ed. New York : Simon & Schuster for Young Readers, c1999.
*TC BS580.N6 G47 1999*

**NOAH (BIBLICAL FIGURE).**
Gerstein, Mordicai. Noah and the great flood. 1st ed. New York : Simon & Schuster for Young Readers, c1999.
*TC BS580.N6 G47 1999*

**NOAH (BIBLICAL FIGURE) - JUVENILE LITERATURE.**
Gerstein, Mordicai. Noah and the great flood. 1st ed. New York : Simon & Schuster for Young Readers, c1999.
*TC BS580.N6 G47 1999*

**Noah Webster and the American dictionary.**
Micklethwait, David. Jefferson, N.C. : McFarland, c2000.
*TC PE65.W5 M53 2000*

**NOAH'S ARK.**
Gerstein, Mordicai. Noah and the great flood. 1st ed. New York : Simon & Schuster for Young Readers, c1999.
*TC BS580.N6 G47 1999*

**NOAH'S ARK - JUVENILE LITERATURE.**
Gerstein, Mordicai. Noah and the great flood. 1st ed. New York : Simon & Schuster for Young Readers, c1999.
*TC BS580.N6 G47 1999*

**Nobrow.**
Seabrook, John. 1st ed. New York : A.A. Knopf ; Distributed by Random House, 2000.
*TC P94.65.U6 S4 2000*

**Nochlin, Linda.** Representing women / Linda Nochlin. New York : Thames and Hudson, 1999. 272 p. : ill. ; 24 cm. (Interplay, arts, history, theory) Includes bibliographical references (p. 239-261) and index. ISBN 0-500-01904-5 DDC 757/.4/09034
*1. Women in art. 2. Painting, Modern - 19th century. 3. Painting, Modern - 20th century. I. Title. II. Series.*
*TC ND1460.W65 N63 1999*

**NOCTURNAL ANIMALS.**
Fraser, Mary Ann. Where are the night animals? 1st ed. New York : HarperCollins Publishers, c1999.
*TC QL755.5 .F735 1999*

**NOCTURNAL ANIMALS - JUVENILE LITERATURE.**
Fraser, Mary Ann. Where are the night animals? 1st ed. New York : HarperCollins Publishers, c1999.
*TC QL755.5 .F735 1999*

**Noden, Harry R.** Image grammar : using grammatical structures to teach writing / Harry R. Noden. Portsmouth, NH : Heinemann, 1999. x, 214 p. ; 24cm+ 1computer optical disc. Includes bibliographical references (p.203-213). ISBN 0-86709-466-4 DDC 808/.071/2
*1. Creative writing (Secondary education) 2. English language - Grammar - Study and teaching (Secondary) I. Title.*
*TC LB1631 .N62 1999*

**Noe, Raymond A.**
Human resource management. 3rd ed. Boston : Irwin/McGraw-Hill, 2000.
*TC HF5549.2.U5 H8 2000*

**NOISE. See SILENCE.**

**Nolan, James F., 1950-.**
Levin, James, 1946- Principles of classroom management. 3rd ed. Boston : Allyn and Bacon, c2000.
*TC LB3013 .L475 2000*

Teachers and educational change : the lived experience of secondary school restructuring / James Nolan, Jr., and Denise G. Meister. Albany : State University of New York Press, c2000. xi, 237 p. ; 24 cm. (SUNY series, restructuring and school change) Includes bibliographical references (p. 225-231) and index. ISBN 0-7914-4699-9 (alk. paper) ISBN 0-7914-4700-6 (pbk. : alk. paper) DDC 373.11/06
*1. High school teachers - United States - Case studies. 2. Educational change - United States - Case studies. 3. Teacher participation in administration - United States - Case studies. 4. School improvement programs - United States - Case studies. I. Meister, Denise G., 1951- II. Title. III. Series.*
*TC LB1777.2 .N64 2000*

**Noland, Richard W.** Sigmund Freud revisited / Richard W. Noland. New York : Twayne Publishers, c1999. xv, 167 p. : ill. ; 22 cm. (Twayne's world authors series ; TWAS 885. German literature) Includes bibliographical references (p. 148-153) and index. ISBN 0-8057-1684-X (alk. paper) DDC 150.19/52/092
*1. Freud, Sigmund - 1856-1939. 2. Psychoanalysts - Austria - Biography. I. Title. II. Series: Twayne's world authors series ; TWAS 885. III. Series: Twayne's world authors series. German literature.*
*TC BF109.F74 N65 1999*

**Nolet, Victor.**
Howell, Kenneth W. Curriculum-based evaluation. 3rd ed. Belmont, CA. : Wadsworth, c2000.
*TC LB3060.32.C74 H68 2000*

**Nolin, Dennis, ill.**
Turner, Ann Warren. Red flower goes West. 1st ed. New York : Hyperion Books for Children, c1999.
*TC PZ7.T8535 Rf 1999*

**NOMADS. See IRISH TRAVELLERS (NOMADIC PEOPLE).**

**NOMENCLATURE - HANDBOOKS.**
Golper, Lee Ann C., 1948- Sourcebook for medical speech pathology. 2nd ed. San Diego, Calif. : Singular Pub. Group, c1998.

*TC RC423 .G64 1998*

**NOMESH.**
Smith, Richard Mason, 1881- From infancy to childhood. Boston : Atlantic monthly press, [c1925]
*TC RJ61 .S675*

**NOMINATIONS FOR OFFICE. See POLITICAL CONVENTIONS.**

**NON-CUSTODIAL PUNISHMENTS. See ALTERNATIVES TO IMPRISONMENT.**

**NON-FORMAL EDUCATION. See also POPULAR EDUCATION.**
Skiba, Michaeline. A naturalistic inquiry of the relationship between organizational change and informal learning in the workplace. 1999.
*TC 06 no. 11180*

Weintraub, Robert Steven. Informal learning in the workplace through desktop technology. 1998.
*TC 06 no. 11003*

**NON-FORMAL EDUCATION - INDIA - CONGRESSES.**
Open learning system. New Delhi : Lancer International, c1989.
*TC LC5808.I4 O64 1989*

**NON-GRADED SCHOOLS. See NONGRADED SCHOOLS.**

**NON-PROFIT ORGANIZATIONS. See NONPROFIT ORGANIZATIONS.**

**NON-PROFIT SECTOR. See NONPROFIT ORGANIZATIONS.**

**NON-PROFITS. See NONPROFIT ORGANIZATIONS.**

**NON-VIOLENCE. See NONVIOLENCE.**

**NONBOOK MATERIALS. See MAPS.**

**NONCONSENSUAL SEXUAL INTERCOURSE. See RAPE.**

**None of the above.**
Owen, David, 1955- Rev. and updated. Lanham, Md. : Rowman & Littlefield Publishers, c1999.
*TC LB2353.57 .O94 1999*

**NONFICTION FILMS. See DOCUMENTARY FILMS.**

**NONFORMAL EDUCATION. See NON-FORMAL EDUCATION.**

**NONGRADED SCHOOLS - HANDBOOKS, MANUALS, ETC.**
The multiage handbook. Peterborough, NH : Society for Developmental Education, c1996.
*TC LB1029.N6 M754 1996*

**Nonlinear dynamics.**
Heath, Richard A. Mahwah, N.J. : London : L. Erlbaum Associates, 2000.
*TC BF39 .H35 2000*

**NONLINEAR THEORIES. See CHAOTIC BEHAVIOR IN SYSTEMS.**

**NONLUMINOUS MATTER (ASTRONOMY). See DARK MATTER (ASTRONOMY).**

**Nonparametric methods in statistics.**
Fraser, D. A. S. (Donald Alexander Stuart), 1925- New York, Wiley [1957]
*TC QA276 .F66 1957*

**NONPARAMETRIC STATISTICS.**
Fraser, D. A. S. (Donald Alexander Stuart), 1925- Nonparametric methods in statistics. New York, Wiley [1957]
*TC QA276 .F66 1957*

**NONPROFIT ORGANIZATIONS - COMPUTER NETWORK RESOURCES.**
Bergan, Helen, 1937- Where the information is. Alexandria, VA : BioGuide Press, c1996.
*TC HD62.6 .B47 1996*

**NONPROFIT ORGANIZATIONS - FINANCE.**
Grace, Kay Sprinkel. Beyond fund raising. New York : Wiley, c1997.
*TC HG4027.65 .G73 1997*

**NONPROFIT ORGANIZATIONS - INFORMATION SERVICES.**
Bergan, Helen, 1937- Where the information is. Alexandria, VA : BioGuide Press, c1996.
*TC HD62.6 .B47 1996*

**NONPROFIT ORGANIZATIONS - MANAGEMENT.**
The Jossey-Bass handbook of nonprofit leadership and

management. 1st ed. San Francisco : Jossey-Bass, c1994.
*TC HD62.6 .J67 1994*

Malaro, Marie C. Museum governance. Washington : Smithsonian Institution Press, c1994.
*TC AM121 .M35 1994*

Oster, Sharon M. Strategic management for nonprofit organizations. New York : Oxford University Press, 1995.
*TC HD62.6 .O87 1995*

**NONPROFIT ORGANIZATIONS - UNITED STATES.**
American Assembly (93rd : 1998 : Los Angeles, Calif.) Trust, service, and the common purpose. Indianapolis, IN : Indiana University Center on Philanthropy ; New York, NY : American Assembly, [1998]
*TC HD62.6 .A44 1998*

De Pree, Max. Leading without power. 1st ed. San Francisco, Calif. : Jossey-Bass, c1997.
*TC HN90.V64 D4 1997*

Mixer, Joseph R., 1923- Principles of professional fundraising. 1st ed. San Francisco : Jossey-Bass, c1993.
*TC HV41.9.U5 M58 1993*

**NONPROFIT ORGANIZATIONS - UNITED STATES - CONGRESSES.**
Nonprofits and government. Washington, DC : Urban Institute Press, 1999.
*TC HD62.6 .N694 1999*

**NONPROFIT ORGANIZATIONS - UNITED STATES - FINANCE.**
Seltzer, Michael, 1947- Securing your organization's future. New York, N.Y. : Foundation Center, 1987.
*TC HV41.9.U5 S45 1987*

**NONPROFIT SECTOR.** *See* **NONPROFIT ORGANIZATIONS.**

**NONPROFITS.** *See* **NONPROFIT ORGANIZATIONS.**

**Nonprofits and government :** collaboration and conflict / Elizabeth Boris, ed. Washington, DC : Urban Institute Press, 1999. xii, 383 p. : ill., map ; 23 cm. "Twelve papers ... prepared for "Nonprofit Organizations and the Government: The Challenge of Civil Society," a conference sponsored by the Center on Nonprofits and Philanthropy at the Urban Institute, in Washington, DC, on June 9-9, 1998"--P. . Includes bibliographical references and index. ISBN 0-87766-686-5 ISBN 0-87766-687-3 (pbk.) DDC 061/.3
*1. Nonprofit organizations - United States - Congresses. 2. Administrative agencies - United States - Congresses. 3. Public-private sector cooperation - United States - Congresses. 4. Democracy - United States - Congresses. I. Boris, Elizabeth T. II. Urban Institute. III. Center on Nonprofits and Philanthropy (Urban Institute)*
*TC HD62.6 .N694 1999*

**Nonreactive measures in the social sciences** / Eugene T. [i.e. J.] Webb ... [et al.]. 2nd ed. Boston : Houghton Mifflin, c1981. x, 394 p. ; 22 cm. Previous ed.: Unobtrusive measures. 1966. Includes bibliographical references (p.331-378) and index. ISBN 0-395-30767-8 (pbk.) DDC 300/.72
*1. Social sciences - Research. I. Webb, Eugene J., 1933- II. Title: Unobtrusive measures.*
*TC H62 .N675 1981*

**NONSELFGOVERNING TERRITORIES.** *See* **COLONIES.**

**NONTRADITIONAL EDUCATION.** *See* **ALTERNATIVE EDUCATION.**

**NONVERBAL COMMUNICATION.** *See* **EXPRESSION.**

**NONVIOLENCE.**
Ackerman, Peter. Strategic nonviolent conflict. Westport, Conn. : Praeger, 1994.
*TC JC328.3 .A28 1994*

Nonviolence in theory and practice. Belmont, Calif. : Wadsworth Pub. Co., c1990.
*TC HM278 .N67 1990*

**NONVIOLENCE - ENCYCLOPEDIAS.**
Protest, power, and change. New York : Garland Pub., 1997.
*TC HM278 .P76 1997*

**NONVIOLENCE IN LITERATURE.**
True, Michael. An energy field more intense than war. 1st ed. Syracuse, N.Y. : Syracuse University Press, 1995.
*TC PS169.N65 T78 1995*

**Nonviolence in theory and practice** / edited by Robert L. Holmes. Belmont, Calif. : Wadsworth Pub. Co., c1990. xi, 208 p. ; 24 cm. Bibliography: p. [207]-208. ISBN 0-534-12180-2 DDC 303.6/1
*1. Nonviolence. 2. Passive resistance. 3. Pacifism. I. Holmes, Robert L.*
*TC HM278 .N67 1990*

**NONVIOLENCE - STUDY AND TEACHING (MIDDLE SCHOOL) - UNITED STATES.**
Promoting nonviolence in early adolescence. New York : Kluwer Academic/Plenum Publishers, c2000.
*TC HM1126 .P76 2000*

**Noon, J. Mitchell.** Counselling and helping carers / J. Mitchell Noon ; medical advisor, Alastair Macdonald. Leicester : BPS Books, 1999. xii, 143 p. ; 22 cm. (Communication and counselling in health care series) At foot of t.p.: British Psychological Society. Includes bibliographical references (p. [135]-139) and index. ISBN 1-85433-272-4 DDC 362.104256
*1. Health counseling. 2. Caregivers. I. British Psychological Society. II. Title. III. Series: Communication and counselling in health care.*
*TC R727.4 .N66 1999*

**Noordenbos, Greta.**
The prevention of eating disorders. New York : New York University Press, 1998.
*TC RC552.E18 P74 1998*

**Norcross, John C., 1957-.**
Psychologists' desk reference. New York : Oxford University Press, 1998.
*TC RC467.2 .P78 1998*

**Nord, Michael B.** Music in the classroom (MITC) : designing a world wide web professional development resources for the integration of music into elementary classrooms / by Michael B. Nord. 1998. xi, 339 leaves ; 29 cm. + 1 computer disc. Accompanying CD-ROM has title: MITC, site prototypes. Issued also on microfilm. Thesis (Ed.D.)--Teachers College, Columbia University, 1998. Includes bibliographical references (leaves 159-167).
*1. Elementary schools - Curricula - New York (State) - New York - Case studies. 2. School music - Instruction and study - New York (State) - New York - Case studies. 3. School music - Computer-assisted instruction. 4. Interdisciplinary approach in education - New York (State) - New York - Case studies. 5. Human-computer interaction. 6. Learning, Psychology of. 7. Instructional systems - Design. 8. Constructivism (Education). I. Title. II. Title: Designing a world wide web professional development resources for integration of music into elementary classrooms III. Title: MITC, site prototypes*
*TC 06 no. 10974*

**NORM BASED TESTS.** *See* **NORM-REFERENCED TESTS.**

**NORM-REFERENCED TESTS - UNITED STATES.**
Taylor, Kathe. Children at the center. Portsmouth, NH : Heinemann, c1998.
*TC LB3060.57 .T39 1998*

**Norman Rockwell's world -- an American dream** [videorecording] / a Concepts Unlimited Production ; director, Robert Deubel ; conceived and written by Gaby Monet. [Chicago, Ill] : Home Vision, 1987, c1972. 1 videocassette (24 min.) : sd., col. with b&w sequences ; 1/2 in. (Portrait of an artist) VHS, Stereo, Hi-fi. Catalogued from credits and container. Narrated by Norman Rockwell. Editor, Burt Rashby ; original music by John Kander ; lyrics by John Kander and Fred Ebb ; music arranged and conducted by Harold Hastings. "Academy Award Best Short Subject--Live Action MCMLXXII."--Container. "NOR 01".--Container. Produced by Concepts Unlimited in 1972. Adolescent through adult. SUMMARY: A study of Norman Rockwell as man and artist. Shows how he documented American life over six decades in the pictures of the children, families, and friends from his world. ISBN 0-7800-0138-9
*1. Rockwell, Norman, -- 1894- 2. Painting, American. 3. Painting, Modern - 20th century - United States. 4. Painters - United States - Biography. 5. Documentary films. 6. Biographical films. I. Rockwell, Norman, 1894- II. Deubel, Robert. III. Monet, Gaby. IV. Home Vision (Firm) V. Concepts Unlimited. VI. Title: American dream [videorecording] VII. Series.*
*TC ND237.R68 N6 1987*

**Norman, Wallace.**
Chadwick, Annie. Showbiz bookkeeper. Dorset, Vermont : Theatre Directories, 1992, c1991.
*TC HF5686.P24 C53 1991*

**NORSEMEN.** *See* **NORTHMEN.**

**Norsk lektorlag.**
Den Høgre skolen Oslo, Steenske forlag.

**Nortel North America.**
The emerging world of wireless communications.

Nashville, TN : Institute for Information Studies, 1996.
*TC TK5103.2 .E44 1996*

**North African textiles.**
Spring, Christopher. Washington, D.C. : Smithsonian Institution Press, c1995.
*TC NK8887.6 .S68 1995*

**NORTH AMERICAN INDIANS.** *See* **INDIANS OF NORTH AMERICA.**

**A North American rain forest scrapbook.**
Wright-Frierson, Virginia. New York : Walker and Co., 1999.
*TC QH105.W2 W75 1999*

**North Atlantic Treaty Organization. Committee on the Challenges of Modern Society.**
Air pollution modeling and its application XII. New York : Plenum Press, c1998.
*TC TD881 .A47523 1998*

**North, Brian, 1950-** The development of a common framework scale of language proficiency / Brian North. New York : P. Lang, c2000. xviii, 459 p. ; 24 cm. (Theoretical studies in second language acquisition ; vol. 8) Includes bibliographical references (p.[417]-459). ISBN 0-8204-4852-4 (alk. paper)
*1. Language and languages - Ability testing. 2. Scaling (Social sciences) 3. Communicative competence. I. Title. II. Series.*
*TC P53.4 .N67 2000*

**North Central Regional Education Laboratory (U.S.).**
Plugging in :. Washington, D.C. : NEKIA Communications ; Oak Brook, Ill. : North Central Regional Educational Laboratory, [1995]. ([1999]).
*TC LB1028.3 .P584 1995*

**North, John David.**
Between demonstration and imagination. Leiden, Netherlands ; Boston : Brill, 1999.
*TC QB15 .B56 1999*

**North, Michael, 1954-.**
Art markets in Europe, 1400-1800. Aldershot ; Brookfield : Ashgate, c1998.
*TC N8600 .A737 1998*

**North, Stephen M.** Refiguring the Ph.D. in English studies : writing, doctoral education, and the fusion-based curriculum / Stephen M. North ; with Barbara A. Chepaitis ... [et al.]. Urbana, Ill. : National Council of Teachers of English, c2000. xix, 319 p. ; 22 cm. (Refiguring English studies) Includes bibliographical references and index. ISBN 0-8141-3977-9 (pbk. : alk. paper) DDC 820/.71/174743
*1. English philology - Study and teaching (Graduate) - New York (State) - Albany. 2. State University of New York at Albany - Graduate work. I. Chepaitis, Barbara. II. Title. III. Series.*
*TC PE69.A47 N67 2000*

**Northam, W. Leland.**
Ramírez de Mellor, Elva Fun with English. Pupil's ed. Mexico : McGraw-Hill c1987
*TC PE1129.S8 .R35 1987*

Ramírez de Mellor, Elva Fun with english. Mexico : McGraw-Hill c1987
*TC PE1129.S8 .R35 1987*

**NORTHEASTERN STATES.** *See* **NEW ENGLAND.**

**Northeastern University studies in rehabilitation** (no. 8) Craddock, George W. Social disadvantagement and dependency: Lexington, Mass., Heath Lexington Books [1970]
*TC HD7256.U6 C438*

(no. 9) Spencer, Gary. Structure and dynamics of social intervention; Lexington, Mass., Heath Lexington Books [1970]
*TC HV91 .S63*

**NORTHERN IRELAND - HISTORY - 1969-1994.**
Wright, Frank, 1948- Two lands on one soil. New York : St. Martin's Press, 1996.
*TC DA990.U46 W756 1996*

**NORTHERN LIGHTS.** *See* **AURORAS.**

**Northern Policy, Review, Research Advisory Network on Education and Training.**
Changing international aid to education. Paris : Unesco Pub./NORRAG, 1999.
*TC LC2607 .C42 1999*

**NORTHERN TIER (MIDDLE EAST).** *See* **MIDDLE EAST.**

**NORTHMEN.** *See* **VIKINGS.**

**NORTHMEN - FOOD - JUVENILE LITERATURE.**
Martell, Hazel. Food & feasts with the Vikings. Parsippany, N.J. : New Discovery Books, c1995.

**TC DL65 .M359 1995**

**NORTHMEN - SOCIAL LIFE AND CUSTOMS - JUVENILE LITERATURE.**
Martell, Hazel. Food & feasts with the Vikings. Parsippany, N.J. : New Discovery Books, c1995.
**TC DL65 .M359 1995**

**Northwestern University studies in phenomenology & existential philosophy.**
Merleau-Ponty, Maurice, 1908-1961. The primacy of perception, and other essays on phenomenological psychology, the philosophy of art, history, and politics. [Evanston, Ill.] : Northwestern University Press, 1964.
**TC B2430.M378 E5 1964**

Merleau-Ponty, Maurice, 1908-1961. [Sens et non-sens. English] Sense and non-sense. [Evanston, Ill.] Northwestern University Press, 1964.
**TC B2430.M379 S43 1964**

**The Norton anthology of African American literature** / Henry Louis Gates, Jr., general editor; Nellie Y. McKay, general editor. 1st ed. New York : W.W. Norton & Co., c1997. xliv, 2665 p. ; 25 cm. Includes bibliographical references (p. 2625-2648) and index. ISBN 0-393-04001-1 DDC 810.8/0896073
*1. American literature - Afro-American authors. 2. Afro-Americans - Literary collections. I. Gates, Henry Louis. II. McKay, Nellie Y.*
**TC PS508.N3 N67 1996**

**Norton history of science**
Grattan-Guinness, I. [Fontana history of the mathematical sciences] The Norton history of the mathematical sciences. 1st American ed. New York : W.W. Norton, 1998.
**TC QA21 .G695 1998**

**The Norton history of the mathematical sciences.**
Grattan-Guinness, I. [Fontana history of the mathematical sciences] 1st American ed. New York : W.W. Norton, 1998.
**TC QA21 .G695 1998**

**Norton, M. Scott.** Resource allocation : managing money and people / by M. Scott Norton, Larry K. Kelly. Larchmont, N.Y. : Eye on Education, c1997. vi, 170 p. : ill. ; 24 cm. (The school leadership library) Includes bibliographical references. ISBN 1-88300-135-8 DDC 371.2/00973
*1. School management and organization - United States. 2. School personnel management - United States. 3. Public schools - United States - Business management. I. Kelly, Larry K., 1936- II. Title. III. Series.*
**TC LB2805 .N73 1997**

**Norwich, Brahm.** Education and psychology in interaction : working with uncertainty in interconnected fields / Brahm Norwich. London ; New York : Routledge, 2000. ix, 259 p. : ill. ; 25 cm. (Routledge research in education ; 3) Includes bibliographical references (p. [238]-249) and index. ISBN 0-415-22431-4 (alk. paper) DDC 370.15
*1. Educational psychology. I. Title. II. Series: Routledge research in education.*
**TC LB1051 .N645 2000**

**NOSTALGIA.**
Coontz, Stephanie. The way we never were. New York, NY : BasicBooks, c1992.
**TC HQ535 .C643 1992**

**NOT-FOR-PROFIT ORGANIZATIONS.** *See* **NONPROFIT ORGANIZATIONS.**

**Not just any medical school.**
Davenport, Horace Willard, 1912- Ann Arbor : University of Michigan Press, c1999.
**TC R747.U6834 D38 1999**

**Not of pure blood.**
Kinsbruner, Jay. Durham : Duke University Press, 1996.
**TC F1983.B55 K56 1996**

**Not to be modern [videorecording].**
The Amish [videorecording]. Oak Forest, IL : MPI Home Video, 1988.

The Amish [videorecording]. Oak Forest, Ill. : MPI Home Video, c1988.
**TC BX8129.A5 A5 1988**

**NOTES, NURSES'.** *See* **NURSING RECORDS.**

**Notre Dame conferences in medieval studies**
(9.) Learning institutionalized. Notre Dame, Ind. : University of Notre Dame Press, c2000.
**TC LA177 .L43 2000**

**Notre Dame story, 1842-1934.**
Burns, Robert E., 1927- Being Catholic, being

American. Notre Dame, Ind. : University of Notre Dame Press, c1999.
**TC LD4113 .B87 1999**

**NOTTINGHAM, SHERIFF OF (LEGENDARY CHARACTER).** *See* **SHERIFF OF NOTTINGHAM (LEGENDARY CHARACTER).**

**Nova (Television program).**
In search of human origins [videorecording]. [Boston, Mass.] : WGBH Educational Foundation, c1994.
**TC GN281 .I45 1994**

**Novak, David, 1941-** Covenantal rights : a study in Jewish political theory / David Novak. Princeton, N.J. : Princeton University Press, 2000. xii, 240 p. ; 24 cm. (Includes bibliographical references (p. [219]-231) and index. ISBN 0-691-02680-7 (cl : alk. paper)
*1. Civil rights (Jewish law) 2. Jews - Politics and government - Philosophy. 3. Human rights - Religious aspects - Judaism - History of doctrines. I. Title. II. Series.*
**TC KC3 .N68 2000**

**Novak, Dori E.** Help! It's an indoor recess day / Dori E. Novak. Thousand Oaks, Calif. : Corwin Press, c2000. xiii, 72 p. : ill. ; 29 cm. ISBN 0-7619-7527-6 (cloth : alk. paper) ISBN 0-7619-7528-4 (pbk. : alk. paper) DDC 372.12/44
*1. Recesses. 2. Play. I. Title.*
**TC LB3033 .N68 2000**

**Novak, Joseph Donald.**
Assessing science understanding :. San Diego, Calif. London : Academic, 2000.
**TC Q181 .A87 2000**

**Novartis Foundation for Gerontological Research.**
Attention, space, and action. Oxford ; New York : Oxford University Press, 1999.
**TC QP405 .A865 1999**

**NOVELISTS.** *See* **FICTION.**

**NOVELLAS (SHORT NOVELS).** *See* **FICTION.**

**NOVELS.** *See* **FICTION.**

**NOVELTY BOOKS.** *See* **TOY AND MOVABLE BOOKS.**

**Novogrodsky, Charles, 1946-.**
Thomas, Barb, 1946- Combatting racism in the workplace. Toronto : Cross Cultural Communication Centre, c1983.
**TC HD4903.5.C3 T56 1983**

**Novotny, Jeanne.**
Schoolcraft, Victoria. A nuts-and-bolts approach to teaching nursing. 2nd ed. New York : Springer Pub. Co., c2000.
**TC RT71 .S26 2000**

**Now we read, we see, we speak.**
Purcell-Gates, Victoria. Mahwah, N.J. : L. Erlbaum Associates, Publishers, 2000.
**TC LC155.S22 P87 2000**

**Nowhere to grow.**
Whitbeck, Les B. New York : Aldine de Gruyer, 1999.
**TC HV4505 .W43 1999**

**Noyelle, Thierry J.**
Stanback, Thomas M. Cities in transition. Totowa, N.J. : Allanheld, Osmun, 1982.
**TC HD5724 .S649 1982**

**NPOS.** *See* **NONPROFIT ORGANIZATIONS.**

**NSF Science and Technology Center in Discrete Mathematics and Theoretical Computer Science.**
Discrete mathematics in the schools. Providence, R.I. : American Mathematical Society, National Council of Teachers of Mathematics, c1997.
**TC QA11.A1 D57 1997**

**The NSFRE/Wiley fund development series**
Grace, Kay Sprinkel. Beyond fund raising. New York : Wiley, c1997.
**TC HG4027.65 .G73 1997**

**NSTA guide to school science facilities.**
Biehle, James T. Arlington, VA : National Science Teachers Association, c1999.
**TC Q183.3.A1 B54 1999**

**NSTA handbook.**
National Science Teachers Association. Washington, D.C. : The Association,
**TC Q145 .N38 1999**

**NTC's beginner's Italian and English dictionary** / editor, Raffaele A. Dioguardi ; general editor, Frank R. Abate. Lincolnwood, Ill. : NTC Pub. Group, c1995. 444 p. : ill., map ; 22 cm. (NTC language dictionaries) ISBN 0-8442-8443-2 DDC 453/.21
*1. Italian language - Dictionaries - English. 2. English*

language - Dictionaries - Italian. I. Dioguardi, Raffaele A. II. Title: National Textbook Company's beginner's Italian and English dictionary III. Title: Beginner's Italian and English dictionary IV. Series: National Textbook language dictionaries.
**TC PC1640 .N83 1995**

**NTC's Italian grammar.**
Lamping, Alwena. Lincolnwood, Ill., U.S.A. : NTC Pub. Group, 1998.
**TC PC1112 .L34 1998**

**NUCLEAR ARMS CONTROL.** *See* **NUCLEAR WEAPONS.**

**NUCLEAR DISARMAMENT.** *See* **ANTINUCLEAR MOVEMENT; NUCLEAR WEAPONS.**

**NUCLEAR FACILITIES.** *See* **ANTINUCLEAR MOVEMENT.**

**NUCLEAR FREEZE MOVEMENT.** *See* **ANTINUCLEAR MOVEMENT.**

**NUCLEAR POWER PLANTS.** *See* **ANTINUCLEAR MOVEMENT.**

**Nuclear rites.**
Gusterson, Hugh. "First paperback printing 1998". Berkeley : University of California Press, 1998.
**TC U264.4.C2 G87 1998**

**NUCLEAR WARFARE.** *See also* **NUCLEAR WEAPONS.**
Fate of the earth [videorecording]. [New York, N.Y.?] : Unapix Entertainment, Inc. [distributor], c1996.
**TC QB631.2 .F3 1996**

**NUCLEAR WEAPONS - ACCIDENTS - FICTION.**
Burdick, Eugene. Fail-safe. 1st Ecco ed. Hopewell, N.J. : Ecco Press ; New York, NY : Distributed by W.W. Norton, 1999.
**TC PS3552.U7116 F35 1999**

**NUCLEAR WEAPONS - RESEARCH - SOCIAL ASPECTS - CALIFORNIA - LIVERMORE.**
Gusterson, Hugh. Nuclear rites. "First paperback printing 1998". Berkeley : University of California Press, 1998.
**TC U264.4.C2 G87 1998**

**NUDE IN ART.** *See* **FIGURE DRAWING; PHOTOGRAPHY OF THE NUDE.**

**NUDE PHOTOGRAPHY.** *See* **PHOTOGRAPHY OF THE NUDE.**

**Nugent, Patricia Mary, 1944-** Test success : test-taking techniques for beginning nursing students / Patricia M. Nugent, Barbara A. Vitale. 3rd ed. Philadelphia : F.A. Davis, c2000. xviii, 359 p. ; 26 cm. Includes bibliographical references and index. ISBN 0-8036-0524-2 (pbk.)
*1. Nursing - Examination Questions. 2. Educational Measurement. I. Vitale, Barbara Ann, 1944- II. Title. III. Title: Test-taking techniques for beginning nursing students*
**TC RT55 .N77 2000**

**NUISANCES.** *See* **ODORS.**

**NUMBER ABILITY.** *See* **MATHEMATICAL ABILITY.**

**Number concepts** [videorecording] / Video Tutor, Inc. Princeton, N.J. : Video Tutor, 1988. 1 videocassette (VHS) (44 min.) : sd., col. ; 1/2 in. + 1 student workbook & pre/post test system ([12] p. ; 19 cm.). (Video tutor instructional series) (A mathematics series) Title on container: Basic number concepts [videorecording]. Title on cassette label: Video Tutor Inc. presents basic number concepts [videorecording]. VHS. Catalogued from credits, cassette label and container. John Hall, instructor. For grades 5-9 math classes. SUMMARY: A no-frills coverage of such basics as rounding decimals, changing decimals to fractions and finding the least common denominator.
*1. Fractions. 2. Decimal fractions. I. Hall, John. II. Video Tutor. III. Title: Basic number concepts [videorecording] IV. Title: Video Tutor Inc. presents basic number concepts [videorecording] V. Series. VI. Series: A mathematics series*
**TC QA117 .N8 1988**

**Number concepts** [videorecording] / Video Tutor, Inc. Princeton, N.J. : Video Tutor, 1988. 1 videocassette (VHS) (44 min.) : sd., col. ; 1/2 in. + 1 student workbook & pre/post test system ([12] p. ; 19 cm.). (Video tutor instructional series) (A mathematics series) Title on container: Basic number concepts [videorecording]. Title on cassette label: Video Tutor Inc. presents basic number concepts [videorecording]. VHS. Catalogued from credits, cassette label and container. John Hall, instructor. For grades 5-9 math classes. SUMMARY: A no-frills coverage of such basics as rounding decimals, changing decimals to fractions and finding the least common denominator.
*1. Fractions. 2. Decimal fractions. 3. Arithmetic - Problems,*

*exercises, etc. I. Hall, John. II. Video Tutor. III. Title: Basic number concepts [videorecording] IV. Title: Video Tutor Inc. presents basic number concepts [videorecording] V. Series. VI. Series: A mathematics series*
*TC QA117 .N8 1988*

**NUMBER THEORY.** *See* **FIBONACCI NUMBERS; NUMERATION.**

**NUMBERS, RATIONAL.** *See* **FRACTIONS.**

**NUMBERS, REAL.** *See* **ARITHMETIC.**

**Numeracy and beyond.**
Hughes, Martin, 1949 May 15- Buckingham [England] : Philadelphia : Open University Press, 2000.
*TC QA135.5 .H844 2000*

**NUMERACY - AUSTRALIA.**
Literacy and numeracy in Australian schools. Canberra : Australian Gov. Pub. Service, 1976-
*TC LA2102 .L57 1976*

**NUMERACY - AUSTRALIA - ADDRESSES, ESSAYS, LECTURES.**
Bourke, S. F. The mastery of literacy and numeracy. Canberra : Australian Govt. Pub. Service, 1977.
*TC LA2102 .B68 1977*

**NUMERALS.**
Marsh, Valerie. Storytelling with shapes & numbers. Ft. Atkinson, Wis. : Alleyside Press, c1999.
*TC LB1042 .M2874 1999*

**NUMERATION - STUDY AND TEACHING.**
Future basics. Golden, Colo. : National Council of Supervisors of Mathematics, c1998.
*TC QA141 .C43 1998*

**Nunan, David.** Second language teaching & learning / David Nunan. Boston, Mass. : Heinle & Heinle Publishers, c1999. vi, 330 p. : ill. ; 24 cm. Includes bibliographical references and index. ISBN 0-8384-0838-9
*1. Language acquisition. 2. Second language acquisition. 3. Language and languages - Study and teaching. 4. Second language acquisition. 5. Language and languages - Study and teaching. I. Title. II. Title: Second language teaching and learning*
*TC P118.2 .N86 1999*

**Nunes, Terezinha.**
Learning to read. Dordrecht ; Boston : Kluwer Academic Publishers, 1999.
*TC LB1050.2 .L42 1999*

**NUPTIALITY.** *See* **MARRIAGE.**

**Nureyev.**
Solway, Diane. Nureyev, his life. 1st ed. New York : William Morrow, c1998.
*TC GV1785.N8 S66 1998*

**Nureyev, his life.**
Solway, Diane. 1st ed. New York : William Morrow, c1998.
*TC GV1785.N8 S66 1998*

**NUREYEV, RUDOLF, 1938-.**
Solway, Diane. Nureyev, his life. 1st ed. New York : William Morrow, c1998.
*TC GV1785.N8 S66 1998*

**Nürnberger, Marianne, 1956-**
[Tanz ist die Sprache der Götter. English]
Dance is the language of the gods : the Chitrasena School and the traditional roots of Sri Lankan stage-dance / Marianne Nürnberger. Amsterdam : VU University Press, 1998. xxvi, 282 p. : ill. ; 24 cm. (Sri Lanka studies ; 5) (h) Includes bibliographical references (p. [259]-265) and index. ISBN 90-5383-579-2
*1. Dance - Sri Lanka. 2. Dance - Sri Lanka - Religious aspects. 3. Sri Lanka - Religious life and customs. I. Title. II. Series.*
*TC GV1703.S74 .N8713 1998*

**NURSE ADMINISTRATORS.**
Grossman, Sheila. The new leadership challenge. Philadelphia : F.A. Davis, c2000.
*TC RT89 .G77 2000*

Simms, Lillian M. (Lillian Margaret) The professional practice of nursing administration. 3rd ed. Albany, NY : Delmar Publishers, c2000.
*TC RT89 .S58 2000*

Traynor, Michael, 1956- Managerialism and nursing. London ; New York : Routledge, 1999.
*TC RT86.45 .T73 1999*

**NURSE ADMINISTRATORS - GREAT BRITAIN.**
Traynor, Michael, 1956- Managerialism and nursing. London ; New York : Routledge, 1999.
*TC RT86.45 .T73 1999*

**NURSE ADMINISTRATORS - ORGANIZATION & ADMINISTRATION.**
McGuffin, Jo A. The nurse's guide to successful management. St. Louis, Mo. : Mosby, c1999.
*TC RT89 .M436 1999*

**NURSE ADMINISTRATORS - UNITED STATES.**
Finkler, Steven A. Financial management for nurse managers and executives. 2nd ed. Philadelphia ; London : W.B. Saunders, c2000.
*TC RT86.7 .F46 2000*

**NURSE ADMINISTRATORS - UNITED STATES.**
Fressola, Maria C. How nurse executives learned to become leaders. 1998.
*TC 06 no. 11115*

Fressola, Maria C. How nurse executives learned to become leaders. 1998.
*TC 06 no. 11115*

**NURSE AND PATIENT.**
Binnie, Alison. Freedom to practise. Oxford ; Boston : Butterworth-Heinemann, 1999.
*TC RT41 .B56 1999*

Libster, Martha. Demonstrating care. Albany, NY : Delmar Thomson Learning, 2000.
*TC RT86 .L535 2000*

O'Brien, Mary Elizabeth. Spirituality in nursing. Sudbury, Mass. : Jones and Bartlett Pub., c1999.
*TC RT85.2 .O37 1999*

**NURSE CLINICIANS.** *See* **NURSE PRACTITIONERS.**

**NURSE EXECUTIVES.** *See* **NURSE ADMINISTRATORS.**

**NURSE MANAGERS.** *See* **NURSE ADMINISTRATORS.**

**NURSE-PATIENT RELATIONS.**
Libster, Martha. Demonstrating care. Albany, NY : Delmar Thomson Learning, 2000.
*TC RT86 .L535 2000*

**NURSE PRACTITIONERS.**
Nurse practitioner's clinical companion. Springhouse, Pa. : Springhouse Corp., c2000.
*TC RT82.8 .N8638 2000*

**Nurse practitioner's clinical companion.** Springhouse, Pa. : Springhouse Corp., c2000. x, 470 p. : ill. ; 21 cm. Includes bibliographical references and indexes. ISBN 1-58255-006-9 (alk. paper)
*1. Nurse practitioners - Handbooks, manuals, etc. 2. Clinical medicine - Handbooks, manuals, etc. 3. Nurse Practitioners. 4. Clinical Medicine. 5. Nursing Care. I. Springhouse Corporation.*
*TC RT82.8 .N8638 2000*

**NURSE PRACTITIONERS - EXAMINATION QUESTIONS.**
Family nurse practitioner certification review. St. Louis : Mosby, c1999.
*TC RT120.F34 F353 1998*

**NURSE PRACTITIONERS - EXAMINATIONS, QUESTIONS, ETC.**
Family nurse practitioner certification review. St. Louis : Mosby, c1999.
*TC RT120.F34 F353 1998*

**NURSE PRACTITIONERS - HANDBOOKS, MANUALS, ETC.**
Nurse practitioner's clinical companion. Springhouse, Pa. : Springhouse Corp., c2000.
*TC RT82.8 .N8638 2000*

**NURSE PRACTITIONERS - PSYCHOLOGY.**
Fenichel, Ann. The relationship between health care clinicians' relational abilities and psychosocial orientation to patient care, and patient adherence with medical treatment. 1998.
*TC 085 F352*

**NURSERY RHYMES.** *See also* **LULLABIES.**
Dana, Katharine Floyd, 1835-1886. Over in the meadow. New York : Scholastic, c1992
*TC PZ8.3.D2 Ov 1992*

Dana, Katharine Floyd, 1835-1886. Over in the meadow. New York : Scholastic, c1992
*TC PZ8.3.D2 Ov 1992*

Ivimey, John W. (John William), b. 1868. [Complete version of ye Three blind mice] Three blind mice. New York : G.P. Putnam's Sons, c1991.
*TC PZ8.3.I83 Th 1991*

Ivimey, John W. (John William), b. 1868. [Complete version of ye Three blind mice] Three blind mice. New York : G.P. Putnam's Sons, c1991.
*TC PZ8.3.I83 Th 1991*

**NURSERY SCHOOLS.** *See also* **DAY CARE CENTERS; EDUCATION, PRESCHOOL; KINDERGARTEN.**
Yardley, Alice. Reaching out. London : Evans Bros., 1970.
*TC LB1140 .Y35*

**NURSERY SCHOOLS - CURRICULA.**
Lavatelli, Celia Stendler, 1911- Piaget's theory applied to an early childhood curriculum. [1st ed.]. Boston : American Science and Engineering, [c1970].
*TC LB1140.2 .L3*

**NURSERY SCHOOLS - GREAT BRITAIN.**
Thompson, Linda, 1949- Young bilingual children in nursery school. Clevedon, UK ; Buffalo, NY : Multilingual Matters, c2000.
*TC LC3723 .T47 2000*

**NURSERY SCHOOLS - UNITED STATES - ADMINISTRATION.**
Click, Phyllis. Administration of schools for young children. 5th ed. Albany, NY : Delmar, 1999.
*TC LB2822.7 .C55 1999*

**NURSERY STOCK.** *See* **TREES.**

**NURSES.** *See also* **NURSE ADMINISTRATORS; NURSE PRACTITIONERS.**
Russell, Graham, 1954- Essential psychology for nurses and other health professionals. London ; New York : Routledge, c1999.
*TC R726.7 .R87 1999*

**NURSES AND NURSING.** *See* **NURSES; NURSING.**

**NURSES - CONNECTICUT - ATTITUDES.**
Abate, Ellen C. Personal characteristics of nurses and their influence on professional autonomy. 1998.
*TC 06 no. 11009*

**NURSES - ENGLAND - BIOGRAPHY.**
Dossey, Barbara Montgomery. Florence Nightingale. Springhouse, PA : Springhouse Corp., c2000.
*TC RT37.N5 D67 2000*

**NURSES - IN-SERVICE TRAINING.**
Integrating community service into nursing education. New York, NY : Springer Pub. Co., c1999.
*TC RT76 .I55 1999*

**Nurse's legal handbook.** 4th ed. Springhouse, Pa. : Springhouse Corp., c2000. x, 422 p. : ill. ; 21 cm. Includes bibliographical references and indexes. ISBN 0-87434-991-5 (alk. paper)
*1. Nursing - Practice - United States. 2. Nursing ethics. 3. Nursing - Law and legislation - United States. 4. Ethics, Nursing. 5. Legislation, Nursing - United States. 6. Malpractice - United States - legislation. 7. Malpractice - United States - nurses' instruction. I. Springhouse Corporation. II. Title: Practices.*
*TC RT86.7 .N88 2000*

**NURSES - LEGAL STATUS, LAWS, ETC.** *See* **NURSING - LAW AND LEGISLATION.**

**NURSES - NEW YORK (STATE) - ATTITUDES.**
Abate, Ellen C. Personal characteristics of nurses and their influence on professional autonomy. 1998.
*TC 06 no. 11009*

**NURSES' NOTES.** *See* **NURSING RECORDS.**

**NURSES - PROFESSIONAL ETHICS.** *See* **NURSING ETHICS.**

**NURSES - STANDARDS.**
American Nurses Association. Task Force on Staff Privileges. Guidelines for appointment of nurses for individual practice privileges in health care organizations. Kansas City, MO : American Nurses Association, Commission on Nursing Service, 1978.
*TC RT104 .A44 1978*

**NURSES - SUPERVISION OF - GREAT BRITAIN.**
Traynor, Michael, 1956- Managerialism and nursing. London ; New York : Routledge, 1999.
*TC RT86.45 .T73 1999*

**NURSING.** *See also* **COMMUNICATION IN NURSING; FAMILY NURSING; INDUSTRIAL NURSING; INTENSIVE CARE NURSING; MILITARY NURSING; PEDIATRIC NURSING; PRACTICAL NURSING; PSYCHIATRIC NURSING; REHABILITATION NURSING.**
American Nurses Association. Task Force on Staff Privileges. Guidelines for appointment of nurses for individual practice privileges in health care organizations. Kansas City, MO : American Nurses Association, Commission on Nursing Service, 1978.

*TC RT104 .A44 1978*

American Nurses Association. Task Force on Staff Privileges. Guidelines for appointment of nurses for individual practice privileges in health care organizations. Kansas City, MO : American Nurses Association, Commission on Nursing Service, 1978.
*TC RT104 .A44 1978*

Binnie, Alison. Freedom to practise. Oxford ; Boston : Butterworth-Heinemann, 1999.
*TC RT41 .B56 1999*

Binnie, Alison. Freedom to practise. Oxford ; Boston : Butterworth-Heinemann, 1999.
*TC RT41 .B56 1999*

Concept development in nursing. 2nd ed. Philadelphia : Saunders, c2000.
*TC RT84.5 .C6624 2000*

Grodner, Michele. Foundations and clinical applications of nutrition. 2nd ed. St. Louis, Mo. : Mosby, c2000.
*TC RM216 .G946 2000*

The Inc. [Los Angeles, CA : Inc. Publishing,

Kim, Hesook Suzie. The nature of theoretical thinking in nursing. 2nd ed. New York : Springer Pub. Co., c2000.
*TC RT84.5 .K545 2000*

Lashley, Felissa R., 1941- Clinical genetics in nursing practice. 2nd ed. New York : Springer, c1998.
*TC RB155 .L37 1998*

Nursing procedures. 3rd ed. Springhouse, Pa. : Springhouse Corp., c2000.
*TC RT41 .N886 2000*

Poirrier, Gail P. Service learning. Boston : Jones and Bartlett Publishers, 2001.
*TC RT73 .P64 2001*

Reflective practice in nursing. 2nd ed. Oxford ; Malden, MA : Blackwell Scientific, 2000.
*TC RT73 .R3461 2000*

**NURSING - ADMINISTRATION.** See **NURSING SERVICES - ADMINISTRATION.**

**NURSING ADMINISTRATION.** See **NURSING SERVICES - ADMINISTRATION.**

**Nursing administration in the 21st century.**
Allison, Sarah E. Thousand Oaks : Sage Publications, c1999.
*TC RT89 .A435 1999*

**Nursing administration in the twenty-first century.**
Allison, Sarah E. Nursing administration in the 21st century. Thousand Oaks : Sage Publications, c1999.
*TC RT89 .A435 1999*

**NURSING ADMINISTRATORS.** See **NURSE ADMINISTRATORS.**

**NURSING AGENCIES.** See **NURSING SERVICES.**

**Nursing and the experience of illness :**
phenomenology in practice / edited by Irena Madjar & JoAnn Walton ; with a foreword by Max van Manen. London ; New York : Routledge, 1999. xvi, 198 p. ; 22 cm. Includes bibliographical references and index. ISBN 0-415-20782-7 (hbk) ISBN 0-415-20783-5 (pbk) DDC 610.73/019
*1. Nursing - Psychological aspects. 2. Phenomenology. 3. Nursing - Research. 4. Mind and body. 5. Nursing Care - psychology. 6. Patients - psychology. 7. Mind-Body Relations (Metaphysics) 8. Nursing Methodology Research. I. Madjar, Irena. II. Walton, Jo Ann.*
*TC RT86 .N886 1999*

**NURSING - BIBLIOGRAPHY.**
Clamp, Cynthia G. L. Resources for nursing research. 3rd ed. London ; Thousand Oaks, Calif. : Sage, 1999.
*TC Z6675.N7 C53 1999*

**NURSING - BIBLIOGRAPHY OF BIBLIOGRAPHIES.**
Clamp, Cynthia G. L. Resources for nursing research. 3rd ed. London ; Thousand Oaks, Calif. : Sage, 1999.
*TC Z6675.N7 C53 1999*

**Nursing care.**
Bedside nurse. New York, National Federation of Licensed Practical Nurses, Inc., 1968-72.

**NURSING CARE.**
Nurse practitioner's clinical companion. Springhouse, Pa. : Springhouse Corp., c2000.
*TC RT82.8 .N8638 2000*

Nursing procedures. 3rd ed. Springhouse, Pa. : Springhouse Corp., c2000.

*TC RT41 .N886 2000*

**NURSING CARE - METHODS.**
Libster, Martha. Demonstrating care. Albany, NY : Delmar Thomson Learning, 2000.
*TC RT86 .L535 2000*

**NURSING CARE - PSYCHOLOGY.**
Nursing and the experience of illness. London ; New York : Routledge, 1999.
*TC RT86 .N886 1999*

**NURSING - DIRECTORIES.**
Hospital progress. St. Louis [etc.] Catholic Health Association of the United States [etc.]

**Nursing documentation :** legal focus across practice settings / [edited by] Sue E. Meiner. Thousand Oaks, Calif. : Sage Publications, c1999. xiii, 294 p. : ill., forms ; 27 cm. Includes bibliographical references (p. 269-277) and index. ISBN 0-7619-1071-9 (c : alk. paper) ISBN 0-7619-1072-7 (p : alk. paper) DDC 610.73
*1. Nursing records - Miscellanea - Handbooks, manuals, etc. 2. Nursing - Law and legislation - Handbooks, manuals, etc. 3. Communication in nursing - Miscellanea - Handbooks, manuals, etc. 4. Liability, Legal - Miscellanea - Handbooks, manuals, etc. 5. Nursing Records - legislation & jurisprudence - United States. 6. Liability, Legal - United States. 7. Risk Management. 8. Communication. I. Meiner, Sue.*
*TC RT50 .N87 1999*

**Nursing education monographs**
Christy, Teresa E. Cornerstone for nursing education. New York : Teachers College Press, Columbia University, [1969]
*TC RT81.N3 C45*

**NURSING ETHICS.** See also **MEDICAL ETHICS.**
Bishop, Anne H., 1935- 2nd ed. Sudbury, Mass. : Jones and Bartlett, c2001.
*TC RT85 .B57 2001*

**NURSING ETHICS.**
Bandman, Elsie L. Nursing ethics through the life span. 3rd ed. Norwalk, Conn. : Appleton & Lange, c1995.
*TC RT85 .B33 1995*

Nurse's legal handbook. 4th ed. Springhouse, Pa. : Springhouse Corp., c2000.
*TC RT86.7 .N88 2000*

**Nursing ethics through the life span.**
Bandman, Elsie L. 3rd ed. Norwalk, Conn. : Appleton & Lange, c1995.
*TC RT85 .B33 1995*

**NURSING ETHICS - UNITED STATES.**
Lederer, Jane. Participation in active euthanasia and assisted suicide and attitudes and interpersonal values of physicians and nurses. 1996.
*TC 06 no. 10849*

**NURSING ETHICS - UNITED STATES - HISTORY.**
Smalls, Sadie Marian. Anna Caroline Maxwell's contributions to nursing. 1996.
*TC 06 no. 10698*

**NURSING - EXAMINATION QUESTIONS.**
Nugent, Patricia Mary, 1944- Test success. 3rd ed. Philadelphia : F.A. Davis, c2000.
*TC RT55 .N77 2000*

**NURSING - HISTORY - ENCYCLOPEDIAS.**
Snodgrass, Mary Ellen. Historical encyclopedia of nursing. Santa Barbara, Calif. : ABC-CLIO, 1999.
*TC RT31 .S66 1999*

Snodgrass, Mary Ellen. Historical encyclopedia of nursing. Santa Barbara, Calif. : ABC-CLIO, 1999.
*TC RT31 .S66 1999*

**NURSING HOME PATIENTS - MENTAL HEALTH.**
Hartz, Gary W. Psychosocial intervention in long-term care. New York : Haworth Press, c1997.
*TC RC451.4.N87 H37 1997*

**NURSING HOME RESIDENTS.** See **NURSING HOME PATIENTS.**

**NURSING HOMES - PATIENTS.** See **NURSING HOME PATIENTS.**

**NURSING LAW.** See **NURSING - LAW AND LEGISLATION.**

**NURSING - LAW AND LEGISLATION - HANDBOOKS, MANUALS, ETC.**
Nursing documentation. Thousand Oaks, Calif. : Sage Publications, c1999.
*TC RT50 .N87 1999*

**NURSING - LAW AND LEGISLATION - UNITED STATES.**
Nurse's legal handbook. 4th ed. Springhouse, Pa. : Springhouse Corp., c2000.
*TC RT86.7 .N88 2000*

**Nursing leadership, management & research.**
Grant, Ann Boyle. Springhouse, Pa. : Springhouse Corp., c1999.
*TC RT89 .G727 1999*

**Nursing leadership, management, and research.**
Grant, Ann Boyle. Nursing leadership, management & research. Springhouse, Pa. : Springhouse Corp., c1999.
*TC RT89 .G727 1999*

**NURSING MANAGERS.** See **NURSE ADMINISTRATORS.**

**NURSING METHODOLOGY RESEARCH.**
Nursing and the experience of illness. London ; New York : Routledge, 1999.
*TC RT86 .N886 1999*

**NURSING MODELS.**
Tiffany, Constance Rimmer. Planned change theories for nursing. Thousand Oaks : Sage Publications, c1998.
*TC RT89 .T54 1998*

**NURSING - MORAL AND ETHICAL ASPECTS.**
See also **NURSING ETHICS.**
O'Brien, Mary Elizabeth. Spirituality in nursing. Sudbury, Mass. : Jones and Bartlett Pub., c1999.
*TC RT85.2 .O37 1999*

**NURSING - ORGANIZATION & ADMINISTRATION - GREAT BRITAIN.**
Traynor, Michael, 1956- Managerialism and nursing. London : New York : Routledge, 1999.
*TC RT86.45 .T73 1999*

**NURSING - ORGANIZATION & ADMINISTRATION - OUTLINES.**
Grant, Ann Boyle. Nursing leadership, management & research. Springhouse, Pa. : Springhouse Corp., c1999.
*TC RT89 .G727 1999*

**NURSING - PERIODICALS.**
Association of Rehabilitation Nurses. ARN journal. [Glenview, Ill.] Association of Rehabilitation Nurses.

**NURSING - PERIODICALS.**
Hospital progress. St. Louis [etc.] Catholic Health Association of the United States [etc.]

**NURSING - PERIODICALS.**
Hospital progress. St. Louis [etc.] Catholic Health Association of the United States [etc.]

**NURSING - PERIODICALS.**
Journal of nursing scholarship. Indianapolis, IN : JNS Publication Office, 2000-
*TC RT1 .I42*

Journal of nursing scholarship. Indianapolis, IN : JNS Publication Office, 2000-
*TC RT1 .I42*

Journal of psychiatric nursing. [Bordentown, N.J., etc., S. James Pub. Co., etc.]

**NURSING - PHILOSOPHY.**
Allison, Sarah E. Nursing administration in the 21st century. Thousand Oaks : Sage Publications, c1999.
*TC RT89 .A435 1999*

Brencick, Janice M. Philosophy of nursing. Albany : State University of New York Press, c2000.
*TC RT84.5 .B74 2000*

Concept development in nursing. 2nd ed. Philadelphia : Saunders, c2000.
*TC RT84.5 .C6624 2000*

Kim, Hesook Suzie. The nature of theoretical thinking in nursing. 2nd ed. New York : Springer Pub. Co., c2000.
*TC RT84.5 .K545 2000*

Libster, Martha. Demonstrating care. Albany, NY : Delmar Thomson Learning, 2000.
*TC RT86 .L535 2000*

Nursing theories. New York : Springer Pub. Co., c1999.
*TC RT84.5 .N8795 1999*

O'Brien, Mary Elizabeth. Spirituality in nursing. Sudbury, Mass. : Jones and Bartlett Pub., c1999.
*TC RT85.2 .O37 1999*

Reflective practice in nursing. 2nd ed. Oxford ; Malden, MA : Blackwell Scientific, 2000.

*TC RT73 .R3461 2000*
Rubenfeld, M. Gaie. Critical thinking in nursing. 2nd ed. Philadelphia : Lippincott, c1999.
*TC RT84.5 .R83 1999*

**NURSING - PLANNING.**
Tiffany, Constance Rimmer. Planned change theories for nursing. Thousand Oaks : Sage Publications, c1998.
*TC RT89 .T54 1998*

**NURSING - PRACTICE.** *See* **NURSE PRACTITIONERS.**

**NURSING - PRACTICE - UNITED STATES.**
Nurse's legal handbook. 4th ed. Springhouse, Pa. : Springhouse Corp., c2000.
*TC RT86.7 .N88 2000*

**NURSING - PROBLEMS.**
Rubenfeld, M. Gaie. Critical thinking in nursing. 2nd ed. Philadelphia : Lippincott, c1999.
*TC RT84.5 .R83 1999*

**NURSING - PROBLEMS, EXERCISES, ETC.**
Rubenfeld, M. Gaie. Critical thinking in nursing. 2nd ed. Philadelphia : Lippincott, c1999.
*TC RT84.5 .R83 1999*

**Nursing procedures.** 3rd ed. Springhouse, Pa. : Springhouse Corp., c2000. xi, 802 p. : ill. ; 24 cm. Includes bibliographical references and index. ISBN 0-87434-978-8 (alk. paper)
*1. Nursing. 2. Nursing Care. I. Springhouse Corporation.*
*TC RT41 .N886 2000*

**NURSING PROCESS.** *See* **NURSING.**

**NURSING PROCESS.**
Grodner, Michele. Foundations and clinical applications of nutrition. 2nd ed. St. Louis, Mo. : Mosby, c2000.
*TC RM216 .G946 2000*
Rubenfeld, M. Gaie. Critical thinking in nursing. 2nd ed. Philadelphia : Lippincott, c1999.
*TC RT84.5 .R83 1999*

**NURSING - PSYCHOLOGICAL ASPECTS.**
Abate, Ellen C. Personal characteristics of nurses and their influence on professional autonomy. 1998.
*TC 06 no. 11009*
Libster, Martha. Demonstrating care. Albany, NY : Delmar Thomson Learning, 2000.
*TC RT86 .L535 2000*
Nursing and the experience of illness. London ; New York : Routledge, 1999.
*TC RT86 .N886 1999*
Russell, Graham, 1954- Essential psychology for nurses and other health professionals. London ; New York : Routledge, c1999.
*TC R726.7 .R87 1999*

**NURSING RECORDS - LEGISLATION & JURISPRUDENCE - UNITED STATES.**
Nursing documentation. Thousand Oaks, Calif. : Sage Publications, c1999.
*TC RT50 .N87 1999*

**NURSING RECORDS - MISCELLANEA - HANDBOOKS, MANUALS, ETC.**
Nursing documentation. Thousand Oaks, Calif. : Sage Publications, c1999.
*TC RT50 .N87 1999*

**NURSING - RELIGIOUS ASPECTS - CHRISTIANITY.**
O'Brien, Mary Elizabeth. Spirituality in nursing. Sudbury, Mass. : Jones and Bartlett Pub., c1999.
*TC RT85.2 .O37 1999*

**NURSING RESEARCH.** *See also* **NURSING - RESEARCH.**
Polit-O'Hara, Denise. 6th ed. Philadelphia : Lippincott, c1999.
*TC RT81.5 .P64 1999*

**NURSING - RESEARCH.**
Dempsey, Patricia Ann. Using nursing research. 5th ed. Baltimore, Md. : Lippincott, c2000.
*TC RT81.5 .D46 2000*

**NURSING RESEARCH.**
Dempsey, Patricia Ann. Using nursing research. 5th ed. Baltimore, Md. : Lippincott, c2000.
*TC RT81.5 .D46 2000*

**NURSING - RESEARCH.**
Nursing and the experience of illness. London ; New York : Routledge, 1999.
*TC RT86 .N886 1999*

**NURSING - RESEARCH - BIBLIOGRAPHY.**
Clamp, Cynthia G. L. Resources for nursing research. 3rd ed. London : Thousand Oaks, Calif. : Sage, 1999.
*TC Z6675.N7 C53 1999*

**NURSING RESEARCH - BIBLIOGRAPHY.**
Clamp, Cynthia G. L. Resources for nursing research. 3rd ed. London : Thousand Oaks, Calif. : Sage, 1999.
*TC Z6675.N7 C53 1999*

**Nursing research digest** / Joyce J. Fitzpatrick, editor. New York : Springer Pub. Co., c1999. xvi, 308 p. ; 23 cm. Mini-version of Encyclopedia of nursing research--Pref. Includes bibliographical references (p. 285-306) and index. ISBN 0-8261-1292-7 (softcover) DDC 610.73/07/2
*1. Nursing - Research - Encyclopedias. 2. Nursing Research - Encyclopedias - English. I. Fitzpatrick, Joyce J., 1944- II. Title: Encyclopedia of nursing research.*
*TC RT81.5 .N8736 1999*

**NURSING - RESEARCH - ENCYCLOPEDIAS.**
Nursing research digest. New York : Springer Pub. Co., c1999.
*TC RT81.5 .N8736 1999*

**NURSING RESEARCH - ENCYCLOPEDIAS - ENGLISH.**
Nursing research digest. New York : Springer Pub. Co., c1999.
*TC RT81.5 .N8736 1999*

**NURSING - RESEARCH - HANDBOOKS, MANUALS, ETC.**
Handbook of clinical nursing research. Thousand Oaks, Calif. : Sage Publications, c1999.
*TC RT81.5 .H25 1999*

**NURSING - RESEARCH - METHODOLOGY.**
Munhall, Patricia L. Qualitative research proposals and reports. Sudbury, MA : Jones and Bartlett, 2000.
*TC RT81.5 .M854 2000*
Polit-O'Hara, Denise. Nursing research. 6th ed. Philadelphia : Lippincott, c1999.
*TC RT81.5 .P64 1999*
Roper, Janice M. Ethnography in nursing research. Thousand Oaks, Calif. : Sage Publications, c2000.
*TC RT81.5 .R66 2000*
Streubert, Helen J. Qualitative research in nursing. 2nd ed. Philadelphia : Lippincott, c1999.
*TC RT81.5 .S78 1999*

**NURSING RESEARCH - METHODS.**
Polit-O'Hara, Denise. Nursing research. 6th ed. Philadelphia : Lippincott, c1999.
*TC RT81.5 .P64 1999*
Streubert, Helen J. Qualitative research in nursing. 2nd ed. Philadelphia : Lippincott, c1999.
*TC RT81.5 .S78 1999*

**NURSING - RESEARCH - OUTLINE, SYLLABI, ETC.**
Grant, Ann Boyle. Nursing leadership, management & research. Springhouse, Pa. : Springhouse Corp., c1999.
*TC RT89 .G727 1999*

**NURSING RESEARCH - OUTLINES.**
Grant, Ann Boyle. Nursing leadership, management & research. Springhouse, Pa. : Springhouse Corp., c1999.
*TC RT89 .G727 1999*

**NURSING SCHOOLS - UNITED STATES - CURRICULA - HISTORY.**
Smalls, Sadie Marian. Anna Caroline Maxwell's contributions to nursing. 1996.
*TC 06 no. 10698*

**NURSING SCHOOLS - UNITED STATES - DIRECTORIES.**
Annual guide to graduate nursing education programs. New York, N.Y. : National League for Nursing Press, c1995-
*TC RT75 .A5*
Official guide to undergraduate nursing schools. Sudbury, Mass. : Jones and Bartlett Publishers, c2000.
*TC RT75.4 .O4 2000*

**NURSING SCHOOLS - UNITED STATES - HISTORY.**
Smalls, Sadie Marian. Anna Caroline Maxwell's contributions to nursing. 1996.
*TC 06 no. 10698*

**NURSING SERVICE ADMINISTRATION.** *See* **NURSING SERVICES - ADMINISTRATION.**

**NURSING SERVICES - ADMINISTRATION.**
Allison, Sarah E. Nursing administration in the 21st century. Thousand Oaks : Sage Publications, c1999.

*TC RT89. A435 1999*
Fressola, Maria C. How nurse executives learned to become leaders. 1998.
*TC 06 no. 11115*
Fressola, Maria C. How nurse executives learned to become leaders. 1998.
*TC 06 no. 11115*
Grossman, Sheila. The new leadership challenge. Philadelphia : F.A. Davis, c2000.
*TC RT89 .G77 2000*
Huber, Diane. Leadership and nursing care management. 2nd ed. Philadelphia : W.B. Saunders, c2000.
*TC RT89 .H83 2000*
Marriner-Tomey, Ann, 1943- Guide to nursing management and leadership. 6th ed. St. Louis, Mo. : Mosby, 2000.
*TC RT89.3 M37 2000*
McGuffin, Jo A. The nurse's guide to successful management. St. Louis, Mo. : Mosby, c1999.
*TC RT89 .M436 1999*

**NURSING SERVICES - ADMINISTRATION - OUTLINE, SYLLABI, ETC.**
Grant, Ann Boyle. Nursing leadership, management & research. Springhouse, Pa. : Springhouse Corp., c1999.
*TC RT89 .G727 1999*

**NURSING SERVICES - BUSINESS MANAGEMENT.**
Finkler, Steven A. Financial management for nurse managers and executives. 2nd ed. Philadelphia ; London : W.B. Saunders, c2000.
*TC RT86.7 .F46 2000*

**NURSING SERVICES - FORECASTING.**
Allison, Sarah E. Nursing administration in the 21st century. Thousand Oaks : Sage Publications, c1999.
*TC RT89. A435 1999*

**NURSING SERVICES - GREAT BRITAIN - ADMINISTRATION.**
Traynor, Michael, 1956- Managerialism and nursing. London ; New York : Routledge, 1999.
*TC RT86.45 .T73 1999*

**NURSING SERVICES - GREAT BRITAIN - PERSONNEL MANAGEMENT.**
Traynor, Michael, 1956- Managerialism and nursing. London ; New York : Routledge, 1999.
*TC RT86.45 .T73 1999*

**NURSING SERVICES - ORGANIZATION & ADMINISTRATION - LEADERSHIP.**
Huber, Diane. Leadership and nursing care management. 2nd ed. Philadelphia : W.B. Saunders, c2000.
*TC RT89 .H83 2000*

**NURSING SERVICES - STANDARDS.**
American Nurses Association. Task Force on Staff Privileges. Guidelines for appointment of nurses for individual practice privileges in health care organizations. Kansas City, MO : American Nurses Association, Commission on Nursing Service, 1978.
*TC RT104 .A44 1978*

**NURSING SERVICES - UNITED STATES - ADMINISTRATION.**
Huber, Diane. Leadership and nursing care management. 2nd ed. Philadelphia : W.B. Saunders, c2000.
*TC RT89 .H83 2000*

**NURSING - SOCIAL ASPECTS.**
Abate, Ellen C. Personal characteristics of nurses and their influence on professional autonomy. 1998.
*TC 06 no. 11009*

**NURSING STAFF - ORGANIZATION & ADMINISTRATION.**
McGuffin, Jo A. The nurse's guide to successful management. St. Louis, Mo. : Mosby, c1999.
*TC RT89 .M436 1999*

**NURSING STAFF - STANDARDS.**
American Nurses Association. Task Force on Staff Privileges. Guidelines for appointment of nurses for individual practice privileges in health care organizations. Kansas City, MO : American Nurses Association, Commission on Nursing Service, 1978.
*TC RT104 .A44 1978*

**NURSING - STUDY & TEACHING.**
Schoolcraft, Victoria. A nuts-and-bolts approach to teaching nursing. 2nd ed. New York : Springer Pub. Co., c2000.

*TC RT71 .S26 2000*

## NURSING - STUDY AND TEACHING.
Gaberson, Kathleen B. Clinical teaching strategies in nursing. New York : Springer, c1999.
*TC RT73 .G26 1999*

Poirrier, Gail P. Service learning. Boston : Jones and Bartlett Publishers, 2001.
*TC RT73 .P64 2001*

Reflective practice in nursing. 2nd ed. Oxford ; Malden, MA : Blackwell Scientific, 2000.
*TC RT73 .R3461 2000*

## NURSING - STUDY AND TEACHING (CONTINUING EDUCATION).
Integrating community service into nursing education. New York, NY : Springer Pub. Co., c1999.
*TC RT76 .I55 1999*

Ulrich, Deborah L. Interactive group learning. New York : Springer, c1999.
*TC RT76 .U46 1999*

## NURSING - STUDY AND TEACHING (GRADUATE) - UNITED STATES - DIRECTORIES.
Annual guide to graduate nursing education programs. New York, N.Y. : National League for Nursing Press, c1995-
*TC RT75 .A5*

## NURSING, SUPERVISORY.
Grossman, Sheila. The new leadership challenge. Philadelphia : F.A. Davis, c2000.
*TC RT89 .G77 2000*

Marriner-Tomey, Ann, 1943- Guide to nursing management and leadership. 6th ed. St. Louis, Mo. : Mosby, 2000.
*TC RT89.3 M37 2000*

## NURSING, SUPERVISORY - LEADERSHIP.
Huber, Diane. Leadership and nursing care management. 2nd ed. Philadelphia : W.B. Saunders, c2000.
*TC RT89 .H83 2000*

## NURSING, SUPERVISORY - ORGANIZATION & ADMINISTRATION.
McGuffin, Jo A. The nurse's guide to successful management. St. Louis, Mo. : Mosby, c1999.
*TC RT89 .M436 1999*

**Nursing theories :** conceptual and philosophical foundations / Hesook Suzie Kim, Ingrid Kollak, editors. New York : Springer Pub. Co., c1999. xiii, 223 p. ; 24 cm. Includes bibliographical references and index. ISBN 0-8261-1287-0 (hardcover) DDC 610.73/01
*1. Nursing - Philosophy. 2. Nursing Theory. 3. Models, Nursing. 4. Philosophy, Nursing. I. Kim, Hesook Suzie. II. Kollak, Ingrid.*
*TC RT84.5 .N8795 1999*

## NURSING THEORY.
Libster, Martha. Demonstrating care. Albany, NY : Delmar Thomson Learning, 2000.
*TC RT86 .L535 2000*

Nursing theories. New York : Springer Pub. Co., c1999.
*TC RT84.5 .N8795 1999*

## NURSING - UNITED STATES - HISTORY.
Smalls, Sadie Marian. Anna Caroline Maxwell's contributions to nursing. 1996.
*TC 06 no. 10698*

## NURSING - UNITED STATES - PERIODICALS.
Journal of nursing scholarship. Indianapolis, IN : JNS Publication Office, 2000-
*TC RT1 .I42*

**Nurturing independent learners.**
Meichenbaum, Donald. Cambridge, Mass. : Brookline Books, c1998.
*TC LB1031.4 .M45 1998*

**Nurturing inquiry.**
Pearce, Charles R. Portsmouth, NH : Heinemann, c1999.
*TC LB1584 .P34 1999*

**Nussbaum, Felicity.**
Defects. Ann Arbor : University of Michigan Press, c2000.
*TC HV1568.25.G7 D44 1999*

**Nussbaum, Jon F.**
Communication and aging. 2nd ed. Mahwah, NJ ; London : L. Erlbaum, 2000.
*TC HQ1064.U5 C5364 2000*

**Nussbaum, Martha Craven, 1947-** Women and human development : the capabilities approach / Martha C. Nussbaum. Cambridge, U.K. ; New York : Cambridge University Press, 2000. xxi, 312 p. ; 24 cm. (The John Robert Seeley lectures) Includes bibliographical references and indexes. ISBN 0-521-66086-6 (hbk.) DDC 305.42/09172/4
*1. Women in development. 2. Women - Developing countries. I. Title. II. Series.*
*TC HQ1240 .N87 2000*

## NUTRITION. *See also* DIET; FOOD; FOOD HABITS; FOOD PREFERENCES; MALNUTRITION.
Grodner, Michele. Foundations and clinical applications of nutrition. 2nd ed. St. Louis, Mo. : Mosby, c2000.
*TC RM216 .G946 2000*

## NUTRITION.
Biochemical and physiological aspects of human nutrition. Philadelphia : W.B. Saunders, c1999.
*TC QP141 .B57 1999*

Clinical nutrition. 2nd ed. Philadelphia : Saunders, 1993.
*TC RM224 .P24 1993*

Energy-yielding macronutrients and energy metabolism in sports nutrition. Boca Raton, Fla. ; London : CRC Press, c2000.
*TC QP176 .E546 2000*

Evolutionary aspects of nutrition and health. Basel ; New York : Karger, c1999.
*TC QP141 .E95 1999*

Evolutionary aspects of nutrition and health. Basel ; New York : Karger, c1999.
*TC QP141 .E95 1999*

Goldfein, Juli Ann. The importance of shape and weight in normal-weight women with bulimia nervosa, restrained eaters (dieters), and normal controls (Non-dieters). 1997.
*TC 085 G5675*

Grodner, Michele. Foundations and clinical applications of nutrition. 2nd ed. St. Louis, Mo. : Mosby, c2000.
*TC RM216 .G946 2000*

Groff, James L. Advanced nutrition and human metabolism. 3rd ed. Belmont, CA : West/Wadsworth, c2000.
*TC QP141 .G76 2000*

McMurray, Robert G. Concepts in fitness programming. Boca Raton : CRC Press, c1999.
*TC QP301 .M3754 1999*

Morgan, Brian L. G. Brainfood. Tucson, Ariz. : Body Press, c1987.
*TC QP376 .M62 1987*

Nutrition and exercise immunology. Boca Raton, Fla. ; London : CRC Press, c2000.
*TC QP301 .N875 2000*

Nutrition and immunology. Totowa, N.J. : Humana Press, c2000.
*TC QP141 .N7767 2000*

Nutrition and immunology. Totowa, N.J. : Humana Press, c2000.
*TC QP141 .N7767 2000*

Nutrition in sport. Osney Mead, Oxford ; Malden, MA : Blackwell Science, 2000.
*TC QP141 .N793 2000*

The nutty, nougat-filled world of human nutrition [videorecording]. [Arlington, Va.] : Cerebellum Corp., c1998.
*TC QP141 .N8 1998*

Rinzler, Carol Ann. The new complete book of food. New York : Facts on File, c1999.
*TC TX353 .R525 1999*

Wildman, Robert E. C., 1964- Advanced human nutrition. Boca Raton : CRC Press, c2000.
*TC QP141 .W512 2000*

Wildman, Robert E. C., 1964- Advanced human nutrition. Boca Raton : CRC Press, c2000.
*TC QP141 .W512 2000*

**Nutrition and disease prevention.**
The nutty, nougat-filled world of human nutrition [videorecording]. [Arlington, Va.] : Cerebellum Corp., c1998.
*TC QP141 .N8 1998*

**Nutrition and exercise immunology** / [edited by] David C. Nieman, Bente Klarlund Pedersen. Boca Raton, Fla. ; London : CRC Press, c2000. 191 p. : ill. ; 25 cm. (Nutrition in exercise and sport) Includes bibliographical references and index. ISBN 0-8493-0741-4 (alk. paper) DDC 616.07/9
*1. Exercise - Immunological aspects. 2. Nutrition. I. Nieman, David C., 1950- II. Pedersen, Bente Klarlund. 1956- III. Series.*
*TC QP301 .N875 2000*

## Nutrition and health (Totowa, N.J.)
The management of eating disorders and obesity. Totowa, N.J. : Humana Press, c1999.
*TC RC552.E18 M364 1999*

**Nutrition and immunology :** principles and practice / edited by M. Eric Gershwin, J. Bruce German, Carl L. Keen. Totowa, N.J. : Humana Press, c2000. xiv, 505 p. : ill. ; 29 cm. Includes bibliographical references and index. ISBN 0-89603-719-3 (alk. paper) DDC 612.3/9
*1. Nutrition. 2. Immunity - Nutritional aspects. 3. Nutrition. 4. Nutritional Requirements. 5. Immunity. I. Gershwin, M. Eric, 1946- II. German, J. Bruce. III. Keen, Carl L.*
*TC QP141 .N7767 2000*

## NUTRITION AND STATE. *See* NUTRITION POLICY.

## NUTRITION - ATLASES.
Human nutrition and obesity. Philadelphia : Current Medicine, 1999.
*TC RC620.5 .H846 1999*

Human nutrition and obesity. Philadelphia : Current Medicine, 1999.
*TC RC620.5 .H846 1999*

## NUTRITION COUNSELING.
The nutty, nougat-filled world of human nutrition [videorecording]. [Arlington, Va.] : Cerebellum Corp., c1998.
*TC QP141 .N8 1998*

## NUTRITION DISORDERS. *See also* MALNUTRITION; OBESITY.
The nutty, nougat-filled world of human nutrition [videorecording]. [Arlington, Va.] : Cerebellum Corp., c1998.
*TC QP141 .N8 1998*

## NUTRITION DISORDERS - ATLASES.
Human nutrition and obesity. Philadelphia : Current Medicine, 1999.
*TC RC620.5 .H846 1999*

## NUTRITION DISORDERS - ETIOLOGY.
Evolutionary aspects of nutrition and health. Basel ; New York : Karger, c1999.
*TC QP141 .E95 1999*

**Nutrition for serious athletes.**
Benardot, Dan, 1949- Champaign, IL ; Leeds, U.K. : Human Kinetics, c2000.
*TC TX361.A8 B45 2000*

**Nutrition in exercise and sport**
Di Pasquale, Mauro G. Amino acids and proteins for the athlete. Boca Raton : CRC Press, c1997.
*TC QP551 .D46 1997*

Energy-yielding macronutrients and energy metabolism in sports nutrition. Boca Raton, Fla. ; London : CRC Press, c2000.
*TC QP176 .E546 2000*

Nutrition and exercise immunology. Boca Raton, Fla. ; London : CRC Press, c2000.
*TC QP301 .N875 2000*

**Nutrition in sport** / edited by Ron J. Maughan. Osney Mead, Oxford ; Malden, MA : Blackwell Science, 2000. 680 p. : ill. ; 26 cm. (Encyclopedia of sports medicine ; v. 7) "An IOC Medical Commission publication in collaboration with the International Federation of Sports Medicine." Includes bibliographical references and index. ISBN 0-632-05094-2 DDC 616.3/9/0088796
*1. Nutrition. 2. Energy metabolism. 3. Exercise - Physiological aspects. 4. Athletes - Nutrition. I. Maughan, Ron J. II. IOC Medical Commission. III. International Federation of Sports Medicine. IV. Series.*
*TC QP141 .N793 2000*

## NUTRITION - MORAL AND ETHICAL ASPECTS.
Coveney, John. Food, morals and meaning. London ; New York : Routledge, 2000.
*TC TX357 .C59 2000*

## NUTRITION - NURSES' INSTRUCTION.
Grodner, Michele. Foundations and clinical applications of nutrition. 2nd ed. St. Louis, Mo. : Mosby, c2000.
*TC RM216 .G946 2000*

## NUTRITION OF CHILDREN. *See* CHILDREN - NUTRITION.

**NUTRITION POLICY.**
Ford, Brian J. (Brian John), 1939- The future of food. London : Thames & Hudson, c2000.
*TC RA601 .F65 2000*

**NUTRITION POLICY - CHINA.**
Feeding China's little emperors. Stanford, Calif. : Stanford University Press, 2000.
*TC TX361.C5 F44 2000*

**NUTRITION POLICY - DEVELOPING COUNTRIES.**
Foster, Phillips, 1931- The world food problem. 2nd ed. Boulder : Lynne Rienner Publishers, 1999.
*TC HD9018.D44 F68 1999*

**NUTRITION POLICY - UNITED STATES.**
Sims, Laura S., 1943- The politics of fat. Armonk, N.Y. : M.E. Sharpe, c1998.
*TC TX360.U6 S58 1998*

**NUTRITION - PSYCHOLOGICAL ASPECTS.** *See also* **FOOD PREFERENCES.**
Working with groups to explore food & body connections. Duluth, Minn. : Whole Person Associates, c1996.
*TC RC552.E18 W67 1996*

**NUTRITION - SOCIAL ASPECTS.**
Coveney, John. Food, morals and meaning. London ; New York : Routledge, 2000.
*TC TX357 .C59 2000*

Interpreting weight. New York : Aldine de Gruyter, c1999.
*TC RA645.O23 I55 1999*

Weighty issues. Hawthorne, N.Y. : Aldine de Gruyter, c1999.
*TC RA645.O23 W45 1999*

**NUTRITION - SOCIAL ASPECTS - CONGRESSES.**
Heidelberger Ernährungsforum (5th : 1998 : Heidelberg) Food quality, nutrition, and health. Berlin ; New York : Springer, 2000.
*TC RA784 .H42 2000*

**NUTRITION - STUDY AND TEACHING (ELEMENTARY).**
Ubbes, Valerie A. Literature links for nutrition and health. Boston : Allyn and Bacon, c2000.
*TC TX364 .U253 2000*

**NUTRITION - STUDY AND TEACHING (SECONDARY).**
Toner, Patricia Rizzo, 1952- Diet and nutrition activities. West Nyack, N.Y. : Center for Applied Research in Education, c1993.
*TC QP143 .T65 1993*

**Nutritional aspects of HIV infection** / edited by Tracie L. Miller and Sherwood L. Gorbach. London ; New York : Arnold : Co-published in the United States by Oxford University Press, 1999. viii, 216 p. : ill. ; 28 cm. Includes bibliographical references and index. ISBN 0-340-74195-3 DDC 616.97/92
*1. AIDS (Disease) - Nutritional aspects. 2. AIDS (Disease) - Diet therapy. 3. AIDS (Disease) - Complications. 4. HIV Infections - complications. 5. Gastrointestinal Diseases - complications. 6. Opportunistic Infections - complications. 7. Diet Therapy. I. Miller, Tracie L. II. Gorbach, Sherwood L., 1934-*
*TC RC607.A26 N895 1998*

**NUTRITIONAL REQUIREMENTS.**
Nutrition and immunology. Totowa, N.J. : Humana Press, c2000.
*TC QP141 .N7767 2000*

**NUTRITIONALLY INDUCED DISEASES.**
Evolutionary aspects of nutrition and health. Basel ; New York : Karger, c1999.
*TC QP141 .E95 1999*

**A nuts-and-bolts approach to teaching nursing.**
Schoolcraft, Victoria. 2nd ed. New York : Springer Pub. Co., c2000.
*TC RT71 .S26 2000*

**Nutta, Joyce W.**
Virtual instruction. Englewood, Colo. : Libraries Unlimited, 1999.
*TC LC5803.C65 V57 1999*

**The nutty, nougat-filled world of human nutrition** [videorecording] / The Standard Deviants' ; produced by Beth Bickford ; script by Van Jordan ; The Standard Deviants Academic Team: content writer, Roberta Donahue, lead professor, Sharlene Holladay, adjunct professor, Wayne C. Miller ; directed by Joseph Doria. [Arlington, Va.] : Cerebellum Corp., c1998. 1 videocassette (136 min.) : sd., col. ; 1/2 in. + 2 cards ([4] p. : ill. ; 18 cm.). Title on container and cassette label:

Standard Deviants' present Human nutrition [videorecording]. VHS. Catalogued from credits and container and cassette label. The Standard Deviants'. Supervising graphic artist: Shawn Batts; edited by Reem Mishal, Julie Ann Naff; music: The Music Bakery; comic writing by Igor Torgeson; assistant director: Tony Deller, Dall Brown. Running time on container: 1 hour, 30 minutes; actual running time: 2 hours, 36 mins. For students of nutrition. SUMMARY: A fast-paced, entertaining, in-depth tutorial in nutrition from A-Z. At times, technical but always entertaining, the video is full of visuals to aid the memory. Winner of 1997 and 1998 Telly awards for best education video, this video is recommended by over 500 professionals. CONTENTS: Part 1. Introduction to nutrition -- Part 2. The Remarkable Body -- Part 3. Macronutrients -- Part 4. Micronutrients -- Part 5. Water -- Part 6. Energy balance, weight control, metabolism -- Part 7. Nutrition and disease prevention. ISBN 1-58198-032-9
*1. Nutrition. 2. Nutrition disorders. 3. Nutrition counseling. 4. Human physiology. 5. Water - Physiological effect. 6. Metabolism. 7. Food habits. 8. Diet. I. Bickford, Beth. II. Jordan, Van. III. Donahue, Roberta. IV. Holladay, Sharlene. V. Miller, Wayne C. VI. Doria, Joseph. VII. Standard Deviants (Performing Group) VIII. Cerebellum Corporation. IX. Title: Introduction to nutrition. X. Title: The remarkable body. XI. Title: Macronutrients. XII. Title: Micronutrients XIII. Title: Water. XIV. Title: Energy balance, weight control, metabolism. XV. Title: Nutrition and disease prevention. XVI. Title: Standard Deviants' present Human nutrition [videorecording] XVII. Title: Human nutrition [videorecording]*
*TC QP141 .N8 1998*

**Nuyts, Jan.**
Language and conceptualization. 1st paperback ed. Cambridge [England] ; New York : Cambridge University Press, 1999.
*TC P37 .L354 1999*

**NVQS (GREAT BRITAIN).** *See* **NATIONAL VOCATIONAL QUALIFICATIONS (GREAT BRITAIN).**

**Nye, Naomi Shihab.** Benito's dream bottle / by Naomi Shihab Nye ; pictures by Yu Cha Pak. 1st ed. New York : Simon & Schuster Books for Young Readers, c1995. 1 v. (unpaged) : ill. col. ; 21 x 26 cm. SUMMARY: Fearing that his grandmother has stopped dreaming, Benito helps her to fill her "dream bottle" once more. ISBN 0-02-768467-9 DDC [E]
*1. Dreams - Fiction. 2. Grandmothers - Fiction. I. Pak, Yu Cha, ill. II. Title.*
*TC PZ7.N976 Be 1995*

**NYMPHAEA (ARCHITECTURE).** *See* **FOUNTAINS.**

**Nystul, Michael S.**
**Art and science of counseling and psychotherapy.** Nystul, Michael S. Introduction to counseling. Boston : Allyn and Bacon, c1999.
*TC BF637.C6 N97 1999*

Introduction to counseling : an art and science perspective / Michael S. Nystul. Boston : Allyn and Bacon, c1999. xvii, 494 p. : ill. ; 25 cm. Rev. ed. of: The art and science of counseling and psychotherapy, c1993. Includes bibliographical references (p. 420-422) and indexes. ISBN 0-205-26827-7 DDC 158/.3
*1. Counseling. 2. Psychotherapy. I. Nystul, Michael S. Art and science of counseling and psychotherapy. II. Title.*
*TC BF637.C6 N97 1999*

**Ó Flatharta, Antoine.** The prairie train / written by Antoine Ó Flatharta ; illustrated by Eric Rohmann. New York : Crown Publishers, 1997. 1v. (unpaged) : col. ill. ; 21 cm. SUMMARY: As a young Irish immigrant boy travels by steam-engine across the American prairie to a new life, memories of the old country pull at his heart. ISBN 0-517-70988-0 (trade) ISBN 0-517-70989-9 (lib. bdg.) DDC [Fic]
*1. Immigrants - Fiction. 2. Locomotives - Fiction. 3. Railroads - Trains - Fiction. I. Rohmann, Eric, ill. II. Title.*
*TC PZ7.O331275 Pr 1997*

**Oakes, Jeannie.**
Becoming good American schools. 1st ed. San Francisco : Jossey-Bass, c2000.
*TC LB2822.82 .B44 2000*

**Oakes, Jill E. (Jill Elizabeth), 1952-** Spirit of Siberia : traditional native life, clothing, and footwear / Jill Oakes and Rick Riewe. Washington, D.C. : Smithsonian Institution Press, 1998. viii, 215 p. : ill. (some col.), maps ; 27 cm. Published in association with the Bata Shoe Museum, Toronto, Canada. Includes bibliographical references (p. 198-205) and index.
*1. Indigenous peoples - Russia (Federation) - Siberia. 2. Indigenous peoples - Material culture - Russia (Federation) - Siberia. 3. Footwear - Russia (Federation) - Siberia. 4. Ethnology - Russia (Federation) - Siberia. 5. Siberia (Russia) - Social life and customs. I. Riewe, R. R. (Roderick R.) II. Title.*

*TC DK758 .O24 1998*

**Oakhill, Jane.**
Reading development and the teaching of reading. Oxford, UK ; Malden, Mass. : Blackwell Publishers, 1999.
*TC LB1050.2 .R424 1999*

**OAKHURST PRESBYTERIAN CHURCH (DECATUR, GA.).**
Stroupe, Nibs. While we run this race. Maryknoll, N.Y. : Orbis Books, c1995.
*TC BX8949.D43 S77 1995*

**Oakland Intermediate School District (Oakland County, Mich.).**
Reforming the Electoral College [videorecording]. [Boulder, Colo.? : Social Science Education Consortium?], c1996.
*TC H62.5.U5 R4 1996*

**OATHS.** *See* **LOYALTY OATHS.**

**Oauknin, Marc-Alain.**
**[Mystères de l'alphabet. English]**
The mysteries of the alphabet : the origins of writing / Marc-Alain Ouaknin ; translated from the French by Josephine Bacon. 1st ed. New York : Abbeville Press, c1999. 381 p. : ill. ; 22 cm. Includes bibliographical references (p. 372-375). ISBN 0-7892-0523-8 ISBN 0-7892-0521-1 (pbk.) DDC 411
*1. Alphabet - History. 2. Writing - History. I. Title.*
*TC P211 .O913 1999*

**OBE (EDUCATION).** *See* **COMPETENCY BASED EDUCATION.**

**OBEDIENCE.**
Compliance and the law; Beverly Hills, Sage Publications [1972]
*TC K376 .C66*

Obedience to authority. Mahwah, N.J. ; London : Lawrence Erlbaum Associates, 2000.
*TC HM1251 .O24 2000*

**Obedience to authority :** current perspectives on the Milgram paradigm / edited by Thomas Blass. Mahwah, N.J. ; London : Lawrence Erlbaum Associates, 2000. xiii, 251 p. : ill. ; 24 cm. Includes bibliographical references and indexes. ISBN 0-8058-2737-4 (alk. paper) DDC 303.3/6
*1. Milgram, Stanley. - Obedience to authority. 2. Authority. 3. Obedience. I. Blass, Thomas.*
*TC HM1251 .O24 2000*

**Oberg, Steven Lynn.**
Shields, Carolyn M. Year-round schooling. Lanham, Md. : Scarecrow Press, 2000.
*TC LB3034 .S55 2000*

**Oberlin College.**
The Amish [videorecording]. Oak Forest, IL : MPI Home Video, 1988.

The Amish [videorecording]. Oak Forest, Ill. : MPI Home Video, c1988.
*TC BX8129.A5 A5 1988*

**OBESITY - ATLASES.**
Human nutrition and obesity. Philadelphia : Current Medicine, 1999.
*TC RC620.5 .H846 1999*

Human nutrition and obesity. Philadelphia : Current Medicine, 1999.
*TC RC620.5 .H846 1999*

**OBESITY - CONTROL.** *See* **WEIGHT LOSS.**

**OBESITY IN ADOLESCENCE.**
Nichter, Mimi. Fat talk. Cambridge, Mass. : Harvard University Press, 2000.
*TC RJ399.C6 N53 2000*

**OBESITY IN CHILDREN - PATIENTS.** *See* **OVERWEIGHT CHILDREN.**

**OBESITY - PREVENTION.**
Lean, Michael E. J. Clinical handbook of weight management. London : Martin Dunitz, Ltd. ; Malden, MA : distributed in the USA, Canada and Brazil by Blackwell Science, Ltd., c1998.
*TC RC628 .L436 1998*

The management of eating disorders and obesity. Totowa, N.J. : Humana Press, c1999.
*TC RC552.E18 M364 1999*

**OBESITY - PREVENTION & CONTROL.**
Lean, Michael E. J. Clinical handbook of weight management. London : Martin Dunitz, Ltd. ; Malden, MA : distributed in the USA, Canada and Brazil by Blackwell Science, Ltd., c1998.
*TC RC628 .L436 1998*

**OBESITY - PSYCHOLOGICAL ASPECTS.**
Solovay, Sondra, 1970- Tipping the scales of justice.
Amherst, N.Y. : Prometheus Books, 2000.
*TC BF697.5.B63 S65 2000*

**OBESITY - SOCIAL ASPECTS.**
Interpreting weight. New York : Aldine de Gruyter,
c1999.
*TC RA645.O23 I55 1999*

Solovay, Sondra, 1970- Tipping the scales of justice.
Amherst, N.Y. : Prometheus Books, 2000.
*TC BF697.5.B63 S65 2000*

Weighty issues. Hawthorne, N.Y. : Aldine de Gruyter,
c1999.
*TC RA645.O23 W45 1999*

**OBESITY - SOCIAL ASPECTS - UNITED
STATES.**
Berg, Francie M. Women afraid to eat. Hettinger,
ND : Healthy Weight Network, c2000.
*TC RC552.O25 B47 2000*

**OBESITY - THERAPY.**
Lean, Michael E. J. Clinical handbook of weight
management. London : Martin Dunitz, Ltd. ; Malden,
MA : distributed in the USA, Canada and Brazil by
Blackwell Science, Ltd., c1998.
*TC RC628 .L436 1998*

The management of eating disorders and obesity.
Totowa, N.J. : Humana Press, c1999.
*TC RC552.E18 M364 1999*

**OBESITY - UNITED STATES.**
Berg, Francie M. Women afraid to eat. Hettinger,
ND : Healthy Weight Network, c2000.
*TC RC552.O25 B47 2000*

**OBJECT (AESTHETICS) - EXHIBITIONS.**
Modernstarts. New York : Museum of Modern Art :
Distributed by Harry N. Abrams, c1999.
*TC N620.M9 M63 1999*

**OBJECT ATTACHMENT.**
Empirical perspectives on object relations theory. 1st
ed. Washington, DC : American Psychological
Association, c1994.
*TC BF175.5.O24 E85 1994*

**Object ID.**
Thornes, Robin. Introduction to Object ID. [Los
Angeles] : Getty Information Institute, c1999.
*TC N3998 .T457 1999*

**OBJECT RELATIONS (PSYCHOANALYSIS).** *See
also* **INTERPERSONAL RELATIONS.**
Empirical perspectives on object relations theory. 1st
ed. Washington, DC : American Psychological
Association, c1994.
*TC BF175.5.O24 E85 1994*

Golden, Valerie. Significant others' perceptions of the
effects of their partners' psychotherapy. 1998.
*TC 085 G566*

**OBJECT RELATIONS THEORY
(PSYCHOANALYSIS).** *See* **OBJECT
RELATIONS (PSYCHOANALYSIS).**

**OBJECT-TEACHING.** *See* **PROJECT METHOD
IN TEACHING.**

**OBJECTIONS (EVIDENCE).** *See* **CONFIDENTIAL
COMMUNICATIONS.**

**OBJECTIVES, EDUCATIONAL.** *See*
**EDUCATION - AIMS AND OBJECTIVES.**

**OBJECTS, RELIGIOUS.** *See* **RELIGIOUS
ARTICLES.**

**OBLIGATION.** *See* **RESPONSIBILITY.**

**OBLIQUE PROJECTION.**
Willats, John. Art and representation. Princeton, N.J. :
Princeton University Press, c1997.
*TC N7430.5 .W55 1997*

**O'Boyle, Ciaran A.**
Individual quality of life. Amsterdam : Harwood
Academic, c1999.
*TC RA407 .I54 1999*

**O'Brien, Gregory.**
Developmental disability and behaviour. London,
England : Mac Keith Press, 2000.
*TC RJ506.D47 D48 2000*

**O'Brien, Karen M.**
Hill, Clara E. Helping skills. 1st ed. Washington, DC :
American Psychological Association, c1999.
*TC BF637.C6 H46 1999*

**O'Brien, Lawrence J.** Bad medicine : how the
American medical establishment is ruining our
healthcare system / Lawrence J. O'Brien. Amherst,

N.Y. : Prometheus Books, c1999. 283 p. ; 24 cm.
Includes bibliographical references and index. ISBN 1-57392-
260-9 DDC 362.1/0973
*1. Medical care - United States. 2. Medical economics - United
States. 3. Health care reform - United States. I. Title.*
*TC RA395.A3 O28 1999*

**O'Brien, Mary Elizabeth.** Spirituality in nursing :
standing on holy ground / Mary Elizabeth O'Brien.
Sudbury, Mass. : Jones and Bartlett Pub., c1999. xvii,
298 p. ; 23 cm. Includes bibliographical references and index.
ISBN 0-7637-0644-2 DDC 610.73/01
*1. Nursing - Religious aspects - Christianity. 2. Nursing -
Moral and ethical aspects. 3. Nursing - Philosophy. 4. Nurse
and patient. I. Title.*
*TC RT85.2 .O37 1999*

**O'Brien, Nancy P.** Education, a guide to reference and
information sources / Nancy Patricia O'Brien. 2nd ed.
Englewood, Colo. : Libraries Unlimited, 2000. xv, 189
p. ; 25 cm. (Reference sources in the social sciences series)
Spine title: Education. Rev. ed. of: Education, a guide to
reference and information sources / Lois J. Buttlar. 1989.
Includes indexes. ISBN 1-56308-626-3 DDC 016.37
*1. Education - Reference books - Bibliography. 2. Education -
Bibliography. 3. Social sciences - Reference books -
Bibliography. 4. Social sciences - Bibliography. I. Buttlar,
Lois, 1934- Education, a guide to reference and information
sources. II. Title. III. Title: Education IV. Series.*
*TC Z5811 .B89 2000*

**O'Brien, Patrick, 1960-** Gigantic! : how big were the
dinosaurs? / Patrick O'Brien. 1st ed. New York :
Henry Holt, 1999. 1 v. (unpaged) : col. ill. ; 26 cm. Includes
one poster attached to inside back cover. SUMMARY:
Explains the names of fourteen dinosaurs, from Stegosaurus to
Compsognathus, and describes their physical characteristics,
size, and probable behavior. ISBN 0-8050-5738-2 (hardcover :
alk. paper) DDC 567.9
*1. Dinosaurs - Size - Juvenile literature. 2. Dinosaurs. I. Title.*
*TC QE862.D5 O27 1999*

**O'Brien, Robert, 1932-** The encyclopedia of
understanding alcohol and other drugs / Robert
O'Brien, Morris Chafetz, Sidney Cohen ; June
Lazerus, Robert Lazow, general editors. New York,
NY : Facts on File, c1999. 2 v. (505, 1108) : ill., maps ; 24
cm. Includes bibliographical references (p. 1006-1037) and
index. ISBN 0-8160-3971-2 (vol. 1 : acid-free paper) ISBN
0-8160-3972-0 (vol. 2 : acid-free paper) ISBN 0-8160-3970-4
(set : acid-free paper) DDC 362.29
*1. Alcoholism - Encyclopedias. 2. Drug abuse - Encyclopedias.
I. Chafetz, Morris E. II. Cohen, Sidney, 1910- III. Title. IV.
Title: Understanding alcohol and other drugs V. Title: Alcohol
and other drugs*
*TC HV5017 .O37 1999*

**O'Brien, Thomas V., 1958-** The politics of race and
schooling : public education in Georgia, 1900-1961 /
Thomas B. O'Brien. Lanham, Md. : Lexington Books,
c1999. xvii, 229 p. ; 24 cm. Includes bibliographical references
(p. 209-221) and index. ISBN 0-7391-0060-2 (alk. paper) DDC
306.43
*1. Discrimination in education - Georgia - History - 20th
century. 2. Education - Social aspects - Georgia - History -
20th century. 3. Politics and education - Georgia - History -
20th century. I. Title.*
*TC LC212.22.G46 O37 1999*

**O'Brien, Tim. 1958-.**
Special needs and the beginning teacher. London ;
New York : Continuum, 2000.
*TC LC4036.G7 S684 2000*

**O'Brien, William Hayes.**
Haynes, Stephen N. Principles and practice of
behavioral assessment. New York ; London : Kluwer
Academic/Plenum, c2000.
*TC BF176.5 .H39 2000*

**OBSERVATION (EDUCATIONAL METHOD).** *See
also* **INTERACTION ANALYSIS IN
EDUCATION.**
Arias, Rafael. Analysis of discourse in an ESL peer-
mentoring teacher group. 1999.
*TC 06 no. 10791*

Frank, Carolyn. Ethnographic eyes. Portsmouth, NH :
Heinemann, c1999.
*TC LB1027.28 .F73 1999*

Trawick-Smith, Jeffrey W. Early childhood
development. 2nd ed. Upper Saddle River, N.J. :
Merrill, c2000.
*TC LB1115 .T73 2000*

**OBSERVATION (EDUCATIONAL METHODS) -
NEW YORK (STATE).**
Southworth, Robert A. Evidence of student learning
and implications for alternative policies that support
instructional use of assessment. 1999.

*TC 06 no. 11218*

**OBSERVATION (PSYCHOLOGY).** *See*
**PARTICIPANT OBSERVATION.**

**OBSESSION (PSYCHOLOGY).** *See* **OBSESSIVE-
COMPULSIVE DISORDER.**

**OBSESSIVE-COMPULSIVE DISORDER.** *See also*
**COMPULSIVE BEHAVIOR.**
Step on a crack [videorecording]. Boston, MA :
Fanlight Productions, 1996.
*TC RC533 .S7 1996*

**OBSESSIVE-COMPULSIVE DISORDER - CASE
STUDIES.**
Step on a crack [videorecording]. Boston, MA :
Fanlight Productions, 1996.
*TC RC533 .S7 1996*

**OBSESSIVE-COMPULSIVE DISORDER -
DIAGNOSIS.**
Neurotic, stress-related, and somatoform disorders
[videorecording]. Princeton, N.J. : Films for the
Humanities & Sciences, 1998.
*TC RC530 .N4 1998*

**OBSESSIVE-COMPULSIVE DISORDER -
PATIENTS.**
Neurotic, stress-related, and somatoform disorders
[videorecording]. Princeton, N.J. : Films for the
Humanities & Sciences, 1998.
*TC RC530 .N4 1998*

**OBSESSIVE-COMPULSIVE DISORDER -
TREATMENT.**
Step on a crack [videorecording]. Boston, MA :
Fanlight Productions, 1996.
*TC RC533 .S7 1996*

**OBSESSIVE-COMPULSIVE NEUROSES.** *See*
**OBSESSIVE-COMPULSIVE DISORDER.**

**OBSESSIVE-COMPULSIVE NEUROSIS.** *See*
**OBSESSIVE-COMPULSIVE DISORDER.**

**OBSTETRICS - PERIODICALS.**
Clinical obstetrics and gynecology. [New York]
Hoeber Medical Division, Harper & Row.

**OBSTETRICS - SURGERY.** *See*
**AMNIOCENTESIS.**

**OCCASIONALISM.** *See* **DUALISM.**

**OCCIDENTAL ART.** *See* **ART.**

**OCCIDENTAL CIVILIZATION.** *See*
**CIVILIZATION, WESTERN.**

**OCCULTISM.** *See also* **MAGIC; WITCHCRAFT.**
Schick, Theodore. How to think about weird things.
2nd ed. Mountain View, Calif. : Mayfield Pub., c1999.
*TC BC177 .S32 1999*

**OCCULTISM IN LITERATURE.**
Williams, John Tyerman. Pooh and the millennium.
1st American ed. New York : Dutton Books, 1999.
*TC PR6025.I65 Z975 1999*

**OCCULTISTS.** *See* **WITCHES.**

**OCCUPATION, CHOICE OF.** *See* **VOCATIONAL
GUIDANCE.**

**OCCUPATION THERAPY.** *See* **OCCUPATIONAL
THERAPY.**

**OCCUPATIONAL APTITUDE TESTS.** *See also*
**VOCATIONAL QUALIFICATIONS.**
Prediger, D. J. Basic structure of work-relevant
abilities. Iowa City, Iowa : ACT, 1998.
*TC LB3051 .A3 no. 98-9*

**OCCUPATIONAL ASPIRATIONS.** *See*
**VOCATIONAL INTERESTS.**

**OCCUPATIONAL CHOICE.** *See* **VOCATIONAL
GUIDANCE.**

**OCCUPATIONAL DISEASES - EPIDEMIOLOGY.**
Vetter, Norman. Epidemiology and public health
medicine. Edinburgh ; New York : Churchill
Livingstone, 1999.
*TC RA427 .V48 1999*

**OCCUPATIONAL HAZARDS, PREVENTION OF.**
*See* **INDUSTRIAL SAFETY.**

**OCCUPATIONAL HEALTH AND SAFETY.** *See*
**INDUSTRIAL SAFETY.**

**OCCUPATIONAL HEALTH NURSING.** *See*
**INDUSTRIAL NURSING.**

**OCCUPATIONAL LITERACY.** *See* **WORKPLACE
LITERACY.**

**OCCUPATIONAL MOBILITY.** *See* **CAREER CHANGES.**

**OCCUPATIONAL MOBILITY - PSYCHOLOGICAL ASPECTS.**
Sosin, Adrienne. Achieving styles preferences of students in an urban graduate teacher education program. 1996.
*TC 06 no. 10701*

**OCCUPATIONAL MOBILITY - UNITED STATES.**
Bates, Timothy Mason. Race, self-employment, and upward mobility. Washington, D.C. : Woodrow Wilson Center Press ; Baltimore : Johns Hopkins University Press, c1997.
*TC HD8037.U5 B384 1997*

**OCCUPATIONAL PSYCHIATRY.** *See* **INDUSTRIAL PSYCHIATRY.**

**OCCUPATIONAL SAFETY AND HEALTH.** *See* **INDUSTRIAL SAFETY.**

**OCCUPATIONAL SATISFACTION.** *See* **JOB SATISFACTION.**

**OCCUPATIONAL STRESS.** *See* **JOB STRESS.**

**OCCUPATIONAL THERAPISTS.** *See* **OCCUPATIONAL THERAPY ASSISTANTS.**

**OCCUPATIONAL THERAPY.** *See also* **HANDICRAFT.**
Barlow, Tracie. The COTA in the schools. San Antonio, Texas : Therapy Skill Builders, c1999.
*TC RM735 .B37 1999*

Smith, Irmhild Wrede. The effect of structured exercise and structured reminiscing on agitation and aggression in geriatric psychiatric patients. 1996.
*TC 06 no. 10700*

**OCCUPATIONAL THERAPY ASSISTANTS - HANDBOOKS, MANUALS,ETC.**
Barlow, Tracie. The COTA in the schools. San Antonio, Texas : Therapy Skill Builders, c1999.
*TC RM735 .B37 1999*

**OCCUPATIONAL THERAPY - PRACTICE.**
Barlow, Tracie. The COTA in the schools. San Antonio, Texas : Therapy Skill Builders, c1999.
*TC RM735 .B37 1999*

**OCCUPATIONAL TRAINING.** *See also* **EMPLOYEES - TRAINING OF; NON-FORMAL EDUCATION; TRAINING NEEDS.**
Garrick, John. Informal learning in the workplace. London ; New York : Routledge, 1998.
*TC HF5549.5.T7 G344 1998*

Skiba, Michaeline. A naturalistic inquiry of the relationship between organizational change and informal learning in the workplace. 1999.
*TC 06 no. 11180*

Weintraub, Robert Steven. Informal learning in the workplace through desktop technology. 1998.
*TC 06 no. 11003*

**OCCUPATIONAL TRAINING - ECONOMIC ASPECTS.**
Vocational education and training reform. Washington, D.C. : World Bank/Oxford University Press, 2000.
*TC LC1044 .V62 2000*

**OCCUPATIONAL TRAINING - EVALUATION.**
Grubb, W. Norton. The roles of evaluation for vocational education and training. London : Kogan Page ; Sterling, VA : Distributed in the US by Stylus Pub. Inc., 1999.
*TC LC1044 .G78 1999*

**OCCUPATIONAL TRAINING - GERMANY (EAST).**
Evans, Karen, 1949- Learning and work in the risk society. New York : St. Martin's Press, 2000.
*TC HD6278.G4 E93 2000*

**OCCUPATIONAL TRAINING - GOVERNMENT POLICY - GREAT BRITAIN.**
Ainley, Patrick. Learning policy. Basingstoke, Hampshire : Macmillan Press ; New York : St. Martin's Press, 1999.
*TC LC93.G7 A76 1999*

**OCCUPATIONAL TRAINING - GREAT BRITAIN.**
Bennett, Neville. Skills development in higher education and employment. Buckingham [England] ; Philadelphia : Society for Research into Higher Education & Open University Press, 2000.
*TC LB1027.47 .B46 2000*

**OCCUPATIONAL TRAINING - JAPAN.**
Vocational education in the industrialization of Japan. Tokyo : United Nations University, c1987.

*TC LC1047.J3 V63 1987*

**OCCUPATIONS.** *See also* **HANDICRAFT; PROFESSIONS; VOCATIONAL GUIDANCE; VOCATIONAL INTERESTS; VOCATIONAL QUALIFICATIONS; WORK.**
Career discovery encyclopedia. 4th ed. Chicago : Ferguson Pub. Co., 2000.
*TC HF5381.2 .C37 2000*

Gibbons, Gail. Say woof!. 1st ed. New York : Macmillan ; Toronto : Maxwell Macmillan Canada ; New York : Maxwell Macmillan International, c1992.
*TC SF756 .G53 1992*

Tropea, Judith. A day in the life of a museum curator. Mahwah, N.J. : Troll Associates, c1991.
*TC QE22.E53 T76 1991*

**OCCUPATIONS - HANDBOOKS, MANUALS, ETC.**
Encyclopedia of careers and vocational guidance. 11th ed. Chicago : Ferguson Pub. Co., 2000.
*TC HF5381 .E52 2000*

**OCCUPATIONS - NEW YORK (STATE) - NEW YORK - CASE STUDIES.**
Howell, Ron. One hundred jobs :b a panorama of work in the American city. New York : New Press : Distributed by W.W. Norton, 1999.
*TC HF5382.5.U6 N37 1999*

**OCCUPATIONS - SOVIET UNION - JUVENILE POETRY.**
Mayakovsky, Vladimir, 1893-1930. Kem byt'? [Moskva] : Gosudarstvennoe izdatel'stvo, 1929.
*TC PN6110.O32 M39 1929 Rus*

**OCD (DISEASE).** *See* **OBSESSIVE-COMPULSIVE DISORDER.**

**OCEAN.**
Markle, Sandra. Down, down, down in the ocean. New York : Walker, 1999.
*TC QH541.5.S3 M2856 1999*

**OCEANIA - SOCIAL LIFE AND CUSTOMS - ENCYCLOPEDIAS.**
Werness, Hope B. The Continuum encyclopedia of native art. New York : Continuum, 2000.
*TC E98.A7 W49 2000*

**OCEANIA - STATISTICS - HISTORY.**
Mitchell, B. R. (Brian R.) International historical statistics, Africa, Asia & Oceania, 1750-1993. 3rd ed. London : Macmillan Reference ; New York : Ggrove's Dictionaries[division of Stockton Press], 1998.
*TC HA1107 .M54 1998*

**OCEANIAN AMERICANS.** *See* **PACIFIC ISLANDER AMERICANS.**

**OCEANICA.** *See* **OCEANIA.**

**OCEANOGRAPHY.**
The blue planet [videorecording]. [New York, N.Y.?] : Unapix Entertainment, Inc. [distributor], c1996.
*TC QB631.2 .B5 1996*

**Ochieng', William Robert, 1943-.**
Decolonization & independence in Kenya, 1940-93. London : J. Currey ; Athens : Ohio University Press, 1995.
*TC DT433.58 .D4 1995*

**Ochoa, Salvador Hector.**
Education of Hispanics in the United States. New York : AMS Press, c1999.
*TC LC4091 .R417 1999*

Education of Hispanics in the United States. New York : AMS Press, c1999.
*TC LC4091 .R417 1999*

**Ochsner, Mindy Blaise.** Something rad & risqu'e : a feminist poststructuralist study of gender in an urban kindergarten class / by Mindy Blaise Ochsner. 1999. ix, 335 leaves ; 29 cm. Typescript; issued also on microfilm. Thesis (Ed.D.)--Teachers College, Columbia University, 1999. Includes bibliographical references (leaves 313-329).
*1. Sex differences (Psychology) in children. 2. Identity (Psychology) in children. 3. Education, Primary - Social aspects - New York (State) - New York - Case studies. 4. Sex role in children. 5. Discursive psychology. 6. Feminist theory. 7. Feminism and education. 8. Poststructuralism. I. Title. II. Title: Feminist poststructuralist study of gender in an urban kindergarten classroom*
*TC 06 no. 11208*

**O'Connell, Bill.** Solution-focused therapy / Bill O'Connell. London ; Thousand Oaks, Calif. : Sage Publications, 1998. xiii, 160 p. ; 23 cm. (Brief therapies series) Includes bibliographical references (p. [147]-154) and

indexes. ISBN 0-7619-5274-8 ISBN 0-7619-5275-6 (pbk.) DDC 616.89/14
*1. Solution-focused therapy. I. Title. II. Series.*
*TC RC489.S65 O26 1998*

**O'Connell, Susan.** Introduction to problem solving : strategies for the elementary math classroom / Susan O'Connell. Portsmouth, NH : Heinemann, c2000. xi, 190 p. : ill. ; 28 cm. Includes bibliographical references (p. 189-190). ISBN 0-325-00199-5 DDC 370.15/24
*1. Problem solving - Study and teaching (Elementary) I. Title.*
*TC QA63 .O36 2000*

**O'Connor, Kevin J.** The play therapy primer / Kevin J. O'Connor. 2nd ed. New York : John Wiley & Sons, c2000. xii, 478 p. ; 25 cm. Includes bibliographical references (p. 435-453) and indexes. ISBN 0-471-24873-8 (cloth : alk. paper) DDC 615.8/5153/083
*1. Play therapy. I. Title.*
*TC RJ505.P6 O26 2000*

**O'Connor, Maureen.**
Hackney Downs. London ; New York : Cassell, 1999.
*TC LF795.L66 H33 1999*

**OĆonnor-Pirkle, Marilyn.** Tracking systemic change in an interagency partnership : the case of Herkimer County / by Marilyn OĆonnor-Pirkle. 1996. ix, 245 leaves : ill. ; 29 cm. Includes tables. Typescript; issued also on microfilm. Thesis (Ed.D.)--Teachers College, Columbia University, 1996. Includes bibliographical references (leaves 229-232).
*1. Social service - New York (State) - Herkimer County - Case studies. 2. Community and school - New York (State) - Herkimer County - Case studies. 3. School management and organization - New York (State) - Herkimer County - Case studies. 4. Educational surveys - New York (State) - Herkimer County - Case studies. 5. Herkimer County (N.Y.) I. Title.*
*TC 06 no. 10677*

Tracking systemic change in an interagency partnership : the case of Herkimer County / by Marilyn OĆonnor-Pirkle. 1996. ix, 245 leaves : ill. ; 29 cm. Includes tables. Typescript; issued also on microfilm. Thesis (Ed.D.)--Teachers College, Columbia University, 1996. Includes bibliographical references (leaves 229-232).
*1. Social service - New York (State) - Herkimer County - Case studies. 2. Community and school - New York (State) - Herkimer County - Case studies. 3. School management and organization - New York (State) - Herkimer County - Case studies. 4. Educational surveys - New York (State) - Herkimer County - Case studies. 5. Herkimer County (N.Y.) I. Title.*
*TC 06 no. 10677*

**Oddone-Paolucci, Elizabeth.**
The changing family and child development. Aldershot : Ashgate, c2000.
*TC HQ518 .C478 2000*

**Odegaard, Charles E.** A pilgrimage through universities / Charles E. Odegaard ; with a foreword by Richard McCormick and a postscript by Keith Benson. Seattle : University of Washington Press, c1999. ix, 203 p., [16] p. of plates : ill. 24 cm. ISBN 0-295-97760-4 (alk. paper) DDC 378/.0092
*1. Odegaard, Charles E. 2. University of Washington - Presidents - Biography. 3. College administrators - United States - Biography. I. Title.*
*TC LD5752.1 .O34 1999*

**ODEGAARD, CHARLES E.**
Odegaard, Charles E. A pilgrimage through universities. Seattle : University of Washington Press, c1999.
*TC LD5752.1 .O34 1999*

**O'DELL, SCOTT, 1898-1989.**
**ISLAND OF THE BLUE DOLPHINS.**
Beech, Linda Ward. Island of the blue dolphins by Scott O'Dell. New York : Scholastic, c1997.
*TC LB1573 .B438 1997*

**Odent, Michel, 1930-** The scientification of love. London ; New York : Free Association Books, 1999. x, 115 p. ; 23 cm. Includes bibliographical references and index. ISBN 1-85343-476-0
*1. Love. 2. Love - Physiological aspects. 3. Infants (Newborn) - Psychology. 4. Emotions in infants. I. Title.*
*TC BF575.L8 O33 1999*

**O'Donnell, Angela M.**
Cognitive perspectives on peer learning. Mahwah, N.J. : L. Erlbaum, 1999.
*TC LB1031.5 .C65 1999*

**O'Donnell, James, 1951-.**
Becoming and unbecoming white. Westport, Conn. : Bergin & Garvey, 1999.
*TC E184.A1 B29 1999*

**O'Donnell, Michael P.** Becoming a reader : a developmental approach to reading instruction / Michael P. O'Donnell, Margo Wood. 2nd ed. Boston :

Allyn and Bacon, c1999. xiii, 386 p. : ill. ; 24 cm. Includes bibliographical references and indexes. ISBN 0-205-27901-5 DDC 428.4/3
*1. Developmental reading. 2. Individualized reading instruction. 3. Reading comprehension. 4. Reading - Remedial teaching. I. Wood, Margo. 1939- II. Title.*
**TC LB1050.53 .O35 1999**

**O'Donoghue, T. A. (Tom A.), 1953-** The Catholic Church and the secondary school curriculum in Ireland, 1922-1962 / Thomas A. O'Donoghue. New York : P. Lang, c1999. 183 p. ; 25 cm. (Irish studies, 1043-5743 ; vol. 5) Includes bibliographical references (p. [155]-174) and index. ISBN 0-8204-4424-3 (hardbound : alk. paper) DDC 373.19/09417
*1. Catholic high schools - Ireland - Curricula - History - 20th century. 2. Education, Secondary - Ireland - Curricula - History - 20th century. 3. Education and state - Ireland - History - 20th century. I. Title. II. Series: Irish studies (New York, N.Y.) ; vol. 5.*
**TC LC506.G72 I745 1999**

**O'Donohue, William.** Management and administration skills for the mental health professional. San Diego, Calif. London : Academic, c1999.
**TC RA790 .M325 1999**

**ODONTOGRAPHY.** *See* **TEETH.**

**ODONTOLOGY.** *See* **TEETH.**

**ODORS.** *See* **PERFUMES.**

**ODORS - FICTION.**
Nikly, Michelle. [Royaume des parfums. English] The perfume of memory. 1st American ed. New York : A.A. Levine Books, 1998.
**TC PZ7.N585 Pe 1998**

**Odyssey.**
Sebesta, Sam Leaton. Orlando, Fla. : Harcourt Brace Jovanovich, c1982.
**TC PE1117 .O39 1982**

Sebesta, Sam Leaton. 2nd ed. Orlando, Fla. : Harcourt Brace Jovanovich, c1986.
**TC PE1117 .O39 1986**

**Odyssey :** an HBJ literature program / Sam Leaton Sebesta, general consultant. Teacher's ed. Orlando, Fla. : Harcourt Brace Jovanovich, c1986. v. : col. ill. ; 24 cm. Includes index. CONTENTS: Level 1. Star light, star bright (preprimer) ; Hello and good-bye (primer) ; Where the clouds go (reader) -- level 2. The heart of the woods -- level 3. Under the midnight stars -- level 4. Across wide fields -- level 5. East of the sun -- level 6. At the edge of the world -- level 7. Ride the silver seas -- level 8. Another earth, another sky. ISBN 0-15-333368-5 (level 7) ISBN 0-15-333369-3 (level 8)
*1. Readers (Elementary) 2. Reading (Elementary) I. Sebesta, Sam Leaton.*
**TC PE1117 .O39 1982 Teacher's Ed.**

**OECD COUNTRIES - SOCIAL POLICY.**
A caring world. Paris : The Organisation, c1999.
**TC HN17.5 .C323 1999**

**OECD database [computer file].**
Education at a glance [computer file]. Ottawa, Ont. : Ivation Datasystems Inc. ; Paris, France : OECD,
**TC LB2846 .E2473**

**OECD education database [computer file].**
Education at a glance [computer file]. Ottawa, Ont. : Ivation Datasystems Inc. ; Paris, France : OECD,
**TC LB2846 .E2473**

**OECD education indicators [computer file].**
Education at a glance [computer file]. Ottawa, Ont. : Ivation Datasystems Inc. ; Paris, France : OECD,
**TC LB2846 .E2473**

**OECD indicators [computer file].**
Education at a glance [computer file]. Ottawa, Ont. : Ivation Datasystems Inc. ; Paris, France : OECD,
**TC LB2846 .E2473**

**OECD MEMBER COUNTRIES.** *See* **OECD COUNTRIES.**

**OECOLOGY.** *See* **ECOLOGY.**

**Oelkers, Jürgen, 1947-.**
Dewey and European education. Dordrecht : Kluwer Academic Publishers, c2000.
**TC LB875.D5 D47 2000**

**Oermann, Marilyn H.**
Gaberson, Kathleen B. Clinical teaching strategies in nursing. New York : Springer, c1999.
**TC RT73 .G26 1999**

**Of colors and things.**
Hoban, Tana. 1st Tupelo Board Book ed. New York : Tupelo Books, 1998.

**Of the conduct of the understanding.**
Locke, John, 1632-1704. [Some thoughts concerning education] Some thoughts concerning education ; Indianapolis : Hackett Pub. Co., c1996.
**TC LB475.L6 L63 1996**

**Fate of the earth** [videorecording] / a production of WQED Pittsburgh in association with the National Academy of Sciences ; series producer, Gregory Andorfer ; producer, Robin Bates ; written by Robin Bates, Chip Walter. [New York, N.Y.?] : Unapix Entertainment, Inc. [distributor], c1996. 1 videocassette (57 min.) : sd., col. ; 1/2 in. (Planet Earth ; 7) At head of title: Unapix Consumer Products feature presentation [videorecording]. VHS. Catalogued from credits and container. Narrator, Richard Kiley. Sound, Kenneth Love... [et al.]; photography by Norris Brock... [et al.]; music, Jack Tillar and William Loose. "Major funding by the Annenberg/CPB Project"--Container. Originally produced in 1986. For adolescent through adult. SUMMARY: Explores the Gaia hypothesis, ie., the role of life in shaping the Earth and its future. Asks whether humans are a threat to Earth, or whether they are emerging as the brain or nervous system of its great organism. Looks at the importance of the rainforest to the health of the planet, the implications of new discoveries that indicate life may be billion years older then previously thought, and revelations about the global consequences of "nuclear winter" and "ultraviolet spring." Asks if humans have any real choice in the fate of the earth.
*1. Earth sciences. 2. Earth. 3. Geology. 4. Nuclear warfare. 5. Ecology. 6. Nature - Effect of human beings on. 7. Gaia hypothesis. 8. Documentary television programs. I. Andorfer, Gregory. II. Bates, Robin. III. Walter, Chip. IV. Kiley, Richard. V. WQED (Television station : Pittsburgh, Pa.) VI. National Academy of Sciences (U.S.) VII. Annenberg/CPB Project. VIII. Unapix Entertainment, Inc. IX. Unapix Consumer Products. X. Title: Unapix Consumer Products feature presentation [videorecording] XI. Series.*
**TC QB631.2 .F3 1996**

**O'Farrell, Clare.**
Taught bodies. New York : P. Lang, c2000.
**TC LB14.7 .T38 2000**

**O'Farrell, Patrick James.** UNSW, a portrait : the University of New South Wales, 1949-1999 / Patrick O'Farrell. Sydney, Australia : UNSW Press, 1999. 307 p. : ill. ; 27 cm. Includes bibliographical references (p. [286]-297) and index. ISBN 0-86840-417-9 ISBN 0-86840-617-1 (boxed numbered ed.)
*1. University of New South Wales - History. I. Title. II. Title: University of New South Wales, a portrait*
**TC LG715.K4 O42 1999**

**OFF-RESERVATION BOARDING SCHOOLS.** *See* **INDIANS OF NORTH AMERICA - EDUCATION.**

**OFFENDERS, SEX.** *See* **SEX OFFENDERS.**

**OFFENSES AGAINST PUBLIC SAFETY.** *See* **RIOTS.**

**OFFENSES AGAINST THE PERSON.** *See* **HOMICIDE; KIDNAPPING; MURDER; RAPE; SEX CRIMES; SUICIDE.**

**OFFICE BUILDINGS.**
Seibold, J,otto. Going to the Getty. Los Angeles : J. Paul Getty Museum, c1997.
**TC NA6813.U6 L678 1997**

**"Office of Citizen" [videorecording].**
A case study in teaching to civic standards using a portfolio approach 1996 : "Office of Citizen". [Boulder, Colo.] : Social Science Education Consortium, c1997.
**TC LC1091 .C37 1997**

**OFFICE POLITICS.**
Haass, Richard. The bureaucratic entrepreneur. Washington, D.C. : Brookings Institution, c1999.
**TC JF1351 .H2 1999**

**OFFICE PRACTICE - AUTOMATION.** *See* **ELECTRONIC DATA PROCESSING.**

**Official bulletin (New York (State). Dept. of Health).**
[Health news (Albany, N.Y. : 1916)] Health news. Albany, N.Y. : The Dept., 1916-1916.

**Official guide to undergraduate nursing schools /** NLN Research and Evaluation Division. Sudbury, Mass. : Jones and Bartlett Publishers, c2000. xi, 1007 p. ; 28 cm. + 1 laser optical disc (4 1/2 in.). Includes index. SUMMARY: An NLN publication including profiles of two-year, three-year, and four-year nursing schools. ISBN 0-7637-1108-X (pbk).
*1. Nursing schools - United States - Directories. I. National League for Nursing. Research and Evaluation Division.*

**Official knowledge.**
Apple, Michael W. 2nd ed. New York : Routledge, 2000.
**TC LC89 .A815 2000**

**OFFICIAL LANGUAGES.** *See* **LANGUAGE POLICY.**

**OGBU, JOHN U.**
Berube, Maurice R. Eminent educators. Westport, Conn. : Greenwood Press, 2000.
**TC LB875.D5 B47 2000**

**Ogletree, Billy T.**
Bridging the family-professional gap. Springfield, Ill. : Charles C. Thomas, c1999.
**TC HV888.5 .B74 1999**

**Ogot, Bethwell A.**
Decolonization & independence in Kenya, 1940-93. London : J. Currey ; Athens : Ohio University Press, 1995.
**TC DT433.58 .D4 1995**

**O'Grady, Jean, 1943-.**
Addison, Margaret, 1868-1940. Diary of a European tour, 1900. Montréal : McGill-Queen's University Press, c1999.
**TC LE3.T619 A33 1999**

**Oh!.**
Henkes, Kevin. New York : Greenwillow Books, 1999.
**TC PZ8.3.H4165 Oh 1999**

**Ohanian, Susan.** Standards, plain English, and The ugly duckling : lessons about what teachers really do. [Bloomington, Ind.] : Published by the Phi Delta Kappa Educational Foundation in cooperation with the John Dewey Project on Progressive Education, [Burlington, Vt.], c1998. 73 p. ; 23 cm. ISBN 0-87367-809-5 DDC 370/.9
*1. Educational change - United States.*
**TC LA217.2 .O33 1998**

**O'Hanlon, William Hudson.**
Rowan, Tim, 1952- Solution-oriented therapy for chronic and severe mental illness. New York : Wiley, c1999.
**TC RC480.53 .R69 1999**

**O'Hara, Mark.** Teaching 3-8 : : meeting the standards for initial teacher training and induction / Mark O'Hara. London ; New York : Continuum, 2000. xiii, 176 p. : ill. ; 25 cm. Includes bibliographical references (p. 173-174) and index. ISBN 0-8264-4843-7
*1. Teachers - Training of - Great Britain. 2. Preschool teaching - Great Britain. 3. Elementary school teaching - Great Britain. I. Title. II. Title: Teaching three to eight.*
**TC LB1725.G7 O36 2000**

**O'Hara, Megan.**
Jernegan, Laura, b. 1862. A whaling captain's daughter. Mankato, Minn. : Blue Earth Books, c2000.
**TC G545 .J47 2000**

Wister, Sarah, 1761-1804. A colonial Quaker girl. Mankato, Minn. : Blue Earth Books, c2000.
**TC F158.44 .W75 2000**

**Ohio State University. Bureau of Educational Research.**
Cowley, William Harold, 1889- The personnel bibliographical index. Columbus, Ohio : The Ohio State University, 1932.
**TC Z5814.P8 C8**

**Ohio University. College of Fine Arts.**
[Wide angle (Online)] Wide angle [computer file]. Baltimore, Md. : John Hopkins University Press, c1996-
**TC EJOURNALS**

**OIIA satellite town meeting.**
Public charter schools : new choices in public education (May 3, 2000 : Washington, D.C.) Public charter schools [videorecording]. [Washington, D.C.] : U.S. Dept. of Education, [2000].
**TC LB2806.36 .P9 2000**

(72.) Modernizing schools : technology and buildings for a new century (September 19, 2000 : Washington, D.C.) Modernizing schools [videorecording]. [Washington, D.C.] : U.S. Dept. of Education, [2000].
**TC LB3205 .M64 2000**

(72.) Modernizing schools : technology and buildings for a new century (September 19, 2000 : Washington, D.C.) Modernizing schools [videorecording]. [Washington, D.C.] : U.S. Dept. of Education, [2000].

*TC LB3205 .M64 2000*

**OIL PAINTING.** *See* **PAINTING.**

**OILSEED PLANTS.** *See* **PEANUTS.**

**O'Keefe, Deborah.** Good girl messages : how young women were misled by their favorite books / Deborah O'Keefe. New York : Continuum, 2000. 212 p. ; 24 cm. Includes index. ISBN 0-8264-1236-X (alk. paper) DDC 810.9/352054
*1. Children's stories, American - History and criticism. 2. Girls in literature. 3. Children's stories, English - History and criticism. 4. Young women - Books and reading. 5. Conduct of life in literature. 6. Girls - Books and reading. 7. Sex role in literature. I. Title.*
*TC PS374.G55 O44 2000*

**O'Keeffe.**
Georgia O'Keeffe [videorecording]. [Boston?] : Home Vision ; c1977.
*TC ND237.O5 G4 1977*

**O'Keeffe, Georgia, 1887-1986.**
Georgia O'Keeffe [videorecording]. [Boston?] : Home Vision ; c1977.
*TC ND237.O5 G4 1977*

**O'KEEFFE, GEORGIA, 1887-1986.**
Georgia O'Keeffe [videorecording]. [Boston?] : Home Vision ; c1977.
*TC ND237.O5 G4 1977*

**Okihiro, Gary Y., 1945-** Stories lives : Japanese American students and World War II / Gary Y. Okihiro ; with a contribution by Leslie A. Ito. Seattle : University of Washington Press, 1999. xiv, 182 p., [8] p. of plates : ill. ; 23 cm. (The Scott and Laurie Oki series in Asian American studies) Includes bibliographical references (p. 167-173) and index. ISBN 0-295-97764-7 (cloth : alk. paper) ISBN 0-295-97796-5 (pbk. : alk. paper) DDC 940.53/089/956073
*1. World War, 1939-1945 - Japanese Americans. 2. Japanese American college students - Social conditions. 3. Japanese American college students - Economic conditions. 4. Racism - United States - History - 20th century. 5. United States - Race relations. I. Ito, Leslie A. II. Title. III. Series.*
*TC D753.8 .O38 1999*

**OKLAHOMA - HISTORY - LAND RUSH, 1889 - FICTION.**
Thomas, Joyce Carol. I have heard of a land. 1st ed. [New York] : HarperCollins Publishers, c1998.
*TC PZ7.T36696 Iae 1998*

**OKLAHOMA - HISTORY - LAND RUSH, 1889 - JUVENILE FICTION.**
Thomas, Joyce Carol. I have heard of a land. 1st ed. [New York] : HarperCollins Publishers, c1998.
*TC PZ7.T36696 Iae 1998*

**OKLAHOMA LAND RUSH OF 1889.** *See* **OKLAHOMA - HISTORY - LAND RUSH, 1889.**

**Olaya, Clara Inés.**
Valette, Jean Paul. Spanish for mastery. Lexington, Mass. : D.C. Heath, c1980.
*TC PC4112 .V29 1980*

**OLD AGE.** *See* **AGED; AGING.**

**OLD AGE ASSISTANCE.** *See* **AGED - MEDICAL CARE.**

**OLD-AGE ASSISTANCE - ELIGIBILITY.**
Schorr, Alvin Louis, 1921- Filial responsibility in the modern American family. [Washington] U.S. Dept. of Health, Education, and Welfare, Social Security Administration, Division of Program Research [1960]
*TC HV75 .S36 1960*

**OLD AGE - FICTION.**
Schachner, Judith Byron. The Grannyman. 1st ed. New York : Dutton Children's Books, c1999.
*TC PZ7.S3286 Gr 1999*

**OLD AGE - PSYCHOLOGICAL ASPECTS.** *See also* **AGED - PSYCHOLOGY.**
Aging and saging [videorecording]. Princeton, NJ : Films for the Humanities & Sciences : Distributed by Canadian Broadcasting Corporation, 1998.
*TC BF724.55.A35 A35 1998*

**OLD AGE - RELIGIOUS ASPECTS.**
Aging and saging [videorecording]. Princeton, NJ : Films for the Humanities & Sciences : Distributed by Canadian Broadcasting Corporation, 1998.
*TC BF724.55.A35 A35 1998*

**OLD AGE - SOCIAL ASPECTS - UNITED STATES.**
Communication and aging. 2nd ed. Mahwah, NJ ; London : L. Erlbaum, 2000.

*TC HQ1064.U5 C5364 2000*

**OLD AGE, SURVIVORS AND DISABILITY INSURANCE.** *See* **SOCIAL SECURITY.**

**Old Dry Frye.**
Johnson, Paul Brett. New York : Scholastic Press, 1999.
*TC PZ8.1.J635 Ol 1999*

**Old Elm speaks.**
George, Kristine O'Connell. New York : Clarion Books, c1998.
*TC PS3557.E488 O4 1998*

**OLD MEN.** *See* **AGED MEN.**

**OLD ORDER AMISH.** *See* **AMISH.**

**Old souls.**
Black, Helen K., 1952- New York : A. de Gruyter, c2000.
*TC HQ1064.U6 P424 2000*

**Old-time schools and school-books.**
Johnson, Clifton, 1865-1940. Detroit : Omnigraphics, 1999.
*TC LA206 .J6 1999*

**OLD WOMEN.** *See* **AGED WOMEN.**

**Oldenski, Thomas.**
Catholic school leadership. London ; New York : Falmer Press, 2000.
*TC LC501 .C3484 2000*

**Oldenziel, Ruth, 1958-** Making technology masculine : men, women and modern machines in America, 1870-1945 / Ruth Oldenziel. Amsterdam : Amsterdam University Press, c1999. 271 p. : ill. ; 24 cm. Includes bibliographical references (p. [232]-261) and index. ISBN 90-5356-381-4
*1. Labor - United States - History. 2. Labor - North America - History. 3. Human-machine systems - United States - History. 4. Sexual division of labor - United States - History. 5. Women - Employment - United States - History. I. Title.*
*TC HD8072 .O57 1999*

**OLDER MEN.** *See* **AGED MEN.**

**OLDER PERSONS.** *See* **AGED.**

**OLDER WOMEN.** *See* **AGED WOMEN.**

**Oldfather, Penny.** Learning through children's eyes : social constructivism and the desire to learn / Penny Oldfather and Jane West with Jennifer White and Jill Wilmarth. 1st ed. Washington, DC : American Psychological Association, c1999. x, 218 p. ; 28 cm. (Psychology in the classroom) Includes bibliographical references. ISBN 1-55798-587-1 (pbk. : alk. paper) DDC 370.15/23
*1. Learning, Psychology of. 2. Motivation in education. 3. Cognition in children. 4. Social interaction in children. 5. Constructivism (Education) I. West, Jane, 1960- II. Title. III. Series.*
*TC LB1060 .O43 1999*

**O'Leary, Charles J.** Counselling couples and families : a person-centred approach / Charles J. O'Leary. London : SAGE, 1999. xiii, 162 p. ; 25 cm. Includes bibliographical references and index. ISBN 0-7619-5790-1 ISBN 0-7619-5791-X (pbk.) DDC 361.06
*1. Family counseling. 2. Family counseling. I. Title.*
*TC RC488.5 .O394 1999*

**Olien, Rebecca.** Walk this way! : classroom hikes to learning / Rebecca Olien. Portsmouth, NH : Heinemann, c1998. ix, 94 p. : ill. ; 23 cm. "Beeline books." Includes bibliographical references. ISBN 0-325-00022-0 (alk. paper) DDC 371.3/84
*1. Outdoor education. 2. Hiking. 3. Nature study. I. Title.*
*TC LB1047 .O55 1998*

**Oliva, Peter F.** Supervision for today's schools / Peter F. Oliva, George E. Pawlas. 6th ed. New York ; Chichester [England] : J. Wiley & Sons, c2001. 1 v. (various pagings) : ill. ; 25 cm. "Wiley Education"--Cover. Includes bibliographical references and indexes. ISBN 0-471-36435-5 (cloth : alk. paper) DDC 371.2
*1. School supervision - United States. I. Pawlas, George. II. Title.*
*TC LB2806.4 .O43 2001*

**Olivardia, Roberto, 1972-.**
Pope, Harrison. The Adonis complex. New York : Free Press, 2000.
*TC BF697.5.B635 2000*

**Oliveira, Nicolas de.** Installation art / Nicolas de Oliveira, Nicola Oxley, Michael Petry ; with texts by Michael Archer. London : Thames and Hudson, 1994. 208 p. : ill. (some col.) ; 29 cm. Includes bibliographical references (p. 188-194) and index. ISBN 0-500-23672-0
*1. Installations (Art) 2. Art, Modern - 20th century. I. Oxley, Nicola. II. Petry, Michael. III. Archer, Michael. IV. Title.*

*TC N6494.E O4 1994*

**Oliver, Frank H.** Fellow beggars : the history of fund raising campaigning in U.S. higer education / by Frank H. Oliver. 1999. 314 leaves : ill. ; 29 cm. Typescript; issued also on microfilm. Thesis (Ed.D.)--Teachers College, Columbia University, 1999. Includes bibliographical references (leaves 297-312).
*1. Fund raising - United States - History. 2. Education, Higher - United State - Finance - History. 3. Universities and colleges - United States - Finance - History. 4. State universities and colleges - United States - Finance - History. 5. Teacher turnover - United States. 6. Endowments - United States - History. 7. Education, Higher - Law and legislation - United States - History. I. Title. II. Title: History of fund raising campaigning in U.S higher education*
*TC 06 no.11157*

**Oliver, Paul.**
Lifelong and continuing education :. Aldershot, Hants, England ; Brookfield, Vt. : Ashgate, c1999.
*TC LC5215 L464 1999*

**Olivera, Fernando, ill.**
Cruz Martinez, Alejandro, d. 1987. [Mujer que brillaba aún más que el sol. English & Spanish] The woman who outshone the sun. San Francisco, Calif. : Children's Book Press, c1991.
*TC F1221.Z3 C78 1991*

**Olivier, Katherine.**
Götz, Stephan, 1960- [New Yorker Künstler in ihren Ateliers. English] American artists in their New York studios. Cambridge [Mass.] : Center for Conservation and Technical Studies, Harvard University Art Museums ; Stuttgart : Daco-Verlag Günter Bläse, c1992.
*TC N6535.N5 G6813 1992*

**Olkowski, Dorothea.** Gilles Deleuze and the ruin of representation / Dorothea Olkowski. Berkeley : University of California Press, c1999. xiii, 298 p. : ill. ; 24 cm. Includes bibliographical references (p. 279-290) and index. ISBN 0-520-21691-1 (alk. paper) ISBN 0-520-21693-8 (pbk. : alk. paper) DDC 111/.85
*1. Kelly, Mary, - 1941- - Criticism and interpretation. 2. Deleuze, Gilles - Contributions in logic. 3. Feminism and art. 4. Psychoanalysis and art. I. Title.*
*TC N6537.K42 O44 1999*

**Ollendick, Thomas H.**
Handbook of psychotherapies with children and families. New York ; London : Kluwer Academic/Plenum Publishers, c1999.
*TC RJ504 .H3619 1999*

**Oller, D. Kimbrough.** The emergence of the speech capacity / D. Kimbrough Oller. Mahwah, N.J. : Lawrence Erlbaum Associates, 2000. xvii, 428 p. ; 24 cm. Includes bibliographical references (p. 365-395) and indexes. ISBN 0-8058-2628-9 (alk. paper) ISBN 0-8058-2629-7 (pbk. : alk. paper) DDC 401/.93
*1. Language acquisition. 2. Oral communication. 3. Animal communication. 4. Primates. 5. Language and languages - Origin. I. Title.*
*TC P118 .O43 2000*

**Olley, J. Gregory.**
Baroff, George S. Mental retardation. 3rd ed. Philadelphia, Pa. : Brunner/Mazel, c1999.
*TC RC570 .B27 1999*

**Olmstead, Andrea.** Juilliard : a history / Andrea Olmstead. Urbana : University of Illinois Press, c1999. 368 p. : ill. ; 25 cm. (Music in American life) Includes bibliographical references and index. ISBN 0-252-02487-7 (cloth) DDC 780/.71/17471
*1. Juilliard School. 2. Conservatories of music - New York (State) - New York. I. Title. II. Series.*
*TC MT4.N5 J846 1999*

**Olmsted, Patricia P.**
Families speak. Ypsilanti, Mich. : High/Scope Press, c1994.
*TC LB1139.23 .F36 1994*

How nations serve young children. Ypsilanti, Mich. : High/Scope Press, c1989.
*TC HQ778.5 .H69 1989*

**Olsen, Victoria C.**
On the market. 1st Riverhead ed. New York : Riverhead Books, 1997.
*TC LB2331.72 .O5 1997*

**Olson, David R., 1935-.**
Minds in the making. Oxford ; Malden, Mass. : Blackwell, 2000.
*TC BF723.C5 M56 2000*

**Olson, Gary A., 1954-.**
Race, rhetoric, and the postcolonial. Albany : State University of New York Press, c1999.

*TC P301.5.P67 R33 1999*

**Olson, Ivan, 1931-** The arts and critical thinking in
American education / Ivan Olson : Ralph A. Smith,
advisory editor. Westport, Conn. : Bergin & Garvey,
2000. xii, 142 p. : ill., map ; 25 cm. Includes bibliographical
references (p. [131]-138) and index. ISBN 0-89789-694-7 (alk.
paper) ISBN 0-313-30844-6 (alk. paper) DDC 111/.85
*1. Aesthetics. 2. Critical thinking. 3. Creative thinking. 4. Art -
Philosophy. I. Title.*
*TC BH39 .O45 2000*

**Olson, Judy L.** Teaching children and adolescents with
special needs / Judy L. Olson and Jennifer M. Platt.
3rd ed. Upper Saddle River, N.J. : Merrill, c2000. x,
427 p. : ill. ; 24 cm. Includes bibliographical references (p.
372-405) and indexes. ISBN 0-13-099949-0 (pbk) DDC 371.9
*1. Special education. 2. Teaching. 3. Classroom management.
I. Platt, Jennifer M., 1945- II. Title.*
*TC LC3969 .O47 2000*

**Olson, Mary E.**
Feminism, community, and communication. New
York ; London : Haworth Press, c2000.
*TC RC488.5 .F43 2000*

**Olszewski-Kubilius, Paula.**
Investigating creativity in youth. Cresskill, N.J. :
Hampton Press, c1999.
*TC BF723.C7 I58 1999*

**Olutoye, Ọmọtayọ.**
Issues on examination malpractices in Nigeria :.
Ikere-Ekiti [Nigeria] : Ondo State College of
Education, c1998.
*TC LB3058.N6 I848 1998*

**OLYMPIC GAMES.** *See* **OLYMPICS.**

**The Olympic games.**
Toohey, K. (Kristine). Oxon, UK ; New York, NY :
CABI Pub., c2000.
*TC GV721.5 .T64 1999*

**OLYMPIC GAMES (ANCIENT).**
Swaddling, Judith. The ancient Olympic games. 2nd
ed. Austin : University of Texas Press, 1999, c1980.
*TC GV23 .S9 1999*

**OLYMPICS.** *See* **OLYMPIC GAMES (ANCIENT).**

**OLYMPICS - HISTORY.**
Chronicle of the Olympics, 1896-2000. 1st American
ed. New York : DK Pub., c1998.
*TC GV721.5 .C474 1998*

Toohey, K. (Kristine). The Olympic games :. Oxon,
UK ; New York, NY : CABI Pub., c2000.
*TC GV721.5 .T64 1999*

**OLYMPICS - PICTORIAL WORKS.**
Chronicle of the Olympics, 1896-2000. 1st American
ed. New York : DK Pub., c1998.
*TC GV721.5 .C474 1998*

**OLYMPICS - POLITICAL ASPECTS - HISTORY.**
Senn, Alfred Erich. Power, politics, and the Olympic
Games. Champaign, IL : Human Kinetics, c1999.
*TC GV721.5 .S443 1999*

**OLYMPICS - RECORDS.**
Chronicle of the Olympics, 1896-2000. 1st American
ed. New York : DK Pub., c1998.
*TC GV721.5 .C474 1998*

**OLYMPICS - SOCIAL ASPECTS.**
Toohey, K. (Kristine). The Olympic games :. Oxon,
UK ; New York, NY : CABI Pub., c2000.
*TC GV721.5 .T64 1999*

**O'Malley, Kevin, 1961-** Bud / Kevin O'Malley. New
York : Walker, 2000. 1v. (unpaged) : col. ill. ; 29 cm.
SUMMARY: The orderly Sweet-Williams are dismayed at
their son's fondness for the messy pastime of gardening. ISBN
0-8027-8718-5 (hardcover) ISBN 0-8027-8719-3 (reinforced)
DDC [E]
*1. Orderliness - Fiction. 2. Parent and child - Fiction. 3.
Gardening - Fiction. 4. Grandfathers - Fiction. 5.
Rhinoceroses - Fiction. I. Title.*
*TC PZ7.O526 Bu 2000*

**O'Meally, Robert G., 1948-.**
The jazz cadence of American culture. New York :
Columbia University Press, c1998.
*TC ML3508 .J38 1998*

**Omori, Chizuko.**
Rabbit in the moon [videorecording]. San Francisco,
Calif. : Wabi-Sabi Productions, 1999.
*TC D753.8 .R3 1999*

**Omori, Emiko.**
Rabbit in the moon [videorecording]. San Francisco,
Calif. : Wabi-Sabi Productions, 1999.
*TC D753.8 .R3 1999*

**Omura, James.**
Rabbit in the moon [videorecording]. San Francisco,
Calif. : Wabi-Sabi Productions, 1999.
*TC D753.8 .R3 1999*

**On becoming a language educator :** personal essays on
professional development / edited by Christine
Pearson Casanave, Sandra R. Schecter. Mahwah, NJ :
Lawrence Erlbaum, 1997. xxi, 243 p. ; 24 cm.
Includes bibliographical references and index. ISBN
0-8058-2263-1 (alk. paper) ISBN 0-8058-2264-X (pbk. : alk.
paper) DDC 407/.1/1
*1. Language teachers - Training of. I. Casanave, Christine
Pearson, 1944- II. Schecter, Sandra.*
*TC P53.85 .O5 1997*

**On becoming Cuban.**
Pérez, Louis A., 1943- Chapel Hill : University of
North Carolina Press, c1999.
*TC F1760 .P47 1999*

**On being a teacher.**
Kottler, Jeffrey A. 2nd ed. Thousand Oaks, Calif. :
Corwin Press, c2000.
*TC LB1025.3 .Z44 2000*

**On display.**
Skaggs, Gayle, 1952- Jefferson, NC : McFarland,
c1999.
*TC Z675.S3 S5975 1999*

**On exhibit.**
Black, Barbara J., 1962- Charlottesville ; London :
University Press of Virginia, 2000.
*TC AM43.L6 B53 2000*

**On holy ground.**
Sullivan, John P. (John Peter) Lanham : University
Press of America, c1998.
*TC RC489.R46 S84 1998*

**On Jung.**
Stevens, Anthony. 2nd ed. Princeton, N.J. : Princeton
University Press, 1999.
*TC BF173 .S828 1999*

**On knowing.**
Bruner, Jerome Seymour. Cambridge, Belknap Press
of Harvard University Press, 1962.
*TC LB885 .B778*

**ON-LINE DATA PROCESSING.** *See* **ONLINE
DATA PROCESSING.**

**ON-LINE DATA PROCESSING - PERIODICALS.**
Online information review. Bradford, West
Yorkshire : MCB University Press, 2000-

**On pictures and paintings** [videorecording] / written
and presented by Charles Harrison ; series producer,
Nick Levinson ; producer, Jeremy Cooper ; a
production for the Open University, BBC ; publication
aided y Espace Video Européen. Peasmarsh, East
Sussex, Eng. : Ho-Ho-kus, NJ : Roland Collection,
1992. 1 videocassette (VHS) (25 min.) : sd. ; 1/2 in. (Modern
art, practices & debates (Television program)) VHS.
Catalogued from credits, cassette label and container.
Presenter: Charles Harrison. Camera, Derek Firmin; sound,
Mike Heald. On container spine: 551. "Publication aided by
Espace Video Européen..."--Credits. 18 to adult. SUMMARY:
Charles Harrison examines works in the Tate Gallery in
London, exploring different ways of thinking about art and
representation. He discusses the philosophy of modernism
versus realism and abstraction versus the ffigurative.
*1. Painting. Modernism - 20th century. 2. Painting, Abstract. 3.
Cubism. 4. Modernism (Art) 5. Modernism (Aesthetics) 6.
Realism in art. 7. Art - Philosophy. I. Harrison, Charles, 1942-
II. Levinson, Nick. III. Cooper, Jeremy. IV. Anthony Roland
Collection of Film on Art. V. Open University. VI. British
Broadcasting Corporation. VII. Espace Video Europeén. VIII.
Series.*
*TC ND195.O45 1992*

**On reflection.**
Miller, Jonathan, 1934- London : National Gallery
Publications ; [New Haven, Conn.] : Distributed by
Yale University Press, c1998.
*TC N8224.M6 M54 1998*

**On solid ground.**
Taberski, Sharon. Portsmouth, NH : Heinemann, c
2000.
*TC LB1525 .T32 2000*

**On the dark side.**
Stephen Hawking's universe [videorecording].
[Alexandria, Va.] : PBS Video; Burbank, CA :
Distributed by Warner Home Video, c1997.
*TC QB982 .S7 1997*

**ON-THE-JOB STRESS.** *See* **JOB STRESS.**

**ON-THE-JOB TRAINING.** *See* **EMPLOYEES -
TRAINING OF.**

**On the market :** surviving the academic job search /
edited by Christina Boufis and Victoria C. Olsen. 1st
Riverhead ed. New York : Riverhead Books, 1997. xv,
381 p. ; 21 cm. Includes bibliographical references. ISBN 1-
57322-626-2 DDC 378.1/2/02373
*1. College teachers - Employment - United States. 2. College
teachers - Selection and appointment - United States. 3. Job
hunting - United States. I. Boufis, Christina. II. Olsen, Victoria
C.*
*TC LB2331.72 .O5 1997*

**On the origins of human emotions.**
Turner, Jonathan H. Stanford, Calif. : Stanford
University Press, c2000.
*TC BF531 .T87 2000*

**On their way.**
Fraser, Jane. Portsmouth, NH : Heinemann, c1994.
*TC LB1576 .F72 1994*

**Ondo State College of Education.**
Issues on examination malpractices in Nigeria :.
Ikere-Ekiti [Nigeria] : Ondo State College of
Education, c1998.
*TC LB3058.N6 I848 1998*

**One-computer classroom.**
Kahn, Jessica L. Ideas and strategies for the one-
computer classroom. Eugene, OR : International
Society for Technology in Education, c1998.
*TC LB1028.5 .K25 1998*

**ONE-FAMILY HOUSES.** *See* **ARCHITECTURE,
DOMESTIC; DWELLINGS.**

**One hundred and one fingerplays, stories, and songs
to use with finger puppets.**
Briggs, Diane. 101 fingerplays, stories, and songs to
use with finger puppets. Chicago : American Library
Association, 1999.
*TC GV1218.F5 B74 1999*

**One hundred and one things to do with a baby.**
Ormerod, Jan. 101 things to do with a baby. 1st U.S.
ed. New York : Lothrop, Lee & Shepard, c1984.
*TC PZ7.O634 Aad 1984*

**One hundred and one ways to integrate personal
development into core curriculum.**
Conroy, Mary Ann. 101 ways to integrate personal
development into core curriculum. Lanham :
University Press of America, c2000.
*TC LC311 .C65 2000*

**One hundred clear grammar tests.**
Folse, Keith S. 100 clear grammar tests. Ann Arbor :
University of Michigan Press, c2000.
*TC PE1128.A2 F646 2000*

**One hundred jobs :b a panorama of work in the
American city.**
Howell, Ron. New York : New Press : Distributed by
W.W. Norton, 1999.
*TC HF5382.5.U6 N37 1999*

**One hundred most popular children's authors.**
McElmeel, Sharron L. 100 most popular children's
authors. Englewood, Colo. : Libraries Unlimited,
1999.
*TC PS490 .M39 1999*

**One hundred one fingerplays, stories, and songs to
use with finger puppets.**
Briggs, Diane. 101 fingerplays, stories, and songs to
use with finger puppets. Chicago : American Library
Association, 1999.
*TC GV1218.F5 B74 1999*

**One hundred one things to do with a baby.**
Ormerod, Jan. 101 things to do with a baby. 1st U.S.
ed. New York : Lothrop, Lee & Shepard, c1984.
*TC PZ7.O634 Aad 1984*

**One hundred one ways to integrate personal
development into core curriculum.**
Conroy, Mary Ann. 101 ways to integrate personal
development into core curriculum. Lanham :
University Press of America, c2000.
*TC LC311 .C65 2000*

**One hundred twenty-four high-impact letters for
busy principals.**
Grady, Marilyn L. 124 high-impact letters for busy
principals. Thousand Oaks, Calif. : Corwin Press,
c2000.
*TC LB2831.9 .G72 2000*

**ONE-ROOM SCHOOLS.** *See* **RURAL SCHOOLS.**

**ONE-TEACHER SCHOOLS.** *See* **RURAL
SCHOOLS.**

**One thousand French words.**
1,000 French words. Princeton, N.J. : Berlitz Kids,
Berlitz Pub. Co., 1998.
*TC PC2680 .A15 1998*

**One thousand German words.**
1,000 German words. Princeton, N.J. : Berlitz Kids,
c1998.
*TC PF3629 .A14 1998*

**One thousand Spanish words.**
1,000 Spanish words. Princeton, N.J. : Berlitz Kids,
c1998.
*TC PC4680 .A13 1998*

**One to ten and back again.**
1 to 10 and back again. Los Angeles : J. Paul Getty
Museum, c1999.
*TC QA113 .A14 1998*

**O'Neil, Judith Ann.** The role of the learning advisor in
action learning / Judith Ann O'Neil. 1999. xv, 277
leaves ; 29 cm. Typescript; issued also on microfilm. Thesis
(Ed.D.) -- Teachers College, Columbia University, 1999.
Includes bibliographical references (leaves 231-248).
*1. Consultants - In-service training. 2. Active learning. 3.
Action research in education. 4. Participant observation. 5.
Interaction analysis in education. 6. Interviewing. I. Title.*
*TC 06 no. 11156*

**O'Neil, Wayne A.**
The generative study of second language acquisition.
Mahwah, N.J. : L. Erlbaum, 1998.
*TC P118.2 .G46 1998*

**Ong, Walter J.** Orality and literacy : the technologizing
of the word / Walter J. Ong. London ; New York :
Routledge, 1988. x, 201 p. ; 20 cm. (New accents)
Originally published: London ; New York : Methuen, 1982.
Includes bibliographical references (p. [180]-195) and index.
"Reprinted 1989, 1990 (twice), 1991, 1993, 1995, 1996, 1997,
1999 (twice)."-- T.p. verso ISBN 0-416-71370-X ISBN
0-415-02796-9 pbk.) DDC 001.54
*1. Language and culture. 2. Oral tradition. 3. Writing. 4.
Oral-formulaic analysis. I. Title. II. Series: New accents
(Routledge (Firm))*
*TC P35 .O5 1988*

**Onion John.**
Krumgold, Joseph, 1908- New York, N.Y. : Thomas
Y. Crowell Company, 1959.
*TC XFK942*

**Online & CD-ROM review.**
Online information review. Bradford, West
Yorkshire : MCB University Press, 2000-

**Online competitive intelligence.**
Burwell, Helen P. Tempe, AZ : Facts on Demand
Press, c1999.
*TC HD38.7 .B974 1999*

**ONLINE DATA PROCESSING.**
Barnicle, Katherine Ann. Evaluation of the interaction
between users of screen reading technology and
graphical user interface elements. 1999.
*TC 085 B265*

Language learning online. Austin : Labyrinth
Publications, c1998.
*TC PE1128.A2 L2955 1998*

Taking flight with OWLs. Mahwah, N.J. : Lawrence
Erlbaum Associates, Publishers, 2000.
*TC PE1404 .T24 2000*

**ONLINE DATA PROCESSING - STUDY AND
TEACHING.**
The online writing classroom. Cresskill, N.J. :
Hampton Press, c2000.
*TC PE1404 .O45 2000*

**Online education resources.**
Bigham, Vicki Smith. The Prentice Hall directory of
online education resources. Paramus, N.J. : Prentice
Hall, c1998.
*TC LB1044.87 .B54 1998*

**Online information review.** Bradford, West Yorkshire :
MCB University Press, 2000- v. ; 28 cm. Frequency:
Bimonthly. Vol. 24, no. 1 (2000)- . "The international journal
of digital information research and use." Title from cover.
Indexed by: Chemical abstracts 0009-2258. Online version
available through World Wide Web. Available in other form:
Online information review (Online). Continues: Online & CD-
ROM review ISSN: 1353-2642 (OCoLC)27743281
(DLC)   93657043. ISSN 1468-4527
*1. Information storage and retrieval systems - Periodicals. 2.
On-line data processing - Periodicals. I. Title: Online
information review (Online) II. Title: Online & CD-ROM
review*

**Online information review (Online).**
Online information review. Bradford, West
Yorkshire : MCB University Press, 2000-

**ONLINE PUBLICATIONS.**  *See* **ELECTRONIC
PUBLICATIONS.**

**The online teaching guide : :** a handbook of attitudes,
strategies, and techniques for the virtual classroom /
Ken W. White, Bob H. Weight, [editors]. Boston,
Mass. : Allyn and Bacon, c2000. xv, 192 p. ; 24 cm.
Includes bibliographical references and index. ISBN 0-205-
29531-2
*1. College teaching - Computer network resources. 2.
Education, Higher - Computer-assisted instruction. I. White,
Ken W. II. Weight, Bob H.*
*TC LB1044.87 .O45 1999*

**The online writing classroom** / edited by Susanmarie
Harrington, Rebecca Rickly, Michael Day. Cresskill,
N.J. : Hampton Press, c2000. xii, 396 p. : ill. ; 24 cm.
(Instructional and information technology) Includes
bibliographical references and indexes. ISBN 1-57273-271-7
ISBN 1-57273-272-5 (pbk.) DDC 808/.042/0285
*1. English language - Rhetoric - Study and teaching - Data
processing. 2. English language - Rhetoric - Computer network
resources. 3. Report writing - Study and teaching - Data
processing. 4. English language - Computer-assisted
instruction. 5. Report writing - Computer network resources. 6.
Online data processing - Study and teaching. I. Harrington,
Susanmarie. II. Rickly, Rebecca. III. Day, Michael. IV. Series.*
*TC PE1404 .O45 2000*

**Ontario Institute for Studies in Education.**
Livingstone, D. W. Public attitudes towards education
in Ontario, 1996. Toronto : OISE/UT in association
with University of Toronto Press, 1997.
*TC LA418.06 L58 1997*

**ONTOGENY.**  *See* **DEVELOPMENTAL BIOLOGY.**

**ONTOLOGY.**  *See* **IDENTITY.**

**Onwumechili, Chuka.** African democratization and
military coups / Chuka Onwumechili ; foreword by
Emmanuel A. Erskine. Westport, Conn. : Praeger,
1998. xii, 121 p. ; 25 cm. Includes bibliographical references
(p. [111]-114) and index. ISBN 0-275-96325-X (alk. paper)
DDC 322/.5/096
*1. Civil-military relations - Africa. 2. Democracy - Africa. 3.
Democratization - Africa. 4. Coups d'état - Africa. I. Title.*
*TC JQ1873.5.C58 O58 1998*

**Opdycke, Sandra.**
Miringoff, Marc L. The social health of the nation.
New York : Oxford University Press, 1999.
*TC HN59.2 .M57 1999*

No one was turned away : the role of public hospitals
in New York City since 1900 / Sandra Opdycke. New
York : Oxford University Press, 1999. x, 244 p. : ill.,
map ; 24 cm. Includes bibliographical references (p. 225-235)
and index. ISBN 0-19-511950-9 (alk. paper) DDC 362.1/1/
09747109049
*1. Public hospitals - New York (State) - New York - History -
20th century. 2. Hospital care - New York (State) - New York -
History - 20th century. 3. Multihospital systems - New York
(State) - New York - History - 20th century. 4. Public welfare -
New York (State) - New York - History - 20th century. I. Title.*
*TC RA982.N49 O63 1999*

The Routledge historical atlas of women in America /
Sandra Opdycke. New York : Routledge, 2000. 144 p. :
ill., maps ; 26 cm. (Routledge atlases of American history)
Includes bibliographical references (p. 134-137) and index.
ISBN 0-415-92132-5 (cloth : alk. paper) ISBN 0-415-92138-4
(pbk. : alk. paper) DDC 973/.082
*1. Women - United States - History - Atlases. I. Title. II. Series.*
*TC HQ1410 .P68 2000*

**Open and distance learning in the developing world.**
Perraton, H. D. London ; New York : Routledge,
2000.
*TC LC5808.D48 P47 2000*

**Open and distance learning series.**
Changing university teaching :. London : Kogan
Page ; Sterling, VA : Stylus Pub., 2000.
*TC LB2331 .C53 2000*

Inglis, Alistair. Delivering digitally. London : Kogan
Page, c1999.
*TC LB1044.87 .I545 1999*

Morgan, Chris. Assessing open and distance learners.
London : Kogan Page ; Sterling, VA : Stylus Pub.,
1999.
*TC LC5800 .M67 1999*

Simpson, Ormond. Supporting students in open and
distance learning. London : Kogan Page, 2000.

**Open court Publishing Company.**
Phonics review kit [kit]. Chicago, Ill. : Open Court
Pub. Co., c1995.
*TC LB1573.3 .P45 1995*

Pocket chart kit [kit]. Chicago, Ill. : Open Court
Publishing Company, c1995.
*TC LB1573.3 .P6 1995*

Teacher toolbox [kit]. Chicago, Ill. : Open Court Pub.
Co., c1995.
*TC LB1573.3 .T4 1995*

**[Open doors (New York, N.Y.)]** Open doors. New
York, N.Y. : Institute of International Education, v. :
ill. ; 28 cm. Frequency: Annual. Began with 1954-55. Subtitle:
Report on international educational exchange, <1997-98->
Some vols. accompanied by diskettes. Description based on:
1991/92. Vol. designation applies to academic year. Some vols.
accompanied by disk. Also available on the Internet via the
World Wide Web. URL: http://iserver.iie.org/opendoors/disk
Continues: Education for one world (DLC)  49048862
(OCoLC)7903086. ISSN 0078-5172 DDC 370.19/62/0973021
*1. Educational exchanges - United States - Statistics -
Periodicals. 2. Intellectual cooperation - Periodicals. 3.
Students, Foreign - United States - Statistics. I. Institute of
International Education (New York, N.Y.) II. Title: Education
for one world*
*TC LB2283 .I615*

**Open doors :** report on international educational
exchange. [New York, N.Y.] : Institute of
International Education, 1954- v. : ill. ; 28 cm. 1954/55- .
Subtitle varies. Continues: Institute of International Education
(New York, N.Y.). Education for one world; annual census of
foreign students in the United States. ISSN 0078-5172 DDC
378.3
*1. Educational exchanges - United States - Statistics. 2.
Intellectual cooperation - Statistics. 3. Students, Foreign -
United States - Statistics. I. Institute of International Education
(New York, N.Y.) II. Title: Institute of International Education
(New York, N.Y.). Education for one world; annual census of
foreign students in the United States.*
*TC LB2283 .I615*

**OPEN FORUM.**  *See* **FORUMS (DISCUSSION AND
DEBATE).**

**Open house.**
Ierley, Merritt. 1st ed. New York : Henry Holt and
Co., 1999.
*TC NA7205 .I35 1999*

**OPEN LEARNING.**  *See also* **ADULT
EDUCATION; DISTANCE EDUCATION;
INDEPENDENT STUDY.**
McConnell, David, 1951- Implementing computer
supported cooperative learning.. 2nd ed. London :
Kogan Page, 2000.
*TC LB1032 .M38 2000*

Morgan, Chris. Assessing open and distance learners.
London : Kogan Page ; Sterling, VA : Stylus Pub.,
1999.
*TC LC5800 .M67 1999*

Simpson, Ormond. Supporting students in open and
distance learning. London : Kogan Page, 2000.
*TC LC5800 .S56 2000*

Staff development in open and flexible learning.
London ; New York : Routledge, 1998.
*TC LC5800 .S83 1998*

**OPEN LEARNING - COMPUTER NETWORK
RESOURCES.**
Inglis, Alistair. Delivering digitally. London : Kogan
Page, c1999.
*TC LB1044.87 .I545 1999*

**OPEN LEARNING - DEVELOPING COUNTRIES.**
Perraton, H. D. Open and distance learning in the
developing world. London ; New York : Routledge,
2000.
*TC LC5808.D48 P47 2000*

**Open learning system :** concept and future / K. Sudha
Rao, ed. New Delhi : Lancer International, c1989. xv,
148 p. : ill. ; 23 cm. Papers presented at a seminar organized by
the India International Centre, 13-14 January 1987. Includes
bibliographies. ISBN 81-7062-062-7
*1. Distance education - India - Congresses. 2. Non-formal
education - India - Congresses. 3. Educational technology -
India - Congresses. I. Sudha Rao, K. II. India International
Centre.*
*TC LC5808.I4 O64 1989*

**Open linguistics series**
Culturally speaking. London ; New York :
Continuum ; [New York] : [Cassell], 2000.
*TC GN345.6 .C86 2000*

*TC LC5800 .S56 2000*

Genre and institutions. London ; Washington :
Cassell, 1997.
*TC P302.84 .G46 1997*

Painter, Clare, 1947- Learning through language in
early childhood. London ; New York : Cassell, 1999.
*TC LB1139.5.L35 P35 1999*

Researching language in schools and communities.
London ; Washington [D.C.] : Cassell, 2000.
*TC P53 .R463 2000*

**OPEN PLAN SCHOOLS.** *See* **FREE SCHOOLS;
INDIVIDUALIZED INSTRUCTION.**

**OPEN PRICE SYSTEM.** *See* **COMPETITION.**

**OPEN SPACE, FEAR OF.** *See* **AGORAPHOBIA.**

**OPEN SPACES, FEAR OF.** *See* **AGORAPHOBIA.**

**Open University.**
Gender and the interpretation of emotion
[videorecording]. Princeton, NJ : Films for the
Humanities & Sciences, c1997.
*TC BF592.F33 G4 1997*

Making sense of social development. London : New
York : Routledge in association with the Open
University, 1999.
*TC HQ783 .L57 1999*

Morgan, Chris. Assessing open and distance learners.
London : Kogan Page ; Sterling, VA : Stylus Pub.,
1999.
*TC LC5800 .M67 1999*

On pictures and paintings [videorecording].
Peasmarsh, East Sussex, Eng. ; Ho-Ho-kus, NJ :
Roland Collection, 1992.
*TC ND195.O45 1992*

**Opening gambits.**
Armstrong, Peter S. Northvale, N.J. : J. Aronson,
1999.
*TC BF175.4.C68 .A76 1999*

**Opening out**
Seshadri-Crooks, Kalpana. Desiring whiteness.
London ; New York : Routledge, 2000.
*TC BF175.4.R34 S47 2000*

**OPERA - COSTUME.** *See* **COSTUME.**

**OPERATING SYSTEMS (COMPUTERS).**
Carling, M. Linux system administration.
Indianapolis, IN : New Riders, c2000.
*TC QA76.76.O63 C3755 2000*

Kirch, Olaf. Linux network administrator's guide. 2nd
ed. Cambridge, Mass. : O'Reilly, 2000.
*TC QA76.76.O63 K566 2000*

Maximum Linux security. Indianapolis, Ind. : Sams,
c2000.
*TC QA76.9.A25 M385 2000*

Maxwell, Steven. Red hat linux network management
tools. New York : McGraw Hill, c2000.
*TC QA76.76.O63 M373339 2000*

Pitts, David. Red Hat Linux 6 unleashed.
[Indianapolis, Ind.] : SAMS, c1999.
*TC QA76.76.O63 P56148 1999*

Red Hat Linux :. Indianapolis, Ind. : Que : Macmillan
USA, c2000.
*TC QA76.76.O63 R43 2000*

Unix and Windows 2000 handbook. Upper Saddle
River, NJ : Prentice Hall, 2000.
*TC QA76.76.O63 U58 2000*

**OPERATOR-MACHINE SYSTEMS.** *See* **HUMAN-
MACHINE SYSTEMS.**

**OPERETTAS.** *See* **MUSICALS.**

**OPHTHALMIC LENSES.** *See* **EYEGLASSES.**

**OPINION, PUBLIC.** *See* **PUBLIC OPINION.**

**Opitz, Michael F.**
Literacy instruction for culturally and linguistically
diverse students. Newark, Del. : International Reading
Association, c1998.
*TC LC3731 .L566 1998*

Rhymes & reasons : literature and language play for
phonological awareness / Michael F. Opitz.
Portsmouth, NH : Heinemann, c2000. v, 170 p. ; 23 cm.
Includes bibliographical references (p. 157-160) and index.
ISBN 0-325-00246-0 (pbk.) DDC 372.46/5044
*1. Language arts (Primary) 2. Phonetics - Study and teaching
(Primary) 3. Children's literature - Study and teaching
(Primary) 4. Education, Primary - Activity programs. I. Title.
II. Title: Rhymes and reasons*

*TC LB1528 .O65 2000*

**OPIUM HABIT.**
Keys, David Patrick, 1955- Confronting the drug
control establishment. Albany, N.Y. : State University
of New York Press, c2000.
*TC HM1031.L56 K49 2000*

**Oppenheimer, Louis.**
How children understand war and peace. 1st ed. San
Francisco : Jossey-Bass, c1999.
*TC JZ5534 .H69 1999*

**OPPORTUNISTIC INFECTIONS -
COMPLICATIONS.**
Nutritional aspects of HIV infection. London ; New
York : Arnold : Co-published in the United States by
Oxford University Press, 1999.
*TC RC607.A26 N895 1998*

**Opportunities in psychology careers.**
Super, Donald E. (Donald Edwin), 1910- New York,
Educational Books Division of Universal Pub. and
Distributing Corp. [1968]
*TC BF76 .S8 1968*

**Opportunity house.**
Angrosino, Michael V. Walnut Creek, CA : AltaMira
Press, c1998.
*TC HV3006.A4 A48 1998*

**Opposing viewpoints series**
Male/female roles. San Diego, Calif. : Greenhaven
Press, c2000.
*TC HQ1075 .M353 2000*

**Opposing viewpoints series (Unnumbered)**
Affirmative action. San Diego, Calif. : Greenhaven
Press, 2000.
*TC JC599.U5 A34685 2000*

Gangs. San Diego, CA : Greenhaven Press, c1996.
*TC HV6437 .G36 1996*

Male/female roles. San Diego, Calif. : Greenhaven
Press, c2000.
*TC HQ1075 .M353 2000*

Poverty. San Diego, CA : Greenhaven Press, c1994.
*TC HC110.P6 P63 1994*

Welfare. San Diego, CA : Greenhaven Press, c1997.
*TC HV95 .W453 1997*

**Opposites.**
Demi. [Opposites] Demi's opposites. New York :
Grosset & Dunlap, c1987.
*TC PE1591 .D43 1987*

**OPPOSITIONAL DEFIANT DISORDER IN
ADOLESCENCE.**
Bustamante, Eduardo M. Treating the disruptive
adolescent. Northvale, NJ : Jason Aronson, c2000.
*TC RJ506.O66 B87 2000*

**OPPOSITIONAL DEFIANT DISORDER IN
CHILDREN.**
Understanding the defiant child [videorecording].
New York : Guilford Publications, c1997.
*TC HQ755.7 .U63 1997*

**OPTICAL ILLUSIONS.**
Krauss, Rosalind E. The optical unconscious. 1st MIT
Press pbk. ed. Cambridge, Mass. : MIT Press, 1994.
*TC N7430.5 .K73 1994*

Willats, John. Art and representation. Princeton, N.J. :
Princeton University Press, c1997.
*TC N7430.5 .W55 1997*

**OPTICAL STORAGE DEVICES.** *See* **CD-ROMS.**

**The optical unconscious.**
Krauss, Rosalind E. 1st MIT Press pbk. ed.
Cambridge, Mass. : MIT Press, 1994.
*TC N7430.5 .K73 1994*

**OPTICIANRY.** *See* **EYEGLASSES.**

**OPTICS.** *See* **COLOR.**

**OPTICS, PSYCHOLOGICAL.** *See* **VISUAL
PERCEPTION.**

**OPTIMALITY THEORY (LINGUISTICS).**
Tesar, Bruce. Learnability in optimality theory.
Cambridge, Mass. : MIT Press, c2000.
*TC P158.42 .T47 2000*

**OPTIMISM.**
Optimism & pessimism. 1st ed. Washington, DC :
American Psychological Association, c2001.
*TC BF698.35.O57 O68 2001*

**Optimism & pessimism** : implications for theory,
research, and practice / edited by Edward C. Chang.
1st ed. Washington, DC : American Psychological
Association, c2001. xxi, 395 p. : ill. ; 27 cm. Includes

bibliographical references and indexes. ISBN 1-55798-691-6
DDC 149/.5
*1. Optimism. 2. Pessimism. I. Chang, Edward C. (Edward
Chin-Ho) II. Title: Optimism and pessimism*
*TC BF698.35.O57 O68 2001*

**Optimism and pessimism.**
Optimism & pessimism. 1st ed. Washington, DC :
American Psychological Association, c2001.
*TC BF698.35.O57 O68 2001*

**OPTIMIZATION (LINGUISTICS).** *See*
**OPTIMALITY THEORY (LINGUISTICS).**

**Options for teaching**
([14]) Teaching Shakespeare through performance.
New York : Modern Language Association of
America, 1999.
*TC PR2987 .T366 1999*

(15) Teaching the literatures of early America. New
York : Modern Language Association of America,
1999.
*TC PS186 .T43 1999*

**Opto-electronic storage.**
Weber, Hartmut. Washington, DC : Commission on
Preservation and Access, 1993.
*TC Z678.93.O7 W4315 1993*

**OPTOELECTRONIC DEVICES.** *See*
**TELEVISION.**

**Oral and nonverbal expression.**
Muse, Ivan. Princeton, NJ : Eye On Education, c1996.
*TC P95 .M86 1996*

**ORAL COMMUNICATION.** *See also*
**CONVERSATION ANALYSIS; DIALOGUE
ANALYSIS; SPEECH.**
Jauregi Ondarra, Kristi. Collaborative negotiation of
meaning. Amsterdam ; Atlanta, GA : Rodopi, 1997.
*TC P118.2 .J38 1997*

Muse, Ivan. Oral and nonverbal expression. Princeton,
NJ : Eye On Education, c1996.
*TC P95 .M86 1996*

Oller, D. Kimbrough. The emergence of the speech
capacity. Mahwah, N.J. : Lawrence Erlbaum
Associates, 2000.
*TC P118 .O43 2000*

O'Shaughnessy, Douglas, 1950- Speech
communications. 2nd ed. New York : IEEE Press,
c2000.
*TC P95 .O74 2000*

Talk, work, and institutional order. Berlin ; New
York : Mouton de Gruyter, 1999.
*TC P95 .T286 1999*

**ORAL COMMUNICATION - SOCIAL ASPECTS.**
Gordon, Tatiana. Russian language directives. 1998.
*TC 06 no. 10940*

**ORAL COMMUNICATION - STUDY AND
TEACHING.**
Guillot, Marie-Noëlle, 1955- Fluency and its teaching.
Clevedon, England ; Philadelphia, Pa. : Multilingual
Matters, c1999.
*TC P53.6 .G85 1999*

**ORAL COMMUNICATION - STUDY AND
TEACHING (ELEMENTARY) - GREAT
BRITAIN.**
An Introduction to oracy. London : Cassell, 1998.
*TC P95.4.G7 I58 1998*

**ORAL-FORMULAIC ANALYSIS.**
Ong, Walter J. Orality and literacy. London ; New
York : Routledge, 1988.
*TC P35 .O5 1988*

**ORAL HABITS.** *See* **FOOD HABITS; SMOKING.**

**ORAL INTERPRETATION.** *See*
**STORYTELLING.**

**ORAL INTERPRETATION OF FICTION.** *See*
**STORYTELLING.**

**ORAL LITERATURE.** *See* **FOLK LITERATURE.**

**ORAL READING - ABILITY TESTING.**
Running records. York, Me. : Stenhouse Publishers ,
2000.
*TC LB1525 R75 2000*

**ORAL TRADITION.** *See also* **FOLKLORE.**
Ong, Walter J. Orality and literacy. London ; New
York : Routledge, 1988.
*TC P35 .O5 1988*

Traditional storytelling today. Chicago : Fitzroy
Dearborn Publishers, 1999.

*TC GR72 .T73 1999*

**ORAL TRANSMISSION.** *See* **ORAL COMMUNICATION.**

**Orality and literacy.**
Ong, Walter J. London ; New York : Routledge, 1988.
*TC P35 .O5 1988*

**Orange, Carolyn.** 25 biggest mistakes teachers make and how to avoid them / Carolyn Orange. Thousand Oaks Calif. : Corwin Press, c2000. xiii, 193 p. : ill. ; 26 cm. Includes bibliographical references and index. ISBN 0-7619-7516-0 (alk. paper) ISBN 0-7619-7517-9 (pbk. : alk. paper) DDC 371.102/3
*1. Teacher-student relationships - United States - Case studies. 2. Effective teaching - United States - Case studies. 3. Interaction analysis in education - Case studies. I. Title. II. Title: Twenty-five biggest mistakes teachers make and how to avoid them*
*TC LB1033 .O73 2000*

**Orange, Graham.**
International perspectives on tele-education and virtual learning environments. Aldershot : Ashgate, 2000.
*TC LB1044.87 .I55 2000*

**ORANGEBURG (S.C.) - SOCIAL CONDITIONS.**
Mack, Kibibi Voloria C. Parlor ladies and ebony drudges. 1st ed. Knoxville : University of Tennessee Press, c1999.
*TC F279.O6 M33 1999*

**ORATORIOS - VOCAL SCORES WITH PIANO.**
Mendelssohn-Bartholdy, Felix, 1809-1847. [Paulus. Vocal score. English] Saint Paul; New York, G. Schirmer [19--]
*TC M2003.M53 S35*

**ORATORY.** *See* **EXPRESSION.**

**ORBS.** *See* **GLOBES.**

**ORCHARD HOUSE MUSEUM (CONCORD, MASS.).**
West, Patricia, 1958- Domesticating history. Washington [D.C.] : Smithsonian Institution Press, c1999.
*TC E159 .W445 1999*

**ORDER.** *See* **ORDERLINESS.**

**ORDERLINESS - FICTION.**
Cummings, Pat. Clean your room, Harvey Moon!. New York : Macmillan/McGraw-Hill School Pub. Co., c1991.
*TC PZ8.3.C898 Cl 1991*

O'Malley, Kevin, 1961- Bud. New York : Walker, 2000.
*TC PZ7.O526 Bu 2000*

Prigger, Mary Skillings. Aunt Minnie McGranahan. New York : Clarion Books, c1999.
*TC PZ7.P93534 Au 1999*

**Ordinary people, extraordinary lives.**
Bernhardt, Debra E. New York : New York University Press, c2000.
*TC HD8085.N53 B47 2000*

**Ordinary resurrections.**
Kozol, Jonathan. 1st ed. New York : Crown Publishers, c2000.
*TC HQ792.U5 K69 2000*

**Oregon Coordinating Council of Social Hygiene and Family Life.**
The Family life coordinator. Eugene, Ore. : E. C. Brown Trust Foundation.

**Oregon Public Broadcasting.**
Teen killers [videorecording]. Princeton, NJ : Films for the Humanities and Sciences, c1998-1999.
*TC HV9067.H6 T4 1999*

**Oregon. State Board of Higher Education.**
The High school. Eugene, Ore.

**Oregon State College. Graduate School.**
Improving college and university teaching. [Corvallis : Graduate School, Oregon State College,

**Oregon State University. Graduate School.**
Improving college and university teaching. [Corvallis : Graduate School, Oregon State College,

**O'Reilly, Mark F.**
Leslie, Julian C. Behavior analysis. Amsterdam, Netherlands : Harwood Academic Publishers, c1999.
*TC BF199 .L47 1999*

**O'Reilly, Meg.**
Morgan, Chris. Assessing open and distance learners. London : Kogan Page ; Sterling, VA : Stylus Pub., 1999.

*TC LC5800 .M67 1999*

**Orenstein, Myrna.** Smart but stuck : what every therapist needs to know about learning disabilities and imprisoned intelligence / Myrna Orenstein. New York : Haworth Press, c2000. xvii, 241 p. ; 23 cm. Includes bibliographical references (p. 225-233) and index. ISBN 0-7890-0853-X (alk. paper) ISBN 0-7890-0888-2 (pbk. : alk. paper) DDC 616.85/889
*1. Learning disabled - Psychology. 2. Learning disabled - Mental health. 3. Learning disabled - Intelligence levels. 4. Learning disabilities. I. Title.*
*TC RC394.L37 O74 2000*

**ORGANIC ARCHITECTURE - CUBA - HAVANA.**
Loomis, John A., 1951- Revolution of forms. New York : Princeton Architectural Press, c1999.
*TC NA6602.A76 L66 1999*

**ORGANIC COMPOUNDS.** *See* **PROTEINS.**

**Organic disorders** [videorecording] / a presentation of Films for the Humanities & Sciences ; University of Sheffield ; produced and directed by Steve Collier ; written by Dr. Steve Peters : Sheffield University Television. Princeton, N.J. : Films for the Humanities & Sciences, 1998. 1 videocassette (36 min.) : sd., col. ; 1/2 in. (Differential diagnosis in psychiatry) Series subtitle: Visual aid based on ICD 10. VHS. Catalogued from credits and container. Commentary: John Graham Davies. Sound: Ken Hardy; cameras: Jackie Jones, Mark Parkin, Gary Wraith; graphics: Sean Purcell. Originally produced 1995-1997 at the University of Sheffield. "Clinical features of myotonic dystrophy and Huntington's disease" included in list of complete series on container no longer part of series. For students of psychiatry, clinical psychology and social work, and counselling. SUMMARY: "This program demonstrates clinical organic disorders, their characteristics, and differential diagnoses. Divided into the two categories of dementia and delirium, the disorders discussed include... dementia disorders... Alzheimer's, Pick's disease, Huntington's disease, Parkinson's disease, Creutzfeldt-Jakob disease, and HIV dementia. Delirium disorders include organic amnestic syndrome, organic personality disorder, frontal lobe syndrome, primary cerebral disease, systemic disease, endocrine disorders, exogenous toxic disorders, and temporal lobe epilepsy."--Container.
*1. Dementia - Diagnosis. 2. Dementia - Patients. 3. Presenile dementia - Diagnosis. 4. Presenile dementia - Patients. 5. AIDS dementia complex - Diagnosis. 6. AIDS dementia complex - Patients. 7. Delirium - Diagnosis. 8. Delirium - Patients. 9. Psychological manifestation of general diseases. 10. Temporal lobe epilepsy - Diagnosis. 11. Temporal lobe epilepsy - Patients. 12. Hyperthyroidism - Diagnosis. 13. Hyperthyroidism - Patients. 14. Diagnosis, Differential. I. Peters, Steve, Dr. II. Collier, Steve. III. Davies, John Graham. IV. University of Sheffield. V. Sheffield University Television. VI. Films for the Humanities (Firm) VII. Title: Visual aid based on ICD 10 VIII. Series.*
*TC RC521 .O7 1998*

**Organisation for Economic Co-operation and Development.**
A caring world. Paris : The Organisation, c1999.
*TC HN17.5 .C323 1999*

Education at a glance [computer file]. Ottawa, Ont. : Ivation Datasystems Inc. ; Paris, France : OECD, 2000.
*TC LB2846 .E2473*

Inclusive education at work. Paris : Organisation for Economic Co-operation and Development, 1999.
*TC LC4015 .I525 1999*

International Adult Literacy Survey. Literacy in the information age. Paris : Organisation for Economic Co-operation and Development; Ottawa : Statistics Canada, 2000.
*TC LC149 .L59 2000*

Measuring student knowledge and skills. Paris : Organisation for Economic Co-operation and Development, c1999.
*TC LB3051 .M43 1999*

Organisation for Economic Co-operation and Development .(Paris) Measuring student knowledge and skills. Paris : Organisation for Economic Co-operation and Development, 2000.
*TC LB3051 .M44 2000*

**ORGANISATION FOR ECONOMIC CO-OPERATION AND DEVELOPMENT COUNTRIES.** *See* **OECD COUNTRIES.**

**Organisation for Economic Co-operation and Development. Directorate for Education, Employment, Labour, and Social Affairs. Statistics and Indicators Division.**
Measuring student knowledge and skills. Paris : Organisation for Economic Co-operation and Development, c1999.

*TC LB3051 .M43 1999*

**Organisation for Economic Co-operation and Development (Paris)** The appraisal of investments in educational facilities / Organisation for Economic Co-operation and Development. Paris : Organisation for Economic Co-operation and Development, 2000. 234 p. ; 23 cm. ISBN 92-64-17036-7 DDC 370
*1. Education - Economic aspects. 2. Education - Finance. 3. Capital investments. I. Title.*
*TC LB2342.3 .A7 2000*

From initial education to working life : Making transitions work / Organisation for Economic Co-operation and Development. Paris : Organisation for Economic Co-operation and Development, 2000. 203 p. : ill. ; 27 cm. (Education and skills) ISBN 92-64-17631-4 DDC 370
*1. School-to-work transition. 2. Career education. I. Title. II. Series.*
*TC LC1037 .O74 2000*

Measuring student knowledge and skills : The PISA 2000 assessment of reading, mathematical and scientific literacy / Organisation for Economic Co-operation and Development. Paris : Organisation for Economic Co-operation and Development, 2000. 104 p. ; 27 cm. (Education and Skills) ISBN 92-64-17646-2 DDC 370
*1. Program for International Student Assessment. 2. Educational tests and measurements. 3. Competency based education - OECD countries. 4. Educational evaluation. 5. Academic achievement - Evaluation. I. Organisation for Economic Co-operation and Development. II. Title. III. Series.*
*TC LB3051 .M44 2000*

**Organising feminisms.**
Morley, Louise, 1954- New York : St. Martin's Press, 1999.
*TC LC197 .M67 1999*

**ORGANISTS - FICTION.**
Ketcham, Sallie. Bach's big adventure. New York : Orchard Books, 1999.
*TC PZ7.K488 Bac 1999*

**ORGANIZATION.** *See also* **COMMUNICATION IN ORGANIZATIONS; INTERORGANIZATIONAL RELATIONS; MANAGEMENT; ORGANIZATIONAL BEHAVIOR; ORGANIZATIONAL CHANGE; ORGANIZATIONAL EFFECTIVENESS.**
Wheatley, Margaret J. Leadership and the new science. 2nd ed. San Francisco : Berrett-Koehler Publishers, c1999.
*TC HD57.7 .W47 1999*

**ORGANIZATION DEVELOPMENT.** *See* **ORGANIZATIONAL CHANGE.**

**The organization of attachment relationships :** maturation, culture, and context / edited by Patricia McKinsey Crittenden, Angelika Hartl Claussen. New York : Cambridge University Press, 2000. xii, 432 p. : ill. ; 24 cm. Includes bibliographical references. ISBN 0-521-58002-1 (hardbound) DDC 155
*1. Attachment behavior. 2. Attachment behavior in children. I. Crittenden, Patricia McKinsey. II. Claussen, Angelika Hartl.*
*TC BF575.A86.O74 2000*

**ORGANIZATION - RESEARCH.**
Doing research that is useful for theory and practice. Lanham, Md. ; Oxford : Lexington Books, c1999.
*TC HD58.7 .D65 1999*

**ORGANIZATION, SOCIAL.** *See* **SOCIAL STRUCTURE.**

**ORGANIZATIONAL BEHAVIOR.**
Collins, David, 1966- Organizational change. New York : Routledge, 1998.
*TC HD58.8 .C642 1998*

Social dreaming @ work. London : Karnac Books, 1998.
*TC BF1078 .S55 1998*

**ORGANIZATIONAL BEHAVIOR - EUROPE.**
Introduction to work and organizational psychology. Malden, Mass. : Blackwell, 1999.
*TC HF5548.8 .I576 1999*

**ORGANIZATIONAL BEHAVIOR - PSYCHOLOGICAL ASPECTS.**
Industrial and organizational psychology. Oxford, UK ; Malden, Mass. : Blackwell Business, 2000.
*TC HF5548.8 .I5233 2000*

**ORGANIZATIONAL BEHAVIOR - RESEARCH.**
Doing research that is useful for theory and practice. Lanham, Md. ; Oxford : Lexington Books, c1999.
*TC HD58.7 .D65 1999*

**ORGANIZATIONAL BEHAVIOR - UNITED STATES.**
Addressing cultural issues in organizations. Thousand Oaks, Calif. : Sage Publications, 2000.
*TC E184.A1 A337 2000*

**ORGANIZATIONAL CAREER DEVELOPMENT.** *See* **CAREER DEVELOPMENT.**

**Organizational change.**
Collins, David, 1966- New York : Routledge, 1998.
*TC HD58.8 .C642 1998*

**ORGANIZATIONAL CHANGE.**
Allen, Kathleen E. Systemic leadership. Lanham, Md. : University Press of America, c2000.
*TC HD57.7 .A42 2000*

The dance of change. 1st ed. New York : Currency/ Doubleday, 1999.
*TC HD58.82 .D36 1999*

Gateways to democracy. San Francisco : Jossey-Bass, 1999.
*TC LB2328.N53 1999*

Gilley, Jerry W. Organizational learning, performance, and change. Cambridge, Mass. : Perseus, c2000.
*TC HF5549.5.M3 G555 2000*

Leading beyond the walls. 1st ed. San Francisco : Jossey-Bass, c1999.
*TC HD57.7 .L4374 1999*

Maddock, Su. Challenging women. London ; Thousand Oaks, Calif. : Sage, 1999.
*TC HQ1236 .M342 1999*

Michel, Patrick. Using action research for school restructuring and organizational change. 2000.
*TC 06 no. 11295*

Michel, Patrick. Using action research for school restructuring and organizational change. 2000.
*TC 06 no. 11295*

Organizational change & gender equity. Thousand Oaks : Sage Publications, c2000.
*TC HD58.8 .O7289 2000*

Skiba, Michaeline. A naturalistic inquiry of the relationship between organizational change and informal learning in the workplace. 1999.
*TC 06 no. 11180*

Skyhooks for leadership. New York : AMACOM, American Management Association, c1999.
*TC HD58.8 .S577 1999*

Tiffany, Constance Rimmer. Planned change theories for nursing. Thousand Oaks : Sage Publications, c1998.
*TC RT89 .T54 1998*

**Organizational change & gender equity :** international perspectives on fathers and mothers at the workplace / editors, Linda L. Haas, Philip Hwang, Graeme Russell. Thousand Oaks : Sage Publications, c2000. xii, 291 p. ; 23 cm. Includes bibliographical references and indexes. ISBN 0-7619-1044-1 ISBN 0-7619-1045-X DDC 331.25
*1. Organizational change. 2. Work and family. 3. Parents - Employment. 4. Sexual division of labor. I. Haas, Linda. II. Hwang, Philip O. III. Russell, Graeme, 1947- IV. Title: Organizational change and gender equity*
*TC HD58.8 .O7289 2000*

**Organizational change and gender equity.**
Organizational change & gender equity. Thousand Oaks : Sage Publications, c2000.
*TC HD58.8 .O7289 2000*

**ORGANIZATIONAL CHANGE - DATA PROCESSING.**
Groth, Lars. Future organizational design. Chichester ; New York : Wiley, c1999.
*TC HD30.2 .G76 1999*

**ORGANIZATIONAL CHANGE - MANAGEMENT.**
Schwartz, Peter. The art of the long view. 1st Currency pbk. ed. New York : Currency Doubleday ; 1996.
*TC HD30.28 .S316 1996*

**ORGANIZATIONAL CHANGE - SOCIAL ASPECTS.**
Collins, David, 1966- Organizational change. New York : Routledge, 1998.
*TC HD58.8 .C642 1998*

**ORGANIZATIONAL CHANGE - UNITED STATES.**
Employee training and U.S. competitiveness. Boulder : Westview Press, 1991.

*TC HF5549.5.T7 E46 1991*

**ORGANIZATIONAL COMMUNICATION.** *See* **COMMUNICATION IN ORGANIZATIONS.**

**Organizational communication and change** / edited by Philip J. Salem. Cresskill, N.J. : Hampton Press, 1999. xiv, 395 p. : ill. ; 23 cm. (Hampton Press communication series) Includes bibliographical references (p. 335-378) and index. ISBN 1-57273-116-8 ISBN 1-57273-117-6 DDC 658.4/5
*1. Communication in organizations. I. Salem, Philip J. II. Series.*
*TC HD30.3 .O722 1999*

**ORGANIZATIONAL DEVELOPMENT.** *See* **ORGANIZATIONAL CHANGE.**

**ORGANIZATIONAL EFFECTIVENESS.**
Birnbaum, Robert. Management fads in higher education. San Francisco : Jossey-Bass, 2000.
*TC LB2341 .B49 2000*

Gilley, Jerry W. Organizational learning, performance, and change. Cambridge, Mass. : Perseus, c2000.
*TC HF5549.5.M3 G555 2000*

Lipman-Blumen, Jean. Hot groups. New York : Oxford University Press, 1999.
*TC HD58.9 .L56 1999*

Sauquet, Alfonso. Conflict and team learning:. 2000.
*TC 06 no. 11308*

Skyhooks for leadership. New York : AMACOM, American Management Association, c1999.
*TC HD58.8 .S577 1999*

Tobe, Dorothy Echols. The development of cognitive leadership frames among African American female college presidents. 1999.
*TC 06 no. 11187*

**ORGANIZATIONAL EFFECTIVENESS - NEW JERSEY - CASE STUDIES.**
Fleck, Mary B. Elementary principals' use of student assessment information. 1999.
*TC 06 no. 11113*

**ORGANIZATIONAL EFFECTIVENESS - PSYCHOLOGICAL ASPECTS.**
Bazigos, Michael Nicholas. The relationship of upward feedback disparities to leader performance. 1999.
*TC 085 B33*

**ORGANIZATIONAL INNOVATION.** *See* **ORGANIZATIONAL CHANGE.**

**ORGANIZATIONAL INNOVATION.**
Shelton, Patrick J. Measuring and improving patient satisfaction. Gaithersburg, Md. : Aspen Publishers, 2000.
*TC RA399.A1 S47 2000*

**Organizational learning.**
Schwandt, David R. Boca Raton, Fla. : St. Lucie Press, c2000.
*TC HD58.82 .S39 2000*

The dance of change. 1st ed. New York : Currency/ Doubleday, 1999.
*TC HD58.82 .D36 1999*

Garvin, David A. Learning in action. Boston, Mass. : Harvard Business School Press, 2000.
*TC HD58.82 .G37 2000*

Gilley, Jerry W. Organizational learning, performance, and change. Cambridge, Mass. : Perseus, c2000.
*TC HF5549.5.M3 G555 2000*

Raelin, Joseph A., 1948- Work based learning. Reading, MA : Addison-Wesley, 1999.
*TC HD30.4 .R33 1999*

Schwandt, David R. Organizational learning. Boca Raton, Fla. : St. Lucie Press, c2000.
*TC HD58.82 .S39 2000*

**ORGANIZATIONAL LEARNING - CASE STUDIES.**
Business-driven action learning. New York : St. Martin's Press, 2000.
*TC HD58.82 .B87 2000*

Garvin, David A. Learning in action. Boston, Mass. : Harvard Business School Press, 2000.
*TC HD58.82 .G37 2000*

**Organizational learning, performance, and change.**
Gilley, Jerry W. Cambridge, Mass. : Perseus, c2000.
*TC HF5549.5.M3 G555 2000*

**ORGANIZATIONAL LEARNING - SPAIN - CASE STUDIES.**
Sauquet, Alfonso. Conflict and team learning:. 2000.
*TC 06 no. 11308*

**Organizational oversight.**
Erlandson, David A. Princeton, NJ : Eye on Education, c1996.
*TC LB2805 .E75 1996*

**ORGANIZATIONAL SOCIOLOGY.** *See also* **BUREAUCRACY.**
Collins, David, 1966- Organizational change. New York : Routledge, 1998.
*TC HD58.8 .C642 1998*

**ORGANIZATIONAL STRESS.** *See* **JOB STRESS.**

**ORGANIZATIONS.** *See* **ASSOCIATIONS, INSTITUTIONS, ETC.**

**ORGANIZATIONS, BUSINESS.** *See* **BUSINESS ENTERPRISES.**

**ORGANIZATIONS, INTERNATIONAL.** *See* **INTERNATIONAL AGENCIES.**

**ORGANIZATIONS, NONPROFIT.** *See* **NONPROFIT ORGANIZATIONS.**

**Organizing wonder.**
Hall, Jody S. Portsmouth, NH : Heinemann, c1998.
*TC LB1585.3 .H35 1998*

**ORGASM.**
Hite, Shere. The Hite report on male sexuality. 1st Ballantine Book ed. New York : Ballantine Books, 1982.
*TC HQ28 .H57 1982*

**ORGASM, FEMALE.**
Hite, Shere. The Hite report. New York : Dell, 1987.
*TC HQ29 .H57 1987*

**ORIENT.** *See* **ASIA, SOUTHEASTERN; EAST ASIA; MIDDLE EAST.**

**Orientalism and the shaping of American culture, 1776-1882.**
Tchen, John Kuo Wei. New York before Chinatown. Baltimore : Johns Hopkins University Press, 1999.
*TC DS706 .T4 1999*

**ORIENTATION.** *See* **ORIENTATION (PHYSIOLOGY); ORIENTATION (PSYCHOLOGY).**

**ORIENTATION (LIBRARY USE).** *See* **LIBRARY ORIENTATION.**

**ORIENTATION OF TEACHERS.** *See* **TEACHER ORIENTATION.**

**ORIENTATION (PHYSIOLOGY).**
Berthoz, A. [Sens du Mouvement. English] The brain's sense of movement. Cambridge, Mass. : Harvard University Press, 2000.
*TC QP493 .B47 2000*

**ORIENTATION (PSYCHOLOGY) - CONGRESSES.**
International Symposium on Attention and Performance (11th : 1984 : Eugene, Or.) Attention and performance XI. Hillsdale, N.J. : L. Erlbaum Associates, 1985.
*TC BF321 .A82 1985*

**ORIENTATION, SEXUAL.** *See* **SEXUAL ORIENTATION.**

**ORIGIN OF SPECIES.** *See* **EVOLUTION (BIOLOGY).**

**Original finger calculation.**
Pai, Hang Young. Chisanbop. Teacher's annotated ed. New York : American Book Co., 1980.
*TC QA115 .P23 1980 Teacher's Ed.*

Pai, Hang Young. Chisanbop. New York : American Book Co., 1980.
*TC QA115 .P23 1980*

Pai, Hang Young. Chisanbop. New York : American Book Co., 1980.
*TC QA115 .P231 1980*

Pai, Hang Young. Chisanbop. Teacher's annotated ed. New York : American Book Co., 1980.
*TC QA115 .P231 1980 Teacher's Ed.*

**ORIGINALITY.** *See* **CREATION (LITERARY, ARTISTIC, ETC.).**

**ORIGINALITY IN ART.**
Krauss, Rosalind E. Bachelors. Cambridge, Mass. : MIT Press, c1999.
*TC NX180.F4 K73 1999*

**Origins and development of schizophrenia :** advances in experimental psychopathology / edited by Mark F. Lenzenweger and Robert H. Dworkin. Washington, DC : American Psychological Association, c1998. xxvii, 557 p. : ill. ; 24 cm. Includes bibliographical references and indexes. ISBN 1-55798-497-2 (cloth : alk. paper) DDC 616.89/82071
*1. Schizophrenia - Etiology. I. Lenzenweger, Mark F. II. Dworkin, Robert H.*
**TC RC514 .O75 1998**

**Origins of impressionism.**
Tinterow, Gary. New York : Metropolitan Museum of Art : Distributed by H.N. Abrams, c1994.
**TC ND547.5.I4 L6913 1994**

**Origins of mass communications research during the American Cold War.**
Glander, Timothy Richard, 1960- Mahwah, N.J. ; London : L. Erlbaum, 2000.
**TC P91.5.U5 G57 2000**

**The origins of photojournalism in America.**
Carlebach, Michael L. Washington : Smithsonian Institution Press, c1992.
**TC TR820 .C357 1992**

**Origins of teacher education at Calvin College, 1900-1930.**
DeBoer, Peter P. Lewiston : E. Mellen Press, c1991.
**TC LD785 .D43 1991**

**O'Riordan, Mary.** Strategic use of transfer and explicit linguistic knowledge : a study of twelve Spanish-speaking college students / by Mary O'Riordan. 1998. ix, 192 leaves ; 29 cm. Typescript; issued also on microfilm. Thesis (Ed.D.)--Teachers College, Columbia University, 1998. Includes bibliographical references (leaves 140-157).
*1. English language - Study and teaching (Higher) - Spanish speakers. 2. Second language acquisition - Methodology. 3. Language transfer (Language learning). 4. Interlanguage (Language learning). 5. English language - Errors of usage. I. Title.*
**TC 06 no. 10975**

**Orivel, François.**
Problems and prospects in European education. Westport, Conn. : Praeger, 2000.
**TC LC191.8. E85 P86 2000**

**Orlikoff, Robert F.**
Baken, R. J. (Ronald J.), 1943- Clinical measurement of speech and voice. 2nd ed. San Diego : Singular Thomson Learning, c2000.
**TC RC423 .B28 2000**

**Orlovsky, G. N. (Grigorii Nikolaevich)** Neuronal control of locomotion : from mollusc to man / G.N. Orlovsky, T.G. Deliagina, and S. Grillner. Oxford ; New York : Oxford University Press, 1999. xiv, 322 p. : ill. ; 24 cm. Includes bibliographical references (p. [263]-316) and index. ISBN 0-19-852405-6 DDC 573.7/9281
*1. Locomotion - Regulation. 2. Efferent pathways. 3. Physiology, Comparative. I. Deliagina, T. G. II. Grillner, Sten, 1941- III. Title.*
**TC QP303 .O75 1999**

**Orme,Michael, 1940-.**
Fundacion Dr. Antonio Esteve. Symposium (7th : 1996 : Sitges, Spain) The clinical pharmacology of sport and exercise. Amsterdam ; New York : Elsevier Science B.V., Excerpta Medica, 1997.
**TC RC1230 .F86 1996**

**Ormerod, Jan.** 101 things to do with a baby / Jan Ormerod. 1st U.S. ed. New York : Lothrop, Lee & Shepard, c1984. [32] p. : col. ill. ; 31 cm. SUMMARY: A six-year-old girl tells 101 things she can do with her baby brother. ISBN 0-688-03801-8 ISBN 0-688-03802-6 (lib. bdg.) DDC [E]
*1. Babies - Fiction. 2. Brothers and sisters - Fiction. I. Title. II. Title: One hundred one things to do with a baby. III. Title: One hundred and one things to do with a baby.*
**TC PZ7.O634 Aad 1984**

**Ormond, Richard.**
Sargent, John Singer, 1856-1925. John Singer Sargent. Princeton : Princeton University Press, 1998.
**TC ND237.S3 A4 1998a**

**Ormrod, David.**
Art markets in Europe, 1400-1800. Aldershot ; Brookfield : Ashgate, c1998.
**TC N8600 .A737 1998**

**ORNITHOLOGY. See BIRDS.**

**OROZCO, JOSÉ CLEMENTE, 1883-1949 - CRITICISM AND INTERPRETATION.**
Folgarait, Leonard. Mural painting and social revolution in Mexico, 1920-1940. Cambridge ; New York, NY : Cambridge University Press, 1998.

**TC ND2644 .F63 1998**

**ORPHAN ASYLUMS. See ORPHANAGES.**

**ORPHANAGES - CHINA.**
Evans, Karin. The lost daughters of China. New York : J.P. Tarcher/Putnam, c2000.
**TC HV1317 .E93 2000**

**ORPHANAGES - UNITED STATES - HISTORY.**
Crenson, Matthew A., 1943- Building the invisible orphanage. Cambridge, Mass. : Harvard University Press, 1998.
**TC HV91 .C74 1998**

**ORPHANS AND ORPHAN-ASYLUMS. See ORPHANAGES; ORPHANS.**

**ORPHANS - ARIZONA - CLIFTON - HISTORY - 20TH CENTURY.**
Gordon, Linda. The great Arizona orphan abduction. Cambridge, Mass. : Harvard University Press, 1999.
**TC F819.C55 G67 1999**

**ORPHANS - FICTION.**
Prigger, Mary Skillings. Aunt Minnie McGranahan. New York : Clarion Books, c1999.
**TC PZ7.P93534 Au 1999**

Rodowsky, Colby F. The Turnabout Shop. 1st ed. New York : Farrar, Straus and Giroux, c1998.
**TC PZ7.R6185 Tu 1998**

**Orr, Marion, 1962-** Black social capital : the politics of school reform in Baltimore, 1986-1998 / Marion Orr. Lawrence : University Press of Kansas, c1999. xiv, 241 p. : ill., maps ; 23 cm. (Studies in government and public policy) Includes bibliographical references (p. 197-229) and index. ISBN 0-7006-0981-4 (cloth : alk. paper) ISBN 0-7006-0982-2 (pbk. : alk. paper) DDC 371.829/60730752/6
*1. Afro-Americans - Education - Maryland - Baltimore - History - 20th century. 2. Educational change - Political aspects - Maryland - Baltimore - Case studies. I. Title. II. Series.*
**TC LC2803.B35 O77 1999**

**Orsini, Alfonso J.** The color of excellence : faculty diversity at American independent schools / by Alfonso J. Orsini. 1999. xviii, 260 leaves : ill. ; 29 cm. Typescript; issued also on microfilm. Thesis (Ed.D.)--Teachers College, Columbia University, 1999. Includes bibliographical references (leaves 232-245).
*1. Private schools - United States - Faculty. 2. Minority teachers - United State - Recruiting. 3. Minority teachers - United States - Selection and appointment. 4. Multicultural education - United States. 5. Teacher turnover - United States. I. National Association of Independent Schools. II. Title. III. Title: Faculty diversity at American independent schools*
**TC 06 no. 11209**

**Országos Pedagógiai Könyvtár és Múzeum.**
Felkai, László. Zsidó iskolázás Magyarországon, 1780-1990. Budapest : Országos Pedagógiai Könyvtár és Múzeum, [1998]
**TC LC746.H8 F455 1998**

**Ort, Suzanne Wichterle.** Standards in practice : a study of a New York City high school's struggle for excellence and equity and its relationship to policy / by Suzanne Wichterle Ort. 1999. 394 leaves ; 29 cm. Typescript; issued also on microfilm. Thesis (Ed.D.)--Teachers College, Columbia University, 1999. Includes bibliographical references (leaves 373-388).
*1. Education - Standards - New York (State) - New York. 2. Educational tests and measurements - New York (State) - Validity. 3. Grading and marking (Students) - New York (State) - Evaluation. 4. Teacher effectiveness - New York (State) I. Title. II. Title: Study of a New York City high school's struggle for excellence and equity and its relationship to policy*
**TC 06 no. 11210**

**ORTHOEPY. See PHONETICS.**

**Ortiz, Samuel O., 1958-.**
Flanagan, Dawn P. The Wechsler intelligence scales and Gf-Gc theory. Boston ; London : Allyn and Bacon, c2000.
**TC BF432.5.W4 F53 2000**

**ORYCTOLAGUS CUNICULUS. See RABBITS.**

**The Oryx guide to natural history.**
Barnes-Svarney, Patricia L. Phoenix, Ariz. : Oryx Press, 1999.
**TC QH45.2 .B37 1999**

**Osakwe, Mabel.** Poetrymate 1 : a guide to poetry teaching and learning for junior secondary schools / by Mabel Osakwe. Enugu, Nigeria : Fourth Dimension Publishing Co., 1996. vii, 108 p. : ill. ; 22 cm. Cover title: Poetrymate. Includes bibliographical references (p. 98-99). ISBN 978-156-417-2 DDC 821/.007/12
*1. Poetry - Study and teaching (Secondary) 2. English poetry - Study and teaching (Secondary) 3. Folk poetry, African - Study*

*and teaching (Secondary) I. Title. II. Title: Poetrymate III. Title: Poetrymate one IV. Title: Guide to poetry teaching and learning for junior secondary schools*
**TC PN1101 .O73 1996**

**Osborn, Cynthia J.**
Davis, Thomas E., Ph. D. The solution-focused school counselor. Philadelphia ; Hove [England] : Accelerated Development/Taylor & Francis Group, c2000.
**TC LB1027.5 .D335 2000**

**Osborn, Terry A., 1966-** Critical reflection and the foreign language classroom / Terry A. Osborn. Westport, Conn. ; London : Bergin & Garvey, 2000. xvi, 143 p. : ill. ; 25 cm. (Critical studies in education and culture series, 1064-8615) Includes bibliographical references (p. [127]-139) and index. ISBN 0-89789-681-5 (alk. paper) DDC 418/.0071/073
*1. Language and languages - Study and teaching - United States. I. Title. II. Series.*
**TC P57.U7 O78 2000**

**Osborne, Margery D.** Examining science teaching in elementary school from the perspective of a teacher and learner / by Margery D. Osborne. New York : Falmer Press, 1999. vi, 255 p. : ill. ; 23 cm. (Garland reference library of social science ; v. 1140. Critical education practice ; v. 18) Includes bibliographical references (p. [245]-250) and index. ISBN 0-8153-2569-X (alk. paper) DDC 372.3/5
*1. Science - Study and teaching. 2. Instructional systems - Design. I. Title. II. Series: Garland reference library of social science ; v. 1140. III. Series: Garland reference library of social science. Critical education practice ; vol. 18.*
**TC LB1585 .O77 1999**

**Osgood, Robert L.** For "children who vary from the normal type" : special education in Boston, 1838-1930 / Robert L. Osgood. Washington, D.C. : Gallaudet University Press, c2000. viii, 214 p. : ill. ; 25 cm. Includes bibliographical references (p. 179-205) and index. ISBN 1-56368-089-0 DDC 371.9/09744/61
*1. Special education - Massachusetts - Boston - History - 19th century. 2. Special education - Massachusetts - Boston - History - 20th century. 3. Education - Massachusetts - Boston - History - 19th century. 4. Education - Massachusetts - Boston - History - 20th century. I. Title.*
**TC LC3983.B7 O84 2000**

**Osguthorpe, Russell T.** Balancing the tensions of change : eight keys to collaborative educational renewal / Russell T. Osguthorpe, Robert S. Patterson. Thousand Oaks, Calif. : Corwin Press, c1998. xxii, 128 p. : ill. ; 24 cm. Includes bibliographical references (p. 118-122)and index. ISBN 0-8039-6699-7 (cloth : alk. paper) ISBN 0-8039-6700-4 (pbk. : alk. paper) DDC 378.1/03
*1. College-school cooperation. 2. Educational change. 3. Interorganizational relations. I. Patterson, Robert S. II. Title.*
**TC LB2331.53 .O74 1998**

**O'Shaughnessy, Brian.** Consciousness and the world / Brian O'Shaughnessy. Oxford : Clarendon Press ; New York : Oxford University Press, 2000. viii, 705 p. ; ill. ; 25 cm. Includes bibliographical references and index. ISBN 0-19-823893-2 (hardcover : alk. paper) DDC 126
*1. Consciousness. I. Title.*
**TC B808.9 .O74 2000**

**O'Shaughnessy, Douglas, 1950-** Speech communications : human and machine / Douglas O'Shaughnessy. 2nd ed. New York : IEEE Press, c2000. xxv, 547 p. : ill. ; 27 cm. Includes bibliographical references (p. 469-535) and index. ISBN 0-7803-3449-3 DDC 302.2/244
*1. Oral communication. 2. Speech processing systems. I. Title.*
**TC P95 .O74 2000**

**O'Shea, Dorothy J.**
Families and teachers of individuals with disabilities. Boston ; London : Allyn and Bacon, c2001.
**TC LC3969 .F34 2001**

**Osofsky, Joy D.**
Handbook of infant mental health. New York : Wiley, c2000.
**TC RJ502.5 .H362 2000**

**Osokoya, Israel O. (Israel Olu).** Writing and teaching history : a guide to advanced study / by Israel Opeolu Osokoya. Ibadan : Laurel Educational Publishers, 1996. 202 p. : ill. ; 23 cm. Includes bibliographical references (p. 195-198) and index. ISBN 978-31062-6-0 (limb.) ISBN 978-31062-5-2 (cased)
*1. Historiography. 2. History - Study and teaching. I. Title.*
**TC D13 .O86 1996**

**Osso, Rafael.** Handbook of emerging communications technologies : the next decade / editor, Rafael Osso. Boca Raton, Fla. : CRC Press, 2000. 400 p. : ill. ; 24 cm. (CRC Press advanced and emerging communications technologies series) Includes bibliographical references and

index. ISBN 0-8493-9594-1 (alk. paper) DDC 621.382
*1. Telecommunication - Technological innovations. I. Title. II. Series.*
**TC TK5105 .O62 2000**

**Ostenfeld, Erik Nis.** Ancient Greek psychology and the modern mind-body debate / Erik Ostenfeld. Aarhus, Denmark : Aarhus University Press, 1987. 109 p. ; 22 cm. Bibliography: p. 101-106. Includes indexes. ISBN 87-7288-010-4 (pbk.) DDC 128/.2/0938
*1. Mind and body - History. 2. Dualism - History. 3. Plato - Contributions in philosophy of mind. 4. Aristotle - Contributions in philosophy of mind. 5. Descartes, René, - 1596-1650 - Contributions in philosophy of mind. I. Title.*
**TC BF161 .O88 1987**

**Oster, Sharon M.** Strategic management for nonprofit organizations : theory and cases / Sharon M. Oster. New York : Oxford University Press, 1995. ix, 350 p. : ill. ; 24 cm. Includes bibliographical references (p. 333-344) and index. ISBN 0-19-508503-5 DDC 658.4/012
*1. Nonprofit organizations - Management. 2. Strategic planning. I. Title.*
**TC HD62.6 .O87 1995**

**Osterink, Carole.**
Daniel, Claire, 1936- The great big book of fun phonics activities. New York : Scholastic professional books, c1999.
**TC LB1525.3 .D36 1999**

**Österreichische Galerie Belvedere.**
America. Munich, Germany ; London ; New York : Prestel, c1999.
**TC ND210 .A724 1999**

**Ostroff, Frank.** The horizontal organization : what the organization of the future looks like and how it delivers value to customers / Frank Ostroff. New York : Oxford University Press, 1999. xiv, 257 p. : ill. ; 24 cm. Includes bibliographical references (p. 235-241) and index. ISBN 0-19-512138-4 DDC 658.4/02
*1. Teams in the workplace. 2. Management - Employee participation. I. Title.*
**TC HD66 .O68 1999**

**Ostrower, Francie.** Why the wealthy give : the culture of elite philanthropy / Francie Ostrower. Princeton, N.J. : Princeton University Press, c1995. xii, 190 p. ; 24 cm. Includes bibliographical references (p. [177]-183) and index. ISBN 0-691-04434-1 (cloth : alk. paper) DDC 361.7/4
*1. Philanthropists - New York (State) - New York. 2. Charities - New York (State) - New York. 3. Voluntarism - New York (State) - New York. 4. Elite (Social sciences) - New York (State) - New York. I. Title.*
**TC HV99.N59 O85 1995**

**O'Sullivan, Edmund, 1938-** Transformative learning : educational vision for the 21st century / Edmund O'Sullivan. London ; New York : Zed Books ; New York : Distributed in USA exclusively by St. Martin's Press, 1999. xv, 304 p. ; 24 cm. Includes bibliographical references. ISBN 1-85649-698-8 ISBN 1-85649-699-6 (pbk.) DDC 370.11/5
*1. Critical pedagogy. 2. Environmentalism. 3. Education - Economic aspects. 4. Postmodernism and education. I. Title.*
**TC LC196 .O7 1999**

**O'Sullivan, Eoin.**
Raftery, Mary. Suffer the little children. Dublin, Ireland : New Island, 1999.
**TC HV9148.A5 R33 1999**

**Osunde, Egerton Oyenmwense, 1950-** Understanding student teaching : case studies of experiences and suggestions for survival / Egerton O. Osunde. Lanham, Md. : University Press of America, 1999. xii, 141 p. : ill. ; 23 cm. Includes bibliographical references (p.134-138) and index. ISBN 0-7618-1498-1 (alk. paper) ISBN 0-7618-1499-X (pbk. : alk. paper) DDC 370/.71
*1. Student teaching - United States - Case studies. I. Title.*
**TC LB2157.U5 O78 1999**

**Otero, George G.**
Drum, Jan. Global winners. Yarmouth, Me. : Intercultural Press, c1994.
**TC LC1099.3 .D78 1994**

**The other Freud.**
DiCenso, James, 1957- London ; New York : Routledge, 1999.
**TC BF175.4.R44 D53 1999**

**OTHER MINDS (THEORY OF KNOWLEDGE).**
Joffe, Hélène. Risk and 'the other'. Cambridge, U.K. ; New York : Cambridge University Press, 1999.
**TC HM256 .J63 1999**

**Otobre, Frances M.**
The role of measurement and evaluation in education policy. Paris : Unesco Pub., 1999.
**TC LB3051 .R653 1999**

**O'Toole, James.** Leadership A to Z : a guide for the appropriately ambitious / James O'Toole. 1st ed. San Francisco, CA : Jossey-Bass Publishers, c1999. xii, 336 p. ; 21 cm. Includes bibliographical references. ISBN 0-7879-4658-3
*1. Leadership. 2. Decision making. 3. Executive ability. 4. Management. I. Title.*
**TC HD57.7 .O87 1999**

**Ottenberg, Simon.** New traditions from Nigeria : seven artists of the Nsukka group / Simon Ottenberg. Washington, DC : Smithsonian Institution Press, c1997. xvii, 302 p. : ill (some col.), col maps. ; 28 cm. Includes bibliographical references (p. 281-297) and index. ISBN 1-56098-800-2 (alk. paper) DDC 709/.669/409045
*1. Art, Nigerian - Nigeria - Nsukka. 2. Art, Modern - 20th century - Nigeria - Nsukka. 3. Art, Igbo - Influence. 4. Artists - Nigeria - Nsukka - Attitudes. I. Title.*
**TC N7399.N52 N786 1997**

**Ottenburg, Susan D.** Education today : parent involvement handbook / by Susan D. Ottenbourg ; edited by J. Lynn McBrien & Carroll T. Miller. 2nd. ed. Boston : Educational Publishing Group, Education Today, c1996. 106 p. : ill. ; 22 cm. Includes bibiographical references. ISBN 0-9644461-2-x
*1. Home and school - United States - Handbooks, manuals, etc. 2. Education - Parent participation - United States - Handbooks, manuals, etc. I. McBrien, J. Lynn. II. Miller, Carrol T. III. Title. IV. Title: Parent involvement, handbook*
**TC LC225.3 .O88 1996**

**Otterbourg, Susan D.** Using technology to strengthen employee and family involvement in education / by Susan D. Otterbourg. [New York] : Conference Board, c1998. 42 p. : col. ill., col. ports. ; 27 cm. (Research report / The Conference Board ; 1223-98-RR) Title from caption--p. [3]. Includes bibliographical references. ISBN 0-8237-0672-9 (pbk.)
*1. Educational technology - United States. 2. Industry and education - United States. 3. Community and school - United States. 4. Education - United States - Parent participation. 5. Educational planning - United States. I. Conference Board. II. Title. III. Series: Conference Board report ; no. 1223-98-RR.*
**TC LB1028.3 .O88 1998**

**Otto, Carolyn.** Pioneer church / Carolyn Otto ; illustrated by Megan Lloyd. 1st ed. New York : Henry Holt, 1999 1 v. (unpaged) : col. ill. ; 29 cm. SUMMARY: In the mid-1700s, four families build a log church on a hill in central Pennsylvania, and congregations worship in it and its replacement up through World War II. Based on the history of Old Zion church in Brickerville, Pennsylvania. ISBN 0-8050-2554-5 DDC [E]
*1. Church buildings - Fiction. 2. Pennsylvania - History - Fiction. I. Lloyd, Megan, ill. II. Title.*
**TC PZ7.O8794 Pi 1999**

**Our friends at the bank** [videorecording] / executive producer, Greg Lanning ; directed by Peter Chappell. New York, NY : First Run/Icarus Films, 1997. 1 videocassette (84 min., 27 sec.) : sd., col. ; 1/2 in. VHS. SUMMARY: Filmed over a period of 14 months, documents the negotiations between the World Bank and Uganda in an attempt to understand and describe the relationship and its implications for Uganda. Describes the activities of James Wolfensohn, president of the World Bank, and Yoweri Museweri [sic], leader of Uganda. Time on container: 90 minutes. Film produced by IBT, JBA Production, La Sept Arte Documentaries Department, Channel 4. Silver Award Winner, 1998 FIPA; Library Jury Prize Winner, 1998 Cinéma du Réel; 1998 Media Nord Sud.
*1. World Bank. 2. Economic development projects - Uganda. 3. Uganda - Economic conditions - 1979- 4. Uganda - Social conditions - 1979- 5. Wolfensohn, James D. 6. Museveni, Yoweri, - 1944- I. Lanning, Greg. II. Chappell, Peter, 1948- III. First Run/Icarus Films.*
**TC HG3881.5.W57 O87 1997**

**Our land, our time.**
Conlin, Joseph Robert. Annotated teacher's ed. San Diego : Coronado Publishers, c1987.
**TC E178.1 .C762 1987**

**Our nation's history.**
Napp, John L. Baltimore, Md. : Media Materials, c1989.
**TC E178.3 .N36 1998**

Napp, John L. Baltimore, Md. : Media Materials, c1989.
**TC E178.3 .N36 1998**

Napp, John L. Baltimore, Md. : Media Materials, c1989.
**TC E178.3 .N36 1998**

**Our only May Amelia.**
Holm, Jennifer L. 1st ed. New York : HarperCollinsPublishers, c1999.

**Our public schools.**
Schneider, Frank. Mobile, Ala. : Factor Press, 2000.
**TC LA217.2 .S34 2000**

**Our sexuality.**
Crooks, Robert, 1941- 7th ed. Pacific Grove, CA : Brooks/Cole Pub. Co., c1999.
**TC HQ21 .C698 1999**

**Out & about campus :** personal accounts by lesbian, gay, bisexual & transgendered college students / edited by Kim Howard and Annie Stevens. 1st ed. Los Angeles : Alyson Books, 2000. xiv, 304 p. ; 23 cm. Includes bibliographical references. ISBN 1-55583-480-9 (pbk.) DDC 378.1/9826/64
*1. Gay college students - United States - Biography. 2. Lesbian college students - United States - Biography. 3. Bisexual college students - United States - Biography. 4. Transsexualism - United States - Case studies. 5. Homosexuality and education - United States - Case studies. I. Howard, Kim, 1971- II. Stevens, Annie. III. Title: Out and about campus*
**TC LC2574.6 .O87 2000**

**Out and about campus.**
Out & about campus. 1st ed. Los Angeles : Alyson Books, 2000.
**TC LC2574.6 .O87 2000**

**Out and about :** teacher's planning guide. New York : Macmillan/McGraw-Hill, c1997. 224, T18 p. : ill. (some col.) ; 31 cm. (Spotlight on literacy ; Gr.1 L.2) (The road to independent reading) Includes index. ISBN 0-02-181151-2
*1. Reading (Primary) 2. Language arts (Primary) I. Series. II. Series: The road to independent reading*
**TC LB1576 .S66 1997 Gr.1 L.2**

**OUT-OF-PRINT BOOKS.** *See* **REPRINTS (PUBLICATIONS).**

**OUT-OF-PRINT BOOKS - BIBLIOGRAPHY.**
Guide to reprints. Munich : K.G. Saur, 2000-
**TC Z1036 .G8**

**Out of work.**
Vedder, Richard K. New York : Holmes & Meier, 1993.
**TC HD7096.U5 V43 1993**

**OUTCOME ASSESSEMENT (MEDICAL CARE).**
Measuring outcomes in speech-language pathology. New York : Thieme, 1998.
**TC RC423 .M39 1997**

**OUTCOME ASSESSMENT.**
The use of psychological testing for treatment planning and outcome assessment. 2nd ed. Mahwah, N.J. : Lawrence Erlbaum Associates, c1999.
**TC RC473.P79 U83 1999**

**Outcome assessment in residential treatment** / Steven I. Pfeiffer, editor. New York : Haworth Press, c1996. xiv, 99 p. : ill. ; 23 cm. "Has also been published as Residential treatment for children & youth, volume 13, number 4 1996"-- T.p. verso. Includes bibliographical references and index. ISBN 1-56024-839-4 (acid-free paper) DDC 618.92/8914
*1. Child psychotherapy - Residential treatment. 2. Outcome assessment (Medical care) I. Pfeiffer, Steven I.*
**TC RJ504.5 .O98 1996**

**OUTCOME ASSESSMENT (MEDICAL CARE).**
Outcome assessment in residential treatment. New York : Haworth Press, c1996.
**TC RJ504.5 .O98 1996**

The use of psychological testing for treatment planning and outcome assessment. 2nd ed. Mahwah, N.J. : Lawrence Erlbaum Associates, c1999.
**TC RC473.P79 U83 1999**

**OUTCOME ASSESSMENT (MEDICAL CARE) - HANDBOOKS, MANUALS, ETC.**
Hawkins, Robert P., 1931- Measuring behavioral health outcomes. New York : Kluwer Academic/ Plenum Publishers, c1999.
**TC RJ503.5 .H39 1999**

**OUTCOME-BASED EDUCATION.** *See* **COMPETENCY BASED EDUCATION.**

**OUTCOME EVALUATION (MEDICAL CARE).** *See* **OUTCOME ASSESSMENT (MEDICAL CARE).**

**OUTCOME MEASURES (MEDICAL CARE).** *See* **OUTCOME ASSESSMENT (MEDICAL CARE).**

**OUTCOMES ASSESSMENT (MEDICAL CARE).** *See* **OUTCOME ASSESSMENT (MEDICAL CARE).**

**OUTCOMES-BASED EDUCATION.** *See* COMPETENCY BASED EDUCATION.

**OUTCOMES MEASUREMENT (MEDICAL CARE).** *See* OUTCOME ASSESSMENT (MEDICAL CARE).

**OUTCOMES RESEARCH (MEDICAL CARE).** *See* OUTCOME ASSESSMENT (MEDICAL CARE).

**OUTDOOR EDUCATION.**
Olien, Rebecca. Walk this way!. Portsmouth, NH : Heinemann, c1998.
*TC LB1047 .O55 1998*

**OUTDOOR LIFE.** *See* SPORTS.

**OUTERCOATS.** *See* COATS.

**Outline of education in Japan, 1997.** Tōkyō : Government of Japan, Ministry of Education, Science, Sports and Culture, 1996. iv, 107, 66 p. : ill. ; 30 cm. Japanese and English. This publication is a reproduction by the Asian/Pacific Cultural Center for Unesco, Tokyo, of "Development of Education in Japan 1994-1996 -- Report for Submission to the 45th Session of the International Conference on Education"-- t.p. verso. ISBN 4-946438-11-4
*1. Education - Japan.*
*TC LA1312 .O87 1996*

**Outlines of a philosophy of art.**
Collingwood, R. G. (Robin George), 1889-1943. Bristol : Thoemmes, 1994, c1925.
*TC N70 .C6 1994*

**OUTPATIENTS - PSYCHOLOGY.**
Baker, Susan Keane. Managing patient expectations. San Francisco : Jossey Bass Publishers, 1998.
*TC R727.3 .B28 1998*

**Outreach scholarship**
(2) Lerner, Richard M. Family diversity and family policy. Boston ; London : Kluwer Academic, c1999.
*TC HQ535 .L39 1999*

(4) Transforming social inquiry, transforming social action. Boston ; London : Kluwer Academic, c2000.
*TC LC238 .T73 2000*

**Outside and inside kangaroos.**
Markle, Sandra. 1st ed. New York, N.Y. : Atheneum Books for Young Readers, c1999.
*TC QL737.M35 M272 1999*

**Ovando, Carlos Julio.**
The politics of multiculturalism and bilingual education. Boston : McGraw-Hill, c2000.
*TC LC1099.3 .P64 2000*

**Ovando, Martha N., 1954-.**
Owen, Jane C., 1948- Superintendent's guide to creating community. Lanham, Md. : Scarecrow Press, 2000.
*TC LB2831.72 . O94 2000*

**Over exposed :** essays on contemporary photography / edited by Carol Squiers. New York : New Press, c1999. 330 p. : ill : c 24 cm. Includes bibliographical references. CONTENTS: Introduction / Carol Squiers -- Ectoplasm : photography in the digital age / Geoffrey Batchen -- Mirrors and window shoppers : lesbians, photography, and the politics of visibility / Deborah Bright -- Newton's gravity / Victor Burgin -- Krysztof Wodiczko's homeless projection and the site of urban revitalization / Rosalyn Deutsche -- Instability and dispersion / Timothy Druckrey -- OI : opportunistic identification, open identification in PWA portraiture / Jan Zita Grover -- On the dissecting table : the unnatural coupling of surrealism and photography / Andy Grundberg -- Adjusting the focus for an indigenous presence / Theresa Harlan -- Playing with dolls / Silvia Kolbowski -- A note on photography and the simulacral / Rosalind Krauss -- Mortal coil : eros and diaspora in the photographs of Rotimi Fani-Kayode / Kobena Mercer -- Photography and fetish / Christian Metz -- Selling green / Kathy Myers -- Missing women : rethinking early thoughts on images of women / Griselda Pollock -- Living with contradictions : critical practices in the age of supply-side aesthetics / Abigail Solomon-Godeau -- Class struggle : the invention of paparazzi photography and the death of Diana, Princess of Wales / Carol Squiers -- The pleasures of looking : the Attorney General's Commission on Pornography versus visual images / Carole S. Vance. ISBN 1-56584-522-6 (pbk.)
*1. Photography, Artistic. I. Squiers, Carol, 1948- II. Title: Overexposed III. Title: Essays on contemporary photography*
*TC TR642 .O94 1999*

**Over in the meadow.**
Dana, Katharine Floyd, 1835-1886. New York : Scholastic, c1992
*TC PZ8.3.D2 Ov 1992*

**OVERACTIVE CHILDREN.** *See* HYPERACTIVE CHILDREN.

**Overall, Lyn.**
Teaching in primary schools. London : Cassell, 1998.
*TC LB1776.T43 1998*

**OVERCOATS.** *See* COATS.

**Overexposed.**
Over exposed. New York : New Press, c1999.
*TC TR642 .O94 1999*

**OVERLAND JOURNEYS TO THE PACIFIC.**
Hester, Sallie. A covered wagon girl. Mankato, Minn. : Blue Earth Books, c2000.
*TC F593 .H47 2000*

**OVERLAND JOURNEYS TO THE PACIFIC - FICTION.**
Turner, Ann Warren. Red flower goes West. 1st ed. New York : Hyperion Books for Children, c1999.
*TC PZ7.T8535 Rf 1999*

**OVERLAND JOURNEYS TO THE PACIFIC - JUVENILE LITERATURE.**
Hester, Sallie. A covered wagon girl. Mankato, Minn. : Blue Earth Books, c2000.
*TC F593 .H47 2000*

**OVERPOPULATION.**
Ehrlich, Paul R. The population explosion. New York : Simon and Schuster, c1990.
*TC HB871 .E33 1990*

**OVERSEAS STUDENTS.** *See* RETURNED STUDENTS.

**OVERWEIGHT.** *See* OBESITY.

**OVERWEIGHT CHILDREN - PSYCHOLOGY.**
Solovay, Sondra, 1970- Tipping the scales of justice. Amherst, N.Y. : Prometheus Books, 2000.
*TC BF697.5.B63 S65 2000*

**OVERWEIGHT PERSONS.** *See* OVERWEIGHT CHILDREN; OVERWEIGHT WOMEN.

**OVERWEIGHT WOMEN - PSYCHOLOGY.**
Berg, Francie M. Women afraid to eat. Hettinger, ND : Healthy Weight Network, c2000.
*TC RC552.O25 B47 2000*

**OVERWEIGHT WOMEN - UNITED STATES.**
Berg, Francie M. Women afraid to eat. Hettinger, ND : Healthy Weight Network, c2000.
*TC RC552.O25 B47 2000*

**Ovesey, Lionel, joint author.**
Kardiner, Abram, 1891- The mark of oppression; [1st ed.]. New York, Norton [1951]
*TC E185.625 .K3*

**Owen, Bruce M.** The Internet challenge to television / Bruce M. Owen. Cambridge, Mass. : Harvard University Press, 1999. xii, 372 p. : ill. ; 24 cm. Includes bibliographical references (p. 352-365) and index. Table of contents URL: http://lcweb.loc.gov/catdir/toc/98-39236.html ISBN 0-674-87299-1 (alk. paper) DDC 384.55/0973
*1. Television broadcasting - United States - Forecasting. 2. Digital television - Economic aspects - United States - Forecasting. 3. Digital video - Economic aspects - United States - Forecasting. 4. Telecommunication - United States - Forecasting. 5. Mass media - Audiences. 6. World Wide Web. I. Title.*
*TC HE8700.8 .O826 1999*

**Owen, David, 1955-** None of the above : the truth behind the SATs / David Owen with Marilyn Doerr. Rev. and updated. Lanham, Md. : Rowman & Littlefield Publishers, c1999. xix, 323 p. ; 25 cm. (Culture and education series) Includes bibliographical references and index. ISBN 0-8476-9506-9 (alk. paper) ISBN 0-8476-9507-7 (pbk. : alk. paper) DDC 378.1/662
*1. Scholastic Aptitude Test. 2. Prediction of scholastic success - Evaluation. I. Doerr, Marilyn. II. Title. III. Series.*
*TC LB2353.57 .O94 1999*

**Owen, Jane C., 1948-** Superintendent's guide to creating community / Jane C. Owen and Martha N. Ovando. Lanham, Md. : Scarecrow Press, 2000. 169 p. : ill. ; 24 cm. Includes bibliographical references and index. ISBN 0-8108-3763-3 (cloth : alk. paper) ISBN 0-8108-3764-1 (pbk. : alk. paper) DDC 371.2/011
*1. School superintendents - United States - Case studies. I. Ovando, Martha N., 1954- II. Title.*
*TC LB2831.72 . O94 2000*

**OWLS - JUVENILE POETRY.**
If the owl calls again. 1st ed. New York : M.K. McElderry Books ; Toronto : Collier Macmillan ; New York : Maxwell Macmillan, c1990.
*TC PN6109.97 .I3 1990*

**OWLS - PICTORIAL WORKS.**
[Nature study class, P.S. 165] [picture] 1935.
*TC BE5564*

[Nature study class, P.S. 165] [picture] 1935.
*TC BE5564*

[Nature study class, P.S. 165] [picture] 1935.
*TC BE5564*

**OWLS - POETRY.**
If the owl calls again. 1st ed. New York : M.K. McElderry Books ; Toronto : Collier Macmillan ; New York : Maxwell Macmillan, c1990.
*TC PN6109.97 .I3 1990*

**OWNERSHIP OF FIREARMS.** *See* FIREARMS OWNERSHIP.

**OWNERSHIP OF SLAVES.** *See* SLAVERY.

**Oxford applied linguistics**
Skehan, Peter. A cognitive approach to language learning. Oxford ; New York : Oxford University Press, 1998.
*TC P118.2 .S567 1998*

**The Oxford companion to food.**
Davidson, Alan, 1924- Oxford : Oxford University Press, 1999.
*TC TX349 .D38 1999*

**Oxford early music series (Unnumbered)**
Toft, Robert. Heart to heart. Oxford ; New York : Oxford University Press, 2000.
*TC MT823 .T64 2000*

**Oxford figures :** 800 years of the mathematical sciences / edited by John Fauvel, Raymond Flood and Robin Wilson. Oxford ; New York : Oxford University Press, 2000. 296 p. : ill. ; 26 cm. Includes bibliographical references (p. 272-288) and index. ISBN 0-19-852309-2 DDC 510/.71/142574
*1. University of Oxford - History. 2. Mathematics - Study and teaching (Higher) - England - Oxford - History. 3. Mathematics - England - Oxford - History. 4. Mathematicians - England - Oxford - Intellectual life. 5. Mathematicians - England - Oxford - Social life and customs. I. Fauvel, John. II. Flood, Raymond. III. Wilson, Robin J.*
*TC QA14.G73 O947 2000*

**The Oxford handbook of memory** / edited by Endel Tulving, Fergus I.M. Craik. Oxford ; New York : Oxford University Press, 2000. xiv, 700 p. : ill. ; 27 cm. Includes bibliographical references and indexes. ISBN 0-19-512265-8 (alk. paper) DDC 153.1/2
*1. Memory - Handbooks, manuals, etc. I. Tulving, Endel. II. Craik, Fergus I. M.*
*TC BF371 .O84 2000*

**Oxford historical monographs**
Palmowski, Jan. Urban liberalism in imperial Germany. Oxford ; New York : Oxford University Press, 1999.
*TC DD901.F78 P35 1999*

**Oxford psychology series**
(no. 30) Laming, D. R. J. (Donald Richard John) The measurement of sensation. Oxford ; New York : Oxford University Press, 1997.
*TC QP435 .L34 1997*

**Oxford science publications**
Laming, D. R. J. (Donald Richard John) The measurement of sensation. Oxford ; New York : Oxford University Press, 1997.
*TC QP435 .L34 1997*

**Oxford studies in comparative education**
(v. 8, no. 2.) Processes of transition in education systems. Wallingford : Symposium, 1998.
*TC LC71 .P7 1998*

(v.9, no.1.) Comparing standards internationally. Wallingford : Symposium, 1999.
*TC QA11 .C64 1999*

**Oxford television studies**
Seiter, Ellen, 1957- Television and new media audiences. Oxford ; New York : Clarendon Press, 1998.
*TC PN1992.3.U5 S35 1998*

**Oxley, Nicola.**
Oliveira, Nicolas de. Installation art. London : Thames and Hudson, 1994.
*TC N6494.E O4 1994*

**Oyama, Susan.** Evolution's eye : a systems view of the biology-culture divide / Susan Oyama. Durham, NC : Duke University Press, 2000. 274 p. ; 24 cm. (Science and cultural theory) Includes bibliographical references (p.[234-259]) and index. ISBN 0-8223-2436-9 (cloth : alk. paper) ISBN 0-8223-2472-5 (paper : alk. paper) DDC 155.7

*1. Developmental psychology. 2. Genetic psychology. 3. System theory. I. Title. II. Series.*
**TC BF713 .O93 2000**

**Ozga, Jennifer.** Policy research in educational settings : : contested terrain / Jenny Ozga. Buckingham [England] ; Philadelphia : Open University Press, 2000. xiii, 146 p. ; 24 cm. (Doing qualitative research in educational settings). Includes bibliographical references (p. [132]-139) and index. ISBN 0-335-20296-9 (hb) ISBN 0-335-20295-0 (pb)
*1. Education - Research - Great Britain - Methodology. 2. Education and state - Research - Great Britain - Methodology. 3. Action research in education - Great Britain. 4. Critical pedagogy - Great Britain. I. Title. II. Series.*
**TC LB1028.25.G7 O93 2000**

**Pace, Robert.** Teachers guide / [by]Robert Pace. Katonah, N.Y. : Lee Roberts Music publications, 1983. v. : ill., music ; 23 x 31 cm. SUMMARY: On cover and title page: "music for piano", "creative music", "theory papers" and "finger builders".
*1. Piano - Studies and exercises. 2. Piano music - Teaching pieces. 3. Piano - Fingering. 4. Piano - Instruction and study. I. Title.*
**TC MT245 .P32 1983**

**Pacey, Arnold.** Meaning in technology / Arnold Pacey. Cambridge, Mass. : MIT Press, c1999. viii, 264 p. ; 24 cm. Includes bibliographical references (p. [223]-253) ISBN 0-262-16182-6 (hc : alk. paper) DDC 601
*1. Technology - Philosophy. 2. Technology - Social aspects. I. Title.*
**TC T14 .P28 1999**

**Pachler, Norbert.**
Learning to teach using ICT in the secondary school. London ; New York : Routledge, 1999.
**TC LB1028.5 .L3884 1999**

Teaching modern foreign languages at advanced level. London ; New York : Routledge, 1999.
**TC PB35 .T42 1999**

**PACIFIC AMERICANS.** *See* **PACIFIC ISLANDER AMERICANS.**

**PACIFIC ISLAND AMERICANS.** *See* **PACIFIC ISLANDER AMERICANS.**

**PACIFIC ISLANDER AMERICANS - COUNSELING OF.**
Asian and Pacific Islander Americans :. Commack, N.Y. : Nova Science Publishers, 1999.
**TC RC451.5.A75 A83 1999**

**PACIFIC ISLANDER AMERICANS - PSYCHOLOGY.**
Asian and Pacific Islander Americans :. Commack, N.Y. : Nova Science Publishers, 1999.
**TC RC451.5.A75 A83 1999**

**PACIFIC ISLANDER AMERICANS - UNITED STATES.** *See* **PACIFIC ISLANDER AMERICANS.**

**PACIFIC ISLANDERS - UNITED STATES.** *See* **PACIFIC ISLANDER AMERICANS.**

**Pacific Northwest Council of Family Relations.**
The Family life coordinator. Eugene, Ore. : E. C. Brown Trust Foundation.

**PACIFIC SETTLEMENT OF INTERNATIONAL DISPUTES.**
Miall. Hugh. Contemporary conflict resolution. Cambridge, UK : Polity Press ; Malden, MA : Blackwell, 1999.
**TC JZ6010 .M53 1999**

**PACIFISM.** *See also* **NONVIOLENCE.**
Nonviolence in theory and practice. Belmont, Calif. : Wadsworth Pub. Co., c1990.
**TC HM278 .N67 1990**

**PACIFISTS.** *See* **WOMEN PACIFISTS.**

**PACIFISTS - BIOGRAPHY.**
True, Michael. To construct peace. Mystic, Conn. : Twenty-Third Publications, c1992.
**TC JX1962.A2 T783 1992**

**Pack-Brown, Sherlon P.** Images of me : a guide to group work with African-American women / Sherlon P. Pack-Brown, Linda E. Whittington-Clark, Woodrow M. Parker. Boston : Allyn and Bacon, c1998. xviii, 286 p. ; 24 cm. Includes bibliographical references and index. ISBN 0-205-17184-2 DDC 362.83/54/ 08996073
*1. Afro-American women - Counseling of. 2. Social work with women - United States. 3. Cross-cultural counseling - United States. 4. Social group work - United States. 5. Group psychotherapy - United States. I. Whittington-Clark, Linda E. II. Parker, Woodrow M. III. Title.*

**TC HV1445 .P33 1998**

**PACS (PICTURE ARCHIVING AND COMMUNICATION SYSTEMS).** *See* **PICTURE ARCHIVING AND COMMUNICATION SYSTEMS.**

**Padak, Nancy.**
Rasinski, Timothy V. Effective reading strategies. 2nd ed. Upper Saddle River, N.J. : Merrill, c2000.
**TC LB1050.5 .R33 2000**

**Padden, Carol, joint author.**
Baker-Shenk, Charlotte Lee. American sign language. Silver Spring, Md. : T. J. Publishers, c1978, 1979 printing.
**TC HV2474 .B29**

**Paddor, Scott.**
The American Revolution. [videorecording]. New York, N.Y. : A&E Home Video, c1994.
**TC E208 .A447 1994**

**Padilla, Genaro M., 1949-.**
Power, race, and gender in academe. New York : Modern Language Association, 2000.
**TC LC3727 .P69 2000**

**PAEDIATRICS.** *See* **PEDIATRICS.**

**Page, Nick.** Music as a way of knowing / Nick Page. York, Me. : Stenhouse Publishers ; Los Angeles, Calif. : Galef Institute, c1995. 76 p. : ill. ; 28 cm. (Strategies for teaching and learning professional library) Includes bibliographical references (p. 69-74). ISBN 1-57110-052-0 (alk. paper) DDC 780/.7
*1. Music - Instruction and study. 2. School music - Instruction and study. 3. Child development. I. Series.*
**TC MT1 .P234 1995**

**Page, Randy M.** Fostering emotional well-being in the classroom / Randy M. Page, Tana S. Page. 2nd ed. Sudbury, Mass. ; London : Jones and Bartlett Publishers, c2000. xv, 336 p. : ill. ; 23 cm. (The Jones and Bartlett series in health sciences) Includes bibliographical references and index. ISBN 0-7637-1264-7 DDC 371.7/13
*1. Students - Mental health. 2. Mental health promotion. 3. Self-esteem in children. 4. Self-esteem in adolescence. 5. Classroom environment. I. Page, Tana S. II. Title. III. Series.*
**TC LB3430 .P34 2000**

Meeks, Linda Brower. Comprehensive school health education. 2nd edition. Blacklick, OH : Meeks Heit Pub. Co., c1996.
**TC RA440.3.U5 M445 1996**

**Page, Tana S.**
Page, Randy M. Fostering emotional well-being in the classroom. 2nd ed. Sudbury, Mass. ; London : Jones and Bartlett Publishers, c2000.
**TC LB3430 .P34 2000**

**Page to screen :** taking literacy into the electronic era / edited by Ilana Snyder ; [Michael Joyce ... et al.]. London ; New York : Routledge, 1998. xxxvi, 260 p. : ill. ; 23 cm. Includes bibliographical references and index. ISBN 0-415-17464-3 (hbk) ISBN 0-415-17465-1 (pbk) DDC 371.33
*1. Computers and literacy. 2. Educational technology. 3. Hypertext systems. I. Snyder, Ilana, 1949- II. Joyce, Michael, 1945-*
**TC LC149.5 .P35 1998**

**PAGE, WALTER HINES, 1855-1918.**
Hendrick, Burton Jesse, 1870-1949. The life and letters of Walter H. Page. Garden City, N.Y. : Doubleday, Page & Co., 1925.
**TC E664.P15 H45 1925**

**PAGEANTS.** *See* **FESTIVALS.**

**PAGEANTS - POLITICAL ASPECTS - UNITED STATES - HISTORY.**
Lorini, Alessandra, 1949- Rituals of race. Charlottesville : University Press of Virginia, 1999.
**TC E185.61 .L675 1999**

**Pagliano, Paul.** Multisensory environments / Paul Pagliano. London : David Fulton, 1999. xii, 164 p. ; 24 cm. Includes bibliographical references (p. [154]-161) and index. ISBN 1-85346-553-4
*1. Sensory stimulation. 2. Special education. I. Title.*
**TC LC3965 .P345 1999**

**Pagliaro, Ann M.** Substance use among women : a reference and resource guide / Ann Maria Pagliaro and Louis A. Pagliaro. Philadelphia, PA : Brunner/ Mazel, c2000. xix, 349 p. : ill. ; 24 cm. Includes bibliographical references and index. ISBN 1-58391-035-2 (case) DDC 362.29/082/0973
*1. Women - Substance use - United States. 2. Substance abuse - United States. I. Pagliaro, Louis A. II. Title.*
**TC RC564.5.W65 P34 2000**

**Pagliaro, Louis A.**
Pagliaro, Ann M. Substance use among women. Philadelphia, PA : Brunner/Mazel, c2000.
**TC RC564.5.W65 P34 2000**

**Pai, Hang Young.** Chisanbop finger calculation method : manual for subtraction and division created by Sung Jin Pai and Hang Young Pai / written by Hang Young Pai ; edited by John Leonard. New York : McCormick-Mathers Pub. Co., 1981. viii, 166 p. : ill. ; 24 cm. ISBN 0-278-54556-4
*1. Arithmetic. 2. Finger calculation. I. Pai, Sung Jin. II. Leonard, John, 1938- III. Title. IV. Title: Finger calculation method : manual for subtraction and division*
**TC QA115 .P23 1981**

Chisanbop : original finger calculation created by Sung Jin Pai and Hang Young Pai / written by Hang Young Pai ; edited by John Leonard. Teacher's annotated ed. New York : American Book Co., 1980. v., : ill. ; 28 cm. CONTENTS: [v. 1]. Subtraction stage one part A -- [v. 2]. Subtraction stage one part B. ISBN 0-278-54551-3 (Part A) ISBN 0-278-54554-8 (Part B)
*1. Arithmetic. 2. Finger calculation. I. Pai, Sung Jin. II. Leonard, John, 1938- III. Title. IV. Title: Original finger calculation*
**TC QA115 .P23 1980 Teacher's Ed.**

Chisanbop : original finger calculation created by Sung Jin Pai and Hang Young Pai / written by Hang Young Pai ; edited by John Leonard. New York : American Book Co., 1980. v. : ill. ; 28 cm. CONTENTS: [v. 1]. Subtraction stage one part A -- [v. 2]. Subtraction stage one part B. ISBN 0-278-54547-5 (Part A) ISBN 0-278-54549-1 (Part B)
*1. Arithmetic. 2. Finger calculation. I. Pai, Sung Jin. II. Leonard, John, 1938- III. Title. IV. Title: Original finger calculation*
**TC QA115 .P23 1980**

Chisanbop : original finger calculation created by Sung Jin Pai and Hang Young Pai / written by Hang Young Pai ; edited by John Leonard. New York : American Book Co., 1980. v. : ill. ; 28 cm. CONTENTS: [v. 1]. Addition and multiplication stage one -- [v. 2]. Addition and multiplication stage two. ISBN 0-278-54546-7 (Stage one) ISBN 0-278-54548-3 (Stage two)
*1. Arithmetic. 2. Finger calculation. I. Pai, Sung Jin. II. Leonard, John, 1938- III. Title. IV. Title: Original finger calculation*
**TC QA115 .P231 1980**

Chisanbop : original finger calculation created by Sung Jin Pai and Hang Young Pai / written by Hang Young Pai ; edited by John Leonard. Teacher's annotated ed. New York : American Book Co., 1980. v. : ill. ; 28 cm. CONTENTS: [v. 1]. Addition and multiplication stage one -- [v. 2]. Addition and multiplication stage two. ISBN 0-278-54550-5 (Stage one) ISBN 0-278-54552-1 (Stage two)
*1. Arithmetic. 2. Finger calculation. I. Pai, Sung Jin. II. Leonard, John, 1938- III. Title. IV. Title: Original finger calculation*
**TC QA115 .P231 1980 Teacher's Ed.**

**Pai, Sung Jin.**
Pai, Hang Young. Chisanbop finger calculation method. New York : McCormick-Mathers Pub. Co., 1981.
**TC QA115 .P23 1981**

Pai, Hang Young. Chisanbop. Teacher's annotated ed. New York : American Book Co., 1980.
**TC QA115 .P23 1980 Teacher's Ed.**

Pai, Hang Young. Chisanbop. New York : American Book Co., 1980.
**TC QA115 .P23 1980**

Pai, Hang Young. Chisanbop. New York : American Book Co., 1980.
**TC QA115 .P231 1980**

Pai, Hang Young. Chisanbop. Teacher's annotated ed. New York : American Book Co., 1980.
**TC QA115 .P231 1980 Teacher's Ed.**

**Paideia agonistes.**
Grote, John E. Lanham, Md. : University Press of America, c2000.
**TC LC1011 .G76 2000**

**Paige, John Rhodes.** Preserving order amid chaos : the survival of schools in Uganda, 1971-1986 / John Rhodes Paige. New York : Berghahn Books, 2000. xvi, 208 p. ; 22 cm. Includes bibliographical references and index. ISBN 1-57181-213-X (alk. paper) DDC 373.6761
*1. Education, Secondary - Uganda - Kabarole District - History - 20th century. 2. Education and State - Uganda - Case studies. I. Title.*
**TC LA1567 .P25 2000**

**Paik, Nam June, 1932-.**
Processing the signal [videorecording]. Cicero, Ill. :
Roland Collection of Films on Art, c1989.
*TC N6494.V53 P7 1989*

**Pailliotet, Ann Watts.**
Reconceptualizing literacy in the media age.
Stamford, Conn. : Jai Press, c2000.
*TC LB1050 .A38 v.7*

**PAIN.** *See* SUFFERING.

**PAIN - NURSING.**
Key aspects of comfort. New York : Springer Pub.
Co., c1989.
*TC RT87.P35 K48 1989*

**Paine, Crispin.**
Godly things. New York : Leicester University Press,
2000.
*TC BL45 .G63 2000*

**PAINTED CEILINGS.** *See* MURAL PAINTING
AND DECORATION.

**Painter, Clare, 1947-** Learning through language in
early childhood / Clare Painter. London ; New York :
Cassell, 1999. vii, 356 p. : ill. ; 24 cm. (Open linguistics
series) Includes bibliographical references (p. [335]-350) and
index. ISBN 0-304-70056-8 (hardcover) DDC 372.62
*1. Language experience approach in education - Longitudinal
studies. 2. Language arts (Early childhood) - Longitudinal
studies. 3. Language acquisition - Longitudinal studies. 4.
Constructivism (Education) - Longitudinal studies. I. Title. II.
Series: Open linguistics series.*
*TC LB1139.5.L35 P35 1999*

**PAINTERS.** *See* EXPATRIATE PAINTERS.

**PAINTERS, AFRO-AMERICAN.** *See* AFRO-
AMERICAN PAINTERS.

**PAINTERS - BELGIUM - BIOGRAPHY.**
Monsieur René Magritte [videorecording]. [Chicago,
Ill.] : Home Vision [distributor], c1978.
*TC ND673.M35 M6 1978*

**PAINTERS - FRANCE - BIOGRAPHY.**
Marc Chagall [videorecording]. [Chicago, Ill.] : Home
Vision [distributor], c1985.
*TC ND699.C5 C5 1985*

Matisse, voyages [videorecording]. [Chicago, Ill.] :
Home Vision ; [S.l.] : Distributed worldwide by RM
Associates, c1989.
*TC ND553.M37 M37 1989*

Picasso [videorecording]. Chicago, IL : Home Vision,
c1986.
*TC N6853.P5 P52 1986*

Seurat [videorecording]. West Long Branch, NJ :
Kultur, c1999.
*TC ND553.S5 S5 1999*

**PAINTERS' MATERIALS.** *See* ARTISTS'
MATERIALS.

**PAINTERS - MEXICO - BIOGRAPHY.**
Hamill, Pete, 1935- Diego Rivera. New York : Harry
N. Abrams, 1999.
*TC ND259.R5 H28 1999*

**The painters of the Wagilag sisters story 1937-1997 /**
Wally Caruana, Nigel Lendon, editors. Canberra,
ACT : The National Gallery of Australia, 1997. 174 p. :
chiefly col. ill., map ; 30 cm. Exhibition held at the National
Gallery of Australia, Canberra, 13 September to 23 November
1997. Includes bibliographical references (p. 161-164). ISBN
0-642-13068-X DDC 759.99429/5
*1. Painting, Australian aboriginal - Australia - Arnhem Land
(N.T.) - Exhibitions. 2. Australian aborigines - Australia -
Arnhem Land (N.T.) - Art - Exhibitions. I. Caruana, Wally. II.
Lendon, Nigel. III. National Gallery of Australia.*
*TC ND1101 .P395 1997*

**PAINTERS - RUSSIAN S.F.S.R. - BIOGRAPHY.**
Marc Chagall [videorecording]. [Chicago, Ill.] : Home
Vision [distributor], c1985.
*TC ND699.C5 C5 1985*

**PAINTERS - SPAIN - BIOGRAPHY.**
Picasso [videorecording]. Chicago, IL : Home Vision,
c1986.
*TC N6853.P5 P52 1986*

**PAINTERS' SPOUSES - UNITED STATES -
BIOGRAPHY.**
Tomkins, Calvin, 1925- Living well is the best
revenge. 1998 Modern Library ed. New York :
Modern Library, c1998.
*TC ND237.M895 T66 1998*

**PAINTERS - UNITED STATES.** *See* AFRO-
AMERICAN PAINTERS.

**PAINTERS - UNITED STATES - BIOGRAPHY.**
Andy Warhol [videorecording]. [Chicago, IL] : Home
Vision [distributor], cc1987.
*TC N6537.W28 A45 1987*

Andy Warhol [videorecording]. [Chicago, IL] : Home
Vision [distributor], cc1987.
*TC N6537.W28 A45 1987*

Jackson Pollock [videorecording]. [Chicago, Ill.] :
Home Vision ; [S.l.] : Distributed Worldwide by RM
Associates, c1987.
*TC ND237.P73 J3 1987*

Mary Cassatt [videorecording]. [Chicago, Ill.]: Home
Vision, c1977.
*TC ND237.C3 M37 1977*

Norman Rockwell's world -- an American dream
[videorecording]. [Chicago, Ill] : Home Vision, 1987,
c1972.
*TC ND237.R68 N6 1987*

Roy Lichtenstein [videorecording]. [Chicago, IL] :
Home Vision ; [S.l.] : distributed worldwide by RM
Asssociates, c1991.
*TC ND237.L627 R6 1991*

Sawin, Martica. Nell Blaine. 1st ed. New York :
Hudson Hills Press ; [Lanham, MD] : Distributed in
the USA, its territories and possessions, and Canada
by National Book Network, c1998.
*TC ND237.B597 S28 1998*

Tomkins, Calvin, 1925- Living well is the best
revenge. 1998 Modern Library ed. New York :
Modern Library, c1998.
*TC ND237.M895 T66 1998*

**PAINTERS' WIVES.** *See* PAINTERS' SPOUSES.

**PAINTING.** *See also* EXPRESSIONISM (ART);
IMPRESSIONISM (ART); MURAL
PAINTING AND DECORATION;
WATERCOLOR PAINTING.
Elkins, James, 1955- What painting is. New York :
Routledge, 1999.
*TC ND1135 .E44 1999*

**PAINTING - 19TH CENTURY - FRANCE -
EXHIBITIONS.**
Tinterow, Gary. Origins of impressionism. New
York : Metropolitan Museum of Art : Distributed by
H.N. Abrams, c1994.
*TC ND547.5.I4 L6913 1994*

**PAINTING, ABSTRACT.**
On pictures and paintings [videorecording].
Peasmarsh, East Sussex, Eng. ; Ho-Ho-kus, NJ :
Roland Collection, 1992.
*TC ND195.O45 1992*

**PAINTING, AMERICAN.**
Norman Rockwell's world -- an American dream
[videorecording]. [Chicago, Ill] : Home Vision, 1987,
c1972.
*TC ND237.R68 N6 1987*

**PAINTING, AMERICAN - EXHIBITIONS.**
America. Munich, Germany ; London ; New York :
Prestel, c1999.
*TC ND210 .A724 1999*

**PAINTING AND LITERATURE.** *See* ART AND
LITERATURE.

**PAINTING - AUSTRALIA - ADELAIDE (S.
AUST.) - EXHIBITIONS.**
Dreamings of the desert. Adelaide : The Gallery,
c1996.
*TC ND1101 .D74 1996*

**PAINTING, AUSTRALIAN.**
Smith, Bernard, 1916- Australian painting, 1788-
1990. 3rd ed. Melbourne ; New York : Oxford
University Press, 1992.
*TC ND1100 .S553 1992*

**PAINTING, AUSTRALIAN ABORIGINAL.**
Contemporary aboriginal painting. East Roseville,
Australia : Craftsmen House, c1993.
*TC ND1101 .C66 1993*

**PAINTING, AUSTRALIAN ABORIGINAL -
AUSTRALIA - ARNHEM LAND (N.T.) -
EXHIBITIONS.**
The painters of the Wagilag sisters story 1937-1997.
Canberra, ACT : The National Gallery of Australia,
1997.
*TC ND1101 .P395 1997*

**PAINTING, AUSTRALIAN ABORIGINAL -
AUSTRALIA - WESTERN DESERT (W.A.) -
EXHIBITIONS.**
Dreamings of the desert. Adelaide : The Gallery,
c1996.

*TC ND1101 .D74 1996*

**Painting by numbers :** Komar and Melamid's scientific
guide to art / edited by JoAnn Wypijewski. Berkeley :
University of California Press, [1999] 203 p. : ill. (some
col.), col. maps ; 22 x 28 cm. Originally published: 1st ed. New
York : Farrar Straus Giroux, c1997. [Selections. col.]. ISBN 0-520-21861-2
(pbk. : alk. paper) DDC 750/.1
*1. Painting - United States - Public opinion. 2. Public opinion -
United States. 3. Painting - Public opinion. I. Komar, Vitaly.
II. Melamid, Aleksandr. III. Wypijewski, JoAnn.*
*TC ND1140 .P26 1999*

**PAINTING - CALIFORNIA - MALIBU -
JUVENILE LITERATURE.**
J. Paul Getty Museum. A is for artist. Los Angeles : J.
Paul Getty Museum, c1997.
*TC N582.M25 A513 1997*

**PAINTING, DECORATIVE.** *See* MURAL
PAINTING AND DECORATION.

**PAINTING - EARLY WORKS TO 1800.**
Diderot, Denis, 1713-1784. [Selections. English.
1995] Diderot on art. New Haven : Yale University
Press, 1995.
*TC N6846 .D4613 1995*

**PAINTING, FRENCH.**
Adams, Steven. The Barbizon school & the origins of
impressionism. 1st ed. London : Phaidon, c1994.
*TC N6847.5.B3 A28 1994*

**PAINTING, FRENCH - EXHIBITIONS.**
Art in the making, Impressionism. London : National
Gallery, in association with Yale University Press,
c1991.
*TC ND547.5.I4 I4472 1991*

The New painting. San Francisco, CA : Fine Arts
Museums of San Francisco, c1996.
*TC ND547.5.I4 N38 1996*

Tinterow, Gary. Origins of impressionism. New
York : Metropolitan Museum of Art : Distributed by
H.N. Abrams, c1994.
*TC ND547.5.I4 L6913 1994*

**PAINTING, ISRAELI - FOREIGN INFLUENCES.**
Fuhrer, Ronald. Israeli painting. Woodstock, N.Y. :
Overlook Press in association with Ronald Lauder,
1998.
*TC ND977 .F85 1998*

**PAINTING, ISRAELI - THEMES, MOTIVES.**
Fuhrer, Ronald. Israeli painting. Woodstock, N.Y. :
Overlook Press in association with Ronald Lauder,
1998.
*TC ND977 .F85 1998*

**PAINTING, JAPANESE - EXHIBITIONS.**
Twelve centuries of Japanese art from the Imperial
collections. Washington, DC : Freer Gallery of Art
and the Arthur M. Sackler Gallery, Smithsonian
Institution Press, c1997.
*TC ND1457.J32 W377 1997*

**PAINTING, MODERN.**
Bell, Julian, 1952- What is painting? New York :
Thames and Hudson, 1999.
*TC ND1140 .B45 1999*

**PAINTING, MODERN - 19TH CENTURY.**
Nochlin, Linda. Representing women. New York :
Thames and Hudson, 1999.
*TC ND1460.W65 N63 1999*

**PAINTING, MODERN - 19TH CENTURY -
FRANCE.**
Adams, Steven. The Barbizon school & the origins of
impressionism. 1st ed. London : Phaidon, c1994.
*TC N6847.5.B3 A28 1994*

Impressionism [videorecording]. [London] : The
National Gallery ; Tillingham, Peasmarsh, East
Sussex, England : Ho-Ho-Kus, NJ : Distributed by
The Roland Collection, c1990.
*TC ND547.5.I4 A7 1990*

Seurat [videorecording]. West Long Branch, NJ :
Kultur, c1999.
*TC ND553.S5 S5 1999*

**PAINTING, MODERN - 19TH CENTURY -
FRANCE - EXHIBITIONS.**
Art in the making, Impressionism. London : National
Gallery, in association with Yale University Press,
c1991.
*TC ND547.5.I4 I4472 1991*

The New painting. San Francisco, CA : Fine Arts
Museums of San Francisco, c1996.
*TC ND547.5.I4 N38 1996*

**PAINTING, MODERN - 19TH CENTURY - UNITED STATES - EXHIBITIONS.**
America. Munich, Germany ; London : New York : Prestel, c1999.
*TC ND210 .A724 1999*

**PAINTING, MODERN - 20TH CENTURY.**
Nochlin, Linda. Representing women. New York : Thames and Hudson, 1999.
*TC ND1460.W65 N63 1999*

On pictures and paintings [videorecording].
Peasmarsh, East Sussex, Eng. ; Ho-Ho-kus, NJ : Roland Collection, 1992.
*TC ND195.O45 1992*

**PAINTING, MODERN - 20TH CENTURY - AUSTRALIA.**
Contemporary aboriginal painting. East Roseville, Australia : Craftsmen House, c1993.
*TC ND1101 .C66 1993*

**PAINTING, MODERN - 20TH CENTURY - FRANCE.**
Picasso [videorecording]. Chicago, IL : Home Vision, c1986.
*TC N6853.P5 P52 1986*

**PAINTING, MODERN - 20TH CENTURY - ISRAEL - THEMES, MOTIVES.**
Fuhrer, Ronald. Israeli painting. Woodstock, N.Y. : Overlook Press in association with Ronald Lauder, 1998.
*TC ND977 .F85 1998*

**PAINTING, MODERN - 20TH CENTURY - MEXICO.**
The frescoes of Diego Rivera [videorecording]. [Detroit, Mich.] : Founders Society, Detroit Institute of Arts ; [Chicago, Ill.?] : Home Vision [distributor], c1986.
*TC ND259.R5 F6 1986*

**PAINTING, MODERN - 20TH CENTURY - SPAIN.**
Picasso [videorecording]. Chicago, IL : Home Vision, c1986.
*TC N6853.P5 P52 1986*

**PAINTING, MODERN - 20TH CENTURY - UNITED STATES.**
Norman Rockwell's world -- an American dream [videorecording]. [Chicago, Ill] : Home Vision, 1987, c1972.
*TC ND237.R68 N6 1987*

**Painting on the left.**
Lee, Anthony W., 1960- Berkeley : University of California Press, c1999.
*TC ND259.R5 L44 1999*

**PAINTING - PHILOSOPHY.**
Bell, Julian, 1952- What is painting? New York : Thames and Hudson, 1999.
*TC ND1140 .B45 1999*

**PAINTING, PREHISTORIC.** *See* ROCK PAINTINGS.

**PAINTING, PRIMITIVE.** *See* PAINTING.

**PAINTING - PUBLIC OPINION.**
Painting by numbers. Berkeley : University of California Press, [1999]
*TC ND1140 .P26 1999*

**PAINTING - TECHNIQUE.**
Buechner, Thomas S. How I paint. New York : Harry N. Abrams, 2000.
*TC ND237.B8827 A4 2000*

Dunning, William V., 1933- Changing images of pictorial space. 1st ed. Syracuse : Syracuse University Press, 1991.
*TC ND1475 .D86 1991*

Italian painting before 1400 [videorecording]. [London] : The National Gallery, c1989.
*TC ND1575 .I87 1989*

Italian painting before 1400 [videorecording]. [London] : The National Gallery, c1989.
*TC ND1575 .I87 1989*

**Painting the musical city.**
Cassidy, Donna. Washington, DC : Smithsonian Institution Press, c1997.
*TC ML85 .C37 1997*

**PAINTING - THEMES, MOTIVES.**
Barber, Antonia, 1932- Apollo & Daphne. Los Angeles : J. Paul Getty Museum, 1998.
*TC ND1420 .B37 1998*

**PAINTING - UNITED STATES - PUBLIC OPINION.**
Painting by numbers. Berkeley : University of California Press, [1999]

*TC ND1140 .P26 1999*

**PAINTINGS.** *See* PAINTING.

**PAINTINGS, AMERICAN.** *See* PAINTING, AMERICAN.

**PAINTINGS, AUSTRALIAN (ABORIGINAL).** *See* PAINTING, AUSTRALIAN ABORIGINAL.

**PAINTINGS, FRENCH.** *See* PAINTING, FRENCH.

**PAINTINGS, MODERN.** *See* PAINTING, MODERN.

**Paintings of Chaim Soutine.**
Kleebblatt, Norman L. An expressionist in Paris. Munich ; New York : Jewish Museum, c1998.
*TC ND553.S7 A4 1998*

**PAINTINGS, ROCK.** *See* ROCK PAINTINGS.

**PAIRED-ASSOCIATION LEARNING.** *See* SIMILARITY (PSYCHOLOGY).

**Pak, Soyung.** Dear Juno / by Soyung Pak : illustrated by Susan Kathleen Hartung. New York : Viking, 1999. 1 v. (unpaged) : col. ill. ; 21 x 26 cm. SUMMARY: Although Juno, a Korean American boy, cannot read the letter he receives from his grandmother in Seoul, he understands what it means from the photograph and dried flower that are enclosed and decides to send a similar letter back to her. ISBN 0-670-88252-6 (hc.) DDC [Fic]
*1. Grandmothers - Fiction. 2. Letters - Fiction. 3. Korean Americans - Fiction. I. Hartung, Susan Kathleen, ill. II. Title.*
*TC PZ7.P173 De 1999*

**Pak, Yu Cha, ill.**
Nye, Naomi Shihab. Benito's dream bottle. 1st ed. New York : Simon & Schuster Books for Young Readers, c1995.
*TC PZ7.N976 Be 1995*

**Pakistan. Bureau of Educational Planning and Management.**
Pakistan education statistics. Islamabad : Bureau of Educational Planning and Management and Central Bureau of Education, Ministry of Education,
*TC LA1155 .P37 1995*

**Pakistan. Central Bureau of Education.**
Pakistan education statistics. Islamabad : Bureau of Educational Planning and Management and Central Bureau of Education, Ministry of Education,
*TC LA1155 .P37 1995*

**Pakistan. Central Bureau of Education. Sector H-9.**
Pakistan education statistics. Islamabad : Bureau of Educational Planning and Management and Central Bureau of Education, Ministry of Education,
*TC LA1155 .P37 1995*

**Pakistan education statistics.** Islamabad : Bureau of Educational Planning and Management and Central Bureau of Education, Ministry of Education, v. ; 24-29 cm. Frequency: Irregular. Description based on: 1947/48 to 1972/73. Issued by: Research Wing, Ministry of Education, Govt. of Pakistan, <1947/1979->; by: Ministry of Education, Central Bureau of Education, Sector H-9, <1985/86 and 1986/87->. DDC 370/.9549/1021
*1. Education - Pakistan - Statistics - Periodicals. I. Pakistan. Bureau of Educational Planning and Management. II. Pakistan. Central Bureau of Education. III. Pakistan. Ministry of Education. Research Wing. IV. Pakistan. Central Bureau of Education. Sector H-9.*
*TC LA1155 .P37 1995*

**Pakistan. Ministry of Education. Research Wing.**
Pakistan education statistics. Islamabad : Bureau of Educational Planning and Management and Central Bureau of Education, Ministry of Education,
*TC LA1155 .P37 1995*

**PAKISTAN - SOCIAL LIFE AND CUSTOMS - JUVENILE FICTION.**
English, Karen. Nadia's hands. 1st ed. Honesdale, PA : Boyds Mills Press, 1999.
*TC PZ7.E7232 Na 1999*

**Pal, Leslie Alexander, 1954-.**
Digital democracy. Toronto ; New York : Oxford University Press, 1998.
*TC JC421 .D55 1998*

**Paladino, Catherine.**
Land, sea & sky. 1st ed. Boston : Joy Street Books, c1993.
*TC PS595.N22 L36 1993*

**PALEONTOLOGISTS - UNITED STATES - BIOGRAPHY - JUVENILE LITERATURE.**
Tropea, Judith. A day in the life of a museum curator. Mahwah, N.J. : Troll Associates, c1991.
*TC QE22.E53 T76 1991*

**PALEONTOLOGY.**
Tropea, Judith. A day in the life of a museum curator. Mahwah, N.J. : Troll Associates, c1991.
*TC QE22.E53 T76 1991*

**Paley, Nicholas.** Questions of you and the struggle of collaborative life / Nicholas Paley and Janice Jipson. New York : P. Lang, c2000. xii, 190 p. ; 23 cm. (Counterpoints; 1058-1634 ; vol. 104) Includes bibliographical references (p. [165]-176). ISBN 0-8204-4251-8 (alk. paper) DDC 370/.7/2
*1. Education - Research - Methodology. I. Jipson, Janice. II. Title. III. Series: Counterpoints (New York, N.Y.) ; vol. 104.*
*TC LB1028 .P233 2000*

**Paley, Vivian Gussin, 1929-** White teacher / Vivian Gussin Paley. Cambridge, Mass. : Harvard University Press, 2000. xx, 136 p. ; 21 cm. Reprint with a new preface. Previously published: Cambridge : Harvard University Press, c1989. ISBN 0-674-00273-3 DDC 371.8299/073
*1. Afro-Americans - Education (Elementary) 2. Kindergarten - United States. 3. Classroom management - United States. I. Title.*
*TC LC2771 .P34 2000*

**Palmer, Barbara Martin, ed.**
College reading. Carrollton, GA : The College Reading Association, 1999.
*TC LB2395 .C64 1999*

**PALMER MEMORIAL INSTITUTE (SEDALIA, N.C.).**
Wadelington, Charles Weldon. Charlotte Hawkins Brown & Palmer Memorial Institute. Chapel Hill ; London : University of North Carolina Press, c1999.
*TC LA2317.B598 W33 1999*

**Palmer, Richard. ed.**
Hogben, Lancelot Thomas,d1895- Science for the citizen; [2d ed.]. New York, W. W. Norton & Co. c1938.
*TC Q162 .H7 1938*

**Palmer, Wayne.**
The Internet in action for math & science K-6 [videorecording]. [New York] : Thirteen-WNET ; [Alexandria, Va. : distributed by] PBS Video, c1998.
*TC LB1044.87 .I45 1998*

**Palmisano, Joseph M.**
Reference library of Black America. Detroit, MI : Gale Group : Distributed by African American Pub., Proteus Enterprises, c2000.
*TC E185 .R44 2000*

**Palmowski, Jan.** Urban liberalism in imperial Germany : Frankfurt am Main, 1866-1914 / Jan Palmowski. Oxford ; New York : Oxford University Press, 1999. xiv, 391 p. : ill. ; 23 cm. (Oxford historical monographs) Includes bibliographical references (p. [345]-384) and index. ISBN 0-19-820750-6 (alk. paper) DDC 320.51/0943/416409434
*1. Liberalism - Germany - Frankfurt am Main - History - 19th century. 2. Frankfurt am Main (Germany) - Politics and government. 3. Middle class - Germany - Frankfurt am Main - History - 19th century. 4. Political parties - Germany - Frankfurt am Main - History - 19th century. I. Title. II. Series.*
*TC DD901.F78 P35 1999*

**Palmquist, Mike.**
Transitions. Greenwich, Conn. : Ablex Pub. Corp., c1998.
*TC PE1404 .T74 1998*

**Pan American Union. Division of Intellectual Cooperation.** Lectura para maestros. Washingon, D.C., Oficina de Cooperación Intelectual, Unión Panamericana, 193 - v. 28cm. núm. 1- . Mimeographed. Manifold copy.
*1. Education - Latin America. I. Title.*

**Panas, Jerold.** Megagifts : who gives them, who gets them / Jerold Panas. Chicago, Ill. : Pluribus Press, c1984. vi, 231 p. : ill. ; 23 cm. ISBN 0-931028-39-6 DDC 361.7/0973
*1. Endowments - United States. 2. Gifts - United States. I. Title.*
*TC HV41 .P34 1984*

**Panda, Santosh K. (Santosh Kumar), 1959-.**
Staff development in higher and distance education. New Delhi : Aravali Books International, 1997.
*TC LB2331 .S692 1997*

**Pandey, Janak, 1945-.**
Handbook of cross-cultural psychology. 2nd ed. Boston : Allyn and Bacon, c1997.
*TC GN502 .H36 1997*

**Panel discussion.**
Race, ethnicity and culture in the visual arts. New York : American Council for the Arts, c1993.
*TC N70 .R32 1993*

**PANEL PAINTING, ITALIAN - ITALY - TUSCANY.**
Italian painting before 1400 [videorecording].
[London] : The National Gallery, c1989.

Italian painting before 1400 [videorecording].
[London] : The National Gallery, c1989.
*TC ND1575 .I87 1989*

**PANEL PAINTING, MEDIEVAL - ITALY - TUSCANY.**
Italian painting before 1400 [videorecording].
[London] : The National Gallery, c1989.

Italian painting before 1400 [videorecording].
[London] : The National Gallery, c1989.
*TC ND1575 .I87 1989*

**Paniagua, Freddy A.**
Handbook of multicultural mental health :. San
Diego : Academic Press, c2000.
*TC RC455.4 .H36 2000*

**PANIC DISORDERS.** *See* **AGORAPHOBIA.**

**PANIC DISORDERS - DIAGNOSIS.**
Neurotic, stress-related, and somatoform disorders
[videorecording]. Princeton, N.J. : Films for the
Humanities & Sciences, 1998.
*TC RC530 .N4 1998*

**PANIC DISORDERS - PATIENTS.**
Challenge cases [videorecording]. Princeton, N.J. :
Films for the Humanities & Sciences, 1998.
*TC RC455.2.C4 C4 1998*

Neurotic, stress-related, and somatoform disorders
[videorecording]. Princeton, N.J. : Films for the
Humanities & Sciences, 1998.
*TC RC530 .N4 1998*

**Pankake, Anita M., 1947-** Implementation : making
things happen / Anita M. Pankake. Larchmont, NY :
Eye on Education, c1998. xiii, 162 p. : ill. ; 24 cm. (The
school leadership library) Includes bibliographical references
(p. 157-162). ISBN 1-88300-153-6 DDC 371.2
*1. School management and organization - United States. 2.
Educational change - United States. 3. Educational
leadership - United States. I. Title. II. Series.*
*TC LB2805 .P32 1998*

**Panorama of work in the American city.**
Howell, Ron. One hundred jobs :b a panorama of
work in the American city. New York : New Press :
Distributed by W.W. Norton, 1999.
*TC HF5382.5.U6 N37 1999*

**Panter-Brick, Catherine, 1959-.**
Hormones, health, and behavior. Cambridge ; New
York : Cambridge University Press, 1999.
*TC QP356.45 .H67 1999*

**PANTOMIME.** *See* **BALLET.**

**PANTOMIMES WITH MUSIC.** *See* **PAGEANTS.**

**Panulla, Sharon.**
ADHD [videorecording]. New York, NY : Guilford
Publications, Inc., c1992.
*TC RJ506.H9 A3 1992*

**Panzer, Mary.** Mathew Brady and the image of history /
Mary Panzer ; withh an essay by Jeana K. Foley.
Washington, D.C. : Smithsonian Institution Press for
the National Portrait Gallery, c1997. xxiii, 232 p. : ill. ;
29 cm. An exhibition at the National Portrait Gallery, Sept. 26,
1997-Jan. 4, 1998; Fogg Art Museum, Harvard University, Jan.
22-April 15, 1998;; International Center of Photography,
Midtown New York City, May 1-July 19, 1998. Includes
bibliographical references and index. ISBN 1-56098-793-6
(alk. paper) DDC 770/.92
*1. Brady, Mathew B.,- 1823 (ca.)-1896 - Exhibitions. 2.
Photographers - United States - Biography - Exhibitions. 3.
Portrait photography - United States - History - Exhibitions. 4.
United States - History - Civil War, 1861-1865 - Photography -
Exhibitions. I. Foley, Jeana Kae. II. National Portrait Gallery
(Smithsonian Institution) III. Fogg Art Museum. IV.
International Center of Photography. V. Title.*
*TC TR140.B7 P36 1997*

**Paolucci-Whitcomb, Phyllis.**
Idol, Lorna. Collaborative consultation. 3rd ed.
Austin, Tex. : PRO-ED, c2000.
*TC LC4019 .I35 2000*

**paorama of work in the American city.**
Howell, Ron. One hundred jobs :b a panorama of
work in the American city. New York : New Press :
Distributed by W.W. Norton, 1999.
*TC HF5382.5.U6 N37 1999*

**PAPER.** *See* **PARCHMENT.**

**Paper bag puppets.**
Druce, Arden. Lanham, MD : Scarecrow Press, 1999.

*TC Z718.3 .D78 1999*

**PAPER - CONSERVATION AND RESTORATION - CONGRESSES.**
Institute of Paper Conservation. Modern works,
modern problems? [England] : Institute of Paper
Conservation, c1994.
*TC N8560 .I59 1994*

**PAPER WORK.**
Marsh, Valerie. Storytelling with shapes & numbers.
Ft. Atkinson, Wis. : Alleyside Press, c1999.
*TC LB1042 .M2874 1999*

**PAPERS.** *See* **PAPER.**

**Papers and discussants' comments.**
Bilingualism Through the Classroom : Strategies and
Practices (1995 : Universiti Brunei Darussalam)
Bilingualism through the classroom : strategies and
practices. [Bandar Seri Begawan : Universiti Brunei
Darussalam, 1995]
*TC P115 .B57 1995*

**Papp, Peggy.**
Couples on the fault line. New York, NY : Guilford
Press, 2000.
*TC RC488.5 .C6435 2000*

**PARACENTESIS.** *See* **AMNIOCENTESIS.**

**Paradigm debates in curriculum and supervision :**
modern and postmodern perspectives / edited by
Jeffrey Glanz, Linda S. Behar-Horenstein ; foreword
by Robert J. Starratt. Westport, Conn. ; London :
Bergin & Garvey, 2000. xvi, 294 p. : ill. ; 25 cm. Includes
bibliographical references and index. ISBN 0-89789-624-6
(alk. paper) DDC 371.2/03
*1. School supervision - Social aspects. 2. Curriculum
planning - Social aspects. 3. Postmodernism and education. 4.
Multicultural education. I. Glanz, Jeffrey. II. Behar-
Horenstein, Linda S.*
*TC LB2806.4 .P37 2000*

**Paradise Films.**
Ecole 27 [videorecording]. Bruxelles : Paradise
Films ; New York, N.Y. : [distributed by] First Run/
Icarus Films, 1997, c1996.
*TC LC746.P7 E2 1997*

**The paradox of plenty :** hunger in a bountiful world /
edited by Douglas H. Boucher. Oakland, Calif. : Food
First Books, c1999. xviii, 342 p. : ill., maps ; 23 cm.
Includes bibliographical references. ISBN 0-935028-71-4 DDC
363.8/09172/4
*1. Peasantry - Developing countries - Economic conditions. 2.
Poverty - Developing countries. 3. Food supply - Developing
countries. 4. Income distribution - Developing countries. 5.
Agriculture - Economic aspects - Developing countries. 6.
Economic assistance. 7. International trade - Moral and
ethical aspects. I. Boucher, Douglas H.*
*TC HD1542 .P37 1999*

**The paradox of social order.**
Moessinger, Pierre. [Irrationalité individuelle et ordre
social. English] New York : Aldine de Gruyter, c2000.
*TC HM1276 .M6413 2000*

**Parallax (Baltimore, Md.)**
Landow, George P. Hypertext 2.0. Rev., amplified ed.
Baltimore : Johns Hopkins University Press, 1997.
*TC PN81 .L28 1997*

**PARALYSIS, CEREBRAL.** *See* **CEREBRAL PALSY.**

**PARALYSIS, CEREBRAL - PERIODICALS.**
Cerebral palsy review. Wichita, Kan., Institute of
Logopedics.

**PARALYSIS, SPASTIC.** *See* **CEREBRAL PALSY.**

**PARAMETER ESTIMATION.**
Du, Zuru. Modeling conditional item dependencies
with a three-parameter logistic testlet model. 1998.
*TC 085 D84*

**PARAMILITARY MILITIA MOVEMENT.** *See*
**MILITIA MOVEMENTS.**

**PARANOIA - PATIENTS.**
Challenge cases [videorecording]. Princeton, N.J. :
Films for the Humanities & Sciences, 1998.
*TC RC455.2.C4 C4 1998*

**PARANOID SCHIZOPHRENIA - DIAGNOSIS.**
Schizophrenia and delusional disorders
[videorecording]. Princeton, N.J. : Films for the
Humanities & Sciences, 1998.
*TC RC514 .S3 1998*

**PARANOID SCHIZOPHRENIA - PATIENTS.**
Schizophrenia and delusional disorders
[videorecording]. Princeton, N.J. : Films for the
Humanities & Sciences, 1998.

*TC RC514 .S3 1998*

**PARAPHILIA.** *See* **PSYCHOSEXUAL DISORDERS.**

**PARAPROFESSIONALS IN EDUCATION.** *See*
**TEACHERS' ASSISTANTS.**

**PARAPSYCHOLOGY.** *See also* **MENTAL HEALING.**
Schick, Theodore. How to think about weird things.
2nd ed. Mountain View, Calif. : Mayfield Pub., c1999.
*TC BC177 .S32 1999*

**PARASITIC PLANTS.** *See* **FUNGI.**

**PARASOLS.** *See* **UMBRELLAS AND PARASOLS.**

**Paratore, Jeanne R.** What should we expect of family
literacy? : experiences of Latino children whose
parents participate in an intergenerational literacy
project / Jeanne R. Paratore, Gigliana Melzi, Barbara
Krol-Sinclair. Newark, Del. : International Reading
Association ; Chicago , Ill. : National Reading
Conference, c1999. xiii, 138 p. ; 23 cm. (Literacy studies
series) Includes bibliographical references (p. 128-131) and
indexes. ISBN 0-87207-246-0 DDC 372.119/2
*1. Family literacy programs - United States - Case studies. 2.
Reading - Parent participation - United States - Case studies.
3. English language - Study and teaching - United States -
Spanish speakers - Case studies. 4. Hispanic American
children - Education (Elementary) - Case studies. 5. Children
of immigrants - Education (Elementary) - United States - Case
studies. 6. Education, Bilingual - United States - Case studies.
I. Melzi, Gigliana. II. Krol-Sinclair, Barbara. III. Title. IV.
Series.*
*TC LC151 .P37 1999*

**Parchment.**
Haines, Betty M. Northampton [England] : Leather
Conservation Centre, 1999.
*TC TS1165 .H35 1999*

**PARCHMENT.**
Haines, Betty M. Parchment. Northampton
[England] : Leather Conservation Centre, 1999.
*TC TS1165 .H35 1999*

**PARCHMENT - CONSERVATION AND RESTORATION.**
Haines, Betty M. Parchment. Northampton
[England] : Leather Conservation Centre, 1999.
*TC TS1165 .H35 1999*

**PARCHMENT - CONSERVATION AND RESTORATION - BIBLIOGRAPHY.**
Ralston, Nicola L. Parchment/vellum conservation
survey and bibliography. Edinburgh : Historic
Scotland : Crown Copyright, c2000.
*TC Z701.4.I5 R35 2000*

**PARCHMENT - PRESERVATION - BIBLIOGRAPHY.**
Ralston, Nicola L. Parchment/vellum conservation
survey and bibliography. Edinburgh : Historic
Scotland : Crown Copyright, c2000.
*TC Z701.4.I5 R35 2000*

**Parchment/vellum conservation survey and bibliography.**
Ralston, Nicola L. Edinburgh : Historic Scotland :
Crown Copyright, c2000.
*TC Z701.4.I5 R35 2000*

Ralston, Nicola L. Parchment/vellum conservation
survey and bibliography. Edinburgh : Historic
Scotland : Crown Copyright, c2000.
*TC Z701.4.I5 R35 2000*

**Parent & educators' drug reference.**
Agins, Alan P. Cranston, R.I. : PRN Press, c1999.
*TC RJ560 .A35 1999*

**PARENT AND CHILD.** *See also* **ADOPTION;
CHILD ABUSE; FATHER AND CHILD;
MOTHER AND CHILD; PARENT AND
TEENAGER; PARENTING;
STEPCHILDREN; STEPMOTHERS.**
Berger, Elizabeth. Raising children with character.
Northvale, N.J. : J. Aronson, c1999.
*TC BF723.P4 B47 1999*

Cavell, Timothy A. Working with parents of
aggressive children. 1st ed. Washington, DC :
American Psychological Association, 2000.
*TC RJ506.A35 C38 2000*

Cerruto, Audra. The effects of training on theory of
mind tasks with children who are deaf. 1999.
*TC 085 C34*

Colin, Virginia L. Human attachment. Philadelphia :
Temple University Press, c1996.

*Parent and child*

**TC BF575.A86 C65 1996**
Family and peers. Westport, Conn. : Praeger, 2000.
**TC HQ755.85 .F365 2000**

Golombok, Susan. Parenting. London ; Philadelphia : Routledge, 2000.
**TC HQ755.8 .G655 2000**

Nevas, Debra Baron. Factors affecting parental attitudes toward a child's therapist and therapy. 1997.
**TC 085 N401**

Power, Thomas George, 1954- Play and exploration in children and animals. Mahwah, N.J. : L. Erlbaum Associates, 2000.
**TC BF717 .P69 2000**

Sayles, Mary Buell, 1878- Substitute parents, New York, The Commonwealth fund; London, H. Milford, Oxford University Press, 1936.
**TC HV875 .S3**

Understanding the defiant child [videorecording]. New York : Guilford Publications, c1997.
**TC HQ755.7 .U63 1997**

Wolfe, David A. Child abuse. 2nd ed. Thousands Oaks, Calif. : Sage Publications, 1999.
**TC HV6626.5 .W58 1999**

**PARENT AND CHILD - CHINA - HONG KONG.**
Lam-Chan, Gladys Lan Tak. Parenting in stepfamilies. Aldershot ; Brookfield USA : Ashgate, c1999.
**TC HQ759.92 .L34 1999**

**PARENT AND CHILD - FICTION.**
Cadnum, Michael. Rundown. New York : Viking, c1999.
**TC PZ7.C11724 Ru 1999**

Collins, Pat Lowery. Signs and wonders. Boston : Houghton Mifflin, 1999.
**TC PZ7.C69675 Si 1999**

Cooney, Caroline B. Tune in anytime. New York : Delacorte Press, 1999.
**TC PZ7.C7834 Tu 1999**

Gordon, Amy, 1949- When JFK was my father. Boston : Houghton Mifflin, 1999.
**TC PZ7.G65 Wh 1999**

Griffin, Adele. Dive. 1st ed. New York : Hyperion Books for Children, 1999.
**TC PZ7.G881325 Di 1999**

O'Malley, Kevin, 1961- Bud. New York : Walker, 2000.
**TC PZ7.O526 Bu 2000**

Weeks, Sarah. Regular Guy. 1st ed. New York : Laura Geringer Book, c1999.
**TC PZ7.W42215 Rg 1999**

**PARENT AND CHILD (LAW). See STEPCHILDREN.**

**PARENT AND CHILD (LAW) - UNITED STATES.**
Field, Martha A. Equal treatment for people with mental retardation. Cambridge, Mass. ; London : Harvard University Press, 1999.
**TC KF480 .F54 1999**

Schorr, Alvin Louis, 1921- Filial responsibility in the modern American family. [Washington] U.S. Dept. of Health, Education, and Welfare, Social Security Administration, Division of Program Research [1960]
**TC HV75 .S36 1960**

**PARENT AND CHILD - PSYCHOLOGICAL ASPECTS.**
Flynn, Bernadette Marie. The teacher-child relationship, temperament, and coping in children with developmental disabilities. 2000.
**TC 06 no. 11267**

**PARENT AND TEENAGER.**
Smith, Mieko Kotake. Adolescents with emotional and behavioral disabilities. Lewiston, NY : E. Mellen Press, c1998.
**TC RJ503 .S63 1998**

**PARENT AND TEENAGER - UNITED STATES.**
Adolescents and their families. New York : Garland Pub., 1999.
**TC HQ796 .A33533 1999**

**Parent articles about ADHD** / edited by Clare B. Jones, H. Russell Searight, Magda A. Urban. San Antonio, Texas : Communication Skill Builders, c1999. vii, 192 p. : ill. ; 28 cm. "Reproducible articles". Includes bibliographical references. ISBN 0-7616-6751-2
*1. Attention-deficit hyperactivity disorder. I. Jones, Clare B. II. Searight, H. Russell. III. Urban, Magda A.*

**TC RJ506.H9 P37 1999**

**PARENT BEHAVIOR. See PARENTING.**

**Parent-child activity pad.**
Making choices. Lexington, Mass. : D.C. Heath & co., c1986.
**TC PE1121 .M34 1986 Activity Pad**

**PARENT-CHILD INTERACTION THERAPY.**
Cavell, Timothy A. Working with parents of aggressive children. 1st ed. Washington, DC : American Psychological Association, 2000.
**TC RJ506.A35 C38 2000**

**PARENT-CHILD RELATIONS. See PARENT AND CHILD.**

**PARENT-CHILD RELATIONS.**
Adolescent siblings in stepfamilies. Chicago, Ill. : University of Chicago Press, 1999.
**TC LB1103.S6 v.64 no. 4**

**PARENT DEATH. See PARENTS - DEATH.**

**PARENT EDUCATION. See PARENTING - STUDY AND TEACHING.**

**Parent grief.**
Rosenblatt, Paul C. Philadelphia ; Hove [England] : Brunner/Mazel, c2000.
**TC BF575.G7 R673 2000**

**Parent involvement, handbook.**
Ottenberg, Susan D. Education today. 2nd. ed. Boston : Educational Publishing Group, Education Today, c1996.
**TC LC225.3 .O88 1996**

**PARENT INVOLVEMENT IN CHILDREN'S EDUCATION. See EDUCATION - PARENT PARTICIPATION.**

**PARENT INVOLVEMENT IN CHILDREN'S READING. See READING - PARENT PARTICIPATION.**

**PARENT INVOLVEMENT IN EARLY CHILDHOOD EDUCATION. See EARLY CHILDHOOD EDUCATION - PARENT PARTICIPATION.**

**PARENT INVOLVEMENT IN ELEMENTARY EDUCATION. See EDUCATION, ELEMENTARY - PARENT PARTICIPATION.**

**PARENT INVOLVEMENT IN PRESCHOOL EDUCATION. See EDUCATION, PRESCHOOL - PARENT PARTICIPATION.**

**PARENT INVOLVEMENT IN SCHOOL ADMINISTRATION. See SCHOOL MANAGEMENT AND ORGANIZATION - PARENT PARTICIPATION.**

**PARENT INVOLVEMENT IN SPECIAL EDUCATION. See SPECIAL EDUCATION - PARENT PARTICIPATION.**

**PARENT PARTICIPATION IN CHILDREN'S EDUCATION. See EDUCATION - PARENT PARTICIPATION.**

**PARENT PARTICIPATION IN CHILDREN'S READING. See READING - PARENT PARTICIPATION.**

**PARENT PARTICIPATION IN EARLY CHILDHOOD EDUCATION. See EARLY CHILDHOOD EDUCATION - PARENT PARTICIPATION.**

**PARENT PARTICIPATION IN ELEMENTARY EDUCATION. See EDUCATION, ELEMENTARY - PARENT PARTICIPATION.**

**PARENT PARTICIPATION IN PRESCHOOL EDUCATION. See EDUCATION, PRESCHOOL - PARENT PARTICIPATION.**

**PARENT PARTICIPATION IN SCHOOL ADMINISTRATION. See SCHOOL MANAGEMENT AND ORGANIZATION - PARENT PARTICIPATION.**

**PARENT PARTICIPATION IN SPECIAL EDUCATION. See SPECIAL EDUCATION - PARENT PARTICIPATION.**

**Parent power.**
Power, Brenda Miller. Portsmouth, NH : Heinemann, c1999.
**TC LC225.3 .P69 1999**

**PARENT-TEACHER CONFERENCES.**
Seligman, Milton, 1937- Conducting effective conferences with parents of children with disabilities. New York : Guilford Press, c2000.

**TC LC4019 .S385 2000**

**PARENT-TEACHER RELATIONSHIPS. See also HOME AND SCHOOL.**
Hornby, Garry. Improving parental involvement. London : Cassell, 2000.
**TC LC225 .H67 2000**

Ryan, Daniel Prentice. Gay/lesbian parents and school personnel. 1998.
**TC 06 no. 10988**

**PARENT-TEACHER RELATIONSHIPS - UNITED STATES.**
Families and teachers of individuals with disabilities. Boston : London : Allyn and Bacon, c2001.
**TC LC3969 .F34 2001**

Gestwicki, Carol, 1940- Home, school, and community relations. 4th ed. Albany, NY : Delmar Publishers, c2000.
**TC LC225.3 .G47 2000**

Power, Brenda Miller. Parent power. Portsmouth, NH : Heinemann, c1999.
**TC LC225.3 .P69 1999**

Wilde, Jerry, 1962- An educators guide to difficult parents. Huntington, N.Y. : Kroshka Books, c2000.
**TC LC225.3 .W54 2000**

**PARENT-TEACHER RELATIONSHIPS - UNITED STATES - CASE STUDIES.**
Harry, Beth. Building cultural reciprocity with families. Baltimore, Md. : P.H. Brookes Pub. Co., c1999.
**TC LC3969 .H377 1999**

**PARENT-TEENAGER RELATIONS. See PARENT AND TEENAGER.**

**PARENTAL BEHAVIOR IN ANIMALS. See also ANIMALS - INFANCY.**
Hrdy, Sarah Blaffer, 1946- Mother nature. 1st ed. New York : Pantheon Books, c1999.
**TC HQ759 .H784 1999**

Jenkins, Martin. The emperor's egg. 1st U.S. ed. Cambridge, Mass. : Candlewick Press, 1999.
**TC QL696.S473 J45 1999**

**PARENTAL BEHAVIOR IN ANIMALS - JUVENILE LITERATURE.**
Jenkins, Martin. The emperor's egg. 1st U.S. ed. Cambridge, Mass. : Candlewick Press, 1999.
**TC QL696.S473 J45 1999**

**PARENTAL BEHAVIOR IN HUMANS. See PARENTING.**

**PARENTAL DEATH. See PARENTS - DEATH.**

**PARENTAL DEPRIVATION. See also PATERNAL DEPRIVATION.**
Clarke, Ann M. (Ann Margaret) Early experience and the life path. London ; Philadelphia : Jessica Kingsley, 2000.
**TC BF721 .C5457 2000**

**PARENTAL INFLUENCES.**
Tucker, Gina Marie. Discipline. 1998.
**TC 06 no. 10999**

**PARENTAL INVOLVEMENT IN CHILDREN'S EDUCATION. See EDUCATION - PARENT PARTICIPATION.**

**PARENTAL INVOLVEMENT IN CHILDREN'S READING. See READING - PARENT PARTICIPATION.**

**PARENTAL INVOLVEMENT IN EARLY CHILDHOOD EDUCATION. See EARLY CHILDHOOD EDUCATION - PARENT PARTICIPATION.**

**PARENTAL INVOLVEMENT IN ELEMENTARY EDUCATION. See EDUCATION, ELEMENTARY - PARENT PARTICIPATION.**

**PARENTAL INVOLVEMENT IN PRESCHOOL EDUCATION. See EDUCATION, PRESCHOOL - PARENT PARTICIPATION.**

**PARENTAL INVOLVEMENT IN SCHOOL ADMINISTRATION. See SCHOOL MANAGEMENT AND ORGANIZATION - PARENT PARTICIPATION.**

**PARENTAL INVOLVEMENT IN SPECIAL EDUCATION. See SPECIAL EDUCATION - PARENT PARTICIPATION.**

**PARENTAL LEAVE. See MATERNITY LEAVE.**

**PARENTAL LEAVE - LAW AND LEGISLATION - UNITED STATES.**
Commission on Family and Medical Leave (U.S.) A

Workable balance. Washington, DC : Commission on Leave ; Women's Bureau, U.S. Dept. of Labor, [1996]
*TC HD5115.6.U5 C66 1996*

**PARENTAL LEAVE - UNITED STATES.**
Commission on Family and Medical Leave (U.S.) A Workable balance. Washington, DC : Commission on Leave ; Women's Bureau, U.S. Dept. of Labor, [1996]
*TC HD5115.6.U5 C66 1996*

**PARENTAL PARTICIPATION IN CHILDREN'S EDUCATION.** *See* **EDUCATION - PARENT PARTICIPATION.**

**PARENTAL PARTICIPATION IN CHILDREN'S READING.** *See* **READING - PARENT PARTICIPATION.**

**PARENTAL PARTICIPATION IN EARLY CHILDHOOD EDUCATION.** *See* **EARLY CHILDHOOD EDUCATION - PARENT PARTICIPATION.**

**PARENTAL PARTICIPATION IN ELEMENTARY EDUCATION.** *See* **EDUCATION, ELEMENTARY - PARENT PARTICIPATION.**

**PARENTAL PARTICIPATION IN PRESCHOOL EDUCATION.** *See* **EDUCATION, PRESCHOOL - PARENT PARTICIPATION.**

**PARENTAL PARTICIPATION IN SCHOOL ADMINISTRATION.** *See* **SCHOOL MANAGEMENT AND ORGANIZATION - PARENT PARTICIPATION.**

**PARENTAL PARTICIPATION IN SPECIAL EDUCATION.** *See* **SPECIAL EDUCATION - PARENT PARTICIPATION.**

**PARENTERAL FEEDING.**
Clinical nutrition. 2nd ed. Philadelphia : Saunders, 1993.
*TC RM224 .P24 1993* ·

**Parenteral nutrition.**
Clinical nutrition. 2nd ed. Philadelphia : Saunders, 1993.
*TC RM224 .P24 1993*

**PARENTERAL NUTRITION.**
Clinical nutrition. 2nd ed. Philadelphia : Saunders, 1993.
*TC RM224 .P24 1993*

**PARENTHOOD.** *See* **MOTHERHOOD; PARENTING.**

**PARENTHOOD - UNITED STATES - LONGITUDINAL STUDIES.**
Cowan, Carolyn Pape. When partners become parents. Mahwah, NJ : Lawrence Erlbaum Associates, 1999.
*TC HQ755.8 .C68 1999*

**Parenting.**
Golombok, Susan. London ; Philadelphia : Routledge, 2000.
*TC HQ755.8 .G655 2000*

Dacey, John S. Your anxious child. 1st ed. San Francisco : Jossey-Bass, c2000.
*TC BF723.A5 D33 2000*

Golombok, Susan. Parenting. London ; Philadelphia : Routledge, 2000.
*TC HQ755.8 .G655 2000*

Greenspan, Stanley I. Building healthy minds. Cambridge, MA : Perseus, 1999.
*TC HQ772 .G672 1999*

Handbook of infant mental health. New York : Wiley, c2000.
*TC RJ502.5 .H362 2000*

Levin, Diane E. Remote control childhood? Washington, D.C. : National Association for the Education of Young Children, c1998.
*TC P94.5.C55 L48 1998*

Understanding the defiant child [videorecording]. New York : Guilford Publications, c1997.
*TC HQ755.7 .U63 1997*

**PARENTING - BIBLIOGRAPHY.**
Infants & toddlers. 2nd ed. Seattle, Wash. : Resourse Pathways, 1999.
*TC HQ755.8 .I54 1999*

**PARENTING - CHINA - HONG KONG.**
Lam-Chan, Gladys Lan Tak. Parenting in stepfamilies. Aldershot ; Brookfield USA : Ashgate, c1999.
*TC HQ759.92 .L34 1999*

**Parenting education and support :** new opportunities / edited by Sheila Wolfendale and Hetty Einzig. London : David Fulton, c1999. viii, 168 p. : ill. ; 24 cm.

(Home and school--a working alliance) Includes bibliographical references and index. CONTENTS: Parenting education and the Social Policy Agenda / Gillian Pugh -- Review of the field : current trends, concepts and issues / Hetty Einzig -- Families and society : change and continuity / Janet Walker -- Parents as key determinants in planning and delivering parenting education and support programmes : an inclusive ideology / Sheila Wolfendale -- Being a parent : influences and effects upon parenting from the media / Lucy McCarraher -- Going critical : childhood, parenthood and the labour market / Peter Moss -- The emotional education of parents : attachment theory and emotional literacy / James Park -- Supporting parents through parenting programmes / Bopinder Samra -- Support for parents at significant times of transition / Sonya Hinton -- Parenting education and support : issues in multi-agency collaboration / Peter Jones -- 'She wants you to think for yourself, she doesn't want to give you the answers all the time' : parents on parenting education and support / Roger Grimshaw. ISBN 1-85346-579-8
*1. Parenting - Study and teaching - Great Britain. I. Einzig, Hetty. II. Wolfendale, Sheila, 1939- III. Series.*
*TC HQ755.7 .P374 1999*

**Parenting in stepfamilies.**
Lam-Chan, Gladys Lan Tak. Aldershot ; Brookfield USA : Ashgate, c1999.
*TC HQ759.92 .L34 1999*

**PARENTING OF TEENAGERS.** *See* **PARENT AND TEENAGER.**

**PARENTING, PART-TIME.** *See* **SINGLE PARENTS.**

**PARENTING - PSYCHOLOGY.**
Understanding the defiant child [videorecording]. New York : Guilford Publications, c1997.
*TC HQ755.7 .U63 1997*

**PARENTING - STUDY AND TEACHING - GREAT BRITAIN.**
Parenting education and support. London : David Fulton, c1999.
*TC HQ755.7 .P374 1999*

**PARENTING - STUDY AND TEACHING - PERIODICALS.**
[Child study (New York, N.Y.)] Child study. [New York City] : Federation for Child Study, 1925-1960.

**PARENTING - UNITED STATES.**
Elder, Glen H. Children of the land. Chicago : University of Chicago Press, 2000.
*TC HQ796 .E525 2000*

Hill, Shirley A. (Shirley Ann), 1947- African American children. Thousand Oaks, Calif. : Sage Publications, c1999.
*TC E185.86 .H665 1999*

Hoffman, Lois Norma Wladis, 1929- Mothers at work. Cambridge ; New York : Cambridge University Press, 1999.
*TC HQ759.48 .H63 1999*

Variability in the social construction of the child. San Francisco : Jossey-Bass, 2000.
*TC BF723.S62 .V37 2000*

**PARENTS.** *See also* **DIVORCED PARENTS; FATHERS; GAY PARENTS; GRANDPARENTS; HANDICAPPED PARENTS; MOTHERS; SINGLE PARENTS; STEPPARENTS.**
Parents' magazine. New York.

**PARENTS AND CHILDREN.** *See* **PARENT AND CHILD.**

**Parents and schools.**
Cutler, William W. Chicago : University of Chicago Press, 2000.
*TC LC225.3 .C86 2000*

**PARENTS AND TEACHERS.** *See* **PARENT-TEACHER RELATIONSHIPS.**

**PARENTS' AND TEACHERS' ASSOCIATIONS.** *See* **HOME AND SCHOOL.**

**Parents' and teachers' guides**
(no. 4) Knight, Pamela, 1940- The care and education of a deaf child. Clevedon [England] ; Buffalo [N.Y.] : Multilingual Matters, c1999.
*TC HV2716 .K65 1999*

**PARENTS AND TEENAGERS.** *See* **PARENT AND TEENAGER.**

**Parents as partners in education.**
Berger, Eugenia Hepworth. 5th ed. Upper Saddle River, N.J. : Merrill, c2000.
*TC LC225.3 .B47 2000*

**PARENTS - ATTITUDES.**
Nevas, Debra Baron. Factors affecting parental attitudes toward a child's therapist and therapy. 1997.
*TC 085 N401*

**PARENTS' CHOICE OF SCHOOL.** *See* **SCHOOL CHOICE.**

**PARENTS - DEATH - PSYCHOLOGICAL ASPECTS.**
Christ, Grace Hyslop. Healing children's grief. New York ; Oxford : Oxford University Press, 2000.
*TC BF723.G75 C58 2000*

**PARENTS - EMPLOYMENT.**
Organizational change & gender equity. Thousand Oaks : Sage Publications, c2000.
*TC HD58.8 .O7289 2000*

**PARENTS - EMPLOYMENT - FOREIGN COUNTRIES.**
Pollock, David C. The third culture kid experience. Yarmouth, Me. : Intercultural Press, c1999.
*TC HQ784.S56 P65 1999*

**Parents' magazine.** New York. v. ill. 28 cm. v. 1-53, no. 10; Oct. 1926-Oct. 1978. Title varies: Oct. 1926-July 1929, Children: the magazine for parents; Aug. 1953-Nov. 1959, Parents magazine and family home guide; Dec. 1959-June 1977, Parents magazine and better homemaking. Continued by: Parents; ISSN: 0195-0967. (IEN)AAN0160. ISSN 0161-4193
*1. Child development - Periodicals. 2. Child care - Periodicals. I. Title: Children: the magazine for parents. Oct. 1926-July 1929. II. Title: Parents magazine and family home guide. Aug. 1953-Nov. 1959. III. Title: Parents magazine and better homemaking. Dec. 1959-June 1977. IV. Title: Parents.*

**Parents magazine and better homemaking. Dec. 1959-June 1977.**
Parents' magazine. New York.

**Parents magazine and family home guide. Aug. 1953-Nov. 1959.**
Parents' magazine. New York.

**PARENTS OF DEAF CHILDREN.**
The deaf child in the family and at school. Mahwah, N.J. : Lawrence Erlbaum Associates, 2000.
*TC HV2392.2 .D43 2000*

**PARENTS OF EXCEPTIONAL CHILDREN - GREAT BRITAIN - BIOGRAPHY.**
Gregory, Jane, 1960- Bringing up a challenging child at home. London ; Philadelphia : Jessica Kingsley Publishers, 2000.
*TC HQ759.913 .G74 2000*

**PARENTS OF HANDICAPPED CHILDREN - COUNSELING OF.**
Seligman, Milton, 1937- Conducting effective conferences with parents of children with disabilities. New York : Guilford Press, c2000.
*TC LC4019 .S385 2000*

**PARENTS OF HANDICAPPED CHILDREN - SERVICES FOR - MEXICO.**
Helping individuals with disabilities and their families. Tempe, Ariz. : Bilingual Review/Press, c1999.
*TC LC4035.M6 H45 1999*

**PARENTS OF HANDICAPPED CHILDREN - SERVICES FOR - UNITED STATES.**
Bridging the family-professional gap. Springfield, Ill. : Charles C. Thomas, c1999.
*TC HV888.5 .B74 1999*

Helping individuals with disabilities and their families. Tempe, Ariz. : Bilingual Review/Press, c1999.
*TC LC4035.M6 H45 1999*

**PARENTS OF HANDICAPPED CHILDREN - UNITED STATES - FINANCE, PERSONAL.**
Pierangelo, Roger. Complete guide to special education transition services. West Nyack, NY : Center for Applied Research in Education, c1997.
*TC HV1569.3.Y68 P55 1997*

**PARENTS - PSYCHOLOGY.**
Golombok, Susan. Parenting. London ; Philadelphia : Routledge, 2000.
*TC HQ755.8 .G655 2000*

**PARENTS, SINGLE.** *See* **SINGLE PARENTS.**

**PARENTS - UNITED STATES - FINANCE, PERSONAL.**
Kane, Thomas J. The price of admission. Washington, D.C. : Brookings Institution Press ; New York : Russell Sage Foundation, c1999.
*TC LB2342 .K35 1999*

**PARENTS - UNITED STATES - LONGITUDINAL STUDIES.**
Cowan, Carolyn Pape. When partners become parents. Mahwah, NJ : Lawrence Erlbaum Associates, 1999.
*TC HQ755.8 .C68 1999*

**Pargament, Kenneth I. (Kenneth Ira), 1950-.**
Forgiveness. New York : Guilford Press, c1999.
*TC BF637.F67 F67 1999*

**Pari, Caroline.**
Education is politics. Portsmouth, NH : Boynton/Cook, c1999.
*TC LC196.5.U6 E36 1999*

**Paris 1900 :** the "American school" at the Universal Exposition / edited by Diane P. Fischer ; with essays by Linda J. Docherty ... [et al.]. New Brunswick, N.J. : Rutgers University Press ; Montclair, N.J. : Montclair Art Museum, c1999. xxii, 232 p. : ill. (some col.) ; 29 cm. Catalog of an exhibition held at the Montclair Art Museum and four other museums. Includes bibliographical references (p. 220-221) and index. ISBN 0-8135-2640-X (cloth : alk. paper) ISBN 0-8135-2641-8 (pbk. : alk. paper) DDC 709/.73/07444361
*1. Art, American - Exhibitions. 2. Art, Modern - 19h century - United States - Exhibitions. 3. Exposition universelle internationale de 1900 (Paris, France) I. Fischer, Diane Pietrucha. II. Docherty, Linda Jones. III. Montclair Art Museum.*
*TC N6510 .P28 1999*

**Paris, Bernard J.**
Horney, Karen, 1885-1952. The therapeutic process. New Haven : Yale University Press, c1999.
*TC RC509 .H674 1999*

The unknown Karen Horney. New Haven : Yale University Press, c2000.
*TC BF173 .U55 2000*

**Paris cat.**
Baker, Leslie A. 1st ed. Boston, Mass. : Little, Brown, c1999.
*TC PZ7.B1744 Par 1999*

**PARIS (FRANCE) - DESCRIPTION AND TRAVEL.**
Paris [videorecording]. New York, NY : V.I.E.W. Video, c1996.
*TC DC707 .P3 1996*

**PARIS (FRANCE) - FICTION.**
Baker, Leslie A. Paris cat. 1st ed. Boston, Mass. : Little, Brown, c1999.
*TC PZ7.B1744 Par 1999*

**PARIS (FRANCE) - HISTORY.**
Paris [videorecording]. New York, NY : V.I.E.W. Video, c1996.
*TC DC707 .P3 1996*

**Paris, Joel, 1940-** Myths of childhood / Joel Paris. Philadelphia, PA : Brunner/Mazel, c2000. xvii, 227 p. ; 23 cm. Includes bibliographical references (p. 201-219) and index. ISBN 0-87630-966-X (alk. paper) DDC 155
*1. Developmental psychology. 2. Nature and nurture. 3. Psychology, Pathological - Etiology. I. Title.*
*TC BF713 .P37 2000*

**Paris** [videorecording] : city of light / an LDJ production ; written and produced by Leah Jay ; directed and edited by Lou Tyrrell. New York, NY : V.I.E.W. Video, c1996. 1 videocassette (58 min.) : sd., col. ; 1/2 in. (View Video art series) (Museum city video) Subtitle on container: Tour of the city seen through the eys of its artists, architects and poet. VHS, Hi-fi, Stereo. Catalogued from credits and container. Narrators: Richard Levine, Kate Fuglei. Camera, Lou Tyrrell ; music, Lou Garisto. For adolescent through adult. SUMMARY: Traces Paris' history and culture through its architecture, monuments, museums and its most notable citizens. Stroll through the stately Luxembourg Gardens and the Rive Gauche, explore the gothic splendor of the Church of Notre Dame, and marvel at the masterpieces of French impressionism.
*1. Paris (France) - Description and travel. 2. Art - France - Paris. 3. Art museums - France - Paris. 4. Historic buildings - France - Paris. 5. Paris (France) - History. I. Jay, Leah. II. Tyrrell, Lou. III. Levine, Richard. IV. Fuglei, Kate. V. LDJ Productions Inc. VI. View Video. VII. Title: City of light [videorecording] VIII. Title: Tour of the city seen through the eys of its artists, architects and poet IX. Series. X. Series: Art series (View Video)*
*TC DC707 .P3 1996*

**PARISH SCHOOLS. See CHURCH SCHOOLS.**

**Park, Clara C., 1944-.**
Asian-American education. Westport, Conn. : Bergin & Garvey, 1999.
*TC LC2632 .A847 1999*

**Park, Denise C.**
Cognitive aging. Philadelphia, PA : Psychology Press, c2000.
*TC BF724.85.C64 A35 2000*

**Park, Namgi.**
Higher education in Korea. New York : Falmer Press, 2000.
*TC LA1333 .H54 2000*

**Parkay, Forrest W.**
Curriculum planning. 7th ed. Boston : Allyn and Bacon, c2000.
*TC LB2806.15 .C868 2000*

**Parke, Ross D.**
Hetherington, E. Mavis (Eileen Mavis), 1926- Child psychology. 5th ed. Boston : McGraw-Hill College, c1999.
*TC BF721 .H418 1999*

**Parker, Glenn M., 1938-** Cross-functional teams : working with allies, enemies, and other strangers / Glenn M. Parker. 1st ed. San Francisco, Calif. : Jossey-Bass, c1994. xxiv, 228 p. ; 24 cm. (The Jossey-Bass management series) Includes bibliographical references (p. 213-220) and index. ISBN 1-55542-609-3 DDC 658.4/02
*1. Cross-functional teams. 2. Intergroup relations. 3. Interorganizational relations. 4. Complex organizations. I. Title. II. Series.*
*TC HD66 .P345 1994*

**Parker, Ian. 1956-.**
Cyberpsychology. New York : Routledge, 1999.
*TC HM1033 .C934 1999*

**Parker, Ian, 1956-.**
Social constructionism, discourse, and realism. London ; Thousand Oaks, Calif. : SAGE Publications, 1998.
*TC HM251 .S671163 1998*

**Parker, James D. A. (James Donald Alexander), 1959-.**
The handbook of emotional intelligence. 1st ed. San Francisco, Calif. : Jossey-Bass, c2000.
*TC BF576 .H36 2000*

**Parker-Jenkins, Marie.** Sparing the rod : schools, discipline and children's rights / Marie Parker-Jenkins. Stoke-on-Trent : Trentham, 1999. xv, 195 p. ; 24 cm. Includes bibliographical references (p. 179-192) and index. Table of contents URL: http://www.mannlib.cornell.edu/cgi-bin/toc.cgi?arh9787 ISBN 1-85856-160-4 ISBN 1-85856-159-0 (pbk) DDC 371.5
*1. School discipline. 2. Children - Legal status, laws, etc. I. Title.*
*TC LB3012 .P37 1999*

**Parker, Laurence.**
Race is-- race isn't. Boulder, CO : Westview Press, c1999.
*TC LC3731 .R27 1999*

**Parker, Michael, 1958-.**
Ethics and community in the health care professions. London ; New York : Routledge, 1999.
*TC R725.5 .E87 1999*

**Parker, Nancy Winslow, ill.**
Blood, Charles L., 1929- The goat in the rug. New York : Four Winds Press, 1976.
*TC PZ7.B6227 Go 1976*

**Parker, Robert Andrew, ill.**
Bierhorst, John. The people with five fingers. New York : Marshall Cavendish, 2000.
*TC E78.C15 B523 2000*

**Parker, Woodrow M.**
Pack-Brown, Sherlon P. Images of me. Boston : Allyn and Bacon, c1998.
*TC HV1445 .P33 1998*

**Parkin, Alan J.** Memory, a guide for professionals / Alan J. Parkin. Chichester, England ; New York : J. Wiley, c1999. 160 p. : ill. ; 23 cm. Includes bibliographical references and index. ISBN 0-471-98302-0 (pbk.) DDC 153.1/2
*1. Memory. I. Title.*
*TC BF371 .P275 1999*

**PARKS - FICTION.**
Day, Alexandra. Carl's afternoon in the park. 1st ed. New York : Farrar, Straus & Giroux, 1991.
*TC PZ7.D32915 Cars 1991*

**Parks, Stephen, 1963-** Class politics : the movement for the students' right to their own language / Stephen Parks. Urbana, Ill. : National Council of Teachers of English, c2000. xviii, 353 p. ; 22 cm. (Refiguring English studies, 1037-9637) Includes bibliographical references and index. ISBN 0-8141-0678-1 DDC 808/.042/071073
*1. English language - Rhetoric - Study and teaching - Political*

aspects - United States. 2. Academic writing - Study and teaching (Higher) - Political aspects - United States. 3. Education, Higher - Political aspects - United States. 4. College students - United States - Political activity. 5. College students - United States - Language. 6. Interdisciplinary approach in education. I. Title. II. Series.
*TC PE1405.U6 P3 2000*

**Parks, Theodore E.**
Looking at looking. Thousand Oaks, Calif. : London : Sage Publications, c2001.
*TC BF241 .L64 2001*

**Parkyn, George W.** Success and failure at the university. Wellington, New Zealand Council for Educational Research, 1959-67. 2 v. : ill. ; 23 cm. (Educational research series, no. 38, 46) Bibliographical footnotes. CONTENTS: v. 1. Academic performance and the entrance standard.--v. 2. The problem of failure. DDC 371.2/6
*1. Prediction of scholastic success. I. Title. II. Series.*
*TC LB1131 .P29*

**PARLIAMENT, MEMBERS OF. See LEGISLATORS.**

**PARLIAMENTS. See LEGISLATIVE BODIES.**

**Parlor ladies and ebony drudges.**
Mack, Kibibi Voloria C. 1st ed. Knoxville : University of Tennessee Press, c1999.
*TC E279.06 M33 1999*

**PAROCHIAL SCHOOLS. See CHURCH SCHOOLS.**

**PAROUSIA (PHILOSOPHY). See MIND AND BODY.**

**Parpart, Jane L.**
Great ideas for teaching about Africa. Boulder : Lynne Rienner, 1999.
*TC DT19.9.U5 G74 1999*

**Parr, Susie, 1953-** Talking about aphasia : living with loss of language after stroke / Susie Parr, Sally Byng, and Sue Gilpin ; with Chris Ireland. Buckingham ; Philadelphia : Open University Press, 1997. xiii, 144 p. : ill. ; 24 cm. Includes bibliographical references (p. [143]-144). ISBN 0-335-19937-2 (hb) ISBN 0-335-19936-4 (pb) DDC 362.1/968552
*1. Aphasia. 2. Aphasia - Case studies. 3. Cerebrovascular disease - Complications. I. Byng, Sally, 1956- II. Gilpin, Sue. III. Ireland, Chris. IV. Title.*
*TC RC425 .P376 1997*

**Parrett, William.**
Barr, Robert D. Hope fulfilled for at-risk and violent youth. 2nd ed. Boston ; London : Allyn and Bacon, c2001.
*TC LC4802 .B37 2001*

Heart of the country [videorecording]. [New York, NY : First Run/Icarus Films, 1998].
*TC LB1565.H6 H3 1998*

**Parrish Art Museum.**
De Salvo, Donna M. Past imperfect. Southampton, N.Y. : Parrish Art Museum, in association with the New Press, New York, N.Y., c1993.
*TC N750 .D4*

**PARRISH ART MUSEUM - EXHIBITIONS.**
De Salvo, Donna M. Past imperfect. Southampton, N.Y. : Parrish Art Museum, in association with the New Press, New York, N.Y., c1993.
*TC N750 .D4*

**Parry, Kate.**
Culture, literacy, and learning English. Portsmouth, NH : Boynton/Cook Publishers, c1998.
*TC PE1130.C4 C85 1998*

From testing to assessment. London ; New York : Longman, 1994.
*TC PE1128.A2 F778 1994*

**Parsons, Kermit C. (Kermit Carlyle), 1927-.**
Stein, Clarence S. The writings of Clarence S. Stein. Baltimore, Md. : Johns Hopkins University Press, 1998.
*TC NA9108 .S83 1998*

**Parsons, Lynne.**
Hill, Fran, 1950- Teamwork in the management of emotional and behavioural difficulties. London : David Fulton, 2000.
*TC LC4803.G7 H54 2000*

**Parsons, William Barclay, 1955-** The enigma of the oceanic feeling : revisioning the psychoanalytic theory of mysticism / William B. Parsons. New York : Oxford University Press, 1999. ix, 252 p. ; 24 cm. Includes bibliographical references (p. 225-237) and index. ISBN 0-19-511508-2 (hardcover : alk. paper) DDC 291.4/22/019

*1. Psychoanalysis and religion. 2. Freud. Sigmund. - 1856-1939. I. Title.*
*TC BF175.4.R44 P37 1999*

**PART-TIME COLLEGE TEACHERS.** *See* **COLLEGE TEACHERS, PART-TIME.**

**PARTIAL HEARING.** *See* **HEARING IMPAIRED.**

**Partial recall** / edited by Lucy R. Lippard ; with essays on photographs of Native North Americans by Suzanne Benally ... [et al.] ; preface by Leslie Marmon Silko. 1st ed. New York : New Press : Distributed by W.W. Norton & Co., Inc., 1992. 199 p. : ill. ; 28 cm. Includes bibliographical references (p. 195). ISBN 1-56584-016-X ISBN 1-56584-041-0 (pbk.) DDC 970.004/97
*1. Indians of North America - Portraits. 2. Indians of North America - Pictorial works. 3. Indians of North America - Ethnic identity. I. Lippard, Lucy R. II. Benally, Suzanne.*
*TC E89 .P33 1992*

**PARTIALLY HEARING.** *See* **HEARING IMPAIRED.**

**PARTIALLY SEEING.** *See* **VISUALLY HANDICAPPED.**

**PARTIALLY-SEEING CHILDREN.** *See* **VISUALLY HANDICAPPED CHILDREN.**

**PARTIALLY SIGHTED.** *See* **VISUALLY HANDICAPPED.**

**PARTICIPANT OBSERVATION.**
O'Neil, Judith Ann. The role of the learning advisor in action learning. 1999.
*TC 06 no. 11156*

**PARTICIPANT OBSERVATION - PSYCHOLOGICAL ASPECTS.**
Behar, Ruth, 1956- The vulnerable observer. Boston : Beacon Press, c1996.
*TC GN346.4 .B44 1996*

**PARTICIPANT RESEARCH.** *See* **PARTICIPANT OBSERVATION.**

**PARTICIPATION BOOKS.** *See* **TOY AND MOVABLE BOOKS.**

**Participation in active euthanasia and assisted suicide and attitudes and interpersonal values of physicians and nurses.**
Lederer, Jane. 1996.
*TC 06 no. 10849*

**PARTICIPATION, POLITICAL.** *See* **POLITICAL PARTICIPATION.**

**PARTICIPATION, SOCIAL.** *See* **SOCIAL PARTICIPATION.**

**Participatory evaluation research in an urban middle school.**
Talking across boundaries. [New York] : [Bruner Foundation], 1996.
*TC LB1623.5 .T35 1996*

**PARTICIPATORY RESEARCH.** *See* **PARTICIPANT OBSERVATION.**

**PARTIES.** *See* **ENTERTAINING.**

**PARTIES - FICTION.**
Reid, Barbara. The party. New York : Scholastic Press, 1999.
*TC PZ8.3.R2665 Pat 1999*

**PARTIES, POLITICAL.** *See* **POLITICAL PARTIES.**

**PARTIES TO ACTIONS.** *See* **INTERVENTION (CIVIL PROCEDURE).**

**Partington, Alan.** Patterns and meanings : using corpora for English language research and teaching / Alan Partington. Amsterdam : Philadelphia : J. Benjamins Pub., c1998. vii, 162 p. ; 23 cm. (Studies in corpus linguistics, 1388-0373 ; v. 2) Includes bibliographical references (p. 151-158) and index. ISBN 1-55619-343-2 (alk. paper) ISBN 1-55619-396-3 (pbk. : alk. paper) DDC 420/.285
*1. English language - Research - Data processing. 2. English language - Discourse analysis - Data processing. 3. English language - Study and teaching - Data processing. 4. Computational linguistics. I. Title. II. Series.*
*TC PE1074.5 .P37 1998*

**Partnering dance and education.**
Hanna, Judith Lynne. Champaign, IL : Human Kinetics, c1999.
*TC GV1589 .H35 1999*

**Partners in progress** : strengthening the superintendent-board relationship / Rebecca Van der Bogert, editor-in-chief ; Matthew King, editor. San Francisco, Calif. : Jossey-Bass Inc., c1999. [6], 85 p. ; 23 cm. (New directions for school leadership, 1089-5612 ; no. 12) "Summer 1999." "Sponsored by the International Network

of Principals' Centers"--Cover. Includes bibliographical references and index.
*1. Special education - United States. I. King, Matthew Jay. II. Van der Bogert. Rebecca. III. Harvard University. Graduate School of Education. International Network of Principals' Centers. IV. Series: New directions for school leadership ; no. 12*
*TC LC3981 .P27 1999*

**The partnership model in human services.**
Darling, Rosalyn Benjamin. New York : Kluwer Academic/Plenum Publishers, c2000.
*TC HV43 .D2 2000*

**Partnerships in research, clinical, and educational settings** / edited by Roger Bibace, James J. Dillon, and Barbara Noel Dowds. Stamford, Conn. : Ablex Pub., c1999. xxvi, 317 p. ; 24 cm. (Advances in applied developmental psychology ; vol. 18) Includes bibliographical references and indexes. ISBN 1-56750-454-X (cloth) ISBN 1-56750-455-8 (pbk.) DDC 302
*1. Interpersonal relations. 2. Research - Psychological aspects. 3. Research - Social aspects. 4. Teacher-student relationships. 5. Physician and patient. I. Bibace. Roger. II. Dillon. James J. III. Dowds. Barbara Noel. IV. Series: Advances in applied developmental psychology (1993) ; v. 18.*
*TC HM1106 .P37 1999*

**Partnerships of possibility.**
Edgoose, Julian Miles. 1999.
*TC 085 E117*

**Partridge, Elizabeth.**
Dorothea Lange--a visual life. Washington : Smithsonian Institution Press, c1994.
*TC TR140.L3 D67 1994*

**The party.**
Reid, Barbara. New York : Scholastic Press, 1999.
*TC PZ8.3.R2665 Pat 1999*

**PASADENA (CALIF.) - BUILDINGS, STRUCTURES, ETC.**
Wyllie, Romy. Caltech's architectural heritage. Los Angeles : Balcony Press, c2000.
*TC NA6603 .W95 2000*

**Pass public issues discussion [videorecording] : Electoral College : Paul Dain at Andover High School in Michigan 1996.**
Reforming the Electoral College [videorecording]. [Boulder, Colo.? : Social Science Education Consortium?], c1996.
*TC H62.5.U5 R4 1996*

**Passages.**
Richards, J. C. (Jack Croft), 1943- Cambridge : Cambridge University Press, 2000.
*TC PE1128 .R4599 2000*

Richards, Jack C. Cambridge, U.K. ; New York : Cambridge University Press, 2000.
*TC PE1128 .R4599 2000*

**Passages to modernity.**
Uno, Kathleen S., 1951- Honolulu : University of Hawai'i Press, c1999.
*TC HQ778.7.J3 U56 1999*

**Passing and pedagogy.**
Caughie, Pamela L., 1953- Urbana : University of Illinois Press, c1999.
*TC PN61 .C38 1999*

**PASSING (IDENTITY).**
Caughie, Pamela L., 1953- Passing and pedagogy. Urbana : University of Illinois Press, c1999.
*TC PN61 .C38 1999*

**PASSING (IDENTITY) IN LITERATURE.**
Caughie, Pamela L., 1953- Passing and pedagogy. Urbana : University of Illinois Press, c1999.
*TC PN61 .C38 1999*

**PASSIONS.** *See* **EMOTIONS.**

**Passions, pedagogies, and 21st century technologies** / edited by Gail E. Hawisher, Cynthia L. Selfe. Logan : Utah State University Press ; Urbana, Ill. : National Council of Teachers of English, c1999. 452 p. : ill. ; 23 cm. Includes bibliographical references (p. [425]-[441]) and index. ISBN 0-87421-258-8 DDC 808/.042/07
*1. English language - Rhetoric - Study and teaching - Technological innovations. 2. English language - Rhetoric - Study and teaching - Data processing. 3. English language - Composition and exercises - Data processing. 4. Academic writing - Study and teaching - Technological innovations. 5. Academic writing - Study and teaching - Data processing. 6. Information technology. I. Hawisher, Gail E. II. Selfe, Cynthia L., 1951- III. National Council of Teachers of English. IV. Title: Passions, pedagogies, and twenty-first century technologies*
*TC PE1404 .P38 1999*

**Passions, pedagogies, and twenty-first century technologies.**
Passions, pedagogies, and 21st century technologies. Logan : Utah State University Press ; Urbana, Ill. : National Council of Teachers of English, c1999.
*TC PE1404 .P38 1999*

**PASSIVE RESISTANCE.**
Nonviolence in theory and practice. Belmont, Calif. : Wadsworth Pub. Co., c1990.
*TC HM278 .N67 1990*

**Past imperfect.**
De Salvo, Donna M. Southampton, N.Y. : Parrish Art Museum, in association with the New Press, New York, N.Y., c1993.
*TC N750 .D4*

**The past in the present.**
McCandless, Amy Thompson, 1946- Tuscaloosa : University of Alabama Press, c1999.
*TC LC1756 .M24 1999*

**Past masters (InteLex Corporation).**
Dewey, John, 1859-1952. The correspondence of John Dewey. [computer file]. Windows version. Charlottesville, VA : InteLex Corp., 1999- Computer data and program.
*TC B945.D44 A4 1999*

Dewey, John, 1859-1952. [Works.] The collected works of John Dewey, 1882-1953. [computer file]. Windows version. Charlottesville, VA : InteLex Corp, 1997, c1992. Computer program.
*TC LB875 .D363 1997*

**PASTA PRODUCTS - FICTION.**
Wright, Alexandra. Alice in Pastaland. Watertown, Mass. : Charlesbridge, 1997.
*TC PZ7.W9195 Al 19997*

**PASTIMES.** *See* **SPORTS.**

**Pastor, Maria del Pilar.**
Milbank Memorial Library story hour [videorecording]. [New York : Milbank Memorial Library, 1999].
*TC Z718.3 .M5 1999 Series 3 Prog. 11*

**PASTORAL ART - UNITED STATES.**
Kinsey, Joni. Plain pictures. Washington, : Published for the University of Iowa Museum of Art by the Smithsonian Institution Press, 1996.
*TC N8214.5.U6 K56 1996*

**PASTORAL COUNSELING - GREAT BRITAIN.**
King, Gail, 1949- Counselling skills for teachers. Buckingham [England] ; Philadelphia : Open University Press, 1999.
*TC LB1620.53.G7 K56 1999*

**PASTORAL PSYCHOLOGY.** *See* **PASTORAL COUNSELING.**

**Patel, Kant, 1946-.**
Rushefsky, Mark E., 1945- Politics, power & policy making. Armonk, N.Y. : M.E. Sharpe, c1998.
*TC RA395.A3 R855 1998*

**PATENT LAWS AND LEGISLATION.** *See* **COPYRIGHT.**

**PATERNAL BEHAVIOR IN ANIMALS.** *See* **PARENTAL BEHAVIOR IN ANIMALS.**

**PATERNAL DEPRIVATION - UNITED STATES.**
The role of the father in child development. 3rd ed. New York : Wiley, c1997
*TC HQ756 .R64 1997*

**PATERNITY.** *See* **PARENT AND CHILD (LAW).**

**PATERSON, KATHERINE. THE GREAT GILLY HOPKINS.**
Beech, Linda Ward. The great Gilly Hopkins by Katherine Paterson. New York : Scholastic, c1998.
*TC LB1573 .B439 1998*

**PATHOGENIC BACTERIA.** *See* **BACTERIAL DISEASES.**

**PATHOGNOMY.** *See* **EMOTIONS.**

**PATHOLOGICAL EATING.** *See* **EATING DISORDERS.**

**Pathological gambling.**
Castellani, Brian, 1966- Albany : State University of New York Press, c2000.
*TC RC569.5.G35 C37 2000*

**PATHOLOGICAL PSYCHOLOGY.** *See* **PSYCHOLOGY, PATHOLOGICAL.**

**PATHOLOGY.** *See* **DISEASES; MEDICINE; MEDICINE, PREVENTIVE.**

**Pathology and the postmodern :** mental illness as discourse and experience / edited by Dwight Fee. London ; Thousand Oaks : SAGE, 2000. xiii, 271 p. ; 24 cm. (Inquiries in social construction) Includes bibliographical references and index. ISBN 0-7619-5252-7 ISBN 0-7619-5253-5 (pbk.) DDC 616.89 DDC 616.89
*1. Mental illness. 2. Postmodernism. 3. Psychology, Pathological. I. Fee, Dwight. II. Series.*
**TC BF636 .P38 2000**

**Pathways into the Jungian world :** phenomenology and analytical psychology / edited by Roger Brooke. London ; New York : Routledge, 2000. xv, 278 p. : ill. ; 25 cm. Includes bibliographical references and index. ISBN 0-415-16998-4 (hbk.) ISBN 0-415-16999-2 (pbk.) DDC 150.19/54
*1. Psychoanalysis. 2. Jungian psychology. 3. Existential phenomenology. I. Brooke, Roger, 1953-*
**TC BF175 .P29 2000**

**Pathways to culture :** readings on teaching culture in the foreign language class / edited by Paula R. Heusinkveld. Yarmouth, ME : Intercultural Press, c1997. xxxii, 666 p. ; 24 cm. Includes bibliographical references and indexes. ISBN 1-87786-448-X DDC 418/.007
*1. Language and languages - Study and teaching. 2. Language and culture - Study and teaching. I. Heusinkveld, Paula Rae.*
**TC P53 .P37 1997**

**PATIENT AND MEDICAL PERSONNEL.** *See* **MEDICAL PERSONNEL AND PATIENT.**

**PATIENT CARE - PSYCHOLOGY - NURSES' INSTRUCTION.**
Russell, Graham, 1954- Essential psychology for nurses and other health professionals. London ; New York : Routledge, c1999.
**TC R726.7 .R87 1999**

**PATIENT-CENTERED CARE.**
Binnie, Alison. Freedom to practise. Oxford ; Boston : Butterworth-Heinemann, 1999.
**TC RT41 .B56 1999**

**PATIENT COMPLIANCE.**
Fenichel, Ann. The relationship between health care clinicians' relational abilities and psychosocial orientation to patient care, and patient adherence with medical treatment. 1998.
**TC 085 F352**

**PATIENT COMPLIANCE - PSYCHOLOGY.**
Russell, Graham, 1954- Essential psychology for nurses and other health professionals. London ; New York : Routledge, c1999.
**TC R726.7 .R87 1999**

**PATIENT EDUCATION.** *See also* **INFORMED CONSENT (MEDICAL LAW).**
Redman, Barbara Klug. Women's health needs in patient education. New York : Springer Pub. Co., c1999.
**TC R727.4 .R43 1999**

**PATIENT EDUCATION.**
Redman, Barbara Klug. Women's health needs in patient education. New York : Springer Pub. Co., c1999.
**TC R727.4 .R43 1999**

**PATIENT OUTCOME ASSESSMENT.** *See* **OUTCOME ASSESSMENT (MEDICAL CARE).**

**PATIENT PARTICIPATION.**
Baker, Susan Keane. Managing patient expectations. San Francisco : Jossey Bass Publishers, 1998.
**TC R727.3 .B28 1998**

**PATIENT PARTICIPATION.**
Bohart, Arthur C. How clients make therapy work. 1st ed. Washington, DC : American Psychological Association, c1999.
**TC RC480.5 .B64 1999**

**PATIENT SATISFACTION.**
Baker, Susan Keane. Managing patient expectations. San Francisco : Jossey Bass Publishers, 1998.
**TC R727.3 .B28 1998**

**PATIENT SATISFACTION.**
Baker, Susan Keane. Managing patient expectations. San Francisco : Jossey Bass Publishers, 1998.
**TC R727.3 .B28 1998**

Quality of life from nursing and patient perspectives. Sudbury, Mass. ; London : Jones and Bartlett, c1998.
**TC RC262 .Q34 1998**

**PATIENT SATISFACTION.**
Shelton, Patrick J. Measuring and improving patient satisfaction. Gaithersburg, Md. : Aspen Publishers, 2000.

**TC RA399.A1 S47 2000**

**PATIENT SATISFACTION.**
Shelton, Patrick J. Measuring and improving patient satisfaction. Gaithersburg, Md. : Aspen Publishers, 2000.
**TC RA399.A1 S47 2000**

**PATIENT SATISFACTION - TESTING.**
Gill, Kenneth Joseph. Social psychological artifacts in the measurement of consumer satisfaction with health care. 1996.
**TC 085 G396**

**PATIENTS.** *See* **HOSPITAL PATIENTS; MEDICAL PERSONNEL AND PATIENT; NURSING HOME PATIENTS; SICK.**

**PATIENTS IN PSYCHIATRIC HOSPITALS.** *See* **PSYCHIATRIC HOSPITAL PATIENTS.**

**PATIENTS - PSYCHOLOGY.**
Nursing and the experience of illness. London ; New York : Routledge, 1999.
**TC RT86 .N886 1999**

**PATIENTS - PSYCHOLOGY.**
Russell, Graham, 1954- Essential psychology for nurses and other health professionals. London ; New York : Routledge, c1999.
**TC R726.7 .R87 1999**

**PATRIARCHY.** *See* **FAMILY.**

**Patrick, Cynthia L.**
Calfee, Robert C. Teach your children well. Stanford, CA : Stanford Alumni Association, c1995.
**TC LB2822.82 .C32 1995**

**Patrick's dinosaurs on the Internet.**
Carrick, Carol. New York : Clarion Books, 1999.
**TC PZ7.C2344 Patf 1999**

**Patrinos, Harry Anthony.** Decentralization of education : demand-side financing / Harry Anthony Patrinos, David Lakshmanan Ariasingam. Washington, D.C. : World Bank, c1997. vii, 50 p. : ill. ; 23 cm. (Directions in development) Includes bibliographical references (p. 47-50). ISBN 0-8213-3930-3 (pbk.) DDC 379.1/2/091724
*1. Education - Developing countries - Finance. 2. Federal aid to education - Developing countries. 3. Educational vouchers - Developing countries. I. Ariasingam, David Lakshmanan. 1963- II. Title. III. Series: Directions in development (Washington, D.C.)*
**TC LB2826.6.D44 P38 1997**

**PATRIOTISM.** *See* **NATIONALISM.**

**Patriotism, politics, and popular liberalism in nineteenth-century Mexico.**
Thomson, Guy P. C., 1949- Wilmington, De. : Scholarly Resources, 1999.
**TC F1326.L83 T5 1999**

**PATRONAGE OF ART.** *See* **ART PATRONAGE.**

**PATTERN.** *See* **EXAMPLE.**

**PATTERN PERCEPTION - CONGRESSES.**
International Federation of Classification Societies. Conference. 5th, 1996, Kobe, Japan. Data science, classification, and related methods :. Tokyo ; New York : Springer, c1998.
**TC QA278 I53 1996**

MLDM'99 (1999 : Leipzig, Germany) Machine learning and data mining in pattern recognition. Berlin ; New York : Springer, c1999.
**TC Q327 .M56 1999**

**PATTERN RECOGNITION.** *See* **PATTERN PERCEPTION.**

**Patterns and meanings.**
Partington, Alan. Amsterdam ; Philadelphia : J. Benjamins Pub., c1998.
**TC PE1074.5 .P37 1998**

**Patterson, Lewis E.** The counseling process / Lewis E. Patterson, Elizabeth Reynolds Welfel. 5th ed. Belmont, CA : Brooks/Cole - Wadsworth, 1999. xi. 369 p. ; 24 cm. Includes bibliographical references and indexes. ISBN 0-534-35866-7 (pbk. : alk. paper) DDC 158/.3
*1. Counseling. I. Welfel, Elizabeth Reynolds, 1949- II. Title.*
**TC BF637.C6 P325 1999**

**Patterson, Robert S.**
Osguthorpe, Russell T. Balancing the tensions of change. Thousand Oaks, Calif. : Corwin Press, c1998.
**TC LB2331.53 .O74 1998**

**Paul Dain at Andover High School in Michigan [videorecording].**
Reforming the Electoral College [videorecording]. [Boulder, Colo.? : Social Science Education Consortium?], c1996.

**TC H62.5.U5 R4 1996**

**Paul, Dierdre Glenn, 1964-** Raising Black children who love reading and writing : a guide from birth through grade six / Dierdre Glenn Paul ; foreword by Catherine Dorsey-Gaines. Westport, Conn. : Bergin & Garvey, 2000. xvii, 168 p. : ill. ; 24 cm. Includes bibliographical references (p. [161]-164) and index. ISBN 0-89789-555-X (alk. paper) DDC 649/.58
*1. Afro-Americans - Education (Elementary) 2. Afro-Americans - Education (Early childhood) 3. Language arts (Elementary) - United States. 4. Language arts (Early childhood) - United States. I. Title.*
**TC LC2778.L34 P28 2000**

**Paul, James L.**
Stories out of school. Stamford, Conn. : Ablex Pub., c2000.
**TC LC196 .S6994 2000**

**Paul, Nora.** Great scouts! : cyberguides for subject searching on the Web / by Nora Paul & Margot Williams ; edited by Paula Hane. Medford, NJ : Information Today, c1999. xiii, 343 p. ; 24 cm. ISBN 0-910965-27-7 (pbk.) DDC 025.04
*1. Internet searching. I. Williams, Margot. II. Hane, Paula. III. Title.*
**TC ZA4201 .P38 1999**

**Paul, Susan, fl. 1837.** Memoir of James Jackson, the attentive and obedient scholar, who died in Boston, October 31, 1833, aged six years and eleven months / by his teacher, Miss Susan Paul ; edited by Lois Brown. Cambridge, MA : Harvard University Press, 2000. ix, 169 p. : ill. map. ; 20 cm. (The John Harvard library) Originally published in 1835. Includes bibliographical references. DDC 974.4/6100496073/0092
*1. Jackson, James - 1826-1833. 2. Afro-American children - Massachusetts - Boston - Biography. 3. Free Afro-Americans - Massachusetts - Boston - Biography. 4. Boston (Mass.) - Biography. 5. Afro-American children - Education - Massachusetts - Boston - History - 19th century. 6. Afro-American children - Massachusetts - Boston - Social conditions - 19th century. I. Brown, Lois, 1966- II. Title. III. Title: Memoir of James Jackson IV. Series.*
**TC F73.9.N4 P38 2000**

**Pauline.**
Hallensleben, Georg. New York : Farrar, Straus & Giroux, c1999.
**TC PZ7.H15425 Pau 1999**

**PAULSEN, GARY. HATCHET.**
Beech, Linda Ward. Hatchet by Gary Paulsen. New York : Scholastic, c1998.
**TC LB1573 .B4310 1998**

Soldier's heart : a novel of the Civil War / Gary Paulsen. New York : Delacorte Press, c1998. xv, 106 p. : ill. map ; 20 cm. "Being the story of the enlistment and due service of the boy Charley Goddard in the First Minnesota Volunteers." SUMMARY: Eager to enlist, fifteen-year-old Charley has a change of heart after experiencing both the physical horrors and mental anguish of Civil War combat. ISBN 0-385-32498-7 DDC [Fic]
*1. United States - History - Civil War, 1861-1865 - Juvenile fiction. 2. United States - History - Civil War, 1861-1865 - Fiction. 3. Post-traumatic stress disorder - Fiction. I. Title.*
**TC PZ7.P2843 So 1998**

**Paulson, Ronald.**
Hogarth, William, 1697-1764. The analysis of beauty. New Haven, Conn. : Published for the Paul Mellon Centre for British Art by Yale University Press, c1997.
**TC BH181 .H6 1997**

**PAUPERISM.** *See* **POOR.**

**Pauwels, Colleen Kristl, 1946-** Legal research : traditional sources, new technologies / Colleen Kristl Pauwels, Linda K. Fariss, Keith Buckley ; introduction by Fred H. Cate. Bloomington, Ind. : Phi Delta Kappa Educational Foundation, c1999. 91 p. ; 23 cm. Includes bibliographical references. ISBN 0-87367-814-1 DDC 340/.07/2073
*1. Legal research - United States. I. Fariss, Linda K., 1951- II. Buckley, Keith. III. Title.*
**TC KF240 .P38 1999**

**Pawlas, George.**
Oliva, Peter F. Supervision for today's schools. 6th ed. New York ; Chichester [England] : J. Wiley & Sons, c2001.
**TC LB2806.4 .O43 2001**

**Payne, C. F., ill.**
Moss, Marissa. True heart. 1st ed. San Diego : Silver Whistle, c1999.
**TC PZ7.M8535 Tr 1999**

**Payne Educational Sociology Foundation.**
The Journal of educational sociology. [New York : American Viewpoint Society, Inc., 1927-1963]

[Journal of educational sociology (Online)] The journal of educational sociology [computer file]. New York, N.Y. : American Viewpoint Society, Inc., 1927-1963.
*TC EJOURNALS*

**Payne, Joseph N. (Joseph Neal)** Elementary mathematics 4 / [by] Joseph N. Payne [and others] in consultation with John R. Clark. Teachers' ed. New York : Harcourt, Brace & World, 1966. T59, v, 346 p. : ill. (some col.) : 24 cm. Includes index. CONTENTS: Part one. Teaching mathematics in grade 4 -- Part two. Pupil's textbook pages with answers and teaching suggestions.
*1. Arithmetic - Problems, exercises, etc. 2. Arithmetic - Study and teaching (Elementary) I. Title: Elementary mathematics four*
*TC QA107 .E43 1966 Teacher's Ed.*

**PBL (PROBLEM-BASED LEARNING).** *See* **PROBLEM-BASED LEARNING.**

**PBS Video.**
Stephen Hawking's universe [videorecording]. [Alexandria, Va.] : PBS Video; Burbank, CA : Distributed by Warner Home Video, c1997.
*TC QB982 .S7 1997*

**A PC for the teacher.**
Brownell, Gregg. Belmont, CA : Wadsworth Pub. Co., c1999.
*TC LB1028.43 .B755 1999*

**Pcholko, A.S.**
Russian grade 3 mathematics. Chicago : University of Chicago School of Mathematics Project, 1992.
*TC QA14.R9 R8811 1992*

**PCS (MICROCOMPUTERS).** *See* **MICROCOMPUTERS.**

**PEACE.** *See also* **INTERNATIONAL EDUCATION; SOCIOLOGY, MILITARY; WAR; WOMEN AND PEACE; YOUTH AND PEACE.**
Miall, Hugh. Contemporary conflict resolution. Cambridge, UK : Polity Press ; Malden, MA : Blackwell, 1999.
*TC JZ6010 .M53 1999*

**Peace and power.**
Chinn, Peggy L. 5th ed. Boston : Jones and Bartlett Publishers, c2001.
*TC HQ1426 .W454 2001*

**PEACE AND WOMEN.** *See* **WOMEN AND PEACE.**

**PEACE AND YOUTH.** *See* **YOUTH AND PEACE.**

**PEACE MOVEMENTS IN LITERATURE.**
True, Michael. An energy field more intense than war. 1st ed. Syracuse, N.Y. : Syracuse University Press, 1995.
*TC PS169.N65 T78 1995*

**PEACE OF MIND.** *See* **CONTENTMENT.**

**PEACE OFFICERS.** *See* **POLICE.**

**PEACE - STUDY AND TEACHING.**
How children understand war and peace. 1st ed. San Francisco : Jossey-Bass, c1999.
*TC JZ5534 .H69 1999*

**PEACE - STUDY AND TEACHING - UNITED STATES.**
The developmental process of positive attitudes and mutual respect. Lewiston, N.Y. : E. Mellen Press, c1999.
*TC LB2822.82 .D49 1999*

Peacebuilding for adolescents. New York : P. Lang, c1999.
*TC JZ5534 .P43 1999*

**Peacebuilding for adolescents :** strategies for educators and community leaders / edited by Linda Rennie Forcey and Ian Murray Harris. New York : P. Lang, c1999. xi, 364 p. : ill. ; 23 cm. (Adolescent cultures, school & society, 1091-1464 ; vol. 2) Includes bibliographical references (p. [331]-339) and index. ISBN 0-8204-3745-X (alk. paper) DDC 327.1/72/07
*1. Peace - Study and teaching - United States. 2. Youth and peace - United States. 3. School violence - United States - Prevention. I. Forcey, Linda Rennie. II. Harris, Ian M., 1943- III. Series.*
*TC JZ5534 .P43 1999*

**PEACEFUL COEXISTENCE.** *See* **INTERNATIONAL RELATIONS; PEACE; WORLD POLITICS - 1945-.**

**Peak with books.**
Nelsen, Marjorie R. 3rd ed. Thousand Oaks, Calif. : Corwin Press, c1999.
*TC Z1037.A1 N347 1999*

**PEANUT BUTTER.**
Robbins, Ken. Make me a peanut butter sandwich and a glass of milk. New York : Scholastic, c1992.
*TC TX814.5.P38 R63 1992*

**PEANUT BUTTER - JUVENILE LITERATURE.**
Robbins, Ken. Make me a peanut butter sandwich and a glass of milk. New York : Scholastic, c1992.
*TC TX814.5.P38 R63 1992*

**PEANUT PRODUCTS.** *See* **PEANUT BUTTER.**

**PEANUTS.**
Robbins, Ken. Make me a peanut butter sandwich and a glass of milk. New York : Scholastic, c1992.
*TC TX814.5.P38 R63 1992*

**PEANUTS - JUVENILE LITERATURE.**
Robbins, Ken. Make me a peanut butter sandwich and a glass of milk. New York : Scholastic, c1992.
*TC TX814.5.P38 R63 1992*

**Pearce, Benjamin W.** Senior living communities : operations management and marketing for assisted living, congregate, and continuing care retirement communities / Benjamin W. Pearce. Baltimore : Johns Hopkins University Press, 1998. xi, 353 p. : ill. ; 28 cm. Includes bibliographical references (p. 347) and index. ISBN 0-8018-5961-1 (pbk. : alk. paper) DDC 362.1/6/068
*1. Congregate housing - United States - Management. 2. Life care communities - United States - Management. 3. Aged - Care - United States. 4. Frail elderly - Care - United States. I. Title.*
*TC HD7287.92.U54 P4 1998*

**Pearce, Charles R.** Nurturing inquiry : real science for the elementary classroom / Charles R. Pearce ; foreword by Wendy Saul. Portsmouth, NH : Heinemann, c1999. xii, 148 p. : ill. ; 24 cm. Includes bibliographical references (p. 141-144) and index. ISBN 0-325-00135-9 DDC 372.3/5/044
*1. Science - Study and teaching (Elementary) 2. Science - Methodology. I. Title.*
*TC LB1584 .P34 1999*

**Pearce, Susan M.** Archaeological curatorship / Susan M. Pearce. Washington, D.C. : Smithsonian Institution Press, 1996. xvi, 223 p. : ill. ; 24 cm. (Leicester Museum Studies Series) Includes bibliographical references (p. 208-219) and index. ISBN 1-56098-632-8
*1. Museums - Administration. 2. Archaeological museums and collections - Administration. 3. Archaeological museums and collections - Great Britain - Administration. 4. Archaeology - History - Sources - Exhibitions - Handbooks, manuals, etc. 5. Museum techniques. I. Title. II. Series.*
*TC AM7 .P43 1996*

**Pearl, Judea.** Causality : models, reasoning, and inference / Judea Pearl. Cambridge ; New York : Cambridge University Press, 2000. xvi, 384 p. : ill. ; 26 cm. Includes bibliographical references (p. 359-373) and indexes. ISBN 0-521-77362-8 (hardback) DDC 122
*1. Causation. 2. Probabilities. I. Title.*
*TC BD541 .P43 2000*

**Pearlin, Leonard I. (Leonard Irving), 1924-.**
Caregiving systems. Hillsdale, N.J. : L. Erlbaum Associates, 1993.
*TC HV1451 .C329 1993*

**Pearlman, Ellen.**
Sikes, Alfred C. Fast forward. 1st ed. New York : William Morrow, 2000.
*TC HM851 .S545 2000*

**The pearly gates of cyberspace.**
Wertheim, Margaret. 1st ed. New York : W.W. Norton, c1999.
*TC QA76.9.C66 W48 1999*

**Pearson, Jacqueline, 1949-** Women's reading in Britain, 1750-1835 : a dangerous recreation / Jacqueline Pearson. Cambridge, UK ; New York : Cambridge University Press, 1999. x, 300 p. ; 24 cm. Includes bibliographical references (p. 221-284) and index. ISBN 0-521-58439-6 DDC 828/.608099287
*1. English prose literature - 18th century - History and criticism. 2. Women - Great Britain - Books and reading - History - 18th century. 3. English prose literature - 19th century - History and criticism. 4. Women - Great Britain - Books and reading - History - 19th century. 5. Women and literature - Great Britain - History - 18th century. 6. Women and literature - Great Britain - History - 19th century. 7. Authors and readers - Great Britain - History - 18th century. 8. Authors and readers - Great Britain - History - 19th century. 9. Literature - Appreciation - Great Britain - History. 10. Books and reading in literature. I. Title.*

**Pearson, Jennifer.** Terms in context / Jennifer Pearson. Amsterdam ; Philadelphia : J. Benjamins, c1998. xii, 242 p. ; 23 cm. (Studies in corpus linguistics, 1388-0373 ; v. 1) Based on the author's thesis. Includes bibliographical references (p. [211]-222) and index. ISBN 1-55619-342-4 (alk. paper) DDC 401/.4
*1. Terms and phrases - Data processing. 2. Semantics. 3. Lexicography. I. Title. II. Series.*
*TC P305.18.D38 P4 1998*

**Pearson, John.**
Telematics in education. 1st ed. Amsterdam ; New York ; Oxford : Pergamon, 1999.
*TC LB1044.84 .T48 1999*

**Pearson, P. David.**
Handbook of reading research. New York : Longman, c1984-<2000 >
*TC LB1050 .H278 2000*

**Pearson, Ruth.**
Feminist visions of development. London ; New York : Routledge, c1998.
*TC HQ1240 .F464 1998*

**Peasant and French.**
Lehning, James R., 1947- Cambridge [England] ; New York : Cambridge University Press, 1995.
*TC DC34 .L5 1995*

**PEASANT ART.** *See* **FOLK ART.**

**PEASANT UPRISINGS - EL SALVATOR - HISTORY.**
Ripton, John R. Export agriculture and social crisis. 1997.
*TC 085 R48*

**PEASANTRY.** *See* **PEASANT UPRISINGS.**

**PEASANTRY - DEVELOPING COUNTRIES - ECONOMIC CONDITIONS.**
The paradox of plenty. Oakland, Calif. : Food First Books, c1999.
*TC HD1542 .P37 1999*

**PEASANTRY - EL SALVATOR - HISTORY.**
Ripton, John R. Export agriculture and social crisis. 1997.
*TC 085 R48*

**PEASANTRY - FRANCE - POLITICAL ACTIVITY.**
Lehning, James R., 1947- Peasant and French. Cambridge [England] ; New York : Cambridge University Press, 1995.
*TC DC34 .L5 1995*

**PEASANTS.** *See* **PEASANTRY.**

**PEASANTS' UPRISINGS.** *See* **PEASANT UPRISINGS.**

**Peat, F. David, 1938-** Infinite potential : the life and times of David Bohm / F. David Peat. Reading, Mass. : Addison Wesley, c1997. viii, 353 p. : ill. ; 24 cm. (Helix books) Includes bibliographical references and index. ISBN 0-201-40635-7 DDC 530/.092
*1. Bohm, David. 2. Physicists - United States - Biography. I. Title.*
*TC QC16.B627 P43 1997*

**Peatling, John H.** Career development : designing self / John H. Peatling, David V. Tiedeman. Muncie, Ind. : Accelerated Development, c1977. ix, 230 p. ; 23 cm. Includes bibliographical references (p.213-216) and index. ISBN 0-915202-09-3 DDC 158
*1. Self. 2. Personality. 3. Psychology - Data processing. 4. Group theory. 5. Vocational guidance. I. Tiedeman, David V., joint author. II. Title.*
*TC BF697 .P384*

**PEB papers**
Programme on Educational Building. Strategic asset management for tertiary institutions. Paris : Organisation for Economic Co-operation and Development, c1999.
*TC LB3223 .P76 1999*

**Peccei, Jean Stilwell.** Child language / Jean Stilwell Peccei. 2nd ed. London ; New York : Routledge, 1999. ix, 116 p. ; 25 cm. (Language workbooks) Includes bibliographical references (p. 89-93) and index. ISBN 0-415-19836-4 DDC 401/.93
*1. Language acquisition. I. Title. II. Series.*
*TC P118 .P38 1999*

**PECK, ALICE, 1855-1943.**
McLeod, Ellen Mary Easton, 1945- In good hands. Montreal ; Ithaca : Published for Carleton University by McGill-Queen's University Press, c1999.
*TC NK841 .M38 1999*

**Peck, Bob, 1945-.**
Picasso [videorecording]. Chicago, IL : Home Vision, c1986.
*TC N6853.P5 P52 1986*

**Peck, David R.** American ethnic literatures : native American, African American, Chicano/Latino, and Asian American writers and their backgrounds : an annotated bibliography / David R. Peck. Pasadena, Calif. : Salem Press, c1992. xii, 218 p. ; 24 cm. (Magill bibliographies) Includes index. ISBN 0-89356-684-5 (alk. paper) DDC 016.8109/920693
*1. American literature - Minority authors - Bibliography. 2. Hispanic Americans in literature - Bibliography. 3. Asian Americans in literature - Bibliography. 4. Afro-Americans in literature - Bibliography. 5. Ethnic groups in literature - Bibliography. 6. Indians in literature - Bibliography. I. Title. II. Series.*
*TC Z1229.E87 P43 1992*

**Pecora, Norma Odom.**
Growing up girls. New York : P. Lang, c1999.
*TC HQ798 .G76 1999*

**The pedagogical contract.**
Too, Yun Lee. Ann Arbor: University of Michigan Press, c2000.
*TC LB1033 .T66 2000*

**Pedagogical pleasures.**
McWilliam, Erica. New York ; Canterbury [England] : P. Lang, c1999.
*TC LB1775 .M319 1999*

**PEDAGOGY.** *See* **EDUCATION; EDUCATION - STUDY AND TEACHING; TEACHING.**

**Pedagogy of freedom.**
Freire, Paulo, 1921- [Pedagogia de autonomia. English] Lanham : Rowman & Littlefield Publishers, c1998.
*TC LC196 .F73713 1998*

**PEDDLERS AND PEDDLING - FICTION.**
Schur, Maxine. [Shnook the peddler] The peddler's gift. 1st ed. New York : Dial Books for Young Readers, 1999.
*TC PZ7.S3964 Pe 1999*

**The peddler's gift.**
Schur, Maxine. [Shnook the peddler] 1st ed. New York : Dial Books for Young Readers, 1999.
*TC PZ7.S3964 Pe 1999*

**Peden, Creighton, 1935-.**
Freedom, equality, and social change. Lewiston : E. Mellen Press, c1989.
*TC HM216 .F83 1989*

Rights, justice, and community. Lewiston, N.Y., USA : Edwin Mellen Press, c1992.
*TC HM216 .R56 1992*

**Pedersen, Bente Klarlund, 1956-.**
Nutrition and exercise immunology. Boca Raton, Fla. ; London : CRC Press, c2000.
*TC QP301 .N875 2000*

**Pederson, Eric.**
Language and conceptualization. 1st paperback ed. Cambridge [England] ; New York : Cambridge University Press, 1999.
*TC P37 .L354 1999*

**PEDIATRIC AIDS.** *See* **AIDS (DISEASE) IN CHILDREN.**

**PEDIATRIC CLINICS.** *See* **CHILD GUIDANCE CLINICS.**

**PEDIATRIC MENTAL HEALTH.** *See* **CHILD MENTAL HEALTH.**

**PEDIATRIC NEUROLOGY.** *See* **CHILD PSYCHIATRY; COMMUNICATIVE DISORDERS IN CHILDREN.**

**PEDIATRIC NEUROLOGY - DIAGNOSIS.**
Dubowitz, Lilly M. S. The neurological assessment of the preterm and full-term newborn infant. 2nd ed. London : Mac Keith, 1999.
*TC RJ486 .D85 1999*

**PEDIATRIC NEUROPSYCHIATRY.**
The effects of early adversity on neurobehavioral development. Mahwah, N.J. : L. Erlbaum Associates, 2000.
*TC RJ499 .E34 2000*

**PEDIATRIC NEUROPSYCHOLOGY.**
Bruer, John T., 1949- The myth of the first three years. New York : Free Press, c1999.
*TC BF318 .B79 1999*

Shore, Rima. Rethinking the brain. New York : Families and Work Institute, c1997.

*TC RJ486.5 .S475 1997*

**Pediatric neuroscience.**
Child's brain. Basel, New York, Karger.

**PEDIATRIC NURSING.**
Pringle, Sheila M. Promoting the health of children. St. Louis : Mosby, 1982.
*TC RJ101 .P66 1982*

Pringle, Sheila M. Promoting the health of children. St. Louis : Mosby, 1982.
*TC RJ101 .P66 1982*

**PEDIATRIC NURSING - HANDBOOKS, MANUALS, ETC.**
Pocket reference for Pediatric primary care. Philadelphia : London : Saunders, c2001.
*TC RJ45 .P525 2001*

**PEDIATRIC NUTRITION.** *See* **CHILDREN - NUTRITION.**

**PEDIATRIC PHARMACOLOGY.** *See also* **PEDIATRIC PSYCHOPHARMACOLOGY.**
Brown, Ronald T. Medications for school-age children. New York : Guilford Press, c1998.
*TC RJ560 .B76 1998*

**Pediatric primary care.**
Pocket reference for Pediatric primary care. Philadelphia ; London : Saunders, c2001.
*TC RJ45 .P525 2001*

**PEDIATRIC PSYCHIATRY.** *See* **CHILD PSYCHIATRY.**

**PEDIATRIC PSYCHOPHARMACOLOGY - POPULAR WORKS.**
Wilens, Timothy E. Straight talk about psychiatric medications for kids . New York : Guilford Press, c1999.
*TC RJ504.7 .W54 1999*

**PEDIATRIC PSYCHOPHARMACOLOGY - SOCIAL ASPECTS.**
Roemmelt, Arthur F., 1944- Haunted children. Albany : State University of New York Press, c1998.
*TC RJ504 .R64 1998*

**PEDIATRICS.** *See also* **CHILDREN - DISEASES; CHILDREN - HEALTH AND HYGIENE.**
20 common problems in pediatrics. New York : McGraw-Hill, Health Professions Division, c2001.
*TC RJ45.T9 2001*

**PEDIATRICS - HANDBOOKS, MANUALS, ETC.**
Pocket reference for Pediatric primary care. Philadelphia : London : Saunders, c2001.
*TC RJ45 .P525 2001*

**PEDIATRICS - UNITED STATES - HANDBOOKS.**
Pocket reference for Pediatric primary care. Philadelphia : London : Saunders, c2001.
*TC RJ45 .P525 2001*

**PEDIGREES.** *See* **GENEALOGY.**

**PEDOLOGY (CHILD STUDY).** *See* **CHILDREN.**

**Peer coaching for educators.**
Gottesman, Barbara Little. 2nd ed. Lanham, Md. : Scarecrow Press, 2000.
*TC LB1029.T4 G68 2000*

**PEER COUNSELING OF STUDENTS.**
Ender, Steven C. Students helping students. 1st ed. San Francisco : Jossey-Bass Publishers, c2000.
*TC LB1027.5 .E52 2000*

Gilhooley, James. Using peer mediation in classrooms and schools. Thousand Oaks, Calif. : Corwin Press, c2000.
*TC LB1027.5 .G48 2000*

Wittenberg, Lauren G. Peer education in eating disorder prevention. 1999.
*TC RC552.E18 W56 1999*

**Peer education in eating disorder prevention.**
Wittenberg, Lauren G. 1999.
*TC RC552.E18 W56 1999*

**PEER-GROUP TUTORING OF STUDENTS.**
Ender, Steven C. Students helping students. 1st ed. San Francisco : Jossey-Bass Publishers, c2000.
*TC LB1027.5 .E52 2000*

Gillespie, Paula. The Allyn and Bacon guide to peer tutoring. Boston : Allyn & Bacon, c2000.
*TC LB1031.5 .G55 2000*

**PEER-GROUP TUTORING OF STUDENTS - CALIFORNIA - CASE STUDIES.**
Samway, Katharine Davies. Buddy reading. Portsmouth, NH : Heinemann, c1995.
*TC LB1031.5 .S36 1995*

**PEER-GROUP TUTORING OF STUDENTS - CONGRESSES.**
Cognitive perspectives on peer learning. Mahwah, N.J. : L. Erlbaum, 1999.
*TC LB1031.5 .C65 1999*

**PEER PRESSURE IN ADOLESCENCE - BERMUDA ISLANDS.**
Tucker, Gina Marie. Discipline. 1998.
*TC 06 no. 10999*

**PEER REVIEW.**
Arias, Rafael. Analysis of discourse in an ESL peer-mentoring teacher group. 1999.
*TC 06 no. 10791*

**Peeters, Theo.** Autism : medical and educational aspects / T. Peeters, C. Gillberg. 2nd ed. London : Whurr Publishers, 1999. viii, 126 p. : ill. ; 24 cm. Includes bibliographical references (p. 117-119) and index. ISBN 1-86156-093-1
*1. Autism. 2. Autistic children - Education. 3. Autism. 4. Education, Special - methods. I. Gillberg, Christopher, 1950- II. Title.*
*TC RJ506.A9 P44 1999*

**Peiperl, Maury.**
Career frontiers. New York : Oxford University Press 2000.
*TC HF5549.5.C35 C367 2000*

**PEIRCE, CHARLES S. (CHARLES SANDERS), 1839-1914.**
Moorjani, Angela B. Beyond fetishism and other excursions in psychopragmatics. New York : St. Martin's Press, 2000.
*TC BF175.4.C84 M663 2000*

**Peist, Linda.**
Glass, Laurie. Read! read! read!. Thousand Oaks, Calif. : Corwin Press, c2000.
*TC LB1050.2 .G54 2000*

**Peller, Jane E.**
Walter, John L., 1945- Recreating brief therapy. New York : W.W. Norton & Co., 2000.
*TC RC480.5 .W276 2000*

**Pelletier, Carol Marra.** A handbook of techniques and strategies for coaching student teachers / Carol Marra Pelletier. 2nd ed. Boston : Allyn and Bacon, 1999. xx, 297 p. ; 28 cm. Includes bibliographical references. ISBN 0-205-30361-7 DDC 370/.71
*1. Student teachers - Training of - United States - Handbooks, manuals, etc. I. Title.*
*TC LB2157.U5 P38 1999*

**Pellett, Gail.**
The hijacked brain [videorecording]. Princeton, NJ : Films for the Humanities & Sciences, c1998.
*TC RC564 .H5 1998*

**Pellicer, Leonard O.** Caring enough to lead : schools and the sacred trust / Leonard O. Pellicer. Thousand Oaks, Calif. : Corwin Press, c1999. xvii, 126 p. ; 24 cm. Includes bibliographical references (125-126). ISBN 0-8039-6754-3 (acid-free paper) ISBN 0-8039-6755-1 (acid free paper) DDC 371.2
*1. Educational leadership - United States. 2. School management and organization - United States. 3. School principals - United States. 4. School administrators - United States. I. Title.*
*TC LB2805 .P375 1999*

**Pels, Winslow, 1947- ill.**
Mayer, Marianna. Iron John. New York : Morrow Junior Books, 1998.
*TC PZ8.M4514 Ir 1998*

**Pelton, Joseph N.** e-Sphere : the rise of the world-wide mind / Joseph N. Pelton ; foreword by Arthur C. Clarke. Westport, Conn. ; London : Quorum Books, 2000. xiv, 262 p. : ill. ; 25 cm. Includes bibliographical references (p. [249]-253) and index. ISBN 1-56720-390-6 (alk. paper) DDC 302.2
*1. Communication, International. 2. Communication - Technological innovations. 3. Telecommunication systems. I. Title.*
*TC P96.I5 P33 2000*

**Pemberton, John, 1928-.**
Fagg, William Buller. Yoruba, sculpture of West Africa. 1st ed. New York : Knopf : Distributed by Random House, 1982.
*TC NB1099.N5 F34*

**PENAL INSTITUTIONS.** *See* **REFORMATORIES.**

**PENGUINS - FICTION.**
Wiesmüller, Dieter. [Pin Kaiser und Fip Husar English] The adventures of Marco and Polo. New York : Walker & Co., 2000.
*TC PZ7.W6366 Ad 2000*

**PENGUINS - HABITS AND BEHAVIOR.**
Jenkins, Martin. The emperor's egg. 1st U.S. ed.
Cambridge, Mass. : Candlewick Press, 1999.
*TC QL696.S473 J45 1999*

**PENGUINS - JUVENILE POETRY.**
Sierra, Judy. Antarctic antics. 1st ed. San Diego :
Harcourt Brace & Co., c1998.
*TC PS3569.I39 A53 1998*

**PENGUINS - POETRY.**
Sierra, Judy. Antarctic antics. 1st ed. San Diego :
Harcourt Brace & Co., c1998.
*TC PS3569.I39 A53 1998*

**Penman, Robyn.** Reconstructing communicating :
looking to a future / Robyn Penman. Mahwah, N.J. ;
London : Lawrence Erlbaum Associates, 2000. vii, 169
p. ; 24 cm. (LEA's communication series) Includes
bibliographical references (p. 151-160) and indexes. ISBN
0-8058-3648-9 (alk. paper) DDC 302.2
*1. Interpersonal communication. 2. Communication - Study
and teaching. I. Title. II. Series.*
*TC BF637.C45 P435 2000*

**PENMANSHIP.** *See* WRITING.

**Penn, Alan, 1926-** Targeting schools : drill, militarism,
and imperialism / Alan Penn. London ; Portland, OR :
Woburn Press, 1999. 210 p. ; 23 cm. (Woburn education
series, 1462-2076) Includes bibliographical references (p.
181-197) and index. ISBN 0-7130-0217-4 (cloth : alk. paper)
ISBN 0-7130-4038-6 (pbk. : alk. paper) DDC 372.86/044/0941
*1. Physical education for children - Great Britain - History. 2.
Drill and minor tactics - History. 3. Militarism - Great
Britain - History. 4. Education, Elementary - Great Britain -
History. I. Title. II. Series.*
*TC GV443 .P388 1999*

**Penn, Helen.**
Early childhood services. Buckingham [England] ;
Philadelphia, PA : Open University Press, 2000.
*TC LB1139.3.E85 E35 2000*

**Penn working papers in educational linguistics -fall
1991.**
Working papers in educational linguistics.
[Philadelphia]: Language in Education Division,
Graduate School of Education, University of
Pennsylvania,
*TC P40.8 .W675*

**Pennartz, Paul.** The domestic domain : : chances,
choices and strategies of family households / Paul
Pennartz, Anke Niehof. Aldershot, Hants, England ;
Brookfield, Vt. : Ashgate, c1999. xii, 241 p. : ill. ; 23 cm.
Includes bibliographical references (p. 219-241). ISBN 0-
7546-1011-X
*1. Family. 2. Households. I. Niehof, Anke. 1948- II. Title.*
*TC HQ728 .P46 1999*

**Pennsylvania Academy of the Fine Arts.** Eakins and
the photograph : works by Thomas Eakins and his
circle in the collection of the Pennsylvania Academy
of the Fine Arts / [edited by] Susan Danly and Cheryl
Leibold ; with essays by Elizabeth Johns, Anne
McCauley, and Mary Panzer. Washington : Published
for the Pennsylvania Academy of the Fine Arts by the
Smithsonian Institution Press, c1994. x, 235 p. : ill. ; 25
x 26 cm. Includes bibliographical references (p. 231-232) and
index. ISBN 1-56098-352-3 (alk. paper) ISBN 1-56098-353-1
(pbk. : alk. paper) DDC 779/.092
*1. Eakins, Thomas. - 1844-1916 - Catalogues raisonnés. 2.
Bregler, Charles - Photograph collections - Catalogs. 3.
Photographs - Private collections - Pennsylvania -
Philadelphia - Catalogs. 4. Pennsylvania Academy of the Fine
Arts - Photograph collections - Catalogs. I. Danly, Susan. II.
Leibold, Cheryl. III. Title.*
*TC TR652 .P46 1994*

**PENNSYLVANIA ACADEMY OF THE FINE
ARTS - PHOTOGRAPH COLLECTIONS -
CATALOGS.**
Pennsylvania Academy of the Fine Arts. Eakins and
the photograph. Washington : Published for the
Pennsylvania Academy of the Fine Arts by the
Smithsonian Institution Press, c1994.
*TC TR652 .P46 1994*

**PENNSYLVANIA - HISTORY.**
Dickinson College. The Spahr lectures, Dickinson
College, Carlisle, Pa., : Dickinson College 1970.
*TC LD1663 .A5 1970*

**PENNSYLVANIA - HISTORY - FICTION.**
Otto, Carolyn. Pioneer church. 1st ed. New York :
Henry Holt, 1999.
*TC PZ7.O8794 Pi 1999*

**Pennsylvania school directory.**
MDR's school directory. Pennsylvania. Shelton, CT :
Market Data Retrieval, 1995-

*TC L903.P4 M37*

**PENOLOGY.** *See* REFORMATORIES.

**Penpals :** teacher's planning guide. New York :
Macmillan/McGraw-Hill, c1997. 1 v. (various pagings) :
col. ill. ; 31 cm. (Spotlight on literacy ; Gr.2 l.7 u.1) (The road
to independent reading) Includes index. ISBN 0-02-181161-x
*1. Language arts (Primary) 2. Reading (Primary) I. Series. II.
Series: The road to independent reading*
*TC LB1576 .S66 1997 Gr.2 l.7 u.1*

**PENSÉE CRITIQUE - ÉTUDE ET
ENSEIGNEMENT (PRIMAIRE).**
McDiarmid, Tami, 1960- Critical challenges for
primary students, Burnaby, B.C. : Field Relations and
Teacher In-Service Education, Faculty of Education,
Simon Fraser University, c1996.
*TC LB1590.3 .M36 1996*

**PENSIONS.** *See* SOCIAL SECURITY.

**Penso, Dorothy E.** Keyboarding skills for children with
disabilities / Dorothy E. Penso ; consulting editor in
occupational therapy Clephane Hume. London ;
Philadelphia, Pa. : Whurr, 1999. iv, 218 p. : ill. ; 25 cm.
Includes bibliographical references and index. ISBN 1-86156-
101-6
*1. Electronic data processing - Keyboarding. 2. Learning
disabled children - Computer-assisted education - Congresses.
I. Hume, Clephane. II. Title.*
*TC LC4024 .P467 1999*

**Pentathlon.**
The Journal of health and physical education. Ann
Arbor, Mich., : American Physical Education
Association,

**People and the land.** New York, Noble and Noble
[1974] 352 p. col. illus. 26 cm. (The Noble and Noble basal
social studies series. Man and his world) SUMMARY:
Describes a variety of cultures, including the Tasadays,
Eskimos, and Ashantis, emphasizing the relationship of people
to the land on which they live. ISBN 0-8107-2556-8 (lib. bdg.)
DDC 301.2
*1. Ethnology - Juvenile literature. 2. Human ecology - Juvenile
literature. 3. Ethnology. 4. Ecology.*
*TC GN330 .P445*

**People come first :** user-centered academic library
service / edited by Dale S. Montanelli & Patricia F.
Stenstrom. Chicago : Association of College and
Research Libraries, 1999. viii, 194 p. ; 23 cm. (ACRL
publications in librarianship ; no. 53) Includes bibliographical
references and index. ISBN 0-8389-7999-8 (alk. paper) DDC
027.7
*1. Academic libraries - United States. 2. Libraries and
readers - United States. I. Montanelli, Dale S. II. Stenstrom,
Patricia. III. Series.*
*TC Z674 .A75*

**PEOPLE, MARRIED.** *See* MARRIED PEOPLE.

**People, places, things.**
Modernstarts. New York : Museum of Modern Art :
Distributed by Harry N. Abrams, c1999.
*TC N620.M9 M63 1999*

**People skills for young adults.**
Csóti, Márianna. London ; Philadelphia : Jessica
Kingsley, 2000.
*TC HQ799.7 .C76 2000*

**PEOPLE WITH AIDS.** *See* AIDS (DISEASE) -
PATIENTS.

**The people with five fingers.**
Bierhorst, John. New York : Marshall Cavendish,
2000.
*TC E78.C15 B523 2000*

**PEOPLE'S HIGH SCHOOLS.** *See* FOLK HIGH
SCHOOLS.

**Peplau, Letitia Anne.**
Gender, culture, and ethnicity. Mountain View,
Calif. : Mayfield Pub. Co., c1999.
*TC HQ1181.U5 G45 1999*

**Pepperell, Sandy.**
Mathematics in the primary school. 2nd ed. London :
D. Fulton, 1999.
*TC QA135.5 .M36934 1999*

**Peppiatt, Michael.**
Farr, Dennis, 1929- Francis Bacon. New York : Harry
N. Abrams in association with the Trust for Museum
Exhibitions, 1999.
*TC ND497.B16 A4 1999*

**PERCENTS.**
Percents [videorecording]. Princeton, N.J. : Video
Tutor, 1988.
*TC QA117.P4 1988*

**Percents** [videorecording] / Video Tutor, Inc. Princeton,
N.J. : Video Tutor, 1988. 1 videocassette (VHS) (69 min.) :
sd., col. ; 1/2 in. + 1 student workbook & pre/post test system
([24] p. ; 19 cm.). (Video tutor instructional series) (A
mathematics series) Title on container: Basic pre-algebra
[videorecording]. Title on voice-over: Video Tutor introduces
pre-algebra [videorecording]. Title on cassette label Video
Tutor Inc. presents basic pre-algebra [videorecording]. VHS.
Catalogued from credits, cassette label and container. John
Hall, instructor. For grades 5-9 math classes. SUMMARY:
Covers addition, subtraction, multiplication, and division of
signed numbers, simple equations, adding, subtracting,
multiplying and dividing monomials, and adding and
subtracting polynomials.
*1. Algebra. I. Hall, John. II. Video Tutor. III. Title: Basic pre-
algebra [videorecording] IV. Title: Video Tutor introduces
pre-algebra [videorecording] V. Title: Video Tutor Inc.
presents basic pre-algebra [videorecording] VI. Series. VII.
Series: A mathematics series*

**Percents** [videorecording] / Video Tutor, Inc. Princeton,
N.J. : Video Tutor, 1988. 1 videocassette (VHS) (34 min.) :
sd., col. ; 1/2 in. + 1 student workbook & pre/post test system
([10] p. ; 19 cm.). (Video tutor instructional series) (A
mathematics series) Title on container: Basic percents
[videorecording]. Title on voice-over: Video Tutor introduces
percents [videorecording]. Title on cassette label: Video Tutor
Inc. presents basic percents [videorecording]. VHS. Catalogued
from credits, cassette label and container. John Hall, instructor.
For grades 5-9 math classes. SUMMARY: Covers converting
percents to decimals and decimals to percents, converting
fractions to percents and percents to fractions, finding a percent
of a number, finding the total number when the percent is
known.
*1. Percents. I. Hall. John. II. Video Tutor. III. Title: Basic
percents [videorecording] IV. Title: Video Tutor introduces
percents [videorecording] V. Title: Video Tutor Inc. presents
basic percents [videorecording] VI. Series. VII. Series: A
mathematics series*
*TC QA117.P4 1988*

**PERCEPTION.** *See also* AUDITORY
PERCEPTION; CONSCIOUSNESS; MENTAL
REPRESENTATION; PATTERN
PERCEPTION; PERCEPTUAL-MOTOR
PROCESSES; RISK PERCEPTION;
SELECTIVITY (PSYCHOLOGY); SELF-
PERCEPTION; SIMILARITY
(PSYCHOLOGY); SOCIAL PERCEPTION;
VISUAL PERCEPTION.
Perception, cognition, and language. Cambridge,
Mass. : MIT, c2000.
*TC BF455 .P389 2000*

**Perception and communication.**
Broadbent, Donald E. (Donald Eric) New York,
Pergamon Press, 1958.
*TC BF38 .B685*

**Perception, cognition, and language :** essays in honor
of Henry and Lila Gleitman / edited by Barbara
Landau ... [et al.]. Cambridge, Mass. : MIT, c2000. x,
360 p. ; 24 cm. "A Bradford book." Includes bibliographical
references and index. ISBN 0-262-12228-6 (alk. paper) DDC
153
*1. Psycholinguistics. 2. Language acquisition. 3. Cognition. 4.
Perception. 5. Gleitman, Henry. I. Gleitman, Henry. II.
Gleitman, Lila R. III. Landau, Barbara, 1949-*
*TC BF455 .P389 2000*

**PERCEPTION - CONGRESSES.**
International Conference on Perception and Action
(10th : 1999 : Edinburgh, Scotland) Studies in
perception and action V. Mahwah, N.J. : L. Erlbaum
Associates, 1999.
*TC BF295 .I57 1999*

**PERCEPTION IN CHILDREN.** *See* FORM
PERCEPTION IN CHILDREN.

**PERCEPTION IN INFANTS.**
Gibson, Eleanor Jack. An ecological approach to
perceptual learning and development. Oxford ; New
York : Oxford University Press, 2000.
*TC BF720.P47 G53 2000*

**PERCEPTION (PHILOSOPHY).**
Merleau-Ponty, Maurice, 1908-1961.
[Phénoménologie de la perception. English]
Phenomenology of perception. London ; New York :
Routledge, 1962.
*TC B829.5 .M413 1962*

**PERCEPTION, RISK.** *See* RISK PERCEPTION.

**PERCEPTION, SELECTIVE.** *See* SELECTIVITY
(PSYCHOLOGY).

**PERCEPTION - SEX DIFFERENCES -
RESEARCH.**
Gender and the interpretation of emotion

[videorecording]. Princeton, NJ : Films for the Humanities & Sciences, c1997.
*TC BF592.F33 G4 1997*

**PERCEPTUAL CONTROL THEORY.**
Control of human behavior, mental processes, and consciousness. Mahwah, N.J. : Lawrence Erlbaum Associates, c2000.
*TC BF611 .C67 2000*

**PERCEPTUAL LEARNING.**
Gibson, Eleanor Jack. An ecological approach to perceptual learning and development. Oxford ; New York : Oxford University Press, 2000.
*TC BF720.P47 G53 2000*

**PERCEPTUAL-MOTOR LEARNING.** *See also*
**PHYSICAL EDUCATION FOR CHILDREN.**
Umansky, Warren. Young children with special needs. 3rd ed. Upper Saddle River, N.J. : Merrill, c1998.
*TC LC4031 .U425 1998*

**PERCEPTUAL-MOTOR PROCESSES -
CONGRESSES.**
International Conference on Perception and Action (10th : 1999 : Edinburgh, Scotland) Studies in perception and action V. Mahwah, N.J. : L. Erlbaum Associates, 1999.
*TC BF295 .I57 1999*

**PERCEPTUALLY HANDICAPPED CHILDREN.**
*See* **CHILDREN, BLIND; CHILDREN, DEAF;
HEARING IMPAIRED CHILDREN;
VISUALLY HANDICAPPED CHILDREN.**

**PERCUSSION INSTRUMENTS.**
Maffit, Rocky, 1952- Rhythm & beauty :. New York : Watson-Guptill Publications, c1999.
*TC ML1030 .M34 1999*

**PERCUSSION INSTRUMENTS - INSTRUCTION
AND STUDY.**
Cook, Gary, 1951- Teaching percussion. 2nd ed. New York : Schirmer Books ; London : Prentice Hall International, c1997.
*TC MT655 .C67 1997*

**PERCUSSION (MUSICAL INSTRUMENTS).** *See*
**PERCUSSION INSTRUMENTS.**

**Perera, Juan.**
Down syndrome. London : Whurr, 1999.
*TC RC571 .D675 1999*

**Pérez, Louis A., 1943-** On becoming Cuban : identity, nationality, and culture / Louis A. Pérez, Jr. Chapel Hill : University of North Carolina Press, c1999. xiv, 579 p. : ill., 1 map ; 25 cm. (H. Eugene and Lillian Youngs Lehman series) Includes bibliographical references (p. [517]-569) and index. ISBN 0-8078-2487-9 (alk. paper) DDC 972.91
*1. Cuba - Civilization - American influences. 2. Nationalism - Cuba - History. 3. Cuba - Relations - United States. 4. United States - Relations - Cuba. I. Title. II. Series.*
*TC F1760 .P47 1999*

**Pérez Pereira, Miguel.** Language development and social interaction in blind children / Miguel Pérez-Pereira, Gina Conti-Ramsden. Hove, UK : Psychology Press, c1999. x, 197 p. : ill. ; 24 cm. (Essays in developmental psychology.) Includes bibliographical references (p. 169-187) and indexes. ISBN 0-86377-795-3
*1. Children, Blind - Language. 2. Social interaction in children. I. Conti-Ramsden, Gina. II. Title. III. Series.*
*TC P118 .P37 1999*

**Perez, Ruperto M.**
Handbook of counseling and psychotherapy with lesbian, gay, and bisexual clients. 1st ed. Washington, DC ; London : American Psychological Association, c2000.
*TC BF637.C6 H3125 2000*

**Perfect, Timothy J.**
Models of cognitive aging. Oxford ; New York : Oxford University Press, 2000.
*TC BF724.55.C63 M63 2000*

**PERFECTIONISM (PERSONALITY TRAIT).**
Lippert, Robin Alissa. Conflating the self with the body. 1999.
*TC 085 L655*

**Perform it!.**
Croteau, Jan Helling. Portsmouth, NH : Heinemann, c2000.
*TC PN3157 .C76 2000*

**PERFORMANCE.** *See also* **ACHIEVEMENT
MOTIVATION.**
Haass, Richard. The bureaucratic entrepreneur. Washington, D.C. : Brookings Institution, c1999.

*TC JF1351 .H2 1999*

**PERFORMANCE ART.** *See also* **PERFORMING
ARTS; STREET ART.**
Rinehart, Robert E., 1951- Players all. Bloomington : Indiana University Press, c1998.
*TC GV706.5 .R56 1998*

**PERFORMANCE ART - UNITED STATES.**
Garoian, Charles R., 1943- Performing pedagogy. Albany, N.Y. : State University of New York Press, 1999.
*TC NX504 .G37 1999*

**Performance-based curriculum for music and the
visual arts.**
Burz, Helen L. Thousand Oaks, Calif. : Corwin Press, c1999.
*TC LB1591 .B84 1999*

**PERFORMANCE-BASED EDUCATION.** *See*
**COMPETENCY BASED EDUCATION.**

**Performance-based learning and assessment in
middle school science.**
Hibbard, K. Michael. Larchmont, NY : Eye On Education, 2000.
*TC Q181 .H52 2000*

**PERFORMANCE - CONGRESSES.**
International Symposium on Attention and Performance (11th : 1984 : Eugene, Or.) Attention and performance XI. Hillsdale, N.J. : L. Erlbaum Associates, 1985.
*TC BF321 .A82 1985*

**PERFORMANCE CONTRACTS IN EDUCATION.**
*See* **COMPETENCY BASED EDUCATION.**

**PERFORMANCE IN CHILDREN.**
Cerruto, Audra. The effects of training on theory of mind tasks with children who are deaf. 1999.
*TC 085 C34*

**PERFORMANCE MOTIVATION.** *See*
**ACHIEVEMENT MOTIVATION.**

**PERFORMANCE - PERIODICALS.**
Improving human performance. Washington, National Society for Performance and Instruction [etc.]

**PERFORMANCE PRACTICE (MUSIC) -
FRANCE - 20TH CENTURY.**
Gingerich, Carol Joy. The French piano style of Fauré and Debussy. 1996.
*TC 06 no. 10644*

**PERFORMANCE STANDARDS.**
Mohrman, Allan M. Designing performance appraisal systems. 1st ed. San Francisco : Jossey-Bass Publishers, 1989.
*TC HF5549.5.P35 M64 1989*

**PERFORMERS.** *See* **ENTERTAINERS.**

**PERFORMING ARTISTS.** *See* **ENTERTAINERS.**

**PERFORMING ARTS.** *See* **DANCE; MOTION
PICTURES; PAGEANTS; PERFORMANCE
ART; THEATER.**

**PERFORMING ARTS AND CHILDREN.**
Taylor, Bruce D. The arts equation. New York, N.Y. : Back Stage Books, c1999.
*TC N350 .T38 1999*

**PERFORMING ARTS - FINANCE.**
Vogel, Harold L. (Harold Leslie), 1946- Entertainment industry economics. 4th ed. Cambridge [England] ; New York, NY, USA : Cambridge University Press, 1998.
*TC PN1590.F55 V6 1998*

**PERFORMING ARTS - STUDY AND TEACHING.**
Taylor, Bruce D. The arts equation. New York, N.Y. : Back Stage Books, c1999.
*TC N350 .T38 1999*

**Performing pedagogy.**
Garoian, Charles R., 1943- Albany, N.Y. : State University of New York Press, 1999.
*TC NX504 .G37 1999*

**PERFORMING PRACTICE (MUSIC).** *See*
**PERFORMANCE PRACTICE (MUSIC).**

**The perfume of memory.**
Nikly, Michelle. [Royaume des parfums. English] 1st American ed. New York : A.A. Levine Books, 1998.
*TC PZ7.N585 Pe 1998*

**PERFUMERY.** *See* **PERFUMES.**

**PERFUMES - FICTION.**
Nikly, Michelle. [Royaume des parfums. English] The perfume of memory. 1st American ed. New York : A.A. Levine Books, 1998.

*TC PZ7.N585 Pe 1998*

**Peril and promise.**
The Task Force on Higher Education and Society. Washington, DC: World Bank, 2000.
*TC LC2610 .I53 2000*

**Perillo, Marie.**
Processing the signal [videorecording]. Cicero, Ill. : Roland Collection of Films on Art, c1989.
*TC N6494.V53 P7 1989*

**PERIODIC LAW.**
Stephen Hawking's universe [videorecording]. [Alexandria, Va.] : PBS Video; Burbank, CA : Distributed by Warner Home Video, c1997.
*TC QB982 .S7 1997*

**PERIODICAL.**
The Hospital world. Toronto : [Canadian Hospital Association?], 1912-1923.

International audiology. Leiden, Netherlands : International Society of Audiology, 1962-1970.

**PERIODICALS.**
Indian journal of educational research. Bombay, Asia Publishing House.

**PERIODICALS - INDEXES - COMPUTER
NETWORK RESOURCES.**
Junior edition [computer file] [Farmington Hills, Mi.] : The Gale Group, c1999. Computer data.

Kids edition [computer file] [Farmington Hills, Mi.] : The Gale Group, c1999. Computer data.

**Peripheral and spinal mechanisms in the neural
control of movement** / edited by M.D. Binder. Amsterdam ; Oxford : Elsevier, 1999. xvi, 482 p. : ill. ; 27 cm. (Progress in brain research ; v. 123) "Presentations made at a Society for Neuroscience Satellite Symposium held from November 4-6, 1998 at the University of Arizona in Tuscon". - pref. Includes bibliographical references and index. ISBN 0-444-50288-2 ISBN 0-444-80104-9 (series) DDC 612.76
*1. Human locomotion - Congresses. 2. Spine - Movements - Congresses. 3. Neural networks (Neurobiology) - Congresses. I. Binder, Marc D. II. Series: Progress in brain research ; v. 123*
*TC QP376.A1 P7 1999*

**Peripheral vision.**
Green, Charles. Roseville East, N.S.W. : Craftsman House, 1995.
*TC N7400.2 .G74 1995*

**PERISSODACTYLA.** *See* **RHINOCEROSES.**

**Perkins, David N.** Archimedes' bathtub : the art and logic of breakthrough thinking / David Perkins. 1st ed. New York : W.W. Norton, c2000. x, 292 p. : ill. ; 22 cm. Includes bibliographical references and index. ISBN 0-393-04795-4
*1. Thought and thinking. 2. Inspiration. 3. Creative thinking. I. Title. II. Title: Art and logic of breakthrough thinking*
*TC BF441 .P47 2000*

**Perkins, Michael.**
New directions in language development and disorders. New York : Kluwer Academic/Plenum Publishers, c2000.
*TC P118 .N49 2000*

**Perkins, Revere D. (Revere Dale)** Deixis, grammar, and culture / Revere D. Perkins. Amsterdam ; Philadelphia : J. Benjamins Pub. co., 1992. 245 p. : ill. ; 23 cm. (Typological studies in language ; v. 24) Includes bibliographical references (p. [229]-235) and index. ISBN 1-55619-412-9 (hb.) ISBN 1-55619-413-7 (pbk. : alk. paper) ISBN 90-272-2909-0 (hb.) ISBN 90-272-2910-4 (pb. : European : alk. paper) DDC 306.4/4
*1. Language and culture. 2. Grammar, Comparative and general - Deixis. 3. Linguistic change. I. Title. II. Series.*
*TC P35 .P47 1992*

**Perlmutter, Philip.** Legacy of hate : a short history of ethnic, religious, and racial prejudice in America / Philip Perlmutter. Armonk, N.Y. ; London : M.E. Sharpe, c1999. xvii, 325 p. ; 24 cm. Includes bibliographical references (p. 269-313) and index. CONTENTS: 1. The Seeds of Contempt -- 2. The Weeds of Contempt -- 3. Proliferation of People and Problems -- 4. The Expansion of Democratic Pluralism -- 5. The Teaching of Contempt -- 6. The Future of Minority Progress -- 7. Notes. ISBN 0-7656-0406-X (hardcover : alk. paper) DDC 305.8/00973 DDC 305.8/00973
*1. Hate - United States. 2. Prejudices - United States. 3. Racism - United States. 4. Discrimination - Religious aspects - United States. 5. United States - Race relations. 6. United States - Social conditions. I. Title. II. Title: Divided we fall.*
*TC BF575.H3 P47 1999*

**PERMANENT EDUCATION.** *See* **CONTINUING EDUCATION.**

**Permissible advantage?.**
Peshkin, Alan. Mahwah, N.J. ; London : L. Erlbaum Associates, 2001.
*TC LC58.4 .P58 2001*

**Perna, Phyllis A.**
The Psychological meaning of chaos. 1st ed. Washington, D.C. : American Psychological Association, c1997.
*TC RC437.5 .P762 1997*

**Perner, Petra.**
MLDM'99 (1999 : Leipzig, Germany) Machine learning and data mining in pattern recognition. Berlin ; New York : Springer, c1999.
*TC Q327 .M56 1999*

**Perraton, H. D.** Open and distance learning in the developing world / Hilary Perraton. London ; New York : Routledge, 2000. x, 228 p. : ill. ; 24 cm. (Routledge studies in distance education) Includes bibliographical references (p. [209]-222) and index. ISBN 0-415-19418-0 (hbk : alk. paper) ISBN 0-415-19419-9 (pbk. : alk. paper) DDC 371.3/5/091724
*1. Distance education - Developing countries. 2. Open learning - Developing countries. I. Title. II. Series.*
*TC LC5808 .D48 P47 2000*

**Perrett, Angelina, 1960-.**
Daines, Brian. Psychodynamic approaches to sexual problems. Buckingham ; Philadelphia : Open University Press, 2000.
*TC RC557 .D35 2000*

**Perrig, Walter J.**
Control of human behavior, mental processes, and consciousness. Mahwah, N.J. : Lawrence Erlbaum Associates, c2000.
*TC BF611 .C67 2000*

**Perrone, Vito.**
Jackson, Carlton. Two centuries of progress. 3rd ed. Mission Hills, CA : Glencoe/McGraw-Hill, 1991.
*TC E178.1 .J321 1991*

**Perrucci, Robert.** The new class society / Robert Perrucci and Earl Wysong. Lanham, Md. : Rowman & Littlefield, 1999. xiii, 299 p. : ill. ; 23 cm. Includes bibliographical references (p. 277-292) and index. ISBN 0-8476-9172-1 (alk. paper) ISBN 0-8476-9173-X (pbk. : alk. paper) DDC 305.5/0973
*1. Social classes - United States. 2. United States - Social conditions - 1980- I. Wysong, Earl, 1944- II. Title.*
*TC HN90.S6 P47 1999*

**Perrucci, Robert, comp.** The triple revolution: social problems in depth [compiled by] Robert Perrucci [and] Marc Pilisuk. Boston, Little, Brown [1968] xiv, 689 p. 21 cm. Includes bibliographies. DDC 309.1/73
*1. United States - Social conditions - 1945- 1. Pilisuk, Marc, joint comp. II. Title.*
*TC HN65 .P4*

**Perry, Elisabeth Israels.**
Cayton, Andrew R. L. (Andrew Robert Lee), 1954- America. Upper Saddle River, N.J. : Prentice Hall, c1998.
*TC E178.1 .C364 1998*

Cayton, Andrew R. L. (Andrew Robert Lee), 1954- America. Teacher's ed. Upper Saddle River, N.J.. : Prentice Hall, c1998.
*TC E178.1 .C364 1998 Teacher's Ed.*

Cayton, Andrew R. L. (Andrew Robert Lee), 1954- America. Upper Saddle River, N.J. : Prentice Hall, c1998.
*TC E178.1 .C3643 1998*

Cayton, Andrew R. L. (Andrew Robert Lee), 1954- America. Upper Saddle River, N.J. : Prentice Hall, c1998.
*TC E178.1 .C3643 1998*

Cayton, Andrew R. L. (Andrew Robert Lee), 1954- America. Teacher's ed. Upper Saddle River, N.J.. : Prentice Hall, c1998.
*TC E178.1 .C3643 1998 Teacher's Ed.*

Cayton, Andrew R. L. (Andrew Robert Lee), 1954- America. Upper Saddle River, N.J. : Prentice Hall, c1998.
*TC E178.1 .C3643 1998*

Cayton, Andrew R. L. (Andrew Robert Lee), 1954- America. Teacher's ed. Upper Saddle River, N.J.. : Prentice Hall, c1998.
*TC E178.1 .C364 1998 Teacher's Ed.*

Cayton, Andrew R. L. (Andrew Robert Lee), 1954- America. Upper Saddle River, N.J. : Prentice Hall, c1998.
*TC E178.1 .C364 1998*

Cayton, Andrew R. L. (Andrew Robert Lee), 1954- America. Teacher's ed. Upper Saddle River, N.J.. : Prentice Hall, c1998.
*TC E178.1 .C3645 1998 Teacher's Ed.*

Cayton, Andrew R. L. (Andrew Robert Lee), 1954- America. Upper Saddle River, N.J. : Prentice Hall, c1998.
*TC E178.1 .C3645 1998*

Cayton, Andrew R. L. (Andrew Robert Lee), 1954- America. Upper Saddle River, N.J. : Prentice Hall, c1998.
*TC E178.1 .C3645 1998*

Cayton, Andrew R. L. (Andrew Robert Lee), 1954- America. Teacher's ed. Upper Saddle River, N.J.. : Prentice Hall, c1998.
*TC E178.1 .C364 1998 Teacher's Ed.*

Cayton, Andrew R. L. (Andrew Robert Lee), 1954- America. Upper Saddle River, N.J.. : Prentice Hall, c1998.
*TC E178.1 .C364 1998*

Cayton, Andrew R. L. (Andrew Robert Lee), 1954- America. Upper Saddle River, N.J. : Prentice Hall, c1998.
*TC E178.1 .C364 1998*

Cayton, Andrew R. L. (Andrew Robert Lee), 1954- America. Teacher's ed. Upper Saddle River, N.J.. : Prentice Hall, c1998.
*TC E178.1 .C3644 1998 Teacher's Ed.*

Cayton, Andrew R. L. (Andrew Robert Lee), 1954- America. Upper Saddle River, N.J. : Prentice Hall, c1998.
*TC E178.1 .C364 1998*

Cayton, Andrew R. L. (Andrew Robert Lee), 1954- America. Upper Saddle River, N.J. : Prentice Hall, c1998.
*TC E178.1 .C3644 1998*

Cayton, Andrew R. L. (Andrew Robert Lee), 1954- America. Upper Saddle River, N.J. : Prentice Hall, c1998.
*TC E178.1 .C3644 1998*

**Perry, Phyllis Jean.** Myths, legends & tales / Phyllis J. Perry. Ft. Atkinson, Wis. : Alleyside Press, c1999. 102 p. ; 28 cm. Includes bibliographical references (p. 95) and indexes. ISBN 1-57950-017-X (pbk. : alk. paper) DDC 016.3982
*1. Mythology - Juvenile literature - Bibliography. 2. Legends - Bibliography. 3. Mythology - Study and teaching (Elementary) 4. Legends - Study and teaching (Elementary) I. Title. II. Title: Myths. legends. and tales*
*TC Z7836 .P47 1999*

**Perry, Rebecca, ill.**
Riddle-me rhymes. 1st ed. New York : M.K. McElderry Books ; Toronto : Maxwell Macmillan Canada ; New York : Maxwell Macmillan International, c1994.
*TC PN6371.5 .R53 1994*

**Perry, Sarah.** If... / by Sarah Perry. Malibu, Calif. : J.P. Getty Museum ; Venice, Calif. : Children's Library Press, c1995. 1 v. (unpaged) : col. ill. ; 27 cm. SUMMARY: Illustrations present such imaginative possibilities as worms with wheels, caterpillar toothpaste, and whales in outer space. ISBN 0-89236-321-5 DDC [E]
*1. Imagination - Fiction. I. Title.*
*TC PZ7.P43595 If 1995*

**PERSEVERATION (PSYCHOLOGY).** *See* **MEMORY.**

**PERSISTENCE.**
Dixon, Jerome C. A qualitative study of perceptions of external factors that influence the persistence of Black males at a predominantly white four-year state college. 1999.
*TC 06 no. 11050*

**Person-centered counseling and Christian spirituality.**
Thorne, Brian, 1937- Person-centred counselling and Christian spirituality :. London : Whurr Publishers, 1998.
*TC BF637.C6 T496 1998*

**Person-centred counselling and Christian spirituality.**
Thorne, Brian, 1937- London : Whurr Publishers, 1998.
*TC BF637.C6 T496 1998*

**Person-environment psychology : new directions and perspectives** / edited by W. Bruce Walsh, Kenneth H. Craik, Richard H. Price. 2nd ed. Mahwah, N.J. : L. Erlbaum, 2000. xi, 345 p. : ill., maps ; 23 cm. Includes bibliographical references and indexes. ISBN 0-8058-2470-7 (hardcover : alk. paper) ISBN 0-8058-2471-5 (pbk. : alk. paper) DDC 155.9
*1. Environmental psychology. I. Walsh, W. Bruce, 1937- II. Craik. Kenneth H. III. Price. Richard H.*
*TC BF353 .P43 2000*

**PERSON SCHEMAS.** *See* **BODY IMAGE.**

**The personal and the political.**
Boehmer, Ulrike, 1959- Albany, NY : State University of New York Press, c2000.
*TC RC280.B8 B62 2000*

**PERSONAL BODY CARE.** *See* **HYGIENE.**

**Personal characteristics of nurses and their influence on professional autonomy.**
Abate, Ellen C. 1998.
*TC 06 no. 11009*

**PERSONAL CLEANLINESS.** *See* **HYGIENE.**

**Personal computer for the teacher.**
Brownell, Gregg. A PC for the teacher. Belmont, CA : Wadsworth Pub. Co., c1999.
*TC LB1028.43 .B755 1999*

**PERSONAL COMPUTERS.** *See* **MICROCOMPUTERS.**

**PERSONAL CONDUCT.** *See* **CONDUCT OF LIFE.**

**Personal construct counselling in action.**
Fransella, Fay. 2nd ed. London ; Thousand Oaks, Calif. : Sage Publications, 2000.
*TC BF698.9.P47 F73 2000*

**PERSONAL CONSTRUCT PSYCHOLOGY.** *See* **PERSONAL CONSTRUCT THEORY.**

**PERSONAL CONSTRUCT THEORY.**
Fransella, Fay. Personal construct counselling in action. 2nd ed. London ; Thousand Oaks, Calif. : Sage Publications, 2000.
*TC BF698.9.P47 F73 2000*

Ravenette, Tom. Personal construct theory in educational psychology :. London : Whurr, c1999.
*TC LB1027.55 .R38 1999*

**Personal construct theory in educational psychology.**
Ravenette, Tom. London : Whurr, c1999.
*TC LB1027.55 .R38 1999*

**PERSONAL CONSTRUCT THEORY - PHILOSOPHY.**
Warren, William, 1942- Philosophical dimensions of personal construct psychology. London ; New York : Routledge, 1998.
*TC BF698.9.P47 W37 1998*

**PERSONAL CONSTRUCT THERAPY.**
Constructions of disorder. 1st ed. Washington, DC : American Psychological Association, c2000.
*TC RC437.5 .C647 2000*

Fransella, Fay. Personal construct counselling in action. 2nd ed. London ; Thousand Oaks, Calif. : Sage Publications, 2000.
*TC BF698.9.P47 F73 2000*

**PERSONAL DEVELOPMENT.** *See* **MATURATION (PSYCHOLOGY); SUCCESS.**

**PERSONAL FINANCE.** *See* **FINANCE, PERSONAL.**

**PERSONAL FINANCIAL PLANNING.** *See* **FINANCE, PERSONAL.**

**PERSONAL GROWTH.** *See* **MATURATION (PSYCHOLOGY); SELF-ACTUALIZATION (PSYCHOLOGY); SUCCESS.**

**PERSONAL HEALTH.** *See* **HEALTH.**

**PERSONAL HEALTH SERVICES.** *See* **MEDICAL CARE.**

**Personal history & health.**
Srole, Leo. New Brunswick, N.J. : Transaction Publishers, c1998.
*TC RA790.6 .S7 1998*

**Personal history and health.**
Srole, Leo. Personal history & health. New Brunswick, N.J.. : Transaction Publishers, c1998.
*TC RA790.6 .S7 1998*

**PERSONAL HYGIENE.** *See* **HYGIENE.**

## PERSONAL INFORMATION MANAGEMENT. *See* TIME MANAGEMENT.

**Personal issues in human sexuality.**
Gordon, Sol, 1923- Boston : Allyn and Bacon, 1986.
*TC HQ35.2 .G67 1986*

## PERSONAL LIBERTY. *See* LIBERTY.

**Personal motivation.**
Cavalier, Robert P., 1933- Westport, Conn. ; London : Praeger, 2000.
*TC BF503 .C39 2000*

## PERSONAL RADIOTELEPHONE. *See* CITIZENS BAND RADIO.

## PERSONAL RELATIONS. *See* INTERPERSONAL RELATIONS.

## PERSONAL TIME MANAGEMENT. *See* TIME MANAGEMENT.

## PERSONALISM.
Baker, Lynne Rudder, 1944- Persons and bodies. New York : Cambridge University Press, 2000.
*TC B105.B64 B35 2000*

## PERSONALITY. *See also* ADAPTABILITY (PSYCHOLOGY); ADJUSTMENT (PSYCHOLOGY); BODY IMAGE; CHARACTER; IDENTITY (PSYCHOLOGY); MOOD (PSYCHOLOGY); PERSONAL CONSTRUCT THEORY; RESILIENCE (PERSONALITY TRAIT); SELF; TEMPERAMENT; TYPOLOGY (PSYCHOLOGY).
Curcio, John J. Relationships among administrator personality, perceptions of feedback source credibility, and attitudes toward program feedback. 1999.
*TC 085 C92*

Emmons, Robert A. The psychology of ultimate concerns. New York : Guilford Press, c1999.
*TC BF505.G6 E58 1999*

Gillett, Grant, 1950- The mind and its discontents. Oxford ; New York : Oxford University Press, c1999.
*TC BD418.3 .G555 1999*

Handbook of personality. 2nd ed. New York : Guilford Press, c1999.
*TC BF698 .H335 1999*

Murphy, Lois Barclay, 1902- The individual child. Washington : Department of Health Education, and Welfare : for sale by the Supt. of Docs., U. S. Govt. Print. Off., 1973.

Peatling, John H. Career development. Muncie, Ind. : Accelerated Development, c1977.
*TC BF697 .P384*

Personality development. London ; New York : Routledge, 1999.
*TC BF175.45 .P47 1999*

Shoham, S. Giora, 1929- Personality and deviance. Westport, Conn. : Praeger, 2000.
*TC BF698 .S5186 2000*

Waddell, Margot, 1946- Inside lives. New York : Routledge, 1998.
*TC BF175.45 .W33 1998*

Wexberg, Erwin, 1889- Individual psychology, New York, Cosmopolitan Book Corporation, 1929.
*TC BF175 .W48*

## PERSONALITY AND COGNITION. *See* COGNITIVE STYLES.

## PERSONALITY AND CREATIVE ABILITY.
Brink, Andrew. The creative matrix. New York : Peter Lang, c2000.
*TC BF698.9.C74 B75 2000*

## PERSONALITY AND CULTURE.
Harrington, Charles C. Psychological anthropology and education. New York : AMS Press, c1979.
*TC GN502 .H37*

Lynn, Richard. Personality and national character [1st ed.]. Oxford, New York, Pergamon Press [1971]
*TC BF698.9.C8 L9 1971*

## PERSONALITY AND CULTURE - ABSTRACTS.
Harrington, Charles C. Psychological anthropology and education. New York : AMS Press, c1979.
*TC GN502 .H37*

## PERSONALITY AND CULTURE - CROSS-CULTURAL STUDIES.
Berry, John W. comp. Culture and cognition: readings in cross-cultural psychology, London, Methuen [1974]
*TC BF311 .B48*

**Personality and deviance.**
Shoham, S. Giora, 1929- Westport, Conn. : Praeger, 2000.
*TC BF698 .S5186 2000*

## PERSONALITY AND EMOTIONS.
Watson, David. Mood and temperament. New York ; London : Guilford Press, c2000.
*TC BF698.9.E45 W38 2000*

**Personality and national character.**
Lynn, Richard. [1st ed.]. Oxford, New York, Pergamon Press [1971]
*TC BF698.9.C8 L9 1971*

## PERSONALITY ASSESSMENT. *See also* PERSONALITY TESTS.
Aiken, Lewis R., 1931- 3rd rev. ed. Seattle ; Toronto : Hogrefe & Huber Publishers, 1999.
*TC BF698.4 .A54 1999*

## PERSONALITY ASSESSMENT.
Aiken, Lewis R., 1931- Personality assessment. 3rd rev. ed. Seattle ; Toronto : Hogrefe & Huber Publishers, 1999.
*TC BF698.4 .A54 1999*

## PERSONALITY ASSESSMENT.
Clinician's guide to neuropsychological assessment. 2nd ed. Mahwah, N.J. : Lawrence Erlbaum Associates, c2000.
*TC RC386.6.N48 G85 2000*

## PERSONALITY ASSESSMENT.
Handbook of cross-cultural and multicultural personality assessment. Mahwah, N.J. ; London : Lawrence Erlbaum Associates, 2000.
*TC RC473.P79 H36 2000*

Leary, Timothy. Politics of self-determination. Berkeley, Ca. ; Ronin Pub., c2000.
*TC BF723.P4 L43 2000*

Problems and solutions in human assessment. Boston : Kluwer Academic Publishers, c2000.
*TC BF698.4 .P666 2000*

## PERSONALITY ASSESSMENT - ADDRESSES, ESSAYS, LECTURES.
Personality assessment in organizations. New York : Praeger, 1985.
*TC HF5548.8 .P3995 1985*

## PERSONALITY ASSESSMENT - CHILD.
Play diagnosis and assessment. 2nd ed. New York : John Wiley & Sons, c2000.
*TC RJ505.P6 P524 1999*

**Personality assessment in organizations** / edited by H. John Bernardin and David A. Bownas. New York : Praeger, 1985. ix, 322 p. : ill. ; 24 cm. "Praeger special studies." Includes bibliographies and indexes. ISBN 0-03-072023-0 (alk. paper) DDC 158.7
*1. Psychology, Industrial - Addresses, essays, lectures. 2. Personality assessment - Addresses, essays, lectures. I. Bernardin, H. John. II. Bownas, David A.*
*TC HF5548.8 .P3995 1985*

## PERSONALITY ASSESSMENT - INFANT.
Play diagnosis and assessment. 2nd ed. New York : John Wiley & Sons, c2000.
*TC RJ505.P6 P524 1999*

## PERSONALITY - CONGRESSES.
Temperament and personality development across the life span. Mahwah, NJ : L. Erlbaum Associates, 2000.
*TC BF798 .T46 2000*

## PERSONALITY DEVELOPMENT.
Berger, Elizabeth. Raising children with character. Northvale, N.J. : J. Aronson, c1999.
*TC BF723.P4 B47 1999*

Leary, Timothy. Politics of self-determination. Berkeley, Ca. ; Ronin Pub., c2000.
*TC BF723.P4 L43 2000*

**Personality development :** a psychoanalytic perspective / edited by Debbie Hindle and Marta Vaciago Smith. London ; New York : Routledge, 1999. xiii, 200 p. ; 23 cm. Includes bibliographical references (p. [177]-189) and index. ISBN 0-415-17957-2 (hbk.) ISBN 0-415-17958-0 (pbk.) DDC 155.2/5
*1. Psychoanalysis. 2. Developmental psychology. 3. Personality. I. Hindle, Debbie, 1949- II. Smith, Marta Vaciago, 1944-*
*TC BF175.45 .P47 1999*

**Personality development in adolescence :** a cross national and life span perspective / edited by Eva Elisabeth Aspaas Skoe and Anna Louise von der Lippe. London ; New York : Routledge, c1998. xvii, 218 p. : ill. ; 23 cm. (Adolescence and society) "Primarily papers presented at the seminar ... May 1994, at the University of Tromsø"--Introd. Includes bibliographical references and index. ISBN 0-415-13505-2 ISBN 0-415-13506-0 (pbk.) DDC 155.5/1825
*1. Personality in adolescence - Cross-cultural studies. I. Skoe, Eva Elisabeth Aspaas, 1944- II. Lippe, Anna Louise von der. III. Series.*
*TC BF724.3.P4 P47 1998*

## PERSONALITY DIAGNOSIS. *See* PERSONALITY ASSESSMENT.

## PERSONALITY DISORDERS. *See* ANTISOCIAL PERSONALITY DISORDERS; BORDERLINE PERSONALITY DISORDER.

## PERSONALITY - DISORDERS. *See* PERSONALITY DISORDERS.

## PERSONALITY DISORDERS. *See also* PSYCHOSEXUAL DISORDERS; SUBSTANCE ABUSE.
Millon, Theodore. Personality disorders in modern life. New York ; Chichester [England] : John Wiley & Sons, c2000.
*TC RC554 .M537 2000*

## PERSONALITY DISORDERS.
Millon, Theodore. Personality disorders in modern life. New York ; Chichester [England] : John Wiley & Sons, c2000.
*TC RC554 .M537 2000*

Millon, Theodore. Personality-guided psychotherapy. New York : J. Wiley, c1999.
*TC RC480.5 .M54 1999*

## PERSONALITY DISORDERS.
Wexberg, Erwin, 1889- Individual psychology, New York, Cosmopolitan Book Corporation, 1929.
*TC BF175 .W48*

## PERSONALITY DISORDERS - CASE STUDIES.
Goldberg, Arnold, 1929- Being of two minds. Hillsdale, NJ : Analytic Press, 1999.
*TC RC569.5.M8 G65 1999*

## PERSONALITY DISORDERS - DIAGNOSIS.
Personality disorders [videorecording]. Princeton, N.J. : Films for the Humanities & Sciences, 1998.
*TC RC554 .P4 1998*

**Personality disorders in modern life.**
Millon, Theodore. New York ; Chichester [England] : John Wiley & Sons, c2000.
*TC RC554 .M537 2000*

## PERSONALITY, DISORDERS OF. *See* PERSONALITY DISORDERS.

## PERSONALITY DISORDERS - PATIENTS.
Personality disorders [videorecording]. Princeton, N.J. : Films for the Humanities & Sciences, 1998.
*TC RC554 .P4 1998*

## PERSONALITY DISORDERS - TREATMENT.
Davidson, Kate M. Cognitive therapy for personality disorders :. Oxford ; Boston : Butterworth-Heinemann, 2000.
*TC RC554 .D38 2000*

Magnavita, Jeffrey J. Relational therapy for personality disorders. New York : Wiley, c2000.
*TC RC554 .M228 2000*

## PERSONALITY DISORDERS - TREATMENT - HANDBOOKS, MANUALS, ETC.
Millon, Theodore. Personality-guided psychotherapy. New York : J. Wiley, c1999.
*TC RC480.5 .M54 1999*

**Personality disorders** [videorecording] / a presentation of Films for the Humanities & Sciences ; University of Sheffield ; produced and directed by Steve Collier ; written by Dr. Steve Peters : Sheffield University Television. Princeton, N.J. : Films for the Humanities & Sciences, 1998. 1 videocassette (26 min.) : sd., col. ; 1/2 in. (Differential diagnosis in psychiatry) VHS. Catalogued from credits and container. Commentary: John Graham Davies. Sound: Ken Hardy; cameras: Jackie Jones, Mark Parkin, Gary Wraith; graphics: Sean Purcell. Series subtitle: A visual aid based on ICD 10. Originally produced 1995-1997 at the University of Sheffield. "Clinical features of myotonic dystrophy and Huntington's disease" included in list of complete series on container no longer part of series. For students of psychiatry, clinical psychology and social work, and counselling. SUMMARY: "Personality disorders come in various varieties and degrees of severity, including persistent, ingrained behavior patterns; extreme deviant behavior; and problems in social functioning. Histrionic disorder, anankastic disorder, anxiety disorder, and dependent disorder are the common categories. This program looks at the most common disorders: paranoid..., dissocial, and emotionally unstable. It describes their symptoms and criteria for diagnosis. Patients exhibit the symptoms in interviews conducted by psychiatrists."--Container.

*1. Personality disorders - Diagnosis. 2. Personality disorders - Patients. 3. Antisocial personality disorder - Patients. 4. Antisocial personality disorder - Patients. 5. Diagnosis, Differential. I. Peters, Steve, Dr. II. Collier, Steve. III. Davies, John Graham. IV. University of Sheffield. V. Sheffield University Television. VI. Films for the Humanities (Firm) VII. Series.*
**TC RC554 .P4 1998**

**PERSONALITY EVALUATION.** *See* PERSONALITY ASSESSMENT.

**Personality-guided psychotherapy.**
Millon, Theodore. New York : J. Wiley, c1999.
**TC RC480.5 .M54 1999**

**PERSONALITY - HEALTH ASPECTS.**
Chiozza, Luis A. Why do we fall ill? Madison, Conn. : Psychosocial Press, c1999.
**TC R726.7 .C48 1999**

**PERSONALITY IN ADOLESCENCE - CROSS-CULTURAL STUDIES.**
Personality development in adolescence. London ; New York : Routledge, c1998.
**TC BF724.3.P4 P47 1998**

**PERSONALITY (LAW).** *See* CONFIDENTIAL COMMUNICATIONS; PRIVACY, RIGHT OF.

**PERSONALITY, MULTIPLE.** *See* MULTIPLE PERSONALITY.

**PERSONALITY - PERIODICALS.**
Character and personality. Durham, N.C. : Duke Univ. Press, 1932-1945.

Journal of projective techniques. Glendale, Calif. : Society for Projective Techniques and Rorschach Institute, 1950-c1963.

**PERSONALITY - PHYSIOLOGICAL ASPECTS.**
Grigsby, Jim. Neurodynamics of personality. New York : Guilford Press, 2000.
**TC BF698.9.B5 G741 2000**

**PERSONALITY - PHYSIOLOGY.**
Grigsby, Jim. Neurodynamics of personality. New York : Guilford Press, 2000.
**TC BF698.9.B5 G741 2000**

**PERSONALITY - RELIGIOUS ASPECTS.**
Emmons, Robert A. The psychology of ultimate concerns. New York : Guilford Press, c1999.
**TC BF505.G6 E58 1999**

**PERSONALITY - RESEARCH - METHODOLOGY.**
Handbook of research methods in social and personality psychology. Cambridge, U.K. ; New York : Cambridge University Press, 2000.
**TC HM1019 .H36 2000**

**PERSONALITY - SOCIAL ASPECTS.**
Shoham, S. Giora, 1929- Personality and deviance. Westport, Conn. : Praeger, 2000.
**TC BF698 .S5186 2000**

**PERSONALITY TESTS.** *See also* MINNESOTA MULTIPHASIC PERSONALITY INVENTORY.
Craig, Robert J., 1941- Interpreting personality tests. New York : J. Wiley & Sons, c1999.
**TC BF698.5 .C73 1999**

Testing and assessment in counseling practice. 2nd ed. Mahwah, N.J. : L. Erlbaum Associates, 2000.
**TC BF176 .T423 2000**

**PERSONALITY TESTS - PERIODICALS.**
Journal of projective techniques & personality assessment. Glendale, Calif.

**PERSONALITY THEORY.** *See* PERSONALITY.

**PERSONALITY (THEORY OF KNOWLEDGE).** *See* SELF-KNOWLEDGE, THEORY OF.

**PERSONALITY TRAITS.** *See* PERSONALITY.

**Personalized instruction** : changing classroom practice / by James W. Keefe and John M. Jenkins. Larchmont, N.Y. : Eye on Education, c2000. xvi, 239 p. ; 23 cm. Includes bibliographical references and index. ISBN 1-88300-186-2 DDC 371.34/9
*1. Individualized instruction - United States. 2. School management and organization - United States. I. Jenkins, John M. II. Title.*
**TC LB1031 .K383 2000**

**Personalizing evaluation.**
Kushner, Saville. London ; Thousand Oaks, Calif. : SAGE, 2000.
**TC LB2822.75 .K87 2000**

**PERSONNALITÉ - ÉVALUATION.**
Aiken, Lewis R., 1931- Personality assessment. 3rd rev. ed. Seattle : Toronto : Hogrefe & Huber Publishers, 1999.
**TC BF698.4 .A54 1999**

**PERSONNEL.** *See* EMPLOYEES.

**PERSONNEL ADMINISTRATION.** *See* PERSONNEL MANAGEMENT.

**PERSONNEL ADMINISTRATION, HOSPITAL - METHODS.**
McGuffin, Jo A. The nurse's guide to successful management. St. Louis, Mo. : Mosby, c1999.
**TC RT89 .M436 1999**

**The personnel bibliographical index.**
Cowley, William Harold, 1889- Columbus, Ohio : The Ohio State University, 1932.
**TC Z5814.P8 C8**

**Personnel journal.**
Journal of personnel research. Baltimore : Williams & Wilkins Co., -1927.

**PERSONNEL MANAGEMENT.** *See also* AFFIRMATIVE ACTION PROGRAMS; CAREER DEVELOPMENT; DIVERSITY IN THE WORKPLACE; EMPLOYEES; PSYCHOLOGY, INDUSTRIAL.
Spector, Paul E. Industrial and organizational psychology. 2nd ed. New York : John Wiley, 2000.
**TC HF5548.8 .S625 2000**

**PERSONNEL MANAGEMENT - HANDBOOKS, MANUALS, ETC.**
The IEBM handbook of human resource management. 1st ed. London ; Boston : International Thomson Business Press, 1998.
**TC HF5549.17 .I33 1998**

**PERSONNEL MANAGEMENT - PERIODICALS.**
Journal of personnel research. Baltimore : Williams & Wilkins Co., -1927.

**PERSONNEL MANAGEMENT - UNITED STATES.**
Human resource management. 3rd ed. Boston : Irwin/McGraw-Hill, 2000.
**TC HF5549.2.U5 H8 2000**

**PERSONNEL PROCEDURE MANUALS.** *See* PERSONNEL MANAGEMENT - HANDBOOKS, MANUALS, ETC.

**Personnel Research Federation (U.S.).**
Journal of personnel research. Baltimore : Williams & Wilkins Co., -1927.

**PERSONNEL SERVICE IN EDUCATION.** *See also* EDUCATIONAL COUNSELING.
National Association for Women Deans, Administrators & Counselors. Journal. [Washington, D.C. : National Association for Women Deans, Administrators, & Counselors]

**PERSONNEL SERVICE IN ELEMENTARY EDUCATION.** *See* COUNSELING IN ELEMENTARY EDUCATION.

**PERSONNEL SERVICE IN HIGHER EDUCATION.** *See* COUNSELING IN HIGHER EDUCATION.

**PERSONNEL SERVICE IN SECONDARY EDUCATION.** *See* COUNSELING IN SECONDARY EDUCATION.

**PERSONNEL STAFFING AND SCHEDULING - ORGANIZATION & ADMINISTRATION - NURSES' INSTRUCTION.**
Staffing management and methods. San Francisco : Jossey-Bass, 2000.
**TC RT89.3 .S72 2000**

**PERSONOLOGY.** *See* PERSONALITY.

**PERSONS.** *See* ARTISTS; ATTENTION-DEFICIT-DISORDERED ADULTS; BISEXUALS; CELEBRITIES; EMPLOYEES; EXILES; GAYS; GIFTED PERSONS; HEROES; HOMELESS PERSONS; HUMAN BEINGS; IMMIGRANTS; INTELLECTUALS; PACIFISTS; PATIENTS; PERSONALITY; REFUGEES; STUDENTS; SUCCESSFUL PEOPLE; TRANSSEXUALS.

**Persons and bodies.**
Baker, Lynne Rudder, 1944- New York : Cambridge University Press, 2000.
**TC B105.B64 B35 2000**

**PERSONS, MARRIED.** *See* MARRIED PEOPLE.

**PERSONS WITH AIDS.** *See* AIDS (DISEASE) - PATIENTS.

**PERSPECTIVE.** *See also* DRAWING.
Willats, John. Art and representation. Princeton, N.J. : Princeton University Press, c1997.
**TC N7430.5 .W55 1997**

**Perspectives in cognitive neuroscience**
Berthoz, A. [Sens du Mouvement. English] The brain's sense of movement. Cambridge, Mass. : Harvard University Press, 2000.
**TC QP493 .B47 2000**

**Perspectives in critical thinking** : essays by teachers in theory and practice / edited by Danny Weil and Holly Kathleen Anderson. New York : P. Lang, c2000. xiv, 220 p. : ill. ; 23 cm. (Counterpoints; vol. 110) Includes bibliographical references. DDC 370.15/2
*1. Critical thinking - Study and teaching. 2. Critical pedagogy. I. Weil, Danny K., 1953- II. Anderson, Holly Kathleen, 1952- III. Series: Counterpoints (New York, N.Y.); vol. 110.*
**TC LB1590.3 .P476 2000**

**Perspectives on behavioral self-regulation** / edited by Robert S. Wyer. Mahwah, N.J. : Lawrence Erlbaum Associates, 1999. viii, 316 p. : ill. ; 24 cm. (Advances in social cognition ; v. 12) Lead article by Charles S. Carver and Michael F. Scheier. Includes bibliographical references and indexes. ISBN 0-8058-2588-6 ISBN 0-8058-2589-4 (pbk.)
*1. Self-perception. 2. Human behavior. I. Wyer, Robert S. II. Carver, Charles S. III. Scheier, Michael.*
**TC HM291 A345 1999**

**Perspectives on behaviour.**
Ayers, Harry. 2nd ed. London : David Fulton, 2000.
**TC LC4801 .A94 2000**

**Perspectives on cognitive science**
(v. 2) Perspectives on cognitive science. Stamford, Conn. : Ablex Pub. Corp., c1999.
**TC BF311 .P373 1999**

**Perspectives on cognitive science** : theories, experiments, and foundations / edited by Janet Wiles, Terry Dartnall. Stamford, Conn. : Ablex Pub. Corp., c1999. vi, 364 p. : ill. ; 23 cm. (Perspectives on cognitive science ; v. 2) Includes bibliographical references and indexes. ISBN 1-56750-382-9 (hardcover) ISBN 1-56750-383-7 (pbk.) DDC 153
*1. Cognition. 2. Cognitive psychology. 3. Cognitive science. 4. Artificial intelligence. I. Wiles, Janet. II. Dartnall, Terry, 1943- III. Series.*
**TC BF311 .P373 1999**

**Perspectives on creativity**
Creativity and giftedness in culturally diverse students. Cresskill, N.J. : Hampton Press, c2000.
**TC LC3993.2 .C74 2000**

Investigating creativity in youth. Cresskill, N.J. : Hampton Press, c1999.
**TC BF723.C7 I58 1999**

Khatena, Joe. Enhancing creativity of gifted children. Cresskill, N.J. : Hampton Press, c2000.
**TC LC3993 .K56 2000**

**Perspectives on economics series**
Schultz, T. Paul. Economics of population. Reading, MA : Addison-Wesley, c1981.
**TC HB849.41 .S38**

**Perspectives on fundamental processes in intellectual functioning** / edited by Sal Soraci, William J. McIlvane. Stamford, Conn. : Ablex Pub. Corp., c1998- v. <1- > : ill. (some col.) ; 23 cm. Includes bibliographical references and index. PARTIAL CONTENTS: v. 1. A survey of research approaches. ISBN 1-56750-358-6 (hardcover : v. 1) ISBN 1-56750-359-4 (pbk. : v. 1) DDC 153
*1. Human information processing. 2. Intellect. 3. Psychology, Comparative. I. Soraci, Sal. II. McIlvane, William J.*
**TC BF444 .P42 1998**

**Perspectives on plagiarism and intellectual property in a postmodern world** / Lise Buranen and Alice M. Roy, editors ; foreword by Andrea Lunsford. Albany : State University of New York Press, c1999. xxii, 302 p. ; 24 cm. Includes bibliographical references (p. 273-292) and index. ISBN 0-7914-4079-6 ISBN 0-7914-4080-X (pbk.) DDC 808
*1. Plagiarism. 2. Intellectual property. I. Buranen, Lise, 1954- II. Roy, Alice Myers.*
**TC PN167 .P47 1999**

**Perspectives on scholarly misconduct in the sciences** / edited by John M. Braxton. Columbus : Ohio State University Press, c1999. vi, 342 p. : ill. ; 24 cm. Includes bibliographical references and index. ISBN 0-8142-0815-0 (acid-free paper) DDC 174/.95
*1. Scientists - Moral and ethical aspects. 2. Self-control. 3. Scientists - Discipline. 4. Research - Social aspects. I. Braxton, John M.*

**TC Q147 .P47 1999**

**Perspectives on shared reading.**
Fisher, Bobbi. Portsmouth, NH : Heinemann, c2000.
**TC LB1573 .F528 2000**

**Perspectives on spiritual well-being and aging** / edited by James A. Thorson. Springfield, Ill. : Charles C. Thomas, c2000. xx, 210 p. ; 26 cm. Includes bibliographic references and index. ISBN 0-398-07037-7 (cloth) ISBN 0-398-07038-5 (paper) DDC 200/.84/6
*1. Aged - Religious life. 2. Aged - Psychology. 3. Aging - Religious aspects. I. Thorson, James A., 1946-*
**TC BL625.4 .P47 2000**

**Perspectives on writing**
(v. 3) History, reflection, and narrative. Stamford, Conn. : Ablex Pub., c1999.
**TC PE1405.U6 H56 1999**

**Persuasion.**
Karlins, Marvin. 2d ed. New York, Springer Pub. Co. [1970]
**TC BF637.P4 K27 1970**

**PERSUASION (PSYCHOLOGY).** *See also* **INFLUENCE (PSYCHOLOGY).**
Attitudes, behavior, and social context. Mahwah, N.J. : L. Erlbaum Associates, 2000.
**TC HM132 .B48 1998**

Gass, Robert H. Persuasion, social influence, and compliance gaining. Boston : Allyn and Bacon, c1999.
**TC BF637.P4 G34 1999**

Haass, Richard. The bureaucratic entrepreneur. Washington, D.C. : Brookings Institution, c1999.
**TC JF1351 .H2 1999**

Karlins, Marvin. Persuasion; 2d ed. New York, Springer Pub. Co. [1970]
**TC BF637.P4 K27 1970**

Shell, G. Richard, 1949- Bargaining for advantage. New York : Viking, 1999.
**TC BF637.N4 S44 1999**

**PERSUASION (RHETORIC).**
Gordon, Tatiana. Russian language directives. 1998.
**TC 06 no. 10940**

**Persuasion, social influence, and compliance gaining.**
Gass, Robert H. Boston : Allyn and Bacon, c1999.
**TC BF637.P4 G34 1999**

**Pervin, Lawrence A.**
Handbook of personality. 2nd ed. New York : Guilford Press, c1999.
**TC BF698 .H335 1999**

**Pervola, Cindy, 1956-** How to get a job if you're a teenager / Cindy Pervola and Debby Hobgood. Fort Atkinson, Wis. : Alleyside Press, 1998. 62 p. : ill. ; 28 cm. Includes bibliographical references and index. SUMMARY: A basic job skills guide for teenagers with appendices of additional resources and web sites for job searches. ISBN 1-57950-013-7 (soft : alk. paper) DDC 650.14/0835
*1. Applications for positions. 2. Job hunting. 3. Vocational guidance. 4. Employment interviewing. 5. Business etiquette. 6. Teenagers - Employment. 7. Applications for positions. 8. Job hunting. 9. Vocational guidance. 10. Employment interviewing. I. Hobgood, Debby, 1964- II. Title.*
**TC HF5383 .P44 1998**

**Peschl, Markus F.**
Understanding representation in the cognitive sciences. New York : Kluwer Academic/Plenum Publishers, c1999.
**TC BF316.6 U63 1999**

**Pescosolido, Bernice A.**
The social worlds of higher education :. Thousand Oaks, Calif. : Pine Forge Press, [1999].
**TC LB2331 .S573 1999 sampler**

**Peshkin, Alan. Permissible advantage?** : the moral consequences of elite schooling / Alan Peshkin. Mahwah, N.J. ; London : L. Erlbaum Associates, 2001. xiv, 135 p. ; 24 cm. (Sociocultural, political, and historical studies in education) Includes bibliographical references (p. 127-130) and indexes. ISBN 0-8058-2466-9 (hbk. : alk. paper) ISBN 0-8058-2467-7 (pbk. : alk. paper) DDC 373.2/22
*1. Preparatory schools - Moral and ethical aspects - United States. 2. Preparatory schools - United States - Case studies. I. Title. II. Series.*
**TC LC58.4 .P58 2001**

**PESSIMISM.**
Optimism & pessimism. 1st ed. Washington, DC : American Psychological Association, c2001.
**TC BF698.35.O57 O68 2001**

**Peter, Beate.**
Wiesmüller, Dieter. [Pin Kaiser und Fip Husar English] The adventures of Marco and Polo. New York : Walker & Co., 2000.
**TC PZ7.W6366 Ad 2000**

**Peter F. Drucker Foundation for Nonprofit Management.**
Leading beyond the walls. 1st ed. San Francisco : Jossey-Bass, c1999.
**TC HD57.7 .L4374 1999**

**Peter Spier's circus!.**
Spier, Peter. [Circus!] 1st ed. New York : Doubleday, c1992.
**TC PZ7.S7544 Cj 1992**

**Peterat, Linda, 1946-** Making textile studies matter : inside outstanding school programs / Linda Peterat. Vancouver : Pacific Educational Press, 1999. 223 p. ; 23 cm. Includes bibliographical references and index. ISBN 1-89576-637-0 DDC 646/.071/2712
*1. Home economics - Study and teaching (Secondary) - Canada, Western. 2. Clothing and dress - Study and teaching (Secondary) - Canada, Western. 3. Textile fabrics - Study and teaching (Secondary) - Canada, Western. I. Title.*
**TC TX340 .P47 1999**

**Petermann, Franz.**
Developmental psychopathology. Australia : Harwood Academic Publishers, c1997.
**TC RJ499 .D48 1997**

**Peters, Cynthia.** Deaf American literature : from carnival to the canon / Cynthia Peters. Washington, D.C. : Gallaudet University Press, 2000. vii, 217 p. ; 24 cm. Based on the author's thesis, George Washington University, 1996. Includes bibliographical references and index. ISBN 1-56368-094-7 (alk. paper) DDC 419
*1. American Sign Language. 2. Interpreters for the deaf. I. Title.*
**TC HV2471 .P38 2000**

**Peters, Dorothy.** Taking cues from kids : how they think, what to do about it / Dorothy Peters ; foreword by Deborah Meier. Portsmouth, NH : Heinemann, c2000. xviii, 184 p. : ill. ; 23 cm. Includes bibliographical references (p. 172-175) and index. ISBN 0-325-00210-X (alk. paper) DDC 372.1102/3
*1. Classroom management. 2. Teacher-student relationships. 3. Education, Elementary - Activity programs. I. Title.*
**TC LB3013 .P43 2000**

**Peters, John Durham.** Speaking into the air : a history of the idea of communication / John Durham Peters. Chicago : University of Chicago Press, 1999. x, 293 p. ; 24 cm. Includes bibliographical references and index. ISBN 0-226-66276-4 (alk. paper) DDC 302.2/01
*1. Communication - Philosophy - History. I. Title.*
**TC P90 .P388 1999**

**Peters, Max, 1906-** Algebra : a modern approach [by] Max Peters [and] William L. Schaaf. 2d ed. Princeton, N.J., Van Nostrand 1968. v. : ill. ; 25 cm. (DVN program in modern mathematics) Copy 2 has at its end "Answers to odd-numbered problems" (p. 1-28). Includes index.
*1. Algebra. 2. Plane trigonometry. I. Schaaf, William Leonard, 1898- joint author. II. Title.*
**TC QA152 .P4562 1968**

Algebra and trigonometry : a modern approach [by] Max Peters [and] William L. Schaaf. Princeton, N.J., Van Nostrand 1965. v. ; ill. ; 25 cm. (DVN program in modern mathematics) Includes index.
*1. Algebra. 2. Plane trigonometry. I. Schaaf, William Leonard, 1898- joint author. II. Title.*
**TC QA152 .P4562 1965**

**Peters, Michael (Michael A.), 1948-.**
After the disciplines. Westport, Conn. : Bergin & Garvey, 1999.
**TC LB2362.N45 A48 1999**

Education policy. Cheltenham, UK : Northampton, MA : Edward Elgar Pub., c1999.
**TC LC71 .E32 1999**

Wittgenstein : philosophy, postmodernism, pedagogy / Michael Peters and James Marshall. Westport, Conn. : Bergin & Garvey, 1999. xvi, 227 p. ; 24 cm. (Critical studies in education and culture series, 1064-8615) Includes bibliographical references (p. [207]-219) and index. ISBN 0-89789-480-4 (alk. paper) DDC 192
*1. Wittgenstein, Ludwig, - 1889-1951. 2. Postmodernism. 3. Education - Philosophy. I. Marshall, James (James D.) II. Title. III. Series.*
**TC B3376.W564 P388 1999**

**Peters, Steve, Dr.**
Challenge cases [videorecording]. Princeton, N.J. : Films for the Humanities & Sciences, 1998.
**TC RC455.2.C4 C4 1998**

Disorders due to psychoactive substance abuse [videorecording]. Princeton, N.J. : Films for the Humanities & Sciences, 1998.
**TC RC564 .D5 1998**

Mood disorders [videorecording]. Princeton, N.J. : Films for the Humanities & Sciences, 1998.
**TC RC537 .M6 1998**

Neurotic, stress-related, and somatoform disorders [videorecording]. Princeton, N.J. : Films for the Humanities & Sciences, 1998.
**TC RC530 .N4 1998**

Organic disorders [videorecording]. Princeton, N.J. : Films for the Humanities & Sciences, 1998.
**TC RC521 .O7 1998**

Personality disorders [videorecording]. Princeton, N.J. : Films for the Humanities & Sciences, 1998.
**TC RC554 .P4 1998**

Schizophrenia and delusional disorders [videorecording]. Princeton, N.J. : Films for the Humanities & Sciences, c1998.
**TC RC514 .S3 1998**

**Petersen, Per Serritslev.**
Literary pedagogics after deconstruction. Aarhus, Denmark : Aarhus University Press, 1992.
**TC PR33 .L58 1992**

**Peterson, Brian H.**
Sport photography today! [videorecording]. Minneapolis, Minn. : Media Loft, c1992.
**TC TR821 .S64 1992**

**Peterson, Candida D. (Candida Clifford).**
Children's understanding of biology and health. 1st ed. Cambridge, U.K. ; New York : Cambridge University Press, 1999.
**TC BF723.C5 C514 1999**

**Peterson, Carolyn Sue, 1938-** Story programs : a source book of materials / Carolyn Sue Peterson and Ann D. Fenton ; revised and edited by Stefani Koorey. 2nd ed. Lanham, Md. : Scarecrow Press, 2000. x, 359 p. : ill. ; 28 cm. (School library media series ; 10) Includes bibliographical references and index. ISBN 0-8108-3207-0 pbk. : alk. paper) DDC 372.67/7
*1. Storytelling. 2. Activity programs in education. I. Fenton, Ann D. II. Koorey, Stefani, 1959- III. Title. IV. Series: School library media series ; no. 10.*
**TC LB1042 .P47 2000**

**Peterson, Donald R. (Donald Robert), 1923-**
Educating professional psychologists : history and guiding conception / Donald R. Peterson. 1st ed. Washington, D.C. : American Psychological Association, c1997. xx, 281 p. ; 26 cm. Includes bibliographical references (p. 253-271) and index. ISBN 1-55798-420-4 (pbk.) DDC 150/.71/173
*1. Psychologists - Training of - United States. I. Title.*
**TC BF80.7.U6 P48 1997**

**Peterson, John L.**
Handbook of HIV prevention. New York : Kluwer/Plenum, 2000.
**TC RA644.A25 H365 2000**

**Peterson, Jordan B.** Maps of meaning : the architecture of belief / Jordan B. Peterson. New York : Routledge, 1999. xxii, 541 p. : ill. ; 23 cm. Includes bibliographical references (p. 503-512) and index. ISBN 0-415-92221-6 (hardcover) ISBN 0-415-92222-4 (pbk) DDC 150/.1
*1. Archetype (Psychology) 2. Meaning (Psychology) I. Title.*
**TC BF175.5.A72 P48 1999**

**Peterson, Keith.**
Drever, Mina. Teaching English in primary classrooms. Stoke on Trent, Staffordshire, England : Trentham Books, 1999.
**TC LB1576 .D749 1999**

**Peterson, Kent D.**
Deal, Terrence E. Shaping school culture. 1st ed. San Francisco : Jossey-Bass Publishers, c1999.
**TC LB2805 .D34 1999**

**Peterson, Nadene.** The role of work in people's lives : applied career counseling and vocational psychology / Nadene Peterson, Roberto Cortéz González. Australia ; Belmont, Calif. : Wadsworth Pub. Co., c2000. xi, 580 p. : ill. ; 24 cm. Includes bibliographical references and index. ISBN 0-534-34688-X DDC 158.7
*1. Vocational guidance. 2. Work - Psychological aspects. I. González, Roberto Cortéz. II. Title.*
**TC HF5381 .P483 2000**

**Peterson, Patricia M.**
Boschee, Floyd. School bond success. 1st ed. Lancaster, Pa. : Technomic Publishing Co., c1999.
**TC LB2825 .B63 1999**

**Peterson, Susan Louise, 1960-** Why children make up stories : a practical guide to help adults recognize the underlying reasons children make up stories / Susan Louise Peterson. San Francisco ; London : International Scholars Publications, 1999. 97 p. ; 22 cm. Includes bibliographical references (p. [99]) and index. ISBN 1-57309-381-5 (hbk. : alk. paper) ISBN 1-57309-382-3 (pbk. : alk. paper) DDC 155.4/136
*1. Interpersonal communication in children. 2. Children and adults. I. Title.*
**TC BF723.C57 P47 1999**

**Petitot, Jean, 1944-.**
Naturalizing phenomenology. Stanford, Calif. : Stanford University Press, c1999.
**TC B829.5 .N38 1999**

**Petkoski, Djordjija B.** Learning together with clients : private sector development training and consulting in economies in transition / Djordjija Petkoski. Washington, D.C. : World Bank, c1997. viii, 67 p. ; 28 cm. (EDI case studies) "Economic Development Institute of the World Bank"--Cover. Includes bibliographical references.
*1. Privatization - Developing countries. 2. Economic development projects - Developing countries. 3. Training needs - Developing countries. I. Economic Development Institute (Washington, D.C.) II. Title. III. Series.*
**TC HQ4420.8.P48 1997**

**Petocz, Agnes.** Freud, psychoanalysis, and symbolism / Agnes Petocz. Cambridge ; New York : Cambridge University Press, 1999. xi, 284 p. ; 24 cm. Includes bibliographical references (p. 269-277) and index. ISBN 0-521-59152-X (hardback) DDC 150.19/52
*1. Freud, Sigmund, - 1856-1939. 2. Symbolism (Psychology) 3. Psychoanalysis. I. Title.*
**TC BF109.F74 P48 1999**

**Petrides, Lisa Ann, 1961-.**
Cases studies on information technology in higher education. Hershey, PA : Idea Group Pub., c2000.
**TC LB2395.7 .C39 2000**

**PETROGLYPHS. See ROCK PAINTINGS.**

**Petronio, Sandra Sporbert.**
Balancing the secrets of private disclosures. Mahwah, N.J. : Lawrence Erlbaum Associates, Publishers, 2000.
**TC BF697.5.S427 B35 2000**

**Petrou, Maria.**
MLDM'99 (1999 : Leipzig, Germany) Machine learning and data mining in pattern recognition. Berlin ; New York : Springer, c1999.
**TC Q327 .M56 1999**

**Petry, Michael.**
Oliveira, Nicolas de. Installation art. London : Thames and Hudson, 1994.
**TC N6494.E O4 1994**

**Pettegree, Andrew.**
Anglo-Dutch Historical Conference (13th : 1997) The education of a Christian society. Aldershot, Hants, England ; Brookfield, Vt. : Ashgate, c1999.
**TC BR377 .E38 1999**

**Pettit, Elinor.**
Design dialogues. New York : Allworth Press, c1998.
**TC NK1390 .D473 1998**

**Petty, Kate.** Horse heroes : true stories of amazing horses / written by Kate Petty. 1st American ed. New York : DK Pub., c1999. 48 p. : ill. (some col.), maps ; 24 cm. (Eyewitness readers. Level 4) SUMMARY: Tells seven stories of heroic and amazing horses. ISBN 0-7894-4001-6 (hardcover) ISBN 0-7894-4000-8 (pbk.) DDC 636.1
*1. Horses - Biography - Juvenile literature. 2. Horses. I. Title. II. Series.*
**TC SF302 .P47 1999**

**Pexman, Penny M.**
Nicol, Adelheid A. M. Presenting your findings. 1st ed. Washington, DC : American Psychological Association, c1999.
**TC HA31 .N53 1999**

**Pezone, Mike.**
Democratic dialogue with special needs students. [Boulder, Colo.] : Social Science Education Consortium, c1997.
**TC LC4069.3 .D4 1997**

**Pfaffenberger, Bryan, 1949-** Mastering GNOME / Bryan Pfaffenberger. San Francisco, CA : Sybex, Inc., 1999. xlii, 821 p. : ill. ; 23 cm. + 1 computer laser optical disc (4 3/4 in.). ISBN 0-7821-2625-1 DDC 005.4/37
*1. Graphical user interfaces (Computer systems) 2. Application program interfaces (Computer software) 3. Linux. I. Title.*
**TC QA76.9.U83 P453 1999**

**Pfeifer, Rolf, 1947-** Understanding intelligence / Rolf Pfeifer and Christian Scheier ; with figures by Alex Riegler and cartoons by Isabelle Follath. Cambridge, Mass. : MIT Press, c1999. xx, 697 p. : ill. ; 26 cm. Includes bibliographical references and indexes. ISBN 0-262-16181-8 (hc : alk. paper) DDC 006.3
*1. Artificial intelligence. 2. Cognitive science. 3. Expert systems (Computer science) I. Scheier, Christian. II. Title.*
**TC Q335 .P46 1999**

**Pfeiffer, Steven I.**
Inclusion practices with special needs students. New York : Haworth Press, c1999.
**TC LC1201 .I538 1999**

Outcome assessment in residential treatment. New York : Haworth Press, c1996.
**TC RJ504.5 .O98 1996**

**PH. D. DEGREE. See DOCTOR OF PHILOSOPHY DEGREE.**

**PHANTOMS. See GHOSTS.**

**Phantoms in the brain.**
Ramachandran, V. S. 1st ed. New York : William Morrow, c1998.
**TC RC351 .R24 1998**

**PHARMACEUTICAL INDUSTRY - LAW AND LEGISLATION. See DRUGS - LAW AND LEGISLATION.**

**PHARMACEUTICAL POLICY. See DRUGS - LAW AND LEGISLATION.**

**PHARMACEUTICALS. See DRUGS.**

**PHARMACOKINETICS.**
Pharmacology in exercise and sports. Boca Raton : CRC Press, c1996.
**TC QP301 .P53 1996**

**PHARMACOLOGY. See also DRUGS; PSYCHOPHARMACOLOGY.**
Pharmacology in exercise and sports. Boca Raton : CRC Press, c1996.
**TC QP301 .P53 1996**

**Pharmacology & toxicology (Boca Raton, Fla.)**
Pharmacology in exercise and sports. Boca Raton : CRC Press, c1996.
**TC QP301 .P53 1996**

**PHARMACOLOGY, CLINICAL.**
Pharmacology in exercise and sports. Boca Raton : CRC Press, c1996.
**TC QP301 .P53 1996**

**Pharmacology in exercise and sports** / edited by Satu M. Somani. Boca Raton : CRC Press, c1996. 359 p. : ill. ; 25 cm. (Pharmacology and toxicology) Includes bibliographical references and index. ISBN 0-8493-8540-7 (acid-free paper) DDC 615/.7
*1. Exercise - Physiological aspects. 2. Drug interactions. 3. Doping in sports. 4. Pharmacology. 5. Pharmacology, Clinical. 6. Exercise - physiology. 7. Pharmacokinetics. I. Somani, Satu M. II. Series: Pharmacology & toxicology (Boca Raton, Fla.)*
**TC QP301 .P53 1996**

**PHARMACOPOEIAS. See DRUGS.**

**PHARMACY. See DRUGS.**

**PHD DEGREE. See DOCTOR OF PHILOSOPHY DEGREE.**

**Phelan, Jo C.**
Handbook of the sociology of mental health. New York : Kluwer Academic/Plenum Publishers, c1999.
**TC RC455 .H2874 1999**

**PHENOMENOLOGY.**
Merleau-Ponty, Maurice, 1908-1961. [Phénoménologie de la perception. English] Phenomenology of perception. London ; New York : Routledge, 1962.
**TC B829.5 .M413 1962**

Merleau-Ponty, Maurice, 1908-1961. Phenomenology of perception. London : Routledge & K. Paul ; New Jersey : Humanities Press, 1986, c1962.
**TC B829.5 .M413 1986**

Merleau-Ponty, Maurice, 1908-1961. The primacy of perception, and other essays on phenomenological psychology, the philosophy of art, history, and politics. [Evanston, Ill.] : Northwestern University Press, 1964.
**TC B2430.M378 E5 1964**

Merleau-Ponty, Maurice, 1908-1961. [Sens et non-sens. English] Sense and non-sense. [Evanston, Ill.] Northwestern University Press, 1964.

**TC B2430.M379 S43 1964**

Naturalizing phenomenology. Stanford, Calif. : Stanford University Press, c1999.
**TC B829.5 .N38 1999**

Nursing and the experience of illness. London ; New York : Routledge, 1999.
**TC RT86 .N886 1999**

**Phenomenology of perception.**
Merleau-Ponty, Maurice, 1908-1961. [Phénoménologie de la perception. English] London ; New York : Routledge, 1962.
**TC B829.5 .M413 1962**

Merleau-Ponty, Maurice, 1908-1961. London : Routledge & K. Paul ; New Jersey : Humanities Press, 1986, c1962.
**TC B829.5 .M413 1986**

**Phi Delta Kappa.**
Time and learning :. Bloomington, IN : Phi Delta Kappa International, c1998.
**TC LB3032 .T562 1998**

**Phi Delta Kappa. Educational Foundation.**
Baker, Justine C. A neural network guide to teaching. Bloomington, Ind. : Phi Delta Kappa Educational Foundation, c1998.
**TC LB1057 .B35 1998**

Baldwin, Harmon A. (Harmon Arthur), 1922- Planning for disaster. 2nd ed. Bloomington, Ind. : Phi Delta Kappa Educational Foundation, c1999.
**TC LB2864.5 .B35 1999**

Baldwin, John. Education and welfare reform. Bloomington, Ind. : Phi Delta Kappa Educational Foundation, c1993.
**TC LC4033.S61 B34 1993**

Fersh, Seymour. Integrating the trans-national/cultural dimension. Bloomington, Ind. : Phi Delta Kappa Educational Foundation, c1993.
**TC LC1090 .F47 1993**

Sparzo, Frank J. The ABC's of behavior change. Bloomington, Ind., U.S.A. : Phi Delta Kappa Educational Foundation, c1999.
**TC LB1060.2 .S62 1999**

**Phi Delta Kappa international studies in education**
Ashmore, Rhea A. Teacher education in the People's Republic of China. Bloomington, Ind., U.S.A. : Phi Delta Kappa Educational Foundation, c1997.
**TC LB1727.C5 A85 1997**

Dichanz, Horst, 1937- Changing traditions in Germany's public schools. Bloomington, Ind. : Phi Delta Kappa Educational Foundation, c1998.
**TC LA723 .D53 1998**

Innovation in Russian schools. Bloomington, Ind. : Phi Delta Kappa Educational Foundation, c1997.
**TC LB1027 .I6575 1997**

**PHILADELPHIA (PA.) - HISTORY - REVOLUTION, 1775-1783 - PERSONAL NARRATIVES - JUVENILE LITERATURE.**
Wister, Sarah, 1761-1804. A colonial Quaker girl. Mankato, Minn. : Blue Earth Books, c2000.
**TC F158.44 .W75 2000**

**PHILADELPHIA (PA.) - HISTORY - REVOLUTION, 1775-1783 - SOCIAL ASPECTS - JUVENILE LITERATURE.**
Wister, Sarah, 1761-1804. A colonial Quaker girl. Mankato, Minn. : Blue Earth Books, c2000.
**TC F158.44 .W75 2000**

**PHILADELPHIA (PA.) - SOCIAL CONDITIONS.**
Anderson, Elijah. Code of the street. 1st ed. New York : W.W Norton, c1999.
**TC F158.9.N4 A52 1999**

**PHILADELPHIA (PA.) - SOCIAL LIFE AND CUSTOMS.**
Anderson, Elijah. Code of the street. 1st ed. New York : W.W Norton, c1999.
**TC F158.9.N4 A52 1999**

**PHILANTHROPISTS. See WOMEN PHILANTHROPISTS.**

**PHILANTHROPISTS - NEW YORK (STATE) - NEW YORK.**
Ostrower, Francie. Why the wealthy give. Princeton, N.J. : Princeton University Press, c1995.
**TC HV99.N59 O85 1995**

**PHILANTHROPISTS - UNITED STATES.**
Prince, Russ Alan, 1958- The seven faces of philanthropy. 1st ed. San Francisco : Jossey-Bass, c1994.

*Philanthropy*

*TC HV41.9.U5 P74 1994*

## PHILANTHROPY. *See* CHARITIES; CHARITY ORGANIZATION; ENDOWMENTS; SOCIAL SERVICE.

**Philanthropy and the nonprofit sector in a changing America.**
American Assembly (93rd : 1998 : Los Angeles, Calif.) Trust, service, and the common purpose. Indianapolis, IN : Indiana University Center on Philanthropy ; New York, NY : American Assembly, [1998]
*TC HD62.6 .A44 1998*

**Philip Lief Group.**
American Jewish desk reference. 1st ed. New York : Random House, 1999.
*TC E184.35 .A44 1999*

## PHILIPPINES - PERIODICALS.
Baguio tech journal. [Baguio City, Philippines : Baguio Tech.,

**Philippot, Pierre, 1960-.**
The social context of nonverbal behavior. Cambridge, U.K. ; New York : Cambridge University Press ; Paris : Editions de la Maison des Sciences de l'Homme, 1999.
*TC BF637.N66 S63 1999*

**Phillips Academy.**
General education in school and college. Cambridge : Harvard University Press, 1952.
*TC 372G28*

Montgomery, Susan J., 1947- New York : Princeton Architectural Press, 2000.
*TC LD7501.A5 M65 2000*

**Phillips Academy, Andover, Mass. Addison Gallery of American Art.**
Hofmann, Hans, 1880-1966. Search for the real, [Rev. ed.]. Cambridge, Mass., M.I.T. Press [c1967]
*TC N7445 .H76 1967*

Hofmann, Hans, 1880-1966. Search for the real, [Rev. ed.]. Cambridge, Mass., M.I.T. Press [c1967]
*TC N7445 .H76 1967*

## PHILLIPS ACADEMY - BUILDINGS - GUIDEBOOKS.
Montgomery, Susan J., 1947- Phillips Academy. New York : Princeton Architectural Press, 2000.
*TC LD7501.A5 M65 2000*

## PHILLIPS ACADEMY - BUILDINGS - PICTORIAL WORKS.
Montgomery, Susan J., 1947- Phillips Academy. New York : Princeton Architectural Press, 2000.
*TC LD7501.A5 M65 2000*

**Phillips, D. C. (Denis Charles), 1938-.**
Constructivism in education. Chicago, Ill. : NSSE : Distributed by the University of Chicago Press, 2000.
*TC LB5 .N25 99th pt. 1*

**Phillips, David, 1944 Dec. 15-.**
Comparing standards internationally. Wallingford : Symposium, 1999.
*TC QA11 .C64 1999*

Processes of transition in education systems. Wallingford : Symposium, 1998.
*TC LC71 .P7 1998*

**Phillips, Deborah.**
Quality in child care. Washington, D.C. : National Association for the Education of Young Children, c1987.
*TC HQ778.7.U6 Q35 1987*

**Phillips, Diane.** Projects with young learners / Diane Phillips, Sarah Burwood & Helen Dunford. Oxford ; New York : Oxford University Press, c1999. 152 p. : ill. ; 28 cm. (Resource books for teachers.) Includes bibliographical references and indexes. ISBN 0-19-437221-9
*1. English language - Study and teaching (Elementary). I. Burwood, Sarah. II. Dunford, Helen. III. Title. IV. Series.*
*TC LB1576 .P577 1999*

**Phillips, Francis R.** Creating an education system for England and Wales / Francis R. Phillips. Lewiston, N.Y. : E. Mellen Press, 1992. ii, 197 p. ; 24 cm. (Welsh studies ; v. 8) Includes bibliographical references (p. [179]-187) and index. ISBN 0-7734-9528-2 DDC 372.942
*1. Education, Elementary - England - History - 19th century. 2. Education, Elementary - Wales - History - 19th century. 3. Education and state - England - History - 19th century. 4. Church and education - England - History - 19th century. I. Title. II. Series.*
*TC LA633 .P48 1992*

**Phillips, James B.** Accent : each his own : any human to another : promised land ; variables / James B. Phillips, James Pike, & Olive Stafford Niles. Glenview, Ill. : Scott, Foresman, 1972. 1 v. (various pagings) : ill. (some col.) ; 24 cm. (Galaxy series) Includes index.
*1. Readers. I. Pike, James. II. Niles, Olive S. III. Title. IV. Series.*
*TC PE1121 .P54 1972*

**Phillips, June K.**
Foreign language standards. Lincolnwood, Ill., U.S.A. : National Textbook Company in conjunction with the American Council on the Teaching of Foreign Languages, c1999.
*TC P53 .F674 1999*

**Phillips, Katharine A.**
Pope, Harrison. The Adonis complex. New York : Free Press, 2000.
*TC BF697.5.B635 2000*

## PHILLIPS, MAY, 1856-1937.
McLeod, Ellen Mary Easton, 1945- In good hands. Montreal : Ithaca : Published for Carleton University by McGill-Queen's University Press, c1999.
*TC NK841 .M38 1999*

**Phillips, Robert, 1959-.**
Issues in history teaching. London ; New York : Routledge, 2000.
*TC D16.2 .I88 2000*

**Phillips, Sarah.** Drama with children / Sarah Phillips. Oxford ; New York : Oxford University Press, c1999. 151 p. : ill. ; 28 cm. (Resource books for teachers.) Includes bibliographical references (p. [149]-151) and indexes. ISBN 0-19-437220-0
*1. Drama in education. 2. English language - Study and teaching (Elementary) - Activity programs. I. Title. II. Series.*
*TC PN3171 .P45 1999*

**Phillipson, Robert.**
Rights to language. Mahwah, N.J. : L. Erlbaum Associates, 2000.
*TC P119.3 .R54 2000*

## PHILOLOGY. *See* GRAMMAR, COMPARATIVE AND GENERAL; LANGUAGE AND LANGUAGES; LITERATURE.

## PHILOLOGY, CLASSICAL. *See* CLASSICAL PHILOLOGY.

## PHILOLOGY, MEDIEVAL. *See* PHILOLOGY, MODERN.

## PHILOLOGY, MODERN - PERIODICALS.
Levende talen magazine. Amsterdam : Vereniging van Leraren in Levenden Talen, 2000-

**Philosophers and religious leaders** / edited by Christian D. von Dehsen ; writers, Scott L. Harris ... [et al.]. Phoenix, Ariz. : Oryx Press, 1999. x, 246 p. : ill. ; 29 cm. (Lives and legacies) Series subtitle: Encyclopedia of people who changed the world. Includes bibliographical references (p. 231-234) and index. ISBN 1-57356-152-5 (alk. paper) DDC 109/.2
*1. Philosophers - Biography - Encyclopedias. 2. Religious biography - Encyclopedias. I. Von Dehsen, Christian D. II. Harris, Scott L. III. Title: Encyclopedia of people who changed the world. IV. Series.*
*TC B104 .P48 1999*

## PHILOSOPHERS - BIOGRAPHY - ENCYCLOPEDIAS.
Philosophers and religious leaders. Phoenix, Ariz. : Oryx Press, 1999.
*TC B104 .P48 1999*

## PHILOSOPHERS - UNITED STATES - BIOGRAPHY.
Schilpp, Paul Arthur, 1897- Reminiscing. Carbondale, IL : Published for the College of Liberal Arts of Southern Illinois University at Carbondale by Southern Illinois University Press, c1996.
*TC B945.S28 A3 1996*

## PHILOSOPHERS - UNITED STATES - CORRESPONDENCE.
Dewey, John, 1859-1952. The correspondence of John Dewey. [computer file]. Windows version. Charlottesville, VA : InteLex Corp., 1999- Computer data and program.
*TC B945.D44 A4 1999*

**Philosophical & cultural values.**
Crawford, George, 1937- Larchmont, NY : Eye On Education, c2000.
*TC LB2831.92 .C72 2000*

**Philosophical and cultural values.**
Crawford, George, 1937- Philosophical & cultural values. Larchmont, NY : Eye On Education, c2000.

*TC LB2831.92 .C72 2000*

**Philosophical and ethical problems in mental handicap** / Peter Byrne.
Byrne, Peter, 1950- New York : St. Martin's Press , 2000.
*TC HV3004 .B95 2000*

## PHILOSOPHICAL ANTHROPOLOGY. *See* HUMANISM; MIND AND BODY; PHILOSOPHY OF MIND.

## PHILOSOPHICAL COUNSELING. *See also* CONDUCT OF LIFE.
Schuster, Shlomit C., 1951- Philosophy practice. Westport, Conn. : London : Praeger, 1999.
*TC BJ1595.5 .S38 1999*

**Philosophical dimensions of personal construct psychology.**
Warren, William, 1942- London ; New York : Routledge, 1998.
*TC BF698.9.P47 W37 1998*

**Philosophical documents in education** / edited by Ronald F. Reed, Tony W. Johnson. 2nd ed. New York : Longman, c2000. xvii, 301 p. ; 24 cm. Includes bibliographical references and indexes. ISBN 0-8013-3316-4 DDC 370/.1
*1. Education - Philosophy. I. Reed, Ronald F. II. Johnson, Tony W.*
*TC LB7 .P5432 2000*

## PHILOSOPHICAL GRAMMAR. *See* GRAMMAR, COMPARATIVE AND GENERAL.

**Philosophical psychopathology. Disorders in mind**
When self-consciousness breaks. Cambridge, Mass. : MIT Press, c2000.
*TC RC553.A84 S74 2000*

**Philosophical studies in contemporary culture**
(ol. v 7) Schwartz, David T. Art, education, and the democratic commitment. Dordrecht ; Boston : Kluwer Academic Publishers, c2000.
*TC NX720 .S33 2000*

**Philosophische Studien (Leipzig, Germany).**
Archiv für die gesamte Psychologie. Leipzig : W. Englemann, 1903-1969.

**Philosophizing art.**
Danto, Arthur Coleman, 1924- Berkeley : University of California Press, c1999.
*TC N71 .D33 1999*

## PHILOSOPHY. *See also* ACT (PHILOSOPHY); AESTHETICS; BELIEF AND DOUBT; BODY, HUMAN (PHILOSOPHY); CONSCIOUSNESS; CONSTRUCTIVISM (PHILOSOPHY); DUALISM; ETHICS; EVOLUTION; HUMANISM; INTENTIONALITY (PHILOSOPHY); INTUITION; KNOWLEDGE, THEORY OF; LOGIC; MEANING (PHILOSOPHY); MEMORY (PHILOSOPHY); PERCEPTION; PERCEPTION (PHILOSOPHY); PHILOSOPHY OF MIND; PSYCHOLOGY; REFLECTION (PHILOSOPHY); REPRESENTATION (PHILOSOPHY); THOUGHT AND THINKING; TRANSCENDENCE (PHILOSOPHY).
Between demonstration and imagination. Leiden, Netherlands : Boston : Brill, 1999.
*TC QB15 .B56 1999*

## PHILOSOPHY, AMERICAN. *See* NAVAJO PHILOSOPHY.

**Philosophy and computing.**
Floridi, Luciano, 1964- London ; New York: Routledge, 1999.
*TC QA76.167 .F56 1999*

## PHILOSOPHY AND SCIENCE. *See* SCIENCE - PHILOSOPHY.

**Philosophy and the arts in Central Europe, 1500-1700.**
Freedman, Joseph S. Aldershot : Ashgate, 1999.
*TC B52.3.C36 F74 1999*

## PHILOSOPHY - BIOGRAPHY. *See* PHILOSOPHERS.

## PHILOSOPHY - COLLECTED WORKS.
Dewey, John, 1859-1952. [Works.] The collected works of John Dewey, 1882-1953. [computer file]. Windows version. Charlottesville, VA : InteLex Corp, 1997, c1992. Computer program.
*TC LB875 .D363 1997*

## PHILOSOPHY - DICTIONARIES.
The Cambridge dictionary of philosophy. 2nd ed.

Cambridge ; New York : Cambridge University Press, 1999.
*TC B41 .C35 1999*

**PHILOSOPHY, DOCTOR OF.** *See* **DOCTOR OF PHILOSOPHY DEGREE.**

**PHILOSOPHY, EUROPEAN.**
The Edinburgh encyclopedia of Continental philosophy. Edinburgh : University Press, c1999.
*TC B831.2 E35 1999*

**PHILOSOPHY, MODERN.** *See also* **SEMANTICS (PHILOSOPHY).**
Humanism and early modern philosophy. London ; New York : Routledge, 2000.
*TC B821 .H657 2000*

**PHILOSOPHY, MODERN - 18TH CENTURY.** *See* **ENLIGHTENMENT.**

**PHILOSOPHY, MODERN - 20TH CENTURY.** *See* **POSTMODERNISM.**

**PHILOSOPHY, MODERN - PERIODICALS.**
Foundations of language; Dordrecht, Holland, Reidel.

**PHILOSOPHY, MORAL.** *See* **ETHICS.**

**PHILOSOPHY, NATURAL.** *See* **PHYSICS.**

**PHILOSOPHY, NAVAJO.** *See* **NAVAJO PHILOSOPHY.**

**PHILOSOPHY, NURSING.**
Bishop, Anne H., 1935- Nursing ethics. 2nd ed. Sudbury, Mass. : Jones and Bartlett, c2001.
*TC RT85 .B57 2001*

Kim, Hesook Suzie. The nature of theoretical thinking in nursing. 2nd ed. New York : Springer Pub. Co., c2000.
*TC RT84.5 .K545 2000*

Nursing theories. New York : Springer Pub. Co., c1999.
*TC RT84.5 .N8795 1999*

Reflective practice in nursing. 2nd ed. Oxford ; Malden, MA : Blackwell Scientific, 2000.
*TC RT73 .R3461 2000*

**Philosophy of higher education series**
(1.) The university and the knowledge society. Bemmel [Netherlands] : Concorde Publishing House, 1998.
*TC LB2322.2 .U55 1998*

**A philosophy of mass art.**
Carroll, Noël (Noël E.) Oxford : Clarendon Press ; New York : Oxford University Press, 1998.
*TC NX180.M3 C37 1998*

**PHILOSOPHY OF MIND.** *See also* **COGNITIVE SCIENCE.**
Cerruto, Audra. The effects of training on theory of mind tasks with children who are deaf. 1999.
*TC 085 C34*

Flanagan, Owen J. Dreaming souls. Oxford ; New York : Oxford University Press, 2000.
*TC BF1091 .F58 2000*

Gillett, Grant, 1950- The mind and its discontents. Oxford ; New York : Oxford University Press, c1999.
*TC BD418.3 .G555 1999*

Glynn, Ian. An anatomy of thought. Oxford ; New York : Oxford University Press, [1999].
*TC QP360 .G595 1999*

Rowlands, Mark. The body in mind. Cambridge, U.K. ; New York : Cambridge University Press, 1999.
*TC BD418.3 .R78 1999*

Scruton, Roger. Art and imagination. South Bend, Ind. : St. Augustine's Press, 1998.
*TC BH301.J8 S37 1998*

Wagman, Morton. The human mind according to artificial intelligence. Westport, Conn. : Praeger, 1999.
*TC Q335 .W342 1999*

**PHILOSOPHY OF MIND IN CHILDREN.**
Children's reasoning and the mind. Hove : Psychology, c2000.
*TC BF723.R4 C555 2000*

Minds in the making. Oxford ; Malden, Mass. : Blackwell, 2000.
*TC BF723.C5 M56 2000*

**Philosophy of mind series**
Flanagan, Owen J. Dreaming souls. Oxford ; New York : Oxford University Press, 2000.
*TC BF1091 .F58 2000*

**Philosophy of moral education series**
(1.) Moral sensibilities and education. Bemmel : Concorde Pub. House, 1999-
*TC BF723.M54 M684 1999*

**Philosophy of nursing.**
Brencick, Janice M. Albany : State University of New York Press, c2000.
*TC RT84.5 .B74 2000*

**PHILOSOPHY OF PSYCHIATRY.** *See* **PSYCHIATRY - PHILOSOPHY.**

**The philosophy of religious education.**
Iheoma, E. O. Enugu, Nigeria : Fourth Dimension Pub., 1997.
*TC BV1464 .I44 1997*

**PHILOSOPHY OF TEACHING.** *See* **EDUCATION - PHILOSOPHY.**

**PHILOSOPHY - PERIODICALS.**
[Journal of the history of ideas (Online)] Journal of the history of ideas [computer file]. Baltimore, MD : Journal of the History of Ideas, Inc., c1996-
*TC EJOURNALS*

**Philosophy practice.**
Schuster, Shlomit C., 1951- Westport, Conn. ; London : Praeger, 1999.
*TC BJ1595.5 .S38 1999*

**PHILOSOPHY - QUOTATIONS, MAXIMS, ETC.**
Historical dictionary of quotations in cognitive science. Westport, Conn. : Greenwood Press, 2000.
*TC PN6084.C545 H57 2000*

**PHILOSOPHY - STUDY AND TEACHING - EUROPE, CENTRAL - HISTORY.**
Freedman, Joseph S. Philosophy and the arts in Central Europe, 1500-1700. Aldershot : Ashgate, 1999.
*TC B52.3.C36 F74 1999*

**Phim, Toni Samantha, 1957-** Dance in Cambodia / Toni Samantha Phim and Ashley Thompson. [Kuala Lumpur] Malaysia ; Oxford ; New York : Oxford University Press, 1999. xii, 91 p., [16] p. of plates : ill. (some col.) ; 21 cm. (Images of Asia) Includes bibliographical references (p. 85-86) and index. ISBN 983-56-0059-7 DDC 792.8/09596
1. Dance - Cambodia. 2. Cambodia - Social life and customs. I. Thompson, Ashley, 1965- II. Title. III. Series.
*TC GV1703.C3 P55 1999*

**PHINN, GERVASE.** Young readers and their books : suggestions and strategies for using texts in the literacy hour. London : David Fulton, 2000. viii, 136 p. ; 25 cm. Includes bibliographical references and index. ISBN 1-85346-681-6
1. Children's literature - Study and teaching (Elementary)
*TC LB1575 .P45 2000*

**PHOBIAS.** *See* **AGORAPHOBIA; HOMOPHOBIA; XENOPHOBIA.**

**PHOBIAS - DIAGNOSIS.**
Neurotic, stress-related, and somatoform disorders [videorecording]. Princeton, N.J. : Films for the Humanities & Sciences, 1998.
*TC RC530 .N4 1998*

**PHOBIAS - TREATMENT.**
Step on a crack [videorecording]. Boston, MA : Fanlight Productions, 1996.
*TC RC533 .S7 1996*

**PHOBIC DISORDERS.** *See* **PHOBIAS.**

**PHOBIC NEUROSES.** *See* **PHOBIAS.**

**PHONATION DISORDERS.** *See* **VOICE DISORDERS.**

**PHONATORY DISORDERS.** *See* **VOICE DISORDERS.**

**PHONETICS.** *See also* **SPEECH; VOICE.**
Coarticulation. Cambridge, U.K. ; New York : Cambridge University Press, 1999.
*TC QP306 .C68 1999*

Goldsworthy, Candace L. Sourcebook of phonological awareness activities. San Diego : Singular Pub. Group, c1998.
*TC LB1050.5 .G66 1998*

Gunning, Thomas G. Phonological awareness and primary phonics. Boston : Allyn and Bacon, c2000.
*TC P221 .G85 2000*

**PHONETICS - STUDY AND TEACHING (PRIMARY).**
Opitz, Michael F. Rhymes & reasons. Portsmouth, NH : Heinemann, c2000.
*TC LB1528 .O65 2000*

**PHONICS.** *See* **READING - PHONETIC METHOD.**

**Phonics review kit** [kit] / Open Court Publishing Company ; [program authors: Marilyn Jager Adams ... [et al.]]. Chicago, Ill. : Open Court Pub. Co., c1995. 1 kit (1 sound cassette (analog, 1 7/8 ips); Learning Framework Cards [1,1a-5]; Phonics Review Cards [24 lessons]; Sound Spelling Cards; Step-by-Step Practice Stories; Phonics Review (activity sheets); Individual Sound Cards; Outlaw Work Flash Cards; Phonemic Awareness Cards; 1 guide (46 p. : ill. ; 28 cm.)) in box (24 x 31 x 11 cm.). (Collections for Young Scholars) Catalogued from container and guide. Title from container; statement of reponsibility from container and title page of guide. For second and third grades reading classes. SUMMARY: Sound recording offers additional aural support for those who need it. It offers an aural version of the short, interactive stories used to introduce the sounds on the Sound/Spelling Cards. Library lacking Step-by-Step Practice Stories, Individual Sound Cards, Outlaw Word Flash Cards, Phonemic Awareness Cards and all Sound/Spelling Cards save one. ISBN 0-8126-1244-2 (cassette) ISBN 0-8126-1239-6 (guide) ISBN 0-8126-1233-7 (Learning Framework cards) ISBN 0-8126-1252-3 (Learning Framework cards) ISBN 0-8126-1233-7 (Sound/Spelling card) ISBN 0-8126-1232-9 (Phonics Review cards)
1. Reading (Elementary) - Phonetic method. 2. Reading - Aids and devices. 3. English language - Phonemics - Study and teaching (Primary) 4. Education (Primary) - Activity programs. I. Adams, Marilyn Jager. II. Open Court Publishing Company. III. Series.
*TC LB1573.3 .P45 1995*

**Phonics they use.**
Cunningham, Patricia Marr. 3rd ed. New York : Longman, c2000.
*TC LB1573.3 .C86 2000*

**Phonological awareness activities.**
Goldsworthy, Candace L. Sourcebook of phonological awareness activities. San Diego : Singular Pub. Group, c1998.
*TC LB1050.5 .G66 1998*

**Phonological awareness and primary phonics.**
Gunning, Thomas G. Boston : Allyn and Bacon, c2000.
*TC P221 .G85 2000*

**PHONOLOGY.** *See* **PHONETICS.**

**PHOTO JOURNALISM.** *See* **PHOTOJOURNALISM.**

**PHOTOGRAPH COLLECTIONS - ILLINOIS - CHICAGO - CATALOGS.**
Museum of Contemporary Photography (Columbia College (Chicago, Ill.)) Photography's multiple roles. Chicago : Museum of Contemporary Photography, Columbia College ; New York : Dap, Inc., c1998.
*TC TR187 .M87 1998*

**PHOTOGRAPHERS.** *See* **WOMEN PHOTOGRAPHERS.**

**Photographers at work**
Roma, Thomas. Sunset Park. Washington : Smithsonian Institution Press, c1998.
*TC TR680 .R675 1998*

**PHOTOGRAPHERS - UNITED STATES - BIOGRAPHY - EXHIBITIONS.**
Panzer, Mary. Mathew Brady and the image of history. Washington, D.C. : Smithsonian Institution Press for the National Portrait Gallery, c1997.
*TC TR140.B7 P36 1997*

**PHOTOGRAPHIC CRITICISM.**
Museum of Contemporary Photography (Columbia College (Chicago, Ill.)) Photography's multiple roles. Chicago : Museum of Contemporary Photography, Columbia College ; New York : Dap, Inc., c1998.
*TC TR187 .M87 1998*

**PHOTOGRAPHS - CONSERVATION AND RESTORATION.**
Keefe, Laurence E. The life of a photograph. 2nd ed. Boston : Focal Press, c1990.
*TC TR465 .K44 1990*

**PHOTOGRAPHS - FICTION.**
Vincent, Gabrielle. [Ernest et Célestine chez le photographe. English] Smile, Ernest and Celestine. 1st American ed. New York : Greenwillow Books, c1982.
*TC PZ7.V744 Sm 1982*

**PHOTOGRAPHS - PRIVATE COLLECTIONS.** *See* **PHOTOGRAPH COLLECTIONS.**

**PHOTOGRAPHS - PRIVATE COLLECTIONS - PENNSYLVANIA - PHILADELPHIA - CATALOGS.**
Pennsylvania Academy of the Fine Arts. Eakins and the photograph. Washington : Published for the

Pennsylvania Academy of the Fine Arts by the Smithsonian Institution Press, c1994.
*TC TR652 .P46 1994*

**PHOTOGRAPHS - TRIMMING, MOUNTING, ETC.**
Keefe, Laurence E. The life of a photograph. 2nd ed. Boston : Focal Press, c1990.
*TC TR465 .K44 1990*

**PHOTOGRAPHY.** *See also* **CINEMATOGRAPHY; DOCUMENTARY PHOTOGRAPHY; PORTRAIT PHOTOGRAPHY.**
Entz, Susan. Picture this. Thousand Oaks, Calif. : Corwin Press, c2000.
*TC LB1043.67 .E58 2000*

Symbolic imprints. Aarhus : Aarhus University Press, c1999.
*TC TR145 .S96 1999*

**PHOTOGRAPHY, ABSTRACT.** *See* **PHOTOMONTAGE.**

**PHOTOGRAPHY - AESTHETICS.** *See* **PHOTOGRAPHY, ARTISTIC.**

**PHOTOGRAPHY - ANIMATED PICTURES.** *See* **CINEMATOGRAPHY.**

**PHOTOGRAPHY, ARTISTIC.**
Over exposed. New York : New Press, c1999.
*TC TR642 .O94 1999*

The power of idea : [videorecording]. Minneapolis, Minn. : Media Loft, c1992.
*TC TR690 .P5 1992*

The sight and insight of Ernst Haas [videorecording]. Minneapolis, Minn. : Media Loft, 1992.
*TC TR647.H3 S5 1992*

**PHOTOGRAPHY, ARTISTIC - AUSTRALIA.**
Alexander, George, 1949- Julie Rrap. [Sidney] : Piper Press, 1998.
*TC TR654 .A44 1998*

**PHOTOGRAPHY, ARTISTIC - EXHIBITIONS.**
National Museum of American Art (U.S.) American photographs. Washington, D.C. : National Museum of American Art, Smithsonian Institution : Smithsonian Institution Press, c1996.
*TC TR645.W18 N37 1996*

**PHOTOGRAPHY, ARTISTIC - PHILOSOPHY.**
The sight and insight of Ernst Haas [videorecording]. Minneapolis, Minn. : Media Loft, 1992.
*TC TR647.H3 S5 1992*

**PHOTOGRAPHY, COMPOSITE.** *See* **PHOTOMONTAGE.**

**PHOTOGRAPHY, DOCUMENTARY.** *See* **DOCUMENTARY PHOTOGRAPHY.**

**PHOTOGRAPHY FOR THE PRESS.** *See* **PHOTOJOURNALISM.**

**PHOTOGRAPHY, HANDWORKED.** *See* **PHOTOMONTAGE.**

**PHOTOGRAPHY - HISTORY.**
Sculpture and photography. Cambridge, [England] ; New York : Cambridge University Press, 1998.
*TC TR658.3 .S38 1998*

**PHOTOGRAPHY IN ETHNOLOGY.**
Spirit capture. Washington : Smithsonian Institution Press in association with the National Museum of the American Indian, Smithsonian Institution, c1998.
*TC E77.5 .S65 1998*

**PHOTOGRAPHY IN ETHNOLOGY - INDONESIA - BAYUNG GEDÉ (BALI).**
Sullivan, Gerald. Margaret Mead, Gregory Bateson, and Highland Bali. Chicago, IL : University of Chicago Press, 1999.
*TC GN635.I65 S948 1999*

**PHOTOGRAPHY, JOURNALISTIC.** *See* **PHOTOJOURNALISM.**

**PHOTOGRAPHY - MOTION PICTURES.** *See* **CINEMATOGRAPHY.**

**PHOTOGRAPHY OF FAMILIES.**
Kuhn, Annette. Family secrets. London ; New York : Verso, 1995.
*TC CT274 .K84 1995*

**PHOTOGRAPHY OF MEN - HISTORY.**
Cooper, Emmanuel. Fully exposed. 2nd ed. London ; New York : Routledge, c1995.
*TC TR674 .C66 1995*

**PHOTOGRAPHY OF SCULPTURE.**
Sculpture and photography. Cambridge, [England] ; New York : Cambridge University Press, 1998.

*TC TR658.3 .S38 1998*

**PHOTOGRAPHY OF SPORTS.**
Sport photography today! [videorecording]. Minneapolis, Minn. : Media Loft, c1992.
*TC TR821 .S64 1992*

**PHOTOGRAPHY OF THE MALE.** *See* **PHOTOGRAPHY OF MEN.**

**PHOTOGRAPHY OF THE NUDE - HISTORY.**
Cooper, Emmanuel. Fully exposed. 2nd ed. London ; New York : Routledge, c1995.
*TC TR674 .C66 1995*

**PHOTOGRAPHY, PICTORIAL.** *See* **PHOTOGRAPHY, ARTISTIC.**

**PHOTOGRAPHY - PORTRAITS.** *See* **PORTRAIT PHOTOGRAPHY.**

**PHOTOGRAPHY - TECHNIQUE.**
Luciana, James. The art of enhanced photography :. Gloucester, Mass. : Rockport Publishers, c1999.
*TC TR654 .L83 1999*

**PHOTOGRAPHY - THERAPEUTIC USE.**
Jackson, Eve, 1949- Learning disability in focus. London ; Philadelphia : Jessica Kingsley, c1999.
*TC RC489.P56 J33 1999*

**PHOTOGRAPHY - UNITED STATES.**
Museum of Contemporary Photography (Columbia College (Chicago, Ill.)) Photography's multiple roles. Chicago : Museum of Contemporary Photography, Columbia College ; New York : Dap, Inc., c1998.
*TC TR187 .M87 1998*

**PHOTOGRAPHY - UNITED STATES - HISTORY - 19TH CENTURY - EXHIBITIONS.**
National Museum of American Art (U.S.) American photographs. Washington, D.C. : National Museum of American Art, Smithsonian Institution : Smithsonian Institution Press, c1996.
*TC TR645.W18 N37 1996*

**Photography's multiple roles.**
Museum of Contemporary Photography (Columbia College (Chicago, Ill.)) Chicago : Museum of Contemporary Photography, Columbia College ; New York : Dap, Inc., c1998.
*TC TR187 .M87 1998*

**PHOTOJOURNALISM.**
The power of idea : [videorecording]. Minneapolis, Minn. : Media Loft, c1992.
*TC TR690 .P5 1992*

Sport photography today! [videorecording]. Minneapolis, Minn. : Media Loft, c1992.
*TC TR821 .S64 1992*

**PHOTOJOURNALISM - UNITED STATES - HISTORY.**
Carlebach, Michael L. American photojournalism comes of age. Washington : Smithsonian Institution Press, c1997.
*TC TR820 .C356 1997*

Carlebach, Michael L. The origins of photojournalism in America. Washington : Smithsonian Institution Press, c1992.
*TC TR820 .C357 1992*

**Photomontage.**
Golding, Stephen. Rockport, Massachusetts : Rockport Pub. Cincinnati, Ohio : North Light Books [distributor], c1997.
*TC TR685 .G64 1997*

Golding, Stephen. Photomontage :. Rockport, Massachusetts : Rockport Pub. Cincinnati, Ohio : North Light Books [distributor], c1997.
*TC TR685 .G64 1997*

**PHOTOMONTAGE - POLITICAL ASPECTS.**
Photomontage today, Peter Kennard [videorecording]. [London] : Art Council of Great Britain ; Ho-Ho-Kus, N.J. : [distributed by] Anthony Roland Collection of Films on Art, c1982.
*TC TR685 .P45 1982*

**PHOTOMONTAGE - SOCIAL ASPECTS.**
Photomontage today, Peter Kennard [videorecording]. [London] : Art Council of Great Britain ; Ho-Ho-Kus, N.J. : [distributed by] Anthony Roland Collection of Films on Art, c1982.
*TC TR685 .P45 1982*

**Photomontage today, Peter Kennard**
[videorecording] / Arts Council of Great Britain ; produced by TV Co-op, Television Co-operative [logo] ; production group, Ken Guest, Hamilton Hawksworth, Brian Hulls (Good News Productions) ; directed and produced, Chris Rodrigues, Rod Stoneman ; texts adapted from Michel Butor ... [et

al.]. [London] : Art Council of Great Britain ; Ho-Ho-Kus, N.J. : [distributed by] Anthony Roland Collection of Films on Art, c1982. 1 videocassette (35 min.) : sd., col. with b&w sequences ; 1/2 in. (Art tapes series / Television Co-operative ; 1) VHS, NTSC. Catalogued from credits, cassette label and container. Place of distribution from cassette label; addresses for the Roland Collection on container: Peasmarsh, East Sussex, England and Ho-Ho-Kus, NJ. Voices over, Hilary Thompson, Marc Karlin. Music, Simon Brint. "For John Heartfield, 1891-1968."--Opening credits. On spine of container and cassette case: "667." Age 14 and up. SUMMARY: "This program will investigate a particular form of photomontage, that which is directed toward political use. It will concentrate on the work of Peter Kennard as an example of one photomontagist working in Britain today. The questions his work raises are relevant to a wide range of issues connecting art and politics"--Voiceover introd.
*1. Photomontage - Political aspects. 2. Photomontage - Social aspects. 3. Art - Political aspects. 4. Social problems in art. 5. Kennard, Peter. 6. Documentary films. I. Kennard, Peter. II. Guest, Ken. III. Hawksworth, Hamilton. IV. Hulls, Brian. V. Rodrigues, Chris. VI. Stoneman, Rod. VII. Butor, Michael. VIII. Thompson, Hilary. IX. Karlin, Marc. X. Heartfield, John, 1891-1968. XI. Television Co-operative. XII. Arts Council of Great Britain. XIII. Anthony Roland Collection of Film on Art. XIV. Series: Art tapes series ; 1.*
*TC TR685 .P45 1982*

**PHOTOS.** *See* **PHOTOGRAPHS.**

**PHRENOLOGY.** *See* **MIND AND BODY.**

**Phtiaka, Helen.** Special kids for special treatment?, or, How special do you need to be to find yourself in a special school? / Helen Phtiaka. London ; Washington, D.C. : Falmer Press, 1997, xiv, 239 p. ; 24 cm. Includes bibliographical references (p. 219-233) and index. ISBN 0-7507-0618-X (paper : alk. paper) ISBN 0-7507-0725-9 (cased : alk. paper) DDC 371.93/0941
*1. Problem children - Education - Great Britain - Case studies. 2. Teacher-student relationships - Great Britain - Case studies. I. Title. II. Title: Special kids for special treatment? III. Title: How special do you need to be to find yourself in a special school?*
*TC LC4803.G7 P58 1998*

**PHYLOGENY.** *See* **EVOLUTION (BIOLOGY).**

**Physical and chemical characteristics of parchment and the materials used in its conservation.**
Haines, Betty M. Parchment. Northampton [England] : Leather Conservation Centre, 1999.
*TC TS1165 .H35 1999*

**PHYSICAL ANTHROPOLOGY.** *See also* **HUMAN BEHAVIOR; HUMAN MECHANICS; RACE.**
Hormones, health, and behavior. Cambridge ; New York : Cambridge University Press, 1999.
*TC QP356.45 .H67 1999*

**PHYSICAL-APPEARANCE-BASED BIAS.**
Solovay, Sondra, 1970- Tipping the scales of justice. Amherst, N.Y. : Prometheus Books, 2000.
*TC BF697.5.B63 S65 2000*

**Physical Best activity guide.**
Physical Best (Program) Champaign, IL : Human Kinetics, c1999.
*TC GV365 .P4993 1999*

**Physical Best (Program)** Physical Best activity guide : secondary level / American Alliance for Health, Physical Education, Recreation, and Dance. Champaign, IL : Human Kinetics, c1999. ix, 228 p. : ill. ; 28 cm. Includes bibliographical references (p. 213-215). ISBN 0-88011-971-3 DDC 613.7/043
*1. Physical education and training - Study and teaching (Secondary) - United States. I. American Alliance for Health, Physical Education, Recreation, and Dance. II. Title.*
*TC GV365 .P4993 1999*

Physical education for lifelong fitness : the Physical Best teacher's guide / American Alliance for Health, Physical Education, Recreation, and Dance. Champaign, Ill. : Human Kinetics, c1999. x, 397 p. : ill. ; 28 cm. Includes bibliographical references (p. 387-391) and index. ISBN 0-88011-983-7 DDC 613.7
*1. Physical education and training - Study and teaching - United States. 2. Physical fitness - Study and teaching - United States. I. American Alliance for Health, Physical Education, Recreation, and Dance. II. Title. III. Title: Physical Best teacher's guide*
*TC GV365 .P4992 1999*

**Physical Best teacher's guide.**
Physical Best (Program) Physical education for lifelong fitness. Champaign, Ill. : Human Kinetics, c1999.
*TC GV365 .P4992 1999*

**PHYSICAL CULTURE.** *See* **PHYSICAL EDUCATION AND TRAINING.**

**PHYSICAL CULTURE PHOTOGRAPHY.** *See* **PHOTOGRAPHY OF MEN.**

**PHYSICAL DIAGNOSIS.** *See* **NEUROLOGIC EXAMINATION.**

**PHYSICAL EDUCATION AND TRAINING.** *See* **COLLEGE SPORTS; EXERCISE; MOVEMENT EDUCATION; PHYSICAL EDUCATION FOR CHILDREN; PHYSICAL FITNESS; SCHOOL SPORTS; SPORTS.**

**PHYSICAL EDUCATION AND TRAINING.**
Foss, Merle L., 1936- Fox's physiological basis for exercise and sport. 6th ed. / Merle L. Foss, Steven J. Keteyian. Boston, Mass. : WCB/McGraw-Hill, c1998.
*TC RC1235 .F65 1998*

**PHYSICAL EDUCATION AND TRAINING - AUSTRALIA.**
Senior physical education. Champaign, IL : Human Kinetics, c1999.
*TC GV315 .S434 1999*

**PHYSICAL EDUCATION AND TRAINING - AUSTRALIA - HISTORY - 19TH CENTURY.**
Kirk, David, 1958- Schooling bodies. London ; Washington, D.C. : Leicester University Press, 1998.
*TC GV315 .K57 1998*

**PHYSICAL EDUCATION AND TRAINING - AUSTRALIA - HISTORY - 20TH CENTURY.**
Kirk, David, 1958- Schooling bodies. London ; Washington, D.C. : Leicester University Press, 1998.
*TC GV315 .K57 1998*

**PHYSICAL EDUCATION AND TRAINING - CHINA - HISTORY.**
Sport and physical education in China. London ; New York : Routledge, 1999.
*TC GV651 .S655 1999*

**PHYSICAL EDUCATION AND TRAINING - CURRICULA.**
V'elez Arias, Hiram Oscar. A multi-case study of physical education teachers and working conditions in inner-city schools /by Hiram Oscar V'elez Arias. 1998.
*TC 06 no. 11001*

**PHYSICAL EDUCATION AND TRAINING - ENGLAND - BRIGHTON.**
Webb, Ida M. The challenge of change in physical education :. London : Falmer Press, 1999.
*TC GV246.E3 B79 1999*

**PHYSICAL EDUCATION AND TRAINING - EQUIPMENT AND SUPPLIES.**
Davison, Bev, 1957- Creative physical activities and equipment. Champaign, IL : Human Kinetics, c1998.
*TC GV745 .D38 1998*

**PHYSICAL EDUCATION AND TRAINING - GREAT BRITAIN - HISTORY - 19TH CENTURY.**
Kirk, David, 1958- Schooling bodies. London ; Washington, D.C. : Leicester University Press, 1998.
*TC GV315 .K57 1998*

**PHYSICAL EDUCATION AND TRAINING - GREAT BRITAIN - HISTORY - 20TH CENTURY.**
Kirk, David, 1958- Schooling bodies. London ; Washington, D.C. : Leicester University Press, 1998.
*TC GV315 .K57 1998*

**PHYSICAL EDUCATION AND TRAINING - MEDICAL ASPECTS.** *See* **SPORTS MEDICINE.**

**PHYSICAL EDUCATION AND TRAINING - PERIODICALS.**
The Journal of health and physical education. Ann Arbor, Mich., : American Physical Education Association,

Medicine and science in sports. Madison, Wisc.

**PHYSICAL EDUCATION AND TRAINING - STUDY AND TEACHING.**
Martin, Robert J. A study of the reflective practices of physical education student teachers. 1998.
*TC 06 no. 11031*

**PHYSICAL EDUCATION AND TRAINING - STUDY AND TEACHING (ELEMENTARY).**
Bailey, Richard. Teaching physical education 5-11. New York : Continuum, 2000.
*TC GV443 .B34 2000*

Schiemer, Suzann, 1956- Assessment strategies for elementary physical education. Champaign, IL ; Leeds, U.K. : Human Kinetics, c2000.

*TC GV436 .S27 2000*

**PHYSICAL EDUCATION AND TRAINING - STUDY AND TEACHING - GREAT BRITAIN.**
Learning and teaching in physical education. London ; Philadelphia, PA : Falmer Press, 1999.
*TC GV361 .L42 1999*

**PHYSICAL EDUCATION AND TRAINING - STUDY AND TEACHING (SECONDARY) - UNITED STATES.**
Physical Best (Program) Physical Best activity guide. Champaign, IL : Human Kinetics, c1999.
*TC GV365 .P4993 1999*

**PHYSICAL EDUCATION AND TRAINING - STUDY AND TEACHING - UNITED STATES.**
Metzler, Michael W., 1952- Instructional models for physical education. Boston : Allyn and Bacon, c2000.
*TC GV363 .M425 2000*

Physical Best (Program) Physical education for lifelong fitness. Champaign, Ill. : Human Kinetics, c1999.
*TC GV365 .P4992 1999*

**PHYSICAL EDUCATION AND TRAINING - TEACHER TRAINING.** *See* **PHYSICAL EDUCATION TEACHERS - TRAINING OF.**

**PHYSICAL EDUCATION FACILITIES.** *See* **SWIMMING POOLS.**

**PHYSICAL EDUCATION FOR CHILDREN.** *See also* **MOVEMENT EDUCATION.**
Bailey, Richard. Teaching physical education 5-11. New York : Continuum, 2000.
*TC GV443 .B34 2000*

Colvin, A. Vonnie, 1951- Teaching the nuts and bolts of physical education. Champaign, IL : Human Kinetics, c2000.
*TC GV443 .C59 2000*

Lichtman, Brenda, 1948- More innovative games. Champaign, IL : Human Kinetics, c1999.
*TC GV443 .L516 1999*

**PHYSICAL EDUCATION FOR CHILDREN - GREAT BRITAIN - HISTORY.**
Penn, Alan, 1926- Targeting schools. London ; Portland, OR : Woburn Press, 1999.
*TC GV443 .P388 1999*

**PHYSICAL EDUCATION FOR CHILDREN - STUDY AND TEACHING.**
Allison, Pamela C. Constructing children's physical education experiences. Boston : Allyn and Bacon, 2000.
*TC GV363 .A512 2000*

**PHYSICAL EDUCATION FOR CHILDREN - UNITED STATES - CASE STUDIES.**
Sammann, Patricia, 1951- Active youth. Champaign, IL : Human Kinetics, c1998.
*TC GV443 .A27 1998*

**PHYSICAL EDUCATION FOR HANDICAPPED PERSONS.**
Block, Martin E., 1958- A teacher's guide to including students with disabilities in general physical education. 2nd ed. Baltimore, Md. : Paul H. Brookes Pub. Co., c2000.
*TC GV445 .B56 2000*

**Physical education for lifelong fitness.**
Physical Best (Program) Champaign, Ill. : Human Kinetics, c1999.
*TC GV365 .P4992 1999*

**PHYSICAL EDUCATION FOR TEACHERS - TRAINING OF.**
Bailey, Richard. Teaching physical education 5-11. New York : Continuum, 2000.
*TC GV443 .B34 2000*

**PHYSICAL EDUCATION FOR WOMEN.** *See* **SPORTS FOR WOMEN.**

**PHYSICAL EDUCATION TEACHERS - GREAT BRITAIN.**
Learning and teaching in physical education. London ; Philadelphia, PA : Falmer Press, 1999.
*TC GV361 .L42 1999*

**PHYSICAL EDUCATION TEACHERS - IN-SERVICE TRAINING.**
Martin, Robert J. A study of the reflective practices of physical education student teachers. 1998.
*TC 06 no. 11031*

**PHYSICAL EDUCATION TEACHERS - NEW JERSEY - ATTITUDES.**
V'elez Arias, Hiram Oscar. A multi-case study of physical education teachers and working conditions in

inner-city schools /by Hiram Oscar V'elez Arias. 1998.
*TC 06 no. 11001*

**PHYSICAL EDUCATION TEACHERS - TRAINING OF.**
Allison, Pamela C. Constructing children's physical education experiences. Boston : Allyn and Bacon, 2000.
*TC GV363 .A512 2000*

**PHYSICAL EDUCATION TEACHERS - TRAINING OF - ENGLAND - BRIGHTON.**
Webb, Ida M. The challenge of change in physical education :. London : Falmer Press, 1999.
*TC GV246.E3 B79 1999*

**PHYSICAL EDUCATION TEACHERS - TRAINING OF - UNITED STATES.**
Metzler, Michael W., 1952- Instructional models for physical education. Boston : Allyn and Bacon, c2000.
*TC GV363 .M425 2000*

**PHYSICAL ENDURANCE.** *See* **PHYSICAL FITNESS.**

**PHYSICAL FITNESS.**
Battinelli, Thomas. Physique, fitness, and performance. Boca Raton : CRC Press, c2000.
*TC QP301 .B364 2000*

McMurray, Robert G. Concepts in fitness programming. Boca Raton : CRC Press, c1999.
*TC QP301 .M3754 1999*

Shephard, Roy J. Aging, physical activity, and health. Champaign, IL : Human Kinetics, c1997.
*TC QP86 .S478 1997*

White, Timothy P. The wellness guide to lifelong fitness. New York : Rebus : Distributed by Random House, c1993.
*TC RA781 .W47 1993*

**PHYSICAL FITNESS FOR THE AGED - UNITED STATES.**
Active older adults. Champaign, IL : Human Kinetics, c1999.
*TC GV482.6 .A38 1999*

**PHYSICAL FITNESS FOR WOMEN.**
Goldfein, Juli Ann. The importance of shape and weight in normal-weight women with bulimia nervosa, restrained eaters (dieters), and normal controls (Non-dieters). 1997.
*TC 085 G5675*

**PHYSICAL FITNESS - STUDY AND TEACHING - UNITED STATES.**
Physical Best (Program) Physical education for lifelong fitness. Champaign, Ill. : Human Kinetics, c1999.
*TC GV365 .P4992 1999*

**PHYSICAL FITNESS - TESTING.**
Schiemer, Suzann, 1956- Assessment strategies for elementary physical education. Champaign, IL ; Leeds, U.K. : Human Kinetics, c2000.
*TC GV436 .S27 2000*

**PHYSICAL SCIENCES.** *See also* **ASTRONOMY; EARTH SCIENCES; PHYSICS.**
Marshall, Robert H. AGS physical science. Circle Pines, Minn. : AGS, American Guidance Service, c1997.
*TC QC23 .M37 1997*

Marshall, Robert H. AGS physical science. Teacher's ed. Circle Pines, Minn. : AGS, American Guidance Service, c1997.
*TC QC23 .M37 1997 Teacher's Ed.*

**PHYSICAL SCIENCES - RESEARCH - METHODOLOGY.**
Theses and dissertations. Lanham, Md. : University Press of America, 1997.
*TC LB2369 .T44 1997*

**PHYSICAL SCIENCES - STUDY AND TEACHING (ELEMENTARY).**
Marshall, Robert H. AGS physical science. Teacher's ed. Circle Pines, Minn. : AGS, American Guidance Service, c1997.
*TC QC23 .M37 1997 Teacher's Ed.*

**PHYSICAL SCIENTISTS.** *See* **PHYSICISTS.**

**PHYSICAL STAMINA.** *See* **PHYSICAL FITNESS.**

**PHYSICAL THERAPY.** *See also* **OCCUPATIONAL THERAPY.**
Journal of the American Physical Therapy Association. [New York, N.Y.] : The Association, [1962-1963]

**Physical therapy review.**
Journal of the American Physical Therapy
Association. [New York, N.Y.] : The Association,
[1962-1963]

**PHYSICAL TRAINING.** *See* **PHYSICAL
EDUCATION AND TRAINING.**

**PHYSICALLY CHALLENGED.** *See*
**PHYSICALLY HANDICAPPED.**

**PHYSICALLY DISABLED.** *See* **PHYSICALLY
HANDICAPPED.**

**PHYSICALLY HANDICAPPED.** *See* **HEARING
IMPAIRED; VISUALLY HANDICAPPED.**

**PHYSICALLY HANDICAPPED -
BIBLIOGRAPHY - PERIODICALS.**
American journal of care for cripples. New York :
Douglas McMurtie, 1914-1919.

**PHYSICALLY HANDICAPPED CHILDREN.** *See*
**CHILDREN, BLIND; CHILDREN, DEAF;
VISUALLY HANDICAPPED CHILDREN.**

**PHYSICALLY HANDICAPPED CHILDREN -
PERIODICALS.**
The Crippled child. Chicago [etc.] National Society
for Crippled Children and Adults [etc.]

**PHYSICALLY HANDICAPPED - FICTION.**
Kirk, Daniel. Breakfast at the Liberty Diner. 1st ed.
New York : Hyperion Books for Children, c1997.
*TC PZ7.K6339 Br 1997*

**PHYSICALLY HANDICAPPED - PERIODICALS.**
American journal of care for cripples. New York :
Douglas McMurtie, 1914-1919.

**PHYSICALLY HANDICAPPED TEENAGERS -
EDUCATION.**
Bridges to independence [videorecording. Burbank,
CA : RCA/Columbia Pictures Home Video ; [S.l. :
Distributed by] Rank Video Services Production,
c1991.
*TC HV1646 .B7 1991*

**PHYSICALLY HANDICAPPED WOMEN -
UNITED STATES - BIOGRAPHY.**
Frank, Gelya, 1948- Venus on wheels. Berkeley,
Calif. : University of California Press, c2000.
*TC HV3021.W66 F73 2000*

**PHYSICALLY HANDICAPPED WOMEN -
UNITED STATES - SOCIAL CONDITIONS.**
Frank, Gelya, 1948- Venus on wheels. Berkeley,
Calif. : University of California Press, c2000.
*TC HV3021.W66 F73 2000*

**PHYSICIAN AND PATIENT.**
Baker, Susan Keane. Managing patient expectations.
San Francisco : Jossey Bass Publishers, 1998.
*TC R727.3 .B28 1998*

Partnerships in research, clinical, and educational
settings. Stamford, Conn. : Ablex Pub., c1999.
*TC HM1106 .P37 1999*

**PHYSICIAN-ASSISTED SUICIDE.** *See* **ASSISTED
SUICIDE.**

**PHYSICIAN-PATIENT RELATIONS.**
Baker, Susan Keane. Managing patient expectations.
San Francisco : Jossey Bass Publishers, 1998.
*TC R727.3 .B28 1998*

**PHYSICIAN-PATIENT RELATIONS -
CONGRESSES.**
The therapeutic alliance. Madison, Conn. :
International Universities Press, c2000.
*TC RC489.T66 T468 2000*

**PHYSICIANS.** *See* **MEDICINE.**

**PHYSICIANS' ASSISTANTS.** *See* **NURSE
PRACTITIONERS.**

**PHYSICIANS - PSYCHOLOGY.**
Fenichel, Ann. The relationship between health care
clinicians' relational abilities and psychosocial
orientation to patient care, and patient adherence with
medical treatment. 1998.
*TC 085 F352*

**PHYSICIANS - UNITED STATES -
PROFESSIONAL ETHICS.**
Lederer, Jane. Participation in active euthanasia and
assisted suicide and attitudes and interpersonal values
of physicians and nurses. 1996.
*TC 06 no. 10849*

**PHYSICISTS - UNITED STATES - BIOGRAPHY.**
Peat, F. David, 1938- Infinite potential. Reading,
Mass. : Addison Wesley, c1997.
*TC QC16.B627 P43 1997*

**PHYSICS.** *See* **ELECTRICITY; MATTER.**

**PHYSICS - EXPERIMENTS.** *See* **ELECTRICITY -
EXPERIMENTS.**

**PHYSICS - METHODOLOGY.**
Miller, Arthur I. Insights of genius. 1st MIT Press
pbk. ed. Cambridge, Mass. : MIT Press, 2000.
*TC QC6 .M44 2000*

**PHYSIOLOGICAL ACOUSTICS.** *See* **HEARING.**

**PHYSIOLOGICAL ASPECTS OF EXERCISE.** *See*
**EXERCISE - PHYSIOLOGICAL ASPECTS.**

**Physiological basis for exercise and sport.**
Foss, Merle L., 1936- Fox's physiological basis for
exercise and sport. 6th ed. / Merle L. Foss, Steven J.
Keteyian. Boston, Mass. : WCB/McGraw-Hill, c1998.
*TC RC1235 .F65 1998*

Muller, Susan. Student study guide to accompany
Fox's physiological basis for exercise and sport. 6th
ed. Boston, Mass. : WCB/McGraw-Hill, c1998.
*TC RC1235 .F65 1998 guide*

**PHYSIOLOGICAL PSYCHOLOGY.** *See*
**PSYCHOPHYSIOLOGY.**

**PHYSIOLOGICAL STRESS.** *See* **STRESS
(PHYSIOLOGY).**

**PHYSIOLOGY.** *See* **BLOOD - CIRCULATION;
FATIGUE; GROWTH; HEALTH;
NUTRITION; ORIENTATION
(PHYSIOLOGY); PREGNANCY;
PSYCHOPHYSIOLOGY.**

**The physiology and pathophysiology of exercise
tolerance** / edited by Jürgen M. Steinacker and Susan
A. Ward. New York : Plenum Press, c1996. xii, 333 p. :
ill. ; 26 cm. "Proceedings of the International Symposium on
the Physiology and Pathophysiology of Exercise Tolerance
held September 21-24, 1994 in Ulm, Germany"--T.p. verso.
Includes bibliographical references and index. ISBN 0-306-
45492-0 DDC 612/.044
*1. Exercise - Physiological aspects - Congresses. 2. Fatigue -
Congresses. 3. Muscles - Physiology - Congresses. 4. Muscles -
Pathophysiology - Congresses. 5. Stauch, Martin - Congresses.
6. Exercise Tolerance - physiology - congresses. 7. Exercise -
physiology - congresses. I. Steinacker, Jürgen M. II. Ward,
Susan A. III. International Symposium on the Physiology and
Pathophysiology of Exercise Tolerance (1994 : Ulm, Germany)*
*TC QP301 .P576 1996*

**PHYSIOLOGY, COMPARATIVE.**
Orlovsky, G. N. (Grigoriĭ Nikolaevich) Neuronal
control of locomotion. Oxford ; New York : Oxford
University Press, 1999.
*TC QP303 .O75 1999*

**PHYSIOLOGY, COMPARATIVE - POPULAR
WORKS.**
Widmaier, Eric P. Why geese don't get obese (and we
do). New York : W. H. Freeman, c1998.
*TC QP33 .W53 1998*

**PHYSIOPHILOSOPHY.** *See* **NATURAL
HISTORY.**

**PHYSIOPSYCHOLOGY.** *See*
**PSYCHOPHYSIOLOGY.**

**Physique, fitness, and performance.**
Battinelli, Thomas. Boca Raton : CRC Press, c2000.
*TC QP301 .B364 2000*

**PHYSIQUE PHOTOGRAPHY.** *See*
**PHOTOGRAPHY OF MEN.**

**PIAGET, JEAN, 1896-.**
Feldberg, Suzanne. A comparison of different types of
mathematical problem-solving hints selected by
concrete and formal operational subjects in a
hypercard environment. 1998.
*TC 085 F316*

Lavatelli, Celia Stendler, 1911- Piaget's theory
applied to an early childhood curriculum. [1st ed.].
Boston : American Science and Engineering, [c1970].
*TC LB1140.2 .L3*

**Piaget, Jean, 1896-1980.**
**[Représentation du monde chez l'enfant. English]**
The child's conception of the world. Translated by
Joan and Andrew Tomlinson. Paterson, N.J.,
Littlefield, Adams, 1960. ix, 397 p. 20 cm.
(International library of psychology, philosophy and
scientific method) Includes index. Translation of La
représentation du monde chez l'enfant. "Gift from Professor
Maxine Greene"
*1. Child development. I. Title. II. Series: International library
of psychology, philosophy, and scientific method.*
*TC BF721 .P513 1960*

**PIAGET, JEAN 1896-1980.**
Andersen, Christopher Lawrence. A microgenetic
study of science reasoning in social context. 1998.
*TC 085 An2305*

**PIAGETIAN THEORY OF COGNITIVE
DEVELOPMENT.** *See* **CONSTRUCTIVISM
(EDUCATION).**

**Piaget's theory applied to an early childhood
curriculum.**
Lavatelli, Celia Stendler, 1911- [1st ed.]. Boston :
American Science and Engineering, [c1970].
*TC LB1140.2 .L3*

**PIANO - FINGERING.**
Pace, Robert. Teachers guide. Katonah, N.Y. : Lee
Roberts Music publications, 1983.
*TC MT245 .P32 1983*

**PIANO - INSTRUCTION AND STUDY.**
Fink, Seymour. Mastering piano technique. Portland,
Or.: Amadeus Press, c1992.
*TC MT220 .F44 1992*

Lyke, James. Creative piano teaching. 3rd ed.
Champaign, Ill. : Stipes Pub. Co., c1996.
*TC MT220 .L95 1996*

Pace, Robert. Teachers guide. Katonah, N.Y. : Lee
Roberts Music publications, 1983.
*TC MT245 .P32 1983*

Teaching piano. New York ; London : Yorktown
Music Press, Inc., c1981.
*TC MT220 .T25*

**PIANO - INSTRUCTION AND STUDY - FICTION.**
Purdy, Carol. Mrs. Merriwether's musical cat. New
York : Putnam, c1994.
*TC PZ7.P9745 Mr 1994*

**PIANO MUSIC (2 HANDS).** *See* **PIANO MUSIC.**

**PIANO MUSIC - BIBLIOGRAPHY.**
Friskin, James, 1886-1967. Music for the piano; New
York, Dover Publications [1973]
*TC ML128.P3 F7 1973*

Teaching piano. New York ; London : Yorktown
Music Press, Inc., c1981.
*TC MT220 .T25*

**PIANO MUSIC - BIBLIOGRAPHY - GRADED
LISTS.**
Teaching piano. New York ; London : Yorktown
Music Press, Inc., c1981.
*TC MT220 .T25*

**PIANO MUSIC - INTERPRETATION
(PHRASING, DYNAMICS, ETC.).**
Schenker, Heinrich, 1868-1935. [Kunst des Vortrags.
English] The art of performance. New York : Oxford
University Press, 2000.
*TC MT220 .S24513 2000*

**PIANO MUSIC, JUVENILE.**
James, Phoebe L. Accompaniments for rhythmic
expressions. [Los Angeles? : s.n.], c1946.
*TC M1993.J18 A3*

**PIANO MUSIC - TEACHING PIECES.**
Pace, Robert. Teachers guide. Katonah, N.Y. : Lee
Roberts Music publications, 1983.
*TC MT245 .P32 1983*

**PIANO - PERFORMANCE.**
Schenker, Heinrich, 1868-1935. [Kunst des Vortrags.
English] The art of performance. New York : Oxford
University Press, 2000.
*TC MT220 .S24513 2000*

**PIANO - PRACTICING.** *See* **PIANO -
INSTRUCTION AND STUDY.**

**PIANO - STUDIES AND EXERCISES.**
Gingerich, Carol Joy. The French piano style of Fauré
and Debussy. 1996.
*TC 06 no. 10644*

Pace, Robert. Teachers guide. Katonah, N.Y. : Lee
Roberts Music publications, 1983.
*TC MT245 .P32 1983*

**Pianta, Robert C.**
The transition to kindergarten. Baltimore : P.H.
Brookes Pub., c1999.
*TC LB1205 .T72 1999*

**Piantanida, Maria.** The qualitative dissertation : a guide
for students and faculty / Maria Piantanida, Noreen B.
Garman. Thousand Oaks, Calif. : Corwin Press,
c1999. xix, 273 p. : ill. ; 26 cm. Includes bibliographical
references (p. 257-266) and index. ISBN 0-8039-6688-1
(acid-free paper) ISBN 0-8039-6689-X (acid-free paper) DDC
808/.02

*1. Dissertations, Academic. 2. Research - Methodology. I. Garman, Noreen B. II. Title.*
*TC LB2369 .P48 1999*

**Picard, Beriau.**
Step on a crack [videorecording]. Boston, MA : Fanlight Productions, 1996.
*TC RC533 .S7 1996*

**PICASSO, PABLO, 1881-1973.**
Picasso [videorecording]. Chicago, IL : Home Vision, c1986.
*TC N6853.P5 P52 1986*

**Picasso** [videorecording] / commentary written by Waldemar Januszczak ; director, Didier Baussy ; produced by RM Arts ... [et al.] in association with Channel Four. Chicago, IL : Home Vision, c1986. 1 videocassette (ca. 81 min.) : sd., col. ; 1/2 in. (Portrait of an artist) At head of title: Public Media Incorporated... Home Vision... [videorecording]. VHS. Catalogued from credits and container. Dates vary: copyright notice on container and videocassette label, 1985. Narrator, Bob Peck. Camera: Frédéric Variot; editor: Delphine Desfons; sound: Bertrand Lendos. "A Public Media Incorporated Release... A film by Didier Baussy-Oulianoff... Devised by Didier Baussy-Oulianoff and Marie-Louise [i.e. Laure] Bernadac."-- Container. Adolescent through adult. SUMMARY: Contains works Picasso felt to be his own personal legacy to the world, filmed both in the vaults of the Palais de Tokyo and during the hanging of the new collection in the Musee Picasso. ISBN 0-7800-1856-7
*1. Picasso, Pablo, - 1881-1973. 2. Painters - France - Biography. 3. Painters - Spain - Biography. 4. Sculptors - France - Biography. 5. Sculptors - Spain - Biography. 6. Painting, Modern - 20th century - France. 7. Painting, Modern - 20th century - Spain. 8. Sculpture, Modern - 20th century - France. 9. Sculpture, Modern - 20th century - Spain. 10. Documentary films. 11. Biographical films. I. Baussy, Didier. II. Januszczak, Waldemar. III. Peck, Bob, 1945- IV. Bernadac Marie-Laure. V. Home Vision (Firm) VI. Musée Picasso (Paris, France) VII. Musée d'art et d'essai (Paris, France) VIII. RM Arts (Firm). IX. Channel Four (Great Britain). X. Public Media Incorporated (Wilmette, Ill.) XI. Title: Public Media Incorporated... Home Vision... [videorecording] XII. Series.*
*TC N6853.P5 P52 1986*

**Piccinin, Sergio.**
Using consultants to improve teaching. San Francisco : Jossey-Bass, c1999.
*TC LB2799.2 .U83 1999*

**Pick, Anne D.**
Gibson, Eleanor Jack. An ecological approach to perceptual learning and development. Oxford ; New York : Oxford University Press, 2000.
*TC BF720.P47 G53 2000*

**Pickering, David, 1958-** A dictionary of folklore / David Pickering. New York, N.Y. : Facts on File, 1999. viii, 324 p. ; 24 cm. (Facts on File library of world literature) "First published in Great Britain as The Cassell dictionary of folklore"--T.p. verso. ISBN 0-8160-4250-0
*1. Folklore - Dictionaries. 2. Mythology - Dictionaries. I. Facts on File, Inc. II. Title.*
*TC GR35 .P53 1999*

**PICK'S DISEASE OF THE BRAIN.** *See* **PRESENILE DEMENTIA.**

**A pictorial history of the University of Georgia.**
Boney, F. N. 2nd ed. Athens : University of Georgia Press, c2000.
*TC LD1983 .B6 2000*

**PICTORIAL PHOTOGRAPHY.** *See* **PHOTOGRAPHY, ARTISTIC.**

**PICTURE ARCHIVING AND COMMUNICATION SYSTEMS - UNITED STATES.**
Delivering digital images. Los Angeles, Calif. : Getty Information Institute, 1998.
*TC N59 .D45 1998*

**PICTURE BOOKS - BIBLIOGRAPHY.**
Matulka, Denise I. Picture this. Westport, Conn. : Greenwood Press, 1997.
*TC Z1033.P52 M37 1997*

**PICTURE BOOKS FOR CHILDREN - EDUCATIONAL ASPECTS.**
What's in the picture? London : P. Chapman Pub. Ltd., c1998.
*TC LB1044.9.P49 W52 1998*

**PICTURE BOOKS FOR CHILDREN - PSYCHOLOGICAL ASPECTS.**
Spitz, Ellen Handler, 1939- Inside picture books. New Haven : Yale University Press, c1999.
*TC BF456.R2 S685 1999*

**PICTURE BOOKS FOR CHILDREN - UNITED STATES - BOOK REVIEWS.**
Cianciolo, Patricia J. Informational picture books for children. Chicago : American Library Association, 2000.
*TC Z1037.A1 C54 1999*

**PICTURE DICTIONARIES.**
French picture dictionary. Princeton : Berlitz Kids, Berlitz Pub. Co., c1997.
*TC PC2629 .F74 1997*

German picture dictionary. Princeton, NJ : Berlitz Pub. Co., 1997.
*TC PF3629 .G47 1997*

Inglés. Princeton [NJ] : Berlitz Pub. Co., 1997.
*TC PE1628.5 .I54 1997*

**PICTURE DICTIONARIES, ENGLISH.**
French picture dictionary. Princeton : Berlitz Kids, Berlitz Pub. Co., c1997.
*TC PC2629 .F74 1997*

German picture dictionary. Princeton, NJ : Berlitz Pub. Co., 1997.
*TC PF3629 .G47 1997*

Spanish picture dictionary. Princeton [N.J.] : Berlitz Kids, c1997.
*TC PC4629 .S63 1997*

**PICTURE DICTIONARIES, ENGLISH - JUVENILE LITERATURE.**
Spanish picture dictionary. Princeton [N.J.] : Berlitz Kids, c1997.
*TC PC4629 .S63 1997*

**PICTURE DICTIONARIES, FRENCH.**
French picture dictionary. Princeton : Berlitz Kids, Berlitz Pub. Co., c1997.
*TC PC2629 .F74 1997*

French picture dictionary. Princeton : Berlitz Kids, Berlitz Pub. Co., c1997.
*TC PC2629 .F74 1997*

**PICTURE DICTIONARIES, GERMAN.**
1,000 German words. Princeton, N.J. : Berlitz Kids, c1998.
*TC PF3629 .A14 1998*

German picture dictionary. Princeton, NJ : Berlitz Pub. Co., 1997.
*TC PF3629 .G47 1997*

German picture dictionary. Princeton, NJ : Berlitz Pub. Co., 1997.
*TC PF3629 .G47 1997*

**PICTURE DICTIONARIES, ITALIAN - JUVENILE LITERATURE.**
Italian picture dictionary. Princeton, NJ : Berlitz Kids, c1997.
*TC PC1629 .I73 1997*

**PICTURE DICTIONARIES, SPANISH.**
Inglés. Princeton [NJ] : Berlitz Pub. Co., 1997.
*TC PE1628.5 .I54 1997*

Spanish picture dictionary. Princeton [N.J.] : Berlitz Kids, c1997.
*TC PC4629 .S63 1997*

**PICTURE DICTIONARIES, SPANISH - JUVENILE LITERATURE.**
Spanish picture dictionary. Princeton [N.J.] : Berlitz Kids, c1997.
*TC PC4629 .S63 1997*

**PICTURE-GALLERIES.** *See* **ART MUSEUMS.**

**PICTURE POSTCARDS.** *See* **POSTCARDS.**

**PICTURE POSTERS.** *See* **POSTERS.**

**PICTURE PUZZLES.**
Steiner, Joan (Joan Catherine) Look-alikes, jr.. 1st ed. Boston : Little, Brown, c1999.
*TC GV1507.P47 S747 1999*

Wick, Walter. I spy treasure hunt. New York : Scholastic, c1999.
*TC GV1507.P47 W5296 1999*

**PICTURE PUZZLES - JUVENILE LITERATURE.**
Steiner, Joan (Joan Catherine) Look-alikes, jr.. 1st ed. Boston : Little, Brown, c1999.
*TC GV1507.P47 S747 1999*

Wick, Walter. I spy treasure hunt. New York : Scholastic, c1999.
*TC GV1507.P47 W5296 1999*

**Picture the Middle Ages.**
Honan, Linda. Amawalk, N.Y. : Golden Owl Pub. Co. : Higgins Armory Museum, c1994.

*TC CB351 .H58 1994*

**Picture this.**
Entz, Susan. Thousand Oaks, Calif. : Corwin Press, c2000.
*TC LB1043.67 .E58 2000*

Matulka, Denise I. Westport, Conn. : Greenwood Press, 1997.
*TC Z1033.P52 M37 1997*

**Picture this century.**
Woolf, Felicity. New York : Doubleday Book for Young Readers, c1992.
*TC N6490 .W66 1992*

**PICTURE-WRITING.** *See* **ROCK PAINTINGS.**

**PICTURED ROCKS.** *See* **ROCK PAINTINGS.**

**PICTURES.** *See* **ILLUSTRATION OF BOOKS; PHOTOGRAPHS; PORTRAITS; POSTERS.**

**PICTURES IN EDUCATION.**
Entz, Susan. Picture this. Thousand Oaks, Calif. : Corwin Press, c2000.
*TC LB1043.67 .E58 2000*

**PICTURES IN EDUCATION - UNITED STATES - DATA PROCESSING.**
Delivering digital images. Los Angeles, Calif. : Getty Information Institute, 1998.
*TC N59 .D45 1998*

**PICTURES - TRIMMING, MOUNTING, ETC.** *See* **PHOTOGRAPHS - TRIMMING, MOUNTING, ETC.**

**Picturing us :** African American identity in photography / edited by Deborah Willis. New York : New Press ; Distributed by W.W. Norton & Co., c1994. xiii, 209 p. : ill. ; 25 cm. Includes bibliographical references. ISBN 1-56584-107-7 DDC 770/.89/96073
*1. Portrait photography. 2. Afro-Americans - Portraits. I. Willis-Thomas, Deborah, 1948-*
*TC TR680 .P53 1994*

**Picus, Larry, 1954-.**
Where does the money go? Thousand Oaks, Calif. : Corwin Press, c1996.
*TC LB2825 .W415 1996*

**Piedmont, Ralph L., 1958-** The revised NEO Personality Inventory : clinical and research applications / Ralph L. Piedmont. New York : Plenum Press, c1998. xx, 286 p. : ill. ; 24 cm. (The Plenum series in social/clinical psychology) Includes bibliographical references (p. 255-275) and indexes. ISBN 0-306-45943-4 DDC 155.2/83
*1. NEO Personality Inventory. 2. NEO Five-Factor Inventory. I. Title. II. Series.*
*TC BF698.8.N46 P54 1998*

**Piekutowski, Lynna, 1951-.**
Remembering the boys. Kent, OH : Kent State University Press, c2000.
*TC D811.A2 R46 2000*

**Piele, Linda J.**
Rubin, Rebecca B. Communication research. 5th ed. Belmont, CA : Wadsworth Thomson Learning, 1999.
*TC P91.3 .R83 1999*

**Pierangelo, Roger.** Complete guide to special education transition services : ready-to-use help and materials for successful transitions from school to adulthood / Roger Pierangelo, Rochelle Crane. West Nyack, NY : Center for Applied Research in Education, c1997. xix, 249 p. ; 28 cm. Includes bibliographical references and index. ISBN 0-87628-274-5 DDC 371.91
*1. Handicapped youth - Services for - United States. 2. Handicapped youth - Vocational education - United States. 3. Vocational guidance for the handicapped - United States. 4. School-to-work transition - United States. 5. Parents of handicapped children - United States - Finance, Personal. I. Crane, Rochelle. II. Title. III. Title: Special education transition services*
*TC HV1569.3.Y68 P55 1997*

The special education yellow pages / Roger Pierangelo, Rochelle Crane. Upper Saddle River, N.J. : Merrill, c2000. xxx, 214 p. ; 26 cm. Includes bibliographical references (p. 201-206) and index. ISBN 0-13-020309-2 (pbk.) DDC 371.9/025/73
*1. Special education - United States - Directories. 2. Handicapped children - Services for - United States - Directories. I. Crane, Rochelle. II. Title.*
*TC LC4031 .P488 2000*

**Pierce, Roberta B.** Speech-language pathologist's guide to home health care / Roberta B. Pierce. San Diego : Academic Press, c2000. ix, 222 p. ; 28 cm. Includes bibliographical references (p. 215-218) and index. ISBN 0-12-554830-3
*1. Speech therapy - Handbooks, manuals, etc. 2. Home care services - Handbooks, manuals, etc. I. Title.*

*Pierce, Roxanne Heide.*

*TC RC423 .P54 2000*

**Pierce, Roxanne Heide.**
Heide, Florence Parry. It's about time!. New York : Clarion Books, c1999.
*TC PS3558.E427 I77 1999*

**Pierce, W. David.** Behavior analysis and learning / W. David Pierce & W. Frank Epling. 2nd ed. Upper Saddle River, N.J. : Prentice Hall, c1999. xvii, 444 p. : ill. ; 25 cm. Includes bibliographical references (p. 404-427) and indexes. ISBN 0-13-080743-5 DDC 150.19/434
*1. Behaviorism (Psychology) 2. Learning, Psychology of. I. Epling, W. Frank. II. Title.*
*TC BF199 .P54 1999*

**Pierre Bourdieu :** language, culture, and education : theory into practice / Michael Grenfell, Michael Kelly, eds. Bern ; New York : P. Lang, c1999. 333 p. : ill. ; 23 cm. Includes bibliographical references. ISBN 0-8204-4602-5 (US) ISBN 3-906763-02-1 DDC 306/.01
*1. Bourdieu, Pierre. 2. Culture - Philosophy. 3. Language and culture. 4. Sociolinguistics. 5. Language and education. 6. Educational sociology. I. Grenfell, Michael, 1953- II. Kelly, Michael, 1946-*
*TC HM621 .P54 1999*

**Pierson, Herbert D. (Herbert DeLeon), 1941-.**
Learner-directed assessment in ESL. Mahwah, N.J. : Lawrence Erlbaum Associates, 2000.
*TC PE1128.A2 L359 2000*

**Piet Mondrian, 1872-1944** / Yve-Alain Bois, ... [et al.] Milan : Leonardo Arte, 1994. 400 p. : ill. (some col.) ; 31 cm. Includes bibliographical references (p.393-399) Published to accompany an exhibition marking the 50th anniversary of Mondrian's death. Exhibition held at Haags Gemeentemuseum, Dec. 18-Apr. 30, 1995; National Gallery of Art, June 11-Sept. 4, 1995; Museum of Modern Art, Oct. 1-Jan. 23, 1996. ISBN 88-7813-506-2
*1. Mondrian, Piet, - 1872-1944. I. Mondrian, Piet, 1872-1944. II. Bois, Yve Alain. III. Haags Gemeentemuseum. IV. National Gallery of Art (U.S.) V. Museum of Modern Art (New York, N.Y.)*
*TC N6953.M64 A4 1994*

**PIETISM.** *See* **EVANGELICALISM.**

**PIGMENTS.** *See also* **DYES AND DYEING.**
Bomford, David. Colour. London : National Gallery Company ; [New Haven, Conn.] : Distributed by Yale Universtiy Press, 2000.
*TC ND1489 B66 2000*

**Pignataro, Anna, 1965- ill.**
Thompson, Colin (Colin Edward) Unknown. New York : Walker & Co., 2000.
*TC PZ7.T371424 Un 2000*

**PIGS - FICTION.**
Marshall, James, 1942- Swine lake. 1st ed. [New York] : Harper Collins Publishers, 1999.
*TC PZ7.M35672 Sw 1999*

Steer, Dugald. Just one more story. New York : Dutton Children's Books, 1999.
*TC PZ7.S81534 Ju 1999*

**Pike, Beth.**
Glass, Laurie. Read! read! read!. Thousand Oaks, Calif. : Corwin Press, c2000.
*TC LB1050.2 .G54 2000*

**Pike, James.**
Phillips, James B. Accent. Glenview, Ill. : Scott, Foresman, 1972.
*TC PE1121 .P54 1972*

**Pikulski, John J.**
Cooper, J. David (James David), 1942- Discover : Grade 1, level 1.5, [Themes 9 and 10]. Boston : Houghton Mifflin, 1997.
*TC LB1575.8 .C6616 1997*

**Pilcher, Jane.**
Gender and qualitative research. Aldershot, Hants, England ; Brookfield, Vt., USA : Avebury, c1996.
*TC HQ1075 .G4617 1996*

**Pilgreen, Janice L.** The SSR handbook : how to organize and manage a sustained silent reading program / Janice J. Pilgreen ; foreword by Stephen D. Krashen. Portsmouth, NH : Boynton/Cook Publishers, c2000. xviii, 142 p. : ill. ; 24 cm. Includes bibliographical references (p. 133-137) and index. ISBN 0-86709-462-1 DDC 428.4
*1. Silent reading - Handbooks, manuals, etc. I. Title.*
*TC LB1050.55 .P55 2000*

**Pilgrim New Media, Inc.**
Her heritage [computer file]. Cambridge, MA : Pilgrim New Media, c1994. Interactive multimedia.
*TC HQ1412 .A43 1994*

**A pilgrimage through universities.**
Odegaard, Charles E. Seattle : University of Washington Press, c1999.
*TC LD5752.1 .O34 1999*

**Pilisuk, Marc, joint comp.**
Perrucci, Robert, comp. The triple revolution: Boston, Little, Brown [1968]
*TC HN65 .P4*

**Pilkey, Dav, 1966-** Captain Underpants and the invasion of the incredibly naughty cafeteria ladies from outer space ... : the third epic novel / by Dav Pilkey. New York : Blue Sky Press, c1999. 134 p. : ill. ; 22 cm. SUMMARY: Only Captain Underpants can stop the three evil space aliens who have invaded Jerome Horwitz Elementary School and turned everyone into lunchroom zombie nerds. ISBN 0-439-04995-4 DDC [Fic]
*1. Schools - Fiction. 2. School principals - Fiction. 3. Heroes - Fiction. 4. Cartoons and comics - Fiction. 5. Humorous stories. I. Title.*
*TC PZ7.P63123 Cat 1999*

**Pilkey, Dav, 1966- ill.**
Denim, Sue, 1966- Make way for Dumb Bunnies. New York : Blue Sky Press, c1996.
*TC PZ7.D4149 Mak 1996*

**Pillow, Wanda S.**
Working the ruins. New York ; London : Routledge, 2000.
*TC LC197 .W67 2000*

**Pimentel, Susan.**
Doyle, Denis P. Raising the standard. 2nd ed. Thousand Oaks, Calif. : Corwin Press, c1999.
*TC LB2822.82 .D69 1999*

**Pinar, William.**
Contemporary curriculum discourses. New York : P. Lang, c1999.
*TC LB2806.15 .C6753 1999*

**PINDARS.** *See* **PEANUTS.**

**PINDAS.** *See* **PEANUTS.**

**PINDERS.** *See* **PEANUTS.**

**Pines, Robert.**
Teaching to teach. Washington, DC : National Education Association, 1999.
*TC LB1715 .T436 1999*

**Pinkava, Joanne.**
Barlow, Tracie. The COTA in the schools. San Antonio, Texas : Therapy Skill Builders, c1999.
*TC RM735 .B37 1999*

**Pinkerson, Daphne.**
The politics of addiction [videorecording]. Princeton, NJ : Films for the Humanities & Sciences, c1998.
*TC RC564 .P59 1998*

**Pinnell, Gay Su.**
Fountas, Irene C. Matching books to readers :. Portsmouth, NH : Heinemann, c1999.
*TC LB1573 .F68*

McCarrier, Andrea. Interactive writing. Portsmouth, NH : Heinemann, c2000.
*TC LB1139.5.L35 M39 2000*

Word matters : teaching phonics and spelling in the reading/writing classroom / Gay Su Pinnell and Irene C. Fountas ; with a chapter by Mary Ellen Giacobbe. Portsmouth, NH : Heinemann, c1998. xviii, 401 p. : ill. ; 28 cm. Includes bibliographical references (p. 395-396) and index. ISBN 0-325-00051-4 (alk. paper) DDC 372.46/5
*1. Reading - Phonetic method. 2. English language - Orthography and spelling - Study and teaching. 3. Language arts. I. Fountas, Irene C. II. Giacobbe, Mary Ellen. III. Title.*
*TC LB1573.3 .P55 1998*

**Pintrich, Paul R.**
Handbook of self-regulation. San Diego : Academic, 2000.
*TC BF632 .H254 2000*

**PIONEER CHILDREN - WEST (U.S.) - DIARIES - JUVENILE LITERATURE.**
Hester, Sallie. A covered wagon girl. Mankato, Minn. : Blue Earth Books, c2000.
*TC F593 .H47 2000*

**Pioneer church.**
Otto, Carolyn. 1st ed. New York : Henry Holt, 1999
*TC PZ7.O8794 Pi 1999*

**A pioneer farm girl.**
Gillespie, Sarah (Sarah L.) Mankato, Minn. : Blue Earth Books, c2000.
*TC F629.M28 G55 2000*

**PIONEER LIFE.** *See* **FRONTIER AND PIONEER LIFE.**

**Pioneering deans of women.**
Nidiffer, Jana, 1957- New York ; London : Teachers College Press, c2000.
*TC LC1620 .N53 2000*

**PIONEERS.** *See* **FRONTIER AND PIONEER LIFE; PIONEER CHILDREN.**

**Pioneers in popular culture studies** / edited by Ray B. Browne and Michael T. Marsden. Bowling Green, OH : Bowling Green State University Popular Press, c1999. 234 p. : ill. ; 24 cm. Includes bibliographical references. ISBN 0-87972-775-6 ISBN 0-87972-776-4 (pbk.) DDC 306.4/0973
*1. Popular culture - United States - Study and teaching. 2. United States - Intellectual life - 20th century. 3. Intellectuals - United States - Biography. I. Browne, Ray Broadus. II. Marsden, Michael T.*
*TC E169.04 .P563 1999*

**Pippitt, Mary.**
Samway, Katharine Davies. Buddy reading. Portsmouth, NH : Heinemann, c1995.
*TC LB1031.5 .S36 1995*

**Piran, Niva.**
Preventing eating disorders. Philadelphia, PA : Brunner/Mazel, c1999.
*TC RC552.E18 P744 1999*

**PISCES.** *See* **FISHES.**

**Piskunov, A. I. (Aleksei Ivanovich).**
Ushinskii, K. D. (Konstantin Dmitrievich), 1824-1870. [Selected works. English. 1975] K. D. Ushinsky. Moscow : Progress, 1975.
*TC LB675 .U8213 1975*

**Piskurich, George M.** Rapid instructional design : learning ID fast and right / George M. Piskurich. San Francisco, Calif. : Jossey-Bass, c2000. xvii, 297 p. ; 24 cm. Includes index. ISBN 0-7879-4721-0 (acid-free paper) DDC 371.33
*1. Instructional systems - Design. I. Title.*
*TC LB1028.38 .P57 2000*

**PISSARRO, CAMILLE, 1830-1903.**
Impressionism [videorecording]. [London] : The National Gallery ; Tillingham, Peasmarsh, East Sussex, England : Ho-Ho-Kus, NJ : Distributed by The Roland Collection, c1990.
*TC ND547.5.I4 A7 1990*

**Pitch in :** teacher's planning guide. New York : Macmillan/McGraw-Hill, c1997. 1 v. (various pagings) : col. ill. ; 31 cm. (Spotlight on literacy ; Gr.4 l.10 u.4) (The road to independent reading) Includes index. ISBN 0-02-181175-x
*1. Language arts (Elementary) 2. Reading (Elementary) I. Series. II. Series: The road to independent reading*
*TC LB1576 .S66 1997 Gr.4 l.10 u.4*

**Pitman, Mary Anne.**
Caring as tenacity. Cresskill, N.J. : Hampton Press, c2000.
*TC LC5131 .C35 2000*

**Pitt Latin American series**
Casanovas, Joan. Bread, or bullets!. Pittsburgh : University of Pittsburgh Press, c1998.
*TC HD8206 .C33 1998*

**Pittinsky, Todd L.**
Levine, James A. Working fathers. Reading, Mass. : Addison-Wesley, c1997.
*TC HQ756 .L474 1997*

**Pitts, David.** Red Hat Linux 6 unleashed / David Pitts, Bill Ball, et al. [Indianapolis, Ind.] : SAMS, c1999. xxxvi, 1252 p. : ill. ; 24 cm. + 1 computer optical disc (4 3/4 in.). ISBN 0-672-31689-7 DDC 005.4/469
*1. Linux. 2. Operating systems (Computers) I. Ball, Bill. II. Title.*
*TC QA76.76.O63 P56148 1999*

**Pittsburgh-Konstanz Colloquium in the Philosophy of Science (4th : 1997 : University of Pittsburgh).**
Science at century's end. Pittsburgh, Pa. : University of Pittsburgh Press, c2000.
*TC Q175 .S4193 2000*

**Pittsburgh-Konstanz series in the philosophy and history of science**
Science at century's end. Pittsburgh, Pa. : University of Pittsburgh Press, c2000.
*TC Q175 .S4193 2000*

**Pivot of the universe.**
Amanat, Abbas. Berkeley : University of California Press, c1997.
*TC DS307.N38 A63 1997*

**PLACEMENT BUREAUS.** *See* **EMPLOYMENT AGENCIES.**

**Placing aesthetics.**
Wood, Robert E., 1934- Athens, OH : Ohio University Press, c1999.
*TC BH81 .W66 1999*

**PLAGIARISM.**
Perspectives on plagiarism and intellectual property in a postmodern world. Albany : State University of New York Press, c1999.
*TC PN167 .P47 1999*

**The plague stone.**
White, Gillian, 1945- Large print ed. Thorndike, Me., USA : G.K. Hall ; Bath, Avon, England : Chivers Press, 1996, c1990.
*TC PR6073.H4925 P58 1996*

**Plain pictures.**
Kinsey, Joni. Washington, : Published for the University of Iowa Museum of Art by the Smithsonian Institution Press, 1996.
*TC N8214.5.U6 K56 1996*

**Plainville, U.S.A.**
Withers, Carl. New York : Columbia University Press, [c1945]
*TC HN57 .W58 1945*

**Planalp, Sally, 1950-** Communicating emotion : social, moral, and cultural processes / Sally Planalp. Cambridge ; New York : Cambridge University Press ; Paris : Editions de la Maison des sciences de l'homme, 1999. xv, 295 p. : ill. ; 23 cm. (Studies in emotion and social interaction) Includes bibliographical references (p. 243-275) and indexes. ISBN 0-521-55315-6 (hardcover) ISBN 0-521-55741-0 (pbk.) DDC 302.2
*1. Expression. 2. Emotions. 3. Interpersonal communication. 4. Emotions - Social aspects. I. Title. II. Series.*
*TC BF591 .P57 1999*

**PLANE TRIGONOMETRY.**
Peters, Max, 1906- Algebra. 2d ed. Princeton, N.J., Van Nostrand 1968.
*TC QA152 .P4562 1968*

Peters, Max, 1906- Algebra and trigonometry. Princeton, N.J., Van Nostrand 1965.
*TC QA152 .P4562 1965*

**PLANES (AIRPLANES).** *See* **AIRPLANES.**

**Planet Earth**
(1) The living machine [videorecording]. [New York, N.Y.?] : Unapix Entertainment, Inc. [distributor], c1996.
*TC QB631.2 .L5 1996*

(2) The blue planet [videorecording]. [New York, N.Y.?] : Unapix Entertainment, Inc. [distributor], c1996.
*TC QB631.2 .B5 1996*

(3) The climate puzzle [videorecording]. [New York, N.Y.?] : Unapix Entertainment, Inc. [distributor], c1996.
*TC QB631.2 .C5 1996*

(4) Tales from other worlds [videorecording]. [New York, N.Y.?] : Unapix Entertainment, Inc. [distributor], c1996.
*TC QB631.2 .T3 1996*

(4) Tales from other worlds [videorecording]. [New York, N.Y.?] : Unapix Entertainment, Inc. [distributor], c1996.
*TC QB631.2 .T3 1996*

(5) The solar sea [videorecording]. [New York, N.Y.?] : Unapix Entertainment, Inc. [distributor], c1996.
*TC QB631.2 .S6 1996*

(6) Gifts from the earth [videorecording]. [New York, N.Y.?] : Unapix Entertainment, Inc. [distributor], c1996.
*TC QB631.2 .G5 1996*

(7) Fate of the earth [videorecording]. [New York, N.Y.?] : Unapix Entertainment, Inc. [distributor], c1996.
*TC QB631.2 .F3 1996*

**Planned change theories for nursing.**
Tiffany, Constance Rimmer. Thousand Oaks : Sage Publications, c1998.
*TC RT89 .T54 1998*

**PLANNED PARENTHOOD.** *See* **BIRTH CONTROL.**

**PLANNING.** *See* **CITY PLANNING; CURRICULUM PLANNING; ECONOMIC POLICY; EDUCATIONAL PLANNING;**

**HEALTH PLANNING; LESSON PLANNING; STRATEGIC PLANNING.**

**Planning a course.**
Forsyth, Ian. The complete guide to teaching a course. 2nd ed. London : Kogan Page ; Sterling, VA : Stylus Publishing, 1999.
*TC LB1025.3 .F67 1999*

**Planning an appropriate curriculum for the under fives.**
Rodger, Rosemary, 1946- London : David Fulton, 1999.
*TC LB1140.25.G7 R64 1999*

**Planning for disaster.**
Baldwin, Harmon A. (Harmon Arthur), 1922- 2nd ed. Bloomington, Ind. : Phi Delta Kappa Educational Foundation, c1999.
*TC LB2864.5 .B35 1999*

**PLANNING, STRATEGIC.** *See* **STRATEGIC PLANNING.**

**PLANS.** *See* **MAPS.**

**PLANS, MANAGED CARE (MEDICAL CARE).** *See* **MANAGED CARE PLANS (MEDICAL CARE).**

**PLANT PRODUCTS INDUSTRY.** *See* **TOBACCO INDUSTRY.**

**PLANTATIONS - VIRGINIA.** *See* **MOUNT VERNON (VA. : ESTATE).**

**PLANTS.** *See* **FLOWERS; TREES.**

**PLANTS IN ART.**
Flora and fauna in Mughal art. [Bombay] : Marg Publications, c1999.
*TC N7302 .F567 1999*

**PLANTS, INDUSTRIAL.** *See* **FACTORIES.**

**PLANTS, PROTECTION OF.** *See* **SCARECROWS.**

**PLANTS, SMOKABLE.** *See* **TOBACCO.**

**PLASTIC FILMS.**
Schlichting, Carl. Working with polyethylene foam and fluted plastic sheet. Ottawa, Ontario, Canada : Canadian Conservation Institute, Dept. of Canadian Heritage, 1994.
*TC N8554 T25 no.14*

**PLASTIC FOAMS.**
Schlichting, Carl. Working with polyethylene foam and fluted plastic sheet. Ottawa, Ontario, Canada : Canadian Conservation Institute, Dept. of Canadian Heritage, 1994.
*TC N8554 T25 no.14*

**PLASTIC SURGEONS.** *See* **SURGERY, PLASTIC.**

**PLASTIC SURGERY.** *See* **SURGERY, PLASTIC.**

**PLATE TECTONICS.**
The living machine [videorecording]. [New York, N.Y.?] : Unapix Entertainment, Inc. [distributor], c1996.
*TC QB631.2 .L5 1996*

Gifts from the earth [videorecording]. [New York, N.Y.?] : Unapix Entertainment, Inc. [distributor], c1996.
*TC QB631.2 .G5 1996*

**PLATEAUS - ALGERIA.** *See* **TASSILI-N-AJJER (ALGERIA).**

**PLATO - CONTRIBUTIONS IN PHILOSOPHY OF MIND.**
Ostenfeld, Erik Nis. Ancient Greek psychology and the modern mind-body debate. Aarhus, Denmark : Aarhus University Press, 1987.
*TC BF161 .O88 1987*

**Platt, Jennifer M., 1945-.**
Olson, Judy L. Teaching children and adolescents with special needs. 3rd ed. Upper Saddle River, N.J. : Merrill, c2000.
*TC LC3969 .O47 2000*

**Platt, Stephen.**
Researching health promotion. London ; New York : Routledge, 2000.
*TC RA427.8 .R47 2000*

**PLAY.**
Brown, Victoria (Victoria L.) The dramatic difference. Portsmouth, NH : Heinemann, c1999.
*TC PN3171 .B76 1999*

Novak, Dori E. Help! It's an indoor recess day. Thousand Oaks, Calif. : Corwin Press, c2000.

*TC LB3033 .N68 2000*

Play and literacy in early childhood. Mahwah, N.J. : Lawrence Erlbaum Associates, Publishers, 2000.
*TC LB1140.35.P55 P557 2000*

**Play and exploration in children and animals.**
Power, Thomas George, 1954- Mahwah, N.J. : L. Erlbaum Associates, 2000.
*TC BF717 .P69 2000*

**Play and literacy in early childhood :** research from multiple perspectives / edited by Kathleen A. Roskos, James F. Christie. Mahwah, N.J. : Lawrence Erlbaum Associates, Publishers, 2000. xxiv, 278 p. : ill. ; 24 cm. Includes bibliographical references (p. 241-263) and indexes. ISBN 0-8058-2964-4 (alk. paper) ISBN 0-8058-2965-2 (pbk. : alk. paper) DDC 372.21
*1. Play. 2. Language arts (Early childhood) I. Roskos, Kathy. II. Christie, James F.*
*TC LB1140.35.P55 P557 2000*

**PLAY AND PLAYTHINGS.**
Play diagnosis and assessment. 2nd ed. New York : John Wiley & Sons, c2000.
*TC RJ505.P6 P524 1999*

**PLAY BEHAVIOR IN ANIMALS.**
Power, Thomas George, 1954- Play and exploration in children and animals. Mahwah, N.J. : L. Erlbaum Associates, 2000.
*TC BF717 .P69 2000*

**Play diagnosis and assessment** / edited by Karen Gitlin-Weiner, Alice Sandgrund, Charles Schaefer. 2nd ed. New York : John Wiley & Sons. xvi, 775 p. : ill. ; 26 cm. Schaefer's name appears first on earlier edition. Includes bibliographical references and indexes. ISBN 0-471-25457-6 (cloth : alk. paper) DDC 618.92/89075
*1. Play therapy. 2. Play - Psychological aspects. 3. Child psychology. 4. Mental Disorders - diagnosis. 5. Mental Disorders - Child. 6. Mental Disorders - Infant. 7. Personality Assessment - Child. 8. Personality Assessment - Infant. 9. Play and Playthings. I. Sandgrund, Alice. II. Schaefer, Charles E.*
*TC RJ505.P6 P524 1999*

**PLAY - FICTION.**
Chichester Clark, Emma. More!. 1st American ed. New York : Doubleday Books for Young Readers/ Bantam Doubleday Dell Pub., 1999.
*TC PZ7.C4335 Mo 1999*

George, Jean Craighead, 1919- Snow Bear. 1st ed. New York : Hyperion Books for Children, 1999.
*TC PZ7.G2933 Sn 1999*

Henkes, Kevin. Oh!. New York : Greenwillow Books, 1999.
*TC PZ8.3.H4165 Oh 1999*

**PLAY - PSYCHOLOGICAL ASPECTS.**
Play diagnosis and assessment. 2nd ed. New York : John Wiley & Sons, c2000.
*TC RJ505.P6 P524 1999*

Power, Thomas George, 1954- Play and exploration in children and animals. Mahwah, N.J. : L. Erlbaum Associates, 2000.
*TC BF717 .P69 2000*

**Play, school, and society.**
Mead, George Herbert, 1863-1931. New York : Peter Lang, c1999.
*TC HQ782 .M43 1999*

**PLAY - SOCIAL ASPECTS.**
Girls, boys, books, toys. Baltimore : Johns Hopkins University Press, 1999.
*TC PN1009.5.S48 G57 1999*

Mead, George Herbert, 1863-1931. Play, school, and society. New York : Peter Lang, c1999.
*TC HQ782 .M43 1999*

**PLAY THERAPY.**
O'Connor, Kevin J. The play therapy primer. 2nd ed. New York : John Wiley & Sons, c2000.
*TC RJ505.P6 O26 2000*

Play diagnosis and assessment. 2nd ed. New York : John Wiley & Sons, c2000.
*TC RJ505.P6 P524 1999*

Theraplay. Northvale, N.J. : J. Aronson, c2000.
*TC RJ505.P6 T485 2000*

**The play therapy primer.**
O'Connor, Kevin J. 2nd ed. New York : John Wiley & Sons, c2000.
*TC RJ505.P6 O26 2000*

**Players all.**
Rinehart, Robert E., 1951- Bloomington : Indiana University Press, c1998.
*TC GV706.5 .R56 1998*

**PLAYERS, MUSICAL INSTRUMENT.** *See* MUSICIANS.

**PLAYGROUNDS.** *See* PARKS.

**PLAYS.** *See* DRAMA.

**PLAYS FOR CHILDREN.** *See* CHILDREN'S PLAYS.

**Please, please, please.**
Vail, Rachel. New York : Scholastic, c1998.
*TC PZ7.V1916 Pl 1998*

**PLEASURE.** *See also* PAIN.
Greenfield, Susan. The private life of the brain. New York : John Wiley, c2000.
*TC BF515 G74 2000*

McWilliam, Erica. Pedagogical pleasures. New York ; Canterbury [England] : P. Lang, c1999.
*TC LB1775 .M319 1999*

**PLEBISCITE.** *See* MINORITIES.

**Plecas, Jennifer, ill.**
Cowley, Joy. Agapanthus Hum and the eyeglasses. New York : Philomel Books, c1999.
*TC PZ7.C8375 Ag 1999*

**The Plenum series in behavioral psychophysiology and medicine**
Handbook of health promotion and disease prevention. New York : Kluwer Academic/Plenum Publishers, c1999.
*TC RA427.8 .H36 1999*

**The Plenum series in social/clinical psychology**
Piedmont, Ralph L., 1958- The revised NEO Personality Inventory. New York : Plenum Press, c1998.
*TC BF698.8.N46 P54 1998*

**Pleydell, Sarah.**
Brown, Victoria (Victoria L.) The dramatic difference. Portsmouth, NH : Heinemann, c1999.
*TC PN3171 .B76 1999*

**Pliszka, Steven R.** ADHD with comorbid disorders : clinical assessment and management / Steven R. Pliszka, Caryn L. Carlson, James M. Swanson. New York : Guilford Press, c1999. x, 325 p. : ill. ; 25 cm. Attention deficit hyperactivity disorder with comorbid disorders. Includes bibliographical references (p. 271-316) and index. ISBN 1-57230-478-2 DDC 618.92
*1. Attention-deficit hyperactivity disorder. 2. Comorbidity. 3. Attention Deficit Disorder with Hyperactivity - diagnosis. 4. Attention Deficit Disorder with Hyperactivity - therapy. 5. Comorbidity. I. Carlson, Caryn L. II. Swanson, James M. III. Title. IV. Title: Attention deficit hyperactivity disorder with comorbid disorders*
*TC RJ506.H9 P55 1999*

**Plomin, Robert, 1948-.**
Reiss, David, 1937- The relationship code. Cambridge, Mass. : London : Harvard University Press, c2000.
*TC BF724 .R39 2000*

**Plotkin, H. C. (Henry C.)** Evolution in mind : an introduction to evolutionary psychology / Henry Plotkin. Cambridge, Mass. : Harvard University Press, 1998. ix, 276 p. ; 24 cm. Includes bibliographical references and index. ISBN 0-674-27120-3 (hardcover)
*1. Genetic psychology. I. Title.*
*TC BF701 .P57 1998*

**Plots of enlightenment.**
Barney, Richard A., 1955- Stanford, Calif. : Stanford University Press, c1999.
*TC PR858.E38 B37 1999*

**Plugging in :** : choosing and using educational technology / Beau Fly Jones ... [et al.]. Washington, D.C. : NEKIA Communications ; Oak Brook, Ill. : North Central Regional Educational Laboratory, [1995]. ([1999]). 46 p. : ill. ; 28 cm. Funded in part by the U.S. Department of Education. RP91002001-RP91002010.
*1. Educational technology. 2. Technology in education. I. Jones, Beau Fly. II. North Central Regional Education Laboratory (U.S.)*
*TC LB1028.3 .P584 1995*

**Plunkett, Kim.** Preliminary approaches to language development / Kim Plunkett. Aarhus, Denmark : Aarhus University Press, c1985. vi, 154 p. : ill. ; 22 cm. (Psykologisk serie = Psychology series, 0901-1021 ; 1) Bibliography: p. 143-145. Includes index. ISBN 87-7288-001-5 (pbk.)
*1. Language acquisition. 2. Psycholinguistics. I. Title. II. Series: Psychology series (Arhus, Denmark) ; 1.*
*TC P118 .P6 1985*

**PLURALISM (SOCIAL SCIENCES).** *See also* ETHNICITY; MULTICULTURALISM.
(Re)visioning composition textbooks. Albany : State University of New York Press, c1999.
*TC PE1404 .R46 1999*

**PLURALISM (SOCIAL SCIENCES) - CANADA - COMPUTER NETWORK RESOURCES - DIRECTORIES.**
Gregory, Vicki L., 1950- Multicultural resources on the Internet. The United States and Canada. Englewood, Colo. : Libraries Unlimited, 1999.
*TC E184.A1 G874 1999*

**PLURALISM (SOCIAL SCIENCES) - RELIGIOUS ASPECTS.**
Fukuyama, Mary A. Integrating spirituality into multicultural counseling. Thousand Oaks, Calif. : Sage Publications, c1999.
*TC BF637.C6 F795 1999*

**PLURALISM (SOCIAL SCIENCES) - STUDY AND TEACHING.**
Garcia, Ricardo L. Teaching for diversity. Bloomington, Ind. : Phi Delta Kappa Educational Foundation, 1998.
*TC LC1099.3 .G367 1998*

**PLURALISM (SOCIAL SCIENCES) - STUDY AND TEACHING (PRESCHOOL) - CANADA.**
Chud, Gyda. Early childhood education for a multicultural society. [Vancouver] : Western Education Development Group, Faculty of Education, The University of British Columbia, c1985.
*TC LC1099 .C494 1985*

**PLURALISM (SOCIAL SCIENCES) - UNITED STATES.**
Addressing cultural issues in organizations. Thousand Oaks, Calif. : Sage Publications, 2000.
*TC E184.A1 A337 2000*

Campbell, Duane E. Choosing democracy. 2nd ed. Upper Saddle River, N.J. : Merrill, c2000.
*TC LC1099.3 .C36 2000*

The challenge of permanency planning in a multicultural society. c1997.
*TC HV741 .C378 1997*

Lerner, Richard M. Family diversity and family policy. Boston ; London : Kluwer Academic, c1999.
*TC HQ535 .L39 1999*

Problems and issues of diversity in the United States. Westport, Conn. : Bergin & Garvey, 1999.
*TC E184.A1 P76 1999*

**PLURALISM (SOCIAL SCIENCES) - UNITED STATES - COMPUTER NETWORK RESOURCES - DIRECTORIES.**
Gregory, Vicki L., 1950- Multicultural resources on the Internet. The United States and Canada. Englewood, Colo. : Libraries Unlimited, 1999.
*TC E184.A1 G874 1999*

**PLURALISM (SOCIAL SCIENCES) - UNITED STATES - STUDY AND TEACHING.**
Teaching the literatures of early America. New York : Modern Language Association of America, 1999.
*TC PS186 .T43 1999*

**Plutchik, Robert.** Foundations of experimental research. New York, Harper & Row [1968] xiii, 290 p. illus. 21 cm. (Harper's experimental psychology series) Bibliography: p. 257-266. DDC 152
*1. Psychology, Experimental. I. Title.*
*TC BF181 .P56*

**Pocket chart kit** [kit] / Open Court Publishing Company. Chicago, Ill. : Open Court Publishing Company, c1995. 1 kit (233 Word cards; 96 Pocket Chart Letter cards; 211 Picture cards; 1 Pickled Peppers book in container (22 x 27 x 11 cm.) + 1 card holder (139 x 36 cm.). (Collections for Young Scholars) Title from container. For the primary grades. SUMMARY: For use with the card holder, to be hung on the wall, which has 10 rows clear plastic pockets for forming sentences with the flash cards. Library lacking 211 Picture cards, Pickled Peppers book and green nylon card holder. ISBN 0-8126-0474-1 (Pocket letter cards) ISBN 0-8126-0408-3 (Word cards) ISBN 0-8126-0426-1 (Picture cards) ISBN 0-8126-0430-X (Book)
*1. Reading (Primary) 2. Reading - Phonetic method. 3. Language arts (Primary) I. Open Court Publishing Company. II. Series.*
*TC LB1573.3 .P6 1995*

**POCKET COMPANIONS.** *See* HANDBOOKS, VADE-MECUMS, ETC.

**Pocket dictionary of audiology.**
Mendel, Lisa Lucks. Singular's pocket dictionary of audiology. San Diego : Singular Pub. Group, c1999.

*TC RF290 .M4642 1999*

**Pocket guides (National Gallery (Great Britain))**
Bomford, David. Colour. London : National Gallery Company ; [New Haven, Conn.] : Distributed by Yale Universtiy Press, 2000.
*TC ND1489 B66 2000*

**The pocket mentor.**
Niebrand, Chris. Boston, Mass. : Allyn and Bacon, 2000.
*TC LB1775.2 .N54 2000*

**Pocket reference for Pediatric primary care /** Catherine E. Burns ... [et al.]. Philadelphia ; London : Saunders, c2001. xx, 568 p. : ill. ; 20 cm. Includes bibliographical references and index. ISBN 0-7216-8466-1 DDC 618.92
*1. Pediatrics - Handbooks, manuals, etc. 2. Pediatric nursing - Handbooks, manuals, etc. 3. Pediatrics - United States - Handbooks. 4. Primary Health Care - United States - Handbooks. I. Burns, Catherine E. II. Title: Pediatric primary care.*
*TC RJ45 .P525 2001*

**Pockets**
Farndon, John. Volcanoes. 1st American ed. New York : DK Pub., 1998.
*TC QE522 .F37 1998*

**Podesta, Connie.** Life would be easy if it weren't for other people / Connie Podesta, with Vicki Sanderson ; illustrations by M. Loys Raymer. Thousand Oaks, Calif. : Corwin Press, c1999. v, 194 p. : ill. ; 24 cm. Includes index. ISBN 0-8039-6864-7 (alk. paper) ISBN 0-8039-6865-5 (alk. paper) DDC 158.2
*1. Interpersonal conflict. 2. Interpersonal communication. 3. Interpersonal relations. I. Sanderson, Vicki. II. Title.*
*TC BF637.I48 P63 1999*

**PODICIPEDIDAE.** *See* GREBES.

**PODICIPEDIFORMES.** *See* GREBES.

**Podis, JoAnne M.**
Working with student writers. New York : P. Lang, c1999.
*TC PE1404 .W66 1999*

**Podis, Leonard A.**
Working with student writers. New York : P. Lang, c1999.
*TC PE1404 .W66 1999*

**Podro, Michael.** Depiction / Michael Podro. New Haven, CT : Yale University Press, c1998. viii, 193 p. : ill. (some col.) ; 25 cm. Includes bibliographical references (p. [180]-189) and index. ISBN 0-300-06914-6 (cloth : alk. paper) DDC 701/.15
*1. Artists - Psychology. 2. Visual perception. 3. Imagery (Psychology) in art. I. Title.*
*TC N71 .P64 1998*

**Podsen, India, 1945-** Coaching & mentoring first-year and student teachers / by India J. Podsen, Vicki M. Denmark. Larchmont, NY : Eye On Education, c2000. xix, 188 p. ; 28 cm. Includes bibliographical references. ISBN 1-88300-180-3 DDC 370/.71
*1. Mentoring in education - United States. 2. Student teachers - United States. 3. First year teachers - United States. I. Denmark, Vicki M., 1957- II. Title. III. Title: Coaching and mentoring first-year and student teachers*
*TC LB1731.4 .P63 2000*

Written expression. Larchmont, NY : Eye on Education, c1997.
*TC PN145 .W78 1997*

**Podwal, Mark H., 1945- ill.**
Sobel, Ileene Smith. Moses and the angels. New York : Delacorte Press, c1999.
*TC BM580 .S55 1999*

**POEA INDIANS.** *See* MACUNA INDIANS.

**POEMS.** *See* POETRY.

**Poems for fathers /** selected by Myra Cohn Livingston ; illustrated by Robert Casilla. 1st ed. New York : Holiday House, c1989. 32 p. : col. ill. ; 24 cm. SUMMARY: Eighteen poems by English and American authors celebrate fathers--sometimes humorously, sometimes poignantly. ISBN 0-8234-0729-2 DDC 811/.008/03520431
*1. Fathers - Juvenile poetry. 2. Children's poetry, American. 3. Children's poetry, English. 4. Fathers - Poetry. 5. American poetry - Collections. 6. English poetry - Collections. I. Livingston, Myra Cohn. II. Casilla, Robert, ill.*
*TC PS595.F39 P64 1989*

**POÉSIE - ÉTUDE ET ENSEIGNEMENT (SECONDAIRE).**
Leggo, Carleton Derek, 1953- Teaching to wonder. Vancouver : Pacific Educational Press, c1997.
*TC PN1101 .L43 1997*

**POETICS.** *See* **POETRY - AUTHORSHIP.**

**POETRY - AUTHORSHIP - STUDY AND TEACHING.**
Wormser, Baron. Teaching the art of poetry. Mahwah, N.J. : Lawrence Erlbaum Assoc., 2000.
*TC PN1101 .W67 2000*

**POETRY - COLLECTIONS.**
Earth, air, fire & water. Rev. ed. New York, N.Y. : Harper & Row, c1989.
*TC PN6101 .E37 1989*

Earth, air, fire & water. Rev. ed. New York, N.Y. : Harper & Row, c1989.
*TC PN6101 .E37 1989*

If the owl calls again. 1st ed. New York : M.K. McElderry Books ; Toronto : Collier Macmillan ; New York : Maxwell Macmillan, c1990.
*TC PN6109.97 .I3 1990*

A journey through time in verse and rhyme. Rev. ed. Edinburgh : Floris Books, 1998.
*TC PN6109.97 .J68 1998*

My mane catches the wind. 1st ed. New York: Harcourt Brace Jovanovich, c1979.
*TC PN6110.H7 M9*

Riddle-me rhymes. 1st ed. New York : M.K. McElderry Books ; Toronto : Maxwell Macmillan Canada ; New York : Maxwell Macmillan International, c1994.
*TC PN6371.5 .R53 1994*

Time is the longest distance. 1st ed. New York, NY : HarperCollins, c1991.
*TC PN6109.97 .T56 1991*

**POETRY - PHILOSOPHY.** *See* **POETRY.**

**POETRY - STUDY AND TEACHING.**
Wormser, Baron. Teaching the art of poetry. Mahwah, N.J. : Lawrence Erlbaum Assoc., 2000.
*TC PN1101 .W67 2000*

**POETRY - STUDY AND TEACHING (ELEMENTARY) - GREAT BRITAIN.**
Carter, Dennis. Teaching poetry in the primary school. London : David Fulton, 1998.
*TC LB1575 .C27 1998*

**POETRY - STUDY AND TEACHING (SECONDARY).**
Leggo, Carleton Derek, 1953- Teaching to wonder. Vancouver : Pacific Educational Press, c1997.
*TC PN1101 .L43 1997*

Osakwe, Mabel. Poetrymate 1. Enugu, Nigeria : Fourth Dimension Publishing Co., 1996.
*TC PN1101 .O73 1996*

**Poetrymate.**
Osakwe, Mabel. Poetrymate 1. Enugu, Nigeria : Fourth Dimension Publishing Co., 1996.
*TC PN1101 .O73 1996*

**Poetrymate 1.**
Osakwe, Mabel. Enugu, Nigeria : Fourth Dimension Publishing Co., 1996.
*TC PN1101 .O73 1996*

**Poetrymate one.**
Osakwe, Mabel. Poetrymate 1. Enugu, Nigeria : Fourth Dimension Publishing Co., 1996.
*TC PN1101 .O73 1996*

**POETS, ENGLISH - 19TH CENTURY - BIOGRAPHY.**
Elledge, Paul. Lord Byron at Harrow School. Baltimore : Johns Hopkins University Press, c2000.
*TC PR4382 .E36 2000*

**Poirrier, Gail P.** Service learning : curricular applications in nursing / Gail P. Poirrier. Boston : Jones and Bartlett Publishers, 2001. xiii, 142 p. : ill. ; 23 cm. Includes bibliographical references and index. ISBN 0-7637-1429-1 DDC 610.73/071
*1. Nursing - Study and teaching. 2. Student service. 3. Community health nursing. 4. Nursing. 5. Community Health Nursing. I. Title.*
*TC RT73 .P64 2001*

**Poitier, Sidney.** Bridges to independence [videorecording. Burbank, CA : RCA/Columbia Pictures Home Video ; [S.l. : Distributed by] Rank Video Services Production, c1991.
*TC HV1646 .B7 1991*

**Polacco, Patricia.** Welcome Comfort / Patricia Polacco. New York : Philomel Books, 1999. 1 v. (unpaged) : col. ill. ; 28 cm. SUMMARY: Welcome Comfort, a lonely foster child, is assured by his friend the school custodian that there is a Santa Claus, but he does not discover the truth until one

wondrous and surprising Christmas Eve. ISBN 0-399-23169-2 DDC [E]
*1. Santa Claus - Juvenile fiction. 2. Santa Claus - Fiction. 3. Christmas - Fiction. 4. Foster home care - Fiction. I. Title.*
*TC PZ7.P75186 Wg 1999*

**Poland, Blake D.** Settings for health promotion. Thousand Oaks, Calif. : Sage Publications, Inc., c2000.
*TC RA427.8 .S48 2000*

**POLAND - HISTORY - REVOLUTION, 1905-1907.**
Blobaum, Robert. Rewolucja. Ithaca : Cornell University Press, 1995.
*TC DK4385 .B57 1995*

**Poland. Ministerstwo Oświaty i Wychowania.**
Języki obce w szkole. Warszawa : Wydawn. Szkolne i Pedagogiczne,

**POLAND - POLITICS AND GOVERNMENT - 1989-.**
Adolescent development and rapid social change. Albany : State University of New York Press, c2000.
*TC HQ799.H8 A35 2000*

**POLAR BEAR - FICTION.**
De Beer, Hans. [Kleine Eisbär und der Angsthase. English] Little Polar Bear and the brave little hare. New York : North-South Books, 1998.
*TC PZ7.D353 Liv 1998*

George, Jean Craighead, 1919- Snow Bear. 1st ed. New York : Hyperion Books for Children, 1999.
*TC PZ7.G2933 Sn 1999*

**POLAR LIGHTS.** *See* **AURORAS.**

**POLAR REGIONS.** *See* **ANTARCTICA; ARCTIC REGIONS.**

**POLES - UNITED STATES.** *See* **POLISH AMERICANS.**

**Polette, Nancy.** Gifted books, gifted readers : literature activities to excite young minds / Nancy J. Polette. Englewood, Colo. : Libraries Unlimited, 2000. xi, 282 p. : ill. ; 28 cm. Includes bibliographical references and index. ISBN 1-56308-822-3 DDC 371.95
*1. Literature - Study and teaching (Elementary) - United States. 2. Reading (Elementary) - United States. 3. Gifted children - Education (Elementary) - United States. 4. Gifted children - United States - Books and reading. I. Title.*
*TC LB1575.5.U5 P64 2000*

**POLICE - ILLINOIS - CHICAGO.**
Walker, Daniel, 1922- Rights in conflict; convention week in Chicago, August, 25-29, 1968; New York : Dutton, c1968.
*TC F548.52 .W3 1968c*

**POLICE - LEGAL STATUS, LAWS, ETC.** *See* **POLICE.**

**POLICE OFFICERS.** *See* **POLICE.**

**POLICEMEN.** *See* **POLICE.**

**Policy and practice in higher education.**
Bleiklie, Ivar, 1948- London ; Phildadelphia : J. Kingsley Publishers, 2000.
*TC LC178.N8 B44 2000*

**Policy entrepreneurs and school choice.**
Mintrom, Michael, 1963- Washington, DC : Georgetown University Press, c2000.
*TC LB1027.9 .M57 2000*

**Policy essay**
(no. 26) Nelson, Joan M. Reforming health and education. Washington, DC : Overseas Development Council ; Baltimore, MD : Distributed by the Johns Hopkins University Press, c1999.
*TC HG3881.5.W57 N447 1999*

**POLICY-MAKING.** *See* **POLICY SCIENCES.**

**POLICY, MEDICAL.** *See* **MEDICAL POLICY.**

**Policy, pedagogy, and social inequality.**
Herideen, Penelope E., 1960- Westport, Conn. : Bergin & Garvey, 1998.
*TC LB2328.15.U6 H47 1998*

**Policy research in educational settings.**
Ozga, Jennifer. Buckingham [England] ; Philadelphia : Open University Press, 2000.
*TC LB1028.25.G7 O93 2000*

**POLICY SCIENCES.**
Mintrom, Michael, 1963- Policy entrepreneurs and school choice. Washington, DC : Georgetown University Press, c2000.
*TC LB1027.9 .M57 2000*

**POLICY SCIENCES - MATHEMATICAL MODELS.**
Greenberger, Martin, 1931- Models in the policy process. New York : Russell Sage Foundation : [distributed by Basic Books], c1976.
*TC H61 .G667*

**POLICY SCIENTISTS.** *See* **SOCIAL SCIENTISTS.**

**POLISH AMERICANS - FICTION.**
Recorvits, Helen. Goodbye, Walter Malinski. 1st ed. New York : Farrar, Straus and Giroux, c1999.
*TC PZ7.R24435 Go 1999*

**POLISH AMERICANS - UNITED STATES.** *See* **POLISH AMERICANS.**

**Polit-O'Hara, Denise.** Nursing research : principles and methods / Denise F. Polit, Bernadette P. Hungler. 6th ed. Philadelphia : Lippincott, c1999. xviii, 757 p. : ill. (some col.) ; 25 cm. Includes bibliographical references and indexes. ISBN 0-7817-1562-8 (alk. paper) DDC 610.73/072
*1. Nursing - Research - Methodology. 2. Nursing Research - methods. I. Hungler, Bernadette P. II. Title.*
*TC RT81.5 .P64 1999*

**POLITICAL ACTIVISTS.** *See* **POLITICAL PARTICIPATION; WOMEN POLITICAL ACTIVISTS.**

**POLITICAL ACTIVISTS - UNITED STATES - BIOGRAPHY.**
Connerly, Ward, 1939- Creating equal. San Francisco : Encounter Books, 2000.
*TC E185.97 .C74 2000*

**POLITICAL ACTIVISTS - YUGOSLAVIA - BELGRADE (SERBIA) - ATTITUDES.**
[Ajmo, ajde, svi u šetnju. English.] Protest in Belgrade. Budapest, Hungary ; New York, NY, USA : Central European University Press, 1999.
*TC DR2044 .A3913 1999*

**POLITICAL ACTIVITY.** *See* **POLITICAL PARTICIPATION.**

**POLITICAL BEHAVIOR.** *See* **POLITICAL PARTICIPATION.**

**POLITICAL CONSULTANTS.** *See* **POLITICIANS.**

**POLITICAL CONVENTIONS.** *See* **POLITICAL PARTIES.**

**POLITICAL CONVENTIONS - UNITED STATES.**
Kirkpatrick, Jeane J. The new Presidential elite. New York : Russell Sage Foundation : [distributed by Basic Books], c1976.
*TC JK1764 .K57*

**POLITICAL CRIMES AND OFFENSES.** *See* **INSURGENCY.**

**POLITICAL ECONOMY.** *See* **ECONOMICS.**

**Political economy of health care series**
Kenig, Sylvia. Who plays? who pays? who cares? Amityville, N.Y. : Baywood Pub. Co., c1992.
*TC RA790.6 .K46 1992*

**The political economy of hope and fear.**
Andrews, Marcellus, 1956- New York : New York University Press, c1999.
*TC E185.8 .A77 1999*

**POLITICAL ETHICS.** *See* **CIVICS.**

**POLITICAL EXTREMISM.** *See* **RADICALISM.**

**POLITICAL FICTION.**
Burdick, Eugene. Fail-safe. 1st Ecco ed. Hopewell, N.J. : Ecco Press ; New York, NY : Distributed by W.W. Norton, 1999.
*TC PS3552.U7116 F35 1999*

**POLITICAL HISTORY.** *See* **WORLD POLITICS.**

**POLITICAL LEADERSHIP - MEXICO - PUEBLA (STATE) - HISTORY - 19TH CENTURY.**
Thomson, Guy P. C., 1949- Patriotism, politics, and popular liberalism in nineteenth-century Mexico. Wilmington, De. : Scholarly Resources, 1999.
*TC F1326.L83 T5 1999*

**POLITICAL PARTICIPATION.** *See also* **POLITICAL ACTIVISTS.**
Kane, Francis, 1944- Neither beasts nor gods. Dallas : Southern Methodist University Press, 1998.
*TC JC330.15 .K36 1998*

**POLITICAL PARTICIPATION - UNITED STATES.**
Kirkpatrick, Jeane J. The new Presidential elite. New York : Russell Sage Foundation : [distributed by Basic Books], c1976.
*TC JK1764 .K57*

Schachter, Hindy Lauer. Reinventing government or reinventing ourselves. Albany : State University of New York Press, c1997.
*TC JK1764 .S35 1997*

**POLITICAL PARTIES.** *See* **POLITICAL CONVENTIONS.**

**POLITICAL PARTIES - GERMANY - FRANKFURT AM MAIN - HISTORY - 19TH CENTURY.**
Palmowski, Jan. Urban liberalism in imperial Germany. Oxford ; New York : Oxford University Press, 1999.
*TC DD901.F78 P35 1999*

**POLITICAL PERSECUTION.** *See* **CIVIL RIGHTS.**

**POLITICAL POSTERS, RUSSIAN.**
Bonnell, Victoria E. Iconography of power. Berkeley : University of California Press, c1997.
*TC DK266.3 .B58 1997*

**POLITICAL POWER.** *See* **POWER (SOCIAL SCIENCES).**

**POLITICAL PSYCHOLOGY.** *See* **POLITICAL SOCIALIZATION; PUBLIC OPINION.**

**POLITICAL REFUGEES - UNITED STATES.**
Gonzalez-Pando, Miguel. The Cuban Americans. Westport, Conn. : Greenwood Press, 1998.
*TC E184.C97 G64 1998*

**POLITICAL REFUGEES - UNITED STATES - EXHIBITIONS.**
Exiles + emigrés. Los Angeles, Calif. : Los Angeles County Museum of Art ; New York : H.N. Abrams, c1997.
*TC N6512 .E887 1997*

**Political relationship and narrative knowledge.**
Armitage, Peter B., 1939- Westport, Conn. : Bergin & Garvey, 2000.
*TC LC93.G7 A86 2000*

**POLITICAL RIGHTS.** *See* **CITIZENSHIP; POLITICAL PARTICIPATION.**

**POLITICAL SCIENCE.** *See* **AUTHORITARIANISM; BUREAUCRACY; CHRISTIANITY AND POLITICS; CITIZENSHIP; CIVICS; CONSERVATISM; COUPS D'ÉTAT; EQUALITY; HINDUISM AND POLITICS; IMPERIALISM; ISLAM AND POLITICS; LIBERALISM; LIBERTY; MONARCHY; NATIONALISM; POLITICAL PARTIES; POWER (SOCIAL SCIENCES); PUBLIC ADMINISTRATION; PUBLIC OPINION; RADICALISM; RELIGION AND POLITICS; STATE GOVERNMENTS; WORLD POLITICS.**

**POLITICAL SCIENCE - PHILOSOPHY.**
Tarcov, Nathan. Locke's education for liberty. Lanham, Md. : Lexington Books, c1999.
*TC LB475.L72 T27 1999*

**POLITICAL SCIENCE - RELIGIOUS ASPECTS.** *See* **RELIGION AND POLITICS.**

**POLITICAL SCIENCE - STUDY AND TEACHING (HIGHER) - SASKATCHEWAN - SASKATOON - HISTORY.**
Spafford, Shirley. No ordinary academics. Toronto : University of Toronto Press, 1999.
*TC HB74.9.C3 S62 1999*

**POLITICAL SCIENCE - STUDY AND TEACHING (SECONDARY) - UNITED STATES.**
Caliendo, Stephen M., 1971- Teachers matter. Westport, Conn. : Praeger, 2000.
*TC JA88.U6 C24 2000*

**POLITICAL SOCIALIZATION.**
Civic education across countries. Amsterdam, the Netherlands : International Association for the Evaluation of Educational Achievement, c1999.
*TC JA86 .C6 1999*

**POLITICAL SOCIALIZATION - EUROPE, EASTERN.**
Adolescent development and rapid social change. Albany : State University of New York Press, c2000.
*TC HQ799.H8 A35 2000*

**POLITICAL SOCIALIZATION - UNITED STATES.**
Caliendo, Stephen M., 1971- Teachers matter. Westport, Conn. : Praeger, 2000.
*TC JA88.U6 C24 2000*

**POLITICAL SOCIOLOGY.** *See* **POLITICAL SOCIALIZATION.**

**POLITICAL THEORY.** *See* **POLITICAL SCIENCE.**

**POLITICAL THOUGHT.** *See* **POLITICAL SCIENCE.**

**POLITICAL VIOLENCE.** *See* **RIOTS.**

**POLITICIANS.** *See* **WOMEN POLITICIANS.**

**POLITICIANS - MEXICO - BIOGRAPHY.**
Llinás Alvarez, Edgar. Vida y obra de Ramón Beteta. 1. ed. México : [s.n.], 1996 (México, D.F. : Impresora Galve)
*TC F1234.B56 L5 1996*

**POLITICS.** *See* **POLITICAL SCIENCE.**

**POLITICS AND ART.** *See* **ART AND STATE; ART - POLITICAL ASPECTS.**

**POLITICS AND CHRISTIANITY.** *See* **CHRISTIANITY AND POLITICS.**

**POLITICS AND CULTURE.** *See also* **POLITICS AND LITERATURE.**
Giroux, Henry A. Stealing innocence. 1st ed. New York : St. Martin's Press, 2000.
*TC HM621 .G57 2000*

**POLITICS AND CULTURE - UNITED STATES.**
Bad subjects. New York : New York University Press, c1998.
*TC E169.12 .B26 1998*

**POLITICS AND CULTURE - UNITED STATES - HISTORY - CONGRESSES.**
Democracy & the arts. Ithaca : Cornell University Press, c1999.
*TC NX180.S6 D447 1999*

**POLITICS AND EDUCATION.**
Politics, education and citizenship. London ; New York : Falmer Press, 2000.
*TC LC1091 .P54 2000*

Rufo-Lignos, Patricia Marie. Towards a new topology of public and private schools. 1999.
*TC 06 no. 11170*

Rufo-Lignos, Patricia Marie. Towards a new typology of public and private schools. 1999.
*TC 06 no. 11170*

**POLITICS AND EDUCATION - AFRICA - HISTORY.**
Bassey, Magnus O. Western education and political domination in Africa. Westport, CT : Bergin & Garvey, 1999.
*TC LC95.A2 B37 1999*

**POLITICS AND EDUCATION - CHINA - HISTORY - 20TH CENTURY.**
Reynolds, Barbara G. Reform and education. 1999.
*TC 06 no. 11166*

**POLITICS AND EDUCATION - GEORGIA - HISTORY - 20TH CENTURY.**
O'Brien, Thomas V., 1958- The politics of race and schooling. Lanham, Md. : Lexington Books, c1999.
*TC LC212.22.G46 O37 1999*

**POLITICS AND EDUCATION - GREAT BRITAIN.**
Armitage, Peter B., 1939- Political relationship and narrative knowledge. Westport, Conn. : Bergin & Garvey, 2000.
*TC LC93.G7 A86 2000*

Education policy and contemporary politics. Basingstoke, Hampshire : Macmillan, 1999.
*TC LC93.G7 E382 1999*

**Politics and education in Israel.**
Swirski, Shlomo. New York : Falmer Press, 1999.
*TC LC94.I75 S95 1999*

**POLITICS AND EDUCATION - ISRAEL.**
Swirski, Shlomo. Politics and education in Israel. New York : Falmer Press, 1999.
*TC LC94.I75 S95 1999*

**POLITICS AND EDUCATION - NORTH CAROLINA - HISTORY - 20TH CENTURY.**
Billingsley, William J., 1953- Communists on campus. Athens, Ga. ; London : University of Georgia Press, c1999.
*TC LC72.3.N67 B55 1999*

**POLITICS AND EDUCATION - UNITED STATES.**
Critical ethnicity. Lanham, Md. : Rowman & Littlefield, c1999.
*TC LC212.2 .C75 1999*

Engel, Michael, 1944- The struggle for control of public education. Philadelphia, Pa. : Temple University Press, c2000.

*TC LA217.2 .E533 2000*

In defense of good teaching. York, Me. : Stenhouse Publishers, c1998.
*TC LB1050.35 .I5 1998*

Kimball, Roger, 1953- Tenured radicals. Rev. ed., with a new introd. by the author, 1st Elephant pbk. ed. Chicago : Elephant Paperbacks, 1998.
*TC LC1023 .K56 1998*

Knowledge and power in the global economy. Mahwah, N.J. : L. Erlbaum Associates, 2000.
*TC LC66 .K66 2000*

The politics of multiculturalism and bilingual education. Boston : McGraw-Hill, c2000.
*TC LC1099.3 .P64 2000*

Rediscovering the democratic purposes of education. Lawrence : University Press of Kansas, c2000.
*TC LC89 .R43 2000*

Wong, Kenneth K., 1955- Funding public schools. Lawrence : University Press of Kansas, c1999.
*TC LB2825 .W56 1999*

**POLITICS AND HINDUISM.** *See* **HINDUISM AND POLITICS.**

**POLITICS AND ISLAM.** *See* **ISLAM AND POLITICS.**

**POLITICS AND LITERATURE - GREAT BRITAIN - HISTORY - 17TH CENTURY.**
Wheale, Nigel. Writing and society. London ; New York : Routledge, 1999.
*TC PR438.P65 W75 1999*

**POLITICS AND LITERATURE - UNITED STATES - HISTORY.**
True, Michael. An energy field more intense than war. 1st ed. Syracuse, N.Y. : Syracuse University Press, 1995.
*TC PS169.N65 T78 1995*

**POLITICS AND RELIGION.** *See* **RELIGION AND POLITICS.**

**Politics, education and citizenship** / edited by Mal Leicester, Celia Modgil and Sohan Modgil. London ; New York : Falmer Press, 2000. viii, 261 p. ; 29 cm. (Education, culture, and values ; v. 6) Includes bibliographical references and index. ISBN 0-7507-1007-1 (hc.) DDC 306.43
1. Citizenship - Study and teaching. 2. Politics and education. I. Leicester, Mal. II. Modgil, Celia. III. Modgil, Sohan. IV. Series.
*TC LC1091 .P54 2000*

**POLITICS IN ART.** *See* **STREET ART.**

**Politics, love, and divorce in urban and rural China, 1949-1964.**
Diamant, Neil Jeffrey, 1964- Revolutionizing the family. Berkeley : University of California Press, c2000.
*TC HQ684 .D53 2000*

**The politics of addiction** [videorecording] / a production of Public Affairs Television ; a presentation of Thirteen/WNET New York ; produced by Daphne Pinkerson, Marc Levin ; directed by Marc Levin. Princeton, NJ : Films for the Humanities & Sciences, c1998. 1 videocassette (57 min.) : sd., col. with b&w sequences ; 1/2 in. (The Moyers collection) (Close to home. Moyers on addiction) Title on cassette label: Close to home, the politics of addiction [videorecording]. VHS. Catalogued from credits and cassette label and container. Host: Bill Moyers. Director of photography, Mark Benjamin ; edited by Rob Kuhns ; series music composed by Richard Fiocca. For adolescents through adult. SUMMARY: Members of Congress, doctors, policy activists and recovering people have joined to push for a new policy on drugs. This program looks at Prop 200 and Arizona's recent struggle to find an alternative to current policies. Policies for alcohol and the tobacco industry are also discussed.
*1. Drug abuse - Government policy - Arizona. 2. Drug abuse - Government policy - United States. 3. Narcotic addicts - Rehabilitation. 4. Alcoholics - Rehabilitation. 5. Tobacco industry - Government policy - United States. 6. United States - Officials and employees - Interviews. I. Moyers, Bill D. II. Pinkerson, Daphne. III. Levin, Marc, 1951- IV. Public Affairs Television (Firm) V. WNET (Television station : New York, N.Y.) VI. Films for the Humanities (Firm) VII. Title: Close to home, the politics of addiction [videorecording] VIII. Series. IX. Series: Close to home (Series)*
*TC RC564 .P59 1998*

**The politics of faculty unionization.**
Arnold, Gordon B., 1954- Westport, Conn. ; London : Bergin & Garvey, 2000.
*TC LB2335.865.U6 A75 2000*

**The politics of fat.**
Sims, Laura S., 1943- Armonk, N.Y. : M.E. Sharpe,
c1998.
*TC TX360.U6 S58 1998*

**The politics of knowledge.**
Lagemann, Ellen Condliffe, 1945- 1st ed.
Middletown, Conn. : Wesleyan University Press,
c1989.
*TC HV97.C3 L34 1989*

**The politics of multiculturalism and bilingual
education :** students and teachers caught in the cross
fire / editors, Carlos J. Ovando, Peter McLaren.
Boston : McGraw-Hill, c2000. xxiv, 240 p. : ill. ; 24 cm.
Includes bibliographical references and index. ISBN 0-07-
366076-0 DDC 370.117/0973
*1. Multicultural education - United States. 2. Education.
Bilingual - United States. 3. Politics and education - United
States. I. Ovando, Carlos Julio. II. McLaren, Peter, 1948-*
*TC LC1099.3 .P64 2000*

**The politics of Muslim cultural reform.**
Khalid, Adeeb, 1964- Berkeley : University of
California Press, c1998.
*TC BP63.A34 K54 1998*

**The politics of professionalism :** teachers and the
curriculum / Gary McCulloch, Gill Helsby and Peter
Knight. London : Continuum, 2000. vi, 136 p. ; 24 cm.
Includes bibliographical references (p. [125]-134) and index.
ISBN 0-8264-4798-8 ISBN 0-8264-4814-3 (pbk.) DDC
375.00941
*1. Education. 2. Teachers - Professional ethics. 3. Teacher
participation in curriculum planning - Great Britain. I. Helsby,
Gill. II. Knight, Peter, 1947- III. Title.*
*TC LB1779 .M33 2000*

**The politics of psychoanalysis.**
Frosh, Stephen. 2nd ed. New York : New York
University Press, 1999.
*TC BF173 .F92 1999* ·

**The politics of pure science.**
Greenberg, Daniel S., 1931- New ed. / with
introductory essays by John Maddox and Steven
Shapin and a new afterword by the author. Chicago :
University of Chicago Press, 1999.
*TC Q127.U6 G68 1999*

**The politics of race and schooling.**
O'Brien, Thomas V., 1958- Lanham, Md. : Lexington
Books, c1999.
*TC LC212.22.G46 O37 1999*

**The politics of school choice.**
Morken, Hubert. Lanham, Md. : Rowman &
Littlefield Publishers, c1999.
*TC LB1027.9 .M68 1999*

**Politics of self-determination.**
Leary, Timothy. Berkeley, Ca. ; Ronin Pub., c2000.
*TC BF723.P4 L43 2000*

**Politics of the new learning environment.**
Elliott, Geoffrey, Dr. Lifelong learning. London ;
Philadelphia : Jessica Kingsley Publishers, c1999.
*TC LB1060 .E447 1999*

**The politics of visual language.**
Roots, James, 1955- Ottawa : Carleton University
Press, 1999.
*TC HV2395 R66 1999*

**Politics, power & policy making.**
Rushefsky, Mark E., 1945- Armonk, N.Y. : M.E.
Sharpe, c1998.
*TC RA395.A3 R855 1998*

**Politics, power, and policy making.**
Rushefsky, Mark E., 1945- Politics, power & policy
making. Armonk, N.Y. : M.E. Sharpe, c1998.
*TC RA395.A3 R855 1998*

**POLITICS, PRACTICAL. See POLITICAL
PARTICIPATION; POLITICS AND
EDUCATION; WOMEN IN POLITICS.**

**POLITICS, PRACTICAL - RELIGIOUS ASPECTS.
See RELIGION AND POLITICS.**

**Pollack, Dennis R.**
Kosmoski, Georgia J. Managing difficult, frustrating,
and hostile conversations. Thousand Oaks, Calif. :
Sage Publications, c2000.
*TC LB3011.5 .K67 2000*

**Pollard, Diane.**
African-centered schooling in theory and practice.
Westport, Conn. ; London : Bergin & Garvey, 2000.
*TC LC2731 .A35 2000*

**Pollock, David C.** The third culture kid experience :
growing up among worlds / David C. Pollock and
Ruth E. Van Reken. Yarmouth, Me. : Intercultural

Press, c1999. xxv, 333 p. : ill. ; 22 cm. Includes
bibliographical references (p.319-333). ISBN 1-87786-472-2
DDC 303.3/2
*1. Social interaction in children - Foreign countries. 2. Social
skills in children - Foreign countries. 3. Children - Travel -
Foreign countries. 4. Children - Foreign countries - Attitudes.
5. Intercultural communication - Foreign countries. 6.
Parents - Employment - Foreign countries. I. Van Reken, Ruth
E., 1945- II. Title.*
*TC HQ784.S56 P65 1999*

**Pollock, Jackson, 1912-1956.**
Jackson Pollock [videorecording]. [Chicago, Ill.] :
Home Vision ; [S.l.] : Distributed Worldwide by RM
Associates, c1987.
*TC ND237.P73 J3 1987*

Varnedoe, Kirk, 1946- Jackson Pollock. New York :
Museum of Modern Art ; Distributed in the U.S. and
Canada by Harry N. Abrams, c1998.
*TC ND237.P73 A4 1998*

**POLLOCK, JACKSON, 1912-1956.**
Jackson Pollock [videorecording]. [Chicago, Ill.] :
Home Vision ; [S.l.] : Distributed Worldwide by RM
Associates, c1987.
*TC ND237.P73 J3 1987*

**POLLOCK, JACKSON, 1912-1956 -
EXHIBITIONS.**
Varnedoe, Kirk, 1946- Jackson Pollock. New York :
Museum of Modern Art ; Distributed in the U.S. and
Canada by Harry N. Abrams, c1998.
*TC ND237.P73 A4 1998*

**POLLUTANTS, AIR. See AIR - POLLUTION.**

**POLLUTION. See AIR - POLLUTION.**

**Polly, Jean Armour.** The Internet kids & family yellow
pages / Jean Armour Polly. Millenium ed. Berkeley,
Calif. : Osborne McGraw-Hill, c2000. xxxvi, 828 p. :
ill. ; 26 cm. + 1 computer laser optical disc (4 3/4 in.). Includes
indexes. ISBN 0-07-212185-8
*1. Web sites - Directories. 2. Children's Web sites -
Directories. I. Title. II. Title: Internet kids and family yellow
pages*
*TC ZA4226 .P6 2000*

**Polman, Joseph L., 1965-** Designing project-based
science : connecting learners through guided inquiry /
Joseph L. Polman ; foreword by Roy Pea. New York ;
London : Teachers College Press, c2000. xiv, 220 p. :
ill. ; 24 cm. (Ways of knowing in science series) Includes
bibliographical references (p. 207-214) and index. ISBN
0-8077-3913-8 (hbk.) ISBN 0-8077-3912-X (pbk.) DDC 507/
.1/2
*1. Science - Study and teaching (Secondary) - Methodology. 2.
Science - Study and teaching - Activity programs. I. Title. II.
Series.*
*TC Q181 .P4694 2000*

**Polska Akademia Nauk. Zakład Socjologii i Historii
Kultury.**
Kultura i społeczeństwo. Warszawa [Państwowe
Wydawn. Naukowe]

**POLYGLOT MATERIALS.**
Bruegel, Jan, 1568-1625. Where's the bear? Los
Angeles : J. Paul Getty Museum, c1997.
*TC QL49 .B749 1997*

Evans, Lezlie. Can you count ten toes? Boston,
Mass. : Houghton Mifflin, 1999.
*TC QA113 .E84 1999*

**POLYHEDRA. See TOPOLOGY.**

**POLYNESIANS. See MAORI (NEW ZEALAND
PEOPLE).**

**POLYNEURITIC NEUROSIS. See KORSAKOFF'S
SYNDROME.**

**Pombal, paradox of the Enlightenment.**
Maxwell, Kenneth, 1941- Cambridge [England] ; New
York, NY : Cambridge University Press, 1995.
*TC DP641 .M39 1995*

**POMBAL, SEBASTIÃO JOSÉ DE CARVALHO E
MELO, MARQUÊS DE, 1699-1782.**
Maxwell, Kenneth, 1941- Pombal, paradox of the
Enlightenment. Cambridge [England] ; New York,
NY : Cambridge University Press, 1995.
*TC DP641 .M39 1995*

**Pomerantz, Charlotte.** The chalk doll / by Charlotte
Pomerantz ; pictures by Frané Lessac. New York :
Lippincott, c1989. 30 p. : col. ill. ; 46 x 38 cm.
SUMMARY: Rosy's mother remembers the pleasures of her
childhood in Jamaica and the very special dolls she used to
play with. ISBN 0-02-109110-2
*1. Dolls - Fiction. 2. Mothers and daughters - Fiction. 3.
Jamaica - Fiction. I. Lessac, Frané, ill. II. Title.*

*TC PZ7.P77 Ch 1989*

**Pomeroy, Karen.**
Heller, Steven. Design literacy. New York : Allworth
Press, c1997.
*TC NC998 .H45 1997*

**Pomeroy, Wardell Baxter.**
Kinsey, Alfred C. (Alfred Charles), 1894-1956.
Sexual behavior in the human male. Bloomington,
Ind. : Indiana University Press, [1998].
*TC HQ28 .K55 1998*

**POMO BASKETS - JUVENILE LITERATURE.**
Sullivan, Missy. The Native American look book.
New York : The New Press, 1996.
*TC E98.A7 S93 1996*

**POMO INDIANS - BASKET MAKING. See POMO
BASKETS.**

**PONIES.**
Henderson, Carolyn. Horse & pony breeds. 1st
American ed. New York, N.Y. : DK Pub., 1999.
*TC SF291 .H365 1999*

Henderson, Carolyn. Horse & pony care. 1st
American ed. New York : DK Pub., 1999.
*TC SF302 .H425 1999*

**PONIES - JUVENILE LITERATURE.**
Henderson, Carolyn. Horse & pony breeds. 1st
American ed. New York, N.Y. : DK Pub., 1999.
*TC SF291 .H365 1999*

Henderson, Carolyn. Horse & pony care. 1st
American ed. New York : DK Pub., 1999.
*TC SF302 .H425 1999*

**Ponzetti, James J.**
Encyclopedia of human emotions. New York :
Macmillan Reference USA, c1999.
*TC BF531 .E55 1999*

**Pooh and the millennium.**
Williams, John Tyerman. 1st American ed. New
York : Dutton Books, 1999.
*TC PR6025.I65 Z975 1999*

**POOH BEAR (FICTITIOUS CHARACTER). See
WINNIE-THE-POOH (FICTITIOUS
CHARACTER).**

**Poole, Michael.**
The IEBM handbook of human resource management.
1st ed. London ; Boston : International Thomson
Business Press, 1998.
*TC HF5549.17 .I33 1998*

**Pooley, Pam Newman.**
The Internet in action for math & science 7-12
[videorecording]. [New York] : Thirteen-WNET ;
[Alexandria, Va. : distributed by] PBS Video, c1997.
*TC LB1044.87 .I453 1997*

The Internet in action for math & science K-6
[videorecording]. [New York] : Thirteen-WNET ;
[Alexandria, Va. : distributed by] PBS Video, c1998.
*TC LB1044.87 .I45 1998*

**POOLS, SWIMMING. See SWIMMING POOLS.**

**POOR. See also POOR AGED; POOR CHILDREN;
POVERTY; RURAL POOR; URBAN POOR.**
Poverty. San Diego, CA : Greenhaven Press, c1994.
*TC HC110.P6 P63 1994*

**POOR AGED - NEW JERSEY - CASE STUDIES.**
Black, Helen K., 1952- Old souls. New York : A. de
Gruyter, c2000.
*TC HQ1064.U6 P424 2000*

**POOR AGED - PENNSYLVANIA -
PHILADELPHIA METROPOLITAN AREA -
CASE STUDIES.**
Black, Helen K., 1952- Old souls. New York : A. de
Gruyter, c2000.
*TC HQ1064.U6 P424 2000*

**POOR CHILDREN - DEVELOPING
COUNTRIES - FAMILY RELATIONSHIPS.**
Strengthening the family. Tokyo ; New York : United
Nations University Press, c1995.
*TC HQ727.9 .S77 1995*

**POOR CHILDREN - ECONOMIC CONDITIONS.
See POOR CHILDREN.**

**POOR CHILDREN - EDUCATION.**
Flaxman, Erwin. Youth mentoring: New York, N.Y. :
ERIC Clearinghouse on Urban Education, 1988.
*TC LC4065 .F53 1988*

**POOR CHILDREN - EDUCATION (PRIMARY) -
ILLINOIS - CHICAGO - CASE STUDIES.**
Barone, Diane M. Resilient children. Newark, Del. :

International Reading Association ; Chicago : National Reading Conference, c1999.
*TC LC4806.4 .B37 1999*

## POOR CHILDREN - EDUCATION - UNITED STATES.
Reaching and teaching children who are victims of poverty. Lewiston, N.Y. ; Lampeter, Wales : E. Mellen Press, c1999.
*TC LC4091 .R38 1999*

## POOR CHILDREN - NAIROBI - PICTORIAL WORKS.
Shootback. London : Booth-Clibborn, 1999.
*TC HV4160.5.N34 S45 1999*

## POOR CHILDREN - UNITED STATES - PSYCHOLOGY.
Luthar, Suniya S. Poverty and children's adjustment. Thousand Oaks, Calif. : Sage Publications, c1999.
*TC HV741 .L88 1999*

## POOR - DEVELOPING COUNTRIES - HEALTH ASPECTS - CASE STUDIES.
Dying for growth. Monroe, Me. : Common Courage Press, c2000.
*TC RA418.5.P6 D95 2000*

## POOR - DEVELOPING COUNTRIES - NUTRITION.
Foster, Phillips, 1931- The world food problem. 2nd ed. Boulder : Lynne Rienner Publishers, 1999.
*TC HD9018.D44 F68 1999*

## POOR - ECONOMIC CONDITIONS. See POOR.

## POOR - HEALTH AND HYGIENE. See POOR - MEDICAL CARE.

## POOR - HEALTH AND HYGIENE - CASE STUDIES.
Dying for growth. Monroe, Me. : Common Courage Press, c2000.
*TC RA418.5.P6 D95 2000*

## POOR LAWS. See PUBLIC WELFARE - LAW AND LEGISLATION.

## POOR - LEGAL STATUS, LAWS, ETC. See PUBLIC WELFARE - LAW AND LEGISLATION.

## POOR - MEDICAL CARE. See POOR - HEALTH AND HYGIENE.

## POOR - MEDICAL CARE - CASE STUDIES.
Dying for growth. Monroe, Me. : Common Courage Press, c2000.
*TC RA418.5.P6 D95 2000*

## POOR - MEDICAL CARE - ECONOMIC ASPECTS - DEVELOPING COUNTRIES - CASE STUDIES.
Dying for growth. Monroe, Me. : Common Courage Press, c2000.
*TC RA418.5.P6 D95 2000*

## POOR RELIEF. See CHARITIES; PUBLIC WELFARE.

## POOR - SERVICES FOR. See CHARITIES.

## POOR - UNITED STATES.
Chamberlin, J. Gordon (John Gordon) Upon whom we depend. New York : Peter Lang, c1999.
*TC HC110.P6 C326 1999*

Poverty. San Diego, CA : Greenhaven Press, c1994.
*TC HC110.P6 P63 1994*

Shorris, Earl, 1936- Riches for the poor. New York : W.W. Norton, 2000.
*TC HV4045 .S464 2000*

**Poorly performing staff and how to manage them :** capability, competence, and motivation / edited by Tessa Atton and Brian Fidler. London ; New York : Routledge, 1999. xii, 214 p. ; 24 cm. Includes bibliographical references (p.203-206 ) and index. ISBN 0-415-19817-8 DDC 371.14/4/0941
*1. Teacher effectiveness - Great Britain. 2. Teachers - Rating of - Great Britain. 3. School personnel management - Great Britain. 4. Teacher-principal relationships - Great Britain. I. Atton, Tessa. II. Fidler, Brian.*
*TC LB2832.4.G7 P66 1999*

**Poortinga, Ype H., 1939-.**
Handbook of cross-cultural psychology. 2nd ed. Boston : Allyn and Bacon, c1997.
*TC GN502 .H36 1997*

## POP ART - UNITED STATES.
Andy Warhol [videorecording]. [Chicago, IL] : Home Vision [distributor],cc1987.
*TC N6537.W28 A45 1987*

Roy Lichtenstein [videorecording]. [Chicago, IL] : Home Vision ; [S.l.] : distributed worldwide by RM Asssociates, c1991.
*TC ND237.L627 R6 1991*

## POP CULTURE. See POPULAR CULTURE.

## POP-UP BOOKS. See TOY AND MOVABLE BOOKS.

**Pope, Harrison.** The Adonis complex : the secret crisis of male body obsession / Harrison G. Pope, Jr., Katharine A. Phillips, Roberto Olivardia. New York : Free Press, 2000. xv, 286 p. : ill. ; 25 cm. Includes bibliographical references and index. ISBN 0-684-86910-1 DDC 155.3/32
*1. Body image in men. 2. Self-esteem in men. I. Phillips, Katharine A. II. Olivardia, Roberto, 1972- III. Title.*
*TC BF697.5.B635 2000*

**Pope, Kenneth S.** The MMPI, MMPI-2, & MMPI-A in court : a practical guide for expert witnesses and attorneys / Kenneth S. Pope, James N. Butcher, Joyce Seelen. 2nd ed. Washington, DC : American Psychological Association, 2000. xviii, 473 p. : ill. ; 29 cm. Includes bibliographical references (p. 431-475) and index. ISBN 1-55798-590-1 DDC 347.73/67
*1. Psychology, Forensic. 2. Evidence, Expert - United States. 3. Psychological tests - Law and legislation - United States. 4. Minnesota Multiphasic Personality Inventory. I. Title. II. Title: MMPI, MMPI-2, and MMPI-A in court*
*TC KF8965 .P66 1999*

**Popham, W. James.** Modern educational measurement : practical guidelines for educational leaders / W. James Popham. 3rd ed. Boston : Allyn and Bacon, c2000. xii, 466 p. : ill. ; 24 cm. Includes bibliographical references and index. ISBN 0-205-28770-0 DDC 371.26
*1. Educational tests and measurements. I. Title.*
*TC LB3051 .P6143 2000*

**Popkewitz, Thomas S.**
Educational knowledge. Albany : State University of New York Press, c2000.
*TC LC71 .L335 2000*

## POPPER, KARL RAIMUND, SIR, 1902-.
Improving education. London ; New York : Cassell, 1999.
*TC LB7 .I48 1999*

**Popping, Roel.** Computer-assisted text analysis / Roel Popping. Thousand Oaks, Calif. ; London : SAGE, c2000. x, 229 p. ; 24 cm. (New technologies for social research) Includes bibliographical references and indexes. ISBN 0-7619-5378-7 ISBN 0-7619-5379-5 (pbk.) DDC 300.285633
*1. Research - Data processing. 2. Discourse analysis - Data processing. 3. Social sciences - Methodology - Data processing. I. Title. II. Series: New technologies for social research*
*TC P302 .P636 2000*

**Popplestone, John A.** An illustrated history of American psychology / John A. Popplestone, Marion White McPherson. 2nd ed. Akron, Ohio : The University of Akron Press, c1999. xiv, 222 p. : ill. ; 28 cm. "To gather archival materials, we have drawn on the holdings of several universities, numerous archives, and various commercial companies, but the major source of materials is the Archives of the History of American Psychology, the University of Akron"--p. xiii. Includes bibliographical references (p. 205-213) and index. ISBN 1-88483-639-9
*1. Psychology - United States - History. 2. Psychologists - United States - History. I. McPherson, Marion White. II. Archives of the History of American Psychology (University of Akron) III. Title.*
*TC BF108.U5 P67 1999*

**Poppy's puppet.**
Gauch, Patricia Lee. 1st ed. New York : Holt, 1999.
*TC PZ7.G2315 Po 1999*

## POPULAR ARTS. See POPULAR CULTURE.

**Popular authors series**
McElmeel, Sharron L. 100 most popular children's authors. Englewood, Colo. : Libraries Unlimited, 1999.
*TC PS490 .M39 1999*

## POPULAR CULTURE. See also FADS; POPULAR LITERATURE.
Carroll, Noël (Noël E.) A philosophy of mass art. Oxford : Clarendon Press ; New York : Oxford University Press, 1998.
*TC NX180.M3 C37 1998*

Jarrett, Michael, 1953- Drifting on a read. Albany, N.Y. : State University of New York Press, 1999.

*TC ML3849 .J39 1999*

## POPULAR CULTURE - GREAT BRITAIN - HISTORY - 19TH CENTURY.
Black, Barbara J., 1962- On exhibit. Charlottesville ; London : University Press of Virginia, 2000.
*TC AM43.L6 B53 2000*

## POPULAR CULTURE - HISTORY - 20TH CENTURY.
Television and common knowledge. New York : Routledge, 1999.
*TC PN1992.6 .T379 1999*

**Popular culture in the classroom.**
Alvermann, Donna E. Newark, Del. : International Reading Association ; Chicago, Ill. : National Reading Conference, c1999.
*TC P91.3 .A485 1999*

## POPULAR CULTURE - MUSEUMS - GREAT BRITAIN.
Moore, Kevin, 1960- Museums and popular culture. London ; New York : Leicester University Press, 1997.
*TC AM41 .M66 1997*

## POPULAR CULTURE - MUSEUMS - UNITED STATES - HISTORY.
Alexander, Edward P. (Edward Porter), 1907- The museum in America. Walnut Creek : AltaMira Press, c1997.
*TC AM11 .A55 1997*

## POPULAR CULTURE - POLITICAL ASPECTS - UNITED STATES - HISTORY.
Lorini, Alessandra, 1949- Rituals of race. Charlottesville : University Press of Virginia, 1999.
*TC E185.61 .L675 1999*

## POPULAR CULTURE - PSYCHOLOGICAL ASPECTS - ENGLAND.
The Block reader in visual culture. London ; New York : Routledge, 1996.
*TC N72.S6 B56 1996*

## POPULAR CULTURE - STUDY AND TEACHING.
Alvermann, Donna E. Popular culture in the classroom. Newark, Del. : International Reading Association ; Chicago, Ill. : National Reading Conference, c1999.
*TC P91.3 .A485 1999*

## POPULAR CULTURE - UNITED STATES.
Giroux, Henry A. Channel surfing. 1st ed. New York : St. Martin's Press, 1997.
*TC HQ799.7 .G57 1997*

Holtzman, Linda, 1949- Media messages. Armonk, NY : M.E. Sharpe, 2000.
*TC P94.5.M552 U646 2000*

Seabrook, John. Nobrow. 1st ed. New York : A.A. Knopf ; Distributed by Random House, 2000.
*TC P94.65.U6 S4 2000*

## POPULAR CULTURE - UNITED STATES - HISTORY - 20TH CENTURY.
Cassidy, Donna. Painting the musical city. Washington, DC : Smithsonian Institution Press, c1997.
*TC ML85 .C37 1997*

Rollin, Lucy. Twentieth-century teen culture by the decades. Westport, Conn. ; London : Greenwood Press, 1999.
*TC HQ799.U65 R65 1999*

## POPULAR CULTURE - UNITED STATES - STUDY AND TEACHING.
Pioneers in popular culture studies. Bowling Green, OH : Bowling Green State University Popular Press, c1999.
*TC E169.04 .P563 1999*

## POPULAR EDUCATION. See also CRITICAL PEDAGOGY.
Freire, Paulo, 1921- [Pedagogia de autonomia. English] Pedagogy of freedom. Lanham : Rowman & Littlefield Publishers, c1998.
*TC LC196 .F73713 1998*

Roberts, Peter, 1963- Education, literacy, and humanization. Westport, Conn. : Bergin & Garvey, 2000.
*TC LB880.F732 R62 2000*

## POPULAR EDUCATION - UNITED STATES.
Critical education in the new information age. Lanham, Md. : Rowman & Littlefield, c1999.
*TC LC196.5.U6 C745 1999*

Robbins, Carol Braswell. An examination of critical feminist pedagogy in practice. 1999.

*TC 06 no. 11067*

## POPULAR LITERATURE - STORIES, PLOTS, ETC.
Herald, Diana Tixier. Genreflecting. 5th ed. Englewood, CO : Libraries Umlimited, 2000.
*TC PS374.P63 H47 2000*

**POPULAR MUSIC.** *See* **BLUES (MUSIC).**

**POPULAR NAMES OF ANIMALS.** *See* **ZOOLOGY - NOMENCLATURE (POPULAR).**

## POPULATION.
Population growth, structure and distribution. New York : United Nations, 1999.
*TC HB871.P6675 1999*

Review and appraisal of the progress made in achieving the goals and objectives of the Programme of Action of the International Conference on Population and Development. New York : United Nations, 1999.
*TC HB849 .R48 1999*

**Population and economic change in developing countries.**
Conference on Population and Economic Change in Less Developed Countries (1976 : Philadelphia, Pa.) Chicago : University of Chicago Press, 1980.
*TC HB849 .C59 1976*

**POPULATION BIOLOGY.** *See* **ECOLOGY.**

**POPULATION CONTROL.** *See* **BIRTH CONTROL.**

## POPULATION - ECONOMIC ASPECTS.
Schultz, T. Paul. Economics of population. Reading, MA : Addison-Wesley, c1981.
*TC HB849.41 .S38*

## POPULATION - ECONOMIC ASPECTS - CONGRESSES.
Conference on Population and Economic Change in Less Developed Countries (1976 : Philadelphia, Pa.) Population and economic change in developing countries. Chicago : University of Chicago Press, 1980.
*TC HB849 .C59 1976*

**The population explosion.**
Ehrlich, Paul R. New York : Simon and Schuster, c1990.
*TC HB871 .E33 1990*

**POPULATION - FORECASTING.** *See* **POPULATION FORECASTING.**

## POPULATION FORECASTING.
Population growth, structure and distribution. New York : United Nations, 1999.
*TC HB871.P6675 1999*

## POPULATION FORECASTING - STATISTICS - PERIODICALS.
World population prospects. New York : United Nations, 1985-
*TC HA154 .W6*

## POPULATION FORECASTING - UNITED STATES.
America's demographic tapestry. New Brunswick, N.J. : Rutgers University Press, c1999.
*TC HB3505 .A683 1999*

**POPULATION GEOGRAPHY.** *See* **EMIGRATION AND IMMIGRATION.**

**POPULATION GROWTH.** *See* **POPULATION.**

**Population growth, structure and distribution :** the concise report / Department of Economic and Social Affairs, Population Division. New York : United Nations, 1999. vi, 41 p. : ill., map ; 22 cm. ([Population studies ; no. 181]) "ST/ESA/SER.A/181" "United Nations publication, Sales No. E.99.XIII.15"--T.p. verso. Includes bibliographical references (p. 39-41). ISBN 92-1-151338-3
*1. Population. 2. Age distribution (Demography) 3. Population forecasting. I. United Nations. Dept. of Economic and Social Affairs. Population Division. II. Series: Population studies (New York, N.Y.) ; no. 181.*
*TC HB871.P6675 1999*

## POPULATION POLICY.
Review and appraisal of the progress made in achieving the goals and objectives of the Programme of Action of the International Conference on Population and Development. New York : United Nations, 1999.
*TC HB849 .R48 1999*

**POPULATION PROJECTIONS.** *See* **POPULATION FORECASTING.**

## POPULATION - STATISTICS - PERIODICALS.
World population prospects. New York : United Nations, 1985-
*TC HA154 .W6*

**Population studies (New York, N.Y.)**
World population prospects. New York : United Nations, 1985-
*TC HA154 .W6*

(no. 181.) Population growth, structure and distribution. New York : United Nations, 1999.
*TC HB871.P6675 1999*

**POPULATIONS, HUMAN.** *See* **POPULATION.**

## PORCELAIN - HISTORY.
Munsterberg, Hugo, 1916- World ceramics. New York : Penguin Studio Books, c1998.
*TC NK3780 .M86 1998*

## PORRO, RICARDO, 1925-.
Loomis, John A., 1951- Revolution of forms. New York : Princeton Architectural Press, c1999.
*TC NA6602.A76 L66 1999*

## PORTA WESTFALICA (CONCENTRATION CAMP).
Madsen, Benedicte, 1943- Survival in the organization. Aarhus [Denmark] ; Oakville, Conn. : Aarhus University Press, c1996.
*TC D805.G3 M24 1996*

**The portable lawyer for mental health professionals.**
Bernstein, Barton E. New York : J. Wiley, c1998.
*TC KF3828.Z9 B47 1998*

**Portable Stanford Book Series**
Calfee, Robert C. Teach your children well. Stanford, CA : Stanford Alumni Association, c1995.
*TC LB2822.82 .C32 1995*

**Porter, Dorothy, 1953-** Health, civilization, and the state : a history of public health from ancient to modern times / Dorothy Porter. London ; New York : Routledge, 1999. 376 p. ; 24 cm. Includes bibliographical references and index. ISBN 0-415-12244-9 (hbk) ISBN 0-415-20036-9 (pbk) DDC 362.1/09
*1. Public health - Social aspects - Europe - History. 2. Public health - Social aspects - North America - History. 3. Public health - Political aspects - Europe - History. 4. Public Health - Political aspects - North America - History. 5. Social medicine - Europe - History. 6. Social medicine - North America - History. I. Title.*
*TC RA424 .P67 1999*

**Porter, James.** Reschooling and the global future : politics, economics and the english experience / James Porter. Wallingford, U.K. : Symposium Books ; c1999. 128 p. ; 24 cm. (Monographs in International Education) Includes bibliographical references and index. ISBN 1-87392-753-3
*1. Global method of teaching. 2. Education and state. I. Title. II. Series.*
*TC LB1029.G55 P67 1999*

**Porter, Louise, 1958-** Behaviour in schools : theory and practice for teachers / Louise Porter. Buckingham [England] ; Philadelphia : Open University Press, 2000. x, 331 p. ; 24 cm. Includes bibliographical references (p. 307-320) and index. ISBN 0-335-20668-9 (pbk) DDC 371.39/3
*1. School discipline. 2. Classroom management. 3. Behavior modification. I. Title.*
*TC LB3012 .P65 2000*

**Porter, Robert.**
Race, ethnicity and culture in the visual arts. New York : American Council for the Arts, c1993.
*TC N70 .R32 1993*

**Porter, Rosalie Pedalino. 1931-.**
Educating language-minority children. New Brunswick (U.S.A.) : Transaction Publishers, c2000.
*TC LC3731 .E374 2000*

**Portfolio and performance assessment in teacher education** / Dorothy M. Campbell ... [et al.]. Boston : Allyn and Bacon, c2000. xiv, 154 p. ; 23 cm. Includes bibliographical references (p. 153-154). ISBN 0-205-30850-3 DDC 370/.71/55
*1. Portfolios in education. 2. Teachers - Rating of. 3. Teachers - Training of. I. Campbell, Dorothy M.*
*TC LB1728 .P667 2000*

**The portfolio project.**
Underwood, Terry. Urbana, Ill. : National Council of Teachers of English, c1999.
*TC LB1029.P67 U53 1999*

**The portfolio standard :** how students can show us what they know and are able to do / edited by Bonnie S. Sunstein and Jonathan H. Lovell ; foreword by Donald Graves. Portsmouth, NH : Heinemann, c2000.

xxii, 248 p. : ill. ; 23 cm. Includes bibliographical references and index. ISBN 0-325-00234-7 DDC 371.39+
*1. Portfolios in education - Standards - United States. I. Sunstein, Bonnie S. II. Lovell, Jonathan H.*
*TC LB1029.P67 P69 2000*

**Portfolios across the curriculum and beyond** / Donna J. Cole ... [et al]. 2nd ed. Thousand Oaks, Calif. : Corwin Press, 2000. xii, 92 p. 22cm. Rev. ed. of: Portfolios across the curriculum and beyond / Donna J. Cole, Charles W. Ryan, Fran Kick. Includes bibliographical references. ISBN 0-7619-7533-0 (alk. paper) ISBN 0-7619-7534-9 (pbk. : alk. paper) DDC 371.27
*1. Portfolios in education - United States. 2. Educational tests and measurements - United States. I. Cole, Donna J.*
*TC LB1029.P67 C65 2000*

## PORTFOLIOS IN EDUCATION.
Portfolio and performance assessment in teacher education. Boston : Allyn and Bacon, c2000.
*TC LB1728 .P667 2000*

## PORTFOLIOS IN EDUCATION - CALIFORNIA - CASE STUDIES.
Underwood, Terry. The portfolio project. Urbana, Ill. : National Council of Teachers of English, c1999.
*TC LB1029.P67 U53 1999*

## PORTFOLIOS IN EDUCATION - CALIFORNIA - HANDBOOKS, MANUALS, ETC.
Assessing literacy with the Learning Record. Portsmouth, NH : Heinemann, c1999.
*TC LB1029.P67 B37 1999b*

Barr, Mary A. (Mary Anderson) Assessing literacy with the Learning Record. Portsmouth, NH : Heinemann, c1999.
*TC LB1029.P67 B37 1999*

## PORTFOLIOS IN EDUCATION - STANDARDS - UNITED STATES.
The portfolio standard. Portsmouth, NH : Heinemann, c2000.
*TC LB1029.P67 P69 2000*

## PORTFOLIOS IN EDUCATION - UNITED STATES.
The example school portfolio. Larchmont, N.Y. : Eye On Education, 2000.
*TC LB2822.82 .E92 2000*

Mabry, Linda. Portfolios plus. Thousand Oaks, Calif. : Corwin Press, c1999.
*TC LB3051 .M4243 1999*

Portfolios across the curriculum and beyond. 2nd ed. Thousand Oaks, Calif. : Corwin Press, 2000.
*TC LB1029.P67 C65 2000*

Wyatt, Robert Lee, 1940- So you have to have a portfolio. Thousand Oaks, Calif. : Corwin Press, c1999.
*TC LB1728 .W93 1999*

**Portfolios plus.**
Mabry, Linda. Thousand Oaks, Calif. : Corwin Press, c1999.
*TC LB3051 .M4243 1999*

**Porton, Harriet.**
Adolescent behavior and society. 5th ed. Boston : McGraw-Hill, c1998.
*TC HQ796 .A3338 1998*

**Portrait of addiction** [videorecording] / a presentation of Films for the Humanities & Sciences ; a production of Public Affairs Television, Inc. ; a presentation of Thirteen/WNET New York ; produced and directed by Amy Schatz. Princeton, NJ : Films for the Humanities & Sciences, c1998. 1 videocassette (57 min.) : sd., col. ; 1/2 in. (The Moyers collection) (Close to home. Moyers on addiction) Title on cassette label: Close to home, portrait of addiction [videorecording]. VHS. Catalogued from credits and cassette label. "FFH 7859"--Cassette label. Host, Bill Moyers. Editors, Lawrence Silk, Tim Squyres ; director of photography, Joel Shapiro ; music, Richard Fiocca ; audio, Gary Silver. For adolescents through adult. SUMMARY: Nine men and women, all recovering from drug/ alcohol addiction, tell their stories. They speak of the euphoria experienced on drugs and alcohol, the escape from pain, and the Pavlovian responses. From the euphoria of heroin to the ease of socializing with alcohol to the social beginning and paranoid ending of cocaine addiction, they discuss why they got hooked and how they kicked their habits. Finding they were not alone was powerful for some; finding a higher being worked for others. All nine are in recovery and their stories are inspirational.
*1. Alcoholics - Rehabilitation. 2. Narcotic addicts - Rehabilitation. 3. Alcoholics - Interviews. 4. Narcotic addicts - Interviews. 5. Alcoholism - Psychological aspects. 6. Drug abuse - Psychological aspects. 7. Narcotic habit - Psychological aspects. 8. Heroin habit - Psychological aspects. 9. Cocaine habit - Psychological aspects. I. Moyers, Bill D. II.*

*Schatz, Amy. III. Films for the Humanities (Firm) IV. Public Affairs Television (Firm) V. WNET (Television station : New York, N.Y.) VI. Title: Close to home, portrait of addiction [videorecording] VII. Series. VIII. Series: Close to home (Series)*
*TC HV5801 .P6 1998*

**Portrait of addiction** [videorecording] / a presentation of Films for the Humanities & Sciences : a production of Public Affairs Television, Inc. ; a presentation of Thirteen/WNET New York ; produced and directed by Amy Schatz. Princeton, NJ : Films for the Humanities & Sciences, c1998. 1 videocassette (57 min.) : sd., col. ; 1/2 in. (The Moyers collection) (Close to home. Moyers on addiction) Title on cassette label: Close to home, portrait of addiction [videorecording]. VHS. Catalogued from credits and cassette label and container. "FFH 7859"-- Cassette label. Host, Bill Moyers. Editors, Lawrence Silk, Tim Squyres ; director of photography, Joel Shapiro ; music, Richard Fiocca ; audio, Gary Silver. For adolescents through adult. SUMMARY: Nine men and women, all recovering from drug/alcohol addiction, tell their stories. They speak of the euphoria experienced on drugs and alcohol, the escape from pain, and the Pavlovian responses. From the euphoria of heroin to the ease of socializing with alcohol to the social beginning and paranoid ending of cocaine addiction, they discuss why they got hooked and how they kicked their habits. Finding they were not alone was powerful for some; finding a higher being worked for others. All nine are in recovery and their stories are inspirational.
*1. Alcoholics - Rehabilitation. 2. Narcotic addicts - Rehabilitation. 3. Alcoholics - Interviews. 4. Narcotic addicts - Interviews. 5. Alcoholism - Psychological aspects. 6. Drug abuse - Psychological aspects. 7. Narcotic habit - Psychological aspects. 8. Heroin habit - Psychological aspects. 9. Cocaine habit - Psychological aspects. 10. Substance abuse - Psychological aspects. I. Moyers, Bill D. II. Schatz, Amy. III. Films for the Humanities (Firm) IV. Public Affairs Television (Firm) V. WNET (Television station : New York, N.Y.) VI. Title: Close to home, portrait of addiction [videorecording] VII. Series. VIII. Series: Close to home (Series)*
*TC RC564 .P6 1998*

**Portrait of an artist**
Andy Warhol [videorecording]. [Chicago, IL] : Home Vision [distributor],cc1987.
*TC N6537.W28 A45 1987*

Andy Warhol [videorecording]. [Chicago, IL] : Home Vision [distributor],cc1987.
*TC N6537.W28 A45 1987*

The frescoes of Diego Rivera [videorecording]. [Detroit, Mich.] : Founders Society, Detroit Institute of Arts ; [Chicago, Ill.?] : Home Vision [distributor], c1986.
*TC ND259.R5 F6 1986*

Georgia O'Keeffe [videorecording]. [Boston?] : Home Vision : c1977.
*TC ND237.O5 G4 1977*

Jackson Pollock [videorecording]. [Chicago, Ill.] : Home Vision : [S.l.] : Distributed Worldwide by RM Associates, c1987.
*TC ND237.P73 J3 1987*

Mary Cassatt [videorecording]. [Chicago, Ill.]: Home Vision, c1977.
*TC ND237.C3 M37 1977*

Matisse, voyages [videorecording]. [Chicago, Ill.] : Home Vision : [S.l.] : Distributed worldwide by RM Associates, c1989.
*TC ND553.M37 M37 1989*

Nevelson in process [videorecording]. Chicago, IL : Public Media Inc., 1977.
*TC NB237.N43 N43 1977*

Norman Rockwell's world -- an American dream [videorecording]. [Chicago, Ill] : Home Vision, 1987, c1972.
*TC ND237.R68 N6 1987*

Picasso [videorecording]. Chicago, IL : Home Vision, c1986.
*TC N6853.P5 P52 1986*

Roy Lichtenstein [videorecording]. [Chicago, IL] : Home Vision ; [S.l.] : distributed by RM Asssociates, c1991.
*TC ND237.L627 R6 1991*

(v. 11) Monsieur René Magritte [videorecording]. [Chicago, Ill.] : Home Vision [distributor], c1978.
*TC ND673.M35 M6 1978*

(v. 13) Marc Chagall [videorecording]. [Chicago, Ill.] : Home Vision [distributor], c1985.

*TC ND699.C5 C5 1985*

**PORTRAIT PAINTING, AUSTRALIAN - HISTORY.**
Ross, Peter. Let's face it. Sydney, Australia : Art Gallery of New South Wales, 1999.
*TC ND1327.A86 R67 1999*

**PORTRAIT PAINTING - AWARDS - AUSTRALIA.** *See* ARCHIBALD PRIZE.

**PORTRAIT PHOTOGRAPHY.**
Matthews, Sandra. Pregnant pictures. New York : Routledge, 2000.
*TC TR681.P67 M38 2000*

Picturing us. New York : New Press : Distributed by W.W. Norton & Co., c1994.
*TC TR680 .P53 1994*

**PORTRAIT PHOTOGRAPHY - NEW YORK (STATE) - NEW YORK.**
Roma, Thomas. Sunset Park. Washington : Smithsonian Institution Press, c1998.
*TC TR680 .R675 1998*

**PORTRAIT PHOTOGRAPHY - UNITED STATES - HISTORY - EXHIBITIONS.**
Panzer, Mary. Mathew Brady and the image of history. Washington, D.C. : Smithsonian Institution Press for the National Portrait Gallery, c1997.
*TC TR140.B7 P36 1997*

Portraits.
Kimmelman, Michael. 1st ed. New York : Random House, c1998.
*TC N71 .K56 1998*

Portraits by Ingres.
Ingres, Jean-Auguste-Dominique, 1780-1867. New York : Metropolitan Museum of Art : Distributed by Harry N. Abrams, c1999.
*TC ND1329.I53 A4 1999*

Portraits of native Americans : 23 postcards from the Field Museum : photographs from the 1904 Louisiana Purchase Exposition / [photographs by Charles H. Carpenter ; introduction by Brenda Child]. New York : New Press : Distributed by W.W. Norton, c1994. [48] p. : chiefly ill. ; 14 x 22 cm. ISBN 1-56584-160-3
*1. Indians of North America - Pictorial works. 2. Carpenter, Charles H. 3. Postcards. I. Carpenter, Charles H. II. Child, Brenda. III. Field Museum of Natural History. IV. Louisiana Purchase Exposition (1904 : Saint Louis, Mo.)*
*TC TR140.C388 C48*

**PORTRAITS - SOCIAL ASPECTS.**
Lawrence-Lightfoot, Sara, 1944- The art and science of portraiture. 1st ed. San Francisco : Jossey-Bass, c1997.
*TC H62 .L33 1997*

**PORTRAITURE.** *See* PORTRAIT PHOTOGRAPHY; PORTRAITS.

**PORTUGAL - POLITICS AND GOVERNMENT - 1750-1777.**
Maxwell, Kenneth, 1941- Pombal, paradox of the Enlightenment. Cambridge [England] ; New York, NY : Cambridge University Press, 1995.
*TC DP641 .M39 1995*

**Portz, John, 1953-** City schools and city politics : institutions and leadership in Pittsburgh, Boston, and St. Louis / John Portz, Lana Stein, and Robin R. Jones. Lawrence : University Press of Kansas, c1999. viii, 199 p. : ill. ; 24 cm. (Studies in government and public policy) Includes bibliographical references (p. 171-191) and index. ISBN 0-7006-0979-2 (cloth : alk. paper) ISBN 0-7006-0980-6 (paper : alk. paper) DDC 370/.9173/2
*1. Education. Urban - Political aspects - United States - Case studies. 2. Urban policy - United States - Case studies. 3. Educational change - United States - Case studies. 4. Educational leadership - United States - Case studies. I. Stein, Lana, 1946- II. Jones, Robin R., 1946- III. Title. IV. Series.*
*TC LC5131 .P67 1999*

**POSADAS (SOCIAL CUSTOM) - FICTION.**
De Paola, Tomie. The night of Las Posadas. New York : Putnam's, 1999.
*TC PZ7.D439 Ni 1999*

**Poshyananda, Apinan, 1956-.**
Contemporary art in Asia. New York : Asia Society Galleries : Distributed by Harry N. Abrams, c1996.
*TC N7262 .C655 1996*

**POSITION ANALYSIS.** *See* TOPOLOGY.

**POSITION, BODY.** *See* POSTURE.

**Positive classroom management.**
DiGiulio, Robert C., 1949- 2nd ed. Thousand Oaks, CA. : Corwin Press, c2000.

*TC LB3013 .D54 2000*

**POSITIVE-HISTORICAL JUDAISM.** *See* CONSERVATIVE JUDAISM.

**Positive pupil management and motivation.**
McNamara, Eddie. London : David Fulton, 1999.
*TC LB3013 .M336 1999*

**Posner, George J.** Field experience : a guide to reflective teaching / George J. Posner. 5th ed. New York : Longman, c2000. xiv, 160 p. : ill. ; 24 cm. Includes bibliographical references and index. ISBN 0-8013-3079-3 (pbk.) DDC 370/.71
*1. Student teaching. 2. Teaching - Vocational guidance. 3. Teachers - Training of. I. Title.*
*TC LB2157.A3 P6 2000*

**Posner, Marc.** Preventing school injuries : a comprehensive guide for school administrators, teachers, and staff / Marc Posner. New Brunswick, N.J. ; London : Rutgers University Press, c2000. xii, 241 p. : ill. ; 24 cm. Includes bibliographical references (p. [217]-234) and index. ISBN 0-8135-2748-1 (hbk. : alk. paper) ISBN 0-8135-2749-X (pbk. : alk. paper) DDC 363.11/9371
*1. School accidents - United States - Prevention. I. Title.*
*TC LB2864.6.A25 P67 2000*

**Posner, Michael I.**
International Symposium on Attention and Performance (11th : 1984 : Eugene, Or.) Attention and performance XI. Hillsdale, N.J. : L. Erlbaum Associates, 1985.
*TC BF321 .A82 1985*

**Possessions.**
Thomas, Nicholas. New York, N.Y. : Thames and Hudson, c1999.
*TC N5313 .T46 1999*

**Possible lives.**
Rose, Mike. New York, N.Y. : Penguin Books, 1996.
*TC LA217.2 R7 1996*

**POST CARDS.** *See* POSTCARDS.

**Post-contemporary interventions**
Beverley, John. Subalternity and representation. Durham [N.C.] ; London : Duke University Press, 1999.
*TC HM1136 .B48 1999*

**POST-GRADUATE STUDENTS.** *See* GRADUATE STUDENTS.

**POST HIGH SCHOOL EDUCATION.** *See* POSTSECONDARY EDUCATION.

**Post-hospital care for the elderly.**
Brown, Gloria M. 1997.
*TC 06 no. 10759*

**POST-IMPRESSIONISM (ART).** *See* EXPRESSIONISM (ART); IMPRESSIONISM (ART).

**POST-MODERNISM.** *See* POSTMODERNISM.

**POST-SECONDARY EDUCATION.** *See* POSTSECONDARY EDUCATION.

**Post-structural study of child-centered pedagogy in kindergarten classroom.**
Ryan, Sharon Kaye. Freedom to choice. 1998.
*TC 06 no. 11034*

**POST-TRAUMATIC STRESS DISORDER.** *See also* POST-TRAUMATIC STRESS DISORDER IN CHILDREN.
Horowitz, Mardi Jon, 1934- Stress response syndromes. 3rd ed. Northvale, N.J. : J. Aronson, c1997.
*TC RC552.P67 H67 1997*

**POST-TRAUMATIC STRESS DISORDER - CASE STUDIES.**
Horowitz, Mardi Jon, 1934- Stress response syndromes. 3rd ed. Northvale, N.J. : J. Aronson, c1997.
*TC RC552.P67 H67 1997*

**POST-TRAUMATIC STRESS DISORDER - DIAGNOSIS.**
Neurotic, stress-related, and somatoform disorders [videorecording]. Princeton, N.J. : Films for the Humanities & Sciences, 1998.
*TC RC530 .N4 1998*

**POST-TRAUMATIC STRESS DISORDER - FICTION.**
Paulsen, Gary. Soldier's heart. New York : Delacorte Press, c1998.
*TC PZ7.P2843 So 1998*

**POST-TRAUMATIC STRESS DISORDER IN CHILDREN - EL SALVADOR.**
Flores, Joaquín Evelio. Psychological effects of the

civil war on children from rural communities of El Salvador.
*TC 083 F67*

**POST-TRAUMATIC STRESS DISORDER - PATIENTS.**
Neurotic, stress-related, and somatoform disorders [videorecording]. Princeton, N.J. : Films for the Humanities & Sciences, 1998.
*TC RC530 .N4 1998*

**POST-TRAUMATIC STRESS DISORDER - TREATMENT.**
Group psychotherapy for psychological trauma. New York : Guilford Press, c2000.
*TC RC552.P67 G76 2000*

**POST-TRAUMATIC STRESS DISORDER - UNITED STATES.**
Gewirtz, Abigail Hadassah. Coping strategies and stage of change among Vietnam combat veterans diagnosed with posttraumatic stress disorder and comorbid substance use disorders. 1997.
*TC 085 G338*

**POSTAL CARDS.** *See* **POSTCARDS.**

**POSTAL STATIONERY.** *See* **POSTCARDS.**

**Postbaccalaureate futures :** new markets, resources, and credentials / edited by Kay J. Kohl and Jules B. LaPidus. Phoenix, AZ : Oryx Press, 2000. xviii, 276 p. : ill. ; 23 cm. (American Council on Education/Oryx Press series on higher education) Includes index. ISBN 1-57356-360-9 (alk. paper) DDC 378.1/55/0973
*1. Universities and colleges - United States - Graduate work - Congresses. 2. Continuing education - United States - Congresses. 3. Education, Higher - Economic aspects - United States - Congresses. I. Kohl, Kay Jordan, 1940- II. LaPidus, Jules B. III. Series.*
*TC LB2371.4 .P68 2000*

**POSTCARDS.**
Portraits of native Americans. New York : New Press : Distributed by W.W. Norton, c1994.
*TC TR140.C388 C48*

**POSTCARDS - HISTORY - 19TH CENTURY - THEMES, MOTIVES.**
Delivering views. Washington [D.C.] : Smithsonian Institution Press, c1998.
*TC NC1872 .D46 1998*

**POSTCARDS - HISTORY - 20TH CENTURY - THEMES, MOTIVES.**
Delivering views. Washington [D.C.] : Smithsonian Institution Press, c1998.
*TC NC1872 .D46 1998*

**POSTCOLONIALISM.** *See also* **DECOLONIZATION.**
Beverley, John. Subalternity and representation. Durham [N.C.] : London : Duke University Press, 1999.
*TC HM1136 .B48 1999*

Race, rhetoric, and the postcolonial. Albany : State University of New York Press, c1999.
*TC P301.5.P67 R33 1999*

**Poster art in Australia.**
Butler, Roger. Canberra : National Gallery of Australia, 1993.
*TC NC1807.A78 B88 1993*

**Poster book**
Contemporary aboriginal painting. East Roseville, Australia : Craftsmen House, c1993.
*TC ND1101 .C66 1993*

**POSTERS.** *See* **COMMERCIAL ART.**

**POSTERS - 19TH CENTURY - AUSTRALIA - EXHIBITIONS.**
Butler, Roger. Poster art in Australia. Canberra : National Gallery of Australia, 1993.
*TC NC1807.A78 B88 1993*

**POSTERS - 20TH CENTURY - AUSTRALIA - EXHIBITIONS.**
Butler, Roger. Poster art in Australia. Canberra : National Gallery of Australia, 1993.
*TC NC1807.A78 B88 1993*

**POSTERS - AUSTRALIA - CANBERRA (A.C.T.) - EXHIBITIONS.**
Butler, Roger. Poster art in Australia. Canberra : National Gallery of Australia, 1993.
*TC NC1807.A78 B88 1993*

**POSTERS, AUSTRALIAN - EXHIBITIONS.**
Butler, Roger. Poster art in Australia. Canberra : National Gallery of Australia, 1993.
*TC NC1807.A78 B88 1993*

**POSTGRADUATE STUDENTS.** *See* **GRADUATE STUDENTS.**

**Posthospital care for the elderly.**
Brown, Gloria M. Post-hospital care for the elderly. 1997.
*TC 06 no. 10759*

**Postlethwaite, T. Neville.**
Ross, Kenneth N. (Kenneth Norman), 1947- Indicators of the quality of education. Paris : International Institute for Educational Planning, 1992.
*TC LA1592 .R67 1992*

**Postmodern dilemmas.**
Jagodzinski, Jan, 1953- Mahwah, N.J. : Lawrence Erlbaum Associates, 1997.
*TC N7445.2 .J34 1997*

**The postmodern educator :** arts-based inquiries and teacher development / coedited by C.T. Patrick Diamond and Carol A. Mullen. New York : P. Lang, c1999. xxxi, 466 p. : ill. ; 24 cm. (Counterpoints ; vol. 89) Includes bibliographical references and index. ISBN 0-8204-4101-5 (pbk. : alk. paper) DDC 370/.71
*1. Teachers - Training of. 2. Teachers - In-service training. 3. Arts - Study and teaching. 4. Postmodernism and education. 5. Action research in education. I. Diamond, C. T. Patrick. II. Mullen, Carol A. III. Series: Counterpoints (New York, N.Y.) ; vol. 89.*
*TC LB1707 .P67 1999*

**POSTMODERNISM.**
Clough, Patricia Ticineto, 1945- Autoaffection. Minneapolis : University of Minnesota Press, c2000.
*TC HM846 .C56 2000*

Curriculum in the postmodern condition. New York : P. Lang, c2000.
*TC LB2806.15 .C694 2000*

Jagodzinski, Jan, 1953- Postmodern dilemmas. Mahwah, N.J. : Lawrence Erlbaum Associates, 1997.
*TC N7445.2 .J34 1997*

Pathology and the postmodern. London ; Thousand Oaks : SAGE, 2000.
*TC BF636 .P38 2000*

Peters, Michael (Michael A.), 1948- Wittgenstein. Westport, Conn. : Bergin & Garvey, 1999.
*TC B3376.W564 P388 1999*

Smith, Bernard, 1916- Modernism's history. New Haven : Yale University Press, 1998.
*TC N6494.M64 S65 1998*

Vital signs. Edinburgh : Edinburgh University Press, c1998.
*TC HQ1190 .V56 1998*

Vital signs. Edinburgh : Edinburgh University Press, c1998.
*TC HQ1190 .V56 1998*

**POSTMODERNISM AND EDUCATION.**
After the disciplines. Westport, Conn. : Bergin & Garvey, 1999.
*TC LB2362.N45 A48 1999*

Barnett, Ronald, 1947- Realizing the university in an age of supercomplexity. Philadelphia, PA : Society for Research into Higher Education & Open University Press, 1999.
*TC LB2322.2 .B37 1999*

Barone, Tom. Aesthetics, politics, and educational inquiry. New York : P. Lang, 2000.
*TC LB1028 .B345 2000*

Core texts in conversation . Lanham, MD : University Press of America, 2000.
*TC LB2361.5 .C68 2000*

Curriculum in the postmodern condition. New York : P. Lang, c2000.
*TC LB2806.15 .C694 2000*

Hicks, D. Emily. Ninety-five languages and seven forms of intelligence. New York : P. Lang, c1999.
*TC LC196 .H53 1999*

O'Sullivan, Edmund, 1938- Transformative learning. London ; New York : Zed Books ; New York : Distributed in USA exclusively by St. Martin's Press, 1999.
*TC LC196 .O7 1999*

Paradigm debates in curriculum and supervision. Westport, Conn. ; London : Bergin & Garvey, 2000.
*TC LB2806.4 .P37 2000*

The postmodern educator. New York : P. Lang, c1999.

*TC LB1707 .P67 1999*

Scheurich, James Joseph, 1944- Research method in the postmodern. London ; Washington, DC : Falmer Press, 1997.
*TC LB1028 .S242 1997*

Trifonas, Peter Pericles, 1960- The ethics of writing. Lanham, Md. : Oxford : Rowman & Littlefield, c2000.
*TC LB14.7 .T75 2000*

Working the ruins. New York : London : Routledge, 2000.
*TC LC197 .W67 2000*

**POSTMODERNISM (LITERATURE).**
Literature and the child. Iowa City : University of Iowa Press, c1999.
*TC PR990 .L58 1999*

Young, R. V., 1947- At war with the word. Wilmington, Del. : ISI Books, 1999.
*TC PN94 .Y68 1999*

**POSTMODERNISM (PHILOSOPHY).** *See* **POSTMODERNISM.**

**POSTMODERNISM - PSYCHOLOGICAL ASPECTS.**
Constructions of disorder. 1st ed. Washington, DC : American Psychological Association, c2000.
*TC RC437.5 .C647 2000*

**POSTON RELOCATION CENTER (POSTON, ARIZ.).**
Rabbit in the moon [videorecording]. San Francisco, Calif. : Wabi-Sabi Productions, 1999.
*TC D753.8 .R3 1999*

**POSTS, MILITARY.** *See* **MILITARY BASES.**

**POSTSECONDARY EDUCATION.** *See* **EDUCATION, HIGHER.**

**POSTSECONDARY EDUCATION - UNITED STATES.**
Adelman, Clifford. Answers in the tool box. Washington, DC : U.S. Dept. of Education, Office of Educational Research and Improvement, [1999]
*TC LB2390 .A34 1999*

Gray, Kenneth C. Getting real. Thousand Oaks, Calif. : Corwin Press, c2000.
*TC HF5382.5.U5 G676 2000*

**POSTSTRUCTURALISM.**
Clough, Patricia Ticineto, 1945- Autoaffection. Minneapolis : University of Minnesota Press, c2000.
*TC HM846 .C56 2000*

Ochsner, Mindy Blaise. Something rad & risqu'e. 1999.
*TC 06 no. 11208*

Working the ruins. New York ; London : Routledge, 2000.
*TC LC197 .W67 2000*

**Posttenure faculty development.**
Alstete, Jeffrey W. San Fransisco, [Calif.] : Jossey-Bass c2000.
*TC LB2335.7 .A47 2000*

**POSTTRAUMATIC STRESS DISORDER.** *See* **POST-TRAUMATIC STRESS DISORDER.**

**POSTURE - MATHEMATICAL MODELS.**
Biomechanics and neural control of posture and movement. New York : Springer, 2000.
*TC QP303 .B5684 2000*

**POTABLE LIQUIDS.** *See* **BEVERAGES.**

**POTABLES.** *See* **BEVERAGES.**

**POTATOES.**
Meltzer, Milton, 1915- The amazing potato. 1st ed. New York, NY : HarperCollins, c1992.
*TC SB211.P8 M53 1992*

**POTATOES - HISTORY - JUVENILE LITERATURE.**
Meltzer, Milton, 1915- The amazing potato. 1st ed. New York, NY : HarperCollins, c1992.
*TC SB211.P8 M53 1992*

**POTATOES - JUVENILE LITERATURE.**
Meltzer, Milton, 1915- The amazing potato. 1st ed. New York, NY : HarperCollins, c1992.
*TC SB211.P8 M53 1992*

**POTATOES - SOCIAL ASPECTS - JUVENILE LITERATURE.**
Meltzer, Milton, 1915- The amazing potato. 1st ed. New York, NY : HarperCollins, c1992.
*TC SB211.P8 M53 1992*

**Potter, Allison.**
Ballet class for beginners [videorecording]. W. Long Branch, NJ : Kultur, c1981.
*TC GV1589 .B3 1981*

**Potter, Beatrix, 1866-1943.**
Lane, Margaret, 1907- The Beatrix Potter country cookery book. London : F. Warne, 1981.
*TC TX717 .L355 1981*

**Potter, Giselle, ill.**
Fleming, Candace. When Agnes caws. 1st ed. New York : Atheneum Books for Young Readers, 1999.
*TC PZ7.F59936 Wh 1999*

**The potter's art.**
Glassie, Henry H. Philadelphia : Material Culture ; Bloomington : Indiana University Press, 1999.
*TC NK4235 .G54 1999*

**POTTERS - NORTH CAROLINA - WINSTON-SALEM - HISTORY - 18TH CENTURY.**
South, Stanley A. Historical archaeology in Wachovia. New York : Kluwer Academic/Plenum Publishers, c1999.
*TC F264.W8 S66 1999*

**POTTERY.** *See* PORCELAIN.

**POTTERY - 20TH CENTURY - AUSTRALIA.**
Mansfield, Janet. Contemporary ceramic art in Australia and New Zealand. Roseville East, NSW : Craftsman House, 1995.
*TC NK4179 .M36 1995*

**POTTERY - 20TH CENTURY - NEW ZEALAND.**
Mansfield, Janet. Contemporary ceramic art in Australia and New Zealand. Roseville East, NSW : Craftsman House, 1995.
*TC NK4179 .M36 1995*

**POTTERY, AMERICAN.** *See* ZUNI POTTERY.

**POTTERY, AUSTRALIAN.**
Mansfield, Janet. Contemporary ceramic art in Australia and New Zealand. Roseville East, NSW : Craftsman House, 1995.
*TC NK4179 .M36 1995*

**POTTERY, COLONIAL - NORTH CAROLINA - WINSTON-SALEM.**
South, Stanley A. Historical archaeology in Wachovia. New York : Kluwer Academic/Plenum Publishers, c1999.
*TC F264.W8 S66 1999*

**POTTERY CRAFT.**
Speight, Charlotte F., 1919- Hands in clay. 4th ed. Mountain View, Calif. : Mayfield, c1999.
*TC TT920 .S685 1999*

**POTTERY - CROSS-CULTURAL STUDIES.**
Glassie, Henry H. The potter's art. Philadelphia : Material Culture ; Bloomington : Indiana University Press, 1999.
*TC NK4235 .G54 1999*

**POTTERY - HISTORY.**
Munsterberg, Hugo, 1916- World ceramics. New York : Penguin Studio Books, c1998.
*TC NK3780 .M86 1998*

Pottery in the making. Washington, D.C. : Smithsonian Institution Press, c1997.
*TC NK3780 .P68 1997*

**Pottery in the making :** ceramic traditions / edited by Ian Freestone and David Gaimster. Washington, D.C. : Smithsonian Institution Press, c1997. 240 p. : ill. (some col.) ; 28 cm. Includes bibliographical references (p. 224-235) and index. ISBN 1-56098-797-9
*1. Pottery - History. I. Freestone, Ian. II. Gaimster, David R. M.*
*TC NK3780 .P68 1997*

**POTTERY, MANDINGO.**
Frank, Barbara E. Mande potters & leatherworkers. Washington, D.C. : Smithsonian Institution Press, 1998.
*TC DT474.6.M36 F73 1998*

**POTTERY, NEW ZEALAND.**
Mansfield, Janet. Contemporary ceramic art in Australia and New Zealand. Roseville East, NSW : Craftsman House, 1995.
*TC NK4179 .M36 1995*

**POTTERY, ORIENTAL.**
Wood, Nigel. Chinese glazes. Philadelphia, Pa. : University of Pennylvania Press, 1999.
*TC TP812 .W65 1999*

**POTTERY, PRIMITIVE.** *See* POTTERY.

**POTTERY, ZUNI.** *See* ZUNI POTTERY.

**Potthoff, Bradley J.**
Savage, Tom V. Effective teaching in elementary social studies. 4th ed. Upper Saddle River, N.J. : Merrill, c2000.
*TC LB1584 .S34 2000*

**Pound, Carole.**
The aphasia therapy file. Hove : Psychology Press, c1999.
*TC RC425 .A665 1999*

**Pour un monde solidaire : le nouvel agenda social.**
A caring world. Paris : The Organisation, c1999.
*TC HN17.5 .C323 1999*

**Pourciau, Lester J., 1936-.**
Ethics and electronic information in the twenty-first century. West Lafayette, Ind. : Purdue University Press, c1999.
*TC T58.5 .E77 1999*

**POVERTY.** *See also* POOR.
Poverty. San Diego, CA : Greenhaven Press, c1994.
*TC HC110.P6 P63 1994*

**Poverty and children's adjustment.**
Luthar, Suniya S. Thousand Oaks, Calif. : Sage Publications, c1999.
*TC HV741 .L88 1999*

**Poverty and turbulence.**
Leventhal, Tama. 1999.
*TC 085 L5515*

**POVERTY - DEVELOPING COUNTRIES.**
The paradox of plenty. Oakland, Calif. : Food First Books, c1999.
*TC HD1542 .P37 1999*

**POVERTY LAW.** *See* PUBLIC WELFARE - LAW AND LEGISLATION.

**Poverty :** opposing viewpoints / David L. Bender & Bruno Leone, series editors, Katie de Koster, book editor, Bruno Leone, assistant editor. San Diego, CA : Greenhaven Press, c1994. 288 p. : ill. ; 22 cm. (Opposing viewpoints series) Includes bibliographical references (280-282) and index. SUMMARY: A collection of articles debating issues related to poverty in America, including its causes, how it affects minorities, government policies, and how poverty can be reduced. ISBN 1-56510-066-2 (lib. : acid-free paper) ISBN 1-56510-065-4 (pbk. : acid-free paper) DDC 362.5/0973
*1. Poor - United States. 2. Economic assistance, Domestic - United States. 3. Public welfare - United States. 4. Poor. 5. Poverty. 6. Public welfare. I. De Koster, Katie, 1948- II. Leone, Bruno, 1939- III. Series: Opposing viewpoints series (Unnumbered)*
*TC HC110.P6 P63 1994*

**POVERTY - UNITED STATES.**
Andrulis, Dennis P. Managed care and the inner city. San Francisco : Jossey-Bass, 1999.
*TC RA413.5.U5 A57 1999*

Chamberlin, J. Gordon (John Gordon) Upon whom we depend. New York : Peter Lang, c1999.
*TC HC110.P6 C326 1999*

Shorris, Earl, 1936- Riches for the poor. New York : W.W. Norton, 2000.
*TC HV4045 .S464 2000*

**POVERTY - UNITED STATES - PSYCHOLOGICAL ASPECTS.**
Luthar, Suniya S. Poverty and children's adjustment. Thousand Oaks, Calif. : Sage Publications, c1999.
*TC HV741 .L88 1999*

**Powell, Gary N.**
Handbook of gender & work. Thousand Oaks, CA : Sage Publications, Inc., c1999.
*TC HQ1233 .H33 1999*

**Powell, Rebecca, 1949-** Literacy as a moral imperative : facing the challenges of a pluralistic society / Rebecca Powell. Lanham, Md. : Rowman & Littlefield Publishers, c1999. ix, 151 p. ; 24 cm. (Culture and education series) Includes bibliographical references (p. 129-140) and index. ISBN 0-8476-9459-3 (pbk. :alk. paper) ISBN 0-8476-9458-5 (hardcover : alk. paper) DDC 302.2/244
*1. Literacy - Social aspects - United States. 2. Moral education - United States. 3. Critical pedagogy - United States. 4. Education - Aims and objectives - United States. I. Title. II. Series.*
*TC LC151 .P69 1999*

**Powell, Richard R., 1951-** Classrooms under the influence : addicted families, addicted students / Richard R. Powell, Stanley J. Zehm, Jeffrey A. Kottler. Newbury Park, Calif. : Corwin Press, c1995. xiv, 152 p. ; 24 cm. Includes bibliographical references (p. 148-152). ISBN 0-8039-6101-4 (acid-free paper) ISBN 0-8039-6102-2 (pbk. : acid-free paper) DDC 371.7/84

*1. Students - Substance use. 2. Substance abuse - Psychological aspects. 3. Problem families - Psychological aspects. 4. Compulsive behavior - Social aspects. 5. Problem children - Education. I. Zehm, Stanley J. II. Kottler, Jeffrey A. III. Title.*
*TC HV5824.Y68 P69 1995*

**Powell, Stuart, 1949-** Returning to study : a guide for professionals / Stuart Powell. Buckingham ; Philadelphia : Open University Press, c1999. xi, 141 p. ; 23 cm. Includes bibliographical references (p. [132]-134) and index. ISBN 0-335-20131-8 (pb) ISBN 0-335-20132-6 (hb) DDC 374/.941
*1. Adult education - Great Britain. 2. Education, Higher - Great Britain. 3. Continuing education - Great Britain. 4. Report writing. I. Title.*
*TC LC5256.G7 P66 1999*

**Power and ideology in American sport.**
Sage, George Harvey. 2nd ed. Champaign, IL : Human Kinetics, c1998.
*TC GV706.5 .S228 1998*

**Power, Brenda Miller.**
Hubbard, Ruth, 1950- The art of classroom inquiry. Portsmouth, N.H. : Heinemann, c1993.
*TC LB1028 .H78 1993*

Parent power : energizing home-school communication / Brenda Power with Mary Bagley ... [et al.]. Portsmouth, NH : Heinemann, c1999. 1 v. (various pagings) : ill. ; 28 cm. + 1 computer laser optical disc (4 3/4 in.). System requirements for accompanying computer disc: Windows 95 or better ; Macintosh System 7 or better. Parent essay masters are in English and Spanish. ISBN 0-325-00155-3 (pbk./CD-ROM : alk. paper) DDC 371.19/2
*1. Home and school - United States. 2. Parent-teacher relationships - United States. 3. Education - Parent participation - United States. I. Bagley, Mary, 1958- II. Title.*
*TC LC225.3 .P69 1999*

**Power grab.**
Moo, G. Gregory. Washington, D.C. : Regnery Pub. ; Lanham, MD : Distributed to the trade by National Book Network, c1999.
*TC LB2844.53.U6 M66 1999*

**Power in the blood :** a handbook on AIDS, politics, and communication / edited by William N. Elwood. Mahwah, N.J. : Erlbaum, 1999. xvii, 442 p. ; 27 cm. (Lea's communication series) Includes bibliographical references and indexes. ISBN 0-8058-2906-7 (alk. paper) DDC 362.1/969792/00973
*1. AIDS (Disease) - Social aspects - United States. I. Elwood, William N. II. Series.*
*TC RA644.A25 P69 1999*

**The power of idea :** professionalism and marketing in photographic communication [videorecording] / research and interviews, R. Smith Schuneman, Rich Clarkson ; script, Marisha Chamberlain ; series director, Patricia Ward Schuneman ; photography: James Balog ... [et al.] in association with Black Star ; produced by Media Loft, Inc. Minneapolis, Minn. : Media Loft, c1992. 1 videocassette (31 min.) : sd., col. ; 1/2 in. (Media Loft educational-awareness presentation) (Great photographers ; v.10) Title on container and cassette label: Power of idea : professionalism and marketing in photography [videorecording]. VHS. Catalogued from credits and container and cassette label. Host and presenter, Howard Chapnick. Videography, John Junis, Ace Allgood; video editing, Ace Allgood, R. Smith Schuneman. "TV-29-VHS."--Container. For general audiences. SUMMARY: Howard Chapnick, former president of Black Star photographic agency, and one of America's foremost photographic representatives, gives tips to photographers on how and where to sell their work in commercial markets. He discusses how to get started and establish credibility, and shows the work of successful photographers and describing how they "made it", while giving a tour of agencies like Black Star, Contact Press and Woodfin Camp's offices in New York. Chapnick's philosophy is that the photographer should have something unique to say with passion and commitment.
*1. Chapnick, Howard. 2. Photography, Artistic. 3. Commercial photography. 4. Photojournalism. 5. Documentary photography. I. Chapnick, Howard. II. Clarkson, Rich. III. Schuneman, R. Smith. IV. Schuneman, Pat Ward. V. Chamberlain, Marisha. VI. Balog, James. VII. Media Loft (Firm) VIII. Title: Power of idea : professionalism and marketing in photography [videorecording] IX. Title: Professionalism and marketing in photographic communication [videorecording] X. Title: Professionalism and marketing in photography [videorecording] XI. Series. XII. Series: Educational/awareness presentation.*
*TC TR690 .P5 1992*

**Power of idea : professionalism and marketing in photography [videorecording].**
The power of idea : [videorecording]. Minneapolis, Minn. : Media Loft, c1992.

**TC TR690 .P5 1992**

**The power of pride.**
Marks, Carole. 1st ed. New York : Crown Publishers, c1999.
*TC E185.6 .M35 1999*

**The power of the inner judge.**
Wurmser, Leon. [Flucht vor dem Gewissen. English]
Northvale, N.J. : Jason Aronson Inc., c2000.
*TC RC530 .W8713 2000*

**Power performance for singers.**
Emmons, Shirlee. New York : Oxford University Press, 1998.
*TC MT892 .E55 1998*

**Power plays.**
Alper, Gerald. San Francisco : International Scholars Publications, 1998.
*TC BF632.5 .A465 1998*

**Power, politics, and crime.**
Chambliss, William J. Boulder, CO : Westview Press, c1999.
*TC HV6789 .C395 1999*

**Power, politics, and the Olympic Games.**
Senn, Alfred Erich. Champaign, IL : Human Kinetics, c1999.
*TC GV721.5 .S443 1999*

**POWER (PSYCHOLOGY).** *See also* **CONTROL (PSYCHOLOGY).**
Gauchet, Marcel. [La pratique de l'esprit humain. English] Madness and democracy. Princeton, N.J. : Princeton University Press, c1999.
*TC RC439 .G2813 1999*

**Power, race, and gender in academe :** strangers in the tower? / edited by Shirley Geok-Lin Lim and Maria Herrera-Sobek ; contributing editor, Genaro Padilla ; with the assistance of Susan Y. Najita. New York : Modern Language Association, 2000. ix, 212 p. ; 24 cm. Includes bibliographical references and index. ISBN 0-87352-269-9 (cloth) ISBN 0-87352-270-2 (paper) DDC 378.1/2/089
*1. Minority college teachers - United States. 2. Women college teachers - United States. 3. Minority college teachers - Selection and appointment - United States. 4. Women college teachers - Selection and appointment - United States. 5. Discrimination in higher education - United States. I. Lim, Shirley. II. Herrera-Sobek, María. III. Padilla, Genaro M., 1949-*
*TC LC3727 .P69 2000*

**POWER (SOCIAL SCIENCES).** *See also* **CONSENSUS (SOCIAL SCIENCES); ELITE (SOCIAL SCIENCES); SOCIAL STATUS.**
Ackerman, Peter. Strategic nonviolent conflict. Westport, Conn. : Praeger, 1994.
*TC JC328.3 .A28 1994*

Dean, Mitchell, 1955- Governmentality. London ; Thousand Oaks, Calif. : Sage Publications, 1999.
*TC HN49.P6 D43 1999*

Dean, Mitchell, 1955- Governmentality. London ; Thousand Oaks, Calif. : Sage Publications, 1999.
*TC HN49.P6 D43 1999*

Gauchet, Marcel. [La pratique de l'esprit humain. English] Madness and democracy. Princeton, N.J. : Princeton University Press, c1999.
*TC RC439 .G2813 1999*

Gendering elites. Houndmills, Basingstoke, Hampshire : Macmillan Press ; New York : St. Martin's Press, 2000.
*TC HM1261 .G46 2000*

Jordan, Tim, 1959- Cyberpower. London ; New York : Routledge, 1999.
*TC ZA4375 .J67 1999*

McGettigan, Timothy. Utopia on wheels. Lanham, MD : University Press of America, c1999.
*TC HM1256 .M34 1999*

**POWER (SOCIAL SCIENCES) - GREAT BRITAIN - HISTORY - 20TH CENTURY.**
Bush, Julia. Edwardian ladies and imperial power. London ; New York : Leicester University Press, 2000.
*TC DA16 .B87 2000*

**Power, Thomas George, 1954-** Play and exploration in children and animals / Thomas G. Power. Mahwah, N.J. : L. Erlbaum Associates, 2000. xiii, 497 p. : ill. ; 24 cm. Includes bibliographical references (p. 397-473) and indexes. ISBN 0-8058-2241-0 (cloth : alk. paper) ISBN 0-8058-2242-9 (paper : alk. paper) DDC 155.4/18
*1. Play - Psychological aspects. 2. Parent and child. 3. Play behavior in animals. 4. Psychology, Comparative. I. Title.*

**TC BF717 .P69 2000**

**Powerful middle schools : teaching and learning for adolescents [videorecording].**
Powerful middle schools : teaching and learning for young adolescents (2000) Powerful middle schools [videorecording]. [Washington, D.C.?] : U.S. Dept. of Education, [2000].
*TC LB1623 .P6 2000*

**Powerful middle schools : teaching and learning for young adolescents (2000)** Powerful middle schools [videorecording] : teaching and learning for young adolescents / [presented by] The U.S. Department of Education in partnership with the National Alliance of Business and the U.S. Chamber of Commerce and the Committee for Economic Development. [Washington, D.C.?] : U.S. Dept. of Education, [2000], 1 videocassette (ca. 60 min.) : sd., col. : 1/2 in. (Satellite town meeting) Title on voice-over: Powerful middle schools : teaching and learning for adolescents [videorecording]. VHS. Catalogued from credits and data sheet. Closed captioned. Host, U.S, Secretary of Education, Richard Riley; co-host, Judith Johnson; moderator, Nancy Mathis. A call in and live web-cast Satellite Town Meeting held on Tuesday, February 15, 2000 from 8:00 to 9:00 P.M. (E.T.). For middle school educators and parents of children aged 10-14. SUMMARY: Hosted by U.S. Secretary of Education, Richard Riley, co-hosted by Judith Johnson, Deputy Assistant Secretary of Education, and moderated by Nancy Mathis, broadcast on February 15, 2000, with provisions for call-in questions, a panel of middle school educators and a parent discuss the primary importance of middle school educationand the needs peculiar to the middle school student. Middle school students make decisions that will affect not only their high school education, but their lives, thus middle schools must maintain high expectations and high standards with advanced courses, learning communities for the needy students, egalitarian education for all,and community and parental engagement in the educational process. Two video clips are shown of outstanding middle schools-- the Barren County Middle School in Kentucky and Handshaw Middle School in Modesto, California. A live web-cast with interactive on-line discussion is operational at ali.apple.com.
*1. Middle schools - United States. 2. Middle school students - United States. 3. Middle school teachers - United States. 4. Middle school principals - United States. 5. Education, Elementary - Parent participation - United States. 6. Education. Elementary - Aims and objectives - United States. 7. Teachers - In-service training - United States. 8. Community and school - United States. 9. Education - Standards - United States. 10. Teachers - In-service training - United States. 11. Home and school - United States. 12. Video recordings for the hearing impaired. I. Mathis, Nancy. II. Riley, Richard W. (Richard Wilson) III. Johnson, Judith. IV. United States. Dept. of Education. V. Committee for Economic Development. VI. National Alliance of Business. VII. Chamber of the United States of America. VIII. Title. IX. Title: Teaching and learning for young adolescents [videorecording] X. Title: Powerful middle schools : teaching and learning for adolescents [videorecording] XI. Title: Teaching and learning for adolescents [videorecording] XII. Series.*
*TC LB1623 .P6 2000*

**Powerful middle schools [videorecording].**
Powerful middle schools : teaching and learning for young adolescents (2000) [Washington, D.C.?] : U.S. Dept. of Education, [2000].
*TC LB1623 .P6 2000*

**Powerful programming for student learning :** approaches that make a difference / Debora L. Liddell, Jon P. Lund, editors. San Francisco : Jossey-Bass, c2000. 107 p. ; 23 cm. (New directions for student services, 0164-7970 ; no. 90) (Jossey-Bass higher and adult education series) "Summer 2000" Includes bibliographical references and index. ISBN 0-7879-5443-8
*1. Counseling in higher education - United States. 2. College students - United States. I. Liddell, Debora L. II. Lund, Jon P. III. Series. IV. Series: New directions for student services ; no. 90*
*TC LB2343 .P643 2000*

**Powerful writing/responsible teaching.**
Lensmire, Timothy J., 1961- New York : Teachers College Press, c2000.
*TC LB1576 .L42 2000*

**Powers, Roger S.**
Protest, power, and change. New York : Garland Pub., 1997.
*TC HM278 .P76 1997*

**Powers, Stephen, 1936-.**
Watson, Linda R., 1950- Deaf and hearing impaired pupils in mainstream schools. London : David Fulton, c1999.
*TC LC1203.G7 W387 1999*

**POW'S.** *See* **PRISONERS OF WAR.**

**Poznańska drukarnia naukowa**
Gontarczyk, Ewa. Kobiecość i męskość jako kategorie społeczno-kulturowe w studiach feministycznych. Poznań : Eruditus, 1995.
*TC HQ1181.P7 G66 1995*

**PR in practice series**
Green, Andy. Creativity in public relations. London ; Dover, N.H. : Kogan Page, c1999.
*TC HD59 .G744 1999*

**PRACTICAL ANATOMY.** *See* **HUMAN DISSECTION.**

**Practical approaches to using learning styles in higher education** / edited by Rita Dunn and Shirley A. Griggs. Westport, Conn. : Bergin & Garvey, 2000. xi, 269 p. : ill. ; 24 cm. Includes bibliographical references (p. [247]-259) and index. ISBN 0-89789-703-X (alk. paper) DDC 378.1/70281
*1. Study skills. 2. Education, Higher. I. Dunn. Rita Stafford. 1930- II. Griggs, Shirley A.*
*TC LB2395 .P69 2000*

**The practical art of suicide assessment.**
Shea, Shawn C. New York ; Chichester [England] : John Wiley, c1999.
*TC RC569 .S46 1999*

**Practical/Forecast for home economics 1963-66.**
Forecast for home economics. Teacher edition of Co-ed. Dayton, Ohio, Scholastic Magazine.

**Practical fun activities to enhance motor skills and improve tactile and concept awareness.**
Flowers, Toni. Reaching the child with autism through art. Arlington, TX : Future Education, c1992.
*TC LC4717 .F56 2000*

**A Practical guide to arts participation research** / [AMS Planning & Research Corp., author]. Washington, DC : National Endowment for the Arts, [1995] iii, 88 p. : ill. ; 28 cm. (Research Division report ; #30) Includes bibliographical references (p. 85-88). DDC 700/.1/030973
*1. Arts audiences - United States. 2. Arts surveys - United States. I. AMS Planning & Research Corp. II. Series: Research Division report (National Endowment for the Arts. Research Division) ; 30.*
*TC NX220 .P73 1995*

**Practical home economics.**
Home economics news. Peoria, Ill. : Published by the Manual Arts Press, [1930-1932].

**Practical intelligence in everyday life** / Robert J. Sternberg ... [et al.]. Cambridge, UK ; New York, NY : Cambridge University Press, 2000. xiv, 288 p. : ill. ; 23 cm. Includes bibliographical references (p. 225-254) and index. ISBN 0-521-65056-9 ISBN 0-521-65958-2 (pbk.)
*1. Intellect. I. Sternberg, Robert J.*
*TC BF431 .P64 2000*

**PRACTICAL JOKES - FICTION.**
Naylor, Phyllis Reynolds. A traitor among the boys. New York : Delacorte Press, 1999.
*TC PZ7.N24 Tpr 1999*

**PRACTICAL NURSING - PERIODICALS.**
Bedside nurse. New York, National Federation of Licensed Practical Nurses, Inc., 1968-72.

**Practical pedagogy for the Jewish classroom.**
Kohn, Daniel B., 1963- Westport, Conn. : Greenwood Press, 1999.
*TC BM108 .K65 1999*

**The practical researcher.**
Dunn, Dana. Boston : McGraw-Hill College, c1999.
*TC BF76.5 .D864 1999*

**Practical resources for the mental health professional.**
Effective brief therapies :. San Diego : Academic Press, c2000.
*TC RC480.55 .E376 2000*

Management and administration skills for the mental health professional. San Diego, Calif. London : Academic, c1999.
*TC RA790 .M325 1999*

**Practical skills for counselors**
Bemak, Fred. Violent and aggressive youth. Thousand Oaks, Calif. ; London : Corwin Press, c2000.
*TC LB3013.3 .B45 2000*

Winslade, John. Narrative counseling in schools. Thousand Oaks, Calif. : Corwin Press, c1999.
*TC LB1027.5 .W535 1999*

**Practical statistics for educators.**
Ravid, Ruth. 2nd ed. Lanham, Md. : University Press of America, c2000.

**Practical steps to the research process for high school.**
Stanley, Deborah B. Englewood, Colo. : Libraries Unlimited, 1999.
*TC Z711.2 .S72 1999*

**Practical visionaries :** women, education, and social progress, 1790-1930 / edited by Mary Hilton and Pam Hirsch. Harlow, England : Longman, 2000. xiii, 252 p. : ill. ; 24 cm. (Women and men in history) Includes bibliographical references (p. 235-240) and index. ISBN 0-582-40431-2 (pb) DDC 371.82/0941/0903
*1. Women - Education - Great Britain - History - 18th century. 2. Women - Education - Great Britain - History - 19th century. 3. Women - Education - Great Britain - History - 20th century. 4. Women in education - History. 5. Women educators - Biography. I. Hilton, Mary, 1946- II. Hirsch, Pam. III. Series.*
*TC LC2042 .P72 2000*

**Practical work in science education : :** recent research studies. 1. ed. Frederiksberg, Denmark : Roskilde University Press ; Dordrecht, Holland : Kluwer Acdemic, 1999. 331 p. ; 23 cm. Includes bibliographical references. ISBN 87-7867-079-9
*1. Science - Study and teaching - Research. I. Leach, John.*
*TC Q181 .P73 1999*

**Practice guideline for the treatment of patients with eating disorders** / American Psychiatric Association ; Work Group on Eating Disorders. 2nd ed. Washington, D.C. : American Psychiatric Association, c2000. vii, 76 p. ; 28 cm. (American Psychiatric Association practice guidelines) Includes bibliographical references (p. 60-76). ISBN 0-89042-314-8
*1. Eating disorders - Treatment. I. American Psychiatric Association. Work Group on Eating Disorders. II. Series.*
*TC RC552.E18 P73 2000*

**The practice of counselling in primary care** / edited by Robert Bor and Damian McCann. London : Thousand Oaks, Calif. : SAGE Publications, 1999. xii, 251 p. ; 24 cm. Includes bibliographical references and index. ISBN 0-7619-5879-7 ISBN 0-7619-5880-0 (pbk) DDC 362.104256
*1. Health counseling. 2. Primary care (Medicine) 3. Sick - Counseling of. 4. Counseling. 5. Primary Health Care. I. Bor, Robert. II. McCann, Damian.*
*TC R727.4 .P733 1999*

**PRACTICE OF LAW.** *See* **TRIAL PRACTICE.**

**PRACTICE (PSYCHOLOGY).**
Practitioner's guide to evaluating change with neuropsychological assessment instruments. New York : Kluwer Academic/Plenum Publishers, c2000.
*TC RC386.6.N48 P73 2000*

**PRACTICE TEACHING.** *See* **STUDENT TEACHING.**

**Practices.**
Nurse's legal handbook. 4th ed. Springhouse, Pa. : Springhouse Corp., c2000.
*TC RT86.7 .N88 2000*

**Practicing feminist ethics in psychology** / edited by Mary M. Brabeck. 1st ed. Washington, DC : American Psychological Association, c2000. xi, 285 p. ; 26 cm. (Psychology of women book series) Includes bibliographical references and indexes. ISBN 1-55798-623-1 (cloth : alk. paper) ISBN 1-55798-635-5 (pbk. : alk. paper) DDC 174/.915/082
*1. Feminist psychology. 2. Feminism. 3. Women - Psychology. I. Brabeck, Mary M. II. Series.*
*TC BF201.4 .P73 2000*

**Practicing harm reduction psychotherapy.**
Denning, Patt, 1950- New York : Guilford Press, 2000.
*TC RC564 .D44 2000*

**Practicing what we preach :** preparing middle level educators / Samuel Totten ... [et al.]. New York : Falmer Press, 1999. xx, 466 p. ; 23 cm. (Garland reference library of social science ; 1193. Source books on education ; v. 56) Includes bibliographical references and indexes. ISBN 0-8153-3166-5 (alk. paper) DDC 370/.71/1
*1. Middle school teachers - Training of - United States. I. Totten, Samuel. II. Series: Garland reference library of social science ; v. 1193. III. Series: Garland reference library of social science. Source books on education ; vol. 56.*
*TC LB1735.5 .P73 1999*

**PRACTICUMS.** *See* **INTERNSHIP PROGRAMS; STUDENT TEACHING.**

**Practising identities :** power and resistance / edited by Sasha Roseneil and Julie Seymour. New York : St. Martin's Press, 1999. xii, 257 p. ill., ; 23 cm. (Explorations in sociology) Includes bibliographical references (p. 246-248) and index. ISBN 0-312-22227-0 (cloth) DDC 305.3

*1. Group identity. 2. Identity (Psychology) I. Roseneil, Sasha, 1966- II. Seymour, Julie. III. Series.*
*TC HM131 .P677 1999*

**Practitioner-based enquiry.**
Murray, Louis, 1944- London : New York : Falmer Press, 2000.
*TC LB1028.24 .M87 2000*

**The practitioner inquiry series**
Ballenger, Cynthia. Teaching other people's children. New York : Teachers College Press, c1999.
*TC LC3746 .B336 1999*

Fishman, Stephen M. Unplayed tapes. Urbana, Ill. : National Council of Teachers of English ; New York : Teachers College Press, c2000.
*TC LB1028.24 .F52 2000*

**The Practitioner inquiry series**
From another angle. New York : Teachers College Press, c2000.
*TC LB1117 .F735 2000*

**The practitioner inquiry series**
Newman, Judith, 1943- Tensions of teaching. New York ; London : Teachers College Press, c1998.
*TC LB1025.3 .N49 1998*

Ritchie, Joy S. Teacher narrative as critical inquiry. New York : Teachers College Press, c2000.
*TC LA2311 .R58 2000*

**Practitioner's guide to evaluating change with neuropsychological assessment instruments** / edited by Robert J. McCaffrey, Kevin Duff, and Holly James Westervelt. New York : Kluwer Academic/Plenum Publishers, c2000. xiv, 552 p. ; 26 cm. (Critical issues in neuropsychology series) Includes bibliographical references (p. 517-541) and index. ISBN 0-306-46361-X DDC 616.8/0475
*1. Review Literature. 2. Neuropsychological tests. 3. Neuropsychological Tests. 4. Nervous System Diseases - diagnosis. 5. Neuropsychology - methods. 6. Practice (Psychology). I. McCaffrey, Robert J. II. Duff, Kevin, 1968- III. Westervelt, Holly James, 1969- IV. Series : Critical issues in neuropsychology*
*TC RC386.6.N48 P73 2000*

**Prado, C. G.** The last choice : preemptive suicide in advanced age / C.G. Prado. 2nd ed. Westport, Conn. : Greenwood Press, 1998. xiv, 188 p. ; 25 cm. (Contributions in philosophy, 0084-926X ; no. 63) Includes bibliographical references (p. [159]-183) and index. ISBN 0-313-30584-6 (alk. paper) DDC 362.28/084/6
*1. Aged - Suicidal behavior. 2. Suicide - Moral and ethical aspects. 3. Euthanasia - Moral and ethical aspects. I. Title. II. Series.*
*TC HV6545.2 .P7 1998*

**Praeger series in applied psychology**
Family and peers. Westport, Conn. : Praeger, 2000.
*TC HQ755.85 .F365 2000*

**Prætorius, Nini.** Principles of cognition, language and action : essays on the foundations of a science of psychology / by N. Prætorius. Dordrecht, The Netherlands ; Boston [Mass., U.S.] : Kluwer Academic Publishers, c2000. xxii, 492 p. ; 25 cm. Includes bibliographical references (p. 483-488) and index. ISBN 0-7923-6230-6 (hb : alk. paper) DDC 150/.1
*1. Psychology - Philosophy. I. Title.*
*TC BF38 .P67 2000*

**Prager, Jeffrey, 1948-** Presenting the past : psychoanalysis and the sociology of misremembering / Jeffrey Prager. Cambridge, Mass. : Harvard University Press, 1998. 261 p. ; 21 cm. Includes bibliographical references (p. 223-249) and index. ISBN 0-674-56641-6 (alk. paper) DDC 153.1/2
*1. Psychoanalysis and culture. 2. Memory. 3. Memory - Case studies. 4. False memory syndrome. 5. False memory syndrome - Case studies. I. Title.*
*TC BF175.4.C84 P73 1998*

**PRAGMATICS.**
Li, Duan-Duan. Expressing needs and wants in a second language. 1998.
*TC 06 no. 10958*

The semantics/pragmatics interface from different points of view. 1st ed. Oxford, UK ; New York : Elsevier, 1999.
*TC P325 .S3814 1999*

**Pragmatics & beyond**
(new ser. 56) Tanaka, Hiroko. Turn-taking in Japanese conversation. Amsterdam ; Philadelphia, PA : John Benjamins Pub. Co., c1999.
*TC PL640.5 .T36 1999*

(new ser. 64) Svennevig, Jan. Getting acquainted in conversation. Amsterdam ; Philadelphia : J. Benjamins Pub. Co., c1999.

*TC P95.45 .S89 1999*

**PRAGMATISM.**
Roskelly, Hephzibah. Reason to believe. Albany : State University of New York Press, c1998.
*TC PE1404 .R67 1998*

**The prairie train.**
Ó Flatharta, Antoine. New York : Crown Publishers, 1997.
*TC PZ7.O331275 Pr 1997*

**Prairie visions.**
Gard, Robert E. (Robert Edward), 1910- Ashland, Wis. : Heartland Press, c1987.
*TC PS3513.A612 P7 1987*

**PRAIRIES - BIOGRAPHIES.**
Gard, Robert E. (Robert Edward), 1910- Prairie visions. Ashland, Wis. : Heartland Press, c1987.
*TC PS3513.A612 P7 1987*

**PRAIRIES - BIOGRAPHY.**
Gard, Robert E. (Robert Edward), 1910- Prairie visions. Ashland, Wis. : Heartland Press, c1987.
*TC PS3513.A612 P7 1987*

**PRAIRIES IN ART.**
Kinsey, Joni. Plain pictures. Washington, : Published for the University of Iowa Museum of Art by the Smithsonian Institution Press, 1996.
*TC N8214.5.U6 K56 1996*

**PRAIRIES - MOEURS ET COUTUMES.**
Gard, Robert E. (Robert Edward), 1910- Prairie visions. Ashland, Wis. : Heartland Press, c1987.
*TC PS3513.A612 P7 1987*

**PRAIRIES - SOCIAL LIFE AND CUSTOMS.**
Gard, Robert E. (Robert Edward), 1910- Prairie visions. Ashland, Wis. : Heartland Press, c1987.
*TC PS3513.A612 P7 1987*

**Pratt, John, 1945-.**
Improving education. London ; New York : Cassell, 1999.
*TC LB7 .I48 1999*

**PRAYER - FICTION.**
Michelson, Richard. Grandpa's gamble. New York : Marshall Cavendish, 1999.
*TC PZ7.M581915 Gr 1999*

**PRAYERS.** *See* **PRAYER.**

**Pre-algebra** [videorecording] / Video Tutor, Inc. Princeton, N.J. : Video Tutor, 1988. 1 videocassette (VHS) (69 min.) : sd., col. ; 1/2 in. + 1 student workbook & pre/post test system ([24] p. ; 19 cm.). (Video tutor instructional series) (A mathematics series) Title on container: Basic pre-algebra [videorecording]. Title on voice-over: Video Tutor introduces pre-algebra [videorecording]. Title on cassette label Video Tutor Inc. presents basic pre-algebra [videorecording]. VHS. Catalogued from credits, cassette label and container. John Hall, instructor. For grades 5-9 math classes. SUMMARY: Covers addition, subtraction, multiplication, and division of signed numbers, simple equations, adding, subtracting, multiplying and dividing monomials, and adding and subtracting polynomials.
*1. Algebra. I. Hall, John. II. Video Tutor. III. Title: Basic pre-algebra [videorecording] IV. Title: Video Tutor introduces pre-algebra [videorecording] V. Title: Video Tutor Inc. presents basic pre-algebra [videorecording] VI. Series. VII. Series: A mathematics series*
*TC QA152.2 .P6 1988*

**PRE-COLUMBIAN ART.** *See* **INDIAN ART.**

**PRE-COLUMBIAN INDIANS.** *See* **INDIANS; INDIANS OF MEXICO.**

**Pre-primary education in Nigeria** / edited by B.O. Igboabuchi, Eze Denco. Onitsha [Nigeria] : Lincel, 1998. 267 p. ; 22 cm. Proceedings of a conference. Includes bibliographical references. CONTENTS: Headstart stimulation : a psychoheuristic approach to pre-primary education in Nigeria / N.N. Okoye -- The philosophical and historical antecedents of pre-primary education in Nigeria / S.N. Okonkwo -- Socio-economic issues in pre-primary education in Nigeria / Emma Obasi -- Early childhood education and the Nigerian environment / Ebele J. Madueweesi -- In the tradition of renowned educators / B.O. Igboabuchi -- Strategies for effective teaching and learning in pre-primary education / B.O. Ayozie -- Concretion and concretizations' strategy in the curriculum and methodology of pre-primary education / Eze Denco -- Play method in pre-primary education : implications for curriculum implementation / Ndudi Jem Mbakwem -- Turning pre-primary school children on to science through play / Ofoefuna Julie O. -- The role of music in the all-round development of the nursery child / Onwuekwe, Agatha Ijeoma -- Supervision of instruction : a neglected strategy for effective teaching and learning in pre-primary education / Ezeani, L.U. -- The national policy on education : implications for effective pre-primary science

teaching / Mike A. Maduabum -- Strategies for teaching pre-primary (nursery and kindergarten) mathematics / S.U. Ekeada -- Strategies for effective teaching and learning in the pre-primary education : the primacy of language in learning / A.F. Obi-Okoye -- Quality of teaching in star private nursery and primary schools in CONTENTS: Anambra State / N.O. Nwankpa -- Characteristics of pre-school children / Damian C. Anuka -- Proposed physical education programme for pre-schoolers / Amaefunah, P.O. -- Strategies for effective teaching and learning of good health habits in pre-primary education / Ibeagha, E.J. -- Educational technology in pre-primary education / Dorothy A. Onyejemezi -- Use of picture books and displays for effective teaching and learning in pre-primary education / E.S. Anaehobi -- The pre-primary school teacher / Akude, Ikechukwu -- Educational technology in pre-primary educa[t]ion / Betty C. Eboh -- New technologies for teaching and learning in pre-primary education / S. Nnaemeka Mbiko -- Management of nursery school staff personnel in Anambra State / F.N.J. Eresimadu -- Some guidelines for the establishment and operation of a standard pre-primary (nursery) school / B.C. Iloral -- The curriculum of nursery and kindergarten programmes / Ogunyiriofo Okoroh -- Model activities for nursery school moral training / Ugoeze N. Eneogwe -- The individualized modular format of instruction / M.O. Ofoefuna -- Towards establishment of functional nursery schools in Nigeria / G.O. Eneasator -- Pre-primary education in Nigeria : challenges for the government / V. Nonyelum Ezike -- Establishment of pre-primary schools in Nigeria / H.O.N. Bosah.
*1. Education, Preschool - Nigeria - Congresses. I. Igboabuchi, B. O. II. Denco, Eze.*
**TC LB1140.25.N6 P74 1998**

**PRECEDENCE.** *See* **GENEALOGY.**

**PRECIPITATION (METEOROLOGY).** *See* **SNOW.**

**PRECOLUMBIAN ART.** *See* **INDIAN ART.**

**PRECOLUMBIAN INDIANS.** *See* **INDIANS; INDIANS OF MEXICO.**

**PREDICTION OF SCHOLASTIC SUCCESS.**
Parkyn, George W. Success and failure at the university. Wellington, New Zealand Council for Educational Research, 1959-67.
**TC LB1131 .P29**

**PREDICTION OF SCHOLASTIC SUCCESS - EVALUATION.**
Owen, David, 1955- None of the above. Rev. and updated. Lanham, Md. : Rowman & Littlefield Publishers, c1999.
**TC LB2353.57 .O94 1999**

**PREDICTION (PSYCHOLOGY).**
Rydberg, Sven. Bias in prediction on correction methods. Stockholm, Almqvist & Wiksell [1963]
**TC HA31.2 .R93**

**Prediger, D. J.** Basic structure of work-relevant abilities / Dale J. Prediger. Iowa City, Iowa : ACT, 1998. iv, 33 p. : ill. ; 28 cm. (ACT research report series ; 98-9.) "October 1998"--Cover. Includes bibliographical references (p. 22-25).
*1. Occupational aptitude tests. 2. Ability - Testing. 3. Vocational evaluation. I. Title. II. Series.*
**TC LB3051 .A3 no. 98-9**

**Preece, Julia.** Combating social exclusion in university adult education / Julia Preece. Aldershot ; Brookfield, Vt. : Ashgate, c1999. ix, 179 p. : ill. ; 22 cm. (Interdisciplinary research series in ethnic, gender and class relations) Includes bibliographical references (p. 163-174) and index. ISBN 0-7546-1150-7 DDC 378.41
*1. Adult education - Great Britain. 2. Education, Higher - Great Britain. 3. Marginality, Social - Great Britain. I. Title. II. Series.*
**TC LC5256.G7 P84 1999**

Using Foucault and feminist theory to explain why some adults are excluded from British university education / Julia Preece. Lewiston, N.Y. : E. Mellen Press, c1999. xiv, 326 p. ; 24 cm. Includes bibliographical references (p. [313]-326). ISBN 0-7734-8001-3 DDC 378.1/75
*1. University extension - Great Britain - Case studies. 2. Women - Education (Continuing education) - Great Britain - Case studies. 3. Foucault, Michel - Contributions in feminist theory. I. Title.*
**TC LC6256.G7 P74 1999**

**PREGNANCY.** *See* **PREGNANT WOMEN; TEENAGE PREGNANCY.**

**PREGNANCY, ADOLESCENT.** *See* **TEENAGE PREGNANCY.**

**PREGNANCY - FICTION.**
Caseley, Judith. Losing Louisa. 1st ed. New York : Farrar, Straus and Giroux, c1999.
**TC PZ7.C2677 Lo 1999**

**PREGNANCY IN ADOLESCENCE.** *See* **TEENAGE PREGNANCY.**

**PREGNANCY - PREVENTION.** *See* **BIRTH CONTROL.**

**PREGNANCY, TEENAGE.** *See* **TEENAGE PREGNANCY.**

**PREGNANT GIRLS IN THE SCHOOLS.** *See* **PREGNANT SCHOOLGIRLS.**

**Pregnant pictures.**
Matthews, Sandra. New York : Routledge, 2000.
**TC TR681.P67 M38 2000**

**PREGNANT SCHOOLGIRLS.** *See* **TEENAGE PREGNANCY.**

**PREGNANT SCHOOLGIRLS - EDUCATION - SOCIAL ASPECTS - BRITISH COLUMBIA - CASE STUDIES.**
Kelly, Deirdre M. Pregnant with meaning. New York : P. Lang, c2000.
**TC LC4094.2.B8 K45 2000**

**PREGNANT SCHOOLGIRLS - UNITED STATES.**
United States. Congress. Senate. Committee on Labor and Public Welfare. Subcommittee on Health. School-age mother and child health act, 1975. Washington : U.S. Govt. Print. Off., 1976.
**TC KF26 .L354 1975**

**Pregnant with meaning.**
Kelly, Deirdre M. New York : P. Lang, c2000.
**TC LC4094.2.B8 K45 2000**

**PREGNANT WOMEN.** *See* **MOTHERS; PREGNANT SCHOOLGIRLS.**

**PREGNANT WOMEN - PORTRAITS.**
Matthews, Sandra. Pregnant pictures. New York : Routledge, 2000.
**TC TR681.P67 M38 2000**

**PREHISTORIC ANIMALS.**
Lessem, Don. Dinosaurs to dodos. 1st ed. New York : Scholastic Reference, 1999.
**TC QE842 .L47 1999**

**PREHISTORIC ARCHAEOLOGY.** *See* **PREHISTORIC PEOPLES.**

**PREHISTORIC ART.** *See* **ART, PREHISTORIC.**

**PREHISTORIC HUMAN BEINGS.** *See* **PREHISTORIC PEOPLES.**

**PREHISTORIC HUMANS.** *See* **PREHISTORIC PEOPLES.**

**PREHISTORIC PEOPLES.**
In search of human origins [videorecording]. [Boston, Mass.] : WGBH Educational Foundation, c1994.
**TC GN281 .I45 1994**

**PREHISTORIC PEOPLES - FICTION.**
Brooke, William J. A is for aarrgh!. 1st ed. New York : HarperCollinsPublishers, 1999.
**TC PZ7.B78977 Ig 1999**

**Prehistoric rock paintings of the Sahara.**
Tassili N'Ajjer [videorecording]. [S.l.] : Editions Cinégraphiques ; Northbrook, Ill. : [distributed by] the Roland Collection, c1968.
**TC N5310.5.A4 T3 1968**

**PREHISTORY.** *See* **PREHISTORIC PEOPLES.**

**PREJUDGMENTS.** *See* **PREJUDICES.**

**PREJUDICE.** *See also* **PREJUDICES.**
Flippen, Annette Rose. Similarity versus motive as explanations for ingroup bias. 1996.
**TC 085 F65**

**PREJUDICE IN TESTING.** *See* **TEST BIAS.**

**PREJUDICES.** *See* **RACISM.**

**PREJUDICES AND ANTIPATHIES.** *See* **PREJUDICES.**

**PREJUDICES - FICTION.**
Bat-Ami, Miriam. Two suns in the sky. 1st ed. [Chicago, IL] : Front Street/Cricket Books, 1999.
**TC PZ7.B2939 Tw 1999**

Fuchshuber, Annegert. [Karlinchen. English] Carly. 1st ed. New York : The Feminist Press, c1997.
**TC PZ7.F94 Car 1997**

Naylor, Phyllis Reynolds. Walker's Crossing. New York : Atheneum Books for Young Readers, c1999.
**TC PZ7.N24 Wai 1999**

**PREJUDICES - PUERTO RICO - HISTORY - 19TH CENTURY.**
Kinsbruner, Jay. Not of pure blood. Durham : Duke University Press, 1996.

**TC F1983.B55 K56 1996**

**PREJUDICES - STUDY AND TEACHING (ELEMENTARY) - UNITED STATES.**
Teaching for a tolerant world, grades K-6. Urbana, Ill. : National Council of Teachers of English, c1999.
**TC HM1271 .T43 1999**

**PREJUDICES - UNITED STATES.**
Perlmutter, Philip. Legacy of hate. Armonk, N.Y. ; London : M.E. Sharpe, c1999.
**TC BF575.H3 P47 1999**

**Preliminary approaches to language development.**
Plunkett, Kim. Aarhus, Denmark : Aarhus University Press, c1985.
**TC P118 .P6 1985**

**PREMARITAL COUNSELING.** *See* **MARRIAGE COUNSELING.**

**PRENATAL DIAGNOSIS.** *See* **AMNIOCENTESIS.**

**PRENATAL INFLUENCES.**
The effects of early adversity on neurobehavioral development. Mahwah, N.J. : L. Erlbaum Associates, 2000.
**TC RJ499 .E34 2000**

Janov, Arthur. The biology of love. Amherst, N.Y. : Prometheus Books, 2000.
**TC BF720.E45 .J36 2000**

**PRENATAL SUBSTANCE ABUSE VICTIMS.** *See* **CHILDREN OF PRENATAL SUBSTANCE ABUSE.**

**Prendiville, Francis, 1949-.**
Toye, Nigel, 1949- Drama and traditional story for the early years. London ; New York : Routledge, 2000.
**TC PN3171 .T695 2000**

**The Prentice Hall directory of online education resources.**
Bigham, Vicki Smith. Paramus, N.J. : Prentice Hall, c1998.
**TC LB1044.87 .B54 1998**

**Prentice Hall studies in writing and culture**
Teaching critical thinking. Englewood Cliffs, N.J. : Prentice Hall, c1993.
**TC LB1590.3 .T4 1993**

**Prentice Hall world geography.**
Baerwald, Thomas John. Englewood Cliffs, N.J. : Prentice Hall, c1992.
**TC G128 .B34 1992**

**PREP SCHOOLS.** *See* **PREPARATORY SCHOOLS.**

**Preparation, collaboration, and emphasis on the family in school counseling for the new millennium** / [edited by] Gwendolyn M. Duhon and Tony Manson. Lewiston : E. Mellen Press, c2000. ii, 294 p. ; 235 cm. (Mellen studies in education ; v. 48) Includes bibliographical references. ISBN 0-7734-7847-7 DDC 371.4
*1. Educational counseling - United States. 2. Cross-cultural counseling - United States. 3. Home and school - United States. I. Duhon, Gwendolyn M. II. Manson, Tony. III. Series.*
**TC LB1027.5 .P6525 2000**

**PREPARATORY SCHOOLS - MORAL AND ETHICAL ASPECTS - UNITED STATES.**
Peshkin, Alan. Permissible advantage? Mahwah, N.J. ; London : L. Erlbaum Associates, 2001.
**TC LC58.4 .P58 2001**

**PREPARATORY SCHOOLS - UNITED STATES - CASE STUDIES.**
Peshkin, Alan. Permissible advantage? Mahwah, N.J. ; London : L. Erlbaum Associates, 2001.
**TC LC58.4 .P58 2001**

**The Prepare Curriculum.**
Goldstein, Arnold P. Revised ed. Champaign, Ill. : Research Press, c1999.
**TC HM299 .G65 1999**

**Preparing a course.**
Forsyth, Ian. The complete guide to teaching a course. 2nd ed. London : Kogan Page ; Sterling, VA : Stylus Publishing, 1999.
**TC LB1025.3 .F67 1999**

**Preparing a nation's teachers :** models for English and foreign language programs / edited by Phyllis Franklin, David Laurence and Elizabeth B. Welles. New York : Modern Language Association of America, 1999. xiv, 423 p. ; 23 cm. Includes bibliographical references. CONTENTS: Preface: The School Reform Movement and Higher Education / Phyllis Franklin, David Laurence and Elizabeth B. Welles -- Introduction: What Happens Next? and How? and Why? / Donald Gray -- I. Model Programs -- Reports from English Departments. Illinois State University - Renewing the Nexus: Strengthening Connections

across the English Education Program. Indiana University, Bloomington - Watch This Space; or, Why We Have Not Revised the Teacher Education Program - Yet. New Mexico State University, Las Cruces - Defining the Secondary School English Education Camel. Norfolk State University - Preparing Secondary School English Teachers. University of Iowa - Educating Teachers of English. University of Virginia - Fit Teachers Though Few -- Reports from Foreign Language Departments. Arizona State University, Tempe - Teacher Education Program Reform: A Case in Point. California State University, Long Beach - Creating Teaching Communities: A Model for Reform and Ongoing Renewal. University of Georgia - The Perils of an Integrated Curriculum; or, How a Team Talked for One Year and Almost Communicated ... University of North Carolina, Greensboro - Integrated Perspectives: An Exemplary Program. University of South Florida - A Curricular Response to a Market Survey of Teachers' Needs. University of Virginia - Teaching and the Open Horizon -- II. Assessment Issues. CONTENTS: Assessment: A Blessing or Bane for Teachers of English? / Edward M. White and Volney S. White. Issues for Foreign Language Departments and Prospective Teachers / Judith E. Liskin-Gasparro -- III. Unresolved Questions. Changing Teacher Preparation for a Changing Student Body / Reed Way Dasenbrock. Connecting Universities and Schools: A Case Study / Harold J. Kolb, Jr. Great Expectations, Hard Times / Deborah K. Woelflein. Stories in Contact: Teacher Research in the Academy / Sarah Michaels. Facing Our Professional Others: Border Crossing in Teacher Education / Bob Broad. Closely Reading Ourselves: Teaching English and the Education of Teachers / James Marshall. Challenges of Teaching Literature: Reflections on the MLA Teacher Education Project / David A. Fein. Teaching Literature in the Foreign Language Classroom: Where Have We Been and Where Do We Go Now? / Doris Y. Kadish -- App. Baseline Studies. ISBN 0-87352-374-1 (pbk.) DDC 428/.0071/173 DDC 428/.0071/173
*1. English teachers - Training of - United States. 2. Language teachers - Training of - United States. 3. English philology - Study and teaching (Higher) - United States. 4. Language and languages - Study and teaching (Higher) - United States. I. Franklin, Phyllis. II. Laurence, David Ernst. III. Welles, Elizabeth B.*
**TC PE68.U5 P74 1999**

**Preparing America's teachers.**
Cruickshank, Donald R. Bloomington, Ind. : Phi Delta Kappa Educational Foundation, c1996.
**TC LB1715 .C86 1996**

**Preparing humanistic teachers for troubled children** / Peter Knoblock ... [et al.]. Syracuse, N.Y. : Division of Special Education and Rehabilitation, Syracuse University, [1974?] v, 135 p. : ill. ; 23 cm. Cover title. Includes bibliographical references. DDC 371.9/3
*1. Problem children - Education. 2. Education, Humanistic. I. Knoblock, Peter, 1934- II. Syracuse University. Division of Special Education and Rehabilitation.*
**TC LC4801 .P73**

**Preparing teachers for inclusive education :** case pedagogies and curricula for teacher educators / edited by Suzanne E. Wade. Mahwah, N.J. : L. Erlbaum Associates, 2000. xiv, 242 p. ; 23 cm. "This volume ... is designed to accompany Inclusive education : a casebook and readings for prospective and practicing teachers"--Pref. Includes bibliographical references and indexes. ISBN 0-8058-2509-6 (pbk. : alk. paper) DDC 371.9/046
*1. Inclusive education - United States - Case studies. 2. Inclusive education - Study and teaching - United States - Curricula. 3. Teachers of handicapped children - Training of - United States. I. Wade, Suzanne E.*
**TC LC1201 .P74 2000**

**Preparing to teach writing.**
Williams, James D. (James Dale), 1949- 2nd ed. Mahwah, N.J. : Lawrence Erlbaum Associates, 1998.
**TC PE1404 .W54 1998**

**Preparing your campus for a networked future** / Mark A. Luker, editor ; foreword by Graham B. Spanier. 1st ed. San Francisco : Jossey-Bass, c2000. xxv, 109 p. : ill. ; 23 cm. (EDUCAUSE leadership strategies ; no. 1) Includes bibliographical references and index. ISBN 0-7879-4734-2 (pbk. : alk. paper) DDC 378/.0025/678
*1. Universities and colleges - Computer networks - United States. 2. Internet (Computer network) in education - United States. I. Luker, Mark A., 1947- II. EDUCAUSE (Association) III. Series.*
**TC LB2395.7 .P74 2000**

**PRESBYTERIANS, AFRO-AMERICAN.** *See* **AFRO-AMERICAN PRESBYTERIANS.**

**PRESBYTERIANS, NEGRO.** *See* **AFRO-AMERICAN PRESBYTERIANS.**

**PRESBYTERIANS - UNITED STATES.** *See* **AFRO-AMERICAN PRESBYTERIANS.**

**PRESCHOOL CHILDREN - NEW YORK (STATE) - NEW YORK - PSYCHOLOGY.**
Flynn, Bernadette Marie. The teacher-child relationship, temperament, and coping in children with developmental disabilities. 2000.
*TC 06 no. 11267*

**PRESCHOOL CHILDREN - SERVICES FOR.** *See* **LIBRARIES - SERVICES TO PRESCHOOL CHILDREN.**

**PRESCHOOL EDUCATION.** *See* **EDUCATION, PRESCHOOL.**

**PRESCHOOL READERS.** *See* **READERS.**

**PRESCHOOL TEACHING - GREAT BRITAIN.**
O'Hara, Mark. Teaching 3-8 :. London ; New York : Continuum, 2000.
*TC LB1725.G7 O36 2000*

**PRESCHOOLERS.** *See* **PRESCHOOL CHILDREN.**

Prescott, Andrew.
Towards the digital library. London : The British Library, 1998.
*TC Z664.B75 T683 1998*

**PRESCRIPTIONS, DRUG.**
Cost benefit analysis of heroin maintenance treatment. Basel ; New York : Karger, c2000.
*TC RC568.H4 C67 2000*

**The presence of the past.**
Rosenzweig, Roy. New York : Columbia University Press, c1998.
*TC E179.5 .R67 1998*

**PRESENILE DEMENTIA.** *See* **ALZHEIMER'S DISEASE.**

**PRESENILE DEMENTIA - DIAGNOSIS.**
Organic disorders [videorecording]. Princeton, N.J. : Films for the Humanities & Sciences, 1998.
*TC RC521 .O7 1998*

**PRESENILE DEMENTIA - PATIENTS.**
Organic disorders [videorecording]. Princeton, N.J. : Films for the Humanities & Sciences, 1998.
*TC RC521 .O7 1998*

**Presenting Tanya, the Ugly Duckling.**
Gauch, Patricia Lee. New York : Philomel Books, c1999.
*TC PZ7.G2315 Pr 1999*

**Presenting the past.**
Prager, Jeffrey, 1948- Cambridge, Mass. : Harvard University Press, 1998.
*TC BF175.4.C84 P73 1998*

**Presenting your findings.**
Nicol, Adelheid A. M. 1st ed. Washington, DC : American Psychological Association, c1999.
*TC HA31 .N53 1999*

**PRESENTS.** *See* **GIFTS.**

**PRESERVATION OF BOOKS.** *See* **BOOKS - CONSERVATION AND RESTORATION.**

**PRESERVICE TEACHERS.** *See* **STUDENT TEACHERS.**

**Preserving order amid chaos.**
Paige, John Rhodes. New York : Berghahn Books, 2000.
*TC LA1567 .P25 2000*

**PRESIDENTS, COLLEGE.** *See* **COLLEGE PRESIDENTS.**

**PRESS.** *See* **PERIODICALS; PUBLIC OPINION.**

**PRESS LAW.** *See* **PRIVACY, RIGHT OF.**

**PRESS PHOTOGRAPHY.** *See* **PHOTOJOURNALISM.**

**PRESTIGE.** *See* **SOCIAL STATUS.**

Preston, Tim. The lonely scarecrow / by Tim Preston ; illustrated by Maggie Kneen. 1st American ed. New York : Dutton Children's Books, 1999. 1 v. (unpaged) : col. ill. ; 22 cm. Embossed illustrations. SUMMARY: A lonely scarecrow with a scary face has trouble making friends with the animals who surround him, until a heavy snowfall transforms him into a jolly snowman. ISBN 0-525-46080-2 (hc) DDC [E]
*1. Scarecrows - Fiction. 2. Loneliness - Fiction. 3. Animals - Fiction. 4. Snowmen - Fiction. I. Kneen, Maggie, ill. II. Title.*
*TC PZ7.P9237 Lo 1999*

Prestoungrange, Gordon.
The virtual learning organization. London ; New York : Continuum, 2000.
*TC LC5215 .V574 2000*

**PRETTY-SHIELD (CROW INDIAN).**
Snell, Alma Hogan. Grandmother's grandchild. Lincoln : University of Nebraska Press, c2000.
*TC E99.C92 S656 2000*

**Prevatt, Frances F., 1955-.**
Casebook in family therapy. Belmont : Brooks/Cole, c1999.
*TC RC488.5 .C369 1999*

**Preventing classroom discipline problems.**
Seeman, Howard. 3rd ed. Lanham, Md. : Scarecrow Press, 2000.
*TC LB3013 .S44 2000*

**Preventing eating disorders :** a handbook of interventions and special challenges / edited by Niva Piran, Michael P. Levine, Catherine Steiner-Adair. Philadelphia, PA : Brunner/Mazel, c1999. xxii, 347 p. : ill. ; 26 cm. Includes bibliographical references and indexes. ISBN 0-87630-968-6 (alk. paper) DDC 618.92/8526
*1. Eating disorders - Prevention - Handbooks, manuals, etc. 2. Eating disorders in adolescence - Prevention - Handbooks, manuals, etc. 3. Eating disorders in children - Prevention - Handbooks, manuals, etc. I. Piran, Niva. II. Levine, Michael P. III. Steiner-Adair, Catherine.*
*TC RC552.E18 P744 1999*

**Preventing school failure.**
Lovitt, Thomas C. 2nd ed. Austin, Tex. : Pro-Ed. : c2000.
*TC LC146.6 .L68 2000*

**Preventing school injuries.**
Posner, Marc. New Brunswick, N.J. ; London : Rutgers University Press, c2000.
*TC LB2864.6.A25 P67 2000*

**Preventing student violence :** what schools can do / Kris Bosworth, editor. Bloomington, IN (P.O. Box 789, Bloomington 47402-0789) : Phi Delta Kappa International, c1999. 321 p. : ill. ; 28 cm. (Hot topics series ; [no. 17]) "June 1999" Includes bibliographical references. DDC 373.17/82/0973
*1. School violence - United States - Prevention. 2. Students - Crimes against - United States - Prevention. I. Bosworth, Kris. II. Series. III. Series: Hot topics series ; no. 17*
*TC LB3013.3 .P755 1999*

**Prevention in practice library**
Becker, Evvie. High-risk sexual behavior. New York : Plenum Press, c1998.
*TC HQ60.7.U6 B43 1998*

Promoting nonviolence in early adolescence. New York : Kluwer Academic/Plenum Publishers, c2000.
*TC HM1126 .P76 2000*

**PREVENTION OF DISEASE.** *See* **MEDICINE, PREVENTIVE.**

**PREVENTION OF DRUG ABUSE.** *See* **DRUG ABUSE - PREVENTION.**

**The prevention of eating disorders** / edited by Walter Vandereycken and Greta Noordenbos. New York : New York University Press, 1998. xii, 232 p. : ill. ; 23 cm. (Studies in eating disorders) Includes bibliographical references and index. ISBN 0-8147-8798-3 (cloth) ISBN 0-8147-8799-1 (pbk.) DDC 616.85/2605
*1. Eating disorders - Prevention. I. Vandereycken, Walter, 1949- II. Noordenbos, Greta. III. Series.*
*TC RC552.E18 P74 1998*

**PREVENTION OF INDUSTRIAL ACCIDENTS.** *See* **INDUSTRIAL SAFETY.**

**PREVENTION OF OCCUPATIONAL HAZARDS.** *See* **INDUSTRIAL SAFETY.**

**PREVENTION OF SUICIDE.** *See* **SUICIDE - PREVENTION.**

**Preventive approaches in couples therapy** / edited by Rony Berger, Mo Therese Hannah. Philadelphia : Brunner/Mazel, 1999. xxi, 442 p. ; 24 cm. Includes bibliographical references and index. ISBN 0-87630-876-0 (casebound) DDC 616.89/156
*1. Marital psychotherapy - Handbooks, manuals, etc. 2. Family psychotherapy - Handbooks, manuals, etc. 3. Marriage counseling - Handbooks, manuals, etc. I. Berger, Rony. II. Hannah, Mo Therese.*
*TC RC488.5 .P74 1999*

**PREVENTIVE HEALTH SERVICES.** *See* **HEALTH EDUCATION; HEALTH PROMOTION; MEDICINE, PREVENTIVE.**

**PREVENTIVE HEALTH SERVICES - AUSTRALIA - MARKETING.**
Health promotion strategies & methods. Rev. ed. Sydney ; New York : McGraw-Hill, c1999.
*TC RA427.8 .H527 1999*

**PREVENTIVE MEDICINE.** *See* **MEDICINE, PREVENTIVE.**

**PREVENTIVE MEDICINE.**
Handbook of health promotion and disease prevention. New York : Kluwer Academic/Plenum Publishers, c1999.
*TC RA427.8 .H36 1999*

**PREVENTIVE MEDICINE PHYSICIANS.** *See* **MEDICINE, PREVENTIVE.**

**Prezant, Fran.**
Marshak, Laura E. Disability and the family life cycle. New York : Basic Books, c1999.
*TC HV1568 .M277 1999*

**Price, Janet.**
Vital signs. Edinburgh : Edinburgh University Press, c1998.
*TC HQ1190 .V56 1998*

**The price of admission.**
Kane, Thomas J. Washington, D.C. : Brookings Institution Press ; New York : Russell Sage Foundation, c1999.
*TC LB2342 .K35 1999*

**Price, Richard H.**
Person-environment psychology. 2nd ed. Mahwah, N.J. : L. Erlbaum, 2000.
*TC BF353 .P43 2000*

**Price, Sylvia Anderson.**
Simms, Lillian M. (Lillian Margaret) The professional practice of nursing administration. 3rd ed. Albany, NY : Delmar Publishers, c2000.
*TC RT89 .S58 2000*

**Prickett, Jeanne Glidden.**
Hand in hand. New York : AFB Press, c1995.
*TC HV1597.2 .H342 1995*

**Pridmore, Pat, 1947-** Children as partners for health : a critical review of the child-to-child approach / Pat Pridmore and David Stephens. London ; New York : Zed Books ; New York : Distributed exclusively in the USA by St. Martin's Press, 2000. xii, 194 p. : ill. ; 22 cm. Includes bibliographical references (p. 176-187) and index. ISBN 1-85649-635-X ISBN 1-85649-636-8 (limp)
*1. School children - Health and hygiene - Case studies. 2. Health education - Case studies. I. Stephens, David. II. Title.*
*TC LB1587.A3 P75 2000*

**Prigger, Mary Skillings.** Aunt Minnie McGranahan / by Mary Skillings Prigger ; illustrated by Betsy Lewin. New York : Clarion Books, c1999. 31 p. : col. ill. ; 26 cm. SUMMARY: The townspeople in St. Clere, Kansas, are sure it will never work out when the neat and orderly spinster, Minnie McGranahan, takes her nine orphaned nieces and nephews into her home in 1920. ISBN 0-395-82270-X DDC [E]
*1. Orderliness - Fiction. 2. Aunts - Fiction. 3. Orphans - Fiction. I. Lewin, Betsy, ill. II. Title.*
*TC PZ7.P93534 Au 1999*

**The primacy of perception, and other essays on phenomenological psychology, the philosophy of art, history, and politics.**
Merleau-Ponty, Maurice, 1908-1961. [Evanston, Ill.] : Northwestern University Press, 1964.
*TC B2430.M378 E5 1964*

**PRIMARY CARE (MEDICINE).**
Handbook of psychological assessment in primary care settings. Mahwah, NJ : Lawrence Erlbaum Associates, Publishers, 2000.
*TC RC469 .H374 2000*

The practice of counselling in primary care. London ; Thousand Oaks, Calif. : SAGE Publications, 1999.
*TC R727.4 .P733 1999*

**PRIMARY CARE (MEDICINE) - RESEARCH - METHODOLOGY.**
Doing qualitative research. 2nd ed. Thousand Oaks, Calif. : Sage Publications, c1999
*TC R853.S64 D65 1999*

**The primary curriculum :** learning from international perspectives / edited by Janet Moyles and Linda Hargreaves, New York ; London : Routledge, 1998. 226 p. ; illus., ; 24 cm. Includes bibliographical references and index. ISBN 0-415-15832-X DDC 372.19
*1. Education, Elementary - Curricula - Cross-cultural studies. 2. Curriculum planning - Cross-cultural studies. 3. Curriculum change - Cross-cultural studies. I. Moyles, Janet R. II. Hargreaves, Linda.*
*TC LB1570 .P678 1998*

**Primary documents in American history and contemporary issues**
Stein, Laura W., 1963- Sexual harassment in America. Westport, Conn. : Greenwood Press, 1999.

*TC KF3467 .S74 1999*

**PRIMARY EDUCATION.** *See* **EDUCATION, PRIMARY.**

**PRIMARY EDUCATION (GREAT BRITAIN).** *See* **EDUCATION, ELEMENTARY.**

**Primary education, popular educator.**
The Grade teacher. Boston, Mass. : Educational Pub. Co., -c1972.

The Grade teacher. Boston, Mass. : Educational Pub. Co., -c1972.

**PRIMARY HEALTH CARE.**
The practice of counselling in primary care. London ; Thousand Oaks, Calif. : SAGE Publications, 1999.
*TC R727.4 .P733 1999*

**PRIMARY HEALTH CARE - UNITED STATES - HANDBOOKS.**
Pocket reference for Pediatric primary care. Philadelphia ; London : Saunders, c2001.
*TC RJ45 .P525 2001*

**PRIMARY MEDICAL CARE.** *See* **PRIMARY CARE (MEDICINE).**

**PRIMARY PREVENTION.**
Leutholtz, Brian C. Exercise and disease management. Boca Raton : CRC Press, c1999.
*TC RM725 .L45 1999*

Redman, Barbara Klug. Women's health needs in patient education. New York : Springer Pub. Co., c1999.
*TC R727.4 .R43 1999*

**PRIMARY READERS.** *See* **READERS (PRIMARY).**

**PRIMARY SCHOOL STUDENTS.** *See* **SCHOOL CHILDREN.**

**The primary triangle.**
Fivaz-Depeursinge, Elisabeth. New York : Basic Books, c1999.
*TC HQ755.85 .F583 1999*

**PRIMATES.** *See also* **MONKEYS.**
Oller, D. Kimbrough. The emergence of the speech capacity. Mahwah, N.J. : Lawrence Erlbaum Associates, 2000.
*TC P118 .O43 2000*

**Prime movers.**
Mazo, Joseph H. 2nd revised edition. Princeton, NJ. : Princeton Book Co. Pub., c2000.
*TC GV1783 .M347 2000*

**A primer for child psychotherapists.**
Siskind, Diana. Northvale, NJ : Jason Aronson, c1999.
*TC RJ504 .S543 1999*

**PRIMERS.** *See* **READERS (PRIMARY).**

**Primers for prudery :** sexual advice to Victorian America / edited by Ronald G. Walters. Updated ed. Baltimore : Johns Hopkins University Press, 2000. xv, 185 p. ; 21 cm. Includes bibliographical references and index. ISBN 0-8018-6348-1 (alk. paper) DDC 306.7/0973
*1. Sex customs - United States - History. 2. Sex instruction - United States - History. 3. Family - United States - History. 4. Sex Education - United States. 5. Sex - United States. 6. Family - United States. 7. United States - Moral conditions. I. Walters, Ronald G.*
*TC HQ18.U5 P75 2000*

**PRINCE GEORGE'S COUNTY (MD.) - BIOGRAPHY.**
Kohn, Howard. We had a dream. New York : Simon & Schuster, 1998.
*TC F187.P9 K64 1998*

**PRINCE GEORGE'S COUNTY (MD.) - RACE RELATIONS.**
Kohn, Howard. We had a dream. New York : Simon & Schuster, 1998.
*TC F187.P9 K64 1998*

**Prince, Russ Alan, 1958-** The seven faces of philanthropy : a new approach to cultivating major donors / Russ Alan Prince, Karen Maru File. 1st ed. San Francisco : Jossey-Bass, c1994. xvi, 219 p. : ill. ; 24 cm. (The Jossey-Bass nonprofit sector series) Includes bibliographical references (207-211) and index. ISBN 0-7879-0008-7 (acid-free paper) DDC 361.7/068/1
*1. Fund raising - United States. 2. Philanthropists - United States. I. File, Karen. II. Title. III. Series.*
*TC HV41.9.U5 P74 1994*

**Princess Ka'iulani.**
Linnea, Sharon. Grand Rapids, Mich. : Eerdmans Books for Young Readers, 1999.
*TC DU627.17.K3 L56 1999*

**Princess Sonora and the long sleep.**
Levine, Gail Carson. 1st ed. New York : HarperCollins Publishers, c1999.
*TC PZ8.L4793 Pq 1999*

**PRINCESSES - HAWAII - BIOGRAPHY - JUVENILE LITERATURE.**
Linnea, Sharon. Princess Ka'iulani. Grand Rapids, Mich. : Eerdmans Books for Young Readers, 1999.
*TC DU627.17.K3 L56 1999*

**Princeton Review cracking the GRE literature in English.**
Cracking the GRE literature in English subject test. New York : Random House, 1996-
*TC LB2367.4 .L58*

**Princeton Review (Firm).**
Cracking the GRE literature in English subject test. New York : Random House, 1996-
*TC LB2367.4 .L58*

**PRINCIPAL-TEACHER RELATIONSHIPS.** *See* **TEACHER-PRINCIPAL RELATIONSHIPS.**

**PRINCIPALS AND TEACHERS.** *See* **TEACHER-PRINCIPAL RELATIONSHIPS.**

**PRINCIPALS, ELEMENTARY SCHOOL.** *See* **ELEMENTARY SCHOOL PRINCIPALS.**

**PRINCIPALS, HIGH SCHOOL.** *See* **HIGH SCHOOL PRINCIPALS.**

**PRINCIPALS - ILLINOIS - CASE STUDIES.**
Lyman, Linda L. How do they know you care? New York : Teachers College Press, c2000.
*TC LB2831.924.I3 L96 2000*

**PRINCIPALS, MIDDLE SCHOOL.** *See* **MIDDLE SCHOOL PRINCIPALS.**

**Principals of dynamic schools.**
Rallis, Sharon F. 2nd ed. Thousand Oaks, Calif. : Corwin Press, c2000.
*TC LB2831.92 .G65 2000*

**PRINCIPALS, SCHOOL.** *See* **SCHOOL PRINCIPALS.**

**PRINCIPALS, SECONDARY SCHOOL.** *See* **HIGH SCHOOL PRINCIPALS.**

**PRINCIPALS, SENIOR HIGH SCHOOL.** *See* **HIGH SCHOOL PRINCIPALS.**

**The principalship.**
Drake, Thelbert L. 5th ed. Upper Saddle River, N.J. : Merrill, c1999.
*TC LB2831.92 .D73 1999*

Sergiovanni, Thomas J. 4th ed. Boston : Allyn & Bacon, c2001.
*TC LB2831.92 .S47 2001*

Speck, Marsha. Upper Saddle River, N.J. : Merrill, c1999.
*TC LB1738.5 .S64 1999*

**Principle & practice in applied linguistics :** studies in honour of H.G. Widdowson / editors, Guy Cook, Barbara Seidlhofer. Oxford : Oxford University Press, 1995. xi, 431 p. : ill. ; 24 cm. Principle and practice in applied linguistics. Includes bibliographical references and index. ISBN 0-19-442147-3 (cased) ISBN 0-19-442148-1 (pbk) DDC 418
*1. Widdowson, H. G. 2. Applied linguistics. I. Widdowson, H. G. II. Cook, Guy. III. Seidlhofer, Barbara. IV. Title: Principle and practice in applied linguistics*
*TC P129 .P75 1995*

**Principle and practice in applied linguistics.**
Principle & practice in applied linguistics. Oxford : Oxford University Press, 1995.
*TC P129 .P75 1995*

**Principles and applications of assessment in counseling.**
Whiston, Susan C., 1953- Australia ; U.S. : Brooks/Cole, c2000.
*TC BF637.C6 W467 2000*

**PRINCIPLES AND PARAMETERS (LINGUISTICS).**
Cook, V. J. (Vivian James), 1940- Chomsky's universal grammar. 2nd [updated] ed. Oxford, OX, UK ; Cambridge, Mass., USA : Blackwell Publishers, 1996.
*TC P85.C47 C66 1996*

Functional categories, argument structure and parametric variation. Edinburgh : Centre for Cognitive Study, University of Edinburgh, c1994.
*TC P151 .F86 1994*

**Principles and practice of behavioral assessment.**
Haynes, Stephen N. New York ; London : Kluwer Academic/Plenum, c2000.
*TC BF176.5 .H39 2000*

**Principles and standards for school mathematics.**
Reston, VA : National Council of Teachers of Mathematics, c2000. xv, 402 p. : ill. (some col.) ; 28 cm. Includes bibliographical references (p. 383-390). ISBN 0-87353-480-8 DDC 510/.71
*1. Mathematics - Study and teaching - United States - Standards. I. National Council of Teachers of Mathematics.*
*TC QA13 .P735 2000*

**Principles of classroom management.**
Levin, James, 1946- 3rd ed. Boston : Allyn and Bacon, c2000.
*TC LB3013 .L475 2000*

**Principles of cognition, language and action.**
Prætorius, Nini. Dordrecht, The Netherlands ; Boston [Mass., U.S.] : Kluwer Academic Publishers, c2000.
*TC BF38 .P67 2000*

**Principles of language learning and teaching.**
Brown, H. Douglas, 1941- 2nd ed. Englewood Cliffs, N.J. : Prentice-Hall, c1987.
*TC P51 .B775 1987*

**Principles of power.**
Brunner, C. Cryss. Albany, NY : State University of New York Press, c2000.
*TC LB2831.72 .B78 2000*

**Principles of professional fundraising.**
Mixer, Joseph R., 1923- 1st ed. San Francisco : Jossey-Bass, c1993.
*TC HV41.9.U5 M58 1993*

**Principles of psychophysiology.**
Handbook of psychophysiology. 2nd ed. Cambridge, UK ; New York, NY, USA : Cambridge University Press, 2000.
*TC QP360 .P7515 2000*

**Pringle, Sheila M.** Promoting the health of children : a guide for caretakers and health care professionals / Sheila M. Pringle, Brenda E. Ramsey. St. Louis : Mosby, 1982. xi, 275 p. : ill. ; 28 cm. Includes bibliographical references (p.258-265) and index. ISBN 0-8016-4048-2 (pbk.) DDC 613/.0432
*1. Children - Health and hygiene. 2. Child development. 3. Children - Diseases. 4. Pediatric nursing. 5. Pediatric nursing. I. Ramsey, Brenda E., 1928- II. Title.*
*TC RJ101 .P66 1982*

**PRINT FINISHING PROCESSES.** *See* **BOOKBINDING.**

**PRINT GALLERIES.** *See* **ART GALLERIES, COMMERCIAL.**

**PRINT MAKERS.** *See* **PRINTMAKERS.**

**PRINTED EPHEMERA - UNITED STATES - HISTORY.**
Fenn, Patricia. Rewards of merit. [Schoharie, N.Y.] : Ephemera Society of America ; Charlottesville [Va.] : Distributed by Howell Press, Inc., c1994.
*TC LA230 .F46 1994*

**PRINTING, EPHEMERAL.** *See* **PRINTED EPHEMERA.**

**PRINTING - GREAT BRITAIN - HISTORY - 17TH CENTURY.**
Wheale, Nigel. Writing and society. London ; New York : Routledge, 1999.
*TC PR438.P65 W75 1999*

**PRINTING - HISTORY.** *See* **VELLUM PRINTED BOOKS.**

**PRINTING - HISTORY - PERIODICALS.**
The East Asian library journal. Princeton, N.J. : Gest Library of Princeton University, c1994-
*TC Z733.G47 G46*

**PRINTING, PRACTICAL.** *See* **PRINTING.**

**PRINTMAKERS - AUSTRALIA - BIOGRAPHY - HISTORY AND CRITICISM.**
Grishin, Sasha. Australian printmaking in the 1990s. Sydney, NSW : Craftsman House : G+B Arts International, c1997.
*TC NE789.4 .G74 1997*

**PRINTMAKERS - UNITED STATES - INDEXES.**
Bryce, Betty Kelly, 1942- American printmakers, 1946-1996. Lanham, Md. : Scarecrow Press, 1999.
*TC NE508 .B76 1999*

**PRINTS.** *See* **ETCHING; LITHOGRAPHY.**

**PRINTS - 20TH CENTURY - AUSTRALIA - THEMES, MOTIVES.**
Grishin, Sasha. Australian printmaking in the 1990s.

Sydney, NSW : Craftsman House : G+B Arts International, c1997.
*TC NE789.4 .G74 1997*

**PRINTS - 20TH CENTURY - ENGLAND.**
Etching [videorecording]. Northbrook, Ill. ; Peasmarsh, East Sussex, Eng. : Roland Collection of Films on Art, c1990.
*TC NE2043 .E87 1990*

**PRINTS - 20TH CENTURY - GREAT BRITAIN.**
Screen printing [videorecording]. [Northbrook?], Ill. ; Peasmarsh, East Sussex, Eng. : Roland Collection of Films on Art, c1992.
*TC NE2238.G7 S4 1992*

**PRINTS - 20TH CENTURY - UNITED STATES - INDEXES.**
Bryce, Betty Kelly, 1942- American printmakers, 1946-1996. Lanham, Md. : Scarecrow Press, 1999.
*TC NE508 .B76 1999*

**PRINTS, AMERICAN - INDEXES.**
Bryce, Betty Kelly, 1942- American printmakers, 1946-1996. Lanham, Md. : Scarecrow Press, 1999.
*TC NE508 .B76 1999*

**PRINTS, AUSTRALIAN - NEW SOUTH WALES - SYDNEY - EXHIBITIONS.**
Art Gallery of New South Wales. Australian prints from the gallery's collection. Sydney : Art Gallery of New South Wales, c1998.
*TC NE789 .A77 1998*

**PRINTS, AUSTRALIAN - THEMES, MOTIVES.**
Grishin, Sasha. Australian printmaking in the 1990s. Sydney, NSW : Craftsman House : G+B Arts International, c1997.
*TC NE789.4 .G74 1997*

**PRINTS - GALLERIES AND MUSEUMS.** *See* **ART GALLERIES, COMMERCIAL.**

**PRINTS - TECHNIQUE.**
Etching [videorecording]. Northbrook, Ill. ; Peasmarsh, East Sussex, Eng. : Roland Collection of Films on Art, c1990.
*TC NE2043 .E87 1990*

Screen printing [videorecording]. [Northbrook?], Ill. ; Peasmarsh, East Sussex, Eng. : Roland Collection of Films on Art, c1992.
*TC NE2238.G7 S4 1992*

**Prior, Pauline.** Gender and mental health / Pauline M. Prior. New York : New York University Press, 1999. x, 198 p. ; 23 cm. Includes bibliographical references and indexes. ISBN 0-8147-6674-9 (hardcover : alk. paper) ISBN 0-8147-6675-7 (pbk. : alk. paper) DDC 616.89
*1. Mental illness - Sex factors. 2. Social psychiatry. 3. Mental health policy. 4. Mentally ill - Services for. 5. Mental illness - Sex factors. 6. Mentally ill women - Services for. I. Title.*
*TC RC455.4.S45 P75 1999*

**PRISON ALTERNATIVES.** *See* **ALTERNATIVES TO IMPRISONMENT.**

**PRISONERS OF WAR - DENMARK - BIOGRAPHY.**
Madsen, Benedicte, 1943- Survival in the organization. Aarhus [Denmark] ; Oakville, Conn. : Aarhus University Press, c1996.
*TC D805.G3 M24 1996*

**PRISONERS OF WAR - GERMANY - BIOGRAPHY.**
Madsen, Benedicte, 1943- Survival in the organization. Aarhus [Denmark] ; Oakville, Conn. : Aarhus University Press, c1996.
*TC D805.G3 M24 1996*

**PRISONS.** *See* **REFORMATORIES.**

**PRIVACY.**
Balancing the secrets of private disclosures. Mahwah, N.J. : Lawrence Erlbaum Associates, Publishers, 2000.
*TC BF697.5.S427 B35 2000*

**PRIVACY, RIGHT OF.** *See* **CONFIDENTIAL COMMUNICATIONS.**

**PRIVACY, RIGHT OF - UNITED STATES.**
Garfinkel, Simson. Database nation. 1st ed. Beijing ; Cambridge : O'Reilly, c2000.
*TC JC596.2.U5 G37 2000*

**PRIVATE ART COLLECTIONS.** *See* **ART - PRIVATE COLLECTIONS.**

**PRIVATE ART COLLECTIONS IN ART.** *See* **ART - PRIVATE COLLECTIONS.**

**PRIVATE COLLECTIONS OF ART.** *See* **ART - PRIVATE COLLECTIONS.**

**PRIVATE DUTY NURSING.**
American Nurses Association. Task Force on Staff Privileges. Guidelines for appointment of nurses for individual practice privileges in health care organizations. Kansas City, MO : American Nurses Association, Commission on Nursing Service, 1978.
*TC RT104 .A44 1978*

**PRIVATE FOUNDATIONS.** *See* **ENDOWMENTS.**

**The private life of the brain.**
Greenfield, Susan. New York : John Wiley, c2000.
*TC BF515 G74 2000*

**PRIVATE NONPROFIT SOCIAL WORK.** *See* **CHARITIES.**

**PRIVATE PRACTICE - STANDARDS.**
American Nurses Association. Task Force on Staff Privileges. Guidelines for appointment of nurses for individual practice privileges in health care organizations. Kansas City, MO : American Nurses Association, Commission on Nursing Service, 1978.
*TC RT104 .A44 1978*

**PRIVATE PREPARATORY SCHOOLS.** *See* **PREPARATORY SCHOOLS.**

**PRIVATE-PUBLIC PARTNERSHIPS.** *See* **PUBLIC-PRIVATE SECTOR COOPERATION.**

**PRIVATE-PUBLIC SECTOR COOPERATION.** *See* **PUBLIC-PRIVATE SECTOR COOPERATION.**

**PRIVATE RADIOTELEPHONE.** *See* **CITIZENS BAND RADIO.**

**PRIVATE SCHOOLS.** *See* **CHURCH SCHOOLS; PREPARATORY SCHOOLS.**

**PRIVATE SCHOOLS - DEVELOPING COUNTRIES - CASE STUDIES.**
Tooley, James. The global education industry. London : Institute of Economic Affairs ; Washington, DC : International Finance Corporation, World Bank, 1999.
*TC LC57.5 .T667 1999*

**PRIVATE SCHOOLS - DEVELOPING COUNTRIES - FINANCE - CASE STUDIES.**
Tooley, James. The global education industry. London : Institute of Economic Affairs ; Washington, DC : International Finance Corporation, World Bank, 1999.
*TC LC57.5 .T667 1999*

**PRIVATE SCHOOLS - LAW AND LEGISLATION - UNITED STATES.**
Mawdsley, Ralph D. Legal problems of religious and private schools. 4th ed. Dayton, OH : Education Law Association, c2000.
*TC KF4124.5 .M38 2000*

**PRIVATE SCHOOLS - UNITED STATES.**
Rufo-Lignos, Patricia Marie. Towards a new topology of public and private schools. 1999.
*TC 06 no. 11170*

Rufo-Lignos, Patricia Marie. Towards a new typology of public and private schools. 1999.
*TC 06 no. 11170*

**PRIVATE SCHOOLS - UNITED STATES - FACULTY.**
Orsini, Alfonso J. The color of excellence. 1999.
*TC 06 no. 11209*

**Private screenings.**
Simon, John Ivan. New York, Macmillan [1967]
*TC PN1995 .S495*

**PRIVATELY PRINTED BOOKS.** *See* **VELLUM PRINTED BOOKS.**

**PRIVATISATION.** *See* **PRIVATIZATION.**

**PRIVATIZATION - DEVELOPING COUNTRIES.**
Petkoski, Djordjija B. Learning together with clients. Washington, D.C. : World Bank, c1997.
*TC HQ4420.8.P48 1997*

**PRIVATIZATION IN EDUCATION.** *See also* **CHARTER SCHOOLS.**
Rufo-Lignos, Patricia Marie. Towards a new topology of public and private schools. 1999.
*TC 06 no. 11170*

Rufo-Lignos, Patricia Marie. Towards a new typology of public and private schools. 1999.
*TC 06 no. 11170*

Tooley, James. Reclaiming education. London ; New York : Cassell, 2000.

**TC LC71 .T65 2000**

**PRIVATIZATION IN EDUCATION - GREAT BRITAIN.**
Tooley, James. Reclaiming education. London ; New York : Cassell, 2000.
**TC LC71 .T65 2000**

**PRIVATIZATION IN EDUCATION - UNITED STATES.**
Education's big gamble [videorecording]. New York, NY : Merrow Report, c1997.
**TC LB2806.36 .E3 1997**

Good, Thomas L., 1943- The great school debate. Mahwah, N.J. : L. Erlbaum Associates, 2000.
**TC LB2806.36 .G66 2000**

Public charter schools : new choices in public education (May 3, 2000 : Washington, D.C.) Public charter schools [videorecording]. [Washington, D.C.] : U.S. Dept. of Education, [2000].
**TC LB2806.36 .P9 2000**

**PRIVATIZATION OF EDUCATION.** *See* **PRIVATIZATION IN EDUCATION.**

**PRIVATIZATION OF SCHOOLING.** *See* **PRIVATIZATION IN EDUCATION.**

**Privatizing government**
Restructuring education. Westport, Conn. : Praeger, 2000.
**TC LB2822.82 . R45 2000**

**PRIVILEGED COMMUNICATIONS (CONFIDENTIAL COMMUNICATIONS).** *See* **CONFIDENTIAL COMMUNICATIONS.**

**PROBABILITIES.** *See also* **MATHEMATICAL STATISTICS; RISK.**
Everitt, Brian. Chance rules. New York : Copernicus, c1999.
**TC QA273 .E84 1999**

Pearl, Judea. Causality. Cambridge ; New York : Cambridge University Press, 2000.
**TC BD541 .P43 2000**

Roeper, Peter. Probability theory and probability logic. Toronto ; Buffalo : University of Toronto Press, c1999.
**TC BC141 .R64 1999**

**PROBABILITIES - STUDY AND TEACHING (ELEMENTARY).**
Cuomo, Celia, 1956- In all probability. Berkeley, CA : Lawrence Hall of Science, University of California, Berkeley, c1998.
**TC QA276.18 .C866 1998**

**Probability theory and probability logic.**
Roeper, Peter. Toronto ; Buffalo : University of Toronto Press, c1999.
**TC BC141 .R64 1999**

**Probability theory and probability semantics.**
Roeper, Peter. Probability theory and probability logic. Toronto ; Buffalo : University of Toronto Press, c1999.
**TC BC141 .R64 1999**

**PROBATION, ACADEMIC.** *See* **COLLEGE ATTENDANCE.**

**PROBE Team (India).**
Public report on basic education in India. New Delhi ; Oxford : Oxford University Press, c1999.
**TC LA1151 .P83 1999**

**Problem analysis.**
Achilles, Charles M. Larchmont, NY : Eye on Education, c1997.
**TC LB2806 .A25 1997**

**PROBLEM-BASED LEARNING.**
Problem-based learning. Mahwah, N.J. : L. Erlbaum Associates, 2000.
**TC LB1027.42 .P78 2000**

Problem-based learning in higher education. Buckingham ; Philadelphia, PA : Society for Research into Higher Education : Open University Press, 2000.
**TC LB1027.42 .S28 2000**

Speck, Marsha. The principalship. Upper Saddle River, N.J. : Merrill, c1999.
**TC LB1738.5 .S64 1999**

**Problem-based learning :** a research perspective on learning interactions / edited by Dorothy H. Evensen, Cindy E. Hmelo. Mahwah, N.J. : L. Erlbaum Associates, 2000. xiii, 362 p. : ill. ; 24 cm. Includes bibliographical references and indexes. ISBN 0-8058-2644-0 (cloth : alk. paper) ISBN 0-8058-2645-9 (paper : alk. paper) DDC 371.39

1. Problem-based learning. 2. Learning - Research. I. Evensen, Dorothy H. II. Hmelo, Cindy E.
**TC LB1027.42 .P78 2000**

**Problem-based learning in higher education :** untold stories / Maggi Savin-Baden. Buckingham ; Philadelphia, PA : Society for Research into Higher Education : Open University Press, 2000. 161 p. : ill. ; 23 cm. Includes bibliographical references (p. [151]-156) and index. ISBN 0-335-20338-8 (hardbound) ISBN 0-335-20337-X (pbk.) DDC 378.1/7
1. Problem-based learning. 2. Education, Higher. 3. Adult learning. I. Title.
**TC LB1027.42 .S28 2000**

**PROBLEM-BASED LEARNING - UNITED STATES.**
Cunningham, William G. Educational administration. Boston ; London : Allyn & Bacon, c2000.
**TC LB1738.5 .C86 2000**

**PROBLEM CHILDREN.** *See* **BEHAVIOR DISORDERS IN CHILDREN.**

**PROBLEM CHILDREN - BEHAVIOR MODIFICATION.**
Ayers, Harry. Perspectives on behaviour. 2nd ed. London : David Fulton, 2000.
**TC LC4801 .A94 2000**

Sparzo, Frank J. The ABC's of behavior change. Bloomington, Ind., U.S.A. : Phi Delta Kappa Educational Foundation, c1999.
**TC LB1060.2 .S62 1999**

**PROBLEM CHILDREN - BEHAVIOR MODIFICATION - UNITED STATES.**
Behavioral management in the public schools. Westport, Conn. ; London : Praeger, 1999.
**TC LB1060.2 .B44 1999**

**PROBLEM CHILDREN - EDUCATION.** *See also* **TEACHERS OF PROBLEM CHILDREN.**
Ayers, Harry. Perspectives on behaviour. 2nd ed. London : David Fulton, 2000.
**TC LC4801 .A94 2000**

Monograph in behavioral disorders. Severe behavior disorders of children and youth. Reston, Va. : Council for Children with Behavioral Disorders, c1978-1986.
**TC BF721 .M65**

Powell, Richard R., 1951- Classrooms under the influence. Newbury Park, Calif. : Corwin Press, c1995.
**TC HV5824.Y68 P69 1995**

Preparing humanistic teachers for troubled children. Syracuse, N.Y. : Division of Special Education and Rehabilitation, Syracuse University, [1974?]
**TC LC4801 .P73**

**PROBLEM CHILDREN - EDUCATION - GREAT BRITAIN - CASE STUDIES.**
Phtiaka, Helen. Special kids for special treatment?, or, How special do you need to be to find yourself in a special school? London ; Washington, D.C. : Falmer Press, 1997.
**TC LC4803.G7 P58 1998**

**PROBLEM CHILDREN - EDUCATION - GREAT BRITAIN - MANAGEMENT.**
Hill, Fran, 1950- Teamwork in the management of emotional and behavioural difficulties. London : David Fulton, 2000.
**TC LC4803.G7 H54 2000**

**PROBLEM CHILDREN - EDUCATION (PRESCHOOL).**
Barnett, David W., 1946- Designing preschool interventions. New York : Guilford Press, 1999.
**TC LC4801 .B36 1999**

**PROBLEM CHILDREN - EDUCATION - UNITED STATES.**
Barr, Robert D. Hope fulfilled for at-risk and violent youth. 2nd ed. Boston ; London : Allyn and Bacon, c2001.
**TC LC4802 .B37 2001**

McEwan, Elaine K., 1941- Managing unmanageable students. Thousand Oaks, Calif. : Corwin Press, c2000.
**TC LC4801.5 .M39 2000**

Vallecorsa, Ada, 1948- Students with mild disabilities in general education settings. Upper Saddle River, N.J. : Merrill, c2000.
**TC LC4705 .V35 2000**

Williams, Thomas L., 1946- The directory of programs for students at risk. Larchmont, N.Y. : Eye on Education, c1999.

**TC LC4091 .W55 1999**

**PROBLEM CHILDREN - EDUCATION - UNITED STATES - CASE STUDIES.**
Murphy, John J. (John Joseph), 1955- Brief intervention for school problems. New York : Guilford Press, c1997.
**TC LC4802 .M87 1997**

**PROBLEM CHILDREN - INSTITUTIONAL CARE.**
Residential education as an option for at-risk youth. New York : Haworth Press, c1996.
**TC HV862 .R473 1996**

**PROBLEM CHILDREN - INSTITUTIONAL CARE - IRELAND - HISTORY.**
Raftery, Mary. Suffer the little children. Dublin, Ireland : New Island, 1999.
**TC HV9148.A5 R33 1999**

**PROBLEM CHILDREN - SERVICES FOR - UNITED STATES.**
Kampwirth, Thomas J. Collaborative consultation in the schools. Upper Saddle River, N.J. : Merrill, c1999.
**TC LB1027.5 .K285 1999**

**PROBLEM CHILDREN - SERVICES FOR - UNITED STATES - CASE STUDIES.**
Murphy, John J. (John Joseph), 1955- Brief intervention for school problems. New York : Guilford Press, c1997.
**TC LC4802 .M87 1997**

**PROBLEM CHILDREN, TEACHERS OF.** *See* **TEACHERS OF PROBLEM CHILDREN.**

**PROBLEM CHILDREN - UNITED STATES - HISTORY - 20TH CENTURY.**
Jones, Kathleen W. Taming the troublesome child. Cambridge, Mass : Harvard University Press, 1999.
**TC RJ501.A2 J64 1999**

**PROBLEM DRINKERS.** *See* **ALCOHOLICS.**

**PROBLEM FAMILIES.**
Walsh, Froma. Strengthening family resilience. New York : Guilford Press, c1998.
**TC RC489.F33 W34 1998**

**PROBLEM FAMILIES - COUNSELING OF.** *See* **FAMILY COUNSELING.**

**PROBLEM FAMILIES - PSYCHOLOGICAL ASPECTS.**
Powell, Richard R., 1951- Classrooms under the influence. Newbury Park, Calif. : Corwin Press, c1995.
**TC HV5824.Y68 P69 1995**

**PROBLEM FAMILIES - UNITED STATES.**
Whitbeck, Les B. Nowhere to grow. New York : Aldine de Gruyter, 1999.
**TC HV4505 .W43 1999**

**PROBLEM FAMILY.** *See* **PROBLEM FAMILIES.**

**PROBLEM SOLVING.** *See also* **CONFLICT MANAGEMENT; GROUP PROBLEM SOLVING; PROBLEM-BASED LEARNING.**
Achilles, Charles M. Problem analysis. Larchmont, NY : Eye on Education, c1997.
**TC LB2806 .A25 1997**

Billstein, Rick. A problem solving approach to mathematics for elementary school teachers. 5th ed. Reading, Mass. : Addison-Wesley, c1993.
**TC QA135.5 .B49 1993**

Denton, D. Keith. The toolbox for the mind. Milwaukee, WI : ASQ Quality Press, c1999.
**TC HD53 .D46 1999**

Dombroski, Ann P. Administrative problem solving. 1999.
**TC 06 no. 11104**

Dombroski, Ann P. Administrative problem solving. 1999.
**TC 06 no. 11104**

Kepner, Charles Higgins, 1922- The new rational manager. Princeton, N.J. (P.O. Box 704, Research Rd., Princeton 08540) : Princeton Research Press, c1981.
**TC HD31 .K456 1981**

Mayer, Bernard S., 1946- The dynamics of conflict resolution. 1st ed. San Francisco : Jossey-Bass Publishers, c2000.
**TC BF637.148 M39 2000**

Sweeney, Jim, 1937- Judgment. Larchmont, NY : Eye on Education, c1997.

*TC LB2806 .S88 1997*

Tillett, Gregory, Ph. D. Resolving conflict :. 2nd ed. Oxford ; New York : Oxford University Press, 1999.
*TC HM132 .T55 1999*

**Problem solving & comprehension.**
Whimbey, Arthur. Problem solving and comprehension. 6th ed. Mahwah, N.J. : Lawrence Erlbaum Associates, 1999.
*TC BF449 .W45 1999*

**A problem solving approach to mathematics for elementary school teachers.**
Billstein, Rick. 5th ed. Reading, Mass. : Addison-Wesley, c1993.
*TC QA135.5 .B49 1993*

**PROBLEM SOLVING, GROUP.** *See* **GROUP PROBLEM SOLVING.**

**PROBLEM SOLVING IN CHILDREN.**
Goodman, Jan M. Group solutions : : [Teacher's guide]. Rev. Berkeley, Calif. : Lawrence Hall of Science, University of California, 1997, c1992.
*TC QA8.7 .G5 1997*

**PROBLEM SOLVING - NURSES' INSTRUCTION.**
Rubenfeld, M. Gaie. Critical thinking in nursing. 2nd ed. Philadelphia : Lippincott, c1999.
*TC RT84.5 .R83 1999*

**PROBLEM SOLVING - PROBLEMS, EXERCISES, ETC.**
Whimbey, Arthur. Problem solving and comprehension. 6th ed. Mahwah, N.J. : Lawrence Erlbaum Associates, 1999.
*TC BF449 .W45 1999*

**PROBLEM SOLVING - STUDY AND TEACHING.**
Feldberg, Suzanne. A comparison of different types of mathematical problem-solving hints selected by concrete and formal operational subjects in a hypercard environment. 1998.
*TC 085 F316*

**PROBLEM SOLVING - STUDY AND TEACHING (ELEMENTARY).**
O'Connell, Susan. Introduction to problem solving. Portsmouth, NH : Heinemann, c2000.
*TC QA63 .O36 2000*

**PROBLEM SOLVING - STUDY AND TEACHING (MIDDLE SCHOOL) - NEW YORK (STATE) - CASE STUDIES.**
Carr, Richard John. The application of multimedia in arts-integrated curricula. 1998.
*TC 06 no. 10919*

**PROBLEM YOUTH - BEHAVIOR MODIFICATION.**
Sparzo, Frank J. The ABC's of behavior change. Bloomington, Ind., U.S.A. : Phi Delta Kappa Educational Foundation, c1999.
*TC LB1060.2 .S62 1999*

**PROBLEM YOUTH - COUNSELING OF.**
Bertolino, Bob. 1965- Therapy with troubled teenagers. New York : Wiley, c1999.
*TC RJ506.P63 B475 1999*

**PROBLEM YOUTH - EDUCATION - UNITED STATES.**
Barr, Robert D. Hope fulfilled for at-risk and violent youth. 2nd ed. Boston ; London : Allyn and Bacon, c2001.
*TC LC4802 .B37 2001*

**PROBLEM YOUTH - EDUCATION - UNITED STATES - CASE STUDIES.**
Goodman, Greg S., 1949- Alternatives in education. New York : P. Lang, c1999.
*TC LC46.4 .G66 1999*

**PROBLEM YOUTH - INSTITUTIONAL CARE.**
Residential education as an option for at-risk youth. New York : Haworth Press, c1996.
*TC HV862 .R473 1996*

**PROBLEM YOUTH - INSTITUTIONAL CARE - IRELAND - HISTORY.**
Raftery, Mary. Suffer the little children. Dublin, Ireland : New Island, 1999.
*TC HV9148.A5 R33 1999*

**PROBLEM YOUTH - LONGITUDINAL STUDIES.**
Smith, Mieko Kotake. Adolescents with emotional and behavioral disabilities. Lewiston, NY : E. Mellen Press, c1998.
*TC RJ503 .S63 1998*

**PROBLEM YOUTH - REHABILITATION.**
Davis, Daniel Leifeld. The aggressive adolescent. New York : Haworth Press, 1999.

*TC RJ506.V56 D38 1999*

**PROBLEM YOUTH - UNITED STATES - HISTORY - 20TH CENTURY.**
Jones, Kathleen W. Taming the troublesome child. Cambridge, Mass : Harvard University Press, 1999.
*TC RJ501.A2 J64 1999*

**Problems and issues of diversity in the United States /**
edited by Larry L. Naylor. Westport, Conn. : Bergin & Garvey, 1999. xi, 215 p. ; 25 cm. Includes bibliographical references (p. [187]-197) and index. ISBN 0-89789-615-7 (alk. paper) ISBN 0-89789-616-5 (pbk. : alk. paper) DDC 305.8/ 00973
*1. Pluralism (Social sciences) - United States. 2. United States - Race relations. 3. United States - Ethnic relations. I. Naylor, Larry L.*
*TC E184.A1 P76 1999*

**Problems and prospects in European education /**
edited by Elizabeth Sherman Swing, Jürgen Schriewer, and François Orivel. Westport, Conn. : Praeger, 2000. viii, 287 p. ; ill ; 25 cm. Includes bibliographical references and index. ISBN 0-275-95202-9 (alk. paper) DDC 370/.94
*1. Education - Social aspects - Europe. 2. Education - Economic aspects - Europe. I. Swing, Elizabeth Sherman. II. Schriewer, Jürgen. III. Orivel, François.*
*TC LC191.8. E85 P86 2000*

**Problems and solutions in human assessment :**
honoring Douglas N. Jackson at seventy / edited by Richard D. Goffin, Edward Helmes. Boston : Kluwer Academic Publishers, c2000. xxiv, 357 p. : ill. ; 24 cm. Includes bibliographical references and index. ISBN 0-7923-7768-0 (alk. paper) DDC 155.2/8
*1. Personality assessment. I. Jackson, Douglas Northrop, 1929- II. Goffin, Richard D., 1956- III. Helmes, Edward, 1949-*
*TC BF698.4 .P666 2000*

**PROBOSCIDEA.** *See* **ELEPHANTS.**

**The proceedings of the twenty-ninth Annual Child Language Research Forum.**
Child Language Research Forum (29th : 1997 : Stanford University) [Stanford] : Published for the Stanford Linguistics Association by the Center for the Study of Language and Information, c1998.
*TC P118 .C4558 1997*

**The process of group psychotherapy :** systems for analyzing change / edited by Ariadne P. Beck and Carol M. Lewis. Washington, DC : American Psychological Association, c2000. xx, 494 p. : ill. ; 26 cm. Includes bibliographical references and index. ISBN 1-55798-658-4 (alk. paper)
*1. Group psychotherapy. 2. Psychotherapy, Group. 3. Group Processes. I. Beck, Ariadne P. II. Lewis, Carol M. III. American Psychological Association.*
*TC RC488 .P75 2000*

**Processes of transition in education systems /** edited by Elizabeth A. McLeish & David Phillips. Wallingford : Symposium, 1998. 102 p. : ill. ; 24 cm. (Oxford studies in comparative education, 0961-2149 ; v. 8, no. 2) Includes bibliographical references. ISBN 1-87392-748-7 DDC 371
*1. Education and state. I. McLeish, Elizabeth A. II. Phillips, David, 1944 Dec. 15- III. Series: Oxford studies in comparative education v. 8, no. 2.*
*TC LC71 .P7 1998*

**PROCESSING (LIBRARIES).** *See* **CATALOGING.**

**Processing the signal** [videorecording] / conceived, produced and directed by Marcello Dantas ; co-produced by Arena Cultural Center. Cicero, Ill. : Roland Collection of Films on Art, c1989. 1 videocassette (38 min.) : sd., col. ; 1/2 in. At head of title: Anthony Roland Collection of Films on Art. VHS, NTSC. Cataloged from credits, cassette label and container. Place of distribution from cassette label; addresses for the Roland Collection on container: Peasmarsh, East Sussex and Ho-Ho-Kus, NJ. Participants: Peer Bode, Paul Garrin, Kit Fitgerald, John Hanhardt, Nam June Paik, Marie Perillo, Zbigniew Rybczynski, John Sanborn, Ira Schneider, Bill Viola, Reynold Weidenaar, Dean Winkler. Director of photography, Olivier Pfeiffer; sound, Ken D'Oronzio. Awards: Line Golden Eagle, Washington, DC, Best Video on Art, New York, Best Video, Paris, Best Production, Brazil. On spine of container and cassette case: "618". Age 11 to adult. SUMMARY: "A documentary made in America in 1988 and 1989 that brings together some of the most innovatory artists of video art-- Bill Viola, Nam June Paik, Kit Fitzgerald, Paul Garrin, John Sanborn, Mary Perillo and Zbigniew Rybczynski among others. Covering video installations, 'satellite art', video performance and the penetration of video art into conventional television, Processing the Signal is a discussion about these artists' ideas and opinions."--Container.
*1. Video art. 2. Documentary films. I. Dantas, Marcello. II. Bode, Peer. III. Garrin, Paul IV. Fitzgrald Kit. V. Hanhardt,*

*John G. VI. Paik, Nam June, 1932- VII. Perillo, Marie. VIII. Rybczynski, Zbigniew. IX. Sanborn, John X. Schneider, Ira. XI. Viola, Bill, 1951- XII. Weidenaar, Reynold, 1945- XIII. Winkler, Dean. XIV. Anthony Roland Collection of Film on Art. XV. Arena Cultural Center (Rio de Janeiro, Brazil) XVI. Title: Anthony Roland Collection of Films on Art*
*TC N6494.V53 P7 1989*

**PROCESSIONS.** *See* **FESTIVALS; PAGEANTS.**

Prochner, Lawrence.
Early childhood care and education in Canada. Vancouver : UBC Press, c2000.
*TC LB1139.3.C2 E27 2000*

**Proctor, Brigid.** Group supervision : a guide to creative practice / Brigid Proctor. London ; Thousand Oaks : SAGE Publications, 2000. viii, 222 p. : ill. ; 23 cm. (Counselling supervision) Includes bibliographical references and index. ISBN 0-7619-5978-5 ISBN 0-7619-5979-3 (pbk.)
*1. Counselors - Supervision of. 2. Psychotherapists - Supervision of. I. Title. II. Series.*
*TC BF637.C6 P95176 2000*

**Proctor, Robert E., 1945-** Defining the humanities : how rediscovering a tradition can improve our schools : with a curriculum for today's students / Robert E. Proctor. 2nd ed. Bloomington : Indiana University Press, c1998. xxviii, 239 p. ; 25 cm. Rev. ed. of: Education's great amnesia. c1988. Includes bibliographical references (p. 222-230) and index. ISBN 0-253-33421-7 (cloth : alk. paper) ISBN 0-253-21219-7 (pbk. : alk. paper) DDC 001.3/09
*1. Learning and scholarship - History. 2. Humanities - Study and teaching - United States. 3. Education, Humanistic - United States. I. Proctor, Robert E., 1945- Education's great amnesia. II. Title.*
*TC AZ221 .P75 1998*

**Education's great amnesia.**
Proctor, Robert E., 1945- Defining the humanities. 2nd ed. Bloomington : Indiana University Press, c1998.
*TC AZ221 .P75 1998*

**Proctor, Robert W.**
Capaldi, E. John. Contextualism in psychological research? Thousand Oaks, Calif. : Sage, c1999.
*TC BF315.2 .C37 1999*

**PRODIGIES, CHILD.** *See* **GIFTED CHILDREN.**

**PRODIGIES (PERSONS).** *See* **GIFTED PERSONS.**

**PRODUCE TRADE.** *See* **FOOD SUPPLY.**

**PRODUCE TRADE - LAW AND LEGISLATION.** *See* **FOOD LAW AND LEGISLATION.**

**PRODUCERS, MOTION PICTURE.** *See* **MOTION PICTURE PRODUCERS AND DIRECTORS.**

**PRODUCT MANAGEMENT.**
Denton, D. Keith. The toolbox for the mind. Milwaukee, WI : ASQ Quality Press, c1999.
*TC HD53 .D46 1999*

**PRODUCTION ECONOMICS, AGRICULTURAL.** *See* **AGRICULTURE - ECONOMIC ASPECTS.**

**PRODUCTIVITY, EDUCATIONAL.** *See* **EDUCATIONAL PRODUCTIVITY.**

**Proett, Jackie, 1926-** The writing process in action : a handbook for teachers / Jackie Proett, Kent Gill. Urbana, Ill. : National Council of Teachers of English, c1986. vii, 59 p. : ill. ; 28 cm. Bibliography: p. 59. ISBN 0-8141-5872-2 (pbk.) DDC 428/.007/12
*1. English language - Study and teaching (Secondary) - United States. 2. English language - United States - Composition and exercises. 3. Report writing - Study and teaching (Secondary) I. Gill, Kent, 1928- II. Title.*
*TC LB1631 .P697 1986*

**Professional burnout :** recent developments in theory and research / edited by Wilmar B. Schaufeli, Christina Maslach, Tadeusz Marek. Washington, DC : Taylor & Francis, c1993. xii, 299 p. : ill. ; 24 cm. (Series in applied psychology ; 1048-8146) Includes bibliographical references (p. 261-292) and index. ISBN 1-56032-262-4 (alk. paper) DDC 158.7
*1. Burn out (Psychology) 2. Job stress. 3. Stress (Psychology) 4. Burnout, Professional - congresses. I. Schaufeli, Wilmar, 1953- II. Maslach, Christina. III. Marek, Tadeusz. IV. Series: Series in applied psychology (New York, N.Y.)*
*TC BF481 .P77 1993*

**Professional counseling :** transitioning into the next millennium / edited, authored by Charlotte G. Dixon and William G. Emener. Springfield, Ill. : C.C. Thomas, Publishers, c1999. xvi, 178 p. ; 26 cm. Includes bibliographical references and indexes. ISBN 0-398-06985-9 (cloth) ISBN 0-398-06986-7 (paper) DDC 158/.3
*1. Counseling. I. Dixon, Charlotte G. II. Emener, William G. (William George)*

*TC BF637.C6 D56 1999*

**Professional development guide for educators** /
editors, Paul Gorski, Gene-Tey Shin, and Martha
Green. Washington, D.C. : National Education
Association of the United States, 2000. 134 p. ; 23 cm.
(The multicultural resource series ; v. 1) Includes
bibliographical references. DDC 370.117/0973
*1. Multicultural education - United States. 2. Teachers - United
States - Case studies. I. Shin, Gene-Tey. II. Gorski, Paul. III.
Green, Martha. IV. National Education Association of the
United States. V. Series.*
*TC LC1099.3 .P755 1999*

**Professional development opportunities in Turkish
schools.**
Seferoglu, Süleyman Sadi. Elementary school teacher
development. 1996.
*TC 06 no. 10693*

**A professional development school partnership.**
Campoy, Renee W. Westport, Conn. : Bergin &
Garvey, 2000.
*TC LB2154.A3 C36 2000*

**PROFESSIONAL DEVELOPMENT SCHOOLS.**
*See* **LABORATORY SCHOOLS.**

**Professional development series for elementary and
middle school math and science teachers
[videorecording].**
The Internet in action for math & science K-6
[videorecording]. [New York] : Thirteen-WNET ;
[Alexandria, Va. : distributed by] PBS Video, c1998.
*TC LB1044.87 .I45 1998*

**Professional development series for middle and high
school math and science teachers [videorecording].**
The Internet in action for math & science 7-12
[videorecording]. [New York] : Thirteen-WNET ;
[Alexandria, Va. : distributed by] PBS Video, c1997.
*TC LB1044.87 .I453 1997*

**PROFESSIONAL EDUCATION.** *See also*
**MEDICAL EDUCATION; TECHNICAL
EDUCATION.**
Business education and training. Lanham, Md. :
University Press of America, c1997-<c2000 >
*TC LC1059 .B87*

Charting a course for continuing professional
education :. San Francisco : Jossey-Bass, c2000.
*TC LC1072.C56 C55 2000*

**PROFESSIONAL EDUCATION - GREAT
BRITAIN.**
Bennett, Neville. Skills development in higher
education and employment. Buckingham [England] ;
Philadelphia : Society for Research into Higher
Education & Open University Press, 2000.
*TC LB1027.47 .B46 2000*

**PROFESSIONAL EDUCATION OF WOMEN.** *See*
**WOMEN - EDUCATION (HIGHER).**

**PROFESSIONAL EDUCATION - UNITED
STATES.**
Schmidt, Jeff, 1946- Disciplined minds. Lanham,
Md. : Oxford : Rowman & Littlefield, c2000.
*TC HT687 .S35 2000*

**PROFESSIONAL EMPLOYEES.** *See*
**BUSINESSPEOPLE; HUMAN SERVICES
PERSONNEL; MEDICAL PERSONNEL.**

**PROFESSIONAL EMPLOYEES - TRAINING OF.**
Business education and training. Lanham, Md. :
University Press of America, c1997-<c2000 >
*TC LC1059 .B87*

Skiba, Michaeline. A naturalistic inquiry of the
relationship between organizational change and
informal learning in the workplace. 1999.
*TC 06 no. 11180*

**PROFESSIONAL ETHICS.** *See also* **BUSINESS
ETHICS; CONFIDENTIAL
COMMUNICATIONS; MEDICAL ETHICS;
NURSING ETHICS.**
Carr, David, 1944- Professionalism and ethics in
teaching. London ; New York : Routledge, 2000.
*TC LB1779 .C37 2000*

Davis, Michael, 1943- Ethics and the university.
London ; New York : Routledge, 1999.
*TC LB2324 .D38 1999*

Ethics and community in the health care professions.
London ; New York : Routledge, 1999.
*TC R725.5 .E87 1999*

**PROFESSIONAL ETHICS.**
Ethics and community in the health care professions.
London ; New York : Routledge, 1999.

*TC R725.5 .E87 1999*

**Professional growth of two multidisciplinary teams
within a professional development school.**
Rutter, Alison Lee. 1999.
*TC 06 no. 11171*

**Professional growth series**
Bucher, Katherine Toth, 1947- Information
technology for schools. 2nd ed. Worthington, Ohio :
Linworth Pub., c1998.
*TC Z675.S3 B773 1998*

Littlejohn, Carol. Keep talking that book!.
Worthington, Ohio : Linworth Pub., 2000.
*TC Z716.3 .L58 2000*

Littlejohn, Carol. Talk that book! booktalks to
promote reading. Worthington, Ohio : Linworth
Publishing, 1999.
*TC Z1037.A2 L58 1999*

**Professional issues for teachers and student
teachers** / edited by Mike Cole. London : David
Fulton, 1999. xii, 116 p. ; 26 cm. Includes bibliographical
references and index. ISBN 1-85346-581-X
*1. Teachers - Great Britain. 2. Student teachers - Great
Britain. I. Cole, Mike, 1946-*
*TC LB1775.4.G7 P73 1999*

**Professional issues in speech-language pathology and
audiology.**
Silverman, Franklin H., 1933- Boston : Allyn and
Bacon, c1999.
*TC RC428.5 .S55 1999*

**PROFESSIONAL LABORATORY EXPERIENCES
(EDUCATION).** *See* **STUDENT TEACHING.**

**PROFESSIONAL LIABILITY.** *See*
**MALPRACTICE.**

**The professional practice of nursing administration.**
Simms, Lillian M. (Lillian Margaret) 3rd ed. Albany,
NY : Delmar Publishers, c2000.
*TC RT89 .S58 2000*

**The professional practices in adult education and
human resource development series**
Whitson, Donna L. Accessing information in a
technological age. Original ed. Malabar, Fla. : Krieger
Pub. Co., 1997.
*TC ZA3075 .W48 1997*

**PROFESSIONAL SECRETS.** *See* **CONFIDENTIAL
COMMUNICATIONS.**

**PROFESSIONAL SERVICES.** *See* **PROFESSIONS.**

**PROFESSIONAL SOCIALIZATION - UNITED
STATES.**
Boice, Robert. Advice for new faculty members.
Boston : London : Allyn and Bacon, c2000.
*TC LB1778.2 .B63 2000*

**The professional vocalist.**
Lebon, Rachel L., 1951- Lanham, Md. : Scarecrow
Press, 1999.
*TC MT855 .L43 1999*

**Professionalism and ethics in teaching.**
Carr, David, 1944- London ; New York : Routledge,
2000.
*TC LB1779 .C37 2000*

**Professionalism and marketing in photographic
communication [videorecording].**
The power of idea : [videorecording]. Minneapolis,
Minn. : Media Loft, c1992.
*TC TR690 .P5 1992*

**Professionalism and marketing in photography
[videorecording].**
The power of idea : [videorecording]. Minneapolis,
Minn. : Media Loft, c1992.
*TC TR690 .P5 1992*

**Professionalism, boundaries, and the workplace** /
edited by Nigel Malin. New York : Routledge, 2000.
x, 271 p. : ill. ; 24 cm. A collection of 15 chapters by university
contributors. Includes bibliographical references and index.
ISBN 0-415-19262-5 ISBN 0-415-19263-3 (pbk.) DDC
361.3/2/0941
*1. Social workers - Great Britain. 2. Social workers -
Professional ethics - Great Britain. 3. Social service - Great
Britain. 4. Human services personnel - Professional ethics -
Great Britain. 5. Medical personnel - Professional ethics -
Great Britain. 6. Counselors - Professional ethics - Great
Britain. 7. Counseling - Great Britain. I. Malin, Nigel.*
*TC HV10.5 .P74 2000*

**PROFESSIONALS.** *See* **PROFESSIONAL
EMPLOYEES.**

**PROFESSIONS.** *See* **ENGINEERS;
INTERPROFESSIONAL RELATIONS;
PROFESSIONAL SOCIALIZATION;
SCIENTISTS; VOCATIONAL GUIDANCE;
WOMEN IN THE PROFESSIONS.**

**PROFESSIONS - SOCIAL ASPECTS - UNITED
STATES.**
Schmidt, Jeff, 1946- Disciplined minds. Lanham,
Md. ; Oxford : Rowman & Littlefield, c2000.
*TC HT687 .S35 2000*

**PROFESSIONS - TORT LIABILITY.** *See*
**MALPRACTICE.**

**PROFESSORS.** *See* **COLLEGE TEACHERS.**

**PROFESSORS OF EDUCATION.** *See* **TEACHER
EDUCATORS.**

**PROFESSORS OF TEACHING.** *See* **TEACHER
EDUCATORS.**

**Professors who believe :** the spiritual journeys of
Christian faculty / edited by Paul M. Anderson.
Downers Grove, Ill. : InterVarsity Press, c1998. 238
p. ; 23 cm. Includes bibliographical references. ISBN
0-8308-1599-6 (paper : alk. paper) DDC 270/.088/372
*1. Christian biography - United States. 2. Christian college
teachers - United States - Biography. I. Anderson, Paul M.,
1938-*
*TC BR569 .P76 1998*

**PROFICIENCY.** *See* **ABILITY.**

**PROFIT.** *See* **CAPITALISM; RISK.**

**PROGNOSIS OF SCHOLASTIC SUCCESS.** *See*
**PREDICTION OF SCHOLASTIC SUCCESS.**

**PROGRAM EVALUATION IN EDUCATION.** *See*
**EDUCATIONAL EVALUATION.**

**PROGRAM EVALUATION - METHODS.**
Evaluating health promotion. Oxford ; New York :
Oxford University Press, 2000.
*TC RA427.8 .E95 2000*

**PROGRAM FOR INTERNATIONAL STUDENT
ASSESSMENT.**
Organisation for Economic Co-operation and
Development (Paris) Measuring student knowledge
and skills. Paris : Organisation for Economic Co-
operation and Development, 2000.
*TC LB3051 .M44 2000*

**PROGRAMED INSTRUCTION.** *See*
**PROGRAMMED INSTRUCTION.**

**PROGRAMME D'ÉTUDES - ÉVALUATION.**
Werner, Walter. Collaborative assessment of school-
based projects. Vancouver : Pacific Educational Press,
c1991.
*TC LB2822.8 .W47 1991*

**PROGRAMME FOR INTERNATIONAL
STUDENT ASSESSMENT.**
Measuring student knowledge and skills. Paris :
Organisation for Economic Co-operation and
Development, c1999.
*TC LB3051 .M43 1999*

**Programme on Educational Building.** Strategic asset
management for tertiary institutions. Paris :
Organisation for Economic Co-operation and
Development, c1999. 71 p. : ill. ; 28 cm. (PEB papers)
Includes bibliographical references. Published in French under
the title: La gestion stratégique des établissements
d'enseignement supérieur. "Based on the proceedings of a
two-day international workshop organised under the auspices
of the OECD Programmes on Educational Building (PEB) and
on Institutional Management in Higher Education (IMHE) for
institutional and system managers responsible for infrastructure
investment and management ... July 1998 in Sydney,
Australia" --p. 5. Other editions available: La gestion
stratégique des biens en capital des établissements
d'enseignement supérieur 9264270140 fre. ISBN 92-64-
17014-6 DDC 330
*1. College facilities - Management - Congresses. I. Title. II.
Title: La gestion stratégique des biens en capital des
établissements d'enseignement supérieur fre III. Series.*
*TC LB3223 .P76 1999*

**Programme on Institutional Management in Higher
Education.**
The response of higher education institutions to
regional needs. Paris : Organisation for Economic
Co-operation and Development, 1999.
*TC LC237 .R47 1999*

**Programme on the International Rights of the Child
(Series)**
Children's rights and traditional values. Aldershot ;
Brookfield, USA : Ashgate/Dartmouth, c1998.

*TC K639 .A55 1998*

**PROGRAMMED INSTRUCTION.** *See*
**COMPUTER-ASSISTED INSTRUCTION.**

**PROGRAMMED INSTRUCTION -**
**PERIODICALS.**
Improving human performance. Washington, National
Society for Performance and Instruction [etc.]

**A programmed introduction to research.**
Levine, Samuel, 1927- Belmont, Calif., Wadsworth
Pub. Co. [1968]
*TC BF76.5 .L44*

**PROGRAMMED LEARNING.** *See*
**PROGRAMMED INSTRUCTION.**

**PROGRAMMED TEXTBOOKS.** *See*
**PROGRAMMED INSTRUCTION.**

**PROGRAMMING (ELECTRONIC COMPUTERS).**
*See* **COMPUTER SOFTWARE.**

**PROGRAMS, ACADEMIC.** *See* **DISSERTATIONS,**
**ACADEMIC.**

**PROGRAMS, APPRENTICESHIP.** *See*
**APPRENTICESHIP PROGRAMS.**

**PROGRAMS, COLLEGE STUDENT**
**DEVELOPMENT.** *See* **COLLEGE STUDENT**
**DEVELOPMENT PROGRAMS.**

**PROGRAMS, INTERNSHIP.** *See* **INTERNSHIP**
**PROGRAMS.**

**PROGRAMS, MANAGED CARE (MEDICAL**
**CARE).** *See* **MANAGED CARE PLANS**
**(MEDICAL CARE).**

**PROGRAMS, MEDIA.** *See* **MEDIA PROGRAMS**
**(EDUCATION).**

**PROGRAMS, SCHOOL IMPROVEMENT.** *See*
**SCHOOL IMPROVEMENT PROGRAMS.**

**PROGRAMS, TELEVISION.** *See* **TELEVISION**
**PROGRAMS.**

**PROGRAMS, TWELVE-STEP.** *See* **TWELVE-**
**STEP PROGRAMS.**

**Progress in brain research**
(v. 123) Peripheral and spinal mechanisms in the
neural control of movement. Amsterdam ; Oxford :
Elsevier, 1999.
*TC QP376.A1 P7 1999*

**Progress in infancy research.** Mahwah, NJ : Lawrence
Erlbaum Associates, 2000- [v.] : ill. ; 24 cm. Frequency:
Annual. Vol. 1- . ISSN 1527-5884
*1. Infant psychology - Periodicals. 2. Animals - Infancy -*
*Periodicals. 3. Child development - Periodicals.*
*TC BF719 .P76*

**Progress in preventing AIDS? :** dogma, dissent, and
innovation : global perspectives / edited by David
Buchanan and George Cernada. Amityville, N.Y. :
Baywood Pub. Co., 1998. vii, 359 p. : ill. ; 23 cm. Includes
bibliographical references and index. ISBN 0-89503-176-0
(cloth : acid-free paper) DDC 362.1/969792
*1. AIDS (Disease) - Prevention. 2. AIDS (Disease) - Social*
*aspects. 3. AIDS (Disease) - Political aspects. I. Buchanan,*
*David Ross. II. Cernada, George Peter.*
*TC RA644.A25 P7655 1998*

**Progress in understanding reading.**
Stanovich, Keith E., 1950- New York : Guilford
Press, c2000.
*TC LB1050 .S723 2000*

**The progress of nations.** New York, NY : UNICEF,
1993- v. : ill. ; 30 cm. Frequency: Annual. 1993- . Issues for
<1995-> also available via the World Wide Web. Issued also in
Spanish with title: El progreso de las naciones, 1999-> URL:
http://www.unicef.org/apublic/ Other editions available:
Progress of nations. Spanish. Progreso de las naciones
(DLC)sn 99037046. Available in other form: Progress of
nations (Online) (OCoLC)37592418.
*1. Children - Health and hygiene - Statistics - Periodicals. 2.*
*Children - Nutrition - Statistics - Periodicals. 3. Education -*
*Statistics - Periodicals. 4. Sanitation - Statistics - Periodicals.*
*5. Women - Social conditions - Statistics - Periodicals. 6.*
*Health status indicators - Periodicals. I. UNICEF. II. Title:*
*Progress of nations. Spanish. Progreso de las naciones III.*
*Title: Progress of nations (Online)*
*TC RA407.A1 P76*

**Progress of nations (Online).**
The progress of nations. New York, NY : UNICEF,
1993-
*TC RA407.A1 P76*

**Progress of nations. Spanish. Progreso de las**
**naciones.**

The progress of nations. New York, NY : UNICEF,
1993-
*TC RA407.A1 P76*

**Progression in primary design and technology.**
Bold, Christine. London : David Fulton, 1999.
*TC LB1541 .B65 1999*

**PROGRESSIVE EDUCATION.**
Revisiting a progressive pedagogy. Albany : State
University of New York Press, c2000.
*TC LB1117 .R44 2000*

**Progressive Education Association.**
Frontiers of democracy. New York, Progressive
Education Association, etc., 1934-

**PROGRESSIVE EDUCATION - UNITED STATES.**
Berube, Maurice R. Eminent educators. Westport,
Conn. : Greenwood Press, 2000.
*TC LB875.D5 B47 2000*

Higher education for democracy. New York : P. Lang,
c1999.
*TC LD2001.G452 .S33 1999*

**PROGRESSIVE EDUCATION - UNITED**
**STATES - HISTORY.**
Beineke, John A. And there were giants in the land.
New York : P. Lang, c1998.
*TC LB875.K54 B44 1998*

**PROGRESSIVISM IN EDUCATION.** *See*
**PROGRESSIVE EDUCATION.**

**PROHIBITED BOOKS.** *See* **CENSORSHIP.**

**Project 2061 (American Association for the**
**Advancement of Science).**
Dialogue on early childhood science, mathematics,
and technology education. Washington, DC :
American Association for the Advancement of
Science/Project 2061, 1999.
*TC LB1139.5.S35 D53 1999*

**PROJECT METHOD IN TEACHING.** *See also*
**ACTIVITY PROGRAMS IN EDUCATION.**
Kent, Richard Burt. Beyond room 109. Portsmouth,
NH : Heinemann, 2000.
*TC LB1049 .K45 2000*

**PROJECT METHOD IN TEACHING -**
**HANDBOOKS, MANUALS, ETC.**
Wee, Patricia Hachten, 1948- Independent projects,
step by step. Lanham, MD : Scarecrow Press, c2000.
*TC LB1620 .W42 2000*

**PROJECT METHOD IN TEACHING -**
**PERIODICALS.**
Building America. [New York : Published for the
Dept. of Supervision and Curriculum Development by
the Society for Curriculum Study, Inc. ; distributed by
Americana Corporation, 1935-

**PROJECT METHOD IN TEACHING - UNITED**
**STATES.**
Art works!. Portsmouth, NH : Heinemann, c1999.
*TC LB1628.5 .A78 1999*

**PROJECT METHOD IN TEACHING - UNITED**
**STATES - HANDBOOKS, MANUALS, ETC.**
Jackman, Hilda L. Sing me a story! Tell me a song!.
Thousand Oaks, Calif. : Corwin Press, c1999.
*TC LB1139.35.A37 J33 1999*

**Project Muse.**
[American quarterly (Online)] American quarterly
[computer file]. Baltimore, Md. : Johns Hopkins
University Press, c1996-
*TC EJOURNALS*

[Journal of the history of ideas (Online)] Journal of
the history of ideas [computer file]. Baltimore, MD :
Journal of the History of Ideas, Inc., c1996-
*TC EJOURNALS*

[Lion and the unicorn (Baltimore, Md. : Online)] The
lion and the unicorn [computer file]. Baltimore, MD :
Johns Hopkins University Press, c1995-
*TC EJOURNALS*

[Review of higher education (Online)] The review of
higher education [computer file]. Baltimore, Md. :
Johns Hopkins University Press, c1996-
*TC EJOURNALS*

[Reviews in American history (Online)] Reviews in
American history [computer file]. Baltimore, MD :
Johns Hopkins University Press, c1995-
*TC EJOURNALS*

[Theatre journal (Online)] Theatre journal [computer
file]. Baltimore, Md. : Johns Hopkins University
Press, c1996-

*TC EJOURNALS*
[Wide angle (Online)] Wide angle [computer file].
Baltimore, Md. : John Hopkins University Press,
c1996-
*TC EJOURNALS*

**Project on Technology Transfer, Transformation,**
**and Development: the Japanese Experience**
**(United Nations University).**
Vocational education in the industrialization of Japan.
Tokyo : United Nations University, c1987.
*TC LC1047.J3 V63 1987*

**PROJECT SAFE.**
Changing lives [videorecording]. Princeton, NJ :
Films for the Humanities & Sciences, c1998.
*TC RC564 .C54 1998*

**PROJECT-TEACHING.** *See* **PROJECT METHOD**
**IN TEACHING.**

**PROJECTIVE TECHNIQUES.** *See* **RORSCHACH**
**TEST.**

**PROJECTS, ECONOMIC DEVELOPMENT.** *See*
**ECONOMIC DEVELOPMENT PROJECTS.**

**Projects with young learners.**
Phillips, Diane. Oxford ; New York : Oxford
University Press, c1999.
*TC LB1576 .P577 1999*

**PROKARYOTES.** *See* **BACTERIA.**

**The promise quilt.**
Ransom, Candice F., 1952- New York : Walker and
Co., 1999.
*TC PZ7.R1743 Pr 1999*

**Promising practices in recruitment, remediation, and**
**retention** / Gerald H. Gaither, editor. San Francisco,
Calif. : Jossey-Bass, c1999. 136 p. ; 23 cm. (New
directions for higher education, 0271-0560 ; no. 108, Winter
1999) "Winter 1999" Includes bibliographical references and
index. ISBN 0-7879-4860-8
*1. Universities and colleges - United States - Admission. 2.*
*Dropouts - Prevention. 3. Remedial teaching. I. Gaither,*
*Gerald H. II. Series: New directions for higher education ; no.*
*108.*
*TC LB2331.72 .N48 1999*

**Promoting acceptance of children with disabilities.**
MacCuspie, P. Ann (Patricia Ann), 1950- Halifax,
N.S. : Atlantic Provinces Special Education Authority,
c1996.
*TC LC4301 .M33 1996*

**Promoting children's learning from birth to five.**
Anning, Angela, 1944- Buckingham [England] ;
Philadelphia : Open University Press, 1999.
*TC LB1139.3.G7 A55 1999*

**Promoting equality in secondary schools** / edited by
Dave Hill and Mike Cole. London ; New York :
Cassell, 1999. xvi, 352 p. : ill. ; 23 cm. (Introduction to
education) Includes bibliographical references and indexes.
ISBN 0-304-70256-0 ISBN 0-304-70257-9 (pbk.) DDC
373.0115
*1. Discrimination in education - Great Britain. 2. Educational*
*equalization - Great Britain. I. Hill, Dave, 1945- II. Cole,*
*Mike, 1946- III. Series.*
*TC LC212.3.G7 P77 1999*

**Promoting health in multicultural populations :** a
handbook for practitioners / [edited by] Robert M.
Huff, Michael V. Kline. Thousand Oaks, Calif. : Sage
Publications, c1999. xvii, 554 p. ; 26 cm. Includes
bibliographical references and indexes. ISBN 0-7619-0182-5
(cloth : acid-free paper) ISBN 0-7619-0183-3 (pbk. : acid-free
paper) DDC 362.1/089/00973
*1. Minorities - Medical care - United States. 2. Health*
*promotion - United States. 3. Transcultural medical care -*
*United States. I. Huff, Robert M. II. Kline, Michael V.*
*TC RA448.4 .P76 1999*

**Promoting healthy behavior :** how much freedom?
whose responsibility? / edited by Daniel Callahan.
Washington, D.C. : Georgetown University Press,
c2000. xi, 186 p. ; 24 cm. (Hastings Center studies in ethics)
Includes bibliographical references and index. ISBN
0-87840-762-6 (cloth : alk. paper) DDC 613
*1. Health promotion - Social aspects. 2. Health promotion -*
*Moral and ethical aspects. I. Callahan, Daniel, 1930- II.*
*Series.*
*TC RA427.8 .P766 2000*

**Promoting literacy in grades 4-9 :** a handbook for
teachers and administrators / edited by Karen D.
Wood, Thomas S. Dickinson. Boston ; London : Allyn
and Bacon, c2000. ix, 453 p. : ill. ; 24 cm. Includes
bibliographical references and indexes. ISBN 0-205-28314-4
DDC 372.6
*1. Language arts (Elementary) - Handbooks, manuals, etc. 2.*

Language arts (Middle school) - Handbooks, manuals, etc. 3. Literacy programs - United States. I. Wood, Karen D. II. Dickinson, Thomas S.
**TC LB1576 .P76 2000**

**Promoting mental, emotional, and social health.**
Weare, Katherine, 1950- London ; New York : Routledge, 2000.
**TC LB3430 .W42 2000**

**Promoting nonviolence in early adolescence :** responding in peaceful and positive ways / Aleta Lynn Meyer ... [et al.]. New York : Kluwer Academic/ Plenum Publishers, c2000. xii, 128 p. ; 24 cm. (Prevention in practice library) Includes bibliographical references (p. 119-124) and index. ISBN 0-306-46385-7 (hardbound) ISBN 0-306-46386-5 (pbk.) DDC 303.6/9/071273
*1. Conflict management - Study and teaching (Middle school) - United States. 2. Nonviolence - Study and teaching (Middle school) - United States. 3. Interpersonal conflict in adolescence - United States - Prevention. I. Meyer, Aleta Lynn. II. Series.*
**TC HM1126 .P76 2000**

**Promoting quality in learning :** does England have the answer? / Patricia Broadfoot ... [et al.]. London ; New York : Cassell, 2000. viii, 280 p. ; 24 cm. Includes bibliographical references and index. ISBN 0-304-70684-1 DDC 370.941
*1. Education - England. 2. Education - France. 3. Comparative education. I. Broadfoot, Patricia.*
**TC LA632.b.P76 2000**

**Promoting the health of children.**
Pringle, Sheila M. St. Louis : Mosby, 1982.
**TC RJ101 .P66 1982**

**Promoting your school.**
Warner, Carolyn. 2nd ed. Thousand Oaks, Calif. : Corwin Press, c2000.
**TC LB2847 .W36 2000**

**PROMOTION OF HEALTH.** *See* **HEALTH PROMOTION.**

**PROPAGANDA.** *See* **PERSUASION (PSYCHOLOGY); PUBLIC OPINION.**

**PROPERTY.** *See* **CULTURAL PROPERTY; WEALTH.**

**PROPERTY, LITERARY.** *See* **COPYRIGHT.**

**Prophetic insight.**
Bracey, Earnest N. Lanham : University Press of America, c1999.
**TC LC2781 .B73 1999**

**PROPORTION.** *See* **AESTHETICS; RATIO AND PROPORTION.**

**PROPORTION (ART).** *See* **COMPOSITION (ART).**

**PROPOSAL WRITING FOR GRANTS - UNITED STATES.**
Ferguson, Jacqueline. Grants for special education and rehabilitation. 4th ed. Gaithersburg, MD : Aspen Publishers, Inc., 2000.
**TC LB2825 .F424 2000**

**PROPOSAL WRITING FOR GRANTS - UNITED STATES - HANDBOOKS, MANUALS, ETC.**
Geever, Jane C. The Foundation Center's guide to proposal writing. Rev. ed. New York : Foundation Center, c1997.
**TC HG177.5.U6 G44 1997**

**PROPOSAL WRITING IN EDUCATION - UNITED STATES.**
Ferguson, Jacqueline. Grants for special education and rehabilitation. 4th ed. Gaithersburg, MD : Aspen Publishers, Inc., 2000.
**TC LB2825 .F424 2000**

**PROPOSAL WRITING IN RESEARCH.**
Theses and dissertations. Lanham, Md. : University Press of America, 1997.
**TC LB2369 .T44 1997**

**PROPRIETARY RIGHTS.** *See* **INTELLECTUAL PROPERTY.**

**PROPRIOCEPTION.** *See also* **ORIENTATION (PHYSIOLOGY).**
Berthoz, A. [Sens du Mouvement. English] The brain's sense of movement. Cambridge, Mass. : Harvard University Press, 2000.
**TC QP493 .B47 2000**

Proprioception and neuromuscular control in joint stability. [Champaign, IL] : Human Kinetics, c2000.
**TC QP454 .P77 2000**

**Proprioception and neuromuscular control in joint stability /** Scott M. Lephart, Freddie H. Fu, editors. [Champaign, IL] : Human Kinetics, c2000. xxiv, 439

p. : ill. ; 29 cm. Includes bibliographical references. ISBN 0-88011-864-4 DDC 612.7/5
*1. Proprioception. 2. Motor ability. 3. Joints - Pathophysiology. I. Lephart, Scott M., 1961- II. Fu, Freddie H.*
**TC QP454 .P77 2000**

**PROSE LITERATURE.** *See* **FICTION.**

**Prospect Archives and Center for Education and Research.**
From another angle. New York : Teachers College Press, c2000.
**TC LB1117 .F735 2000**

**PROSPECT SCHOOL (NORTH BENNINGTON, VT.).**
From another angle. New York : Teachers College Press, c2000.
**TC LB1117 .F735 2000**

**PROSPECTING (FUND RAISING).** *See* **FUND RAISING.**

**Prospects for tomorrow.**
Ford, Brian J. (Brian John), 1939- The future of food. London : Thames & Hudson, c2000.
**TC RA601 .F65 2000**

Scanning the future. New York : Thames & Hudson, c1999.
**TC CB161 .S44 1999**

**PROSTHESIS.** *See* **HEARING AIDS.**

**PROSTHESIS FITTING - METHODS.**
Venema, Ted. Compression for clinicians. San Diego, Calif. : Singular Pub. Group, c1998.
**TC RF300 .V46 1998**

**PROSTITUTION.** *See* **SEX CRIMES; TEENAGE PROSTITUTION.**

**PROSTITUTION, JUVENILE.** *See* **TEENAGE PROSTITUTION.**

**Protecting human subjects :** departmental subject pools and institutional review boards / edited by Garvin Chastain and R. Eric Landrum. 1st ed. Washington, DC : American Psychological Association, c1999. x, 228 p. ; 23 cm. Includes bibliographical references and index. ISBN 1-55798-575-8 (pbk.) DDC 174/.915
*1. Human experimentation in psychology - Moral and ethical aspects. 2. Psychology - Research - Moral and ethical aspects. I. Chastain, Garvin D. II. Landrum, R. Eric.*
**TC BF181 .P65 1999**

**PROTECTION OF CHILDREN.** *See* **CHILD WELFARE.**

**PROTECTION OF ENVIRONMENT.** *See* **ENVIRONMENTAL PROTECTION.**

**PROTEIDS.** *See* **PROTEINS.**

**PROTEINS IN HUMAN NUTRITION.**
Di Pasquale, Mauro G. Amino acids and proteins for the athlete. Boca Raton : CRC Press, c1997.
**TC QP551 .D46 1997**

**PROTEINS - METABOLISM.**
Welle, Stephen. Human protein metabolism. New York : Springer, c1999.
**TC QP551 .W43 1999**

**Protest in Belgrade.**
[Ajmo, ajde, svi u šetnju. English.] Budapest, Hungary ; New York, NY, USA : Central European University Press, 1999.
**TC DR2044 .A3913 1999**

**PROTEST MOVEMENT, ANTINUCLEAR.** *See* **ANTINUCLEAR MOVEMENT.**

**PROTEST MOVEMENTS.**
Ackerman, Peter. Strategic nonviolent conflict. Westport, Conn. : Praeger, 1994.
**TC JC328.3 .A28 1994**

**PROTEST MOVEMENTS (CIVIL RIGHTS).** *See* **CIVIL RIGHTS MOVEMENTS.**

**PROTEST MOVEMENTS - YUGOSLAVIA.**
[Ajmo, ajde, svi u šetnju. English.] Protest in Belgrade. Budapest, Hungary ; New York, NY, USA : Central European University Press, 1999.
**TC DR2044 .A3913 1999**

**Protest, power, and change :** an encyclopedia of nonviolent action from ACT-UP to women's suffrage / editors, Roger S. Powers, William B. Vogele ; associate editors, Christopher Kruegler, Ronald M. McCarthy. New York : Garland Pub., 1997. xxv, 610 p. : ill. ; 26 cm. (Garland reference library of the humanities ; vol. 1625) Includes bibliographical references and index. ISBN 0-8153-0913-9 (acid-free paper) DDC 303.61/03

*1. Nonviolence - Encyclopedias. I. Powers, Roger S. II. Vogele, William B. III. Kruegler, Christopher. IV. McCarthy, Ronald M. V. Series.*
**TC HM278 .P76 1997**

**PROTESTANT REFORMATION.** *See* **REFORMATION.**

**PROTESTANTISM.** *See* **EVANGELICALISM; REFORMATION.**

**PROTESTANTISM, EVANGELICAL.** *See* **EVANGELICALISM.**

**PROTESTERS, STUDENT.** *See* **STUDENT PROTESTERS.**

**Provenzo, Eugene F.** The Internet and the World Wide Web for preservice teachers / Eugene F. Provenzo, Jr. Boston : Allyn & Bacon, c1999. x, 138 p. : ill. ; 24 cm. Includes bibliographical references (p. [137]-138). ISBN 0-205-28857-X
*1. Internet (Computer network) in education. 2. World Wide Web. 3. Education - Curricula - Computer network resources. I. Title.*
**TC LB1044.87 .P763 1999**

**Provet, Anne Gersony.**
Donahue, Paul J. Mental health consultation in early childhood. Baltimore, MD : Paul H. Brookes Publishing, 2000.
**TC RJ499 .D595 2000**

**Providing culturally relevant adult education :** a challenge for the twenty-first century / Talmadge C. Guy, editor. San Francisco : Jossey Bass, c1999. 106 p. : ill. ; 23 cm. (New directions for adult and continuing education, 1052-2891 ; no. 82) "Summer 1999" Includes bibliographical references and index. CONTENTS: Culture as context for adult education : the need for culturally relevant adult education / Talmadge C. Guy -- Adult learning : moving toward more inclusive theories and practices / Donna D. Amstutz -- Giving voice : inclusion of Afro-American students' polyrhythmic realities in adult basic education / Vanessa Sheared -- The quest for visibility in adult education : the Hispanic experience / Jorge Jeria -- Navajo language and culture in adult education / Louise Lockhart -- Creating a culturally relevant challenge for African American adult education / Elizabeth A. Peterson --Culturally relevant adult education : key themes and common purposes / Talmadge C. Guy. ISBN 0-7879-1167-4
*1. Adult education. 2. Adult learning. I. Guy, Talmadge C. II. Series.*
**TC LC5219 .P76 1999**

**PROVINCIAL GOVERNMENTS.** *See* **STATE GOVERNMENTS.**

**Proweller, Amira.** Constructing female identities : meaning making in an upper middle class youth culture / Amira Proweller. Albany : State University of New York Press, c1998. xi, 284 p. ; 24 cm. (SUNY series, power, social identity, and education) Includes bibliographical references (p. 235-277) and index. ISBN 0-7914-3771-X (hc : alk. paper) ISBN 0-7914-3772-8 (pbk. : alk. paper) DDC 371.822
*1. Teenage girls - Education (Secondary) - Social aspects - United States. 2. Middle class women - Education (Secondary) - United States. 3. Women - Socialization - United States. 4. Women - Identity. I. Title. II. Series.*
**TC LC1755 .P76 1998**

**PROXEMIC BEHAVIOR.** *See* **SPATIAL BEHAVIOR.**

**Prussin, Labelle.** African nomadic architecture : space, place, and gender / Labelle Prussin. Washington : Smithsonian Institution Press : National Museum of African Art, c1995. xxii, 245 p., [16] p. of plates : ill. (some col.), maps (some col.) ; 29 cm. Includes bibliographical references (p. 223-232) and index. DDC 728
*1. Tents - Africa, Northeast. 2. Architecture, Domestic - Africa, Northeast. 3. Vernacular architecture - Africa, Northeast. I. Title.*
**TC NA7461.A1 P78 1995**

**Przetwarzanie informacji społecznych dla ocen moralnych u uczniów klas młodszoszkolnych.**
Gaweł-Luty, Elżbieta. Słupsk : Wyższa Szkoła Pedagogiczna w Słupsku, 1996.
**TC LC314.P7 G37 1996**

**PSEUDO-CLASSICISM.** *See* **CLASSICISM.**

**PSEUDO-ROMANTICISM.** *See* **ROMANTICISM.**

**PSYCHAGOGY.** *See* **PSYCHOLOGY, APPLIED; PSYCHOTHERAPY.**

**PSYCHIATRIC AIDES.** *See* **PSYCHIATRIC NURSING.**

**Psychiatric and behavioural disorders in developmental disabilities and mental retardation /** edited by Nick Bouras. Cambridge, UK ; New York,

NY, USA : Cambridge University Press, 1999. xv, 464 p. : ill. ; 24 cm. Include bibliographical references and index. ISBN 0-521-64395-3 (pbk.) DDC 616.89
*1. Mentally handicapped - Mental health. 2. Mentally handicapped - Mental health services. 3. Mental Retardation. 4. Mental Disorders. 5. Developmental Disabilities. 6. Behavior. I. Bouras. Nick.*
*TC RC451.4.M47 P77 1999*

**PSYCHIATRIC CARE.** *See* **MENTAL HEALTH SERVICES.**

**PSYCHIATRIC DRUGS.** *See* **PSYCHOTROPIC DRUGS.**

**PSYCHIATRIC ERRORS.** *See* **FALSE MEMORY SYNDROME.**

**PSYCHIATRIC HOSPITAL CARE.**
Gauchet, Marcel. [La pratique de l'esprit humain. English] Madness and democracy. Princeton, N.J. : Princeton University Press, c1999.
*TC RC439 .G2813 1999*

**PSYCHIATRIC HOSPITAL PATIENTS - NEW JERSEY.**
Smith, Irmhild Wrede. The effect of structured exercise and structured reminiscing on agitation and aggression in geriatric psychiatric patients. 1996.
*TC 06 no. 10700*

**Psychiatric interview of children and adolescents.**
Cepeda, Claudio, 1942- Concise guide to the psychiatric interview of children and adolescents. Washington, DC : American Psychiatric Press, c2000.
*TC RJ503.6 .C46 2000*

**PSYCHIATRIC NURSING - PERIODICALS.**
Journal of psychiatric nursing. [Bordentown, N.J., etc., S. James Pub. Co., etc.]

**PSYCHIATRIC PERSONNEL.** *See* **MENTAL HEALTH PERSONNEL.**

**PSYCHIATRIC RATING SCALES.**
The use of psychological testing for treatment planning and outcome assessment. 2nd ed. Mahwah, N.J. : Lawrence Erlbaum Associates, c1999.
*TC RC473.P79 U83 1999*

**PSYCHIATRIC RATING SCALES - UNITED STATES.**
Gallagher, Trish. Arousal patterns, emotion identification, and cognitive style in depressed and nondepressed inner-city adolescent Latinas. 1997.
*TC 085 G136*

**PSYCHIATRIC RESEARCH.** *See* **PSYCHIATRY - RESEARCH.**

**PSYCHIATRIC SERVICES.** *See* **MENTAL HEALTH SERVICES.**

**PSYCHIATRIC STATUS RATING SCALES.** *See also* **PSYCHIATRIC RATING SCALES.**
Assessment in geriatric psychopharmacology. New Canaan, Conn. : Mark Powley Associates, 1983.
*TC WT150 .A846 1983*

**PSYCHIATRISTS.** *See* **PSYCHOANALYSTS.**

**PSYCHIATRY.** *See also* **ADOLESCENT PSYCHIATRY; CHILD PSYCHIATRY; CLINICAL PSYCHOLOGY; GERIATRIC PSYCHIATRY; INDUSTRIAL PSYCHIATRY; MENTAL HEALTH; MENTAL ILLNESS; PSYCHOLOGY, PATHOLOGICAL; PSYCHOTHERAPY; SOCIAL PSYCHIATRY.**
Psychiatry and religion. 1st ed. Washington, DC : American Psychiatric Press, c2000.
*TC RC455.4.R4 P755 2000*

**PSYCHIATRY AND RELIGION.**
Psychiatry and religion. 1st ed. Washington, DC : American Psychiatric Press, c2000.
*TC RC455.4.R4 P755 2000*

**Psychiatry and religion :** the convergence of mind and spirit / edited by James K. Boehnlein. 1st ed. Washington, DC : American Psychiatric Press, c2000. xx, 196 p. : ill. ; 24 cm. (Issues in psychiatry) Includes bibliographical references and index. ISBN 0-88048-920-0 (acid-free paper) DDC 616.89
*1. Psychiatry and religion. 2. Religion and Psychology. 3. Mental Disorders - therapy. 4. Psychiatry. I. Boehnlein, James K. II. Series.*
*TC RC455.4.R4 P755 2000*

**PSYCHIATRY, CHILD.** *See* **CHILD PSYCHIATRY.**

**PSYCHIATRY - CONGRESSES.**
Basic and clinical science of mental and addictive disorders. Basel ; New York : Karger, c1997.
*TC RC327 .B37 1997*

**PSYCHIATRY, CROSS-CULTURAL.** *See* **PSYCHIATRY, TRANSCULTURAL.**

**PSYCHIATRY - CROSS-CULTURAL STUDIES.** *See* **PSYCHIATRY, TRANSCULTURAL.**

**PSYCHIATRY - DICTIONARIES.**
Cardwell, Mike. The dictionary of psychology. London ; Chicago : Fitzroy Dearborn Publishers, 1999, c1996.
*TC BF31 .C33 1999*

**PSYCHIATRY - DICTIONARY.**
Cardwell, Mike. The dictionary of psychology. London ; Chicago : Fitzroy Dearborn Publishers, 1999, c1996.
*TC BF31 .C33 1999*

**PSYCHIATRY - DIFFERENTIAL THERAPEUTICS.**
The use of psychological testing for treatment planning and outcome assessment. 2nd ed. Mahwah, N.J. : Lawrence Erlbaum Associates, c1999.
*TC RC473.P79 U83 1999*

**PSYCHIATRY, GERIATRIC.** *See* **GERIATRIC PSYCHIATRY.**

**PSYCHIATRY - HISTORY.**
Bromberg, Walter, 1900- The mind of man. 4th ed. New York : Harper & Brothers, 1937.
*TC RC480 .B7*

**PSYCHIATRY, INFANT.** *See* **INFANT PSYCHIATRY.**

**PSYCHIATRY - METHODS - ADOLESCENCE - HANDBOOKS.**
Cepeda, Claudio, 1942- Concise guide to the psychiatric interview of children and adolescents. Washington, DC : American Psychiatric Press, c2000.
*TC RJ503.6 .C46 2000*

**PSYCHIATRY - METHODS - CHILD - HANDBOOKS.**
Cepeda, Claudio, 1942- Concise guide to the psychiatric interview of children and adolescents. Washington, DC : American Psychiatric Press, c2000.
*TC RJ503.6 .C46 2000*

**PSYCHIATRY - METHODS - CHILD, PRESCHOOL - HANDBOOKS.**
Cepeda, Claudio, 1942- Concise guide to the psychiatric interview of children and adolescents. Washington, DC : American Psychiatric Press, c2000.
*TC RJ503.6 .C46 2000*

**PSYCHIATRY - PERIODICALS.**
Journal of psycho-asthenics. Faribault, Minn. : Association of American Institutions for Feeble-Minded, [1896-1918]

**PSYCHIATRY - PHILOSOPHY.**
Gillett, Grant, 1950- The mind and its discontents. Oxford ; New York : Oxford University Press, c1999.
*TC BD418.3 .G555 1999*

Grant, Brian W., 1939- The condition of madness. Lanham, Md : University Press of America, 1999.
*TC RC437.5 .G73 1999*

The Psychological meaning of chaos. 1st ed. Washington, D.C. : American Psychological Association, c1997.
*TC RC437.5 .P762 1997*

**PSYCHIATRY - PUBLIC OPINION.**
Wahl, Otto F. Telling is risky business. New Brunswick, N.J. ; London : Rutgers University Press, c1999.
*TC RC454.4 .W327 1999*

**PSYCHIATRY - RESEARCH - METHODOLOGY.**
Chen, Sheying. Measurement and analysis in psychosocial research. Aldershot, Hants, UK ; Brookfield USA : Avebury, c1997.
*TC RC473.P79 C46 1997*

**PSYCHIATRY, SOCIAL.** *See* **SOCIAL PSYCHIATRY.**

**PSYCHIATRY, TRANSCULTURAL.**
Intercultural therapy. [2nd ed.]. Oxford ; Malden, MA : Blackwell Science, 2000.
*TC RC455.4.E8 I57 2000*

**PSYCHIATRY, TRANSCULTURAL - UNITED STATES.**
Handbook of multicultural mental health :. San Diego : Academic Press, c2000.
*TC RC455.4 .H36 2000*

**PSYCHIC ENERGIZERS.** *See* **ANTIDEPRESSANTS.**

**PSYCHIC HEALING.** *See* **MENTAL HEALING.**

**PSYCHIC TRAUMA IN CHILDREN.**
[Kindheit und Trauma. English.] Childhood and trauma. Aldershot, Hants, UK ; Brookfield, Vt., USA : Ashgate, c1999.
*TC RJ506.P66 K613 1999*

**PSYCHIC TRAUMA - TREATMENT.**
Dalenberg, Constance J. Countertransference and the treatment of trauma. 1st ed. Washington, D.C. : American Psychological Association, c2000.
*TC RC489.C68 D37 2000*

Group psychotherapy for psychological trauma. New York : Guilford Press, c2000.
*TC RC552.P67 G76 2000*

**PSYCHOACOUSTICS.**
Gelfand, Stanley A., 1948- Hearing. 3rd ed., rev. and expanded. New York : Marcel Dekker, c1998.
*TC QP461 .G28 1998*

**PSYCHOACTIVE DRUGS.** *See* **PSYCHOTROPIC DRUGS.**

**PSYCHOANALYSIS.** *See also* **ARCHETYPE (PSYCHOLOGY); CHILD ANALYSIS; COUNTERTRANSFERENCE (PSYCHOLOGY); OBJECT RELATIONS (PSYCHOANALYSIS); PSYCHOANALYTIC INTERPRETATION; PSYCHOHISTORY; PSYCHOLOGY, PATHOLOGICAL; SYMBOLISM (PSYCHOLOGY).**
Armstrong, Peter S. Opening gambits. Northvale, N.J. : J. Aronson, 1999.
*TC BF175.4.C68 A76 1999*

Barzilai, Shuli. Lacan and the matter of origins. Stanford, Calif. : Stanford University Press, 1999.
*TC BF17 .B2145 1999*

Billig, Michael. Freudian repression. New York : Cambridge University Press, 1999.
*TC BF175.5.R44 B55 1999*

Brink, Andrew. The creative matrix. New York : Peter Lang, c2000.
*TC BF698.9.C74 B75 2000*

Britzman, Deborah P., 1952- Lost subjects, contested objects. Albany : State University of New York Press, c1998.
*TC LB1060 .B765 1998*

Caper, Robert. Immaterial facts. London ; New York : Routledge, 2000.
*TC BF173 .C35 2000*

Cioffi, Frank. Freud and the question of pseudoscience. Chicago : Open Court, c1998.
*TC BF173 .C495 1998*

Dalenberg, Constance J. Countertransference and the treatment of trauma. 1st ed. Washington, D.C. : American Psychological Association, c2000.
*TC RC489.C68 D37 2000*

Dilman, İlham. Raskolnikov's rebirth. Chicago : Open Court, c2000.
*TC BF47 .D55 2000*

Dufresne, Todd, 1966- Tales from the Freudian crypt. Stanford, Calif. : Stanford University Press, 2000.
*TC BF175.5.D4 D84 2000*

Forrester, John. Dispatches from the Freud wars. Cambridge, Mass. : Harvard University Press, 1997.
*TC BF175 .F646 1997*

Forrester, John. The seductions of psychoanalysis. 1st pbk. ed. Cambridge ; New York : Cambridge University Press, 1991 (1992 printing)
*TC RC504 .F63 1991*

Freud, Sigmund, 1856-1939. The ego and the id and other works. London : Hogarth Press, 1957.
*TC BF173.F645 1957*

Freud, Sigmund, 1856-1939. [Sammlung kleiner schriften zur neurosenlehre. eng] Collected papers. 1st American ed. New York : Basic Books, 1959.
*TC BF173 .F672 1959*

Frosh, Stephen. The politics of psychoanalysis. 2nd ed. New York : New York University Press, 1999.
*TC BF173 .F92 1999*

Hoffman, Irwin Z. Ritual and spontaneity in the psychoanalytic process. Hillsdale, NJ : Analytic Press, c1998.
*TC BF175.4.C68 H64 1998*

Horney, Karen, 1885-1952. The therapeutic process. New Haven : Yale University Press, c1999.

*TC RC509 .H674 1999*

Humor and psyche. Hillsdale, NJ : Analytic Press, c1999.
*TC BF175 .H85 1999*

Jung on film [videorecording]. [Chicago, Ill.?] : Public Media Video, c1990.
*TC BF109.J8 J4 1990*

Jung on film [videorecording]. [Chicago, Ill.?] : Public Media Video, c1990.
*TC BF109.J8 J4 1990*

Jungian thought in the modern world. London ; New York : Free Association, 2000.
*TC BF173.J85 J85 2000*

Kainer, Rochelle G. K., 1936- The collapse of the self and its therapeutic restoration. Hillsdale, NJ ; London : Analytic Press, 1999.
*TC RC489.S43 K35 1999*

Kohon, Gregorio No lost certainties to be recovered. London : Karnac Books, 1999.
*TC BF173 .K64 1999*

Pathways into the Jungian world. London ; New York : Routledge, 2000.
*TC BF175 .P29 2000*

Personality development. London ; New York : Routledge, 1999.
*TC BF175.45 .P47 1999*

Petocz, Agnes. Freud, psychoanalysis, and symbolism. Cambridge ; New York : Cambridge University Press, 1999.
*TC BF109.F74 P48 1999*

Psychoanalysis and culture. New York : Routledge, 1999.
*TC BF175 .P79 1999*

Psychoanalysis and woman. New York : New York University Press, 2000.
*TC BF175.5.S48 P795 2000*

Rubin, Jeffrey B. A psychoanalysis for our time. New York : New York University Press, c1998.
*TC BF173 .R76 1998*

Shengold, Leonard. Soul murder revisited. New Haven, CT : Yale University Press, 1999.
*TC RC569.5.C55 S53 1999*

Stevens, Anthony. On Jung. 2nd ed. Princeton, N.J. : Princeton University Press, 1999.
*TC BF173 .S828 1999*

The unknown Karen Horney. New Haven : Yale University Press, c2000.
*TC BF173 .U55 2000*

Waddell, Margot, 1946- Inside lives. New York : Routledge, 1998.
*TC BF175.45 .W33 1998*

Weber, Samuel M. [Freud-Legende. English] The legend of Freud. Expanded ed. Stanford, Calif. : Stanford University Press, 2000, c1982.
*TC BF173.F85 W2813 2000*

Winter, Sarah. Freud and the institution of psychoanalytic knowledge. Stanford, Calif. : Stanford University Press, 1999.
*TC BF173 .W5485 1999*

Woodruff, Debra, 1967- General family functioning, parental bonding, and attachment style. 1998.
*TC 085 W858*

## PSYCHOANALYSIS AND ART.
Olkowski, Dorothea. Gilles Deleuze and the ruin of representation. Berkeley : University of California Press, c1999.
*TC N6537.K42 O44 1999*

Segal, Hanna. Dream, phantasy, and art. London ; New York : Tavistock/Routledge, 1991.
*TC BF1078 .S375 1991*

## PSYCHOANALYSIS AND CULTURE.
Clough, Patricia Ticineto, 1945- Autoaffection. Minneapolis : University of Minnesota Press, c2000.
*TC HM846 .C56 2000*

Moorjani, Angela B. Beyond fetishism and other excursions in psychopragmatics. New York : St. Martin's Press, 2000.
*TC BF175.4.C84 M663 2000*

Prager, Jeffrey, 1948- Presenting the past. Cambridge, Mass. : Harvard University Press, 1998.
*TC BF175.4.C84 P73 1998*

**Psychoanalysis and culture** : a Kleinian perspective. New York : Routledge, 1999. xiii, 226 p. ; 22 cm. Includes bibliographical references and index. ISBN

0-415-92687-4 (cloth) ISBN 0-415-92688-2 (paper) DDC 150.1
*1. Psychoanalysis I. Bell, David*
*TC BF175 .P79 1999*

## PSYCHOANALYSIS AND FEMINISM.
Hughes, Judith M. Freudian analysts/feminist issues. New Haven [Conn.] : Yale University Press, c1999.
*TC BF175.4.F45 H84 1999*

Psychoanalysis and woman. New York : New York University Press, 2000.
*TC BF175.5.S48 P795 2000*

## PSYCHOANALYSIS AND HOMOSEXUALITY - CASE STUDIES.
Therapeutic perspectives on working with lesbian, gay and bisexual clients. Buckingham [England] ; Philadelphia : Open University Press, 2000.
*TC RC451.4.G39 T476 2000*

## PSYCHOANALYSIS AND LITERATURE.
Rollin, Lucy. Psychoanalytic responses to children's literature. Jefferson, N.C. : McFarland, c1999.
*TC PR990 .R65 1999*

## PSYCHOANALYSIS AND RACISM.
Seshadri-Crooks, Kalpana. Desiring whiteness. London ; New York : Routledge, 2000.
*TC BF175.4.R34 S47 2000*

## PSYCHOANALYSIS AND RELIGION.
DiCenso, James, 1957- The other Freud. London ; New York : Routledge, 1999.
*TC BF175.4.R44 D53 1999*

Parsons, William Barclay, 1955- The enigma of the oceanic feeling. New York : Oxford University Press, 1999.
*TC BF175.4.R44 P37 1999*

**Psychoanalysis and woman** : a reader / edited by Shelley Saguaro. New York : New York University Press, 2000. xii, 354 p. ; 25 cm. Includes bibliographical references (p. [337]-344) and index. ISBN 0-8147-9770-9 (alk. paper) ISBN 0-8147-9771-7 (pbk. : alk. paper) DDC 155.3/33
*1. Sex (Psychology) 2. Psychoanalysis. 3. Women and psychoanalysis. 4. Psychoanalysis and feminism. I. Saguaro, Shelley.*
*TC BF175.5.S48 P795 2000*

**A psychoanalysis for our time.**
Rubin, Jeffrey B. New York : New York University Press, c1998.
*TC BF173 .R76 1998*

## PSYCHOANALYSIS - FRANCE.
Shepherdson, Charles. Vital signs. New York : Routledge, 2000.
*TC BF173 .S4975 2000*

## PSYCHOANALYSIS - HISTORY.
Forrester, John. Dispatches from the Freud wars. Cambridge, Mass. : Harvard University Press, 1997.
*TC BF175 .F646 1997*

Safouan, Moustafa. [Jacques Lacan et la question de la formation des analystes. English] Jacques Lacan and the question of psychoanalytic training. New York : St. Martin's Press, 2000.
*TC BF173.L15 S2414 2000*

Schwartz, Joseph. Cassandra's daughter. 1st American ed. New York : Viking, 1999.
*TC BF173 .S387 1999*

Stepansky, Paul E. Freud, surgery, and the surgeons. Hillsdale, NJ : Analytic Press, 1999.
*TC RC506 .S733 1999*

Winter, Sarah. Freud and the institution of psychoanalytic knowledge. Stanford, Calif. : Stanford University Press, 1999.
*TC BF173 .W5485 1999*

## PSYCHOANALYSIS - HISTORY - CONGRESSES.
The Hartmann era. New York : Other Press, 2000.
*TC BF173 .B4675 2000*

## PSYCHOANALYSIS IN HISTORIOGRAPHY. *See* PSYCHOHISTORY.

## PSYCHOANALYSIS - PHILOSOPHY.
Stepansky, Paul E. Freud, surgery, and the surgeons. Hillsdale, NJ : Analytic Press, 1999.
*TC RC506 .S733 1999*

## PSYCHOANALYSIS - STUDY AND TEACHING.
Safouan, Moustafa. [Jacques Lacan et la formation des analystes. English] Jacques Lacan and the question of psychoanalytic training. New York : St. Martin's Press, 2000.
*TC BF173.L15 S2414 2000*

## PSYCHOANALYSIS - UNITED STATES.
Buse, William Joseph. The alternate session. 1999.
*TC 085 B9603*

## PSYCHOANALYSTS - AUSTRIA - BIOGRAPHY.
Noland, Richard W. Sigmund Freud revisited. New York : Twayne Publishers, c1999.
*TC BF109.F74 N65 1999*

## PSYCHOANALYSTS - SWITZERLAND - BIOGRAPHY.
Stevens, Anthony. On Jung. 2nd ed. Princeton, N.J. : Princeton University Press, 1999.
*TC BF173 .S828 1999*

## PSYCHOANALYSTS - SWITZERLAND - INTERVIEWS.
Jung on film [videorecording]. [Chicago, Ill.?] : Public Media Video, c1990.
*TC BF109.J8 J4 1990*

Jung on film [videorecording]. [Chicago, Ill.?] : Public Media Video, c1990.
*TC BF109.J8 J4 1990*

## PSYCHOANALYSTS - TRAINING OF - UNITED STATES.
Buse, William Joseph. The alternate session. 1999.
*TC 085 B9603*

## PSYCHOANALYSTS - UNITED STATES - BIOGRAPHY.
Funk, Rainer. Erich Fromm. New York : Continuum, 2000.
*TC BF109.F76 F8413 2000*

Wheelis, Allen, 1915- The listener. New York : W.W. Norton, 1999.
*TC BF109.W44 A3 1999*

## PSYCHOANALYTIC COUNSELING.
Armstrong, Peter S. Opening gambits. Northvale, N.J. : J. Aronson, 1999.
*TC BF175.4.C68 A76 1999*

Hoffman, Irwin Z. Ritual and spontaneity in the psychoanalytic process. Hillsdale, NJ : Analytic Press, c1998.
*TC BF175.4.C68 H64 1998*

## PSYCHOANALYTIC INTERPRETATION.
Forrester, John. Dispatches from the Freud wars. Cambridge, Mass. : Harvard University Press, 1997.
*TC BF175 .F646 1997*

## PSYCHOANALYTIC INTERPRETATION - UNITED STATES.
Buse, William Joseph. The alternate session. 1999.
*TC 085 B9603*

**Psychoanalytic responses to children's literature.**
Rollin, Lucy. Jefferson, N.C. : McFarland, c1999.
*TC PR990 .R65 1999*

## PSYCHOANALYTIC THEORY.
Wurmser, Leon. [Flucht vor dem Gewissen. English] The power of the inner judge. Northvale, N.J. : Jason Aronson Inc., c2000.
*TC RC530 .W8713 2000*

## PSYCHOANALYTIC THERAPY.
Stepansky, Paul E. Freud, surgery, and the surgeons. Hillsdale, NJ : Analytic Press, 1999.
*TC RC506 .S733 1999*

## PSYCHOANALYTIC THERAPY - CASE STUDIES.
Goldberg, Arnold, 1929- Being of two minds. Hillsdale, NJ : Analytic Press, 1999.
*TC RC569.5.M8 G65 1999*

## PSYCHOANALYTIC THERAPY - CONGRESSES.
The therapeutic alliance. Madison, Conn. : International Universities Press, c2000.
*TC RC489.T66 T468 2000*

## PSYCHOANALYTIC THERAPY - METHODS.
Wurmser, Leon. [Flucht vor dem Gewissen. English] The power of the inner judge. Northvale, N.J. : Jason Aronson Inc., c2000.
*TC RC530 .W8713 2000*

## PSYCHOBIOLOGY. *See also* PSYCHOPHYSIOLOGY.
The Journal of comparative and physiological psychology. Baltimore, 1921-82.

## PSYCHOBIOLOGY.
Environmental influences: New York, Rockefeller University Press ; Russell Sage Foundation, 1968.
*TC BF353 .E5*

**Psychobiology 1921-1946.**
The Journal of animal behavior. Cambridge, Mass., H. Holt and Company; [etc., etc., 1911-17]

## PSYCHODIAGNOSTICS. *See also* BEHAVIORAL ASSESSMENT; PERSONALITY ASSESSMENT; PSYCHIATRIC RATING SCALES.

Assessment in geriatric psychopharmacology. New Canaan, Conn. : Mark Powley Associates, 1983.
*TC WT150 .A846 1983*

Whiston, Susan C., 1953- Principles and applications of assessment in counseling. Australia ; U.S. : Brooks/Cole, c2000.
*TC BF637.C6 W467 2000*

## PSYCHODIAGNOSTICS - HANDBOOKS, MANUALS, ETC.

Handbook of assessment in clinical gerontology. New York : Wiley, 1999.
*TC RC451.4.A5 H358 1999*

Handbook of psychological assessment in primary care settings. Mahwah, NJ : Lawrence Erlbaum Associates, Publishers, 2000.
*TC RC469 .H374 2000*

## PSYCHODRAMA.

Beyond talk therapy. 1st ed. Washington, DC : American Psychological Association, c1999.
*TC RC489.A72 B49 1999*

Blatner, Adam. Foundations of psychodrama. 4th ed. New York : Springer Pub. Co,. c2000.
*TC RC489.P7 B475 2000*

[Group psychotherapy.] Psychodrama and sociodrama in American education. New York Beacon House, 1949.

Newham, Paul, 1962- Using voice and theatre in therapy. London ; Philadelphia, Pa. : Jessica Kingsley Publishers, 1999.
*TC RZ999 .N437 1999*

## Psychodrama and sociodrama in American education.

[Group psychotherapy.] New York Beacon House, 1949.

## PSYCHODRAMA - CASE REPORT.

Beyond talk therapy. 1st ed. Washington, DC : American Psychological Association, c1999.
*TC RC489.A72 B49 1999*

## Psychodynamic approaches to sexual problems.

Daines, Brian. Buckingham ; Philadelphia : Open University Press, 2000.
*TC RC557 .D35 2000*

## PSYCHODYNAMIC PSYCHOTHERAPY.

Comparative approaches in brief dynamic psychotherapy. New York : Haworth Press, c1999.
*TC RC480.55 .C658 1999*

Daines, Brian. Psychodynamic approaches to sexual problems. Buckingham ; Philadelphia : Open University Press, 2000.
*TC RC557 .D35 2000*

Gartner, Richard B. Betrayed as boys. New York : Guilford Press, c1999.
*TC RC569.5.A28 G37 1999*

Magnavita, Jeffrey J. Relational therapy for personality disorders. New York : Wiley, c2000.
*TC RC554 .M228 2000*

## Psychodynamic treatment of the severe neuroses.

Wurmser, Leon. [Flucht vor dem Gewissen. English] The power of the inner judge. Northvale, N.J. : Jason Aronson Inc., c2000.
*TC RC530 .W8713 2000*

## The psychoeducational assessment of preschool children / edited by Bruce A. Bracken. 3rd ed.

Boston : Allyn and Bacon, c2000. viii, 488 p. : ill. ; 25 cm. Includes bibliographical references and indexes. ISBN 0-205-29021-3 (hard) DDC 372.126
*1. Child development - Evaluation. 2. Ability - Testing. 3. Readiness for school. I. Bracken, Bruce A.*
*TC LB1115 .P963 2000*

## PSYCHOGERIATRICS. *See* GERIATRIC PSYCHIATRY.

## PSYCHOHISTORY - PERIODICALS.

History of childhood quarterly. [Broadway, N.Y., Atcom]

## PSYCHOLANALYSIS AND PHILOSOPHY.

The analytic Freud. London ; New York : Routledge, 2000.
*TC BF109.F74 A84 2000*

## PSYCHOLINGUISTICS. *See also* CREATIVITY (LINGUISTICS); GENERATIVE GRAMMAR; LANGUAGE ACQUISITION; RACISM IN LANGUAGE; THOUGHT AND THINKING.

Ableman, Paul. The secret of consciousness. London ; New York : Marion Boyars, 1999.
*TC BF311 .A195 1999*

Chomsky, Noam. Language and mind. Enl. ed. New York : Harcourt Brace Jovanovich, [1972].
*TC P106 .C52 1972*

Dorsey, John Morris, 1900- Psychology of language; Detroit, Center for Health Education [1971]
*TC P106 .D64*

Gordon, Tatiana. Russian language directives. 1998.
*TC 06 no. 10940*

Language and conceptualization. 1st paperback ed. Cambridge [England] ; New York : Cambridge University Press, 1999.
*TC P37 .L354 1999*

Perception, cognition, and language. Cambridge, Mass. : MIT, c2000.
*TC BF455 .P389 2000*

Plunkett, Kim. Preliminary approaches to language development. Aarhus, Denmark : Aarhus University Press, c1985.
*TC P118 .P6 1985*

Skehan, Peter. A cognitive approach to language learning. Oxford ; New York : Oxford University Press, 1998.
*TC P118.2 .S567 1998*

## PSYCHOLINGUISTICS, DEVELOPMENTAL. *See* LANGUAGE ACQUISITION.

## Psychological abstracts.

Cumulative subject index to Psychological abstracts. Washington, D.C. : American Psychological Association, 1971-
*TC BF1 .P652*

Cumulative subject index to Psychological abstracts. Washington, D.C. : American Psychological Association, 1971-
*TC BF1 .P652*

## PSYCHOLOGICAL ABSTRACTS - INDEXES.

Cumulative subject index to Psychological abstracts. Washington, D.C. : American Psychological Association, 1971-
*TC BF1 .P652*

## PSYCHOLOGICAL ADAPTATION.

Chrispin, Marie C. Resilient adaptation of church-affiliated young Haitian immigrants. 1998.
*TC 06 no. 11015*

## PSYCHOLOGICAL ANTHROPOLOGY. *See* ETHNOPSYCHOLOGY.

## Psychological anthropology and education.

Harrington, Charles C. New York : AMS Press, c1979.
*TC GN502 .H37*

## PSYCHOLOGICAL ASSESSMENT. *See* PSYCHODIAGNOSTICS; PSYCHOLOGICAL TESTS.

## Psychological detachment from school.

Smith, Hawthorne Emery. 1999.
*TC 085 Sm586*

## The psychological dimension of foreign policy.

De Rivera, Joseph. Columbus, Ohio, C. E. Merrill Pub. Co. [1968]
*TC JX1255 .D45*

## Psychological effects of the civil war on children from rural communities of El Salvador.

Flores, Joaquín Evelio.
*TC 083 F67*

## PSYCHOLOGICAL EXPERIMENTATION ON HUMANS. *See* HUMAN EXPERIMENTATION IN PSYCHOLOGY.

## Psychological experiments on the Internet / edited by Michael H. Birnbaum. San Diego : Academic Press, c2000. xx, 317 p. : ill. ; 24 cm. Includes bibliographical references and index. CONTENTS: Contributors -- Introduction to psychological experiments on the internet -- Sect. I. General issues. Ch. 1. Decision making in the lab and on the web / Michael H. Birnbaum ; Ch. 2. Validity of web-based psychological research / John H. Krantz and Reeshad Dalal ; Ch. 3. A brief history of web experimenting / Jochen Musch and Ulf-Dietrich Reips ; Ch. 4. The web experiment method: advantages, disadvantages, and solutions / Ulf-Dietrich Reips -- Sect. II. Individual differences and cross-cultural studies. Ch. 5. Potential of the internet for personality research / Tom Buchanan ; Ch. 6. Human sexual behavior: a comparison of college and internet surveys / Robert D. Bailey, Winona E. Foote, and Barbara Throckmorton ; Ch. 7. An intercultural examination of facial features communicating

surprise / Donatella Pagani and Luigi Lombardi ; Ch. 8. What are computing experiences good for?: a case study in online research / John H. Mueller, D. Michele Jacobsen, and Ralf Schwarzer -- Sect. III. Computer techniques for internet experimentation. Ch. 9. PsychExps: an online psychology laboratory / Kenneth O. McGraw, Mark D. Tew, and John E. Williams ; Ch. 10. Techniques for creating and using web questionnaires in research and teaching / Jonathan Baron and Michael Siepman ; Ch. 11. The Cognitive Psychology Online Laboratory / Gregory Francis, Ian Neath, and Aimee Surprenant ; Ch. 12. The server side of psychology web experiments / William CONTENTS: C. Schmidt -- Glossary of web terms -- Index. ISBN 0-12-099980-3
*1. Internet (Computer network) in experimental psychology. 2. Human experimentation in psychology - Data processing. I. Birnbaum, Michael H.*
*TC BF198.7 .P79 2000*

## PSYCHOLOGICAL FICTION, ENGLISH - HISTORY AND CRITICISM.

Barney, Richard A., 1955- Plots of enlightenment. Stanford, Calif. : Stanford University Press, c1999.
*TC PR858.E38 B37 1999*

## Psychological interventions and research with Latino populations / edited by Jorge G. García, María Cecilia Zea. Boston : Allyn and Bacon, c1997. xx, 284 p. : ill. ; 25 cm. Includes bibliographical references and indexes. ISBN 0-205-16095-6 DDC 362.2/08968073
*1. Hispanic Americans - Mental health services. 2. Hispanic Americans - Psychology. 3. Hispanic Americans - Health risk assessment. I. García, Jorge G. II. Zea, María Cecilia.*
*TC RC451.5.H57 P77 1997*

## PSYCHOLOGICAL MANIFESTATION OF GENERAL DISEASES.

Organic disorders [videorecording]. Princeton, N.J. : Films for the Humanities & Sciences, 1998.
*TC RC521 .O7 1998*

## PSYCHOLOGICAL MANIFESTATIONS OF GENERAL DISEASES. *See* DELIRIUM.

## The Psychological meaning of chaos : translating theory into practice / edited by Frank Masterpasqua, Phyllis A. Perna. 1st ed. Washington, D.C. : American Psychological Association, c1997. xv, 323 p. ; 26 cm. Includes bibliographical references and index. ISBN 1-55798-429-8 DDC 616.89/001
*1. Psychiatry - Philosophy. 2. Psychotherapy - Philosophy. 3. Chaotic behavior in systems - Miscellanea. I. Masterpasqua, Frank. II. Perna, Phyllis A.*
*TC RC437.5 .P762 1997*

## PSYCHOLOGICAL MEASUREMENT. *See* PSYCHOMETRICS.

## The psychological mystique.

Justman, Stewart. Evanston, Ill. : Northwestern University Press, 1998.
*TC BF38 .J87 1998*

## Psychological perspectives on self and identity / edited by Abraham Tesser, Richard B. Felson, and Jerry M. Suls. 1st ed. Washington, DC : American Psychological Association, c2000. x, 252 p. : ill. ; 27 cm. Includes bibliographical references and indexes. ISBN 1-55798-678-9 DDC 155.2
*1. Self - Social aspects. I. Tesser, Abraham. II. Felson, Richard B. III. Suls, Jerry M.*
*TC BF697 .P765 2000*

## Psychological problems of ageing : assessment, treatment and care / edited by Robert T. Woods. Chichester ; New York : Wiley, c1999. xiv, 352 p. : ill. ; 23 cm. (The Wiley series in clinical psychology) Includes bibliographical references and index. ISBN 0-471-97434-X (pbk.) DDC 618.97/689
*1. Aged - Mental health. 2. Aging - Psychological aspects. 3. Psychotherapy for the aged. 4. Geriatric psychiatry. I. Woods, Robert T. II. Series.*
*TC RC451.4.A5 P7774 1999*

## PSYCHOLOGICAL RESEARCH. *See* PSYCHOLOGY - RESEARCH.

## PSYCHOLOGICAL SCALING. *See* PSYCHOMETRICS.

## PSYCHOLOGICAL STATISTICS. *See* PSYCHOMETRICS.

## PSYCHOLOGICAL STRESS. *See* STRESS (PSYCHOLOGY).

## Psychological testing and assessment.

Aiken, Lewis R., 1931- 10th ed. Boston : Allyn and Bacon, c2000.
*TC BF176 .A48 2000*

## PSYCHOLOGICAL TESTS. *See also* CLINICAL PSYCHOLOGY; EDUCATIONAL TESTS AND MEASUREMENTS; INTELLIGENCE TESTS; PERSONALITY TESTS;

## PREDICTION (PSYCHOLOGY); PSYCHODIAGNOSTICS; PSYCHOMETRICS.

Aiken, Lewis R., 1931- Psychological testing and assessment. 10th ed. Boston : Allyn and Bacon, c2000.
*TC BF176 .A48 2000*

Aiken, Lewis R., 1931- comp. Readings in psychological and educational testing, Boston, Allyn and Bacon [1973]
*TC LB3051 .A5625*

Assessment in geriatric psychopharmacology. New Canaan, Conn. : Mark Powley Associates, 1983.
*TC WT150 .A846 1983*

Assessment in geriatric psychopharmacology. New Canaan, Conn. : Mark Powley Associates, 1983.
*TC WT150 .A846 1983*

Corcoran, Kevin (Kevin J.) Measures for clinical practice. 3rd ed. New York ; London : Free Press, c2000.
*TC BF176 .C66 2000*

Drummond, Robert J. Appraisal procedures for counselors and helping professionals. 4th ed. Upper Saddle River, N.J. : Merrill, c2000.
*TC BF176 .D78 2000*

Gutin, Nina J. Differential object representations in inpatients with narcissistic and borderline personality disorders and normal controls. 1997.
*TC 085 G975*

Handbook of psychological assessment. 3rd ed. Amsterdam ; New York : Pergamon, 2000.
*TC BF39 .H2645 2000*

Key readings in testing. 1st ed. Tucson, Ariz. : P. Juul Press, c1985.
*TC BF176 .K48 1985*

Kline, Paul. The handbook of psychological testing. 2nd ed. London ; New York : Routledge, 2000.
*TC BF176 .K575 2000*

Sax, Gilbert. The construction and analysis of educational and psychological tests: Madison, Wisconsin : College Printing and Typing Co., 1962.
*TC BF39 .S27*

Testing and assessment in counseling practice. 2nd ed. Mahwah, N.J. : L. Erlbaum Associates, 2000.
*TC BF176 .T423 2000*

The use of psychological testing for treatment planning and outcome assessment. 2nd ed. Mahwah, N.J. : Lawrence Erlbaum Associates, c1999.
*TC RC473.P79 U83 1999*

Walsh, W. Bruce, 1936- Tests and assessment. 4th ed. Upper Saddle River, N.J. : Prentice Hall, c2001.
*TC BF176 .W335 2001*

## PSYCHOLOGICAL TESTS - EVALUATION.

Christiansen, Harley Duane. Basic background for test interpretation. 1st ed. Tucson, Ariz. : P. Juul Press, c1981.
*TC BF176 .C472*

## PSYCHOLOGICAL TESTS FOR CHILDREN. See also EDUCATIONAL TESTS AND MEASUREMENTS.

Johnson, Orval G., 1917- Tests and measurements in child development: [1st ed.]. San Francisco, Jossey-Bass, 1971.
*TC BF722 .J64*

## PSYCHOLOGICAL TESTS FOR MINORITIES. See MINORITIES - PSYCHOLOGICAL TESTING.

## PSYCHOLOGICAL TESTS - INTERPRETATION.

Scientist-practitioner perspectives on test interpretation. Boston, Mass. : Allyn and Bacon, c1999.
*TC BF176 .S37 1999*

## PSYCHOLOGICAL TESTS - LAW AND LEGISLATION - UNITED STATES.

Pope, Kenneth S. The MMPI, MMPI-2, & MMPI-A in court. 2nd ed. Washington, DC : American Psychological Association, 2000.
*TC KF8965 .P66 1999*

## PSYCHOLOGICAL TESTS - PROBLEMS, EXERCISES, ETC.

Cohen, Ronald Jay. Sixty-five exercises in psychological testing and assessment. 2nd ed. Mountain View, CA : Mayfield, c1992.
*TC BF176 .C64 1992*

## PSYCHOLOGICAL TESTS - SOCIAL ASPECTS.

Key readings in testing. 1st ed. Tucson, Ariz. : P. Juul Press, c1985.

## *TC BF176 .K48 1985*

**Psychological theories of drinking and alcoholism /** edited by Kenneth E. Leonard, Howard T. Blane. 2nd ed. New York : Guilford Press, c1999. x, 467 p. : ill. (some col.) ; 25 cm. (The Guilford substance abuse series) Includes bibliographical references and index. ISBN 1-57230-410-3 (alk. paper) DDC 616.86/1/0019
*1. Alcoholism - Psychological aspects. 2. Drinking of alcoholic beverages - Psychological aspects. 3. Alcohol Drinking. 4. Alcoholism - psychology. I. Leonard, Kenneth E. II. Blane. Howard T., 1926- III. Series.*
*TC HV5045 .P74 1999*

## PSYCHOLOGICAL THEORY.

Grigsby, Jim. Neurodynamics of personality. New York : Guilford Press, 2000.
*TC BF698.9.B5 G741 2000*

## PSYCHOLOGICAL TYPES. See TYPOLOGY (PSYCHOLOGY).

## PSYCHOLOGISTS - BIOGRAPHY.

A history of geropsychology in autobiography. 1st ed. Washington, DC ; London : American Psychological Association, c2000.
*TC BF724.8 .H57 2000*

**Psychologists' desk reference /** editors, Gerald P. Koocher, John C. Norcross, Sam S. Hill III. New York : Oxford University Press, 1998. xx, 613 p. : ill. ; 26 cm. Includes bibliographical references and index. ISBN 0-19-511186-9 (acid-free) DDC 616.89
*1. Clinical psychology - Handbooks, manuals, etc. I. Koocher, Gerald P. II. Norcross, John C., 1957- III. Hill, Sam S.*
*TC RC467.2 .P78 1998*

## PSYCHOLOGISTS - PROFESSIONAL ETHICS.

Ethical conflicts in psychology. 2nd ed. Washington, DC : American Psychological Association, c1999.
*TC BF76.4 .E814 1999*

Kitchener, Karen S. Foundations of ethical practice, research, and teaching in psychology. Mahwah, N.J. : L. Erlbaum, 2000.
*TC BF76.4 .K58 2000*

Nagy, Thomas F. Ethics in plain English. 1st ed. Washington, DC : London : American Psychological Association, c2000.
*TC BF76.4 .N34 2000*

## PSYCHOLOGISTS - TRAINING OF - UNITED STATES.

Peterson, Donald R. (Donald Robert), 1923- Educating professional psychologists. 1st ed. Washington, D.C. : American Psychological Association, c1997.
*TC BF80.7.U6 P48 1997*

## PSYCHOLOGISTS - UNITED STATES - HISTORY.

Popplestone, John A. An illustrated history of American psychology. 2nd ed. Akron, Ohio : The University of Akron Press, c1999.
*TC BF108.U5 P67 1999*

## PSYCHOLOGY. See also ADJUSTMENT (PSYCHOLOGY); ADOLESCENT PSYCHOLOGY; AFFECT (PSYCHOLOGY); AGGRESSIVENESS (PSYCHOLOGY); ASSERTIVENESS (PSYCHOLOGY); ATTENTION; ATTITUDE (PSYCHOLOGY); BEHAVIORISM (PSYCHOLOGY); BELIEF AND DOUBT; CHANGE (PSYCHOLOGY); CHILD PSYCHOLOGY; CHOICE (PSYCHOLOGY); CLINICAL PSYCHOLOGY; COGNITION; CONSCIOUSNESS; CONSTRUCTIVISM (PSYCHOLOGY); CONTEXT EFFECTS (PSYCHOLOGY); CONTROL (PSYCHOLOGY); DEVELOPMENTAL PSYCHOLOGY; DISCURSIVE PSYCHOLOGY; DRAWING, PSYCHOLOGY OF; EDUCATIONAL PSYCHOLOGY; EMOTIONS; ETHNOPSYCHOLOGY; HUMAN BEHAVIOR; IMAGINATION; INFLUENCE (PSYCHOLOGY); INTELLECT; KNOWLEDGE, THEORY OF; LOGIC; LOSS (PSYCHOLOGY); MATURATION (PSYCHOLOGY); MEANING (PSYCHOLOGY); MEMORY; MENTAL HEALTH; MOTIVATION (PSYCHOLOGY); NEW THOUGHT; ORIENTATION (PSYCHOLOGY); PERCEPTION; PERSONAL CONSTRUCT THEORY; PERSONALITY; PREDICTION (PSYCHOLOGY); PROBLEM SOLVING; PSYCHOANALYSIS; PSYCHOLOGY, APPLIED; SELF-ACCEPTANCE; SOCIAL INTERACTION; SOCIAL PSYCHOLOGY; SPATIAL BEHAVIOR; STRESS

## (PSYCHOLOGY); SYMBOLISM (PSYCHOLOGY); TEMPERAMENT; THOUGHT AND THINKING; TRANSPERSONAL PSYCHOLOGY; TYPOLOGY (PSYCHOLOGY); VALUES.

Friedberg, Felix. Caveat homo sapiens. Lanham, Md. ; Oxford : University Press of America, c2000.
*TC BF41 .F75 2000*

Leslie, Julian C. Behavior analysis. Amsterdam, Netherlands : Harwood Academic Publishers, c1999.
*TC BF199 .L47 1999*

Psychology today. 7th ed. New York : McGraw-Hill, c1991.
*TC BF121 .P85 1991*

Russell, Graham, 1954- Essential psychology for nurses and other health professionals. London ; New York : Routledge, c1999.
*TC R726.7 .R87 1999*

Scheibe, Karl E., 1937- The drama of everyday life. Cambridge, Mass. : Harvard University Press, 2000.
*TC BF121 .S328 2000*

Smith, John L., 1945- The psychology of action. New York : St. Martin's Press, 2000.
*TC BF121 .S56 2000*

Thorndike, Edward L. (Edward Lee), 1874-1949. Human nature and the social order Cambridge, Mass., M.I.T. Press [1969]
*TC BF121 .T442*

## PSYCHOLOGY, ABNORMAL. See PSYCHOLOGY, PATHOLOGICAL.

## PSYCHOLOGY - AFRICA, SUB-SAHARAN.

Holdstock, T. Len. Re-examining psychology. London ; New York : Routledge, 2000.
*TC BF108.A3 .H65 2000*

## Psychology and African Americans.

Jenkins, Adelbert H. 2nd ed. Boston : Allyn and Bacon, 1995.
*TC E185.625 .J47 1995*

## PSYCHOLOGY AND PHILOSOPHY.

Macnamara, John. Through the rearview mirror. Cambridge, Mass. : MIT Press, 1999.
*TC BF105 .M33 1999*

## PSYCHOLOGY AND RELIGION. See also PSYCHOLOGY, RELIGIOUS.

Metzner, Ralph. Green psychology. Rochester, Vt. : Park Street Press, c1999.
*TC BF353.5.N37 M47 1999*

## PSYCHOLOGY, APPLIED. See also BEHAVIOR MODIFICATION; CLINICAL PSYCHOLOGY; COMMUNITY PSYCHOLOGY; COUNSELING; INTERVIEWING; NEGOTIATION; PERSUASION (PSYCHOLOGY); PSYCHOLOGY, INDUSTRIAL; SCHOOL PSYCHOLOGY.

Handbook of counseling psychology. 3rd ed. New York : J. Wiley, c2000.
*TC BF637.C6 H315 2000*

## PSYCHOLOGY, APPLIED - MORAL AND ETHICAL ASPECTS.

Kendler, Howard H., 1919- Amoral thoughts about morality. Springfield, Ill. : C.C. Thomas, c2000.
*TC BF76.4 .K47 2000*

## PSYCHOLOGY, APPLIED - SOCIAL ASPECTS.

Kendler, Howard H., 1919- Amoral thoughts about morality. Springfield, Ill. : C.C. Thomas, c2000.
*TC BF76.4 .K47 2000*

## PSYCHOLOGY, APPLIED - STUDY AND TEACHING - AUDIO-VISUAL AIDS - VIDEO CATALOGS.

Videos in psychology. 1st ed. Washington, DC : American Psychological Association, c2000.
*TC BF80.3 .V53 2000*

## PSYCHOLOGY, APPLIED - VOCATIONAL GUIDANCE.

The applied psychologist. 2nd ed. Buckingham [England] ; Philadelphia : Open University Press, 2000.
*TC BF76 .A63 2000*

## PSYCHOLOGY - AUTHORSHIP.

Guide to publishing in psychology journals. Cambridge, U.K. ; New York : Cambridge University Press, 2000.
*TC BF76.8 .G85 2000*

Journals in psychology. 5th ed. Washington, D.C. : American Psychological Association, c1997.

TC BF76.8 J655 1997

**PSYCHOLOGY - BIOGRAPHICAL METHODS.**
Gray, Barry, 1944- Lifemaps of people with learning
difficulties. London ; Philadelphia : Jessica Kingsley,
1999.
*TC HV3004 .G73 1999*

**PSYCHOLOGY, CHILD.** *See* **CHILD
PSYCHOLOGY.**

**PSYCHOLOGY, CLINICAL.** *See also* **CLINICAL
PSYCHOLOGY.**
Clinical counselling in context. London ; New York :
Routledge, 1999.
*TC RC466 .C55 1999*

**PSYCHOLOGY, CLINICAL - CHILD.**
Handbook of research in pediatric and clinical child
psychology. New York : Kluwer Academic/Plenum
Publishers, c 2000.
*TC RJ499.3 .H367 2000*

**PSYCHOLOGY, CLINICAL HEALTH.** *See*
**CLINICAL HEALTH PSYCHOLOGY.**

**PSYCHOLOGY, COMPARATIVE.** *See also*
**HUMAN BEHAVIOR.**
Animal models of human emotion and cognition. 1st
ed. Washington, DC : American Psychological
Association, c1999.
*TC BF671 .A55 1999*

The evolution of cognition. Cambridge, Mass. : MIT
Press, c2000.
*TC BF701 .E598 2000*

Handbook of intelligence. Cambridge : New York :
Cambridge University Press, 2000.
*TC BF431 .H31865 2000*

Perspectives on fundamental processes in intellectual
functioning. Stamford, Conn. : Ablex Pub. Corp.,
c1998-
*TC BF444 .P42 1998*

Power, Thomas George, 1954- Play and exploration in
children and animals. Mahwah, N.J. : L. Erlbaum
Associates, 2000.
*TC BF717 .P69 2000*

Weisfeld, Glenn, 1943- Evolutionary principles of
human adolescence. New York, NY : Basic Books,
1999.
*TC BF724 .W35 1999*

Wyrwicka, Wanda. Conditioning. New Brunswick,
N.J. : Transaction Publishers, c2000.
*TC BF319 .W94 2000*

**PSYCHOLOGY, COMPARATIVE -
PERIODICALS.**
The Journal of animal behavior. Cambridge, Mass., H.
Holt and Company; [etc., etc., 1911-17]

The Journal of comparative and physiological
psychology. Baltimore, 1921-82.

**PSYCHOLOGY, CROSS-CULTURAL.** *See*
**ETHNOPSYCHOLOGY.**

**PSYCHOLOGY - DATA PROCESSING.**
Peatling, John H. Career development. Muncie, Ind. :
Accelerated Development, c1977.
*TC BF697 .P384*

**PSYCHOLOGY - DATA PROCESSING -
PERIODICALS.**
[Computers in human behavior (Online)] Computers
in human behavior [computer file]. New York :
Elsevier Science.
*TC EJOURNALS*

**PSYCHOLOGY - DENMARK.**
Essays in general psychology. Aarhus : Aarhus
University Press, c1989.
*TC BF38 .E78 1989*

**PSYCHOLOGY - DICTIONARIES.**
Baker encyclopedia of psychology & counseling. 2nd
ed. Grand Rapids, Mich. : Baker Books, c1999.
*TC BF31 .B25 1999*

Cardwell, Mike. The dictionary of psychology.
London ; Chicago : Fitzroy Dearborn Publishers,
1999, c1996.
*TC BF31 .C33 1999*

Corsini, Raymond J. The dictionary of psychology.
Philadelphia, PA : Brunner/Mazel, Taylor & Francis,
c1999.
*TC BF31 .C72 1999*

Encyclopedia of mental health. San Diego : Academic
Press, c1998.

TC RA790.5 .E53 1998

**PSYCHOLOGY - DICTIONARY.**
Cardwell, Mike. The dictionary of psychology.
London ; Chicago : Fitzroy Dearborn Publishers,
1999, c1996.
*TC BF31 .C33 1999*

**PSYCHOLOGY, EDUCATIONAL.** *See*
**EDUCATIONAL PSYCHOLOGY.**

**PSYCHOLOGY - ENCYCLOPEDIAS.**
The Corsini encyclopedia of psychology and
behavioral science. 3rd ed. New York : Wiley, 2000.
*TC BF31 .E52 2000*

**PSYCHOLOGY - ENCYCLOPEDIAS.**
Encyclopedia of mental health. San Diego : Academic
Press, c1998.
*TC RA790.5 .E53 1998*

**PSYCHOLOGY - ENCYCLOPEDIAS.**
Encyclopedia of psychology. Washington, D.C. :
American Psychological Association, 2000.
*TC BF31 .E52 2000*

**PSYCHOLOGY, ETHNIC.** *See*
**ETHNOPSYCHOLOGY.**

**PSYCHOLOGY, EXPERIMENTAL.** *See also*
**HUMAN EXPERIMENTATION IN
PSYCHOLOGY.**
Dunn, Dana. The practical researcher. Boston :
McGraw-Hill College, c1999.
*TC BF76.5 .D864 1999*

Laming, D. R. J. (Donald Richard John) The
measurement of sensation. Oxford ; New York :
Oxford University Press, 1997.
*TC QP435 .L34 1997*

Plutchik, Robert. Foundations of experimental
research. New York, Harper & Row [1968]
*TC BF181 .P56*

**PSYCHOLOGY - EXPERIMENTS.** *See* **HUMAN
EXPERIMENTATION IN PSYCHOLOGY.**

**Psychology focus**
Hartley, James, Ph. D. Learning and studying.
London ; New York : Routledge, 1998.
*TC BF318 .H365 1998*

**PSYCHOLOGY, FORENSIC.**
Pope, Kenneth S. The MMPI, MMPI-2, & MMPI-A
in court. 2nd ed. Washington, DC : American
Psychological Association, 2000.
*TC KF8965 .P66 1999*

Towl, Graham J. The handbook of psychology for
forensic practitioners. London ; New York :
Routledge, 1996.
*TC RA1148 .T69 1996*

**PSYCHOLOGY, HEALTH.** *See* **CLINICAL
HEALTH PSYCHOLOGY.**

**PSYCHOLOGY - HISTORY.**
Leahey, Thomas Hardy. A history of psychology. 5th
ed. Upper Saddle River, N.J. : Prentice Hall, c2000.
*TC BF81 .L4 2000*

Macnamara, John. Through the rearview mirror.
Cambridge, Mass. : MIT Press, 1999.
*TC BF105 .M33 1999*

**PSYCHOLOGY - HISTORY - 20TH CENTURY.**
Halliwell, Martin. Romantic science and the
experience of self. Aldershot, Hants ; Brookfield, Vt. :
Ashgate, c1999.
*TC BF697 R6375 1999*

**PSYCHOLOGY - HISTORY - PERSONAL
NARRATIVES.**
A history of geropsychology in autobiography. 1st ed.
Washington, DC ; London : American Psychological
Association, c2000.
*TC BF724.8 .H57 2000*

**PSYCHOLOGY IN ART.**
Rollin, Lucy. Psychoanalytic responses to children's
literature. Jefferson, N.C. : McFarland, c1999.
*TC PR990 .R65 1999*

**Psychology in economics and business**
Antonides, Gerrit, 1951- 2nd rev. ed. Dordrecht,
Netherlands ; Boston : Kluwer Academic, c1996.
*TC HB74.P8 A64 1996*

**PSYCHOLOGY IN LITERATURE.**
Rollin, Lucy. Psychoanalytic responses to children's
literature. Jefferson, N.C. : McFarland, c1999.
*TC PR990 .R65 1999*

**Psychology in the classroom**
Oldfather, Penny. Learning through children's eyes.

1st ed. Washington, DC : American Psychological
Association, c1999.
*TC LB1060 .O43 1999*

**PSYCHOLOGY - INDEXES.**
Cumulative subject index to Psychological abstracts.
Washington, D.C. : American Psychological
Association, 1971-
*TC BF1 .P652*

**PSYCHOLOGY, INDUSTRIAL.** *See also*
**INDUSTRIAL PSYCHIATRY; JOB STRESS;
ORGANIZATIONAL BEHAVIOR.**
Industrial and organizational psychology. Oxford,
UK ; Malden, Mass. : Blackwell Business, 2000.
*TC HF5548.8 .I5233 2000*

Multilevel theory, research, and methods in
organizations. 1st ed. San Francisco : Jossey-Bass,
c2000.
*TC HF5548.8 .M815 2000*

Social dreaming @ work. London : Karnac Books,
1998.
*TC BF1078 .S55 1998*

Spector, Paul E. Industrial and organizational
psychology. 2nd ed. New York : John Wiley, 2000.
*TC HF5548.8 .S625 2000*

**PSYCHOLOGY, INDUSTRIAL - ADDRESSES,
ESSAYS, LECTURES.**
Personality assessment in organizations. New York :
Praeger, 1985.
*TC HF5548.8 .P3995 1985*

**PSYCHOLOGY, INDUSTRIAL - EUROPE.**
Introduction to work and organizational psychology.
Malden, Mass. : Blackwell, 1999.
*TC HF5548.8 .I576 1999*

**PSYCHOLOGY - MATHEMATICAL MODELS -
CONGRESSES.**
Recent progress in mathematical psychology.
Mahwah, N.J. : L. Erlbaum, 1998.
*TC BF39 .R35 1998*

**PSYCHOLOGY - MATHEMATICAL MODELS -
PERIODICALS.**
Journal of mathematical psychology. New York,
Academic Press.

**PSYCHOLOGY - MEASUREMENT.** *See*
**PSYCHOMETRICS.**

**PSYCHOLOGY - METHODOLOGY.** *See also*
**BEHAVIORAL ASSESSMENT;
PSYCHOLOGICAL TESTS;
PSYCHOMETRICS.**
Essays in general psychology. Aarhus : Aarhus
University Press, c1989.
*TC BF38 .E78 1989*

**PSYCHOLOGY, MILITARY.**
Bourke, Joanna. An intimate history of killing. [New
York, NY] : Basic Books, c1999.
*TC U22.3 .B68 1999*

**PSYCHOLOGY - MORAL AND ETHICAL
ASPECTS.**
Ethical conflicts in psychology. 2nd ed. Washington,
DC : American Psychological Association, c1999.
*TC BF76.4 .E814 1999*

Kendler, Howard H., 1919- Amoral thoughts about
morality. Springfield, Ill. : C.C. Thomas, c2000.
*TC BF76.4 .K47 2000*

Kitchener, Karen S. Foundations of ethical practice,
research, and teaching in psychology. Mahwah, N.J. :
L. Erlbaum, 2000.
*TC BF76.4 .K58 2000*

Nagy, Thomas F. Ethics in plain English. 1st ed.
Washington, DC ; London : American Psychological
Association, c2000.
*TC BF76.4 .N34 2000*

**PSYCHOLOGY, NATIONAL.** *See*
**ETHNOPSYCHOLOGY.**

**PSYCHOLOGY - NURSES' INSTRUCTION.**
Russell, Graham, 1954- Essential psychology for
nurses and other health professionals. London ; New
York : Routledge, c1999.
*TC R726.7 .R87 1999*

**The psychology of action.**
Smith, John L., 1945- New York : St. Martin's Press,
2000.
*TC BF121 .S56 2000*

**The psychology of couples and illness :** theory,
research, & practice / edited by Karen B. Schmaling
and Tamara Goldman Sher. 1st ed. Washington,
D.C. : American Psychological Association, c2000.

xvi, 407 p. : ill. ; 26 cm. Includes bibliographical references and indexes. ISBN 1-55798-649-5 (cloth) DDC 155.6/45 *1. Married people - Health and hygiene. 2. Unmarried couples - Health and hygiene. 3. Intimacy (Psychology) - Health aspects. 4. Sick - Family relationships. I. Schmaling, Karen B. II. Sher, Tamara Goldman.*
*TC R726.5 .P785 2000*

**The psychology of high abilities.**
Howe, Michael J. A., 1940- New York : New York University Press, 1999.
*TC BF723.A25 H69 1999*

**Psychology of language.**
Dorsey, John Morris, 1900- Detroit, Center for Health Education [1971]
*TC P106 .D64*

**PSYCHOLOGY OF LEARNING.** *See* **LEARNING, PSYCHOLOGY OF.**

**Psychology of learning for instruction.**
Driscoll, Marcy Perkins. 2nd ed. Boston : London : Allyn and Bacon, c2000.
*TC LB1060 .D75 2000*

**PSYCHOLOGY OF RELIGION.** *See* **PSYCHOLOGY, RELIGIOUS.**

**The psychology of saving.**
Wärneryd, Karl Erik, 1927- Northampton, Mass. : E. Elgar, c1999.
*TC HB822 .W37 1999*

**Psychology of the home.**
Gunter, Barrie. London ; Philadelphia : Whurr, c2000.
*TC GT165.5 .G86 2000*

**Psychology of the image.**
Forrester, Michael A. London ; Philadelphia : Routledge, 2000.
*TC BF367 .F675 2000*

**The psychology of the Internet.**
Wallace, Patricia M. Cambridge ; New York : Cambridge University Press, 1999.
*TC BF637.C45 W26 1999*

**The psychology of ultimate concerns.**
Emmons, Robert A. New York : Guilford Press, c1999.
*TC BF505.G6 E58 1999*

**Psychology of women book series**
Practicing feminist ethics in psychology. 1st ed. Washington, DC : American Psychological Association, c2000.
*TC BF201.4 .P73 2000*

**PSYCHOLOGY, PATHOLOGICAL.** *See also*
**ACTING OUT (PSYCHOLOGY); AFFECTIVE DISORDERS; BRAIN DAMAGE; BRAIN - DISEASES; CHILD PSYCHOPATHOLOGY; COGNITION DISORDERS; COMPULSIVE BEHAVIOR; DISSOCIATIVE DISORDERS; EATING DISORDERS; MENTAL HEALTH; MENTAL ILLNESS; MENTAL RETARDATION; NEUROSES; PANIC DISORDERS; PARANOIA; PERSONALITY DISORDERS; PSYCHIATRY; PSYCHIC TRAUMA; PSYCHOANALYSIS; PSYCHOSES.**
Gender and its effects on psychopathology. Washington, DC : American Psychiatric Press, c2000.
*TC RC455.4.S45 G465 2000*

Pathology and the postmodern. London ; Thousand Oaks : SAGE, 2000.
*TC BF636 .P38 2000*

Shapiro, David, 1926- Dynamics of character. New York : Basic Books, c2000.
*TC RC455.5.T45 .S46 2000*

Wexberg, Erwin, 1889- Individual psychology, New York, Cosmopolitan Book Corporation, 1929.
· *TC BF175 .W48*

**PSYCHOLOGY, PATHOLOGICAL - DICTIONARIES.**
Baker encyclopedia of psychology & counseling. 2nd ed. Grand Rapids, Mich. : Baker Books, c1999.
*TC BF31 .B25 1999*

**PSYCHOLOGY, PATHOLOGICAL - ETIOLOGY.**
Adversity, stress, and psychopathology. New York : Oxford University Press, 1998.
*TC RC455.4.S87 A39 1998*

Paris, Joel, 1940- Myths of childhood. Philadelphia, PA : Brunner/Mazel, c2000.
*TC BF713 .P37 2000*

**PSYCHOLOGY, PATHOLOGICAL - RESEARCH.** *See* **PSYCHIATRY - RESEARCH.**

**PSYCHOLOGY - PERIODICALS.**
Archiv für die gesamte Psychologie. Leipzig : W. Englemann, 1903-1969.

Character and personality. Durham, N.C. : Duke Univ. Press, 1932-1945.

Journal of consulting psychology. [Lancaster, Pa., etc.] American Psychological Association.

**PSYCHOLOGY - PERIODICALS - PUBLISHING - DIRECTORIES.**
Journals in psychology. 5th ed. Washington, D.C. : American Psychological Association, c1997.
*TC BF76.8 J655 1997*

**PSYCHOLOGY - PERIODICALS - PUBLISHING - UNITED STATES - DIRECTORIES.**
Journals in psychology. 5th ed. Washington, D.C. : American Psychological Association, c1997.
*TC BF76.8 J655 1997*

**PSYCHOLOGY - PHILOSOPHY.** *See also*
**ACTION THEORY.**
Combs, Arthur W. (Arthur Wright), 1912- Being and becoming. New York : Springer Pub. Co., c1999.
*TC BF38 .C715 1999*

Elster, Jon, 1940- Ulysses unbound. Cambridge, U.K. ; New York : Cambridge University Press, 2000.
*TC BF441 .E45 2000*

Empathy and agency. Boulder, Colo. ; Oxford : Westview Press, 2000.
*TC BF64 .E67 2000*

Essays in general psychology. Aarhus : Aarhus University Press, c1989.
*TC BF38 .E78 1989*

Justman, Stewart. The psychological mystique. Evanston, Ill. : Northwestern University Press, 1998.
*TC BF38 .J87 1998*

Prætorius, Nini. Principles of cognition, language and action. Dordrecht, The Netherlands ; Boston [Mass., U.S.] : Kluwer Academic Publishers, c2000.
*TC BF38 .P67 2000*

Roszak, Theodore, 1933- The gendered atom. Berkeley, Calif. : Conari Press, 1999.
*TC BF64 .R69 1999*

**PSYCHOLOGY - PHILOSOPHY - CONGRESSES.**
The societal subject. Aarhus C, Denmark : Aarhus University Press, c1993.
*TC B105.A35 S68 1991*

**PSYCHOLOGY, PHYSIOLOGICAL.** *See* **PSYCHOPHYSIOLOGY.**

**PSYCHOLOGY, PRACTICAL.** *See* **PSYCHOLOGY, APPLIED.**

**PSYCHOLOGY - PROBLEMS, EXERCISES, ETC.**
Activities handbook for the teaching of psychology. Washington, D.C. : American Psychological Association, c1981-<c1999 >
*TC BF78 .A28*

**PSYCHOLOGY - QUOTATIONS, MAXIMS, ETC.**
Historical dictionary of quotations in cognitive science. Westport, Conn. : Greenwood Press, 2000.
*TC PN6084.C545 H57 2000*

**PSYCHOLOGY, RACIAL.** *See* **ETHNOPSYCHOLOGY.**

**PSYCHOLOGY, RELIGIOUS.**
Dilman, İlham. Raskolnikov's rebirth. Chicago : Open Court, c2000.
*TC BF47 .D55 2000*

**PSYCHOLOGY, RELIGIOUS - UNITED STATES - HISTORY.**
Taylor, Eugene. Shadow culture Washington, D.C. : Counterpoint, c1999.
*TC BL2525 .T39 1999*

**PSYCHOLOGY - RESEARCH.** *See* **HUMAN EXPERIMENTATION IN PSYCHOLOGY.**

**PSYCHOLOGY - RESEARCH - METHODOLOGY.**
Chen, Sheying. Mastering research. Chicago : Nelson-Hall, c1998.
*TC BF76.5 .C44 1998*

Dunn, Dana. The practical researcher. Boston : McGraw-Hill College, c1999.
*TC BF76.5 .D864 1999*

Transpersonal research methods for the social sciences. Thousand Oaks, Calif. : Sage Publications, c1998.

*TC BF76.5 .T73 1998*

**PSYCHOLOGY - RESEARCH - MORAL AND ETHICAL ASPECTS.**
Kitchener, Karen S. Foundations of ethical practice, research, and teaching in psychology. Mahwah, N.J. : L. Erlbaum, 2000.
*TC BF76.4 .K58 2000*

Protecting human subjects. 1st ed. Washington, DC : American Psychological Association, c1999.
*TC BF181 .P65 1999*

**PSYCHOLOGY - RESEARCH - PROGRAMMED INSTRUCTION.**
Levine, Samuel, 1927- A programmed introduction to research Belmont, Calif., Wadsworth Pub. Co. [1968]
*TC BF76.5 .L44*

**PSYCHOLOGY - SCALING.** *See* **PSYCHOMETRICS.**

**PSYCHOLOGY, SCHOOL.** *See* **SCHOOL PSYCHOLOGY.**

**Psychology series (Arhus, Denmark)**
(1.) Plunkett, Kim. Preliminary approaches to language development. Aarhus, Denmark : Aarhus University Press, c1985.
*TC P118 .P6 1985*

**PSYCHOLOGY, SEXUAL.** *See* **SEX (PSYCHOLOGY).**

**PSYCHOLOGY, SOCIAL.** *See also* **SOCIAL PSYCHOLOGY.**
Genius and eminence. 2nd ed. Oxford ; New York : Pergamon Press, 1992.
*TC BF412 .G43 1992*

**PSYCHOLOGY - SOCIAL ASPECTS.**
Kendler, Howard H., 1919- Amoral thoughts about morality. Springfield, Ill. : C.C. Thomas, c2000.
*TC BF76.4 .K47 2000*

**PSYCHOLOGY - STATISTICAL METHODS.**
McDonald, Roderick P. Test theory. Mahwah, N.J. ; London : L. Erlbaum Associates, 1999.
*TC BF39 .M175 1999*

Rosenthal, Robert, 1933- Contrasts and effect sizes in behavioral research. Cambridge, U.K. ; New York : Cambridge University Press, 2000.
*TC BF39.2.A52 R67 2000*

**PSYCHOLOGY - STATISTICS.** *See* **PSYCHOMETRICS.**

**PSYCHOLOGY - STUDY AND TEACHING.**
Activities handbook for the teaching of psychology. Washington, D.C. : American Psychological Association, c1981-<c1999 >
*TC BF78 .A28*

**PSYCHOLOGY - STUDY AND TEACHING - ACTIVITY PROGRAMS.**
Handbook of demonstrations and activities in the teaching of psychology. 2nd ed. Mahwah, N.J. : Lawrence Erlbaum Associates, c2000.
*TC BF77 .H265 2000*

**PSYCHOLOGY - STUDY AND TEACHING - AUDIO-VISUAL AIDS - VIDEO CATALOGS.**
Videos in psychology. 1st ed. Washington, DC : American Psychological Association, c2000.
*TC BF80.3 .V53 2000*

**PSYCHOLOGY - STUDY AND TEACHING - AUDIO-VISUAL METHODS.**
Handbook of demonstrations and activities in the teaching of psychology. 2nd ed. Mahwah, N.J. : Lawrence Erlbaum Associates, c2000.
*TC BF77 .H265 2000*

**PSYCHOLOGY - STUDY AND TEACHING (GRADUATE).**
Keith-Spiegel, Patricia. The complete guide to graduate school admission. 2nd ed. Mahwah, N.J. ; London : L. Erlbaum Associates, 2000.
*TC BF77 .K35 2000*

**PSYCHOLOGY - STUDY AND TEACHING (GRADUATE) - CANADA - DIRECTORIES.**
[Graduate study in psychology (1992)] Graduate study in psychology. Washington, D.C. : American Psychological Association, c1992-
*TC BF77 .G73*

**PSYCHOLOGY - STUDY AND TEACHING (GRADUATE) - UNITED STATES - DIRECTORIES.**
[Graduate study in psychology (1992)] Graduate study in psychology. Washington, D.C. : American Psychological Association, c1992-
*TC BF77 .G73*

## PSYCHOLOGY - STUDY AND TEACHING (HIGHER).
Handbook of demonstrations and activities in the teaching of psychology. 2nd ed. Mahwah, N.J. : Lawrence Erlbaum Associates, c2000.
*TC BF77 .H265 2000*

Teaching introductory psychology. 1st ed. Washington, DC : American Psychological Association, c1997.
*TC BF77 .T42 1997*

## PSYCHOLOGY - STUDY AND TEACHING - MORAL AND ETHICAL ASPECTS.
Kitchener, Karen S. Foundations of ethical practice, research, and teaching in psychology. Mahwah, N.J. : L. Erlbaum, 2000.
*TC BF76.4 .K58 2000*

## PSYCHOLOGY - STUDY AND TEACHING - SIMULATION METHODS.
Handbook of demonstrations and activities in the teaching of psychology. 2nd ed. Mahwah, N.J. : Lawrence Erlbaum Associates, c2000.
*TC BF77 .H265 2000*

**Psychology today :** an introduction / Richard R. Bootzin ... [et al.]. 7th ed. New York : McGraw-Hill, c1991. 1 v. (various pagings) : ill. (some col.) ; 29 cm. Includes bibliographical references and indexes. ISBN 0-07-006539-X DDC 150
*1. Psychology. I. Bootzin, Richard R., 1940-*
*TC BF121 .P85 1991*

## PSYCHOLOGY, TRANSPERSONAL. See TRANSPERSONAL PSYCHOLOGY.

## PSYCHOLOGY - UNITED STATES - AUTHORSHIP.
Journals in psychology. 5th ed. Washington, D.C. : American Psychological Association, c1997.
*TC BF76.8 J655 1997*

## PSYCHOLOGY - UNITED STATES - HISTORY.
Popplestone, John A. An illustrated history of American psychology. 2nd ed. Akron, Ohio : The University of Akron Press, c1999.
*TC BF108.U5 P67 1999*

## PSYCHOLOGY - VOCATIONAL GUIDANCE.
The applied psychologist. 2nd ed. Buckingham [England] ; Philadelphia : Open University Press, 2000.
*TC BF76 .A63 2000*

Super, Donald E. (Donald Edwin), 1910- Opportunities in psychology careers, New York, Educational Books Division of Universal Pub. and Distributing Corp. [1968]
*TC BF76 .S8 1968*

**Psychometic methods : item response theory for psychologists.**
Embretson, Susan E. Item response theory for psychologists. Mahwah, N.J. : Lawrence Erlbaum Associates, Publishers, 2000.
*TC BF39 .E495 2000*

## PSYCHOMETRICS. See also EDUCATIONAL TESTS AND MEASUREMENTS; PSYCHOLOGY - MATHEMATICAL MODELS.
Chen, Sheying. Measurement and analysis in psychosocial research. Aldershot, Hants, UK ; Brookfield USA : Avebury, c1997.
*TC RC473.P79 C46 1997*

Christiansen, Harley Duane. Basic background for test interpretation. 1st ed. Tucson, Ariz. : P. Juul Press, c1981.
*TC BF176 .C472*

Du, Zuru. Modeling conditional item dependencies with a three-parameter logistic testlet model. 1998.
*TC 085 D84*

EDENBOROUGH, ROBERT. Using psychometrics. 2nd ed. London ; Dover, NH : Kogan Page, 1999.
*TC BF39 .E34 1999*

Embretson, Susan E. Item response theory for psychologists. Mahwah, N.J. : Lawrence Erlbaum Associates, Publishers, 2000.
*TC BF39 .E495 2000*

Handbook of psychological assessment. 3rd ed. Amsterdam ; New York : Pergamon, 2000.
*TC BF39 .H2645 2000*

Heath, Richard A. Nonlinear dynamics. Mahwah, N.J. ; London : L. Erlbaum Associates, 2000.
*TC BF39 .H35 2000*

Kline, Paul. The handbook of psychological testing. 2nd ed. London ; New York : Routledge, 2000.

*TC BF176 .K575 2000*

McDonald, Roderick P. Test theory. Mahwah, N.J. ; London : L. Erlbaum Associates, 1999.
*TC BF39 .M175 1999*

Rosenthal, Robert, 1933- Contrasts and effect sizes in behavioral research. Cambridge, U.K. ; New York : Cambridge University Press, 2000.
*TC BF39.2.A52 R67 2000*

Sax, Gilbert. The construction and analysis of educational and psychological tests: Madison, Wisconsin : College Printing and Typing Co., 1962.
*TC BF39 .S27*

Walsh, W. Bruce, 1936- Tests and assessment. 4th ed. Upper Saddle River, N.J. : Prentice Hall, c2001.
*TC BF176 .W335 2001*

## PSYCHOMETRICS - CONGRESSES.
Recent progress in mathematical psychology. Mahwah, N.J. : L. Erlbaum, 1998.
*TC BF39 .R35 1998*

## PSYCHOMETRICS - PERIODICALS.
Journal of mathematical psychology. New York, Academic Press.

## PSYCHOMETRICS - PROBLEMS, EXERCISES, ETC.
Cohen, Ronald Jay. Sixty-five exercises in psychological testing and assessment. 2nd ed. Mountain View, CA : Mayfield, c1992.
*TC BF176 .C64 1992*

## PSYCHOMETRY (PSYCHOPHYSICS). See PSYCHOMETRICS.

## PSYCHOMOTOR EPILEPSY. See TEMPORAL LOBE EPILEPSY.

## PSYCHONEUROENDOCRINOLOGY.
Hormones, health, and behavior. Cambridge ; New York : Cambridge University Press, 1999.
*TC QP356.45 .H67 1999*

## PSYCHONEUROSES. See NEUROSES.

## PSYCHOPATHIC PERSONALITY. See ANTISOCIAL PERSONALITY DISORDERS.

**Psychopathological disorders in childhood.**
Group for the Advancement of Psychiatry. Committee on Child Psychiatry. [New York, 1966]
*TC RJ499 .G76*

## PSYCHOPATHOLOGY. See PSYCHOLOGY, PATHOLOGICAL.

## PSYCHOPATHOLOGY, CHILD. See CHILD PSYCHOPATHOLOGY.

## PSYCHOPATHOLOGY IN CHILDREN. See CHILD PSYCHOPATHOLOGY.

## PSYCHOPHARMACEUTICALS. See PSYCHOTROPIC DRUGS.

## PSYCHOPHARMACOLOGY. See also PEDIATRIC PSYCHOPHARMACOLOGY; PSYCHOTROPIC DRUGS.
Assessment in geriatric psychopharmacology. New Canaan, Conn. : Mark Powley Associates, 1983.
*TC WT150 .A846 1983*

Keen, Ernest, 1937- Chemicals for the mind. Westport, Conn. ; London : Praeger, 2000.
*TC RM315 .K44 2000*

Tasman, Allan, 1947- The doctor-patient relationship in pharmacotherapy. New York : Guilford Press, c2000.
*TC RC483.3 .T375 2000*

## PSYCHOPHARMACOLOGY - IN OLD AGE.
Assessment in geriatric psychopharmacology. New Canaan, Conn. : Mark Powley Associates, 1983.
*TC WT150 .A846 1983*

## PSYCHOPHYSIOLOGY. See also MIND AND BODY; MOVEMENT, PSYCHOLOGY OF; NEUROPSYCHOLOGY; SENSES AND SENSATION.
Handbook of psychophysiology. 2nd ed. Cambridge, UK ; New York, NY, USA : Cambridge University Press, 2000.
*TC QP360 .P7515 2000*

## PSYCHOPHYSIOLOGY - CROSS-CULTURAL STUDIES.
Tiago de Melo, Janine, 1969- Factors relating to Hispanic and non-Hispanic White Americans' willingness to seek psychotherapy. 1998.
*TC 085 T43*

## PSYCHOPHYSIOLOGY - HANDBOOKS, MANUALS, ETC.
Handbook of psychophysiology. 2nd ed. Cambridge, UK ; New York, NY, USA : Cambridge University Press, 2000.
*TC QP360 .P7515 2000*

## PSYCHOSES. See ALCOHOLIC PSYCHOSES; DEMENTIA; MANIA; MANIC-DEPRESSIVE ILLNESS; PARANOIA; SCHIZOPHRENIA.

## PSYCHOSES - DIAGNOSIS.
Disorders due to psychoactive substance abuse [videorecording]. Princeton, N.J. : Films for the Humanities & Sciences, 1998.
*TC RC564 .D5 1998*

Insight and psychosis. New York : Oxford University Press, 1998.
*TC RC512 .I49 1998*

## PSYCHOSES - PATIENTS.
Disorders due to psychoactive substance abuse [videorecording]. Princeton, N.J. : Films for the Humanities & Sciences, 1998.
*TC RC564 .D5 1998*

## PSYCHOSEXUAL DEVELOPMENT.
Constructing gender and difference. Cresskill, N.J. : Hampton Press, c1999.
*TC BF723.S42 C66 1999*

## PSYCHOSEXUAL DISORDERS - TREATMENT.
Daines, Brian. Psychodynamic approaches to sexual problems. Buckingham ; Philadelphia : Open University Press, 2000.
*TC RC557 .D35 2000*

## PSYCHOSIS. See PSYCHOSES.

**Psychosocial intervention in long-term care.**
Hartz, Gary W. New York : Haworth Press, c1997.
*TC RC451.4.N87 H37 1997*

**Psychosocial process.**
Issues in child mental health. [New York, Human Sciences Press]

## PSYCHOTECHNICS. See PSYCHOLOGY, INDUSTRIAL.

## PSYCHOTHERAPIST AND PATIENT. See also COUNTERTRANSFERENCE (PSYCHOLOGY); THERAPEUTIC ALLIANCE.
For love or money. New York : Haworth Press, c1999.
*TC RC489.F45 F67 1999*

Golden, Valerie. Significant others' perceptions of the effects of their partners' psychotherapy. 1998.
*TC 085 G566*

Tasman, Allan, 1947- The doctor-patient relationship in pharmacotherapy. New York : Guilford Press, c2000.
*TC RC483.3 .T375 2000*

Therapeutic perspectives on working with lesbian, gay and bisexual clients. Buckingham [England] : Philadelphia : Open University Press, 2000.
*TC RC451.4.G39 T476 2000*

Wosket, Val, 1954- The therapeutic use of self. New York : Routledge, 1999.
*TC RC480.5 .W67 1999*

## PSYCHOTHERAPISTS - ATTITUDES.
Nevas, Debra Baron. Factors affecting parental attitudes toward a child's therapist and therapy. 1997.
*TC 085 N401*

## PSYCHOTHERAPISTS - FEES.
For love or money. New York : Haworth Press, c1999.
*TC RC489.F45 F67 1999*

**The psychotherapist's guide to human memory.**
Jones, Janet L. New York : Basic Books, c1999.
*TC BF371 .J66 1999*

## PSYCHOTHERAPISTS - PROFESSIONAL ETHICS.
Cohen, Elliot D. The virtuous therapist. Belmont, CA : Brooks/Cole Wadworth, 1999.
*TC BF637.C6 C46 1999*

## PSYCHOTHERAPISTS - PSYCHOLOGY.
Wosket, Val, 1954- The therapeutic use of self. New York : Routledge, 1999.
*TC RC480.5 .W67 1999*

## PSYCHOTHERAPISTS - RELIGIOUS LIFE.
Sullivan, John P. (John Peter) On holy ground. Lanham : University Press of America, c1998.
*TC RC489.R46 S84 1998*

## PSYCHOTHERAPISTS - SUPERVISION OF.
Proctor, Brigid. Group supervision. London ; Thousand Oaks : SAGE Publications, 2000.
*TC BF637.C6 P95176 2000*

Taking supervision forward. London : Sage, 2000.
*TC BF637.C6 T35 2000*

Taking supervision forward. London : Sage, 2000.
*TC BF637.C6 T35 2000*

## PSYCHOTHERAPISTS - TRAINING OF.
Schapira, Sylvie K., 1940- Choosing a counselling or psychotherapy training. London ; New York : Routledge, 2000.
*TC BF637.C6 S355 2000*

## PSYCHOTHERAPY. *See also* CHILD PSYCHOTHERAPY; FEMINIST THERAPY; GROUP PSYCHOTHERAPY; OCCUPATIONAL THERAPY.
Heine, Ralph W. Englewood Cliffs, N.J., Prentice-Hall [1971]
*TC RC480 .H42*

## PSYCHOTHERAPY.
Bohart, Arthur C. How clients make therapy work. 1st ed. Washington, DC : American Psychological Association, c1999.
*TC RC480.5 .B64 1999*

Brems, Christiane. Dealing with challenges in psychotherapy and counseling. Belmont, Calif. : Wadsworth Pub., Brooks/Cole, c2000.
*TC BF637.C6 B723 2000*

Canino, Ian A. Culturally diverse children and adolescents. 2nd ed. New York : Guilford Press, c2000.
*TC RJ507.M54 C36 2000*

Cave, Sue, 1949- Therapeutic approaches in psychology. London ; New York : Routledge, 1999.
*TC RC480 .C37 1999*

Corey, Gerald. Theory and practice of counseling and psychotherapy. 6th ed. Stamford, Conn : Brooks/Cole, 2000.
*TC BF637.C6 C574 2000*

Denning, Patt, 1950- Practicing harm reduction psychotherapy. New York : Guilford Press, 2000.
*TC RC564 .D44 2000*

Goldberg, Marilee C. The art of the question. New York : Wiley, c1998.
*TC RC489.N47 G65 1998*

Golden, Valerie. Significant others' perceptions of the effects of their partners' psychotherapy. 1998.
*TC 085 G566*

Handbook of counseling and psychotherapy with lesbian, gay, and bisexual clients. 1st ed. Washington, DC ; London : American Psychological Association, c2000.
*TC BF637.C6 H3125 2000*

Handbook of psychological change :. New York : John Wiley & Sons, c2000.
*TC RC480 .H2855 2000*

Heine, Ralph W. Psychotherapy Englewood Cliffs, N.J., Prentice-Hall [1971]
*TC RC480 .H42*

Howatt, William A. The human services counseling toolbox. Belmont, CA : Brooks/Cole-Wadsworth, c2000.
*TC BF637.C6 H677 2000*

Intercultural therapy. [2nd ed.]. Oxford ; Malden, MA : Blackwell Science, 2000.
*TC RC455.4.E8 I57 2000*

Jones, Janet L. The psychotherapist's guide to human memory. New York : Basic Books, c1999.
*TC BF371 .J66 1999*

Nystul, Michael S. Introduction to counseling. Boston : Allyn and Bacon, c1999.
*TC BF637.C6 N97 1999*

Reconciling empirical knowledge and clinical experience. 1st ed. Washington, DC : American Psychological Association, c1999.
*TC RC480 .R395 1999*

Reconciling empirical knowledge and clinical experience. 1st ed. Washington, DC : American Psychological Association, c1999.
*TC RC480 .R395 1999*

Robinson, Tracy L. The convergence of race, ethnicity, and gender. Upper Saddle River, N.J. : Merrill, c2000.

*TC BF637.C6 R583 2000*

Schapira, Sylvie K., 1940- Choosing a counselling or psychotherapy training. London ; New York : Routledge, 2000.
*TC BF637.C6 S355 2000*

Walter, John L., 1945- Recreating brief therapy. New York : W.W. Norton & Co., 2000.
*TC RC480.5 .W276 2000*

Weissman, Myrna M. Comprehensive guide to interpersonal psychotherapy. New York: Basic Books, c2000.
*TC RC480.8 .W445 2000*

Writing and healing. Urbana, Ill. : National Council of Teachers of English, c2000.
*TC RC489.W75 W756 2000*

## PSYCHOTHERAPY AND PATIENT.
Weissman, Myrna M. Comprehensive guide to interpersonal psychotherapy. New York: Basic Books, c2000.
*TC RC480.8 .W445 2000*

## PSYCHOTHERAPY - CONGRESSES.
Ericksonian approaches to hypnosis and psychotherapy. New York : Brunner/Mazel, c1982.
*TC RC490.5.E75 E75*

Ericksonian approaches to hypnosis and psychotherapy. New York : Brunner/Mazel, c1982.
*TC RC490.5.E75 E75*

## PSYCHOTHERAPY - CROSS-CULTURAL STUDIES.
Ivey, Allen E. Counseling and psychotherapy. 4th ed. Boston : Allyn and Bacon, c1997.
*TC BF637.C6 I93 1997*

Seeley, Karen M. Cultural psychotherapy. Northvale, N.J. : Jason Aronson, c2000.
*TC RC455.4.E8 S44 2000*

Tiago de Melo, Janine, 1969- Factors relating to Hispanic and non-Hispanic White Americans' willingness to seek psychotherapy. 1998.
*TC 085 T43*

## PSYCHOTHERAPY - DICTIONARIES.
Baker encyclopedia of psychology & counseling. 2nd ed. Grand Rapids, Mich. : Baker Books, c1999.
*TC BF31 .B25 1999*

Key words in multicultural interventions. Westport, Conn. : Greenwood Press, 1999.
*TC BF637.C6 K493 1999*

## PSYCHOTHERAPY ETHICS. *See* PSYCHOTHERAPY - MORAL AND ETHICAL ASPECTS.

## PSYCHOTHERAPY FOR THE AGED.
Psychological problems of ageing. Chichester ; New York : Wiley, c1999.
*TC RC451.4.A5 P7774 1999*

## PSYCHOTHERAPY - GOVERNMENT POLICY - UNITED STATES.
Counseling and the therapeutic state. New York : Aldine de Gruyter, c1999.
*TC HV95 .C675 1999*

## PSYCHOTHERAPY, GROUP.
The process of group psychotherapy. Washington, DC : American Psychological Association, c2000.
*TC RC488 .P75 2000*

## PSYCHOTHERAPY - HANDBOOKS, MANUALS, ETC.
Millon, Theodore. Personality-guided psychotherapy. New York : J. Wiley, c1999.
*TC RC480.5 .M54 1999*

## PSYCHOTHERAPY - HISTORY.
Bromberg, Walter, 1900- The mind of man. Harper colophon ed. New York : Harper & Row, 1963.
*TC RC480 .B7 1963*

## PSYCHOTHERAPY - IN ADOLESCENCE.
Gardner, Richard A. Developmental conflicts and diagnostic evaluation in adolescent psychotherapy. Northvale, N.J. : J. Aronson, c1999.
*TC RJ503 .G376 1999*

Innovative psychotherapy techniques in child and adolescent therapy. 2nd ed. New York : Wiley, c1999.
*TC RJ504 .I57 1999*

## PSYCHOTHERAPY - IN ADULTHOOD.
Gartner, Richard B. Betrayed as boys. New York : Guilford Press, c1999.
*TC RC569.5.A28 G37 1999*

## PSYCHOTHERAPY - IN INFANCY & CHILDHOOD.
Innovative psychotherapy techniques in child and adolescent therapy. 2nd ed. New York : Wiley, c1999.
*TC RJ504 .I57 1999*

**Psychotherapy in the age of accountability.**
Johnson, Lynn D. 1st ed. New York : W.W. Norton & Co., c1995.
*TC RC480.55 .J64 1995*

## PSYCHOTHERAPY - METHODOLOGY.
Druss, Richard G., 1933- Listening to patients :. Oxford ; New York : Oxford University Press, 2000.
*TC RC480.8 .D78 2000*

Handbook of psychological change :. New York : John Wiley & Sons, c2000.
*TC RC480 .H2855 2000*

Wosket, Val, 1954- The therapeutic use of self. New York : Routledge, 1999.
*TC RC480.5 .W67 1999*

## PSYCHOTHERAPY - METHODS.
Clinical counselling in context. London ; New York : Routledge, 1999.
*TC RC466 .C55 1999*

Gauchet, Marcel. [La pratique de l'esprit humain. English] Madness and democracy. Princeton, N.J. : Princeton University Press, c1999.
*TC RC439 .G2813 1999*

Hays, Kate F. Working it out. 1st ed. Washington, DC : American Psychological Association, c1999.
*TC RC489.E9 H39 1999*

Innovative psychotherapy techniques in child and adolescent therapy. 2nd ed. New York : Wiley, c1999.
*TC RJ504 .I57 1999*

Millon, Theodore. Personality-guided psychotherapy. New York : J. Wiley, c1999.
*TC RC480.5 .M54 1999*

Sexual harassment in the workplace and academia. 1st ed. Washington, DC : American Psychiatric Press, c1996.
*TC RC560.S47 S495 1996*

Sommers-Flanagan, Rita, 1953- Clinical interviewing. 2nd ed. New York : Wiley, c1999.
*TC RC480.7 .S66 1999*

Tobin, David L. Coping strategies therapy for bulimia nervosa. Washington, DC : American Psychological Association, c2000.
*TC RC552.B84 T63 2000*

## PSYCHOTHERAPY - METHODS - ADOLESCENCE.
Handbook of psychotherapies with children and families. New York ; London : Kluwer Academic/ Plenum Publishers, c1999.
*TC RJ504 .H3619 1999*

## PSYCHOTHERAPY - METHODS - CASE REPORT.
Beyond talk therapy. 1st ed. Washington, DC : American Psychological Association, c1999.
*TC RC489.A72 B49 1999*

## PSYCHOTHERAPY - METHODS - CHILD.
Handbook of psychotherapies with children and families. New York ; London : Kluwer Academic/ Plenum Publishers, c1999.
*TC RJ504 .H3619 1999*

## PSYCHOTHERAPY - MORAL AND ETHICAL ASPECTS.
Cohen, Elliot D. The virtuous therapist. Belmont, CA : Brooks/Cole Wadworth, 1999.
*TC BF637.C6 C46 1999*

## PSYCHOTHERAPY - MORAL AND ETHICAL ASPECTS - CASE STUDIES.
Cohen, Elliot D. The virtuous therapist. Belmont, CA : Brooks/Cole Wadworth, 1999.
*TC BF637.C6 C46 1999*

## PSYCHOTHERAPY - PHILOSOPHY.
Burston, Daniel, 1954- The crucible of experience. Cambridge, Mass. : Harvard University Press, c2000.
*TC RC438.6.L34 B86 2000*

Constructions of disorder. 1st ed. Washington, DC : American Psychological Association, c2000.
*TC RC437.5 .C647 2000*

The Psychological meaning of chaos. 1st ed. Washington, D.C. : American Psychological Association, c1997.
*TC RC437.5 .P762 1997*

## PSYCHOTHERAPY - RELIGIOUS ASPECTS.
Integrating spirituality into treatment. 1st ed.
Washington, DC : American Psychological
Association, c1999.
*TC RC489.R46 I58 1999*

Sullivan, John P. (John Peter) On holy ground.
Lanham : University Press of America, c1998.
*TC RC489.R46 S84 1998*

## PSYCHOTHERAPY - TERMINATION.
Murdin, Lesley. How much is enough? London ; New
York : Routledge, 2000.
*TC RC489.T45 M87 2000*

**PSYCHOTIC CHILDREN.** *See* **MENTALLY ILL
CHILDREN.**

**PSYCHOTIC DISORDERS.** *See* **PSYCHOSES.**

## PSYCHOTIC DISORDERS - PSYCHOLOGY.
Insight and psychosis. New York : Oxford University
Press, 1998.
*TC RC512 .I49 1998*

**PSYCHOTROPIC DRUGS.** *See*
**ANTIDEPRESSANTS;
PSYCHOPHARMACOLOGY.**

## PSYCHOTROPIC DRUGS - EFFECTIVENESS.
Mood disorders. Basel ; New York : Karger, c1997.
*TC RC483 .M6 1997*

## PSYCHOTROPIC DRUGS - THERAPEUTIC USE.
Assessment in geriatric psychopharmacology. New
Canaan, Conn. : Mark Powley Associates, 1983.
*TC WT150 .A846 1983*

## PSYCHOTROPIC DRUGS - THERAPEUTIC USE.
Mood disorders. Basel ; New York : Karger, c1997.
*TC RC483 .M6 1997*

**PSYCHOTROPIC PLANTS.** *See* **PSYCHOTROPIC
DRUGS; TOBACCO.**

## PTOLEMY, 2ND CENT.
Stephen Hawking's universe [videorecording].
[Alexandria, Va.] : PBS Video; Burbank, CA :
Distributed by Warner Home Video, c1997.
*TC QB982 .S7 1997*

**PTSD (PSYCHIATRY).** *See* **POST-TRAUMATIC
STRESS DISORDER.**

**PUBERTY.** *See* **ADOLESCENCE.**

## Pubic Media Incorporated (Wilmette, Ill.).
Jung on film [videorecording]. [Chicago, Ill.?] : Public
Media Video, c1990.
*TC BF109.J8 J4 1990*

Jung on film [videorecording]. [Chicago, Ill.?] : Public
Media Video, c1990.
*TC BF109.J8 J4 1990*

## PUBLIC ADMINISTRATION. *See also*
**ADMINISTRATIVE AGENCIES;
BUREAUCRACY; PERSONNEL
MANAGEMENT; PUBLIC RECORDS.**
Haass, Richard. The bureaucratic entrepreneur.
Washington, D.C. : Brookings Institution, c1999.
*TC JF1351 .H2 1999*

## PUBLIC ADMINISTRATION - DATA
PROCESSING - CONGRESSES.
Digital democracy. London ; New York : Routledge,
1999.
*TC JF1525.A8 D54 1999*

## PUBLIC ADMINISTRATION - STUDY AND
TEACHING - UNITED STATES.
Teaching public administration and public policy.
Huntington, N.Y. : Nova Science Publishers, c1999.
*TC JF1338.A3 U59 1999*

## PUBLIC ADMINISTRATION - UNITED STATES -
HISTORY.
Schachter, Hindy Lauer. Reinventing government or
reinventing ourselves. Albany : State University of
New York Press, c1997.
*TC JK1764 .S35 1997*

## Public Affairs Television (Firm).
Changing lives [videorecording]. Princeton, NJ :
Films for the Humanities & Sciences, c1998.
*TC RC564 .C54 1998*

The hijacked brain [videorecording]. Princeton, NJ :
Films for the Humanities & Sciences, c1998.
*TC RC564 .H5 1998*

The next generation [videorecording]. Princeton, NJ :
Films for the Humanities & Sciences, c1998.
*TC RC564 .N4 1998*

The politics of addiction [videorecording]. Princeton,
NJ : Films for the Humanities & Sciences, c1998.

*TC RC564 .P59 1998*
Portrait of addiction [videorecording]. Princeton, NJ :
Films for the Humanities & Sciences, c1998.
*TC HV5801 .P6 1998*

Portrait of addiction [videorecording]. Princeton, NJ :
Films for the Humanities & Sciences, c1998.
*TC RC564 .P6 1998*

## Public and private responsibilities in long-term care :
finding the balance / edited by Leslie C. Walker,
Elizabeth H. Bradley, and Terrie Wetle. Baltimore :
Johns Hopkins University Press, 1998. xv, 206 p. ; 24
cm. Includes bibliographical references and index. ISBN
0-8018-5901-8 (alk. paper) DDC 362.1/6/0973
*1. Long-term care of the sick - United States - Finance. 2.
Long-term care of the sick - Government policy - United States.
3. Insurance, Long-term care - United States. I. Walker, Leslie
C., 1962- II. Bradley, Elizabeth H., 1962- III. Wetle, Terrie
Todd, 1946-*
*TC RA644.6 .P8 1998*

**PUBLIC ART.** *See* **PUBLIC SCULPTURE.**

**PUBLIC ASSISTANCE.** *See* **PUBLIC WELFARE.**

## PUBLIC ASSISTANCE - RECIPIENTS.
Schorr, Alvin Louis, 1921- Filial responsibility in the
modern American family. [Washington] U.S. Dept. of
Health, Education, and Welfare, Social Security
Administration, Division of Program Research [1960]
*TC HV75 .S36 1960*

## Public attitudes towards education in Ontario, 1996.
Livingstone, D. W. Toronto : OISE/UT in association
with University of Toronto Press, 1997.
*TC LA418.06 L58 1997*

**PUBLIC BUILDINGS.** *See* **SCHOOL BUILDINGS.**

**PUBLIC CHARITIES.** *See* **PUBLIC WELFARE.**

## Public charter schools : new choices in public
education (May 3, 2000 : Washington, D.C.) Public
charter schools [videorecording] : new choices in
public education / [presented by the] U.S. Department
of Education, [Washington, D.C.] : U.S. Dept. of
Education, [2000]. 1 videocassette (ca. 60 min.) : sd., col. ;
1/2 in. (Satellite town meeting) VHS. Catalogued from credits
and data sheet. Closed captioned. Host, U.S Deputy Secretary
of Education, Frank Holleman; co-host, Judith Johnson,
Deputy Assistant Secretary for Elementary and Secondary
Education; moderator, Barbara Harrison. A call-in Satellite
Town meeting held in Washington, D.C., Wednesday, May 3,
2000, 4:00-5:00 P.M. (ET). For educators, parents and
students. SUMMARY: Moderated by Barbara Harrison and
hosted by Deputy Secretary of Education, Frank Holleman, the
panel features spokespersons for charter schools across the
country.  Linda Carlson, a parent, represents Mountain View
Core Knowledge Charter School in Canon City, Colorado.
Bob DeBoer, director, represents New Visions School in
Minneapolis, Minnesota. Carmen NNamdi, director,
represents Nataki Talibah Schoolhouse of Detroit in Detroit,
Michigan. Irasema Salcido, principal, represents Cesar Chavez
Public Policy High School. And Glenn Schneider, group
director, corporate services, represents Ryder System Inc., a
corporate-run charter school in Miami, Florida. Contains video
clips of Fenten Avenue Charter School in Lakeview Terrace,
California and a couple of charter school student testimonials
from students in Minnesota.
*1. Charter schools - United States. 2. Privatization in
education - United States. 3. Education, Elementary - United
States. 4. Education, Secondary - United States. 5. Video
recordings for the hearing impaired. I. Harrison, Barbara. II.
Holleman, Frank. III. Johnson, Judith. IV. United States. Dept.
of Education. V. Title. VI. Title: New choices in public
education [videorecording] VII. Series: OIIA satellite town
meeting.*
*TC LB2806.36 .P9 2000*

## Public charter schools [videorecording].
Public charter schools : new choices in public
education (May 3, 2000 : Washington, D.C.)
[Washington, D.C.] : U.S. Dept. of Education, [2000].
*TC LB2806.36 .P9 2000*

**PUBLIC COMMUNITY COLLEGES.** *See*
**COMMUNITY COLLEGES.**

**PUBLIC CORPORATIONS.** *See*
**CORPORATIONS.**

**PUBLIC DEMONSTRATIONS.** *See*
**DEMONSTRATIONS.**

**PUBLIC FORUMS.** *See* **FORUMS (DISCUSSION
AND DEBATE).**

## Public funding for the arts.
Resource development handbook. [Washington,
D.C.] : National Assembly of Local Arts Agencies,
Institute for Community Development and the Arts,
1995.

*TC NX110 .R47 1995*
## PUBLIC GOODS.
Global public goods. New York : Oxford University
Press, 1999.
*TC HB846.5 .G55 1999*

## PUBLIC HEALTH. *See also* COMMUNITY
HEALTH SERVICES; ENVIRONMENTAL
HEALTH; FOOD ADULTERATION AND
INSPECTION; HEALTH FACILITIES;
HEALTH PLANNING; MEDICAL CARE;
MEDICINE, PREVENTIVE; MENTAL
HEALTH; SANITATION; SOCIAL
MEDICINE.
Tulchinsky, Theodore H. The new public health. San
Diego, Calif. : London : Academic Press, c2000.
*TC RA425 .T85 2000*

## PUBLIC HEALTH.
Tulchinsky, Theodore H. The new public health. San
Diego, Calif. : London : Academic Press, c2000.
*TC RA425 .T85 2000*

## PUBLIC HEALTH.
Tulchinsky, Theodore H. The new public health. San
Diego, Calif. : London : Academic Press, c2000.
*TC RA425 .T85 2000*

Vetter, Norman. Epidemiology and public health
medicine. Edinburgh ; New York : Churchill
Livingstone, 1999.
*TC RA427 .V48 1999*

**PUBLIC HEALTH ADMINISTRATION.** *See*
**HEALTH SERVICES ADMINISTRATION.**

**PUBLIC HEALTH - GOVERNMENT POLICY.** *See*
**MEDICAL POLICY.**

## PUBLIC HEALTH - HISTORY.
Tulchinsky, Theodore H. The new public health. San
Diego, Calif. ; London : Academic Press, c2000.
*TC RA425 .T85 2000*

## PUBLIC HEALTH - HISTORY - UNITED STATES.
Bennett, James T. From pathology to politics. New
Brunswick [N.J.] (U.S.A.) : Transaction Publishers,
c2000.
*TC RA445 .B45 2000*

## PUBLIC HEALTH - INDIA - HISTORY.
Harrison, Mark, lecturer. Climates & constitutions :.
New Delhi ; New York : Oxford University Press,
c1999.
*TC RA395.I5 H37 1999*

**PUBLIC HEALTH - LAW AND LEGISLATION.**
*See* **PUBLIC HEALTH LAWS.**

**PUBLIC HEALTH LAWS.** *See* **DRUGS - LAW
AND LEGISLATION; SMOKING - LAW AND
LEGISLATION.**

## PUBLIC HEALTH LAWS - UNITED STATES.
United States. Congress. Senate. Committee on Labor
and Public Welfare. Subcommittee on Health.
School-age mother and child health act, 1975.
Washington : U.S. Govt. Print. Off., 1976.
*TC KF26 .L354 1975*

**PUBLIC HEALTH - METHODOLOGY.** *See*
**HEALTH STATUS INDICATORS.**

## PUBLIC HEALTH - NEW YORK
METROPOLITAN AREA - DIRECTORIES.
The CARES directory in electronic form [computer
file] Maywood, NJ : ACIT.
*TC HV99.N59 S58*

## PUBLIC HEALTH - NEW YORK (STATE) -
STATISTICS.
Maternal, child and adolescent health profile. Albany,
N.Y. : New York State Dept. of Health, 1996.
*TC HV742.N7 B83 1996*

**PUBLIC HEALTH NURSING.** *See* **INDUSTRIAL
NURSING.**

**PUBLIC HEALTH PERSONNEL.** *See* **HEALTH
REFORMERS.**

**PUBLIC HEALTH - PLANNING.** *See* **HEALTH
PLANNING.**

## PUBLIC HEALTH - POLITICAL ASPECTS -
EUROPE - HISTORY.
Porter, Dorothy, 1953- Health, civilization, and the
state. London ; New York : Routledge, 1999.
*TC RA424 .P67 1999*

## PUBLIC HEALTH - POLITICAL ASPECTS -
NORTH AMERICA - HISTORY.
Porter, Dorothy, 1953- Health, civilization, and the
state. London ; New York : Routledge, 1999.
*TC RA424 .P67 1999*

**PUBLIC HEALTH - POLITICAL ASPECTS -
UNITED STATES.**
Rovner, Julie. Health care policy and politics A to Z.
Washington, DC : CQ Press, 2000.
*TC RA395.A3 R685 1999*

**Public health reports.**
United States. Health Services and Mental Health
Administration. Health services reports. Rockville,
Md.

**PUBLIC HEALTH SERVICES.** *See* **PUBLIC
HEALTH.**

**PUBLIC HEALTH - SOCIAL ASPECTS -
EUROPE - HISTORY.**
Porter, Dorothy, 1953- Health, civilization, and the
state. London ; New York : Routledge, 1999.
*TC RA424 .P67 1999*

**PUBLIC HEALTH - SOCIAL ASPECTS - NORTH
AMERICA - HISTORY.**
Porter, Dorothy, 1953- Health, civilization, and the
state. London ; New York : Routledge, 1999.
*TC RA424 .P67 1999*

**PUBLIC HEALTH - SOCIAL ASPECTS - UNITED
STATES.**
The society and population health reader. Volume I.
New York, N.Y. : The New Press, c1999.
*TC RA418 .S6726 1999*

**PUBLIC HEALTH - SOCIAL ASPECTS - UNITED
STATES - HISTORY.**
Bennett, James T. From pathology to politics. New
Brunswick [N.J.] (U.S.A.) : Transaction Publishers,
c2000.
*TC RA445 .B45 2000*

**PUBLIC HEALTH - SURVEYS.** *See* **HEALTH
SURVEYS.**

**PUBLIC HEALTH SURVEYS.** *See* **HEALTH
SURVEYS.**

**PUBLIC HEALTH - UNITED STATES.**
Rovner, Julie. Health care policy and politics A to Z.
Washington, DC : CQ Press, 2000.
*TC RA395.A3 R685 1999*

**PUBLIC HEALTH - UNITED STATES - HISTORY.**
Bennett, James T. From pathology to politics. New
Brunswick [N.J.] (U.S.A.) : Transaction Publishers,
c2000.
*TC RA445 .B45 2000*

**PUBLIC HEALTH - UNITED STATES -
STATISTICS.**
Health and healthcare in the United States. 1st ed.
Lanham, MD : Bernan Press : Nationshealth Corp.,
c1999.
*TC HA214 .H435 1999*

Health and healthcare in the United States. 1st ed.
Lanham, MD : Bernan Press : Nationshealth Corp.,
c1999.
*TC HA214 .H435 1999*

**PUBLIC HEALTH - UNITED STATES -
STATISTICS - PERIODICALS.**
Health, education, and welfare indicators.
Washington, D.C. : U.S. Dept. of Health, Education
and Welfare : For sale by the Supt. of Docs., U.S.
G.P.O., 1960-[1967]

**PUBLIC HOSPITALS - NEW YORK (STATE) -
NEW YORK - HISTORY - 20TH CENTURY.**
Opdycke, Sandra. No one was turned away. New
York : Oxford University Press, 1999.
*TC RA982.N49 O63 1999*

**PUBLIC HYGIENE.** *See* **PUBLIC HEALTH.**

**PUBLIC INSTITUTIONS.** *See* **INSTITUTIONAL
CARE; LIBRARIES; MUSEUMS; PUBLIC
HOSPITALS; REFORMATORIES;
SCHOOLS; UNIVERSITIES AND
COLLEGES.**

**PUBLIC INSTITUTIONS - LAW AND
LEGISLATION.** *See* **EDUCATIONAL LAW
AND LEGISLATION.**

**PUBLIC INTEREST.**
Kane, Francis, 1944- Neither beasts nor gods. Dallas :
Southern Methodist University Press, 1998.
*TC JC330.15 .K36 1998*

**Public issues discussion** [videorecording] : Diana Hess
at Denver High School 1997 / produced by the Social
Science Education Consortium. [Boulder, Colo.] :
Social Science Education Consortium, c1997. 1
videocassette (42 min.) : sd., col. ; 1/2 in. VHS. Catalogued
from credits and cassette label. Title from cassette label. Guest
presenter, Diana Hess; law class teacher, Dr. Deanna Morrison.
Video production by Vicki Murray-Kurzban. For educators,

especially high school Social Studies teachers. SUMMARY:
Diana Hess, guest presenter in Dr. Deanna Morrison's law
class at Denver East High School, leads a discussion on
doctor-assisted suicide. First laying the ground rules for a
successful discussion, she elicits opinions on this controversial
topic and teaches the class what a successful discussion is.
Doctor-assisted suicide is thus viewed from many angles with
diverse opinions expressed based on the student's prior
research. CONTENTS: A public issues discussion: Diana Hess,
Guest Presenter; Dr. Deanna Morrison's Law Class, Denver
East High School, February 1997 -- Generating criteria --
Setting up the discussion and reviewing the case -- Assessment.
*1. Social sciences - Study and teaching (Secondary) - United
States - Problems, exercises, etc. 2. Social sciences and ethics -
Study and teaching (Secondary) - Colorado - Denver -
Problems, exercises, etc. 3. DiscussionxStudy and teaching
(Secondary) - Colorado - Denver - Problems, exercises, etc. 4.
Assisted suicide - Law and legislation - United States - Study
and teaching (Secondary) - Colorado - Denver - Problems,
exercises, etc. 5. Constitutional law - United States - Study and
teaching (Secondary) - Colorado - Denver - Problems,
exercises, etc. I. Hess, Diana. II. Morrison, Deanna. III. Social
Science Education Consortium. IV. Title: Diana Hess at
Denver High School 1997 [videorecording]*
*TC H62.3 .P4 1997*

**PUBLIC JUNIOR COLLEGES.** *See* **COMMUNITY
COLLEGES.**

**Public key cryptosystems.**
Chacko, Mathew Vadakkan. 1998.
*TC 085 C35*

**PUBLIC LAW.** *See* **CITIZENSHIP;
CONSTITUTIONAL LAW.**

**The public leadership of women of faith.**
Henderson, Katharine Rhodes. 2000.
*TC 06 no. 11276*

**PUBLIC LIBRARIES - SERVICES TO COLLEGES
AND UNIVERSITIES.** *See* **ACADEMIC
LIBRARIES.**

**PUBLIC LIBRARIES - SERVICES TO
ILLITERATE PERSONS - UNITED STATES.**
Talan, Carole. Founding and funding family literacy
programs. New York : Neal-Schuman, c1999.
*TC Z716.45 .T35 1999*

**PUBLIC LIBRARIES - SERVICES TO
PRESCHOOL CHILDREN.** *See* **LIBRARIES -
SERVICES TO PRESCHOOL CHILDREN.**

**PUBLIC LIBRARIES - UNITED STATES -
HISTORY - 19TH CENTURY.**
Breisch, Kenneth A. Henry Hobson Richardson and
the small public library in America. Cambridge,
Mass. : MIT Press, c1997.
*TC Z679.2.U54 B74 1997*

**PUBLIC LIMITED COMPANIES.** *See*
**CORPORATIONS.**

**PUBLIC MANAGEMENT.** *See* **PUBLIC
ADMINISTRATION.**

**Public Media Incorporated... Home Vision...
[videorecording].**
Picasso [videorecording]. Chicago, IL : Home Vision,
c1986.
*TC N6853.P5 P52 1986*

**Public Media Incorporated (Wilmette, Ill.).**
Jackson Pollock [videorecording]. [Chicago, Ill.] :
Home Vision ; [S.l.] : Distributed Worldwide by RM
Associates, c1987.
*TC ND237.P73 J3 1987*

Mary Cassatt [videorecording]. [Chicago, Ill.]: Home
Vision, c1977.
*TC ND237.C3 M37 1977*

Nevelson in process [videorecording]. Chicago, IL :
Public Media Inc., 1977.
*TC NB237.N43 N43 1977*

Picasso [videorecording]. Chicago, IL : Home Vision,
c1986.
*TC N6853.P5 P52 1986*

Roy Lichtenstein [videorecording]. [Chicago, IL] :
Home Vision ; [S.l.] : distributed worldwide by RM
Asssociates, c1991.
*TC ND237.L627 R6 1991*

**Public Media Video (Firm).**
Jung on film [videorecording]. [Chicago, Ill.?] : Public
Media Video, c1990.
*TC BF109.J8 J4 1990*

Jung on film [videorecording]. [Chicago, Ill.?] : Public
Media Video, c1990.

*TC BF109.J8 J4 1990*

**PUBLIC MEETINGS.** *See* **DEMONSTRATIONS.**

**PUBLIC OFFICERS.** *See* **LOCAL OFFICIALS
AND EMPLOYEES; PUBLIC
ADMINISTRATION.**

**PUBLIC OPINION.** *See also* **ATTITUDE
(PSYCHOLOGY).**
Splichal, Slavko. Lanham, Md. : Rowman &
Littlefield, 1999.
*TC HM261 .S7515 1999*

**PUBLIC OPINION.**
Shamir, Jacob. The anatomy of public opinion. Ann
Arbor, Mich. : University of Michigan Press, c2000.
*TC HM236 .S5 2000*

Splichal, Slavko. Public opinion. Lanham, Md. :
Rowman & Littlefield, 1999.
*TC HM261 .S7515 1999*

**PUBLIC OPINION - GREAT BRITAIN.**
Weber, Sandra. That's funny, you don't look like a
teacher!. London ; Washington, D.C. : Falmer Press,
1995.
*TC LB1775.4.G7 W43 1995*

**PUBLIC OPINION - NEW YORK (STATE) - NEW
YORK - HISTORY - 18TH CENTURY.**
Tchen, John Kuo Wei. New York before Chinatown.
Baltimore : Johns Hopkins University Press, 1999.
*TC DS706 .T4 1999*

**PUBLIC OPINION - NEW YORK (STATE) - NEW
YORK - HISTORY - 19TH CENTURY.**
Tchen, John Kuo Wei. New York before Chinatown.
Baltimore : Johns Hopkins University Press, 1999.
*TC DS706 .T4 1999*

**PUBLIC OPINION - ONTARIO.**
Livingstone, D. W. Public attitudes towards education
in Ontario, 1996. Toronto : OISE/UT in association
with University of Toronto Press, 1997.
*TC LA418.06 L58 1997*

**PUBLIC OPINION POLLS.**
Splichal, Slavko. Public opinion. Lanham, Md. :
Rowman & Littlefield, 1999.
*TC HM261 .S7515 1999*

**PUBLIC OPINION - UNITED STATES.**
Caliendo, Stephen M., 1971- Teachers matter.
Westport, Conn. : Praeger, 2000.
*TC JA88.U6 C24 2000*

Klages, Mary. Woeful afflictions. Philadelphia :
University of Pennsylvania Press, c1999.
*TC HV1553 .K53 1999*

Painting by numbers. Berkeley : University of
California Press, [1999]
*TC ND1140 .P26 1999*

**PUBLIC PLACES.** *See* **PUBLIC SPACES.**

**Public policy and social welfare**
(v. 21) The challenge of diversity. Aldershot,
England ; Brookfield, Vt. : Avebury, 1996.
*TC JV225 .C530 1996*

**PUBLIC POLICY MANAGEMENT.** *See* **POLICY
SCIENCES.**

**PUBLIC-PRIVATE PARTNERSHIPS.** *See*
**PUBLIC-PRIVATE SECTOR
COOPERATION.**

**PUBLIC-PRIVATE SECTOR COLLABORATION.**
*See* **PUBLIC-PRIVATE SECTOR
COOPERATION.**

**PUBLIC-PRIVATE SECTOR COOPERATION -
UNITED STATES - CONGRESSES.**
Nonprofits and government. Washington, DC : Urban
Institute Press, 1999.
*TC HD62.6 .N694 1999*

**PUBLIC RECORDS - LAW AND LEGISLATION -
UNITED STATES.**
Foerstel, Herbert N. Freedom of information and the
right to know. Westport, Conn. : Greenwood Press,
1999.
*TC KF5753 .F64 1999*

**PUBLIC RELATIONS.** *See also* **PUBLIC
OPINION.**
Green, Andy. Creativity in public relations. London ;
Dover, N.H. : Kogan Page, c1999.
*TC HD59 .G744 1999*

**Public relations for school leaders.**
Hughes, Larry W., 1931- Boston ; London : Allyn and
Bacon, c2000.
*TC LB2847 .H84 2000*

**Public relations in educational organizations.**
Public relations in schools. 2nd ed. Upper Saddle River, N.J. : Merrill, c2000.
*TC LB2847 .P82 2000*

**Public relations in schools** / Theodore J. Kowalski. 2nd ed. Upper Saddle River, N.J. : Merrill, c2000. xxv, 390 p. ; 25 cm. Rev. ed. of: Public relations in educational organizations. c1996. Includes bibliographical references. ISBN 0-13-974411-8 DDC 659.2/9371
*1. Schools - Public relations. 2. Schools - Public relations - Case studies. 3. School management and organization. 4. School management and organization - Case studies. 5. Community and school. 6. Community and school - Case studies. I. Kowalski, Theodore J. II. Title: Public relations in educational organizations.*
*TC LB2847 .P82 2000*

**PUBLIC RELATIONS - PUBLIC ADMINISTRATION.** *See* GOVERNMENT PUBLICITY.

**PUBLIC RELATIONS - SCHOOLS.** *See* PARENT-TEACHER RELATIONSHIPS.

**PUBLIC RELIEF.** *See* PUBLIC WELFARE.

**Public report on basic education in India** / the PROBE Team in association with Centre for Development Economics. New Delhi ; Oxford : Oxford University Press, c1999. 156 p. : ill., maps ; 28 cm. Includes bibliographical references. ISBN 0-19-564870-6
*1. Basic education - India. 2. Education - Social aspects - India. 3. Education - Economic aspects - India. I. PROBE Team (India). II. Delhi School of Economics. Centre for Development Economics.*
*TC LA1151 .P83 1999*

**Public school 165 (New York, N.Y.) ISSN: Pictorial works.**
[Nature study class, P.S. 165] [picture] 1935.
*TC BE5564*

**PUBLIC SCHOOL 165 (NEW YORK, N.Y.) - PICTORIAL WORKS.**
[Nature study class, P.S. 165] [picture] 1935.
*TC BE5564*

[Nature study class, P.S. 165] [picture] 1935.
*TC BE5564*

**Public-school journal.**
Illinois school journal. Normal, Ill. : [s.n.], 1881/82-1889.

**PUBLIC SCHOOL LIBRARIES.** *See* SCHOOL LIBRARIES.

**PUBLIC-SCHOOL MUSIC.** *See* SCHOOL MUSIC.

**PUBLIC SCHOOLS.** *See* EVENING AND CONTINUATION SCHOOLS; HIGH SCHOOLS; RELIGION IN THE PUBLIC SCHOOLS; SCHOOLS; SUBURBAN SCHOOLS.

**PUBLIC SCHOOLS - BUSINESS MANAGEMENT.** *See* EDUCATION - FINANCE.

**PUBLIC SCHOOLS - DECENTRALIZATION - UNITED STATES.**
Balancing local control and state responsibility for K-12 education. Larchmont, NY : Eye on Education, 2000.
*TC LC89 .B35 2000*

**PUBLIC SCHOOLS - EMPLOYEES - ACCIDENTS.** *See* SCHOOL ACCIDENTS.

**PUBLIC SCHOOLS - FINANCE.** *See* EDUCATION - FINANCE.

**PUBLIC SCHOOLS - GERMANY.**
Dichanz, Horst, 1937- Changing traditions in Germany's public schools. Bloomington, Ind. : Phi Delta Kappa Educational Foundation, c1998.
*TC LA723 .D53 1998*

**Public schools in the making of black masculinity.**
Ferguson, Ann Arnett, 1940- Bad boys. Ann Arbor : University of Michigan Press, c2000.
*TC LC2771 .F47 2000*

**PUBLIC SCHOOLS - LAW AND LEGISLATION.** *See* EDUCATIONAL LAW AND LEGISLATION.

**PUBLIC SCHOOLS - MICHIGAN - HAMTRAMCK - PERIODICALS.**
Hamtramck public school bulletin. Hamtramck, Mich. : Board of Education,

**PUBLIC SCHOOLS - MINNESOTA.**
Randall, Ruth E. School choice. Bloomington, Ind. : National Educational Service, 1991.
*TC LB1027.9 .R36 1991*

**PUBLIC SCHOOLS - NBUSINESS MANAGEMENT.**
Michel, Patrick. Using action research for school restructuring and organizational change. 2000.
*TC 06 no. 11295*

**PUBLIC SCHOOLS - NEW YORK (STATE) - NEW YORK.**
Wright, Stanley Nathaniel. The Beacon model. 1998.
*TC 06 no. 11007*

**PUBLIC SCHOOLS - NEW YORK (STATE) - NEW YORK - ADMINISTRATION.**
Curcio, John J. Relationships among administrator personality, perceptions of feedback source credibility, and attitudes toward program feedback. 1999.
*TC 085 C92*

**PUBLIC SCHOOLS - POLITICAL ASPECTS - GREAT BRITAIN.**
State schools. London ; Portland, OR : Woburn Press, 1999.
*TC LC93.G7 S73 1999*

**PUBLIC SCHOOLS - SOCIAL ASPECTS - UNITED STATES.**
Behavioral management in the public schools. Westport, Conn. ; London : Praeger, 1999.
*TC LB1060.2 .B44 1999*

Fennimore, Beatrice Schneller. Talk matters. New York ; London : Teachers College Press, c2000.
*TC LB1033.5 F46 2000*

**PUBLIC SCHOOLS - UNITED STATES.**
Becoming good American schools. 1st ed. San Francisco : Jossey-Bass, c2000.
*TC LB2822.82 .B44 2000*

Bracey, Gerald W. (Gerald Watkins) Bail me out. Thousand Oaks, Calif. : Corwin Press, c2000.
*TC LA217.2 .B72 2000*

Bracey, Gerald W. (Gerald Watkins) The truth about America's schools. Bloomington, Ind. : Phi Delta Kappa Educational Foundation, c1997.
*TC LA217.2 .B75 1997*

Engel, Michael, 1944- The struggle for control of public education. Philadelphia, Pa. : Temple University Press, c2000.
*TC LA217.2 .E533 2000*

Lieberman, Ann. Teachers--transforming their world and their work. New York : Teachers College Press ; Alexandria, Va. : Association for Supervision and Curriculum Development, c1999.
*TC LB1025.3 .L547 1999*

Macedo, Stephen, 1957- Diversity and distrust. Cambridge, Mass. ; London : Harvard University Press, 2000.
*TC LA217.2 .M33 2000*

Randall, Ruth E. School choice. Bloomington, Ind. : National Educational Service, 1991.
*TC LB1027.9 .R36 1991*

Rufo-Lignos, Patricia Marie. Towards a new topology of public and private schools. 1999.
*TC 06 no. 11170*

Rufo-Lignos, Patricia Marie. Towards a new typology of public and private schools. 1999.
*TC 06 no. 11170*

Schneider, Frank. Our public schools. Mobile, Ala. : Factor Press, 2000.
*TC LA217.2 .S34 2000*

**PUBLIC SCHOOLS - UNITED STATES - BUSINESS MANAGEMENT.**
Norton, M. Scott. Resource allocation. Larchmont, N.Y. : Eye on Education, c1997.
*TC LB2805 .N73 1997*

**PUBLIC SCHOOLS - UNITED STATES - CASE STUDIES.**
Rose, Mike. Possible lives. New York, N.Y. : Penguin Books, 1996.
*TC LA217.2 R7 1996*

**PUBLIC SCHOOLS - UNITED STATES - CURRICULA - CENSORSHIP.**
Brinkley, Ellen Henson, 1944- Caught off guard. Boston : Allyn and Bacon, c1999.
*TC LC72.2 .B75 1999*

**PUBLIC SCHOOLS - UNITED STATES - EVALUATION.**
Gross, Martin L. (Martin Louis), 1925- The conspiracy of ignorance. New York : HarperCollins, c1999.
*TC LA217.2 .G76 1999*

Kearns, David T. A legacy of learning. Washington, D.C. : Brookings Institution Press, c2000.
*TC LA217.2 .K43 2000*

**PUBLIC SCHOOLS - UNITED STATES - FINANCE.**
Balancing local control and state responsibility for K-12 education. Larchmont, NY : Eye on Education, 2000.
*TC LC89 .B35 2000*

**PUBLIC SCHOOLS - UNITED STATES - HISTORY.**
Michel, Patrick. Using action research for school restructuring and organizational change. 2000.
*TC 06 no. 11295*

Moo, G. Gregory. Power grab. Washington, D.C. : Regnery Pub. ; Lanham, MD : Distributed to the trade by National Book Network, c1999.
*TC LB2844.53.U6 M66 1999*

**PUBLIC SCHOOLS - UNITED STATES - HISTORY - 1945-1953.**
Foster, Stuart J., 1960- Red alert!. New York ; Canterbury [England] : P. Lang, c2000.
*TC LC72.2 .F67 2000*

**PUBLIC SCHOOLS - UNITED STATES - HISTORY - 20TH CENTURY.**
Ravitch, Diane. Left back. New York : Simon & Schuster, c2000.
*TC LA216 .R28 2000*

**PUBLIC SCHOOLS - WISCONSIN - MILWAUKEE - LONGITUDINAL STUDIES.**
African-centered schooling in theory and practice. Westport, Conn. ; London : Bergin & Garvey, 2000.
*TC LC2731 .A35 2000*

**PUBLIC SCULPTURE.** *See* MONUMENTS.

**Public sculpture and the civic ideal in New York City, 1890-1930.**
Bogart, Michele Helene, 1952- 1st Smithsonian ed. Washington, D.C. : Smithsonian Institution Press, 1997.
*TC NB235.N5 B64 1997*

**PUBLIC SCULPTURE - AUSTRALIA.**
Hedger, Michael. Public sculpture in Australia. Roseville East, NSW : Distributed by Craftsman House ; United States : G+B Arts International, c1995.
*TC NB1100 .H44 1995*

**Public sculpture in Australia.**
Hedger, Michael. Roseville East, NSW : Distributed by Craftsman House ; United States : G+B Arts International, c1995.
*TC NB1100 .H44 1995*

**PUBLIC SCULPTURE - NEW YORK (STATE) - NEW YORK - THEMES, MOTIVES.**
Bogart, Michele Helene, 1952- Public sculpture and the civic ideal in New York City, 1890-1930. 1st Smithsonian ed. Washington, D.C. : Smithsonian Institution Press, 1997.
*TC NB235.N5 B64 1997*

**PUBLIC SECTOR MANAGEMENT.** *See* PUBLIC ADMINISTRATION.

**PUBLIC SERVICES (LIBRARIES).** *See* LIBRARIES AND READERS.

**PUBLIC SPACES - PSYCHOLOGICAL ASPECTS.**
Fullilove, Mindy Thompson. The house of Joshua. Lincoln, NE : University of Nebraska Press, c1999.
*TC BF353 .F85 1999*

**PUBLIC SPEAKING.** *See* EXPRESSION.

**PUBLIC TWO-YEAR COLLEGES.** *See* COMMUNITY COLLEGES.

**PUBLIC UNIVERSITIES AND COLLEGES.** *See* COMMUNITY COLLEGES; STATE UNIVERSITIES AND COLLEGES.

**PUBLIC UTILITIES.** *See* CORPORATIONS; RAILROADS.

**PUBLIC WELFARE.** *See also* AID TO FAMILIES WITH DEPENDENT CHILDREN PROGRAMS; CHILD WELFARE; COMMUNITY ORGANIZATION; FAMILY POLICY; INSTITUTIONAL CARE; SOCIAL MEDICINE.
Poverty. San Diego, CA : Greenhaven Press, c1994.
*TC HC110.P6 P63 1994*

**PUBLIC WELFARE - GOVERNMENT POLICY.** *See* PUBLIC WELFARE.

**PUBLIC WELFARE - GOVERNMENT POLICY - UNITED STATES.**
Welfare, the family, and reproductive behavior. Washington, D.C. : National Academy Press, 1998.
*TC HV91 .W478 1998*

**PUBLIC WELFARE - LAW.** *See* **PUBLIC WELFARE - LAW AND LEGISLATION.**

**PUBLIC WELFARE - LAW AND LEGISLATION - UNITED STATES.**
Baldwin, John. Education and welfare reform. Bloomington, Ind. : Phi Delta Kappa Educational Foundation, c1993.
*TC LC4033.S61 B34 1993*

Welfare. San Diego, CA : Greenhaven Press, c1997.
*TC HV95 .W453 1997*

**PUBLIC WELFARE - NEW YORK (STATE) - NEW YORK - HISTORY - 20TH CENTURY.**
Opdycke, Sandra. No one was turned away. New York : Oxford University Press, 1999.
*TC RA982.N49 O63 1999*

**PUBLIC WELFARE - PERIODICALS.**
American economic security. Washington, Chamber of Commerce of the United States of America.

**PUBLIC WELFARE REFORM.** *See* **PUBLIC WELFARE.**

**PUBLIC WELFARE - UNITED STATES.**
Baldwin, John. Education and welfare reform. Bloomington, Ind. : Phi Delta Kappa Educational Foundation, c1993.
*TC LC4033.S61 B34 1993*

Counseling and the therapeutic state. New York : Aldine de Gruyter, c1999.
*TC HV95 .C675 1999*

Kahn, Alfred J., 1919- Big cities in the welfare transition. New York City : Cross-National Studies Research Program, Columbia University School of Social Work, 1998.
*TC HV91 .K27 1998*

Poverty. San Diego, CA : Greenhaven Press, c1994.
*TC HC110.P6 P63 1994*

Schorr, Alvin Louis, 1921- Filial responsibility in the modern American family. [Washington] U.S. Dept. of Health, Education, and Welfare, Social Security Administration, Division of Program Research [1960]
*TC HV75 .S36 1960*

**PUBLIC WELFARE - UNITED STATES - HISTORY.**
Crenson, Matthew A., 1943- Building the invisible orphanage. Cambridge, Mass. : Harvard University Press, 1998.
*TC HV91 .C74 1998*

**PUBLIC WELFARE - UNITED STATES - PERIODICALS.**
American economic security. Washington, Chamber of Commerce of the United States of America.

**PUBLIC WELFARE - UNITED STATES - PHILOSOPHY.**
Welfare. San Diego, CA : Greenhaven Press, c1997.
*TC HV95 .W453 1997*

**PUBLIC WELFARE - UNITED STATES - STATISTICS - PERIODICALS.**
Health, education, and welfare indicators. Washington, D.C. : U.S. Dept. of Health, Education and Welfare : For sale by the Supt. of Docs., U.S. G.P.O., 1960-[1967]

**PUBLICATIONS, ELECTRONIC.** *See* **ELECTRONIC PUBLICATIONS.**

**Publications in creativity research**
Creativity, spirituality, and transcendence. Stamford, Conn. : Ablex, c2000.
*TC BF411 .C76 2000*

Khatena, Joe. Developing creative talent in art. Stamford, Conn. : Ablex Publ., c1999.
*TC NX164.C47 K53 1999*

**Publications of the Society for Psychological Anthropology**
([10]) Biocultural approaches to the emotions. Cambridge, U.K. ; New York : Cambridge University Press, 1999.
*TC GN502 .B53 1999*

**PUBLICATIONS, ONLINE.** *See* **ELECTRONIC PUBLICATIONS.**

**PUBLICITY.** *See* **PUBLIC OPINION.**

**PUBLICITY, GOVERNMENT.** *See* **GOVERNMENT PUBLICITY.**

**PUBLISHERS AND PUBLISHING - GREAT BRITAIN - HISTORY - 17TH CENTURY.**
Wheale, Nigel. Writing and society. London ; New York : Routledge, 1999.
*TC PR438.P65 W75 1999*

**PUBLISHERS AND PUBLISHING - UNITED STATES - DIRECTORIES.**
El-Hi textbooks in print. New York, N.Y. : Bowker, 1970-
*TC Z5813 .A51*

**Puckett, Margaret B.** Authentic assessment of the young child : celebrating development and learning / Margaret B. Puckett, Janet K. Black. 2nd ed. Upper Saddle River, N.J. : Merrill, c2000. xv, 384 p. : ill. ; 24 cm. Includes bibliographical references (p. 357-370) and indexes. ISBN 0-13-080271-9 DDC 372.126/4
*1. Educational tests and measurements. 2. Early childhood education - Evaluation. 3. Child development - Evaluation. I. Black, Janet K. II. Title.*
*TC LB3051 .P69 2000*

**PUEBLA (MEXICO : STATE) - POLITICS AND GOVERNMENT.**
Thomson, Guy P. C., 1949- Patriotism, politics, and popular liberalism in nineteenth-century Mexico. Wilmington, De. : Scholarly Resources, 1999.
*TC F1326.L83 T5 1999*

**PUEBLO CULTURE.** *See* **PUEBLO INDIANS.**

**PUEBLO INDIANS.** *See also* **TEWA INDIANS.**
Hazen-Hammond, Susan. Thunder Bear and Ko. 1st ed. New York : Dutton Children's Books, 1999.
*TC E99.T35 H36 1999*

**PUEBLO INDIANS - JUVENILE LITERATURE.**
Hazen-Hammond, Susan. Thunder Bear and Ko. 1st ed. New York : Dutton Children's Books, 1999.
*TC E99.T35 H36 1999*

**PUERICULTURE.** *See* **CHILDREN - HEALTH AND HYGIENE.**

**PUERTO RICAN CHILDREN - LITERARY COLLECTIONS.**
Growing up Puerto Rican. 1st ed. New York : Morrow, c1997.
*TC PS508.P84 G76 1997*

**PUERTO RICAN CHILDREN - UNITED STATES.** *See* **PUERTO RICAN CHILDREN.**

**Puerto Rican students in U.S. schools** / edited by Sonia Nieto, Mahwah, NJ : Lawrence Erlbaum Associates, 2000. xvi, 354 p. ; 23 cm. Includes bibliographical references and index. ISBN 0-8058-2764-1 (alk. paper) ISBN 0-8058-2765-X (pbk. : alk. paper) DDC 371.82968/7295
*1. Puerto Ricans - Education - United States. 2. Puerto Ricans - United States - Social conditions. I. Nieto, Sonia.*
*TC LC2692 .P82 2000*

**PUERTO RICAN YOUTH - LITERARY COLLECTIONS.**
Growing up Puerto Rican. 1st ed. New York : Morrow, c1997.
*TC PS508.P84 G76 1997*

**PUERTO RICANS - EDUCATION - UNITED STATES.**
Puerto Rican students in U.S. schools. Mahwah, NJ : Lawrence Erlbaum Associates, 2000.
*TC LC2692 .P82 2000*

**Puerto Ricans, from island to mainland.**
Kurtis, Arlene Harris. New York : J. Messner, c1969.
*TC F1958.3 .K8*

**PUERTO RICANS - UNITED STATES.**
Kurtis, Arlene Harris. Puerto Ricans, from island to mainland. New York : J. Messner, c1969.
*TC F1958.3 .K8*

**PUERTO RICANS - UNITED STATES - JUVENILE LITERATURE.**
Kurtis, Arlene Harris. Puerto Ricans, from island to mainland. New York : J. Messner, c1969.
*TC F1958.3 .K8*

**PUERTO RICANS - UNITED STATES - LITERARY COLLECTIONS.**
Growing up Puerto Rican. 1st ed. New York : Morrow, c1997.
*TC PS508.P84 G76 1997*

**PUERTO RICANS - UNITED STATES - SOCIAL CONDITIONS.**
Puerto Rican students in U.S. schools. Mahwah, NJ : Lawrence Erlbaum Associates, 2000.
*TC LC2692 .P82 2000*

**PUERTO RICO - HISTORY.**
Kurtis, Arlene Harris. Puerto Ricans, from island to mainland. New York : J. Messner, c1969.
*TC F1958.3 .K8*

**PUERTO RICO - HISTORY - JUVENILE LITERATURE.**
Kurtis, Arlene Harris. Puerto Ricans, from island to mainland. New York : J. Messner, c1969.
*TC F1958.3 .K8*

**PUERTO RICO - HISTORY - TO 1898.**
Kinsbruner, Jay. Not of pure blood. Durham : Duke University Press, 1996.
*TC F1983.B55 K56 1996*

**PUERTO RICO - RACE RELATIONS.**
Kinsbruner, Jay. Not of pure blood. Durham : Duke University Press, 1996.
*TC F1983.B55 K56 1996*

**PUFFINS.**
McMillan, Bruce. Nights of the pufflings. Boston : Houghton Mifflin Co., 1995.
*TC QL696.C42 M39 1995*

**PUFFINS - ICELAND - JUVENILE LITERATURE.**
McMillan, Bruce. Nights of the pufflings. Boston : Houghton Mifflin Co., 1995.
*TC QL696.C42 M39 1995*

**PULMONARY VENTILATORS.** *See* **RESPIRATORS (MEDICAL EQUIPMENT).**

**Punished by rewards.**
Kohn, Alfie. Boston : Houghton Mifflin Co., 1999, c1993.
*TC BF505.R48 K65 1999*

**PUNISHMENT.** *See* **ALTERNATIVES TO IMPRISONMENT.**

**Punishment and aversive stimulation in special education** : legal, theoretical and practical issues in their use with emotionally disturbed children and youth / Frank H. Wood and K. Charlie Lakin, editors. Reston, Va. : Council for Exceptional Children, 1982. 124 p. ; 22 cm. Includes bibliographical references. Reprint. Originally published : Minneapolis, Minn. : Advanced Institute for Trainers of Teachers for Seriously Emotionally Disturbed Children and Youth, 1978.
*1. Mentally ill children - Education - Addresses, essays, lectures. 2. Rewards and punishments in education - Addresses, essays, lectures. 3. Punishment (Psychology) - Addresses, essays, lectures. I. Wood, Frank H. (Frank Henderson), 1929- II. Lakin, Charlie K.*
*TC LC4169 .P8 1982*

**PUNISHMENT (PSYCHOLOGY).** *See* **REWARDS AND PUNISHMENTS IN EDUCATION.**

**PUNISHMENT (PSYCHOLOGY) - ADDRESSES, ESSAYS, LECTURES.**
Punishment and aversive stimulation in special education. Reston, Va. : Council for Exceptional Children, 1982.
*TC LC4169 .P8 1982*

**PUPIL-TEACHER RELATIONSHIPS.** *See* **TEACHER-STUDENT RELATIONSHIPS.**

**PUPILS.** *See* **SCHOOL CHILDREN; STUDENTS.**

**Pupipat, Apisak.** Scientific writing and publishing in English in Thailand : the perceptions of Thai scientists and editors / by Apisak Pupipat. 1998. xi, 196 leaves ; 29 cm. Typescript; issued also on microfilm. Thesis (Ed.D.)--Teachers College, Columbia University, 1998. Includes bibliographical references (leaves 166-185).
*1. English language - Written English - Thailand. 2. Scientists - Thailand. 3. Technical writing - Study and teaching (Higher) 4. English language - Technical English - Study and teaching - Thailand. 5. Academic writing - Study and teaching (Higher) - Thailand. 6. Language and languages - Variation. 7. Interference (Linguistics) I. Title.*
*TC 06 no. 10981*

**PUPPET PLAYS, AMERICAN - NEW YORK (STATE) - NEW YORK.**
Milbank Memorial Library story hour [videorecording]. [New York : Milbank Memorial Library, 1999].
*TC Z718.3 .M5 1999 Series 3 Prog. 11*

**PUPPET THEATER.** *See* **PUPPETS.**

**PUPPET THEATER IN EDUCATION - UNITED STATES.**
Druce, Arden. Paper bag puppets. Lanham, MD : Scarecrow Press, 1999.
*TC Z718.3 .D78 1999*

**PUPPETS.** *See* **LIBRARIES AND PUPPETS.**

**PUPPETS AND LIBRARIES.** *See* **LIBRARIES AND PUPPETS.**

**PUPPETS AND PUPPET-PLAYS.** *See* **PUPPETS.**

**PUPPETS AND PUPPET-PLAYS IN EDUCATION.** *See* **PUPPET THEATER IN EDUCATION.**

**PUPPETS - FICTION.**
Gauch, Patricia Lee. Poppy's puppet. 1st ed. New York : Holt, 1999.
*TC PZ7.G2315 Po 1999*

**Purcell-Gates, Victoria.** Now we read, we see, we speak : portrait of literacy development in an adult Freirean-based class / Victoria Purcell-Gates, Robin A. Waterman. Mahwah, N.J. : L. Erlbaum Associates, Publishers, 2000. xvii, 256 p. : ill. ; 24 cm. Includes bibliographical references (p. 239-245) and indexes. ISBN 0-8058-3469-9 (alk. paper) ISBN 0-8058-3470-2 (pbk. : alk. paper) DDC 302.2/244
*1. Freire, Paulo. - 1921- 2. Functional literacy - El Salvador - Case studies. 3. Literacy programs - El Salvador - Case studies. 4. Critical pedagogy - El Salvador - Case studies. I. Waterman, Robin. II. Title.*
*TC LC155.S22 P87 2000*

**Purdue University.**
First stage. Lafayette, Ind. : Purdue University, c1961-c1967.

**Purdue University. Dept. of English.**
Journal of developmental reading. [Layfayette, Ind. : Dept. of English, Purdue University], c1957-1964.

**Purdy, Carol.** Mrs. Merriwether's musical cat / Carol Purdy ; illustrated by Petra Mathers. New York : Putnam, c1994. 1 v. (unpaged) : col. ill. ; 28 cm. SUMMARY: Mrs. Merriwether takes in a stray cat that proves to have an amazing effect on her piano students. ISBN 0-399-22543-9 DDC [E]
*1. Piano - Instruction and study - Fiction. 2. Cats - Fiction. I. Mathers, Petra, ill. II. Title.*
*TC PZ7.P9745 Mr 1994*

**Purdy, Laura Martha.**
Embodying bioethics. Lanham : Rowman & Littlefield Publishers, c1999.
*TC QH332 .E43 1999*

**PURE FOOD.** *See* **FOOD ADULTERATION AND INSPECTION; FOOD LAW AND LEGISLATION.**

**The pure food, drink, and drug crusaders, 1879-1914.**
Goodwin, Lorine Swainston, 1925- Jefferson, N.C. : McFarland, 1999.
*TC HD9000.9.U5 G66 1999*

**Purkey, William Watson.** What students say to themselves : internal dialogue and school success / William Watson Purkey. Thousand Oaks, Calif. : Corwin Press, c2000. x, 110 p. : ill. ; 24 cm. Includes bibliographical references (p. 92-103) and index. ISBN 0-8039-6694-6 (hbk. : alk. paper) ISBN 0-8039-6695-4 (pbk. : alk. paper) DDC 371.8
*1. Academic achievement - Psychological aspects. 2. Students - Psychology. 3. Self-perception. 4. Motivation in education. I. Title.*
*TC LB1062.6 .P87 2000*

**PURPOSES, EDUCATIONAL.** *See* **EDUCATION - AIMS AND OBJECTIVES.**

**Putnam and Pennyroyal.**
Jennings, Patrick. 1st ed. New York : Scholastic Press, 1999.
*TC PZ7.J4298715 Co 1999*

**PUZZLES.** *See* **PICTURE PUZZLES.**

**PWAS.** *See* **AIDS (DISEASE) - PATIENTS.**

**Pylyshyn, Zenon W., 1937-.**
What is cognitive science? Malden, Mass. : Blackwell, 1999.
*TC BF311 .W48 1999*

**PYROTECHNICS.** *See* **FIREWORKS.**

**Pyshkalo, A.M.**
Russian grade 3 mathematics. Chicago : University of Chicago School of Mathematics Project, 1992.
*TC QA14.R9 R8811 1992*

**QUAKERS.**
Wister, Sarah, 1761-1804. A colonial Quaker girl. Mankato, Minn. : Blue Earth Books, c2000.
*TC F158.44 .W75 2000*

**QUAKERS - PENNSYLVANIA - PHILADELPHIA REGION - DIARIES - JUVENILE LITERATURE.**
Wister, Sarah, 1761-1804. A colonial Quaker girl. Mankato, Minn. : Blue Earth Books, c2000.

*TC F158.44 .W75 2000*

**QUALIFICATIONS, VOCATIONAL.** *See* **VOCATIONAL QUALIFICATIONS.**

**The qualitative dissertation.**
Piantanida, Maria. Thousand Oaks, Calif. : Corwin Press, c1999.
*TC LB2369 .P48 1999*

**Qualitative education and development.**
Majasan, James. Ibadan : Spectrum Books Limited : Channel Islands, UK : In association with Safari Books (Export) ; Oxford, UK : African Books Collective Ltd. (Distributor), 1998.
*TC LC2605 .M32 1998*

**Qualitative research.**
Handbook of qualitative research. 2nd ed. Thousand Oaks, Calif. : Sage Publications, c2000.
*TC H62 .H2455 2000*

**QUALITATIVE RESEARCH.**
Munhall, Patricia L. Qualitative research proposals and reports. Sudbury, MA : Jones and Bartlett, 2000.
*TC RT81.5 .M854 2000*

Roper, Janice M. Ethnography in nursing research. Thousand Oaks, Calif. : Sage Publications, c2000.
*TC RT81.5 .R66 2000*

**Qualitative research and case study applications in education.**
Merriam, Sharan B. 2nd ed. San Francisco : Jossey-Bass Publishers, c1998.
*TC LB1028 .M396 1998*

**Qualitative research in nursing.**
Streubert, Helen J. 2nd ed. Philadelphia : Lippincott, c1999.
*TC RT81.5 .S78 1999*

**Qualitative research methods**
(v. 16.) Morgan, David L. Focus groups as qualitative research / David L. Morgan. 2nd ed. Thousand Oaks, Calif. : Sage Publications, c1997.
*TC H61.28 .M67 1997*

**Qualitative research proposals and reports.**
Munhall, Patricia L. Sudbury, MA : Jones and Bartlett, 2000.
*TC RT81.5 .M854 2000*

**Qualitative research :** the emotional dimension / edited by Keith Carter, Sara Delamont. Aldershot, Hants, England : Brookfield, Vt. : Avebury, c1996. xv, 138 p. ; 23 cm. (Cardiff papers in qualitative research) Includes bibliographical references. ISBN 1-85972-263-6 DDC 300/.72
*1. Social sciences - Research. 2. Emotions - Research. I. Carter, Keith. II. Delamont, Sara, 1947- III. Series.*
*TC H62 .Q355 1996*

**QUALITATIVE RESEARCH - UNITED STATES.**
Multiple and intersecting identities in qualitative research. Mahwah, N.J. ; London : L. Erlbaum Associates, 2001.
*TC LB1028.25.U6 M85 2001*

**Qualitative studies series**
(3) Scheurich, James Joseph, 1944- Research method in the postmodern. London ; Washington, DC : Falmer Press, 1997.
*TC LB1028 .S242 1997*

**A qualitative study of perceptions of external factors that influence the persistence of Black males at a predominantly white four-year state college.**
Dixon, Jerome C. 1999.
*TC 06 no. 11050*

**QUALITY ASSURANCE, HEALTH CARE.**
Streubert, Helen J. Qualitative research in nursing. 2nd ed. Philadelphia : Lippincott, c1999.
*TC RT81.5 .S78 1999*

**QUALITY ASSURANCE, HEALTH CARE - ORGANIZATION & ADMINISTRATION.**
Shelton, Patrick J. Measuring and improving patient satisfaction. Gaithersburg, Md. : Aspen Publishers, 2000.
*TC RA399.A1 S47 2000*

**Quality circle time in the secondary school.**
Mosley, Jenny. London : David Fulton, 1999.
*TC LB1032 .M67 1999*

**QUALITY CIRCLES.**
Cole, Robert E. Managing quality fads. New York : Oxford University Press, 1999.
*TC HD66 .C539 1999*

**QUALITY CIRCLES - UNITED STATES - HISTORY.**
Cole, Robert E. Managing quality fads. New York : Oxford University Press, 1999.

*TC HD66 .C539 1999*

**QUALITY CONTROL.** *See* **QUALITY CIRCLES.**

**QUALITY CONTROL CIRCLES.** *See* **QUALITY CIRCLES.**

**Quality human resources leadership.**
Weller, L. David. Lanham, Md. : Scarecrow Press, 2000.
*TC LB2831.92 .W45 2000*

**Quality in child care :** what does research tell us? / Deborah A. Phillips, editor. Washington, D.C. : National Association for the Education of Young Children, c1987. xi, 127 p. : ill. ; 23 cm. (NAEYC ; #140) (Research monographs of the National Association for the Education of Young Children ; v. 1) Includes bibliographies and indexes. ISBN 0-935989-08-0 (pbk.) DDC 362.7/12
*1. Child care - United States. 2. Child care - United States - Evaluation. I. Phillips, Deborah. II. National Association for the Education of Young Children. III. Series. IV. Series: NAEYC (Series) ; #140.*
*TC HQ778.7.U6 Q35 1987*

**QUALITY MANAGEMENT, TOTAL.** *See* **TOTAL QUALITY MANAGEMENT.**

**QUALITY OF FOOD.** *See* **FOOD - QUALITY.**

**QUALITY OF LIFE.** *See also* **HEALTH STATUS INDICATORS; QUALITY OF WORK LIFE; SOCIAL INDICATORS.**
Individual quality of life. Amsterdam : Harwood Academic, c1999.
*TC RA407 .I54 1999*

The many dimensions of aging. New York : Springer Pub., c2000.
*TC HQ1061 .M337 2000*

Quality of life from nursing and patient perspectives. Sudbury, Mass. ; London : Jones and Bartlett, c1998.
*TC RC262 .Q34 1998*

**QUALITY OF LIFE - EVALUATION.**
Individual quality of life. Amsterdam : Harwood Academic, c1999.
*TC RA407 .I54 1999*

**Quality of life from nursing and patient perspectives :** theory, research, practice / Cynthia R. King & Pamela S. Hinds, editors. Sudbury, Mass. ; London : Jones and Bartlett, c1998. xxv, 390 p. : ill. ; 24 cm. (Jones and Bartlett series in oncology) Includes bibliographical references and index. ISBN 0-7637-0628-0 DDC 610.73/698
*1. Cancer - Psychological aspects. 2. Cancer - Social aspects. 3. Quality of life. 4. Cancer - Nursing. 5. Neoplasms - nursing. 6. Quality of Life - nurses' instruction. 7. Patient Satisfaction. 8. Research. I. King, Cynthia R. II. Hinds, Pamela S. III. Series.*
*TC RC262 .Q34 1998*

**QUALITY OF LIFE - NURSES' INSTRUCTION.**
Quality of life from nursing and patient perspectives. Sudbury, Mass. ; London : Jones and Bartlett, c1998.
*TC RC262 .Q34 1998*

**QUALITY OF PRODUCTS.** *See* **FOOD - QUALITY.**

**Quality of students of color efort on a predominantly white college and the internal environmental elements that influence involvement.**
Capeheart-Meningall, Jennifer. 1998.
*TC 06 no. 10874*

**QUALITY OF WORK LIFE.** *See* **JOB SATISFACTION.**

**QUALITY OF WORK LIFE - UNITED STATES.**
Schmidt, Jeff, 1946- Disciplined minds. Lanham, Md. ; Oxford : Rowman & Littlefield, c2000.
*TC HT687 .S35 2000*

**QUALITY OF WORKING LIFE.** *See* **QUALITY OF WORK LIFE.**

**Quandt, Richard E.**
Technology and scholarly communication. Berkeley, Calif. : University of California Press ; [Pittsburgh?] : Published in association with the Andrew K. Mellon Foundation, c1999.
*TC Z479 .T43 1999*

**Quann, Steve.** Learning computers, speaking English : cooperative activities for learning English and basic word processing / Steve Quann and Diana Satin. Ann Arbor : University of Michigan Press, c2000. xv, 186 p. : ill. ; 28 cm. "For intermediate ESL/EFL students"--cover. System requirements for accompanying computer disk: IBM-compatible PC; Windows. SUMMARY: Leads high-beginning and intermediate ESL students through cooperative computer-based activities that combine language learning with training in basic computer skills and word processing. ISBN 0-472-

08655-3 ISBN 0-472-08683-9 (set)
1. *English language - Study and teaching - Foreign speakers.*
2. *English language - Computer-assisted instruction for foreign speakers. 3. Word processing in education.I. Satin, Diana. II. Title.*
**TC PE1128.A2 .Q83 2000**

**Quantitative naturalistic research.**
Butler, John M. Englewood Cliffs, N.J., Prentice-Hall [1963]
**TC BF39 .B83**

**Quantum chaos.**
Stöckmann, Hans-Jürgen, 1945- Cambridge [England] ; New York : Cambridge University Press, 1999.
**TC QC174.17.C45 S84 1999**

**QUANTUM CHAOS.**
Stöckmann, Hans-Jürgen, 1945- Quantum chaos. Cambridge [England] ; New York : Cambridge University Press, 1999.
**TC QC174.17.C45 S84 1999**

**Quantum teaching.**
DePorter, Bobbi. Boston, Mass. : Allyn and Bacon, c1999.
**TC LB1027 .D418 1999**

**QUANTUM THEORY.**
Stephen Hawking's universe [videorecording]. [Alexandria, Va.] : PBS Video; Burbank, CA : Distributed by Warner Home Video, c1997.
**TC QB982 .S7 1997**

Wheatley, Margaret J. Leadership and the new science. 2nd ed. San Francisco : Berrett-Koehler Publishers, c1999.
**TC HD57.7 .W47 1999**

**Quarterly bulletin of fundamental education.**
Fundamental education. [Paris, France : Unesco, 1949-1952].

**QUASARS.**
Stephen Hawking's universe [videorecording]. [Alexandria, Va.] : PBS Video; Burbank, CA : Distributed by Warner Home Video, c1997.
**TC QB982 .S7 1997**

Stephen Hawking's universe [videorecording]. [Alexandria, Va.] : PBS Video; Burbank, CA : Distributed by Warner Home Video, c1997.
**TC QB982 .S7 1997**

**Quay, Suzanne.**
Deuchar, M. (Margaret) Bilingual acquisition. Oxford ; New York : Oxford University Press, 2000.
**TC P118 .D439 2000**

**QUÉBEC (PROVINCE) - HISTORY.**
Neatby, Nicole, 1962- Carabins ou activistes? Montréal ; Ithaca : McGill-Queen's University Press, [1999?], c1997.
**TC LA418.Q8 N42 1999**

**Queen, J. Allen.** Curriculum practice in the elementary and middle school / J. Allen Queen. Upper Saddle River, N.J. : Merrill, 1999. xvi, 320 p. : ill. ; 24 cm. Includes bibliographical references and indexes. ISBN 0-02-397051-0 DDC 375/.001
1. *Education, Elementary - United States - Curricula. 2. Middle school education - United States - Curricula. 3. Curriculum planning - United States. 4. Instructional systems - Design. 5. Curriculum change - United States. I. Title.*
**TC LB1570 .Q45 1999**

**QUEEN'S UNIVERSITY (KINGSTON, ONT.). SCHOOL OF BUSINESS - HISTORY.**
Daub, Mervin, 1943- Getting down to business. Montreal ; Ithaca : McGill-Queen's University Press, c1999.
**TC HF1134.Q442 D38 1999**

**Queering elementary education :** advancing the dialogue about sexualities and schooling / edited by William J. Letts IV and James T. Sears. Lanham, Md. ; Oxford : Rowman & Littlefield, c1999. xviii, 291 p. ; 24 cm. (Curriculum, cultures, and (homo)sexualities) Includes bibliographical references (p. 263-275) and index. ISBN 0-8476-9368-6 (cloth : alk. paper) ISBN 0-8476-9369-4 (paper : alk. paper) DDC 371/.01/1
1. *Homosexuality and education - United States. 2. Education, Elementary - Social aspects - United States. 3. Education, Elementary - United States - Curricula. 4. Sex instruction - United States. I. Letts, William J., 1965- II. Sears, James T. (James Thomas), 1951- III. Series.*
**TC LC192.6 .Q85 1999**

**Quehl, Gary H.** Fifty years of innovations in undergraduate education : change and stasis in the pursuit of quality / Gary H. Quehl, William H. Bergquist and Joseph L. Subbiondo. Indianapolis, Ind : USA Group Foundation, c1999. 60 p. ; 28 cm.

(USAGroup Foundation new agenda series ; v.1, no.4 (Oct. 1999).) Cover title. Includes bibliographical references (p. 59)
1. *Educational innovations - United States. 2. Education, Higher - United States - History - 20th century.I. Bergquist. William H. II. Subbiondo.Joseph L. III. USAGroup Foundation. IV. Title. V. Series.*
**TC LB1027.3 .Q43 1999**

**Quenk, Naomi L., 1936-** Essentials of Myers-Briggs type indicator assessment / Naomi L. Quenk. New York : J. Wiley & Sons, 2000. x, 197 p. : ill. ; 22 cm. (Essentials of psychological assessment series) Includes bibliographical references (p. 181-192) and index. ISBN 0-471-33239-9 (paper : alk. paper) DDC 155.2/83
1. *Myers-Briggs Type Indicator. 2. Typology (Psychology) I. Title. II. Series.*
**TC BF698.8.M94 Q45 2000**

**QUERIES.** *See* **QUESTIONS AND ANSWERS.**

**Quesnell, Quentin.** The strange disappearance of Sophia Smith / Quentin Quesnell. Northampton [Mass.] : Smith College, c1999. xxvi, 250 p. : ill. map ; 26 cm. Includes bibliographical references and index. ISBN 0-87391-048-6
1. *Smith, Sophia, - 1796-1870. 2. Smith College - Biography. 3. Smith College - History. 4. Greene, John Morton, - 1830-1919. 5. Hanscom, Elizabeth Deering, - 1865-1960 - Sophia Smith and the beginnings of Smith College. 6. Sex role - United States - Historiography. 7. Women - United States - Historiography. 8. Women - United States - Biography. 9. Women's colleges - Massachusetts - Northampton - History. I. Title. II. Title: Sophia Smith*
**TC LD7152.65.S45 Q84 1999**

**Quest for silence.**
Wilmer, Harry A., 1917- Einsiedeln, Switzerland : Daimon, c2000.
**TC BJ1499.S5 W556 2000**

**Questar Video, Inc.**
Headline stories of the century [videorecording]. Chicago, IL. : Distributed by Questar Video, Inc., c1992.
**TC D743 .H42 1992**

**QUESTION BOXES.** *See* **QUESTIONS AND ANSWERS.**

**QUESTIONING.** *See also* **INTERVIEWING.**
Ball, Wanda H., 1953- Socratic seminars in the block. Larchmont, N.Y. : Eye On Education, 2000.
**TC LB1027.44 .B35 2000**

Chuska, Kenneth R. Improving classroom questions. Bloomington, Ind. : Phi Delta Kappa Educational Foundation, 1995.
**TC LB1027.44 .C58 1995**

**Questioning outside the lines.**
Interdisciplinary general education. New York, NY : College Board Publications, c1999.
**TC LB2361 .I43 1999**

**QUESTIONING - STUDY AND TEACHING (MIDDLE SCHOOL) - UNITED STATES - PROBLEMS, EXERCISES, ETC.**
Socratic seminar [videorecording]. [Boulder, Colo.] : Social Science Education Consortium, c1997.
**TC LB1027.44 .S6 1997**

**QUESTIONING - STUDY AND TEACHING (SECONDARY) - UNITED STATES - PROBLEMS, EXERCISES, ETC.**
Socratic seminar [videorecording]. [Boulder, Colo.] : Social Science Education Consortium, c1997.
**TC LB1027.44 .S6 1997**

**QUESTIONING - THERAPEUTIC USE.**
Goldberg, Marilee C. The art of the question. New York : Wiley, c1998.
**TC RC489.N47 G65 1998**

**QUESTIONS AND ANSWERS.** *See also* **EXAMINATIONS.**
January, Brendan, 1972- The New York Public Library amazing mythology. New York : Wiley, 2000.
**TC BL311 .J36 2000**

**QUESTIONS AND ANSWERS - FICTION.**
Camp, Lindsay. Why? New York : Putnam, c1998.
**TC PZ7.C1475 Wf 1998**

**Questions of you and the struggle of collaborative life.**
Paley, Nicholas. New York : P. Lang, c2000.
**TC LB1028 .P233 2000**

**Quicke, John, 1941-** A curriculum for life : schools for a democratic learning society / John Quicke. Buckingham ; Philadelphia : Open University Press, 1999. viii, 184 p. ; 24 cm. Includes bibliographical references (p. ) and index. ISBN 0-335-20298-5 ISBN 0-335-20297-7 (pbk.) DDC 375/.000941

1. *Education - Great Britain - Curricula. 2. Curriculum change - Great Britain. 3. Democracy - Study and teaching - Great Britain. I. Title.*
**TC LB1564.G7 Q85 1999**

**Quigley, Jean.** The grammar of autobiography : a developmental account / Jean Quigley. Mahwah, N.J. : Lawrence Erlbaum Associates, c2000. xiv, 232 p. ; 24 cm. Includes bibliographical references (p. 203-219) and index. ISBN 0-8058-3483-4 DDC 425
1. *English language - Modality. 2. English language - Grammar. 3. Children - Language. 4. Narration (Rhetoric) 5. Autobiography. I. Title.*
**TC PE1315.M6 Q54 2000**

**QUINARY SYSTEM.**
Speiser, R. (Robert) Five women build a number system. Stamford, Conn. : Ablex Pub., c2000.
**TC QA135.5 .S5785 2000**

**Quinn, Aidan.**
The Irish in America [videorecording]. [New York, N.Y.] : A&E Home Video ; New York, N.Y. : Distributed by the New Video Group, 1997.
**TC E184.16 I6 1997**

**Quinn, Susan.**
Jazz dance class [videorecording]. W. Long Branch, NJ : Kultur, [1992?]
**TC GV1784 .J3 1992**

**Quisenberry, Nancy L.**
Educators healing racism. Reston, VA : Association of Teacher Educators ; Olney, MD : Association for Childhood Education International, c1999.
**TC LC212.2 .E38 1999**

**Quist, Hubert Oswald.** Secondary education and nation-building : a study of Ghana, 1951-1991 / by Hubert Oswald Quist. 1999. xxii, 404 leaves ; 29 cm. Typescript; issued also on microfilm. Thesis (Ph.D.) -- Columbia University, 1999. Includes bibliographical references (leaves 360-153)
1. *Education - Ghana - History. 2. Education, Secondary - Ghana - History. 3. Ghana - Politics and government. 4. Economic development - Effect of education on. 5. Nationalism and education - Ghana. 6. Religion in the public schools - Ghana. 7. Nkrumah, Kwame, - 1909-1972 8. Rawlings, Jerry, - 1947- I. Title. II. Title: Secondary education and nation building, a study of Ghana, 1951-1991*
**TC 085 Q52**

**QUIZ BOOKS.** *See* **QUESTIONS AND ANSWERS.**

**Quong, Terry.** Values based strategic planning : : a dynamic approach for schools / Terry Quong, Allan Walker, Kenneth Stott. Singapore ; New York : Prentice Hall, 1998. vii, 232 p. : ill. ; 23 cm. Includes bibliographical references (p. 215-221) and index. ISBN 0-13-081926-3
1. *Educational planning. 2. Strategic planning. 3. School management and organization. I. Walker. Allan. II. Stott, Kenneth. III. Title.*
**TC LB2806 .Q86 1998**

**QUOTATIONS, ENGLISH.**
Lordahl, Jo Ann. Reflections for busy educators. Thousand Oaks, Calif. : Corwin Press, c1995.
**TC PN6084.E38 L67 1995**

**R.**
Dombroski, Ann P. Administrative problem solving. 1999.
**TC 06 no. 11104**

**RABBINICAL LITERATURE.** *See* **MOSES (BIBLICAL LEADER) IN RABBINICAL LITERATURE.**

**Rabbit in the moon [videorecording] : a documentary/memoir.**
Rabbit in the moon [videorecording]. San Francisco, Calif. : Wabi-Sabi Productions, 1999.
**TC D753.8 .R3 1999**

**Rabbit in the moon** [videorecording] / a Wabi-Sabi production ; a film by Emiko Omori ; directed, written, and narrated by Emiko Omori ; produced by Emiko Omori, Chizuko Omori. San Francisco, Calif. : Wabi-Sabi Productions, 1999. 1 videocassette (85 min.) : sd., col. and b&w ; 1/2 in. Title on container: Rabbit in the moon [videorecording] : a documentary/memoir. VHS. Cataloguued from credits, cassette label and container. Narrator: Emiko Omori; commentary: Chizuko Omori, Frank Emi, Aiko Yoshinaga-Herzig, James Hirabayashi, Hisaye Yamamoto, Shosuke Sasaki, Ernest Besig, Harry Ueno, Mits Koshiyama, Frank Miyamoto, Hiroshi Kashiwagi, James Omura. Editors, Pat Jackson, Emiko Omori; camera, Witt Monts, Emiko Omori; original music by Janice Giteck. Winner, Best Documentary Cinematography, Sundance Film Festival 1999. Silver Apple Award 1999, National Educational Media Network. SUMMARY: A documentary/memoir about the lingering effects of the World War II internment of the

Japanese American community. Visually stunning and emotionally compelling, the film examines issues that ultimately created deep rifts within the Japanese American community, reveals the racist subtext of the loyalty questionnaire and exposes the absurdity of the military draft within the camps. These testimonies are linked by the filmmakers' own experiences in the camps and placed in a larger historical context by the director.
*1. Manzanar War Relocation Center. 2. Heart Mountain Relocation Center (Wyo.) 3. Tule Lake Relocation Center (Calif.) 4. Poston Relocation Center (Poston. Ariz.) 5. Japanese Americans - Evacuation and relocation. 1942-1945. 6. Japanese Americans - Evacuation and relocation. 1942-1945 - Personal narratives. 7. Japanese Americans - Evacuation and relocation. 1942-1945 - Psychological aspects. 8. Concentration camps - United States. 9. Concentration camps - California. 10. Concentration camps - Arizona. 11. Concentration camps - Wyoming. 12. World War, 1939-1945 - Draft resisters. 13. World War, 1939-1945 - Participation, Japanese American. 14. World War, 1939-1945 - Japanese Americans - Personal narratives. 15. Japanese American Citizens' League. 16. Loyalty oaths - United States. 17. Documentary television programs. 18. Autobiography. I. Omori, Emiko. II. Omori, Chizuko. III. Emi, Frank. IV. Yoshinaga-Herzig, Aiko. V. Hirabayashi, James. VI. Yamamoto, Hisaye. VII. Sasaki, Shosuke. VIII. Besig, Ernest. IX. Ueno, Harry Y. (Harry Yoshio), 1907- X. Koshiyama, Mits. XI. Miyamoto, Frank. XII. Kashiwagi, Hiroshi. XIII. Omura. James. XIV. Wabi-Sabi Productions (Firm) XV. Title: Rabbit in the moon [videorecording] : a documentary/memoir*
**TC D753.8 .R3 1999**

**RABBITS AS PETS.** *See* **RABBITS.**

**RABBITS - FICTION.**
Denim, Sue, 1966- Make way for Dumb Bunnies. New York : Blue Sky Press, c1996.
**TC PZ7.D4149 Mak 1996**

McCarty, Peter. Little bunny on the move. 1st ed. New York : Holt, 1999.
**TC PZ7.M47841327 Li 1999**

**Rabil, Alison.** Content, context, and continuity : the Yale report of 1828, its impact on antebellum higher education with implications for contemporary liberal arts programs / by Alison Rabil. 1998. vii, 216 leaves ; 29 cm. Issued also on microfilm. Thesis (Ed.D.)--Teachers College, Columbia University, 1998. Includes bibliographical references (leaves 204-211).
*1. Yale University - History. 2. Yale report of 1828. 3. Universities and colleges - United States - History. 4. Universities and colleges - United States - Curricula - History. 5. Classical education - United States - History. 6. Education, Humanistic - United States - History. 7. Social ethics - Study and teaching (Higher) - United States - History. I. Title. II. Title: Yale report of 1828, its impact on antebellum higher education with implications for contemporary liberal arts programs*
**TC 06 no. 10901**

**Rabins, Peter V.**
Mace, Nancy L. The 36-hour day. 3rd ed. Baltimore : Johns Hopkins University Press, c1999.
**TC RC523 .M33 1999**

**Raboteau, Albert J.** A fire in the bones : reflections on African-American religious history / Albert J. Raboteau. Boston : Beacon Press, c1995. xi, 224 p. ; 22 cm. Includes bibliographical references (p. [197]-214) and index. ISBN 0-8070-0932-6 DDC 277.3/08/08996073
*1. Afro-Americans - Religion. 2. United States - Church history. I. Title.*
**TC BR563.N4 R24 1995**

**Rabow, Jerome.** Tutoring matters : everything you always wanted to know about how to tutor / Jerome Rabow, Tiffani Chin, Nima Fahimian. Philadelphia : Temple University Press, 1999. xxiv, 188 p. ; 20 cm. Includes bibliographical references. ISBN 1-56639-695-6 (alk. paper) ISBN 1-56639-696-4 (pbk. : alk. paper) DDC 371.39/4
*1. Tutors and tutoring - United States - Handbooks, manuals, etc. I. Chin, Tiffani. II. Fahimian, Nima. III. Title.*
**TC LC41 .R33 1999**

**RACE.**
Banton, Michael P. Racial theories. 2nd ed. Cambridge ; New York : Cambridge University Press, 1998.
**TC HT1521 .B345 1998**

**Race and American culture**
Witt, Doris. Black hunger. New York : Oxford University Press, 1999.
**TC E185.86 .W58 1999**

**Race and class in the American criminal justice system.**
Cole, David. No equal justice. New York : The New Press : Distributed by W. W. Norton, c1999.

**Race and ethnicity in multi-ethnic schools.**
Ryan, James, 1952 Oct. 18- Clevedon [England] : Philadelphia : Multilingual Matters, c1999.
**TC LC3734 .R93 1999**

**RACE AWARENESS.** *See also* **BLACKS - RACE IDENTITY; ETHNIC ATTITUDES.**
Seshadri-Crooks, Kalpana. Desiring whiteness. London ; New York : Routledge, 2000.
**TC BF175.4.R34 S47 2000**

**RACE AWARENESS IN CHILDREN - UNITED STATES.**
Wright, Marguerite A. I'm chocolate, you're vanilla. 1st paperback ed. San Francisco : Jossey-Bass, 2000.
**TC BF723.R3 W75 2000**

**RACE AWARENESS - UNITED STATES.**
Addressing cultural issues in organizations. Thousand Oaks, Calif. : Sage Publications, 2000.
**TC E184.A1 A337 2000**
Capeheart-Meningall, Jennifer. Quality of students of color efort on a predominantly white college and the internal environmental elements that influence involvement. 1998.
**TC 06 no. 10874**

**RACE AWARENESS - UNITED STATES - CASE STUDIES.**
Weiler, Jeanne. Codes and contradictions. Albany : State University of New York Press, c2000.
**TC LC1755 .W45 2000**

**RACE BIAS.** *See* **RACE DISCRIMINATION; RACISM.**

**RACE DISCRIMINATION - CALIFORNIA.**
Connerly, Ward, 1939- Creating equal. San Francisco : Encounter Books, 2000.
**TC E185.97 .C74 2000**

**RACE DISCRIMINATION - CANADA.**
Racism and education. Ottawa : Canadian Teachers' Federation, 1992.
**TC LC212.3.C3 R32 1992**

**RACE DISCRIMINATION - COMPUTER NETWORK RESOURCES.**
Race in cyberspace. New York ; London : Routledge, 2000.
**TC HT1523 .R252 2000**

**RACE DISCRIMINATION IN CRIMINAL JUSTICE ADMINISTRATION.** *See* **DISCRIMINATION IN CRIMINAL JUSTICE ADMINISTRATION.**

**RACE DISCRIMINATION IN EDUCATION.** *See* **DISCRIMINATION IN EDUCATION.**

**RACE DISCRIMINATION IN EMPLOYMENT.** *See* **DISCRIMINATION IN EMPLOYMENT.**

**RACE DISCRIMINATION IN HIGHER EDUCATION.** *See* **DISCRIMINATION IN HIGHER EDUCATION.**

**RACE DISCRIMINATION IN MEDICAL CARE.** *See* **DISCRIMINATION IN MEDICAL CARE.**

**RACE DISCRIMINATION IN MEDICAL EDUCATION.** *See* **DISCRIMINATION IN MEDICAL EDUCATION.**

**RACE DISCRIMINATION - POLITICAL ASPECTS - UNITED STATES - HISTORY - 20TH CENTURY.**
Cochran, David Carroll. The color of freedom. Albany : State University of New York Press, c1999.
**TC E185.615 .C634 1999**

**RACE DISCRIMINATION - SOUTH AFRICA.**
Ford, Richard B., 1935- Tradition and change in four societies; New York, Holt, Rinehart and Winston, 1968.
**TC HT1521 .F6 1968**

**RACE DISCRIMINATION - UNITED STATES.** *See also* **AFRO-AMERICANS - CIVIL RIGHTS.**
Cole, David. No equal justice. New York : The New Press : Distributed by W. W. Norton, c1999.
**TC HV9950 .C65 1999**

Connerly, Ward, 1939- Creating equal. San Francisco : Encounter Books, 2000.
**TC E185.97 .C74 2000**

**Race, ethnicity and culture in the visual arts** : January 8, 1992, Whitney Museum of American Art, New York City / participants, Kinshasha Holman Conwill ... [et al.] New York : American Council for the Arts, c1993. 11 p. : ports. ; 28 cm. Cover title. Edited by Robert Porter. "This panel discussion was organized by

**TC HV9950 .C65 1999**

ArtTable, Inc. ... publication of these proceedings is made possible by the generous support of the Nathan Cummings Foundation." "A panel discussion."
*1. Race relations - Art. 2. Art and race. I. Porter. Robert. II. Conwill, Kinshasha Holman. III. ArtTable, Inc. IV. Nathan Cummings Foundation. V. Whitney Museum of American Art. VI. Title: Panel discussion.*
**TC N70 .R32 1993**

**RACE IMPROVEMENT.** *See* **EUGENICS.**

**Race in contemporary Brazil** : from indifference to inequality / edited by Rebecca Reichmann. University Park, Pa. : Pennsylvania State University Press, 1999. xiv, 290 p. ; 24 cm. Includes bibliographical references (p. 251-272) and index. ISBN 0-271-01905-0 (cloth : alk. paper) DDC 305.896081
*1. Blacks - Brazil - Social conditions. 2. Women, Black - Brazil - Social conditions. 3. Brazil - Race relations. 4. Racism - Brazil. I. Reichmann. Rebecca Lynn.*
**TC F2659.N4 R245 1999**

**Race in cyberspace** / edited by Beth E. Kolko, Lisa Nakamura, Gilbert B. Rodman. New York : London : Routledge, 2000. vii, 247 p. : ill. ; 24 cm. Includes bibliographical references and index. ISBN 0-415-92162-7 (hbk.) ISBN 0-415-92163-5 (pbk.) DDC 025.06/3058
*1. Race discrimination - Computer network resources. 2. Computer networks - Social aspects. 3. Cyberspace - Social aspects. 4. Internet (Computer network) - Social aspects. 5. Social interaction - Computer network resources. I. Kolko, Beth E. II. Nakamura, Lisa. III. Rodman, Gilbert B., 1965-*
**TC HT1523 .R252 2000**

**RACE IN LITERATURE - STUDY AND TEACHING.**
Making Mark Twain work in the classroom. Durham [N.C.] : Duke University Press, 1999.
**TC PS1338 .M23 1999**

**Race is-- race isn't** : critical race theory and qualitative studies in education / edited by Laurence Parker, Donna Deyhle, Sofia Villenas. Boulder, CO : Westview Press, c1999. ix, 284 p. ; 24 cm. Includes bibliographical references and index. ISBN 0-8133-9069-9 (alk. paper) DDC 306.43
*1. Minorities - Education - United States. 2. Racism - United States. 3. United States - Race relations. 4. Discrimination in education - United States. I. Parker, Laurence. II. Deyhle, Donna. III. Villenas, Sofia A.*
**TC LC3731 .R27 1999**

**Race on the Agenda (Organization).**
Richardson, Robin. Inclusive schools, inclusive society. Stoke on Trent, Staffordshire, England : Trentham Books, 1999.
**TC LC212.3.G7 R523 1999**

**Race, Phil.** 500 tips on group learning / Phil Race. London : Kogan Page, 2000. viii, 135 p. ; 24 cm. Includes bibliographical references and index. ISBN 0-7494-2884-8
*1. Group work in education. 2. Learning, Psychology of. 3. Group relations training. I. Title. II. Title: Five hundred tips on group learning.*
**TC LB1032 .A15 2000**

**Race, Philip.** 500 computing tips for teachers and lecturers / Phil Race & Steve McDowell. 2nd ed. London : Kogan Page ; Sterling, VA : Stylus Pub., 1999. vi, 131 p. ; 24 cm. Previous ed.: 1996. Includes bibliographical references (p. 119-120) and index. ISBN 0-7494-3150-4
*1. Education - Data processing. 2. Computer-assisted instruction. I. McDowell, Steve. II. Title. III. Title: Five hundred computing tips for teachers and lecturers.*
**TC LB1028.43 .R33 1999**

Brown, Sally A. 500 tips for teachers. 2nd ed. London : Kogan Page ; Sterling, VA : Stylus Pub., 1998.
**TC LB3013 .B76 1998**

Computer-assisted assessment in higher education. London : Kogan Page, 1999.
**TC LB2366 .C65 1999**

**RACE PREJUDICE.** *See* **RACISM.**

**RACE PROBLEMS.** *See* **RACE RELATIONS.**

**RACE - PSYCHOLOGICAL ASPECTS.**
Seshadri-Crooks, Kalpana. Desiring whiteness. London ; New York : Routledge, 2000.
**TC BF175.4.R34 S47 2000**

**RACE PSYCHOLOGY.** *See* **ETHNOPSYCHOLOGY.**

**RACE QUESTION.** *See* **RACE RELATIONS.**

**RACE RELATIONS.** *See also* **ETHNIC RELATIONS; MASS MEDIA AND RACE RELATIONS; MINORITIES; RACISM.**
Banton, Michael P. Racial theories. 2nd ed.

Cambridge ; New York : Cambridge University Press, 1998.
*TC HT1521 .B345 1998*

Camara, Evandro de Morais, 1946- The cultural one or the racial many. Aldershot, Hants, England ; Brookfield, Vt., USA : Ashgate, c1997.
*TC HT1521 .C343 1997*

Race, rhetoric, and the postcolonial. Albany : State University of New York Press, c1999.
*TC P301.5.P67 R33 1999*

**RACE RELATIONS AND MASS MEDIA.** *See* **MASS MEDIA AND RACE RELATIONS.**

**RACE RELATIONS - ART.**
Race, ethnicity and culture in the visual arts. New York : American Council for the Arts, c1993.
*TC N70 .R32 1993*

**RACE RELATIONS IN LITERATURE.**
Mensh, Elaine, 1924- Black, white, and Huckleberry Finn. Tuscaloosa : University of Alabama Press, c2000.
*TC PS1305 .M46 2000*

**RACE RELATIONS (IN RELIGION, FOLKLORE, ETC.).** *See* **RACE RELATIONS - RELIGIOUS ASPECTS.**

**RACE RELATIONS IN SCHOOL MANAGEMENT.** *See* **SCHOOL INTEGRATION; SEGREGATION IN EDUCATION.**

**RACE RELATIONS REFORMERS.** *See* **CIVIL RIGHTS WORKERS.**

**RACE RELATIONS - RELIGIOUS ASPECTS - PRESBYTERIAN CHURCH.**
Stroupe, Nibs. While we run this race. Maryknoll, N.Y. : Orbis Books, c1995.
*TC BX8949.D43 S77 1995*

**Race, rhetoric, and the postcolonial** / edited by Gary A. Olson, Lynn Worsham. Albany : State University of New York Press, c1999. xv, 259 p. ; 24 cm. Includes bibliographical references (p. [241]-249) and index. ISBN 0-7914-4173-3 (hc : alk. paper) ISBN 0-7914-4174-1 (pbk. : alk. paper) DDC 808
*1. Rhetoric - Political aspects. 2. Race relations. 3. Feminist theory. 4. Postcolonialism. 5. Intellectuals - Interviews. I. Olson, Gary A., 1954- II. Worsham, Lynn., 1953-*
*TC P301.5.P67 R33 1999*

**Race, self-employment, and upward mobility.**
Bates, Timothy Mason. Washington, D.C. : Woodrow Wilson Center Press ; Baltimore : Johns Hopkins University Press, c1997.
*TC HD8037.U5 B384 1997*

**RACES OF MAN.** *See* **ETHNOLOGY.**

**Rachlin, Howard, 1935-** Behavior and learning / Howard Rachlin. San Francisco : W. H. Freeman, c1976. xvi, 613 p. : ill. ; 24 cm. Includes bibliographies and index. ISBN 0-7167-0568-0 DDC 156/.3/15
*1. Conditioned response. 2. Behavior modification. 3. Behavior. 4. Learning. I. Title.*
*TC BF319 .R327*

The science of self-control / Howard Rachlin. Cambridge, Mass. : Harvard University Press, 2000. 220 p. : ill. ; 24 cm. Includes bibliographical references (p. [207]-215) and index. ISBN 0-674-00093-5 (alk. paper) DDC 153.8
*1. Self-control. 2. Habit. I. Title.*
*TC BF632 .R3 2000*

**Racial and ethnic minority psychology series**
Valencia, Richard R. Intelligence testing and minority students. Thousand Oaks, Calif. : Sage Publications, [2000]
*TC BF431.5.U6 V35 2000*

**RACIAL BIAS.** *See* **RACE DISCRIMINATION; RACISM.**

**RACIAL DISCRIMINATION.** *See* **RACE DISCRIMINATION.**

**Racial identification and self-concept issues in biracial adolescent girls.**
Harrison, Patricia M. Racial identification and self-concept issues in biracial Black/White adolescent girls. 1997.
*TC 085 H247*

**Racial identification and self-concept issues in biracial Black/White adolescent girls.**
Harrison, Patricia M. 1997.
*TC 085 H247*

**RACIAL IDENTITY OF BLACKS.** *See* **BLACKS - RACE IDENTITY.**

**Racial situations.**
Hartigan, John, 1964- Princeton, N.J. : Princeton University Press, c1999.
*TC F574.D49 A1 1999*

**Racial theories.**
Banton, Michael P. 2nd ed. Cambridge ; New York : Cambridge University Press, 1998.
*TC HT1521 .B345 1998*

**RACIALLY MIXED CHILDREN - ATTITUDES.**
Wright, Marguerite A. I'm chocolate, you're vanilla. 1st paperback ed. San Francisco : Jossey-Bass, 2000.
*TC BF723.R3 W75 2000*

**RACIALLY MIXED CHILDREN - BIOGRAPHY.**
Souls looking back. New York : Routledge, 1999.
*TC E185.625 .S675 1999*

**RACIALLY MIXED CHILDREN - ETHNIC IDENTITY.**
Wright, Marguerite A. I'm chocolate, you're vanilla. 1st paperback ed. San Francisco : Jossey-Bass, 2000.
*TC BF723.R3 W75 2000*

**RACIALLY MIXED CHILDREN - PSYCHOLOGY.**
Wright, Marguerite A. I'm chocolate, you're vanilla. 1st paperback ed. San Francisco : Jossey-Bass, 2000.
*TC BF723.R3 W75 2000*

**RACIALLY MIXED CHILDREN - RACE IDENTITY - CASE STUDIES.**
Souls looking back. New York : Routledge, 1999.
*TC E185.625 .S675 1999*

**RACIALLY MIXED CHILDREN - SOCIAL CONDITIONS - CASE STUDIES.**
Souls looking back. New York : Routledge, 1999.
*TC E185.625 .S675 1999*

**RACIALLY MIXED CHILDREN - UNITED STATES - JUVENILE LITERATURE.**
Nash, Renea D. Everything you need to know about being a biracial/biethnic teen. 1st ed. New York : Rosen Pub. Group, 1995.
*TC HQ77.9 .N39 1995*

**RACIALLY MIXED PEOPLE - BIOGRAPHY.**
Nash, Gary B. Forbidden love. 1st ed. New York : H. Holt, 1999.
*TC E184.M47 N47 1999*

**RACIALLY MIXED PEOPLE - FICTION.**
Katz, Karen. The colors of us. 1st ed. New York : H. Holt, 1999.
*TC PZ7.K15745 Co 1999*

**RACIALLY MIXED PEOPLE - LATIN AMERICA.** *See* **MESTIZOS.**

**RACIALLY MIXED PEOPLE - SOUTH AFRICA.** *See* **COLORED PEOPLE (SOUTH AFRICA).**

**RACIALLY MIXED PEOPLE - UNITED STATES - PSYCHOLOGY.**
Harrison, Patricia M. Racial identification and self-concept issues in biracial Black/White adolescent girls. 1997.
*TC 085 H247*

**RACIALLY MIXED PEOPLE - UNITED STATES - RACE IDENTITY.**
Harrison, Patricia M. Racial identification and self-concept issues in biracial Black/White adolescent girls. 1997.
*TC 085 H247*

**RACING - FICTION.**
Dodds, Dayle Ann. The Great Divide. 1st ed. Cambridge, MA : Candlewick Press, 1999.
*TC PZ8.3.D645 Gr 1999*

**RACISM.** *See also* **RACE RELATIONS.**
Education and racism :. Aldershot ; Brookfield, Vt. : Ashgate, c1999.
*TC LC212.3.G7E48 1999*

Mio, Jeffrey Scott. Resistance to multiculturalism :. Philadelphia, PA : Brunner/Mazel, c2000.
*TC HM1271 .M56 2000*

**Racism and education :** different perspectives and experiences. Ottawa : Canadian Teachers' Federation, 1992. iii, 108, 108, iii p. ; 28 cm. Title on added t. p., inverted: Racisme et l'éducation. Includes bibliographical references. Text in English and French. ISBN 0-88989-261-X DDC 370.19/342/0971
*1. Discrimination in education - Canada. 2. Race discrimination in education - Canada. 3. Multicultural education - Canada. I. Canadian Teachers' Federation. II. Title: Racisme et l'éducation*

*TC LC212.3.C3 R32 1992*

**RACISM AND LANGUAGE.** *See* **RACISM IN LANGUAGE.**

**RACISM - BRAZIL.**
Race in contemporary Brazil. University Park, Pa. : Pennsylvania State University Press, 1999.
*TC F2659.N4 R245 1999*

**RACISM - CROSS-CULTURAL STUDIES.**
Comparative perspectives on racism. Aldershot, Hants, UK ; Burlington, VT, USA : Ashgate, c2000.
*TC GN269 .C646 2000*

**RACISM - FICTION.**
Cooney, Caroline B. Burning up. New York : Delacorte Press, c1999.
*TC PZ7.C7834 Bu 1999*

**RACISM - GREAT BRITAIN.**
Dadzie, Stella, 1952- Toolkit for tackling racism in schools. Stoke on Trent, Staffordshire, England : Trentham Books, 2000.
*TC LC212.3.G7 D339 2000*

**RACISM IN LANGUAGE.**
Shiffrin, Steven H., 1941- Dissent, injustice, and the meanings of America. Princeton, N.J. : Princeton University Press, c1999.
*TC KF4772 .S448 1999*

**RACISM IN LANGUAGE - DICTIONARIES.**
Herbst, Philip. The color of words. Yarmouth, Me., USA : Intercultural Press, [1997]
*TC E184.A1 H466 1997*

**RACISM IN LITERATURE.**
MacCann, Donnarae. White supremacy in children's literature. New York : Garland Pub., 1998.
*TC PS173.N4 M33 1998*

**RACISM IN PSYCHOLOGY.**
Holdstock, T. Len. Re-examining psychology. London ; New York : Routledge, 2000.
*TC BF108.A3 .H65 2000*

**RACISM - NEW YORK (STATE) - NEW YORK - HISTORY - 20TH CENTURY.**
Edgell, Derek. The movement for community control of New York City's schools, 1966-1970. Lewiston, N.Y. : E. Mellen Press, c1998.
*TC LB2862 .E35 1998*

**RACISM - POLITICAL ASPECTS - UNITED STATES - HISTORY - 20TH CENTURY.**
Cochran, David Carroll. The color of freedom. Albany : State University of New York Press, c1999.
*TC E185.615 .C634 1999*

Without justice for all. Boulder, Colo. : Westview Press, 1999.
*TC E185.615 .W57 1999*

**RACISM - PUERTO RICO - HISTORY - 19TH CENTURY.**
Kinsbruner, Jay. Not of pure blood. Durham : Duke University Press, 1996.
*TC F1983.B55 K56 1996*

**RACISM - SOCIAL ASPECTS - UNITED STATES - HISTORY - 20TH CENTURY.**
Witt, Doris. Black hunger. New York : Oxford University Press, 1999.
*TC E185.86 .W58 1999*

**RACISM - UNITED STATES.**
Becoming and unbecoming white. Westport, Conn. : Bergin & Garvey, 1999.
*TC E184.A1 B29 1999*

Campbell, Duane E. Choosing democracy. 2nd ed. Upper Saddle River, N.J. : Merrill, c2000.
*TC LC1099.3 .C36 2000*

Giroux, Henry A. Channel surfing. 1st ed. New York : St. Martin's Press, 1997.
*TC HQ799.7 .G57 1997*

Perlmutter, Philip. Legacy of hate. Armonk, N.Y. ; London : M.E. Sharpe, c1999.
*TC BF575.H3 P47 1999*

Race is-- race isn't. Boulder, CO : Westview Press, c1999.
*TC LC3731 .R27 1999*

Whiteness. Lanham, [Md.] : Rowman & Littlefield, c1999.
*TC E184.A1 W399 1999*

**RACISM - UNITED STATES - CASE STUDIES.**
Educators healing racism. Reston, VA : Association of Teacher Educators ; Olney, MD : Association for Childhood Education International, c1999.
*TC LC212.2 .E38 1999*

Rothenberg, Paula S., 1943- Invisible privilege. Lawrence : University Press of Kansas, c2000.
*TC E185.615 .R68 2000*

**RACISM - UNITED STATES - DICTIONARIES.**
Herbst, Philip. The color of words. Yarmouth, Me., USA : Intercultural Press, [1997]
*TC E184.A1 H466 1997*

**RACISM - UNITED STATES - HISTORY - 20TH CENTURY.**
Okihiro, Gary Y., 1945- Stories lives. Seattle : University of Washington Press, 1999.
*TC D753.8 .O38 1999*

**Racisme et l'éducation.**
Racism and education. Ottawa : Canadian Teachers' Federation, 1992.
*TC LC212.3.C3 R32 1992*

**RACIST LANGUAGE.** *See* **RACISM IN LANGUAGE.**

**RACIST SPEECH.** *See* **HATE SPEECH.**

**Raczynski, James M.**
Handbook of health promotion and disease prevention. New York : Kluwer Academic/Plenum Publishers, c1999.
*TC RA427.8 .H36 1999*

**Radest, Howard B., 1928-** From clinic to classroom : medical ethics and moral education / Howard B. Radest. Westport, Conn. ; London : Praeger, 2000. xiii, 199 p. ; 25 cm. Includes bibliographical references (p. [191]-195) and index. ISBN 0-275-96194-X (alk. paper) DDC 174/.2
*1. Medical ethics. 2. Moral education. I. Title.*
*TC R725.5 .R33 2000*

**Radford, Andrew.**
Linguistics. Cambridge, UK ; New York, NY : Cambridge University Press, 1999.
*TC P121 .L528 1999*

**Radical education in the rural South.**
Cobb, William H. Detroit : Wayne State University Press, 2000.
*TC LD1276 .C63 2000*

**RADICAL PEDAGOGY.** *See* **CRITICAL PEDAGOGY.**

**RADICALISM - UNITED STATES.**
Kimball, Roger, 1953- Tenured radicals. Rev. ed., with a new introd. by the author, 1st Elephant pbk. ed. Chicago : Elephant Paperbacks, 1998.
*TC LC1023 .K56 1998*

**RADICALS (CHEMISTRY).** *See* **FREE RADICALS (CHEMISTRY).**

**RADIO ADDRESSES, DEBATES, ETC.** *See* **FORUMS (DISCUSSION AND DEBATE).**

**RADIO AUTHORSHIP.**
Edmonds, Robert. Scriptwriting for the audio-visual media. New York : Teachers College Press, c1978.
*TC PN1991.7 .E3*

**RADIO - BROADCASTING.** *See* **RADIO BROADCASTING.**

**RADIO BROADCASTING - PERIODICALS.**
Journal of broadcasting. Phila., Pa.[etc.] Association for Professional Broadcasting Education.

**RADIO, CITIZENS BAND.** *See* **CITIZENS BAND RADIO.**

**RADIO CONTROL.** *See* **CITIZENS BAND RADIO.**

**RADIO INDUSTRY AND TRADE.** *See* **RADIO BROADCASTING.**

**RADIO PROGRAMS.** *See* **TALK SHOWS.**

**RADIO STATIONS.** *See* **COLLEGE RADIO STATIONS.**

**RADIO TALK SHOWS.** *See* **TALK SHOWS.**

**Radio-Télévision belge de la communauté culturelle française.**
Ecole 27 [videorecording]. Bruxelles : Paradise Films ; New York, N.Y. : [distributed by] First Run/Icarus Films, 1997, c1996.
*TC LC746.P7 E2 1997*

**RADIO VISION.** *See* **TELEVISION.**

**RADIOTELEPHONE.** *See* **CITIZENS BAND RADIO.**

**Radó, Tibor, 1895-1965.** Length and area. New York, American Mathematical Society, 1948. 572 p. 26 cm. (American Mathematical Society. Colloquium publications, v.30) "An amplification of ... four Colloquium lectures ... deliver[ed] at the annual meeting of the American Mathematical Society in Chicago, November 1945." Includes Bibliographical references ( p. 562-569 ) and index. DDC 513.83
*1. Topology I. Title. II. Series: Colloquium publications (American Mathematical Society) v.30*
*TC QA611 .R3*

**Radstone, Susannah.**
Memory and methodology. Oxford ; New York : Berg, 2000.
*TC BD181.7 .M46 2000*

**RAE, LESLIE.** Using activities in training and development. 2nd ed. London : Kogan Page ; Sterling, VA : Stylus Pub., 1999. x, 222 p. ; 24 cm. Includes bibliographical references and index. ISBN 0-7494-3102-4 DDC 371.3
*1. Active learning*
*TC LB1027.23 .R34 1999*

**Raeff, Catherine.**
Variability in the social construction of the child. San Francisco : Jossey-Bass, 2000.
*TC BF723.S62 .V37 2000*

**Raelin, Joseph A., 1948-** Work based learning : the new frontier of management development / Joseph A. Raelin. Reading, MA : Addison-Wesley, 1999. xii, 281 p. : ill. ; 21 cm. (Addison-Wesley series on organization development) Includes bibliographical references (p.240-265) and index. ISBN 0-201-43388-5 DDC 658.4/07124
*1. Executives - Training of. 2. Employees - Training of. 3. Organizational learning. I. Title. II. Series.*
*TC HD30.4 .R33 1999*

**Raffaelli, Marcela, 1960-.**
Homeless and working youth around the world. San Francisco : Jossey-Bass, 1999.
*TC HV4493 .H655 1999*

**Rafoth, Mary Ann.** Inspiring independent learning : successful classroom strategies / Mary Ann Rafoth. Washington, DC : National Education Association of the United States, 1999. 151 p. ; 23 cm. (Inspired classroom series) Includes bibliographical references (p. 147-149). ISBN 0-8106-2954-2 DDC 371.39/43
*1. Independent study. 2. Educational tests and measurements. I. Title. II. Series.*
*TC LB1049 .R35 1999*

**Raftery, Mary.** Suffer the little children : the inside story of Ireland's industrial schools / Mary Raftery & Eoin O'Sullivan. Dublin, Ireland : New Island, 1999. 424 p. : ill. ; 22 cm. Includes bibliographical references (p. 402-412) and index. ISBN 1-87459-783-9
*1. Reformatories - Ireland - History. 2. Trade schools - Ireland - History. 3. Problem children - Institutional care - Ireland - History. 4. Problem youth - Institutional care - Ireland - History. I. O'Sullivan, Eoin. II. Title.*
*TC HV9148.A5 R33 1999*

**RAGE.** *See* **ANGER.**

**Raggatt, Peter C. M.** Government, markets and vocational qualifications : an anatomy of policy / Peter Raggatt and Steve Williams. London ; New York : Falmer Press, 1999. ix, 220 p. ; 24 cm. Includes bibliographical references (p. [201]-213) and index. ISBN 0-7507-0917-0 (hbk. : alk. paper) ISBN 0-7507-0916-2 (pbk. : alk. paper) DDC 331.11/42/0941
*1. Vocational qualifications - Great Britain. 2. National Vocational Qualifications (Great Britain) I. Williams, Steve, 1968- II. Title.*
*TC HF5381.6 .R34 1999*

**Ragged Dick.**
Alger, Horatio, 1832-1899. Ragged Dick, or, Street life in New York with the boot-blacks. New York, N.Y. : Penguin Group, c1990.
*TC PS1029.A3 R34 1990*

**Ragged Dick, or, Street life in New York with the boot-blacks.**
Alger, Horatio, 1832-1899. New York, N.Y. : Penguin Group, c1990.
*TC PS1029.A3 R34 1990*

**Ragno, Nancy N.** World of language / Nancy Nickell Ragno, Marian Davies Toth, Betty G. Gray ; contributing author, Elfrieda Hiebert ... [et al.]. [Teacher ed.]. Morristown, NJ : Silver Burdett & Ginn, c1990. 9 v. : col. ill ; 28 cm. For grades K-8. Author's name appear in different order in some volumes. Includes bibliographical references and indexes. ISBN 0-382-10671-7 (level 2) ISBN 0-382-10673-3 (level 4) ISBN 0-382-10676-8 (level 6)
*1. Language arts (Elementary) 2. English language - Study and teaching (Elementary) 3. English language - Study and teaching (Primary) I. Toth, Marian Davies. II. Gray, Betty G. III. Hiebert, Elfrieda. IV. Silver Burdett & Ginn. V. Title.*

World of language / Nancy Nickell Ragno, Marian Davies Toth, Betty G. Gray ; contributing author, Elfrieda Hiebert ... [et al.]. [Teacher ed.]. Morristown, NJ : Silver Burdett & Ginn, c1990. 9 v. : col. ill ; 28 cm. For grades K-8. Author's name appear in different order in some volumes. Includes bibliographical references and indexes. ISBN 0-382-10671-7 (level 2) ISBN 0-382-10673-3 (level 4) ISBN 0-382-10676-8 (level 6)
*1. Language arts (Elementary) 2. English language - Study and teaching (Elementary) 3. English language - Study and teaching (Primary) I. Toth, Marian Davies. II. Gray, Betty G. III. Hiebert, Elfrieda. IV. Silver Burdett & Ginn. V. Title.*

**Ragno, Nancy Nickell.** World of language / Nancy Nickell Ragno, Marian Davies Toth, Betty G. Gray ; contributing author, Elfrieda Hiebert ... [et al.]. Needham, Ma. : Silver Burdett Ginn, c1996. 9 v. : col. ill ; 28 cm. For grades K-8. Authors' names appear in different order in some volumes. Includes indexes. For grade 7 only 1993 ed. available. ISBN 0-382-25165-2 (level 1) ISBN 0-382-25166-0 (level 2) ISBN 0-382-25168-7 (level 3) ISBN 0-382-25101-6 (level 4) ISBN 0-382-25170-9 (level 5) ISBN 0-382-25171-7 (level 6) ISBN 0-382-25104-0 (level 7) ISBN 0-382-25173-3 (level 8)
*1. Language arts (Elementary) 2. English language - Study and teaching (Elementary) 3. English language - Study and teaching (Primary) I. Toth, Marian Davies. II. Gray, Betty G. III. Hiebert, Elfrieda. IV. Silver Burdett Ginn (Firm) V. Title.*
*TC LB1576 .S4471 1996*

World of language / Nancy Nickell Ragno, Marian Davies Toth, Betty G. Gray ; contributing author, Elfrieda Hiebert ... [et al.]. Needham, Mass. : Silver Burdett Ginn, c1996. 9 v. : col. ill ; 28 cm. For grades K-8. Authors' names appear in different order in some volumes. Includes indexes. For grade 7 only 1993 ed. available. ISBN 0-382-25165-2 (Gr. 1) ISBN 0-382-25166-0 (Gr. 2) ISBN 0-382-25168-7 (Gr. 3) ISBN 0-382-25101-6 (Gr. 4) ISBN 0-382-25170-9 (Gr. 5) ISBN 0-382-25171-7 (Gr. 6) ISBN 0-382-25104-0 (Gr. 7) ISBN 0-382-25173-3 (Gr. 8)
*1. Language arts (Elementary) 2. English language - Study and teaching (Elementary) 3. English language - Study and teaching (Primary) I. Toth, Marian Davies. II. Gray, Betty G. III. Hiebert, Elfrieda. IV. Silver Burdett Ginn (Firm) V. Title.*
*TC LB1576 .S4471 1996*

World of language. Needham, Mass. : Silver Burdett Ginn, c1996.
*TC LB1576 .S4471 1996*

World of language. Teacher ed. Needham, Mass. : Silver Burdett Ginn, c1996.
*TC LB1576 .S4471 1996 Teacher Ed.*

**Ragoné, Helena.**
Situated lives. New York : Routledge, 1997.
*TC GN479.65 .S57 1997*

**Rahman, Tariq.** Language, education, and culture / Tariq Rahman. Islamabad : Sustainable Development Policy Institute ; Karachi : Oxford Uinversity Press, 1999. xvi, 318 p. ; 22 cm. Includes bibliographical references (p. 296-310) and index. ISBN 0-19-579146-0
*1. Language policy - Pakistan. 2. Language and education - Pakistan. 3. Language and culture - Pakistan. I. Title.*
*TC P119.32.P18 R35 1999*

**Rai, Kul B.** Affirmative action and the university : race, ethnicity, and gender in higher education employment / Kul B. Rai and John W. Critzer. Lincoln : University of Nebraska Press, 2000. xxiii, 250 p. ; 24 cm. Includes bibliographical references (p.[223]-245) and index. ISBN 0-8032-3934-3 (cloth : alk. paper) DDC 378.1/2
*1. Discrimination in higher education - United States. 2. Minority college teachers - Employment - United States. 3. Minority college administrators - Employment - United States. 4. Affirmative action programs - United States. I. Critzer, John W., 1947- II. Title.*
*TC LC212.42 .R35 2000*

**RAIL LINES.** *See* **RAILROADS.**

**RAIL TRANSPORTATION.** *See* **RAILROADS.**

**RAILROAD LINES.** *See* **RAILROADS.**

**RAILROAD TRANSPORTATION.** *See* **RAILROADS.**

**RAILROADS - EMPLOYEES.** *See* **LOCOMOTIVE ENGINEERS.**

**RAILROADS - FICTION.**
Kay, Verla. Iron horses. New York : Putnam, c1999.
*TC PZ8.3.K225 Ir 1999*

**RAILROADS - ROLLING-STOCK.** *See*
**LOCOMOTIVES.**

**RAILROADS - TRAINS - FICTION.**
Ó Flatharta, Antoine. The prairie train. New York :
Crown Publishers, 1997.
*TC PZ7.O331275 Pr 1997*

**RAILWAYS.** *See* **RAILROADS.**

**RAIN FOREST ECOLOGY - WASHINGTON
(STATE).**
Wright-Frierson, Virginia. A North American rain
forest scrapbook. New York : Walker and Co., 1999.
*TC QH105.W2 W75 1999*

**RAIN FOREST ECOLOGY - WASHINGTON
(STATE) - OLYMPIC PENINSULA -
JUVENILE LITERATURE.**
Wright-Frierson, Virginia. A North American rain
forest scrapbook. New York : Walker and Co., 1999.
*TC QH105.W2 W75 1999*

**RAIN FORESTS - WASHINGTON (STATE).**
Wright-Frierson, Virginia. A North American rain
forest scrapbook. New York : Walker and Co., 1999.
*TC QH105.W2 W75 1999*

**RAIN FORESTS - WASHINGTON (STATE) -
OLYMPIC PENINSULA - JUVENILE
LITERATURE.**
Wright-Frierson, Virginia. A North American rain
forest scrapbook. New York : Walker and Co., 1999.
*TC QH105.W2 W75 1999*

**Rainbird, Helen.**
Apprenticeship. London : Kogan Page, c1999.
*TC HD4885.G7 A67 1999*

**Rainbow of mathematics.**
Grattan-Guinness, I. [Fontana history of the
mathematical sciences] The Norton history of the
mathematical sciences. 1st American ed. New York :
W.W. Norton, 1998.
*TC QA21 .G695 1998*

**The rainbow tulip.**
Mora, Pat. New York : Viking, 1999.
*TC PZ7.M78819 Rai 1999*

**RAINFORESTS.** *See* **RAIN FORESTS.**

**RAINSTORMS.** *See* **THUNDERSTORMS.**

**Raising Black children who love reading and writing.**
Paul, Dierdre Glenn, 1964- Westport, Conn. :
Bergin & Garvey, 2000.
*TC LC2778.L34 P28 2000*

**Raising children with character.**
Berger, Elizabeth. Northvale, N.J. : J. Aronson, c1999.
*TC BF723.P4 B47 1999*

**Raising healthy Black and biracial children in a
race-conscious world.**
Wright, Marguerite A. I'm chocolate, you're vanilla.
1st paperback ed. San Francisco : Jossey-Bass, 2000.
*TC BF723.R3 W75 2000*

**RAISING OF CHILDREN.** *See* **CHILD REARING.**

**Raising standards in American health care.**
Sherman, V. Clayton. 1st ed. San Francisco : Jossey-
Bass, c1999.
*TC RA395.A3 S483 1999*

**Raising the standard.**
Doyle, Denis P. 2nd ed. Thousand Oaks, Calif. :
Corwin Press, c1999.
*TC LB2822.82 .D69 1999*

**The Raj at table.**
Burton, David, 1952- London ; Boston : Faber, 1994.
*TC TX724.5.I4 B87 1993*

**Rajput, J. S.** Education in a changing world : fallacies
and forces / J.S. Rajput. New Delhi : Vikas Pub.
House ; Distributors, UBS Publishers' Distributors,
1999. x, 262 p. ; 22 cm. SUMMARY: In the Indian context.
Includes bibliographical references and index. ISBN 81-259-
0657-6 DDC 370/.954
*1. Educational change - India. 2. Education - India. I. Title.*
*TC LA1151 .R343 1999*

**Rallis, Sharon F.** Principals of dynamic schools : taking
charge of change / Sharon F. Rallis, Ellen B.
Goldring. 2nd ed. Thousand Oaks, Calif. : Corwin
Press, c2000. xvii, 174 p. : ill. ; 25 cm. Rev. ed. of:
Principals of dynamic schools / Ellen B. Goldring, Sharon F.
Rallis. 1993. Includes bibliographical references (p. 149-167)
and index. ISBN 0-7619-7609-4 (cloth: acid-free paper) ISBN
0-7619-7610-8 (pbk.: acid-free paper) DDC 371.2/012/0973
*1. School principals - United States. 2. School management*

and organization - United States. 3. Educational leadership -
United States. I. Goldring, Ellen B. (Ellen Borish), 1957- II.
Goldring. Ellen B. (Ellen Borish), 1957- Principals of dynamic
schools. III. Title.
*TC LB2831.92 .G65 2000*

**Ralston, Nicola L.** Parchment/vellum conservation
survey and bibliography / [author, Nicola L. Ralston].
Edinburgh : Historic Scotland : Crown Copyright,
c2000. viii, 40 p. : ill. ; 28 cm. (Historic Scotland technical
advice notes) At head of title: Reference. "Commissioned by
Technical Conservation Research and Education Division."
Includes bibliographical references. ISBN 1-900168-90-1
(pbk.)
*1. Parchment - Preservation - Bibliography. 2. Parchment -
Conservation and restoration - Bibliography. 3. Vellum printed
books - Preservation - Bibliography. 4. Vellum printed books -
Conservation and restoration - Bibliography. 5. Archival
materials - Conservation and restoration - Study and teaching.
I. Historic Scotland. II. Title. III. Title: Parchment vellum
conservation survey and bibliography IV. Series.*
*TC Z701.4.I5 R35 2000*

**Ram Dass.**
Aging and saging [videorecording]. Princeton, NJ :
Films for the Humanities & Sciences : Distributed by
Canadian Broadcasting Corporation, 1998.
*TC BF724.55.A35 A35 1998*

**Ramachandran, V. S.** Phantoms in the brain : probing
the mysteries of the human mind / V.S.
Ramachandran, and Sandra Blakeslee. 1st ed. New
York : William Morrow, c1998. xix, 328 p. : ill. ; 25 cm.
Includes bibliographical references (p. 299-313) and index.
ISBN 0-688-15247-3 (alk. paper) DDC 612.8/2
*1. Neurology - Popular works. 2. Brain - Popular works. 3.
Neurosciences - Popular works. I. Blakeslee, Sandra. II. Title.*
*TC RC351 .R24 1998*

**Ramesh, M., 1960-** Welfare capitalism in southeast
Asia : social security, health, and education policies /
M. Ramesh with Mukul G. Asher. New York : St.
Martin's Press, c2000. xii, 217 p. ; 23 cm. (International
political economy series) Includes bibliographical references
(p. 196-213) and index. ISBN 0-312-23016-8 DDC 361.6/1/
0959
*1. Asia, Southeastern - Social policy - Case studies. 2. Asia,
Southeastern - Economic conditions - Case studies. 3. Social
security - Asia, Southeastern - Case studies. 4. Medical policy -
Asia, Southeastern - Case studies. 5. Education and state -
Asia, Southeastern - Case studies. I. Asher, Mukul G. II. Title.
III. Series.*
*TC HN690.8.A8 R35 2000*

**Ramey, Craig T.**
Ramey, Sharon L. Going to school. New York :
Goddard Press ; Lanham, MD : Distributed to the
trade by National Book Network, c1999.
*TC LB1139.35.P37 R26 1999*

**Ramey, Sharon L.** Going to school : how to help your
child succeed : a handbook for parents of children
ages 3-8 / Sharon L. Ramey, Craig T. Ramey. New
York : Goddard Press ; Lanham, MD : Distributed to
the trade by National Book Network, c1999. x, 277 p. :
ill. ; 26 cm. (Goddard parenting guides) Includes
bibliographical references (p. [276]-277). ISBN 0-9666397-3-1
*1. Early childhood education - Parent participation -
Handbooks, manuals, etc. 2. Home and school - Handbooks,
manuals, etc. 3. Child development - Handbooks, manuals, etc.
I. Ramey, Craig T. II. Title. III. Series.*
*TC LB1139.35.P37 R26 1999*

**Ramírez de Mellor, Elva** Fun with English / Elva
Ramírez de Mellor, Jacqueline Flamm, W. Leland
Northam Pupil's ed. Mexico : McGraw-Hill c1987 v. :
ill. (some col.) ; 21 x 27 cm. For grade K-6. ISBN 968-451-
'915-x
*1. English language - Problems, exercises, etc. 2. English
language - Textbooks for foreign speakers. 3. Language arts
(Elementary) I. Flamm, Jacqueline, 1940- II. Northam, W.
Leland*
*TC PE1129.S8 .R35 1987*

Fun with english : teacher's guide/ Elva Ramírez de
Mellor, Jacqueline Flamm, W. Leland Northam.
Mexico : McGraw-Hill c1987 v. : ill. (some col.) ; 21 x 27
cm. For grade K-6. ISBN 968-451-940-0 (Book 1) ISBN
968-451-942-7 (Book 3) ISBN 968-451-943-5 (Book 4) ISBN
968-451-945-1 (Book 5) ISBN 968-451-947-8 (Book 6)
*1. English language - Study and teaching (Elementary) 2.
English language - Textbooks for foreign speakers. 3.
Language arts (Elementary) I. Flamm, Jacqueline, 1940- II.
Northam, W. Leland III. Title.*
*TC PE1129.S8 .R35 1987*

**Rampley, Matthew.** Nietzsche, aesthetics, and
modernity / Matthew Rampley. Cambridge, U.K. ;
New York : Cambridge University Press, 2000. xi, 286
p. ; 23 cm. Includes bibliographical references (p. 263-275)
and index. ISBN 0-521-65155-7 (hb) DDC 111/.85/092

*1. Nietzsche, Friedrich Wilhelm, - 1844-1900 - Aesthetics. 2.
Aesthetics, Modern. I. Title.*
*TC B3318.A4 R36 2000*

**Ramsbotham, Oliver.**
Miall, Hugh. Contemporary conflict resolution.
Cambridge, UK : Polity Press ; Malden, MA :
Blackwell, 1999.
*TC JZ6010 .M53 1999*

**Ramsden, Paul.** Learning to lead in higher education /
Paul Ramsden. London ; New York : Routledge,
1998. xv, 288 p. : ill. ; 24 cm. Includes bibliographical
references (p. 276-282) and index. ISBN 0-415-15199-6 ISBN
0-415-15200-3 (pbk.) DDC 378.1/01
*1. Education, Higher - Administration. 2. Educational
leadership. I. Title.*
*TC LB2341 .R32 1998*

**Ramsey, Brenda E., 1928-.**
Pringle, Sheila M. Promoting the health of children.
St. Louis : Mosby, 1982.
*TC RJ101 .P66 1982*

**Ramsey, Katherine D., 1944-.**
A middle mosaic. Urbana, Ill. : National Council of
Teachers of English, c2000.
*TC LB1631 .A2 2000*

**Ramsey, William L.** Modern earth science : teacher's
resource book / William L. Ramsey ... [et. al.] Austin,
Tex. : Holt, Rinehart and Winston, Inc., c1989. 1 v.
(various pagings) : ill. ; 29 cm. Title from cover. CONTENTS:
[1] Teacher's resource guide -- [2] Laboratory investigations --
[3] Long-range investigations -- [4] Tests -- [5] Review. ISBN
0-03-021868-3
*1. Geology - Study and teaching (Secondary). 2. Earth
sciences - Study and teaching (Secondary).*
*TC QE28 .R35 1989 Teacher's Resource Book*

Modern earth science / William L. Ramsey ... [et. al.]
Austin, Tex. : Holt, Rinehart and Winston, Inc.,
c1989. xv, 592 p. : col. ill. ; 26 cm. Includes index. ISBN 0-
03-004449-9
*1. Geology. 2. Earth sciences.*
*TC QE28 .R35 1989*

**RANCH LIFE - WYOMING - FICTION.**
Naylor, Phyllis Reynolds. Walker's Crossing. New
York : Atheneum Books for Young Readers, c1999.
*TC PZ7.N24 Wai 1999*

**RAND, AYN - AESTHETICS.**
Torres, Louis, 1938- What art is. Chicago, Ill. : Open
Court, c2000.
*TC PS3535.A547 Z9 2000*

**Rand Corporation.**
Berends, Mark, 1962- Assessing the progress of New
American Schools. Santa Monica, CA : RAND, 1999.
*TC LB2822.82 .B45 1999*

Kirby, Sheila Nataraj, 1946- Staffing at-risk school
districts in Texas. Santa Monica, CA : Rand, 1999.
*TC LB2833.3.T4 K57 1999*

**Rand, Ted, ill.**
Ross, Alice. Jezebel's spooky spot. 1st ed. New
York : Dutton Children's Books, 1999.
*TC PZ7.R719694 Jf 1999*

**Randall, E. Vance.**
Accuracy or advocacy. Thousand Oaks, Calif. :
Corwin Press, c1999.
*TC LB1028 .A312 1999*

**Randall, Ruth E.** School choice : issues and answers /
Ruth E. Randall, Keith Geiger ; foreword by Rudy
Perpich. Bloomington, Ind. : National Educational
Service, 1991. x, 233 p. ; 23 cm. Includes bibliographical
references. CONTENTS: Why choice? -- Choice without
losers : a comprehensive approach / Keith Geiger -- Issues
included in legislative bills -- Case study : choice for students
and parents in Minnesota -- Challenges in choice programs --
Appendix A: NEA criteria for developing and implementing
choice plans. ISBN 1-87963-902-5 DDC 379.1/11/0973
*1. School choice - Minnesota. 2. School choice - United States.
3. Public schools - Minnesota. 4. Public schools - United
States. I. Geiger, Keith. II. Title.*
*TC LB1027.9 .R36 1991*

**Random House children's encyclopedia.**
Children's illustrated encyclopedia. [2nd] rev. ed.
New York : DK Pub., 1998.
*TC AG5 .C535 1998*

**RANDOM SAMPLING.** *See* **SAMPLING
(STATISTICS).**

**Ranger, T. O. (Terence O.)** Are we not also men? : the
Samkange family & African politics in Zimbabwe,
1920-64 / Terrence Ranger. Harare : Baobab ;
Portsmouth, NH : Heinemann, 1995. x, 211 p. : ill. ; 24
cm. (Social history of Africa) Includes bibliographical

references and indexes. ISBN 0-435-08975-7 ISBN 0-435-08977-3 (pbk.) DDC 968.91/0099
*1. Samkange family. 2. Zimbabwe - Politics and government - 1890-1965. 3. Methodist Church - Zimbabwe - History. 4. Zimbabwe - Church history. I. Title. II. Series.*
*TC DT2974 .R36 1995*

**RANK.** *See* **SOCIAL CLASSES.**

**Rank Video Services America.**
Bridges to independence [videorecording]. Burbank, CA : RCA/Columbia Pictures Home Video ; [S.l. : Distributed by] Rank Video Services Production, c1991.
*TC HV1646 .B7 1991*

Bright beginnings [videorecording. Burbank, CA : RCA/Columbia Pictures Home Video ; [S.l. : Distributed by] Rank Video Services America, c1991.
*TC HV1642 .B67 1991*

Touch 'n' go [videorecording. Burbank, Calif. : Columbia Tristar Home Video ; [S.l. : Distributed by] Rank Video Services Production, c1991.
*TC HV1626 .T6 1991*

**Rankin, Elizabeth Deane.**
Becker, Evvie. High-risk sexual behavior. New York : Plenum Press, c1998.
*TC HQ60.7.U6 B43 1998*

**Rannveig Traustadóttir, 1950-.**
Women with intellectual disabilities. London ; Philadelphia : Jessica Kingsley Publishers, 2000.
*TC HV3009.5.W65 W66 2000*

**Ransom, Candice F., 1952-** The promise quilt / Candice F. Ransom ; illustrations by Ellen Beier. New York : Walker and Co., 1999. 1v. (unpaged) :bcol. ill. ; 29 cm.
SUMMARY: After her father leaves the family farm on Lost Mountain to be General Lee's guide, Addie finds ways to remember him--even when he does not return at the end of the war. ISBN 0-8027-8694-4 (hardcover) ISBN 0-8027-8695-2 (reinforced) DDC [Fic]
*1. Virginia - History - Civil War, 1861-1865 - Juvenile fiction. 2. Virginia - History - Civil War, 1861-1865 - Fiction. 3. United States - History - Civil War, 1861-1865 - Fiction. 4. Family life - Virginia - Fiction. I. Beier, Ellen, ill. II. Title.*
*TC PZ7.R1743 Pr 1999*

**RAPE.** *See* **ACQUAINTANCE RAPE.**

**RAPE - FICTION.**
Cadnum, Michael. Rundown. New York : Viking, c1999.
*TC PZ7.C11724 Ru 1999*

**RAPE - LAW AND LEGISLATION.** *See* **RAPE.**

**RAPE TRAUMA SYNDROME.**
d·a·t·e rape [videorecording]. [Charleston, WV] : Cambridge Educational, c1994.
*TC RC560.R36 D3 1994*

**RAPE VICTIMS.** *See* **MALE RAPE VICTIMS.**

**RAPE VICTIMS - PSYCHOLOGY.**
d·a·t·e rape [videorecording]. [Charleston, WV] : Cambridge Educational, c1994.
*TC RC560.R36 D3 1994*

**Rapee, Ronald M.**
Treating anxious children and adolescents. Oakland, CA : New Harbinger Publications, c2000.
*TC RJ504.A58 T74 2000*

**Raphael, Jacqueline.**
Haines, Dawn Denham. Writing together. 1st ed. New York : Berkley Pub. Group, 1997.
*TC PN145 .H28 1997*

**Raphael, Matthew J.** Bill W. and Mr. Wilson : the legend and life of A.A.'s cofounder / Matthew J. Raphael. Amherst : University of Massachusetts Press, c2000. xiv, 206 p. ; 24 cm. Includes bibliographical references and index. ISBN 1-55849-245-3 (alk. paper) DDC 362.292/86/092
*1. W., Bill. 2. Alcoholics - Biography. 3. Alcoholics Anonymous. I. Title. II. Title: Bill W. and Mister Wilson*
*TC HV5032.W19 R36 2000*

**Rapid instructional design.**
Piskurich, George M. San Francisco, Calif. : Jossey-Bass, c2000.
*TC LB1028.38 .P57 2000*

**Rapoport, Robert N.** Families, children, and the quest for a global ethic / Robert N. Rapoport. Aldershot ; Brookfield, Vt. : Ashgate, c1997. 191 p. ; 23 cm. Includes bibliographical references (p. 175-191). ISBN 1-85972-287-3 DDC 306.85
*1. Family. 2. Family - Moral and ethical aspects. 3. Social values. 4. Social ethics. I. Title.*
*TC HQ518 .R36 1997*

**Rapp, Rayna.** Testing women, testing the fetus : the social impact of amniocentesis in America / Rayna Rapp. New York : Routledge, 1999. xiii, 361 p. ; 24 cm. (The anthropology of everyday life) Includes bibliographical references (p. [330]-352) and index. ISBN 0-415-91644-5 (hb : alk. paper) ISBN 0-415-91645-3 (pbk. : alk. paper) DDC 618.3/204275
*1. Amniocentesis - Social aspects - United States. I. Title. II. Series.*
*TC RG628.3.A48 R37 1999*

**Rappaport, Julian.**
Handbook of community psychology. New York ; London : Kluwer Academic/Plenum, c2000.
*TC RA790.55 .H36 2000*

**Rappaport, Karen.**
Directory of schools for alternative and complementary health care. 2nd ed. Phoenix, AZ : Oryx Press, 1999.
*TC R733.D59 D59 1999*

**RARE BOOKS.** *See* **VELLUM PRINTED BOOKS.**

**Rarick, G. Lawrence (George Lawrence), 1911- joint author.**
Francis, Robert Jay. Motor characteristics of the mentally retarded, [Washington] U.S. Dept. of Health, Education, and Welfare, Office of Education [1960]
*TC RJ499 .F7 1960*

**Raschka, Christopher, ill.**
Hooks, Bell. Happy to be nappy. 1st ed. New York : Hyperion Books for Children, 1999.
*TC PZ7.H7663 Hap 1999*

**Rasinski, Timothy V.** Effective reading strategies : teaching children who find reading difficult / Timothy Rasinski, Nancy Padak. 2nd ed. Upper Saddle River, N.J. : Merrill, c2000. xx, 341 p. : ill. ; 24 cm. Rev. ed. of: Holistic reading strategies. c1995. Includes bibliographical references (p. [321]-329) and indexes . ISBN 0-13-099669-6 DDC 372.43
*1. Reading - Remedial teaching. 2. Developmental reading. I. Padak, Nancy. II. Rasinski, Timothy V. Holistic reading strategies. III. Title.*
*TC LB1050.5 .R33 2000*

**Holistic reading strategies.**
Rasinski, Timothy V. Effective reading strategies. 2nd ed. Upper Saddle River, N.J. : Merrill, c2000.
*TC LB1050.5 .R33 2000*

**Raskin, Jonathan D.**
Constructions of disorder. 1st ed. Washington, DC : American Psychological Association, c2000.
*TC RC437.5 .C647 2000*

**Raskolnikov's rebirth.**
Dilman, Ilham. Chicago : Open Court, c2000.
*TC BF47 .D55 2000*

**Rasool, Joan.** Multicultural education in middle and secondary classrooms : meeting the challenge of diversity and change / Joan A. Rasool, A. Cheryl Curtis. Belmont, CA : Wadsworth, c2000. xviii, 414 p. ; 24 cm. Includes bibliographical references and index. ISBN 0-534-50847-2 DDC 370.117/0973 DDC 370.117
*1. Multicultural education - United States - Curricula. 2. Middle school education - United States - Curricula. 3. Education, Secondary - United States - Curricula. I. Curtis, A. Cheryl. II. Title.*
*TC LC1099.3 .R38 2000*

**Rassool, Naz, 1949-** Literacy for sustainable development in the age of information / Naz Rassool. Clevedon [England] ; Philadelphia : Multilingual Matters, c1999. xvi, 264 p. ; 21 cm. (The language and education library ; 14) Includes bibliographical references (p. 244-258) and index. ISBN 1-85359-432-6 (pbk.) ISBN 1-85359-433-4 (hbk.) DDC 302.2/244
*1. Literacy - Social aspects. 2. Sociolinguistics. 3. Information technology - Social aspects. 4. Functional literacy. 5. Sustainable development. I. Title. II. Series.*
*TC LC149 .R37 1999*

**Rathvon, Natalie.** Effective school interventions : strategies for enhancing academic achievement and social competence / Natalie Rathvon. New York : Guilford Press, c1999. xvi, 366 p. ; 24 cm. (The Guilford school practitioner series) Includes bibliographical references (p. 335-357) and index. ISBN 1-57230-409-X (alk. paper) DDC 371.9/046
*1. Inclusive education - United States. 2. Classroom management - United States. 3. Behavior modification - United States. 4. Academic achievement - United States. 5. Social skills - Study and teaching - United States. I. Title. II. Series.*
*TC LC1201 .R38 1999*

**RATING SCALES, PSYCHIATRIC.** *See* **PSYCHIATRIC RATING SCALES.**

**RATIO AND PROPORTION - STUDY AND TEACHING (ELEMENTARY).**
Lamon, Susan J., 1949- More. Mahwah, N.J. : L. Erlbaum Associates, 1999.
*TC QA137 .L34 1999*

**RATIOCINATION.** *See* **REASONING.**

**Rationales for teaching young adult literature** / edited by Louann Reid, with Jamie Hayes Neufeld. Portland, Me. : Calendar Islands Publishers, 1999. vii, 216 p. ; 23 cm. Includes bibliographical references. ISBN 1-89305-604-X DDC 809/.89283
*1. Young adult literature - Study and teaching (Secondary) 2. Teenagers - Books and reading. I. Reid, Louann. II. Neufeld, Jamie.*
*TC PN59 .R33 1999*

**RATIONALISM.** *See* **BELIEF AND DOUBT; ENLIGHTENMENT; INTUITION.**

**RATIONALISM - PSYCHOLOGICAL ASPECTS.**
Elster, Jon, 1940- Ulysses unbound. Cambridge, U.K. ; New York : Cambridge University Press, 2000.
*TC BF441 .E45 2000*

**RATIONALIZATION OF INDUSTRY.** *See* **INDUSTRIAL MANAGEMENT.**

**Rationing education.**
Gillborn, David. Buckingham [England] ; Philadelphia : Open University Press, 2000.
*TC LC213.3.G73 L664 2000*

**Ratner, Nan Bernstein.**
Methods for studying language production. Mahwah, N.J. : Lawrence Erlbaum Associates, 2000.
*TC P118 .M47 2000*

Stuttering research and practice. Mahwah, N.J. : Erlbaum, 1999.
*TC RC424 .S786 1999*

**Rauschenberg, Robert, 1925-.**
Hopps, Walter. Robert Rauschenberg. New York : Guggenheim Museum, c1997.
*TC N6537.R27 H66 1997*

**RAUSCHENBERG, ROBERT, 1925 - - EXHIBITIONS.**
Hopps, Walter. Robert Rauschenberg. New York : Guggenheim Museum, c1997.
*TC N6537.R27 H66 1997*

**Ravenette, Tom.** Personal construct theory in educational psychology : : a practitioner's view / Tom Ravenette. London : Whurr, c1999. xi, 281 p. : ill. ; 24 cm. Includes bibliographical references (p. 270-273) and index. ISBN 1-86156-121-0
*1. School psychology. 2. Educational psychology. 3. Personal construct theory. I. Title.*
*TC LB1027.55 .R38 1999*

**Ravenhill, Philip L.** Dreams and reverie : images of otherworld mates among the Baule, West Africa / Philip L. Ravenhill. Washington : Smithsonian Institution Press, c1996. xv, 102 p. : col. ill. ; 26 cm. Includes bibliographical references (p. 99-102). ISBN 1-56098-650-6 (cloth : alk. paper) DDC 730/.89/963385
*1. Wood sculpture, Baoulé. 2. Sculpture, Primitive - Côte d'Ivoire. 3. Sex in art. 4. Man-woman relationships - Côte d'Ivoire. I. Title.*
*TC NB1255.C85 R38 1996*

**Ravid, Ruth.** Practical statistics for educators / Ruth Ravid. 2nd ed. Lanham, Md. : University Press of America, c2000. xiii, 368 p. : ill. ; 23 cm. Includes index. ISBN 0-7618-1594-5 (pbk.) DDC 370.21
*1. Educational statistics - Study and teaching. 2. Educational tests and measurements. I. Title.*
*TC LB2846 .R33 2000*

**Ravitch, Diane.**
Brookings papers on education policy, 2000. Washington, D.C. : Brookings Institution Press, c2000.
*TC LC89 .B7472 2000*

City schools. Baltimore : Johns Hopkins University Press, c2000.
*TC LC5133.N4 C57 2000*

Left back : a century of failed school reforms / Diane Ravitch. New York : Simon & Schuster, c2000. 555 p. ; 24 cm. Includes bibliographical references (p. 529-531) and index. ISBN 0-684-84417-6 DDC 370/.973
*1. Education - United States - History - 20th century. 2. Educational change - United States - History - 20th century. 3. Public schools - United States - History - 20th century. I. Title.*
*TC LA216 .R28 2000*

**Raviv, Amiram.**
How children understand war and peace. 1st ed. San Francisco : Jossey-Bass, c1999.

*TC JZ5534 .H69 1999*

**Rawlings, Carol Miller.** The lion, the witch and the wardrobe by C. S. Lewis / written by Carol Miller Rawlings. New York : Scholastic, c1997. 16 p. : ill. ; 28 cm. (Scholastic literature guide. Grades 4-8.) "Author biography, chapter summaries, discussion questions, vocabulary builders, assessment strategies, reproducibles, cross-curricular activities for students of all learning styles."-- Cover. ISBN 0-590-36647-5
*1. Lewis, C. S. - (Clive Staples), - 1898-1963. - The lion, the witch and the wardrobe. 2. Children's literature - Study and teaching. 3. Reading (Elementary) I. Title. II. Series.*
*TC LB1573 .R38 1997*

**RAWLINGS, JERRY, 1947-.**
Quist, Hubert Oswald. Secondary education and nation-building. 1999.
*TC 085 Q52*

**Ray, Heidi.**
Lazear, David G. Eight ways of knowing. 3rd ed. Arlington Heights, Ill. : SkyLight Training and Pub., c1999.
*TC LB1060 .L39 1999*

**Ray, Michael L.**
Goleman, Daniel. The creative spirit. New York, N.Y., U.S.A. : Dutton, c1992.
*TC BF408 .G57 1992*

**Ray, R. Glenn.** The facilitative leader : behaviors that enable success / R. Glenn Ray. Upper Saddler River, NJ : Prentice Hall, c1999. xiii, 173 p. : ill. ; 24 cm. Includes bibliographical references (p. 165-168) and index. ISBN 0-13-895228-0 DDC 658.4/092
*1. Group facilitation. 2. Leadership. I. Title.*
*TC HD66 .R3918 1999*

**Rayevsky, Robert, ill.**
Hodges, Margaret, 1911- Joan of Arc. 1st ed. New York : Holiday House, c1999.
*TC DC103.5 .H64 1999*

**Raymond, Susan Ueber.**
Science, technology, and the economic future. New York : New York Academy of Sciences, c1998.
*TC HD82 .S35 1998*

**Raymont, Thomas, 1864-** A history of the education of young children,. London ; New York : Longmans, Green and co., [1937] xi, 352 p. ; 19 cm. "First published 1937." Includes bibliographical references and index.
*1. Education. 2. Education - History. I. Title.*
*TC LA21 .R37*

**RCA/Columbia Pictures Home Video.**
Bright beginnings [videorecording. Burbank, CA : RCA/Columbia Pictures Home Video ; Toluca Lake, CA : [Distributed by] Corporate Productions, c1991.
*TC HV1642 .B67 1991*

Bright beginnings [videorecording. Burbank, CA : RCA/Columbia Pictures Home Video ; [S.l. : Distributed by] Rank Video Services America, c1991.
*TC HV1642 .B67 1991*

Brighter visions [videorecording. Burbank, CA : RCA/Columbia Pictures Home Video ; Toluca Lake, CA : [Distributed by] Corporate Productions, c1991.
*TC HV1597.5 .B67 1991*

**RCA/Columbia Pictures of America.**
Bridges to independence [videorecording. Burbank, CA : RCA/Columbia Pictures Home Video ; [S.l. : Distributed by] Rank Video Services Production, c1991.
*TC HV1646 .B7 1991*

Work sight [videorecording]. Burbank, Ca. : RCA/Columbia Pictures Home Video, c1991.
*TC HV1652 .W6 1991*

**Re-examining psychology.**
Holdstock, T. Len. London ; New York : Routledge, 2000.
*TC BF108.A3 .H65 2000*

**(Re)visioning composition textbooks :** conflicts of culture, ideology, and pedagogy / edited by Xin Liu Gale and Frederic G. Gale ; foreword by Gary A. Olson. Albany : State University of New York Press, c1999. xi, 274 p. ; 24 cm. Includes bibliographical references and index. ISBN 0-7914-4121-0 (hardcover : alk. paper) ISBN 0-7914-4122-9 (pbk. : alk. paper) DDC 808/.042/0711
*1. English language - Rhetoric - Textbooks - History - 20th century. 2. English language - Rhetoric - Study and teaching - Social aspects. 3. English language - Rhetoric - Study and teaching - Political aspects. 4. English language - Rhetoric - Textbooks - Publishing. 5. Report writing - Study and teaching. 6. Pluralism (Social sciences) 7. Culture conflict. I. Gale, Xin Liu, 1952- II. Gale, Fredric G., 1933- III. Title: Revisioning composition textbooks*

*TC PE1404 .R46 1999*

**Rea-Dickins, Pauline.**
Managing evaluation and innovation in language teaching. New York : Longman, 1998.
*TC P53.63 .M36 1998*

**Reaching and teaching children who are victims of poverty** / edited by Alice Duhon-Ross. Lewiston, N.Y. : Lampeter, Wales : E. Mellen Press, c1999. xi, 206 p. : 24 cm. (Symposium series ; v. 55) Includes bibliographical references. ISBN 0-7734-7964-3 DDC 371.826/942
*1. Poor children - Education - United States. 2. Educational equalization - United States. I. Duhon-Ross, Alice. II. Series: Symposium series (Edwin Mellen Press) ; v. 55.*
*TC LC4091 .R38 1999*

**Reaching out.**
Yardley, Alice. London : Evans Bros., 1970.
*TC LB1140 .Y35*

**Reaching out.** New York, N.Y. : American Book Company, c1980. 96 p. : ill. ; 22x28 cm. (American readers ; K-2) ISBN 0-278-45988-9
*1. Readers (Prmimary) I. Series.*
*TC PE1119 .R42 1980*

**Reaching out.** Teacher's ed. New York, N.Y. : American Book Company, c1980. xiv, 210 p. : ill. ; 22x28 cm. (American readers ; K-2) Includes index. ISBN 0-278-46010-0
*1. Readers (Primary) 2. Reading (Primary) I. Series.*
*TC PE1119 .R42 1980 Teacher's Ed.*

**Reaching out.** Teacher's ed. Lexington, Mass. : D.C. Heath and Company, c1983. xxxii, 236 p. : ill. ; 22x28 cm. (American readers ; K-2) Includes index. ISBN 0-669-04920-4
*1. Readers (Primary) 2. Reading (Primary) I. Series.*
*TC PE1119 .R42 1983 Teacher's Ed.*

**Reaching out.** Teacher's ed. Lexington, Mass. : D.C. Heath and Company, c1986. T30, 325 p. : ill. ; 22x28 cm. (American readers ; K-2) Includes index. ISBN 0-669-08043-8
*1. Readers (Primary) 2. Reading (Primary) I. Series.*
*TC PE1119 .R42 1986 Teacher's Ed.*

**Reaching out in family therapy.**
Boyd-Franklin, Nancy. New York : Guilford Press, 2000.
*TC RC488.5 .B678 2000*

**Reaching potentials** / Sue Bredekamp and Teresa Rosegrant, editors. Washington, DC : National Association for the Education of Young Children, c1992-<1995> [v.2] : ill. ; 28 cm. (NAEYC ; #225, 227) "A 1991-92 NAEYC comprehensive membership benefit." Includes bibliographical references. CONTENTS: v. 1. Appropriate curriculum and assessment for young children -- v. 2. Transforming early childhood curriculum and assessment. ISBN 0-935989-53-6 (v.1) ISBN 0-935989-73-0 (v.2) DDC 372.19
*1. Early childhood education - United States - Curricula. 2. Curriculum planning - United States. I. Bredekamp, Sue. II. Rosegrant, Teresa Jane, 1949- III. Series: NAEYC (Series) ; #225, 227.*
*TC LB1140.23 .R36 1992*

**Reaching the child with autism through art.**
Flowers, Toni. Arlington, TX : Future Education, c1992.
*TC LC4717 .F56 2000*

**Reaching up for manhood.**
Canada, Geoffrey. Boston : Beacon Press, c1998.
*TC HQ775 .C35 1998*

**Read all about it :** teacher's planning guide. New York : Macmillan/McGraw-Hill, c1997. 320, T114 p. : ill. (some col.) ; 31 cm. (Spotlight on literacy ; Gr.1 l.1) (The road to independent reading) ISBN 0-02-181150-4
*1. Reading (Primary) 2. Language arts (Primary) I. Series. II. Series: The road to independent reading*
*TC LB1576 .S66 1997 Gr.1 l.1*

**Read and wonder**
Casey, Patricia. My cat Jack. 1st U.S. ed. Cambridge, Mass. : Candlewick Press, c1994.
*TC PZ7.C2679 My 1994*

**Read, Donald A., comp.** Humanistic education sourcebook / edited by Donald A. Read, Sidney B. Simon ; with an introd. by Don Hamachek. Englewood Cliffs, N.J. : Prentice-Hall, [1975] xiv, 482 p. ; 23 cm. Bibliography: p. 479-482. ISBN 0134477146. ISBN 0-13-447706-5 (pbk.) DDC 370.11/2
*1. Education, Humanistic - Addresses, essays, lectures. I. Simon, Sidney B., joint comp. II. Title.*
*TC LC1011 .R38*

**Read, Michelle Riordan.**
Sean's story [videorecording]. Princeton, N.J. : Films for the Humanities & Sciences ; [S.l. : distributed by] ABC Multimedia : Capital Cities/ABC, c1994.

*TC LC1203.M3 .S39 1994*

**READ perspectives**
(v. 6.) Educating language-minority children. New Brunswick (U.S.A.) : Transaction Publishers, c2000.
*TC LC3731 .E374 2000*

**Read! read! read!.**
Glass, Laurie. Thousand Oaks, Calif. : Corwin Press, c2000.
*TC LB1050.2 .G54 2000*

**Readence, John E., 1947-.**
Tierney, Robert J. Reading strategies and practices. 5th ed. Boston : Allyn and Bacon, c2000.
*TC LB1050 .T57 2000*

**Reader on finance in higher education.**
ASHE reader on finance in higher education. Needham Heights, MA : Ginn Press, c1986.
*TC LB2342 .A76 1990*

**READER-RESPONSE CRITICISM.**
Hancock, Marjorie R. A celebration of literature and response. Upper Saddle River, N.J. : Merrill, c2000.
*TC LB1575 .H36 2000*

**READERS.**
Phillips, James B. Accent. Glenview, Ill. : Scott, Foresman, 1972.
*TC PE1121 .P54 1972*

**READERS - 1950-.**
Dixson, Robert James. Easy reading selections in English; Rev. ed. [New York] Regents Pub. Co. [c1971]
*TC PE1128.A2 D5 1971*

**READERS AND AUTHORS.** *See* AUTHORS AND READERS.

**READERS AND LIBRARIES.** *See* LIBRARIES AND READERS.

**READERS (ELEMENTARY).**
Botel, Morton. Communicating. Lexington, Mass. : D. C. Heath, c1973.
*TC PE1121 .B67 1973 Bk A*

Botel, Morton. Communicating. Lexington, Mass. : D. C. Heath, c1973.
*TC PE1121 .B67 1973*

Changing views. Teacher's ed. Lexington, Mass. : D.C. Heath and Company, c1983.
*TC PE1121 .C52 1983 Teacher's Ed.*

Changing views. Teacher's ed. Lexington, Mass. : D.C. Heath and Company, c1983.
*TC PE1121 .C52 1983 Teacher's Ed. Workbook*

Clearing paths. New York, N.Y. : American Book Company, c1980
*TC PE1121 .C63 1980*

Clearing paths. Lexington, Mass. : D.C. Heath and Company, c1983.
*TC PE1121 .C63 1983*

Clearing paths. Teacher's ed. New York, N.Y. : American Book Company, c1980
*TC PE1121 .C63 1980 Teacher's Ed. Workbook*

Clearing paths. Teacher's ed. Lexington, Mass. : D.C. Heath and Company, c1983.
*TC PE1121 .C63 1983 Teacher's Ed. Workbook*

Crossing boundaries. Teacher's ed. Lexington, Mass. : D.C. Heath and Company, c1983.
*TC PE1121 .C76 1983 Teacher's Ed. Workbook*

M. Margaret Michael, Sister, O.P. This is our land. New ed. Boston, Mass. : Ginn and Company, 1955.
*TC PE1121 .M52 1955*

Making choices. Teacher's ed. New York, N.Y. : American Book Company, c1980.
*TC PE1121 .M34 1980 Teacher's Ed.*

Making choices. New York, N.Y. : American Book Company, c1980.
*TC PE1121 .M34 1980*

Making choices. Teacher's ed. Lexington, Mass. : D.C. Heath & co., c1986.
*TC PE1121 .M34 1986 Teacher's Ed.*

Making choices. Lexington, Mass. : D.C. Heath & co., c1986.
*TC PE1121 .M34 1986*

Making choices. Lexington, Mass. : D.C. Heath & co., c1986.
*TC PE1121 .M34 1986 Activity Pad*

Making choices. Lexington, Mass. : D.C. Heath & Co., c1986.

*TC PE1121 .M34 1986 Skills Pad*

Making choices. Lexington, Mass. : D.C. Heath & co., c1986.
*TC PE1121 .M34 1986 Resource Binder*

Making choices. Teacher's ed. New York, N.Y. : American Book Company, c1980.
*TC PE1121 .M34 1980 Teacher's Ed. Workbook*

Making choices. Teacher's ed. Lexington, Mass. : D.C. Heath & co., c1986.
*TC PE1121 .M34 1986 Teacher's Ed. Workbook*

Meeting challenges. Teacher's ed. New York, N.Y. : American Book Co., c1980.
*TC PE1121 .M43 1980 Teacher's Ed.*

Meeting challenges. Lexington, Mass. : D. C. Heath and Company, c1983.
*TC PE1121 .M43 1983*

Meeting challenges. Teacher's ed. Lexington, Mass. : D.C. Heath and Company, c1983.
*TC PE1121 .M43 1983 Teacher's Ed.*

Meeting challenges. Lexington, Mass. : D.C. Heath and Company, c1983.
*TC PE1121 .M43 1983*

Meeting challenges. Teacher's ed. Lexington, Mass. : D.C. Heath and Company, c1986.
*TC PE1121 .M43 1986 Teacher's Ed.*

Meeting challenges. Lexington, Mass. : D.C. Heath and Company, c1986.
*TC PE1121 .M43 1986*

Meeting challenges. Lexington, Mass. : D. C. Heath and Company, c1986.
*TC PE1121 .M43 1986 Skills Pad*

Meeting challenges. Teacher's ed. Lexington, Mass. : D. C. Heath and Company, c1983.
*TC PE1121 .M43 1983 Teacher's Ed. Workbook*

Meeting challenges. Teacher's ed. Lexington, Mass. : D.C. Heath and Company, c1986.
*TC PE1121 .M43 1986 Teacher's Ed. Workbook*

Moving on. Lexington, Mass. : D.C. Heath, c1983.
*TC PE1117 .M68 1983*

Moving on. Lexington, Mass. : D.C. Heath, c1983.
*TC PE1117 .M68 1983*

Nelson, Joan Meeting challenges. Lexington, Mass. : D. C. Heath and Company, c1983.
*TC PE1121 .M43 1983*

Odyssey. Teacher's ed. Orlando, Fla. : Harcourt Brace Jovanovich, c1982.
*TC PE1117 .O39 1982 Teacher's Ed.*

Roberts, Paul. The Roberts English series. Teacher's ed. New York : Harcourt, Brace & World c<1966-  >
*TC PE1112 .R6 Teacher's edition*

Roberts, Paul. The Roberts English series. Teacher's ed. New York : Harcourt, Brace & World c<1966-  >
*TC PE1112 .R6 Teacher's edition*

Sebesta, Sam Leaton. Odyssey. Orlando, Fla. : Harcourt Brace Jovanovich, c1982.
*TC PE1117 .O39 1982*

Sebesta, Sam Leaton. Odyssey. 2nd ed. Orlando, Fla. : Harcourt Brace Jovanovich, c1986.
*TC PE1117 .O39 1986*

Workbook for making choices. Teacher's ed. Lexington, Mass. : D.C. Heath Company, c1983.
*TC PE1121 .M34 1983 Teacher's Ed. Workbook*

## READERS - EMIGRATION AND IMMIGRATION.
New immigrants in the United States. Cambridge, U.K. ; New York : Cambridge University Press, 2000.
*TC PE1128 .N384 1999*

**Reader's guide to lesbian and gay studies** / editor, Timothy Murphy. Chicago : Fitzroy Dearborn Publishers, 2000. xxviii, 720 p. ; 29 cm. Includes bibliographical references and index. ISBN 1-57958-142-0
*1. Gay and lesbian studies. 2. Gay and lesbian studies - Bibliography. I. Murphy, Timothy F., 1955- II. Title: Lesbian and gay studies*
*TC HQ75.15 .R43 2000*

## READERS - IMMIGRANTS.
New immigrants in the United States. Cambridge, U.K. : New York : Cambridge University Press, 2000.
*TC PE1128 .N384 1999*

## READERS (PRIMARY).
Building dreams. New York, N.Y. : American Book Company, c1980.
*TC PE1119 .B84 1980*

Building dreams. Teacher's ed. New York, N.Y. : American Book Company, c1980.
*TC PE1119 .B84 1980 Teacher's Ed.*

Building dreams. Lexington, Mass. : D.C. Heath and Company, c1983.
*TC PE1119 .B84 1983*

Building dreams. Teacher's ed. Lexington, Mass. : D.C. Heath and Company, c1986.
*TC PE1119 .B84 1986 Teacher's Ed.*

Building dreams. Teacher's ed. New York, N.Y. : American Book Company, c1980.
*TC PE1119 .B84 1980 Teacher's Ed. Workbook*

Building dreams. Teacher's Ed. Lexington, Mass. : D.C. Heath and Company, c1983.
*TC PE1119 .B84 1983 Teacher's Ed. Workbook*

Catching glimpses. Teacher's ed. Lexington, Mass. : D.C. Heath & co., c1986.
*TC PE1119 .C37 1986 Teacher's Ed.*

Catching glimpses. Teacher's ed. Lexington, Mass. : D.C. Heath & Co., c1983.
*TC PE1119 .C37 1983 Teacher's Ed. Workbook*

Clearing paths. Teacher's ed. New York, NY : American Book Company, c1980
*TC PE1119 .C63 1980 Teacher's Ed.*

Climbing up. New York, N.Y. : American Book Company, c1980.
*TC PE1119 .C54 1980*

Finding places. Teacher's ed. New York, N.Y. : American Book Company, c1980.
*TC PE1119 .F56 1980 Teacher's Ed.*

Finding places. New York, NY : American Book Company, c1980.
*TC PE1119 .F56 1980*

Finding places. Lexington, Mass. : D.C. Heath and Company, c1983.
*TC PE1119 .F56 1983*

Finding places. Teacher's ed. Lexington, Mass. : D.C. Heath and Company, c1983.
*TC PE1119 .F56 1983 Teacher's Ed.*

Finding places. Teacher's ed. Lexington, Mass. : D.C. Heath and Company, c1986.
*TC PE1119 .F56 1986 Teacher's Ed.*

Finding places. Teacher's ed. New York, N.Y. : American Book Company, c1980.
*TC PE1119 .F56 1980 Teacher's Ed. Workbook*

Finding places. Teacher's ed. Lexington, Mass. : D.C. Heath and Company, c1983.
*TC PE1119 .F56 1983 Teacher's Ed. Workbook*

Going far. New York, N.Y. : American Book Company, c1980.
*TC PE1119 .G64 1980*

Looking out. Climbing up. Going far. Teacher's ed. New York, N.Y. : American Book Cpmpany, c1980.
*TC PE1119 .L66 1980 Teacher's Ed.*

Looking out. Climbing up. Going far. Teacher's ed. Lexington, Mass. : D.C. Heath and Cpmpany, c1986.
*TC PE1119 .L66 1986 Teacher's Ed.*

Looking out. Climbing up. Going far. Teacher's ed. New York, N.Y. : American Book Company, c1980.
*TC PE1119 .L66 1980 Teacher's Ed. Workbook*

Looking out. Climbing up. Going far. Teacher's ed. Lexington, Mass. : D.C. Heath and Cpmpany, c1983.
*TC PE1119 .L66 1983 Teacher's Ed. Workbook*

Marching along. Teacher's ed. New York, N.Y. : American Book Company, c1980.
*TC PE1119 .M37 1980 Teacher's Ed.*

Marching along. New York, N.Y. : American Book Company, c1980.
*TC PE1119 .M37 1980*

Marching along. Teacher's ed. Lexington, Mass. : D.C. Heath and Company, c1983.
*TC PE1119 .M37 1983 Teacher's Ed.*

Marching along. Lexington, Mass. : D.C. Heath and Company, c1983.
*TC PE1119 .M37 1983*

Marching along. Teacher's ed. Lexington, Mass. : D.C. Heath and Company, c1986.
*TC PE1119 .M37 1986 Teacher's Ed.*

Marching along. Teacher's ed. New York, N.Y. : D.C. Heath and Company, c1983.
*TC PE1119 .M37 1980 Teacher's Ed. Workbook*

Marching along. Teacher's ed. Lexington, Mass. : D.C. Heath and Company, c1983.

Moving on. Lexington, Mass. : D.C. Heath, c1983.
*TC PE1119 .M68 1986 Teacher's Ed.*

Moving on. Lexington, Mass. : D.C. Heath, c1983.
*TC PE1119 .M68 1983 Teacher's Ed. Workbook*

Reaching out. Teacher's ed. New York, N.Y. : American Book Company, c1980.
*TC PE1119 .R42 1980 Teacher's Ed.*

Reaching out. Teacher's ed. Lexington, Mass. : D.C. Heath and Company, c1983.
*TC PE1119 .R42 1983 Teacher's Ed.*

Reaching out. Teacher's ed. Lexington, Mass. : D.C. Heath and Company, c1986.
*TC PE1119 .R42 1986 Teacher's Ed.*

Starting off. Teacher's ed. Lexington, Mass. : D.C. Heath and Company, c1986.
*TC PE1119 .S82 1986 Teacher's Ed.*

Turning corners. New York, N.Y. : American Book Company, c1980.
*TC PE1119 .T87 1980*

Turning corners. Teacher's ed. New York, N.Y. : American Book Company, c1980.
*TC PE1119 .T87 1980 Teacher's Ed.*

Turning corners. Teacher's ed. New York, N.Y. : American Book Company, c1980.
*TC PE1119 .T87 1980 Teacher's Ed.*

Turning corners. Lexington, Mass. : D.C. Heath and Company, c1983.
*TC PE1119 .T87 1983*

Turning corners. Teacher's ed. Lexington, Mass. : D.C. Heath and Company, c1986.
*TC PE1119 .T87 1986 Teacher's Ed.*

Turning corners. Teacher's ed. New York, N.Y. : American Book Company, c1980.
*TC PE1119 .T87 1980 Teacher's Ed. Workbook*

Turning corners. Teacher's ed. Lexington, Mass. : D.C. Heath and Company, c1983.
*TC PE1119 .T87 1983 Teacher's Ed. Workbook*

Warming up. Teacher's ed. New York, N.Y. : American Book Company, c1980.
*TC PE1119 .W37 1980 Teacher's Ed.*

Warming up. New York, N.Y. : American Book Company, c1980.
*TC PE1119 .W37 1980*

Warming up. Teacher's ed. Lexington, Mass. : D.C. Heath and Company, c1983.
*TC PE1119 .W37 1983 Teacher's Ed.*

Warming up. Teacher's ed. Lexington, Mass. : D.C. Heath and Company, c1986.
*TC PE1119 .W37 1986 Teacher's Ed.*

## READERS (PRMIMARY).
Reaching out. New York, N.Y. : American Book Company, c1980.
*TC PE1119 .R42 1980*

**Readers, teachers, learners.**
Brozo, William G. 3rd ed. Upper Saddle River, N.J. : Merrill, c1999.
*TC LB1632 .B7 1999*

## READINESS FOR SCHOOL.
The psychoeducational assessment of preschool children. 3rd ed. Boston : Allyn and Bacon, c2000.
*TC LB1115 .P963 2000*

## READING. *See also* BOOKS AND READING; CONTENT AREA READING; EXPRESSION; ORAL READING; SILENT READING.
Bloom, Harold. How to read and why. New York : Scribner, c2000.
*TC LB1050 .B56 2000*

Carver, Ronald P. The causes of high and low reading achievement. Mahway, N.J. : Lawrence Erlbaum Associates, 2000.
*TC LB1050.2 .C27 2000*

Cooper, J. David (James David), 1942- Literacy. 4th ed. Boston : Houghton Mifflin Co., c2000.
*TC LB1050.45 .C76 2000*

The explicit teaching of reading. Newark, Del. : International Reading Association, c1999.
*TC LB1573 .E96 1999*

Handbook of reading research. New York : Longman, c1984-<2000  >
*TC LB1050 .H278 2000*

Issues and trends in literacy education. 2nd ed. Boston : Allyn and Bacon, c2000.

TC LB1576 .I87 2000

Learning to read. Dordrecht ; Boston : Kluwer Academic Publishers, 1999.
TC LB1050.2 .L42 1999

May, Frank B. Unraveling the seven myths of reading. Boston : Allyn and Bacon, c2001.
TC LB1050.2 .M364 2001

Reading development and the teaching of reading. Oxford, UK ; Malden, Mass. : Blackwell Publishers, 1999.
TC LB1050.2 .R424 1999

Reutzel, D. Ray (Douglas Ray), 1953- Balanced reading strategies and practices. Upper Saddle river, N.J. : Merrill, c1999.
TC LB1050 .R477 1999

Stanovich, Keith E., 1950- Progress in understanding reading. New York : Guilford Press, c2000.
TC LB1050 .S723 2000

Tierney, Robert J. Reading strategies and practices. 5th ed. Boston : Allyn and Bacon, c2000.
TC LB1050 .T57 2000

**READING - ABILITY TESTING.**
Gillet, Jean Wallace. Understanding reading problems. 5th ed. New York ; Harlow, England : Longman, c2000.
TC LB1050.46 .G55 2000

Hill, Clifford. Children and reading tests. Stamford, Conn. : Ablex Pub. Corp., c2000.
TC LB1050.46 .H55 2000

Reading assessment. Newark, Del. : International Reading Association, c1999.
TC LB1573 .R2793 1999

Running records. York, Me. : Stenhouse Publishers , 2000.
TC LB1525 R75 2000

Walker, Barbara J., 1946- Diagnostic teaching of reading. 4th ed. Upper Saddle River, NJ : Merrill, c2000.
TC LB1050.5 .W35 2000

**READING - ABILITY TESTING - UNITED STATES.**
Hargis, Charles H. Teaching and testing in reading. Springfield, Ill. : C.C. Thomas, c1999.
TC LB1050 .H29 1999

**READING - ABILITY TESTING - UNITED STATES - CASE STUDIES.**
Simmons, Jay, 1947- You never asked me to read. Boston : Allyn and Bacon, c2000.
TC LB1050.46 .S535 2000

**READING (ADULT EDUCATION).**
Mellgren, Lars. New horizons in English, [workbooks]. Reading, Mass. : Addison-Wesley Pub. Co., 1973-c1978.
TC PE1128 .M38

**READING (ADULT EDUCATION) - STUDY AND TEACHING. See READING (ADULT EDUCATION).**

**READING - AIDS AND DEVICES.**
Phonics review kit [kit]. Chicago, Ill. : Open Court Pub. Co., c1995.
TC LB1573.3 .P45 1995

Teacher toolbox [kit]. Chicago, Ill. : Open Court Pub. Co., c1995.
TC LB1573.3 .T4 1995

**READING ALOUD. See ORAL READING.**

**READING AND BOOKS. See BOOKS AND READING.**

**Reading and writing in elementary classrooms :**
strategies and obervations / Patricia M. Cunningham ... [et al.]. 4th ed. New York : Longman, c2000. 1 v. (various pagings) : ill. ; 24 cm. Includes bibliographical references and index. ISBN 0-8013-3063-7 (hardcover) DDC 372.4
1. Reading (Elementary) 2. English language - Composition and exercises - Study and teaching (Elementary) 3. Language arts (Elementary) I. Cunningham. Patricia Marr.
TC LB1573 .R279 2000

**Reading and writing in the time of Jesus.**
Millard, A. R. (Alan Ralph) New York : New York University Press, 2000.
TC BS2555.5 .M55 2000

**Reading assessment :** principles and practices for elementary teachers : a collection of articles from The reading teacher / Shelby J. Barrentine, editor. Newark, Del. : International Reading Association, c1999. vi,

271 p. : ill. ; 26 cm. Includes bibliographical references and index. ISBN 0-87207-250-9 (pbk.) DDC 372.4
1. Reading (Elementary) 2. Reading - Ability testing. I. Barrentine, Shelby J. II. International Reading Association. III. Title: Reading teacher.
TC LB1573 .R2793 1999

**Reading between the signs.**
Mindess, Anna. Yarmouth, Me. : Intercultural Press, c1999.
TC HV2402 .M56 1999

**READING, CHOICE OF. See BOOKS AND READING.**

**READING CIRCLES. See GROUP READING.**

**READING - CODE EMPHASIS APPROACHES. See READING - PHONETIC METHOD.**

**READING COMPREHENSION.**
Biemiller, Andrew, 1939- Language and reading success. Cambridge, Mass. : Brookline Books, c1999.
TC LB1139.L3 B48 1999

Carver, Ronald P. The causes of high and low reading achievement. Mahway, N.J. : Lawrence Erlbaum Associates, 2000.
TC LB1050.2 .C27 2000

Cooper, J. David (James David), 1942- Literacy. 4th ed. Boston : Houghton Mifflin Co., c2000.
TC LB1050.45 .C76 2000

May, Frank B. Unraveling the seven myths of reading. Boston : Allyn and Bacon, c2001.
TC LB1050.2 .M364 2001

O'Donnell, Michael P. Becoming a reader. 2nd ed. Boston : Allyn and Bacon, c1999.
TC LB1050.53 .O35 1999

Tierney, Robert J. Reading strategies and practices. 5th ed. Boston : Allyn and Bacon, c2000.
TC LB1050 .T57 2000

Walker, Barbara J., 1946- Diagnostic teaching of reading. 4th ed. Upper Saddle River, NJ : Merrill, c2000.
TC LB1050.5 .W35 2000

**READING COMPREHENSION - ABILITY TESTING.**
Hill, Clifford. Children and reading tests. Stamford, Conn. : Ablex Pub. Corp., c2000.
TC LB1050.46 .H55 2000

Tian, Shiau-ping. TOEFL reading comprehension. 2000.
TC 06 no. 11316

**READING COMPREHENSION - UNITED STATES.**
Reading for meaning. New York ; London : Teachers College Press, c2000.
TC LB1050.45 .R443 2000

**READING - COMPUTER-ASSISTED INSTRUCTION.**
Jody, Marilyn, 1932- Using computers to teach literature. 2nd ed. Urbana, Ill. : National Council of Teachers of English, c1998.
TC LB1050.37 .J63 1998

**READING - CONGRESSES.**
Claremont Reading Conference. Yearbook. Claremont, Calif. : Claremont Graduate School Curriculum Laboratory, c1961-
TC BF456.R2 A24

**READING, CONTENT AREA. See CONTENT AREA READING.**

**Reading counts.**
Borasi, Raffaella. New York ; London : Teachers College Press, c2000.
TC QA11 .B6384 2000

**Reading development and the teaching of reading :** a psychological perspective / [edited by] Jane Oakhill and Roger Beard. Oxford, UK ; Malden, Mass. : Blackwell Publishers, 1999. xix, 238 p. ; 24 cm. Includes bibliographical references and index. ISBN 0-631-20681-7 (hbk. : alk. paper) ISBN 0-631-20682-5 (pbk. : alk. paper) DDC 428/.4
1. Reading. 2. Reading, Psychology of. I. Oakhill, Jane. II. Beard, Roger.
TC LB1050.2 .R424 1999

**READING DEVICES FOR THE DISABLED. See BLIND, APPARATUS FOR THE.**

**READING DISABILITY. See also DYSLEXIA.**
Carver, Ronald P. The causes of high and low reading achievement. Mahway, N.J. : Lawrence Erlbaum Associates, 2000.

TC LB1050.2 .C27 2000

Goldsworthy, Candace L. Sourcebook of phonological awareness activities. San Diego : Singular Pub. Group, c1998.
TC LB1050.5 .G66 1998

Learning to read. Dordrecht ; Boston : Kluwer Academic Publishers, 1999.
TC LB1050.2 .L42 1999

May, Frank B. Unraveling the seven myths of reading. Boston : Allyn and Bacon, c2001.
TC LB1050.2 .M364 2001

Teaching struggling readers. Newark, Del. : International Reading Association, c1998.
TC LB1050.5 .T437 1998

Walton, Margaret. Teaching reading and spelling to dyslexic children. London : D. Fulton, 1998.
TC LC4708 .W35 1998

What reading research tells us about children with diverse learning needs. Mahwah, N.J. : Erlbaum, 1998.
TC LB1050.5 .W47 1998

**READING (EARLY CHILDHOOD).**
Children achieving. Newark, Del. : International Reading Association, c1998.
TC LB1139.5.R43 C55 1998

Stirring the waters. Portsmouth, NH : Heinemann, c1999.
TC LB1139.5.L35 S85 1999

**READING (EARLY CHILDHOOD) - COMPUTER-ASSISTED INSTRUCTION.**
Casey, Jean Marie. Early literacy. Rev. ed. Englewood, Colo. : Libraries Unlimited, 2000.
TC LB1139.5.L35 C37 2000

**READING (EARLY CHILDHOOD) - GREAT BRITAIN.**
MALLETT, MARGARET. Young researchers. London ; New York : Routledge, 1999.
TC LB1576 .M3627 1999

**READING (EARLY CHILDHOOD) - STUDY AND TEACHING. See READING (EARLY CHILDHOOD).**

**READING (EARLY CHILDHOOD) - UNITED STATES.**
Dorn, Linda J. Apprenticeship in literacy. York, Me. : Stenhouse Publishers, c1998.
TC LB1139.5.L35 D67 1998

McGee, Lea M. Literacy's beginnings. 3rd ed. Boston ; London : Allyn and Bacon, c2000.
TC LB1139.5.R43 M33 2000

**READING (ELEMENTARY).**
Assessment as inquiry. Urbana, Ill. : National Council of Teachers of English, 1999.
TC LB3051 .A76665 1999

Beech, Linda Ward. The cay by Theodore Taylor. New York : Scholastic, c1997.
TC LB1573 .B4312 1997

Beech, Linda Ward. Danny the champion of the world by Roald Dahl. New York : Scholastic, c1997.
TC LB11573 .B431 1997

Beech, Linda Ward. Danny the champion of the world by Roald Dahl. New York : Scholastic, c1997.
TC LB1573 .B431 1997

Beech, Linda Ward. The diary of a young girl by Anne Frank. New York : Scholastic, c1998.
TC LB1573 .B433 1998

Beech, Linda Ward. The great fire by Jim Murphy. New York : Scholastic, c1996.
TC LB11573 .B437 1996

Beech, Linda Ward. The great fire by Jim Murphy. New York : Scholastic, c1996.
TC LB1573 .B437 1996

Beech, Linda Ward. The great Gilly Hopkins by Katherine Paterson. New York : Scholastic, c1998.
TC LB1573 .B439 1998

Beech, Linda Ward. Guests by Michael Dorris. New York, NY : Scholastic, c1996.
TC LB1573 .B432 1996

Beech, Linda Ward. Hatchet by Gary Paulsen. New York : Scholastic, c1998.
TC LB1573 .B4310 1998

Beech, Linda Ward. Island of the blue dolphins by Scott O'Dell. New York : Scholastic, c1997.

*TC LB1573 .B438 1997*

Beech, Linda Ward. Julie of the wolves by Jean Craighead George. New York : Scholastic, c1996.
*TC LB1573 .B434 1996*

Beech, Linda Ward. Maniac Magee by Jerry Spinelli. New York : Scholastic, c1997.
*TC LB1573 .B4311 1997*

Beech, Linda Ward. Sarah, plain and tall by Patricia MacLachlan. New York : Scholastic, c1996.
*TC LB1573 .B436 1996*

Beech, Linda Ward. Tuck everlasting by Natalie Babbitt. New York : Scholastic, c1997.
*TC LB1573 .B43 1997*

Beech, Linda Ward. A wrinkle in time by Madeleine L'Engle. New York : Scholastic, c1997.
*TC LB1573 .B435 1997*

Biemiller, Andrew, 1939- Language and reading success. Cambridge, Mass. : Brookline Books, c1999.
*TC LB1139.L3 B48 1999*

Call it courage. New York : Macmillan/McGraw-Hill, c1997.
*TC LB1576 .S66 1997 Gr.6 l.12 u.6*

Changing views. Teacher's ed. Lexington, Mass. : D.C. Heath and Company, c1983.
*TC PE1121 .C52 1983 Teacher's Ed.*

Changing views. Teacher's ed. Lexington, Mass. : D.C. Heath and Company, c1983.
*TC PE1121 .C52 1983 Teacher's Ed. Workbook*

Clearing paths. Teacher's ed. New York, N.Y. : American Book Company, c1980
*TC PE1121 .C63 1980 Teacher's Ed. Workbook*

Clearing paths. Teacher's ed. Lexington, Mass. : D.C. Heath and Company, c1983.
*TC PE1121 .C63 1983 Teacher's Ed. Workbook*

Coming home. New York : Macmillan/McGraw-Hill, c1997.
*TC LB1576 .S66 1997 Gr.6 l.12 u.5*

Cooper, J. David (James David), 1942- Discover : Grade 1, level 1.5, [Themes 9 and 10]. Boston : Houghton Mifflin, 1997.
*TC LB1575.8 .C6616 1997*

Cramer, Ronald L. The spelling connection. New York : Guilford Press, c1998.
*TC LB1574 .C65 1998*

Crossing boundaries. Teacher's ed. Lexington, Mass. : D.C. Heath and Company, c1983.
*TC PE1121 .C76 1983 Teacher's Ed. Workbook*

Dare to discover. New York : Macmillan/McGraw-Hill, c1997.
*TC LB1576 .S66 1997 Gr.6 l.12 u.2*

Fisher, Bobbi. Perspectives on shared reading. Portsmouth, NH : Heinemann, c2000.
*TC LB1573 .F528 2000*

Fountas, Irene C. Matching books to readers :. Portsmouth, NH : Heinemann, c1999.
*TC LB1573 .F68*

Getting to know you. New York : Macmillan/McGraw-Hill, c1997.
*TC LB1576 .S66 1997 Gr.5 l.11 u.4*

Golden, Joanne Marie, 1949- Storymaking in elementary and middle school classrooms. Mahwah, N.J. : L. Erlbaum Associates, 2000.
*TC LB1042 .G54 2000*

Grugeon, Elizabeth. The art of storytelling for teachers and pupils. London : David Fulton, 2000.
*TC LB1042 .G78 2000*

Gunning, Thomas G. Creating literacy instruction for all children. 3rd ed. Boston : Allyn and Bacon, c2000.
*TC LB1573 .G93 2000*

Gutner, Howard. Caddie Woodlawn by Carol Ryrie Brink. New York : Scholastic, c1997.
*TC LB1573 .G87 1997*

Harris, Albert Josiah. How to increase reading ability, a guide to individualized and remedial methods. 2d ed., rev. and enl. London : New York[etc.] : Longmans, Green and Co., 1947.
*TC 372.4H2421*

Hoffman, James V. Balancing principles for teaching elementary reading. Mahwah, N.J. : L. Erlbaum Associates, c2000.
*TC LB1573 . H459 2000*

Jobe, Ron. Reluctant readers. Markham, Ont. : Pembroke Pub., 1999.

*TC LB1573 .J58 1999*

Make a wish. New York : Macmillan/McGraw-Hill. c1997.
*TC LB1576 .S66 1997 Gr.4 l.10 u.1*

Making choices. Teacher's ed. New York, N.Y. : American Book Company, c1980.
*TC PE1121 .M34 1980 Teacher's Ed.*

Making choices. Teacher's ed. Lexington, Mass. : D.C. Heath & co., c1986.
*TC PE1121 .M34 1986 Teacher's Ed.*

Making choices. Lexington, Mass. : D.C. Heath & co., c1986.
*TC PE1121 .M34 1986 Resource Binder*

Making choices. Teacher's ed. New York, N.Y. : American Book Company, c1980.
*TC PE1121 .M34 1980 Teacher's Ed. Workbook*

Making choices. Teacher's ed. Lexington, Mass. : D.C. Heath & co., c1986.
*TC PE1121 .M34 1986 Teacher's Ed. Workbook*

Making the grade. New York : Macmillan/McGraw-Hill, c1997.
*TC LB1576 .S66 1997 Gr.6 l.12 u.1*

McCarthy, Tara. My brother Sam is dead by James Lincoln Collier and Christopher Collier. New York : Scholastic, c1997.
*TC LB1573 .M32 1997*

Meeting challenges. Teacher's ed. New York, N.Y. : American Book Co., c1980.
*TC PE1121 .M43 1980 Teacher's Ed.*

Meeting challenges. Teacher's ed. Lexington, Mass. : D.C. Heath and Company, c1983.
*TC PE1121 .M43 1983 Teacher's Ed.*

Meeting challenges. Teacher's ed. Lexington, Mass. : D.C. Heath and Company, c1986.
*TC PE1121 .M43 1986 Teacher's Ed.*

Meeting challenges. Lexington, Mass. : D. C. Heath and Company, c1986.
*TC PE1121 .M43 1986 Skills Pad*

Meeting challenges. Teacher's ed. Lexington, Mass. : D. C. Heath and Company, c1983.
*TC PE1121 .M43 1983 Teacher's Ed. Workbook*

Meeting challenges. Teacher's ed. Lexington, Mass. : D.C. Heath and Company, c1986.
*TC PE1121 .M43 1986 Teacher's Ed. Workbook*

Memories to keep. New York : Macmillan/McGraw-Hill, c1997.
*TC LB1576 .S66 1997 Gr.4 l.10 u.5*

Moving on. Lexington, Mass. : D.C. Heath, c1983.
*TC PE1117 .M68 1983*

Moving on. Lexington, Mass. : D.C. Heath, c1983.
*TC PE1117 .M68 1983*

Naturally. New York : Macmillan/McGraw-Hill, c1997.
*TC LB1576 .S66 1997 Gr.4 l.10 u.2*

Odyssey. Teacher's ed. Orlando, Fla. : Harcourt Brace Jovanovich, c1982.
*TC PE1117 .O39 1982 Teacher's Ed.*

Pitch in. New York : Macmillan/McGraw-Hill, c1997.
*TC LB1576 .S66 1997 Gr.4 l.10 u.5*

Rawlings, Carol Miller. The lion, the witch and the wardrobe by C. S. Lewis. New York : Scholastic, c1997.
*TC LB1573 .R38 1997*

Reading and writing in elementary classrooms. 4th ed. New York : Longman, c2000.
*TC LB1573 .R279 2000*

Reading assessment. Newark, Del. : International Reading Association, c1999.
*TC LB1573 .R2793 1999*

Scenes of wonder. New York : Macmillan/McGraw-Hill, c1997.
*TC LB1576 .S66 1997 Gr.5 l.11 u.1*

Take the high road. New York : Macmillan/McGraw-Hill, c1997.
*TC LB1576 .S66 1997 Gr.5 l.11 u.5*

That's what friends are for. New York : Macmillan/McGraw-Hill, c1997.
*TC LB1576 .S66 1997 Gr.4 l.10 u.3*

Time & time again. New York : Macmillan/McGraw-Hill, c1997.

*TC LB1576 .S66 1997 Gr.6 l.12 u.4*

Tips for the reading team. Newark, Del. : International Reading Association, c1998.
*TC LB1573 .T57 1998*

Twice-told tales. New York : Macmillan/McGraw-Hill, c1997.
*TC LB1576 .S66 1997 Gr.4 l.10 u.6*

Unlikely heroes. New York : Macmillan/McGraw-Hill, c1997.
*TC LB1576 .S66 1997 Gr.6 l.12 u.3*

Winning attitudes. New York : Macmillan/McGraw-Hill, c1997.
*TC LB1576 .S66 1997 Gr.5 l.11 u.3*

Workbook for making choices. Teacher's ed. Lexington, Mass. : D.C. Heath Company, c1983.
*TC PE1121 .M34 1983 Teacher's Ed. Workbook*

Worlds of change. New York : Macmillan/McGraw-Hill, c1997.
*TC LB1576 .S66 1997 Gr.5 l.11 u.2*

Zoom in. New York : Macmillan/McGraw-Hill, c1997.
*TC LB1576 .S66 1997 Gr.5 l.11 u.6*

**READING (ELEMENTARY) - CALIFORNIA - CASE STUDIES.**
Samway, Katharine Davies. Buddy reading. Portsmouth, NH : Heinemann, c1995.
*TC LB1031.5 .S36 1995*

**READING (ELEMENTARY) - CHINA.**
Ingulsrud, John E. Learning to read in China. Lewiston, N.Y. ; Lampeter, Wales : Mellen, c1999.
*TC LB1577.C48 I54 1999*

**READING (ELEMENTARY) - GREAT BRITAIN.**
Improving literacy in the primary school. London ; New York : Routledge, 1998.
*TC LB1573 .I56 1998*

MALLETT, MARGARET. Young researchers. London ; New York : Routledge, 1999.
*TC LB1576 .M3627 1999*

**READING (ELEMENTARY) - PHONETIC METHOD.** *See also* **READING - PHONETIC METHOD.**
Daniel, Claire, 1936- The great big book of fun phonics activities. New York : Scholastic professional books, c1999.
*TC LB1525.3 .D36 1999*

Phonics review kit [kit]. Chicago, Ill. : Open Court Pub. Co., c1995.
*TC LB1573.3 .P45 1995*

**READING (ELEMENTARY) - PROBLEMS, EXERCISES, ETC.**
Making choices. Lexington, Mass. : D.C. Heath & co., c1986.
*TC PE1121 .M34 1986 Activity Pad*

Making choices. Lexington, Mass. : D.C. Heath & Co., c1986.
*TC PE1121 .M34 1986 Skills Pad*

**READING (ELEMENTARY) - RESEARCH - UNITED STATES.**
National Reading Panel (U.S.) Report of the National Reading Panel : teaching children to read. [Washington, D.C.?] : National Institute of Child Health and Human Development, National Institutes of Health, [2000]
*TC LB1050 .N335 2000*

**READING (ELEMENTARY) - STUDY AND TEACHING.** *See* **READING (ELEMENTARY).**

**READING (ELEMENTARY) - UNITED STATES.**
Calkins, Lucy McCormick. The art of teaching reading. 1st ed. New York ; London : Longman, c2001.
*TC LB1573 .C185 2001*

Carr, Janine Chappell. A child went forth. Portsmouth, NH : Heinemann, 1999.
*TC LB1576 .C31714 1999*

Engaging young readers. New York : Guilford Press, c2000.
*TC LB1573 .E655 2000*

Fraser, Jane. On their way. Portsmouth, NH : Heinemann, c1994.
*TC LB1576 .F72 1994*

Gunning, Thomas G. Best books for building literacy for elementary school children. Boston : Allyn and Bacon, 2000.

*TC LB1573 .B47 2000*

Polette, Nancy. Gifted books, gifted readers. Englewood, Colo. : Libraries Unlimited, 2000.
*TC LB1575.5.U5 P64 2000*

The teaching of reading in Spanish to the bilingual student = 2nd ed. Mahwah, N.J. : L. Erlbaum Associates, 1998.
*TC LB1573 .T365 1998*

**Reading for meaning :** fostering comprehension in the middle grades / edited by Barbara M. Taylor, Michael F. Graves & Paul van den Broek. New York ; London : Teachers College Press, c2000. x, 206 p. : ill. ; 24 cm. (Language and literacy series) Includes bibliographical references and index. ISBN 0-8077-3897-2 (hbk.) ISBN 0-8077-3896-4 (pbk.) DDC 428.4/3/0712
*1. Reading comprehension - United States. 2. Reading (Middle school) - United States. I. Taylor, Barbara (Barbara M.) II. Graves, Michael F. III. Broek, Paul van den. IV. Series: Language and literacy series (New York, N.Y.)*
*TC LB1050.45 .R443 2000*

**Reading for understanding :** a guide to improving reading in middle and high school classrooms / Ruth Schoenbach ... [et al.]. 1st ed. San Francisco, Calif. : Jossey-Bass Publishers, c1999. xxv, 193 p. : ill. ; 28 cm. (The Jossey-Bass education series) Includes bibliographical references. ISBN 0-7879-5045-9 (pbk. : alk. paper) DDC 428.4/071/2
*1. Reading (Secondary) - United States. 2. Reading (Middle school) - United States. I. Schoenbach, Ruth. II. Series.*
*TC LB1632 .R357 1999*

**READING GROUPS.** *See* **GROUP READING.**

**READING HABITS.** *See* **BOOKS AND READING.**

**READING (HIGHER EDUCATION).**
College reading. Carrollton, GA : The College Reading Association, 1999.
*TC LB2395 .C64 1999*

The subject is reading. Portsmouth, NH : Heinemann c2000.
*TC LB2395.3 .S82 2000*

**READING (HIGHER EDUCATION) - STUDY AND TEACHING.** *See* **READING (HIGHER EDUCATION).**

**READING (HIGHER EDUCATION) - UNITED STATES - HANDBOOKS, MANUALS, ETC.**
Handbook of college reading and study strategy research. Mahwah, N.J. : Lawrence Erlbaum Associates, c2000.
*TC LB2395.3 .H36 2000*

**Reading in series :** a selection guide to books for children / editor, Catherine Barr, contributing editor, Rebecca L. Thomas ; foreword by Barbara Barstow. New Providence, N.J. : R.R. Bowker, c1999. xvi, 596 p. : ill. ; 27 cm. Includes indexes. ISBN 0-8352-4011-8 DDC 016.813008/09282
*1. Children's stories, American - Bibliography. 2. Children's literature in series - Bibliography. 3. Children's libraries - Book selection. I. Barr, Catherine, 1951-*
*TC Z1037 .R36 1999*

**READING INTERESTS.** *See also* **BOOKS AND READING.**
Herald, Diana Tixier. Genreflecting. 5th ed. Englewood, CO : Libraries Unlimited, 2000.
*TC PS374.P63 H47 2000*

**READING INTERESTS OF CHILDREN.** *See* **CHILDREN - BOOKS AND READING.**

**READING (KINDERGARTEN).**
Arnold, Virginia A. Macmillan predictable big books:. New York : Macmillan Publishing Co., 1990.
*TC LB1181.2 .A76 1990*

**READING (KINDERGARTEN) - STUDY AND TEACHING.** *See* **READING (KINDERGARTEN).**

**READING (KINDERGARTEN) - UNITED STATES.**
Morrow, Lesley Mandel. Literacy instruction in half-and whole-day kindergarten. Newark, Del. : International Reading Association ; Chicago, Ill. : National Reading Conference, c1998.
*TC LB1181.2 .M67 1998*

**READING - LANGUAGE EXPERIENCE APPROACH.**
The changing face of whole language. Newark, Del. : International Reading Association ; Victoria, Australia : Australian Literacy Educators' Association, c1997.
*TC LB1050.35 .C43 1997*

Wilde, Sandra. Miscue analysis made easy. Portsmouth, NH : Heinemann, c2000.
*TC LB1050.33 .W54 2000*

**READING - LANGUAGE EXPERIENCE APPROACH - RESEARCH.**
Coles, Gerald. Misreading reading. Portsmouth, NH : Heinemann, c2000.
*TC LB1050.6 .C65 2000*

**READING (MIDDLE SCHOOL).**
Golden, Joanne Marie, 1949- Storymaking in elementary and middle school classrooms. Mahwah, N.J. : L. Erlbaum Associates, 2000.
*TC LB1042 .G54 2000*

**READING (MIDDLE SCHOOL) - STUDY AND TEACHING.** *See* **READING (MIDDLE SCHOOL).**

**READING (MIDDLE SCHOOL) - UNITED STATES.**
Reading for meaning. New York ; London : Teachers College Press, c2000.
*TC LB1050.45 .R443 2000*

Reading for understanding. 1st ed. San Francisco, Calif. : Jossey-Bass Publishers, c1999.
*TC LB1632 .R357 1999*

**READING - MISCELLANEA.**
Fry, Edward Bernard, 1925- The reading teacher's book of lists. 3rd ed. Englewood Cliffs, NJ : Prentice Hall, c1993.
*TC LB1050.2 .F79 1993*

Fry, Edward Bernard, 1925- The reading teacher's book of lists. 4th ed. Paramus, N.J. : Prentice Hall, c2000.
*TC LB1050.2 .F79 2000*

**Reading National geographic.**
Lutz, Catherine. Chicago : University of Chicago Press, 1993.
*TC G1.N275 L88 1993*

**READING, ORAL.** *See* **ORAL READING.**

**READING OUT LOUD.** *See* **ORAL READING.**

**READING - PARENT PARTICIPATION.**
Fisher, Bobbi. Perspectives on shared reading. Portsmouth, NH : Heinemann, c2000.
*TC LB1573 .F528 2000*

Spitz, Ellen Handler, 1939- Inside picture books. New Haven : Yale University Press, c1999.
*TC BF456.R2 S685 1999*

Taylor, Denny, 1947- Family literacy. Portsmouth, NH : Heinemann, c1998.
*TC LC149 .T37 1998*

**READING - PARENT PARTICIPATION - UNITED STATES.**
Nelsen, Marjorie R. Peak with books. 3rd ed. Thousand Oaks, Calif. : Corwin Press, c1999.
*TC Z1037.A1 N347 1999*

Thomas, Adele, 1942- Families at school. Newark, Del. : International Reading Association, c1999.
*TC LC151 .T563 1999*

**READING - PARENT PARTICIPATION - UNITED STATES - CASE STUDIES.**
Glass, Laurie. Read! read! read!. Thousand Oaks, Calif. : Corwin Press, c2000.
*TC LB1050.2 .G54 2000*

Paratore, Jeanne R. What should we expect of family literacy? Newark, Del. : International Reading Association : Chicago , Ill. : National Reading Conference, c1999.
*TC LC151 .P37 1999*

**READING - PERIODICALS.**
Journal of developmental reading. [Layfayette, Ind. : Dept. of English, Purdue University], c1957-1964.

The Journal of the reading specialist. Bethlehem, Pa. : The Association, c1962-

**READING - PHONETIC METHOD.**
Blachman, Benita A. Road to the code. Baltimore : Paul H. Brookes, c2000.
*TC LB1139.L3 B53 2000*

Cunningham, Patricia Marr. Phonics they use. 3rd ed. New York : Longman, c2000.
*TC LB1573.3 .C86 2000*

Dombey, Henrietta. Whole to part phonics. London : Centre for Language in Primary Education : Language Matters, c1998.
*TC LB1573.3 .D66 1998*

Gunning, Thomas G. Phonological awareness and primary phonics. Boston : Allyn and Bacon, c2000.

*TC P221 .G85 2000*

Pinnell, Gay Su. Word matters. Portsmouth, NH : Heinemann, c1998.
*TC LB1573.3 .P55 1998*

Pocket chart kit [kit]. Chicago, Ill. : Open Court Publishing Company, c1995.
*TC LB1573.3 .P6 1995*

Words their way. 2nd ed. Upper Saddle River, N.J. : Merrill, c2000.
*TC LB1050.44 .B43 2000*

**READING - PHONETIC METHOD - RESEARCH.**
Coles, Gerald. Misreading reading. Portsmouth, NH : Heinemann, c2000.
*TC LB1050.6 .C65 2000*

**READING - PHONETIC METHOD - STUDY AND TEACHING (HIGHER).**
Fox, Barbara J. Word identification strategies. 2nd ed. Upper Saddle River, N.J. : Merrill, c2000.
*TC LB1050.34 .F69 2000*

**READING - PHONETIC METHOD - UNITED STATES.**
Gunning, Thomas G. Building words. Boston ; London : Allyn and Bacon, c2001.
*TC LB1573.3 .G83 2001*

**READING (PRIMARY).**
Arnold, Virginia A. Macmillan predictable big books:. New York : Macmillan Publishing Co., 1990.
*TC LB1181.2 .A76 1990*

Better together. New York : Macmillan/McGraw-Hill, c1997.
*TC LB1576 .S66 1997 Gr.2 l.6 u.3*

Building dreams. Teacher's ed. New York, N.Y. : American Book Company, c1980.
*TC PE1119 .B84 1980 Teacher's Ed.*

Building dreams. Teacher's ed. Lexington, Mass. : D.C. Heath and Company, c1986.
*TC PE1119 .B84 1986 Teacher's Ed.*

Building dreams. Teacher's ed. New York, N.Y. : American Book Company, c1980.
*TC PE1119 .B84 1980 Teacher's Ed. Workbook*

Building dreams. Teacher's Ed. Lexington, Mass. : D.C. Heath and Company, c1983.
*TC PE1119 .B84 1983 Teacher's Ed. Workbook*

Catching glimpses. Teacher's ed. Lexington, Mass. : D.C. Heath & co., c1986.
*TC PE1119 .C37 1986 Teacher's Ed.*

Catching glimpses. Teacher's ed. Lexington, Mass. : D.C. Heath & co., c1983.
*TC PE1119 .C37 1983 Teacher's Ed. Workbook*

Clearing paths. Teacher's ed. New York, NY : American Book Company, c1980
*TC PE1119 .C63 1980 Teacher's Ed.*

Community spirit. New York : Macmillan/McGraw-Hill, c1997.
*TC LB1576 .S66 1997 Gr.3 l.9 u.1*

Daniel, Claire, 1936- The great big book of fun phonics activities. New York : Scholastic professional books, c1999.
*TC LB1525.3 .D36 1999*

Eureka. New York : Macmillan/McGraw-Hill, c1997.
*TC LB1576 .S66 1997 Gr.2 l.6 u.2*

Family album. New York : Macmillan/McGraw-Hill, c1997.
*TC LB1576 .S66 1997 Gr.3 l.8 u.3*

Family fun:. New York : Macmillan/McGraw-Hill, c1997.
*TC LB1576 .S66 1997 Gr.2 l.6 u.1*

Finding places. Teacher's ed. New York, N.Y. : American Book Company, c1980.
*TC PE1119 .F56 1980 Teacher's Ed.*

Finding places. Teacher's ed. Lexington, Mass. : D.C. Heath and Company, c1983.
*TC PE1119 .F56 1983 Teacher's Ed.*

Finding places. Teacher's ed. Lexington, Mass. : D.C. Heath and Company, c1986.
*TC PE1119 .F56 1986 Teacher's Ed.*

Finding places. Teacher's ed. New York, N.Y. : American Book Company, c1980.
*TC PE1119 .F56 1980 Teacher's Ed. Workbook*

Finding places. Teacher's ed. Lexington, Mass. : D.C. Heath and Company, c1983.

*TC PE1119 .F56 1983 Teacher's Ed. Workbook*

Forces of nature. New York : Macmillan/McGraw-Hill, c1997.
*TC LB1576 .S66 1997 Gr.3 L9 u.2*

Good thinking. New York : Macmillan/McGraw-Hill, c1997.
*TC LB1576 .S66 1997 Gr.3 L8 u.1*

Hand in hand. New York : Macmillan/McGraw-Hill, c1997.
*TC LB1576 .S66 1997 Gr.2 L7 u.2*

Hart-Hewins, Linda. Better books! Better readers!. York, Me. : Stenhouse Publishers ; Markham, Ont. : Pembroke Publishers, c1999.
*TC LB1525 .H26 1999*

Let's pretend. New York : Macmillan/McGraw-Hill, c1997.
*TC LB1576 .S66 1997 Gr.1 L5 u.1*

Looking out. Climbing up. Going far. Teacher's ed. New York, N.Y. : American Book Cpmpany, c1980.
*TC PE1119 .L66 1980 Teacher's Ed.*

Looking out. Climbing up. Going far. Teacher's ed. Lexington, Mass. : D.C. Heath and Cpmpany, c1986.
*TC PE1119 .L66 1986 Teacher's Ed.*

Looking out. Climbing up. Going far. Teacher's ed. New York, N.Y. : American Book Company, c1980.
*TC PE1119 .L66 1980 Teacher's Ed. Workbook*

Looking out. Climbing up. Going far. Teacher's ed. Lexington, Mass. : D.C. Heath and Cpmpany, c1983.
*TC PE1119 .L66 1983 Teacher's Ed. Workbook*

Marching along. Teacher's ed. New York, N.Y. : American Book Company, c1980.
*TC PE1119 .M37 1980 Teacher's Ed.*

Marching along. Teacher's ed. Lexington, Mass. : D.C. Heath and Company, c1983.
*TC PE1119 .M37 1983 Teacher's Ed.*

Marching along. Teacher's ed. Lexington, Mass. : D.C. Heath and Company, c1986.
*TC PE1119 .M37 1986 Teacher's Ed.*

Marching along. Teacher's ed. New York, N.Y. : D.C. Heath and Company, c1983.
*TC PE1119 .M37 1980 Teacher's Ed. Workbook*

Marching along. Teacher's ed. Lexington, Mass. : D.C. Heath and Company, c1983.
*TC PE1119 .M37 1983 Teacher's Ed. Workbook*

Moving on. Lexington, Mass. : D.C. Heath, c1983.
*TC PE1119 .M68 1986 Teacher's Ed.*

Moving on. Lexington, Mass. : D.C. Heath, c1983.
*TC PE1119 .M68 1983 Teacher's Ed. Workbook*

Out and about. New York : Macmillan/McGraw-Hill, c1997.
*TC LB1576 .S66 1997 Gr.1 L.2*

Penpals. New York : Macmillan/McGraw-Hill, c1997.
*TC LB1576 .S66 1997 Gr.2 L7 u.1*

Pocket chart kit [kit]. Chicago, Ill. : Open Court Publishing Company, c1995.
*TC LB1573.3 .P6 1995*

Reaching out. Teacher's ed. New York, N.Y. : American Book Company, c1980.
*TC PE1119 .R42 1980 Teacher's Ed.*

Reaching out. Teacher's ed. Lexington, Mass. : D.C. Heath and Company, c1983.
*TC PE1119 .R42 1983 Teacher's Ed.*

Reaching out. Teacher's ed. Lexington, Mass. : D.C. Heath and Company, c1986.
*TC PE1119 .R42 1986 Teacher's Ed.*

Read all about it. New York : Macmillan/McGraw-Hill, c1997.
*TC LB1576 .S66 1997 Gr.1 l.1*

See for yourself. New York : Macmillan/McGraw-Hill, c1997.
*TC LB1576 .S66 1997 Gr.3 L8 u.2*

Something new. New York : Macmillan/McGraw-Hill, c1997.
*TC LB1576 .S66 1997 Gr.1 L.3*

Starting off. Teacher's ed. Lexington, Mass. : D.C. Heath and company, c1986.
*TC PE1119 .S82 1986 Teacher's Ed.*

Surprises along the way:. New York : Macmillan/McGraw-Hill, c1997.
*TC LB1576 .S66 1997 Gr.1 L4 u.2*

Take a closer look. New York : Macmillan/McGraw-Hill, c1997.

*TC LB1576 .S66 1997 Gr.1 L.4 u.1*

Teamwork. New York : Macmillan/McGraw-Hill, c1997.
*TC LB1576 .S66 1997 Gr.3 l.9 u.3*

True-blue friends. New York : Macmillan/McGraw-Hill, c1997.
*TC LB1576 .S66 1997 Gr.1 L.5 u.2*

Turning corners. Teacher's ed. Lexington, Mass. : D.C. Heath and Company, c1986.
*TC PE1119 .T87 1986 Teacher's Ed.*

Turning corners. Teacher's ed. New York, N.Y. : American Book Company, c1980.
*TC PE1119 .T87 1980 Teacher's Ed. Workbook*

Turning corners. Teacher's ed. Lexington, Mass. : D.C. Heath and Company, c1983.
*TC PE1119 .T87 1983 Teacher's Ed. Workbook*

Warming up. Teacher's ed. New York, N.Y. : American Book Company, c1980.
*TC PE1119 .W37 1980 Teacher's Ed.*

Warming up. Teacher's ed. Lexington, Mass. : D.C. Heath and Company, c1983.
*TC PE1119 .W37 1983 Teacher's Ed.*

Warming up. Teacher's ed. Lexington, Mass. : D.C. Heath and Company, c1986.
*TC PE1119 .W37 1986 Teacher's Ed.*

**READING (PRIMARY) - GREAT BRITAIN.**
Teaching through texts. London ; New York : Routledge, 1999.
*TC LB1573 .T39 1999*

**READING (PRIMARY) - ILLINOIS - CHICAGO - CASE STUDIES.**
Barone, Diane M. Resilient children. Newark, Del. : International Reading Association ; Chicago : National Reading Conference, c1999.
*TC LC4806.4 .B37 1999*

**READING (PRIMARY) - PHONETIC METHOD.**
Teacher toolbox [kit]. Chicago, Ill. : Open Court Pub. Co., c1995.
*TC LB1573.3 .T4 1995*

**READING (PRIMARY) - STUDY AND TEACHING. See READING (PRIMARY).**

**READING (PRIMARY) - UNITED STATES.**
Stull, Elizabeth Crosby. Let's read!. West Nyack, NY : Center for Applied Research in Education, c2000.
*TC LB1573 .S896 2000*

Taberski, Sharon. On solid ground. Portsmouth, NH : Heinemann, c 2000.
*TC LB1525 .T32 2000*

**READING (PRIMARY) - UNITED STATES - LANGUAGE EXPERIENCE APPROACH.**
Taberski, Sharon. On solid ground. Portsmouth, NH : Heinemann, c 2000.
*TC LB1525 .T32 2000*

**READING PROGRAMS (LITERACY). See LITERACY PROGRAMS.**

**READING PROMOTION. See BOOKS AND READING.**

**READING, PSYCHOLOGY OF.**
Case studies in the neuropsychology of reading. Hove, East Sussex : Psychology Press, c2000.
*TC RC394.W6 .C37 2000*

Harris, Albert Josiah. How to increase reading ability, a guide to individualized and remedial methods. 2d ed., rev. and enl. London ; New York[etc.] : Longmans, Green and Co., 1947.
*TC 372.4H2421*

Learning to read. Dordrecht ; Boston : Kluwer Academic Publishers, 1999.
*TC LB1050.2 .L42 1999*

Reading development and the teaching of reading. Oxford, UK ; Malden, Mass. : Blackwell Publishers, 1999.
*TC LB1050.2 .R424 1999*

Stanovich, Keith E., 1950- Progress in understanding reading. New York : Guilford Press, c2000.
*TC LB1050 .S723 2000*

**READING PUBLIC. See BOOKS AND READING; LIBRARIES AND READERS.**

**Reading rainbow book**
Knowlton, Jack. Maps & globes. New York : HarperCollins, c1985.
*TC GA105.6 .K58 1985*

**READING - REMEDIAL TEACHING.**
Converging methods for understanding reading and dyslexia. Cambridge, Mass. : London : MIT Press, c1999.
*TC LB1050.5 .C662 1999*

Gillet, Jean Wallace. Understanding reading problems. 5th ed. New York ; Harlow, England : Longman, c2000.
*TC LB1050.46 .G55 2000*

Goldsworthy, Candace L. Sourcebook of phonological awareness activities. San Diego : Singular Pub. Group, c1998.
*TC LB1050.5 .G66 1998*

Learning to read. Dordrecht ; Boston : Kluwer Academic Publishers, 1999.
*TC LB1050.2 .L42 1999*

O'Donnell, Michael P. Becoming a reader. 2nd ed. Boston : Allyn and Bacon, c1999.
*TC LB1050.53 .O35 1999*

Rasinski, Timothy V. Effective reading strategies. 2nd ed. Upper Saddle River, N.J. : Merrill, c2000.
*TC LB1050.5 .R33 2000*

Reutzel, D. Ray (Douglas Ray), 1953- Balanced reading strategies and practices. Upper Saddle river, N.J. : Merrill, c1999.
*TC LB1050 .R477 1999*

Shanker, James L. Locating and correcting reading difficulties. 7th ed. Upper Saddle River, N.J. : Merrill, c1998.
*TC LB1050.5 .E38 1998*

Teaching struggling readers. Newark, Del. : International Reading Association, c1998.
*TC LB1050.5 .T437 1998*

Walker, Barbara J., 1946- Diagnostic teaching of reading. 4th ed. Upper Saddle River, NJ : Merrill, c2000.
*TC LB1050.5 .W35 2000*

What reading research tells us about children with diverse learning needs. Mahwah, N.J. : Erlbaum, 1998.
*TC LB1050.5 .W47 1998*

**READING RESEARCH. See also READING - RESEARCH.**
Handbook of reading research. New York : Longman, c1984-<2000 >
*TC LB1050 .H278 2000*

**READING - RESEARCH.**
Coles, Gerald. Misreading reading. Portsmouth, NH : Heinemann, c2000.
*TC LB1050.6 .C65 2000*

Elley, Warwick B. How in the world do students read? Hamburg : The International Association for the Evaluation of Educational Achievement, [1992]
*TC LB1050.6 .E55 1992*

What reading research tells us about children with diverse learning needs. Mahwah, N.J. : Erlbaum, 1998.
*TC LB1050.5 .W47 1998*

**READING - RESEARCH - METHODOLOGY.**
Handbook of reading research. New York : Longman, c1984-<2000 >
*TC LB1050 .H278 2000*

**READING ROOMS - PICTORIAL WORKS.**
[Teachers College Library. [picture] 1940.
*TC TCX/H5*

**READING (SECONDARY EDUCATION). See READING (SECONDARY).**

**READING (SECONDARY) - GREAT BRITAIN.**
Dean, Geoff. Teaching reading in secondary schools. London : David Fulton, 2000.
*TC LB1632 .D43 2000*

Literacy in the secondary school. London : David Fulton, 2000.
*TC LB1632 .L587 2000*

**READING (SECONDARY) - STUDY AND TEACHING. See READING (SECONDARY).**

**READING (SECONDARY) - UNITED STATES.**
Brozo, William G. Readers, teachers, learners. 3rd ed. Upper Saddle River, N.J. : Merrill, c1999.
*TC LB1632 .B7 1999*

Reading for understanding. 1st ed. San Francisco, Calif. : Jossey-Bass Publishers, c1999.
*TC LB1632 .R357 1999*

**Reading strategies and practices.**
Tierney, Robert J. 5th ed. Boston : Allyn and Bacon, c2000.
*TC LB1050 .T57 2000*

**READING - STUDY AND TEACHING.** *See* **READING.**

**READING - STUDY AND TEACHING (ADULT EDUCATION).** *See* **READING (ADULT EDUCATION).**

**READING - STUDY AND TEACHING (EARLY CHILDHOOD).** *See* **READING (EARLY CHILDHOOD).**

**READING - STUDY AND TEACHING (ELEMENTARY).** *See* **READING (ELEMENTARY).**

**READING - STUDY AND TEACHING (HIGHER EDUCATION).** *See* **READING (HIGHER EDUCATION).**

**READING - STUDY AND TEACHING (KINDERGARTEN).** *See* **READING (KINDERGARTEN).**

**READING - STUDY AND TEACHING (MIDDLE SCHOOL).** *See* **READING (MIDDLE SCHOOL).**

**READING - STUDY AND TEACHING (PRIMARY).** *See* **READING (PRIMARY).**

**READING - STUDY AND TEACHING (SECONDARY).** *See* **READING (SECONDARY).**

**READING, SUBJECT-MATTER.** *See* **CONTENT AREA READING.**

**Reading teacher.**
Reading assessment. Newark, Del. : International Reading Association, c1999.
*TC LB1573 .R2793 1999*

Teaching struggling readers. Newark, Del. : International Reading Association, c1998.
*TC LB1050.5 .T437 1998*

**READING TEACHERS.**
Dugan, JoAnn R. Advancing the world of literacy. Carrollton, Ga. : College Reading Association, 1999.
*TC LB2395 .C62 1999*

**The reading teacher's book of lists.**
Fry, Edward Bernard, 1925- 3rd ed. Englewood Cliffs, NJ : Prentice Hall, c1993.
*TC LB1050.2 .F79 1993*

Fry, Edward Bernard, 1925- 4th ed. Paramus, N.J. : Prentice Hall, c2000.
*TC LB1050.2 .F79 2000*

**READING, TEACHERS OF.** *See* **READING TEACHERS.**

**READING TEACHERS - TRAINING OF.**
Running records. York, Me. : Stenhouse Publishers , 2000.
*TC LB1525 R75 2000*

**Reading team.**
Tips for the reading team. Newark, Del. : International Reading Association, c1998.
*TC LB1573 .T57 1998*

**READING - UNITED STATES.**
Hargis, Charles H. Teaching and testing in reading. Springfield, Ill. : C.C. Thomas, c1999.
*TC LB1050 .H29 1999*

Literacy instruction for culturally and linguistically diverse students. Newark, Del. : International Reading Association, c1998.
*TC LC3731 .L566 1998*

National Reading Panel (U.S.) Report of the National Reading Panel : teaching children to read. [Washington, D.C.?] : National Institute of Child Health and Human Development, National Institutes of Health, [2000]
*TC LB1050 .N335 2000*

**READING - UNITED STATES - LANGUAGE EXPERIENCE APPROACH.**
In defense of good teaching. York, Me. : Stenhouse Publishers, c1998.
*TC LB1050.35 .I5 1998*

**READING - UNITED STATES - LANGUAGE EXPERIENCE APPROACH - RELIGIOUS ASPECTS.**
In defense of good teaching. York, Me. : Stenhouse Publishers, c1998.
*TC LB1050.35 .I5 1998*

**READING - WHOLE LANGUAGE APPROACH.** *See* **READING - LANGUAGE EXPERIENCE APPROACH.**

**Reading with Alice.**
Campbell, Robin, 1937- Literacy from home to school :. Stoke on Trent, Staffordshire, Eng. : Trentham Books, 1999.
*TC LB1140.2 .C35 1999*

**Reading world.**
The Journal of the reading specialist. Bethlehem, Pa. : The Association, c1962-

**Readings and cases in educational psychology.**
Readings in educational psychology. 2nd ed. Boston : Allyn and Bacon, c1998.
*TC LB1051 .R386 1998*

**Readings for anthropology and education 1-.**
Harrington, Charles C. New York, MSS Educational Publishing Co. [c1971-
*TC LB45 .H3*

**Readings in anthropology of human movement**
(no. 2) Williams, Drid, 1928- Anthropology and human movement. Lanham, Md. ; London : Scarecrow Press, 2000.
*TC GV1595 .W53 2000*

**Readings in attitude theory and measurement** / edited by Martin Fishbein. New York: Wiley, 1967. vii, 499 p. : ill ; 26 cm. Photocopy. Ann Arbor, Mich. : University Microfilms International, 1992. 26 cm. Includes bibliographical references and index. ISBN 0-471-26055-X
*1. Attitude (Psychology) I. Fishbein, Martin. II. Title. III. Title: Attitude theory and measurement.*
*TC BF323.C5 F5*

**Readings in discipline-based art education :** a literature of educational reform / edited by Ralph A. Smith. Reston, Va. : National Art Education Assoc., c2000. xix, 429 p. : ill. ; 23 cm. Includes bibliographical references. ISBN 1-89016-012-1
*1. Getty Center for Education in the Arts. 2. Art - Study and teaching - Philosophy. 3. Educational change. 4. Museums - Educational aspects. I. Smith, Ralph Alexander. II. National Art Education Association.*
*TC N87 .R43 2000*

**Readings in educational psychology** / [edited by] Anita E. Woolfolk. 2nd ed. Boston : Allyn and Bacon, c1998. v, 266 p. : ill. ; 28 cm. Rev. ed. of: Readings and cases in educational psychology. c1993. Includes bibliographical references. ISBN 0-205-27889-2 (pbk.) DDC 370.15
*1. Educational psychology. 2. Educational psychology - Case studies. I. Woolfolk, Anita. II. Title: Readings and cases in educational psychology.*
*TC LB1051 .R386 1998*

**Readings in psychological and educational testing.**
Aiken, Lewis R., 1931- comp. Boston, Allyn and Bacon [1973]
*TC LB3051 .A5625*

**Readings on equal education**
(v. 16) Education of Hispanics in the United States. New York : AMS Press, c1999.
*TC LC4091 .R417 1999*

(v. 16) Education of Hispanics in the United States. New York : AMS Press, c1999.
*TC LC4091 .R417 1999*

**Ready-to-use activities & materials for improving content reading skills.**
Miller, Wilma H. West Nyack, NY : Center For Applied Research in Education, c1999.
*TC LB1576 .M52 1999*

**Ready-to-use activities and materials for improving content reading skills.**
Miller, Wilma H. Ready-to-use activities & materials for improving content reading skills. West Nyack, NY : Center For Applied Research in Education, c1999.
*TC LB1576 .M52 1999*

**Ready-to-use fundamental motor skills & movement activities for young children.**
Landy, Joanne M. West Nyack, NY : Center for Applied Research in Education, c1999.
*TC GV452 .L355 1999*

**Ready-to-use world geography activities for grades 5-12.**
Silver, James F. West Nyack, N.Y. : Center for Applied Research in Education, 1992.
*TC G73 .S45 1992*

**Reaffirming higher education.**
Neusner, Jacob, 1932- New Brunswick, U.S.A. : Transaction Publishers, c2000.

*TC LA227.4 .N47 2000*

**Reagan, Timothy G.** Becoming a reflective educator : how to build a culture of inquiry in the schools / Timothy G. Reagan, Charles W. Case, John W. Brubacher. 2nd ed. Thousand Oaks Calif. : Sage Publications, c2000. xiv, 170 p. ; 24 cm. Brubacher's name appears first on the earlier edition. Includes bibliographical references (p. 151-160) and index. ISBN 0-7619-7552-7 (alk. paper) ISBN 0-7619-7553-5 (pbk. : alk. paper) DDC 371.102
*1. Teaching. 2. Teaching - Case studies. 3. Teachers - Case studies. 4. School management and organization - Case studies. 5. Inquiry (Theory of knowledge) I. Case, Charles W. II. Brubacher, John W. III. Title.*
*TC LB1025.3 .R424 2000*

**Real analysis.**
Stahl, Saul. New York : J. Wiley, c1999.
*TC QA300 .S882 1999*

**Real language series**
Rethinking language and gender research. London ; New York : Longman, 1996.
*TC P120.S48 R48 1996*

**Real-life case studies for school administrators.**
Hayes, William, 1938- Lanham, Md. : Scarecrow Press, c2000.
*TC LB2806 .H39 2000*

**Real-life case studies for teachers.**
Hayes, William, 1938- Lanham, Md. : Scarecrow Press, 2000.
*TC LB1775.2 .H39 2000*

**REAL PROPERTY.** *See* **INHERITANCE AND SUCCESSION.**

**The real work of leaders.**
Laurie, Donald L. Cambridge, Mass. : Perseus Pub., 2000.
*TC HD57.7 .L387 2000*

**Real-world readings in art education :** things your professor never told you / edited by Dennis E. Fehr ... [et al.]. New York : Falmer Press, c2000. xvii, 176 p. : ill. ; 23 cm. (Garland reference library of social science ; v. 1444. Thinking and teaching ; v. 1) Includes bibliographical references and index. ISBN 0-8153-3477-X (alk. paper) DDC 707/.1
*1. Art - Study and teaching (Elementary) - United States. 2. Art - Study and teaching (Secondary) - United States. I. Fehr, Dennis Earl, 1952- II. Series: Garland reference library of social science ; v. 1444. III. Series: Garland reference library of social science. Thinking and teaching ; v. 1.*
*TC N353 .R43 2000*

**REALISM.** *See also* **DUALISM; RATIONALISM.**
Kirk, Robert, 1933- Relativism and reality. London ; New York : Routledge, 1999.
*TC B835 .K57 1999*

**REALISM IN ART.**
On pictures and paintings [videorecording]. Peasmarsh, East Sussex, Eng. ; Ho-Ho-kus, NJ : Roland Collection, 1992.
*TC ND195.O45 1992*

**REALITY.** *See* **KNOWLEDGE, THEORY OF.**

**Realizing the university in an age of supercomplexity.**
Barnett, Ronald, 1947- Philadelphia, PA : Society for Research into Higher Education & Open University Press, 1999.
*TC LB2322.2 .B37 1999*

**REAM, VINNIE, 1847-1914 - FICTION.**
Sappey, Maureen Stack, 1952- Letters from Vinnie. Asheville, NC : Front Street, 1999.
*TC PZ7.S2388 Le 1999*

**REAM, VINNIE, 1847-1914 - JUVENILE FICTION.**
Sappey, Maureen Stack, 1952- Letters from Vinnie. Asheville, NC : Front Street, 1999.
*TC PZ7.S2388 Le 1999*

**Reardon, Mark.**
DePorter, Bobbi. Quantum teaching. Boston, Mass. : Allyn and Bacon, c1999.
*TC LB1027 .D418 1999*

**Reardon, Robert C.**
Career development and planning. Belmont, CA ; London : Brooks/Cole/Thomson Learning, c2000.
*TC HF5381 .C265275 2000*

**REARING OF CHILDREN.** *See* **CHILD REARING.**

**REASON.** *See* **REASONING.**

**Reason to believe.**
Roskelly, Hephzibah. Albany : State University of New York Press, c1998.
*TC PE1404 .R67 1998*

**REASONING.** *See also* **LOGIC.**
Felton, Mark Kenji. Metacognitive reflection and strategy development in argumentive discourse. 1999.
*TC 085 F34*

Flaton, Robin Anne. Effect of deliberation on juror reasoning. 1999.
*TC 085 F612*

Johnson, Ralph H. Manifest rationality. Mahwah, N.J. : London : Lawrence Erlbaum Associates, 2000.
*TC BC177 .J54 2000*

Locke, John, 1632-1704. [Some thoughts concerning education] Some thoughts concerning education ; Indianapolis : Hackett Pub. Co., c1996.
*TC LB475.L6 L63 1996*

**REASONING - CONGRESSES.**
Cognition, agency, and rationality. Boston : Kluwer Academic, 1999.
*TC BC177 .C45 1999*

**REASONING IN CHILDREN.**
Children's reasoning and the mind. Hove : Psychology, c2000.
*TC BF723.R4 C555 2000*

The child's world. Camberwell, Vic. : ACER Press, 2000.
*TC BF723.C5 C467 2000*

Rights and wrongs. San Francisco, [CA] : Jossey-Bass, c2000.
*TC BF723.M54 L38 2000*

**REASONING - PROBLEMS, EXERCISES, ETC.**
Whimbey, Arthur. Problem solving and comprehension. 6th ed. Mahwah, N.J. : Lawrence Erlbaum Associates, 1999.
*TC BF449 .W45 1999*

Yang, Fang-Ying. An analysis of 12th grade students' reasoning styles and competencies when presented with an environmental problem in a social and scientific context. 1999.
*TC 06 no. 11076*

**REASONING (PSYCHOLOGY).**
Baynes, Joyce Frisby. The development of a van Hiele-based summer geometry program and its impact on student van Hiele level and achievement in high school geometry. 1998.
*TC 06 no. 10915*

Deductive reasoning and strategies. Mahwah, N.J. : L. Erlbaum Associates, 2000.
*TC BF442 .D43 2000*

Elster, Jon, 1940- Ulysses unbound. Cambridge, U.K. ; New York : Cambridge University Press, 2000.
*TC BF441 .E45 2000*

**REASONING (PSYCHOLOGY) - CASE STUDIES.**
Andersen, Christopher Lawrence. A microgenetic study of science reasoning in social context. 1998.
*TC 085 An2305*

**REASONING - STUDY AND TEACHING (SECONDARY) - TAIWAN.**
Yang, Fang-Ying. An analysis of 12th grade students' reasoning styles and competencies when presented with an environmental problem in a social and scientific context. 1999.
*TC 06 no. 11076*

**Rebecca Horn.**
Horn, Rebecca, 1944- [Stuttgart] : Edition Cantz, 1993.
*TC NB573.H78 H785 1993*

**Rebecca of Sunnybrook Farm.**
Wiggin, Kate Douglas Smith, 1856-1923. Boston, New York [etc.] : Houghton, Mifflin Company, [c1903] (Cambridge, Mass. : Riverside Press)
*TC PZ7.W638 Re 1903*

**REBELLIONS.** *See* **INSURGENCY.**

**REBELS (SOCIAL PSYCHOLOGY).** *See* **ALIENATION (SOCIAL PSYCHOLOGY).**

**Rebore, Ronald W.** Human resources administration in education : a management approach / Ronald W. Rebore. 6th ed. Boston ; London : Allyn and Bacon, c2001. viii, 376 p. : ill. ; 25 cm. Includes bibliographical references and indexes. Rev. ed. of: Personnel administration in education. 5th ed. 1998. ISBN 0-205-32212-3 (alk. paper) DDC 371.2/01/0973
*1. School personnel management - United States. I. Rebore, Ronald W. Personnel administration in education. II. Title.*
*TC LB2831.58 .R43 2001*

**Personnel administration in education.**
Rebore, Ronald W. Human resources administration in education. 6th ed. Boston ; London : Allyn and Bacon, c2001.
*TC LB2831.58 .R43 2001*

**Rebuilding urban neighborhoods :** achievements, opportunities, and limits / W. Dennis Keating, Norman Krumholz, editors. Thousand Oaks, Calif. : Sage Publications, c1999. xv, 236 p. : ill., maps ; 24 cm. (Cities & planning series) Includes bibliographical references and index. ISBN 0-7619-0691-6 (cloth : alk. paper) ISBN 0-7619-0692-4 (pbk. : alk. paper) DDC 307.3/416/0973
*1. Urban renewal - United States. I. Keating, W. Dennis (William Dennis) II. Krumholz, Norman. III. Series.*
*TC HT175 .R425 1999*

**RECALL (PSYCHOLOGY).** *See* **RECOLLECTION (PSYCHOLOGY).**

**Recasting the past.**
Barnhouse, Rebecca. Portsmouth, NH : Boynton/Cook Publishers, c2000.
*TC PN3443 .B37 2000*

**Recent advances in the measurement of acceptance and rejection in the peer system** / Antonius H.N. Cillessen, Willliam M. Bukowski, editors. San Francisco : Jossey-Bass Publishers, c2000. 98 p. : ill. ; 23 cm. (New directions for child and adolescent development, 1520-3247 ; no. 88) "Summer 2000." Includes bibliographical references and index. CONTENTS: Conceptualizing and measuring peer acceptance and rejection / Antonius H.N. Cillessen, William M. Bukowski -- Pages from a sociometric notebook : an analysis of nomination and rating scale measures of acceptance, rejection, and social preference / William M. Bukowski ... [et al.] -- Recent advances in measurement theory and the use of sociometric techniques / Robert Terry -- A ratings-based approach to two-dimensional sociometric status determination / Gerard H. Maassen ... [et al.] -- Stability of sociometric categories / Antonius H.N. Cillessen, William M. Bukowski, Gerbert J.T. Haselager. ISBN 0-7879-1255-7
*1. Interpersonal relations in children - Statistical methods. 2. Interpersonal relations in adolescence - Statistical methods. 3. Social desirability in children - Statistical methods. 4. Social desirability in adolescence - Statistical methods. 5. Sociometry. I. Cillessen, Antonius H. II. Bukowski, William M. III. Series.*
*TC BF723.I65 R4 2000*

**Recent books on international relations.**
Foreign affairs. New York : Council on Foreign Relations, 1922-

**Recent progress in mathematical psychology** / edited by Cornelia E. Dowling, Fred S. Roberts, Peter Theuns. Mahwah, N.J. : L. Erlbaum, 1998. xviii, 338 p. : ill. ; 24 cm. (Scientific psychology series) Chiefly papers originally presented at the July 1992 meeting of the European Mathematical Psychology Group in Brussels. Includes bibliographical references and indexes. ISBN 0-8058-1975-4 (hardcover : alk. paper) DDC 150/.1/51
*1. Psychology - Mathematical models - Congresses. 2. Psychometrics - Congresses. I. Dowling, Cornelia E. II. Roberts, Fred S. III. Theuns, Peter. IV. Series.*
*TC BF39 .R35 1998*

**RECESSES.**
Novak, Dori E. Help! It's an indoor recess day. Thousand Oaks, Calif. : Corwin Press, c2000.
*TC LB3033 .N68 2000*

**RECESSIONS.** *See* **DEPRESSIONS.**

**Reclaiming education.**
Tooley, James. London ; New York : Cassell, 2000.
*TC LC71 .T65 2000*

**RECOGNITION (PSYCHOLOGY).** *See* **RECOLLECTION (PSYCHOLOGY).**

**RECOLLECTION (PSYCHOLOGY).**
Stratification in cognition and consciousness. Amsterdam ; Philadelphia : J. Benjamins, c1999.
*TC BF444 .S73 1999*

**Recollections.**
Middleton, Bernard C., 1924- New Castle, Del. : Oak Knoll Press, 2000.
*TC Z269.2.M53 A3 2000*

**Recommended books in Spanish for children and young adults, 1996 through 1999.**
Schon, Isabel. Lanham, Md. : Scarecrow Press, 2000.
*TC Z1037.7 .S387 2000*

**Reconceptualizing literacy in the media age** / edited by Ann Watts Pailliotet, Peter B. Mosenthal. Stamford, Conn. : Jai Press, c2000. 451 p. : ill. ; 24 cm. (Advances in reading/language research ; vol. 7) Includes bibliographical references. ISBN 0-7623-0264-X
*1. Literacy. I. Pailliotet, Ann Watts. II. Mosenthal, Peter. III. Series.*
*TC LB1050 .A38 v.7*

**Reconceptualizing the literacies in adolescents' lives** / Donna E. Alvermann ... [et al.]. Mahwah, N.J. : L. Erlbaum Associates, 1998. xxiii, 383 p. : ill. ; 26 cm. Includes bibliographical references and indexes. ISBN 0-8058-2559-2 (alk. paper) ISBN 0-8058-2560-6 (pbk. : alk. paper) DDC 428/.0071/2
*1. Language arts (Secondary) - Social aspects - United States. 2. Literacy - Social aspects - United States. 3. Critical pedagogy - United States. I. Alvermann, Donna E.*
*TC LB1631 .R296 1998*

**Reconciling empirical knowledge and clinical experience :** the art and science of psychotherapy / edited by Stephen Soldz, Leigh McCullough. 1st ed. Washington, DC : American Psychological Association, c1999. vii, 286 p. ; 26 cm. Includes bibliographical references and index. ISBN 1-55798-603-7 DDC 616.89/14
*1. Psychotherapy. 2. Evidence-based medicine. 3. Psychotherapy. 4. Evidence-Based Medicine. 5. Research. I. Soldz, Stephen. II. McCullough, Leigh.*
*TC RC480 .R395 1999*

**Reconstructing America (Series)**
(no. 2.) Fuke, Richard Paul, 1940- Imperfect equality. New York : Fordham University Press, 1999.
*TC E185.93.M2 F85 1999*

**Reconstructing communicating.**
Penman, Robyn. Mahwah, N.J. ; London : Lawrence Erlbaum Associates, 2000.
*TC BF637.C45 P435 2000*

**Reconstructing the common good in education :** coping with intractable American dilemmas / edited by Larry Cuban and Dorothy Shipps. Stanford, Calif. : Stanford University Press, c2000. xvi, 283 p. ; 24 cm. In honor of David B. Tyack, upon his retirement from the Vida Jacks Professorship of Education at Stanford University in September 2000. Includes bibliographical references (p. [231]-274) and index. ISBN 0-8047-3862-9 (hbk. : alk. paper) ISBN 0-8047-3863-7 (pbk. : alk. paper) DDC 370/.973
*1. Education - United States. 2. Educational change - United States. 3. Education - Social aspects - United States. I. Tyack, David B. II. Cuban, Larry. III. Shipps, Dorothy.*
*TC LA212 .R42 2000*

**RECONSTRUCTION (1914-1939).** *See* **PEACE.**

**Reconstruction after the war.**
National Institute of Social Sciences. Journal of the National Institute of Social Sciences. [New York]

**RECONSTRUCTION - FICTION.**
Hansen, Joyce. The heart calls home. New York : Walker & Company, 1999.
*TC PZ7.H19825 He 1999*

**RECONSTRUCTION - JUVENILE FICTION.**
Hansen, Joyce. The heart calls home. New York : Walker & Company, 1999.
*TC PZ7.H19825 He 1999*

**RECONSTRUCTION - MARYLAND.**
Fuke, Richard Paul, 1940- Imperfect equality. New York : Fordham University Press, 1999.
*TC E185.93.M2 F85 1999*

**RECONSTRUCTION - UNITED STATES.** *See* **RECONSTRUCTION.**

**RECONSTRUCTIVE SURGERY.** *See* **SURGERY, PLASTIC.**

**RECORDS.** *See* **PUBLIC RECORDS.**

**Recorvits, Helen.** Goodbye, Walter Malinski / Helen Recorvits ; pictures by Lloyd Bloom. 1st ed. New York : Farrar, Straus and Giroux, c1999. 85 p. : ill. ; 20 cm. SUMMARY: In 1934, even though life is hard for Wanda Malinski and her family, she enjoys school, good times with her best friend, and a special relationship with her older brother. ISBN 0-374-32747-5 DDC [Fic]
*1. Brothers and sisters - Fiction. 2. Family life - Fiction. 3. Depressions - 1929 - Fiction. 4. Death - Fiction. 5. Polish Americans - Fiction. I. Bloom, Lloyd, ill. II. Title.*
*TC PZ7.R24435 Go 1999*

**RECOVERED MEMORY.** *See also* **FALSE MEMORY SYNDROME.**
Cameron, Catherine. Resolving childhood trauma. Thousand Oaks, Calif. : Sage Publications, c2000.
*TC RC569.5.A28 C35 2000*

**RECOVERING ADDICTS.** *See also* **RECOVERING ALCOHOLICS.**
Granfield, Robert, 1955- Coming clean. New York ; London : New York University Press, c1999.
*TC HV4998 .G73 1999*

**RECOVERING ADDICTS - INTERVIEWS.**
Changing lives [videorecording]. Princeton, NJ : Films for the Humanities & Sciences, c1998.

administration in education. 6th ed. Boston ; London : Allyn and Bacon, c2001.
*TC LB2831.58 .R43 2001*

*TC RC564 .C54 1998*

**RECOVERING ALCOHOLICS - INTERVIEWS.**
Changing lives [videorecording]. Princeton, NJ : Films for the Humanities & Sciences, c1998.
*TC RC564 .C54 1998*

**RECOVERY MOVEMENT.**
Communication in recovery. Cresskill, N.J. : Hampton Press, c1999.
*TC HV4998 .C64 1999*

**Recreating brief therapy.**
Walter, John L., 1945- New York : W.W. Norton & Co., 2000.
*TC RC480.5 .W276 2000*

**RECREATION.** *See* **COMMUNITY ORGANIZATION; LEISURE; PLAY; POPULAR CULTURE; SPORTS; VACATIONS.**

**RECREATION AREAS.** *See* **PARKS.**

**RECREATION - RESEARCH.**
Riddick, Carol Cutler. Evaluative research in recreation, park, and sport settings. [Champaign, Ill.? : Sagamore Publishing], c1999.
*TC GV181.46 .R533 1999*

**RECREATION - SOCIOLOGICAL ASPECTS.**
Rojek, Chris. Leisure and culture. Houndmills [England] : Macmillan Press ; New York : St. Martin's Press, 2000.
*TC GV14.45 .R657 2000*

**RECREATIONAL THERAPY.** *See* **PSYCHODRAMA.**

**RECREATIONS.** *See* **PLAY; SCHOOLS - EXERCISES AND RECREATIONS; SPORTS.**

**RECURRENT EDUCATION.** *See* **CONTINUING EDUCATION.**

**Recurrent education and socioeconomic success.**
Tuijnman, Albert. [Stockholm] : Institute of International Education, University of Stockholm, c1986.
*TC LC5215 .T84 1986*

**Red alert!.**
Foster, Stuart J., 1960- New York ; Canterbury [England] : P. Lang, c2000.
*TC LC72.2 .F67 2000*

**Red flower goes West.**
Turner, Ann Warren. 1st ed. New York : Hyperion Books for Children, c1999.
*TC PZ7.T8535 Rf 1999*

**Red Hat Linux 6 unleashed.**
Pitts, David. [Indianapolis, Ind.] : SAMS, c1999.
*TC QA76.76.O63 P56148 1999*

**Red Hat Linux : :** installation and configuration handbook / Duane Hellums ... [et al.]. Indianapolis, Ind. : Que : Macmillan USA, c2000. xix, 757 p. : ill. ; 24 cm. 1 computer laser optical disc (4 3/4 in.). Includes index. System requirements for accompanying disc: CD-ROM drive. ISBN 0-7897-2181-3 (pbk.)
*1. Linux (Computer file). 2. Operating systems (Computers). I. Hellums, Duane. II. Title: Red Hat Linux version 6.0.*
*TC QA76.76.O63 R43 2000*

**Red hat linux network management tools.**
Maxwell, Steven. New York : McGraw Hill, c2000.
*TC QA76.76.O63 M373339 2000*

**Red Hat Linux version 6.0.**
Red Hat Linux :. Indianapolis, Ind. : Que : Macmillan USA, c2000.
*TC QA76.76.O63 R43 2000*

**The Red Queen.**
Ridley, Matt. New York : Penguin Books, 1995.
*TC GN365.9 .R53 1995*

**The red string.**
Blair, Margot. Malibu, Calif. : J. Paul Getty Museum and Childrens Library Press, c1996.
*TC PZ7.B537865 Re 1996*

**Reddy, Linda A.**
Inclusion practices with special needs students. New York : Haworth Press, c1999.
*TC LC1201 .I538 1999*

**Redefining fatherhood.**
Dowd, Nancy E., 1949- New York : New York University Press, 2000.
*TC HQ756 .D588 2000*

**Redeker, Gisela.**
Discourse and perspective in cognitive linguistics. Amsterdam ; Philadelphia : J. Benjamins, c1997.

*TC P165 .D57 1997*

**REDEMPTIONERS.** *See* **INDENTURED SERVANTS.**

**REDEVELOPMENT, URBAN.** *See* **CITY PLANNING.**

**Redirectional method.**
Rosen, Sidney M. Toward a gang solution. [Norman, Okla.?] NRC Youth Services, 1996.
*TC HV6439.U7 R67 1996*

**Rediscovering San Cristóbal Canyon.**
Laborde, Ilia M. 1996.
*TC 06 no. 10660*

Laborde, Ilia M. 1996.
*TC 06 no. 10660*

**Rediscovering the democratic purposes of education** / edited by Lorraine M. McDonnell, P. Michael Timpane, and Roger Benjamin. Lawrence : University Press of Kansas, c2000. viii, 280 p. ; 24 cm. (Studies in government and public policy) Includes bibliographical references (p. 243-265) and index. ISBN 0-7006-1026-X (cloth : alk. paper) ISBN 0-7006-1027-8 (paper : alk. paper) DDC 370.11
*1. Politics and education - United States. 2. Education - Aims and objectives - United States. 3. Democracy - Study and teaching - United States. I. McDonnell, Lorraine, 1947- II. Timpane, P. Michael, 1934- III. Benjamin, Roger W. IV. Series.*
*TC LC89 .R43 2000*

**Redman, Barbara Klug.** Women's health needs in patient education / Barbara K. Redman. New York : Springer Pub. Co., c1999. xv, 171 p. ; 24 cm. (Springer series, focus on women) Includes bibliographical references and index. ISBN 0-8261-1264-1 (hardcover) DDC 615.5/071/082
*1. Patient education. 2. Women - Health and hygiene. 3. Women's Health. 4. Patient Education. 5. Primary Prevention. I. Title. II. Series: Springer series, focus on women (Unnumbered)*
*TC R727.4 .R43 1999*

**REDUCING.** *See* **WEIGHT LOSS.**

**REDUCING DIETS.**
Nichter, Mimi. Fat talk. Cambridge, Mass. : Harvard University Press, 2000.
*TC RJ399.C6 N53 2000*

**Reducing urban unemployment.**
McCarthy, William H. Washington, D.C. : National League of Cities, c1985.
*TC HD5724 .M34 1985*

**REDUCTION OF WEIGHT.** *See* **WEIGHT LOSS.**

**Reece, Robert M.**
Treatment of child abuse. Baltimore, Md. ; London : Johns Hopkins University Press, 2000.
*TC RJ375 .T74 2000*

**Reed, Adolph L., 1947-.**
Without justice for all. Boulder, Colo. : Westview Press, 1999.
*TC E185.615 .W57 1999*

**Reed, Carol J., 1937-** Teaching with power : shared decision-making and classroom practice / Carol J. Reed ; foreword by Ann Lieberman. New York : Teachers College Press, c2000. xiii, 193 p. ; 24 cm. (The series on school reform) Includes bibliographical references and index. ISBN 0-8077-3941-3 (cloth) ISBN 0-8077-3940-5 (pbk.) DDC 371.1/06
*1. Teacher participation in administration - United States. 2. Decision making - United States. 3. School management and organization - United States. 4. Teaching - United States. 5. Educational change - United States. I. Title. II. Series.*
*TC LB2806.45 .R44 2000*

**Reed, Peter.**
Modernstarts. New York : Museum of Modern Art : Distributed by Harry N. Abrams, c1999.
*TC N620.M9 M63 1999*

**Reed, Roger G., 1950-.**
Montgomery, Susan J., 1947- Phillips Academy. New York : Princeton Architectural Press, 2000.
*TC LD7501.A5 M65 2000*

**Reed, Ronald F.**
Philosophical documents in education. 2nd ed. New York : Longman, c2000.
*TC LB7 .P5432 2000*

**Reed-Scott, Jutta, 1936-.**
Library storage facilities, management, and services. Washington, DC : Association of Research Libraries, Office of Leadership and Management Services, 1999.
*TC Z675.S75 L697 1999*

**Reed-Victor, Evelyn, 1947-.**
Educating homeless students. Larchmont, N.Y. : Eye On Education, c2000.
*TC LC5144.2 .E385 2000*

**Reeves, Mona Rabun.** I had a cat / by Mona Rabun Reeves ; illustrated by Julie Downing. 1st American ed. New York : Bradbury Press, c1989. [32] p. : col. ill. ; 25 cm. SUMMARY: The owner of a cat, dog, bird, ape, frog, elk, deer, and a multitude of other animals finds new homes for all but one. ISBN 0-02-775731-5 DDC [E]
*1. Animals - Fiction. 2. Stories in rhyme. I. Downing, Julie, ill. II. Title.*
*TC PZ8.3.R263 Iah 1989*

**REFERENCE BOOKS.** *See* **ENCYCLOPEDIAS AND DICTIONARIES.**

**Reference books on family issues**
(v. 27) Infancy and culture. New York : Falmer Press, 1999.
*TC GN482 .I53 1999*

**Reference library of Black America** / edited by Jessie Carney Smith [and] Joseph M. Palmisano. Detroit, MI : Gale Group ; Distributed by African American Pub., Proteus Enterprises, c2000. 5 v. : ill., maps ; 29 cm. "Based on the eighth edition of The African American almanac..."--Introd. Includes bibliographical references and index. CONTENTS: v. 1. Chronology -- African-American firsts -- Significant documents in African-American history -- African-American landmarks -- v. 2. Africa and the Black diaspora -- Africans in America: 1600 to 1900 -- Civil rights -- Black nationalism -- National organizations -- Law -- v. 3. Politics -- Population -- Employment and income -- Entrepreneurship -- The family -- Education -- Religion -- Literature -- v. 4. Media -- Film and television -- Drama, comedy, and dance -- Classical music -- Sacred music traditions -- v. 5. Blues and jazz -- Popular music -- Visual and applied arts -- Science and technology -- Sports -- Military. ISBN 0-7876-4363-7 (set) ISBN 0-7876-4364-5 (v. 1) ISBN 0-7876-4365-3 (v. 2) ISBN 0-7876-4366-1 (v. 3) ISBN 0-7876-4367-X (v. 4) ISBN 0-7876-4368-8 (v. 5)
*1. Afro-Americans - Encyclopedias. I. Smith, Jessie Carney. II. Palmisano, Joseph M. III. Title: Black America*
*TC E185 .R44 2000*

**REFERENCE MATERIALS.** *See* **REFERENCE SOURCES.**

**REFERENCE RESOURCES.** *See* **REFERENCE SOURCES.**

**Reference Service Press (El Dorado Hills, Calif.).**
Financial aid for African Americans. El Dorado Hills, Calif. : Reference Service Press, c1997-
*TC LB2338 .F5643*

**Reference sources in the social sciences series**
O'Brien, Nancy P. Education, a guide to reference and information sources. 2nd ed. Englewood, Colo. : Libraries Unlimited, 2000.
*TC Z5811 .B89 2000*

**REFERENCE SOURCES - JUVENILE LITERATURE - COMPUTER NETWORK RESOURCES.**
Junior edition [computer file] [Farmington Hills, Mi.] : The Gale Group, c1999. Computer data.

Kids edition [computer file] [Farmington Hills, Mi.] : The Gale Group, c1999. Computer data.

**Refiguring English studies**
North, Stephen M. Refiguring the Ph.D. in English studies. Urbana, Ill. : National Council of Teachers of English, c2000.
*TC PE69.A47 N67 2000*

Parks, Stephen, 1963- Class politics. Urbana, Ill. : National Council of Teachers of English, c2000.
*TC PE1405.U6 P3 2000*

Writing and healing. Urbana, Ill. : National Council of Teachers of English, c2000.
*TC RC489.W75 W756 2000*

**Refiguring the Ph.D. in English studies.**
North, Stephen M. Urbana, Ill. : National Council of Teachers of English, c2000.
*TC PE69.A47 N67 2000*

**Reflecting on practice in elementary school mathematics** : readings from NCTM's school-based journals and other publications / edited by Anne R. Teppo. Reston, Va. : National Council of Teachers of Mathematics, c1999. vii, 256 p. : ill. ; 28 cm. Includes bibliographical references. ISBN 0-87353-477-8 DDC 372.7/0973
*1. Mathematics - Study and teaching (Elementary) - United States. I. Teppo, Anne R.*
*TC QA135.5 .R426 1999*

## REFLECTION (OPTICS) IN ART.
Miller, Jonathan, 1934- On reflection. London : National Gallery Publications ; [New Haven, Conn.] : Distributed by Yale University Press, c1998.
*TC N8224.M6 M54 1998*

## REFLECTION (PHILOSOPHY) - CONGRESSES.
A middle mosaic. Urbana, Ill. : National Council of Teachers of English, c2000.
*TC LB1631 .A2 2000*

## REFLECTION (THEORY OF KNOWLEDGE). See SELF-KNOWLEDGE, THEORY OF.

## REFLECTIONS.
Miller, Jonathan, 1934- On reflection. London : National Gallery Publications ; [New Haven, Conn.] : Distributed by Yale University Press, c1998.
*TC N8224.M6 M54 1998*

**Reflections and connections :** essays in honor of Kenneth S. Goodman's influence on language education / edited by Ann M. Marek, Carole Edelsky. Cresskill, N.J. : Hampton Press, c1999. xiv, 429 p. ; 24 cm. Includes bibliographical references. ISBN 1-57273-157-5 (alk. paper) ISBN 1-57273-158-3 (alk. paper) DDC 418/.007
*1. Language and languages - Study and teaching. 2. Goodman, Kenneth S. - Influence. I. Marek, Ann M. II. Edelsky, Carole. III. Goodman, Kenneth S.*
*TC P51 .R36 1999*

**Reflections for busy educators.**
Lordahl, Jo Ann. Thousand Oaks, Calif. : Corwin Press, c1995.
*TC PN6084.E38 L67 1995*

**Reflections of a culture broker.**
Kurin, Richard, 1950- Washington, D.C. : Smithsonian Institution Press, c1997.
*TC GN36.U62 D5775 1997*

**Reflections of first-year teachers on school culture :** questions, hopes, and challenges / edited by Rebecca Van Der Bogert, Morgaen L. Donaldson, and Brian Poon. San Francisco : Jossey-Bass Inc., 1999. 76 p. ; 23 cm. (New directions for school leadership, 1089-5612 ; no. 11, Spring 1999) "Sponsored by the International Network of Principals' Centers"--on cover. Includes index. ISBN 0-7879-4701-6
*1. First year teachers - Attitudes. 2. Classroom environment. I. Harvard University. Graduate School of Education. International Network of Principals' Centers. II. Van der Bogert, Rebecca. III. Series: New directions for school leadership ; no. 11.*
*TC LB2844.1.N4 R44 1999*

**Reflections on statistics :** learning, teaching, and assessment in grades K-12 / edited by Susanne P. Lajoie. Mahwah, N.J. : L. Erlbaum, 1998. xxi, 336 p. : ill. ; 24 cm. (The Studies in mathematical thinking and learning series) Includes bibliographical references and indexes. ISBN 0-8058-1971-1 (cloth : alk. paper) ISBN 0-8058-1972-X (paper : alk. paper) DDC 519.5/071
*1. Mathematical statistics - Study and teaching. I. Lajoie, Susanne. II. Series: Studies in mathematical thinking and learning.*
*TC QA276.18 .R44 1998*

**Reflections on understanding and welcoming immigrants and refugees.**
Who are my sisters and brothers? Washington, D.C. : The Conference, c1996.
*TC BX1795.E44 W46 1996*

**Reflective history series**
Curriculum and consequence. New York : Teachers College Press, c2000.
*TC LB1570 .C88379 2000*

**Reflective practice in nursing :** the growth of the professional practitioner / edited by Sarah Burns and Chris Bulman. 2nd ed. Oxford ; Malden, MA : Blackwell Scientific, 2000. xiv, 199 p. ; 24 cm. Includes bibliographical references and index. ISBN 0-632-05291-0 (pbk.)
*1. Nursing - Study and teaching. 2. Nursing - Philosophy. 3. Self-evaluation. 4. Self-knowledge, Theory of 5. Education, Nursing. 6. Nursing. 7. Philosophy, Nursing. I. Burns, Sarah, DN. II. Bulman, Chris.*
*TC RT73 .R3461 2000*

## REFLEXIVE KNOWLEDGE. See SELF-KNOWLEDGE, THEORY OF.

**Reflexive methodology.**
Alvesson, Mats, 1956- London ; Thousand Oaks, Calif. : SAGE, 2000.
*TC H61 .A62 2000*

**Reform and education.**
Reynolds, Barbara G. 1999.
*TC 06 no. 11166*

## REFORM, EDUCATION. See EDUCATIONAL CHANGE.

## REFORM OF HEALTH CARE DELIVERY. See HEALTH CARE REFORM.

## REFORM OF MEDICAL CARE DELIVERY. See HEALTH CARE REFORM.

## REFORM SCHOOLS. See REFORMATORIES.

## REFORM, SOCIAL. See SOCIAL PROBLEMS.

## REFORMATION - GREAT BRITAIN.
Anglo-Dutch Historical Conference (13th : 1997) The education of a Christian society. Aldershot, Hants, England ; Brookfield, Vt. : Ashgate, c1999.
*TC BR377 .E38 1999*

## REFORMATION - HISTORY. See REFORMATION.

## REFORMATION - NETHERLANDS.
Anglo-Dutch Historical Conference (13th : 1997) The education of a Christian society. Aldershot, Hants, England ; Brookfield, Vt. : Ashgate, c1999.
*TC BR377 .E38 1999*

## REFORMATORIES. See JUVENILE DELINQUENCY.

## REFORMATORIES - IRELAND - HISTORY.
Raftery, Mary. Suffer the little children. Dublin, Ireland : New Island, 1999.
*TC HV9148.A5 R33 1999*

## REFORMERS. See HEALTH REFORMERS; SOCIAL REFORMERS.

**Reforming a college :** the University of Tennessee story / edited by Richard Wisniewski. New York : P. Lang, c2000. viii, 203 p. ; 23 cm. (Higher ed ; vol. 4) Includes bibliographical references (p. [201]-203). ISBN 0-8204-4551-7 (alk. paper) DDC 378.768/85
*1. University of Tennessee. Knoxville - History. 2. Educational change - Tennessee. I. Wisniewski, Richard. II. Series.*
*TC LD5293 .R44 2000*

**Reforming American education from the bottom to the top** / edited by Evans Clinchy. Portsmouth, NH : Heinemann, c1999. xviii, 206 p. ; 23 cm. Includes bibliographical references and index. ISBN 0-325-00174-X DDC 370/.973
*1. Educational change - United States. 2. Education - Aims and objectives - United States. 3. Educational planning - United States. I. Clinchy, Evans.*
*TC LA210 .R44 1999*

**Reforming college composition :** writing the wrongs / edited by Ray Wallace, Alan Jackson, and Susan Lewis Wallace. Westport, Conn. : Greenwood Press, 2000. xxx, 268 p. ; 24 cm. (Contributions to the study of education, 0196-707X ; no. 79) Includes bibliographical references and index. ISBN 0-313-31093-9 (acid-free paper) DDC 808/.042
*1. English language - Rhetoric - Study and teaching. 2. Report writing - Study and teaching (Higher) 3. Educational change. I. Wallace, Ray. II. Jackson, Alan, 1957- III. Wallace, Susan Lewis. IV. Series.*
*TC PE1404 .R383 2000*

**Reforming health and education.**
Nelson, Joan M. Washington, DC : Overseas Development Council ; Baltimore, MD : Distributed by the Johns Hopkins University Press, c1999.
*TC HG3881.5.W57 N447 1999*

**Reforming the Electoral College** [videorecording] / Michigan Social Studies Education Project ; video production director, Rockland L. Richardson ; produced by: Oakland Schools, School Support Services, Carol Klenow, Linda Erkkila. [Boulder, Colo.? : Social Science Education Consortium?], c1996. 1 videocassette (27 min.) : sd., col. ; 1/2 in. Title on cassette label: Pass public issues discussion [videorecording] : Electoral College : Paul Dain at Andover High School in Michigan 1996. VHS. Catalogued from credits and cassette label. Paul Dain, Social Studies teacher, and his class at Andover High School, Bloomfield Hills, MI. Edited by Rockland L. Richardson; camera: Rockland L. Richardson, Mark Hansen; project director, Michael Yocum. "This video is part of Powerful and Authentic Social Studies (PASS) the professional development program of the Michigan Social Studies Education Project." For Social Studies teachers.
SUMMARY: Paul Dain conducts his class on the Electoral College by presenting the class with problems/questions to discuss in small groups and then come together to discuss as a whole.
*1. Social sciences - Study and teaching (Secondary) - Michigan - Bloomfield. I. Richardson, Rockland L. II. Klenow, Carol. III. Erkkila, Linda. IV. Oakland Intermediate School District (Oakland County, Mich.) V. Social Science Education Consortium. VI. Michigan Social Studies Education Project. VII. Title: Pass public issues discussion [videorecording] :*

*Electoral College : Paul Dain at Andover High School in Michigan 1996 VIII. Title: Paul Dain at Andover High School in Michigan [videorecording]*
*TC H62.5.U5 R4 1996*

**Reframing health behavior change with behavioral economics** / edited by Warren K. Bickel, Rudy E. Vuchinich. Mahwah, N.J. ; London : Lawrence Erlbaum, 2000. xxiii, 417 p. ; 24 cm. Includes bibliographical references and indexes. ISBN 0-8058-2733-1 (cloth : alk. paper) DDC 338.4/33621
*1. Health behavior - Economic aspects. 2. Medicine and psychology. I. Bickel, Warren K. II. Vuchinich, Rudy E. (Rudy Eugene), 1949-*
*TC RA776.9 .R433 2000*

## REFUGEES - EDUCATION.
Education as a humanitarian response. London ; Herndon, VA : Cassell ; [s.l.] : UNESCO International Bureau of Education, 1998.
*TC LC3719 .E37 1998*

## REFUGEES - FICTION.
Bat-Ami, Miriam. Two suns in the sky. 1st ed. [Chicago, IL] : Front Street/Cricket Books, 1999.
*TC PZ7.B2939 Tw 1999*

## REFUGEES, JEWISH - NEW YORK (STATE) - OSWEGO - JUVENILE FICTION.
Bat-Ami, Miriam. Two suns in the sky. 1st ed. [Chicago, IL] : Front Street/Cricket Books, 1999.
*TC PZ7.B2939 Tw 1999*

## REFUGEES - LEGAL STATUS, LAWS, ETC. - UNITED STATES - CONGRESSES.
National Legal Conference on Immigration and Refugee Policy (6th : 1983 : Washington, D.C.) Immigration and refugee policy. 1st ed. New York : Center for Migration Studies, 1984.
*TC KF4819.A2 N375 1983*

## REFUGEES, POLITICAL. See EXILES; REFUGEES, JEWISH.

## REFUGEES, POLITICAL - LEGAL STATUS, LAWS, ETC. See EMIGRATION AND IMMIGRATION LAW.

## REFUGEES, RELIGIOUS. See EMIGRATION AND IMMIGRATION - RELIGIOUS ASPECTS.

## REFUGEES - RELIGIOUS LIFE.
Who are my sisters and brothers? Washington, D.C. : The Conference, c1996.
*TC BX1795.E44 W46 1996*

## REFUGEES - SERVICES FOR - UNITED STATES.
Scheinfeld, Daniel, 1933- Strengthening refugee families. Chicago, Ill. : Lyceum Books, c1997.
*TC HV640.4.U54 S34 1997*

**Regan, Laura, ill.**
Lesser, Carolyn. Spots. 1st ed. San Diego : Harcourt Brace, c1999.
*TC QA113 .L47 1999*

## REGIONAL DEVELOPMENT. See COMMUNITY DEVELOPMENT; RURAL DEVELOPMENT.

## REGIONAL EDUCATIONAL LABORATORIES. See DEMONSTRATION CENTERS IN EDUCATION.

## REGIONAL MEDICAL PROGRAMS. See COMMUNITY HEALTH SERVICES.

## REGIONAL PLANNING. See CITY PLANNING; RURAL DEVELOPMENT.

**Regional studies series (Englewood Cliffs, N.J.)**
Regional studies series. Englewood Cliffs, N.J. : Globe Book Co., c1993.
*TC LC1090 .R43 1993*

**Regional studies series :** New York state teacher's resource manual / Englewood Cliffs, N.J. : Globe Book Co., c1993. vi, 298 p. : ill. ; 28 cm. (Regional studies series) ISBN 0-8359-0441-5
*1. International education - Study and teaching. I. Series: Regional studies series (Englewood Cliffs, N.J.)*
*TC LC1090 .R43 1993*

## REGIONALISM IN ARCHITECTURE.
Abel, Chris. Architecture and identity. 2nd ed. Oxford : Boston : Architectural Press, 2000.
*TC NA2500 .A392 2000*

## REGISTER (LINGUISTICS). See SUBLANGUAGE.

## REGRESSION ANALYSIS.
Applied regression analysis and other multivariable methods. 3rd ed. / David G. Kleinbaum ... [et al.]. Pacific Grove : Duxbury Press, c1998.

*TC QA278 .A665 1998*

Eye, Alexander von. Regression analysis for social sciences. San Diego, Calif. : Academic Press, c1998.
*TC HA31.3 .E94 1998*

**Regression analysis for social sciences.**
Eye, Alexander von. San Diego, Calif. : Academic Press, c1998.
*TC HA31.3 .E94 1998*

**Regular Guy.**
Weeks, Sarah. 1st ed. New York : Laura Geringer Book, c1999.
*TC PZ7.W42215 Rg 1999*

**REGULATORY AGENCIES.** *See* **ADMINISTRATIVE AGENCIES.**

**REHABILITATION.** *See* **MEDICAL REHABILITATION; VOCATIONAL REHABILITATION.**

**REHABILITATION MEDICINE.** *See* **MEDICAL REHABILITATION.**

**Rehabilitation nursing.**
Association of Rehabilitation Nurses. ARN journal. [Glenview, Ill.] Association of Rehabilitation Nurses.

**REHABILITATION NURSING - PERIODICALS.**
Association of Rehabilitation Nurses. ARN journal. [Glenview, Ill.] Association of Rehabilitation Nurses.

**REHABILITATION - PERIODICALS.**
Association of Rehabilitation Nurses. ARN journal. [Glenview, Ill.] Association of Rehabilitation Nurses.

**REHABILITATION - PERIODICALS.**
Cerebral palsy journal. Wichita, Kan., Institute of Logopedics, inc.

Cerebral palsy review. Wichita, Kan., Institute of Logopedics.

**REHABILITATION, RURAL.** *See* **RURAL DEVELOPMENT.**

**REHABILITATION, VOCATIONAL.** *See* **VOCATIONAL REHABILITATION.**

**Rehabilitative audiology** : children and adults / editors, Jerome G. Alpiner, Patricia A. McCarthy. 3rd ed. Philadelphia, PA : Lippincott Williams & Wilkins, c2000. xii, 690 p. : ill. ; 26 cm. Includes bibliographical references and indexes. ISBN 0-683-30652-9 DDC 617.8/9
*1. Hearing impaired - Rehabilitation. 2. Deaf - Rehabilitation. 3. Audiology. I. Alpiner, Jerome G., 1932- II. McCarthy, Patricia A.*
*TC RF297 .R44 2000*

**REHABILITATIVE COUNSELING - CASE STUDIES.**
Wanting to talk. London : Whurr, c1998.
*TC RC423 .W26 1998*

**Reichmann, Rebecca Lynn.**
Race in contemporary Brazil. University Park, Pa. : Pennsylvania State University Press, 1999.
*TC F2659.N4 R245 1999*

**Reid, Barbara.** The party / Barbara Reid. New York : Scholastic Press, 1999. 1v. (unpaged) : col. ill. ; 27 cm. SUMMARY: Two sisters don't want to go the annual family summer party, but after they get there, they have so much fun they do not want to leave. ISBN 0-590-97801-2 DDC [E]
*1. Family life - Fiction. 2. Parties - Fiction. 3. Stories in rhyme. I. Title.*
*TC PZ8.3.R2665 Pat 1999*

**Reid, Charles R.** Education and evolution : school instruction and the human future / Charles R. Reid. Lanham, Md. ; Oxford : University Press of America, c2000. xx, 245 p. ; 24 cm. Includes bibliographical references (p. 213-230) and index. ISBN 0-7618-1595-3 (cloth : alk. paper) DDC 370/.973
*1. Education - Social aspects - United States. 2. Education - Aims and objectives - United States. I. Title.*
*TC LC191.4 .R43 2000*

**Reid, D. Kim.**
Fahey, Kathleen R. Language development, differences, and disorders. Austin, Tex. : PRO-ED, c2000.
*TC LB1139.L3 F35 2000*

**Reid, Gavin, 1950-** Dyslexia : a practitioner's handbook / Gavin Reid. Chichester ; New York : J. Wiley, c1998. vii, 250 p. : ill. ; 25 cm. Includes bibliographical references (p. [213]-234) and index. ISBN 0-471-97391-2 (pbk. : alk. paper) DDC 371.91/44
*1. Dyslexic children - Education - Handbooks, manuals, etc. 2. Dyslexic children - Ability testing - Handbooks, manuals, etc. 3. Curriculum planning - Handbooks, manuals, etc. I. Title.*

*TC LC4708 .R45 1998*

**Reid, Ken.** Tackling truancy in schools : a practical manual for primary and secondary schools / Ken Reid. London ; New York : Routledge, 2000. viii, 353 p. : ill. ; 30 cm. Includes bibliographical references (p. [348]-[350]) and index. ISBN 0-415-20508-5 (pbk. : alk. paper) DDC 371.2/95/0941
*1. School attendance - Great Britain - Handbooks, manuals, etc. I. Title.*
*TC LB3081 .R446 2000*

Truancy and schools / Ken Reid. London : New York : Routledge, 1999. xii, 338 p. : ill. ; 24 cm. Includes bibliographical references (p. [334]-335) and index. ISBN 0-415-20509-3 (pb. : alk. paper) DDC 371.2/95/0941
*1. School attendance - Great Britain. 2. Education and state - Great Britain. I. Title.*
*TC LB3081 .R45 1999*

**Reid, Louann.**
Rationales for teaching young adult literature. Portland, Me. : Calendar Islands Publishers, 1999.
*TC PN59 .R33 1999*

**Reig, Howard.**
Headline stories of the century [videorecording]. Chicago, IL. : Distributed by Questar Video, Inc., c1992.
*TC D743 .H42 1992*

**Reilly, Thomas, 1941-.**
Fundacion Dr. Antonio Esteve. Symposium (7th : 1996 : Sitges, Spain) The clinical pharmacology of sport and exercise. Amsterdam ; New York : Elsevier Science B.V., Excerpta Medica, 1997.
*TC RC1230 .F86 1996*

**Reiner Moritz Associates.**
Jackson Pollock [videorecording]. [Chicago, Ill.] : Home Vision ; [S.l.] : Distributed Worldwide by RM Associates, c1987.
*TC ND237.P73 J3 1987*

Roy Lichtenstein [videorecording]. [Chicago, IL] : Home Vision ; [S.l.] : distributed worldwide by RM Asssociates, c1991.
*TC ND237.L627 R6 1991*

**REINFORCEMENT (PSYCHOLOGY).** *See* **FEEDBACK (PSYCHOLOGY); PUNISHMENT (PSYCHOLOGY); REWARD (PSYCHOLOGY).**

**Reinhartz, Judy.**
Beach, Don M. Supervisory leadership. Boston : Allyn and Bacon, c2000.
*TC LB2806.4 .B433 2000*

**Reinventing fundraising.**
Shaw, Sondra C., 1936- 1st ed. San Francisco : Jossey-Bass Publishers, c1995.
*TC HV41.9.U5 S53 1995*

**Reinventing government or reinventing ourselves.**
Schachter, Hindy Lauer. Albany : State University of New York Press, c1997.
*TC JK1764 .S35 1997*

**Reis, David.**
Adolescent siblings in stepfamilies. Chicago, Ill. : University of Chicago Press, 1999.
*TC LB1103.S6 v.64 no. 4*

**Reis, Harry T.**
Handbook of research methods in social and personality psychology. Cambridge, U.K. ; New York : Cambridge University Press, 2000.
*TC HM1019 .H36 2000*

**Reischl, Uwe, 1945-.**
Gross, Clifford M. The new idea factory. Columbus, OH : Battelle Press, c2000.
*TC HD53 .G75 2000*

**Reise, Steve.**
Embretson, Susan E. Item response theory for psychologists. Mahwah, N.J. : Lawrence Erlbaum Associates, Publishers, 2000.
*TC BF39 .E495 2000*

**Reiser, Lynn.** Earthdance / by Lynn Reiser. New York : Greenwillow Books, 1999. 1v. (npaged) : ill. ; 29 cm. SUMMARY: As Terra performs her part in a school show about the Earth and the solar system, her mother, who is an astronaut, is hurrying back from space with a special ending for the production. ISBN 0-688-16326-2 (trade : alk. paper) ISBN 0-688-16327-0 (lib. bdg. : alk. paper) DDC [E]
*1. Earth - Fiction. 2. Schools - Fiction. I. Title.*
*TC PZ7.R27745 Ear 1999*

**Reiss, Albert J.**
Understanding and preventing violence. Washington, D.C. : National Academy Press, 1993-1994.

*TC HN90.V5 U53 1993*

**Reiss, David, 1937-** The relationship code : deciphering genetic and social influences on adolescent development / David Reiss, with Jenae M. Neiderhiser, E. Mavis Hetherington, Robert Plomin. Cambridge, Mass. ; London : Harvard University Press, c2000. xviii, 532 p. : ill. ; 25 cm. (Adolescent lives ; 1) Includes bibliographical references (p. 489-510) and indexes. ISBN 0-674-00054-4 (alk. paper) DDC 155.5
*1. Adolescent psychology. I. Neiderhiser, Jenae M. II. Hetherington, E. Mavis (Eileen Mavis), 1926- III. Plomin, Robert, 1948- IV. Title. V. Series.*
*TC BF724 .R39 2000*

**Reiss, Donna, 1944-.**
Learning literature in an era of change. Sterling, Va. : Stylus Pub., c2000.
*TC PN59 .L39 2000*

**Reiss, Oscar, 1925-** Medicine in colonial America / Oscar Reiss. Lanham : University Press of America, 2000. xi, 518 p. ; 24 cm. Includes bibliographical references and index. ISBN 0-7618-1576-7 (cloth : alk. paper)
*1. History of Medicine, 17th Cent. - United States. 2. History of Medicine, 18th Cent. - United States. 3. Colonialism - history - United States. I. Title.*
*TC RC151 .R44 2000*

**Reitz, Charles.** Art, alienation, and the humanities : a critical engagement with Herbert Marcuse / Charles Reitz. Albany : State University of New York Press, c2000. xiv, 336 p. ; 23 cm. (SUNY series, the philosophy of education) (SUNY series in the philosophy of the social sciences) Includes bibliographical references (p. 311-324) and index. ISBN 0-7914-4461-9 (HC : acid-free paper) ISBN 0-7914-4462-7 (PB : acid-free paper) DDC 111/.85/092
*1. Marcuse, Herbert, - 1898- - Aesthetics. 2. Education - Philosophy. I. Title. II. Series. III. Series: SUNY series in philosophy of education.*
*TC B945.M2984 R45 2000*

**Rekindling the flame.**
Brock, Barbara L. Thousand Oaks, Calif. : Corwin Press, c2000.
*TC LB2840.2 .B76 2000*

**Relation between preferred subject matter and the formal artistic characteristics of children's drawing.**
Tuman, Donna M. Gender difference in form and content. 1998.
*TC 06 no. 11000*

**Relational perspectives book series**
(v. 15) Kainer, Rochelle G. K., 1936- The collapse of the self and its therapeutic restoration. Hillsdale, NJ ; London : Analytic Press, 1999.
*TC RC489.S43 K35 1999*

**Relational therapy for personality disorders.**
Magnavita, Jeffrey J. New York : Wiley, c2000.
*TC RC554 .M228 2000*

**RELATIONS AMONG ETHNIC GROUPS.** *See* **ETHNIC RELATIONS.**

**RELATIONS, INTERGENERATIONAL.** *See* **INTERGENERATIONAL RELATIONS.**

**RELATIONS, INTERGROUP.** *See* **INTERGROUP RELATIONS.**

**RELATIONS, INTERPERSONAL.** *See* **INTERPERSONAL RELATIONS.**

**RELATIONS, RACE.** *See* **RACE RELATIONS.**

**RELATIONSHIP ADDICTION.**
Feeney, Don J., 1948- Entrancing relationships. Westport, Conn. : Praeger, 1999.
*TC RC552.R44 F44 1999*

**The relationship between health care clinicians' relational abilities and psychosocial orientation to patient care, and patient adherence with medical treatment.**
Fenichel, Ann. 1998.
*TC 085 F352*

**The relationship code.**
Reiss, David, 1937- Cambridge, Mass. ; London : Harvard University Press, c2000.
*TC BF724 .R39 2000*

**The relationship of upward feedback disparities to leader performance.**
Bazigos, Michael Nicholas. 1999.
*TC 085 B33*

**Relationships among administrator personality, perceptions of feedback source credibility, and attitudes toward program feedback.**
Curcio, John J. 1999.

*TC 085 C92*

**Relationships and communication activities.**
Toner, Patricia Rizzo, 1952- West Nyack, N.Y. :
Center for Applied Research in Education, c1993.
*TC HM132 .T663 1993*

**RELATIONSHIPS BETWEEN HEALTH
FACILITIES.** *See* HEALTH FACILITIES -
AFFILIATIONS.

**RELATIONSHIPS, HUMAN-ANIMAL.** *See*
HUMAN-ANIMAL RELATIONSHIPS.

**RELATIONSHIPS, INTERPERSONAL.** *See*
INTERPERSONAL RELATIONS.

**RELATIONSHIPS, MAN-WOMAN.** *See* MAN-
WOMAN RELATIONSHIPS.

**Relativism and reality.**
Kirk, Robert, 1933- London ; New York : Routledge,
1999.
*TC B835 .K57 1999*

**RELATIVITY.**
Capaldi, E. John. Contextualism in psychological
research? Thousand Oaks, Calif. : Sage, c1999.
*TC BF315.2 .C37 1999*

Kirk, Robert, 1933- Relativism and reality. London ;
New York : Routledge, 1999.
*TC B835 .K57 1999*

**RELAXATION.**
Smith, Jonathan C. ABC relaxation theory. New
York : Springer Pub., c1999.
*TC BF637.R45 S549 1999*

**RELIABILITY.** *See* HONESTY.

**RELIEF (AID).** *See* CHARITIES; PUBLIC
WELFARE.

**RELIEF STATIONS (FOR THE POOR).** *See*
SOCIAL SERVICE.

**RELIGION.** *See* ART AND RELIGION;
ATHEISM; BELIEF AND DOUBT; GOD;
MISSIONS; MYTHOLOGY; PSYCHOLOGY,
RELIGIOUS; RATIONALISM; RELIGIONS;
RELIGIOUS ARTICLES; RELIGIOUS
FUNDAMENTALISM; WOMEN AND
RELIGION.

**RELIGION AND ART.** *See* ART AND RELIGION.

**RELIGION AND CULTURE.**
Fukuyama, Mary A. Integrating spirituality into
multicultural counseling. Thousand Oaks, Calif. :
Sage Publications, c1999.
*TC BF637.C6 F795 1999*

Kelly, Gerard, 1959- Retrofuture. Downers Grove,
Ill. : InterVarsity Press, c1999.
*TC HN17.5 .K439 1999*

**RELIGION AND POLITICS.**
Henderson, Katharine Rhodes. The public leadership
of women of faith. 2000.
*TC 06 no. 11276*

**RELIGION AND POLITICS - UNITED STATES.**
Spinner-Halev, Jeff. Surviving diversity. Baltimore :
Johns Hopkins University Press, 2000.
*TC BL2525 .S588 2000*

**RELIGION AND PSYCHOLOGY.**
Psychiatry and religion. 1st ed. Washington, DC :
American Psychiatric Press, c2000.
*TC RC455.4.R4 P755 2000*

**RELIGION, COMPARATIVE.** *See* RELIGIONS.

**Religion in America series (Oxford University Press)**
Bramadat, Paul A. The church on the world's turf.
Oxford ; New York : Oxford University Press, 2000.
*TC BV970.16 B73 2000*

**RELIGION IN THE PUBLIC SCHOOLS - GHANA.**
Quist, Hubert Oswald. Secondary education and
nation-building. 1999.
*TC 085 Q52*

**RELIGION - MUSEUMS.**
Godly things. New York : Leicester University Press,
2000.
*TC BL45 .G63 2000*

**RELIGION - PHILOSOPHY.** *See* KNOWLEDGE,
THEORY OF (RELIGION).

**RELIGION - POLITICAL ASPECTS.** *See*
RELIGION AND POLITICS.

**RELIGION, PRIMITIVE.** *See* RELIGION.

**RELIGION - PSYCHOLOGICAL ASPECTS.** *See*
PSYCHOLOGY, RELIGIOUS.

**RELIGION - PSYCHOLOGY.** *See* PSYCHOLOGY,
RELIGIOUS.

**RELIGION - STUDY AND TEACHING
(HIGHER) - UNITED STATES - HISTORY.**
Hart, D. G. (Darryl G.) The university gets religion.
Baltimore, Md. : Johns Hopkins University Press,
1999.
*TC BL41 .H38 1999*

**RELIGION - STUDY AND TEACHING
(SECONDARY) - GREAT BRITAIN.**
Wright, Andrew, 1958- Learning to teach religious
education in the secondary school. London ; New
York : Routledge, 2000.
*TC LC410.G7 W75 2000*

**RELIGIONS.** *See* CHRISTIANITY AND OTHER
RELIGIONS; HINDUISM; ISLAM; JUDAISM;
MYTHOLOGY; RELIGION; SHAMANISM.

**RELIGIONS - BIOGRAPHY.** *See* RELIGIOUS
BIOGRAPHY.

**RELIGIONS, COMPARATIVE.** *See* RELIGIONS.

**RELIGIONS - POLITICAL ASPECTS.** *See*
RELIGION AND POLITICS.

**RELIGIONS - PSYCHOLOGICAL ASPECTS.** *See*
PSYCHOLOGY, RELIGIOUS.

**RELIGIONS - PSYCHOLOGY.** *See*
PSYCHOLOGY, RELIGIOUS.

**RELIGIONS - RELATIONS.**
Eck, Diana L. Encountering God. Boston : Beacon
Press, c1993.
*TC BR127 .E25 1993*

**RELIGIOUS ART OBJECTS.** *See* RELIGIOUS
ARTICLES.

**RELIGIOUS ARTICLES - MUSEUMS.**
Godly things. New York : Leicester University Press,
2000.
*TC BL45 .G63 2000*

**RELIGIOUS BELIEF.** *See* BELIEF AND DOUBT.

**RELIGIOUS BIOGRAPHY.** *See* CHRISTIAN
BIOGRAPHY.

**RELIGIOUS BIOGRAPHY - ENCYCLOPEDIAS.**
Philosophers and religious leaders. Phoenix, Ariz. :
Oryx Press, 1999.
*TC B104 .P48 1999*

**RELIGIOUS CEREMONIES.** *See* RITES AND
CEREMONIES.

**RELIGIOUS DENOMINATIONS.** *See*
RELIGIONS.

**RELIGIOUS EDUCATION.** *See also* CHRISTIAN
EDUCATION; JEWISH RELIGIOUS
EDUCATION; MORAL EDUCATION;
RELIGION IN THE PUBLIC SCHOOLS;
TEACHING, FREEDOM OF.
Spiritual and religious education. London ; New
York : Falmer Press, 2000.
*TC BL42 .S68 2000*

**RELIGIOUS EDUCATION - ENGLAND.**
Levitt, Mairi. Nice when they are young. Aldershot,
Hants, England ; Brookfield, Vt. : Avebury, c1996.
*TC BV1475.2 .L45 1996*

**RELIGIOUS EDUCATION - GREAT BRITAIN.**
Wright, Andrew, 1958- Learning to teach religious
education in the secondary school. London ; New
York : Routledge, 2000.
*TC LC410.G7 W75 2000*

**Religious education in the early years.**
Ashton, Elizabeth, lecturer. London ; New York :
Routledge, 2000.
*TC BV1475.2 .A84 2000*

**RELIGIOUS EDUCATION, JEWISH.** *See* JEWISH
RELIGIOUS EDUCATION.

**RELIGIOUS EDUCATION OF CHILDREN.** *See*
RELIGION IN THE PUBLIC SCHOOLS.

**RELIGIOUS EDUCATION - PERIODICALS.**
[Christian education (Chicago, Ill.)] Christian
education. Chicago : [Council of Church Boards of
Education in the United States of America,    -1952]

The christian scholar. [Somerville, N.J., etc.]

**RELIGIOUS EDUCATION - PHILOSOPHY.**
Iheoma, E. O. The philosophy of religious education.
Enugu, Nigeria : Fourth Dimension Pub., 1997.
*TC BV1464 .I44 1997*

**RELIGIOUS FUNDAMENTALISM -
COMPARATIVE STUDIES.**
Marty, Martin E., 1928- The glory and the power.
Boston : Beacon Press, c1992.
*TC BL238 .M37 1992*

**RELIGIOUS GOODS.** *See* RELIGIOUS
ARTICLES.

**RELIGIOUS KNOWLEDGE, THEORY OF.** *See*
KNOWLEDGE, THEORY OF (RELIGION).

**RELIGIOUS LIFE.** *See* SPIRITUAL LIFE.

**RELIGIOUS OBJECTS.** *See* RELIGIOUS
ARTICLES.

**RELIGIOUS PSYCHOLOGY.** *See* PSYCHOLOGY,
RELIGIOUS.

**RELIGIOUS RITES.** *See* RITES AND
CEREMONIES.

**RELIGIOUS SOCIAL WORK.** *See* CHURCH
CHARITIES.

**RELOCATION OF JAPANESE AMERICANS,
1942-1945.** *See* JAPANESE AMERICANS -
EVACUATION AND RELOCATION, 1942-
1945.

**Reluctant readers.**
Jobe, Ron. Markham, Ont. : Pembroke Pub., 1999.
*TC LB1573 .J58 1999*

**Remaking health care in America :** building organized
delivery systems / Stephen M. Shortell ... et al. 1st ed.
San Francisco : Jossey-Bass Publishers, c1996. xxv,
370 p. : ill. ; 24 cm. Includes bibliographical references (p.
337-352) and index. ISBN 0-7879-0227-6 (acid-free paper)
DDC 362.1/0973
*1. Medical care - United States. 2. Health facilities -
Affiliations - United States. 3. Health services administration -
United States. I. Shortell, Stephen M. (Stephen Michael), 1944-*
*TC RA395.A3 R46 1996*

**Remaking relapse prevention with sex offenders :** a
sourcebook / D. Richard Laws, Stephen M. Hudson,
Tony Ward, editors. Thousand Oaks, Calif. : Sage
Publications, c2000. xiv, 559 p. ; 25 cm. Includes
bibliographical references and index. ISBN 0-7619-1887-6
(cloth : alk. paper) DDC 616.85/83
*1. Sex offenders - Rehabilitation. 2. Sex crimes - Prevention. I.
Laws, D. Richard. II. Hudson, Stephen M. III. Ward, Tony.*
*TC RC560.S47 R46 2000*

**REMAND HOMES.** *See* REFORMATORIES.

**The remarkable body.**
The nutty, nougat-filled world of human nutrition
[videorecording]. [Arlington, Va.] : Cerebellum Corp.,
c1998.
*TC QP141 .N8 1998*

**REMARRIAGE - UNITED STATES.**
Ganong, Lawrence H. Changing families, changing
responsibilities. Mahwah, N.J. : Lawrence Erlbaum
Associates, 1999.
*TC HQ834 .G375 1999*

**REMEDIAL EDUCATION.** *See* REMEDIAL
TEACHING.

**Remedial education and grading.**
Chen, Sheying. New York : the City University of
New York, 1999.
*TC LB1029.R4 C54 1999*

**REMEDIAL INSTRUCTION.** *See* REMEDIAL
TEACHING.

**REMEDIAL LANGUAGE ARTS.** *See* LANGUAGE
ARTS - REMEDIAL TEACHING.

**REMEDIAL TEACHING.** *See also* LANGUAGE
ARTS - REMEDIAL TEACHING; TUTORS
AND TUTORING.
Harris, Albert Josiah. How to increase reading ability,
a guide to individualized and remedial methods. 2d
ed., rev. and enl. London ; New York[etc.] :
Longmans, Green and Co., 1947.
*TC 372.4H2421*

Promising practices in recruitment, remediation, and
retention. San Francisco, Calif. : Jossey-Bass, c1999.
*TC LB2331.72 .N48 1999*

Shapiro, Edward S. (Edward Steven), 1951-
Academic skills problems workbook. New York :
Guilford Press, c1996.
*TC LB1029.R4 S52 1996*

**REMEDIAL TEACHING - UNITED STATES -
CASE STUDIES.**
Chen, Sheying. Remedial education and grading. New
York : the City University of New York, 1999.

**TC LB1029.R4 C54 1999**

**Remediation.**
Bolter, J. David, 1951- Cambridge, Mass. : MIT Press, c1999.
*TC P96.T42 B59 1998*

**Remembering the boys :** a collection of letters, a gathering of memories / edited by Lynna Piekutowski. Kent, OH : Kent State University Press, c2000. xxvi, 299 p. : ill. ; 26 cm. ISBN 0-87338-664-7 DDC 940.54/8173
*1. World War, 1939-1945 - Personal narratives, American. 2. Western Reserve Academy - Alumni and alumnae - Correspondence. 3. Western Reserve Academy - Faculty - Correspondence. I. Piekutowski, Lynna, 1951-*
*TC D811.A2 R46 2000*

**Reminiscing.**
Schilpp, Paul Arthur, 1897- Carbondale, IL : Published for the College of Liberal Arts of Southern Illinois University at Carbondale by Southern Illinois University Press, c1996.
*TC B945.S28 A3 1996*

**REMINISCING IN OLD AGE.**
Smith, Irmhild Wrede. The effect of structured exercise and structured reminiscing on agitation and aggression in geriatric psychiatric patients. 1996.
*TC 06 no. 10700*

**Remote control childhood?.**
Levin, Diane E. Washington, D.C. : National Association for the Education of Young Children, c1998.
*TC P94.5.C55 L48 1998*

**REMOTE STORAGE FOR LIBRARIES.** *See* **LIBRARIES, STORAGE.**

**Remy, Richard C.** Government in the United States / Richard C. Remy, senior author ; Larry Elowitz, William Berlin. New York : Scribner educational publishers, 1987. xiv, 808 p., R-42 : ill. (some col.) ; 27 cm. Includes index. ISBN 0-02-151140-3
*1. United States - Politics and government. I. Elowitz, Larry. II. Berlin, William S. III. Title.*
*TC JK274 .R54 1987*

**RENAISSANCE.** *See also* **CIVILIZATION, MEDIEVAL; CIVILIZATION, MODERN; HUMANISM; MIDDLE AGES.**
Carlino, Andrea, 1960- [Fabbrica del corpo. English] Books of the body. Chicago : University of Chicago Press, c1999.
*TC QM33.4 .C3613 1999*

**Renaissance women in science.**
Van der Does, Louise Q. Lanham, Md. : University Press of America, c1999.
*TC Q141 .V25 1999*

**RENEWABLE ENERGY SOURCES.** *See* **SOLAR ENERGY.**

**RENEWAL OF COPYRIGHT.** *See* **COPYRIGHT - DURATION.**

**Renewing American schools**
Teaching transformed. Boulder, Colo. ; Oxford : Westview Press, 2000.
*TC LB2822.82 .T44 2000*

**Renn, Ortwin.**
Cross-cultural risk perception. Dordrecht ; Boston ; London : Kluwer Academic, c2000.
*TC HM1101 .C76 2000*

**Renner, Michael. 1957-.**
Brown, Lester Russell, 1934- Vital signs 2000 :. New York : Norton, c2000.
*TC HD75.6 .B768 2000*

**RENOIR, AUGUSTE, 1841-1919.**
Impressionism [videorecording]. [London] : The National Gallery ; Tillingham, Peasmarsh, East Sussex, England : Ho-Ho-Kus, NJ : Distributed by The Roland Collection, c1990.
*TC ND547.5.I4 A7 1990*

**RENOWN.** *See* **FAME.**

**Renpenning, Kathie McLaughlin.**
Allison, Sarah E. Nursing administration in the 21st century. Thousand Oaks : Sage Publications, c1999.
*TC RT89. A435 1999*

**Renstrom, Peter G., 1943-** Constitutional rights sourcebook / Peter G. Renstrom. Santa Barbara, Calif. : ABC-CLIO, 1999. xxi, 770 p. ; 26 cm. Includes bibliographical references and index. ISBN 1-57607-061-1 DDC 342.73/02
*1. Constitutional law - United States. I. Title.*
*TC KF4550.Z9 R463 1999*

**Rentel, Victor M.**
Themes and issues in faculty development. Lanham, MD : University Press of America, 1999.
*TC LB1738 .T54 1999*

**Renwick Gallery.** Skilled work : American craft in the Renwick Gallery, National Museum of American Art, Smithsonian Institution. Washington, D.C. : Smithsonian Institution Press, c1998. 191 p. : ill. (some col.) ; 31 cm. ISBN 1-56098-831-2 ISBN 1-56098-806-1 (pbk.) DDC 745/.0973/074753
*1. Renwick Gallery - Catalogs. 2. Decorative arts - United States - Catalogs. 3. Decorative arts - Washington (D.C.) - Catalogs. I. Title.*
*TC NK460.W3 R467 1998*

**RENWICK GALLERY - CATALOGS.**
Renwick Gallery. Skilled work. Washington, D.C. : Smithsonian Institution Press, c1998.
*TC NK460.W3 R467 1998*

**Renz, Loren.** Arts funding : an update on foundation trends / Loren Renz, Steven Lawrence ; research assistants, Elizabeth Cuccaro, Meredith Gerson. 3rd ed. [New York, N.Y.] : Foundation Center, c1998. x, 69 p. : ill. ; 28 cm. Includes bibliographical references. "The Foundation Center in cooperation with Grantmakers in the Arts"--Cover. ISBN 0-87954-813-4 (pbk.)
*1. Arts - United States - Finance. I. Renz, Loren. II. Lawrence, Steven. III. Foundation Center. IV. Grantmakers in the Arts. V. Title. VI. Title: Update on foundation trends.*
*TC NX711.U5 R4 1998*

Renz, Loren. Arts funding. 3rd ed. [New York, N.Y.] : Foundation Center, c1998.
*TC NX711.U5 R4 1998*

**Reorganizing secondary education.**
Thayer, Vivian Trow, 1886- New York, Appleton-Century [c1939]
*TC LB1607 .T5*

**Repair and binding of old Chinese books.**
The East Asian library journal. Princeton, N.J. : Gest Library of Princeton University, c1994-
*TC Z733.G47 G46*

**REPATRIATION.** *See* **PRISONERS OF WAR.**

**Repertoire, authenticity, and instruction.**
Damm, Robert J., 1964- New York ; London : Garland Pub., 2000.
*TC MT3.U6 O53 2000*

**REPERTORY GRID TECHNIQUE.** *See* **PERSONAL CONSTRUCT THEORY.**

**Report (Group for the Advancement of Psychiatry : 1984)**
(no. 143.) In the long run--longitudinal studies of psychopathology in children. Washington, DC : American Psychiatric Press, c1999.
*TC RC321 .G7 no. 143*

**Report of the National Reading Panel : teaching children to read.**
National Reading Panel (U.S.) [Washington, D.C.?] : National Institute of Child Health and Human Development, National Institutes of Health, [2000]
*TC LB1050 .N335 2000*

**Report of the Secretary's Task Force on Black & Minority Health.**
United States. Dept. of Health and Human Services. Task Force on Black and Minority Health. Washington, D.C. : U.S. Dept. of Health and Human Services, [1985-<1986 >
*TC RA448.5.N4 U55 1985*

**Report to Congress on family and medical leave policies.**
Commission on Family and Medical Leave (U.S.) A Workable balance. Washington, DC : Commission on Leave ; Women's Bureau, U.S. Dept. of Labor, [1996]
*TC HD5115.6.U5 C66 1996*

**REPORT WRITING.**
Bankhead, Elizabeth. Write it!. 2nd ed./MLA version. Englewood, Colo. : Libraries Unlimited, c1999.
*TC LB1047.3 .W75 1999*

Duncan, Donna. I-Search, you search, we all to learn to research. New York : Neal-Schuman Publishers, 2000.
*TC Z711.2 .D86 2000*

Powell, Stuart, 1949- Returning to study. Buckingham ; Philadelphia : Open University Press, c1999.
*TC LC5256.G7 P66 1999*

**REPORT WRITING - COMPUTER-ASSISTED INSTRUCTION.**
Coogan, David. Electronic writing centers. Stamford, Conn. : Ablex Pub. Corp., c1999.

**TC PE1404 .C6347 1999**

Taking flight with OWLs. Mahwah, N.J. : Lawrence Erlbaum Associates, Publishers, 2000.
*TC PE1404 .T24 2000*

Transitions. Greenwich, Conn. : Ablex Pub. Corp., c1998.
*TC PE1404 .T74 1998*

**REPORT WRITING - COMPUTER NETWORK RESOURCES.**
The online writing classroom. Cresskill, N.J. : Hampton Press, c2000.
*TC PE1404 .O45 2000*

**REPORT WRITING - COMPUTER NETWORK RESOURCES - HANDBOOKS, MANUALS, ETC.**
Ruszkiewicz, John J., 1950- Bookmarks. New York ; Harlow, England : Longman, c2000.
*TC LB2369 .R88 2000*

**REPORT WRITING - HANDBOOKS, MANUALS, ETC.**
Ruszkiewicz, John J., 1950- Bookmarks. New York ; Harlow, England : Longman, c2000.
*TC LB2369 .R88 2000*

Thomas, R. Murray (Robert Murray), 1921- Theses and dissertations. Westport, Conn. : Bergin & Garvey, 2000.
*TC LB2369 .T458 2000*

**REPORT WRITING - PROBLEMS, EXERCISES, ETC.**
Literacies. 2nd ed. New York : W.W. Norton, c2000.
*TC PE1417 .L62 2000*

**REPORT WRITING - STUDY AND TEACHING.**
Babin, Edith H. Contemporary composition studies. Westport, Conn. : Greenwood Press, 1999.
*TC PE1404 .B23 1999*

Comp tales. New York : Longman, c2000.
*TC PE1404 .C617 2000*

Elbow, Peter. Everyone can write. New York : Oxford University Press, 2000.
*TC PE1404 .E42 2000*

Kaufer, David S. Designing interactive worlds with words. Mahwah, N.J. : Lawrence Erlbaum Associates, 2000.
*TC PE1404 .K38 2000*

(Re)visioning composition textbooks. Albany : State University of New York Press, c1999.
*TC PE1404 .R46 1999*

A Rhetoric of doing. Carbondale : Southern Illinois University Press, c1992.
*TC PE1404 .R496 1992*

Romano, Tom. Blending genre, altering style. Portsmouth, NH : Boynton/Cook ; Heinemann, c2000.
*TC PE1404 .R635 2000*

Roskelly, Hephzibah. Reason to believe. Albany : State University of New York Press, c1998.
*TC PE1404 .R67 1998*

Self-assessment and development in writing. Cresskill, N.J. : Hampton Press, c2000.
*TC PE1404 .S37 2000*

A sourcebook for responding to student writing. Cresskill, N.J. : Hampton Press, c1999.
*TC PE1404 .S683 1999*

Stories from the center. Urbana, Ill. National Council of Teachers of English, c2000.
*TC PE1404 .S834 2000*

Transitions. Greenwich, Conn. : Ablex Pub. Corp., c1998.
*TC PE1404 .T74 1998*

Working with student writers. New York : P. Lang, c1999.
*TC PE1404 .W66 1999*

Writing across languages. Stamford, Conn. : Ablex Pub., c2000.
*TC PB36 .W77 2000*

The writing teacher's sourcebook. 4th ed. New York : Oxford University Press, 2000.
*TC PE1404 .W74 2000*

**REPORT WRITING - STUDY AND TEACHING - DATA PROCESSING.**
Coogan, David. Electronic writing centers. Stamford, Conn. : Ablex Pub. Corp., c1999.
*TC PE1404 .C6347 1999*

The online writing classroom. Cresskill, N.J. : Hampton Press, c2000.

*TC PE1404 .O45 2000*

Taking flight with OWLs. Mahwah, N.J. : Lawrence Erlbaum Associates, Publishers, 2000.
*TC PE1404 .T24 2000*

**REPORT WRITING - STUDY AND TEACHING (HIGHER).**
The Allyn & Bacon sourcebook for college writing teachers. Boston ; London : Allyn and Bacon, 2000.
*TC PE1404 .A45 2000*

Reforming college composition. Westport, Conn. : Greenwood Press, 2000.
*TC PE1404 .R383 2000*

**REPORT WRITING - STUDY AND TEACHING (HIGHER) - MORAL AND ETHICAL ASPECTS.**
Ethical issues in college writing. New York ; Canterbury [England] : Peter Lang, c1999.
*TC PE1404 .E84 1999*

**REPORT WRITING - STUDY AND TEACHING (HIGHER) - UNITED STATES.**
Comp tales. New York : Longman, c2000.
*TC PE1404 .C617 2000*

**REPORT WRITING - STUDY AND TEACHING - PSYCHOLOGICAL ASPECTS.**
Davis, D. Diane (Debra Diane), 1963- Breaking up (at) totality. Carbondale : Southern Illinois University Press, c2000.
*TC PE1404 .D385 2000*

**REPORT WRITING - STUDY AND TEACHING - RESEARCH.**
Williams, James D. (James Dale), 1949- Preparing to teach writing. 2nd ed. Mahwah, N.J. : Lawrence Erlbaum Associates, 1998.
*TC PE1404 .W54 1998*

**REPORT WRITING - STUDY AND TEACHING (SECONDARY).**
Proett, Jackie, 1926- The writing process in action. Urbana, Ill. : National Council of Teachers of English, c1986.
*TC LB1631 .P697 1986*

**REPORT WRITING - STUDY AND TEACHING - SOCIAL ASPECTS.**
Davis, D. Diane (Debra Diane), 1963- Breaking up (at) totality. Carbondale : Southern Illinois University Press, c2000.
*TC PE1404 .D385 2000*

**REPORT WRITING - STUDY AND TEACHING - TECHNOLOGICAL INNOVATIONS.**
Transitions. Greenwich, Conn. : Ablex Pub. Corp., c1998.
*TC PE1404 .T74 1998*

**REPORT WRITING - STUDY AND TEACHING - UNITED STATES - HISTORY.**
History, reflection, and narrative. Stamford, Conn. : Ablex Pub., c1999.
*TC PE1405.U6 H56 1999*

**REPORT WRITING - UNITED STATES.**
Lane, Nancy D. Techniques for student research. New York : Neal-Schuman Publishers, 2000.
*TC Z710 .L36 2000*

**REPOSITORY LIBRARIES.** *See* **LIBRARIES, STORAGE.**

**Repp, Alan C.**
Functional analysis of problem behavior. Belmont, CA : Wadsworth Pub. Co., c1999.
*TC RC473.B43 F85 1999*

**REPRESENTATION, MENTAL.** *See* **MENTAL REPRESENTATION.**

**REPRESENTATION (PHILOSOPHY).**
Danto, Arthur Coleman, 1924- The body/body problem. Berkeley : University of California Press, c1999.
*TC B105.R4 D36 1999*

Kaufer, David S. Designing interactive worlds with words. Mahwah, N.J. : Lawrence Erlbaum Associates, 2000.
*TC PE1404 .K38 2000*

**REPRESENTATIONALISM (PHILOSOPHY).** *See* **REPRESENTATION (PHILOSOPHY).**

**REPRESENTATIONISM (PHILOSOPHY).** *See* **REPRESENTATION (PHILOSOPHY).**

**REPRESENTATIVE GOVERNMENT AND REPRESENTATION.** *See* **LEGISLATIVE BODIES.**

**REPRESENTATIVES IN CONGRESS (UNITED STATES).** *See* **LEGISLATORS - UNITED STATES.**

**Representing women.**
Nochlin, Linda. New York : Thames and Hudson, 1999.
*TC ND1460.W65 N63 1999*

**REPRESSION (PSYCHOLOGY).**
Billig, Michael. Freudian repression. New York : Cambridge University Press, 1999.
*TC BF175.5.R44 B55 1999*

**REPRINT EDITIONS.** *See* **REPRINTS (PUBLICATIONS).**

**Reprints from the Bulletin of the American Mathematical Society.**
Bulletin (new series) of the American Mathematical Society. Providence, R.I. : The Society, 1979-

**REPRINTS (PUBLICATIONS).** *See* **OUT-OF-PRINT BOOKS.**

**REPRINTS (PUBLICATIONS) - BIBLIOGRAPHY.**
Guide to reprints. Munich : K.G. Saur, 2000-
*TC Z1036 .G8*

**Reproducible activities for the classroom.**
Teaching government and citizenship using the Internet. Rev. ed. viii, 112 p. : ill. ; 28 cm.
*TC H61.95 .T43 2000*

**REPRODUCTION.** *See also* **HUMAN REPRODUCTION; PREGNANCY.**
Generations at risk. Cambridge, Mass. : MIT Press, c1999.
*TC RA1224.2 .G46 1999*

**REPRODUCTION, ASEXUAL.** *See* **CLONING.**

**REPRODUCTION (PSYCHOLOGY).** *See* **IMAGINATION; MEMORY.**

**REPRODUCTIVE TOXICOLOGY.**
Generations at risk. Cambridge, Mass. : MIT Press, c1999.
*TC RA1224.2 .G46 1999*

**REPTILES, FOSSIL.** *See* **DINOSAURS.**

**Requirements for certification.**
Requirements for certification of teachers, counselors, librarians, administrators for elementary and secondary schools. Chicago : University of Chicago Press, 1989-
*TC LB1171 .W6*

Woellner, Elizabeth H. Chicago : University of Chicago Press, 1935-
*TC LB1771 .W6*

**Requirements for certification of teachers, counselors, librarians, administrators for elementary and secondary schools.**
Woellner, Elizabeth H. Requirements for certification: Chicago : University of Chicago Press, 1935-
*TC LB1771 .W6*

**Requirements for certification of teachers, counselors, librarians, administrators for elementary and secondary schools.** Chicago : University of Chicago Press, 1989- v. ; 28 cm. Frequency: Annual. 54th ed. (1989-90)- . Requirements for certification. Continues: Requirements for certification : teachers, counselors, librarians, administrators for elementary schools, secondary schools, junior colleges ISSN: 1048-9371 (DLC)sn 89038314 (OCoLC)4698056. ISSN 1047-7071 DDC 371
1. Librarians - Certification - United States - Periodicals. 2. Teachers - Certification - United States - Periodicals. 3. Student counselors - Certification - United States - Periodicals. 4. School administrators - Certification - United States - Periodicals. I. Title: Requirements for certification II. Title: Requirements for certification : teachers, counselors, librarians, administrators for elementary schools, secondary schools, junior colleges
*TC LB1171 .W6*

**Requirements for certification : teachers, counselors, librarians, administrators for elementary schools, secondary schools, junior colleges.**
Requirements for certification of teachers, counselors, librarians, administrators for elementary and secondary schools. Chicago : University of Chicago Press, 1989-
*TC LB1171 .W6*

**Requirements for teaching certificates 1935-1938.**
Woellner, Elizabeth H. Requirements for certification: Chicago : University of Chicago Press, 1935-
*TC LB1771 .W6*

**Reschooling and the global future.**
Porter, James. Wallingford, U.K. : Symposium Books ; c1999.
*TC LB1029.G55 P67 1999*

**RESCUE OF JEWS, 1939-1945.** *See* **WORLD WAR, 1939-1945 - JEWS - RESCUE.**

**RESEARCH.** *See also* **EVALUATION; LEARNING AND SCHOLARSHIP; LEGAL RESEARCH.**
Bankhead, Elizabeth. Write it!. 2nd ed./MLA version. Englewood, Colo. : Libraries Unlimited, c1999.
*TC LB1047.3 .W75 1999*

Handbook of qualitative research. 2nd ed. Thousand Oaks, Calif. : Sage Publications, c2000.
*TC H62 .H2455 2000*

Quality of life from nursing and patient perspectives. Sudbury, Mass. ; London : Jones and Bartlett, c1998.
*TC RC262 .Q34 1998*

Reconciling empirical knowledge and clinical experience. 1st ed. Washington, DC : American Psychological Association, c1999.
*TC RC480 .R395 1999*

Whitson, Donna L. Accessing information in a technological age. Original ed. Malabar, Fla. : Krieger Pub. Co., 1997.
*TC ZA3075 .W48 1997*

**Research and advanced technology for digital libraries.**
ECDL '99 (3rd : 1999 : Paris, France) Berlin ; New York : Springer, c1999.
*TC ZA4080 .E28 1999*

**Research and scholarship in composition**
(4) Assessment of writing. New York : Modern Language Association of America, 1996.
*TC PE1404 .A88 1996*

**Research as social change.**
Schratz, Michael, 1952- London ; New York : Routledge, 1995.
*TC H62 .S33984 1995*

**RESEARCH - COMPUTER NETWORK RESOURCES.**
Henninger, Maureen, 1940- Don't just surf. 2nd ed. Sydney : UNSW Press, 1999.
*TC ZA4201 .H46 1999*

**RESEARCH - COMPUTER NETWORK RESOURCES - HANDBOOKS, MANUALS, ETC.**
Ruszkiewicz, John J., 1950- Bookmarks. New York ; Harlow, England : Longman, c2000.
*TC LB2369 .R88 2000*

**RESEARCH - DATA PROCESSING.**
Popping, Roel. Computer-assisted text analysis. Thousand Oaks, Calif. ; London : SAGE, c2000.
*TC P302 .P636 2000*

**RESEARCH DESIGN.**
Streubert, Helen J. Qualitative research in nursing. 2nd ed. Philadelphia : Lippincott, c1999.
*TC RT81.5 .S78 1999*

**Research Division report (National Endowment for the Arts. Research Division)**
(30.) A Practical guide to arts participation research. Washington, DC : National Endowment for the Arts, [1995]
*TC NX220 .P73 1995*

**RESEARCH ETHICS.** *See* **RESEARCH - MORAL AND ETHICAL ASPECTS.**

**RESEARCH - EUROPE.**
Geuna, Aldo, 1965- The economics of knowledge production. Cheltenham, UK ; Northampton, MA : E. Elgar, c1999.
*TC Q180.E9 G48 1999*

**RESEARCH - FINANCE.**
Analyzing costs in higher education. San Francisco, Calif. : Jossey-Bass Publishers, c2000.
*TC LB2342 .A68 2000*

**RESEARCH - HANDBOOKS, MANUALS, ETC.**
Ruszkiewicz, John J., 1950- Bookmarks. New York ; Harlow, England : Longman, c2000.
*TC LB2369 .R88 2000*

**Research in ethnic relations series**
Camara, Evandro de Morais, 1946- The cultural one or the racial many. Aldershot, Hants, England ; Brookfield, Vt., USA : Ashgate, c1997.
*TC HT1521 .C343 1997*

**RESEARCH IN HIGHER EDUCATION.** *See* **EDUCATION, HIGHER - RESEARCH.**

**Research in migration and ethnic relations series**
Comparative perspectives on racism. Aldershot, Hants, UK ; Burlington, VT, USA : Ashgate, c2000.
*TC GN269 .C646 2000*

Education and racism :. Aldershot ; Brookfield, Vt. : Ashgate, c1999.
*TC LC212.3.G7E48 1999*

Education and racism :. Aldershot ; Brookfield, Vt. : Ashgate, c1999.
*TC LC212.3.G7E48 1999*

**Research in science education in Europe** / edited by M. Bandiera ... [et al.]. Dordrecht : Boston, Mass. : Kluwer Academic Publishers, c1999. xii, 317 p. : ill. ; 25 cm. Includes bibliographical references and indexes. ISBN 0-7923-5699-3 (hardbound : alk. paper) DDC 507.1/04
*1. Science - Study and teaching - Research - Europe. I. Bandiera, M.*
*TC Q183.4.E85 R467 1999*

**RESEARCH, INDUSTRIAL.** *See* **INVENTIONS; TECHNOLOGICAL INNOVATIONS; TECHNOLOGY TRANSFER.**

**Research into classroom processes;** recent developments and next steps. Ian Westbury & Arno A. Bellack, editors. New York, Teachers College Press, 1971. x, 279 p. 24 cm. (Theory and research in teaching) Bibliography: p. 259-274. DDC 370/.78
*1. Education - Research - Addresses, essays, lectures. 2. Teaching - Addresses, essays, lectures. 3. Interaction analysis in education - Addresses, essays, lectures. I. Westbury, Ian, ed. II. Bellack, Arno A., ed. III. Series.*
*TC LB1028 .W488*

**RESEARCH, LEGAL.** *See* **LEGAL RESEARCH.**

**Research Libraries Group.**
Kenney, Anne R., 1950- Moving theory into practice. Mountain View, CA : Research Libraries Group, 2000.
*TC Z681.3.D53 K37*

**RESEARCH LIBRARIES - UNITED STATES - CONGRESSES.**
Technology and scholarly communication. Berkeley, Calif. : University of California Press ; [Pittsburgh?] : Published in association with the Andrew K. Mellon Foundation, c1999.
*TC Z479 .T43 1999*

**Research method in the postmodern.**
Scheurich, James Joseph, 1944- London ; Washington, DC : Falmer Press, 1997.
*TC LB1028 .S242 1997*

**RESEARCH - METHODOLOGY.**
Henninger, Maureen, 1940- Don't just surf. 2nd ed. Sydney : UNSW Press, 1999.
*TC ZA4201 .H46 1999*

Integrating quantitative and qualitative methods in research. Lanham, Md. ; Oxford : University Press of America, c2000.
*TC Q175 .I1513 2000*

Piantanida, Maria. The qualitative dissertation. Thousand Oaks, Calif. : Corwin Press, c1999.
*TC LB2369 .P48 1999*

**RESEARCH - METHODS.**
Handbook of research in pediatric and clinical child psychology. New York : Kluwer Academic/Plenum Publishers, c 2000.
*TC RJ499.3 .H367 2000*

**Research methods in applied settings.**
Gliner, Jeffrey A. Mahwah, N.J. : Lawrence Erlbaum, 2000.
*TC H62 .G523 2000*

**Research methods in education.**
Wiersma, William. 7th ed. Boston : Allyn and Bacon, c2000.
*TC LB1028 .W517 2000*

**Research monographs of the National Association for the Education of Young Children**
(v. 1) Quality in child care. Washington, D.C. : National Association for the Education of Young Children, c1987.
*TC HQ778.7.U6 Q35 1987*

**RESEARCH - MORAL AND ETHICAL ASPECTS - UNITED STATES.**
Davis, Michael, 1943- Ethics and the university. London ; New York : Routledge, 1999.
*TC LB2324 .D38 1999*

**RESEARCH - NETHERLANDS - PERIODICALS.**
Higher education and research in the Netherlands. The Hague, Netherlands Foundation for International Cooperation.

**Research on effective models for teacher education** / editors, D. John McIntyre, David M. Byrd. Thousand Oaks, Calif. : Corwin Press, Inc., c2000. xii, 256 p. : ill. ; 24 cm. (Teacher education yearbook ; 8) Includes bibliographical references. ISBN 0-7619-7615-9 ISBN 0-7619-7616-7 (pbk.)
*1. Teachers - Training of - Research. I. McIntyre, D. John. II. Byrd, David M. III. Series.*
*TC LB1715 .R42 2000*

**Research on men and masculinities series**
(11) Masculinities at school. Thousand Oaks, Calif. : SAGE, c2000.
*TC LC1390 .M37 2000*

**Research on professional development schools** / editors, David M. Byrd, D. John McIntyre. Thousand Oaks, Calif. : Corwin Press, c1999. xii, 276 p. ; 24 cm. (Teacher education yearbook ; 7) Includes bibliographical references and index. ISBN 0-8039-6829-9 ISBN 0-8039-6830-2 (pbk)
*1. Teachers - Training of - United States. 2. Educational change - United States. 3. Laboratory schools - United States. 4. College-school cooperation - United States. 5. Action research in education - United States. I. Byrd, David M. II. McIntyre, D. John. III. Association of Teacher Educators. IV. Series.*
*TC LB2154.A3 R478 1999*

**Research on schooling in Nigeria :** introductory readings / [edited by Babatunde Ipaye]. Ondo [Nigeria] : Centre for Research on Schooling, Adeyemi College of Education, 1995. iii, 251 p. ; 21 cm. Includes bibliographical references.
*1. Education, Elementary - Nigeria - Research. 2. Education, Secondary - Nigeria - Research. 3. Education - Nigeria. I. Ipaye, J. B. (J. Babatunde)*
*TC LB1028.25.N6 R477 1995*

**Research on socialization of young children in the Nordic countries :** an annotated and selected bibliography / edited by Berit Elgaard, Ole Langsted and Dion Sommer. Aarhus : Aarhus University Press, c1989. v, 160 p. : ill. ; 22 cm. Covers Denmark, Finland, Iceland, Norway and Sweden. Includes indexes. ISBN 87-7288-175-5 DDC 016.3033/2/0948
*1. Socialization - Bibliography. 2. Children - Scandinavia - Social conditions - Bibliography. 3. Child development - Scandinavia - Bibliography. I. Elgaard, Berit. II. Langsted, Ole. III. Sommer, Dion.*
*TC Z7164.S678 R47 1989*

**RESEARCH PAPER WRITING.** *See* **REPORT WRITING.**

**RESEARCH - POPULAR WORKS.**
The Horizons of health. Cambridge, Mass. : Harvard University Press, 1977.
*TC R850 .H67*

**RESEARCH - PSYCHOLOGICAL ASPECTS.**
Partnerships in research, clinical, and educational settings. Stamford, Conn. : Ablex Pub., c1999.
*TC HM1106 .P37 1999*

**RESEARCH - SOCIAL ASPECTS.**
Partnerships in research, clinical, and educational settings. Stamford, Conn. : Ablex Pub., c1999.
*TC HM1106 .P37 1999*

Perspectives on scholarly misconduct in the sciences. Columbus : Ohio State University Press, c1999.
*TC Q147 .P47 1999*

**Research strategies in the social sciences :** a guide to new approaches / edited by Elinor Scarbrough and Eric Tanenbaum. Oxford [England] ; New York : Oxford University Press, 1998. xiv, 316 p. : ill. ; 24 cm. Includes bibliographical references and indexes. ISBN 0-19-829238-4 (alk. paper) ISBN 0-19-829237-6 (pbk. : alk. paper) DDC 300/.7/2
*1. Social sciences - Research - Methodology. 2. Social sciences - Methodology. 3. Social sciences - Research - Data processing. I. Scarbrough, Elinor. II. Tanenbaum, Eric.*
*TC H62 .R4614 1998*

**RESEARCH - STUDY AND TEACHING.**
Handbook for teaching statistics and research methods. 2nd ed. Mahwah, N.J. : Lawrence Erlbaum Associates, c1999.
*TC QA276.18 .H36 1999*

Small, Ruth V. Turning kids on to research. Englewood, Colo. : Libraries Unlimited, 2000.
*TC LB1065 .S57 2000*

**RESEARCH TEAMS.** *See* **RESEARCH.**

**RESEARCH - UNITED STATES.**
Transforming social inquiry, transforming social action. Boston ; London : Kluwer Academic, c2000.
*TC LC238 .T73 2000*

What is institutional research all about ? San Francisco, Calif. : Jossey-Bass Publishers, c1999.
*TC LB2326.3 .W43 1999*

**RESEARCH - UNITED STATES - TECHNOLOGICAL INNOVATIONS.**
How technology is changing institutional research. San Francisco, Calif. : Jossey-Bass Publishers, c1999.
*TC LB2326.3 .H69 1999*

**Research with children :** perspectives and practices / edited by Pia Christensen and Allison James. New York : Falmer Press, 2000. xii, 272 p. ; 24 cm. Includes bibliographical references and index. ISBN 0-7507-0975-8 (hb : alk. paper) ISBN 0-7507-0974-X (pb : alk. paper) DDC 305.23/072
*1. Children - Research - Methodology. 2. Child development - Research. 3. Adolescent psychology - Research. I. Christensen, Pia Monrad. II. James, Allison.*
*TC HQ767.85 .R48 1999*

**Researching children's perspectives.**
Lewis, Ann, 1950- Buckingham ; Philadelphia : Open University Press, 2000.
*TC HQ767.85 .L49 2000*

**Researching health promotion** / edited by Jonathan Watson and Stephen Platt. London ; New York : Routledge, 2000. xiii, 279 p. : ill. ; 23 cm. Includes bibliographical references and index. ISBN 0-415-21590-0 (hbk.) ISBN 0-415-21591-9 (pbk.) DDC 613/.072
*1. Health promotion - Research. I. Watson, Jonathan, 1960- II. Platt, Stephen.*
*TC RA427.8 .R47 2000*

**Researching language in schools and communities :** functional linguistic perspectives / edited by Len Unsworth. London ; Washington [D.C.] : Cassell, 2000. ix, 311 p. : ill., map ; 25 cm. (Open linguistics series) Includes bibliographical references and index. ISBN 0-304-70244-7 (hardback) ISBN 0-304-70245-5 (paperback) DDC 410/.1/8
*1. Linguistics - Research. 2. Functionalism (Linguistics) I. Unsworth, Len. II. Series: Open linguistics series.*
*TC P53 .R463 2000*

**Researching school experience :** ethnographic studies of teaching and learning / edited by Martyn Hammersley ; contributors, Jennifer Nias ... [et al.]. London ; New York : Falmer Press, 1999. vi, 223 p. ; 25 cm. Includes bibliographical references (p. [204]-214) and index. ISBN 0-7507-0915-4 (hbk.) ISBN 0-7507-0914-6 (pbk.) DDC 306.43/2
*1. Teaching - Social aspects. 2. Teachers - Social conditions. 3. Learning. 4. Educational sociology. 5. Ethnology. I. Hammersley, Martyn. II. Nias, Jennifer.*
*TC LB1027 .R453 1999*

**RESEMBLANCE (PHILOSOPHY).** *See* **IDENTITY.**

**The reshaping of psychoanalysis**
(vol. 10) Brink, Andrew. The creative matrix. New York : Peter Lang, c2000.
*TC BF698.9.C74 B75 2000*

**RESIDENCES.** *See* **ARCHITECTURE, DOMESTIC; DWELLINGS; HOUSING.**

**RESIDENTIAL BUILDINGS.** *See* **DWELLINGS.**

**Residential education as an option for at-risk youth** / Jerome Beker, Douglas Magnuson, editors. New York : Haworth Press, c1996. xv, 133 p. ; 22 cm. Also published as: Residential treatment for children & youth, v. 13, no. 3, 1996. Includes bibliographical references and index. ISBN 1-56024-818-1 (alk. paper) DDC 362.7/4
*1. Problem children - Institutional care. 2. Problem youth - Institutional care. I. Beker, Jerome. II. Magnuson, Douglas. III. Title: Residential treatment for children & youth. Vol. 13, no. 4.*
*TC HV862 .R473 1996*

**Residential treatment for children & youth. Vol. 13, no. 4.**
Residential education as an option for at-risk youth. New York : Haworth Press, c1996.
*TC HV862 .R473 1996*

**RESIDENTS OF NURSING HOMES.** *See* **NURSING HOME PATIENTS.**

**Resilience across contexts :** family, work, culture, and community / edited by Ronald D. Taylor and Margaret C. Wang. Mahwah, NJ : Lawrence Erlbaun, 2000. xiii, 386 p. ; 23 cm. Includes bibliographical references and indexes. ISBN 0-8058-3347-1 (alk. paper) DDC 306.85/0973
*1. Family - United States. I. Wang, Margaret C. II. Taylor, Ronald D., 1958-*
*TC HQ535 .R47 2000*

**RESILIENCE (PERSONALITY TRAIT).**
Stress, coping, and health in families. Thousand Oaks, Calif. : Sage Publications, c1998.

**TC RC455.4.F3 S79 1998**
Walsh, Froma. Strengthening family resilience. New York : Guilford Press, c1998.
**TC RC489.F33 W34 1998**

**Resiliency in families series (Thousand Oaks, Calif.)**
(v. 1.) Stress, coping, and health in families. Thousand Oaks, Calif. : Sage Publications, c1998.
**TC RC455.4.F3 S79 1998**

**RESILIENCY (PERSONALITY TRAIT).** *See* **RESILIENCE (PERSONALITY TRAIT).**

**Resilient adaptation of church-affiliated young Haitian immigrants.**
Chrispin, Marie C. 1998.
**TC 06 no. 11015**

**Resilient children.**
Barone, Diane M. Newark, Del. : International Reading Association ; Chicago : National Reading Conference, c1999.
**TC LC4806.4 .B37 1999**

**Resistance to multiculturalism.**
Mio, Jeffrey Scott. Philadelphia, PA : Brunner/Mazel, c2000.
**TC HM1271 .M56 2000**

**Resisting gender.**
Unger, Rhoda Kesler. London ; Thousand Oaks, Calif. : Sage Publications, 1998.
**TC BF201.4 .U544 1998**

**Resisting linguistic imperialism in English teaching.**
Canagarajah, A. Suresh. Oxford : Oxford University Press, 1999.
**TC PE1068.S7 C36 1999**

**Resnick-West, Susan M., 1951-.**
Mohrman, Allan M. Designing performance appraisal systems. 1st ed. San Francisco : Jossey-Bass Publishers, 1989.
**TC HF5549.5.P35 M64 1989**

**Resolving childhood trauma.**
Cameron, Catherine. Thousand Oaks, Calif. : Sage Publications, c2000.
**TC RC569.5.A28 C35 2000**

**Resolving conflict.**
Tillett, Gregory, Ph. D. 2nd ed. Oxford ; New York : Oxford University Press, 1999.
**TC HM132 .T55 1999**

**RESORT ARCHITECTURE - WHITE MOUNTAINS (N.H. AND ME.) - HISTORY.**
Tolles, Bryant Franklin, 1939- The grand resort hotels of the White Mountains. 1st ed. Boston : D.R. Godine, 1995.
**TC TX909 .T58 1995**

**Resource allocation.**
Norton, M. Scott. Larchmont, N.Y. : Eye on Education, c1997.
**TC LB2805 .N73 1997**

**RESOURCE ALLOCATION.**
Where does the money go? Thousand Oaks, Calif. : Corwin Press, c1996.
**TC LB2825 .W415 1996**

**Resource books for teachers**
The Internet. Oxford ; New York : Oxford University Press, c2000.
**TC TK5105.875.I57 I57 2000**

Phillips, Diane. Projects with young learners. Oxford ; New York : Oxford University Press, c1999.
**TC LB1576 .P577 1999**

Phillips, Sarah. Drama with children. Oxford ; New York : Oxford University Press, c1999.
**TC PN3171 .P45 1999**

**Resource development handbook : untapped public funding for the arts** / compiled and edited by Dian Magie. [Washington, D.C.] : National Assembly of Local Arts Agencies, Institute for Community Development and the Arts, 1995. 148 p. : ill. ; 28 cm. CONTENTS: 1. Summer and after-school youth arts programs -- 2. Innovative local and state puclic funding for the arts -- 3. Arts programs that address social issues -- 4. Cultural tourism and economic impact -- 5. Arts technology.
*1. Art commissions - United States - Directories. 2. Community art projects - United States - Directories. 3. Art in education - United States. I. Magie, Dian. II. National Assembly for Local Arts Agencies. III. Institute for Community Development and the Arts. IV. Title: Untapped public funding for the arts V. Title: Public funding for the arts*
**TC NX110 .R47 1995**

**A resource guide for secondary school teaching.**
Kim, Eugene C. 5th ed. New York : Macmillan Pub. Co., c1991.

**TC LB1737.A3 K56 1991 5th ed.**

**Resource materials for teachers**
Ayers, Harry. Perspectives on behaviour. 2nd ed. London : David Fulton, 2000.
**TC LC4801 .A94 2000**

Hill, Fran, 1950- Teamwork in the management of emotional and behavioural difficulties. London : David Fulton, 2000.
**TC LC4803.G7 H54 2000**

**Resource Pathways guidebook**
Infants & toddlers. 2nd ed. Seattle, Wash. : Resourse Pathways, 1999.
**TC HQ755.8 .I54 1999**

**Resources for nursing research.**
Clamp, Cynthia G. L. 3rd ed. London ; Thousand Oaks, Calif. : Sage, 1999.
**TC Z6675.N7 C53 1999**

**Resources in education.**
[ERIC (SilverPlatter International : Online)] The ERIC database [computer file]. WebSPIRS version 3.1. [Norwood, MA] : SilverPlatter International,
**TC NETWORKED RESOURCES**

**Resources in Education.**
Resources in education. Semiannual index. Phoenix, AZ : Oryx Press,
**TC Z5813 .R42**

**RESOURCES IN EDUCATION - INDEXES.**
Resources in education. Semiannual index. Phoenix, AZ : Oryx Press,
**TC Z5813 .R42**

**Resources in education.** Semiannual index : RIE. Phoenix, AZ : Oryx Press, v. ; 28 cm. Frequency: Semiannual. RIE. Description based on: Vol. 31 (Jan.-June 1996). Description based on Vol. 31 (Jan.-June 1996). Cumulative index to: Resources in education. Continues the semiannual index published by the Dept. of Education, Office of Educational Research and Improvement. Resources in Education ISSN: 0098-0897 (DLC) 75644211. ISSN 1082-8915 DDC 016
*1. Education - Research - Bibliography - Periodicals. 2. Education - Bibliography - Periodicals. 3. Resources in education - Indexes. I. Title: RIE II. Title: Resources in Education*
**TC Z5813 .R42**

**RESPECT FOR PERSONS.** *See* **SELF-ESTEEM.**

**RESPECT - STUDY AND TEACHING - UNITED STATES.**
Annual State of American Education Address (7th : February 22, 2000 : Durham, N.C.) The seventh annual state of American education address [videorecording. [Washington, D.C. : U.S. Dept. of Education], 2000.

**RESPIRATION, ARTIFICIAL.**
Tracheostomy and ventilator dependency. New York : Thieme, 2000.
**TC RF517 .T734 2000**

**RESPIRATORS.** *See* **RESPIRATORS (MEDICAL EQUIPMENT).**

**RESPIRATORS (MEDICAL EQUIPMENT).**
Tracheostomy and ventilator dependency. New York : Thieme, 2000.
**TC RF517 .T734 2000**

**RESPIRATORY ORGANS.** *See* **LARYNX.**

**RESPIRATORY THERAPY - EQUIPMENT AND SUPPLIES.** *See* **RESPIRATORS (MEDICAL EQUIPMENT).**

**The response of higher education institutions to regional needs.** Paris : Organisation for Economic Co-operation and Development, 1999. 149 p. : ill. ; 23 cm. At head of title: Programme on Institutional Management in Higher Education. Published in French under the title: Les établissements d'enseignement supérieur face aux besoins régionaux. Includes bibliographical references (p. 147-149). ISBN 92-64-17143-6 (pbk.)
*1. Community and college - Case studies. 2. Community development - Case studies. 3. Economic development - Effect of education on - Case studies. 4. Education, Higher - Economic aspects - Case studies. I. Programme on Institutional Management in Higher Education.*
**TC LC237 .R47 1999**

**RESPONSIBILITY.** *See also* **EDUCATIONAL ACCOUNTABILITY.**
Sabini, John, 1947- Emotion, character, and responsibility. New York : Oxford University Press, 1998.

**TC BF531 .S23 1998**

**RESPONSIBILITY - STUDY AND TEACHING - UNITED STATES.**
Annual State of American Education Address (7th : February 22, 2000 : Durham, N.C.) The seventh annual state of American education address [videorecording. [Washington, D.C. : U.S. Dept. of Education], 2000.

**REST.** *See* **FATIGUE.**

**RESTAURANTS.** *See* **COFFEE SHOPS; DINERS (RESTAURANTS).**

**RESTORATION OF BOOKS.** *See* **BOOKS - CONSERVATION AND RESTORATION.**

**RESTRICTED LANGUAGE.** *See* **SUBLANGUAGE.**

**Restructuring education : innovations and evaluations of alternative systems** / edited by Simon Hakim, Daniel J. Ryan, and Judith C. Stull ; foreword by Lamar Alexander. Westport, Conn. : Praeger, 2000. xi, 270 p. ; 24 cm. (Privatizing government, 1087-5603) Includes bibliographical references and index. ISBN 0-275-95176-6 (alk. paper) DDC 379.1/11
*1. School improvement programs - United States. 2. Educational innovations - United States. 3. School choice - United States. I. Hakim, Simon. II. Ryan, Daniel J., 1956- III. Stull, Judith C., 1944- IV. Series.*
**TC LB2822.82 . R45 2000**

**Results-based leadership.**
Ulrich, David, 1953- Boston : Harvard Business School Press, 1999.
**TC HD57.7 .U45 1999**

**RETAIL STORES.** *See* **STORES, RETAIL.**

**RETAIL TRADE.** *See* **STORES, RETAIL.**

**RETAIL TRADE - UNITED STATES.**
Employee training and U.S. competitiveness. Boulder : Westview Press, 1991.
**TC HF5549.5.T7 E46 1991**

**RETAILING.** *See* **RETAIL TRADE.**

**Retallick, John, 1945-.**
Learning communities in education. London ; New York : Routledge, 1999.
**TC LB14.7 .L43 1999**

**Retamal, Gonzalo.**
Education as a humanitarian response. London ; Herndon, VA : Cassell ; [s.l.] : UNESCO International Bureau of Education, 1998.
**TC LC3719 .E37 1998**

**RETARDATION, MENTAL.** *See* **MENTAL RETARDATION.**

**RETARDED CHILDREN.** *See* **MENTALLY HANDICAPPED CHILDREN.**

**Retarded isn't stupid, mom!.**
Kaufman, Sandra Z., 1928- Rev. ed. Baltimore : P.H. Brookes Pub., 1999.
**TC HV894 .K383 1999**

**RETARDED PERSONS.** *See* **MENTALLY HANDICAPPED.**

**Retelling stories, framing culture.**
Stephens, John, 1944- New York : Garland Pub., 1998.
**TC PN1009.A1 S83 1998**

**RETENTION (PSYCHOLOGY).** *See* **MEMORY.**

**Retherford, Kristine S., 1950-** Guide to analysis of language transcripts / Kristine S. Retherford. 2nd ed. Eau Claire, WI : Thinking Publications, 1993. xi, 283 p. : ill. ; 28 cm. Previous ed. entered under: Stickler, Kristine Retherford. Includes bibliographical references (p. 277-282). ISBN 0-930599-87-X DDC 401/.9
*1. Children - Language - Evaluation. I. Title.*
**TC RJ496.L35 S84 1993**

**Rethinking childhood**
(vol. 11) Lopez, Marianne Exum, 1960- When discourses collide. New York : P. Lang, c1999.
**TC HQ792.U5 L665 1999**

(vol. 4) Landscapes in early childhood education. New York : P. Lang, 2000.
**TC LB1139.23 .L26 2000**

(vol. 5) Schmidt, Patricia Ruggiano, 1944- Cultural conflict and struggle. New York : P. Lang, c1998.
**TC LB1181 .S36 1998**

**Rethinking higher education.**
Lange, Thomas, 1967- London : IEA Education and Training Unit, 1998.

*TC LB2342.2.G7 L364 1998*

**Rethinking how art is taught.**
Walling, Donovan R., 1948- Thousand Oaks, Calif. :
Corwin Press, c2000.
*TC N85 .W35 2000*

**Rethinking language and gender research :** theory
and practice / edited by Victoria L. Bergvall, Janet M.
Bing, Alice F. Freed. London ; New York : Longman,
1996. xi, 303 p. ; 23 cm. (Real language series) Selected rev.
papers, with one additional paper, of a conference held during
the 1993 Linguistic Institute in Columbus, Ohio, July 16-19,
1993; the conference was sponsored by the Committee on the
Status of Women in Linguistics of the Linguistic Society of
America. Includes bibliographical references and index. ISBN
0-582-26574-6 (cased) ISBN 0-582-26573-8 (paper) DDC
306.4/4
*1. Language and languages - Sex differences - Congresses. I.
Bergvall, Victoria L. (Victoria Lee), 1956- II. Bing, Janet
Mueller, 1937- III. Freed. Alice F., 1946- IV. Series.*
*TC P120.S48 R48 1996*

**Rethinking pastoral care** / edited by Úna M. Collins
and Jean McNiff. London ; New York : Routledge,
1999. xv, 217 p. ; 24 cm. Includes bibliographical references
(p. 209-214) and index. ISBN 0-415-19441-5 (hbk. : alk.
paper) ISBN 0-415-19442-3 (pbk. : alk. paper) DDC 373.14/
046/09417
*1. Counseling in secondary education - Ireland - Case studies.
2. Teacher-student relationships - Ireland - Case studies. 3.
Tutors and tutoring - Ireland - Case studies. 4. Action research
in education - Ireland - Case studies. I. Collins, Úna M. II.
McNiff, Jean.*
*TC LB1620.53.I73 R48 1999*

**Rethinking student conduct in higher education.**
Dannells, Michael. From discipline to development.
Washington, DC : George Washington University,
Graduate School of Education and Human
Development, [1997]
*TC LB2344 .D36 1997*

**Rethinking the brain.**
Shore, Rima. New York : Families and Work
Institute, c1997.
*TC RJ486.5 .S475 1997*

**Rethinking theory**
Justman, Stewart. The psychological mystique.
Evanston, Ill. : Northwestern University Press, 1998.
*TC BF38 .J87 1998*

**Reticker, Gini.**
New school order [videorecording]. New York : First
Run/Icarus Films, 1996.
*TC LB2831.583.P4 N4 1996*

**RETIRED MILITARY PERSONNEL.** *See*
VETERANS.

**RETIREMENT COMMUNITIES.** *See* LIFE CARE
COMMUNITIES.

**RETRIBUTION.** *See* REVENGE.

**RETRIEVAL OF INFORMATION.** *See*
INFORMATION RETRIEVAL.

**Retrofuture.**
Kelly, Gerard, 1959- Downers Grove, Ill. :
InterVarsity Press, c1999.
*TC HN17.5 .K439 1999*

**Rettig, Michael D., 1950-** Scheduling strategies for
middle schools / by Michael D. Rettig and Robert
Lynn Canady. Larchmont, NY : Eye On Education,
2000. xviii, 262 p. : ill. ; 26 cm. Includes bibliographical
references. ISBN 1-88300-167-6 DDC 373.12/42
*1. Block scheduling (Education) - United States. 2. Middle
schools - United States. I. Canady, Robert Lynn. II. Title.*
*TC LB3032.2 .R48 2000*

**The return of the god of wealth.**
Ikels, Charlotte. Stanford, Calif. : Stanford University
Press, c1996.
*TC HC428.C34 I38 1996*

**RETURNED STUDENTS - UNITED STATES.**
Hess, J. Daniel (John Daniel), 1937- Studying
abroad/learning abroad. Yarmouth, Me., USA :
Intercultural Press, c1997.
*TC LB2375 .H467 1997*

**Returning from the brink of suicide [videorecording].**
The Choice of a lifetime [videorecording]. Hohokus,
NJ : New Day Films, c1996.
*TC RC569 .C45 1996*

**Returning to study.**
Powell, Stuart, 1949- Buckingham ; Philadelphia :
Open University Press, c1999.
*TC LC5256.G7 P66 1999*

**Reunion.**
Fishel, Elizabeth. 1st ed. New York : Random House,
c2000.
*TC LD7501.N494 F575 2000*

**REUNIONS.** *See* CLASS REUNIONS.

**REUNIONS, CLASS.** *See* CLASS REUNIONS.

**Reutzel, D. Ray (Douglas Ray), 1953-** Balanced
reading strategies and practices : assessing and
assisting readers with special needs / D. Ray Reutzel,
Robert B. Cooter, Jr. Upper Saddle river, N.J. :
Merrill, c1999. xiii, 418 p. : ill. ; 24 cm. Includes
bibliographical references and indexes. ISBN 0-02-324715-0
DDC 372.43
*1. Reading. 2. Reading - Remedial teaching. 3. Child
development. I. Cooter. Robert B. II. Title.*
*TC LB1050 .R477 1999*

**REVENGE - FICTION.**
Moeyaert, Bart. [Blote handen. English] Bare hands.
1st ed. Asheville, N.C. : Front Street, 1998.
*TC PZ7.M7227 Bar 1998*

**REVERSE DISCRIMINATION - UNITED
STATES.**
Affirmative action. San Diego, Calif. : Greenhaven
Press, 2000.
*TC JC599.U5 A34685 2000*

**Review and appraisal of the progress made in
achieving the goals and objectives of the
Programme of Action of the International
Conference on Population and Development :** 1999
report / Department of Economic and Social Affairs,
Population Division. New York : United Nations,
1999. viii, 100 p. : ill. ; 28 cm. "ST/ESA/SER.A/182."
"United Nations publication, Sales No. E.99.XIII.16"--T.p.
verso. Includes bibliographical references. ISBN 92-1-
151339-1
*1. Population. 2. Population policy. 3. Emigration and
immigration. 4. Women - Health and hygiene. 5. International
Conference on Population and Development - (1994 : - Cairo,
Egypt) I. United Nations. Dept. of Economic and Social
Affairs. Population Division.*
*TC HB849 .R48 1999*

**REVIEW LITERATURE.**
Practitioner's guide to evaluating change with
neuropsychological assessment instruments. New
York : Kluwer Academic/Plenum Publishers, c2000.
*TC RC386.6.N48 P73 2000*

**Review of higher education.**
[Review of higher education (Online)] The review of
higher education [computer file]. Baltimore, Md. :
Johns Hopkins University Press, c1996-
*TC EJOURNALS*

**[Review of higher education (Online)]** The review of
higher education [computer file]. Baltimore, Md. :
Johns Hopkins University Press, c1996- Frequency:
Quarterly. 20.1 (fall 1996)- . Title from title screen. Hypertext
(electronic journal), with links to text and non-text files. Also
available in a print ed. System requirements: World Wide Web
browser software. Mode of access: Internet via World Wide
Web. Issued by: Association for the Study of Higher
Education; digitized and made available by: Project Muse.
URL: http://muse.jhu.edu/journals/
review%5Fof%5Fhigher%5Feducation/ Available in other
form: Review of higher education ISSN: 0162-5748
(DLC) 81642863 (OCoLC)4179660. ISSN 1090-7009 DDC
378
*1. Education, Higher - United States - Periodicals. I.
Association for the Study of Higher Education. II. Project
Muse. III. Title: Review of higher education*
*TC EJOURNALS*

**REVIEWS.** *See* BOOKS - REVIEWS.

**Reviews in American history.**
[Reviews in American history (Online)] Reviews in
American history [computer file]. Baltimore, MD :
Johns Hopkins University Press, c1995-
*TC EJOURNALS*

**[Reviews in American history (Online)]** Reviews in
American history [computer file]. Baltimore, MD :
Johns Hopkins University Press, c1995- Frequency:
Quarterly. 23.1 (Mar. 1995)- . Title from title screen. Text
(electronic journal) Also available in a print ed. Mode of
access: Internet via World Wide Web. Digitized and made
available by: Project Muse. URL: http://muse.jhu.edu/
journals/reviews%5Fin%5Famerican%5Fhistory/ Available in
other form: Reviews in American history ISSN: 0048-7511
(DLC) 72013938 (OCoLC)1783629. ISSN 1080-6628 DDC
973
*1. United States - History - Book reviews - Periodicals. I.
Project Muse. II. Title: Reviews in American history*
*TC EJOURNALS*

**REVIEWS, LAW.** *See* LAW REVIEWS.

**Reviews (New York, N.Y.) <1995->.**
[Lancet (North American ed.)] The lancet. North
American ed. Boston : Little, Brown and Co., c1966-

**The revised NEO Personality Inventory.**
Piedmont, Ralph L., 1958- New York : Plenum Press,
c1998.
*TC BF698.8.N46 P54 1998*

**Revisioning composition textbooks.**
(Re)visioning composition textbooks. Albany : State
University of New York Press, c1999.
*TC PE1404 .R46 1999*

**Revisiting a progressive pedagogy :** the
developmental-interaction approach / edited by Nancy
Nager and Edna K. Shapiro. Albany : State University
of New York Press, c2000. ix, 313 p. : ill. ; 24 cm. (SUNY
series, early childhood education) Includes bibliographical
references and index. ISBN 0-7914-4467-8 (alk. paper) ISBN
0-7914-4468-6 (pbk. : alk. paper) DDC 372.21
*1. Child development. 2. Progressive education. 3. Social
sciences - Study and teaching (Early childhood education) 4.
Early childhood teachers. 5. Early childhood teachers -
Training of. 6. Home and school. I. Nager, Nancy, 1951- II.
Shapiro. Edna Kaufman, 1925- III. Series.*
*TC LB1117 .R44 2000*

**REVIVAL MOVEMENTS (ART).** *See*
NEOCLASSICISM (ART); ROMANESQUE
REVIVAL (ARCHITECTURE).

**REVOLUTION, AMERICAN.** *See* UNITED
STATES - HISTORY - REVOLUTION, 1775-
1783.

**Revolution of forms.**
Loomis, John A., 1951- New York : Princeton
Architectural Press, c1999.
*TC NA6602.A76 L66 1999*

**Revolution [videorecording].**
Africans in America [videorecording]. [Boston,
Mass.] : WGBH Educational Foundation ; South
Burlington, VT : WGBH Boston Video [distributor],
c1998.
*TC E441 .A47 1998*

**REVOLUTIONARY WAR, AMERICAN.** *See*
UNITED STATES - HISTORY -
REVOLUTION, 1775-1783.

**Revolutionizing the family.**
Diamant, Neil Jeffrey, 1964- Berkeley : University of
California Press, c2000.
*TC HQ684 .D53 2000*

**REVOLUTIONS.** *See* COUPS D'ÉTAT;
INSURGENCY; PEASANT UPRISINGS.

**REVOLUTIONS AND SOCIALISM.**
James, C. L. R. (Cyril Lionel Robert), 1901- Marxism
for our times. Jackson, Miss: University Press of
Mississippi, c1999.
*TC HX44 .J25 1999*

**Revolutions of the heart.**
Langford, Wendy, 1960- London ; New York :
Routledge, 1999.
*TC BF575.L8 L266 1999*

**Revue internationale de pédagogie.**
Internationale Zeitschrift für
Erziehungswissenschaft = Köln : J.P. Bachem,

**Revue universitaire de Liège.**
Association des amis de l'Université de Liège.
Bulletin trimestriel. Liège.

**REWARD (PSYCHOLOGY).** *See also* REWARD
(PSYCHOLOGY) IN CHILDREN.
Kohn, Alfie. Punished by rewards. Boston : Houghton
Mifflin Co., 1999, c1993.
*TC BF505.R48 K65 1999*

**REWARD (PSYCHOLOGY) IN CHILDREN -
UNITED STATES - HISTORY.**
Fenn, Patricia. Rewards of merit. [Schoharie, N.Y.] :
Ephemera Society of America ; Charlottesville [Va.] :
Distributed by Howell Press, Inc., c1994.
*TC LA230 .F46 1994*

**REWARDS AND PUNISHMENTS IN
EDUCATION - ADDRESSES, ESSAYS,
LECTURES.**
Punishment and aversive stimulation in special
education. Reston, Va. : Council for Exceptional
Children, 1982.
*TC LC4169 .P8 1982*

**REWARDS AND PUNISHMENTS IN
EDUCATION - UNITED STATES.**
Cangelosi, James S. Classroom management

strategies. 3rd ed. White Plains, N.Y. : Longman, c1997.
*TC LB3013 .C3259 1997*

Cangelosi, James S. Classroom management strategies. 4th ed. New York : J. Wiley, c2000.
*TC LB3013 .C3259 2000*

**Rewards of merit.**
Fenn, Patricia. [Schoharie, N.Y.] : Ephemera Society of America ; Charlottesville [Va.] : Distributed by Howell Press, Inc., c1994.
*TC LA230 .F46 1994*

**Rewolucja.**
Blobaum, Robert. Ithaca : Cornell University Press, 1995.
*TC DK4385 .B57 1995*

**Reynolds, Arthur J.** Success in early intervention : the Chicago child parent centers / by Arthur J. Reynolds ; foreword by Edward Zigler. Lincoln, Neb. : University of Nebraska Press, c2000. xxviii, 261 p. : ill. ; 23 cm. (Child, youth, and family services.) Includes bibliographical references (p. 237-250) and indexes. ISBN 0-8032-3936-X (cloth : alk. paper) DDC 362.7/086/940977311
*1. Child-Parent Center Program (Chicago, Ill.) 2. Socially handicapped children - Services for - Illinois - Chicago. 3. Socially handicapped children - Education (Early childhood) - Illinois - Chicago. 4. Socially handicapped children - Illinois - Chicago - Longitudinal studies. 5. Early childhood education - Illinois - Chicago. 6. Early childhood education - Parent participation - Illinois - Chicago. I. Title. II. Series.*
*TC HV743.C5 R48 2000*

**Reynolds, Barbara G.** Reform and education : an exploration of the influence of Deng Xiaoping's ideas on current primary education policy, curricula and textbooks in China / by Barbara Gwyneth Reynolds. 1999. v, 215 leaves ; 29 cm. Issued also on microfilm. Thesis (Ed.D.)--Teachers College, Columbia University, 1999. Includes bibliographical references (leaves 180-185).
*1. Deng, Xiaoping, - 1904- 2. Educators - China - Biography. 3. Education - China - History - 20th century. 4. Education, Elementary - China - Aims and objections - Curricula. 5. Social sciences - China - Textbooks. 6. Education - China - Philosophy - History - 20th century. 7. Educational change - China - 20th century. 8. Politics and education - China - History - 20th century. I. Title. II. Title: Influence of Deng Xiaoping's ideas on current primary education policy, curricula and textbooks in China*
*TC 06 no. 11166*

**Reynolds, Cecil R., 1952-.**
Encyclopedia of special education. 2nd ed. New York : J. Wiley & Sons, c2000.
*TC LC4007 .E53 2000*

**Reynolds, David, 1949-.**
The international handbook of school effectiveness research. London ; New York : Falmer Press, 2000.
*TC LB2822.75 .I59 2000*

**Reynolds, David R.** There goes the neighborhood : rural school consolidation at the grass roots in early twentieth-century Iowa / by David R. Reynolds. Iowa City : University of Iowa Press, 1999. xii, 306 p. : ill., maps ; 25 cm. Includes bibliographical references (p. 289-298) and index. ISBN 0-87745-693-3 (cloth : alk. paper) DDC 379.1/535
*1. Schools - Centralization - Iowa - History - 20th century. 2. Rural schools - Iowa - History - 20th century. I. Title.*
*TC LB2861 .R49 1999*

**Reynolds, Janice.**
Hand in hand [videorecording]. New York, N.Y. : AFB Press, c1995.
*TC HV1597.2 .H3 1995*

Making the most of early communication [videorecording]. New York, NY : Distributed by AFB Press, c1997.
*TC HV1597.2 .M3 1997*

**Reynolds, John S., 1931-.**
Achilles, Charles M. Problem analysis. Larchmont, NY : Eye on Education, c1997.
*TC LB2806 .A25 1997*

**RHETORIC.** *See also* **CRITICISM; EXPRESSION; NARRATION (RHETORIC).**
Inventing a discipline. Urbana, Ill. : National Council of Teachers of English, c2000.
*TC PN175 .I58 2000*

A Rhetoric of doing. Carbondale : Southern Illinois University Press, c1992.
*TC PE1404 .R496 1992*

**RHETORIC - DATA PROCESSING.**
Welch, Kathleen E. Electric rhetoric. Cambridge, Mass. : MIT Press, c1999.
*TC P301.5.D37 W45 1999*

**Rhetoric, knowledge, and society**
Worlds apart. Mahwah, N.J. : L. Erlbaum Associates, 1999.
*TC PE1404 .W665 1999*

**RHETORIC - MORAL AND ETHICAL ASPECTS.**
Ethical issues in college writing. New York ; Canterbury [England] : Peter Lang, c1999.
*TC PE1404 .E84 1999*

**A Rhetoric of doing :** essays on written discourse in honor of James L. Kinneavy / edited by Stephen P. Witte, Neil Nakadate, Roger D. Cherry. Carbondale : Southern Illinois University Press, c1992. vi, 376 p. ; 26 cm. Includes bibliographical references. ISBN 0-8093-1531-9 (cloth) ISBN 0-8093-1532-7 (pbk.) DDC 808
*1. English language - Rhetoric - Study and teaching. 2. Report writing - Study and teaching. 3. Written communication. 4. Discourse analysis. 5. Rhetoric. I. Kinneavy, James L., 1920- II. Witte, Stephen P. (Stephen Paul), 1943- III. Nakadate, Neil. IV. Cherry, Roger Dennis.*
*TC PE1404 .R496 1992*

**RHETORIC - POLITICAL ASPECTS.**
Race, rhetoric, and the postcolonial. Albany : State University of New York Press, c1999.
*TC P301.5.P67 R33 1999*

**RHETORIC - STUDY AND TEACHING.** *See* **WRITING CENTERS.**

**RHETORIC - STUDY AND TEACHING - AUDIO-VISUAL AIDS.**
Welch, Kathleen E. Electric rhetoric. Cambridge, Mass. : MIT Press, c1999.
*TC P301.5.D37 W45 1999*

**Rhetorical philosophy and theory**
Davis, D. Diane (Debra Diane), 1963- Breaking up (at) totality. Carbondale : Southern Illinois University Press, c2000.
*TC PE1404 .D385 2000*

**RHINOCERI.** *See* **RHINOCEROSES.**

**RHINOCEROS.** *See* **RHINOCEROSES.**

**RHINOCEROS FAMILY.** *See* **RHINOCEROSES.**

**RHINOCEROSES - FICTION.**
O'Malley, Kevin, 1961- Bud. New York : Walker, 2000.
*TC PZ7 .O526 Bu 2000*

**RHINOCEROTIDAE.** *See* **RHINOCEROSES.**

**RHINOS.** *See* **RHINOCEROSES.**

**Rhoades, Gary.** Managed professionals : unionized faculty and restructuring academic labor / Gary Rhoades. Albany : State University of New York Press, c1998. x, 351 p. ; 25 cm. (SUNY series, frontiers in education) Includes bibliographical references (p. 321-339) and index. ISBN 0-7914-3715-9 (hardcover : alk. paper) ISBN 0-7914-3716-7 (pbk. : alk. paper) DDC 378.1/22
*1. College teachers - United States. 2. College teachers - Salaries, etc. - United States. 3. College teachers' unions - United States. 4. Collective bargaining - College teachers - United States. 5. College teachers, Part-time - Salaries, etc. - United States. 6. Universities and colleges - United States - Administration. I. Title. II. Series.*
*TC LB2331.72 .R56 1998*

**Rhoton, Jack** Issues in science education / Jack Rhoton, Patricia Bowers editors. Arlington, Va. : National Science Teachers Association: National Science Education Leadership Association, c1997. vi, 227 p. : 23 cm. Includes bibliographical references. ISBN 0-87355-137-0
*1. Science - Study and teaching - United States. 2. Life sciences - Study and teaching - United States. I. Bowers, Patricia joint editor. II. Title.*
*TC Q181 .R56 1996*

**Rhymes & reasons.**
Opitz, Michael F. Portsmouth, NH : Heinemann, c2000.
*TC LB1528 .O65 2000*

**Rhymes and reasons.**
Opitz, Michael F. Rhymes & reasons. Portsmouth, NH : Heinemann, c2000.
*TC LB1528 .O65 2000*

**Rhyming dictionary.**
Young, Sue, 1932- The Scholastic rhyming dictionary. New York : Scholastic Reference, c1994.
*TC PE1519 .Y684 1994*

**RHYMING GAMES - STUDY AND TEACHING (PRIMARY).**
Teacher toolbox [kit]. Chicago, Ill. : Open Court Pub. Co., c1995.
*TC LB1573.3 .T4 1995*

**Rhyn, Heinz, 1960-.**
Dewey and European education. Dordrecht : Kluwer Academic Publishers, c2000.
*TC LB875.D5 D47 2000*

**Rhys, C. S.**
Functional categories, argument structure and parametric variation. Edinburgh : Centre for Cognitive Study, University of Edinburgh, c1994.
*TC P151 .F86 1994*

**Rhythm & beauty.**
Maffit, Rocky, 1952- New York : Watson-Guptill Publications, c1999.
*TC ML1030 .M34 1999*

**Riba, Michelle B.**
Tasman, Allan, 1947- The doctor-patient relationship in pharmacotherapy. New York : Guilford Press, c2000.
*TC RC483.3 .T375 2000*

**RIBBON.** *See* **RIBBONS.**

**Ribbon rescue.**
Munsch, Robert N., 1945- New York : Scholastic, 1999.
*TC PZ7.M927 Ri 1999*

**RIBBONS - FICTION.**
Munsch, Robert N., 1945- Ribbon rescue. New York : Scholastic, 1999.
*TC PZ7.M927 Ri 1999*

**Ricci, Fred.**
DiVincenzo, Joe. Group decision making. [S.l.] : NEA Professional Library : NEA Affiliate Capacity Building, c1999.
*TC LB2806 .D58 1999*

**The Rice Institute pamphlet.** Houston, Tex. : The Institute, 1915-1961. 47 v. : ill., ports. ; 23 cm. Frequency: Quarterly, 1916-1961. Former frequency: Eight no. a year, 1915. Vol. 1, no. 3 (June 1915)-v. 47, no. 4 (Jan. 1961). Vols. for 1915-Apr. 1960 published by Rice Institute; for July 1960-Jan. 1961, by William Marsh Rice University. Vols. 1 (1915)-47 (1961). 1 v. Continues: Rice Institute pamphlets ISSN: 0097-4390 (DLC)sf 85003084 (OCoLC)12119895. Continued by: Rice University studies ISSN: 0035-4996 (DLC) 16007786 (OCoLC)3220941. ISSN 0097-4390
*1. Music - united states I. William M. Rice Institute. II. Rice University. III. Title: Rice Institute pamphlets IV. Title: Rice University studies*
*TC AS36 .W65*

**Rice Institute pamphlets.**
The Rice Institute pamphlet. Houston, Tex. : The Institute, 1915-1961.
*TC AS36 .W65*

**Rice-Maximin, Edward Francis, 1941-.**
Buhle, Paul, 1944- William Appleman Williams. New York : Routledge, 1995.
*TC E175.5.W55 B84 1995*

**Rice, Patricia C.**
Strategies in teaching anthropology. Upper Saddle River, N.J. : Prentice Hall, c2000.
*TC GN43 .S77 2000*

**Rice University.**
The Rice Institute pamphlet. Houston, Tex. : The Institute, 1915-1961.
*TC AS36 .W65*

**Rice University studies.**
The Rice Institute pamphlet. Houston, Tex. : The Institute, 1915-1961.
*TC AS36 .W65*

**Rich, Yisrael.**
Enhancing education in heterogeneous schools. Ramat-Gan : Bar-Ilan University Press, [1997]
*TC LC214 .E54 1997*

**Richard Strauss.**
Kennedy, Michael, 1926- Cambridge, UK : New York, NY, USA : Cambridge University Press, 1999.
*TC ML410.S93 K46 1999*

**Richards, Caroline Cowles, 1842-1913.** A nineteenth-century schoolgirl : the diary of Caroline Cowles Richards, 1852-1855 / edited by Kerry A. Graves ; foreword by Suzanne L. Bunkers. Mankato, Minn. : Blue Earth Books, c2000. 32 p. : ill. (some col.) ; 24 cm. (Diaries, letters, and memoirs) Includes bibliographical references (p. 31) and index. SUMMARY: The diary of a ten-year-old girl who lived in western New York during the 1850s records her family and school life, clothing, transportation, and views on women's rights. Includes sidebars, activities, and a timeline related to this era. ISBN 0-7368-0342-4 DDC 974.7/86
*1. Richards, Caroline Cowles, - 1842-1913 - Diaries - Juvenile literature. 2. Girls - New York (State) - Canandaigua*

*Diaries - Juvenile literature. 3. Canandaigua (N.Y.) - Social life and customs - 19th century - Juvenile literature. 4. Canandaigua (N.Y.) - Biography - Juvenile literature. 5. Richards, Caroline Cowles. - 1842-1913. 6. New York (State) - Social life and customs. 7. Diaries. 8. Women - Biography. I. Graves, Kerry. II. Title. III. Series.*
**TC F129.C2 R53 2000**

**RICHARDS, CAROLINE COWLES, 1842-1913.**
Richards, Caroline Cowles, 1842-1913. A nineteenth-century schoolgirl. Mankato, Minn. : Blue Earth Books, c2000.
**TC F129.C2 R53 2000**

**RICHARDS, CAROLINE COWLES, 1842-1913 - DIARIES - JUVENILE LITERATURE.**
Richards, Caroline Cowles, 1842-1913. A nineteenth-century schoolgirl. Mankato, Minn. : Blue Earth Books, c2000.
**TC F129.C2 R53 2000**

**Richards, J. C. (Jack Croft), 1943-** Passages : an upper-level multi-skills course : teacher's manual 2 / Jack C. Richards, Chuck Sandy. Cambridge : Cambridge University Press, 2000. xvii, 208 p. : 26 cm. ISBN 0521564670(pbk.) DDC 428.24071
*1. English language - Study and teaching - North America - Foreign speakers. 2. English language - Problems, exercises, etc. I. Sandy, Chuck. II. Title.*
**TC PE1128 .R4599 2000**

**Richards, Jack C.** The language teaching matrix / Jack C. Richards. Cambridge [England] ; New York : Cambridge University Press, 1990. ix, 185 p. : ill. ; 24 cm. (Cambridge language teaching library) Includes bibliographical references (p. 167-176). ISBN 0-521-38408-7 ISBN 0-521-38794-9 (pbk.) DDC 418/.007
*1. Language and languages - Study and teaching. I. Title. II. Series.*
**TC P51 .R48 1990**

Passages : an upper-level multi-skills course : student's book 2 / Jack C. Richards & Chuck Sandy. Cambridge, U.K. : New York : Cambridge University Press, 2000. ix, 118 p. : ill. (some col.) ; 28 cm. ISBN 0-521-56471-9 (pbk.) DDC 428.2/4
*1. English language - Textbooks for foreign speakers. 2. English language - Problems, exercises, etc. I. Sandy, Chuck. II. Title.*
**TC PE1128 .R4599 2000**

**Richards, Janet C.** Elementary literacy lessons : cases and commentaries from the field / Janet C. Richards and Joan P. Gipe. Mahwah, N.J. : L. Erlbaum Associates, 2000. xix, 231 p. ; 28 cm. Includes bibliographical references (p. 221-224) and index. ISBN 0-8058-2988-1 (paper : alk. paper) DDC 372.6/044
*1. Language arts (Elementary) - United States - Case studies. 2. Student teachers - United States - Case studies. I. Gipe, Joan P. II. Title.*
**TC LB1576 .R517 2000**

**Richardson, Bonnie.** Factors influencing the sexual and contraceptive behavior of sexually abused adolescents of color : an investigation of self-efficacy, stages of change and perceived risk / by Bonnie Richardson. 1999. viii, 168 leaves ; 29 cm. Typescript; issued also on microfilm. Thesis (Ed.D.)--Teachers College, Columbia University, 1999. Includes bibliographical references (leaves 109-115).
*1. Afro-American teenage girls - Sexual behavior. 2. Hispanic American teenagers - Sexual behavior. 3. Teenage pregnancy - Psychological aspects. 4. Sexually abused children - Mental health. 5. Teenage pregnancy - Prevention - Services for. 6. Contraception. 7. Self-efficacy. I. Title.*
**TC 06 no. 11167**

**RICHARDSON, H. H. (HENRY HOBSON), 1838-1886.**
Breisch, Kenneth A. Henry Hobson Richardson and the small public library in America. Cambridge, Mass. : MIT Press, c1997.
**TC Z679.2.U54 B74 1997**

**Richardson, Irv, 1956-.**
The multiage handbook. Peterborough, NH : Society for Developmental Education, c1996.
**TC LB1029.N6 M754 1996**

**Richardson, John G.** Common, delinquent, and special : the institutional shape of special education / John G. Richardson. New York : Falmer Press, 1999. xx, 217 p. ; 23 cm. (Studies in the history of education ; v. 9) Includes bibliographical references (p. 177-207) and index. ISBN 0-8153-3077-4 (alk. paper) DDC 371.0/0973
*1. Special education - United States - History - 19th century. 2. Special education - United States - History - 20th century. I. Title. II. Series: Studies in the history of education (Falmer Press) ; v.9.*
**TC LC3981 .R525 1999**

**Richardson, Lewis Fry, 1881-1953.** Statistics of deadly quarrels. Edited by Quincy Wright and C.C. Lienau. Pacific Grove, Ca. Boxwood Press [1960] xlvi, 373 p. : port., diagrs. ; 24 cm. Includes index. Includes bibliographies. DDC 355.01
*1. Sociology, Military - Mathematical models. 2. Homicide - Statistics. 3. Military history - Statistics. I. Wright, Quincy, 1890-1970. II. Lienau. C. C. III. Title.*
**TC U21.7 .R5 1960**

**Richardson, Robin.** Inclusive schools, inclusive society : race and identity on the agenda / written and compiled for Race on the Agenda by Robin Richardson and Angela Wood. Stoke on Trent, Staffordshire, England : Trentham Books, 1999. x, 86 p. : ill. ; 30 cm. "Produced by Race on the Agenda in partnership with Association of London Government and Save the Children." Includes bibliographical references (p. 83-86). ISBN 1-85856-203-1
*1. Minorities - Education - Great Britain. 2. Discrimination in education - Great Britain. 3. Students, Black - Great Britain. I. Wood, Angela. II. Race on the Agenda (Organization) III. Association of London Government. IV. Save the Children Fund (Great Britain) V. Title.*
**TC LC212.3.G7 R523 1999**

**Richardson, Rockland L.**
Reforming the Electoral College [videorecording]. [Boulder, Colo.? : Social Science Education Consortium?], c1996.
**TC H62.5.U5 R4 1996**

**RICHES. See WEALTH.**

**Riches for the poor.**
Shorris, Earl, 1936- New York : W.W. Norton, 2000.
**TC HV4045 .S464 2000**

**Richgels, Donald J., 1949-.**
McGee, Lea M. Literacy's beginnings. 3rd ed. Boston ; London : Allyn and Bacon, c2000.
**TC LB1139.5.R43 M33 2000**

**Richmond, Alison.**
Institute of Paper Conservation. Modern works, modern problems? [England] : Institute of Paper Conservation, c1994.
**TC N8560 .I59 1994**

**Rickel, Annette U., 1941-.**
Becker, Evvie. High-risk sexual behavior. New York : Plenum Press, c1998.
**TC HQ60.7.U6 B43 1998**

**Rickels, Laurence A.**
Acting out in groups. Minneapolis, Minn. ; London : University of Minnesota Press, c1999.
**TC RC569.5.A25 A28 1999**

**Ricken, Robert.** The high school principal's calendar : a month-by-month planner for the school year / Robert Ricken, Richard Simon, and Michael Terc. Thousand Oaks, Calif. : Corwin Press, c2000. xviii, 171 p. : ill. ; 30 cm. ISBN 0-7619-7654-X (cloth : alk. paper) ISBN 0-7619-7655-8 (pbk. : alk. paper) DDC 373.12/012
*1. Schedules, School - United States - Handbooks, manuals, etc. 2. High school principals - United States - Handbooks, manuals, etc. I. Simon, Richard, 1951- II. Terc, Michael. III. Title.*
**TC LB3032 .R53 2000**

**Rickford, John R., 1949-** Spoken soul : the story of Black English / John Russell Rickford and Russell John Rickford ; foreword by Geneva Smitherman. New York ; Chichester [England] : Wiley, c2000. xii, 267 p., [8] p. of plates : ill. ; 24 cm. Includes bibliographical references (p. 231-258) and index. ISBN 0-471-32356-X (cloth) DDC 427/.089/96073
*1. Black English - United States. 2. English language - Spoken English - United States. 3. English language - Social aspects - United States. 4. Afro-Americans - Language. I. Rickford, Russell J. II. Title.*
**TC PE3102.N42 R54 2000**

**Rickford, Russell J.**
Rickford, John R., 1949- Spoken soul. New York ; Chichester [England] : Wiley, c2000.
**TC PE3102.N42 R54 2000**

**Rickly, Rebecca.**
The online writing classroom. Cresskill, N.J. : Hampton Press, c2000.
**TC PE1404 .O45 2000**

**Rīdashippu kōdō no kagaku.**
Misumi, Jūji, 1924-
**TC HM141 .M48 1978**

**Riddell, Sheila.**
Gender, policy and educational change :. London ; New York : Routledge, 2000.
**TC LC213.3.G7 G48 2000**

**Ridden, G. M.**
Gray, Barry, 1944- Lifemaps of people with learning difficulties. London : Philadelphia : Jessica Kingsley, 1999.
**TC HV3004 .G73 1999**

**Riddick, Carol Cutler.** Evaluative research in recreation, park, and sport settings : searching for useful information / Carol Cutler Riddick and Ruth V. Russell. [Champaign, Ill.? : Sagamore Publishing], c1999. viii, 392 p. : ill. ; 26 cm. Includes bibliographical references and index. ISBN 1-57167-245-1
*1. Recreation - Research. 2. Leisure - Research. I. Russell, Ruth V., 1948- II. Title.*
**TC GV181.46 .R533 1999**

**Riddle me rhymes.**
Riddle-me rhymes. 1st ed. New York : M.K. McElderry Books ; Toronto : Maxwell Macmillan Canada ; New York : Maxwell Macmillan International, c1994.
**TC PN6371.5 .R53 1994**

**Riddle-me rhymes** / selected by Myra Cohn Livingston ; illustrated by Rebecca Perry. 1st ed. New York : M.K. McElderry Books ; Toronto : Maxwell Macmillan Canada ; New York : Maxwell Macmillan International, c1994. 90 p. : ill. ; 22 cm. Includes indexes. ISBN 0-689-50602-3 DDC 398.6
*1. Riddles, Juvenile. 2. Riddles. 3. Poetry - Collections. I. Livingston, Myra Cohn. II. Perry, Rebecca, ill. III. Title: Riddle me rhymes.*
**TC PN6371.5 .R53 1994**

**RIDDLES.**
Riddle-me rhymes. 1st ed. New York : M.K. McElderry Books ; Toronto : Maxwell Macmillan Canada ; New York : Maxwell Macmillan International, c1994.
**TC PN6371.5 .R53 1994**

Swann, Brian. The house with no door. 1st ed. San Diego : Harcourt Brace & Company., c1998.
**TC PS3569.W256 H6 1998**

Swann, Brian. The house with no door. 1st ed. San Diego : Harcourt Brace & Company., c1998.
**TC PS3569.W256 H6 1998**

**RIDDLES, JUVENILE.**
Riddle-me rhymes. 1st ed. New York : M.K. McElderry Books ; Toronto : Maxwell Macmillan Canada ; New York : Maxwell Macmillan International, c1994.
**TC PN6371.5 .R53 1994**

**Riddles of culture [videorecording].**
Harris, Marvin, 1927- Cows, pigs, wars & witches. [1st ed.]. New York : Random House, c1974.
**TC GN320 .H328 1974**

**Rider, Betty L.**
Diversity in technology education. New York : Glencoe, c1998.
**TC T61 .A56 47th 1998**

Diversity in technology education. New York : Glencoe, c1998.
**TC T61 .A56 47th 1998**

**Rider, Pam.**
Singh, Sadanand. Illustrated dictionary of speech-language pathology. San Diego : Singular Pub. Group, c2000.
**TC RC423 .S533 2000**

**RIDGEVIEW INSTITUTE.**
Changing lives [videorecording]. Princeton, NJ : Films for the Humanities & Sciences, c1998.
**TC RC564 .C54 1998**

**RIDICULOUS, THE. See WIT AND HUMOR.**

**RIDING. See HORSEMANSHIP.**

**RIDING, EASTERN. See HORSEMANSHIP.**

**RIDING, ENGLISH. See HORSEMANSHIP.**

**Ridley, Matt.** The Red Queen : sex and the evolution of human nature / Matt Ridley. New York : Penguin Books, 1995. ix, 405 p. ; 21 cm. Includes bibliographical references (p. [369]-393) and index. ISBN 0-14-024548-0 (pbk.)
*1. Human evolution. 2. Social evolution. 3. Sex. I. Title.*
**TC GN365.9 .R53 1995**

**RIE.**
Resources in education. Semiannual index. Phoenix, AZ : Oryx Press,
**TC Z5813 .R42**

**Rieger, Oya Y.**
Kenney, Anne R., 1950- Moving theory into practice. Mountain View, CA : Research Libraries Group, 2000.

*TC Z681.3.D53 K37*

**Riegler, Alex.**
Understanding representation in the cognitive sciences. New York : Kluwer Academic/Plenum Publishers, c1999.
*TC BF316.6 U63 1999*

**Riester, Albert E., 1941-.**
Special education. San Francisco : EMText, c1992.
*TC LC3981 .S63 1992*

**Riewe, R. R. (Roderick R.).**
Oakes, Jill E. (Jill Elizabeth), 1952- Spirit of Siberia. Washington, D.C. : Smithsonian Institution Press, c1998.
*TC DK758 .O24 1998*

**Rigby, Ken.**
Children's peer relations. London ; New York : Routledge, 1998.
*TC BF723.I646 C47 1998*

**Riggenbach, Heidi.** Discourse analysis in the language classroom / Heidi Riggenbach. Ann Arbor : University of Michigan Press, c1999- v. <1 > : ill. ; 26 cm. Includes bibliographical references. "A Michigan teacher resource" CONTENTS: v. 1. The spoken language. ISBN 0-472-08541-7 (v. 1) DDC 418/.007
*1. Discourse analysis. 2. Language and languages - Study and teaching. I. Title.*
*TC P53.2965 .R54 1999*

**Riggio, Milla Cozart.**
Teaching Shakespeare through performance. New York : Modern Language Association of America, 1999.
*TC PR2987 .T366 1999*

**Riggs, Karen E.** Mature audiences : television in the lives of elders / Karen E. Riggs. New Brunswick, N.J. : Rutgers University Press, c1998. xiv, 197 p. ; 24 cm. (Communications, media and culture) Includes bibliographical references (p. 177-190) and index. ISBN 0-8135-2539-X (alk. paper) ISBN 0-8135-2540-3 (pbk : alk. paper) DDC 306.4/85/0846
*1. Television and the aged - United States. 2. Mass media and the aged - United States. 3. Aged - United States - Psychology. 4. Aged - Communication - United States. I. Title. II. Series.*
*TC HQ1064.U5 R546 1998*

**Riggs, Kevin John.**
Children's reasoning and the mind. Hove : Psychology, c2000.
*TC BF723.R4 C555 2000*

**Right hemisphere damage.**
Myers, Penelope S. San Diego : Singular Pub., c1999.
*TC RC423 .M83 1999*

**RIGHT OF PRIVACY.** *See* **PRIVACY, RIGHT OF.**

**RIGHT (POLITICAL SCIENCE).** *See* **CONSERVATISM.**

**RIGHT TO BEAR ARMS.** *See* **FIREARMS - LAW AND LEGISLATION.**

**RIGHT TO DIE.** *See* **EUTHANASIA; SUICIDE.**

**RIGHT TO DIE - MORAL AND ETHICAL ASPECTS.**
Lederer, Jane. Participation in active euthanasia and assisted suicide and attitudes and interpersonal values of physicians and nurses. 1996.
*TC 06 no. 10849*

**RIGHT TO EDUCATION.**
Spring, Joel H. The universal right to education. Mahwah, N.J. ; London : Lawrence Erlbaum Associates, 2000.
*TC LC213 .S67 2000*

**Right to feel better [videorecording].**
Depression in older adults [videorecording]. Boston, MA : Fanlight Productions ; [Chicago, Ill.] : Distributed by Terra Nova Films, Inc., 1997.
*TC RC537.5 .D4 1997*

**RIGHT TO KEEP ARMS.** *See* **FIREARMS - LAW AND LEGISLATION.**

**RIGHT TO KNOW.** *See* **FREEDOM OF INFORMATION.**

**RIGHT TO LABOR.** *See* **UNEMPLOYMENT.**

**Right versus wrong.**
Stilwell, Barbara M. Right vs. wrong-- . Bloomington : Indiana University Press, c2000.
*TC BJ1471 .S69 2000*

**Right vs. wrong - .**
Stilwell, Barbara M. Bloomington : Indiana University Press, c2000.
*TC BJ1471 .S69 2000*

**RIGHTEOUS GENTILES IN THE HOLOCAUST.** *See* **WORLD WAR, 1939-1945 - JEWS - RESCUE.**

**Rights and wrongs :** how children and young adults evaluate the world / Marta Laupa, editor. San Francisco, [CA] : Jossey-Bass, c2000. 96 p. ; 23 cm. (New directions for child and adolescent development, 1520-3247 ; no. 89) "Fall 2000" Includes bibliographical references and index. CONTENTS: Children's thinking about truth : a parallel to social domain judgments? / Charles W. Kalish -- Similarities and differences in children's reasoning about morality and mathematics / Marta Laupa -- Values and truths : the making and judging of moral decisions / Cecilia Wainryb -- The aretaic domain and its relation to the deontic domain in moral reasoning / Orlando Lourenço -- Distinguishing necessary and contingent knowledge / Joe Becker -- 'Is' and ought', fact and value : a relational developmental perspective / Willis F. Overton. ISBN 0-7879-1256-5
*1. Judgment. 2. Moral development. 3. Reasoning in children. 4. Child development. 5. Child psychology. I. Laupa, Marta. II. Series.*
*TC BF723.M54 L38 2000*

**RIGHTS, CIVIL.** *See* **CIVIL RIGHTS.**

**RIGHTS, HUMAN.** *See* **HUMAN RIGHTS.**

**Rights in conflict; convention week in Chicago, August, 25-29, 1968.**
Walker, Daniel, 1922- New York : Dutton, c1968.
*TC F548.52 .W3 1968c*

**Rights, justice, and community** / edited by Creighton Peden and John K. Roth. Lewiston, N.Y., USA : Edwin Mellen Press, c1992. 485 p. ; 24 cm. (Social philosophy today ; no. 7) Papers presented at the Fourth International Conference on Social Philosophy, held in Oxford, England, during the summer of 1988, sponsored by the North American Society for Social Philosophy. Includes bibliographical references. ISBN 0-7734-9599-1 DDC 303.3/72
*1. Social justice - Congresses. 2. Human rights - Congresses. 3. Social problems - Congresses. 4. Social sciences - Philosophy - Congresses. I. Peden, Creighton, 1935- II. Roth, John K. III. Series.*
*TC HM216 .R56 1992*

**Rights, not roses.**
Deslippe, Dennis A. (Dennis Arthur), 1961- Urbana : University of Illinois Press, c2000.
*TC HD6079.2.U5 D47 2000*

**RIGHTS OF MAN.** *See* **HUMAN RIGHTS.**

**RIGHTS OF WOMEN.** *See* **WOMEN'S RIGHTS.**

**RIGHTS, PROPRIETARY.** *See* **INTELLECTUAL PROPERTY.**

**Rights to language :** equity, power, and education : celebrating the 60th birthday of Tove Skutnabb-Kangas / edited by Robert Phillipson. Mahwah, N.J. : L. Erlbaum Associates, 2000. 310 p. : ill. ; 24 cm. Includes bibliographical references (p. [289]-303) and index. ISBN 0-8058-3346-3 (hc. : alk. paper) ISBN 0-8058-3835-X (pbk.) DDC 306.44
*1. Language policy. 2. Language and education. 3. Language planning. 4. Human rights. I. Skutnabb-Kangas, Tove. II. Phillipson, Robert.*
*TC P119.3 .R54 2000*

**RIGIDITY (PSYCHOLOGY).** *See* **STEREOTYPE (PSYCHOLOGY).**

**Riker, Thad Weed, 1880-1952.** The story of modern Europe / by T.W. Riker ; edited by Howard R. Anderson. Boston : Houghton, Mifflin, 1942. vi, 382, iii, viii p. ill., maps, ports ; 27 cm. Includes bibliographies and index.
*1. History, Modern. 2. Europe - History. I. Anderson, Howard R. (Howard Richmond), 1898- ed. II. Title.*
*TC D209 .R48*

**Riley, Linda Capus.** Elephants swim / by Linda Capus Riley ; illustrated by Steve Jenkins. Boston : Houghton Mifflin, 1995. 1 v. unpaged : col. ill. ; 23 x 26 cm. ISBN 0-395-73654-4 DDC 591.1/852
*1. Swimming - Juvenile literature. 2. Animal swimming. I. Jenkins, Steve, 1952- ill. II. Title.*
*TC QP310.S95 R55 1995*

**Riley, Richard W. (Richard Wilson).**
Annual State of American Education Address (7th : February 22, 2000 : Durham, N.C.) The seventh annual state of American education address [videorecording]. [Washington, D.C. : U.S. Dept. of Education], 2000.
Modernizing schools : technology and buildings for a new century (September 19, 2000 : Washington, D.C.) Modernizing schools [videorecording]. [Washington, D.C.] : U.S. Dept. of Education, [2000].

*TC LB3205 .M64 2000*

Modernizing schools : technology and buildings for a new century (September 19, 2000 : Washington, D.C.) Modernizing schools [videorecording]. [Washington, D.C.] : U.S. Dept. of Education, [2000].
*TC LB3205 .M64 2000*

Powerful middle schools : teaching and learning for young adolescents (2000) Powerful middle schools [videorecording]. [Washington, D.C.?] : U.S. Dept. of Education, [2000].
*TC LB1623 .P6 2000*

**Riley, Shirley, 1949-.**
Davies, Ian, 1957- Good citizenship and educational provision. London ; New York : Falmer Press, c1999.
*TC LC1091 .D28 1999*

**Rimer, Barbara K.**
Health behavior and health education. 2nd ed. San Francisco : Jossey-Bass, 1997.
*TC RA776.9 .H434 1997*

**Rinehart, Robert E., 1951-** Players all : performances in contemporary sport / Robert E. Rinehart. Bloomington : Indiana University Press, c1998. xvi, 188 p. ; 25 cm. (Drama and performance studies) Includes bibliographical references (p. 139-179) and index. ISBN 0-253-33426-8 (alk. paper) ISBN 0-253-21223-5 (pbk. : alk. paper) DDC 796
*1. Sports - Sociological aspects. 2. Performance art. I. Title. II. Series.*
*TC GV706.5 .R56 1998*

**Riner, Phillip S., 1950-** Successful teaching in the elementary classroom / Phillip S. Riner. Upper Saddle River, N.J. : Merrill, c2000. xvi, 432 p. ; 24 cm. Includes bibliographical references and indexes. ISBN 0-02-401613-6 DDC 372.1102
*1. Elementary school teaching - United States. 2. Elementary school teachers - United States. I. Title.*
*TC LB1555 .R53 2000*

**Ring of earth.**
Yolen, Jane. 1st ed. San Diego : Harcourt Brace Jovanovich, c1986.
*TC PS3575.O43 R5 1986*

**Rink, Deane.**
The climate puzzle [videorecording]. [New York, N.Y.?] : Unapix Entertainment, Inc. [distributor], c1996.
*TC QB631.2 .C5 1996*

**Rintelmann, William F.**
Musiek, Frank E. Contemporary perspectives in hearing assessment. Boston : Allyn and Bacon, 1999.
*TC RF294 .M87 1999*

**Rinzler, Carol Ann.** The new complete book of food : a nutritional, medical, and culinary guide / Carol Ann Rinzler ; with an introduction by Jane E. Brody ; foreword by Michael D. Jensen. New York : Facts on File, c1999. xvii, 440 p. ; 25 cm. Includes bibliographical references (p. 415-427) and index. ISBN 0-8160-3987-9 (cloth : alk. paper) ISBN 0-8160-3988-7 (paper : alk. paper) DDC 641.3
*1. Food. 2. Nutrition. I. Title.*
*TC TX353 .R525 1999*

**RÍO BRAVO DEL NORTE.** *See* **RIO GRANDE.**

**Rio Grande.**
Lourie, Peter. 1st ed. Honesdale, Pa. : Boyds Mills Press, 1999.
*TC F392.R5 L68 1999*

**RIO GRANDE - JUVENILE LITERATURE.**
Lourie, Peter. Rio Grande :. 1st ed. Honesdale, Pa. : Boyds Mills Press, 1999.
*TC F392.R5 L68 1999*

**RIO GRANDE. <JUVENILE SUBJECT HEADING>.**
Lourie, Peter. Rio Grande :. 1st ed. Honesdale, Pa. : Boyds Mills Press, 1999.
*TC F392.R5 L68 1999*

**RIO GRANDE VALLEY - JUVENILE LITERATURE.**
Lourie, Peter. Rio Grande :. 1st ed. Honesdale, Pa. : Boyds Mills Press, 1999.
*TC F392.R5 L68 1999*

**RIO GRANDE VALLEY. <JUVENILE SUBJECT HEADING>.**
Lourie, Peter. Rio Grande :. 1st ed. Honesdale, Pa. : Boyds Mills Press, 1999.
*TC F392.R5 L68 1999*

**RIO GRANDE VALLEY, LOWER (TEX.).** *See* **LOWER RIO GRANDE VALLEY (TEX.).**

**Riordan, James, 1936-.**
Sport and physical education in China. London ; New York : Routledge, 1999.
*TC GV651 .S655 1999*

**Riordan, Robert C.**
Steinberg, Adria. Schooling for the real world. 1st ed. San Francisco : Jossey-Bass, c1999.
*TC LC1037.5 .S843 1999*

**RIOTS. *See* DEMONSTRATIONS.**

**Riots and rebellion.**
Masotti, Louis H. Beverly Hills, Calif., Sage Publications [1968]
*TC HV6477 .M37*

**RIOTS - ILLINOIS - CHICAGO.**
Walker, Daniel, 1922- Rights in conflict; convention week in Chicago, August, 25-29, 1968; New York : Dutton, c1968.
*TC F548.52 .W3 1968c*

**RIOTS - U.S.**
Masotti, Louis H. Riots and rebellion; Beverly Hills, Calif., Sage Publications [1968]
*TC HV6477 .M37*

**Ripoll, Ignacio.**
Leutholtz, Brian C. Exercise and disease management. Boca Raton : CRC Press, c1999.
*TC RM725 .L45 1999*

**Ripton, John R.** Export agriculture and social crisis : El Salvador to 1972 / John R. Ripton. 1997. iii, 305 leaves ; 29 cm. Issued also on microfilm. Thesis (Ph.D.)-- Columbia University, 1997. Includes bibliographical references (leaves 295-305).
*1. Agriculture - Economic aspects - El Salvador - History. 2. Agriculture - Political aspects - El Salvador - History. 3. Developing countries - Economic integration. 4. Peasantry - El Salvador - History. 5. Peasant uprisings - El Salvador - History. I. Title.*
*TC 085 R48*

**The rise of the network society.**
Castells, Manuel. 2nd ed. Malden, MA : Blackwell Publishers, 2000.
*TC HC79.I55 C373 2000*

**Risinger, C. Frederick.**
Surfing social studies. Washington, DC : National Council for the Social Studies, c1999.
*TC LB1044.87 .S97 1999*

**Risjord, Norman K.** History of the American people / Norman K. Risjord. New York : Holt, Rinehart, and Winston, c1986. xvi, 879 p. : ill. (some col.) , maps ; 27 cm. Includes bibliographical references and index. ISBN 0-03-002657-1
*1. United States - History. I. Title.*
*TC E178.1 .R597 1986*

**RISK. *See* PROBABILITIES.**

**Risk and sociocultural theory :** new directions and perspectives / edited by Deborah Lupton. Cambridge, U.K. ; New York : Cambridge University Press, 1999. ix, 191 p. ; 23 cm. Includes bibliographical references and index. ISBN 0-521-64207-8 (hb) ISBN 0-521-64554-9 (pb) DDC 302/.12
*1. Risk - Sociological aspects. 2. Risk perception - Social aspects. I. Lupton, Deborah.*
*TC HM1101 .R57 1999*

**Risk and 'the other'.**
Joffe, Hélène. Cambridge, U.K. ; New York : Cambridge University Press, 1999.
*TC HM256 .J63 1999*

**RISK AWARENESS. *See* RISK PERCEPTION.**

**RISK MANAGEMENT.**
Nursing documentation. Thousand Oaks, Calif. : Sage Publications, c1999.
*TC RT50 .N87 1999*

**RISK PERCEPTION.**
Cross-cultural risk perception. Dordrecht ; Boston ; London : Kluwer Academic, c2000.
*TC HM1101 .C76 2000*

Joffe, Hélène. Risk and 'the other'. Cambridge, U.K. ; New York : Cambridge University Press, 1999.
*TC HM256 .J63 1999*

**RISK PERCEPTION - CROSS-CULTURAL STUDIES.**
Cross-cultural risk perception. Dordrecht ; Boston ; London : Kluwer Academic, c2000.
*TC HM1101 .C76 2000*

**RISK PERCEPTION - SOCIAL ASPECTS.**
Risk and sociocultural theory. Cambridge, U.K. ; New York : Cambridge University Press, 1999.

*TC HM1101 .R57 1999*

**RISK - SOCIOLOGICAL ASPECTS.**
Cross-cultural risk perception. Dordrecht ; Boston ; London : Kluwer Academic, c2000.
*TC HM1101 .C76 2000*

Risk and sociocultural theory. Cambridge, U.K. ; New York : Cambridge University Press, 1999.
*TC HM1101 .R57 1999*

**Ritchie, Joy S.** Teacher narrative as critical inquiry : rewriting the script / Joy S. Ritchie and David E. Wilson with Ruth Kupfer ... [et al.] ; foreword by Bonnie Sunstein. New York : Teachers College Press, c2000. xiii, 200 p. ; 24 cm. (The practitioner inquiry series) Includes bibliographical references (p. 183-187) and index. ISBN 0-8077-3961-8 (cloth : alk. paper) ISBN 0-8077-3960-X (pbk. : alk. paper) DDC 371.1/0092/2
*1. Teachers - United States - Biography. 2. Education - United States - Biographical methods. 3. Teaching - United States. I. Wilson, David E., 1955- II. Title. III. Series.*
*TC LA2311 .R58 2000*

**Ritchie, Ron, 1952-.**
Bell, Derek, 1950- Towards effective subject leadership in the primary school. Buckingham [England] ; Philadelphia : Open University Press, c1999.
*TC LB2832.4.G7 B45 1999*

**RITES AND CEREMONIES - UNITED STATES.**
Harris, Neil, 1938- Building lives. New Haven [Conn.] ; London : Yale University Press, c1999.
*TC NA2543.S6 H37 1999*

**The rites of men.**
Burstyn, Varda. Toronto ; Buffalo : University of Toronto Press, 1999.
*TC GV706.5 .B87 1999*

**RITES OF PASSAGE. *See* RITES AND CEREMONIES.**

**RITUAL. *See* RITES AND CEREMONIES.**

**Ritual and spontaneity in the psychoanalytic process.**
Hoffman, Irwin Z. Hillsdale, NJ : Analytic Press, c1998.
*TC BF175.4.C68 H64 1998*

**Ritual, ceremonies, and cultural meaning in higher education.**
Manning, Kathleen, 1954- Westport, Conn. : Bergin & Garvey, 2000.
*TC LC191.9 .M26 2000*

**RITUALISM. *See* RITES AND CEREMONIES.**

**Rituals of race.**
Lorini, Alessandra, 1949- Charlottesville : University Press of Virginia, 1999.
*TC E185.61 .L675 1999*

**River winding.**
Zolotow, Charlotte, 1915- 1st ed. New York : Crowell, [1978]
*TC PZ8.3.Z6 Ri 1978*

**Rivera, Diego, 1886-1957.**
The frescoes of Diego Rivera [videorecording]. [Detroit, Mich.] : Founders Society, Detroit Institute of Arts ; [Chicago, Ill.?] : Home Vision [distributor], c1986.
*TC ND259.R5 F6 1986*

**RIVERA, DIEGO, 1886-1957.**
The frescoes of Diego Rivera [videorecording]. [Detroit, Mich.] : Founders Society, Detroit Institute of Arts ; [Chicago, Ill.?] : Home Vision [distributor], c1986.
*TC ND259.R5 F6 1986*

Hamill, Pete, 1935- Diego Rivera. New York : Harry N. Abrams, 1999.
*TC ND259.R5 H28 1999*

**RIVERA, DIEGO, 1886-1957 - CRITICISM AND INTERPRETATION.**
Folgarait, Leonard. Mural painting and social revolution in Mexico, 1920-1940. Cambridge ; New York, NY : Cambridge University Press, 1998.
*TC ND2644 .F63 1998*

**RIVERA, DIEGO, 1886-1957 - POLITICAL AND SOCIAL VIEWS.**
Lee, Anthony W., 1960- Painting on the left. Berkeley : University of California Press, c1999.
*TC ND259.R5 L44 1999*

**Rivera [videorecording].**
The frescoes of Diego Rivera [videorecording]. [Detroit, Mich.] : Founders Society, Detroit Institute of Arts ; [Chicago, Ill.?] : Home Vision [distributor], c1986.

*TC ND259.R5 F6 1986*

**RIVERS - FICTION.**
Greene, Carol. Sunflower Island. 1st ed. New York : HarperCollins, c1999.
*TC PZ7.G82845 Sl 1999*

**RIVERS - MEXICO. *See* RIO GRANDE.**

**RIVERS - UNITED STATES. *See* RIO GRANDE.**

**The Riverside literature series :**
([no.] 264) Wiggin, Kate Douglas Smith, 1856-1923. Rebecca of Sunnybrook Farm. Boston, New York [etc.] : Houghton, Mifflin Company, [c1903] (Cambridge, Mass. : Riverside Press)
*TC PZ7.W638 Re 1903*

**Riviere, Joan, 1883- tr.**
Freud, Sigmund, 1856-1939. [Sammlung kleiner schriften zur neurosenlehre. eng] Collected papers. 1st American ed. New York : Basic Books, 1959.
*TC BF173 .F672 1959*

**Riviere, Joan, trans.**
Freud, Sigmund, 1856-1939. The ego and the id and other works. London : Hogarth Press, 1957.
*TC BF173.F645 1957*

**Rivkin, Mary S.**
Harlan, Jean Durgin. Science experiences for the early childhood years. 7th ed. Upper Saddle River, N.J. : Merrill, c2000.
*TC LB1139.5.S35 H37 2000*

**RM Arts (Firm).**
Andy Warhol [videorecording]. [Chicago, IL] : Home Vision [distributor],cc1987.
*TC N6537.W28 A45 1987*

Andy Warhol [videorecording]. [Chicago, IL] : Home Vision [distributor],cc1987.
*TC N6537.W28 A45 1987*

Jackson Pollock [videorecording]. [Chicago, Ill.] : Home Vision ; [S.l.] : Distributed Worldwide by RM Associates, c1987.
*TC ND237.P73 J3 1987*

Marc Chagall [videorecording]. [Chicago, Ill.] : Home Vision [distributor], c1985.
*TC ND699.C5 C5 1985*

Matisse, voyages [videorecording]. [Chicago, Ill.] : Home Vision ; [S.l.] : Distributed worldwide by RM Associates, c1989.
*TC ND553.M37 M37 1989*

Picasso [videorecording]. Chicago, IL : Home Vision, c1986.
*TC N6853.P5 P52 1986*

Roy Lichtenstein [videorecording]. [Chicago, IL] : Home Vision ; [S.l.] : distributed worldwide by RM Asssociates, c1991.
*TC ND237.L627 R6 1991*

**R.M. Productions.**
Monsieur René Magritte [videorecording]. [Chicago, Ill.] : Home Vision [distributor], c1978.
*TC ND673.M35 M6 1978*

**RNS. *See* NURSES.**

**The road to independent reading**
Better together. New York : Macmillan/McGraw-Hill, c1997.
*TC LB1576 .S66 1997 Gr.2 l.6 u.3*

Call it courage. New York : Macmillan/McGraw-Hill, c1997.
*TC LB1576 .S66 1997 Gr.6 l.12 u.6*

Coming home. New York : Macmillan/McGraw-Hill, c1997.
*TC LB1576 .S66 1997 Gr.6 l.12 u.5*

Community spirit. New York : Macmillan/McGraw-Hill, c1997.
*TC LB1576 .S66 1997 Gr.3 l.9 u.1*

Dare to discover. New York : Macmillan/McGraw-Hill, c1997.
*TC LB1576 .S66 1997 Gr.6 l.12 u.2*

Eureka. New York : Macmillan/McGraw-Hill, c1997.
*TC LB1576 .S66 1997 Gr.2 l.6 u.2*

Family album. New York : Macmillan/McGraw-Hill, c1997.
*TC LB1576 .S66 1997 Gr.3 l.8 u.3*

Family fun:. New York : Macmillan/McGraw-Hill, c1997.
*TC LB1576 .S66 1997 Gr.2 l.6 u.1*

Forces of nature. New York : Macmillan/McGraw-Hill, c1997.

*TC LB1576 .S66 1997 Gr.3 l.9 u.2*

Getting to know you. New York : Macmillan/
McGraw-Hill, c1997.
*TC LB1576 .S66 1997 Gr.5 l.11 u.4*

Good thinking. New York : Macmillan/McGraw-Hill,
c1997.
*TC LB1576 .S66 1997 Gr.3 l.8 u.1*

Hand in hand. New York : Macmillan/McGraw-Hill,
c1997.
*TC LB1576 .S66 1997 Gr.2 l.7 u.2*

Let's pretend. New York : Macmillan/McGraw-Hill,
c1997.
*TC LB1576 .S66 1997 Gr.1 l.5 u.1*

Make a wish. New York : Macmillan/McGraw-Hill,
c1997.
*TC LB1576 .S66 1997 Gr.4 l.10 u.1*

Making the grade. New York : Macmillan/McGraw-
Hill, c1997.
*TC LB1576 .S66 1997 Gr.6 l.12 u.1*

Memories to keep. New York : Macmillan/McGraw-
Hill, c1997.
*TC LB1576 .S66 1997 Gr.4 l.10 u.5*

Naturally. New York : Macmillan/McGraw-Hill,
c1997.
*TC LB1576 .S66 1997 Gr.4 l.10 u.2*

Out and about. New York : Macmillan/McGraw-Hill,
c1997.
*TC LB1576 .S66 1997 Gr.1 l.2*

Penpals. New York : Macmillan/McGraw-Hill, c1997.
*TC LB1576 .S66 1997 Gr.2 l.7 u.1*

Pitch in. New York : Macmillan/McGraw-Hill, c1997.
*TC LB1576 .S66 1997 Gr.4 l.10 u.4*

Read all about it. New York : Macmillan/McGraw-
Hill, c1997.
*TC LB1576 .S66 1997 Gr.1 l.1*

Scenes of wonder. New York : Macmillan/McGraw-
Hill, c1997.
*TC LB1576 .S66 1997 Gr.5 l.11 u.1*

See for yourself. New York : Macmillan/McGraw-
Hill, c1997.
*TC LB1576 .S66 1997 Gr.3 l.8 u.2*

Something new. New York : Macmillan/McGraw-
Hill, c1997.
*TC LB1576 .S66 1997 Gr.1 l.3*

Surprises along the way:. New York : Macmillan/
McGraw-Hill, c1997.
*TC LB1576 .S66 1997 Gr.1 l.4 u.2*

Take a closer look. New York : Macmillan/McGraw-
Hill, c1997.
*TC LB1576 .S66 1997 Gr.1 l.4 u.1*

Take the high road. New York : Macmillan/McGraw-
Hill, c1997.
*TC LB1576 .S66 1997 Gr.5 l.11 u.5*

Teamwork. New York : Macmillan/McGraw-Hill,
c1997.
*TC LB1576 .S66 1997 Gr.3 l.9 u.3*

That's what friends are for. New York : Macmillan/
McGraw-Hill, c1997.
*TC LB1576 .S66 1997 Gr.4 l.10 u.3*

Time & time again. New York : Macmillan/McGraw-
Hill, c1997.
*TC LB1576 .S66 1997 Gr.6 l.12 u.4*

True-blue friends. New York : Macmillan/McGraw-
Hill, c1997.
*TC LB1576 .S66 1997 Gr.1 l.5 u.2*

Twice-told tales. New York : Macmillan/McGraw-
Hill, c1997.
*TC LB1576 .S66 1997 Gr.4 l.10 u.6*

Unlikely heroes. New York : Macmillan/McGraw-
Hill, c1997.
*TC LB1576 .S66 1997 Gr.6 l.12 u.3*

Winning attitudes. New York : Macmillan/McGraw-
Hill, c1997.
*TC LB1576 .S66 1997 Gr.5 l.11 u.3*

Worlds of change. New York : Macmillan/McGraw-
Hill, c1997.
*TC LB1576 .S66 1997 Gr.5 l.11 u.2*

Zoom in. New York : Macmillan/McGraw-Hill,
c1997.
*TC LB1576 .S66 1997 Gr.5 l.11 u.6*

**Roaring 20's [picture].**
Roaring twenties [picture]. Amawalk, NY : Jackdaw
Publications, c1997.
*TC E784 .R6 1997*

**ROARING TWENTIES.** *See* **NINETEEN
TWENTIES.**

**Roaring twenties** [picture]. Amawalk, NY : Jackdaw
Publications, c1997. 12 posters : b&w ; 43 x 56 cm. +
1 leaflet ([6] p. : ill. ; 28 cm.). (Jackdaw photo
collections ; S-PC 103) Compiled by Enid Goldberg &
Norman Itzkowitz. SUMMARY: 12 historical photo-
posters depicting cultural, sports, political, s cientific
and popular scenes from the roaring twenties.
CONTENTS: 1. The symbol of the 1920's-- flappers
dancing the Charleston -- 2. Driving for fun: a Ford
Motor car, 1926 -- 3. Charles Lindbergh and The Spirit
of St. Louis, 1927 -- 4. Movie star Charlie Chaplin in
The Gold Rush, 1925 -- 5. Lou Gehrig and Babe Ruth,
"The Home Run Twins," 1927 -- 6. Marble
Championship, Philadelphia, PA, 1926 -- 7. The
wireless: listening to the radio, 1923 -- 8. Prohibition
agents raid a still, Washington, DC, 1922 -- 9. Terror in
the US: The Ku Klux Klan, Freeport, NY, 1923 -- 10.
Scientist George Washington Carver, circa 1922 -- 11.
Women demand the Right to Vote-- and get it in 1920 --
12. The end of an era: the start of the Great Depression,
1929. ISBN 1-56696-159-9
*1. United States - Civilization - 1918-1945 - Pictorial works. 2.
United States - History - 1919-1933 - Pictorial works. 3.
Nineteen twenties - Economic aspects - Pictorial works. 4.
Nineteen twenties - Political aspects - Pictorial works. 5.
Nineteen twenties - Social aspects - Pictorial works. 6.
Documentary photography - United States. I. Goldberg, Enid.
II. Itzkowitz, Norman. III. Jackdaw Publications. IV. Title:
Roaring 20's [picture] V. Series.*
*TC E784 .R6 1997*

**ROBBERS AND OUTLAWS - FICTION.**
Cadnum, Michael. In a dark wood. New York :
Orchard Books, c1998.
*TC PZ7.C11724 In 1998*

**ROBBINS, BRIAN.** Inclusive mathematics 5-11.
London ; New York : Continuum, 2000. 168 p. ; 22 cm.
(Special needs in ordinary schools) ISBN 0-304-70703-1
*1. Mathematics - Study and teaching (Elementary)*
*TC QA135.5 .R63 2000*

**Robbins, Carol Braswell.** An examination of critical
feminist pedagogy in practice / by Carol Braswell
Robbins. 1999. x, 322 leaves ; 29 cm. Typescript; issued
also on microfilm. Thesis (Ed.D.)--Teachers College,
Columbia University, 1999. Includes bibliographical
references (leaves 241-247).
*1. Critical pedagogy - United States. 2. Popular education -
United States. 3. Multicultural education - United States. 4.
Adult education - United States. 5. Feminism - United States. 6.
Feminist theory - United States. 7. Afro-American women
college teachers - United States. 8. Johnson, Bonnie. 9. Freire,
Paulo. - 1921- 10. Knowledge, Theory of. I. Title.*
*TC 06 no. 11067*

**Robbins, Keith.** Appeasement / Keith Robbins. Oxford,
UK ; New York, NY, USA : B. Blackwell, 1988. 89
p. ; 20 cm. (Historical Association studies) Bibliography: p.
84-87. Includes index. ISBN 0-631-16013-2 (pbk.) DDC
940.53/112
*1. Great Britain - Foreign relations - Germany. 2. Great
Britain - Foreign relations - 1936-1945. 3. Germany - Foreign
relations - Great Britain. 4. Germany - Foreign relations -
1933-1945. 5. World War, 1939-1945 - Causes. I. Title. II.
Series.*
*TC DA47.2 .R62 1988*

**Robbins, Ken.** Make me a peanut butter sandwich and a
glass of milk / Ken Robbins. New York : Scholastic,
c1992. 1 v. (unpaged) : col. ill. ; 23 x 29 cm. SUMMARY:
Text and hand-tinted photographs show how each part of a
peanut butter sandwich and milk lunch is made, from field, to
store, to table. ISBN 0-590-43550-7 DDC 641.6/56596
*1. Peanut butter - Juvenile literature. 2. Bread - Juvenile
literature. 3. Wheat - Juvenile literature. 4. Peanuts - Juvenile
literature. 5. Milk - Juvenile literature. 6. Peanut butter. 7.
Bread. 8. Wheat. 9. Peanuts. 10. Milk. I. Title.*
*TC TX814.5.P38 R63 1992*

**Robbins, Pamela.** Thinking inside the block schedule :
strategies for teaching in extended periods of time /
Pam Robbins, Gayle Gregory, Lynne Herndon.
Thousand Oaks, Calif. : Corwin Press, c2000. xiv, 209
p. ; il. ; 30 cm. Includes bibliographical references (p. 197-
199) and index. ISBN 0-8039-6782-9 (cloth: acid-free paper)
ISBN 0-8039-6783-7 (pbk.: acid-free paper) DDC 371.2/42
*1. Block scheduling (Education) 2. Lesson planning. 3.
Classroom management. I. Gregory, Gayle. II. Herndon,
Lynne. III. Title.*
*TC LB3032.2 .R63 2000*

**Robert F. Wagner Labor Archives.**
Bernhardt, Debra E. Ordinary people, extraordinary
lives. New York : New York University Press, c2000.

*TC HD8085.N53 B47 2000*

**Robert Rauschenberg.**
Hopps, Walter. New York : Guggenheim Museum,
c1997.
*TC N6537.R27 H66 1997*

**Roberts, Albert R.**
Crisis intervention handbook. 2nd ed. Oxford ; New
York : Oxford University Press, 2000.
*TC RC480.6 .C744 2000*

**Roberts, Celia, 1947-.**
Talk, work, and institutional order. Berlin ; New
York : Mouton de Gruyter, 1999.
*TC P95 .T286 1999*

**The Roberts English series.**
Roberts, Paul. Teacher's ed. New York : Harcourt,
Brace & World c<1966- >
*TC PE1112 .R6 Teacher's edition*

Roberts, Paul. Teacher's ed. New York : Harcourt,
Brace & World c<1966- >
*TC PE1112 .R6 Teacher's edition*

**Roberts, Fred S.**
Discrete mathematics in the schools. Providence,
R.I. : American Mathematical Society, National
Council of Teachers of Mathematics, c1997.
*TC QA11.A1 D57 1997*

Recent progress in mathematical psychology.
Mahwah, N.J. : L. Erlbaum, 1998.
*TC BF39 .R35 1998*

**Roberts, J. T. (John T.)** Two French language teaching
reformers reassessed : Claude Marcel and François
Gouin / J.T. Roberts. Lewiston [N.Y.] : E. Mellen
Press, c1999. xx, 173 p. ; 24 cm. (Studies in linguistics and
semiotics ; v. 2) Includes bibliographical references and index.
ISBN 0-7734-7988-0 DDC 418/.007
*1. Languages, Modern - Study and teaching. 2. Marcel,
Claude, - 19th cent. 3. Gouin, François, - 1831-1896. I. Title.
II. Title: 2 French language teaching reformers reassessed III.
Series.*
*TC PB35 .R447 1999*

**Roberts, Jon H.** The sacred and the secular university /
Jon H. Roberts and James Turner ; with an
introduction by John F. Wilson. Princeton, N.J. :
Princeton University Press, c2000. xii, 184 p. ; 24 cm.
Includes bibliographical references (p. [123]-175) and index.
ISBN 0-691-01556-2 (cl) DDC 378.73/09/034
*1. Universities and colleges - United States - History - 19th
century. 2. Universities and colleges - United States - History -
20th century. 3. Secularism - United States - History. 4.
Humanities - Study and teaching (Higher) - United States. 5.
Science - Study and teaching (Higher) - United States. I.
Turner, James, 1946- II. Title.*
*TC LA636.7 .R62 2000*

**Roberts, Kim P.**
Children's source monitoring. Mahwah, N.J. ;
London : Lawrence Erlbaum Associates, 2000.
*TC BF723.M4 C45 2000*

**Roberts, Mark S.**
Allison, David B. Disordered mother or disordered
diagnosis? :. Hillsdale, NJ : Analytic Press, 1998.
*TC RC569.5.M83 A38 1998*

**Roberts, Michael C.**
Beyond appearance. 1st ed. Washington, DC :
American Psychological Association, c1999.
*TC HQ798 .B43 1999*

**Roberts, Nancy, 1938-.**
Modeling and simulation in science and mathematics
education. New York : Springer, c1999.
*TC Q181 .M62 1999*

**Roberts, Patricia, 1936-** Language arts and
environmental awareness : 100+ integrated books and
activities for children / Patricia L. Roberts. New
Haven, Conn. : Linnet Professional Publications,
1998. xv, 295 p. : ill. ; 24 cm. Includes bibliographical
references and indexes. ISBN 0208024271(alk. paper) ISBN
0-208-02436-0 (pbk.: alk. paper) DDC 016.3723/57
*1. Environmental education - Bibliography. 2. Environmental
sciences - Study and teaching (Elementary) - Bibliography. 3.
Language arts (Elementary) - Bibliography. I. Title.*
*TC Z5863.E55 R63 1998*

**Roberts, Paul.** The Roberts English series : a lingustics
program / by Paul Roberts. Teacher's ed. New York :
Harcourt, Brace & World c<1966- > v. : col. ill. ; 24
cm. Volume 9 reads "Teacher's manual."
*1. English language - Grammar - 1950- 2. English language -
Composition and exercises. 3. English language - Study and
teaching (Elementary) 4. Readers (Elementary) I. Title.*
*TC PE1112 .R6 Teacher's edition*

The Roberts English series : a linsgustics program / by Paul Roberts. Teacher's ed. New York : Harcourt, Brace & World c<1966-   > v. : col. ill. ; 24 cm. Volume 9 reads "Teacher's manual".
*1. English language - Grammar - 1950- 2. English language - Composition and exercises. 3. English language - Study and teaching (Elementary) 4. Readers (Elementary) I. Title.*
**TC PE1112 .R6 Teacher's edition**

**Roberts, Peter, 1963-** Education, literacy, and humanism : exploring the work of Paulo Freire / Peter Roberts. Westport, Conn. : Bergin & Garvey, 2000. xiv, 173 p. ; 24 cm. (Critical studies in education and culture series, 1064-8615) Includes bibliographical references (p. [157]-167) and index. ISBN 0-89789-571-1 (alk. paper) DDC 370/.1
*1. Freire, Paulo, - 1921- 2. Education - Philosophy. 3. Popular education. 4. Critical pedagogy. I. Title. II. Series.*
**TC LB880.F732 R62 2000**

**Robertson, Alice.**
Teaching in the 21st century. New York : Falmer Press, 1999.
**TC PE1404 .T394 1999**

**Robertson, Douglas S.** The new renaissance : computers and the next level of civilization / Douglas S. Robertson. New York : Oxford University Press, 1998. 200 p. ; 22 cm. Includes bibliographical references (p. [189]-192) and index. ISBN 0-19-512189-9 (alk. paper) DDC 303.48/34
*1. Computers and civilization.*
**TC QA76.9.C66 R618 1998**

**Robertson, Ian H., 1951-.**
Cognitive neurorehabilitation. Cambridge, UK ; New York : Cambridge University Press, c1999.
**TC RC553.C64 C654 1999**

**Robertson, Judith P., 1951-.**
Teaching for a tolerant world, grades K-6. Urbana, Ill. : National Council of Teachers of English, c1999.
**TC HM1271 .T43 1999**

**Robertson, Margaret.**
The child's world. Camberwell, Vic. : ACER Press, 2000.
**TC BF723.C5 C467 2000**

**Robertson, Ritchie.**
Freud, Sigmund, 1856-1939 The interpretation of dreams. Oxford ; New York : Oxford University Press, 1999.
**TC BF1078 .F72 1999**

**Robertson, Una A.** An illustrated history of the housewife, 1650-1950 / Una A Robertson. New York : St. Martin's Press, 1997. xii, 204 p. : ill. ; 26 cm. Includes bibliographical references (p. 189-200) and index. ISBN 0-312-17712-7 (cloth) DDC 305.43/649/0941
*1. Housewives - Great Britain - History. I. Title.*
**TC HD8039.H842 G77 1997**

**Robillard, Douglas.**
Dimensions of managing academic affairs in the community college. San Francisco : Jossey-Bass, 2000.
**TC LB2341 .D56 2000**

**ROBIN HOOD. *See* ROBIN HOOD (LEGENDARY CHARACTER).**

**ROBIN HOOD (LEGENDARY CHARACTER) - FICTION.**
Cadnum, Michael. In a dark wood. New York : Orchard Books, c1998.
**TC PZ7.C11724 In 1998**

**ROBIN HOOD (LEGENDARY CHARACTER) - JUVENILE FICTION.**
Cadnum, Michael. In a dark wood. New York : Orchard Books, c1998.
**TC PZ7.C11724 In 1998**

**Robins, Kevin.** Times of the technoculture : from the information society to the virtual life / Kevin Robins and Frank Webster. London ; New York : Routledge, 1999. viii, 318 p. ; 24 cm. (Comedia) Includes bibliographical references and index. ISBN 0-415-16115-0 (hbk) ISBN 0-415-16116-9 (pbk) DDC 303.48/33
*1. Information technology - Social aspects. 2. Information society. 3. Communication and culture. I. Webster, Frank. II. Title. III. Series.*
**TC T58.5 .R65 1999**

**Robinson, Anna Bess.** Leadership development in women's civic organizations / by Anna Bess Robinson. 1999. 248 leaves ; 29 cm. Typescript; issued also on microfilm. Thesis (Ed.D.)--Teachers College, Columbia University, 1999. Includes bibliographical references (leaves 222-229).
*1. Women volunteers in social services - New York (State) - Suffolk County. 2. Women civic leaders - New York (State) -*

*Suffolk County - Training of. 3. Leadership in women - New York (State) - Suffolk County. 4. Women civic leaders - New York (State) - Suffolk County. 5. Voluntarism. 6. Civic leaders - Training of. 7. Self-actualization (Psychology) I. Title.*
**TC 06 no. 11168**

**Robinson, Catherine A.** Tradition and liberation : the Hindu tradition in the Indian women's movement / Catherine A. Robinson. New York : St. Martin's Press, 1999. x, 230 p. ; 23 cm. Includes bibliographical references (p. 201-224) and index. ISBN 0-312-22718-3 (cloth) DDC 305.42/0954
*1. Feminism - South Asia - History - 20th century. 2. Women and religion - South Asia - History. 3. Women in Hinduism - India - History. 4. Hinduism and politics - India - History. 5. Women in politics - South Asia - History - 20th century. I. Title.*
**TC HQ1735.3 .R63 1999**

**Robinson, Denise L.**
Family nurse practitioner certification review. St. Louis : Mosby, c1999.
**TC RT120.F34 F353 1998**

**Robinson, James F.**
Jazz dance class [videorecording]. W. Long Branch, NJ : Kultur, [1992?]
**TC GV1784 .J3 1992**

**Robinson, Kim Stanley.** Antarctica / Kim Stanley Robinson. New York : Bantam Books, c1998. 511 p. : maps ; 25 cm. ISBN 0-553-10063-7 DDC 813/.54
*1. Ecology - Antarctica - Fiction. 2. Mineral resources conservation - Antarctica - Fiction. 3. Antarctica - Fiction. I. Title.*
**TC PS3568.O2893 A82 1998**

**Robinson, Richard David, 1940-.**
Issues and trends in literacy education. 2nd ed. Boston : Allyn and Bacon, c2000.
**TC LB1576 .I87 2000**

**Robinson, Tracy L.** The convergence of race, ethnicity, and gender : multiple identities in counseling / Tracy L. Robinson, Mary F. Howard-Hamilton. Upper Saddle River, N.J. : Merrill, c2000. xv, 338 p. ; 24 cm. Includes bibliographical references and indexes. ISBN 0-02-402481-3 DDC 158/.3
*1. Cross-cultural counseling. 2. Psychotherapy. I. Howard-Hamilton, Mary F. II. Title.*
**TC BF637.C6 R583 2000**

**Robitaille, David F.**
Curriculum frameworks for mathematics and science. Vancouver, Canada : Pacific Educational Press, c1993.
**TC QA11 .C87 1993**

National contexts for mathematics & science education. Vancouver : Pacific Educational Press, 1997.
**TC Q181 N37 1997**

**Robles de Melendez, Wilma J.** Teaching social studies in early education / by Wilma J. Robles de Melendez, Vesna Beck, Melba Fletcher. Albany, NY : Delmar Thomson Learning, c2000. xvii, 299 p. : ill. ; 23 cm. Includes bibliographical references. ISBN 0-7668-0288-4 DDC 372.83
*1. Social sciences - Study and teaching (Early childhood) - United States. I. Beck, Vesna. II. Fletcher, Melba. III. Title.*
**TC LB1139.5.S64 R62 2000**

**The Robot in the garden :** telerobotics and telepistemology in the age of the Internet / edited by Ken Goldberg. Cambridge, Mass. : MIT Press, 2000. xix, 366 p. : ill. ; 24 cm. (Leonardo (Series) (Cambridge, Mass.)) Includes bibliographical references and index. ISBN 0-262-07203-3 (alk. paper)
*1. Robotics. 2. Knowledge, Theory of. I. Goldberg, Ken. II. Title: Telerobotics and telepistemology in the age of the internet III. Series.*
**TC TJ211 .R537 2000**

**ROBOTICS. *See also* ROBOTS.**
The Robot in the garden. Cambridge, Mass. : MIT Press, 2000.
**TC TJ211 .R537 2000**

**ROBOTS - FICTION.**
Joyce, William. Rolie Polie Olie. 1st ed. New York : Laura Geringer Book, c1999.
**TC PZ8.3.J835 Ro 1999**

**Robson, Emanuel W., 1897-** The film answers back : an historical appreciation of the cimena / by E.W. & M.M. Robson. London : John Lane, [1947] 336 p. : front., plates ; 22 cm. "First published in 1939."
*1. Motion pictures - History. I. Robson, Mary Major, 1901- II. Title. III. Title: Historical appreciation of the cinema*
**TC PN1993.5.A1 R6 1947**

**Robson, Mary Major, 1901-.**
Robson, Emanuel W., 1897- The film answers back. London : John Lane, [1947]
**TC PN1993.5.A1 R6 1947**

**Roche, Denis, ill.**
Evans, Lezlie. Can you count ten toes? Boston, Mass. : Houghton Mifflin, 1999.
**TC QA113 .E84 1999**

**Rochester Symposium on Developmental Psychopathology (Series)**
(v. 8.) Developmental perspectives on trauma. Rochester, N.Y., USA : University of Rochester Press, 1997.
**TC RJ499 .D4825 1997**

**ROCK DRAWINGS. *See* ROCK PAINTINGS.**

**Rock, Irvin.**
Looking at looking. Thousand Oaks, Calif. ; London : Sage Publications, c2001.
**TC BF241 .L64 2001**

**ROCK PAINTINGS. *See* CAVE PAINTINGS.**

**ROCK PAINTINGS - ALGERIA - TASSILI-N-AJJER.**
Tassili N'Ajjer [videorecording]. [S.l.] : Editions Cinégraphiques ; Northbrook, Ill. : [distributed by] the Roland Collection, c1968.
**TC N5310.5.A4 T3 1968**

**Rockefeller University.**
Environmental influences: New York, Rockefeller University Press ; Russell Sage Foundation, 1968.
**TC BF353 .E5**

**ROCKETS (AERONAUTICS). *See* INTERPLANETARY VOYAGES.**

**Rockwell, Norman, 1894-.**
Norman Rockwell's world -- an American dream [videorecording]. [Chicago, Ill] : Home Vision, 1987, c1972.
**TC ND237.R68 N6 1987**

**ROCKWELL, NORMAN, 1894-.**
Norman Rockwell's world -- an American dream [videorecording]. [Chicago, Ill] : Home Vision, 1987, c1972.
**TC ND237.R68 N6 1987**

**Rodd, Jillian.** Leadership in early childhood : the pathway to professionalism / Jillian Rodd. 2nd edition. New York : Teachers College Press, 1998. xix, 212 p. ; 22 cm. (Early childhood education series) Includes bibliographical references and index. ISBN 0-8077-3776-3
*1. Early childhood educators - Training of - Australia. 2. Educational leadership - Australia. I. Title. II. Series.*
**TC LB1776.4.A8 R63 1998**

**Rodeheffer, Jane Kelley.**
Core texts in conversation . Lanham, MD : University Press of America, 2000.
**TC LB2361.5 .C68 2000**

**RODENTS. *See* MICE.**

**Rodger, Rosemary, 1946-** Planning an appropriate curriculum for the under fives / Rosemary Rodger. London : David Fulton, 1999. 163 p. : ill. ; 25 cm. (Early years.) Includes bibliographical references and index. ISBN 1-85346-550-X
*1. Education, Preschool - Great Britain - Curricula. I. Title. II. Series: Early years (London, England).*
**TC LB1140.25.G7 R64 1999**

**Rodgers, Beth L.**
Concept development in nursing. 2nd ed. Philadelphia : Saunders, c2000.
**TC RT84.5 .C6624 2000**

**Rodis, Pano.**
Learning disabilities and life stories. Boston : Allyn and Bacon, c2001.
**TC LC4818.38 .L42 2001**

**Rodman, Gilbert B., 1965-.**
Race in cyberspace. New York ; London : Routledge, 2000.
**TC HT1523 .R252 2000**

**Rodowsky, Colby F.** The Turnabout Shop / Colby Rodowsky. 1st ed. New York : Farrar, Straus and Giroux, c1998. 135 p. ; 22 cm. SUMMARY: In "conversations" with her dead mother, fifth-grader Livvy records her adjustment to living in Baltimore with a woman she had never met, and she comes to see the wisdom of her mother's choice as she gets to know the woman's large, loving family. ISBN 0-374-37889-4 DDC [Fic]
*1. Mothers and daughters - Fiction. 2. Death - Fiction. 3. Grief - Fiction. 4. Orphans - Fiction. I. Title.*
**TC PZ7.R6185 Tu 1998**

**Rodrigues, Chris.**
Photomontage today, Peter Kennard [videorecording]. [London] : Art Council of Great Britain ; Ho-Ho-Kus, N.J. : [distributed by] Anthony Roland Collection of Films on Art, c1982.
*TC TR685 .P45 1982*

**Rodriguez, Kathryn.**
The viola [videorecording]. Van Nuys, CA : Backstage Pass Productions ; Canoga Park, Calif. : [Distributed by] MVP Home Entertainment, c1991.
*TC MT285 .V5 1991*

The viola [videorecording]. Van Nuys, CA : Backstage Pass Productions ; Canoga Park, Calif. : [Distributed by] MVP Home Entertainment, c1995.
*TC MT285 .V5 1995*

**Rodriguez, Roberto.**
Connect with English [videorecording]. S. Burlington, Vt. : The Annenberg/CPB Collection, c1997.
*TC PE1128 .C66 1997*

**Roe, William Henry, 1917-.**
Drake, Thelbert L. The principalship. 5th ed. Upper Saddle River, N.J. : Merrill, c1999.
*TC LB2831.92 .D73 1999*

**Roehampton Institute. Centre for Mathematics Education.**
Mathematics in the primary school. 2nd ed. London : D. Fulton, 1999.
*TC QA135.5 .M36934 1999*

**Roehmann, Franz L.**
Music and child development. St. Louis, Mo. : MMB Music, c1990.
*TC ML3820 .M87 1990*

**Roemmelt, Arthur F., 1944-** Haunted children : rethinking medication of common psychological disorders / Arthur F. Roemmelt. Albany : State University of New York Press, c1998. xiii, 196 p. ; 24 cm. (SUNY series in transpersonal and humanistic psychology) Includes index. ISBN 0-7914-3885-6 (hardcover : alk. paper) ISBN 0-7914-3886-4 (pbk. : alk. paper) DDC 618.92/8914
*1. Child psychotherapy - Case studies. 2. Child psychotherapy - Philosophy. 3. Pediatric psychopharmacology - Social aspects. I. Title. II. Series.*
*TC RJ504 .R64 1998*

**Roeper, Peter.** Probability theory and probability logic / P. Roeper and H. Leblanc. Toronto ; Buffalo : University of Toronto Press, c1999. xii, 240 p. : ill. ; 24 cm. (Toronto studies in philosophy) Spine title: Probability theory and probability semantics. Includes bibliographical references (p. [231]-233) and indexes. ISBN 0-8020-0807-0
*1. Probabilities. 2. Semantics (Philosophy) 3. Logic. I. Leblanc, Hugues, 1924- II. Title. III. Title: Probability theory and probability semantics IV. Series.*
*TC BC141 .R64 1999*

**Roff, Sandra Shoiock.** From the Free Academy to CUNY : illustrating public higher education in New York City, 1847-1997 / Sandra Shoiock Roff, Anthony M. Cucchiara, Barbara J. Dunlap. New York : Fordham University Press, c2000. viii, 146 p. : ill. ; 25 cm. Includes bibliographical references (p. [133]-138) and index. ISBN 0-8232-2019-2 (hc) ISBN 0-8232-2020-6 (pbk.) DDC 378.747/1
*1. City University of New York - History. 2. Education, Higher - New York (State) - New York - History. I. Cucchiara, Anthony M. II. Dunlap, Barbara J. III. Title.*
*TC LD3835 .R64 2000*

**Rogers, Derek.** First break [videorecording]. Boston, MA : Fanlight Productions, c1997.
*TC RC465 .F5 1997*

First break [videorecording]. Boston, MA : Fanlight Productions, c1997.
*TC RC465 .F5 1997*

First break [videorecording]. Boston, MA : Fanlight Productions, c1997.
*TC RC465 .F5 1997*

**Rogers, Jackie, ill.**
Gould, Deborah Lee. Brendan's best-timed birthday. New York : Bradbury Press, 1988.
*TC PZ7.G723 Br 1988*

**Rogers, Joel, 1952-.**
Will standards save public education? Boston : Beacon Press, c2000.
*TC LB3060.83 .W55 2000*

**Rogers, Lester Brown, 1875-** Story of nations / Lester B. Rogers, Fay Adams, Walker Brown. New York : H.Holt, 1965. vi, 802 p. : ill. (some col.), maps (some col.) ; 24 cm. Includes index.
*1. World history. I. Adams, Fay Greene, 1903- II. Brown, Walker, 1894- III. Title.*

**Rogers, Richard Randall.** The impact of gay identity and perceived milieu toward gay employees on job involvement and organizational commitment of gay men / by Richard Randall Rogers. 1998. vi, 134 leaves ; 29 cm. Typescript; issued also on microfilm. Thesis (Ph.D.)--Columbia University, 1998. Includes bibliographical references (leaves 109-118).
*1. Gay men - United States. 2. Homosexuality in the workplace - United States. 3. Work - Psychological aspects. 4. Coming out (Sexual orientation). 5. Social interaction - Psychological aspects. 6. Commitment (Psychology). 7. Job satisfaction. 8. Job enrichment. 9. Social surveys. I. Title. II. Title: Job involvement and organizational commitment of gay men*
*TC 085 R635*

**Rogovin, Paula.** Classroom interviews : a world of learning / Paula Rogovin. Portsmouth, NH : Heinemann, c1998. xix, 153 p. : ill. ; 22 cm. (Teacher to teacher) Includes bibliographical references (p. 143-150). ISBN 0-325-00047-6 (alk. paper) DDC 372.19
*1. Education, Primary - Activity programs - United States. 2. Interviewing - Study and teaching (Primary) - United States. 3. Community - Study and teaching (Primary) - United States. 4. Curriculum planning - United States. 5. Language experience approach in education - United States. I. Title. II. Series: Teacher to teacher series.*
*TC LB1537 .R58 1998*

**Rohmann, Eric, ill.**
Ó Flatharta, Antoine. The prairie train. New York : Crown Publishers, 1997.
*TC PZ7.O331275 Pr 1997*

**Rohmer, Harriet.**
Cruz Martinez, Alejandro, d. 1987. [Mujer que brillaba aún más que el sol. English & Spanish] The woman who outshone the sun. San Francisco, Calif. : Children's Book Press, c1991.
*TC F1221.Z3 C78 1991*

**Rohrmann, Bernd.**
Cross-cultural risk perception. Dordrecht ; Boston ; London : Kluwer Academic, c2000.
*TC HM1101 .C76 2000*

**Rojek, Chris.** Leisure and culture / Chris Rojek. Houndmills [England] : Macmillan Press : New York : St. Martin's Press, 2000. ix, 234 p. ; 23 cm. Includes bibliographical references (p. 215-226) and index. ISBN 0-333-68000-6 (Macmillan : cloth) ISBN 0-333-68001-4 (Macmillan : paper) ISBN 0-312-22591-1 (St. Martin's : cloth) DDC 306.4/812
*1. Leisure - Sociological aspects. 2. Recreation - Sociological aspects. I. Title.*
*TC GV14.45 .R657 2000*

**Rojstaczer, Stuart.** Gone for good : tales of university life after the golden age / Stuart Rojstaczer. Oxford : Oxford University Press, 1999. x, 187 p. ; 24 cm. ISBN 0-19-512682-3 (alk. paper) DDC 378.73
*1. Education, Higher - United States. 2. College teaching - United States. I. Title.*
*TC LA227.4 .R65 1999*

**Roland, Anthony.**
What is a good drawing? [videorecording]. Peasmarsh, East Sussex, Eng. : Ho-Ho-Kus, NJ : Roland Collection, [1980-1986?].
*TC NC703 .W45 1980*

**Roland, Henry Montagu.**
What is a good drawing? [videorecording]. Peasmarsh, East Sussex, Eng. : Ho-Ho-Kus, NJ : Roland Collection, [1980-1986?].
*TC NC703 .W45 1980*

**ROLE CONFLICT.**
Newman, Stephanie. Self-silencing, depression, gender role, and gender role conflict in women and men. 1997.
*TC 085 N47*

**The role of measurement and evaluation in education policy** / edited by Frances M. Ottobre. Paris : Unesco Pub., 1999. 108 p. : ill. ; 30 cm. (Educational studies and documents ; 69) Includes bibliographical references. DDC 370
*1. Educational tests and measurements. 2. Education and state. I. Otobre, Frances M. II. Unesco. III. Series.*
*TC LB3051 .R653 1999*

**The role of the father in child development** / edited by Michael E. Lamb. 3rd ed. New York : Wiley, c1997 x, 416 p. ; 26 cm. Includes bibliographical references (p.[309]-397) and indexes. ISBN 0-471-11771-4 (cloth : alk. paper) DDC 306.874/2
*1. Fathers. 2. Father and child - United States. 3. Paternal deprivation - United States. 4. Single-parent families - United States. I. Lamb, Michael E., 1953-*

**The role of the learning advisor in action learning.**
O'Neil, Judith Ann. 1999.
*TC 06 no. 11156*

**The Role of theory in sex research** / John Bancroft, editor. Bloomington, IN : Indiana University Press, 2000. ix, 366 p. : 24 cm. (The Kinsey Institute series ; v. 6) Proceedings from a conference held at the Kinsey Institute on May 14-17, 1998, in Bloomington, Indiana. Includes bibliographical references and index. ISBN 0-253-33706-2 (cloth) DDC 306.7/072
*1. Sexology - Research - Congresses. 2. Sex - Congresses. I. Bancroft, John. II. Kinsey Institute for Research in Sex, Gender, and Reproduction. III. Series.*
*TC HQ60 .R65 2000*

**The role of work in people's lives.**
Peterson, Nadene. Australia ; Belmont, Calif. : Wadsworth Pub. Co., c2000.
*TC HF5381 .P483 2000*

**The role student aid plays in enrollment management** / Michael D. Coomes, editor. San Francisco : Jossey-Bass Publishers, 2000. 102 p. : ill. ; 23 cm. (New directions for student services, 0164-7970 ; no. 89) Includes bibliographical references and index. CONTENTS: The historical roots of enrollment management / Michael D. Coomes -- Federal and state aid in the 1900s: a policy context for enrollment management / Shirley A. Ort -- Enrollment management, institutional resources, and the private college / Joseph A. Russo, Michael D. Coomes -- Alternative financing methods for college / Robert DeBard -- The impact of student aid on recruitment and retention: what the research indicates / Edward P. St.John -- The role of financial aid in enrollment management / Don Hossler -- Recommended reading / Marie T. Saddlemire. ISBN 0-7879-5378-4
*1. Universities and colleges - United States - Admissions. 2. Student financial aid administration - United States. 3. Student aid - United States. 4. Universities and colleges - United States - Finance. I. Coomes, Michael D., 1951- II. Series: New directions for student services ; no. 89.*
*TC LB2337.4 .R655 2000*

**The roles of evaluation for vocational education and training.**
Grubb, W. Norton. London : Kogan Page ; Sterling, VA : Distributed in the US by Stylus Pub. Inc., 1999.
*TC LC1044 .G78 1999*

**Rolie Polie Olie.**
Joyce, William. 1st ed. New York : Laura Geringer Book, c1999.
*TC PZ8.3.J835 Ro 1999*

**Rollin, Lucy.** Psychoanalytic responses to children's literature / by Lucy Rollin and Mark I. West. Jefferson, N.C. : McFarland, c1999. xii, 178 p. ; 24 cm. Includes bibliographical references (p. 171-173) and index. ISBN 0-7864-0674-7 (lib. bdg. : alk. paper) DDC 820.9/9282/019
*1. Children's literature, English - History and criticism. 2. Children's literature - Illustrations - Psychological aspects. 3. Children's literature, American - History and criticism. 4. Children's literature - Psychological aspects. 5. Psychoanalysis and literature. 6. Psychology in literature. 7. Psychology in art. I. West, Mark I. II. Title.*
*TC PR990 .R65 1999*

Twentieth-century teen culture by the decades : a reference guide / Lucy Rollin. Westport, Conn. ; London : Greenwood Press, 1999. xiv, 396 p. : ill. ; 25 cm. Includes bibliographical references and index. ISBN 0-313-30223-5 (alk. paper) DDC 305.235/0973/0904
*1. Teenagers - United States - History - 20th century. 2. Teenagers - United States - Social life and customs. 3. Popular culture - United States - History - 20th century. I. Title. II. Title: 20th-century teen culture by the decades*
*TC HQ799.U65 R65 1999*

**Roma, Thomas.** Sunset Park / photographs by Thomas Roma. Washington : Smithsonian Institution Press, c1998. 63 p. : ill. ; 25 cm. (Photographers at work) "Published in association with Constance Sullivan Editions." ISBN 1-56098-643-3 (paper : alk. paper) DDC 779/.2/092
*1. Portrait photography - New York (State) - New York. 2. Swimming pools - New York (State) - New York - Pictorial works. 3. Roma, Thomas. 4. Sunset Park (New York, N.Y.) - Pictorial works. I. Title. II. Series.*
*TC TR680 .R675 1998*

**ROMA, THOMAS.**
Roma, Thomas. Sunset Park. Washington : Smithsonian Institution Press, c1998.
*TC TR680 .R675 1998*

**ROMAN ALPHABET.** *See* **ALPHABET.**

**ROMAN MUSIC.** *See* **MUSIC, GREEK AND ROMAN.**

**ROMANESQUE REVIVAL (ARCHITECTURE) - UNITED STATES.**
Breisch, Kenneth A. Henry Hobson Richardson and the small public library in America. Cambridge, Mass. : MIT Press, c1997.
*TC Z679.2.U54 B74 1997*

**Romano, Tom.** Blending genre, altering style : writing multigenre papers / Tom Romano. Portsmouth, NH : Boynton/Cook ; Heinemann, c2000. xi, 189 p. ; 24 cm. Includes bibliographical references (p. 181-184). ISBN 0-86709-478-8 DDC 808/.042/071
*1. English language - Rhetoric - Study and teaching. 2. Creative writing - Study and teaching. 3. Report writing - Study and teaching. 4. English language - Style. 5. Literary form. I. Title.*
*TC PE1404 .R635 2000*

**Romantic science and the experience of self.**
Halliwell, Martin. Aldershot, Hants ; Brookfield, Vt. : Ashgate, c1999.
*TC BF697 R6375 1999*

**ROMANTICISM.**
Literature and the child. Iowa City : University of Iowa Press, c1999.
*TC PR990 .L58 1999*

Roskelly, Hephzibah. Reason to believe. Albany : State University of New York Press, c1998.
*TC PE1404 .R67 1998*

**ROMANTICISM IN ART.**
Tekiner, Deniz. Modern art and the Romantic vision. Lanham, Md. : University Press of America, c2000.
*TC N6465.R6 T43 2000*

**ROMANTICISM IN LITERATURE.** *See* **ROMANTICISM.**

**ROMANTICISM - INFLUENCE.**
Halliwell, Martin. Romantic science and the experience of self. Aldershot, Hants ; Brookfield, Vt. : Ashgate, c1999.
*TC BF697 R6375 1999*

**Rombeau, John L.**
Clinical nutrition. 2nd ed. Philadelphia : Saunders, 1993.
*TC RM224 .P24 1993*

**ROME - CIVILIZATION.**
The eye expanded. Berkeley : University of California Press, c1999.
*TC DE59 .E93 1999*

Hemelrijk, Emily Ann, 1953- Matrona docta. London ; New York : Routledge, 1999.
*TC HQ1136 .H45 1999*

**ROME - CIVILIZATION - PROBLEMS, EXERCISES, ETC.**
Jenney, Charles. Third year Latin. Newton, Mass. : Allyn and Bacon, c1987.
*TC PA2087.5 .J462 1987*

**ROME - SOCIAL LIFE AND CUSTOMS.**
Hemelrijk, Emily Ann, 1953- Matrona docta. London ; New York : Routledge, 1999.
*TC HQ1136 .H45 1999*

**Romiette and Julio.**
Draper, Sharon M. (Sharon Mills) 1st ed. New York : Atheneum Books for Young Readers, 1999.
*TC PZ7.D78325 Ro 1999*

**Ronald, Kate.**
Roskelly, Hephzibah. Reason to believe. Albany : State University of New York Press, c1998.
*TC PE1404 .R67 1998*

**Rondal, J. A.**
Down syndrome. London : Whurr, 1999.
*TC RC571 .D675 1999*

**Roney, Christopher R. J.**
Sorrentino, Richard M. The uncertain mind. Philadelphia : Psychology Press, c2000.
*TC BF697 .S674 2000*

**Ronning, Royce R.**
Bruning, Roger H. Cognitive psychology and instruction. 3rd ed. Upper Saddle River, N.J. : Merrill, c1999.
*TC LB1060 .B786 1999*

**Room, Adrian.**
Dictionary of confusable words. Chicago, IL : Fitzroy Dearborn Publ., 2000.
*TC PE1591 .D53 2000*

**A room full of mirrors.**
Ikeda, Keiko. Stanford, Calif. : Stanford University Press; 1998.
*TC LB3618 .I54 1998*

**ROOMS.** *See* **CLASSROOMS; READING ROOMS.**

**ROOSEVELT, ELEANOR, 1884-1962 - FICTION.**
Ryan, Pam Muñoz. Amelia and Eleanor go for a ride. New York : Scholastic Press, 1999.
*TC PZ7.R9553 Am 1999*

**ROOSEVELT, ELEANOR, 1884-1962 - JUVENILE FICTION.**
Ryan, Pam Muñoz. Amelia and Eleanor go for a ride. New York : Scholastic Press, 1999.
*TC PZ7.R9553 Am 1999*

**ROOSEVELT, FRANKLIN D. (FRANKLIN DELANO), 1882-1945 - FICTION.**
Kirk, Daniel. Breakfast at the Liberty Diner. 1st ed. New York : Hyperion Books for Children, c1997.
*TC PZ7.K6339 Br 1997*

**Root-Bernstein, Michèle.**
Root-Bernstein, Robert Scott. Sparks of genius. Boston, Mass. : Houghton Mifflin Co., 1999.
*TC BF408 R66 1999*

**Root-Bernstein, Robert Scott.** Sparks of genius : the thirteen thinking tools of the world's most creative people / Robert and Michèle Root-Bernstein. Boston, Mass. : Houghton Mifflin Co., 1999. viii, 401 p. : ill. ; 24 cm. Includes bibliographical references (p. [344]-364) and index. ISBN 0-395-90771-3 DDC 153.3/5
*1. Creative thinking. I. Root-Bernstein, Michèle. II. Title.*
*TC BF408 R66 1999*

**Root, Kimberly Bulcken, ill.**
Schur, Maxine. [Shnook the peddler] The peddler's gift. 1st ed. New York : Dial Books for Young Readers, 1999.
*TC PZ7.S3964 Pe 1999*

**Root, Phyllis.** Soup for supper / by Phyllis Root ; illustrated by Sue Truesdell. 1st ed. New York : Harper & Row, c1986. 24 p., [1] p. of plates : col. ill. ; 24 cm. SUMMARY: A wee small woman catches a giant taking the vegetables from her garden and finds that they can share both vegetable soup and friendship. ISBN 0-06-025070-4 ISBN 0-06-025071-2 (lib. bdg.) DDC [E]
*1. Giants - Fiction. 2. Vegetables - Fiction. 3. Soups - Fiction. I. Truesdell, Sue, ill. II. Title.*
*TC PZ7.R6784 So 1986*

**Rootman, I.**
Settings for health promotion. Thousand Oaks, Calif. : Sage Publications, Inc., c2000.
*TC RA427.8 .S48 2000*

**Roots, James, 1955-** The politics of visual language : deafness, language choice, and political socialization / by James Roots. Ottawa : Carleton University Press, 1999. Includes bibliographical references. ISBN 0-88629-345-6 DDC 361.4/2
*1. Deaf - Means of communication. 2. Deafness - Social aspects. I. Title.*
*TC HV2395 R66 1999*

**ROPE JUMPING.** *See* **ROPE SKIPPING.**

**ROPE SKIPPING - FICTION.**
Millen, C. M. The low-down laundry line blues. Boston : Houghton Mifflin, 1999.
*TC PZ7.M6035 Lo 1999*

**Roper, Janice M.** Ethnography in nursing research / by Janice M. Roper, Jill Shapira. Thousand Oaks, Calif. : Sage Publications, c2000. x, 150 p. ; 22 cm. (Methods in nursing research ; v. 1) Includes bibliographical references (p. 135-141) and indexes. ISBN 0-7619-0873-0 (acid-free paper) ISBN 0-7619-0874-9 (pbk. : acid-free paper) DDC 610.73/072
*1. Nursing - Research - Methodology. 2. Ethnology. 3. Qualitative research. I. Shapira, Jill. II. Title. III. Series.*
*TC RT81.5 .R66 2000*

**RORSCHACH INKBLOT TEST.** *See* **RORSCHACH TEST.**

**Rorschach research exchange and journal of projective techniques.**
Journal of projective techniques. Glendale, Calif. : Society for Projective Techniques and Rorschach Institute, 1950-c1963.

**Rorschach research exchange and journal of projective techniques, 1947-1949.**
Journal of projective techniques & personality assessment. Glendale, Calif.

**Rorschach research exchange, Sept. 1936-1946.**
Journal of projective techniques & personality assessment. Glendale, Calif.

**RORSCHACH TEST - PERIODICALS.**
Journal of projective techniques. Glendale, Calif. : Society for Projective Techniques and Rorschach Institute, 1950-c1963.

Journal of projective techniques & personality assessment. Glendale, Calif.

**Rosa, Peter, 1951-.**
Educating entrepreneurs for wealth creation. Aldershot, Hants, England ; Brookfield, USA : Ashgate, 1998.
*TC HF1106 .E378 1998*

**Rosaen, Cheryl L.**
Guiding teacher learning. Washington. DC : AACTE, c1997.
*TC LB1731 .G85 1997*

**Rosch, Lee J., joint author.**
Ball, Grant T. Civics. Fifth edition. Chicago, Ill. : Follett Pub. Co., c1978.
*TC H62 .B34 1978*

**Rose, Jennifer S.**
Multivariate applications in substance use research. Mahwah, N.J. : Lawrence Erlbaum Associates, 2000.
*TC HV5809 .M84 2000*

**Rose, Mike.** Possible lives : the promise of public education in America / Mike Rose. New York, N.Y. : Penguin Books, 1996. 454 p. ; 24 cm. Includes bibliographical references (p. [437]-450). ISBN 0-14-023617-1 (pbk.)
*1. Public schools - United States - Case studies. I. Title.*
*TC LA217.2 R7 1996*

**Rosegrant, Teresa Jane, 1949-.**
Reaching potentials. Washington, DC : National Association for the Education of Young Children, c1992-<1995>
*TC LB1140.23 .R36 1992*

**Rosen, Efrem, 1933 - .**
Teaching children about health. Englewood, Colo. : Morton Pub., 1999.
*TC LB1587.A3 T43 1999*

**Rosen, Michael, 1946-** A Thanksgiving wish / Michael J. Rosen ; painting by John Thompson. New York : Blue Sky Press, c1999. 1 v. (various pagings). : col. ill. ; 29 cm. SUMMARY: When Amanda's grandmother dies and the extended family tries to recreate her famous Thanksgiving meal, friends and neighbors pitch in to help carry on Bubbe's traditions. ISBN 0-590-25563-0 DDC [Fic]
*1. Grandmothers - Fiction. 2. Thanksgiving Day - Fiction. 3. Neighbors - Fiction. I. Thompson, John, 1940- ill. II. Title.*
*TC PZ7.R71867 Tf 1999*

**Rosen, Sidney M.** Toward a gang solution : the redirectional method / Sidney M. Rosen, Pasimi V. Hingano, Deborah L.K. Spencer. [Norman, Okla.?] NRC Youth Services, 1996. 86 p. : ill. ; 23 cm. Includes bibliographical references (p. 85-86)
*1. Gangs. 2. Gangs - Hawaii - Case studies. 3. Juvenile delinquency. 4. Juvenile delinquency - Hawaii - Case studies. 5. Violence - United States - Prevention. 6. Violence - United States - Prevention - Case studies. 7. Intervention (Civil procedure) I. Hingano, Pasimi V. II. Spencer, Deborah L. K. III. Title. IV. Title: Redirectional method*
*TC HV6439.U7 R67 1996*

**Rosenberg, Karen F.**
Groza, Victor, 1956- Clinical and practice issues in adoption. Westport, Conn. : Praeger, 1998.
*TC HV875 .G776 1998*

**Rosenberg, Liz.** The silence in the mountains / by Liz Rosenberg ; illustrations by Chris Soentpiet. 1st American ed. New York : Orchard Books, c1999. 1 v. (unpaged) : col. ill. ; 29 cm. SUMMARY: When his family leaves their war-torn country to come to live in America, a young boy has trouble adjusting, until his grandfather helps him find what he had missed most. ISBN 0-531-30084-6 (tr. : alk. paper) ISBN 0-531-33084-2 (lib. ed. : alk. paper) DDC [Fic]
*1. Emigration and immigration - Fiction. 2. Family life - Fiction. 3. Grandfathers - Fiction. I. Soentpiet, Chris K., ill. II. Title.*
*TC PZ7.R71894 Si 1999*

**Rosenberg, Mindy Susan.**
Rossman, B. B. Robbie. Children and interparental violence. Philadelphia, Pa. : London : Brunner/Mazel, c2000.
*TC HQ784.V55 R675 2000*

**Rosenblatt, Paul C.** Parent grief : narratives of loss and relationship / written by Paul C. Rosenblatt. Philadelphia ; Hove [England] : Brunner/Mazel, c2000. xv, 252 p. ; 24 cm. (The series in death, dying and bereavement, 1091-5427) Includes bibliographical references and index. ISBN 1-58391-033-6 (hbk. : alk. paper) ISBN

1-58391-034-4 (pbk. : alk. paper) DDC 155.9/37/085
*1. Grief. 2. Bereavement - Psychological aspects. 3. Children - Death - Psychological aspects. 4. Children - Death - Psychological aspects - Case studies. 5. Loss (Psychology) I. Title. II. Series.*
*TC BF575.G7 R673 2000*

**Rosencrans, Gladys.** The spelling book : teaching children how to spell, now what to spell / Gladys Rosencrans. Newark, Del. : International Reading Association, c1998. viii, 141, 36 p. : ill. ; 27 cm. Includes bibliographical references (p. 127-128) and index. ISBN 0-87207-192-8 (pbk.) DDC 372.63/2
*1. English language - Orthography and spelling - Study and teaching (Elementary) I. Title.*
*TC LB1574 .R654 1998*

**Rosencrans, Kendra.**
Berg, Francie M. Women afraid to eat. Hettinger, ND : Healthy Weight Network, c2000.
*TC RC552.O25 B47 2000*

**Roseneil, Sasha, 1966-.**
Practising identities. New York : St. Martin's Press, 1999.
*TC HM131 .P677 1999*

**Rosenstein, Joseph G.**
Discrete mathematics in the schools. Providence, R.I. : American Mathematical Society, National Council of Teachers of Mathematics, c1997.
*TC QA11.A1 D57 1997*

**Rosenthal, Robert, 1933-** Contrasts and effect sizes in behavioral research : a correlational approach / Robert Rosenthal, Ralph L. Rosnow, Donald B. Rubin. Cambridge, U.K. ; New York : Cambridge University Press, 2000. x, 212 p. : ill. ; 26 cm. Includes bibliographical references (p. 205-207) and index. ISBN 0-521-65258-8 (hbk.) ISBN 0-521-65980-9 (pbk.) DDC 150/.7/27
*1. Psychometrics. 2. Analysis of variance. 3. Psychology - Statistical methods. 4. Social sciences - Statistical methods. I. Rosnow, Ralph L. II. Rubin, Donald B. III. Title.*
*TC BF39.2.A52 R67 2000*

**Rosenzweig, Mark R.**
History of the International Union of Psychological Science (IUPsyS). Hove, East Sussex : Psychology Press, 2000.
*TC BF11 .H57 2000*

**Rosenzweig, Roy.** The presence of the past : popular uses of history in American life / Roy Rosenzweig and David Thelen. New York : Columbia University Press, c1998. x, 291 p. ; 24 cm. Includes bibliographical references (p. [261]-284) and index. ISBN 0-231-11148-7 (alk. paper) DDC 973/.01
*1. United States - History - Philosophy. 2. Memory - Social aspects - United States. 3. National characteristics, American. 4. United States - Social life and customs. 5. Interviews - United States. I. Thelen, David P. (David Paul) II. Title.*
*TC E179.5 .R67 1998*

**Rosier, Katherine Brown.** Mothering inner-city children : the early school years / Katherine Brown Rosier. New Brunswick, NJ : Rutgers University Press, 2000. x, 301 p. ; 24 cm. Includes bibliographical references and index. ISBN 0-8135-2796-1 (cloth : alk. paper) DDC 362.83 DDC 362.83
*1. Socially handicapped women - Indiana - Indianapolis - Interviews. 2. Women heads of households - Indiana - Indianapolis - Interviews. 3. Afro-American single mothers - Indiana - Indianapolis - Interviews. 4. Socially handicapped children - Indiana - Indianapolis - Case studies. 5. Socially handicapped children - Education - Indiana - Indianapolis - Case studies. 6. Education - Parent participation - Indiana - Indianapolis - Case studies. 7. Child rearing - Indiana - Indianapolis - Case studies. I. Title.*
*TC HV1447.I53 R67 2000*

**Roskelly, Hephzibah.** Reason to believe : romanticism, pragmatism, and the possibility of teaching / Hephzibah Roskelly and Kate Ronald. Albany : State University of New York Press, c1998. xiv, 187 p. ; 24 cm. Includes bibliographical references (p. 167-176) and index. ISBN 0-7914-3795-7 (hc) ISBN 0-7914-3796-5 (pb) DDC 808/.042/071
*1. English language - Rhetoric - Study and teaching. 2. Report writing - Study and teaching. 3. Romanticism. 4. Pragmatism. I. Ronald, Kate. II. Title.*
*TC PE1404 .R67 1998*

**Roskos, Kathy.**
Children achieving. Newark, Del. : International Reading Association, c1998.
*TC LB1139.5.R43 C55 1998*

Play and literacy in early childhood. Mahwah, N.J. : Lawrence Erlbaum Associates, Publishers, 2000.

*TC LB1140.35.P55 P557 2000*

**Rosner, Mary.**
History, reflection, and narrative. Stamford, Conn. : Ablex Pub., c1999.
*TC PE1405.U6 H56 1999*

**Rosnow, Ralph L.**
Rosenthal, Robert, 1933- Contrasts and effect sizes in behavioral research. Cambridge, U.K. ; New York : Cambridge University Press, 2000.
*TC BF39.2.A52 R67 2000*

**Ross, Alice.** Jezebel's spooky spot / Alice Ross & Kent Ross ; illustrated by Ted Rand. 1st ed. New York : Dutton Children's Books, 1999. 1 v. (unpaged) : col. ill. ; 29 cm. SUMMARY: When Jezebel's Papa goes to war, she finds a special place in the woods to do battle with her own fears. ISBN 0-525-45448-9 DDC [Fic]
*1. Separation anxiety - Fiction. 2. Fear - Fiction. 3. Fathers and daughters - Fiction. 4. Afro-Americans - Fiction. I. Ross, Kent. II. Rand, Ted, ill. III. Title.*
*TC PZ7.R719694 Jf 1999*

**Ross, Alistair, 1946-** Curriculum : construction and critique / Alistair Ross. New York : Falmer Press, 2000. xiii, 187 p. : ill. ; 26 cm. (Master classes in education series) Includes bibliographical references (p. 161-176) and index. ISBN 0-7507-0797-6 (hbk.) ISBN 0-7507-0621-X (pbk.) DDC 375/.001/0941
*1. Education - Curricula - Social aspects - Great Britain. 2. Curriculum planning - Social aspects - Great Britain. I. Title. II. Series.*
*TC LB1564.G7 R66 2000*

**Ross, Doran H., joint author.**
Cole, Herbert M. The arts of Ghana. Los Angeles : Museum of Cultural History, University of California, c1977.
*TC NX589.6.G5 C64*

**Ross, Heidi A., 1954-.**
The ethnographic eye. New York : Falmer Press, 2000.
*TC LB45 .E837 2000*

**Ross, Karen, 1957-.**
Woodward, Diana, 1948- Managing equal opportunities in higher education. Buckingham [England] ; Philadelphia : Society for Research into Higher Education : Open University Press, 2000.
*TC LC213.3.G7 W66 2000*

**Ross, Kenneth N. (Kenneth Norman), 1947-** Indicators of the quality of education : a summary of a national study of primary schools in Zimbabwe / by Kenneth N. Ross, T. Neville Postlethwaite. Paris : International Institute for Educational Planning, 1992. v, 67 p. : ill. ; 21 cm. (IIEP research report ; no. 96) Includes bibliographical references (p. 67).
*1. Education, Primary - Zimbabwe. I. Postlethwaite, T. Neville. II. Title. III. Series: IIEP research report ; 96.*
*TC LA1592 .R67 1992*

**Ross, Kent.**
Ross, Alice. Jezebel's spooky spot. 1st ed. New York : Dutton Children's Books, 1999.
*TC PZ7.R719694 Jf 1999*

**Ross, Peter.** Let's face it : the history of the Archibald Prize / Peter Ross. Sydney, Australia : Art Gallery of New South Wales, 1999. 147 p. : col. ill. ; 32 cm. Includes index. ISBN 0-7313-8966-2 ISBN 0-7313-8942-5 (pbk)
*1. Archibald Prize - History. 2. Portrait painting, Australian - History. 3. Art - Competitions - Australia - History. I. Art Gallery of New South Wales. II. Title.*
*TC ND1327.A86 R67 1999*

**Ross, Tony, ill.**
Camp, Lindsay. Why? New York : Putnam, c1998.
*TC PZ7.C1475 Wf 1998*

**Rosser, Sue Vilhauer.** Women, science, and society : the crucial union / Sue V. Rosser. New York : Teachers College Press, c2000. x, 166 p. : ill.; 24 cm. (Athene series) Includes bibliographical references (p. 115-156) and index. ISBN 0-8077-3943-X (cloth : acid-free paper) ISBN 0-8077-3942-1 (paper : acid-free paper) DDC 570/.82
*1. Women life scientists. 2. Women's studies. 3. Feminism. I. Title. II. Series.*
*TC QH305.5 .R67 2000*

**Rosser, Vicki J.**
Understanding the work and career paths of midlevel administrators. San Francisco : Jossey-Bass, 2000.
*TC LB2341 .N5111 2000*

**Rossi, Peter Henry, 1921-** Evaluation : a systematic approach / Peter H. Rossi, Howard E. Freeman, Mark W. Lipsey. 6th ed. Thousand Oaks, Calif. : Sage Publications, c1999. x, 500 p. : ill. ; 25 cm. Includes bibliographical references (p. 451-475) and index. CONTENTS: Programs, policies, and evaluation -- Tailoring

evaluations -- Identifying issues and formulating questions -- Needs assessment -- Expressing and assessing program theory -- Assessing program process and performance -- Strategies for impact assessment -- Randomized designs for impact assessment -- Quasi-experimental impact assessments -- Assessment of full-coverage programs -- Measuring efficiency -- The social context of evaluation. ISBN 0-7619-0893-5 (acid-free paper) DDC 361.6/1/072
*1. Evaluation research (Social action programs) I. Freeman, Howard E. II. Lipsey, Mark W. III. Title.*
*TC H62 .R666 1999*

**Rossīa, obrazovanie v perekhodnyi period.**
Russia, education in the transition = [S.l.] : The World Bank, ECA Country Development III, Human Resources Division, 1995.
*TC LA839.2 .R87 1995*

**Rosskopf, Allen.**
Marshall, Robert H. AGS earth science. Circle Pines, Minn. : AGS, American Guidance Service, c1997.
*TC QE28 .M37 1997*

Marshall, Robert H. AGS earth science. Teacher's ed. Circle Pines, Minn. : AGS, American Guidance Service, c1997.
*TC QE28 .M37 1997 Teacher's Ed.*

**Rossman, B. B. Robbie.** Children and interparental violence : the impact of exposure / B.B. Robbie Rossman, Honore M. Hughes, Mindy S. Rosenberg. Philadelphia, Pa. ; London : Brunner/Mazel, c2000. xi, 172 p. ; 25 cm. Includes bibliographical references and index. ISBN 0-87630-958-9 (hbk. : alk. paper) DDC 362.82/92
*1. Children and violence. 2. Family violence. 3. Family violence - Prevention. I. Hughes, Honore M. II. Rosenberg, Mindy Susan. III. Title.*
*TC HQ784.V55 R675 2000*

**Rossman, Gretchen B.**
Marshall, Catherine. Designing qualitative research. 3rd ed. Thousand Oaks, Calif. : Sage Publications, c1999.
*TC H62 .M277 1999*

**Rost, Joseph C. (Joseph Clarence), 1931-** Leadership for the twenty-first century / Joseph C. Rost ; foreword by James MacGregor Burns. New York : Praeger, 1991. xv, 220 p. : ill. ; 24 cm. Includes bibliographical references (p. [189]-213) and index. ISBN 0-275-93670-8 (alk. paper) ISBN 0-275-94610-X (pbk.) DDC 303.3/4
*1. Leadership. I. Title. II. Title: Leadership for the 21st century.*
*TC HM141 .R685 1991*

**Roszak, Theodore, 1933-** The gendered atom : reflections on the sexual psychology of science / Theodore Roszak ; foreword by Jane Goodall. Berkeley, Calif. : Conari Press, 1999. xiv, 174 p. ; 20 cm. Includes bibliographical references. ISBN 1-57324-171-7 (hardcover) DDC 501
*1. Science and psychology. 2. Psychology - Philosophy. 3. Sex (Psychology) 4. Feminist psychology. I. Title.*
*TC BF64 .R69 1999*

**Rotenberg, Ken J.**
Lonliness in childhood and adolescence. New York : Cambridge University Press, 1999.
*TC BF723.L64 L64 1999*

**Roth, Jeffrey A., 1945-.**
Understanding and preventing violence. Washington, D.C. : National Academy Press, 1993-1994.
*TC HN90.V5 U53 1993*

**Roth, John K.**
Rights, justice, and community. Lewiston, N.Y., USA : Edwin Mellen Press, c1992.
*TC HM216 .R56 1992*

**Rothberg, Donald Jay.**
Ken Wilber in dialogue. 1st Quest ed. Wheaton, Ill. : Theosophical Pub. House, 1998.
*TC BF204.7 .K46 1998*

**Rothblum, Esther D.**
Learning from our mistakes. New York : Haworth Press, c1998.
*TC RC489.F45 L43 1998*

**Rothenberg, Paula S., 1943-** Invisible privilege : a memoir about race, class, and gender / Paula Rothenberg. Lawrence : University Press of Kansas, c2000. x, 229 p. ; 23 cm. Includes bibliographical references. ISBN 0-7006-1004-9 (alk. paper) DDC 305.8/00973
*1. Rothenberg, Paula S. - 1943- - Childhood and youth. 2. Racism - United States - Case studies. 3. Social classes - United States - Case studies. 4. Sex role - United States - Case studies. 5. Jewish women - United States - Biography. 6. United States - Race relations - Case studies. I. Title.*
*TC E185.615 .R68 2000*

**ROTHENBERG, PAULA S., 1943 - -CHILDHOOD AND YOUTH.**
Rothenberg, Paula S., 1943- Invisible privilege. Lawrence : University Press of Kansas, c2000.
*TC E185.615 .R68 2000*

**Rothko, Mark, 1903-1970.** Mark Rothko : the works on canvas : catalogue raisonné / David Anfam. New Haven : Yale University Press ; Washington, D.C. : National Gallery of Art, c1998. 708 p. : ill. (chiefly col.) ; 31 cm. Includes bibliographical references (p. 681-696) and index. ISBN 0-300-07489-1 (cloth) DDC 759.13
*1. Rothko, Mark, - 1903-1970 - Catalogues raisonnés. I. Anfam, David. II. Title. III. Title: Works on canvas*
*TC ND237.R725 A4 1998*

**ROTHKO, MARK, 1903-1970 - CATALOGUES RAISONNÉS.**
Rothko, Mark, 1903-1970. Mark Rothko. New Haven : Yale University Press ; Washington, D.C. : National Gallery of Art, c1998.
*TC ND237.R725 A4 1998*

**ROTHKO, MARK, 1903-1970 - EXHIBITIONS.**
Weiss, Jeffrey. Mark Rothko. Washington : National Gallery of Art ; New Haven, Conn. : Yale University Press, c1998.
*TC N6537.R63 A4 1998*

**Rothman, Robert, 1959-.**
Testing, teaching, and learning. Washington, D.C. : National Academy Press, c1999.
*TC LC3981 .T4 1999*

**Rothstein, Laura F.** Special education law / Laura F. Rothstein. New York : Longman, 2000. xxi, 342 p. ; 24 cm. Includes bibliographical references and index. ISBN 0-8013-1961-7 (alk. paper) DDC 344.73/0791
*1. Special education - Law and legislation - United States. I. Title.*
*TC KF4210 .R68 2000*

**Rottweiler, Gail Price.**
Cutchin, Kay Lynch. Landscapes and language. Cambridge, UK ; New York, NY, USA : Cambridge University Press, 1999.
*TC PE1128 .C88 1999*

**Rouse, Martyn.**
Special education and school reform in the United States and Britain. London ; New York : Routledge, 2000.
*TC LC3986.G7 S64 2000*

**Rousmaniere, Kate, 1958-.**
Silences & images. New York : P. Lang, c1999.
*TC LA128 .S55 1999*

**The routes of resistance.**
Kenny, Máirín. Aldershot, Hants, England ; Brookfield, Vt. : Ashgate, c1997.
*TC LC3650.I74 K45 1997*

**The Routledge atlas of African American history.**
Earle, Jonathan. New York : Routledge, 2000.
*TC E185 .E125 2000*

**Routledge atlases of American history**
Earle, Jonathan. The Routledge atlas of African American history. New York : Routledge, 2000.
*TC E185 .E125 2000*

Opdycke, Sandra. The Routledge historical atlas of women in America. New York : Routledge, 2000.
*TC HQ1410 .P68 2000*

**The Routledge historical atlas of women in America.**
Opdycke, Sandra. New York : Routledge, 2000.
*TC HQ1410 .P68 2000*

**Routledge international companion to education /** edited by Bob Moon, Miriam Ben-Peretz and Sally Brown. London ; New York : Routledge, 2000. xv, 1006 p. : ill. ; 26 cm. Includes bibliographical references and index. ISBN 0-415-11814-x
*1. Education. I. Moon, Bob, 1945- II. Ben-Peretz, Miriam. III. Brown, Sally.*
*TC LB7 .R688 2000*

**Routledge modular psychology**
Cave, Sue, 1949- Therapeutic approaches in psychology. London ; New York : Routledge, 1999.
*TC RC480 .C37 1999*

Wren, Kevin, 1947- Social influences. London ; New York : Routledge, 1999.
*TC HM1176 .W74 1999*

**Routledge research in education.**
Norwich, Brahm. Education and psychology in interaction. London ; New York : Routledge, 2000.
*TC LB1051 .N645 2000*

(1) Learning communities in education. London ; New York : Routledge, 1999.

*TC LB14.7 .L43 1999*

(3) Bottery, Mike. Teachers and the state. London ; New York : Routledge, c2000.
*TC LB1775.4.G7 B68 2000*

**Routledge studies in distance education**
Perraton, H. D. Open and distance learning in the developing world. London ; New York : Routledge, 2000.
*TC LC5808.D48 P47 2000*

Staff development in open and flexible learning. London ; New York : Routledge, 1998.
*TC LC5800 .S83 1998*

**Routledge studies in social and political thought**
(17) Goffman and social organization. London ; New York : Routledge, 1999.
*TC HM291 .G57 1999*

**Routman, Regie.** Conversations : strategies for teaching, learning, and evaluating / Regie Routman. Portsmouth, NH : Heinemann, c2000. xlii, 613, 240b p. : ill. 24 cm. Includes bibliographical references (p.603-613) and index. ISBN 0-325-00109-X DDC 372.6/044
*1. Language arts (Elementary) 2. Effective teaching. 3. Educational tests and measurements. I. Title.*
*TC LB1576 .R757 1999*

**Rovner, Julie.** Health care policy and politics A to Z / Julie Rovner. Washington, DC : CQ Press, 2000. xii, 244 p. : ill. ; 24 cm. Includes bibliographical references and index. ISBN 1-56802-437-1 DDC 362.1/0973
*1. Medical policy - United States. 2. Medical care - Political aspects - United States. 3. Public health - Political aspects - United States. 4. Health Policy - United States. 5. Public Health - United States. I. Title.*
*TC RA395.A3 R685 1999*

**Rowan, Kate.** I know how we fight germs / Kate Rowan ; illustrated by Katharine McEwen. Cambridge, Mass. : Candlewick Press, 1999. 25, [5] p. : col. ill. ; 26 cm. (Sam's science) SUMMARY: Sam and his mother talk about germs, viruses, and bacteria, including how the body fights harmful germs and uses germs that are helpful. ISBN 0-7636-0503-4 (alk. paper) DDC 616.07/9
*1. Immunity - Juvenile literature. 2. Infection - Juvenile literature. 3. Bacteria - Juvenile literature. 4. Bacteria. 5. Viruses. I. McEwen, Katharine, ill. II. Title. III. Series: Rowan, Kate. Sam's science.*
*TC QR57 .R69 1999*

**Sam's science.**
Rowan, Kate. I know how we fight germs. Cambridge, Mass. : Candlewick Press, 1999.
*TC QR57 .R69 1999*

**Rowan, Tim, 1952-** Solution-oriented therapy for chronic and severe mental illness / Tim Rowan and Bill O'Hanlon. New York : Wiley, c1999. xiv, 177 p. ; 23 cm. Includes bibliographical references (p. 165-167) and index. ISBN 0-471-18362-8 (cloth : alk. paper) DDC 616.89/1
*1. Mentally ill - Rehabilitation. 2. Solution-focused therapy. I. O'Hanlon, William Hudson. II. Title.*
*TC RC480.53 .R69 1999*

**Rowell, Loring B.** Human cardiovascular control / Loring B. Rowell. New York : Oxford University Press, 1993. xv, 500 p. : ill. ; 24 cm. Includes bibliographical references and index. ISBN 0-19-507362-2 (cloth : acid-free paper) DDC 612.1/3
*1. Blood - Circulation - Regulation. 2. Blood pressure - Regulation. 3. Adaptation, Physiological. 4. Cardiovascular System - physiology. 5. Exercise. 6. Hemodynamics. I. Title.*
*TC QP109 .R68 1993*

**Rowland, William G.**
A First dictionary of cultural literacy. Boston : Houghton Mifflin, 1989.
*TC AG105 .F43 1989*

**Rowlands, Mark.** The body in mind : understanding cognitive processes / Mark Rowlands. Cambridge, U.K. ; New York : Cambridge University Press, 1999. x, 270 p. ; 23 cm. (Cambridge studies in philosophy) Includes bibliographical references (p. 258-266) and index. ISBN 0-521-65274-X (hb) DDC 128/.2
*1. Philosophy of mind. 2. Mind and body. 3. Cognition. 4. Externalism (Philosophy of mind) I. Title. II. Series.*
*TC BD418.3 .R78 1999*

**Rowling, J. K.** Harry Potter and the Chamber of Secrets / by J.K. Rowling. New York : Arthur A. Levine Books, 1999. 341 p. : ill. ; 24 cm. Sequel to: Harry Potter and the sorcerer's stone. SUMMARY: When the Chamber of Secrets is opened again at the Hogswart School for Witchcraft and Wizardry, second-year student Harry Potter finds himself in danger from a dark power that has once more been unleashed on the school. ISBN 0-439-06486-4 (hardcover) DDC [Fic]
*1. Wizards - Fiction. 2. Magic - Fiction. 3. Schools - Fiction. 4. England - Fiction. I. Title.*

*TC PZ7.R7968 Har 1999*

Harry Potter and the prisoner of Azkaban / by J.K. Rowling. New York : Arthur A. Levine Books, 1999. 435 p. : ill. ; 24 cm. Sequel to: Harry Potter and the Chamber of Secrets. SUMMARY: During his third year at Hogwarts School for Witchcraft and Wizardry, Harry Potter must confront the devious and dangerous wizard responsible for his parents' deaths. ISBN 0-439-13635-0 (hc) ISBN 0-439-13636-9 (pb) DDC [Fic]
*1. Wizards - Fiction. 2. Magic - Fiction. 3. Schools - Fiction. 4. England - Fiction. I. Title.*
*TC PZ7.R79835 Ham 1999*

Harry Potter and the sorcerer's stone / by J.K. Rowling ; illustrations by Mary GrandPré. 1st American ed. New York : A.A. Levine Books, 1998. vi, 309 p. : ill. ; 24 cm. Sequel: Harry Potter and the Chamber of Secrets. SUMMARY: Rescued from the outrageous neglect of his aunt and uncle, a young boy with a great destiny proves his worth while attending Hogwarts School for Wizards and Witches. ISBN 0-590-35340-3 (hardcover) ISBN 0-590-35342-X (pbk.) DDC [Fic]
*1. Witches - Fiction. 2. Wizards - Fiction. 3. Schools - Fiction. 4. England - Fiction. I. GrandPré, Mary, ill. II. Title.*
*TC PZ7.R79835 Har 1998*

**Roy, Alice Myers.**
Perspectives on plagiarism and intellectual property in a postmodern world. Albany : State University of New York Press, c1999.
*TC PN167 .P47 1999*

**Roy, Ashok.**
Bomford, David. Colour. London : National Gallery Company ; [New Haven, Conn.] : Distributed by Yale Universtiy Press, 2000.
*TC ND1489 B66 2000*

**Roy, Beth.** Bitters in the honey : tales of hope and disappointment across divides of race and time / Beth Roy. Fayetteville : University of Arkansas Press, 1999. vi, 400 p. ; 24 cm. Includes bibliographical references (p. [385]-397) and index. ISBN 1-55728-553-5 (cloth : alk. paper) ISBN 1-55728-554-3 (paper : alk. paper) DDC 379.2/ 63/0976773
*1. Central High School (Little Rock, Ark.) - History - 20th century 2. School integration - Arkansas - Little Rock - History. I. Title.*
*TC LC214.23.L56 R69 1999*

**Roy, Cynthia B., 1950-.**
Innovative practices for teaching sign language interpreters. Washington, D.C. : Gallaudet University Press, 2000.
*TC HV2402 .I56 2000*

**Roy Lichtenstein** [videorecording] / produced and directed by Chris Hunt ; edited and presented by Melvyn Bragg. [Chicago, IL] : Home Vision ; [S.l.] : distributed worldwide by RM Asssociates, c1991. 1 videocassette (51 min.) : sd., col. ; 1/2 in. (Portrait of an artist) At head of title: Home Vision... presents an RM Arts Production [videorecording]. VHS. Catalogued from credits and container. Title from container. Editor, Ian Pitch. "An Iambic Production for LWT."--Credits. "LIC 010"--Container. "A Public Media Incoporated Release."--Container.7 Originally presented on the television program South Bank Show. For adolescents through adult. SUMMARY: A profile of American Pop Art artist Roy Lichtenstein's life and work. Lichetenstein talks about his current work, the Pop Art explosion, and the history of Western art. ISBN 0-7800-0751-4
*1. Lichtenstein, Roy, - 1923- 2. Pop art - United States. 3. Comic books, strips, etc., in art. 4. Painters - United States - Biography. 5. Documentary television programs. 6. Biographical films. I. Hunt, Chris. II. Bragg, Melvyn, 1931- III. Lichtenstein, Roy, 1923- IV. Iambic Productions (Firm) V. Home Vision (Firm) VI. RM Arts (Firm) VII. London Weekend Television, ltd. VIII. Public Media Incorporated (Wilmette, Ill.) IX. Reiner Moritz Associates. X. Title: South Bank show (Television program) XI. Title: Home Vision... presents an RM Arts Production [videorecording] XII. Series.*
*TC ND237.L627 R6 1991*

**Royal Anthropological Institute of Great Britain and Ireland.**
[Journal of the Royal Anthropological Institute of Great Britain and Ireland (Online)] The journal of the Royal Anthropological Institute of Great Britain and Ireland [computer file]. London [England] : The Institute, 1907-1965.
*TC EJOURNALS*

**Royal education.**
Gordon, Peter, 1927- London ; Portland, OR : Frank Cass, 1999.
*TC LC4945.G72 G67 1999*

**Royal Society (Great Britain).**
Attention, space, and action. Oxford ; New York : Oxford University Press, 1999.

*TC QP405 .A865 1999*

**ROYALISTS.** *See* **MONARCHY.**

**ROYALTY.** *See* **PRINCESSES.**

**Rozmajzl, Michon.** Music fundamentals, methods, and materials for the elementary classroom teacher / Michon Rozmajzl, René Boyer-Alexander. 3rd ed. New York ; Harlow, England : Longman, c2000. xx, 394 p. : ill., music ; 28 cm. Includes bibliographical references and index. ISBN 0-8013-3081-5 DDC 372.87/044
*1. School music - Instruction and study - United States. I. Boyer-Alexander, René. II. Title.*
*TC MT1 .R85 2000*

**R.R. Bowker Company.**
Bowker's directory of audiocassettes for children. New Providence, N.J. : R.R. Bowker, c1998-
*TC ZA4750 .B69*

**RUBBER-SHEET GEOMETRY.** *See* **TOPOLOGY.**

**RUBBER STAMP PRINTING.**
Taormina, Grace. The complete guide to rubber stamping. New York : Watson-Guptill Publications, c1996.
*TC TT867 .T36 1996*

**Ruben, Douglas H.**
Behavioral management in the public schools. Westport, Conn. ; London : Praeger, 1999.
*TC LB1060.2 .B44 1999*

**Rubenfeld, M. Gaie.** Critical thinking in nursing : an interactive approach / M. Gaie Rubenfeld, Barbara K. Scheffer ; illustrations by Mark Steele. 2nd ed. Philadelphia : Lippincott, c1999. xxv, 438 p. : ill. ; 23 cm. Includes bibliographical references (p. 419-424) and index. ISBN 0-7817-1634-9 (paper : alk. paper) DDC 610.73
*1. Nursing - Philosophy. 2. Critical thinking. 3. Nursing - Problems, exercises, etc. 4. Nursing Process. 5. Problem Solving - nurses' instruction. 6. Nursing - problems. I. Scheffer, Barbara K. II. Title.*
*TC RT84.5 .R83 1999*

**Rubenstein, William B.**
AIDS agenda. 1st ed. New York : New Press, c1992.
*TC RA644.A25 A33214 1992*

**Rubin, Alan M., 1949-.**
Rubin, Rebecca B. Communication research. 5th ed. Belmont, CA : Wadsworth Thomson Learning, 1999.
*TC P91.3 .R83 1999*

**Rubin, Donald B.**
Rosenthal, Robert, 1933- Contrasts and effect sizes in behavioral research. Cambridge, U.K. ; New York : Cambridge University Press, 2000.
*TC BF39.2.A52 R67 2000*

**Rubin, Dorothy.** Teaching elementary language arts : a balanced approach / Dorothy Rubin. 6th ed. Boston : Allyn and Bacon, c2000. xxv, 470 p. : ill. ; 24 cm. Includes bibliographical references and index. ISBN 0-205-29372-7 DDC 372.6/044
*1. Language arts (Elementary) I. Title.*
*TC LB1576 .R773 2000*

**Rubin, Jeffrey B.** A psychoanalysis for our time : exploring the blindness of the seeing I / Jeffrey B. Rubin. New York : New York University Press, c1998. xiv, 255 p. ; 23 cm. Includes bibliographical references (p. 223-245) and index. ISBN 0-8147-7491-1 (alk. paper) DDC 150/.195
*1. Psychoanalysis. I. Title.*
*TC BF173 .R76 1998*

**Rubin, Rebecca B.** Communication research : strategies and sources / Rebecca B. Rubin, Alan M. Rubin, Linda J. Piele. 5th ed. Belmont, CA : Wadsworth Thomson Learning, 1999. xv, 317 p. ; 24 cm. Includes bibliographical references and indexes. ISBN 0-534-56169-1 (alk. paper) DDC 302.2/072
*1. Communication - Research - Methodology. I. Rubin, Alan M., 1949- II. Piele, Linda J. III. Title.*
*TC P91.3 .R83 1999*

**Rubinstein, Robert L.**
Black, Helen K., 1952- Old souls. New York : A. de Gruyter, c2000.
*TC HQ1064.U6 P424 2000*

The many dimensions of aging. New York : Springer Pub., c2000.
*TC HQ1061 .M337 2000*

**Rudd, M. David.**
Suicide science. Boston ; London : Kluwer Academic Publishers, c2000.
*TC RC569 .S9368 2000*

**Ruddiman, Ken.** Strategic management of college premises / Ken Ruddiman. London : Falmer, 1999. ix, 78 p. : ill. ; 24 cm. (Managing colleges effectively series ; 4)

Includes index. ISBN 0-7507-0966-9
*1. College facilities - Great Britain. 2. Universities and colleges - Great Britain - Administration. I. Title. II. Series.*
*TC LB3223.5.G7 R84 1999*

**Rudnick, Stephen.** Teaching middle school mathematics. Boston : Allyn and Bacon, c2000.
*TC QA11 .K818 2000*

**Ruetsche, Laura.**
Science at century's end. Pittsburgh, Pa. : University of Pittsburgh Press, c2000.
*TC Q175 .S4193 2000*

**Rufo-Lignos, Patricia Marie.** Towards a new topology of public and private schools / by Patricia Marie Rufo-Lignos. 1999. xi, 256 leaves : ill. ; 29 cm. Typescript; issued also on microfilm. Thesis (Ed.D.)--Teachers College, Columbia University, 1999. Includes bibliographical references (leaves 240-250).
*1. Public schools - United States. 2. Private schools - United States. 3. Charter schools - United States. 4. School choice. 5. Privatization in education. 6. Politics and education. 7. School management and organization. 8. Education - United States - Finance. I. Title.*
*TC 06 no. 11170*

Towards a new typology of public and private schools / by Patricia Marie Rufo-Lignos. 1999. xi, 256 leaves : ill. ; 29 cm. Typescript; issued also on microfilm. Thesis (Ed.D.)--Teachers College, Columbia University, 1999. Includes bibliographical references (leaves 240-250).
*1. Public schools - United States. 2. Private schools - United States. 3. Charter schools - United States. 4. School choice. 5. Privatization in education. 6. Politics and education. 7. School management and organization. 8. Education - United States - Finance. I. Title.*
*TC 06 no. 11170*

**RUG MANUFACTURE.** *See* **RUGS.**

**Rugh, Andrea B.** Teaching practices to increase student achievement : evidence form Pakistan / Andrea B. Rugh ; with Ahmed Nawaz Malik and R.A. Farooq. Cambridge, Mass. : B.R.I.D.G.E.S. Basic Research and Implementation in Developing Education Systems, [1991]. v, 32 p. : ill. ; 28 cm. (BRIDGES research report series, no. 8.) "A project of the Harvard Institute for International Development, the Harvard Graduate School of Education, and the Office of Education, Bureau for Science and Technology, United States Agency for International Development"--Cover. "March 1991." Includes bibliographical references ( p. 32).
*1. Teaching. 2. Teachers - Pakistan. 3. Academic achievement - Pakistan. I. Malik, Ahmed Nawaz. II. Farooq, R. A. III. Title. IV. Series.*
*TC LB1025.2 .R83 1991*

**RUGS - FICTION.**
Blood, Charles L., 1929- The goat in the rug. New York : Four Winds Press, 1976.
*TC PZ7.B6227 Go 1976*

**RUINS.** *See* **EXCAVATIONS (ARCHAEOLOGY).**

**Ruiz de Austri, Maite.**
Comics, the 9th art [videorecording]. [S.l.] : EPISA : Cicero, Ill. : [Distributed by] The Roland Collection, 1990.
*TC PN6710 .C6 1990*

**Rummel, R. J. (Rudolph J.), 1932-** The dimensions of nations [by] R. J. Rummel. Beverly Hills, Sage Publications [1972] 512 p. illus. 25 cm. ([His Dimensions of nations series, v. 1]) Bibliography: p. 425-438. ISBN 0-8039-0170-4 DDC 327/.07/2
*1. International relations - Research. 2. Factor analysis. I. Title.*
*TC JX1291 .R84*

**RUNAWAY TEENAGERS - CALIFORNIA - LOS ANGELES.**
Children of the night [videorecording]. [Charleston, W.V.] : Cambridge Educational, c1994.
*TC HV1435.C3 C45 1994*

Children of the night [videorecording]. [Charleston, W.V.] : Cambridge Educational, c1994.
*TC HV1435.C3 C45 1994*

Children of the night [videorecording]. [Charleston, W.V.] : Cambridge Educational, c1994.
*TC HV1435.C3 C45 1994*

Starting over [videorecording]. [Charleston, W.V.] : Cambridge Educational, c1994.
*TC HV1435.C3 S7 1994*

**RUNAWAY TEENAGERS - DRUG USE - UNITED STATES.**
Children of the night [videorecording]. [Charleston, W.V.] : Cambridge Educational, c1994.

*TC HV1435.C3 C45 1994*

Starting over [videorecording]. [Charleston, W.V.] : Cambridge Educational, c1994.
*TC HV1435.C3 S7 1994*

**RUNAWAY TEENAGERS - EMPLOYMENT - UNITED STATES.**
Starting over [videorecording]. [Charleston, W.V.] : Cambridge Educational, c1994.
*TC HV1435.C3 S7 1994*

**RUNAWAY TEENAGERS - FLORIDA - FORT LAUDERDALE.**
Starting over [videorecording]. [Charleston, W.V.] : Cambridge Educational, c1994.
*TC HV1435.C3 S7 1994*

**RUNAWAY TEENAGERS - NEW YORK (STATE) - NEW YORK.**
Children of the night [videorecording]. [Charleston, W.V.] : Cambridge Educational, c1994.
*TC HV1435.C3 C45 1994*

Children of the night [videorecording]. [Charleston, W.V.] : Cambridge Educational, c1994.
*TC HV1435.C3 C45 1994*

Children of the night [videorecording]. [Charleston, W.V.] : Cambridge Educational, c1994.
*TC HV1435.C3 C45 1994*

Starting over [videorecording]. [Charleston, W.V.] : Cambridge Educational, c1994.
*TC HV1435.C3 S7 1994*

**RUNAWAY TEENAGERS - UNITED STATES.**
Whitbeck, Les B. Nowhere to grow. New York : Aldine de Gruyter, 1999.
*TC HV4505 .W43 1999*

**RUNAWAY TEENAGERS - UNITED STATES - FAMILY RELATIONSHIPS.**
Children of the night [videorecording]. [Charleston, W.V.] : Cambridge Educational, c1994.
*TC HV1435.C3 C45 1994*

Children of the night [videorecording]. [Charleston, W.V.] : Cambridge Educational, c1994.
*TC HV1435.C3 C45 1994*

Children of the night [videorecording]. [Charleston, W.V.] : Cambridge Educational, c1994.
*TC HV1435.C3 C45 1994*

Starting over [videorecording]. [Charleston, W.V.] : Cambridge Educational, c1994.
*TC HV1435.C3 S7 1994*

Whitbeck, Les B. Nowhere to grow. New York : Aldine de Gruyer, 1999.
*TC HV4505 .W43 1999*

**RUNAWAY TEENAGERS - UNITED STATES - SOCIAL CONDITIONS.**
Children of the night [videorecording]. [Charleston, W.V.] : Cambridge Educational, c1994.
*TC HV1435.C3 C45 1994*

Children of the night [videorecording]. [Charleston, W.V.] : Cambridge Educational, c1994.
*TC HV1435.C3 C45 1994*

Children of the night [videorecording]. [Charleston, W.V.] : Cambridge Educational, c1994.
*TC HV1435.C3 C45 1994*

Starting over [videorecording]. [Charleston, W.V.] : Cambridge Educational, c1994.
*TC HV1435.C3 S7 1994*

**RUNAWAY YOUTH.** *See* **RUNAWAY TEENAGERS.**

**RUNAWAYS - FICTION.**
Curtis, Christopher Paul. Bud, not Buddy. New York : Delacorte Press, 1999.
*TC PZ7.C94137 Bu 1999*

**Rundown.**
Cadnum, Michael. New York : Viking, c1999.
*TC PZ7.C11724 Ru 1999*

**Running away, dropping out**
Children of the night [videorecording]. [Charleston, W.V.] : Cambridge Educational, c1994.
*TC HV1435.C3 C45 1994*

Children of the night [videorecording]. [Charleston, W.V.] : Cambridge Educational, c1994.
*TC HV1435.C3 C45 1994*

Starting over [videorecording]. [Charleston, W.V.] : Cambridge Educational, c1994.
*TC HV1435.C3 S7 1994*

**Running away, dropping out series**
Children of the night [videorecording]. [Charleston, W.V.] : Cambridge Educational, c1994.
*TC HV1435.C3 C45 1994*

**Running records :** a self tutoring guide / Peter H. Johnston. York, Me. : Stenhouse Publishers , 2000. 1 sound cassette : analog, 1 7/8 ips + includes: 1 guide book (ix, 53 p., 22 cm.). Title from container.
*1. Reading - Ability testing. 2. Oral reading - Ability testing. 3. Reading teachers - Training of. I. Johnston, Peter H. II. Title.*
*TC LB1525 R75 2000*

**RUNS (RIVERS).** *See* **RIVERS.**

**Rural America in transition.**
Nagy, Martin. Washington, DC : NALAA, 1996.
*TC NX798 .N3 1996*

**RURAL ARCHITECTURE.** *See* **ARCHITECTURE, DOMESTIC.**

**RURAL COMMUNITY DEVELOPMENT.** *See* **RURAL DEVELOPMENT.**

**RURAL DEVELOPMENT - CITIZEN PARTICIPATION.** *See* **RURAL DEVELOPMENT.**

**RURAL DEVELOPMENT - SOCIAL ASPECTS.** *See* **RURAL DEVELOPMENT.**

**RURAL DEVELOPMENT - UNITED STATES.**
Nagy, Martin. Rural America in transition. Washington, DC : NALAA, 1996.
*TC NX798 .N3 1996*

**RURAL ECONOMIC DEVELOPMENT.** *See* **RURAL DEVELOPMENT.**

**RURAL HIGH SCHOOLS.** *See* **RURAL SCHOOLS.**

**RURAL LIFE.** *See* **COUNTRY LIFE; FARM LIFE.**

**RURAL POOR - ECONOMIC CONDITIONS.** *See* **RURAL POOR.**

**RURAL POOR - SOUTHERN STATES.**
Abbott, Shirley Womenfolks, growing up down South. Boston : Houghton Mifflin, c1998.
*TC HQ1438.S63 A33 1998*

**RURAL POPULATION.** *See* **PEASANTRY.**

**RURAL POVERTY.** *See* **RURAL POOR.**

**RURAL SCHOOLS - IOWA - HISTORY - 20TH CENTURY.**
Reynolds, David R. There goes the neighborhood. Iowa City : University of Iowa Press, 1999.
*TC LB2861 .R49 1999*

**RURAL WOMEN - MEXICO - MEXQUITIC - SOCIAL CONDITIONS - CASE STUDIES.**
Behar, Ruth, 1956- Translated woman. Boston : Beacon Press, c1993.
*TC HQ1465.M63 B44 1993*

**RURAL WOMEN - NEW ENGLAND - HISTORY.**
Kelly, Catherine E. In the New England fashion. Ithaca, N.Y. : Cornell University Press, 1999.
*TC HQ1438.N35 K45 1999*

**RURAL WOMEN - SOUTHERN STATES.**
Abbott, Shirley Womenfolks, growing up down South. Boston : Houghton Mifflin, c1998.
*TC HQ1438.S63 A33 1998*

**Ruse, Michael.** Mystery of mysteries : is evolution a social construction? / Michael Ruse. Cambridge, Mass. : Harvard University Press, 1999. viii, 296 p. : ill., ports. ; 25 cm. Includes bibliographical references (p. 259-275) and index. ISBN 0-674-46706-X (alk. paper) DDC 576.8/01
*1. Evolution (Biology) - Philosophy. 2. Science - Philosophy. 3. Biologists. 4. Scientists. I. Title.*
*TC QH360.5 .R874 1999*

**Rush, A. John.** Mood disorders. Basel ; New York : Karger, c1997.
*TC RC483 .M6 1997*

**Rushefsky, Mark E., 1945-** Politics, power & policy making : the case of health care reform in the 1990s / Mark E. Rushefsky, Kant Patel. Armonk, N.Y. : M.E. Sharpe, c1998. xii, 312 p. ; 24 cm. Includes bibliographical references (p. 273-296) and index. ISBN 1-56324-955-3 (c : alk. paper) ISBN 1-56324-956-1 (p : alk. paper) DDC 362.1/0973
*1. Health care reform - United States. I. Patel, Kant, 1946- II. Title. III. Title: Politics, power, and policy making*
*TC RA395.A3 R855 1998*

**Rushing, W. Jackson.** Native American art in the twentieth century. London ; New York : Routledge, 1999.
*TC E98.A7 R89 1999*

Shared visions. 1st New Press ed. New York : New Press ; Distributed by Norton, [1993], c1991.
*TC N6538.A4 A7 1993*

**Russ, Sandra Walker.**
Handbook of psychotherapies with children and families. New York : London : Kluwer Academic/ Plenum Publishers, c1999.
*TC RJ504 .H3619 1999*

**Russell, Andrew. 1958-.**
Contraception across cultures :. Oxford ; New York : Berg, 2000.
*TC RG136 .C574 2000*

**Russell, Graeme, 1947-.**
Organizational change & gender equity. Thousand Oaks : Sage Publications, c2000.
*TC HD58.8 .O7289 2000*

**Russell, Graham, 1954-** Essential psychology for nurses and other health professionals / Graham Russell. London ; New York : Routledge, c1999. xiv, 203 p. : ill. ; 24 cm. Includes bibliographical references and index. ISBN 0-415-18888-1 (hbk.) ISBN 0-415-18889-X (pbk.) DDC 616.89
*1. Clinical health psychology. 2. Patients - Psychology. 3. Nursing - Psychological aspects. 4. Psychology. 5. Nurses. 6. Psychology - nurses' instruction. 7. Patient Care - psychology - nurses' instruction. 8. Health Promotion. 9. Patient Compliance - psychology. 10. Allied Health Personnel. I. Title.*
*TC R726.7 .R87 1999*

**Russell, Lynne, ill.**
Hoffman, Mary, 1945- Three wise women. 1st ed. New York : Phyllis Fogelman Books, 1999.
*TC PZ7.H67562 Th 1999*

**Russell, Ruth V., 1948-.**
Riddick, Carol Cutler. Evaluative research in recreation, park, and sport settings. [Champaign, Ill.? : Sagamore Publishing], c1999.
*TC GV181.46 .R533 1999*

**Russell Sage Foundation.**
Environmental influences: New York, Rockefeller University Press ; Russell Sage Foundation, 1968.
*TC BF353 .E5*

Kirkpatrick, Jeane J. The new Presidential elite. New York : Russell Sage Foundation : [distributed by Basic Books], c1976.
*TC JK1764 .K57*

**Technical report on the social consequences of testing**
(no. 3.) The Use of standardized ability tests in American secondary schools and their impact on students, teachers, and administrators New York] Russell Sage Foundation [1965]
*TC LB3051 .R914*

**Russia, education in the transition** = Rossiña, obrazovanie v perekhodnyi period / The World Bank. [S.l.] : The World Bank, ECA Country Development III, Human Resources Division, 1995. xxiv, 73, [26], xxviii, 29-154 p. : maps ; 29 cm. Added title page title: Rossiña, obrazovanie v perekhodnyi period. Two identical maps bound in the end of both English and Russian sections of the book.
*1. Educational change - Russia (Federation) - 1991- 2. Education - Aims and objectives - Russia (Federation) 3. Educational innovations - Russia (Federation) I. World Bank. Europe and Central Asia Region. Country Dept. III. Human Resources Division. II. Title: Education in the transition III. Title: Rossiña, obrazovanie v perekhodnyi period*
*TC LA839.2 .R87 1995*

**Russia (Federation). Ministerstvo obrazovaniña.**
[Geografiña v shkole (Moscow, Russia)] Geografiña v shkole. Moskva : Gos. ucheb.-pedagog. izd-vo, 1934-

**RUSSIAN CHILDREN'S POETRY.** *See* **CHILDREN'S POETRY, RUSSIAN.**

**Russian grade 3 mathematics** / A.S. Pcholko, M.A. Bantova, M.I. Moro, and A.M. Pyshkalo ; translator, Robert H. Silverman ; translation editor, Steven R. Young. Chicago : University of Chicago School of Mathematics Project, 1992. x, 283 p. : ill. ; 26 cm. (UCSMP Textbook Translations) ISBN 0-936745-52-5
*1. Mathematics - Study and teaching (Elementary) - Soviet Union. 2. Mathematics - Soviet Union - Textbooks. I. Moro, M. I. II. Bantova, M. A. III. Pcholko, A.S. IV. Pyshkalo, A.M. V. Silverman, Robert H. VI. Young, Steven R. VII. Series.*
*TC QA14.R9 R8811 1992*

**Russian language directives.**
Gordon, Tatiana. 1998.
*TC 06 no. 10940*

**RUSSIAN LANGUAGE - DISCOURSE ANALYSIS.**
Gordon, Tatiana. Russian language directives. 1998.

*TC 06 no. 10940*

**RUSSIAN POETRY.** *See* **CHILDREN'S POETRY, RUSSIAN.**

**Russian S.F.S.R. Ministerstvo prosveshcheniña.**
[Geografiña v shkole (Moscow, Russia)] Geografiña v shkole. Moskva : Gos. ucheb.-pedagog. izd-vo, 1934-

**Russian S.F.S.R. Narodnyi komissariat prosveshcheniña.**
[Geografiña v shkole (Moscow, Russia)] Geografiña v shkole. Moskva : Gos. ucheb.-pedagog. izd-vo, 1934-

**RUSTIN, BAYARD, 1912-1987.**
Haskins, James, 1941- Bayard Rustin. 1st ed. New York : Hyperion Books for Children, c1997.
*TC E185.97.R93 H37 1997*

**RUSTIN, BAYARD, 1912-1987 - JUVENILE LITERATURE.**
Haskins, James, 1941- Bayard Rustin. 1st ed. New York : Hyperion Books for Children, c1997.
*TC E185.97.R93 H37 1997*

**Ruszkiewicz, John J., 1950-** Bookmarks : a guide to research and writing / by John Ruszkiewicz, Janice R. Walker. New York ; Harlow, England : Longman, c2000. xx, 355 p. : ill. ; 24 cm. Includes index. ISBN 0-321-02393-5 DDC 808/.027
*1. Report writing - Handbooks, manuals, etc. 2. Report writing - Computer network resources - Handbooks, manuals, etc. 3. Research - Handbooks, manuals, etc. 4. Research - Computer network resources - Handbooks, manuals, etc. I. Walker, Janice R. II. Title.*
*TC LB2369 .R88 2000*

**Rutgers invitational symposium on education series**
Cognitive perspectives on peer learning. Mahwah, N.J. : L. Erlbaum, 1999.
*TC LB1031.5 .C65 1999*

**RUTGERS UNIVERSITY - FACULTY - CASE STUDIES.**
Ernest, Ivan. Faculty evaluation of post-tenure review at a research university. 1999.
*TC 06 no. 11110*

**Rutherford, Anna.**
Teaching post-colonialism and post-colonial literatures. Aarhus, Denmark ; Oakville, Conn. : Aarhus University Press, c1997.
*TC PR9080.A53 T43 1997*

**Rutherford, William E.**
The current state of interlanguage. Amsterdam ; Philadelphia : J. Benjamins, c1995.
*TC P118.2 .C867 1995*

**Rutter, Alison Lee.** Professional growth of two multidisciplinary teams within a professional development school / by Alison Lee Rutter. 1999. 282 leaves ; 29 cm. Typescript; issued also on microfilm. Thesis (Ed.D.)--Teachers College, Columbia University, 1999. Includes bibliographical references (leaves 252-261).
*1. Middle school teachers - Attitudes. 2. Middle school teachers - In-service training. 3. Effective teaching. 4. Teaching teams. 5. Faculty integration. 6. Action research in education. I. Title.*
*TC 06 no. 11171*

**Ryan, Allan J.** The trickster shift : humour and irony in contemporary native art / Allan J. Ryan. Vancouver, BC : UBC Press ; Seattle : University of Washington Press, c1999. xv, 303 p. : col. ill. ; 29 cm. Includes bibliographical references (p. 285-291) and index. ISBN 0-7748-0704-0 (Canada : alk. paper) ISBN 0-295-97816-3 (U.S. : alk. paper) DDC 704.03/97071
*1. Indian art - Canada. 2. Indian paintings - Canada. 3. Tricksters in art. 4. Art criticism - Canada. I. Title.*
*TC E78.C2 R93 1999*

**Ryan, Angela Shen.**
The challenge of permanency planning in a multicultural society. New York : Haworth Press, c1997.
*TC HV741 .C378 1997*

**Ryan, Anne.**
Art Gallery of New South Wales. Australian drawings from the gallery's collection. Sydney : Art Gallery of New South Wales, 1997.
*TC NC369 .A78 1997*

Art Gallery of New South Wales. Australian prints from the gallery's collection. Sydney : Art Gallery of New South Wales, c1998.
*TC NE789 .A77 1998*

Sport photography today! [videorecording]. Minneapolis, Minn. : Media Loft, c1992.
*TC TR821 .S64 1992*

**Ryan, Daniel J., 1956-.**
Restructuring education. Westport, Conn. : Praeger, 2000.
*TC LB2822.82 . R45 2000*

**Ryan, Daniel Prentice.** Gay/lesbian parents and school personnel : the contexts that inhibit or support the home/school partnership / by Daniel Prentice Ryan. 1998. xi, 199 leaves ; 29 cm. Typescript; issued also on microfilm. Thesis (Ed.D.)--Teachers College, Columbia University, 1998. Includes bibliographical references (leaves 180-183).
*1. Gay parents - United States. 2. Children of gay parents - United States. 3. Home and school - United States. 4. Parent-teacher relationships. 5. Education - Parent participation - Psychological aspects. 6. School management and organization - Parent participation - United States. I. Title. II. Title: Gay-lesbian parents and school personnel*
*TC 06 no. 10988*

**Ryan, James, 1952 Oct. 18-** Race and ethnicity in multi-ethnic schools : a critical case study / James Ryan. Clevedon [England] ; Philadelphia : Multilingual Matters, c1999. v, 218 p. ; 21 cm. (The language and education library ; 15) Includes bibliographical references (p. 208-218). ISBN 1-85359-446-6 (pbk.) ISBN 1-85359-447-4 (hard) DDC 373.1829
*1. Minorities - Education (Secondary) - Canada - Case studies. 2. Discrimination in education - Canada - Case studies. 3. Multicultural education - Canada - Case studies. 4. Critical pedagogy - Canada - Case studies. 5. Ethnicity - Canada - Case studies. I. Title. II. Series.*
*TC LC3734 .R93 1999*

**Ryan, Katherine E.**
Evaluation as a democratic process. San Francisco, CA : Jossey-Bass, c2000.
*TC LB2806 .E79 2000*

**Ryan, Pam Muñoz.** Amelia and Eleanor go for a ride / by Pam Muñoz Ryan ; illustrated by Brian Selznick. New York : Scholastic Press, 1999. 1v. (unpaged) : col. ill. ; 27 cm. SUMMARY: A fictionalized account of the night Amelia Earhart flew Eleanor Roosevelt over Washington, D.C. in an airplane. ISBN 0-590-96075-X (alk. paper) DDC [Fic]
*1. Earhart, Amelia. - 1897-1937 - Juvenile fiction. 2. Roosevelt, Eleanor, - 1884-1962 - Juvenile fiction. 3. Earhart, Amelia, - 1897-1937 - Fiction. 4. Roosevelt, Eleanor, - 1884-1962 - Fiction. I. Selznick, Brian, ill. II. Title.*
*TC PZ7.R9553 Am 1999*

**Ryan, Paul, 1947-.**
Grubb, W. Norton. The roles of evaluation for vocational education and training. London : Kogan Page ; Sterling, VA : Distributed in the US by Stylus Pub. Inc., 1999.
*TC LC1044 .G78 1999*

**Ryan, Sharon Kaye.** Freedom to choice : a post-structural study of child-centered pedagogy in kindergarten classroom / by Sharon Kaye Ryan. 1998. ix, 370 leaves ; 29 cm. Issued also on microfilm. Thesis (Ed.D.)--Teachers College, Columbia University, 1998. Includes bibliographical references (leaves 352-365).
*1. Early childhood education - New York (State) - New York - Philosophy - Case studies. 2. Early childhood education - New York (State) - New York - Curricula - Case studies. 3. Activity programs in education. 4. Classroom environment. 5. Group work in education. 6. Learning, Psychology of. 7. Education, Primary - Experimental methods. I. Title. II. Title: Post-structural study of child-centered pedagogy in kindergarten classroom*
*TC 06 no. 11034*

**Ryan, Yoni.**
Supervising postgraduates from non-English speaking backgrounds. Buckingham ; Philadelphia : Society for Research into Higher Education : Open University Press, 1999.
*TC LB2343 .S86 1999*

**Rybczynski, Zbigniew.**
Processing the signal [videorecording]. Cicero, Ill. : Roland Collection of Films on Art, c1989.
*TC N6494.V53 P7 1989*

**Rydberg, Sven.** Bias in prediction on correction methods. Stockholm, Almqvist & Wiksell [1963] xv, 248 p. diagrs., tables. 22 cm. (Stockholm studies in educational psychology, 7) Akademisk avhandling-Stockholm. Extra t.p., with thesis statement, inserted.
*1. Prediction (Psychology) 2. Statistics. 3. Sampling (Statistics) I. Title. II. Series: Acta Universitatis Stockholmiensis. Stockholm studies in educational psychology ; 7.*
*TC HA31.2 .R93*

**Rydell, C. Peter.**
Vernez, Georges. Closing the education gap. Santa Monica, CA : RAND, 1999.
*TC LC213.2 .V47 1999*

**Ryff, Carol D.**
The self and society in aging processes. New York : Springer Pub., c1999.
*TC HQ1061 .S438 1999*

**Rylant, Cynthia.** Henry and Mudge and the wild wind : the twelfth book of their adventures / story by Cynthia Rylant ; pictures by Suçie Stevenson. 1st ed. New York : Bradbury Press ; Toronto : Maxwell Macmillan Canada ; New York : Maxwell Macmillan International, c1993. 40 p. : col. ill. ; 22 cm. (The Henry and Mudge books) SUMMARY: Henry and his big dog Mudge try to keep busy inside the house during a thunderstorm. ISBN 0-02-778014-7 DDC [E]
*1. Dogs - Fiction. 2. Thunderstorms - Fiction. I. Stevenson, Suçie, ill. II. Title. III. Series: Rylant, Cynthia. Henry and Mudge books.*
*TC PZ7.R982 Heb 1992*

**Henry and Mudge books.**
Rylant, Cynthia. Henry and Mudge and the wild wind. 1st ed. New York : Bradbury Press ; Toronto : Maxwell Macmillan Canada ; New York : Maxwell Macmillan International, c1993.
*TC PZ7.R982 Heb 1992*

**Ryndak, Diane Lea, 1952-.**
Alper, Sandra K. Alternate assessment of students with disabilities in inclusive settings. Boston ; London : Allyn and Bacon, c2001.
*TC LC4031 .A58 2001*

**Gifts from the earth** [videorecording] / a production of WQED Pittsburgh in association with the National Academy of Sciences ; series producer, Gregory Andorfer ; producer, Theodore Thomas ; written by Theodore Thomas. [New York, N.Y.?] : Unapix Entertainment, Inc. [distributor], c1996. 1 videocassette (57 min.) : sd., col. ; 1/2 in. (Planet Earth ; 6) At head of title: Unapix Consumer Products feature presentation [videorecording]. VHS. Catalogued from credits and container. Narrator, Richard Kiley. Sound, Aerlyn Weissman; photography by Orlando Bagwell... [et al.]; music, Jack Tillar and William Loose. "Major funding by the Annenberg/CPB Project"--Container. Originally produced in 1986. For adolescent through adult. SUMMARY: Examines how mankind has been made aware that earth is a closed system and its resources are finite. Questions what treasures lay hidden beneath the Red Sea and Antartic ice cap, how the theory of plate tectonics has revolutionized the search for minerals and energy, and if mankind is ruining the land and running out of water.
*1. Human ecology. 2. Earth. 3. Natural resources. 4. Plate tectonics. 5. Documentary television programs. I. Andorfer, Gregory. II. Thomas, Theodore, 1951- III. Kiley, Richard. IV. WQED (Television station : Pittsburgh, Pa.) V. National Academy of Sciences (U.S.) VI. Unapix Entertainment, Inc. VIII. Unapix Consumer Products. IX. Title: Unapix Consumer Products feature presentation [videorecording] X. Series.*
*TC QB631.2 .G5 1996*

**SA99 10.**
Text in education and society. Singapore : Singapore University Press ; Singapore ; River Edge, N.J. : World Scientific, c1998.
*TC P40.8 .T48 1998*

**Saaf, Donald, ill.**
Ziefert, Harriet. Animal music. Boston : Houghton Mifflin, 1999.
*TC PZ8.3.Z47 An 1999*

**Sabini, John, 1947-** Emotion, character, and responsibility / John Sabini, Maury Silver. New York : Oxford University Press, 1998. vi, 175 p. ; 22 cm. Includes bibliographical references and index. ISBN 0-19-512167-8 (hardcover : alk. paper) DDC 152.4
*1. Emotions. 2. Character. 3. Responsibility. I. Silver, Maury, 1944- II. Title.*
*TC BF531 .S23 1998*

**Saccardi, Marianne.**
Jody, Marilyn, 1932- Using computers to teach literature. 2nd ed. Urbana, Ill. : National Council of Teachers of English, c1998.
*TC LB1050.37 .J63 1998*

**Sachar, Louis, 1954-** Sideways stories from Wayside School / Louis Sachar ; illustrated by Julie Brinckloe. New York : Morrow Junior Books, 1998. 124 p. : ill. ; 22 cm. SUMMARY: Humorous episodes from the classroom on the thirtieth floor of Wayside School, which was accidentally built sideways with one classroom on each story. ISBN 0-688-16086-7 DDC [Fic]
*1. Schools - Fiction. 2. Humorous stories. I. Brinckloe, Julie, ill. II. Title.*
*TC PZ7.S1185 Si 1998*

**Sacks, Peter.** Standardized minds : the high price of America's testing culture and what we can do to change it / Peter Sacks. Cambridge, Mass. : Perseus Books, c1999. xii, 351 p. ; 25 cm. Includes bibliographical references (p. 317-334) and index. ISBN 0-7382-0243-6
*1. Educational tests and measurements - United States. I. Title.*
*TC LB4051 .S22 1999*

**SACKTER, BILL.**
Walz, Thomas, 1933- The unlikely celebrity. Carbondale : Southern Illinois University Press, c1998.
*TC HV3006.S33 W35 1998*

**SACRAMENTS.** *See* **MARRIAGE.**

**The sacred and the secular university.**
Roberts, Jon H. Princeton, N.J. : Princeton University Press, c2000.
*TC LA636.7 .R62 2000*

**Sacred dreams :** women and the superintendency / edited by C. Cryss Brunner. Albany : State University of New York Press, c1999. xvi, 231 p. : ill. ; 24 cm. (SUNY series in women in education) Includes bibliographical references and index. ISBN 0-7914-4159-8 (hc.) ISBN 0-7914-4160-1 (pbk.) DDC 371.2/011
*1. Women school superintendents - United States. I. Brunner, C. Cryss. II. Series.*
*TC LB2831.72 .S23 1999*

**SACRED VOCAL MUSIC.** *See* **ORATORIOS.**

**Sadlak, Jan.**
Higher education research. 1st ed. Oxford ; [New York] : Pergamon, published for the IAU Press, 2000.
*TC LB2326.3 .H548 2000*

**Sadler, D. Royce (David Royce)** Managing your academic career : strategies for success / D. Royce Sadler. St Leonards, N.S.W., Australia : Allen & Unwin, 1999. xiv, 209 p. ; 20 cm. Includes bibliographical references (p. 203-204) and index. ISBN 1-86448-984-7
*1. College teachers - Employment. 2. College teaching - Vocational guidance. I. Title.*
*TC LB1778 .S23 1999*

**SADNESS.** *See* **DEPRESSION, MENTAL; MELANCHOLY.**

**Sadovnik, Alan R.** Exploring education : an introduction to the foundations of education / Alan R. Sadovnik, Peter W. Cookson, Jr., Susan F. Semel. Boston : Allyn and Bacon, c1994. xvi, 589 p. : ill. ; 24 cm. Includes bibliographical references and index. ISBN 0-205-14191-9 DDC 370/.973
*1. Education - United States. 2. Educational sociology - United States. 3. Education - United States - Philosophy. I. Cookson, Peter W. II. Semel, Susan F., 1941- III. Title.*
*TC LB17 .S113 1994*

Exploring education : an introduction to the foundations of education / Alan R. Sadovnik, Peter W. Cookson, Jr., Susan F. Semel. 2nd ed. Boston : Allyn and Bacon, 2000. xviii, 588 p. ; 24 cm. Includes bibliographical references and index. ISBN 0-205-29016-7 DDC 370/.973
*1. Education - United States. 2. Educational sociology - United States. 3. Education - United States - Philosophy. I. Cookson, Peter W. II. Semel, Susan F., 1941- III. Title.*
*TC LA217.2 . S23 2000*

**SAFETY EDUCATION - UNITED STATES - PROBLEMS, EXERCISES, ETC.**
Toner, Patricia Rizzo, 1952- Consumer health and safety activities. West Nyack, N.Y. : Center for Applied Research in Education, c1993.
*TC RA440.3.U5 T66 1993*

**SAFETY ENGINEERING.** *See* **INDUSTRIAL SAFETY.**

**SAFETY, INDUSTRIAL.** *See* **INDUSTRIAL SAFETY.**

**SAFETY MEASURES.** *See* **INDUSTRIAL SAFETY.**

**SAFETY OF WORKERS.** *See* **INDUSTRIAL SAFETY.**

**SAFETY REGULATIONS.** *See* **FIREARMS - LAW AND LEGISLATION.**

**Safouan, Moustafa.**
**[Jacques Lacan et la question de la formation des analystes. English]**
Jacques Lacan and the question of psychoanalytic training / Moustapha Safouan ; translated and introduced by Jacqueline Rose. New York : St. Martin's Press, 2000. 132 p. ; 23 cm. (Language, discourse, society) Includes bibliographical references and index. ISBN 0-312-23117-2 (cloth) DDC 150.19/5/0711
*1. Lacan, Jacques, - 1901- 2. Psychoanalysis - Study and teaching. 3. Psychoanalysis - History. I. Title. II. Series: Language, discourse, society.*

*TC BF173.L15 S2414 2000*

**Sagawa, Shirley, 1961-** Common interest, common good : creating value through business and social sector partnerships / Shirley Sagawa, Eli Segal. Boston : Harvard Business School Press, c2000. xxv, 278 p. ; 24 cm. Includes bibliographical references (p. 247-264) and index. ISBN 0-87584-848-6 DDC 658.4/08
*1. Social responsibility of business - United States. 2. Social service - United States. 3. Charities - United States. I. Segal, Eli. 1943- II. Title.*
*TC HD60.5.U5 S24 2000*

**Sage, George Harvey.** Power and ideology in American sport : a critical perspective / George H. Sage. 2nd ed. Champaign, IL : Human Kinetics, c1998. xiii, 335 p. : ill. ; 23 cm. Includes bibliographical references (p. 295-326) and index. ISBN 0-88011-660-9 (pbk.) DDC 306.4/83/0973
*1. Sports - Social aspects - United States. I. Title.*
*TC GV706.5 .S228 1998*

**Sage, James.** The little band / James Sage ; illustrated by Keiko Narahashi. 1st ed. New York : M.K. McElderry Books ; Toronto : Collier Macmillan Canada ; New York : Maxwell Macmillan International Pub. Group, c1991. [25] p. : col. ill. ; 28 cm. SUMMARY: A little band marches through town delighting everyone with its beautiful music. ISBN 0-689-50516-7 DDC [E]
*1. Bands (Music) - Fiction. I. Narahashi, Keiko, ill. II. Title.*
*TC PZ7.S1304 Li 1991*

**SAGGERS.** *See* **POTTERY.**

**Saguaro, Shelley.** Psychoanalysis and woman. New York : New York University Press, 2000.
*TC BF175.5.S48 P795 2000*

**Saigh, Robert A.** The international dictionary of data communications / Robert A. Saigh. Chicago : Glenlake Pub. Co. ; New York : American Management Association, c1998. 409 p. ; 24 cm. Appendices (p. 323-409) contain addresses, telephone numbers, and Internet sites for relevant publications, organizations, and meetings. ISBN 1-88899-828-8 ISBN 0-8144-0469-3 ISBN 1-88496-475-3 (library ed.) DDC 004.6/03
*1. Data transmission systems - Dictionaries. 2. Computer networks - Dictionaries. I. Title.*
*TC TK5102 .S25 1998*

**Sailor Song.** Jewell, Nancy. New York : Clarion Books, c1999.
*TC PZ7.J55325 Sai 1999*

**SAILORS - FICTION.** Jewell, Nancy. Sailor Song. New York : Clarion Books, c1999.
*TC PZ7.J55325 Sai 1999*

**SAILORS' LIFE.** *See* **SEAFARING LIFE.**

**SAINT NICHOLAS' DAY.** *See* **SANTA CLAUS.**

**Saint Paul.** Mendelssohn-Bartholdy, Felix, 1809-1847. [Paulus. Vocal score. English] New York, G. Schirmer [19--]
*TC M2003.M53 S35*

**SAINTS.** *See also* **CHRISTIAN SAINTS.** Hodges, Margaret, 1911- Joan of Arc. 1st ed. New York : Holiday House, c1999.
*TC DC103.5 .H64 1999*

**Saito, Akiko, 1964-.** Bartlett, culture and cognition. [London] : Psychology Press ; [New York] : [Routledge], 2000.
*TC BF311 .B2885 2000*

**Sakari, Mary Dayton, 1941-.** Jobe, Ron. Reluctant readers. Markham, Ont. : Pembroke Pub., 1999.
*TC LB1573 .J58 1999*

**Salacuse, Jeswald W.** The wise advisor : what every professional should know about consulting and counseling / Jeswald W. Salacuse. Westport, Conn. : Praeger, 2000. x, 133 p. 24 cm. Includes bibliographical references and index. ISBN 0-275-96725-5 (alk. paper) ISBN 0-275-96726-3 (pbk. alk. paper) DDC 158/.3
*1. Consultants. 2. Counseling. 3. Helping behavior. I. Title.*
*TC BF637.C56 .S26 2000*

**Salary bulletin May 1953-June 1953.** The classroom teacher. Berkeley, Calif., Berkeley Federation of Teachers Local 1078.

**SALEM (MASS.) - RACE RELATIONS - JUVENILE LITERATURE.** Forten, Charlotte L. A free Black girl before the Civil War. Mankato, Minn. : Blue Earth Books, c2000.
*TC F74.S1 F67 2000*

**SALEM (MASS.) - SOCIAL LIFE AND CUSTOMS - JUVENILE LITERATURE.** Forten, Charlotte L. A free Black girl before the Civil War. Mankato, Minn. : Blue Earth Books, c2000.
*TC F74.S1 F67 2000*

**Salem, Philip J.** Organizational communication and change. Cresskill, N.J. : Hampton Press, 1999.
*TC HD30.3 .O722 1999*

**SALES.** *See* **CONSIGNMENT SALES.**

**SALES PROMOTION.** *See* **EXHIBITIONS.**

**Saletu, Bernd.** Basic and clinical science of mental and addictive disorders. Basel ; New York : Karger, c1997.
*TC RC327 .B37 1997*

**Salisbury, Jane.** Gender, policy and educational change :. London ; New York : Routledge, 2000.
*TC LC213.3.G7 G48 2000*

**Säljö, Roger, 1948-.** Learning sites. 1st ed. Amsterdam ; New York : Pergamon, 1999.
*TC LB1060 .L4245 1999*

**Salkind, Neil J.** Nathan, Peter E. Treating mental disorders. New York : Oxford University Press, 1999.
*TC RC480.515 .N38 1999*

**Salmon, Gilly.** E-moderating : the key to teaching and learning online / Gilly Salmon. London : Kogan Page ; Sterling, VA : Stylus, 2000. xii, 180 p. ; 24 cm. Includes bibliographical references (p. 173-176) and index. ISBN 0-7494-3110-5 DDC 371.358
*1. College teaching - Computer network resources. 2. Education, Higher - Computer-assisted instruction. 3. Internet in education. 4. Effective teaching. 5. Distance education. I. Title. II. Title: Key to teaching and learning online III. Title: Key to teaching and learning on-line*
*TC LB1044.87 .S25 2000*

**Salmon, Shirley J.** The Artificial larynx handbook. New York : Grune & Stratton, c1978.
*TC RF538 .A77*

**SALON (EXHIBITION : PARIS, FRANCE).** Diderot, Denis, 1713-1784. [Selections. English. 1995] Diderot on art. New Haven : Yale University Press, 1995.
*TC N6846 .D4613 1995*

**The salsa-riffic world of Spanish** [videorecording] / [presented by] the Standard Deviants ; produced by Christopher Mattingly, Lara Derby ; directed by Robert Deege ; script by Kristie Wingenbach. [Arlington, Va.] : Cerebellum Corp., c1998. 2 videocassettes (176 min.) : sd., col. ; 1/2 in. + 2 guides ([4] p. ; 18 x 11 folded to 9 x 11 cm.). (Standard Deviants video course review) At head of title: Standard Deviants video course review presents ... Title on container: Standard Deviants present Spanish [videorecording]. VHS. Catalogued from credits and container. Executive producers, Chip Paucek, James Rena ; supervising editors, Joseph Braband, Nic Dipalma ; editors, Kelly Markham, Scott Stuckey ; comedy writers, Igor Torgeson, Matt Clark, Matt Flanagan, Kristie Wingenbach ; supervising graphic artist, Shawn Batts ; graphic artist, Bryan Cung ; music, Music Bakery. Cast: Standard Deviants: Gelila Asres, Ashley Flemming, Tessa Munro, Herschel Bleefeld, Shawn Powell, Deena Rubinson, Kerry Washington, Chas Mastin, Walter Mastrapa, Brad Aldous, Jeremy Klavens, Lara Derby, Andrew Wynn, Shannon Ward, Mariam Aschir, Tanya Munro. For beginning Spanish students. SUMMARY: The Standard Deviants use humor to explain the basics of the Spanish language in this video course review for college students. CONTENTS: Part 1: I. Oh, yeah, you can speak Spanish ; II. Articles and pronouns ; III. The verbs "ser" and "estar" -- Part 2: I. Really basic stuff ; II. Some grammatical stuff ; III. Verb that word! ; IV. A little more grammar and some easy stuff. ISBN 1-88615-634-4 (pt. 1) ISBN 1-88615-635-2 (pt. 2)
*1. Spanish language - Study and teaching. I. Deege, Robert. II. Mattingly, Christopher. III. Derby, Lara. IV. Wingenbach, Kristie. V. Standard Deviants (Performing Group) VI. Cerebellum Corporation. VII. Title: Standard Deviants video course review presents ... VIII. Title: Standard Deviants present Spanish [videorecording] IX. Series.*
*TC PC4112.7 .S25 1998*

**Salsbury, Robert E.** Mitchell, Bruce M. Encyclopedia of multicultural education. Westport, Conn. : Greenwood Press, 1999.
*TC LC1099.3 .M58 1999*

Mitchell, Bruce M. Multicultural education in the U.S.. Westport, Conn. ; London : Greenwood Press, 2000.

*TC LC1099.3 .M59 2000*

**Saltin, Bengt, 1935-.** Exercise and circulation in health and disease. Champaign, IL : Leeds, U.K. : Human Kinetics, c2000.
*TC QP301 .E9346 2000*

**Saltveit, Elin Kordahl, 1964-** Hit enter : 50+ computer projects for K-5 classrooms / Elin Kordahl Saltveit. Portsmouth, NH : Heinemann, c1999. x, 84 p. : ill. ; 24 cm. "Beeline books." ISBN 0-325-00081-6 (alk. paper) DDC 372.133/4
*1. Education, Elementary - Computer-assisted instruction. 2. Computers - Study and teaching (Elementary) I. Title.*
*TC LB1028.5 .S233 1999*

**Salvisberg, Paul von, 1855-1925.** Hochschul-Nachrichten. München : Academischer Verlag,

**SAMKANGE FAMILY.** Ranger, T. O. (Terence O.) Are we not also men? Harare : Baobab ; Portsmouth, NH : Heinemann, 1995.
*TC DT2974 .R36 1995*

**Sammann, Patricia, 1951-** Active youth : ideas for implementing CDC physical activity promotion guidelines / Patricia Sammann, writer. Champaign, IL : Human Kinetics, c1998. ix, 156 p. : ill. ; 24 cm. Includes bibliographical references (p. 155). ISBN 0-88011-669-2 DDC 613.7
*1. Physical education for children - United States - Case studies. I. Human Kinetics (Organization)*
*TC GV443 .A27 1998*

**Sammlung Göschen** (Bd. 1229/1229a) Atteslander, Peter M., 1926- Methoden der empirischen Sozialforschung. Berlin : De Gruyter, 1969.
*TC H62 .A8*

**Sammons, Pam.** School effectiveness : coming of age in the twenty-first century / Pam Sammons. Lisse, Netherlands ; Abingdon [England] ; Exton, PA : Swets & Zeitlinger Publishers, c1999. xiv, 396 p. : ill. ; 25 cm. (Contexts of learning) Includes bibliographical references (p. 361-387) and index. ISBN 90-265-1549-9 (hbk) ISBN 90-265-1550-2 (pbk) DDC 379.1/58
*1. Educational evaluation - Great Britain. 2. Educational accountability - Great Britain. 3. School improvement programs - Great Britain - Evaluation. 4. Education - Standards - Great Britain. I. Title. II. Series.*
*TC LB2822.75 .S24 1999*

**Samper, Diego.** Arhem, Kaj. Makuna. Washington : Smithsonian Institution Press, c1998.
*TC F2270.2.M33 A68 1998*

**SAMPLING (STATISTICS).** *See also* **MATHEMATICAL STATISTICS.** Dombroski, Ann P. Administrative problem solving. 1999.
*TC 06 no. 11104*

Rydberg, Sven. Bias in prediction on correction methods. Stockholm, Almqvist & Wiksell [1963]
*TC HA31.2 .R93*

**Samuel, David.** Memory : how we use it, lose it, and can improve it / David Samuel. New York : New York University Press, c1999. x, 128 p. ; 24 cm. Includes bibliographical references (p. [122]) and index. ISBN 0-8147-8145-4 (cloth : alk. paper) DDC 612.8/2
*1. Memory - Physiological aspects. I. Title.*
*TC QP406 .S26 1999*

**Samuels, Linda S.** Girls can succeed in science! : antidotes for science phobia in boys and girls / Linda S. Samuels. Thousand Oaks, Calif. : Corwin Press, c1999. xii, 228 p. : ill. ; 29 cm. Includes bibliographical references (p. 223-224) and index. ISBN 0-8039-6730-6 (acid-free paper) ISBN 0-8039-6731-4 (pbk. : acid-free paper) DDC 507.1
*1. Women science students - Study and teaching. 2. Science teachers - Training of - Handbooks, manuals, etc. 3. Science - Study and teaching (Secondary) - Activity programs. 4. Science - Study and teaching (Higher) - Activity programs. I. Title.*
*TC Q181 .S19 1999*

**Samway, Katharine Davies.** Buddy reading : cross-age tutoring in a multicultural school / Katharine Davies Samway, Gail Whang, Mary Pippitt. Portsmouth, NH : Heinemann, c1995. ix, 145 p. : ill. ; 26 cm. Includes bibliographical references (p. 145). ISBN 0-435-08840-8 (acid-free paper) DDC 371.3/94
*1. Peer-group tutoring of students - California - Case studies. 2. Reading (Elementary) - California - Case studies. 3. Literacy programs - California - Case studies. 4. Education, Bilingual - California - Case studies. 5. Interpersonal*

relations - California - Case studies. I. Whang, Gail. II.
Pippitt, Mary. III. Title.
*TC LB1031.5 .S36 1995*

**SAN CRISTÓBAL CANYON (P.R.) -
ENVIRONMENTAL CONDITIONS.**
Laborde, Ilia M. Rediscovering San Cristóbal Canyon.
1996.
*TC 06 no. 10660*

Laborde, Ilia M. Rediscovering San Cristóbal Canyon.
1996.
*TC 06 no. 10660*

**San Diego Museum of Art.**
Carbone, Teresa A. Eastman Johnson. New York :
Brooklyn Museum of Art in association with Rizzoli
International Publications, 1999.
*TC ND237.J7 A4 1999*

**Sanborn, John.**
Processing the signal [videorecording]. Cicero, Ill. :
Roland Collection of Films on Art, c1989.
*TC N6494.V53 P7 1989*

**Sanchez, Enrique O., 1942- ill.**
Figueredo, D. H., 1951- When this world was new. 1st
ed. New York : Lee & Low Books, 1999.
*TC PZ7.F488 Wh 1999*

**Sanchez, Valerie A., 1960-.**
Field, Martha A. Equal treatment for people with
mental retardation. Cambridge, Mass. ; London :
Harvard University Press, 1999.
*TC KF480 .F54 1999*

**A sanctuary of their own :** intellectual refugees in the
academy / Raphael Sassower. Lanham, Md. :
Rowman & Littlefield, c2000. xxi, 113 p. ; 23 cm.
(Critical perspectives series) Includes bibliographical
references (p. 97-103) and index. ISBN 0-8476-9842-4 (cloth :
alk. paper) ISBN 0-8476-9843-2 (paper : alk. paper) DDC
378.73
*1. Education, Higher - Social aspects - United States. 2.
Education, Higher - Economic aspects - United States. 3.
Education, Higher - Aims and objectives - United States. 4.
University autonomy - United States. I. Title. II. Series.*
*TC LC191.9 .S28 2000*

**Sand, Barbara Lourie.** Teaching genius : Dorothy
DeLay and the making of a musician / by Barbara
Lourie Sand. Portland, Or. : Amadeus Press, 2000. 240
p. : ill. ; 24 cm. Includes bibliographical references (p. 235-
236) and index. ISBN 1-57467-052-2 DDC 787.2/092
*1. DeLay, Dorothy, - 1917- 2. Violin teachers - United States -
Biography. I. Title.*
*TC ML423.D35 S36 2000*

**Sandbank, Audrey C., 1935-.**
Twin and triplet psychology. London ; New York :
Routledge, 1999.
*TC BF723.T9 T85 1999*

**Sandburg, Carl, 1878-1967.** The Huckabuck family and
how they raised popcorn in Nebraska and quit and
came back / Carl Sandburg ; pictures by David Small.
1st ed. New York : Farrar Strauss Giroux, c1999. 1 v.
(unpaged) : col. ill. ; 30 cm. "The text was originally published
in 1923 by Harcourt, Brace & Company in the book Rootabaga
stories by Carl Sandburg." SUMMARY: After the popcorn the
Huckabucks had raised explodes in a fire and Pony Pony
Huckabuck finds a silver buckle inside a squash, the family
decides it is time for a change. ISBN 0-374-33511-7 DDC
[Fic]
*1. Humorous stories. I. Small, David, 1945- ill. II. Title.*
*TC PZ7.S1965 Hu 1999*

**Sandbye, Mette.**
Symbolic imprints. Aarhus : Aarhus University Press,
c1999.
*TC TR145 .S96 1999*

**Sandelands, Eric.**
Teare, Richard. The virtual university. London ; New
York : Cassell, 1998.
*TC LC5215 .T42 1998*

The virtual learning organization. London ; New
York : Continuum, 2000.
*TC LC5215 .V574 2000*

**Sanders, Catherine M.** Grief : the mourning after :
dealing with adult bereavement / Catherine M.
Sanders. 2nd ed. New York : J. Wiley, c1999. xix, 316
p. ; 25 cm. Includes bibliographical references (p. 287-302)
and index. ISBN 0-471-12777-9 (hardcover : alk. paper) DDC
155.9/37
*1. Bereavement - Psychological aspects. 2. Grief. I. Title.*
*TC BF575.G7 S26 1999*

**Sanders, James R.** Evaluating school programs : an
educator's guide / James R. Sanders. 2nd ed.
Thousand Oaks, Calif. : Corwin Press, c2000. vii, 80
p. : ill. ; 29 cm. Includes bibliographical references (p. 75-76)

and index. ISBN 0-7619-7502-0 (c : alk. paper) ISBN
0-7619-7503-9 (p : alk. paper) DDC 379.1/58
*1. Educational evaluation - United States - Handbooks,
manuals, etc. I. Title.*
*TC LB2822.75 .S26 2000*

**Sanders, Liz.**
How technology is changing institutional research.
San Francisco, Calif. : Jossey-Bass Publishers, c1999.
*TC LB2326.3 .H69 1999*

**Sanderson, Robert.**
Minogue, Coll. Wood-fired ceramics. London : A & C
Black ; Philadelphia : University of Pennsylvania
Press, 2000.
*TC TP841 .M57 2000*

**Sanderson, Vicki.**
Podesta, Connie. Life would be easy if it weren't for
other people. Thousand Oaks, Calif. : Corwin Press,
c1999.
*TC BF637.I48 P63 1999*

**Sandgrund, Alice.**
Play diagnosis and assessment. 2nd ed. New York :
John Wiley & Sons, c2000.
*TC RJ505.P6 P524 1999*

**Sandhu, Daya Singh. 1943-.**
Asian and Pacific Islander Americans :. Commack,
N.Y. : Nova Science Publishers, 1999.
*TC RC451.5.A75 A83 1999*

**SANDIEGO, CARMEN (FICTITIOUS
CHARACTER).**
Carmen Sandiego [computer file]. Novato, Calif. :
Brøderbund Software, 1998. Computer data and
program.
*TC QA115 .C37 1998*

**Sands, Deanna J.** Inclusive education for the 21st
century / Deanna J. Sands, Elizabeth B. Kozleski,
Nancy K. French. Belmont, CA : Wadsworth/
Thomson Learning, 2000. xvi, 431 p. : ill. ; 26 cm.
Includes bibliographical references (p.397-421) and index.
ISBN 0-534-23820-3 DDC 371.9/046
*1. Inclusive education - United States. 2. Handicapped
students - Education - United States. 3. Educational change -
United States. I. Kozleski, Elizabeth B. II. French, Nancy K.
III. Title. IV. Title: Inclusive education for the twenty-first
century*
*TC LC1201 .S27 2000*

**Sandy, Chuck.**
Richards, J. C. (Jack Croft), 1943- Passages.
Cambridge : Cambridge University Press, 2000.
*TC PE1128 .R4599 2000*

Richards, Jack C. Passages. Cambridge, U.K. ; New
York : Cambridge University Press, 2000.
*TC PE1128 .R4599 2000*

**Sanger, Martha Frick Symington.** Henry Clay Frick :
an intimate portrait / Martha Frick Symington Sanger.
1st ed. New York : Abbeville Press Publishers, c1998.
599 p. : ill. (some col.) ; 28 cm. Includes bibliographical
references (p. 564-588) and index. ISBN 0-7892-0500-9 DDC
338.092
*1. Frick, Henry Clay, - 1849-1919. 2. Businessmen - United
States - Biography. 3. Capitalists and financiers - United
States - Biography. I. Title.*
*TC HC102.5.F75 S32 1998*

**Sanguineti, Vincenzo R.** Landscapes in my mind : the
origins and structure of the subjective experience /
Vincenzo R. Sanguineti. Madison, Conn. :
Psychosocial Press, c1999. xvi, 181 p. : ill. ; 23 cm.
Includes bibliographical references (p. 167-170) and indexes.
ISBN 1-88784-125-3 DDC 155.2
*1. Subjectivity. I. Title.*
*TC BF697 .S2394 1999*

**SANITARY AFFAIRS.** *See* **PUBLIC HEALTH;
SANITATION.**

**SANITARY CHEMISTRY.** *See* **FOOD
ADULTERATION AND INSPECTION.**

**SANITARY ENGINEERING.** *See* **SANITATION.**

**SANITATION.** *See* **HYGIENE; PUBLIC HEALTH.**

**SANITATION SERVICES.** *See* **SANITATION.**

**SANITATION - STATISTICS - PERIODICALS.**
The progress of nations. New York, NY : UNICEF,
1993-
*TC RA407.A1 P76*

**Sankar, Andrea.** Dying at home : a family guide for
caregiving / Andrea Sankar. Rev. and updated ed.
Baltimore, Md.: Johns Hopkins University Press,
1999. xxv, 298 p. ; 24 cm. (A Johns Hopkins Press health
book) Includes bibliographical references and index. ISBN
0-8018-6202-7 (alk. paper) ISBN 0-8018-6203-5 (pbk. : alk.

paper) DDC 362.1/75
*1. Terminally ill - Home care. I. Title. II. Series.*
*TC R726.8 .S26 1999*

**Sanlo, Ronni L., 1947-** Unheard voices : the effects of
silence on lesbian and gay educators / Ronni L. Sanlo.
Westport, Conn. ; London : Bergin & Garvey, 1999.
xxi, 148 p. ; 25 cm. Includes bibliographical references (p.
[131]-139) and index. ISBN 0-89789-640-8 (alk. paper) DDC
371.1/008/664
*1. Lesbian teachers - Florida - Interviews. 2. Gay teachers -
Florida - Interviews. I. Title.*
*TC LB2844.1.G39 S36 1999*

**SANTA CLAUS - FICTION.**
Polacco, Patricia. Welcome Comfort. New York :
Philomel Books, 1999.
*TC PZ7.P75186 Wg 1999*

**SANTA CLAUS - JUVENILE FICTION.**
Polacco, Patricia. Welcome Comfort. New York :
Philomel Books, 1999.
*TC PZ7.P75186 Wg 1999*

**SANTA FE (N.M.) - FICTION.**
De Paola, Tomie. The night of Las Posadas. New
York : Putnam's, 1999.
*TC PZ7.D439 Ni 1999*

**Santería aesthetics in contemporary Latin American
art** / edited by Arturo Lindsay. Washington :
Smithsonian Institution Press, c1996. xxvii, 306 p. : ill.
(some col.), maps ; 27 cm. Includes bibliographical references
and index. ISBN 1-56098-644-1 (alk. paper) ISBN
1-56098-615-8 (alk. paper) DDC 701/.04
*1. Art and religion - Latin America. 2. Santería in art. 3.
Yoruba (African people) - Religion - Influence. 4. Art,
Modern - 20th century - Latin America. I. Lindsay, Arturo.*
*TC N72.R4 S26 1996*

**SANTERIA IN ART.**
Santería aesthetics in contemporary Latin American
art. Washington : Smithsonian Institution Press,
c1996.
*TC N72.R4 S26 1996*

**SAPES Trust.**
Mahlase, Shirley Motleke. The careers of women
teachers under apartheid. Harare : SAPES Books,
c1997.
*TC LB2832.4.S6 M35 1997*

**Saport, Linda, ill.**
All the pretty little horses. New York : Clarion Books,
c1999.
*TC PZ8.3 .A4165 1999*

**Sappey, Maureen Stack, 1952-** Letters from Vinnie /
Maureen Stack Sappey. Asheville, NC : Front Street,
1999. 248 p. ; 24 cm. SUMMARY: A fictionalized account of
the Washington, D.C., Civil War years experienced by Vinnie
Ream the sculptress, best known for the statue of Abraham
Lincoln that is in the Capitol building. ISBN 1-88691-031-6
(alk. paper) DDC [Fic]
*1. Ream, Vinnie, - 1847-1914 - Juvenile fiction. 2. Washington,
D.C. - History - Civil War, 1861-1865 - Juvenile fiction. 3.
Ream, Vinnie, - 1847-1914 - Fiction. 4. Washington, D.C. -
History - Civil War, 1861-1865 - Fiction. 5. United States -
History - Civil War, 1861-1865 - Fiction. 6. Sculptors -
Fiction. 7. Lincoln, Abraham, - 1809-1865 - Fiction. 8.
Letters - Fiction. I. Title.*
*TC PZ7.S2388 Le 1999*

**Sarah, plain and tall by Patricia MacLachlan.**
Beech, Linda Ward. New York : Scholastic, c1996.
*TC LB1573 .B436 1996*

**Sarangi, Srikant, 1956-.**
Talk, work, and institutional order. Berlin ; New
York : Mouton de Gruyter, 1999.
*TC P95 .T286 1999*

**Saraswati, T. S.**
Culture, socialization and human development. New
Delhi ; Thousand Oaks, CA : Sage Publications,
c1999.
*TC HQ783 .C85 1999*

**Sargent, John Singer, 1856-1925.** John Singer Sargent /
edited by Elaine Kilmurray and Richard Ormond.
Princeton : Princeton University Press, 1998. 285 p. :
ill. (some col.), ports. ; 30 cm. "This catalogue is published to
accompany the exhibition at Tate Gallery, London 15 Oct.
1998-17 Jan. 1999, and touring to National Gallery of Art,
Washington 21 Feb.-31 May 1999; Museum of Fine Arts,
Boston 23 June-26 Sept. 1999"--T.p. verso. Includes
bibliographical references (p. 278-280) and index.
CONTENTS: Directors' Foreword -- Acknowledgements --
John Singer Sargent : a biographical sketch / Richard
Ormond -- Sargent's art / Richard Ormond -- Sargent in
public : on the Boston murals / Mary Crawford Volk --
Catalogue -- Chronology -- Select bibliography -- Index. ISBN
0-691-00434-X DDC 759.13

1. Sargent, John Singer, - 1856-1925 - Exhibitions. I. Kilmurray, Elaine. II. Ormond, Richard. III. Volk, Mary Crawford. IV. Tate Gallery. V. National Gallery of Art (U.S.) VI. Museum of Fine Arts, Boston. VII. Title.
*TC ND237.S3 A4 1998a*

Little, Carl. The watercolors of John Singer Sargent. Berkeley : University of California Press, c1998.
*TC ND1839.S32 L58 1998*

**SARGENT, JOHN SINGER, 1856-1925 - CRITICISM AND INTERPRETATION.**
Little, Carl. The watercolors of John Singer Sargent. Berkeley : University of California Press, c1998.
*TC ND1839.S32 L58 1998*

**SARGENT, JOHN SINGER, 1856-1925 - EXHIBITIONS.**
Ferber, Linda S. Masters of color and light. Washington : Brooklyn Museum of Art in Association with Smithsonian Institution Press, c1998.
*TC ND1807 .F47 1998*

Sargent, John Singer, 1856-1925. John Singer Sargent. Princeton : Princeton University Press, 1998.
*TC ND237.S3 A4 1998a*

**Sarkisian, Ellen.** Teaching American students : a guide for international faculty and teaching assistants in colleges and universities / Ellen Sarkisian. Rev. ed. Cambridge, Mass. : The President and Fellows of Harvard University, Derek Bok Center for Teaching and Learning, 1997, c1990. 109 p. : ill. ; 26 cm. Includes bibliographical references and index. Copy 2 (112 p.) is special edition for Harvard. Contains references to Harvard University: GLossary of Harvard Terms -- Resources for Faculty and Teaching Assistants in the Faculty of Arts and Sciences at Harvard -- Peer Counseling Organizations at Harvard.
1. Teachers, Foreign - United States - Handbooks, manuals, etc. 2. Graduate teaching assistants - United States - Handbooks, manuals, etc. 3. College teaching - United States. I. Harvard University. Derek Bok Center for Teaching and Learning. II. Title.
*TC LB1738 .S371 1997*

**Sarnecky, Mary T.** A history of the U.S. Army Nurse Corps / Mary T. Sarnecky. Philadelphia : University of Pennsylvania Press, c1999. xiv, 518 p. : ill. ; 25 cm. (Studies in health, illness, and caregiving) Includes bibliographical references and index. ISBN 0-8122-3502-9 (alk. paper) DDC 355.3/45
1. United States. - Army Nurse Corps - History. 2. Military nursing - United States - History. I. Title. II. Series.
*TC UH493 .S27 1999*

**Saru no nigirimeshi saiban.**
Uchida, Yoshiko. The two foolish cats. New York : M.K. McElderry Books, c1987.
*TC PZ8.1.U35 Tw 1987*

**Sasaki, Miyuki, 1959-** Second language proficiency, foreign language aptitude, and intelligence : quantitative and qualitative analyses / Miyuki Sasaki. New York : P. Lang, c1999. xii, 155 p. : ill. ; 23 cm. (Theoretical studies in second language acquisition ; vol. 6) Includes bibliographical references (p. [137]-149) and index. ISBN 0-8204-2497-8 DDC 418/.0076
1. Language and languages - Ability testing. 2. Second language acquisition. 3. Intellect. 4. English language - Study and teaching (Higher) - Japanese speakers. I. Title. II. Series.
*TC P53.4 .S27 1999*

**Sasaki, Shosuke.**
Rabbit in the moon [videorecording]. San Francisco, Calif. : Wabi-Sabi Productions, 1999.
*TC D753.8 .R3 1999*

**Satellite town meeting**
Annual State of American Education Address (7th : February 22, 2000 : Durham, N.C.) The seventh annual state of American education address [videorecording]. [Washington, D.C. : U.S. Dept. of Education], 2000.

Powerful middle schools : teaching and learning for young adolescents (2000) Powerful middle schools [videorecording]. [Washington, D.C.?] : U.S. Dept. of Education, [2000].
*TC LB1623 .P6 2000*

**SATELLITES.** See MOON.

**Sateren, Shelley Swanson.**
Bircher, William, 1845-1917. A Civil War drummer boy. Mankato, Minn. : Blue Earth Books, c2000.
*TC E601 .B605 2000*

**Sathre, Vivian.** Three kind mice / written by Vivian Sathre ; illustrated by Rodger Wilson. 1st ed. San Diego : Harcourt Brace, c1997. 1 v. (unpaged) : col. ill. ; 21 x 29 cm. SUMMARY: Three kind mice bake a birthday cake surprise for their mysterious friend. ISBN 0-15-201266-4

DDC [E]
1. Mice - Fiction. 2. Baking - Fiction. 3. Birthdays - Fiction. 4. Stories in rhyme. I. Wilson, Rodger, 1947- ill. II. Title.
*TC PZ8.3.S238 Th 1997*

**Satin, Diana.**
Quann, Steve. Learning computers, speaking English. Ann Arbor : University of Michigan Press, c2000.
*TC PE1128.A2 .Q83 2000*

**SATISFACTION.** See CONTENTMENT; JOB SATISFACTION; PATIENT SATISFACTION; SELF-REALIZATION.

**Sato, Takahiko.**
Heart of the country [videorecording]. [New York, NY : First Run/Icarus Films, 1998].
*TC LB1565.H6 H3 1998*

**Satter, Beryl, 1959-** Each mind a kingdom : American women, sexual purity, and the New Thought movement, 1875-1920 / Beryl Satter. Berkeley : University of California Press, c1999. xii, 382 p. : ill. ; 23 cm. Includes bibliographical references (p. 333-357) and index. ISBN 0-520-21765-9 (alk. paper) DDC 289.9/8/0973
1. New Thought - History. 2. Women - Religious life - United States. 3. Eddy, Mary Baker, - 1821-1910. 4. Christian Science - United States - History. 5. Twelve-step programs - History. 6. United States - Church history. 7. Sex role - United States - History. 8. Feminism - United States - History. 9. Sex customs - United States - History. 10. United States - Civilization - 1865-1918. 11. United States - Intellectual life - 1865-1918. I. Title.
*TC BF639 .S124 1999*

**Saturday school.**
Keating, Tom, 1941- Bloomington, Ind. : Phi Delta Kappa Educational Foundation, c1999.
*TC LC212.23.D43 K42 1999*

**SAUCERS, FLYING.** See UNIDENTIFIED FLYING OBJECTS.

**Sauls, Samuel J.** The culture of American college radio / Samuel J. Sauls. 1st ed. Ames : Iowa State University Press, 2000. xii, 216 p. : ill. ; 26 cm. Includes bibliographical references and index. ISBN 0-8138-2068-5 DDC 384.54/53
1. College radio stations - United States. I. Title.
*TC PN1991.67.C64 S38 2000*

**Sauquet, Alfonso.** Conflict and team learning: multiple case study in three organizations in Spain / Alfonso Sauquet. 2000. xi, 397 p. ; 29 cm. Issued also on microfilm. Includes tables. Thesis (Ed.D.) -- Teachers College, Columbia University, 2000. Includes bibliographical references (leaves 347-366)
1. Organizational effectiveness. 2. Communication in organizations - Spain. 3. Conflict management - Spain - Case studies. 4. Group work in education - Spain - Case studies. 5. Team learning approach in education - Spain - Case studies. 6. Organizational learning - Spain - Case studies. I. Title. II. Title: Multiple case study in three organizations in Spain
*TC 06 no. 11308*

**Sauter, Steven L., 1946-.**
Work and well-being. Washington, DC : American Psychological Association, c1992.
*TC RC967.5 .W67 1992*

**Savage inequalities.**
Kozol, Jonathan. 1st Harper Perennial ed. New York : HarperPerennial, 1992.
*TC LC4091 .K69 1992*

**Savage, John F., 1938-** For the love of literature : children & books in the elementary years / John F. Savage. Boston : McGraw-Hill, c2000. xviii, 412 p. : ill. (some col.) ; 24 cm. Includes bibliographical references and indexes. ISBN 0-07-290534-4 (alk. paper) DDC 372.64/044
1. Children's literature - Study and teaching (Elementary) 2. Children's literature - History and criticism. 3. Children's literature - Bibliography. 4. Children - Books and reading. I. Title.
*TC LB1575 .S28 2000*

**Savage, Tom V.**
**Discipline for self control.**
Savage, Tom V. Teaching self-control through management and discipline. 2nd ed. Boston : London : Allyn and Bacon, c1999.
*TC LB3012.2 .S38 1999*

Effective teaching in elementary social studies / by Tom V. Savage, David G. Armstrong ; [editor, Bradley J. Potthoff]. 4th ed. Upper Saddle River, N.J. : Merrill, c2000. xix, 507 p. : ill. ; 25 cm. Includes bibliographical references and indexes. ISBN 0-13-082622-7 DDC 372.83/044
1. Social sciences - Study and teaching (Elementary) - United States. I. Armstrong, David G. II. Potthoff, Bradley J. III. Title.

**TC LB1584 .S34 2000**

Teaching self-control through management and discipline / Tom V. Savage. 2nd ed. Boston : London : Allyn and Bacon, c1999. x, 258 p. : ill., forms ; 23 cm. Rev. ed. of: Discipline for self-control. c1991. Includes bibliographical references and index. ISBN 0-205-28819-7 DDC 371.102/4
1. Classroom management - United States. 2. School discipline - United States. 3. Self-control - United States. I. Savage, Tom V. Discipline for self-control. II. Title.
*TC LB3012.2 .S38 1999*

**SAVANNA ECOLOGY - AFRICA.**
Dunphy, Madeleine. Here is the African savanna. 1st ed. New York : Hyperion Books for Children, c1999.
*TC QH194 .D86 1999*

**SAVANNA ECOLOGY - AFRICA - JUVENILE LITERATURE.**
Dunphy, Madeleine. Here is the African savanna. 1st ed. New York : Hyperion Books for Children, c1999.
*TC QH194 .D86 1999*

**Save the Children Fund (Great Britain).**
Richardson, Robin. Inclusive schools, inclusive society. Stoke on Trent, Staffordshire, England : Trentham Books, 1999.
*TC LC212.3.G7 R523 1999*

**SAVING AND INVESTMENT - PSYCHOLOGICAL ASPECTS.**
Wärneryd, Karl Erik, 1927- The psychology of saving. Northampton, Mass. : E. Elgar, c1999.
*TC HB822 .W37 1999*

**Savitt, Sam.**
My mane catches the wind. 1st ed. New York: Harcourt Brace Jovanovich, c1979.
*TC PN6110.H7 M9*

**Sawin, Martica.** Nell Blaine : her art and life / by Martica Sawin. 1st ed. New York : Hudson Hills Press ; [Lanham, MD] : Distributed in the USA, its territories and possessions, and Canada by National Book Network, c1998. 153 p. : ill. (some col.) ; 29 cm. Includes bibliographical references (p. 146-149) and index. ISBN 1-55595-113-9 (cloth : alk. paper) DDC 759.13
1. Blaine, Nell, - 1922- 2. Painters - United States - Biography. I. Blaine, Nell, 1922- II. Title.
*TC ND237.B597 S28 1998*

**Sawyer, Ann Elisabeth.** Developments in elementary mathematics teaching / Ann Elisabeth Sawyer ; with a foreword by Hildegarde Howden. Portsmouth, NH : Heinemann, c1995. ix, 214 p. : ill. ; 23 cm. Includes bibliographical references (p. [207]-210) and index. ISBN 0-435-08371-6 DDC 372.7/0941
1. Mathematics - Study and teaching (Elementary) - Great Britain - Case studies. I. Title.
*TC QA135.5 .S278 1995*

**Sawyer, Diane, 1945-.**
Heroin [videorecording]. [Princeton, N.J.] : Films for the Humanities & Sciences, c1998.
*TC HV5822.H4 H4 1998*

**Sawyer, Michael G.**
Brown, Ronald T. Medications for school-age children. New York : Guilford Press, c1998.
*TC RJ560 .B76 1998*

**Sawyer, Robin G.**
Gilbert, Glen G. (Glen Gordon), 1946- Health education. 2nd ed. Sudbury, Mass. : Jones and Bartlett, c2000.
*TC RA440.5 .G48 2000*

**Sawyer, Walter.** Growing up with literature / Walter E. Sawyer ; foreword by Francis P. Hodge ; illustrations by Sally Newcomb. 3rd ed. Albany, N.Y. : Delmar, c2000. xv, 304 p. : ill ; 24 cm. Includes bibliographical references and indexes. ISBN 0-7668-0369-4 DDC 372.21/0973
1. Children's literature - Study and teaching (Preschool) - United States. 2. Children - Books and reading. 3. Early childhood education - United States - Curricula. I. Title.
*TC LB1140.5.L3 S28 2000*

**Sax, Gilbert.** The construction and analysis of educational and psychological tests : a laboratory manual. Madison, Wisconsin : College Printing and Typing Co., 1962. 74 p. ill. ; 28 cm. Includes bibliography.
1. Psychometrics 2. Psychological tests. I. Title.
*TC BF39 .S27*

**SAXOPHONE AND PIANO MUSIC (JAZZ).** See JAZZ.

**Say woof!.**
Gibbons, Gail. 1st ed. New York : Macmillan ; Toronto : Maxwell Macmillan Canada ; New York : Maxwell Macmillan International, c1992.

*TC SF756 .G53 1992*

**Saye, Jerry D.** Manheimer's cataloging and classification / by Jerry D. Saye with April J. Bohannan ; MARC formatting with the assistance of Terri O. Saye. 4th ed., rev. and expanded. New York : Marcel Dekker, c2000. xiv, 395 p. : ill. ; 26 cm. + 1 computer optical disc (4 3/4 in.). (Books in library and information science ; v. 59) Includes bibliographical references. System requirements for accompanying disc: IBM PC and compatible systems. ISBN 0-8247-9476-1 (alk. paper) DDC 025.3/076
*1. Cataloging - United States - Problems, exercises, etc. 2. Classification - Books - Problems, exercises, etc. I. Bohannan, April. II. Title. III. Series.*
*TC Z693 .S28 2000*

**Sayer, John, 1931-** The General Teaching Council / John Sayer. London : Cassell, 2000. ix, 195 p. ; 25 cm. Includes bibliographical references (p. [183]-187) and indexes. ISBN 0-304-70562-4
*1. General Teaching Council for England. 2. General Teaching Council for Wales. 3. Teaching - Great Britain. I. Title.*
*TC LB1775.4.G7 S39 2000*

**Sayers, Janet.** Boy crazy : remembering adolescence, therapies, and dreams / Janet Sayers. London ; New York : Routledge, 1998. viii, 185 p. ; 24 cm. Includes bibliographical references and index. ISBN 0-415-19084-3 (hbk) ISBN 0-415-19085-1 (pbk.) DDC 155.5
*1. Adolescent psychology. 2. Adolescent analysis. I. Title.*
*TC BF724 .S325 1998*

**Sayles, Elizabeth, ill.**
Mora, Pat. The rainbow tulip. New York : Viking, 1999.
*TC PZ7.M78819 Rai 1999*

**Sayles, Mary Buell, 1878-** Substitute parents, a study of foster families, by Mary Buell Sayles. New York, The Commonwealth fund; London, H. Milford, Oxford University Press, 1936. viii, 309 p. 24 cm. DDC 362.73
*1. Adoption. 2. Child welfare. 3. Parent and child. I. Title.*
*TC HV875 .S3*

**Sayre, April Pulley.** Home at last : a song of migration / April Pulley Sayre ; illustrations by Alix Berenzy. 1st ed. New York : Holt, 1998. 1 v. (unpaged) : col. ill. ; 21 x 27 cm. SUMMARY: Describes how a variety of creatures, including a butterfly, a sea turtle, a caribou herd, and an Arctic tern, find their ways home. ISBN 0-8050-5154-6 (alk. paper) DDC 591.56/8
*1. Animal migration - Juvenile literature. 2. Animals - Migration. I. Berenzy, Alix, ill. II. Title.*
*TC QL754 .S29 1998*

**SCALE ANALYSIS (PSYCHOLOGY).**
Foye, Stephanie Diane. Using item response theory methods to explore the effect of item wording on Likert data. 1997.
*TC 085 F82*

**SCALE ANALYSIS (SOCIAL SCIENCES).** *See* **SCALING (SOCIAL SCIENCES).**

**SCALES OF MEASUREMENT.** *See* **SCALING (SOCIAL SCIENCES).**

**Scales, Peter, 1949-** Developmental assets : a synthesis of the scientific research on adolescent development / Peter C. Scales and Nancy Leffert ; foreword by Richard M. Lerner. Minneapolis : Search Institute, c1999. xvi, 279 p. : ill. ; 23 cm. Includes bibliographical references (p. 223-266) and index. ISBN 1-57482-338-8 (acid-free paper) DDC 305.235/5
*1. Adolescent psychology. I. Leffert, Nancy, 1949- II. Lerner, Richard M. III. Title.*
*TC BF724 .S327 1999*

**SCALES, PSYCHIATRIC RATING.** *See* **PSYCHIATRIC RATING SCALES.**

**SCALES, RATING (PSYCHIATRY).** *See* **PSYCHIATRIC RATING SCALES.**

**SCALING, PSYCHOLOGICAL.** *See* **PSYCHOMETRICS.**

**SCALING (SOCIAL SCIENCES).** *See also* **PSYCHOMETRICS.**
Chen, Sheying. Measurement and analysis in psychosocial research. Aldershot, Hants, UK ; Brookfield USA : Avebury, c1997.
*TC RC473.P79 C46 1997*

Foye, Stephanie Diane. Using item response theory methods to explore the effect of item wording on Likert data. 1997.
*TC 085 F82*

North, Brian, 1950- The development of a common framework scale of language proficiency. New York : P. Lang, c2000.

*TC P53.4 .N67 2000*

**Scalora, Suza.** The fairies : photographic evidence of the existence of another world / by Suza Scalora. New York : Joanna Cotler Books, c1999. 1 v. (unpaged) : col. ill. ; 29 cm. SUMMARY: After mysteriously receiving a copy of an old manuscript, an archeologist sets off around the world to photograph and document the existence of a variety of fairies. ISBN 0-06-028234-7 DDC [Fic]
*1. Fairies - Fiction. I. Title.*
*TC PZ7.S27915 Fai 1999*

**SCALP.** *See* **HAIR.**

**Scandinavian Seminar College.**
Grundtvig's ideas in North America. Copenhagen, Denmark : Danske Selskab, 1983.
*TC LB675.G832 G79 1983*

**Scanlon, Eileen.**
Communicating science. London ; New York : Routledge in association with The Open University, 1999.
*TC Q223 .C6542 1999*

**Scanning the future :** 20 eminent thinkers on the world of tomorrow / edited and introduced by Yorick Blumenfeld. New York : Thames & Hudson, c1999. 304 p. ; 22 cm. (Prospects for tomorrow) ISBN 0-500-28045-2 (pbk)
*1. Twenty-first century - Forecasts. 2. Forecasting. 3. Technological forecasting. 4. Social change. 5. Civilization, Modern. I. Blumenfeld, Yorick. II. Series.*
*TC CB161 .S44 1999*

**Scarbrough, Elinor.**
Research strategies in the social sciences. Oxford [England] ; New York : Oxford University Press, 1998.
*TC H62 .R4614 1998*

**SCARECROWS - FICTION.**
Preston, Tim. The lonely scarecrow. 1st American ed. New York : Dutton Children's Books, 1999.
*TC PZ7.P9237 Lo 1999*

**Scarry, Elaine.**
Memory, brain, and belief. Cambridge, Mass. ; London : Harvard University Press, 2000.
*TC QP406 .M44 2000*

**Scattered.**
Maté, Gabor. 1st American ed. New York, N.Y., U.S.A. : Dutton, 1999.
*TC RJ506.H9 M42326 1999*

**Scenario educational software.**
Keegan, Mark. Englewood Cliffs, N.J. : Educational Technology Publications, c1995.
*TC LB1028.6 .K44 1995*

**Scenes of wonder :** teacher's planning guide. New York : Macmillan/McGraw-Hill, c1997. 1 v. (various pagings) : col. ill. ; 31 cm. (Spotlight on literacy ; Gr.5 l.11 u.1) (The road to independent reading) Includes index. ISBN 0-02-181179-2
*1. Language arts (Elementary) 2. Reading (Elementary) I. Series. II. Series: The road to independent reading*
*TC LB1576 .S66 1997 Gr.5 l.11 u.1*

**SCENTS.** *See* **ODORS.**

**Schaaf, William Leonard, 1898- joint author.**
Peters, Max, 1906- Algebra. 2d ed. Princeton, N.J., Van Nostrand 1968.
*TC QA152 .P4562 1968*

Peters, Max, 1906- Algebra and trigonometry. Princeton, N.J., Van Nostrand 1965.
*TC QA152 .P4562 1965*

**Schachner, Judith Byron.** The Grannyman / by Judith Byron Schachner. 1st ed. New York : Dutton Children's Books, c1999. 1 v. (unpaged) : col. ill. ; 28 cm. SUMMARY: Simon the cat is so old that most of his parts have stopped working, but just when he is ready to breathe his last breath, his family brings home a new kitten for him to raise. ISBN 0-525-46122-1 (hardcover) DDC [E]
*1. Cats - Fiction. 2. Old age - Fiction. I. Title.*
*TC PZ7.S3286 Gr 1999*

**Schachter, Hindy Lauer.** Reinventing government or reinventing ourselves : the role of citizen owners in making a better government / Hindy Lauer Schachter. Albany : State University of New York Press, c1997. x, 138 p. ; 24 cm. (SUNY series in public administration) Includes bibliographical references (p. 119-134) and index. ISBN 0-7914-3155-X (hb. : alk. paper) ISBN 0-7914-3156-8 (pbk. : alk. paper) DDC 353.07/5
*1. Political participation - United States. 2. Administrative agencies - United States - Reorganization. 3. Administrative agencies - United States - Management. 4. Government publicity - United States. 5. Public administration - United*

States - History. 6. Bureau of Municipal Research (New York, N.Y.) - History. I. Title. II. Series.
*TC JK1764 .S35 1997*

**Schachter, Pam Brown, 1952-.**
Making the most of early communication [videorecording]. New York, NY : Distributed by AFB Press, c1997.
*TC HV1597.2 .M3 1997*

**Schachter-Shalomi, Zalman. 1924-.**
Aging and saging [videorecording]. Princeton, NJ : Films for the Humanities & Sciences : Distributed by Canadian Broadcasting Corporation, 1998.
*TC BF724.55.A35 A35 1998*

**Schacter, Daniel L.**
Memory, brain, and belief. Cambridge, Mass. ; London : Harvard University Press, 2000.
*TC QP406 .M44 2000*

**Schaefer, Charles E.**
Innovative psychotherapy techniques in child and adolescent therapy. 2nd ed. New York : Wiley, c1999.
*TC RJ504 .I57 1999*

Play diagnosis and assessment. 2nd ed. New York : John Wiley & Sons, c2000.
*TC RJ505.P6 P524 1999*

**Schaefer, Judy.**
Socratic seminar [videorecording]. [Boulder, Colo.] : Social Science Education Consortium, c1997.
*TC LB1027.44 .S6 1997*

**Schaeken, Walter.**
Deductive reasoning and strategies. Mahwah, N.J. : L. Erlbaum Associates, 2000.
*TC BF442 .D43 2000*

**Schaie, K. Warner (Klaus Warner), 1928-.**
Caregiving systems. Hillsdale, N.J. : L. Erlbaum Associates, 1993.
*TC HV1451 .C329 1993*

Handbook of theories of aging. New York : Springer Pub. Co., c1999.
*TC HQ1061 .H3366 1999*

**Schaler, Jeffrey A.** Addiction is a choice / Jeffrey A. Schaler. Chicago, Ill. : Open Court, 2000. xviii, 179 p. ; 23 cm. Includes bibliographical references and index. ISBN 0-8126-9403-1 (alk. paper) ISBN 0-8126-9404-X (pbk. : alk. paper) DDC 362.29
*1. Substance abuse. 2. Compulsive behavior. 3. Choice (Psychology) I. Title.*
*TC HV4998 .S33 2000*

**Schank, Roger C., 1946-.**
**Dynamic memory.**
Schank, Roger C., 1946- Dynamic memory revisited. [2nd ed.]. Cambridge : New York : Cambridge University Press, 1999.
*TC BF371 .S365 1999*

Dynamic memory revisited / Roger C. Schank. [2nd ed.]. Cambridge ; New York : Cambridge University Press, 1999. xii, 302 p. : ill. ; 23 cm. Includes bibliographical references (p. 289-298) and index. ISBN 0-521-63302-8 (hardcover) ISBN 0-521-63398-2 (pbk.) DDC 153.1
*1. Memory. 2. Learning, Psychology of. I. Schank, Roger C., 1946- Dynamic memory. II. Title.*
*TC BF371 .S365 1999*

**Schapira, Sylvie K., 1940-** Choosing a counselling or psychotherapy training : a practical guide / Sylvie K. Schapira. London ; New York : Routledge, 2000. ix, 244 p. ; 23 cm. Includes bibliographical references and index. ISBN 0-415-20846-7 (pbk.) DDC 158/.3/071
*1. Counselors - Training of. 2. Counseling. 3. Psychotherapists - Training of. 4. Psychotherapy. I. Title.*
*TC BF637.C6 S355 2000*

**Schapiro, Meyer, 1904-.**
**Selections. 1977. Braziller**
(4.) Schapiro, Meyer, 1904- Theory and philosophy of art. New York : George Braziller, 1994.
*TC N66 .S345 1994*

(5.) Schapiro, Meyer, 1904- Worldview in painting--Art and Society. 1st ed. New York, N.Y. : George Braziller, 1999.
*TC N72.S6 S313 1999*

Theory and philosophy of art : style, artist, and society / Meyer Schapiro. New York : George Braziller, 1994. vii, 253 p. : ill. ; 24 cm. (Selected papers ; 4) Includes bibliographical references and index. ISBN 0-8076-1356-8 ISBN 0-8076-1357-6 (pbk.) DDC 701
*1. Art - Philosophy. 2. Art and society. 3. Art and religion. I. Title. II. Series: Schapiro, Meyer, 1904- Selections. 1977. Braziller ; 4.*

*TC N66 .S345 1994*

Words, script, and pictures : semiotics of visual
language / Meyer Schapiro. New York, NY : George
Braziller, 1996. 199 p. : ill. ; 24 cm. ISBN 0-8076-1416-5
DDC 302.23/014
*1. Visual communication. 2. Semiotics. I. Title.*
*TC P93.5 .S33 1996*

Worldview in painting-Art and Society / Meyer
Schapiro. New York : George Braziller,
1999. 256 p. : ill. ; 24 cm. (Selected papers ; [5]) Series
numbering from book jacket. Includes bibliographical
references and index. ISBN 0-8076-1450-5 DDC 701/.03
*1. Art and society. I. Title. II. Series: Schapiro, Meyer, 1904-
Selections. 1977. Braziller ; 5.*
*TC N72.S6 S313 1999*

**Schapiro, Renie.**
The definition of death. Baltimore : Johns Hopkins
University Press, 1999.
*TC RA1063 .D44 1999*

**Schapiro, Steven A., 1950-.**
Higher education for democracy. New York : P. Lang,
c1999.
*TC LD2001.G452 .S33 1999*

**Scharrer, Erica.**
Comstock, George A. Television. San Diego :
Academic Press, c1999.
*TC PN1992.6 .C645 1999*

**Schatz, Amy.**
Portrait of addiction [videorecording]. Princeton, NJ :
Films for the Humanities & Sciences, c1998.
*TC HV5801 .P6 1998*

Portrait of addiction [videorecording]. Princeton, NJ :
Films for the Humanities & Sciences, c1998.
*TC RC564 .P6 1998*

**Schaufeli, Wilmar, 1953-.**
Professional burnout. Washington, DC : Taylor &
Francis, c1993.
*TC BF481 .P77 1993*

**Schechter, John Mendell.**
Music in Latin American culture. New York :
Schirmer Books, c1999.
*TC ML199 .M86 1999*

**Schecter, David.**
Cruz Martinez, Alejandro, d. 1987. [Mujer que
brillaba aún más que el sol. English & Spanish] The
woman who outshone the sun. San Francisco, Calif. :
Children's Book Press, c1991.
*TC F1221.Z3 C78 1991*

**Schecter, Sandra.**
On becoming a language educator. Mahwah, NJ :
Lawrence Erlbaum, 1997.
*TC P53.85 .O5 1997*

**SCHEDULED TRIBES (INDIA).** *See* **INDIA -
SCHEDULED TRIBES.**

**SCHEDULES, SCHOOL - NEW JERSEY.**
Campbell, Delois. High school students' perceptions
of the impact of block scheduling on instructional
effectiveness. 1999.
*TC 06 no. 11089*

**SCHEDULES, SCHOOL - UNITED STATES.**
Block scheduling. Bloomington, IN : Phi Delta Phi
International, c1999.
*TC LB3032.2 .B47 1999*

The dimensions of time and the challenge of school
reform. Albany : State University of New York Press,
c2000.
*TC LB3032 .D55 2000*

Time and learning :. Bloomington, IN : Phi Delta
Kappa International, c1998.
*TC LB3032 .T562 1998*

**SCHEDULES, SCHOOL - UNITED STATES -
HANDBOOKS, MANUALS, ETC.**
Ricken, Robert. The high school principal's calendar.
Thousand Oaks, Calif. : Corwin Press, c2000.
*TC LB3032 .R53 2000*

**Scheduling for success.**
Time and learning :. Bloomington, IN : Phi Delta
Kappa International, c1998.
*TC LB3032 .T562 1998*

**Scheduling strategies for middle schools.**
Rettig, Michael D., 1950- Larchmont, NY : Eye On
Education, 2000.
*TC LB3032.2 .R48 2000*

**SCHEDULING - UNITED STATES.**
Erlandson, David A. Organizational oversight.
Princeton, NJ : Eye on Education, c1996.

*TC LB2805 .E75 1996*

**Scheffer, Barbara K.**
Rubenfeld, M. Gaie. Critical thinking in nursing. 2nd
ed. Philadelphia : Lippincott, c1999.
*TC RT84.5 .R83 1999*

**Scheibe, Karl E., 1937-** The drama of everyday life /
Karl E. Scheibe. Cambridge, Mass. : Harvard
University Press, 2000. xii, 281 p. : ill. ; 24 cm. Includes
bibliographical references (p. [259]-271) and index. ISBN
0-674-00231-8 (alk. paper) DDC 150
*1. Psychology. I. Title.*
*TC BF121 .S328 2000*

**Scheidecker, David, 1950-** Bringing out the best in
students : how legendary teachers motivate kids /
David Scheidecker, William Freeman. Thousand
Oaks, Calif. : Corwin Press, c1999. xiv, 151 p. : ill. ; 24
cm. CONTENTS: Piecing together the personality puzzle --
Nothing succeeds like success -- Establishing high
expectations -- Practicing skillful communication -- From
chaos to organization -- Recognizing and promoting
excellence -- Motivating high student achievement --
Developing powerful classroom management skills --
Becoming a legend. ISBN 0-8039-6756-X (cloth : acid-free
paper) ISBN 0-8039-6757-8 (pbk. : acid-free paper) DDC
370.15/4
*1. Motivation in education. 2. Effective teaching. I. Freeman,
William, 1951- II. Title.*
*TC LB1065 .S344 1999*

**Scheidenhelm, Carol.**
Hoffman, Eric. An introduction to teaching
composition in an electronic environment. Needham
Heights, Mass. : Allyn & Bacon, c2000.
*TC LB1028.3 .H63 2000*

**Scheier, Christian.**
Pfeifer, Rolf, 1947- Understanding intelligence.
Cambridge, Mass. : MIT Press, c1999.
*TC Q335 .P46 1999*

**Scheier, Michael.**
Perspectives on behavioral self-regulation. Mahwah,
N.J. : Lawrence Erlbaum Associates, 1999.
*TC HM291 A345 1999*

**Scheinfeld, Daniel, 1933-** Strengthening refugee
families : designing programs for refugee and other
families in need / Daniel Scheinfeld and Lorraine B.
Wallach, with Trudi Langendorf. Chicago, Ill. :
Lyceum Books, c1997. x, 235 p. : ill. ; 22 cm. Includes
bibliographical references (p. 235). ISBN 0-925065-13-7
(pbk.) DDC 362.87/8/0973
*1. Refugees - Services for - United States. 2. Family services -
United States. I. Wallach, Lorraine B. II. Langendorf, Trudi,
1955- III. Title.*
*TC HV640.4.U54 S34 1997*

**Schenker, Heinrich, 1868-1935.**
**[Kunst des Vortrags. English]**
The art of performance / Heinrich Schenker ; edited
by Heribert Esser ; translated by Irene Schreier
Scott. New York : Oxford University Press, 2000.
xxvii, 101 p. : facsims., music ; 25 cm. An unfinished work
edited from the author's papers in the New York Public
Library and the University of California at Riverside.
Includes bibliographical references and index. CONTENTS:
Musical composition and performance -- Mode of notation
and performance -- The technique of playing the piano --
Non legato -- Legato -- Staccato -- Fingering -- Dynamics --
Tempo and tempo modifications -- Rests -- The
performance of older music -- On practicing. ISBN 0-19-
512254-2 DDC 786.2/193
*1. Piano - Performance. 2. Piano music - Interpretation
(Phrasing, dynamics, etc.) 3. Music - Performance. I. Esser,
Heribert. II. Title.*
*TC MT220 .S24513 2000*

**Scherer, Marge, 1945-.**
A better beginning. Alexandria, Va. : Association for
Supervision and Curriculum Development, c1999.
*TC LB2844.1.N4 B48 1999*

**Schermer, Victor L.**
Group psychotherapy for psychological trauma. New
York : Guilford Press, c2000.
*TC RC552.P67 G76 2000*

**Scherrer, Christian P.**
Ethnicity and intra-state conflict. Aldershot, Hants,
England : Brookfield, Vt., USA : Ashgate, c1999.
*TC GN495.6 .E83 1999*

**Schettler, Ted.**
Generations at risk. Cambridge, Mass. : MIT Press,
c1999.
*TC RA1224.2 .G46 1999*

**Scheuch, Nannette S.**
Gilhooley, James. Using peer mediation in classrooms

and schools. Thousand Oaks, Calif. : Corwin Press,
c2000.
*TC LB1027.5 .G48 2000*

**Scheurich, James Joseph, 1944-** Research method in
the postmodern / James Joseph Scheurich. London ;
Washington, DC : Falmer Press, 1997. vii, 189 p. ; 25
cm. (Qualitative studies series ; 3) Includes bibliographical
references and index. ISBN 0-7507-0709-7 (cased) ISBN
0-7507-0645-7 (pbk.) DDC 370/.7
*1. Education - Research - Philosophy. 2. Education -
Research - Methodology. 3. Postmodernism and education. I.
Title. II. Series.*
*TC LB1028 .S242 1997*

**Schick, Theodore.** How to think about weird things :
critical thinking for a new age / Theodore Schick, Jr.,
Lewis Vaughn ; foreword by Martin Gardner. 2nd ed.
Mountain View, Calif. : Mayfield Pub., c1999. xv, 300
p. : ill. ; 24 cm. Includes bibliographical references and index.
ISBN 0-7674-0013-5 (alk. paper) DDC 001.9/01
*1. Critical thinking. 2. Parapsychology. 3. Occultism. 4.
Mysticism. 5. Miracles. 6. Curiosities and wonders. I. Vaughn,
Lewis. II. Title.*
*TC BC177 .S32 1999*

**Schiemer, Suzann, 1956-** Assessment strategies for
elementary physical education / Suzann Schiemer.
Champaign, IL ; Leeds, U.K. : Human Kinetics,
c2000. ix, 143 p. : ill., forms ; 28 cm. Includes bibliographical
references (p. 141). ISBN 0-88011-569-6 DDC 372.86
*1. Physical fitness - Testing. 2. Physical education and
training - Study and teaching (Elementary) I. Title.*
*TC GV436 .S27 2000*

**Schiller, Ellen P.**
Contemporary special education research. Mahwah,
N.J. : Lawrence Erlbaum, c2000.
*TC LC4019 .C575 2000*

**Schilpp, Madelon Golden.**
Schilpp, Paul Arthur, 1897- Reminiscing. Carbondale,
IL : Published for the College of Liberal Arts of
Southern Illinois University at Carbondale by
Southern Illinois University Press, c1996.
*TC B945.S28 A3 1996*

**Schilpp, Paul Arthur, 1897-** Reminiscing :
autobiographical notes / Paul Arthur Schilpp with
Madelon Golden Schilpp. Carbondale, IL : Published
for the College of Liberal Arts of Southern Illinois
University at Carbondale by Southern Illinois
University Press, c1996. x, 163 p. : ill. ; 22 cm. ISBN
0-8093-2028-2 (alk. paper) DDC 191
*1. Schilpp, Paul Arthur, - 1897- 2. Philosophers - United
States - Biography. I. Schilpp, Madelon Golden. II. Title.*
*TC B945.S28 A3 1996*

**SCHILPP, PAUL ARTHUR, 1897-.**
Schilpp, Paul Arthur, 1897- Reminiscing. Carbondale,
IL : Published for the College of Liberal Arts of
Southern Illinois University at Carbondale by
Southern Illinois University Press, c1996.
*TC B945.S28 A3 1996*

**Schindler, S. D., ill.**
Kay, Verla, Gold fever. New York : Putnam's, c1999.
*TC PZ8.3.K225 Go 1999*

Simon, Seymour. The invisible man and other cases.
Rev. ed. New York : Morrow Junior Books, c1998.
*TC PZ7.S60573 In 1998*

**Schirmer, Barbara R.** Language and literacy
development in children who are deaf / Barbara R.
Schirmer. 2nd ed. Boston : Allyn and Bacon, 2000. xi,
278 p. : ill. ; 24 cm. Includes bibliographical references and
index. ISBN 0-205-31493-7 DDC 305.9/08162
*1. Deaf - Means of communication - Study and teaching
(Elementary) 2. Deaf children - Language. 3. Deaf -
Education. I. Title.*
*TC HV2443 .S33 2000*

**SCHIZO-AFFECTIVE PSYCHOSIS.** *See*
**SCHIZOAFFECTIVE DISORDERS.**

**SCHIZOAFFECTIVE DISORDERS - DIAGNOSIS.**
Schizophrenia and delusional disorders
[videorecording]. Princeton, N.J. : Films for the
Humanities & Sciences, c1998.
*TC RC514 .S3 1998*

**SCHIZOAFFECTIVE DISORDERS - PATIENTS.**
Schizophrenia and delusional disorders
[videorecording]. Princeton, N.J. : Films for the
Humanities & Sciences, c1998.
*TC RC514 .S3 1998*

**SCHIZOAFFECTIVE PSYCHOSIS.** *See*
**SCHIZOAFFECTIVE DISORDERS.**

**SCHIZOAFFECTIVE SCHIZOPHRENIA.** *See*
**SCHIZOAFFECTIVE DISORDERS.**

## SCHIZOHRENIA.
First break [videorecording]. Boston, MA : Fanlight Productions, c1997.
*TC RC465 .F5 1997*

First break [videorecording]. Boston, MA : Fanlight Productions, c1997.
*TC RC465 .F5 1997*

## SCHIZOPHRENIA. See also PARANOID SCHIZOPHRENIA; SCHIZOAFFECTIVE DISORDERS.
Bell, Lisa M. Frontal lobe dysfunction in first episode Schizophrenia. 1998.
*TC 085 B3995*

Shapiro, David, 1926- Dynamics of character. New York : Basic Books, c2000.
*TC RC455.5.T45 .S46 2000*

When the brain goes wrong [videorecording]. Short version. Boston, MA : Fanlight Productions [dist.], c1992.
*TC RC386 .W54 1992*

### Schizophrenia and delusional disorders
[videorecording] / a presentation of Films for the Humanities & Sciences ; University of Sheffield ; produced and directed by Steve Collier ; written by Dr. Steve Peters. Princeton, N.J. : Films for the Humanities & Sciences, c1998. 1 videocassette (46 min.) : sd., col. ; 1/2 in. (Differential diagnosis in psychiatry) VHS. Catalogued from credits and container. Commentary by John Graham Davies. Sound: Ken Hardy; cameras: Jackie Jones, Mark Parkin, Gary Wraith; graphics: Sean Purcell. Series subtitle: A visual aid based on ICD 10. "Clinical features of myotonic dystrophy and Huntington's disease" included in list of complete series on container no longer part of series. For students of psychiatry, clinical psychology and social work, and counselling. SUMMARY: "Schizophrenia, acute and transient psychoses, persistent delusional disorders, and schizoaffective disorders are examined in this program. Their principal abnormalities are divided into the following psychiatric phenomena: disordered thinking, delusions, hallucinations, and abnormal behavior. Specific symptoms of each disorder are discussed. Particular symptoms to look for in patient interviews are provided, along with criteria for diagnosing each disorder."--Container.
*1. Schizophrenia - Diagnosis. 2. Schizophrenia - Patients. 3. Paranoid schizophrenia - Diagnosis. 4. Paranoid schizophrenia - Patients. 5. Schizoaffective disorders - Diagnosis. 6. Schizoaffective disorders - Patients. 7. Hallucinations and illusions. 8. Delusions. 9. Diagnosis, Differential. I. Peters, Steve, Dr. II. Collier, Steve. III. Davies, John Graham. IV. University of Sheffield. V. Films for the Humanities (Firm) VI. Series.*
*TC RC514 .S3 1998*

## SCHIZOPHRENIA - DIAGNOSIS.
Schizophrenia and delusional disorders [videorecording]. Princeton, N.J. : Films for the Humanities & Sciences, c1998.
*TC RC514 .S3 1998*

## SCHIZOPHRENIA - ETIOLOGY.
Origins and development of schizophrenia. Washington, DC : American Psychological Association, c1998.
*TC RC514 .O75 1998*

## SCHIZOPHRENIA, PARANOID. See PARANOID SCHIZOPHRENIA.

## SCHIZOPHRENIA - PATIENTS. See also SCHIZOPHRENICS.
Schizophrenia and delusional disorders [videorecording]. Princeton, N.J. : Films for the Humanities & Sciences, c1998.
*TC RC514 .S3 1998*

## SCHIZOPHRENIC DISORDERS. See SCHIZOPHRENIA.

## SCHIZOPHRENICS - CASE STUDIES.
First break [videorecording]. Boston, MA : Fanlight Productions, c1997.
*TC RC465 .F5 1997*

First break [videorecording]. Boston, MA : Fanlight Productions, c1997.
*TC RC465 .F5 1997*

## SCHIZOPHRENICS - FAMILY RELATIONSHIPS.
First break [videorecording]. Boston, MA : Fanlight Productions, c1997.
*TC RC465 .F5 1997*

First break [videorecording]. Boston, MA : Fanlight Productions, c1997.
*TC RC465 .F5 1997*

## SCHIZOPHRENICS - INTERVIEWS.
First break [videorecording]. Boston, MA : Fanlight Productions, c1997.

---

First break [videorecording]. Boston, MA : Fanlight Productions, c1997.
*TC RC465 .F5 1997*

## SCHIZOPHRENIFORM PSYCHOSIS, AFFECTIVE TYPE. See SCHIZOAFFECTIVE DISORDERS.

## SCHIZOTYPAL PERSONALITY DISORDER. See SCHIZOPHRENIA.

**Schlanger, Dean J.** An exploration of school belongingness : ethnicity, mediating factors, and fostering activities in a multicultural, middle-class, suburban middle school / Dean J. Schlanger. 1998. x, 189 leaves : ill. ; 29 cm. Issued also on microfilm. Thesis (Ed.D.)--Teachers College, Columbia University, 1998. Includes bibliographical references (leaves 155-165).
*1. Middle school students - New York (State) - Social aspects. 2. Minority students - New York (State) - Attitudes - Case studies. 3. Alienation (Social psychology) 4. Intercultural communication - New York (State) - Case studies. 5. Interpersonal relations - New York (State) - Case studies. 6. School environment - New York (State) - Case studies. 7. Multicultural education. I. Title.*
*TC 06 no. 10993*

**Schleicher, Andreas.**
Measuring student knowledge and skills. Paris : Organisation for Economic Co-operation and Development, c1999.
*TC LB3051 .M43 1999*

**Schlichting, Carl.** Working with polyethylene foam and fluted plastic sheet / by Carl Schlichting. Ottawa, Ontario, Canada : Canadian Conservation Institute, Dept. of Canadian Heritage, 1994. 19, 20 p. : ill. ; 28 cm. (Technical bulletin (Canadian Conservation Institute), 0706-4152 ; no. 14.) Text in English and French with French text on inverted pages. Title on added t.p. : Travail de la mousse de polyéthylène et des feuilles de plastique cannelées. "Cat. No. NM 95/55-14-1994." ISBN 0-662-61042-3
*1. Museum conservation methods. 2. Museums - Furniture, equipment, etc. 3. Plastic foams. 4. Plastic films. 5. Art - Exhibition techniques. I. Title. II. Title: Travail de la mousse de polyéthylène et des feuilles de plastique cannelées. III. Series.*
*TC N8554 T25 no.14*

**Schloss, Cynthia N.**
Alper, Sandra K. Alternate assessment of students with disabilities in inclusive settings. Boston ; London : Allyn and Bacon, c2001.
*TC LC4031 .A58 2001*

**Schmaling, Karen B.**
The psychology of couples and illness. 1st ed. Washington, D.C. : American Psychological Association, c2000.
*TC R726.5 .P785 2000*

**Schmidt, Gary D.** Anson's way / Gary D. Schmidt. New York : Clarion Books, c1999. 213 p. ; 22 cm. SUMMARY: While serving as a British Fencible to maintain the peace in eighteenth-century Ireland, Anson finds that his sympathy for a hedge master, a teacher devoted to teaching Irish children their forbidden language and culture, places him in conflict with the law of King George II. ISBN 0-395-91529-5 DDC [Fic]
*1. Ireland - History - 18th century - Juvenile fiction. 2. Ireland - History - 18th century - Fiction. 3. Fathers and sons - Fiction. 4. Identity - Fiction. I. Title.*
*TC PZ7.S3527 An 1999*

**Schmidt, Jan Zlotnik.**
Wise women. New York ; London : Routledge, 2000.
*TC LB2837 .W58 2000*

**Schmidt, Jeff, 1946-** Disciplined minds : a critical look at salaried professionals and the soul-battering system that shapes their lives / Jeff Schmidt. Lanham, Md. ; Oxford : Rowman & Littlefield, c2000. viii, 293 p. : ill. ; 24 cm. Includes bibliographical references and index. ISBN 0-8476-9364-3 (cloth : alk. paper) DDC 305.5/53/0973
*1. Professions - Social aspects - United States. 2. Professional education - United States. 3. Quality of work life - United States. I. Title.*
*TC HT687 .S35 2000*

**Schmidt, John J., 1946-** Counseling in schools : essential services and comprehensive programs / John J. Schmidt. 3rd ed. Boston : Allyn and Bacon, c2000. xi, 355 p. : ill. ; 25 cm. Includes bibliographical references (p. 332-345) and indexes. ISBN 0-205-28879-0 DDC 371.4
*1. Educational counseling - United States. 2. Student counselors - United States. 3. Counseling in elementary education - United States. 4. Counseling in middle school education - United States. 5. Counseling in secondary education - United States. I. Title.*

---

*TC LB1027.5 .S2585 1999*

**Schmidt, Mary.** Index to nineteenth century American art periodicals / Mary Morris Schmidt. Madison, CT : Sound View Press, c1999. 2 v. ; 29 cm. CONTENTS: Vol. I Citations -- vol. II Author/subject index. ISBN 0-932087-56-6
*1. Art - Periodicals - Indexes. 2. American periodicals - Indexes.*
*TC N1 Sch5*

**Schmidt, Patricia Ruggiano, 1944-** Cultural conflict and struggle : literacy learning in a kindergarten program / Patricia Ruggiano Schmidt. New York : P. Lang, c1998. xviii, 160 p. : ill ; 23 cm. (Rethinking childhood ; vol. 5) Includes bibliographical references (p. [139]-151) and index. ISBN 0-8204-3757-3 (alk. paper) DDC 372.21/8
*1. Children - New York (State) - Language - Case studies. 2. Kindergarten - Social aspects - New York (State) - Case studies. 3. Asian-American children - Education - New York (State) - Case studies. 4. Socialization - New York (State) - Case studies. 5. Education, Bilingual - New York (State) - Case studies. 6. Multicultural education - New York (State) - Case studies. I. Title. II. Series.*
*TC LB1181 .S36 1998*

**Schmidt, William H.**
Facing the consequences. Dordrecht ; Boston : Kluwer Academic Publishers, c1999.
*TC QA13 .F33 1999*

**Schminke, Marshall.**
Managerial ethics. Mahwah, N.J. : Lawrence Erlbaum Assocs., 1998.
*TC HF5387 .M3345 1998*

**Schneider, Barbara.**
Csikszentmihalyi, Mihaly. Becoming adult. New York : Basic Books, 2000.
*TC HQ796 .C892 2000*

**Schneider, Elke.** Multisensory structured metacognitive instruction : an approach to teaching a foreign language to at-risk students / Elke Schneider. Frankfurt am Main ; New York : P. Lang, c1999. xvii, 305 p. : ill. ; 21 cm. (Theorie und Vermittlung der Sprache ; Bd. 30) Includes bibliographical references (p. 221-274) and index. ISBN 0-8204-3595-3 DDC 418/.007
*1. Language and languages - Study and teaching - Psychological aspects. 2. Language and languages - Study and teaching (Higher) 3. Learning disabilities. 4. Metacognition. I. Title. II. Series.*
*TC P53.7 .S357 1999*

**Schneider, Frank.** Our public schools : a pearl of great price / Frank Schneider. Mobile, Ala. : Factor Press, 2000. 169 p. ; 22 cm. Includes bibliographical references and index. ISBN 1-88765-019-9
*1. Public schools - United States. 2. Educational change - United States. 3. Education - Aims and objectives - United States. I. Title.*
*TC LA217.2 .S34 2000*

**Schneider, Ira.**
Processing the signal [videorecording]. Cicero, Ill. : Roland Collection of Films on Art, c1989.
*TC N6494.V53 P7 1989*

**Schneider, Jane, 1938-.**
Cloth and human experience. Washington : Smithsonian Institution Press, c1989.
*TC GT525 .C57 1989*

**Schneider, Kim.**
Hand in hand [videorecording]. New York, N.Y. : AFB Press, c1995.
*TC HV1597.2 .H3 1995*

Making the most of early communication [videorecording]. New York, NY : Distributed by AFB Press, c1997.
*TC HV1597.2 .M3 1997*

**Schneider, Mark, 1946-** Choosing schools : consumer choice and the quality of American schools / Mark Schneider, Paul Teske, Melissa Marschall. Princeton, N.J. ; Oxford : Princeton University Press, c2000. xi, 315 p. : ill. ; 25 cm. Includes bibliographical references (p. [285]-305) and index. ISBN 0-691-05057-0 (cl : alk. paper) DDC 379.1/11/0973
*1. School choice - United States. I. Teske, Paul Eric. II. Marschall, Melissa, 1968- III. Title.*
*TC LB1027.9 .S32 2000*

**Schnotz, Wolfgang, 1946-.**
New perspectives on conceptual change. 1st ed. Amsterdam ; New York ; Oxford : Pergamon, 1999.
*TC LB1062 .N49 1999*

**Schoenbach, Ruth.**
Reading for understanding. 1st ed. San Francisco, Calif. : Jossey-Bass Publishers, c1999.

*TC LB1632 .R357 1999*

**Schoener, Allon.**
Harlem on my mind : cultural capital of Black
America, 1900-1968. New York : New Press :
Distributed by W.W. Norton & Co., c1995.
*TC F128.68.H3 S3 1995*

**SCHOLARLY ELECTRONIC PUBLISHING -
UNITED STATES - CONGRESSES.**
Technology and scholarly communication. Berkeley,
Calif. : University of California Press ; [Pittsburgh?] :
Published in association with the Andrew K. Mellon
Foundation, c1999.
*TC Z479 .T43 1999*

**SCHOLARLY WEB SITES - DIRECTORIES.**
The School administrator's handbook of essential
Internet sites. Fourth ed. Gaithersburg, MD : Aspen
Publishers.
*TC TK5105.875.I57 S3 2000*

**SCHOLARLY WRITING.** *See* **ACADEMIC
WRITING.**

**SCHOLARS.** *See* **HISTORIANS;
PHILOSOPHERS.**

**SCHOLARS, AMERICAN - DIRECTORIES.**
Directory of American scholars. 9th ed. / edited by
Rita C. Velazquez. Detroit, Mich. : Gale Group, 1999.
*TC LA2311 .D57 1999*

**SCHOLARSHIP.** *See* **LEARNING AND
SCHOLARSHIP.**

**SCHOLARSHIP FUNDS.** *See* **SCHOLARSHIPS.**

**SCHOLARSHIPS.** *See* **STUDENT FINANCIAL
AID ADMINISTRATION.**

**Scholarships for a better world.**
Weinstein, Miriam (Miriam H.) Making a difference.
Rev. & exp. 2nd ed. Gabriola Island, BC, Can. : New
Society Publishers, 2000.
*TC LB2338 W45 2000*

**SCHOLARSHIPS - UNITED STATES.** *See* **AFRO-
AMERICAN COLLEGE STUDENTS -
SCHOLARSHIPS, FELLOWSHIPS, ETC.;
AFRO-AMERICANS - SCHOLARSHIPS,
FELLOWSHIPS, ETC.**

**SCHOLARSHIPS - UNITED STATES -
DIRECTORIES.**
Weinstein, Miriam (Miriam H.) Making a difference.
Rev. & exp. 2nd ed. Gabriola Island, BC, Can. : New
Society Publishers, 2000.
*TC LB2338 W45 2000*

**SCHOLASTIC ACHIEVEMENT.** *See* **ACADEMIC
ACHIEVEMENT.**

**SCHOLASTIC APTITUDE TEST.**
Owen, David, 1955- None of the above. Rev. and
updated. Lanham, Md. : Rowman & Littlefield
Publishers, c1999.
*TC LB2353.57 .O94 1999*

**Scholastic encyclopedia of the Civil War.**
Clinton, Catherine, 1952- New York : Scholastic
Reference, 1999.
*TC E468 .C67 1999*

**Scholastic encyclopedia of the United States at war.**
English, June, 1955- New York : Scholastic, 1998.
*TC E181 .E64 1998*

**Scholastic encyclopedia of U.S. at war.**
English, June, 1955- Scholastic encyclopedia of the
United States at war. New York : Scholastic, 1998.
*TC E181 .E64 1998*

**SCHOLASTIC FAILURE.** *See* **SCHOOL
FAILURE.**

**Scholastic Inc.**
Young, Sue, 1932- The Scholastic rhyming dictionary.
New York : Scholastic Reference, c1994.
*TC PE1519 .Y684 1994*

**Scholastic literature guide. Grades 4-8.**
Beech, Linda Ward. The cay by Theodore Taylor.
New York : Scholastic, c1997.
*TC LB1573 .B4312 1997*

Beech, Linda Ward. Danny the champion of the world
by Roald Dahl. New York : Scholastic, c1997.
*TC LB11573 .B431 1997*

Beech, Linda Ward. Danny the champion of the world
by Roald Dahl. New York : Scholastic, c1997.
*TC LB1573 .B431 1997*

Beech, Linda Ward. The diary of a young girl by
Anne Frank. New York : Scholastic, c1998.

*TC LB1573 .B433 1998*

Beech, Linda Ward. The great fire by Jim Murphy.
New York : Scholastic, c1996.
*TC LB11573 .B437 1996*

Beech, Linda Ward. The great fire by Jim Murphy.
New York : Scholastic, c1996.
*TC LB1573 .B437 1996*

Beech, Linda Ward. The great Gilly Hopkins by
Katherine Paterson. New York : Scholastic, c1998.
*TC LB1573 .B439 1998*

Beech, Linda Ward. Guests by Michael Dorris. New
York, NY : Scholastic, c1996.
*TC LB1573 .B432 1996*

Beech, Linda Ward. Hatchet by Gary Paulsen. New
York : Scholastic, c1998.
*TC LB1573 .B4310 1998*

Beech, Linda Ward. Island of the blue dolphins by
Scott O'Dell. New York : Scholastic, c1997.
*TC LB1573 .B438 1997*

Beech, Linda Ward. Julie of the wolves by Jean
Craighead George. New York : Scholastic, c1996.
*TC LB1573 .B434 1996*

Beech, Linda Ward. Maniac Magee by Jerry Spinelli.
New York : Scholastic, c1997.
*TC LB1573 .B4311 1997*

Beech, Linda Ward. Sarah, plain and tall by Patricia
MacLachlan. New York : Scholastic, c1996.
*TC LB1573 .B436 1996*

Beech, Linda Ward. Tuck everlasting by Natalie
Babbitt. New York : Scholastic, c1997.
*TC LB1573 .B43 1997*

Beech, Linda Ward. A wrinkle in time by Madeleine
L'Engle. New York : Scholastic, c1997.
*TC LB1573 .B435 1997*

Gutner, Howard. Caddie Woodlawn by Carol Ryrie
Brink. New York : Scholastic, c1997.
*TC LB1573 .G87 1997*

McCarthy, Tara. My brother Sam is dead by James
Lincoln Collier and Christopher Collier. New York :
Scholastic, c1997.
*TC LB1573 .M32 1997*

Rawlings, Carol Miller. The lion, the witch and the
wardrobe by C. S. Lewis. New York : Scholastic,
c1997.
*TC LB1573 .R38 1997*

**The Scholastic rhyming dictionary.**
Young, Sue, 1932- New York : Scholastic Reference,
c1994.
*TC PE1519 .Y684 1994*

**SCHOLASTIC SUCCESS.** *See* **ACADEMIC
ACHIEVEMENT.**

**SCHOLASTIC SUCCESS, PREDICTION OF.** *See*
**PREDICTION OF SCHOLASTIC SUCCESS.**

**Scholes, Robert J.** A linguistic approach to reading and
writing / Robert James Scholes. Lewiston, N.Y. : E.
Mellen Press, c1999. ii, 136 p. : ill. ; 24 cm. (Studies in
linguistics and semiotics ; v. 3) Includes bibliographical
references (p. 129-136). ISBN 0-7734-7919-8 DDC 302.2/244
*1. Written communication. 2. Speech. 3. Literacy. I. Title. II.
Series.*
*TC P211 .S383 1999*

**Scholnick, Ellin Kofsky.**
Toward a feminist developmental psychology. New
York : Routledge, 2000.
*TC BF713 .T66 2000*

**Schomburg Center for Research in Black Culture.**
The New York Public Library African American Desk
Reference. New york : Wiley, c1999.
*TC E185 .N487 1999*

The New York Public Library African American Desk
Reference. New york : Wiley, c1999.
*TC E185 .N487 1999*

**Schon, Isabel.** Recommended books in Spanish for
children and young adults, 1996 through 1999 / Isabel
Schon. Lanham, Md. : Scarecrow Press, 2000. x, 362
p. ; 23 cm. Includes indexes. ISBN 0-8108-3840-0 (alk. paper)
DDC 011.62
*1. Children's literature, Spanish - Bibliography. 2. Children's
literature, Spanish American - Bibliography. 3. Young adult
literature, Spanish - Bibliography. 4. Young adult literature,
Spanish American - Bibliography. 5. Children's literature -
Translations into Spanish - Bibliography. 6. Young adult
literature - Translations into Spanish - Bibliography. 7.
Children's libraries - Book lists. 8. Children - Books and
reading. I. Title.*

*TC Z1037.7 .S387 2000*

**School & college.**
The High school quarterly. Athens, Ga. : University of
Georgia, 1912-[1936]

**School & society.**
Intellect. [New York, Society for the Advancement of
Education]

**School 27 [videorecording].**
Ecole 27 [videorecording]. Bruxelles : Paradise
Films ; New York, N.Y. : [distributed by] First Run/
Icarus Films, 1997, c1996.
*TC LC746.P7 E2 1997*

**SCHOOL ACCIDENTS - UNITED STATES -
PREVENTION.**
Posner, Marc. Preventing school injuries. New
Brunswick, N.J. ; London : Rutgers University Press,
c2000.
*TC LB2864.6.A25 P67 2000*

**SCHOOL ADMINISTRATION.** *See* **SCHOOL
MANAGEMENT AND ORGANIZATION.**

**SCHOOL ADMINISTRATORS.** *See* **SCHOOL
PRINCIPALS; SCHOOL
SUPERINTENDENTS; WOMEN SCHOOL
ADMINISTRATORS.**

**SCHOOL ADMINISTRATORS -
CERTIFICATION - UNITED STATES -
PERIODICALS.**
Requirements for certification of teachers, counselors,
librarians, administrators for elementary and
secondary schools. Chicago : University of Chicago
Press, 1989-
*TC LB1171 .W6*

**SCHOOL ADMINISTRATORS - GREAT
BRITAIN.**
Law, Sue. Educational leadership and learning.
Buckingham [England] ; Philadelphia : Open
University Press, 2000.
*TC LB2900.5 .L39 1999*

**The School administrator's handbook of essential
Internet sites.** Fourth ed. Gaithersburg, MD : Aspen
Publishers. v. ; 26 cm. Frequency: Annual. Description based
on 4th ed. (2000). ISSN 1530-7409
*1. School management and organization - Computer network
resources - Directories. 2. Education - Computer network
resources - Directories. 3. Scholarly Web sites - Directories. 4.
Internet in education. 5. Web sites - Directories.*
*TC TK5105.875.I57 S3 2000*

**SCHOOL ADMINISTRATORS - HANDBOOKS,
MANUALS, ETC.**
Written expression. Larchmont, NY : Eye on
Education, c1997.
*TC PN145 .W78 1997*

**SCHOOL ADMINISTRATORS - NEW YORK
(STATE) - NEW YORK.**
Wright, Stanley Nathaniel. The Beacon model. 1998.
*TC 06 no. 11007*

**SCHOOL ADMINISTRATORS - NEW YORK
(STATE) - NEW YORK - ATTITUDES.**
Curcio, John J. Relationships among administrator
personality, perceptions of feedback source
credibility, and attitudes toward program feedback.
1999.
*TC 085 C92*

**SCHOOL ADMINISTRATORS - TRAINING OF -
UNITED STATES.**
Cunningham, William G. Educational administration.
Boston ; London : Allyn & Bacon, c2000.
*TC LB1738.5 .C86 2000*

**SCHOOL ADMINISTRATORS - UNITED
STATES.**
Durocher, Elizabeth Antointette. Leadership
orientations of school administrators. 1995.
*TC 06 no. 10583a*

Gallagher, Karen S. Shaping school policy. Newbury
Park, Calif. : Corwin Press, c1992.
*TC LC89 .G35 1992*

Kosmoski, Georgia J. Managing difficult, frustrating,
and hostile conversations. Thousand Oaks, Calif. :
Sage Publications, c2000.
*TC LB3011.5 .K67 2000*

Pellicer, Leonard O. Caring enough to lead. Thousand
Oaks, Calif. : Corwin Press, c1999.
*TC LB2805 .P375 1999*

**SCHOOL ADMINISTRATORS - UNITED
STATES - CASE STUDIES.**
Case studies for school administrators. 1st ed.
Lancaster, PA : Technomic Pub. Co., c1999.

**TC LB2806 .C316 1999**

Hayes, William, 1938- Real-life case studies for school administrators. Lanham, Md. : Scarecrow Press, c2000.
**TC LB2806 .H39 2000**

Hughes, Larry W., 1931- Public relations for school leaders. Boston ; London : Allyn and Bacon, c2000.
**TC LB2847 .H84 2000**

**School-age mother and child health act, 1975.**
United States. Congress. Senate. Committee on Labor and Public Welfare. Subcommittee on Health. Washington : U.S. Govt. Print. Off., 1976.
**TC KF26 .L354 1975**

**SCHOOL-AGE MOTHERS.** *See* **TEENAGE MOTHERS.**

**School and college placement 1940-Dec.1951.**
Journal of college placement. [Philadelphia, Pa. etc.], The College Placement Council, inc. [etc.].

**SCHOOL AND COMMUNITY.** *See* **COMMUNITY AND SCHOOL.**

**The school and community relations.**
Bagin, Don, 1938- 7th ed. Boston ; London : Allyn and Bacon, c2001.
**TC LC221 .G35 2001**

**SCHOOL AND HOME.** *See* **HOME AND SCHOOL.**

**School and home (Atlanta, Ga.).**
Home, school, and community. Atlanta, Ga. : Georgia Council of Social Agencies, 1923-1926.

**School and society.**
Feinberg, Walter, 1937- 3rd ed. New York : Teachers College Press, c1998.
**TC LC191 .F4 1998**

**SCHOOL ARCHITECTURE.** *See* **SCHOOL BUILDINGS.**

**SCHOOL ASSEMBLY.** *See* **SCHOOLS - EXERCISES AND RECREATIONS.**

**SCHOOL ATHLETICS.** *See* **SCHOOL SPORTS.**

**SCHOOL ATTENDANCE.** *See* **HIGH SCHOOL ATTENDANCE; SCHOOL DAY; VACATIONS.**

**SCHOOL ATTENDANCE - COLLEGE.** *See* **COLLEGE ATTENDANCE.**

**SCHOOL ATTENDANCE - GREAT BRITAIN.**
Reid, Ken. Truancy and schools. London ; New York : Routledge, 1999.
**TC LB3081 .R45 1999**

Vernon, Jeni. Maintaining children in school. London : National Children's Bureau Enterprises, c1998.
**TC LB3081 .V47 1998**

**SCHOOL ATTENDANCE - GREAT BRITAIN - HANDBOOKS, MANUALS, ETC.**
Reid, Ken. Tackling truancy in schools. London ; New York : Routledge, 2000.
**TC LB3081 .R446 2000**

**SCHOOL ATTENDANCE - HIGH SCHOOL.** *See* **HIGH SCHOOL ATTENDANCE.**

**SCHOOL AUTONOMY.** *See* **UNIVERSITY AUTONOMY.**

**School-based management.**
Abu-Duhou, Ibtisam. Paris : International Institute for Educational Planning (IIEP) ; Paris : Unesco, 1999.
**TC LB5 .F85 1999**

**SCHOOL-BASED MANAGEMENT.**
Abu-Duhou, Ibtisam. School-based management. Paris : International Institute for Educational Planning (IIEP) ; Paris : Unesco, 1999.
**TC LB5 .F85 1999**

**SCHOOL-BASED MANAGEMENT - GREAT BRITAIN.**
Joyce, Bruce R. The new structure of school improvement. Buckingham [England] ; Philadelphia : Open University Press, 1999.
**TC LB2822.84.G7 J69 1999**

**SCHOOL-BASED MANAGEMENT - UNITED STATES.**
Joyce, Bruce R. The new structure of school improvement. Buckingham [England] ; Philadelphia : Open University Press, 1999.
**TC LB2822.84.G7 J69 1999**

**SCHOOL BOARDS.** *See* **SCHOOL DISTRICTS.**

**SCHOOL BOARDS - GREAT BRITAIN.**
Creese, Michael. Improving schools and governing bodies. London ; New York : Routledge, 1999.
**TC LB2822.84.G7 C75 1999**

Education year book. [London, England] : Councils and Education Press, 1979-
**TC L915 .E4**

**SCHOOL BOARDS - POLITICAL ASPECTS - UNITED STATES.**
New school order [videorecording]. New York : First Run/Icarus Films, 1996.
**TC LB2831.583.P4 N4 1996**

**SCHOOL BOARDS - UNITED STATES.**
Gallagher, Karen S. Shaping school policy. Newbury Park, Calif. : Corwin Press, c1992.
**TC LC89 .G35 1992**

**School bond success.**
Boschee, Floyd. 1st ed. Lancaster, Pa. : Technomic Publishing Co., c1999.
**TC LB2825 .B63 1999**

**SCHOOL BONDS - UNITED STATES.**
Boschee, Floyd. School bond success. 1st ed. Lancaster, Pa. : Technomic Publishing Co., c1999.
**TC LB2825 .B63 1999**

**SCHOOL-BOOKS.** *See* **TEXTBOOKS.**

**SCHOOL BUILDINGS.** *See* **CLASSROOMS; COLLEGE BUILDINGS.**

**SCHOOL BUILDINGS - CONTRACTS AND SPECIFICATIONS.** *See* **SCHOOL BUILDINGS - SPECIFICATIONS.**

**SCHOOL BUILDINGS - GREAT BRITAIN - COSTS.**
Spon's building costs guide for educational premises. 2nd ed. London : E & FN SPON, 1999.
**TC LB3219.G7 S67 1999**

**SCHOOL BUILDINGS - GREAT BRITAIN - STATISTICS.**
Spon's building costs guide for educational premises. 2nd ed. London : E & FN SPON, 1999.
**TC LB3219.G7 S67 1999**

**SCHOOL BUILDINGS - SPECIFICATIONS - GREAT BRITAIN.**
Spon's building costs guide for educational premises. 2nd ed. London : E & FN SPON, 1999.
**TC LB3219.G7 S67 1999**

**SCHOOL BUILDINGS - UNITED STATES - MAINTENANCE AND REPAIR.**
Modernizing schools : technology and buildings for a new century (September 19, 2000 : Washington, D.C.) Modernizing schools [videorecording]. [Washington, D.C.] : U.S. Dept. of Education, [2000].
**TC LB3205 .M64 2000**

Modernizing schools : technology and buildings for a new century (September 19, 2000 : Washington, D.C.) Modernizing schools [videorecording]. [Washington, D.C.] : U.S. Dept. of Education, [2000].
**TC LB3205 .M64 2000**

**SCHOOL CALENDARS.** *See* **SCHEDULES, SCHOOL.**

**SCHOOL CENTRALIZATION.** *See* **SCHOOLS - CENTRALIZATION.**

**SCHOOL CHILDREN.** *See* **LIBRARY ORIENTATION FOR SCHOOL CHILDREN.**

**SCHOOL CHILDREN - COUNSELING OF.** *See* **COUNSELING IN ELEMENTARY EDUCATION.**

**SCHOOL CHILDREN - HEALTH AND HYGIENE - CASE STUDIES.**
Pridmore, Pat, 1947- Children as partners for health. London ; New York : Zed Books ; New York : Distributed exclusively in the USA by St. Martin's Press, 2000.
**TC LB1587.A3 P75 2000**

**SCHOOL CHILDREN - HEALTH AND HYGIENE - GREAT BRITAIN - HANDBOOKS, MANUALS, ETC.**
Medical Officers of Schools Association. Handbook of school health. 18th ed. Stoke-on-Trent : Trentham, 1998.
**TC LB3409.G7 H36 1998**

**SCHOOL CHILDREN - LIBRARY ORIENTATION.** *See* **LIBRARY ORIENTATION FOR SCHOOL CHILDREN.**

**SCHOOL CHILDREN - MENTAL HEALTH.**
House, Alvin E. DSM-IV diagnosis in the schools. New York : Guilford Press, c1999

**TC RJ503.5 .H68 1999**

Theraplay. Northvale, N.J. : J. Aronson, c2000.
**TC RJ505.P6 T485 2000**

Weare, Katherine, 1950- Promoting mental, emotional, and social health. London ; New York : Routledge, 2000.
**TC LB3430 .W42 2000**

**SCHOOL CHILDREN - MENTAL HEALTH SERVICES - UNITED STATES.**
Marks, Edward S. Entry strategies for school consultation. New York : Guilford Press, c1995.
**TC LB2799.2 .M36 1995**

**SCHOOL CHILDREN - UNITED STATES - BOOKS AND READING.**
Taberski, Sharon. On solid ground. Portsmouth, NH : Heinemann, c 2000.
**TC LB1525 .T32 2000**

**SCHOOL CHILDREN - VERMONT - BENNINGTON.**
From another angle. New York : Teachers College Press, c2000.
**TC LB1117 .F735 2000**

**School choice.**
Randall, Ruth E. Bloomington, Ind. : National Educational Service, 1991.
**TC LB1027.9 .R36 1991**

Rufo-Lignos, Patricia Marie. Towards a new topology of public and private schools. 1999.
**TC 06 no. 11170**

Rufo-Lignos, Patricia Marie. Towards a new typology of public and private schools. 1999.
**TC 06 no. 11170**

**School choice and social controversy :** politics, policy, and law / Stephen D. Sugarman, Frank R. Kemerer, editors. Washington, D.C. : Brookings Institution Press, c1999. vii, 378 p. ; 23 cm. Includes bibliographical references and index. ISBN 0-8157-8276-4 (alk. paper) ISBN 0-8157-8275-6 (pbk. : alk. paper) DDC 379.1/11/0973
*1. School choice - Social aspects - United States. 2. School choice - Law and legislation - United States. 3. Education and state - United States. I. Sugarman, Stephen D. II. Kemerer, Frank R.*
**TC LB1027.9 .S352 1999**

**School choice and social justice.**
Brighouse, Harry. Oxford ; New York : Oxford University Press, 2000.
**TC LB1027.9 .B75 2000**

**SCHOOL CHOICE - LAW AND LEGISLATION - UNITED STATES.**
School choice and social controversy. Washington, D.C. : Brookings Institution Press, c1999.
**TC LB1027.9 .S352 1999**

Viteritti, Joseph P., 1946- Choosing equality. Washington, D.C. : Brookings Institution Press, c1999.
**TC LB1027.9 .V58 1999**

**SCHOOL CHOICE - MINNESOTA.**
Randall, Ruth E. School choice. Bloomington, Ind. : National Educational Service, 1991.
**TC LB1027.9 .R36 1991**

**SCHOOL CHOICE - NEW ZEALAND - LONGITUDINAL STUDIES.**
Trading in futures. Buckingham [England] ; Philadelphia : Open University Press, 1999.
**TC LB2826.6.N45 T73 1999**

**SCHOOL, CHOICE OF.** *See* **SCHOOL CHOICE.**

**SCHOOL CHOICE - POLITICAL ASPECTS - UNITED STATES.**
Morken, Hubert. The politics of school choice. Lanham, Md. : Rowman & Littlefield Publishers, c1999.
**TC LB1027.9 .M68 1999**

**SCHOOL CHOICE - SOCIAL ASPECTS.**
Brighouse, Harry. School choice and social justice. Oxford ; New York : Oxford University Press, 2000.
**TC LB1027.9 .B75 2000**

**SCHOOL CHOICE - SOCIAL ASPECTS - UNITED STATES.**
School choice and social controversy. Washington, D.C. : Brookings Institution Press, c1999.
**TC LB1027.9 .S352 1999**

**SCHOOL CHOICE - UNITED STATES.**
Engel, Michael, 1944- The struggle for control of public education. Philadelphia, Pa. : Temple University Press, c2000.
**TC LA217.2 .E533 2000**

Good, Thomas L., 1943- The great school debate. Mahwah, N.J. : L. Erlbaum Associates, 2000.
*TC LB2806.36 .G66 2000*

Mintrom, Michael, 1963- Policy entrepreneurs and school choice. Washington, DC : Georgetown University Press, c2000.
*TC LB1027.9 .M57 2000*

Morken, Hubert. The politics of school choice. Lanham, Md. : Rowman & Littlefield Publishers, c1999.
*TC LB1027.9 .M68 1999*

Randall, Ruth E. School choice. Bloomington, Ind. : National Educational Service, 1991.
*TC LB1027.9 .R36 1991*

Restructuring education. Westport, Conn. : Praeger, 2000.
*TC LB2822.82 . R45 2000*

Schneider, Mark, 1946- Choosing schools. Princeton, N.J. ; Oxford : Princeton University Press, c2000.
*TC LB1027.9 .S32 2000*

Viteritti, Joseph P., 1946- Choosing equality. Washington, D.C. : Brookings Institution Press, c1999.
*TC LB1027.9 .V58 1999*

**SCHOOL CHOICE - WISCONSIN - MILWAUKEE - CASE STUDIES.**
Witte, John F. The market approach to education. Princeton, N.J. : Princeton University Press, c2000.
*TC LB2828.85.W6 W58 2000*

School climate : measuring, improving, and sustaining healthy learning environments / edited by H. Jerome Freiberg. London ; Philadelphia : Falmer Press, 1999.
x, 230 p. : ill. ; 25 cm. Includes bibliographical references and index. ISBN 0-7507-0641-4 (cased : alk. paper) ISBN 0-7507-0642-2 (paper : alk. paper)
*1. School environment - Evaluation. 2. Classroom environment - Evaluation. 3. Learning. I. Freiberg, H. Jerome.*
*TC LC210 .S35 1999*

**SCHOOL-COLLEGE COOPERATION.** *See* **COLLEGE-SCHOOL COOPERATION.**

**SCHOOL-COLLEGE PARTNERSHIPS.** *See* **COLLEGE-SCHOOL COOPERATION.**

**SCHOOL COUNSELING.** *See* **EDUCATIONAL COUNSELING.**

School counseling for the 21st century.
Baker, Stanley B., 1935- School counseling for the twenty-first century. 3rd ed. Upper Saddle River, N.J. : Merrill, c2000.
*TC LB1731.75 .B35 2000*

School counseling for the twenty-first century.
Baker, Stanley B., 1935- 3rd ed. Upper Saddle River, N.J. : Merrill, c2000.
*TC LB1731.75 .B35 2000*

**SCHOOL COUNSELORS.** *See* **STUDENT COUNSELORS.**

**SCHOOL CRISIS MANAGEMENT - UNITED STATES.**
Trump, Kenneth S. Classroom killers? hallway hostages? Thousand Oaks, Calif. : Corwin Press, c2000.
*TC LB2866.5 .T78 2000*

**SCHOOL DAY - UNITED STATES.**
Morrow, Lesley Mandel. Literacy instruction in half- and whole-day kindergarten. Newark, Del. : International Reading Association ; Chicago, Ill. : National Reading Conference, c1998.
*TC LB1181.2 .M67 1998*

**SCHOOL DECENTRALIZATION.** *See* **SCHOOLS - DECENTRALIZATION.**

**SCHOOL DESEGREGATION.** *See* **SCHOOL INTEGRATION.**

School development series
Clarke, Paul, 1961- Learning schools, learning systems. London ; New York : Continuum, 2000.
*TC LB1027 .C468 2000*

School directory. Connecticut.
MDR's school directory. Connecticut. Shelton, CT : Market Data Retrieval, c1995-
*TC L903.C8 M37*

School directory. New Jersey.
MDR's school directory. New Jersey. Shelton, CT : Market Data Retrieval, c1995-
*TC L903.N5 M37*

School directory. New York.
MDR's school directory. New York. Shelton, CT : Market Data Retrieval, c1995-
*TC L903.N7 M37*

School directory. Pennsylvania.
MDR's school directory. Pennsylvania. Shelton, CT : Market Data Retrieval, 1995-
*TC L903.P4 M37*

**SCHOOL DISCIPLINE.** *See also* **CLASSROOM MANAGEMENT; COLLEGE DISCIPLINE; REWARDS AND PUNISHMENTS IN EDUCATION.**
Beyond behaviorism. Boston : Allyn and Bacon, c 1999.
*TC LB3013 .B42 1999*

Campbell, Jack, Ed. D. Student discipline and classroom management. Springfield, Ill. : C.C. Thomas, c1999.
*TC LB3012 .C34 1999*

Charles, C. M. The synergetic classroom. New York : Longman, c2000.
*TC LB3013 .C4653 2000*

Council of Europe. Council for Cultural Co-operation. Bullying in schools. Strasbourg : Council of Europe Publishing, 1999.
*TC BF637.B85 B842 1999*

Jones, Vernon F., 1945- Comprehensive classroom management. 6th ed. Boston : Allyn and Bacon, c2001.
*TC LB3013 . J66 2001*

Koshewa, Allen. Discipline and democracy. Portsmouth, NH : Heinemann, c1999.
*TC LB3011 .K66 1999*

Parker-Jenkins, Marie. Sparing the rod. Stoke-on-Trent : Trentham, 1999.
*TC LB3012 .P37 1999*

Porter, Louise, 1958- Behaviour in schools. Buckingham [England] ; Philadelphia : Open University Press, 2000.
*TC LB3012 .P65 2000*

School discipline. Ann Arbor, Mich. : University of Michigan School of Education, 1989.
*TC LB3011 .S425*

Sparzo, Frank J. The ABC's of behavior change. Bloomington, Ind., U.S.A. : Phi Delta Kappa Educational Foundation, c1999.
*TC LB1060.2 .S62 1999*

**SCHOOL DISCIPLINE - BERMUDA ISLANDS.**
Tucker, Gina Marie. Discipline. 1998.
*TC 06 no. 10999*

School discipline : contemporary issues in law & policy / Charles B. Vergon, editor. Ann Arbor, Mich. : University of Michigan School of Education, 1989.
vii, 214 p. ; 23 cm. 1989 Education Law Institute. Includes bibliographical references.
*1. School discipline. I. Vergon, Charles B. II. University of Michigan. School of Education.*
*TC LB3011 .S425*

**SCHOOL DISCIPLINE - UNITED STATES.**
Hyman, Irwin A. Dangerous schools. 1st ed. San Francisco : Jossey-Bass Publishers, c1999.
*TC LB3013 .H897 1999*

Savage, Tom V. Teaching self-control through management and discipline. 2nd ed. Boston ; London : Allyn and Bacon, c1999.
*TC LB3012.2 .S38 1999*

Tauber, Robert T. Classroom management. 3rd ed. Westport, Conn. : Bergin & Garvey, 1999.
*TC LB3011 .T38 1999*

Tomal, Daniel R. Discipline by negotiation. 1st ed. Lancaster, Pa. : Technomic Pub. Co., c1999.
*TC LB3011.5 .T66 1999*

**SCHOOL DISTRICTS.** *See* **SCHOOL BOARDS.**

**SCHOOL DISTRICTS - CONNECTICUT - DIRECTORIES.**
MDR's school directory. Connecticut. Shelton, CT : Market Data Retrieval, c1995-
*TC L903.C8 M37*

**SCHOOL DISTRICTS - NEW JERSEY - DIRECTORIES.**
MDR's school directory. New Jersey. Shelton, CT : Market Data Retrieval, c1995-
*TC L903.N5 M37*

**SCHOOL DISTRICTS - NEW YORK - DIRECTORIES.**

MDR's school directory. New York. Shelton, CT : Market Data Retrieval, c1995-
*TC L903.N7 M37*

**SCHOOL DISTRICTS - PENNSYLVANIA - DIRECTORIES.**
MDR's school directory. Pennsylvania. Shelton, CT : Market Data Retrieval, 1995-
*TC L903.P4 M37*

**SCHOOL DISTRICTS - UNITED STATES.**
Capper, Colleen A., 1960- Meeting the needs of students of all abilities. Thousand Oaks, Calif. : Corwin Press, c2000.
*TC LC1201 .C36 2000*

**SCHOOL DROPOUTS.** *See* **DROPOUTS.**

School effectiveness.
Sammons, Pam. Lisse, Netherlands ; Abingdon [England] ; Exton, PA : Swets & Zeitlinger Publishers, c1999.
*TC LB2822.75 .S24 1999*

**SCHOOL EMPLOYEES.** *See* **TEACHERS.**

**SCHOOL ENDOWMENTS.** *See* **ENDOWMENTS.**

**SCHOOL ENROLLMENT - CONNECTICUT - STATISTICS - PERIODICALS.**
MDR's school directory. Connecticut. Shelton, CT : Market Data Retrieval, c1995-
*TC L903.C8 M37*

**SCHOOL ENROLLMENT - ECONOMIC ASPECTS - CAMEROON.**
Amin, Martin E. (Martin Efuetngu) Trends in the demand for primary education in Cameroon. Lanham, MD : University Press of America, 1999.
*TC LC137.C36 A55 1999*

**SCHOOL ENROLLMENT - NEW JERSEY - STATISTICS - PERIODICALS.**
MDR's school directory. New Jersey. Shelton, CT : Market Data Retrieval, c1995-
*TC L903.N5 M37*

**SCHOOL ENROLLMENT - NEW YORK - STATISTICS - PERIODICALS.**
MDR's school directory. New York. Shelton, CT : Market Data Retrieval, c1995-
*TC L903.N7 M37*

**SCHOOL ENROLLMENT - PENNSYLVANIA - STATISTICS - PERIODICALS.**
MDR's school directory. Pennsylvania. Shelton, CT : Market Data Retrieval, 1995-
*TC L903.P4 M37*

**SCHOOL ENROLLMENT - SOCIAL ASPECTS - CAMEROON.**
Amin, Martin E. (Martin Efuetngu) Trends in the demand for primary education in Cameroon. Lanham, MD : University Press of America, 1999.
*TC LC137.C36 A55 1999*

**SCHOOL ENVIRONMENT.** *See also* **CLASSROOM ENVIRONMENT.**
Deal, Terrence E. Shaping school culture. 1st ed. San Francisco : Jossey-Bass Publishers, c1999.
*TC LB2805 .D34 1999*

Graham, Sheila L. Urban minority gifted students. 1999.
*TC 06 no. 11119*

Learning communities in education. London ; New York : Routledge, 1999.
*TC LB14.7 .L43 1999*

Masculinities at school. Thousand Oaks, Calif. : SAGE, c2000.
*TC LC1390 .M37 2000*

Smith, Hawthorne Emery. Psychological detachment from school. 1999.
*TC 085 Sm586*

Whitaker, Todd, 1959- Motivating and inspiring teachers. Larchmont, N.Y. : Eye on Education, c2000.
*TC LB2840 .W45 2000*

**SCHOOL ENVIRONMENT - EVALUATION.**
Dickerson, Pless Moore. Haitian students' perception of a school as a community of support. 1998.
*TC 06 no. 11018*

Dickerson, Pless Moore. Haitian students' perception of a school as a community of support. 1998.
*TC 06 no. 11018*

Dickerson, Pless Moore. Haitian students' perception of a school as a community of support. 1998.
*TC 06 no. 11018*

School climate. London ; Philadelphia : Falmer Press, 1999.

TC *LC210 .S35 1999*

**SCHOOL ENVIRONMENT - GREAT BRITAIN.**
Klein, Reva Defying disaffection. Staffordshire, England : Trentham Books, 1999.
TC *LC4091 .K53 1999*

**SCHOOL ENVIRONMENT - HISTORY - CONGRESSES.**
Silences & images. New York : P. Lang, c1999.
TC *LA128 .S55 1999*

**SCHOOL ENVIRONMENT - NEW YORK (STATE) - CASE STUDIES.**
Schlanger, Dean J. An exploration of school belongingness. 1998.
TC *06 no. 10993*

**SCHOOL ENVIRONMENT - UNITED STATES.**
Hoyle, John. Interpersonal sensitivity. Larchmont, NY : Eye on Education, c1997.
TC *LB2831.92.U6 H67 1997*

Klein, Reva Defying disaffection. Staffordshire, England : Trentham Books, 1999.
TC *LC4091 .K53 1999*

**SCHOOL ENVIRONMENT - UNITED STATES - HISTORY - CONGRESSES.**
Silences & images. New York : P. Lang, c1999.
TC *LA128 .S55 1999*

**SCHOOL EXCURSIONS.** *See* **SCHOOL FIELD TRIPS.**

**School executives magazine.**
American educational digest. [Crawfordsville, Ind. : Educational Digest Co., 1923-1928]

**School experiences of gay and lesbian youth** : the invisible minority / Mary B. Harris, editor. New York : Harrington Park Press, c1997. xxii, 115 p. ; 22 cm. "Simultaneously issued by The Haworth Press, Inc., under the same title, as a special issue of the Journal of gay & lesbian social services, volume 7, number 4, 1997." Includes bibliographical references and index. DDC 371.826/64 *1. Gay students - United States. 2. Lesbian students - United States. 3. Homophobia - United States. I. Harris, Mary B. (Mary Bierman), 1943- II. Title: Journal of gay & lesbian social services, v. 7, no. 4.*
TC *LC2575 .S36 1997*

**SCHOOL FACILITIES.** *See* **COLLEGE FACILITIES; SCHOOL BUILDINGS; SCHOOLS - FURNITURE, EQUIPMENT, ETC.**

**SCHOOL FACITILIES - UNITED STATES - DESIGN AND CONSTRUCTION.**
Modernizing schools : technology and buildings for a new century (September 19, 2000 : Washington, D.C.) Modernizing schools [videorecording]. [Washington, D.C.] : U.S. Dept. of Education, [2000].
TC *LB3205 .M64 2000*

Modernizing schools : technology and buildings for a new century (September 19, 2000 : Washington, D.C.) Modernizing schools [videorecording]. [Washington, D.C.] : U.S. Dept. of Education, [2000].
TC *LB3205 .M64 2000*

**SCHOOL FAILURE - GREAT BRITAIN.**
Sharp, Mavis, 1945- The management of failing DipSW students. Aldershot ; Brookfield, Vt. : Ashgate, c1999.
TC *HV11.8.G7 S53 1999*

**SCHOOL FAILURE - UNITED STATES.**
Gross, Martin L. (Martin Louis), 1925- The conspiracy of ignorance. New York : HarperCollins, c1999.
TC *LA217.2 .G76 1999*

**SCHOOL FIELD TRIPS - PUERTO RICO.**
Laborde, Ilia M. Rediscovering San Cristóbal Canyon. 1996.
TC *06 no. 10660*

Laborde, Ilia M. Rediscovering San Cristóbal Canyon. 1996.
TC *06 no. 10660*

**SCHOOL FINANCE.** *See* **EDUCATION - FINANCE.**

**A school for healing.**
Kennedy, Rosa L., 1938- New York : P. Lang, c1999.
TC *LC46.4 .K46 1999*

**SCHOOL FUNDS.** *See* **PUBLIC SCHOOLS.**

**SCHOOL FURNITURE.** *See* **SCHOOLS - FURNITURE, EQUIPMENT, ETC.**

**SCHOOL GOVERNORS.** *See* **SCHOOL BOARDS.**

**SCHOOL GUIDANCE.** *See* **EDUCATIONAL COUNSELING.**

**SCHOOL HEALTH SERVICES - GREAT BRITAIN - HANDBOOKS, MANUALS, ETC.**
Medical Officers of Schools Association. Handbook of school health. 18th ed. Stoke-on-Trent : Trentham, 1998.
TC *LB3409.G7 H36 1998*

**SCHOOL-HOUSES.** *See* **SCHOOL BUILDINGS.**

**SCHOOL HYGIENE.** *See* **SCHOOL CHILDREN - HEALTH AND HYGIENE; SCHOOL HEALTH SERVICES.**

**SCHOOL IMPROVEMENT PROGRAMS.** *See also* **SCHOOL SUPPORT TEAMS.**
Chall, Jeanne Sternlicht, 1921- The academic achievement challenge. New York ; London : Guilford Press, c2000.
TC *LB2822.8 .C49 2000*

Combating educational disadvantage. London ; New York : Falmer Press, 2000.
TC *LC4065 .C66 1999*

Leithwood, Kenneth A. Changing leadership for changing times. Buckingham ; Philadelphia : Open University Press, 1999.
TC *LB2805 .L358 1999*

**SCHOOL IMPROVEMENT PROGRAMS - CANADA - ONTARIO - CASE STUDIES.**
Fink, Dean, 1936- Good schools/real schools. New York : Teachers College Press, c2000.
TC *LB2822.84.C2 F56 2000*

**SCHOOL IMPROVEMENT PROGRAMS - ENGLAND - ESSEX.**
Supporting improving primary schools. London ; New York : Falmer Press, 2000.
TC *LB2822.84.E64 S86 1999*

**SCHOOL IMPROVEMENT PROGRAMS - EVALUATION.**
Werner, Walter. Collaborative assessment of school-based projects. Vancouver : Pacific Educational Press, c1991.
TC *LB2822.8 .W47 1991*

**SCHOOL IMPROVEMENT PROGRAMS - GREAT BRITAIN.**
Brighouse, Tim. How to improve your school. London ; New York : Routledge, 1999.
TC *LB2822.84.G7 B75 1999*

Creese, Michael. Improving schools and governing bodies. London ; New York : Routledge, 1999.
TC *LB2822.84.G7 C75 1999*

Field, Kit. Effective subject leadership. London ; New York : Routledge, 2000.
TC *LB2806.15 .F54 2000*

Harris, Alma, 1958- Teaching and learning in the effective school. Aldershot, England ; Brookfield, Vt. : Ashgate, c1999.
TC *LB2822.84.G7 H37 1999*

Hoy, Charles, 1939- Improving quality in education. London ; New York : Falmer Press, 2000.
TC *LB2822.84.G7 H69 1999*

Joyce, Bruce R. The new structure of school improvement. Buckingham [England] ; Philadelphia : Open University Press, 1999.
TC *LB2822.84.G7 J69 1999*

Special education and school reform in the United States and Britain. London ; New York : Routledge, 2000.
TC *LC3986.G7 S64 2000*

**SCHOOL IMPROVEMENT PROGRAMS - GREAT BRITAIN - CASE STUDIES.**
Improving schools. Buckingham [England] ; Philadelphia : Open University Press, 1999.
TC *LB2822.84.G7 I68 1999*

**SCHOOL IMPROVEMENT PROGRAMS - GREAT BRITAIN - EVALUATION.**
Sammons, Pam. School effectiveness. Lisse, Netherlands ; Abingdon [England] ; Exton, PA : Swets & Zeitlinger Publishers, c1999.
TC *LB2822.75 .S24 1999*

**SCHOOL IMPROVEMENT PROGRAMS - KENTUCKY - CASE STUDIES.**
Accountability, assessment, and teacher commitment. Albany, N.Y. : State University of New York Press, 2000.
TC *LB2806.22 .A249 2000*

**SCHOOL IMPROVEMENT PROGRAMS - NEW YORK (STATE).**
Mahammad, Hasna. Multicultural education. 1998.
TC *06 no. 11033*

**SCHOOL IMPROVEMENT PROGRAMS - NEW ZEALAND - CASE STUDIES.**
Fiske, Edward B. When schools compete. Washington, D.C. : Brookings Institution Press, c2000.
TC *LB2822.84.N45 F58 2000*

**SCHOOL IMPROVEMENT PROGRAMS - OECD COUNTRIES - CASE STUDIES.**
Motivating students for lifelong learning. Paris : Organisation for Economic Co-operation and Development, c2000.
TC *LB1065 .M669 2000*

**SCHOOL IMPROVEMENT PROGRAMS - RESEARCH - UNITED STATES.**
An educators' guide to schoolwide reform. Arlington, Va. : Educational Research Service, c1999.
TC *LB2806.35 .E38 1999*

**SCHOOL IMPROVEMENT PROGRAMS - UNITED STATES.**
Becoming good American schools. 1st ed. San Francisco : Jossey-Bass, c2000.
TC *LB2822.82 .B44 2000*

Creating new schools. New York ; London : Teachers College Press, c2000.
TC *LB2822.82 .C76 2000*

The developmental process of positive attitudes and mutual respect. Lewiston, N.Y. : E. Mellen Press, c1999.
TC *LB2822.82 .D49 1999*

The example school portfolio. Larchmont, N.Y. : Eye On Education, 2000.
TC *LB2822.82 .E92 2000*

Improving student learning. Washington, D.C. : National Academy Press, c1999.
TC *LB1028.25.U6 I66 1999*

Joyce, Bruce R. The new structure of school improvement. Buckingham [England] ; Philadelphia : Open University Press, 1999.
TC *LB2822.84.G7 J69 1999*

McNeil, Linda M. Contradictions of school reform. New York : Routledge, 2000.
TC *LB3060.83 .M38 2000*

Michel, Patrick. Using action research for school restructuring and organizational change. 2000.
TC *06 no. 11295*

Restructuring education. Westport, Conn. : Praeger, 2000.
TC *LB2822.82 . R45 2000*

Sergiovanni, Thomas J. The principalship. 4th ed. Boston : Allyn & Bacon, c2001.
TC *LB2831.92 .S47 2001*

Special education and school reform in the United States and Britain. London ; New York : Routledge, 2000.
TC *LC3986.G7 S64 2000*

Steinberg, Adria. Schooling for the real world. 1st ed. San Francisco : Jossey-Bass, c1999.
TC *LC1037.5 .S843 1999*

Teaching transformed. Boulder, Colo. ; Oxford : Westview Press, 2000.
TC *LB2822.82 .T44 2000*

Tye, Barbara Benham, 1942- Hard truths. New York : Teachers College Press, c2000.
TC *LB2822.82 .T94 2000*

**SCHOOL IMPROVEMENT PROGRAMS - UNITED STATES - CASE STUDIES.**
Doyle, Denis P. Raising the standard. 2nd ed. Thousand Oaks, Calif. : Corwin Press, c1999.
TC *LB2822.82 .D69 1999*

Nolan, James F., 1950- Teachers and educational change. Albany : State University of New York Press, c2000.
TC *LB1777.2 .N64 2000*

**SCHOOL IMPROVEMENT PROGRAMS - UNITED STATES - EVALUATION.**
Berends, Mark, 1962- Assessing the progress of New American Schools. Santa Monica, CA : RAND, 1999.
TC *LB2822.82 .B45 1999*

**SCHOOL INSPECTION.** *See* **SCHOOL MANAGEMENT AND ORGANIZATION.**

**SCHOOL INTEGRATION.** *See also*
    **SEGREGATION IN EDUCATION.**
    Enhancing education in heterogeneous schools.
    Ramat-Gan : Bar-Ilan University Press, [1997]
    *TC LC214 .E54 1997*

**SCHOOL INTEGRATION - ARKANSAS - LITTLE**
    **ROCK - HISTORY.**
    Roy, Beth. Bitters in the honey. Fayetteville :
    University of Arkansas Press, 1999.
    *TC LC214.23.L56 R69 1999*

**SCHOOL INTEGRATION - ARKANSAS - LITTLE**
    **ROCK - HISTORY - 20TH CENTURY.**
    Counts, I. Wilmer (Ira Wilmer), 1931- A life is more
    than a moment. Bloomington, IN : Indiana University
    Press, c1999.
    *TC LC214.23.L56 C68 1999*

    Understanding the Little Rock crisis. Fayetteville,
    Ark : University of Arkansas Press, 1999.
    *TC LC214.23.L56 U53 1999*

**SCHOOL INTEGRATION - NEW ZEALAND -**
    **CASE STUDIES.**
    Thrupp, Martin, 1964- Schools making a difference--
    let's be realistic!. Buckingham [England] ;
    Philadelphia : Open University Press, 1999.
    *TC LB2822.75 .T537 1999*

**SCHOOL INTEGRATION - TEXAS - HOUSTON -**
    **HISTORY.**
    Kellar, William Henry, 1952- Make haste slowly. 1st
    ed. College Station : Texas A&M University Press,
    c1999.
    *TC LC214.23.H68 K45 1999*

**SCHOOL INTEGRATION - UNITED STATES.** *See*
    **AFRO-AMERICANS - EDUCATION.**

**SCHOOL LAW.** *See* **EDUCATIONAL LAW AND**
    **LEGISLATION.**

**School law letter.**
    The bi-weekly school law letter. Laramie, Wyo. :
    Published by R.R. Hamilton, 1951-1955.

**SCHOOL LEADERSHIP.** *See* **EDUCATIONAL**
    **LEADERSHIP.**

**The school leadership library**
    Achilles, Charles M. Problem analysis. Larchmont,
    NY : Eye on Education, c1997.
    *TC LB2806 .A25 1997*

**The School leadership library**
    Crawford, George, 1937- Philosophical & cultural
    values. Larchmont, NY : Eye On Education, c2000.
    *TC LB2831.92 .C72 2000*

**School leadership library**
    Crow, Gary Monroe, 1947- Leadership. Princeton,
    NJ : Eye on Education, c1996.
    *TC LB2831.92 .C76 1996*

    Erlandson, David A. Organizational oversight.
    Princeton, NJ : Eye on Education, c1996.
    *TC LB2805 .E75 1996*

**The school leadership library**
    Hoyle, John. Interpersonal sensitivity. Larchmont,
    NY : Eye on Education, c1997.
    *TC LB2831.92.U6 H67 1997*

    Keefe, James W. Instruction and the learning
    environment. Larchmont, NY : Eye On Education,
    c1997.
    *TC LB2806.4 .K44 1997*

    Muse, Ivan. Oral and nonverbal expression. Princeton,
    NJ : Eye On Education, c1996.
    *TC P95 .M86 1996*

    Norton, M. Scott. Resource allocation. Larchmont,
    N.Y. : Eye on Education, c1997.
    *TC LB2805 .N73 1997*

    Pankake, Anita M., 1947- Implementation.
    Larchmont, NY : Eye on Education, c1998.
    *TC LB2805 .P32 1998*

    Short, Paula M. Information collection. Larchmont,
    NY : Eye on Education, c1998.
    *TC LB1028.27.U6 S46 1998*

    Sweeney, Jim, 1937- Judgment. Larchmont, NY : Eye
    on Education, c1997.
    *TC LB2806 .S88 1997*

**School leadership library**
    Thompson, David P., 1959- Motivating others.
    Princeton, NJ : Eye On Education, c1996.
    *TC LB2831.58 .T56 1996*

**The school leadership library**
    Ward, Mary Ann, 1946- Student guidance and

development. Larchmont, N.Y. : Eye On Education,
    c1998.
    *TC LB1027.5 .W356 1998*

    Ward, Michael E., 1953- Delegation and
    empowerment. Larchmont, NY : Eye on Education,
    c1999.
    *TC LB2831.92 .W37 1999*

    Written expression. Larchmont, NY : Eye on
    Education, c1997.
    *TC PN145 .W78 1997*

**SCHOOL LIBRARIES.** *See* **ELEMENTARY**
    **SCHOOL LIBRARIES; HIGH SCHOOL**
    **LIBRARIES; INSTRUCTIONAL MATERIALS**
    **CENTERS.**

**SCHOOL LIBRARIES (ELEMENTARY**
    **SCHOOL).** *See* **ELEMENTARY SCHOOL**
    **LIBRARIES.**

**SCHOOL LIBRARIES (HIGH SCHOOL).** *See*
    **HIGH SCHOOL LIBRARIES.**

**SCHOOL LIBRARIES - UNITED STATES.**
    Skaggs, Gayle, 1952- On display. Jefferson, NC :
    McFarland, c1999.
    *TC Z675.S3 S5975 1999*

    Zweizig, Douglas. Lessons from library power.
    Englewood, Colo. : Libraries Unlimited, 1999.
    *TC Z675.S3 Z94 1999*

**SCHOOL LIBRARIES - UNITED STATES -**
    **ADMINISTRATION.**
    Woolls, Blanche. The school library media manager.
    2nd ed. Englewood, CO : Libraries Unlimited, 1999.
    *TC Z675.S3 W8735 1999*

**SCHOOL LIBRARIES - UNITED STATES - DATA**
    **PROCESSING.**
    Bucher, Katherine Toth, 1947- Information
    technology for schools. 2nd ed. Worthington, Ohio :
    Linworth Pub., c1998.
    *TC Z675.S3 B773 1998*

**SCHOOL LIBRARIES - UNITED STATES -**
    **FINANCE.**
    Zweizig, Douglas. Lessons from library power.
    Englewood, Colo. : Libraries Unlimited, 1999.
    *TC Z675.S3 Z94 1999*

**The school library media manager.**
    Woolls, Blanche. 2nd ed. Englewood, CO : Libraries
    Unlimited, 1999.
    *TC Z675.S3 W8735 1999*

**School library media series**
    (no. 10.) Peterson, Carolyn Sue, 1938- Story
    programs. 2nd ed. Lanham, Md. : Scarecrow Press,
    2000.
    *TC LB1042 .P47 2000*

    (no. 15) Druce, Arden. Paper bag puppets. Lanham,
    MD : Scarecrow Press, 1999.
    *TC Z718.3 .D78 1999*

    (no. 18) Cooper, Cathie Hilterbran, 1953- Color and
    shape books for all ages. Lanham, Md. ; London :
    Scarecrow Press, 2000.
    *TC QC496 .C66 2000*

**SCHOOL LIFE.** *See* **STUDENTS.**

**SCHOOL MANAGEMENT AND**
    **ORGANIZATION.** *See also* **ARTICULATION**
    **(EDUCATION); CLASS SIZE; CLASSROOM**
    **MANAGEMENT; EDUCATIONAL**
    **ACCELERATION; ELEMENTARY SCHOOL**
    **ADMINISTRATION; SCHEDULES,**
    **SCHOOL; SCHOOL ADMINISTRATORS;**
    **SCHOOL ATTENDANCE; SCHOOL**
    **BOARDS; SCHOOL CRISIS MANAGEMENT;**
    **SCHOOL DISCIPLINE; SCHOOL**
    **DISTRICTS; SCHOOL IMPROVEMENT**
    **PROGRAMS; SCHOOL MANAGEMENT**
    **TEAMS; SCHOOL PERSONNEL**
    **MANAGEMENT; SCHOOL SUPERVISION;**
    **SCHOOL-BASED MANAGEMENT;**
    **TEACHER PARTICIPATION IN**
    **ADMINISTRATION.**
    Abu-Duhou, Ibtisam. School-based management.
    Paris : International Institute for Educational Planning
    (IIEP); Paris : Unesco, 1999.
    *TC LB5 .F85 1999*

    Dombroski, Ann P. Administrative problem solving.
    1999.
    *TC 06 no. 11104*

    Dombroski, Ann P. Administrative problem solving.
    1999.

*TC 06 no. 11104*

    Dunklee, Dennis R. You sound taller on the telephone.
    Thousand Oaks, Calif. : Corwin Press, c1999.
    *TC LB2831.9 .D85 1999*

    Images of educational change. Buckingham
    [England] ; Philadelphia : Open University Press,
    2000.
    *TC LB2805 .I415 2000*

    Kohn, Alfie. What to look for in a classroom. 1st ed.
    San Francisco : Jossey-Bass, c1998.
    *TC LB1775 .K643 1998*

    Leithwood, Kenneth A. Changing leadership for
    changing times. Buckingham ; Philadelphia : Open
    University Press, 1999.
    *TC LB2805 .L358 1999*

    Michel, Patrick. Using action research for school
    restructuring and organizational change. 2000.
    *TC 06 no. 11295*

    Public relations in schools. 2nd ed. Upper Saddle
    River, N.J. : Merrill, c2000.
    *TC LB2847 .P82 2000*

    Quong, Terry. Values based strategic planning :.
    Singapore ; New York : Prentice Hall, 1998.
    *TC LB2806 .Q86 1998*

    Rufo-Lignos, Patricia Marie. Towards a new topology
    of public and private schools. 1999.
    *TC 06 no. 11170*

    Rufo-Lignos, Patricia Marie. Towards a new typology
    of public and private schools. 1999.
    *TC 06 no. 11170*

    Speck, Marsha. The principalship. Upper Saddle
    River, N.J. : Merrill, c1999.
    *TC LB1738.5 .S64 1999*

    Values and educational leadership. Albany : State
    University of New York Press, c1999.
    *TC LB2806 .V25 1999*

    The values of educational administration. London :
    Falmer, 1999.
    *TC LB2806 .V255 1999*

    Welsh, Thomas. Decentralization of education. Paris :
    International Institute for Educational Planning (IIEP);
    Paris : UNESCO, 1999.
    *TC LB5 .F85 v.64*

    Whitaker, Todd, 1959- Motivating and inspiring
    teachers. Larchmont, N.Y. : Eye on Education, c2000.
    *TC LB2840 .W45 2000*

**SCHOOL MANAGEMENT AND**
    **ORGANIZATION - AFRICA, SUB-SAHARAN.**
    Schooling in sub-Saharan Africa. New York : Garland
    Pub., 1998.
    *TC LA1501 .S35 1998*

**SCHOOL MANAGEMENT AND**
    **ORGANIZATION - CANADA - ONTARIO -**
    **CASE STUDIES.**
    Fink, Dean, 1936- Good schools/real schools. New
    York : Teachers College Press, c2000.
    *TC LB2822.84.C2 F56 2000*

**SCHOOL MANAGEMENT AND**
    **ORGANIZATION - CASE STUDIES.**
    Public relations in schools. 2nd ed. Upper Saddle
    River, N.J. : Merrill, c2000.
    *TC LB2847 .P82 2000*

    Reagan, Timothy G. Becoming a reflective educator.
    2nd ed. Thousand Oaks Calif. : Sage Publications,
    c2000.
    *TC LB1025.3 .R424 2000*

**SCHOOL MANAGEMENT AND**
    **ORGANIZATION - COMPUTER NETWORK**
    **RESOURCES - DIRECTORIES.**
    The School administrator's handbook of essential
    Internet sites. Fourth ed. Gaithersburg, MD : Aspen
    Publishers.
    *TC TK5105.875.I57 S3 2000*

**SCHOOL MANAGEMENT AND**
    **ORGANIZATION - CROSS-CULTURAL**
    **STUDIES.**
    Educational knowledge. Albany : State University of
    New York Press, c2000.
    *TC LC71 .L335 2000*

**SCHOOL MANAGEMENT AND**
    **ORGANIZATION - DECISION MAKING.**
    DiVincenzo, Joe. Group decision making. [S.l.] : NEA
    Professional Library : NEA Affiliate Capacity
    Building, c1999.
    *TC LB2806 .D58 1999*

Sweeney, Jim, 1937- Judgment. Larchmont, NY : Eye on Education, c1997.
*TC LB2806 .S88 1997*

## SCHOOL MANAGEMENT AND ORGANIZATION - GREAT BRITAIN.

Helsby, Gill. Changing teachers' work. Buckingham [England] ; Philadelphia : Open University Press, 1999.
*TC LA635 .H375 1999*

An inspector calls :. London : Kogan Page, 1999.
*TC LB2900.5 .I58 1999*

Law, Sue. Educational leadership and learning. Buckingham [England] ; Philadelphia : Open University Press, 2000.
*TC LB2900.5 .L39 1999*

Leading schools in times of change. Buckingham [England] ; Philadelphia : Open University Press, 2000.
*TC LB2900.5 .L45 2000*

Thody, Angela. Leadership of schools. London ; Herndon, Va. : Cassell, 1997.
*TC LB2831.726.G7 T56 1997*

Walsh, Mike. Building a successful school. London : Kogan Page, 1999.
*TC LB2900.5 .W37 1999*

## SCHOOL MANAGEMENT AND ORGANIZATION - GREAT BRITAIN - CASE STUDIES.

Improving schools. Buckingham [England] ; Philadelphia : Open University Press, 1999.
*TC LB2822.84.G7 I68 1999*

## SCHOOL MANAGEMENT AND ORGANIZATION - GREAT BRITAIN - CROSS-CULTURAL STUDIES.

Enhancing educational excellence, equity, and efficiency. Dordrecht ; Boston : Kluwer Academic Publishers, c1999.
*TC LB2921 .E54 1999*

## SCHOOL MANAGEMENT AND ORGANIZATION - HANDBOOKS, MANUALS, ETC.

Callison, William. Elementary school principal's handbook. Lancaster, Pa. : Technomic, c1999.
*TC LB2822.5 .C34 1999*

## SCHOOL MANAGEMENT AND ORGANIZATION - LAW AND LEGISLATION - UNITED STATES - CASES.

Imber, Michael. Education law. 2nd ed. Mahwah, N.J. : Lawrence Erlbaum Associates, 2000.
*TC KF4118 .I43 2000*

## SCHOOL MANAGEMENT AND ORGANIZATION - NETHERLANDS - CROSS-CULTURAL STUDIES.

Enhancing educational excellence, equity, and efficiency. Dordrecht ; Boston : Kluwer Academic Publishers, c1999.
*TC LB2921 .E54 1999*

## SCHOOL MANAGEMENT AND ORGANIZATION - NEW JERSEY.

Campbell, Delois. High school students' perceptions of the impact of block scheduling on instructional effectiveness. 1999.
*TC 06 no. 11089*

## SCHOOL MANAGEMENT AND ORGANIZATION - NEW YORK (STATE) - HERKIMER COUNTY - CASE STUDIES.

OConnor-Pirkle, Marilyn. Tracking systemic change in an interagency partnership. 1996.
*TC 06 no. 10677*

OConnor-Pirkle, Marilyn. Tracking systemic change in an interagency partnership. 1996.
*TC 06 no. 10677*

## SCHOOL MANAGEMENT AND ORGANIZATION - NEW YORK (STATE) - NEW YORK.

Curcio, John J. Relationships among administrator personality, perceptions of feedback source credibility, and attitudes toward program feedback. 1999.
*TC 085 C92*

## SCHOOL MANAGEMENT AND ORGANIZATION - OHIO - COLUMBUS.

Columbus (Ohio). Board of Education. Rules, 1905, 1910, 1922. Columbus : [s.n.], 1905-1922.
*TC 379.7830C722*

## SCHOOL MANAGEMENT AND ORGANIZATION - PARENT PARTICIPATION - NEW YORK (STATE) -

## NEW YORK - HISTORY - 20TH CENTURY.

Edgell, Derek. The movement for community control of New York City's schools, 1966-1970. Lewiston, N.Y. : E. Mellen Press, c1998.
*TC LB2862 .E35 1998*

## SCHOOL MANAGEMENT AND ORGANIZATION - PARENT PARTICIPATION - UNITED STATES.

Ryan, Daniel Prentice. Gay/lesbian parents and school personnel. 1998.
*TC 06 no. 10988*

## SCHOOL MANAGEMENT AND ORGANIZATION - RESEARCH - UNITED STATES.

An educators' guide to schoolwide reform. Arlington, Va. : Educational Research Service, c1999.
*TC LB2806.35 .E38 1999*

## SCHOOL MANAGEMENT AND ORGANIZATION - SCOTLAND.

Scottish education. Edinburgh : Edinburgh University Press, c1999.
*TC LA652 .S34 1999*

## SCHOOL MANAGEMENT AND ORGANIZATION - STUDY AND TEACHING (HIGHER) - UNITED STATES.

Cunningham, William G. Educational administration. Boston ; London : Allyn & Bacon, c2000.
*TC LB1738.5 .C86 2000*

## SCHOOL MANAGEMENT AND ORGANIZATION - UNITED STATES.

Bauer, Anne M. Inclusion 101. Baltimore, Md. : P.H. Brookes Pub., c1999.
*TC LC1201 .B38 1999*

Capper, Colleen A., 1960- Meeting the needs of students of all abilities. Thousand Oaks, Calif. : Corwin Press, c2000.
*TC LC1201 .C36 2000*

Catholic school leadership. London ; New York : Falmer Press, 2000.
*TC LC501 .C3484 2000*

Challenges and opportunities for education in the 21st century. Lewiston, NY : Edwin Mellen Press, c1999.
*TC LA209.2 .C45 1999*

Education's big gamble [videorecording]. New York, NY : Merrow Report, c1997.
*TC LB2806.36 .E3 1997*

Erlandson, David A. Organizational oversight. Princeton, NJ : Eye on Education, c1996.
*TC LB2805 .E75 1996*

Kampwirth, Thomas J. Collaborative consultation in the schools. Upper Saddle River, N.J. : Merrill, c1999.
*TC LB1027.5 .K285 1999*

Lashway, Larry. Measuring leadership. Eugene, OR : ERIC Clearinghouse on Educational Management, University of Oregon, 1999.
*TC LB2806 .L28 1999*

Michel, Patrick. Using action research for school restructuring and organizational change. 2000.
*TC 06 no. 11295*

Norton, M. Scott. Resource allocation. Larchmont, N.Y. : Eye on Education, c1997.
*TC LB2805 .N73 1997*

Pankake, Anita M., 1947- Implementation. Larchmont, NY : Eye on Education, c1998.
*TC LB2805 .P32 1998*

Pellicer, Leonard O. Caring enough to lead. Thousand Oaks, Calif. : Corwin Press, c1999.
*TC LB2805 .P375 1999*

Personalized instruction. Larchmont, N.Y. : Eye on Education, c2000.
*TC LB1031 .K383 2000*

Rallis, Sharon F. Principals of dynamic schools. 2nd ed. Thousand Oaks, Calif. : Corwin Press, c2000.
*TC LB2831.92 .G65 2000*

Reed, Carol J., 1937- Teaching with power. New York : Teachers College Press, c2000.
*TC LB2806.45 .R44 2000*

Sergiovanni, Thomas J. The principalship. 4th ed. Boston : Allyn & Bacon, c2001.
*TC LB2831.92 .S47 2001*

Shields, Carolyn M. Year-round schooling. Lanham, Md. : Scarecrow Press, 2000.
*TC LB3034 .S55 2000*

Tye, Barbara Benham, 1942- Hard truths. New York : Teachers College Press, c2000.

*TC LB2822.82 .T94 2000*

## SCHOOL MANAGEMENT AND ORGANIZATION - UNITED STATES - CASE STUDIES.

Case studies for school administrators. 1st ed. Lancaster, PA : Technomic Pub. Co., c1999.
*TC LB2806 .C316 1999*

Case studies of the superintendency. Lanham, Md. : Scarecrow Press, c2000.
*TC LB2831.72 .C38 2000*

Hayes, William, 1938- Real-life case studies for school administrators. Lanham, Md. : Scarecrow Press, c2000.
*TC LB2806 .H39 2000*

## SCHOOL MANAGEMENT AND ORGANIZATION - UNITED STATES - CROSS-CULTURAL STUDIES.

Enhancing educational excellence, equity, and efficiency. Dordrecht ; Boston : Kluwer Academic Publishers, c1999.
*TC LB2921 .E54 1999*

## SCHOOL MANAGEMENT AND ORGANIZATION - UNITED STATES - DECISION MAKING.

Achilles, Charles M. Problem analysis. Larchmont, NY : Eye on Education, c1997.
*TC LB2806 .A25 1997*

Short, Paula M. Information collection. Larchmont, NY : Eye on Education, c1998.
*TC LB1028.27.U6 S46 1998*

## SCHOOL MANAGEMENT AND ORGANIZATION - UNITED STATES - HANDBOOKS, MANUALS, ETC.

Callison, William. Elementary school principal's handbook. Lancaster, Pa. : Technomic, c1999.
*TC LB2822.5 .C34 1999*

Dunklee, Dennis R. If you want to lead, not just manage. Thousand Oaks, Calif. : Corwin Press, c2000.
*TC LB2831.92 .D85 2000*

## SCHOOL MANAGEMENT TEAMS - GREAT BRITAIN - CASE STUDIES.

Wallace, Mike. Senior management teams in primary schools. London ; New York : Routledge, 1999.
*TC LB2806.3 .W37 1999*

**SCHOOL MEDIA CENTERS.** See INSTRUCTIONAL MATERIALS CENTERS.

**SCHOOL MEDIA PROGRAMS.** See MEDIA PROGRAMS (EDUCATION).

## SCHOOL MUSIC - COMPUTER-ASSISTED INSTRUCTION.

Nord, Michael B. Music in the classroom (MITC). 1998.
*TC 06 no. 10974*

## SCHOOL MUSIC - INSTRUCTION AND STUDY.

Blackburn, Lois. Whole music. Portsmouth, N.H. : Heinemann, c1998.
*TC MT1 .B643 1998*

Haines, B. Joan E. (Beatrice Joan Elizabeth), 1920- Leading young children to music. 6th ed. Upper Saddle River, NJ : Merrill, c2000.
*TC MT1 .H13 2000*

Page, Nick. Music as a way of knowing. York, Me. : Stenhouse Publishers ; Los Angeles, Calif. : Galef Institute, c1995.
*TC MT1 .P234 1995*

Singing development. London : Roehampton Institute, Centre for Advanced Studies in Music Education, Faculty of Education, [1997?]
*TC MT898 .S55 1997*

## SCHOOL MUSIC - INSTRUCTION AND STUDY - ACTIVITY PROGRAMS.

Bitz, Michael Eric. A description and investigation of strategies for teaching classroom music improvisation. 1998.
*TC 06 no. 11012*

## SCHOOL MUSIC - INSTRUCTION AND STUDY - NEW YORK (STATE) - NEW YORK.

Bitz, Michael Eric. A description and investigation of strategies for teaching classroom music improvisation. 1998.
*TC 06 no. 11012*

## SCHOOL MUSIC - INSTRUCTION AND STUDY - NEW YORK (STATE) - NEW YORK - CASE STUDIES.

Nord, Michael B. Music in the classroom (MITC). 1998.

*TC 06 no. 10974*

**SCHOOL MUSIC - INSTRUCTION AND STUDY - OKLAHOMA.**
Damm, Robert J., 1964- Repertoire, authenticity, and instruction. New York ; London : Garland Pub., 2000.
*TC MT3.U6 O53 2000*

**SCHOOL MUSIC - INSTRUCTION AND STUDY - UNITED STATES.**
Hall, Louis O. Strategies for teaching. Reston, VA : Music Educators National Conference, c1997.
*TC MT1.H136 S77 1997*

Rozmajzl, Michon. Music fundamentals, methods, and materials for the elementary classroom teacher. 3rd ed. New York ; Harlow, England : Longman, c2000.
*TC MT1 .R85 2000*

**SCHOOL NURSING.**
Brown, Ronald T. Medications for school-age children. New York : Guilford Press, c1998.
*TC RJ560 .B76 1998*

**School of Education bulletin.**
The University of Michigan School of Education bulletin. [Ann Arbor] : The School, 1929-1964.

**SCHOOL OPERATION POLICIES.** *See* **SCHOOL MANAGEMENT AND ORGANIZATION.**

**SCHOOL ORGANIZATION.** *See* **SCHOOL MANAGEMENT AND ORGANIZATION.**

**SCHOOL PERSONNEL ADMINISTRATION.** *See* **SCHOOL PERSONNEL MANAGEMENT.**

**SCHOOL PERSONNEL MANAGEMENT.** *See* **COLLEGE PERSONNEL MANAGEMENT; TEACHER-ADMINISTRATOR RELATIONSHIPS; TEACHER-PRINCIPAL RELATIONSHIPS.**

**SCHOOL PERSONNEL MANAGEMENT - GREAT BRITAIN.**
Poorly performing staff and how to manage them. London : New York : Routledge, 1999.
*TC LB2832.4.G7 P66 1999*

**SCHOOL PERSONNEL MANAGEMENT - UNITED STATES.**
Castetter, William Benjamin, 1914- The human resource function in educational administration. 7th ed. Upper Saddle River, N.J. : Merrill, c2000.
*TC LB2831.58 .C37 2000*

Herman, Jerry John, 1930- School planning & personnel. Lancaster, Pa. : Technomic Pub. Co., c1999.
*TC LB2831.58 .H47 1999*

Norton, M. Scott. Resource allocation. Larchmont, N.Y. : Eye on Education, c1997.
*TC LB2805 .N73 1997*

Rebore, Ronald W. Human resources administration in education. 6th ed. Boston ; London : Allyn and Bacon, c2001.
*TC LB2831.58 .R43 2001*

Weller, L. David. Quality human resources leadership :. Lanham, Md. : Scarecrow Press, 2000.
*TC LB2831.92 .W45 2000*

**SCHOOL PERSONNEL MANAGEMENT - UNITED STATES - PSYCHOLOGICAL ASPECTS.**
Thompson, David P., 1959- Motivating others. Princeton, NJ : Eye On Education, c1996.
*TC LB2831.58 .T56 1996*

**School planning & personnel.**
Herman, Jerry John, 1930- Lancaster, Pa. : Technomic Pub. Co., c1999.
*TC LB2831.58 .H47 1999*

**School planning and personnel.**
Herman, Jerry John, 1930- School planning & personnel. Lancaster, Pa. : Technomic Pub. Co., c1999.
*TC LB2831.58 .H47 1999*

**SCHOOL PLAYS.** *See* **CHILDREN'S PLAYS.**

**SCHOOL PRINCIPALS.** *See also* **ELEMENTARY SCHOOL PRINCIPALS; HIGH SCHOOL PRINCIPALS; MIDDLE SCHOOL PRINCIPALS; WOMEN SCHOOL PRINCIPALS.**
Dunklee, Dennis R. You sound taller on the telephone. Thousand Oaks, Calif. : Corwin Press, c1999.
*TC LB2831.9 .D85 1999*

**SCHOOL PRINCIPALS - CORRESPONDENCE - HANDBOOKS, MANUALS, ETC.**
Grady, Marilyn L. 124 high-impact letters for busy

principals. Thousand Oaks, Calif. : Corwin Press, c2000.
*TC LB2831.9 .G72 2000*

**SCHOOL PRINCIPALS - FICTION.**
Pilkey, Dav, 1966- Captain Underpants and the invasion of the incredibly naughty cafeteria ladies from outer space .... New York : Blue Sky Press, c1999.
*TC PZ7.P63123 Cat 1999*

**SCHOOL PRINCIPALS - PROFESSIONAL ETHICS - UNITED STATES.**
Crawford, George, 1937- Philosophical & cultural values. Larchmont, NY : Eye On Education, c2000.
*TC LB2831.92 .C72 2000*

**SCHOOL PRINCIPALS - QUOTATIONS.**
What every principal would like to say-- and what to say next time. Thousand Oaks, Calif. : Corwin Press, c2000.
*TC LB2831.9 .W53 2000*

**SCHOOL PRINCIPALS - TRAINING OF.**
Speck, Marsha. The principalship. Upper Saddle River, N.J. : Merrill, c1999.
*TC LB1738.5 .S64 1999*

**SCHOOL PRINCIPALS - UNITED STATES.**
Achilles, Charles M. Problem analysis. Larchmont, NY : Eye on Education, c1997.
*TC LB2806 .A25 1997*

Crow, Gary Monroe, 1947- Leadership. Princeton, NJ : Eye on Education, c1996.
*TC LB2831.92 .C76 1996*

Drake, Thelbert L. The principalship. 5th ed. Upper Saddle River, N.J. : Merrill, c1999.
*TC LB2831.92 .D73 1999*

Dyer, Karen M. The intuitive principal. Thousand Oaks, Calif. : Corwin Press, c2000.
*TC LB2831.92 .D94 2000*

Erlandson, David A. Organizational oversight. Princeton, NJ : Eye on Education, c1996.
*TC LB2805 .E75 1996*

Pellicer, Leonard O. Caring enough to lead. Thousand Oaks, Calif. : Corwin Press, c1999.
*TC LB2805 .P375 1999*

Rallis, Sharon F. Principals of dynamic schools. 2nd ed. Thousand Oaks, Calif. : Corwin Press, c2000.
*TC LB2831.92 .G65 2000*

Sergiovanni, Thomas J. The principalship. 4th ed. Boston : Allyn & Bacon, c2001.
*TC LB2831.92 .S47 2001*

Short, Paula M. Information collection. Larchmont, NY : Eye on Education, c1998.
*TC LB1028.27.U6 S46 1998*

Villani, Susan. Are you sure you're the principal? Thousand Oaks, Calif. : Corwin Press, c1999.
*TC LB2831.92 .V55 1999*

Ward, Michael E., 1953- Delegation and empowerment. Larchmont, NY : Eye on Education, c1999.
*TC LB2831.92 .W37 1999*

What principals should know about--. Springfield, Ill. : C.C. Thomas, c2000.
*TC LB2831.92 .W52 2000*

**SCHOOL PRINCIPALS - UNITED STATES - ATTITUDES.**
Hoyle, John. Interpersonal sensitivity. Larchmont, NY : Eye on Education, c1997.
*TC LB2831.92.U6 H67 1997*

**SCHOOL PRINCIPALS - UNITED STATES - HANDBOOKS, MANUALS, ETC.**
Dunklee, Dennis R. If you want to lead, not just manage. Thousand Oaks, Calif. : Corwin Press, c2000.
*TC LB2831.92 .D85 2000*

**SCHOOL PRIVATIZATION.** *See* **PRIVATIZATION IN EDUCATION.**

**SCHOOL PROSE.** *See* **COLLEGE PROSE.**

**SCHOOL PSYCHOLOGY.**
Branwhite, Tony. Helping adolescents in school. Westport, Conn. ; London : Praeger, 2000.
*TC LB1027.55 .B72 2000*

Council of Europe. Council for Cultural Co-operation. Bullying in schools. Strasbourg : Council of Europe Publishing, 1999.
*TC BF637.B85 B842 1999*

Ravenette, Tom. Personal construct theory in educational psychology :. London : Whurr, c1999.

*TC LB1027.55 .R38 1999*

**SCHOOL PSYCHOLOGY - HANDBOOKS, MANUALS, ETC.**
Conducting school-based assessments of child and adolescent behavior. New York : Guilford Press, c2000.
*TC LB1124 .C66 2000*

**SCHOOL REFORM.** *See* **EDUCATIONAL CHANGE.**

**School, reform and society in the new Russia.**
Webber, Stephen L., 1967- Houndmills [England] : Macmillan Press ; New York : St. Martin's Press in association with Centre for Russian and East European Studies, University of Birmingham, 2000.
*TC LA839.2 .W4 2000*

**SCHOOL REPORTS.** *See* **GRADING AND MARKING (STUDENTS).**

**SCHOOL REUNIONS.** *See* **CLASS REUNIONS.**

**SCHOOL SCHEDULES.** *See* **SCHEDULES, SCHOOL.**

**School science facilities.**
Biehle, James T. NSTA guide to school science facilities. Arlington, VA : National Science Teachers Association, c1999.
*TC Q183.3.A1 B54 1999*

**SCHOOL SELF-IMPROVEMENT PROGRAMS.** *See* **SCHOOL IMPROVEMENT PROGRAMS.**

**SCHOOL SIZE.** *See* **CLASS SIZE.**

**SCHOOL SOCIAL WORK - UNITED STATES.**
Allen-Meares, Paula, 1948- Social work services in schools. 3rd ed. Boston : Allyn and Bacon, c2000.
*TC LB3013.4 .A45 2000*

Collaborative practice. Westport, Conn. ; London : Praeger, 1999.
*TC HV741 .C5424 1999*

**SCHOOL SPORTS.** *See* **COLLEGE SPORTS.**

**SCHOOL SPORTS - UNITED STATES - JUVENILE LITERATURE.**
Hastings, Penny. Sports for her. Westport, Conn. ; London : Greenwood Press, 1999.
*TC GV709.18.U6 H37 1999*

**SCHOOL STORIES.**
Jones, Jennifer B. Dear Mrs. Ryan, you're ruining my life. New York : Walker & Co., 2000.
*TC PZ7.J7203 De 2000*

**SCHOOL STUDY TRIPS.** *See* **SCHOOL FIELD TRIPS.**

**SCHOOL SUPERINTENDENTS.** *See also* **WOMEN SCHOOL SUPERINTENDENTS.**
Cuban, Larry. Urban school chiefs under fire. Chicago : University of Chicago Press, 1976.
*TC LB2831.7 .C82*

**SCHOOL SUPERINTENDENTS AND PRINCIPALS.** *See* **SCHOOL PRINCIPALS; SCHOOL SUPERINTENDENTS.**

**SCHOOL SUPERINTENDENTS - GREAT BRITAIN.**
Thody, Angela. Leadership of schools. London ; Herndon, Va. : Cassell, 1997.
*TC LB2831.726.G7 T56 1997*

**SCHOOL SUPERINTENDENTS - TENNESSEE - BIOGRAPHY.**
McGarrh, Kellie, d. 1995. Kellie McGarrh's hangin' in tough. New York : P. Lang, c2000.
*TC LA2317.D6185 M34 2000*

**SCHOOL SUPERINTENDENTS - UNITED STATES - CASE STUDIES.**
Case studies of the superintendency. Lanham, Md. : Scarecrow Press, c2000.
*TC LB2831.72 .C38 2000*

Owen, Jane C., 1948- Superintendent's guide to creating community. Lanham, Md. : Scarecrow Press, 2000.
*TC LB2831.72 . O94 2000*

**SCHOOL SUPERVISION.** *See also* **SCHOOL SUPERVISORS.**
Wiles, Jon. Supervision. 5th ed. Upper Saddle River, N.J. : Merrill, c2000.
*TC LB2806.4 .W55 2000*

**SCHOOL SUPERVISION - PLANNING.**
Zepeda, Sally J., 1956- Supervision and staff development on the block. Larchmont, N.Y. : Eye On Education, c2000.
*TC LB3032.2 .Z46 2000*

**SCHOOL SUPERVISION - SOCIAL ASPECTS.**
Paradigm debates in curriculum and supervision.
Westport, Conn. : London : Bergin & Garvey, 2000.
*TC LB2806.4 .P37 2000*

**SCHOOL SUPERVISION - UNITED STATES.**
Beach, Don M. Supervisory leadership. Boston :
Allyn and Bacon, c2000.
*TC LB2806.4 .B433 2000*

Glatthorn, Allan A., 1924- Differentiated supervision.
2nd ed. Alexandria, Va. : Association for Supervision
and Curriculum Development, c1997.
*TC LB2806.4 .G548 1997*

Keefe, James W. Instruction and the learning
environment. Larchmont, NY : Eye On Education,
c1997.
*TC LB2806.4 .K44 1997*

Oliva, Peter F. Supervision for today's schools. 6th
ed. New York ; Chichester [England] : J. Wiley &
Sons, c2001.
*TC LB2806.4 .O43 2001*

Sergiovanni, Thomas J. The principalship. 4th ed.
Boston : Allyn & Bacon, c2001.
*TC LB2831.92 .S47 2001*

Sullivan, Susan, 1943- Supervision that improves
teaching. Thousand Oaks, Calif. : Corwin Press,
c2000.
*TC LB2806.4 .S85 2000*

**SCHOOL SUPERVISION - UNITED STATES -
CASE STUDIES.**
Improved test scores, attitudes, and behaviors in
America's schools. Westport, Conn. : Bergin &
Garvey, 1999.
*TC LB2806.4 .I56 1999*

**SCHOOL SUPERVISORS - UNITED STATES -
CASE STUDIES.**
Improved test scores, attitudes, and behaviors in
America's schools. Westport, Conn. : Bergin &
Garvey, 1999.
*TC LB2806.4 .I56 1999*

**SCHOOL SUPPLIES.** *See* **SCHOOLS -
FURNITURE, EQUIPMENT, ETC.**

**SCHOOL SUPPORT TEAMS - UNITED STATES.**
Snell, Martha E. Collaborative teaming. Baltimore :
Paul H. Brookes Pub., c2000.
*TC LC1201 .S64 2000*

**SCHOOL SURVEYS.** *See* **EDUCATIONAL
SURVEYS.**

**SCHOOL TAXES.** *See* **EDUCATION - FINANCE.**

**SCHOOL TEACHING.** *See* **TEACHING.**

**SCHOOL-TO-CAREERS PROGRAMS.** *See*
**SCHOOL-TO-WORK TRANSITION.**

**SCHOOL-TO-WORK PROGRAMS.** *See*
**SCHOOL-TO-WORK TRANSITION.**

**SCHOOL-TO-WORK TRANSITION.**
Connecting mathematics and science to workplace
contexts. Thousand Oaks, Calif. : Corwin Press,
c1999.
*TC QA11 .C655 1999*

Organisation for Economic Co-operation and
Development (Paris) From initial education to
working life. Paris : Organisation for Economic Co-
operation and Development, 2000.
*TC LC1037 .O74 2000*

**SCHOOL-TO-WORK TRANSITION - EUROPE.**
Bridging the skills gap between work and education.
Dordrecht ; Boston : Kluwer Academic Publishers,
c1999.
*TC LC5056.A2 B75 1999*

**SCHOOL-TO-WORK TRANSITION - UNITED
STATES.**
Hughes, Carolyn, 1946- The transition handbook.
Baltimore : P.H. Brookes Pub., c2000.
*TC LC4019 .H84 2000*

Pierangelo, Roger. Complete guide to special
education transition services. West Nyack, NY :
Center for Applied Research in Education, c1997.
*TC HV1569.3.Y68 P55 1997*

Steinberg, Adria. Schooling for the real world. 1st ed.
San Francisco : Jossey-Bass, c1999.
*TC LC1037.5 .S843 1999*

**SCHOOL-TO-WORK TRANSITION - UNITED
STATES - CONGRESSES.**
Transitions to adulthood in a changing economy.
Westport, Conn. : Praeger, c1999.

*TC HQ799.7 .T73 1999*

**SCHOOL TRUSTEES.** *See* **SCHOOL BOARDS.**

**School twenty-seven [videorecording].**
Ecole 27 [videorecording]. Bruxelles : Paradise
Films ; New York, N.Y. : [distributed by] First Run/
Icarus Films, 1997, c1996.
*TC LC746.P7 E2 1997*

**SCHOOL-UNIVERSITY COOPERATION.** *See*
**COLLEGE-SCHOOL COOPERATION.**

**SCHOOL VANDALISM.** *See* **SCHOOL
VIOLENCE.**

**SCHOOL VIOLENCE.** *See* **STUDENTS - CRIMES
AGAINST.**

**SCHOOL VIOLENCE - TEXAS - PREVENTION.**
Turk, William L. When juvenile crime comes to
school. Lewiston, NY : E. Mellen Press, 1999.
*TC HV6250.4.S78 T87 1999*

**SCHOOL VIOLENCE - UNITED STATES.**
Hyman, Irwin A. Dangerous schools. 1st ed. San
Francisco : Jossey-Bass Publishers, c1999.
*TC LB3013 .H897 1999*

**SCHOOL VIOLENCE - UNITED STATES -
PREVENTION.**
Bemak, Fred. Violent and aggressive youth. Thousand
Oaks, Calif. : London : Corwin Press, c2000.
*TC LB3013.3 .B45 2000*

Capozzoli, Thomas. Kids killing kids. Boca Raton,
Fla. : London : St. Lucie Press, c2000.
*TC LB3013.3 .C37 2000*

Peacebuilding for adolescents. New York : P. Lang,
c1999.
*TC JZ5534 .P43 1999*

Preventing student violence. Bloomington, IN (P.O.
Box 789, Bloomington 47402-0789) : Phi Delta
Kappa International, c1999.
*TC LB3013.3 .P755 1999*

Trump, Kenneth S. Classroom killers? hallway
hostages? Thousand Oaks, Calif. : Corwin Press,
c2000.
*TC LB2866.5 .T78 2000*

Turk, William L. When juvenile crime comes to
school. Lewiston, NY : E. Mellen Press, 1999.
*TC HV6250.4.S78 T87 1999*

**SCHOOL VOUCHERS.** *See* **EDUCATIONAL
VOUCHERS.**

**SCHOOL YEAR.** *See also* **SCHEDULES, SCHOOL.**
Special days and weeks for planning the school
calendar. Arlington, Va. : Educational Research
Service.
*TC LB3525 .S63*

**SCHOOLBOOKS.** *See* **TEXTBOOKS.**

**Schoolcraft, Victoria.** A nuts-and-bolts approach to
teaching nursing / Victoria Schoolcraft ; with Jeanne
Novotny. 2nd ed. New York : Springer Pub. Co.,
c2000. xvi, 183 p. ; 24 cm. (Springer series on the teaching of
nursing.) Includes bibliographical references and index.
CONTENTS: Making clinical assignments -- Supervising a
clinical group -- Designing a learning contract -- Teaching
students to work in groups -- Planning to give a lecture --
Planning a successful seminar -- Course design,
implementation, and evaluation -- Textbook and reading
assignment selection -- Designing and grading a major
assignment -- Designing and grading a minor assignment --
Test construction and analysis -- Using technology to facilitate
learning -- Guiding independent study -- Helping students to
improve their writing skills. ISBN 0-8261-6601-6 (hardcover)
*1. Nursing - Study & teaching. I. Novotny, Jeanne. II. Title. III.
Series: Springer series on the teaching of nursing
(Unnumbered).*
*TC RT71 .S26 2000*

**SCHOOLGIRLS AS MOTHERS.** *See* **TEENAGE
MOTHERS.**

**SCHOOLHOUSES.** *See* **SCHOOL BUILDINGS.**

**Schooling as a ritual performance.**
McLaren, Peter, 1948- 3rd ed. Lanham, Md. :
Rowman & Littlefield, c1999.
*TC LC504.3.T67 M35 1999*

**Schooling at-risk Native American children.**
Clay, Cheryl D., 1947- New York : Garland Pub.,
1998.
*TC E99.U8 C53 1998*

**Schooling bodies.**
Kirk, David, 1958- London ; Washington, D.C. :
Leicester University Press, 1998.

*TC GV315 .K57 1998*

**Schooling for the real world.**
Steinberg, Adria. 1st ed. San Francisco : Jossey-Bass,
c1999.
*TC LC1037.5 .S843 1999*

**SCHOOLING, HOME.** *See* **HOME SCHOOLING.**

**Schooling in sub-Saharan Africa :** contemporary
issues and future concerns / edited by Cynthia
Szymanski Sunal. New York : Garland Pub., 1998.
xxv, 246 p. ; 23 cm. (Garland reference library of social
sciences ; vol. 952. Reference books in international
education ; vol. 41) Includes bibliographical references and
index. ISBN 0-8153-1645-3 (alk. paper) DDC 370/.967
*1. Education - Africa, Sub-Saharan. 2. School management and
organization - Africa, Sub-Saharan. 3. Education - Africa,
Sub-Saharan - Curricula. I. Sunal, Cynthia S. II. Series:
Garland reference library of social science ; v. 952. III. Series:
Garland reference library of social science. Reference books in
international education ; vol. 41.*
*TC LA1501 .S35 1998*

**SCHOOLS.** *See* **ALTERNATIVE SCHOOLS; ART
SCHOOLS; BOARDING SCHOOLS;
CHARTER SCHOOLS; CONSERVATORIES
OF MUSIC; EDUCATION; ELEMENTARY
SCHOOLS; EVENING AND CONTINUATION
SCHOOLS; HIGH SCHOOLS;
INSTRUCTIONAL MATERIALS CENTERS;
JUNIOR HIGH SCHOOLS; LABORATORY
SCHOOLS; MANUAL TRAINING; MIDDLE
SCHOOLS; NURSERY SCHOOLS; PRIVATE
SCHOOLS; PUBLIC SCHOOLS; RURAL
SCHOOLS; SUBURBAN SCHOOLS; SUNDAY
SCHOOLS; TRADE SCHOOLS;
UNIVERSITIES AND COLLEGES; YEAR-
ROUND SCHOOLS.**

**Schools and community.**
Arthur, James, 1957- London : New York : Falmer
Press, 2000.
*TC LC221.4.G7 A78 2000*

**Schools and societies.**
Brint, Steven G. Thousand Oaks : Pine Forge Press,
c1998.
*TC LC191.4 .B75 1998*

**Schools and the social development of young
Australians.** Melbourne, Vic. : Australian Council for
Educational Research, 1998. xxix, 162 p. ; 25 cm. ISBN
0-86431-300-4
*1. Socialization - Australia. I. Ainley, John.*
*TC LC192.4 .S36 1998*

**SCHOOLS - CANADA - ONTARIO -
SOCIOLOGICAL ASPECTS - CASE
STUDIES.**
Fink, Dean, 1936- Good schools/real schools. New
York : Teachers College Press, c2000.
*TC LB2822.84.C2 F56 2000*

**SCHOOLS - CENTRALIZATION.** *See* **SCHOOL
DISTRICTS.**

**SCHOOLS - CENTRALIZATION - IOWA -
HISTORY - 20TH CENTURY.**
Reynolds, David R. There goes the neighborhood.
Iowa City : University of Iowa Press, 1999.
*TC LB2861 .R49 1999*

**SCHOOLS - CONNECTICUT - DIRECTORIES.**
MDR's school directory. Connecticut. Shelton, CT :
Market Data Retrieval, c1995-
*TC L903.C8 M37*

**SCHOOLS - CURRICULA.** *See* **EDUCATION -
CURRICULA.**

**SCHOOLS - DATA PROCESSING -
PERIODICALS.**
Journal of educational data processing. [Malibu,
Calif., etc., Educational Systems Corp.]

**SCHOOLS - DECENTRALIZATION - NEW YORK
(STATE) - NEW YORK - HISTORY - 20TH
CENTURY.**
Edgell, Derek. The movement for community control
of New York City's schools, 1966-1970. Lewiston,
N.Y. : E. Mellen Press, c1998.
*TC LB2862 .E35 1999*

**SCHOOLS - DECENTRALIZATION - SOCIAL
ASPECTS - CONNECTICUT - NEW HAVEN
METROPOLITAN AREA - CASE STUDIES.**
McDermott, Kathryn A., 1969- Controlling public
education. Lawrence : University Press of Kansas,
c1999.
*TC LC213.23.N39 M34 1999*

**SCHOOLS, DENOMINATIONAL.** *See* **CHURCH SCHOOLS.**

**SCHOOLS - EQUIPMENT AND SUPPLIES.** *See* **SCHOOLS - FURNITURE, EQUIPMENT, ETC.**

**SCHOOLS - EVALUATION - RESEARCH.**
The international handbook of school effectiveness research. London ; New York : Falmer Press, 2000.
*TC LB2822.75 .I59 2000*

**SCHOOLS - EXERCISES AND RECREATIONS - UNITED STATES.**
Heflick, David. How to make money performing in schools. Orient, Wash. : Silcox Productions, c1996.
*TC LB3015 .H428 1996*

**SCHOOLS - FICTION.**
Carrick, Carol. Patrick's dinosaurs on the Internet. New York : Clarion Books, 1999.
*TC PZ7.C2344 Patf 1999*

Draper, Sharon M. (Sharon Mills) Romiette and Julio. 1st ed. New York : Atheneum Books for Young Readers, 1999.
*TC PZ7.D78325 Ro 1999*

Gordon, Amy, 1949- When JFK was my father. Boston : Houghton Mifflin, 1999.
*TC PZ7.G65 Wh 1999*

Mills, Claudia. You're a brave man, Julius Zimmerman. 1st ed. New York : Farrar Straus Giroux, c1999.
*TC PZ7.M63963 Yo 1999*

Mora, Pat. The rainbow tulip. New York : Viking, 1999.
*TC PZ7.M78819 Rai 1999*

Pilkey, Dav, 1966- Captain Underpants and the invasion of the incredibly naughty cafeteria ladies from outer space .... New York : Blue Sky Press, c1999.
*TC PZ7.P63123 Cat 1999*

Reiser, Lynn. Earthdance. New York : Greenwillow Books, 1999.
*TC PZ7.R27745 Ear 1999*

Rowling, J. K. Harry Potter and the Chamber of Secrets. New York : Arthur A. Levine Books, 1999.
*TC PZ7.R7968 Har 1999*

Rowling, J. K. Harry Potter and the prisoner of Azkaban. New York : Arthur A. Levine Books, 1999.
*TC PZ7.R79835 Ham 1999*

Rowling, J. K. Harry Potter and the sorcerer's stone. 1st American ed. New York : A.A. Levine Books, 1998.
*TC PZ7.R79835 Har 1998*

Sachar, Louis, 1954- Sideways stories from Wayside School. New York : Morrow Junior Books, 1998.
*TC PZ7.S1185 Si 1998*

Sheldon, Dyan. Confessions of a teenage drama queen. 1st ed. Cambridge, Mass. : Candlewick Press, 1999.
*TC PZ7.S54144 Co 1999*

Vail, Rachel. If you only knew. 1st ed. New York : Scholastic, c1998.
*TC PZ7.V1916 If 1998*

Vail, Rachel. Please, please, please. New York : Scholastic, c1998.
*TC PZ7.V1916 Pl 1998*

**SCHOOLS - FINANCE.** *See* **EDUCATION - FINANCE.**

**Schools for the mathematically talented in the former Soviet Union.**
Tokar, Inna. 1999.
*TC 085 T572*

**SCHOOLS - FURNITURE, EQUIPMENT, ETC. - DIRECTORIES.**
New York public school administrators' business directory. Hackettstown, NJ : Kinsley Publications.
*TC LB3280 .N4*

**SCHOOLS IN LITERATURE.**
Keroes, Jo. Tales out of school. Carbondale : Southern Illinois University Press, c1999.
*TC PS374.T43 K47 1999*

**SCHOOLS - INSPECTION.** *See* **SCHOOL MANAGEMENT AND ORGANIZATION.**

**SCHOOLS, JEWISH.** *See* **JEWISH DAY SCHOOLS; JEWISH RELIGIOUS SCHOOLS.**

**SCHOOLS - JEWS.** *See* **JEWISH DAY SCHOOLS; JEWISH RELIGIOUS SCHOOLS.**

**SCHOOLS - LAW AND LEGISLATION.** *See* **EDUCATIONAL LAW AND LEGISLATION.**

**Schools making a difference - let's be realistic!.**
Thrupp, Martin, 1964- Buckingham [England] ; Philadelphia : Open University Press, 1999.
*TC LB2822.75 .T537 1999*

**SCHOOLS - MANAGEMENT AND ORGANIZATION.** *See* **SCHOOL MANAGEMENT AND ORGANIZATION.**

**SCHOOLS - NEW JERSEY - DIRECTORIES.**
MDR's school directory. New Jersey. Shelton, CT : Market Data Retrieval, c1995-
*TC L903.N5 M37*

**SCHOOLS - NEW YORK - DIRECTORIES.**
MDR's school directory. New York. Shelton, CT : Market Data Retrieval, c1995-
*TC L903.N7 M37*

**SCHOOLS - NEW YORK (STATE) - DIRECTORIES.**
New York public school administrators' business directory. Hackettstown, NJ : Kinsley Publications.
*TC LB3280 .N4*

**SCHOOLS, NONGRADED.** *See* **NONGRADED SCHOOLS.**

**SCHOOLS, NURSING - UNITED STATES - DIRECTORIES.**
Annual guide to graduate nursing education programs. New York, N.Y. : National League for Nursing Press, c1995-
*TC RT75 .A5*

**SCHOOLS OF NURSING.** *See* **NURSING SCHOOLS.**

**SCHOOLS OF SOCIOLOGY.** *See* **CHICAGO SCHOOL OF SOCIOLOGY; FRANKFURT SCHOOL OF SOCIOLOGY.**

**SCHOOLS - OPENING EXERCISES.** *See* **SCHOOLS - EXERCISES AND RECREATIONS.**

**SCHOOLS, PAROCHIAL.** *See* **CHURCH SCHOOLS.**

**SCHOOLS - PENNSYLVANIA - DIRECTORIES.**
MDR's school directory. Pennsylvania. Shelton, CT : Market Data Retrieval, 1995-
*TC L903.P4 M37*

**SCHOOLS - PERSONNEL MANAGEMENT.** *See* **SCHOOL PERSONNEL MANAGEMENT.**

**SCHOOLS, PRIVATE.** *See* **PRIVATE SCHOOLS.**

**SCHOOLS - PUBLIC RELATIONS.**
Public relations in schools. 2nd ed. Upper Saddle River, N.J. : Merrill, c2000.
*TC LB2847 .P82 2000*

**SCHOOLS - PUBLIC RELATIONS - CASE STUDIES.**
Public relations in schools. 2nd ed. Upper Saddle River, N.J. : Merrill, c2000.
*TC LB2847 .P82 2000*

**SCHOOLS - PUBLIC RELATIONS - UNITED STATES.**
Bagin, Don, 1938- The school and community relations. 7th ed. Boston ; London : Allyn and Bacon, c2001.
*TC LC221 .G35 2001*

Conners, Gail A. Good news!. Thousand Oaks, Calif. : Corwin Press, c2000.
*TC LB2847 .C65 2000*

Warner, Carolyn. Promoting your school. 2nd ed. Thousand Oaks, Calif. : Corwin Press, c2000.
*TC LB2847 .W36 2000*

**SCHOOLS - PUBLIC RELATIONS - UNITED STATES - CASE STUDIES.**
Hughes, Larry W., 1931- Public relations for school leaders. Boston ; London : Allyn and Bacon, c2000.
*TC LB2847 .H84 2000*

**SCHOOLS - RECREATIONS.** *See* **SCHOOLS - EXERCISES AND RECREATIONS.**

**SCHOOLS, RURAL.** *See* **RURAL SCHOOLS.**

**SCHOOLS - SCHEDULES.** *See* **SCHEDULES, SCHOOL.**

**SCHOOLS - SECURITY MEASURES - UNITED STATES.**
Trump, Kenneth S. Classroom killers? hallway

hostages? Thousand Oaks, Calif. : Corwin Press, c2000.
*TC LB2866.5 .T78 2000*

**SCHOOLS - SELECTION.** *See* **SCHOOL CHOICE.**

**SCHOOLS - SOCIOLOGICAL ASPECTS.**
Weare, Katherine, 1950- Promoting mental, emotional, and social health. London ; New York : Routledge, 2000.
*TC LB3430 .W42 2000*

**SCHOOLS - STANDARDS - VERMONT - BENNINGTON.**
From another angle. New York : Teachers College Press, c2000.
*TC LB1117 .F735 2000*

**SCHOOLS, SUBURBAN.** *See* **SUBURBAN SCHOOLS.**

**Schools transformed for the 21st century.**
Barnes, Barbara. Torrance, Calif. : Griffin Pub. Group, c1999.
*TC LA217.2 .B39 1999*

**Schools transformed for the twenty-first century.**
Barnes, Barbara. Schools transformed for the 21st century. Torrance, Calif. : Griffin Pub. Group, c1999.
*TC LA217.2 .B39 1999*

**SCHOOLS, UNGRADED.** *See* **NONGRADED SCHOOLS.**

**SCHOOLS - UNITED STATES - SAFETY MEASURES.**
Baldwin, Harmon A. (Harmon Arthur), 1922- Planning for disaster. 2nd ed. Bloomington, Ind. : Phi Delta Kappa Educational Foundation, c1999.
*TC LB2864.5 .B35 1999*

Capozzoli, Thomas. Kids killing kids. Boca Raton, Fla. ; London : St. Lucie Press, c2000.
*TC LB3013.3 .C37 2000*

Hyman, Irwin A. Dangerous schools. 1st ed. San Francisco : Jossey-Bass Publishers, c1999.
*TC LB3013 .H897 1999*

**SCHOOLS - UNITED STATES - SOCIOLOGICAL ASPECTS.**
Brint, Steven G. Schools and societies. Thousand Oaks : Pine Forge Press, c1998.
*TC LC191.4 .B75 1998*

**Schools we need.**
Hirsch, E. D. (Eric Donald), 1928- The schools we need and why we don't have them. 1st Anchor Books ed. New York : Anchor Books/Doubleday, 1999.
*TC LA210 .H57 1999*

**The schools we need and why we don't have them.**
Hirsch, E. D. (Eric Donald), 1928- 1st Anchor Books ed. New York : Anchor Books/Doubleday, 1999.
*TC LA210 .H57 1999*

**SCHOOLTEACHING.** *See* **TEACHING.**

**Schoolwide and classroom management.**
Froyen, Len A. 3rd ed. Upper Saddle River, N.J. : Merrill, c1999.
*TC LB3013 .F783 1999*

**Schoolwide test preparation.**
Smith, Steven H. [Arlington, Va.] : Educational Research Service, c2000.
*TC LB2806.22 .S65 2000*

**Schöpf, Christine.**
LifeScience. Wien ; New York : Springer, 1999.
*TC T14.5 L54 1999*

**Schopler, Janice H.**
Support groups. New York : Haworth Press, c1995.
*TC HV45 .S896 1995*

**Schorr, Alvin Louis, 1921-** Filial responsibility in the modern American family. An evaluation of current practice of filial responsibility in the United States and the relationship to it of social security programs. [Washington] U.S. Dept. of Health, Education, and Welfare, Social Security Administration, Division of Program Research [1960] v, 45 p. ; 23 cm. References: p. 41-45.
*1. Public welfare - United States. 2. Public assistance - Recipients. 3. Old-age assistance - Eligibility. 4. Parent and child (Law) - United States. 5. Family welfare - United States. I. Title.*
*TC HV75 .S36 1960*

**Schoub, B. D.** AIDS & HIV in perspective : a guide to understanding the virus and its consequences / Barry D. Schoub. 2nd ed. Cambridge ; New York, NY : Cambridge University Press, 1999. xix, 274 p. : ill. ; 24 cm. Includes bibliographical references (p. 258-265) and index. ISBN 0-521-62150-X (hardback) ISBN 0-521-62766-4 (pbk.)

DDC 616.97/92
*1. AIDS (Disease) 2. Acquired Immunodeficiency Syndrome. 3. HIV Infections. I. Title. II. Title: AIDS and HIV in perspective*
**TC RC607.A26 S3738 1999**

**Schraagen, Jan Maarten.**
Cognitive task analysis. Mahwah, N.J. : L. Erlbaum Associates, 2000.
**TC BF311 .C55345 2000**

**Schramm, Carl J.**
Health care and its costs. 1st ed. New York : Norton, c1987.
**TC RA395.A3 H392 1987**

**Schratz, Michael, 1952-** Research as social change : new opportunities for qualitative research / Michael Schratz and Rob Walker. London ; New York : Routledge, 1995. vi, 182 p. : ill. ; 25 cm. Includes bibliographical references (p. [175]-179) and index. ISBN 0-415-11868-9 ISBN 0-415-11869-7 (pbk.) DDC 300/.72
*1. Social sciences - Research - Methodology. I. Walker, Rob, 1943- II. Title.*
**TC H62 .S33984 1995**

**Schraw, Gregory J.**
Bruning, Roger H. Cognitive psychology and instruction. 3rd ed. Upper Saddle River, N.J. : Merrill, c1999.
**TC LB1060 .B786 1999**

**Schriewer, Jürgen.**
Problems and prospects in European education. Westport, Conn. : Praeger, 2000.
**TC LC191.8. E85 P86 2000**

**Schroots, J. J. F.**
A history of geropsychology in autobiography. 1st ed. Washington, DC ; London : American Psychological Association, c2000.
**TC BF724.8 .H57 2000**

**Schrum, Stephen Alan, 1957-.**
Theatre in cyberspace. New York : P. Lang, c1999.
**TC PN2075 .T54 1999**

**Schubert, J. Daniel.**
Knowledge and power in higher education. New York ; London : Teachers College Press, c2000.
**TC LC171 .K62 2000**

**Schubert, William Henry.**
Marshall, J. Dan. Turning points in curriculum. Upper Saddle River, N.J. : Merrill, c2000.
**TC LB1570 .M36675 2000**

**Schuh, John H.**
Creating successful partnerships between academic and student affairs. San Francisco : Jossey-Bass Publishers, 1999.
**TC LB2342.9 .C75 1999**

**Schultz, Jeffrey Alan, 1946-.**
Break throughs [videorecording]. Boston, MA : Fanlight Productions, c1998.
**TC LC4717.5 .B7 1998**

**Schultz, Mindella.** Comparative political systems; an inquiry approach. New York, Holt, Rinehart and Winston [1967] xiv, 304 p. illus. 24 cm. (Holt social studies curriculum) Includes bibliographies. DDC 320.3
*1. United States - Politics and government - 1945-1989. 2. Soviet Union - Politics and government - 1945-1991. I. Title.*
**TC JF51 .S34 1967**

**Schultz, T. Paul.** Economics of population / T. Paul Schultz. Reading, MA : Addison-Wesley, c1981. xi, 240 p. : ill. ; 24 cm. (Perspectives on economics series) Includes bibliographies and index. ISBN 0-201-08371-X DDC 330.9
*1. Population - Economic aspects. I. Title. II. Series.*
**TC HB849.41 .S38**

**Schulz, Jane B., 1924-.**
Bridging the family-professional gap. Springfield, Ill. : Charles C. Thomas, c1999.
**TC HV888.5 .B74 1999**

**Schumacker, Randall E.** A beginner's guide to structural equation modeling / Randall E. Schumacker, Richard G. Lomax. Mahwah, N.J. : L. Erlbaum Associates, 1996. xvi, 288 p. : ill. ; 24 cm. Includes bibliographical references and indexes. ISBN 0-8058-1766-2 (cloth : alk. paper) ISBN 0-8058-1767-0 (pbk. : alk. paper) DDC 519.5/35
*1. Multivariate analysis. 2. Social sciences - Statistical methods. I. Lomax, Richard G. II. Title.*
**TC QA278 .S36 1996**

**Schumm, Jeanne Shay, 1947-.**
Vaughn, Sharon, 1952- Teaching exceptional, diverse, and at-risk students in the general education classroom. 2nd ed. Boston : Allyn and Bacon, 2000.

**TC LC3981 .V28 2000**

**Schuneman, Pat Ward.**
The power of idea : [videorecording]. Minneapolis, Minn. : Media Loft, c1992.
**TC TR690 .P5 1992**

Sport photography today! [videorecording]. Minneapolis, Minn. : Media Loft, c1992.
**TC TR821 .S64 1992**

**Schuneman, R. Smith.**
The filming of a television commercial [videorecording]. Minneapolis, Minn. : Media Loft, c1992.
**TC HF6146.T42 F5 1992**

The power of idea : [videorecording]. Minneapolis, Minn. : Media Loft, c1992.
**TC TR690 .P5 1992**

Sport photography today! [videorecording]. Minneapolis, Minn. : Media Loft, c1992.
**TC TR821 .S64 1992**

The sight and insight of Ernst Haas [videorecording]. Minneapolis, Minn. : Media Loft, 1992.
**TC TR647.H3 S5 1992**

**Schunk, Dale H.** Learning theories : an educational perspective / Dale H. Schunk. 3rd ed. Upper Saddle River, N.J. : Merrill, c2000. xx, 522 p. : ill. ; 25 cm. Includes bibliographical references and index. ISBN 0-13-010850-2 DDC 370.15/23
*1. Learning. 2. Cognition. 3. Learning, Psychology of. I. Title.*
**TC LB1060 .S37 2000**

**Schur, Maxine.**
**[Shnook the peddler]**
The peddler's gift / Maxine Rose Schur ; pictures by Kimberly Bulcken Root. 1st ed. New York : Dial Books for Young Readers, 1999. 1 v. (unpaged) : col. ill. ; 24 x 27 cm. SUMMARY: A young boy in turn-of-the-century rural Russia learns that appearances are often deceiving after he steals and then tries to return a dreidel to the traveling peddler Shnook. ISBN 0-8037-1978-7 (trade) DDC [Fic]
*1. Peddlers and peddling - Fiction. 2. Jews - Russia - Fiction. I. Root, Kimberly Bulcken, ill. II. Title.*
**TC PZ7.S3964 Pe 1999**

**Schurer, Heinz.** GER Bulletin [London, German educational reconstruction, 1946] 23, [1] p. 22 cm. (German educational reconstruction. [Publications] No. 5) "References and annotations": p. 23. DDC 027.443
*1. Libraries - Germany. I. Title. II. Series: German educational reconstruction. Publications. No.5.*

**Schuster, Christof.**
Eye, Alexander von. Regression analysis for social sciences. San Diego, Calif. : Academic Press, c1998.
**TC HA31.3 .E94 1998**

**Schuster, Shlomit C., 1951-** Philosophy practice : an alternative to counseling and psychotherapy / Shlomit C. Schuster. Westport, Conn. ; London : Praeger, 1999. 207 p. ; 25 cm. Includes bibliographical references (p. [187]-200) and index. ISBN 0-275-96541-4 (alk. paper) DDC 100
*1. Philosophical counseling. I. Title.*
**TC BJ1595.5 .S38 1999**

**Schutte, Nicola S. (Nicola Susanne)** Measuring emotional intelligence and related constructs / Nicola S. Schutte and John M. Malouff. Lewiston, N.Y. ; Lampeter, Wales : E. Mellen Press, c1999. ix, 212 p. ; 24 cm. Includes bibliographical references and index. ISBN 0-7734-7876-0 DDC 152.4
*1. Emotions - Measurement. 2. Emotions and cognition. 3. Emotions - Social aspects. I. Malouff, John M. II. Title.*
**TC BF576.3 .S38 1999**

**Schuyler, Gwyer.**
Trends in community college curriculum. San Francisco : Jossey-Bass, c1999.
**TC LB2328.15.U6 T75 1999**

**Schwandt, David R.** Organizational learning : from world-class theories to global best practices / David R. Schwandt, Michael J. Marquardt ; foreword by Betty S. Beene. Boca Raton, Fla. : St. Lucie Press, c2000. xviii, 258 p. : ill. ; 24 cm. Includes bibliographical references and index. ISBN 1-57444-259-7 (alk. paper) DDC 658.3/124
*1. Organizational learning. I. Marquardt, Michael J. II. Title.*
**TC HD58.82 .S39 2000**

**Schwartz, David T.** Art, education, and the democratic commitment : a defence of state support for the arts / by David T. Schwartz. Dordrecht ; Boston : Kluwer Academic Publishers, c2000. xi, 180 p. ; 25 cm. (Philosophical studies in contemporary culture ; ol. v 7) Includes bibliographical references (p. 173-180) and index. ISBN 0-7923-6292-6 (alk. paper) DDC 700/.1/03

*1. Federal aid to the arts - Philosophy. 2. Art and state - Philosophy. I. Title. II. Series.*
**TC NX720 .S33 2000**

**Schwartz, Ira M.** Kids raised by the government / Ira M. Schwartz and Gideon Fishman ; Simon Hakim, advisory editor. Westport, Conn. : Praeger, 1999. 150 p. : ill. ; 25 cm. Includes bibliographical references and index. ISBN 0-275-96264-4 (acid-free paper) DDC 362.7/0973
*1. Child welfare - United States. 2. Child welfare - Michigan. 3. Foster children - United States. 4. Foster children - Michigan. I. Fishman, Gideon. 1945- II. Title.*
**TC HV741 .S367 1999**

**Schwartz, Joseph.** Cassandra's daughter : a history of psychoanalysis / Joseph Schwartz. 1st American ed. New York : Viking, 1999. 339 p. ; 24 cm. Includes bibliographical references (p. 285-327) and index. ISBN 0-670-88623-8 DDC 150.19/5/09
*1. Psychoanalysis - History. I. Title.*
**TC BF173 .S387 1999**

**Schwartz, Peter.** The art of the long view : paths to strategic insight for yourself and your company / Peter Schwartz. 1st Currency pbk. ed. New York : Currency Doubleday ; 1996. xvi, 272 p. ; 24 cm. Includes bibliographical references (p. [256]-258) and index. ISBN 0-385-26732-0 DDC 658.4/012
*1. Strategic planning. 2. Business forecasting. 3. Organizational change - Management. I. Title.*
**TC HD30.28 .S316 1996**

**Schwartz, Peter, 1946-** When good companies do bad things : responsibility and risk in an age of globalization / Peter Schwartz and Blair Gibb. New York : John Wiley, c1999. xiv, 194 p. : ill. ; 25 cm. Includes bibliographical references (p. 183-187) and index. ISBN 0-471-32332-2 (cloth : alk. paper) DDC 658.4/08
*1. Social responsibility of business. 2. International business enterprises. I. Gibb, Blair, 1947- II. Title.*
**TC HD60 .S39 1999**

**Schwartz, Phyllis B. (Phyllis Benna).**
Critical challenges in social studies for junior high students. Burnaby, B.C. : Field Relations and Teacher In-Service Education, Faculty of Education, Simon Fraser University, 1996.
**TC D16.2 .C75 1996**

**Schwarz, Gretchen, 1952-** Teacher lore and professional development for school reform / written and edited by Gretchen Schwarz and Joye Alberts. Westport, Conn : Bergin & Garvey, 1998. xiii, 189 p. ; 25 cm. Includes bibliographical references (p. [175]-181) and index. ISBN 0-89789-509-6 (alk. paper) DDC 371.1/00973
*1. Teachers - United States. 2. Teachers - United States - Biography. 3. Storytelling - United States. 4. Teachers - In-service training - United States. 5. Educational change - United States. I. Alberts, Joye, 1951- II. Title.*
**TC LB1775.2 .S38 1998**

**Schwarz, Norbert, Dr. phil.**
Cognitive aging. Philadelphia, PA : Psychology Press, c2000.
**TC BF724.85.C64 A35 2000**

**Schwehn, Mark R., 1945-.**
Everyone a teacher. Notre Dame, Ind. : University of Notre Dame Press, c2000.
**TC LB1025.3 .E87 2000**

**Schweitzer, Robert, 1950-.**
Elphinstone, Leonie. How to get a research degree. St. Leonards, Australia : Allen & Unwin, 1998.
**TC LB2371 .E46 1998**

**Schweizer, Heidi.** Designing and teaching an on-line course : : spinning your web classroom / Heidi Schweizer. Boston : Allyn & Bacon, c1999. 121 p. : ill. ; 28 cm. Includes bibliographical references (p. 121). ISBN 0-205-30321-8
*1. Distance education. 2. Internet (Computer network) in education. 3. World Wide Web (Information retrieval system). 4. Education - Curricula - Computer network resources. 5. Educational technology. I. Title.*
**TC LB1028.3 .S377 1999**

**Schwieger, Ruben D.** Teaching elementary school mathematics : a problem-solving approach / Ruben D. Schwieger. Belmont, CA : Wadsworth Pub., 1999. xv, 365 p. : ill. ; 24 cm. Includes bibliographical references and index. ISBN 0-8273-8164-6 DDC 372.7/044
*1. Mathematics - Study and teaching (Elementary) I. Title.*
**TC QA135.5 .S329 1999**

**Schwille, John.**
Civic education across countries. Amsterdam, the Netherlands : International Association for the Evaluation of Educational Achievement, c1999.
**TC JA86 .C6 1999**

**Sci-fi aesthetics** / guest-edited by Rachel Armstrong. London : Academy Group Ltd. ; Lanham, Md. : Distributed in the USA by National Book Network, c1997. vii, [1], 88 p. : ill. (some col.) ; 30 cm. (Art & design profile ; no. 56) (Art & design, 0267-3991 ; v. 12, no. 9/10) Caption title. Includes bibliographical references. ISBN 0-471-97855-8
*1. Science fiction in art. 2. Fantasy in art. I. Armstrong, Rachel. II. Series. III. Series: Art & design, 0267-3991 ; v. 12, no. 9/10.*
*TC N8217.F28 S34 1994*

**SCIENCE.** *See also* COGNITIVE SCIENCE; COMPUTER SCIENCE; ENVIRONMENTAL SCIENCES; LIFE SCIENCES; MATHEMATICS; NATURAL HISTORY; PHYSICAL SCIENCES; TECHNOLOGY; ZOOLOGY.
Anfinson, Olaf P. Understanding the physical sciences. Boston, Allyn and Bacon, 1963.
*TC Q162 .A54*

Hogben, Lancelot Thomas,d1895- Science for the citizen; [2d ed.]. New York, W. W. Norton & Co. c1938.
*TC Q162 .H7 1938*

Mallinson, George G. Silver Burdett science. Morristown, N.J. : Silver Burdett, c1987.
*TC Q161 .M34 1987*

Silver Burdett science [grade 6]. Centennial ed. Morristown, NJ : Silver Burdett, c1985.
*TC lb*

Silver Burdett science [grade 6]. Centennial ed. Morristown, NJ : Silver Burdett, c1985.
*TC lb*

**Science & technology education library**
(v. 6) Examining pedagogical content knowledge. Dordrecht ; London : Kluwer Academic, c1999.
*TC Q181 .E93 1999*

(v. 8) Learning from others. Dordrecht [Netherlands] ; Boston : Kluwer Academic Publishers, c2000.
*TC LB43 .L42 2000*

**SCIENCE - ABILITY TESTING.**
Assessment in primary school science. London : Commonwealth Secretariat, c1998.
*TC LB1585 .A87 1998*

**Science activities for elementary students.**
Lorbeer, George C. 11th ed. Boston : McGraw-Hill, c2000.
*TC LB1585.3 .L67 2000*

**Science and cultural theory**
Oyama, Susan. Evolution's eye. Durham, NC : Duke University Press, 2000.
*TC BF713 .O93 2000*

**SCIENCE AND LAW.** *See* EVOLUTION - STUDY AND TEACHING - LAW AND LEGISLATION.

**SCIENCE AND PSYCHOLOGY.**
Empathy and agency. Boulder, Colo. ; Oxford : Westview Press, 2000.
*TC BF64 .E67 2000*

Roszak, Theodore, 1933- The gendered atom. Berkeley, Calif. : Conari Press, 1999.
*TC BF64 .R69 1999*

**SCIENCE AND SOCIETY.** *See* SCIENCE - SOCIAL ASPECTS.

**SCIENCE AND STATE.** *See also* MEDICAL POLICY.
Science, technology, and the economic future. New York : New York Academy of Sciences, c1998.
*TC HD82 .S35 1998*

**SCIENCE AND STATE - EUROPE.**
Geuna, Aldo, 1965- The economics of knowledge production. Cheltenham, UK ; Northampton, MA : E. Elgar, c1999.
*TC Q180.E9 G48 1999*

**SCIENCE AND STATE - UNITED STATES.**
Greenberg, Daniel S., 1931- The politics of pure science. New ed. / with introductory essays by John Maddox and Steven Shapin and a new afterword by the author. Chicago : University of Chicago Press, 1999.
*TC Q127.U6 G68 1999*

Guston, David H. Between politics and science. Cambridge, U.K. ; New York, NY : Cambridge University Press, 2000.

*TC Q127.U6 G87 2000*

Harnessing science and technology for America's economic future. Washington, D.C. : National Academy Press, c1999.
*TC Q127.U5 H37 1999*

**SCIENCE AND THE HUMANITIES.**
Høyrup, Jens. Human sciences. Albany, NY : State University of New York Press, c2000.
*TC AZ103 .H69 2000*

**SCIENCE, APPLIED.** *See* TECHNOLOGY.

**Science at century's end** : philosophical questions on the progress and limits of science / edited by Martin Carrier, Gerald J. Massey, and Laura Ruetsche. Pittsburgh, Pa. : University of Pittsburgh Press, c2000. xii, 385 p. : ill. ; 24 cm. (Pittsburgh-Konstanz series in philosophy and history of science) "Fourth Pittsburgh-Konstanz Colloquium held in Pittsburgh, October 3-7, 1997"--Pref. Includes bibliographical references and index. ISBN 0-8229-4121-X (alk. paper) DDC 501
*1. Science - Philosophy - Congresses. I. Carrier, Martin. II. Massey, Gerald J. III. Ruetsche, Laura. IV. Pittsburgh-Konstanz Colloquium in the Philosophy of Science (4th : 1997 : University of Pittsburgh) V. Series.*
*TC Q175 .S4193 2000*

**SCIENCE - AUTHORSHIP.** *See* TECHNICAL WRITING.

**SCIENCE - COMPUTER SIMULATION.**
Modeling and simulation in science and mathematics education. New York : Springer, c1999.
*TC Q181 .M62 1999*

**SCIENCE - DATABASES.**
SIRS researcher [computer file] [Boca Raton, Fla.] : SIRS Mandarin,
*TC NETWORKED RESOURCE*

**Science discoveries on the net.**
Fredericks, Anthony D. Englewood, Colo. : Libraries Unlimited, 2000.
*TC Q182.7 .F73 2000*

**Science experiences for the early childhood years.**
Harlan, Jean Durgin. 7th ed. Upper Saddle River, N.J. : Merrill, c2000.
*TC LB1139.5.S35 H37 2000*

**SCIENCE - EXPERIMENTS.**
Abruscato, Joseph. Whizbangers and wonderments. Boston : Allyn and Bacon, c2000.
*TC Q182.3 .A27 2000*

**SCIENCE FICTION.** *See also* INTERPLANETARY VOYAGES.
Lasky, Kathryn. Star split. 1st ed. New York : Hyperion Books for Children, 1999.
*TC PZ7.L3274 St 1999*

Tomorrowland. New York : Scholastic Press, 1999.
*TC PZ5 .T6235 1999*

**SCIENCE FICTION, AMERICAN.**
Tomorrowland. New York : Scholastic Press, 1999.
*TC PZ5 .T6235 1999*

**SCIENCE FICTION, AMERICAN - HISTORY AND CRITICISM.**
Young adult science fiction. Westport, Conn. : Greenwood Press, 1999.
*TC PS374.S35 Y63 1999*

**SCIENCE FICTION IN ART.**
Sci-fi aesthetics. London : Academy Group Ltd. ; Lanham, Md. : Distributed in the USA by National Book Network, c1997.
*TC N8217.F28 S34 1994*

**Science for all.**
Brock, W. H. (William Hodson) Brookfield, VT : Variorum, 1996.
*TC Q127.G5 B76 1996*

**Science for children.**
Jacobson, Willard J. Englewood Cliffs, N.J. : Prentice-Hall, c1980.
*TC LB1585 .J32*

**Science for the citizen.**
Hogben, Lancelot Thomas,d1895- [2d ed.]. New York, W. W. Norton & Co. c1938.
*TC Q162 .H7 1938*

**Science fun with toys.**
Sills, Thomas W. 1st ed. Chicago : Dearborn Resources, c1999.
*TC LB1029.T6 S54 1999*

**SCIENCE - GOVERNMENT POLICY.** *See* SCIENCE AND STATE.

**SCIENCE - GREAT BRITAIN - HISTORY - 19TH CENTURY.**
Brock, W. H. (William Hodson) Science for all. Brookfield, VT : Variorum, 1996.
*TC Q127.G5 B76 1996*

**SCIENCE - HISTORY.**
Hogben, Lancelot Thomas,d1895- Science for the citizen; [2d ed.]. New York, W. W. Norton & Co. c1938.
*TC Q162 .H7 1938*

**Science in the elementary and middle school.**
Wolfinger, Donna M. New York : Longman, c2000.
*TC LB1585.3 .W65 2000*

**SCIENCE - INDEXES.**
SIRS researcher [computer file] [Boca Raton, Fla.] : SIRS Mandarin,
*TC NETWORKED RESOURCE*

**SCIENCE - JUVENILE LITERATURE.** *See* NATURE STUDY.

**SCIENCE, MENTAL.** *See* PSYCHOLOGY.

**SCIENCE - METHODOLOGY.** *See also* LOGIC; SCIENTISM.
Miller, Arthur I. Insights of genius. 1st MIT Press pbk. ed. Cambridge, Mass. : MIT Press, 2000.
*TC QC6 .M44 2000*

Pearce, Charles R. Nurturing inquiry. Portsmouth, NH : Heinemann, c1999.
*TC LB1584 .P34 1999*

**SCIENCE - METHODOLOGY - EARLY WORKS TO 1800.**
Bacon, Francis, 1561-1626. The advancement of learning. Oxford : Clarendon, 2000.
*TC B1191 .K545 2000*

**SCIENCE - MISCELLANEA.**
Wynn, Charles M. The five biggest ideas in science. New York : Wiley, c1997.
*TC Q163 .W99 1997*

Wynn, Charles M. The five biggest ideas in science. New York : Wiley, c1997.
*TC Q163 .W99 1997*

**SCIENCE, MORAL.** *See* ETHICS.

**SCIENCE MUSEUMS.** *See* NATURAL HISTORY MUSEUMS.

**SCIENCE NEWS.**
Communicating science. London ; New York : Routledge in association with The Open University, 1999.
*TC Q223 .C6542 1999*

**SCIENCE OF LANGUAGE.** *See* LINGUISTICS.

**SCIENCE OF SCIENCE.** *See* SCIENCE.

**The science of self-control.**
Rachlin, Howard, 1935- Cambridge, Mass. : Harvard University Press, 2000.
*TC BF632 .R3 2000*

**SCIENCE - PERIODICALS.**
L'Enseignement des sciences. [Paris]

**SCIENCE - PHILOSOPHY.**
Ruse, Michael. Mystery of mysteries. Cambridge, Mass. : Harvard University Press, 1999.
*TC QH360.5 .R874 1999*

**SCIENCE - PHILOSOPHY - CONGRESSES.**
Science at century's end. Pittsburgh, Pa. : University of Pittsburgh Press, c2000.
*TC Q175 .S4193 2000*

**SCIENCE POLICY.** *See* SCIENCE AND STATE.

**SCIENCE, POLITICAL.** *See* POLITICAL SCIENCE.

**SCIENCE - POLITICAL ASPECTS - UNITED STATES.**
Greenberg, Daniel S., 1931- The politics of pure science. New ed. / with introductory essays by John Maddox and Steven Shapin and a new afterword by the author. Chicago : University of Chicago Press, 1999.
*TC Q127.U6 G68 1999*

**Science, politics, and universities in Europe, 1600-1800.**
Gascoigne, John, Ph. D. Aldershot [England] ; Brookfield, Vt. : Ashgate, c1998.
*TC LA621.5 .G37 1998*

**SCIENCE POLITIQUE.**
Digital democracy. Toronto ; New York : Oxford University Press, 1998.

*TC JC421 .D55 1998*

**SCIENCE - PROBLEMS, EXERCISES, ETC. - FICTION.**
Simon, Seymour. The invisible man and other cases. Rev. ed. New York : Morrow Junior Books, c1998.
*TC PZ7.S60573 In 1998*

**SCIENCE - PUBLIC OPINION - CONGRESSES.**
The thirteenth labor. Amsterdam : Gordon and Breach Publishers, c1999.
*TC Q181.3 .T45 1999*

**SCIENCE - RESEARCH.** *See* **RESEARCH.**

**SCIENCE RESEARCH.** *See* **RESEARCH.**

**SCIENCE - RESEARCH GRANTS - DIRECTORIES.**
GrantFinder. Science. New York : St. Martin's Press, c2000.
*TC LB2338 .G652 2000*

**SCIENCE - RESEARCH - STUDY AND TEACHING.**
Houser, Rick. Counseling and educational research. Thousand Oaks, Calif. : Sage Publications, c1998.
*TC Q180.A1 H595 1998*

**SCIENCE - SOCIAL ASPECTS.**
Dhingra, Koshi. An ethnographic study of the construction of science on television. 1999.
*TC 06 no. 11101*

Geisler, Eliezer, 1942- The metrics of science and technology. Westport, Conn. : Quorum Books, 2000.
*TC Q175.5 .G43 2000*

**SCIENCE - SOCIAL ASPECTS - CONGRESSES.**
The thirteenth labor. Amsterdam : Gordon and Breach Publishers, c1999.
*TC Q181.3 .T45 1999*

**SCIENCE - SOCIAL ASPECTS - GREAT BRITAIN - HISTORY - 19TH CENTURY.**
Brock, W. H. (William Hodson) Science for all. Brookfield, VT : Variorum, 1996.
*TC Q127.G5 B76 1996*

**SCIENCE STUDENTS.** *See* **WOMEN SCIENCE STUDENTS.**

**SCIENCE - STUDY AND TEACHING.** *See also* **NATURE STUDY.**
Assessing science understanding :. San Diego, Calif. London : Academic, 2000.
*TC Q181 .A87 2000*

Curriculum frameworks for mathematics and science. Vancouver, Canada : Pacific Educational Press, c1993.
*TC QA11 .C87 1993*

Dhingra, Koshi. An ethnographic study of the construction of science on television. 1999.
*TC 06 no. 11101*

Examining pedagogical content knowledge. Dordrecht : London : Kluwer Academic, c1999.
*TC Q181 .E93 1999*

Johnston, Jane, 1954- Enriching early scientific learning. Philadelphia : Open University Press, 1999.
*TC Q181 .J58 1999*

National contexts for mathematics & science education. Vancouver : Pacific Educational Press, 1997.
*TC Q181 N37 1997*

Osborne, Margery D. Examining science teaching in elementary school from the perspective of a teacher and learner. New York : Falmer Press, 1999.
*TC LB1585 .O77 1999*

Science, technology, and society. New York : Kluwer Academic/Plenum, c2000.
*TC Q181 .S38225 1999*

Tsai, Chin-Chung. The interrelationships between junior high school students' scientific epistemologicl beliefs, learning environment preferences and their cognitive structure outcomes. 1996.
*TC 06 no. 10713*

The wonderworld of science. New York : Scribner, c1952.
*TC Q161.2 .W66 1952*

**SCIENCE - STUDY AND TEACHING - ACTIVITY PROGRAMS.**
Polman, Joseph L., 1965- Designing project-based science. New York ; London : Teachers College Press, c2000.
*TC Q181 .P4694 2000*

**SCIENCE - STUDY AND TEACHING - ACTIVITY PROGRAMS - UNITED STATES - HANDBOOKS, MANUALS, ETC.**
Lorbeer, George C. Science activities for elementary students. 11th ed. Boston : McGraw-Hill, c2000.
*TC LB1585.3 .L67 2000*

**SCIENCE - STUDY AND TEACHING - AIDS AND DEVICES - PRUCHASING - UNITED STATES.**
Center for Science, Mathematics, and Engineering Education. Committee on Developing the Capacity to Select Effective Instructional Materials. Selecting instructional materials. Washington, D.C. : National Academy Press, c1999.
*TC LB1585.3 .C45 1999*

**SCIENCE - STUDY AND TEACHING - COMPUTER NETWORK RESOURCES.**
Fredericks, Anthony D. Science discoveries on the net. Englewood, Colo. : Libraries Unlimited, 2000.
*TC Q182.7 .F73 2000*

**SCIENCE - STUDY AND TEACHING - CONGRESSES.**
The thirteenth labor. Amsterdam : Gordon and Breach Publishers, c1999.
*TC Q181.3 .T45 1999*

**SCIENCE - STUDY AND TEACHING (EARLY CHILDHOOD).**
Harlan, Jean Durgin. Science experiences for the early childhood years. 7th ed. Upper Saddle River, N.J. : Merrill, c2000.
*TC LB1139.5.S35 H37 2000*

Johnston, Jane, 1954- Enriching early scientific learning. Philadelphia : Open University Press, 1999.
*TC Q181 .J58 1999*

Lind, Karen. Exploring science in early childhood. 3rd ed. Albany, NY ; London : Delmar/Thomson Learning, c2000.
*TC LB1532 .L47 2000*

Siraj-Blatchford, John, 1952- Supporting science, design and technology in the early years. Philadelphia, Pa. : Open University Press, 1999.
*TC T65.3 .S55 1999*

**SCIENCE - STUDY AND TEACHING (EARLY CHILDHOOD) - ACTIVITY PROGRAMS.**
Johnston, Jane, 1954- Enriching early scientific learning. Philadelphia : Open University Press, 1999.
*TC Q181 .J58 1999*

**SCIENCE - STUDY AND TEACHING (EARLY CHILDHOOD) - UNITED STATES.**
Dialogue on early childhood science, mathematics, and technology education. Washington, DC : American Association for the Advancement of Science/Project 2061, 1999.
*TC LB1139.5.S35 D53 1999*

**SCIENCE - STUDY AND TEACHING (ELEMENTARY).**
Abruscato, Joseph. Teaching children science. 5th ed. Boston : Allyn and Bacon, c2000.
*TC LB1585 .A29 2000*

Andersen, Christopher Lawrence. A microgenetic study of science reasoning in social context. 1998.
*TC 085 An2305*

Assessment in primary school science. London : Commonwealth Secretariat, c1998.
*TC LB1585 .A87 1998*

Biehle, James T. NSTA guide to school science facilities. Arlington, VA : National Science Teachers Association, c1999.
*TC Q183.3.A1 B54 1999*

DiscoveryWorks. Parsippany, N.J. : Silver Burdett Ginn, c1996-
*TC LB1585 .D574 1996*

DiscoveryWorks. Parsippany, N.J. : Silver Burdett Ginn, c1996
*TC LB1585 .D574 1996 Teaching Guide Gr. 4*

DiscoveryWorks. Parsippany, N.J. : Silver Burdett Ginn, c1996
*TC LB1585 .D574 1996 Teaching Guide Gr. 5*

DiscoveryWorks. Parsippany, N.J. : Silver Burdett Ginn, c1996
*TC LB1585 .D574 1996 Teaching Guide Gr. 6*

DiscoveryWorks. Parsippany, N.J. : Silver Burdett Ginn, c1996
*TC LB1585 .D574 1996 Teaching Guide Gr. 1*

DiscoveryWorks. Parsippany, N.J. : Silver Burdett Ginn, c1996

DiscoveryWorks. Parsippany, N.J. : Silver Burdett Ginn, c1996
*TC LB1585 .D574 1996 Teaching Guide Gr. 2*

DiscoveryWorks. Parsippany, N.J. : Silver Burdett Ginn, c1996
*TC LB1585 .D574 1996 Teaching Guide Gr. 3*

DiscoveryWorks. Parsippany, NJ : Silver Burdett Ginn, c1996-
*TC LB1585 .D574 1996*

DiscoveryWorks. Parsippany, N.J. : Silver Burdett Ginn, c1996-
*TC LB1585 .D574 1996 Workbook*

Pearce, Charles R. Nurturing inquiry. Portsmouth, NH : Heinemann, c1999.
*TC LB1584 .P34 1999*

Sills, Thomas W. Science fun with toys. 1st ed. Chicago : Dearborn Resources, c1999.
*TC LB1029.T6 S54 1999*

Silver Burdett science [grade 6]. Centennial ed. Morristown, NJ : Silver Burdett, c1985.
*TC lb*

Silver Burdett science [grade 6]. Centennial ed. Morristown, NJ : Silver Burdett, c1985.
*TC lb*

What is visual literacy? York, Maine : Stenhouse Pub., c1996.
*TC LB1068 .W45 1996*

**SCIENCE - STUDY AND TEACHING (ELEMENTARY) - COMPUTER NETWORK RESOURCES.**
The Internet in action for math & science K-6 [videorecording]. [New York] : Thirteen-WNET ; [Alexandria, Va. : distributed by] PBS Video, c1998.
*TC LB1044.87 .I45 1998*

**SCIENCE - STUDY AND TEACHING (ELEMENTARY) - HANDBOOK, MANUALS, ETC.**
Jacobson, Willard J. Science for children. Englewood Cliffs, N.J. : Prentice-Hall, c1980.
*TC LB1585 .J32*

**SCIENCE - STUDY AND TEACHING (ELEMENTARY) - UNITED STATES.**
Exploring science in the library. Chicago : American Library Association, 2000.
*TC Z675.S3 E97 2000*

Hall, Jody S. Organizing wonder. Portsmouth, NH : Heinemann, c1998.
*TC LB1585.3 .H35 1998*

Martin, David Jerner. Elementary science methods. 2nd ed. Belmont, CA : Wadsworth, c2000.
*TC LB1585.3 .M37 2000*

Wolfinger, Donna M. Science in the elementary and middle school. New York : Longman, c2000.
*TC LB1585.3 .W65 2000*

**SCIENCE - STUDY AND TEACHING (ELEMENTARY) - UNITED STATES - HANDBOOKS, MANUALS, ETC.**
Lorbeer, George C. Science activities for elementary students. 11th ed. Boston : McGraw-Hill, c2000.
*TC LB1585.3 .L67 2000*

**SCIENCE - STUDY AND TEACHING - EUROPE - CONGRESSES.**
The challenges of science education. Strasbourg : Council of Europe Pub., c1999.
*TC Q183.4.E85 C475 1999*

**SCIENCE - STUDY AND TEACHING - GREAT BRITAIN - HISTORY - 19TH CENTURY.**
Brock, W. H. (William Hodson) Science for all. Brookfield, VT : Variorum, 1996.
*TC Q127.G5 B76 1996*

**SCIENCE - STUDY AND TEACHING (HIGHER) - ACTIVITY PROGRAMS.**
Samuels, Linda S. Girls can succeed in science!. Thousand Oaks, Calif. : Corwin Press, c1999.
*TC Q181 .S19 1999*

**SCIENCE - STUDY AND TEACHING (HIGHER) - UNITED STATES.**
Roberts, Jon H. The sacred and the secular university. Princeton, N.J. : Princeton University Press, c2000.
*TC LA636.7 .R62 2000*

Transforming undergraduate education in science, mathematics, engineering, and technology. Washington, DC : National Academy Press, 1999.

*TC Q183.3.A1 T73 1999*

**SCIENCE - STUDY AND TEACHING (MIDDLE SCHOOL) - CASE STUDIES.**
Cases in middle and secondary science education. Upper Saddle River, N.J. : Merrill, c2000.
*TC Q181 .C348 2000*

**SCIENCE - STUDY AND TEACHING (MIDDLE SCHOOL) - COMPUTER NETWORK RESOURCES.**
The Internet in action for math & science 7-12 [videorecording]. [New York] : Thirteen-WNET ; [Alexandria, Va. : distributed by] PBS Video, c1997.
*TC LB1044.87 .I453 1997*

The Internet in action for math & science K-6 [videorecording]. [New York] : Thirteen-WNET ; [Alexandria, Va. : distributed by] PBS Video, c1998.
*TC LB1044.87 .I45 1998*

**SCIENCE - STUDY AND TEACHING (MIDDLE SCHOOL) - UNITED STATES.**
Hibbard, K. Michael. Performance-based learning and assessment in middle school science. Larchmont, NY : Eye On Education, 2000.
*TC Q181 .H52 2000*

**SCIENCE - STUDY AND TEACHING (MIDDLE SCHOOL) - UNITED STATES.**
Hurd, Paul DeHart, 1905- Transforming middle school science education. New York : Teachers College Press, c2000.
*TC LB1585.3 .H89 2000*

**SCIENCE - STUDY AND TEACHING (MIDDLE SCHOOL) - UNITED STATES.**
Wolfinger, Donna M. Science in the elementary and middle school. New York : Longman, c2000.
*TC LB1585.3 .W65 2000*

**SCIENCE - STUDY AND TEACHING (MIDDLE SCHOOL) - UNITED STATES - CASE STUDIES.**
Linn, Marcia C. Computers, teachers, peers. Mahwah, N.J. : L. Erlbaum Associates, 2000.
*TC LB1585.3 .L56 2000*

**SCIENCE - STUDY AND TEACHING - PHILOSOPHY.**
Constructivism in science education. Dordrecht ; Boston : Kluwer Academic, c1998.
*TC Q181 .C612 1998*

**SCIENCE - STUDY AND TEACHING (PRESCHOOL) - UNITED STATES.**
Martin, David Jerner. Elementary science methods. 2nd ed. Belmont, CA : Wadsworth, c2000.
*TC LB1585.3 .M37 2000*

**SCIENCE - STUDY AND TEACHING (PRIMARY).**
Charlesworth, Rosalind. Math and science for young children. 3rd ed. Albany, NY : Delmar Publishers, c1999.
*TC QA135.5 .C463 1999*

Lind, Karen. Exploring science in early childhood. 3rd ed. Albany, NY ; London : Delmar/Thomson Learning, c2000.
*TC LB1532 .L47 2000*

**SCIENCE - STUDY AND TEACHING - RESEARCH.**
Handbook of research design in mathematics and science education. Mahwah, N.J. : Lawrence Erlbaum, 1999.
*TC QA11 .H256 1999*

Practical work in science education :. 1. ed. Frederiksberg, Denmark : Roskilde University Press ; Dordrecht, Holland : Kluwer Acdemic, 1999.
*TC Q181 .P73 1999*

**SCIENCE - STUDY AND TEACHING - RESEARCH - EUROPE.**
Research in science education in Europe. Dordrecht ; Boston, Mass. : Kluwer Academic Publishers, c1999.
*TC Q183.4.E85 R467 1999*

**SCIENCE - STUDY AND TEACHING (SECONDARY).**
Biehle, James T. NSTA guide to school science facilities. Arlington, VA : National Science Teachers Association, c1999.
*TC Q183.3.A1 B54 1999*

Connecting mathematics and science to workplace contexts. Thousand Oaks, Calif. : Corwin Press, c1999.
*TC QA11 .C655 1999*

Modeling and simulation in science and mathematics education. New York : Springer, c1999.

*TC Q181 .M62 1999*

**SCIENCE - STUDY AND TEACHING (SECONDARY) - ACTIVITY PROGRAMS.**
Samuels, Linda S. Girls can succeed in science!. Thousand Oaks, Calif. : Corwin Press, c1999.
*TC Q181 .S19 1999*

**SCIENCE - STUDY AND TEACHING (SECONDARY) - CASE STUDIES.**
Cases in middle and secondary science education. Upper Saddle River, N.J. : Merrill, c2000.
*TC Q181 .C348 2000*

Wiltshire, Michael A. Integrating mathematics and science for below average ninth grade students. 1997.
*TC 06 no. 10847*

**SCIENCE - STUDY AND TEACHING (SECONDARY) - COMPUTER NETWORK RESOURCES.**
The Internet in action for math & science 7-12 [videorecording]. [New York] : Thirteen-WNET ; [Alexandria, Va. : distributed by] PBS Video, c1997.
*TC LB1044.87 .I453 1997*

**SCIENCE - STUDY AND TEACHING (SECONDARY) - METHODOLOGY.**
Polman, Joseph L., 1965- Designing project-based science. New York ; London : Teachers College Press, c2000.
*TC Q181 .P4694 2000*

**SCIENCE - STUDY AND TEACHING (SECONDARY) - TAIWAN - RESEARCH.**
Yang, Fang-Ying. An analysis of 12th grade students' reasoning styles and competencies when presented with an environmental problem in a social and scientific context. 1999.
*TC 06 no. 11076*

**SCIENCE - STUDY AND TEACHING (SECONDARY) - UNITED STATES - CASE STUDIES.**
Linn, Marcia C. Computers, teachers, peers. Mahwah, N.J. : L. Erlbaum Associates, 2000.
*TC LB1585.3 .L56 2000*

**SCIENCE - STUDY AND TEACHING - STANDARDS - UNITED STATES.**
Inquiry and the National Science Education Standards. Washington, D.C. : National Academy Press, c2000.
*TC LB1585.3 .I57 2000*

**SCIENCE - STUDY AND TEACHING - TECHNOLOGICAL INNOVATIONS.**
Innovations in science and mathematics education. Mahwah, N.J. : L. Erlbaum, 2000.
*TC Q181 .I654 1999*

**SCIENCE - STUDY AND TEACHING - UNITED STATES.**
Bybee, Rodger W. Achieving scientific literacy. Portsmouth, NH : Heinemann, c1997.
*TC Q183.3.A1 B92 1997*

Designing mathematics or science curriculum programs. Washington, D.C. : National Academy Press, 1999.
*TC Q183.3.A1 D46 1999*

Enhancing program quality in science and mathematics. Thousand Oaks, Calif. : Corwin Press, c1999.
*TC LB1585.3 .E55 1999*

Facing the consequences. Dordrecht ; Boston : Kluwer Academic Publishers, c1999.
*TC QA13 .F33 1999*

Global perspectives for local action. Washington, D.C. : National Academy Press, 1999.
*TC LB1583.3 .G56 1999*

Lynch, Sharon J. Equity and science education reform. Mahwah, N.J. ; London : L. Erlbaum Associates, 2000.
*TC LB1585.3 .L96 2000*

Rhoton, Jack Issues in science education. Arlington, Va. National Science Teachers Association: National Science Education Leadership Association, c1997.
*TC Q181 .R56 1996*

**SCIENCE - STUDY AND TEACHING - UNITED STATES - AIDS AND DEVICES.**
Center for Science, Mathematics, and Engineering Education. Committee on Developing the Capacity to Select Effective Instructional Materials. Selecting instructional materials. Washington, D.C. : National Academy Press, c1999.
*TC LB1585.3 .C45 1999*

**SCIENCE - STUDY AND TEAHCING (ELEMENTARY).**
Holt science. New York : Holt, Rinehart and Winston, c1986.
*TC Q161.2 .A27 1986*

Holt science. New York : Holt, Rinehart and Winston, c1986.
*TC Q161.2 .A27 1986*

**SCIENCE TEACHERS - IN-SERVICE TRAINING - UNITED STATES.**
Enhancing program quality in science and mathematics. Thousand Oaks, Calif. : Corwin Press, c1999.
*TC LB1585.3 .E55 1999*

**SCIENCE TEACHERS - TRAINING OF.**
Examining pedagogical content knowledge. Dordrecht ; London : Kluwer Academic, c1999.
*TC Q181 .E93 1999*

Johnston, Jane, 1954- Enriching early scientific learning. Philadelphia : Open University Press, 1999.
*TC Q181 .J58 1999*

**SCIENCE TEACHERS - TRAINING OF - HANDBOOKS, MANUALS, ETC.**
Samuels, Linda S. Girls can succeed in science!. Thousand Oaks, Calif. : Corwin Press, c1999.
*TC Q181 .S19 1999*

**Science, technology, and society :** a sourcebook on research and practice / edited by David D. Kumar and Daryl E. Chubin. New York : Kluwer Academic/ Plenum, c2000. xii, 308 p. : ill. ; 23 cm. (Innovations in science education and technology) Includes bibliographical references and index. ISBN 0-306-46173-0 DDC 303.48/3
*1. Science - Study and teaching. I. Kumar, David D. II. Chubin, Daryl E. III. Series.*
*TC Q181 .S38225 1999*

**Science, technology, and the economic future** / edited by Susan U. Raymond. New York : New York Academy of Sciences, c1998. xi, 224 p. : ill. ; 23 cm. ISBN 1-57331-147-2
*1. Economic development. 2. Economic policy. 3. Science and state. I. Raymond, Susan Ueber.*
*TC HD82 .S35 1998*

**SCIENCE - UNITED STATES - COMPUTER-ASSISTED INSTRUCTION.**
Network science, a decade later. Mahwah, N.J. : Lawrence Erlbaum, 2000.
*TC LB1583.3 .N48 2000*

**SCIENCE - UNITED STATES - ECONOMIC ASPECTS.**
Harnessing science and technology for America's economic future. Washington, D.C. : National Academy Press, c1999.
*TC Q127.U5 H37 1999*

**ScienceDirect.**
[Computers in human behavior (Online)] Computers in human behavior [computer file]. New York : Elsevier Science,
*TC EJOURNALS*

**Sciencedirect.**
[Economics of education review (Online)] Economics of education review [computer file]. Oxford ; New York : Pergamon,
*TC EJOURNALS*

**ScienceDirect.**
[English for specific purposes (New York, N.Y. : Online)] English for specific purposes [computer file]. Oxford ; New York : Pergamon,
*TC EJOURNALS*

**Sciencedirect.**
[International journal of educational development (Online)] International journal of educational development [computer file]. Oxford ; New York : Pergamon,
*TC EJOURNALS*

**SCIENCES.** *See* **SCIENCE.**

**SCIENCES DE LA POLITIQUE.**
Digital democracy. Toronto ; New York : Oxford University Press, 1998.
*TC JC421 .D55 1998*

**Sciences et L'Enseignement des sciences.**
L'Enseignement des sciences. [Paris]

**SCIENCES, LIFE.** *See* **LIFE SCIENCES.**

**SCIENCES, SOCIAL.** *See* **SOCIAL SCIENCES.**

**SCIENCES SOCIALES - ÉTUDE ET ENSEIGNEMENT.**
The Canadian anthology of social studies. Vancouver : Pacific Educational Press, c1999.

## TC H62.5.C3 C32 1999

**SCIENCES SOCIALES - ÉTUDE ET ENSEIGNEMENT - CANADA.**
Trends & issues in Canadian social studies. Vancouver : Pacific Educational Press, c1997.
*TC LB1584.5.C3 T74 1997*

**Scientific discovery processes in humans and computers.**
Wagman, Morton. Westport. CT : Praeger, 2000.
*TC Q180.55.D57 W34 2000*

**SCIENTIFIC EDUCATION.** *See* SCIENCE - STUDY AND TEACHING.

**SCIENTIFIC ENGLISH.** *See* ENGLISH LANGUAGE - TECHNICAL ENGLISH.

**Scientific foundations of cognitive theory and therapy of depression.**
Clark. David A., 1954- New York : John Wiley, c1999.
*TC RC537 .C53 1999*

**SCIENTIFIC MANAGEMENT.** *See* INDUSTRIAL MANAGEMENT.

**SCIENTIFIC METHOD.** *See* SCIENCE - METHODOLOGY.

**Scientific psychology series**
Recent progress in mathematical psychology. Mahwah, N.J. : L. Erlbaum, 1998.
*TC BF39 .R35 1998*

Uttal, William R. The war between mentalism and behaviorism. Mahwah, N.J. ; London : Lawrence Erlbaum Associates, Publishers, 2000.
*TC BF199 .U77 2000*

**SCIENTIFIC RESEARCH.** *See* RESEARCH.

**SCIENTIFIC WRITING.** *See* TECHNICAL WRITING.

**Scientific writing and publishing in English in Thailand.**
Pupipat, Apisak. 1998.
*TC 06 no. 10981*

**The scientification of love.**
Odent, Michel, 1930- London ; New York : Free Association Books, 1999.
*TC BF575.L8 O33 1999*

**SCIENTISM - POLITICAL ASPECTS.**
Knowledge and power in higher education. New York : London : Teachers College Press, c2000.
*TC LC171 .K62 2000*

**The scientist in the crib.**
Gopnik, Alison. New York : William Morrow & Co., 1999.
*TC BF311 .G627 1999*

**Scientist-practitioner perspectives on test interpretation** / edited by James W. Lichtenberg, Rodney K. Goodyear. Boston, Mass. : Allyn and Bacon, c1999, xv, 192 p. : ill. ; 23 cm. Includes bibliographical references and indexes. ISBN 0-205-17481-7 DDC 150/.28/7
*1. Psychological tests - Interpretation. I. Lichtenberg. James W. II. Goodyear, Rodney K.*
*TC BF176 .S37 1999*

**SCIENTISTS.** *See also* ANTHROPOLOGISTS; LIFE SCIENTISTS; MATHEMATICIANS; SOCIAL SCIENTISTS; WOMEN SCIENTISTS.
Ruse, Michael. Mystery of mysteries. Cambridge, Mass. : Harvard University Press, 1999.
*TC QH360.5 .R874 1999*

**SCIENTISTS - DISCIPLINE.**
Perspectives on scholarly misconduct in the sciences. Columbus : Ohio State University Press, c1999.
*TC Q147 .P47 1999*

**SCIENTISTS - EUROPE - BIOGRAPHY.**
Gascoigne, John, Ph. D. Science, politics, and universities in Europe, 1600-1800. Aldershot [England] ; Brookfield, Vt. : Ashgate, c1998.
*TC LA621.5 .G37 1998*

**SCIENTISTS - MORAL AND ETHICAL ASPECTS.**
Perspectives on scholarly misconduct in the sciences. Columbus : Ohio State University Press, c1999.
*TC Q147 .P47 1999*

**SCIENTISTS - THAILAND.**
Pupipat, Apisak. Scientific writing and publishing in English in Thailand. 1998.
*TC 06 no. 10981*

**SCIENTISTS - VOCATIONAL GUIDANCE.**
Enhancing the postdoctoral experience for scientists and engineers. Washington, DC : National Academy Press, 2000.
*TC Q147 .E53 2000*

**SCOPES, JOHN THOMAS - TRIALS, LITIGATION, ETC.**
Larson, Edward J. (Edward John) Summer for the gods. New York : BasicBooks, c1997.
*TC KF224.S3 L37 1997*

**SCOTLAND - HISTORY - 18TH CENTURY - FICTION.**
Curry, Jane Louise. A Stolen life. New York : McElderry Books, 1999.
*TC PZ7.C936 St 1999*

**The Scott and Laurie Oki series in Asian American studies**
Okihiro, Gary Y., 1945- Stories lives. Seattle : University of Washington Press, 1999.
*TC D753.8 .O38 1999*

**Scott, Jack, Ph.D.** Students with autism : characteristics and instructional programming for special educators / by Jack Scott, Claudia Clark, and Michael Brady. San Diego : Singular Pub. Group, 2000. xi, 435 p. ; 23 cm. Includes bibliographical references and index. ISBN 1-56593-630-2 (softcover : alk. paper) DDC 371.94
*1. Autistic children - Education - United States. 2. Autism - United States. I. Clark, Claudia, 1950- II. Brady, Michael P. III. Title.*
*TC LC4718 .S36 2000*

**Scott, Michael (Michael G.).**
Educating entrepreneurs for wealth creation. Aldershot, Hants, England ; Brookfield, USA : Ashgate, 1998.
*TC HF1106 .E378 1998*

**Scott, Randolph.**
Ballroom dancing for beginners [videorecording]. W. Long Branch, N.J. Kultur, c1993.
*TC GV1753.7 .B3 1993*

Ballroom dancing for beginners [videorecording]. W. Long Branch, N.J. Kultur, c1993.
*TC GV1753.7 .B3 1993*

**Scott, Ray.**
Sport photography today! [videorecording]. Minneapolis, Minn. : Media Loft, c1992.
*TC TR821 .S64 1992*

**Scotti, Joseph R.**
Behavioral intervention. Baltimore, Md. : Paul H. Brookes Pub., c1999.
*TC BF637.B4 B452 1999*

**Scottish education** / edited by T.G.K. Bryce and W.M. Humes. Edinburgh : Edinburgh University Press, c1999. xvi, 1040 p. : 25 cm. Includes bibliographical references and index. ISBN 0-7486-0980-6 ISBN 0-7486-0980-6 DDC 370/.9411
*1. Education - Scotland. 2. School management and organization - Scotland. 3. Education and state - Scotland. I. Bryce. T. G. K. II. Humes. Walter M.*
*TC LA652 .S34 1999*

**SCRAPBOOKS.**
Wright-Frierson, Virginia. A North American rain forest scrapbook. New York : Walker and Co., 1999.
*TC QH105.W2 W75 1999*

**SCREEN PRINTING.** *See* SERIGRAPHY.

**Screen printing** [videorecording] / produced and directed, Gavin Nettleton ; written by Harvey Daniels, Terry Gravett, Gavin Nettleton ; produced by Brighton Polytechnic Media Services. [Northbrook?], Ill. ; Peasmarsh, East Sussex, Eng. : Roland Collection of Films on Art, c1992. 1 videocassette (33 min.) : sd., col. ; 1/2 in. Title on cassette label: Screenprinting [videorecording]. At head of title: Anthony Roland Collection of Films on Art. VHS. Catalogued from credits, cassette label and container. Narrator, Barbara Myers. Graphics by Judy Herbert. Addresses of the Roland Collection on container: Ho-Ho-Kus, N.J. and Peasmarsh, East Sussex, Eng. For students of screen printing. SUMMARY: Follows the creation of a work. Covers the use of basic equipment, stencils, direct photo emulsion, washing and preparing the mesh, applying the emulsion, exposing it in the print down frame with UV light and then washing out the unexposed areas, retouching and printing the next color, inks and bases for printing, racking and removal of the stencil and cleaning the screen. Shows the work of Brendan Neilan, Sue Gollifer, Terry Gravett and Harvey Daniels.
*1. Serigraphy - Technique. 2. Serigraphy - 20th century - Great Britain. 3. Prints - Technique. 4. Prints - 20th century - Great Britain. 5. Art, Modern - 20th century - Great Britain. I. Daniels, Harvey, 1936- II. Gravett, Terry. III. Nettleton, Gavin. rt IV. Myers, Barbara. V. Neilan, Brendan. VI. Gollifer, Sue.*

*VII. Gravett, Terry. VIII. Daniels, Harvey, 1936- IX. Anthony Roland Collection of Film on Art. X. Brighton Polytechnic. Media Services. XI. Title: Screenprinting [videorecording] XII. Title: Anthony Roland Collection of Films on Art*
*TC NE2238.G7 S4 1992*

**Screenprinting [videorecording].**
Screen printing [videorecording]. [Northbrook?], Ill. ; Peasmarsh, East Sussex, Eng. : Roland Collection of Films on Art, c1992.
*TC NE2238.G7 S4 1992*

**Scribble scrabble - teaching children to become successful readers and writers.**
Meier, Daniel R. New York : Teachers College Press, c2000.
*TC LB1140.5.L3 M45 2000*

**Scribner, Jay Paredes, 1963-.**
Case studies of the superintendency. Lanham, Md. : Scarecrow Press, c2000.
*TC LB2831.72 .C38 2000*

**Scrimshaw, Susan.**
Handbook of social studies in health and medicine. London ; Thousand Oaks, Calif. : Sage Publications, 2000.
*TC RA418 .H36 2000*

**Scripts, grooves, and writing machines.**
Gitelman, Lisa. Stanford, Calif. : Stanford University Press, c1999.
*TC P96.T422 U6343*

**Scriptwriting for the audio-visual media.**
Edmonds, Robert. New York : Teachers College Press, c1978.
*TC PN1991.7 .E3*

**SCROLLS, JAPANESE - EXHIBITIONS.**
Twelve centuries of Japanese art from the Imperial collections. Washington, DC : Freer Gallery of Art and the Arthur M. Sackler Gallery, Smithsonian Institution Press, c1997.
*TC ND1457.J32 W377 1997*

**SCROLLS - PRIVATE COLLECTIONS - JAPAN - EXHIBITIONS.**
Twelve centuries of Japanese art from the Imperial collections. Washington, DC : Freer Gallery of Art and the Arthur M. Sackler Gallery, Smithsonian Institution Press, c1997.
*TC ND1457.J32 W377 1997*

**Scruton, Roger.** The aesthetic understanding : essays in the philosophy of art and culture / Roger Scruton. South Bend, Ind. : St. Augustine's Press, 1998. 286 p. : ill. ; 23 cm. (Carthage reprint) Originally published: London ; New York : Methuen, 1983. Includes bibliographical references and index. ISBN 1-89031-802-7 (pbk. : alk. paper) DDC 111/.85
*1. Aesthetics. I. Title. II. Series.*
*TC BH39 .S38 1998*

Art and imagination : a study in the philosophy of mind / Roger Scruton. South Bend, Ind. : St. Augustine's Press, 1998. viii, 256 p. : ill. ; 24 cm. Originally published: London : Methuen, 1974. Includes bibliographical references (p. [250]-253) and index. ISBN 1-89031-800-0 (cloth : alk. paper) DDC 111/.85
*1. Judgment (Aesthetics) 2. Philosophy of mind. 3. Empiricism. I. Title.*
*TC BH301.J8 S37 1998*

**Scudder, John R., 1926-.**
Bishop, Anne H., 1935- Nursing ethics. 2nd ed. Sudbury, Mass. : Jones and Bartlett, c2001.
*TC RT85 .B57 2001*

**Scudder, Rogers V.**
Jenney, Charles. First year Latin workbook. Newton, Mass. : Allyn and Bacon, c1987.
*TC PA2087.5 .J46 1987*

Jenney, Charles. Fourth year Latin. Needham, Mass. : Prentice Hall, c1990.
*TC PA2087.5 .J463 1990*

Jenney, Charles. Third year Latin. Newton, Mass. : Allyn and Bacon, c1987.
*TC PA2087.5 .J462 1987*

**SCULPTORS.** *See* WOMEN SCULPTORS.

**SCULPTORS - FICTION.**
Sappey, Maureen Stack, 1952- Letters from Vinnie. Asheville, NC : Front Street, 1999.
*TC PZ7.S2388 Le 1999*

**SCULPTORS - FRANCE - BIOGRAPHY.**
Picasso [videorecording]. Chicago, IL : Home Vision, c1986.
*TC N6853.P5 P52 1986*

**SCULPTORS - SPAIN - BIOGRAPHY.**
Picasso [videorecording]. Chicago, IL : Home Vision,
c1986.
*TC N6853.P5 P52 1986*

**SCULPTORS - UNITED STATES - BIOGRAPHY.**
Nevelson in process [videorecording]. Chicago, IL :
Public Media Inc., 1977.
*TC NB237.N43 N43 1977*

**SCULPTRESSES.** *See* **WOMEN SCULPTORS.**

**SCULPTURE.** *See* **MONUMENTS; PUBLIC
SCULPTURE.**

**SCULPTURE, AFRICAN - EXHIBITIONS.**
Sieber, Roy, 1923- African art in the cycle of life.
Washington, D.C. : Published for the National
Museum of African Art by the Smithsonian Press,
c1987.
*TC NB1091.65 .S54 1987*

**SCULPTURE, AMERICAN.**
Dabakis, Melissa. Visualizing labor in American
sculpture. New York : Cambridge University Press,
1999.
*TC NB1952.L33 D24 1999*

**SCULPTURE AND LITERATURE.** *See* **ART AND
LITERATURE.**

**Sculpture and photography** : envisioning the third
dimension / edited by Geraldine A. Johnson.
Cambridge, [England] ; New York : Cambridge
University Press, 1998. xvi, 255 p. : ill. ; 26 cm. Includes
bibliographical references and index. ISBN 0-521-62137-2
(hardback) DDC 779/.973
*1. Photography of sculpture. 2. Photography - History. I.
Johnson, Geraldine A.*
*TC TR658.3 .S38 1998*

**SCULPTURE - AUSTRALIA.**
Hedger, Michael. Public sculpture in Australia.
Roseville East, NSW : Distributed by Craftsman
House ; United States : G+B Arts International,
c1995.
*TC NB1100 .H44 1995*

**SCULPTURE, BLACK - MEXICO -
EXHIBITIONS.**
Catlett, Elizabeth, 1915- Elizabeth Catlett sculpture.
[Purchase, N.Y.] : Neuberger Museum of Art,
Purchase College, State University of New York :
Seattle : Distributed by University of Washington
Press, c1998.
*TC NB259.C384 A4 1998*

**SCULPTURE, MODERN - 19TH CENTURY -
UNITED STTES.**
Dabakis, Melissa. Visualizing labor in American
sculpture. New York : Cambridge University Press,
1999.
*TC NB1952.L33 D24 1999*

**SCULPTURE, MODERN - 20TH CENTURY -
FRANCE.**
Picasso [videorecording]. Chicago, IL : Home Vision,
c1986.
*TC N6853.P5 P52 1986*

**SCULPTURE, MODERN - 20TH CENTURY -
SPAIN.**
Picasso [videorecording]. Chicago, IL : Home Vision,
c1986.
*TC N6853.P5 P52 1986*

**SCULPTURE, MODERN - 20TH CENTURY -
UNITED STATES.**
Dabakis, Melissa. Visualizing labor in American
sculpture. New York : Cambridge University Press,
1999.
*TC NB1952.L33 D24 1999*

Nevelson in process [videorecording]. Chicago, IL :
Public Media Inc., 1977.
*TC NB237.N43 N43 1977*

**SCULPTURE, PRIMITIVE - AFRICA, SUB-
SAHARAN - EXHIBITIONS.**
Sieber, Roy, 1923- African art in the cycle of life.
Washington, D.C. : Published for the National
Museum of African Art by the Smithsonian Press,
c1987.
*TC NB1091.65 .S54 1987*

**SCULPTURE, PRIMITIVE - CÔTE D'IVOIRE.**
Ravenhill, Philip L. Dreams and reverie. Washington :
Smithsonian Institution Press, c1996.
*TC NB1255.C85 R38 1996*

**SCULPTURE, PRIMITIVE - GHANA.**
Fagg, William Buller. Yoruba, sculpture of West
Africa. 1st ed. New York : Knopf : Distributed by
Random House, 1982.

*TC NB1099.N5 F34*

**SCULPTURE, PRIMITIVE - NIGERIA.**
Fagg, William Buller. Yoruba, sculpture of West
Africa. 1st ed. New York : Knopf : Distributed by
Random House, 1982.
*TC NB1099.N5 F34*

**SCULPTURE, PRIMITIVE - TOGO.**
Fagg, William Buller. Yoruba, sculpture of West
Africa. 1st ed. New York : Knopf : Distributed by
Random House, 1982.
*TC NB1099.N5 F34*

**SCULPTURE, PUBLIC.** *See* **PUBLIC
SCULPTURE.**

**SCULPTURE, YORUBA.**
Fagg, William Buller. Yoruba, sculpture of West
Africa. 1st ed. New York : Knopf : Distributed by
Random House, 1982.
*TC NB1099.N5 F34*

**Scutt, William R.**
The violin [videorecording]. Van Nuys, CA :
Backstage Pass Productions ; Canoga Park, Calif. :
[Distributed by] MVP, c1998.
*TC MT265 .V5 1998*

**SEA-FISHERIES.** *See* **FISHERIES.**

**SEA LIFE.** *See* **SEAFARING LIFE.**

**SEA POETRY.**
Livingston, Myra Cohn. Sea songs. 1st ed. New
York : Holiday House, c1986.
*TC PS3562.I945 S4 1986*

**SEA POETRY, AMERICAN.**
Livingston, Myra Cohn. Sea songs. 1st ed. New
York : Holiday House, c1986.
*TC PS3562.I945 S4 1986*

**SEA-SHORE.** *See* **SEASHORE.**

**Sea songs.**
Livingston, Myra Cohn. 1st ed. New York : Holiday
House, c1986.
*TC PS3562.I945 S4 1986*

**Seabrook, John.** Nobrow : the culture of marketing, the
marketing of culture / John Seabrook. 1st ed. New
York : A.A. Knopf ; Distributed by Random House,
2000. 215 p. ; 22 cm. ISBN 0-375-40504-6 (cloth) ISBN
0-375-70451-5 (pbk.) DDC 302.23/0973
*1. Mass media and culture - United States. 2. Popular culture -
United States. I. Title.*
*TC P94.65.U6 S4 2000*

**Seabury, Marcia Bundy.**
Interdisciplinary general education. New York, NY :
College Board Publications, c1999.
*TC LB2361 .I43 1999*

**SEAFARING LIFE.**
Jernegan, Laura, b. 1862. A whaling captain's
daughter. Mankato, Minn. : Blue Earth Books, c2000.
*TC G545 .J47 2000*

**SEAFARING LIFE - JUVENILE LITERATURE.**
Jernegan, Laura, b. 1862. A whaling captain's
daughter. Mankato, Minn. : Blue Earth Books, c2000.
*TC G545 .J47 2000*

**Seagull beach.**
Wallace, Karen. A day at Seagull beach. 1st American
ed. New York : DK Pub., 1999.
*TC PZ10.3.W1625 Se 1999*

**SEAMEN.** *See* **SAILORS.**

**Sean's story** [videorecording] : a lesson in life / ABC
News ; produced by Michelle Riordan Read ; directed
by Roger Goodman ; senior producer, Rudy Bednar ;
writer, Ed Fields ; a presentation of Films for the
Humanities & Sciences. Princeton, N.J. : Films for the
Humanities & Sciences ; [S.l. : distributed by] ABC
Multimedia : Capital Cities/ABC, c1994. 1 videocassette
(52 min.) : sd., col. ; 1/2 in. VHS. Catalogued from credits and
container. Originally produced for the television program
Turning point. Reporter: Meredith Vieira. Photographs, Gino
Bruno; editor, Sharon Kaufman. For high school and adult
viewers. SUMMARY: Reports on the issue of the inclusion of
mentally and physically challenged children in the Baltimore
County (Maryland) public school system. Sean Begg, an
eight-year-old boy with Down's syndrome, is followed through
first grade in a public school; his experience is contrasted to
that of Bobby Shriver, also with Down's syndrome, who stays
in a special education school.
*1. Inclusive education - Maryland. 2. Mainstreaming in
education - Maryland. 3. Mentally handicapped children -
Education (Elementary) - Maryland. 4. Handicapped children -
Education (Elementary) - Maryland. 5. Down syndrome -
Maryland. 6. Documentary television programs. I. Vieira,
Meredith. II. Goodman, Roger. III. Read, Michelle Riordan.*

*IV. Bednar, Rudy. V. Fields, Ed. VI. ABC News. VII. Films for
the Humanities (firm) VIII. ABC Multimedia. IX. Capital
Cities/ABC, Inc. X. Title: Turning point (Television program)
XI. Title: Lesson in life [videorecording]*
*TC LC1203.M3 .S39 1994*

**Search for the real.**
Hofmann, Hans, 1880-1966. [Rev. ed.]. Cambridge,
Mass., M.I.T. Press [c1967]
*TC N7445 .H76 1967*

Hofmann, Hans, 1880-1966. [Rev. ed.]. Cambridge,
Mass., M.I.T. Press [c1967]
*TC N7445 .H76 1967*

**Searight, H. Russell.**
Parent articles about ADHD. San Antonio, Texas :
Communication Skill Builders, c1999.
*TC RJ506.H9 P37 1999*

**Searle, Dennis.**
Hughes, Margaret, 1941- The violent E and other
tricky sounds. York, Me. : Stenhouse Publishers ;
Markham, Ontario : Pembroke Publishers Limited,
c1997.
*TC LB1574 .H84 1997*

**Sears, A. M. (Alan Murray), 1954-.**
Trends & issues in Canadian social studies.
Vancouver : Pacific Educational Press, c1997.
*TC LB1584.5.C3 T74 1997*

**Sears, James T. (James Thomas), 1951-.**
Marshall, J. Dan. Turning points in curriculum. Upper
Saddle River, N.J. : Merrill, c2000.
*TC LB1570 .M36675 2000*

Queering elementary education. Lanham, Md. ;
Oxford : Rowman & Littlefield, c1999.
*TC LC192.6 .Q85 1999*

**SEASHORE - FICTION.**
Wallace, Karen. A day at Seagull beach. 1st American
ed. New York : DK Pub., 1999.
*TC PZ10.3.W1625 Se 1999*

**SEASONS - JUVENILE POETRY.**
Jacobs, Leland B. (Leland Blair), 1907- Just around
the corner. New York : H. Holt, 1993.
*TC PS3560.A2545 J87 1993*

Livingston, Myra Cohn. Cricket never does. New
York : Margaret K. McElderry Books, c1997.
*TC PS3562.I945 C75 1997*

The sky is full of song. 1st ed. New York : Harper &
Row, c1983.
*TC PS595.S42 S5 1983*

Yolen, Jane. Ring of earth. 1st ed. San Diego :
Harcourt Brace Jovanovich, c1986.
*TC PS3575.O43 R5 1986*

**SEASONS - POETRY.**
Jacobs, Leland B. (Leland Blair), 1907- Just around
the corner. New York : H. Holt, 1993.
*TC PS3560.A2545 J87 1993*

Livingston, Myra Cohn. Cricket never does. New
York : Margaret K. McElderry Books, c1997.
*TC PS3562.I945 C75 1997*

The sky is full of song. 1st ed. New York : Harper &
Row, c1983.
*TC PS595.S42 S5 1983*

Yolen, Jane. Ring of earth. 1st ed. San Diego :
Harcourt Brace Jovanovich, c1986.
*TC PS3575.O43 R5 1986*

**Seattle Art Museum.**
Carbone, Teresa A. Eastman Johnson. New York :
Brooklyn Museum of Art in association with Rizzoli
International Publications, 1999.
*TC ND237.J7 A4 1999*

**Sebba, Leslie.**
Children's rights and traditional values. Aldershot ;
Brookfield, USA : Ashgate/Dartmouth, c1998.
*TC K639 .A55 1998*

**Sebesta, Sam Leaton.** Odyssey : an HBJ literature
program / Sam Leaton Sebesta. Orlando, Fla. :
Harcourt Brace Jovanovich, c1982. v. : col. ill. ; 24 cm.
Includes index. CONTENTS: [Level 1.] Star light, star bright
(preprimer) ; Hello and good-bye (primer) ; Where the clouds
go (reader) -- [level 2.] Under the midnight stars -- [level 3.]
Under the midnight stars -- [level 4.] Across wide fields --
[level 5.] East of the sun -- [level 6.] At the edge of the
world -- [level 7.] Ride the silver seas -- [level 8.] Another
earth, another sky. ISBN 0-15-333358-8 (level 7) ISBN
0-15-333359-6 (level 8)
*1. Readers (Elementary) I. Title.*
*TC PE1117 .O39 1982*

Odyssey : an HBJ literature program / Sam Leaton Sebesta. 2nd ed. Orlando, Fla. : Harcourt Brace Jovanovich, c1986. v. : col. ill. ; 24 cm. For grades K-6. CONTENTS: [Level 1.] Star light, star bright (preprimer) ; Hello and good-bye (primer) ; Where the clouds go (reader) -- [level 2.] The heart of the woods -- [level 3.] Under the midnight stars -- [level 4.] Across wide fields -- [level 5.] East of the sun -- [level 6.] At the edge of the world. ISBN 0-15-333256-5 (level 5) ISBN 0-15-333257-3 (level 6) *1. Readers (Elementary) I. Title.*
*TC PE1117 .O39 1986*

Odyssey. Teacher's ed. Orlando, Fla. : Harcourt Brace Jovanovich, c1982.
*TC PE1117 .O39 1982 Teacher's Ed.*

**Sebrechts, Jadwiga, 1953-.**
Coming into her own. San Francisco, Calif. : Jossey-Bass, c1999.
*TC LC1503 .C65 1999*

**SECOND CAREERS.** *See* **CAREER CHANGES.**

**Second chance? [videorecording].**
Teen killers [videorecording]. Princeton, NJ : Films for the Humanities and Sciences, c1998-1999.
*TC HV9067.H6 T4 1999*

**SECOND GENERATION CHILDREN.** *See* **CHILDREN OF IMMIGRANTS.**

**SECOND GRADE (EDUCATION) - UNITED STATES.**
Fraser, Jane. On their way. Portsmouth, NH : Heinemann, c1994.
*TC LB1576 .F72 1994*

**SECOND LANGUAGE ACQUISITION.**
Brisk, Maria. Literacy and bilingualism. Mahwah, N.J. : L. Erlbaum Associates, c2000.
*TC LC3731 .B684 2000*

Cary, Stephen. Working with second language learners. Portsmouth, NH : Heinemann, c2000.
*TC P53 .C286 2000*

Culture in second language teaching and learning. Cambridge, U.K. ; New York : Cambridge University Press, 1999.
*TC P53 .C77 1999*

The current state of interlanguage. Amsterdam ; Philadelphia : J. Benjamins, c1995.
*TC P118.2 .C867 1995*

Educating language-minority children. New Brunswick (U.S.A.) : Transaction Publishers, c2000.
*TC LC3731 .E374 2000*

Ellis, Rod. Learning a second language through interaction. Amsterdam ; Philadelphia : J. Benjamins, c1999.
*TC P118.2 .E38 1999*

Language transfer in language learning. Rev. ed. with corrections. Amsterdam ; Philadelphia : J. Benjamins Pub. Co., 1994.
*TC P118.25 .L36 1994*

Li, Duan-Duan. Expressing needs and wants in a second language. 1998.
*TC 06 no. 10958*

Markee, Numa. Conversation analysis. Mahwah, N.J. : L. Erlbaum Associates, c2000.
*TC P95.45 .M35 2000*

McKay, Heather, 1950- Teaching adult second language learners. Cambridge ; New York : Cambridge University Press, 1999.
*TC P53 .M33 1999*

Nunan, David. Second language teaching & learning. Boston, Mass. : Heinle & Heinle Publishers, c1999.
*TC P118.2 .N86 1999*

Nunan, David. Second language teaching & learning. Boston, Mass. : Heinle & Heinle Publishers, c1999.
*TC P118.2 .N86 1999*

Sasaki, Miyuki, 1959- Second language proficiency, foreign language aptitude, and intelligence. New York : P. Lang, c1999.
*TC P53.4 .S27 1999*

Second language acquisition and linguistic theory. Malden, Mass. : Blackwell, 2000.
*TC P118.2 .S425 2000*

Skehan, Peter. A cognitive approach to language learning. Oxford ; New York : Oxford University Press, 1998.
*TC P118.2 .S567 1998*

Writing across languages. Stamford, Conn. : Ablex Pub., c2000.

**Second language acquisition and linguistic theory** / edited by John Archibald. Malden, Mass. : Blackwell, 2000. vii, 256 p. : ill. ; 25 cm. Includes bibliographical references and index. ISBN 0-631-20591-8 (alk. paper) ISBN 0-631-20592-6 (pbk. : alk. paper) DDC 401/.93 *1. Second language acquisition. I. Archibald. John.*
*TC P118.2 .S425 2000*

**Second language acquisition and the critical period hypothesis** / edited by David Birdsong. Mahwah, N.J. : Erlbaum, 1999. ix, 191 p. ; 24 cm. (Second language acquisition research) Chiefly papers presented at a conference held Aug. 1996, Jyväskylä, Finland. Includes bibliographical references and indexes. ISBN 0-8058-3084-7 (alk. paper) DDC 401/.93
*1. Second language acquisition - Congresses. I. Series.*
*TC P118.2 .S428 1999*

**SECOND LANGUAGE ACQUISITION - CHINA - METHODOLOGY.**
Ting, Yenren, 1948- Learning English text by heart in a Chinese university. [New York : Columbia University], 1999.
*TC 085 T438*

**SECOND LANGUAGE ACQUISITION - COMPUTER-ASSISTED INSTRUCTION.**
Language learning online. Austin : Labyrinth Publications, c1998.
*TC PE1128.A2 L2955 1998*

**SECOND LANGUAGE ACQUISITION - CONGRESSES.**
The generative study of second language acquisition. Mahwah, N.J. : L. Erlbaum, 1998.
*TC P118.2 .G46 1998*

Second language acquisition and the critical period hypothesis. Mahwah, N.J. : Erlbaum, 1999.
*TC P118.2 .S428 1999*

**SECOND LANGUAGE ACQUISITION - METHODOLOGY.**
O'Riordan, Mary. Strategic use of transfer and explicit linguistic knowledge. 1998.
*TC 06 no. 10975*

**Second language acquisition research**
Markee, Numa. Conversation analysis. Mahwah, N.J. : L. Erlbaum Associates, c2000.
*TC P95.45 .M35 2000*

Second language acquisition and the critical period hypothesis. Mahwah, N.J. : Erlbaum, 1999.
*TC P118.2 .S428 1999*

**SECOND LANGUAGE ACQUISITION - RESEARCH.**
Jauregi Ondarra, Kristi. Collaborative negotiation of meaning. Amsterdam ; Atlanta, GA : Rodopi, 1997.
*TC P118.2 J38 1997*

**SECOND LANGUAGE ACQUISITION - RESEARCH - METHODOLOGY.**
Tian, Shiau-ping. TOEFL reading comprehension. 2000.
*TC 06 no. 11316*

**SECOND LANGUAGE AQUISITION.**
Cava, Margaret T. Second language learner strategies and the unsuccessful second language writer. 1999.
*TC 085 C295*

**Second language learner strategies and the unsuccessful second language writer.**
Cava, Margaret T. 1999.
*TC 085 C295*

**SECOND LANGUAGE LEARNING.** *See* **SECOND LANGUAGE ACQUISITION.**

**Second language proficiency, foreign language aptitude, and intelligence.**
Sasaki, Miyuki, 1959- New York : P. Lang, c1999.
*TC P53.4 .S27 1999*

**Second language teaching & learning.**
Nunan, David. Boston, Mass. : Heinle & Heinle Publishers, c1999.
*TC P118.2 .N86 1999*

**Second language teaching and learning.**
Nunan, David. Second language teaching & learning. Boston, Mass. : Heinle & Heinle Publishers, c1999.
*TC P118.2 .N86 1999*

**Second sight :** stories for a new millennium / Avi ... [et al.]. New York : Philomel Books, 1999. 122 p. ; 22 cm. CONTENTS: Oswin's millennium / Avi -- The beginning of time / Janet Taylor Lisle -- Clay / Rita Williams-Garcia -- Rob Austin and the millennium bug / Madeleine L'Engle -- I believe? / Nancy Springer -- Horizon / Michael Cadnum -- Tomorrow / Natalie Babbitt -- The three-century woman /

Richard Peck. ISBN 0-399-23458-6 DDC [Fic] *1. Children's stories, American. 2. Short stories. 3. Short stories. I. Avi. 1937-*
*TC PZ5 .S4375 1999*

**Second year Latin.**
Jenney, Charles. Jenney's second year Latin. Newton, Mass. : Allyn and Bacon, c1987.
*TC PA2087.5 .J461 1987*

**Secondary and middle school teaching methods.**
Clark, Leonard H. 7th ed. Englewood Cliffs, N.J. : Merrill, c1996.
*TC LB1737.A3 C53 1996*

**SECONDARY EDUCATION.** *See* **EDUCATION, SECONDARY.**

**Secondary education and nation-building.**
Quist, Hubert Oswald. 1999.
*TC 085 Q52*

**Secondary education and nation building, a study of Ghana, 1951-1991.**
Quist, Hubert Oswald. Secondary education and nation-building. 1999.
*TC 085 Q52*

**SECONDARY EDUCATION COUNSELING.** *See* **COUNSELING IN SECONDARY EDUCATION.**

**SECONDARY EDUCATION GUIDANCE.** *See* **COUNSELING IN SECONDARY EDUCATION.**

**SECONDARY SCHOOL DROPOUTS.** *See* **HIGH SCHOOL DROPOUTS.**

**SECONDARY SCHOOL PRINCIPALS.** *See* **HIGH SCHOOL PRINCIPALS.**

**SECONDARY SCHOOL TEACHERS.** *See* **HIGH SCHOOL TEACHERS.**

**SECONDARY SCHOOL TEACHING.** *See* **HIGH SCHOOL TEACHING.**

**SECONDARY SCHOOLS.** *See* **EDUCATION, SECONDARY; HIGH SCHOOLS; PRIVATE SCHOOLS; PUBLIC SCHOOLS.**

**SECRECY.** *See also* **CONFIDENTIAL COMMUNICATIONS.**
Balancing the secrets of private disclosures. Mahwah, N.J. : Lawrence Erlbaum Associates, Publishers, 2000.
*TC BF697.5.S427 B35 2000*

**SECRECY - LAW AND LEGISLATION.** *See* **PRIVACY, RIGHT OF.**

**The secret garden cookbook.**
Cotler, Amy. 1st ed. New York : HarperCollins Publishers. c1999.
*TC TX717 .C588 1999*

**The secret of consciousness.**
Ableman, Paul. London ; New York : Marion Boyars, 1999.
*TC BF311 .A195 1999*

**SECRETS, PROFESSIONAL.** *See* **CONFIDENTIAL COMMUNICATIONS.**

**Sector 7.**
Wiesner, David. New York : Clarion Books, c1999.
*TC PZ7.W6367 Se 1999*

**Sector seven.**
Wiesner, David. Sector 7. New York : Clarion Books, c1999.
*TC PZ7.W6367 Se 1999*

**The secular mind.**
Coles, Robert. Princeton, N.J. : Princeton University Press, c1999.
*TC BL2760 .C65 1999*

**SECULARISM.** *See* **ATHEISM.**

**SECULARISM - UNITED STATES.**
Coles, Robert. The secular mind. Princeton, N.J. : Princeton University Press, c1999.
*TC BL2760 .C65 1999*

**SECULARISM - UNITED STATES - HISTORY.**
Roberts, Jon H. The sacred and the secular university. Princeton, N.J. : Princeton University Press, c2000.
*TC LA636.7 .R62 2000*

**SECULARIZATION (THEOLOGY).** *See* **SECULARISM.**

**Securing the future :** investing in children from birth to college / Sheldon Danziger and Jane Waldfogel, editors. New York : Russell Sage Foundation, c2000. xv, 330 p. : ill. ; 25 cm. (The Ford Foundation series on asset building) Includes bibliographical references and index.

CONTENTS: Foreword / Melvin L. Oliver -- Introduction: Investing in Children: What Do We Know? What Should We Do? / Sheldon Danziger and Jane Waldfogel -- Ch. 1. Trends in and Consequences of Investments in Children / Lisa M. Lynch -- Ch. 2. Rethinking Education and Training Policy: Understanding the Sources of Skill Formation in a Modern Economy / James J. Heckman and Lance Lochner -- Ch. 3. Pathways to Early Child Health and Development / Barry Zuckerman and Robert Kahn -- Ch. 4. Early Childhood Experiences and Developmental Competence / Sharon Landesman Ramey and Craig T. Ramey -- Ch. 5. Schooling's Influences on Motivation and Achievement / Jacquelynne S. Eccles and Allan Wigfield -- Ch. 6. Promoting Positive Outcomes for Youth: Resourceful Families and Communities / Margaret Beale Spencer and Dena Phillips Swanson -- Ch. 7. The Neighborhood Context of Investing in Children: Facilitating Mechanisms and Undermining Risks / Robert J. Sampson -- Ch. 8. The Transition from School to Work: Is there a Crisis? What Can Be Done? / Debra Donahoe and Marta Tienda -- Ch. 9. New Directions in Job Training Strategies for the Disadvantaged / Hillard Pouncy -- Ch. 10. Who is Getting a College Education? Family Background and the Growing Gaps in Enrollment / David T. Ellwood and Thomas J. Kane. ISBN 0-87154-899-2 DDC 362.7/0973 DDC 362.7/0973
*1. Child welfare - United States. 2. Children - United States - Social conditions. 3. Children - Government policy - United States. 4. Youth - United States - Social conditions. 5. Youth - Government policy - United States. I. Danziger, Sheldon. II. Waldfogel, Jane. III. Series.*
**TC HV741 .S385 2000**

**Securing your organization's future.**
Seltzer, Michael, 1947- New York, N.Y. : Foundation Center, 1987.
**TC HV41.9.U5 S45 1987**

**SECURITY, INTERNATIONAL.** *See* PEACE.

**SECURITY OF COMPUTER SYSTEMS.** *See* COMPUTER SECURITY.

**SECURITY SYSTEMS.** *See* COMPUTER SECURITY; POLICE.

**The seductions of psychoanalysis.**
Forrester, John. 1st pbk. ed. Cambridge ; New York : Cambridge University Press, 1991 (1992 printing)
**TC RC504 .F63 1991**

**See for yourself** : teacher's planning guide. New York : Macmillan/McGraw-Hill, c1997. 1 v. (various pagings) : col. ill. ; 31 cm. (Spotlight on literacy ; Gr.3 l.8 u.2) (The road to independent reading) Includes index. ISBN 0-02-181166-0
*1. Language arts (Primary) 2. Reading (Primary) I. Series. II. Series: The road to independent reading*
**TC LB1576 .S66 1997 Gr.3 l.8 u.2**

**See, Prudence, ill.**
Cotler, Amy. The secret garden cookbook. 1st ed. New York : HarperCollins Publishers, c1999.
**TC TX717 .C588 1999**

**Seeing Australia.**
Sullivan, Graeme, 1951- Annandale, NSW, Australia : Piper Press, 1994.
**TC N7400.2 .S85 1994**

**Seeing is believing.**
Stephen Hawking's universe [videorecording]. [Alexandria, Va.] : PBS Video; Burbank, CA : Distributed by Warner Home Video, c1997.
**TC QB982 .S7 1997**

**Seeley, Karen M.** Cultural psychotherapy : working with culture in the clinical encounter / Karen M. Seeley. Northvale, N.J. : Jason Aronson, c2000. xi, 266 p. ; 24 cm. Includes bibliographical references (p. [247]-260) and index. ISBN 0-7657-0224-X DDC 616.89/14
*1. Cultural psychiatry. 2. Psychotherapy - Cross-cultural studies. 3. Ethnopsychology. I. Title.*
**TC RC455.4.E8 S44 2000**

**Seelye, H. Ned.**
Experiential activities for intercultural learning. Yarmouth, Me., USA : Intercultural Press, c1996-
**TC LC1099.3 .E97 1996**

**Seeman, Howard.** Preventing classroom discipline problems : a classroom management handbook. 3rd ed. Lanham, Md. : Scarecrow Press, 2000. xxi, 475 p. : ill. ; 24 cm. Includes bibliographical references (p. 465-470) and index. ISBN 1-56676-834-9 DDC 371.1024
*1. Classroom management. I. Title.*
**TC LB3013 .S44 2000**

**Seferoglu, Süleyman Sadi.** Elementary school teacher development : a study of professional development opportunities in Turkish schools / by Süleyman Sadi Seferoglu. 1996. xi, 207 leaves ; 29 cm. Typescript; issued also on microfilm. Thesis (Ed.D.)--Teachers College, Columbia University, 1996. Includes bibliographical references (leaves 175-182).

*1. Elementary school teachers - Turkey - Ankara. 2. Elementary school teachers - In-service training - Turkey - Ankara. 3. Elementary school teachers - Attitudes - Turkey - Ankara. 4. Mentoring in education - Turkey - Ankara. 5. Interpersonal relations - Turkey - Ankara. 6. Ankara (Turkey) I. Title. II. Title: Professional development opportunities in Turkish schools*
**TC 06 no. 10693**

**Sefton-Green, Julian.**
Digital diversions. London : UCL Press, 1998.
**TC QA76.575 .D536 1998**

**Segal, Bernard, 1936-.**
Conducting drug abuse research with minority populations. New York : Haworth Press, c1999.
**TC HV5824.E85 C66 1999**

**Segal, Eli, 1943-.**
Sagawa, Shirley, 1961- Common interest, common good. Boston : Harvard Business School Press, c2000.
**TC HD60.5.U5 S24 2000**

**Segal, Hanna.** Dream, phantasy, and art / Hanna Segal. London ; New York : Tavistock/Routledge, 1991. xiii, 120 p. ; 24 cm. (New library of psychoanalysis ; 12) Includes bibliographical references (p. 110-113) and indexes. DDC 154.6/3
*1. Dreams. 2. Fantasy. 3. Psychoanalysis and art. I. Title. II. Series.*
**TC BF1078 .S375 1991**

**Segal, Marcia Texler.**
Social change for women and children. Stamford, Conn. : JAI Press, 2000.
**TC HQ1421 .S68 2000**

**Segaller Films.**
Jung on film [videorecording]. [Chicago, Ill.?] : Public Media Video, c1990.
**TC BF109.J8 J4 1990**

Jung on film [videorecording]. [Chicago, Ill.?] : Public Media Video, c1990.
**TC BF109.J8 J4 1990**

**Segan, Philip.**
The teaching of reading in Spanish to the bilingual student = 2nd ed. Mahwah, N.J. : L. Erlbaum Associates, 1998.
**TC LB1573 .T365 1998**

**SEGREGATION.** *See* APARTHEID; MINORITIES.

**SEGREGATION IN EDUCATION.** *See* DISCRIMINATION IN EDUCATION; SCHOOL INTEGRATION.

**SEGREGATION IN EDUCATION - ISRAEL.**
Swirski, Shlomo. Politics and education in Israel. New York : Falmer Press, 1999.
**TC LC94.I75 S95 1999**

**SEGREGATION IN EDUCATION - LAW AND LEGISLATION - UNITED STATES - HISTORY.**
Whitman, Mark, 1937- The irony of desegregation law. Princeton, NJ : M. Wiener, c1998.
**TC KF4155 .I76 1997**

**SEGREGATION IN EDUCATION - PERIODICALS.**
Integrated education. [Amherst, Mass., etc., Center for Equal Education, School of Education, University of Massachusetts, etc.]

**SEGREGATION IN EDUCATION - UNITED STATES - HISTORY.**
Spring, Joel H. Deculturalization and the struggle for equality. 3rd ed. Boston : McGraw-Hill, c2001.
**TC LC3731 .S68 2000**

**Seibold, J.otto.** Going to the Getty : a book about the Getty Center in Los Angeles / J. Otto Seibold and Vivian Walsh. Los Angeles : J. Paul Getty Museum, c1997. 1 v. (unpaged) : col. ill. ; 32 cm. ISBN 0-89236-493-9
*1. Getty Center (Los Angeles, Calif.) - Juvenile literature. 2. Art centers - California - Los Angeles - Juvenile literature. 3. Los Angeles (Calif.) - Buildings, structures, etc. - Juvenile literature. 4. Getty Center (Los Angeles, Calif.) 5. Art centers. 6. Office buildings. I. Walsh, Vivian. II. Title.*
**TC NA6813.U6 L678 1997**

**Seidlhofer, Barbara.**
Principle & practice in applied linguistics. Oxford : Oxford University Press, 1995.
**TC P129 .P75 1995**

**Seidman, Edward.**
Handbook of community psychology. New York ; London : Kluwer Academic/Plenum, c2000.
**TC RA790.55 .H36 2000**

**Seiter, Ellen, 1957-** Television and new media audiences / Ellen Seiter. Oxford ; New York : Clarendon Press, 1998. 154 p. : ill. ; 25 cm. (Oxford television studies) Includes bibliographical references (p. [141]-148) and index. ISBN 0-19-871141-9 (hardcover : alk. paper) ISBN 0-19-871141-7 (pbk. : alk. paper) DDC 302.23/45/0973
*1. Television viewers - United States - Attitudes. 2. Television viewers - Research - United States. 3. Television viewers - Social aspects - United States. I. Title. II. Series.*
**TC PN1992.3.U5 S35 1998**

**Seiter, John S.**
Gass, Robert H. Persuasion, social influence, and compliance gaining. Boston : Allyn and Bacon, c1999.
**TC BF637.P4 G34 1999**

**Seivewright, Nicholas.** Community treatment of drug misuse : more than methadone / Nicholas Seivewright. Cambridge, UK ; New York : Cambridge University Press, 2000. xvi, 243 p. ; 23 cm. Includes bibliographical references and index. ISBN 0-521-59091-4 (hardback) ISBN 0-521-66562-0 (paperback) DDC 362.2
*1. Drug abuse - Treatment. 2. Substance-Related Disorders - therapy. I. Title.*
**TC RC564 .S45 2000**

**Seldenrijk, R.**
Meaningful care. Dordrecht ; Boston ; London : Kluwer Academic Publishers, c2000.
**TC HV3004 .M34 2000**

**Selecting books for the elementary school library media center.**
Van Orden, Phyllis. New York : Neal-Schuman Publishers, c2000.
**TC Z675.S3 V36 2000**

**Selecting instructional materials.**
Center for Science, Mathematics, and Engineering Education. Committee on Developing the Capacity to Select Effective Instructional Materials. Washington, D.C. : National Academy Press, c1999.
**TC LB1585.3 .C45 1999**

**SELECTIVITY (PSYCHOLOGY) - CONGRESSES.**
International Symposium on Attention and Performance (11th : 1984 : Eugene, Or.) Attention and performance XI. Hillsdale, N.J. : L. Erlbaum Associates, 1985.
**TC BF321 .A82 1985**

**SELENOLOGY.** *See* MOON.

**SELF.** *See also* BODY, HUMAN; CONSCIOUSNESS; IDENTITY (PSYCHOLOGY); MIND AND BODY; PERSONALITY; THOUGHT AND THINKING.
Holstein, James A. The self we live by. New York : Oxford University Press, 2000.
**TC BF697.5.S65 H65 2000**

Kainer, Rochelle G. K., 1936- The collapse of the self and its therapeutic restoration. Hillsdale, NJ ; London : Analytic Press, 1999.
**TC RC489.S43 K35 1999**

Peatling, John H. Career development. Muncie, Ind. : Accelerated Development, c1977.
**TC BF697 .P384**

Psychological perspectives on self and identity. 1st ed. Washington, DC : American Psychological Association, c2000.
**TC BF697 .P765 2000**

The self in social psychology. Philadelphia ; Hove [England] : Psychology Press, c1999.
**TC HM1033 .S35 1999**

Seligman, A. Modernity's wager. Princeton, NJ : Princeton University Press, 2000.
**TC HM1251 .S45 2000**

Stevens, Anthony. The two million-year-old self. New York : Fromm International Publishing, 1997.
**TC BF175.5.A72 S75 1997**

When self-consciousness breaks. Cambridge, Mass. : MIT Press, c2000.
**TC RC553.A84 S74 2000**

**SELF-ACCEPTANCE.**
Lippert, Robin Alissa. Conflating the self with the body. 1999.
**TC 085 L655**

Magno, Joseph. Self-love. Lanham, Md. ; Oxford : University Press of America, c2000.
**TC BF575.L8 M29 2000**

## SELF-ACCEPTANCE - FICTION.
Mills, Claudia. You're a brave man, Julius Zimmerman. 1st ed. New York : Farrar Straus Giroux, c1999.
*TC PZ7.M63963 Yo 1999*

Shavick, Andrea. You'll grow soon, Alex. New York : Walker, 2000.
*TC PZ7.S5328 Yo 2000*

## SELF-ACTUALIZATION (PSYCHOLOGY).
Emmons, Robert A. The psychology of ultimate concerns. New York : Guilford Press, c1999.
*TC BF505.G6 E58 1999*

Fosha, Diana. The transforming power of affect. 1st ed. New York : BasicBooks, 2000.
*TC BF637.C4 F67 2000*

Heath, Douglas H. Morale, culture, and character. 1st ed. Bryn Mawr, PA : Conrow Pub. House, c1999.
*TC LC311 .H43 1999*

Robinson, Anna Bess. Leadership development in women's civic organizations. 1999.
*TC 06 no. 11168*

## SELF-ACTUALIZATION (PSYCHOLOGY) IN OLD AGE.
Hillman, James. The force of character. 1st ed. New York : Random House, c1999.
*TC BF724.85.S45 H535 1999b*

## SELF-ACTUALIZATION (PSYCHOLOGY) - SOCIAL ASPECTS.
Hall, C. Margaret (Constance Margaret) Heroic self. Springfield, Ill. : C.C. Thomas, c1998.
*TC RC489.S62 H35 1998*

Lippert, Robin Alissa. Conflating the self with the body. 1999.
*TC 085 L655*

**The self-altering process.**
Walters, Glenn D. Westport, Conn. : Praeger, 2000.
*TC BF637.C4 W35 2000*

**The self and society in aging processes** / Carol D. Ryff, Victor W. Marshall, editors. New York : Springer Pub., c1999. xi, 491 p. : ill. ; 24 cm. Includes bibliographical references and index. ISBN 0-8261-1267-6 (hardcover) DDC 305.26
*1. Aging - Social aspects. 2. Aging - Psychological aspects. 3. Aged - Social conditions. 4. Aged - Psychology. 5. Gerontology. I. Ryff, Carol D. II. Marshall, Victor W.*
*TC HQ1061 .S438 1999*

**Self-assessment and development in writing** : a collaborative inquiry / edited by Jane Bowman Smith, Kathleen Blake Yancey. Cresskill, N.J. : Hampton Press, c2000. xv, 184 p. ; 24 cm. (Written language series) Includes bibliographical references and indexes. ISBN 1-57273-146-X (hbk.) ISBN 1-57273-147-8 (pbk.) DDC 808/.042/07
*1. English language - Rhetoric - Study and teaching. 2. Report writing - Study and teaching. 3. Students - Self rating of. I. Smith, Jane Bowman. II. Yancey, Kathleen Blake. 1950- III. Series.*
*TC PE1404 .S37 2000*

## SELF-AWARENESS. See SELF-PERCEPTION.

**Self-awareness** : its nature and development / edited by Michel Ferrari, Robert J. Sternberg. New York : Guilford Press, c1998. xiv, 430 p. : ill. ; 24 cm. Includes bibliographical references and index. ISBN 1-57230-317-4 (alk. paper) DDC 126
*1. Self-perception. I. Ferrari, M. D. II. Sternberg, Robert J.*
*TC BF697.5.S43 S434 1998*

## SELF-CARE, HEALTH.
Granfield, Robert, 1955- Coming clean. New York : London : New York University Press, c1999.
*TC HV4998 .G73 1999*

Mendoza, Maria Adalia. A study to compare inner city Black men and women completers and non-attenders of diabetes self-care classes. 1999.
*TC 06 no. 11206*

## SELF-CONCEPT. See SELF-PERCEPTION.

## SELF CONCEPT - CONGRESSES.
Memory, brain, and belief. Cambridge, Mass. ; London : Harvard University Press, 2000.
*TC QP406 .M44 2000*

**Self-construal as a moderator of the effects of task and reward interdependence of group performance.**
Katz, Tal Y. 1999.
*TC 085 K1524*

## SELF-CONTROL.
Control of human behavior, mental processes, and consciousness. Mahwah, N.J. : Lawrence Erlbaum Associates, c2000.
*TC BF611 .C67 2000*

Handbook of self-regulation. San Diego : Academic, 2000.
*TC BF632 .H254 2000*

Perspectives on scholarly misconduct in the sciences. Columbus : Ohio State University Press, c1999.
*TC Q147 .P47 1999*

Rachlin, Howard, 1935- The science of self-control. Cambridge, Mass. : Harvard University Press, 2000.
*TC BF632 .R3 2000*

## SELF-CONTROL IN CHILDREN.
Bronson, Martha. Self-regulation in early childhood. New York : London : Guilford Press, c2000.
*TC BF723.S25 B76 2000*

## SELF-CONTROL - UNITED STATES.
Savage, Tom V. Teaching self-control through management and discipline. 2nd ed. Boston ; London : Allyn and Bacon, c1999.
*TC LB3012.2 .S38 1999*

## SELF-CULTURE. See also OPEN LEARNING.
Individualisation. Oxford : Modern English Publications, 1982.
*TC LC32 .I53 1982*

**Self-deception.**
Fingarette, Herbert. Berkeley, Calif. ; London : University of California Press, 2000.
*TC BF697 .F47 2000*

Fingarette, Herbert. Self-deception. Berkeley, Calif. ; London : University of California Press, 2000.
*TC BF697 .F47 2000*

## SELF-DEFEATING BEHAVIOR.
McWhorter, John H. Losing the race. New York : Free Press, c2000.
*TC E185.625 .M38 2000*

## SELF-DESTRUCTIVE BEHAVIOR.
Between the lines [videorecording]. Boston, MA : Fanlight Productions, c1997.
*TC RC552.S4 B4 1997*

## SELF-DETERMINATION.
Handbook of self-regulation. San Diego : Academic, 2000.
*TC BF632 .H254 2000*

## SELF-DETERMINATION (PSYCHOLOGY). See AUTONOMY (PSYCHOLOGY).

## SELF-DIRECTED LEARNING. See ADULT LEARNING.

## SELF-DIRECTION (PSYCHOLOGY). See AUTONOMY (PSYCHOLOGY).

## SELF-DISCIPLINE. See SELF-CONTROL.

## SELF-DISCLOSURE.
Balancing the secrets of private disclosures. Mahwah, N.J. : Lawrence Erlbaum Associates, Publishers, 2000.
*TC BF697.5.S427 B35 2000*

**Self efficacy.**
Eisenberger, Joanne, 1942- Larchmont, N.Y. : Eye On Education, c2000.
*TC LC4705 .C67 2000*

## SELF-EFFICACY.
Grice, Marthe Jane. Attachment, race, and gender in late life. 1999.
*TC 085 G865*

Richardson, Bonnie. Factors influencing the sexual and contraceptive behavior of sexually abused adolescents of color. 1999.
*TC 06 no. 11167*

Yamusah, Salifu. An investigation of the relative effectiveness of the composite approach and the phenomenological method for enhancing self-esteem in adults with mental retardation. 1998.
*TC 085 Y146*

## SELF-EMPLOYED AFRO-AMERICANS.
Bates, Timothy Mason. Race, self-employment, and upward mobility. Washington, D.C. : Woodrow Wilson Center Press ; Baltimore : Johns Hopkins University Press, c1997.
*TC HD8037.U5 B384 1997*

## SELF-EMPLOYED ASIAN AMERICANS.
Bates, Timothy Mason. Race, self-employment, and upward mobility. Washington, D.C. : Woodrow Wilson Center Press ; Baltimore : Johns Hopkins University Press, c1997.
*TC HD8037.U5 B384 1997*

## SELF-ESTEEM.
Bea, Holly, 1956- My spiritual alphabet book. Tiburon, Calif. : H.J. Kramer, c2000.
*TC BL625.5 .B43 1999*

Yamusah, Salifu. An investigation of the relative effectiveness of the composite approach and the phenomenological method for enhancing self-esteem in adults with mental retardation. 1998.
*TC 085 Y146*

## SELF-ESTEEM IN ADOLESCENCE.
Mosley, Jenny. Quality circle time in the secondary school :. London : David Fulton, 1999.
*TC LB1032 .M67 1999*

Page, Randy M. Fostering emotional well-being in the classroom. 2nd ed. Sudbury, Mass. ; London : Jones and Bartlett Publishers, c2000.
*TC LB3430 .P34 2000*

Toner, Patricia Rizzo, 1952- Stress-management and self-esteem activities. West Nyack, N.Y. : Center for Applied Research in Education, c1993.
*TC RA785 .T65 1993*

## SELF-ESTEEM IN ADOLESCENCE - STUDY AND TEACHING (SECONDARY).
Herod, Leslie. Discovering me. Boston, MA : Allyn and Bacon, c1999.
*TC BF724.3.S36 H47 1999*

## SELF-ESTEEM IN CHILDREN.
Page, Randy M. Fostering emotional well-being in the classroom. 2nd ed. Sudbury, Mass. ; London : Jones and Bartlett Publishers, c2000.
*TC LB3430 .P34 2000*

Solovay, Sondra, 1970- Tipping the scales of justice. Amherst, N.Y. : Prometheus Books, 2000.
*TC BF697.5.B63 S65 2000*

## SELF-ESTEEM IN MEN.
Pope, Harrison. The Adonis complex. New York : Free Press, 2000.
*TC BF697.5.B635 2000*

## SELF-ESTEEM IN WOMEN - UNITED STATES.
Empowering women of color. New York : Columbia University Press, c1999.
*TC HV1445 .E45 1999*

## SELF-ESTEEM IN YOUNG ADULTS - UNITED STATES.
Csóti, Márianna. People skills for young adults. London ; Philadelphia : Jessica Kingsley, 2000.
*TC HQ799.7 .C76 2000*

## SELF-ESTEEM - SEX DIFFERENCES.
Lippert, Robin Alissa. Conflating the self with the body. 1999.
*TC 085 L655*

## SELF-ESTEEM - STUDY AND TEACHING - UNITED STATES.
The developmental process of positive attitudes and mutual respect. Lewiston, N.Y. : E. Mellen Press, c1999.
*TC LB2822.82 .D49 1999*

## SELF-EVALUATION. See also SELF-PERCEPTION.
Bazigos, Michael Nicholas. The relationship of upward feedback disparities to leader performance. 1999.
*TC 085 B33*

Martin, Robert J. A study of the reflective practices of physical education student teachers. 1998.
*TC 06 no. 11031*

Martin, Robert J. A study of the reflective practices of physical education student teachers. 1998.
*TC 06 no. 11031*

Reflective practice in nursing. 2nd ed. Oxford ; Malden, MA : Blackwell Scientific, 2000.
*TC RT73 .R3461 2000*

Zersen, David John. Independent learning among clergy. 1998.
*TC 06 no. 11008*

## SELF-EVALUATION IN EDUCATION. See EDUCATIONAL EVALUATION.

## SELF-FULFILLING PROPHECY.
How expectancies shape experience. 1st ed. Washington, DC : American Psychological Association, c1999.
*TC BF323.E8 H69 1999*

## SELF-FULFILLMENT. See SELF-REALIZATION.

**SELF-HELP DEVICES FOR THE DISABLED.** *See also* **BLIND, APPARATUS FOR THE.**
King, Thomas W. Modern Morse code in rehabilitation and education. Boston : Allyn and Bacon, c2000.
*TC HV1569.5 .K55 2000*

**SELF-HELP GROUPS.**
Mendoza, Maria Adalia. A study to compare inner city Black men and women completers and non-attenders of diabetes self-care classes. 1999.
*TC 06 no. 11206*

**SELF-HELP GROUPS - UNITED STATES.**
Support groups. New York : Haworth Press, c1995.
*TC HV45 .S896 1995*

**SELF-HELP TECHNIQUES.** *See* **SELF-MANAGEMENT (PSYCHOLOGY); TWELVE-STEP PROGRAMS.**

**SELF - HISTORY - 20TH CENTURY.**
Halliwell, Martin. Romantic science and the experience of self. Aldershot, Hants ; Brookfield, Vt. : Ashgate, c1999.
*TC BF697 R6375 1999*

**SELF IMAGE.** *See* **SELF-PERCEPTION.**

**SELF-IMPROVEMENT.** *See* **SELF-ACTUALIZATION (PSYCHOLOGY); SUCCESS.**

**SELF IN LITERATURE.**
McCallum, Robyn. Ideologies of identity in adolescent fiction. New York : Garland Pub., 1999.
*TC PN3443 .M38 1999*

**The self in social psychology** / edited by Roy F. Baumeister. Philadelphia ; Hove [England] : Psychology Press, c1999. ix, 492 p. : ill. ; 25 cm. (Key readings in social psychology) Includes bibliographical references and indexes. ISBN 0-86377-572-1 (hbk. : alk. paper) ISBN 0-86377-573-X (pbk. : alk. paper) DDC 302.5
*1. Social psychology. 2. Self. I. Baumeister, Roy F. II. Series.*
*TC HM1033 .S45 1999*

**SELF-INJURIOUS BEHAVIOR.**
Hyman, Jane Wegscheider. Women living with self-injury. Philadelphia : Temple University Press, 1999.
*TC RC552.S4 H95 1999*

**SELF-KILLING.** *See* **SUICIDE.**

**SELF-KNOWLEDGE, THEORY OF.**
Martin, Robert J. A study of the reflective practices of physical education student teachers. 1998.
*TC 06 no. 11031*

Reflective practice in nursing. 2nd ed. Oxford ; Malden, MA : Blackwell Scientific, 2000.
*TC RT73 .R3461 2000*

**Self-love.**
Magno, Joseph. Lanham, Md. ; Oxford : University Press of America, c2000.
*TC BF575.L8 M29 2000*

**SELF-LOVE (PSYCHOLOGY).** *See* **SELF-ACCEPTANCE; SELF-ESTEEM.**

**SELF-MANAGEMENT (PSYCHOLOGY).**
Granfield, Robert, 1955- Coming clean. New York ; London : New York University Press, c1999.
*TC HV4998 .G73 1999*

**SELF-MASTERY.** *See* **SELF-CONTROL.**

**SELF-MUTILATION.**
Between the lines [videorecording]. Boston, MA : Fanlight Productions, c1997.
*TC RC552.S4 B4 1997*

Hyman, Jane Wegscheider. Women living with self-injury. Philadelphia : Temple University Press, 1999.
*TC RC552.S4 H95 1999*

**SELF-ORGANIZING SYSTEMS.** *See also* **ARTIFICIAL INTELLIGENCE.**
Wheatley, Margaret J. Leadership and the new science. 2nd ed. San Francisco : Berrett-Koehler Publishers, c1999.
*TC HD57.7 .W47 1999*

**SELF-PERCEPTION.** *See also* **BODY IMAGE.**
Abate, Ellen C. Personal characteristics of nurses and their influence on professional autonomy. 1998.
*TC 06 no. 11009*

Eddy, Jennifer B.K. Multiple intelligences, styles, and proficiency. 1999.
*TC 085 E10*

Katz, Tal Y. Self-construal as a moderator of the effects of task and reward interdependence of group performance. 1999.

*TC 085 K1524*

Perspectives on behavioral self-regulation. Mahwah, N.J. : Lawrence Erlbaum Associates, 1999.
*TC HM291 A345 1999*

Purkey, William Watson. What students say to themselves. Thousand Oaks, Calif. : Corwin Press, c2000.
*TC LB1062.6 .P87 2000*

Self-awareness. New York : Guilford Press, c1998.
*TC BF697.5.S43 S434 1998*

When self-consciousness breaks. Cambridge, Mass. : MIT Press, c2000.
*TC RC553.A84 S74 2000*

Woo, Kimberley Ann. "Double happiness," double jeopardy. 1999.
*TC 06 no. 11075*

**SELF-PERCEPTION - FICTION.**
Borden, Louise. A. Lincoln and me. New York : Scholastic, 1999.
*TC PZ7.B64827 An 1999*

Gauch, Patricia Lee. Presenting Tanya, the Ugly Duckling. New York : Philomel Books, c1999.
*TC PZ7.G2315 Pr 1999*

Gordon, Amy, 1949- When JFK was my father. Boston : Houghton Mifflin, 1999.
*TC PZ7.G65 Wh 1999*

Many, Paul. My life, take two. New York : Walker & Co., 2000.
*TC PZ7.M3212 My 2000*

**SELF-PERCEPTION IN ADOLESCENCE.**
Smith, Hawthorne Emery. Psychological detachment from school. 1999.
*TC 085 Sm586*

**SELF-PERCEPTION IN ADOLESCENCE - UNITED STATES.**
Harrison, Patricia M. Racial identification and self-concept issues in biracial Black/White adolescent girls. 1997.
*TC 085 H247*

**SELF-PERCEPTION IN TEENAGERS.** *See* **SELF-PERCEPTION IN ADOLESCENCE.**

**SELF-PERCEPTION IN WOMEN.**
Miller, Estelle L. Fears expressed by female reentry students at an urban community college : qualitative study. 1997.
*TC 06 no. 10864*

**SELF (PHILOSOPHY).** *See* **SELF-KNOWLEDGE, THEORY OF.**

**SELF-PRESENTATION.**
Weber, Robert J. (Robert John), 1936- The created self. 1st ed. New York ; London : W.W. Norton, c2000.
*TC BF697.5.S44 W43 2000*

**SELF PSYCHOLOGY.**
Greif, Gary F. The tragedy of the self. Lanham, Md. ; Oxford : University Press of America, c2000.
*TC BF175.5.S44 G74 2000*

Yamusah, Salifu. An investigation of the relative effectiveness of the composite approach and the phenomenological method for enhancing self-esteem in adults with mental retardation. 1998.
*TC 085 Y146*

**SELF-REALIZATION - FICTION.**
Gauch, Patricia Lee. Poppy's puppet. 1st ed. New York : Holt, 1999.
*TC PZ7.G2315 Po 1999*

**SELF-REALIZATION (PSYCHOLOGY).** *See* **SELF-ACTUALIZATION (PSYCHOLOGY).**

**Self-regulation in early childhood.**
Bronson, Martha. New York ; London : Guilford Press, c2000.
*TC BF723.S25 B76 2000*

**SELF-RESPECT.** *See* **SELF-ESTEEM.**

**SELF-RESPECT IN ADOLESCENCE.** *See* **SELF-ESTEEM IN ADOLESCENCE.**

**SELF-RESPECT IN TEENAGERS.** *See* **SELF-ESTEEM IN ADOLESCENCE.**

**SELF-RESPECT IN WOMEN.** *See* **SELF-ESTEEM IN WOMEN.**

**Self-silencing, depression, gender role, and gender role conflict in women and men.**
Newman, Stephanie. 1997.
*TC 085 N47*

**SELF - SOCIAL ASPECTS.**
Holstein, James A. The self we live by. New York : Oxford University Press, 2000.
*TC BF697.5.S65 H65 2000*

Psychological perspectives on self and identity. 1st ed. Washington, DC : American Psychological Association, c2000.
*TC BF697 .P765 2000*

**SELF-SUPPORTED STUDY.** *See* **OPEN LEARNING.**

**SELF-UNDERSTANDING.** *See* **SELF-PERCEPTION.**

**The self we live by.**
Holstein, James A. New York : Oxford University Press, 2000.
*TC BF697.5.S65 H65 2000*

**SELF-WORTH.** *See* **SELF-ESTEEM.**

**Selfe, Cynthia L., 1951-.**
Global literacies and the World-Wide Web. London ; New York : Routledge, 2000.
*TC P94.6 .G58 2000*

Passions, pedagogies, and 21st century technologies. Logan : Utah State University Press ; Urbana, Ill. : National Council of Teachers of English, c1999.
*TC PE1404 .P38 1999*

Technology and literacy in the twenty-first century : the importance of paying attention / Cynthia L. Selfe ; with a foreword by Hugh Burns. Carbondale : Southern Illinois University Press, c1999. xxiii, 182 p. ; 22 cm. (Studies in writing and rhetoric) Includes bibliographical references (p. 165-176) and index. ISBN 0-8093-2269-2 (pbk. : alk. paper) DDC 371.33/4
*1. Computers and literacy - United States. 2. Technological literacy - United States. 3. Literacy - Social aspects - United States. I. Title. II. Series: Studies in writing & rhetoric.*
*TC LC149.5 .S45 1999*

**Seligman, A.** Modernity's wager : authority, the self, and transcendence. Princeton, NJ : Princeton University Press, 2000. xii, 177 p. ; 24 cm. Includes bibliographical references and index. ISBN 0-691-05061-9 (CL : alk. paper) DDC 303.3/6
*1. Authority. 2. Self. 3. Transcendence (Philosophy) I. Title.*
*TC HM1251 .S45 2000*

**Seligman, Milton, 1937-** Conducting effective conferences with parents of children with disabilities : a guide for teachers / Milton Seligman. New York : Guilford Press, c2000. xiii, 303 p. ; 23 cm. Includes bibliographical references (p. 277-292) and index. ISBN 1-57230-553-3 (hc.) ISBN 1-57230-537-1 (pbk.) DDC 371.103
*1. Handicapped children - Education. 2. Parents of handicapped children - Counseling of. 3. Parent-teacher conferences. I. Title.*
*TC LC4019 .S385 2000*

Marshak, Laura E. Disability and the family life cycle. New York : Basic Books, c1999.
*TC HV1568 .M277 1999*

**Selinger, Michelle, 1950-.**
Telematics in education. 1st ed. Amsterdam ; New York ; Oxford : Pergamon, 1999.
*TC LB1044.84 .T48 1999*

**Selinker, Larry, 1937-.**
The current state of interlanguage. Amsterdam ; Philadelphia : J. Benjamins, c1995.
*TC P118.2 .C867 1995*

Language transfer in language learning. Rev. ed. with corrections. Amsterdam ; Philadelphia : J. Benjamins Pub. Co., 1994.
*TC P118.25 .L36 1994*

**SELLING.** *See* **PEDDLERS AND PEDDLING.**

**Selling out.**
Wakefield, Dan. 1st ed. Boston : Little, Brown, c1985.
*TC PS3573.A413 S44 1985*

**Seltzer, Isadore, ill.**
Gross, Ruth Belov. What's on my plate? 1st American ed. New York : Macmillan, c1990.
*TC TX355 .G795 1990*

**Seltzer, Michael, 1947-** Securing your organization's future : a complete guide to fundraising strategies / Michael Seltzer. New York, N.Y. : Foundation Center, 1987. xiv, 514 p. : ill. ; 24 cm. Includes bibliographies and index. ISBN 0-87954-190-3 (pbk.) DDC 658.1/5224
*1. Fund raising - United States. 2. Fund raising - Law and legislation - United States. 3. Nonprofit organizations - United States - Finance. I. Title.*
*TC HV41.9.U5 S45 1987*

**Selznick, Brian, ill.**
Ryan, Pam Muñoz. Amelia and Eleanor go for a ride. New York : Scholastic Press, 1999.
*TC PZ7.R9553 Am 1999*

**Semali, Ladislaus, 1946-.**
What is indigenous knowledge? New York : Falmer Press, 1999.
*TC GN476 .W47 1999*

**SEMANTICS.** *See also* **COMPONENTIAL ANALYSIS (LINGUISTICS); DISCOURSE ANALYSIS; INDEXICALS (SEMANTICS); SUBLANGUAGE.**
Alston, William P. Illocutionary acts and sentence meaning. Ithaca : Cornell University Press, 2000.
*TC P95.55 .A47 2000*

Bloom, Paul, 1963- How children learn the meanings of words. Cambridge, MA : MIT Press, c2000.
*TC P118 .B623 2000*

Nida, Eugène Albert, 1914- Componential analysis of meaning. The Hague : Mouton, 1975.
*TC P325 .N5*

Pearson, Jennifer. Terms in context. Amsterdam ; Philadelphia : J. Benjamins, c1998.
*TC P305.18.D38 P4 1998*

The semantics/pragmatics interface from different points of view. 1st ed. Oxford, UK ; New York : Elsevier, 1999.
*TC P325 .S3814 1999*

**SEMANTICS - DATA PROCESSING.**
Lorenz, Gunter R. Adjective intensification--learners versus native speakers. Amsterdam ; Atlanta, GA : Rodopi, 1999.
*TC PE1074.5 .L67 1999*

**SEMANTICS (LOGIC).** *See* **SEMANTICS (PHILOSOPHY).**

**SEMANTICS (PHILOSOPHY).** *See also* **INDEXICALS (SEMANTICS); MEANING (PHILOSOPHY); SPEECH ACTS (LINGUISTICS).**
Roeper, Peter. Probability theory and probability logic. Toronto ; Buffalo : University of Toronto Press, c1999.
*TC BC141 .R64 1999*

**The semantics/pragmatics interface from different points of view** / edited by Ken Turner. 1st ed. Oxford, UK ; New York : Elsevier, 1999. x, 491 p. ; 23 cm. (Current research in the semantics/pragmatics interface ; v. 1) Includes bibliographical references and indexes. ISBN 0-08-043080-5 DDC 401/.43
*1. Semantics. 2. Pragmatics. 3. Discourse analysis. I. Turner, Ken (Ken P.) II. Series.*
*TC P325 .S3814 1999*

**SEMASIOLOGY.** *See* **SEMANTICS.**

**SEMEIOTICS.** *See* **SEMANTICS (PHILOSOPHY).**

**Semel, Susan F., 1941-.**
Sadovnik, Alan R. Exploring education. Boston : Allyn and Bacon, c1994.
*TC LB17 .S113 1994*

Sadovnik, Alan R. Exploring education. 2nd ed. Boston : Allyn and Bacon, 2000.
*TC LA217.2 . S23 2000*

**SEMIC ANALYSIS.** *See* **COMPONENTIAL ANALYSIS (LINGUISTICS).**

**SEMINARS - STUDY AND TEACHING (MIDDLE SCHOOL) - UNITED STATES - PROBLEMS, EXERCISES, ETC.**
Socratic seminar [videorecording]. [Boulder, Colo.] : Social Science Education Consortium, c1997.
*TC LB1027.44 .S6 1997*

**SEMINARS - STUDY AND TEACHING (SECONDARY) - UNITED STATES - PROBLEMS, EXERCISES, ETC.**
Socratic seminar [videorecording]. [Boulder, Colo.] : Social Science Education Consortium, c1997.
*TC LB1027.44 .S6 1997*

**SEMIOLOGY (SEMANTICS).** *See* **SEMANTICS.**

**SEMIOTICS.** *See also* **DISCOURSE ANALYSIS; SEMANTICS (PHILOSOPHY).**
Berthoff, Ann E. The mysterious barricades. Toronto ; Buffalo : University of Toronto Press, c1999.
*TC P106 .B463 1999*

Moorjani, Angela B. Beyond fetishism and other excursions in psychopragmatics. New York : St. Martin's Press, 2000.

*TC BF175.4.C84 M663 2000*
Schapiro, Meyer, 1904- Words, script, and pictures. New York, NY : George Braziller, 1996.
*TC P93.5 .S33 1996*

**SEMITES.** *See* **JEWS.**

**SEMITES - RELIGION.** *See* **JUDAISM.**

**SEMOLINA PRODUCTS.** *See* **PASTA PRODUCTS.**

**SENATORS (UNITED STATES).** *See* **LEGISLATORS - UNITED STATES.**

**The SENCO handbook.**
Cowne, Elizabeth A. 2nd ed. London : D. Fulton Publishers, 1998.
*TC LC3986.G7 C69 1998*

**Sendak, Maurice, ill.**
Marshall, James, 1942- Swine lake. 1st ed. [New York] : Harper Collins Publishers, 1999.
*TC PZ7.M35672 Sw 1999*

**Seneca, Joseph J., 1943-.**
America's demographic tapestry. New Brunswick, N.J. : Rutgers University Press, c1999.
*TC HB3505 .A683 1999*

**SENESCENCE.** *See* **AGING; OLD AGE.**

**Senge, Peter M.**
The dance of change. 1st ed. New York : Currency/Doubleday, 1999.
*TC HD58.82 .D36 1999*

**SENILE DEMENTIA.** *See* **ALZHEIMER'S DISEASE.**

**SENILE DEMENTIA - PATIENTS - HOME CARE.**
Mace, Nancy L. The 36-hour day. 3rd ed. Baltimore : Johns Hopkins University Press, c1999.
*TC RC523 .M33 1999*

**SENILE PSYCHOSES.** *See* **SENILE DEMENTIA.**

**SENILITY.** *See* **SENILE DEMENTIA.**

**SENIOR CITIZENS.** *See* **AGED.**

**SENIOR CLASS (HIGH SCHOOL).** *See* **TWELFTH GRADE (EDUCATION).**

**SENIOR HIGH SCHOOL PRINCIPALS.** *See* **HIGH SCHOOL PRINCIPALS.**

**SENIOR HIGH SCHOOL TEACHERS.** *See* **HIGH SCHOOL TEACHERS.**

**Senior living communities.**
Pearce, Benjamin W. Baltimore : Johns Hopkins University Press, 1998.
*TC HD7287.92.U54 P4 1998*

**Senior management teams in primary schools.**
Wallace, Mike. London ; New York : Routledge, 1999.
*TC LB2806.3 .W37 1999*

**Senior physical education :** an integrated approach / David Kirk ... [et al.]. [Mac illustrators, Denise Lowry, Jennifer Delmotte ; line artist, Robert Sabas ; medical illustrator, Roger Phillips]. Champaign, IL : Human Kinetics, c1999. xv, 215 p. : ill. ; 28 cm. Includes bibliographical references (p. 193) and index. ISBN 0-88011-788-5 DDC 613.7/071/294
*1. Physical education and training - Australia. I. Kirk, David, 1958-*
*TC GV315 .S434 1999*

**SENIORS, HIGH SCHOOL.** *See* **HIGH SCHOOL SENIORS.**

**SENIORS (OLDER PERSONS).** *See* **AGED.**

**Senn, Alfred Erich.** Power, politics, and the Olympic Games / Alfred Erich Senn. Champaign, IL : Human Kinetics, c1999. xx, 315 p. : ill. ; 23 cm. Includes bibliographical references (p. 289-299) and index. ISBN 0-88011-958-6 DDC 796.48
*1. Olympics - Political aspects - History. 2. Sports and state - History. 3. Brundage, Avery. 4. International Olympic Committee - History. I. Title.*
*TC GV721.5 .S443 1999*

**SENSATION.** *See* **SENSES AND SENSATION.**

**Sense and non-sense.**
Merleau-Ponty, Maurice, 1908-1961. [Sens et non-sens. English] [Evanston, Ill.] Northwestern University Press, 1964.
*TC B2430.M379 S43 1964*

**A sense of place.**
Feldman, Lynne B. Tuscaloosa, Ala. ; London : University of Alabama Press, c1999.
*TC F334.B69 N437 1999*

**SENSE ORGANS.** *See* **EAR.**

**SENSES AND SENSATION.** *See* **CONTROL (PSYCHOLOGY); HEARING; ORIENTATION (PHYSIOLOGY); ORIENTATION (PSYCHOLOGY); PAIN; PERCEPTION.**

**SENSES AND SENSATION - TESTING.**
Laming, D. R. J. (Donald Richard John) The measurement of sensation. Oxford ; New York : Oxford University Press, 1997.
*TC QP435 .L34 1997*

**SENSITIVITY TRAINING.** *See* **GROUP RELATIONS TRAINING.**

**SENSORY-MOTOR PROCESSES.** *See* **PERCEPTUAL-MOTOR PROCESSES.**

**SENSORY STIMULATION.**
Pagliano, Paul. Multisensory environments. London : David Fulton, 1999.
*TC LC3965 .P345 1999*

**SENSUALITY.** *See* **SEX (PSYCHOLOGY).**

**Senter, Gail W.** Charles, C. M. Elementary classroom management. 2nd ed. White Plains, N.Y. : Longman, c1995.
*TC LB3013 .C465 1995*

**Seo, Kyoung-Hye.** Children's construction of personal meanings of mathematical symbolism in a reform-oriented classroom / by Kyoung-Hye Seo. 2000. iv, 231 leaves : ill. ; 29 cm. Issued also on microfilm. Thesis (Ed.D.)--Teachers College, Columbia University, 2000. Includes bibliographical references (leaves 221-227).
*1. Mathematical notation. 2. Mathematics - Study and teaching (Elementary) - Case studies. 3. Communication in education. 4. Learning, Psychology of. 5. Symbolism (Psychology). I. Title.*
*TC 06 no. 11310*

**Separate by degree.**
Miller-Bernal, Leslie, 1946- New York : P. Lang, c2000.
*TC LC1601 .M55 2000*

**SEPARATE DEVELOPMENT (RACE RELATIONS).** *See* **APARTHEID.**

**SEPARATION ANXIETY - FICTION.**
Ross, Alice. Jezebel's spooky spot. 1st ed. New York : Dutton Children's Books, 1999.
*TC PZ7.R719694 Jf 1999*

**SEPARATION ANXIETY IN CHILDREN.**
Attachment disorganization. New York ; London : Guilford Press, c1999.
*TC RJ507.A77 A87 1999*

**SEPARATION OF CHURCH AND STATE.** *See* **CHURCH AND STATE.**

**SEPT (Television station : France).**
Matisse, voyages [videorecording]. [Chicago, Ill.] : Home Vision ; [S.l.] : Distributed worldwide by RM Associates, c1989.
*TC ND553.M37 M37 1989*

**SEQUENCE, FIBONACCI.** *See* **FIBONACCI NUMBERS.**

**SERFDOM.** *See* **SLAVERY.**

**Serfozo, Mary.** What's what? a guessing game/ Mary Serfozo ; illustrated by Keiko Narahashi. 1st ed. New York, NY : Margaret K. McElderry Books, c1996. 1 v. (unpaged) : col. ill. ; 23 cm. SUMMARY: Illustrations and rhyming text provide examples of what is soft and hard, warm and cold, wet and dry, long and short, and light and dark and describe how a puppy is all these things at once. ISBN 0-689-80653-1 DDC [E]
*1. English language - Synonyms and antonyms - Fiction. 2. Dogs - Fiction. 3. Afro-Americans - Fiction. I. Narahashi, Keiko, ill. II. Title.*
*TC PZ7.S482 Wg 1996*

**Sergiovanni, Thomas J.** The principalship : a reflective practice perspective / Thomas J. Sergiovanni. 4th ed. Boston : Allyn & Bacon, c2001. xv, 25 cm. Includes bibliographical references and index. ISBN 0-205-32185-2 DDC 371.2/012/0973
*1. School principals - United States. 2. Educational leadership - United States. 3. School management and organization - United States. 4. School supervision - United States. 5. School improvement programs - United States. I. Title.*
*TC LB2831.92 .S47 2001*

**SERIAL.**
The Hospital world. Toronto : [Canadian Hospital Association?], 1912-1923.

International audiology. Leiden, Netherlands : International Society of Audiology, 1962-1970.

**SERIAL PICTURE BOOKS.** *See* **COMIC BOOKS, STRIPS, ETC.**

**SERIAL PUBLICATIONS.** *See* **PERIODICALS.**

**Serie Divulgación (INTERCOOP, Editora Cooperativa Ltda.)**
Kaplan de Drimer, Alicia. Los amigos del Hada Melina. Buenos Aires : Intercoop Editora Cooperativa, [1995?]-1998.
*TC PQ7798.21.A64 A65 1995*

**Series in affective science**
Anxiety, depression, and emotion. Oxford ; New York : Oxford University Press, 2000.
*TC RC531 .A559 2000*

**Series in applied psychology (New York, N.Y.)**
Professional burnout. Washington, DC : Taylor & Francis, c1993.
*TC BF481 .P77 1993*

**Series in Continental thought**
(26) Wood, Robert E., 1934- Placing aesthetics. Athens, OH : Ohio University Press, c1999.
*TC BH81 .W66 1999*

**The series in death, dying and bereavement**
Rosenblatt, Paul C. Parent grief. Philadelphia ; Hove [England] : Brunner/Mazel, c2000.
*TC BF575.G7 R673 2000*

**Series in health and social justice**
Dying for growth. Monroe, Me. : Common Courage Press, c2000.
*TC RA418.5.P6 D95 2000*

**Series in Russian and East European studies.**
Holmes, Larry E. (Larry Eugene), 1942- Stalin's school. Pittsburgh, Pa. : University of Pittsburgh Press, c1999.
*TC LF4435.M657 H65 1999*

**Series on alcohol in society.**
Alcohol and emerging markets. Philadelphia, Penn : Brunner/Mazel, 1998.
*TC HD9350.6 .A4 1998*

Heath, Dwight B. Drinking occasions. Philadelphia : Brunner/Mazel, c2000.
*TC GT2884 .H4 2000*

**Series on biophysics and biocybernetics**
(vol. 8.) International School of Biocybernetics (1997 : Naples, Italy) Neuronal bases and psychological aspects of consiousness. Singapore ; River Edge, N.J : World Scientific, c1999.
*TC QP411 .I56 1997*

**Series on literacy**
The future of literacy in a changing world. Rev. ed. Cresskill, N.J. : Hampton Press, c1998.
*TC LC149 .F87 1998*

**The series on school reform**
Adams, Jacob E. Taking charge of curriculum. New York : Teachers College Press, c2000.
*TC LB2806.15 .A35 2000*

Chazan, Daniel. Beyond formulas in mathematics and teaching. New York : Teachers College Press, c2000.
*TC QA159 .C48 2000*

Fink, Dean, 1936- Good schools/real schools. New York : Teachers College Press, c2000.
*TC LB2822.84.C2 F56 2000*

Lieberman, Ann. Teachers--transforming their world and their work. New York : Teachers College Press ; Alexandria, Va. : Association for Supervision and Curriculum Development, c1999.
*TC LB1025.3 .L547 1999*

Reed, Carol J., 1937- Teaching with power. New York : Teachers College Press, c2000.
*TC LB2806.45 .R44 2000*

**Series paper (Gannett Foundation)**
Nancy Hanks lecture on arts and public policy. [New York, NY] : American Council for the Arts, <1988->
*TC NX730 .N25*

**SERIES (PUBLICATIONS).** *See* **CHILDREN'S LITERATURE IN SERIES.**

**SERIGRAPHS (PRINTS).** *See* **SERIGRAPHY.**

**SERIGRAPHY - 20TH CENTURY - GREAT BRITAIN.**
Screen printing [videorecording]. [Northbrook?], Ill. ; Peasmarsh, East Sussex, Eng. : Roland Collection of Films on Art, c1992.
*TC NE2238.G7 S4 1992*

**SERIGRAPHY - TECHNIQUE.**
Screen printing [videorecording]. [Northbrook?], Ill. ; Peasmarsh, East Sussex, Eng. : Roland Collection of Films on Art, c1992.
*TC NE2238.G7 S4 1992*

**SERVANTS, INDENTURED.** *See* **INDENTURED SERVANTS.**

**SERVICE IN EDUCATION - PERIODICALS.**
Journal of college placement. [Philadelphia, Pa. etc.], The College Placement Council, inc. [etc.]

**SERVICE INDUSTRIES.** *See* **EMPLOYMENT AGENCIES.**

**SERVICE INDUSTRIES - UNITED STATES.**
Employee training and U.S. competitiveness. Boulder : Westview Press, 1991.
*TC HF5549.5.T7 E46 1991*

Stanback, Thomas M. Cities in transition. Totowa, N.J. : Allanheld, Osmun, 1982.
*TC HD5724 .S649 1982*

**SERVICE INDUSTRIES WORKERS.** *See* **SHOE SHINERS.**

**SERVICE LEARNING.** *See also* **STUDENT SERVICE.**
Poirrier, Gail P. Boston : Jones and Bartlett Publishers, 2001.
*TC RT73 .P64 2001*

**Service learning across the curriculum :** case applications in higher education. Lanham, Md. : University Press of America, c2000. vi, 166 p. ; 24 cm. Includes bibliographical references and index. ISBN 0-7618-1583-X (cloth : alk. ppr.) ISBN 0-7618-1584-8 (pbk. : alk. ppr.) DDC 371.1
*1. Student service - United States - Case studies. I. Madden, Steven J.*
*TC LC221 .S47 2000*

**SERVICE, STUDENT.** *See* **STUDENT SERVICE.**

**Service to users with disabilities.**
DeCandido, GraceAnne A. Transforming libraries. Washington, D.C. : Association of Research Libraries, Office of Leadership and Management Services, c1999.
*TC Z711.92.H3 D43 1999*

**SERVICES FOR ABUSED WIVES.** *See* **ABUSED WIVES - SERVICES FOR.**

**SERVICES FOR HANDICAPPED CHILDREN.** *See* **HANDICAPPED CHILDREN - SERVICES FOR.**

**SERVICES, HUMAN.** *See* **HUMAN SERVICES.**

**SERVICES, NURSING.** *See* **NURSING SERVICES.**

**Servis, Joan.** Celebrating the fourth : ideas and inspiration for teachers of grade four / Joan Servis ; foreword by Regie Routman. Portsmouth, NH : Heinemann, c1999. xiv, 154 p. : ill. ; 24 cm. Includes bibliographical references (p. 143-147) and index. ISBN 0-325-00145-6 DDC 372.24/2
*1. Fourth grade (Education) - United States. I. Title.*
*TC LB1571 4th .S47 1999*

**SERVITUDE.** *See* **SLAVERY.**

**Seshadri-Crooks, Kalpana.** Desiring whiteness : a Lacanian analysis of race / Kalpana Seshadri-Crooks. London ; New York : Routledge, 2000. ix, 182 p. : ill. ; 24 cm. (Opening out) Includes bibliographical references (p. [168]-175) and index. ISBN 0-415-19254-4 ISBN 0-415-19255-2 DDC 155.8/2
*1. Psychoanalysis and racism. 2. Race - Psychological aspects. 3. Race awareness. 4. Lacan, Jacques, - 1901- I. Title. II. Series.*
*TC BF175.4.R34 S47 2000*

**SET THEORY.** *See* **ARITHMETIC; TOPOLOGY.**

**Settersten, Richard A.** Lives in time and place : the problems and promises of developmental science / Richard A. Settersten. Amityville, N.Y. : Baywood Pub., c1999. vi, 318 p. : ill. ; 24 cm. (Society and aging series) Includes bibliographical references (p. 257-296) and indexes. ISBN 0-89503-200-7 (hardcover) DDC 155
*1. Developmental psychology. 2. Life cycle, Human. I. Title. II. Series.*
*TC BF713 .S48 1999*

**Settings for health promotion :** linking theory and practice / Blake D. Poland, Lawrence W. Green, Irving Rootman, editors. Thousand Oaks, Calif. : Sage Publications, Inc., c2000. viii, 373 p. ; 24 cm. Includes bibliographical references and index. ISBN 0-8039-7418-3 (acid-free paper) ISBN 0-8039-7419-1 (acid-free paper) DDC 613

*1. Health promotion. 2. Social medicine. 3. Health Promotion. I. Poland, Blake D. II. Green, Lawrence W. III. Rootman, I.*
*TC RA427.8 .S48 2000*

**SETTLEMENT HOUSES.** *See* **SOCIAL SETTLEMENTS.**

**SETTLEMENTS, SOCIAL.** *See* **SOCIAL SETTLEMENTS.**

**Seurat, Georges, 1859-1891.**
Seurat [videorecording]. West Long Branch, NJ : Kultur, c1999.
*TC ND553.S5 S5 1999*

**SEURAT, GEORGES, 1859-1891.**
Seurat [videorecording]. West Long Branch, NJ : Kultur, c1999.
*TC ND553.S5 S5 1999*

**Seurat** [videorecording] / Kultur ; written by Dave Manson ; producer, Lara Lowe ; editor, Chris Gormlie. West Long Branch, NJ : Kultur, c1999. 1 videocassette (50 min.) : sd., col. with b&w sequences ; 1/2 in. (The Impressionists) (The great artists) VHS, Hi-fi. Catalogued from credits and container. Narrator: John Viner. Original music, Paul Farrer; expert analysis: David Addison, Bill Cummings ; Carole Guberman. For adolescents through adult. SUMMARY: Art historians, David Addison, Bill Cummings and Carole Gubernman, analyze Seurat's work and discuss his life and contributions to art history, tracing the influences of ancient Egyptian art and poster art on his work, describing his legacy of art as a "scientific exploration, and his development of pointillism. They further explain how Seurat's philosophy of the colors mixing in the eye rather than on the palette, the philosophy of pointilism, is his unique contribution to the world of art. ISBN 0-7697-7035-5
*1. Seurat, Georges. - 1859-1891. 2. Painters - France - Biography. 3. Painting, Modern - 19th century - France. I. Seurat, Georges, 1859-1891. II. Lowe, Lara. III. Manson, Dave. IV. Viner, John. V. Gormlie, Chris. VI. Kultur International Films. VII. Cromwell Productions. VIII. Series. IX. Series: The great artists*
*TC ND553.S5 S5 1999*

**SEUSS, DR. - JUVENILE SOFTWARE.**
Dr. Seuss kindergarten [computer file] Windows / Macintosh CD-ROM ; v. 1.0. Novato, CA : Brøderbund, c1998.
*TC LB1195 .D77 1998*

**The seven faces of philanthropy.**
Prince, Russ Alan, 1958- 1st ed. San Francisco : Jossey-Bass, c1994.
*TC HV41.9.U5 P74 1994*

**SEVEN LIBERAL ARTS.** *See* **EDUCATION, MEDIEVAL.**

**Seven short films about brain disorders [videorecording].**
When the brain goes wrong [videorecording]. Short version. Boston, MA : Fanlight Productions [dist.], c1992.
*TC RC386 .W54 1992*

**The seventh annual state of American education address [videorecording.**
Annual State of American Education Address (7th : February 22, 2000 : Durham, N.C.) [Washington, D.C. : U.S. Dept. of Education], 2000.

**Severe behavior disorders of children and youth.**
Monograph in behavioral disorders. Severe behavior disorders of children and youth. Reston, Va. : Council for Children with Behavioral Disorders, c1978-1986.
*TC BF721 .M65*

**Sevig, Todd D.**
Fukuyama, Mary A. Integrating spirituality into multicultural counseling. Thousand Oaks, Calif. : Sage Publications, c1999.
*TC BF637.C6 F795 1999*

**Sewell, Donna N.**
Taking flight with OWLs. Mahwah, N.J. : Lawrence Erlbaum Associates, Publishers, 2000.
*TC PE1404 .T24 2000*

**Sewell, James.**
Ballet class [videorecording]. W. Long Branch, NJ : Kultur, c1984.
*TC GV1589 .B33 1984*

**Sewell, Karen.**
Break throughs [videorecording]. Boston, MA : Fanlight Productions, c1998.
*TC LC4717.5 .B7 1998*

**SEX.** *See also* **MASS MEDIA AND SEX; SEX INSTRUCTION; SEXOLOGY.**
Crooks, Robert, 1941- Our sexuality. 7th ed. Pacific Grove, CA : Brooks/Cole Pub. Co., c1999.

*TC HQ21 .C698 1999*

Gordon, Sol, 1923- Personal issues in human sexuality. Boston : Allyn and Bacon, 1986.
*TC HQ35.2 .G67 1986*

Just sex. Lanham, MD : Rowman & Littlefield, 2000.
*TC HQ21 .J87 1999*

Mead, Margaret, 1901-1978. Male and female. London : Victor Gollancz, c1949.
*TC HQ21 .M464 1949*

Mead, Margaret, 1901-1978. Male and female. London : Victor Gollancz, c1949.
*TC HQ21 .M464 1949*

Ridley, Matt. The Red Queen :. New York : Penguin Books, 1995.
*TC GN365.9 .R53 1995*

Wilson, John, 1928- Learning to love. Houndmills [England] : Macmillan Press ; New York : St. Martin's Press, 2000.
*TC BF575.L8 .W555 2000*

**Sex and age distributions of population.**
World population prospects. New York : United Nations, 1985-
*TC HA154 .W6*

**SEX AND LAW.** *See* **ARTIFICIAL INSEMINATION, HUMAN - LAW AND LEGISLATION; SEX CRIMES; STERILIZATION, EUGENIC.**

**SEX AND LAW - UNITED STATES.**
Levesque, Roger J. R. Adolescents, sex, and the law. 1st ed. Washington, DC : American Psychological Association, c2000.
*TC KF479 .L48 2000*

**SEX AND MASS MEDIA.** *See* **MASS MEDIA AND SEX.**

**Sex, art, and audience.**
Fleming, Bruce. New York ; Canterbury [England] : P. Lang, c2000.
*TC GV1588.3 .F54 2000*

**SEX. BEHAVIOR.**
Gordon, Sol, 1923- Personal issues in human sexuality. Boston : Allyn and Bacon, 1986.
*TC HQ35.2 .G67 1986*

**SEX BEHAVIOR - PSYCHOLOGY.**
Sexual aggression. 1st ed. Washington, DC : American Psychiatric Press, c1999.
*TC RC560.S47 S488 1999*

**SEX BEHAVIOR SURVEYS.** *See* **SEXUAL BEHAVIOR SURVEYS.**

**SEX - CONGRESSES.**
The Role of theory in sex research. Bloomington, IN : Indiana University Press, 2000.
*TC HQ60 .R65 2000*

**SEX COUNSELING.** *See* **MARRIAGE COUNSELING; SEX INSTRUCTION.**

**SEX COUNSELING - UNITED STATES.**
Becker, Evvie. High-risk sexual behavior. New York : Plenum Press, c1998.
*TC HQ60.7.U6 B43 1998*

**SEX CRIMES.** *See also* **CHILD SEXUAL ABUSE; INCEST; RAPE; SEX AND LAW.**
Sexual aggression. 1st ed. Washington, DC : American Psychiatric Press, c1999.
*TC RC560.S47 S488 1999*

**SEX CRIMES - PREVENTION.**
Remaking relapse prevention with sex offenders. Thousand Oaks, Calif. : Sage Publications, c2000.
*TC RC560.S47 R46 2000*

**SEX CRIMINALS.** *See* **SEX OFFENDERS.**

**SEX CUSTOMS.**
Just sex. Lanham, MD : Rowman & Littlefield, 2000.
*TC HQ21 .J87 1999*

**SEX CUSTOMS - UNITED STATES.**
Crooks, Robert, 1941- Our sexuality. 7th ed. Pacific Grove, CA : Brooks/Cole Pub. Co., c1999.
*TC HQ21 .C698 1999*

Ericksen, Julia A., 1941- Kiss and tell. Cambridge, Mass. : Harvard University Press, 1999.
*TC HQ18.U5 E75 1999*

**SEX CUSTOMS - UNITED STATES - HISTORY.**
Primers for prudery. Updated ed. Baltimore : Johns Hopkins University Press, 2000.
*TC HQ18.U5 P75 2000*

Satter, Beryl, 1959- Each mind a kingdom. Berkeley : University of California Press, c1999.

*TC BF639 .S124 1999*

**SEX DIFFERENCES.**
Gender and society. Oxford ; New York : Oxford University Press, 2000.
*TC HQ1075 .G4619 2000*

**Sex differences in cognitive abilities.**
Halpern, Diane F. 3rd ed. Mahwah, N.J. : L. Erlbaum Associates, 2000.
*TC BF311 .H295 2000*

**SEX DIFFERENCES IN EDUCATION - ENGLAND - LONDON - CROSS-CULTURAL STUDIES.**
Making spaces. New York : St. Martin's Press, 2000.
*TC LC208.4 .M35 2000*

**SEX DIFFERENCES IN EDUCATION - FINLAND - HELSINKI - CROSS-CULTURAL STUDIES.**
Making spaces. New York : St. Martin's Press, 2000.
*TC LC208.4 .M35 2000*

**SEX DIFFERENCES IN EDUCATION - GREAT BRITAIN.**
Gender in the secondary curriculum. London ; New York : Routledge, 1998.
*TC LC212.93.G7 G46 1998*

Whatever happened to equal opportunities in schools? Buckingham [England] ; Philadelphia : Open University Press, 2000.
*TC LC213.3.G7 W53 2000*

**SEX DIFFERENCES IN EDUCATION - SOCIAL ASPECTS.**
Masculinities at school. Thousand Oaks, Calif. : SAGE, c2000.
*TC LC1390 .M37 2000*

**SEX DIFFERENCES IN EDUCATION - SOCIAL ASPECTS - FRANCE - HISTORY - 19TH CENTURY.**
Knottnerus, J. David. The social worlds of male and female children in the nineteenth century French educational system. Lewiston, N.Y. ; Lampeter, Wales : Edwin Mellen Press, c1999.
*TC LC191.8.F8 K66 1999*

**SEX DIFFERENCES IN EDUCATION - UNITED STATES.**
Campbell, Duane E. Choosing democracy. 2nd ed. Upper Saddle River, N.J. : Merrill, c2000.
*TC LC1099.3 .C36 2000*

Grossman, Herbert, 1934- Achieving educational equality. Springfield, Ill. : C.C. Thomas, c1998.
*TC LC213.2 .G76 1998*

**SEX DIFFERENCES (PSYCHOLOGY).** *See also* **SEX ROLE.**
The Developmental social psychology of gender. Mahwah, N.J. : Lawrence Erlbaum, c2000.
*TC HQ1075 .D47 2000*

Gender and its effects on psychopathology. Washington, DC : American Psychiatric Press, c2000.
*TC RC455.4.S45 G465 2000*

Grice, Marthe Jane. Attachment, race, and gender in late life. 1999.
*TC 085 G865*

Halpern, Diane F. Sex differences in cognitive abilities. 3rd ed. Mahwah, N.J. : L. Erlbaum Associates, 2000.
*TC BF311 .H295 2000*

Just sex. Lanham, MD : Rowman & Littlefield, 2000.
*TC HQ21 .J87 1999*

Sosin, Adrienne. Achieving styles preferences of students in an urban graduate teacher education program. 1996.
*TC 06 no. 10701*

**SEX DIFFERENCES (PSYCHOLOGY) IN CHILDREN.**
Constructing gender and difference. Cresskill, N.J. : Hampton Press, c1999.
*TC BF723.S42 C66 1999*

Ochsner, Mindy Blaise. Something rad & risqu'e. 1999.
*TC 06 no. 11208*

Tuman, Donna M. Gender difference in form and content. 1998.
*TC 06 no. 11000*

**SEX DIFFERENCES (PSYCHOLOGY) IN OLD AGE.**
Hatch, Laurie Russell. Beyond gender differences. Amityville, N.Y. : Baywood Pub., c2000.

*TC HQ1061 .H375 2000*

**SEX DISCRIMINATION.** *See also* **SEX DISCRIMINATION AGAINST WOMEN; SEX DISCRIMINATION IN EMPLOYMENT.**
Just sex. Lanham, MD : Rowman & Littlefield, 2000.
*TC HQ21 .J87 1999*

**SEX DISCRIMINATION AGAINST WOMEN - LAW AND LEGISLATION - UNITED STATES.**
Manegold, Catherine S. In glory's shadow. 1st ed. New York : Alfred A. Knopf, 1999.
*TC KF228.C53 M36 1999*

**SEX DISCRIMINATION AGAINST WOMEN - UNITED STATES.**
Deslippe, Dennis A. (Dennis Arthur), 1961- Rights, not roses. Urbana : University of Illinois Press, c2000.
*TC HD6079.2.U5 D47 2000*

**SEX DISCRIMINATION IN EDUCATION - COMMONWEALTH COUNTRIES.**
Leo-Rhynie, Elsa. Gender mainstreaming in education. London : Commonwealth Secretariat, c1999.
*TC LC2572 .L46 1999*

**SEX DISCRIMINATION IN EDUCATION - EUROPE.**
Gender, policy and educational change :. London ; New York : Routledge, 2000.
*TC LC213.3.G7 G48 2000*

**SEX DISCRIMINATION IN EDUCATION - GREAT BRITAIN.**
Gender, policy and educational change :. London ; New York : Routledge, 2000.
*TC LC213.3.G7 G48 2000*

Whatever happened to equal opportunities in schools? Buckingham [England] ; Philadelphia : Open University Press, 2000.
*TC LC213.3.G7 W53 2000*

**SEX DISCRIMINATION IN EDUCATION - TANZANIA - KILIMANJARO REGION.**
Stambach, Amy, 1966- Lessons from Mount Kilimanjaro. New York : Routledge, 2000.
*TC LA1844.K54 S72 2000*

**SEX DISCRIMINATION IN EMPLOYMENT.** *See* **SEX ROLE IN THE WORK ENVIRONMENT; SEXUAL DIVISION OF LABOR; WOMEN - EMPLOYMENT.**

**SEX DISCRIMINATION IN EMPLOYMENT - LAW AND LEGISLATION - UNITED STATES - HISTORY - SOURCES.**
Stein, Laura W., 1963- Sexual harassment in America. Westport, Conn. : Greenwood Press, 1999.
*TC KF3467 .S74 1999*

**SEX DISCRIMINATION IN EMPLOYMENT - UNITED STATES.**
Deslippe, Dennis A. (Dennis Arthur), 1961- Rights, not roses. Urbana : University of Illinois Press, c2000.
*TC HD6079.2.U5 D47 2000*

**SEX DISCRIMINATION IN HIGHER EDUCATION - LAW AND LEGISLATION - UNITED STATES.**
Manegold, Catherine S. In glory's shadow. 1st ed. New York : Alfred A. Knopf, 1999.
*TC KF228.C53 M36 1999*

**SEX DISCRIMINATION IN HIGHER EDUCATION - SOUTH AFRICA.**
Makosana, I. Nokuzola Zola, Social factors in the positioning of black women in South African universities. 1997.
*TC 06 no. 10825*

**SEX DISCRIMINATION IN HIGHER EDUCATION - SOUTH CAROLINA - CHARLESTON.**
Manegold, Catherine S. In glory's shadow. 1st ed. New York : Alfred A. Knopf, 1999.
*TC KF228.C53 M36 1999*

**SEX DISCRIMINATION IN MEDICINE.**
Gender inequalities in health. Buckingham [England] ; Philadelphia : Open University Press, 2000.
*TC RA564.85 .G4653 2000*

**Sex ed.**
Eberwein, Robert T., 1940- New Brunswick, N.J. : Rutgers University Press, 1999.
*TC HQ56 .E19 1999*

**SEX EDUCATION.** *See* **SEX INSTRUCTION.**

**Sex education activities.**
Toner, Patricia Rizzo, 1952- West Nyack, N.Y. : Center for Applied Research in Education, c1993.

*TC HQ35 .T65 1993*

**Sex education in secondary schools.**
Harrison, Jennifer, 1949- Buckingham [England] ;
Philadelphia : Open University Press, 2000.
*TC HQ57.6.G7 H37 2000*

**SEX EDUCATION - UNITED STATES.**
Primers for prudery. Updated ed. Baltimore : Johns
Hopkins University Press, 2000.
*TC HQ18.U5 P75 2000*

**SEX - ENCYCLOPEDIAS.**
Ellis, Albert, ed. The encyclopedia of sexual behavior,
[1st ed.]. New York, Hawthorn books [1961-1964]
*TC HQ9 .E4*

**SEX FACTORS.**
Gender and its effects on psychopathology.
Washington, DC : American Psychiatric Press, c2000.
*TC RC455.4.S45 G465 2000*

**SEX (GENDER).** *See* **SEX.**

**SEX HYGIENE.** *See* **HYGIENE, SEXUAL.**

**SEX IDENTITY (GENDER IDENTITY).** *See*
**GENDER IDENTITY.**

**SEX IN ART.**
Ravenhill, Philip L. Dreams and reverie. Washington :
Smithsonian Institution Press, c1996.
*TC NB1255.C85 R38 1996*

**SEX IN DANCE.**
Fleming, Bruce. Sex, art, and audience. New York ;
Canterbury [England] : P. Lang, c2000.
*TC GV1588.3 .F54 2000*

**SEX INSTRUCTION.** *See also* **HYGIENE,
SEXUAL; SEX COUNSELING.**
Gordon, Sol, 1923- Personal issues in human
sexuality. Boston : Allyn and Bacon, 1986.
*TC HQ35.2 .G67 1986*

McKay, Alexander, 1962- Sexual ideology and
schooling. London, Ont. : Althouse Press, 1998.
*TC HQ57.3 .M34 1998*

**SEX INSTRUCTION FOR TEENAGERS.**
Toner, Patricia Rizzo, 1952- Sex education activities.
West Nyack, N.Y. : Center for Applied Research in
Education, c1993.
*TC HQ35 .T65 1993*

**SEX INSTRUCTION FOR TEENAGERS - UNITED
STATES - HISTORY.**
Moran, Jeffrey P. Teaching sex. Cambridge, Mass. :
Harvard University Press, 2000.
*TC HQ57.5.A3 M66 2000*

**SEX INSTRUCTION - GREAT BRITAIN.**
Harrison, Jennifer, 1949- Sex education in secondary
schools. Buckingham [England] ; Philadelphia : Open
University Press, 2000.
*TC HQ57.6.G7 H37 2000*

**SEX INSTRUCTION - JUVENILE LITERATURE.**
*See* **SEX INSTRUCTION FOR TEENAGERS.**

**SEX INSTRUCTION - PERIODICALS.**
Journal of social hygiene. New York : American
Social Hygiene Association,

**SEX INSTRUCTION - UNITED STATES.**
Queering elementary education. Lanham, Md. :
Oxford : Rowman & Littlefield, c1999.
*TC LC192.6 .Q85 1999*

**SEX INSTRUCTION - UNITED STATES -
HISTORY.**
Eberwein, Robert T., 1940- Sex ed. New Brunswick,
N.J. : Rutgers University Press, 1999.
*TC HQ56 .E19 1999*

Moran, Jeffrey P. Teaching sex. Cambridge, Mass. :
Harvard University Press, 2000.
*TC HQ57.5.A3 M66 2000*

Primers for prudery. Updated ed. Baltimore : Johns
Hopkins University Press, 2000.
*TC HQ18.U5 P75 2000*

**SEX - MORAL AND ETHICAL ASPECTS.** *See*
**SEXUAL ETHICS.**

**SEX - MORAL AND RELIGIOUS ASPECTS.** *See*
**SEXUAL ETHICS.**

**SEX OFFENDERS.** *See also* **TEENAGE SEX
OFFENDERS.**
Sexual aggression. 1st ed. Washington, DC :
American Psychiatric Press, c1999.
*TC RC560.S47 S488 1999*

**SEX OFFENDERS - MENTAL HEALTH
SERVICES - UNITED STATES.**

Juvenile sex offenders [videorecording]. Princeton,
N.J. : Films of the Humanities & Sciences, c1998.
*TC HV9067.S48 J8 1998*

**SEX OFFENDERS - REHABILITATION.**
Remaking relapse prevention with sex offenders.
Thousand Oaks, Calif. : Sage Publications, c2000.
*TC RC560.S47 R46 2000*

**SEX OFFENDERS - REHABILITATION - UNITED
STATES.**
Juvenile sex offenders [videorecording]. Princeton,
N.J. : Films of the Humanities & Sciences, c1998.
*TC HV9067.S48 J8 1998*

**SEX OFFENDERS - UNITED STATES -
PSYCHOLOGY.**
Juvenile sex offenders [videorecording]. Princeton,
N.J. : Films of the Humanities & Sciences, c1998.
*TC HV9067.S48 J8 1998*

**SEX OFFENSES.** *See* **SEX CRIMES.**

**SEX OFFENSES - PSYCHOLOGY.**
Sexual aggression. 1st ed. Washington, DC :
American Psychiatric Press, c1999.
*TC RC560.S47 S488 1999*

**SEX - PSYCHOLOGICAL ASPECTS.** *See* **SEX
(PSYCHOLOGY).**

**SEX (PSYCHOLOGY).** *See also* **GENDER
IDENTITY; MASCULINITY; SEX
DIFFERENCES (PSYCHOLOGY); SEX
ROLE; SEXUAL ORIENTATION.**
Hite, Shere. The Hite report on male sexuality. 1st
Ballantine Book ed. New York : Ballantine Books,
1982.
*TC HQ28 .H57 1982*

Psychoanalysis and woman. New York : New York
University Press, 2000.
*TC BF175.5.S48 P795 2000*

Roszak, Theodore, 1933- The gendered atom.
Berkeley, Calif. : Conari Press, 1999.
*TC BF64 .R69 1999*

**SEX - RESEARCH.** *See* **SEXOLOGY -
RESEARCH.**

**SEX RESEARCH.** *See* **SEXOLOGY - RESEARCH.**

**SEX ROLE.** *See also* **SEXUAL DIVISION OF
LABOR.**
The Developmental social psychology of gender.
Mahwah, N.J. : Lawrence Erlbaum, c2000.
*TC HQ1075 .D47 2000*

Dryden, Caroline. Being married, doing gender.
London ; New York : Routledge, 1999.
*TC HQ734 .D848 1999*

Gender and society. Oxford ; New York : Oxford
University Press, 2000.
*TC HQ1075 .G4619 2000*

Halpern, Diane F. Sex differences in cognitive
abilities. 3rd ed. Mahwah, N.J. : L. Erlbaum
Associates, 2000.
*TC BF311 .H295 2000*

Hatch, Laurie Russell. Beyond gender differences.
Amityville, N.Y. : Baywood Pub., c2000.
*TC HQ1061 .H375 2000*

Male/female roles. San Diego, Calif. : Greenhaven
Press, c2000.
*TC HQ1075 .M353 2000*

Montagu, Ashley, 1905- The natural superiority of
women. 5th ed. Walnut Creek, Calif. : AltaMira Press,
c1999.
*TC HQ1206 .M65 1999*

Tumin, Melvin Marvin, 1919- Male and female in
today's world. New York : Harcourt Brace
Jovanovich, c1980.
*TC GN479.65 .T95 1980*

Unger, Rhoda Kesler. Resisting gender. London ;
Thousand Oaks, Calif. : Sage Publications, 1998.
*TC BF201.4 .U544 1998*

**SEX ROLE - AFRICA, WEST.**
Frank, Barbara E. Mande potters & leatherworkers.
Washington, D.C. : Smithsonian Institution Press,
1998.
*TC DT474.6.M36 F73 1998*

**SEX ROLE - CROSS-CULTURAL STUDIES.**
Situated lives. New York : Routledge, 1997.
*TC GN479.65 .S57 1997*

**SEX ROLE - DEVELOPING COUNTRIES.**
Feminist visions of development. London ; New
York : Routledge, c1998.

*TC HQ1240 .F464 1998*

**SEX ROLE - ENGLAND - LONDON.**
Gatter, Philip. Identity and sexuality. New York :
Cassell, 1999.
*TC HQ1075.5.G7 G37 1999*

**SEX ROLE - FICTION.**
Holm, Jennifer L. Our only May Amelia. 1st ed. New
York : HarperCollinsPublishers, c1999.
*TC PZ7.H732226 Ou 1999*

Moss, Marissa. True heart. 1st ed. San Diego : Silver
Whistle, c1999.
*TC PZ7.M8535 Tr 1999*

**SEX ROLE IN ART.**
Frank, Barbara E. Mande potters & leatherworkers.
Washington, D.C. : Smithsonian Institution Press,
1998.
*TC DT474.6.M36 F73 1998*

**SEX ROLE IN CHILDREN.**
Constructing gender and difference. Cresskill, N.J. :
Hampton Press, c1999.
*TC BF723.S42 C66 1999*

Ochsner, Mindy Blaise. Something rad & risqu'e.
1999.
*TC 06 no. 11208*

Tuman, Donna M. Gender difference in form and
content. 1998.
*TC 06 no. 11000*

**SEX ROLE IN LITERATURE.**
O'Keefe, Deborah. Good girl messages. New York :
Continuum, 2000.
*TC PS374.G55 O44 2000*

**SEX ROLE IN LITERATURE - STUDY AND
TEACHING.**
Making Mark Twain work in the classroom. Durham
[N.C.] : Duke University Press, 1999.
*TC PS1338 .M23 1999*

**SEX ROLE IN MASS MEDIA - UNITED STATES.**
Calvert, Sandra L. Children's journeys through the
information age. 1st ed. Boston : McGraw-Hill
College, c1999.
*TC HQ784.T4 C24 1999*

**SEX ROLE IN THE WORK ENVIRONMENT.** *See
also* **SEX DISCRIMINATION IN
EMPLOYMENT; SEXUAL HARASSMENT.**
Handbook of gender & work. Thousand Oaks, CA :
Sage Publications, Inc., c1999.
*TC HQ1233 .H33 1999*

Maddock, Su. Challenging women. London ;
Thousand Oaks, Calif. : Sage, 1999.
*TC HQ1236 .M342 1999*

**SEX ROLE IN THE WORK ENVIRONMENT -
UNITED STATES.**
Cleveland, Jeanette. Women and men in
organizations. Mahwah, N.J. ; London : Lawrence
Erlbaum Associates, 2000.
*TC HD6060.65.U5 C58 2000*

**SEX ROLE - RESEARCH.**
Gender and qualitative research. Aldershot, Hants,
England ; Brookfield, Vt., USA : Avebury, c1996.
*TC HQ1075 .G4617 1996*

**SEX ROLE - RESEARCH - UNITED STATES.**
Gender, culture, and ethnicity. Mountain View,
Calif. : Mayfield Pub. Co., c1999.
*TC HQ1181.U5 G45 1999*

**SEX ROLE - UNITED STATES.**
Male/female roles. San Diego, Calif. : Greenhaven
Press, c2000.
*TC HQ1075 .M353 2000*

Situated lives. New York : Routledge, 1997.
*TC GN479.65 .S57 1997*

**SEX ROLE - UNITED STATES - CASE STUDIES.**
Rothenberg, Paula S., 1943- Invisible privilege.
Lawrence : University Press of Kansas, c2000.
*TC E185.615 .R68 2000*

**SEX ROLE - UNITED STATES -
HISTORIOGRAPHY.**
Quesnell, Quentin. The strange disappearance of
Sophia Smith. Northampton [Mass.] : Smith College,
c1999.
*TC LD7152.65.S45 Q84 1999*

**SEX ROLE - UNITED STATES - HISTORY.**
Satter, Beryl, 1959- Each mind a kingdom. Berkeley :
University of California Press, c1999.
*TC BF639 .S124 1999*

**SEX - STUDY AND TEACHING.** *See* **SEX INSTRUCTION.**

**SEX SURVEYS.** *See* **SEXUAL BEHAVIOR SURVEYS.**

**SEX THERAPY.** *See also* **PSYCHOSEXUAL DISORDERS.**
Daines, Brian. Psychodynamic approaches to sexual problems. Buckingham ; Philadelphia : Open University Press, 2000.
*TC RC557 .D35 2000*

**SEX - UNITED STATES.**
Primers for prudery. Updated ed. Baltimore : Johns Hopkins University Press, 2000.
*TC HQ18.U5 P75 2000*

**SEXISM.** *See also* **SEX ROLE.**
Girls, boys, books, toys. Baltimore : Johns Hopkins University Press, 1999.
*TC PN1009.5.S48 G57 1999*

**SEXISM IN EDUCATION.**
Tuman, Donna M. Gender difference in form and content. 1998.
*TC 06 no. 11000*

**SEXISM IN HIGHER EDUCATION - UNITED STATES - CASE STUDIES.**
Brodie, Laura Fairchild. Breaking out. 1st ed. New York : Pantheon Books, c2000.
*TC LC212.862 .B75 2000*

**SEXISM IN LANGUAGE.** *See* **LANGUAGE AND LANGUAGES - SEX DIFFERENCES.**

**SEXISM IN LITERATURE.**
Girls, boys, books, toys. Baltimore : Johns Hopkins University Press, 1999.
*TC PN1009.5.S48 G57 1999*

**SEXISM IN RELIGION.** *See* **WOMEN AND RELIGION.**

**SEXOLOGY.** *See also* **SEX.**
Money, John, 1921- The lovemap guidebook. New York : Continuum, c1999.
*TC BF692 .M57 1999*

**SEXOLOGY - RESEARCH.**
Gender and qualitative research. Aldershot, Hants, England ; Brookfield, Vt., USA : Avebury, c1996.
*TC HQ1075 .G4617 1996*

Hillman, Jennifer L. Clinical perspectives on elderly sexuality. New York : Kluwer Academic/Plenum Publishers, c2000.
*TC HQ30 .H55 2000*

**SEXOLOGY - RESEARCH - CONGRESSES.**
The Role of theory in sex research. Bloomington, IN : Indiana University Press, 2000.
*TC HQ60 .R65 2000*

**SEXOLOGY - UNITED STATES - HISTORY - 20TH CENTURY.**
Ericksen, Julia A., 1941- Kiss and tell. Cambridge, Mass. : Harvard University Press, 1999.
*TC HQ18.U5 E75 1999*

**SEXUAL ABUSE.** *See* **SEX CRIMES.**

**SEXUAL ABUSE OF CHILDREN.** *See* **CHILD SEXUAL ABUSE.**

**SEXUAL ABUSE VICTIMS.** *See also* **ADULT CHILD SEXUAL ABUSE VICTIMS; INCEST VICTIMS; RAPE VICTIMS; SEXUALLY ABUSED CHILDREN.**
Bohmer, Carol. The wages of seeking help. Westport, Conn. ; London : Praeger, 2000.
*TC RC560.S44 B57 2000*

**Sexual aggression** / edited by Jon A. Shaw. 1st ed. Washington, DC : American Psychiatric Press, c1999. xv, 343 p. ; 24 cm. Includes bibliographical references and index. ISBN 0-88048-757-7 DDC 616.85/82
*1. Sex crimes. 2. Sex offenders. 3. Child sexual abuse. 4. Sex Offenses - psychology. 5. Violence. 6. Child Abuse, Sexual - psychology. 7. Sex Behavior - psychology. I. Shaw, Jon A.*
*TC RC560.S47 S488 1999*

**SEXUAL ATTRACTION.**
Money, John, 1921- The lovemap guidebook. New York : Continuum, c1999.
*TC BF692 .M57 1999*

**SEXUAL BEHAVIOR.** *See* **SEX; SEX CUSTOMS; SEXUAL ETHICS.**

**Sexual behavior in the human female** / by the staff of the Institute for Sex Research, Indiana University, Alfred C. Kinsey ... [et al.] ; with a new introduction by John Bancroft. Bloomington, Ind. : Indiana University Press, [1998] xxx, 842 p. : ill. ; 24 cm.
Originally published: Philadelphia : W.B. Saunders Co., 1953.

Includes bibliographical references (p. 763-810) and index. ISBN 0-253-33411-X (cloth : alk. paper) DDC 306.7/082
*1. Women - Sexual behavior. I. Kinsey, Alfred C. (Alfred Charles), 1894-1956. II. Institute for Sex Research.*
*TC HQ29 .S487 1998*

**Sexual behavior in the human male.**
Kinsey, Alfred C. (Alfred Charles), 1894-1956. Bloomington, Ind. : Indiana University Press, [1998].
*TC HQ28 .K55 1998*

**SEXUAL BEHAVIOR, PSYCHOLOGY OF.** *See* **SEX (PSYCHOLOGY).**

**SEXUAL BEHAVIOR SURVEYS - UNITED STATES.**
Ericksen, Julia A., 1941- Kiss and tell. Cambridge, Mass. : Harvard University Press, 1999.
*TC HQ18.U5 E75 1999*

Hite, Shere. The Hite report. New York : Dell, 1987.
*TC HQ29 .H57 1987*

**Sexual bullying.**
Duncan, Neil, 1956- London ; New York : Routledge, 1999.
*TC LC212.83.G7 D85 1999*

**SEXUAL CHILD ABUSE.** *See* **CHILD SEXUAL ABUSE.**

**SEXUAL CRIMES.** *See* **SEX CRIMES.**

**SEXUAL DELINQUENCY.** *See* **SEX CRIMES.**

**SEXUAL DEVIATION.** *See* **PSYCHOSEXUAL DISORDERS.**

**SEXUAL DISEASES.** *See* **SEXUALLY TRANSMITTED DISEASES.**

**SEXUAL DISORDERS.** *See* **PSYCHOSEXUAL DISORDERS.**

**SEXUAL DIVISION OF LABOR.** *See also* **SEX DISCRIMINATION IN EMPLOYMENT.**
Organizational change & gender equity. Thousand Oaks : Sage Publications, c2000.
*TC HD58.8 .O7289 2000*

**SEXUAL DIVISION OF LABOR - AFRICA, WEST.**
Frank, Barbara E. Mande potters & leatherworkers. Washington, D.C. : Smithsonian Institution Press, 1998.
*TC DT474.6.M36 F73 1998*

**SEXUAL DIVISION OF LABOR - UNITED STATES.**
Williams, Joan, 1952- Unbending gender. Oxford ; New York : Oxford University Press, c2000.
*TC HD4904.25 .W55 2000*

**SEXUAL DIVISION OF LABOR - UNITED STATES - HISTORY.**
Oldenziel, Ruth, 1958- Making technology masculine. Amsterdam : Amsterdam University Press, c1999.
*TC HD8072 .O57 1999*

**SEXUAL ETHICS.** *See* **BIRTH CONTROL; CONTRACEPTION; SEXUAL HARASSMENT.**

**SEXUAL ETHICS - FICTION.**
Caseley, Judith. Losing Louisa. 1st ed. New York : Farrar, Straus and Giroux, c1999.
*TC PZ7.C2677 Lo 1999*

**SEXUAL ETHICS FOR TEENAGERS - UNITED STATES - HISTORY.**
Moran, Jeffrey P. Teaching sex. Cambridge, Mass. : Harvard University Press, 2000.
*TC HQ57.5.A3 M66 2000*

**SEXUAL ETHICS - STUDY AND TEACHING (SECONDARY) - GREAT BRITAIN.**
Harrison, Jennifer, 1949- Sex education in secondary schools. Buckingham [England] ; Philadelphia : Open University Press, 2000.
*TC HQ57.6.G7 H37 2000*

**SEXUAL ETHICS - UNITED STATES.**
Davis, Michael, 1943- Ethics and the university. London ; New York : Routledge, 1999.
*TC LB2324 .D38 1999*

**SEXUAL HARASSMENT.** *See* **SEX ROLE IN THE WORK ENVIRONMENT.**

**Sexual harassment in America.**
Stein, Laura W., 1963- Westport, Conn. : Greenwood Press, 1999.
*TC KF3467 .S74 1999*

**SEXUAL HARASSMENT IN EDUCATION - GREAT BRITAIN - CASE STUDIES.**
Duncan, Neil, 1956- Sexual bullying. London ; New York : Routledge, 1999.

*TC LC212.83.G7 D85 1999*

**SEXUAL HARASSMENT IN EDUCATION - UNITED STATES.**
Wetzel, Roberta, 1946- Student-generated sexual harassment in secondary schools. Westport, Conn. ; London : Bergin & Garvey, 2000.
*TC LC212.82 .W47 2000*

**SEXUAL HARASSMENT IN SCHOOLS.** *See* **SEXUAL HARASSMENT IN EDUCATION.**

**Sexual harassment in the workplace and academia :** psychiatric issues / edited by Diane K. Shrier. 1st ed. Washington, DC : American Psychiatric Press, c1996. xv, 278 p. : ill. ; 22 cm. (Clinical practice ; no. 38) Includes bibliographical references (p. 245-265) and index. ISBN 0-88048-490-X (acid-free paper) DDC 616.85/83
*1. Sexual harassment - Psychological aspects. 2. Sexual Harassment - psychology. 3. Psychotherapy - methods. 4. Sexual Harassment - United States - legislation. I. Shrier, Diane K. II. Series.*
*TC RC560.S47 S495 1996*

**SEXUAL HARASSMENT - LAW AND LEGISLATION - UNITED STATES - HISTORY - SOURCES.**
Stein, Laura W., 1963- Sexual harassment in America. Westport, Conn. : Greenwood Press, 1999.
*TC KF3467 .S74 1999*

**SEXUAL HARASSMENT - PSYCHOLOGICAL ASPECTS.**
Sexual harassment in the workplace and academia. 1st ed. Washington, DC : American Psychiatric Press, c1996.
*TC RC560.S47 S495 1996*

**SEXUAL HARASSMENT - PSYCHOLOGY.**
Sexual harassment in the workplace and academia. 1st ed. Washington, DC : American Psychiatric Press, c1996.
*TC RC560.S47 S495 1996*

**SEXUAL HARASSMENT - UNITED STATES - LEGISLATION.**
Sexual harassment in the workplace and academia. 1st ed. Washington, DC : American Psychiatric Press, c1996.
*TC RC560.S47 S495 1996*

**SEXUAL HYGIENE.** *See* **HYGIENE, SEXUAL.**

**SEXUAL IDENTITY (GENDER IDENTITY).** *See* **GENDER IDENTITY.**

**Sexual ideology and schooling.**
McKay, Alexander, 1962- London, Ont. : Althouse Press, 1998.
*TC HQ57.3 .M34 1998*

**SEXUAL INTERCOURSE.** *See* **INCEST.**

**SEXUAL OFFENDERS.** *See* **SEX OFFENDERS.**

**SEXUAL OFFENSES.** *See* **SEX CRIMES.**

**SEXUAL ORIENTATION.** *See* **HOMOSEXUALITY.**

**SEXUAL ORIENTATION - MORAL AND ETHICAL ASPECTS.**
Stein, Edward, 1965- The mismeasure of desire. Oxford ; New York : Oxford University Press, 1999.
*TC HQ76.25 .S69 1999*

**SEXUAL ORIENTATION - PHILOSOPHY.**
Stein, Edward, 1965- The mismeasure of desire. Oxford ; New York : Oxford University Press, 1999.
*TC HQ76.25 .S69 1999*

**SEXUAL ORIENTATION - RESEARCH.**
Stein, Edward, 1965- The mismeasure of desire. Oxford ; New York : Oxford University Press, 1999.
*TC HQ76.25 .S69 1999*

**Sexual, physical, and emotional abuse in out-of-home care.**
Johnson, Toni Cavanagh. New York : The Haworth Maltreatment and Trauma Press, c1997.
*TC RJ507.A29 J64 1997*

**SEXUAL PREFERENCE.** *See* **SEXUAL ORIENTATION.**

**SEXUAL PSYCHOLOGY.** *See* **SEX (PSYCHOLOGY).**

**SEXUALITY.** *See* **SEX.**

**SEXUALLY ABUSED CHILDREN.** *See* **ADULT CHILD SEXUAL ABUSE VICTIMS.**

**SEXUALLY ABUSED CHILDREN - MENTAL HEALTH.**
Richardson, Bonnie. Factors influencing the sexual and contraceptive behavior of sexually abused adolescents of color. 1999.

*TC 06 no. 11167*

**SEXUALLY ABUSED PATIENTS.**
Bohmer, Carol. The wages of seeking help. Westport,
Conn. ; London : Praeger, 2000.
*TC RC560.S44 B67 2000*

**SEXUALLY TRANSMITTED DISEASES.** *See also*
HYGIENE, SEXUAL.
Marr, Lisa. Baltimore, Md : The Johns Hopkins
University Press, 1998.
*TC RC200.2 .M27 1998*

**SEXUALLY TRANSMITTED DISEASES -
EPIDEMIOLOGY - UNITED STATES.**
Institute of Medicine (U.S.). Committee on Prevention
and Control of Sexually Transmitted Diseases. The
hidden epidemic. Washington, D.C. : National
Academy Press, 1997.
*TC RA644.V4 I495 1997*

**SEXUALLY TRANSMITTED DISEASES -
POPULAR WORKS.**
Marr, Lisa. Sexually transmitted diseases. Baltimore,
Md : The Johns Hopkins University Press, 1998.
*TC RC200.2 .M27 1998*

**SEXUALLY TRANSMITTED DISEASES -
PREVENTION & CONTROL - UNITED
STATES.**
Institute of Medicine (U.S.). Committee on Prevention
and Control of Sexually Transmitted Diseases. The
hidden epidemic. Washington, D.C. : National
Academy Press, 1997.
*TC RA644.V4 I495 1997*

**SEXUALLY TRANSMITTED DISEASES -
UNITED STATES.**
Becker, Evvie. High-risk sexual behavior. New York :
Plenum Press, c1998.
*TC HQ60.7.U6 B43 1998*

Institute of Medicine (U.S.). Committee on Prevention
and Control of Sexually Transmitted Diseases. The
hidden epidemic. Washington, D.C. : National
Academy Press, 1997.
*TC RA644.V4 I495 1997*

**Seymour, Julie.**
Practising identities. New York : St. Martin's Press,
1999.
*TC HM131 .P677 1999*

**Seymour Simon's book of trucks.**
Simon, Seymour. New York : HarperCollins
Publishers, 2000.
*TC TL230.15 .S56 2000*

**Shaddock, David.** Contexts and connections : an
intersubjective systems approach to couples therapy /
David Shaddock. New York : Basic Books, 2000. xvi,
192 p. ; 24 cm. Includes bibliographical references and index.
ISBN 0-465-09570-4 DDC 616.89/156
*1. Marital psychotherapy. 2. Intersubjectivity. I. Title.*
*TC RC488.5 .S483 2000*

**Shadow culture.**
Taylor, Eugene. Washington, D.C. : Counterpoint,
c1999.
*TC BL2525 .T39 1999*

**The shadow education system.**
Bray, Mark. Paris : Unesco, International Institute for
Educational Planning, 1999.
*TC LC41 .B73 1999*

**SHADOW PUPPETS.**
Ewart, Franzeska G. Let the shadows speak. Stoke on
Trent, Staffordshire, England : Trentham Books,
1998.
*TC PN1979.S5 E8 1998*

**SHADOW SHOWS.**
Ewart, Franzeska G. Let the shadows speak. Stoke on
Trent, Staffordshire, England : Trentham Books,
1998.
*TC PN1979.S5 E8 1998*

**Shakespeare, Tom.**
Barnes, Colin, 1946- Exploring disability. Cambridge,
UK : Polity Press ; Malden, MA : Blackwell
Publishers, 1999.
*TC HV1568 .B35 1999*

**SHAKESPEARE, WILLIAM, 1564-1616 -
DRAMATIC PRODUCTION.**
Teaching Shakespeare through performance. New
York : Modern Language Association of America,
1999.
*TC PR2987 .T366 1999*

**SHAKESPEARE, WILLIAM, 1564-1616 - STAGE
HISTORY.**
Teaching Shakespeare through performance. New

York : Modern Language Association of America,
1999.
*TC PR2987 .T366 1999*

**SHAKESPEARE, WILLIAM, 1564-1616 - STUDY
AND TEACHING.**
Teaching Shakespeare through performance. New
York : Modern Language Association of America,
1999.
*TC PR2987 .T366 1999*

**Shalin, Valerie L.**
Cognitive task analysis. Mahwah, N.J. : L. Erlbaum
Associates, 2000.
*TC BF311 .C55345 2000*

**SHAMANISM - UAUPÉS RIVER VALLEY
(COLOMBIA AND BRAZIL).**
Arhem, Kaj. Makuna. Washington : Smithsonian
Institution Press, c1998.
*TC F2270.2.M33 A68 1998*

**SHAME.** *See* GUILT; STIGMA (SOCIAL
PSYCHOLOGY).

**Shame of the nation [picture].**
Child labor [picture]. Amawalk, NY : Jackdaw
Publications, c1997.
*TC HD6250.U5 C4 1997*

**Shames, George H., 1926-** Counseling the
communicatively disabled and their families : a
manual for clinicians / George H. Shames. Boston ;
London : Allyn and Bacon, c2000. xi, 175 p. ; 23 cm.
Includes bibliographical references (p. 159-162) and index.
ISBN 0-205-30799-X DDC 616.85/50651
*1. Communicative disorders - Patients - Counseling of. I. Title.*
*TC RC428.8 .S53 2000*

**Shamir, Jacob.** The anatomy of public opinion / Jacob
Shamir and Michal Shamir. Ann Arbor, Mich. :
University of Michigan Press, c2000. xiii, 301 p. : ill. ;
23 cm. Includes bibliographical references and indexes. ISBN
0-472-11022-5
*1. Public opinion. I. Shamir, Michal. 1951- II. Title.*
*TC HM236 .S5 2000*

**Shamir, Michal. 1951-.**
Shamir, Jacob. The anatomy of public opinion. Ann
Arbor, Mich. : University of Michigan Press, c2000.
*TC HM236 .S5 2000*

**Shanahan, James.** Television and its viewers :
cultivation theory and research / James Shanahan and
Michael Morgan. Cambridge ; New York : Cambridge
University Press, 1999. xiii, 267 p. : ill. ; 24 cm. Includes
bibliographical references (p. 251-264) and index. ISBN 0-
521-58296-2 ISBN 0-521-58755-7 (pbk.) DDC 302.23/45
*1. Television broadcasting - Social aspects. I. Morgan,
Michael.*
*TC PN1992.6 .S417 1999*

**Shanahan, Michael J.**
Transitions to adulthood in a changing economy.
Westport, Conn. : Praeger, c1999.
*TC HQ799.7 .T73 1999*

**Shanker, James L.** Locating and correcting reading
difficulties / James L. Shanker, Eldon E. Ekwall. 7th
ed. Upper Saddle River, N.J. : Merrill, c1998. xxii, 522
p. : ill. ; 24 cm. Ekwall's name appears first on the 6th edition.
Includes bibliographical references and index. ISBN 0-13-
862962-5 DDC 372.43
*1. Reading - Remedial teaching. I. Ekwall, Eldon E. II. Title.*
*TC LB1050.5 .E38 1998*

**Shannon, Ann.** Keeping score / by Ann Shannon ;
Mathematical Sciences Education Board, Center for
Science, Mathematics, and Engineering Education,
National Research Council. Washington, D.C. :
National Academy Press, 1999. x, 203 p. : ill. ; 26 cm.
(Compass series) (Assessment in practice) Includes
bibliographical references (p.81-85). ISBN 0-309-06535-6
*1. Mathematics - Study and teaching - United States. 2.
Education - Standards - United States. 3. Educational
evaluation - United States. I. National Research Council
(U.S.). Mathematical Sciences Education Board. II. Title. III.
Series.*
*TC QA135.5 .S45 1999x*

**SHAPE.**
Fisher, Leonard Everett. Look around. New York,
N.Y., U.S.A. : Viking Kestrel, 1987.
*TC QA447 .F5 1987*

**SHAPES.**
Marsh, Valerie. Storytelling with shapes & numbers.
Ft. Atkinson, Wis. : Alleyside Press, c1999.
*TC LB1042 .M2874 1999*

**Shaping school culture.**
Deal, Terrence E. 1st ed. San Francisco : Jossey-Bass
Publishers, c1999.

*TC LB2805 .D34 1999*

**Shaping school policy.**
Gallagher, Karen S. Newbury Park, Calif. : Corwin
Press, c1992.
*TC LC89 .G35 1992*

**Shapira, Jill.**
Roper, Janice M. Ethnography in nursing research.
Thousand Oaks, Calif. : Sage Publications, c2000.
*TC RT81.5 .R66 2000*

**Shapiro, David, 1926-** Dynamics of character : self-
regulation in psychopathology / David Shapiro. New
York : Basic Books, c2000. xii, 172 p. ; 25 cm. (Basic
behavioral science) Series statement on jacket. Includes
bibliographical references (p. 161-165) and index. ISBN 0-
465-09571-2 DDC 616.89
*1. Temperament. 2. Psychology, Pathological. 3. Character. 4.
Will. 5. Schizophrenia. I. Title. II. Series.*
*TC RC455.5.T45 .S46 2000*

**Shapiro, David, 1947-.**
Uncontrollable beauty. New York : Allworth Press :
School of Visual Arts, c1998.
*TC BH201 .U53 1998*

**Shapiro, Edna Kaufman, 1925-.**
Revisiting a progressive pedagogy. Albany : State
University of New York Press, c2000.
*TC LB1117 .R44 2000*

**Shapiro, Edward S. (Edward Steven), 1951-**
Academic skills problems workbook / Edward S.
Shapiro. New York : Guilford Press, c1996. vi, 135 p. :
ill. ; 28 cm. (The Guilford school practitioner series) Includes
bibliographical references (p. 135). ISBN 1-57230-107-4
*1. Remedial teaching. 2. Basic education. 3. Educational tests
and measurements. I. Title. II. Series.*
*TC LB1029.R4 S52 1996*

Behavioral assessment in schools. 2nd ed. New York :
Guilford Press, c2000.
*TC LB1124 .B435 2000*

Conducting school-based assessments of child and
adolescent behavior. New York : Guilford Press,
c2000.
*TC LB1124 .C66 2000*

**Shapiro, H. Svi.**
Strangers in the land. New York : Peter Lang, c1999.
*TC E184.36.E84 S77 1999*

**Shaposhnikova, T. D.**
Innovation in Russian schools. Bloomington, Ind. :
Phi Delta Kappa Educational Foundation, c1997.
*TC LB1027 .I6575 1997*

**Shared beliefs in a society.**
Bar-Tal, Daniel. Thousand Oaks, Calif. : Sage
Publications, c2000.
*TC HM1041 .B37 2000*

**Shared visions :** Native American painters and sculptors
in the twentieth century / [edited by] Margaret
Archuleta and Rennard Strickland ; essays by Joy L.
Gritton, W. Jackson Rushing. 1st New Press ed. New
York : New Press : Distributed by Norton, [1993],
c1991. 110 p. : ill. (some col.) ; 31 cm. Catalog of an
exhibition held at the Heard Museum, Phoenix, Ariz., Apr.-
May 1991. Includes bibliographical references (p. 103-108).
ISBN 1-56584-069-0 (pbk.) DDC 704/.0397/0904
*1. Art, Indian - Exhibitions. 2. Art, Modern - 20th century -
United States - Exhibitions. 3. Indians of North America - Art -
Exhibitions. I. Archuleta, Margaret. II. Strickland, Rennard.
III. Gritton, Joy L. IV. Rushing, W. Jackson. V. Heard Museum.*
*TC N6538.A4 A7 1993*

**SHARIA (ISLAMIC LAW).** *See* ISLAMIC LAW.

**SHARING - FICTION.**
Kadono, Eiko. Grandpa's soup. Grand Rapids, MI :
Eerdmans Books for Young Readers, 1999.
*TC PZ7.K1167 Gr 1999*

**Sharing words.**
Flecha, Ramón. [Compartiendo palabras. English]
Lanham, Md. ; Oxford : Rowman & Littlefield
Publishers, c2000.
*TC LB1060 .F5913 2000*

**Sharma, Martha B., 1945-** Using internet primary
sources to teach critical thinking skills in geography /
Martha B. Sharma and Gary S. Elbow. Westport,
Conn. ; London : Greenwood Press, 2000. xv, 165 p. ;
25 cm. (Greenwood professional guides in school librarianship,
1074-150X) Includes bibliographical references and index.
ISBN 0-313-30899-3 (alk. paper) DDC 910/.285
*1. Geography - Study and teaching (Secondary) - Computer
network resources. 2. Internet in education. 3. Critical
thinking - Study and teaching (Secondary) I. Elbow, Gary S. II.
Title. III. Series.*

*TC G73 .S393 2000*

**Sharma, R. (Rajendra), 1959-** The family encyclopedia of health : the complete family reference guide to alternative & orthodox medical diagnosis, treatment & preventative healthcare / Dr. Rajendra Sharma. Boston : Element Books, 1999. xxviii, 692 p. : ill. ; 26 cm. "First published in the U.K. in 1998 by Element Books Limited." Includes bibliographical references and index. ISBN 1-86204-426-0
*1. Medicine, Popular - Encyclopedias. 2. Alternative medicine - Encyclopedias. 3. Health - Encyclopedias. I. Title. II. Title: Complete family reference guide to alternative & orthodoxe medical diagnosis, treatment & preventive healthcare III. Title: Complete family reference guide to alternative and orthodoxe medical diagnosis, treatment and preventive healthcare*
*TC RC81.A2 S53 1999*

**Sharmat, Marjorie Weinman.** The 329th friend / by Marjorie Weinman Sharmat ; ill. by Cyndy Szekeres. New York : Four Winds Press, c1979. [48] p. : col. ill. ; 34 x 45 cm. SUMMARY: Bored with his own company, Emery Raccoon invites 328 guests to lunch but finds that none of them have time to listen to him. ISBN 0-02-109116-1
*1. Friendship - Fiction. 2. Animals - Fiction. I. Szekeres, Cyndy. II. Title.*
*TC PZ7.S5299 Tk 1979*

**Sharp, Mavis, 1945-** The management of failing DipSW students : activities and exercises to prepare practice teachers for work with failing students / Mavis Sharp and Hazel Danbury. Aldershot ; Brookfield, Vt. : Ashgate, c1999. ix, 193 p. : ill. ; 22 cm. Includes bibliographical references (p. 185-187) and index. ISBN 1-85742-437-9 (pbk.) DDC 361.31/2/071141
*1. Social work education - Great Britain. 2. Student teaching - Great Britain. 3. Grading and marking (Students) - Great Britain. 4. Grading and marking (Students) - Great Britain - Problems, exercises, etc. 5. School failure - Great Britain. I. Danbury, Hazel, 1939- II. Title. III. Title: Management of failing Diploma in Social Work students*
*TC HV11.8.G7 S53 1999*

**Sharp, Richard M.** The best Web sites for teachers / Richard M. Sharp, Vicki F. Sharp, Martin G. Levine. 3rd ed. Eugene, OR : International Society for Technology in Education, 2000. 224 p. : ill. ; 28 cm. Includes index. ISBN 1-56484-160-x
*1. Education - Computer network resources - Directories. 2. Web sites - Directories. 3. Internet in education - Directories. I. Sharp, Vicki F. II. Levine, Martin G. III. Title.*
*TC LB1044.87 .S52 2000*

**Sharp, Vicki F.** Computer education for teachers / Vicki Sharp. 3rd ed. Boston, Mass. : McGraw-Hill College, c1999. xvi, 512 p. : ill. ; 24 cm. Includes bibliographical references and index. ISBN 0-07-292458-6 (alk. paper) DDC 370/.285
*1. Education - Data processing. 2. Computers - Study and teaching. 3. Computer-assisted instruction. I. Title.*
*TC LB1028.43 .S55 1999*

Sharp, Richard M. The best Web sites for teachers. 3rd ed. Eugene, OR : International Society for Technology in Education, 2000.
*TC LB1044.87 .S52 2000*

**Sharwood Smith, Michael, 1942-.**
The current state of interlanguage. Amsterdam ; Philadelphia : J. Benjamins, c1995.
*TC P118.2 .C867 1995*

**Shattuck, Roger.** Candor and perversion : literature, education, and the arts / Roger Shattuck. 1st ed. New York : W.W. Norton, c1999. viii, 415 p. : ill. (some col.) ; 24 cm. Includes bibliographical references and index. ISBN 0-393-04807-1 DDC 809
*1. Literature - History and criticism - Theory, etc. 2. American literature - History and criticism. 3. French literature - History and criticism. 4. Education, Higher - United States. 5. Arts - Study and teaching. I. Title.*
*TC PN52 .S53 1999*

**Shaver, Joan.**
Handbook of clinical nursing research. Thousand Oaks, Calif. : Sage Publications, c1999.
*TC RT81.5 .H25 1999*

**Shavick, Andrea.** You'll grow soon, Alex / Andrea Shavick ; illustrations by Russell Ayto. New York : Walker, 2000. 1v. (unpaged) : col. ill. ; 29 cm. SUMMARY: Alex follows the advice of his mother, father, sister, and teacher hoping to grow taller, but it is his very tall uncle's advice that really makes a difference. ISBN 0-8027-8736-3 (hc) DDC [E]
*1. Size - Fiction. 2. Growth - Fiction. 3. Self-acceptance - Fiction. I. Ayto, Russell, ill. II. Title.*
*TC PZ7.S5328 Yo 2000*

**Shaw, Jon A.**
Sexual aggression. 1st ed. Washington, DC : American Psychiatric Press, c1999.
*TC RC560.S47 S488 1999*

**Shaw, Nancy (Nancy E.)** Sheep on a ship / Nancy Shaw ; illustrated by Margot Apple. Boston : Houghton Mifflin, 1989. 32 p. : chiefly col. ill. ; 21 x 22 cm. SUMMARY: Sheep on a deep-sea voyage run into trouble when it storms and are glad to come paddling into port. ISBN 0-395-48160-0 DDC [E]
*1. Ships - Fiction. 2. Sheep - Fiction. 3. Stories in rhyme. I. Apple, Margot, ill. II. Title.*
*TC PZ8.3.S5334 Si 1989*

**Shaw, Simon.**
Towards the digital library. London : The British Library. 1998.
*TC Z664.B75 T683 1998*

**Shaw, Sondra C., 1936-** Reinventing fundraising : realizing the potential of women's philanthropy / Sondra C. Shaw, Martha A. Taylor. 1st ed. San Francisco : Jossey-Bass Publishers, c1995. xxv, 270 p. : ill. ; 24 cm. (The Jossey-Bass nonprofit sector series) Includes bibliographical references (p. 259-263) and index. ISBN 0-7879-0050-8 (acid-free paper) DDC 361.7/068/1
*1. Fund raising - United States. 2. Women philanthropists - United States. I. Taylor, Martha A., 1949- II. Title. III. Series.*
*TC HV41.9.U5 S53 1995*

**Shea, Shawn C.** The practical art of suicide assessment : a guide for mental health professionals and substance abuse counselors / Shawn Christopher Shea. New York ; Chichester [England] : John Wiley, c1999. xvii, 254 p. : ill. ; 24 cm. Includes bibliographical references and index. CONTENTS: Foreword / David A. Jobes -- Pt. 1. The Experience of Suicide: Etiology, Phenomenology, and Risk Factors. 1. Suicide: The Ultimate Paradox. 2. Descent into the Maelstrom: Etiology and Phenomenology of Suicide. 3. Risk Factors: Harbingers of Death -- Pt. 2. Uncovering Suicidal Ideation: Principles, Techniques, and Strategies. 4. Before the Interview Begins: Overcoming the Taboo against Talking about Suicide. 5. Validity Techniques: Simple Tools for Uncovering Complex Secrets. 6. Eliciting Suicidal Ideation: Practical Techniques and Effective Strategies -- Pt. 3. Practical Assessment of Risk: Flexible Strategies and Sound Formulations. 7. Putting It All Together: Safe and Effective Decision Making. ISBN 0-471-18363-6 (pbk. : alk. paper) DDC 616.85/8445 DDC 616.85/8445
*1. Suicide - Risk factors. 2. Suicide - Prevention. I. Title.*
*TC RC569 .S46 1999*

**Shea, Thomas M., 1934-.**
Bauer, Anne M. Inclusion 101. Baltimore, Md. : P.H. Brookes Pub., c1999.
*TC LC1201 .B38 1999*

**SHEEP - FICTION.**
Shaw, Nancy (Nancy E.) Sheep on a ship. Boston : Houghton Mifflin, 1989.
*TC PZ8.3.S5334 Si 1989*

**Sheep on a ship.**
Shaw, Nancy (Nancy E.) Boston : Houghton Mifflin, 1989.
*TC PZ8.3.S5334 Si 1989*

**Sheffield, Linda Jensen, 1949-** Teaching and learning elementary and middle school mathematics / Linda Jensen Sheffield, Douglas E. Cruikshank. 4th ed. New York : Wiley, c2000. viii, 520 p. : ill. ; 28 cm. Cruikshank's name appears first on earlier eds. Includes bibliographical references and index. ISBN 0-471-36546-7 DDC 510/.71/2
*1. Mathematics - Study and teaching (Elementary) 2. Mathematics - Study and teaching (Middle school) I. Cruikshank, Douglas E., 1941- II. Title.*
*TC QA135.5 .S48 2000*

**Sheffield University Television.**
Challenge cases [videorecording]. Princeton, N.J. : Films for the Humanities & Sciences, 1998.
*TC RC455.2.C4 C4 1998*

Disorders due to psychoactive substance abuse [videorecording]. Princeton, N.J. : Films for the Humanities & Sciences, 1998.
*TC RC564 .D5 1998*

Organic disorders [videorecording]. Princeton, N.J. : Films for the Humanities & Sciences, 1998.
*TC RC521 .O7 1998*

Personality disorders [videorecording]. Princeton, N.J. : Films for the Humanities & Sciences, 1998.
*TC RC554 .P4 1998*

**Shelby, Anne.** We keep a store / by Anne Shelby ; illustrated by John Ward. New York : Orchard Books, c1989. 34 p. : col. ill. ; 24 cm. SUMMARY: A small girl describes the many pleasures that accompany running a country store. ISBN 0-531-05856-5 ISBN 0-531-08456-6 (lib. bdg.) DDC [E]

*1. Stores, Retail - Fiction. 2. Country life - Fiction. I. Ward, John (John Clarence), ill. II. Title.*
*TC PZ7.S54125 We 1989*

We keep a store / by Anne Shelby ; paintings by John Ward. New York : Orchard Books, c1990. [32] p. : col. ill. ; 38 x 53 cm. SUMMARY: A small girl describes the many pleasures that accompany running a country store. ISBN 0-02-109104-8
*1. Stores, Retail - Fiction. 2. Country life - Fiction. I. Ward, John (John Clarence), ill. II. Title.*
*TC PZ7 .S54125We 1990*

**Sheldon, Dyan.** Confessions of a teenage drama queen / Dyan Sheldon. 1st ed. Cambridge, Mass. : Candlewick Press, 1999. 272 p. ; 22 cm. SUMMARY: In her first year at a suburban New Jersy high school, Mary Elizabeth Cep, who now calls herself "Lola," sets her sights on the lead in the annual drama production, and finds herself in conflict with the most popular girl in school. ISBN 0-7636-0822-X (hardcover : alk. paper) DDC [Fic]
*1. Identity - Fiction. 2. Interpersonal relations - Fiction. 3. High schools - Fiction. 4. Schools - Fiction. I. Title.*
*TC PZ7.S54144 Co 1999*

**Shell, G. Richard, 1949-** Bargaining for advantage : negotiation strategies for reasonable people / G. Richard Shell. New York : Viking, 1999. xvi, 286 p. : ill ; 24 cm. Includes bibliographical references (p. [275]-277) and index. ISBN 0-670-88133-3 (alk. paper) DDC 302.3
*1. Negotiation. 2. Persuasion (Psychology) I. Title.*
*TC BF637.N4 S44 1999*

**Shell game.**
Boutwell, Clinton E. Bloomington, Ind. : Phi Delta Kappa Educational Foundation, c1997.
*TC LC1085.2 .B68 1997*

**SHELLCRAFT.**
Sohi, Morteza E. Look what I did with a shell!. New York : Walker & Co., 2000.
*TC TT862 .S64 2000*

**SHELLCRAFT - JUVENILE LITERATURE.**
Sohi, Morteza E. Look what I did with a shell!. New York : Walker & Co., 2000.
*TC TT862 .S64 2000*

**Shellenberger, Sylvia.**
McGoldrick, Monica. Genograms. 2nd ed. New York : W.W. Norton, 1999.
*TC RC488.5 .M395 1999*

**SHELLS. See SHELLCRAFT.**

**Shelton, Patrick J.** Measuring and improving patient satisfaction / Patrick J. Shelton. Gaithersburg, Md. : Aspen Publishers, 2000. xxiii, 510 p. : ill. ; 24 cm. Includes bibliographical references and index. ISBN 0-8342-1074-6 DDC 362.1/068/5
*1. Patient satisfaction. 2. Patient Satisfaction. 3. Data Collection - methods. 4. Organizational Innovation. 5. Quality Assurance, Health Care - organization & administration. 6. Staff Development. I. Title.*
*TC RA399.A1 S47 2000*

**Shengold, Leonard.** Soul murder revisited : thoughts about therapy, hate, love, and memory / Leonard Shengold. New Haven, CT : Yale University Press, 1999. viii, 328 p. ; 22 cm. Includes bibliographical references (p. 303-311) and index. ISBN 0-300-07594-4 (alk. paper) DDC 616.85/82239
*1. Adult child abuse victims - Mental health. 2. Psychoanalysis. 3. Child abuse in literature. I. Title.*
*TC RC569.5.C55 S53 1999*

**Shepard, Ernest H. (Ernest Howard), 1879-1976.**
Williams, John Tyerman. Pooh and the millennium. 1st American ed. New York : Dutton Books, 1999.
*TC PR6025.I65 Z975 1999*

**Shephard, Roy J.** Aging, physical activity, and health / Roy J. Shephard. Champaign, IL : Human Kinetics, c1997. viii, 488 p. : ill. ; 24 cm. Includes bibliographical references (p. 377-472) and indexes. ISBN 0-87322-889-8 DDC 613.7/0446
*1. Aging. 2. Physical fitness. 3. Age factors in disease. 4. Exercise for the aged. I. Title.*
*TC QP86 .S478 1997*

**SHEPHERDS. See SHEEP.**

**Shepherdson, Charles.** Vital signs : nature, culture, psychoanalysis / Charles Shepherdson. New York : Routledge, 2000. xv, 256 p. : ill. ; 24 cm. Includes bibliographical references (p. 239-246) and index. ISBN 0-415-90879-5 (hardcover) ISBN 0-415-90880-9 (pbk.) DDC 150.19/5
*1. Psychoanalysis - France. I. Title.*
*TC BF173 .S4975 2000*

**Sher, Tamara Goldman.**
The psychology of couples and illness. 1st ed.

Washington, D.C. : American Psychological Association, c2000.
*TC R726.5 .P785 2000*

**SHERIFF OF NOTTINGHAM (LEGENDARY CHARACTER) - FICTION.**
Cadnum, Michael. In a dark wood. New York : Orchard Books, c1998.
*TC PZ7.C11724 In 1998*

**SHERIFF OF NOTTINGHAM (LEGENDARY CHARACTER) - JUVENILE FICTION.**
Cadnum, Michael. In a dark wood. New York : Orchard Books, c1998.
*TC PZ7.C11724 In 1998*

**Sherlock, Philip Manderson, Sir.** The story of the Jamaican people / Philip Sherlock & Hazel Bennett. Kingston, Jamaica : I. Randle Publishers ; Princeton, N.J. : M. Wiener Publishers, 1998. xiii, 434 p. : ill., maps ; 24 cm. "[Published] in collaboration with the Creative Production and Training Centre Ltd, Kingston, Jamaica." Includes bibliographical references (p. 412-419) and indexes. ISBN 976-8100-30-3 (pbk.) ISBN 976-8123-09-5 (cloth) ISBN 1-55876-146-2 (Wiener : pbk.) ISBN 1-55876-145-4 (Wiener : cloth) DDC 972.92
*1. Jamaica - History. I. Bennett, Hazel. II. Title.*
*TC F1881 .S5 1998*

**Sherman, Francine T., 1955-.**
Transforming social inquiry, transforming social action. Boston ; London : Kluwer Academic, c2000.
*TC LC238 .T73 2000*

**Sherman, Frederick Fairchild.**
Art in America. New York, Frederick Fairchild Sherman.

Art in America and elsewhere. Springfield, Mass., Frederick Fairchild Sherman.

**Sherman, V. Clayton.** Raising standards in American health care : best people, best practices, best results / V. Clayton Sherman. 1st ed. San Francisco : Jossey-Bass, c1999. xxiv, 332 p. : ill. ; 24 cm. (Jossey-Bass health series) Includes bibliographical references (p. 293-301) and index. ISBN 0-7879-4621-4 (hardcover : alk. paper) DDC 362.1/02/1873
*1. Medical care - Standards - United States. 2. Social medicine - Standards - United States. I. Title. II. Series.*
*TC RA395.A3 S483 1999*

**Shields, Carolyn M.** Year-round schooling : promises and pitfalls / Carolyn M. Shields and Steven Lynn Oberg. Lanham, Md. : Scarecrow Press, 2000. xii, 235 p. : ill. ; 24 cm. "Technomic Books." Includes bibliographical references (p. 223-230) and index. ISBN 0-8108-3744-7 (cloth : alk. paper) DDC 371.2/36/0973
*1. Year-round schools - United States. 2. School management and organization - United States. I. Oberg, Steven Lynn. II. Title.*
*TC LB3034 .S55 2000*

**Shiffrin, Steven H., 1941-** Dissent, injustice, and the meanings of America / Steven H. Shiffrin. Princeton, N.J. : Princeton University Press, c1999. xiv, 204 p. ; 24 cm. Includes bibliographical references (p. [131]-197) and index. ISBN 0-691-00142-1 (alk. paper) DDC 342.73/0853
*1. Freedom of speech - United States. 2. Hate speech - United States. 3. Racism in language. I. Title.*
*TC KF4772 .S448 1999*

**Shifrin, Nisson Abramovich, 1892-.**
Mayakovsky, Vladimir, 1893-1930. Kem byt'? [Moskva] : Gosudarstvennoe izdatel'stvo, 1929.
*TC PN6110.O32 M39 1929 Rus*

**Shifting focus.**
Lawyer-Brook, Dianna, 1949- Lanham, Md. ; London : Scarecrow Press, 2000.
*TC LB1044.7 .L313 2000*

**The shifting wind.**
Howard, John R., 1933- Albany : State University of New York Press, c1999.
*TC KF4757 .H69 1999*

**Shildrick, Margrit.**
Vital signs. Edinburgh : Edinburgh University Press, c1998.
*TC HQ1190 .V56 1998*

**Shillcock, Richard.**
Language acquisition. 1st ed. Amsterdam ; New York : North-Holland, 1999.
*TC P118 .L2539 1999*

**Shimin, Symeon, 1902-.**
Krumgold, Joseph, 1908- Onion John. New York, N.Y. : Thomas Y. Crowell Company, 1959.
*TC XFK942*

**Shin, Gene-Tey.**
Professional development guide for educators. Washington, D.C. : National Education Association of the United States, 2000.
*TC LC1099.3 .P755 1999*

**Shinn, Mark R.**
Advanced applications of curriculum-based measurement. New York : Guilford Press, c1998.
*TC LB3060.32.C74 A38 1998*

**SHIPBUILDING.** *See* SHIPS.

**Shipps, Dorothy.**
Reconstructing the common good in education. Stanford, Calif. : Stanford University Press, c2000.
*TC LA212 .R42 2000*

**SHIPS - FICTION.**
Shaw, Nancy (Nancy E.) Sheep on a ship. Boston : Houghton Mifflin, 1989.
*TC PZ8.3.S5334 Si 1989*

**SHIPWRECKS - FICTION.**
Bodkin, Odds. Ghost of the Southern Belle. 1st ed. Boston : Little, Brown, 1999.
*TC PZ7.B6355 Gh 1999*

Greene, Carol. Sunflower Island. 1st ed. New York : HarperCollins, c1999.
*TC PZ7.G82845 Sl 1999*

**Shiva, V. A.** Arts and the Internet : a guide to the revolution / V.A. Shiva. New York : Allworth Press, c1996. 207 p. : ill. ; 23 cm. Includes index. ISBN 1-88055-940-4 (pbk.)
*1. Arts - Computer network resources. 2. Arts - Computer network resources - Directories. 3. Internet (Computer network) I. Title.*
*TC NX260 .S55 1996*

**Shiva, Vandana.** Stolen harvest : the hijacking of the global food supply / by Vandana Shiva. Cambridge, MA : South End Press, c2000. 146 p. ; 23 cm. Includes bibliographical references and index. ISBN 0-89608-608-9 (hbk. : alk. paper) ISBN 0-89608-607-0 (pbk. : alk. paper) DDC 338.4/7664
*1. Food industry and trade. 2. Big business. 3. Food supply. I. Title.*
*TC HD9000.5 .S454 2000*

**SHO'AH (1939-1945).** *See* HOLOCAUST, JEWISH (1939-1945).

**SHOE POLISHERS.** *See* SHOE SHINERS.

**SHOE SHINERS - FICTION.**
Ketteman, Helen. Shoeshine Whittaker. New York : Walker & Co., 1999.
*TC PZ7.K494 Sh 1999*

**Shoemaker, Cynthia.**
**Administration and management of programs for young children.**
Shoemaker, Cynthia. Leadership and management of programs for young children. 2nd ed. Upper Saddle River, N.J. : Merrill, 2000.
*TC LB2822.6 .S567 2000*

Leadership and management of programs for young children / Cynthia C. Jones Shoemaker. 2nd ed. Upper Saddle River, N.J. : Merrill, 2000. xvii, 553 p. : ill. ; 24 cm. Rev. ed. of: Administration and management of programs for young children. c1995. Includes bibliographical references and index. ISBN 0-13-012940-2 (pbk.) DDC 372.12
*1. Early childhood education - United States - Administration. 2. Day care centers - United States - Administration. I. Shoemaker, Cynthia. Administration and management of programs for young children. II. Title.*
*TC LB2822.6 .S567 2000*

**Shoeshine Whittaker.**
Ketteman, Helen. New York : Walker & Co., 1999.
*TC PZ7.K494 Sh 1999*

**Shoham, S. Giora, 1929-** Personality and deviance : development and core dynamics / Shlomo Giora Shoham. Westport, Conn. : Praeger, 2000. 217 p. : ill. ; 25 cm. Includes bibliographical references (p. [209]-214) and index. ISBN 0-275-96683-6 (alk. paper) DDC 155.2
*1. Personality. 2. Personality - Social aspects. 3. Deviant behavior. I. Title.*
*TC BF698 .S5186 2000*

**Shohamy, Elana Goldberg.**
Language policy and pedagogy. Philadelphia : J. Benjamins, c2000.
*TC P53 .L364 2000*

**Shohat, Ella.**
Talking visions. New York, N.Y. : New Museum of Contemporary Art ; Cambridge, Mass. : MIT Press, c1998.
*TC NX180.F4 T36 1998*

**Shootback :** photos by kids from the Nairobi slums / [editor, Lana Wong]. London : Booth-Clibborn, 1999. 1 v. (unpaged) : chiefly col. ill. ; 27 cm. ISBN 1-86154-132-5
*1. Street children - Nairobi - pictorial works. 2. Poor children - Nairobi - pictorial works. 3. Slums - Kenya - Nairobi - pictorial works. 4. Urban poor - Kenya - Nairobi - pictorial works. 5. Nairobi (Kenya) - social conditions - pictorial works. I. Wong, Lana.*
*TC HV4160.5.N34 S45 1999*

**SHOOTING.** *See* FIREARMS.

**SHOPPERS' GUIDES.** *See* CONSUMER EDUCATION.

**SHOPPING.** *See* CONSUMER EDUCATION.

**SHOPPING CENTERS.** *See* RETAIL TRADE; STORES, RETAIL.

**SHOPS.** *See* STORES, RETAIL.

**SHOPS, COFFEE.** *See* COFFEE SHOPS.

**Shor, Ira, 1945-.**
Education is politics. Portsmouth, NH : Boynton/ Cook, c1999.
*TC LC196.5.U6 E36 1999*

**Shore, Bruce M.**
Talents unfolding. 1st ed. Washington, DC : American Psychological Association, c2000.
*TC BF723.G5 T35 2000*

**Shore, Rima.** Rethinking the brain : new insights into early development / by Rima Shore. New York : Families and Work Institute, c1997. xviii, 92 p. : ill. (some col.) ; 27 cm. Notes: p. 81-87. Includes bibliographical references (p. 88-92). ISBN 1-88832-404-X DDC 612.6/5
*1. Pediatric neuropsychology. 2. Brain - Growth. 3. Child development. 4. Child Development. 5. Infant Care. 6. Brain - growth & development. 7. Neuropsychology. 8. Learning - in infancy & childhood. 9. Child development. 10. Infants - Development. 11. Brain. I. Shore, Rima. II. Title.*
*TC RJ486.5 .S475 1997*

Shore, Rima. Rethinking the brain. New York : Families and Work Institute, c1997.
*TC RJ486.5 .S475 1997*

**Shorris, Earl, 1936-.**
**New America blues.**
Shorris, Earl, 1936- Riches for the poor. New York : W.W. Norton, 2000.
*TC HV4045 .S464 2000*

Riches for the poor : the Clemente Course in the Humanities / Earl Shorris. New York : W.W. Norton, 2000. 273 p. ; 21 cm. Rev. ed. of: New America blues. 1997. Includes bibliographical references and index. ISBN 0-393-32066-9 (pbk.) DDC 362.5/0973
*1. Poor - United States. 2. Poverty - United States. I. Shorris, Earl, 1936- . New America blues. II. Title.*
*TC HV4045 .S464 2000*

**Shorrocks-Taylor, Diane.**
Learning from others. Dordrecht [Netherlands] ; Boston : Kluwer Academic Publishers, c2000.
*TC LB43 .L42 2000*

**Short, Deborah.**
Echevarria, Jana, 1956- Making content comprehensible for English language learners. Boston, MA : Allyn and Bacon, 2000.
*TC PE1128.A2 E24 2000*

**Short, Paula M.**
Case studies of the superintendency. Lanham, Md. : Scarecrow Press, c2000.
*TC LB2831.72 .C38 2000*

Information collection : the key to data-based decision making / Paula M. Short, Rick Jay Short, Kenneth Brinson, Jr. Larchmont, NY : Eye on Education, c1998. xii, 130 p. : ill. ; 24 cm. (The school leadership library) Includes bibliographical references. ISBN 1-88300-146-3 DDC 025.06/37
*1. Education - United States - Information services. 2. Information storage and retrieval systems - Education - United States. 3. School management and organization - United States - Decision making. 4. School principals - United States. I. Short, Rick Jay. II. Brinson, Kenneth. 1961- III. Title. IV. Series.*
*TC LB1028.27.U6 S46 1998*

**Short, Rick Jay.**
Short, Paula M. Information collection. Larchmont, NY : Eye on Education, c1998.
*TC LB1028.27.U6 S46 1998*

**SHORT STORIES.**
Second sight. New York : Philomel Books, 1999.
*TC PZ5 .S4375 1999*

Second sight. New York : Philomel Books, 1999.

*Short stories.*

*TC PZ5 .S4375 1999*

Tomorrowland. New York : Scholastic Press, 1999.
*TC PZ5 .T6235 1999*

**SHORT STORIES, AMERICAN - HISTORY AND CRITICISM.**
Short stories in the classroom. Urbana, Ill. : National Council of Teachers of English, c1999.
*TC PS374.S5 S48 1999*

**SHORT STORIES, AMERICAN - STUDY AND TEACHING.**
Short stories in the classroom. Urbana, Ill. : National Council of Teachers of English, c1999.
*TC PS374.S5 S48 1999*

**Short stories in the classroom** / edited by Carole L. Hamilton [and] Peter Kratzke. Urbana, Ill. : National Council of Teachers of English, c1999. xv, 207 p. : ill. ; 27 cm. Includes bibliographical references and index. ISBN 0-8141-0399-5 (pbk.) DDC 813/.0109/0071
*1. Short stories, American - Study and teaching. 2. Short stories, American - History and criticism. I. Hamilton, Carole L., 1951- II. Kratzke, Peter, 1960-*
*TC PS374.S5 S48 1999*

**Shortell, Stephen M. (Stephen Michael), 1944-.**
Remaking health care in America. 1st ed. San Francisco : Jossey-Bass Publishers, c1996.
*TC RA395.A3 R46 1996*

**SHOW-AND-TELL PRESENTATIONS - FICTION.**
Carrick, Carol. Patrick's dinosaurs on the Internet. New York : Clarion Books, 1999.
*TC PZ7.C2344 Patf 1999*

**SHOW BUSINESS.** *See* **PERFORMING ARTS.**

**SHOW BUSINESS PERSONALITIES.** *See* **ENTERTAINERS.**

**SHOW-MEN.** *See* **ENTERTAINERS.**

**Showbiz bookkeeper.**
Chadwick, Annie. Dorset, Vermont : Theatre Directories, 1992, c1991.
*TC HF5686.P24 C53 1991*

**SHOWS, MUSICAL.** *See* **MUSICALS.**

**SHOWS, TELEVISION.** *See* **TELEVISION PROGRAMS.**

**Shribman, David M.**
Miraculously builded in our hearts. Hanover : Dartmouth University Press, 1999.
*TC LD1438 .M573 1999*

**Shrier, Diane K.**
Sexual harassment in the workplace and academia. 1st ed. Washington, DC : American Psychiatric Press, c1996.
*TC RC560.S47 S495 1996*

**Shrum, Judith L.** Teacher's handbook : contextualized language instruction / Judith L. Shrum, Eileen W. Glisan. 2nd ed. Boston, Mass. : Heinle & Heinle, c2000. xvii, 364 p. : ill., maps ; 26 cm. Includes bibliographical references and index. ISBN 0-8384-0879-6 (pbk.) DDC 418/.007
*1. Language and languages - Study and teaching - Handbooks, manuals, etc. I. Glisan, Eileen W. II. Title.*
*TC P51 .S48 2000*

**Shtogren, John A.**
Skyhooks for leadership. New York : AMACOM, American Management Association, c1999.
*TC HD58.8 .S577 1999*

**Shucksmith, Janet, 1953-** Health issues and adolescents : growing up, speaking out / Janet Shucksmith and Leo B. Hendry. London ; New York : Routledge, 1998. vii, 165 p. ; 22 cm. (Adolescence and society) Includes bibliographical references and index. ISBN 0-415-16848-1 (hbk.) ISBN 0-415-16849-X (pbk.) DDC 613/.0433
*1. Teenagers - Health and hygiene. 2. Health attitudes. 3. Teenagers - Attitudes. 4. Health behavior in adolescence. 5. Teenagers - Health and hygiene - Scotland. 6. Health attitudes - Scotland. 7. Teenagers - Scotland - Attitudes. 8. Health behavior in adolescence - Scotland. I. Hendry, Leo B. II. Title. III. Series.*
*TC RJ47.53 .S455 1998*

**Shukri, Shirin J. A.** Social changes and women in the Middle East : state policy, education, economics and development / Shirin J.A. Shukri. Aldershot ; Brookfield, Vt. : Ashgate, c1999. x, 118 p. ; 22 cm. Includes bibliographical references and index. ISBN 1-85972-668-2 DDC 305.486971056
*1. Muslim women - Middle East - Social conditions. 2. Middle East - Social policy. I. Title.*
*TC HQ1726.5 .S58 1999*

**Parisian scholars in the early fourteenth century.**
Courtenay, William J. Cambridge, U.K. ; New York, NY : Cambridge University Press, 1999.
*TC LF2165 .C68 1999*

**SIBERIA.** *See* **SIBERIA (RUSSIA).**

**SIBERIA (R.S.F.S.R.).** *See* **SIBERIA (RUSSIA).**

**SIBERIA (R.S.F.S.R. AND KAZAKH S.S.R.).** *See* **SIBERIA (RUSSIA).**

**SIBERIA (RUSSIA) - SOCIAL LIFE AND CUSTOMS.**
Oakes, Jill E. (Jill Elizabeth), 1952- Spirit of Siberia. Washington, D.C. : Smithsonian Institution Press, c1998.
*TC DK758 .O24 1998*

**SIBIR' (RUSSIA).** *See* **SIBERIA (RUSSIA).**

**SIBLING ABUSE.** *See* **BROTHERS AND SISTERS.**

**SIBLING RELATIONS.** *See* **BROTHERS AND SISTERS.**

**SIBLING RELATIONS.**
Adolescent siblings in stepfamilies. Chicago, Ill. : University of Chicago Press, 1999.
*TC LB1103.S6 v.64 no. 4*

**SIBLING RIVALRY.**
Brothers and sisters. Northvale, N.J. : J. Aronson, c1999.
*TC BF723.S43 B78 1999*

**SIBLINGS.** *See* **BROTHERS AND SISTERS.**

**SICK.** *See* **ADDICTS; DISEASES; MENTALLY ILL; PATIENTS.**

**SICK CHILDREN.** *See* **CHRONICALLY ILL CHILDREN; MENTALLY ILL CHILDREN.**

**SICK CHILDREN - EDUCATION - GREAT BRITAIN.**
The education of children with medical conditions. London : D. Fulton Publishers, 2000.
*TC LC4564.G7 E38 2000*

**SICK - COUNSELING OF.**
The practice of counselling in primary care. London ; Thousand Oaks, Calif. : SAGE Publications, 1999.
*TC R727.4 .P733 1999*

**SICK - FAMILY RELATIONSHIPS.**
The psychology of couples and illness. 1st ed. Washington, D.C. : American Psychological Association, c2000.
*TC R726.5 .P785 2000*

**SICK - FICTION.**
Cherry, Lynne. Who's sick today? 1st ed. New York : Dutton, c1988.
*TC PZ8.3.C427 Wh 1988*

**SICK LEAVE - LAW AND LEGISLATION - UNITED STATES.**
Commission on Family and Medical Leave (U.S.) A Workable balance. Washington, DC : Commission on Leave ; Women's Bureau, U.S. Dept. of Labor, [1996]
*TC HD5115.6.U5 C66 1996*

**SICK LEAVE - UNITED STATES.**
Commission on Family and Medical Leave (U.S.) A Workable balance. Washington, DC : Commission on Leave ; Women's Bureau, U.S. Dept. of Labor, [1996]
*TC HD5115.6.U5 C66 1996*

**SICK - PSYCHOLOGY.**
Chiozza, Luis A. Why do we fall ill? Madison, Conn. : Psychosocial Press, c1999.
*TC R726.7 .C48 1999*

**SICKNESS.** *See* **DISEASES.**

**SICKNESSES.** *See* **DISEASES.**

**Siddiqui, Zillur Rahman.** Visions and revisions : higher education in Bangladesh, 1947-1992 / Zillur Rahman Siddiqui. Dhaka : University Press, 1997. xxiii, 259 p. ; 21 cm. Includes bibliographical references (p. [251]-252) and index. DDC 378.5492
*1. Education, Higher - Bangladesh - History - 20th century. I. Title.*
*TC LA1168 .S53 1997*

**SIDE DRUM.** *See* **SNARE DRUM.**

**SIDEREAL SYSTEM.** *See* **STARS.**

**Sideways stories from Wayside School.**
Sachar, Louis, 1954- New York : Morrow Junior Books, 1998.
*TC PZ7.S1185 Si 1998*

**Sieber, Roy, 1923-** African art in the cycle of life / Roy Sieber and Roslyn Adele Walker. Washington, D.C. : Published for the National Museum of African Art by

the Smithsonian Press, c1987. 155 p. : ill. (some col.) ; 30 cm. "Published in conjunction with an inaugural exhibition, African Art in the Cycle of Life, organized by the National Museum of African Art, September 28, 1987-March 20, 1988"--T.p. verso. Bibliography: p. 149-155. ISBN 0-87474-821-6 (pbk. : alk. paper) ISBN 0-87474-822-4 (hard : alk. paper) DDC 732./2/0967074153
*1. Sculpture, African - Exhibitions. 2. Sculpture, Primitive - Africa, Sub-Saharan - Exhibitions. 3. Art and society - Africa, Sub-Saharan - Exhibitions. I. Walker, Roslyn A. II. National Museum of African Art (U.S.) III. Title.*
*TC NB1091.65 .S54 1987*

**Siegal, Michael.**
Children's understanding of biology and health. 1st ed. Cambridge, U.K. ; New York : Cambridge University Press, 1999.
*TC BF723.C5 C514 1999*

**Siegel, Eli, 1902-.**
Aesthetics.
Kunz, Linda Ann. English modals in American talk shows. 1999.
*TC 06 no. 11136*

**Siegel, Marjorie Gail, 1952-.**
Borasi, Raffaella. Reading counts. New York ; London : Teachers College Press, c2000.
*TC QA11 .B6384 2000*

**SIEGES - VIRGINIA.** *See* **YORKTOWN (VA.) - HISTORY - SIEGE, 1781.**

**Siegler, Robert S.**
Chen, Zhe, 1964- Across the great divide. Oxford : Blackwell, 2000.
*TC LB1103 .S6 v.65 no. 2*

**Sierra, Judy.** Antarctic antics : a book of penguin poems / written by Judy Sierra ; illustrated by Jose Aruego & Ariane Dewey. 1st ed. San Diego : Harcourt Brace & Co., c1998. 1 v. (unpaged) : col. ill. ; 24 x 29 cm. "Gulliver books." SUMMARY: A collection of poems celebrating the habits and habitat of Emperor penguins. ISBN 0-15-201006-8 DDC 811/.54
*1. Penguins - Juvenile poetry. 2. Antarctic regions - Juvenile poetry. 3. Children's poetry, American. 4. Penguins - Poetry. 5. Antarctic regions - Poetry. 6. American poetry. I. Aruego, Jose, ill. II. Dewey, Ariane, ill. III. Title.*
*TC PS3569.I39 A53 1998*

**Sigel, Irving E.**
Development of mental representation. Mahwah, NJ : L. Erlbaum Associates, c1999.
*TC BF723.M43 T47 1999*

**Sigfluence III.**
Loase, John Frederick, 1947- Lanham, Md. : University Press of America, c1996.
*TC BF774 .L63 1996*

**Sigfluence three.**
Loase, John Frederick, 1947- Sigfluence III. Lanham, Md. : University Press of America, c1996.
*TC BF774 .L63 1996*

**Sight lines.**
Kirby, Sandy. Tortola, BVI : Craftsman House in association with Gordon and Breach ; New York : Distributed in the USA by STBS Ltd., 1992.
*TC N72.F45 K57 1992*

**SIGHTINGS OF UNIDENTIFIED FLYING OBJECTS.** *See* **UNIDENTIFIED FLYING OBJECTS - SIGHTINGS AND ENCOUNTERS.**

**Sigma Theta Tau International.**
Journal of nursing scholarship. Indianapolis, IN : JNS Publication Office, 2000-
*TC RT1 .I42*

**Sigmund Freud revisited.**
Noland, Richard W. New York : Twayne Publishers, c1999.
*TC BF109.F74 N65 1999*

**SIGN LANGUAGE.** *See also* **AMERICAN SIGN LANGUAGE.**
Gesture, speech, and sign. Oxford [England] ; New York : Oxford University Press, c1999.
*TC P117 .G469 1999*

The signs of language revisited. Mahwah, N.J. : L.Erlbaum, 2000.
*TC HV2474 .S573 2000*

Uyechi, Linda, 1957- The geometry of visual phonology. Stanford, Calif. : CSLI Publications, 1996.
*TC HV2474 .U88 1996*

**SIGN LANGUAGE - HISTORY.**
Williams, Drid, 1928- Anthropology and human movement. Lanham, Md. ; London : Scarecrow Press, 2000.

**TC GV1595 .W53 2000**

**SIGN LANGUAGE INTERPRETERS.** *See* INTERPRETERS FOR THE DEAF.

**SIGN LANGUAGE - STUDY AND TEACHING - UNITED STATES.**
Innovative practices for teaching sign language interpreters. Washington, D.C. : Gallaudet University Press, 2000.
**TC HV2402 .I56 2000**

**Significant others' perceptions of the effects of their partners' psychotherapy.**
Golden, Valerie. 1998.
**TC 085 G566**

**SIGNIFICS.** *See* SEMANTICS (PHILOSOPHY).

**SIGNS AND SIGNBOARDS.** *See* POSTERS.

**SIGNS AND SYMBOLS.** *See* SEMANTICS (PHILOSOPHY); SIGN LANGUAGE.

**SIGNS AND SYMBOLS IN ART.** *See* SYMBOLISM IN ART.

**Signs and wonders.**
Collins, Pat Lowery. Boston : Houghton Mifflin, 1999.
**TC PZ7.C69675 Si 1999**

**The signs of language revisited :** an anthology to honor Ursula Bellugi and Edward Klima / edited by Karen Emmorey and Harlan Lane. Mahwah, N.J. : L.Erlbaum, 2000. xv, 580 p. : ill. ; 24 cm. Includes bibliographical references and indexes ISBN 0-8058-3246-7 DDC 419
*1. Sign language. 2. American Sign Language. I. Emmorey, Karen. II. Lane, Harlan L. III. Bellugi, Ursula, 1931- IV. Klima, Edward S., 1931-*
**TC HV2474 .S573 2000**

**Sikes, Alfred C.** Fast forward : America's leading experts reveal how the internet is changing your life / [compiled by] Alfred C. Sikes with Ellen Pearlman. 1st ed. New York : William Morrow, 2000. xii, 298 p. ; 25 cm. Includes bibliographical references. ISBN 0-380-97828-8
*1. Internet (Computer network) - Social aspects. I. Pearlman, Ellen. II. Title.*
**TC HM851 .S545 2000**

**Silbereisen, R. K. (Rainer K.), 1944-.**
Growing up in times of social change. New York : Walter de Gruyter, 1999.
**TC HQ799.G5 G76 1999**

Negotiating adolescence in times of social change. Cambridge, U.K. : New York : Cambridge University Press, 2000.
**TC HQ796 .N415 2000**

**SILENCE.**
Wilmer, Harry A., 1917- Quest for silence. Einsiedeln, Switzerland : Daimon, c2000.
**TC BJ1499.S5 W556 2000**

**The silence in the mountains.**
Rosenberg, Liz. 1st American ed. New York : Orchard Books, c1999.
**TC PZ7.R71894 Si 1999**

**SILENCE - RELIGIOUS ASPECTS.**
Wilmer, Harry A., 1917- Quest for silence. Einsiedeln, Switzerland : Daimon, c2000.
**TC BJ1499.S5 W556 2000**

**Silences & images :** the social history of the classroom / edited by Ian Grosvenor, Martin Lawn & Kate Rousmaniere. New York : P. Lang, c1999. vi, 274 p. : ill. ; 23 cm. (History of schools and schooling ; vol. 7) Includes bibliographical references. ISBN 0-8204-3926-6 (pbk. : alk. paper) DDC 370/.009
*1. Classrooms - History - Congresses. 2. School environment - History - Congresses. 3. Education - Social aspects - History - Congresses. 4. Classrooms - United States - History - Congresses. 5. School environment - United States - History - Congresses. 6. Education - Social aspects - United States - History - Congresses. I. Grosvenor, Ian. II. Lawn, Martin. III. Rousmaniere, Kate, 1958- IV. Title: Silences and images V. Series: History of schools and schooling ; v. 7.*
**TC LA128 .S55 1999**

**Silences and images.**
Silences & images. New York : P. Lang, c1999.
**TC LA128 .S55 1999**

**SILENT READING - HANDBOOKS, MANUALS, ETC.**
Pilgreen, Janice L. The SSR handbook. Portsmouth, NH : Boynton/Cook Publishers, c2000.
**TC LB1050.55 .P55 2000**

**Silk, Kenneth R., 1944-.**
Tasman, Allan, 1947- The doctor-patient relationship in pharmacotherapy. New York : Guilford Press, c2000.
**TC RC483.3 .T375 2000**

**SILK SCREEN PRINTING.** *See* SERIGRAPHY.

**SILK SCREEN PROCESS.** *See* SERIGRAPHY.

**Sills, Thomas W.** Science fun with toys : a guide for parents and teachers : with resource descriptions for unique & educational toys / Thomas W. Sills. 1st ed. Chicago : Dearborn Resources, c1999. xvii, 191 p. : ill. ; 22 cm. Includes index. ISBN 0-9644096-2-3 (pbk.)
*1. Educational toys 2. Science - Study and teaching (Elementary) I. Title.*
**TC LB1029.T6 S54 1999**

**Silva, Inigo.**
Comics, the 9th art [videorecording]. [S.l.] : EPISA ; Cicero, Ill. : [Distributed by] The Roland Collection, 1990.
**TC PN6710 .C6 1990**

**Silver Burdett & Ginn.**
Ragno, Nancy N. World of language. [Teacher ed.]. Morristown, NJ : Silver Burdett & Ginn, c1990.

Ragno, Nancy N. World of language. [Teacher ed.]. Morristown, NJ : Silver Burdett & Ginn, c1990.

Ragno, Nancy N. World of language. [Teacher ed.]. Morristown, NJ : Silver Burdett & Ginn, c1990.

**Silver Burdett Company.**
Mallinson, George G. Silver Burdett science. Morristown, N.J. : Silver Burdett, c1987.
**TC Q161 .M34 1987**

**Silver Burdett elementary science program**
Silver Burdett science [grade 6]. Centennial ed. Morristown, NJ : Silver Burdett, c1985.
**TC lb**

Silver Burdett science [grade 6]. Centennial ed. Morristown, NJ : Silver Burdett, c1985.
**TC lb**

**Silver Burdett Ginn (Firm).**
DiscoveryWorks. Parsippany, N.J. : Silver Burdett Ginn, c1996-
**TC LB1585 .D574 1996**

DiscoveryWorks. Parsippany, N.J. : Silver Burdett Ginn, c1996
**TC LB1585 .D574 1996 Teaching Guide Gr. 4**

DiscoveryWorks. Parsippany, N.J. : Silver Burdett Ginn, c1996
**TC LB1585 .D574 1996 Teaching Guide Gr. 5**

DiscoveryWorks. Parsippany, N.J. : Silver Burdett Ginn, c1996
**TC LB1585 .D574 1996 Teaching Guide Gr. 6**

DiscoveryWorks. Parsippany, N.J. : Silver Burdett Ginn, c1996
**TC LB1585 .D574 1996 Teaching Guide Gr. 1**

DiscoveryWorks. Parsippany, N.J. : Silver Burdett Ginn, c1996
**TC LB1585 .D574 1996 Teaching Guide Gr. 2**

DiscoveryWorks. Parsippany, N.J. : Silver Burdett Ginn, c1996
**TC LB1585 .D574 1996 Teaching Guide Gr. 3**

DiscoveryWorks. Parsippany, NJ : Silver Burdett Ginn, c1996-
**TC LB1585 .D574 1996**

DiscoveryWorks. Parsippany, N.J. : Silver Burdett Ginn, c1996-
**TC LB1585 .D574 1996 Workbook**

Ragno, Nancy Nickell. World of language. Needham, Ma. : Silver Burdett Ginn, c1996.
**TC LB1576 .S4471 1996**

Ragno, Nancy Nickell. World of language. Needham, Mass. : Silver Burdett Ginn, c1996.
**TC LB1576 .S4471 1996**

World of language. Needham, Mass. : Silver Burdett Ginn, c1996.
**TC LB1576 .S4471 1996**

World of language. Teacher ed. Needham, Mass. : Silver Burdett Ginn, c1996.
**TC LB1576 .S4471 1996 Teacher Ed.**

**Silver Burdett Ginn science**
DiscoveryWorks. Parsippany, N.J. : Silver Burdett Ginn, c1996-

**TC LB1585 .D574 1996**

DiscoveryWorks. Parsippany, N.J. : Silver Burdett Ginn, c1996
**TC LB1585 .D574 1996 Teaching Guide Gr. 4**

DiscoveryWorks. Parsippany, N.J. : Silver Burdett Ginn, c1996
**TC LB1585 .D574 1996 Teaching Guide Gr. 5**

DiscoveryWorks. Parsippany, N.J. : Silver Burdett Ginn, c1996
**TC LB1585 .D574 1996 Teaching Guide Gr. 6**

DiscoveryWorks. Parsippany, N.J. : Silver Burdett Ginn, c1996
**TC LB1585 .D574 1996 Teaching Guide Gr. 1**

DiscoveryWorks. Parsippany, N.J. : Silver Burdett Ginn, c1996
**TC LB1585 .D574 1996 Teaching Guide Gr. 2**

DiscoveryWorks. Parsippany, N.J. : Silver Burdett Ginn, c1996
**TC LB1585 .D574 1996 Teaching Guide Gr. 3**

DiscoveryWorks. Parsippany, N.J. : Silver Burdett Ginn, c1996
**TC LB1585 .D574 1996 Teaching Guide Gr. K**

DiscoveryWorks. Parsippany, NJ : Silver Burdett Ginn, c1996-
**TC LB1585 .D574 1996**

DiscoveryWorks. Parsippany, N.J. : Silver Burdett Ginn, c1996-
**TC LB1585 .D574 1996 Workbook**

**Silver Burdett science [grade 6]** / George G. Mallinson ... [et. al.]. Centennial ed. Morristown, NJ : Silver Burdett, c1985. v. : ill. (some col.) ; 23-31 cm. (Silver Burdett elementary science program) Includes bibliographical references. ISBN 0-382-13440-0
*1. Science. 2. Science - Study and teaching (Elementary) I. Mallinson, George G. II. Series.*
**TC lb**

**Silver Burdett science [grade 6]** / George G. Mallinson ... [et. al.]. Centennial ed. Morristown, NJ : Silver Burdett, c1985. v. : ill. (some col.) ; 23-31 cm. (Silver Burdett elementary science program) Includes bibliographical references. ISBN 0-382-13440-0
*1. Science. 2. Science - Study and teaching (Elementary) I. Mallinson, George G. II. Series.*
**TC lb**

**Silver, Harold.** English education and the radicals 1780-1850 / Harold Silver. London ; Boston : Routledge & Kegan Paul, 1975. x, 134 p. ; 20 cm. (Students library of education) Bibliography: p. 123-134. ISBN 0-7100-8212-6
*1. Education - England - History. 2. Educational sociology - England - History. I. Title.*
**TC LA631.7 .S45**

**Silver, James F.** Ready-to-use world geography activities for grades 5-12 / James F. Silver ; illustrations and maps by Eileen Gerne Ciavarella. West Nyack, N.Y. : Center for Applied Research in Education, 1992. xvi, 298 p. : ill., maps ; 29 cm. ISBN 0-87628-945-6 DDC 910/.0712
*1. Geography - Study and teaching (Secondary) I. Title.*
**TC G73 .S45 1992**

**Silver, Kenneth E.**
Kleeblatt, Norman L. An expressionist in Paris. Munich ; New York : Jewish Museum, c1998.
**TC ND553.S7 A4 1998**

**Silver, Maury, 1944-.**
Sabini, John, 1947- Emotion, character, and responsibility. New York : Oxford University Press, 1998.
**TC BF531 .S23 1998**

**Silver, Nan.**
Gottman, John Mordechai. Why marriages succeed or fail :. 1st Fireside ed. New York : Fireside, 1995.
**TC HQ536 .G68 1994**

**Silverman, Franklin H., 1933-** Professional issues in speech-language pathology and audiology / Franklin H. Silverman. Boston : Allyn and Bacon, c1999. x, 210 p. ; 23 cm. Includes bibliographical references and index. ISBN 0-205-27470-6 (pbk.) DDC 616.85/5
*1. Speech therapy - Practice. 2. Audiology - Practice. 3. Speech-Language Pathology. 4. Audiology. I. Title.*
**TC RC428.5 .S55 1999**

**Silverman, Phyllis R.** Never too young to know : death in children's lives / Phyllis Rolfe Silverman. New York : Oxford University Press, 2000. xv, 271 p. ; 25 cm. Includes bibliographical references (p. 247-259) and index. ISBN 0-19-510954-6 (alk. paper) ISBN 0-19-510955-4 (pbk. :

**Silverman, Robert H.**
alk. paper) DDC 155.9/37
*1. Children and death. I. Title.*
*TC BF723.D3 S58 2000*

**Silverman, Robert H.**
Moro, M. I. Russian grade 1 mathematics. Chicago :
University of Chicago School of Mathematics Project,
1992.
*TC QA14.R9 R8611 1992*

Moro, M. I. Russian grade 2 mathematics. Chicago :
University of Chicago School of Mathematics Project,
1992.
*TC QA14.R9 R8711 1992*

Russian grade 3 mathematics. Chicago : University of
Chicago School of Mathematics Project, 1992.
*TC QA14.R9 R8811 1992*

**SilverPlatter Information, Inc.**
[LLBA (Online)] LLBA [computer file]. [Norwood,
MA] : SilverPlatter International, [1993- Computer
data and program.

[LLBA (Online)] LLBA [computer file]. [Norwood,
MA] : SilverPlatter International, [1993- Computer
data and program.

[LLBA (Online)] LLBA [computer file]. [Norwood,
MA] : SilverPlatter International, [1993- Computer
data and program.
*TC NETWORKED RESOURCE*

**SilverPlatter International.**
[ERIC (SilverPlatter International : Online)] The
ERIC database [computer file]. WebSPIRS version
3.1. [Norwood, MA] : SilverPlatter International,
*TC NETWORKED RESOURCES*

[ERIC (SilverPlatter International : Online)] The
ERIC database [computer file]. WebSPIRS version
3.1. [Norwood, MA] : SilverPlatter International,
*TC NETWORKED RESOURCES*

**Silverstone, Barbara, 1931-.**
The Lighthouse handbook on vision impairment and
vision rehabilitation. New York, N.Y. : Oxford
University Press, 2000.
*TC RE91 .L54 2000*

**Simek-Morgan, Lynn.**
Ivey, Allen E. Counseling and psychotherapy. 4th ed.
Boston : Allyn and Bacon, c1997.
*TC BF637.C6 I93 1997*

**SIMILARITY (PSYCHOLOGY).**
Flippen, Annette Rose. Similarity versus motive as
explanations for ingroup bias. 1996.
*TC 085 F65*

**Similarity versus motive as explanations for ingroup
bias.**
Flippen, Annette Rose. 1996.
*TC 085 F65*

**Simmons, Deborah C.**
What reading research tells us about children with
diverse learning needs. Mahwah, N.J. : Erlbaum,
1998.
*TC LB1050.5 .W47 1998*

**Simmons, J. L. (Jerry Laird), 1933-.**
McCall, George J. Social psychology, a sociological
approach. New York : Free Press, c1982.
*TC HM251 .M38 1982*

**Simmons, Jay, 1947-** You never asked me to read :
useful assessment of reading and writing problems /
Jay Simmons. Boston : Allyn and Bacon, c2000. xi,
260 p. : ill. ; 24 cm. Includes bibliographical references and
index. ISBN 0-205-28854-5 DDC 428.4/076
*1. Reading - Ability testing - United States - Case studies. 2.
Language arts - Ability testing - United States - Case studies.
3. Educational tests and measurements - United States - Case
studies. 4. Learning disabled children - United States - Case
studies. I. Title.*
*TC LB1050.46 .S535 2000*

**Simms, Lillian M. (Lillian Margaret)** The professional
practice of nursing administration / Lillian M. Simms,
Sylvia A. Price, Naomi E. Ervin. 3rd ed. Albany, NY :
Delmar Publishers, c2000. xvi, 685 p. : ill. ; 25 cm.
Includes bibliographical references and index. ISBN 0-7668-
0790-8
*1. Nurse Administrators. 2. Administrative Personnel. I. Price,
Sylvia Anderson. II. Ervin, Naomi E. III. Title.*
*TC RT89 .S58 2000*

**Simms, Margaret C.**
Job creation. Washington, DC : Joint Center for
Political and Economic Studies ; Lanham, Md. ;
Oxford : University Press of America, c1998.
*TC HD8081.A65 J63 1998*

**Simon, Francesca.** Calling all toddlers / by Francesca
Simon ; illustrated by Susan Winter. 1st American ed.
New York : Orchard Books, 1999. 33 p. : col. ill. ; 27 cm.
SUMMARY: Rhyming verses describe activities that toddlers
enjoy, such as splashing, stomping, and making faces. ISBN
0-531-30120-6 (alk. paper) DDC [E]
*1. Toddlers - Juvenile poetry. 2. Children's poetry, English. 3.
Toddlers - Poetry. 4. English poetry. I. Winter, Susan, ill. II.
Title.*
*TC PZ8.3.S5875 Cal 1999*

**Simon Fraser University. Faculty of Education. Field
Relations and Teacher In-Service Education.**
Critical challenges in social studies for junior high
students. Burnaby, B.C. : Field Relations and Teacher
In-Service Education, Faculty of Education, Simon
Fraser University, 1996.
*TC D16.2 .C75 1996*

Harrison, John, 1951- Critical challenges in social
studies for upper elementary students. Vancouver :
Critical Thinking Cooperative, 1999.
*TC LB1584.5.C3 H37 1999*

McDiarmid, Tami, 1960- Critical challenges for
primary students. Burnaby, B.C. : Field Relations and
Teacher In-Service Education, Faculty of Education,
Simon Fraser University, c1996.
*TC LB1590.3 .M36 1996*

**Simon, John Ivan.** Private screenings [by] John Simon.
New York, Macmillan [1967] 316 p. 22 cm. DDC
791.43/015
*1. Moving-pictures - Reviews. I. Title.*
*TC PN1995 .S495*

**Simon, Richard, 1951-.**
Ricken, Robert. The high school principal's calendar.
Thousand Oaks, Calif. : Corwin Press, c2000.
*TC LB3032 .R53 2000*

**Simon, Rita James.**
A look backward and forward at American
professional women and their families. Lanham :
University Press of America, 1999.
*TC HQ759.48 .L66 1999*

Van der Does, Louise Q. Renaissance women in
science. Lanham, Md. : University Press of America,
c1999.
*TC Q141 .V25 1999*

**Simon, Seymour.**
**Einstein Anderson sees through the invisible man.**
Simon, Seymour. The invisible man and other
cases. Rev. ed. New York : Morrow Junior Books,
c1998.
*TC PZ7.S60573 In 1998*

**Einstein Anderson, science detective**
(#7.) Simon, Seymour. The invisible man and other
cases. Rev. ed. New York : Morrow Junior Books,
c1998.
*TC PZ7.S60573 In 1998*

The invisible man and other cases / by Seymour
Simon : illustrated by S.D. Schindler. Rev. ed. New
York : Morrow Junior Books, c1998. 88 p. : ill. ; 22 cm.
(Einstein Anderson, science detective ; #7) "First published in
1983 by Viking Penguin under the title 'Einstein Anderson
sees through the invisible man'"--T.p. verso. SUMMARY: The
sixth grade science sleuth solves ten more puzzling cases, one
involving an allergic monster, and another an invisible man.
ISBN 0-688-14447-0 DDC [Fic]
*1. Science - Problems, exercises, etc. - Fiction. I. Schindler, S.
D., ill. II. Simon, Seymour. Einstein Anderson sees through the
invisible man. III. Title. IV. Series: Simon, Seymour. Einstein
Anderson, science detective ; #7.*
*TC PZ7.S60573 In 1998*

Seymour Simon's book of trucks. New York :
HarperCollins Publishers, 2000. 1v. (unpaged) : col. ill. ;
24 cm. SUMMARY: Describes various kinds of trucks and
their functions, including a log truck, cement mixer truck, and
sanitation truck. ISBN 0-06-028473-0 ISBN 0-06-028481-1
(lib. bdg.) DDC 629.224
*1. Trucks - Juvenile literature. 2. Trucks. I. Title. II. Title: Book
of trucks*
*TC TL230.15 .S56 2000*

**Simon, Sidney B., joint comp.**
Read, Donald A., comp. Humanistic education
sourcebook. Englewood Cliffs, N.J. : Prentice-Hall,
[1975]
*TC LC1011 .R38*

**Simonian, Susan J.**
Directory of internship and post-doctoral fellowships
in clinical child/pediatric psychology, 1997. [Mahwah,
N.J. : Lawrence Erlbaum Associates, c1997].
*TC RJ503.3 .D57 1997*

**Simonson, Michael R.**
Teaching and learning at a distance. Upper Saddle
River, N.J. : Merrill, c2000.
*TC LC5800 .T43 2000*

**A simple justice** : the challenge of small schools / edited
by William Ayers, Michael Klonsky, and Gabrielle
Lyon. New York : Teachers College Press, 2000. ix,
198 p. ; 24 cm. (The teaching for social justice series) Includes
bibliographical references and index. ISBN 0-8077-3963-4
(alk. paper) ISBN 0-8077-3962-6 (pbk. :alk.paper) DDC 371
*1. Educational equalization - United States. 2. Small schools -
United States. 3. Social justice - Study and teaching - United
States. I. Ayers, William, 1944- II. Klonsky, Michael. III. Lyon,
Gabrielle. IV. Series.*
*TC LC213.2 .S56 2000*

**Simpson, Colin, 1960-.**
Williams, Donald. Art now. Sydney ; New York :
McGraw-Hill Book Co., c1996.
*TC N6490 .W49 1996*

**Simpson, Michele L.**
Brozo, William G. Readers, teachers, learners. 3rd ed.
Upper Saddle River, N.J. : Merrill, c1999.
*TC LB1632 .B7 1999*

**Simpson, Ormond.** Supporting students in open and
distance learning. London : Kogan Page, 2000. v, 186
p. ; 24 cm. (Open and distance learning series) Includes
bibliographical references and index. ISBN 0-7494-3082-6
DDC 378.175
*1. Distance education. 2. Open learning. 3. Educational
technology. I. Title. II. Series.*
*TC LC5800 .S56 2000*

**Sims, Laura S., 1943-** The politics of fat : food and
nutrition policy in America / Laura S. Sims. Armonk,
N.Y. : M.E. Sharpe, c1998. xiv, 311 p. : ill. ; 24 cm.
Includes bibliographical references(p. 299-301) and index.
ISBN 0-7656-0193-1 (cloth : alk. paper) ISBN 0-7656-0194-X
(pbk. : alk. paper) DDC 363.8/56/0973
*1. Nutrition policy - United States. 2. Food - Fat content. 3.
Lipids in human nutrition. I. Title.*
*TC TX360.U6 S58 1998*

**Sims, Lowery Stokes.**
Catlett, Elizabeth, 1915- Elizabeth Catlett sculpture.
[Purchase, N.Y.] : Neuberger Museum of Art,
Purchase College, State University of New York ;
Seattle : Distributed by University of Washington
Press, c1998.
*TC NB259.C384 A4 1998*

**Simulating nonmodel-fitting responses in a CAT
environment.**
Yi, Qing. Iowa City, Iowa : ACT, 1998.
*TC LB3051 .A3 no. 98-10*

**SIMULATION METHODS. See ARTIFICIAL
INTELLIGENCE.**

**SIN. See GUILT.**

**SINCERITY. See HONESTY.**

**Sinclair, Ruth.**
Clark, Alison. The child in focus. London : National
Children's Bureau Enterprise, c1999.
*TC KD785 .C43 1999*

Vernon, Jeni. Maintaining children in school.
London : National Children's Bureau Enterprises,
c1998.
*TC LB3081 .V47 1998*

**Sing me a story! Tell me a song!.**
Jackman, Hilda L. Thousand Oaks, Calif. : Corwin
Press, c1999.
*TC LB1139.35.A37 J33 1999*

**Singelis, Theodore M.**
Teaching about culture, ethnicity & diversity.
Thousand Oaks : Sage Publications, c1998.
*TC HM101 .T38 1998*

**Singer, Alan.**
Democratic dialogue with special needs students.
[Boulder, Colo.] : Social Science Education
Consortium, c1997.
*TC LC4069.3 .D4 1997*

**Singer, Bennett L.**
42 up. New York : The New Press : Distributed by
W.W. Norton, c1998.
*TC HQ792.G7 A18 1998*

**Singer, Edward.** 20th century revolutions in
technology / Edward Nathan Singer. Commack, NY :
Nova Science Pub., 1998. xviii, 440 p. : ill. ; 27 cm.
Includes bibliographical references and index. ISBN 1-56072-
432-3 DDC 609/.04
*1. Technological innovations - History - 20th century. 2.
Technology - History - 20th century. 3. Inventions - History -*

20th century. I. Title. II. Title: Twentieth century revolutions in technology
*TC T173.8 .S568 1998*

**Singer, Maxine.**
Center for Science, Mathematics, and Engineering Education. Committee on Developing the Capacity to Select Effective Instructional Materials. Selecting instructional materials. Washington, D.C. : National Academy Press, c1999.
*TC LB1585.3 .C45 1999*

**Singer-Nourie, Sarah.**
DePorter, Bobbi. Quantum teaching. Boston, Mass. : Allyn and Bacon, c1999.
*TC LB1027 .D418 1999*

**Singh, Rajendra Pal, 1932-** The Indian teacher [by] R. P. Singh. Delhi, National [Pub. House, 1969] xi, 186 p. 22 cm. Bibliography: p. [180]-182.
*1. Teachers - India. I. Title.*

**Singh, Sadanand.** Illustrated dictionary of speech-language pathology / Sadanand Singh, Raymond D. Kent : with contributions from Pam Rider. San Diego : Singular Pub. Group, c2000. ix, 287 p. : ill. ; 26 cm. Cover title: Singular's illustrated dictionary of speech-language pathology. Also published in paperback under title: Singular's pocket dictionary of speech-language pathology. Includes bibliographical references (p. 287). CONTENTS: Appendices: A. Abbreviations, acronyms, and initializations -- B. The international phonetic alphabet -- C. List of illustrations -- D. A Poor man's tour of physical quantities and units. ISBN 1-56593-988-3 (alk. paper) ISBN 0-7693-0048-0 (pbk. : alk. paper) DDC 616.8/55/003
*1. Speech disorders - Dictionaries. 2. Language disorders - Dictionaries. 3. Speech Disorders - Dictionary - English. 4. Language Disorders - Dictionary - English. 5. Speech-Language Pathology - Dictionary - English. I. Kent, Raymond D. II. Rider, Pam. III. Singh, Sadanand. Singular's pocket dictionary of speech-language pathology. IV. Title. V. Title: Singular's illustrated dictionary of speech-language pathology*
*TC RC423 .S533 2000*

Mendel, Lisa Lucks. Singular's pocket dictionary of audiology. San Diego : Singular Pub. Group, c1999.
*TC RF290 .M4642 1999*

**Singular's pocket dictionary of speech language pathology.**
Singh, Sadanand. Illustrated dictionary of speech-language pathology. San Diego : Singular Pub. Group, c2000.
*TC RC423 .S533 2000*

**SINGING.** *See* **CHORAL SINGING; VOICE.**

**Singing development :** childhood & change : an overview. London : Roehampton Institute, Centre for Advanced Studies in Music Education, Faculty of Education, [1997?] 38 p. : ill. ; 30 cm. Cover title. Includes bibliographical references. ISBN 1-87195-470-3
*1. Singing - Instruction and study - Juvenile. 2. Music - Physiological aspects. 3. Voice. 4. School music - Instruction and study. I. Centre for Advanced Studies in Music Education. Faculty of Education.*
*TC MT898 .S55 1997*

**SINGING - DICTION.**
Adams, David, 1950- A handbook of diction for singers. New York : Oxford University Press, 1999.
*TC MT883 .A23 1999*

**SINGING - HISTORY.**
Stark, James A. (James Arthur), 1938- Bel canto. Toronto : University of Toronto Press, c1999.
*TC MT823 S795 1999*

**SINGING - INSTRUCTION AND STUDY.**
Lebon, Rachel L., 1951- The professional vocalist. Lanham, Md. : Scarecrow Press, 1999.
*TC MT855 .L43 1999*

**SINGING - INSTRUCTION AND STUDY - ENGLAND - HISTORY - 18TH CENTURY.**
Toft, Robert. Heart to heart. Oxford ; New York : Oxford University Press, 2000.
*TC MT823 .T64 2000*

**SINGING - INSTRUCTION AND STUDY - ENGLAND - HISTORY - 19TH CENTURY.**
Toft, Robert. Heart to heart. Oxford ; New York : Oxford University Press, 2000.
*TC MT823 .T64 2000*

**SINGING - INSTRUCTION AND STUDY - JUVENILE.**
Singing development. London : Roehampton Institute, Centre for Advanced Studies in Music Education, Faculty of Education, [1997?]
*TC MT898 .S55 1997*

**SINGING - PSYCHOLOGICAL ASPECTS.**
Emmons, Shirlee. Power performance for singers. New York : Oxford University Press, 1998.
*TC MT892 .E55 1998*

**SINGING - VOCATIONAL GUIDANCE.**
Lebon, Rachel L., 1951- The professional vocalist. Lanham, Md. : Scarecrow Press, 1999.
*TC MT855 .L43 1999*

**SINGLE CELL PROTEINS.** *See* **FOOD SUPPLY.**

**SINGLE MOTHERS, AFRO-AMERICAN.** *See* **AFRO-AMERICAN SINGLE MOTHERS.**

**SINGLE MOTHERS - UNITED STATES.** *See* **AFRO-AMERICAN SINGLE MOTHERS.**

**SINGLE-PARENT FAMILIES.**
Maass, Vera Sonja. Counseling single parents. New York : Springer Pub. Co., c2000.
*TC HQ759.915 .M23 2000*

**SINGLE-PARENT FAMILIES - UNITED STATES.**
The role of the father in child development. 3rd ed. New York : Wiley, c1997
*TC HQ756 .R64 1997*

**SINGLE-PARENT FAMILY.** *See* **SINGLE PARENTS.**

**SINGLE PARENTS.** *See also* **DIVORCED PARENTS.**
Kinnear, Karen L. Santa Barbara, Calif. : ABC-CLIO, c1999.
*TC HQ759.915 .K56 1999*

**SINGLE PARENTS.**
Golombok, Susan. Parenting. London ; Philadelphia : Routledge, 2000.
*TC HQ755.8 .G655 2000*

Grounded for life [videorecording]. Charleston, WV : Cambridge Research Group, Ltd., 1988.
*TC HQ759.4 .G7 1988*

**SINGLE PARENTS - COUNSELING OF.**
Maass, Vera Sonja. Counseling single parents. New York : Springer Pub. Co., c2000.
*TC HQ759.915 .M23 2000*

**SINGLE PARENTS - UNITED STATES - HANDBOOKS, MANUALS, ETC.**
Kinnear, Karen L. Single parents. Santa Barbara, Calif. : ABC-CLIO, c1999.
*TC HQ759.915 .K56 1999*

**Singleton, Laurel R., 1950-** H is for history : using children's literature to develop historical understandings / by Laurel R. Singleton. Boulder, Colo. : Social Science Education Consortium, 1995. iii, 111 p. : ill. ; 28 cm. Includes bibliographical references and index. ISBN 0-89994-385-3
*1. History - Study and teaching (Elementary) - United States. 2. United States - History - Study and teaching (Elementary) - Juvenile literature. 3. History in literature. 4. Children's literature - Study and teaching (Elementary) - United States. I. Title. II. Title: Using children's literature to develop historical understandings*
*TC LB1582.U6 S56 1995*

**A Singular audiology text.**
Counseling for hearing aid fittings. San Diego : Singular Pub. Group, c1999.
*TC RF300 .C68 1999*

**Singular audiology text**
The efferent auditory system. San Diego : Singular Pub. Group, c1999.
*TC RF286.5 .E36 1999*

**A Singular audiology text**
Gerber, Sanford E. Etiology and prevention of communicative disorders. 2nd ed. San Diego : Singular Pub. Group, c1998.
*TC RJ496.C67 G47 1998*

Venema, Ted. Compression for clinicians. San Diego, Calif. : Singular Pub. Group, c1998.
*TC RF300 .V46 1998*

**Singular audiology text.**
Venema, Ted. Compression for clinicians. San Diego, Calif. : Singular Pub. Group, c1998.
*TC RF300 .V46 1998*

Vonlanthen, A. (Andy), 1961- Hearing instrument technology for the hearing healthcare professional. 2nd ed. San Diego : Singular Pub. Group, c2000.
*TC RF300 .V66 2000*

**Singular impressions.**
Moser, Joann. Washington : Published for the National Museum of American Art by Smithsonian Institution Press, c1997.

*TC NE2245.U54 M67 1997*

**Singular textbook series**
Webster, Douglas B., 1934- Neuroscience of communication. 2nd ed. San Diego : Singular Publishing Group, c1999.
*TC QP355.2 .W43 1999*

**SINGULARITIES, NAKED (COSMOLOGY).** *See* **NAKED SINGULARITIES (COSMOLOGY).**

**Singular's illustrated dictionary of speech-language pathology.**
Singh, Sadanand. Illustrated dictionary of speech-language pathology. San Diego : Singular Pub. Group, c2000.
*TC RC423 .S533 2000*

**Singular's pocket dictionary of audiology.**
Mendel, Lisa Lucks. San Diego : Singular Pub. Group, c1999.
*TC RF290 .M4642 1999*

**SINO-TIBETAN LANGUAGES.** *See* **CHINESE LANGUAGE.**

**SIOUAN INDIANS.** *See* **CROW INDIANS.**

**Sipiora, Phillip.**
Ethical issues in college writing. New York : Canterbury [England] : Peter Lang, c1999.
*TC PE1404 .E84 1999*

**SIQUEIROS, DAVID ALFARO - CRITICISM AND INTERPRETATION.**
Folgarait, Leonard. Mural painting and social revolution in Mexico, 1920-1940. Cambridge ; New York, NY : Cambridge University Press, 1998.
*TC ND2644 .F63 1998*

**Siraj-Blatchford, Iram.** Supporting identity, diversity and language in the early years / Iram Siraj-Blatchford and Priscilla Clarke. Buckingham [England] ; Philadelphia : Open University Press, 2000. ix, 147 p. : ill. ; 24 cm. (Supporting early learning) Includes bibliographical references (p. [132]-139) and index. ISBN 0-335-20435-X (hbk.) ISBN 0-335-20434-1 (pbk.) DDC 372.21/0941
*1. Early childhood education - Great Britain. 2. Child care - Great Britain. 3. Language acquisition. 4. Multicultural education - Great Britain. 5. Educational equalization - Great Britain. I. Clarke, Priscilla, 1943- II. Title. III. Series: Supporting early learning.*
*TC LB1139.3.G7 S57 2000*

**Siraj-Blatchford, John, 1952-** Supporting science, design and technology in the early years / John Siraj-Blatchford and Iain MacLeod-Brudenell. Philadelphia, Pa. : Open University Press, 1999. xii, 143 p. : ill. ; 23 cm. (Supporting early learning) Includes bibliographical references (p. [136]-141) and index. ISBN 0-335-19943-7 ISBN 0-335-19942-9 (pbk.) DDC 372.3/5
*1. Technology - Study and teaching (Early childhood) 2. Science - Study and teaching (Early childhood) I. MacLeod-Brudenell, Iain. II. Title. III. Series.*
*TC T65.3 .S55 1999*

**SIRS knowledge source [computer file].**
SIRS researcher [computer file] [Boca Raton, Fla.] : SIRS Mandarin,
*TC NETWORKED RESOURCE*

**SIRS Mandarin, Inc.**
SIRS researcher [computer file] [Boca Raton, Fla.] : SIRS Mandarin,
*TC NETWORKED RESOURCE*

**SIRS researcher** [computer file] [Boca Raton, Fla.] : SIRS Mandarin, Mode of access: World Wide Web. Subscription and registration are required for access. Searchable HTML-encoded indexed citations, abstracts, full text. System requirements: Internet connectivity, World Wide Web browser. Title from main search screen viewed April 4, 2000. Accessed through the SIRS knowledge source web interface. SUMMARY: Features current news, world almanac excerpts, world maps, "spotlight of the month," and publications directory.
*1. Social sciences - Indexes. 2. Social problems - Indexes. 3. Science - Indexes. 4. World history - Indexes. 5. Social sciences - Databases. 6. Social problems - Databases. 7. Science - Databases. 8. World history - Databases. 9. World politics - Databases. I. SIRS Mandarin, Inc. II. Title: SIRS knowledge source [computer file]*
*TC NETWORKED RESOURCE*

**Siskind, Diana.** A primer for child psychotherapists / Diana Siskind. Northvale, NJ : Jason Aronson, c1999. x, 271 p. ; 24 cm. Includes bibliographical references (p. [263]-264) and index. ISBN 0-7657-0233-9 DDC 618.92/8914
*1. Child psychotherapy. 2. Children - Diseases - Treatment. 3. Child psychiatry. I. Title.*
*TC RJ504 .S543 1999*

**Siskind, Theresa Gayle, 1951-** Cases for middle school educators / Theresa Gayle Siskind. Lanham. Md. : London : Scarecrow Press, 2000. ix, 134 p. : forms ; 23 cm. Includes bibliographical references (p. 131-132) and index. ISBN 0-8108-3762-5 (pbk. : alk. paper) DDC 373.236/0973
*1. Middle schools - United States - Case studies. 2. Middle school teachers - United States - Case studies. I. Title.*
*TC LC1623.5 .S57 2000*

**Sissel, Peggy A.** Staff, parents, and politics in Head Start : a case study in unequal power, knowledge, and material sources / Peggy A. Sissel. New York : London : Falmer Press, 2000. xv, 321 p. ; 23 cm. (Garland reference library of social science ; v. 1188. Studies in education/politics ; v. 4) Includes bibliographical references (p. 291-309) and indexes. ISBN 0-8153-3103-7 (hbk. : alk. paper) ISBN 0-8153-3110-X (pbk. : alk. paper) DDC 372.21
*1. Head Start Program (U.S.) 2. Head Start programs - United States - Case studies. I. Title. II. Series: Garland reference library of social science ; v. 1188. III. Series: Garland reference library of social science. Studies in education/politics ; vol. 4.*
*TC LC4091 .S49 2000*

**SISTERS AND BROTHERS.** *See* **BROTHERS AND SISTERS.**

**SISTERS - FICTION.**
Couloumbis, Audrey. Getting near to baby. New York : Putnam, 1999.
*TC PZ7.C8305 Gg 1999*

Millen, C. M. The low-down laundry line blues. Boston : Houghton Mifflin, 1999.
*TC PZ7.M6035 Lo 1999*

Naylor, Phyllis Reynolds. A traitor among the boys. New York : Delacorte Press, 1999.
*TC PZ7.N24 Tpr 1999*

**SITE-BASED MANAGEMENT (SCHOOL MANAGEMENT).** *See* **SCHOOL-BASED MANAGEMENT.**

**SITES, EXCAVATION (ARCHAEOLOGY).** *See* **EXCAVATIONS (ARCHAEOLOGY).**

**Situated literacies** : reading and writing in context / edited by David Barton, Mary Hamilton and Roz Ivanič. London ; New York : Routledge, 2000. xv, 222 p. ; 24 cm. (Literacies) Includes bibliographical references and index. ISBN 0-415-20670-7 (hbk) ISBN 0-415-20671-5 (pbk) DDC 302.2/244
*1. Literacy - Social aspects. 2. Discourse analysis. I. Barton, David, 1949- II. Hamilton, Mary, 1949- III. Ivanič, Roz. IV. Series.*
*TC LC149 .S52 2000*

**Situated lives** : gender and culture in everyday life / edited by Louise Lamphere, Helena Ragoné, and Patricia Zavella. New York : Routledge, 1997. 493 p. : ill. ; 26 cm. Includes bibliographical references and index. ISBN 0-415-91806-5 ISBN 0-415-91807-3 (pbk.) DDC 305.3
*1. Sex role - Cross-cultural studies. 2. Social change - Cross-cultural studies. 3. United States - Social conditions - 1980- 4. Sex role - United States. 5. Feminist anthropology. I. Lamphere, Louise. II. Ragoné, Helena. III. Zavella, Patricia.*
*TC GN479.65 .S57 1997*

**Sivonen, Seppo.** White-collar or hoe handle : African education under British colonial policy, 1920-1945 / Seppo Sivonen. Helsinki : Suomen Historiallinen Seura, [1995] 264 p. : ill. ; 25 cm. (Bibliotheca historica, 1238-3503 ; 4) Includes bibliographical references (p. 249-261) and index. ISBN 951-710-016-7
*1. Education - Africa - History - 20th century. 2. Education and state - Africa - History - 20th century. 3. Great Britain - Colonies - Africa - History - 20th century. 4. Educational planning - Africa - History - 20th century. 5. Africa - Politics and government - To 1945. I. Title. II. Series: Bibliotheca historica (Helsinki, Finland) ; 4.*
*TC LA1531 .S58 1995*

**Six strategies for promoting educational equity.** Law and school reform. New Haven [Conn.] : Yale University Press, c1999.
*TC LC213.2. L38 1999*

**Six urban community college systems.** Gateways to democracy. San Francisco : Jossey-Bass, 1999.
*TC LB2328.N53 1999*

**SIXTH GRADE (EDUCATION) - CURRICULA.** What your sixth grader needs to know. New York : Doubleday, c1993.
*TC LB1571 6th .W43 1993*

**Sixty-five exercises in psychological testing and assessment.** Cohen, Ronald Jay. 2nd ed. Mountain View, CA : Mayfield, c1992.

*TC BF176 .C64 1992*

**SIZE - FICTION.**
Shavick, Andrea. You'll grow soon, Alex. New York : Walker, 2000.
*TC PZ7.S5328 Yo 2000*

**Skaggs, Gayle, 1952-** On display : 25 themes to promote reading / by Gayle Skaggs. Jefferson, NC : McFarland, c1999. vi, 162 p. : ill. ; 23 cm. Includes index. ISBN 0-7864-0657-7 (sewn softcover) DDC 027.8/074/73
*1. School libraries - United States. 2. Library exhibits - United States. 3. Displays in education. I. Title.*
*TC Z675.S3 S5975 1999*

**Skehan, Peter.** A cognitive approach to language learning / Peter Skehan. Oxford ; New York : Oxford University Press, 1998. iii, 324 p. ; 24 cm. (Oxford applied linguistics) Includes bibliographical references (p. [295]-313) and index. ISBN 0-19-437217-0
*1. Second language acquisition. 2. Cognition. 3. Psycholinguistics. I. Title. II. Series.*
*TC P118.2 .S567 1998*

**SKELETON.** *See* **SPINE.**

**SKEPTICISM.** *See* **BELIEF AND DOUBT.**

**SKETCHING.** *See* **DRAWING.**

**Skiba, Michaeline.** A naturalistic inquiry of the relationship between organizational change and informal learning in the workplace / by Michaeline Skiba. 1999. ix, 328 leaves ; 29 cm. Typescript; issued also on microfilm. Thesis (Ed.D.)--Teachers College, Columbia University, 1999. Includes bibliographical references (leaves 282-292).
*1. Organizational change. 2. Downsizing of organizations. 3. Non-formal education. 4. Occupational training. 5. Professional employees - Training of. 6. Executives - Attitudes. I. Title.*
*TC 06 no. 11180*

**SKILL.** *See* **ABILITY.**

**SKILLED LABOR.** *See* **ARTISANS.**

**Skilled work.**
Renwick Gallery. Washington, D.C. : Smithsonian Institution Press, c1998.
*TC NK460.W3 R467 1998*

**SKILLS.** *See* **ABILITY.**

**Skills development in higher education and employment.**
Bennett, Neville. Buckingham [England] ; Philadelphia : Society for Research into Higher Education & Open University Press, 2000.
*TC LB1027.47 .B46 2000*

**Skills for living.**
Smead, Rosemarie, 1943- Champaign, IL : Research Press, c1990.
*TC BF637.C6 M67 1990*

**SKILLS, SOCIAL.** *See* **SOCIAL SKILLS.**

**SKILLS, TEST-TAKING.** *See* **TEST-TAKING SKILLS.**

**SKILLS TRAINING.** *See* **TRAINING.**

**SKINHEADS.** *See* **WHITE SUPREMACY MOVEMENTS.**

**SKIPPING ROPE.** *See* **ROPE SKIPPING.**

**Skoe, Eva Elisabeth Aspaas, 1944-.** Personality development in adolescence. London ; New York : Routledge, c1998.
*TC BF724.3.P4 P47 1998*

**Sköldberg, Kaj, 1942-.** Alvesson, Mats, 1956- Reflexive methodology. London ; Thousand Oaks, Calif. : SAGE, 2000.
*TC H61 .A62 2000*

**Skoleforum 75.- arg.; 1976-.** Den Høgre skolen Oslo, Steenske forlag.

**Skolnick, Donna.** Fraser, Jane. On their way. Portsmouth, NH : Heinemann, c1994.
*TC LB1576 .F72 1994*

**Skrtic, Thomas M.** Special education & student disability. 4th ed. Denver, Colo. : Love Pub. Co., c1995.
*TC LC3965 .E87 1995*

**Skutnabb-Kangas, Tove.** Linguistic genocide in education, or worldwide diversity and human rights? / Tove Skutnabb-Kangas. Mahwah, N.J. : L. Erlbaum Associates, 2000. xxxiii, 785 p. ; 24 cm. Includes bibliographical references (p. 669-736) and indexes. ISBN 0-8058-3467-2 (cloth : alk. paper) ISBN 0-8058-3468-0 (pbk. : alk. paper) DDC 306.44

*1. Language and education. 2. Language and culture. 3. Language policy. 4. Multiculturalism. 5. Human rights. I. Title.*
*TC P40.8 .S58 2000*

Rights to language. Mahwah, N.J. : L. Erlbaum Associates, 2000.
*TC P119.3 .R54 2000*

**The sky is full of song** / selected by Lee Bennett Hopkins ; illustrated by Dirk Zimmer. 1st ed. New York : Harper & Row, c1983. 46 p. : col. ill. ; 19 cm. "A Charlotte Zolotow book." SUMMARY: An anthology of poems celebrating the seasons. Includes index. ISBN 0-06-022582-3 ISBN 0-06-022583-1 (lib. bdg.) DDC 811/.008/033
*1. Seasons - Juvenile poetry. 2. Children's poetry, American. 3. Seasons - Poetry. 4. American poetry - Collections. I. Hopkins, Lee Bennett. II. Zimmer, Dirk, ill.*
*TC PS595.S42 S5 1983*

**SKY - JUVENILE POETRY.**
Livingston, Myra Cohn. Sky songs. 1st ed. New York : Holiday House, c1984.
*TC PS3562.I945 S5 1984*

**SKY - POETRY.**
Livingston, Myra Cohn. Sky songs. 1st ed. New York : Holiday House, c1984.
*TC PS3562.I945 S5 1984*

**Sky songs.**
Livingston, Myra Cohn. 1st ed. New York : Holiday House, c1984.
*TC PS3562.I945 S5 1984*

**Skyhooks for leadership** : a new framework that brings together five decades of thought : from Maslow to Senge / John A. Shtogren, editor. New York : AMACOM, American Management Association, c1999. xii, 416 p. : ill. ; 24 cm. Includes bibliographical references (p. [401]-408) and index. ISBN 0-8144-0516-9 DDC 658.4/092
*1. Organizational change. 2. Leadership. 3. Organizational effectiveness. I. Shtogren, John A.*
*TC HD58.8 .S577 1999*

**SLAVE KEEPING.** *See* **SLAVERY.**

**SLAVE LABOR.** *See* **INDENTURED SERVANTS.**

**Slave missions and the Black church in the antebellum South.**
Cornelius, Janet Duitsman. Columbia : University of South Carolina Press, c1999.
*TC E449 .C82 1999*

**SLAVERY.** *See* **SLAVES.**

**SLAVERY AND THE CHURCH - SOUTHERN STATES - HISTORY - 19TH CENTURY.**
Cornelius, Janet Duitsman. Slave missions and the Black church in the antebellum South. Columbia : University of South Carolina Press, c1999.
*TC E449 .C82 1999*

**SLAVERY - ANTI-SLAVERY MOVEMENTS.** *See* **ANTISLAVERY MOVEMENTS.**

**SLAVERY - CUBA - HISTORY - 19TH CENTURY.**
Casanovas, Joan. Bread, or bullets!. Pittsburgh : University of Pittsburgh Press, c1998.
*TC HD8206 .C33 1998*

**SLAVERY - ECONOMIC ASPECTS - UNITED STATES - HISTORY.**
Africans in America [videorecording]. [Boston, Mass.] : WGBH Educational Foundation ; South Burlington, VT : WGBH Boston Video [distributor], c1998.
*TC E441 .A47 1998*

**SLAVERY - ECONOMIC ASPECTS - VIRGINIA - HISTORY.**
Africans in America [videorecording]. [Boston, Mass.] : WGBH Educational Foundation ; South Burlington, VT : WGBH Boston Video [distributor], c1998.
*TC E441 .A47 1998*

**SLAVERY - FICTION.**
McGill, Alice. Molly Bannaky. Boston, Mass. : Houghton Mifflin, 1999.
*TC PZ7.M478468 Mol 1999*

**SLAVERY IN THE UNITED STATES.** *See* **SLAVERY - UNITED STATES.**

**SLAVERY - JUSTIFICATION.**
Africans in America [videorecording]. [Boston, Mass.] : WGBH Educational Foundation ; South Burlington, VT : WGBH Boston Video [distributor], c1998.
*TC E441 .A47 1998*

**SLAVERY - UNITED STATES.** *See* **SOUTHERN STATES - HISTORY.**

**SLAVERY - UNITED STATES - HISTORY.**
Africans in America [videorecording]. [Boston, Mass.] : WGBH Educational Foundation : South Burlington, VT : WGBH Boston Video [distributor], c1998.
*TC E441 .A47 1998*

**SLAVERY - VIRGINIA - HISTORY.**
Africans in America [videorecording]. [Boston, Mass.] : WGBH Educational Foundation : South Burlington, VT : WGBH Boston Video [distributor], c1998.
*TC E441 .A47 1998*

**SLAVES.** *See* **FREEDMEN; WOMEN SLAVES.**

**SLAVES, AFRO-AMERICAN.** *See* **SLAVES - UNITED STATES.**

**SLAVES - RELIGIOUS LIFE - SOUTHERN STATES - HISTORY - 19TH CENTURY.**
Cornelius, Janet Duitsman. Slave missions and the Black church in the antebellum South. Columbia : University of South Carolina Press, c1999.
*TC E449 .C82 1999*

**SLAVES - UNITED STATES - BIOGRAPHY.**
Jacobs, Harriet A. (Harriet Ann), 1813-1897. Incidents in the life of a slave girl : written by herself. Cambridge, Mass. : Harvard University Press, 2000.
*TC E444.J17 A3 2000c*

**SLAVES - UNITED STATES - BIOGRAPHY - HISTORY AND CRITICISM.**
Approaches to teaching Narrative of the life of Frederick Douglass. New York : Modern Language Association of America, 1999.
*TC E449.D75 A66 1999*

**SLAVES - UNITED STATES - SOCIAL CONDITIONS.**
Jacobs, Harriet A. (Harriet Ann), 1813-1897. Incidents in the life of a slave girl : written by herself. Cambridge, Mass. : Harvard University Press, 2000.
*TC E444.J17 A3 2000c*

**SLAVES, WOMEN.** *See* **WOMEN SLAVES.**

**SLAVES' WRITINGS, AMERICAN - STUDY AND TEACHING.**
Approaches to teaching Narrative of the life of Frederick Douglass. New York : Modern Language Association of America, 1999.
*TC E449.D75 A66 1999*

**SLAVIC LANGUAGES, EASTERN.** *See* **RUSSIAN LANGUAGE.**

**Slee, Phillip T.** Children's peer relations. London ; New York : Routledge, 1998.
*TC BF723.I646 C47 1998*

**SLEEP.** *See also* **DREAMS.**
Kajikawa, Kimiko. Sweet dreams. 1st ed. New York : Henry Holt, c1999.
*TC QL755.3 .K36 1999*

**SLEEP BEHAVIOR IN ANIMALS - JUVENILE LITERATURE.**
Kajikawa, Kimiko. Sweet dreams. 1st ed. New York : Henry Holt, c1999.
*TC QL755.3 .K36 1999*

**Sleeping Beauty. English.**
Levine, Gail Carson. Princess Sonora and the long sleep. 1st ed. New York : HarperCollins Publishers, c1999.
*TC PZ8.L4793 Pq 1999*

**SLEEPING-SICKNESS.** *See* **EPIDEMIC ENCEPHALITIS.**

**SLEEPING SICKNESS, VIRAL.** *See* **EPIDEMIC ENCEPHALITIS.**

**Slevin, James.** The internet and society / James Slevin. Malden, MA : Polity Press, 2000. xi, 266 p. ; 24 cm. Includes bibliographical references and index. ISBN 0-7456-2086-8 (plpc : alk. paper) ISBN 0-7456-2087-6 (pbk. : alk. paper) DDC 303.48/33
*1. Internet (Computer network) - Social aspects. 2. Computers and civilization. 3. Information society. I. Title.*
*TC HM851 .S58 2000*

**SLIMMING.** *See* **WEIGHT LOSS.**

**Slingerland, Beth H.** A multi-sensory approach to language arts for specific language disability children / Beth H. Slingerland. Cambridge, Mass. : Educators Pub. Service, c1976-<c1981 > v. <book [2]-3 > : ill. ; 26 cm. Book 2 has title: Basics in scope and sequence of a multi-sensory approach to language arts for specific language disability children. Includes bibliographies. PARTIAL CONTENTS: --[book 2] A guide for primary teachers in the second-year continuum.--book 3. A guide for elementary

teachers. ISBN 0-8388-1480-8 (v. 2) DDC 371.9/14
*1. Learning disabled children - Education - Language arts. 2. Learning disabilities. 3. Language disorders in children. I. Title. II. Title: Basics in scope and sequence of a multi-sensory approach to language arts for specific language disability children.*
*TC LC4704.85 .S59 1976*

**Slips of the ear.**
Bond, Zinny S. (Zinny Sans), 1940- San Diego, Calif. : London : Academic, c1999.
*TC P37.5.S67 B66 1999*

**Slipware.**
Eden, Michael, 1955- London : A & C Black ; Philadelphia, Pa. : University of Pennslvania Press, 1999.
*TC NK4285 .E33 1999*

**SLIPWARE.**
Eden, Michael, 1955- Slipware. London : A & C Black ; Philadelphia, Pa. : University of Pennslvania Press, 1999.
*TC NK4285 .E33 1999*

**The Slow learner project.**
Herriot, Sarah T. [Stanford, Calif.: Leland Stanford Junior University; 1967]
*TC QA11 .S25 no.5*

**SLOW-LEARNING ADULTS.** *See* **LEARNING DISABLED.**

**SLOW LEARNING CHILDREN.**
Wiltshire, Michael A. Integrating mathematics and science for below average ninth grade students. 1997.
*TC 06 no. 10847*

**SLOYD.** *See* **HANDICRAFT; MANUAL TRAINING.**

**SLP assistant in the schools.**
Thomas, Alice F. [San Antonio, Tex.] : Communication Skill Builders, c1999.
*TC LB3454 .T46 1999*

**SLUM CLEARANCE.** *See* **CITY PLANNING; HOUSING; SLUMS.**

**SLUMBER SONGS.** *See* **LULLABIES.**

**SLUMS - KENYA - NAIROBI - PICTORIAL WORKS.**
Shootback. London : Booth-Clibborn, 1999.
*TC HV4160.5.N34 S45 1999*

**Smagorinsky, Peter.**
Vygotskian perspectives on literacy research. Cambridge, U.K. ; New York : Cambridge University Press, 2000.
*TC LB1060 .V95 2000*

**SMALL AND MEDIUM-SIZED BUSINESS.** *See* **SMALL BUSINESS.**

**SMALL AND MEDIUM-SIZED ENTERPRISES.** *See* **SMALL BUSINESS.**

**SMALL ARMS.** *See* **FIREARMS.**

**SMALL BUSINESS - MANAGEMENT.**
Heflick, David. How to make money performing in schools. Orient, Wash. : Silcox Productions, c1996.
*TC LB3015 .H428 1996*

**SMALL BUSINESS - UNITED STATES.**
Hollenbeck, Kevin. Classrooms in the workplace. Kalamazoo, Mich. : W.E. Upjohn Institute for Employment Research, 1993.
*TC HF5549.5.T7 H598 1993*

**SMALL COLLEGES - NORTHEASTERN STATES - HISTORY - CASE STUDIES.**
Miller-Bernal, Leslie, 1946- Separate by degree. New York : P. Lang, c2000.
*TC LC1601 .M55 2000*

**SMALL COMPUTERS.** *See* **MICROCOMPUTERS.**

**Small, David, 1945- ill.**
Sandburg, Carl, 1878-1967. The Huckabuck family and how they raised popcorn in Nebraska and quit and came back. 1st ed. New York : Farrar Strauss Giroux, c1999.
*TC PZ7.S1965 Hu 1999*

**A small, good thing.**
Hawkins, Anne Hunsaker, 1944- New York : W.W. Norton, 2000.
*TC RJ387.A25 H39 2000*

**SMALL GROUPS.** *See also* **GROUP RELATIONS TRAINING.**
Vorwerg, Manfred. Sozialpsychologische Strukturanalysen des Kollektivs. Berlin, Deutscher Verlag der Wissenschaften, 1966.

*TC HM291 .V6*

**SMALL LIBRARIES - UNITED STATES - HISTORY - 19TH CENTURY.**
Breisch, Kenneth A. Henry Hobson Richardson and the small public library in America. Cambridge, Mass. : MIT Press, c1997.
*TC Z679.2.U54 B74 1997*

**Small, Ruth V.** Turning kids on to research : the power of motivation / Ruth V. Small, Marilyn P. Arnone. Englewood, Colo. : Libraries Unlimited, 2000. xv, 198 p. : ill. ; 28 cm. (Information literacy series) Includes bibliographical references and index. ISBN 1-56308-782-0 DDC 370.15/4
*1. Motivation in education. 2. Research - Study and teaching. 3. Information retrieval - Study and teaching. I. Arnone, Marilyn P. II. Title. III. Series.*
*TC LB1065 .S57 2000*

**SMALL SCHOOLS - UNITED STATES.**
Creating new schools. New York ; London : Teachers College Press, c2000.
*TC LB2822.82 .C76 2000*

A simple justice. New York : Teachers College Press, 2000.
*TC LC213.2 .S56 2000*

**SMALL SCULPTURE.** *See* **FIGURINES.**

**SMALL TOWNS.** *See* **CITIES AND TOWNS.**

**Smalling, Walter.**
Montgomery, Susan J., 1947- Phillips Academy. New York : Princeton Architectural Press, 2000.
*TC LD7501.A5 M65 2000*

**Smalls, Sadie Marian.** Anna Caroline Maxwell's contributions to nursing : 1880-1904 / by Sadie Marian Smalls. 1996. vi, 192 p. ; 29 cm. Typescript; issued also on microfilm. Thesis (Ed.D.)--Teachers College, Columbia University. 1996. Includes bibliographical references (leaves 144-150).
*1. Maxwell, Anna Caroline - Biography. 2. Maxwell, Anna Caroline - Contributions in nursing services. 3. Nursing - United States - History. 4. Nursing ethics - United States - History. 5. Nursing schools - United States - History. 6. Nursing schools - United States - Curricula - History. I. Title.*
*TC 06 no. 10698*

**Smallwood, W. Norman.**
Ulrich, David, 1953- Results-based leadership. Boston : Harvard Business School Press, 1999.
*TC HD57.7 .U45 1999*

**Smart but stuck.**
Orenstein, Myrna. New York : Haworth Press, c2000.
*TC RC394.L37 O74 2000*

**Smead, Rosemarie, 1943-** Skills for living : group counseling activities for young adolescents / Rosemarie S. Morganett. Champaign, IL : Research Press, c1990. ix, 229 p. : ill. ; 28 cm. Includes bibliographical references. ISBN 0-87822-318-5 (pbk.) DDC 616./89152
*1. Group counseling. I. Title.*
*TC BF637.C6 M67 1990*

**SMELL.** *See* **ODORS.**

**SMELLS.** *See* **ODORS.**

**SMES (SMALL BUSINESS).** *See* **SMALL BUSINESS.**

**Smile, Ernest and Celestine.**
Vincent, Gabrielle. [Ernest et Célestine chez le photographe. English] 1st American ed. New York : Greenwillow Books, c1982.
*TC PZ7.V744 Sm 1982*

**Smith, Adam, 1723-1790.** An inquiry into the nature and causes of the wealth of nations / by Adam Smith ; edited by Edwin Cannan ; with a new preface by George J. Stigler. Chicago : University of Chicago Press, 1976. liv, 524, 568 p. ; 21 cm. Reprint of the 1904 ed. published by Methuen & Co., London. Includes Bibliographical references (p.563-568) and index. ISBN 0-226-76374-9 DDC 330.15/3
*1. Economics. I. Title. II. Title: Wealth of nations.*
*TC HB161 .S65 1976*

**Smith, Barbara, 1949 Dec. 28-.**
Teaching in the 21st century. New York : Falmer Press, 1999.
*TC PE1404 .T394 1999*

**Smith, Bernard, 1916-** Australian painting, 1788-1990 / Bernard Smith with the three additional chapters on Australian painting since 1970 by Terry Smith. 3rd ed. Melbourne ; New York : Oxford University Press, 1992. xi, 592 p. : ill. (some col.) ; 26 cm. Includes bibliographical references (p. 565-567) and index. Publisdhed

in paperback 1992. ISBN 0-19-553476-X DDC 759.994
*1. Painting, Australian. I. Smith, Terry (Terry E.) II. Title.*
**TC ND1100 .S553 1992**

Modernism's history : a study in twentieth-century art
and ideas / Bernard Smith. New Haven : Yale
University Press, 1998. vi, 376 p. ; 24 cm. Includes
bibliographical references (p. [346]-364) and index. ISBN 0-
300-07392-5 DDC 709/.04
*1. Modernism (Art) 2. Postmodernism. 3. Art, Modern - 20th
century. I. Title.*
**TC N6494.M64 S65 1998**

**Smith, Charles W., 1938-** Market values in American
higher education : the pitfalls and promises / Charles
W. Smith. Lanham, Md. ; Oxford : Rowman &
Littlefield, 2000. xii, 168 p. ; 24 cm. Includes
bibliographical references (p. 151-164) and index. ISBN
0-8476-9563-8 (cloth : alk. paper) ISBN 0-8476-9564-6
(paper : alk. paper) DDC 338.4/337873
*1. Education, Higher - United States - Finance. 2. College
costs - United States. 3. Education, Higher - Economic
aspects - United States. I. Title.*
**TC LB2342 .S55 2000**

**Smith, Clagett G., 1930- comp.** Conflict resolution:
contributions of the behavioral sciences. Clagett G.
Smith, editor. Notre Dame [Ind.] University of Notre
Dame Press [1971] xvii, 553 p. 27 cm. Includes
bibliographical references. ISBN 0-268-00448-X DDC 301.6/3
*1. International relations - Research. 2. Conflict (Psychology).
I. Title.*
**TC JX1291 .S45**

**SMITH COLLEGE - BIOGRAPHY.**
Quesnell, Quentin. The strange disappearance of
Sophia Smith. Northampton [Mass.] : Smith College,
c1999.
**TC LD7152.65.S45 Q84 1999**

**SMITH COLLEGE - HISTORY.**
Quesnell, Quentin. The strange disappearance of
Sophia Smith. Northampton [Mass.] : Smith College,
c1999.
**TC LD7152.65.S45 Q84 1999**

**Smith, Constance, 1949-** Art marketing 101 : a
handbook for the fine artist / [Constance Smith] 2nd
ed. Penn Valley, Calif. : ArtNetwork, c1997. 328 p. :
ill. ; 26 cm. Includes bibliographical references and index.
ISBN 0-940899-32-9 (pbk.)
*1. Art - Economic aspects. 2. Art - Marketing. I. Title. II. Title:
Art marketing one hundred one III. Title: Art marketing one
hundred and one*
**TC N8353 .S63 1997**

**Smith, Darren James, 1960-** Stepping inside the
classroom through personal narratives / Darren James
Smith. Lanham, Md. : University Press of America,
1999. xxxviii, 164 p. ; 22 cm. Includes bibliographical
references. ISBN 0-7618-1411-6 (cloth : alk. paper) DDC
373.1102
*1. High school teaching - United States - Longitudinal studies.
2. Social sciences - Study and teaching (Secondary) - United
States - Longitudinal studies. 3. Education - United States -
Experimental methods - Longitudinal studies. 4. Smith, Darren
James, - 1960- I. Title.*
**TC LB1737.U6 S55 1999**

**SMITH, DARREN JAMES, 1960-.**
Smith, Darren James, 1960- Stepping inside the
classroom through personal narratives. Lanham, Md. :
University Press of America, 1999.
**TC LB1737.U6 S55 1999**

**Smith, David Barton.** Health care divided : race and
healing a nation / David Barton Smith. Ann Arbor :
University of Michigan Press, 1999. x, 386 p. : ill. ; 24
cm. Includes bibliographical references (p. 337-371) and index.
CONTENTS: Race and health care in the United States --
Attending the birth of the struggle -- The North Carolina
campaign -- The federal offensive -- The federal retreat --
What happened and what didn't? -- Race and long-term care --
Race and prenatal care -- Healing a nation. ISBN 0-472-
10991-X (cloth : alk. paper) DDC 362.1/089/96073
*1. Discrimination in medical care - United States. 2. Afro-
Americans - Medical care. I. Title.*
**TC RA448.5.N4 S63 1999**

**Smith, David Livingstone, 1953-** Freud's philosophy of
the unconscious / by David Livingstone Smith.
Dordrecht ; Boston : Kluwer, 1999. 221 p. ; 25 cm.
(Studies in cognitive systems ; v. 23) Includes bibliographical
references (p. [198]-211) and index. ISBN 0-7923-5882-1
DDC 127
*1. Freud, Sigmund, - 1856-1939. 2. Subconsciousness. I. Title.
II. Series.*
**TC BF173.F85 S615 1999**

**Smith, David T., 1935- joint author.**
Sussman, Marvin B. The family and inheritance New
York, Russell Sage Foundation, 1970.

**TC KFO142 .S9**

**Smith, Deborah Deutsch.** Introduction to special
education : teaching in an age of opportunity /
Deborah Deutsch Smith. 4th ed. Boston : Allyn and
Bacon, c2001. xxvi, 629 p. : ill. (some col.) ; 27 cm.
Includes bibliographical references and indexes. ISBN 0-205-
29222-4 DDC 371.9/0973
*1. Special education - United States. I. Title.*
**TC LC3981 .S56 2001**

**Smith, Elaine M., 1942-.**
Bethune, Mary McLeod, 1875-1955. [Selections.
1999] Mary McLeod Bethune. Bloomington : Indiana
University Press, c1999.
**TC E185.97.B34 A25 1999**

**Smith, Ethel Morgan, 1952-** From whence cometh my
help : the African American community at Hollins
College / Ethel Morgan Smith. Columbia ; London :
University of Missouri Press, c2000. xiii, 147 p. : ill. ; 25
cm. Includes bibliographical references (p. 133-140) and index.
ISBN 0-8262-1260-3 (alk. paper) DDC 975.5/792
*1. Afro-Americans - Virginia - History. 2. Afro-
Americans - Virginia - Hollins - Biography. 3. Hollins (Va.) -
History. 4. Hollins (Va.) - Race relations. 5. Hollins College -
Biography. 6. Hollins College - History. I. Title.*
**TC F234.H65 S55 2000**

**Smith, Greg, M. A.**
Goffman and social organization. London ; New
York ; Routledge, 1999.
**TC HM291 .G57 1999**

**Smith, Hawthorne Emery.** Psychological detachment
from school : its effects on the academic achievement
of black adolescent students in inner-city schools / by
Hawthorne Emery Smith. 1999. x, 229 leaves ; 29 cm.
Issued also on microfilm. Thesis (Ph.D.)--Columbia
University, 1999. Includes bibliographical references (leaves
169-205).
*1. African American students - Education (Secondary) - New
York (State) - New York. 2. High school students - Attitudes -
New York (State) - New York. 3. Academic achievements -
Psychological aspects. 4. African American students - Racial
identity. 5. Self-perception in adolescence. 6. Social
perception. 7. School environment. 8. East Harlem (New York,
N.Y.) I. Title.*
**TC 085 Sm586**

**Smith, Helen, 1951-.**
Benchmarking and threshold standards in higher
education. London : Kogan Page, c1999.
**TC LB2341.8.G7 B463 1999**

**Smith, Henrietta M.**
The Coretta Scott King awards book, 1970-1999.
Chicago : American Library Association, 1999.
**TC Z1037.A2 C67 1999**

**Smith, Irmhild Wrede.** The effect of structured
exercise and structured reminiscing on agitation and
aggression in geriatric psychiatric patients / by Irmhild
Wrede Smith. 1996. vii, 240 leaves : ill. ; 29 cm.
Typescript; issued also on microfilm. Thesis (Ed.D.)--Teachers
College, Columbia University, 1996. Includes bibliographical
references (leaves 73-87).
*1. Psychiatric hospital patients - New Jersey. 2. Aged men -
New Jersey. 3. Aggressiveness (Psychology) 4. Mentally
handicapped aged - Services for - New Jersey. 5. Exercise
therapy for the aged - New Jersey. 6. Reminiscing in old age. 7.
Geriatric psychiatry. 8. Occupational therapy. I. Title.*
**TC 06 no. 10700**

**Smith, Jane Bowman.**
Self-assessment and development in writing.
Cresskill, N.J. : Hampton Press, c2000.
**TC PE1404 .S37 2000**

**Smith, Jane W. (Jane Wilcox)** AGS United States
government / by Jane W. Smith, Carol Sullivan. Circle
Pines, Minn. : AGS, American Guidance Service,
1997. ix, 342 p. : ill. ; 24 cm. Includes index. ISBN 0-7854-
0882-7
*1. United States - Politics and government. I. Sullivan, Carol.
II. Title. III. Title: American Guidance Service United States
government*
**TC JK40 .S639 1997**

AGS United States government / by Jane W. Smith,
Carol Sullivan. Teacher's ed. Circle Pines, Minn. :
AGS, American Guidance Service, 1997. T16, x, 356
p. : ill. ; 29 cm. Includes index. ISBN 0-7854-0884-3
*1. United States - Politics and government. I. Sullivan, Carol.
II. Title. III. Title: American Guidance Service United States
government*
**TC JK40 .S639 1997 Teacher's Ed.**

**Smith, Jason.**
National Gallery of Victoria. In relief. Melbourne :
National Gallery of Victoria, c1997.

**TC NE1190.25 .G72 1997**

**Smith, Jeffery, 1961-.**
Smith, Jeffery, 1961- Where the roots reach for water.
New York : North Point Press, 1999.
**TC BF575.M44 S55 1999**

Where the roots reach for water : a personal and
natural history of melancholia / Jeffery Smith. New
York : North Point Press, 1999. 292 p. ; 24 cm. ISBN
0-86547-542-3 (hardcover : alk. paper) DDC 616.85/27
*1. Melancholy. 2. Depression, Mental. 3. Melancholy - History.
4. Adjustment (Psychology) I. Smith, Jeffery, 1961- II. Title.*
**TC BF575.M44 S55 1999**

**Smith, Jessie Carney.**
Reference library of Black America. Detroit, MI :
Gale Group ; Distributed by African American Pub.,
Proteus Enterprises, c2000.
**TC E185 .R44 2000**

**Smith, John L., 1945-** The psychology of action / John
L. Smith. New York : St. Martin's Press, 2000. xiv,
240 p. : ill. ; 23 cm. Includes bibliographical references and
index. ISBN 0-312-23066-4 (cloth) DDC 150
*1. Psychology. 2. Human behavior. I. Title.*
**TC BF121 .S56 2000**

**Smith, Jonathan C.** ABC relaxation theory : an
evidence-based approach / Jonathan C. Smith. New
York : Springer Pub., c1999. xv, 216 p. ; 24 cm. Spine
title: ABC relaxation. Includes bibliographical references (p.
133-137) and index. ISBN 0-8261-1283-8 DDC 613.7/9
*1. Relaxation. I. Title. II. Title: ABC relaxation*
**TC BF637.R45 S549 1999**

**Smith, Llewellyn.**
Africans in America [videorecording]. [Boston,
Mass.] : WGBH Educational Foundation ; South
Burlington, VT : WGBH Boston Video [distributor],
c1998.
**TC E441 .A47 1998**

**Smith, Mark, 1956-** Neal-Schuman Internet policy
handbook for libraries / Mark Smith. New York :
Neal-Schuman, c1999. vii, 219 p. : ill. ; 28 cm. (Neal-
Schuman NetGuide series) Includes bibliographical references
and index. ISBN 1-55570-345-3 (pbk.) DDC 025/.00285
*1. Internet access for library users - United States. I. Title. II.
Title: Internet policy handbook for libraries III. Series: Neal-
Schuman net-guide series.*
**TC Z692.C65 S66 1999**

**Smith, Marta Vaciago, 1944-.**
Personality development. London ; New York :
Routledge, 1999.
**TC BF175.45 .P47 1999**

**Smith, Mieko Kotake.** Adolescents with emotional and
behavioral disabilities : transition to adulthood /
Mieko Kotake Smith. Lewiston, NY : E. Mellen Press,
c1998. xii, 98 p. : ill. ; 24 cm. (Studies in health and human
services ; v. 31) Includes bibliographical references (p. 89-95)
and index. ISBN 0-7734-8286-5 (hardcover) DDC 616.89/
00835
*1. Mentally handicapped teenagers - Longitudinal studies. 2.
Problem youth - Longitudinal studies. 3. Adulthood -
Psychological aspects - Longitudinal studies. 4. Adolescent
psychology. 5. Parent and teenager. I. Title. II. Series.*
**TC RJ503 .S63 1998**

**Smith, Neil.**
Harrison, John, 1951- Critical challenges in social
studies for upper elementary students. Vancouver :
Critical Thinking Cooperative, 1999.
**TC LB1584.5.C3 H37 1999**

**Smith, Ralph Alexander.**
Readings in discipline-based art education. Reston,
Va. : National Art Education Assoc., c2000.
**TC N87 .R43 2000**

**Smith, Richard Mason, 1881-** From infancy to
childhood : the child from two to six years / by
Richard M. Smith. Boston : Atlantic monthly press,
[c1925] ix p., 2 leaves, [3]-105, [1] p. ; 17 cm. Diagrams on
lining-papers. Includes index.
*1. Book 2. nomesh 3. Children - Care and hygiene. I. Title.*
**TC RJ61 .S675**

**Smith, Robert** Schools, politics and society :
elementary education in Wales, 1870-1902. Cardiff :
University of Wales Press, 1999. x, 301 p. ; 23 cm.
(Studies in Welsh history ; 15) Includes bibliographical
references and index. ISBN 0-7083-1535-6 DDC 372.9
*1. Education, Elementary - Wales - History - 19th century.*
**TC LA663 .S65 1999**

**Smith, Rogers M., 1953-.**
Klinkner, Philip A. The unsteady march. Chicago :
University of Chicago Press, c1999.
**TC E185 .K55 1999**

**Smith, Ruth B.**
Social work in pediatrics. New York : Haworth Press, c1995.
*TC HV688.U5 S63 1995*

**SMITH, SOPHIA, 1796-1870.**
Quesnell, Quentin. The strange disappearance of Sophia Smith. Northampton [Mass.] : Smith College, c1999.
*TC LD7152.65.S45 Q84 1999*

**Smith, Stacy, 1968-.**
Foundational perpectives in multiculural education. New York : Longman, c2000.
*TC LC196 .F68 2000*

**Smith, Steven H.** Schoolwide test preparation : one elementary school's instructional approach that dramatically raised standardized test scores / by Stephen H. Smith. [Arlington, Va.] : Educational Research Service, c2000. ix, 113 p. : ill. ; 28 cm. (ERS monograph)
*1. Educational accountability - Idaho - Twin Falls. 2. Educational tests and measurements - Idaho - Twin Falls. 3. Educational evaluation - Idaho - Twin Falls. I. Educational Research Service (Arlington, Va.) II. Title. III. Series.*
*TC LB2806.22 .S65 2000*

**Smith, Susan C.** The forgotten mourners : guidelines for working with bereaved children / Susan C. Smith. 2nd ed. London ; Philadelphia : Jessica Kingsley Publishers, 1999. 114 p. : ill. ; 22 cm. "First edition by Margaret Pennells and Susan Smith published in 1995"--T.p. verso. Includes bibliographical references (p. 103-109) and index. ISBN 1-85302-758-8 (pbk. : alk. paper) DDC 155.9/37/083
*1. Bereavement in children. 2. Grief in children. 3. Children and death. 4. Children - Counseling of. I. Title.*
*TC BF723.G75 P46 1999*

**Smith, Terry Jo.**
Stories out of school. Stamford, Conn. : Ablex Pub., c2000.
*TC LC196 .S6994 2000*

**Smith, Terry (Terry E.).**
Smith, Bernard, 1916- Australian painting, 1788-1990. 3rd ed. Melbourne ; New York : Oxford University Press, 1992.
*TC ND1100 .S553 1992*

**Smith, William L., 1956-** Families and communes : an examination of nontraditional lifestyles / William L. Smith. Thousand Oaks, Calif. : Sage Publications, c1999. xiii, 161 p. : ill. ; 24 cm. (Understanding families) Includes bibliographical references (p. 139-147) and indexes. ISBN 0-7619-1073-5 (alk. paper) ISBN 0-7619-1074-3 (pbk. : alk. paper) DDC 307.77/4/0973
*1. Communal living - United States - History. 2. Collective settlements - United States - History. 3. Family - United States - History. 4. Alternative lifestyles - United States - History. I. Title. II. Series.*
*TC HQ971 .S55 1999*

**Smitherman, Geneva, 1940-** Black talk : words and phrases from the hood to the amen corner / Geneva Smitherman. Rev. ed. Boston : Houghton Mifflin, 2000. xii, 305 p. : ill. ; 21 cm. ISBN 0-395-96919-0 DDC 427/.089/96073
*1. Afro-Americans - Languages - Dictionaries. 2. English language - United States - Glossaries, vocabularies, etc. 3. English language - United States - Slang - Dictionaries. 4. Black English - United States - Dictionaries. 5. Americanisms - Dictionaries. I. Title.*
*TC PE3102.N4 S65 2000*

Talkin that talk : language, culture, and education in African America / Geneva Smitherman. London ; New York : Routledge, 2000. xvi, 457 p. : ill. ; 25 cm. Includes bibliographical references (p. [400]-429) and index. ISBN 0-415-20864-5 (hbk.) ISBN 0-415-20865-3 (pbk.) DDC 427/.973/08996073
*1. Afro-Americans - Language. 2. Afro-Americans - Education - Language arts. 3. Afro-Americans - Social life and customs. 4. Black English. 5. Americanisms. I. Title. II. Title: Talking that talk*
*TC PE3102.N4 S63 2000*

**SMITHSONIAN INSTITUTION.**
Exhibiting dilemmas. Washington, D.C. : Smithsonian Insitution Press, c1997.
*TC AM151 .E96 1997*

**SMITHSONIAN INSTITUTION - MANAGEMENT.**
Kurin, Richard, 1950- Reflections of a culture broker. Washington, D.C. : Smithsonian Institution Press, c1997.
*TC GN36.U62 D5775 1997*

**SMITHSONIAN INSTITUTION - PUBLIC RELATIONS.**
Kurin, Richard, 1950- Reflections of a culture broker.

Washington, D.C. : Smithsonian Institution Press, c1997.
*TC GN36.U62 D5775 1997*

**Smithsonian series in ethnographic inquiry**
Cloth and human experience. Washington : Smithsonian Institution Press, c1989.
*TC GT525 .C57 1989*

**SMOKING.** *See* **TOBACCO HABIT.**

**Smoking** / Carol Wekesser, book editor. San Diego, CA : Greenhaven Press, c1997. 192 p. : ill. ; 25 cm. (Current controversies) Includes bibliographical references (p. 183-184) and index. ISBN 1-56510-534-6 (lib. bdg. : alk. paper) ISBN 1-56510-533-8 (pbk. : alk. paper) DDC 362.29/6/0973
*1. Smoking - United States. 2. Tobacco - Health aspects. 3. Tobacco habit - United States. 4. Tobacco industry - Corrupt practices - United States. 5. Smoking - United States - Prevention. 6. Teenagers - Tobacco use - United States - Prevention. 7. Smoking - Law and legislation - United States. I. Wekesser, Carol, 1963- II. Series.*
*TC HV5760 .S663 1997*

**SMOKING - COSTS.**
Valuing the cost of smoking. Boston : Kluwer Academic Publishers, 1999.
*TC HV5735 .V35 1999*

**SMOKING - ECONOMIC ASPECTS.**
Valuing the cost of smoking. Boston : Kluwer Academic Publishers, 1999.
*TC HV5735 .V35 1999*

**SMOKING - HEALTH ASPECTS - COSTS.**
Valuing the cost of smoking. Boston : Kluwer Academic Publishers, 1999.
*TC HV5735 .V35 1999*

**SMOKING - LAW AND LEGISLATION - UNITED STATES.**
Smoking. San Diego, CA : Greenhaven Press, c1997.
*TC HV5760 .S663 1997*

**SMOKING - PREVENTION.**
The next generation [videorecording]. Princeton, NJ : Films for the Humanities & Sciences, c1998.
*TC RC564 .N4 1998*

**SMOKING - UNITED STATES.**
Smoking. San Diego, CA : Greenhaven Press, c1997.
*TC HV5760 .S663 1997*

**SMOKING - UNITED STATES - ENCYCLOPEDIAS.**
Hirschfelder, Arlene B. Encyclopedia of smoking and tobacco. Phoenix, AZ : Oryx Press, 1999.
*TC HV5760 .H57 1999*

**SMOKING - UNITED STATES - PREVENTION.**
Smoking. San Diego, CA : Greenhaven Press, c1997.
*TC HV5760 .S663 1997*

**Smolensky, Paul, 1955-.**
Tesar, Bruce. Learnability in optimality theory. Cambridge, Mass. : MIT Press, c2000.
*TC P158.42 .T47 2000*

**SMPTE journal.**
Journal of the SMPTE. New York, N.Y. : SMPTE, 1956-1975.

**SMPTE journal (1955).**
Journal of the SMPTE. New York, N.Y. : SMPTE, 1956-1975.

**SMSG Reports**
(no. 5.) Herriot, Sarah T. The Slow learner project: [Stanford, Calif.: Leland Stanford Junior University; 1967]
*TC QA11 .S25 no.5*

**Smulyan, Lisa.** Balancing acts : women principals at work / Lisa Smulyan. Albany : State University of New York Press, c2000. vii, 245 p. ; 24 cm. (SUNY series in women in education) Includes bibliographical references (p. 227-236) and index. ISBN 0-7914-4517-8 (alk. paper) ISBN 0-7914-4518-6 (pbk. : alk. paper) DDC 371.2/012/082
*1. Women school principals - United States - Case studies. 2. Educational leadership - United States - Case studies. I. Title. II. Series: SUNY series in women in education.*
*TC LB2831.92 .S58 2000*

**SNAPSHOTS.** *See* **PHOTOGRAPHS.**

**SNARE DRUM - INSTRUCTION AND STUDY.**
The drums [videorecording]. Van Nuys, CA : Backstage Pass Productions ; Canoga Park, Calif. : [Distributed by] MVP Home Entertainment, c1998.
*TC MT662.3 .S6 1998*

**SNARE DRUM - STUDIES AND EXERCISES.**
The drums [videorecording]. Van Nuys, CA : Backstage Pass Productions ; Canoga Park, Calif. : [Distributed by] MVP Home Entertainment, c1998.

*TC MT662.3 .S6 1998*

**Snare drums for beginners [videorecording].**
The drums [videorecording]. Van Nuys, CA : Backstage Pass Productions ; Canoga Park, Calif. : [Distributed by] MVP Home Entertainment, c1998.
*TC MT662.3 .S6 1998*

**Snell, Alma Hogan.** Grandmother's grandchild : my Crow Indian life / Alma Hogan Snell ; edited by Becky Matthews. Lincoln : University of Nebraska Press, c2000. xvii, 213 p. : ill., maps ; 24 cm. (American Indian lives) Includes bibliographical references and index. ISBN 0-8032-4277-8 (cl : alk. paper) DDC 978.6/0049752/0092
*1. Snell, Alma Hogan. 2. Crow Indians - Biography. 3. Pretty-shield (Crow Indian) 4. Crow women - Biography. I. Matthews, Becky. II. Title. III. Series.*
*TC E99.C92 S656 2000*

**SNELL, ALMA HOGAN.**
Snell, Alma Hogan. Grandmother's grandchild. Lincoln : University of Nebraska Press, c2000.
*TC E99.C92 S656 2000*

**Snell, Martha E.** Collaborative teaming / by Martha E. Snell and Rachel Janney with contributions from Johnna Elliot ... [et al.]. Baltimore : Paul H. Brookes Pub., c2000. ix, 158 p. : ill. ; 25 cm. (Teachers' guides to inclusive practices) Includes bibliographical references (p. 151-152) and index. ISBN 1-55766-353-X (pbk.) DDC 378.14/8
*1. Inclusive education - United States. 2. School support teams - United States. 3. Home and school - United States. I. Janney, Rachel. II. Elliot, Johnna. III. Title. IV. Series.*
*TC LC1201 .S64 2000*

Instruction of students with severe disabilities. 5th ed. Upper Saddle River, N.J. : Merrill, c2000.
*TC LC4031 .I572 2000*

Janney, Rachel. Behavioral support. Baltimore, Md. ; London : Paul H. Brookes Pub., c2000.
*TC LB1060.2 .J26 2000*

Janney, Rachel. Modifying schoolwork. Baltimore, Md. : Paul H. Brookes Pub., c2000.
*TC LC1201 .J26 2000*

Social relationships and peer support / by Martha E. Snell and Rachel Janney with contributions from Laura K. Vogtle, Kenna M. Colley, Monica Delano. Baltimore, Md. ; London : Paul H. Brookes Pub. Co., c2000. ix, 188 p. : ill., forms ; 26 cm. (Teachers' guides to inclusive practices) Includes bibliographical references (p. 153-162) and index. ISBN 1-55766-356-4 DDC 371.826/94
*1. Socially handicapped children - Education - United States. 2. Social skills - Study and teaching - United States. 3. Inclusive education - United States. I. Vogtle, Laura K. II. Colley, Kenna M. III. Delano, Monica. IV. Title.*
*TC LC4069 .S54 2000*

**Snick, Anne.** Women in educational [sic] policy-making : a qualitative and quantitative analysis of the situation in the E.U. / Anne Snick & Agnes de Munter. Leuven, Belgium : Leuven University Press, 1999. 24 cm. (Studia paedagogica ; new series 24) Cover title: Women in educational policy-making. Includes bibliographical references (p. [81]-86). ISBN 90-6186-952-8 DDC 379.4
*1. Education and state - European Union countries. 2. Education - European Union countries - Decision making. 3. Women in education - European Union countries. I. Munter, Agnes de. II. Title. III. Title: Women in educational policy-making IV. Series: Studia paedagogica (Louvain. Belgium) ; nieuwe reeks 24.*
*TC LC93.A2 S56 1999*

**Snijders, Tom A. B.** Multilevel analysis : an introduction to basic and advanced multilevel modeling / Tom A. B. Snijders and Roel J. Bosker. Thousand Oaks, Calif. ; London : SAGE, 1999. [ix], 266 p. : ill. ; 24 cm. ISBN 0-7619-5889-4 ISBN 0-7619-5890-8 (pbk.)
*1. Mathematical models. 2. Multivariate analysis. I. Bosker, R. J. (Roel J.) II. Title.*
*TC QA278 .S645 1999*

**Snipt, J. (Joke).**
Klaassen, R. G. Effective lecturing behaviour in English-medium instruction. Delft, Netherlands : Delft University Press, 1999.
*TC LB2393 .K53 1999*

**Snodgrass, Dawn M., 1955-** Collaborative learning in middle and secondary schools : applications and assessments / Dawn M. Snodgrass, Mary M. Bevevino. Larchmont, N.Y. : Eye On Education, 2000. ix, 178 p. : ill. ; 28 cm. Includes bibliographical references (p. 167-174) and index. ISBN 1-88300-184-6 DDC 371.39/5
*1. Group work in education - United States. 2. Middle school*

*education - United States. 3. Education, Secondary - United States. 4. Educational tests and measurements - United States. I. Bevevino, Mary M. II. Title.*
**TC LB1032 .S62 2000**

**Snodgrass, Mary Ellen.** Historical encyclopedia of nursing / Mary Ellen Snodgrass. Santa Barbara, Calif. : ABC-CLIO, 1999. xvii, 254 p. : ill. ; 27 cm. Includes bibliographical references and index. SUMMARY: An encyclopedia covering the history of nursing, spanning topics from abortion to World War II. ISBN 1-57607-086-7 (alk. paper) DDC 610.73/09
*1. Nursing - History - Encyclopedias. 2. Nursing - History - Encyclopedias. I. Title.*
**TC RT31 .S66 1999**

**Snook, Pamela A.**
Hyman, Irwin A. Dangerous schools. 1st ed. San Francisco : Jossey-Bass Publishers, c1999.
**TC LB3013 .H897 1999**

**Snow Bear.**
George, Jean Craighead, 1919- 1st ed. New York : Hyperion Books for Children, 1999.
**TC PZ7.G2933 Sn 1999**

**SNOW - FICTION.**
Figueredo, D. H., 1951- When this world was new. 1st ed. New York : Lee & Low Books, 1999.
**TC PZ7.F488 Wh 1999**

Henkes, Kevin. Oh!. New York : Greenwillow Books, 1999.
**TC PZ8.3.H4165 Oh 1999**

**Snowling, Margaret J.** Dyslexia / Margaret J. Snowling. 2nd ed. Malden, MA : Blackwell Publishers, 2000. xiv, 253 p. ; 23 cm. Includes bibliographical references and index. ISBN 0-631-22144-1 (alk. paper) ISBN 0-631-20574-8 (alk. paper) DDC 618.92/8553
*1. Dyslexia. 2. Cognition disorders in children.*
**TC RJ496.A5 S65 2000**

**SNOWMEN - FICTION.**
Preston, Tim. The lonely scarecrow. 1st American ed. New York : Dutton Children's Books, 1999.
**TC PZ7.P9237 Lo 1999**

**Snyder, C. R.**
Handbook of psychological change :. New York : John Wiley & Sons, c2000.
**TC RC480 .H2855 2000**

**Snyder, C. R. (Charles Richard).**
Handbook of hope. San Diego, Calif. : Academic, 2000.
**TC BF575.H56 H36 2000**

**Snyder, Craig W.**
Gordon, Sol, 1923- Personal issues in human sexuality. Boston : Allyn and Bacon, 1986.
**TC HQ35.2 .G67 1986**

**Snyder, Ilana, 1949-.**
Page to screen. London ; New York : Routledge, 1998.
**TC LC149.5 .P35 1998**

**Snyder, Jack W.**
Spandorfer, Merle, 1934- Making art safely. New York : Van Nostrand Reinhold, c1993.
**TC RC963.6.A78 S62 1993**

**Snyder, Mary Gail.**
Blakely, Edward James, 1938- Fortress America. Washington, D.C. : Brookings Institution Press, c1997.
**TC HT169.59.U6 B53 1997**

**So much to say :** adolescents, bilingualism, and ESL in the secondary school / Christian J. Faltis, Paula M. Wolfe, editors. New York : Teachers College Press, c1999. x, 296 p. : ill. ; 24 cm. (Language and literacy series) Includes bibliographical references and index. ISBN 0-8077-3797-6 (cloth : acid-free paper) ISBN 0-8077-3796-8 (pbk. : acid-free paper) DDC 428/.007
*1. English language - Study and teaching (Secondary) - Foreign speakers. 2. English language - Study and teaching (Secondary) - United States. 3. Education, Bilingual - United States. 4. Bilingualism - United States. I. Faltis, Christian, 1950- II. Wolfe, Paula M. III. Series: Language and literacy series (New York, N.Y.)*
**TC PE1128.A2 S599 1999**

**So what?.**
Brandy, Tim. Portsmouth, NH : Heinemann, c1999.
**TC QA135.5 .B6785 1999**

**So you have to have a portfolio.**
Wyatt, Robert Lee, 1940- Thousand Oaks, Calif. : Corwin Press, c1999.
**TC LB1728 .W93 1999**

**So you want to be a professor?.**
Vesilind, P. Aarne. Thousand Oaks, Calif. : Sage Publications, c2000.
**TC LB1778.2 .V47 2000**

**Sobal, Jeffery, 1950-.**
Interpreting weight. New York : Aldine de Gruyter, c1999.
**TC RA645.O23 I55 1999**

Weighty issues. Hawthorne, N.Y. : Aldine de Gruyter, c1999.
**TC RA645.O23 W45 1999**

**Sobel, Ileene Smith.** Moses and the angels / by Ileene Smith Sobel ; paintings by Mark Podwal ; with an introduction by Elie Wiesel. New York : Delacorte Press, c1999. xii, 64 p. : col. ill. ; 23 cm. Includes bibliographical references (p. 63-64). SUMMARY: Describes the events in the life of Moses and the presence of angels as a sign of God's special relationship to this prophet. ISBN 0-385-32612-2 DDC 296.1/9
*1. Moses - (Biblical leader) - Juvenile literature. 2. Moses (Biblical leader) in rabbinical literature - Juvenile literature. 3. Bible. - O.T. - Biography - Juvenile literature. 4. Angels (Judaism) - Juvenile literature. 5. Moses - (Biblical leader) 6. Angels. I. Podwal, Mark H., 1945- ill. II. Title.*
**TC BM580 .S55 1999**

**Sobo, Elisa Janine. 1963-.**
Contraception across cultures :. Oxford ; New York : Berg, 2000.
**TC RG136 .C574 2000**

**Sobol, Joseph Daniel.** The storytellers' journey : an American revival / Joseph Daniel Sobol. Urbana : University of Illinois Press, c1999. xvi, 265 p. : ill. ; 24 cm. Includes bibliographical references (p. [241]-260) and index. CONTENTS: Preface -- Acknowledgments -- Introduction -- The archetype of the storyteller -- The motif of serendipity in the birth of the storytelling revival -- From serendipity to ceremony: the traditionalization of the national storytelling festival -- The storyteller's journey: the national storytelling festival as ritualization of the revival mythos -- Alternative models of community: dynamics of local, regional, and national storytelling revival associations -- "Blood on the porch": the Protestant Reformation of NAPPS -- Concluding thoughts and stories with morals: reflections on an American revival -- Bibliography -- Index. ISBN 0-252-02436-2 (acid-free paper) ISBN 0-252-06746-0 (pbk. : acid-free paper) DDC 808.5/43/0973
*1. Storytelling - United States. 2. National Storytelling Festival. I. Title.*
**TC GR72.3 .S62 1999**

**SOCCER - HISTORY.**
Giulianotti, Richard, 1966- Football. Cambridge, UK : Polity Press ; Malden, MA : Blackwell Publishers, 1999.
**TC GV943.9.S64 G576 1999**

**SOCCER - SOCIAL ASPECTS.**
Giulianotti, Richard, 1966- Football. Cambridge, UK : Polity Press ; Malden, MA : Blackwell Publishers, 1999.
**TC GV943.9.S64 G576 1999**

**SOCE (AFRICAN PEOPLE). See MANDINGO (AFRICAN PEOPLE).**

**SOCIAL ABILITY. See SOCIAL SKILLS.**

**SOCIAL ACCOUNTING. See QUALITY OF LIFE; SOCIAL INDICATORS.**

**SOCIAL ACTION. See EVALUATION RESEARCH (SOCIAL ACTION PROGRAMS).**

**SOCIAL ACTION - SCHOLARSHIPS, FELLOWSHIPS, ETC. - DIRECTORIES.**
Weinstein, Miriam (Miriam H.) Making a difference. Rev. & exp. 2nd ed. Gabriola Island, BC, Can. : New Society Publishers, 2000.
**TC LB2338 W45 2000**

**SOCIAL ACTION - UNITED STATES.**
Loeb, Paul Rogat, 1952- Soul of a citizen. 1st St. Martin's Griffin ed. New York : St. Martin's Griffin, 1999.
**TC HN65 .L58 1999**

Transforming social inquiry, transforming social action. Boston ; London : Kluwer Academic, c2000.
**TC LC238 .T73 2000**

**SOCIAL ALIENATION. See ALIENATION (SOCIAL PSYCHOLOGY).**

**Social and political studies from Hong Kong**
Lam-Chan, Gladys Lan Tak. Parenting in stepfamilies. Aldershot ; Brookfield USA : Ashgate, c1999.

**TC HQ759.92 .L34 1999**

**SOCIAL ANTHROPOLOGY. See ETHNOLOGY.**

**SOCIAL APPROVAL. See SOCIAL DESIRABILITY.**

**SOCIAL AREAS. See PUBLIC SPACES.**

**SOCIAL BEHAVIOR. See INTERPERSONAL RELATIONS.**

**SOCIAL BEHAVIOR DISORDERS - GENETICS - CONGRESSES.**
Genetics of criminal and antisocial behaviour. Chichester ; New York : Wiley, 1996.
**TC HV6047 .G46 1996**

**Social biology.**
Eugenics quarterly. New York : American Eugenics Society, [1954]-c1968.

**SOCIAL CASE WORK. See also COUNSELING; FAMILY SOCIAL WORK; INTERVIEWING.**
Darling, Rosalyn Benjamin. The partnership model in human services. New York : Kluwer Academic/Plenum Publishers, c2000.
**TC HV43 .D2 2000**

**SOCIAL CASE WORK - STUDY AND TEACHING. See SOCIAL WORK EDUCATION.**

**SOCIAL CASE WORK - UNITED STATES - CASE STUDIES.**
McWilliam, P. J. Lives in progress. Baltimore : P.H. Brookes, c2000.
**TC HV741 .M3128 2000**

**SOCIAL CHANGE.**
Kelly, Gerard, 1959- Retrofuture. Downers Grove, Ill. : InterVarsity Press, c1999.
**TC HN17.5 .K439 1999**

Miles, Steven. Youth lifestyles in a changing world. Buckingham ; Philadelphia : Open University Press, 2000.
**TC HQ796 .M4783 2000**

Negotiating adolescence in times of social change. Cambridge, U.K. ; New York : Cambridge University Press, 2000.
**TC HQ796 .N415 2000**

Scanning the future. New York : Thames & Hudson, c1999.
**TC CB161 .S44 1999**

Tiffany, Constance Rimmer. Planned change theories for nursing. Thousand Oaks : Sage Publications, c1998.
**TC RT89 .T54 1998**

**SOCIAL CHANGE - CONGRESSES.**
Freedom, equality, and social change. Lewiston : E. Mellen Press, c1989.
**TC HM216 .F83 1989**

**SOCIAL CHANGE - CROSS-CULTURAL STUDIES.**
Situated lives. New York : Routledge, 1997.
**TC GN479.65 .S57 1997**

**SOCIAL CHANGE - EUROPE, EASTERN.**
Adolescent development and rapid social change. Albany : State University of New York Press, c2000.
**TC HQ799.H8 A35 2000**

**Social change for women and children** / edited by Vasilikie Demos, Marcia Texler Segal. Stamford, Conn. : JAI Press, 2000. xix, 359 p. : ill. ; 24 cm. (Advances in gender research) Includes bibliographical references and index. Series numbering supplied by vendor.
*1. Women - United States - Social conditions. 2. Women - Latin America - Social conditions. 3. Children - Social conditions. 4. Social change - United States. I. Demos, Vasilikie. II. Segal, Marcia Texler. III. Series: Advances in gender research ; v. 4*
**TC HQ1421 .S68 2000**

**Social change in global perspective**
Coquery-Vidrovitch, Catherine. [Africaines. English] African women. Boulder, Colo. : WestviewPress, 1997.
**TC HQ1787 .C6613 1997**

**SOCIAL CHANGE - MEXICO.**
Guevara-Vázquez, Fabián. El indigena en la novela de la Revolucion Mexicana. 1999.
**TC 085 G934**

**SOCIAL CHANGE - TAIWAN - TAIPEI.**
Marsh, Robert Mortimer. The great transformation. Armonk, N.Y. : M.E. Sharpe, c1996.
**TC HN749.T35 M37 1996**

**SOCIAL CHANGE - UNITED STATES.**
Gordon, Jacob U. Black leadership for social change. Westport, Conn. : Greenwood Press, 2000.
*TC E185.615 .G666 2000*

Social change for women and children. Stamford, Conn. : JAI Press, 2000.
*TC HQ1421 .S68 2000*

**SOCIAL CHANGE - UNITED STATES - CROSS-CULTURAL STUDIES.**
Clauss, Caroline Seay. Degrees of distance. 1999.
*TC 085 C58*

**Social changes and women in the Middle East.**
Shukri, Shirin J. A. Aldershot : Brookfield, Vt. : Ashgate, c1999.
*TC HQ1726.5 .S58 1999*

**SOCIAL CLASSES.** *See* ELITE (SOCIAL SCIENCES); INTELLECTUALS; MIDDLE CLASS; POOR; UPPER CLASS; WORKING CLASS.

**SOCIAL CLASSES - CUBA - HISTORY - 19TH CENTURY.**
Casanovas, Joan. Bread, or bullets!. Pittsburgh : University of Pittsburgh Press, c1998.
*TC HD8206 .C33 1998*

**SOCIAL CLASSES IN LITERATURE - STUDY AND TEACHING.**
Making Mark Twain work in the classroom. Durham [N.C.] : Duke University Press, 1999.
*TC PS1338 .M23 1999*

**SOCIAL CLASSES - SOUTH CAROLINA - ORANGEBURG - HISTORY.**
Mack, Kibibi Voloria C. Parlor ladies and ebony drudges. 1st ed. Knoxville : University of Tennessee Press, c1999.
*TC F279.O6 M33 1999*

**SOCIAL CLASSES - UNITED STATES.**
Campbell, Duane E. Choosing democracy. 2nd ed. Upper Saddle River, N.J. : Merrill, c2000.
*TC LC1099.3 .C36 2000*

Chamberlin, J. Gordon (John Gordon) Upon whom we depend. New York : Peter Lang, c1999.
*TC HC110.P6 C326 1999*

Holtzman, Linda, 1949- Media messages. Armonk, NY : M.E. Sharpe, 2000.
*TC P94.5.M552 U646 2000*

Perrucci, Robert. The new class society. Lanham, Md. : Rowman & Littlefield, 1999.
*TC HN90.S6 P47 1999*

**SOCIAL CLASSES - UNITED STATES - CASE STUDIES.**
Rothenberg, Paula S., 1943- Invisible privilege. Lawrence : University Press of Kansas, c2000.
*TC E185.615 .R68 2000*

**SOCIAL COGNITION.** *See* SOCIAL PERCEPTION.

**SOCIAL COMPETENCE.** *See* SOCIAL SKILLS.

**SOCIAL CONDITIONS.** *See* SOCIAL HISTORY.

**SOCIAL CONFLICT.** *See also* CONFLICT MANAGEMENT.
Wagner Pacifici, Robin Erica. Theorizing the standoff. Cambridge : Cambridge University Press, 2000.
*TC HM1121 .W34 2000*

**SOCIAL CONFLICT - CASE STUDIES.**
Social conflicts and collective identities. Lanham, Md. : Oxford : Rowman & Littlefield Publishers, c2000.
*TC HM1121 .S63 2000*

**SOCIAL CONFLICT - ULSTER (NORTHERN IRELAND AND IRELAND).**
Wright, Frank, 1948- Two lands on one soil. New York : St. Martin's Press, 1996.
*TC DA990.U46 W756 1996*

**SOCIAL CONFLICT - UNITED STATES - CASE STUDIES.**
Wagner Pacifici, Robin Erica. Theorizing the standoff. Cambridge : Cambridge University Press, 2000.
*TC HM1121 .W34 2000*

**Social conflicts and collective identities** / edited by Patrick G. Coy and Lynne M. Woehrle ; associate editors, Bruce W. Dayton ... [et al.]. Lanham, Md. ; Oxford : Rowman & Littlefield Publishers, c2000. x, 218 p. : maps ; 24 cm. Includes bibliographical references and index. ISBN 0-7425-0050-0 (hbk. : alk. paper) ISBN 0-7425-0051-9 (pbk. : alk. paper) DDC 303.6
*1. Social conflict - Case studies. 2. Group identity - Case studies. I. Coy, Patrick G. II. Woehrle, Lynne M., 1965-*

*TC HM1121 .S63 2000*

**Social constructionism, discourse, and realism** / edited by Ian Parker. London : Thousand Oaks, Calif. : SAGE Publications, 1998. xii, 159 p. ; 24 cm. (Inquiries in social construction) Includes bibliographical references and index. ISBN 0-7619-5376-0 ISBN 0-7619-5377-9 (pbk.)
*1. Social psychology. 2. Subjectivity. 3. Discourse analysis. 4. Social sciences - Philosophy. I. Parker, Ian, 1956- II. Series.*
*TC HM251 .S671163 1998*

**The social context of nonverbal behavior** / edited by Pierre Philippot, Robert S. Feldman, Erik J. Coats. Cambridge, U.K. ; New York : Cambridge University Press ; Paris : Editions de la Maison des Sciences de l'Homme, 1999. xiii, 431 p. : ill. ; 24 cm. (Studies in emotion and social interaction) Includes bibliographical references and indexes. ISBN 0-521-58371-3 (hardcover) ISBN 0-521-58666-6 (pbk.) DDC 153.6/9
*1. Body language. I. Philippot, Pierre, 1960- II. Feldman, Robert S. (Robert Stephen), 1947- III. Coats, Erik J., 1968- IV. Series: Studies in emotion and social interaction.*
*TC BF637.N66 S63 1999*

**SOCIAL CONTRACT.** *See* CIVIL SOCIETY.

**SOCIAL CONTROL.** *See* LIBERTY.

**SOCIAL DANCING.** *See* BALLROOM DANCING.

**SOCIAL DARWINISM.**
Cziko, Gary. The things we do. Cambridge, Mass. : MIT Press, c2000.
*TC HM1033 .C95 2000*

**SOCIAL DEMOCRACY.** *See* SOCIALISM.

**SOCIAL DESIRABILITY.** *See* SOCIAL DESIRABILITY IN CHILDREN.

**SOCIAL DESIRABILITY IN ADOLESCENCE - STATISTICAL METHODS.**
Recent advances in the measurement of acceptance and rejection in the peer system. San Francisco : Jossey-Bass Publishers, c2000.
*TC BF723.165 R4 2000*

**SOCIAL DESIRABILITY IN ADOLESCENCE - TESTING.**
Halperin, Jane Carol. The influence of causal attributions on the psychological adjustment of post-treatment adolescent cancer survivors. 1999.
*TC 085 H155*

**SOCIAL DESIRABILITY IN CHILDREN - STATISTICAL METHODS.**
Recent advances in the measurement of acceptance and rejection in the peer system. San Francisco : Jossey-Bass Publishers, c2000.
*TC BF723.165 R4 2000*

**SOCIAL DESIRABILITY - TESTING.**
Gill, Kenneth Joseph. Social psychological artifacts in the measurement of consumer satisfaction with health care. 1996.
*TC 085 G396*

**Social dimensions of information technology** : issues for the new millennium / [edited by] G. David Garson. Hershey, Pa. : Ideas Group Pub., 2000. 362 p. : ill. ; 25 cm. Includes bibliographical references and index. ISBN 1-87828-986-1 (pbk.) DDC 303.48/33
*1. Information technology - Social aspects. 2. Information society. 3. Computers and civilization. I. Garson, G. David.*
*TC HM851 .S63 2000*

**Social disadvantagement and dependency.**
Craddock, George W. Lexington, Mass., Heath Lexington Books [1970]
*TC HD7256.U6 C438*

**SOCIAL DISTANCE.** *See also* SOCIAL ISOLATION.
Clauss, Caroline Seay. Degrees of distance. 1999.
*TC 085 C58*

**Social dreaming @ work** / edited by W. Gordon Lawrence ; introduction by David Armstrong. London : Karnac Books, 1998. xxi, 198 p. : ill. ; 23 cm. Includes bibliographical references (p. 183-188) and index. ISBN 1-85575-209-3
*1. Dreams. 2. Organizational behavior. 3. Social groups. 4. Interpersonal relations. 5. Psychology, Industrial. I. Lawrence, W. Gordon. II. Title: Social dreaming at work*
*TC BF1078 .S55 1998*

**Social dreaming at work.**
Social dreaming @ work. London : Karnac Books, 1998.
*TC BF1078 .S55 1998*

**SOCIAL DRINKING.** *See* DRINKING OF ALCOHOLIC BEVERAGES.

**SOCIAL EDUCATION.** *See* SOCIAL SKILLS - STUDY AND TEACHING; SOCIAL WORK WITH YOUTH; SOCIALIZATION.

**SOCIAL EQUALITY.** *See* EQUALITY.

**SOCIAL ETHICS.** *See also* CIVICS; COMMUNITARIANISM; SOCIAL SCIENCES AND ETHICS.
Rapoport, Robert N. Families, children, and the quest for a global ethic. Aldershot ; Brookfield, Vt. : Ashgate, c1997.
*TC HQ518 .R36 1997*

**SOCIAL ETHICS - CONGRESSES.**
Freedom, equality, and social change. Lewiston : E. Mellen Press, c1989.
*TC HM216 .F83 1989*

**SOCIAL ETHICS - STUDY AND TEACHING.**
White, Patricia, 1937- Civic virtues and public schooling. New York : Teachers College Press, c1996.
*TC LC1011 .W48 1996*

**SOCIAL ETHICS - STUDY AND TEACHING (HIGHER) - UNITED STATES - HISTORY.**
Rabil, Alison. Content, context, and continuity. 1998.
*TC 06 no. 10901*

**SOCIAL EVOLUTION.** *See also* SOCIAL CHANGE.
Jolly, Alison. Lucy's legacy. Cambridge, Mass. ; London : Harvard University Press, 1999.
*TC GN281 .J6 1999*

Ridley, Matt. The Red Queen :. New York : Penguin Books, 1995.
*TC GN365.9 .R53 1995*

**Social factors in the positioning of black women in South African universities.**
Makosana, I. Nokuzola Zola. 1997.
*TC 06 no. 10825*

**SOCIAL GEOGRAPHY.** *See* HUMAN GEOGRAPHY.

**SOCIAL GROUP WORK - UNITED STATES.**
Pack-Brown, Sherlon P. Images of me. Boston : Allyn and Bacon, c1998.
*TC HV1445 .P33 1998*

Support groups. New York : Haworth Press, c1995.
*TC HV45 .S896 1995*

**SOCIAL GROUPS.** *See also* ELITE (SOCIAL SCIENCES); NEIGHBORHOOD; SOCIAL PARTICIPATION; SOCIAL PSYCHOLOGY.
Brown, Rupert, 1950- Group processes. 2nd ed. Oxford ; Malden, Mass. : Blackwell Publishers, 2000.
*TC HM131 .B726 2000*

Flippen, Annette Rose. Similarity versus motive as explanations for ingroup bias. 1996.
*TC 085 F65*

Goffman and social organization. London ; New York : Routledge, 1999.
*TC HM291 .G57 1999*

Leonard-Barton, Dorothy. When sparks fly. Boston, Mass. : Harvard Business School Press, 1999.
*TC HD53 .L46 1999*

Misumi, Jūji, 1924- Rīdashippu kōdō no kagaku =
*TC HM141 .M48 1978*

Social dreaming @ work. London : Karnac Books, 1998.
*TC BF1078 .S55 1998*

Social identity. Malden, MA : Blackwell Publishers, 1999.
*TC HM131 .S58433 1999*

Ulrich, Deborah L. Interactive group learning. New York : Springer, c1999.
*TC RT76 .U46 1999*

**SOCIAL GROUPS - PSYCHOLOGICAL ASPECTS.**
Attitudes, behavior, and social context. Mahwah, N.J. : L. Erlbaum Associates, 2000.
*TC HM132 .B48 1998*

**SOCIAL HANDICAPPED CHILDREN - EDUCATION (EARLY CHILDHOOD) - COLORADO.**
Clay, Cheryl D., 1947- Schooling at-risk Native American children. New York : Garland Pub., 1998.
*TC E99.U8 C53 1998*

**The social health of the nation.**
Miringoff, Marc L. New York : Oxford University Press, 1999.
*TC HN59.2 .M57 1999*

**SOCIAL HISTORY.** *See* QUALITY OF LIFE; SOCIAL CHANGE; SOCIAL INDICATORS; SOCIAL PROBLEMS.

**SOCIAL HISTORY - 20TH CENTURY.**
Kelly, Gerard, 1959- Retrofuture. Downers Grove, Ill. : InterVarsity Press, c1999.
*TC HN17.5 .K439 1999*

**SOCIAL HISTORY - MEDIEVAL, 500-1500 - JUVENILE LITERATURE.**
Martell, Hazel. Food & feasts with the Vikings. Parsippany, N.J. : New Discovery Books, c1995.
*TC DL65 .M359 1995*

**SOCIAL HISTORY - MODERN, 1500-.** *See* SOCIAL HISTORY.

**Social history of Africa**
Freund, Bill. Insiders and outsiders. Portsmouth, NH : Heinemann, c1995.
*TC HD8801.Z8 D8725 1995*

Ranger, T. O. (Terence O.) Are we not also men? Harare : Baobab ; Portsmouth, NH : Heinemann, 1995.
*TC DT2974 .R36 1995*

**SOCIAL HISTORY - PERIODICALS.**
Building America. [New York : Published for the Dept. of Supervision and Curriculum Development by the Society for Curriculum Study, Inc. ; distributed by Americana Corporation, 1935-

**SOCIAL HYGIENE.** *See also* HYGIENE, SEXUAL; PUBLIC HEALTH.
Journal of social hygiene. New York : American Social Hygiene Association,

**Social hygiene news.**
Journal of social hygiene. New York : American Social Hygiene Association,

**Social hygiene papers.**
Journal of social hygiene. New York : American Social Hygiene Association,

**SOCIAL IDENTITY.** *See* GROUP IDENTITY.

**Social identity :** context, commitment, content / edited by Naomi Ellemers, Russell Spears, and Bertjan Doosje. Malden, MA : Blackwell Publishers, 1999. ix, 273 p. : ill. ; 25 cm. Includes bibliographical references (p. [230]-265) and index. ISBN 0-631-20690-6 (alk. paper) ISBN 0-631-20691-4 (alk. paper) DDC 302.4
*1. Group identity. 2. Social groups. 3. Intergroup relations. 4. Social perception. 5. Context effects (Psychology) I. Ellemers, Naomi. II. Spears, Russell. III. Doosje, Bertjan.*
*TC HM131 .S58433 1999*

**SOCIAL INDICATORS.** *See* HEALTH STATUS INDICATORS.

**SOCIAL INDICATORS - STATISTICS.** *See* SOCIAL INDICATORS.

**SOCIAL INDICATORS - UNITED STATES.**
Miringoff, Marc L. The social health of the nation. New York : Oxford University Press, 1999.
*TC HN59.2 .M57 1999*

**SOCIAL INFLUENCE.**
Attitudes, behavior, and social context. Mahwah, N.J. : L. Erlbaum Associates, 2000.
*TC HM132 .B48 1998*

Bissonnette, Madeline Monaco. Adolescents' perspectives about the environmental impacts of food production practices. 1999.
*TC 06 no. 11084*

Loase, John Frederick, 1947- Sigfluence III. Lanham, Md. : University Press of America, c1996.
*TC BF774 .L63 1996*

Wren, Kevin, 1947- Social influences. London ; New York : Routledge, 1999.
*TC HM1176 .W74 1999*

**Social influences.**
Wren, Kevin, 1947- London ; New York : Routledge, 1999.
*TC HM1176 .W74 1999*

**SOCIAL INSTITUTIONS.** *See* FAMILY; SOCIAL STRUCTURE.

**SOCIAL INSURANCE.** *See* SOCIAL SECURITY.

**SOCIAL INTEGRATION.**
The challenge of diversity. Aldershot, England ; Brookfield, Vt. : Avebury, 1996.
*TC JV225 .C530 1996*

Dickerson, Pless Moore. Haitian students' perception of a school as a community of support. 1998.

*TC 06 no. 11018*

Dickerson, Pless Moore. Haitian students' perception of a school as a community of support. 1998.
*TC 06 no. 11018*

Dickerson, Pless Moore. Haitian students' perception of a school as a community of support. 1998.
*TC 06 no. 11018*

**SOCIAL INTERACTION.** *See also* GROUP RELATIONS TRAINING; INTERACTION ANALYSIS IN EDUCATION; INTERGROUP RELATIONS; SOCIAL SKILLS.
Behaving badly. 1st ed. Washington, D.C. : American Psychological Association, 2001.
*TC HM1106 .B45 2001*

Chrispin, Marie C. Resilient adaptation of church-affiliated young Haitian immigrants. 1998.
*TC 06 no. 11015*

Dixon, Jerome C. A qualitative study of perceptions of external factors that influence the persistence of Black males at a predominantly white four-year state college. 1998.
*TC 06 no. 11050*

Goffman and social organization. London ; New York : Routledge, 1999.
*TC HM291 .G57 1999*

Hollander, Edwin Paul, 1927- Leaders, groups, and influence New York, Oxford University Press, 1964.
*TC HM141 .H58*

Talk, work, and institutional order. Berlin ; New York : Mouton de Gruyter, 1999.
*TC P95 .T286 1999*

Vorwerg, Manfred. Sozialpsychologische Strukturanalysen des Kollektivs. Berlin, Deutscher Verlag der Wissenschaften, 1966.
*TC HM291 .V6*

Wheeler, Ladd, 1937- Interpersonal influence. Boston, Allyn and Bacon [1970]
*TC HM291 .W35*

**SOCIAL INTERACTION - COMPUTER NETWORK RESOURCES.**
Race in cyberspace. New York ; London : Routledge, 2000.
*TC HT1523 .R252 2000*

**SOCIAL INTERACTION IN ADOLESCENCE.**
Family and peers. Westport, Conn. : Praeger, 2000.
*TC HQ755.85 .F365 2000*

Mosley, Jenny. Quality circle time in the secondary school :. London : David Fulton, 1999.
*TC LB1032 .M67 1999*

**SOCIAL INTERACTION IN CHILDREN.**
Family and peers. Westport, Conn. : Praeger, 2000.
*TC HQ755.85 .F365 2000*

Light, Paul. Social processes in children's learning. Cambridge, U.K. ; New York : Cambridge University Press, 1999.
*TC LB1060 .L533 1999*

Oldfather, Penny. Learning through children's eyes. 1st ed. Washington, DC : American Psychological Association, c1999.
*TC LB1060 .O43 1999*

Pérez Pereira, Miguel. Language development and social interaction in blind children. Hove, UK : Psychology Press, c1999.
*TC P118 .P37 1999*

**SOCIAL INTERACTION IN CHILDREN - FOREIGN COUNTRIES.**
Pollock, David C. The third culture kid experience. Yarmouth, Me. : Intercultural Press, c1999.
*TC HQ784.S56 P65 1999*

**SOCIAL INTERACTION IN CHILDREN - INDIA.**
Culture, socialization and human development. New Delhi ; Thousand Oaks, CA : Sage Publications, c1999.
*TC HQ783 .C85 1999*

**SOCIAL INTERACTION IN LITERATURE.**
McCallum, Robyn. Ideologies of identity in adolescent fiction. New York : Garland Pub., 1999.
*TC PN3443 .M38 1999*

**SOCIAL INTERACTION - PSYCHOLOGICAL ASPECTS.**
Rogers, Richard Randall. The impact of gay identity and perceived milieu toward gay employees on job involvement and organizational commitment of gay men. 1998.
*TC 085 R635*

**SOCIAL INTERACTION - UNITED STATES.**
Flaton, Robin Anne. Effect of deliberation on juror reasoning. 1999.
*TC 085 F612*

**SOCIAL ISOLATION.** *See* ALIENATION (SOCIAL PSYCHOLOGY); LONELINESS; MARGINALITY, SOCIAL.

**SOCIAL ISOLATION - GREAT BRITAIN.**
Hayton, Annette. Tackling disaffection and social exclusion. London : Kogan Page, 1999.
*TC LC93.G7 H39 1999*

**SOCIAL JUSTICE.**
Edgoose, Julian Miles. Partnerships of possibility. 1999.
*TC 085 E117*

**SOCIAL JUSTICE - CONGRESSES.**
Rights, justice, and community. Lewiston, N.Y., USA : Edwin Mellen Press, c1992.
*TC HM216 .R56 1992*

**SOCIAL JUSTICE IN LITERATURE.**
True, Michael. An energy field more intense than war. 1st ed. Syracuse, N.Y. : Syracuse University Press, 1995.
*TC PS169.N65 T78 1995*

**SOCIAL JUSTICE - STUDY AND TEACHING - UNITED STATES.**
A simple justice. New York : Teachers College Press, 2000.
*TC LC213.2 .S56 2000*

**SOCIAL LEGISLATION.** *See* LABOR LAWS AND LEGISLATION; PUBLIC WELFARE - LAW AND LEGISLATION; SOCIAL SECURITY.

**The social life of information.**
Brown, John Seely. Boston : Harvard Business School Press, c2000.
*TC HM851 .B76 2000*

**SOCIAL MARGINALITY.** *See* MARGINALITY, SOCIAL.

**SOCIAL MEDICINE.** *See also* MEDICAL ETHICS; SOCIAL PSYCHIATRY; TRANSCULTURAL MEDICAL CARE.
Fenichel, Ann. The relationship between health care clinicians' relational abilities and psychosocial orientation to patient care, and patient adherence with medical treatment. 1998.
*TC 085 F352*

Handbook of social studies in health and medicine. London ; Thousand Oaks, Calif. : Sage Publications, 2000.
*TC RA418 .H36 2000*

Loue, Sana. Gender, ethnicity, and health research. New York : Kluwer Academic/Plenum Publishers, c1999.
*TC RA448.4 .L68 1999*

Settings for health promotion. Thousand Oaks, Calif. : Sage Publications, Inc., c2000.
*TC RA427.8 .S48 2000*

**SOCIAL MEDICINE - EUROPE - HISTORY.**
Porter, Dorothy, 1953- Health, civilization, and the state. London ; New York : Routledge, 1999.
*TC RA424 .P67 1999*

**SOCIAL MEDICINE - NORTH AMERICA - HISTORY.**
Porter, Dorothy, 1953- Health, civilization, and the state. London ; New York : Routledge, 1999.
*TC RA424 .P67 1999*

**SOCIAL MEDICINE - RESEARCH - METHODOLOGY.**
Doing qualitative research. 2nd ed. Thousand Oaks, Calif. : Sage Publications, c1999
*TC R853.S64 D65 1999*

**SOCIAL MEDICINE - STANDARDS - UNITED STATES.**
Sherman, V. Clayton. Raising standards in American health care. 1st ed. San Francisco : Jossey-Bass, c1999.
*TC RA395.A3 S483 1999*

**SOCIAL MEDICINE - UNITED STATES.**
Bennett, James T. From pathology to politics. New Brunswick [N.J.] (U.S.A.) : Transaction Publishers, c2000.
*TC RA445 .B45 2000*

**SOCIAL MOBILITY.** *See* OCCUPATIONAL MOBILITY.

**SOCIAL MOVEMENTS.** *See also* **ANTINUCLEAR MOVEMENT; ANTISLAVERY MOVEMENTS; CIVIL RIGHTS MOVEMENTS; ENVIRONMENTALISM; GAY LIBERATION MOVEMENT; LABOR MOVEMENT; MILITIA MOVEMENTS; PROTEST MOVEMENTS; WHITE SUPREMACY MOVEMENTS.**
Global visions. 1st ed. Boston : South End Press, c1993.
*TC HF1359 .G58 1993*

Hetherington, Kevin. Expressions of identity. London ; Thousand Oaks, Calif. : Sage Publications, 1998.
*TC HM131 .H3995 1998*

**SOCIAL NETWORKS.** *See* **BUSINESS NETWORKS.**

**SOCIAL ORGANIZATION.** *See* **SOCIAL STRUCTURE.**

**SOCIAL PARTICIPATION.** *See also* **POLITICAL PARTICIPATION; SOCIAL GROUPS.**
Hall, C. Margaret (Constance Margaret) Heroic self. Springfield, Ill. : C.C. Thomas, c1998.
*TC RC489.S62 H35 1998*

**SOCIAL PARTICIPATION - UNITED STATES.**
Loeb, Paul Rogat, 1952- Soul of a citizen. 1st St. Martin's Griffin ed. New York : St. Martin's Griffin, 1999.
*TC HN65 .L58 1999*

**SOCIAL PERCEPTION.** *See also* **ATTRIBUTION (SOCIAL PSYCHOLOGY); GROUP RELATIONS TRAINING.**
Bar-Tal, Daniel. Shared beliefs in a society. Thousand Oaks, Calif. : Sage Publications, c2000.
*TC HM1041 .B37 2000*

Bazigos, Michael Nicholas. The relationship of upward feedback disparities to leader performance. 1999.
*TC 085 B33*

Chen, Zhe, 1964- Across the great divide. Oxford : Blackwell, 2000.
*TC LB1103 .S6 v.65 no. 2*

Emotion and social judgments. 1st ed. Oxford ; New York : Pergamon Press, 1991.
*TC BF531 .E4834 1991*

Feeling and thinking. Cambridge, U.K. ; New York : Cambridge University Press ; Paris : Editions de la Maison des Sciences de l'Homme, 2000.
*TC BF531 .F44 2000*

McGarty, Craig. Categorization in social psychology. London ; Thousand Oaks, Calif. : SAGE Publications, 1999.
*TC BF445 .M34 1999*

Smith, Hawthorne Emery. Psychological detachment from school. 1999.
*TC 085 Sm586*

Social identity. Malden, MA : Blackwell Publishers, 1999.
*TC HM131 .S58433 1999*

**SOCIAL PERCEPTION - ISRAEL.**
Bar-Tal, Daniel. Shared beliefs in a society. Thousand Oaks, Calif. : Sage Publications, c2000.
*TC HM1041 .B37 2000*

**SOCIAL PHILOSOPHY.** *See* **SOCIAL SCIENCES - PHILOSOPHY.**

**Social philosophy today**
(no. 2) Freedom, equality, and social change. Lewiston : E. Mellen Press, c1989.
*TC HM216 .F83 1989*

(no. 7) Rights, justice, and community. Lewiston, N.Y., USA : Edwin Mellen Press, c1992.
*TC HM216 .R56 1992*

**SOCIAL PLANNING.** *See* **COMMUNITY DEVELOPMENT.**

**SOCIAL POLICY.** *See also* **ECONOMIC POLICY; EDUCATION AND STATE; FAMILY POLICY; MEDICAL POLICY; MULTICULTURALISM; NUTRITION POLICY; SOCIAL ACTION; URBAN POLICY.**
Grimshaw, Jennie. Employment and health. London : British Library, 1999.
*TC HF5548.85 .G75 1999*

**SOCIAL PREDICTION.** *See* **POPULATION FORECASTING; SOCIAL INDICATORS.**

**SOCIAL PROBLEMS.** *See* **CHURCH AND SOCIAL PROBLEMS; CRIME; ETHNIC RELATIONS; RACE RELATIONS; SOCIAL ACTION; SOCIAL ETHICS.**

**Social problems and social issues**
Counseling and the therapeutic state. New York : Aldine de Gruyter, c1999.
*TC HV95 .C675 1999*

Interpreting weight. New York : Aldine de Gruyter, c1999.
*TC RA645.O23 I55 1999*

Weighty issues. Hawthorne, N.Y. : Aldine de Gruyter, c1999.
*TC RA645.O23 W45 1999*

**SOCIAL PROBLEMS AND THE CHURCH.** *See* **CHURCH AND SOCIAL PROBLEMS.**

**SOCIAL PROBLEMS - CONGRESSES.**
Rights, justice, and community. Lewiston, N.Y., USA : Edwin Mellen Press, c1992.
*TC HM216 .R56 1992*

**SOCIAL PROBLEMS - DATABASES.**
SIRS researcher [computer file] [Boca Raton, Fla.] : SIRS Mandarin,
*TC NETWORKED RESOURCE*

**SOCIAL PROBLEMS IN ART.**
Photomontage today, Peter Kennard [videorecording]. [London] : Art Council of Great Britain ; Ho-Ho-Kus, N.J. : [distributed by] Anthony Roland Collection of Films on Art, c1982.
*TC TR685 .P45 1982*

**SOCIAL PROBLEMS IN EDUCATION.** *See* **EDUCATIONAL SOCIOLOGY.**

**SOCIAL PROBLEMS - INDEXES.**
SIRS researcher [computer file] [Boca Raton, Fla.] : SIRS Mandarin,
*TC NETWORKED RESOURCE*

**SOCIAL PROBLEMS - PERIODICALS.**
Building America. [New York : Published for the Dept. of Supervision and Curriculum Development by the Society for Curriculum Study, Inc. ; distributed by Americana Corporation, 1935-

Journal of social hygiene. New York : American Social Hygiene Association,

**Social processes in children's learning.**
Light, Paul. Cambridge, U.K. ; New York : Cambridge University Press, 1999.
*TC LB1060 .L533 1999*

**SOCIAL PSYCHIATRY.**
Hacking, Ian. Mad travelers. Charlottesville, Va. : University Press of Virginia, 1998.
*TC RC553.F83 H33 1998*

Handbook of the sociology of mental health. New York : Kluwer Academic/Plenum Publishers, c1999.
*TC RC455 .H2874 1999*

Prior, Pauline. Gender and mental health. New York : New York University Press, 1999.
*TC RC455.4.S45 P75 1999*

**SOCIAL PSYCHIATRY - GERMANY - HISTORY - 16TH CENTURY.**
Midelfort, H. C. Erik A history of madness in sixteenth-century Germany. Stanford, Calif. : Stanford University Press, c1999.
*TC RC450.G3 M528 1999*

**SOCIAL PSYCHIATRY - UNITED STATES.**
Kenig, Sylvia. Who plays? who pays? who cares? Amityville, N.Y. : Baywood Pub. Co., c1992.
*TC RA790.6 .K46 1992*

**Social psychological artifacts in the measurement of consumer satisfaction with health care.**
Gill, Kenneth Joseph. 1996.
*TC 085 G396*

**SOCIAL PSYCHOLOGISTS - UNITED STATES - BIOGRAPHY.**
Keys, David Patrick, 1955- Confronting the drug control establishment. Albany, N.Y. : State University of New York Press, c2000.
*TC HM1031.L56 K49 2000*

**SOCIAL PSYCHOLOGY.** *See also* **ALIENATION (SOCIAL PSYCHOLOGY); ATTRIBUTION (SOCIAL PSYCHOLOGY); COMMUNITY PSYCHOLOGY; COOPERATIVENESS; INTERPERSONAL RELATIONS; INTERVIEWING; ORGANIZATIONAL BEHAVIOR; PUBLIC OPINION; SOCIAL CONFLICT; SOCIAL DESIRABILITY; SOCIAL INTERACTION; SOCIAL**

**ISOLATION; SOCIAL PSYCHIATRY; STEREOTYPE (PSYCHOLOGY); STIGMA (SOCIAL PSYCHOLOGY); VIOLENCE.**
Acting out in groups. Minneapolis, Minn. ; London : University of Minnesota Press, c1999.
*TC RC569.5.A25 A28 1999*

Bar-Tal, Daniel. Shared beliefs in a society. Thousand Oaks, Calif. : Sage Publications, c2000.
*TC HM1041 .B37 2000*

Brumfitt, Shelagh. The social psychology of communication impairment. London : Whurr, 1999.
*TC HM251 .B758 1999*

Cziko, Gary. The things we do. Cambridge, Mass. : MIT Press, c2000.
*TC HM1033 .C95 2000*

The Developmental social psychology of gender. Mahwah, N.J. : Lawrence Erlbaum, c2000.
*TC HQ1075 .D47 2000*

Greif, Gary F. The tragedy of the self. Lanham, Md. ; Oxford : University Press of America, c2000.
*TC BF175.5.S44 G74 2000*

Homeless and working youth around the world. San Francisco : Jossey-Bass, 1999.
*TC HV4493 .H655 1999*

Joffe, Hélène. Risk and 'the other'. Cambridge, U.K. ; New York : Cambridge University Press, 1999.
*TC HM256 .J63 1999*

Kinloch, Graham Charles. The comparative understanding of intergroup realtions [i.e. relations]. Boulder, CO : Westview Press, 1999.
*TC HM131 .K495 1999*

McCall, George J. Social psychology, a sociological approach. New York : Free Press, c1982.
*TC HM251 .M38 1982*

The message within. Philadelphia, Pa. : Psychology Press, 2000.
*TC BF697 .M457 2000*

Moessinger, Pierre. [Irrationalité individuelle et ordre social. English] The paradox of social order. New York : Aldine de Gruyter, c2000.
*TC HM1276 .M6413 2000*

The self in social psychology. Philadelphia ; Hove [England] : Psychology Press, c1999.
*TC HM1033 .S45 1999*

Social constructionism, discourse, and realism. London ; Thousand Oaks, Calif. : SAGE Publications, 1998.
*TC HM251 .S671163 1998*

Social psychology and cultural context. Thousand Oaks, Calif. : Sage Publications, c1999.
*TC HM1033 .S64 1999*

Splichal, Slavko. Public opinion. Lanham, Md. : Rowman & Littlefield, 1999.
*TC HM261 .S7515 1999*

Teen violence [videorecording]. Princeton, NJ : Films for the Humanities & Sciences, c1998.
*TC RJ506.V56 T44 1998*

Vorwerg, Manfred. Sozialpsychologische Strukturanalysen des Kollektivs. Berlin, Deutscher Verlag der Wissenschaften, 1966.
*TC HM291 .V6*

**Social psychology, a sociological approach.**
McCall, George J. New York : Free Press, c1982.
*TC HM251 .M38 1982*

**Social psychology and cultural context** / John Adamopoulos, Yoshihisa Kashima, editors. Thousand Oaks, Calif. : Sage Publications, c1999. xiv, 305 p. : ill. ; 26 cm. (Cross-cultural psychology series ; v. 4) Includes bibliographical references (p. 247-287). ISBN 0-7619-0637-1 (alk. paper) ISBN 0-7619-0638-X (alk. paper) DDC 302
*1. Social psychology. 2. Ethnopsychology. 3. Context effects (Psychology) I. Adamopoulos, John. II. Kashima, Yoshihisa, 1957- III. Title. IV. Series.*
*TC HM1033 .S64 1999*

**The social psychology of communication impairment.**
Brumfitt, Shelagh. London : Whurr, 1999.
*TC HM251 .B758 1999*

**SOCIAL PSYCHOLOGY - RESEARCH.**
Foye, Stephanie Diane. Using item response theory methods to explore the effect of item wording on Likert data. 1997.
*TC 085 F82*

**SOCIAL PSYCHOLOGY - RESEARCH - METHODOLOGY.**
Handbook of research methods in social and personality psychology. Cambridge, U.K. ; New York : Cambridge University Press, 2000.
*TC HM1019 .H36 2000*

**SOCIAL PSYCHOLOGY - UNITED STATES.**
Edmund W. Gordon. Stamford, Conn. : Jai Press, c2000.
*TC HM1033 .E35 2000*

**SOCIAL PSYCHOTECHNICS.** *See* **PSYCHOLOGY, APPLIED.**

**SOCIAL REFORM.** *See* **SOCIAL PROBLEMS.**

**SOCIAL REFORMERS.** *See* **CIVIC LEADERS; CIVIL RIGHTS WORKERS; FEMINISTS; WOMEN SOCIAL REFORMERS.**

**SOCIAL REFORMERS - GREAT BRITAIN.**
Finlayson, Geoffrey B. A. M. Decade of reform; New York, Norton [1970]
*TC HN385 .F54 1970*

**Social relationships and peer support.**
Snell, Martha E. Baltimore, Md. ; London : Paul H. Brookes Pub. Co., c2000.
*TC LC4069 .S54 2000*

**Social research and educational studies series**
(20) Murray, Louis, 1944- Practitioner-based enquiry. London ; New York : Falmer Press, 2000.
*TC LB1028.24 .M87 2000*

**SOCIAL RESPONSIBILITY, CORPORATE.** *See* **SOCIAL RESPONSIBILITY OF BUSINESS.**

**SOCIAL RESPONSIBILITY OF BUSINESS.** *See also* **INDUSTRIES - SOCIAL ASPECTS.**
Schwartz, Peter, 1946- When good companies do bad things. New York : John Wiley, c1999.
*TC HD60 .S39 1999*

**SOCIAL RESPONSIBILITY OF BUSINESS - CONGRESSES.**
Education, leadership, and business ethics. Boston, MA : Kluwer Academic Publishers, c1998.
*TC HF5387 .E346 1998*

**SOCIAL RESPONSIBILITY OF BUSINESS - UNITED STATES.**
Sagawa, Shirley, 1961- Common interest, common good. Boston : Harvard Business School Press, c2000.
*TC HD60.5.U5 S24 2000*

**SOCIAL RESPONSIBILITY OF INDUSTRY.** *See* **SOCIAL RESPONSIBILITY OF BUSINESS.**

**SOCIAL ROLE.** *See also* **SEX ROLE.**
Goffman and social organization. London ; New York : Routledge, 1999.
*TC HM291 .G57 1999*

**SOCIAL SCIENCE.** *See* **SOCIAL SCIENCES.**

**Social Science Education Consortium.**
A case study in teaching to civic standards using a portfolio approach 1996 : "Office of Citizen". [Boulder, Colo.] : Social Science Education Consortium, c1997.
*TC LC1091 .C37 1997*

Democratic dialogue with special needs students. [Boulder, Colo.] : Social Science Education Consortium, c1997.
*TC LC4069.3 .D4 1997*

Democratic dialogue with special needs students. [Boulder, Colo.] : Social Science Education Consortium, c1997.

Public issues discussion [videorecording] : Diana Hess at Denver High School 1997. [Boulder, Colo.] : Social Science Education Consortium, c1997.
*TC H62.3 .P4 1997*

Reforming the Electoral College [videorecording]. [Boulder, Colo.? : Social Science Education Consortium?], c1996.
*TC H62.5.U5 R4 1996*

Socratic seminar [videorecording]. [Boulder, Colo.] : Social Science Education Consortium, c1997.

Socratic seminar [videorecording]. [Boulder, Colo.] : Social Science Education Consortium, c1997.
*TC LB1027.44 .S6 1997*

We the people simulated congressional hearing [videorecording]. [Boulder, Colo.] : Social Science Education Consortium, c1997.
*TC KF4208.5.L3 W4 1997*

**Social science reference sources.**
Li, Tze-chung, 1927- 3rd ed. Westport, Conn. : Greenwood Press, 2000.

*TC Z7161.A1 L5 2000*

**SOCIAL SCIENCE RESEARCH.** *See* **SOCIAL SCIENCES - RESEARCH.**

**SOCIAL SCIENCES.** *See also* **CIVICS; CROSS-CULTURAL STUDIES; ECONOMICS; GERONTOLOGY; HUMAN BEHAVIOR; LIBERALISM; PLURALISM (SOCIAL SCIENCES); POLITICAL SCIENCE; POWER (SOCIAL SCIENCES); SOCIOLOGY.**
GrantFinder : Social sciences. New York, NY : St. Martin's Press,
*TC LB2337.2 .G7 2000*

**SOCIAL SCIENCES.**
Handbook of qualitative research. 2nd ed. Thousand Oaks, Calif. : Sage Publications, c2000.
*TC H62 .H2455 2000*

**SOCIAL SCIENCES.**
Thorndike, Edward L. (Edward Lee), 1874-1949. Human nature and the social order Cambridge, Mass., M.I.T. Press [1969]
*TC BF121 .T442*

**SOCIAL SCIENCES AND ETHICS - STUDY AND TEACHING (SECONDARY) - COLORADO - DENVER - PROBLEMS, EXERCISES, ETC.**
Public issues discussion [videorecording] : Diana Hess at Denver High School 1997. [Boulder, Colo.] : Social Science Education Consortium, c1997.
*TC H62.3 .P4 1997*

Socratic seminar [videorecording]. [Boulder, Colo.] : Social Science Education Consortium, c1997.

**SOCIAL SCIENCES AND PSYCHOANALYSIS.**
Frosh, Stephen. The politics of psychoanalysis. 2nd ed. New York : New York University Press, 1999.
*TC BF173 .F92 1999*

**SOCIAL SCIENCES - BIBLIOGRAPHY.**
Li, Tze-chung, 1927- Social science reference sources. 3rd ed. Westport, Conn. : Greenwood Press, 2000.
*TC Z7161.A1 L5 2000*

O'Brien, Nancy P. Education, a guide to reference and information sources. 2nd ed. Englewood, Colo. : Libraries Unlimited, 2000.
*TC Z5811 .B89 2000*

**SOCIAL SCIENCES - BIBLIOGRAPHY OF BIBLIOGRAPHIES.**
Li, Tze-chung, 1927- Social science reference sources. 3rd ed. Westport, Conn. : Greenwood Press, 2000.
*TC Z7161.A1 L5 2000*

**SOCIAL SCIENCES - CHINA - TEXTBOOKS.**
Reynolds, Barbara G. Reform and education. 1999.
*TC 06 no. 11166*

**SOCIAL SCIENCES - COMPUTER NETWORK RESOURCES.**
Surfing social studies. Washington, DC : National Council for the Social Studies, c1999.
*TC LB1044.87 .S97 1999*

**SOCIAL SCIENCES - COMPUTER NETWORK RESOURCES - DIRECTORIES.**
Millhorn, Jim, 1953- Student's companion to the World Wide Web. Lanham, Md. ; London : Scarecrow Press, 1999.
*TC H61.95 .M55 1999*

Teaching government and citizenship using the Internet. Rev. ed. viii, 112 p. : ill. ; 28 cm.
*TC H61.95 .T43 2000*

**SOCIAL SCIENCES - COMPUTER NETWORK RESOURCES - REVIEWS.**
Teaching government and citizenship using the Internet. Rev. ed. viii, 112 p. : ill. ; 28 cm.
*TC H61.95 .T43 2000*

**SOCIAL SCIENCES - DATA PROCESSING.**
Information technology and scholarship. Oxford : Oxford University Press for the British Academy, c1999.
*TC AZ186 .I556 1999*

Information technology and scholarship. Oxford : Oxford University Press for the British Academy, c1999.
*TC AZ186 .I556 1999*

**SOCIAL SCIENCES - DATABASES.**
SIRS researcher [computer file] [Boca Raton, Fla.] : SIRS Mandarin,
*TC NETWORKED RESOURCE*

**SOCIAL SCIENCES - ENGLISH-SPEAKING COUNTRIES - TERMINOLOGY.**
Knapp, Sara D. The contemporary thesaurus of search

terms and synonyms. 2nd ed. Phoenix, Ariz. : Oryx Press, 2000.
*TC ZA4060 .K58 2000*

**SOCIAL SCIENCES - FIELD WORK.** *See* **PARTICIPANT OBSERVATION.**

**SOCIAL SCIENCES - INDEXES.**
SIRS researcher [computer file] [Boca Raton, Fla.] : SIRS Mandarin,
*TC NETWORKED RESOURCE*

**SOCIAL SCIENCES - METHODOLOGY.** *See also* **SCALING (SOCIAL SCIENCES).**
Atteslander, Peter M., 1926- Methoden der empirischen Sozialforschung. Berlin : De Gruyter, 1969.
*TC H62 .A8*

Hammersley, Martyn. Taking sides in social research. London ; New York : Routledge, 2000.
*TC H62 .H2338 2000*

Krueger, Richard A. Focus groups. 3rd ed. Thousand Oaks, Calif. : Sage Publications, c2000.
*TC H61.28 .K78 2000*

Lawrence-Lightfoot, Sara, 1944- The art and science of portraiture. 1st ed. San Francisco : Jossey-Bass, c1997.
*TC H62 .L33 1997*

Memory and methodology. Oxford ; New York : Berg, 2000.
*TC BD181.7 .M46 2000*

Memory and methodology. Oxford ; New York : Berg, 2000.
*TC BD181.7 .M46 2000*

Research strategies in the social sciences. Oxford [England] ; New York : Oxford University Press, 1998.
*TC H62 .R4614 1998*

**SOCIAL SCIENCES - METHODOLOGY - DATA PROCESSING.**
Popping, Roel. Computer-assisted text analysis. Thousand Oaks, Calif. ; London : SAGE, c2000.
*TC P302 .P636 2000*

**SOCIAL SCIENCES - PERIODICALS.**
Centro sociale. Roma.

Civilisations. Bruxelles, Institut International des Civilisations Différentes.

[Humanitas (Pretoria, South Africa)] Humanitas. [Pretoria, South African Human Sciences Research Council]

National Institute of Social Sciences. Journal of the National Institute of Social Sciences. [New York]

**SOCIAL SCIENCES - PHILOSOPHY.**
Social constructionism, discourse, and realism. London ; Thousand Oaks, Calif. : SAGE Publications, 1998.
*TC HM251 .S671163 1998*

**SOCIAL SCIENCES - PHILOSOPHY - CONGRESSES.**
Rights, justice, and community. Lewiston, N.Y., USA : Edwin Mellen Press, c1992.
*TC HM216 .R56 1992*

**SOCIAL SCIENCES - REFERENCE BOOKS - BIBLIOGRAPHY.**
Li, Tze-chung, 1927- Social science reference sources. 3rd ed. Westport, Conn. : Greenwood Press, 2000.
*TC Z7161.A1 L5 2000*

O'Brien, Nancy P. Education, a guide to reference and information sources. 2nd ed. Englewood, Colo. : Libraries Unlimited, 2000.
*TC Z5811 .B89 2000*

**SOCIAL SCIENCES - RESEARCH.** *See* **EVALUATION RESEARCH (SOCIAL ACTION PROGRAMS).**

**Social sciences research.**
Staines, Gail M., 1961- Lanham, Md. ; London : Scarecrow Press, 2000.
*TC H62 .S736 2000*

**SOCIAL SCIENCES - RESEARCH.**
Atteslander, Peter M., 1926- Methoden der empirischen Sozialforschung. Berlin : De Gruyter, 1969.
*TC H62 .A8*

Bell, Judith, 1930- Doing your research project. 3rd ed. Buckingham [England] ; Philadelphia : Open University Press, 1999.

*TC LB1028 .B394 1999*

Collaborative inquiry in practice. Thousand Oaks [Calif.] : Sage Publications, c2000.
*TC H62 .C5657 2000*

Gliner, Jeffrey A. Research methods in applied settings. Mahwah, N.J. : Lawrence Erlbaum, 2000.
*TC H62 .G523 2000*

Hammersley, Martyn. Taking sides in social research. London ; New York : Routledge, 2000.
*TC H62 .H2338 2000*

Handbook of qualitative research. 2nd ed. Thousand Oaks, Calif. : Sage Publications, c2000.
*TC H62 .H2455 2000*

Lawrence-Lightfoot, Sara, 1944- The art and science of portraiture. 1st ed. San Francisco : Jossey-Bass, c1997.
*TC H62 .L33 1997*

Nonreactive measures in the social sciences. 2nd ed. Boston : Houghton Mifflin, c1981.
*TC H62 .N675 1981*

Qualitative research. Aldershot, Hants, England ; Brookfield, Vt. : Avebury, c1996.
*TC H62 .Q355 1996*

Thomas, Susan J. Designing surveys that work!. Thousand Oaks, Calif. : Corwin Press, c1999.
*TC H62 .T447 1999*

### SOCIAL SCIENCES - RESEARCH - DATA PROCESSING.
Research strategies in the social sciences. Oxford [England] ; New York : Oxford University Press, 1998.
*TC H62 .R4614 1998*

### SOCIAL SCIENCES - RESEARCH GRANTS.
GrantFinder : Social sciences. New York, NY : St. Martin's Press,
*TC LB2337.2 .G7 2000*

### SOCIAL SCIENCES - RESEARCH - METHODOLOGY.
Alvesson, Mats, 1956- Reflexive methodology. London ; Thousand Oaks, Calif. : SAGE, 2000.
*TC H61 .A62 2000*

Bell, Judith, 1930- Doing your research project. 3rd ed. Buckingham [England] ; Philadelphia : Open University Press, 1999.
*TC LB1028 .B394 1999*

Chen, Sheying. Mastering research. Chicago : Nelson-Hall, c1998.
*TC BF76.5 .C44 1998*

DeVault, Marjorie L., 1950- Liberating method. Philadelphia : Temple University Press, 1999.
*TC HQ1180 .D48 1999*

Doing qualitative research. 2nd ed. Thousand Oaks, Calif. : Sage Publications, c1999
*TC R853.S64 D65 1999*

Marshall, Catherine. Designing qualitative research. 3rd ed. Thousand Oaks, Calif. : Sage Publications, c1999.
*TC H62 .M277 1999*

Morgan, David L. Focus groups as qualitative research / David L. Morgan. 2nd ed. Thousand Oaks, Calif. : Sage Publications, c1997.
*TC H61.28 .M67 1997*

Research strategies in the social sciences. Oxford [England] ; New York : Oxford University Press, 1998.
*TC H62 .R4614 1998*

Schratz, Michael, 1952- Research as social change. London ; New York : Routledge, 1995.
*TC H62 .S33984 1995*

Staines, Gail M., 1961- Social sciences research. Lanham, Md. ; London : Scarecrow Press, 2000.
*TC H62 .S736 2000*

Theses and dissertations. Lanham, Md. : University Press of America, 1997.
*TC LB2369 .T44 1997*

Transpersonal research methods for the social sciences. Thousand Oaks, Calif. : Sage Publications, c1998.
*TC BF76.5 .T73 1998*

### SOCIAL SCIENCES - RESEARCH - UNITED STATES.
Transforming social inquiry, transforming social action. Boston ; London : Kluwer Academic, c2000.
*TC LC238 .T73 2000*

### SOCIAL SCIENCES - STATISTICAL METHODS.
Byrne, Barbara M. Structural equation modeling with LISREL, PRELIS, and SIMPLIS. Mahwah, N.J. : L. Erlbaum Associates, 1998.
*TC QA278 .B97 1998*

Eye, Alexander von. Regression analysis for social sciences. San Diego, Calif. : Academic Press, c1998.
*TC HA31.3 .E94 1998*

McDonald, Roderick P. Test theory. Mahwah, N.J. ; London : L. Erlbaum Associates, 1999.
*TC BF39 .M175 1999*

Rosenthal, Robert, 1933- Contrasts and effect sizes in behavioral research. Cambridge, U.K. ; New York : Cambridge University Press, 2000.
*TC BF39.2.A52 R67 2000*

Schumacker, Randall E. A beginner's guide to structural equation modeling. Mahwah, N.J. : L. Erlbaum Associates, 1996.
*TC QA278 .S36 1996*

### SOCIAL SCIENCES - STUDY AND TEACHING.
See also SOCIAL WORK EDUCATION.
The Canadian anthology of social studies. Vancouver : Pacific Educational Press, c1999.
*TC H62.5.C3 C32 1999*

Fersh, Seymour. Integrating the trans-national/cultural dimension. Bloomington, Ind. : Phi Delta Kappa Educational Foundation, c1993.
*TC LC1090 .F47 1993*

Surfing social studies. Washington, DC : National Council for the Social Studies, c1999.
*TC LB1044.87 .S97 1999*

### SOCIAL SCIENCES - STUDY AND TEACHING - CANADA.
Trends & issues in Canadian social studies. Vancouver : Pacific Educational Press, c1997.
*TC LB1584.5.C3 T74 1997*

### SOCIAL SCIENCES - STUDY AND TEACHING (EARLY CHILDHOOD EDUCATION).
Revisiting a progressive pedagogy. Albany : State University of New York Press, c2000.
*TC LB1117 .R44 2000*

### SOCIAL SCIENCES - STUDY AND TEACHING (EARLY CHILDHOOD) - UNITED STATES.
Robles de Melendez, Wilma J. Teaching social studies in early education. Albany, NY : Delmar Thomson Learning, c2000.
*TC LB1139.5.S64 R62 2000*

### SOCIAL SCIENCES - STUDY AND TEACHING (ELEMENTARY).
Fennessey, Sharon M. History in the spotlight. Portsmouth, NH : Heinemann, c2000.
*TC PN3171 .F46 2000*

Harrison, John, 1951- Critical challenges in social studies for upper elementary students. Vancouver : Critical Thinking Cooperative, 1999.
*TC LB1584.5.C3 H37 1999*

### SOCIAL SCIENCES - STUDY AND TEACHING (ELEMENTARY) - COMPUTER NETWORK RESOURCES.
Fredericks, Anthony D. Social studies discoveries on the net. Englewood, Colo. : Libraries Unlimited, 2000.
*TC LB1584 .F6597 2000*

### SOCIAL SCIENCES - STUDY AND TEACHING (ELEMENTARY) - UNITED STATES.
Fredericks, Anthony D. More social studies through children's literature. Englewood, Colo. : Teacher Ideas Press, 2000.
*TC LB1584 .F659 2000*

Savage, Tom V. Effective teaching in elementary social studies. 4th ed. Upper Saddle River, N.J. : Merrill, c2000.
*TC LB1584 .S34 2000*

Zarrillo, James. Teaching elementary social studies. Upper Saddle River, N.J. : Merrill, c2000.
*TC LB1584 .Z27 2000*

### SOCIAL SCIENCES - STUDY AND TEACHING (ELEMENTARY) - UNITED STATES - COMPUTER NETWORK RESOURCES.
Fredericks, Anthony D. Social studies discoveries on the net. Englewood, Colo. : Libraries Unlimited, 2000.
*TC LB1584 .F6597 2000*

### SOCIAL SCIENCES - STUDY AND TEACHING (HIGHER).
Staines, Gail M., 1961- Social sciences research. Lanham, Md. ; London : Scarecrow Press, 2000.
*TC H62 .S736 2000*

### SOCIAL SCIENCES - STUDY AND TEACHING (MIDDLE SCHOOL) - UNITED STATES - PROBLEMS, EXERCISES, ETC.
Socratic seminar [videorecording]. [Boulder, Colo.] : Social Science Education Consortium, c1997.
*TC LB1027.44 .S6 1997*

### SOCIAL SCIENCES - STUDY AND TEACHING - PERIODICALS.
Historical outlook. Philadelphia, Pa. : McKinley Pub. Co., c1918-c1933.

### SOCIAL SCIENCES - STUDY AND TEACHING (SECONDARY) - MICHIGAN - BLOOMFIELD.
Reforming the Electoral College [videorecording]. [Boulder, Colo.? : Social Science Education Consortium?], c1996.
*TC H62.5.U5 R4 1996*

### SOCIAL SCIENCES - STUDY AND TEACHING (SECONDARY) - TAIWAN - RESEARCH.
Yang, Fang-Ying. An analysis of 12th grade students' reasoning styles and competencies when presented with an environmental problem in a social and scientific context. 1999.
*TC 06 no. 11076*

### SOCIAL SCIENCES - STUDY AND TEACHING (SECONDARY) - UNITED STATES.
Teaching government and citizenship using the Internet. Rev. ed. viii, 112 p. : ill. ; 28 cm.
*TC H61.95 .T43 1997*

Zevin, Jack. Social studies for the twenty-first century. 2nd ed. Mahwah, N.J. : L. Erlbaum Associates, c2000.
*TC H62.5.U5 Z48 2000*

### SOCIAL SCIENCES - STUDY AND TEACHING (SECONDARY) - UNITED STATES - LONGITUDINAL STUDIES.
Smith, Darren James, 1960- Stepping inside the classroom through personal narratives. Lanham, Md. : University Press of America, 1999.
*TC LB1737.U6 S55 1999*

### SOCIAL SCIENCES - STUDY AND TEACHING (SECONDARY) - UNITED STATES - PROBLEMS, EXERCISES, ETC.
Public issues discussion [videorecording] : Diana Hess at Denver High School 1997. [Boulder, Colo.] : Social Science Education Consortium, c1997.
*TC H62.3 .P4 1997*

Socratic seminar [videorecording]. [Boulder, Colo.] : Social Science Education Consortium, c1997.

Socratic seminar [videorecording]. [Boulder, Colo.] : Social Science Education Consortium, c1997.
*TC LB1027.44 .S6 1997*

### SOCIAL SCIENCES - STUDY AND TEACHING - UNITED STATES.
Democratic dialogue with special needs students. [Boulder, Colo.] : Social Science Education Consortium, c1997.
*TC LC4069.3 .D4 1997*

### SOCIAL SCIENTISTS. See SOCIOLOGISTS.

### SOCIAL SCIENTISTS - UNITED STATES - BIOGRAPHY.
Bornet, Vaughn Davis, 1917- An independent scholar in twentieth century America. Talent, Or. : Bornet Books, 1995.
*TC H59.B63 A3 1995*

### SOCIAL SECURITY. See FAMILY POLICY.

### SOCIAL SECURITY - ASIA, SOUTHEASTERN - CASE STUDIES.
Ramesh, M., 1960- Welfare capitalism in southeast Asia. New York : St. Martin's Press, c2000.
*TC HN690.8.A8 R35 2000*

### SOCIAL SECURITY - PERIODICALS.
American economic security. Washington, Chamber of Commerce of the United States of America.

### SOCIAL SECURITY - UNITED STATES - PERIODICALS.
American economic security. Washington, Chamber of Commerce of the United States of America.

### SOCIAL SERVICE. See also ABUSED WIVES - SERVICES FOR; CHARITIES; COMMUNITY ORGANIZATION; MEDICAL SOCIAL WORK; PUBLIC WELFARE; SCHOOL SOCIAL WORK; SOCIAL CASE WORK; SOCIAL GROUP WORK; STUDENT AFFAIRS SERVICES; STUDENT SERVICE.
Integrating community service into nursing education. New York, NY : Springer Pub. Co., c1999.

*TC RT76 .I55 1999*

**SOCIAL SERVICE AGENCIES.** *See* **SOCIAL SERVICE.**

**SOCIAL SERVICE - CASES.** *See* **SOCIAL CASE WORK.**

**SOCIAL SERVICE - CONTRACT SERVICES.** *See* **SOCIAL SERVICE - CONTRACTING OUT.**

**SOCIAL SERVICE - CONTRACTING OUT - UNITED STATES.**
United States. General Accounting Office. Child welfare. Washington, D.C. (P.O. Box 37050, Washington, D.C. 20013) : The Office, [1998]
*TC HV741 .U525 1998a*

**SOCIAL SERVICE - FINANCE.** *See* **FUND RAISING.**

**SOCIAL SERVICE - GREAT BRITAIN.**
Professionalism, boundaries, and the workplace. New York : Routledge, 2000.
*TC HV10.5 .P74 2000*

**SOCIAL SERVICE, MEDICAL.** *See* **MEDICAL SOCIAL WORK.**

**SOCIAL SERVICE - NEW YORK (CITY) - DIRECTORIES.**
The CARES directory in electronic form [computer file] Maywood, NJ : ACIT,
*TC HV99.N59 S58*

**SOCIAL SERVICE - NEW YORK METROPOLITAN AREA - DIRECTORIES.**
The CARES directory in electronic form [computer file] Maywood, NJ : ACIT,
*TC HV99.N59 S58*

**SOCIAL SERVICE - NEW YORK (STATE) - HERKIMER COUNTY - CASE STUDIES.**
OĆonnor-Pirkle, Marilyn. Tracking systemic change in an interagency partnership. 1996.
*TC 06 no. 10677*

OĆonnor-Pirkle, Marilyn. Tracking systemic change in an interagency partnership. 1996.
*TC 06 no. 10677*

**SOCIAL SERVICE - RESEARCH.** *See* **EVALUATION RESEARCH (SOCIAL ACTION PROGRAMS).**

**SOCIAL SERVICE, SCHOOL.** *See* **SCHOOL SOCIAL WORK.**

**SOCIAL SERVICE - STUDY AND TEACHING.** *See* **SOCIAL WORK EDUCATION.**

**SOCIAL SERVICE - UNITED STATES.**
Sagawa, Shirley, 1961- Common interest, common good. Boston : Harvard Business School Press, c2000.
*TC HD60.5.U5 S24 2000*

**SOCIAL SERVICE - UNITED STATES - CASE STUDIES.**
Spencer, Gary. Structure and dynamics of social intervention; Lexington, Mass., Heath Lexington Books [1970]
*TC HV91 .S63*

**SOCIAL SETTLEMENTS - ILLINOIS - CHICAGO - HISTORY.**
Jackson, Shannon, 1967- Lines of activity. Ann Arbor : University of Michigan Press, c2000.
*TC HV4196.C4 J33 2000*

**SOCIAL SETTLEMENTS - UNITED STATES - BIBLIOGRAPHY.**
Barbuto, Domenica M., 1951- The American settlement movement. Westport, Conn. : Greenwood Press, 1999.
*TC Z7164.S665 B37 1999*

**The social shaping of technology** / edited by Donald MacKenzie and Judy Wajcman. 2nd ed. Buckingham [England] ; Philadelphia : Open University Press, c1999. xvii, 462 p. : ill. ; 25 cm. Includes bibliographical references (p. [443]-451) and index. ISBN 0-335-19914-3 (hc) ISBN 0-335-19913-5 (pbk.) DDC 306.4/6
*1. Technology - Social aspects. I. MacKenzie, Donald A. II. Wajcman, Judy.*
*TC T14.5 .S6383 1999*

**SOCIAL SKILLS.** *See* **SOCIAL SKILLS IN CHILDREN.**

**SOCIAL SKILLS IN CHILDREN.**
Education for spiritual, moral, social and cultural development. London ; New York : Continuum, 2000.
*TC LC268 .E384 2000*

Variability in the social construction of the child. San Francisco : Jossey-Bass, 2000.

*TC BF723.S62 .V37 2000*

**SOCIAL SKILLS IN CHILDREN - COLORADO.**
Clay, Cheryl D., 1947- Schooling at-risk Native American children. New York : Garland Pub., 1998.
*TC E99.U8 C53 1998*

**SOCIAL SKILLS IN CHILDREN - FOREIGN COUNTRIES.**
Pollock, David C. The third culture kid experience. Yarmouth, Me. : Intercultural Press, c1999.
*TC HQ784.S56 P65 1999*

**SOCIAL SKILLS - STUDY AND TEACHING.**
Bridges to independence [videorecording. Burbank, CA : RCA/Columbia Pictures Home Video ; [S.l. : Distributed by] Rank Video Services Production, c1991.
*TC HV1646 .B7 1991*

Goldstein, Arnold P. The Prepare Curriculum. Revised ed. Champaign, Ill. : Research Press, c1999.
*TC HM299 .G65 1999*

**SOCIAL SKILLS - STUDY AND TEACHING (SECONDARY) - UNITED STATES.**
Kessler, Rachael, 1946- The soul of education. Alexandria, Va. : Association for Supervision and Curriculum Development, c2000.
*TC LB1072 .K48 2000*

**SOCIAL SKILLS - STUDY AND TEACHING - UNITED STATES.**
Rathvon, Natalie. Effective school interventions. New York : Guilford Press, c1999.
*TC LC1201 .R38 1999*

Snell, Martha E. Social relationships and peer support. Baltimore, Md. ; London : Paul H. Brookes Pub. Co., c2000.
*TC LC4069 .S54 2000*

**SOCIAL SKILLS TRAINING.** *See* **SOCIAL SKILLS - STUDY AND TEACHING.**

**SOCIAL SKILLS - UNITED STATES.**
Csóti, Márianna. People skills for young adults. London ; Philadelphia : Jessica Kingsley, 2000.
*TC HQ799.7 .C76 2000*

**SOCIAL STATUS.** *See* **SOCIAL CLASSES.**

**SOCIAL STATUS - UNITED STATES - STATISTICS.**
The society and population health reader. Volume I. New York, N.Y. : The New Press, c1999.
*TC RA418 .S6726 1999*

**SOCIAL STRATIFICATION.** *See* **SOCIAL CLASSES.**

**SOCIAL STRUCTURE.**
Dean, Mitchell, 1955- Governmentality. London ; Thousand Oaks, Calif. : Sage Publications, 1999.
*TC HN49.P6 D43 1999*

Dean, Mitchell, 1955- Governmentality. London ; Thousand Oaks, Calif. : Sage Publications, 1999.
*TC HN49.P6 D43 1999*

Goffman and social organization. London ; New York : Routledge, 1999.
*TC HM291 .G57 1999*

**Social structure and aging**
Caregiving systems. Hillsdale, N.J. : L. Erlbaum Associates, 1993.
*TC HV1451 .C329 1993*

**SOCIAL STRUCTURE - UGANDA.**
Gitta, Cosmas. International human rights. 1998.
*TC 085 G4398*

**SOCIAL STUDIES.** *See also* **SOCIAL SCIENCES.**
Historical outlook. Philadelphia, Pa. : McKinley Pub. Co., c1918-c1933.

**Social studies discoveries on the net.**
Fredericks, Anthony D. Englewood, Colo. : Libraries Unlimited, 2000.
*TC LB1584 .F6597 2000*

**Social studies for the twenty-first century.**
Zevin, Jack. 2nd ed. Mahwah, N.J. : L. Erlbaum Associates, c2000.
*TC H62.5.U5 Z48 2000*

**SOCIAL STUDIES - STUDY AND TEACHING (SECONDARY).**
Critical challenges in social studies for junior high students. Burnaby, B.C. : Field Relations and Teacher In-Service Education, Faculty of Education, Simon Fraser University, 1996.
*TC D16.2 .C75 1996*

**SOCIAL SURVEYS.** *See also* **EDUCATIONAL SURVEYS; FAMILY LIFE SURVEYS; SEXUAL BEHAVIOR SURVEYS.**
Rogers, Richard Randall. The impact of gay identity and perceived milieu toward gay employees on job involvement and organizational commitment of gay men. 1998.
*TC 085 R635*

Thomas, Susan J. Designing surveys that work!. Thousand Oaks, Calif. : Corwin Press, c1999.
*TC H62 .T447 1999*

Withers, Carl. Plainville, U.S.A.. New York : Columbia University Press, [c1945]
*TC HN57 .W58 1945*

**SOCIAL TENSIONS.** *See* **SOCIAL CONFLICT.**

**SOCIAL THEORY.** *See* **SOCIAL SCIENCES - PHILOSOPHY.**

**Social theory, education, and cultural change**
Globalization and education. New York : Routledge, 1999.
*TC LC191 .G545 1999*

**SOCIAL VALUES.**
Bar-Tal, Daniel. Shared beliefs in a society. Thousand Oaks, Calif. : Sage Publications, c2000.
*TC HM1041 .B37 2000*

Moessinger, Pierre. [Irrationalité individuelle et ordre social. English] The paradox of social order. New York : Aldine de Gruyter, c2000.
*TC HM1276 .M6413 2000*

Rapoport, Robert N. Families, children, and the quest for a global ethic. Aldershot ; Brookfield, Vt. : Ashgate, c1997.
*TC HQ518 .R36 1997*

**SOCIAL VALUES - UNITED STATES.**
Hall, John A., 1949- Is America breaking apart? Princeton, NJ : Princeton University Press, c1999.
*TC HN59.2 .H34 1999*

**SOCIAL WELFARE.** *See* **CHARITIES; PUBLIC WELFARE; SOCIAL PROBLEMS; SOCIAL SERVICE.**

**SOCIAL WORK.** *See* **SOCIAL SERVICE.**

**SOCIAL WORK EDUCATION.**
Darling, Rosalyn Benjamin. The partnership model in human services. New York : Kluwer Academic/ Plenum Publishers, c2000.
*TC HV43 .D2 2000*

**SOCIAL WORK EDUCATION - GREAT BRITAIN.**
Sharp, Mavis, 1945- The management of failing DipSW students. Aldershot ; Brookfield, Vt. : Ashgate, c1999.
*TC HV11.8.G7 S53 1999*

**Social work in pediatrics** / Ruth B. Smith, Helen G. Clinton, editors. New York : Haworth Press, c1995. 136 p. : ill. ; 23 cm. "Has also been published as Social work in health care, volume 21, number 1 1995"--T.p. verso. Includes bibliographical references. ISBN 1-56024-765-7 (alk. paper) DDC 362.1/0425
*1. Medical social work - United States. 2. Social work with children - United States. 3. Chronically ill children - Services for - United States. I. Smith, Ruth B. II. Clinton, Helen G.*
*TC HV688.U5 S63 1995*

**Social work services in schools.**
Allen-Meares, Paula, 1948- 3rd ed. Boston : Allyn and Bacon, c2000.
*TC LB3013.4 .A45 2000*

**SOCIAL WORK WITH ALCOHOLICS - GREAT BRITAIN.**
Thom, Betsy. Dealing with drink. London ; New York : Free Association Books, 1999.
*TC HV5283.G6 T56 1999*

**SOCIAL WORK WITH CHILDREN.** *See* **CHILD WELFARE.**

**SOCIAL WORK WITH CHILDREN - GREAT BRITAIN.**
Vernon, Jeni. Maintaining children in school. London : National Children's Bureau Enterprises, c1998.
*TC LB3081 .V47 1998*

**SOCIAL WORK WITH CHILDREN - ILLINOIS - CHICAGO.**
McMahon, Anthony. Damned if you do, damned if you don't. Aldershot, England ; Brookfield, USA : Ashgate, 1998.
*TC HV743.C5 M35 1998*

**SOCIAL WORK WITH CHILDREN -
RESEARCH - METHODOLOGY.**
Eisikovits, Rivka Anne. The anthropology of child
and youth care work. New York : Haworth Press,
c1997.
*TC HV713 .E47 1997*

**SOCIAL WORK WITH CHILDREN - UNITED
STATES.**
The challenge of permanency planning in a
multicultural society. New York : Haworth Press,
c1997.
*TC HV741 .C378 1997*

Social work in pediatrics. New York : Haworth Press,
c1995.
*TC HV688.U5 S63 1995*

**SOCIAL WORK WITH CHILDREN - UNITED
STATES - CASE STUDIES.**
McWilliam, P. J. Lives in progress. Baltimore : P.H.
Brookes, c2000.
*TC HV741 .M3128 2000*

**SOCIAL WORK WITH FAMILIES.** *See* **FAMILY
SOCIAL WORK.**

**SOCIAL WORK WITH HANDICAPPED
CHILDREN.**
Interdisciplinary clinical assessment of young children
with developmental disabilities. Baltimore : Paul H.
Brookes Pub. Co., c2000.
*TC HV891 .I58 2000*

Lava, Valerie Forkin. Early intervention. 1998.
*TC 06 no. 11140*

Middleton, Laura. Disabled children. Malden, Mass. :
Blackwell Sciences, 1999.
*TC HV888 .M53 1999*

**SOCIAL WORK WITH MINORITIES - GREAT
BRITAIN.**
Banks, Nick. White counsellors--Black clients.
Aldershot, Hants, England ; Brookfield, Vt. : Ashgate,
c1999.
*TC HV3177.G7 B36 1999*

**SOCIAL WORK WITH MINORITIES -
ILLINOIS - CHICAGO.**
McMahon, Anthony. Damned if you do, damned if
you don't. Aldershot, England ; Brookfield, USA :
Ashgate, 1998.
*TC HV743.C5 M35 1998*

**SOCIAL WORK WITH MINORITIES - UNITED
STATES.**
The challenge of permanency planning in a
multicultural society. New York : Haworth Press,
c1997.
*TC HV741 .C378 1997*

**SOCIAL WORK WITH THE AGED.**
Nemeroff, Robin. Stress, social support, and
psychological distress in late life. 1999.
*TC 085 N341*

**SOCIAL WORK WITH THE MENTALLY
HANDICAPPED - PSYCHOLOGICAL
ASPECTS.**
Gray, Barry, 1944- Lifemaps of people with learning
difficulties. London ; Philadelphia : Jessica Kingsley,
1999.
*TC HV3004 .G73 1999*

**SOCIAL WORK WITH WOMEN - UNITED
STATES.**
Empowering women of color. New York : Columbia
University Press, c1999.
*TC HV1445 .E45 1999*

Pack-Brown, Sherlon P. Images of me. Boston : Allyn
and Bacon, c1998.
*TC HV1445 .P33 1998*

**SOCIAL WORK WITH YOUTH.** *See* **CHILD
WELFARE.**

**SOCIAL WORK WITH YOUTH - GREAT
BRITAIN.**
Vernon, Jeni. Maintaining children in school.
London : National Children's Bureau Enterprises,
c1998.
*TC LB3081 .V47 1998*

**SOCIAL WORK WITH YOUTH - RESEARCH -
METHODOLOGY.**
Eisikovits, Rivka Anne. The anthropology of child
and youth care work. New York : Haworth Press,
c1997.
*TC HV713 .E47 1997*

**SOCIAL WORKERS - GREAT BRITAIN.**
Professionalism, boundaries, and the workplace. New
York : Routledge, 2000.

*TC HV10.5 .P74 2000*

**SOCIAL WORKERS - ILLINOIS - CHICAGO.**
McMahon, Anthony. Damned if you do, damned if
you don't. Aldershot, England ; Brookfield, USA :
Ashgate, 1998.
*TC HV743.C5 M35 1998*

**SOCIAL WORKERS - PROFESSIONAL ETHICS -
GREAT BRITAIN.**
Professionalism, boundaries, and the workplace. New
York : Routledge, 2000.
*TC HV10.5 .P74 2000*

**The social worlds of higher education : :** handbook for
teaching in a new century / [editors], Bernice A.
Pescosolido, Ronald Aminzade. Thousand Oaks,
Calif. : Pine Forge Press, [1999]. 102 p. ; 24 cm. "This is
a preview--or a 'sampler'--of some of the essays contained in
the final product that will be published February 22, 1999."--P.
[2] of cover. Includes bibliographical references.
*1. College teaching - Social aspects - United States. 2. College
teachers - United States - Social conditions. 3. Education,
Higher - Social aspects - United States. 4. Educational
change - United States. I. Pescosolido, Bernice A. II.
Aminzade, Ronald, 1949-*
*TC LB2331 .S573 1999 sampler*

**The social worlds of male and female children in the
nineteenth century French educational system.**
Knottnerus, J. David. Lewiston, N.Y. ; Lampeter,
Wales : Edwin Mellen Press, c1999.
*TC LC191.8.F8 K66 1999*

**SOCIALISM.** *See also* **ANARCHISM;
COLLECTIVE SETTLEMENTS; MIXED
ECONOMY.**
James, C. L. R. (Cyril Lionel Robert), 1901- Marxism
for our times. Jackson, Miss: University Press of
Mississippi, c1999.
*TC HX44 .J25 1999*

**SOCIALISM - FRANCE - HISTORY.**
Gordon, Felicia. Early French feminisms, 1830-1940.
Cheltenham, U.K. ; Brookfield, Vt. : Edward Elgar,
c1996.
*TC HQ1615.A3 G67 1996*

**SOCIALISM - PERIODICALS.**
Frontiers of democracy. New York, Progressive
Education Association, etc., 1934-

**SOCIALIST MOVEMENTS.** *See* **SOCIALISM.**

**SOCIALISTS.** *See* **WOMEN SOCIALISTS.**

**SOCIALIZATION.** *See also* **ASSIMILATION
(SOCIOLOGY); COGNITION AND
CULTURE; POLITICAL SOCIALIZATION;
PROFESSIONAL SOCIALIZATION; SOCIAL
SKILLS; WOMEN - SOCIALIZATION.**
Asher, Nina. Margins, center, and the spaces in-
between. 1999.
*TC 06 no. 11080*

Barnett, David W., 1946- Designing preschool
interventions. New York : Guilford Press, 1999.
*TC LC4801 .B36 1999*

The deaf child in the family and at school. Mahwah,
N.J. : Lawrence Erlbaum Associates, 2000.
*TC HV2392.2 .D43 2000*

Flaxman, Erwin. Youth mentoring: New York, N.Y. :
ERIC Clearinghouse on Urban Education, 1988.
*TC LC4065 .F53 1988*

Human cognition and social agent technology.
Amsterdam ; Philadelphia : John Benjamins, c2000.
*TC BF311 .H766 2000*

Hutcheon, Pat Duffy. Building character and culture.
Westport, Conn. : Praeger, 1999.
*TC HQ783 .H88 1999*

Mead, George Herbert, 1863-1931. Play, school, and
society. New York : Peter Lang, c1999.
*TC HQ782 .M43 1999*

Thomas, R. Murray (Robert Murray), 1921- Human
development theories. Thousand Oaks : Sage
Publications, c1999.
*TC HQ783 .T57 1999*

Wyness, Michael G. Contesting childhood. London ;
New York : Falmer Press, 2000.
*TC HQ767.9 .W96 2000*

**SOCIALIZATION - AUSTRALIA.**
Schools and the social development of young
Australians. Melbourne, Vic. : Australian Council for
Educational Research, 1998.
*TC LC192.4 .S36 1998*

**SOCIALIZATION - BIBLIOGRAPHY.**
Research on socialization of young children in the
Nordic countries. Aarhus : Aarhus University Press,
c1989.
*TC Z7164.S678 R47 1989*

**SOCIALIZATION - CROSS-CULTURAL
STUDIES - ADDRESSES, ESSAYS,
LECTURES.**
Harrington, Charles C. Cross cultural approaches to
learning. New York : MSS Informationc c1973.
*TC GN488.5 .H33 1973*

**SOCIALIZATION - INDIA.**
Culture, socialization and human development. New
Delhi ; Thousand Oaks, CA : Sage Publications,
c1999.
*TC HQ783 .C85 1999*

**SOCIALIZATION - NEW YORK (STATE) - CASE
STUDIES.**
Schmidt, Patricia Ruggiano, 1944- Cultural conflict
and struggle. New York : P. Lang, c1998.
*TC LB1181 .S36 1998*

**SOCIALIZATION, POLITICAL.** *See* **POLITICAL
SOCIALIZATION.**

**SOCIALIZATION - UNITED STATES.**
Hill, Shirley A. (Shirley Ann), 1947- African
American children. Thousand Oaks, Calif. : Sage
Publications, c1999.
*TC E185.86 .H665 1999*

**SOCIALLY DISADVANTAGED.** *See* **SOCIALLY
HANDICAPPED.**

**SOCIALLY HANDICAPPED.** *See*
**MARGINALITY, SOCIAL.**

**SOCIALLY HANDICAPPED CHILDREN -
EDUCATION.**
Combating educational disadvantage. London ; New
York : Falmer Press, 2000.
*TC LC4065 .C66 1999*

**SOCIALLY HANDICAPPED CHILDREN -
EDUCATION (EARLY CHILDHOOD) -
CROSS-CULTURAL STUDIES.**
Effective early education. New York : Falmer Press,
1999.
*TC LB1139.23 .E44 1999*

**SOCIALLY HANDICAPPED CHILDREN -
EDUCATION (EARLY CHILDHOOD) -
ILLINOIS - CHICAGO.**
Reynolds, Arthur J. Success in early intervention.
Lincoln, Neb. : University of Nebraska Press, c2000.
*TC HV743.C5 R48 2000*

**SOCIALLY HANDICAPPED CHILDREN -
EDUCATION - GREAT BRITAIN.**
Klein, Reva Defying disaffection. Staffordshire,
England : Trentham Books, 1999.
*TC LC4091 .K53 1999*

Morgan, Sally, 1951- Care about education. London :
DfEE, 1999.
*TC HV59 .M67 1999*

**SOCIALLY HANDICAPPED CHILDREN -
EDUCATION - HUNGARY.**
Disadvantaged youth project. Budapest : Ministry of
Labour, 1998.
*TC LC4096.H9 D57 1998*

**SOCIALLY HANDICAPPED CHILDREN -
EDUCATION - INDIANA - INDIANAPOLIS -
CASE STUDIES.**
Rosier, Katherine Brown. Mothering inner-city
children. New Brunswick, NJ : Rutgers University
Press, 2000.
*TC HV1447.I53 R67 2000*

**SOCIALLY HANDICAPPED CHILDREN -
EDUCATION - NORTH CAROLINA -
CHARLOTTE - CASE STUDIES.**
Dunlap, Katherine M. Family empowerment. New
York ; London : Garland Pub., 2000.
*TC LB1140.35.P37 D86 2000*

**SOCIALLY HANDICAPPED CHILDREN -
EDUCATION (PRESCHOOL) - UNITED
STATES.** *See* **HEAD START PROGRAMS.**

**SOCIALLY HANDICAPPED CHILDREN -
EDUCATION (SECONDARY) - UNITED
STATES - CASE STUDIES.**
Corwin, Miles. And still we rise. 1st ed. New York :
Bard, 2000.
*TC LC3993.9 .C678 2000*

**SOCIALLY HANDICAPPED CHILDREN -
EDUCATION - UNITED STATES.**
Barr, Robert D. Hope fulfilled for at-risk and violent

youth. 2nd ed. Boston ; London : Allyn and Bacon, c2001.
*TC LC4802 .B37 2001*

Bartolomé, Lilia I. The misteaching of academic discourses. Boulder, Colo. : Westview Press, 1998.
*TC LB1033.5 .B37 1998*

Chalker, Christopher S. Effective alternative education programs. Lancaster, Pa. : Technomic, c1999.
*TC LC4091 .C5 1999*

Democratic dialogue with special needs students. [Boulder, Colo.] : Social Science Education Consortium, c1997.
*TC LC4069.3 .D4 1997*

Educating the disadvantaged, 1972-1973. New York : AMS Press, c1976.
*TC LC4091 .F52 1976*

Flaxman, Erwin, comp. Educating the disadvantaged, 1971-1972. New York : AMS Press, [c1973]
*TC LC4091 .F52 1973*

Grossman, Herbert, 1934- Achieving educational equality. Springfield, Ill. : C.C. Thomas, c1998.
*TC LC213.2 .G76 1998*

Klein, Reva Defying disaffection. Staffordshire, England : Trentham Books, 1999.
*TC LC4091 .K53 1999*

Kozol, Jonathan. Savage inequalities. 1st Harper Perennial ed. New York : HarperPerennial, 1992.
*TC LC4091 .K69 1992*

Snell, Martha E. Social relationships and peer support. Baltimore, Md. ; London : Paul H. Brookes Pub. Co., c2000.
*TC LC4069 .S54 2000*

Vaughn, Sharon, 1952- Teaching exceptional, diverse, and at-risk students in the general education classroom. 2nd ed. Boston : Allyn and Bacon, 2000.
*TC LC3981 .V28 2000*

Williams, Thomas L., 1946- The directory of programs for students at risk. Larchmont, N.Y. : Eye on Education, c1999.
*TC LC4091 .W55 1999*

**SOCIALLY HANDICAPPED CHILDREN - ILLINOIS - CHICAGO - LONGITUDINAL STUDIES.**
Reynolds, Arthur J. Success in early intervention. Lincoln, Neb. : University of Nebraska Press, c2000.
*TC HV743.C5 R48 2000*

**SOCIALLY HANDICAPPED CHILDREN - INDIANA - INDIANAPOLIS - CASE STUDIES.**
Rosier, Katherine Brown. Mothering inner-city children. New Brunswick, NJ : Rutgers University Press, 2000.
*TC HV1447.I53 R67 2000*

**SOCIALLY HANDICAPPED CHILDREN - NEW YORK (STATE) - NEW YORK.**
Kozol, Jonathan. Ordinary resurrections. 1st ed. New York : Crown Publishers, c2000.
*TC HQ792.U5 K69 2000*

**SOCIALLY HANDICAPPED CHILDREN - SERVICES FOR - ILLINOIS - CHICAGO.**
Reynolds, Arthur J. Success in early intervention. Lincoln, Neb. : University of Nebraska Press, c2000.
*TC HV743.C5 R48 2000*

**SOCIALLY HANDICAPPED CHILDREN - SERVICES FOR - UNITED STATES.**
Caring as tenacity. Cresskill, N.J. : Hampton Press, c2000.
*TC LC5131 .C35 2000*

**SOCIALLY HANDICAPPED CHILDREN - UNITED STATES - ATTITUDES.**
Democratic dialogue with special needs students. [Boulder, Colo.] : Social Science Education Consortium, c1997.
*TC LC4069.3 .D4 1997*

**SOCIALLY HANDICAPPED CHILDREN - UNITED STATES - PSYCHOLOGY.**
Luthar, Suniya S. Poverty and children's adjustment. Thousand Oaks, Calif. : Sage Publications, c1999.
*TC HV741 .L88 1999*

**SOCIALLY HANDICAPPED - EDUCATION - INDIA.**
Kinjaram, Ramaiah. Educational performance of scheduled castes. New Delhi : APH Pub. Corp., [1998?]
*TC LC4097.14 K55 1998*

**SOCIALLY HANDICAPPED - EDUCATION - INDIA - STATISTICS.**
Kinjaram, Ramaiah. Educational performance of scheduled castes. New Delhi : APH Pub. Corp., [1998?]
*TC LC4097.14 K55 1998*

**SOCIALLY HANDICAPPED - EMPLOYMENT.** *See* **HARD-CORE UNEMPLOYED.**

**SOCIALLY HANDICAPPED - PITTSBURG, CALIF.**
Craddock. George W. Social disadvantagement and dependency: Lexington, Mass., Heath Lexington Books [1970]
*TC HD7256.U6 C438*

**SOCIALLY HANDICAPPED WOMEN - INDIANA - INDIANAPOLIS - INTERVIEWS.**
Rosier, Katherine Brown. Mothering inner-city children. New Brunswick, NJ : Rutgers University Press, 2000.
*TC HV1447.I53 R67 2000*

**SOCIALLY HANDICAPPED YOUTH.**
Flaxman, Erwin. Youth mentoring: New York, N.Y. : ERIC Clearinghouse on Urban Education, 1988.
*TC LC4065 .F53 1988*

**SOCIALLY HANDICAPPED YOUTH - EDUCATION - UNITED STATES.**
Barr, Robert D. Hope fulfilled for at-risk and violent youth. 2nd ed. Boston ; London : Allyn and Bacon, c2001.
*TC LC4802 .B37 2001*

**SOCIALLY HANDICAPPED YOUTH - EDUCATION - UNITED STATES - CASE STUDIES.**
Kennedy, Rosa L., 1938- A school for healing. New York : P. Lang, c1999.
*TC LC46.4 .K46 1999*

**The societal impact of technology.**
Katsikides, Savvas. Aldershot, Hants, England ; Brookfield, Vt. : Ashgate, c1998.
*TC T14.5 .K373 1998*

**The societal subject** / edited by Niels Engelsted ... [et al.]. Aarhus C, Denmark : Aarhus University Press, c1993. 296 p. : ill. ; 24 cm. "The 14 articles presented are enlarged and revised versions of papers and commentaries delivered at the 2nd Danish Conference of Activity Theory held at Roesnaes, Denmark, 1991"--Introd. Includes bibliographical references. CONTENTS: At a crossroads : an introduction / Niels Engelsted -- Conation, cognition, and consciousness / Henrik Poulsen -- The elements of psychology / Jens Mammen -- The conscious body : birth of consciousness, a theoretical synthesis / Mogens Hansen -- Relating subject and society : a critical appraisal / Erik Axel & Morten Nissen -- The psychodynamics of activities and life projects / Preben Bertelsen -- Methods, focus of interest, and theory in humanistic research / Eric Schultz -- A platform for modern didactics in a postmodern society, and an example / Mads Hermansen -- Activity and the disembedding of human capacities in modernity / Arne Poulsen -- Conceptualizing fundamental social processes : the path to the comprehension of entrepreneurship? / Ole Elstrup Rasmussen -- Societal anomia and the psychological turn of the mass / Benny Karpatschof -- Notes on communication, activity theory, and zone of proximal development / Aksel Mortensen -- Where does personality go, when the child goes to school? / Kirsten Baltzer -- Foundations for investigating the role of culture in Danish school teaching / Mariane Hedegaard & Seth Chaiklin -- Pedagogical intervention and youth development : theory and practice in a pedagogical youth-evaluation project / Sven Mørch & Søren Frost. ISBN 87-7288-113-5 (alk. paper) DDC 150
*1. Act (Philosophy) - Congresses. 2. Psychology - Philosophy - Congresses. I. Engelsted, Niels. II. Danish Conference of Activity Theory (2nd : 1991)*
*TC B105.A35 S68 1991*

**Société du savoir et gestion des connaissances fre.**
Centre for Educational Research and Innovation. Knowledge management in the learning society. Paris : Organisation for Economic Co-operation and Development, 2000.
*TC HD30.2 .C462 2000*

**Societe nationale de television en couleur "Antenne 2".**
Monsieur René Magritte [videorecording]. [Chicago, Ill.] : Home Vision [distributor], c1978.
*TC ND673.M35 M6 1978*

**Société pédagogique de la Suisse romande.**
L'Éducateur et bulletin corporatif. Lausanne,

**SOCIETIES.** *See* **ASSOCIATIONS, INSTITUTIONS, ETC.**

**SOCIETIES, NURSING - UNITED STATES - PERIODICALS.**
Journal of nursing scholarship. Indianapolis, IN : JNS Publication Office, 2000-
*TC RT1 .I42*

**SOCIETIES - UNITED STATES.**
Buse, William Joseph. The alternate session. 1999.
*TC 085 B9603*

**Society and aging series**
The gerontological prism. Amityville, N.Y. : Baywood Pub., c2000.
*TC HQ1061 .G416 2000*

Hatch, Laurie Russell. Beyond gender differences. Amityville, N.Y. : Baywood Pub., c2000.
*TC HQ1061 .H375 2000*

Settersten, Richard A. Lives in time and place. Amityville, N.Y. : Baywood Pub., c1999.
*TC BF713 .S48 1999*

**SOCIETY AND ARCHITECTURE.** *See* **ARCHITECTURE AND SOCIETY.**

**SOCIETY AND ART.** *See* **ART AND SOCIETY.**

**SOCIETY AND DANCE.** *See* **DANCE - SOCIAL ASPECTS.**

**SOCIETY AND DRUG ABUSE.** *See* **DRUG ABUSE - SOCIAL ASPECTS.**

**SOCIETY AND EDUCATION.** *See* **EDUCATIONAL SOCIOLOGY.**

**SOCIETY AND LANGUAGE.** *See* **SOCIOLINGUISTICS.**

**SOCIETY AND LITERATURE.** *See* **LITERATURE AND SOCIETY.**

**The society and population health reader.** Volume I : income inequality and health / edited by Ichirō Kawachi, Bruce P. Kennedy, and Richard G. Wilkinson. New York, N.Y. : The New Press, c1999. xxxvi, 505 p. : ill. ; 24 cm. Income inequality and health. Includes bibliographies. ISBN 1-56584-526-9
*1. Public health - Social aspects - United States. 2. Social status - United States - Statistics. 3. Income distribution - United States - Statistics. I. Kawachi, Ichirō. II. Kennedy, Bruce P. III. Wilkinson, Richard G. IV. Title: Income inequality and health*
*TC RA418 .S6726 1999*

**SOCIETY AND TELECOMMUNICATION.** *See* **TELECOMMUNICATION - SOCIAL ASPECTS.**

**SOCIETY AND THE ARTS.** *See* **ARTS AND SOCIETY.**

**SOCIETY AND WAR.** *See* **WAR AND SOCIETY.**

**Society for Curriculum Study.**
Building America. [New York : Published for the Dept. of Supervision and Curriculum Development by the Society for Curriculum Study, Inc. ; distributed by Americana Corporation, 1935-

**Society for Intercultural Education, Training, and Research.**
[International journal of intercultural relations (Online)] International journal of intercultural relations [computer file]. Oxford ; New York : Pergamon,
*TC EJOURNALS*

**Society for Projective Techniques.**
Journal of projective techniques. Glendale, Calif. : Society for Projective Techniques and Rorschach Institute, 1950-c1963.

Journal of projective techniques & personality assessment. Glendale, Calif.

**Society for Projective Techniques and Rorschach Institute.**
Journal of projective techniques. Glendale, Calif. : Society for Projective Techniques and Rorschach Institute, 1950-c1963.

**Society for Research in Child Development.**
Adolescent siblings in stepfamilies. Chicago, Ill. : University of Chicago Press, 1999.
*TC LB1103.S6 v.64 no. 4*

Chen, Zhe, 1964- Across the great divide. Oxford : Blackwell, 2000.
*TC LB1103 .S6 v.65 no. 2*

**Society for Research into Higher Education.**
Bennett, Neville. Skills development in higher education and employment. Buckingham [England] ; Philadelphia : Society for Research into Higher Education & Open University Press, 2000.

*TC LB1027.47 .B46 2000*

**Society for the Advancement of Education.**
Intellect. [New York, Society for the Advancement of Education]

**Society for the Promotion of Education in India.**
The geography teacher, India. Madras : The Society for the Promotion of Education in India, 1965-

**SOCIETY, HIGH.** *See* UPPER CLASS.

**SOCIETY OF FRIENDS.** *See* QUAKERS.

**Society of Motion Picture and Television Engineers.**
Journal of the SMPTE. New York, N.Y. : SMPTE, 1956-1975.

**Society of Pediatric Psychology.**
Directory of internship and post-doctoral fellowships in clinical child/pediatric psychology, 1997. [Mahwah, N.J. : Lawrence Erlbaum Associates, c1997].
*TC RJ503.3 .D57 1997*

**SOCIO-ECONOMIC STATUS.** *See* SOCIAL STATUS.

**SOCIOBIOLOGY.**
Cziko, Gary. The things we do. Cambridge, Mass. : MIT Press, c2000.
*TC HM1033 .C95 2000*

Wright, Robert, 1957- The moral animal. 1st Vintage books ed. New York : Vintage Books, 1995, c1994.
*TC GN365.9 .W75 1995*

**Sociocultural, political, and historical studies in education**
Glander, Timothy Richard, 1960- Origins of mass communications research during the American Cold War. Mahwah, N.J. ; London : L. Erlbaum, 2000.
*TC P91.5.U5 G57 2000*

Indigenous educational models for contemporary practice. Mahwah, N.J.·: L. Erlbaum Associates, 2000.
*TC LC3719 .I53 2000*

Knowledge and power in the global economy. Mahwah, N.J. : L. Erlbaum Associates, 2000.
*TC LC66 .K66 2000*

Peshkin, Alan. Permissible advantage? Mahwah, N.J. ; London : L. Erlbaum Associates, 2001.
*TC LC58.4 .P58 2001*

Spring, Joel H. The universal right to education. Mahwah, N.J. ; London : Lawrence Erlbaum Associates, 2000.
*TC LC213 .S67 2000*

**SOCIOECONOMIC STATUS.** *See* SOCIAL STATUS.

**Sociolinguistic theory.**
Chambers, J. K. Oxford, UK ; Cambridge, Mass., USA : Blackwell, 1995.
*TC P40 .C455 1995*

**SOCIOLINGUISTICS.** *See also* LINGUISTIC MINORITIES; LITERATURE AND SOCIETY; RACISM IN LANGUAGE.
Bernstein, Basil B. Pedagogy, symbolic control, and identity. Lanham, Md. : Rowman & Littlefield, 2000.
*TC LC191 .B456 2000*

Bernstein, Basil B. The structuring of pedagogic discourse. London ; New York : Routledge, 1990.
*TC P40 .B39 1990*

Chambers, J. K. Sociolinguistic theory. Oxford, UK ; Cambridge, Mass., USA : Blackwell, 1995.
*TC P40 .C455 1995*

Fischer, Steven R. A history of language. London : Reaktion Books, 1999.
*TC P140 .F57 1999*

How and why language matters in evaluation. San Francisco, CA : Jossey-Bass, c2000.
*TC H62 .H67 2000*

Ingulsrud, John E. Learning to read in China. Lewiston, N.Y. : Lampeter, Wales : Mellen, c1999.
*TC LB1577.C48 I54 1999*

Li, Duan-Duan. Expressing needs and wants in a second language. 1998.
*TC 06 no. 10958*

Pierre Bourdieu. Bern ; New York : P. Lang, c1999.
*TC HM621 .P54 1999*

Rassool, Naz, 1949- Literacy for sustainable development in the age of information. Clevedon [England] ; Philadelphia : Multilingual Matters, c1999.

*TC LC149 .R37 1999*

Text in education and society. Singapore : Singapore University Press ; Singapore ; River Edge, N.J. : World Scientific, c1998.
*TC P40.8 .T48 1998*

**SOCIOLINGUISTICS - CONGRESSES.**
Vygotskian perspectives on literacy research. Cambridge, U.K. ; New York : Cambridge University Press, 2000.
*TC LB1060 .V95 2000*

**SOCIOLINGUISTICS - NEW YORK (STATE) - NEW YORK.**
The multilingual Apple. Berlin ; New York : Mouton de Gruyter, 1997.
*TC P40.5.L56 M8 1997*

**SOCIOLINGUISTICS - PERIODICALS.**
Working papers in educational linguistics. [Philadelphia]: Language in Education Division, Graduate School of Education, University of Pennsylvania.
*TC P40.8 .W675*

**SOCIOLINGUISTICS - UNITED STATES.**
Asian-American education. Westport, Conn. : Bergin & Garvey, 1999.
*TC LC2632 .A847 1999*

Fennimore, Beatrice Schneller. Talk matters. New York ; London : Teachers College Press, c2000.
*TC LB1033.5 F46 2000*

**Sociological Abstracts, Inc.**
[LLBA (Online)] LLBA [computer file]. [Norwood, MA] : SilverPlatter International, [1993- Computer data and program.

[LLBA (Online)] LLBA [computer file]. [Norwood, MA] : SilverPlatter International, [1993- Computer data and program.

[LLBA (Online)] LLBA [computer file]. [Norwood, MA] : SilverPlatter International, [1993- Computer data and program.
*TC NETWORKED RESOURCE*

**Sociological imagination and structural change**
Moessinger, Pierre. [Irrationalité individuelle et ordre social. English] The paradox of social order. New York : Aldine de Gruyter, c2000.
*TC HM1276 .M6413 2000*

**SOCIOLOGICAL JURISPRUDENCE.**
Compliance and the law; Beverly Hills, Sage Publications [1972]
*TC K376 .C66*

**SOCIOLOGICAL RESEARCH.** *See* SOCIOLOGY - RESEARCH.

**SOCIOLOGISTS - UNITED STATES - BIOGRAPHY.**
Keys, David Patrick, 1955- Confronting the drug control establishment. Albany, N.Y. : State University of New York Press, c2000.
*TC HM1031.L56 K49 2000*

**SOCIOLOGY.** *See also* CHICAGO SCHOOL OF SOCIOLOGY; COMMUNICATION; COMMUNITY; CONSERVATISM; EDUCATIONAL SOCIOLOGY; EQUALITY; ETHNIC RELATIONS; INFORMATION SOCIETY; MARGINALITY, SOCIAL; POPULATION; POWER (SOCIAL SCIENCES); RACE RELATIONS; SOCIAL CONFLICT; SOCIAL ETHICS; SOCIAL GROUPS; SOCIAL HISTORY; SOCIAL MEDICINE; SOCIAL PSYCHOLOGY; SOCIAL STRUCTURE; SOCIALIZATION; SOCIOLINGUISTICS; WAR AND SOCIETY.
Arendt, Hannah. The human condition. 2nd ed. / introduction by Margaret Canovan. Chicago : University of Chicago Press, 1998.
*TC HM211 .A7 1998*

Critical sociology. Harmondsworth : New York [etc.] : Penguin, 1976.
*TC HM24 .C74*

**SOCIOLOGY AND ARCHITECTURE.** *See* ARCHITECTURE AND SOCIETY.

**SOCIOLOGY AND ART.** *See* ART AND SOCIETY.

**SOCIOLOGY AND LITERATURE.** *See* LITERATURE AND SOCIETY.

**SOCIOLOGY AND THE ARTS.** *See* ARTS AND SOCIETY.

**SOCIOLOGY - BIBLIOGRAPHY - PERIODICALS.**

International bibliography of anthropology = London : New York : Routledge, 1999-
*TC Z7161 .I593*

**SOCIOLOGY, CHRISTIAN.** *See* SOCIAL ETHICS.

**SOCIOLOGY, EDUCATIONAL.** *See* EDUCATIONAL SOCIOLOGY.

**Sociology for a new century**
Brint, Steven G. Schools and societies. Thousand Oaks : Pine Forge Press, c1998.
*TC LC191.4 .B75 1998*

**SOCIOLOGY - FRANCE - HISTORY.**
Swartz, David, 1945- Culture & power. Chicago : University of Chicago Press, 1997.
*TC HM22.F8 S93 1997*

**SOCIOLOGY - GERMANY (WEST) - HISTORY.**
Critical sociology. Harmondsworth ; New York [etc.] : Penguin, 1976.
*TC HM24 .C74*

**SOCIOLOGY - ILLINOIS - CHICAGO - HISTORY.**
Abbott, Andrew. Department & discipline. Chicago, IL : University of Chicago Press, c1999.
*TC HM22.U5 A23 1999*

**SOCIOLOGY LITERATURE.** *See* SOCIOLOGY - BIBLIOGRAPHY.

**SOCIOLOGY - METHODOLOGY.**
Swartz, David, 1945- Culture & power. Chicago : University of Chicago Press, 1997.
*TC HM22.F8 S93 1997*

**SOCIOLOGY, MILITARY.** *See* CIVIL-MILITARY RELATIONS; MILITARISM; WAR AND SOCIETY.

**SOCIOLOGY, MILITARY - MATHEMATICAL MODELS.**
Richardson, Lewis Fry, 1881-1953. Statistics of deadly quarrels. Pacific Grove, Ca. Boxwood Press [1960]
*TC U21.7 .R5 1960*

**SOCIOLOGY OF CULTURE.** *See* CULTURE.

**SOCIOLOGY OF DISABILITY.**
Barnes, Colin, 1946- Exploring disability. Cambridge, UK : Polity Press ; Malden, MA : Blackwell Publishers, 1999.
*TC HV1568 .B35 1999*

Marks, Deborah, 1964- Disability. London ; New York : Routledge, 1999.
*TC HV1568.2 .M37 1999*

**SOCIOLOGY OF DISABILITY - STUDY AND TEACHING.** *See* DISABILITY STUDIES.

**SOCIOLOGY OF DISABILITY - UNITED STATES.**
Frank, Gelya, 1948- Venus on wheels. Berkeley, Calif. : University of California Press, c2000.
*TC HV3021.W66 F73 2000*

**SOCIOLOGY OF DISABLEMENT.** *See* SOCIOLOGY OF DISABILITY.

**Sociology of education.**
The Journal of educational sociology. [New York : American Viewpoint Society, Inc., 1927-1963]

**Sociology of education (Online).**
[Journal of educational sociology (Online)] The journal of educational sociology [computer file]. New York, N.Y. : American Viewpoint Society, Inc., 1927-1963.
*TC EJOURNALS*

**SOCIOLOGY OF IMPAIRMENT.** *See* SOCIOLOGY OF DISABILITY.

**SOCIOLOGY OF LANGUAGE.** *See* SOCIOLINGUISTICS.

**SOCIOLOGY OF SCIENCE.** *See* SCIENCE - SOCIAL ASPECTS.

**A sociology of sport.**
Nixon, Howard L., 1944- Belmont : Wadsworth Pub. Co., c1996.
*TC GV706.5 .N58 1996*

**SOCIOLOGY - PERIODICALS.**
Frontiers of democracy. New York, Progressive Education Association, etc., 1934-

**SOCIOLOGY - PHILOSOPHY.** *See* ACTION THEORY.

**SOCIOLOGY - RESEARCH - METHODOLOGY.**
Streubert, Helen J. Qualitative research in nursing. 2nd ed. Philadelphia : Lippincott, c1999.

*TC RT81.5 .S78 1999*

**SOCIOLOGY, RURAL.** *See* **COMMUNITY.**

**SOCIOLOGY - UNITED STATES.**
Hall, John A., 1949- Is America breaking apart?
Princeton, NJ : Princeton University Press, c1999.
*TC HN59.2 .H34 1999*

**SOCIOLOGY - UNITED STATES - HISTORY.**
Abbott, Andrew. Department & discipline. Chicago,
IL : University of Chicago Press, c1999.
*TC HM22.U5 A23 1999*

**SOCIOLOGY - UNITED STATES -**
**PERIODICALS - HISTORY.**
Abbott, Andrew. Department & discipline. Chicago,
IL : University of Chicago Press, c1999.
*TC HM22.U5 A23 1999*

**SOCIOLOGY, URBAN.** *See* **CITIES AND TOWNS;**
**CITY AND TOWN LIFE; URBAN POLICY;**
**URBAN RENEWAL.**

**SOCIOMETRY.** *See also* **PSYCHODRAMA.**
Recent advances in the measurement of acceptance
and rejection in the peer system. San Francisco :
Jossey-Bass Publishers, c2000.
*TC BF723.I65 R4 2000*

**SOCIOPATHIC PERSONALITY.** *See*
**ANTISOCIAL PERSONALITY DISORDERS.**

**The sociopolitics of English language teaching** / edited
by Joan Kelly Hall and William G. Eggington.
Clevedon : Buffalo [N.Y.] : Multilingual Matters,
c2000. xiv, 251 p. : ill. ; 22 cm. (Bilingual education and
bilingualism ; 21) Includes bibliographical references (p. 226-
239) and index. ISBN 1-85359-437-7 (alk. paper) ISBN
1-85359-436-9 (pbk. : alk. paper) DDC 428/.0071
*1. English language - Study and teaching - Foreign speakers.*
*2. English language - Study and teaching - Social aspects -*
*United States. 3. English language - Study and teaching -*
*Political aspects - United States. 4. Education, Bilingual -*
*United States. I. Hall, Joan Kelly. II. Eggington, William. III.*
*Series: Bilingual education and bilingualism ; 21*
*TC PE1128.A2 S5994 2000*

**SOCRATES - CONTRIBUTIONS IN EDUCATION.**
Too, Yun Lee. The pedagogical contract. Ann Arbor:
University of Michigan Press, c2000.
*TC LB1033 .T66 2000*

**SOCRATIC METHOD.** *See* **QUESTIONING.**

**Socratic seminar** [videorecording] : Zola, Schaefer,
perspectives on (on Instruction & Assessment) 1996 /
produced by the Social Science Education
Consortium. [Boulder, Colo.] : Social Science
Education Consortium, c1997. 1 videocassette (60 min.) :
sd., col. ; 1/2 in. VHS. Catalogued from credits and cassette
label. Title from cassette label. New Vista High School teacher,
John Zola; Campus Middle School teacher, Judy Schaefer.
Video production by Vicki Murray-Kurzban. For educators,
especially high school and elemtary Social Studies teachers.
SUMMARY: Teachers, John Zola and Judy Schaefer, use the
Socratic Seminar to teach Social Studies. Zola opens up a
seminar on "The Pledge of Allegiance" and its meaning to his
class at New Vista High School. Schaefer uses the texts, 'We
the People" and "April Morning" for a seminar in American
History at Campus Middle School. Both teachers discuss the
advantages and permutations of using the Socratic Seminar
method. CONTENTS: A public issues discussion: Diana Hess,
Guest Presenter; Dr. Deanna Morrison's Law Class, Denver
East High School, February 1997 -- Generating criteria --
Setting up the discussion and reviewing the case -- Assessment.
*1. Social sciences - Study and teaching (Secondary) - United*
*States - Problems, exercises, etc. 2. Social sciences and ethics -*
*Study and teaching (Secondary) - Colorado - Denver -*
*Problems, exercises, etc. 3. DiscussionxStudy and teaching*
*(Secondary) - Colorado - Denver - Problems, exercises, etc. 4.*
*Assisted suicide - Law and legislation - United States - Study*
*and teaching (Secondary) - Colorado - Denver - Problems,*
*exercises, etc. 5. Constitutional law - United States - Study and*
*teaching (Secondary) - Colorado - Denver - Problems,*
*exercises, etc. I. Hess, Diana. II. Morrison, Deanna. III. Social*
*Science Education Consortium.*

**Socratic seminar** [videorecording] : Zola, Schaefer,
perspectives on (on Instruction & Assessment) 1996 /
produced by the Social Science Education
Consortium. [Boulder, Colo.] : Social Science
Education Consortium, c1997. 1 videocassette (60 min.) :
sd., col. ; 1/2 in. VHS. Catalogued from credits and cassette
label. Title from cassette label. New Vista High School teacher,
John Zola; Campus Middle School teacher, Judy Schaefer.
Video production by Vicki Murray-Kurzban. For educators,
especially high school and elementary Social Studies teachers.
SUMMARY: Teachers, John Zola and Judy Schaefer, use the
Socratic Seminar to teach Social Studies. Zola opens up a
seminar on "The Pledge of Allegiance" and its meaning to his
class at New Vista High School. Schaefer uses the texts, 'We

the People" and "April Morning" for a seminar in American
History at Campus Middle School. Both teachers discuss the
advantages and permutations of using the Socratic Seminar
method. CONTENTS: Teaching and assessing Socratic
Seminars, Zola: a case study; Context for a Socratic Seminar
using 'The Pledge of Allegiance", New Vista High School;
Norms and expectations -- Role of teacher -- Self-assessment/
Reflection -- Context for a Socratic Seminar using "We the
People" and "April Morning", Campus Middle School --
Setting expectations -- Discussion - Role of teacher --
Assessment -- Teacher's reflection in the Socratic Seminar --
Issues and perspectives in teaching and assessing discussion --
Student perspectives -- Two teacher's perspectives, Judy
Schaefer and John Zola -- Classroom discussion, Campus
Middle School -- Classroom discussion, New Vista High
School -- Teacher's perspectives on assessment.
*1. Social sciences - Study and teaching (Secondary) - United*
*States - Problems, exercises, etc. 2. Social sciences - Study and*
*teaching (Middle school) - United States - Problems, exercises,*
*etc. 3. Questioning - Study and teaching (Secondary) - United*
*States - Problems, exercises, etc. 4. Questioning - Study and*
*teaching (Middle school) - United States - Problems, exercises,*
*etc. 5. Seminars - Study and teaching (Secondary) - United*
*States - Problems, exercises, etc. 6. Seminars - Study and*
*teaching (Middle school) - United States - Problems, exercises,*
*etc. 7. United States - History - Study and teaching (Middle*
*school - United Staes - Problems, exercises, etc. 8. Civics -*
*Study and teaching (Secondary) - United States. I. Zola, John.*
*II. Schaefer, Judy. III. Social Science Education Consortium.*
*TC LB1027.44 .S6 1997*

**Socratic seminars in the block.**
Ball, Wanda H., 1953- Larchmont, N.Y. : Eye On
Education, 2000.
*TC LB1027.44 .B35 2000*

**Soentpiet, Chris K., ill.**
McGill, Alice. Molly Bannaky. Boston, Mass. :
Houghton Mifflin, 1999.
*TC PZ7.M478468 Mol 1999*

Rosenberg, Liz. The silence in the mountains. 1st
American ed. New York : Orchard Books, c1999.
*TC PZ7.R71894 Si 1999*

**Soete, George J.**
Management of library security. Washington, DC :
Systems and Procedures Exchange Center, Office of
Leadership and Management Services, Association of
Research Libraries, c1999.
*TC Z679.6 .M26 1999*

Managing the licensing of electronic products.
Washington, DC : Systems and Procedures Exchange
Center, Office of Leadership and Management
Service, Association of Research Libraries, c1999.

Managing the licensing of electronic products.
Washington, DC : Systems and Procedures Exchange
Center, Office of Leadership and Management
Service, Association of Research Libraries, c1999.

Managing the licensing of electronic products.
Washington, DC : Systems and Procedures Exchange
Center, Office of Leadership and Management
Service, Association of Research Libraries, c1999.
*TC HF5429.255 .M26 1999*

**Soft boundaries.**
Detels, Claire Janice, 1953- Westport, Conn. :
Bergin & Garvey, 1999.
*TC LB1591.5.U6 D48 1999*

**SOFT COMPUTING.** *See* **EXPERT SYSTEMS**
**(COMPUTER SCIENCE); NEURAL**
**NETWORKS (COMPUTER SCIENCE).**

**SOFTWARE, COMPUTER.** *See* **COMPUTER**
**SOFTWARE.**

**SOFTWARE FOR CHILDREN.** *See* **CHILDREN'S**
**SOFTWARE.**

**Soguel, Nils C.**
Valuing the cost of smoking. Boston : Kluwer
Academic Publishers, 1999.
*TC HV5735 .V35 1999*

**Sohi, Morteza E.** Look what I did with a shell! /
Morteza E. Sohi. New York : Walker & Co., 2000. 1v.
(unpaged) : col. ill. ; 23 cm. (NatureCraft series) SUMMARY:
Demonstrates how to make animal figurines and decorative
objects with shells. Includes a field guide to the shells used.
ISBN 0-8027-8722-3 ISBN 0-8027-8723-1 (rein) DDC 745.55
*1. Shellcraft - Juvenile literature. 2. Figurines - Juvenile*
*literature. 3. Shellcraft. 4. Handicraft. I. Title. II. Series.*
*TC TT862 .S64 2000*

**Sokolowski, David.**
Core texts in conversation . Lanham, MD : University
Press of America, 2000.
*TC LB2361.5 .C68 2000*

**SOLANUM.** *See* **POTATOES.**

**SOLANUM TUBEROSUM.** *See* **POTATOES.**

**SOLAR ENERGY - FICTION.**
Weeks, Sarah. Little factory. 1st ed. [New York] :
Laura Geringer book, c1998.
*TC PZ7.W4125 Li 1998*

**SOLAR POWER.** *See* **SOLAR ENERGY.**

**SOLAR RADIATION.** *See* **SOLAR ENERGY.**

**The solar sea** [videorecording] / a production of WQED
Pittsburgh in association with the National Academy
of Sciences ; series producer, Gregory Andorfer ;
producer, Georgann Kane ; written by Georgann
Kane. [New York, N.Y.?] : Unapix Entertainment,
Inc. [distributor], c1996. 1 videocassette (60 min.) : sd.,
col. ; 1/2 in. (Planet Earth ; 5) At head of title: Unapix
Consumer Products feature presentation [videorecording].
VHS. Catalogued from credits and container. Narrator, Richard
Kiley. Sound, Ken King, Beverly Johnson; photography by
Orlando Bagwell, Christopher Woods, Norris Brock; music by
Jack Tillar and William Loose. "Major funding by the
Annenberg/CPB Project"--Container. For adolescent through
adult. SUMMARY: Discusses the sun's effect on the earth and
its weather and how scientists analyze tree and rock remains to
record the sun's history.
*1. Sun. 2. Earth. 3. Sunspots. 4. Documentary television*
*programs. I. Andorfer, Gregory. II. Kane, Georgann. III. Kiley,*
*Richard. IV. WQED (Television station : Pittsburgh, Pa.) V.*
*National Academy of Sciences (U.S.) VI. Annenberg/CPB*
*Project. VII. Unapix Entertainment, Inc. VIII. Unapix*
*Consumer Products. IX. Title: Unapix Consumer Products*
*feature presentation [videorecording] X. Series.*
*TC QB631.2 .S6 1996*

**SOLAR SYSTEM.**
Tales from other worlds [videorecording]. [New York,
N.Y.?] : Unapix Entertainment, Inc. [distributor],
c1996.
*TC QB631.2 .T3 1996*

Tales from other worlds [videorecording]. [New York,
N.Y.?] : Unapix Entertainment, Inc. [distributor],
c1996.
*TC QB631.2 .T3 1996*

**SOLDIERS.** *See* **BOYS AS SOLDIERS; WOMEN**
**SOLDIERS.**

**SOLDIERS, AFRO-AMERICAN.** *See* **AFRO-**
**AMERICAN SOLDIERS.**

**SOLDIERS - DRILL.** *See* **DRILL AND MINOR**
**TACTICS.**

**Soldier's heart.**
Paulsen, Gary. New York : Delacorte Press, c1998.
*TC PZ7.P2843 So 1998*

**SOLDIERS' MONUMENTS.** *See* **WAR**
**MEMORIALS.**

**SOLDIERS - UNITED STATES.** *See* **AFRO-**
**AMERICAN SOLDIERS.**

**Soldz, Stephen.**
Reconciling empirical knowledge and clinical
experience. 1st ed. Washington, DC : American
Psychological Association, c1999.
*TC RC480 .R395 1999*

**SOLITUDE.** *See* **LONELINESS.**

**Solley, Bobbie A.**
Writers' workshop. Boston ; London : Allyn and
Bacon, c2000.
*TC LB1576 .W734 2000*

**Solomon-Godeau, Abigail.** Male trouble : : a crisis in
representation / Abigail Solomon-Godeau. London :
Thames and Hudson, c1997. 264 p. : ill. ; 24 cm. Includes
bibliographical references and index. ISBN 0-500-01765-4
*1. Neoclassicism (Art) - France - Themes, motives. 2. Male*
*nude in art. 3. Masculinity (Psychology) in art. 4. Feminist art*
*criticism. I. Title.*
*TC N6847.5.N35 S64 1997*

**Solomon, Hester.**
Jungian thought in the modern world. London ; New
York : Free Association, 2000.
*TC BF173.J85 J85 2000*

**Solomon, Judith.**
Attachment disorganization. New York ; London :
Guilford Press, c1999.
*TC RJ507.A77 A87 1999*

**Solomon R. Guggenheim Museum.**
Hopps, Walter. Robert Rauschenberg. New York :
Guggenheim Museum, c1997.
*TC N6537.R27 H66 1997*

**Solomon, Robert C.** A better way to think about business : how personal integrity leads to corporate success / Robert C. Solomon. New York : Oxford University Press, 1999. xxiv, 145 p. ; 22 cm. Includes bibliographical references (p. [125]-141) and index. ISBN 0-19-511238-5 (alk. paper) DDC 174/.4
*1. Business ethics. I. Title.*
**TC HF5387 .S612 1999**

**Solovay, Sondra, 1970-** Tipping the scales of justice : fighting weight-based discrimination / Sondra Solovay. Amherst, N.Y. : Prometheus Books, 2000. 261 p. ; 23 cm. Includes bibliographical references and index. ISBN 1-57392-764-3 (paper) DDC 306.4
*1. Body image. 2. Overweight children - Psychology. 3. Obesity - Psychological aspects. 4. Obesity - Social aspects. 5. Self-esteem in children. 6. Body image - Social aspects. 7. Physical-appearance-based bias. 8. Discrimination against overweight persons. I. Title.*
**TC BF697.5.B63 S65 2000**

**Soltis, Jonas F.**
Feinberg, Walter, 1937- School and society. 3rd ed. New York : Teachers College Press, c1998.
**TC LC191 .F4 1998**

**SOLUTION-FOCUSED BRIEF THERAPY.**
Davis, Thomas E., Ph. D. The solution-focused school counselor. Philadelphia ; Hove [England] : Accelerated Development/Taylor & Francis Group, c2000.
**TC LB1027.5 .D335 2000**

Littrell, John M., 1944- Brief counseling in action. 1st ed. New York : W. W. Norton, c1998.
**TC RC480.55 .L58 1998**

McNeilly, Robert B. Healing the whole person. New York ; Chichester [England] : John Wiley & Sons, c2000.
**TC RC489.S65 M38 2000**

**The solution-focused school counselor.**
Davis, Thomas E., Ph. D. Philadelphia ; Hove [England] : Accelerated Development/Taylor & Francis Group, c2000.
**TC LB1027.5 .D335 2000**

**Solution-focused therapy.**
O'Connell, Bill. London ; Thousand Oaks, Calif. : Sage Publications, 1998.
**TC RC489.S65 O26 1998**

**SOLUTION-FOCUSED THERAPY.**
Bertolino, Bob, 1965- Therapy with troubled teenagers. New York : Wiley, c1999.
**TC RJ506.P63 B475 1999**

O'Connell, Bill. Solution-focused therapy. London ; Thousand Oaks, Calif. : Sage Publications, 1998.
**TC RC489.S65 O26 1998**

Rowan, Tim, 1952- Solution-oriented therapy for chronic and severe mental illness. New York : Wiley, c1999.
**TC RC480.53 .R69 1999**

**Solution-oriented therapy for chronic and severe mental illness.**
Rowan, Tim, 1952- New York : Wiley, c1999.
**TC RC480.53 .R69 1999**

**Solving problems in the teaching of literacy**
Engaging young readers. New York : Guilford Press, c2000.
**TC LB1573 .E655 2000**

**Solway, Diane.** Nureyev, his life / Diane Solway. 1st ed. New York : William Morrow, c1998. x, 625 p., [32] p. of plates : ill. ; 25 cm. Includes bibliographical references (p. [553]-601) and index. ISBN 0-688-12873-4 (alk. paper) DDC 792.8/028/092
*1. Nureyev, Rudolf. - 1938- 2. Ballet dancers - Russia (Federation) - Biography. I. Title. II. Title: Nureyev*
**TC GV1785.N8 S66 1998**

**Somani, Satu M.**
Pharmacology in exercise and sports. Boca Raton : CRC Press, c1996.
**TC QP301 .P53 1996**

**SOMATAFORM DISORDER - DIAGNOSIS.**
Neurotic, stress-related, and somatoform disorders [videorecording]. Princeton, N.J. : Films for the Humanities & Sciences, 1998.
**TC RC530 .N4 1998**

**SOMATAFORM DISORDER - PATIENTS.**
Neurotic, stress-related, and somatoform disorders [videorecording]. Princeton, N.J. : Films for the Humanities & Sciences, 1998.
**TC RC530 .N4 1998**

**SOMATOPSYCHICS.** *See* **MIND AND BODY; PSYCHOPHYSIOLOGY.**

**SOMATOTYPES.**
Battinelli, Thomas. Physique, fitness, and performance. Boca Raton : CRC Press, c2000.
**TC QP301 .B364 2000**

**Some thoughts concerning education.**
Locke, John, 1632-1704. [Some thoughts concerning education] Indianapolis : Hackett Pub. Co., c1996.
**TC LB475.L6 L63 1996**

**Some thoughts concerning education ; and, Of the conduct of the understanding.**
Locke, John, 1632-1704. [Some thoughts concerning education] Some thoughts concerning education ; Indianapolis : Hackett Pub. Co., c1996.
**TC LB475.L6 L63 1996**

**Somerville, Iain.**
Leading beyond the walls. 1st ed. San Francisco : Jossey-Bass, c1999.
**TC HD57.7 .L4374 1999**

**SOMESTHESIA.** *See* **TOUCH.**

**Something new :** teacher's planning guide. New York : Macmillan/McGraw-Hill, c1997, 224, T18 p. : ill. (some col.) ; 31 cm. (Spotlight on literacy ; Gr.1 l.3) (The road to independent reading) Includes index.
*1. Reading (Primary) 2. Language arts (Primary) I. Series. II. Series: The road to independent reading*
**TC LB1576 .S66 1997 Gr.1 L3**

**Something rad & risqu'e.**
Ochsner, Mindy Blaise. 1999.
**TC 06 no. 11208**

**Sommer, Dion.**
Research on socialization of young children in the Nordic countries. Aarhus : Aarhus University Press, c1989.
**TC Z7164.S678 R47 1989**

**Sommers-Flanagan, John, 1957-.**
**Foundations of therapeutic interviewing.**
Sommers-Flanagan, Rita, 1953- Clinical interviewing. 2nd ed. New York : Wiley, c1999.
**TC RC480.7 .S66 1999**

Sommers-Flanagan, Rita, 1953- Clinical interviewing. 2nd ed. New York : Wiley, c1999.
**TC RC480.7 .S66 1999**

**Sommers-Flanagan, Rita, 1953-** Clinical interviewing / Rita Sommers-Flanagan and John Sommers-Flanagan. 2nd ed. New York : Wiley, c1999. xii, 436 p. : ill. ; 26 cm. Rev. ed. of: Foundations of therapeutic interviewing / John Sommers-Flanagan. c1993. "Published simultaneously in Canada"--T.p. verso. Includes bibliographical references and indexes. ISBN 0-471-29567-1 (acid-free paper) DDC 616.89/075
*1. Interviewing in mental health. 2. Interviewing in psychiatry. 3. Interview, Psychological - methods. 4. Psychotherapy - methods. I. Sommers-Flanagan, John, 1957- II. Sommers-Flanagan, John, 1957- Foundations of therapeutic interviewing. III. Title.*
**TC RC480.7 .S66 1999**

**Song of the earth.**
Hefling, Stephen E. Mahler, Das Lied von der Erde = Cambridge, UK ; New York : Cambridge University Press, c2000.
**TC MT121.M34 H44 2000**

**SONGBIRDS.** *See* **BIRDSONGS.**

**SONGS.** *See also* **CHILDREN'S SONGS; FOLK SONGS; LULLABIES.**
All the pretty little horses. New York : Clarion Books, c1999.
**TC PZ8.3 .A4165 1999**

**SONGS - FICTION.**
Jewell, Nancy. Sailor Song. New York : Clarion Books, c1999.
**TC PZ7.J55325 Sai 1999**

**SONGS - JUVENILE.** *See* **CHILDREN'S SONGS.**

**SONGS WITH VARIOUS ACC.** *See* **SONGS.**

**SONGWRITERS.** *See* **COMPOSERS.**

**Sonnenberg, Frank A.**
Chapman, Gretchen B., 1965- Decision making in health care. New York : Cambridge University Press, 2000.
**TC R723.5 .C48 2000**

**SONS.** *See* **FATHERS AND SONS; MOTHERS AND SONS.**

**SONS AND FATHERS.** *See* **FATHERS AND SONS.**

**SONS AND MOTHERS.** *See* **MOTHERS AND SONS.**

**Sophia Smith.**
Quesnell, Quentin. The strange disappearance of Sophia Smith. Northampton [Mass.] : Smith College, c1999.
**TC LD7152.65.S45 Q84 1999**

**Sorace, Antonella.**
Language acquisition. 1st ed. Amsterdam ; New York : North-Holland, 1999.
**TC P118 .L2539 1999**

**Soraci, Sal.**
Perspectives on fundamental processes in intellectual functioning. Stamford, Conn. : Ablex Pub. Corp., c1998-
**TC BF444 .P42 1998**

**SORCERERS.** *See* **WIZARDS.**

**SORCERY.** *See* **MAGIC; WITCHCRAFT.**

**Sorrentino, Richard M.** The uncertain mind : individual differences in facing the unknown / Richard M. Sorrentino, Christopher R.J. Roney. Philadelphia : Psychology Press, c2000. x, 194 p. : ill. ; 25 cm. (Essays in social psychology, 1367-5826) Includes bibliographical references (p. [173]-186) and index. ISBN 0-86377-691-4 (case : alk. paper) DDC 155.2/32
*1. Individual differences. 2. Certainty. 3. Uncertainty. I. Roney, Christopher R. J. II. Title. III. Series.*
**TC BF697 .S674 2000**

**SORROW.** *See* **GRIEF.**

**Sosa, Ernest.**
Cognition, agency, and rationality. Boston : Kluwer Academic, 1999.
**TC BC177 .C45 1999**

**Sosa, Maria.**
Exploring science in the library. Chicago : American Library Association, 2000.
**TC Z675.S3 E97 2000**

**Sosin, Adrienne.** Achieving styles preferences of students in an urban graduate teacher education program / by Adrienne Sosin. 1996. viii, 147 : ill. ; 29 cm. Typescript; issued also on microfilm. Thesis (Ed.D.)-- Teachers College, Columbia University, 1996. Includes bibliographical references (117-147).
*1. Education - Study and teaching (Graduate) - New York (State) 2. Achievement motivation - Psychological aspects. 3. Minorities - Education (Graduate) - New York (State) 4. Achievement motivation - Psychological aspects. 5. Occupational mobility - Psychological aspects. 6. Study skills. 7. Sex differences (Psychology) 8. Learning strategies. 9. Environmental impact analysis. I. Title.*
**TC 06 no. 10701**

**SOSSE (AFRICAN PEOPLE).** *See* **MANDINGO (AFRICAN PEOPLE).**

**Soto, Julie.**
Infants & toddlers. 2nd ed. Seattle, Wash. : Resourse Pathways, 1999.
**TC HQ755.8 .I54 1999**

**SOUL.** *See also* **PERSONALITY; PSYCHOLOGY.**
Miller, John P., 1943- Education and the soul. Albany : State University of New York Press, c2000.
**TC LC268 .M52 2000**

**Soul murder revisited.**
Shengold, Leonard. New Haven, CT : Yale University Press, 1999.
**TC RC569.5.C55 S53 1999**

**Soul of a citizen.**
Loeb, Paul Rogat, 1952- 1st St. Martin's Griffin ed. New York : St. Martin's Griffin, 1999.
**TC HN65 .L58 1999**

**The soul of education.**
Kessler, Rachael, 1946- Alexandria, Va. : Association for Supervision and Curriculum Development, c2000.
**TC LB1072 .K48 2000**

**Souls looking back :** life stories of growing up Black / Andrew Garrod ... [et al.], eds ; foreword by James P. Comer. New York : Routledge, 1999. xxvi, 300 p. ; 23 cm. Includes bibliographical references (p. [281]-289) and index. ISBN 0-415-92061-2 (hc.) ISBN 0-415-92062-0 (pbk.) DDC 305.235
*1. Afro-American youth - Race identity - Case studies. 2. Afro-American youth - Biography. 3. Afro-American youth - Social conditions - Case studies. 4. Racially mixed children - Race identity - Case studies. 5. Racially mixed children - Biography. 6. Racially mixed children - Social conditions - Case studies. 7. United States - Race relations - Case studies. 8. Canada - Race relations - Case studies. 9. West Indies - Race relations - Case studies. I. Garrod, Andrew, 1937-*

*TC E185.625 .S675 1999*

**SOUND.** *See* **PHONETICS.**

**SOUND PERCEPTION.** *See* **AUDITORY PERCEPTION.**

**The sound that jazz makes.**
Weatherford, Carole Boston, 1956- New York : Walker & Co., c2000.
*TC ML3506 .W42 2000*

**Soundings.**
The christian scholar. [Somerville, N.J., etc.]

**Soup for supper.**
Root, Phyllis. 1st ed. New York : Harper & Row, c1986.
*TC PZ7.R6784 So 1986*

**SOUPS - FICTION.**
Kadono, Eiko. Grandpa's soup. Grand Rapids, MI : Eerdmans Books for Young Readers, 1999.
*TC PZ7.K1167 Gr 1999*

Root, Phyllis. Soup for supper. 1st ed. New York : Harper & Row, c1986.
*TC PZ7.R6784 So 1986*

**Source book.**
The CARES directory in electronic form [computer file] Maywood, NJ : ACIT,
*TC HV99.N59 S58*

**Sourcebook for college writing teachers.**
The Allyn & Bacon sourcebook for college writing teachers. Boston ; London : Allyn and Bacon, 2000.
*TC PE1404 .A45 2000*

**Sourcebook for medical speech pathology.**
Golper, Lee Ann C., 1948- 2nd ed. San Diego, Calif. : Singular Pub. Group, c1998.
*TC RC423 .G64 1998*

**A sourcebook for responding to student writing /**
edited by Richard Straub. Cresskill, N.J. : Hampton Press, c1999. vii, 230 p. ; 23 cm. Includes bibliographical references (p. [213]-219). ISBN 1-57273-236-9 (pbk.) DDC 808/.042/0711
*1. English language - Rhetoric - Study and teaching. 2. Report writing - Study and teaching. 3. Grading and marking (Students) 4. College prose - Evaluation. I. Straub, Richard.*
*TC PE1404 .S683 1999*

**Sourcebook of phonological awareness activities.**
Goldsworthy, Candace L. San Diego : Singular Pub. Group, c1998.
*TC LB1050.5 .G66 1998*

**SOUTH AFRICA - BIOGRAPHY.**
McCord, Margaret (McCord Nixon) The calling of Katie Makanya. New York : J. Wiley, 1995.
*TC CT1929.M34 M38 1995*

**South Africa. Dept. of Bantu Education.**
Educamus. Pretoria : Govt. Printer, [1978-

**SOUTH AFRICA. DEPT. OF BANTU EDUCATION - PERIODICALS.**
Educamus. Pretoria : Govt. Printer, [1978-

**South Africa. Dept. of Education and Training.**
Educamus. Pretoria : Govt. Printer, [1978-

**SOUTH AFRICA. DEPT. OF EDUCATION AND TRAINING - PERIODICALS.**
Educamus. Pretoria : Govt. Printer, [1978-

**SOUTH AFRICA - SOCIAL CONDITIONS.**
Hlatshwayo, Simphiwe A. (Simphiwe Abner) Education and independence. Westport, Conn : Greenwood Press, 2000.
*TC LA1536 .H53 2000*

**SOUTH AFRICANS, AFRIKAANS-SPEAKING.**
*See* **AFRIKANERS.**

**South Bank show (Television program).**
Andy Warhol [videorecording]. [Chicago, IL] : Home Vision [distributor],cc1987.
*TC N6537.W28 A45 1987*

Andy Warhol [videorecording]. [Chicago, IL] : Home Vision [distributor],cc1987.
*TC N6537.W28 A45 1987*

Jackson Pollock [videorecording]. [Chicago, Ill.] : Home Vision : [S.l.] : Distributed Worldwide by RM Associates, c1987.
*TC ND237.P73 J3 1987*

Roy Lichtenstein [videorecording]. [Chicago, IL] : Home Vision : [S.l.] : distributed worldwide by RM Asssociates, c1991.
*TC ND237.L627 R6 1991*

**South Carolina Educational Technology Plan.**
[Columbia, S.C.] : South Carolina State Dept. of Education, [1995] 73, [7], S1-S36 p. : ill. ; 28 cm. "November 1995." Includes bibliographical references (p. 61-64).
*1. Educational technology - South Carolina - Planning. I. South Carolina. State Dept. of Education.*
*TC LB1028.3 .S628 1995*

**South Carolina Educational Television Network.**
Education's big gamble [videorecording]. New York, NY : Merrow Report, c1997.
*TC LB2806.36 .E3 1997*

**SOUTH CAROLINA - FICTION.**
Hansen, Joyce. The heart calls home. New York : Walker & Company, 1999.
*TC PZ7.H19825 He 1999*

**South Carolina. State Dept. of Education.**
South Carolina Educational Technology Plan. [Columbia, S.C.] : South Carolina State Dept. of Education. [1995]
*TC LB1028.3 .S628 1995*

**SOUTH EAST ASIA.** *See* **ASIA, SOUTHEASTERN.**

**SOUTH PACIFIC.** *See* **OCEANIA.**

**SOUTH PACIFIC REGION.** *See* **OCEANIA.**

**SOUTH SEA ISLANDS.** *See* **OCEANIA.**

**SOUTH SEAS.** *See* **OCEANIA.**

**South, Stanley A.** Historical archaeology in Wachovia : excavating eighteenth-century Bethabara and Moravian pottery / Stanley South. New York : Kluwer Academic/Plenum Publishers, c1999. xv, 442 p. : ill., maps ; 26 cm. Includes bibliographical references (p. 401-403) and index. ISBN 0-306-45658-3 DDC 975.6/67
*1. Moravians - North Carolina - Winston-Salem - Antiquities. 2. Moravians - North Carolina - Winston-Salem - History - 18th century. 3. Potters - North Carolina - Winston-Salem - History - 18th century. 4. Pottery, Colonial - North Carolina - Winston-Salem. 5. Archaeology and history - North Carolina - Winston-Salem. 6. Excavations (Archaeology) - North Carolina - Winston-Salem. 7. Winston-Salem (N.C.) - Antiquities. 8. Winston-Salem (N.C.) - Church history. I. Title.*
*TC F264.W8 S66 1999*

**SOUTH, THE.** *See* **SOUTHERN STATES.**

**SOUTH WEST ASIA.** *See* **MIDDLE EAST.**

**SOUTHEAST ASIA.** *See* **ASIA, SOUTHEASTERN.**

**SOUTHEASTERN ASIA.** *See* **ASIA, SOUTHEASTERN.**

**SOUTHEASTERN STATES.** *See* **SOUTHERN STATES.**

**Southern Africa Regional Institute for Policy Studies.**
Mahlase, Shirley Motleke. The careers of women teachers under apartheid. Harare : SAPES Books, c1997.
*TC LB2832.4.S6 M35 1997*

**Southern Africa specialised studies series**
Mahlase, Shirley Motleke. The careers of women teachers under apartheid. Harare : SAPES Books, c1997.
*TC LB2832.4.S6 M35 1997*

**Southern Association of Colleges and Secondary Schools. Commission on Accredited Schools of the Southern States.**
The High school quarterly. Athens, Ga. : University of Georgia, 1912-[1936]

**SOUTHERN OSCILLATION.**
Broad, Kenneth. Climate, culture, and values. 1999.
*TC 085 B7775*

**Southern school work.**
Journal of the Louisiana Teachers' Association. [Baton Rouge] : The Association, [1923-1932], (Baton Rouge, La. : Gladney's Print Shop)

**SOUTHERN STATES - CHURCH HISTORY - 19TH CENTURY.**
Cornelius, Janet Duitsman. Slave missions and the Black church in the antebellum South. Columbia : University of South Carolina Press, c1999.
*TC E449 .C82 1999*

**SOUTHERN STATES - HISTORY - 1775-1865.**
Cornelius, Janet Duitsman. Slave missions and the Black church in the antebellum South. Columbia : University of South Carolina Press, c1999.
*TC E449 .C82 1999*

**SOUTHERN STATES - HISTORY - 1865-1877.** *See* **RECONSTRUCTION.**

**SOUTHERN STATES - HISTORY - CIVIL WAR, 1861-1865.** *See* **UNITED STATES - HISTORY - CIVIL WAR, 1861-1865.**

**SOUTHERN STATES - SOCIAL CONDITIONS.**
Abbott, Shirley Womenfolks, growing up down South. Boston : Houghton Mifflin, c1998.
*TC HQ1438.S63 A33 1998*

**SOUTHWEST ASIA.** *See* **MIDDLE EAST.**

**SOUTHWEST PACIFIC REGION.** *See* **OCEANIA.**

**Southworth, Geoff.**
Supporting improving primary schools. London ; New York : Falmer Press, 2000.
*TC LB2822.84.E64 S86 1999*

**Southworth, Robert A.** Evidence of student learning and implications for alternative policies that support instructional use of assessment : a survey of teacher opinion and reported practice concerning the use of student assessment / by Robert A. Southworth. 1999. xiii, 355 leaves ; 29 cm. Typescript; issued also on microfilm. Thesis (Ed.D.)--Teachers College, Columbia University, 1999. Includes bibliographical references (leaves 326-347).
*1. Educational tests and measurements - New York (State) - Validity. 2. Grading and marking (Students) - New York (State) - Evaluation. 3. Teacher effectiveness - New York (State) 4. Teachers - New York (State) - Attitudes. 5. Observation (Educational methods) - New York (State) 6. Educational accountability - New York (State) 7. Competency based educational tests - New York (State) I. Title. II. Title: Survey of teacher opinion and reported practice concerning the use of student assessment*
*TC 06 no. 11218*

**Soutine, Chaim, 1893-1943.**
Kleeblatt, Norman L. An expressionist in Paris. Munich ; New York : Jewish Museum, c1998.
*TC ND553.S7 A4 1998*

**SOUTINE, CHAIM, 1893-1943 - EXHIBITIONS.**
Kleeblatt, Norman L. An expressionist in Paris. Munich ; New York : Jewish Museum, c1998.
*TC ND553.S7 A4 1998*

**Sovak, Jan, 1953- ill.**
Lessem, Don. Dinosaurs to dodos. 1st ed. New York : Scholastic Reference, 1999.
*TC QE842 .L47 1999*

**SOVEREIGNTY.** *See* **DECOLONIZATION.**

**SOVIET CENTRAL ASIA.** *See* **ASIA, CENTRAL.**

**SOVIET UNION - ECONOMIC POLICY - 1917-1928.**
Clark, Charles E., 1960- Uprooting otherness. Selinsgrove [Pa.] : Susquehanna University Press ; London : Associated University Presses, c2000.
*TC LC156.S65 C56 2000*

**SOVIET UNION - FOREIGN RELATIONS - UNITED STATES - FICTION.**
Burdick, Eugene. Fail-safe. 1st Ecco ed. Hopewell, N.J. : Ecco Press ; New York, NY : Distributed by W.W. Norton, 1999.
*TC PS3552.U7116 F35 1999*

**Soviet Union. Gosudarstvennyĭ komitet po narodnomu obrazovaniiu.**
[Geografiia v shkole (Moscow, Russia)] Geografiia v shkole. Moskva : Gos. ucheb.-pedagog. izd-vo, 1934-

**Soviet Union. Ministerstvo prosveshcheniia.**
[Geografiia v shkole (Moscow, Russia)] Geografiia v shkole. Moskva : Gos. ucheb.-pedagog. izd-vo, 1934-

**SOVIET UNION - POLITICS AND GOVERNMENT - 1917-1936 - POSTERS.**
Bonnell, Victoria E. Iconography of power. Berkeley : University of California Press, c1997.
*TC DK266.3 .B58 1997*

**SOVIET UNION - POLITICS AND GOVERNMENT - 1936-1953 - POSTERS.**
Bonnell, Victoria E. Iconography of power. Berkeley : University of California Press, c1997.
*TC DK266.3 .B58 1997*

**SOVIET UNION - POLITICS AND GOVERNMENT - 1945-1991.**
Schultz, Mindella. Comparative political systems; New York, Holt, Rinehart and Winston [1967]
*TC JF51 .S34 1967*

**SOVIET UNION - RELIGION.**
Husband, William. "Godless communists". DeKalb : Northern Illinois University Press, 2000.
*TC BL2765.S65 H87 2000*

**Sowell, Evelyn J.** Curriculum : an integrative introduction / Evelyn J. Sowell ; [editor, Debra A. Stollenwerk ; illustrations, Tom Kennedy, Janet Bidwell]. 2nd ed. Upper Saddle River, N.J. : Merrill,

c2000. xii, 388 p. : ill. ; 25 cm. Includes bibliographical references (p. 366-377) and indexes. ISBN 0-13-080700-1 DDC 375/.001
*1. Curriculum planning. 2. Educational change. 3. Teaching - Aids and devices. I. Stollenwerk, Debra A. II. Title.*
**TC LB2806.15 .S69 2000**

**Sozialpsychologische Strukturanalysen des Kollektivs.**
Vorwerg, Manfred. Berlin, Deutscher Verlag der Wissenschaften, 1966.
**TC HM291 .V6**

**SPACE AND TIME.** *See* **CYBERSPACE; NAKED SINGULARITIES (COSMOLOGY); SPATIAL BEHAVIOR.**

**SPACE (ART).**
Dunning, William V., 1933- Changing images of pictorial space. 1st ed. Syracuse : Syracuse University Press, 1991.
**TC ND1475 .D86 1991**

**SPACE BEHAVIOR.** *See* **SPATIAL BEHAVIOR.**

**SPACE FLIGHT.** *See* **INTERPLANETARY VOYAGES.**

**SPACE PERCEPTION IN CHILDREN.**
Newcombe, Nora S. Making space. Cambridge, Mass. : MIT Press, 2000.
**TC BF723.S63 N49 2000**

**SPACE SCIENCES.** *See* **ASTRONOMY.**

**SPACE TRAVEL.** *See* **INTERPLANETARY VOYAGES.**

**Spackman, Jeff, ill.**
Hubbell, Patricia. Boo!. 1st ed. New York : Marshall Cavendish, 1998.
**TC PS3558.U22 B66 1998**

**Spafford, Shirley.** No ordinary academics : economics and political science at the University of Saskatchewan, 1910-1960 / Shirley Spafford. Toronto : University of Toronto Press, 1999. ix, 272 p. 16 p. of plates ; 24 cm. Includes bibliographical references and index. ISBN 0-8020-4437-9 DDC 330/.071/1712425
*1. University of Saskatchewan - Dept. of Political Economy - History. 2. Economics - Study and teaching (Higher) - Saskatchewan - Saskatoon - History. 3. Political science - Study and teaching (Higher) - Saskatchewan - Saskatoon - History. 4. College teachers - Saskatchewan - Saskatoon. I. Title.*
**TC HB74.9.C3 S62 1999**

**Spahr, James R.**
Education's big gamble [videorecording]. New York, NY : Merrow Report, c1997.
**TC LB2806.36 .E3 1997**

**The Spahr lectures, Dickinson College.**
Dickinson College. Carlisle, Pa., : Dickinson College 1970.
**TC LD1663 .A5 1970**

**SPAIN - COLONIES - AMERICA - ADMINISTRATION.**
Casanovas, Joan. Bread, or bullets!. Pittsburgh : University of Pittsburgh Press, c1998.
**TC HD8206 .C33 1998**

**Spandorfer, Merle, 1934-** Making art safely : alternative methods and materials in drawing, painting, printmaking, graphic design, and photography / Merle Spandorfer, Deborah Curtiss, Jack Snyder. New York : Van Nostrand Reinhold, c1993. xvi, 255 p. : ill. (some col.) ; 29 cm. Includes bibliographical references (p. 245-246) and index. ISBN 0-442-23489-9 DDC 363.11/976
*1. Artists - Health and hygiene. 2. Artists' materials - Safety measures. I. Curtiss, Deborah, 1937- II. Snyder, Jack W. III. Title.*
**TC RC963.6.A78 S62 1993**

**Spangle, Michael.**
Isenhart, Myra Warren. Collaborative approaches to resolving conflict. Thousand Oaks, Calif. : Sage Publications, c2000.
**TC HM1126 .I74 2000**

**SPANIARDS - FICTION.**
Zamorano, Ana. Let's eat!. New York : Scholastic Press, 1997.
**TC PZ7.Z25455 Le 1997**

**SPANISH AMERICAN CHILDREN'S LITERATURE.** *See* **CHILDREN'S LITERATURE, SPANISH AMERICAN.**

**SPANISH AMERICAN LITERATURE.** *See* **CHILDREN'S LITERATURE, SPANISH AMERICAN; YOUNG ADULT LITERATURE, SPANISH AMERICAN.**

**SPANISH AMERICAN YOUNG ADULT LITERATURE.** *See* **YOUNG ADULT LITERATURE, SPANISH AMERICAN.**

**SPANISH AMERICANS IN THE UNITED STATES.** *See* **HISPANIC AMERICANS.**

**SPANISH AMERICANS (LATIN AMERICA).** *See* **HISPANIC AMERICANS.**

**Spanish and academic achievement among Midwest Mexican youth.**
MacGregor-Mendoza, Patricia, 1963- New York ; London : Garland Pub., 1999.
**TC LC2686.4 .M33 1999**

**SPANISH CHILDREN'S LITERATURE.** *See* **CHILDREN'S LITERATURE, SPANISH.**

**Spanish for mastery.**
Valette, Jean Paul. Lexington, Mass. : D.C. Heath, c1980.
**TC PC4112 .V29 1980**

**Spanish grammar in review.**
Chastain, Kenneth. Lincolnwood, Ill., USA : National Textbook Co., c1994.
**TC PC4112 .C4 1994**

**SPANISH LANGUAGE - DICTIONARIES.** *See* **PICTURE DICTIONARIES, SPANISH.**

**SPANISH LANGUAGE - DICTIONARIES, JUVENILE - ENGLISH.**
Spanish picture dictionary. Princeton [N.J.] : Berlitz Kids, c1997.
**TC PC4629 .S63 1997**

**SPANISH LANGUAGE - GLOSSARIES, VOCABULARIES, ETC. - JUVENILE LITERATURE.**
1,000 palabras en inglés. Princeton : Berlitz Kids, c1998.
**TC PC4680 .A12 1998**

1,000 Spanish words. Princeton, N.J. : Berlitz Kids, c1998.
**TC PC4680 .A13 1998**

**SPANISH LANGUAGE - GRAMMAR.**
Chastain, Kenneth. Spanish grammar in review. Lincolnwood, Ill., USA : National Textbook Co., c1994.
**TC PC4112 .C4 1994**

Turk, Laurel Herbert, 1903- El español al día. 5th ed. Lexington, Mass. : D.C. Heath, c1979.
**TC PC4111 .T87 1979**

Turk, Laurel Herbert, 1903- El español al día. Revised ed. Lexington, Mass. : D.C. Heath, c1974.
**TC PC4111 .T87 1974**

Valette, Jean Paul. Spanish for mastery. Lexington, Mass. : D.C. Heath, c1980.
**TC PC4112 .V29 1980**

**SPANISH LANGUAGE - GRAMMAR - 1950-.**
Jarvis, Ana C. Getting along in Spanish. Lexington, Mass. : D.C. Heath, c1984.
**TC PC4121 .J37 1984**

**SPANISH LANGUAGE MATERIALS - BILINGUAL.**
1,000 Spanish words. Princeton, N.J. : Berlitz Kids, c1998.
**TC PC4680 .A13 1998**

Cruz Martinez, Alejandro, d. 1987. [Mujer que brillaba aún más que el sol. English & Spanish] The woman who outshone the sun. San Francisco, Calif. : Children's Book Press, c1991.
**TC F1221.Z3 C78 1991**

Inglés. Princeton [NJ] : Berlitz Pub. Co., 1997.
**TC PE1628.5 .I54 1997**

Spanish picture dictionary. Princeton [N.J.] : Berlitz Kids, c1997.
**TC PC4629 .S63 1997**

**SPANISH LANGUAGE - STUDY AND TEACHING.**
The salsa-riffic world of Spanish [videorecording]. [Arlington, Va.] : Cerebellum Corp., c1998.
**TC PC4112.7 .S25 1998**

**SPANISH LANGUAGE - STUDY AND TEACHING (ELEMENTARY) - UNITED STATES.**
The teaching of reading in Spanish to the bilingual student = 2nd ed. Mahwah, N.J. : L. Erlbaum Associates, 1998.
**TC LB1573 .T365 1998**

**SPANISH LANGUAGE - STUDY AND TEACHING (HIGHER) - ENGLISH SPEAKERS.**

Eddy, Jennifer B.K. Multiple intelligences, styles, and proficiency. 1999.
**TC 085 E10**

**SPANISH LANGUAGE - STUDY AND TEACHING - MIDDLE WEST - CASE STUDIES.**
MacGregor-Mendoza, Patricia, 1963- Spanish and academic achievement among Midwest Mexican youth. New York ; London : Garland Pub., 1999.
**TC LC2686.4 .M33 1999**

**SPANISH LANGUAGE - TEXTBOOKS FOR FOREIGN SPEAKERS - ENGLISH.**
Jarvis, Ana C. Getting along in Spanish. Lexington, Mass. : D.C. Heath, c1984.
**TC PC4121 .J37 1984**

Turk, Laurel Herbert, 1903- El español al día. 5th ed. Lexington, Mass. : D.C. Heath, c1979.
**TC PC4111 .T87 1979**

Turk, Laurel Herbert, 1903- El español al día. Revised ed. Lexington, Mass. : D.C. Heath, c1974.
**TC PC4111 .T87 1974**

Turk, Laurel Herbert, 1903- El español al día. 4th ed. Lexington, Mass., Heath [1973]
**TC PC4112 .T766 1973 Teacher's Ed.**

Valette, Jean Paul. Spanish for mastery. Lexington, Mass. : D.C. Heath, c1980.
**TC PC4112 .V29 1980**

**SPANISH LITERATURE.** *See* **CHILDREN'S LITERATURE, SPANISH; YOUNG ADULT LITERATURE, SPANISH.**

**SPANISH PICTURE DICTIONARIES.** *See* **PICTURE DICTIONARIES, SPANISH.**

**Spanish picture dictionary.** Princeton [N.J.] : Berlitz Kids, c1997. 128 p. : col. ill. ; 32 cm. Includes index. SUMMARY: Provides over 1,000 entries for terms in English and Spanish with sentences in both languages to show proper usage. ISBN 2-8315-6257-0 DDC 863/.21
*1. Picture dictionaries, Spanish - Juvenile literature. 2. Picture dictionaries, English - Juvenile literature. 3. Spanish language - Dictionaries, Juvenile - English. 4. English language - Dictionaries, Juvenile - Spanish. 5. Picture dictionaries, Spanish. 6. Picture dictionaries, English. 7. Spanish language materials - Bilingual.*
**TC PC4629 .S63 1997**

**SPANISH SPEAKING PEOPLE (UNITED STATES).** *See* **HISPANIC AMERICANS.**

**SPANISH SURNAMED PEOPLE (UNITED STATES).** *See* **HISPANIC AMERICANS.**

**SPANISH YOUNG ADULT LITERATURE.** *See* **YOUNG ADULT LITERATURE, SPANISH.**

**Sparing the rod.**
Parker-Jenkins, Marie. Stoke-on-Trent : Trentham, 1999.
**TC LB3012 .P37 1999**

**Sparks, Elizabeth E.**
Lerner, Richard M. Family diversity and family policy. Boston ; London : Kluwer Academic, c1999.
**TC HQ535 .L39 1999**

**Sparks-Langer, Georgea M.**
Teaching as decision making. Upper Saddle River, N.J. : Prentice Hall, c2000.
**TC LB1607.5 .T43 2000**

**Sparks of genius.**
Root-Bernstein, Robert Scott. Boston, Mass. : Houghton Mifflin Co., 1999.
**TC BF408 R66 1999**

**Sparrow, William Anthony, 1955-.**
Energetics of human activity. Champaign, IL : Human Kinetics, c2000.
**TC QP301 .E568 2000**

**Sparzo, Frank J.** The ABC's of behavior change / by Frank J. Sparzo. Bloomington, Ind., U.S.A. : Phi Delta Kappa Educational Foundation, c1999. 91 p. : ill. ; 23 cm. Includes bibliographical references. ISBN 0-87367-816-8 (pbk.)
*1. Behavior modification. 2. Behavior therapy for children. 3. Behavior therapy for teenagers. 4. Problem children - Behavior modification. 5. Problem youth - Behavior modification. 6. School discipline. I. Phi Delta Kappa. Educational Foundation. II. Title.*
**TC LB1060.2 .S62 1999**

**SPASMS.** *See* **EPILEPSY.**

**Spastic review 1940-49.**
Cerebral palsy review. Wichita, Kan., Institute of Logopedics.

**Spastic review v.1-10, 1940-1949.**
Cerebral palsy journal. Wichita, Kan., Institute of
Logopedics, inc.

**SPATIAL ANALYSIS (STATISTICS).** *See*
**CLUSTER ANALYSIS.**

**SPATIAL BEHAVIOR.** *See* **AGORAPHOBIA;**
**HUMAN TERRITORIALITY; ORIENTATION**
**(PSYCHOLOGY).**

**SPATIAL BEHAVIOR - CALIFORNIA - CASE**
**STUDIES.**
Childress, Herb, 1958- Landscapes of betrayal,
landscapes of joy. Albany [N.Y.] : State University of
New York Press, c2000.
*TC HQ796 .C458237 2000*

**SPATIALLY-ORIENTED BEHAVIOR.** *See*
**SPATIAL BEHAVIOR.**

**SPEAKING.** *See* **RHETORIC; VOICE.**

**Speaking into the air.**
Peters, John Durham. Chicago : University of Chicago
Press, 1999.
*TC P90 .P388 1999*

**Speaking of emotions :** conceptualisation and
expression / edited by Angeliki Athanasiadou,
Elżbieta Tabakowska. Berlin ; New York : Mouton de
Gruyter, 1998. xxii, 444 p. : ill. ; 23 cm. (Cognitive
linguistics research ; 10) Includes bibliographical references
and index. ISBN 3-11-015767-5 (hardcover : alk. paper) DDC
306.44
*1. Language and emotion. 2. Expression. I. Athanasiadou,*
*Angeliki. II. Tabakowska, Elżbieta. III. Series.*
*TC BF591 .S64 1998*

**Speaking worlds.**
Dunt, Lesley, 1944- Parkville, Vic. : History
Department, The University of Melbourne, c1993.
*TC LA2101 .D96 1993*

**Spears, Russell.**
Social identity. Malden, MA : Blackwell Publishers,
1999.
*TC HM131 .S58433 1999*

**Spec flyer**
(240) Marketing and public relations activities in
ARL Libraries. Washington, DC : Association of
Research Libraries, Office of Leadership and
Management Services, c1999.
*TC Z176.3 .M2875 1999*

**SPEC flyer**
(242) Library storage facilities, management, and
services. Washington, DC : Association of
Research Libraries, Office of Leadership and
Management Services, 1999.
*TC Z675.S75 L697 1999*

(247) Management of library security. Washington,
DC : Systems and Procedures Exchange Center,
Office of Leadership and Management Services,
Association of Research Libraries, c1999.
*TC Z679.6 .M26 1999*

(248) Managing the licensing of electronic
products. Washington, DC : Systems and
Procedures Exchange Center, Office of Leadership
and Management Service, Association of Research
Libraries, c1999.
*TC HF5429.255 .M26 1999*

**Spec flyer**
(no. 248.) Managing the licensing of electronic
products. Washington, DC : Systems and
Procedures Exchange Center, Office of Leadership
and Management Service, Association of Research
Libraries, c1999.

(no. 248.) Managing the licensing of electronic
products. Washington, DC : Systems and
Procedures Exchange Center, Office of Leadership
and Management Service, Association of Research
Libraries, c1999.

**Spec kit**
(240) Marketing and public relations activities in
ARL Libraries. Washington, DC : Association of
Research Libraries, Office of Leadership and
Management Services, c1999.
*TC Z176.3 .M2875 1999*

**SPEC kit**
(242) Library storage facilities, management, and
services. Washington, DC : Association of
Research Libraries, Office of Leadership and
Management Services, 1999.
*TC Z675.S75 L697 1999*

(243.) DeCandido, GraceAnne A. Transforming
libraries. Washington, D.C. : Association of

Research Libraries, Office of Leadership and
Management Services, c1999.
*TC Z711.92.H3 D43 1999*

(247) Management of library security. Washington,
DC : Systems and Procedures Exchange Center,
Office of Leadership and Management Services,
Association of Research Libraries, c1999.
*TC Z679.6 .M26 1999*

**Spec kit**
(248) Managing the licensing of electronic
products. Washington, DC : Systems and
Procedures Exchange Center, Office of Leadership
and Management Service, Association of Research
Libraries, c1999.

(248) Managing the licensing of electronic
products. Washington, DC : Systems and
Procedures Exchange Center, Office of Leadership
and Management Service, Association of Research
Libraries, c1999.

**SPEC kit**
(248) Managing the licensing of electronic
products. Washington, DC : Systems and
Procedures Exchange Center, Office of Leadership
and Management Service, Association of Research
Libraries, c1999.
*TC HF5429.255 .M26 1999*

**The special child.**
Furneaux, Barbara. Harmondsworth : Penguin, 1969.
*TC LC4661 .F87*

**SPECIAL COLLECTIONS IN LIBRARIES.** *See*
**LIBRARIES - SPECIAL COLLECTIONS.**

**Special days and weeks for planning the school**
**calendar.** Arlington, Va. : Educational Research
Service, v. ; 28 cm. (ERS information aid) Description based
on: 1982-83. Subseries of: ERS information aid. Continues:
Special days and weeks observed by schools.
*1. School year. 2. Holidays - United States - Chronology. I.*
*Educational Research Service (Arlington, Va.) II. Title: ERS*
*information aid III. Title: Special days and weeks observed by*
*schools. IV. Series.*
*TC LB3525 .S63*

**Special days and weeks observed by schools.**
Special days and weeks for planning the school
calendar. Arlington, Va. : Educational Research
Service.
*TC LB3525 .S63*

**SPECIAL DISTRICTS.** *See* **SCHOOL DISTRICTS.**

**SPECIAL EDUCATION.**
Gibb, Gordon S. Guide to writing quality
individualzed education programs :. Boston : Allyn
and Bacon, c2000.
*TC LC4019 .G43 2000*

Hand in hand [videorecording]. New York, N.Y. :
AFB Press, c1995.
*TC HV1597.2 .H3 1995*

Making the most of early communication
[videorecording]. New York, NY : Distributed by
AFB Press, c1997.
*TC HV1597.2 .M3 1997*

Olson, Judy L. Teaching children and adolescents
with special needs. 3rd ed. Upper Saddle River, N.J. :
Merrill, c2000.
*TC LC3969 .O47 2000*

Pagliano, Paul. Multisensory environments. London :
David Fulton, 1999.
*TC LC3965 .P345 1999*

Special education & student disability. 4th ed. Denver,
Colo. : Love Pub. Co., c1995.
*TC LC3965 .E87 1995*

Steiner, Rudolf, 1861-1925. [Heilpädagogischer Kurs.
English] Education for special needs. [New ed.].
London : Rudolf Steiner Press, 1998.
*TC LB1029.W34 S73 1998*

**Special education & student disability :** an
introduction : traditional, emerging, and alternative
perspectives / edited by Edward L. Meyen, Thomas
M. Skrtic. 4th ed. Denver, Colo. : Love Pub. Co.,
c1995. xvii, 830 p. : ill. ; 24 cm. Rev. ed. of: Exceptional
children and youth, an introduction. 1988. Includes
bibliographical references and indexes. ISBN 0-89108-231-X
DDC 371.9
*1. Special education. 2. Handicapped children - Education. I.*
*Meyen, Edward L. II. Skrtic, Thomas M. III. Title: Exceptional*
*children and youth, an introduction. IV. Title: Special*
*education and student disability.*
*TC LC3965 .E87 1995*

**SPECIAL EDUCATION - ACTIVITY**
**PROGRAMS.**
Creativity in the classroom. Burbank, CA : Disney
Learning Partnership, c1999.
*TC LB1062 .C7 1999*

**Special education and school reform in the United**
**States and Britain** / edited by Margaret J.
McLaughlin and Martyn Rouse. London ; New York :
Routledge, 2000. xii, 201 p. : ill. ; 24 cm. Includes
bibliographical references and index. ISBN 0-415-19757-0
(pbk. : alk. paper) DDC 371.9/0941
*1. Special education - Great Britain. 2. Special education -*
*United States. 3. School improvement programs - Great*
*Britain. 4. School improvement programs - United States. I.*
*McLaughlin, Margaret J. II. Rouse, Martyn.*
*TC LC3986.G7 S64 2000*

**Special education and student disability.**
Special education & student disability. 4th ed. Denver,
Colo. : Love Pub. Co., c1995.
*TC LC3965 .E87 1995*

**SPECIAL EDUCATION - ART.**
Henley, David R. Exceptional children: exceptional
art. Worcester, Mass. : Davis Publications, c1992.
*TC RJ505.A7 H46 1992*

**Special education: forward trends.**
Forward trends. London, National Council for Special
Education [etc.]

**SPECIAL EDUCATION - GOVERNMENT**
**POLICY - UNITED STATES.**
Testing, teaching, and learning. Washington, D.C. :
National Academy Press, c1999.
*TC LC3981 .T4 1999*

**SPECIAL EDUCATION - GREAT BRITAIN.**
Beveridge, Sally. Special educational needs in
schools. 2nd ed. London ; New York : Routledge,
1999.
*TC LC3986.G7 B48 1999*

The education of children with medical conditions.
London : D. Fulton Publishers, 2000.
*TC LC4564.G7 E38 2000*

Special education and school reform in the United
States and Britain. London ; New York : Routledge,
2000.
*TC LC3986.G7 S64 2000*

Special education re-formed. London ; New York :
Falmer Press, 2000.
*TC LC1203.G7 S72 1999*

**SPECIAL EDUCATION - GREAT BRITAIN -**
**ADMINISTRATION - HANDBOOKS,**
**MANUALS, ETC.**
Cowne, Elizabeth A. The SENCO handbook. 2nd ed.
London : D. Fulton Publishers, 1998.
*TC LC3986.G7 C69 1998*

**SPECIAL EDUCATION - GREAT BRITAIN -**
**HANDBOOKS, MANUALS, ETC.**
Fox, Glenys. A handbook for learning support
assistants. London : D. Fulton Publishers, 1998.
*TC LB2844.1.A8 F68 1998*

**SPECIAL EDUCATION - GREAT BRITAIN -**
**PHILOSOPHY.**
Theorising special education. London ; New York :
Routledge, 1998.
*TC LC3986.G7 T54 1998*

**Special education law.**
Rothstein, Laura F. New York : Longman, 2000.
*TC KF4210 .R68 2000*

**SPECIAL EDUCATION - LAW AND**
**LEGISLATION - UNITED STATES.**
Fiedler, Craig R. Making a difference. Boston ;
London : Allyn and Bacon, c2000.
*TC LC4031 .F52 2000*

**SPECIAL EDUCATION - LAW AND**
**LEGISLATION - UNITED STATES.**
Kelman, Mark. Jumping the queue. Cambridge,
Mass. : Harvard University Press, 1997.
*TC KF4215 .K45 1997*

**SPECIAL EDUCATION - LAW AND**
**LEGISLATION - UNITED STATES.**
Rothstein, Laura F. Special education law. New
York : Longman, 2000.
*TC KF4210 .R68 2000*

**SPECIAL EDUCATION - MASSACHUSETTS -**
**BOSTON - HISTORY - 19TH CENTURY.**
Osgood, Robert L. For "children who vary from the
normal type". Washington, D.C. : Gallaudet
University Press, c2000.
*TC LC3983.B7 O84 2000*

**SPECIAL EDUCATION - MASSACHUSETTS - BOSTON - HISTORY - 20TH CENTURY.**
Osgood, Robert L. For "children who vary from the normal type". Washington, D.C. : Gallaudet University Press, c2000.
*TC LC3983.B7 O84 2000*

**SPECIAL EDUCATION - NEW YORK (STATE) - NEW YORK - CASE STUDIES.**
Fleischer, Lee. Living in contradiction. 1998.
*TC 06 no. 11021*

**SPECIAL EDUCATION - PARENT PARTICIPATION.**
Bright beginnings [videorecording. Burbank, CA : RCA/Columbia Pictures Home Video ; Toluca Lake, CA : [Distributed by] Corporate Productions, c1991.
*TC HV1642 .B67 1991*

Bright beginnings [videorecording. Burbank, CA : RCA/Columbia Pictures Home Video ; [S.l. : Distributed by] Rank Video Services America, c1991.
*TC HV1642 .B67 1991*

Hand in hand [videorecording]. New York, N.Y. : AFB Press, c1995.
*TC HV1597.2 .H3 1995*

Making the most of early communication [videorecording]. New York, NY : Distributed by AFB Press, c1997.
*TC HV1597.2 .M3 1997*

**SPECIAL EDUCATION - PARENT PARTICIPATION - UNITED STATES - CASE STUDIES.**
Harry, Beth. Building cultural reciprocity with families. Baltimore, Md. : P.H. Brookes Pub. Co., c1999.
*TC LC3969 .H377 1999*

Kalyanpur, Maya. Culture in special education. Baltimore, Md. : P.H. Brookes Pub., c1999.
*TC LC3969 .K35 1999*

**Special education re-formed** : beyond rhetoric? / edited by Harry Daniels. London ; New York : Falmer Press, 2000. ix, 283 p. : 24 cm. (New millennium series) Includes bibliographical references and index. ISBN 0-7507-0893-X (alk. paper) ISBN 0-7507-0892-1 (pbk. : alk. paper) DDC 371.95/2
*1. Inclusive education - Great Britain. 2. Special education - Great Britain. I. Daniels, Harry. II. Series.*
*TC LC1203.G7 S72 1999*

**SPECIAL EDUCATION - RESEARCH - UNITED STATES - METHODOLOGY.**
Contemporary special education research. Mahwah, N.J. : Lawrence Erlbaum, c2000.
*TC LC4019 .C575 2000*

**SPECIAL EDUCATION - SOCIAL ASPECTS - UNITED STATES - CASE STUDIES.**
Kalyanpur, Maya. Culture in special education. Baltimore, Md. : P.H. Brookes Pub., c1999.
*TC LC3969 .K35 1999*

**SPECIAL EDUCATION - STANDARDS - UNITED STATES.**
Testing, teaching, and learning. Washington, D.C. : National Academy Press, c1999.
*TC LC3981 .T4 1999*

**SPECIAL EDUCATION - STUDY AND TEACHING - UNITED STATES.**
Meese, Ruth Lyn. Teaching learners with mild disabilities. 2nd ed. Belmont, CA : Wadsworth/Thomson Learning, c2001.
*TC LC4031 .M44 2001*

**SPECIAL EDUCATION TEACHERS - TRAINING OF.**
Friend, Marilyn Penovich, 1953- Interactions. 3rd ed. New York : Longman, 1999.
*TC LC3969.45 .F75 1999*

**SPECIAL EDUCATION TEACHERS - UNITED STATES.**
Families and teachers of individuals with disabilities. Boston ; London : Allyn and Bacon, c2001.
*TC LC3969 .F34 2001*

**SPECIAL EDUCATION TEACHERS - UNITED STATES - BIOGRAPHY.**
Ballenger, Cynthia. Teaching other people's children. New York : Teachers College Press, c1999.
*TC LC3746 .B336 1999*

**Special education** : the challenge of the future / edited by Karen A. Waldron, Albert E. Riester, John H. Moore. San Francisco : EMText, c1992. x, 242 p. ; 23 cm. Includes bibliographical references and index. ISBN 0-7734-1936-5 DDC 371.9/0973
*1. Special education - United States. 2. Special education -*

United States - Evaluation. I. Waldron, Karen A., 1945- II. Riester, Albert E., 1941- III. Moore, John H., 1938-
*TC LC3981 .S63 1992*

**Special education transition services.**
Pierangelo, Roger. Complete guide to special education transition services. West Nyack, NY : Center for Applied Research in Education, c1997.
*TC HV1569.3.Y68 P55 1997*

**SPECIAL EDUCATION - UNITED STATES.**
Bigge, June L. Curriculum, assessment, and instruction for students with disabilities. Belmont, CA : Wadsworth Pub., c1999.
*TC LC4031 .B46 1999*

Heward, William L., 1949- Exceptional children. 6th ed. Upper Saddle River, N.J. : Merrill, c2000.
*TC LC3981 .H49 2000*

Instruction of students with severe disabilities. 5th ed. Upper Saddle River, N.J. : Merrill, c2000.
*TC LC4031 .I572 2000*

Law and school reform. New Haven [Conn.] : Yale University Press, c1999.
*TC LC213.2. L38 1999*

Lewis, Rena B. Teaching special students in general education classrooms. 5th ed. Upper Saddle River, N.J. : Merrill, c1999.
*TC LC1201 .L48 1999*

Lovitt, Thomas C. Preventing school failure. 2nd ed. Austin, Tex. : Pro-Ed. : c2000.
*TC LC146.6 .L68 2000*

McGregor, Gail Inclusive schooling practices. [S.l.] : Allegheny University of Health Sciences ; Baltimore : Distributed exclusively by Paul H. Brookes Publishing, c1998.
*TC LC4031 .M394 1998*

Partners in progress. San Francisco, Calif. : Jossey-Bass Inc., c1999.
*TC LC3981 .P27 1999*

Smith, Deborah Deutsch. Introduction to special education. 4th ed. Boston : Allyn and Bacon, c2001.
*TC LC3981 .S56 2001*

Special education and school reform in the United States and Britain. London ; New York : Routledge, 2000.
*TC LC3986.G7 S64 2000*

Special education. San Francisco : EMText, c1992.
*TC LC3981 .S63 1992*

Successful inclusive teaching. 3rd ed. Boston : Allyn and Bacon, c2000.
*TC LC1201 .S93 2000*

Taylor, Ronald L., 1949- Assessment of exceptional students. 5th ed. Boston : Allyn and Bacon, c2000.
*TC LC4031 .T36 2000*

Vaughn, Sharon, 1952- Teaching exceptional, diverse, and at-risk students in the general education classroom. 2nd ed. Boston : Allyn and Bacon, 2000.
*TC LC3981 .V28 2000*

**SPECIAL EDUCATION - UNITED STATES - COMPUTER-ASSISTED INSTRUCTION.**
Birnbaum, Barry W. Connecting special education and technology for the 21st century. Lewiston, N.Y. ; Lampeter, Wales : E. Mellen Press, c1999.
*TC LC3969.5 .B57 1999*

**SPECIAL EDUCATION - UNITED STATES - DIRECTORIES.**
Pierangelo, Roger. The special education yellow pages. Upper Saddle River, N.J. : Merrill, c2000.
*TC LC4031 .P488 2000*

**SPECIAL EDUCATION - UNITED STATES - ENCYCLOPEDIAS.**
Encyclopedia of special education. 2nd ed. New York : J. Wiley & Sons, c2000.
*TC LC4007 .E53 2000*

**SPECIAL EDUCATION - UNITED STATES - EVALUATION.**
Special education. San Francisco : EMText, c1992.
*TC LC3981 .S63 1992*

**SPECIAL EDUCATION - UNITED STATES - FINANCE.**
Ferguson, Jacqueline. Grants for special education and rehabilitation. 4th ed. Gaithersburg, MD : Aspen Publishers, Inc., 2000.
*TC LB2825 .F424 2000*

**SPECIAL EDUCATION - UNITED STATES - HISTORY - 19TH CENTURY.**
Richardson, John G. Common, delinquent, and special. New York : Falmer Press, 1999.

*TC LC3981 .R525 1999*

**SPECIAL EDUCATION - UNITED STATES - HISTORY - 20TH CENTURY.**
Richardson, John G. Common, delinquent, and special. New York : Falmer Press, 1999.
*TC LC3981 .R525 1999*

**SPECIAL EDUCATION - VOCATIONAL GUIDANCE - UNITED STATES.**
Westling, David L. Teaching students with severe disabilities. 2nd ed. Upper Saddle River, N.J. : Merrill, c2000.
*TC LC4031 .W47 2000*

**The special education yellow pages.**
Pierangelo, Roger. Upper Saddle River, N.J. : Merrill, c2000.
*TC LC4031 .P488 2000*

**Special educational needs in schools.**
Beveridge, Sally. 2nd ed. London ; New York : Routledge, 1999.
*TC LC3986.G7 B48 1999*

**Special kids for special treatment?.**
Phtiaka, Helen. Special kids for special treatment?, or, How special do you need to be to find yourself in a special school? London ; Washington, D.C. : Falmer Press, 1997.
*TC LC4803.G7 P58 1998*

**Special kids for special treatment?, or, How special do you need to be to find yourself in a special school?.**
Phtiaka, Helen. London ; Washington, D.C. : Falmer Press, 1997.
*TC LC4803.G7 P58 1998*

**SPECIAL LANGUAGE.** *See* **SUBLANGUAGE.**

**SPECIAL LIBRARIES.** *See* **CHILDREN'S LIBRARIES.**

**Special needs and the beginning teacher** / edited by Peter Benton and Tim O'Brien. London ; New York : Continuum, 2000. x, 213 p. : ill. ; 22 cm. (Special needs in ordinary schools.) Includes bibliographical references (p. [204]-210) and index. ISBN 0-8264-4889-5 (pbk.)
*1. Handicapped children - Education - Great Britain. 2. Teachers of handicapped children - Training of - Great Britain. I. Benton, Peter. II. O'Brien, Tim. 1958- III. Series.*
*TC LC4036.G7 S684 2000*

**Special needs in ordinary schools**
Croll, Paul. Special needs in the primary school. London : Cassell, 2000.
*TC LC4036.G6 C763 2000*

Special needs and the beginning teacher. London ; New York : Continuum, 2000.
*TC LC4036.G7 S684 2000*

**Special needs in the primary school.**
Croll, Paul. London : Cassell, 2000.
*TC LC4036.G6 C763 2000*

**Special publication (Royal Society of Chemistry (Great Britain))**
(no. 244.) Lipids in health and nutrition. Cambridge : Royal Society of Chemistry, c1999.
*TC QP751 .L57 1999*

**Special report (Carnegie Foundation for the Advancement of Teaching)**
The international academic profession. Princeton, N.J. : Carnegie Foundation for the Advancement of Teaching, c1996.
*TC LB1778 .I54 1996*

**SPECIALISTS.** *See* **COMMUNICATION SPECIALISTS; CONSULTANTS; INTELLECTUALS.**

**SPECIALIZATION.** *See* **EXPERTISE.**

**SPECIALIZED AGENCIES OF THE UNITED NATIONS.** *See* **INTERNATIONAL AGENCIES.**

**Specific language impairment in children** / Heather K. J. van der Lely, guest editor. Hillsdale, N.J. : Lawrence Erlbaum , 1998. p. [83]-344 : ill. ; 24 cm. Language acquisition: a journal of developmental linguistics, v.7 no. 2-4, 1998. Includes bibliographical references. Supplement to: Language acquisition: a journal of developmental linguistics ISSN: 1048-9223. ISSN 1048-9223
*1. Language disorders in children. 2. Language acquisition. 3. Language development in children. I. Van der Lely, Heather K. J. II. Title. III. Title: Language acquisition: a journal of developmental linguistics*
*TC RJ496.L35 S643 1998*

**SPECIMENS, ARCHAEOLOGICAL.** *See* **ANTIQUITIES.**

**Speck, Bruce W.** Grading students' classroom writing : issues and strategies / Bruce W. Speck ; prepared by ERIC HE, ERIC Clearinghouse on Higher Education, The George Washington University, in cooperation with ASHE, Association for the Study of Higher Education. Washington, DC : Graduate School of Education and Human Development, The George Washington University, 2000. xiii, 117 p. ; 24 cm. (ASHE-ERIC higher education report, 0884-0040 ; v. 27, no. 3) "Prepared by ERIC HE, ERIC Clearinghouse on Higher Education, The George Washington University, in cooperation with ASHE, Association for the Study of Higher Education." Includes bibliographical references (p. 85-98) and index. CONTENTS: The writing process and grading students' writing -- Constructing writing assignments -- Fairness and professional judgment -- Including students in the assessment of writing -- Providing feedback for revision : reading and responding to students' writing -- Conclusion and recommendations -- Appendix: Example of a student's paper with effective written comments. ISBN 1-87838-091-5 (pbk.) *1. English language - Composition and exercises - Ability testing. 2. Grading and marking (Students) I. ERIC Clearinghouse on Higher Education. II. American Association for the Study of Higher Education. III. Title. IV. Series.*
*TC LB1576 .S723 2000*

**Speck, Marsha.** The principalship : building a learning community / Marsha Speck ; [editor, Debra A. Stollenwerk ; illustrations, Tom Kennedy]. Upper Saddle River, N.J. : Merrill, c1999. xiv, 240 p. : ill. ; 23 cm. Includes bibliographical references and index. ISBN 0-13-440686-9 DDC 371.2/012
*1. School principals - Training of. 2. School management and organization. 3. Community and school. 4. Problem-based learning. I. Stollenwerk, Debra A. II. Title.*
*TC LB1738.5 .S64 1999*

**SPECTACLES.** *See* **EYEGLASSES.**

**SPECTERS.** *See* **GHOSTS.**

**Spector, Paul E.** Industrial and organizational psychology : research and practice / Paul E. Spector. 2nd ed. New York : John Wiley, 2000. xxiii, 376 p. : ill. ; 25 cm. Includes bibliographical references (p. 335-352) and index. ISBN 0-471-24373-6 (cloth : alk. paper) DDC 158.7
*1. Psychology, Industrial. 2. Personnel management. I. Title.*
*TC HF5548.8 .S625 2000*

**SPECTRES.** *See* **GHOSTS.**

**SPEECH.** *See also* **PHONETICS; SPEECH ACTS (LINGUISTICS); VERBAL BEHAVIOR; VOICE.**
Gesture, speech, and sign. Oxford [England] ; New York : Oxford University Press, c1999.
*TC P117 .G469 1999*

The neurocognition of language. Oxford ; New York : Oxford University Press, 1999.
*TC QP399 .N483 1999*

Scholes, Robert J. A linguistic approach to reading and writing. Lewiston, N.Y. : E. Mellen Press, c1999.
*TC P211 .S383 1999*

**SPEECH ACT THEORY (LINGUISTICS).** *See* **SPEECH ACTS (LINGUISTICS).**

**SPEECH ACTS (LINGUISTICS).**
Alston, William P. Illocutionary acts and sentence meaning. Ithaca : Cornell University Press, 2000.
*TC P95.55 .A47 2000*

Gordon, Tatiana. Russian language directives. 1998.
*TC 06 no. 10940*

Li, Duan-Duan. Expressing needs and wants in a second language. 1998.
*TC 06 no. 10958*

**SPEECH, ALARYNGEAL.**
Boone, Daniel R. The voice and voice therapy. 6th ed. Boston ; London : Allyn & Bacon, c2000.
*TC RF540 .B66 2000*

**SPEECH COMMUNICATION.** *See* **ORAL COMMUNICATION.**

**Speech communications.**
O'Shaughnessy, Douglas, 1950- 2nd ed. New York : IEEE Press, c2000.
*TC P95 .O74 2000*

**SPEECH CORRECTION.** *See* **SPEECH THERAPY.**

**SPEECH DEFECTS.** *See* **SPEECH DISORDERS.**

**SPEECH DISORDERS.** *See* **APHASIA; STUTTERING; VOICE DISORDERS.**

**SPEECH DISORDERS.**
Diagnosis in speech-language pathology. 2nd ed. San Diego : Singular, c2000.

*TC RC423 .D473 2000*

**SPEECH DISORDERS - CHILD.**
Love, Russell J. Childhood motor speech disability. 2nd ed. Boston ; London : Allyn and Bacon, c2000.
*TC RJ496.S7 L68 2000*

**SPEECH DISORDERS - DIAGNOSIS.**
Baken, R. J. (Ronald J.), 1943- Clinical measurement of speech and voice. 2nd ed. San Diego : Singular Thomson Learning, c2000.
*TC RC423 .B28 2000*

Diagnosis in speech-language pathology. 2nd ed. San Diego : Singular, c2000.
*TC RC423 .D473 2000*

**SPEECH DISORDERS - DICTIONARIES.**
Singh, Sadanand. Illustrated dictionary of speech-language pathology. San Diego : Singular Pub. Group, c2000.
*TC RC423 .S533 2000*

**SPEECH DISORDERS - DICTIONARY - ENGLISH.**
Singh, Sadanand. Illustrated dictionary of speech-language pathology. San Diego : Singular Pub. Group, c2000.
*TC RC423 .S533 2000*

**SPEECH DISORDERS IN CHILDREN.**
Love, Russell J. Childhood motor speech disability. 2nd ed. Boston ; London : Allyn and Bacon, c2000.
*TC RJ496.S7 L68 2000*

**SPEECH DISORDERS IN CHILDREN - CASE STUDIES.**
Chiat, Shula. Understanding children with language problems. Oxford [England] ; New York : Cambridge University Press, 2000.
*TC RJ496.L35 C46 2000*

**SPEECH DISORDERS IN CHILDREN - TREATMENT.** *See* **SPEECH THERAPY FOR CHILDREN.**

**SPEECH, DISORDERS OF.** *See* **SPEECH DISORDERS.**

**SPEECH DISORDERS - PATIENTS - COUNSELING OF - CASE STUDIES.**
Wanting to talk. London : Whurr, c1998.
*TC RC423 .W26 1998*

**SPEECH DISORDERS - THERAPY.**
Klein, Harriet B. Intervention planning for adults with communication problems : Volume 2. Boston : Allyn and Bacon, c1999.
*TC RC423 .K57 1999*

Measuring outcomes in speech-language pathology. New York : Thieme, 1998.
*TC RC423 .M39 1997*

**SPEECH DISORDERS - TREATMENT.** *See* **SPEECH THERAPY.**

**SPEECH EVENTS (LINGUISTICS).** *See* **SPEECH ACTS (LINGUISTICS).**

**SPEECH, FREEDOM OF.** *See* **FREEDOM OF SPEECH.**

**SPEECH, HATE.** *See* **HATE SPEECH.**

**SPEECH-LANGUAGE PATHOLOGISTS.** *See* **SPEECH THERAPISTS.**

**Speech-language pathologist's guide to home health care.**
Pierce, Roberta B. San Diego : Academic Press, c2000.
*TC RC423 .P54 2000*

**SPEECH-LANGUAGE PATHOLOGY.**
Diagnosis in speech-language pathology. 2nd ed. San Diego : Singular, c2000.
*TC RC423 .D473 2000*

Measuring outcomes in speech-language pathology. New York : Thieme, 1998.
*TC RC423 .M39 1997*

Silverman, Franklin H., 1933- Professional issues in speech-language pathology and audiology. Boston : Allyn and Bacon, c1999.
*TC RC428.5 .S55 1999*

**Speech-language pathology assistant in the schools.**
Thomas, Alice F. SLP assistant in the schools. [San Antonio, Tex.] : Communication Skill Builders, c1999.
*TC LB3454 .T46 1999*

**SPEECH-LANGUAGE PATHOLOGY - DICTIONARY - ENGLISH.**
Singh, Sadanand. Illustrated dictionary of speech-

language pathology. San Diego : Singular Pub. Group, c2000.
*TC RC423 .S533 2000*

**SPEECH-LANGUAGE PATHOLOGY - HANDBOOKS.**
Golper, Lee Ann C., 1948- Sourcebook for medical speech pathology. 2nd ed. San Diego, Calif. : Singular Pub. Group, c1998.
*TC RC423 .G64 1998*

**SPEECH-LANGUAGE THERAPISTS.** *See* **SPEECH THERAPISTS.**

**Speech/language therapists and teachers working together.**
McCartney, Elspeth. London : Whurr, 1999.
*TC LB3454 .M32 1999*

**SPEECH - MEASUREMENT.**
Baken, R. J. (Ronald J.), 1943- Clinical measurement of speech and voice. 2nd ed. San Diego : Singular Thomson Learning, c2000.
*TC RC423 .B28 2000*

**SPEECH PATHOLOGISTS.** *See* **SPEECH THERAPISTS.**

**SPEECH PATHOLOGY.** *See* **SPEECH DISORDERS.**

**SPEECH PERCEPTION.**
Bond, Zinny S. (Zinny Sans), 1940- Slips of the ear. San Diego, Calif. ; London : Academic, c1999.
*TC P37.5.S67 B66 1999*

**SPEECH - PHYSIOLOGICAL ASPECTS.**
Coarticulation. Cambridge, U.K. ; New York : Cambridge University Press, 1999.
*TC QP306 .C68 1999*

**SPEECH PROCESSING SYSTEMS.**
O'Shaughnessy, Douglas, 1950- Speech communications. 2nd ed. New York : IEEE Press, c2000.
*TC P95 .O74 2000*

**SPEECH PRODUCTION MEASUREMENT.**
Baken, R. J. (Ronald J.), 1943- Clinical measurement of speech and voice. 2nd ed. San Diego : Singular Thomson Learning, c2000.
*TC RC423 .B28 2000*

**SPEECH-READING.** *See* **DEAF - MEANS OF COMMUNICATION.**

**SPEECH THERAPISTS.**
Golper, Lee Ann C., 1948- Sourcebook for medical speech pathology. 2nd ed. San Diego, Calif. : Singular Pub. Group, c1998.
*TC RC423 .G64 1998*

**SPEECH THERAPISTS - GREAT BRITAIN.**
McCartney, Elspeth. Speech/language therapists and teachers working together. London : Whurr, 1999.
*TC LB3454 .M32 1999*

**SPEECH THERAPISTS - UNITED STATES.**
Thomas, Alice F. SLP assistant in the schools. [San Antonio, Tex.] : Communication Skill Builders, c1999.
*TC LB3454 .T46 1999*

**SPEECH THERAPY.**
The aphasia therapy file. Hove : Psychology Press, c1999.
*TC RC425 .A665 1999*

The aphasia therapy file. Hove : Psychology Press, c1999.
*TC RC425 .A665 1999*

Golper, Lee Ann C., 1948- Sourcebook for medical speech pathology. 2nd ed. San Diego, Calif. : Singular Pub. Group, c1998.
*TC RC423 .G64 1998*

**SPEECH THERAPY - EVALUATION.**
Measuring outcomes in speech-language pathology. New York : Thieme, 1998.
*TC RC423 .M39 1997*

**SPEECH THERAPY FOR CHILDREN.**
Fahey, Kathleen R. Language development, differences, and disorders. Austin, Tex. : PRO-ED, c2000.
*TC LB1139.L3 F35 2000*

Goldsworthy, Candace L. Sourcebook of phonological awareness activities. San Diego : Singular Pub. Group, c1998.
*TC LB1050.5 .G66 1998*

**SPEECH THERAPY FOR CHILDREN - UNITED STATES.**
Thomas, Alice F. SLP assistant in the schools. [San

Antonio, Tex.] : Communication Skill Builders,
c1999.
*TC LB3454 .T46 1999*

### SPEECH THERAPY - GREAT BRITAIN.
McCartney, Elspeth. Speech/language therapists and
teachers working together. London : Whurr, 1999.
*TC LB3454 .M32 1999*

### SPEECH THERAPY - HANDBOOKS, MANUALS, ETC.
Pierce, Roberta B. Speech-language pathologist's
guide to home health care. San Diego : Academic
Press, c2000.
*TC RC423 .P54 2000*

### SPEECH THERAPY - METHODS.
Goldsworthy, Candace L. Sourcebook of phonological
awareness activities. San Diego : Singular Pub.
Group, c1998.
*TC LB1050.5 .G66 1998*

Stuttering and related disorders of fluency. 2nd ed.
New York : Thieme Medical Publishers, 1999.
*TC RC424 .S768 1998*

### SPEECH THERAPY - PRACTICE.
Silverman, Franklin H., 1933- Professional issues in
speech-language pathology and audiology. Boston :
Allyn and Bacon, c1999.
*TC RC428.5 .S55 1999*

### SPEED PERCEPTION. *See* MOTION PERCEPTION (VISION).

Speight, Charlotte F., 1919- Hands in clay / Charlotte
F. Speight, John Toki. 4th ed. Mountain View, Calif. :
Mayfield, c1999. xi, 518 p., [32] p. of plates : ill. (some
col.), maps ; 28 cm. Includes bibliographical references and
index. ISBN 0-7674-0501-3 DDC 738
*1. Pottery craft. I. Toki, John. II. Title.*
*TC TT920 .S685 1999*

Speiser, R. (Robert) Five women build a number
system / by Robert Speiser and Chuck Walter.
Stamford, Conn. : Ablex Pub., c2000. xiv, 145 p. : ill. ;
24 cm. (Mathematics, learning, and cognition) Includes
bibliographical references (p. 131-137) and indexes. ISBN
1-56750-464-7 (cloth) ISBN 1-56750-465-5 (paper) DDC 510
*1. Mathematics - Study and teaching (Elementary) 2. Quinary
system. I. Walter, Chuck. II. Title. III. Series.*
*TC QA135.5 .S5785 2000*

### SPELLERS.
Gentry, J. Richard Spelling connections. Columbus,
Ohio : Zaner Bloser, c1996.
*TC LB1574 .G46 1996 Gr. 1*

Gentry, J. Richard Spelling connections. Columbus,
Ohio : Zaner Bloser, c1996.
*TC LB1574 .G46 1996 Gr. 3*

Gentry, J. Richard Spelling connections. Columbus,
Ohio : Zaner Bloser, c1996.
*TC LB1574 .G46 1996 Gr. 5*

### Spelling.
Westwood, Peter S. Camberwell, Vic. : ACER Press,
1999.
*TC LB1574 .W47 1999*

### The spelling book.
Rosencrans, Gladys. Newark, Del. : International
Reading Association, c1998.
*TC LB1574 .R654 1999*

### The spelling connection.
Cramer, Ronald L. New York : Guilford Press, c1998.
*TC LB1574 .C65 1998*

### SPELLING DISABILITY.
Walton, Margaret. Teaching reading and spelling to
dyslexic children. London : D. Fulton, 1998.
*TC LC4708 .W35 1998*

### SPELLS. *See* MAGIC.

Spencer, Deborah L. K.
Rosen, Sidney M. Toward a gang solution. [Norman,
Okla.?] NRC Youth Services, 1996.
*TC HV6439.U7 R67 1996*

Spencer, Gary. Structure and dynamics of social
intervention; a comparative study of the reduction of
dependency in three low-income housing projects.
Lexington, Mass., Heath Lexington Books [1970]
xviii, 153 p. illus. 24 cm. (Northeastern University studies in
rehabilitation no. 9) Bibliography: p. [151]-153. DDC 362.5/
0973
*1. Social service - United States - Case studies. 2. Vocational
rehabilitation - United States - Case studies. I. Title. II. Series.*
*TC HV91 .S63*

Spencer-Oatey, Helen, 1952-.
Culturally speaking. London ; New York :
Continuum ; [New York] : [Cassell], 2000.

*TC GN345.6 .C86 2000*

Spencer, Patricia Elizabeth.
The deaf child in the family and at school. Mahwah,
N.J. : Lawrence Erlbaum Associates, 2000.
*TC HV2392.2 .D43 2000*

Sperber, Dan.
Metarepresentations. Oxford ; New York : Oxford
University Press, c2000.
*TC BF316.6 .M48 2000*

### SPHENISCIDAE. *See* PENGUINS.

### SPHENISCIFORMES. *See* PENGUINS.

### SPHERE. *See* CIRCLE.

Spiegelman, Ronnie.
Ballet class [videorecording]. W. Long Branch, NJ :
Kultur, c1984.
*TC GV1589 .B33 1984*

Spier, Peter.
[Circus!]
Peter Spier's circus!. 1st ed. New York :
Doubleday, c1992. 1 v. (unpaged) : col. ill. ; 27 cm. "A
Doubleday book for young readers." SUMMARY: A
traveling circus arrives, sets up its village of tents, performs
for the crowd, and then moves on again. ISBN 0-385-
41969-4 ISBN 0-385-41970-8 (lib. bdg.) DDC [E]
*1. Circus - Fiction. I. Title. II. Title: Circus!*
*TC PZ7.S7544 Cj 1992*

Spillman, Diana M.
Ubbes, Valerie A. Literature links for nutrition and
health. Boston : Allyn and Bacon, c2000.
*TC TX364 .U253 2000*

### SPINAL COLUMN. *See* SPINE.

### Spindler anthology.
Spindler, George Dearborn. Fifty years of
anthropology and education, 1950-2000. Mahwah,
N.J. L.Erlbaum Associates, 2000.
*TC LB45 .S66 2000*

Spindler, George Dearborn. Fifty years of
anthropology and education, 1950-2000 : a Spindler
anthology / George and Louise Spindler ; edited by
George Spindler. Mahwah, N.J. L.Erlbaum
Associates, 2000. xx, 434 p. : ill. ; 24 cm. Includes
bibliographical references (p.409-415) and indexes. ISBN
0-8058-3495-8 (cloth) DDC 306.43
*1. Educational anthropology. 2. Educational sociology. I.
Spindler, Louise S. II. Title. III. Title: Spindler anthology IV.
Title: Fifty years of anthropology and education, 1950-2000.*
*TC LB45 .S66 2000*

Spindler, Louise S.
Spindler, George Dearborn. Fifty years of
anthropology and education, 1950-2000. Mahwah,
N.J. L.Erlbaum Associates, 2000.
*TC LB45 .S66 2000*

### SPINE - MOVEMENTS - CONGRESSES.
Peripheral and spinal mechanisms in the neural
control of movement. Amsterdam ; Oxford : Elsevier,
1999.
*TC QP376.A1 P7 1999*

### SPINELLI, JERRY, 1940- /. MANIAC MAGEE.
Beech, Linda Ward. Maniac Magee by Jerry
Spinelli. New York : Scholastic, c1997.
*TC LB1573 .B4311 1997*

Spinner-Halev, Jeff. Surviving diversity : religion and
democratic citizenship / Jeff Spinner-Halev.
Baltimore : Johns Hopkins University Press, 2000. x,
246 p. ; 24 cm. Includes bibliographical references (p. [221]-
240) and index. ISBN 0-8018-6346-5 (alk. paper) DDC
323.44/2/0973
*1. Religion and politics - United States. 2. Conservatism -
Religious aspects. I. Title.*
*TC BL2525 .S588 2000*

### SPIRAL GALAXIES.
Stephen Hawking's universe [videorecording].
[Alexandria, Va.] : PBS Video; Burbank, CA :
Distributed by Warner Home Video, c1997.
*TC QB982 .S7 1997*

### SPIRIT. *See* CONSCIOUSNESS.

Spirit capture : photographs from the National Museum
of the American Indian / edited by Tim Johnson.
Washington : Smithsonian Institution Press in
association with the National Museum of the
American Indian, Smithsonian Institution, c1998. xvii,
205 p. : ill. (some col.) ; 27 cm. Includes bibliographical
references (p. 193-195) and index. ISBN 1-56098-924-6
(cloth : alk. paper) ISBN 1-56098-765-0 (paper : alk. paper)
DDC 779/.997000497
*1. Indians of North America - Pictorial works. 2. Indians -*

*Pictorial works. 3. Photography in ethnology. 4. National
Museum of the American Indian (U.S.) I. Johnson, Tim, 1947-
II. National Museum of the American Indian (U.S.)*
*TC E77.5 .S65 1998*

Spirit of Siberia.
Oakes, Jill E. (Jill Elizabeth), 1952- Washington,
D.C. : Smithsonian Institution Press, c1998.
*TC DK758 .O24 1998*

Spiritual and religious education / edited by Mal
Leicester, Celia Modgil and Sohan Modgil. London ;
New York : Falmer Press, 2000. viii, 240 p. ; 29 cm.
(Education, culture, and values ; v. 5) Includes bibliographical
references and index. ISBN 0-7507-1006-3 DDC 291.7/5
*1. Spiritual formation. 2. Religious education. I. Leicester,
Mal. II. Modgil, Celia. III. Modgil, Sohan. IV. Series.*
*TC BL42 .S68 2000*

### SPIRITUAL BIOGRAPHY. *See* RELIGIOUS BIOGRAPHY.

### SPIRITUAL FORMATION.
Education for spiritual, moral, social and cultural
development. London ; New York : Continuum, 2000.
*TC LC268 .E384 2000*

Miller, John P., 1943- Education and the soul.
Albany : State University of New York Press, c2000.
*TC LC268 .M52 2000*

Spiritual and religious education. London ; New
York : Falmer Press, 2000.
*TC BL42 .S68 2000*

Stewart, Therese Marie Klein. The challenges to
sustaining Unification faith and the spiritual quest
after seminary. 1996.
*TC 06 no. 10751*

### SPIRITUAL HEALING. *See* CHRISTIAN SCIENCE.

### SPIRITUAL LIFE. *See also* SPIRITUALITY.
Luke, Helen M., 1904- Such stuff as dreams are made
on. New York : Parabola Books, c2000.
*TC BF1091 .L82 2000*

Sullivan, John P. (John Peter) On holy ground.
Lanham : University Press of America, c1998.
*TC RC489.R46 S84 1998*

### SPIRITUAL LIFE - CHRISTIANITY. *See* MONASTIC AND RELIGIOUS LIFE.

### SPIRITUAL LIFE - STUDY AND TEACHING.
Addressing the spiritual dimensions of adult
learning :. San Francisco : Jossey Bass, 2000.
*TC LC5219 .A25 2000*

### SPIRITUAL-MINDEDNESS. *See* SPIRITUALITY.

Spiritual vision for every teacher and parent.
Groome, Thomas H. Educating for life. Allen, Tex. :
T. More, c1998.
*TC BV1471.2 .G6874 1998*

### SPIRITUALISM IN ART.
Drury, Nevill, 1947- Fire and shadow. Roseville East,
NWS : Craftsman House [Australia : United States :
G + B Arts International [distributor], c1996.
*TC N7400.2 .D78 1996*

### SPIRITUALITY. *See also* SPIRITUAL LIFE.
Creativity, spirituality, and transcendence. Stamford,
Conn. : Ablex, c2000.
*TC BF411 .C76 2000*

Fukuyama, Mary A. Integrating spirituality into
multicultural counseling. Thousand Oaks, Calif. :
Sage Publications, c1999.
*TC BF637.C6 F795 1999*

Integrating spirituality into treatment. 1st ed.
Washington, DC : American Psychological
Association, c1999.
*TC RC489.R46 I58 1999*

Spirituality, ethics, and relationship in adulthood :
clinical and theoretical explorations / edited by Melvin
E. Miller & Alan N. West. Madison, Conn. :
Psychosocial Press, c2000. xiii, 413 p. ; 24 cm. Chiefly
papers presented at the Society for Research in Adult
Development Symposia, 1994 to 1996. Includes
bibliographical references and indexes. ISBN 1-88784-129-6
DDC 155.6
*1. Adulthood - Psychological aspects - Congresses. 2.
Maturation (Psychology) - Congresses. I. Miller, Melvin E. II.
West, Alan N.*
*TC BF724.5 .S68 2000*

Spirituality in nursing.
O'Brien, Mary Elizabeth. Sudbury, Mass. : Jones and
Bartlett Pub., c1999.
*TC RT85.2 .O37 1999*

**SPIRITUALITY (IN RELIGIOUS ORDERS, CONGREGATIONS, ETC.).** *See* MONASTIC AND RELIGIOUS LIFE.

**SPIRITUALITY - STUDY AND TEACHING (HIGHER).**
The academy and the possibility of belief. Cresskill, N.J. : Hampton Press, c2000.
*TC LB2324 .A27 2000*

**SPIRITUALITY - UNITED STATES - HISTORY.**
Taylor, Eugene. Shadow culture Washington, D.C. : Counterpoint, c1999.
*TC BL2525 .T39 1999*

**Spitz, Ellen Handler, 1939-** Inside picture books / Ellen Handler Spitz. New Haven : Yale University Press, c1999. xxii, 230 p. : ill. ; 25 cm. Includes bibliographical references (p. 217-225) and index. ISBN 0-300-07602-9 (alk. paper) DDC 028.5/01/9
*1. Children - Books and reading - Psychological aspects. 2. Picture books for children - Psychological aspects. 3. Reading - Parent participation. I. Title.*
*TC BF456.R2 S685 1999*

**Splain, D. Michael.**
Hartz, Gary W. Psychosocial intervention in long-term care. New York : Haworth Press, c1997.
*TC RC451.4.N87 H37 1997*

**Splichal, Slavko.** Public opinion : developments and controversies in the Twentieth Century / Slavko Splichal. Lanham, Md. : Rowman & Littlefield, 1999. xi, 367 p. 23 cm. (Critical media studies) Includes bibliographical references and index. ISBN 0-8476-9162-4 (cloth : alk. paper) ISBN 0-8476-9163-2 (pbk. : alk. paper) DDC 303.3/8
*1. Public opinion. 2. Public opinion polls. 3. Social psychology. I. Title. II. Series.*
*TC HM261 .S7515 1999*

**SPLIT PERSONALITY.** *See* MULTIPLE PERSONALITY.

**Spodek, Howard, 1941-** The world's history / Howard Spodek. Combined ed. Upper Saddle River, NJ : Prentice Hall, 1998. 1 v. (various pagings) : ill. (some col.), col. maps ; 26 cm. Includes bibliographical references and index. ISBN 0-13-644469-5 DDC 909
*1. World history. I. Title.*
*TC D20 .S77 1998*

**SPOKEN ENGLISH.** *See* ENGLISH LANGUAGE - SPOKEN ENGLISH.

**Spoken soul.**
Rickford, John R., 1949- New York ; Chichester [England] : Wiley, c2000.
*TC PE3102.N42 R54 2000*

**Spolsky, Bernard.**
Concise encyclopedia of educational linguistics. Amsterdam ; New York : Elsevier, 1999.
*TC P40.8 .C66 1999*

**Spon's building costs guide for educational premises** / edited by Barnsley and Partners. 2nd ed. London : E & FN SPON, 1999. xv, 277 p. : ill. ; 22 x 30 cm. ISBN 0-419-23310-5
*1. School buildings - Great Britain - Costs. 2. School buildings - Specifications - Great Britain. 3. School buildings - Great Britain - Statistics. I. Barnsley and Partners. II. Title: Building costs guide for educational premises*
*TC LB3219.G7 S67 1999*

**Sporn, Barbara.** Adaptive university structures : an analysis of adaptation to socioeconomic environments of US and European universities / Barbara Sporn. London ; Philadelphia : Jessica Kingsley, c1999. 320 p. : ill. ; 24 cm. (Higher education series ; 54.) Includes bibliographical references (p. 291-309) and indexes. ISBN 1-85302-781-2 DDC 378.1
*1. Educational change - Europe. 2. Educational change - United States. 3. Education, Higher - Aims and objectives. 4. Universities and colleges - Sociological aspects. 5. Universities and colleges - Europe - Administration. 6. Universities and colleges - United States - Administration. I. Title. II. Series.*
*TC LB2322.2 .S667 1999*

**Sport and physical education in China** / [edited by] James Riordan and Robin Jones. London ; New York : Routledge, 1999. xviii, 278 p. ill. ; 24 cm. (ISCPES book series) Includes bibliographical references and index. ISBN 0-419-24750-5 (hardbound) ISBN 0-419-22030-5 (pbk.) DDC 613.7/0951
*1. Sports - China - History. 2. Physical education and training - China - History. I. Riordan, James, 1936- II. Jones, Robin (Robin E.) III. Series.*
*TC GV651 .S655 1999*

**SPORTING GOODS.** *See also* BALLS (SPORTING GOODS).

Davison, Bev, 1957- Creative physical activities and equipment. Champaign, IL : Human Kinetics, c1998.
*TC GV745 .D38 1998*

**Sporting Goods Manufacturers Association (U.S.).**
Active older adults. Champaign, IL : Human Kinetics, c1999.
*TC GV482.6 .A38 1999*

**SPORTS.** *See also* DOPING IN SPORTS; OLYMPICS; PHYSICAL EDUCATION AND TRAINING; RACING; SCHOOL SPORTS.
Foss, Merle L., 1936- Fox's physiological basis for exercise and sport. 6th ed. / Merle L. Foss, Steven J. Keteyian. Boston, Mass. : WCB/McGraw-Hill, c1998.
*TC RC1235 .F65 1998*

**SPORTS AND STATE - HISTORY.**
Senn, Alfred Erich. Power, politics, and the Olympic Games. Champaign, IL : Human Kinetics, c1999.
*TC GV721.5 .S443 1999*

**SPORTS - ANTHROPOLOGICAL ASPECTS.**
Games, sports and cultures. Oxford ; New York : Berg, 2000.
*TC GV706.5 .G36 2000*

**SPORTS - CHINA - HISTORY.**
Sport and physical education in China. London ; New York : Routledge, 1999.
*TC GV651 .S655 1999*

**SPORTS - CROSS-CULTURAL STUDIES.**
Games, sports and cultures. Oxford ; New York : Berg, 2000.
*TC GV706.5 .G36 2000*

**SPORTS FACILITIES.** *See* SWIMMING POOLS.

**Sports for her.**
Hastings, Penny. Westport, Conn. ; London : Greenwood Press, 1999.
*TC GV709.18.U6 H37 1999*

**SPORTS FOR THE HANDICAPPED - UNITED STATES.**
Fink, Dale Borman, 1949- Making a place for kids with disabilities. Westport, Conn. : Praeger, 2000.
*TC GV183.6 .F56 2000*

**SPORTS FOR WOMEN.**
Hastings, Penny. Sports for her. Westport, Conn. ; London : Greenwood Press, 1999.
*TC GV709.18.U6 H37 1999*

**SPORTS FOR WOMEN - UNITED STATES - JUVENILE LITERATURE.**
Hastings, Penny. Sports for her. Westport, Conn. ; London : Greenwood Press, 1999.
*TC GV709.18.U6 H37 1999*

**Sports Illustrated photographers shooting the Olympics [videorecording].**
Sport photography today! [videorecording]. Minneapolis, Minn. : Media Loft, c1992.
*TC TR821 .S64 1992*

**SPORTS ILLUSTRATED (TIME, INC.).**
Sport photography today! [videorecording]. Minneapolis, Minn. : Media Loft, c1992.
*TC TR821 .S64 1992*

**SPORTS INJURIES.**
Sports injuries sourcebook ; 1st ed. Detroit, MI : Omnigraphics, c1999.
*TC RD97 .S736 1999*

**Sports injuries sourcebook ;** basic consumer health information about common sports injuries ... / edited by Heather E. Aldred. 1st ed. Detroit, MI : Omnigraphics, c1999. xiv, 606 p. ; 24 cm. (Health reference series) Includes bibliographical references and index. ISBN 0-7808-0218-7 (lib. bdg. : alk. paper) DDC 617.1/027
*1. Sports injuries. 2. Sports medicine. 3. Wounds and injuries. 4. Athletic Injuries. 5. Sports Medicine. I. Aldred, Heather E. TC RD97 .S736 1999*

**SPORTS - LITERARY COLLECTIONS.**
Crossing boundaries. Champaign, IL : Human Kinetics, c1999.
*TC PN6071.S62 C76 1999*

**SPORTS - MEDICAL ASPECTS.** *See* SPORTS MEDICINE.

**SPORTS MEDICINE.** *See* DOPING IN SPORTS.

**SPORTS MEDICINE.**
Foss, Merle L., 1936- Fox's physiological basis for exercise and sport. 6th ed. / Merle L. Foss, Steven J. Keteyian. Boston, Mass. : WCB/McGraw-Hill, c1998.
*TC RC1235 .F65 1998*

**SPORTS MEDICINE.**
Karlsson, Jan, 1940- Antioxidants and exercise. Champaign, IL : Human Kinetics, c1997.

*TC RB170 .K37 1997*
Sports injuries sourcebook ; 1st ed. Detroit, MI : Omnigraphics, c1999.
*TC RD97 .S736 1999*

**SPORTS MEDICINE.**
Sports injuries sourcebook ; 1st ed. Detroit, MI : Omnigraphics, c1999.
*TC RD97 .S736 1999*

**SPORTS MEDICINE - CONGRESSES.**
Fundacion Dr. Antonio Esteve. Symposium (7th : 1996 : Sitges, Spain) The clinical pharmacology of sport and exercise. Amsterdam ; New York : Elsevier Science B.V., Excerpta Medica, 1997.
*TC RC1230 .F86 1996*

**SPORTS MEDICINE - PERIODICALS.**
Canadian journal of applied sport sciences = Windsor, Ont. : Canadian Association of Sports Sciences,

Medicine and science in sports. Madison, Wisc.

**SPORTS - PERIODICALS.**
Canadian journal of applied sport sciences = Windsor, Ont. : Canadian Association of Sports Sciences,

**SPORTS PERSONNEL.** *See* ATHLETES.

**Sports Photography today! [videorecording] : Sports Illustrated photographers shooting the Olympics.**
Sport photography today! [videorecording]. Minneapolis, Minn. : Media Loft, c1992.
*TC TR821 .S64 1992*

**SPORTS - PHYSIOLOGICAL ASPECTS.**
Foss, Merle L., 1936- Fox's physiological basis for exercise and sport. 6th ed. / Merle L. Foss, Steven J. Keteyian. Boston, Mass. : WCB/McGraw-Hill, c1998.
*TC RC1235 .F65 1998*

Muller, Susan. Student study guide to accompany Fox's physiological basis for exercise and sport. 6th ed. Boston, Mass. : WCB/McGraw-Hill, c1998.
*TC RC1235 .F65 1998 guide*

**SPORTS - PHYSIOLOGY - CONGRESSES.**
Fundacion Dr. Antonio Esteve. Symposium (7th : 1996 : Sitges, Spain) The clinical pharmacology of sport and exercise. Amsterdam ; New York : Elsevier Science B.V., Excerpta Medica, 1997.
*TC RC1230 .F86 1996*

**SPORTS - PSYCHOLOGICAL ASPECTS.**
Eitzen, D. Stanley. Fair and foul. Lanham, Md. : Rowman & Littlefield Publishers, c1999.
*TC GV706.5 .E567 1999*

**SPORTS SCIENCES.** *See* PHYSICAL FITNESS; SPORTS MEDICINE.

**SPORTS - SOCIAL ASPECTS.**
Burstyn, Varda. The rites of men. Toronto ; Buffalo : University of Toronto Press, 1999.
*TC GV706.5 .B87 1999*

**SPORTS - SOCIAL ASPECTS - UNITED STATES.**
Sage, George Harvey. Power and ideology in American sport. 2nd ed. Champaign, IL : Human Kinetics, c1998.
*TC GV706.5 .S228 1998*

**SPORTS - SOCIOLOGICAL ASPECTS.**
Eitzen, D. Stanley. Fair and foul. Lanham, Md. : Rowman & Littlefield Publishers, c1999.
*TC GV706.5 .E567 1999*

Games, sports and cultures. Oxford ; New York : Berg, 2000.
*TC GV706.5 .G36 2000*

Giulianotti, Richard, 1966- Football. Cambridge, UK : Polity Press ; Malden, MA : Blackwell Publishers, 1999.
*TC GV943.9.S64 G576 1999*

Nixon, Howard L., 1944- A sociology of sport. Belmont : Wadsworth Pub. Co., c1996.
*TC GV706.5 .N58 1996*

Rinehart, Robert E., 1951- Players all. Bloomington : Indiana University Press, c1998.
*TC GV706.5 .R56 1998*

**SPORTS - TRAINING.** *See* PHYSICAL EDUCATION AND TRAINING.

**SPORTS TRAINING.** *See* PHYSICAL EDUCATION AND TRAINING.

**SPORTS - UNITED STATES - RELIGIOUS ASPECTS - HISTORY.**
Ladd, Tony. Muscular Christianity. Grand Rapids, Mich. : Baker Books, c1999.
*TC GV706.42 .L34 1999*

**Spotlight on literacy**
  (Gr.1 l.1) Read all about it. New York :
  Macmillan/McGraw-Hill, c1997.
  *TC LB1576 .S66 1997 Gr.1 l.1*

  (Gr.1 l.2) Out and about. New York : Macmillan/
  McGraw-Hill, c1997.
  *TC LB1576 .S66 1997 Gr.1 l.2*

  (Gr.1 l.3) Something new. New York : Macmillan/
  McGraw-Hill, c1997.
  *TC LB1576 .S66 1997 Gr.1 l.3*

  (Gr.1 l.4 u.1) Take a closer look. New York :
  Macmillan/McGraw-Hill, c1997.
  *TC LB1576 .S66 1997 Gr.1 l.4 u.1*

  (Gr.1 l.4 u.2) Surprises along the way:. New York :
  Macmillan/McGraw-Hill, c1997.
  *TC LB1576 .S66 1997 Gr.1 l.4 u.2*

  (Gr.1 l.5 u.1) Let's pretend. New York :
  Macmillan/McGraw-Hill, c1997.
  *TC LB1576 .S66 1997 Gr.1 l.5 u.1*

  (Gr.1 l.5 u.2) True-blue friends. New York :
  Macmillan/McGraw-Hill, c1997.
  *TC LB1576 .S66 1997 Gr.1 l.5 u.2*

  (Gr.2 l.6 u.1) Family fun:. New York : Macmillan/
  McGraw-Hill, c1997.
  *TC LB1576 .S66 1997 Gr.2 l.6 u.1*

  (Gr.2 l.6 u.2) Eureka. New York : Macmillan/
  McGraw-Hill, c1997.
  *TC LB1576 .S66 1997 Gr.2 l.6 u.2*

  (Gr.2 l.6 u.3) Better together. New York :
  Macmillan/McGraw-Hill, c1997.
  *TC LB1576 .S66 1997 Gr.2 l.6 u.3*

  (Gr.2 l.7 u.1) Penpals. New York : Macmillan/
  McGraw-Hill, c1997.
  *TC LB1576 .S66 1997 Gr.2 l.7 u.1*

  (Gr.2 l.7 u.2) Hand in hand. New York :
  Macmillan/McGraw-Hill, c1997.
  *TC LB1576 .S66 1997 Gr.2 l.7 u.2*

  (Gr.3 l.8 u.1) Good thinking. New York :
  Macmillan/McGraw-Hill, c1997.
  *TC LB1576 .S66 1997 Gr.3 l.8 u.1*

  (Gr.3 l.8 u.2) See for yourself. New York :
  Macmillan/McGraw-Hill, c1997.
  *TC LB1576 .S66 1997 Gr.3 l.8 u.2*

  (Gr.3 l.8 u.3) Family album. New York :
  Macmillan/McGraw-Hill, c1997.
  *TC LB1576 .S66 1997 Gr.3 l.8 u.3*

  (Gr.3 l.9 u.1) Community spirit. New York :
  Macmillan/McGraw-Hill, c1997.
  *TC LB1576 .S66 1997 Gr.3 l.9 u.1*

  (Gr.3 l.9 u.2) Forces of nature. New York :
  Macmillan/McGraw-Hill, c1997.
  *TC LB1576 .S66 1997 Gr.3 l.9 u.2*

  (Gr.3 l.9 u.3) Teamwork. New York : Macmillan/
  McGraw-Hill, c1997.
  *TC LB1576 .S66 1997 Gr.3 l.9 u.3*

  (Gr.4 l.10 u.1) Make a wish. New York :
  Macmillan/McGraw-Hill, c1997.
  *TC LB1576 .S66 1997 Gr.4 l.10 u.1*

  (Gr.4 l.10 u.2) Naturally. New York : Macmillan/
  McGraw-Hill, c1997.
  *TC LB1576 .S66 1997 Gr.4 l.10 u.2*

  (Gr.4 l.10 u.3) That's what friends are for. New
  York : Macmillan/McGraw-Hill, c1997.
  *TC LB1576 .S66 1997 Gr.4 l.10 u.3*

  (Gr.4 l.10 u.4) Pitch in. New York : Macmillan/
  McGraw-Hill, c1997.
  *TC LB1576 .S66 1997 Gr.4 l.10 u.4*

  (Gr.4 l.10 u.5) Memories to keep. New York :
  Macmillan/McGraw-Hill, c1997.
  *TC LB1576 .S66 1997 Gr.4 l.10 u.5*

  (Gr.4 l.10 u.6) Twice-told tales. New York :
  Macmillan/McGraw-Hill, c1997.
  *TC LB1576 .S66 1997 Gr.4 l.10 u.6*

  (Gr.5 l.11 u.1) Scenes of wonder. New York :
  Macmillan/McGraw-Hill, c1997.
  *TC LB1576 .S66 1997 Gr.5 l.11 u.1*

  (Gr.5 l.11 u.2) Worlds of change. New York :
  Macmillan/McGraw-Hill, c1997.
  *TC LB1576 .S66 1997 Gr.5 l.11 u.2*

  (Gr.5 l.11 u.3) Winning attitudes. New York :
  Macmillan/McGraw-Hill, c1997.

  (Gr.5 l.11 u.4) Getting to know you. New York :
  Macmillan/McGraw-Hill, c1997.
  *TC LB1576 .S66 1997 Gr.5 l.11 u.4*

  (Gr.5 l.11 u.5) Take the high road. New York :
  Macmillan/McGraw-Hill, c1997.
  *TC LB1576 .S66 1997 Gr.5 l.11 u.5*

  (Gr.5 l.11 u.6) Zoom in. New York : Macmillan/
  McGraw-Hill, c1997.
  *TC LB1576 .S66 1997 Gr.5 l.11 u.6*

  (Gr.6 l.12 u.1) Making the grade. New York :
  Macmillan/McGraw-Hill, c1997.
  *TC LB1576 .S66 1997 Gr.6 l.12 u.1*

  (Gr.6 l.12 u.2) Dare to discover. New York :
  Macmillan/McGraw-Hill, c1997.
  *TC LB1576 .S66 1997 Gr.6 l.12 u.2*

  (Gr.6 l.12 u.3) Unlikely heroes. New York :
  Macmillan/McGraw-Hill, c1997.
  *TC LB1576 .S66 1997 Gr.6 l.12 u.3*

  (Gr.6 l.12 u.4) Time & time again. New York :
  Macmillan/McGraw-Hill, c1997.
  *TC LB1576 .S66 1997 Gr.6 l.12 u.4*

  (Gr.6 l.12 u.5) Coming home. New York :
  Macmillan/McGraw-Hill, c1997.
  *TC LB1576 .S66 1997 Gr.6 l.12 u.5*

  (Gr.6 l.12 u.6) Call it courage. New York :
  Macmillan/McGraw-Hill, c1997.
  *TC LB1576 .S66 1997 Gr.6 l.12 u.6*

**Spots.**
  Lesser, Carolyn. 1st ed. San Diego : Harcourt Brace,
  c1999.
  *TC QA113 .L47 1999*

**SPOUSES.** *See* **MARRIED PEOPLE.**

**Spriestersbach, D. C.**
  Diagnosis in speech-language pathology. 2nd ed. San
  Diego : Singular, c2000.
  *TC RC423 .D473 2000*

**Spring, Christopher.** North African textiles /
  Christopher Spring & Julie Hudson. Washington,
  D.C. : Smithsonian Institution Press, c1995. 143 p. : ill.
  (some col.) ; 28 cm. Includes bibliographical references (p.
  140-141) and index. ISBN 1-56098-666-2 DDC 746/.0961
  *1. Textile fabrics - Africa, North. 2. Textile fabrics, Islamic -*
  *Africa, North. 3. Costume - Africa, North. I. Hudson, Julie. II.*
  *Title.*
  *TC NK8887.6 .S68 1995*

**SPRING - FOLKLORE.** *See* **MAY DAY.**

**Spring, Joel H.** Deculturalization and the struggle for
  equality : a brief history of the education of dominated
  cultures in the United States / Joel Spring. 3rd ed.
  Boston : McGraw-Hill, c2001. xii, 125 p. ; 24 cm.
  Includes bibliographical references and index. ISBN
  0-07-232275-6 (pbk. : alk. paper) DDC 371.829
  *1. Minorities - Education - United States - History. 2.*
  *Discrimination in education - United States - History. 3.*
  *Segregation in education - United States - History. 4.*
  *Multicultural education - United States - History. I. Title.*
  *TC LC3731 .S68 2001*

  The universal right to education : justification,
  definition, and guidelines / Joel Spring. Mahwah,
  N.J. ; London : Lawrence Erlbaum Associates, 2000.
  x, 191 p. ; 24 cm. (Sociocultural, political, and historical
  studies in education) Includes bibliographical references (p.
  165-178) and index. ISBN 0-8058-3547-4 (hbk. : alk. paper)
  ISBN 0-8058-3548-2 (pbk. : alk. paper) DDC 379.2/6
  *1. Right to education. 2. Human rights - Study and teaching. I.*
  *Title. II. Series.*
  *TC LC213 .S67 2000*

**SPRING WHEAT.** *See* **WHEAT.**

**Springer, Jane.**
  Thomas, Barb, 1946- Combatting racism in the
  workplace. Toronto : Cross Cultural Communication
  Centre, c1983.
  *TC HD4903.5.C3 T56 1983*

**Springer, Judith W., 1938-.**
  American Society for Training and Development.
  Issues in career and human resource development.
  Madison, Wisc. : American Society for Training and
  Development, c1980.
  *TC HF5549.5.T7 A59 1980*

**Springer series, focus on women (Unnumbered)**
  Redman, Barbara Klug. Women's health needs in
  patient education. New York : Springer Pub. Co.,
  c1999.
  *TC R727.4 .R43 1999*

**Springer series on the teaching of nursing**
  Gaberson, Kathleen B. Clinical teaching strategies in
  nursing. New York : Springer, c1999.
  *TC RT73 .G26 1999*

  Integrating community service into nursing education.
  New York, NY : Springer Pub. Co., c1999.
  *TC RT76 .I55 1999*

**Springer series on the teaching of nursing**
  **(Unnumbered).**
  Schoolcraft, Victoria. A nuts-and-bolts approach to
  teaching nursing. 2nd ed. New York : Springer Pub.
  Co., c2000.
  *TC RT71 .S26 2000*

**Springer texts in statistics**
  Bilodeau, Martin, 1961- Theory of multivariate
  statistics. New York : Springer, c1999.
  *TC QA278 .B55 1999*

**Springhouse Corporation.**
  Nurse practitioner's clinical companion. Springhouse,
  Pa. : Springhouse Corp., c2000.
  *TC RT82.8 .N8638 2000*

  Nurse's legal handbook. 4th ed. Springhouse, Pa. :
  Springhouse Corp., c2000.
  *TC RT86.7 .N88 2000*

  Nursing procedures. 3rd ed. Springhouse, Pa. :
  Springhouse Corp., c2000.
  *TC RT41 .N886 2000*

**Springhouse notes**
  Grant, Ann Boyle. Nursing leadership, management &
  research. Springhouse, Pa. : Springhouse Corp.,
  c1999.
  *TC RT89 .G727 1999*

**Sprog og kulturmøde**
  (22.) Interactional perspectives on LSP. Aalborg
  Øst, Denmark : Centre for Languages and
  Intercultural Studies, Aalborg University, 1997.
  *TC P120.S9 I58 1997*

**Spruijt-Metz, Donna.** Adolescence, affect and health /
  Donna Spruijt-Metz. Hove : Psychology Press, for the
  European Association for Research on Adolescence,
  1999. xvii, 221 p. : ill. ; 25 cm. (Studies in adolescent
  development.) Includes bibliographical references and index.
  ISBN 0-86377-518-7
  *1. Adolescent psychology. 2. Health education (Secondary). 3.*
  *Teenagers - Health and hygiene. I. European Association for*
  *Research on Adolescence. II. Title. III. Series.*
  *TC RJ47.53 .S67 1999*

**Spurlin, William J., 1954-.**
  Lesbian and gay studies and the teaching of English.
  Urbana, Ill. : National Council of Teachers of English,
  2000.
  *TC PE66 .L45 2000*

**Spurlock, Jeanne.**
  Canino, Ian A. Culturally diverse children and
  adolescents. 2nd ed. New York : Guilford Press,
  c2000.
  *TC RJ507.M54 C36 2000*

**Squiers, Carol, 1948-.**
  Over exposed. New York : New Press, c1999.
  *TC TR642 .O94 1999*

**Sreberny, Annabelle.**
  Gender, politics and communication. Cresskill, N.J. :
  Hampton Press, c2000.
  *TC P94.5.W65 G46 2000*

**SRI LANKA - RELIGIOUS LIFE AND CUSTOMS.**
  Nürnberger, Marianne, 1956- [Tanz ist die Sprache
  der Götter. English] Dance is the language of the
  gods. Amsterdam : VU University Press, 1998.
  *TC GV1703.S74 .N8713 1998*

**Sri Lanka studies in the humanities and the social**
  **sciences**
  (5.) Nürnberger, Marianne, 1956- [Tanz ist die
  Sprache der Götter. English] Dance is the language
  of the gods. Amsterdam : VU University Press,
  1998.
  *TC GV1703.S74 .N8713 1998*

**Srole, Leo.** Personal history & health : the Midtown
  Longitudinal Study, 1954-1974 / Leo Srole, Ernest
  Joel Millman. New Brunswick, N.J. : Transaction
  Publishers, c1998. x, 204 p. ; 24 cm. Includes
  bibliographical references and index. ISBN 1-56000-325-1
  (alk. paper) DDC 362.2/0422
  *1. Mental health - United States - Longitudinal studies. 2.*
  *Mental illness - United States - Longitudinal studies. 3. Mental*
  *illness - Forecasting - Longitudinal studies. I. Millman, Ernest*
  *Joel. II. Title. III. Title: Personal history and health*
  *TC RA790.6 .S7 1998*

**The SSR handbook.**
Pilgreen, Janice L. Portsmouth, NH : Boynton/Cook Publishers, c2000.
*TC LB1050.55 .P55 2000*

**St. Andrews studies in Reformation history**
Anglo-Dutch Historical Conference (13th : 1997) The education of a Christian society. Aldershot, Hants, England : Brookfield, Vt. : Ashgate, c1999.
*TC BR377 .E38 1999*

**St. Christopher's Hospital for Children (Philadelphia, Pa.).**
Symposium on Issues in Human Development (1967 : Philadelphia) Issues in human development: Washington, For sale by the Supt. of Docs., U. S. Govt. Print. Off. [1970?]
*TC RJ131.A1 S93 1967*

**St. Paul.**
Mendelssohn-Bartholdy, Felix, 1809-1847. [Paulus. Vocal score. English] Saint Paul; New York, G. Schirmer [19--]
*TC M2003.M53 S35*

**St. Pierre, Elizabeth.**
Working the ruins. New York ; London : Routledge, 2000.
*TC LC197 .W67 2000*

**Staatspersonalverband des Kantons Luzern.**
Korrespondenz-blatt. Luzern : Luzerner Staatspersonalverband, 1947-

**Stacey, David, 1955-.**
Nash, Walter. Creating texts. London ; New York : Longman, 1997.
*TC PE1408 .N22 1997*

**Stack, Robert.**
Bright beginnings [videorecording. Burbank, CA : RCA/Columbia Pictures Home Video ; Toluca Lake, CA : [Distributed by] Corporate Productions, c1991.
*TC HV1642 .B67 1991*

Bright beginnings [videorecording. Burbank, CA : RCA/Columbia Pictures Home Video ; [S.l. : Distributed by] Rank Video Services America, c1991.
*TC HV1642 .B67 1991*

**Staff and education development series (New Delhi, India)**
Staff development in higher and distance education. New Delhi : Aravali Books International, 1997.
*TC LB2331 .S692 1997*

**Staff and educational development series.**
Benchmarking and threshold standards in higher education. London : Kogan Page, c1999.
*TC LB2341.8.G7 B463 1999*

Computer-assisted assessment in higher education. London : Kogan Page, 1999.
*TC LB2366 .C65 1999*

Inspiring students :. London : Kogan Page, 1999.
*TC LB1065 .I57 1999*

**STAFF DEVELOPMENT.**
Shelton, Patrick J. Measuring and improving patient satisfaction. Gaithersburg, Md. : Aspen Publishers, 2000.
*TC RA399.A1 S47 2000*

**Staff development in higher and distance education /** edited by Santosh Panda. New Delhi : Aravali Books International, 1997. x, 231 p. ; 25 cm. ([Staff and educational development series]) Series statement from jacket. Includes bibliographical references and index. SUMMARY: In the Indian context; contributed articles. ISBN 81-86880-00-3
*1. College teaching - India. 2. College teachers - In-service training - India. 3. Education, Higher - India. 4. Universities and colleges - India. 5. Continuing education - India. I. Panda, Santosh K. (Santosh Kumar), 1959- II. Series: Staff and education development series (New Delhi, India)*
*TC LB2331 .S692 1997*

**Staff development in open and flexible learning /** edited by Colin Latchem and Fred Lockwood. London ; New York : Routledge, 1998. xxv, 286 p. ; ill. ; 25 cm. (Routledge studies in distance education) Includes bibliographical references and indexes. ISBN 0-415-17376-0 (HB) ISBN 0-415-17390-6 (PB) DDC 378/.03
*1. Distance education. 2. Open learning. 3. College teachers - In-service training. I. Latchem, C. R. (Colin R.) II. Lockwood, Fred. III. Series.*
*TC LC5800 .S83 1998*

**Staff, parents, and politics in Head Start.**
Sissel, Peggy A. New York ; London : Falmer Press, 2000.
*TC LC4091 .S49 2000*

**Staffing at-risk school districts in Texas.**
Kirby, Sheila Nataraj, 1946- Santa Monica, CA : Rand, 1999.
*TC LB2833.3.T4 K57 1999*

**STAFFING INDUSTRY.** *See* **EMPLOYMENT AGENCIES.**

**Staffing management and methods :** tools and techniques for nursing leaders / Maryann F. Fralic, editor. San Francisco : Jossey-Bass, 2000. xxviii, 220 p. : ill. ; 23 cm. (AONE management series) Includes bibliographical references and index. ISBN 0-7879-5536-1
*1. Personnel Staffing and Scheduling - organization & administration - Nurses' Instruction. I. Fralic, Maryann F. II. American Organization of Nurse Executives. III. Series.*
*TC RT89.3 .S72 2000*

**STAGE.** *See* **ACTING; DRAMA; THEATER.**

**STAGE COSTUME.** *See* **COSTUME.**

**Stage, Frances K.**
Linking theory to practice. 2nd ed. Philadelphia, Pa. : Taylor and Francis, 2000.
*TC LB2342.9 .L56 2000*

**Stahl, Saul.** Real analysis : a historical approach / Saul Stahl. New York : J. Wiley, c1999. xiii, 269 p. : ill. ; 24 cm. "A Wiley-Interscience publication." Includes bibliographical references (p. [264]-[266]) and index. ISBN 0-471-31852-3 (cloth : alk. paper) DDC 515
*1. Mathematical analysis. 2. Functions of real variables. I. Title.*
*TC QA300 .S882 1999*

**Staines, Gail M., 1961-** Social sciences research : writing strategies for students / Gail M. Staines, Mark Bonacci, and Katherine Johnson. Lanham, Md. ; London : Scarecrow Press, 2000. x, 107 p. : ill. ; 23 cm. Includes bibliographical references (p. 103) and index. ISBN 0-8108-3686-6 (hbk.) ISBN 0-8108-3716-1 (pbk.) DDC 300/.7/2
*1. Social sciences - Research - Methodology. 2. Social sciences - Study and teaching (Higher) I. Bonacci, Mark A. II. Johnson, Katherine. 1958- III. Title.*
*TC H62 .S736 2000*

**Stalin's school.**
Holmes, Larry E. (Larry Eugene), 1942- Pittsburgh, Pa. : University of Pittsburgh Press, c1999.
*TC LF4435.M657 H65 1999*

**Stambach, Amy, 1966-** Lessons from Mount Kilimanjaro : schooling, community, and gender in East Africa / Amy Stambach. New York : Routledge, 2000. xv, 206 p. : ill., 1 map ; 23 cm. Includes bibliographical references (p. 187-199) and index. ISBN 0-415-92582-7 (hb) ISBN 0-415-92583-5 (pb) DDC 306.43/09678/26
*1. Education - Social aspects - Tanzania - Kilimanjaro Region. 2. Sex discrimination in education - Tanzania - Kilimanjaro Region. 3. Educational anthropology - Tanzania - Kilimanjaro Region. I. Title. II. Title: Mount Kilimanjaro*
*TC LA1844.K54 S72 2000*

**STAMINA, PHYSICAL.** *See* **PHYSICAL FITNESS.**

**STAMMERING.** *See* **STUTTERING.**

**Stanback, Thomas M.** Cities in transition : changing job structures in Atlanta, Denver, Buffalo, Phoenix, Columbus (Ohio), Nashville, Charlotte / Thomas M. Stanback, Jr., Thierry J. Noyelle ; foreword by Eli Ginzberg. Totowa, N.J. : Allanheld, Osmun, 1982. xv, 180 p. ; 24 cm. (LandMark studies) (Conservation of human resources series ; 15) Includes bibliographical references (p.71-173) and index. ISBN 0-86598-080-2 DDC 331.11/8/0973
*1. Labor supply - United States. 2. United States - Economic conditions - Regional disparities. 3. Income distribution - United States. 4. Labor mobility - United States. 5. Working class - United States. 6. White collar workers - United States. 7. Service industries - United States. 8. Metropolitan areas - United States. I. Noyelle, Thierry J. II. Title. III. Series.*
*TC HD5724 .S649 1982*

**Standard Deviants (Performing Group).**
The nutty, nougat-filled world of human nutrition [videorecording]. [Arlington, Va.] : Cerebellum Corp., c1998.
*TC QP141 .N8 1998*

The salsa-riffic world of Spanish [videorecording]. [Arlington, Va.] : Cerebellum Corp., c1998.
*TC PC4112.7 .S25 1998*

**Standard Deviants' present Human nutrition [videorecording].**
The nutty, nougat-filled world of human nutrition [videorecording]. [Arlington, Va.] : Cerebellum Corp., c1998.
*TC QP141 .N8 1998*

**Standard Deviants present Spanish [videorecording].**
The salsa-riffic world of Spanish [videorecording]. [Arlington, Va.] : Cerebellum Corp., c1998.
*TC PC4112.7 .S25 1998*

**Standard Deviants video course review**
The salsa-riffic world of Spanish [videorecording]. [Arlington, Va.] : Cerebellum Corp., c1998.
*TC PC4112.7 .S25 1998*

**Standard Deviants video course review presents ...**
The salsa-riffic world of Spanish [videorecording]. [Arlington, Va.] : Cerebellum Corp., c1998.
*TC PC4112.7 .S25 1998*

**STANDARD LANGUAGE.**
Milroy, James. Authority in language. 3rd ed. London [England] ; New York : Routledge, 1999.
*TC P368 .M54 1999*

**Standardized minds.**
Sacks, Peter. Cambridge, Mass. : Perseus Books, c1999.
*TC LB4051 .S22 1999*

**Standards.**
Lockwood, Anne Turnbaugh. Thousand Oaks, Calif. : Corwin Press, c1998.
*TC LB3060.83 .L63 1998*

**STANDARDS AND STANDARDIZATION IN EDUCATION.** *See* **EDUCATION - STANDARDS.**

**Standards-based K-12 language arts curriculum :** a focus on performance / William J. Agnew, editor. Boston : Allyn and Bacon, c2000. xviii, 174 p. ; 24 cm. Includes bibliographical references (p.170 ) and index. ISBN 0-205-28971-1 DDC 428/.0071
*1. Language arts - United States. 2. Language arts - Standards - United States. I. Agnew, William J.*
*TC LB1576 .S747 2000*

**Standards in practice.**
Ort, Suzanne Wichterle. 1999.
*TC 06 no. 11210*

**Standards in the classroom.**
Kordalewski, John. New York ; London : Teachers College Press, c2000.
*TC LB3060.83 .K67 2000*

**Stanford, Lynn.**
Ballet class [videorecording]. W. Long Branch, NJ : Kultur, c1984.
*TC GV1589 .B33 1984*

**Stanford, Michael. 1923-.**
A First dictionary of cultural literacy. Boston : Houghton Mifflin, 1989.
*TC AG105 .F43 1989*

**Stanford University.**
Joncas, Richard, 1953- 1st ed. New York : Princeton Architectural Press, 1999.
*TC LD3031 .J65 1999*

**STANFORD UNIVERSITY - BUILDINGS.**
Joncas, Richard, 1953- Stanford University. 1st ed. New York : Princeton Architectural Press, 1999.
*TC LD3031 .J65 1999*

**STANFORD UNIVERSITY - BUILDINGS - HISTORY.**
Joncas, Richard, 1953- Stanford University. 1st ed. New York : Princeton Architectural Press, 1999.
*TC LD3031 .J65 1999*

**STANFORD UNIVERSITY - BUILDINGS - PICTORIAL WORKS.**
Joncas, Richard, 1953- Stanford University. 1st ed. New York : Princeton Architectural Press, 1999.
*TC LD3031 .J65 1999*

**STANFORD UNIVERSITY - GUIDEBOOKS.**
Joncas, Richard, 1953- Stanford University. 1st ed. New York : Princeton Architectural Press, 1999.
*TC LD3031 .J65 1999*

**Stanford University. School of Education.**
Junior college journal. Washington, D.C. [etc.]

**Stanley, Deborah B.** Practical steps to the research process for high school / Deborah B. Stanley. Englewood, Colo. : Libraries Unlimited, 1999. xvii, 230 p. : ill. ; 28 cm. (Information literacy series) Includes bibliographical references (p. 227-228) and index. ISBN 1-56308-762-6 DDC 027.62/6
*1. Library orientation for high school students - United States. I. Title. II. Series.*
*TC Z711.2 .S72 1999*

**Stanovich, Keith E., 1950-** Progress in understanding reading : scientific foundations and new frontiers / Keith E. Stanovich ; foreword by Isabel L. Beck. New York : Guilford Press, c2000. xxiii, 536 p. ; 25 cm.

Includes bibliographical references (p. 421-511) and indexes. ISBN 1-57230-564-9 (cloth) ISBN 1-57230-565-7 (pbk.) DDC 428.4
*1. Reading. 2. Reading. Psychology of. I. Title.*
**TC LB1050 .S723 2000**

**Star split.**
Lasky, Kathryn. 1st ed. New York : Hyperion Books for Children, 1999.
**TC PZ7.L3274 St 1999**

**Stark, James A. (James Arthur), 1938-** Bel canto : a history of vocal pedagogy / James Stark. Toronto : University of Toronto Press, c1999. xxv, 325 p. : ill. ; 24 cm. Includes bibliographical references (p. [267]-299) and index. ISBN 0-8020-4703-3 DDC 783/.043/09
*1. Singing - History. 2. Bel canto. 3. Chant - Histoire. 4. Bel canto. I. Title.*
**TC MT823 S795 1999**

**Stark, Peggy L., 1949-.**
Erlandson, David A. Organizational oversight. Princeton, NJ : Eye on Education, c1996.
**TC LB2805 .E75 1996**

**Starke, Linda.**
Brown, Lester Russell, 1934- Vital signs 2000 :. New York : Norton, c2000.
**TC HD75.6 .B768 2000**

**Starkey, Margaret M.**
Christ, Henry I. (Henry Irving), 1915- Modern English in action. Lexington, Mass. : D. C. Heath, 1975
**TC PE1112 .C47 1975**

**Starr, Irving S.**
Clark, Leonard H. Secondary and middle school teaching methods. 7th ed. Englewood Cliffs, N.J. : Merrill, c1996.
**TC LB1737.A3 C53 1996**

**STARS.** *See also* **BLACK HOLES (ASTRONOMY).**
Stephen Hawking's universe [videorecording]. [Alexandria, Va.] : PBS Video; Burbank, CA : Distributed by Warner Home Video, c1997.
**TC QB982 .S7 1997**

**STARS - CONSTITUTION.**
Stephen Hawking's universe [videorecording]. [Alexandria, Va.] : PBS Video; Burbank, CA : Distributed by Warner Home Video, c1997.
**TC QB982 .S7 1997**

**Starting off.** Teacher's ed. Lexington, Mass. : D.C. Heath and Company, c1986. T30, 375 p. : ill. (some col.) ; 22x28 cm. (Heath American readers ; R) Includes index. ISBN 0-669-08044-6
*1. Readers (Primary) 2. Reading (Primary) I. Series.*
**TC PE1119 .S82 1986 Teacher's Ed.**

**Starting over** [videorecording] : the long road back / producer & director, Janet Gardner ; screenwriter, Janet Gardner ; Cambridge Educational. [Charleston, W.V.] : Cambridge Educational, c1994. 1 videorecording (35 min.) : sd., col. ; 1/2 in. (Running away, dropping out) At head of title: Cambridge Educational. VHS. Catalogued from credits, cassette label and container. Narrator, Eric Conger. Children of the Night music written and performed by Richard Marx, Chi-Boy Productions; directors of photography, Len McClure, Jim Nickless; audio, Isak Ben Meir, Chris Nickless, Michael Greene; editors, Janet Gardner, Jessie Weiner, Marlo Paoll. Copyright holder: Cambridge Research Group, Ltd. "FFH 8078"--Label mounted on container. For pre-adolescents through adult. SUMMARY: Follows kids as they turn their lives around, become drug-free, change their attitudes and get jobs. Portraits three programs: Angel's Flight Shelter in Los Angeles, California, Covenant House in New York and Children of the Night in Van Nuys, California. Residents and counselors describe the rules and way of life in each shelter. Also depicts the homeless job situation in Fort Lauderdale, Florida.
*1. Runaway teenagers - California - Los Angeles. 2. Runaway teenagers - New York (State) - New York. 3. Runaway teenagers - Florida - Fort Lauderdale. 4. Homeless youth - California - Los Angeles. 5. Homeless youth - New York (State) - New York. 6. Homeless youth - Florida - Fort Lauderdale. 7. Homeless youth - Employment - United States. 8. Homeless youth - Drug use - United States. 9. Teenage prostitution - United States. 10. Runaway teenagers - United States - Family relationships. 11. Runaway teenagers - United States - Social conditions. 12. Runaway teenagers - Employment - United States. 13. Runaway teenagers - Drug use - United States. 14. Angel's Flight Shelter (Los Angeles, Calif.) 15. Covenant House (New York, N.Y.) 16. Children of the Night (Van Nuys, Calif.) 17. Documentary films. I. Gardner, Janet. II. Conger, Eric. III. Cambridge Educational (Firm) IV. Cambridge Research Group, Ltd. V. Title: Cambridge Educational VI. Title: Long road back [videorecording] VII. Series.*

**TC HV1435.C3 S7 1994**

**STARVATION.** *See* **MALNUTRITION.**

**Starving for salvation.**
Lelwica, Michelle Mary. New York : Oxford University Press, 1999.
**TC RC552.E18 L44 1999**

**STATE AND ART.** *See* **ART AND STATE.**

**STATE AND CHURCH.** *See* **CHURCH AND STATE.**

**STATE AND EDUCATION.** *See* **EDUCATION AND STATE.**

**STATE AND ENVIRONMENT.** *See* **ENVIRONMENTAL POLICY.**

**STATE AND FAMILY.** *See* **FAMILY POLICY.**

**STATE AND HIGHER EDUCATION.** *See* **HIGHER EDUCATION AND STATE.**

**STATE AND INSURANCE.** *See* **SOCIAL SECURITY.**

**STATE AND ISLAM.** *See* **ISLAM AND STATE.**

**STATE AND LANGUAGE.** *See* **LANGUAGE POLICY.**

**STATE AND MEDICINE.** *See* **MEDICAL POLICY.**

**STATE AND NUTRITION.** *See* **NUTRITION POLICY.**

**STATE AND SCIENCE.** *See* **SCIENCE AND STATE.**

**STATE AND SPORTS.** *See* **SPORTS AND STATE.**

**STATE ARTS AGENCIES.** *See* **ART COMMISSIONS.**

**STATE BOARDS OF EDUCATION.** *See* **SCHOOL BOARDS.**

**STATE COLLEGES.** *See* **STATE UNIVERSITIES AND COLLEGES.**

**STATE GOVERNMENTS.** *See* **STATE-LOCAL RELATIONS.**

**STATE GOVERNMENTS - UNITED STATES - OFFICIALS AND EMPLOYEES - DIRECTORIES.**
CSG state directory. Directory I, Elective officials. Lexington, Ky. : The Council, c1998-
**TC JK2403 .S69**

CSG state directory. Directory III, Administrative officials. Lexington, Ky. : The Council, c1998-
**TC JK2403 .B6**

**State leadership directory. Directory I, State elective officials.**
CSG state directory. Directory I, Elective officials. Lexington, Ky. : The Council, c1998-
**TC JK2403 .S69**

**State leadership directory. Directory II, State legislative leadership, committees & staff.**
CSG state directory. Directory II, Legislative leadership, committees & staff. Lexington, Ky. : Council of State Governments, c1998-
**TC JK2495 .S688**

**State leadership directory. Directory III, State administrative officials classified by function.**
CSG state directory. Directory III, Administrative officials. Lexington, Ky. : The Council, c1998-
**TC JK2403 .B6**

**STATE-LOCAL RELATIONS - UNITED STATES.**
Kahn, Alfred J., 1919- Big cities in the welfare transition. New York City : Cross-National Studies Research Program, Columbia University School of Social Work, 1998.
**TC HV91 .K27 1998**

**STATE MINISTRIES.** *See* **EXECUTIVE DEPARTMENTS.**

**State of health series**
The global challenge of health care rationing. Buckingham [England] : Philadelphia : Open University Press, 2000.
**TC RA394.9 .G56 2000**

**STATE PARKS.** *See* **PARKS.**

**STATE PLANNING.** *See* **ECONOMIC POLICY.**

**State schools :** new Labour and the Conservative legacy / edited by Clyde Chitty and John Dunford. London ; Portland, OR : Woburn Press, 1999. viii, 168 p. ; 24 cm. (Woburn education series) Includes bibliographical references (p. [159]-163) and index. ISBN 0-7130-0214-X (cloth) ISBN 0-7130-4034-3 (pbk.) DDC 371.01/0941

*1. Public schools - Political aspects - Great Britain. 2. Education and state - Great Britain. I. Chitty, Clyde. II. Dunford, J. E. III. Series.*
**TC LC93.G7 S73 1999**

**STATE, THE.** *See* **CHURCH AND STATE; ISLAM AND STATE; POLITICAL SCIENCE; SCIENCE AND STATE.**

**STATE UNIVERSITIES AND COLLEGES - UNITED STATES - FINANCE - HISTORY.**
Oliver, Frank H. Fellow beggars. 1999.
**TC 06 no.11157**

**STATE UNIVERSITY OF NEW YORK AT ALBANY - GRADUATE WORK.**
North, Stephen M. Refiguring the Ph.D. in English studies. Urbana, Ill. : National Council of Teachers of English, c2000.
**TC PE69.A47 N67 2000**

**STATEHOOD (AMERICAN POLITICS).** *See* **STATE GOVERNMENTS.**

**STATESMEN.** *See* **LEGISLATORS; POLITICIANS.**

**STATESMEN - PORTUGAL - BIOGRAPHY.**
Maxwell, Kenneth, 1941- Pombal, paradox of the Enlightenment. Cambridge [England] ; New York, NY : Cambridge University Press, 1995.
**TC DP641 .M39 1995**

**STATESWOMEN.** *See* **STATESMEN.**

**STATICS AND DYNAMICS (SOCIAL SCIENCES).** *See* **ECONOMIC DEVELOPMENT.**

**STATIONS, MILITARY.** *See* **MILITARY BASES.**

**Statistical abstract of education, science, and culture.**
Statistical abstract of education, science, sports, and culture. [Tokyo] : Research and Statistics Planning Division, Minister's Secretariat, Ministry of Education, Science, Sports, and Culture, 1996-
**TC LA1310 .S73**

**Statistical abstract of education, science, and culture.**
[Tokyo] : Research and Statistics Division, Minister's Secretariat, Ministry of Education, Science, and Culture, Japan, v. ; 19 cm. Description based on: 1979 ed. Continued by: Statistical abstract of education, science, sports, and culture (DLC) 99124428 (OCoLC)35594476. DDC 370/.952
*1. Education - Japan - Statistics - Periodicals. 2. Japan - Statistics - Periodicals. I. Japan. Monbushō. Daijin Kanbō. Chōsa Tōkeika. II. Title: Statistical abstract of education, science, sports, and culture*
**TC LA1310 .S73**

**Statistical abstract of education, science, sports, and culture.**
Statistical abstract of education, science, and culture. [Tokyo] : Research and Statistics Division, Minister's Secretariat, Ministry of Education, Science, and Culture, Japan,
**TC LA1310 .S73**

**Statistical abstract of education, science, sports, and culture.** [Tokyo] : Research and Statistics Planning Division, Minister's Secretariat, Ministry of Education, Science, Sports, and Culture, 1996- v. ; 19 cm. Frequency: Annual. 1996 ed-. - Continues: Statistical abstract of education, science, and culture (OCoLC)7620353 (DLC) 81642696. DDC 370/.952
*1. Education - Japan - Statistics - Periodicals. 2. Japan - Statistics - Periodicals. I. Japan. Monbushō. Daijin Kanbō. Chōsa Tōkei Kikakuka. II. Title: Statistical abstract of education, science, and culture*
**TC LA1310 .S73**

**STATISTICAL ANALYSIS.** *See* **STATISTICS.**

**Statistical analysis report (National Center for Education Statistics)**
Vocational education in the United States. Washington, DC : U.S. Dept. of Education, Office of Educational Research and Improvement : For sale by the U.S. G.P.O., Supt. of Docs., [2000]
**TC LC1045 .V5874 2000**

**STATISTICAL DATA.** *See* **STATISTICS.**

**STATISTICAL DIAGRAMS.** *See* **STATISTICS - CHARTS, DIAGRAMS, ETC.**

**Statistical handbook on consumption and wealth in the United States** / edited by Chandrika Kaul and Valerie Tomaselli-Moschovitis. Phoenix, Ariz. : Oryx Press, 1999. xviii, 290 p. : ill. ; 29 cm. Includes index. ISBN 1-57356-251-3 (alk. paper) DDC 339.4/1/0973021
*1. Consumption (Economics) - United States - Statistics. 2. Wealth - United States - Statistics. I. Kaul, Chandrika. II. Tomaselli-Moschovitis, Valerie.*

*TC HC110.C6 S73 1999*

**Statistical handbook on racial groups in the United States.**
Heaton, Tim B. Phoenix, AZ : Oryx Press, 2000.
*TC E184.A1 H417 2000*

**The statistical handbook on technology.**
Berinstein, Paula. Phoenix, AZ : Oryx Press, 1999.
*TC T21 .B47 1999*

**STATISTICAL INFERENCE.** *See*
**MATHEMATICAL STATISTICS;**
**PROBABILITIES.**

**STATISTICAL METHODS.** *See* **STATISTICS.**

**Statistical yearbook of the Republic of China.** [Taipei]
Directorate-General of Budget, Accounting &
Statistics, Executive Yuan, Republic of China. v. ill. 30
cm. Frequency: Annual. 1975- . ISSN 0256-7857 DDC 315.1/
249
*1. Taiwan - Statistics - Periodicals. I. China (Republic : 1949-
). Chu chi ch'u.*

**[Statistical yearbook (Unesco)]** Statistical yearbook =
Annuaire statistique / Unesco. [Paris : Unesco], 1987-
v. ; 27-29 cm. Frequency: Annual. 1963- . Annuaire statistique.
Other title: Anuario estadístico 1976- . Other title: Unesco
statistical yearbook. SUMMARY: "Reference tables,
education, science and technology, and culture and
communication." Text in English and French. Continues: Basic
facts and figures (Unesco). ISSN 0082-7541
*1. Intellectual life - Statistics - Periodicals. 2. Literacy -
Statistics - Periodicals. I. Unesco. II. Title: Annuaire
statistique III. Title: Anuario estadístico 1976- IV. Title:
Unesco statistical yearbook V. Title: Basic facts and figures
(Unesco)*
*TC AZ361 .U45*

**STATISTICS.** *See also* **EDUCATIONAL**
**STATISTICS; MATHEMATICAL**
**STATISTICS; NUMERACY; SAMPLING**
**(STATISTICS).**
Andersen, Christopher Lawrence. A microgenetic
study of science reasoning in social context. 1998.
*TC 085 An2305*

Kendall, Maurice G. (Maurice George), 1907- The
advanced theory of statistics. 4th ed. London, C.
Griffin, 1948.
*TC QA276 .K4262 1948*

Kendall, Maurice George. The advanced theory of
statistics. 3d ed. New York, Hafner Pub. Co., 1951.
*TC QA276 .K38 1951*

Rydberg, Sven. Bias in prediction on correction
methods. Stockholm, Almqvist & Wiksell [1963]
*TC HA31.2 .R93*

**Statistics and neural networks :** advances at the
interface / edited by J.W. Kay and D.M. Titterington.
Oxford ; New York : Oxford University Press, 1999.
xvii, 260 p. : ill. ; 24 cm. Includes bibliographical references
and index. ISBN 0-19-852422-6 DDC 519.5/0285/632
*1. Mathematical statistics. 2. Neural computers. 3. Neural
networks (Computer science) I. Kay, J. W. (Jim W.) II.
Titterington, D. M.*
*TC QA276 .S78343 1999*

**Statistics Canada.**
International Adult Literacy Survey. Literacy in the
information age. Paris : Organisation for Economic
Co-operation and Development; Ottawa : Statistics
Canada, 2000.
*TC LC149 .L59 2000*

**STATISTICS - CHARTS, DIAGRAMS, ETC.**
Nicol, Adelheid A. M. Presenting your findings. 1st
ed. Washington, DC : American Psychological
Association, c1999.
*TC HA31 .N53 1999*

**STATISTICS - CHARTS, TABLES, ETC.** *See*
**STATISTICS - CHARTS, DIAGRAMS, ETC.**

**STATISTICS - HISTORY.**
Mitchell, B. R. (Brian R.) International historical
statistics. 4th ed. London : Macmillan Reference ;
New YorkGrove Dictionaries[division of : Stockton
Press], 1998.
*TC HA1107 .M55 1998*

**STATISTICS, MATHEMATICAL.** *See*
**MATHEMATICAL STATISTICS.**

**Statistics of deadly quarrels.**
Richardson, Lewis Fry, 1881-1953. Pacific Grove, Ca.
Boxwood Press [1960]
*TC U21.7 .R5 1960*

**STATISTICS OF SAMPLING.** *See* **SAMPLING**
**(STATISTICS).**

**Statistics on the table.**
Stigler, Stephen M. Cambridge, Mass. : Harvard
University Press, 1999.
*TC QA276.15 .S755 1999*

**STATISTICS - STUDY AND TEACHING.**
Handbook for teaching statistics and research
methods. 2nd ed. Mahwah, N.J. : Lawrence Erlbaum
Associates, c1999.
*TC QA276.18 .H36 1999*

**STATUE OF LIBERTY (NEW YORK, N.Y.).**
Maestro, Betsy. The story of the Statue of Liberty.
New York : Lothrop, Lee & Shepard Books, 1986.
*TC NB553.B3 A75 1986*

Maestro, Betsy. The story of the Statue of Liberty.
New York : Lothrop, Lee & Shepard Books, 1986.
*TC NB553.B3 A75 1986*

**STATUE OF LIBERTY (NEW YORK, N.Y.) -**
**JUVENILE LITERATURE.**
Maestro, Betsy. The story of the Statue of Liberty.
New York : Lothrop, Lee & Shepard Books, 1986.
*TC NB553.B3 A75 1986*

**STATUE OF LIBERTY (NEW YORK, N.Y.) -**
**POSTERS.**
Ellis Island [picture]. Amawalk, NY : Jackdaw
Publications, c1997.
*TC TR820.5 .E4 1997*

**STATUES.** *See also* **MONUMENTS; SCULPTURE.**
Maestro, Betsy. The story of the Statue of Liberty.
New York : Lothrop, Lee & Shepard Books, 1986.
*TC NB553.B3 A75 1986*

**STATUES - NEW YORK (STATE).** *See* **STATUE**
**OF LIBERTY (NEW YORK, N.Y.).**

**STATUETTES.** *See* **FIGURINES.**

**STATURE.** *See* **POSTURE.**

**STATURE, TALL.** *See* **GIANTS.**

**A status report on contemporary criminal justice**
**education.**
Nemeth, Charles P., 1951- Lewiston, NY, USA : E.
Mellen Press, c1989.
*TC HV7419.5 .N45 1989*

**STATUS, SOCIAL.** *See* **SOCIAL STATUS.**

**STAUCH, MARTIN - CONGRESSES.**
The physiology and pathophysiology of exercise
tolerance. New York : Plenum Press, c1996.
*TC QP301 .P576 1996*

**Stauffer, Marilyn H. Karrenbrock, 1936-.**
Gregory, Vicki L., 1950- Multicultural resources on
the Internet. The United States and Canada.
Englewood, Colo. : Libraries Unlimited, 1999.
*TC E184.A1 G874 1999*

**STD (DISEASES).** *See* **SEXUALLY**
**TRANSMITTED DISEASES.**

**STDS (DISEASES).** *See* **SEXUALLY**
**TRANSMITTED DISEASES.**

**Stealing innocence.**
Giroux, Henry A. 1st ed. New York : St. Martin's
Press, 2000.
*TC HM621 .G57 2000*

**Stearns, Peter N.**
World history in documents. New York : New York
University Press, c1998.
*TC D5 .W67 1998*

**Steele, Brenton H., 1942-.**
Deegan, William L. Translating theory into practice.
1st ed. [Columbus, Ohio] : National Association of
Student Personnel Administrators, c1985.
*TC LB2343 .D356 1985*

**Steele, Christy.**
Berry, Carrie, b. 1854. A Confederate girl. Mankato,
Minn. : Blue Earth Books, c2000.
*TC E605 .B5 2000*

Forten, Charlotte L. A free Black girl before the Civil
War. Mankato, Minn. : Blue Earth Books, c2000.
*TC F74.S1 F67 2000*

Hester, Sallie. A covered wagon girl. Mankato,
Minn. : Blue Earth Books, c2000.
*TC F593 .H47 2000*

**Steer, Dugald.** Just one more story / by Dugald Steer ;
illustrated by Elisabeth Moseng. New York : Dutton
Children's Books, 1999. 1 v. (unpaged) : col. ill. ; 27 cm.
Four booklets (11 cm.) are attached to pages through book.
"First published in Great Britain by Templar Publishing by
1999" -- Opposite of T.p. SUMMARY: Mother Pig reads
bedtime stories to her little pigs, including "The Pig Prince,"
"The Ugly Pigling," "Piggerella," and "the Prince and the

Porker." ISBN 0-525-46215-5 DDC [E]
*1. Toy and movable books - Specimens. 2. Bedtime - Fiction. 3.
Pigs - Fiction. 4. Books and reading - Fiction. 5. Fairy tales. 6.
Toy and movable books. I. Moseng, Elisabeth, ill. II. Title.*
*TC PZ7.S81534 Ju 1999*

**Steffen, Sally A.**
Ericksen, Julia A., 1941- Kiss and tell. Cambridge,
Mass. : Harvard University Press, 1999.
*TC HQ18.U5 E75 1999*

**Steffen, Thomas, Dr.**
Cost benefit analysis of heroin maintenance treatment.
Basel ; New York : Karger, c2000.
*TC RC568.H4 C67 2000*

**Steffy, Betty E.**
Life cycle of the career teacher. [Indianapolis, Ind.] :
Kappa Delta Pi ; Thousand Oaks, Calif. : Corwin
Press, c2000.
*TC LB1775.2 .L54 2000*

**Stefik, Mark.** The Internet edge : social, legal and
technological challenges for a networked world /
Mark Stefik. Cambridge, Mass. : MIT Press, c1999.
xviii, 320 p. ; 24 cm. Includes bibliographical references and
index. ISBN 0-262-19418-X DDC 306.4/6
*1. Internet (Computer network) - Social aspects. 2. Computers
and civilization. 3. Information society. I. Title.*
*TC HM851 .S74 1999*

**Stegner, Wallace Earle, 1909-** Angle of repose /
Wallace Stegner. New York : Modern Library, 2000.
ix, 632 p. ; 21 cm. ISBN 0-679-60338-7 (alk. paper) DDC
813/.52
*1. Domestic fiction. 2. Married people - Fiction. 3.
Grandparents - Fiction. 4. Aged - Fiction. 5. California -
Fiction. I. Title.*
*TC PS3537.T316 A8 2000*

**Stein, Astrid von.**
Understanding representation in the cognitive
sciences. New York : Kluwer Academic/Plenum
Publishers, c1999.
*TC BF316.6 U63 1999*

**Stein, Clarence S.** The writings of Clarence S. Stein :
architect of the planned community / edited by Kermit
Carlyle Parsons. Baltimore, Md. : Johns Hopkins
University Press, 1998. xxxvi, 717 p. : ill. ; 26 cm.
"Published in cooperation with the Center for American Places,
Harrisonburg, Virginia." Includes bibliographical references (p.
681-687) and index. ISBN 0-8018-5756-2 (acid-free paper)
DDC 711/.45
*1. City planning - United States - History - 20th century. 2.
Architecture, Modern - 20th century - United States. 3. Stein,
Clarence S. 4. Architects - United States - Biography. I.
Parsons, Kermit C. (Kermit Carlyle), 1927- II. Title. III. Title:
Clarence S. Stein*
*TC NA9108 .S83 1998*

**STEIN, CLARENCE S.**
Stein, Clarence S. The writings of Clarence S. Stein.
Baltimore, Md. : Johns Hopkins University Press,
1998.
*TC NA9108 .S83 1998*

**Stein, Edward, 1965-** The mismeasure of desire : the
science, theory, and ethics of sexual orientation /
Edward Stein. Oxford ; New York : Oxford University
Press, 1999. xi, 388 p. : ill. ; 24 cm. (Ideologies of desire)
Includes bibliographical references (p. 349-381) and index.
ISBN 0-19-509995-8 DDC 306.76/6
*1. Homosexuality - Research. 2. Homosexuality - Philosophy.
3. Homosexuality - Moral and ethical aspects. 4. Sexual
orientation - Research. 5. Sexual orientation - Philosophy. 6.
Sexual orientation - Moral and ethical aspects. I. Title. II.
Series.*
*TC HQ76.25 .S69 1999*

**Stein, Herbert, 1916-** What I think : essays on
economics, politics, and life / Herbert Stein.
Washington, D.C. : AEI Press, 1998. xi, 260 p. : ill. ; 24
cm. Includes bibliographical references. ISBN 0-8447-4097-7
(cloth : alk. paper) ISBN 0-8447-4098-5 (pbk. : alk. paper)
DDC 330.973/09
*1. United States - Economic conditions - 1945- 2. United
States - Economic policy - 1945- 3. United States - Politics and
government - 20th century. I. Title.*
*TC HC106.5 .S784 1998*

**Stein, Joan W** The family as a unit of study and
treatment, by Joan W. Stein; edited by Trova K.
Hutchins with the collaboration of Josephine Anna
Bates, Manzer J. Griswold [and] Robert Wesley
Macdonald. [Seattle] Regional Rehabilitation
Research Institute, University of Washington, School
of Social Work [1970] iii, 93 p. ; 23 cm. (Washington
(State) University. Regional Rehabilitation Research Institute.
Monograph 1) On cover: Region IX, Rehabilitation Research
Institute, University of Washington. "This investigation was
supported, in part, by Research grant no. RD-2104-G from the

Social and Rehabilitation Service, Department of Health, Education, and Welfare." Bibliography: p. 87-93.
*1. Family psychotherapy I. Hutchins, Trova K ed. II. Title. III. Series.*
**TC RC488.5 .S88**

**Stein, Lana, 1946-.**
Portz, John, 1953- City schools and city politics. Lawrence : University Press of Kansas, c1999.
**TC LC5131 .P67 1999**

**Stein, Laura W., 1963-** Sexual harassment in America : a documentary history / Laura W. Stein. Westport, Conn. : Greenwood Press, 1999. xxv, 297 p. ; 24 cm. (Primary documents in American history and contemporary issues, 1069-5605) Includes bibliographical references and index. ISBN 0-313-30184-0 (alk. paper) DDC 344.7301/4133
*1. Sexual harassment - Law and legislation - United States - History - Sources. 2. Sex discrimination in employment - Law and legislation - United States - History - Sources. I. Title. II. Series.*
**TC KF3467 .S74 1999**

**Stein, Mary Kay.**
Implementing standards-based mathematics instruction. New York : Teachers College Press, c2000.
**TC QA135.5 .I525 2000**

**Stein, Morris Isaac, 1921-.**
Evocative images. 1st ed. Washington, DC : American Psychological Association, c1999.
**TC BF698.8.T5 E96 1999**

**Stein, Sherman K.** Archimedes : what did he do besides cry eureka? / Sherman Stein. Washington, D.C. : Mathematical Association of America, c1999. x, 155 p. : ill. ; 23 cm. (Classroom resource materials) Includes bibliographical references (p. 149-152) and index. ISBN 0-88385-718-9 (pbk.)
*1. Archimedes. 2. Mathematics, Greek. I. Title. II. Series.*
**TC QA31 .S84 1999** ·

**Steinacker, Jürgen M.**
The physiology and pathophysiology of exercise tolerance. New York : Plenum Press, c1996.
**TC QP301 .P576 1996**

**Steinbach, Rosanne, 1942-.**
Leithwood, Kenneth A. Changing leadership for changing times. Buckingham ; Philadelphia : Open University Press, 1999.
**TC LB2805 .L358 1999**

**Steinberg, Adria.** CityWorks : exploring your community : a workbook / Adria Steinberg and David Stephen. New York : New Press, c1999. 184 p. : ill. ; 24 cm. City works : exploring your community. ISBN 1-56584-416-5
*1. Community - Study and teaching (Secondary) I. Stephen, David. II. Title. III. Title: City works : exploring your community*
**TC LC1036 .S74 1999**

Schooling for the real world : the essential guide to rigorous and relevant learning / Adria Steinberg, Kathleen Cushman, Robert Riordan ; with foreword by Theodore R. Sizer. 1st ed. San Francisco : Jossey-Bass, c1999. xxi, 105 p. ; 28 cm. (The Jossey-Bass education series) Includes bibliographical references (p. 94-98) and index. URL: http://www.JosseyBass.com/catalog/isbn/0-7879-5041-6/ CONTENTS: Two visions, one purpose -- Teaching and learning in real-world contexts -- Changing the whole school -- Creating circles of community support -- Resources for practitioners. ISBN 0-7879-5041-6 (perm. paper) DDC 370.11/3/0973
*1. School-to-work transition - United States. 2. Career education - United States. 3. School improvement programs - United States. I. Cushman, Kathleen. II. Riordan, Robert C. III. Title. IV. Series.*
**TC LC1037.5 .S843 1999**

**Steinberg, Laurence D., 1952-** Adolescence / Laurence Steinberg. 5th ed. Boston : McGraw-Hill College, c1999. xxii, 519 p. : ill. (some col.) ; 27 cm. Includes bibliographical references (p. 436-494) and indexes. ISBN 0-07-001323-3
*1. Adolescent psychology. I. Title.*
**TC BF724 .S75 1999**

**Steinberg, Shirley R., 1952-.**
Kincheloe, Joe L. The stigma of genius. New York ; Canterbury [England] : P. Lang, c1999.
**TC LB875.E562 K56 1999**

Thinking queer. New York : Peter Lang, c2000.
**TC LC192.6 .T55 2000**

**Steiner-Adair, Catherine.**
Preventing eating disorders. Philadelphia, PA : Brunner/Mazel, c1999.
**TC RC552.E18 P744 1999**

**Steiner, Joan (Joan Catherine)** Look-alikes, jr. / Joan Steiner ; photography by Thomas Lindley. 1st ed. Boston : Little, Brown, c1999. 1 v. : col. ill. ; 32 cm. SUMMARY: Simple verses challenge readers to identify the everyday objects used to construct eleven three-dimensional scenes, including a house, kitchen, bedroom, school bus, train, farm, and rocket. ISBN 0-316-81307-9 DDC 793.73
*1. Picture puzzles - Juvenile literature. 2. Picture puzzles. I. Lindley, Thomas, ill. II. Title. III. Title: Look-alikes, junior*
**TC GV1507.P47 S747 1999**

**Steiner, Rudolf, 1861-1925.**
**Curative education.**
Steiner, Rudolf, 1861-1925. [Heilpädagogischer Kurs. English] Education for special needs. [New ed.]. London : Rudolf Steiner Press, 1998.
**TC LB1029.W34 S73 1998**

**[Heilpädagogischer Kurs. English]**
Education for special needs : the curative education course : twelve lectures for doctors and teachers given at Dornach between 25 June and 7 July 1924 / Rudolf Steiner. [New ed.]. London : Rudolf Steiner Press, 1998. vii, 232 p., [15] p. of plates : ill. (some col.) ; 22 cm. Previous ed.: i.e. 2nd ed. 1993; 1st ed. published as Curative education. 1972. Includes index. Translated from the German. ISBN 1-85584-042-1 DDC 371.39
*1. Steiner, Rudolf, - 1861-1925 - Contributions in special education. 2. Special education. 3. Waldorf method of education. 4. Handicapped children - Education. I. Steiner, Rudolf, 1861-1925. Curative education. II. Title.*
**TC LB1029.W34 S73 1998**

**[Konferenzen mit den Lehrern der Freien Waldorfschule in Stuttgart. English]**
Faculty meetings with Rudolf Steiner / Rudolf Steiner ; translated by Robert Lathe & Nancy Parsons Whittaker. Hudson, NY : Anthroposophic Press, c1998. 2 v. (xxxviii, 811 p.) : ill. ; 22 cm. (Foundations of Waldorf education ; 8) Includes bibliographical references (v. 2, p. [791]-798) and index. CONTENTS: v. 1. 1919-1922 -- v. 2. 1922-1924. ISBN 0-88010-458-9 (set) ISBN 0-88010-421-X (v. 1 : pbk.) ISBN 0-88010-452-X (v. 2 : pbk.) DDC 371.39
*1. Freie Waldorfschule. 2. Freie Waldorfschule - Faculty. 3. Steiner, Rudolf, - 1861-1925. 4. Waldorf method of education. 5. Anthroposophy. I. Title. II. Series.*
**TC LF3195.S834 S8413 1998**

**STEINER, RUDOLF, 1861-1925.**
Steiner, Rudolf, 1861-1925. [Konferenzen mit den Lehrern der Freien Waldorfschule in Stuttgart. English] Faculty meetings with Rudolf Steiner. Hudson, NY : Anthroposophic Press, c1998.
**TC LF3195.S834 S8413 1998**

**STEINER, RUDOLF, 1861-1925 - CONTRIBUTIONS IN SPECIAL EDUCATION.**
Steiner, Rudolf, 1861-1925. [Heilpädagogischer Kurs. English] Education for special needs. [New ed.]. London : Rudolf Steiner Press, 1998.
**TC LB1029.W34 S73 1998**

**Steiner, Stanley F.**
Freirean pedagogy, praxis, and possibilities. New York : Falmer Press, 2000.
**TC LC196 .F76 2000**

**Steininger, Otto.**
Kale, Shelly. My museum journal. Los Angeles, CA : J. Paul Getty Museum, c2000.
**TC N7440 .K35 2000**

**Stemple, Joseph C.** Clinical voice pathology : theory and management / Joseph C. Stemple, Leslie Glaze, Bernice Klaben Gerdemann. 3rd ed. San Diego : Singular Pub. Group, c2000. xiii, 544 p. : ill. (some col.) ; 23 cm. Includes bibliographical references and index. ISBN 0-7693-0005-7 (soft cover : alk. paper) DDC 616.85/5
*1. Voice disorders. 2. Voice Disorders. I. Glaze, Leslie E. II. Gerdeman, Bernice K. III. Title.*
**TC RF510 .S74 2000**

**STENCIL PRINTING. See SERIGRAPHY.**

**STENCIL WORK. See SERIGRAPHY.**

**Stenhouse Publishers.**
What is visual literacy? York, Maine : Stenhouse Pub., c1996.
**TC LB1068 .W45 1996**

**Stenross, Barbara, 1946-** Missed connections : hard of hearing in a hearing world / Barbara Stenross. Philadelphia : Temple University Press, 1999. xii, 139 p. : ill. ; 22 cm. Includes bibliographical references (p. 123-124) and index. Table of Contents URL: http://lcweb.loc.gov/catdir/toc/98030716.html ISBN 1-56639-681-6 (alk. paper) ISBN 1-56639-682-4 (pbk. : alk. paper) DDC 362.1/978/092

*1. Stenross, Barbara. - 1946- 2. Hearing impaired - United States - Biography. I. Title.*
**TC RF291 .S74 1999**

**STENROSS, BARBARA, 1946-.**
Stenross, Barbara, 1946- Missed connections. Philadelphia : Temple University Press, 1999.
**TC RF291 .S74 1999**

**Stenstrom, Patricia.**
People come first. Chicago : Association of College and Research Libraries, 1999.
**TC Z674 .A75**

**Step on a crack** [videorecording] / written, produced and directed by Arlene Lorre. Boston, MA : Fanlight Productions, 1996. 1 videocassette (ca. 28 min.) : sd., col. ; 1/2 in. Subtitle on container: Video on obsessive compulsive disorder [videorecording]. VHS. Catalogued from credits and container. Editor, Beriau Picard ; audio, Wolf Bukowski ; music composed and performed by Stan Ayeroff. For adolescents through adult. SUMMARY: Six individuals discuss how obsessive compulsive disorder has affected their lives and how they have come to manage the disorder through medication, psychotherapy and behavioral therapy. ISBN 1-57295-222-9
*1. Obsessive-compulsive disorder. 2. Obsessive-compulsive disorder - Treatment. 3. Obsessive-compulsive disorder - Case studies. 4. Phobias - Treatment. I. Lorre, Arlene. II. Picard, Beriau. III. Bukowski, Wolf. IV. Ayeroff, Stan. V. Fanlight Productions. VI. Alef Pictures. VII. Title: Video on obsessive compulsive disorder [videorecording]*
**TC RC533 .S7 1996**

**STEP-PARENTS. See STEPPARENTS.**

**Stepansky, Paul E.** Freud, surgery, and the surgeons / Paul E. Stepansky. Hillsdale, NJ : Analytic Press, 1999. xix, 260 p. ; 24 cm. Includes bibliographical references and index. ISBN 0-88163-289-9 DDC 616.89/17
*1. Psychoanalysis - Philosophy. 2. Psychoanalysis - History. 3. Freud, Sigmund. - 1856-1939 - Views on surgery. 4. Surgery. 5. Metaphor. 6. Freud, Sigmund. - 1856-1939. 7. Psychoanalytic Therapy. 8. Surgery. 9. Metaphor. I. Title.*
**TC RC506 .S733 1999**

**STEPCHILDREN. See STEPMOTHERS.**

**STEPCHILDREN - CHINA - HONG KONG - FAMILY RELATIONSHIPS.**
Lam-Chan, Gladys Lan Tak. Parenting in stepfamilies. Aldershot ; Brookfield USA : Ashgate, c1999.
**TC HQ759.92 .L34 1999**

**STEPFAMILIES - CHINA - HONG KONG.**
Lam-Chan, Gladys Lan Tak. Parenting in stepfamilies. Aldershot ; Brookfield USA : Ashgate, c1999.
**TC HQ759.92 .L34 1999**

**STEPFAMILIES - FICTION.**
Delton, Judy. Angel spreads her wings. Boston : Houghton Mifflin, 1999.
**TC PZ7.D388 Anf 1999**

Griffin, Adele. Dive. 1st ed. New York : Hyperion Books for Children, 1999.
**TC PZ7.G881325 Di 1999**

**STEPFATHERS. See STEPCHILDREN.**

**Stephen, David.**
Steinberg, Adria. CityWorks. New York : New Press, c1999.
**TC LC1036 .S74 1999**

**Stephen Hawking's universe (Television program).**
Stephen Hawking's universe [videorecording]. [Alexandria, Va.] : PBS Video; Burbank, CA : Distributed by Warner Home Video, c1997.
**TC QB982 .S7 1997**

**Stephen Hawking's universe** [videorecording] / a Thirteen/WNET Associates/David Filkin Enterprises co-production in association with BBC-TV ; series producer, David Filkin ; series director, Philip Martin. [Alexandria, Va.] : PBS Video; Burbank, CA : Distributed by Warner Home Video, c1997. 3 videocassettes (360 min.) : sd., col. ; 1/2 in. VHS. Stereo. Catalogued from credits and container; cataloging based on volume 1. Closed captioned. Narrated by Frank Langella. Editor, Scott McEwing; camera, Jeff Baynes Piers Lello; sound, David Lindsay; music, Cynthia Millar. For general audiences. SUMMARY: Presents the latest advances in cosmological thought by one of today's most renowned scientists, Stephen Hawkings, including the mathematics of astronomy, the Big Bang theory of creation, the nature of matter, the discovery and implications of dark matter, quasars and black holes, and the question of how the Big Bang began. CONTENTS: v.1. Prog. 1. Seeing is believing; Prog. 2 The big bang (120 min.) -- v.2. Prog. 3. Cosmic alchemy; Prog. 4. On the dark side (120 min.) -- v.3. Prog. 5. Black holes and

beyond; Prog. 6. An answer to everything (120 min.) ISBN 0-7806-2023-2 (set) ISBN 0-7806-2024-0 (v. 1) ISBN 0-7806-2025-9 (v. 2) ISBN 0-7806-2026-7 (v. 3)
*1. Hawking, S. W. - (Stephen W.) 2. Cosmology. 3. Ptolemy, - 2nd cent. 4. Newton, Isaac. - Sir. - 1642-1727. 5. Einstein, Albert. - 1879-1955. 6. Hubble, Edwin Powell. - 1889-1953. 7. Big bang theory. 8. Expanding universe. 9. Superstring theories. 10. Unified field theories. 11. Interstellar matter. 12. Matter - Constitution. 13. Matter. 14. Chemical elements. 15. Periodic law. 16. Stars - Constitution. 17. Celestial mechanics. 18. Stars. 19. Dark matter (Astronomy) 20. Black holes (Astronomy) 21. Gravitational collapse. 22. Spiral galaxies. 23. Unified field theories. 24. Quantum theory. 25. Naked singularities (Cosmology) 26. Astronomy - Mathematics. 27. Cosmology - Mathematics. 28. Quasars. 29. Inflationary universe. 30. Life on other planets. 31. Quasars. 32. Astrophysics. 33. Video recordings for the hearing impaired. I. Martin, Philip, 1938- II. Hawking, S. W. (Stephen W.) III. Filkin, David. IV. Langella, Frank. V. WNET (Television station : New York, N.Y.) VI. Uden Associates. VII. David Filkin Enterprises. VIII. British Broadcasting Corporation. Television Service. IX. PBS Video. X. Warner Home Video (Firm) XI. Title: Stephen Hawking's universe (Television program) XII. Title: Seeing is believing. XIII. Title: Big bang. XIV. Title: Cosmic alchemy. XV. Title: On the dark side. XVI. Title: Black holes and beyond. XVII. Title: Answer to everything. XVIII. Title: Universe*
**TC QB982 .S7 1997**

**Stephens, Brad.**
Junion-Metz, Gail, 1947- Creating a power web site. New York : Neal-Schuman, c1998.
**TC Z674.75.W67 J86 1998**

**Stephens, David.**
Pridmore, Pat, 1947- Children as partners for health. London ; New York : Zed Books ; New York : Distributed exclusively in the USA by St. Martin's Press, 2000.
**TC LB1587.A3 P75 2000**

**Stephens, Diane.**
Assessment as inquiry. Urbana, Ill. : National Council of Teachers of English, 1999.
**TC LB3051 .A76665 1999**

**Stephens, John, 1944-** Retelling stories, framing culture : traditional story and metanarratives in children's literature / John Stephens, Robyn McCallum. New York : Garland Pub., 1998. xi, 316 p. ; 23 cm. (Garland reference library of the humanities ; v. 1975. Children's literature and culture ; v. 5) Includes bibliographical references (p. [293]-307) and index. ISBN 0-8153-1298-9 (alk. paper) DDC 809/.89282
*1. Children's literature - History and criticism. I. McCallum, Robyn. II. Title. III. Series: Garland reference library of the humanities ; vol. 1975. IV. Series: Garland reference library of the humanities. Children's literature and culture ; v. 5.*
**TC PN1009.A1 S83 1998**

**STEPMOTHERS. See STEPCHILDREN.**

**STEPMOTHERS - CHINA - HONG KONG - FAMILY RELATIONSHIPS.**
Lam-Chan, Gladys Lan Tak. Parenting in stepfamilies. Aldershot ; Brookfield USA : Ashgate, c1999.
**TC HQ759.92 .L34 1999**

**STEPPARENTS. See STEPMOTHERS.**

**STEPPARENTS - CHINA - HONG KONG.**
Lam-Chan, Gladys Lan Tak. Parenting in stepfamilies. Aldershot ; Brookfield USA : Ashgate, c1999.
**TC HQ759.92 .L34 1999**

**Stepping inside the classroom through personal narratives.**
Smith, Darren James, 1960- Lanham, Md. : University Press of America, 1999.
**TC LB1737.U6 S55 1999**

**STEPS, TWELVE (SELF-HELP). See TWELVE-STEP PROGRAMS.**

**Sterba, James P.**
Freedom, equality, and social change. Lewiston : E. Mellen Press, c1989.
**TC HM216 .F83 1989**

**Stereotype activation and inhibition** / edited by Robert S. Wyer, Jr. Mahwah, N.J. : L. Erlbaum Associates, 1998. viii, 269 p. : ill. ; 24 cm. (Advances in social cognition, v. 11.) "Lead article by Galen V. Bodenhausen, C. Neil Macrae"--Cover. Includes bibliographical references and indexes. ISBN 0-8058-2338-7 (cloth) ISBN 0-8058-2339-5 (paper)
*1. Stereotype (Psychology). I. Wyer, Robert S. II. Bodenhausen, Galen Von. 1961- III. Macrae, C. Neil. IV. Series.*
**TC BF323.S63 S75 1998**

**STEREOTYPE (PSYCHOLOGY).** *See also* **STIGMA (SOCIAL PSYCHOLOGY).**
Flippen, Annette Rose. Similarity versus motive as explanations for ingroup bias. 1996.
**TC 085 F65**

Mahammad, Hasna. Multicultural education. 1998.
**TC 06 no. 11033**

Mio, Jeffrey Scott. Resistance to multiculturalism :. Philadelphia, PA : Brunner/Mazel, c2000.
**TC HM1271 .M56 2000**

Stereotype activation and inhibition. Mahwah, N.J. : L. Erlbaum Associates, 1998.
**TC BF323.S63 S75 1998**

**STEREOTYPE (PSYCHOLOGY) IN MASS MEDIA.**
Growing up girls. New York : P. Lang, c1999.
**TC HQ798 .G76 1999**

**STEREOTYPE (PSYCHOLOGY) - STUDY AND TEACHING (HIGHER) - ACTIVITY PROGRAMS.**
Teaching about culture, ethnicity & diversity. Thousand Oaks : Sage Publications, c1998.
**TC HM101 .T38 1998**

**STEREOTYPED BEHAVIOR. See STEREOTYPE (PSYCHOLOGY).**

**STERILIZATION (BIRTH CONTROL). See STERILIZATION, EUGENIC.**

**STERILIZATION, EUGENIC - LAW AND LEGISLATION - UNITED STATES.**
Field, Martha A. Equal treatment for people with mental retardation. Cambridge, Mass. : London : Harvard University Press, 1999.
**TC KF480 .F54 1999**

**STERILIZATION OF CRIMINALS AND DEFECTIVES. See STERILIZATION, EUGENIC.**

**Stern, Marc A.**
Global public goods. New York : Oxford University Press, 1999.
**TC HB846.5 .G55 1999**

**Stern, Paul C., 1944-.**
The aging mind: opportunities in cognitive research. Washington, D.C. : National Academy Press, c2000.
**TC BF724.55 .C63 A48 2000**

**Stern, Robert A. M.** New York 1880 : architecture and urbanism in the gilded age / Robert A.M. Stern, Thomas Mellins, and David Fishman. New York, N.Y. : Monacelli Press, 1999. 1164 p. : ill. ; 29 cm. Includes bibliographical references (p. 1031-1130) and index. ISBN 1-58093-027-1 DDC 720/.9747/109034
*1. Eclecticism in architecture - New York (State) - New York. 2. Architecture, Modern - 19th century - New York (State) - New York. 3. City planning - New York (State) - New York - History - 19th century. 4. New York (N.Y.) - Buildings, structures, etc. I. Mellins, Thomas. II. Fishman, David. III. Title.*
**TC NA735.N5 S727 1999**

**Sternberg, Robert J.**
Guide to publishing in psychology journals. Cambridge, U.K. ; New York : Cambridge University Press, 2000.
**TC BF76.8 .G85 2000**

Handbook of creativity. Cambridge, U.K. ; New York : Cambridge University Press, 1999.
**TC BF408 .H285 1999**

Handbook of intelligence. Cambridge ; New York : Cambridge University Press, 2000.
**TC BF431 .H31865 2000**

Practical intelligence in everyday life. Cambridge, UK : New York, NY : Cambridge University Press, 2000.
**TC BF431 .P64 2000**

Self-awareness. New York : Guilford Press, c1998.
**TC BF697.5.S43 S434 1998**

Teaching introductory psychology. 1st ed. Washington, DC : American Psychological Association, c1997.
**TC BF77 .T42 1997**

**STEROIDS. See LIPIDS.**

**Stevens, Annie.**
Out & about campus. 1st ed. Los Angeles : Alyson Books, 2000.
**TC LC2574.6 .O87 2000**

**Stevens, Anthony.** On Jung / Anthony Stevens. 2nd ed. Princeton, N.J. : Princeton University Press, 1999. xii, 311 p. : ill. ; 22 cm. (Princeton paperbacks) "An updated

edition with a reply to Jung's critics." Includes bibliographical references (p. 295-300) and index. ISBN 0-691-01048-X (pbk. : alk. paper) DDC 150.19/54/092
*1. Jung, C. G. - (Carl Gustav), - 1875-1961. 2. Psychoanalysis. 3. Psychoanalysts - Switzerland - Biography. 4. Developmental psychology. I. Title.*
**TC BF173 .S828 1999**

The two million-year-old self / Anthony Stevens ; foreword by David H. Rosen. New York : Fromm International Publishing, 1997. xvi, 140 p. ; 21 cm. (Carolyn and Ernest Fay series in analytical psychology ; no. 3) Originally published : College Station : Texas A&M University Press, c1993. Includes bibliographical references (p. [130]-134) and index. ISBN 0-88064-214-9 DDC 155.2
*1. Archetype (Psychology) 2. Self. 3. Civilization, Modern - 20th century - Psychological aspects. 4. Dreams - Therapeutic use. 5. Jungian psychology. I. Title. II. Series.*
**TC BF175.5.A72 S75 1997**

**Stevens, David.**
Forsyth, Ian. The complete guide to teaching a course. 2nd ed. London : Kogan Page ; Sterling, VA : Stylus Publishing, 1999.
**TC LB1025.3 .F67 1999**

**Stevens, David, 1954-.**
Grigsby, Jim. Neurodynamics of personality. New York : Guilford Press, 2000.
**TC BF698.9.B5 G741 2000**

**Stevens, Ed.** Due process and higher education : a systemic approach to fair decision making / Ed Stevens Washington, DC : Graduate School of Education and Human Development, George Washington University, [1999] xi, 145 p. ; 23 cm. (ASHE-ERIC higher education report, 0884-0040 ; v. 27, no. 2) Includes bibliographical references (p. 115-124) and index. CONTENTS: Overview of due process in higher education -- Systemic approach to due process in higher education -- Conclusion. ISBN 1-87838-090-7
*1. Universities and colleges - Law and legislation - United States. 2. Universities and colleges - United States. 3. Due process of law. 4. Education, Higher. I. ERIC Clearinghouse on Higher Education. II. Association for the Study of Higher Education. III. Title. IV. Series: ASHE-ERIC higher education report ; vol. 27, no. 2.*
**TC LB2344 .S73 1999**

**Stevens, Janet.** Animal fair / adopted and illustrated by Janet Stevens. New York : Holiday House, c1981. [32] p. : col. ill. ; 24 cm. SUMMARY: A retelling of a traditional song in which a little boy is awakened by a friendly panda who takes him to the animal fair. ISBN 0-8234-0388-2 (lib. bdg.) DDC 811/.54; 784.4
*1. Folk songs - Texts. 2. Folk songs. 3. Animals - Poetry. I. Title.*
**TC PZ8.3.S844 An**

**Stevens, Kate.** Doing postgraduate research in Australia / Kate Stevens and Christine Asmar. Melbourne : Melbourne University Press, 1999. xviii, 117 p. : ill. ; 22 cm. Includes bibliographical references and index. ISBN 0-522-84880-X
*1. Universities and colleges - Australia - Graduate work - Handbooks, manuals, etc. 2. Graduate students - Australia - Handbooks, manuals, etc. I. Asmar, Christine. II. Title.*
**TC LB2371.6.A7 S74 1999**

**Stevenson, James, 1929-** Don't make me laugh / James Stevenson. 1st ed. New York : Farrar, Straus and Giroux, c1999. 1 v. (unpaged) : col. ill. ; 29 cm. "Frances Foster books." SUMMARY: Readers are requested not to laugh or do anything to influence the behavior of various animal characters in this book. ISBN 0-374-31827-1 DDC [E]
*1. Laughter - Fiction. 2. Behavior - Fiction. 3. Animals - Fiction. I. Title.*
**TC PZ7.S84748 Do 1999**

**Stevenson, Suçie, ill.**
Rylant, Cynthia. Henry and Mudge and the wild wind. 1st ed. New York : Bradbury Press : Toronto : Maxwell Macmillan Canada ; New York : Maxwell Macmillan International, c1993.
**TC PZ7.R982 Heb 1992**

**Stewart, Ian, 1940-** Transactional analysis counselling in action / Ian Stewart. 2nd ed. London : SAGE, 2000. xv, 198 p. : ill. ; 23 cm. (Counselling in action.) Previous ed.: 1989. Includes bibliographical references and index. ISBN 0-7619-6318-9 ISBN 0-7619-6319-7 (pbk.)
*1. Counseling. 2. Transactional analysis. I. Title. II. Series.*
**TC RC489.T7 S74 2000**

**Stewart, John Robert, 1941-.**
Bridges not walls. 7th ed. Boston : McGraw Hill College, c1999.
**TC BF637.C45 B74 1999**

**Stewart, Therese Marie Klein.** The challenges to sustaining Unification faith and the spiritual quest after seminary / by Therese Marie Klein Stewart.

1996. vi, 194 leaves ; 29 cm. Issued also on microfilm. Thesis (Ed.D.)--Teachers College, Columbia University, 1996. Includes bibliographical references (leaves 183-188).
*1. Unification Church - Clergy - United States - Psychological aspects. 2. Spiritual formation. 3. Moral development. I. Unification Theological Seminary. II. Title.*
**TC 06 no. 10751**

**Stewig, John W.** Language arts in the early childhood classroom / John Warren Stewig, Mary Jett-Simpson. Belmont [Calif.] : Wadsworth Pub. Co., c1995. xii, 324 p. : ill. ; 25 cm. Includes bibliographical references and index. ISBN 0-534-25080-7 (alk. paper) DDC 372.6
*1. Language arts (Preschool) 2. Early childhood education. 3. Children - Books and reading. 4. Curriculum planning. I. Jett-Simpson, Mary, 1938- II. Title.*
**TC LB1140.5.L3 S72 1995**

**Stichting voor Internationale Samenwerking der Nederlandse Universiteiten en Hogescholen.** Higher education and research in the Netherlands. The Hague, Netherlands Foundation for International Cooperation.

**Stiefelmeyer, Betty L.**
Thomas, Adele, 1942- Families at school. Newark, Del. : International Reading Association, c1999.
**TC LC151 .T56 1999**

Thomas, Adele, 1942- Families at school. Newark, Del. : International Reading Association, c1999.
**TC LC151 .T563 1999**

**STIEGLITZ, ALFRED, 1864-1946.**
Georgia O'Keeffe [videorecording]. [Boston?] : Home Vision ; c1977.
**TC ND237.O5 G4 1977**

**Stierer, Barry.**
Student writing in higher education. Philadelphia, Pa. : Open University Press, c2000.
**TC PE1404 .S84 2000**

**Stigler, Stephen M.** Statistics on the table : the history of statistical concepts and methods / Stephen M. Stigler. Cambridge, Mass. : Harvard University Press, 1999. ix, 488 p. : ill. ; 25 cm. Includes bibliographical references (p. 433-475) and index. ISBN 0-674-83601-4 (alk. paper) DDC 519.5/09
*1. Mathematical statistics - History. I. Title.*
**TC QA276.15 .S755 1999**

**The stigma of genius.**
Kincheloe, Joe L. New York ; Canterbury [England] : P. Lang, c1999.
**TC LB875.E562 K56 1999**

**STIGMA (SOCIAL PSYCHOLOGY).**
Lippert, Robin Alissa. Conflating the self with the body. 1999.
**TC 085 L655**

Wahl, Otto F. Telling is risky business. New Brunswick, N.J. ; London : Rutgers University Press, c1999.
**TC RC454.4 .W327 1999**

**Still, Julie.**
The library Web. Medford, NJ : Information Today, 1997.
**TC Z674.75.W67 L53 1997**

**Stilwell, Barbara M.** Right vs. wrong-- : raising a child with a conscience / Barbara M. Stilwell, Matthew R. Galvin, S. Mark Kopta. Bloomington : Indiana University Press, c2000. xiii, 235 p. : ill. ; 24 cm. Includes bibliographical references and index. ISBN 0-253-33709-7 (cloth : alk. paper) ISBN 0-253-21368-1 (pbk. : alk. paper) DDC 649/.7
*1. Conscience. 2. Moral development. 3. Moral education (Elementary) 4. Moral education (Secondary) I. Galvin, Matthew. II. Kopta, Stephen M., 1951- III. Title. IV. Title: Right versus wrong*
**TC BJ1471 .S69 2000**

**Stimolo, Bob.** Introduction to school marketing / Bob Stimolo, Lynn Vosburgh. [Haddam], Conn. : School Market Research Institute, c1989. xv, 107 p. : ill. ; 23 cm. Includes bibliographical references and index. ISBN 0-9622067-0-9
*1. Teaching - Aids and devices - Marketing. 2. Instructional materials industry. 3. Direct marketing. I. Vosburgh, Lynn. II. Title.*
**TC HF5415.122 .S75 1989**

**Stipanuk, Martha H.**
Biochemical and physiological aspects of human nutrition. Philadelphia : W.B. Saunders, c1999.
**TC QP141 .B57 1999**

**Stirring the waters** : the influence of Marie Clay / edited by Janet S. Gaffney, Billie J. Askew. Portsmouth, NH : Heinemann, c1999. xiv, 289 p. : ill. ; 24 cm. Includes bibliographical references. ISBN 0-325-

00207-X DDC 372.6
*1. Clay, Marie M. 2. Children - Language. 3. Language arts (Early childhood) 4. Reading (Early childhood) I. Gaffney, Janet S. II. Askew, Billie J.*
**TC LB1139.5.L35 S85 1999**

**STOCK COMPANIES.** *See* **CORPORATIONS.**

**STOCK CORPORATIONS.** *See* **CORPORATIONS.**

**STOCK MARKET CRASH, 1929.** *See* **DEPRESSIONS - 1929.**

**Stockard, Olivia.** The write approach : techniques for effective business writing / Olivia Stockard. San Diego, Calif. : Academic Press, c1999. viii, 190 p. : ill. ; 23 cm. Includes bibliographical references (p. 185) and index. ISBN 0-12-671545-9 DDC 808/.06665
*1. Business writing. I. Title.*
**TC HF5718.3 .S764 1999**

**Stockdale, Margaret S.**
Cleveland, Jeanette. Women and men in organizations. Mahwah, N.J. ; London : Lawrence Erlbaum Associates, 2000.
**TC HD6060.65.U5 C58 2000**

**Stocker, Gerfried.**
LifeScience. Wien ; New York : Springer, 1999.
**TC T14.5 L54 1999**

**Stockholms universitet. Institutionen för internationell pedagogik.**
Tuijnman, Albert. Recurrent education and socioeconomic success. [Stockholm] : Institute of International Education, University of Stockholm, c1986.
**TC LC5215 .T84 1986**

**Stockley, Michele.** Art investigator / Michele Stockley. Port Melbourne, Vic. : Heinemann, 1998. iv, 268 p. : ill. (chiefly col.) ; 28 cm. Bibliography: p. 262. Includes index. ISBN 0-85859-833-7
*1. Art - History. I. Title.*
**TC N5300 .S915 1998**

**Stöckmann, Hans-Jürgen, 1945-** Quantum chaos : an introduction / Hans-Jürgen Stöckmann. Cambridge [England] ; New York : Cambridge University Press, 1999. xi, 368 p. : ill. ; 26 cm. Includes bibliographical references (p. 344-364) and index. ISBN 0-521-59284-4 (hb) DDC 530.12
*1. Quantum chaos. I. Title.*
**TC QC174.17.C45 S84 1999**

**STOCKMEN (ANIMAL INDUSTRY).** *See* **COWBOYS.**

**STOCKS.** *See* **CORPORATIONS.**

**Stoff, Michael B.**
Davidson, James West. The American nation. Annotated teacher's ed. Upper Saddle River, N.J. : Prentice Hall, c1998.
**TC E178.1 .D22 1998 Teacher's Ed.**

**Stolen harvest.**
Shiva, Vandana. Cambridge, MA : South End Press, c2000.
**TC HD9000.5 .S454 2000**

**A Stolen life.**
Curry, Jane Louise. New York : McElderry Books, 1999.
**TC PZ7.C936 St 1999**

**Stolk, Joop.**
Meaningful care. Dordrecht ; Boston ; London : Kluwer Academic Publishers, c2000.
**TC HV3004 .M34 2000**

**Stoll, Clifford.** High tech heretic : why computers don't belong in the classroom and other reflections by a computer contrarian / Clifford Stoll. 1st ed. New York : Doubleday, c1999. xv, 221 p. ; 25 cm. Includes index. ISBN 0-385-48975-7
*1. Computer-assisted instruction. 2. Computers and civilization. 3. Internet (Computer network) in education. I. Title.*
**TC LB1028.5 .S77 1999**

**Stollenwerk, Debra A.**
Goethals, M. Serra, 1934- Student teaching. Upper Saddle River, N.J. : Merrill, c2000.
**TC LB2157.A3 G57 2000**

Henderson, James George. Transformative curriculum leadership. 2nd ed. Upper Saddle River, N.J. : Merrill, c2000.
**TC LB1570 .H45 2000**

Marshall, J. Dan. Turning points in curriculum. Upper Saddle River, N.J. : Merrill, c2000.

**TC LB1570 .M36675 2000**

McEwan, Barbara, 1946- The art of classroom management. Upper Saddle River, N.J. : Merrill, c2000.
**TC LB3013 .M383 2000**

Morrison, Gary R. Integrating computer technology into the classroom. Upper Saddle River, N.J. : Merrill, c1999.
**TC LB1028.5 .M6373 1999**

Sowell, Evelyn J. Curriculum. 2nd ed. Upper Saddle River, N.J. : Merrill, c2000.
**TC LB2806.15 .S69 2000**

Speck, Marsha. The principalship. Upper Saddle River, N.J. : Merrill, c1999.
**TC LB1738.5 .S64 1999**

**Stone, Howard W.** Depression and hope : new insights for pastoral counseling / Howard W. Stone. Minneapolis : Fortress Press, c1998. xiii, 161 p. ; 22 cm. Includes bibliographical references (p. 153-160) and index. ISBN 0-8006-3139-0 (alk. paper) DDC 259/.425
*1. Depressed persons - Pastoral counseling of. 2. Depression. Mental - Religious aspects - Christianity. I. Title.*
**TC BV4461 .S76 1998**

**Stone, M. W. F. (Martin William Francis), 1965-.** Humanism and early modern philosophy. London ; New York : Routledge, 2000.
**TC B821 .H657 2000**

**Stone, Randi.** Best classroom practices : what award-winning elementary teachers do / Randi Stone. Thousand Oaks, Calif. : Corwin Press, c1999. xiii, 217 p. : ill. ; 25 cm. Includes bibliographical references. ISBN 0-8039-6758-6 (cloth: acid-free paper) ISBN 0-8039-6759-4 (pbk.: acid-free paper) DDC 372.11/0973
*1. Elementary school teachers - United States - Case studies. 2. Elementary school teaching - United States - Case studies. I. Title.*
**TC LB1776.2 .S86 1999**

**Stoneman, Rod.**
Photomontage today, Peter Kennard [videorecording]. [London] : Art Council of Great Britain ; Ho-Ho-Kus, N.J. : [distributed by] Anthony Roland Collection of Films on Art, c1982.
**TC TR685 .P45 1982**

**STONEWORK, DECORATIVE.** *See* **SCULPTURE.**

**Stop the bus.**
Deuschle, C. (Constance) Lanham, Md. : University Press of America, c2000.
**TC LB1027.5 .D4567 2000**

**Stoppard, Janet M. (Janet Mary), 1945-**
Understanding depression : feminist social constructivist approaches / Janet M. Stoppard. London ; New York : Routledge, 2000. ix, 239 p. ; 25 cm. (Women and psychology) Includes bibliographical references (p. 216-229) and index. ISBN 0-415-16562-8 (hbk.) ISBN 0-415-16563-6 (pbk.) DDC 616.85/27/0082
*1. Depression in women - Social aspects. 2. Feminist psychology. I. Title. II. Series.*
**TC RC537 .S82 2000**

**STORAGE LIBRARIES.** *See* **LIBRARIES, STORAGE.**

**STORES, RETAIL - FICTION.**
Shelby, Anne. We keep a store. New York : Orchard Books, c1989.
**TC PZ7.S54125 We 1989**

Shelby, Anne. We keep a store. New York : Orchard Books, c1990.
**TC PZ7 .S54125We 1990**

**STORIES.** *See* **FICTION.**

**Stories from the center** : connecting narrative and theory in the writing center / edited by Lynn Craigue Briggs, Meg Woolbright. Urbana, Ill. National Council of Teachers of English, c2000. xvi, 129 p. ; 22 cm. Includes bibliographical references and index. ISBN 0-8141-4746-1 DDC 808/.042/07
*1. English language - Rhetoric - Study and teaching. 2. Report writing - Study and teaching. 3. English teachers - Attitudes. 4. Teacher-student relationships. 5. Writing centers. I. Briggs, Lynn Craigue. 1960- II. Woolbright, Meg, 1955-*
**TC PE1404 .S834 2000**

**STORIES IN RHYME.**
Brown, Ruth. Mad summer night's dream. 1st American ed. New York : Dutton Children's Books, 1999.
**TC PZ8.3.B8155 Mad 1999**

Cherry, Lynne. Who's sick today? 1st ed. New York : Dutton, c1988.

*Stories in rhyme.*

*TC PZ8.3.C427 Wh 1988*

Dodds, Dayle Ann. The Great Divide. 1st ed. Cambridge, MA : Candlewick Press, 1999.
*TC PZ8.3.D645 Gr 1999*

Garne, S. T. By a blazing blue sea. San Diego : Harcourt Brace & Co., 1999.
*TC PZ8.3.G1866 By 1999*

Grossman, Bill. Donna O'Neeshuck was chased by some cows. 1st ed. [New York] : Harper & Row, c1988.
*TC PZ8.3.G914 Do 1988*

Henkes, Kevin. Oh!. New York : Greenwillow Books, 1999.
*TC PZ8.3.H4165 Oh 1999*

Joyce, William. Rolie Polie Olie. 1st ed. New York : Laura Geringer Book, c1999.
*TC PZ8.3.J835 Ro 1999*

Kay, Verla. Gold fever. New York : Putnam's, c1999.
*TC PZ8.3.K225 Go 1999*

Kay, Verla. Iron horses. New York : Putnam, c1999.
*TC PZ8.3.K225 Ir 1999*

Martin, Bill, 1916- Brown bear, brown bear, what do you see? New York : H. Holt, 1992.
*TC PZ8.3.M418 Br 1992*

Mathis, Melissa Bay. Animal house. 1st ed. New York : Simon & Schuster Books for Young Readers, 1999.
*TC PZ8.3.M4265 Ap 1999*

Reeves, Mona Rabun. I had a cat. 1st American ed. New York : Bradbury Press, c1989.
*TC PZ8.3.R263 Iah 1989*

Reid, Barbara. The party. New York : Scholastic Press, 1999.
*TC PZ8.3.R2665 Pat 1999*

Sathre, Vivian. Three kind mice. 1st ed. San Diego : Harcourt Brace, c1997.
*TC PZ8.3.S238 Th 1997*

Shaw, Nancy (Nancy E.) Sheep on a ship. Boston : Houghton Mifflin, 1989.
*TC PZ8.3.S5334 Si 1989*

Willard, Nancy. The tale I told Sasha. 1st ed. Boston : Little, Brown, c1999.
*TC PZ8.3.W668 Tal 1999*

Yolen, Jane. Mouse's birthday. New York : Putnam's, c1993.
*TC PZ8.3.Y76 Mo 1993*

Ziefert, Harriet. Animal music. Boston : Houghton Mifflin, 1999.
*TC PZ8.3.Z47 An 1999*

**Stories lives.**
Okihiro, Gary Y., 1945- Seattle : University of Washington Press, 1999.
*TC D753.8 .O38 1999*

**Stories out of school :** memories and reflections on care and cruelty in the classroom / edited by James Paul and Terry Jo Smith. Stamford, Conn. : Ablex Pub., c2000. xii, 162 p. ; 24 cm. (Contemporary studies in social and policy issues in education) Includes bibliographical references and indexes. ISBN 1-56750-476-0 ISBN 1-56750-477-9 (pbk.) DDC 370.11/5
*1. Critical pedagogy. 2. Teacher-student relationships. 3. Classroom environment. I. Paul, James L. II. Smith, Terry Jo. III. Series.*
*TC LC196 .S6994 2000*

**STORIES WITHOUT WORDS.**
Blair, Margot. The red string. Malibu, Calif. : J. Paul Getty Museum and Childrens Library Press, c1996.
*TC PZ7.B537865 Re 1996*

Blake, Quentin. Clown. 1st American ed. New York : H. Holt, 1996.
*TC PZ7.B56 Cl 1996*

Collington, Peter. The tooth fairy. 1st U.S. ed. New York : Knopf ; Distributed by Random House, 1995.
*TC PZ7.C686 To 1995*

Hutchins, Pat, 1942- Changes, changes. New York, Macmillan c1971.
*TC PZ8.9 .H95 1971*

Hutchins, Pat, 1942- Changes, changes. New York, Macmillan c1971.
*TC PZ8.9.H95 Ch 1971*

Wiesner, David. Sector 7. New York : Clarion Books, c1999.

*TC PZ7.W6367 Se 1999*

**STORMS. *See* THUNDERSTORMS.**

**A story, a story.**
Haley, Gail E. 2nd Aladdin Books ed. New York : Aladdin Books, 1988, c1970.
*TC PZ8.1.H139 St 1988*

**Story, Jennifer.**
Assessment as inquiry. Urbana, Ill. : National Council of Teachers of English, 1999.
*TC LB3051 .A76665 1999*

**The story of a second chance school.**
Baldwin, John. Education and welfare reform. Bloomington, Ind. : Phi Delta Kappa Educational Foundation, c1993.
*TC LC4033.S61 B34 1993*

**Story of Lucy.**
In search of human origins [videorecording]. [Boston, Mass.] : WGBH Educational Foundation, c1994.
*TC GN281 .I45 1994*

**Story of man's conquest of mental illness.**
Bromberg, Walter, 1900- The mind of man. 4th ed. New York : Harper & Brothers, 1937.
*TC RC480 .B7*

**The story of modern Europe.**
Riker, Thad Weed, 1880-1952. Boston : Houghton, Mifflin, 1942.
*TC D209 .R48*

**Story of nations.**
Rogers, Lester Brown, 1875- New York : H.Holt, 1965.
*TC D21 .R63 1965*

**The story of the Jamaican people.**
Sherlock, Philip Manderson, Sir. Kingston, Jamaica : I. Randle Publishers ; Princeton, N.J. : M. Wiener Publishers, 1998.
*TC F1881 .S5 1998*

**The story of the Statue of Liberty.**
Maestro, Betsy. New York : Lothrop, Lee & Shepard Books, 1986.
*TC NB553.B3 A75 1986*

**Story programs.**
Peterson, Carolyn Sue, 1938- 2nd ed. Lanham, Md. : Scarecrow Press, 2000.
*TC LB1042 .P47 2000*

**STORY-TELLING. *See* STORYTELLING.**

**Storymaking in elementary and middle school classrooms.**
Golden, Joanne Marie, 1949- Mahwah, N.J. : L. Erlbaum Associates, 2000.
*TC LB1042 .G54 2000*

**The storytellers' journey.**
Sobol, Joseph Daniel. Urbana : University of Illinois Press, c1999.
*TC GR72.3 .S62 1999*

**STORYTELLING. *See also* CHILDREN'S STORIES; FOLKLORE.**
Clandinin, D. Jean. Narrative inquiry. 1st ed. San Francisco : Jossey-Bass Inc., c2000.
*TC LB1028 .C55 2000*

Golden, Joanne Marie, 1949- Storymaking in elementary and middle school classrooms. Mahwah, N.J. : L. Erlbaum Associates, 2000.
*TC LB1042 .G54 2000*

Grugeon, Elizabeth. The art of storytelling for teachers and pupils. London : David Fulton, 2000.
*TC LB1042 .G78 2000*

Lipkin, Lisa. Bringing the story home. New York : W.W. Norton & Co., c2000.
*TC LB1042 .L515 2000*

Marsh, Valerie. Storytelling with shapes & numbers. Ft. Atkinson, Wis. : Alleyside Press, c1999.
*TC LB1042 .M2874 1999*

Peterson, Carolyn Sue, 1938- Story programs. 2nd ed. Lanham, Md. : Scarecrow Press, 2000.
*TC LB1042 .P47 2000*

Traditional storytelling today. Chicago : Fitzroy Dearborn Publishers, 1999.
*TC GR72 .T73 1999*

**STORYTELLING - FICTION.**
Jennings, Patrick. Putnam and Pennyroyal. 1st ed. New York : Scholastic Press, 1999.
*TC PZ7.J4298715 Co 1999*

**STORYTELLING - NEW YORK (STATE) - NEW YORK.**
Milbank Memorial Library story hour

[videorecording]. [New York : Milbank Memorial Library, 1999].
*TC Z718.3 .M5 1999 Series 3 Prog. 11*

Milbank Memorial Library story hour [videorecording]. [New York : Milbank Memorial Library, 1999]
*TC Z718.3 .M5 1999 Series 3 Prog. 6*

**STORYTELLING - STUDY AND TEACHING (PRIMARY).**
Teacher toolbox [kit]. Chicago, Ill. : Open Court Pub. Co., c1995.
*TC LB1573.3 .T4 1995*

**STORYTELLING - THERAPEUTIC USE.**
Constructions of disorder. 1st ed. Washington, DC : American Psychological Association, c2000.
*TC RC437.5 .C647 2000*

Winslade, John. Narrative counseling in schools. Thousand Oaks, Calif. : Corwin Press, c1999.
*TC LB1027.5 .W535 1999*

**STORYTELLING - UNITED STATES.**
Cullum, Carolyn N. The storytime sourcebook. 2nd ed. New York ; London : Neal-Schuman Publishers, c1999.
*TC Z718.3 .C85 1999*

Druce, Arden. Paper bag puppets. Lanham, MD : Scarecrow Press, 1999.
*TC Z718.3 .D78 1999*

Madigan, Dan. The writing lives of children. York, ME : Stenhouse Publishers, 1997.
*TC LB1042 .M24 1997*

Marsh, Valerie. True tales of heroes & heroines. Fort Atkinson, Wis. : Alleyside Press, c1999.
*TC CT85 .M37 1999*

Schwarz, Gretchen, 1952- Teacher lore and professional development for school reform. Westport, Conn : Bergin & Garvey, 1998.
*TC LB1775.2 .S38 1998*

Sobol, Joseph Daniel. The storytellers' journey. Urbana : University of Illinois Press, c1999.
*TC GR72.3 .S62 1999*

**Storytelling with shapes & numbers.**
Marsh, Valerie. Ft. Atkinson, Wis. : Alleyside Press, c1999.
*TC LB1042 .M2874 1999*

**Storytelling with shapes and numbers.**
Marsh, Valerie. Storytelling with shapes & numbers. Ft. Atkinson, Wis. : Alleyside Press, c1999.
*TC LB1042 .M2874 1999*

**The storytime sourcebook.**
Cullum, Carolyn N. 2nd ed. New York ; London : Neal-Schuman Publishers, c1999.
*TC Z718.3 .C85 1999*

**Stotsky, Sandra.**
What's at stake in the K-12 standards wars. New York : P. Lang, 2000.
*TC LB3060.83 .W53 2000*

**Stott, Kenneth.**
Quong, Terry. Values based strategic planning :. Singapore ; New York : Prentice Hall, 1998.
*TC LB2806 .Q86 1998*

**Strachey, Alix, tr.**
Freud, Sigmund, 1856-1939. [Sammlung kleiner schriften zur neurosenlehre. eng] Collected papers. 1st American ed. New York : Basic Books, 1959.
*TC BF173 .F672 1959*

**Strachey, James, tr.**
Freud, Sigmund, 1856-1939. [Sammlung kleiner schriften zur neurosenlehre. eng] Collected papers. 1st American ed. New York : Basic Books, 1959.
*TC BF173 .F672 1959*

**Straight talk about psychiatric medications for kids.**
Wilens, Timothy E. New York : Guilford Press, c1999.
*TC RJ504.7 .W54 1999*

**Strang, Thomas J. K.** Controlling museum fungal problems / by Thomas J.K. Strang and John E. Dawson. Ottawa : Canadian Conservation Institute, Department of Communications, [1991] 8, 8, p. ; 28 cm. (Technical bulletin / Canadian Conservation Institute, 0706-4152 ; no. 12) Text in English and French with French text on inverted pages. Title on added t.p.: Le contrôle des moisissures dans les musées. Includes bibliographical references (p. 7-8). DDC 580
*1. Museums - Environmental aspects. 2. Fungi - Control. 3. Museum conservation methods. I. Dawson, John E. II. Canadian Conservation Institute. III. Title. IV. Title: Le*

*controle des moisissures dans les musées.* V. Series: Technical bulletin (Canadian Conservation Institute) ; no. 12
*TC TH9031 .S75 1991*

**Strange, Charles Carney.** Educating by design : creating campus learning environments that work / C. Carney Strange, James H. Banning ; consulting editor, Ursula Delworth. 1st ed. San Francisco : Jossey-Bass, c2001. xx, 251 p. ; 24 cm. (The Jossey-Bass higher and adult education series) Includes bibliographical references (p. 221-239) and indexes. CONTENTS: Physical environments: the role of design and space -- Aggregate environments: the impact of human characteristics -- Organizational environments: how institutional goals are achieved -- Constructed environments: different views through different eyes -- Promoting safety and inclusion -- Encouraging participation and involvement -- Building a community of learners -- Considering computer-mediated environments -- Designing for education: campus assessment and action. ISBN 0-7879-1046-5 DDC 378.1/98 DDC 378.1/98
*1. College environment - United States. 2. Campus planning - United States. 3. College students - United States - Attitudes. I. Banning, James H. II. Title. III. Series.*
*TC LB2324 .S77 2001*

**The strange disappearance of Sophia Smith.**
Quesnell, Quentin. Northampton [Mass.] : Smith College, c1999.
*TC LD7152.65.S45 Q84 1999*

**Strangers in the land :** pedagogy, modernity, and Jewish identity / edited by H. Svi Shapiro. New York : Peter Lang, c1999. xiv, 350 p. ; 23 cm. (Counterpoints ; vol. 46) Includes bibliographical references and index. ISBN 0-8204-3689-5 (pbk. : alk. paper) DDC 305.892/4073
*1. Jews - United States - Identity. 2. Jews - Education - United States - Philosophy. 3. Jewish teachers - United States - Attitudes. 4. Critical pedagogy - United States. 5. Education - Social aspects - United States. 6. Jews - United States - Intellectual life. 1. Shapiro, H. Svi. II. Series: Counterpoints (New York, N.Y.) ; vol. 46.* '
*TC E184.36.E84 S77 1999*

**STRATEGIC ALLIANCES (BUSINESS).** *See* **BUSINESS NETWORKS.**

**Strategic asset management for tertiary institutions.**
Programme on Educational Building. Paris : Organisation for Economic Co-operation and Development, c1999.
*TC LB3223 .P76 1999*

**STRATEGIC MANAGEMENT.** *See* **STRATEGIC PLANNING.**

**Strategic management for nonprofit organizations.**
Oster, Sharon M. New York : Oxford University Press, 1995.
*TC HD62.6 .O87 1995*

**Strategic management of college premises.**
Ruddiman, Ken. London : Falmer, 1999.
*TC LB3223.5.G7 R84 1999*

**Strategic nonviolent conflict.**
Ackerman, Peter. Westport, Conn. : Praeger, 1994.
*TC JC328.3 .A28 1994*

**STRATEGIC PLANNING.**
Oster, Sharon M. Strategic management for nonprofit organizations. New York : Oxford University Press, 1995.
*TC HD62.6 .O87 1995*

Quong, Terry. Values based strategic planning :. Singapore ; New York : Prentice Hall, 1998.
*TC LB2806 .Q86 1998*

Schwartz, Peter. The art of the long view. 1st Currency pbk. ed. New York : Currency Doubleday ; 1996.
*TC HD30.28 .S316 1996*

**STRATEGIC PLANNING - GREAT BRITAIN.**
Watson, David, 1949- Managing strategy. Buckingham [England] ; Philadelphia : Open University Press, 2000.
*TC LB2341.8.G7 W28 2000*

**Strategic use of transfer and explicit linguistic knowledge.**
O'Riordan, Mary. 1998.
*TC 06 no. 10975*

**Strategies for developing emergent literacy.**
Miller, Wilma H. 1st ed. Boston : McGraw-Hill, c2000.
*TC LB1139.5.L35 M55 2000*

**Strategies for energizing large classes : from small groups to learning communities** / Jean MacGregor ... [et al.], editors. San Francisco, Calif. : Jossey-Bass, 2000. 97 p. : ill. ; 23 cm. (New directions for teaching and learning, 0271-0633 ; no. 81) "Spring 2000."

Includes bibliographical references and index. ISBN 0-7879-5337-7
*1. Interdisciplinary approach in education - United States. 2. Team learning approach in education. 3. Classroom learning centers. 4. Communication in education. I. MacGregor, Jean. II. Series. III. Series: New directions for teaching and learning ; . no. 81*
*TC LB2361.5 .S77 2000*

**Strategies for nurse educators.**
Ulrich, Deborah L. Interactive group learning. New York : Springer, c1999.
*TC RT76 .U46 1999*

**Strategies for teachers.**
Eggen, Paul D., 1940- 4th ed. Boston : Allyn and Bacon, 2001.
*TC LB1027.3 .E44 2001*

**Strategies for teaching.**
Hall, Louis O. Reston, VA : Music Educators National Conference, c1997.
*TC MT1.H136 S77 1997*

**Strategies for teaching and learning professional library.**
Page, Nick. Music as a way of knowing. York, Me. : Stenhouse Publishers ; Los Angeles, Calif. : Galef Institute, c1995.
*TC MT1 .P234 1995*

**Strategies in teaching anthropology** / edited by Patricia C. Rice and David W. McCurdy ; foreword by Conrad P. Kottak ; introduction by Yolanda T. Moses. Upper Saddle River, N.J. : Prentice Hall, c2000. xvi, 181 p. : ill. ; 28 cm. Includes bibliographical references.
*1. Anthropology - Study and teaching - United States. I. Rice, Patricia C. II. McCurdy, David W. III. Kottak, Conrad Phillip. IV. Moses, Yolanda T.*
*TC GN43 .S77 2000*

**Strathern, Marilyn.**
Audit cultures. London ; New York : Routledge, 2000.
*TC LB2324 .A87 2000*

**Stratification in cognition and consciousness** / [edited by] Bradford H. Challis, Boris M. Velichkovsky. Amsterdam ; Philadelphia : J. Benjamins, c1999. viii, 293 p. : ill. ; 23 cm. (Advances in consciousness research, 1381-589X ; v. 15) Includes bibliographical references and indexes. ISBN 90-272-5135-5 (Eur. : pbk. : alk. paper) ISBN 1-55619-195-2 (US. : pbk. : alk. paper) DDC 153
*1. Information processing. 2. Categorization (Psychology) 3. Visual perception. 4. Recollection (Psychology) 5. Memory. I. Challis, Bradford H. II. Velichkovskiĭ, B. M. (Boris Mitrofanovich) III. Series.*
*TC BF444 .S73 1999*

**STRATIFICATION, SOCIAL.** *See* **SOCIAL CLASSES.**

**Straub, Richard.**
A sourcebook for responding to student writing. Cresskill, N.J. : Hampton Press, c1999.
*TC PE1404 .S683 1999*

**Straub, Richard O. (Richard Otto)** Study guide : to accompany Kathleen Strassen Berger : The developing person through the life span, fourth ed. / Richard O. Straub. New York : Worth Publishers, 1998. xvi, 380 p. ; 28 cm. ISBN 1-57259-225-7
*1. Developmental psychology - Problems, exercises, etc. I. Berger, Kathleen Stassen. The developing person through the life span. 4th edition II. Title.*
*TC BF713 .B463 1998 Guide*

Study guide : to accompany Kathleen Strassen Berger : The developing person through the life span, fourth ed. / Richard O. Straub. New York : Worth Publishers, 1998. xvi, 380 p. ; 28 cm. ISBN 1-57259-225-7
*1. Developmental psychology - Problems, exercises, etc. I. Berger, Kathleen Stassen. The developing person through the life span. 4th edition II. Title.*
*TC BF713 .B463 1998 Guide*

Study guide : to accompany Kathleen Strassen Berger : The developing person through the life span / Richard O. Straub. New York : Worth Publishers, 1998. xvi, 380 p. ; 28 cm. ISBN 1-57259-225-7
*1. Developmental psychology - Problems, exercises, etc. I. Berger, Kathleen Stassen. The developing person through the life span. 4th edition II. Title.*
*TC BF713 .B463 1998 guide*

**STRAUSS, RICHARD, 1864-1949.**
Kennedy, Michael, 1926- Richard Strauss. Cambridge, UK ; New York, NY, USA : Cambridge University Press, 1999.
*TC ML410.S93 K46 1999*

**Stray, Christopher.** Classics transformed : schools, universities, and society in England, 1830-1960 / Christopher Stray. Oxford : Clarendon Press ; New York : Oxford University Press, 1998. xii, 336 p. : ill. ; 23 cm. Includes bibliographical references (p. [298]-329) and index. ISBN 0-19-815013-X (h/b : acid-free paper) DDC 480/.07/041
*1. Classical philology - Study and teaching - England - History. 2. Classical philology - Study and teaching - History - 19th century. 3. Classical philology - Study and teaching - History - 20th century. 4. Classical education - England - History - 19th century. 5. Classical education - England - History - 20th century. 6. England - Civilization - Classical influences. 7. England - Social conditions - 19th century. 8. England - Social conditions - 20th century. 9. Educational sociology - England. 10. Classicism - England. I. Title.*
*TC PA78.E53 S87 1998*

**Straylight Media, Inc.**
What is visual literacy? York, Maine : Stenhouse Pub., c1996.
*TC LB1068 .W45 1996*

**STREAMS.** *See* **RIVERS.**

**Streb, Richard W.** Life and death aboard the U.S.S. Essex / by Richard W. Streb. Pittsburgh, Pa. : Dorrance Pub. Co., c1999. xiii, 347 p. : ill. ; 23 cm. ISBN 0-8059-4605-5
*1. Essex (Aircraft carrier) 2. World War, 1939-1945 - Aerial operations, American. 3. World War, 1939-1945 - Naval operations, American. 4. World War, 1939-1945 - Pacific Ocean. 5. World War, 1939-1945 - Personal narratives, American. I. Title.*
*TC D774.E7 S77 1999*

**STREET ART - CALIFORNIA - SAN FRANCISCO.**
Lee, Anthony W., 1960- Painting on the left. Berkeley : University of California Press, c1999.
*TC ND259.R5 L44 1999*

**Street, Brian V.**
Students writing in the university. Amsterdam ; Philadelphia : John Benjamins Pub., c1999.
*TC PE1405.G7 S78 1999*

**STREET CHILDREN - BRAZIL - SOCIAL CONDITIONS.**
Children on the streets of the Americas. London ; New York : Routledge, 2000.
*TC HV887.B8 C475 2000*

**STREET CHILDREN - CUBA - SOCIAL CONDITIONS.**
Children on the streets of the Americas. London ; New York : Routledge, 2000.
*TC HV887.B8 C475 2000*

**STREET CHILDREN - EDUCATION - BRAZIL.**
Children on the streets of the Americas. London ; New York : Routledge, 2000.
*TC HV887.B8 C475 2000*

**STREET CHILDREN - EDUCATION - CUBA.**
Children on the streets of the Americas. London ; New York : Routledge, 2000.
*TC HV887.B8 C475 2000*

**STREET CHILDREN - EDUCATION - UNITED STATES.**
Children on the streets of the Americas. London ; New York : Routledge, 2000.
*TC HV887.B8 C475 2000*

**STREET CHILDREN - NAIROBI - PICTORIAL WORKS.**
Shootback. London : Booth-Clibborn, 1999.
*TC HV4160.5.N34 S45 1999*

**STREET CHILDREN - SERVICES FOR - BRAZIL - CASE STUDIES.**
Children on the streets of the Americas. London ; New York : Routledge, 2000.
*TC HV887.B8 C475 2000*

**STREET CHILDREN - SERVICES FOR - CUBA - CASE STUDIES.**
Children on the streets of the Americas. London ; New York : Routledge, 2000.
*TC HV887.B8 C475 2000*

**STREET CHILDREN - SERVICES FOR - UNITED STATES - CASE STUDIES.**
Children on the streets of the Americas. London ; New York : Routledge, 2000.
*TC HV887.B8 C475 2000*

**STREET CHILDREN - SOCIAL CONDITIONS.**
Homeless and working youth around the world. San Francisco : Jossey-Bass, 1999.
*TC HV4493 .H655 1999*

**STREET CHILDREN - UNITED STATES - SOCIAL CONDITIONS.**
Children on the streets of the Americas. London ; New York : Routledge, 2000.
*TC HV887.B8 C475 2000*

**STREET DECORATION - INDIA - PICTORIAL WORKS.**
Dawson, Barry. Street graphics India. London : Thames & Hudson, 1999.
*TC NC998.6.I6 D38 1999*

Dawson, Barry. Street graphics India. London : Thames & Hudson, 1999.
*TC NC998.6.I6 D38 1999*

**STREET FIGHTING (MILITARY SCIENCE).** *See* **RIOTS.**

**STREET GANGS.** *See* **GANGS.**

**Street graphics India.**
Dawson, Barry. London : Thames & Hudson, 1999.
*TC NC998.6.I6 D38 1999*

**STREET KIDS.** *See* **STREET CHILDREN.**

**Street life in New York with the boot-blacks.**
Alger, Horatio, 1832-1899. Ragged Dick, or, Street life in New York with the boot-blacks. New York, N.Y. : Penguin Group, c1990.
*TC PS1029.A3 R34 1990*

**STREET LITERATURE.** *See* **PRINTED EPHEMERA.**

**STREET PEOPLE.** *See* **HOMELESS PERSONS.**

**STREET YOUTH.** *See* **HOMELESS YOUTH.**

**Streets as art galleries.**
Butler, Roger. Poster art in Australia. Canberra : National Gallery of Australia, 1993.
*TC NC1807.A78 B88 1993*

**Strengthening family resilience.**
Walsh, Froma. New York : Guilford Press, c1998.
*TC RC489.F33 W34 1998*

**Strengthening refugee families.**
Scheinfeld, Daniel, 1933- Chicago, Ill. : Lyceum Books, c1997.
*TC HV640.4.U54 S34 1997*

**Strengthening the family :** implications for international development / Marian F. Zeitlin ... [et al.]. Tokyo ; New York : United Nations University Press, c1995. viii, 268 p. : ill. ; 24 cm. Includes bibliographical references. "UNUP-890"--T.p. verso. "03500 P"--T.p. verso. CONTENTS: Social change and the family -- Economic perspectives on the family -- Psychological approaches to the family -- Perspectives from international development assistance and from family programmes -- The Javanese family -- The Yoruba family : kinship, socialization, and child development -- Structural models of family social health theory -- Synthesis of concepts and research needs -- Policy and programme recommendations. ISBN 92-808-0890-7 DDC 306.85/09172/4
*1. Family - Developing countries. 2. Family policy - Developing countries. 3. Child development - Developing countries. 4. Poor children - Developing countries - Family relationships. 5. Economic development - Social aspects. 6. Family - Research. I. Zeitlin. Marian F. II. United Nations University.*
*TC HQ727.9 .S77 1995*

**Strenski, Ellen, 1942-.**
IFIP TC3 WG3.2/3.6 International Working Conference on Building University Electronic Educational Environments (1999 : Irvine, Calif.) Building university electronic educational environments. Boston : Kluwer Academic Publishers, c2000.
*TC LC5803.C65 .I352 2000*

**Stress & strategy.**
Fisher, S. (Shirley) Stress and strategy. London ; Hillsdale, N.J. : Lawrence Erlbaum Associates, c1986.
*TC BF575.S75 F52 1986*

**Stress and emotion.**
Lazarus, Richard S. New York : Springer Pub. Co., c1999.
*TC BF575.S75 L315 1999*

**Stress and health :** research and clinical applications / edited by Dianna T. Kenny... [et al.]. Amsterdam : Harwood Academic ; Abingdon : Marston, 2000. xiii, 468 p. : ill. ; 25 cm. Includes bibliographical references and index. ISBN 90-5702-376-8 DDC 616.98
*1. Stress management. 2. Stress (Physiology) 3. Job stress - Health aspects. 4. Stress (Psychology) - Health aspects. I. Kenny, Dianna T.*
*TC RA785 .S774 2000*

**Stress and strategy.**
Fisher, S. (Shirley) London ; Hillsdale, N.J. : Lawrence Erlbaum Associates, c1986.
*TC BF575.S75 F52 1986*

**Stress, coping, and health in families :** sense of coherence and resiliency / editors, Hamilton I. McCubbin ... [et al.]. Thousand Oaks, Calif. : Sage Publications, c1998. viii, 313 p. : ill. ; 24 cm. (Resiliency in families series ; v. 1) "Originally published by the Board of Regents of the University of Wisconsin System and the Center for Excellence in Family Studies, 1994, under the title of Sense Of Coherence and Resiliency: Stress, Coping, and Health"--T.p. verso. Includes bibliographical references and index. ISBN 0-7619-1396-3 (hbk. : acid-free paper) ISBN 0-7619-1397-1 (pbk. : acid-free paper) DDC 155.9/24
*1. Family - Mental health. 2. Family - Health and hygiene. 3. Stress (Psychology) 4. Adjustment (Psychology) 5. Resilience (Personality trait) 6. Life cycle. Human. I. McCubbin. Hamilton I. II. Series: Resiliency in families series (Thousand Oaks. Calif.) ; v. 1.*
*TC RC455.4.F3 S79 1998*

**STRESS DISORDER, POST-TRAUMATIC.** *See* **POST-TRAUMATIC STRESS DISORDER.**

**Stress free teaching.**
Joseph, Russell. London ; Sterling, VA : Kogan Page, 2000.
*TC LB2840.2 .J67 2000*

**STRESS IN CHILDREN.** *See also* **POST-TRAUMATIC STRESS DISORDER IN CHILDREN.**
The effects of early adversity on neurobehavioral development. Mahwah, N.J. : L. Erlbaum Associates, 2000.
*TC RJ499 .E34 2000*

**Stress in college athletics.**
Humphrey, James Harry, 1911- New York : Haworth Press, c2000.
*TC GV347 .H86 2000*

**STRESS IN OLD AGE.**
Nemeroff, Robin. Stress, social support, and psychological distress in late life. 1999.
*TC 085 N341*

**STRESS MANAGEMENT.**
Joseph, Russell. Stress free teaching :. London ; Sterling, VA : Kogan Page, 2000.
*TC LB2840.2 .J67 2000*

Stress and health. Amsterdam : Harwood Academic ; Abingdon : Marston, 2000.
*TC RA785 .S774 2000*

**Stress-management and self-esteem activities.**
Toner, Patricia Rizzo, 1952- West Nyack, N.Y. : Center for Applied Research in Education, c1993.
*TC RA785 .T65 1993*

**STRESS MANAGEMENT FOR TEENAGERS.**
Toner, Patricia Rizzo, 1952- Stress-management and self-esteem activities. West Nyack, N.Y. : Center for Applied Research in Education, c1993.
*TC RA785 .T65 1993*

**STRESS MANAGEMENT - GREAT BRITAIN.**
Edworthy, Ann, 1952- Managing stress. Buckingham [England] ; Philadelphia : Open University Press, 2000.
*TC LB2333.3 .E39 2000*

**STRESS MANAGEMENT IN CHILDREN.**
Dacey, John S. Your anxious child. 1st ed. San Francisco : Jossey-Bass, c2000.
*TC BF723.A5 D33 2000*

**STRESS MANAGEMENT IN TEENAGERS.**
Dacey, John S. Your anxious child. 1st ed. San Francisco : Jossey-Bass, c2000.
*TC BF723.A5 D33 2000*

**STRESS (PHYSIOLOGY).** *See also* **JOB STRESS.**
Adversity, stress, and psychopathology. New York : Oxford University Press, 1998.
*TC RC455.4.S87 A39 1998*

Stress and health. Amsterdam : Harwood Academic ; Abingdon : Marston, 2000.
*TC RA785 .S774 2000*

**STRESS, PSYCHOLOGICAL - IN INFANCY & CHILDHOOD - CONGRESSES.**
Developmental perspectives on trauma. Rochester, N.Y., USA : University of Rochester Press, 1997.
*TC RJ499 .D4825 1997*

**STRESS (PSYCHOLOGY).** *See also* **ANXIETY; BURN OUT (PSYCHOLOGY); JOB STRESS; LIFE CHANGE EVENTS; POST-TRAUMATIC STRESS DISORDER.**

Adversity, stress, and psychopathology. New York : Oxford University Press, 1998.
*TC RC455.4.S87 A39 1998*

Chrispin, Marie C. Resilient adaptation of church-affiliated young Haitian immigrants. 1998.
*TC 06 no. 11015*

Fisher, S. (Shirley) Stress and strategy. London ; Hillsdale, N.J. : Lawrence Erlbaum Associates, c1986.
*TC BF575.S75 F52 1986*

Hammond, Kenneth R. Judgments under stress. New York : Oxford University Press, 2000.
*TC BF441 .H27 2000*

Humphrey, James Harry, 1911- Stress in college athletics. New York : Haworth Press, c2000.
*TC GV347 .H86 2000*

Lazarus, Richard S. Stress and emotion. New York : Springer Pub. Co., c1999.
*TC BF575.S75 L315 1999*

Professional burnout. Washington, DC : Taylor & Francis, c1993.
*TC BF481 .P77 1993*

Stress, coping, and health in families. Thousand Oaks, Calif. : Sage Publications, c1998.
*TC RC455.4.F3 S79 1998*

**STRESS (PSYCHOLOGY) - HEALTH ASPECTS.**
Stress and health. Amsterdam : Harwood Academic ; Abingdon : Marston, 2000.
*TC RA785 .S774 2000*

**STRESS (PSYCHOLOGY) - SOCIAL ASPECTS.**
Grimshaw, Jennie. Employment and health. London : British Library, 1999.
*TC HF5548.85 .G75 1999*

**Stress response syndromes.**
Horowitz, Mardi Jon, 1934- 3rd ed. Northvale, N.J. : J. Aronson, c1997.
*TC RC552.P67 H67 1997*

**Stress, social support, and psychological distress in late life.**
Nemeroff, Robin. 1999.
*TC 085 N341*

**STRESSFUL EVENTS.** *See* **LIFE CHANGE EVENTS.**

**STRESSFUL LIFE EVENTS.** *See* **LIFE CHANGE EVENTS.**

**Streubert, Helen J.** Qualitative research in nursing : advancing the humanistic imperative / Helen J. Streubert, Dona R. Carpenter. 2nd ed. Philadelphia : Lippincott, c1999. xxi, 344 p. : ill. ; 23 cm. Includes bibliographical references and index. ISBN 0-7817-1628-4 (alk. paper) DDC 610.73/07/2
*1. Nursing - Research - Methodology. 2. Sociology - Research - Methodology. 3. Nursing Research - methods. 4. Research Design. 5. Quality Assurance. Health Care. 6. Ethics. Nursing. I. Carpenter. Dona Rinaldi. II. Title.*
*TC RT81.5 .S78 1999*

**Streznewski, Marylou Kelly, 1934-** Gifted grownups : the mixed blessings of extraordinary potential / Marylou Kelly Streznewski. New York : J. Wiley, c1999. xii, 292 p. ; 24 cm. Includes bibliographical references (p. 277-290). ISBN 0-471-29580-9 (hardcover : alk. paper) DDC 153.9/8
*1. Gifted persons. 2. Gifted persons - Case studies. 3. Creative ability - Social aspects. I. Title.*
*TC BF412 .S77 1999*

**Strickland, Dorothy S.**
Morrow, Lesley Mandel. Literacy instruction in half- and whole-day kindergarten. Newark, Del. : International Reading Association ; Chicago, Ill. : National Reading Conference, c1998.
*TC LB1181.2 .M67 1998*

**Strickland, James.**
Strickland, Kathleen. Making assessment elementary. Portsmouth, NH : Heinemann, 2000.
*TC LB3051 .S873 1999*

**Strickland, Kathleen.** Making assessment elementary / Kathleen and James Strickland. Portsmouth, NH : Heinemann, 2000. xiii, 193 p. : ill. ; 28 cm. + 1computer optical disc (4 3/4 in). Includes bibliographical references (p.185-190) and index. ISBN 0-325-00200-2 DDC 371.27
*1. Educational tests and measurements - United States. 2. Examinations - United States. 3. Education, Elementary - United States. I. Strickland, James. II. Title.*
*TC LB3051 .S873 1999*

**Strickland, Rennard.**
Shared visions. 1st New Press ed. New York : New Press : Distributed by Norton, [1993], c1991.

*TC N6538.A4 A7 1993*

STRIGES. *See* OWLS.

STRIGIFORMES. *See* OWLS.

STRING - FICTION.
Blair, Margot. The red string. Malibu, Calif. : J. Paul Getty Museum and Childrens Library Press, c1996.
*TC PZ7.B537865 Re 1996*

STRINGED INSTRUMENTS, BOWED. *See* VIOLA; VIOLIN; VIOLONCELLO.

Stringfield, Sam.
Enhancing educational excellence, equity, and efficiency. Dordrecht ; Boston : Kluwer Academic Publishers, c1999.
*TC LB2921 .E54 1999*

STROKE. *See* CEREBROVASCULAR DISEASE.

Strong, David, 1955-.
Technology and the good life? Chicago ; London : University of Chicago Press, 2000.
*TC T14 .T386 2000*

Strong feelings.
Elster, Jon, 1940- Cambridge, Mass. : MIT Press, c1999.
*TC BF531 .E475 1999*

Strong, James H., 1950-.
Educating homeless students. Larchmont, N.Y. : Eye On Education, c2000.
*TC LC5144.2 .E385 2000*

Stroupe, Nibs. While we run this race : confronting the power of racism in a southern church / Nibs Stroupe and Inez Fleming. Maryknoll, N.Y. : Orbis Books, c1995. xii, 174 p. : ill. ; 22 cm. Includes bibliographical references (p. 173-174). ISBN 1-57075-000-9 (pbk.) DDC 261.8/348/009758225
*1. Race relations - Religious aspects - Presbyterian Church. 2. Oakhurst Presbyterian Church (Decatur, Ga.) 3. Decatur (Ga.) - Church history - 20th century. 4. Georgia - Church history - 20th century. 5. Fleming, Inez. 6. Afro-American Presbyterians - Georgia - Decatur - Biography. 7. Decatur (Ga.) - Race relations. 8. Georgia - Race relations. I. Fleming, Inez. II. Title.*
*TC BX8949.D43 S77 1995*

STRUCTURAL ADJUSTMENT (ECONOMIC POLICY) - AFRICA.
A thousand flowers. Trenton, NJ : Africa World Press, c2000, [1999].
*TC LC67.68.A35 T56 2000*

Structural equation modeling with LISREL, PRELIS, and SIMPLIS.
Byrne, Barbara M. Mahwah, N.J. : L. Erlbaum Associates, 1998.
*TC QA278 .B97 1998*

STRUCTURAL LINGUISTICS. *See* FUNCTIONALISM (LINGUISTICS).

STRUCTURAL UNEMPLOYMENT - UNITED STATES.
McCarthy, William H. Reducing urban unemployment. Washington, D.C. : National League of Cities, c1985.
*TC HD5724 .M34 1985*

Structure and dynamics of social intervention.
Spencer, Gary. Lexington, Mass., Heath Lexington Books [1970]
*TC HV91 .S63*

The structure of English.
DeCarrico, Jeanette S. Ann Arbor, Mich. : University of Michigan Press ; Wantage : University Presses Marketing, 2000.
*TC PE1112 .D43 2000*

The structure of schooling : readings in the sociology of education / [compiled by] Richard Arum and Irenee R. Beattie. Mountain View, Calif. : Mayfield Pub. Co., 1999. x, 516 p. ; 24 cm. Includes bibliographical references. ISBN 0-7674-1070-X DDC 306.43
*1. Educational sociology. 2. Education - Social aspects. I. Arum, Richard. II. Beattie, Irenee R.*
*TC LC189 .S87 1999*

The structuring of pedagogic discourse.
Bernstein, Basil B. London ; New York : Routledge, 1990.
*TC P40 .B39 1990*

The struggle for control of public education.
Engel, Michael, 1944- Philadelphia, Pa. : Temple University Press, c2000.
*TC LA217.2 .E533 2000*

A struggle to survive : funding higher education in the next century / editors, David S. Honeyman, James L. Wattenbarger, Kathleen C. Westbrook. Thousand Oaks, Calif. : Corwin Press, c1996. xiii, 245 p. : ill. ; 23 cm. (Annual yearbook of the American Education Finance Association ; 17th) Includes bibliographical references and index. CONTENTS: The financing of higher education -- The value of investments in higher education -- State funding formulas -- Accountability and quality evaluation in higher education -- Benefit and retirement issues in higher education -- Responsibility-centered management -- Funding public education with a state lottery -- Funding for community colleges -- Funding the multipurpose community college in an era of consolidation -- Competition for limited resources. ISBN 0-8039-6530-3 (acid-free paper) DDC 379.1/18/0973
*1. Education, Higher - United States - Finance. 2. Government aid to higher education - United States. I. Honeyman, David Smith. II. Wattenbarger, James Lorenzo, 1922- III. Westbrook, Kathleen C. IV. Series.*
*TC LB2342 .S856 1996*

Strzelecki, Piotr.
Ecole 27 [videorecording]. Bruxelles : Paradise Films ; New York, N.Y. : [distributed by] First Run/ Icarus Films, 1997, c1996.
*TC LC746.P7 E2 1997*

Stubbs, Michael, 1947- Text and corpus analysis : computer-assisted studies of language and culture / Michael Stubbs. Oxford, OX, UK ; Cambridge, Mass., USA : Blackwell Publishers, c1996. xix, 267 p. ; 23 cm. (Language in society ; 23) Includes bibliographical references (p. [245]-258) and indexes. ISBN 0-631-19511-4 (acid-free paper) ISBN 0-631-19512-0 (pbk. : acid-free paper) DDC 401/.41
*1. Discourse analysis. 2. Discourse analysis - Data processing. 3. Language and culture. 4. English language - Modality. I. Title. II. Series: Language in society (Oxford, England) ; 23.*
*TC P302 .S773 1996*

STUDENT ACHIEVEMENT. *See* ACADEMIC ACHIEVEMENT.

STUDENT ACTIVISM. *See* STUDENT MOVEMENTS.

STUDENT ACTIVITIES. *See* COLLEGE STUDENT DEVELOPMENT PROGRAMS; SCHOOL FIELD TRIPS; STUDENT UNIONS.

STUDENT ACTIVITIES - UNITED STATES.
Heflick, David. How to make money performing in schools. Orient, Wash. : Silcox Productions, c1996.
*TC LB3015 .H428 1996*

Komives, Susan R., 1946- Exploring leadership. 1st ed. San Francisco : Jossey-Bass Publishers, c1998.
*TC LB3605 .K64 1998*

Student development in college unions and student activities. Bloomington, Ind. : Association of College Unions-International, c1996.
*TC LB2343.4 .S84 1996*

Ward, Mary Ann, 1946- Student guidance and development. Larchmont, N.Y. : Eye On Education, c1998.
*TC LB1027.5 .W356 1998*

STUDENT ACTIVITIES - UNITED STATES - MANAGEMENT.
Barr, Margaret J. The handbook of student affairs administration. 2nd ed. San Francisco : Jossey-Bass, c2000.
*TC LB2342.92 .B37 2000*

Creating successful partnerships between academic and student affairs. San Francisco : Jossey-Bass Publishers, 1999.
*TC LB2342.9 .C75 1999*

Student affairs administration.
Barr, Margaret J. The handbook of student affairs administration. 2nd ed. San Francisco : Jossey-Bass, c2000.
*TC LB2342.92 .B37 2000*

STUDENT AFFAIRS SERVICES. *See* COUNSELING IN HIGHER EDUCATION.

STUDENT AFFAIRS SERVICES - GREAT BRITAIN - ADMINISTRATION.
Gledhill, John M., 1948- Managing students. Buckingham ; Philadelphia : Open University Press, 1999.
*TC LB2341.8.G7 G54 1996*

STUDENT AFFAIRS SERVICES - UNITED STATES.
Barr, Margaret J. The handbook of student affairs administration. 2nd ed. San Francisco : Jossey-Bass, c2000.
*TC LB2342.92 .B37 2000*

Creating successful partnerships between academic and student affairs. San Francisco : Jossey-Bass Publishers, 1999.
*TC LB2342.9 .C75 1999*

STUDENT AFFAIRS SERVICES - UNITED STATES - CASE STUDIES.
Linking theory to practice. 2nd ed. Philadelphia, Pa. : Taylor and Francis, 2000.
*TC LB2342.9 .L56 2000*

STUDENT AID. *See also* SCHOLARSHIPS; STUDENT FINANCIAL AID ADMINISTRATION.
GrantFinder. Arts and humanities. New York, NY : St. Martin's Press, 2000.
*TC LB2337.2 .G72*

STUDENT AID - DIRECTORIES.
GrantFinder. Science. New York : St. Martin's Press, c2000.
*TC LB2338 .G652 2000*

GrantFinder : Arts and humanities. New York, NY : St. Martin's Press, 2000.
*TC LB2337.2 .G72*

GrantFinder : Medicine. New York, NY : St. Martin's Press,
*TC LB2337.2 .G73*

GrantFinder : Social sciences. New York, NY : St. Martin's Press,
*TC LB2337.2 .G7 2000*

STUDENT AID - UNITED STATES.
Kane, Thomas J. The price of admission. Washington, D.C. : Brookings Institution Press ; New York : Russell Sage Foundation, c1999.
*TC LB2342 .K35 1999*

The role student aid plays in enrollment management. San Francisco : Jossey-Bass Publishers, 2000.
*TC LB2337.4 .R655 2000*

STUDENT AID - UNITED STATES - DIRECTORIES.
Financial aid for African Americans. El Dorado Hills, Calif. : Reference Service Press, c1997-
*TC LB2338 .F5643*

STUDENT ASPIRATIONS - UNITED STATES.
Ward, Mary Ann, 1946- Student guidance and development. Larchmont, N.Y. : Eye On Education, c1998.
*TC LB1027.5 .W356 1998*

STUDENT ASSISTANCE PROGRAMS - UNITED STATES.
Ward, Mary Ann, 1946- Student guidance and development. Larchmont, N.Y. : Eye On Education, c1998.
*TC LB1027.5 .W356 1998*

STUDENT ASSISTANCE PROGRAMS - UNITED STATES - CASE STUDIES.
Murphy, John J. (John Joseph), 1955- Brief intervention for school problems. New York : Guilford Press, c1997.
*TC LC4802 .M87 1997*

STUDENT-ATHLETES. *See* COLLEGE ATHLETES.

STUDENT ATTENDANCE. *See* SCHOOL ATTENDANCE.

STUDENT CHEATING. *See* CHEATING (EDUCATION).

Student cheating and plagiarism in the Internet era.
Lathrop, Ann. Englewood, Colo. : Libraries Unlimited, 2000.
*TC LB3609 .L28 2000*

STUDENT COMMUNITY SERVICE. *See* STUDENT SERVICE.

STUDENT COUNSELING. *See* EDUCATIONAL COUNSELING.

STUDENT COUNSELORS. *See* FACULTY ADVISORS.

STUDENT COUNSELORS - CERTIFICATION - UNITED STATES - PERIODICALS.
Requirements for certification of teachers, counselors, librarians, administrators for elementary and secondary schools. Chicago : University of Chicago Press, 1989-
*TC LB1171 .W6*

STUDENT COUNSELORS - PERIODICALS.
Focus on guidance. Denver, Love Publishing Co.

**STUDENT COUNSELORS, TRAINING OF.** *See*
**STUDENT COUNSELORS - TRAINING OF.**

**STUDENT COUNSELORS - TRAINING OF -**
**UNITED STATES.**
Baker, Stanley B., 1935- School counseling for the
twenty-first century. 3rd ed. Upper Saddle River,
N.J. : Merrill, c2000.
*TC LB1731.75 .B35 2000*

**STUDENT COUNSELORS - UNITED STATES.**
Schmidt, John J., 1946- Counseling in schools. 3rd ed.
Boston : Allyn and Bacon, c1999.
*TC LB1027.5 .S2585 1999*

**STUDENT COUNSELORS - UNITED STATES -**
**HANDBOOKS, MANUALS, ETC.**
Deuschle, C. (Constance) Stop the bus. Lanham, Md. :
University Press of America, c2000.
*TC LB1027.5 .D4567 2000*

**Student development.**
Student development in college unions and student
activities. Bloomington, Ind. : Association of College
Unions-International, c1996.
*TC LB2343.4 .S84 1996*

**Student development in college unions and student**
**activities** / edited by Nancy Davis Metz.
Bloomington, Ind. : Association of College Unions-
International, c1996. vii, 141 p. ; 28 cm. (ACUI classics)
Spine title: Student development. Includes bibliographical
references. ISBN 0-923276-06-8 DDC 378.1/94
*1. College student development programs - United States. 2.*
*Student unions - United States. 3. Student activities - United*
*States. I. Metz, Nancy Davis. II. Association of College*
*Unions-International. III. Title: Student development IV.*
*Series.*
*TC LB2343.4 .S84 1996*

**STUDENT DEVELOPMENT PROGRAMS,**
**COLLEGE.** *See* **COLLEGE STUDENT**
**DEVELOPMENT PROGRAMS.**

**STUDENT DISCIPLINE.** *See* **SCHOOL**
**DISCIPLINE.**

**Student discipline and classroom management.**
Campbell, Jack, Ed. D. Springfield, Ill. : C.C.
Thomas, c1999.
*TC LB3012 .C34 1999*

**STUDENT DISHONESTY.** *See* **CHEATING**
**(EDUCATION).**

**STUDENT ENROLLMENT.** *See* **SCHOOL**
**ENROLLMENT.**

**STUDENT EXCHANGE PROGRAMS - UNITED**
**STATES.**
Hansel, Bettina G. The exchange student survival kit.
Yarmouth, ME : Intercultural Press, c1993.
*TC LB1696 .H36 1993*

**STUDENT EXCHANGES.** *See* **STUDENT**
**EXCHANGE PROGRAMS.**

**STUDENT EXPENDITURES.** *See* **COLLEGE**
**COSTS.**

**STUDENT FINANCIAL AID.** *See* **STUDENT AID.**

**STUDENT FINANCIAL AID ADMINISTRATION -**
**UNITED STATES.**
The role student aid plays in enrollment management.
San Francisco : Jossey-Bass Publishers, 2000.
*TC LB2337.4 .R655 2000*

**STUDENT FINANCIAL ASSISTANCE.** *See*
**STUDENT AID.**

**Student-generated sexual harassment in secondary**
**schools.**
Wetzel, Roberta, 1946- Westport, Conn. ; London :
Bergin & Garvey, 2000.
*TC LC212.82 .W47 2000*

**STUDENT GUIDANCE.** *See* **EDUCATIONAL**
**COUNSELING; VOCATIONAL GUIDANCE.**

**Student guidance & development.**
Ward, Mary Ann, 1946- Student guidance and
development. Larchmont, N.Y. : Eye On Education,
c1998.
*TC LB1027.5 .W356 1998*

**Student guidance and development.**
Ward, Mary Ann, 1946- Larchmont, N.Y. : Eye On
Education, c1998.
*TC LB1027.5 .W356 1998*

**STUDENT HEALTH SERVICES - METHODS.**
Brief Alcohol Screening and Intervention for College
Students (BASICS). New York : Guilford Press,
c1999.
*TC HV5135 .B74 1998*

**STUDENT LEARNING.**
Involving commuter students in learning. San
Francisco, Calif. : Jossey-Bass, 2000.
*TC LB2343.6 .I68 2000*

**STUDENT LIFE AND CUSTOMS.** *See* **STUDENTS.**

**STUDENT LOAN FUNDS.** *See* **SCHOLARSHIPS;**
**STUDENT AID.**

**STUDENT MOVEMENTS.** *See* **STUDENT**
**PROTESTERS.**

**STUDENT MOVEMENTS - QUÉBEC**
**(PROVINCE) - MONTRÉAL - HISTORY.**
Neatby, Nicole, 1962- Carabins ou activistes?
Montréal ; Ithaca : McGill-Queen's University Press,
[1999?], c1997.
*TC LA418.Q8 N42 1999*

**STUDENT PARTICIPATION IN CURRICULUM**
**PLANNING - UNITED STATES.**
Mallery, Anne L. Creating a catalyst for thinking.
Boston : Allyn and Bacon, c2000.
*TC LB2806.15 .M34 2000*

**Student perceptions of their educational experiences**
**at Satellite Academy High School and their former**
**schools.**
Dreyer, Susan T. 1999.
*TC 06 no. 11105*

**Student Personnel Association for Teacher**
**Education. Journal.**
The Humanist educator. [Washington, American
Personnel and Guidance Association]

**STUDENT PERSONNEL SERVICES.** *See*
**STUDENT AFFAIRS SERVICES.**

**STUDENT PLANS.** *See* **STUDENT ASPIRATIONS.**

**STUDENT PROTEST.** *See* **STUDENT**
**MOVEMENTS.**

**STUDENT PROTESTERS.** *See* **STUDENT**
**MOVEMENTS.**

**STUDENT PROTESTERS - YUGOSLAVIA -**
**BELGRADE (SERBIA) - ATTITUDES.**
[Ajmo, ajde, svi u šetnju. English.] Protest in
Belgrade. Budapest, Hungary ; New York, NY, USA :
Central European University Press, 1999.
*TC DR2044 .A3913 1999*

**STUDENT SERVICE.**
Poirrier, Gail P. Service learning. Boston : Jones and
Bartlett Publishers, 2001.
*TC RT73 .P64 2001*

**STUDENT SERVICE - UNITED STATES.**
Building bridges. Washington, DC : National Council
for the Social Studies, 2000.

Colleges and universities as citizens. Boston : Allyn
and Bacon, c1999.
*TC LC220.5 .C644 1999*

Combining service and learning in higher education.
Santa Monica, CA : RAND Education, 1999.
*TC LC220.5 .C646 1999*

**STUDENT SERVICE - UNITED STATES - CASE**
**STUDIES.**
Service learning across the curriculum. Lanham, Md. :
University Press of America, c2000.
*TC LC221 .S47 2000*

**Student study guide, the American nation.**
The American nation. Upper Saddle River, N.J. :
Prentice Hall, c1998.
*TC E178.1 .D22 1998 Study Guide*

**Student study guide to accompany Fox's**
**physiological basis for exercise and sport.**
Muller, Susan. 6th ed. Boston, Mass. : WCB/
McGraw-Hill, c1998.
*TC RC1235 .F65 1998 guide*

**STUDENT-TEACHER RELATIONSHIPS.** *See*
**TEACHER-STUDENT RELATIONSHIPS.**

**STUDENT TEACHERS.**
Martin, Robert J. A study of the reflective practices of
physical education student teachers. 1998.
*TC 06 no. 11031*

**STUDENT TEACHERS - GREAT BRITAIN.**
Professional issues for teachers and student teachers.
London : David Fulton, 1999.
*TC LB1775.4.G7 P73 1999*

**STUDENT TEACHERS - TRAINING OF - UNITED**
**STATES - CASE STUDIES.**
Guiding teacher learning. Washington. DC : AACTE,
c1997.
*TC LB1731 .G85 1997*

**STUDENT TEACHERS - TRAINING OF - UNITED**
**STATES - HANDBOOKS, MANUELS, ETC.**
Pelletier, Carol Marra. A handbook of techniques and
strategies for coaching student teachers. 2nd ed.
Boston : Allyn and Bacon, 1999.
*TC LB2157.U5 P38 1999*

**STUDENT TEACHERS - UNITED STATES.**
Podsen, India, 1945- Coaching & mentoring first-year
and student teachers. Larchmont, NY : Eye On
Education, c2000.
*TC LB1731.4 .P63 2000*

**STUDENT TEACHERS - UNITED STATES - CASE**
**STUDIES.**
Richards, Janet C. Elementary literacy lessons.
Mahwah, N.J. : L. Erlbaum Associates, 2000.
*TC LB1576 .R517 2000*

**Student teaching.**
Goethals, M. Serra, 1934- Upper Saddle River, N.J. :
Merrill, c2000.
*TC LB2157.A3 G57 2000*

Lawrence, Alexandria Teresa. Cooperating teachers'
perceptions of the nature and quality of professional
development in a professional development school
collaboration. 1999.
*TC 06 no. 11141*

Lawrence, Alexandria Teresa. Cooperating teachers'
perceptions of the nature and quality of professional
development in a professional development school
collaboration. 1999.
*TC 06 no. 11141*

Lawrence, Alexandria Teresa. Cooperating teachers'
perceptions of the nature and quality of professional
development in a professional development school
collaboration. 1999.
*TC 06 no. 11141*

Posner, George J. Field experience. 5th ed. New
York : Longman, c2000.
*TC LB2157.A3 P6 2000*

**STUDENT TEACHING - GREAT BRITAIN.**
Sharp, Mavis, 1945- The management of failing
DipSW students. Aldershot ; Brookfield, Vt. :
Ashgate, c1999.
*TC HV11.8.G7 S53 1999*

**STUDENT TEACHING - HANDBOOKS,**
**MANUALS, ETC.**
Goethals, M. Serra, 1934- Student teaching. Upper
Saddle River, N.J. : Merrill, c2000.
*TC LB2157.A3 G57 2000*

**STUDENT TEACHING - UNITED STATES - CASE**
**STUDIES.**
Osunde, Egerton Oyenmwense, 1950- Understanding
student teaching. Lanham, Md. : University Press of
America, 1999.
*TC LB2157.U5 O78 1999*

**STUDENT-TO-STUDENT TUTORING.** *See*
**PEER-GROUP TUTORING OF STUDENTS.**

**STUDENT UNIONS - UNITED STATES.**
Student development in college unions and student
activities. Bloomington, Ind. : Association of College
Unions-International, c1996.
*TC LB2343.4 .S84 1996*

**STUDENT UNREST.** *See* **STUDENT**
**MOVEMENTS.**

**STUDENT VICTIMS OF CRIME.** *See*
**STUDENTS - CRIMES AGAINST.**

**STUDENT VIOLENCE.** *See* **SCHOOL VIOLENCE.**

**Student writing in higher education** : new contexts /
edited by Mary R. Lea and Barry Stierer.
Philadelphia, Pa. : Open University Press, c2000. ix,
205 p. ; 23 cm. Includes bibliographical references (p. [196]-
202) and index. ISBN 0-335-20408-2 (hb) ISBN
0-335-20407-4 (pbk.) DDC 808/.042/0711
*1. English language - Rhetoric - Study and teaching. 2.*
*Interdisciplinary approach in education. 3. Academic writing -*
*Study and teaching. I. Lea, Mary R. (Mary Rosalind), 1950- II.*
*Stierer, Barry.*
*TC PE1404 .S84 2000*

**STUDENTS.** *See* **AFRO-AMERICAN STUDENTS;**
**AMERICAN STUDENTS; COLLEGE**
**STUDENTS; DROPOUTS; EDUCATION;**
**GAY STUDENTS; HIGH SCHOOL STUDENTS; HANDICAPPED**
**STUDENTS; HIGH SCHOOL STUDENTS;**
**JEWISH STUDENTS; JUNIOR HIGH**
**SCHOOL STUDENTS; LESBIAN STUDENTS;**
**MIDDLE SCHOOL STUDENTS; MINORITY**
**STUDENTS; PREGNANT SCHOOLGIRLS;**
**SCHOOL CHILDREN.**

**STUDENTS, BLACK - GREAT BRITAIN.**
Richardson, Robin. Inclusive schools, inclusive society. Stoke on Trent, Staffordshire, England : Trentham Books, 1999.
*TC LC212.3.G7 R523 1999*

**Student's companion to the World Wide Web.**
Millhorn, Jim, 1953- Lanham, Md. ; London : Scarecrow Press, 1999.
*TC H61.95 .M55 1999*

**STUDENTS - CONDUCT OF LIFE.** *See* **CHEATING (EDUCATION).**

**STUDENTS - COUNSELING OF.** *See* **EDUCATIONAL COUNSELING.**

**STUDENTS - CRIMES AGAINST.** *See* **SCHOOL VIOLENCE.**

**STUDENTS - CRIMES AGAINST - TEXAS.**
Turk, William L. When juvenile crime comes to school. Lewiston, NY : E. Mellen Press, 1999.
*TC HV6250.4.S78 T87 1999*

**STUDENTS - CRIMES AGAINST - UNITED STATES - PREVENTION.**
Preventing student violence. Bloomington, IN (P.O. Box 789, Bloomington 47402-0789) : Phi Delta Kappa International, c1999.
*TC LB3013.3 .P755 1999*

**STUDENTS - CRIMES AGAINST - UNITED STATES - STATES.**
Turk, William L. When juvenile crime comes to school. Lewiston, NY : E. Mellen Press, 1999.
*TC HV6250.4.S78 T87 1999*

**STUDENTS - DISCIPLINE.** *See* **SCHOOL DISCIPLINE.**

**STUDENTS, FOREIGN.** *See* **FOREIGN STUDY; RETURNED STUDENTS.**

**STUDENTS, FOREIGN - COUNSELING OF.**
Supervising postgraduates from non-English speaking backgrounds. Buckingham ; Philadelphia : Society for Research into Higher Education : Open University Press, 1999.
*TC LB2343 .S86 1999*

**STUDENTS, FOREIGN - GREAT BRITAIN.**
Humfrey, Christine, 1947- Managing international students. Philadelphia, Penn : Society for Research into Higher Education & Open University Press, 1999.
*TC LB2376.6.G7 H86 1999*

**STUDENTS, FOREIGN - UNITED STATES - STATISTICS.**
[Open doors (New York, N.Y.)] Open doors. New York, N.Y. : Institute of International Education,
*TC LB2283 .I615*

Open doors. [New York, N.Y.] : Institute of International Education, 1954-
*TC LB2283 .I615*

**STUDENTS - GRADING AND MARKING.** *See* **GRADING AND MARKING (STUDENTS).**

**STUDENTS, GRADUATE.** *See* **GRADUATE STUDENTS.**

**Students helping students.**
Ender, Steven C. 1st ed. San Francisco : Jossey-Bass Publishers, c2000.
*TC LB1027.5 .E52 2000*

**STUDENTS, HISPANIC AMERICAN.** *See* **HISPANIC AMERICAN STUDENTS.**

**STUDENTS, INTERCHANGE OF.** *See* **STUDENT EXCHANGE PROGRAMS.**

**STUDENTS, INTERNATIONAL.** *See* **STUDENTS, FOREIGN.**

**STUDENTS - INTERVIEWS.**
McCaslin, Mary M. Listening in classrooms. 1st ed. New York : HarperCollins College Publishers, c1996.
*TC LB1033 .M34 1996*

**The student's introduction to Mathematica.**
Torrence, Bruce F. (Bruce Follett), 1963- Cambridge ; New York : Cambridge University Press, 1999.
*TC QA76.95 .T67 1999*

**STUDENTS, JEWISH.** *See* **JEWISH STUDENTS.**

**STUDENTS - MENTAL HEALTH.**
Page, Randy M. Fostering emotional well-being in the classroom. 2nd ed. Sudbury, Mass. ; London : Jones and Bartlett Publishers, c2000.
*TC LB3430 .P34 2000*

**Students on the margins.**
Hutchinson, Jaylynne N., 1954- Albany : State University of New York Press, c1999.

*TC LA210 .H88 1999*

**STUDENTS - PSYCHOLOGY.**
Brief Alcohol Screening and Intervention for College Students (BASICS). New York : Guilford Press, c1999.
*TC HV5135 .B74 1998*

**STUDENTS - PSYCHOLOGY.**
Masculinities at school. Thousand Oaks, Calif. : SAGE, c2000.
*TC LC1390 .M37 2000*

Purkey, William Watson. What students say to themselves. Thousand Oaks, Calif. : Corwin Press, c2000.
*TC LB1062.6 .P87 2000*

**STUDENTS - QUÉBEC (PROVINCE) - MONTRÉAL - POLITICAL ACTIVITY - HISTORY.**
Neatby, Nicole, 1962- Carabins ou activistes? Montréal ; Ithaca : McGill-Queen's University Press, [1999?], c1997.
*TC LA418.Q8 N42 1999*

**STUDENTS - RATING OF.** *See also* **EDUCATIONAL TESTS AND MEASUREMENTS; GRADING AND MARKING (STUDENTS).**
Hunt, Gilbert. Effective teaching. 3rd ed. Springfield, Ill. : C.C. Thomas Publisher, c1999.
*TC LB1025.3 .H86 1999*

**STUDENTS - SELF RATING OF.**
Self-assessment and development in writing. Cresskill, N.J. : Hampton Press, c2000.
*TC PE1404 .S37 2000*

**STUDENTS - SERVICES FOR - UNITED STATES.**
Collaborative practice. Westport, Conn. ; London : Praeger, 1999.
*TC HV741 .C5424 1999*

**STUDENTS - SEXUAL BEHAVIOR.**
Just sex. Lanham, MD : Rowman & Littlefield, 2000.
*TC HQ21 .J87 1999*

**STUDENTS - SUBSTANCE USE.**
Powell, Richard R., 1951- Classrooms under the influence. Newbury Park, Calif. : Corwin Press, c1995.
*TC HV5824.Y68 P69 1995*

**STUDENTS - UNITED STATES.** *See also* **HISPANIC AMERICAN STUDENTS.**
Hutchinson, Jaylynne N., 1954- Students on the margins. Albany : State University of New York Press, c1999.
*TC LA210 .H88 1999*

**STUDENTS - UNITED STATES - ATTITUDES.**
Heath, Douglas H. Assessing schools of hope. 1st ed. Bryn Mawr, PA : Conrow Pub. House, c1999.
*TC LB2822.75 .H42 1999*

**STUDENTS - VIOLENCE AGAINST - UNITED STATES.**
Hyman, Irwin A. Dangerous schools. 1st ed. San Francisco : Jossey-Bass Publishers, c1999.
*TC LB3013 .H897 1999*

**Students with autism.**
Scott, Jack, Ph. D. San Diego : Singular Pub. Group, 2000.
*TC LC4718 .S36 2000*

**Students with mild disabilities in general education settings.**
Vallecorsa, Ada, 1948- Upper Saddle River, N.J. : Merrill, c2000.
*TC LC4705 .V35 2000*

**Students writing in the university** : cultural and epistemological issues / edited by Carys Jones, Joan Turner, Brian Street. Amsterdam ; Philadelphia : John Benjamins Pub., c1999. xxiv, 231 p. : ill. ; 23 cm. (Studies in written language and literacy, 0929-7324 ; v. 8) Includes bibliographical references and index. ISBN 90-272-1801-3 (Eur. : hbk. : alk. paper) ISBN 1-55619-386-6 (U.S. : hbk. : alk. paper) DDC 808/.042/071141
*1. English language - Rhetoric - Study and teaching - Great Britain. 2. Academic writing - Study and teaching - Great Britain. 3. College students - Great Britain - Social conditions. 4. College students - Great Britain - Language. I. Jones, Carys. II. Turner, Joan, 1951- III. Street, Brian V. IV. Series.*
*TC PE1405.G7 S78 1999*

**Studia paedagogica (Louvain, Belgium)**
(nieuwe reeks 24.) Snick, Anne. Women in educational [sic] policy-making. Leuven, Belgium : Leuven University Press, 1999.
*TC LC93.A2 S56 1999*

**Studien zur Bildungsgeschichte im 17. Jahrhundert.**
Helmer, Karl. Umbruch zur Moderne. 1. Aufl. Sankt Augustin : Academia, 1994.
*TC LA116 .H445 1994*

**Studies in adolescent development.**
Spruijt-Metz, Donna. Adolescence, affect and health. Hove : Psychology Press, for the European Association for Research on Adolescence, 1999.
*TC RJ47.53 .S67 1999*

**Studies in bilingualism**
(v. 17) Ellis, Rod. Learning a second language through interaction. Amsterdam ; Philadelphia : J. Benjamins, c1999.
*TC P118.2 .E38 1999*

**Studies in church history. Subsidia**
(11) The medieval church. Woodbridge, Suffolk ; Rochester, NY : Published for the Ecclesiastical History Society by the Boydell Press, 1999.
*TC BR270 .M43 1999*

**Studies in classification, data analysis, and knowledge organization.**
International Federation of Classification Societies. Conference. 5th, 1996, Kobe, Japan. Data science, classification, and related methods :. Tokyo ; New York : Springer, c1998.
*TC QA278 I53 1996*

**Studies in cognitive systems**
(v. 23) Smith, David Livingstone, 1953- Freud's philosophy of the unconscious. Dordrecht ; Boston : Kluwer, 1999.
*TC BF173.F85 S615 1999*

**Studies in composition and rhetoric**
(vol. 1) Ethical issues in college writing. New York ; Canterbury [England] : Peter Lang, c1999.
*TC PE1404 .E84 1999*

**Studies in corpus linguistics**
(v. 1) Pearson, Jennifer. Terms in context. Amsterdam : Philadelphia : J. Benjamins, c1998.
*TC P305.18.D38 P4 1998*

(v. 2) Partington, Alan. Patterns and meanings. Amsterdam ; Philadelphia : J. Benjamins Pub., c1998.
*TC PE1074.5 .P37 1998*

**Studies in crime and public policy**
Zimring, Franklin E. American youth violence. New York : Oxford University Press, 1998.
*TC HV9104 .Z57 1998*

**Studies in curriculum theory**
Cultures of curriculum. Mahwah, N.J. ; London : L. Erlbaum Associates, 2000.
*TC LB2806.15 .C73 2000*

Doll, Mary Aswell. Like letters in running water. Mahwah, N.J. ; London : L. Erlbaum Publishers, 2000.
*TC LB1575 .D64 2000*

Jagodzinski, Jan, 1953- Postmodern dilemmas. Mahwah, N.J. : Lawrence Erlbaum Associates, 1997.
*TC N7445.2 .J34 1997*

**Studies in dance**
(v. 1) Hagood, Thomas K. A history of dance in American higher education. Lewiston, N.Y. : E. Mellen Press, c2000.
*TC GV1589 .H33 2000*

**Studies in dance history (Unnumbered)**
Limón, José. José Limón. Hanover, NH : University Press of New England, [1998?]
*TC GV1785.L515 A3 1998*

**Studies in discourse and grammar**
(v. 8) Mori, Junko. Negotiating agreement and disagreement in Japanese. Amsterdam ; Philadelphia, Pa. : J. Benjamins Pub. Co., c1999.
*TC PL611.C6 M67 1999*

**Studies in eating disorders**
The prevention of eating disorders. New York : New York University Press, 1998.
*TC RC552.E18 P74 1998*

**Studies in education**
(no. 6) Lange, Thomas, 1967- Rethinking higher education. London : IEA Education and Training Unit, 1998.
*TC LB2342.2.G7 L364 1998*

**Studies in educational gerontology**
(4) Glendenning, Frank. Teaching and learning in later life. Aldershot, Hants, Eng. ; Burlington, Vt. : Ashgate / Arena, c2000.
*TC LC5457 .G54 2000*

## Studies in emotion and social interaction
Berkowitz, Leonard, 1926- Causes and consequences of feelings. Cambridge, U.K. ; New York : Cambridge University Press ; Paris : Editions de la Maison des sciences de l'homme, 2000.
*TC BF531 .B45 2000*

Planalp, Sally, 1950- Communicating emotion. Cambridge ; New York : Cambridge University Press ; Paris : Editions de la Maison des sciences de l'homme, 1999.
*TC BF591 .P57 1999*

The social context of nonverbal behavior. Cambridge, U.K. ; New York : Cambridge University Press ; Paris : Editions de la Maison des Sciences de l'Homme, 1999.
*TC BF637.N66 S63 1999*

## Studies in emotion and social interaction. Second series
Feeling and thinking. Cambridge, U.K. ; New York : Cambridge University Press ; Paris : Editions de la Maison des Sciences de l'Homme, 2000.
*TC BF531 .F44 2000*

Gender and emotion. New York : Cambridge University Press, 1999.
*TC BF591 .G45 1999*

Kövecses, Zoltán. Metaphor and emotion. Cambridge ; New York : Cambridge University Press ; Paris : Editions de la Maison des Sciences de l'Homme, 2000.
*TC BF582 .K68 2000*

Wierzbicka, Anna. Emotions across languages and cultures. Cambridge : Cambridge University Press, 1999.
*TC BF531 .W54 1999*

## Studies in European cultural transition
(v. 2) Halliwell, Martin. Romantic science and the experience of self. Aldershot, Hants ; Brookfield, Vt. : Ashgate, c1999.
*TC BF697 R6375 1999*

## Studies in fuzziness and soft computing
(vol. 36) Innovative teaching and learning. Heidelberg [Germany] ; New York : Physica-Verlag, c2000.
*TC QA76.76.E95 I54 2000*

## Studies in gender and history series
Heathorn, Stephen J., 1965- For home, country, and race. Toronto : University of Toronto Press, 1999.
*TC LC93.E5 H42 1999*

## Studies in government and public policy
McDermott, Kathryn A., 1969- Controlling public education. Lawrence : University Press of Kansas, c1999.
*TC LC213.23.N39 M34 1999*

Orr, Marion, 1962- Black social capital. Lawrence : University Press of Kansas, c1999.
*TC LC2803.B35 O77 1999*

Portz, John, 1953- City schools and city politics. Lawrence : University Press of Kansas, c1999.
*TC LC5131 .P67 1999*

Rediscovering the democratic purposes of education. Lawrence : University Press of Kansas, c2000.
*TC LC89 .R43 2000*

Wong, Kenneth K., 1955- Funding public schools. Lawrence : University Press of Kansas, c1999.
*TC LB2825 .W56 1999*

## Studies in health and human services
(v. 31) Smith, Mieko Kotake. Adolescents with emotional and behavioral disabilities. Lewiston, NY : E. Mellen Press, c1998.
*TC RJ503 .S63 1998*

(v. 36) Clinical psychology in Ireland. Lewiston, N.Y. : E. Mellen, 2000.
*TC RC466.83.I73 C56 2000*

## Studies in health, illness, and caregiving
Fairman, Julie. Critical care nursing. Philadelphia : University of Pennsylvania Press, c1998.
*TC RT120.I5 F34 1998*

Sarnecky, Mary T. A history of the U.S. Army Nurse Corps. Philadelphia : University of Pennsylvania Press, c1999.
*TC UH493 .S27 1999*

## Studies in inclusive education series
Inclusive education. London ; Philadelphia : Falmer Press, 1999.
*TC LC1200 .I53 1999*

Moore, Alex, 1947- Teaching multicultured students. London ; New York : Falmer Press, 1999.
*TC LC3736.G6 M66 1999*

## Studies in language & literature
Fiction, literature and media. Amsterdam : Amsterdam University Press, c1999.
*TC LB1575.8 .F53 1999*

## Studies in linguistics and semiotics
(v. 2) Roberts, J. T. (John T.) Two French language teaching reformers reassessed. Lewiston [N.Y.] : E. Mellen Press, c1999.
*TC PB35 .R447 1999*

(v. 3) Scholes, Robert J. A linguistic approach to reading and writing. Lewiston, N.Y. : E. Mellen Press, c1999.
*TC P211 .S383 1999*

## Studies in mathematical thinking and learning
Designing learning environments for developing understanding of geometry and space. Mahwah, N.J. : Lawrence Erlbaum, c1998.
*TC QA461 .L45 1998*

Ma, Liping. Knowing and teaching elementary mathematics. Mahwah, N.J. : Lawrence Erlbaum Associates, 1999.
*TC QA135.5 .M22 1999*

Martin, Danny Bernard. Mathematics success and failure among African-American youth. Mahwah, N.J. : Lawrence Erlbaum, 2000.
*TC QA13 .M145 2000*

Reflections on statistics. Mahwah, N.J. : L. Erlbaum, 1998.
*TC QA276.18 .R44 1998*

## Studies in musical genesis and structure.
Zychowicz, James L. Mahler's Fourth symphony. New York : Oxford University Press, 2000.
*TC MT130.M25 Z93 2000*

## Studies in perception and action V.
International Conference on Perception and Action (10th : 1999 : Edinburgh, Scotland) Mahwah, N.J. : L. Erlbaum Associates, 1999.
*TC BF295 .I57 1999*

## Studies in risk and uncertainty
Valuing the cost of smoking. Boston : Kluwer Academic Publishers, 1999.
*TC HV5735 .V35 1999*

## Studies in Russian and East European history and society
Webber, Stephen L., 1967- School, reform and society in the new Russia . Houndmills [England] : Macmillan Press ; New York : St. Martin's Press in association with Centre for Russian and East European Studies, University of Birmingham, 2000.
*TC LA839.2 .W4 2000*

## Studies in social and political theory
(v. 3) Freedom, equality, and social change. Lewiston : E. Mellen Press, c1989.
*TC HM216 .F83 1989*

## Studies in the history of education (Falmer Press)
(v. 9.) Richardson, John G. Common, delinquent, and special. New York : Falmer Press, 1999.
*TC LC3981 .R525 1999*

## Studies in the spectator role.
Benton, Michael, 1939- London ; New York : Routledge, 2000.
*TC PR51.G7 B46 2000*

## Studies in theoretical psycholinguistics
(v. 13) Lillo-Martin, Diane C. (Diane Carolyn), 1959- Universal grammar and American sign language. Dordrecht ; Boston : Kluwer Academic Publishers, c1991.
*TC HV2474 .L55 1991*

## Studies in world peace
(v. 11) The developmental process of positive attitudes and mutual respect. Lewiston, N.Y. : E. Mellen Press, c1999.
*TC LB2822.82 .D49 1999*

## Studies in writing & rhetoric.
Selfe, Cynthia L., 1951- Technology and literacy in the twenty-first century. Carbondale : Southern Illinois University Press, c1999.
*TC LC149.5 .S45 1999*

## Studies in written language and literacy
(v. 8) Students writing in the university. Amsterdam ; Philadelphia : John Benjamins Pub., c1999.
*TC PE1405.G7 S78 1999*

## Studies on modern China
Benson, Linda. China's last Nomads. Armonk, N.Y. : M.E. Sharpe, c1998.
*TC DS731.K38 B46 1998*

## Studies on the history of Quebec.
Neatby, Nicole, 1962- Carabins ou activistes? Montréal ; Ithaca : McGill-Queen's University Press, [1999?], c1997.
*TC LA418.Q8 N42 1999*

## Studies on the history of society and culture
(27) Bonnell, Victoria E. Iconography of power. Berkeley : University of California Press, c1997.
*TC DK266.3 .B58 1997*

**STUDY ABROAD.** *See* **FOREIGN STUDY.**

**STUDY AND TEACHING - PERIODICALS.**
L'Enseignement des sciences. [Paris]

**STUDY, COURSES OF.** *See* **EDUCATION - CURRICULA.**

## Study guide.
Straub, Richard O. (Richard Otto) New York : Worth Publishers, 1998.
*TC BF713 .B463 1998 Guide*

Straub, Richard O. (Richard Otto) New York : Worth Publishers, 1998.
*TC BF713 .B463 1998 Guide*

Straub, Richard O. (Richard Otto) New York : Worth Publishers, 1998.
*TC BF713 .B463 1998 guide*

**STUDY, INDEPENDENT.** *See* **INDEPENDENT STUDY.**

**STUDY, METHOD OF.** *See* **STUDY SKILLS.**

**STUDY METHODS.** *See* **STUDY SKILLS.**

## Study of a New York City high school's struggle for excellence and equity and its relationship to policy.
Ort, Suzanne Wichterle. Standards in practice. 1999.
*TC 06 no. 11210*

## A study of the reflective practices of physical education student teachers.
Martin, Robert J. 1998.
*TC 06 no. 11031*

## Study of the sexes in a changing world.
Mead, Margaret, 1901-1978. Male and female. London : Victor Gollancz, c1949.
*TC HQ21 .M464 1949*

Mead, Margaret, 1901-1978. Male and female. London : Victor Gollancz, c1949.
*TC HQ21 .M464 1949*

**STUDY SKILLS.** *See also* **HOMEWORK; INDEPENDENT STUDY.**
Banner, James M., 1935- The elements of learning. New Haven, Conn. : Yale University Press, c1999.
*TC LB1060 .B36 1999*

Baynes, Joyce Frisby. The development of a van Hiele-based summer geometry program and its impact on student van Hiele level and achievement in high school geometry. 1998.
*TC 06 no. 10915*

Elphinstone, Leonie. How to get a research degree. St. Leonards, Australia : Allen & Unwin, 1998.
*TC LB2371 .E46 1998*

Hartley, James, Ph. D. Learning and studying. London ; New York : Routledge, 1998.
*TC BF318 .H365 1998*

Individualisation. Oxford : Modern English Publications, 1982.
*TC LC32 .I53 1982*

Practical approaches to using learning styles in higher education. Westport, Conn. : Bergin & Garvey, 2000.
*TC LB2395 .P69 2000*

Sosin, Adrienne. Achieving styles preferences of students in an urban graduate teacher education program. 1996.
*TC 06 no. 10701*

Tsai, Chin-Chung. The interrelationships between junior high school students' scientific epistemologicl beliefs, learning environment preferences and their cognitive structure outcomes. 1996.
*TC 06 no. 10713*

**STUDY SKILLS - UNITED STATES - HANDBOOKS, MANUALS, ETC.**
Handbook of college reading and study strategy research. Mahwah, N.J. : Lawrence Erlbaum Associates, c2000.

*TC LB2395.3 .H36 2000*

**A study to compare inner city Black men and women completers and non-attenders of diabetes self-care classes.**
Mendoza, Maria Adalia. 1999.
*TC 06 no. 11206*

**Study to teach :** a guide to studying in teacher education / edited by Steve Herne, John Jessel, and Jenny Griffiths. London ; New York : Routledge, 2000. xii, 198 p. ; 24 cm. Includes bibliographical references and index. ISBN 0-415-19112-2 (pbk. : alk. paper) DDC 370/.71
*1. Teachers - Training of. 2. Teaching. 3. Learning. I. Herne, Steve, 1950- II. Jessel, John. III. Griffiths, Jenny, 1943-*
*TC LB1707 .S88 2000*

**STUDY TRIPS, SCHOOL.** *See* **SCHOOL FIELD TRIPS.**

**Studying abroad/learning abroad.**
Hess, J. Daniel (John Daniel), 1937- Yarmouth, Me., USA : Intercultural Press, c1997.
*TC LB2375 .H467 1997*

**Stueber, Karsten R.**
Empathy and agency. Boulder, Colo. ; Oxford : Westview Press, 2000.
*TC BF64 .E67 2000*

**Stull, Elizabeth Crosby.** Let's read! : a complete month-by-month activities program for beginning readers / Elizabeth Crosby Stull. West Nyack, NY : Center for Applied Research in Education, c2000. xlii, 501 p. : ill. ; 28 cm. Includes bibliographical references (495-501). ISBN 0-87628-489-6 DDC 372.4
*1. Reading (Primary) - United States. 2. Education, Primary - Activity programs - United States. I. Title.*
*TC LB1573 .S896 2000*

**Stull, Judith C., 1944-.**
Restructuring education. Westport, Conn. : Praeger, 2000.
*TC LB2822.82 . R45 2000*

**Stump, Colleen Shea.**
Bigge, June L. Curriculum, assessment, and instruction for students with disabilities. Belmont, CA : Wadsworth Pub., c1999.
*TC LC4031 .B46 1999*

**Sturge, Theodore.** The conservation of leather artefacts : case studies from the Leather Conservation Centre / Theodore Sturge. London : The Leather Conservation Centre, 2000. 40 p. : ill. (some col.) ; 30 cm. Includes bibliographical references (p. 38) and index. ISBN 0-946072-06-x
*1. Leather - Conservation and restoration. 2. Leather work - Conservation and restoration. I. Leather Conservation Centre. II. Title.*
*TC N8555 .S8 2000*

**Sturtridge, Gill.**
Individualisation. Oxford : Modern English Publications, 1982.
*TC LC32 .I53 1982*

**Stuss, Donald T.**
Cognitive neurorehabilitation. Cambridge, UK ; New York : Cambridge University Press, c1999.
*TC RC553.C64 C654 1999*

**STUTTERING.**
Stuttering and related disorders of fluency. 2nd ed. New York : Thieme Medical Publishers, 1999.
*TC RC424 .S768 1998*

Stuttering research and practice. Mahwah, N.J. : Erlbaum, 1999.
*TC RC424 .S786 1999*

Stuttering research and practice. Mahwah, N.J. : Erlbaum, 1999.
*TC RC424 .S786 1999*

**Stuttering and related disorders of fluency** / [editor] Richard F. Curlee. 2nd ed. New York : Thieme Medical Publishers, 1999. xi, 307 p. : ill. ; 26 cm. Includes bibliographical references and index. ISBN 0-86577-764-0 DDC 616.85/54
*1. Stuttering. 2. Stuttering - therapy. 3. Speech Therapy - methods. I. Curlee, Richard F. (Richard Frederick), 1935-*
*TC RC424 .S768 1998*

**Stuttering research and practice :** bridging the gap / edited by Nan Bernstein Ratner, E. Charles Healey. Mahwah, N.J. : Erlbaum, 1999. 260 p. : ill. ; 25 cm. Includes bibliographical references and index. ISBN 0-8058-2458-8 (c : alk. paper) ISBN 0-8058-2459-6 (pbk. : alk. paper) DDC 616.85/54
*1. Stuttering. 2. Stuttering. I. Ratner, Nan Bernstein. II. Healey, E. Charles.*

*TC RC424 .S786 1999*

**STUTTERING - THERAPY.**
Stuttering and related disorders of fluency. 2nd ed. New York : Thieme Medical Publishers, 1999.
*TC RC424 .S768 1998*

**STUTTERING - TREATMENT - CONGRESSES.**
Treatment efficacy for stuttering. San Diego, Calif. : Singular Pub. Group, c1998.
*TC RC424 .T698 1998*

**STYLE, LITERARY.** *See* **CRITICISM; LITERATURE, EXPERIMENTAL; LITERATURE - HISTORY AND CRITICISM; RHETORIC.**

**STYLES, COGNITIVE.** *See* **COGNITIVE STYLES.**

**STYLES, LIFE.** *See* **LIFESTYLES.**

**Styles, Morag.**
Teaching through texts. London ; New York : Routledge, 1999.
*TC LB1573 .T39 1999*

**Su, Xiaojun.**
Culture, literacy, and learning English. Portsmouth, NH : Boynton/Cook Publishers, c1998.
*TC PE1130.C4 C85 1998*

**Suárez-Richard, Frederick, 1941-.**
Valette, Jean Paul. Spanish for mastery. Lexington, Mass. : D.C. Heath, c1980.
*TC PC4112 .V29 1980*

**Subalternity and representation.**
Beverley, John. Durham [N.C.] ; London : Duke University Press, 1999.
*TC HM1136 .B48 1999*

**Subbiondo, Joseph L.**
Quehl, Gary H. Fifty years of innovations in undergraduate education. Indianapolis, Ind : USA Group Foundation, c1999.
*TC LB1027.3 .Q43 1999*

**SUBCHAPTER C CORPORATIONS.** *See* **CORPORATIONS.**

**SUBCONSCIOUSNESS.** *See also* **ARCHETYPE (PSYCHOLOGY); DREAMS.**
Clough, Patricia Ticineto, 1945- Autoaffection. Minneapolis : University of Minnesota Press, c2000.
*TC HM846 .C56 2000*

MacIntyre, Alasdair C. The unconscious. Bristol, England : Thoemmes Press, 1997, c1958.
*TC BF315 .M23 1997*

Smith, David Livingstone, 1953- Freud's philosophy of the unconscious. Dordrecht ; Boston : Kluwer, 1999.
*TC BF173.F85 S615 1999*

**SUBCULTURE.**
Digital diversions. London : UCL Press, 1998.
*TC QA76.575 .D536 1998*

**SUBJECT CATALOGING.** *See* **CLASSIFICATION - BOOKS.**

**SUBJECT DICTIONARIES.** *See* **ENCYCLOPEDIAS AND DICTIONARIES.**

**The subject is reading :** essays by teachers and students / edited by Wendy Bishop. Portsmouth, NH : Heinemann c2000. xiii, 257 p. ; 23 cm. Includes bibliographical references. ISBN 0-86709-472-9 (alk. paper) DDC 428.4/071/1
*1. Reading (Higher education) I. Bishop, Wendy.*
*TC LB2395.3 .S82 2000*

**Subject leader's handbooks.**
Wintle, Mike. Coordinating assessment practice across the primary school. London : Philadelphia, PA : Falmer Press, 1999.
*TC LB3060.37 .W56 1999*

**SUBJECT-MATTER READING.** *See* **CONTENT AREA READING.**

**SUBJECTIVITY.**
The message within. Philadelphia, Pa. : Psychology Press, 2000.
*TC BF697 .M457 2000*

Sanguineti, Vincenzo R. Landscapes in my mind. Madison, Conn. : Psychosocial Press, c1999.
*TC BF697 .S2394 1999*

Social constructionism, discourse, and realism. London ; Thousand Oaks, Calif. : SAGE Publications, 1998.
*TC HM251 .S671163 1998*

**SUBJECTIVITY IN LITERATURE.**
McCallum, Robyn. Ideologies of identity in adolescent fiction. New York : Garland Pub., 1999.
*TC PN3443 .M38 1999*

**SUBLANGUAGE.** *See* **TERMS AND PHRASES.**

**SUBLANGUAGE - CONGRESSES.**
Interactional perspectives on LSP. Aalborg Øst, Denmark : Centre for Languages and Intercultural Studies, Aalborg University, 1997.
*TC P120.S9 I58 1997*

**SUBORDINATION OF WOMEN.** *See* **SEX DISCRIMINATION AGAINST WOMEN; SEX ROLE.**

**SUBSISTENCE ECONOMY.** *See* **POVERTY.**

**SUBSTANCE ABUSE.** *See also* **ALCOHOLISM; DRUG ABUSE; TOBACCO HABIT.**
Changing lives [videorecording]. Princeton, NJ : Films for the Humanities & Sciences, c1998.
*TC RC564 .C54 1998*

Schaler, Jeffrey A. Addiction is a choice. Chicago, Ill. : Open Court, 2000.
*TC HV4998 .S33 2000*

When the brain goes wrong [videorecording]. Short version. Boston, MA : Fanlight Productions [dist.], c1992.
*TC RC386 .W54 1992*

**SUBSTANCE ABUSE - COMPLICATIONS - PREVENTION.**
Denning, Patt, 1950- Practicing harm reduction psychotherapy. New York : Guilford Press, 2000.
*TC RC564 .D44 2000*

**SUBSTANCE ABUSE - ECONOMIC ASPECTS - UNITED STATES - CONGRESSES.**
The economic analysis of substance use and abuse. Chicago : University of Chicago Press, 1999.
*TC HV4999.2 .E25 1999*

**SUBSTANCE ABUSE - ETIOLOGY.**
Elster, Jon, 1940- Strong feelings. Cambridge, Mass. : MIT Press, c1999.
*TC BF531 .E475 1999*

**SUBSTANCE ABUSE IN PREGNANCY.** *See* **CHILDREN OF PRENATAL SUBSTANCE ABUSE.**

**SUBSTANCE ABUSE - LONGITUDINAL STUDIES - STATISTICAL METHODS.**
Multivariate applications in substance use research. Mahwah, N.J. : Lawrence Erlbaum Associates, 2000.
*TC HV5809 .M84 2000*

**SUBSTANCE ABUSE - PATIENTS - COUNSELING OF.**
Miller, Geraldine A., 1955- Learning the language of addiction counseling. Boston : Allyn and Bacon, c1999.
*TC RC564 .M536 1999*

**SUBSTANCE ABUSE - PHYSIOLOGICAL ASPECTS - RESEARCH.**
The hijacked brain [videorecording]. Princeton, NJ : Films for the Humanities & Sciences, c1998.
*TC RC564 .H5 1998*

**SUBSTANCE ABUSE - PHYSIOLOGICAL EFFECT - RESEARCH.**
The hijacked brain [videorecording]. Princeton, NJ : Films for the Humanities & Sciences, c1998.
*TC RC564 .H5 1998*

**Substance abuse prevention activities.**
Toner, Patricia Rizzo, 1952- West Nyack. N.Y. : Center for Applied Research in Education, c1993.
*TC HV4999.2 .T66 1993*

**SUBSTANCE ABUSE - PREVENTION - STUDY AND TEACHING (ELEMENTARY).**
Weinstein, Sanford. The educator's guide to substance abuse prevention. Mahwah, N.J. : Lawrence Erlbaum Publishers, 1999.
*TC HV5808 .W45 1999*

**SUBSTANCE ABUSE - PREVENTION - STUDY AND TEACHING (SECONDARY) - UNITED STATES.**
Toner, Patricia Rizzo, 1952- Substance abuse prevention activities. West Nyack, N.Y. : Center for Applied Research in Education, c1993.
*TC HV4999.2 .T66 1993*

**SUBSTANCE ABUSE - PSYCHOLOGICAL ASPECTS.**
Portrait of addiction [videorecording]. Princeton, NJ : Films for the Humanities & Sciences, c1998.
*TC RC564 .P6 1998*

Powell, Richard R., 1951- Classrooms under the influence. Newbury Park, Calif. : Corwin Press, c1995.
*TC HV5824.Y68 P69 1995*

**SUBSTANCE ABUSE - RESEARCH.**
Multivariate applications in substance use research. Mahwah, N.J. : Lawrence Erlbaum Associates, 2000.
*TC HV5809 .M84 2000*

**SUBSTANCE ABUSE - SOCIAL ASPECTS.**
Denning, Patt, 1950- Practicing harm reduction psychotherapy. New York : Guilford Press, 2000.
*TC RC564 .D44 2000*

**SUBSTANCE ABUSE - TREATMENT.**
Denning, Patt, 1950- Practicing harm reduction psychotherapy. New York : Guilford Press, 2000.
*TC RC564 .D44 2000*

Twerski, Abraham J. Substance-abusing high achievers. Northvale, N.J. : Aronson, 1998.
*TC RC564.5.S83 T94 1998*

**SUBSTANCE ABUSE - TREATMENT - UNITED STATES.**
Bridges to recovery. New York ; London : Free Press, c2000.
*TC HV5199.5 .B75 2000*

Gewirtz, Abigail Hadassah. Coping strategies and stage of change among Vietnam combat veterans diagnosed with posttraumatic stress disorder and comorbid substance use disorders. 1997.
*TC 085 G338*

**SUBSTANCE ABUSE - UNITED STATES.**
The next generation [videorecording]. Princeton, NJ : Films for the Humanities & Sciences, c1998.
*TC RC564 .N4 1998*

Pagliaro, Ann M. Substance use among women. Philadelphia, PA : Brunner/Mazel, c2000.
*TC RC564.5.W65 P34 2000*

**Substance-abusing high achievers.**
Twerski, Abraham J. Northvale, N.J. : Aronson, 1998.
*TC RC564.5.S83 T94 1998*

**SUBSTANCE ADDICTION.** See **SUBSTANCE ABUSE.**

**SUBSTANCE (PHILOSOPHY).** See **MATTER.**

**SUBSTANCE-RELATED DISORDERS - THERAPY.**
Seivewright, Nicholas. Community treatment of drug misuse. Cambridge, UK ; New York : Cambridge University Press, 2000.
*TC RC564 .S45 2000*

**Substance use among women.**
Pagliaro, Ann M. Philadelphia, PA : Brunner/Mazel, c2000.
*TC RC564.5.W65 P34 2000*

**Substitute parents.**
Sayles, Mary Buell, 1878- New York, The Commonwealth fund; London, H. Milford, Oxford University Press, 1936.
*TC HV875 .S3*

**SUBSTITUTIONS (MATHEMATICS).** See **GROUP THEORY.**

**The subtlety of emotions.**
Ben-Ze'ev, Aharon. Cambridge, Mass. ; London : MIT Press, c2000.
*TC BF531 .B43 2000*

**Subtractive schooling.**
Valenzuela, Angela. Albany : State University of New York Press, c1999.
*TC LC2683.4 .V35 1999*

**SUBURBAN LIFE IN ART.**
McAuliffe, Chris. Art and suburbia. Roseville East, NSW : Craftsman House, c1996.
*TC N7400.2 .M32 1996*

**SUBURBAN SCHOOLS - UNITED STATES.**
New school order [videorecording]. New York : First Run/Icarus Films, 1996.
*TC LB2831.583.P4 N4 1996*

**SUBURBS - AUSTRALIA - HISTORY.**
McAuliffe, Chris. Art and suburbia. Roseville East, NSW : Craftsman House, c1996.
*TC N7400.2 .M32 1996*

**Succeeding in an academic career :** a guide for faculty of color / edited by Mildred García ; foreword by Yolanda Moses. Westport, Conn. : Greenwood Press, 2000. xix, 164 p. ; 25 cm. (The Greenwood educators' reference collection, 1056-2192) Includes bibliographical references and index. ISBN 0-313-29906-4 (alk. paper) DDC 378.1/2/08996073

*1. Universities and colleges - United States - Faculty - Case studies. 2. Minority college teachers - United States - Case studies. 3. Afro-American college teachers - Case studies. I. García, Mildred. II. Series.*
*TC LB2331.72 .S83 2000*

**SUCCESS.** See also **ACADEMIC ACHIEVEMENT; SELF-REALIZATION.**
Dixon, Jerome C. A qualitative study of perceptions of external factors that influence the persistence of Black males at a predominantly white four-year state college. 1999.
*TC 06 no. 11050*

**Success and failure at the university.**
Parkyn, George W. Wellington, New Zealand Council for Educational Research, 1959-67.
*TC LB1131 .P29*

**Success in early intervention.**
Reynolds, Arthur J. Lincoln, Neb. : University of Nebraska Press, c2000.
*TC HV743.C5 R48 2000*

**SUCCESS - PSYCHOLOGICAL ASPECTS.**
Loase, John Frederick, 1947- Sigfluence III. Lanham, Md. : University Press of America, c1996.
*TC BF774 .L63 1996*

McWhorter, John H. Losing the race. New York : Free Press, c2000.
*TC E185.625 .M38 2000*

**SUCCESS - UNITED STATES.**
Elder, Glen H. Children of the land. Chicago : University of Chicago Press, 2000.
*TC HQ796 .E525 2000*

**Successful inclusion.**
Kochhar, Carol. 2nd ed. Upper Saddle River, NJ : Prentice Hall, c2000.
*TC LC1201 .K63 2000*

**Successful inclusive teaching :** proven ways to detect and correct special needs / edited by Joyce S. Choate. 3rd ed. Boston : Allyn and Bacon, c2000. xviii, 478 p. : ill., forms ; 28 cm. Includes bibliographical references and index. ISBN 0-205-30621-7 DDC 371.9/046/0973
*1. Inclusive education - United States. 2. Special education - United States. 3. Handicapped children - Education - United States. I. Choate, Joyce S.*
*TC LC1201 .S93 2000*

**SUCCESSFUL PEOPLE - SUBSTANCE USE.**
Twerski, Abraham J. Substance-abusing high achievers. Northvale, N.J. : Aronson, 1998.
*TC RC564.5.S83 T94 1998*

**Successful school.**
Walsh, Mike. Building a successful school. London : Kogan Page, 1999.
*TC LB2900.5 .W37 1999*

**Successful schools**
(v. 2) Gallagher, Karen S. Shaping school policy. Newbury Park, Calif. : Corwin Press, c1992.
*TC LC89 .G35 1992*

**Successful teaching in the elementary classroom.**
Riner, Phillip S., 1950- Upper Saddle River, N.J. : Merrill, c2000.
*TC LB1555 .R53 2000*

**SUCCESSION, INTESTATE.** See **INHERITANCE AND SUCCESSION.**

**Such stuff as dreams are made on.**
Luke, Helen M., 1904- New York : Parabola Books, c2000.
*TC BF1091 .L82 2000*

**Suchodolski, Bogdan, ed.**
Kwartalnik pedagogiczny. [Warszawa] Państwowe Wydawn. Naukowe.

**Sudha Rao, K.**
Open learning system. New Delhi : Lancer International, c1989.
*TC LC5808.I4 O64 1989*

**Sudol, Ronald A., 1943-.**
The literacy connection. Cresskill, N.J. : Hampton Press, c1999.
*TC LC151 .L482 1999*

**Sudzina, Mary R.**
Case study applications for teacher education. Boston : Allyn and Bacon, c1999.
*TC LB1715 .S796 1999*

**Suffer the little children.**
Raftery, Mary. Dublin, Ireland : New Island, 1999.
*TC HV9148.A5 R33 1999*

**SUFFERING.** See **LONELINESS; PAIN.**

**SUFFERING - PSYCHOLOGICAL ASPECTS.**
Adversity, stress, and psychopathology. New York : Oxford University Press, 1998.
*TC RC455.4.S87 A39 1998*

**Sugar, Max, 1925-.**
The adolescent in group and family therapy. 2nd ed. Northvale, NJ : Jason Aronson, 1999.
*TC RJ505.G7 A36 1999*

**Sugarman, Stephen D.**
School choice and social controversy. Washington, D.C. : Brookings Institution Press, c1999.
*TC LB1027.9 .S352 1999*

**SUGGESTION - CONGRESSES.**
The therapeutic alliance. Madison, Conn. : International Universities Press, c2000.
*TC RC489.T66 T468 2000*

**SUICIDAL BEHAVIOR.** See **SUICIDE.**

**SUICIDE.** See also **ASSISTED SUICIDE.**
Life-threatening behavior. [New York, Behavioral Publications, inc.]

**SUICIDE.**
The Harvard Medical School guide to suicide assessment and intervention. 1st ed. San Francisco : Jossey-Bass, c1999.
*TC RC569 .H37 1999*

Suicide science. Boston ; London : Kluwer Academic Publishers, c2000.
*TC RC569 .S9368 2000*

**Suicide assessment and intervention.**
The Harvard Medical School guide to suicide assessment and intervention. 1st ed. San Francisco : Jossey-Bass, c1999.
*TC RC569 .H37 1999*

**SUICIDE IN LITERATURE.**
Berman, Jeffrey, 1945- Surviving literary suicide. Amherst : University of Massachusetts Press, c1999.
*TC PS169.S85 B47 1999*

**SUICIDE - MORAL AND ETHICAL ASPECTS.**
Prado, C. G. The last choice. 2nd ed. Westport, Conn. : Greenwood Press, 1998.
*TC HV6545.2 .P7 1998*

**SUICIDE - PERIODICALS.**
Life-threatening behavior. [New York, Behavioral Publications, inc.]

**SUICIDE - PERIODICALS.**
Life-threatening behavior. [New York, Behavioral Publications, inc.]

**SUICIDE - PERSONAL NARRATIVES.**
The Choice of a lifetime [videorecording]. Hohokus, NJ : New Day Films, c1996.
*TC RC569 .C45 1996*

**SUICIDE PREVENTION.** See **SUICIDE - PREVENTION.**

**SUICIDE - PREVENTION.**
The Harvard Medical School guide to suicide assessment and intervention. 1st ed. San Francisco : Jossey-Bass, c1999.
*TC RC569 .H37 1999*

Johnson, Wanda Yvonne, 1936- Youth suicide. Bloomington, Ind. : Phi Delta Kappa Educational Foundation, c1999.
*TC HV6546 .J645 1999*

Shea, Shawn C. The practical art of suicide assessment. New York ; Chichester [England] : John Wiley, c1999.
*TC RC569 .S46 1999*

**SUICIDE - PREVENTION - PERIODICALS.**
Life-threatening behavior. [New York, Behavioral Publications, inc.]

**SUICIDE - RISK FACTORS.**
Shea, Shawn C. The practical art of suicide assessment. New York ; Chichester [England] : John Wiley, c1999.
*TC RC569 .S46 1999*

**Suicide science :** expanding the boundaries / [edited] by Thomas Joiner, M. David Rudd. Boston ; London : Kluwer Academic Publishers, c2000. 278 p. : ill. ; 25 cm. Includes bibliographical references. CONTENTS: 1. New Life in Suicide Science / Thomas Joiner -- 2. Decades of Suicide Research: Wherefrom and Whereto? / David Lester -- 3. The Hopelessness Theory of Suicidality / Lyn Y. Abramson, Lauren B. Alloy and Michael E. Hogan / [et al.] -- 4. Escaping the Self Consumes Regulatory Resources: A Self-Regulatory Model of Suicide / Kathleen D. Vohs and Roy F. Baumeister -- 5. Toward an Integrated Theory of Suicidal

Behaviors: Merging the Hopelessness, Self-Discrepancy, and Escape Theories / Michelle M. Cornette, Lyn Y. Abramson and Anna M. Bardone -- 6. Shame, Guilt, and Suicide / Mark E. Hastings, Lisa M. Northman and June P. Tangney -- 7. Mood Regulation and Suicidal Behavior / Salvatore J. Catanzaro -- 8. Desperate Acts for Desperate Times: Looming Vulnerability and Suicide / John H. Riskind, Daniel G. Long and Nathan L. Williams / [et al.] -- 9. Suicide and Panic Disorder: Integration of the Literature and New Findings / Norman B. Schmidt, Kelly Woolaway-Bickel and Mark Bates -- 10. Suicide Risk in Externalizing Syndromes: Temperamental and Neurobiological Underpinnings / Edelyn Verona and Christopher J. Patrick -- 11. Studying Interpersonal Factors in Suicide: Perspectives from Depression Research / Joanne Davila and Shannon E. Daley -- 12. Gender, Social Roles, and Suicidal Ideation and Attempts in a General Population Sample / Natalie Sachs-Ericsson -- 13. CONTENTS: Suicidal Behavior in African American Women with a History of Childhood Maltreatment / Sharon Young, Heather Twomey and Nadine J. Kaslow -- 14. Issues in the Evaluation of Youth Suicide Prevention Initiatives / John Kalafat -- 15. Recognition and Treatment of Suicidal Youth: Broadening Our Research Agenda / Cheryl A. King and Michele Knox -- 16. A Conceptual Scheme for Assessing Treatment Outcome in Suicidality / M. David Rudd. ISBN 0-7923-7845-8 (alk. paper) DDC 616.85/8445 DDC 616.85/8445
*1. Suicide. I. Joiner, Thomas E. II. Rudd, M. David.*
*TC RC569 .S9368 2000*

**SUICIDE - UNITED STATES.**
Jamison, Kay R. Night falls fast. 1st ed. New York : Knopf ; Distributed by Random House, 1999.
*TC RC569 .J36 1999*

**Sullivan, Carol.**
Smith, Jane W. (Jane Wilcox) AGS United States government. Circle Pines, Minn. : AGS, American Guidance Service, 1997.
*TC JK40 .S639 1997*

Smith, Jane W. (Jane Wilcox) AGS United States government. Teacher's ed. Circle Pines, Minn. : AGS, American Guidance Service, 1997.
*TC JK40 .S639 1997 Teacher's Ed.*

**Sullivan, Charles Wm. (Charles William), 1944-.**
Young adult science fiction. Westport, Conn. : Greenwood Press, 1999.
*TC PS374.S35 Y63 1999*

**Sullivan, Gerald.** Margaret Mead, Gregory Bateson, and Highland Bali : fieldwork photographs of Bayung Gedé, 1936-1939. Chicago, IL : University of Chicago Press, 1999. ix, 213 p. : ill. ; 25 cm. Includes bibliographical references. ISBN 0-226-38434-9 (cloth) DDC 306/.09598/6
*1. Photography in ethnology - Indonesia - Bayung Gedé (Bali) 2. Ethnology - Indonesia - Bayung Gedé (Bali) - Field work. 3. Mead, Margaret. - 1901-1978 - Photograph collections. 4. Bateson, Gregory - Photograph collections. 5. Bayung Gedé (Bali, Indonesia) - Social life and customs.*
*TC GN635.I65 S948 1999*

**Sullivan, Graeme, 1951-** Seeing Australia : views of artists and artwriters / Graeme Sullivan. Annandale, NSW, Australia : Piper Press, 1994. 176 p. : col. ill. ; 30 cm. Includes bibliographical references and index. ISBN 0-9587984-2-7 DDC 700/.994
*1. Art, Australian - Themes, motives. 2. Art, Modern - 20th century - Australia - Themes, motives. 3. Artists - Australia - Biography. I. Title.*
*TC N7400.2 .S85 1994*

**Sullivan, John P. (John Peter)** On holy ground : the impact of psychotherapists' spirituality on their practice / John P. Sullivan. Lanham : University Press of America, c1998. xvi, 120 p. : ill. ; 23 cm. Based on the author's thesis (doctoral)--California School of Professional Psychology. Includes bibliographical references (p. 111-116) and index. ISBN 0-7618-1176-1 (hardcover : alk. paper) ISBN 0-7618-1177-X (pbk. : alk. paper) DDC 616.89/14
*1. Psychotherapy - Religious aspects. 2. Psychotherapists - Religious life. 3. Spiritual life. I. Title.*
*TC RC489.R46 S84 1998*

**Sullivan, Missy.** The Native American look book : art and activities from the Brooklyn Museum / Missy Sullivan ... [et al.]. New York : The New Press, 1996. 46 p. : ill. (some col.) ; 29 cm. "Based upon an original program created by Dorothea Basile." Includes bibliographical references. SUMMARY: Introduces Native American art and culture by examining a Kwakiutl whale mask, a Zuni water jar, and a Pomo basket at the Brooklyn Museum. ISBN 1-56584-022-4 (hardcover) DDC 730/.089/979
*1. Indian art - North America - Juvenile literature. 2. Kwakiutl wood-carving - Juvenile literature. 3. Zuni pottery - Juvenile literature. 4. Pomo baskets - Juvenile literature. 5. Indian art - North America. 6. Indians of North America - Social life and customs. 7. Art appreciation. I. Brooklyn Museum. II. Title.*

*TC E98.A7 S93 1996*

**Sullivan, Susan, 1943-** Supervision that improves teaching : strategies and techniques / Susan Sullivan, Jeffrey Glanz ; foreword by Karen Osterman. Thousand Oaks, Calif. : Corwin Press, c2000. xvi, 189 p. : ill. ; 29 cm. Includes bibliographical references (p. 177-183) and index. ISBN 0-8039-6724-1 (alk. paper) ISBN 0-8039-6725-X (alk. paper) DDC 371.2/03
*1. School supervision - United States. 2. Teacher effectiveness - United States. 3. Effective teaching - United States. I. Glanz, Jeffrey. II. Title.*
*TC LB2806.4 .S85 2000*

**Sullo, Robert A., 1951-** The inspiring teacher : new beginnings for the 21st century / Robert A. Sullo. Washington, D.C. : National Education Association of the United States, c1999. 167 p. : ill. ; 23 cm. (The inspired classroom series) Includes bibliographical references (p. 161-165). ISBN 0-8106-2955-0 DDC 371.102
*1. Teaching. 2. Effective teaching. I. Title. II. Series.*
*TC LB1025.3 .S85 1999*

**Suls, Jerry M.**
Psychological perspectives on self and identity. 1st ed. Washington, DC : American Psychological Association, c2000.
*TC BF697 .P765 2000*

**Sumara, Dennis J., 1958-.**
Davis, Brent. Engaging minds. Mahwah, N.J. : L. Erlbaum Associates, 2000.
*TC LB1060 .D38 2000*

**SUMMER EMPLOYMENT.** *See* **TEACHERS - SUPPLEMENTARY EMPLOYMENT.**

**Summer for the gods.**
Larson, Edward J. (Edward John) New York : BasicBooks, c1997.
*TC KF224.S3 L37 1997*

**SUMMER OLYMPICS.** *See* **OLYMPICS.**

**SUMMER SCHOOLS.** *See* **UNIVERSITY EXTENSION.**

**Summerhill at 70** [videorecording] / a presentation of Films for the Humanities & Sciences ; a Middlemarch film for Channel Four ; producer, Belinda Allen ; directed, photographed and recorded by Peter Getzels and Harriet Gordon Getzels. Princeton, N.J. : Films for the Humanities, c1992. 1 videocassette (52 min.) : sd., col. ; 1/2 in. VHS. Catalogued from credits and container. Assistant producer, Felicity Nock; film editor, Dai Vaughn. Contains coarse language and incidents of animal cruelty. SUMMARY: A.S. Neill founded Summerhill school in 1921 as a place where children should have complete freedom to be themselves, a self-governing community with tribunals in which the vote of a child and headmistress are equal. The program shows life at Summerhill during one and a half terms of the 70th year of this radical educational experiment, where children make the rules, classes are optional and "pairing off" is par for the course. Do the children learn on their own or is it chaos? Foul language, constant battles, and animal cruelty are among some of the more distressing results captured on this revealing film.
*1. Summerhill School. 2. Free schools - England - Leiston. 3. Neill, Alexander Sutherland. - 1883-1973. I. Allen, Belinda. II. Vaughan, Dai. III. Getzels, Peter. IV. Getzels, Harriet Gordon. V. Films for the Humanities (Firm) VI. Middlemarch Films. VII. Channel Four (Great Britain) VIII. Title: Summerhill at seventy [videorecording]*
*TC LF795.L692953 S9 1992*

**Summerhill at seventy** [videorecording].
Summerhill at 70 [videorecording]. Princeton, N.J. : Films for the Humanities, c1992.
*TC LF795.L692953 S9 1992*

**SUMMERHILL SCHOOL.**
Summerhill at 70 [videorecording]. Princeton, N.J. : Films for the Humanities, c1992.
*TC LF795.L692953 S9 1992*

**Summers, Ian R.**
Martin, Michael, OBE. Dictionary of hearing. London : Whurr, 1999.
*TC QP461 .M375 1999*

**Summers, Randal W., 1946-.**
Managing colleges and universities. Westport, Conn. : Bergin & Garvey, 2000.
*TC LB2341 .M2779 2000*

**SUN.**
The solar sea [videorecording]. [New York, N.Y.?] : Unapix Entertainment, Inc. [distributor], c1996.
*TC QB631.2 .S6 1996*

**Sunal, Cynthia S.**
Schooling in sub-Saharan Africa. New York : Garland Pub., 1998.

*TC LA1501 .S35 1998*

**SUNBELT STATES.** *See* **SOUTHERN STATES.**

**SUNDAY SCHOOLS - UNITED STATES - HISTORY.**
Fenn, Patricia. Rewards of merit. [Schoharie, N.Y.] : Ephemera Society of America ; Charlottesville [Va.] : Distributed by Howell Press, Inc., c1994.
*TC LA230 .F46 1994*

**Sunflower Island.**
Greene, Carol. 1st ed. New York : HarperCollins, c1999.
*TC PZ7.G82845 Sl 1999*

**Sunset Park.**
Roma, Thomas. Washington : Smithsonian Institution Press, c1998.
*TC TR680 .R675 1998*

**SUNSET PARK (NEW YORK, N.Y.) - PICTORIAL WORKS.**
Roma, Thomas. Sunset Park. Washington : Smithsonian Institution Press, c1998.
*TC TR680 .R675 1998*

**SUNSPOTS.**
The solar sea [videorecording]. [New York, N.Y.?] : Unapix Entertainment, Inc. [distributor], c1996.
*TC QB631.2 .S6 1996*

**Sunstein, Bonnie S.**
The portfolio standard. Portsmouth, NH : Heinemann, c2000.
*TC LB1029.P67 P69 2000*

**SUNY series, early childhood education**
Revisiting a progressive pedagogy. Albany : State University of New York Press, c2000.
*TC LB1117 .R44 2000*

**SUNY series, frontiers in education**
Educational knowledge. Albany : State University of New York Press, c2000.
*TC LC71 .L335 2000*

Grass roots and glass ceilings. Albany : State University of New York Press, c1999.
*TC LC212.42 .G73 1999*

Rhoades, Gary. Managed professionals. Albany : State University of New York Press, c1998.
*TC LB2331.72 .R56 1998*

**SUNY series, identities in the classroom**
Bloom, Leslie Rebecca. Under the sign of hope. Albany, N.Y. : State University of New York Press, c1998.
*TC HQ1185 .B56 1998*

Henry, Annette, 1955- Taking back control. Albany : State University of New York Press, c1998.
*TC LB1775.4.C2 H45 1998*

**SUNY series in Afro-American studies**
Cochran, David Carroll. The color of freedom. Albany : State University of New York Press, c1999.
*TC E185.615 .C634 1999*

Howard, John R., 1933- The shifting wind. Albany : State University of New York Press, c1999.
*TC KF4757 .H69 1999*

**SUNY series in deviance and social control**
Keys, David Patrick, 1955- Confronting the drug control establishment. Albany, N.Y. : State University of New York Press, c2000.
*TC HM1031.L56 K49 2000*

**SUNY series in dream studies**
Bulkeley, Kelly, 1962- Visions of the night. Albany, NY : State University of New York Press, c1999.
*TC BF1091 .B94 1999*

**SUNY series in educational leadership.**
Values and educational leadership. Albany : State University of New York Press, c1999.
*TC LB2806 .V25 1999*

**SUNY series in environmental and architectural phenomenology**
Childress, Herb, 1958- Landscapes of betrayal, landscapes of joy. Albany [N.Y.] : State University of New York Press, c2000.
*TC HQ796 .C458237 2000*

**SUNY series in philosophy of education.**
Reitz, Charles. Art, alienation, and the humanities. Albany : State University of New York Press, c2000.
*TC B945.M2984 R45 2000*

**SUNY series in public administration**
Schachter, Hindy Lauer. Reinventing government or reinventing ourselves. Albany : State University of New York Press, c1997.

**TC JK1764 .S35 1997**

**SUNY series in teacher preparation and development.**
Collaborative reform and other improbable dreams.
Albany, N.Y. : State University of New York Press,
2000.
**TC LB2154.A3 C65 2000**

**SUNY series in the anthropology of work**
Wilkinson-Weber, Clare M. Embroidering lives.
Albany, N.Y. : State University of New York Press,
c1999.
**TC HD6073.T42 1483 1999**

**SUNY series in the philosophy of the social sciences**
Reitz, Charles. Art, alienation, and the humanities.
Albany : State University of New York Press, c2000.
**TC B945.M2984 R45 2000**

**SUNY series in transpersonal and humanistic psychology**
Roemmelt, Arthur F., 1944- Haunted children.
Albany : State University of New York Press, c1998.
**TC RJ504 .R64 1998**

**SUNY series in women in education**
Gardiner, Mary E., 1953- Coloring outside the lines.
Albany : State University of New York Press, c2000.
**TC LB2831.82 .G37 2000**

Sacred dreams. Albany : State University of New
York Press, c1999.
**TC LB2831.72 .S23 1999**

Smulyan, Lisa. Balancing acts. Albany : State
University of New York Press, c2000.
**TC LB2831.92 .S58 2000**

**SUNY series, innovations in curriculum**
Curriculum, culture, and art education. Albany :
State University of New York Press, c1998.
**TC N85 .C87 1998**

Curriculum politics, policy, practice. Albany : State
University of New York Press, c2000.
**TC LC71.3 .C87 2000**

Garoian, Charles R., 1943- Performing pedagogy.
Albany, N.Y. : State University of New York Press,
1999.
**TC NX504 .G37 1999**

**SUNY series, interruptions -- border testimony(ies) and critical discourse/s**
Brown, Stephen Gilbert. Words in the wilderness.
Albany : State University of New York Press, c2000.
**TC E99.A86 B76 2000**

**SUNY series, Interruptions -- Border testimony(ies) and Critical Discourse/s**
Garoian, Charles R., 1943- Performing pedagogy.
Albany, N.Y. : State University of New York Press,
1999.
**TC NX504 .G37 1999**

**SUNY series, power, social identity, and education**
Proweller, Amira. Constructing female identities.
Albany : State University of New York Press, c1998.
**TC LC1755 .P76 1998**

Weiler, Jeanne. Codes and contradictions. Albany :
State University of New York Press, c2000.
**TC LC1755 .W45 2000**

**SUNY series, restructuring and school change**
Accountability, assessment, and teacher commitment.
Albany, N.Y. : State University of New York Press,
2000.
**TC LB2806.22 A249 2000**

The dimensions of time and the challenge of school
reform. Albany : State University of New York Press,
c2000.
**TC LB3032 .D55 2000**

Nolan, James F., 1950- Teachers and educational
change. Albany : State University of New York Press,
c2000.
**TC LB1777.2 .N64 2000**

**SUNY series, social context of education.**
Valenzuela, Angela. Subtractive schooling. Albany :
State University of New York Press, c1999.
**TC LC2683.4 .V35 1999**

**SUNY series, Studies in scientific and technical communication**
Johnson, Robert R., 1951- User-centered technology.
Albany : State University of New York Press, c1998.
**TC QA76.9.U83 J64 1998**

**SUNY series, the social context of education.**
Jenoure, Terry. Navigators. Albany, NY : State
University of New York Press, c2000.

**TC NX396.5 .J45 2000**

**SUNY series, urban voices, urban visions**
Hutchinson, Jaylynne N., 1954- Students on the
margins. Albany : State University of New York
Press, c1999.
**TC LA210 .H88 1999**

**Super, Charles M.**
Variability in the social construction of the child. San
Francisco : Jossey-Bass, 2000.
**TC BF723.S62 .V37 2000**

**Super, Donald E. (Donald Edwin), 1910-**
Opportunities in psychology careers, by Donald E.
Super. New York, Educational Books Division of
Universal Pub. and Distributing Corp. [1968] 110 p. 20
cm. (Vocational guidance manuals) 1955 ed. published under
title: Opportunities in psychology; 3d ed. (c1976) published
under title: Opportunities in psychology careers today.
Bibliography: p. 108. DDC 150/.23
*1. Psychology - Vocational guidance. I. Title.*
**TC BF76 .S8 1968**

**SUPER-EGO.**
Wurmser, Leon. [Flucht vor dem Gewissen. English]
The power of the inner judge. Northvale, N.J. : Jason
Aronson Inc., c2000.
**TC RC530 .W8713 2000**

Wurmser, Leon. [Flucht vor dem Gewissen. English]
The power of the inner judge. Northvale, N.J. : Jason
Aronson Inc., c2000.
**TC RC530 .W8713 2000**

**SUPEREGO.**
Wurmser, Leon. [Flucht vor dem Gewissen. English]
The power of the inner judge. Northvale, N.J. : Jason
Aronson Inc., c2000.
**TC RC530 .W8713 2000**

**SUPEREROGATION.** *See* **RESPONSIBILITY.**

**SUPERHEROES.** *See* **HEROES.**

**SUPERHIGHWAY, INFORMATION.** *See*
**INFORMATION SUPERHIGHWAY.**

**Superintendent's guide to creating community.**
Owen, Jane C., 1948- Lanham, Md. : Scarecrow
Press, 2000.
**TC LB2831.72 . O94 2000**

**SUPERINTENDENTS OF SCHOOLS.** *See*
**SCHOOL SUPERINTENDENTS.**

**SUPERIOR CHILDREN.** *See* **GIFTED
CHILDREN.**

**The superior student in American higher education.**
Cohen, Joseph W., ed. New York : McGraw-Hill,
[c1966]
**TC 371.95C66**

**SUPERREALISM.** *See* **SURREALISM.**

**SUPERSTRING THEORIES.**
Stephen Hawking's universe [videorecording].
[Alexandria, Va.] : PBS Video; Burbank, CA :
Distributed by Warner Home Video, c1997.
**TC QB982 .S7 1997**

**Supervising postgraduates from non-English
speaking backgrounds** / edited by Yoni Ryan and
Ortrun Zuber-Skerritt. Buckingham ; Philadelphia :
Society for Research into Higher Education : Open
University Press, 1999. xi, 193 p. ; 23 cm. Includes
bibliographical references and index. ISBN 0-335-20372-8
(hb) ISBN 0-335-20371-X (pb) DDC 378.1/94046
*1. Faculty advisors. 2. Graduate students - Counseling of. 3.
Students, Foreign - Counseling of. 4. Teacher-student
relationships. 5. English language - Study and teaching -
Foreign speakers. I. Ryan, Yoni. II. Zuber-Skerritt, Ortrun.*
**TC LB2343 .S86 1999**

**Supervision.**
Wiles, Jon. 5th ed. Upper Saddle River, N.J. : Merrill,
c2000.
**TC LB2806.4 .W55 2000**

**Supervision and staff development in the block.**
Zepeda, Sally J., 1956- Larchmont, N.Y. : Eye On
Education, c2000.
**TC LB3032.2 .Z46 2000**

**Supervision for today's schools.**
Oliva, Peter F. 6th ed. New York : Chichester
[England] : J. Wiley & Sons, c2001.
**TC LB2806.4 .O43 2001**

**SUPERVISION OF FIRST YEAR TEACHERS.** *See*
**FIRST YEAR TEACHERS - SUPERVISION
OF.**

**SUPERVISION OF NURSES.** *See* **NURSES -
SUPERVISION OF.**

**SUPERVISION OF SCHOOLS.** *See* **SCHOOL
SUPERVISION.**

**Supervision that improves teaching.**
Sullivan, Susan, 1943- Thousand Oaks, Calif. :
Corwin Press, c2000.
**TC LB2806.4 .S85 2000**

**Supervisory leadership.**
Beach, Don M. Boston : Allyn and Bacon, c2000.
**TC LB2806.4 .B433 2000**

**SUPERVISORY NURSING.** *See* **NURSING
SERVICES - ADMINISTRATION.**

**SUPPLY AND DEMAND.** *See* **COMPETITION.**

**SUPPLY AND DEMAND FOR LABOR.** *See*
**LABOR MARKET.**

**Support groups :** current perspectives on theory and
practice / Maeda J. Galinsky, Janice H. Schopler,
editors. New York : Haworth Press, c1995. 123 p. ; 23
cm. "Has also been published as Social work with groups,
volume 18, number 1 1995"--T.p. verso. Includes
bibliographical references and index. ISBN 1-56024-763-0
(alk. paper) DDC 361.4
*1. Social group work - United States. 2. Self-help groups -
United States. I. Galinsky, Maeda J. II. Schopler, Janice H.*
**TC HV45 .S896 1995**

**SUPPORT TEACHERS.** *See* **MASTER
TEACHERS.**

**Supporting early learning.**
Siraj-Blatchford, Iram. Supporting identity, diversity
and language in the early years. Buckingham
[England] ; Philadelphia : Open University Press,
2000.
**TC LB1139.3.G7 S57 2000**

Siraj-Blatchford, John, 1952- Supporting science,
design and technology in the early years. Philadelphia,
Pa. : Open University Press, 1999.
**TC T65.3 .S55 1999**

Whitehead, Marian R. Supporting language and
literacy development in the early years. Buckingham
[England] ; Philadelphia : Open University Press,
1999.
**TC LB1139.5.L35 W53 1999**

**Supporting identity, diversity and language in the
early years.**
Siraj-Blatchford, Iram. Buckingham [England] ;
Philadelphia : Open University Press, 2000.
**TC LB1139.3.G7 S57 2000**

**Supporting improving primary schools** / edited by
Geoff Southworth and Paul Lincoln. London ; New
York : Falmer Press, 2000. 236 p. Includes bibliographical
references and index. ISBN 0-7507-1014-4 (hb : alk. paper)
ISBN 0-7507-1015-2 (pb : alk. paper) DDC 372.9426/7
*1. Essex Primary School Improvement Research and
Development Programme. 2. School improvement programs -
England - Essex. 3. Education, Elementary - England - Essex -
Administration. I. Southworth, Geoff. II. Lincoln, Paul.*
**TC LB2822.84.E64 S86 1999**

**Supporting language and literacy development in the
early years.**
Whitehead, Marian R. Buckingham [England] ;
Philadelphia : Open University Press, 1999.
**TC LB1139.5.L35 W53 1999**

**Supporting science, design and technology in the
early years.**
Siraj-Blatchford, John, 1952- Philadelphia, Pa. : Open
University Press, 1999.
**TC T65.3 .S55 1999**

**Supporting students in open and distance learning.**
Simpson, Ormond. London : Kogan Page, 2000.
**TC LC5800 .S56 2000**

**Surfing social studies :** the Internet book / edited by
Joseph A. Braun, Jr. & Frederick Risinger.
Washington, DC : National Council for the Social
Studies, c1999. 176 p. : ill. ; 24 cm. (NCSS bulletin ; 96)
Includes bibliographical references and index. ISBN 0-87986-
078-2
*1. Social sciences - Study and teaching. 2. Social sciences -
Computer network resources. 3. Internet (Computer network)
in education. I. Braun, Joseph A., 1947- II. Risinger, C.
Frederick. III. Series: Bulletin (National Council for the Social
Studies) ; 96.*
**TC LB1044.87 .S97 1999**

**SURGERY.**
Stepansky, Paul E. Freud, surgery, and the surgeons.
Hillsdale, NJ : Analytic Press, 1999.
**TC RC506 .S733 1999**

Stepansky, Paul E. Freud, surgery, and the surgeons.
Hillsdale, NJ : Analytic Press, 1999.

TC RC506 .S733 1999

**SURGERY, AESTHETIC.** See **SURGERY, PLASTIC.**

**SURGERY, COSMETIC.** See **SURGERY, PLASTIC.**

**SURGERY, PLASTIC - PSYCHOLOGICAL ASPECTS.**
Brook, Barbara, 1949- Feminist perspective on the body. New York : Longman, 1999.
*TC GT495 .B76 1999*

**SURGERY, RECONSTRUCTIVE.** See **SURGERY, PLASTIC.**

**Surprises along the way:** teacher's planning guide. New York : Macmillan/McGraw-Hill, c1997. 1 v. (various pagings) : col. ill. ; 31 cm. (Spotlight on literacy ; Gr.1 l.4 u.2) (The road to independent reading) Includes index. ISBN 0-02-181154-7
*1. Language arts (Primary) 2. Reading (Primary) I. Series. II. Series: The road to independent reading*
*TC LB1576 .S66 1997 Gr.1 L4 u.2*

**SURREALISM.** See **POP ART.**

**SURREALISM IN ART.** See **SURREALISM.**

**SURREALISM - INFLUENCE.**
Krauss, Rosalind E. Bachelors. Cambridge, Mass. : MIT Press, c1999.
*TC NX180.F4 K73 1999*

**Survey of educational research, 1988-92.**
Fifth survey of educational research, 1988-92. New Delhi : National Council of Educational Research and Training, 1997-
*TC LB1028 .F44 1997*

**Survey of nationally recognized school leaders.**
Durocher, Elizabeth Antointette. Leadership orientations of school administrators. 1995.
*TC 06 no. 10583a*

**Survey of research in education.**
Fifth survey of educational research, 1988-92. New Delhi : National Council of Educational Research and Training, 1997-
*TC LB1028 .F44 1997*

**Survey of teacher opinion and reported practice concerning the use of student assessment.**
Southworth, Robert A. Evidence of student learning and implications for alternative policies that support instructional use of assessment. 1999.
*TC 06 no. 11218*

**SURVEYS.** See **ARTS SURVEYS; HEALTH SURVEYS.**

**Survival in the organization.**
Madsen, Benedicte, 1943- Aarhus [Denmark] ; Oakville, Conn. : Aarhus University Press, c1996.
*TC D805.G3 M24 1996*

**Survival skills for scholars**
(v. 19) Carbone, Elisa Lynn. Teaching large classes. Thousand Oaks, Calif. : Sage Publications, c1998.
*TC LB2331 .C336 1998*

**Surviving diversity.**
Spinner-Halev, Jeff. Baltimore : Johns Hopkins University Press, 2000.
*TC BL2525 .S588 2000*

**Surviving in Africa.**
In search of human origins [videorecording]. [Boston, Mass.] : WGBH Educational Foundation, c1994.
*TC GN281 .I45 1994*

**Surviving literary suicide.**
Berman, Jeffrey, 1945- Amherst : University of Massachusetts Press, c1999.
*TC PS169.S85 B47 1999*

**Surviving the age of virtual reality.**
Langan, Thomas. Columbia, Mo. ; London : University of Missouri Press, c2000.
*TC B105.M4 L355 2000*

**SURVIVORS, HOLOCAUST.** See **HOLOCAUST SURVIVORS.**

**Suskin, Albert I.**
Ullman, B. L. (Berthold Louis), 1882-1965. Latin for Americans. Third book. 7th ed. Mission Hills, Calif. : Glencoe, a division of Macmillan Pub. Co., c1990.
*TC PA2087.5 .U399 1990*

**Suskind, Ron.** A hope in the unseen : an American odyssey from the inner city to the Ivy League / Ron Suskind. 1st ed. New York : Broadway Books, c1998. 372 p. ; 25 cm. ISBN 0-7679-0125-8 (hardcover) DDC 371.8/092

*1. Jennings, Cedric Lavar - Childhood and youth. 2. Jennings, Cedric Lavar - Knowledge and learning. 3. Afro-American teenage boys - Education - Washington (D.C.) 4. Frank W. Ballou Senior High School (Washington, D.C.) - Students - Biography. 5. Brown University - Students - Biography. 6. Afro-American college students - Biography. I. Title.*
*TC LC2803.W3 S87 1998*

**Susskind, Lawrence.**
The consensus building handbook. Thousand Oaks, Calif. : Sage Publications, c1999.
*TC HM746 .C66 1999*

**Sussman, Marvin B.** The family and inheritance [by] Marvin B. Sussman, Judith N. Cates [and] David T. Smith. With the collaboration of Lodoska K. Clausen. New York, Russell Sage Foundation, 1970. xiii, 367 p. 24 cm. Bibliography: p. 355-362. ISBN 0-87154-873-9 DDC 347.6/5/09771
*1. Inheritance and succession - Ohio. I. Cates, Judith N., joint author. II. Smith, David T., 1935- joint author. III. Title.*
*TC KFO142 .S9*

**SUSTAINABLE DEVELOPMENT.**
Rassool, Naz, 1949- Literacy for sustainable development in the age of information. Clevedon [England] ; Philadelphia : Multilingual Matters, c1999.
*TC LC149 .R37 1999*

Towards sustainable development. New York, N.Y. : St. Martin's Press, 1999.
*TC HD75.6 .T695 1999*

**SUSTAINABLE DEVELOPMENT - CONGRESSES.**
Forum on Biodiversity (1997 : National Academy of Sciences) Nature and human society. Washington, D.C. : National Academy Press, 2000.
*TC QH541.15.B56 F685 1997*

**SUSTAINABLE ECONOMIC DEVELOPMENT.** See **SUSTAINABLE DEVELOPMENT.**

**Suteev, Vladimir Grigor'evich.**
**Pod gribom.**
Ginsburg, Mirra. Mushroom in the rain. New York : Macmillan/McGraw-Hill, 1974.
*TC PZ10.3 .G455Mu 1974*

**Sutton, Tiffany.** The classification of visual art : a philosophical myth and its history / Tiffany Sutton. Cambridge ; New York : Cambridge University Press, 2000. xii, 184 p. : ill. ; 24 cm. Includes bibliographical references (p. 177-180) and index. ISBN 0-521-77236-2 (hardback) DDC 701/.2
*1. Art - Philosophy. I. Title.*
*TC N66 .S88 2000*

**Suzuki, Lisa A., 1961-.**
Valencia, Richard R. Intelligence testing and minority students. Thousand Oaks, Calif. : Sage Publications, [2000]
*TC BF431.5.U6 V35 2000*

**SUZUKI, SHIN'ICHI, 1898-.**
Barrett, Carolyn M., 1941- The magic of Matsumoto. Palm Springs, CA : ETC Publications, c1995.
*TC MT1 .B325 1995*

**Svanberg, Ingvar, 1953-.**
Benson, Linda. China's last Nomads. Armonk, N.Y. : M.E. Sharpe, c1998.
*TC DS731.K38 B46 1998*

**Svarney, Thomas E.**
Barnes-Svarney, Patricia L. The Oryx guide to natural history. Phoenix, Ariz. : Oryx Press, 1999.
*TC QH45.2 .B37 1999*

**Švec, Juraj.**
Groof, Jan de. Democracy and governance in higher education. The Hague ; Boston : Kluwer Law International, 1998.
*TC LB2341.8.E85 G76 1998*

**Svennevig, Jan.** Getting acquainted in conversation : a study of initial interactions / Jan Svennevig. Amsterdam ; Philadelphia : J. Benjamins Pub. Co., c1999. x, 383 p. : ill. ; 23 cm. (Pragmatics & beyond, 0922-842X ; new ser. 64) Includes bibliographical references (p. [357]-376) and indexes. ISBN 90-272-5078-2 (Eur. : alk. paper) ISBN 1-55619-942-2 (US : alk. paper) DDC 306.44
*1. Conversation analysis. I. Title. II. Series.*
*TC P95.45 .S89 1999*

**Svenska folkhögskolans lärarförbundet.**
Folk-högskolan. Stockholm : Lärarförbundet, 1979-

**Sveriges folkskollärärförbund.**
Folkskollärarnas tidning. Stockholm : Folkskollärarförbund,

**Svinicki, Marilla D. 1946-.**
Teaching and learning on the edge of the millennium :. San Francisco : Jossey-Bass, c1999.
*TC LB2331 .T35 1999*

**Swaddling, Judith.** The ancient Olympic games / Judith Swaddling. 2nd ed. Austin : University of Texas Press, 1999, c1980. 112 p. : ill. ; 25 cm. "Further reading": p. 107-108. Includes index. ISBN 0-292-77751-5 DDC 796.48 DDC S971, 1999
*1. Olympic games (Ancient) I. Title.*
*TC GV23 .S9 1999*

**Swaffar, Janet K.**
Language learning online. Austin : Labyrinth Publications, c1998.
*TC PE1128.A2 L2955 1998*

**Swain, Gladys, 1945-.**
Gauchet, Marcel. [La pratique de l'esprit humain. English] Madness and democracy. Princeton, N.J. : Princeton University Press, c1999.
*TC RC439 .G2813 1999*

**Swain, John, 1948-.**
Therapy and learning difficulties. Boston, Mass : Butterworth-Heinemann, 1999.
*TC HV3008.G7 T48 1999*

**Swann, Brian.** The house with no door : African riddle-poems / Brian Swann ; illustrated by Ashley Bryan. 1st ed. San Diego : Harcourt Brace & Company., c1998. 1 v. (unpaged) : col. ill. ; 27 cm. (Browndeer Press) "Browndeer Press" SUMMARY: A collection of original poems created from riddles of various African tribes. ISBN 0-15-200805-5 DDC 811/.54
*1. Riddles. 2. Folklore - Africa. 3. Children's poetry, American. 4. Riddles. 5. Folklore - Africa. 6. American poetry. I. Bryan, Ashley, ill. II. Title. III. Series.*
*TC PS3569.W256 H6 1998*

**Swann, Joanna.**
Improving education. London ; New York : Cassell, 1999.
*TC LB7 .I48 1999*

**Swanson, James M.**
Pliszka, Steven R. ADHD with comorbid disorders. New York : Guilford Press, c1999.
*TC RJ506.H9 P55 1999*

**Swanson, Jane Laurel.** Career theory and practice : learning through case studies / Jane L. Swanson, Nadya A. Fouad. Thousand Oaks, Calif. : Sage Publications, c1999. xv, 253 p. : ill. ; 26 cm. Includes bibliographical references (p. 221-231) and index. Table of Contents URL: http://lcweb.loc.gov/catdir/toc/99006008.html CONTENTS: Introduction -- The case of Leslie -- Holland's theory -- Theory of work adjustment -- Developmental theories -- Krumboltz's social learning theory -- Social-cognitive career theory -- Gender-aware and feminist approaches -- Culturally appropriate career counseling -- Summary and integration. ISBN 0-7619-1142-1 (acid-free paper) ISBN 0-7619-1143-X (acid-free paper) DDC 158.6
*1. Career development - Case studies. 2. Vocational guidance - Case studies. I. Fouad, Nadya A. II. Title.*
*TC HF5381 .S937 1999*

**Swanwick, Keith.** Teaching music musically / Keith Swanwick. London ; New York : Routledge, 1999. xii, 120 p. : ill., music ; 25 cm. Includes bibliographical references (p. [110]-114) and index. ISBN 0-415-19935-2 (alk. paper) ISBN 0-415-19936-0 (pbk. : alk. paper) DDC 780/.71
*1. Music - Instruction and study. I. Title.*
*TC MT1 .S946 1999*

**Swanwick, Ruth, 1963-.**
Knight, Pamela, 1940- The care and education of a deaf child. Clevedon [England] ; Buffalo [N.Y.] : Multilingual Matters, c1999.
*TC HV2716 .K65 1999*

**Swap, Walter C.**
Leonard-Barton, Dorothy. When sparks fly. Boston, Mass. : Harvard Business School Press, 1999.
*TC HD53 .L46 1999*

**Swartz, David, 1945-** Culture & power : the sociology of Pierre Bourdieu / David Swartz. Chicago : University of Chicago Press, 1997. viii, 333 p. ; 24 cm. Includes bibliographical references (p. 297-317) and indexes. ISBN 0-226-78594-7 (alk. paper) ISBN 0-226-78595-5 (pbk. : alk. paper) DDC 301/.0944
*1. Bourdieu, Pierre. 2. Sociology - France - History. 3. Sociology - Methodology. I. Title. II. Title: Culture and power*
*TC HM22.F8 S93 1997*

**Sweeney, Jim, 1937-** Judgment / Jim Sweeney, Diana Bourisaw. Larchmont, NY : Eye on Education, c1997. xvii, 155 p. : ill. ; 24 cm. (The school leadership library) Subtitle on cover: Making the right calls. Includes bibliographical references (p. 153-155). ISBN 1-88300-137-4 DDC 371.2

*1. School management and organization - Decision making. 2. Judgment. 3. Critical thinking. 4. Problem solving. I. Bourisaw. Diana. 1956- II. Title. III. Title: Making the right calls IV. Series.*
**TC LB2806 .S88 1997**

**Sweet dreams.**
Kajikawa, Kimiko. 1st ed. New York : Henry Holt, c1999.
**TC QL755.3 .K36 1999**

**Sweetow, Robert W.**
Counseling for hearing aid fittings. San Diego : Singular Pub. Group, c1999.
**TC RF300 .C68 1999**

**SWIMMING - JUVENILE LITERATURE.**
Riley, Linda Capus. Elephants swim. Boston : Houghton Mifflin, 1995.
**TC QP310.S95 R55 1995**

**SWIMMING POOLS - NEW YORK (STATE) - NEW YORK - PICTORIAL WORKS.**
Roma, Thomas. Sunset Park. Washington : Smithsonian Institution Press, c1998.
**TC TR680 .R675 1998**

**SWIMMING - STUDY AND TEACHING.**
Neuner, John. Teacher/swimmer :. New York : Jay Street, c1998.
**TC GV837 .N48 1998**

**Swinburn, Kate.**
The aphasia therapy file. Hove : Psychology Press, c1999.
**TC RC425 .A665 1999**

**Swinburne, Stephen R.** Coyote : : North America's dog / by Stephen R. Swinburne. 1st ed. Honesdale, Pa. : Boyds Mill Press, c1999. 32 p. : ill. (some col.), col. map ; 21 x 26 cm. SUMMARY: "An examination of coyotes, their behavior and habitat." ISBN 1-56397-765-6
*1. Coyotes - Juvenile literature. 2. Coyotes. <Juvenile subject heading>. I. Title.*
**TC QL737.C22 S9 1999**

**Swine lake.**
Marshall, James, 1942- 1st ed. [New York] : Harper Collins Publishers, 1999.
**TC PZ7.M35672 Sw 1999**

**Swing, Elizabeth Sherman.**
Problems and prospects in European education. Westport, Conn. : Praeger, 2000.
**TC LC191.8. E85 P86 2000**

**Swirski, Shlomo.** Politics and education in Israel : comparisons with the United States / Shlomo Swirski. New York : Falmer Press, 1999. xv, 296 p. ; 23 cm. (Garland reference library of social science ; v. 946. Studies in education/politics ; v. 3) Includes bibliographical references (p. 255-281) and index. ISBN 0-8153-1616-X (alk. paper) DDC 379.5694
*1. Politics and education - Israel. 2. Discrimination in education - Israel. 3. Education and state - Israel. 4. Segregation in education - Israel. I. Title. II. Series: Garland reference library of social science ; v. 946. III. Series: Garland reference library of social science. Studies in education/ politics ; vol. 3.*
**TC LC94.I75 S95 1999**

**Syder, Diana.**
Wanting to talk. London : Whurr, c1998.
**TC RC423 .W26 1998**

**Sygall, Susan.**
Loud, proud & passionate. 1st ed. Eugene, OR : Mobility International USA, 1997.
**TC HV1569.3.W65 L68 1997**

**Sykes, Sandy.**
Etching [videorecording]. Northbrook, Ill. ; Peasmarsh, East Sussex, Eng. : Roland Collection of Films on Art, c1990.
**TC NE2043 .E87 1990**

**Sylwester, Robert.** A biological brain in a cultural classroom : applying biological research to classroom management / Robert Sylwester. Thousand Oaks, Calif. : Corwin Press, c2000. xi, 148 p. : ill. ; 24 cm. Includes bibliographical references (p. 137-141) and index. CONTENTS: The biological and cultural foundations of classroom management -- The multiple-everything modular bodybrain that schools seek to manage -- Biological and cultural energy in classroom management -- Biological and cultural space in classroom management -- Biological and cultural time in classroom management -- Biological and cultural movement in classroom management -- Biological and cultural range in classroom management. ISBN 0-8039-6744-6 (cloth : alk. paper) ISBN 0-8039-6745-4 (pbk. : alk. paper) DDC 371.102/4
*1. Classroom management - Psychological aspects. 2.*

*Learning - Physiological aspects. 3. Brain. 4. Teacher-student relationships. I. Title.*
**TC LB3011.5 .S95 2000**

**Symbolic imprints :** essays on photography and visual culture / edited by Lars Kiel Bertelsen, Rune Gade, Mette Sandbye ; [translated by Johannes Plesner ... Pauline Cumbers ... Anne Barr]. Aarhus : Aarhus University Press, c1999. 218 p. : ill. ; 25 cm. Includes bibliographical references. ISBN 87-7288-787-7
*1. Photography. 2. Visual communication. I. Bertelsen, Lars Kiel. II. Gade. Rune. 1964- III. Sandbye, Mette.*
**TC TR145 .S96 1999**

**SYMBOLIC INTERACTION.** *See* **SOCIAL INTERACTION.**

**SYMBOLISM.** *See* **SEMANTICS (PHILOSOPHY).**

**SYMBOLISM IN ART - AFRICA - ENCYCLOPEDIAS.**
Werness, Hope B. The Continuum encyclopedia of native art. New York : Continuum, 2000.
**TC E98.A7 W49 2000**

**SYMBOLISM IN ART - NORTH AMERICA - ENCYCLOPEDIAS.**
Werness, Hope B. The Continuum encyclopedia of native art. New York : Continuum, 2000.
**TC E98.A7 W49 2000**

**SYMBOLISM IN ART - OCEANIA - ENCYCLOPEDIAS.**
Werness, Hope B. The Continuum encyclopedia of native art. New York : Continuum, 2000.
**TC E98.A7 W49 2000**

**SYMBOLISM IN LITERATURE.**
Balakian, Anna Elizabeth, 1915- The symbolist movement. 1977 ed. New York : New York University Press, 1977.
**TC PN56.S9 .B3 1977**

**SYMBOLISM IN PSYCHOLOGY.** *See* **SYMBOLISM (PSYCHOLOGY).**

**SYMBOLISM (PSYCHOLOGY).** *See also* **ARCHETYPE (PSYCHOLOGY).**
Moorjani, Angela B. Beyond fetishism and other excursions in psychopragmatics. New York : St. Martin's Press, 2000.
**TC BF175.4.C84 M663 2000**

Petocz, Agnes. Freud, psychoanalysis, and symbolism. Cambridge ; New York : Cambridge University Press, 1999.
**TC BF109.F74 P48 1999**

Seo, Kyoung-Hye. Children's construction of personal meanings of mathematical symbolism in a reform-oriented classroom. 2000.
**TC 06 no. 11310**

**The symbolist movement.**
Balakian, Anna Elizabeth, 1915- 1977 ed. New York : New York University Press, 1977
**TC PN56.S9 .B3 1977**

**Symbolizing and communicating in mathematics classrooms :** perspectives on discourse, tools, and instructional design / edited by Paul Cobb, Erna Yackel, Kay McClain. Mahwah, N.J. : Lawrence Erlbaum Associates, 2000. x, 411 p. : ill. ; 24 cm. Includes bibliographical references and indexes. ISBN 0-8058-2975-X (hb : alk. paper) ISBN 0-8058-2976-8 (pb : alk. paper) DDC 510/.71
*1. Mathematics - Study and teaching. 2. Mathematical notation. I. Cobb, Paul. II. Yackel, Erna. III. McClain, Kay.*
**TC QA11 .S873 2000**

**SYMMETRY.** *See* **AESTHETICS.**

**Symonides, Janusz.**
Human rights. Aldershot, England ; Brookfield, VT : Ashgate/Dartmouth ; Paris : UNESCO Publishing, 1998.
**TC JC571 .H76967 1998**

**SYMPOSIA.** *See* **CONGRESSES AND CONVENTIONS.**

**Symposium on Genetics of Criminal and Antisocial Behaviour (1995 : Ciba Foundation).**
Genetics of criminal and antisocial behaviour. Chichester ; New York : Wiley, 1996.
**TC HV6047 .G46 1996**

**Symposium on Issues in Human Development (1967 : Philadelphia)** Issues in human development; an inventory of problems, unfinished business and directions for research. Victor C. Vaughan, III, scientific editor. Based on a symposium sponsored by Temple University, St. Christopher's Hospital for Children [and] the National Institute of Child Health and Human Development. Washington, For sale by

the Supt. of Docs., U. S. Govt. Print. Off. [1970?] x, 217 p. : ill. ; 27 cm. Includes bibliographies and index.
*1. Children - Growth. 2. Human ecology. I. Vaughan, Victor C.. 1919- II. National Institute of Child Health and Human Development (U.S.) III. St. Christopher's Hospital for Children (Philadelphia, Pa.) IV. Temple University. V. Title.*
**TC RJ131.A1 S93 1967**

**Symposium on Learner Autonomy (1996 : Juväskylä, Finland).**
Learner autonomy in language learning. Frankfurt am Main ; New York : Peter Lang, c1999.
**TC P53 .L378 1999**

**Symposium on Science, Reason, and Modern Democracy.**
Democracy & the arts. Ithaca : Cornell University Press, c1999.
**TC NX180.S6 D447 1999**

**Symposium series (Edwin Mellen Press)**
(v. 55.) Reaching and teaching children who are victims of poverty. Lewiston, N.Y. ; Lampeter, Wales : E. Mellen Press, c1999.
**TC LC4091 .R38 1999**

(v. 60.) Ainsa, Patricia. Teaching children with AIDS. Lewiston, N.Y. ; Lampeter, Wales : Edwin Mellen Press, c2000.
**TC LC4561 .A55 2000**

**SYMPOSIUMS.** *See* **CONGRESSES AND CONVENTIONS.**

**SYMPTOMATOLOGY.** *See* **NAUSEA; PAIN.**

**SYNCRETISM (CHRISTIANITY).** *See* **CHRISTIANITY AND OTHER RELIGIONS.**

**SYNDICALISM.** *See* **SOCIALISM.**

**SYNDROMES.** *See* **BATTERED WOMAN SYNDROME; DOWN SYNDROME; FALSE MEMORY SYNDROME; KORSAKOFF'S SYNDROME.**

**The synergetic classroom.**
Charles, C. M. New York : Longman, c2000.
**TC LB3013 .C4653 2000**

**SYNESTHESIA.** *See* **PERCEPTION.**

**Synon, Mary.**
M. Margaret Michael, Sister, O.P. This is our land. New ed. Boston, Mass. : Ginn and Company, 1955.
**TC PE1121 .M52 1955**

**SYNTACTICS.** *See* **SEMANTICS (PHILOSOPHY).**

**The syntax of American Sign Language :** functional categories and hierarchical structure / Carol Neidle ... [et al.]. Cambridge, Mass. : MIT Press, c2000. x, 229 p. : ill. ; 24 cm. (Language, speech, and communication) Includes bibliographical references (p. [197]-218) and indexes. ISBN 0-262-14067-5 (alk. paper) DDC 419
*1. American Sign Language - Syntax. I. Neidle. Carol Jan. II. Series.*
**TC HV2474 .S994 2000**

**Syracuse studies on peace and conflict resolution**
True, Michael. An energy field more intense than war. 1st ed. Syracuse, N.Y. : Syracuse University Press, 1995.
**TC PS169.N65 T78 1995**

**Syracuse University. Division of Special Education and Rehabilitation.**
Preparing humanistic teachers for troubled children. Syracuse, N.Y. : Division of Special Education and Rehabilitation, Syracuse University, [1974?]
**TC LC4801 .P73**

**SYSTEM SAFETY.** *See* **INDUSTRIAL SAFETY.**

**SYSTEM THEORY.** *See also* **CHAOTIC BEHAVIOR IN SYSTEMS.**
Cain, Michael Scott. The community college in the twenty-first century. Lanham, MD : University Press of America, c1999.
**TC LB2328.15.U6 C33 1999**

Oyama, Susan. Evolution's eye. Durham, NC : Duke University Press, 2000.
**TC BF713 .O93 2000**

**Systemic family therapy.**
Nichols, William C. New York : Guilford Press, c1986.
**TC RC488.5 .N535 1986**

**Systemic leadership.**
Allen, Kathleen E. Lanham, Md. : University Press of America, c2000.
**TC HD57.7 .A42 2000**

**SYSTEMS ENGINEERING.** *See* **HUMAN-MACHINE SYSTEMS.**

**SYSTEMS, EXPERT (COMPUTER SCIENCE).** *See* **EXPERT SYSTEMS (COMPUTER SCIENCE).**

**SYSTEMS, HEALING.** *See* **ALTERNATIVE MEDICINE.**

**SYSTEMS, MANAGED CARE (MEDICAL CARE).** *See* **MANAGED CARE PLANS (MEDICAL CARE).**

**SYSTEMS, MULTIHOSPITAL.** *See* **MULTIHOSPITAL SYSTEMS.**

**Systems of education :** theories, policies and implicit values / edited by Mal Leicester, Celia Modgil and Sohan Modgil. London ; New York : Falmer Press, 2000. xx, 238 p. : ill. ; 29 cm. (Education, culture, and values ; v. 1) Includes bibliographical references and index. ISBN 0-7507-1002-0 (hard) DDC 306.43
*1. Educational sociology. 2. Values - Study and teaching. 3. Multiculturalism. I. Leicester, Mal. II. Modgil, Celia. III. Modgil, Sohan. IV. Series.*
*TC LC191 .S98 2000*

**SYSTEMS SOFTWARE.** *See* **OPERATING SYSTEMS (COMPUTERS).**

**SYSTEMS, THERAPEUTIC.** *See* **ALTERNATIVE MEDICINE.**

**Syverson, Margaret A., 1948-.**
Barr, Mary A. (Mary Anderson) Assessing literacy with the Learning Record. Portsmouth, NH : Heinemann, c1999.
*TC LB1029.P67 B37 1999*

**Szabadi, E. (Elmer).**
Time and behaviour. Amsterdam ; New York : Elsevier, 1997.
*TC BF468 .T538 1997*

**Szekeres, Cyndy.**
Sharmat, Marjorie Weinman. The 329th friend. New York : Four Winds Press, c1979.
*TC PZ7.S5299 Tk 1979*

**Szinovácz, Maximiliane.**
Handbook on grandparenthood. Westport, Conn. : Greenwood Press, 1998.
*TC HQ759.9 .H36 1998*

**Szokolszky, István, 1915-1968.**
Emlékezés Szokolszky Istvánra. [Budapest] : Magyar Pedagógiai Társaság, 1998.
*TC LA2375.H92 S9653 1998*

**SZOKOLSZKY, ISTVÁN, 1915-1968.**
Emlékezés Szokolszky Istvánra. [Budapest] : Magyar Pedagógiai Társaság, 1998.
*TC LA2375.H92 S9653 1998*

**T-GROUPS.** *See* **GROUP RELATIONS TRAINING.**

**Sport photography today!** [videorecording] : with photographs and commentary by Sports Illustrated photographers / program concept, direction, Rich Clarkson ; director, interviews, Jeff Harrington ; producer, R. Smith Schuneman ; script, Gary Lindberg ; series director, Patricia Ward Schuneman ; photography : Brian Lanker... [et al.] ; produced by Media Loft, Inc. Minneapolis, Minn. : Media Loft, c1992. 1 videocassette (31 min.) : sd., col. ; 1/2 in. (Media Loft educational-awareness presentation) (Great photographers ; v.3) Title on container and cassette label: Sports Photography today! [videorecording] : Sports Illustrated photographers shooting the Olympics. VHS. Catalogued from credits and container and cassette label. Host and presenter, Rich Clarkson ; narrator, Ray Scott. Videography, John Junis, Jim Dreher; video editing, John Junis. "TV-28-VHS."--Container. For those interested in sports photography. SUMMARY: Rich Clarkson, head of the faculty for the highlights of the Olympic Sports Photography workshop at a recent U.S. Olympic festival, gives tips on sports photography. Clarkson and other Sports Illustrated photographers, John Biever (expert in football photography), Bill Eppridge, Brian Lanker, Neil Liefer, Ron Modra (best known for his baseball photos), Walter Jooss Jr., Brian Peterson and Anne Ryan demonstrate the key elements in sports photography. Ron Modra and others, including Phil Jache, assistant director of photography at Sports Illustrated, discuss tips for good sports action and feature photography. ISBN 1-88238-603-5
*1. Photography of sports. 2. Commercial photography. 3. Photojournalism. 4. Documentary photography. 5. Sports illustrated (Time, inc.) I. Clarkson, Rich II. Harrington, Jeff. III. Biever, John. IV. Eppridge, Bill. V. Modra, Ron. VI. Lanker, Brian. VII. Liefer, Neil. VIII. Peterson, Brian H. IX. Jooss, Walter. X. Ryan, Anne. XI. Schuneman, R. Smith. XII. Schuneman, Pat Ward. XIII. Lindberg, Gary. XIV. Scott, Ray. XV. Media Loft (Firm) XVI. Title: Sports Photography today!*

[videorecording] : Sports Illustrated photographers shooting the Olympics XVII. Title: Sports Illustrated photographers shooting the Olympics [videorecording] XVIII. Series. XIX. Series: Educational/awareness presentation.
*TC TR821 .S64 1992*

**Taback, Simms.** Joseph had a little overcoat / by Simms Taback. New York : Viking, 1999. [32] p. : col. ill. ; 28 cm. SUMMARY: A very old overcoat is recycled numerous times into a variety of garments. ISBN 0-670-87855-3 (hardcover) DDC [E]
*1. Coats - Fiction. 2. Clothing and dress - Fiction. I. Title.*
*TC PZ7.T1115 Jo 1999*

**Tabakowska, Elżbieta.**
Speaking of emotions. Berlin ; New York : Mouton de Gruyter, 1998.
*TC BF591. S64 1998*

**Taberski, Sharon.** On solid ground : strategies for teaching reading K-3 / Sharon Taberski. Portsmouth, NH : Heinemann, c 2000. xvi, 219 p. : ill. ; 28 cm. Includes bibliographical references (p. 205-208) and index. ISBN 0-325-00227-4 DDC 372.41/6
*1. Reading (Primary) - United States. 2. School children - United States - Books and reading. 3. Reading (Primary) - United States - Language experience approach. I. Title.*
*TC LB1525 .T32 2000*

**TABLE.** *See* **COOKERY; DINNERS AND DINING; FOOD.**

**Tackling disaffection and social exclusion.**
Hayton, Annette. London : Kogan Page, 1999.
*TC LC93.G7 H39 1999*

**Tackling truancy in schools.**
Reid, Ken. London ; New York : Routledge, 2000.
*TC LB3081 .R446 2000*

**TACTICS.** *See* **DRILL AND MINOR TACTICS.**

**TACTILE PERCEPTION.** *See* **TOUCH.**

**TACTUAL PERCEPTION.** *See* **TOUCH.**

**Taddei-Ferretti, C. (Cloe).**
International School of Biocybernetics (1997 : Naples, Italy) Neuronal bases and psychological aspects of consciousness. Singapore ; River Edge, N.J : World Scientific, c1999.
*TC QP411 .I56 1997*

**Tahara, Mildred M., 1941-.**
New trends & issues in teaching Japanese language & culture. Honolulu ; Second Language Teaching and Curriculum, University of Hawai'i at Manoa, 1997.
*TC PL519 .N45 1997*

**Tai, Robert H., 1965-.**
Critical ethnicity. Lanham, Md. : Rowman & Littlefield, c1999.
*TC LC212.2 .C75 1999*

**TAIPEI (TAIWAN) - SOCIAL CONDITIONS.**
Marsh, Robert Mortimer. The great transformation. Armonk, N.Y. : M.E. Sharpe, c1996.
*TC HN749.T35 M37 1996*

**Taiwan in the modern world**
Marsh, Robert Mortimer. The great transformation. Armonk, N.Y. : M.E. Sharpe, c1996.
*TC HN749.T35 M37 1996*

**TAIWAN - STATISTICS - PERIODICALS.**
Statistical yearbook of the Republic of China. [Taipei] Directorate-General of Budget, Accounting & Statistics, Executive Yuan, Republic of China.

**The Taiwanese Americans.**
Ng, Franklin, 1947- Westport, Conn. : Greenwood Press, 1998.
*TC E184.T35 N45 1998*

**TAIWANESE AMERICANS.**
Ng, Franklin, 1947- The Taiwanese Americans. Westport, Conn. : Greenwood Press, 1998.
*TC E184.T35 N45 1998*

**Takahashi, Nobuo, 1939-.**
A Teacher's & textbook writers' handbook on Japan. 5th., rev. printing. Tokyo : International Society for Educational Information, c1993.
*TC DS806 .T34 1993*

**Takayoshi, Pamela.**
Feminist cyberscapes. Stamford, Conn. : Ablex Pub., c1999.
*TC PE1404 .F39 1999*

**Take a closer look :** teacher's planning guide. New York : Macmillan/McGraw-Hill, c1997. 224, T18 p. : ill. (some col.) ; 31 cm. (Spotlight on literacy ; Gr.1 l.4 u.1) (The road to independent reading) Includes index. ISBN 0-02-181153-9

*1. Reading (Primary) 2. Language arts (Primary) I. Series. II. Series: The road to independent reading*
*TC LB1576 .S66 1997 Gr.1 l.4 u.1*

**Take the high road :** teacher's planning guide. New York : Macmillan/McGraw-Hill, c1997. 1 v. (various pagings) : col. ill. ; 31 cm. (Spotlight on literacy ; Gr.5 l.11 u.5) (The road to independent reading) Includes index. ISBN 0-02-181183-0
*1. Language arts (Elementary) 2. Reading (Elementary) I. Series. II. Series: The road to independent reading*
*TC LB1576 .S66 1997 Gr.5 l.11 u.5*

**Taking back control.**
Henry, Annette, 1955- Albany : State University of New York Press, c1998.
*TC LB1775.4.C2 H45 1998*

**Taking charge of curriculum.**
Adams, Jacob E. New York : Teachers College Press, c2000.
*TC LB2806.15 . A35 2000*

**Taking cues from kids.**
Peters, Dorothy. Portsmouth, NH : Heinemann, c2000.
*TC LB3013 .P43 2000*

**Taking flight with OWLs :** examining electronic writing center work / edited by James A. Inman, Donna N. Sewell. Mahwah, N.J. : Lawrence Erlbaum Associates, Publishers, 2000. xxx, 252 p. ; 24 cm. Includes bibliographical references (p. 235-243) and indexes. ISBN 0-8058-3171-1 (acid-free paper) ISBN 0-8058-3172-X (pbk. : acid-free paper) DDC 808/.042/0285
*1. English language - Rhetoric - Study and teaching - Data processing. 2. Report writing - Study and teaching - Data processing. 3. English language - Computer-assisted instruction. 4. Report writing - Computer-assisted instruction. 5. Online data processing. 6. Writing centers. I. Inman, James A. II. Sewell, Donna N.*
*TC PE1404 .T24 2000*

**Taking inquiry outdoors :** reading, writing, and science beyond the classroom walls / edited by Barbara Bourne. York, Me. : Stenhouse Publishers, c2000. x, 142 p. : ill. ; 23 cm. Includes bibliographical references (p. [141]-142). ISBN 1-57110-302-3 DDC 372.3/57
*1. Natural history - Study and teaching (Elementary) - Anecdotes. 2. Natural history - Study and teaching (Elementary) I. Bourne, Barbara.*
*TC QH51 .T35 2000*

**Taking learning to task.**
Vella, Jane Kathryn, 1931- San Francisco, Calif. : Jossey-Bass, c2000.
*TC LC5225.L42 V43 2000*

**Taking sides in social research.**
Hammersley, Martyn. London ; New York : Routledge, 2000.
*TC H62 .H2338 2000*

**Taking supervision forward :** enquiries and trends in counselling and psychotherapy / edited by Barbara Lawton and Colin Feltham. London : Sage, 2000. x, 219 p. ; 24 cm. Includes bibliographic references and index. ISBN 0-7619-6009-0 ISBN 0-7619-6010-4 (pbk.) DDC 361.06
*1. Counselors - Supervision of. 2. Psychotherapists - Supervision of. 3. Counselors - Supervision of. 4. Psychotherapists - Supervision of. I. Feltham, Colin. II. Lawton, Barbara.*
*TC BF637.C6 T35 2000*

**Taking the stress out of teaching.**
Bernard, Michael E. (Michael Edwin), 1950-. Melbourne : Collins Dove, 1990.
*TC LB2840.2 .B47 1990*

**Talab, R. S., 1948-** Commonsense copyright : a guide for educators and librarians / by R.S. Talab. 2nd ed. Jefferson, N.C. : McFarland & Co., 1999. xii, 292 p. : forms ; 23 cm. Includes index. ISBN 0-7864-0675-5 (sewn softcover : alk. paper) DDC 346.7304/82
*1. Copyright - United States - Popular works. 2. Fair use (Copyright) - United States - Popular works. I. Title.*
*TC KF2994 .T36 1999*

**Talan, Carole.** Founding and funding family literacy programs : a how-to-do-it manual for librarians / Carole Talan. New York : Neal-Schuman, c1999. ix, 222 p. : ill. ; 28 cm. (How-to-do-it manuals for librarians ; no. 92) Includes bibliographical references (p. [215]-218) and index. ISBN 1-55570-210-4 DDC 027.6
*1. Libraries and new literates - United States. 2. Family literacy programs - United States. 3. Public libraries - Services to illiterate persons - United States. I. Title. II. Series: How-to-do-it manuals for libraries ; no. 92.*
*TC Z716.45 .T35 1999*

**Talburt, Susan.**
Thinking queer. New York : Peter Lang, c2000.
*TC LC192.6 .T55 2000*

**The tale I told Sasha.**
Willard, Nancy. 1st ed. Boston : Little, Brown, c1999.
*TC PZ8.3.W668 Tal 1999*

**TALENT.** *See* **ABILITY.**

**TALENTED CHILDREN.** *See* **GIFTED CHILDREN.**

**TALENTED PERSONS.** *See* **GIFTED PERSONS.**

**TALENTS.** *See* **ABILITY.**

**Talents unfolding :** cognition and development / edited by Reva C. Friedman, Bruce M. Shore. 1st ed. Washington, DC : American Psychological Association, c2000. xix, 279 p. : ill. ; 26 cm. Includes bibliographical references and indexes. ISBN 1-55798-643-6 (alk. paper) DDC 155.45/5
*1. Gifted children. 2. Gifted persons. I. Friedman, Reva C. II. Shore, Bruce M.*
*TC BF723.G5 T35 2000*

**TALES.** *See also* **FAIRY TALES; LEGENDS.**
Evetts-Secker, Josephine. Father and son tales. Richmond Hill, Ont. : Scholastic Canada, 1998.
*TC GR469 E93 1998*

Mayer, Marianna. Women warriors. New York : Morrow Junior Books, 1999.
*TC PZ8.1.M46 Wo 1999*

Traditional storytelling today. Chicago : Fitzroy Dearborn Publishers, 1999.
*TC GR72 .T73 1999*

**TALES - CALIFORNIA.**
Bierhorst, John. The people with five fingers. New York : Marshall Cavendish, 2000.
*TC E78.C15 B523 2000*

**Tales from other worlds** [videorecording] / a production of WQED Pittsburgh in association with the National Academy of Sciences ; series producer, Gregory Andorfer ; written by Robin Bates and Chip Walter ; producer, Robin Bates. [New York, N.Y.?] : Unapix Entertainment, Inc. [distributor], c1996. 1 videocassette (60 min.) : sd., col. with b&w sequences ; 1/2 in. (Planet Earth ; 4) At head of title: Unapix Consumer Products feature presentation [videorecording]. VHS. Catalogued from credits and container. Narrator, Richard Kiley. Sound, Kenneth Love... [et al.]; photography by Norris Brock... [et al.] ; music by Jack Tillar and William Loose. "Major funding by the Annenberg/CPB Project"--Container. For adolescent through adult. SUMMARY: An explanation of the origins of the planet and solar system. Follows scientists as they attempt to reconstruct the events which led to the creation of the earth. Suggests that bombardments from space affected and shaped the earth's surface and explores reasons for the extinction of the dinosaurs.
*1. Earth. 2. Geology. 3. Earth sciences. 4. Solar system. 5. Astrophysics. 6. Documentary television programs. I. Andorfer, Gregory. II. Bates, Robin. III. Walter. Chip. IV. Kiley, Richard. V. WQED (Television station : Pittsburgh, Pa.) VI. National Academy of Sciences (U.S.) VII. Annenberg/CPB Project. VIII. Unapix Entertainment, Inc. IX. Unapix Consumer Products. X. Title: Unapix Consumer Products feature presentation [videorecording] XI. Series.*
*TC QB631.2 .T3 1996*

**Tales from other worlds** [videorecording] / a production of WQED Pittsburgh in association with the National Academy of Sciences ; series producer, Gregory Andorfer ; written by Robin Bates and Chip Walter ; producer, Robin Bates. [New York, N.Y.?] : Unapix Entertainment, Inc. [distributor], c1996. 1 videocassette (60 min.) : sd., col. with b&w sequences ; 1/2 in. (Planet Earth ; 4) At head of title: Unapix Consumer Products feature presentation [videorecording]. VHS. Catalogued from credits and container. Narrator, Richard Kiley. Sound, Kenneth Love... [et al.] ; photography by Norris Brock... [et al.] ; music by Jack Tillar and William Loose. "Major funding by the Annenberg/CPB Project"--Container. For adolescent through adult. SUMMARY: An explanation of the origins of the planet and solar system. Follows scientists as they attempt to reconstruct the events which led to the creation of the earth. Suggests that bombardments from space affected and shaped the earth's surface and explores reasons for the extinction of the dinosaurs.
*1. Earth. 2. Geology. 3. Earth sciences. 4. Solar system. 5. Astrophysics. 6. Documentary television programs. I. Andorfer, Gregory. II. Bates, Robin. III. Walter. Chip. IV. Kiley, Richard. V. WQED (Television station : Pittsburgh, Pa.) VI. National Academy of Sciences (U.S.) VII. Annenberg/CPB Project. VIII. Unapix Entertainment, Inc. IX. Unapix Consumer Products. X. Title: Unapix Consumer Products feature presentation [videorecording] XI. Series.*
*TC QB631.2 .T3 1996*

**Tales from the Freudian crypt.**
Dufresne, Todd, 1966- Stanford, Calif. : Stanford University Press, 2000.

*TC BF175.5.D4 D84 2000*

**Tales out of school.**
Keroes, Jo. Carbondale : Southern Illinois University Press, c1999.
*TC PS374.T43 K47 1999*

**TALES - STUDY AND TEACHING (ELEMENTARY).**
Barchers, Suzanne I. Multicultural folktales. Englewood, Colo. : Teacher Ideas Press, 2000.
*TC GR43.C4 B39 2000*

Kraus, Anne Marie. Folktale themes and activities for children. Englewood, Colo. : Teacher Ideas Press, c1998-1999.
*TC GR45 .K73 1998*

**Talk matters.**
Fennimore, Beatrice Schneller. New York ; London : Teachers College Press, c2000.
*TC LB1033.5 F46 2000*

**TALK SHOWS - UNITED STATES.**
Kunz, Linda Ann. English modals in American talk shows. 1999.
*TC 06 no. 11136*

**Talk that book! booktalks to promote reading.**
Littlejohn, Carol. Worthington, Ohio : Linworth Publishing, 1999.
*TC Z1037.A2 L58 1999*

**Talk, work, and institutional order :** discourse in medical, mediation, and management settings / edited by Srikant Sarangi, Celia Roberts. Berlin ; New York : Mouton de Gruyter, 1999. xi, 529 p. ; 23 cm. (Language, power, and social process ; 1) Includes bibliographical references and index. ISBN 3-11-015723-3 (cloth : alk. paper) ISBN 3-11-015722-5 (pbk. : alk. paper) DDC 302.2/242
*1. Oral communication. 2. Communication in organizations. 3. Discourse analysis. 4. Social interaction. I. Sarangi, Srikant, 1956- II. Roberts, Celia, 1947- III. Series.*
*TC P95 .T286 1999*

**Talkin that talk.**
Smitherman, Geneva, 1940- London ; New York : Routledge, 2000.
*TC PE3102.N4 S63 2000*

**TALKING.** *See* **SPEECH.**

**Talking about aphasia.**
Parr, Susie, 1953- Buckingham ; Philadelphia : Open University Press, 1997.
*TC RC425 .P376 1997*

**Talking about health and wellness with patients.**
Jonas, Steven. New York : Springer, c2000.
*TC RA427.8 .J66 2000*

**Talking across boundaries :** participatory evaluation research in an urban middle school / edited by Michell Fine ; authored by the Bruner Inquiry Team: Cathie Bell ... [et al.]. [New York] : [Bruner Foundation], 1996. 112 p. ; 29 cm.
*1. Middle schools - United States. 2. Education, Urban - United States. I. Fine, Michell. II. Bell, Cathie. III. Bruner Foundation. IV. Title: Participatory evaluation research in an urban middle school*
*TC LB1623.5 .T35 1996*

**Talking books :** children's authors talk about the craft, creativity, and process of writing / [edited by] James Carter. London ; New York : Routledge, 1999. xv, 266 p. : ill., facsims., ports. ; 26 cm. Includes bibliographical references. CONTENTS: Brian Moses -- Benjamin Zephaniah -- Ian Beck -- Neil Ardley -- Terry Deary -- Helen Cresswell -- Gillian Cross -- Berlie Doherty -- Alan Durant -- Philip Pullman -- Celia Rees -- Norman Silver -- Jacqueline Wilson. ISBN 0-415-19416-4 (alk. paper) ISBN 0-415-19417-2 (pbk. : alk. paper) DDC 809/.89282
*1. Children's literature, English - History and criticism - Theory, etc. 2. Authors, English - 20th century - Biography. 3. Children's literature - Authorship. I. Carter, James, 1959-*
*TC PR990 .T35 1999*

**Talking that talk.**
Smitherman, Geneva, 1940- Talkin that talk. London ; New York : Routledge, 2000.
*TC PE3102.N4 S63 2000*

**Talking visions :** multicultural feminism in a transnational age / Ella Shohat, editor ; foreword by Marcia Tucker. New York, N.Y. : New Museum of Contemporary Art ; Cambridge, Mass. : MIT Press, c1998. xix, 574 p. : ill. ; 25 cm. (Documentary sources in contemporary art ; v. 5) Includes bibliographical references (p. [533]-545) and index. ISBN 0-262-69205-8 (pbk : alk. paper) DDC 700/.82
*1. Feminism and the arts. 2. Arts and society - History - 20th century. 3. Multiculturalism in art. 4. Gender identity in art. I. Shohat, Ella. II. Series.*

*TC NX180.F4 T36 1998*

**Talking with artists.** Volume three : : conversations with Peter Catalanotto, Raúl Colón, Lisa Desimini, Jane Dyer, Kevin Hawkes, G. Brian Karas, Betsy Lewin, Ted Lewin, Keiko Narahashi, Elise Primavera, Anna Rich, Peter Sis, Paul O. Zelinsky / compiled and edited by Pat Cummings. 1st ed. New York : Clarion Books, c1999. 96 p. : ill. (some col.) ; 29 cm. Includes bibliographical references (p. 93-95). SUMMARY: Distinguished picture book artists talk about their early art experiences, answer questions most frequently asked by children, and offer encouragement to aspiring artists. CONTENTS: Peter Catalanotto -- Raul Colon -- Lisa Desimini -- Dane Dyer -- Kevin Hawkes -- G. Brian Karas -- Betsy Lewin -- Ted Lewin -- Keiko Narahashi -- Elise Primavera -- Anna Rich -- Peter Sis -- Paul O. Zelinsky -- Secret techniques -- Books by the artists. ISBN 0-395-89132-9
*1. Illustrators - United States - Biography - Juvenile literature. I. Cummings, Pat.*
*TC NC961.6 .T35 1999*

**Talking with artists.** Volume two : : conversations with Thomas B. Allen, Mary Jane Begin, Floyd Cooper, Julie Downing, Denise Fleming, Sheila Hamanaka, Kevin Henkes, William Joyce, Maira Kalman, Deborah Nourse Lattimore, Brian Pinkney, Vera B. Williams and David Wisniewski / compiled and edited by Pat Cummings. 1st ed. New York : Simon & Schuster Books for Young Readers, c1995. 96 p. : ill. (some col.) ; 29 cm. Includes bibliographical references (p. 93-95). SUMMARY: Distinguished picture book artists talk about their early art experiences, answer questions most frequently asked by children, and offer encouragement to aspiring artists. ISBN 0-689-80310-9
*1. Illustrators - United States - Biography - Juvenile literature. I. Cummings, Pat.*
*TC NC975 .T34 1995*

**TALL TALES.**
Ketteman, Helen. Shoeshine Whittaker. New York : Walker & Co., 1999.
*TC PZ7.K494 Sh 1999*

**Tallman, Karen.**
Bohart, Arthur C. How clients make therapy work. 1st ed. Washington, DC : American Psychological Association, c1999.
*TC RC480.5 .B64 1999*

**Tally, William.**
Brunner, Cornelia, Dr. The new media literacy handbook. New York : Anchor Books, 1999.
*TC LB1028.3 .B77 1999*

**Talmadge, Jonathan.**
Heroin [videorecording]. [Princeton, N.J.] : Films for the Humanities & Sciences, c1998.
*TC HV5822.H4 H4 1998*

**TALMUD TORAHS (SCHOOLS).** *See* **JEWISH RELIGIOUS SCHOOLS.**

**Tamakloe, E. K.** An evaluation of the National Conference on Teacher Education 1986. Accra : Ghana Universities Press, 1997. 92 p. ; 22 cm. "... organized by the Institute of Education of the University of Cape Coast (UCC), and held at the University ... from September 7 to September 15 ..."--Introd. Includes bibliographical references (p. [85]) and index. ISBN 9964-3-0241-X
*1. National Conference on Teacher Education - (1986 : - University of Cape Coast) - Evaluation. I. Title.*
*TC LB1727.G5 T36 1997*

**Tambourine moon.**
Jones, Joy. New York : Simon & Schuster, 1999.
*TC PZ7.J72025 Tam 1999*

**Taming the time stealers.**
Gore, M. C. Thousand Oaks, Calif. : Corwin Press, c1999.
*TC LB2838.8 .G67 1999*

**Taming the troublesome child.**
Jones, Kathleen W. Cambridge, Mass : Harvard University Press, 1999.
*TC RJ501.A2 J64 1999*

**Tamis-LeMonda, Catherine S. (Catherine Susan), 1958-.**
Child psychology. Philadelphia, PA : Psychology Press, c1999.
*TC BF721 .C5155 1999*

**Tan, Elizabeth Bachrach.**
The academy and the possibility of belief. Cresskill, N.J. : Hampton Press, c2000.
*TC LB2324 .A27 2000*

**Tanaka, Hiroko.** Turn-taking in Japanese conversation : a study in grammar and interaction / Hiroko Tanaka. Amsterdam ; Philadelphia, PA : John Benjamins Pub.

Co., c1999. xiii, 242 p. : ill. ; 23 cm. (Pragmatics & beyond, 0922-842X ; new ser. 56) Includes bibliographical references (p. [227]-235) and index. ISBN 1-55619-819-1 (US : alk. paper) ISBN 90-272-5070-7 (Eur.) DDC 495.6/0141
*1. Japanese language - Discourse analysis. 2. Conversation analysis - Japan. 3. Dialogue analysis - Japan. I. Title. II. Series.*
**TC PL640.5 .T36 1999**

**Tancred, Peta, 1937-.**
Adams, Annmarie. Designing women. Toronto : University of Toronto Press, c2000.
**TC NA1997 A32 2000**

**Tandy, Miles.**
Winston, Joe. Beginning drama 4-11. London : David Fulton Publishers, 1998.
**TC PN1701 .W567 1998**

**Tanenbaum, Eric.**
Research strategies in the social sciences. Oxford [England] ; New York : Oxford University Press, 1998.
**TC H62 .R4614 1998**

**Tang, Joyce, 1962-** Doing engineering : the career attainment and mobility of Caucasian, Black, and Asian-American engineers / Joyce Tang. Lanham, Md. ; Oxford : Rowman & Littlefield Publishers, c2000. xx, 242 p. : ill. ; 24 cm. Includes bibliographical references (p. [215]-232) and index. ISBN 0-8476-9464-X (hbk. : alk. paper) ISBN 0-8476-9465-8 (pbk. : alk. paper) DDC 331.12/52/000973
*1. Engineers - Employment - United States. I. Title.*
**TC TA157 .T363 2000**

**[Tanglaw (Manila, Philippines)]** Tanglaw : journal of the College of Education. Manila : The College, 1992-
v. ; 23-29 cm. Vol. 1, no. 1 (May 1992)- . Journal of the College of Education. In English and Tagalog. ISSN 0117-357X
*1. Education - Philippines. I. De la Salle University. College of Education. II. Title: Journal of the College of Education*

**Tannenbaum, Abraham.** Dropout or diploma : a socio-educational analysis of early school withdrawal / [by] Abraham J. Tannenbaum. New York : Teachers College Press, 1966. ix, 36 p., 23 cm. (Urban problems series) Bibliography : p. 34-36. DDC 373.129130973
*1. Elimination (In education) 2. Urban education. I. Title. II. Series: Teachers College. Urban problems series.*
**TC 371.2913T15**

**Tanner, David Earl, 1948-** Assessing academic achievement / David E. Tanner. Boston ; London : Allyn and Bacon, c2001. xvi, 367 p. : ill. ; 24 cm. Includes bibliographical references (p. 348-354) and index. ISBN 0-205-28266-0 (alk. paper) DDC 371.26
*1. Educational evaluation. 2. Academic achievement - Evaluation. I. Title.*
**TC LB2822.75 .T36 2001**

**TANNING.** See **LEATHER.**

**TANOAN INDIANS.** See **TEWA INDIANS.**

**Taormina, Grace.** The complete guide to rubber stamping : design and decorate gifts and keepsakes simply and beautifully with rubber stamps / Grace Taormina. New York : Watson-Guptill Publications, c1996. 160 p. : col. ill. ; 26 cm. (Watson-Guptill crafts) Includes index. ISBN 0-8230-4613-3 (paper) DDC 761
*1. Rubber stamp printing. I. Title. II. Series.*
**TC TT867 .T36 1996**

**Tap dancing for beginners** [videorecording] : with Henry Le Tang / [presented by] the Video Classroom ; producer and director, Lee Kraft. W. Long Branch, NJ : Kultur, c1981. 1 videocassette (22 min.) : sd., col. ; 1/2 in. VHS, Hi-fi, Mono, Stereo-Compatible, Dolby System. Catalogued from credits and container. Instructor: Henry Le Tang ; guest artist: Honi Coles ; student dancer: Cory Beychok. Executive producer, Marc Chase Weinstein. Time listed on container, 31 minutes; actual time, 22 minutes. For the beginning tap dance student. SUMMARY: Master tap choreographer and Le Tang School of Dance owner, Henry Le Tang, teaches the basics of tap dancing with student dancer, Cory Beychok, after a demonstration of legendary tap dancing by the famous Honi Coles. The two finish up the tape by dancing together.
*1. Tap dancing - Study and teaching. I. Le Tang, Henry.4dnc II. Coles, Honi, 1911- III. Beychok, Cory. IV. Kraft, Leland M. V. Kultur International Films. VI. Video Classroom (Firm)*
**TC GV1794 .T3 1981**

**TAP DANCING - STUDY AND TEACHING.**
Tap dancing for beginners [videorecording]. W. Long Branch, NJ : Kultur, c1981.
**TC GV1794 .T3 1981**

**Tappan, Olivia.**
Connect with English [videorecording]. S. Burlington, Vt. : The Annenberg/CPB Collection, c1997.
**TC PE1128 .C66 1997**

**Tarcov, Nathan.**
Locke, John, 1632-1704. [Some thoughts concerning education] Some thoughts concerning education : Indianapolis : Hackett Pub. Co., c1996.
**TC LB475.L6 L63 1996**

Locke's education for liberty / Nathan Tarcov. Lanham, Md. : Lexington Books, c1999. viii, 272 p. ; 23 cm. Originally published: Chicago : University of Chicago Press, c1984. Includes bibliographical references (p. 261-264) and index. ISBN 0-7391-0085-8 (alk. paper) DDC 370/.1
*1. Locke, John - 1632-1704. 2. Education - Philosophy. 3. Liberty. 4. Political science - Philosophy. I. Title.*
**TC LB475.L72 T27 1999**

**Tardif, Jacques, 1947-.**
The challenges of the information and communication technologies facing history teaching. Strasbourg : Council of Europe Pub., c1999.
**TC D424 .C425 1999**

**Targeting schools.**
Penn, Alan, 1926- London ; Portland, OR : Woburn Press, 1999.
**TC GV443 .P388 1999**

**Tarnowski, Kenneth J.**
Directory of internship and post-doctoral fellowships in clinical child/pediatric psychology, 1997. [Mahwah, N.J. : Lawrence Erlbaum Associates, c1997].
**TC RJ503.3 .D57 1997**

**Tashakkori, Abbas.**
Education of Hispanics in the United States. New York : AMS Press, c1999.
**TC LC4091 .R417 1999**

Education of Hispanics in the United States. New York : AMS Press, c1999.
**TC LC4091 .R417 1999**

**TASILI (ALGERIA).** See **TASSILI-N-AJJER (ALGERIA).**

**TASK ANALYSIS.**
Cognitive task analysis. Mahwah, N.J. : L. Erlbaum Associates, 2000.
**TC BF311 .C55345 2000**

**TASK ANALYSIS IN EDUCATION.**
Jonassen, David H., 1947- Task analysis methods for instructional design. Mahwah, N.J. : L. Erlbaum Associates, 1999.
**TC LB1028.38 .J65 1999**

**Task analysis methods for instructional design.**
Jonassen, David H., 1947- Mahwah, N.J. : L. Erlbaum Associates, 1999.
**TC LB1028.38 .J65 1999**

**Tasman, Allan, 1947-** The doctor-patient relationship in pharmacotherapy : improving treatment effectiveness / Allan Tasman, Michelle B. Riba, Kenneth R. Silk. New York : Guilford Press, c2000. ix, 182 p. ; 24 cm. Includes bibliographical references (p. 171-176) and index. ISBN 1-57230-596-7 (cloth) DDC 616.89/18
*1. Psychopharmacology. 2. Psychotherapist and patient. 3. Mental illness - Chemotherapy. I. Riba, Michelle B. II. Silk, Kenneth R., 1944- III. Title.*
**TC RC483.3 .T375 2000**

**TASSILI DES ADJJER (ALGERIA).** See **TASSILI-N-AJJER (ALGERIA).**

**TASSILI DES AJJER PLATEAU (ALGERIA).** See **TASSILI-N-AJJER (ALGERIA).**

**TASSILI-N-AJJER (ALGERIA) - ANTIQUITIES.**
Tassili N'Ajjer [videorecording] : Editions Cinégraphiques ; Northbrook, Ill. : [distributed by] the Roland Collection, c1968.
**TC N5310.5.A4 T3 1968**

**Tassili-n-Ajjer [videorecording].**
Tassili N'Ajjer [videorecording]. [S.l.] : Editions Cinégraphiques ; Northbrook, Ill. : [distributed by] the Roland Collection, c1968.
**TC N5310.5.A4 T3 1968**

**TASSILI N'AHAGGAR (ALGERIA).** See **TASSILI-N-AJJER (ALGERIA).**

**Tassili N'Ajjer** [videorecording] / un film de J. Dominique Lajoux ; réalisé en collaboration avec Michel Meignant ; un produit par Jean Thuillier pour les éditions cinégraphiques ; texte de Max-Pol Fouchet. [S.l.] : Editions Cinégraphiques ; Northbrook, Ill. : [distributed by] the Roland Collection, c1968. 1 videocassette (16 min.) : sd., col. ; 1/2 in. At head of title: Anthony Roland Collection of Films on

Art. Subtitle on cassette label and container: Prehistoric rock paintings of the Sahara. VHS. NTSC. Catalogued from credits, cassette label and container. Credits in French; narration in English. Narrator: auteur, Max-Pol Fouchet. Music by Maurice Le Roux ; edited by J. Dominique Lajoux ; sound engineer, René Hanotel. Place of distribution from cassette label; addresses for the Roland Collection on container: Peasmarsh, East Sussex, England and Ho-Ho-Kus, NJ. On spine of container and cassette case: "10." For high school and up. SUMMARY: Shows the prehistoric rock paintings of the Sahara when the Sahara desert was a garden thousands of years ago. Examines pre-historic rock paintings created over 4,000 years ago by people who inhabited the Tassili n'Ajjer, a group of mountains in the eastern Sahara. Paintings of early man have some mysterious and some recognizable themes painted in earth colors on the stone walls of the cave. At this site hundreds of thousands of paintings and drawings are found from nearly 5,000 years ago. Nowhere else is there such an abundance of prehistoric rock art.
*1. Rock paintings - Algeria - Tassili-n-Ajjer. 2. Cave paintings - Algeria - Tassili-n-Ajjer. 3. Tassili-n-Ajjer (Algeria) - Antiquities. 4. Art, Prehistoric - Algeria - Tassili-n-Ajjer. 5. Documentary films. I. Lajoux, Jean-Dominiques. II. Meignant, Michel, 1936- III. Thuillier, Jean-Paul. IV. Fouchet, Max-Pol. V. Editions Cinégraphiques. VI. Anthony Rolland Collection of Film on Art. VII. Title: Tassili-n-Ajjer [videorecording] VIII. Title: Anthony Roland Collection of Films on Art IX. Title: Prehistoric rock paintings of the Sahara.*
**TC N5310.5.A4 T3 1968**

**Tassinary, Louis G.**
Handbook of psychophysiology. 2nd ed. Cambridge, UK ; New York, NY, USA : Cambridge University Press, 2000.
**TC QP360 .P7515 2000**

**TASTE.** See **FOOD PREFERENCES.**

**TASTE (AESTHETICS).** See **AESTHETICS.**

**Tatai, Zoltán.**
Emlékezés Szokolszky Istvánra. [Budapest] : Magyar Pedagógiai Társaság, 1998.
**TC LA2375.H92 S9653 1998**

**Tate Gallery.**
The dynamics of now. London : Wimbledon School of Art in association with Tate, c2000.
**TC N185 .D96 2000**

Institute of Paper Conservation. Modern works, modern problems? [England] : Institute of Paper Conservation, c1994.
**TC N8560 .I59 1994**

Sargent, John Singer, 1856-1925. John Singer Sargent. Princeton : Princeton University Press, 1998.
**TC ND237.S3 A4 1998a**

Varnedoe, Kirk, 1946- Jackson Pollock. New York : Museum of Modern Art ; Distributed in the U.S. and Canada by Harry N. Abrams, c1998.
**TC ND237.P73 A4 1998**

Whitfield, Sarah, 1942- Bonnard. New York, N.Y. : Harry N. Abrams, 1998.
**TC ND553.B65 W45 1998**

**Tate, Gary.**
The writing teacher's sourcebook. 4th ed. New York : Oxford University Press, 2000.
**TC PE1404 .W74 2000**

**Tate, Marsha Ann.**
Alexander, Janet E. Web wisdom. Mahwah, N.J. : Lawrence Erlbaum Associates, Publishers, 1999.
**TC TK5105.888 .A376 1999**

**Tatto, Maria Teresa.**
Nielsen, H. Dean. The cost-effectiveness of distance education for teacher training. Cambridge, Mass. : B.R.I.D.G.E.S. Basic Research and Implementation in Developing Education Systems, [1991].
**TC LB1731 .N43 1991**

**Tauber, Robert T.**
**Classroom management from A to Z.**
Tauber, Robert T. Classroom management. 3rd ed. Westport, Conn. : Bergin & Garvey, 1999.
**TC LB3011 .T38 1999**

Classroom management : sound theory and effective practice / Robert T. Tauber. 3rd ed. Westport, Conn. : Bergin & Garvey, 1999. xv, 339 p. : ill. ; 25 cm. Rev. ed. of: Classroom management from A to Z. c1990. Includes bibliographical references (p. [311]-327) and indexes. ISBN 0-89789-618-1 (alk. paper) ISBN 0-89789-619-X (pbk. : alk. paper) DDC 371.102/4
*1. Classroom management - United States. 2. School discipline - United States. I. Tauber, Robert T. Classroom management from A to Z. II. Title.*

### *TC LB3011 .T38 1999*

**Taught bodies** / edited by Clare O'Farrell ... [et al.]. New York : P. Lang, c2000. vi, 215 p. ; 23 cm. (Eruptions, 1091-8590 ; vol. 5) Includes bibliographical references. CONTENTS: Sleuthing the body : the deadly thrill of learning / Helen Yeates -- The Kama Sutra as curriculum / Peter Cryle -- Stuck in the missionary position? / Erica McWilliam -- The lecherous professor / Susie O'Brien -- Wicked bodies : towards a critical pedagogy of corporeal differences for performance / Christopher Beckey -- Pedagogy : incomplete, unrequited / Bronwen Levy -- Teaching an embodied aesthetic : towards a different practice of English / Ray Mission and Wendy Morgan -- Making an exhibition of education : the Body at the Art Gallery of New South Wales / Colin Symes -- Practices of the heart : the art of being a good listener / Caroline Hatcher -- Testing the bodies of knowledge / Daphne Meadmore -- Surveillance and student handwriting / Alison Jones -- Iconic (pre)occupations / Denise Kirkpatrick and Stephen Thorpe -- Is there any body out there? : particular bodies in lecturing spaces / Barbara Brook -- Celluloid bodies / Clare O'Farrell. ISBN 0-8204-4297-6 DDC 370/.1
*1. Education - Philosophy. 2. Body, Human (Philosophy) 3. Critical pedagogy. 4. Teaching. I. O'Farrell, Clare. II. Series.*

### *TC LB14.7 .T38 2000*

**TAVERNS (INNS).** *See* **HOTELS.**

**Tavistock Clinic series**
Waddell, Margot, 1946- Inside lives. New York : Routledge, 1998.
### *TC BF175.45 .W33 1998*

**Tawa, Nicholas E.** High-minded and low-down : music in the lives of Americans, 1800-1861 / Nicholas E. Tawa. Boston : Northeastern University Press, c2000. xiii, 350 p. ; 24 cm. Includes bibliographical references (p. 299-343) and index. ISBN 1-55553-443-0 (cloth : alk. paper) ISBN 1-55553-442-2 (paper : alk. paper) DDC/.973/09034
*1. Music - Social aspects - United States. 2. Music - United States - 19th century - History and criticism. I. Title.*

### *TC ML3917.U6 T39 2000*

**TAX-EXEMPT ORGANIZATIONS.** *See* **NONPROFIT ORGANIZATIONS.**

**TAXES, SCHOOL.** *See* **EDUCATION - FINANCE.**

**Taylor, Barbara (Barbara M.).**
Reading for meaning. New York ; London : Teachers College Press, c2000.
### *TC LB1050.45 .R443 2000*

**Taylor, Bruce D.** The arts equation : forging a vital link between performing artists & educators / Bruce D. Taylor. New York, N.Y. : Back Stage Books, c1999. 208 p. : ill. ; 23 cm. Includes index. ISBN 0-8230-8805-7
*1. Art - Study and teaching. 2. Performing arts - Study and teaching. 3. Performing arts and children. 4. Artists as teachers. I. Title.*

### *TC N350 .T38 1999*

**Taylor, Denny, 1947-** Family literacy : young children learning to read and write / Denny Taylor ; foreword by Yetta M. Goodman. Portsmouth, NH : Heinemann, c1998. x, 132 p. : ill. ; 21 cm. Includes bibliographical references (p. [127]-132). ISBN 0-325-00074-3 (alk. paper)
*1. Literacy. 2. Reading - Parent participation. 3. English language - Composition and exercises. I. Title.*

### *TC LC149 .T37 1998*

**Taylor, Eugene.** Shadow culture psychology and spirituality in America / Eugene Taylor. Washington, D.C. : Counterpoint, c1999. xii, 296 p. ; 24 cm. Includes bibliographical references and index. ISBN 1-88717-880-5 (alk. paper) DDC 200/.973
*1. United States - Religion. 2. Spirituality - United States - History. 3. Psychology, Religious - United States - History. I. Title.*

### *TC BL2525 .T39 1999*

**Taylor, George R.** Curriculum models and strategies for educating individuals with disabilities in inclusive classrooms / by George R. Taylor. Springfield, Ill. : C.C. Thomas, Publisher, c1999. xvi, 244 p. ; 27 cm. Includes bibliographical references and indexes. ISBN 0-398-06975-1 (cloth) ISBN 0-398-06976-X (paper) DDC 371.9/044/0973
*1. Handicapped children - Education - United States - Curricula. 2. Inclusive education - United States. I. Title.*

### *TC LC4031 .T33 1999*

Integrating quantitative and qualitative methods in research. Lanham, Md. ; Oxford : University Press of America, c2000.
### *TC Q175 .I1513 2000*

**Taylor, Harriet Peck.** Ulaq and the northern lights / Harriet Peck Taylor. 1st ed. New York : Farrar Straus Giroux, 1998. 1 v. (unpaged) : col. ill. ; 28 cm. Includes bibliographical references. SUMMARY: A curious young fox hears different explanations of the northern lights from the

various animals he encounters. ISBN 0-374-38063-5 DDC [E]
*1. Auroras - Fiction. 2. Foxes - Fiction. 3. Animals - Fiction. I. Title.*

### *TC PZ7.T2135 Ul 1998*

**Taylor, Kathe.** Children at the center : a workshop approach to standardized test preparation, K-8 / Kathe Taylor and Sherry Walton. Portsmouth, NH : Heinemann, c1998. xiii, 130 p. ; 28 cm. Includes bibliographical references. ISBN 0-325-00095-6 (alk. paper) DDC 371.26
*1. Test-taking skills - United States. 2. Demonstration centers in education - United States. 3. Educational tests and measurements - United States. 4. Norm-referenced tests - United States. 5. Education, Elementary - United States - Evaluation. I. Walton, Sherry. II. Title.*

### *TC LB3060.57 .T39 1998*

**Taylor, Kathleen, 1943-** Developing adult learners : strategies for teachers and trainers / Kathleen Taylor, Catherine Marienau, Morris Fiddler. 1st ed. San Francisco : Jossey-Bass, c2000. xx, 391 p. ; 24 cm. (The Jossey-Bass higher and adult education series) Includes bibliographical references (p. 363-372) and indexes. ISBN 0-7879-4573-0 (alk. paper) DDC 374/.13
*1. Adult learning. 2. Learning, Psychology of. I. Marienau, Catherine. II. Fiddler, Morris. III. Title. IV. Series.*

### *TC LC5225.L42 T39 2000*

**Taylor, Martha A., 1949-.**
Shaw, Sondra C., 1936- Reinventing fundraising. 1st ed. San Francisco : Jossey-Bass Publishers, c1995.
### *TC HV41.9.U5 S53 1995*

**Taylor, Michael, 1957-.**
The Amish [videorecording]. Oak Forest, IL : MPI Home Video, 1988.

The Amish [videorecording]. Oak Forest, Ill. : MPI Home Video, c1988.
### *TC BX8129.A5 A5 1988*

**Taylor, Peter G., 1951-** Making sense of academic life : academics, universities, and change / Peter G. Taylor. Philadelphia, PA : Open University Press, 1999. ix, 167 p. ; 23 cm. Includes bibliographical references and index. ISBN 0-335-20185-7 (hard) ISBN 0-335-20184-9 (pbk.) DDC 378.1/2
*1. College teachers. 2. College teaching. 3. Education, Higher - Aims and objectives. 4. Universities and colleges - Administration. 5. Educational change. I. Title.*

### *TC LB1778 .T39 1999*

**Taylor, Ronald D., 1958-.**
Resilience across contexts. Mahwah, NJ : Lawrence Erlbaun, 2000.
### *TC HQ535 .R47 2000*

**Taylor, Ronald L., 1949-** Assessment of exceptional students : educational and psychological procedures / Ronald L. Taylor. 5th ed. Boston : Allyn and Bacon, c2000. xi, 579 p. : ill. ; 25 cm. Includes bibliographical references (p. 528-559) and indexes. ISBN 0-205-30612-8 DDC 371.91/0973
*1. Handicapped children - Education - United States. 2. Handicapped children - Psychological testing - United States. 3. Educational tests and measurements - United States. 4. Special education - United States. I. Title.*

### *TC LC4031 .T36 2000*

**TAYLOR, THEODORE, 1921- /. THE CAY.**
Beech, Linda Ward. The cay by Theodore Taylor. New York : Scholastic, c1997.
### *TC LB1573 .B4312 1997*

**Taylor, William Septimus, 1885, ed.**
Kentucky high school quarterly. Lexington, Ky. : Department of Education, State University of Kentucky, 1915-1927.

**Taymans, Juliana M.**
Kochhar, Carol. Successful inclusion. 2nd ed. Upper Saddle River, NJ : Prentice Hall, c2000.
### *TC LC1201 .K63 2000*

**Tchen, John Kuo Wei.** New York before Chinatown : Orientalism and the shaping of American culture, 1776-1882 / John Kuo Wei Tchen. Baltimore : Johns Hopkins University Press, 1999. xxiv, 385 p. : ill. ; 24 cm. Includes bibliographical references (p. [347]-373) and index. ISBN 0-8018-6006-7 (alk. paper) DDC 303.48/251073
*1. Public opinion - New York (State) - New York - History - 18th century. 2. Public opinion - New York (State) - New York - History - 19th century. 3. China - Foreign public opinion, American - History - 18th century. 4. China - Foreign public opinion, American - History - 19th century. 5. New York (N.Y.) - History - 1775-1865. 6. New York (N.Y.) - History - 1865-1898. I. Title. II. Title: Orientalism and the shaping of American culture, 1776-1882*

### *TC DS706 .T4 1999*

**Tchudi, Stephen, 1942-.**
Tchudi, Susan J. (Susan Jane), 1945- The English language arts handbook. 2nd ed. Portsmouth, NH : Boynton/Cook, c1999.
### *TC LB1576 .T358 1999*

**Tchudi, Susan J. (Susan Jane), 1945-** The English language arts handbook : classroom strategies for teachers / Susan J. Tchudi and Stephen N. Tchudi. 2nd ed. Portsmouth, NH : Boynton/Cook, c1999. x, 278 p. : ill. ; 24 cm. Stephen Tchudi's name appears first on the earlier edition. Includes bibliographical references (p. 269-274) and index. ISBN 0-86709-463-X DDC 428./0071/2
*1. Language arts. 2. English language - Study and teaching. I. Tchudi, Stephen, 1942- II. Title.*

### *TC LB1576 .T358 1999*

**Teach our children well : bringing K-12 education into the 21st century.**
Calfee, Robert C. Teach your children well. Stanford, CA : Stanford Alumni Association, c1995.
### *TC LB2822.82 .C32 1995*

**Teach your children well.**
Calfee, Robert C. Stanford, CA : Stanford Alumni Association, c1995.
### *TC LB2822.82 .C32 1995*

**Teachable movies for elementary and middle school classrooms.**
Hulse, John. Bloomington, Ind. : Phi Delta Kappa Educational Foundation, c1998.
### *TC PN1998 .H76 1998*

**TEACHER-ADMINISTRATOR RELATIONSHIPS - NEW YORK (STATE) - GARDEN CITY - CASE STUDIES.**
Lewis, Lionel S. (Lionel Stanley) When power corrupts. New Brunswick, NJ: Transaction Publishers, c2000.
### *TC LD25.8 .L49 2000*

**TEACHER AIDES.** *See* **TEACHERS' ASSISTANTS.**

**TEACHER APPRAISAL.** *See* **TEACHERS - RATING OF.**

**TEACHER ASSOCIATIONS.** *See* **TEACHERS' UNIONS.**

**TEACHER AUTONOMY.** *See* **TEACHING, FREEDOM OF.**

**The teacher-child relationship, temperament, and coping in children with developmental disabilities.**
Flynn, Bernadette Marie. 2000.
### *TC 06 no. 11267*

**TEACHER CONTRACTS.** *See* **TEACHERS' CONTRACTS.**

**Teacher development**
Louden, William. Understanding teaching. New York : Cassell : Teachers College Press, Teachers College, Columbia University, 1991.
### *TC LB1025.3 .L68 1991*

**TEACHER EDUCATION.** *See* **TEACHERS - TRAINING OF.**

**Teacher education in the Asia-Pacific region :** a comparative study / edited by Paul Morris, John Williamson. New York : Falmer Press, c2000. ix, 322 p. : ill. ; 23 cm. (Garland reference library of social science ; v. 996) (Garland reference library of social science. Reference books in international education ; vol. 48) Includes bibliographical references (p. 289-307) and indexes. ISBN 0-8153-1856-1 (alk. paper) DDC 370/.71/05
*1. Teachers - Training of - Asia - Cross-cultural studies. 2. Teachers - Training of - Pacific Area - Cross-cultural studies. I. Morris, Paul, 1951- II. Williamson, John, 1947- III. Series. IV. Series: Garland reference library of social science. Reference books in international education ; vol. 48*

### *TC LB1727.A69 T42 2000*

**Teacher education in the People's Republic of China.**
Ashmore, Rhea A. Bloomington, Ind., U.S.A. : Phi Delta Kappa Educational Foundation, c1997.
### *TC LB1727.C5 A85 1997*

**Teacher education yearbook**
(7) Research on professional development schools. Thousand Oaks, Calif. : Corwin Press, c1999.
### *TC LB2154.A3 R478 1999*

(8) Research on effective models for teacher education. Thousand Oaks, Calif. : Corwin Press, Inc., c2000.
### *TC LB1715 .R42 2000*

**TEACHER EDUCATORS - BIOGRAPHY.**
International narratives on becoming a teacher educator. Lewiston, N.Y. ; Lampeter, Wales : E. Mellen Press, c2000.

*TC LB1737.5 .I58 2000*

**Teacher Educators for Children with Behavior Disorders.**
Monograph in behavioral disorders. Severe behavior disorders of children and youth. Reston, Va. : Council for Children with Behavioral Disorders, c1978-1986.
*TC BF721 .M65*

**TEACHER EDUCATORS - TRAINING OF.**
International narratives on becoming a teacher educator. Lewiston, N.Y. ; Lampeter,Wales : E. Mellen Press, c2000.
*TC LB1737.5 .I58 2000*

**TEACHER EFFECTIVENESS.** *See also* **EFFECTIVE TEACHING.**
V'elez Arias, Hiram Oscar. A multi-case study of physical education teachers and working conditions in inner-city schools /by Hiram Oscar V'elez Arias. 1998.
*TC 06 no. 11001*

**TEACHER EFFECTIVENESS - GREAT BRITAIN.**
Harris, Alma, 1958- Teaching and learning in the effective school. Aldershot, England ; Brookfield, Vt. : Ashgate, c1999.
*TC LB2822.84.G7 H37 1999*

Poorly performing staff and how to manage them. London ; New York : Routledge, 1999.
*TC LB2832.4.G7 P66 1999*

**TEACHER EFFECTIVENESS - GREAT BRITAIN - CASE STUDIES.**
Failing teachers? London ; New York : Routledge, 2000.
*TC LB1775.4.G7 F35 2000*

**TEACHER EFFECTIVENESS - NEW YORK (STATE).**
Ort, Suzanne Wichterle. Standards in practice. 1999.
*TC 06 no. 11210*

Southworth, Robert A. Evidence of student learning and implications for alternative policies that support instructional use of assessment. 1999.
*TC 06 no. 11218*

**TEACHER EFFECTIVENESS - UNITED STATES.**
Beerens, Daniel R. Evaluating teachers for professional growth. Thousand Oaks, Calif. ; London : Corwin Press, c2000.
*TC LB2838 .B44 2000*

Lieberman, Ann. Teachers--transforming their world and their work. New York : Teachers College Press ; Alexandria, Va. : Association for Supervision and Curriculum Development, c1999.
*TC LB1025.3 .L547 1999*

Sullivan, Susan, 1943- Supervision that improves teaching. Thousand Oaks, Calif. : Corwin Press, c2000.
*TC LB2806.4 .S85 2000*

**TEACHER EVALUATION.** *See* **TEACHERS - RATING OF.**

**Teacher evaluation to enhance professional practice.**
Danielson, Charlotte. Alexandria, Va. : Association for Supervision and Curriculum Development, c2000.
*TC LB2838 .D26 2000*

**Teacher (Greenwich, Conn.).**
The Grade teacher. Boston, Mass. : Educational Pub. Co., -c1972.

The Grade teacher. Boston, Mass. : Educational Pub. Co., -c1972.

**TEACHER INDUCTION.** *See also* **TEACHER ORIENTATION.**
Tickle, Les. Buckingham [England] ; Philadelphia : Open University Press, 2000.
*TC LB1729 .T53 2000*

**Teacher lore and professional development for school reform.**
Schwarz, Gretchen, 1952- Westport, Conn : Bergin & Garvey, 1998.
*TC LB1775.2 .S38 1998*

**TEACHER MORALE.**
Whitaker, Todd, 1959- Motivating and inspiring teachers. Larchmont, N.Y. : Eye on Education, c2000.
*TC LB2840 .W45 2000*

**Teacher narrative as critical inquiry.**
Ritchie, Joy S. New York : Teachers College Press, c2000.
*TC LA2311 .R58 2000*

**TEACHER ORGANIZATIONS.** *See* **TEACHERS' UNIONS.**

**TEACHER ORIENTATION.**
Tickle, Les. Teacher induction. Buckingham [England] ; Philadelphia : Open University Press, 2000.
*TC LB1729 .T53 2000*

**TEACHER ORIENTATION - GREAT BRITAIN.**
Bleach, Kevan. The induction and mentoring of newly qualified teachers :. London : David Fulton, 1999.
*TC LB1729 .B584 1999*

**TEACHER-PARENT RELATIONSHIPS.** *See* **PARENT-TEACHER RELATIONSHIPS.**

**TEACHER PARTICIPATION IN ADMINISTRATION - UNITED STATES.**
Reed, Carol J., 1937- Teaching with power. New York : Teachers College Press, c2000.
*TC LB2806.45 .R44 2000*

**TEACHER PARTICIPATION IN ADMINISTRATION - UNITED STATES - CASE STUDIES.**
Nolan, James F., 1950- Teachers and educational change. Albany : State University of New York Press, c2000.
*TC LB1777.2 .N64 2000*

**TEACHER PARTICIPATION IN CURRICULUM PLANNING - GREAT BRITAIN.**
Bell, Derek, 1950- Towards effective subject leadership in the primary school. Buckingham [England] ; Philadelphia : Open University Press, c1999.
*TC LB2832.4.G7 B45 1999*

Field, Kit. Effective subject leadership. London ; New York : Routledge, 2000.
*TC LB2806.15 .F54 2000*

The politics of professionalism. London : Continuum, 2000.
*TC LB1779 .M33 2000*

**TEACHER PARTICIPATION IN EDUCATIONAL COUNSELING - GREAT BRITAIN.**
King, Gail, 1949- Counselling skills for teachers. Buckingham [England] ; Philadelphia : Open University Press, 1999.
*TC LB1620.53.G7 K56 1999*

**TEACHER PARTICIPATION IN PERSONNEL SERVICE.** *See* **TEACHER PARTICIPATION IN EDUCATIONAL COUNSELING.**

**TEACHER PARTICIPATION IN THE COMMUNITY.** *See* **TEACHERS AND COMMUNITY.**

**TEACHER-PRINCIPAL RELATIONSHIPS.**
Blase, Joseph. Bringing out the best in teachers. 2nd ed. Thousand Oaks, Calif. : Corwin Press, c2000.
*TC LB2840 .B57 2000*

Brock, Barbara L. Rekindling the flame. Thousand Oaks, Calif. : Corwin Press, c2000.
*TC LB2840.2 .B76 2000*

**TEACHER-PRINCIPAL RELATIONSHIPS - GREAT BRITAIN.**
Poorly performing staff and how to manage them. London ; New York : Routledge, 1999.
*TC LB2832.4.G7 P66 1999*

**TEACHER-PRINCIPAL RELATIONSHIPS - UNITED STATES.**
Thompson, David P., 1959- Motivating others. Princeton, NJ : Eye On Education, c1996.
*TC LB2831.58 .T56 1996*

**Teacher professionalism and the challenge of change** / edited by Jim Graham. Stoke-on-Trent, Staffordshire, England : Trentham Books, 1999. ix, 104 p. ; 21 cm. (University of East London studies in education.) Includes bibliographical references and index. ISBN 1-85856-218-X (pbk.)
*1. Teaching - Vocational guidance - Great Britain. 2. Education and state - Great Britain. I. Graham, Jim. 1946- II. Series.*
*TC LB1775.4.G7 T43 1999*

**TEACHER-PUPIL INTERACTION.** *See* **INTERACTION ANALYSIS IN EDUCATION.**

**TEACHER-PUPIL RATIO.** *See* **CLASS SIZE.**

**TEACHER-PUPIL RELATIONSHIPS.** *See* **TEACHER-STUDENT RELATIONSHIPS.**

**TEACHER QUALITY.** *See* **TEACHER EFFECTIVENESS.**

**TEACHER RATING.** *See* **TEACHERS - RATING OF.**

**TEACHER RECRUITMENT.** *See* **TEACHERS - RECRUITING.**

**TEACHER STRESS.** *See* **TEACHERS - JOB STRESS.**

**TEACHER-STUDENT RELATIONSHIPS.** *See also* **CLASSROOM ENVIRONMENT; INTERACTION ANALYSIS IN EDUCATION; STUDENT PARTICIPATION IN CURRICULUM PLANNING.**
Anderson, Dennis S. Mathematics and distance education on the internet. 1999.
*TC 085 An2317*

Babbage, Keen J. High-impact teaching. Lancaster, Pa. : Technomic Pub. Co., c1998.
*TC LB1065 .B23 1998*

Chuska, Kenneth R. Improving classroom questions. Bloomington, Ind. : Phi Delta Kappa Educational Foundation, 1995.
*TC LB1027.44 .C58 1995*

Edgoose, Julian Miles. Partnerships of possibility. 1999.
*TC 085 E117*

Flynn, Bernadette Marie. The teacher-child relationship, temperament, and coping in children with developmental disabilities. 2000.
*TC 06 no. 11267*

Hunt, Gilbert. Effective teaching. 3rd ed. Springfield, Ill. : C.C. Thomas Publisher, c1999.
*TC LB1025.3 .H86 1999*

Johnson, Richard T., 1956- Hands off!. New York ; Canterbury [England] : P. Lang, c2000.
*TC LB1033 .J63 2000*

Kohn, Alfie. What to look for in a classroom. 1st ed. San Francisco : Jossey-Bass, c1998.
*TC LB1775 .K643 1998*

McCaslin, Mary M. Listening in classrooms. 1st ed. New York : HarperCollins College Publishers, c1996.
*TC LB1033 .M34 1996*

Partnerships in research, clinical, and educational settings. Stamford, Conn. : Ablex Pub., c1999.
*TC HM1106 .P37 1999*

Peters, Dorothy. Taking cues from kids. Portsmouth, NH : Heinemann, c2000.
*TC LB3013 .P43 2000*

Stories from the center. Urbana, Ill. National Council of Teachers of English, c2000.
*TC PE1404 .S834 2000*

Stories out of school. Stamford, Conn. : Ablex Pub., c2000.
*TC LC196 .S6994 2000*

Supervising postgraduates from non-English speaking backgrounds. Buckingham ; Philadelphia : Society for Research into Higher Education : Open University Press, 1999.
*TC LB2343 .S86 1999*

Sylwester, Robert. A biological brain in a cultural classroom. Thousand Oaks, Calif. : Corwin Press, c2000.
*TC LB3011.5 .S95 2000*

**TEACHER-STUDENT RELATIONSHIPS - BERMUDA ISLANDS.**
Tucker, Gina Marie. Discipline. 1998.
*TC 06 no. 10999*

**TEACHER-STUDENT RELATIONSHIPS - CASE STUDIES.**
Assessment as inquiry. Urbana, Ill. : National Council of Teachers of English, 1999.
*TC LB3051 .A76665 1999*

**TEACHER-STUDENT RELATIONSHIPS - GREAT BRITAIN - CASE STUDIES.**
Phtiaka, Helen. Special kids for special treatment?, or, How special do you need to be to find yourself in a special school? London ; Washington, D.C. : Falmer Press, 1997.
*TC LC4803.G7 P58 1998*

**TEACHER-STUDENT RELATIONSHIPS IN LITERATURE.**
Keroes, Jo. Tales out of school. Carbondale : Southern Illinois University Press, c1999.
*TC PS374.T43 K47 1999*

**TEACHER-STUDENT RELATIONSHIPS - IRELAND - CASE STUDIES.**
Rethinking pastoral care. London ; New York : Routledge, 1999.
*TC LB1620.53.I73 R48 1999*

## TEACHER-STUDENT RELATIONSHIPS - SOCIAL ASPECTS.
Too, Yun Lee. The pedagogical contract. Ann Arbor: University of Michigan Press, c2000.
*TC LB1033 .T66 2000*

## TEACHER-STUDENT RELATIONSHIPS - UNITED STATES.
Cangelosi, James S. Classroom management strategies. 3rd ed. White Plains, N.Y. : Longman, c1997.
*TC LB3013 .C3259 1997*

Cangelosi, James S. Classroom management strategies. 4th ed. New York : J. Wiley, c2000.
*TC LB3013 .C3259 2000*

Hyman, Irwin A. Dangerous schools. 1st ed. San Francisco : Jossey-Bass Publishers, c1999.
*TC LB3013 .H897 1999*

McEwan, Elaine K., 1941- Managing unmanageable students. Thousand Oaks, Calif. : Corwin Press, c2000.
*TC LC4801.5 .M39 2000*

## TEACHER-STUDENT RELATIONSHIPS - UNITED STATES - CASE STUDIES.
Mirochnik, Elijah, 1952- Teaching in the first person. New York : P. Lang, c2000.
*TC LB1033 .M546 2000*

Orange, Carolyn. 25 biggest mistakes teachers make and how to avoid them. Thousand Oaks Calif. : Corwin Press, c2000.
*TC LB1033 .O73 2000*

## TEACHER-STUDENTS RELATIONSHIPS.
Dreyer, Susan T. Student perceptions of their educational experiences at Satellite Academy High School and their former schools. 1999.
*TC 06 no. 11105*

**Teacher/swimmer.**
Neuner, John. New York : Jay Street, c1998.
*TC GV837 .N48 1998*

**Teacher to teacher series.**
Fraser, Jane. On their way. Portsmouth, NH : Heinemann, c1994.
*TC LB1576 .F72 1994*

Griss, Susan. Minds in motion. Portsmouth, NH : Heinemann, c1998.
*TC LB1592 .G75 1998*

Rogovin, Paula. Classroom interviews. Portsmouth, NH : Heinemann, c1998.
*TC LB1537 .R58 1998*

Teaching with technology. Washington, D.C. : National Education Association of the United States, 1999.
*TC LB1044.88 .T44 1999*

**Teacher toolbox** [kit] / Open Court Publishing Company ; [program authors: Carl Bereiter ... [et al.]]. Chicago, Ill. : Open Court Pub. Co., c1995. 1 kit (1 sound cassette (analog, 1 7/8 ips); Teacher Tool Cards: Songs, Rhymes and games, Classroom Support; Learning Framework Cards 1-12; Reproducible Masters (29 p. :ill. ; 28 cm.); Activity Sheets (29 p. : ill ; 28 cm.); Home/School Connection (15 p. ; 28 cm.); Cumulative Class Folder; Kindergarten Overview Planner (39 p. ; 28 cm.) in box (26 x 31 x 6 cm). (Collections for Young Scholars) Catalogued from container and planner. Title from container; statement of reponsibility from container and title page of planner. For Kindergarten classes. SUMMARY: Teaches phonemic awareness, the alphabetic principle, print awareness, reading and literature, writing, vocabulary, knowledge of the World and cognitive strategies and sturctures-- all through reading aloud, writing, discussion and "Workshop". Uses songs, rhymes and games. Library lacking Learning Framework Card No. 1 ISBN 0-8126-0222-6 (Planner) ISBN 0-8126-0492-x (Teacher Tool Cards) ISBN 0-8126-0403-2 (Teacher Tool Cards) ISBN 0-8126-0492-x (Learning Framework Cards) ISBN 0-8126-0431-8 (Learning Framework Cards) ISBN 0-8126-0427-x (Reproducible Masters) ISBN 0-8126-0406-7 (Activity sheets) ISBN 0-8126-0405-9 (Home/School Connection) ISBN 0-8126-0472-5 (Cumulative Class Folder) ISBN 0-8126-0244-7 (Cassette)
*1. Reading (Primary) - Phonetic method. 2. Reading - Aids and devices. 3. English language - Phonemics - Study and teaching (Primary) 4. Education (Primary) - Activity programs. 5. English language - Rhyme - Study and teaching (Primary) 6. Rhyming games - Study and teaching (Primary) 7. Children's songs - Study and teaching (Primary) 8. Storytelling - Study and teaching (Primary) 9. Lnaguage arts (Primary) I. Bereiter, Carl. II. Open Court Publishing Company. III. Series.*
*TC LB1573.3 .T4 1995*

## TEACHER TRAINING. See TEACHERS - TRAINING OF.

## TEACHER TURNOVER - UNITED STATES.
Oliver, Frank H. Fellow beggars. 1999.
*TC 06 no.11157*

Orsini, Alfonso J. The color of excellence. 1999.
*TC 06 no. 11209*

## TEACHERS. See also COLLEGE TEACHERS; EARLY CHILDHOOD TEACHERS; EDUCATORS; ELEMENTARY SCHOOL TEACHERS; FIRST YEAR TEACHERS; GAY TEACHERS; HIGH SCHOOL TEACHERS; LANGUAGE ARTS TEACHERS; LANGUAGE TEACHERS; MASTER TEACHERS; MATHEMATICS TEACHERS; MIDDLE SCHOOL TEACHERS; MINORITY TEACHERS; PHYSICAL EDUCATION TEACHERS; READING TEACHERS; SCIENCE TEACHERS; SPECIAL EDUCATION TEACHERS; STUDENT TEACHERS; TEACHER EFFECTIVENESS; TEACHER PARTICIPATION IN CURRICULUM PLANNING; TEACHERS OF HANDICAPPED CHILDREN; TEACHERS OF PROBLEM CHILDREN; TEACHERS OF THE BLIND-DEAF; TEACHERS' ASSISTANTS; WOMEN TEACHERS.
Everyone a teacher. Notre Dame, Ind. : University of Notre Dame Press, c2000.
*TC LB1025.3 .E87 2000*

Kohn, Alfie. What to look for in a classroom. 1st ed. San Francisco : Jossey-Bass, c1998.
*TC LB1775 .K643 1998*

Kottler, Jeffrey A. On being a teacher. 2nd ed. Thousand Oaks, Calif. : Corwin Press, c2000.
*TC LB1025.3 .Z44 2000*

**A Teacher's & textbook writers' handbook on Japan** / [writers, Nobuo Takahashi ... [et al.]]. 5th., rev. printing. Tokyo : International Society for Educational Information, c1993. 102 p. : ill., maps ; 26 cm. (Understanding Japan ; no. 66)
*1. Japan - Handbooks, manuals, etc. I. Takahashi, Nobuo, 1939- II. Kokusai Kyōiku Jōhō Sentā. III. Title: Teacher's and textbook writers' handbook on Japan. IV. Series.*
*TC DS806 .T34 1993*

## TEACHERS - ALASKA - BIOGRAPHY.
Brown, Stephen Gilbert. Words in the wilderness. Albany : State University of New York Press, c2000.
*TC E99.A86 B76 2000*

## TEACHERS AND COMMUNITY - HUNGARY.
Gegő, Elek, 1805-1844. Népoktató. Budapest : Országos Pedagógiai Könyvtár és Múzeum, [1997]
*TC LC227 .G44 1997*

**Teachers and educational change.**
Nolan, James F., 1950- Albany : State University of New York Press, c2000.
*TC LB1777.2 .N64 2000*

## TEACHERS AND PARENTS. See PARENT-TEACHER RELATIONSHIPS.

## TEACHERS AND PRINCIPALS. See TEACHER-PRINCIPAL RELATIONSHIPS.

**Teacher's and textbook writers' handbook on Japan.**
A Teacher's & textbook writers' handbook on Japan. 5th., rev. printing. Tokyo : International Society for Educational Information, c1993.
*TC DS806 .T34 1993*

**Teachers and the state.**
Bottery, Mike. London ; New York : Routledge, c2000.
*TC LB1775.4.G7 B68 2000*

## TEACHERS' ASSISTANTS - GREAT BRITAIN - HANDBOOKS, MANUALS, ETC.
Fox, Glenys. A handbook for learning support assistants. London : D. Fulton Publishers, 1998.
*TC LB2844.1.A8 F68 1998*

## TEACHERS - ATTITUDES.
McWilliam, Erica. Pedagogical pleasures. New York ; Canterbury [England] : P. Lang, c1999.
*TC LB1775 .M319 1999*

**Teacher's book: a resource for planning and teaching, level 1.5.**
Cooper, J. David (James David), 1942- Discover : Grade 1, level 1.5 (Themes 9 and 10). Boston : Houghton Mifflin, 1997.
*TC LB1575.8 .C6616 1997*

**Teacher's bookshelf.**
Frontiers of democracy. New York, Progressive Education Association, etc., 1934-

## TEACHERS - CALIFORNIA - PERIODICALS.
The classroom teacher. Berkeley, Calif., Berkeley Federation of Teachers Local 1078.

## TEACHERS - CANADA - CASE STUDIES.
Louden, William. Understanding teaching. New York : Cassell : Teachers College Press, Teachers College, Columbia University, 1991.
*TC LB1025.3 .L68 1991*

## TEACHERS - CASE STUDIES.
Reagan, Timothy G. Becoming a reflective educator. 2nd ed. Thousand Oaks Calif. : Sage Publications, c2000.
*TC LB1025.3 .R424 2000*

## TEACHERS, CERTIFICATION OF. See TEACHERS - CERTIFICATION.

## TEACHERS - CERTIFICATION - UNITED STATES.
Feistritzer, C. Emily. Alternative teacher certification. Washington, D.C. : National Center for Education Information, c2000.
*TC LB1771 .A47 2000*

Woellner, Elizabeth H. Requirements for certification: Chicago : University of Chicago Press, 1935-
*TC LB1771 .W6*

## TEACHERS - CERTIFICATION - UNITED STATES - PERIODICALS.
Requirements for certification of teachers, counselors, librarians, administrators for elementary and secondary schools. Chicago : University of Chicago Press, 1989-
*TC LB1171 .W6*

## TEACHERS - CERTIFICATION - UNITED STATES - STATISTICS.
Feistritzer, C. Emily. Alternative teacher certification. Washington, D.C. : National Center for Education Information, c2000.
*TC LB1771 .A47 2000*

**[Teachers College Library.** Reserve Reading Room] [picture] 1940. 1 digital image (black and white). 1 photograph ; original print, 8 x 10, black and white. Reserve Reading Room, Russell Hall, Third floor. Special Collections Archives, Milbank Memorial Library.
*1. Milbank Memorial Library - Pictorial works. 2. Teachers College (New York, N.Y.) - Buildings - Pictorial works. 3. Reading rooms - Pictorial works. I. Milbank Memorial Library Special Collections.*
*TC TCX/H5*

## TEACHERS COLLEGE (NEW YORK, N.Y.) - BUILDINGS - PICTORIAL WORKS.
[Teachers College Library. [picture] 1940.
*TC TCX/H5*

## TEACHERS COLLEGE STUDENTS - RATING OF - UNITED STATES.
Wyatt, Robert Lee, 1940- So you have to have a portfolio. Thousand Oaks, Calif. : Corwin Press, c1999.
*TC LB1728 .W93 1999*

**Teachers, computers, and curriculum.**
Geisert, Paul. 3rd ed. Boston : Allyn and Bacon, c2000.
*TC LB1028.5 .G42 2000*

## TEACHERS - CONTRACTS. See TEACHERS' CONTRACTS.

## TEACHERS' CONTRACTS - UNITED STATES.
Lieberman, Myron, 1919- Understanding the teacher union contract. New Brunswick, N.J. : Social Philosophy and Policy Foundation : Transaction Publishers, 2000.
*TC KF3409.T4 L54 2000*

## TEACHERS - CROSS-CULTURAL STUDIES.
Bottery, Mike. Teachers and the state. London ; New York : Routledge, c2000.
*TC LB1775.4.G7 B68 2000*

## TEACHERS, EARLY CHILDHOOD. See EARLY CHILDHOOD TEACHERS.

## TEACHERS, ELEMENTARY SCHOOL. See ELEMENTARY SCHOOL TEACHERS.

## TEACHERS - EMPLOYMENT - UNITED STATES - HANDBOOKS, MANUALS, ETC.
Moffatt, Courtney W. How to get a teaching job. Boston ; London : Allyn and Bacon, c2000.
*TC LB1780 .M64 2000*

## TEACHERS, FIRST YEAR. See FIRST YEAR TEACHERS.

**Teachers for Integrated Schools.**
Integrated education. [Amherst, Mass., etc., Center for

Equal Education, School of Education, University of
Massachusetts, etc.]

**TEACHERS, FOREIGN - UNITED STATES -
HANDBOOKS, MANUALS, ETC.**
Sarkisian, Ellen. Teaching American students. Rev.
ed. Cambridge, Mass. : The President and Fellows of
Harvard University, Derek Bok Center for Teaching
and Learning, 1997, c1990.
*TC LB1738 .S371 1997*

**TEACHERS - GHANA - PERIODICALS.**
Ghana teachers' journal. Accra. 1952-1968.

**TEACHERS - GREAT BRITAIN.**
Bottery, Mike. Teachers and the state. London ; New
York : Routledge, c2000.
*TC LB1775.4.G7 B68 2000*

McCartney, Elspeth. Speech/language therapists and
teachers working together. London : Whurr, 1999.
*TC LB3454 .M32 1999*

Professional issues for teachers and student teachers.
London : David Fulton, 1999.
*TC LB1775.4.G7 P73 1999*

**TEACHERS - GREAT BRITAIN - ATTITUDES.**
Davies, Ian, 1957- Good citizenship and educational
provision. London : New York : Falmer Press, c1999.
*TC LC1091 .D28 1999*

**TEACHERS - GREAT BRITAIN - PUBLIC
OPINION.**
Weber, Sandra. That's funny, you don't look like a
teacher!. London ; Washington, D.C. : Falmer Press,
1995.
*TC LB1775.4.G7 W43 1995*

**Teachers guide.**
Pace, Robert. Katonah, N.Y. : Lee Roberts Music
publications, 1983.
*TC MT245 .P32 1983*

**A teacher's guide to including students with
disabilities in general physical education.**
Block, Martin E., 1958- 2nd ed. Baltimore, Md. : Paul
H. Brookes Pub. Co., c2000.
*TC GV445 .B56 2000*

**Teachers' guides to inclusive practices**
Janney, Rachel. Modifying schoolwork. Baltimore,
Md. : Paul H. Brookes Pub., c2000.
*TC LC1201 .J26 2000*

Snell, Martha E. Collaborative teaming. Baltimore :
Paul H. Brookes Pub., c2000.
*TC LC1201 .S64 2000*

**Teacher's handbook.**
Shrum, Judith L. 2nd ed. Boston, Mass. : Heinle &
Heinle, c2000.
*TC P51 .S48 2000*

**TEACHERS, HIGH SCHOOL.** *See* **HIGH
SCHOOL TEACHERS.**

**TEACHERS IN FOREIGN COUNTRIES.** *See*
**TEACHERS, FOREIGN.**

**TEACHERS IN LITERATURE.**
Keroes, Jo. Tales out of school. Carbondale : Southern
Illinois University Press, c1999.
*TC PS374.T43 K47 1999*

**TEACHERS IN MOTION PICTURES.**
Keroes, Jo. Tales out of school. Carbondale : Southern
Illinois University Press, c1999.
*TC PS374.T43 K47 1999*

**TEACHERS - IN-SERVICE TRAINING.**
Clement, Mary C. Building the best faculty. Lanham,
Md. : Scarecrow Press, 2000.
*TC LB2833 .C53 2000*

Nielsen, H. Dean. The cost-effectiveness of distance
education for teacher training. Cambridge, Mass. :
B.R.I.D.G.E.S. Basic Research and Implementation in
Developing Education Systems, [1991].
*TC LB1731 .N43 1991*

The postmodern educator. New York : P. Lang,
c1999.
*TC LB1707 .P67 1999*

Tickle, Les. Teacher induction. Buckingham
[England] ; Philadelphia : Open University Press,
2000.
*TC LB1729 .T53 2000*

Zepeda, Sally J., 1956- Supervision and staff
development in the block. Larchmont, N.Y. : Eye On
Education, c2000.
*TC LB3032.2 .Z46 2000*

**TEACHERS - IN-SERVICE TRAINING - GREAT
BRITAIN - ADMINISTRATION.**
Blandford, Sonia. Managing professional
development in schools. London ; New York :
Routledge, 2000.
*TC LB1731 .B57 2000*

**TEACHERS - IN-SERVICE TRAINING - UNITED
STATES.**
Critical knowledge for diverse teachers & learners.
Washington, DC : AACTE : ERIC, c1997.
*TC LB1715 .C732 1997*

Glatthorn, Allan A., 1924- Differentiated supervision.
2nd ed. Alexandria, Va. : Association for Supervision
and Curriculum Development, c1997.
*TC LB2806.4 .G548 1997*

Guiding teacher learning. Washington. DC : AACTE,
c1997.
*TC LB1731 .G85 1997*

Learning circles. Thousand Oaks, Calif. : Corwin
Press, c1998.
*TC LB1032 .L355 1998*

Powerful middle schools : teaching and learning for
young adolescents (2000) Powerful middle schools
[videorecording]. [Washington, D.C.?] : U.S. Dept. of
Education, [2000].
*TC LB1623 .P6 2000*

Powerful middle schools : teaching and learning for
young adolescents (2000) Powerful middle schools
[videorecording]. [Washington, D.C.?] : U.S. Dept. of
Education, [2000].
*TC LB1623 .P6 2000*

Schwarz, Gretchen, 1952- Teacher lore and
professional development for school reform.
Westport, Conn : Bergin & Garvey, 1998.
*TC LB1775.2 .S38 1998*

**TEACHERS - IN-SERVICE TRAINING - UNITED
STATES - CASE STUDIES.**
Life cycle of the career teacher. [Indianapolis, Ind.] :
Kappa Delta Pi ; Thousand Oaks, Calif. : Corwin
Press, c2000.
*TC LB1775.2 .L54 2000*

UpDrafts. Urbana, Ill. : National Council of Teachers
of English, c2000.
*TC LB1775.2 .U63 2000*

**TEACHERS - INDIA.**
Singh, Rajendra Pal, 1932- The Indian teacher Delhi,
National [Pub. House, 1969]

**TEACHERS - INDIANA - PERIODICALS.**
The Indiana teacher. Indianapolis, Ind. : Indiana State
Teachers Association, 1924-1972.

**TEACHERS, JEWISH.** *See* **JEWISH TEACHERS.**

**TEACHERS - JOB STRESS.**
Brock, Barbara L. Rekindling the flame. Thousand
Oaks, Calif. : Corwin Press, c2000.
*TC LB2840.2 .B76 2000*

Joseph, Russell. Stress free teaching :. London ;
Sterling, VA : Kogan Page, 2000.
*TC LB2840.2 .J67 2000*

**TEACHERS - JOB STRESS - PREVENTION.**
Bernard, Michael E. (Michael Edwin), 1950-. Taking
the stress out of teaching. Melbourne : Collins Dove,
1990.
*TC LB2840.2 .B47 1990*

**TEACHERS - KENTUCKY - CASE STUDIES.**
Accountability, assessment, and teacher commitment.
Albany, N.Y. : State University of New York Press,
2000.
*TC LB2806.22 .A249 2000*

**TEACHERS - LEGAL STATUS, LAWS, ETC.** *See*
**TEACHERS - CERTIFICATION.**

**TEACHERS, MASTER.** *See* **MASTER
TEACHERS.**

**Teachers matter.**
Caliendo, Stephen M., 1971- Westport, Conn. :
Praeger, 2000.
*TC JA88.U6 C24 2000*

**TEACHERS, MIDDLE SCHOOL.** *See* **MIDDLE
SCHOOL TEACHERS.**

**TEACHERS - NEW YORK (STATE) -
ATTITUDES.**
Southworth, Robert A. Evidence of student learning
and implications for alternative policies that support
instructional use of assessment. 1999.
*TC 06 no. 11218*

**TEACHERS' OATHS.** *See* **LOYALTY OATHS.**

**TEACHERS OF EDUCATION.** *See* **TEACHER
EDUCATORS.**

**TEACHERS OF EXCEPTIONAL CHILDREN.** *See*
**SPECIAL EDUCATION TEACHERS.**

**TEACHERS OF GIFTED CHILDREN -
ATTITUDES.**
Tokar, Inna. Schools for the mathematically talented
in the former Soviet Union. 1999.
*TC 085 T572*

**TEACHERS OF HANDICAPPED CHILDREN,
TRAINING OF.** *See* **TEACHERS OF
HANDICAPPED CHILDREN - TRAINING OF.**

**TEACHERS OF HANDICAPPED CHILDREN -
TRAINING OF - GREAT BRITAIN.**
Special needs and the beginning teacher. London ;
New York : Continuum, 2000.
*TC LC4036.G7 S684 2000*

**TEACHERS OF HANDICAPPED CHILDREN -
TRAINING OF - UNITED STATES.**
Preparing teachers for inclusive education. Mahwah,
N.J. : L. Erlbaum Associates, 2000.
*TC LC1201 .P74 2000*

**TEACHERS OF HANDICAPPED CHILDREN -
UNITED STATES.**
Idol, Lorna. Collaborative consultation. 3rd ed.
Austin, Tex. : PRO-ED, c2000.
*TC LC4019 .I35 2000*

**TEACHERS OF HANDICAPPED CHILDREN -
UNITED STATES - CASE STUDIES.**
Inclusive education. Mahwah, N.J. : L. Erlbaum
Associates, c2000.
*TC LC1201 .I527 2000*

**TEACHERS OF PROBLEM CHILDREN -
TRAINING OF - GREAT BRITAIN.**
Hill, Fran, 1950- Teamwork in the management of
emotional and behavioural difficulties. London :
David Fulton, 2000.
*TC LC4803.G7 H54 2000*

**TEACHERS OF THE BLIND-DEAF - TRAINING
OF.**
Hand in hand. New York : AFB Press, c1995.
*TC HV1597.2 .H342 1995*

Hand in hand. New York : AFB Press, c1995.
*TC HV1597.2 .H34 1995*

**TEACHERS - OUT-OF-SCHOOL ACTIVITIES.**
*See* **TEACHERS - SUPPLEMENTARY
EMPLOYMENT.**

**TEACHERS - PAKISTAN.**
Rugh, Andrea B. Teaching practices to increase
student achievement. Cambridge, Mass. :
B.R.I.D.G.E.S. Basic Research and Implementation in
Developing Education Systems, [1991].
*TC LB1025.2 .R83 1991*

**TEACHERS, PART-TIME.** *See* **COLLEGE
TEACHERS, PART-TIME.**

**Teachers' pedagogical thinking :** theoretical
landscapes, practical challenges / Pertti Kansanen ...
[et al.]. New York : P. Lang, 2000. vi, 216 p. ; 24 cm.
(American university studies. Series XIV, Education ; vol. 47)
Includes bibliographical references (p. [195]-212) and index.
ISBN 0-8204-4897-4 (alk. paper) DDC 371.1/001/9
1. Teachers - Psychology. 2. Teaching - Psychological aspects.
I. Kansanen, Pertti, 1940- II. Series.
*TC LB1775 . T4179 2000*

**TEACHERS - PERIODICALS.**
Changing education. Detroit [etc.]

**TEACHERS - PERSONNEL MANAGEMENT.** *See*
**SCHOOL PERSONNEL MANAGEMENT.**

**TEACHERS, PHYSICAL EDUCATION.** *See*
**PHYSICAL EDUCATION TEACHERS.**

**TEACHERS - PROFESSIONAL ETHICS.**
Carr, David, 1944- Professionalism and ethics in
teaching. London ; New York : Routledge, 2000.
*TC LB1779 .C37 2000*

Carr, David, 1944- Professionalism and ethics in
teaching. London ; New York : Routledge, 2000.
*TC LB1779 .C37 2000*

The politics of professionalism. London : Continuum,
2000.
*TC LB1779 .M33 2000*

**TEACHERS - PSYCHOLOGY.**
Hunt, Gilbert. Effective teaching. 3rd ed. Springfield,
Ill. : C.C. Thomas Publisher, c1999.

*TC LB1025.3 .H86 1999*

Teachers' pedagogical thinking. New York : P. Lang, 2000.
*TC LB1775 . T4179 2000*

**TEACHERS, RATING OF.** *See* **TEACHERS - RATING OF.**

**TEACHERS - RATING OF.**
Portfolio and performance assessment in teacher education. Boston : Allyn and Bacon, c2000.
*TC LB1728 .P667 2000*

**TEACHERS - RATING OF - GREAT BRITAIN.**
Poorly performing staff and how to manage them. London ; New York : Routledge, 1999.
*TC LB2832.4.G7 P66 1999*

**TEACHERS - RATING OF - UNITED STATES.**
Beerens, Daniel R. Evaluating teachers for professional growth. Thousand Oaks, Calif. ; London : Corwin Press, c2000.
*TC LB2838 .B44 2000*

Danielson, Charlotte. Teacher evaluation to enhance professional practice. Alexandria, Va. : Association for Supervision and Curriculum Development, c2000.
*TC LB2838 .D26 2000*

**TEACHERS, READING.** *See* **READING TEACHERS.**

**TEACHERS - RECRUITING.**
Clement, Mary C. Building the best faculty. Lanham, Md. : Scarecrow Press, 2000.
*TC LB2833 .C53 2000*

Lawrence, Alexandria Teresa. Cooperating teachers' perceptions of the nature and quality of professional development in a professional development school collaboration. 1999.
*TC 06 no. 11141*

Lawrence, Alexandria Teresa. Cooperating teachers' perceptions of the nature and quality of professional development in a professional development school collaboration. 1999.
*TC 06 no. 11141*

Lawrence, Alexandria Teresa. Cooperating teachers' perceptions of the nature and quality of professional development in a professional development school collaboration. 1999.
*TC 06 no. 11141*

**TEACHERS, SECONDARY SCHOOL.** *See* **HIGH SCHOOL TEACHERS.**

**TEACHERS - SELECTION AND APPOINTMENT.**
*See also* **TEACHER TURNOVER.**
Clement, Mary C. Building the best faculty. Lanham, Md. : Scarecrow Press, 2000.
*TC LB2833 .C53 2000*

**TEACHERS, SENIOR HIGH SCHOOL.** *See* **HIGH SCHOOL TEACHERS.**

**TEACHERS - SOCIAL CONDITIONS.**
Researching school experience. London ; New York : Falmer Press, 1999.
*TC LB1027 .R453 1999*

**TEACHERS - SOCIAL NETWORKS - UNITED STATES.**
Adams, Jacob E. Taking charge of curriculum. New York : Teachers College Press, c2000.
*TC LB2806.15 . A35 2000*

**TEACHERS - SUPPLEMENTARY EMPLOYMENT - UNITED STATES - HANDBOOKS, MANUALS, ETC.**
Zuelke, Dennis C. Educational private practice. Lancaster : Technomic Pub., c1996.
*TC LB2844.1.S86 Z84 1996*

**TEACHERS - TENURE.** *See* **TEACHER TURNOVER.**

**TEACHERS - TIME MANAGEMENT.**
Gore, M. C. Taming the time stealers. Thousand Oaks, Calif. : Corwin Press, c1999.
*TC LB2838.8 .G67 1999*

**TEACHERS - TRAINING OF.** *See* **OBSERVATION (EDUCATIONAL METHOD); STUDENT TEACHING; TEACHER ORIENTATION.**

**TEACHERS, TRAINING OF.** *See* **TEACHERS - TRAINING OF.**

**TEACHERS - TRAINING OF.**
Hinely, Reg. Education in Edge City. 2nd ed. Mahwah, N.J. : L. Erlbaum Associates, 2000.
*TC LB1029.C37 H45 2000*

Institutional issues. London ; New York : Falmer Press, 2000.
*TC LC191 .I495 2000*

Lawrence, Alexandria Teresa. Cooperating teachers' perceptions of the nature and quality of professional development in a professional development school collaboration. 1999.
*TC 06 no. 11141*

Lawrence, Alexandria Teresa. Cooperating teachers' perceptions of the nature and quality of professional development in a professional development school collaboration. 1999.
*TC 06 no. 11141*

Lawrence, Alexandria Teresa. Cooperating teachers' perceptions of the nature and quality of professional development in a professional development school collaboration. 1999.
*TC 06 no. 11141*

Portfolio and performance assessment in teacher education. Boston : Allyn and Bacon, c2000.
*TC LB1728 .P667 2000*

Posner, George J. Field experience. 5th ed. New York : Longman, c2000.
*TC LB2157.A3 P6 2000*

The postmodern educator. New York : P. Lang, c1999.
*TC LB1707 .P67 1999*

Study to teach. London ; New York : Routledge, 2000.
*TC LB1707 .S88 2000*

**TEACHERS - TRAINING OF - AFRICA - CASE STUDIES.**
Democratic teacher education reform in Africa. Boulder, Colo. ; Oxford : Westview Press, 1999.
*TC LB1727.N3 D46 1999*

**TEACHERS - TRAINING OF - ASIA - CROSS-CULTURAL STUDIES.**
Teacher education in the Asia-Pacific region. New York : Falmer Press, c2000.
*TC LB1727.A69 T42 2000*

**TEACHERS - TRAINING OF - CHINA.**
Ashmore, Rhea A. Teacher education in the People's Republic of China. Bloomington, Ind., U.S.A. : Phi Delta Kappa Educational Foundation, c1997.
*TC LB1727.C5 A85 1997*

**TEACHERS - TRAINING OF - COMPUTER-ASSISTED INSTRUCTION.**
Idzal, June M. Multimedia authoring tools and teacher training. 1997.
*TC 06 no. 10816*

**TEACHERS - TRAINING OF - GREAT BRITAIN.**
Bottery, Mike. Teachers and the state. London ; New York : Routledge, c2000.
*TC LB1775.4.G7 B68 2000*

Nicholls, Gill. Learning to teach. London : Kogan Page, 1999.
*TC LB1727.G7 N53 1999*

O'Hara, Mark. Teaching 3-8 :. London ; New York : Continuum, 2000.
*TC LB1725.G7 O36 2000*

**TEACHERS - TRAINING OF - HANDBOOKS, MANUALS, ETC.**
Goethals, M. Serra, 1934- Student teaching. Upper Saddle River, N.J. : Merrill, c2000.
*TC LB2157.A3 G57 2000*

**TEACHERS - TRAINING OF - MICHIGAN - HISTORY.**
DeBoer, Peter P. Origins of teacher education at Calvin College, 1900-1930. Lewiston : E. Mellen Press, c1991.
*TC LD785 .D43 1991*

**TEACHERS - TRAINING OF - NAMIBIA.**
Democratic teacher education reform in Africa. Boulder, Colo. ; Oxford : Westview Press, 1999.
*TC LB1727.N3 D46 1999*

**TEACHERS - TRAINING OF - PACIFIC AREA - CROSS-CULTURAL STUDIES.**
Teacher education in the Asia-Pacific region. New York : Falmer Press, c2000.
*TC LB1727.A69 T42 2000*

**TEACHERS, TRAINING OF - PERIODICALS.**
The Humanist educator. [Washington, American Personnel and Guidance Association]

**TEACHERS - TRAINING OF - RESEARCH.**
Research on effective models for teacher education. Thousand Oaks, Calif. : Corwin Press, Inc., c2000.

*TC LB1715 .R42 2000*

**TEACHERS - TRAINING OF - UNITED STATES.**
Case study applications for teacher education. Boston : Allyn and Bacon, c1999.
*TC LB1715 .S796 1999*

Critical knowledge for diverse teachers & learners. Washington, DC : AACTE : ERIC, c1997.
*TC LB1715 .C732 1997*

Cruickshank, Donald R. Preparing America's teachers. Bloomington, Ind. : Phi Delta Kappa Educational Foundation, c1996.
*TC LB1715 .C86 1996*

Frank, Carolyn. Ethnographic eyes. Portsmouth, NH : Heinemann, c1999.
*TC LB1027.28 .F73 1999*

Gordon, Mordechai. Toward an integrative conception of authority in education. 1997.
*TC 085 G656*

Grossman, Herbert, 1934- Achieving educational equality. Springfield, Ill. : C.C. Thomas, c1998.
*TC LC213.2 .G76 1998*

Research on professional development schools. Thousand Oaks, Calif. : Corwin Press, c1999.
*TC LB2154.A3 R478 1999*

Who learns what from cases and how? Mahwah, N.J. : L. Erlbaum Associates, 1999.
*TC LB1029.C37 W56 1999*

**TEACHERS - TRAINING OF - UNITED STATES - CASE STUDIES.**
Life cycle of the career teacher. [Indianapolis, Ind.] : Kappa Delta Pi ; Thousand Oaks, Calif. : Corwin Press, c2000.
*TC LB1775.2 .L54 2000*

**TEACHERS - TRAINING OF - UNITED STATES - LONGITUDINAL STUDIES.**
Teaching to teach. Washington, DC : National Education Association, 1999.
*TC LB1715 .T436 1999*

**Teachers - transforming their world and their work.**
Lieberman, Ann. New York : Teachers College Press ; Alexandria, Va. : Association for Supervision and Curriculum Development, c1999.
*TC LB1025.3 .L547 1999*

**TEACHERS' UNIONS.** *See* **COLLEGE TEACHERS' UNIONS.**

**Teachers unions and educational reform.**
Conflicting missions? Washington, D.C. : Brookings Institution Press, c2000.
*TC LB2844.53.U62 C66 2000*

**TEACHERS' UNIONS - UNITED STATES.**
Conflicting missions? Washington, D.C. : Brookings Institution Press, c2000.
*TC LB2844.53.U62 C66 2000*

**TEACHERS - UNITED STATES.**
Bracey, Gerald W. (Gerald Watkins) Bail me out. Thousand Oaks, Calif. : Corwin Press, c2000.
*TC LA217.2 .B72 2000*

Draper, Sharon M. (Sharon Mills) Teaching from the heart. Portsmouth, NH : Heinemann, c2000.
*TC LB1775.2 .D72 2000*

Schwarz, Gretchen, 1952- Teacher lore and professional development for school reform. Westport, Conn : Bergin & Garvey, 1998.
*TC LB1775.2 .S38 1998*

**TEACHERS - UNITED STATES - BIOGRAPHY.**
Draper, Sharon M. (Sharon Mills) Teaching from the heart. Portsmouth, NH : Heinemann, c2000.
*TC LB1775.2 .D72 2000*

Ritchie, Joy S. Teacher narrative as critical inquiry. New York : Teachers College Press, c2000.
*TC LA2311 .R58 2000*

Schwarz, Gretchen, 1952- Teacher lore and professional development for school reform. Westport, Conn : Bergin & Garvey, 1998.
*TC LB1775.2 .S38 1998*

**TEACHERS - UNITED STATES - CASE STUDIES.**
Hayes, William, 1938- Real-life case studies for teachers. Lanham, Md. : Scarecrow Press, 2000.
*TC LB1775.2 .H39 2000*

Life cycle of the career teacher. [Indianapolis, Ind.] : Kappa Delta Pi ; Thousand Oaks, Calif. : Corwin Press, c2000.
*TC LB1775.2 .L54 2000*

Professional development guide for educators.
Washington, D.C. : National Education Association of
the United States, 2000.
*TC LC1099.3 .P755 1999*

**TEACHERS - UNITED STATES - HANDBOOKS,
MANUALS, ETC.**
Niebrand, Chris. The pocket mentor. Boston, Mass. :
Allyn and Bacon, 2000.
*TC LB1775.2 .N54 2000*

**TEACHERS - UNITED STATES - PSYCHOLOGY -
CASE STUDIES.**
UpDrafts. Urbana, Ill. : National Council of Teachers
of English, c2000.
*TC LB1775.2 .U63 2000*

**TeacherSource**
Campbell, Cherry. Teaching second-language writing.
Pacific Grove : Heinle & Heinle, c1998.
*TC PE1128.A2 C325 1998*

**TEACHING.** *See also* **AUDIO-VISUAL
EDUCATION; CLASS SIZE; CLASSROOM
MANAGEMENT; COLLEGE TEACHING;
EDUCATION; EFFECTIVE TEACHING;
ELEMENTARY SCHOOL TEACHING;
GROUP WORK IN EDUCATION; HIGH
SCHOOL TEACHING; INSTRUCTIONAL
SYSTEMS; LESSON PLANNING; MASTERY
LEARNING; MIDDLE SCHOOL TEACHING;
PRESCHOOL TEACHING; QUESTIONING;
REMEDIAL TEACHING; STUDENT
TEACHING; TEACHER-STUDENT
RELATIONSHIPS; TEACHING TEAMS;
TRAINING; TUTORS AND TUTORING.**
Anderson, Lorin W. Assessing affective
characteristics in the schools. 2nd ed. Mahwah, NJ :
Lawrence Erlbaum, c2000.
*TC LB3051 .A698 2000*

Baker, Justine C. A neural network guide to teaching.
Bloomington, Ind. : Phi Delta Kappa Educational
Foundation, c1998.
*TC LB1057 .B35 1998*

Baxter Magolda, Marcia B., 1951- Creating contexts
for learning and self-authorship. 1st ed. Nashville
[Tenn.] : Vanderbilt University Press, 1999.
*TC LB1025.3 .B39 1999*

Bickart, Toni S. Building the primary classroom.
Washington, DC : Teaching Strategies ; Portsmouth,
NH : Heinemann, 1999.
*TC LB1507 .B53 1999*

Buckley, Francis J. Team teaching. Thousand Oaks,
Calif. : Sage Publications, c2000.
*TC LB1029.T4 B83 2000*

Chall, Jeanne Sternlicht, 1921- The academic
achievement challenge. New York ; London :
Guilford Press, c2000.
*TC LB2822.8 .C49 2000*

Christenbury, Leila. Making the journey. 2nd ed.
Portsmouth, NH : Boynton/Cook Publishers, c2000.
*TC LB1631 .C4486 2000*

Chuska, Kenneth R. Improving classroom questions.
Bloomington, Ind. : Phi Delta Kappa Educational
Foundation, 1995.
*TC LB1027.44 .C58 1995*

Classroom issues. London ; New York : Falmer Press,
2000.
*TC LC268 .C52 2000*

Daniels, Harvey, 1947- Methods that matter. York,
Me. : Stenhouse Publishers, c1998.
*TC LB1027 .D24 1998*

Davis, Brent. Engaging minds. Mahwah, N.J. : L.
Erlbaum Associates, 2000.
*TC LB1060 .D38 2000*

DePorter, Bobbi. Quantum teaching. Boston, Mass. :
Allyn and Bacon, c1999.
*TC LB1027 .D418 1999*

Driscoll, Marcy Perkins. Psychology of learning for
instruction. 2nd ed. Boston ; London : Allyn and
Bacon, c2000.
*TC LB1060 .D75 2000*

Educational foundations. Upper Saddle River, N.J. :
Merrill, c2000.
*TC LB17 .E393 2000*

Eggen, Paul D., 1940- Strategies for teachers. 4th ed.
Boston : Allyn and Bacon, 2001.
*TC LB1027.3 .E44 2001*

Everyone a teacher. Notre Dame, Ind. : University of
Notre Dame Press, c2000.

*TC LB1025.3 .E87 2000*

Finkel, Donald L., 1943- Teaching with your mouth
shut. Portsmouth, NH Boynton/Cook Publishers,
c2000.
*TC LB1026 .F49 2000*

Freiberg, H. Jerome. Universal teaching strategies. 3rd
ed. Boston : Allyn and Bacon, c2000.
*TC LB1025.3 .F74 2000*

Freire, Paulo, 1921- [Pedagogia de autonomia.
English] Pedagogy of freedom. Lanham : Rowman &
Littlefield Publishers, c1998.
*TC LC196 .F73713 1998*

Hinely, Reg. Education in Edge City. 2nd ed.
Mahwah, N.J. : L. Erlbaum Associates, 2000.
*TC LB1029.C37 H45 2000*

Kincheloe, Joe L. The stigma of genius. New York ;
Canterbury [England] : P. Lang, c1999.
*TC LB875.E562 K56 1999*

Kohn, Alfie. What to look for in a classroom. 1st ed.
San Francisco : Jossey-Bass, c1998.
*TC LB1775 .K643 1998*

Kottler, Jeffrey A. On being a teacher. 2nd ed.
Thousand Oaks, Calif. : Corwin Press, c2000.
*TC LB1025.3 .Z44 2000*

Lazear, David G. Eight ways of knowing. 3rd ed.
Arlington Heights, Ill. : SkyLight Training and Pub.,
c1999.
*TC LB1060 .L39 1999*

McWilliam, Erica. Pedagogical pleasures. New York ;
Canterbury [England] : P. Lang, c1999.
*TC LB1775 .M319 1999*

Newton, Douglas P. Teaching for understanding.
London ; New York : Routledge/Falmer, 2000.
*TC LB1025.3 .N495 2000*

Olson, Judy L. Teaching children and adolescents
with special needs. 3rd ed. Upper Saddle River, N.J. :
Merrill, c2000.
*TC LC3969 .O47 2000*

Reagan, Timothy G. Becoming a reflective educator.
2nd ed. Thousand Oaks Calif. : Sage Publications,
c2000.
*TC LB1025.3 .R424 2000*

Rugh, Andrea B. Teaching practices to increase
student achievement. Cambridge, Mass. :
B.R.I.D.G.E.S. Basic Research and Implementation in
Developing Education Systems, [1991].
*TC LB1025.2 .R83 1991*

Study to teach. London ; New York : Routledge, 2000.
*TC LB1707 .S88 2000*

Sullo, Robert A., 1951- The inspiring teacher.
Washington, D.C. : National Education Association of
the United States, c1999.
*TC LB1025.3 .S85 1999*

Taught bodies. New York : P. Lang, c2000.
*TC LB14.7 .T38 2000*

**Teaching 3-8.**
O'Hara, Mark. London ; New York : Continuum,
2000.
*TC LB1725.G7 O36 2000*

**Teaching Aboriginal studies** / edited by Rhonda
Craven ; endorsed by the National Federation of
Aboriginal Education Consultative Groups. St
Leonards, N.S.W. : Allen & Unwin, 1999. xiii, 298 p. :
ill. ; 26 cm. Includes bibliographical references (p. [280]-287)
and index. ISBN 1-86448-923-5 DDC 305.899150071
*1. Australian aborigines - Study and teaching (Primary) 2.
Australian aborigines - Study and teaching (Secondary) I.
Craven, Rhonda. II. National Federation of Aboriginal
Education Consultative Groups (Australia)*
*TC GN666 .T43 1999*

**Teaching about culture, ethnicity & diversity :**
exercises and planned activities / editor, Theodore M.
Singelis. Thousand Oaks : Sage Publications, c1998.
xii, 255 p. : ill. ; 28 cm. Includes bibliographical references and
index. ISBN 0-7619-0695-9 (pbk. : alk. paper) DDC 306/.071
*1. Culture - Study and teaching (Higher) - Activity programs.
2. Ethnicity - Study and teaching (Higher) - Activity programs.
3. Multiculturalism - Study and teaching (Higher) - Activity
programs. 4. Intercultural communication - Study and teaching
(Higher) - Activity programs. 5. Stereotype (Psychology) -
Study and teaching (Higher) - Activity programs. I. Singelis.
Theodore M. II. Title: Teaching about culture, ethnicity, and
diversity*
*TC HM101 .T38 1998*

**Teaching about culture, ethnicity, and diversity.**
Teaching about culture, ethnicity & diversity.
Thousand Oaks : Sage Publications, c1998.
*TC HM101 .T38 1998*

**TEACHING - ADDRESSES, ESSAYS, LECTURES.**
Learning activity and development. Aarhus : Aarhus
Universit #, 1999.
*TC LB1060 .L43 1999*

Research into classroom processes; New York,
Teachers College Press, 1971.
*TC LB1028 .W488*

**Teaching adult second language learners.**
McKay, Heather, 1950- Cambridge ; New York :
Cambridge University Press, 1999.
*TC P53 .M33 1999*

**TEACHING - AIDS AND DEVICES.** *See also*
EDUCATIONAL TECHNOLOGY; MEDIA
PROGRAMS (EDUCATION); PICTURES IN
EDUCATION; PORTFOLIOS IN
EDUCATION; PROGRAMMED
INSTRUCTION; TELEVISION IN
EDUCATION.
Idzal, June M. Multimedia authoring tools and teacher
training. 1997.
*TC 06 no. 10816*

Sowell, Evelyn J. Curriculum. 2nd ed. Upper Saddle
River, N.J. : Merrill, c2000.
*TC LB2806.15 .S69 2000*

Walmsley, Bonnie Brown. Teaching with favorite
Marc Brown books. New York : Scholastic
Professional Books, c1998.
*TC LB1576 .W258 1998*

**TEACHING - AIDS AND DEVICES -
HANDBOOKS, MANUALS, ETC.**
Lorbeer, George C. Science activities for elementary
students. 11th ed. Boston : McGraw-Hill, c2000.
*TC LB1585.3 .L67 2000*

**TEACHING - AIDS AND DEVICES -
MARKETING.**
Stimolo, Bob. Introduction to school marketing.
[Haddam], Conn. : School Market Research Institute,
c1989.
*TC HF5415.122 .S75 1989*

**TEACHING - AIDS AND DEVICES -
PERIODICALS.**
British journal of educational technology. London,
Councils and Education Press.

K-eight. [Philadelphia, American Pub. Co.]

**Teaching alone, teaching together.**
Bess, James L. 1st ed. San Francisco : Jossey-Bass,
c2000.
*TC LB2331 .B48 2000*

**Teaching American students.**
Sarkisian, Ellen. Rev. ed. Cambridge, Mass. : The
President and Fellows of Harvard University, Derek
Bok Center for Teaching and Learning, 1997, c1990.
*TC LB1738 .S371 1997*

**Teaching and learning at a distance :** foundations of
distance education / Michael Simonson ... [et al.].
Upper Saddle River, N.J. : Merrill, c2000. xiv, 241 p. :
ill. ; 24 cm. Includes bibliographical references and index.
ISBN 0-13-769258-7 (pbk.) DDC 371.3/5
*1. Distance education. I. Simonson, Michael R.*
*TC LC5800 .T43 2000*

**Teaching and learning elementary and middle school
mathematics.**
Sheffield, Linda Jensen, 1949- 4th ed. New York :
Wiley, c2000.
*TC QA135.5 .S48 2000*

**Teaching and learning for adolescents
[videorecording].**
Powerful middle schools : teaching and learning for
young adolescents (2000) Powerful middle schools
[videorecording]. [Washington, D.C.?] : U.S. Dept. of
Education, [2000].
*TC LB1623 .P6 2000*

**Teaching and learning for young adolescents
[videorecording].**
Powerful middle schools : teaching and learning for
young adolescents (2000) Powerful middle schools
[videorecording]. [Washington, D.C.?] : U.S. Dept. of
Education, [2000].
*TC LB1623 .P6 2000*

**Teaching and learning in cities** / editor, James
Learmonth assisted by Lauren Maidment. [S.l.] :
Whitbread, 1993. viii, 238 p. ; 21 cm. (A Whitbread
Education Partnership paper.) ISBN 0-9503360-5-X (pbk)

*1. Education, Urban. I. Learmonth, James, 1939- II. Maidment, Lauren. III. Whitbread Education Partnership.*
*TC LC5115 .T43 1993*

**Teaching and learning in later life.**
Glendenning, Frank. Aldershot, Hants, Eng. ; Burlington, Vt. : Ashgate / Arena, c2000.
*TC LC5457 .G54 2000*

**Teaching and learning in the effective school.**
Harris, Alma, 1958- Aldershot, England ; Brookfield, Vt. : Ashgate, c1999.
*TC LB2822.84.G7 H37 1999*

**Teaching and learning in the first three years of school**
Ashton, Elizabeth, lecturer. Religious education in the early years. London ; New York : Routledge, 2000.
*TC BV1475.2 .A84 2000*

**Teaching and learning mathematics.**
Nickson, Marilyn. London ; New York : Cassell, 2000.
*TC QA11 .N524 2000*

**Teaching and learning on the edge of the millennium : :** building on what we have learned / Marilla D. Svinicki, editor. San Francisco : Jossey-Bass, c1999. 111 p. ; 23 cm. (New directions for teaching and learning; 01647970 no. 80.) "Winter 1999." Includes bibliographical references and index. CONTENTS: Theory and research on learning and teaching -- New directions in learning and motivation / Marilla D. Svinicki -- New directions for theory amd research on teaching: a review of the past twenty years / Michael Theall -- A reprise of popular topics: where are they now? -- Group-based learning / Russell Y. Garth -- Can we teach without communicating? / Jean M. Civikly-Powell -- Teaching for critical thinking: helping college students develop the skills and dispositions of a critical thinker / Diane F. Halpern -- Development and adaptations of the seven principles for good practice in undergraduate education / Arthur W. Chickering, Zelda F. Gamson -- Taking diversity seriously: new developments in teaching for diversity / Laura L.B. Border -- Teaching in the information age: a new look / Michael J. Albright -- And now what? -- New directions for new directions? / Marilla D. Svinicki. ISBN 0-7879-4874-8
*1. College teaching. 2. Learning. I. Svinicki, Marilla D. 1946-*
*II. Series: New directions for teaching and learning ; no.80*
*TC LB2331 .T35 1999*

**Teaching and learning thinking skills** / edited by J.H.M. Hamers, J.E.H. van Luit, and B. Csapó. Lisse [Netherlands] ; Exton, PA : Swets & Zeitlinger, c1999. 360 p. : ill. ; 25 cm. (Contexts of learning) Includes bibliographical references and index. ISBN 90-265-1545-6 (hard) DDC 370.15/2
*1. Thought and thinking - Study and teaching. 2. Learning, Psychology of. 3. Mathematics - Study and teaching (Elementary) I. Hamers, J. H. M. (Jo H. M.), 1945- II. Luit, J. E. H. van, 1953- III. Csapó, Benő. IV. Series.*
*TC LB1590.3 .T36 1999*

**Teaching and testing in reading.**
Hargis, Charles H. Springfield, Ill. : C.C. Thomas, c1999.
*TC LB1050 .H29 1999*

**TEACHING AS A PROFESSION.** *See*
**TEACHING - VOCATIONAL GUIDANCE.**

**Teaching as decision making :** successful practices for the secondary teacher / Georgea M. Sparks-Langer ... [et al.] ; [illustrations, Carlisle Communications]. Upper Saddle River, N.J. : Prentice Hall, c2000. xx, 409 p. : ill. ; 24 cm. Includes bibliographical references and index. ISBN 0-13-950452-4 DDC 373.1102
*1. High school teaching - United States - Decision making. 2. Effective teaching. I. Sparks-Langer, Georgea M.*
*TC LB1607.5 .T43 2000*

**TEACHING - BRITISH COLUMBIA - PERIODICALS.**
Education bulletin of the Faculty and College of Education: Vancouver : University of British Columbia.

**TEACHING - CASE STUDIES.**
Hubbard, Ruth, 1950- The art of classroom inquiry. Portsmouth, N.H. : Heinemann, c1993.
*TC LB1028 .H78 1993*

Louden, William. Understanding teaching. New York : Cassell : Teachers College Press, Teachers College, Columbia University, 1991.
*TC LB1025.3 .L68 1991*

Reagan, Timothy G. Becoming a reflective educator. 2nd ed. Thousand Oaks Calif. : Sage Publications, c2000.
*TC LB1025.3 .R424 2000*

**Teaching children about health :** a multidisciplinary approach / edited by Estelle Weinstein, Efrem Rosen. Englewood, Colo. : Morton Pub., 1999. xvi, 624 p. : ill. ; 24 cm. Includes bibliographical references and index. ISBN 0-89582-439-6
*1. Health education (Elementary) - United States. 2. Interdisciplinary approach in education. 3. Health education - United States - Curricula. I. Weinstein, Estelle. 1937- II. Rosen. Efrem, 1933-- III. Title.*
*TC LB1587.A3 T43 1999*

**Teaching children and adolescents with special needs.**
Olson, Judy L. 3rd ed. Upper Saddle River, N.J. : Merrill, c2000.
*TC LC3969 .O47 2000*

**Teaching children science.**
Abruscato, Joseph. 5th ed. Boston : Allyn and Bacon, c2000.
*TC LB1585 .A29 2000*

**Teaching children to become successful readers and writers.**
Meier, Daniel R. Scribble scrabble--teaching children to become successful readers and writers. New York : Teachers College Press, c2000.
*TC LB1140.5.L3 M45 2000*

**Teaching children to read : an evidence-based assessment of the scientific research literature on reading and its implications for reading instruction.**
National Reading Panel (U.S.) Report of the National Reading Panel : teaching children to read. [Washington, D.C.?] : National Institute of Child Health and Human Development, National Institutes of Health, [2000]
*TC LB1050 .N335 2000*

**Teaching children what matters in math.**
Brandy, Tim. So what? Portsmouth, NH : Heinemann, c1999.
*TC QA135.5 .B6785 1999*

**Teaching children with AIDS.**
Ainsa, Patricia. Lewiston, N.Y. ; Lampeter, Wales : Edwin Mellen Press, c2000.
*TC LC4561 .A55 2000*

**TEACHING - COMPUTER NETWORK RESOURCES.**
Barron, Ann E. The Internet and instruction. 2nd ed. Englewood, Colo. : Libraries Unlimited, 1998.
*TC LB1044.87 .B37 1998*

Joseph, Linda C., 1949- Net curriculum. Medford, N.J. : CyberAge Books, c1999.
*TC LB1044.87 .J67 1999*

Kouki, Rafa. Telelearning via the Internet. Hershey, PA : Idea Group Pub., c1999.
*TC LC5800 .K68 1999*

Web-based learning and teaching technologies. Hershey, PA : London : Idea Group Pub., c2000.
*TC LB1044.87 .W435 2000*

Williams, Bard. The Internet for teachers. 3rd ed. Foster City, CA : IDG Books Worldwide, c1999.
*TC LB1044.87 .W55 1999*

**TEACHING CONTRACTS.** *See* **TEACHERS' CONTRACTS.**

**Teaching critical thinking :** reports from across the curriculum / [edited by] John H. Clarke, Arthur W. Biddle. Englewood Cliffs, N.J. : Prentice Hall, c1993. x, 306 p. : ill. ; 23 cm. (Prentice Hall studies in writing and culture) Includes bibliographical references (p. 305-306). ISBN 0-13-917410-9 DDC 371.3
*1. Critical thinking - Study and teaching. 2. Interdisciplinary approach in education. I. Clarke, John H., 1943- II. Biddle, Arthur W. III. Series.*
*TC LB1590.3 .T4 1993*

**TEACHING - DATA PROCESSING.** *See* **COMPUTER-ASSISTED INSTRUCTION.**

**TEACHING - DECISION MAKING.**
Gore, M. C. Taming the time stealers. Thousand Oaks, Calif. : Corwin Press, c1999.
*TC LB2838.8 .G67 1999*

**TEACHING DEMONSTRATIONS.** *See* **DEMONSTRATION CENTERS IN EDUCATION.**

**Teaching economics to undergraduates :** alternatives to chalk and talk / edited by William E. Becker and Michael Watts. Cheltenham, UK ; Northampton, MA, USA : E. Elgar, c1998. xvi, 274 p. : ill. ; 24 cm. Includes bibliographical references and index. ISBN 1858989728(pbk.) DDC 330/.071/173

*1. Economics - Study and teaching (Higher) - United States. I. Becker, William E. II. Watts, Michael.*
*TC HB74.8 .T4 1998*

**TEACHING EFFECTIVENESS.** *See* **EFFECTIVE TEACHING.**

**Teaching elementary language arts.**
Rubin, Dorothy. 6th ed. Boston : Allyn and Bacon, c2000.
*TC LB1576 .R773 2000*

**Teaching elementary school mathematics.**
Schwieger, Ruben D. Belmont, CA : Wadsworth Pub., 1999.
*TC QA135.5 .S329 1999*

**Teaching elementary social studies.**
Zarrillo, James. Upper Saddle River, N.J. : Merrill, c2000.
*TC LB1584 .Z27 2000*

**TEACHING ENGLISH AS A SECOND LANGUAGE.** *See* **ENGLISH LANGUAGE - STUDY AND TEACHING - FOREIGN SPEAKERS.**

**Teaching English in primary classrooms.**
Drever, Mina. Stoke on Trent, Staffordshire, England : Trentham Books, 1999.
*TC LB1576 .D749 1999*

**Teaching exceptional, diverse, and at-risk students in the general education classroom.**
Vaughn, Sharon, 1952- 2nd ed. Boston : Allyn and Bacon, 2000.
*TC LC3981 .V28 2000*

**Teaching for a tolerant world, grades K-6 :** essays and resources / Judith P. Robertson, editor, and the Committee on Teaching about Genocide and Intolerance of the National Council of Teachers of English. Urbana, Ill. : National Council of Teachers of English, c1999. xi, 464 p. ; 26 cm. Includes bibliographical references and index. ISBN 0-8141-5183-3 (pbk.) DDC 372.83
*1. Toleration - Study and teaching (Elementary) - United States. 2. Prejudices - Study and teaching (Elementary) - United States. 3. Genocide - Study and teaching (Elementary) - United States. 4. Discrimination - Study and teaching (Elementary) - United States. 5. Multicultural education - United States. I. Robertson, Judith P., 1951- II. National Council of Teachers of English. Committee on Teaching about Genocide and Intolerance.*
*TC HM1271 .T43 1999*

**Teaching for diversity.**
Garcia, Ricardo L. Bloomington, Ind. : Phi Delta Kappa Educational Foundation, 1998.
*TC LC1099.3 .G367 1998*

**Teaching for multiple intelligences.**
Lazear, David G. Eight ways of knowing. 3rd ed. Arlington Heights, Ill. : SkyLight Training and Pub., c1999.
*TC LB1060 .L39 1999*

**Teaching for quality learning at university.**
Biggs, John B. (John Burville). Buckingham, UK ; Philadelphia : Society for Research into Higher Education : Open University Press, 1999.
*TC LB2331 .B526 1999*

**The teaching for social justice series**
A simple justice. New York : Teachers College Press, 2000.
*TC LC213.2 .S56 2000*

**Teaching for understanding.**
Newton, Douglas P. London ; New York : Routledge/Falmer, 2000.
*TC LB1025.3 .N495 2000*

**Teaching foreign languages in the block.**
Blaz, Deborah. Larchmont, NY : Eye on Education, c1998.
*TC P51 .B545 1998*

**TEACHING, FREEDOM OF - UNITED STATES.**
Brinkley, Ellen Henson, 1944- Caught off guard. Boston : Allyn and Bacon, c1999.
*TC LC72.2 .B75 1999*

**Teaching from the heart.**
Draper, Sharon M. (Sharon Mills) Portsmouth, NH : Heinemann, c2000.
*TC LB1775.2 .D72 2000*

**Teaching genius.**
Sand, Barbara Lourie. Portland, Or. : Amadeus Press, 2000.
*TC ML423.D35 S36 2000*

**Teaching government and citizenship using the Internet :** reproducible activities for the classroom / Aaron Willis, project editor, George Cassutto, editor ;

contributing writers Betsy Hedberg ... [et al.] Rev. ed. viii, 112 p. : ill. ; 28 cm. Culvar City, CA : Social Studies School Service, 2000. Includes bibliographical references and web addresses. First printing August 1998. ISBN 0-934508-99-2
*1. Social sciences - Computer network resources - Reviews. 2. Social sciences - Computer network resources - Directories. 3. Social sciences - Study and teaching (Secondary) - United States. 4. Internet (Computer network) in education. I. Willis, Aaron. II. Cassutto, George. III. Hedberg, Betsy. IV. Title: Reproducible activities for the classroom*
**TC H61.95 .T43 2000**

### TEACHING - GREAT BRITAIN.
Hart, Susan. Thinking through teaching. London : David Fulton, 2000.
**TC LB1025.3 .H37 2000**

Sayer, John, 1931- The General Teaching Council. London : Cassell, 2000.
**TC LB1775.4.G7 S39 2000**

### TEACHING - HANDBOOKS, MANUALS, ETC.
Brown, Sally A. 500 tips for teachers. 2nd ed. London : Kogan Page ; Sterling, VA : Stylus Pub., 1998.
**TC LB3013 .B76 1998**

Forsyth, Ian. The complete guide to teaching a course. 2nd ed. London : Kogan Page ; Sterling, VA : Stylus Publishing, 1999.
**TC LB1025.3 .F67 1999**

### TEACHING - HISTORY. *See* EDUCATION - HISTORY.

**Teaching in primary schools** / edited by Asher Cashdan and Lyn Overall. London : Cassell, 1998. xvii, 221 p. : ill. ; 25 cm. Includes bibliographical references and index. ISBN 0-304-70361-3 (pbk) ISBN 0-304-70360-5 (hbk)
*1. Elementary school teaching. 2. Education, Elementary - England. 3. Education, Elementary - Wales. I. Cashdan, Asher. II. Overall, Lyn.*
**TC LB1776.T43 1998**

**Teaching in the 21st century** : adapting writing pedagogies to the college curriculum / edited by Alice Robertson and Barbara Smith. New York : Falmer Press, 1999. xxii, 362 p. ; 23 cm. (Garland reference library of social science ; v. 1189. Cultural studies in the classroom ; v. 1) Includes bibliographical references and index. ISBN 0-8153-3152-5 (acid-free paper) DDC 808/.042/07
*1. English language - Rhetoric - Study and teaching. 2. Interdisciplinary approach in education. 3. Academic writing - Study and teaching. 4. Curriculum change. I. Robertson, Alice. II. Smith, Barbara, 1949 Dec. 28- III. Title: Teaching in the twenty-first century IV. Series: Garland reference library of social science ; v. 1189. V. Series: Garland reference library of social science. Cultural studies in the classroom ; v. 1.*
**TC PE1404 .T394 1999**

**Teaching in the first person.**
Mirochnik, Elijah, 1952- New York : P. Lang, c2000.
**TC LB1033 .M546 2000**

**Teaching in the twenty-first century.**
Teaching in the 21st century. New York : Falmer Press, 1999.
**TC PE1404 .T394 1999**

**Teaching introduction to women's studies** : expectations and strategies index / Barbara Scott Winkler and Carolyn DiPalma, co-editors ; foreword by Frances Maher. Westport, Conn. : Bergin & Garvey, 1999. xiv, 273 p. ; 24 cm. Includes bibliographical references. ISBN 0-89789-590-8 (alk. paper) DDC 305.4/07
*1. Women's studies - United States. 2. Women's studies - Study and teaching - United States. I. Winkler, Barbara Scott. II. DiPalma, Carolyn.*
**TC HQ1181.U5 T43 1999**

**Teaching introductory psychology** : survival tips from the experts / edited by Robert J. Sternberg. 1st ed. Washington, DC : American Psychological Association, c1997. xi, 193 p. : ill. ; 26 cm. Includes bibliographical references and index. ISBN 1-55798-417-4 (pbk.) DDC 150/.71/1
*1. Psychology - Study and teaching (Higher) I. Sternberg, Robert J.*
**TC BF77 .T42 1997**

### TEACHING LABORATORIES. *See* STUDENT TEACHING.

**Teaching language arts in middle schools.**
Kingen, Sharon. Mahwah, NJ : Lawrence Erlbaum, 2000.
**TC LB1631 .K493 2000**

**Teaching large classes.**
Carbone, Elisa Lynn. Thousand Oaks, Calif. : Sage Publications, c1998.

**TC LB2331 .C336 1998**

**Teaching learners with mild disabilities.**
Meese, Ruth Lyn. 2nd ed. Belmont, CA : Wadsworth/Thomson Learning, c2001.
**TC LC4031 .M44 2001**

**Teaching, learning & professional development with the Internet.**
Net-working. Dunedin, N.Z. : University of Otago Press, 1999.
**TC LB1044.87 .N47 1999**

**Teaching literature 11-18** / edited by Martin Blocksidge. London & New York : Continuum, 2000. xiii, 145 p. ; 24 cm. Includes index. ISBN 0-8264-4794-5 ISBN 0-8264-4818-6 (pbk.) DDC 820.71241
*1. English literature - Study and teaching (Secondary) - Great Britain. I. Blocksidge, Martin.*
**TC PR51.G7 T43 2000**

### TEACHING MATERIALS. *See* TEACHING - AIDS AND DEVICES.

### TEACHING - METHODS.
Gaberson, Kathleen B. Clinical teaching strategies in nursing. New York : Springer, c1999.
**TC RT73 .G26 1999**

**Teaching middle school mathematics.**
Krulik, Stephen. Boston : Allyn and Bacon, c2000.
**TC QA11 .K818 2000**

**Teaching modern foreign languages at advanced level** / edited by Norbert Pachler. London ; New York : Routledge, 1999. xviii, 355 p. : ill. ; 24 cm. Includes bibliographical references. ISBN 0-415-20314-7 DDC 418/.0071
*1. Languages, Modern - Study and teaching. I. Pachler, Norbert.*
**TC PB35 .T42 1999**

**Teaching multicultured students.**
Moore, Alex, 1947- London ; New York : Falmer Press, 1999.
**TC LC3736.G6 M66 1999**

**Teaching music musically.**
Swanwick, Keith. London ; New York : Routledge, 1999.
**TC MT1 .S946 1999**

**The teaching of reading in Spanish to the bilingual student** = La enseñanza de la lectura en español para el estudiante bilingüe / edited by Angela Carrasquillo, Philip Segan. 2nd ed. Mahwah, N.J. : L. Erlbaum Associates, 1998. xiii, 222 p. ; 23 cm. English and Spanish. Includes bibliographical references and indexes. ISBN 0-8058-2462-6 (pbk. : alk. paper) DDC 372.41/6
*1. Reading (Elementary) - United States. 2. Education, Bilingual - United States. 3. Spanish language - Study and teaching (Elementary) - United States. 4. Hispanic American students - Education. I. Carrasquillo, Angela. II. Segan, Philip. III. Title: Enseñanza de la lectura en español para el estudiante bilingüe*
**TC LB1573 .T365 1998**

**Teaching other people's children.**
Ballenger, Cynthia. New York : Teachers College Press, c1999.
**TC LC3746 .B336 1999**

**Teaching percussion.**
Cook, Gary, 1951- 2nd ed. New York : Schirmer Books ; London : Prentice Hall International, c1997.
**TC MT655 .C67 1997**

### TEACHING - PERIODICALS.
[Journal (Martha Holden Jennings Foundation)] Journal. [Cleveland : The Foundation, 1974-

### TEACHING - PHILOSOPHY.
McHenry, Henry Davis. From cognition to being. Ottawa : University of Ottawa Press, c1999.
**TC LB1025.3 .M36 1999**

**Teaching physical education 5-11.**
Bailey, Richard. New York : Continuum, 2000.
**TC GV443 .B34 2000**

**Teaching piano** : a comprehensive guide and reference book for the instructor / edited by Denes Agay ; associate editor, Hazel Ghazarian Skaggs ; contributing authors, Denes Agay ... [et al.]. New York ; London : Yorktown Music Press, Inc., c1981. 2 v. (687 p.) : music ; 24 cm. Bibliography: v. 2, p. 681-684. Includes indexes. ISBN 0-8256-8039-5
*1. Piano - Instruction and study. 2. Piano music - Bibliography - Graded lists. 3. Piano music - Bibliography. I. Agay, Denes, ed.*
**TC MT220 .T25**

### TEACHING - PLANNING.
Buckley, Francis J. Team teaching. Thousand Oaks, Calif. : Sage Publications, c2000.

**TC LB1029.T4 B83 2000**

**Teaching poetry in the primary school.**
Carter, Dennis. London : David Fulton, 1998.
**TC LB1575 .C27 1998**

### TEACHING post-colonialism.
Teaching post-colonialism and post-colonial literatures. Aarhus, Denmark ; Oakville, Conn. : Aarhus University Press, c1997.
**TC PR9080.A53 T43 1997**

**Teaching post-colonialism and post-colonial literatures** / edited by Anne Collett, Lars Jensen, and Anna Rutherford. Aarhus, Denmark ; Oakville, Conn. : Aarhus University Press, c1997. 207 p. ; 22 cm. (The Dolphin, 0106-4487 ; 27) Spine title: Teaching post-colonialism. Includes bibliographical references. ISBN 87-7288-378-2 DDC 809/.89171241
*1. Commonwealth literature (English) - Study and teaching. 2. Commonwealth countries - In literature - Study and teaching. 3. English literature - 20th century - Study and teaching. 4. Decolonization in literature - Study and teaching. I. Collett, Anne. II. Jensen, Lars. III. Rutherford, Anna. IV. Title: Teaching post-colonialism V. Series: Dolphin (Arhus, Denmark) ; no. 27.*
**TC PR9080.A53 T43 1997**

### TEACHING - PRACTICE - UNITED STATES - HANDBOOKS, MANUALS, ETC.
Zuelke, Dennis C. Educational private practice. Lancaster : Technomic Pub., c1996.
**TC LB2844.1.S86 Z84 1996**

**Teaching practices to increase student achievement.**
Rugh, Andrea B. Cambridge, Mass. : B.R.I.D.G.E.S. Basic Research and Implementation in Developing Education Systems, [1991].
**TC LB1025.2 .R83 1991**

**Teaching prosocial competencies.**
Goldstein, Arnold P. The Prepare Curriculum. Revised ed. Champaign, Ill. : Research Press, c1999.
**TC HM299 .G65 1999**

### TEACHING - PSYCHOLOGICAL ASPECTS.
The intuitive practitioner. Buckingham [England] ; Philadelphia : Open University Press, 2000.
**TC LB1025.3 .I59 2000**

Teachers' pedagogical thinking. New York : P. Lang, 2000.
**TC LB1775 . T4179 2000**

**Teaching public administration and public policy** / Stuart S. Nagel (editor). Huntington, N.Y. : Nova Science Publishers, c1999. xxi, 175 p. : ill. ; 27 cm. Includes bibliographical references and index. ISBN 1-56072-738-1 DDC 351/.071/073
*1. Public administration - Study and teaching - United States. I. Nagel, Stuart S., 1934-*
**TC JF1338.A3 U59 1999**

### TEACHING QUALITY. *See* EFFECTIVE TEACHING.

**Teaching reading and spelling to dyslexic children.**
Walton, Margaret. London : D. Fulton, 1998.
**TC LC4708 .W35 1998**

**Teaching reading in secondary schools.**
Dean, Geoff. London : David Fulton, 2000.
**TC LB1632 .D43 2000**

**Teaching second-language writing.**
Campbell, Cherry. Pacific Grove : Heinle & Heinle, c1998.
**TC PE1128.A2 C325 1998**

**Teaching secondary and middle school mathematics.**
Brahier, Daniel J. Boston : Allyn and Bacon, 2000.
**TC QA11 .B6999 2000**

**Teaching secondary mathematics** / Douglas K. Brumbaugh ... [et al.]. Mahwah, N.J. : L. Erlbaum Associates, 1997. xii, 385 p. : ill. ; 28 cm. Includes bibliographical references and index. ISBN 0-8058-8037-2 (pbk. : alk. paper) DDC 510/.71/2
*1. Mathematics - Study and teaching (Secondary) I. Brumbaugh, Douglas K., 1939-*
**TC QA11 .T357 1997**

**Teaching self-control through management and discipline.**
Savage, Tom V. 2nd ed. Boston ; London : Allyn and Bacon, c1999.
**TC LB3012.2 .S38 1999**

**Teaching sex.**
Moran, Jeffrey P. Cambridge, Mass. : Harvard University Press, 2000.
**TC HQ57.5.A3 M66 2000**

**Teaching Shakespeare through performance** / edited by Milla Cozart Riggio. New York : Modern Language Association of America, 1999. ix, 503 p. ; 24 cm. (Options for teaching, 1079-2562 ; [14]) Includes bibliographical references and index. ISBN 0-87352-372-5 (cloth) ISBN 0-87352-373-3 (paper)
*1. Shakespeare, William, - 1564-1616 - Study and teaching. 2. Shakespeare, William, - 1564-1616 - Dramatic production. 3. Shakespeare, William, - 1564-1616 - Stage history. 4. Theater - Study and teaching. 5. Drama - Study and teaching. 6. Drama in education. I. Riggio, Milla Cozart. II. Series.*
**TC PR2987 .T366 1999**

**TEACHING - SOCIAL ASPECTS.**
Researching school experience. London ; New York : Falmer Press, 1999.
**TC LB1027 .R453 1999**

**TEACHING - SOCIAL ASPECTS - UNITED STATES.**
Bartolomé, Lilia I. The misteaching of academic discourses. Boulder, Colo. : Westview Press, 1998.
**TC LB1033.5 .B37 1998**

Frank, Carolyn. Ethnographic eyes. Portsmouth, NH : Heinemann, c1999.
**TC LB1027.28 .F73 1999**

Gay, Geneva. Culturally responsive teaching. New York : Teachers College Press, c2000.
**TC LC1099.3 .G393 2000**

Gordon, June A., 1950- The color of teaching. London ; New York : RoutledgeFalmer, c2000.
**TC LB2835.25 .G67 2000**

**Teaching social studies in early education.**
Robles de Melendez, Wilma J. Albany, NY : Delmar Thomson Learning, c2000.
**TC LB1139.5.S64 R62 2000**

**Teaching special students in general education classrooms.**
Lewis, Rena B. 5th ed. Upper Saddle River, N.J. : Merrill, c1999.
**TC LC1201 .L48 1999**

**Teaching struggling readers** : articles from The reading teacher / Richard L. Allington, editor. Newark, Del. : International Reading Association, c1998. vi, 311 p. : ill. ; 26 cm. Includes bibliographical references and index. ISBN 0-87207-183-9 DDC 372.43
*1. Reading - Remedial teaching. 2. Reading disability. I. Allington, Richard L. II. Title: Reading teacher.*
**TC LB1050.5 .T437 1998**

**Teaching students with severe disabilities.**
Westling, David L. 2nd ed. Upper Saddle River, N.J. : Merrill, c2000.
**TC LC4031 .W47 2000**

**TEACHING TEAMS.**
Bright beginnings [videorecording. Burbank, CA : RCA/Columbia Pictures Home Video ; Toluca Lake, CA : [Distributed by] Corporate Productions, c1991.
**TC HV1642 .B67 1991**

Bright beginnings [videorecording. Burbank, CA : RCA/Columbia Pictures Home Video ; [S.l. : Distributed by] Rank Video Services America, c1991.
**TC HV1642 .B67 1991**

Buckley, Francis J. Team teaching. Thousand Oaks, Calif. : Sage Publications, c2000.
**TC LB1029.T4 B83 2000**

Rutter, Alison Lee. Professional growth of two multidisciplinary teams within a professional development school. 1999.
**TC 06 no. 11171**

**TEACHING TEAMS - PLANNING.**
Buckley, Francis J. Team teaching. Thousand Oaks, Calif. : Sage Publications, c2000.
**TC LB1029.T4 B83 2000**

**TEACHING TEAMS - UNITED STATES.**
Bess, James L. Teaching alone, teaching together. 1st ed. San Francisco : Jossey-Bass, c2000.
**TC LB2331 .B48 2000**

Collaboration for inclusive education. Boston ; London : Allyn and Bacon, c2000.
**TC LC1201 .C63 2000**

Gottesman, Barbara Little. Peer coaching for educators. 2nd ed. Lanham, Md. : Scarecrow Press, 2000.
**TC LB1029.T4 G68 2000**

Idol, Lorna. Collaborative consultation. 3rd ed. Austin, Tex. : PRO-ED, c2000.
**TC LC4019 .I35 2000**

**Teaching the art of poetry.**
Wormser, Baron. Mahwah, N.J. : Lawrence Erlbaum Assoc., 2000.
**TC PN1101 .W67 2000**

**Teaching the emotionally handicapped child.**
Collins, Christopher G. Danville, Ill. : Interstate Printers & Publishers, c1983.
**TC LC4165 .C62 1983**

**Teaching the Holocaust** : : educational dimensions, principles and practice / edited by Ian Davies. London : Continuum, 2000. xiii, 178 p. ; 24 cm. Includes bibliographical references and index. ISBN 0-8264-4789-9 ISBN 0-8264-4851-8 (pbk.)
*1. Holocaust, Jewish (1939-1945) - Study and teaching. I. Davies, Ian.*
**TC D804.33 .T43 2000**

**Teaching the Internet to library staff and users.**
Hollands, William D. New York : Neal-Schuman, c1999.
**TC ZA4201 .H65 1999**

**Teaching the literatures of early America** / edited by Carla Mulford. New York : Modern Language Association of America, 1999. xii, 402 p. ; 24 cm. (Options for teaching ; 15) Includes bibliographical references and index. ISBN 0-87352-358-X (cloth) ISBN 0-87352-359-8 (pbk.) DDC 810/.7
*1. American literature - Colonial period, ca. 1600-1775 - Study and teaching. 2. American literature - Revolutionary period, 1775-1783 - Study and teaching. 3. Pluralism (Social sciences) - United States - Study and teaching. 4. American literature - Minority authors - Study and teaching. 5. American literature - 1783-1850 - Study and teaching. 6. Decolonization in literature - Study and teaching. 7. Minorities in literature - Study and teaching. 8. United States - History - Revolution, 1775-1783 - Literature and the revolution - Study and teaching. 9. America - Literatures - Study and teaching. I. Mulford, Carla, 1955- II. Series: Options for teaching ; 15*
**TC PS186 .T43 1999**

**Teaching the mother tongue in a multilingual Europe** / edited by Witold Tulasiewicz and Anthony Adams. London : Cassell, 1998. vi, 230 p. : maps ; 26 cm. (Cassell education) Includes bibliographical references (p. [207]-223) and index. ISBN 0-304-33490-1
*1. Native language - Study and teaching - Europe. 2. Linguistic minorities - Education - Europe. I. Tulasiewicz, Witold. II. Adams, Anthony, 1933- III. Series.*
**TC P53.5 .T43 1998**

**Teaching the nuts and bolts of physical education.**
Colvin, A. Vonnie, 1951- Champaign, IL : Human Kinetics, c2000.
**TC GV443 .C59 2000**

**Teaching three to eight.**
O'Hara, Mark. Teaching 3-8 :. London ; New York : Continuum, 2000.
**TC LB1725.G7 O36 2000**

**Teaching through texts** : promoting literacy through popular and literary texts in the primary classroom / [edited by] Holly Anderson and Morag Styles. London ; New York : Routledge, 1999. viii, 169 p. ; 24 cm. Includes bibliographical references and index. ISBN 0-415-20306-6 (hard : alk. paper) ISBN 0-415-20307-4 (pbk. : alk. paper) DDC 372.64/044/0941
*1. Reading (Primary) - Great Britain. 2. Children's literature - Study and teaching (Primary) - Great Britain. 3. Literacy - Great Britain. I. Anderson, Holly, 1949- II. Styles, Morag.*
**TC LB1573 .T39 1999**

**Teaching to promote intellectual and personal maturity** : : incorporating students' worldviews and identities into the learning process / Marcia B. Baxter Magolda, editor. San Francisco : Jossey-Bass, c2000. 104 p. ; 23 cm. (New directions for teaching and learning, no. 82.) "Summer 2000." Includes bibliographical references and index. ISBN 0-7879-5446-2
*1. Learning, Psychology of. 2. College students. 3. College teaching. I. Baxter Magolda, Marcia B. 1951- II. Series: New directions for teaching and learning, no. 82*
**TC LB1060 .T43 2000**

**Teaching to teach** : new partnerships in teacher education / Cherie Major and Robert Pines, editors. Washington, DC : National Education Association, 1999. 215 p. : ill. ; 23 cm. Includes bibliographical references. ISBN 0-8106-2083-9 (pbk.) DDC 370/.71/1
*1. Teachers - Training of - United States - Longitudinal studies. 2. College-school cooperation - United States - Longitudinal studies. 3. National Education Association's Teacher Education Initiative. I. Major, Cherie. II. Pines, Robert. III. National Education Association of the United States.*
**TC LB1715 .T436 1999**

**Teaching to wonder.**
Leggo, Carleton Derek, 1953- Vancouver : Pacific Educational Press, c1997.
**TC PN1101 .L43 1997**

**TEACHING TOYS. See EDUCATIONAL TOYS.**

**Teaching transformed** : achieving excellence, fairness, inclusion, and harmony / Roland G. Tharp ... [et al.]. Boulder, Colo. ; Oxford : Westview Press, 2000. xii, 274 p. ; 24 cm. (Renewing American schools) Includes bibliographical references (p. 247-266) and index. ISBN 0-8133-2268-5 (hbk.) ISBN 0-8133-2269-3 (pbk.) DDC 371.2/00973
*1. School improvement programs - United States. 2. Educational equalization - United States. 3. Inclusive education - United States. I. Tharp, Roland G., 1930- II. Series.*
**TC LB2822.82 .T44 2000**

**TEACHING - UNITED STATES.**
Draper, Sharon M. (Sharon Mills) Teaching from the heart. Portsmouth, NH : Heinemann, c2000.
**TC LB1775.2 .D72 2000**

Gordon, Mordechai. Toward an integrative conception of authority in education. 1997.
**TC 085 G656**

Keefe, James W. Instruction and the learning environment. Larchmont, NY : Eye On Education, c1997.
**TC LB2806.4 .K44 1997**

Kordalewski, John. Standards in the classroom. New York ; London : Teachers College Press, c2000.
**TC LB3060.83 .K67 2000**

Learning circles. Thousand Oaks, Calif. : Corwin Press, c1998.
**TC LB1032 .L355 1998**

Lieberman, Ann. Teachers--transforming their world and their work. New York : Teachers College Press ; Alexandria, Va. : Association for Supervision and Curriculum Development, c1999.
**TC LB1025.3 .L547 1999**

Newman, Judith, 1943- Tensions of teaching. New York ; London : Teachers College Press, c1998.
**TC LB1025.3 .N49 1998**

Reed, Carol J., 1937- Teaching with power. New York : Teachers College Press, c2000.
**TC LB2806.45 .R44 2000**

Ritchie, Joy S. Teacher narrative as critical inquiry. New York : Teachers College Press, c2000.
**TC LA2311 .R58 2000**

Time and learning :. Bloomington, IN : Phi Delta Kappa International, c1998.
**TC LB3032 .T562 1998**

**TEACHING - UNITED STATES - AIDS AND DEVICES.**
Druce, Arden. Paper bag puppets. Lanham, MD : Scarecrow Press, 1999.
**TC Z718.3 .D78 1999**

Miller, Wilma H. Ready-to-use activities & materials for improving content reading skills. West Nyack, NY : Center For Applied Research in Education, c1999.
**TC LB1576 .M52 1999**

Teaching with technology. Washington, D.C. : National Education Association of the United States, 1999.
**TC LB1044.88 .T44 1999**

**TEACHING - UNITED STATES - AIDS AND DEVICES - HANDBOOKS, MANUALS, ETC.**
Lawyer-Brook, Dianna, 1949- Shifting focus. Lanham, Md. : London : Scarecrow Press, 2000.
**TC LB1044.7 .L313 2000**

**TEACHING - UNITED STATES - CASE STUDIES.**
Hayes, William, 1938- Real-life case studies for teachers. Lanham, Md. : Scarecrow Press, 2000.
**TC LB1775.2 .H39 2000**

**TEACHING - UNITED STATES - EVALUATION.**
Danielson, Charlotte. Teacher evaluation to enhance professional practice. Alexandria, Va. : Association for Supervision and Curriculum Development, c2000.
**TC LB2838 .D26 2000**

**TEACHING - UNITED STATES - HANDBOOKS, MANUALS, ETC.**
Niebrand, Chris. The pocket mentor. Boston, Mass. : Allyn and Bacon, 2000.
**TC LB1775.2 .N54 2000**

**TEACHING - UNITED STATES - MARKETING - HANDBOOKS, MANUALS, ETC.**

Zuelke, Dennis C. Educational private practice. Lancaster : Technomic Pub., c1996.
*TC LB2844.1.S86 Z84 1996*

**TEACHING - UNITED STATES - PROBLEMS, EXERCISES, ETC.**
Levin, James, 1946- Principles of classroom management. 3rd ed. Boston : Allyn and Bacon, c2000.
*TC LB3013 .L475 2000*

**TEACHING - VOCATIONAL GUIDANCE.**
Posner, George J. Field experience. 5th ed. New York : Longman, c2000.
*TC LB2157.A3 P6 2000*

**TEACHING - VOCATIONAL GUIDANCE - GREAT BRITAIN.**
Teacher professionalism and the challenge of change. Stoke-on-Trent, Staffordshire, England : Trentham Books, 1999.
*TC LB1775.4.G7 T43 1999*

**TEACHING - VOCATIONAL GUIDANCE - UNITED STATES.**
McNergney, Robert F. Foundations of education. 3rd ed. Boston ; London : Allyn and Bacon, c2001.
*TC LB1775.2 .M32 2001*

**TEACHING - VOCATIONAL GUIDANCE - UNITED STATES - HANDBOOKS, MANUALS, ETC.**
Moffatt, Courtney W. How to get a teaching job. Boston ; London : Allyn and Bacon, c2000.
*TC LB1780 .M64 2000*

**Teaching with favorite Marc Brown books.**
Walmsley, Bonnie Brown. New York : Scholastic Professional Books, c1998.
*TC LB1576 .W258 1998*

**Teaching with power.**
Reed, Carol J., 1937- New York : Teachers College Press, c2000.
*TC LB2806.45 .R44 2000*

**Teaching with technology.** Washington, D.C. : National Education Association of the United States, 1999. 96 p. ; 19 x 24 cm. (Teacher to teacher series) "NEA teacher-to-teacher books." Includes bibliographical references (p. 89-91). ISBN 0-8106-2912-7 (acid-free paper) DDC 371.33
*1. Teaching - United States - Aids and devices. 2. Computer-assisted instruction - United States. 3. Educational technology - United States. I. National Education Association of the United States. II. Series.*
*TC LB1044.88 .T44 1999*

**Teaching with your mouth shut.**
Finkel, Donald L., 1943- Portsmouth, NH Boynton/ Cook Publishers, c2000.
*TC LB1026 .F49 2000*

**Teaching writing.**
Tompkins, Gail E. 3rd ed. Upper Saddle River, N.J. : Merrill, c2000.
*TC LB1576 .T66 2000*

**TEAM LEARNING APPROACH IN EDUCATION.**
Strategies for energizing large classes : from small groups to learning communities. San Francisco, Calif. : Jossey-Bass, 2000.
*TC LB2361.5 .S77 2000*

**TEAM LEARNING APPROACH IN EDUCATION - SPAIN - CASE STUDIES.**
Sauquet, Alfonso. Conflict and team learning:. 2000.
*TC 06 no. 11308*

**TEAM LEARNING APPROACH IN EDUCATION - UNITED STATES.**
Bess, James L. Teaching alone, teaching together. 1st ed. San Francisco : Jossey-Bass, c2000.
*TC LB2331 .B48 2000*

**TEAM MANAGEMENT IN SCHOOLS.** *See* **SCHOOL MANAGEMENT TEAMS.**

**TEAM PROBLEM SOLVING.** *See* **GROUP PROBLEM SOLVING.**

**TEAM TEACHING.** *See also* **TEACHING TEAMS.**
Buckley, Francis J. Thousand Oaks, Calif. : Sage Publications, c2000.
*TC LB1029.T4 B83 2000*

**TEAMS IN THE WORKPLACE.** *See also* **QUALITY CIRCLES.**
Barker, James R. (James Robert), 1957- The discipline of teamwork. Thousand Oaks, Calif. : Sage Publications, Inc., c1999.
*TC HD66 .B364 1999*

Leonard-Barton, Dorothy. When sparks fly. Boston, Mass. : Harvard Business School Press, 1999.

*TC HD53 .L46 1999*

Ostroff, Frank. The horizontal organization. New York : Oxford University Press, 1999.
*TC HD66 .O68 1999*

Wheelan, Susan A. Creating effective teams. Thousand Oaks, Calif. : Sage Publications, c1999.
*TC HD66 .W485 1999*

**Teamwork in the management of emotional and behavioural difficulties.**
Hill, Fran, 1950- London : David Fulton, 2000.
*TC LC4803.G7 H54 2000*

**Teamwork :** teacher's planning guide. New York : Macmillan/McGraw-Hill, c1997. 1 v. (various pagings) : col. ill. ; 31 cm. (Spotlight on literacy ; Gr.3 l.9) (The road to independent reading) Includes index. ISBN 0-02-181170-9
*1. Language arts (Primary) 2. Reading (Primary) I. Series. II. Series: The road to independent reading*
*TC LB1576 .S66 1997 Gr.3 l.9 u.3*

**Teare, Richard.**
The virtual learning organization. London ; New York : Continuum, 2000.
*TC LC5215 .V574 2000*

The virtual university : an action paradigm and process for workplace learning / Richard Teare, David Davies, and Eric Sandelands. London ; New York : Cassell, 1998. 315 p. : ill. ; 25 cm. (Workplace learning series) Includes bibliographical references. ISBN 0-304-70327-3 ISBN 0-304-70324-9 (pbk.)
*1. Adult education. 2. Continuing education. 3. Employees - Training of. 4. Interactive multimedia. I. Davies, David, 1952- II. Sandelands, Eric. III. Title. IV. Series.*
*TC LC5215 .T42 1998*

**Teasdale, G. R. (G. Robert).**
Local knowledge and wisdom in higher education. 1st ed. Oxford : Published for the IAU Press [by] Pergamon, 2000.
*TC GN380 .L63 2000*

**Techknowledgey.**
Campbell, Hope. Managing technology in the early childhood classroom. Westminster, CA : Teacher Created Materials, c1999.
*TC LB1139.35.C64 C36 1999*

**TECHNICAL ASSISTANCE.** *See* **ECONOMIC DEVELOPMENT PROJECTS; EDUCATIONAL ASSISTANCE.**

**TECHNICAL ASSISTANCE - ANTHROPOLOGICAL ASPECTS.** *See* **INTERCULTURAL COMMUNICATION.**

**Technical bulletin (Canadian Conservation Institute)**
(no. 12) Strang, Thomas J. K. Controlling museum fungal problems. Ottawa : Canadian Conservation Institute, Department of Communications, [1991]
*TC TH9031 .S75 1991*

(no. 14.) Schlichting, Carl. Working with polyethylene foam and fluted plastic sheet. Ottawa, Ontario, Canada : Canadian Conservation Institute, Dept. of Canadian Heritage, 1994.
*TC N8554 T25 no.14*

**TECHNICAL CHEMISTRY.** *See* **CHEMISTRY, TECHNICAL.**

**TECHNICAL EDUCATION.** *See* **EVENING AND CONTINUATION SCHOOLS; PROFESSIONAL EDUCATION; VOCATIONAL EDUCATION.**

**TECHNICAL EDUCATION - PERIODICALS.**
Industrial arts magazine. Milwaukee [etc.] Bruce Publishing Co.

Industrial education. Greenwich, Conn., Macmillan Professional Magazines.

**Technical Education Research Centers (U.S.).**
Network science, a decade later. Mahwah, N.J. : Lawrence Erlbaum, 2000.
*TC LB1583.3 .N48 2000*

**TECHNICAL ENGLISH.** *See* **ENGLISH LANGUAGE - TECHNICAL ENGLISH.**

**TECHNICAL INNOVATIONS.** *See* **TECHNOLOGICAL INNOVATIONS.**

**TECHNICAL INSTITUTES - CALIFORNIA - BUILDINGS.** *See* **COLLEGE BUILDINGS - CALIFORNIA.**

**Technical report (University of Hawaii at Manoa. Second Language Teaching & Curriculum Center)**
(#15.) New trends & issues in teaching Japanese language & culture. Honolulu ; Second Language

Teaching and Curriculum, University of Hawai'i at Manoa, 1997.
*TC PL519 .N45 1997*

**TECHNICAL WRITING - STUDY AND TEACHING.**
Worlds apart. Mahwah, N.J. : L. Erlbaum Associates, 1999.
*TC PE1404 .W665 1999*

**TECHNICAL WRITING - STUDY AND TEACHING (HIGHER).**
Pupipat, Apisak. Scientific writing and publishing in English in Thailand. 1998.
*TC 06 no. 10981*

**Techniques for student research.**
Lane, Nancy D. New York : Neal-Schuman Publishers, 2000.
*TC Z710 .L36 2000*

**TECHNOLOGICAL BREAKTHROUGHS.** *See* **TECHNOLOGICAL INNOVATIONS.**

**TECHNOLOGICAL CHANGE.** *See* **TECHNOLOGICAL INNOVATIONS.**

**TECHNOLOGICAL CHANGE IN AGRICULTURE.** *See* **AGRICULTURAL INNOVATIONS.**

**TECHNOLOGICAL CHANGE IN EDUCATION.** *See* **EDUCATIONAL INNOVATIONS.**

**TECHNOLOGICAL FORECASTING.** *See also* **TECHNOLOGY TRANSFER.**
Bell, Trudy E. Engineering tomorrow :. Piscataway, NJ : IEEE Press, c2000.
*TC T174 .B451 2000*

Scanning the future. New York : Thames & Hudson, c1999.
*TC CB161 .S44 1999*

**TECHNOLOGICAL INNOVATIONS.** *See* **AGRICULTURAL INNOVATIONS; CITIES AND TOWNS - EFFECT OF TECHNOLOGICAL INNOVATIONS ON; EDUCATION, HIGHER - EFFECT OF TECHNOLOGICAL INNOVATIONS ON; TECHNOLOGY TRANSFER.**

**TECHNOLOGICAL INNOVATIONS - ECONOMIC ASPECTS - UNITED STATES.**
Critical technologies and competitiveness. Huntington, New York : Nova Science Publishers, c2000.
*TC HC110.T4 C74 2000*

**TECHNOLOGICAL INNOVATIONS - HISTORY.**
Mattelart, Armand. [Mondialisation de la communication. English] Networking the world, 1794-2000. Minneapolis, MN ; London : University of Minnesota Press, c2000.
*TC HE7631 .M37513 2000*

**TECHNOLOGICAL INNOVATIONS - HISTORY - 20TH CENTURY.**
Singer, Edward. 20th century revolutions in technology. Commack, NY : Nova Science Pub., 1998.
*TC T173.8 .S568 1998*

**TECHNOLOGICAL INNOVATIONS - UNITED STATES.**
Employee training and U.S. competitiveness. Boulder : Westview Press, 1991.
*TC HF5549.5.T7 E46 1991*

**TECHNOLOGICAL LITERACY.** *See* **COMPUTER LITERACY; ELECTRONIC INFORMATION RESOURCE LITERACY; MEDIA LITERACY.**

**TECHNOLOGICAL LITERACY - UNITED STATES.**
Selfe, Cynthia L., 1951- Technology and literacy in the twenty-first century. Carbondale : Southern Illinois University Press, c1999.
*TC LC149.5 .S45 1999*

**TECHNOLOGICAL TRANSFER.** *See* **TECHNOLOGY TRANSFER.**

**TECHNOLOGIE DE L'INFORMATION - ASPECT POLITIQUE.**
Digital democracy. Toronto ; New York : Oxford University Press, 1998.
*TC JC421 .D55 1998*

**Technologies of procreation :** kinship in the age of assisted conception / Jeanette Edwards ... [et al.]. 2nd ed. New York : Routledge, 1999. [xiv], 236 p. ; 23 cm. Includes bibliographical references and index. ISBN 0-415-17055-9 ISBN 0-415-17056-7 (pbk.) DDC 304.6/32
*1. Artificial insemination, Human - Social aspects. 2. Kinship.*

3. *Human reproduction - Social aspects.* 4. *Artificial insemination, Human - Law and legislation - Great Britain.* I. *Edwards, Jeanette. 1954-*
**TC HQ761 .T43 1999**

**TECHNOLOGY.** *See also* **CHEMISTRY, TECHNICAL; COMMUNICATION AND TECHNOLOGY; ENGINEERING; HIGH TECHNOLOGY; INDUSTRIAL ARTS; INFORMATION TECHNOLOGY; MATERIAL CULTURE.**
Arendt, Hannah. The human condition. 2nd ed. / introduction by Margaret Canovan. Chicago : University of Chicago Press, 1998.
**TC HM211 .A7 1998**

**Technology and buildings for a new century [videorecording].**
Modernizing schools : technology and buildings for a new century (September 19, 2000 : Washington, D.C.) Modernizing schools [videorecording]. [Washington, D.C.] : U.S. Dept. of Education, [2000].
**TC LB3205 .M64 2000**

Modernizing schools : technology and buildings for a new century (September 19, 2000 : Washington, D.C.) Modernizing schools [videorecording]. [Washington, D.C.] : U.S. Dept. of Education, [2000].
**TC LB3205 .M64 2000**

**TECHNOLOGY AND CIVILIZATION.**
Castells, Manuel. The rise of the network society. 2nd ed. Malden, MA : Blackwell Publishers, 2000.
**TC HC79.I55 C373 2000**

Kelly, Gerard, 1959- Retrofuture. Downers Grove, Ill. : InterVarsity Press, c1999.
**TC HN17.5 .K439 1999**

Wolf, Mark J. P. Abstracting reality. Lanham, Md.: University Press of America, c2000.
**TC HM851 .W65 2000**

**TECHNOLOGY AND COMMUNICATION.** *See* **COMMUNICATION AND TECHNOLOGY.**

**TECHNOLOGY AND INTERNATIONAL AFFAIRS.** *See* **TECHNOLOGY TRANSFER.**

**Technology and literacy in the twenty-first century.**
Selfe, Cynthia L., 1951- Carbondale : Southern Illinois University Press, c1999.
**TC LC149.5 .S45 1999**

**Technology and scholarly communication** / edited by Richard Ekman and Richard E. Quandt. Berkeley, Calif. : University of California Press ; [Pittsburgh?] : Published in association with the Andrew K. Mellon Foundation, c1999. xi, 442 p. ; 24 cm. Papers presented at a conference held April 1997 at Emory University, Atlanta, Ga. Includes bibliographical references (p. 421-427) and index. ISBN 0-520-21762-4 (alk. paper) ISBN 0-520-21763-2 (alk. paper) DDC 686.2/2544
1. *Scholarly electronic publishing - United States - Congresses.* 2. *Libraries - United States - Special collections - Electronic information resources - Congresses.* 3. *Research libraries - United States - Congresses.* I. *Ekman, Richard.* II. *Quandt, Richard E.*
**TC Z479 .T43 1999**

**Technology and society :** a bridge to the 21st century / edited by Linda S. Hjorth ... [et al.]. Upper Saddle River, NJ : Prentice Hall, 2000. xviii, 536 p. : ill. ; 23 cm. ISBN 0-13-618547-9 DDC 303.48/3
1. *Technology - Social aspects.* I. *Hjorth, Linda S.*
**TC T14.5 .T44168 2000**

**TECHNOLOGY AND STATE - UNITED STATES.**
Harnessing science and technology for America's economic future. Washington, D.C. : National Academy Press, c1999.
**TC Q127.U5 H37 1999**

**TECHNOLOGY AND THE ARTS.**
LifeScience. Wien : New York : Springer, 1999.
**TC T14.5 L54 1999**

Wolf, Mark J. P. Abstracting reality. Lanham, Md.: University Press of America, c2000.
**TC HM851 .W65 2000**

**Technology and the good life?** / edited by Eric Higgs, Andrew Light, and David Strong. Chicago : London : University of Chicago Press, 2000. xii, 392 p. ; 24 cm. Includes bibliographical references and index. ISBN 0-226-33386-8 (cloth : alk. paper) ISBN 0-226-33387-6 (paper : alk. paper) DDC 303.48/3
1. *Technology - Philosophy.* 2. *Technology - Social aspects.* I. *Higgs, Eric S.* II. *Light, Andrew, 1966-* III. *Strong, David, 1955-*
**TC T14 .T386 2000**

**Technology and the lifeworld.**
Ihde, Don, 1934- Bloomington : Indiana University Press, c1990.
**TC T14 .I353 1990**

**TECHNOLOGY ASSESSMENT.**
Vision assessment. New York : Springer, 2000.
**TC T174.5 V57 2000**

**TECHNOLOGY - AUTHORSHIP.** *See* **TECHNICAL WRITING.**

**TECHNOLOGY, EDUCATIONAL.** *See* **EDUCATIONAL TECHNOLOGY.**

**TECHNOLOGY - EXHIBITIONS.** *See* **EXHIBITIONS.**

**Technology funding for schools.**
Bauer, David G. 1st ed. San Francisco : Jossey-Bass, c2000.
**TC LB1028.43 .B38 2000**

**TECHNOLOGY - HISTORY - 20TH CENTURY.**
Singer, Edward. 20th century revolutions in technology. Commack, NY : Nova Science Pub., 1998.
**TC T173.8 .S568 1998**

**TECHNOLOGY IN EDUCATION.**
Plugging in :. Washington, D.C. : NEKIA Communications ; Oak Brook, Ill. : North Central Regional Educational Laboratory, [1995]. ([1999]).
**TC LB1028.3 .P584 1995**

**TECHNOLOGY - INTERNATIONAL COOPERATION.** *See* **TECHNOLOGY TRANSFER.**

**TECHNOLOGY - LANGUAGE.** *See* **ENGLISH LANGUAGE - TECHNICAL ENGLISH.**

**TECHNOLOGY, MEDICAL - INSTRUMENTATION.**
Vonlanthen, A. (Andy), 1961- Hearing instrument technology for the hearing healthcare professional. 2nd ed. San Diego : Singular Pub. Group, c2000.
**TC RF300 .V66 2000**

**TECHNOLOGY - PHILOSOPHY.**
Ihde, Don, 1934- Technology and the lifeworld. Bloomington : Indiana University Press, c1990.
**TC T14 .I353 1990**

Pacey, Arnold. Meaning in technology. Cambridge, Mass. : MIT Press, c1999.
**TC T14 .P28 1999**

Technology and the good life? Chicago ; London : University of Chicago Press, 2000.
**TC T14 .T386 2000**

**TECHNOLOGY - PSYCHOLOGICAL ASPECTS.**
Human cognition and social agent technology. Amsterdam ; Philadelphia : John Benjamins, c2000.
**TC BF311 .H766 2000**

**Technology, risk, and society**
(v. 13) Cross-cultural risk perception. Dordrecht ; Boston ; London : Kluwer Academic, c2000.
**TC HM1101 .C76 2000**

**TECHNOLOGY - SOCIAL ASPECTS.**
Clough, Patricia Ticineto, 1945- Autoaffection. Minneapolis : University of Minnesota Press, c2000.
**TC HM846 .C56 2000**

Diversity in technology education. New York : Glencoe, c1998.
**TC T61 .A56 47th 1998**

Diversity in technology education. New York : Glencoe, c1998.
**TC T61 .A56 47th 1998**

Geisler, Eliezer, 1942- The metrics of science and technology. Westport, Conn. : Quorum Books, 2000.
**TC Q175.5 .G43 2000**

Harvey, Kerric. Eden online. Cresskill, N.J. : Hampton Press, c2000.
**TC T14.5 .H367 2000**

Johnson, Robert R., 1951- User-centered technology. Albany : State University of New York Press, c1998.
**TC QA76.9.U83 J64 1998**

Katsikides, Savvas. The societal impact of technology. Aldershot, Hants, England ; Brookfield, Vt. : Ashgate, c1998.
**TC T14.5 .K373 1998**

Lienhard, John H., 1930- The engines of our ingenuity. Oxford ; New York : Oxford University Press, 2000.

**TC T14.5 .L52 2000**
Pacey, Arnold. Meaning in technology. Cambridge, Mass. : MIT Press, c1999.
**TC T14 .P28 1999**

The social shaping of technology. 2nd ed. Buckingham [England] ; Philadelphia : Open University Press, c1999.
**TC T14.5 .S6383 1999**

Technology and society. Upper Saddle River, NJ : Prentice Hall, 2000.
**TC T14.5 .T44168 2000**

Technology and the good life? Chicago ; London : University of Chicago Press, 2000.
**TC T14 .T386 2000**

Vision assessment. New York : Springer, 2000.
**TC T174.5 V57 2000**

**TECHNOLOGY - STUDY AND TEACHING.**
Diversity in technology education. New York : Glencoe, c1998.
**TC T61 .A56 47th 1998**

Diversity in technology education. New York : Glencoe, c1998.
**TC T61 .A56 47th 1998**

**TECHNOLOGY - STUDY AND TEACHING (EARLY CHILDHOOD).**
Siraj-Blatchford, John, 1952- Supporting science, design and technology in the early years. Philadelphia, Pa. : Open University Press, 1999.
**TC T65.3 .S55 1999**

**TECHNOLOGY - STUDY AND TEACHING (EARLY CHILDHOOD) - UNITED STATES.**
Dialogue on early childhood science, mathematics, and technology education. Washington, DC : American Association for the Advancement of Science/Project 2061, 1999.
**TC LB1139.5.S35 D53 1999**

**TECHNOLOGY - STUDY AND TEACHING (ELEMENTARY) - GREAT BRITAIN.**
Bold, Christine. Progression in primary design and technology. London : David Fulton, 1999.
**TC LB1541 .B65 1999**

**TECHNOLOGY - STUDY AND TEACHING (HIGHER) - UNITED STATES.**
Transforming undergraduate education in science, mathematics, engineering, and technology. Washington, DC : National Academy Press, 1999.
**TC Q183.3.A1 T73 1999**

**TECHNOLOGY TRANSFER.** *See* **TECHNOLOGICAL INNOVATIONS.**

**TECHNOLOGY TRANSFER - UNITED STATES.**
Gross, Clifford M. The new idea factory. Columbus, OH : Battelle Press, c2000.
**TC HD53 .G75 2000**

**TECHNOLOGY - UNITED STATES - ECONOMIC ASPECTS.**
Harnessing science and technology for America's economic future. Washington, D.C. : National Academy Press, c1999.
**TC Q127.U5 H37 1999**

**TECHNOLOGY - UNITED STATES - STATISTICS - HANDBOOKS, MANUALS, ETC.**
Berinstein, Paula. The statistical handbook on technology. Phoenix, AZ : Oryx Press, 1999.
**TC T21 .B47 1999**

**Teddlie, Charles.**
The international handbook of school effectiveness research. London : New York : Falmer Press, 2000.
**TC LB2822.75 .I59 2000**

**TEDDY BEARS IN LITERATURE.**
Williams, John Tyerman. Pooh and the millennium. 1st American ed. New York : Dutton Books, 1999.
**TC PR6025.I65 Z975 1999**

**TEEN-AGE.** *See* **ADOLESCENCE.**

**TEEN-AGERS.** *See* **TEENAGERS.**

**Teen killers [videorecording] :** a second chance? / an Oregon Public Broadcasting Production in association with Home Box Office ; a presentation of Films for the Humanities & Sciences ; senior producer, Larry Badger. Princeton, NJ : Films for the Humanities and Sciences, c1998-1999. 1 videorecording (37 min.) : sd., col. ; 1/2 in. At the head of the title: HBO original programming. VHS. Catalogued from credits and container. Sound, Katy Dolan ... [et al.]; editor, Jason Rosenfield; original music composed by Philip Marshall; camera, Greg Bond ... [et al.]. For adolescents through adult. SUMMARY: Originally

produced by HBO in 1998. For three teenage murderers, a controversial therapy program in Oregon offers the hope of rehabilitation and early release from prison. This compelling documentary outlines the brutal killings they commited and shows them in group therapy, where they are forced to confront their crimes through discussions and reenactments. By ceasing their denial, accepting responsibility, and feeling genuine remorse, counselors predict they will be able to reenter society. But is the potential threat to innocent bystanders worth the risk?
*1. Juvenile homicide - United States. 2. Juvenile corrections - Oregon. 3. Murder - United States. 4. Homicide - United States. 5. Murderers - United States. 6. Violent crimes - United States. 7. Documentary television programs. I. Badger, Larry. II. Oregon Public Broadcasting. III. Home Box Office (Firm) IV. Films for the Humanities (Firm) V. Title: American undercover. VI. Title: Second chance? [videorecording] VII. Title: HBO original programming*
**TC HV9067.H6 T4 1999**

**TEEN PREGNANCY.** *See* **TEENAGE PREGNANCY.**

**Teen violence** [videorecording] / :Wot u lookin' at? / a presentation of Films for the Humanities & Sciences ; BBC ; Horizon : written and produced by Oliver James & David Malone. Princeton, NJ : Films for the Humanities & Sciences, c1998. 1 videocassette (60 min.) : sd., col. with b&w sequences ; 1/2 in. VHS. Catalogued from credits and container. Narrator, John Ware. Camera: John Addeley ... [et al.] ; editor, Jana Bennett ; sound, Morton Hardacre, Tim Humphries. For adolescents through adult. SUMMARY: Explores the causes of antisocial behavior in young urban males. Candid interviews with youthful criminals encourage viewers to question whether there is, indeed, such a thing as a "violent gene," and whether violent behavior is linked to low intelligence. Looks for the roots of violence in morality, psychology and biology. Finds a history of abuse in the childhoods of violent teens.
*1. Violence in children. 2. Violence. 3. Violent crimes. 4. Social psychology. 5. Documentary television programs. I. James, Oliver, 1953- II. Malone, David. III. Ware, John. IV. Films for the Humanities (Firm) V. BBC Worldwide Americas, Inc. VI. British Broadcasting Corporation. VII. Horizon Film and Video (Firm) VIII. Title: Wot u lookin' at? [videorecording]*
**TC RJ506.V56 T44 1998**

**TEENAGE BOYS, AFRO-AMERICAN.** *See* **AFRO-AMERICAN TEENAGE BOYS.**

**TEENAGE BOYS - EDUCATION - GREAT BRITAIN.**
Head, John (John O.) Understanding the boys. New York : Falmer Press, 1999.
**TC LC1390 .H43 1999**

**TEENAGE BOYS - GREAT BRITAIN - PHYSIOLOGY.**
Head, John (John O.) Understanding the boys. New York : Falmer Press, 1999.
**TC LC1390 .H43 1999**

**TEENAGE BOYS - GREAT BRITAIN - PSYCHOLOGY.**
Head, John (John O.) Understanding the boys. New York : Falmer Press, 1999.
**TC LC1390 .H43 1999**

**TEENAGE BOYS - GREAT BRITAIN - SOCIAL CONDITIONS.**
Head, John (John O.) Understanding the boys. New York : Falmer Press, 1999.
**TC LC1390 .H43 1999**

**TEENAGE BOYS - UNITED STATES.** *See* **AFRO-AMERICAN TEENAGE BOYS.**

**TEENAGE GANGS.** *See* **GANGS.**

**TEENAGE GIRLS, AFRO-AMERICAN.** *See* **AFRO-AMERICAN TEENAGE GIRLS.**

**TEENAGE GIRLS - ATTITUDES.**
Growing up girls. New York : P. Lang, c1999.
**TC HQ798 .G76 1999**

**TEENAGE GIRLS - EDUCATION - CASE STUDIES.**
Harper, Helen J., 1957- Wild words-dangerous desires. New York : Peter Lang, c2000.
**TC LB1631 .H267 2000**

**TEENAGE GIRLS - EDUCATION (SECONDARY) - SOCIAL ASPECTS - UNITED STATES.**
Proweller, Amira. Constructing female identities. Albany : State University of New York Press, c1998.
**TC LC1755 .P76 1998**

**TEENAGE GIRLS IN POPULAR CULTURE.**
Growing up girls. New York : P. Lang, c1999.
**TC HQ798 .G76 1999**

**TEENAGE GIRLS - LEGAL STATUS, LAWS, ETC. - UNITED STATES.**
United States. Congress. Senate. Committee on Labor and Public Welfare. Subcommittee on Health. School-age mother and child health act, 1975. Washington : U.S. Govt. Print. Off., 1976.
**TC KF26 .L354 1975**

**TEENAGE GIRLS - NUTRITION.**
Nichter, Mimi. Fat talk. Cambridge, Mass. : Harvard University Press, 2000.
**TC RJ399.C6 N53 2000**

**TEENAGE GIRLS - PENNSYLVANIA - PHILADELPHIA REGION - DIARIES - JUVENILE LITERATURE.**
Wister, Sarah, 1761-1804. A colonial Quaker girl. Mankato, Minn. : Blue Earth Books, c2000.
**TC F158.44 .W75 2000**

**TEENAGE GIRLS - PSYCHOLOGY.**
Growing up girls. New York : P. Lang, c1999.
**TC HQ798 .G76 1999**

**TEENAGE GIRLS - UNITED STATES.** *See* **AFRO-AMERICAN TEENAGE GIRLS.**

**TEENAGE GIRLS - UNITED STATES - PSYCHOLOGY.**
Beyond appearance. 1st ed. Washington, DC : American Psychological Association, c1999.
**TC HQ798 .B43 1999**

Harrison, Patricia M. Racial identification and self-concept issues in biracial Black/White adolescent girls. 1997.
**TC O85 H247**

**TEENAGE GIRLS - UNITED STATES - SOCIAL CONDITIONS.**
Beyond appearance. 1st ed. Washington, DC : American Psychological Association, c1999.
**TC HQ798 .B43 1999**

**TEENAGE IMMIGRANTS - TEXAS - LOWER RIO GRANDE VALLEY - PICTORIAL WORKS.**
Anastos, Phillip. Illegal. New York : Rizzoli, 1991.
**TC F392.R5 A53 1991**

**TEENAGE LITERATURE.** *See* **YOUNG ADULT LITERATURE.**

**TEENAGE MOTHERS.**
Grounded for life [videorecording]. Charleston, WV : Cambridge Research Group, Ltd., 1988.
**TC HQ759.4 .G7 1988**

**TEENAGE MOTHERS - EDUCATION - SOCIAL ASPECTS - BRITISH COLUMBIA - CASE STUDIES.**
Kelly, Deirdre M. Pregnant with meaning. New York : P. Lang, c2000.
**TC LC4094.2.B8 K45 2000**

**TEENAGE PARENTS.** *See also* **TEENAGE MOTHERS.**
Grounded for life [videorecording]. Charleston, WV : Cambridge Research Group, Ltd., 1988.
**TC HQ759.4 .G7 1988**

**TEENAGE PREGNANCY.** *See* **PREGNANT SCHOOLGIRLS.**

**TEENAGE PREGNANCY - PREVENTION - SERVICES FOR.**
Richardson, Bonnie. Factors influencing the sexual and contraceptive behavior of sexually abused adolescents of color. 1999.
**TC 06 no. 11167**

**TEENAGE PREGNANCY - PSYCHOLOGICAL ASPECTS.**
Richardson, Bonnie. Factors influencing the sexual and contraceptive behavior of sexually abused adolescents of color. 1999.
**TC 06 no. 11167**

**TEENAGE PREGNANCY - UNITED STATES.**
Becker, Evvie. High-risk sexual behavior. New York : Plenum Press, c1998.
**TC HQ60.7.U6 B43 1998**

**Teenage pregnancy** [videorecording] : afraid to say no!.
Grounded for life [videorecording]. Charleston, WV : Cambridge Research Group, Ltd., 1988.
**TC HQ759.4 .G7 1988**

**TEENAGE PROSTITUTION - UNITED STATES.**
Children of the night [videorecording]. [Charleston, W.V.] : Cambridge Educational, c1994.
**TC HV1435.C3 C45 1994**

Children of the night [videorecording]. [Charleston, W.V.] : Cambridge Educational, c1994.
**TC HV1435.C3 C45 1994**

Children of the night [videorecording]. [Charleston, W.V.] : Cambridge Educational, c1994.
**TC HV1435.C3 C45 1994**

Starting over [videorecording]. [Charleston, W.V.] : Cambridge Educational, c1994.
**TC HV1435.C3 S7 1994**

**TEENAGE SEX OFFENDERS - MENTAL HEALTH SERVICES - UNITED STATES.**
Juvenile sex offenders [videorecording]. Princeton, N.J. : Films of the Humanities & Sciences, c1998.
**TC HV9067.S48 J8 1998**

**TEENAGE SEX OFFENDERS - REHABILITATION - UNITED STATES.**
Juvenile sex offenders [videorecording]. Princeton, N.J. : Films of the Humanities & Sciences, c1998.
**TC HV9067.S48 J8 1998**

**TEENAGE SEX OFFENDERS - UNITED STATES - PSYCHOLOGY.**
Juvenile sex offenders [videorecording]. Princeton, N.J. : Films of the Humanities & Sciences, c1998.
**TC HV9067.S48 J8 1998**

**TEENAGED BOYS.** *See* **TEENAGE BOYS.**

**TEENAGED GIRLS.** *See* **TEENAGE GIRLS.**

**TEENAGER AND PARENT.** *See* **PARENT AND TEENAGER.**

**TEENAGERS.** *See* **ENVIRONMENT AND TEENAGERS; MINORITY TEENAGERS; RUNAWAY TEENAGERS; SEX INSTRUCTION FOR TEENAGERS; SEXUAL ETHICS FOR TEENAGERS; TEENAGE BOYS; TEENAGE GIRLS.**

**TEENAGERS - ALCOHOL USE.**
Windle, Michael T. Alcohol use among adolescents. Thousand Oaks : Sage Publications, c1999.
**TC RJ506.A4 W557 1999**

**TEENAGERS AND DEATH.**
Christ, Grace Hyslop. Healing children's grief. New York ; Oxford : Oxford University Press, 2000.
**TC BF723.G75 C58 2000**

**TEENAGERS AND ENVIRONMENT.** *See* **ENVIRONMENT AND TEENAGERS.**

**TEENAGERS AND PARENTS.** *See* **PARENT AND TEENAGER.**

**TEENAGERS - ATTITUDES.**
Shucksmith, Janet, 1953- Health issues and adolescents. London ; New York : Routledge, 1998.
**TC RJ47.53 .S455 1998**

**TEENAGERS - BOOKS AND READING.**
Rationales for teaching young adult literature. Portland, Me. : Calendar Islands Publishers, 1999.
**TC PN59 .R33 1999**

**TEENAGERS - CALIFORNIA - SOCIAL CONDITIONS - CASE STUDIES.**
Childress, Herb, 1958- Landscapes of betrayal, landscapes of joy. Albany [N.Y.] : State University of New York Press, c2000.
**TC HQ796 .C458237 2000**

**TEENAGERS - DEVELOPMENT.** *See* **ADOLESCENCE.**

**TEENAGERS - DRUG USE - PREVENTION.**
The next generation [videorecording]. Princeton, NJ : Films for the Humanities & Sciences, c1998.
**TC RC564 .N4 1998**

**TEENAGERS - DRUG USE - UNITED STATES.**
Children of the night [videorecording]. [Charleston, W.V.] : Cambridge Educational, c1994.
**TC HV1435.C3 C45 1994**

Children of the night [videorecording]. [Charleston, W.V.] : Cambridge Educational, c1994.
**TC HV1435.C3 C45 1994**

**TEENAGERS, EAST INDIAN AMERICAN.** *See* **EAST INDIAN AMERICAN TEENAGERS.**

**TEENAGERS - EMPLOYMENT.**
Pervola, Cindy, 1956- How to get a job if you're a teenager. Fort Atkinson, Wis. : Alleyside Press, 1998.
**TC HF5383 .P44 1998**

**TEENAGERS - EMPLOYMENT - UNITED STATES.**
Csikszentmihalyi, Mihaly. Becoming adult. New York : Basic Books, 2000.
**TC HQ796 .C892 2000**

**TEENAGERS - GERMANY.**
Growing up in times of social change. New York :
Walter de Gruyter, 1999.
*TC HQ799.G5 G76 1999*

**TEENAGERS, HAITIAN AMERICAN.** *See*
HAITIAN AMERICAN TEENAGERS.

**TEENAGERS - HEALTH AND HYGIENE.**
Shucksmith, Janet, 1953- Health issues and
adolescents. London ; New York : Routledge, 1998.
*TC RJ47.53 .S455 1998*

Spruijt-Metz, Donna. Adolescence, affect and health.
Hove : Psychology Press, for the European
Association for Research on Adolescence, 1999.
*TC RJ47.53 .S67 1999*

**TEENAGERS - HEALTH AND HYGIENE - NEW
YORK (STATE) - STATISTIC.**
Maternal, child and adolescent health profile. Albany,
N.Y. : New York State Dept. of Health, 1996.
*TC HV742.N7 B83 1996*

**TEENAGERS - HEALTH AND HYGIENE -
SCOTLAND.**
Shucksmith, Janet, 1953- Health issues and
adolescents. London ; New York : Routledge, 1998.
*TC RJ47.53 .S455 1998*

**TEENAGERS, HISPANIC AMERICAN.** *See*
HISPANIC AMERICAN TEENAGERS.

**TEENAGERS - HUNGARY.**
Adolescent development and rapid social change.
Albany : State University of New York Press, c2000.
*TC HQ799.H8 A35 2000*

**TEENAGERS - LEGAL STATUS, LAWS, ETC. -
UNITED STATES.**
Levesque, Roger J. R. Adolescents, sex, and the law.
1st ed. Washington, DC : American Psychological
Association, c2000.
*TC KF479 .L48 2000*

**TEENAGERS - MENTAL HEALTH SERVICES.**
*See* COMMUNITY MENTAL HEALTH
SERVICES FOR TEENAGERS.

**TEENAGERS - POLAND.**
Adolescent development and rapid social change.
Albany : State University of New York Press, c2000.
*TC HQ799.H8 A35 2000*

**TEENAGERS - PSYCHOLOGICAL TESTING.**
Hoge, Robert D. Assessing adolescents in educational,
counseling, and other settings. Mahwah, N.J. :
Lawrence Erlbaum Associates, 1999.
*TC BF724.25 .H64 1999*

**TEENAGERS - PSYCHOLOGY.** *See*
ADOLESCENT PSYCHOLOGY.

**TEENAGERS - SCOTLAND - ATTITUDES.**
Shucksmith, Janet, 1953- Health issues and
adolescents. London ; New York : Routledge, 1998.
*TC RJ47.53 .S455 1998*

**TEENAGERS - SEXUAL BEHAVIOR - UNITED
STATES - HISTORY.**
Moran, Jeffrey P. Teaching sex. Cambridge, Mass. :
Harvard University Press, 2000.
*TC HQ57.5.A3 M66 2000*

**TEENAGERS - SUBSTANCE USE -
PREVENTION.**
The next generation [videorecording]. Princeton, NJ :
Films for the Humanities & Sciences, c1998.
*TC RC564 .N4 1998*

**TEENAGERS - TOBACCO USE - PREVENTION.**
The next generation [videorecording]. Princeton, NJ :
Films for the Humanities & Sciences, c1998.
*TC RC564 .N4 1998*

**TEENAGERS - TOBACCO USE - UNITED
STATES - PREVENTION.**
Smoking. San Diego, CA : Greenhaven Press, c1997.
*TC HV5760 .S663 1997*

**TEENAGERS - UNITED STATES.** *See* EAST
INDIAN AMERICAN TEENAGERS;
HAITIAN AMERICAN TEENAGERS;
HISPANIC AMERICAN TEENAGERS.

**TEENAGERS - UNITED STATES - ATTITUDES.**
Csikszentmihalyi, Mihaly. Becoming adult. New
York : Basic Books, 2000.
*TC HQ796 .C892 2000*

**TEENAGERS - UNITED STATES - BOOKS AND
READING.**
Matulka, Denise I. Picture this. Westport, Conn. :
Greenwood Press, 1997.
*TC Z1033.P52 M37 1997*

**TEENAGERS - UNITED STATES - DIARIES.**
Freedom Writers. The Freedom Writers diary. 1st ed.
New York : Doubleday, c1999.
*TC HQ796 .F76355 1999*

**TEENAGERS - UNITED STATES - FAMILY
RELATIONSHIPS.**
Adolescents and their families. New York : Garland
Pub., 1999.
*TC HQ796 .A33533 1999*

**TEENAGERS - UNITED STATES - HISTORY -
20TH CENTURY.**
Rollin, Lucy. Twentieth-century teen culture by the
decades. Westport, Conn. ; London : Greenwood
Press, 1999.
*TC HQ799.U65 R65 1999*

**TEENAGERS - UNITED STATES - INTERVIEWS.**
Lewis, Sydney, 1952- A totally alien life-form. New
York : New Press : Distributed by W.W. Norton,
c1996.
*TC HQ796 .L3995 1996*

**TEENAGERS - UNITED STATES - LIFE SKILLS
GUIDES - JUVENILE LITERATURE.**
Nash, Renea D. Everything you need to know about
being a biracial/biethnic teen. 1st ed. New York :
Rosen Pub. Group, 1995.
*TC HQ77.9 .N39 1995*

**TEENAGERS - UNITED STATES - SOCIAL
CONDITIONS.**
Adolescents and their families. New York : Garland
Pub., 1999.
*TC HQ796 .A33533 1999*

Lewis, Sydney, 1952- A totally alien life-form. New
York : New Press : Distributed by W.W. Norton,
c1996.
*TC HQ796 .L3995 1996*

**TEENAGERS - UNITED STATES - SOCIAL LIFE
AND CUSTOMS.**
Rollin, Lucy. Twentieth-century teen culture by the
decades. Westport, Conn. ; London : Greenwood
Press, 1999.
*TC HQ799.U65 R65 1999*

**TEENAGERS - VOCATIONAL GUIDANCE -
UNITED STATES.**
Csikszentmihalyi, Mihaly. Becoming adult. New
York : Basic Books, 2000.
*TC HQ796 .C892 2000*

**TEENS.** *See* TEENAGERS.

**TEETH - FICTION.**
Collington, Peter. The tooth fairy. 1st U.S. ed. New
York : Knopf ; Distributed by Random House, 1995.
*TC PZ7.C686 To 1995*

**TEGUA INDIANS.** *See* TEWA INDIANS.

**Tehranian, Majid.** Global communication and world
politics : domination, development, and discourse /
Majid Tehranian. Boulder, Colo. : Lynne Rienner
Publishers, 1999. xii, 212 p. ; 24 cm. Includes
bibliographical references (p. 193-204) and index. ISBN
1-55587-373-1 (alk. paper) ISBN 1-55587-708-7 (pbk. : alk.
paper) DDC 302.2
*1. Communication - Political aspects. 2. Communication,
International. 3. World politics - 1989- I. Title.*
*TC P95.8 .T44 1999*

**TEHUA INDIANS.** *See* TEWA INDIANS.

**Teichler, Ulrich.**
Higher education research. 1st ed. Oxford : [New
York] : Pergamon, published for the IAU Press, 2000.
*TC LB2326.3 .H548 2000*

**Tejeda, Carlos, 1968-.**
Charting terrains of Chicana(o)/Latina(o) education.
Cresskill, N.J. : Hampton Press, c2000.
*TC LC2669 .C42 2000*

**Tekiner, Deniz.** Modern art and the Romantic vision /
Deniz Tekiner. Lanham, Md. : University Press of
America, c2000. ix, 119 p. ; 24 cm. Includes bibliographical
references (p. [107]-114) and index. ISBN 0-7618-1528-7
(cloth : alk. paper) ISBN 0-7618-1529-5 (pbk. : alk. paper)
DDC 709/.04
*1. Romanticism in art. 2. Art, Modern - 19th century. 3. Art,
Modern - 20th century. 4. Art and society - History - 19th
century. 5. Art and society - History - 20th century. I. Title.*
*TC N6465.R6 T43 2000*

**TELECOMMUNICATION.** *See also* COMPUTER
NETWORKS; TELEMATICS; TELEVISION.
The emerging world of wireless communications.
Nashville, TN : Institute for Information Studies,
1996.

*TC TK5103.2 .E44 1996*

**TELECOMMUNICATION - HISTORY.**
Hugill, Peter J. Global communications since 1844.
Baltimore, Md. : Johns Hopkins University Press,
c1999.
*TC TK5102.2 .H84 1999*

Mattelart, Armand. [Mondialisation de la
communication. English] Networking the world,
1794-2000. Minneapolis, MN ; London : University of
Minnesota Press, c2000.
*TC HE7631 .M37513 2000*

**TELECOMMUNICATION IN EDUCATION.** *See
also* DISTANCE EDUCATION.
Cook, Deirdre, 1943- Interactive children,
communicative teaching. Buckingham [England] ;
Philadelphia : Open University Press, 1999.
*TC LB1028.46 .C686 1999*

International perspectives on tele-education and
virtual learning environments. Aldershot : Ashgate,
2000.
*TC LB1044.87 .I55 2000*

Telematics in education. 1st ed. Amsterdam ; New
York ; Oxford : Pergamon, 1999.
*TC LB1044.84 .T48 1999*

Virtual instruction. Englewood, Colo. : Libraries
Unlimited, 1999.
*TC LC5803.C65 V57 1999*

**TELECOMMUNICATION IN HIGHER
EDUCATION - CONGRESSES.**
IFIP TC3 WG3.2/3.6 International Working
Conference on Building University Electronic
Educational Environments (1999 : Irvine, Calif.)
Building university electronic educational
environments. Boston : Kluwer Academic Publishers,
c2000.
*TC LC5803.C65 .I352 2000*

IFIP TC3/WG3.3 & WG3.6 Joint Working
Conference on the Virtual Campus: Trends for Higher
Education and Training (1997 : Madrid, Spain) The
virtual campus. 1st ed. London ; New York :
Chapman & Hall on behalf of the International
Federation for Information Processing (IFIP), 1998.
*TC LC5803.C65 I353 1997*

**TELECOMMUNICATION INDUSTRY.** *See*
TELECOMMUNICATION.

**TELECOMMUNICATION - LAW AND
LEGISLATION.** *See* FREEDOM OF
INFORMATION.

**TELECOMMUNICATION - SOCIAL ASPECTS.**
Clough, Patricia Ticineto, 1945- Autoaffection.
Minneapolis : University of Minnesota Press, c2000.
*TC HM846 .C56 2000*

Mitchell, William J. (William John), 1944- E-topia.
Cambridge, Mass. : MIT Press, 1999.
*TC HE7631 .M58 1999*

**TELECOMMUNICATION - SOCIAL ASPECTS -
UNITED STATES.**
Cities in the telecommunications age. New York :
Routledge, 2000.
*TC HT167 .C483 2000*

**TELECOMMUNICATION SYSTEMS.** *See also*
DATA TRANSMISSION SYSTEMS.
Pelton, Joseph N. e-Sphere. Westport, Conn. ;
London : Quorum Books, 2000.
*TC P96.I5 P33 2000*

**TELECOMMUNICATION - TECHNOLOGICAL
INNOVATIONS.**
Osso, Rafael. Handbook of emerging communications
technologies. Boca Raton, Fla. : CRC Press, 2000.
*TC TK5105 .O62 2000*

**TELECOMMUNICATION - UNITED STATES -
FORECASTING.**
Owen, Bruce M. The Internet challenge to television.
Cambridge, Mass. : Harvard University Press, 1999.
*TC HE8700.8 .O826 1999*

**TELECOMMUNICATIONS.** *See*
TELECOMMUNICATION.

**TELECOMMUNNICATION - HISTORY.**
History of the Internet. Santa Barbara, Calif. : ABC-
CLIO, c1999.
*TC TK5105.875.I57 H58 1999*

**TELECOMMUTING.** *See*
TELECOMMUNICATION.

**Telelearning via the Internet.**
Kouki, Rafa. Hershey, PA : Idea Group Pub., c1999.

*TC LC5800 .K68 1999*

**TELEMATICS.** *See also* **COMPUTER-ASSISTED INSTRUCTION; CYBERSPACE; INFORMATION TECHNOLOGY.**
Telematics in education. 1st ed. Amsterdam ; New York ; Oxford : Pergamon, 1999.
*TC LB1044.84 .T48 1999*

**Telematics in education** : trends and issues / edited by Michelle Selinger and John Pearson. 1st ed. Amsterdam ; New York ; Oxford : Pergamon, 1999. xviii, 196 p. : ill. ; 23 cm. Includes bibliographical references and indexes. ISBN 0-08-042788-X DDC 371.3/58
*1. Telecommunication in education. 2. Telematics. I. Selinger, Michelle, 1950- II. Pearson, John.*
*TC LB1044.84 .T48 1999*

**TELEMATICS - SOCIAL ASPECTS.**
Jordan, Tim, 1959- Cyberpower. London ; New York : Routledge, 1999.
*TC ZA4375 .J67 1999*

**TELEOLOGY.** *See* **CREATION; EVOLUTION.**

**TELEPROCESSING MONITORS (COMPUTER PROGRAMS).** *See* **ONLINE DATA PROCESSING.**

**TELEPROCESSING NETWORKS.** *See* **COMPUTER NETWORKS.**

**Telerobotics and telepistemology in the age of the internet.**
The Robot in the garden. Cambridge, Mass. : MIT Press, 2000.
*TC TJ211 .R537 2000*

**TELEVISION.** *See also* **DANCE IN MOTION PICTURES, TELEVISION, ETC.; DIGITAL TELEVISION; INTERACTIVE TELEVISION.**
Comstock, George A. San Diego : Academic Press, c1999.
*TC PN1992.6 .C645 1999*

**TELEVISION ADVERTISING.**
The filming of a television commercial [videorecording]. Minneapolis, Minn. : Media Loft, c1992.
*TC HF6146.T42 F5 1992*

**TELEVISION ADVERTISING AND CHILDREN - UNITED STATES.**
Advertising to children. Thousand Oaks, Calif. : Sage Publications, c1999.
*TC HQ784.T4 A29 1999*

**TELEVISION ADVERTISING DIRECTORS - UNITED STATES.**
The filming of a television commercial [videorecording]. Minneapolis, Minn. : Media Loft, c1992.
*TC HF6146.T42 F5 1992*

**TELEVISION AND CHILDREN.**
Buckingham, David, 1954- The making of citizens. London ; New York : Routledge, 2000.
*TC HQ784.T4 .B847 2000*

**TELEVISION AND CHILDREN - UNITED STATES.**
Calvert, Sandra L. Children's journeys through the information age. 1st ed. Boston : McGraw-Hill College, c1999.
*TC HQ784.T4 C24 1999*

**Television and common knowledge** / edited by Jostein Gripsrud. New York : Routledge, 1999. x, 209 p. : ill. ; 24 cm. Includes bibliographical references and index. ISBN 0-415-18928-4 (hardcover : alk. paper) ISBN 0-415-18929-2 (pbk. : alk. paper) DDC 302.23/45
*1. Television - Social aspects. 2. Knowledge, Sociology of. 3. Popular culture - History - 20th century. I. Gripsrud, Jostein, 1952-*
*TC PN1992.6 .T379 1999*

**Television and new media audiences.**
Seiter, Ellen, 1957- Oxford ; New York : Clarendon Press, 1998.
*TC PN1992.3.U5 S35 1998*

**TELEVISION AND THE AGED - UNITED STATES.**
Riggs, Karen E. Mature audiences. New Brunswick, N.J. : Rutgers University Press, c1998.
*TC HQ1064.U5 R546 1998*

**TELEVISION AUDIENCES.** *See* **TELEVISION VIEWERS.**

**TELEVISION AUTHORSHIP.**
Edmonds, Robert. Scriptwriting for the audio-visual media. New York : Teachers College Press, c1978.
*TC PN1991.7 .E3*

**TELEVISION - BROADCASTING.** *See* **TELEVISION BROADCASTING.**

**TELEVISION BROADCASTING.** *See* **TELEVISION PROGRAMS.**

**TELEVISION BROADCASTING - INFLUENCE.**
Comstock, George A. Television. San Diego : Academic Press, c1999.
*TC PN1992.6 .C645 1999*

**TELEVISION BROADCASTING OF NEWS.**
Buckingham, David, 1954- The making of citizens. London ; New York : Routledge, 2000.
*TC HQ784.T4 .B847 2000*

**TELEVISION BROADCASTING - PERIODICALS.**
Journal of broadcasting. Phila., Pa.[etc.] Association for Professional Broadcasting Education.

**TELEVISION BROADCASTING - SOCIAL ASPECTS.**
Comstock, George A. Television. San Diego : Academic Press, c1999.
*TC PN1992.6 .C645 1999*

Shanahan, James. Television and its viewers. Cambridge ; New York : Cambridge University Press, 1999.
*TC PN1992.6 .S417 1999*

**TELEVISION BROADCASTING - UNITED STATES - FORECASTING.**
Owen, Bruce M. The Internet challenge to television. Cambridge, Mass. : Harvard University Press, 1999.
*TC HE8700.8 .O826 1999*

**TELEVISION, BUSINESS.** *See* **INDUSTRIAL TELEVISION.**

**Television Co-operative.**
Photomontage today, Peter Kennard [videorecording]. [London] : Art Council of Great Britain ; Ho-Ho-Kus, N.J. : [distributed by] Anthony Roland Collection of Films on Art, c1982.
*TC TR685 .P45 1982*

**TELEVISION COMMERCIAL FILMS.**
The filming of a television commercial [videorecording]. Minneapolis, Minn. : Media Loft, c1992.
*TC HF6146.T42 F5 1992*

**TELEVISION - DIRECTION.** *See* **TELEVISION - PRODUCTION AND DIRECTION.**

**TELEVISION DIRECTION.** *See* **TELEVISION - PRODUCTION AND DIRECTION.**

**TELEVISION DOCUMENTARIES.** *See* **DOCUMENTARY TELEVISION PROGRAMS.**

**TELEVISION FANS.** *See* **TELEVISION VIEWERS.**

**TELEVISION IN EDUCATION - PERIODICALS.**
Educational & industrial television. [Ridgefield, Conn. : C.S. Tepfer Pub. Co.,     -c1983]

**TELEVISION IN EDUCATION - UNITED STATES.**
Adams, Dennis M. Media and literacy. 2nd ed. Springfield, Ill. : C.C. Thomas, c2000.
*TC LB1043 .A33 2000*

**TELEVISION IN EDUCATION - UNITED STATES - HANDBOOKS, MANUALS, ETC.**
Lawyer-Brook, Dianna, 1949- Shifting focus. Lanham, Md. ; London : Scarecrow Press, 2000.
*TC LB1044.7 .L313 2000*

**TELEVISION IN EDUCATION - UNITED STATES - HISTORY.**
Moody, Kate. The children of Telstar. 1st ed. New York : Center for Understanding Media : Vantage Press, c1999.
*TC LB1044.7 .M616 1999*

**TELEVISION IN INDUSTRY.** *See* **INDUSTRIAL TELEVISION.**

**TELEVISION IN MANAGEMENT.** *See* **INDUSTRIAL TELEVISION.**

**TELEVISION IN SCIENCE EDUCATION.**
Dhingra, Koshi. An ethnographic study of the construction of science on television. 1999.
*TC 06 no. 11101*

**TELEVISION, INDUSTRIAL.** *See* **INDUSTRIAL TELEVISION.**

**TELEVISION - INDUSTRIAL APPLICATIONS.** *See* **INDUSTRIAL TELEVISION.**

**TELEVISION INDUSTRY.** *See* **TELEVISION BROADCASTING.**

**TELEVISION - PERIODICALS.**
Journal of the SMPTE. New York, N.Y. : SMPTE, 1956-1975.

**TELEVISION PRODUCERS AND DIRECTORS.** *See* **TELEVISION ADVERTISING DIRECTORS.**

**TELEVISION PRODUCTION.** *See* **TELEVISION - PRODUCTION AND DIRECTION.**

**TELEVISION - PRODUCTION AND DIRECTION - HISTORY.**
Moody, Kate. The children of Telstar. 1st ed. New York : Center for Understanding Media : Vantage Press, c1999.
*TC LB1044.7 .M616 1999*

**TELEVISION PROGRAMS.** *See also* **TALK SHOWS.**
Dhingra, Koshi. An ethnographic study of the construction of science on television. 1999.
*TC 06 no. 11101*

**TELEVISION PROGRAMS, DOCUMENTARY.** *See* **DOCUMENTARY TELEVISION PROGRAMS.**

**TELEVISION PROGRAMS - UNITED STATES.**
Kunz, Linda Ann. English modals in American talk shows. 1999.
*TC 06 no. 11136*

**TELEVISION SCRIPTS.** *See* **TELEVISION PROGRAMS.**

**TELEVISION SHOWS.** *See* **TELEVISION PROGRAMS.**

**TELEVISION - SOCIAL ASPECTS.**
Television and common knowledge. New York : Routledge, 1999.
*TC PN1992.6 .T379 1999*

**TELEVISION - SOCIAL ASPECTS - GREAT BRITAIN.**
Gauntlett, David. TV Living. London ; New York : Routledge, 1999.
*TC PN1992.55 .G38 1999*

**TELEVISION TALK SHOWS.** *See* **TALK SHOWS.**

**TELEVISION VIEWERS.**
Dhingra, Koshi. An ethnographic study of the construction of science on television. 1999.
*TC 06 no. 11101*

**TELEVISION VIEWERS - GREAT BRITAIN - ATTITUDES.**
Gauntlett, David. TV Living. London ; New York : Routledge, 1999.
*TC PN1992.55 .G38 1999*

**TELEVISION VIEWERS - RESEARCH - UNITED STATES.**
Seiter, Ellen, 1957- Television and new media audiences. Oxford ; New York : Clarendon Press, 1998.
*TC PN1992.3.U5 S35 1998*

**TELEVISION VIEWERS - SOCIAL ASPECTS - UNITED STATES.**
Seiter, Ellen, 1957- Television and new media audiences. Oxford ; New York : Clarendon Press, 1998.
*TC PN1992.3.U5 S35 1998*

**TELEVISION VIEWERS - UNITED STATES - ATTITUDES.**
Seiter, Ellen, 1957- Television and new media audiences. Oxford ; New York : Clarendon Press, 1998.
*TC PN1992.3.U5 S35 1998*

**TELEVISION WATCHERS.** *See* **TELEVISION VIEWERS.**

**Telling a different story.**
Wilson, Catherine S. New York ; London : Teachers College Press, c2000.
*TC LC5131 .W49 2000*

**Telling is risky business.**
Wahl, Otto F. New Brunswick, N.J. ; London : Rutgers University Press, c1999.
*TC RC454.4 .W327 1999*

**TELLING OF STORIES.** *See* **STORYTELLING.**

**Telling pieces.**
Albers, Peggy. Mahwah, N.J. : L. Erlbaum Associates, 2000.
*TC N362.5 .A43 2000*

**Tellings, Agnes.**
Moral sensibilities and education. Bemmel : Concorde Pub. House, 1999-
*TC BF723.M54 M684 1999*

**Tellings, Agnes. 1954- .**
The university and the knowledge society. Bemmel [Netherlands] : Concorde Publishing House, 1998.
*TC LB2322.2 .U55 1998*

**TEMPER.  *See* ANGER.**

**TEMPERAMENT.  *See also* PERSONALITY; TYPOLOGY (PSYCHOLOGY).**
Shapiro, David, 1926- Dynamics of character. New York : Basic Books, c2000.
*TC RC455.5.T45 .S46 2000*

**Temperament and personality development across the life span** / edited by Victoria J. Molfese, Dennis L. Molfese. Mahwah, NJ : L. Erlbaum Associates, 2000. ix, 301 p. : ill. ; 24 cm. Papers presented at a meeting in 1997. Includes bibliographical references and index. ISBN 0-8058-3338-2 (alk. paper) DDC 155.2/5
*1. Temperament - Congresses. 2. Personality - Congresses. I. Molfese, Dennis L.*
*TC BF798 .T46 2000*

**TEMPERAMENT - CONGRESSES.**
Temperament and personality development across the life span. Mahwah, NJ : L. Erlbaum Associates, 2000.
*TC BF798 .T46 2000*

**TEMPERAMENT IN CHILDREN.**
Flynn, Bernadette Marie. The teacher-child relationship, temperament, and coping in children with developmental disabilities. 2000.
*TC 06 no. 11267*

**TEMPERANCE.  *See* ALCOHOL - PHYSIOLOGICAL EFFECT; ALCOHOLISM; DRINKING OF ALCOHOLIC BEVERAGES; NARCOTIC HABIT.**

**Temple, Charles A., 1947-.**
Gillet, Jean Wallace. Understanding reading problems. 5th ed. New York ; Harlow, England : Longman, c2000.
*TC LB1050.46 .G55 2000*

**Temple, Christine.** Developmental cognitive neuropsychology / Christine M. Temple. Hove, East Sussex, UK : Psychology Press, c1997. viii, 398 p. : ill. ; 24 cm. (Brain damage, behaviour and cognition series) Includes bibliographical references (p. 331-378) and indexes. ISBN 0-86377-400-8 ISBN 0-86377-401-6 (pbk.) DDC 616.85/889
*1. Cognition disorders. 2. Cognitive neuroscience. I. Title. II. Series: Brain damage, behaviour and cognition.*
*TC RC553.C64 T46 1997*

**Temple University.**
Symposium on Issues in Human Development (1967 : Philadelphia) Issues in human development ; Washington, For sale by the Supt. of Docs., U. S. Govt. Print. Off. [1970?]
*TC RJ131.A1 S93 1967*

**TEMPORAL LOBE EPILEPSY - DIAGNOSIS.**
Organic disorders [videorecording]. Princeton, N.J. : Films for the Humanities & Sciences, 1998.
*TC RC521 .O7 1998*

**TEMPORAL LOBE EPILEPSY - PATIENTS.**
Organic disorders [videorecording]. Princeton, N.J. : Films for the Humanities & Sciences, 1998.
*TC RC521 .O7 1998*

**Ten best teaching practices.**
Tileston, Donna Walker. Thousand Oaks, Calif. : Corwin Press, c2000.
*TC LB1775.2 .T54 2000*

**TENSION (PHYSIOLOGY).  *See* STRESS (PHYSIOLOGY).**

**TENSION (PSYCHOLOGY).  *See* STRESS (PSYCHOLOGY).**

**Tensions of teaching.**
Newman, Judith, 1943- New York ; London : Teachers College Press, c1998.
*TC LB1025.3 .N49 1998*

**The tented field.**
Melville, Tom. Bowling Green, OH : Bowling Green State University Popular Press, c1998.
*TC GV928.U6 M45 1998*

**TENTS - AFRICA, NORTHEAST.**
Prussin, Labelle. African nomadic architecture. Washington : Smithsonian Institution Press : National Museum of African Art, c1995.
*TC NA7461.A1 P78 1995*

**TENURE OF COLLEGE TEACHERS.  *See* COLLEGE TEACHERS - TENURE.**

**Tenured radicals.**
Kimball, Roger, 1953- Rev. ed., with a new introd. by the author. 1st Elephant pbk. ed. Chicago : Elephant Paperbacks, 1998.
*TC LC1023 .K56 1998*

**Teppo, Anne R.**
Reflecting on practice in elementary school mathematics. Reston, Va. : National Council of Teachers of Mathematics, c1999.
*TC QA135.5 .R426 1999*

**Ter Wal, Jessika.**
Comparative perspectives on racism. Aldershot, Hants, UK : Burlington, VT, USA : Ashgate, c2000.
*TC GN269 .C646 2000*

**Terc, Michael.**
Ricken, Robert. The high school principal's calendar. Thousand Oaks, Calif. : Corwin Press, c2000.
*TC LB3032 .R53 2000*

**TERM PAPER WRITING.  *See* REPORT WRITING.**

**TERMINAL CARE.  *See* DEATH.**

**TERMINAL CARE - IN INFANCY & CHILDHOOD.**
Judd, Dorothy. Give sorrow words. 2nd ed. New York : Haworth Press, 1995.
*TC RJ249 .J83 1995*

**TERMINAL CARE - PSYCHOLOGY.**
Judd, Dorothy. Give sorrow words. 2nd ed. New York : Haworth Press, 1995.
*TC RJ249 .J83 1995*

**TERMINAL CARE - RELIGIOUS ASPECTS.**
Death. Amsterdam : VU University Press, 1998.
*TC R726.8 .D42 1998*

**TERMINALLY ILL.  *See* DEATH.**

**TERMINALLY ILL - CARE AND TREATMENT.  *See* TERMINAL CARE.**

**TERMINALLY ILL CHILDREN.  *See also* CHILDREN - DEATH.**
Judd, Dorothy. Give sorrow words. 2nd ed. New York : Haworth Press, 1995.
*TC RJ249 .J83 1995*

**TERMINALLY ILL - HOME CARE.**
Sankar, Andrea. Dying at home. Rev. and updated ed. Baltimore, Md.: Johns Hopkins University Press, 1999.
*TC R726.8 .S26 1999*

**TERMINALLY ILL - MEDICAL CARE.  *See also* TERMINAL CARE.**
Death. Amsterdam : VU University Press, 1998.
*TC R726.8 .D42 1998*

**TERMINALLY ILL PARENTS.  *See* PARENTS - DEATH.**

**TERMINALLY ILL - UNITED STATES - PSYCHOLOGY.**
Lederer, Jane. Participation in active euthanasia and assisted suicide and attitudes and interpersonal values of physicians and nurses. 1996.
*TC 06 no. 10849*

**TERMINOLOGY.  *See* TERMS AND PHRASES.**

**TERMITES - ENVIRONMENTAL ASPECTS.**
The climate puzzle [videorecording]. [New York, N.Y.?] : Unapix Entertainment, Inc. [distributor], c1996.
*TC QB631.2 .C5 1996*

**TERMITOMYCES.  *See* TERMITES.**

**TERMS AND PHRASES - DATA PROCESSING.**
Pearson, Jennifer. Terms in context. Amsterdam ; Philadelphia : J. Benjamins, c1998.
*TC P305.18.D38 P4 1998*

**Terms in context.**
Pearson, Jennifer. Amsterdam ; Philadelphia : J. Benjamins, c1998.
*TC P305.18.D38 P4 1998*

**Terra Nova Films.**
Depression in older adults [videorecording]. Boston, MA : Fanlight Productions ; [Chicago, Ill.] : Distributed by Terra Nova Films, Inc., 1997.
*TC RC537.5 .D4 1997*

**TERRESTRIAL GLOBES.  *See* GLOBES.**

**Terrible transformation [videorecording].**
Africans in America [videorecording]. [Boston, Mass.] : WGBH Educational Foundation : South

Burlington, VT : WGBH Boston Video [distributor], c1998.
*TC E441 .A47 1998*

**Terrific connections.**
Buzzeo, Toni. Terrific connections with authors, illustrators, and storytellers. Englewood, Colo. : Libraries Unlimited, 1999.
*TC LB1575.5.U5 B87 1999*

**Terrific connections with authors, illustrators, and storytellers.**
Buzzeo, Toni. Englewood, Colo. : Libraries Unlimited, 1999.
*TC LB1575.5.U5 B87 1999*

**TERRITORIAL BEHAVIOR.  *See* HUMAN TERRITORIALITY.**

**TERRITORIALITY, HUMAN.  *See* HUMAN TERRITORIALITY.**

**Terry, Deborah J.**
Attitudes, behavior, and social context. Mahwah, N.J. : L. Erlbaum Associates, 2000.
*TC HM132 .B48 1998*

**Terry, Michael Bad Hand.** Daily life in a Plains Indian village, 1868 / Michael Bad Hand Terry. 1st American ed. New York : Clarion Books, c1999. 48 p. : ill. (some col.), col. maps ; 28 cm. Includes index. SUMMARY: Depicts the historical background, social organization, and daily life of a Plains Indian village in 1868, presenting interiors, landscapes, clothing, and everyday objects. ISBN 0-395-94542-9 (hardcover) DDC 978/.00497
*1. Indians of North America - Great Plains - History - Juvenile literature. 2. Indians of North America - Material culture - Great Plains - Juvenile literature. 3. Indians of North America - Great Plains - Social life and customs - Juvenile literature. 4. Indians of North America - Great Plains. 1. Title.*
*TC E78.G73 T47 1999*

**Terry, Robert M. (Robert Meredith).**
Foreign language standards. Lincolnwood, Ill., U.S.A. : National Textbook Company in conjunction with the American Council on the Teaching of Foreign Languages, c1999.
*TC P53 .F674 1999*

**Tesar, Bruce.** Learnability in optimality theory / Bruce Tesar and Paul Smolensky. Cambridge, Mass. : MIT Press, c2000. vi, 140 p. : ill. ; 24 cm. Includes bibliographical references (p. [133]-138) and index. ISBN 0-262-20126-7 DDC 401/.93
*1. Optimality theory (Linguistics) 2. Language acquisition. 3. Learning ability. I. Smolensky, Paul, 1955- II. Title.*
*TC P158.42 .T47 2000*

**Teske, Paul Eric.**
Schneider, Mark, 1946- Choosing schools. Princeton, N.J. : Oxford : Princeton University Press, c2000.
*TC LB1027.9 .S32 2000*

**TESL.  *See* ENGLISH LANGUAGE - STUDY AND TEACHING - FOREIGN SPEAKERS; ENGLISH LANGUAGE - TEXTBOOKS FOR FOREIGN SPEAKERS.**

**Tesser, Abraham.**
Psychological perspectives on self and identity. 1st ed. Washington, DC : American Psychological Association, c2000.
*TC BF697 .P765 2000*

**Tessier, Annette.**
Cook, Ruth E. Adapting early childhood curricula for children in inclusive settings. 5th ed. Englewood Cliffs, N.J. : Merrill, c2000.
*TC LC4019.2 .C66 2000*

**Tessler, Richard C.** Family experiences with mental illness / Richard Tessler and Gail Gamache. Westport, Conn. ; London : Auburn House, 2000. xviii, 187 p. : ill. ; 25 cm. Includes bibliographical references (p. [173]-183) and index. ISBN 0-86569-251-3 (hbk. : alk. paper) ISBN 0-86569-252-1 (pbk. : alk. paper) DDC 362.2/0422
*1. Mentally ill - Family relationships. 2. Mental illness. I. Gamache, Gail, 1938- II. Title.*
*TC RC455.4.F3 T46 2000*

**Tessmer, Martin.**
Jonassen, David H., 1947- Task analysis methods for instructional design. Mahwah, N.J. : L. Erlbaum Associates, 1999.
*TC LB1028.38 .J65 1999*

**TEST BIAS - UNITED STATES.**
Measuring up. Boston : Kluwer Academic Publishers, c1999.
*TC LB3051 .M4627 1999*

**Test interpretation.**
Christiansen, Harley Duane. Basic background for test

interpretation. 1st ed. Tucson, Ariz. : P. Juul Press, c1981.
*TC BF176 .C472*

**TEST OF ENGLISH AS A FOREIGN LANGUAGE - STUDY AND TEACHING - TAIWAN.**
Tian, Shiau-ping. TOEFL reading comprehension. 2000.
*TC 06 no. 11316*

**TEST RESULTS.** *See* **EXAMINATIONS - VALIDITY.**

**Test success.**
Nugent, Patricia Mary, 1944- 3rd ed. Philadelphia : F.A. Davis, c2000.
*TC RT55 .N77 2000*

**TEST-TAKING SKILLS.**
Tian, Shiau-ping. TOEFL reading comprehension. 2000.
*TC 06 no. 11316*

**TEST TAKING SKILLS.**
Tian, Shiau-ping. TOEFL reading comprehension. 2000.
*TC 06 no. 11316*

**TEST-TAKING SKILLS - UNITED STATES.**
Taylor, Kathe. Children at the center. Portsmouth, NH : Heinemann, c1998.
*TC LB3060.57 .T39 1998*

**TEST-TAKING STRATEGIES.** *See* **TEST-TAKING SKILLS.**

**Test-taking techniques for beginning nursing students.**
Nugent, Patricia Mary, 1944- Test success. 3rd ed. Philadelphia : F.A. Davis, c2000.
*TC RT55 .N77 2000*

**Test theory.**
McDonald, Roderick P. Mahwah, N.J. ; London : L. Erlbaum Associates, 1999.
*TC BF39 .M175 1999*

**TEST VALIDITY.** *See* **EXAMINATIONS - VALIDITY.**

**TEST WISENESS.** *See* **TEST-TAKING SKILLS.**

**TESTING.** *See* **PSYCHOLOGICAL TESTS.**

**Testing and assessment in counseling practice** / edited by C. Edward Watkins, Jr., Vicki L. Campbell. 2nd ed. Mahwah, N.J. : L. Erlbaum Associates, 2000. xvi, 575 p. : ill. ; 24 cm. (Vocational psychology) Includes bibliographical references and indexes. ISBN 0-8058-2380-8 (alk. paper) ISBN 0-8058-2381-6 (pbk. : alk. paper) DDC 150/.28/7
*1. Psychological tests. 2. Personality tests. 3. Vocational interests - Testing. 4. Counseling. I. Watkins, C. Edward. II. Campbell, Vicki Lynn. III. Series.*
*TC BF176 .T423 2000*

**Testing, friend or foe?.**
Black, P. J. (Paul Joseph), 1930- London ; Washington : Falmer Press, 1998.
*TC LB3056.E54 B53 1998*

**Testing, teaching, and learning** : a guide for states and school districts / Committee on Title I Testing and Assessment, Board on Testing and Assessment, Commission on Behavioral and Social Sciences and Education, National Research Council ; Richard F. Elmore and Robert Rothman, editors. Washington, D.C. : National Academy Press, 2000. xiii, 120 p. ; 28 cm. Includes bibliographical references (p. 102-110) and index. ISBN 0-309-06534-8
*1. Special education - Standards - United States. 2. Compensatory education - Standards - United States. 3. Special education - Government policy - United States. 4. Compensatory education - Government policy - United States. I. Rothman, Robert, 1959- II. Elmore, Richard F. III. National Research Council (U.S.). Committee on Title I Testing and Assessment.*
*TC LC3981 .T4 1999*

**Testing women, testing the fetus.**
Rapp, Rayna. New York : Routledge, 1999.
*TC RG628.3.A48 R37 1999*

**TESTS.** *See* **EXAMINATIONS.**

**Tests and assessment.**
Walsh, W. Bruce, 1936- 4th ed. Upper Saddle River, N.J. : Prentice Hall, c2001.
*TC BF176 .W335 2001*

**Tests and measurements in child development.**
Johnson, Orval G., 1917- [1st ed.]. San Francisco, Jossey-Bass, 1971.
*TC BF722 .J64*

**TESTS AND MEASUREMENTS IN EDUCATION.** *See* **EDUCATIONAL TESTS AND MEASUREMENTS.**

**TESTS, PSYCHOLOGICAL.** *See* **PSYCHOLOGICAL TESTS.**

**TETON INDIANS.**
Left Hand Bull, Jacqueline. Lakota hoop dancer. 1st ed. New York : Dutton Children's Books, c1999.
*TC E99.T34 L43 1999*

**TETON INDIANS - JUVENILE LITERATURE.**
Left Hand Bull, Jacqueline. Lakota hoop dancer. 1st ed. New York : Dutton Children's Books, c1999.
*TC E99.T34 L43 1999*

**Tew, Marilyn.**
Mosley, Jenny. Quality circle time in the secondary school :. London : David Fulton, 1999.
*TC LB1032 .M67 1999*

**TEWA INDIANS - JUVENILE LITERATURE.**
Hazen-Hammond, Susan. Thunder Bear and Ko. 1st ed. New York : Dutton Children's Books, 1999.
*TC E99.T35 H36 1999*

**Text and corpus analysis.**
Stubbs, Michael, 1947- Oxford, OX, UK ; Cambridge, Mass., USA : Blackwell Publishers, c1996.
*TC P302 .S773 1996*

**TEXT-BOOKS.** *See* **TEXTBOOKS.**

**TEXT-BOOKS - BIBLIOGRAPHY - PERIODICALS.**
CAS. Chicago : Curriculum Advisory Service, 1969-1974.

**TEXT-BOOKS - BIBLIOGRPAHY.**
El-Hi textbooks in print. New York, N.Y. : Bowker, 1970-
*TC Z5813 .A51*

**TEXT GRAMMAR.** *See* **DISCOURSE ANALYSIS.**

**Text in education and society** / edited by Desmond Allison ... [et al.]. Singapore : Singapore University Press ; Singapore ; River Edge, N.J. : World Scientific, c1998. xiv, 273 p. ; 26 cm. "Selected papers from an international conference on Language and knowledge: the unpacking of text, which was hosted in September 1996 by the Department of English Language and Literature at the National University of Singapore"--P. [ix]. Includes bibliographical references. ISBN 9971-69-222-8
*1. sa99 10 2. Language and education. 3. Sociolinguistics. I. Allison, Desmond.*
*TC P40.8 .T48 1998*

**TEXTBOOKS.** *See* **READERS.**

**TEXTBOOKS - AUTHORSHIP.**
Naumes, William. The art & craft of case writing. Thousand Oaks, Calif. : Sage Publications, c1999.
*TC LB1029.C37 N38 1999*

**TEXTBOOKS - CENSORSHIP - UNITED STATES.**
Brinkley, Ellen Henson, 1944- Caught off guard. Boston : Allyn and Bacon, c1999.
*TC LC72.2 .B75 1999*

**Textbooks in print.**
El-Hi textbooks in print. New York, N.Y. : Bowker, 1970-
*TC Z5813 .A51*

**TEXTBOOKS - KOREA - HISTORY.**
Lee, Yoonmi. Modern education, textbooks and the image of the nation. New York ; London : Garland Pub., 2000.
*TC LB3048.K6 L44 2000*

**TEXTBOOKS - SOCIAL ASPECTS - KOREA.**
Lee, Yoonmi. Modern education, textbooks and the image of the nation. New York ; London : Garland Pub., 2000.
*TC LB3048.K6 L44 2000*

**TEXTBOOKS - UNITED STATES.**
Johnson, Clifton, 1865-1940. Old-time schools and school-books. Detroit : Omnigraphics, 1999.
*TC LA206 .J6 1999*

**TEXTILE FABRICS.** *See* **INDIAN TEXTILE FABRICS; RIBBONS; RUGS.**

**TEXTILE FABRICS - AFRICA, NORTH.**
Spring, Christopher. North African textiles. Washington, D.C. : Smithsonian Institution Press, c1995.
*TC NK8887.6 .S68 1995*

**TEXTILE FABRICS, INDIAN.** *See* **INDIAN TEXTILE FABRICS.**

**TEXTILE FABRICS, ISLAMIC - AFRICA, NORTH.**
Spring, Christopher. North African textiles. Washington, D.C. : Smithsonian Institution Press, c1995.
*TC NK8887.6 .S68 1995*

**TEXTILE FABRICS, MUSLIM.** *See* **TEXTILE FABRICS, ISLAMIC.**

**TEXTILE FABRICS, NAVAJO.** *See* **NAVAJO TEXTILE FABRICS.**

**TEXTILE FABRICS - SOCIAL ASPECTS.**
Cloth and human experience. Washington : Smithsonian Institution Press, c1989.
*TC GT525 .C57 1989*

**TEXTILE FABRICS - SOUTHWEST, NEW.** *See* **NAVAJO TEXTILE FABRICS.**

**TEXTILE FABRICS - STUDY AND TEACHING (SECONDARY) - CANADA, WESTERN.**
Peterat, Linda, 1946- Making textile studies matter. Vancouver : Pacific Educational Press, 1999.
*TC TX340 .P47 1999*

**TEXTILE FIBERS.** *See* **TEXTILE FABRICS.**

**TEXTILE INDUSTRY.** *See* **WEAVING.**

**TEXTILE INDUSTRY AND FABRICS.** *See* **TEXTILE FABRICS; TEXTILE INDUSTRY.**

**TEXTILE INDUSTRY - EMPLOYEES.** *See* **TEXTILE WORKERS.**

**TEXTILE INDUSTRY - UNITED STATES.**
Employee training and U.S. competitiveness. Boulder : Westview Press, 1991.
*TC HF5549.5.T7 E46 1991*

**TEXTILE MACHINERY - UNITED STATES - HISTORY - PICTORIAL WORKS.**
Mills [picture]. Amawalk, NY : Jackdaw Publications, c1999.
*TC TR820.5 .M5 1999*

**TEXTILE WORKERS - UNITED STATES - HISTORY - PICTORIAL WORKS.**
Mills [picture]. Amawalk, NY : Jackdaw Publications, c1999.
*TC TR820.5 .M5 1999*

**TEXTILES.** *See* **TEXTILE FABRICS.**

**Texts and contexts (Unnumbered)**
Fullilove, Mindy Thompson. The house of Joshua. Lincoln, NE : University of Nebraska Press, c1999.
*TC BF353 .F85 1999*

**THALARCTOS MARITIMUS.** *See* **POLAR BEAR.**

**THALASSARCTOS MARITIMUS.** *See* **POLAR BEAR.**

**THANATOLOGY.** *See* **DEATH.**

**THANKSGIVING DAY - FICTION.**
Rosen, Michael, 1946- A Thanksgiving wish. New York : Blue Sky Press, c1999.
*TC PZ7.R71867 Tf 1999*

**A Thanksgiving wish.**
Rosen, Michael, 1946- New York : Blue Sky Press, c1999.
*TC PZ7.R71867 Tf 1999*

**Tharp, Roland G., 1930-.**
Teaching transformed. Boulder, Colo. ; Oxford : Westview Press, 2000.
*TC LB2822.82 .T44 2000*

**That can't be right!.**
Maylone, Nelson John. Lancaster, PA : Technomic Pub. Co., c1999.
*TC QA43 .M367 1999*

**That's funny, you don't look like a teacher!.**
Weber, Sandra. London ; Washington, D.C. : Falmer Press, 1995.
*TC LB1775.4.G7 W43 1995*

**That's what friends are for** : teacher's planning guide. New York : Macmillan/McGraw-Hill, c1997. 1 v. (various pagings) : col. ill. ; 31 cm. (Spotlight on literacy ; Gr.4 l.10 u.3) (The road to independent reading) Includes index. ISBN 0-02-181174-1
*1. Language arts (Elementary) 2. Reading (Elementary) I. Series. II. Series: The road to independent reading*
*TC LB1576 .S66 1997 Gr.4 l.10 u.3*

**Thayer-Bacon, Barbara J., 1953-** Transforming critical thinking : thinking constructively / Barbara J. Thayer-Bacon ; foreword by Jane Roland Martin. New York : Teachers College Press, c2000. xvi, 199 p. ; 24 cm. Includes bibliographical references (p. 179-189) and index. ISBN 0-8077-3924-3 (paper) ISBN 0-8077-3925-1

(cloth) DDC 160/.82
*1. Critical thinking. 2. Feminist theory. I. Title.*
**TC BC177 .T45 2000**

**Thayer, Vivian Trow, 1886-** Reorganizing secondary education; prepared by V. T. Thayer, Caroline B. Zachry [and] Ruth Kotinsky for the Commission on secondary school curriculum. New York, Appleton-Century [c1939] 483 p. Includes bibliographies.
*1. Education, Secondary. 2. Education - Aims and objectives. 3. Adolescence. I. Zachry, Caroline Beaumont. 1894- joint author. II. Kotinsky, Ruth. 1903- joint author. III. American education fellowship. Commission on the Secondary school curriculum. IV. Title.*
**TC LB1607 .T5**

**The Carnegie series in American education**
Cohen, Joseph W., ed. The superior student in American higher education. New York : McGraw-Hill, [c1966]
**TC 371.95C66**

**The comparative understanding of intergroup relations.**
Kinloch, Graham Charles. The comparative understanding of intergroup realtions [i.e. relations]. Boulder, CO : Westview Press, 1999.
**TC HM131 .K495 1999**

**The family as a unit of study and treatment.**
Stein, Joan W [Seattle] Regional Rehabilitation Research Institute, University of Washington, School of Social Work [1970]
**TC RC488.5 .S88**

**The International Council of Nurses.**
The Inc. [Los Angeles, CA : Inc. Publishing,

**The John D. and Catherine T. MacArthur Foundation series on mental health and development. Studies on successful adolescent development**
Elder, Glen H. Children of the land. Chicago : University of Chicago Press, 2000.
**TC HQ796 .E525 2000**

**The LEA series in personality and clinical psychology**
Handbook of cross-cultural and multicultural personality assessment. Mahwah, N.J. ; London : Lawrence Erlbaum Associates, 2000.
**TC RC473.P79 H36 2000**

**The mothers legacy to her unborn child.**
Jocelin, Elizabeth, 1596-1622. The mothers legacy to her vnborn [i.e. unborn] childe [i.e. child]. Toronto : University of Toronto Press, 2000.
**TC BV4570 .J62 2000**

**The sight and insight of Ernst Haas** [videorecording] : with photographs and commentary by Ernst Haas ; direction and script editing, William Moriarty ; research and interviews, William Moriarity, R. Smith Schuneman ; produced by Media Loft, Inc. Minneapolis, Minn. : Media Loft, 1992. 1 videocassette (49 min.) : sd., col. ; 1/2 in. (Great photographers ; v.2) (Media Loft educational/awareness presentation) Title from opening credits: To dream with open eyes [videorecording]. Title on container and cassette label: Ernst Haas : to dream with open eyes [videorecording]. VHS. Catalogued from credits, container and cassette label. Title only appears in opening credits for part II. Narrated by the late Ernst Haas. Tape editing, Everett LaBuda; closing music, Alexander Haas. "TV-15X-VHS"--Container. For general audiences. SUMMARY: Against a back drop of his photographs, the late Ernst Haas talks about photography in general and his theories in particular. In part I, Haas describes his desire to travel, politically forbidden in his early years, which he later exploited photographically. He discusses his personal approach and philosophy, and how he has trained himself to "see" photographs. He talks about capturing what he calls a "dream-like" state on film-- in essence, an altered, mystical state of awareness. In part II, he describes how the photographer, like the dancer, must "warm up" to prepare for shots and the discipline required in photography. CONTENTS: [Part I.] To dream with open eyes (ca. 28 min.) -- Part II. Expanding photographic vision (ca. 21 min.). ISBN 1-88238-602-7
*1. Haas. Ernst. - 1921- 2. Photography. Artistic. 3. Photography. Artistic - Philosophy. I. Haas. Ernst. 1921- II. Moriarty, William. III. Schuneman. R. Smith. IV. Media Loft (Firm) V. Title: Expanding photgraphic vision [videorecording] VI. Title: To dream with open eyes [videorecording] VII. Title: Ernst Haas : to dream with open eyes [videorecording] VIII. Series. IX. Series: Educational/awareness presentation.*
**TC TR647.H3 S5 1992**

**The Task Force on Higher Education and Society.**
Peril and promise : higher education in developing countries / the Task Force on Higher Education and Society. Washington, DC: World Bank, 2000. 135 p. :

ill. maps ; 29 cm. ISBN 0-8213-4630-X DDC 378/.009172/4
*1. Education. Higher - Developing countries. I. Title.*
**TC LC2610 .I53 2000**

**THEATER.** *See* **ACTING; CHILDREN'S PLAYS.**

**THEATER - COMPUTER NETWORK RESOURCES.**
Theatre in cyberspace. New York : P. Lang, c1999.
**TC PN2075 .T54 1999**

**THEATER - COSTUME.** *See* **COSTUME.**

**THEATER IN EDUCATION.** *See* **DRAMA IN EDUCATION.**

**THEATER - NORTH AMERICA - HISTORY - 19TH CENTURY.**
Theatrical touring and founding in North America. Westport, Conn. : Greenwood Press, 1982.
**TC PN2219.5 .T5 1982**

**THEATER - NORTH AMERICA - HISTORY - 20TH CENTURY.**
Theatrical touring and founding in North America. Westport, Conn. : Greenwood Press, 1982.
**TC PN2219.5 .T5 1982**

**The theater of politics.**
Gorham, Eric B., 1960- Lanham, Md. ; Oxford: Lexington Books, c2000.
**TC LC171 .G56 2000**

**THEATER - PERIODICALS.**
First stage. Lafayette, Ind. : Purdue University, c1961-c1967.

**THEATER - STUDY AND TEACHING.**
Teaching Shakespeare through performance. New York : Modern Language Association of America, 1999.
**TC PR2987 .T366 1999**

**THEATER - STUDY AND TEACHING - INTERACTIVE MULTIMEDIA.**
Theatre in cyberspace. New York : P. Lang, c1999.
**TC PN2075 .T54 1999**

**THEATRE.** *See* **THEATER.**

**Theatre in cyberspace :** issues of teaching, acting and directing / edited by Stephen A. Schrum. New York : P. Lang, c1999. viii, 294 p. ; 23 cm. (Artists and issues in the theatre ; vol. 10) Includes bibliographical references. ISBN 0-8204-4140-6 (alk. paper) DDC 792/.07
*1. Theater - Study and teaching - Interactive multimedia. 2. Acting - Study and teaching - Interactive multimedia. 3. Theater - Computer network resources. 4. Acting - Computer network resources. 5. ATHEMOO. I. Schrum. Stephen Alan. 1957- II. Series.*
**TC PN2075 .T54 1999**

**Theatre journal.**
[Theatre journal (Online)] Theatre journal [computer file]. Baltimore, Md. : Johns Hopkins University Press, c1996-
**TC EJOURNALS**

**[Theatre journal (Online)]** Theatre journal [computer file]. Baltimore, Md. : Johns Hopkins University Press, c1996- Frequency: Quarterly. 48.1 (spring 1996)- . Title from title screen. Access restricted to institutions with a site license for to the Project Muse collection. HTML encoded text and graphic files (electronic journal). Also available in a print ed. Mode of access: Internet via the World Wide Web. System requirements: World Wide Web browser software. Issued on behalf of: Association for Theatre in Higher Education (U.S.); digitized and made available by: Project Muse. URL: http://muse.jhu.edu/journals/theatre%5Fjournal/ Available in other form: Theatre journal ISSN: 0192-2882 (DLC)    79643622 (OCoLC)4799124. ISSN 1086-332X DDC 792
*1. Drama - Periodicals. I. Association for Theatre in Higher Education (U.S.) II. Project Muse. III. Title: Theatre journal*
**TC EJOURNALS**

**THEATRICAL COSTUME.** *See* **COSTUME.**

**Theatrical touring and founding in North America /** edited by L.W. Conolly ; foreword by Michael Sidnell. Westport, Conn. : Greenwood Press, 1982. xiv, 245 p. : ill. ; 24 cm. (Contributions in drama and theatre studies, 0163-3821 ; no. 5) Bibliography: p. [213]-222. Includes index. ISBN 0-313-22595-8 (lib. bdg.) DDC 792/.097
*1. Theater - North America - History - 19th century. 2. Theater - North America - History - 20th century. I. Conolly. L. W. (Leonard W.) II. Series.*
**TC PN2219.5 .T5 1982**

**Their day in the sun.**
Howes, Ruth (Ruth Hege) Philadelphia, PA : Temple University Press, 1999.
**TC QC773.3.U5 H68 1999**

**THEISM.** *See* **ATHEISM; GOD.**

**Thelen, David P. (David Paul).**
Rosenzweig, Roy. The presence of the past. New York : Columbia University Press, c1998.
**TC E179.5 .R67 1998**

**THEMATIC APPERCEPTION TEST.**
Evocative images. 1st ed. Washington, DC : American Psychological Association, c1999.
**TC BF698.8.T5 E96 1999**

Gutin, Nina J. Differential object representations in inpatients with narcissistic and borderline personality disorders and normal controls. 1997.
**TC 085 G975**

**Themes and issues in faculty development :** case studies of innovative practice in teacher education / edited by Victor M. Rentel, Allan Dittmer. Lanham, MD : University Press of America, 1999. xii, 221 p. ; 23 cm. Includes bibliographical references (p.197-213) and index. ISBN 0-7618-1513-9 ISBN 0-7618-1514-7 (pbk.) DDC 378.1/25
*1. College teachers - In-service training - United States - Case studies. I. Rentel, Victor M. II. Dittmer, Allan.*
**TC LB1738 .T54 1999**

**Themes of urban and inner city education**
Charting terrains of Chicana(o)/Latina(o) education. Cresskill, N.J. : Hampton Press, c2000.
**TC LC2669 .C42 2000**

**Theobald, Neil D. (Neil David).**
Balancing local control and state responsibility for K-12 education. Larchmont, NY : Eye on Education, 2000.
**TC LC89 .B35 2000**

**THEOLOGICAL EDUCATION.** *See* **RELIGIOUS EDUCATION.**

**THEOLOGY.** *See* **RELIGION.**

**THEOLOGY, DOCTRINAL.** *See* **HERESIES, CHRISTIAN; KNOWLEDGE, THEORY OF (RELIGION).**

**THEOLOGY, DOCTRINAL - HISTORY - 20TH CENTURY.** *See* **FUNDAMENTALISM.**

**THEOLOGY, PRACTICAL.** *See* **CHRISTIAN EDUCATION; ECCLESIASTICAL LAW; MISSIONS.**

**THEOLOGY - STUDY AND TEACHING.** *See* **CHRISTIAN EDUCATION; TEACHING, FREEDOM OF.**

**Theoretical studies in second language acquisition**
(vol. 6) Sasaki, Miyuki, 1959- Second language proficiency, foreign language aptitude, and intelligence. New York : P. Lang, c1999.
**TC P53.4 .S27 1999**

(vol. 8) North, Brian, 1950- The development of a common framework scale of language proficiency. New York : P. Lang, c2000.
**TC P53.4 .N67 2000**

**Theorie und Vermittlung der Sprache**
(Bd. 30) Schneider, Elke. Multisensory structured metacognitive instruction. Frankfurt am Main ; New York : P. Lang, c1999.
**TC P53.7 .S357 1999**

**Theories of development.**
Crain, William C., 1943- 4th ed. Uppder Saddle River, N.J. : Prentice Hall, c2000.
**TC BF713 .C72 2000**

**Theories of mass communication.**
DeFleur, Melvin L. (Melvin Lawrence), 1923- New York : D. McKay, c1966.
**TC HM258 .D35 1966**

**Theorising special education /** edited by Catherine Clark, Alan Dyson, and Alan Millward. London ; New York : Routledge, 1998. ix, 199 p. ; 24 cm. Includes bibliographical references (p. 174-192) and index. ISBN 0-415-14750-6 (alk. paper) ISBN 0-415-14751-4 (pbk. : alk. paper) DDC 371.9/0941
*1. Special education - Great Britain - Philosophy. I. Clark, Catherine. 1944- II. Dyson, Alan. III. Millward, Alan.*
**TC LC3986.G7 T54 1998**

**Theorizing the standoff.**
Wagner Pacifici, Robin Erica. Cambridge : Cambridge University Press, 2000.
**TC HM1121 .W34 2000**

**THEORY, ACTION.** *See* **ACTION THEORY.**

**Theory and philosophy of art.**
Schapiro, Meyer, 1904- New York : George Braziller, 1994.

Valid Expertise / Ursula W. Goodenough -- 10. Confronting Complexity: A New Meaning to World Literacy / David Chen -- 11. Sciences and the Future of Human Culture / Vilmos Csanyi -- 12. The Guidance System of Higher Mind: Implications for Science and Science Education / David Loye -- 13. A Question of Will, Not Knowledge / Janet Ward -- 14. Some Remarks about Education / Willem Brouwer -- 15. Science Literacy for the 21st Century: The Role of Science Centers / David Ellis -- 16. Networking, Interdisciplinarity, and Scientific/Technical Literacy: Perspectives from the Space Program / E. Julius Dasch -- 17. Why Don't Physics Students Understand Physics? Building a Consensus, Fostering Change / Ronald K. Thornton -- 18. CONTENTS: Toward a Science-Friendly Society / Loyal Rue. ISBN 90-5700-538-7 DDC 500 DDC 500
*1. Science - Study and teaching - Congresses. 2. Science - Social aspects - Congresses. 3. Science - Public opinion - Congresses. I. Chaisson, Eric. II. Kim, T'ae-ch'ang. III. Series.*
***TC Q181.3 .T45 1999***

**Thirty-six hour day.**
Mace, Nancy L. The 36-hour day. 3rd ed. Baltimore : Johns Hopkins University Press, c1999.
***TC RC523 .M33 1999***

**This book is not required.**
Bell, Inge. Rev. ed., new ed. / by Team Bell, Lynette Albovias ... [et al.]. Thousand Oaks, Calif. : Pine Forge Press, c1999.
***TC LA229 .B386 1999***

**This is our land.**
M. Margaret Michael, Sister, O.P. New ed. Boston, Mass. : Ginn and Company, 1955.
***TC PE1121 .M52 1955***

**This is our way.**
Ilan pasin = Queensland : Cairns Regional Gallery, [1998?].
***TC DU125.T67 I53 1998***

**This old man** / illustrated by Carol Jones. 1st American ed. Boston : Houghton Mifflin, 1990. [48] p. : col. ill. ; 19 x 27 cm. "Originally published in Australia in 1990 by Angus & Robertson Publishers"--T.p. verso. SUMMARY: An illustrated version of the traditional counting song. Some pages are die-cut, permitting a portion of the next illustration to be seen. ISBN 0-395-54699-0 DDC [E]
*1. Folk songs, English. 2. Toy and movable books - Specimens. 3. Folk songs. 4. Counting. 5. Toy and movable books. I. Jones, Carol, ill.*
***TC PZ8.3 .T2965 1990b***

**Thody, Angela.** Leadership of schools : chief executives in education / Angela Thody. London ; Herndon, Va. : Cassell, 1997. 228 p. ; 26 cm. (Management and leadership in education) Includes bibliographical references (p. [211]-224) and index. ISBN 0-304-33359-X ISBN 0-304-33360-3 (pbk.) DDC 371.2/011/0941
*1. School superintendents - Great Britain. 2. School management and organization - Great Britain. 3. Educational leadership - Great Britain. I. Title. II. Series: Management and leadership in education series (Cassell Ltd.)*
***TC LB2831.726.G7 T56 1997***

**Thom, Betsy.** Dealing with drink : alcohol and social policy : from treatment to management / Betsy Thom. London ; New York : Free Association Books, 1999. xi, 266 p. ; 24 cm. Includes bibliographical references (p. 233-252) and index. ISBN 1-85343-449-3 (hbk.) ISBN 1-85343-450-7 (pbk.) DDC 362.292/8/0941
*1. Alcoholics - Rehabilitation - Great Britain. 2. Alcoholism - Treatment - Great Britain. 3. Social work with alcoholics - Great Britain. 4. Community health services - Great Britain. I. Title.*
***TC HV5283.G6 T56 1999***

**Thomas, Adele, 1942-** Families at school : a guide for educators / Adele Thomas, Lynn Fazio, Betty L. Stiefelmeyer. Newark, Del. : International Reading Association, c1999. vi, 134 p.: ill. ; 29 cm. Includes bibliographical references (p. 123-126) and index. ISBN 0-87207-195-2 DDC 372.119
*1. Family literacy programs - United States. 2. Home and school - United States. I. Fazio, Lynn. II. Stiefelmeyer, Betty L. III. Title.*
***TC LC151 .T56 1999***

Families at school : a handbook for parents / Adele Thomas, Lynn Fazio, Betty L. Stiefelmeyer. Newark, Del. : International Reading Association, c1999. vi, 89 p. : ill. ; 28 cm. Includes bibliographical references. ISBN 0-87207-248-7 DDC 371.19
*1. Family literacy programs - United States. 2. Home and school - United States. 3. Reading - Parent participation - United States. I. Fazio, Lynn. II. Stiefelmeyer, Betty L. III. Title.*
***TC LC151 .T563 1999***

**Thomas, Alice F.** SLP assistant in the schools / Alice F. Thomas, Kathy L. Webster. [San Antonio, Tex.] : Communication Skill Builders, c1999. 82 p. : ill. ; 23 cm. ISBN from label mounted on p. [4] of cover. Includes bibliographical references (p. 81-82). ISBN 0-12-784454-6
*1. Speech therapy for children - United States. 2. Speech therapists - United States. I. Webster, Kathy L. II. Title. III. Title: Speech-language pathology assistant in the schools.*
***TC LB3454 .T46 1999***

**Thomas, Alma, 1939-.**
Emmons, Shirlee. Power performance for singers. New York : Oxford University Press, 1998.
***TC MT892 .E55 1998***

**Thomas, Barb, 1946-** Combatting racism in the workplace : a course for workers / Barb Thomas and Charles Novogrodsky ; illustrated by Margie Bruun-Meyer ; [edited by Jane Springer]. Toronto : Cross Cultural Communication Centre, c1983. 142 p. : ill. ; 21 cm. Includes bibliographical references. ISBN 0-9691060-2-5 DDC 331.13/3/0971
*1. Discrimination in employment - Canada. 2. Intercultural education - Canada. I. Novogrodsky, Charles, 1946-. II. Springer, Jane. III. Cross Cultural Communication Centre (Toronto, Ont.). IV. Title.*
***TC HD4903.5.C3 T56 1983***

**Thomas, Carol, 1958-** Female forms : experiencing and understanding disability / Carol Thomas. Philadelphia, Pa. : Open University Press, 1999. xi, 174 p. ; 24 cm. (Disability, human rights, and society) Includes bibliographical references. ISBN 0-335-19694-2 ISBN 0-335-19693-4 (pbk.) DDC 362.4/082/0941
*1. Disability studies - Great Britain. 2. Handicapped women - Great Britain. 3. Feminist theory - Great Britain. I. Title. II. Series.*
***TC HV1568.25.G7 T46 1999***

**Thomas, Elwyn.** Culture and schooling : building bridges between research, praxis, and professionalism / Elwyn Thomas. Chichester, West Sussex, England ; New York : J. Wiley & Sons, c2000. xvi, 312 p. : ill. ; 23 cm. (Wiley series in culture and professional practice) Includes bibliographical references (p. [281]-302) and indexes. ISBN 0-471-89788-4 (alk. paper) DDC 306.43
*1. Educational anthropology. 2. Educational sociology. I. Title. II. Series.*
***TC LB45 .T476 2000***

**Thomas, George E.** Building America's first university : an historical and architectural guide to the University of Pennsylvania / George E. Thomas and David B. Brownlee. Philadelphia : University of Pennsylvania Press, c2000. xi, 374 p. : ill. ; 26 cm. "Placeholder art." Includes bibliographical references and index. ISBN 0-8122-3515-0 (alk. paper) DDC 378.748/11
*1. University of Pennsylvania - Buildings - History. I. Brownlee, David Bruce. II. Title.*
***TC LD4531 .T56 1999***

**Thomas, H. G. (Harold G).**
Bligh, Donald, 1936- Understanding higher education. Oxford : Intellect, 1999.
***TC LA637 .B55 1999***

**Thomas, Heather.**
A journey through time in verse and rhyme. Rev. ed. Edinburgh : Floris Books, 1998.
***TC PN6109.97 .J68 1998***

**Thomas, Helen, 1947-** Dance, modernity, and culture : explorations in the sociology of dance / Helen Thomas. London ; New York : Routledge, 1995. x, 206 p. : ill. ; 25 cm. Includes bibliographical references and index. ISBN 0-415-08793-7 ISBN 0-415-08794-5 (pbk.) DDC 306.4/84
*1. Dance - Sociological aspects. 2. Modern dance - Social aspects - United States - History. I. Title.*
***TC GV1588.6 .T46 1995***

**Thomas, J. Lawrence.**
Cummings, Nicholas A. The value of psychological treatment. Phoenix, AZ : Zeig, Tucker & Co., 1999.
***TC RA790.6 .C85 1999***

**Thomas Jefferson and the education of a citizen** / edited by James Gilreath. Washington, DC : Library of Congress, 1999. xv, 382 p. ; 27 cm. Essays published here were selected from a conference, held at the Library of Congress, May 13 to May 15, 1993; cosponsored by the Library's Rare Book and Special Collections Division, the Center for the Book in the Library of Congress, and the Institute of Early American Culture at Williamsburg, Va. Includes bibliographical references and index. ISBN 0-8444-0965-0 (alk. paper) DDC 973.4/6/092
*1. Jefferson, Thomas, - 1743-1826 - Views on citizenship - Congresses. 2. Citizenship - Study and teaching - United States - Congresses. I. Gilreath, James, 1947-*
***TC Z663 .T425 1999***

**Thomas, Joyce Carol.** I have heard of a land / by Joyce Carol Thomas ; illustrated by Floyd Cooper. 1st ed. [New York] : HarperCollins Publishers, c1998. 1 v. (unpaged) : col. ill. ; 26 cm. "Joanna Cotler books." SUMMARY: Describes the joys and hardships experienced by an African-American pioneer woman who staked a claim for free land in the Oklahoma territory. ISBN 0-06-023477-6 ISBN 0-06-023478-4 (lib. bdg.) DDC [E]
*1. Oklahoma - History - Land Rush, 1889 - Juvenile fiction. 2. Oklahoma - History - Land Rush, 1889 - Fiction. 3. Frontier and pioneer life - Fiction. 4. Afro-Americans - Fiction. I. Cooper, Floyd, ill. II. Title.*
***TC PZ7.T36696 Iae 1998***

**Thomas-Larmer, Jennifer.**
The consensus building handbook. Thousand Oaks, Calif. : Sage Publications, c1999.
***TC HM746 .C66 1999***

**Thomas, Nicholas.** Possessions : indigenous art, colonial culture / Nicholas Thomas. New York, N.Y. : Thames and Hudson, c1999. 304 p. : ill. (some col.) ; 24 cm. (Interplay, arts, history, theory) Includes bibliographical references and index. ISBN 0-500-28097-5 (pbk.) DDC 303.482
*1. Folk art - Australia. 2. Folk art - New Zealand. 3. Indigenous peoples - Colonization. 4. Indigenous peoples - Ethnic identity. 5. Australian aborigines - Ethnic identity. 6. Maori (New Zealand people) - Ethnic identity. 7. Art, Modern - 20th century - Primitive influences. I. Title. II. Title: Indigenous art, colonial culture III. Series.*
***TC N5313 .T46 1999***

**Thomas, R. Murray (Robert Murray), 1921-** Human development theories : windows on culture / R. Murray Thomas. Thousand Oaks : Sage Publications, c1999. viii, 271 p. : ill. ; 24 cm. Includes bibliographical references (p. 241-256) and indexes. ISBN 0-7619-2015-3 (alk. paper) DDC 306
*1. Socialization. 2. Cognition and culture. 3. Child development. 4. Developmental psychology. I. Title.*
***TC HQ783 .T57 1999***

Theses and dissertations : a guide to planning, research, and writing / R. Murray Thomas and Dale L. Brubaker. Westport, Conn. : Bergin & Garvey, 2000. x, 294 p. : ill. ; 24 cm. Includes bibliographical references (p. [283]-288) and index. ISBN 0-89789-746-3 (alk. paper) DDC 808/.02
*1. Dissertations, Academic - Handbooks, manuals, etc. 2. Report writing - Handbooks, manuals, etc. I. Brubaker, Dale L. II. Title.*
***TC LB2369 .T458 2000***

**Thomas, Rhys.**
The Irish in America [videorecording]. [New York, N.Y.] : A&E Home Video ; New York, N.Y. : Distributed by the New Video Group, 1997.
***TC E184.I6 I6 1997***

**Thomas, Richard K., 1944-.**
Health and healthcare in the United States. 1st ed. Lanham, MD : Bernan Press : Nationshealth Corp., c1999.
***TC HA214 .H435 1999***

Health and healthcare in the United States. 1st ed. Lanham, MD : Bernan Press : Nationshealth Corp., c1999.
***TC HA214 .H435 1999***

**Thomas-Ružić, Maria.**
Huizenga, Jann. Writing workout. Glenview, Ill. : Scott, Foresman and Co.,cc1990.
***TC PE1128 .H84 1990***

**Thomas, Susan J.** Designing surveys that work! : a step-by-step guide / Susan J. Thomas. Thousand Oaks, Calif. : Corwin Press, c1999. xii, 97 p. : ill. ; 24 cm. ISBN 0-8039-6851-5 (acid-free paper) ISBN 0-8039-6852-3 (pbk. : acid-free paper) DDC 001.4/33
*1. Social sciences - Research. 2. Social surveys. I. Title.*
***TC H62 .T447 1999***

**Thomas, Theodore, 1951-.**
The blue planet [videorecording]. [New York, N.Y.?] : Unapix Entertainment, Inc. [distributor], c1996.
***TC QB631.2 .B5 1996***

Gifts from the earth [videorecording]. [New York, N.Y.?] : Unapix Entertainment, Inc. [distributor], c1996.
***TC QB631.2 .G5 1996***

**Thompson, Ashley, 1965-.**
Phim, Toni Samantha, 1957- Dance in Cambodia. [Kuala Lampur] Malaysia ; Oxford ; New York : Oxford University Press, 1999.
***TC GV1703.C3 P55 1999***

**Thompson, Colin (Colin Edward)** Unknown / Colin
Thompson ; illustrations by Anna Pignataro. New
York : Walker & Co., 2000. 1v. (unpaged) : col. ill. ; 29
cm. SUMMARY: Ignored by prospective human owners who
walk past her cage at the pound, a shy dog with an unusual
name becomes a hero during a lightning storm. ISBN 0-8027-
8730-4 ISBN 0-8027-8731-2 (lib. bdg.) DDC [E]
*1. Dogs - Fiction. 2. Animals - Treatment - Fiction. I.
Pignataro, Anna, 1965- ill. II. Title.*
**TC PZ7.T371424 Un 2000**

**Thompson, David P., 1959-** Motivating others :
creating the conditions / David P. Thompson.
Princeton, NJ : Eye On Education, c1996. xv, 158 p. ;
24 cm. (School leadership library) Includes bibliographical
references. ISBN 1-88300-125-0 DDC 371.2/01
*1. School personnel management - United States -
Psychological aspects. 2. Motivation in education - United
States. 3. Teacher-principal relationships - United States. I.
Title. II. Series.*
**TC LB2831.58 .T56 1996**

**Thompson, Hilary.**
Photomontage today, Peter Kennard [videorecording].
[London] : Art Council of Great Britain ; Ho-Ho-Kus,
N.J. : [distributed by] Anthony Roland Collection of
Films on Art, c1982.
**TC TR685 .P45 1982**

**Thompson, Ian (Frederick Ian).**
Issues in teaching numeracy in primary schools.
Buckingham [England] ; Philadelphia : Open
University Press, 1999.
**TC QA135.5 .I77 1999**

**Thompson, John, 1940- ill.**
Rosen, Michael, 1946- A Thanksgiving wish. New
York : Blue Sky Press, c1999.
**TC PZ7.R71867 Tf 1999**

**Thompson, Linda, 1949-** Young bilingual children in
nursery school / Linda Thompson. Clevedon, UK ;
Buffalo, NY : Multilingual Matters, c2000. viii, 230 p. :
ill., maps ; 21 cm. (Bilingual education and bilingualism ; 18)
Includes bibliographical references (p. 218-226) and index.
ISBN 1-85359-454-7 (hard : alk. paper) ISBN 1-85359-453-9
(pbk. : alk. paper) DDC 370.117/0941
*1. Education, Bilingual - Great Britain. 2. Language arts
(Preschool) - Great Britain. 3. Children of immigrants -
Education (Preschool) - Great Britain. 4. Children of
minorities - Education (Preschool) - Great Britain. 5. Nursery
schools - Great Britain. I. Title. II. Series: Bilingual education
and bilingualism ; 18*
**TC LC3723 .T47 2000**

**Thompson, Mary.**
Contraception across cultures :. Oxford ; New York :
Berg, 2000.
**TC RG136 .C574 2000**

**Thompson, Mary McCaslin.**
The academy and the possibility of belief. Cresskill,
N.J. : Hampton Press, c2000.
**TC LB2324 .A27 2000**

**Thompson, Melvin R.** The implementation of
multicultural curricula in the New York City public
elementary schools / by Melvin R. Thompson. 1999.
ix, 123 leaves ; 29 cm. Issued also on microfilm. Thesis
(Ed.D.)--Teachers College, Columbia University, 1999.
Includes bibliographical references (leaves 109-113).
*1. Multicultural education - New York (State) - New York -
Curricula. 2. Minorities - Education (Elementary) - New York
(State) - New York. 3. Educational equalization. I. New York
(N.Y.). Board of Education. II. Title.*
**TC 06 no. 11186**

**Thompson, Patricia J.**
Environmental education for the 21st century. New
York : Peter Lang, c1997.
**TC GE70 .E5817 1997**

**Thompson, Sheila.** The group context / Sheila
Thompson. London ; Philadelphia : Jessica Kingsley
Publishers, 1999. 229 p. ; 24 cm. (The international library
of group analysis ; 7) Includes bibliographical references (p.
217-220) and indexes. ISBN 1-85302-657-3 (pbk.) DDC 158/
.3
*1. Group counseling. 2. Group psychotherapy. I. Title. II.
Series.*
**TC BF637.C6 T49 1999**

**Thomson, Guy P. C., 1949-** Patriotism, politics, and
popular liberalism in nineteenth-century Mexico :
Juan Francisco Lucas and the Puebla Sierra / Guy P.C.
Thomson, with David G. LaFrance. Wilmington, De. :
Scholarly Resources, 1999. xviii, 420 p. : ill., maps ; 24
cm. Includes bibliographical references (p. 315-396) and index.
ISBN 0-8420-2683-5 (alk. paper) DDC 972/.4804/092 DDC
972/.48
*1. Lucas, Juan Francisco. 2. Lucas, Juan Francisco - Military
leadership. 3. Puebla (Mexico : State) - Politics and*

government. *4. Mexico - History - 19th century. 5. Political
leadership - Mexico - Puebla (State) - History - 19th century.
6. Violence - Mexico - Puebla (State) - History - 19th century.
7. Nationalism - Mexico - Puebla (State) - History - 19th
century. I. LaFrance, David G. (David Gerald), 1948- II. Title.*
**TC F1326.L83 T5 1999**

**Thomson, James A. (James Alick), 1951-.**
International Conference on Perception and Action
(10th : 1999 : Edinburgh, Scotland) Studies in
perception and action V. Mahwah, N.J. : L. Erlbaum
Associates, 1999.
**TC BF295 .I57 1999**

**Thoresen, Carl E.**
Forgiveness. New York : Guilford Press, c1999.
**TC BF637.F67 F67 1999**

**Thorndike, Edward L. (Edward Lee), 1874-1949.**
Human nature and the social order [by] Edward L.
Thorndike. Edited and abridged by Geraldine Jonçich
Clifford. Cambridge, Mass., M.I.T. Press [1969] xxv,
373 p. 24 cm. Bibliography: p. 351-363. ISBN 0-262-20016-3
DDC 301.15
*1. Psychology. 2. Social sciences. I. Clifford, Geraldine
Jonçich. II. Title.*
**TC BF121 .T442**

**Thorne, Brian, 1937-** Person-centred counselling and
Christian spirituality : : the secular and the holy /
Brian Thorne. London : Whurr Publishers, 1998. xi,
163 p. ; 24 cm. (Counselling and psychotherapy series.)
Includes bibliographical references and indexes. ISBN 1-
86156-080-X
*1. Counseling. I. Title. II. Title: Person-centered counseling
and Christian spirituality. III. Series.*
**TC BF637.C6 T496 1998**

**Thornes, Robin.** Introduction to Object ID : guidelines
for making records that describe art, antiques, and
antiquities / Robin Thornes with Peter Dorrell and
Henry Lie. [Los Angeles] : Getty Information
Institute, c1999. ix, 61 p. : ill. ; 25 cm. Includes
bibliographical references (p. 60-61). ISBN 0-89236-572-2
(pbk. : alk. paper) DDC 707/.5/3
*1. Art - Documentation - Standards. 2. Antiques -
Documentation - Standards. 3. Antiquities - Documentation -
Standards. I. Dorrell, Peter G. II. Lie, Henry. III. Title. IV.
Title: Object ID*
**TC N3998 .T457 1999**

**Thornicroft, Graham.**
Mental health in our future cities. Hove, England :
Psychology Press, c1998.
**TC RA790.5 .M4196 1998**

**Thornton, Christopher James.** Truth from trash : how
learning makes sense / Chris Thornton. Cambridge,
Mass. ; London : MIT Press, c2000. x, 204 p. : ill. ; 24
cm. (Complex adaptive systems) Includes bibliographical
references (p. [199]-201) and index. ISBN 0-262-20127-5
(hc. : alk. paper) DDC 006.3/1
*1. Machine learning. I. Title. II. Series.*
**TC Q325.4 .T47 2000**

**Thorogood, Margaret.**
Evaluating health promotion. Oxford ; New York :
Oxford University Press, 2000.
**TC RA427.8 .E95 2000**

**Thorson, James A., 1946-.**
Perspectives on spiritual well-being and aging.
Springfield, Ill. : Charles C. Thomas, c2000.
**TC BL625.4 .P47 2000**

**THOUGHT AND THINKING.** *See also*
**ATTENTION; CREATIVE THINKING;
CRITICAL THINKING; INTELLECT;
LOGIC; MEMORY; PERCEPTION;
REASONING; REASONING
(PSYCHOLOGY); SELF; STEREOTYPE
(PSYCHOLOGY).**
Chomsky, Noam. Language and mind. Enl. ed. New
York : Harcourt Brace Jovanovich, [1972].
**TC P106 .C52 1972**

Claxton, Guy. Wise up. 1st U.S. ed. New York, N.Y. :
Bloomsbury : Distributed to the trade by St. Martin's
Press, 1999.
**TC BF318 .C55 1999**

Clough, Patricia Ticineto, 1945- Autoaffection.
Minneapolis : University of Minnesota Press, c2000.
**TC HM846 .C56 2000**

Cognitive dynamics. Mahwah, N.J. ; London : L.
Erlbaum, 2000.
**TC BF316.6 .C64 2000**

Dewey, John, 1859-1952. How we think. Boston :
Houghton Mifflin, c1998.

**TC BF441 .D43 1998**

Durocher, Elizabeth Antointette. Leadership
orientations of school administrators. 1995.
**TC 06 no. 10583a**

Education, information, and transformation. Upper
Saddle River, N.J. : Merrill, c1999.
**TC BF441 .E25 1999**

Flew, Antony, 1923- [Thinking about thinking] How
to think straight. 2nd ed. Amherst, N.Y. : Prometheus
Books, 1998.
**TC BF455 .F614 1998**

Kinnamon, James C. A comparison of structural
knowledge in eighth graders and college students.
1999.
**TC 085 K6194**

Mind and cognition. 2nd ed. Malden, Mass. :
Blackwell Publishers, 1999.
**TC BF171 .M55 1999**

Perkins, David N. Archimedes' bathtub. 1st ed. New
York : W.W. Norton, c2000.
**TC BF441 .P47 2000**

**THOUGHT AND THINKING - CONGRESSES.**
Metarepresentations. Oxford ; New York : Oxford
University Press, c2000.
**TC BF316.6 .M48 2000**

**THOUGHT AND THINKING - SEX
DIFFERENCES - RESEARCH.**
Gender and the interpretation of emotion
[videorecording]. Princeton, NJ : Films for the
Humanities & Sciences, c1997.
**TC BF592.F33 G4 1997**

**THOUGHT AND THINKING - STUDY AND
TEACHING.**
Eggen, Paul D., 1940- Strategies for teachers. 4th ed.
Boston : Allyn and Bacon, 2001.
**TC LB1027.3 .E44 2001**

Johnson, Andrew P. Up and out :. Boston : Allyn and
Bacon, c2000.
**TC LB1590.3 .J64 2000**

Teaching and learning thinking skills. Lisse
[Netherlands] ; Exton, PA : Swets & Zeitlinger,
c1999.
**TC LB1590.3 .T36 1999**

**THOUGHT INSERTION.**
When self-consciousness breaks. Cambridge, Mass. :
MIT Press, c2000.
**TC RC553.A84 S74 2000**

**THOUGHT, NEW.** *See* **NEW THOUGHT.**

**A thousand flowers :** social struggles against structural
adjustment in African universities / edited by Silvia
Federici, George Caffentzis, Ousseina Alidou.
Trenton, NJ : Africa World Press, c2000, [1999]. xv,
248 p. ; 23 cm. (h) Includes bibliographical references and
index. ISBN 0-86543-772-6 (HB) ISBN 0-86543-773-4 (PB)
DDC 378.6
*1. Education, Higher - Economic aspects - Africa. 2. Structural
adjustment (Economic policy) - Africa. 3. World Bank. 4.
Academic freedom - Africa. I. Federici, Silvia. II. Caffentzis,
Constantine George, 1945- III. Alidou, Ousseina.*
**TC LC67.68.A35 T56 2000**

**Three blind mice.**
Ivimey, John W. (John William), b. 1868. [Complete
version of ye Three blind mice] New York : G.P.
Putnam's Sons, c1991.
**TC PZ8.3.I83 Th 1991**

**Three kind mice.**
Sathre, Vivian. 1st ed. San Diego : Harcourt Brace,
c1997.
**TC PZ8.3.S238 Th 1997**

**Three wise women.**
Hoffman, Mary, 1945- 1st ed. New York : Phyllis
Fogelman Books, 1999.
**TC PZ7.H67562 Th 1999**

**THROAT.** *See* **LARYNX; VOICE.**

**Through the eyes of innocents.**
Werner, Emmy E. Boulder, CO : Westview Press,
2000.
**TC D810.C4 W45 1999**

**Through the rearview mirror.**
Macnamara, John. Cambridge, Mass. : MIT Press,
1999.
**TC BF105 .M33 1999**

**Thrupp, Martin, 1964-** Schools making a difference--
let's be realistic! : school mix, school effectiveness,
and the social limits of reform / Martin Thrupp.
Buckingham [England] ; Philadelphia : Open

University Press, 1999. ix, 225 p. ; 23 cm. Includes bibliographical references and index. ISBN 0-335-20213-6 (hb) ISBN 0-335-20212-8 (pbk.) DDC 306.43/2/0993
*1. Educational evaluation - New Zealand - Case studies. 2. High schools - New Zealand - Sociological aspects - Case studies. 3. High school students - New Zealand - Social conditions - Case studies. 4. School integration - New Zealand - Case studies. 5. Working class - Education (Secondary) - New Zealand - Case studies. 6. Academic achievement - New Zealand - Case studies. 7. Educational change - Social aspects - New Zealand - Case studies. 8. Educational sociology - New Zealand - Case studies. I. Title.*
*TC LB2822.75 .T537 1999*

**Thuillier, Jean-Paul.**
Tassili N'Ajjer [videorecording]. [S.l.] : Editions Cinégraphiques ; Northbrook, Ill. : [distributed by] the Roland Collection, c1968.
*TC N5310.5.A4 T3 1968*

**Thunder Bear and Ko.**
Hazen-Hammond, Susan. 1st ed. New York : Dutton Children's Books, 1999.
*TC E99.T35 H36 1999*

**THUNDER-STORMS.** *See* **THUNDERSTORMS.**

**THUNDERSTORMS - FICTION.**
Rylant, Cynthia. Henry and Mudge and the wild wind. 1st ed. New York : Bradbury Press ; Toronto : Maxwell Macmillan Canada ; New York : Maxwell Macmillan International, c1993.
*TC PZ7.R982 Heb 1992*

**Thurlow, Martha L.**
Elliott, Judy L. Improving test performance of students with disabilities-- on district and state assessments. Thousands Oaks, Calif. : Corwin Press, c2000.
*TC LB3051 .E48 2000*

**Thurlow, Richard.**
Linking literacy and technology. Newark, Del. : International Reading Association, c2000.
*TC LB1576.7 .L56 2000*

**THYROID GLAND - DISEASES.** *See* **HYPERTHYROIDISM.**

**THYROTOXICOSIS.** *See* **HYPERTHYROIDISM.**

**Tiago de Melo, Janine, 1969-** Factors relating to Hispanic and non-Hispanic White Americans' willingness to seek psychotherapy / Janine A. Tiago de Melo. 1998. v, 167 leaves ; 29 cm. Issued also on microfilm. Thesis (Ph.D.)--Columbia University, 1998. Includes bibliographical references (leaves 132-146).
*1. Hispanic Americans - Mental health. 2. Hispanic Americans - Psychology. 3. Acculturation. 4. Help-seeking behavior. 5. Psychotherapy - Cross-cultural studies. 6. Psychophysiology - Cross-cultural studies. I. Title.*
*TC 085 T43*

**Tian, Shiau-ping.** TOEFL reading comprehension : strategies used by Taiwanese students with coaching-school training / by Shiau-ping Tian. 2000. x, 271 leaves ; 29 cm. Issued also on microfilm. Thesis (Ed.D.)--Teachers College, Columbia University, 2000. Includes bibliographical references (leaves 240-255).
*1. Test of English as a Foreign Language - Study and teaching - Taiwan. 2. English language - Study and teaching - Chinese speakers - Taiwan - Case studies. 3. Second language acquisition - Research - Methodology. 4. Reading comprehension - Ability testing. 5. Test-taking skills. 6. Verbal behavior - Reseach. 7. Communication in education - Taiwan - Case studies. 8. Test taking skills. I. Title.*
*TC 06 no. 11316*

**Prentice Hall Latin**
Jenney, Charles. Fourth year Latin. Needham, Mass. : Prentice Hall, c1990.
*TC PA2087.5 .J463 1990*

**Tichen, Angie.**
Binnie, Alison. Freedom to practise. Oxford ; Boston : Butterworth-Heinemann, 1999.
*TC RT41 .B56 1999*

**Tickle, Les.** Teacher induction : the way ahead / Les Tickle. Buckingham [England] ; Philadelphia : Open University Press, 2000. xii, 215 p. ; 24 cm. (Developing teacher education) Includes bibliographical references (p. [191]-206) and index. ISBN 0-335-20178-4 (pb) ISBN 0-335-20179-2 (hb) DDC 371.1
*1. Teacher orientation. 2. First year teachers - Training of. 3. Teachers - In-service training. I. Title. II. Series.*
*TC LB1729 .T53 2000*

**The Ticos.**
Biesanz, Mavis Hiltunen. Boulder, Colo. : Lynne Rienner Publishers, 1999.
*TC F1543 .B563 1999*

**TIDINESS.** *See* **ORDERLINESS.**

**Tidskrift för svenska folkhögskolan.**
Folk-högskolan. Stockholm : Lärarförbundet, 1979-

**Tiedeman, David V., joint author.**
Peatling, John H. Career development. Muncie, Ind. : Accelerated Development, c1977.
*TC BF697 .P384*

**Tierney, Helen.**
Women's studies encyclopedia. Rev. and expanded ed. Westport, Conn. : Greenwood Press, c1999.
*TC HQ1115 .W645 1999*

**Tierney, Robert J.** Reading strategies and practices : a compendium / Robert J. Tierney, John E. Readence. 5th ed. Boston : Allyn and Bacon, c2000. xiii, 530 p. : ill. ; 24 cm. Includes bibliographical references and indexes. ISBN 0-205-29808-7 DDC 428/.43
*1. Reading. 2. Reading comprehension. I. Readence, John E., 1947- II. Title.*
*TC LB1050 .T57 2000*

**Tierney, William G.** Building the responsive campus : creating high performance colleges and universities / William G. Tierney. Thousand Oaks, Calif. : Sage, c1999. vi, 185 p. ; 24 cm. Includes bibliographical references (p. 172-175) and index. CONTENTS: Organizational redesign -- The new face of leadership -- Organizational attention deficit disorder : evaluating high performance -- Faculty productivity and organizational culture -- The chiaroscuro of reform -- The 21st century organization. ISBN 0-7619-0987-7 (hc : acid-free paper) ISBN 0-7619-0988-5 (pbk. : acid-free paper) DDC 378.1/01
*1. Universities and colleges - United States - Administration. 2. Universities and colleges - United States - Faculty. 3. Educational change - United States. I. Title.*
*TC LB2341 .T584 1999*

Faculty productivity :. New York : Falmer Press, 1999.
*TC LB2331.7 .F33 1999*

**Tiffany, Constance Rimmer.** Planned change theories for nursing : review, analysis, and implications / Constance Rimmer Tiffany, Louette R. Johnson Lutjens. Thousand Oaks : Sage Publications, c1998. viii, 408 p. : ill. ; 24 cm. Includes bibliographical references and indexes. ISBN 0-7619-0234-1 (cloth : acid-free paper) ISBN 0-7619-0235-X (pbk. : acid-free paper) DDC 610.73/01
*1. Nursing - Planning. 2. Organizational change. 3. Social change. 4. Nursing models. I. Lutjens, Louette R. Johnson. II. Title.*
*TC RT89 .T54 1998*

**Tileston, Donna Walker.** Ten best teaching practices : how brain research, learning styles, and standards define teaching competencies / Donna Walker Tileston. Thousand Oaks, Calif. : Corwin Press, c2000. xi, 83 p. : ill. ; 29 cm. Includes bibliographical references (p. 75-77) and index. ISBN 0-7619-7584-5 (cloth : alk. paper) ISBN 0-7619-7585-3 (pbk. : alk. paper) DDC 371.102
*1. Effective teaching - United States. 2. Learning. 3. Educational innovations - United States. 4. Educational change - United States. I. Title. II. Title: 10 best teaching practices*
*TC LB1775.2 .T54 2000*

**Tillett, Gregory, Ph. D.** Resolving conflict : : a practical approach / Gregory Tillett. 2nd ed. Oxford ; New York : Oxford University Press, 1999. viii, 248 p. : ill. ; 23 cm. Includes bibliographical references and index. ISBN 0-19-551151-4
*1. Conflict management. 2. Problem solving. 3. Mediation. I. Title.*
*TC HM132 .T55 1999*

**Tillman, Jonathan.**
Get a grip [videorecording]. Racine, WI : S.C. Johnson and Son, Inc., 1999, c1998.
*TC TD170 .G4 1999*

**TIMBER.** *See* **TREES.**

**TIMBER WOLVES.** *See* **WOLVES.**

**TIME.** *See also* **DAY; NIGHT.**
Bennett, Joel B. Time and intimacy. Mahwah, N.J. ; London : Lawrence Erlbaum Associates, 2000.
*TC BF575.I5 B45 2000*

**Time & time again :** teacher's planning guide. New York : Macmillan/McGraw-Hill, c1997. 1 v. (various pagings) : col. ill. ; 31 cm. (Spotlight on literacy ; Gr.6 l.12 u.4) (The road to independent reading) Includes index. ISBN 0-02-183197-1
*1. Language arts (Elementary) 2. Reading (Elementary) I. Series. II. Series: The road to independent reading*
*TC LB1576 .S66 1997 Gr.6 l.12 u.4*

**TIME ALLOCATION.** *See* **TIME MANAGEMENT.**

**Time and behaviour :** psychological and neurobehavioural analyses / edited by C.M. Bradshaw and E. Szabadi. Amsterdam ; New York : Elsevier, 1997. xi, 576 p. : ill. ; 24 cm. (Advances in psychology ; 120) Includes bibliographical references and index. ISBN 0-444-82449-9 (alk. paper) DDC 153.7/53
*1. Time - Psychological aspects. 2. Time perception. 3. Time perception in animals. I. Bradshaw, C. M. (Christopher M.) II. Szabadi, E. (Elmer) III. Series: Advances in psychology (Amsterdam, Netherlands) ; 120.*
*TC BF468 .T538 1997*

**Time and intimacy.**
Bennett, Joel B. Mahwah, N.J. : London : Lawrence Erlbaum Associates, 2000.
*TC BF575.I5 B45 2000*

**Time and learning : :** scheduling for success / Robert L. Kennedy and Ann E. Witcher, editors. Bloomington, IN : Phi Delta Kappa International, c1998. 267 p. : ill. ; 28 cm. (Hot topics series.) "December 1998". Includes bibliographical references (p. 245-267).
*1. Teaching - United States. 2. Schedules, School - United States. 3. Time management. I. Kennedy, Robert Loren. 1951- II. Witcher, Ann E. III. Phi Delta Kappa. IV. Title: Scheduling for success. V. Series.*
*TC LB3032 .T562 1998*

**TIME BUDGETS.** *See* **TIME MANAGEMENT.**

**TIME IN LITERATURE.**
Nikolajeva, Maria. From mythic to linear. Lanham, Md. : Children's Literature Association : Scarecrow Press, 2000.
*TC PN1009.5.T55 N55 2000*

**Time is the longest distance :** an anthology of poems / selected by Ruth Gordon. New York, NY : HarperCollins, c1991. xvii, 74 p. ; 24 cm. "A Charlotte Zolotow book." Includes indexes. SUMMARY: An international anthology of poetry about the timelessness of time. Includes works by such poets as Emily Dickinson, Rumi, Salvatore Quasimodo and Ono no Komachi. ISBN 0-06-022297-2 ISBN 0-06-022424-X (lib. bdg.) DDC 808.81/938
*1. Time - Juvenile poetry. 2. Children's poetry. 3. Time - Poetry. 4. Poetry - Collections. I. Gordon, Ruth, 1933-*
*TC PN6109.97 .T56 1991*

**TIME - JUVENILE POETRY.**
Heide, Florence Parry. It's about time!. New York : Clarion Books, c1999.
*TC PS3558.E427 I77 1999*

Time is the longest distance. 1st ed. New York, NY : HarperCollins, c1991.
*TC PN6109.97 .T56 1991*

**Time, love, memory.**
Weiner, Jonathan. 1st ed. New York : Knopf, 1999.
*TC QH457 .W43 1999*

**TIME MANAGEMENT.** *See* **SCHEDULING.**

**TIME - MANAGEMENT.** *See* **TIME MANAGEMENT.**

**TIME MANAGEMENT.**
Time and learning :. Bloomington, IN : Phi Delta Kappa International, c1998.
*TC LB3032 .T562 1998*

**TIME MANAGEMENT - UNITED STATES.**
The dimensions of time and the challenge of school reform. Albany : State University of New York Press, c2000.
*TC LB3032 .D55 2000*

**TIME MEASUREMENTS.** *See* **CLOCKS AND WATCHES.**

**TIME - ORGANIZATION.** *See* **TIME MANAGEMENT.**

**TIME PERCEPTION.**
Time and behaviour. Amsterdam ; New York : Elsevier, 1997.
*TC BF468 .T538 1997*

**TIME PERCEPTION IN ANIMALS.**
Time and behaviour. Amsterdam ; New York : Elsevier, 1997.
*TC BF468 .T538 1997*

**TIME - POETRY.**
Heide, Florence Parry. It's about time!. New York : Clarion Books, c1999.
*TC PS3558.E427 I77 1999*

Time is the longest distance. 1st ed. New York, NY : HarperCollins, c1991.

*TC PN6109.97 .T56 1991*

**TIME - PSYCHOLOGICAL ASPECTS.**
Time and behaviour. Amsterdam ; New York : Elsevier, 1997.
*TC BF468 .T538 1997*

**Time saver resource binder.**
Making choices. Lexington, Mass. : D.C. Heath & co., c1986.
*TC PE1121 .M34 1986 Resource Binder*

**TIME-SHARING COMPUTER SYSTEMS.** *See* **ONLINE DATA PROCESSING.**

**Time to heal.**
Ludmerer, Kenneth M. Oxford ; New York : Oxford University Press, 1999.
*TC R745 .L843 1999*

**TIME USE.** *See* **TIME MANAGEMENT.**

**TIME - USE OF.** *See* **TIME MANAGEMENT.**

**TIMEPIECES.** *See* **CLOCKS AND WATCHES.**

**Times of the technoculture.**
Robins, Kevin. London ; New York : Routledge, 1999.
*TC T58.5 .R65 1999*

**Timpane, P. Michael, 1934-.**
Rediscovering the democratic purposes of education. Lawrence : University Press of Kansas, c2000.
*TC LC89 .R43 2000*

**TIMSS monograph**
(no. 1) Curriculum frameworks for mathematics and science. Vancouver, Canada : Pacific Educational Press, c1993.
*TC QA11 .C87 1993*

**TINCTORIAL SUBSTANCES.** *See* **DYES AND DYEING.**

**Ting, Yenren, 1948-** Learning English text by heart in a Chinese university : a traditional literacy practice in a modern setting / Yenren Ting. [New York : Columbia University], 1999. ix, 273 leaves ; 28 cm. Issued also on microfilm. Thesis (Ph.D.)--Columbia University, 1999. Includes bibliographical references (leaves 258-265).
*1. Second language acquisition - China - Methodology. 2. English language - Study and teaching - China. 3. Learning, Psychology of. 4. Educational sociology. 5. English language - Study and teaching - China - Chinese speakers. 6. English language - Textbooks - China. 7. Language arts. 8. Educational psychology. I. Title.*
*TC 085 T438*

**Tinterow, Gary.**
Ingres, Jean-Auguste-Dominique, 1780-1867. Portraits by Ingres. New York : Metropolitan Museum of Art ; Distributed by Harry N. Abrams, c1999.
*TC ND1329.I53 A4 1999*

Origins of impressionism / Gary Tinterow and Henri Loyrette. New York : Metropolitan Museum of Art : Distributed by H.N. Abrams, c1994. xvi, 486 p. : ill. (some col.) ; 32 cm. Conjunction with the exhibition held at the Galerie nationales du Grand Palais, April 19-August 8, 1994, and the Metropolitan Museum of Art, New York, September 27, 1994-January 8, 1995. Loyrette's contributions translated from French. Includes bibliographical references (p. 468-473) and index. ISBN 0-87099-717-3 ISBN 0-87099-718-1 (pbk.) ISBN 0-8109-6485-6 (Abrams) DDC 759.4/09/0340747471
*1. Impressionism (Art) - France - Exhibitions. 2. Painting, French - Exhibitions. 3. Painting - 19th century - France - Exhibitions. I. Loyrette, Henri. II. Grand Palais (Paris, France) III. Metropolitan Museum of Art (New York, N.Y.) IV. Title.*
*TC ND547.5.I4 L6913 1994*

**TIPIṬAKA. SUTTAPIṬAKA. KHUDDAKANIKĀYA. JĀTAKA - PARAPHRASES, ENGLISH.**
Lee, Jeanne M. I once was a monkey. 1st ed. New York : Farrar, Straus and Giroux, 1999.
*TC BQ1462.E5 L44 1999*

**Tippett, Donna C.**
Tracheostomy and ventilator dependency. New York : Thieme, 2000.
*TC RF517 .T734 2000*

**Tipping the scales of justice.**
Solovay, Sondra, 1970- Amherst, N.Y. : Prometheus Books, 2000.
*TC BF697.5.B63 S65 2000*

**Tippins, Deborah J.**
Cases in middle and secondary science education. Upper Saddle River, N.J. : Merrill, c2000.
*TC Q181 .C348 2000*

Kincheloe, Joe L. The stigma of genius. New York ; Canterbury [England] : P. Lang, c1999.

*TC LB875.E562 K56 1999*

**Tipps, Steven.**
Kennedy, Leonard M. Guiding children's learning of mathematics. 9th ed. Belmont, CA : Wadsworth/ Thomson Learning, c2000.
*TC QA135.5 .K43 2000*

**Tips for the reading team :** strategies for tutors / Barbara J. Walker, Lesley Mandel Morrow, editors. Newark, Del. : International Reading Association, c1998. iv, 90 p. : ill. ; 23 cm. Includes bibliographical references. ISBN 0-87207-190-1 (pbk.) DDC 372.4
*1. Reading (Elementary) 2. Tutors and tutoring. I. Walker. Barbara J., 1946- II. Morrow, Lesley Mandel. III. Title: Reading team*
*TC LB1573 .T57 1998*

**TIREDNESS.** *See* **FATIGUE.**

**TISSIÉ, PHILIPPE, 1852-1925.**
Hacking, Ian. Mad travelers. Charlottesville, Va. : University Press of Virginia, 1998.
*TC RC553.F83 H33 1998*

**TISSUES.** *See* **MUSCLES.**

**Titchener, Frances B., 1954-.**
The eye expanded. Berkeley : University of California Press, c1999.
*TC DE59 .E93 1999*

**TITLES OF DEGREE.** *See* **DEGREES, ACADEMIC.**

**TITLES OF HONOR AND NOBILITY.** *See* **DEGREES, ACADEMIC.**

**Titone, Connie.**
Women's philosophies of education. Upper Saddle River, N.J. : Merrill, c1999.
*TC LC1752 .T46 1999*

**Titterington, D. M.**
Statistics and neural networks. Oxford ; New York : Oxford University Press, 1999.
*TC QA276 .S78343 1999*

**To construct peace.**
True, Michael. Mystic, Conn. : Twenty-Third Publications, c1992.
*TC JX1962.A2 T783 1992*

**To dream with open eyes [videorecording].**
The sight and insight of Ernst Haas [videorecording]. Minneapolis, Minn. : Media Loft, 1992.
*TC TR647.H3 S5 1992*

**To the zoo :** animal poems / selected by Lee Bennett Hopkins ; illustrated by John Wallner. 1st ed. Boston : Little, Brown, c1992. 32 p. : col. ill. ; 24 cm. SUMMARY: A collection of poems about animals at the zoo, by poets including Myra Cohn Livingston, Theodore Roethke, and Maxine Kumin. ISBN 0-316-37273-0 DDC 811.008/036
*1. Zoo animals - Juvenile poetry. 2. Children's poetry, American. 3. Zoo animals - Poetry. 4. American poetry - Collections. I. Hopkins, Lee Bennett. II. Wallner, John C., ill.*
*TC PS595.Z66 T6 1992*

**To touch the future :** transforming the way teachers are taught: an action agenda for college and university presidents. Washington, D.C. : American Council on Education, c1999. v, 38 p. : col. ill. ; 22 x 28 cm. + Executive summary (5 p. ; 26cm.). Includes bibliographical references (p. 28-30) Executive summary bound in.
*1. College teachers - Training of - United States. 2. College teaching - United States. I. American Council on Education.*
*TC LB1738 .T6 1999*

**TOADSTOOLS.** *See* **MUSHROOMS.**

**TOBACCO HABIT.** *See* **CIGARETTE HABIT; SMOKING.**

**TOBACCO HABIT - PREVENTION.**
The next generation [videorecording]. Princeton, NJ : Films for the Humanities & Sciences, c1998.
*TC RC564 .N4 1998*

**TOBACCO HABIT - UNITED STATES.**
The next generation [videorecording]. Princeton, NJ : Films for the Humanities & Sciences, c1998.
*TC RC564 .N4 1998*

Smoking. San Diego, CA : Greenhaven Press, c1997.
*TC HV5760 .S663 1997*

**TOBACCO HABIT - UNITED STATES - ENCYCLOPEDIAS.**
Hirschfelder, Arlene B. Encyclopedia of smoking and tobacco. Phoenix, AZ : Oryx Press, 1999.
*TC HV5760 .H57 1999*

**TOBACCO - HEALTH ASPECTS.**
Smoking. San Diego, CA : Greenhaven Press, c1997.
*TC HV5760 .S663 1997*

**TOBACCO INDUSTRY - CORRUPT PRACTICES - UNITED STATES.**
Smoking. San Diego, CA : Greenhaven Press, c1997.
*TC HV5760 .S663 1997*

**TOBACCO INDUSTRY - GOVERNMENT POLICY - UNITED STATES.**
The politics of addiction [videorecording]. Princeton, NJ : Films for the Humanities & Sciences, c1998.
*TC RC564 .P59 1998*

**TOBACCO INDUSTRY - UNITED STATES - ENCYCLOPEDIAS.**
Hirschfelder, Arlene B. Encyclopedia of smoking and tobacco. Phoenix, AZ : Oryx Press, 1999.
*TC HV5760 .H57 1999*

**TOBACCO MANUFACTURE AND TRADE.** *See* **TOBACCO INDUSTRY.**

**TOBACCO - PHYSIOLOGICAL EFFECT.** *See also* **TOBACCO HABIT.**
Brigham, Janet. Dying to quit. Washington, D.C. : Joseph Henry Press, 1998.
*TC HV5740 .B75 1998*

**TOBACCO SMOKING.** *See* **SMOKING.**

**TOBACCO USE.** *See* **TOBACCO HABIT.**

**Tobe, Dorothy Echols.** The development of cognitive leadership frames among African American female college presidents / by Dorothy Rchols Tobe. 1999. xii, 263 leaves ; 29 cm. Issued also on microfilm. Thesis (Ed.D.)--Teachers College, Columbia University, 1999. Includes bibliographical references (leaves 210-222).
*1. African American college presidents - United States. 2. Women college presidents - United States. 3. Educational leadership. 4. Leadership - Psychological aspects. 5. Leadership - Social aspects. 6. Interpersonal relations. 7. Organizational effectiveness. I. Title.*
*TC 06 no. 11187*

**Tobin, David L.** Coping strategies therapy for bulimia nervosa / by David L. Tobin. Washington, DC : American Psychological Association, c2000. xvi, 249 p. ; 27 cm. Includes bibliographical references (p. 209-221) and indexes. ISBN 1-55798-638-X (alk. paper) DDC 616.85/263
*1. Bulimia. 2. Eating disorders. 3. Bulimia - therapy. 4. Adaptation, Psychological. 5. Psychotherapy - methods. I. Title.*
*TC RC552.B84 T63 2000*

**Tobin, Joseph Jay.** "Good guys don't wear hats" : children's talk about the media / Joseph Tobin. New York : Teachers College Press, c2000. x, 166 p. : ill. ; 23 cm. Includes bibliographical references and index. ISBN 0-8077-3886-7 (pbk.) ISBN 0-8077-3887-5 (cloth) DDC 302.23/083
*1. Mass media and children. 2. Children - Attitudes. 3. Children - Language. I. Title.*
*TC HQ784.M3 T63 2000*

**Toby.**
Wild, Margaret, 1948- 1st American ed. New York : Ticknor & Fields, 1994.
*TC PZ7.W64574 To 1994*

**TOCQUEVILLE, ALEXIS DE, 1805-1859. ANCIEN RÉGIME ET LA RÉVOLUTION.**
LaCapra, Dominick, 1939- History and reading. Toronto : University of Toronto Press, c2000.
*TC DC36.9.L32 1999*

LaCapra, Dominick, 1939- History and reading. Toronto : University of Toronto Press, c2000.
*TC DC36.9.L32 1999*

**Todd, Anne.**
Berry, Carrie, b. 1854. A Confederate girl. Mankato, Minn. : Blue Earth Books, c2000.
*TC E605 .B5 2000*

**TODD, GARFIELD, 1908-.**
Mungazi, Dickson A. The last British liberals in Africa. Westport, Conn. : Praeger, 1999.
*TC DT2979.T63 M86 1999*

**TODDLERS - JUVENILE POETRY.**
Simon, Francesca. Calling all toddlers. 1st American ed. New York : Orchard Books, 1999.
*TC PZ8.3.S5875 Cal 1999*

**TODDLERS - POETRY.**
Simon, Francesca. Calling all toddlers. 1st American ed. New York : Orchard Books, 1999.
*TC PZ8.3.S5875 Cal 1999*

**TOE DANCING.** *See* **BALLET DANCING.**

**TOEFL reading comprehension.**
Tian, Shiau-ping. 2000.
*TC 06 no. 11316*

**TOEFL (TEST OF ENGLISH AS A FOREIGN LANGUAGE).** *See* **TEST OF ENGLISH AS A FOREIGN LANGUAGE.**

**Toelken, Barre.**
Traditional storytelling today. Chicago : Fitzroy Dearborn Publishers, 1999.
*TC GR72 .T73 1999*

**Toft, Robert.** Heart to heart : expressive singing in England, 1780-1830 / Robert Toft. Oxford ; New York : Oxford University Press, 2000. xv, 198 p. : ill., music ; 24 cm. (Oxford early music series) Includes bibliographical references (p. 183-191) and index. ISBN 0-19-816662-1 DDC 782.04/3/094209033
*1. Singing - Instruction and study - England - History - 18th century. 2. Singing - Instruction and study - England - History - 19th century. I. Title. II. Series: Oxford early music series (Unnumbered)*
*TC MT823 .T64 2000*

**Togher, Leanne.**
Communication disorders following traumatic brain injury. Hove, East Sussex, UK : Psychology Press, c1999.
*TC RD594 .C648 1999*

**TOILET PREPARATIONS.** *See* **PERFUMES.**

**Tokar, Inna.** Schools for the mathematically talented in the former Soviet Union / Inna Tokar. 1999. vii, 275 leaves ; 29 cm. Issued also on microfilm. Thesis (Ph.D.) -- Columbia University, 1999. Includes bibliographical references (leaves 211-219)
*1. Gifted children - Education - Soviet Union. 2. Mathematical ability. 3. Teachers of gifted children - Attitudes. 4. Mathematics - Competitions - Soviet Union. 5. Education and state - Soviet Union. I. Title.*
*TC 085 T572*

**Toki, John.**
Speight, Charlotte F., 1919- Hands in clay. 4th ed. Mountain View, Calif. : Mayfield, c1999.
*TC TT920 .S685 1999*

**TOLERATION.** *See* **ACADEMIC FREEDOM; DISCRIMINATION; TEACHING, FREEDOM OF.**

**TOLERATION - STUDY AND TEACHING (ELEMENTARY) - UNITED STATES.**
Teaching for a tolerant world, grades K-6. Urbana, Ill. : National Council of Teachers of English, c1999.
*TC HM1271 .T43 1999*

**TOLERATION - UNITED STATES.**
Freedom Writers. The Freedom Writers diary. 1st ed. New York : Doubleday, c1999.
*TC HQ796 .F76355 1999*

**Tolles, Bryant Franklin, 1939-** The grand resort hotels of the White Mountains : a vanishing architectural legacy / by Bryant F. Tolles. 1st ed. Boston : D.R. Godine, 1995. 263 p. : ill. ; 29 cm. Includes bibliographical references and index. ISBN 1-56792-026-8 DDC 647.94742/201
*1. Hotels - White Mountains (N.H. and Me.) - History. 2. Resort architecture - White Mountains (N.H. and Me.) - History. I. Title.*
*TC TX909 .T58 1995*

**Tolliver, Joseph A.** Administratively mandated change at Amherst College : student reaction and its effect on student personnel administrators / by Joseph A. Tolliver. 1997. ix, 161 leaves ; 29 cm. Issued also on microfilm. Thesis (Ed.D.)--Teachers College, Columbia University, 1997. Includes bibliographical references (leaves 150-152).
*1. Amherst College - Students. 2. Amherst College - Administration. 3. Greek letter sociaties - History. 4. College students - Attitudes. 5. College students - Social life and customs. 6. Conflict management. I. Amherst College. II. Title.*
*TC 06 no. 10871*

**Tom, Abigail, 1941-.**
McKay, Heather, 1950- Teaching adult second language learners. Cambridge ; New York : Cambridge University Press, 1999.
*TC P53 .M33 1999*

**Tomal, Daniel R.** Discipline by negotiation : methods for managing student behavior / Daniel R. Tomal. 1st ed. Lancaster, Pa. : Technomic Pub. Co., c1999. xviii, 157 p. ; 21 cm. Includes bibliographical references (p. 147-153) and index. ISBN 1-56676-673-7 (pbk. : acid-free paper)
*1. School discipline - United States. 2. Negotiation - United States. 3. Behavior modification - United States. 4. Classroom management - United States. I. Title.*
*TC LB3011.5 .T66 1999*

**Tomaselli-Moschovitis, Valerie.**
Statistical handbook on consumption and wealth in the United States. Phoenix, Ariz. : Oryx Press, 1999.

*TC HC110.C6 S73 1999*

**Tomasello, Michael.** The cultural origins of human cognition / Michael Tomasello. Cambridge, Mass. ; London : Harvard University Press, 1999. vi, 248 p. : ill. ; 22 cm. Includes bibliographical references (p. [219]-240) and index. ISBN 0-674-00070-6 DDC 153
*1. Cognition and culture. 2. Cognition in children. I. Title.*
*TC BF311 .T647 1999*

**Tomasi, Lydio F.**
National Legal Conference on Immigration and Refugee Policy (6th : 1983 : Washington, D.C.) Immigration and refugee policy. 1st ed. New York : Center for Migration Studies, 1984.
*TC KF4819.A2 N375 1983*

**Tomblin, J. Bruce.**
Diagnosis in speech-language pathology. 2nd ed. San Diego : Singular, c2000.
*TC RC423 .D473 2000*

**Tomic, W. (Welko), 1946-.**
Conceptual issues in research on intelligence. Stamford, Conn. : JAI Press , 1998.
*TC BF311 .A38 v. 5 1998*

**Tomkins, Calvin, 1925-** Living well is the best revenge / Calvin Tomkins. 1998 Modern Library ed. New York : Modern Library, c1998. xiv, 172 p. : ill. ; 20 cm. Originally published: New York : Viking Press, 1971. With new introd. ISBN 0-679-60308-5 (acid-free paper) DDC 944/.00413/00922
*1. Murphy, Gerald, - 1888-1964. 2. Murphy, Sara. 3. Painters - United States - Biography. 4. Painters' spouses - United States - Biography. 5. Expatriate painters - France - Biography. I. Title.*
*TC ND237.M895 T66 1998*

**Tomorrowland :** ten stories about the future / compiled by Michael Cart. New York : Scholastic Press, 1999. 1x, 198 p. ; 24 cm. SUMMARY: A collection of ten stories about the future, by such authors as Lois Lowry, Katherine Paterson, and Jon Scieszka. ISBN 0-590-37678-0 DDC [Fic]
*1. Science fiction, American. 2. Children's stories, American. 3. Science fiction. 4. Short stories. I. Cart, Michael.*
*TC PZ5 .T6235 1999*

**Tomorrow's children.**
Eisler, Riane Tennenhaus. Boulder, Colo. ; Oxford : Westview Press, 2000.
*TC LC1023 .E57 2000*

**Tompkins, Gail E.** Teaching writing : balancing process and product / Gail E. Tompkins. 3rd ed. Upper Saddle River, N.J. : Merrill, c2000. xx, 400 p. : ill. ; 24 cm. Includes bibliographical references (p. 377-390) and indexes. ISBN 0-13-955469-6 DDC 372.62/3044
*1. English language - Composition and exercises - Study and teaching (Elementary) 2. Creative writing (Elementary education) I. Title.*
*TC LB1576 .T66 2000*

**Toner, Patricia Rizzo, 1952-** Consumer health and safety activities / Patricia Rizzo Toner. West Nyack, N.Y. : Center for Applied Research in Education, c1993. xvii, 125 p. : ill. ; 28 cm. (Just for the health of it! ; unit 1) "Includes 90 ready-to-use activities and worksheets for grades 7-12." ISBN 0-87628-263-X DDC 613.2
*1. Health education (Secondary) - United States - Problems, exercises, etc. 2. Safety education - United States - Problems, exercises, etc. 3. Consumer education - United States - Problems, exercises, etc. I. Title. II. Series: Toner, Patricia Rizzo, 1952- Just for the health of it! ; unit 1.*
*TC RA440.3.U5 T66 1993*

Diet and nutrition activities / Patricia Rizzo Toner. West Nyack, N.Y. : Center for Applied Research in Education, c1993. x, 150 p. : ill. ; 28 cm. (Just for the health of it! ; unit 2) "Includes 90 ready-to-use worksheets for grades 7-12." ISBN 0-87628-265-6 DDC 613.2/071/2
*1. Nutrition - Study and teaching (Secondary) I. Title. II. Series: Toner, Patricia Rizzo, 1952- Just for the health of it! ; unit 2.*
*TC QP143 .T65 1993*

**Just for the health of it!**
(unit 1.) Toner, Patricia Rizzo, 1952- Consumer health and safety activities. West Nyack, N.Y. : Center for Applied Research in Education, c1993.
*TC RA440.3.U5 T66 1993*

(unit 2.) Toner, Patricia Rizzo, 1952- Diet and nutrition activities. West Nyack, N.Y. : Center for Applied Research in Education, c1993.
*TC QP143 .T65 1993*

(unit 3.) Toner, Patricia Rizzo, 1952- Relationships and communication activities. West Nyack, N.Y. : Center for Applied Research in Education, c1993.

(unit 4.) Toner, Patricia Rizzo, 1952- Sex education activities. West Nyack, N.Y. : Center for Applied Research in Education, c1993.
*TC HQ35 .T65 1993*

(unit 5.) Toner, Patricia Rizzo, 1952- Stress-management and self-esteem activities. West Nyack, N.Y. : Center for Applied Research in Education, c1993.
*TC RA785 .T65 1993*

(unit 6.) Toner, Patricia Rizzo, 1952- Substance abuse prevention activities. West Nyack, N.Y. : Center for Applied Research in Education, c1993.
*TC HV4999.2 .T66 1993*

Relationships and communication activities / Patricia Rizzo Toner. West Nyack, N.Y. : Center for Applied Research in Education, c1993. xi, 109 p. : ill. ; 28 cm. (Just for the health of it! ; unit 3) "Includes 90 ready-to-use worksheets for grades 7-12." ISBN 0-87628-847-6 DDC 302/.071/2
*1. Interpersonal relations - Study and teaching (Secondary) 2. Interpersonal communication - Study and teaching (Secondary) 3. Activity programs in education. I. Title. II. Series: Toner, Patricia Rizzo, 1952- Just for the health of it! ; unit 3.*
*TC HM132 .T663 1993*

Sex education activities / Patricia Rizzo Toner. West Nyack, N.Y. : Center for Applied Research in Education, c1993. xiv, 141 p. : ill. ; 28 cm. (Just for the health of it! ; unit 4) On cover: Includes 90 ready-to-use worksheets for grades 7-12. ISBN 0-87628-851-4 DDC 613.9/07
*1. Sex instruction for teenagers. I. Center for Applied Research in Education. II. Title. III. Series: Toner, Patricia Rizzo, 1952- Just for the health of it! ; unit 4.*
*TC HQ35 .T65 1993*

Stress-management and self-esteem activities / Patricia Rizzo Toner. West Nyack, N.Y. : Center for Applied Research in Education, c1993. x, 102 p. : ill. ; 28 cm. (Just for the health of it! ; unit 5) "Includes 90 ready-to-use activities and worksheets for grades 7-12"--Cover. ISBN 0-87628-874-3 DDC 155.9/042/0835
*1. Stress management for teenagers. 2. Self-esteem in adolescence. 3. Activity programs in education. I. Title. II. Series: Toner, Patricia Rizzo, 1952- Just for the health of it! ; unit 5.*
*TC RA785 .T65 1993*

Substance abuse prevention activities / Patricia Rizzo Toner. West Nyack, N.Y. : Center for Applied Research in Education, c1993. xix, 137 p. : ill. ; 28 cm. (Just for the health of it! ; unit 6) "Includes 90 ready-to-use activities and worksheets for grades 7-12"--Cover. ISBN 0-87628-879-4 DDC 362.29/17/071273
*1. Substance abuse - Prevention - Study and teaching (Secondary) - United States. I. Title. II. Series: Toner, Patricia Rizzo, 1952- Just for the health of it! ; unit 6.*
*TC HV4999.2 .T66 1993*

**Tonken, Phil.**
Headline stories of the century [videorecording]. Chicago, IL. : Distributed by Questar Video, Inc., c1992.
*TC D743 .H42 1992*

**Tønnessen, Finn Egil.**
Dyslexia. Dordrecht ; Boston, Mass : Kluwer Academic, 1999.
*TC RC394 .D9525 1999*

**Tonnsen, Sandra.**
What principals should know about--. Springfield, Ill. : C.C. Thomas, c2000.
*TC LB2831.92 .W52 2000*

**Too scared to learn.**
Horsman, Jenny. Mahwah, N.J. : L. Erlbaum Associates, Publishers, 2000.
*TC LC1481 . H67 2000*

**Too, Yun Lee.** The pedagogical contract : the economies of teaching and learning in the ancient world / by Yun Lee Too. Ann Arbor: University of Michigan Press, c2000. 176 p. ; 24 cm. (The body, in theory) Includes bibliographical references (p. 161-172) and index. ISBN 0-472-11087-X (cloth : alk. paper) DDC 370.11/5
*1. Teacher-student relationships - Social aspects. 2. Socrates - Contributions in education. 3. Critical pedagogy. 4. Education, Greek - Philosophy. I. Title. II. Series.*
*TC LB1033 .T66 2000*

**Toohey, K. (Kristine).** The Olympic games : : a social science perspective / Kristine Toohey and A.J. Veal. Oxon, UK ; New York, NY : CABI Pub., c2000. ix, 276 p. : ill. ; 24 cm. Includes bibliographical references (p. 238-267) and index. ISBN 0-85199-342-7 (alk. paper)
*1. Olympics - Social aspects. 2. Olympics - History. I. Veal, Anthony James. II. Title.*

**TC GV721.5 .T64 1999**

**Toohey, Kelleen, 1950-** Learning English at school : identity, social relations, and classroom practice / Kelleen Toohey. Clevedon, [England] ; Buffalo : Multilingual Matters, 2000. vii, 152 p. : ill. ; 25 cm. (Bilingual education and bilingualism ; 20) Includes bibliographical references (p. 137-147) and index. ISBN 1-85359-481-4 (pbk. : alk. paper) ISBN 1-85359-482-2 (hbk. : alk. paper) DDC 428/.007
*1. English language - Study and teaching - Foreign speakers. 2. English language - Study and teaching - Social aspects. 3. Language and education - United States. 4. Education. Bilingual - United States. I. Title. II. Series.*
**TC PE1128.A2 T63 2000**

**TOOLBOOK.**
Idzal, June M. Multimedia authoring tools and teacher training. 1997.
**TC 06 no. 10816**

**The toolbox for the mind.**
Denton, D. Keith. Milwaukee, WI : ASQ Quality Press, c1999.
**TC HD53 .D46 1999**

**Tooley, James.** The global education industry : lessons from private education in developing countries / James Tooley. London : Institute of Economic Affairs ; Washington, DC : International Finance Corporation, World Bank, 1999. 136 p. ; 22 cm. (IEA studies in education ; no. 7) Includes bibliographical references (p. 134-136). ISBN 0-255-36475-X
*1. Private schools - Developing countries - Case studies. 2. Private schools - Developing countries - Finance - Case studies. 3. Education and state - Developing countries - Case studies. I. Title. II. Series.*
**TC LC57.5 .T667 1999**

Reclaiming education / James Tooley. London : New York : Cassell, 2000. vi, 258 p. : ill ; 24 cm. Includes bibliographical references (p. [241]-250) and index. ISBN 0-304-70567-5 ISBN 0-304-70566-7 (hardback) DDC 379
*1. Education and state. 2. Education and state - Great Britain. 3. Privatization in education. 4. Privatization in education - Great Britain. 5. Educational change. 6. Educational change - Great Britain. I. Title.*
**TC LC71 .T65 2000**

**Toolkit for tackling racism in schools.**
Dadzie, Stella, 1952- Stoke on Trent, Staffordshire, England : Trentham Books, 2000.
**TC LC212.3.G7 D339 2000**

**The tooth fairy.**
Collington, Peter. 1st U.S. ed. New York : Knopf ; Distributed by Random House, 1995.
**TC PZ7.C686 To 1995**

**TOOTH FAIRY - FICTION.**
Collington, Peter. The tooth fairy. 1st U.S. ed. New York : Knopf ; Distributed by Random House, 1995.
**TC PZ7.C686 To 1995**

**TOPOGRAPHIC BRAIN MAPPING.** *See* **BRAIN MAPPING.**

**TOPOLOGY.**
Radó, Tibor, 1895-1965. Length and area. New York, American Mathematical Society, 1948.
**TC QA611 .R3**

**Torbert, William R., 1944-.**
Transforming social inquiry, transforming social action. Boston : London : Kluwer Academic, c2000.
**TC LC238 .T73 2000**

**Toronto studies in philosophy**
Roeper, Peter. Probability theory and probability logic. Toronto ; Buffalo : University of Toronto Press, c1999.
**TC BC141 .R64 1999**

**Toronto studies in semiotics**
Berthoff, Ann E. The mysterious barricades. Toronto ; Buffalo : University of Toronto Press, c1999.
**TC P106 .B463 1999**

**Torrence, Bruce F. (Bruce Follett), 1963-** The student's introduction to Mathematica : a handbook for precalculus, calculus, and linear algebra / Bruce F. Torrence, Eve A. Torrence. Cambridge ; New York : Cambridge University Press, 1999. xvii, 280 p. : ill. ; 24 cm. Includes index. ISBN 0-521-59445-6 (hb) ISBN 0-521-59461-8 (pb) DDC 510/.285/5369
*1. Mathematica (Computer file) 2. Mathematics - Data processing. I. Torrence, Eve A. (Eve Alexandra), 1963- II. Title.*
**TC QA76.95 .T67 1999**

**Torrence, Eve A. (Eve Alexandra), 1963-.**
Torrence, Bruce F. (Bruce Follett), 1963- The student's introduction to Mathematica. Cambridge ; New York : Cambridge University Press, 1999.
**TC QA76.95 .T67 1999**

**Torres, Carlos Alberto.**
Challenges of urban education. Albany : State Unviersity of New York Press, c2000.
**TC LC5131 .C38 2000**

Comparative education. Lanham : Rowman & Littlefield, c1999.
**TC LB43 .C68 1999**

Globalization and education. New York : Routledge, 1999.
**TC LC191 .G545 1999**

**Torres, Louis, 1938-** What art is : the esthetic theory of Ayn Rand / Louis Torres & Michelle Marder Kamhi. Chicago, Ill. : Open Court, c2000. xvi, 523 p. ; 23 cm. Includes bibliographical references (p. [479]-503) and index. ISBN 0-8126-9372-8 (alk. paper) ISBN 0-8126-9373-6 (pbk. : alk.) DDC 813/.52
*1. Rand, Ayn - Aesthetics. 2. Art and literature - United States - History - 20th century. 3. Aesthetics, American. 4. Art in literature. I. Kamhi, Michelle Marder. II. Title.*
**TC PS3535.A547 Z9 2000**

**Torres-Saillant, Silvio.** The Dominican Americans / Silvio Torres-Saillant and Ramona Hernández. Westport, Conn. : Greenwood Press, 1998. xxi, 184 p. : ill. ; 24 cm. (The new Americans, 1092-6364) Includes bibliographical references (p. [161]-171) and index. ISBN 0-313-29839-4 (alk. paper) DDC 973/.04687293
*1. Dominican Americans. I. Hernández, Ramona. II. Title. III. Series: New Americans (Westport, Conn.)*
**TC E184.D6 T67 1998**

**Torres Strait art.**
Ilan pasin = Queensland : Cairns Regional Gallery, [1998?].
**TC DU125.T67 I53 1998**

**TORRES STRAIT ISLANDERS.** *See* **AUSTRALIAN ABORIGINES.**

**TORRES STRAIT ISLANDERS - SOCIAL LIFE AND CUSTOMS - EXHIBITIONS.**
Ilan pasin = Queensland : Cairns Regional Gallery, [1998?].
**TC DU125.T67 I53 1998**

**TORT LIABILITY OF PROFESSIONS.** *See* **MALPRACTICE.**

**TORTS.** *See* **MALPRACTICE.**

**Toscan, Cathy.**
Interactive television. Aalborg, Denmark : Aalborg University Press, 1999.
**TC HE8700.95 .I57 1999**

**TOTAL QUALITY MANAGEMENT.**
Deming, W. Edwards (William Edwards), 1900- The new economics. 2nd ed. Cambridge, Mass. ; London : MIT Press, 2000.
**TC HD62.15 .D46 2000**

Lamm, Sharon Lea. The connection between action reflection learning and transformative learning. 2000.
**TC 06 no. 11230**

**TOTAL QUALITY MANAGEMENT - UNITED STATES.**
Freed, Jann E. A culture for academic excellence. Washington, D.C. : Graduate School of Education and Human Development, George Washington University, 1997.
**TC LB2341 .F688 1997**

**TOTAL QUALITY MANAGEMENT - UNIVERSITIES AND COLLEGES - UNITED STATES.**
Creating successful partnerships between academic and student affairs. San Francisco : Jossey-Bass Publishers, 1999.
**TC LB2342.9 .C75 1999**

**A totally alien life-form.**
Lewis, Sydney, 1952- New York : New Press : Distributed by W.W. Norton, c1996.
**TC HQ796 .L3995 1996**

**Toth, Marian Davies.**
Ragno, Nancy N. World of language. [Teacher ed.]. Morristown, NJ : Silver Burdett & Ginn, c1990.

Ragno, Nancy N. World of language. [Teacher ed.]. Morristown, NJ : Silver Burdett & Ginn, c1990.

Ragno, Nancy N. World of language. [Teacher ed.]. Morristown, NJ : Silver Burdett & Ginn, c1990.

Ragno, Nancy Nickell. World of language. Needham, Ma. : Silver Burdett Ginn, c1996.
**TC LB1576 .S4471 1996**

Ragno, Nancy Nickell. World of language. Needham, Mass. : Silver Burdett Ginn, c1996.

**TC LB1576 .S4471 1996**

World of language. Needham, Mass. : Silver Burdett Ginn, c1996.
**TC LB1576 .S4471 1996**

World of language. Teacher ed. Needham, Mass. : Silver Burdett Ginn, c1996.
**TC LB1576 .S4471 1996 Teacher Ed.**

**Toth, Sheree L.**
Developmental perspectives on trauma. Rochester, N.Y., USA : University of Rochester Press, 1997.
**TC RJ499 .D4825 1997**

**Totten, Samuel.**
Practicing what we preach. New York : Falmer Press, 1999.
**TC LB1735.5 .P73 1999**

**Touch 'n' go** [videorecording / Braille Institute of America]. Burbank, Calif. : Columbia Tristar Home Video ; [S.l. : Distributed by] Rank Video Services Production, c1991. 1 videocassette (27 min.) : sd., col. ; 1/2 in. (Braille Institute insight series) VHS. Catalogued from credits and container. Introduced by Efrem Zimbalist, Jr. Photography: Brad Fowler. Originally produced by the Braille Institute of America by Corporate Productions, Toluca Lake, CA. For teachers, families and professionals working with the blind. SUMMARY: This video shows real-life situations which provide motivation and information on how to move about safely and confidently after loss of sight, using the touch technique and other methods. ISBN 0-8001-0871-x
*1. Blind - Orientation and mobility. 2. Blind - Services for. 3. Blind - Rehabilitation. 4. Visually handicapped - Orientation and mobility. 5. Visually handicapped - Services for. 6. Visually handicapped - Rehabilitation. 7. Documentary television programs. I. Zimbalist, Efrem, 1923- II. Braille Institute of America. III. Columbia Tristar Home Video (Firm) IV. Corporate Productions. V. Rank Video Services America. VI. Series.*
**TC HV1626 .T6 1991**

**TOUCH - PSYCHOLOGICAL ASPECTS.**
Touch, representation, and blindness. Oxford ; New York : Oxford University Press, 2000.
**TC BF275 .T68 2000**

**Touch, representation, and blindness** / edited by Morton A. Heller. Oxford ; New York : Oxford University Press, 2000. 225 p. : ill. ; 24 cm. (Debates in psychology) Includes bibliographical references and index. ISBN 0-19-850388-1 (hbk) ISBN 0-19-850387-3 (pbk.) DDC 152.1/82
*1. Touch - Psychological aspects. 2. Mental representation. 3. Blindness - Psychological aspects. I. Heller, Morton A. II. Series.*
**TC BF275 .T68 2000**

**TOUGHNESS (PERSONALITY TRAIT).** *See* **AGGRESSIVENESS (PSYCHOLOGY).**

**Tour of the city seen through the eyes of its artists, architects and poet.**
Paris [videorecording]. New York, NY : V.I.E.W. Video, c1996.
**TC DC707 .P3 1996**

**Tourse, Robbie W. C. (Robbie Welch Christler).**
Collaborative practice. Westport, Conn. ; London : Praeger, 1999.
**TC HV741 .C5424 1999**

**Touzel, Timothy J.**
Hunt, Gilbert. Effective teaching. 3rd ed. Springfield, Ill. : C.C. Thomas Publisher, c1999.
**TC LB1025.3 .H86 1999**

**Toward a feminist developmental psychology** / edited by Patricia H. Miller and Ellin Kofsky Scholnick. New York : Routledge, 2000. viii, 309 p. ; 24 cm. Includes bibliographical references (p. [255]-295) and index. ISBN 0-415-92178-3 (hb) ISBN 0-415-92177-5 (pb) DDC 155/.082
*1. Developmental psychology. 2. Feminist psychology. I. Miller, Patricia H. II. Scholnick, Ellin Kofsky.*
**TC BF713 .T66 2000**

**Toward a gang solution.**
Rosen, Sidney M. [Norman, Okla.?] NRC Youth Services, 1996.
**TC HV6439.U7 R67 1996**

**Toward a science of consciousness III :** the third Tucson discussions and debates / edited by Stuart R. Hameroff, Alfred W. Kaszniak, and David J. Chalmers. Cambridge, Mass. : MIT Press, c1999. xx, 504 p. : ill. ; 23 cm. (Complex adaptive systems) "A Bradford book." Conference proceedings. Includes bibliographical references and index. ISBN 0-262-58181-7 (alk. paper) DDC 153
*1. Consciousness - Congresses. I. Hameroff, Stuart R. II. Kaszniak, Alfred W., 1949- III. Chalmers, David John, 1966-*

IV. Title: Toward a science of consciousness three V. Title: Third Tucson discussions and debates VI. Series.
**TC BF311 .T67 1999**

**Toward a science of consciousness three.**
Toward a science of consciousness III. Cambridge, Mass. : MIT Press, c1999.
**TC BF311 .T67 1999**

**Toward acceptance :** sexual orientation issues on campus / edited by Vernon A. Wall and Nancy J. Evans. Lanham, Md. : University Press of America, 1999. xiii, 455 p. ; 24 cm. Includes bibliographical references. DDC 378.1/982664
*1. Homosexuality and education - United States. 2. Homophobia in higher education - United States. 3. Gay college students - United States - Social conditions. 4. Bisexual college students - United States - Social conditions. I. Wall, Vernon A. II. Evans, Nancy J., 1947-*
**TC LC192.6 .T69 1999**

**Toward an integrative conception of authority in education.**
Gordon, Mordechai. 1997.
**TC 085 G656**

Gordon, Mordechai. 1997.
**TC 085 G656**

**Towards a new model of governance for universities? :** a comparative view / edited by Dietmar Braun and François-Xavier Merrien. London ; Philadelphia : Jessica Kingsley, c1999. 286 p. : ill. ; 24 cm. (Higher education policy series ; 53) Includes bibliographical references (p. 262-276) and indexes. ISBN 1-85302-773-1 DDC 378.1
*1. Higher education and state. 2. Universities and colleges - Administration. I. Braun, Dietmar. II. Merrien, François-Xavier. III. Series.*
**TC LC171 .T683 1999**

**Towards a new museum.**
Newhouse, Victoria. New York : Monacelli Press, 1998.
**TC NA6695 .N49 1998**

**Towards a new topology of public and private schools.**
Rufo-Lignos, Patricia Marie. 1999.
**TC 06 no. 11170**

**Towards a new typology of public and private schools.**
Rufo-Lignos, Patricia Marie. 1999.
**TC 06 no. 11170**

**Towards a pluralist and tolerant approach to teaching history :** a range of sources and new didactics : symposium, 10-12 December 1998, Brussels, Belgium / keynote address by Marc Ferro ; general report by Henry Frendo. Strasbourg : Council of Europe Pub., c1999. 131 p. ; 21 cm. (Education) "Council for Cultural Co-operation." Includes bibliographical references. ISBN 92-871-4097-9
*1. History - Study and teaching - Europe. 2. Europe - History - 20th century - Study and teaching - Europe - Congresses. I. Ferro, Marc. II. Frendo, Henry. III. Council of Europe. IV. Council of Europe. Council for Cultural Co-operation. V. Title: Learning and teaching about the history of Europe in the 20th century VI. Series: Collection Education (Strasbourg, France)*
**TC D424 .T665 1999**

**Towards effective subject leadership in the primary school.**
Bell, Derek, 1950- Buckingham [England] ; Philadelphia : Open University Press, c1999.
**TC LB2832.4.G7 B45 1999**

**Towards sustainable development :** on the goals of development-and the conditions of sustainability / edited by William M. Lafferty and Oluf Langhelle. New York, N.Y. : St. Martin's Press, 1999. xiii, 270 p. ; 23 cm. Includes bibliographical references (p. 240-255) and index. ISBN 0-312-21669-6 (cloth) DDC 363.7
*1. Sustainable development. 2. Economic development - Environmental aspects. I. Lafferty, William, 1939- II. Langhelle, Oluf.*
**TC HD75.6 .T695 1999**

**Towards the digital library :** the British Library's Initiatives for Access programme / edited by Leona Carpenter, Simon Shaw and Andrew Prescott. London : The British Library, 1998. 256 p., [8] p. of plates : ill. (some col.) ; 25 cm. Includes bibliographical references (p. 247-253). ISBN 0-7123-4540-X
*1. Digital libraries - Great Britain - Planning. 2. British Library - Planning. I. Carpenter, Leona. II. Shaw, Simon. III. Prescott, Andrew. IV. Title: British Library's Initiatives for Access programme*
**TC Z664.B75 T683 1998**

**Towl, Graham J.** The handbook of psychology for forensic practitioners / Graham J. Towl and David A. Crighton. London ; New York : Routledge, 1996. xii, 227 p. : ill. ; 23 cm. Includes bibliographical references (p. [199]-217) and indexes. ISBN 0-415-12887-0 ISBN 0-415-12888-9 (pbk). DDC 614/.1
*1. Psychology, Forensic. 2. Criminal psychology. I. Crighton, David A., 1964- II. Title.*
**TC RA1148 .T69 1996**

**TOWN AND GOWN. *See* COMMUNITY AND COLLEGE.**

**TOWN LIFE. *See* CITY AND TOWN LIFE.**

**Town mouse house.**
Brooks, Nigel. New York : Walker & Co., 2000.
**TC PZ7.B7977 To 2000**

**The town of Hercules.**
Deiss, Joseph Jay. Rev. and expanded. Malibu, Calif. : J. Paul Getty Museum, c1995.
**TC DG70.H5 D4 1995**

**TOWN PLANNING. *See* CITY PLANNING.**

**TOWNS. *See* CITIES AND TOWNS.**

**Townsend, Barbara K.**
Two-year colleges for women and minorities. New York : Falmer Press, 1999.
**TC LB2328.15.U6 T96 1999**

**TOWNSEND HARRIS HIGH SCHOOL (MANHATTAN, NEW YORK, N.Y.) - HISTORY.**
Lebow, Eileen F. The bright boys. Westport, Conn. : Greenwood Press, c2000.
**TC LD7501.N5 T692 2000**

**TOXICOLOGY.**
Generations at risk. Cambridge, Mass. : MIT Press, c1999.
**TC RA1224.2 .G46 1999**

**TOXICS, AIR. *See* AIR - POLLUTION.**

**TOY AND MOVABLE BOOKS.**
Jonas, Ann. Where can it be? 1st ed. New York : Greenwillow Books, c1986.
**TC PZ7.J664 Wi 1986**

Steer, Dugald. Just one more story. New York : Dutton Children's Books, 1999.
**TC PZ7.S81534 Ju 1999**

This old man. 1st American ed. Boston : Houghton Mifflin, 1990.
**TC PZ8.3 .T2965 1990b**

**TOY AND MOVABLE BOOKS - SPECIMENS.**
Jonas, Ann. Where can it be? 1st ed. New York : Greenwillow Books, c1986.
**TC PZ7.J664 Wi 1986**

Steer, Dugald. Just one more story. New York : Dutton Children's Books, 1999.
**TC PZ7.S81534 Ju 1999**

This old man. 1st American ed. Boston : Houghton Mifflin, 1990.
**TC PZ8.3 .T2965 1990b**

**TOY MAKERS. *See* TOYMAKERS.**

**TOY MAKING. *See* TOYMAKERS.**

**Toye, Nigel, 1949-** Drama and traditional story for the early years / Nigel Toye and Francis Prendiville ; foreword by Jonothan Neelands. London ; New York : Routledge, 2000. viii, 257 p. ill. ; 23 cm. Includes bibliographical references (p. [250]-254) and index. ISBN 0-415-19536-5 (pbk. : alk. paper) DDC 372.13/32
*1. Drama in education - Great Britain. 2. Drama - Study and teaching (Early childhood) - Great Britain. I. Prendiville, Francis, 1949- II. Title.*
**TC PN3171 .T695 2000**

**TOYMAKERS - FICTION.**
Gauch, Patricia Lee. Poppy's puppet. 1st ed. New York : Holt, 1999.
**TC PZ7.G2315 Po 1999**

**Toyoda, Toshio, 1925-.**
Vocational education in the industrialization of Japan. Tokyo : United Nations University, c1987.
**TC LC1047.J3 V63 1987**

**TOYS. *See* BLOCKS (TOYS); DOLLS; EDUCATIONAL TOYS.**

**TOYS - FICTION.**
Blake, Quentin. Clown. 1st American ed. New York : H. Holt, 1996.
**TC PZ7.B56 Cl 1996**

Freeman, Don. Corduroy. Harmondsworth, Middlesex ; New York : Puffin Books, 1976.

**TC PZ8.9.F85 C5 1976**

**TOYS - SOCIAL ASPECTS.**
Girls, boys, books, toys. Baltimore : Johns Hopkins University Press, 1999.
**TC PN1009.5.S48 G57 1999**

**TQM (TOTAL QUALITY MANAGEMENT). *See* TOTAL QUALITY MANAGEMENT.**

**Tracey Moffatt.**
Moffatt, Tracey. Annandale, N.S.W., Australia : Piper Press, c1995.
**TC TR647 .M843 1995**

**TRACHEA. *See* LARYNX.**

**Tracheostomy and ventilator dependency :** management of breathing, speaking, and swallowing / [edited by] Donna C. Tippett. New York : Thieme, 2000. xv, 311 p. : ill. ; 26 cm. Includes bibliographical references and index. ISBN 0-86577-774-8 (hard cover) ISBN 3-13-108571-1 DDC 617.5/33
*1. Tracheotomy. 2. Artificial respiration. 3. Respirators (Medical equipment) 4. Tracheostomy - rehabilitation. 5. Respiration, Artificial. I. Tippett, Donna C.*
**TC RF517 .T734 2000**

**TRACHEOSTOMY - REHABILITATION.**
Tracheostomy and ventilator dependency. New York : Thieme, 2000.
**TC RF517 .T734 2000**

**TRACHEOTOMY.**
Tracheotomy and ventilator dependency. New York : Thieme, 2000.
**TC RF517 .T734 2000**

**Trachtenberg, Alan.** Brooklyn Bridge : fact and symbol / Alan Trachtenberg. Phoenix ed. Chicago : University of Chicago Press, 1979. x, 206 p., [4] leaves of plates : ill. ; 23 cm. (A Phoenix book ; P828) Includes bibliographical references and index. ISBN 0-226-81115-8 DDC 624.5/5/097471
*1. Brooklyn Bridge (New York, N.Y.) I. Title.*
**TC TG25.N53 T7 1979**

**Tracking systemic change in an interagency partnership.**
OConnor-Pirkle, Marilyn. 1996.
**TC 06 no. 10677**

OConnor-Pirkle, Marilyn. 1996.
**TC 06 no. 10677**

**TRADE ADJUSTMENT ASSISTANCE. *See* MANPOWER POLICY.**

**TRADE, INTERNATIONAL. *See* INTERNATIONAL TRADE.**

**TRADE SCHOOLS - IRELAND - HISTORY.**
Raftery, Mary. Suffer the little children. Dublin, Ireland : New Island, 1999.
**TC HV9148.A5 R33 1999**

**TRADE-UNIONS - COLLEGE TEACHERS. *See* COLLEGE TEACHERS' UNIONS.**

**TRADE-UNIONS - MINORITY MEMBERSHIP. *See* DISCRIMINATION IN EMPLOYMENT.**

**TRADE-UNIONS - TEACHERS. *See* TEACHERS' UNIONS.**

**TRADES. *See* INDUSTRIAL ARTS; OCCUPATIONS.**

**Trading in futures :** why markets in education don't work / David Hughes ... [et al.]. Buckingham [England] ; Philadelphia : Open University Press, 1999. viii, 193 p. : ill ; 24 cm. Includes bibliographical references and index. ISBN 0-335-20278-0 ISBN 0-335-20277-2 (pbk.) DDC 379.3/2/0993
*1. Education - New Zealand - Finance - Longitudinal studies. 2. School choice - New Zealand - Longitudinal studies. 3. Free markets - New Zealand - Longitudinal studies. I. Hughes, David, 1944-*
**TC LB2826.6.N45 T73 1999**

**Tradition and change in four societies.**
Ford, Richard B., 1935- New York, Holt, Rinehart and Winston, 1968.
**TC HT1521 .F6 1968**

**Tradition and liberation.**
Robinson, Catherine A. New York : St. Martin's Press, 1999.
**TC HQ1735.3 .R63 1999**

**Tradition renewed :** a history of the Jewish Theological Seminary / edited by Jack Wertheimer. 1st ed. New York, N.Y. : The Seminary, 1997. 2 v. : ill. ; 27 cm. Includes bibliographical references and index. CONTENTS: v. 1. The making of an institution of Jewish higher learning -- v. 2. Beyond the academy. ISBN 0-87334-075-2 DDC 296/.071/1747

1. *Jewish Theological Seminary of America - History. 2. Conservative Judaism - United States - History. I. Wertheimer, Jack.*
*TC BM90.J56 T83 1997*

**Traditional buildings of India.**
Cooper, Ilay. New York : Thames and Hudson, c1998.
*TC NA1501 .C58 1998*

**Traditional storytelling today :** an international sourcebook / edited by Margaret Read MacDonald ; contributing editors, John H. McDowell, Linda Dégh, Barre Toelken. Chicago : Fitzroy Dearborn Publishers, 1999. xv, 627 p. ; 26 cm. Includes bibliographical references and index. ISBN 1-57958-011-4
1. *Folklore. 2. Folk literature - Themes, motives. 3. Tales. 4. Storytelling. 5. Oral tradition. I. McDowell, John Holmes, 1946- II. Dégh, Linda. III. Toelken, Barre. IV. MacDonald, Margaret Read, 1940-*
*TC GR72 .T73 1999*

**TRADITIONS.** *See* **FOLKLORE; LEGENDS; RITES AND CEREMONIES.**

**Traditions, tensions.**
Contemporary art in Asia. New York : Asia Society Galleries ; Distributed by Harry N. Abrams, c1996.
*TC N7262 .C655 1996*

**TRAFFIC CONGESTION - FICTION.**
Chwast, Seymour. Traffic jam. Boston : Houghton Mifflin, 1999.
*TC PZ7.C4893 Tr 1999*

**TRAFFIC ENGINEERING.** *See* **TRAFFIC CONGESTION.**

**TRAFFIC FLOW.** *See* **TRAFFIC CONGESTION.**

**Traffic jam.**
Chwast, Seymour. Boston : Houghton Mifflin, 1999.
*TC PZ7.C4893 Tr 1999*

**TRAFFIC JAMS.** *See* **TRAFFIC CONGESTION.**

**Trafton, Paul R.** Learning through problems : number sense and computational strategies : a resource for primary teachers / Paul R. Trafton & Diane Thiessen. Portsmouth, NH : Heinemann, c1999. ix, 116 p. : ill. ; 22 x 28 cm. Includes bibliographical references (p. 115-116). ISBN 0-325-00126-X (pbk. : alk. paper) DDC 372.7/044
1. *Mathematics - Study and teaching (Primary) I. Thiessen, Diane. II. Title.*
*TC QA135.5 .T685 1999*

**The tragedy of the self.**
Greif, Gary F. Lanham, Md. ; Oxford : University Press of America, c2000.
*TC BF175.5.S44 G74 2000*

**Trained nurse and hospital review.**
Industrial nursing. [Chicago : Industrial Medicine Pub. Co.,

**TRAINING.** *See* **EDUCATION; GROUP RELATIONS TRAINING; MANUAL TRAINING; OCCUPATIONAL TRAINING; TEACHING.**

**Training College Association (Great Britain).**
Forum of education. London, Longmans Green.

**TRAINING - GREAT BRITAIN.**
Bennett, Neville. Skills development in higher education and employment. Buckingham [England] ; Philadelphia : Society for Research into Higher Education & Open University Press, 2000.
*TC LB1027.47 .B46 2000*

**TRAINING NEEDS - DEVELOPING COUNTRIES.**
Petkoski, Djordjija B. Learning together with clients. Washington, D.C. : World Bank, c1997.
*TC HQ4420.8.P48 1997*

**TRAINING OF CHILDREN.** *See* **CHILD REARING.**

**TRAINING OF EMPLOYEES.** *See* **EMPLOYEES - TRAINING OF.**

**TRAINING, PHYSICAL.** *See* **PHYSICAL EDUCATION AND TRAINING.**

**TRAINING SCHOOLS FOR NURSES.** *See* **NURSING SCHOOLS.**

**Training teachers in practice.**
Grenfell, Michael, 1953- Clevedon, UK ; Philadelphia : Multilingual Matters, c1998.
*TC P53.85 .G74 1998*

**Training with a beat.**
Millbower, Lenn, 1951- 1st ed. Sterling, Va. : Stylus, c2000.
*TC ML3830 .M73 2000*

**TRAINING WITHIN INDUSTRY.** *See* **EMPLOYEES - TRAINING OF.**

**TRAINS, RAILROAD.** *See* **RAILROADS - TRAINS.**

**A traitor among the boys.**
Naylor, Phyllis Reynolds. New York : Delacorte Press, 1999.
*TC PZ7.N24 Tpr 1999*

**TRAITS, PERSONALITY.** *See* **PERSONALITY.**

**TRANCE.** *See* **HYPNOTISM.**

**TRANS-CULTURAL STUDIES.** *See* **CROSS-CULTURAL STUDIES.**

**TRANS-NATIONAL ADOPTION.** *See* **INTERCOUNTRY ADOPTION.**

**TRANSACTIONAL ANALYSIS.**
Midgley, David. New directions in transactional analysis counselling. London ; New York : Free Association Books, 1999.
*TC RC489.T7M535 1999*

Stewart, Ian, 1940- Transactional analysis counselling in action. 2nd ed. London : SAGE, 2000.
*TC RC489.T7 S74 2000*

**Transactional analysis counselling in action.**
Stewart, Ian, 1940- 2nd ed. London : SAGE, 2000.
*TC RC489.T7 S74 2000*

**TRANSATLANTIC FLIGHTS.**
Burleigh, Robert. Flight. New York : Philomel Books, c1991.
*TC TL540.L5 B83 1991*

**TRANSATLANTIC FLIGHTS - JUVENILE LITERATURE.**
Burleigh, Robert. Flight. New York : Philomel Books, c1991.
*TC TL540.L5 B83 1991*

**TRANSCENDENCE (PHILOSOPHY).**
Seligman, A. Modernity's wager. Princeton, NJ : Princeton University Press, 2000.
*TC HM1251 .S45 2000*

**Transcending boundaries :** writing for a dual audience of children and adults / edited by Sandra L. Beckett. New York : Garland, 1999. xx, 286 p. ; 23 cm. (Garland reference library of the humanities ; v. 2152. Children's literature and culture ; v. 13) Includes bibliographical references (p. 255-272) and index. ISBN 0-8153-3359-5 (acid-free paper) DDC 809/.89282
1. *Children's literature - History and criticism. 2. Children's literature - Authorship. 3. Children - Books and reading. 4. Authors and readers. 5. Books and reading. 6. Authorship. 7. Adulthood. I. Beckett, Sandra L., 1953- II. Series: Garland reference library of the humanities ; vol. 2152. III. Series: Garland reference library of the humanities. Children's literature and culture ; v. 13.*
*TC PN1009.A1 T69 1999*

**TRANSCONTINENTAL JOURNEYS (UNITED STATES).** *See* **OVERLAND JOURNEYS TO THE PACIFIC.**

**TRANSCULTURAL MEDICAL CARE - UNITED STATES.**
Promoting health in multicultural populations. Thousand Oaks, Calif. : Sage Publications, c1999.
*TC RA448.4 .P76 1999*

**TRANSCULTURAL MEDICINE.** *See* **TRANSCULTURAL MEDICAL CARE.**

**TRANSCULTURAL PSYCHIATRY.** *See* **PSYCHIATRY, TRANSCULTURAL.**

**TRANSCULTURAL STUDIES.** *See* **CROSS-CULTURAL STUDIES.**

**TRANSEXUALS.** *See* **TRANSSEXUALS.**

**TRANSFER, LANGUAGE (LANGUAGE LEARNING).** *See* **LANGUAGE TRANSFER (LANGUAGE LEARNING).**

**TRANSFER OF TECHNOLOGY.** *See* **TECHNOLOGY TRANSFER.**

**TRANSFER OF TRAINING.**
Lamm, Sharon Lea. The connection between action reflection learning and transformative learning. 2000.
*TC 06 no. 11230*

An update on adult development theory :. San Francisco, CA : Jossey-Bass Publishers, 1999.
*TC LC5225.L42 U63 1999*

**TRANSFERENCE (PSYCHOLOGY).** *See also* **COUNTERTRANSFERENCE (PSYCHOLOGY).**

Borderline patients :. 1st ed. New York : BasicBooks, c2000.
*TC RC569.5.B67 B685 2000*

**The transformation of collective education in the kibbutz :** the end of utopia? / Werner Fölling, Maria Fölling-Albers (eds.). Frankfurt am Main ; New York : P. Lang, 1999. 245 p. : ill. ; 22 cm. Revised papers from a German-Israeli symposium held July, 1998, at the University of Regensburg. Includes bibliographical references. ISBN 3-631-34297-7 ISBN 0-8204-3647-X (U.S) DDC 371.04/095694
1. *Collective education - Israel. 2. Educational change - Israel. 3. Kibbutzim. I. Fölling, Werner, 1944- II. Fölling-Albers, Maria.*
*TC LC1027.I75 T73 1999*

**TRANSFORMATIONAL GRAMMAR.** *See* **GENERATIVE GRAMMAR.**

**Transformative curriculum leadership.**
Henderson, James George. 2nd ed. Upper Saddle River. N.J. : Merrill, c2000.
*TC LB1570 .H45 2000*

**Transformative learning.**
O'Sullivan, Edmund, 1938- London ; New York : Zed Books ; New York : Distributed in USA exclusively by St. Martin's Press, 1999.
*TC LC196 .O7 1999*

**Transforming critical thinking.**
Thayer-Bacon, Barbara J., 1953- New York : Teachers College Press, c2000.
*TC BC177 .T45 2000*

**Transforming libraries.**
DeCandido, GraceAnne A. Washington, D.C. : Association of Research Libraries, Office of Leadership and Management Services, c1999.
*TC Z711.92.H3 D43 1999*

(8.) DeCandido, GraceAnne A. Transforming libraries. Washington, D.C. : Association of Research Libraries, Office of Leadership and Management Services, c1999.
*TC Z711.92.H3 D43 1999*

**Transforming middle school science education.**
Hurd, Paul DeHart, 1905- New York : Teachers College Press, c2000.
*TC LB1585.3 .H89 2000*

**The transforming power of affect.**
Fosha, Diana. 1st ed. New York : BasicBooks, 2000.
*TC BF637.C4 F67 2000*

**Transforming social inquiry, transforming social action :** new paradigms for crossing the theory/ practice divide in universities and communities / edited by Francine T. Sherman, William R. Torbert. Boston ; London : Kluwer Academic, c2000. xviii, 301 p. : ill. ; 25 cm. (Outreach scholarship ; 4) Includes bibliographical references and index. ISBN 0-7923-7787-7 (alk. paper) DDC 378.1/03
1. *Community and college - United States. 2. Social action - United States. 3. Social sciences - Research - United States. 4. Research - United States. I. Sherman, Francine T., 1955- II. Torbert, William R., 1944- III. Series.*
*TC LC238 .T73 2000*

**Transforming undergraduate education in science, mathematics, engineering, and technology /** Committee on Undergraduate Science Education, Center for Science, Mathematics, and Engineering Education, National Research Council. Washington, DC : National Academy Press, 1999. xiii, 113 p. ; 28 cm. Includes bibliographical references (p. 65-70). ISBN 0-309-06294-2 (perfectbound) DDC 507.1/173
1. *Science - Study and teaching (Higher) - United States. 2. Mathematics - Study and teaching (Higher) - United States. 3. Technology - Study and teaching (Higher) - United States. I. Center for Science, Mathematics, and Engineering Education. Committee on Undergraduate Science Education.*
*TC Q183.3.A1 T73 1999*

**Transforming universities :** changing patterns of governance, structure and learning in Swedish higher education / Marianne Bauer .. [et al.]. London ; Philadelphia : Jessica Kingsley Publishers, 1999. 320 p. : ill. ; 24 cm. (Higher education policy series ; 48) Includes bibliographical references (p. 299-313) and indexes. ISBN 1-85302-675-1
1. *Education, Higher - Sweden. 2. Higher education and state - Sweden 3. Educational change - Sweden I. Bauer, Marianne, 1940- II. Series.*
*TC LA908 .T73 1999*

**Transforming women's education :** the history of women's studies in the University of Wisconsin System. Madison, WI : Office of University Publications for the University of Wisconsin System, Women's Studies Consortium, 1999. iv, 162 p. ; 24 cm.

Includes bibliographical references. ISBN 0-9658834-6-9 (pbk.) DDC 305.4/071/1775
*1. Women's studies - Wisconsin - History. 2. Women - Education (Higher) - Wisconsin - History. 3. University of Wisconsin System - History. I. University of Wisconsin System. Women's Studies Consortium.*
*TC HQ1181.U5 T77 1999*

**TRANSGENIC ORGANISMS.** *See* **GENETIC ENGINEERING.**

**TRANSHUMANISTIC PSYCHOLOGY.** *See* **TRANSPERSONAL PSYCHOLOGY.**

**The transition handbook.**
Hughes, Carolyn, 1946- Baltimore : P.H. Brookes Pub., c2000.
*TC LC4019 .H84 2000*

**TRANSITION, SCHOOL-TO-WORK.** *See* **SCHOOL-TO-WORK TRANSITION.**

**Transition to a market economy in urban China.**
Ikels, Charlotte. The return of the god of wealth. Stanford, Calif. : Stanford University Press, c1996.
*TC HC428.C34 I38 1996*

**The transition to kindergarten** / edited by Robert C. Pianta and Martha J. Cox. Baltimore : P.H. Brookes Pub., c1999. xviii, 395 p. : ill. ; 26 cm. "National Center for Early Development & Learning." "Derived from 'The Transition to kindergarten: a synthesis conference' held at the University of Virginia in Charlottesville on February 18-20, 1998. The conference was conducted under the auspices of the National Center for Early Development and Learning (NCEDL), funded by the U.S. Department fo Education, Office of Educational Research and Improvement,"--Pref. Includes bibliographical references and index. ISBN 1-55766-399-8 (pbk.) DDC 372.21/8 DDC 372.21/8
*1. Kindergarten - United States - Congresses. 2. Early childhood education - United States - Congresses. I. Pianta, Robert C. II. Cox. Martha J. III. National Center for Early Development & Learning (U.S.)*
*TC LB1205 .T72 1999*

**Transitions** : teaching writing in computer-supported and traditional classrooms / by Mike Palmquist ... [et al.]. Greenwich, Conn. : Ablex Pub. Corp., c1998. xxii, 252 p. : ill. ; 24 cm. (New directions in computers & composition studies) Includes bibliographical references (p. 233-246) and indexes. ISBN 1-56750-352-7 ISBN 1-56750-353-5 (pbk.) DDC 808/.042/07
*1. English language - Rhetoric - Study and teaching. 2. English language - Rhetoric - Study and teaching - Technological innovations. 3. Report writing - Study and teaching - Technological innovations. 4. English language - Computer-assisted instruction. 5. Report writing - Computer-assisted instruction. 6. Report writing - Study and teaching. 7. Information technology. I. Palmquist. Mike. II. Series: New directions in computers and composition studies.*
*TC PE1404 .T74 1998*

**Transitions to adulthood in a changing economy** : no work, no family, no future? / edited by Alan Booth, Ann C. Crouter, and Michael J. Shanahan. Westport, Conn. : Praeger, c1999. ix, 279 p. : ill. ; 24 cm. Based on a symposium held at Pennsylvania State University, Oct. 30-31, 1997. Includes bibliographical references and indexes. ISBN 0-275-96238-5 (alk. paper) DDC 305.242
*1. Young adults - United States - Social conditions - Congresses. 2. Young adults - United States - Economic conditions - Congresses. 3. Young adults - Employment - United States - Congresses. 4. Job vacancies - United States - Congresses. 5. School-to-work transition - United States - Congresses. I. Booth. Alan, 1935- II. Crouter, Ann C. III. Shanahan, Michael J.*
*TC HQ799.7 .T73 1999*

**Translated woman.**
Behar, Ruth, 1956- Boston : Beacon Press, c1993.
*TC HQ1465.M63 B44 1993*

**Translating theory into practice.**
Deegan, William L. 1st ed. [Columbus, Ohio] : National Association of Student Personnel Administrators, c1985.
*TC LB2343 .D356 1985*

**TRANSLATORS.** *See* **INTERPRETERS FOR THE DEAF.**

**TRANSLITERATION.** *See* **ALPHABET.**

**TRANSMISSION OF DATA.** *See* **DATA TRANSMISSION SYSTEMS.**

**Transnational associations.**
International transnational associations. [Bruxelles, Union of International Associations]

**Transnational associations <1977, 1984>.**
International transnational associations. [Bruxelles, Union of International Associations]

**TRANSNATIONAL CORPORATIONS.** *See also* **INTERNATIONAL BUSINESS ENTERPRISES.**
University curriculum on transnational corporations. New York : United Nations, 1991.
*TC HD2755.5 .U55 1991*

**TRANSPERSONAL PSYCHOLOGY.**
Fukuyama, Mary A. Integrating spirituality into multicultural counseling. Thousand Oaks, Calif. : Sage Publications, c1999.
*TC BF637.C6 F795 1999*

Ken Wilber in dialogue. 1st Quest ed. Wheaton, Ill. : Theosophical Pub. House, 1998.
*TC BF204.7 .K46 1998*

**TRANSPERSONAL PSYCHOLOGY - RESEARCH - METHODOLOGY.**
Transpersonal research methods for the social sciences. Thousand Oaks, Calif. : Sage Publications, c1998.
*TC BF76.5 .T73 1998*

**Transpersonal research methods for the social sciences** : honoring human experience / [edited by] William Braud, Rosemarie Anderson. Thousand Oaks, Calif. : Sage Publications, c1998. xxxi, 321 p. : ill. ; 24 cm. Includes bibliographical references (p. 287-306) and index. ISBN 0-7619-1012-3 (hardcover : alk. paper) ISBN 0-7619-1013-1 (pbk. : alk. paper) DDC 150.19/8
*1. Psychology - Research - Methodology. 2. Transpersonal psychology - Research - Methodology. 3. Social sciences - Research - Methodology. I. Braud, William. II. Anderson, Rosemarie.*
*TC BF76.5 .T73 1998*

**TRANSPLANTATION OF ORGANS, TISSUES, ETC.** *See* **SURGERY, PLASTIC.**

**TRANSPORT WORKERS.** *See* **SAILORS.**

**TRANSPORTATION.** *See* **RAILROADS.**

**TRANSPORTATION, AUTOMOTIVE.** *See* **TRUCKS.**

**TRANSSEXUALISM - PATIENTS.** *See* **TRANSSEXUALS.**

**TRANSSEXUALISM - UNITED STATES - CASE STUDIES.**
Out & about campus. 1st ed. Los Angeles : Alyson Books, 2000.
*TC LC2574.6 .O87 2000*

**TRANSSEXUALITY.** *See* **TRANSSEXUALISM.**

**TRANSSEXUALS - UNITED STATES - BIOGRAPHY.**
McCloskey, Deirdre N. Crossing. Chicago, Ill. : University of Chicago Press, 1999.
*TC HQ77.8.M39 A3 1999*

**TRANSSEXUALS - UNITED STATES - PSYCHOLOGY.**
McCloskey, Deirdre N. Crossing. Chicago, Ill. : University of Chicago Press, 1999.
*TC HQ77.8.M39 A3 1999*

**TRAUMA, EMOTIONAL.** *See* **PSYCHIC TRAUMA.**

**TRAUMA, PSYCHIC.** *See* **PSYCHIC TRAUMA.**

**TRAUMATIC NEUROSES.** *See* **POST-TRAUMATIC STRESS DISORDER.**

**TRAUMATIC STRESS SYNDROME.** *See* **POST-TRAUMATIC STRESS DISORDER.**

**Trautman, Barbara A.** AGS English to use / by Barbara A. Trautman, David H. Trautman. Teacher's ed. Circle Pines, Minn. : AGS, American Guidance Service, c1998. T16, x, 318 p. : ill. ; 29 cm. Includes index. ISBN 0-7854-1001-5
*1. English language - Usage. 2. English language - Composition and exercises. 3. American Sign Language. 4. English language - Study and teaching (Secondary) I. Trautman, David H. II. Title. III. Title: American Guidance Service English to use*
*TC PE1121 .T72 1998 Teacher's Ed.*

AGS English to use / by Barbara A. Trautman, David H. Trautman. Circle Pines, Minn. : AGS, American Guidance Service, c1998. ix, 292 p. : ill. ; 25 cm. Includes index. ISBN 0-7854-1450-9
*1. English language - Usage. 2. English language - Composition and exercises. 3. American Sign Language. I. Trautman, David H. II. Title. III. Title: American Guidance Service English to use*
*TC PE1121 .T72 1998*

**Trautman, David H.**
Trautman, Barbara A. AGS English to use. Teacher's ed. Circle Pines, Minn. : AGS, American Guidance Service, c1998.
*TC PE1121 .T72 1998 Teacher's Ed.*

Trautman, Barbara A. AGS English to use. Circle Pines, Minn. : AGS, American Guidance Service, c1998.
*TC PE1121 .T72 1998*

**Trautner, Hanns Martin, 1943-.**
The Developmental social psychology of gender. Mahwah, N.J. : Lawrence Erlbaum, c2000.
*TC HQ1075 .D47 2000*

**Travail de la mousse de polyéthylène et des feuilles de plastique cannelées.**
Schlichting, Carl. Working with polyethylene foam and fluted plastic sheet. Ottawa, Ontario, Canada : Canadian Conservation Institute, Dept. of Canadian Heritage, 1994.
*TC N8554 T25 no.14*

**TRAVAILLEURS - ÉDUCATION - ANGLETERRE - HISTOIRE.**
Heathorn, Stephen J., 1965- For home, country, and race. Toronto : University of Toronto Press, 1999.
*TC LC93.E5 H42 1999*

**TRAVELERS, IRISH (NOMADIC PEOPLE).** *See* **IRISH TRAVELLERS (NOMADIC PEOPLE).**

**TRAVELING SALES PERSONNEL.** *See* **PEDDLERS AND PEDDLING.**

**TRAVELLERS, IRISH (NOMADIC PEOPLE).** *See* **IRISH TRAVELLERS (NOMADIC PEOPLE).**

**TRAVELLING PEOPLE, IRISH (NOMADIC PEOPLE).** *See* **IRISH TRAVELLERS (NOMADIC PEOPLE).**

**TRAVELS.** *See* **OVERLAND JOURNEYS TO THE PACIFIC.**

**Trawick-Smith, Jeffrey W.** Early childhood development : a multicultural perspective / Jeffrey Trawick-Smith. 2nd ed. Upper Saddle River, N.J. : Merrill, c2000. xvii, 528 p. : ill. ; 26 cm. Includes bibliographical references (p. 487-509) and indexes. ISBN 0-13-013565-8 DDC 305.23/1
*1. Child development. 2. Early childhood education. 3. Multicultural education. 4. Cognition in children. 5. Observation (Educational method) 6. Handicapped children - Education. I. Title.*
*TC LB1115 .T73 2000*

**Traxler, Mary Ann Duranczyk.**
Turner, Nancy D'Isa. Children's literature for the primary inclusive classroom. Albany, N.Y. : Delmar Publishers, c2000.
*TC LC4028 .T87 2000*

**Traynor, Michael, 1956-** Managerialism and nursing : beyond oppression and profession / Michael Traynor. London ; New York : Routledge, 1999. xiv, 192 p. ; 25 cm. Includes bibliographical references (p. [177]-187) and index. ISBN 0-415-17895-9 (hbk.) ISBN 0-415-17896-7 (pbk.) DDC 362.1/73/068
*1. Nurses - Supervision of - Great Britain. 2. Nursing services - Great Britain - Administration. 3. Interprofessional relations - Great Britain. 4. Nurse administrators - Great Britain. 5. Conflict management - Great Britain. 6. Nursing services - Great Britain - Personnel management. 7. Nursing - organization & administration - Great Britain. 8. Interprofessional Relations. 9. Nurse Administrators. I. Title.*
*TC RT86.45 .T73 1999*

**The treasure chests of mnemosyne** : selected texts on memory theory from Plato to Derrida. Dresden : Verlag der Kunst, 1998. 319 p. : ill. ; 25 cm. Includes bibliographical references. ISBN 90-5701-171-9 DDC 153.1
*1. Memory I. Fleckner, Uwe.*
*TC BF371 .T7413 1998*

**TREASURE, NATIONAL.** *See* **CULTURAL PROPERTY.**

**Treasury of literature ; Readtext series**
Johnson, Eleanor M. (Eleanor Murdoch), 1892-1987. Treat shop. Columbus, Ohio : Charles E. Merrill, c1954.
*TC PE1119 .J63 1954*

**Treat shop.**
Johnson, Eleanor M. (Eleanor Murdoch), 1892-1987. Columbus, Ohio : Charles E. Merrill, c1954.
*TC PE1119 .J63 1954*

**TREATIES.** *See* **CONGRESSES AND CONVENTIONS.**

**Treating anxious children and adolescents** : an evidence-based approach / Ronald M. Rapee ... [et al.]. Oakland, CA : New Harbinger Publications, c2000. vi, 195 p. : ill. ; 26 cm. Includes bibliographical

references. CONTENTS: Ch. 1. Assessment and Diagnosis of Anxiety Disorders -- Ch. 2. Understanding and Treatment of Anxiety in Children -- Ch. 3. Case Studies -- Ch. 4. Getting Started -- Ch. 5. Cognitive Restructuring -- Ch. 6. Relaxation -- Ch. 7. Child Management -- Ch. 8. Exposure -- Ch. 9. Social Skills Training -- Ch. 10. Assertiveness -- Ch. 11. Closure -- App. Running Treatment in Groups. ISBN 1-57224-192-6
*1. Anxiety in children - Treatment. 2. Anxiety in adolescence - Treatment. I. Rapee, Ronald M.*
**TC RJ504.A58 T74 2000**

**Treating borderline states in marriage.**
McCormack, Charles C. Northvale, NJ : Jason Aronson, 2000.
**TC RC488.5 .M392 2000**

**Treating mental disorders.**
Nathan, Peter E. New York : Oxford University Press, 1999.
**TC RC480.515 .N38 1999**

**Treating the disruptive adolescent.**
Bustamante, Eduardo M. Northvale, NJ : Jason Aronson, c2000.
**TC RJ506.O66 B87 2000**

**TREATMENT, CONSENT TO.** *See* **INFORMED CONSENT (MEDICAL LAW).**

**Treatment efficacy for stuttering :** a search for empirical bases / edited by Anne K. Cordes and Roger J. Ingham. San Diego, Calif. : Singular Pub. Group, c1998. xiv, 323 p. : ill. ; 23 cm. Papers based on a 3-day "State-of-the-Art Conference" held at the University of Georgia in March, 1997. Includes bibliographical references and index. ISBN 1-56543-904-X (alk. paper) DDC 616.85/ 5406
*1. Stuttering - Treatment - Congresses. I. Cordes, Anne K. II. Ingham, Roger J., 1945-*
**TC RC424 .T698 1998**

**Treatment of child abuse :** common ground for mental health, medical, and legal practitioners / edited by Robert M. Reece. Baltimore, Md. ; London : Johns Hopkins University Press, 2000. xvii, 378 p. : 26 cm. Includes bibliographical references and index. ISBN 0-8018-6320-1 (alk. paper) DDC 362.76/8/0973
*1. Child abuse - Treatment. 2. Abused children - Rehabilitation. I. Reece, Robert M.*
**TC RJ375 .T74 2000**

**TREATMENT OUTCOME.**
Measuring outcomes in speech-language pathology. New York : Theime, 1998.
**TC RC423 .M39 1997**

**TREE-DWELLINGS.** *See* **TREE HOUSES.**

**TREE HOUSES - FICTION.**
Mathis, Melissa Bay. Animal house. 1st ed. New York : Simon & Schuster Books for Young Readers, 1999.
**TC PZ8.3.M4265 Ap 1999**

**Tree of hope.**
Littlesugar, Amy. New York : Philomel Books, 1999.
**TC PZ7.L7362 Tr 1999**

**TREES - JUVENILE POETRY.**
George, Kristine O'Connell. Old Elm speaks. New York : Clarion Books, c1998.
**TC PS3557.E488 O4 1998**

**TREES - POETRY.**
George, Kristine O'Connell. Old Elm speaks. New York : Clarion Books, c1998.
**TC PS3557.E488 O4 1998**

**Treff, August V.** AGS basic math skills / by August V. Treff and Donald H. Jacobs. Circle Pines, Minn. : AGS, American Guidance Service, c1997. viii, 358 p. : col. ill. ; 25 cm. Includes index. ISBN 0785409165H
*1. Mathematics. I. Jacobs, Donald H. II. Title. III. Title: American Guidance Service basic math skills*
**TC QA107 .T73 1997**

AGS basic math skills / by August V. Treff and Donald H. Jacobs. Teacher's ed. Circle Pines, Minn. : AGS, American Guidance Service, c1997. T16, x, 374 p. : col. ill. ; 29 cm. Includes index. ISBN 0-7854-0443-0
*1. Mathematics. I. Jacobs, Donald H. II. Title. III. Title: American Guidance Service basic math skills*
**TC QA107 .T73 1997 Teacher's Ed.**

**Tregoe, Benjamin B.**
Kepner, Charles Higgins, 1922- The new rational manager. Princeton, N.J. (P.O. Box 704, Research Rd., Princeton 08540) : Princeton Research Press, c1981.
**TC HD31 .K456 1981**

**Treichler, Paula A.** How to have theory in an epidemic : cultural chronicles of AIDS / Paula A. Treichler. Durham : Duke University Press, 1999. xi,

477 p. : ill. ; 24 cm. Includes bibliographical references (p. [387]-451) and index. ISBN 0-8223-2286-2 (cloth : alk. paper) ISBN 0-8223-2318-4 (pbk. : alk. paper) DDC 362.1/969792
*1. AIDS (Disease) - Social aspects. 2. Culture - Philosophy. 3. AIDS (Disease) in mass media. I. Title.*
**TC RA644.A25 T78 1999**

**Treisman, Anne.**
Attention, space, and action. Oxford ; New York : Oxford University Press, 1999.
**TC QP405 .A865 1999**

**Trencher, Susan R.** Mirrored images : American anthropology and American culture, 1960-1980 / Susan R. Trencher. Westport, CT : Bergin & Garvey, 2000. xiii, 217 p. ; 24 cm. Includes bibliographical references (p. [197-209) and index. ISBN 0-89789-673-4 (alk. paper)
*1. Anthropology - United States - History. 2. Anthropology - United States - Philosophy. 3. Ethnology - United States - Philosophy. 4. United States - Civilization - 1945- I. Title.*
**TC GN17.3.U6 T74 2000**

**Trends & issues.**
Trends & issues in postsecondary English studies. Urbana, Ill. : National Council of Teachers of English, c1999-
**TC PE65 .T75**

**Trends & issues in Canadian social studies** / edited by Ian Wright and Alan Sears. Vancouver : Pacific Educational Press, c1997. 384 p. : ill. ; 23 cm. Includes bibliographical references. ISBN 1-89576-633-8 DDC 300/ .71/071
*1. Social sciences - Study and teaching - Canada. 2. Sciences sociales - Étude et enseignement - Canada. I. Sears, A. M. (Alan Murray), 1954- II. Wright, Ian, 1941- III. Title: Trends and issues in Canadian social studies*
**TC LB1584.5.C3 T74 1997**

**Trends & issues in postsecondary English studies.**
Urbana, Ill. : National Council of Teachers of English, c1999- v. : ill. ; 23 cm. Frequency: Annual. 1999- . (Trends and issues in English language arts) Trends and issues in postsecondary English studies. Trends & issues. Trends and issues. ISSN 1527-4241 DDC 808
*1. English philology - Study and teaching (Higher) - Periodicals. 2. English language - Rhetoric - Study and teaching (Higher) - Periodicals. 3. English literature - Study and teaching (Higher) - Periodicals. 4. English language - Study and teaching (Higher) - Periodicals. I. National Council of Teachers of English. II. Title: Trends and issues in postsecondary English studies III. Title: Trends & issues IV. Title: Trends and issues V. Series.*
**TC PE65 .T75**

**Trends and issues.**
Trends & issues in postsecondary English studies. Urbana, Ill. : National Council of Teachers of English, c1999-
**TC PE65 .T75**

**Trends and issues in Canadian social studies.**
Trends & issues in Canadian social studies. Vancouver : Pacific Educational Press, c1997.
**TC LB1584.5.C3 T74 1997**

**Trends and issues in English language arts**
Trends & issues in postsecondary English studies. Urbana, Ill. : National Council of Teachers of English, c1999-
**TC PE65 .T75**

**Trends and issues in postsecondary English studies.**
Trends & issues in postsecondary English studies. Urbana, Ill. : National Council of Teachers of English, c1999-
**TC PE65 .T75**

**Trends in community college curriculum** / Gwyer Schuyler, editor. San Francisco : Jossey-Bass, c1999. 112 p. : ill. ; 23 cm. (New directions for community colleges, 0194-3081 ; no. 108 (Winter 1999)) (Jossey-Bass higher and adult education series) Spine title: Community college curriculum. "Winter 1999" Includes bibliographic references (p. 99-107) and index. CONTENTS: Historical and contemporary view of the community college curriculum / Gwyer Schuyler -- Liberal arts / Florence B. Brawer -- Statistical portrait of the non-liberal arts curriculum / James Palmer -- Dimensions of general education requirements / Paula Zeszotarski -- Interdisciplinary studies in the community colleges / Arianne Abell Walker -- Importance of community college honors programs / Charles Outcalt -- English as a second language in the community college curriculum / Elaine W. Kuo -- Status of multicultural education in the curriculum / William E. Piland, Alexandria Piland, Shelly Hess -- Scratching the surface: distance education in the community colleges / Carol A. Kozeracki -- Sources and information: forces influencing curriculum / Jennifer Rinella Keup. ISBN 0-7879-4849-7 (pbk.)
*1. Community colleges - United States - Curricula. 2. Curriculum planning. 3. Community colleges - Curricula. I.*

*Schuyler, Gwyer. II. Title: Community college curriculum III. Series. IV. Series: New directions for community colleges ; no. 108.*
**TC LB2328.15.U6 T75 1999**

**Trends in linguistics. Studies and monographs**
(26) Linguistic minorities and literacy. Berlin ; New York : Mouton Publishers, 1984.
**TC P119.315 .L56 1984**

**Trends in the demand for primary education in Cameroon.**
Amin, Martin E. (Martin Efuetngu) Lanham, MD : University Press of America, 1999.
**TC LC137.C36 A55 1999**

**Trends in the early careers of life scientists /**
Committee on Dimensions, Causes, and Implications of Recent Trends in the Careers of Life Scientists, Board on Biology, Commission on Life Sciences, Office of Scientific and Engineering Personnel, National Research Council. Washington, DC : National Academy Press, 1998. xv, 178 p. : ill. ; 28 cm. Includes bibliographical references. ISBN 0-309-06180-6 DDC 570/.23/73
*1. Life scientists - Employment - United States. 2. Life scientists - Training of - United States. 3. Life sciences - Vocational guidance - United States. I. National Research Council (U.S.). Committee on Dimensions, Causes, and Implications of Recent Trends in the Careers of Life Scientists.*
**TC QH314 .T74 1998**

**TRIAL BY JURY.** *See* **JURY.**

**TRIAL BY PEERS.** *See* **JURY.**

**TRIAL PRACTICE - UNITED STATES.**
Flaton, Robin Anne. Effect of deliberation on juror reasoning. 1999.
**TC 085 F612**

**TRIALS.** *See* **JURY.**

**TRIBES - INDIA.** *See* **INDIA - SCHEDULED TRIBES.**

**The trickster shift.**
Ryan, Allan J. Vancouver, BC : UBC Press ; Seattle : University of Washington Press, c1999.
**TC E78.C2 R93 1999**

**TRICKSTERS IN ART.**
Ryan, Allan J. The trickster shift. Vancouver, BC : UBC Press ; Seattle : University of Washington Press, c1999.
**TC E78.C2 R93 1999**

**Trifonas, Peter Pericles, 1960-** The ethics of writing : Derrida, deconstruction, and pedagogy / Peter Pericles Trifonas. Lanham, Md. ; Oxford : Rowman & Littlefield, c2000. viii, 200 p. ; 24 cm. (Culture and education series) Includes bibliographical references and index. ISBN 0-8476-9557-3 (hbk. : alk. paper) ISBN 0-8476-9558-1 (pbk. : alk. paper) DDC 370/.1
*1. Education - Philosophy. 2. Derrida, Jacques. 3. Postmodernism and education. 4. Critical pedagogy. 5. Deconstruction. I. Title. II. Series.*
**TC LB14.7 .T75 2000**

Revolutionary pedagogies : cultural politics, instituting education, and the discourse of theory / [edited by] Peter Pericles Trifonas. New York : Routledge, 2000. xxi, 362 p. ; 25 cm. Includes bibliographical references and index. ISBN 0-415-92568-1 (hb : alk. paper) ISBN 0-415-92569-X (pb : alk. paper) DDC 370.11/5
*1. Critical pedagogy. 2. Education - Political aspects. 3. Education - Social aspects. 4. Education - Philosophy.*
**TC LC196 .R48 2000**

**TRINITY.** *See* **GOD.**

**TRINITY COLLEGE (DUBLIN, IRELAND). LIBRARY - HISTORY.**
Essays on the history of Trinity College Library, Dublin. Dublin : Four Courts, c2000.
**TC Z792.5.T75 E87 2000**

**Trinkle, Dennis A., 1968-.**
History.edu. Armonk, N.Y. ; London : M.E. Sharpe, c2001.
**TC D16.3 .H53 2001**

**The triple revolution.**
Perrucci, Robert, comp. Boston, Little, Brown [1968]
**TC HN65 .P4**

**TRIPLETS - PSYCHOLOGY.**
Twin and triplet psychology. London ; New York : Routledge, 1999.
**TC BF723.T9 T85 1999**

**TRISOMY 21.** *See* **DOWN SYNDROME.**

**TRITICUM.** *See* **WHEAT.**

**TRITICUM AESTIVUM.** *See* **WHEAT.**

**TRITICUM SATIVUM.** *See* **WHEAT.**

**TRITICUM VULGARE.** *See* **WHEAT.**

**TRIVIA.** *See* **QUESTIONS AND ANSWERS.**

**Trombone for beginners.**
The trombone [videorecording]. Van Nuys, CA : Backstage Pass Productions ; Canoga Park, Calif. : [Distributed by] MVP, c1998.
*TC MT465 .T7 1998*

**The trombone** [videorecording] / director, Todd Brinegar ; producer, Mark S. Arnett ; a production of Aesthetic Artist Records and Brinegar Video/Film Productions, Inc. in association with Backstage Pass Instructional Video. Van Nuys, CA : Backstage Pass Productions ; Canoga Park, Calif. : [Distributed by] MVP, c1998. 1 videocassette (49 min.) : sd., col. ; 1/2 in. + 1 instruction booklet (4 p. : music ; 18 cm.). (Maestro music instrument instructional video ... for) Title on container: Trombone for beginners. VHS, Hi-Fi, Stereo. Cataloged from credits, cassette label and container. Instructor: Hal Harris. Audio, Mark S. Arnett. For beginners. SUMMARY: Hal Harris teaches the basics of learning to play the trombone, from handling to rudimentary playing, and demonstrates the technique along with one of his pupils. CONTENTS: Trombone assembly -- Holding the trombone -- How it works -- Playing tones -- Warming up -- Finding a teacher -- Slide positions -- Playing notes -- Practicing notes -- Trombone care -- Wrapping it up.
*1. Violin - Instruction and study. 2. Violin - Studies and exercises. I. Harris, Hal. II. Brinegar, Todd. III. Arnett, Mark S. IV. Backstage Pass Productions. V. Aesthetic Artist Records. VI. Brinegar Video/Film Productions, Inc. VII. MVP Home Entertainment (Firm) VIII. Title: Trombone for beginners IX. Series.*
*TC MT465 .T7 1998*

**Tropea, Judith.** A day in the life of a museum curator / by Judith Tropea ; photography by John Halpern. Mahwah, N.J. : Troll Associates, c1991. 32 p. : col. ill. ; 24 cm. SUMMARY: Describes the work of Niles Eldredge, a curator at the American Museum of Natural History, including his field work in search of invertebrate fossils. ISBN 0-8167-2212-9 (lib. bdg.) ISBN 0-8167-2213-7 (pbk.) DDC 562/.074/7471
*1. Eldredge, Niles - Juvenile literature. 2. Paleontologists - United States - Biography - Juvenile literature. 3. Museum curators - United States - Biography - Juvenile literature. 4. Museum techniques - Vocational guidance - Juvenile literature. 5. Museum curators. 6. Paleontology. 7. Occupations. 8. Eldredge, Niles. I. Halpern, John, 1957- ill. II. Title.*
*TC QE22.E53 T76 1991*

**TROPICAL RAIN FOREST ECOLOGY.** *See* **RAIN FOREST ECOLOGY.**

**TROPICAL RAIN FORESTS.** *See* **RAIN FORESTS.**

**Trotzer, James P., 1943-** The counselor and the group : integrating theory, training, and practice / James P. Trotzer. 3rd ed. Philadelphia ; London : Accelerated Development, c1999. xxx, 574 p. : ill. ; 25 cm. Includes bibliographical references (p. 471-490) and index. ISBN 1-56032-699-9 (case : alk. paper) DDC 158/.35
*1. Group counseling. I. Title.*
*TC BF637.C6 T68 1999*

**TROUBLED FAMILIES.** *See* **PROBLEM FAMILIES.**

**TROUBLED YOUTH.** *See* **PROBLEM YOUTH.**

**Troyka, Lynn Quitman, 1938-.**
Carter, Carol. Majoring in the rest of your life. Upper Saddle River, NJ : Prentice Hall, c2000.
*TC HF5382.5.U5 C373 2000*

**Truancy and schools.**
Reid, Ken. London ; New York : Routledge, 1999.
*TC LB3081 .R45 1999*

**TRUANCY (SCHOOLS).** *See* **SCHOOL ATTENDANCE.**

**TRUCK DRIVERS - FICTION.**
Day, Alexandra. Frank and Ernest on the road. New York : Scholastic Inc., c1994.
*TC PZ7.D32915 Frn 1994*

**TRUCKERS.** *See* **TRUCK DRIVERS.**

**TRUCKS.**
Simon, Seymour. Seymour Simon's book of trucks. New York : HarperCollins Publishers, 2000.
*TC TL230.15 .S56 2000*

**TRUCKS - JUVENILE LITERATURE.**
Simon, Seymour. Seymour Simon's book of trucks. New York : HarperCollins Publishers, 2000.

*TC TL230.15 .S56 2000*

**True-blue friends** : teacher's planning guide. New York : Macmillan/McGraw-Hill, c1997. 1 v. (various pagings) : col. ill. ; 31 cm. (Spotlight on literacy ; Gr.1 l.5 u.2) (The road to independent reading) Includes index. ISBN 0-02-181156-3
*1. Language arts (Primary) 2. Reading (Primary) I. Series. II. Series: The road to independent reading*
*TC LB1576 .S66 1997 Gr.1 l.5 u.2*

**True heart.**
Moss, Marissa. 1st ed. San Diego : Silver Whistle, c1999.
*TC PZ7.M8535 Tr 1999*

**True, Michael.** An energy field more intense than war : the nonviolent tradition and American literature / Michael True. 1st ed. Syracuse, N.Y. : Syracuse University Press, 1995. xxiii, 169 p. ; 23 cm. (Syracuse studies on peace and conflict resolution) Includes bibliographical references (p. 145-154) and index. ISBN 0-8156-0367-3 (pbk. : alk. paper) ISBN 0-8156-2679-7 (hard : alk. paper) DDC 810.9/355
*1. American literature - History and criticism. 2. Nonviolence in literature. 3. Social justice in literature. 4. Peace movements in literature. 5. Literature and society - United States - History. 6. Politics and literature - United States - History. I. Title. II. Series.*
*TC PS169.N65 T78 1995*

To construct peace : 30 more justice seekers, peace makers / Michael True. Mystic, Conn. : Twenty-Third Publications, c1992. 190 p. : ports. ; 22 cm. Includes bibliographical references. ISBN 0-89622-487-2 DDC 303.6/6/092273
*1. Pacifists - Biography. I. Title.*
*TC JX1962.A2 T783 1992*

**True tales of heroes & heroines.**
Marsh, Valerie. Fort Atkinson, Wis. : Alleyside Press, c1999.
*TC CT85 .M37 1999*

**True tales of heroes and heroines.**
Marsh, Valerie. True tales of heroes & heroines. Fort Atkinson, Wis. : Alleyside Press, c1999.
*TC CT85 .M37 1999*

**Truesdell, Sue, ill.**
Grossman, Bill. Donna O'Neeshuck was chased by some cows. 1st ed. [New York] : Harper & Row, c1988.
*TC PZ8.3.G914 Do 1988*

Root, Phyllis. Soup for supper. 1st ed. New York : Harper & Row, c1986.
*TC PZ7.R6784 So 1986*

**Trujillo, Armando L.** Chicano empowerment and bilingual education : movimiento politics in Crystal City, Texas / Armando L. Trujillo. New York : Garland Pub., c1998. xvi, 228 p. ; 23 cm. (Latino communities) Includes bibliographical references (p. 209-219) and index. ISBN 0-8153-3169-X (alk. paper) DDC 370.117/5/09764/437
*1. Mexican Americans - Education - Texas - Crystal City. 2. Education, Bilingual - Texas - Crystal City. 3. Mexican Americans - Texas - Crystal City - Politics and government. I. Title. II. Series.*
*TC LC2688.C79 T78 1998*

**Trump, Kenneth S.** Classroom killers? hallway hostages? : how schools can prevent and manage school crises / Kenneth S. Trump. Thousand Oaks, Calif. : Corwin Press, c2000. xx, 161 p. : ill. ; 27 cm. Includes bibliographical references (p. 159-160). ISBN 0-7619-7510-1 (cloth : alk. paper) ISBN 0-7619-7511-X (pbk. : alk. paper) DDC 371.7/82/0973
*1. School crisis management - United States. 2. School violence - United States - Prevention. 3. Schools - Security measures - United States. I. Title.*
*TC LB2866.5 .T78 2000*

**Trust for Museum Exhibitions.**
Farr, Dennis, 1929- Francis Bacon. New York : Harry N. Abrams in association with the Trust for Museum Exhibitions, 1999.
*TC ND497.B16 A4 1999*

**TRUST (PROGRAM).**
The next generation [videorecording]. Princeton, NJ : Films for the Humanities & Sciences, c1998.
*TC RC564 .N4 1998*

**Trust, service, and the common purpose.**
American Assembly (93rd : 1998 : Los Angeles, Calif.) Indianapolis, IN : Indiana University Center on Philanthropy ; New York, NY : American Assembly, [1998]
*TC HD62.6 .A44 1998*

**TRUSTEES, MUSEUM.** *See* **MUSEUM TRUSTEES.**

**TRUSTS AND TRUSTEES.** *See* **GUARDIAN AND WARD; INHERITANCE AND SUCCESSION; MUSEUM TRUSTEES.**

**TRUSTS, INDUSTRIAL.** *See* **COMPETITION; CORPORATIONS; RAILROADS.**

**TRUTH.** *See* **KNOWLEDGE, THEORY OF.**

**The truth about America's schools.**
Bracey, Gerald W. (Gerald Watkins) Bloomington, Ind. : Phi Delta Kappa Educational Foundation, c1997.
*TC LA217.2 .B75 1997*

**Truth from trash.**
Thornton, Christopher James. Cambridge, Mass. ; London : MIT Press, c2000.
*TC Q325.4 .T47 2000*

**TRUTHFULNESS AND FALSEHOOD.** *See* **HONESTY.**

**Tsai, Chin-Chung.** The interrelationships between junior high school students' scientific epistemologicl beliefs, learning environment preferences and their cognitive structure outcomes / by Chin-Chung Tsai. 1996. xvi, 344 leaves : ill. ; 29 cm. Includes tables. Issued also on microfilm. Thesis (Ed.D.) -- Teachers College, Columbia University, 1996. Includes bibliographical references (leaves 286-317)
*1. Constructivism (Education) 2. Science - Study and teaching. 3. Learning, Psychology of. 4. Cognitive learning. 5. High school students - Interviews. 6. Study skills. I. Title.*
*TC 06 no. 10713*

**Tsamasiros, Katherine V.** Using interactive multimedia software to improve cognition of complex imagery in adolescents / by Katherine V. Tsamasiros. 1998. xiii, 209 leaves : ill. ; 29 cm. Issued also on microfilm. Thesis (Ed.D.)--Teachers College, Columbia University, 1998. Includes bibliographical references (leaves 168-183).
*1. Art, Modern - History - Study and teaching (Middle school) - Software. 2. Art appreciation - Study and teaching (Middle school) - Interactive multimedia. 3. Art appreciation - Study and teaching (Middle school) - Software. 4. Imagery (Psychology) 5. Visual perception. 6. Middle school students - New York (State) - New York - Attitudes. 7. Brooklyn (New York, N.Y.) I. Title.*
*TC 06 no. 10905*

**Tsui, Anne S.** Demographic differences in organizations : current research and future directions / Anne S. Tsui and Barbara A. Gutek. Lanham, MD : Lexington Books, 1999. xv, 204 p. : ill. ; 24 cm. Includes bibliographical references (p. 185-197) and index. ISBN 0-7391-0056-4 (cloth : al. paper) DDC 331.11/43
*1. Diversity in the workplace. I. Gutek, Barbara A. II. Title.*
*TC HF5549.5.M5 T75 1999*

**Tuck everlasting by Natalie Babbitt.**
Beech, Linda Ward. New York : Scholastic, c1997.
*TC LB1573 .B43 1997*

**Tucker, Everett Brackin, ed.**
The Journal of Arkansas education. [Little Rock : Arkansas Educational Association, 1923-1975].

**Tucker, Gina Marie.** Discipline : Bermuda high school student, teacher, parent, and administrator perceptions of the causes of misbehavior / by Gina Marie Tucker. 1998. ix, 193 leaves ; 29 cm. Typescript; issued also on microfilm. Thesis (Ed.D.)--Teachers College, Columbia University, 1998. Includes bibliographical references (leaves 182-188).
*1. High school students - Bermuda Islands - Discipline. 2. School discipline - Bermuda Islands. 3. Classroom management - Bermuda Islands. 4. Parental influences. 5. Peer pressure in adolescence - Bermuda Islands. 6. High school attendance - Bermuda Islands. 7. High school teachers - Bermuda Islands - Attitudes. 8. Teacher-student relationships - Bermuda Islands. 9. High schools - Bermuda Islands - Administration. I. Title. II. Title: Bermuda high school student, teacher, parent, and administrator perceptions of the causes of misbehavior*
*TC 06 no. 10999*

**Tuijnman, Albert.** Recurrent education and socioeconomic success : a theoretical and longitudinal analysis / Albert Tuijnman. [Stockholm] : Institute of International Education, University of Stockholm, c1986. x, 145 p. : ill. ; 25 cm. (Master's degree studies from the Institute of International Education ; no 1) Bibliography: p. 130-145. ISBN 91-7146-467-0
*1. Continuing education - Social aspects. 2. Continuing education - Economic aspects. I. Stockholms universitet. Institutionen för internationell pedagogik. II. Title. III. Series.*
*TC LC5215 .T84 1986*

**TUITION.** *See* **COLLEGE COSTS; EDUCATION - FINANCE.**

**Tulasiewicz, Witold.**
Teaching the mother tongue in a multilingual Europe. London : Cassell, 1998.
*TC P53.5 .T43 1998*

**Tulchinsky, Theodore H.** The new public health : an introduction for the 21st century / Theodore H. Tulchinsky, Elena A. Varavikova. San Diego, Calif. ; London : Academic Press, c2000. xxi, 882 p. : ill. ; 24 cm. Includes bibliographical references and index. ISBN 0-12-703350-5 DDC 614
*1. Public health. 2. Medical policy. 3. Public health - History. 4. Public Health. 5. Health Policy. 6. Delivery of Health Care. 7. Economics. Medical. 8. World Health. 9. Public health. 10. Medical policy. I. Varavikova, Elena II. Title.*
*TC RA425 .T85 2000*

**TULE LAKE RELOCATION CENTER (CALIF.).**
Rabbit in the moon [videorecording]. San Francisco, Calif. : Wabi-Sabi Productions, 1999.
*TC D753.8 .R3 1999*

**Tulip Films.**
When the brain goes wrong [videorecording]. Short version. Boston, MA : Fanlight Productions [dist.], c1992.
*TC RC386 .W54 1992*

**Tulving, Endel.**
Memory, consciousness, and the brain. Philadelphia ; London : Psychology Press, c2000.
*TC BF371 .M4483 2000*

The Oxford handbook of memory. Oxford ; New York : Oxford University Press, 2000.
*TC BF371 .O84 2000*

**Tuman, Donna M.** Gender difference in form and content : the relation between preferred subject matter and the formal artistic characteristics of children's drawing. 1998. xix, 305 leaves : ill. ; 29 cm. Typescript; issued also on microfilm. Thesis (Ed.D.)--Teachers College, Columbia University, 1998. Includes bibliographical references (leaves 171-194).
*1. Children's drawings - Psychological aspects - Sex differences. 2. Children's drawings - Themes, motives - Sex differences. 3. Figure drawing - Psychological aspects - Sex differences. 4. Imagery (Psychology) in children - Sex differences. 5. Drawing, Psychology of - Sex differences. 6. Drawing ability in children - Sex differences. 7. Form perception in children - Sex differences. 8. Cognitive styles in children - Sex differences. 9. Art appreciation - Psychological aspects - Sex differences. 10. Sex differences (Psychology) in children. 11. Sex role in children. 12. Sexism in education. 13. Art - Study and teaching (Elementary) - Psychological aspects - Sex differences. I. Title. II. Title: Relation between preferred subject matter and the formal artistic characteristics of children's drawing*
*TC 06 no. 11000*

**Tumin, Melvin Marvin, 1919-** Male and female in today's world / Melvin M. Tumin. New York : Harcourt Brace Jovanovich, c1980. 2 v. : ill. (some col.) ; 23-28 cm. (Foundations in social studies) Includes index. Library has only v. 1 (Student text). PARTIAL CONTENTS: [v. 1. Student text] -- [v. 2]. Teaching guide. ISBN 0-15-379214-0
*1. Sex role. I. Title. II. Series.*
*TC GN479.65 .T95 1980*

**TUMORS.** *See* **CANCER.**

**Tune in anytime.**
Cooney, Caroline B. New York : Delacorte Press, 1999.
*TC PZ7.C7834 Tu 1999*

**Tunnell, Michael O.** Children's literature, briefly / Michael O. Tunnell, James S. Jacobs. 2nd ed. Upper Saddle River, N.J. : Merrill, c2000. xviii, 390 p. : ill. ; 24 cm. + 1 computer optical disk (4 3/4 in.). Rev. ed. of: Children's literature, briefly / James S. Jacobs. 1996. Includes bibliographical references and indexes. ISBN 0-13-096214-7 DDC 809/.89282
*1. Children's literature - Study and teaching. 2. Children's literature - History and criticism. I. Jacobs, James S., 1945- II. Title.*
*TC PN1008.8 .J33 2000*

**Tuomi, Jan.**
Center for Science, Mathematics, and Engineering Education. Committee on Developing the Capacity to Select Effective Instructional Materials. Selecting instructional materials. Washington, D.C. : National Academy Press, c1999.
*TC LB1585.3 .C45 1999*

**Turbill, Jan, edt.**
The changing face of whole language. Newark, Del. : International Reading Association ; Victoria,

Australia : Australian Literacy Educators' Association, c1997.
*TC LB1050.35 .C43 1997*

**Turk, Laurel Herbert, 1903-** El español al día / Laurel H. Turk, Edith M. Allen. 5th ed. Lexington, Mass. : D.C. Heath, c1979. 2 v. : ill. (some col.), music ; 25 cm. Includes index. ISBN 0-669-01647-0 (Bk. 1)
*1. Spanish language - Textbooks for foreign speakers - English. 2. Spanish language - Grammar. I. Allen, Edith M. (Edith Marion), 1902- joint author. II. Title.*
*TC PC4111 .T87 1979*

El español al día / Laurel H. Turk, Edith M. Allen, César A. Muñoz-Plaza. Revised ed. Lexington, Mass. : D.C. Heath, c1974. v. : ill. , maps ; 25 cm. Includes index. ISBN 0-669-94276-5 (Bk. 3)
*1. Spanish language - Textbooks for foreign speakers - English. 2. Spanish language - Grammar. I. Allen, Edith M. (Edith Marion), 1902- II. Muñoz-Plaza, César A. III. Title.*
*TC PC4111 .T87 1974*

El español al día : teacher's edition / [by] Laurel H. Turk [and] Edith M. Allen. 4th ed. Lexington, Mass., Heath [1973] 2 v. : ill. ; 25 cm. "Teacher's edition." ISBN 0-669-82842-4 (v. 1) ISBN 0-669-82875-0 (v. 2) DDC 468/.2/421
*1. Spanish language - Textbooks for foreign speakers - English. I. Allen, Edith M. (Edith Marion), 1902- joint author. II. Title.*
*TC PC4112 .T766 1973 Teacher's Ed.*

**Turk, William L.** When juvenile crime comes to school / William L. Turk. Lewiston, NY : E. Mellen Press, 1999. [xiv], xii, 193 p. : ill. (some col.), map ; 24 cm. (Criminology studies ; v. 7) Includes bibliographical references (p. 173-188) and index. ISBN 0-7734-7979-1 DDC 371.7/82
*1. Students - Crimes against - United States - States. 2. School violence - United States - Prevention. 3. Juvenile delinquency - United States - Prevention. 4. Students - Crimes against - Texas. 5. School violence - Texas - Prevention. 6. Juvenile delinquency - Texas - Prevention. I. Title. II. Series.*
*TC HV6250.4.S78 T87 1999*

**TURKESTAN.** *See* **ASIA, CENTRAL.**

**TURKIC PEOPLES.** *See* **KAZAKHS.**

**Turn-taking in Japanese conversation.**
Tanaka, Hiroko. Amsterdam ; Philadelphia, PA : John Benjamins Pub. Co., c1999.
*TC PL640.5 .T36 1999*

**The Turnabout Shop.**
Rodowsky, Colby F. 1st ed. New York : Farrar, Straus and Giroux, c1998.
*TC PZ7.R6185 Tu 1998*

**Turner, Ann Warren.** Red flower goes West / Ann Turner ; illustrated by Dennis Nolin. 1st ed. New York : Hyperion Books for Children, c1999. 1 v. (unpaged) : col. ill. ; 29 cm. SUMMARY: As they journey west, a family nurtures the red geranium they have carried with them from their old home. ISBN 0-7868-0313-4 ISBN 0-7868-2253-8 DDC [E]
*1. Overland journeys to the Pacific - Fiction. 2. Family life - Fiction. 3. Flowers - Fiction. I. Nolin, Dennis, ill. II. Title.*
*TC PZ7.T8535 Rf 1999*

**Turner, Anthony John.**
Learning, language, and invention. Aldershot, Hampshire, Great Britain : Variorum ; Brookfield, Vt., USA : Ashgate Pub. Co. ; Paris, France : Société internationale de l'Astrolabe, 1994.
*TC AC5 .L38 1994*

**Turner, Caroline Sotello Viernes.** Faculty of color in academe : bittersweet success / Caroline Sotello Viernes Turner, Samuel L. Myers, Jr. Boston : Allyn and Bacon, c2000. xiii, 257 p : ill. ; 24 cm. Includes bibliographical references (p. 239-248) and index. ISBN 0-205-27849-3 DDC 378.1/2
*1. Minority college teachers - Selection and appointment - United States. 2. Afro-American college teachers - Selection and appointment. 3. Hispanic American college teachers - Selection and appointment. I. Myers, Samuel L. II. Title.*
*TC LB2332.72 .T87 2000*

**TURNER, FREDERICK JACKSON, 1861-1932 - EXHIBITIONS.**
White, Richard, 1947- The frontier in American culture. Chicago : The Library ; Berkeley : University of California Press, c1994.
*TC F596 .W562 1994*

**Turner, James, 1946-.**
Roberts, Jon H. The sacred and the secular university. Princeton, N.J. : Princeton University Press, c2000.
*TC LA636.7 .R62 2000*

**Turner, Joan, 1951-.**
Students writing in the university. Amsterdam ; Philadelphia : John Benjamins Pub., c1999.

*TC PE1405.G7 S78 1999*

**Turner, Jonathan H.** On the origins of human emotions : a sociological inquiry into the evolution of human affect / Jonathan H. Turner. Stanford, Calif. : Stanford University Press, c2000. xiii, 189 p. : ill. ; 24 cm. Includes bibliographical references (p. 157-179) and index. ISBN 0-8047-3719-3 (cloth : alk. paper) ISBN 0-8047-3720-7 (pbk. : alk. paper) DDC 304.5
*1. Emotions. 2. Emotions - Social aspects. I. Title.*
*TC BF531 .T87 2000*

**Turner, Ken (Ken P.).**
The semantics/pragmatics interface from different points of view. 1st ed. Oxford, UK ; New York : Elsevier, 1999.
*TC P325 .S3814 1999*

**Turner, Nancy D'Isa.** Children's literature for the primary inclusive classroom / by Nancy D'Isa Turner, Mary Ann Traxler. Albany, N.Y. : Delmar Publishers, c2000. xvii, 234 p. : ill. ; 24 cm. Includes bibliographical references and index. ISBN 0-7668-0345-7 DDC 371.9/04464
*1. Handicapped children - Education (Primary) - United States. 2. Children's literature - Study and teaching (Primary) - United States. 3. Inclusive education - United States. I. Traxler, Mary Ann Duranczyk. II. Title.*
*TC LC4028 .T87 2000*

**Turner, Paul Venable.**
Joncas, Richard, 1953- Stanford University. 1st ed. New York : Princeton Architectural Press, 1999.
*TC LD3031 .J65 1999*

**Turner, Tony, 1935-.**
Learning to teach in the secondary school. 2nd ed. London ; New York : Routledge, 1999.
*TC LB1737.A3 L43 1999*

**Turning corners.** New York, N.Y. : American Book Company, c1980. 287 p. : col. ill. ; 24 cm. (American readers ; 2-2) ISBN 0-278-45817-3
*1. Readers (Primary) I. Series.*
*TC PE1119 .T87 1980*

**Turning corners.** Teacher's ed. New York, N.Y. : American Book Company, c1980. xvi, 496 p. : col. ill. ; 28 cm. (American readers ; 2-2) Includes index. ISBN 0-278-45850-5
*1. Readers (Primary) 2. Readers (Primary) I. Series.*
*TC PE1119 .T87 1980 Teacher's Ed.*

**Turning corners.** Lexington, Mass. : D.C. Heath and Company, c1983. 303 p. : ill. ; 24 cm. (American readers ; 2-2) ISBN 0-669-04999-9
*1. Readers (Primary) I. Series.*
*TC PE1119 .T87 1983*

**Turning corners.** Teacher's ed. Lexington, Mass. : D.C. Heath and Company, c1986. T32, 550 p. : ill. ; 29 cm. (Heath American readers ; 2-2) Includes index. ISBN 0-669-08050-0
*1. Readers (Primary) 2. Reading (Primary) I. Series.*
*TC PE1119 .T87 1986 Teacher's Ed.*

**Turning corners :** workbook. Teacher's ed. New York, N.Y. : American Book Company, c1980. 128 p. : col. ill. ; 28 cm. (American readers ; 2-2) Includes index. ISBN 0-278-45930-7
*1. Readers (Primary) 2. Reading (Primary) I. Series.*
*TC PE1119 .T87 1980 Teacher's Ed. Workbook*

**Turning corners :** workbook. Teacher's ed. Lexington, Mass. : D.C. Heath and Company, c1983. 128 p. : ill. ; 28 cm. (American readers ; 2-2) Includes index. ISBN 0-669-05005-9
*1. Readers (Primary) 2. Reading (Primary) I. Series.*
*TC PE1119 .T87 1983 Teacher's Ed. Workbook*

**Turning kids on to research.**
Small, Ruth V. Englewood, Colo. : Libraries Unlimited, 2000.
*TC LB1065 .S57 2000*

**Turning point (Television program).**
Heroin [videorecording]. [Princeton, N.J.] : Films for the Humanities & Sciences, c1998.
*TC HV5822.H4 H4 1998*

Sean's story [videorecording]. Princeton, N.J. : Films for the Humanities & Sciences : [S.l. : distributed by] ABC Multimedia : Capital Cities/ABC, c1994.
*TC LC1203.M3 .S39 1994*

**Turning points in curriculum.**
Marshall, J. Dan. Upper Saddle River, N.J. : Merrill, c2000.
*TC LB1570 .M36675 2000*

**TURNOVER, TEACHER.** *See* **TEACHER TURNOVER.**

**TUTELAGE.** *See* **GUARDIAN AND WARD.**

**TUTORIAL METHOD IN EDUCATION.** *See* TUTORS AND TUTORING.

**Tutoring matters.**
Rabow, Jerome. Philadelphia : Temple University Press, 1999.
*TC LC41 .R33 1999*

**TUTORS AND TUTORING.** *See also* INDEPENDENT STUDY; INDIVIDUALIZED INSTRUCTION; PEER-GROUP TUTORING OF STUDENTS; REMEDIAL TEACHING.
Bray, Mark. The shadow education system :. Paris : Unesco, International Institute for Educational Planning, 1999.
*TC LC41 .B73 1999*

Gillespie, Paula. The Allyn and Bacon guide to peer tutoring. Boston : Allyn & Bacon, c2000.
*TC LB1031.5 .G55 2000*

Tips for the reading team. Newark, Del. : International Reading Association, c1998.
*TC LB1573 .T57 1998*

Working with student writers. New York : P. Lang, c1999.
*TC PE1404 .W66 1999*

**TUTORS AND TUTORING - HANDBOOKS, MANUALS, ETC.**
Adams, Arlene. Handbook for literacy tutors. Springfield, Ill. : C.C. Thomas, Publisher, c1999.
*TC LB1576 .A3893 1999*

**TUTORS AND TUTORING - IRELAND - CASE STUDIES.**
Rethinking pastoral care. London ; New York : Routledge, 1999.
*TC LB1620.53.I73 R48 1999*

**TUTORS AND TUTORING - MISCELLANEA.**
Fry, Edward Bernard, 1925- The reading teacher's book of lists. 3rd ed. Englewood Cliffs, NJ : Prentice Hall, c1993.
*TC LB1050.2 .F79 1993*

Fry, Edward Bernard, 1925- The reading teacher's book of lists. 4th ed. Paramus, N.J. : Prentice Hall, c2000.
*TC LB1050.2 .F79 2000*

**TUTORS AND TUTORING - UNITED STATES - HANDBOOKS, MANUALS, ETC.**
Rabow, Jerome. Tutoring matters. Philadelphia : Temple University Press, 1999.
*TC LC41 .R33 1999*

**TV.** *See* TELEVISION.

**TV Living.**
Gauntlett, David. London ; New York : Routledge, 1999.
*TC PN1992.55 .G38 1999*

**TWAIN, MARK, 1835-1910.**
**ADVENTURES OF HUCKLEBERRY FINN.**
Making Mark Twain work in the classroom. Durham [N.C.] : Duke University Press, 1999.
*TC PS1338 .M23 1999*

Mensh, Elaine, 1924- Black, white, and Huckleberry Finn. Tuscaloosa : University of Alabama Press, c2000.
*TC PS1305 .M46 2000*

**TWAIN, MARK, 1835-1910 - POLITICAL AND SOCIAL VIEWS.**
Mensh, Elaine, 1924- Black, white, and Huckleberry Finn. Tuscaloosa : University of Alabama Press, c2000.
*TC PS1305 .M46 2000*

**TWAIN, MARK, 1835-1910 - STUDY AND TEACHING.**
Making Mark Twain work in the classroom. Durham [N.C.] : Duke University Press, 1999.
*TC PS1338 .M23 1999*

**Twayne's evolution of modern business series**
Kwolek-Folland, Angel. Incorporating women. New York : Twayne Publishers, 1998.
*TC HD6095 .K85 1998*

**Twayne's world authors series**
(TWAS 885.) Noland, Richard W. Sigmund Freud revisited. New York : Twayne Publishers, c1999.
*TC BF109.F74 N65 1999*

**Twayne's world authors series. German literature.**
Noland, Richard W. Sigmund Freud revisited. New York : Twayne Publishers, c1999.
*TC BF109.F74 N65 1999*

**TWELFTH GRADE (EDUCATION) - UNITED STATES.**
Wee, Patricia Hachten, 1948- Independent projects, step by step. Lanham, MD : Scarecrow Press, c2000.
*TC LB1620 .W42 2000*

**Twelve centuries of Japanese art from the Imperial collections** / introduction by Ann Yonemura ; contributions by Hirabayashi Moritoku ... [et al.]. Washington, DC : Freer Gallery of Art and the Arthur M. Sackler Gallery, Smithsonian Institution Press, c1997. 224 p. : col. ill., col. map ; 34 cm. Catalogue of an exhibition held at the Arthur M Sackler Gallery, Smithsonian Institution, Washington, D.C., Dec. 14, 1997-Mar. 8, 1998. Includes bibliographical references (p. 222-224) and index. ISBN 1-56098-893-2 (hardback) DDC 759.952/074/753
*1. Scrolls, Japanese - Exhibitions. 2. Ink painting, Japanese - Exhibitions. 3. Calligraphy, Japanese - Exhibitions. 4. Painting, Japanese - Exhibitions. 5. Scrolls - Private collections - Japan - Exhibitions. 6. Japan - Kunaichō - Art collections - Exhibitions. I. Hirabayashi, Moritoku, 1933- II. Freer Gallery of Art. III. Arthur M. Sackler Gallery (Smithsonian Institution)*
*TC ND1457.J32 W377 1997*

**TWELVE-STEP PROGRAMS.**
Communication in recovery. Cresskill, N.J. : Hampton Press, c1999.
*TC HV4998 .C64 1999*

**TWELVE-STEP PROGRAMS - HISTORY.**
Satter, Beryl, 1959- Each mind a kingdom. Berkeley : University of California Press, c1999.
*TC BF639 .S124 1999*

**TWELVE STEPS (SELF-HELP).** *See* TWELVE-STEP PROGRAMS.

**TWENTIES (TWENTIETH CENTURY DECADE).** *See* NINETEEN TWENTIES.

**TWENTIETH CENTURY.** *See* CIVILIZATION, MODERN - 20TH CENTURY; NINETEEN TWENTIES.

**Twentieth century actor training** / edited by Alison Hodge. London : New York : Routledge, 2000. xv, 251 p. : ill. ; 24 cm. Includes bibliographical references and index. ISBN 0-415-19451-2 (hc.) ISBN 0-415-19452-0 (pbk.) DDC 792/.028/07
*1. Acting - Study and teaching. I. Hodge, Alison, 1959-*
*TC PN2075 .T94 2000*

**Twentieth century day by day.**
20th century day by day. New York, NY : DK Pub., c1999.
*TC D422 .C53 1999*

**TWENTIETH CENTURY - FORECASTS.**
Kahn, Herman, 1922- The year 2000. New York : Macmillan, c1967.
*TC CB160 .K3 1967*

**Twentieth Century Fund.**
Meyer, Karl Ernest. The art museum. 1st ed. New York : Morrow, 1979.
*TC N510 .M47*

**Twentieth century revolutions in technology.**
Singer, Edward. 20th century revolutions in technology. Commack, NY : Nova Science Pub., 1998.
*TC T173.8 .S568 1998*

**Twentieth-century teen culture by the decades.**
Rollin, Lucy. Westport, Conn. ; London : Greenwood Press, 1999.
*TC HQ799.U65 R65 1999*

**Twenty common problems in pediatrics.**
20 common problems in pediatrics. New York : McGraw-Hill, Health Professions Division, c2001.
*TC RJ45.T9 2001*

**TWENTY-FIRST CENTURY - FORECASTS.**
Bell, Trudy E. Engineering tomorrow :. Piscataway, NJ : IEEE Press, c2000.
*TC T174 .B451 2000*

Drucker, Peter Ferdinand, 1909- Management challenges for the 21st century. 1st ed. New York : HarperBusiness, c1999.
*TC HD30.27 .D78 1999*

The emergence of family into the 21st century. Boston : Jones and Bartlett Publishers ; [New York] : NLN Press, c2001.
*TC HQ535 .E44 2001*

Scanning the future. New York : Thames & Hudson, c1999.
*TC CB161 .S44 1999*

Wallerstein, Immanuel Maurice, 1930- Utopistics, or, Historical choices of the twenty-first century. New York : New Press, 1998.
*TC D860 .W35 1998*

**Twenty-five biggest mistakes teachers make and how to avoid them.**
Orange, Carolyn. 25 biggest mistakes teachers make and how to avoid them. Thousand Oaks Calif. : Corwin Press, c2000.
*TC LB1033 .O73 2000*

**Twenty-six Fairmont Avenue.**
De Paola, Tomie. 26 Fairmount Avenue. New York : G.P. Putnam's Sons, c1999.
*TC PS3554.E11474 Z473 1999*

**Twerski, Abraham J.** Substance-abusing high achievers : addiction as an equal opportunity destroyer / Abraham J. Twerski. Northvale, N.J. : Aronson, 1998. viii, 221 p. ; 23 cm. (Library of substance abuse and addiction treatment) Includes bibliographical references and index. ISBN 0-7657-0110-3 (alk. paper) DDC 362.29
*1. Successful people - Substance use. 2. Substance abuse - Treatment. I. Title. II. Series.*
*TC RC564.5.S83 T94 1998*

**Twice-told tales :** teacher's planning guide. New York : Macmillan/McGraw-Hill, c1997. 1 v. (various pagings) : col. ill. ; 31 cm. (Spotlight on literacy) (The road to independent reading) Includes index. ISBN 0-02-181177-6
*1. Language arts (Elementary) 2. Reading (Elementary) I. Series. II. Series: The road to independent reading*
*TC LB1576 .S66 1997 Gr.4 l.10 u.6*

**Twin and triplet psychology :** a professional guide to working with multiples / edited by Audrey C. Sandbank. London : New York : Routledge, 1999. xvi, 208 p. : ill. ; 23 cm. Includes bibliographical references and index. ISBN 0-415-18397-9 (hardcover) ISBN 0-415-18398-7 (pbk.) DDC 155.44/4
*1. Twins - Psychology. 2. Triplets - Psychology. I. Sandbank, Audrey C., 1935-*
*TC BF723.T9 T85 1999*

**TWINS - PSYCHOLOGY.**
Twin and triplet psychology. London : New York : Routledge, 1999.
*TC BF723.T9 T85 1999*

**TWO-CAREER COUPLES.** *See* DUAL-CAREER FAMILIES.

**Two centuries of progress.**
Jackson, Carlton. 3rd ed. Mission Hills, CA : Glencoe/McGraw-Hill, 1991.
*TC E178.1 .J321 1991*

**TWO-EARNER FAMILIES.** *See* DUAL-CAREER FAMILIES.

**The two foolish cats.**
Uchida, Yoshiko. New York : M.K. McElderry Books, c1987.
*TC PZ8.1.U35 Tw 1987*

**Two French language teaching reformers reassessed.**
Roberts, J. T. (John T.) Lewiston [N.Y.] : E. Mellen Press, c1999.
*TC PB35 .R447 1999*

**Two lands on one soil.**
Wright, Frank, 1948- New York : St. Martin's Press, 1996.
*TC DA990.U46 W756 1996*

**Two lives.**
Mitchell, Lucy (Sprague) 1878- New York, Simon and Schuster, 1953.
*TC HB119.M5 M52*

**The two million-year-old self.**
Stevens, Anthony. New York : Fromm International Publishing, 1997.
*TC BF175.5.A72 S75 1997*

**Two suns in the sky.**
Bat-Ami, Miriam. 1st ed. [Chicago, IL] : Front Street/Cricket Books, 1999.
*TC PZ7.B2939 Tw 1999*

**Two ways to count to ten.**
Dee, Ruby. New York : H. Holt., c1988.
*TC PZ8.1.D378 Tw 1988*

Dee, Ruby. New York : H. Holt., c1988.
*TC PZ8.1.D378 Tw 1988a*

Dee, Ruby. 1st ed. New York : H. Holt., c1988.
*TC PZ8.1.D378 Tw 1988*

**TWO-YEAR COLLEGES.** *See* COMMUNITY COLLEGES; JUNIOR COLLEGES.

**Two-year colleges for women and minorities :** enabling access to the baccalaureate / edited by Barbara Townsend. New York : Falmer Press, 1999. xii, 256 p. ; 24 cm. (Garland reference library of social science ; v. 1195. Garland studies in higher education ; v. 16) Includes bibliographical references and index. ISBN 0-8153-3173-8 (alk. paper) DDC 378.1/543
*1. Community colleges - United States - Case studies. 2. Junior colleges - United States - Case studies. 3. Women - Education (Higher) - United States - Case studies. 4. Minorities - Education (Higher) - United States - Case studies. I. Townsend, Barbara K. II. Series: Garland reference library of social science ; v. 1195. III. Series: Garland reference library of social science. Garland studies in higher education ; vol. 16.*
*TC LB2328.15.U6 T96 1999*

**Twu, Bor-Yaun.**
Chang, Shun-Wen. A comparative study of item exposure control methods in computerized adaptive testing. Iowa City, IA : ACT, Inc., 1998.
*TC LB3051 .A3 no. 98-3*

**Tyack, David B.**
Reconstructing the common good in education. Stanford, Calif. : Stanford University Press, c2000.
*TC LA212 .R42 2000*

**Tye, Barbara Benham, 1942-** Hard truths : uncovering the deep structure of schooling / Barbara Benham Tye ; foreword by Ron Brandt. New York : Teachers College Press, c2000. xi, 204 p. ; 24 cm. Includes bibliographical references (p. 181-194) and index. ISBN 0-8077-3934-0 (cloth : alk. paper) ISBN 0-8077-3933-2 (pbk. : alk. paper) DDC 371.2/00973
*1. School improvement programs - United States. 2. School management and organization - United States. I. Title.*
*TC LB2822.82 .T94 2000*

**Tyman, J. H. P. (John H P).**
Lipids in health and nutrition. Cambridge : Royal Society of Chemistry, c1999.
*TC QP751 .L57 1999*

**TYMMS, PETER.** Baseline assessment and monitoring in primary schools : achievements, attitudes and value-added indicators. London : David Fulton Publishers, 1999. vii, 104 p. ; 30 cm. ISBN 1-85346-591-7 DDC 371.2
*1. Educational tests and measurements - Great Britain.*
*TC LB3060.22 .T96 1999*

**TYPE 1 DIABETES.** *See* **DIABETES.**

**TYPE A BEHAVIOR.** *See* **CORONARY HEART DISEASE; STRESS (PSYCHOLOGY).**

**TYPE (PSYCHOLOGY).** *See* **TYPOLOGY (PSYCHOLOGY).**

**TYPES, MENTAL.** *See* **TYPOLOGY (PSYCHOLOGY).**

**TYPES, PSYCHOLOGICAL.** *See* **TYPOLOGY (PSYCHOLOGY).**

**TYPEWRITERS FOR THE BLIND.** *See* **BLIND, APPARATUS FOR THE.**

**TYPOGRAPHY.** *See* **PRINTING.**

**Typological studies in language**
(v. 24) Perkins, Revere D. (Revere Dale) Deixis, grammar, and culture. Amsterdam ; Philadelphia : J. Benjamins Pub. co., 1992.
*TC P35 .P47 1992*

**TYPOLOGY (PSYCHOLOGY).**
Quenk, Naomi L., 1936- Essentials of Myers-Briggs type indicator assessment. New York : J. Wiley & Sons, 2000.
*TC BF698.8.M94 Q45 1999*

**Tyrrell, Lou.**
Paris [videorecording]. New York, NY : V.I.E.W. Video, c1996.
*TC DC707 .P3 1996*

**UAUPÉS RIVER VALLEY (COLOMBIA AND BRAZIL) - SOCIAL LIFE AND CUSTOMS.**
Arhem, Kaj. Makuna. Washington : Smithsonian Institution Press, c1998.
*TC F2270.2.M33 A68 1998*

**UAUPÉS VALLEY (COLOMBIA AND BRAZIL).** *See* **UAUPÉS RIVER VALLEY (COLOMBIA AND BRAZIL).**

**Ubbes, Valerie A.** Literature links for nutrition and health / Valerie A. Ubbes, Diana M. Spillman. Boston : Allyn and Bacon, c2000. xv, 228 p. : ill. ; 28 cm. Includes bibliographical references and indexes. ISBN 0-205-30954-2
*1. Nutrition - Study and teaching (Elementary) 2. Content area reading. I. Spillman, Diana M. II. Title.*

*TC TX364 .U253 2000*

**UBEA forum.**
Business education forum. Reston, Va., National Business Education Association.

**Uchida, Yoshiko.** The two foolish cats : suggested by a Japanese folktale / Yoshiko Uchida ; illustrated by Margot Zemach. New York : M.K. McElderry Books, c1987. [32] p. : col. ill. ; 46 x34 cm. Based on: Saru no nigirimeshi saiban. SUMMARY: Two foolish cats go to the old monkey of the mountain to settle their quarrel. ISBN 0-02-109113-7
*1. Folklore - Japan. 2. Cats - Folklore. I. Zemach, Margot, ill. II. Title. III. Title: Saru no nigirimeshi saiban IV. Title: 2 foolish cats*
*TC PZ8.1.U35 Tw 1987*

**UCSMP Textbook Translations**
Moro, M. I. Russian grade 1 mathematics. Chicago : University of Chicago School of Mathematics Project, 1992.
*TC QA14.R9 R8611 1992*

Moro, M. I. Russian grade 2 mathematics. Chicago : University of Chicago School of Mathematics Project, 1992.
*TC QA14.R9 R8711 1992*

Russian grade 3 mathematics. Chicago : University of Chicago School of Mathematics Project, 1992.
*TC QA14.R9 R8811 1992*

**Uden Associates.**
Stephen Hawking's universe [videorecording]. [Alexandria, Va.] : PBS Video: Burbank, CA : Distributed by Warner Home Video, c1997.
*TC QB982 .S7 1997*

**Ueno, Harry Y. (Harry Yoshio), 1907-.**
Rabbit in the moon [videorecording]. San Francisco, Calif. : Wabi-Sabi Productions, 1999.
*TC D753.8 .R3 1999*

**Uff, Caroline.** Happy birthday, Lulu! / Caroline Uff. New York : Walker & Company, 2000. 1v. (unpaged) : col. ill. ; 27 cm. SUMMARY: On her birthday, a young girl receives hugs, cards, telephone calls, presents, and a party. ISBN 0-8027-8751-7 DDC [E]
*1. Birthdays - Fiction. I. Title.*
*TC PZ7.U285 Hap 2000*

Lulu's busy day / Caroline Uff. New York : Walker, 2000. 1v. (unpaged) : col. ill. ; 27 cm. SUMMARY: Lulu enjoys many activities during the day, including drawing a picture, visiting the park, and reading a bedtime story. ISBN 0-8027-8716-9 (hc.) ISBN 0-8027-8717-7 DDC [E]
*1. Day - Fiction. I. Title.*
*TC PZ7.U285 Lu 2000*

**UFO ENCOUNTER PHENOMENA.** *See* **UNIDENTIFIED FLYING OBJECTS - SIGHTINGS AND ENCOUNTERS.**

**UFO ENCOUNTERS.** *See* **UNIDENTIFIED FLYING OBJECTS - SIGHTINGS AND ENCOUNTERS.**

**UFO PHENOMENA.** *See* **UNIDENTIFIED FLYING OBJECTS.**

**UFO SIGHTINGS.** *See* **UNIDENTIFIED FLYING OBJECTS - SIGHTINGS AND ENCOUNTERS.**

**UFOLOGY.** *See* **UNIDENTIFIED FLYING OBJECTS.**

**UFOS.** *See* **UNIDENTIFIED FLYING OBJECTS.**

**UGANDA - ECONOMIC CONDITIONS - 1979-.**
Our friends at the bank [videorecording]. New York, NY : First Run/Icarus Films, 1997.
*TC HG3881.5.W57 O87 1997*

**UGANDA - HISTORY.**
Gitta, Cosmas. International human rights. 1998.
*TC 085 G4398*

**UGANDA - SOCIAL CONDITIONS - 1979-.**
Our friends at the bank [videorecording]. New York, NY : First Run/Icarus Films, 1997.
*TC HG3881.5.W57 O87 1997*

**The ugly American.**
Lederer, William J., 1912- 1st ed. New York : Norton, 1958.
*TC PS3523 .E27U35 1958*

**Ulaq and the northern lights.**
Taylor, Harriet Peck. 1st ed. New York : Farrar Straus Giroux, 1998.
*TC PZ7.T2135 Ul 1998*

**Ullberg, Alan D.** Museum trusteeship / by Alan D. Ullberg, with Patricia Ullberg. Washington : American Association of Museums, 1981. xii, 123 p. ;

23 cm. Bibliography: p. 93-117. Includes index.
*1. Museum trustees - Handbooks, manuals, etc. I. Ullberg, Patricia. II. American Association of Museums. III. Title.*
*TC AM121 .U44*

**Ullberg, Patricia.**
Ullberg, Alan D. Museum trusteeship. Washington : American Association of Museums, 1981.
*TC AM121 .U44*

**Ullman, B. L. (Berthold Louis), 1882-1965.** Latin for Americans. First book / B.L. Ullman, Charles Henderson, Jr., Norman E. Henry. 7th ed. Woodland Hills, Calif. : Glencoe, c1990. 4 v. : ill. (some col.) ; 28 cm. Includes index. The size of "First Book" is 24 cm. CONTENTS: [v. 1]. First book -- [v. 2]. Workbook 1 -- [v. 3]. Workbook 1, Teacher's annotated ed. -- [v. 4]. Teacher's resource guide 1. ISBN 0-02-646000-9 (First Book) ISBN 0-02-646002-5 (Workbook 1 Student Text) ISBN 0-02-646003-3 (Workbook 1 Teacher's Annotated Ed.) ISBN 0-02-646001-7 (Teacher's Resource Guide 1) DDC 478.2/421
*1. Latin language - Grammar. 2. Latin language - Readers. I. Henderson, Charles, 1923- II. Henry, Norman E. III. Title.*
*TC PA2087.5 .U339 1990*

Latin for Americans, First book / B.L. Ullman, Charles Henderson, Jr., Norman E. Henry. 7th ed. Woodland Hills, Calif. : Glencoe, c1990. 4 v. : ill. (some col.) ; 28 cm. Includes index. The size of "First Book" is 24 cm. CONTENTS: [v. 1]. First book -- [v. 2]. Workbook 1 -- [v. 3]. Workbook 1, Teacher's annotated ed. -- [v. 4]. Teacher's resource guide 1. ISBN 0-02-646000-9 (First Book) ISBN 0-02-646002-5 (Workbook 1 Student Text) ISBN 0-02-646003-3 (Workbook 1 Teacher's Annotated Ed.) ISBN 0-02-646001-7 (Teacher's Resource Guide 1) DDC 478.2/421
*1. Latin language - Grammar. 2. Latin language - Readers. I. Henderson, Charles, 1923- II. Henry, Norman E. III. Title.*
*TC PA2087.5 .U339 1990 First Book*

Latin for Americans. Second book / B.L. Ullman, Charles Henderson, Jr., Norman E. Henry. 7th ed. Mission Hills, Calif. : Glencoe, c1990. 2 v. : ill. (some col.) ; 24 cm. Includes index. CONTENTS: [1]. Second book--[2]. Workbook 2. ISBN 0-02-646001-7 (First Book) ISBN 0-02-646010-6 (Second Book) ISBN 0-02-646019-x (Third Book)
*1. Latin language - Grammar. 2. Latin language - Readers. I. Henderson, Charles, 1923- II. Henry, Norman E. III. Title.*
*TC PA2087.5 .U339 1990 Teacher's Guide*

Latin for Americans. Second book / B.L. Ullman, Charles Henderson, Jr., Norman E. Henry. 7th ed. Mission Hills, Calif. : Glencoe, c1990. 4 v. : ill. (some col.) ; 24 cm. Includes index. CONTENTS: [1]. Second book -- [2]. Workbook 2. -- [3]. Workbook 2, teacher's annotated ed. -- [4]. Teacher's resource guide 2. ISBN 0-02-646009-2 (Second book) ISBN 0-02-646011-4 (Workbook 2 Student Text) ISBN 0-02-646012-2 (Workbook 2 Teacher's Annotated Ed.) ISBN 0-02-646010-6 (Teacher's Resource Guide 2)
*1. Latin language - Grammar. 2. Latin language - Readers. I. Henderson, Charles, 1923- II. Henry, Norman E. III. Title.*
*TC PA2087.5 .U339 1990*

Latin for Americans. Second book / B.L. Ullman, Charles Henderson, Jr., Norman E. Henry. 7th ed. Mission Hills, Calif. : Glencoe, c1990. 4 v. : ill. (some col.) ; 24 cm. Includes index. CONTENTS: [1]. Second book -- [2]. Workbook 2. -- [3]. Workbook 2, teacher's annotated ed. -- [4]. Teacher's resource guide 2. ISBN 0-02-646009-2 (Second book) ISBN 0-02-646011-4 (Workbook 2 Student Text) ISBN 0-02-646012-2 (Workbook 2 Teacher's Annotated Ed.) ISBN 0-02-646010-6 (Teacher's Resource Guide 2)
*1. Latin language - Grammar. 2. Latin language - Readers. I. Henderson, Charles, 1923- II. Henry, Norman E. III. Title.*
*TC PA2087.5 .U339 1990 Third Book*

Latin for Americans. Second book / B.L. Ullman, Charles Henderson, Jr., Norman E. Henry. 7th ed. Mission Hills, Calif. : Glencoe, c1990. 4 v. : ill. (some col.) ; 24 cm. Includes index. CONTENTS: [1]. Second book -- [2]. Workbook 2. -- [3]. Workbook 2, teacher's annotated ed. -- [4]. Teacher's resource guide 2. ISBN 0-02-646009-2 (Second book) ISBN 0-02-646011-4 (Workbook 2 Student Text) ISBN 0-02-646012-2 (Workbook 2 Teacher's Annotated Ed.) ISBN 0-02-646010-6 (Teacher's Resource Guide 2)
*1. Latin language - Grammar. 2. Latin language - Readers. I. Henderson, Charles, 1923- II. Henry, Norman E. III. Title.*
*TC PA2087.5 .U339 1990 Second Book*

Latin for Americans. Third book / B.L. Ullman, Albert I. Suskin. 7th ed. Mission Hills, Calif. : Glencoe, a division of Macmillan Pub. Co., c1990. v. : ill (some col.) ; 24 cm. Includes bibliographical references (p. 379-383) and index. CONTENTS: [v. 1]. Third book -- [v. 2]. Teacher's resource guide 3. ISBN 0-02-646018-1 (Third Book) ISBN 0-02-646019-x (Teacher's Resource Guide 3) DDC 478.6/421
*1. Latin language - Readers. 2. Latin language - Grammar. I. Suskin, Albert I. II. Title.*

*TC PA2087.5 .U399 1990*

**Ullmann, Elisabeth, 1966-.**
[Kindheit und Trauma. English.] Childhood and trauma. Aldershot, Hants, UK ; Brookfield, Vt., USA : Ashgate, c1999.
*TC RJ506.P66 K613 1999*

**Ulrich, David, 1953-** Results-based leadership / Dave Ulrich, Jack Zenger, Norm Smallwood. Boston : Harvard Business School Press, 1999. xiv, 234 p. ; 24 cm. Includes bibliographical references (p. 217-225) and index. ISBN 0-87584-871-0 (alk. paper) DDC 658.4/092
*1. Leadership. 2. Executive ability. I. Zenger, John H. II. Smallwood, W. Norman. III. Title.*
*TC HD57.7 .U45 1999*

**Ulrich, Deborah L.** Interactive group learning : strategies for nurse educators / Deborah L. Ulrich, Kellie J. Glendon. New York : Springer, c1999. xiii, 115 p. : ill. ; 24 cm. Includes bibliographical references (p. 107-109) and index. ISBN 0-8261-1238-2 DDC 610.73/071/1
*1. Nursing - Study and teaching (Continuing education) 2. Social groups. 3. Education, Nursing - methods. 4. Learning. 5. Group Structure. I. Glendon, Kellie J. II. Title. III. Title: Strategies for nurse educators*
*TC RT76 .U46 1999*

**ULSTER (NORTHERN IRELAND AND IRELAND) - HISTORY.**
Wright, Frank, 1948- Two lands on one soil. New York : St. Martin's Press, 1996.
*TC DA990.U46 W756 1996*

**Ulysses unbound.**
Elster, Jon, 1940- Cambridge, U.K. ; New York : Cambridge University Press, 2000.
*TC BF441 .E45 2000*

**Umansky, Warren.** Young children with special needs / Warren Umansky, Stephen R. Hooper. 3rd ed. Upper Saddle River, N.J. : Merrill, c1998. xv, 448 p. : ill. ; 25 cm. Rev. ed. of: Young children with special needs / Nancy H. Fallen, Warren Umansky. 2nd ed. c1985. Includes bibliographical references and indexes. ISBN 0-13-612052-0 DDC 371.91/0973
*1. Handicapped children - Education - United States. 2. Perceptual-motor learning. 3. Child development - United States. I. Hooper, Stephen R. II. Fallen, Nancy H. Young children with special needs. III. Title.*
*TC LC4031 .U425 1998*

**Umbrella.**
Yashima, Taro, 1908- New York : Viking, 1958.
*TC PZ7.Y212 Um10*

**UMBRELLAS AND PARASOLS - JUVENILLE LITERATURE.**
Yashima, Taro, 1908- Umbrella. New York : Viking, 1958.
*TC PZ7.Y212 Um10*

**Umbruch zur Moderne.**
Helmer, Karl. 1. Aufl. Sankt Augustin : Academia, 1994.
*TC LA116 .H445 1994*

**UMMAH (ISLAM). See ISLAM AND STATE.**

**Unapix Consumer Products.**
The blue planet [videorecording]. [New York, N.Y.?] : Unapix Entertainment, Inc. [distributor], c1996.
*TC QB631.2 .B5 1996*

The climate puzzle [videorecording]. [New York, N.Y.?] : Unapix Entertainment, Inc. [distributor], c1996.
*TC QB631.2 .C5 1996*

The living machine [videorecording]. [New York, N.Y.?] : Unapix Entertainment, Inc. [distributor], c1996.
*TC QB631.2 .L5 1996*

Fate of the earth [videorecording]. [New York, N.Y.?] : Unapix Entertainment, Inc. [distributor], c1996.
*TC QB631.2 .F3 1996*

Gifts from the earth [videorecording]. [New York, N.Y.?] : Unapix Entertainment, Inc. [distributor], c1996.
*TC QB631.2 .G5 1996*

The solar sea [videorecording]. [New York, N.Y.?] : Unapix Entertainment, Inc. [distributor], c1996.
*TC QB631.2 .S6 1996*

Tales from other worlds [videorecording]. [New York, N.Y.?] : Unapix Entertainment, Inc. [distributor], c1996.
*TC QB631.2 .T3 1996*

Tales from other worlds [videorecording]. [New York, N.Y.?] : Unapix Entertainment, Inc. [distributor], c1996.
*TC QB631.2 .T3 1996*

**Unapix Consumer Products feature presentation [videorecording].**
The blue planet [videorecording]. [New York, N.Y.?] : Unapix Entertainment, Inc. [distributor], c1996.
*TC QB631.2 .B5 1996*

The climate puzzle [videorecording]. [New York, N.Y.?] : Unapix Entertainment, Inc. [distributor], c1996.
*TC QB631.2 .C5 1996*

The living machine [videorecording]. [New York, N.Y.?] : Unapix Entertainment, Inc. [distributor], c1996.
*TC QB631.2 .L5 1996*

Fate of the earth [videorecording]. [New York, N.Y.?] : Unapix Entertainment, Inc. [distributor], c1996.
*TC QB631.2 .F3 1996*

Gifts from the earth [videorecording]. [New York, N.Y.?] : Unapix Entertainment, Inc. [distributor], c1996.
*TC QB631.2 .G5 1996*

The solar sea [videorecording]. [New York, N.Y.?] : Unapix Entertainment, Inc. [distributor], c1996.
*TC QB631.2 .S6 1996*

Tales from other worlds [videorecording]. [New York, N.Y.?] : Unapix Entertainment, Inc. [distributor], c1996.
*TC QB631.2 .T3 1996*

**Unapix Entertainment, Inc.**
The blue planet [videorecording]. [New York, N.Y.?] : Unapix Entertainment, Inc. [distributor], c1996.
*TC QB631.2 .B5 1996*

The climate puzzle [videorecording]. [New York, N.Y.?] : Unapix Entertainment, Inc. [distributor], c1996.
*TC QB631.2 .C5 1996*

The living machine [videorecording]. [New York, N.Y.?] : Unapix Entertainment, Inc. [distributor], c1996.
*TC QB631.2 .L5 1996*

Fate of the earth [videorecording]. [New York, N.Y.?] : Unapix Entertainment, Inc. [distributor], c1996.
*TC QB631.2 .F3 1996*

Gifts from the earth [videorecording]. [New York, N.Y.?] : Unapix Entertainment, Inc. [distributor], c1996.
*TC QB631.2 .G5 1996*

The solar sea [videorecording]. [New York, N.Y.?] : Unapix Entertainment, Inc. [distributor], c1996.
*TC QB631.2 .S6 1996*

Tales from other worlds [videorecording]. [New York, N.Y.?] : Unapix Entertainment, Inc. [distributor], c1996.
*TC QB631.2 .T3 1996*

Tales from other worlds [videorecording]. [New York, N.Y.?] : Unapix Entertainment, Inc. [distributor], c1996.
*TC QB631.2 .T3 1996*

**Unbending gender.**
Williams, Joan, 1952- Oxford ; New York : Oxford University Press, c2000.
*TC HD4904.25 .W55 2000*

**The uncertain mind.**
Sorrentino, Richard M. Philadelphia : Psychology Press, c2000.
*TC BF697 .S674 2000*

**UNCERTAINTY. See also RISK.**
Sorrentino, Richard M. The uncertain mind. Philadelphia : Psychology Press, c2000.
*TC BF697 .S674 2000*

**Uncle Sam's K-12 Web.**
Andriot, Laurie. Medford, N.J. : CyberAge Books, 1999.

*TC ZA575 .A53 1999*

**UNCLES - FICTION.**
Jennings, Patrick. Putnam and Pennyroyal. 1st ed. New York : Scholastic Press, 1999.
*TC PZ7.J4298715 Co 1999*

**The unconscious.**
MacIntyre, Alasdair C. Bristol, England : Thoemmes Press, 1997, c1958.
*TC BF315 .M23 1997*

**Uncontrollable beauty :** toward a new aesthetics / edited by Bill Beckley with David Shapiro. New York : Allworth Press : School of Visual Arts, c1998. xxiv, 423 p. ; 24 cm. Includes bibliographical references and index. ISBN 1-88055-990-0 DDC 111/.85
*1. Aesthetics, Modern - 20th century. 2. Art criticism. I. Beckley, Bill, 1946- II. Shapiro, David, 1947-*
*TC BH201 .U53 1998*

**Under the sign of hope.**
Bloom, Leslie Rebecca. Albany, N.Y. : State University of New York Press, c1998.
*TC HQ1185 .B56 1998*

**UNDERDEVELOPED AREAS. See DEVELOPING COUNTRIES.**

**UNDERDEVELOPED COUNTRIES. See DEVELOPING COUNTRIES.**

**UNDEREMPLOYMENT. See UNEMPLOYMENT.**

**UNDERGRADUATES. See COLLEGE STUDENTS.**

**UNDERGROUND, ANTI-COMMUNIST. See ANTI-COMMUNIST MOVEMENTS.**

**UNDERPRIVILEGED. See SOCIALLY HANDICAPPED.**

**UNDERSTANDING. See COMPREHENSION.**

**Understanding adult education and training** / edited by Griff Foley. 2nd ed. St. Leonards, NSW, Australia : Allen & Unwin, 2000. xix, 327 p. : ill. ; 22 cm. Includes bibliographical references (p. 292-320) and indexes. ISBN 1-86508-147-7
*1. Adult education - Australia. 2. Continuing education - Australia. I. Foley, Griff.*
*TC LC5259 U53 2000*

**Understanding alcohol and other drugs.**
O'Brien, Robert, 1932- The encyclopedia of understanding alcohol and other drugs. New York, NY : Facts on File, c1999.
*TC HV5017 .O37 1999*

**Understanding and applying cognitive development theory.**
Love, Patrick G. San Francisco : Jossey-Bass, c1999.
*TC LB2343 .L65 1999*

**Understanding and preventing violence** / Albert J. Reiss, Jr., and Jeffrey A. Roth, editors. Washington, D.C. : National Academy Press, 1993-1994. 4 v. : ill. ; 24 cm. Vol. 2 edited by Albert J. Reiss, Jr., Klaus A. Miczek, and Jeffrey A. Roth. "Panel on the Understanding and Control of Violent Behavior, Committee on Law and Justice, Commission on Behavioral and Social Sciences and Education, National Research Council." Includes bibliographical references and indexes. CONTENTS: [1] [without special title] -- v. 2. Biobehavioral influences -- v. 3. Social influences -- v. 4. Consequences and control. ISBN 0-309-04594-0 (v. 1) ISBN 0-309-04649-1 (v. 2 : pbk.) ISBN 0-309-05080-4 (v. 3 : pbk.) ISBN 0-309-05079-0 (v. 4 : pbk.) DDC 303.6
*1. Violence - United States. 2. Violence - United States - Prevention. 3. Violent crimes - United States. I. Reiss, Albert J. II. Roth, Jeffrey A., 1945- III. Miczek, Klaus A. IV. National Research Council (U.S.). Panel on the Understanding and Control of Violent Behavior.*
*TC HN90.V5 U53 1993*

**Understanding children with language problems.**
Chiat, Shula. Oxford [England] ; New York : Cambridge University Press, 2000.
*TC RJ496.L35 C46 2000*

**Understanding children's literature :** key essays from the International Companion Encyclopedia of Children's Literature / edited by Peter Hunt. London ; New York : Routledge, 1999. x, 188 p. ; 24 cm. Includes bibliographical references (p. [174]-177) and index. ISBN 0-415-19546-2 DDC 809/.89282
*1. Children's literature - History and criticism. I. Hunt, Peter, 1945-*
*TC PN1009.A1 U44 1999*

**Understanding children's worlds**
Harris, Paul. L. The work of the imagination. Oxford : Blackwell Publishers, 2000.

**TC BF723.I5 H37a 2000**

**Understanding depression.**
Ainsworth, Patricia, M.D. Jackson : University Press of Mississippi, c2000.
*TC RC537 .A39 2000*

Stoppard, Janet M. (Janet Mary), 1945- London ; New York : Routledge, 2000.
*TC RC537 .S82 2000*

**Understanding education and policy**
Abowitz, Kathleen Knight. Making meaning of community in an American high school. Cresskill, N.J. : Hampton Press, c2000.
*TC LC311 .A36 2000*

Caring as tenacity. Cresskill, N.J. : Hampton Press, c2000.
*TC LC5131 .C35 2000*

From nihilism to possibility. Cresskill, N.J. : Hampton Press, c1999.
*TC LC5141 .F76 1999*

**Understanding families**
Smith, William L., 1956- Families and communes. Thousand Oaks, Calif. : Sage Publications, c1999.
*TC HQ971 .S55 1999*

(v. 14) Hill, Shirley A. (Shirley Ann), 1947- African American children. Thousand Oaks, Calif. : Sage Publications, c1999.
*TC E185.86 .H665 1999*

**Understanding health and sickness series**
Ainsworth, Patricia, M.D. Understanding depression. Jackson : University Press of Mississippi, c2000.
*TC RC537 .A39 2000*

**Understanding higher education.**
Bligh, Donald, 1936- Oxford : Intellect, 1999.
*TC LA637 .B55 1999*

**Understanding intelligence.**
Pfeifer, Rolf, 1947- Cambridge, Mass. : MIT Press, c1999.
*TC Q335 .P46 1999*

**Understanding Japan**
(no. 66) A Teacher's & textbook writers' handbook on Japan. 5th., rev. printing. Tokyo : International Society for Educational Information, c1993.
*TC DS806 .T34 1993*

**Understanding literacy development.**
Geekie, Peter. Stoke on Trent, England : Trentham Books, 1999.
*TC LC149 .G44 1999*

**Understanding misunderstandings.**
Young, Robert L. (Robert Louis), 1949- 1st ed. Austin : University of Texas Press, 1999.
*TC BF637.C45 Y69 1999*

**Understanding modern telecommunications and the information superhighway.**
Nellist, John G. Boston, Mass. : Artech House, 1999.
*TC TK5105.5 .N45 1999*

**Understanding old age.**
Wilson, Gail. London : Sage, 2000.
*TC HQ1061 .W54 2000*

**Understanding reading problems.**
Gillet, Jean Wallace. 5th ed. New York ; Harlow, England : Longman, c2000.
*TC LB1050.46 .G55 2000*

**Understanding representation in the cognitive sciences :** does representation need reality? / edited by Alexander Riegler, Markus Peschl, and Astrid von Stein. New York : Kluwer Academic/Plenum Publishers, c1999. 307 p. : ill. ; 26 cm. Includes bibliographical references and index. ISBN 0-306-46286-9 DDC 153
*1. Mental representation - Congresses. I. Riegler, Alex. II. Peschl, Markus F. III. Stein, Astrid von.*
*TC BF316.6 U63 1999*

**Understanding student teaching.**
Osunde, Egerton Oyenmwense, 1950- Lanham, Md. : University Press of America, 1999.
*TC LB2157.U5 O78 1999*

**Understanding teaching.**
Louden, William. New York : Cassell : Teachers College Press, Teachers College, Columbia University, 1991.
*TC LB1025.3 .L68 1991*

**Understanding the boys.**
Head, John (John O.) New York : Falmer Press, 1999.
*TC LC1390 .H43 1999*

**Understanding the defiant child** [videorecording] / [presented by] Guilford Publications ; Kevin Dawkins, producer/writer ; Kevin Dawkins Productions. New York : Guilford Publications, c1997. 1 videocassette (ca. 34 min.) : sd., col. ; 1/2 in. + 1 program manual (vii, 28 p. : ill. ; 22 cm.). VHS. Catalogued from credits and container. Author/host: Russell A. Barkley. Graphic design: Lee Dawkins. A companion video specifically designed for teaching parents by the same author is available under the title: Managing the defiant child : a guide to parent training; a video for clinicians is available under the title: Defiant children : a clinician's manual for assessment and parent training. For parents and teachers of ODD and ADD children. SUMMARY: Offering a clear picture of the children who routinely demonstrate negative, hostile, and defiant behavior, this video illuminates the nature and causes of oppositional defiant disorder (ODD). Featuring Dr. Russell Barkley, the video also shows real-life scenes of family interactions and interviews with parents. Dr. Barkley discusses what ODD is according to DSMIV, its causes, the reason for treatment and a model for treatment. ISBN 1-57230-166-X
*1. Oppositional defiant disorder in children. 2. Attention-deficit-disordered children. 3. Behavior disorders in children. 4. Parent and child. 5. Parenting - Psychology. 6. Child rearing. 7. Parenting. I. Barkley, Russell A., 1949- II. Guilford Publications, Inc. III. Kevin Dawkins Productions. IV. Title: Managing the defiant child : a guide to parent training [videorecording] V. Title: Defiant children : a clinician's manual for assessment and parent training.*
*TC HQ755.7 .U63 1997*

**Understanding the Little Rock crisis :** an exercise in remembrance and reconciliation / edited by Elizabeth Jacoway and C. Fred Williams. Fayetteville, Ark : University of Arkansas Press, 1999. vii, 186 p. : ill. ; 24 cm. Includes bibliographical references and index. ISBN 1-55728-529-2 (cloth : alk. paper) ISBN 1-55728-530-6 (paper : alk. paper) DDC 379.2/63/0976773
*1. School integration - Arkansas - Little Rock - History - 20th century. 2. Central High School (Little Rock, Ark.) - History. 3. Afro-Americans - Education - Arkansas - Little Rock - History - 20th century. I. Jacoway, Elizabeth, 1944- II. Williams, C. Fred.*
*TC LC214.23.L56 U53 1999*

**Understanding the physical sciences.**
Anfinson, Olaf P. Boston, Allyn and Bacon, 1963.
*TC Q162 .A54*

**Understanding the teacher union contract.**
Lieberman, Myron, 1919- New Brunswick, N.J. : Social Philosophy and Policy Foundation : Transaction Publishers, 2000.
*TC KF3409.T4 L54 2000*

**Understanding the work and career paths of midlevel administrators** / Linda K. Johnsrud, Vicki J. Rosser, editors. San Francisco : Jossey-Bass, 2000. 125 p. ; 23 cm. (New directions for higher education, 0271-0560 ; no. 111) (Jossey-Bass higher and adult education series) Spine title: Work and career paths of midlevel administrators. "Fall 2000." Includes bibliographical references and index. CONTENTS: Mid-level administrators : what we know / Vicki J. Rosser -- Academic advising / Kathryn Nemeth Tuttle -- Institutional advancement / Jeri L. Kozobarich -- Information technology / David Lassner -- Human resources / Daniel J. Julius -- International student affairs / Melinda Wood, Parandeh Kia -- Enrollment management / Thomas Huddleston, Jr. -- Budget and planning / Patricia N. Haeuser -- Student life and development / Jan Minoru Javinar -- Academic business affairs / Larry M. Dooley -- Institutional research / Deborah Olsen - CONTENTS: Commentary / Linda K. Johnsrud. ISBN 0-7879-5435-7
*1. College administrators - Professional relationships. 2. Middle managers. 3. Universities and colleges - Administration. 4. Universities and colleges - Administration - Vocational guidance. I. Rosser, Vicki J. II. Title: Work and career paths of midlevel administrators III. Series. IV. Series: New directions for higher education ; no. 111*
*TC LB2341 .N5111 2000*

**Underwood, Terry.** The portfolio project : a study of assessment, instruction, and middle school reform / Terry Underwood. Urbana, Ill. : National Council of Teachers of English, c1999. xvi, 259 p. : ill. ; 26 cm. Includes bibliographical references (p. 241-251) and index. "NCTE stock number: 36281-3050"--T.p. verso. ISBN 0-8141-3628-1 (paper) DDC 371.39
*1. Portfolios in education - California - Case studies. 2. Educational tests and measurements - California - Case studies. I. Title.*
*TC LB1029.P67 U53 1999*

**The undiscovered mind.**
Horgan, John, 1953- New York : Free Press, c1999.
*TC RC343 .H636 1999*

**UNDOCUMENTED ALIENS.** *See* **ILLEGAL ALIENS.**

**UNEMPLOYED.** *See* **HARD-CORE UNEMPLOYED; JOB VACANCIES.**

**UNEMPLOYMENT.** *See* **FULL EMPLOYMENT POLICIES; STRUCTURAL UNEMPLOYMENT.**

**UNEMPLOYMENT, STRUCTURAL.** *See* **STRUCTURAL UNEMPLOYMENT.**

**UNEMPLOYMENT - UNITED STATES.**
McCarthy, William H. Reducing urban unemployment. Washington, D.C. : National League of Cities, c1985.
*TC HD5724 .M34 1985*

**UNEMPLOYMENT - UNITED STATES - HISTORY - 20TH CENTURY.**
Vedder, Richard K. Out of work. New York : Holmes & Meier, 1993.
*TC HD7096.U5 V43 1993*

**Unesco.**
Changing international aid to education. Paris : Unesco Pub./NORRAG, 1999.
*TC LC2607 .C42 1999*

Fundamental and adult education. [Paris : Unesco, 1952-1960]

Fundamental education. [Paris, France : Unesco, 1949-1952].

Higher education research. 1st ed. Oxford ; [New York] : Pergamon, published for the IAU Press, 2000.
*TC LB2326.3 .H548 2000*

Human rights. Aldershot, England ; Brookfield, VT : Ashgate/Dartmouth ; Paris : UNESCO Publishing, 1998.
*TC JC571 .H76967 1998*

International bibliography of anthropology = London ; New York : Routledge, 1999-
*TC Z7161 .I593*

Local knowledge and wisdom in higher education. 1st ed. Oxford : Published for the IAU Press [by] Pergamon, 2000.
*TC GN380 .L63 2000*

The role of measurement and evaluation in education policy. Paris : Unesco Pub., 1999.
*TC LB3051 .R653 1999*

[Statistical yearbook (Unesco)] Statistical yearbook = [Paris : Unesco], 1987-
*TC AZ361 .U45*

**Unesco. Regional Office for Education in Asia and the Pacific.**
Grass roots networking for primary education :. Bangkok : Unesco Regional Office for Education in Asia and the Pacific, 1985.
*TC LA1054 .G73 1985*

**Unesco statistical yearbook.**
[Statistical yearbook (Unesco)] Statistical yearbook = [Paris : Unesco], 1987-
*TC AZ361 .U45*

**Unger, Rhoda Kesler.** Resisting gender : twenty-five years of feminist psychology / Rhoda K. Unger. London : Thousand Oaks, Calif. : Sage Publications, 1998. vi, 239 p. ; 23 cm. (Gender and psychology) Includes bibliographical references (p. [213]-233) and index. ISBN 0-8039-7824-3 ISBN 0-8039-7825-1 (pbk.) DDC 150/.82
*1. Feminist psychology. 2. Women - Psychology. 3. Sex role. I. Title. II. Series.*
*TC BF201.4 .U544 1998*

**UNGRADED SCHOOLS.** *See* **NONGRADED SCHOOLS.**

**Unheard voices.**
Sanlo, Ronni L., 1947- Westport, Conn. : London : Bergin & Garvey, 1999.
*TC LB2844.1.G39 S36 1999*

**UNICAMERAL LEGISLATURES.** *See* **LEGISLATIVE BODIES.**

**UNICEF.**
The progress of nations. New York, NY : UNICEF, 1993-
*TC RA407.A1 P76*

**UNIDENTIFIED FLYING OBJECTS.**
Brooks, Philip, 1955- Invaders from outer space. 1st American ed. New York : DK, 1999.
*TC TL789.2 .B76 1999*

**UNIDENTIFIED FLYING OBJECTS - SIGHTINGS AND ENCOUNTERS.** *See* **HUMAN-ALIEN ENCOUNTERS.**

**UNIDENTIFIED FLYING OBJECTS - SIGHTINGS AND ENCOUNTERS - JUVENILE LITERATURE.**
Brooks, Philip, 1955- Invaders from outer space. 1st American ed. New York : DK, 1999.
*TC TL789.2 .B76 1999*

**UNIFICATION CHURCH - CLERGY - UNITED STATES - PSYCHOLOGICAL ASPECTS.**
Stewart, Therese Marie Klein. The challenges to sustaining Unification faith and the spiritual quest after seminary. 1996.
*TC 06 no. 10751*

**Unification Theological Seminary.**
Stewart, Therese Marie Klein. The challenges to sustaining Unification faith and the spiritual quest after seminary. 1996.
*TC 06 no. 10751*

**UNIFIED FIELD THEORIES.**
Combs, Arthur W. (Arthur Wright), 1912- Being and becoming. New York : Springer Pub. Co., c1999.
*TC BF38 .C715 1999*

Stephen Hawking's universe [videorecording]. [Alexandria, Va.] : PBS Video; Burbank, CA : Distributed by Warner Home Video, c1997.
*TC QB982 .S7 1997*

Stephen Hawking's universe [videorecording]. [Alexandria, Va.] : PBS Video; Burbank, CA : Distributed by Warner Home Video, c1997.
*TC QB982 .S7 1997*

**UNIFIED SCIENCE.** *See* **SEMANTICS (PHILOSOPHY).**

**UNIFORMS.** *See* **COSTUME.**

**Union of International Associations.**
International transnational associations. [Bruxelles, Union of International Associations]

**Unions and the rise of working-class feminism 1945-80.**
Deslippe, Dennis A. (Dennis Arthur), 1961- Rights, not roses. Urbana : University of Illinois Press, c2000.
*TC HD6079.2.U5 D47 2000*

**UNIONS, STUDENT.** *See* **STUDENT UNIONS.**

**UNIPOLAR DEPRESSION.** *See* **DEPRESSION, MENTAL.**

**UNITAS FRATRUM.** *See* **MORAVIANS.**

**United Nations. Dept. of Economic and Social Affairs. Population Division.**
Population growth, structure and distribution. New York : United Nations, 1999.
*TC HB871.P6675 1999*

Review and appraisal of the progress made in achieving the goals and objectives of the Programme of Action of the International Conference on Population and Development. New York : United Nations, 1999.
*TC HB849 .R48 1999*

**United Nations. Dept. of International Economic and Social Affairs.**
World population prospects. New York : United Nations, 1985-
*TC HA154 .W6*

**United Nations University.**
Linguistic minorities and literacy. Berlin ; New York : Mouton Publishers, 1984.
*TC P119.315 .L56 1984*

Strengthening the family. Tokyo ; New York : United Nations University Press, c1995.
*TC HQ727.9 .S77 1995*

**United States.**
**Education for All Handicapped Children Act. 1983.**
Collins, Christopher G. Teaching the emotionally handicapped child. Danville, Ill. : Interstate Printers & Publishers, c1983.
*TC LC4165 .C62 1983*

(no. 1) Francis, Robert Jay. Motor characteristics of the mentally retarded, [Washington] U.S. Dept. of Health, Education, and Welfare, Office of Education [1960]
*TC RJ499 .F7 1960*

**United States. Advisory Commission on International Educational and Cultural Affairs.**
International educational and cultural exchange. [Washington, U.S. Advisory Commission on International Educational and Cultural Affairs; for sale by the Supt. of Docs., U.S. Govt. Print. Off.]

**UNITED STATES. AGENCY FOR INTERNATIONAL DEVELOPMENT.**
Basile, Michael L., 1943- The deployment of educational innovation through foreign aid. 1989.
*TC LD3234.M267 B32 1989*

**UNITED STATES. AIR FORCE ROTC.**
Neiberg, Michael S. Making citizen-soldiers. Cambridge, Mass. ; London : Harvard University Press, 2000.
*TC U428.5 .N45 2000*

**UNITED STATES - ANTIQUITIES.** *See* **INDIANS OF NORTH AMERICA - ANTIQUITIES.**

**UNITED STATES - ARMED FORCES - AFRO-AMERICANS.** *See* **AFRO-AMERICAN SOLDIERS.**

**UNITED STATES - ARMED FORCES - OFFICERS - TRAINING OF.**
Neiberg, Michael S. Making citizen-soldiers. Cambridge, Mass. ; London : Harvard University Press, 2000.
*TC U428.5 .N45 2000*

**UNITED STATES. ARMY. MINNESOTA INFANTRY REGIMENT, 2ND (1861-1865) - BIOGRAPHY - JUVENILE LITERATURE.**
Bircher, William, 1845-1917. A Civil War drummer boy. Mankato, Minn. : Blue Earth Books, c2000.
*TC E601 .B605 2000*

**UNITED STATES. ARMY NURSE CORPS - HISTORY.**
Sarnecky, Mary T. A history of the U.S. Army Nurse Corps. Philadelphia : University of Pennsylvania Press, c1999.
*TC UH493 .S27 1999*

**UNITED STATES. ARMY. RESERVE OFFICERS' TRAINING CORPS.**
Neiberg, Michael S. Making citizen-soldiers. Cambridge, Mass. ; London : Harvard University Press, 2000.
*TC U428.5 .N45 2000*

**UNITED STATES - BIOGRAPHY.**
Directory of American scholars. 9th ed. / edited by Rita C. Velazquez. Detroit, Mich. : Gale Group, 1999.
*TC LA2311 .D57 1999*

**UNITED STATES - BIOGRAPHY - PORTRAITS - EXHIBITIONS.**
Beaux, Cecilia, 1855-1942. Cecilia Beaux and the art of portraiture. Washington, DC : Published for the National Portrait Gallery by the Smithsonian Institution Press, 1995.
*TC ND1329.B39 A4 1995*

**UNITED STATES - BIOGRAPHY - STUDY AND TEACHING.**
Druce, Arden. Paper bag puppets. Lanham, MD : Scarecrow Press, 1999.
*TC Z718.3 .D78 1999*

Marsh, Valerie. True tales of heroes & heroines. Fort Atkinson, Wis. : Alleyside Press, c1999.
*TC CT85 .M37 1999*

**United States Catholic Conference. Dept. of Education.**
Who are my sisters and brothers? Washington, D.C. : The Conference, c1996.
*TC BX1795.E44 W46 1996*

**UNITED STATES - CHURCH HISTORY.**
Raboteau, Albert J. A fire in the bones. Boston : Beacon Press, c1995.
*TC BR563.N4 R24 1995*

Satter, Beryl, 1959- Each mind a kingdom. Berkeley : University of California Press, c1999.
*TC BF639 .S124 1999*

**UNITED STATES - CIVILIZATION - 1865-1918.**
Satter, Beryl, 1959- Each mind a kingdom. Berkeley : University of California Press, c1999.
*TC BF639 .S124 1999*

**UNITED STATES - CIVILIZATION - 1918-1945 - PICTORIAL WORKS.**
Roaring twenties [picture]. Amawalk, NY : Jackdaw Publications, c1997.
*TC E784 .R6 1997*

**UNITED STATES - CIVILIZATION - 1945-.**
Trencher, Susan R. Mirrored images. Westport, CT : Bergin & Garvey, 2000.
*TC GN17.3.U6 T74 2000*

**UNITED STATES - CIVILIZATION - 1970-.**
Bad subjects. New York : New York University Press, c1998.

*TC E169.12 .B26 1998*

**UNITED STATES - CIVILIZATION - 19TH CENTURY - CHRONOLOGY.**
Bornstein, Jerry. An American chronology. New York : Neal-Schuman Publishers, 2000.
*TC E169.1 .B758 2000*

**UNITED STATES - CIVILIZATION - 20TH CENTURY - CHRONOLOGY.**
Bornstein, Jerry. An American chronology. New York : Neal-Schuman Publishers, 2000.
*TC E169.1 .B758 2000*

**UNITED STATES - CIVILIZATION - CLASSICAL INFLUENCES.**
Kopff, E. Christian. The devil knows Latin. Wilmington, Del. : ISI Books, 1999.
*TC PA78.U6 K67 1999*

**UNITED STATES - CIVILIZATION - COMPUTER NETWORK RESOURCES - DIRECTORIES.**
Gregory, Vicki L., 1950- Multicultural resources on the Internet. The United States and Canada. Englewood, Colo. : Libraries Unlimited, 1999.
*TC E184.A1 G874 1999*

**UNITED STATES - CIVILIZATION - CONGRESSES.**
Education, leadership, and business ethics. Boston, MA : Kluwer Academic Publishers, c1998.
*TC HF5387 .E346 1998*

**UNITED STATES - CIVILIZATION - JEWISH INFLUENCES - ENCYCLOPEDIAS.**
American Jewish desk reference. 1st ed. New York : Random House, 1999.
*TC E184.35 .A44 1999*

**United States. Congress. House. Committee on Ways and Means. Subcommittee on Human Resources.**
United States. General Accounting Office. Child welfare. Washington, D.C. (P.O. Box 37050, Washington, D.C. 20013) : The Office, [1998]
*TC HV741 .U525 1998a*

**United States. Congress. House. Documents.**
Boy Scouts of America. Annual report of the Boy Scouts of America. Washington, D.C., Govt. Print. Off.
*TC HS3313.B7 A15*

**United States. Congress. Senate. Committee on Labor and Public Welfare. Subcommittee on Health.** School-age mother and child health act, 1975 : hearing before the Subcommittee on Health of the Committee on Labor and Public Welfare, United States Senate, Ninety-fourth Congress, first session, on S. 2538 ... November 4, 1975. Washington : U.S. Govt. Print. Off., 1976. vi, 878 p. : ill. ; 24 cm. Includes bibliographical references and indexes.
*1. Teenage girls - Legal status, laws, etc. - United States. 2. Public health laws - United States. 3. Pregnant schoolgirls - United States. I. Title.*
*TC KF26 .L354 1975*

**UNITED STATES - CONSTITUTIONAL LAW.** *See* **CONSTITUTIONAL LAW - UNITED STATES.**

**UNITED STATES - COPYRIGHT.** *See* **COPYRIGHT - UNITED STATES.**

**UNITED STATES - CULTURAL POLICY.**
Kurin, Richard, 1950- Reflections of a culture broker. Washington, D.C. : Smithsonian Institution Press, c1997.
*TC GN36.U62 D5775 1997*

**UNITED STATES - CULTURAL POLICY - HISTORY - 20TH CENTURY.**
Art matters. New York : New York University Press, c1999.
*TC N72.S6 A752 1999*

**United States. Dept. of Education.**
Annual State of American Education Address (7th : February 22, 2000 : Durham, N.C.) The seventh annual state of American education address [videorecording. [Washington, D.C. : U.S. Dept. of Education], 2000.

Modernizing schools : technology and buildings for a new century (September 19, 2000 : Washington, D.C.) Modernizing schools [videorecording]. [Washington, D.C.] : U.S. Dept. of Education, [2000].
*TC LB3205 .M64 2000*

Modernizing schools : technology and buildings for a new century (September 19, 2000 : Washington, D.C.) Modernizing schools [videorecording]. [Washington, D.C.] : U.S. Dept. of Education, [2000].

*TC LB3205 .M64 2000*
Powerful middle schools : teaching and learning for young adolescents (2000) Powerful middle schools [videorecording]. [Washington, D.C.?] : U.S. Dept. of Education, [2000].
*TC LB1623 .P6 2000*

Public charter schools : new choices in public education (May 3, 2000 : Washington, D.C.) Public charter schools [videorecording]. [Washington, D.C.] : U.S. Dept. of Education, [2000].
*TC LB2806.36 .P9 2000*

**United States. Dept. of Health and Human Services. Task Force on Black and Minority Health.** Report of the Secretary's Task Force on Black & Minority Health. Washington, D.C. : U.S. Dept. of Health and Human Services, [1985-<1986 > <v. 1, 3-4, pts. 1-2; 5-8; in 8 > : ill. ; 28 cm. Vol. 1: August 1985. Vols. 3-8: January 1986. Includes bibliographies. PARTIAL CONTENTS: v. 1. Executive summary -- v. 3. Cancer -- v. 4. Cardiovascular and cerebrovascular disease (2 v.) -- v. 5. Homicide, suicide, and unintentional injuries -- v. 6. Infant mortality and low birthweight -- v. 7. Chemical dependency and diabetes -- v. 8. Hispanic health issues, Inventory of DHHS programs, Survey of non-federal community. DDC 362.1/08996073
*1. Afro-Americans - Health and hygiene - United States. 2. Minorities - Health and hygiene - United States. 3. Afro-Americans - Health and hygiene - United States - Statistics. 4. Minorities - Health and hygiene - United States - Statistics. 5. Mortality - United States - Statistics. 6. United States - Statistics, Medical. 7. United States - Statistics, Vital. I. Title.*
*TC RA448.5.N4 U55 1985*

**United States. Dept. of Health, Education, and Welfare. Office of Program Analysis.** Health, education, and welfare indicators. Washington, D.C. : U.S. Dept. of Health, Education and Welfare : For sale by the Supt. of Docs., U.S. G.P.O., 1960-[1967]

**United States. Dept. of Health, Education, and Welfare. Office of the Secretary.** Health, education, and welfare indicators. Washington, D.C. : U.S. Dept. of Health, Education and Welfare : For sale by the Supt. of Docs., U.S. G.P.O., 1960-[1967]

**UNITED STATES - ECONOMIC CONDITIONS.**
Vedder, Richard K. Out of work. New York : Holmes & Meier, 1993.
*TC HD7096.U5 V43 1993*

**UNITED STATES - ECONOMIC CONDITIONS - 1918-1945.**
Uys, Errol Lincoln. Riding the rails. New York : TV Books ; c1999.
*TC HC106.3 U97 1999*

**UNITED STATES - ECONOMIC CONDITIONS - 1918-1945 - PERIODICALS.**
Building America. [New York : Published for the Dept. of Supervision and Curriculum Development by the Society for Curriculum Study, Inc. ; distributed by Americana Corporation, 1935-

**UNITED STATES - ECONOMIC CONDITIONS - 1918-1945 - POSTERS.**
The depression hits home [picture]. Amawalk, NY : Jackdaw Publications, c1997.
*TC TR820.5 .D4 1997*

**UNITED STATES - ECONOMIC CONDITIONS - 1945-.**
Andrews, Marcellus, 1956- The political economy of hope and fear. New York : New York University Press, c1999.
*TC E185.8 .A77 1999*

Stein, Herbert, 1916- What I think. Washington, D.C. : AEI Press, 1998.
*TC HC106.5 .S784 1998*

**UNITED STATES - ECONOMIC CONDITIONS - PERIODICALS.**
American economic security. Washington, Chamber of Commerce of the United States of America.

**UNITED STATES - ECONOMIC CONDITIONS - REGIONAL DISPARITIES.**
Stanback, Thomas M. Cities in transition. Totowa, N.J. : Allanheld, Osmun, 1982.
*TC HD5724 .S649 1982*

**UNITED STATES - ECONOMIC POLICY.**
Andrews, Marcellus, 1956- The political economy of hope and fear. New York : New York University Press, c1999.
*TC E185.8 .A77 1999*

Welfare. San Diego, CA : Greenhaven Press, c1997.

*TC HV95 .W453 1997*
**UNITED STATES - ECONOMIC POLICY - 1945-.**
Stein, Herbert, 1916- What I think. Washington, D.C. : AEI Press, 1998.
*TC HC106.5 .S784 1998*

**UNITED STATES - EMIGRATION AND IMMIGRATION.**
Gonzalez-Pando, Miguel. The Cuban Americans. Westport, Conn. : Greenwood Press, 1998.
*TC E184.C97 G64 1998*

**UNITED STATES - EMIGRATION AND IMMIGRATION - HISTORY - POSTERS.**
Ellis Island [picture]. Amawalk, NY : Jackdaw Publications, c1997.
*TC TR820.5 .E4 1997*

**UNITED STATES - EMIGRATION AND IMMIGRATION LAW.** *See* **EMIGRATION AND IMMIGRATION LAW - UNITED STATES.**

**UNITED STATES - EMIGRATION AND IMMIGRATION - PROBLEMS, EXERCISES, ETC.**
New immigrants in the United States. Cambridge, U.K. : New York : Cambridge University Press, 2000.
*TC PE1128 .N384 1999*

**UNITED STATES - EMIGRATION AND IMMIGRATION - PUBLIC OPINION - HISTORY.**
Irving, Katrina. Immigrant mothers. Urbana : University of Illinois Press, c2000.
*TC HQ1419 .I75 2000*

**UNITED STATES - EMIGRATION AND IMMIGRATION - RELIGIOUS ASPECTS - CATHOLIC CHURCH.**
Who are my sisters and brothers? Washington, D.C. : The Conference, c1996.
*TC BX1795.E44 W46 1996*

**UNITED STATES - EMPLOYEES.** *See* **UNITED STATES - OFFICIALS AND EMPLOYEES.**

**UNITED STATES - ETHNIC RELATIONS.**
Addressing cultural issues in organizations. Thousand Oaks, Calif. : Sage Publications, 2000.
*TC E184.A1 A337 2000*

Problems and issues of diversity in the United States. Westport, Conn. : Bergin & Garvey, 1999.
*TC E184.A1 P76 1999*

**UNITED STATES - ETHNIC RELATIONS - DICTIONARIES.**
Herbst, Philip. The color of words. Yarmouth, Me., USA : Intercultural Press, [1997]
*TC E184.A1 H466 1997*

**UNITED STATES - ETHNIC RELATIONS - HISTORY.**
Irving, Katrina. Immigrant mothers. Urbana : University of Illinois Press, c2000.
*TC HQ1419 .I75 2000*

**UNITED STATES. FOOD AND DRUGS ACT - HISTORY.**
Goodwin, Lorine Swainston, 1925- The pure food, drink, and drug crusaders, 1879-1914. Jefferson, N.C. : McFarland, 1999.
*TC HD9000.9.U5 G66 1999*

**UNITED STATES - FOREIGN POPULATION.** *See* **IMMIGRANTS - UNITED STATES.**

**UNITED STATES - FOREIGN RELATIONS - GREAT BRITAIN.**
Hendrick, Burton Jesse, 1870-1949. The life and letters of Walter H. Page. Garden City, N.Y. : Doubleday, Page & Co., 1925.
*TC E664.P15 H45 1925*

**UNITED STATES - FOREIGN RELATIONS - SOVIET UNION - FICTION.**
Burdick, Eugene. Fail-safe. 1st Ecco ed. Hopewell, N.J. : Ecco Press ; New York, NY : Distributed by W.W. Norton, 1999.
*TC PS3552.U7116 F35 1999*

**UNITED STATES - FOREIGN RELATIONS - VIETNAM.**
Vietnam [videorecording]. Beverly Hills, CA : CBS/Fox Video, c1981.

**UNITED STATES. FREEDOM OF INFORMATION ACT.**
Foerstel, Herbert N. Freedom of information and the right to know. Westport, Conn. : Greenwood Press, 1999.
*TC KF5753 .F64 1999*

**United States. General Accounting Office.** Child welfare : early experiences implementing a managed care approach : report to the Chairman, Subcommittee on Human Resources, Committee on Ways and Means, House of Representatives / United States General Accounting Office. Washington, D.C. (P.O. Box 37050, Washington, D.C. 20013) : The Office, [1998] 104 p. : ill., form ; 28 cm. Cover title. "October 1998." Includes bibliographical references. "GAO/HEHS-99-8." "B-280259"--P. [1]. Also issued via the Internet.
*1. Child welfare - United States. 2. Social service - Contracting out - United States. 3. Children - Services for - United States - Cost control. 4. Children - Government policy - United States. I. United States. Congress. House. Committee on Ways and Means. Subcommittee on Human Resources. II. Title. III. Title: Early experiences implementing a managed care approach*
*TC HV741 .U525 1998a*

**UNITED STATES - GOVERNMENT.** *See* **UNITED STATES - POLITICS AND GOVERNMENT.**

**UNITED STATES - GOVERNMENT EMPLOYEES.** *See* **UNITED STATES - OFFICIALS AND EMPLOYEES.**

**United States. Health Services and Mental Health Administration.** Health services reports. Rockville, Md. v. 86-89, no. 3; Jan. 1971-May/June 1974. Title varies: HSMHA health reports 1971-Feb. 1972. Vols. for issued as its HSM Supersedes and continues the numbering of U.S. Public Health Service Public health reports. Continued by Public health reports.
*I. Title. II. Title: U.S Public Health Service Public health reports III. Title: U.S Public Health Service Public health reports IV. Title: Public health reports*

**UNITED STATES - HISTORY.**
Cayton, Andrew R. L. (Andrew Robert Lee), 1954- America. Upper Saddle River, N.J. : Prentice Hall, c1998.
*TC E178.1 .C364 1998*

Cayton, Andrew R. L. (Andrew Robert Lee), 1954- America. Teacher's ed. Upper Saddle River, N.J.. : Prentice Hall, c1998.
*TC E178.1 .C364 1998 Teacher's Ed.*

Cayton, Andrew R. L. (Andrew Robert Lee), 1954- America. Upper Saddle River, N.J. : Prentice Hall, c1998.
*TC E178.1 .C3643 1998*

Cayton, Andrew R. L. (Andrew Robert Lee), 1954- America. Upper Saddle River, N.J. : Prentice Hall, c1998.
*TC E178.1 .C3643 1998*

Cayton, Andrew R. L. (Andrew Robert Lee), 1954- America. Teacher's ed. Upper Saddle River, N.J.. : Prentice Hall, c1998.
*TC E178.1 .C3643 1998 Teacher's Ed.*

Cayton, Andrew R. L. (Andrew Robert Lee), 1954- America. Upper Saddle River, N.J. : Prentice Hall, c1998.
*TC E178.1 .C3643 1998*

Cayton, Andrew R. L. (Andrew Robert Lee), 1954- America. Teacher's ed. Upper Saddle River, N.J.. : Prentice Hall, c1998.
*TC E178.1 .C364 1998 Teacher's Ed.*

Cayton, Andrew R. L. (Andrew Robert Lee), 1954- America. Upper Saddle River, N.J. : Prentice Hall, c1998.
*TC E178.1 .C364 1998*

Cayton, Andrew R. L. (Andrew Robert Lee), 1954- America. Teacher's ed. Upper Saddle River, N.J.. : Prentice Hall, c1998.
*TC E178.1 .C3645 1998 Teacher's Ed.*

Cayton, Andrew R. L. (Andrew Robert Lee), 1954- America. Upper Saddle River, N.J. : Prentice Hall, c1998.
*TC E178.1 .C3645 1998*

Cayton, Andrew R. L. (Andrew Robert Lee), 1954- America. Upper Saddle River, N.J. : Prentice Hall, c1998.
*TC E178.1 .C3645 1998*

Cayton, Andrew R. L. (Andrew Robert Lee), 1954- America. Teacher's ed. Upper Saddle River, N.J.. : Prentice Hall, c1998.
*TC E178.1 .C364 1998 Teacher's Ed.*

Cayton, Andrew R. L. (Andrew Robert Lee), 1954- America. Upper Saddle River, N.J.. : Prentice Hall, c1998.
*TC E178.1 .C364 1998*

Cayton, Andrew R. L. (Andrew Robert Lee), 1954-
America. Upper Saddle River, N.J. : Prentice Hall,
c1998.
*TC E178.1 .C364 1998*

Cayton, Andrew R. L. (Andrew Robert Lee), 1954-
America. Teacher's ed. Upper Saddle River, N.J.. :
Prentice Hall, c1998.
*TC E178.1 .C3644 1998 Teacher's Ed.*

Cayton, Andrew R. L. (Andrew Robert Lee), 1954-
America. Upper Saddle River, N.J. : Prentice Hall,
c1998.
*TC E178.1 .C364 1998*

Cayton, Andrew R. L. (Andrew Robert Lee), 1954-
America. Upper Saddle River, N.J. : Prentice Hall,
c1998.
*TC E178.1 .C3644 1998*

Cayton, Andrew R. L. (Andrew Robert Lee), 1954-
America. Upper Saddle River, N.J. : Prentice Hall,
c1998.
*TC E178.1 .C3644 1998*

Cayton, Andrew R. L. (Andrew Robert Lee), 1954-
America. Upper Saddle River, N.J. : Prentice Hall,
c1998.
*TC E178.1 .C3644 1998*

Conlin, Joseph Robert. Our land, our time. Annotated
teacher's ed. San Diego : Coronado Publishers, c1987.
*TC E178.1 .C762 1987*

Davidson, James West. The American nation. Upper
Saddle River, N.J. : Prentice Hall, c1997.
*TC E178.1 .D22 1997*

Jackson, Carlton. Two centuries of progress. 3rd ed.
Mission Hills, CA : Glencoe/McGraw-Hill, 1991.
*TC E178.1 .J321 1991*

King, Wayne E. AGS United States history. Teacher's
ed. Circle Pines, Minn. : AGS, American Guidance
Service, c1998.
*TC E175.8 .K56 1998 Teacher's Ed.*

Napp, John L. AGS United States history. Circle
Pines, Minn. : AGS, American Guidance Service,
c1998.
*TC E178.1 .N36 1998*

Risjord, Norman K. History of the American people.
New York : Holt, Rinehart, and Winston, c1986.
*TC E178.1 .R597 1986*

**UNITED STATES - HISTORY - 1865-1898.** *See*
**RECONSTRUCTION.**

**UNITED STATES - HISTORY - 1865-1898 -
FICTION.**
Hansen, Joyce. The heart calls home. New York :
Walker & Company, 1999.
*TC PZ7.H19825 He 1999*

**UNITED STATES - HISTORY - 1865-1898 -
JUVENILE FICTION.**
Hansen, Joyce. The heart calls home. New York :
Walker & Company, 1999.
*TC PZ7.H19825 He 1999*

**UNITED STATES - HISTORY - 1919-1933 -
PICTORIAL WORKS.**
Roaring twenties [picture]. Amawalk, NY : Jackdaw
Publications, c1997.
*TC E784 .R6 1997*

**UNITED STATES - HISTORY - 1919-1933 -
POSTERS.**
The depression hits home [picture]. Amawalk, NY :
Jackdaw Publications, c1997.
*TC TR820.5 .D4 1997*

**UNITED STATES - HISTORY - 1929-1933.**
Uys, Errol Lincoln. Riding the rails. New York : TV
Books ; c1999.
*TC HC106.3 U97 1999*

**UNITED STATES - HISTORY - 1933-1945 -
POSTERS.**
The depression hits home [picture]. Amawalk, NY :
Jackdaw Publications, c1997.
*TC TR820.5 .D4 1997*

**UNITED STATES - HISTORY - BOOK REVIEWS -
PERIODICALS.**
[Reviews in American history (Online)] Reviews in
American history [computer file]. Baltimore, MD :
Johns Hopkins University Press, c1995-
*TC EJOURNALS*

**UNITED STATES - HISTORY - CIVIL WAR,
1861-1865.**
Clinton, Catherine, 1952- Scholastic encyclopedia of
the Civil War. New York : Scholastic Reference,
1999.

*TC E468 .C67 1999*

**UNITED STATES - HISTORY - CIVIL WAR,
1861-1865 - CORRESPONDENTS.** *See*
**UNITED STATES - HISTORY - CIVIL WAR,
1861-1865 - JOURNALISTS.**

**UNITED STATES - HISTORY - CIVIL WAR,
1861-1865 - DRUMMER BOYS.** *See* **UNITED
STATES - HISTORY - CIVIL WAR, 1861-
1865 - PARTICIPATION, JUVENILE.**

**UNITED STATES - HISTORY - CIVIL WAR,
1861-1865 - ENCYCLOPEDIAS, JUVENILE.**
Clinton, Catherine, 1952- Scholastic encyclopedia of
the Civil War. New York : Scholastic Reference,
1999.
*TC E468 .C67 1999*

**UNITED STATES - HISTORY - CIVIL WAR,
1861-1865 - FICTION.**
Paulsen, Gary. Soldier's heart. New York : Delacorte
Press, c1998.
*TC PZ7.P2843 So 1998*

Ransom, Candice F., 1952- The promise quilt. New
York : Walker and Co., 1999.
*TC PZ7.R1743 Pr 1999*

Sappey, Maureen Stack, 1952- Letters from Vinnie.
Asheville, NC : Front Street, 1999.
*TC PZ7.S2388 Le 1999*

**UNITED STATES - HISTORY - CIVIL WAR,
1861-1865 - JOURNALISTS - JUVENILE
LITERATURE.**
Morrison, Taylor. Civil War artist. Boston : Houghton
Mifflin, 1999.
*TC E468.9 .M86 1999*

**UNITED STATES - HISTORY - CIVIL WAR,
1861-1865 - JUVENILE FICTION.**
Paulsen, Gary. Soldier's heart. New York : Delacorte
Press, c1998.
*TC PZ7.P2843 So 1998*

**UNITED STATES - HISTORY - CIVIL WAR,
1861-1865 - JUVENILE PARTICIPANTS.** *See*
**UNITED STATES - HISTORY - CIVIL WAR,
1861-1865 - PARTICIPATION, JUVENILE.**

**UNITED STATES - HISTORY - CIVIL WAR,
1861-1865 - PARTICIPATION, JUVENILE -
JUVENILE LITERATURE.**
Bircher, William, 1845-1917. A Civil War drummer
boy. Mankato, Minn. : Blue Earth Books, c2000.
*TC E601 .B605 2000*

**UNITED STATES - HISTORY - CIVIL WAR,
1861-1865 - PARTICIPATION, JUVENILE -
POSTERS.**
Civil war [picture]. Amawalk, NY : Jackdaw
Publications, c1999.
*TC TR820.5 .C56 1999*

**UNITED STATES - HISTORY - CIVIL WAR,
1861-1865 - PERSONAL NARRATIVES.**
Berry, Carrie, b. 1854. A Confederate girl. Mankato,
Minn. : Blue Earth Books, c2000.
*TC E605 .B5 2000*

Bircher, William, 1845-1917. A Civil War drummer
boy. Mankato, Minn. : Blue Earth Books, c2000.
*TC E601 .B605 2000*

**UNITED STATES - HISTORY - CIVIL WAR,
1861-1865 - PERSONAL NARRATIVES,
CONFEDERATE - JUVENILE LITERATURE.**
Berry, Carrie, b. 1854. A Confederate girl. Mankato,
Minn. : Blue Earth Books, c2000.
*TC E605 .B5 2000*

**UNITED STATES - HISTORY - CIVIL WAR,
1861-1865 - PERSONAL NARRATIVES -
JUVENILE LITERATURE.**
Bircher, William, 1845-1917. A Civil War drummer
boy. Mankato, Minn. : Blue Earth Books, c2000.
*TC E601 .B605 2000*

**UNITED STATES - HISTORY - CIVIL WAR,
1861-1865 - PHOTOGRAPHY -
EXHIBITIONS.**
Panzer, Mary. Mathew Brady and the image of
history. Washington, D.C. : Smithsonian Institution
Press for the National Portrait Gallery, c1997.
*TC TR140.B7 P36 1997*

**UNITED STATES - HISTORY - CIVIL WAR,
1861-1865 - POSTERS.**
Civil war [picture]. Amawalk, NY : Jackdaw
Publications, c1999.
*TC TR820.5 .C56 1999*

**UNITED STATES - HISTORY - CIVIL WAR,
1861-1865 - PRESS COVERAGE.**
Morrison, Taylor. Civil War artist. Boston : Houghton
Mifflin, 1999.
*TC E468.9 .M86 1999*

**UNITED STATES - HISTORY - CIVIL WAR,
1861-1865 - PRESS COVERAGE - JUVENILE
LITERATURE.**
Morrison, Taylor. Civil War artist. Boston : Houghton
Mifflin, 1999.
*TC E468.9 .M86 1999*

**UNITED STATES - HISTORY - CIVIL WAR,
1861-1865 - RECONSTRUCTION.** *See*
**RECONSTRUCTION.**

**UNITED STATES - HISTORY - CIVIL WAR,
1861-1865 - SOCIAL ASPECTS - JUVENILE
LITERATURE.**
Berry, Carrie, b. 1854. A Confederate girl. Mankato,
Minn. : Blue Earth Books, c2000.
*TC E605 .B5 2000*

**UNITED STATES - HISTORY - COLONIAL
PERIOD, CA. 1600-1775).**
Africans in America [videorecording]. [Boston,
Mass.] : WGBH Educational Foundation ; South
Burlington, VT : WGBH Boston Video [distributor],
c1998.
*TC E441 .A47 1998*

**UNITED STATES - HISTORY - CONGRESSES.**
American studies in eastern Africa. Nairobi : Nairobi
University Press, 1993.
*TC E172.9 .A47 1993*

**UNITED STATES - HISTORY, ECONOMIC.** *See*
**UNITED STATES - ECONOMIC
CONDITIONS.**

**UNITED STATES - HISTORY - ERRORS,
INVENTIONS, ETC.**
Loewen, James W. Lies across America. New York :
New Press : Distributed by W.W. Norton, c1999.
*TC E159 .L64 1999*

**UNITED STATES - HISTORY - JUVENILE
LITERATURE.**
Davidson, James West. The American nation. Upper
Saddle River, N.J. : Prentice Hall, c1997.
*TC E178.1 .D22 1997*

Napp, John L. Our nation's history. Baltimore, Md. :
Media Materials, c1989.
*TC E178.3 .N36 1998*

Napp, John L. Our nation's history. Baltimore, Md. :
Media Materials, c1989.
*TC E178.3 .N36 1998*

Napp, John L. Our nation's history. Baltimore, Md. :
Media Materials, c1989.
*TC E178.3 .N36 1998*

**UNITED STATES - HISTORY, LOCAL -
EXHIBITIONS - HANDBOOKS, MANUALS,
ETC.**
Ideas and images. Walnut Creek, CA : AltaMira
Press, 1997.
*TC E172 .I34 1997*

**UNITED STATES - HISTORY, MILITARY -
ENCYCLOPEDIAS.**
English, June, 1955- Scholastic encyclopedia of the
United States at war. New York : Scholastic, 1998.
*TC E181 .E64 1998*

**UNITED STATES - HISTORY, MILITARY -
ENCYCLOPEDIAS, JUVENILE.**
English, June, 1955- Scholastic encyclopedia of the
United States at war. New York : Scholastic, 1998.
*TC E181 .E64 1998*

**UNITED STATES - HISTORY - PHILOSOPHY.**
Rosenzweig, Roy. The presence of the past. New
York : Columbia University Press, c1998.
*TC E179.5 .R67 1998*

**UNITED STATES - HISTORY, POLITICAL.** *See*
**UNITED STATES - POLITICS AND
GOVERNMENT.**

**UNITED STATES - HISTORY - PORTRAITS.** *See*
**UNITED STATES - BIOGRAPHY -
PORTRAITS.**

**UNITED STATES - HISTORY - PROBLEMS,
EXERCISES, ETC.**
The American nation. Upper Saddle River, N.J. :
Prentice Hall, c1998.
*TC E178.1 .D22 1998 Study Guide*

**UNITED STATES - HISTORY -
RECONSTRUCTION, 1865-1877.** *See*
**RECONSTRUCTION.**

**UNITED STATES - HISTORY - REVOLUTION, 1775-1783.**
The American Revolution. [videorecording]. New York, N.Y. : A&E Home Video, c1994.
*TC E208 .A447 1994*

**UNITED STATES - HISTORY - REVOLUTION, 1775-1783 - FICTION.**
Waters, Kate. Mary Geddy's day :. 1st ed. New York : Scholastic Press, 1999.
*TC PZ7.W26434 Mar 1999*

**UNITED STATES - HISTORY - REVOLUTION, 1775-1783 - LITERATURE AND THE REVOLUTION - STUDY AND TEACHING.**
Teaching the literatures of early America. New York : Modern Language Association of America, 1999.
*TC PS186 .T43 1999*

**UNITED STATES - HISTORY - REVOLUTION, 1775-1783 - PARTICIPATION, AFRO-AMERICAN.**
Cox, Clinton. Come all you brave soldiers. 1st ed. New York : Scholastic Press, 1999.
*TC E269.N3 C69 1999*

**UNITED STATES - HISTORY - REVOLUTION, 1775-1783 - PARTICIPATION, AFRO-AMERICAN - JUVENILE LITERATURE.**
Cox, Clinton. Come all you brave soldiers. 1st ed. New York : Scholastic Press, 1999.
*TC E269.N3 C69 1999*

**UNITED STATES - HISTORY - REVOLUTION, 1775-1783 - PERSONAL NARRATIVES.**
Wister, Sarah, 1761-1804. A colonial Quaker girl. Mankato, Minn. : Blue Earth Books, c2000.
*TC F158.44 .W75 2000*

**UNITED STATES - HISTORY - REVOLUTION, 1775-1783 - PERSONAL NARRATIVES - JUVENILE LITERATURE.**
Wister, Sarah, 1761-1804. A colonial Quaker girl. Mankato, Minn. : Blue Earth Books, c2000.
*TC F158.44 .W75 2000*

**UNITED STATES - HISTORY - REVOLUTION, 1775-1783 - SOCIAL ASPECTS - JUVENILE LITERATURE.**
Wister, Sarah, 1761-1804. A colonial Quaker girl. Mankato, Minn. : Blue Earth Books, c2000.
*TC F158.44 .W75 2000*

**UNITED STATES - HISTORY - STUDY AND TEACHING.**
Creativity in the classroom. Burbank, CA : Disney Learning Partnership, c1999.
*TC LB1062 .C7 1999*

**UNITED STATES - HISTORY - STUDY AND TEACHING (ELEMENTARY) - JUVENILE LITERATURE.**
Singleton, Laurel R., 1950- H is for history. Boulder, Colo. : Social Science Education Consortium, 1995.
*TC LB1582.U6 S56 1995*

**UNITED STATES - HISTORY - STUDY AND TEACHING (MIDDLE SCHOOL - UNITED STAES - PROBLEMS, EXERCISES, ETC.**
Socratic seminar [videorecording]. [Boulder, Colo.] : Social Science Education Consortium, c1997.
*TC LB1027.44 .S6 1997*

**UNITED STATES - HISTORY - STUDY AND TEACHING (SECONDARY).**
Conlin, Joseph Robert. Our land, our time. Annotated teacher's ed. San Diego : Coronado Publishers, c1987.
*TC E178.1 .C762 1987*

Davidson, James West. The American nation. Annotated teacher's ed. Upper Saddle River, N.J. : Prentice Hall, c1997.
*TC E178.1 .D22 1997 Teacher's Ed.*

Davidson, James West. The American nation. Annotated teacher's ed. Upper Saddle River, N.J. : Prentice Hall, c1998.
*TC E178.1 .D22 1998 Teacher's Ed.*

Instructional Objectives Exchange. American history, grades 7-12. Los Angeles : The Exchange, [1968?]
*TC E175.8.I56*

King, Wayne E. AGS United States history. Teacher's ed. Circle Pines, Minn. : AGS, American Guidance Service, c1998.
*TC E175.8 .K56 1998 Teacher's Ed.*

**UNITED STATES - IMMIGRATION.** *See* **UNITED STATES - EMIGRATION AND IMMIGRATION.**

**UNITED STATES - IN ART - EXHIBITIONS.**
America. Munich, Germany ; London ; New York : Prestel, c1999.

*TC ND210 .A724 1999*

**UNITED STATES - INTELLECTUAL LIFE - 1783-1865.**
Brooks, Van Wyck, 1886-1963. The world of Washington Irving, [New York] E. P. Dutton & co., inc. [1944]
*TC PS208 .B7 1944*

**UNITED STATES - INTELLECTUAL LIFE - 1865-1918.**
Satter, Beryl, 1959- Each mind a kingdom. Berkeley : University of California Press, c1999.
*TC BF639 .S124 1999*

**UNITED STATES - INTELLECTUAL LIFE - 20TH CENTURY.**
America, the West, and liberal education. Lanham, Md. : Rowman & Littlefield, c1999.
*TC LC1023 .A44 1999*

Berlinerblau, Jacques. Heresy in the University. New Brunswick, N.J. : Rutgers University Press, c1999.
*TC DF78.B3983 B47 1999*

Bertman, Stephen. Cultural amnesia. Westport, Conn. : London : Praeger, 2000.
*TC HN59.2 .B474 2000*

Pioneers in popular culture studies. Bowling Green, OH : Bowling Green State University Popular Press, c1999.
*TC E169.04 .P563 1999*

**UNITED STATES - INTELLECTUAL LIFE - HISTORY.**
Alexander, Edward P. (Edward Porter), 1907- The museum in America. Walnut Creek : AltaMira Press, c1997.
*TC AM11 .A55 1997*

**UNITED STATES - INTERNATIONAL RELATIONS.**
Basile, Michael L., 1943- The deployment of educational innovation through foreign aid. 1989.
*TC LD3234.M267 B32 1989*

**UNITED STATES - LANGUAGES.** *See* **AMERICAN SIGN LANGUAGE.**

**UNITED STATES - LAW.** *See* **LAW - UNITED STATES.**

**UNITED STATES - LEGISLATIVE BODIES.** *See* **LEGISLATIVE BODIES - UNITED STATES.**

**UNITED STATES - LITERATURES.** *See* **AMERICAN LITERATURE.**

**UNITED STATES - MORAL CONDITIONS.**
Primers for prudery. Updated ed. Baltimore : Johns Hopkins University Press, 2000.
*TC HQ18.U5 P75 2000*

**United States. National Commission on the Causes and Prevention of Violence.**
Walker, Daniel, 1922- Rights in conflict; convention week in Chicago, August, 25-29, 1968; New York : Dutton, 1968.
*TC F548.52 .W3 1968c*

**UNITED STATES. NAVAL RESERVE OFFICERS TRAINING CORPS.**
Neiberg, Michael S. Making citizen-soldiers. Cambridge, Mass. ; London : Harvard University Press, 2000.
*TC U428.5 .N45 2000*

**United States. Office of Educational Research and Improvement.**
Adelman, Clifford. Answers in the tool box. Washington, DC : U.S. Dept. of Education, Office of Educational Research and Improvement, [1999]
*TC LB2390 .A34 1999*

**UNITED STATES - OFFICIALS AND EMPLOYEES - INTERVIEWS.**
The politics of addiction [videorecording]. Princeton, NJ : Films for the Humanities & Sciences, c1998.
*TC RC564 .P59 1998*

**UNITED STATES - PERIODICALS.**
[American quarterly (Online)] American quarterly [computer file]. Baltimore, Md. : Johns Hopkins University Press, c1996-
*TC EJOURNALS*

**UNITED STATES - POLITICS AND GOVERNMENT.**
Remy, Richard C. Government in the United States. New York : Scribner educational publishers, 1987.
*TC JK274 .R54 1987*

Smith, Jane W. (Jane Wilcox) AGS United States government. Circle Pines, Minn. : AGS, American Guidance Service, 1997.

*TC JK40 .S639 1997*

Smith, Jane W. (Jane Wilcox) AGS United States government. Teacher's ed. Circle Pines, Minn. : AGS, American Guidance Service, 1997.
*TC JK40 .S639 1997 Teacher's Ed.*

**UNITED STATES - POLITICS AND GOVERNMENT - 1945-1989.**
Conyers, James E., 1932- Black elected officials. New York : Russell Sage Foundation, c1976.
*TC JK1924 .C65*

Schultz, Mindella. Comparative political systems: New York, Holt, Rinehart and Winston [1967]
*TC JF51 .S34 1967*

**UNITED STATES - POLITICS AND GOVERNMENT - 1989-.**
Bad subjects. New York : New York University Press, c1998.
*TC E169.12 .B26 1998*

Connerly, Ward, 1939- Creating equal. San Francisco : Encounter Books, 2000.
*TC E185.97 .C74 2000*

**UNITED STATES - POLITICS AND GOVERNMENT - 1993-.**
Without justice for all. Boulder, Colo. : Westview Press, 1999.
*TC E185.615 .W57 1999*

**UNITED STATES - POLITICS AND GOVERNMENT - 20TH CENTURY.**
Stein, Herbert, 1916- What I think. Washington, D.C. : AEI Press, 1998.
*TC HC106.5 .S784 1998*

**UNITED STATES - POLITICS AND GOVERNMENT - PHILOSOPHY.**
Hall, John A., 1949- Is America breaking apart? Princeton, NJ : Princeton University Press, c1999.
*TC HN59.2 .H34 1999*

**UNITED STATES - POLITICS AND GOVERNMENT - STUDY AND TEACHING (ELEMENTARY) - SIMULATION METHODS - UNITED STATES.**
We the people simulated congressional hearing [videorecording]. [Boulder, Colo.] : Social Science Education Consortium, c1997.
*TC KF4208.5.L3 W4 1997*

**UNITED STATES - POLITICS AND GOVERNMENT - STUDY AND TEACHING (ELEMENTARY) - UNITED STATES - EVALUATION.**
We the people simulated congressional hearing [videorecording]. [Boulder, Colo.] : Social Science Education Consortium, c1997.
*TC KF4208.5.L3 W4 1997*

**UNITED STATES - POLITICS AND GOVERNMENT - STUDY AND TEACHING (SECONDARY).**
Caliendo, Stephen M., 1971- Teachers matter. Westport, Conn. : Praeger, 2000.
*TC JA88.U6 C24 2000*

**UNITED STATES - POPULAR CULTURE.** *See* **POPULAR CULTURE - UNITED STATES.**

**UNITED STATES - POPULATION.**
America's demographic tapestry. New Brunswick, N.J. : Rutgers University Press, c1999.
*TC HB3505 .A683 1999*

**UNITED STATES - POPULATION POLICY.**
America's demographic tapestry. New Brunswick, N.J. : Rutgers University Press, c1999.
*TC HB3505 .A683 1999*

**UNITED STATES - POPULATION - STATISTICS.**
Heaton, Tim B. Statistical handbook on racial groups in the United States. Phoenix, AZ : Oryx Press, 2000.
*TC E184.A1 H417 2000*

**United States. President's Committee on the Arts and the Humanities.**
Champions of change. Washington, DC : Arts Education Partnership : President's Committee on the Arts and the Humanities, [1999]
*TC NX304.A1 C53 1999*

**UNITED STATES - RACE QUESTION.** *See* **UNITED STATES - RACE RELATIONS.**

**UNITED STATES - RACE RELATIONS.**
Addressing cultural issues in organizations. Thousand Oaks, Calif. : Sage Publications, 2000.
*TC E184.A1 A337 2000*

Becoming and unbecoming white. Westport, Conn. : Bergin & Garvey, 1999.

*TC E184.A1 B29 1999*

Campbell, Duane E. Choosing democracy. 2nd ed. Upper Saddle River, N.J. : Merrill, c2000.
*TC LC1099.3 .C36 2000*

Connerly, Ward, 1939- Creating equal. San Francisco : Encounter Books, 2000.
*TC E185.97 .C74 2000*

Interracial relationships. San Diego : Greenhaven Press, c2000.
*TC HQ1031 .I59 2000*

Klinkner, Philip A. The unsteady march. Chicago : University of Chicago Press, c1999.
*TC E185 .K55 1999*

Nash, Gary B. Forbidden love. 1st ed. New York : H. Holt, 1999.
*TC E184.M47 N47 1999*

Nash, Gary B. Forbidden love. 1st ed. New York : H. Holt, 1999.
*TC E184.M47 N47 1999*

Okihiro, Gary Y., 1945- Stories lives. Seattle : University of Washington Press, 1999.
*TC D753.8 .O38 1999*

Perlmutter, Philip. Legacy of hate. Armonk, N.Y. ; London : M.E. Sharpe, c1999.
*TC BF575.H3 P47 1999*

Problems and issues of diversity in the United States. Westport, Conn. : Bergin & Garvey, 1999.
*TC E184.A1 P76 1999*

Race is-- race isn't. Boulder, CO : Westview Press, c1999.
*TC LC3731 .R27 1999*

Whiteness. Lanham, [Md.] : Rowman & Littlefield, c1999.
*TC E184.A1 W399 1999*

Without justice for all. Boulder, Colo. : Westview Press, 1999.
*TC E185.615 .W57 1999*

**UNITED STATES - RACE RELATIONS - CASE STUDIES.**
Educators healing racism. Reston, VA : Association of Teacher Educators ; Olney, MD : Association for Childhood Education International, c1999.
*TC LC212.2 .E38 1999*

Kohn, Howard. We had a dream. New York : Simon & Schuster, 1998.
*TC F187.P9 K64 1998*

Rothenberg, Paula S., 1943- Invisible privilege. Lawrence : University Press of Kansas, c2000.
*TC E185.615 .R68 2000*

Souls looking back. New York : Routledge, 1999.
*TC E185.625 .S675 1999*

**UNITED STATES - RACE RELATIONS - POLITICAL ASPECTS.**
Lorini, Alessandra, 1949- Rituals of race. Charlottesville : University Press of Virginia, 1999.
*TC E185.61 .L675 1999*

**UNITED STATES - RACE RELATIONS - POLITICAL ASPECTS - HISTORY - 20TH CENTURY.**
Cochran, David Carroll. The color of freedom. Albany : State University of New York Press, c1999.
*TC E185.615 .C634 1999*

**UNITED STATES - RACE RELATIONS - PSYCHOLOGICAL ASPECTS.**
Clauss, Caroline Seay. Degrees of distance. 1999.
*TC 085 C58*

**UNITED STATES - RACE RELATIONS - SOURCES.**
Bethune, Mary McLeod, 1875-1955. [Selections. 1999] Mary McLeod Bethune. Bloomington : Indiana University Press, c1999.
*TC E185.97.B34 A25 1999*

**UNITED STATES - RELATIONS - ASIA - FICTION.**
Lederer, William J., 1912- The ugly American. 1st ed. New York : Norton, 1958.
*TC PS3523 .E27U35 1958*

**UNITED STATES - RELATIONS - CUBA.**
Pérez, Louis A., 1943- On becoming Cuban. Chapel Hill : University of North Carolina Press, c1999.
*TC F1760 .P47 1999*

**UNITED STATES - RELATIONS - FOREIGN COUNTRIES - FICTION.**
Lederer, William J., 1912- The ugly American. 1st ed. New York : Norton, 1958.

*TC PS3523 .E27U35 1958*

**UNITED STATES - RELIGION.**
Taylor, Eugene. Shadow culture Washington, D.C. : Counterpoint, c1999.
*TC BL2525 .T39 1999*

**UNITED STATES - RURAL CONDITIONS.**
Elder, Glen H. Children of the land. Chicago : University of Chicago Press, 2000.
*TC HQ796 .E525 2000*

**UNITED STATES - SANITARY AFFAIRS.** *See* **PUBLIC HEALTH - UNITED STATES.**

**UNITED STATES - SOCIAL CONDITIONS.**
Cavan, Ruth Shonle, 1896- The American family. 3d ed. New York, Crowell [1963]
*TC HQ535 .C33 1963*

Clauss, Caroline Seay. Degrees of distance. 1999.
*TC 085 C58*

Coontz, Stephanie. The way we never were. New York, NY : BasicBooks, c1992.
*TC HQ535 .C643 1992*

Perlmutter, Philip. Legacy of hate. Armonk, N.Y. ; London : M.E. Sharpe, c1999.
*TC BF575.H3 P47 1999*

Wimsatt, William Upski. No more prisons. [New York] : Soft Skull Press, [2000?]
*TC HV9276.5 .W567x 2000*

Withers, Carl. Plainville, U.S.A.. New York : Columbia University Press, [c1945]
*TC HN57 .W58 1945*

**UNITED STATES - SOCIAL CONDITIONS - 1918-1932 - POSTERS.**
The depression hits home [picture]. Amawalk, NY : Jackdaw Publications, c1997.
*TC TR820.5 .D4 1997*

**UNITED STATES - SOCIAL CONDITIONS - 1933-1945 - POSTERS.**
The depression hits home [picture]. Amawalk, NY : Jackdaw Publications, c1997.
*TC TR820.5 .D4 1997*

**UNITED STATES - SOCIAL CONDITIONS - 1945-.**
Perrucci, Robert, comp. The triple revolution: Boston, Little, Brown [1968]
*TC HN65 .P4*

**UNITED STATES - SOCIAL CONDITIONS - 1971-.**
Miringoff, Marc L. The social health of the nation. New York : Oxford University Press, 1999.
*TC HN59.2 .M57 1999*

**UNITED STATES - SOCIAL CONDITIONS - 1980-.**
Bad subjects. New York : New York University Press, c1998.
*TC E169.12 .B26 1998*

Bertman, Stephen. Cultural amnesia. Westport, Conn. ; London : Praeger, 2000.
*TC HN59.2 .B474 2000*

Family ethnicity. 2nd ed. Thousand Oaks, Calif. : Sage Publications, c1999.
*TC E184.A1 F33 1999*

Hall, John A., 1949- Is America breaking apart? Princeton, NJ : Princeton University Press, c1999.
*TC HN59.2 .H34 1999*

Holtzman, Linda, 1949- Media messages. Armonk, NY : M.E. Sharpe, 2000.
*TC P94.5.M552 U646 2000*

Perrucci, Robert. The new class society. Lanham, Md. : Rowman & Littlefield, 1999.
*TC HN90.S6 P47 1999*

Situated lives. New York : Routledge, 1997.
*TC GN479.65 .S57 1997*

Zinn, Maxine Baca, 1942- Diversity in families. 5th ed. New York : Longman, 1998.
*TC HQ536 .Z54 1998*

**UNITED STATES - SOCIAL CONDITIONS - BIBLIOGRAPHY - PERIODICALS.**
Building America. [New York : Published for the Dept. of Supervision and Curriculum Development by the Society for Curriculum Study, Inc. ; distributed by Americana Corporation, 1935-

**UNITED STATES - SOCIAL CONDITIONS - PERIODICALS.**
Building America. [New York : Published for the Dept. of Supervision and Curriculum Development by the Society for Curriculum Study, Inc. ; distributed by Americana Corporation, 1935-

[Journal of intergroup relations (1970)] Journal of intergroup relations. Louisville, KY : National Association of Human Rights Workers,

**UNITED STATES - SOCIAL LIFE AND CUSTOMS.**
Gabaccia, Donna R., 1949- We are what we eat. Cambridge, Mass. : Harvard University Press, 1998.
*TC GT2853.U5 G33 1998*

Harris, Neil, 1938- Building lives. New Haven [Conn.] ; London : Yale University Press, c1999.
*TC NA2543.S6 H37 1999*

Rosenzweig, Roy, The presence of the past. New York : Columbia University Press, c1998.
*TC E179.5 .R67 1998*

**UNITED STATES - SOCIAL LIFE AND CUSTOMS - 1775-1783.**
Wister, Sarah, 1761-1804. A colonial Quaker girl. Mankato, Minn. : Blue Earth Books, c2000.
*TC F158.44 .W75 2000*

**UNITED STATES - SOCIAL LIFE AND CUSTOMS - 1865-1918.**
Lorini, Alessandra, 1949- Rituals of race. Charlottesville : University Press of Virginia, 1999.
*TC E185.61 .L675 1999*

**UNITED STATES - SOCIAL LIFE AND CUSTOMS - PERIODICALS.**
Building America. [New York : Published for the Dept. of Supervision and Curriculum Development by the Society for Curriculum Study, Inc. ; distributed by Americana Corporation, 1935-

**UNITED STATES - SOCIAL POLICY.**
Affirmative action. San Diego, Calif. : Greenhaven Press, 2000.
*TC JC599.U5 A34685 2000*

Crenson, Matthew A., 1943- Building the invisible orphanage. Cambridge, Mass. : Harvard University Press, 1998.
*TC HV91 .C74 1998*

Lagemann, Ellen Condliffe, 1945- The politics of knowledge. 1st ed. Middletown, Conn. : Wesleyan University Press, c1989.
*TC HV97.C3 L34 1989*

Welfare. San Diego, CA : Greenhaven Press, c1997.
*TC HV95 .W453 1997*

**UNITED STATES - SOCIAL POLICY - 1993-.**
Kahn, Alfred J., 1919- Big cities in the welfare transition. New York City : Cross-National Studies Research Program, Columbia University School of Social Work, 1998.
*TC HV91 .K27 1998*

Without justice for all. Boulder, Colo. : Westview Press, 1999.
*TC E185.615 .W57 1999*

**UNITED STATES. SOCIAL SECURITY ADMINISTRATION - PERIODICALS.**
American economic security. Washington, Chamber of Commerce of the United States of America.

**UNITED STATES. SOCIAL SECURITY BOARD - PERIODICALS.**
American economic security. Washington, Chamber of Commerce of the United States of America.

**UNITED STATES - STATISTICS.**
Health and healthcare in the United States. 1st ed. Lanham, MD : Bernan Press : Nationshealth Corp., c1999.
*TC HA214 .H435 1999*

Health and healthcare in the United States. 1st ed. Lanham, MD : Bernan Press : Nationshealth Corp., c1999.
*TC HA214 .H435 1999*

**UNITED STATES - STATISTICS, MEDICAL.**
United States. Dept. of Health and Human Services. Task Force on Black and Minority Health. Report of the Secretary's Task Force on Black & Minority Health. Washington, D.C. : U.S. Dept. of Health and Human Services, [1985-<1986 >
*TC RA448.5.N4 U55 1985*

**UNITED STATES - STATISTICS, VITAL.**
United States. Dept. of Health and Human Services. Task Force on Black and Minority Health. Report of the Secretary's Task Force on Black & Minority Health. Washington, D.C. : U.S. Dept. of Health and Human Services, [1985-<1986 >
*TC RA448.5.N4 U55 1985*

**UNITED STATES - STUDY AND TEACHING - AFRICA, EASTERN - CONGRESSES.**

American studies in eastern Africa. Nairobi : Nairobi University Press, 1993.
*TC E172.9 .A47 1993*

**UNITED STATES. SUPREME COURT - HISTORY.**
Howard, John R., 1933- The shifting wind. Albany : State University of New York Press, c1999.
*TC KF4757 .H69 1999*

**UNITED STATES. SUPREME COURT - PUBLIC OPINION.**
Caliendo, Stephen M., 1971- Teachers matter. Westport, Conn. : Praeger, 2000.
*TC JA88.U6 C24 2000*

**United States. Women's Bureau.**
Commission on Family and Medical Leave (U.S.) A Workable balance. Washington, DC : Commission on Leave : Women's Bureau, U.S. Dept. of Labor, [1996]
*TC HD5115.6.U5 C66 1996*

**United Way of New York City.**
The CARES directory in electronic form [computer file] Maywood, NJ : ACIT,
*TC HV99.N59 S58*

**Universal design in education.**
Bowe, Frank. Westport, Conn. ; London : Bergin & Garvey, 2000.
*TC LB1028.38 .B69 2000*

**Universal grammar and American sign language.**
Lillo-Martin, Diane C. (Diane Carolyn), 1959- Dordrecht ; Boston : Kluwer Academic Publishers, c1991.
*TC HV2474 .L55 1991*

**Universal health care.**
Armstrong, Pat, 1945- New York : New Press : Distributed by W.W. Norton, c1998.
*TC RA412.5.C3 A76 1998*

**UNIVERSAL HISTORY.** *See* **WORLD HISTORY.**

**The universal right to education.**
Spring, Joel H. Mahwah, N.J. ; London : Lawrence Erlbaum Associates, 2000.
*TC LC213 .S67 2000*

**UNIVERSAL SUCCESSION.** *See* **INHERITANCE AND SUCCESSION.**

**Universal teaching strategies.**
Freiberg, H. Jerome. 3rd ed. Boston : Allyn and Bacon, c2000.
*TC LB1025.3 .F74 2000*

**UNIVERSALS (LINGUISTICS).** *See* **COMPONENTIAL ANALYSIS (LINGUISTICS).**

**UNIVERSE.** *See also* **COSMOLOGY.**
Stephen Hawking's universe [videorecording]. [Alexandria, Va.] : PBS Video; Burbank, CA : Distributed by Warner Home Video, c1997.
*TC QB982 .S7 1997*

**UNIVERSITÉ DE LIÈGE - PERIODICALS.**
Association des amis de l'Université de Liège. Bulletin trimestriel. Liège.

**UNIVERSITÉ DE MONTRÉAL - STUDENTS - POLITICAL ACTIVITY - HISTORY.**
Neatby, Nicole, 1962- Carabins ou activistes? Montréal ; Ithaca : McGill-Queen's University Press, [1999?], c1997.
*TC LA418.Q8 N42 1999*

**UNIVERSITÉ DE PARIS - HISTORY.**
Courtenay, William J. Parisian scholars in the early fourteenth century. Cambridge, U.K. ; New York, NY : Cambridge University Press, 1999.
*TC LF2165 .C68 1999*

**UNIVERSITÉS - CANADA - COOPÉRATION INTERNATIONALE.**
A new world of knowledge. Ottawa : International Development Research Centre, c1999.
*TC LC1090 N38 1999*

**UNIVERSITIES AND COLLEGES.** *See* **CATHOLIC UNIVERSITIES AND COLLEGES; CHURCH COLLEGES; COEDUCATION; DIPLOMA MILLS; EDUCATION, HIGHER; JUNIOR COLLEGES; MEDICAL COLLEGES; SMALL COLLEGES; UNIVERSITY EXTENSION; WOMEN'S COLLEGES.**

**UNIVERSITIES AND COLLEGES - ACCREDITATION - UNITED STATES.**
Misrepresentation in the marketplace and beyond. Washington, DC : American Association of Collegiate Registrars and Admissions Officers, 1996.

*TC LB2331.615.U6 M57 1996*

**UNIVERSITIES AND COLLEGES - ADMINISTRATION.** *See also* **COLLEGE ADMINISTRATORS; COLLEGE DISCIPLINE; COLLEGE PERSONNEL MANAGEMENT; COLLEGE PRESIDENTS; DEPARTMENTAL CHAIRMEN (UNIVERSITIES); TEACHER PARTICIPATION IN ADMINISTRATION; UNIVERSITY AUTONOMY.**
Taylor, Peter G., 1951- Making sense of academic life. Philadelphia, PA : Open University Press, 1999.
*TC LB1778 .T39 1999*

Towards a new model of governance for universities? London : Philadelphia : Jessica Kingsley, c1999.
*TC LC171 .T683 1999*

Understanding the work and career paths of midlevel administrators. San Francisco : Jossey-Bass, 2000.
*TC LB2341 .N5111 2000*

**UNIVERSITIES AND COLLEGES - ADMINISTRATION - CASE STUDIES.**
What kind of university? 1st ed. Buckingham ; Philadelphia, PA : Society for Research into Higher Education : Open University Press, 1999.
*TC LB2322.2 .W43 1999*

**UNIVERSITIES AND COLLEGES - ADMINISTRATION - CROSS-CULTURAL STUDIES.**
The adult university. Buckingham [England] ; Philadelphia, PA : Society for Research into Higher Education & Open University Press, 1999.
*TC LC5219 .A35 1999*

**UNIVERSITIES AND COLLEGES - ADMINISTRATION - LAW AND LEGISLATION - UNITED STATES.**
Goonen, Norma M. Higher education administration. Westport, Conn. ; London : Greenwood Press, 1999.
*TC LB2341 .G573 1999*

**UNIVERSITIES AND COLLEGES - ADMINISTRATION - MORAL AND ETHICAL ASPECTS - UNITED STATES.**
Goonen, Norma M. Higher education administration. Westport, Conn. ; London : Greenwood Press, 1999.
*TC LB2341 .G573 1999*

**UNIVERSITIES AND COLLEGES - ADMINISTRATION - PSYCHOLOGICAL ASPECTS.**
Austin, Ann E. Academic workplace. Washington, D.C. : Association for the Study of Higher Education, 1983.
*TC LB2331.7 .A96 1983*

**UNIVERSITIES AND COLLEGES - ADMINISTRATION - VOCATIONAL GUIDANCE.**
Understanding the work and career paths of midlevel administrators. San Francisco : Jossey-Bass, 2000.
*TC LB2341 .N5111 2000*

**UNIVERSITIES AND COLLEGES - ADMISSION.**
Keith-Spiegel, Patricia. The complete guide to graduate school admission. 2nd ed. Mahwah, N.J. ; London : L. Erlbaum Associates, 2000.
*TC BF77 .K35 2000*

**UNIVERSITIES AND COLLEGES, AFRO-AMERICAN.** *See* **AFRO-AMERICAN UNIVERSITIES AND COLLEGES.**

**UNIVERSITIES AND COLLEGES - ALUMNI AND ALUMNAE.** *See* **COLLEGE GRADUATES.**

**UNIVERSITIES AND COLLEGES - ATHLETICS.** *See* **COLLEGE SPORTS.**

**UNIVERSITIES AND COLLEGES - AUSTRALIA - GRADUATE WORK - HANDBOOKS, MANUALS, ETC.**
Stevens, Kate. Doing postgraduate research in Australia. Melbourne : Melbourne University Press, 1999.
*TC LB2371.6.A7 S74 1999*

**UNIVERSITIES AND COLLEGES, BLACK - UNITED STATES.** *See* **AFRO-AMERICAN UNIVERSITIES AND COLLEGES.**

**UNIVERSITIES AND COLLEGES - BRITISH COLUMBIA - CURRICULA.**
McKellin, Karen, 1950- Maintaining the momentum. Victoria, B.C. : British Columbia Centre for International Education, c1998.
*TC LC1090 .M24 1998*

**UNIVERSITIES AND COLLEGES - BUILDINGS.** *See* **COLLEGE BUILDINGS.**

**UNIVERSITIES AND COLLEGES - CANADA - INTERNATIONAL COOPERATION.**
A new world of knowledge. Ottawa : International Development Research Centre, c1999.
*TC LC1090 N38 1999*

**UNIVERSITIES AND COLLEGES - CATALOGS.** *See* **CATALOGS, COLLEGE.**

**UNIVERSITIES AND COLLEGES - COMPUTER NETWORKS - UNITED STATES.**
Preparing your campus for a networked future. 1st ed. San Francisco : Jossey-Bass, c2000.
*TC LB2395.7 .P74 2000*

**UNIVERSITIES AND COLLEGES - CORRUPT PRACTICES.** *See* **DIPLOMA MILLS.**

**UNIVERSITIES AND COLLEGES - CURRICULA.**
General education in school and college. Cambridge : Harvard University Press, 1952.
*TC 372G28*

Nelson, Michael, 1949- Alive at the core. 1st ed. San Francisco : Jossey-Bass, c2000.
*TC AZ183.U5 N45 2000*

**UNIVERSITIES AND COLLEGES - DISSERTATIONS.** *See* **DISSERTATIONS, ACADEMIC.**

**UNIVERSITIES AND COLLEGES - EMPLOYEES - JOB SATISFACTION - UNITED STATES.**
What contributes to job satisfaction among faculty and staff. San Francisco, Calif. : Jossey-Bass Publishers, c2000.
*TC LB2331.7 .W45 2000*

**UNIVERSITIES AND COLLEGES - EUROPE.**
Geuna, Aldo, 1965- The economics of knowledge production. Cheltenham, UK ; Northampton, MA : E. Elgar, c1999.
*TC Q180.E9 G48 1999*

Wasser, Henry Hirsch, 1919- Diversification in higher education. Kassel : Wissenschaftliches Zentrum für Berufs- und Hochschulforschung der Gesamthochschule Kassel, 1999.
*TC LA622 .W37 1999*

**UNIVERSITIES AND COLLEGES - EUROPE - ADMINISTRATION.**
Sporn, Barbara. Adaptive university structures. London ; Philadelphia : Jessica Kingsley, c1999.
*TC LB2322.2 .S667 1999*

**UNIVERSITIES AND COLLEGES - EUROPE - ADMINISTRATION - HISTORY.**
Duryea, E. D. (Edwin D.) The academic corporation. New York : Falmer Press, 2000.
*TC LB2341 .D79 2000*

**UNIVERSITIES AND COLLEGES - EUROPE - CONGRESSES.**
Learning institutionalized. Notre Dame, Ind. : University of Notre Dame Press, c2000.
*TC LA177 .L43 2000*

**UNIVERSITIES AND COLLEGES - EUROPE - HISTORY.**
The medieval church. Woodbridge, Suffolk ; Rochester, NY : Published for the Ecclesiastical History Society by the Boydell Press, 1999.
*TC BR270 .M43 1999*

**UNIVERSITIES AND COLLEGES - EUROPE - PERIODICALS.**
Hochschul-Nachrichten. München : Academischer Verlag,

**UNIVERSITIES AND COLLEGES - EUROPE - SOCIOLOGICAL ASPECTS - HISTORY - 17TH CENTURY.**
Gascoigne, John, Ph. D. Science, politics, and universities in Europe, 1600-1800. Aldershot [England] ; Brookfield, Vt. : Ashgate, c1998.
*TC LA621.5 .G37 1998*

**UNIVERSITIES AND COLLEGES - EUROPE - SOCIOLOGICAL ASPECTS - HISTORY - 18TH CENTURY.**
Gascoigne, John, Ph. D. Science, politics, and universities in Europe, 1600-1800. Aldershot [England] ; Brookfield, Vt. : Ashgate, c1998.
*TC LA621.5 .G37 1998*

**UNIVERSITIES AND COLLEGES - EXAMINATIONS.**
Heywood, John, 1930- Assessment in higher education. London ; Philadelphia : Jessica Kingsley Publishers, 2000.
*TC LB2366 .H49 2000*

**UNIVERSITIES AND COLLEGES -
EXAMINATIONS - DATA PROCESSING.**
Computer-assisted assessment in higher education.
London : Kogan Page, 1999.
*TC LB2366 .C65 1999*

**UNIVERSITIES AND COLLEGES - FACULTY.**
*See* COLLEGE TEACHERS.

**UNIVERSITIES AND COLLEGES - FACULTY -
JOB SATISFACTION - UNITED STATES.**
What contributes to job satisfaction among faculty and
staff. San Francisco, Calif. : Jossey-Bass Publishers,
c2000.
*TC LB2331.7 .W45 2000*

**UNIVERSITIES AND COLLEGES - FACULTY -
UNITED STATES - PROFESSIONAL
ETHICS.**
Ernest, Ivan. Faculty evaluation of post-tenure review
at a research university. 1999.
*TC 06 no. 11110*

**UNIVERSITIES AND COLLEGES - FACULTY -
VOCATIONAL GUIDANCE.**
McCabe, Linda. How to succeed in academics. San
Diego, Calif. : Academic, c2000.
*TC LB2331.7 .M34 2000*

**UNIVERSITIES AND COLLEGES - FINANCE.**
*See also* COLLEGE COSTS; EDUCATIONAL
FUND RAISING.
Analyzing costs in higher education. San Francisco,
Calif. : Jossey-Bass Publishers, c2000.
*TC LB2342 .A68 2000*

**UNIVERSITIES AND COLLEGES -
FORECASTING.**
The university in transformation. Westport, Conn. ;
London : Bergin & Garvey, 2000.
*TC LB2324 .U56 2000*

**UNIVERSITIES AND COLLEGES - FURNITURE,
EQUIPMENT, ETC.** *See* SCHOOLS -
FURNITURE, EQUIPMENT, ETC.

**UNIVERSITIES AND COLLEGES - GRADUATE
WORK.** *See also* GRADUATE STUDENTS.
Elphinstone, Leonie. How to get a research degree. St.
Leonards, Australia : Allen & Unwin, 1998.
*TC LB2371 .E46 1998*

**UNIVERSITIES AND COLLEGES - GRADUATE
WORK - EXAMINATIONS.** *See* GRADUATE
RECORD EXAMINATION.

**UNIVERSITIES AND COLLEGES - GREAT
BRITAIN - ADMINISTRATION.**
Bolton, Allan. Managing the academic unit.
Buckingham [England] ; Philadelphia : Open
University Press, c2000.
*TC LB2341 .B583 2000*

Ruddiman, Ken. Strategic management of college
premises. London : Falmer, 1999.
*TC LB3223.5.G7 R84 1999*

Watson, David, 1949- Managing strategy.
Buckingham [England] ; Philadelphia : Open
University Press, 2000.
*TC LB2341.8.G7 W28 2000*

**UNIVERSITIES AND COLLEGES - GREAT
BRITAIN - FACULTY - HISTORY.**
Annan, Noel Gilroy Annan, Baron, 1916- The dons.
Chicago : University of Chicago Press ; London :
HarperCollins Publishers, 1999.
*TC LB2331.74.G7 A55 1999*

**UNIVERSITIES AND COLLEGES - HONORS
COURSES.** *See* INDEPENDENT STUDY.

**UNIVERSITIES AND COLLEGES - INDIA.**
Staff development in higher and distance education.
New Delhi : Aravali Books International, 1997.
*TC LB2331 .S692 1997*

**UNIVERSITIES AND COLLEGES - LAW AND
LEGISLATION.** *See* UNIVERSITY
AUTONOMY.

**UNIVERSITIES AND COLLEGES - LAW AND
LEGISLATION - NORTH CAROLINA.**
Billingsley, William J., 1953- Communists on
campus. Athens, Ga. ; London : University of Georgia
Press, c1999.
*TC LC72.3.N67 B55 1999*

**UNIVERSITIES AND COLLEGES - LAW AND
LEGISLATION - UNITED STATES.**
Accommodations in higher education under the
Americans with Disabilities Act (ADA) :. DeWitt,
NY : GSI Publications, 2000.
*TC RA1055.5 A28 2000*

Stevens, Ed. Due process and higher education.
Washington, DC : Graduate School of Education and
Human Development, George Washington University,
[1999]
*TC LB2344 .S73 1999*

**UNIVERSITIES AND COLLEGES - MORAL AND
ETHICAL ASPECTS - UNITED STATES -
DIRECTORIES.**
Weinstein, Miriam (Miriam H.) Making a difference.
Rev. & exp. 2nd ed. Gabriola Island, BC, Can. : New
Society Publishers, 2000.
*TC LB2338 W45 2000*

**UNIVERSITIES AND COLLEGES -
NETHERLANDS.**
The university and the knowledge society. Bemmel
[Netherlands] : Concorde Publishing House, 1998.
*TC LB2322.2 .U55 1998*

**UNIVERSITIES AND COLLEGES -
NETHERLANDS - PERIODICALS.**
Higher education and research in the Netherlands. The
Hague, Netherlands Foundation for International
Cooperation.

**UNIVERSITIES AND COLLEGES - NEW
ENGLAND - ADMINISTRATION - CASE
STUDIES.**
Arnold, Gordon B., 1954- The politics of faculty
unionization. Westport, Conn. ; London : Bergin &
Garvey, 2000.
*TC LB2335.865.U6 A75 2000*

**UNIVERSITIES AND COLLEGES - NEW
ZEALAND - CURRICULA.**
After the disciplines. Westport, Conn. : Bergin &
Garvey, 1999.
*TC LB2362.N45 A48 1999*

**UNIVERSITIES AND COLLEGES - PERSONNEL
MANAGEMENT.** *See* COLLEGE
PERSONNEL MANAGEMENT.

**UNIVERSITIES AND COLLEGES -
PHILOSOPHY.**
Barnett, Ronald, 1947- Realizing the university in an
age of supercomplexity. Philadelphia, PA : Society for
Research into Higher Education & Open University
Press, 1999.
*TC LB2322.2 .B37 1999*

The university and the knowledge society. Bemmel
[Netherlands] : Concorde Publishing House, 1998.
*TC LB2322.2 .U55 1998*

**UNIVERSITIES AND COLLEGES - PLANNING.**
*See* CAMPUS PLANNING.

**UNIVERSITIES AND COLLEGES - SOCIAL
ASPECTS - UNITED STATES.**
Bell, Inge. This book is not required. Rev. ed., new
ed. / by Team Bell, Lynette Albovias ... [et al.].
Thousand Oaks, Calif. : Pine Forge Press, c1999.
*TC LA229 .B386 1999*

**UNIVERSITIES AND COLLEGES -
SOCIOLOGICAL ASPECTS.**
Sporn, Barbara. Adaptive university structures.
London ; Philadelphia : Jessica Kingsley, c1999.
*TC LB2322.2 .S667 1999*

**UNIVERSITIES AND COLLEGES - SOUTHERN
STATES - SOCIOLOGICAL ASPECTS -
HISTORY - 20TH CENTURY.**
McCandless, Amy Thompson, 1946- The past in the
present. Tuscaloosa : University of Alabama Press,
c1999.
*TC LC1756 .M24 1999*

**UNIVERSITIES AND COLLEGES - SPORTS.** *See*
COLLEGE SPORTS.

**UNIVERSITIES AND COLLEGES - STUDENTS.**
*See* COLLEGE STUDENTS.

**UNIVERSITIES AND COLLEGES - TEACHERS.**
*See* COLLEGE TEACHERS.

**UNIVERSITIES AND COLLEGES - UNITED
STATES.** *See also* AFRO-AMERICAN
UNIVERSITIES AND COLLEGES.
Bell, Inge. This book is not required. Rev. ed., new
ed. / by Team Bell, Lynette Albovias ... [et al.].
Thousand Oaks, Calif. : Pine Forge Press, c1999.
*TC LA229 .B386 1999*

Dober, Richard P. Campus landscape. New York :
Wiley, c2000.
*TC LB3223.3 .D65 2000*

Neusner, Jacob, 1932- Reaffirming higher education.
New Brunswick, U.S.A. : Transaction Publishers,
c2000.

*TC LA227.4 .N47 2000*

Stevens, Ed. Due process and higher education.
Washington, DC : Graduate School of Education and
Human Development, George Washington University,
[1999]
*TC LB2344 .S73 1999*

Wasser, Henry Hirsch, 1919- Diversification in higher
education. Kassel : Wissenschaftliches Zentrum für
Berufs- und Hochschulforschung der
Gesamthochschule Kassel, 1999.
*TC LA622 .W37 1999*

**UNIVERSITIES AND COLLEGES - UNITED
STATES - ADMINISTRATION.**
ASHE reader on finance in higher education.
Needham Heights, MA : Ginn Press, c1986.
*TC LB2342 .A76 1990*

Becker, Nancy Jane. Implementing technology in
higher education. 1999.
*TC 06 no. 11082*

Goonen, Norma M. Higher education administration.
Westport, Conn. ; London : Greenwood Press, 1999.
*TC LB2341 .G573 1999*

Managing colleges and universities. Westport, Conn. :
Bergin & Garvey, 2000.
*TC LB2341 .M2779 2000*

Rhoades, Gary. Managed professionals. Albany :
State University of New York Press, c1998.
*TC LB2331.72 .R56 1998*

Sporn, Barbara. Adaptive university structures.
London ; Philadelphia : Jessica Kingsley, c1999.
*TC LB2322.2 .S667 1999*

Tierney, William G. Building the responsive campus.
Thousand Oaks, Calif. : Sage, c1999.
*TC LB2341 .T584 1999*

**UNIVERSITIES AND COLLEGES - UNITED
STATES - ADMINISTRATION - HISTORY.**
Duryea, E. D. (Edwin D.) The academic corporation.
New York : Falmer Press, 2000.
*TC LB2341 .D79 2000*

**UNIVERSITIES AND COLLEGES - UNITED
STATES - ADMISSION.**
Latimer, Leah Y. Higher ground. New York : Avon
Books, c1999.
*TC LC2781 .L27 1999*

Promising practices in recruitment, remediation, and
retention. San Francisco, Calif. : Jossey-Bass, c1999.
*TC LB2331.72 .N48 1999*

**UNIVERSITIES AND COLLEGES - UNITED
STATES - ADMISSIONS.**
The role student aid plays in enrollment management.
San Francisco : Jossey-Bass Publishers, 2000.
*TC LB2337.4 .R655 2000*

**UNIVERSITIES AND COLLEGES - UNITED
STATES - CURRICULA.**
After the disciplines. Westport, Conn. : Bergin &
Garvey, 1999.
*TC LB2362.N45 A48 1999*

Core texts in conversation . Lanham, MD : University
Press of America, 2000.
*TC LB2361.5 .C68 2000*

**UNIVERSITIES AND COLLEGES - UNITED
STATES - CURRICULA - EVALUATION -
DIRECTORIES.**
Educational rankings annual. Detroit, MI : Gale
Research, c1991-
*TC LB2331.63 .E34*

**UNIVERSITIES AND COLLEGES - UNITED
STATES - CURRICULA - HISTORY.**
Rabil, Alison. Content, context, and continuity. 1998.
*TC 06 no. 10901*

**UNIVERSITIES AND COLLEGES - UNITED
STATES - DATA PROCESSING.**
Dollars, distance, and online education. Phoenix, Az. :
Oryx Press, 2000.
*TC LB2395.7 .M26 2000*

**UNIVERSITIES AND COLLEGES - UNITED
STATES - DIRECTORIES.**
The adult student's guide. Berkley trade pbk. ed. New
York, N.Y. : Berkley Books, 1999.
*TC L901 .A494 1999*

**UNIVERSITIES AND COLLEGES - UNITED
STATES - EVALUATION.**
Freed, Jann E. A culture for academic excellence.
Washington, D.C. : Graduate School of Education and
Human Development, George Washington University,
1997.

**UNIVERSITY LIBRARIANS.** *See* **COLLEGE LIBRARIANS.**

**UNIVERSITY LIBRARIES.** *See* **ACADEMIC LIBRARIES.**

**University of Alaska Museum. Alaska Center for Documentary Film.**
Heart of the country [videorecording]. [New York, NY : First Run/Icarus Films, 1998].
*TC LB1565.H6 H3 1998*

**University of Baguio journal.**
Baguio tech journal. [Baguio City, Philippines : Baguio Tech.,

**UNIVERSITY OF BRIGHTON. CHELSEA SCHOOL.**
Webb, Ida M. The challenge of change in physical education :. London : Falmer Press, 1999.
*TC GV246.E3 B79 1999*

**University of British Columbia. Faculty and College of Education.**
Education bulletin of the Faculty and College of Education: Vancouver : University of British Columbia.

**UNIVERSITY OF BRITISH COLUMBIA. FACULTY AND COLLEGE OF EDUCATION - PERIODICALS.**
Education bulletin of the Faculty and College of Education: Vancouver : University of British Columbia.

**University of British Columbia. Faculty of Education.**
The Journal of education of the Faculty of Education Vancouver. Vancouver, University of British Columbia, Faculty of Education.

**University of California, Berkeley.**
White, Timothy P. The wellness guide to lifelong fitness. New York : Rebus : Distributed by Random House, c1993.
*TC RA781 .W47 1993*

**University of California, Berkeley, wellness letter.**
White, Timothy P. The wellness guide to lifelong fitness. New York : Rebus : Distributed by Random House, c1993.
*TC RA781 .W47 1993*

**University of California, Los Angeles. Museum of Cultural History.**
Cole, Herbert M. The arts of Ghana. Los Angeles : Museum of Cultural History, University of California, c1977.
*TC NX589.6.G5 C64*

**UNIVERSITY OF CALIFORNIA (SYSTEM). REGENTS - BIOGRAPHY.**
Connerly, Ward, 1939- Creating equal. San Francisco : Encounter Books, 2000.
*TC E185.97 .C74 2000*

**UNIVERSITY OF CALIFORNIA (SYSTEM). REGENTS - TRIALS, LITIGATION, ETC.**
Ball, Howard. The Bakke case. Lawrence, Kan. : University Press of Kansas, 2000.
*TC KF228.B34 B35 2000*

**UNIVERSITY OF CAMBRIDGE - HISTORY - 17TH CENTURY.**
Gascoigne, John, Ph. D. Science, politics, and universities in Europe, 1600-1800. Aldershot [England] ; Brookfield, Vt. : Ashgate, c1998.
*TC LA621.5 .G37 1998*

**UNIVERSITY OF CAMBRIDGE - HISTORY - 18TH CENTURY.**
Gascoigne, John, Ph. D. Science, politics, and universities in Europe, 1600-1800. Aldershot [England] ; Brookfield, Vt. : Ashgate, c1998.
*TC LA621.5 .G37 1998*

**University of Cape Town. Institute of Development and Labour Law.**
Leo-Rhynie, Elsa. Gender mainstreaming in education. London : Commonwealth Secretariat, c1999.
*TC LC2572 .L46 1999*

**UNIVERSITY OF CHICAGO. DEPT. OF SOCIOLOGY - HISTORY.**
Abbott, Andrew. Department & discipline. Chicago, IL : University of Chicago Press, c1999.
*TC HM22.U5 A23 1999*

**UNIVERSITY OF CONNECTICUT.**
Arnold, Gordon B., 1954- The politics of faculty unionization. Westport, Conn. ; London : Bergin & Garvey, 2000.
*TC LB2335.865.U6 A75 2000*

**UNIVERSITY OF DELAWARE - HISTORY.**
Hoffecker, Carol E. Beneath thy guiding hand. Newark, Del. : University of Delaware, c1994.
*TC LD1483 .H64 1994*

**UNIVERSITY OF EAST LONDON.**
Eastern promise. London : Lawrence and Wishart, 2000.
*TC LC238.4.G73 L66 2000*

**University of East London studies in education.**
Teacher professionalism and the challenge of change. Stoke-on-Trent, Staffordshire, England : Trentham Books, 1999.
*TC LB1775.4.G7 T43 1999*

**University of Edinburgh. Centre for Cognitive Science.**
Functional categories, argument structure and parametric variation. Edinburgh : Centre for Cognitive Study, University of Edinburgh, c1994.
*TC P151 .F86 1994*

**University of Georgia.**
Boney, F. N. A pictorial history of the University of Georgia. 2nd ed. Athens : University of Georgia Press, c2000.
*TC LD1983 .B6 2000*

The High school quarterly. Athens, Ga. : University of Georgia, 1912-[1936]

**UNIVERSITY OF GEORGIA - HISTORY.**
Boney, F. N. A pictorial history of the University of Georgia. 2nd ed. Athens : University of Georgia Press, c2000.
*TC LD1983 .B6 2000*

**UNIVERSITY OF GEORGIA - HISTORY - PICTORIAL WORKS.**
Boney, F. N. A pictorial history of the University of Georgia. 2nd ed. Athens : University of Georgia Press, c2000.
*TC LD1983 .B6 2000*

**UNIVERSITY OF HARTFORD - CURRICULA.**
Interdisciplinary general education. New York, NY : College Board Publications, c1999.
*TC LB2361 .I43 1999*

**University of Hartford experience.**
Interdisciplinary general education. New York, NY : College Board Publications, c1999.
*TC LB2361 .I43 1999*

**University of Illinois bulletin.**
University of Illinois (Urbana-Champaign campus). Bureau of Educational Research. Bulletin. Urbana, 1918-47.

**University of Illinois (Urbana-Champaign campus). Bureau of Educational Research.** Bulletin. Urbana, 1918-47. 63 no. illus., tables, diagrs. 23 cm. no. 1-63. (Issued as the university's Bulletin.) Publication suspended, 1933-45.
*1. Education - Research - Illinois. 2. Education - Illinois. I. Title. II. Series: University of Illinois bulletin.*

**University of Iowa. Museum of Art.**
Kinsey, Joni. Plain pictures. Washington, : Published for the University of Iowa Museum of Art by the Smithsonian Institution Press, 1996.
*TC N8214.5.U6 K56 1996*

**University of Kansas bulletin of education.**
Bulletin of education. Lawrence, Kan. : Bureau of School Service and Research, University of Kansas, 1926-1969.

**University of Kansas. Bureau of School Service and Research.**
Bulletin of education. Lawrence, Kan. : Bureau of School Service and Research, University of Kansas, 1926-1969.

**University of Kansas. School of Education.**
Bulletin of education. Lawrence, Kan. : Bureau of School Service and Research, University of Kansas, 1926-1969.

**University of Kentucky. College of Education.**
Kentucky high school quarterly. Lexington, Ky. : Department of Education, State University of Kentucky, 1915-1927.

**University of Kentucky. Dept. of Education.**
Kentucky high school quarterly. Lexington, Ky. : Department of Education, State University of Kentucky, 1915-1927.

**The University of Louisville.**
Cox, Dwayne, 1950- [Lexington] : University Press of Kentucky, c2000.
*TC LD3131.L42 C69 2000*

**UNIVERSITY OF LOUISVILLE - HISTORY.**
Cox, Dwayne, 1950- The University of Louisville. [Lexington] : University Press of Kentucky, c2000.
*TC LD3131.L42 C69 2000*

**University of Massachusetts at Amherst. Center for Equal Education.**
Integrated education. [Amherst, Mass., etc., Center for Equal Education, School of Education, University of Massachusetts, etc.]

**UNIVERSITY OF MASSACHUSETTS (SYSTEM).**
Arnold, Gordon B., 1954- The politics of faculty unionization. Westport, Conn. ; London : Bergin & Garvey, 2000.
*TC LB2335.865.U6 A75 2000*

**University of Melbourne. Dept. of History.**
Dunt, Lesley, 1944- Speaking worlds. Parkville, Vic. : History Department, The University of Melbourne, c1993.
*TC LA2101 .D96 1993*

**University of Michigan. Center for Research on Conflict Resolution.**
McNeil, Elton B., ed. The nature of human conflict. Englewood Cliffs, N.J., Prentice-Hall [1965]
*TC HM36.5 .M25*

**UNIVERSITY OF MICHIGAN - HISTORY.**
Bordin, Ruth Birgitta Anderson, 1917- Women at Michigan. Ann Arbor : University of Michigan Press, c1999.
*TC LD3280 .B67 1999*

Duderstadt, James J., 1942- A university for the 21st century. Ann Arbor, MI : University of Michigan Press, c2000.
*TC LD3280 .D83 2000*

**UNIVERSITY OF MICHIGAN. MEDICAL SCHOOL - HISTORY.**
Davenport, Horace Willard, 1912- Not just any medical school. Ann Arbor : University of Michigan Press, c1999.
*TC R747.U6834 D38 1999*

**University of Michigan. School of Education.**
School discipline. Ann Arbor, Mich. : University of Michigan School of Education, 1989.
*TC LB3011 .S425*

The University of Michigan School of Education bulletin. [Ann Arbor] : The School, 1929-1964.

**The University of Michigan School of Education bulletin.** [Ann Arbor] : The School, 1929-1964. 35 v. ; 23 cm. Frequency: Monthly (Oct.-May). Vol. 1, no. 1 (Oct. 1929)-v. 35, no. 6 (Mar. 1964). School of Education bulletin. Bulletin. Title from caption.
*1. Education - Periodicals. I. University of Michigan. School of Education. II. Title: School of Education bulletin III. Title: Bulletin*

**University of New South Wales, a portrait.**
O'Farrell, Patrick James. UNSW, a portrait. Sydney, Australia : UNSW Press, 1999.
*TC LG715.K4 O42 1999*

**UNIVERSITY OF NEW SOUTH WALES - HISTORY.**
O'Farrell, Patrick James. UNSW, a portrait. Sydney, Australia : UNSW Press, 1999.
*TC LG715.K4 O42 1999*

**UNIVERSITY OF NOTRE DAME - HISTORY.**
Burns, Robert E., 1927- Being Catholic, being American. Notre Dame, Ind. : University of Notre Dame Press, c1999.
*TC LD4113 .B87 1999*

**University of Oregon. School of Education.**
The High school. Eugene, Ore.

**UNIVERSITY OF OXFORD - HISTORY.**
Oxford figures. Oxford ; New York : Oxford University Press, 2000.
*TC QA14.G73 O947 2000*

**UNIVERSITY OF PENNSYLVANIA - BUILDINGS - HISTORY.**
Thomas, George E. Building America's first university. Philadelphia : University of Pennsylvania Press, c2000.
*TC LD4531 .T56 1999*

**University of Pennsylvania. Graduate School of Education. Language in Education Division.**
Working papers in educational linguistics. [Philadelphia]: Language in Education Division, Graduate School of Education, University of Pennsylvania,
*TC P40.8 .W675*

**University of Pittsburgh. Dept. of Black Studies.**
Black lines. [Pittsburgh, Dept. of Black Studies, University of Pittsburgh.

**University of Pittsburgh. Project Talent Office.**
The Use of standardized ability tests in American secondary schools and their impact on students, teachers, and administrators New York] Russell Sage Foundation [1965]
*TC LB3051 .R914*

**University of Pittsburgh. School of Education.**
Journal / University of Pittsburgh, School of Education. [Lancaster, Pa. : The School, 1925- 6 v. : ill. ; 23 cm. Frequency: Bimonthly during the school year. Vol. 1, no. 1 (Sept./Oct. 1925)-v. 6 (May 1931). Other title: University of Pittsburgh School of Education journal. Title from cover. No more published?
*1. Education - Periodicals. 2. Education - United States - Periodicals. I. Title. II. Title: University of Pittsburgh School of Education journal*

**University of Pittsburgh School of Education journal.**
University of Pittsburgh. School of Education. Journal. [Lancaster, Pa. : The School, 1925-

**UNIVERSITY OF RHODE ISLAND.**
Arnold, Gordon B., 1954- The politics of faculty unionization. Westport, Conn. ; London : Bergin & Garvey, 2000.
*TC LB2335.865.U6 A75 2000*

**UNIVERSITY OF SASKATCHEWAN. DEPT. OF POLITICAL ECONOMY - HISTORY.**
Spafford, Shirley. No ordinary academics. Toronto : University of Toronto Press, 1999.
*TC HB74.9.C3 S62 1999*

**University of Sheffield.**
Challenge cases [videorecording]. Princeton, N.J. : Films for the Humanities & Sciences, 1998.
*TC RC455.2.C4 C4 1998*

Disorders due to psychoactive substance abuse [videorecording]. Princeton, N.J. : Films for the Humanities & Sciences, 1998.
*TC RC564 .D5 1998*

Mood disorders [videorecording]. Princeton, N.J. : Films for the Humanities & Sciences, 1998.
*TC RC537 .M6 1998*

Neurotic, stress-related, and somatoform disorders [videorecording]. Princeton, N.J. : Films for the Humanities & Sciences, 1998.
*TC RC530 .N4 1998*

Organic disorders [videorecording]. Princeton, N.J. : Films for the Humanities & Sciences, 1998.
*TC RC521 .O7 1998*

Personality disorders [videorecording]. Princeton, N.J. : Films for the Humanities & Sciences, 1998.
*TC RC554 .P4 1998*

Schizophrenia and delusional disorders [videorecording]. Princeton, N.J. : Films for the Humanities & Sciences, c1998.
*TC RC514 .S3 1998*

**University of Southern California. Dept. of Exceptional Children.**
Annual distinguished lectures in special education and rehabilitation. Los Angeles, Dept. of Exceptional Children, University of Southern California.
*TC LC4019 .D57*

**UNIVERSITY OF TENNESSEE, KNOXVILLE - HISTORY.**
Reforming a college. New York : P. Lang, c2000.
*TC LD5293 .R44 2000*

**University of the State of New York** Bulletin to the schools ... Albany, The University of the State of New York Press [1928- v. illus. 25 cm.
*1. Education - New York (State) 2. Education - Periodicals. I. Title.*

[Inside education (Albany, N.Y.)] Inside education. Albany : New York State Education Dept., 1968-1983.

**University of the State of New York. Annual report.**
[Inside education (Albany, N.Y.)] Inside education. Albany : New York State Education Dept., 1968-1983.

[Inside education (Albany, N.Y.)] Inside education. Albany : New York State Education Dept., 1968-1983.

**University of the State of New York. Bulletin to the schools Oct. 1914-June 1968.**
[Inside education (Albany, N.Y.)] Inside education.

Albany : New York State Education Dept., 1968-1983.

**University of the State of New York. Center for Learning Technologies.**
The ... Educational software preview guide. Redwood City, CA : California TECC Software Library & Clearinghouse,
*TC LB1028.7 .E35*

**University of the State of New York. Office of Communications.**
[Inside education (Albany, N.Y. : 1991)] Inside education. Albany, N.Y. : University of the State of New York, State Education Dept., 1991-

**University of the State of New York. Office of Elementary, Middle, Secondary, and Continuing Education.**
Adapted physical education. Albany, N.Y. : University of the State of New York, State Education Dept., Office of Elementary, Middle, Secondary, and Continuing Education, Office of Vocational and Educational Services for Individuals with Disabilities, 1997.
*TC GV445 .A3 1997*

**University of the State of New York. Office of Vocational and Educational Services for Individuals with Disabilities.**
Adapted physical education. Albany, N.Y. : University of the State of New York, State Education Dept., Office of Elementary, Middle, Secondary, and Continuing Education, Office of Vocational and Educational Services for Individuals with Disabilities, 1997.
*TC GV445 .A3 1997*

**The University of Virginia.**
Hitchcock, Susan Tyler. Charlottesville : University Press of Virginia and University of Virginia Bookstore, 1999.
*TC LD5678 .H58 1999*

**UNIVERSITY OF VIRGINIA - HISTORY.**
Hitchcock, Susan Tyler. The University of Virginia. Charlottesville : University Press of Virginia and University of Virginia Bookstore, 1999.
*TC LD5678 .H58 1999*

**UNIVERSITY OF VIRGINIA - PICTORIAL WORKS.**
Hitchcock, Susan Tyler. The University of Virginia. Charlottesville : University Press of Virginia and University of Virginia Bookstore, 1999.
*TC LD5678 .H58 1999*

**UNIVERSITY OF WASHINGTON - PRESIDENTS - BIOGRAPHY.**
Odegaard, Charles E. A pilgrimage through universities. Seattle : University of Washington Press, c1999.
*TC LD5752.1 .O34 1999*

**UNIVERSITY OF WISCONSIN SYSTEM - HISTORY.**
Transforming women's education. Madison, WI : Office of University Publications for the University of Wisconsin System, Women's Studies Consortium, 1999.
*TC HQ1181.U5 T77 1999*

**University of Wisconsin System. Women's Studies Consortium.**
Transforming women's education. Madison, WI : Office of University Publications for the University of Wisconsin System, Women's Studies Consortium, 1999.
*TC HQ1181.U5 T77 1999*

**UNIVERSITY OFFICIALS.** *See* **COLLEGE ADMINISTRATORS.**

**UNIVERSITY PERSONNEL MANAGEMENT.** *See* **COLLEGE PERSONNEL MANAGEMENT.**

**University placement review.**
Journal of college placement. [Philadelphia, Pa. etc.], The College Placement Council, inc. [etc.]

**UNIVERSITY PRESIDENTS.** *See* **COLLEGE PRESIDENTS.**

**UNIVERSITY RADIO STATIONS.** *See* **COLLEGE RADIO STATIONS.**

**UNIVERSITY SETTLEMENTS.** *See* **SOCIAL SETTLEMENTS.**

**UNIVERSITY SPORTS.** *See* **COLLEGE SPORTS.**

**UNIVERSITY STUDENTS.** *See* **COLLEGE STUDENTS.**

**UNIVERSITY TEACHERS.** *See* **COLLEGE TEACHERS.**

**UNIVERSITY TEACHING.** *See* **COLLEGE TEACHING.**

**UNIVERSITY TOWNS.** *See* **COMMUNITY AND COLLEGE.**

**Unix and Windows 2000 handbook :** planning, integration, and administration / Lonnie Harvel ... [et al.]. Upper Saddle River, NJ : Prentice Hall, 2000. xvii, 679 p. : ill. ; 24 cm. ISBN 0-13-025493-2 (alk. paper) DDC 005.4/476
*1. UNIX (Computer file) 2. Microsoft Windows (Computer file) 3. Operating systems (Computers) I. Harvel, Lonnie.*
*TC QA76.76.O63 U58 2000*

**UNIX (COMPUTER FILE).**
Unix and Windows 2000 handbook. Upper Saddle River, NJ : Prentice Hall, 2000.
*TC QA76.76.O63 U58 2000*

**Unknown.**
Thompson, Colin (Colin Edward) New York : Walker & Co., 2000.
*TC PZ7.T371424 Un 2000*

**The unknown Karen Horney :** essays on gender, culture, and psychoanalysis / edited with introductions by Bernard J. Paris. New Haven : Yale University Press, c2000. xiv, 362 p. ; 24 cm. Includes bibliographical references and index. ISBN 0-300-08042-5 DDC 150.19/5
*1. Psychoanalysis. 2. Horney, Karen, - 1885-1952. I. Paris, Bernard J.*
*TC BF173 .U55 2000*

**The unlikely celebrity.**
Walz, Thomas, 1933- Carbondale : Southern Illinois University Press, c1998.
*TC HV3006.S33 W35 1998*

**Unlikely heroes :** teacher's planning guide. New York : Macmillan/McGraw-Hill, c1997. 1 v. (various pagings) : col. ill. ; 31 cm. (Spotlight on literacy ; Gr.6 l.12 u.3) (The road to independent reading) Includes index. ISBN 0-02-183196-3
*1. Language arts (Elementary) 2. Reading (Elementary) I. Series. II. Series: The road to independent reading*
*TC LB1576 .S66 1997 Gr.6 l.12 u.3*

**Unlocking literacy :** a guide for teachers / edited by Robert Fisher and Mary Williams. London : David Fulton, 2000. xii, 132 p. : ill. ; 25 cm. Includes bibliographical references and index. ISBN 1-85346-652-2
*1. Literacy - Study and teaching - Great Britain. I. Williams, Mary. II. Fisher, Robert, 1943-*
*TC LC149 .U485 2000*

**UNMARRIED COUPLES.** *See* **SINGLE PARENTS.**

**UNMARRIED COUPLES - HEALTH AND HYGIENE.**
The psychology of couples and illness. 1st ed. Washington, D.C. : American Psychological Association, c2000.
*TC R726.5 .P785 2000*

**Unmet need in psychiatry :** problems, resources, responses / edited by Gavin Andrews and Scott Henderson. Cambridge, U.K. ; New York, NY : Cambridge University Press, 2000. xvi, 444 p. : ill. ; 24 cm. Includes bibliographical references and index. ISBN 0-521-66229-X (hb) DDC 362.2
*1. Mental health services - Utilization - Congresses. 2. Medical care - Needs assessment - Congresses. 3. Mental illness - Epidemiology - Congresses. 4. Community Mental Health Services - Congresses. 5. Health Services Needs and Demand - Congresses. 6. Mental Disorders - therapy - Congresses. I. Andrews, Gavin. II. Henderson, Scott, 1935-*
*TC RA790.5 .U565 2000*

**Uno, Kathleen S., 1951-** Passages to modernity : motherhood, childhood, and social reform in early twentieth century Japan / Kathleen S. Uno. Honolulu : University of Hawai'i Press, c1999. x, 237 p. : ill. ; 24 cm. Includes bibliographical references (p. [195]-215) and index. ISBN 0-8248-1619-6 (cloth : alk. paper) ISBN 0-8248-2137-8 (pbk. : alk. paper) DDC 306.874/09520904
*1. Day care centers - Japan - History - 20th century. 2. Child care - Japan - History - 20th century. 3. Mother and child - Japan - History - 20th century. I. Title.*
*TC HQ778.7.J3 U56 1999*

**UNOBSERVED MATTER (ASTRONOMY).** *See* **DARK MATTER (ASTRONOMY).**

**Unobtrusive measures.**
Nonreactive measures in the social sciences. 2nd ed. Boston : Houghton Mifflin, c1981.
*TC H62 .N675 1981*

**Unplayed tapes.**
Fishman, Stephen M. Urbana, Ill. : National Council

of Teachers of English : New York : Teachers College Press, c2000.
*TC LB1028.24 .F52 2000*

**Unraveling 10 controversial issues in education.**
Hot buttons. Bloomington, Ind. : Phi Delta Kappa Educational Foundation, c1997.
*TC LA210 .H68 1997*

**Unraveling the seven myths of reading.**
May, Frank B. Boston : Allyn and Bacon, c2001.
*TC LB1050.2 .M364 2001*

**UNSEEN MATTER (ASTRONOMY).** *See* **DARK MATTER (ASTRONOMY).**

**The unsteady march.**
Klinkner, Philip A. Chicago : University of Chicago Press, c1999.
*TC E185 .K55 1999*

**UNSW, a portrait.**
O'Farrell, Patrick James. Sydney, Australia : UNSW Press, 1999.
*TC LG715.K4 O42 1999*

**Unsworth, Len.**
Researching language in schools and communities. London ; Washington [D.C.] : Cassell, 2000.
*TC P53 .R463 2000*

**Untapped public funding for the arts.**
Resource development handbook. [Washington, D.C.] : National Assembly of Local Arts Agencies, Institute for Community Development and the Arts, 1995.
*TC NX110 .R47 1995*

**UNTOUCHABLES.** *See* **INDIA - SCHEDULED TRIBES.**

**Up and out.**
Johnson, Andrew P. Boston : Allyn and Bacon, c2000.
*TC LB1590.3 .J64 2000*

**Up and running.**
Walton, Richard E. Boston, Mass. : Harvard Business School Press, c1989.
*TC T58.6 .W345 1989*

**Up in the air.**
Livingston, Myra Cohn. 1st ed. New York : Holiday House, c1989.
*TC PS3562.I945 U6 1989*

**An update on adult development theory : :** new ways of thinking about the life course / M. Carolyn Clark, Rosemary S. Caffarella, editors. San Francisco, CA : Jossey-Bass Publishers, 1999. 106 p. ; 23 cm. (New directions for adult and continuing education, no. 84.) New ways of thinking about the life course. "Winter 1999" Includes bibliographical references and index. CONTENTS: Theorizing adult development / M. Carolyn Clark, Rosemary S. Caffarella -- Our complex human body: biological development explored / Vivian W. Mott -- Psychological development: becoming a person / Patricia M. Reeves -- Gender identity and gendered adult development / Jovita M. Ross-Gordon -- Racial and ethnic identity and development / Alicia Fedelina Chavez, Florence Guido-DiBrito -- The development of sexual identity / Kathleen Edwards, Ann K. Brooks -- Development as separation and connection: finding a balance / Kathleen Taylor -- Time as the integrative factor / Sharon B. Merriam --Understanding adult development as narrative / Marsha Rossiter -- The spiritual dimension of adult development / Elizabeth J. Tisdell -- Development and learning: themes and conclusions / Rosemary S. Caffarella, M. Carolyn Clark. ISBN 0-7879-1171-2
*1. Adult learning. 2. Adult education. 3. Meaning (Psychology). 4. Transfer of training. I. Clark, M. Carolyn. II. Caffarella, Rosemary S. (Rosemary Shelley), dd 1946-) III. Title: New ways of thinking about the life course. IV. Series: New directions for adult continuing education ; no.84*
*TC LC5225.L42 U63 1999*

**Update on foundation trends.**
Renz, Loren. Arts funding. 3rd ed. [New York, N.Y.] : Foundation Center, c1998.
*TC NX711.U5 R4 1998*

**Updike, John.** A child's calendar / poems by John Updike ; illustrations by Trina Schart Hyman. <Rev. ed.>. New York : Holiday House, 1999. 1 v. (unpaged) : ill. ; 25 cm. First published by Alfred A. Knopf in 1965 with illustrations by Nancy Ekholm Burkert. The text for this new edition incorporates a number of changes by the author. SUMMARY: A collection of twelve poems describing the activities in a child's life and the changes in the weather as the year moves from January to December. ISBN 0-8234-1445-0 DDC 811/.54
*1. Months - Juvenile poetry. 2. Children's poetry, American. 3. Months - Poetry. 4. American poetry. I. Hyman, Trina Schart, ill. II. Title.*

*TC PS3571.P4 C49 1999*

**UpDrafts :** case studies in teacher renewal / edited by Roy F. Fox. Urbana, Ill. : National Council of Teachers of English, c2000. xli, 193 p. : ill. ; 23 cm. Includes bibliographical references and index. ISBN 0-8141-5575-8 (pbk.) DDC 371.1/001/9
*1. Teachers - United States - Psychology - Case studies. 2. Teachers - In-service training - United States - Case studies. I. Fox, Roy F. II. National Council of Teachers of English. III. Title.*
*TC LB1775.2 .U63 2000*

**UPHOLSTERY.** *See* **FURNITURE.**

**Upon whom we depend.**
Chamberlin, J. Gordon (John Gordon) New York : Peter Lang, c1999.
*TC HC110.P6 C326 1999*

**UPPER CLASS - EDUCATION - GREAT BRITAIN - HISTORY.**
Gordon, Peter, 1927- Royal education. London ; Portland, OR : Frank Cass, 1999.
*TC LC4945.G72 G67 1999*

**UPPER CLASS WOMEN - EDUCATION - ROME - HISTORY.**
Hemelrijk, Emily Ann, 1953- Matrona docta. London ; New York : Routledge, 1999.
*TC HQ1136 .H45 1999*

**UPPER CLASS WOMEN - ROME - HISTORY.**
Hemelrijk, Emily Ann, 1953- Matrona docta. London ; New York : Routledge, 1999.
*TC HQ1136 .H45 1999*

**UPPER CLASS WOMEN - ROME - INTELLECTUAL LIFE.**
Hemelrijk, Emily Ann, 1953- Matrona docta. London ; New York : Routledge, 1999.
*TC HQ1136 .H45 1999*

**UPPER CLASSES.** *See* **UPPER CLASS.**

**Upravlenie nachal'noĭ i sredneĭ shkoly Narkomprosa RSFSR.**
[Geografiia v shkole (Moscow, Russia)] Geografiia v shkole. Moskva : Gos. ucheb.-pedagog. izd-vo, 1934-

**UPRISINGS, PEASANT.** *See* **PEASANT UPRISINGS.**

**Uprooting otherness.**
Clark, Charles E., 1960- Selinsgrove [Pa.] : Susquehanna University Press ; London : Associated University Presses, c2000.
*TC LC156.S65 C56 2000*

**Upton, Clifford Brewster. 1877-** American Arithmetic / Clifford B. Upton, Kenneth G. Fuller, and George H. McMeen. 2nd ed. New York, N.Y. : American Book Company, 1963. v. : ill. (some col.) ; 24 cm. Includes index. CONTENTS: V. 3. Moving ahead -- v. 5. Achieving goals -- v. 6. Broadening knowledge.
*1. Arithmetic. I. Fuller, Kenneth G. II. McMeen, George H. III. Title.*
*TC QA103 .U67 1963*

**Urban affairs annual reviews**
(v. 46.) Affordable housing and urban redevelopment in the United States. Thousand Oaks, Calif. : Sage Publications, c1997.
*TC HD7293 .A55 1997*

**URBAN AREAS.** *See* **CITIES AND TOWNS; METROPOLITAN AREAS.**

**URBAN CHILDREN.** *See* **CITY CHILDREN.**

**URBAN CORES.** *See* **INNER CITIES.**

**URBAN CRIME.** *See* **CRIME.**

**URBAN DESIGN.** *See* **CITY PLANNING.**

**URBAN DEVELOPMENT.** *See* **CITY PLANNING.**

**Urban diversity series**
(no. 97) Flaxman, Erwin. Youth mentoring: New York, N.Y. : ERIC Clearinghouse on Urban Education, 1988.
*TC LC4065 .F53 1988*

**URBAN ECOLOGY.**
Gendering the city. Lanham [Md.] : Rowman & Littlefield, c2000.
*TC HT166 .G4614 2000*

**URBAN EDUCATION.** *See also* **EDUCATION, URBAN.**
Tannenbaum, Abraham. Dropout or diploma. New York : Teachers College Press, 1966.
*TC 371.2913T15*

**URBAN HOUSING.** *See* **HOUSING.**

**Urban Institute.**
Nonprofits and government. Washington, DC : Urban Institute Press, 1999.
*TC HD62.6 .N694 1999*

**URBAN LEGENDS.** *See* **LEGENDS.**

**Urban liberalism in imperial Germany.**
Palmowski, Jan. Oxford ; New York : Oxford University Press, 1999.
*TC DD901.F78 P35 1999*

**URBAN LIFE.** *See* **CITY AND TOWN LIFE.**

**Urban, Magda A.**
Parent articles about ADHD. San Antonio, Texas : Communication Skill Builders, c1999.
*TC RJ506.H9 P37 1999*

**Urban minority gifted students.**
Graham, Sheila L. 1999.
*TC 06 no. 11119*

**URBAN PLANNING.** *See* **CITY PLANNING.**

**URBAN POLICY.** *See* **CITY PLANNING; EDUCATION, URBAN; URBAN RENEWAL.**

**URBAN POLICY - UNITED STATES.**
Affordable housing and urban redevelopment in the United States. Thousand Oaks, Calif. : Sage Publications, c1997.
*TC HD7293 .A55 1997*

Bartlett, Randall, 1945- The crisis of America's cities. Armonk, N.Y. : M.E. Sharpe, c1998.
*TC HT123 .B324 1998*

**URBAN POLICY - UNITED STATES - CASE STUDIES.**
Portz, John, 1953- City schools and city politics. Lawrence : University Press of Kansas, c1999.
*TC LC5131 .P67 1999*

**URBAN POOR - KENYA - NAIROBI - PICTORIAL WORKS.**
Shootback. London : Booth-Clibborn, 1999.
*TC HV4160.5.N34 S45 1999*

**URBAN POOR - MEDICAL CARE - UNITED STATES.**
Andrulis, Dennis P. Managed care and the inner city. San Francisco : Jossey-Bass, 1999.
*TC RA413.5.U5 A57 1999*

**URBAN PROBLEMS.** *See* **URBAN POLICY.**

**URBAN PUBLIC SPACES.** *See* **PUBLIC SPACES.**

**URBAN REDEVELOPMENT.** *See* **URBAN RENEWAL.**

**URBAN RENEWAL.** *See* **CITY PLANNING; COMMUNITY ORGANIZATION; URBAN POLICY.**

**URBAN RENEWAL - ENGLAND - LONDON.**
Eastern promise. London : Lawrence and Wishart, 2000.
*TC LC238.4.G73 L66 2000*

**URBAN RENEWAL - UNITED STATES.**
Affordable housing and urban redevelopment in the United States. Thousand Oaks, Calif. : Sage Publications, c1997.
*TC HD7293 .A55 1997*

Rebuilding urban neighborhoods. Thousand Oaks, Calif. : Sage Publications, c1999.
*TC HT175 .R425 1999*

**Urban school chiefs under fire.**
Cuban, Larry. Chicago : University of Chicago Press, 1976.
*TC LB2831.7 .C82*

**URBAN SPACES.** *See* **PUBLIC SPACES.**

**URBAN WOMEN - SOCIAL CONDITIONS.**
Gendering the city. Lanham [Md.] : Rowman & Littlefield, c2000.
*TC HT166 .G4614 2000*

**URBAN YOUTH.** *See* **CITY CHILDREN.**

**URBAN YOUTH - UNITED STATES.**
Violence and childhood in the inner city. Cambridge, UK ; New York : Cambridge University Press, 1997.
*TC HN90.V5 V532 1997*

**URBAN YOUTH - UNITED STATES - FAMILY RELATIONSHIPS.**
Elder, Glen H. Children of the land. Chicago : University of Chicago Press, 2000.
*TC HQ796 .E525 2000*

**URBANISM.** *See* **CITIES AND TOWNS.**

**Uri, Noel D.**
Huang, Wen-Yuan. The economic and environmental consequences of nutrient management in agriculture. Commack, N.Y. : Nova Science, c1999.
*TC S651 .H826 1999*

**URNINGS.** *See* GAY MEN.

**URSIDAE.** *See* BEARS.

**URSUS.** *See* POLAR BEAR.

**URSUS EOGROENLANDICUS.** *See* POLAR BEAR.

**URSUS GROENLANDICUS.** *See* POLAR BEAR.

**URSUS JENAENSIS.** *See* POLAR BEAR.

**URSUS LABRADORENSIS.** *See* POLAR BEAR.

**URSUS MARINUS.** *See* POLAR BEAR.

**URSUS MARITIMUS.** *See* POLAR BEAR.

**URSUS POLARIS.** *See* POLAR BEAR.

**URSUS SPITZBERGENSIS.** *See* POLAR BEAR.

**URSUS UNGAVENSIS.** *See* POLAR BEAR.

**U.S. Dept. of Education.**
Kirby, Sheila Nataraj, 1946- Staffing at-risk school districts in Texas. Santa Monica, CA : Rand, 1999.
*TC LB2833.3.T4 K57 1999*

**U.S Public Health Service Public health reports.**
United States. Health Services and Mental Health Administration. Health services reports. Rockville, Md.

United States. Health Services and Mental Health Administration. Health services reports. Rockville, Md.

**USA today.**
Intellect. [New York, Society for the Advancement of Education]

**USAGroup Foundation.**
Quehl, Gary H. Fifty years of innovations in undergraduate education. Indianapolis, Ind : USA Group Foundation, c1999.
*TC LB1027.3 .Q43 1999*

**USAGroup Foundation new agenda series**
(v.1, no.4 (Oct. 1999)) Quehl, Gary H. Fifty years of innovations in undergraduate education. Indianapolis, Ind : USA Group Foundation, c1999.
*TC LB1027.3 .Q43 1999*

**Use of language across the primary curriculum** / edited by Eve Bearne. London ; New York : Routledge, 1998. xiv, 286 p. : ill. ; 24 cm. Includes bibliographical references and index. ISBN 0-415-15851-6 (pbk.) DDC 372.6/044
*1. English language - Study and teaching (Elementary) - Great Britain. 2. Interdisciplinary approach in education - Great Britain. I. Bearne, Eve, 1943-*
*TC LB1576 U74 1998*

**The use of psychological testing for treatment planning and outcome assessment** / edited by Mark E. Maruish. 2nd ed. Mahwah, N.J. : Lawrence Erlbaum Associates, c1999. xvi, 1507 p. : ill. ; 27 cm. Includes bibliographical references and indexes. ISBN 0-8058-2761-7 (cloth : alk. paper) DDC 616.89/075
*1. Psychological tests. 2. Mental illness - Diagnosis. 3. Psychiatry - Differential therapeutics. 4. Mental illness - Treatment - Evaluation. 5. Psychiatric rating scales. 6. Outcome assessment (Medical care) 7. Outcome assessment I. Maruish, Mark E. (Mark Edward)*
*TC RC473.P79 U83 1999*

**The Use of standardized ability tests in American secondary schools and their impact on students, teachers, and administrators** [by] Orville G. Brim, Jr. [and others. New York] Russell Sage Foundation [1965] lv, 300, [148] p. 28 cm. (Technical report on the social consequences of testing, no. 3) "Cooperative research project no. 2334, University of Pittsburgh, Project Talent Office ... 1964." Title on spine: The impact of secondary school testing.
*1. Ability - Testing. 2. Educational tests and measurements. I. Brim, Orville Gilbert, 1923- II. University of Pittsburgh. Project Talent Office. III. Title: The impact of secondary school testing. IV. Series: Russell Sage Foundation. Technical report on the social consequences of testing ; no. 3.*
*TC LB3051 .R914*

**USE OF TIME.** *See* TIME MANAGEMENT.

**USEFUL ARTS.** *See* INDUSTRIAL ARTS; TECHNOLOGY.

**User-centered technology.**
Johnson, Robert R., 1951- Albany : State University of New York Press, c1998.

*TC QA76.9.U83 J64 1998*

**USER INTERFACES (COMPUTER SYSTEMS).**
*See also* **GRAPHICAL USER INTERFACES (COMPUTER SYSTEMS).**
Intelligent multimedia information retrieval. Menlo Park, Calif. : AAAI Press ; Cambridge, Mass. : MIT Press, c1997.
*TC QA76.575 .I577 1997*

Johnson, Robert R., 1951- User-centered technology. Albany : State University of New York Press, c1998.
*TC QA76.9.U83 J64 1998*

**The uses of images.**
Gombrich, E. H. (Ernst Hans), 1909- London : Phaidon, 1999.
*TC N72.S6 G66 1999*

**Usher, Robin, 1944-.**
Globalisation and pedagogy. London ; New York : Routledge, 2000.
*TC LC1090 .E33 2000*

**Ushinskiĭ, K. D. (Konstantin Dmitrievich), 1824-1870. [Selected works. English. 1975]**
K. D. Ushinsky : selected works / edited by A. I. Piskunov ; [translated from the Russian by Anatoly Bratov ; compiled and annotated by E. D. Dneprov]. Moscow : Progress, 1975. 378, [3] p. ; 19 cm. Bibliography: p. [81] DDC 370/.92/4
*1. Ushinskiĭ, K. D. - (Konstantin Dmitrievich) - 1824-1870. 2. Education. 3. Education - Russia. I. Piskunov, A. I. (Alekseĭ Ivanovich) II. Title.*
*TC LB675 .U8213 1975*

**USHINSKIĬ, K. D. (KONSTANTIN DMITRIEVICH), 1824-1870.**
Ushinskiĭ, K. D. (Konstantin Dmitrievich), 1824-1870. [Selected works. English. 1975] K. D. Ushinsky. Moscow : Progress, 1975.
*TC LB675 .U8213 1975*

**Using a digital nervous system.**
Gates, Bill, 1955- Business @ the speed of thought. New York, NY : Warner Books, c1999.
*TC HD30.37 .G38 1999*

**Using action research for school restructuring and organizational change.**
Michel, Patrick. 2000.
*TC 06 no. 11295*

Michel, Patrick. 2000.
*TC 06 no. 11295*

**Using art to make art.**
Libby, Wendy M. L. Albany, N.Y. : Delmar Publishers, 2000.
*TC N362 .L49 2000*

**Using children's literature to develop historical understandings.**
Singleton, Laurel R., 1950- H is for history. Boulder, Colo. : Social Science Education Consortium, 1995.
*TC LB1582.U6 S56 1995*

**Using computers to teach literature.**
Jody, Marilyn, 1932- 2nd ed. Urbana, Ill. : National Council of Teachers of English, c1998.
*TC LB1050.37 J63 1998*

**Using consultants to improve teaching** / Christopher Knapper, Sergio Piccinin, editors. San Francisco : Jossey-Bass, c1999. 111 p. ; 23 cm. (New directions for teaching and learning, 0271-0633 ; no. 79, Fall 1999) (Jossey-Bass higher and adult education series) "Fall 1999" Includes bibliographical references and index. ISBN 0-7879-4876-4
*1. Educational consultants - United States. I. Knapper. Christopher. II. Piccinin. Sergio. III. Series. IV. Series: New directions for teaching and learning ; no. 79.*
*TC LB2799.2 .U83 1999*

**Using creative and critical thinking skills to enhance learning.**
Johnson, Andrew P. Up and out :. Boston : Allyn and Bacon, c2000.
*TC LB1590.3 .J64 2000*

**Using exercise in psychotherapy.**
Hays, Kate F. Working it out. 1st ed. Washington, DC : American Psychological Association, c1999.
*TC RC489.E9 H39 1999*

**Using Foucault and feminist theory to explain why some adults are excluded from British university education.**
Preece, Julia. Lewiston, N.Y. : E. Mellen Press, c1999.
*TC LC6256.G7 P74 1999*

**Using interactive multimedia software to improve cognition of complex imagery in adolescents.**
Tsamasiros, Katherine V. 1998.

*TC 06 no. 10905*

**Using internet primary sources to teach critical thinking skills in geography.**
Sharma, Martha B., 1945- Westport, Conn. ; London : Greenwood Press, 2000.
*TC G73 .S393 2000*

**Using item response theory methods to explore the effect of item wording on Likert data.**
Foye, Stephanie Diane. 1997.
*TC 085 F82*

**Using leveled books in guided reading, K-3.**
Fountas, Irene C. Matching books to readers :. Portsmouth, NH : Heinemann, c1999.
*TC LB1573 .F68*

**Using nursing research.**
Dempsey, Patricia Ann. 5th ed. Baltimore, Md. : Lippincott, c2000.
*TC RT81.5 .D46 2000*

**Using peer mediation in classrooms and schools.**
Gilhooley, James. Thousand Oaks, Calif. : Corwin Press, c2000.
*TC LB1027.5 .G48 2000*

**Using technology to strengthen employee and family involvement in education.**
Otterbourg, Susan D. [New York] : Conference Board, c1998.
*TC LB1028.3 .O88 1998*

**Using voice and theatre in therapy.**
Newham, Paul, 1962- London ; Philadelphia, Pa. : Jessica Kingsley Publishers, 1999.
*TC RZ999 .N437 1999*

**USMARC code list for countries** / prepared by Network Development and MARC Standards Office. 1993 ed. Washington, D.C. : Cataloging Distribution Service, Library of Congress, 1993. x, 55 p. ; 28 cm. ISBN 0-8444-0825-5 (pbk.) DDC 025.3/0285
*1. MARC formats - United States. 2. Names, Geographical (Cataloging) - Code words. I. Library of Congress. Network Development and MARC Standards Office.*
*TC Z699.35.M28 U78 1993*

**USMARC code list for geographic areas** / prepared by Network Development and MARC Standards Office. 1998 ed. Washington, D.C. : Cataloging Distribution Service, Library of Congress, 1998. 49 p. ; 28 cm. ISBN 0-8444-0960-X DDC 025.3/16
*1. Names, Geographical (Cataloging) - Code words. 2. MARC formats - United States. I. Library of Congress. Network Development and MARC Standards Office.*
*TC Z695.1.G4 U83 1998*

**USMARC code list for languages** / prepared by Network Development and MARC Standards Office. 1996 ed. Washington, D.C. : Cataloging Distribution Service, Library of Congress, 1996. 139 p. ; 28 cm. ISBN 0-8444-0936-7 DDC 025.3/16
*1. MARC formats - United States. 2. Language and languages - Code words. I. Library of Congress. Network Development and MARC Standards Office.*
*TC Z699.35.M28 U79 1997*

**USMARC code list for relators, sources, description conventions** / prepared by Network Development and MARC Standards Office. 1997 ed. Washington, DC : Cataloging Distribution Service, Library of Congress, 1997. iv, 46 p. ; 28 cm. Includes bibliographical references. ISBN 0-8444-0944-8 (pbk.) DDC 025.3/16
*1. MARC formats - United States. 2. Cataloging - United States - Code words. I. Library of Congress. Network Development and MARC Standards Office.*
*TC Z699.35.M28 U795 1997*

**UTE CHILDREN - EDUCATION (EARLY CHILDHOOD) - COLORADO.**
Clay, Cheryl D., 1947- Schooling at-risk Native American children. New York : Garland Pub., 1998.
*TC E99.U8 C53 1998*

**UTE CHILDREN - SOCIAL CONDITIONS.**
Clay, Cheryl D., 1947- Schooling at-risk Native American children. New York : Garland Pub., 1998.
*TC E99.U8 C53 1998*

**UTE CHILDREN - SOCIALIZATION.**
Clay, Cheryl D., 1947- Schooling at-risk Native American children. New York : Garland Pub., 1998.
*TC E99.U8 C53 1998*

**UTILITARIANISM.** *See* SECULARISM.

**Utilization of evaluative information** / Larry A. Braskamp, Robert D. Brown, guest editors. San Francisco : Jossey-Bass, 1980. xi, 101 p. ; 24 cm. (New directions for program evaluation ; no. 5) Includes bibliographies and index. DDC 361.6/1/072073; 219
*1. Evaluation research (Social action programs) - United*

States - Addresses, essays, lectures. I. Braskamp, Larry A. II. Brown, Robert Donald, 1931- III. Series.
**TC H62.5.U5 U86**

**UTILIZATION OF MEDICAL CARE.** *See* **MEDICAL CARE - UTILIZATION.**

**UTILIZATION OF MENTAL HEALTH SERVICES.** *See* **MENTAL HEALTH SERVICES - UTILIZATION.**

**Utopia on wheels.**
McGettigan, Timothy. Lanham, MD : University Press of America, c1999.
**TC HM1256 .M34 1999**

**Utopistics.**
Wallerstein, Immanuel Maurice, 1930- Utopistics, or, Historical choices of the twenty-first century. New York : New Press, 1998.
**TC D860 .W35 1998**

**Utopistics, or, Historical choices of the twenty-first century.**
Wallerstein, Immanuel Maurice, 1930- New York : New Press, 1998.
**TC D860 .W35 1998**

**Utrecht studies in language and communication**
(11) Jauregi Ondarra, Kristi. Collaborative negotiation of meaning. Amsterdam ; Atlanta, GA : Rodopi, 1997.
**TC P118.2 .J38 1997**

**Uttal, William R.** The war between mentalism and behaviorism : on the accessibility of mental processes / William R. Uttal. Mahwah, N.J. ; London : Lawrence Erlbaum Associates, Publishers, 2000. xviii, 205 p. ; 24 cm. (Scientific psychology series) Includes bibliographical references (p. 190-195) and indexes. ISBN 0-8058-3361-7 (hardcover : alk. paper) DDC 150.19/43
*1. Behaviorism (Psychology) 2. Cognitive psychology. I. Title. II. Series.*
**TC BF199 .U77 2000**

**Utter, Glenn H.** Encyclopedia of gun control and gun rights / Glenn H. Utter. Phoenix, Ariz. : Oryx Press, 2000. xxiii, 376 p. : ill. ; 26 cm. Includes bibliographical references (p. 361-364) and index. ISBN 1-57356-172-X (alk. paper) DDC 363.3/3/097303
*1. Firearms - Law and legislation - United States - Encyclopedia. 2. Gun control - United States - Encyclopedia. I. Title.*
**TC KF3941.A68 U88 2000**

**UXORICIDE.** *See* **CHILDREN OF UXORICIDES.**

**UXORICIDES' CHILDREN.** *See* **CHILDREN OF UXORICIDES.**

**Uyechi, Linda, 1957-** The geometry of visual phonology / Linda Uyechi. Stanford, Calif. : CSLI Publications, 1996. x, 240 p. : ill. ; 24 cm. Revision of author's 1994 thesis. Includes bibliographical references and index. ISBN 1-57586-012-0 ISBN 1-57586-013-9 (hardback) DDC 419
*1. Sign language. 2. American Sign Language. 3. Grammar, Comparative and general - Phonology. I. Title.*
**TC HV2474 .U88 1996**

**Uys, Errol Lincoln.** Riding the rails : teenagers on the move during the Great Depression / Errol Lincoln Uys. New York : TV Books ; c1999. 303 p., [32] p. of plates : ill. ; 24 cm. Includes references and index. ISBN 1-57500-037-7
*1. Depressions - 1929. 2. United States - Economic conditions - 1918-1945. 3. United States - History - 1929-1933.*
**TC HC106.3 U97 1999**

**Užgiris, Ina Č.**
Communication. Stamford, Conn. : Ablex Pub. Corp., c2000.
**TC BF712 .A36 v.19**

**Uzzell, Barbara P.**
International handbook of neuropsychological rehabilitation. New York : Kluwer Academic/Plenum Publishers, c2000.
**TC RC387.5 .I478 2000**

**V GUIDEBOOKS.**
Montgomery, Susan J., 1947- Phillips Academy. New York : Princeton Architectural Press, 2000.
**TC LD7501.A5 M65 2000**

**Vabø, Agnete.**
Bleiklie, Ivar, 1948- Policy and practice in higher education. London ; Phildadelphia : J. Kingsley Publishers, 2000.
**TC LC178.N8 B44 2000**

**VACATION SCHOOLS.**
Baynes, Joyce Frisby. The development of a van Hiele-based summer geometry program and its impact

on student van Hiele level and achievement in high school geometry. 1998.
**TC 06 no. 10915**

**VACATIONS.** *See* **HOLIDAYS.**

**VACATIONS, EMPLOYEE.** *See* **LEAVE OF ABSENCE; SICK LEAVE.**

**VACATIONS - FICTION.**
Delton, Judy. Angel spreads her wings. Boston : Houghton Mifflin, 1999.
**TC PZ7.D388 Anf 1999**

**VADE-MECUMS, ETC.** *See* **HANDBOOKS, VADE-MECUMS, ETC.**

**Vail, Rachel.**
**Friendship ring.**
Vail, Rachel. If you only knew. 1st ed. New York : Scholastic, c1998.
**TC PZ7.V1916 If 1998**

Vail, Rachel. Please, please, please. New York : Scholastic, c1998.
**TC PZ7.V1916 Pl 1998**

If you only knew / Rachel Vail. 1st ed. New York : Scholastic, c1998. 226 p. ; 13 cm. (The friendship ring) SUMMARY: Seventh-grader Zoe, who comes from a big family where she's never had anything all to herself, desperately wants CJ for a best friend, but when CJ reveals that she likes the boy Zoe likes, she must make a choice. ISBN 0-590-03370-0 DDC [Fic]
*1. Friendship - Fiction. 2. Interpersonal relations - Fiction. 3. Schools - Fiction. 4. Family life - Fiction. I. Title. II. Series: Vail, Rachel. Friendship ring.*
**TC PZ7.V1916 If 1998**

Please, please, please / Rachel Vail. New York : Scholastic, c1998. 259 p. ; 14 cm. (The friendship ring) SUMMARY: Twelve-year-old CJ, an accomplished ballet student, struggles with her conflicting desires to continue her ballet study and please her mother or to quit ballet and finally be like all the other kids in school. ISBN 0-590-00327-5 DDC [Fic]
*1. Identity - Fiction. 2. Mothers and daughters - Fiction. 3. Ballet dancing - Fiction. 4. Friendship - Fiction. 5. Schools - Fiction. I. Title. II. Series: Vail, Rachel. Friendship ring.*
**TC PZ7.V1916 Pl 1998**

**Valencia, Richard R.** Intelligence testing and minority students : foundations, performance factors, and assessment issues / Richard R. Valencia, Lisa A. Suzuki. Thousand Oaks, Calif. : Sage Publications, [2000] xxvii, 388 p. : ill. ; 26 cm. (Racial and ethnic minority psychology series) Includes bibliographical references (p. 323-363) and indexes. ISBN 0-7619-1230-4 (alk. paper) DDC 153.9/3/086930973
*1. Minorities - Psychological testing - United States. 2. Intelligence levels - United States. 3. Intelligence tests - United States. 4. Intellect - Genetic aspects. 5. Cognition. I. Suzuki, Lisa A., 1961- II. Title. III. Series.*
**TC BF431.5.U6 V35 2000**

**Valente, Christina M.**
Valente, William D. Law in the schools. 4th ed. Upper Saddle River, N.J. : Merrill, c1998.
**TC KF4119 .V28 1998**

**Valente, William D.** Law in the schools / William D. Valente with Christina M. Valente. 4th ed. Upper Saddle River, N.J. : Merrill, c1998. xviii, 398 p. ; 25 cm. Includes bibliographical references and index. ISBN 0-13-266321-X DDC 344.73/07
*1. Educational law and legislation - United States. I. Valente, Christina M. II. Title.*
**TC KF4119 .V28 1998**

**Valentine, Gill, 1965-.**
Children's geographies. London ; New York : Routledge, 2000.
**TC HQ767.9 .C4559 2000**

**Valenzuela, Angela.** Subtractive schooling : U.S.-Mexican youth and the politics of caring / Angela Valenzuela. Albany : State University of New York Press, c1999. xviii, 328 p. ; 24 cm. (SUNY series, the social context of education) Includes bibliographical references (p. 307-319) and index. ISBN 0-7914-4321-3 (hc : alk. paper) ISBN 0-7914-4322-1 (pb. : alk. paper) DDC 371.829/6872073
*1. Mexican Americans - Education (Secondary) - Texas - Case studies. 2. Children of immigrants - Education (Secondary) - Texas - Case studies. 3. Mexican American youth - Social conditions - Texas - Case studies. I. Title. II. Series: SUNY series, social context of education.*
**TC LC2683.4 .V35 1999**

**Valette, Jean-Paul.** Discovering French. Bleu / Jean-Paul Valette, Rebecca M. Valette. Extended teacher's ed. Evanston, Ill. : McDougal Littell, c1997. 64, Txiv, T397, R51 p. : col. ill., col. maps ; 29 cm. Includes index. ISBN 0-669-43476-0

*1. French language - Textbooks for foreign speakers - English. I. Valette, Rebecca M. II. Title.*
**TC PC1129.E5 V342 1997 Teacher's Ed.**

Discovering French. Rouge / Jean-Paul Valette, Rebecca M. Valette. Evanston, Ill. : McDougal Littell, c1997. xv, 420, R92 p. : col. ill., col. maps ; 27 cm. Includes index. ISBN 0-669-43528-7
*1. French language - Textbooks for foreign speakers - English. I. Valette, Rebecca M. II. Title.*
**TC PC2129.E5 V342 1997**

**Valette, Jean Paul.** Discovering French. Rouge / Jean-Paul Valette, Rebecca M. Valette. Lexington, Mass. : D.C. Heath and Co., c1997. T64, xv, 420, R92 p. : col. ill. ; 27 cm. "Teacher's annotated edition." Includes index. ISBN 0-669-43529-5 DDC 448.2/421
*1. French language - Textbooks for foreign speakers - English. I. Valette, Rebecca M. II. Title.*
**TC PC2129.E5 V342 1997**

Spanish for mastery / Jean-Paul Valette, Rebecca Valette ; contributing writer, Frederick Suárez Richard ; editor-consultants, Teresa Carrera Hanley, Clara Inés Olaya. Lexington, Mass. : D.C. Heath, c1980. 2 v. : ill. (some col.) ; 24 cm. Includes index. SUMMARY: A high school text providing an introduction to the language and culture of the Spanish-speaking world. ISBN 0-669-02206-3 (V. 1) ISBN 0-669-02211-x (V. 2)
*1. Spanish language - Textbooks for foreign speakers - English. 2. Spanish language - Grammar. I. Valette, Rebecca M. II. Suárez-Richard, Frederick, 1941- III. Hanley, Teresa Carrera. IV. Olaya, Clara Inés. V. Title.*
**TC PC4112 .V29 1980**

**Valette, Rebecca M.**
Valette, Jean-Paul. Discovering French. Bleu. Extended teacher's ed. Evanston, Ill. : McDougal Littell, c1997.
**TC PC1129.E5 V342 1997 Teacher's Ed.**

Valette, Jean-Paul. Discovering French. Rouge. Evanston, Ill. : McDougal Littell, c1997.
**TC PC2129.E5 V342 1997**

Valette, Jean-Paul. Discovering French. Rouge. Lexington, Mass. : D.C. Heath and Co., c1997.
**TC PC2129.E5 V342 1997**

Valette, Jean Paul. Spanish for mastery. Lexington, Mass. : D.C. Heath, c1980.
**TC PC4112 .V29 1980**

**VALIDITY OF EXAMINATIONS.** *See* **EXAMINATIONS - VALIDITY.**

**Valiga, Theresa M.**
Grossman, Sheila. The new leadership challenge. Philadelphia : F.A. Davis, c2000.
**TC RT89 .G77 2000**

**Vallecorsa, Ada, 1948-** Students with mild disabilities in general education settings : a guide for special educators / Ada L. Vallecorsa, Laurie U. deBettencourt, Naomi Zigmond ; [editor, Ann Castel Davis]. Upper Saddle River, N.J. : Merrill, c2000. x, 290 p. : ill. ; 24 cm. Includes bibliographical references (p. 265-276) and indexes. ISBN 0-02-422371-9 DDC 371.92/6
*1. Learning disabled children - Education - United States. 2. Problem children - Education - United States. 3. Handicapped children - Education - United States. 4. Mainstreaming in education - United States. I. DeBettencourt, Laurie Ungerleider. II. Zigmond, Naomi, 1941- III. Davis, Ann Castel. IV. Title.*
**TC LC4705 .V35 2000**

**Vallejo, Alejandro.**
Comics, the 9th art [videorecording]. [S.l.] : EPISA ; Cicero, Ill. : [Distributed by] The Roland Collection, 1990.
**TC PN6710 .C6 1990**

**VALLEYS - BRAZIL.** *See* **UAUPÉS RIVER VALLEY (COLOMBIA AND BRAZIL).**

**VALLEYS - COLOMBIA.** *See* **UAUPÉS RIVER VALLEY (COLOMBIA AND BRAZIL).**

**VALLEYS - MEXICO.** *See* **RIO GRANDE VALLEY.**

**VALLEYS - UNITED STATES.** *See* **RIO GRANDE VALLEY.**

**VALLEYS - YUKON TERRITORY.** *See* **KLONDIKE RIVER VALLEY (YUKON).**

**Valmont, William J.**
Linking literacy and technology. Newark, Del. : International Reading Association, c2000.
**TC LB1576.7 .L56 2000**

**Valsiner, Jaan.** Culture and human development : an introduction / Jaan Valsiner. London ; Thousand Oaks, Calif. : Sage, 2000. xiv, 319 p. : ill. ; 26 cm.

Includes bibliographical references (p. [303]-315) and index.
ISBN 0-7619-5683-2 ISBN 0-7619-5684-0 (pbk)
*1. Developmental psychology - Cross-cultural studies. 2.
Ethnopsychology. 3. Child development - Cross-cultural
studies. I. Title.*
**TC BF713 .V35 2000**

**The value of psychological treatment.**
Cummings, Nicholas A. Phoenix, AZ : Zeig,
Tucker & Co., 1999.
**TC RA790.6 .C85 1999**

**VALUES.** *See also* **ETHICS; SOCIAL VALUES.**
Business education and training. Lanham, Md. :
University Press of America, c1997-<c2000   >
**TC LC1059 .B87**

Hammersley, Martyn. Taking sides in social research.
London ; New York : Routledge, 2000.
**TC H62 .H2338 2000**

Values and educational leadership. Albany : State
University of New York Press, c1999.
**TC LB2806 .V25 1999**

The values of educational administration. London :
Falmer, 1999.
**TC LB2806 .V255 1999**

**Values and educational leadership** / edited by Paul T.
Begley. Albany : State University of New York Press,
c1999. xix, 341 p. : ill. ; 24 cm. (SUNY series, educational
leadership) Includes bibliographical references and index.
ISBN 0-7914-4291-8 (hard : alk. paper) ISBN 0-7914-4292-6
(pbk. : alk. paper) DDC 371.2
*1. Educational leadership. 2. School management and
organization. 3. Values. I. Begley, Paul Thomas, 1949- II.
Series: SUNY series in educational leadership.*
**TC LB2806 .V25 1999**

**Values based strategic planning.**
Quong, Terry. Singapore ; New York : Prentice Hall,
1998.
**TC LB2806 .Q86 1998**

**The values of educational administration** / edited by
Paul T. Begley and Pauline E. Leonard. London :
Falmer, 1999. xvii, 263 p. : ill. ; 24 cm. Includes
bibliographical references and index. ISBN 0-7507-0937-5
ISBN 0-7507-0936-7 (pbk.).
*1. Educational leadership. 2. School management and
organization. 3. Values. I. Begley, Paul Thomas, 1949- II.
Leonard, Pauline E.*
**TC LB2806 .V255 1999**

**VALUES - STUDY AND TEACHING.**
Haydon, Graham. Values, virtues and violence.
Oxford : Malden, MA : Blackwell Publishers, 1999.
**TC LC268 .H294 1999**

Institutional issues. London ; New York : Falmer
Press, 2000.
**TC LC191 .I495 2000**

Systems of education. London ; New York : Falmer
Press, 2000.
**TC LC191 .S98 2000**

**VALUES - STUDY AND TEACHING - UNITED
STATES.**
Annual State of American Education Address (7th :
February 22, 2000 : Durham, N.C.) The seventh
annual state of American education address
[videorecording. [Washington, D.C. : U.S. Dept. of
Education], 2000.

**Values, virtues and violence.**
Haydon, Graham. Oxford ; Malden, MA : Blackwell
Publishers, 1999.
**TC LC268 .H294 1999**

**Valuing the cost of smoking** : assessment methods, risk
perception, and policy options / edited by Claude
Jeanrenaud and Nils Soguel. Boston : Kluwer
Academic Publishers, 1999. viii, 218 p. : ill. ; 25 cm.
(Studies in risk and uncertainty) "This volume is the outcome
of a conference held in Lausanne, Switzerland in August
1998"--Introd. Includes bibliographical references. ISBN
0-7923-8644-2 (acid-free paper) DDC 338.4/36797
*1. Smoking - Costs. 2. Smoking - Health aspects - Costs. 3.
Smoking - Economic aspects. I. Jeanrenaud, Claude. II.
Soguel, Nils C. III. Series.*
**TC HV5735 .V35 1999**

**Van de Poel-Knottnerus, Frédérique.**
Knottnerus, J. David. The social worlds of male and
female children in the nineteenth century French
educational system. Lewiston, N.Y. ; Lampeter,
Wales : Edwin Mellen Press, c1999.
**TC LC191.8.F8 K66 1999**

**Van der Bogert, Rebecca.**
Partners in progress. San Francisco, Calif. : Jossey-
Bass Inc., c1999.

**TC LC3981 .P27 1999**
Reflections of first-year teachers on school culture.
San Francisco : Jossey-Bass Inc., 1999.
**TC LB2844.1.N4 R44 1999**

**Van der Does, Louise Q.** Renaissance women in
science / Louise Q. van der Does, Rita J. Simon.
Lanham, Md. : University Press of America, c1999.
iii, 192 p. : ill. ; 24 cm. Includes bibliographical references.
ISBN 0-7618-1480-9 (alk. paper) ISBN 0-7618-1481-7 (pbk. :
alk. paper) DDC 500/.82/0922
*1. Women scientists - Biography. I. Simon, Rita James. II. Title.*
**TC Q141 .V25 1999**

**Van der Lely, Heather K. J.**
Specific language impairment in children. Hillsdale,
N.J. : Lawrence Erlbaum , 1998.
**TC RJ496.L35 S643 1998**

**Van Dusen, Gerald C.** Digital dilemma : issues of
access, cost, and quality in media-enhanced and
distance education / Gerald C. Van Dusen. San
Francisco : Jossey-Bass, c2000. x, 141 p. : ill. ; 23 cm.
(ASHE-ERIC higher education report, 0884-0040 ; v. 27, no.
5) "Prepared ... in cooperation with ERIC Clearinghouse on
Higher Education, the George Washington University,
Association for the Study of Higher Education, Graduate
School of Education and Human Development, the George
Washington University." Includes bibliographical references
(p. 103-120) and index. CONTENTS: Introduction -- Issues of
access and equity -- Issues of cost and affordability -- Issues of
quality and effectiveness -- Conclusions and recommendations.
ISBN 0-7879-5573-6 (pbk.)
*1. Distance education - United States. 2. Educational
technology - United States. 3. Information technology - United
States. I. ERIC Clearinghouse on Higher Education. II.
Association for the Study of Higher Education. III. George
Washington University. Graduate School of Education and
Human Development. IV. Title. V. Series: ASHE-ERIC higher
education report ; vol. 27, no. 5.*
**TC LC5805 .V35 2000**

**Van Engen, John H.**
Learning institutionalized. Notre Dame, Ind. :
University of Notre Dame Press, c2000.
**TC LA177 .L43 2000**

**Van Geel, Tyll.**
Imber, Michael. Education law. 2nd ed. Mahwah,
N.J. : Lawrence Erlbaum Associates, 2000.
**TC KF4118 .I43 2000**

**Van Hiele-based summer geometry program and its
impact on student van Hiele level and achievement
in high school geometryp.**
Baynes, Joyce Frisby. The development of a van
Hiele-based summer geometry program and its impact
on student van Hiele level and achievement in high
school geometry. 1998.
**TC 06 no. 10915**

**Van Hoorn, Judith Lieberman.**
Adolescent development and rapid social change.
Albany : State University of New York Press, c2000.
**TC HQ799.H8 A35 2000**

**Van Orden, Phyllis.** Selecting books for the elementary
school library media center : a complete guide /
Phyllis Van Orden. New York : Neal-Schuman
Publishers, c2000. xvii, 211 p., : col. ill. ; 28 cm. Includes
bibliographical references (p. 183-185) and index. ISBN
1-55570-368-2 (alk. paper) DDC 025.2/1878222
*1. Elementary school libraries - Book selection - United States.
2. Instructional materials centers - Book selection - United
States. I. Title.*
**TC Z675.S3 V36 2000**

**Van Patten, James J.**
Challenges and opportunities for education in the 21st
century. Lewiston, NY : Edwin Mellen Press, c1999.
**TC LA209.2 .C45 1999**

Watersheds in higher education. Lewiston, N.Y. : E.
Mellen Press, c1997.
**TC LA228 .W28 1997**

**Van Reken, Ruth E., 1945-.**
Pollock, David C. The third culture kid experience.
Yarmouth, Me. : Intercultural Press, c1999.
**TC HQ784.S56 P65 1999**

**Van Vliet - , Willem, 1952-.**
Affordable housing and urban redevelopment in the
United States. Thousand Oaks, Calif. : Sage
Publications, c1997.
**TC HD7293 .A55 1997**

**Vancko, Candace Shedd.**
Miller, Richard I. Evaluating, improving, and judging
faculty performance in two-year colleges. Westport,
Conn. ; London : Bergin & Garvey, 2000.

**TC LB2333 .M49 2000**

**Vancouver studies in cognitive science**
(v. 10) Metarepresentations. Oxford ; New York :
Oxford University Press, c2000.
**TC BF316.6 .M48 2000**

**VandenBos, Gary R.**
Videos in psychology. 1st ed. Washington, DC :
American Psychological Association, c2000.
**TC BF80.3 .V53 2000**

**Vanderbilt issues in higher education**
The American college in the nineteenth century. 1st
ed. Nashville : Vanderbilt University Press, 2000.
**TC LA227.1 .A64 2000**

Baxter Magolda, Marcia B., 1951- Creating contexts
for learning and self-authorship. 1st ed. Nashville
[Tenn.] : Vanderbilt University Press, 1999.
**TC LB1025.3 .B39 1999**

**Vandereycken, Walter, 1949-.**
The prevention of eating disorders. New York : New
York University Press, 1998.
**TC RC552.E18 P74 1998**

**Vanderjagt, Arie Johan.**
Between demonstration and imagination. Leiden,
Netherlands ; Boston : Brill, 1999.
**TC QB15 .B56 1999**

**Vanderploeg, Rodney D.**
Clinician's guide to neuropsychological assessment.
2nd ed. Mahwah, N.J. : Lawrence Erlbaum
Associates, c2000.
**TC RC386.6.N48 G85 2000**

**Vanourek, Gregg.**
Finn, Chester E., 1944- Charter schools in action.
Princeton, N.J. : Princeton University Press, c2000.
**TC LB2806.36 .F527 2000**

**VAQUEIROS.** *See* **COWBOYS.**

**VAQUEROS.** *See* **COWBOYS.**

**Varavikova, Elena.**
Tulchinsky, Theodore H. The new public health. San
Diego, Calif. ; London : Academic Press, c2000.
**TC RA425 .T85 2000**

**Vardaman, James M., 1947-.**
Japanese education since 1945. Armonk, N.Y. : M.E.
Sharpe, c1994.
**TC LA1311.82 .J39 1994**

**Varela, Francisco J., 1945-
[Know-how per l'etica. English]**
Ethical know-how : action, wisdom, and cognition /
Francisco J. Varela. Stanford, Calif. : Stanford
University Press, 1999. ix, 85 p. ; 21 cm. (Writing
science) Originally presented as three lectures, delivered at
the Università di Bologna. Includes bibliographical
references (p. 79-85). CONTENTS: Know-how and know-
what -- On ethical expertise -- The embodiment of
emptiness. ISBN 0-8047-3032-6 (cloth : alk. paper) ISBN
0-8047-3033-4 (pbk. : alk. paper) DDC 170
*1. Ethics. 2. Knowledge, Theory of. I. Title. II. Series.*
**TC BJ1012 .V3813 1999**

**Vargas, Luis A., 1951-.**
Koss-Chioino, Joan. Working with Latino youth. 1st
ed. San Francisco : Jossey-Bass, c1999.
**TC RC451.5.H57 K67 1999**

**Variability in the social construction of the child** /
Sara Harkness, Catherine Raeff, Charles M. Super,
eds. San Francisco : Jossey-Bass, 2000. 115 p. ; 23 cm.
(New directions for child and adolescent development, 0195-
2269 ; no. 87) (Jossey-Bass education series) "Spring 2000"
Includes bibliographical references and index. CONTENTS:
Editors' notes / Sara Harkness, Catherine Raeff, Charles M.
Super. -- Independence and interdependence in diverse cultural
contexts / Melanie Killen, Cecilia Wainryb -- Individualism
and the "Western Mind reconsidered : American and Dutch
parents' ethnotheories of the child / Sara Harkness, Charles M.
Super, Nathalie van Tijen. -- Homogeneity and heterogenity in
cultural belief systems / Robin L. Harwood, Axel
Sch"olmerich, Pamela A. Schultze. -- Conceptualizing
interpersonal relationships in the cultural contexts of
individualism and collectivism / Catherine Raeff, Patricia
Marks CONTENTS: Greenfield, Blanca Quiroz -- Uniformity
and diversity in everyday views of the child / Kelvin L.
Seifert. -- Cross-cultural conflict and harmony in the social
construction of the child / Patricia Marks Greenfield, Blanca
Quiroz, Catherine Raeff. ISBN 0-7879-5506-X (pbk.)
*1. Parenting - United States. 2. Child rearing - United States.
3. Child psychology. 4. Developmental psychology. 5. Social
skills in children. 6. Children - Cross-cultural studies. I.
Harkness, Sara. II. Raeff, Catherine. III. Super, Charles M. IV.
Series. V. Series: New directions for child and adolescent
development ; no. 87*

*TC BF723.S62 .V37 2000*

**VARIANCE ANALYSIS.** *See* **ANALYSIS OF VARIANCE.**

**VARIATION (BIOLOGY).** *See* **EVOLUTION.**

**VARIATION (GENETICS).**
Evolutionary aspects of nutrition and health. Basel ; New York : Karger, c1999.
*TC QP141 .E95 1999*

**VARIETY SHOWS (THEATER).** *See* **VAUDEVILLE.**

**VARIETY-THEATERS.** *See* **VAUDEVILLE.**

**Varley, Rosemary.**
Crystal, David, 1941- Introduction to language pathology. 4th ed. London : Whurr Publishers, c1998.
*TC RC423 .C76 1998*

**Varnedoe, Kirk, 1946-** Jackson Pollock / Kirk Varnedoe, with Pepe Karmel. New York : Museum of Modern Art ; Distributed in the U.S. and Canada by Harry N. Abrams, c1998. 336 p. : ill. (some col.), ports. ; 26 x 31 cm. "Published on the occasion of the exhibition Jackson Pollock, organized by Kirk Varnedoe, Chief Curator, with Pepe Karmel, Adjunct Assistant Curator, Department of Painting and Sculpture, The Museum of Modern Art, New York, November 1, 1998 to February 2, 1999. The exhibition travels to the Tate Gallery, London, March 11 to June 6, 1999"--T.p. verso. Includes bibliographical references (p. 330-332) and index. ISBN 0-87070-068-5 (MoMA : cloth) ISBN 0-87070-069-3 (MoMA : pbk.) ISBN 0-8109-6193-8 (Abrams : cloth) ISBN 1-85437-275-0 (Tate : cloth) ISBN 1-85437-276-9 (Tate : pbk.) DDC 759.13
*1. Pollock, Jackson, - 1912-1956 - Exhibitions. I. Karmel, Pepe. II. Pollock, Jackson, 1912-1956. III. Museum of Modern Art (New York, N.Y.) IV. Tate Gallery. V. Title.*
*TC ND237.P73 A4 1998*

Jasper Johns : a retrospective / Kirk Varnedoe ; with an essay by Roberta Bernstein. New York : Museum of Modern Art : Distributed by Harry N. Abrams, c1996. 408 p. : ill. (some col.) ; 32 cm. Published in conjunction with an exhibition at the Museum of Modern Art, New York, Oct. 20, 1996-Jan. 21, 1997. Includes bibliographical references (p. 397-403) and index. ISBN 0-87070-388-9 (MOMA, T&H) ISBN 0-87070-389-7 (MOMA pbk.) ISBN 0-8109-6165-2 (Abrams) DDC 709/.2074
*1. Johns, Jasper, - 1930- - Exhibitions. I. Johns, Jasper, 1930- II. Bernstein, Roberta. III. Museum of Modern Art (New York, N.Y.) IV. Title.*
*TC N6537.J6 A4 1996*

**VASCULAR RESISTANCE.** *See* **BLOOD PRESSURE.**

**VASCULAR SYSTEM.** *See* **CARDIOVASCULAR SYSTEM.**

**VAUDEVILLE - UNITED STATES.**
Gilbert, Douglas, 1889-1948. American vaudeville, its life and times. New York, Dover Publications [c1940, c1968]
*TC PN1967 .G5 1968*

**Vaughan, Dai.**
Summerhill at 70 [videorecording]. Princeton, N.J. : Films for the Humanities, c1992.
*TC LF795.L692953 S9 1992*

**Vaughan, David, 1924-** Merce Cunningham : fifty years / chronicle and commentary by David Vaughan ; edited by Melissa Harris. 1st ed. New York, NY : Aperture, c1997. 315, [4] p. : ill. (some col.) ; 31 cm. Includes bibliographical references (p. 305-306) and index. ISBN 0-89381-624-8 ISBN 0-89381-767-8 (pbk.)
*1. Cunningham, Merce. 2. Dancers - United States - Biography. 3. Choreographers - United States - Biography. 4. Choreography - Pictorial works. I. Harris, Melissa. II. Title.*
*TC GV1785.C85 V38 1997*

**Vaughan, J. G. (John Griffith)** The new Oxford book of food plants / J.G. Vaughan and C. Geissler ; illustrated by B.E. Nicholson ; with additional illustrations by Elisabeth Dowle and Elizabeth Rice. Oxford ; New York : Oxford University Press, 1997. xx, 239 p. : col. ill. ; 26 cm. Rev. and updated ed. of: The Oxford book of food plants / illustrations by B.E. Nicholson. 1969. Includes bibliographical references (p. 227-228) and index. ISBN 0-19-854825-7 (hbk) DDC 633
*1. Food crops. I. Geissler, Catherine. II. Nicholson, Barbara. III. Nicholson, Barbara. Oxford book of food plants. IV. Title.*
*TC SB175 .V38 1997*

**Vaughan, Victor C., 1919-.**
Symposium on Issues in Human Development (1967 : Philadelphia) Issues in human development; Washington, For sale by the Supt. of Docs., U. S. Govt. Print. Off. [1970?]
*TC RJ131.A1 S93 1967*

**Vaughn, Dawn.**
Bankhead, Elizabeth. Write it!. 2nd ed./MLA version. Englewood, Colo. : Libraries Unlimited, c1999.
*TC LB1047.3 .W75 1999*

**Vaughn, Lewis.**
Schick, Theodore. How to think about weird things. 2nd ed. Mountain View, Calif. : Mayfield Pub., c1999.
*TC BC177 .S32 1999*

**Vaughn, Sharon, 1952-.**
Contemporary special education research. Mahwah, N.J. : Lawrence Erlbaum, c2000.
*TC LC4019 .C575 2000*

Teaching exceptional, diverse, and at-risk students in the general education classroom / Sharon Vaughn, Candace S. Bos, Jeanne Shay Schumm. 2nd ed. Boston : Allyn and Bacon, 2000. xxvii 550 p. : ill. (som col.) ; 26 cm. Rev. ed. of: Teaching mainstreamed, diverse, and at-risk students in the general education classroom. c1997. Includes bibliographical references and index. ISBN 0-205-30620-9 (alk. paper) DDC 371.9/046
*1. Mainstreaming in education - United States. 2. Special education - United States. 3. Handicapped children - Education - United States. 4. Socially handicapped children - Education - United States. 5. Learning disabled children - Education - United States. 6. Inclusive education - United States. I. Bos, Candace S., 1950- II. Schumm, Jeanne Shay, 1947- III. Vaughn, Sharon, 1952- Teaching mainstreamed, diverse, and at-risk students in the general education classroom. IV. Title.*
*TC LC3981 .V28 2000*

**Teaching mainstreamed, diverse, and at risk students in the general education classroom.**
Vaughn, Sharon, 1952- Teaching exceptional, diverse, and at-risk students in the general education classroom. 2nd ed. Boston : Allyn and Bacon, 2000.
*TC LC3981 .V28 2000*

**VD (DISEASE).** *See* **SEXUALLY TRANSMITTED DISEASES.**

**Veal, Anthony James.**
Toohey, K. (Kristine). The Olympic games :. Oxon, UK ; New York, NY : CABI Pub., c2000.
*TC GV721.5 .T64 1999*

**Vedder, Richard K.** Out of work : unemployment and government in twentieth-century America / Richard Vedder and Lowell Gallaway ; foreword by Martin Bronfenbrenner. New York : Holmes & Meier, 1993. xv, 336 p. : ill. ; 24 cm. (Independent studies in political economy) Includes bibliographical references (p. 308-328) and index. ISBN 0-8419-1324-2 DDC 331.13/7973/0904
*1. Unemployment - United States - History - 20th century. 2. Employment (Economic theory) 3. United States - Economic conditions. I. Gallaway, Lowell E. (Lowell Eugene), 1930- II. Title. III. Series.*
*TC HD7096.U5 V43 1993*

**VEGETABLES - FICTION.**
Root, Phyllis. Soup for supper. 1st ed. New York : Harper & Row, c1986.
*TC PZ7.R6784 So 1986*

**Velasquez, Eric, ill.**
Weatherford, Carole Boston, 1956- The sound that jazz makes. New York : Walker & Co., c2000.
*TC ML3506 .W42 2000*

**Velazquez, Rita C.**
Directory of American scholars. 9th ed. / edited by Rita C. Velazquez. Detroit, Mich. : Gale Group, 1999.
*TC LA2311 .D57 1999*

**V'elez Arias, Hiram Oscar.** A multi-case study of physical education teachers and working conditions in inner-city schools /by Hiram Oscar V'elez Arias. 1998. xiii, 281 leaves : ill. ; 29 cm. Issued also on microfilm. Thesis (Ed.D.)--Teachers College, Columbia University, 1998. Includes bibliographical references (leaves 245-267).
*1. Education, Urban - New Jersey. 2. Physical education teachers - New Jersey - Attitudes. 3. Physical education and training - Curricula. 4. Effective teaching. 5. Teacher effectiveness. 6. Lesson planning. I. Title.*
*TC 06 no. 11001*

**Velichkovskiĭ, B. M. (Boris Mitrofanovich).**
Stratification in cognition and consciousness. Amsterdam ; Philadelphia : J. Benjamins, c1999.
*TC BF444 .S73 1999*

**Vella, Jane Kathryn, 1931-** Taking learning to task : creative strategies for teaching adults / Jane Vella. San Francisco, Calif. : Jossey-Bass, c2000. xxi, 151 p. ; 23 cm. (The Jossey-Bass higher and adult education series) Includes bibliographical references and index. ISBN 0-7879-5227-3 (alk. paper) DDC 374/.13
*1. Adult learning. 2. Adult education. 3. Learning strategies. I. Title. II. Series.*

*TC LC5225.L42 V43 2000*

**VELLUM.** *See* **PARCHMENT.**

**VELLUM PRINTED BOOKS - CONSERVATION AND RESTORATION - BIBLIOGRAPHY.**
Ralston, Nicola L. Parchment/vellum conservation survey and bibliography. Edinburgh : Historic Scotland : Crown Copyright, c2000.
*TC Z701.4.I5 R35 2000*

**VELLUM PRINTED BOOKS - PRESERVATION - BIBLIOGRAPHY.**
Ralston, Nicola L. Parchment/vellum conservation survey and bibliography. Edinburgh : Historic Scotland : Crown Copyright, c2000.
*TC Z701.4.I5 R35 2000*

**Venema, Ted.** Compression for clinicians / Ted Venema. San Diego, Calif. : Singular Pub. Group, c1998. viii, 153 p. : ill. ; 23 cm. (A Singular audiology text) Includes bibliographical references and index. ISBN 1-56593-973-5 (pbk. : alk. paper) DDC 617.8/9
*1. Hearing aids - Fitting. 2. Compression (Audiology) 3. Hearing aids - Design and construction. 4. Hearing Aids. 5. Prosthesis Fitting - methods. 6. Cochlea - physiology. 7. Loudness Perception. 8. Equipment Design. I. Title. II. Series. III. Series: Singular audiology text.*
*TC RF300 .V46 1998*

**VENEREAL DISEASES.** *See* **SEXUALLY TRANSMITTED DISEASES.**

**VENGEANCE.** *See* **REVENGE.**

**Venn, John.** Assessing students with special needs / John Venn. 2nd ed. Upper Saddle River, N.J. : Merrill, c2000. xv, 656 p. : ill. ; 25 cm. Rev. ed. of: Assessment of students with special needs. c1994. Includes bibliographical references and indexes. ISBN 0-13-781204-3 DDC 371.9
*1. Handicapped children - Education - United States. 2. Educational tests and measurements - United States. 3. Handicapped children - Psychological testing - United States. 4. Behavioral assessment of children - United States. I. Venn, John. Assessment of students with special needs. II. Title.*
*TC LC4031 .V46 2000*

**Assessment of students with special needs.**
Venn, John. Assessing students with special needs. 2nd ed. Upper Saddle River, N.J. : Merrill, c2000.
*TC LC4031 .V46 2000*

**VENTILATORS, MECHANICAL (MEDICAL EQUIPMENT).** *See* **RESPIRATORS (MEDICAL EQUIPMENT).**

**VENTILATORS, PULMONARY.** *See* **RESPIRATORS (MEDICAL EQUIPMENT).**

**Venus on wheels.**
Frank, Gelya, 1948- Berkeley, Calif. : University of California Press, c2000.
*TC HV3021.W66 F73 2000*

**VERBAL BEHAVIOR.** *See* **INTERACTION ANALYSIS IN EDUCATION; VERBAL LEARNING.**

**VERBAL BEHAVIOR - PERIODICALS.**
Journal of verbal learning and verbal behavior. New York, Academic Press.

**VERBAL BEHAVIOR - RESEACH.**
Tian, Shiau-ping. TOEFL reading comprehension. 2000.
*TC 06 no. 11316*

**VERBAL COMMUNICATION.** *See* **ORAL COMMUNICATION.**

**VERBAL LEARNING.** *See* **VERBAL BEHAVIOR.**

**VERBAL LEARNING - PERIODICALS.**
Journal of verbal learning and verbal behavior. New York, Academic Press.

**Verband der Beamten und Angestellten des Kantons Luzern.**
Korrespondenz-blatt. Luzern : Luzerner Staatspersonalverband, 1947-

**Vercoustre, Anne-Marie, 1946-.**
ECDL '99 (3rd : 1999 : Paris, France) Research and advanced technology for digital libraries. Berlin ; New York : Springer, c1999.
*TC ZA4080 .E28 1999*

**Verdejo, Maria Feliza.**
IFIP TC3/WG3.3 & WG3.6 Joint Working Conference on the Virtual Campus: Trends for Higher Education and Training (1997 : Madrid, Spain) The virtual campus. 1st ed. London ; New York : Chapman & Hall on behalf of the International Federation for Information Processing (IFIP), 1998.
*TC LC5803.C65 I353 1997*

**VERDICTS - UNITED STATES.**
Flaton, Robin Anne. Effect of deliberation on juror reasoning. 1999.
*TC 085 F612*

**Vereniging van Leraren in Levende Talen.**
Levende talen magazine. Amsterdam : Vereniging van Leraren in Levenden Talen, 2000-

**Vergon, Charles B.**
School discipline. Ann Arbor, Mich. : University of Michigan School of Education, 1989.
*TC LB3011 .S425*

**Verkuyten, M.**
Comparative perspectives on racism. Aldershot, Hants, UK ; Burlington, VT, USA : Ashgate, c2000.
*TC GN269 .C646 2000*

**Verma, Gajendra K.**
Chinese adolescents in Britain and Hong Kong. Aldershot ; Brookfield, USA : Ashgate, c1999.
*TC DA125.C5 C47 1999*

**Verma, Som Prakash, 1942-.**
Flora and fauna in Mughal art. [Bombay] : Marg Publications, c1999.
*TC N7302 .F567 1999*

**VERNACULAR ARCHITECTURE - AFRICA, NORTHEAST.**
Prussin, Labelle. African nomadic architecture. Washington : Smithsonian Institution Press : National Museum of African Art, c1995.
*TC NA7461.A1 P78 1995*

**VERNACULAR ARCHITECTURE - INDIA.**
Cooper, Ilay. Traditional buildings of India. New York : Thames and Hudson, c1998.
*TC NA1501 .C58 1998*

**VERNACULAR LANGUAGE.** *See* **NATIVE LANGUAGE.**

**Vernez, Georges.** Closing the education gap : benefits and costs / Georges Vernez, Richard A. Krop, Peter Rydell. Santa Monica, CA : RAND, 1999. xxvi, 198 : ill. ; 23 cm. "MR-1036-EDU." Includes bibliographic references. ISBN 0-8330-2748-4 DDC 379.2/6/0973
*1. Educational equalization - United States. 2. Minorities - Education - Economic aspects - United States. I. Krop, Richard A., 1962- II. Rydell, C. Peter. III. Title.*
*TC LC213.2 .V47 1999*

**Vernon, Jeni.** Maintaining children in school : the contribution of social services departments / Jeni Vernon and Ruth Sinclair. London : National Children's Bureau Enterprises, c1998. 60 p. ; 25 cm. "Supported by JR, Joseph Rowntree Foundation, National Children's Bureau." Includes bibliographical references (p. [58]) and index. CONTENTS: Maintaining children in school : a suitable case for social services departments? -- What are SSDs doing? : a picture of emerging developments -- The dynamics of moving forward -- Addressing the issue : some possible approaches -- What makes a difference? : views from the frontline -- Concluding remarks. ISBN 1-900990-43-1 DDC 371.2/94/0941
*1. School attendance - Great Britain. 2. Education and state - Great Britain. 3. Social work with children - Great Britain. 4. Social work with youth - Great Britain. I. Sinclair, Ruth. II. National Children's Bureau. III. Joseph Rowntree Foundation. IV. Title.*
*TC LB3081 .V47 1998*

**Versola, Anna Rhesa.**
Ajmera, Maya. Children from Australia to Zimbabwe. Watertown, Mass. : Charlesbridge, c1997.
*TC GF48 .A45 1997*

**VERTEBRAL COLUMN.** *See* **SPINE.**

**VERTEBRATES.** *See* **BIRDS; FISHES.**

**VERTEBRATES, FOSSIL.**
Lessem, Don. Dinosaurs to dodos. 1st ed. New York : Scholastic Reference. 1999.
*TC QE842 .L47 1999*

**VERTEBRATES, FOSSIL - ENCYCLOPEDIAS, JUVENILE.**
Lessem, Don. Dinosaurs to dodos. 1st ed. New York : Scholastic Reference. 1999.
*TC QE842 .L47 1999*

**VERTICAL INTEGRATION.**
Demetriou, Andrew J. Health care integration. Washington, D.C. : Bureau of National Affairs, Inc., c1996.
*TC KF3825 .D394 1996*

**Vesilind, P. Aarne.** So you want to be a professor? : a handbook for graduate students / by P. Aarne Vesilind. Thousand Oaks, Calif. : Sage Publications, c2000. x, 197 p. ; 23 cm. Includes bibliographical references and index. ISBN 0-7619-1896-5 ISBN 0-7619-1897-3 (pbk.)

DDC 378.1/2
*1. College teaching - Vocational guidance - United States - Handbooks, manuals, etc. 2. College teachers - Employment - United States - Handbooks, manuals, etc. 3. Graduate students - Employment - United States - Handbooks, manuals, etc. I. Title.*
*TC LB1778.2 .V47 2000*

**VESSELS (SHIPS).** *See* **SHIPS.**

**VESTIBULE SCHOOLS.** *See* **EMPLOYEES - TRAINING OF.**

**VETERANS - MENTAL HEALTH - UNITED STATES.**
Gewirtz, Abigail Hadassah. Coping strategies and stage of change among Vietnam combat veterans diagnosed with posttraumatic stress disorder and comorbid substance use disorders. 1997.
*TC 085 G338*

**VETERINARIANS.**
Gibbons, Gail. Say woof!. 1st ed. New York : Macmillan ; Toronto : Maxwell Macmillan Canada ; New York : Maxwell Macmillan International, c1992.
*TC SF756 .G53 1992*

Walker-Hodge, Judith. Animal hospital. 1st American ed. New York : DK Pub., 1999.
*TC SF604.55 .H63 1999*

**VETERINARIANS - JUVENILE LITERATURE.**
Gibbons, Gail. Say woof!. 1st ed. New York : Macmillan ; Toronto : Maxwell Macmillan Canada ; New York : Maxwell Macmillan International, c1992.
*TC SF756 .G53 1992*

**VETERINARY CLINICS.** *See* **VETERINARY HOSPITALS.**

**VETERINARY HOSPITALS.**
Walker-Hodge, Judith. Animal hospital. 1st American ed. New York : DK Pub., 1999.
*TC SF604.55 .H63 1999*

**VETERINARY HOSPITALS - JUVENILE LITERATURE.**
Walker-Hodge, Judith. Animal hospital. 1st American ed. New York : DK Pub., 1999.
*TC SF604.55 .H63 1999*

**VETERINARY MEDICINE.**
Gibbons, Gail. Say woof!. 1st ed. New York : Macmillan ; Toronto : Maxwell Macmillan Canada ; New York : Maxwell Macmillan International, c1992.
*TC SF756 .G53 1992*

**VETERINARY MEDICINE - VOCATIONAL GUIDANCE - JUVENILE LITERATURE.**
Gibbons, Gail. Say woof!. 1st ed. New York : Macmillan ; Toronto : Maxwell Macmillan Canada ; New York : Maxwell Macmillan International, c1992.
*TC SF756 .G53 1992*

**VETERINARY SCIENCE.** *See* **VETERINARY MEDICINE.**

**VETERINARY SURGEONS.** *See* **VETERINARIANS.**

**Vetter, Norman.** Epidemiology and public health medicine / Norman Vetter, Ian Matthews. Edinburgh ; New York : Churchill Livingstone, 1999. 258 p. : ill. ; 25 cm. Includes bibliographical references (p. 251-252) and index. ISBN 0-443-05704-4 DDC 614.4/2
*1. Public health. 2. Epidemiology. 3. Epidemiologic Methods. 4. Epidemiologic Studies. 5. Delivery of Health Care. 6. Environmental Illness - epidemiology. 7. Health Services. 8. Occupational Diseases - epidemiology. I. Matthews, Ian, PhD. II. Title.*
*TC RA427 .V48 1999*

**Vialle, Wilma.**
The many faces of giftedness. Belmont, CA : Wadsworth Pub. Co., c1999.
*TC BF723.G5 M36 1999*

**Vianello, Mino, 1927-.**
Gendering elites. Houndmills, Basingstoke, Hampshire : Macmillan Press ; New York : St. Martin's Press, 2000.
*TC HM1261 .G46 2000*

**VIBRAPHONE AND PIANO MUSIC (JAZZ).** *See* **JAZZ.**

**Vickery, Margaret Birney, 1963-** Buildings for bluestockings : the architecture and social history of women's colleges in late Victorian England / by Margaret Birney Vickery. Newark [Del.] : University of Delaware Press ; London ; Cranbury, NJ : Associated University Presses, c1999. xiii, 200 p., [8] p. of plates : ill. (some col.) ; 27 cm. Includes bibliographical references (p. 179-193) and index. ISBN 0-87413-697-0 (alk. paper) DDC 727/.3/0820942

*1. Women's colleges - England - Buildings. 2. Architecture, Victorian - England. 3. Architecture, Modern - 19th century - England. 4. Women's colleges - Social aspects - England - History - 19th century. I. Title.*
*TC NA6605.G7 V53 1999*

**VICTIMS.** *See* **HOLOCAUST SURVIVORS.**

**VICTIMS OF CHILD ABUSE.** *See* **ABUSED CHILDREN.**

**VICTIMS OF CRIMES.** *See* **ABUSED CHILDREN; ABUSED WOMEN; ADULT CHILD ABUSE VICTIMS; VICTIMS OF FAMILY VIOLENCE.**

**VICTIMS OF FAMILY ABUSE.** *See* **VICTIMS OF FAMILY VIOLENCE.**

**VICTIMS OF FAMILY VIOLENCE.** *See* **ABUSED WIVES.**

**VICTIMS OF FAMILY VIOLENCE - UNITED STATES.**
Gordon, Judith S., 1958- Helping survivors of domestic violence. New York : Garland Pub., 1998.
*TC HV6626.2 .G67 1998*

**VICTIMS OF WIFE ABUSE.** *See* **ABUSED WIVES.**

**VICTORIA COLLEGE (TORONTO, ONT.).**
Addison, Margaret, 1868-1940. Diary of a European tour, 1900. Montréal : McGill-Queen's University Press, c1999.
*TC LE3.T619 A33 1999*

**VICTORIAN ARCHITECTURE.** *See* **ARCHITECTURE, VICTORIAN.**

**VICTORIAN ART.** *See* **ART, VICTORIAN.**

**Victorian literature and culture series**
Black, Barbara J., 1962- On exhibit. Charlottesville ; London : University Press of Virginia, 2000.
*TC AM43.L6 B53 2000*

**The Victorians and the visual imagination**
Flint, Kate. Cambridge, U.K. ; New York : Cambridge University Press, 2000.
*TC N6767 .F58 2000*

**VICTORS.** *See* **CONQUERORS.**

**Victory deferred.**
Andriote, John-Manuel. Chicago : The University of Chicago Press, c1999.
*TC RA644.A25 A523 1999*

**Vida y obra de Ramón Beteta.**
Llinás Alvarez, Edgar. 1. ed. México : [s.n.], 1996 (México, D.F. : Impresora Galve)
*TC F1234.B56 L5 1996*

**Video.**
Donnell Library Center. New York : New York Public Library, 1990.
*TC PN1992.95 .D66*

**Video Aided Instruction, Inc.**
Basic English [videorecording]. [Roslyn Heights, N.Y.] : Video Aided Instruction, [c1995].
*TC PE1128 .B3 1995*

Intermediate English [videorecording]. [Roslyn Heights, N.Y.] : Video Aided Instruction, [c1995].
*TC PE1128 .I5 1995*

**Video Aided Instruction, Inc. presents Basic English [videorecording].**
Basic English [videorecording]. [Roslyn Heights, N.Y.] : Video Aided Instruction, [c1995].
*TC PE1128 .B3 1995*

**Video Aided Instruction, Inc. presents Intermediate English [videorecording].**
Intermediate English [videorecording]. [Roslyn Heights, N.Y.] : Video Aided Instruction, [c1995].
*TC PE1128 .I5 1995*

**VIDEO ART.**
Processing the signal [videorecording]. Cicero, Ill. : Roland Collection of Films on Art, c1989.
*TC N6494.V53 P7 1989*

**Video Classroom (Firm).**
Ballet class for beginners [videorecording]. W. Long Branch, NJ : Kultur, c1981.
*TC GV1589 .B3 1981*

Tap dancing for beginners [videorecording]. W. Long Branch, NJ : Kultur, c1981.
*TC GV1794 .T3 1981*

**Video on obsessive compulsive disorder [videorecording].**
Step on a crack [videorecording]. Boston, MA : Fanlight Productions, 1996.

**TC RC533 .S7 1996**

**VIDEO RECORDINGS - CATALOGS.**
Culturally diverse videos, audios, and CD-ROMS for children and young adults. New York : Neal-Schuman Publishers, 1999.
**TC PN1998 .M85 1999**

Donnell Library Center. Video. New York : New York Public Library, 1990.
**TC PN1992.95 .D66**

**VIDEO RECORDINGS, DOCUMENTARY.** *See* **DOCUMENTARY TELEVISION PROGRAMS.**

**VIDEO RECORDINGS FOR CHILDREN.**
Exploring the English language [videorecording]. [Princeton, N.J.] : Video Tutor ; [Chesterton, Ind.? : Distributed by] Griffin Media Design, 1988, c1986.

Milbank Memorial Library story hour [videorecording]. [New York : Milbank Memorial Library, 1999].
**TC Z718.3 .M5 1999 Series 3 Prog. 11**

Milbank Memorial Library story hour [videorecording]. [New York : Milbank Memorial Library, 1999]
**TC Z718.3 .M5 1999 Series 3 Prog. 6**

**VIDEO RECORDINGS FOR CHILDREN - CATALOGS - PERIODICALS.**
Bowker's directory of videocassettes for children. New Providence, N.J. : R.R. Bowker, c1998-
**TC PN1992.945 .B66**

**VIDEO RECORDINGS FOR THE HEARING IMPAIRED.**
Africans in America [videorecording]. [Boston, Mass.] : WGBH Educational Foundation ; South Burlington, VT : WGBH Boston Video [distributor], c1998.
**TC E441 .A47 1998**

Annual State of American Education Address (7th : February 22, 2000 : Durham, N.C.) The seventh annual state of American education address [videorecording. [Washington, D.C. : U.S. Dept. of Education], 2000.

Break throughs [videorecording]. Boston, MA : Fanlight Productions, c1998.
**TC LC4717.5 .B7 1998**

Hand in hand [videorecording]. New York, N.Y. : AFB Press, c1995.
**TC HV1597.2 .H3 1995**

Making the most of early communication [videorecording]. New York, NY : Distributed by AFB Press, c1997.
**TC HV1597.2 .M3 1997**

Modernizing schools : technology and buildings for a new century (September 19, 2000 : Washington, D.C.) Modernizing schools [videorecording]. [Washington, D.C.] : U.S. Dept. of Education, [2000].
**TC LB3205 .M64 2000**

Modernizing schools : technology and buildings for a new century (September 19, 2000 : Washington, D.C.) Modernizing schools [videorecording]. [Washington, D.C.] : U.S. Dept. of Education, [2000].
**TC LB3205 .M64 2000**

New school order [videorecording]. New York : First Run/Icarus Films, 1996.
**TC LB2831.583.P4 N4 1996**

Powerful middle schools : teaching and learning for young adolescents (2000) Powerful middle schools [videorecording]. [Washington, D.C.?] : U.S. Dept. of Education, [2000].
**TC LB1623 .P6 2000**

Public charter schools : new choices in public education (May 3, 2000 : Washington, D.C.) Public charter schools [videorecording]. [Washington, D.C.] : U.S. Dept. of Education, [2000].
**TC LB2806.36 .P9 2000**

Stephen Hawking's universe [videorecording]. [Alexandria, Va.] : PBS Video; Burbank, CA : Distributed by Warner Home Video, c1997.
**TC QB982 .S7 1997**

When the brain goes wrong [videorecording]. Short version. Boston, MA : Fanlight Productions [dist.], c1992.
**TC RC386 .W54 1992**

**VIDEO TAPES IN EDUCATION.**
Arias, Rafael. Analysis of discourse in an ESL peer-mentoring teacher group. 1999.

---

**TC 06 no. 10791**

**VIDEO TAPES IN SEX INSTRUCTION - UNITED STATES - HISTORY.**
Eberwein, Robert T., 1940- Sex ed. New Brunswick, N.J. : Rutgers University Press, 1999.
**TC HQ56 .E19 1999**

**Video Tutor.**
Decimals [videorecording]. Princeton, N.J. : Video Tutor, 1988.
**TC QA117 .D4 1988**

Fractions [videorecording]. Princeton, N.J. : Video Tutor, 1988.
**TC QA117 .F7 1988**

The high school proficiency test [videorecording]. Princeton, N.J. : Video Tutor, 1988.
**TC QA445 .H5 1988**

Number concepts [videorecording]. Princeton, N.J. : Video Tutor, 1988.
**TC QA117 .N8 1988**

Number concepts [videorecording]. Princeton, N.J. : Video Tutor, 1988.
**TC QA117 .N8 1988**

Percents [videorecording]. Princeton, N.J. : Video Tutor, 1988.

Percents [videorecording]. Princeton, N.J. : Video Tutor, 1988.
**TC QA117.P4 1988**

Pre-algebra [videorecording]. Princeton, N.J. : Video Tutor, 1988.
**TC QA152.2 .P6 1988**

Word problems [videorecording]. Princeton, N.J. : Video Tutor, 1988.
**TC QA139 .W6 1988**

**Video Tutor : exploring the English language [videorecording].**
Exploring the English language [videorecording]. [Princeton, N.J.] : Video Tutor ; [Chesterton, Ind.? : Distributed by] Griffin Media Design, 1988, c1986.

**Video Tutor, Inc.**
Exploring the English language [videorecording]. [Princeton, N.J.] : Video Tutor ; [Chesterton, Ind.? : Distributed by] Griffin Media Design, 1988, c1986.

**Video Tutor Inc. presents basic decimals [videorecording].**
Decimals [videorecording]. Princeton, N.J. : Video Tutor, 1988.
**TC QA117 .D4 1988**

**Video Tutor Inc. presents basic number concepts [videorecording].**
Number concepts [videorecording]. Princeton, N.J. : Video Tutor, 1988.
**TC QA117 .N8 1988**

Number concepts [videorecording]. Princeton, N.J. : Video Tutor, 1988.
**TC QA117 .N8 1988**

**Video Tutor Inc. presents basic percents [videorecording].**
Percents [videorecording]. Princeton, N.J. : Video Tutor, 1988.
**TC QA117.P4 1988**

**Video Tutor Inc. presents basic pre-algebra [videorecording].**
Percents [videorecording]. Princeton, N.J. : Video Tutor, 1988.

Pre-algebra [videorecording]. Princeton, N.J. : Video Tutor, 1988.
**TC QA152.2 .P6 1988**

**Video Tutor Inc. presents basic word problems [videorecording].**
Word problems [videorecording]. Princeton, N.J. : Video Tutor, 1988.
**TC QA139 .W6 1988**

**Video tutor instructional series**
Decimals [videorecording]. Princeton, N.J. : Video Tutor, 1988.
**TC QA117 .D4 1988**

Fractions [videorecording]. Princeton, N.J. : Video Tutor, 1988.
**TC QA117 .F7 1988**

The high school proficiency test [videorecording]. Princeton, N.J. : Video Tutor, 1988.
**TC QA445 .H5 1988**

Number concepts [videorecording]. Princeton, N.J. : Video Tutor, 1988.

---

**TC QA117 .N8 1988**

Number concepts [videorecording]. Princeton, N.J. : Video Tutor, 1988.
**TC QA117 .N8 1988**

Percents [videorecording]. Princeton, N.J. : Video Tutor, 1988.
**TC QA117 .N8 1988**

Percents [videorecording]. Princeton, N.J. : Video Tutor, 1988.
**TC QA117.P4 1988**

Pre-algebra [videorecording]. Princeton, N.J. : Video Tutor, 1988.
**TC QA152.2 .P6 1988**

Word problems [videorecording]. Princeton, N.J. : Video Tutor, 1988.
**TC QA139 .W6 1988**

**Video Tutor introduces decimals [videorecording].**
Decimals [videorecording]. Princeton, N.J. : Video Tutor, 1988.
**TC QA117 .D4 1988**

**Video Tutor introduces fractions [videorecording].**
Fractions [videorecording]. Princeton, N.J. : Video Tutor, 1988.
**TC QA117 .F7 1988**

**Video Tutor introduces percents [videorecording].**
Percents [videorecording]. Princeton, N.J. : Video Tutor, 1988.
**TC QA117.P4 1988**

**Video Tutor introduces pre-algebra [videorecording].**
Percents [videorecording]. Princeton, N.J. : Video Tutor, 1988.

Pre-algebra [videorecording]. Princeton, N.J. : Video Tutor, 1988.
**TC QA152.2 .P6 1988**

**VIDEOCASSETTES FOR CHILDREN.** *See also* **VIDEO RECORDINGS FOR CHILDREN.**
Bowker's directory of videocassettes for children. New Providence, N.J. : R.R. Bowker, c1998-
**TC PN1992.945 .B66**

**VIDEORECORDINGS.** *See* **VIDEO RECORDINGS.**

**VIDEOS.** *See* **VIDEO RECORDINGS.**

**Videos in psychology** : a resource directory / Gary R. VandenBos, editor ; development team, Andrea Brown ... [et al.]. 1st ed. Washington, DC : American Psychological Association, c2000. viii, 188 p. : ill. ; 28 cm. Includes index. ISBN 1-55798-709-2 (alk. paper) DDC 016.15
*1. Psychology - Study and teaching - Audio-visual aids - Video catalogs. 2. Psychology. Applied - Study and teaching - Audio-visual aids - Video catalogs. I. VandenBos, Gary R. II. American Psychological Association.*
**TC BF80.3 .V53 2000**

**Vieira, Meredith.**
Sean's story [videorecording]. Princeton, N.J. : Films for the Humanities & Sciences ; [S.l. : distributed by] ABC Multimedia : Capital Cities/ABC, c1994.
**TC LC1203.M3 .S39 1994**

**Vienna series in theoretical biology**
The evolution of cognition. Cambridge, Mass. : MIT Press, c2000.
**TC BF701 .E598 2000**

**VIETNAM CONFLICT, 1961-1975.** *See* **VIETNAMESE CONFLICT, 1961-1975.**

**VIETNAM - FOREIGN RELATIONS - UNITED STATES.**
Vietnam [videorecording]. Beverly Hills, CA : CBS/ Fox Video, c1981.

**VIETNAM - HISTORY - 1945-1975.** *See also* **VIETNAMESE CONFLICT, 1961-1975.**
Vietnam [videorecording]. [Beverly Hills, Calif.?] : CBS Fox Video : Distributed by Fox Video, c1993.
**TC DS557.7 .V53 1993**

**Vietnam** [videorecording] : chronicle of a war / CBS Fox Video. Beverly Hills, CA : CBS/Fox Video, c1981. 1 videocassette (88 min.) : sd., col. ; 1/2 in. VHS. "An MGM/CBS home video presentation." SUMMARY: Uses television videotape news reports to trace the history of American involvement in Vietnam from the early 1950's to the fall of South Vietnam in 1973.
*1. Vietnamese Conflict, 1961-1975 - United States. 2. United States - Foreign relations - Vietnam. 3. Vietnam - Foreign relations - United States. I. CBS Television Network. II. Cronkite, Walter.*

**Vietnam** [videorecording] : chronicle of a war / CBS Fox Video ; [CBS News]. [Beverly Hills, Calif.?] : CBS Fox Video : Distributed by Fox Video, c1993. 1

videocassette (89 min.) : sd., col. with b&w sequences ; 1/2 in. (CBS News collectors series) VHS. Catalogued from credits and container. Narrator: Walter Cronkite; with correspondents: Ed Bradley, Charles Collingwood, Bruce Dunning, Charles Kuralt, Dan Rather, Eric Sevareid, Mike Wallace. For high school through adult. SUMMARY: Drawing upon the resources of the CBS News Archives, this program traces the history of the devastating conflict of the first televised war. Cast: Narrated by Walter Cronkite. ISBN 0-7939-7049-0 DDC 959.704
*1. Vietnamese Conflict, 1961-1975 - United States. 2. Vietnamese Conflict, 1961-1975 - United States - Public opinion. 3. Vietnam - History - 1945-1975. 4. Documentary television programs. I. Cronkite, Walter. II. CBS News. III. CBS News Archives. IV. CBS Video (Firm) V. Fox Video (Firm) VI. CBS Fox Video. VII. Title: Chronicle of a war [videorecording] VIII. Series.*
*TC DS557.7 .V53 1993*

**VIETNAM WAR, 1961-1975.** *See* **VIETNAMESE CONFLICT, 1961-1975.**

**VIETNAMESE CONFLICT, 1961-1975.**
Bourke, Joanna. An intimate history of killing. [New York, NY] : Basic Books, c1999.
*TC U22.3 .B68 1999*

**VIETNAMESE CONFLICT, 1961-1975 - UNITED STATES.**
Vietnam [videorecording]. Beverly Hills, CA : CBS/ Fox Video, c1981.

Vietnam [videorecording]. [Beverly Hills, Calif.?] : CBS Fox Video : Distributed by Fox Video, c1993.
*TC DS557.7 .V53 1993*

**VIETNAMESE CONFLICT, 1961-1975 - UNITED STATES - PUBLIC OPINION.**
Vietnam [videorecording]. [Beverly Hills, Calif.?] : CBS Fox Video : Distributed by Fox Video, c1993.
*TC DS557.7 .V53 1993*

**VIETNAMESE CONFLICT, 1961-1975 - VETERANS - UNITED STATES.**
Gewirtz, Abigail Hadassan. Coping strategies and stage of change among Vietnam combat veterans diagnosed with posttraumatic stress disorder and comorbid substance use disorders. 1997.
*TC 085 G338*

**VIETNAMESE WAR, 1961-1975.** *See* **VIETNAMESE CONFLICT, 1961-1975.**

**View Video.**
Paris [videorecording]. New York, NY : V.I.E.W. Video, c1996.
*TC DC707 .P3 1996*

**VIEWERS, TELEVISION.** *See* **TELEVISION VIEWERS.**

**VIGILANCE COMMITTEES.** *See* **VIGILANTES.**

**VIGILANTES - ARIZONA - CLIFTON - HISTORY - 20TH CENTURY.**
Gordon, Linda. The great Arizona orphan abduction. Cambridge, Mass. : Harvard University Press, 1999.
*TC F819.C55 G67 1999*

**Vihos, Lisa.**
Kale, Shelly. My museum journal. Los Angeles, CA : J. Paul Getty Museum, c2000.
*TC N7440 .K35 2000*

**VIKING COOKERY.** *See* **COOKERY, VIKING.**

**VIKINGS - FOOD - JUVENILE LITERATURE.**
Martell, Hazel. Food & feasts with the Vikings. Parsippany, N.J. : New Discovery Books, c1995.
*TC DL65 .M359 1995*

**VIKINGS - SOCIAL LIFE AND CUSTOMS.**
Martell, Hazel. Food & feasts with the Vikings. Parsippany, N.J. : New Discovery Books, c1995.
*TC DL65 .M359 1995*

**VIKINGS - SOCIAL LIFE AND CUSTOMS - JUVENILE LITERATURE.**
Martell, Hazel. Food & feasts with the Vikings. Parsippany, N.J. : New Discovery Books, c1995.
*TC DL65 .M359 1995*

**Villamil Tinajero, Josefina.**
Educating Latino students. Lancaster, Pa. : Technomic Pub. Co., c1998.
*TC LC2669 .E37 1998*

Literacy assessment of second language learners. Boston ; London : Allyn and Bacon, c2001.
*TC P53.4 .L58 2001*

**Villani, Susan.** Are you sure you're the principal? : on being an authentic leader / Susan Villani ; foreword by Roland S. Barth. Thousand Oaks, Calif. : Corwin Press, c1999. xx, 99 p. : ill. ; 24 cm. CONTENTS: New person in an old role : multiple images of a principal. First

impressions. Larger than life. Mirror, mirror, on the wall. Finding my way. A little respect -- Working through conflict : power and communication. What are our choices? Lonely at the top. Stuck in righteousness. For the sake of the students. Women as principals. Truth or dare. Knowing when -- Being a leader and being myself : feelings, attitudes, and roles. Symbols communicate more than style. "She smiles too much." Feeling my way. Group member, group leader. Invited out of the lunch box. Share the problem and invest in the solution -- What we have to offer : fitting a school together. Building the school with people. Matching the teachers and the students-- and their parents. Protecting relationships. Revealing the obvious -- Promoting acceptance in the school community : each person's right to belong. First friends. "Just because." Realizing our resources. On common ground. To stand up, to stand behind. Essence. Modeling what's important. Recognizing and owning our part -- Mentors, allies, and friends : support for authentic leadership and vision. In support of leaders. At the core of leadership. Doing something more. Not a fairy godmother. Time well spent. The courage to pursue growth. What we give to each other. Passing the torch and sharing its light. Leading with my voice. ISBN 0-8039-6804-3 (acid-free paper) ISBN 0-8039-6805-1 (pbk. : acid-free paper) DDC 371.2/012
*1. School principals - United States. 2. Women school principals - United States. 3. Educational leadership - United States. I. Title.*
*TC LB2831.92 .V55 1999*

**Villari, Susan, 1957-.**
Just sex. Lanham, MD : Rowman & Littlefield, 2000.
*TC HQ21 .J87 1999*

**VILLAS.** *See* **ARCHITECTURE, DOMESTIC.**

**Villenas, Sofia A.**
Race is-- race isn't. Boulder, CO : Westview Press, c1999.
*TC LC3731 .R27 1999*

**Vincent, Gabrielle.**
**[Ernest et Célestine chez le photographe. English]**
Smile, Ernest and Celestine / Gabrielle Vincent. 1st American ed. New York : Greenwillow Books, c1982. [24] p. : col. ill. ; 23 x 24 cm. Translation of: Ernest et Célestine chez le photographe. SUMMARY: After he explains to Celestine why his collection of photographs does not include her, Ernest remedies the omission. ISBN 0-688-01247-7 ISBN 0-688-01249-3 (lib. bdg.) DDC [E]
*1. Photographs - Fiction. 2. Bears - Fiction. 3. Mice - Fiction. I. Title.*
*TC PZ7.V744 Sm 1982*

**Vincoli, Jeffrey W.**
Lewis' dictionary of occupational and environmental safety and health. Boca Raton : Lewis Publishers, c2000.
*TC T55 .L468 2000*

**Viner, John.**
Seurat [videorecording]. West Long Branch, NJ : Kultur, c1999.
*TC ND553.S5 S5 1999*

**Viney, John.** Drive : what makes a leader in business and beyond / John Viney. 1st U.S. ed. New York, N.Y. : Bloomsbury, 1999. 263 p. : ill. ; 24 cm. Includes index. ISBN 1-58234-025-0
*1. Leadership. 2. Management. 3. Business. 4. Interpersonal relations. I. Title.*
*TC HD57.7 .V564 1999*

**Vinson, Betsy Partin.** Language disorders across the lifespan : an introduction / Betsy Partin Vinson. San Diego : Singular Pub. Group, c1999. xii, 333 p. : ill. ; 25 cm. Includes bibliographical references and index. ISBN 1-56593-977-8 (pbk. : alk. paper) DDC 616.85/5
*1. Language disorders. 2. Language disorders in children. 3. Language disorders in adolescence. 4. Language disorders in old age. I. Title.*
*TC RC423 .V56 1999*

**Viola, Bill, 1951-.**
Processing the signal [videorecording]. Cicero, Ill. : Roland Collection of Films on Art, c1989.
*TC N6494.V53 P7 1989*

**VIOLA DA BRACCIO.** *See* **VIOLA.**

**Viola for beginners.**
The viola [videorecording]. Van Nuys, CA : Backstage Pass Productions ; Canoga Park, Calif. : [Distributed by] MVP Home Entertainment, c1991.
*TC MT285 .V5 1991*

The viola [videorecording]. Van Nuys, CA : Backstage Pass Productions ; Canoga Park, Calif. : [Distributed by] MVP Home Entertainment, c1995.
*TC MT285 .V5 1995*

**VIOLA - INSTRUCTION AND STUDY.**
The viola [videorecording]. Van Nuys, CA :

**Backstage Pass Productions ; Canoga Park, Calif. : [Distributed by] MVP Home Entertainment, c1991.**
*TC MT285 .V5 1991*

The viola [videorecording]. Van Nuys, CA : Backstage Pass Productions ; Canoga Park, Calif. : [Distributed by] MVP Home Entertainment, c1995.
*TC MT285 .V5 1995*

**VIOLA - STUDIES AND EXERCISES.**
The viola [videorecording]. Van Nuys, CA : Backstage Pass Productions ; Canoga Park, Calif. : [Distributed by] MVP Home Entertainment, c1991.
*TC MT285 .V5 1991*

The viola [videorecording]. Van Nuys, CA : Backstage Pass Productions ; Canoga Park, Calif. : [Distributed by] MVP Home Entertainment, c1995.
*TC MT285 .V5 1995*

**The viola** [videorecording] / director, Todd Brinegar ; producer, Mark S. Arnett ; a production of Aesthetic Artist Records and Brinegar Video/Film Productions, Inc. in association with Backstage Pass Instructional Video. Van Nuys, CA : Backstage Pass Productions ; Canoga Park, Calif. : [Distributed by] MVP Home Entertainment, c1991. 1 videocassette (63 min.) : sd., col. ; 1/2 in. + 1 instruction booklet (6 p. ; 18 cm.). (Maestro music instrument instructional video ... for) Title on container: Viola for beginners. VHS, Hi-Fi, Stereo. Cataloged from credits, cassette label and container. Instructor: Kathryn Rodriguez. Audio, Mark S. Arnett. For beginners. SUMMARY: Kathryn Rodriguez teaches the basics of learning to play the viola, from handling to rudimentary playing, and demonstrates the technique along with two of her pupils. CONTENTS: Handling your viola -- Tuning your viola -- Holding your viola -- Playing your viola -- Wrapping it up.
*1. Viola - Instruction and study. 2. Viola - Studies and exercises. I. Rodriguez, Kathryn. II. Brinegar, Todd. III. Arnett, Mark S. IV. Backstage Pass Productions. V. Aesthetic Artist Records. VI. Brinegar Video/Film Productions, Inc. VII. MVP Home Entertainment (Firm) VIII. Title: Viola for beginners IX. Series.*
*TC MT285 .V5 1991*

**The viola** [videorecording] / director, Todd Brinegar ; producer, Mark S. Arnett ; a production of Aesthetic Artist Records and Brinegar Video/Film Productions, Inc. in association with Backstage Pass Instructional Video. Van Nuys, CA : Backstage Pass Productions ; Canoga Park, Calif. : [Distributed by] MVP Home Entertainment, c1995. 1 videocassette (63 min.) : sd., col. ; 1/2 in. + 1 instruction booklet (6 p. : music ; 18 cm.). (Maestro music instrument instructional video ... for) Title on container: Viola for beginners. VHS, Hi-Fi, Stereo. Cataloged from credits, cassette label and container. Instructor: Kathryn Rodriguez. Audio, Mark S. Arnett. For beginners. SUMMARY: Kathryn Rodriguez teaches the basics of learning to play the viola, from handling to rudimentary playing, and demonstrates the technique along with two of her pupils. CONTENTS: Handling your viola -- Tuning your viola -- Holding your viola -- Playing your viola -- Wrapping it up.
*1. Viola - Instruction and study. 2. Viola - Studies and exercises. I. Rodriguez, Kathryn. II. Brinegar, Todd. III. Arnett, Mark S. IV. Backstage Pass Productions. V. Aesthetic Artist Records. VI. Brinegar Video/Film Productions, Inc. VII. MVP Home Entertainment (Firm) VIII. Title: Viola for beginners IX. Series.*
*TC MT285 .V5 1995*

**Violato, Claudio.**
The changing family and child development. Aldershot : Ashgate, c2000.
*TC HQ518 .C478 2000*

**VIOLENCE.** *See also* **CHILDREN AND VIOLENCE; DATING VIOLENCE; FAMILY VIOLENCE; SCHOOL VIOLENCE.**
Sexual aggression. 1st ed. Washington, DC : American Psychiatric Press, c1999.
*TC RC560.S47 S488 1999*

Teen violence [videorecording]. Princeton, NJ : Films for the Humanities & Sciences, c1998.
*TC RJ506.V56 T44 1998*

**Violence and childhood in the inner city** / edited by Joan McCord. Cambridge, UK ; New York : Cambridge University Press, 1997. xiii, 334 p. ; 24 cm. (Cambridge criminology series) Includes bibliographical references and indexes. ISBN 0-521-58326-8 ISBN 0-521-58720-4 (pbk.) DDC 303.6/0973
*1. Violence - United States. 2. Inner cities - United States. 3. Children and violence - United States. 4. Violence in children - United States. 5. City children - United States. 6. Urban youth - United States. I. McCord, Joan. II. Series.*
*TC HN90.V5 V532 1997*

**VIOLENCE AND CHILDREN.** *See* **CHILDREN AND VIOLENCE.**

## VIOLENCE IN ADOLESCENCE.
Davis, Daniel Leifeld. The aggressive adolescent.
New York : Haworth Press, 1999.
*TC RJ506.V56 D38 1999*

## VIOLENCE IN CHILDREN. *See also* CHILDREN AND VIOLENCE.
Cavell, Timothy A. Working with parents of
aggressive children. 1st ed. Washington, DC :
American Psychological Association, 2000.
*TC RJ506.A35 C38 2000*

Teen violence [videorecording]. Princeton, NJ : Films
for the Humanities & Sciences, c1998.
*TC RJ506.V56 T44 1998*

## VIOLENCE IN CHILDREN - UNITED STATES.
Violence and childhood in the inner city. Cambridge,
UK ; New York : Cambridge University Press, 1997.
*TC HN90.V5 V532 1997*

**Violence in families :** assessing prevention and
treatment programs / Rosemary Chalk and Patricia A.
King, editors ; Committee on the Assessment of
Family Violence Interventions, Board on Children,
Youth, and Families, Commission on Behavioral and
Social Sciences and Education, National Research
Council and Institute of Medicine. Washington, D.C. :
National Academy Press, 1998. xvii, 392 p. ; 23 cm.
Includes bibliographical references (p. 319-357) and index.
ISBN 0-309-05496-6 (cloth) DDC 362.82/927/0973
*1. Family violence - United States - Prevention - Evaluation. 2.
Crisis intervention (Mental health services) - United States -
Evaluation. 3. Evaluation research (Social action programs) -
United States. I. Chalk, Rosemary A. II. King, Patricia, 1942-
III. Board on Children, Youth, and Families (U.S.). Committee
on the Assessment of Family Violence Interventions.*
*TC HV6626.2 .V56 1998*

## VIOLENCE IN MASS MEDIA.
Levin, Diane E. Remote control childhood?
Washington, D.C. : National Association for the
Education of Young Children, c1998.
*TC P94.5.C55 L48 1998*

## VIOLENCE IN MASS MEDIA - UNITED STATES.
Calvert, Sandra L. Children's journeys through the
information age. 1st ed. Boston : McGraw-Hill
College, c1999.
*TC HQ784.T4 C24 1999*

## VIOLENCE IN SCHOOLS. *See* SCHOOL VIOLENCE.

## VIOLENCE - MEXICO - PUEBLA (STATE) - HISTORY - 19TH CENTURY.
Thomson, Guy P. C., 1949- Patriotism, politics, and
popular liberalism in nineteenth-century Mexico.
Wilmington, De. : Scholarly Resources, 1999.
*TC F1326.L83 T5 1999*

## VIOLENCE - UNITED STATES.
Guns and violence. San Diego : Greenhaven Press,
c1999.
*TC HV7436 .G8774 1999*

Understanding and preventing violence. Washington,
D.C. : National Academy Press, 1993-1994.
*TC HN90.V5 U53 1993*

Violence and childhood in the inner city. Cambridge,
UK ; New York : Cambridge University Press, 1997.
*TC HN90.V5 V532 1997*

## VIOLENCE - UNITED STATES - PREVENTION.
Garbarino, James. Lost boys. New York : Free Press,
c1999.
*TC HQ799.2.V56 G37 1999*

Rosen, Sidney M. Toward a gang solution. [Norman,
Okla.?] NRC Youth Services, 1996.
*TC HV6439.U7 R67 1996*

Understanding and preventing violence. Washington,
D.C. : National Academy Press, 1993-1994.
*TC HN90.V5 U53 1993*

## VIOLENCE - UNITED STATES - PREVENTION - CASE STUDIES.
Rosen, Sidney M. Toward a gang solution. [Norman,
Okla.?] NRC Youth Services, 1996.
*TC HV6439.U7 R67 1996*

**Violent and aggressive youth.**
Bemak, Fred. Thousand Oaks, Calif. ; London :
Corwin Press, c2000.
*TC LB3013.3 .B45 2000*

## VIOLENT CRIMES.
Teen violence [videorecording]. Princeton, NJ : Films
for the Humanities & Sciences, c1998.
*TC RJ506.V56 T44 1998*

## VIOLENT CRIMES - GOVERNMENT POLICY - UNITED STATES.
Zimring, Franklin E. American youth violence. New
York : Oxford University Press, 1998.
*TC HV9104 .Z57 1998*

## VIOLENT CRIMES - UNITED STATES.
Guns and violence. San Diego : Greenhaven Press,
c1999.
*TC HV7436 .G8774 1999*

Teen killers [videorecording]. Princeton, NJ : Films
for the Humanities and Sciences, c1998-1999.
*TC HV9067.H6 T4 1999*

Understanding and preventing violence. Washington,
D.C. : National Academy Press, 1993-1994.
*TC HN90.V5 U53 1993*

## VIOLENT DEATHS. *See* DROWNING; HOMICIDE; MURDER; SUICIDE.

**The violent E and other tricky sounds.**
Hughes, Margaret, 1941- York, Me. : Stenhouse
Publishers ; Markham, Ontario : Pembroke Publishers
Limited, c1997.
*TC LB1574 .H84 1997*

## VIOLIN - FICTION.
Gray, Libba Moore. When Uncle took the fiddle. New
York : Orchard Books, 1999.
*TC PZ7.G7793 Wh 1999*

**Violin for beginners.**
The violin [videorecording]. Van Nuys, CA :
Backstage Pass Productions ; Canoga Park, Calif. :
[Distributed by] MVP, c1998.
*TC MT265 .V5 1998*

## VIOLIN - INSTRUCTION AND STUDY.
The trombone [videorecording]. Van Nuys, CA :
Backstage Pass Productions ; Canoga Park, Calif. :
[Distributed by] MVP, c1998.
*TC MT465 .T7 1998*

The violin [videorecording]. Van Nuys, CA :
Backstage Pass Productions ; Canoga Park, Calif. :
[Distributed by] MVP, c1998.
*TC MT265 .V5 1998*

## VIOLIN - STUDIES AND EXERCISES.
The trombone [videorecording]. Van Nuys, CA :
Backstage Pass Productions ; Canoga Park, Calif. :
[Distributed by] MVP, c1998.
*TC MT465 .T7 1998*

The violin [videorecording]. Van Nuys, CA :
Backstage Pass Productions ; Canoga Park, Calif. :
[Distributed by] MVP, c1998.
*TC MT265 .V5 1998*

## VIOLIN TEACHERS - UNITED STATES - BIOGRAPHY.
Sand, Barbara Lourie. Teaching genius. Portland, Or. :
Amadeus Press, 2000.
*TC ML423.D35 S36 2000*

**The violin** [videorecording] / director, Todd Brinegar ;
producer, Mark S. Arnett ; a production of Aesthetic
Artist Records and Brinegar Video/Film Productions,
Inc. in association with Backstage Pass Instructional
Video. Van Nuys, CA : Backstage Pass Productions ;
Canoga Park, Calif. : [Distributed by] MVP, c1998. 1
videocassette (45 min.) : sd., col. ; 1/2 in. (Maestro music
instrument instructional video ... for) Title on container: Violin
for beginners. VHS, Hi-Fi, Stereo. Cataloged from credits,
cassette label and container. Instructor: Bill Scutt. Audio, Mark
S. Arnett. For beginners. SUMMARY: Bill Scutt teaches the
basics of learning to play the violin, from handling to
rudimentary playing, and demonstrates the technique along
with two of his pupils. CONTENTS: Introducing the violin --
Proper sizing -- Starting lessons -- Parts of the violin -- Tuning
the violin -- Holding the violin -- Finger placement -- Plucking
the violin -- Variation one -- Another song -- Using the bow --
More bowing -- Maintaining your violin -- All about dots --
Wrapping it up.
*1. Violin - Instruction and study. 2. Violin - Studies and
exercises. I. Scutt, William R. II. Brinegar, Todd. III. Arnett,
Mark S. IV. Backstage Pass Productions. V. Aesthetic Artist
Records. VI. Brinegar Video/Film Productions, Inc. VII. MVP
Home Entertainment (Firm) VIII. Title: Violin for beginners
IX. Series.*
*TC MT265 .V5 1998*

## VIOLONCELLISTS - UNITED STATES - BIOGRAPHY.
Booth, Wayne C. For the love of it. Chicago :
University of Chicago Press, c1999.
*TC ML418.B49 A3 1999*

## VIOLONCELLO - INSTRUCTION AND STUDY.
The cello [videorecording]. Van Nuys, CA :
Backstage Pass Productions ; Canoga Park, Calif. :
[Distributed by] MVP, c1995.

*TC MT305 .C4 1995*

## VIOLONCELLO PLAYERS. *See* VIOLONCELLISTS.

## VIOLONCELLO - STUDIES AND EXERCISES.
The cello [videorecording]. Van Nuys, CA :
Backstage Pass Productions ; Canoga Park, Calif. :
[Distributed by] MVP, c1995.
*TC MT305 .C4 1995*

**Viorst, Judith.** Alexander, who used to be rich last
Sunday / Judith Viorst ; illustrated by Ray Cruz. 1st
ed. New York : Atheneum, 1978. [32] p. : ill. ; 34 x 46
cm. SUMMARY: Although Alexander and his money are
quickly parted, he comes to realize all the things that can be
done with a dollar. ISBN 0-02-109112-9
*1. Finance, Personal - Fiction. 2. Humorous stories. I. Cruz,
Ray. II. Title.*
*TC PZ7.V816 Am 1978*

## VIRAL DISEASES. *See* VIRUS DISEASES.

## VIRAL INFECTIONS. *See* VIRUS DISEASES.

**Virginia Federation of Business and Professional
Women's Clubs.**
Federation notes. [Arlington, Va., Wing Publications.]

## VIRGINIA - HISTORY - CIVIL WAR, 1861-1865 - FICTION.
Ransom, Candice F., 1952- The promise quilt. New
York : Walker and Co., 1999.
*TC PZ7.R1743 Pr 1999*

## VIRGINIA - HISTORY - CIVIL WAR, 1861-1865 - JUVENILE FICTION.
Ransom, Candice F., 1952- The promise quilt. New
York : Walker and Co., 1999.
*TC PZ7.R1743 Pr 1999*

## VIRGINIA - HISTORY - COLONIAL PERIOD, 1600-1775 - FICTION.
Curry, Jane Louise. A Stolen life. New York :
McElderry Books, 1999.
*TC PZ7.C936 St 1999*

## VIRGINIA - HISTORY - COLONIAL PERIOD, CA. 1600-1775.
Africans in America [videorecording]. [Boston,
Mass.] : WGBH Educational Foundation : South
Burlington, VT : WGBH Boston Video [distributor],
c1998.
*TC E441 .A47 1998*

## VIRGINIA MILITARY INSTITUTE - HISTORY - 20TH CENTURY.
Brodie, Laura Fairchild. Breaking out. 1st ed. New
York : Pantheon Books, c2000.
*TC LC212.862 .B75 2000*

**The virtual campus.**
IFIP TC3/WG3.3 & WG3.6 Joint Working
Conference on the Virtual Campus: Trends for Higher
Education and Training (1997 : Madrid, Spain) 1st ed.
London ; New York : Chapman & Hall on behalf of
the International Federation for Information
Processing (IFIP), 1998.
*TC LC5803.C65 I353 1997*

**Virtual instruction :** issues and insights from an
international perspective / [edited by] Carine M.
Feyten, Joyce W. Nutta. Englewood, Colo. : Libraries
Unlimited, 1999. xvi, 262 p. : ill. ; 24 cm. Includes
bibliographical references and index. ISBN 1-56308-714-6
(paper) DDC 371.3/5/0785
*1. Distance education - Computer-assisted instruction. 2.
Telecommunication in education. I. Feyten, Carine M. II.
Nutta, Joyce W.*
*TC LC5803.C65 V57 1999*

**The virtual learning organization :** learning at the
corporate university workplace campus / edited by
Gordon Prestoungrange, Eric Sandelands, Richard
Teare. London ; New York : Continuum, 2000. xxi,
249 p. : ill. ; 25 cm. Includes bibliographical references and
index. ISBN 0-8264-4707-4
*1. Adult education. 2. Continuing education. 3. Employees -
Training of. I. Prestoungrange, Gordon. II. Sandelands, Eric.
III. Teare, Richard.*
*TC LC5215 .V574 2000*

## VIRTUAL LIBRARIES. *See* DIGITAL LIBRARIES.

## VIRTUAL REALITY.
Fink, Jeri. Cyberseduction. Amherst, N.Y. :
Prometheus Books, 1999.
*TC QA76.9.P75 F53 1999*

Hayles, N. Katherine. How we became posthuman.
Chicago, Ill. : University of Chicago Press, 1999.

*TC Q335 .H394 1999*

**VIRTUAL REALITY IN LITERATURE.**
Hayles, N. Katherine. How we became posthuman.
Chicago, Ill. : University of Chicago Press, 1999.
*TC Q335 .H394 1999*

**The virtual university.**
Teare, Richard. London ; New York : Cassell, 1998.
*TC LC5215 .T42 1998*

**The virtuous therapist.**
Cohen, Elliot D. Belmont, CA : Brooks/Cole
Wadworth, 1999.
*TC BF637.C6 C46 1999*

**VIRUS DISEASES IN CHILDREN.** *See* AIDS
(DISEASE) IN CHILDREN.

**VIRUS DISEASES - JUVENILE LITERATURE.**
Berger, Melvin. Germs make me sick!. 1st ed. New
York : Crowell, c1985.
*TC QR57 .B47 1985*

**VIRUS-INDUCED IMMUNOSUPPRESSION.** *See*
AIDS (DISEASE).

**VIRUS INFECTIONS.** *See* VIRUS DISEASES.

**VIRUSES.**
Berger, Melvin. Germs make me sick!. 1st ed. New
York : Crowell, c1985.
*TC QR57 .B47 1985*

Rowan, Kate. I know how we fight germs. Cambridge,
Mass. : Candlewick Press, 1999.
*TC QR57 .R69 1999*

**VIRUSES - JUVENILE LITERATURE.**
Berger, Melvin. Germs make me sick!. 1st ed. New
York : Crowell, c1985.
*TC QR57 .B47 1985*

**VISION.** *See* MOTION PERCEPTION (VISION);
VISUAL PERCEPTION.

**Vision assessment :** shaping technology in 21st century
society towards a repertoire for technology
assessment / John Grin, Armin Grunwald (eds.). New
York : Springer, 2000. x, 192 p. ; 25 cm.
(Wissenschaftsethik und Technikfolgenbeurteilung ; Bd. 4)
Includes bibliographical references. ISBN 3-540-66633-8
(hardcover : alk. paper) DDC 303.48/3
*1. Technology assessment. 2. Technology - Social aspects. I.
Grin, John. II. Grunwald, Armin. III. Series.*
*TC T174.5 V57 2000*

**VISION DISORDERS.** *See also* BLINDNESS.
The Lighthouse handbook on vision impairment and
vision rehabilitation. New York, N.Y. : Oxford
University Press, 2000.
*TC RE91 .L54 2000*

**VISION DISORDERS IN CHILDREN.** *See also*
CHILDREN, BLIND; VISUALLY
HANDICAPPED CHILDREN.
Making the most of early communication
[videorecording]. New York, NY : Distributed by
AFB Press, c1997.
*TC HV1597.2 .M3 1997*

**VISION DISORDERS IN CHILDREN - PATIENTS.**
*See* VISUALLY HANDICAPPED CHILDREN.

**VISION DISORDERS IN OLD AGE.** *See*
VISUALLY HANDICAPPED AGED.

**VISION DISORDERS - PATIENTS.** *See*
VISUALLY HANDICAPPED.

**Vision impairment and vision rehabilitation.**
The Lighthouse handbook on vision impairment and
vision rehabilitation. New York, N.Y. : Oxford
University Press, 2000.
*TC RE91 .L54 2000*

**VISION - PSYCHOLOGICAL ASPECTS.** *See*
VISUAL PERCEPTION.

**VISIONS.** *See* DREAMS.

**Visions and revisions.**
Siddiqui, Zillur Rahman. Dhaka : University Press,
1997.
*TC LA1168 .S53 1997*

**Visions of the night.**
Bulkeley, Kelly, 1962- Albany, NY : State University
of New York Press, c1999.
*TC BF1091 .B94 1999*

**VISITORS, FOREIGN.** *See* STUDENTS,
FOREIGN.

**Visual aid based on ICD 10.**
Challenge cases [videorecording]. Princeton, N.J. :
Films for the Humanities & Sciences, 1998.

*TC RC455.2.C4 C4 1998*
Disorders due to psychoactive substance abuse
[videorecording]. Princeton, N.J. : Films for the
Humanities & Sciences, 1998.
*TC RC564 .D5 1998*

Mood disorders [videorecording]. Princeton, N.J. :
Films for the Humanities & Sciences, 1998.
*TC RC537 .M6 1998*

Organic disorders [videorecording]. Princeton, N.J. :
Films for the Humanities & Sciences, 1998.
*TC RC521 .O7 1998*

**VISUAL ANTHROPOLOGY.** *See*
PHOTOGRAPHY IN ETHNOLOGY.

**VISUAL ARTS.** *See* ART.

**The visual arts.**
Honour, Hugh. 5th ed. New York : Henry N. Abrams,
1999.
*TC N5300 .H68 1999*

**VISUAL COMMUNICATION.** *See also*
COMMERCIAL ART; GRAPHIC ARTS;
WRITTEN COMMUNICATION.
Barnard, Malcolm, 1958- Art, design, and visual
culture. New York : St. Martin's Press, 1998.
*TC N71 .B32 1998*

Looking at looking. Thousand Oaks, Calif. ; London :
Sage Publications, c2001.
*TC BF241 .L64 2001*

Schapiro, Meyer, 1904- Words, script, and pictures.
New York, NY : George Braziller, 1996.
*TC P93.5 .S33 1996*

Symbolic imprints. Aarhus : Aarhus University Press,
c1999.
*TC TR145 .S96 1999*

What is visual literacy? York, Maine : Stenhouse
Pub., c1996.
*TC LB1068 .W45 1996*

**VISUAL CORTEX.**
Zeki, Semir. Inner vision. Oxford ; New York :
Oxford University Press, c1999.
*TC N71 .Z45 1999*

**VISUAL DISCRIMINATION.** *See* VISUAL
PERCEPTION.

**VISUAL EDUCATION.** *See also* AUDIO-VISUAL
EDUCATION; PICTURES IN EDUCATION.
What is visual literacy? York, Maine : Stenhouse
Pub., c1996.
*TC LB1068 .W45 1996*

**Visual journal :** Harlem and D.C. in the thirties and
forties / edited by Deborah Willis and Jane Lusaka.
Washington, DC : Smithsonian Institution Press,
c1996. xiii, 208 p. : ill. ; 24 x 26 cm. Includes bibliographical
references. ISBN 1-56098-691-3 DDC 973/.0496073
*1. Documentary photography - New York (State) - New York -
History - 20th century. 2. Documentary photography -
Washington (D.C.) - History - 20th century. 3. Afro-
Americans - New York (State) - New York - History - 20th
century - Pictorial works. 4. Afro-Americans - Washington
(D.C.) - History - 20th century - Pictorial works. 5. Harlem
(New York, N.Y.) - History - 20th century - Pictorial works. 6.
Washington (D.C.) - History - 20th century - Pictorial works. I.
Willis-Thomas, Deborah, 1948- II. Lusaka, Jane.*
*TC TR820.5 .V57 1996*

**VISUAL LEARNING.**
What is visual literacy? York, Maine : Stenhouse
Pub., c1996.
*TC LB1068 .W45 1996*

**VISUAL LEARNING - UNITED STATES.**
Adams, Dennis M. Media and literacy. 2nd ed.
Springfield, Ill. : C.C. Thomas, c2000.
*TC LB1043 .A33 2000*

**Visual life.**
Dorothea Lange--a visual life. Washington :
Smithsonian Institution Press, c1994.
*TC TR140.L3 D67 1994*

**VISUAL LITERACY.**
What is visual literacy? York, Maine : Stenhouse
Pub., c1996.
*TC LB1068 .W45 1996*

**VISUAL PERCEPTION.** *See also* MOTION
PERCEPTION (VISION).
Dunning, William V., 1933- Changing images of
pictorial space. 1st ed. Syracuse : Syracuse University
Press, 1991.
*TC ND1475 .D86 1991*

Flint, Kate. The Victorians and the visual imagination.
Cambridge, U.K. ; New York : Cambridge University
Press, 2000.
*TC N6767 .F58 2000*

Krauss, Rosalind E. The optical unconscious. 1st MIT
Press pbk. ed. Cambridge, Mass. : MIT Press, 1994.
*TC N7430.5 .K73 1994*

Looking at looking. Thousand Oaks, Calif. ; London :
Sage Publications, c2001.
*TC BF241 .L64 2001*

Podro, Michael. Depiction. New Haven, CT : Yale
University Press, c1998.
*TC N71 .P64 1998*

Stratification in cognition and consciousness.
Amsterdam ; Philadelphia : J. Benjamins, c1999.
*TC BF444 .S73 1999*

Tsamasiros, Katherine V. Using interactive
multimedia software to improve cognition of complex
imagery in adolescents. 1998.
*TC 06 no. 10905*

Willats, John. Art and representation. Princeton, N.J. :
Princeton University Press, c1997.
*TC N7430.5 .W55 1997*

Zeki, Semir. Inner vision. Oxford ; New York :
Oxford University Press, c1999.
*TC N71 .Z45 1999*

**VISUAL PERCEPTION - CONGRESSES.**
Attention, space, and action. Oxford ; New York :
Oxford University Press, 1999.
*TC QP405 .A865 1999*

**VISUAL PERCEPTION - CONGRESSES.**
Attention, space, and action. Oxford ; New York :
Oxford University Press, 1999.
*TC QP405 .A865 1999*

**VISUALIZATION.** *See* IMAGERY
(PSYCHOLOGY).

**Visualizing labor in American sculpture.**
Dabakis, Melissa. New York : Cambridge University
Press, 1999.
*TC NB1952.L33 D24 1999*

**VISUALLY DISABLED.** *See* VISUALLY
HANDICAPPED.

**VISUALLY HANDICAPPED.** *See also* BLIND;
VISUALLY HANDICAPPED AGED.
Barnicle, Katherine Ann. Evaluation of the interaction
between users of screen reading technology and
graphical user interface elements. 1999.
*TC 085 B265*

**VISUALLY HANDICAPPED AGED.** *See* BLIND
AGED.

**VISUALLY HANDICAPPED AGED - SERVICES
FOR.**
Brighter visions [videorecording. Burbank, CA :
RCA/Columbia Pictures Home Video ; Toluca Lake,
CA : [Distributed by] Corporate Productions, c1991.
*TC HV1597.5 .B67 1991*

**VISUALLY HANDICAPPED - BOOKS AND
READING.**
European modernism. New York, N.Y. :
OpticalTouch Systems ; Louisville, Ky. : American
Printing House for the Blind, c1998-1999.
*TC N6758 .A7 1999*

**VISUALLY HANDICAPPED CHILDREN -
EDUCATION.**
Bridges to independence [videorecording. Burbank,
CA : RCA/Columbia Pictures Home Video ; [S.l. :
Distributed by] Rank Video Services Production,
c1991.
*TC HV1646 .B7 1991*

**VISUALLY HANDICAPPED CHILDREN -
EDUCATION (EARLY CHILDHOOD).**
Bright beginnings [videorecording. Burbank, CA :
RCA/Columbia Pictures Home Video ; Toluca Lake,
CA : [Distributed by] Corporate Productions, c1991.
*TC HV1642 .B67 1991*

Bright beginnings [videorecording. Burbank, CA :
RCA/Columbia Pictures Home Video ; [S.l. :
Distributed by] Rank Video Services America, c1991.
*TC HV1642 .B67 1991*

Making the most of early communication
[videorecording]. New York, NY : Distributed by
AFB Press, c1997.
*TC HV1597.2 .M3 1997*

**VISUALLY HANDICAPPED CHILDREN -
LANGUAGE.**
Making the most of early communication

[videorecording]. New York, NY : Distributed by AFB Press, c1997.
*TC HV1597.2 .M3 1997*

**VISUALLY HANDICAPPED CHILDREN - PSYCHOLOGY.**
Making the most of early communication [videorecording]. New York, NY : Distributed by AFB Press, c1997.
*TC HV1597.2 .M3 1997*

**VISUALLY HANDICAPPED CHILDREN - REHABILITATION.**
Making the most of early communication [videorecording]. New York, NY : Distributed by AFB Press, c1997.
*TC HV1597.2 .M3 1997*

**VISUALLY HANDICAPPED - EDUCATION.**
Bridges to independence [videorecording. Burbank, CA : RCA/Columbia Pictures Home Video ; [S.l. : Distributed by] Rank Video Services Production, c1991.
*TC HV1646 .B7 1991*

**VISUALLY HANDICAPPED - EMPLOYMENT.**
Work sight [videorecording]. Burbank, Ca. : RCA/ Columbia Pictures Home Video, c1991.
*TC HV1652 .W6 1991*

**VISUALLY HANDICAPPED - ORIENTATION AND MOBILITY.**
Touch 'n' go [videorecording. Burbank, Calif. : Columbia Tristar Home Video ; [S.l. : Distributed by] Rank Video Services Production, c1991.
*TC HV1626 .T6 1991*

**VISUALLY HANDICAPPED - REHABILITATION.**
The Lighthouse handbook on vision impairment and vision rehabilitation. New York, N.Y. : Oxford University Press, 2000.
*TC RE91 .L54 2000*

Touch 'n' go [videorecording. Burbank, Calif. : Columbia Tristar Home Video ; [S.l. : Distributed by] Rank Video Services Production, c1991.
*TC HV1626 .T6 1991*

**VISUALLY HANDICAPPED - SERVICES FOR.**
Touch 'n' go [videorecording. Burbank, Calif. : Columbia Tristar Home Video ; [S.l. : Distributed by] Rank Video Services Production, c1991.
*TC HV1626 .T6 1991*

**VISUALLY HANDICAPPED - UNITED STATES - BOOKS AND READING.**
Leibs, Andrew. A field guide for the sight-impaired reader. Westport, Conn. ; London : Greenwood Press, 1999.
*TC HV1731 .L45 1999*

**VISUALLY IMPAIRED.** *See* **VISUALLY HANDICAPPED.**

**VITAL SIGNS.** *See also* **BLOOD PRESSURE.**
Shepherdson, Charles. New York : Routledge, 2000.
*TC BF173 .S4975 2000*

**Vital signs 2000.**
Brown, Lester Russell, 1934- New York : Norton, c2000.
*TC HD75.6 .B768 2000*

**Vital signs** : feminist reconfigurations of the bio/logical body / edited by Margrit Shildrick and Janet Price. Edinburgh : Edinburgh University Press, c1998. vii, 256 p. : ill., port. ; 24 cm. Includes bibliographical references and index. ISBN 0-7486-0962-8 (pbk.) ISBN 0-7486-0963-6 (hardback) DDC 305.42/01
*1. Feminist theory. 2. Women - Physiology. 3. Body, Human - Social aspects. 4. Body, Human - Symbolic aspects. 5. Postmodernism. 6. Medical sciences. 7. Body, Human. 8. Postmodernism. 9. Feminist theory. 10. Medical sciences. I. Shildrick, Margrit. II. Price, Janet.*
*TC HQ1190 .V56 1998*

**VITAL STATISTICS.** *See* **AGE DISTRIBUTION (DEMOGRAPHY); POPULATION - STATISTICS.**

**Vitale, Barbara Ann, 1944-.**
Nugent, Patricia Mary, 1944- Test success. 3rd ed. Philadelphia : F.A. Davis, c2000.
*TC RT55 .N77 2000*

**Vitale, Stefano, ill.**
Jewell, Nancy. Sailor Song. New York : Clarion Books, c1999.
*TC PZ7.J55325 Sai 1999*

**VITAMIN B COMPLEX.** *See* **CARNITINE.**

**VITAMIN BT.** *See* **CARNITINE.**

**Viteritti, Joseph P., 1946-** Choosing equality : school choice, the constitution and civil society / Joseph P. Viteritti. Washington, D.C. : Brookings Institution Press, c1999. x, 284 p. ; 24 cm. Includes bibliographical references and index. ISBN 0-8157-9046-5 (alk. paper)
*1. School choice - United States. 2. School choice - Law and legislation - United States. 3. Educational equalization - United States. I. Title.*
*TC LB1027.9 .V58 1999*

City schools. Baltimore : Johns Hopkins University Press, c2000.
*TC LC5133.N4 C57 2000*

**Vittetoe, Craig B.**
Kirby, Anne. Elementary school English. Teachers' ed. Palo Alto, Calif. : Addison-Wesley Publishing Company, 1967.
*TC PE1112 .K57 1967 Teachers' Ed.*

Kirby, Anne. Elementary school English. Palo Alto, Calif. : Addison-Wesley Publishing Company, 1967.
*TC PE1112 .K57 1967*

**Vivas, Julie, 1947- ill.**
Zamorano, Ana. Let's eat!. New York : Scholastic Press, 1997.
*TC PZ7.Z25455 Le 1997*

**Vlaeminke, Meriel.** The English higher grade schools : a lost opportunity / Meriel Vlaeminke. London ; Portland, OR : Woburn Press, 2000. viii, 259 p. ; 24 cm. (Woburn education series, 1462-2076) Includes bibliographical references (p. [231]-251) and index. ISBN 0-7130-0220-4 (cloth) DDC 373.42
*1. Education, Secondary - England - History. 2. Education, Secondary - Social aspects - England. I. Title. II. Series.*
*TC LA634 .V52 2000*

**VOCABULARY.**
1,000 French words. Princeton, N.J. : Berlitz Kids, Berlitz Pub. Co., 1998.
*TC PC2680 .A15 1998*

1,000 German words. Princeton, N.J. : Berlitz Kids, c1998.
*TC PF3629 .A14 1998*

1,000 Spanish words. Princeton, N.J. : Berlitz Kids, c1998.
*TC PC4680 .A13 1998*

**VOCABULARY - JUVENILE FILMS.**
Exploring the English language [videorecording]. [Princeton, N.J.] : Video Tutor ; [Chesterton, Ind.? : Distributed by] Griffin Media Design, 1988, c1986.

**VOCABULARY - STUDY AND TEACHING (ELEMENTARY).**
What is visual literacy? York, Maine : Stenhouse Pub., c1996.
*TC LB1068 .W45 1996*

**VOCAL CULTURE.** *See* **SINGING.**

**VOCAL DUETS, UNACCOMPANIED - BIBLIOGRAPHY.**
Newman, Marilyn Stephanie Mercedes, 1954- Duet literature for female voices with piano, organ or unaccompanied. 1998.
*TC 06 no. 10897*

**VOCAL DUETS WITH KEYBOARD INSTRUMENT - 19TH CENTURY - BIBLIOGRAPHY.**
Newman, Marilyn Stephanie Mercedes, 1954- Duet literature for female voices with piano, organ or unaccompanied. 1998.
*TC 06 no. 10897*

**VOCAL DUETS WITH KEYBOARD INSTRUMENT - 20TH CENTURY - BIBLIOGRAPHY.**
Newman, Marilyn Stephanie Mercedes, 1954- Duet literature for female voices with piano, organ or unaccompanied. 1998.
*TC 06 no. 10897*

**VOCAL MUSIC.** *See* **SONGS.**

**VOCAL MUSIC - HISTORY AND CRITICISM.** *See* **CHORAL MUSIC.**

**VOCAL TECHNIQUE.** *See* **SINGING - INSTRUCTION AND STUDY.**

**VOCATION, CHOICE OF.** *See* **VOCATIONAL GUIDANCE.**

**Vocational and adult education in Europe** / edited by Fons van Wieringen and Graham Attwell. Dordrecht ; Boston ; London : Kluwer Academic, c1999. ix, 441 p. : ill. ; 25 cm. Includes bibliographical references and index. ISBN 0-7923-5975-5 (alk. paper) DDC 370.11/3/094
*1. Vocational education - Europe. 2. Adult education - Europe. I. Wieringen, Fons van. II. Attwell, Graham.*

*TC LC1047.E8 V58 1999*

**VOCATIONAL ASPIRATIONS.** *See* **VOCATIONAL INTERESTS.**

**VOCATIONAL EDUCATION.** *See* **HANDICAPPED YOUTH - VOCATIONAL EDUCATION; MANUAL TRAINING; TECHNICAL EDUCATION; VOCATIONAL REHABILITATION.**

**Vocational education and training.**
Grubb, W. Norton. The roles of evaluation for vocational education and training. London : Kogan Page ; Sterling, VA : Distributed in the US by Stylus Pub. Inc., 1999.
*TC LC1044 .G78 1999*

**Vocational education and training reform** : matching skills to markets and budgets / edited by Indermit S. Gill, Fred Fluitman, and Amit Dar. Washington, D.C. : World Bank/Oxford University Press, 2000. xxiv, 542 p. : ill. ; 24 cm. Includes bibliographical references and index. ISBN 0-19-521590-7 DDC 331.25/92
*1. Vocational education - Economic aspects. 2. Occupational training - Economic aspects. I. Gill, Indermit Singh, 1961- II. Fluitman, Fred. III. Dar, Amit.*
*TC LC1044 .V62 2000*

**VOCATIONAL EDUCATION - ECONOMIC ASPECTS.**
Vocational education and training reform. Washington, D.C. : World Bank/Oxford University Press, 2000.
*TC LC1044 .V62 2000*

**VOCATIONAL EDUCATION - EUROPE.**
Bridging the skills gap between work and education. Dordrecht ; Boston : Kluwer Academic Publishers, c1999.
*TC LC5056.A2 B75 1999*

Vocational and adult education in Europe. Dordrecht ; Boston ; London : Kluwer Academic, c1999.
*TC LC1047.E8 V58 1999*

**VOCATIONAL EDUCATION - EVALUATION.**
Grubb, W. Norton. The roles of evaluation for vocational education and training. London : Kogan Page ; Sterling, VA : Distributed in the US by Stylus Pub. Inc., 1999.
*TC LC1044 .G78 1999*

**VOCATIONAL EDUCATION - GERMANY (EAST).**
Evans, Karen, 1949- Learning and work in the risk society. New York : St. Martin's Press, 2000.
*TC HD6278.G4 E93 2000*

**VOCATIONAL EDUCATION - GREAT BRITAIN.**
Ainley, Patrick. Learning policy. Basingstoke, Hampshire : Macmillan Press ; New York : St. Martin's Press, 1999.
*TC LC93.G7 A76 1999*

**Vocational education in the industrialization of Japan** / edited by Toshio Toyoda. Tokyo : United Nations University, c1987. xii, 267 p. : ill. ; 24 cm. English translation of the essential parts of: Wagakuni rirukii no jitsugyō kyōiku; and: Wagakuni sangyōka to jitsugyō kyōiku. "HSDB-1/10/UNUP-584"--T.p. verso. "United Nations sales no. E.87.III.A.1"--T.p. verso. Includes bibliographical references and index. ISBN 92-808-0584-3 DDC 370.1130952
*1. Vocational education - Japan. 2. Occupational training - Japan. 3. Employees - Training of - Japan. I. Toyoda, Toshio, 1925- II. Project on Technology Transfer, Transformation, and Development: the Japanese Experience (United Nations University)*
*TC LC1047.J3 V63 1987*

**Vocational education in the United States** : toward the year 2000 / Karen Levesque ... [et al.] ; Dawn Nelson, project officer. Washington, DC : U.S. Dept. of Education, Office of Educational Research and Improvement : For sale by the U.S. G.P.O., Supt. of Docs., [2000] xxxiv, 390 p. : ill. ; 28 cm. (Statistical analysis report / National Center for Education Statistics) "February 2000." "NCES 2000-029." Includes bibliographical references (p. 387-390). DDC 370.11/3/0973021
*1. Vocational education - United States - Statistics. I. Levesque, Karen. II. Nelson, Dawn D. III. National Center for Education Statistics. IV. Series: Statistical analysis report (National Center for Education Statistics)*
*TC LC1045 .V5874 2000*

**VOCATIONAL EDUCATION - JAPAN.**
Vocational education in the industrialization of Japan. Tokyo : United Nations University, c1987.
*TC LC1047.J3 V63 1987*

**VOCATIONAL EDUCATION - PERIODICALS.**
Industrial education magazine. Chicago, Ill. : The University of Chicago Press, 1899-1939.

**Vocational education Sept. 1914.**
Industrial education magazine. Chicago, Ill. : The
University of Chicago Press, 1899-1939.

**VOCATIONAL EDUCATION - UNITED STATES -
STATISTICS.**
Vocational education in the United States.
Washington, DC : U.S. Dept. of Education, Office of
Educational Research and Improvement : For sale by
the U.S. G.P.O., Supt. of Docs., [2000]
*TC LC1045 .V5874 2000*

**VOCATIONAL EDUCATIONAL - HUNGARY.**
Disadvantaged youth project. Budapest : Ministry of
Labour, 1998.
*TC LC4096.H9 D57 1998*

**VOCATIONAL EVALUATION.**
Prediger, D. J. Basic structure of work-relevant
abilities. Iowa City, Iowa : ACT, 1998.
*TC LB3051 .A3 no. 98-9*

**VOCATIONAL GUIDANCE.** *See also* **CAREER
CHANGES; CAREER DEVELOPMENT;
EDUCATIONAL COUNSELING; JOB
HUNTING; OCCUPATIONS; PROFESSIONS;
VOCATIONAL INTERESTS; VOCATIONAL
QUALIFICATIONS; VOCATIONAL
REHABILITATION.**
Figler, Howard E. The career counselor's handbook.
Berkeley, Calif. : Ten Speed Press, c1999.
*TC HF5549.5.C35 F54 1999*

Giangrande, Gregory. The liberal arts advantage. New
York : Avon Books, c1998.
*TC HF5382.7 .G53 1998*

Holland, John L. Making vocational choices. 3rd ed.
Odessa, Fla. : Psychological Assessment Resources,
c1997.
*TC HF5381 .H5668 1997*

Peatling, John H. Career development. Muncie, Ind. :
Accelerated Development, c1977.
*TC BF697 .P384*

Pervola, Cindy, 1956- How to get a job if you're a
teenager. Fort Atkinson, Wis. : Alleyside Press, 1998.
*TC HF5383 .P44 1998*

Pervola, Cindy, 1956- How to get a job if you're a
teenager. Fort Atkinson, Wis. : Alleyside Press, 1998.
*TC HF5383 .P44 1998*

Peterson, Nadene. The role of work in people's lives.
Australia ; Belmont, Calif. : Wadsworth Pub. Co.,
c2000.
*TC HF5381 .P483 2000*

**VOCATIONAL GUIDANCE CASE STUDIES.**
Swanson, Jane Laurel. Career theory and practice.
Thousand Oaks, Calif. : Sage Publications, c1999.
*TC HF5381 .S937 1999*

**VOCATIONAL GUIDANCE - CONGRESSES.**
American Society for Training and Development.
Issues in career and human resource development.
Madison, Wisc. : American Society for Training and
Development, c1980.
*TC HF5549.5.T7 A59 1980*

**VOCATIONAL GUIDANCE - DICTIONARIES.**
Career discovery encyclopedia. 4th ed. Chicago :
Ferguson Pub. Co., 2000.
*TC HF5381.2 .C37 2000*

**VOCATIONAL GUIDANCE - DICTIONARIES -
JUVENILE LITERATURE.**
Career discovery encyclopedia. 4th ed. Chicago :
Ferguson Pub. Co., 2000.
*TC HF5381.2 .C37 2000*

**VOCATIONAL GUIDANCE FOR THE
HANDICAPPED.**
Janus, Raizi Abby. Mapping careers with LD and
ADD clients. New York : Columbia University Press,
c1999.
*TC HV1568.5 .J36 1999*

Janus, Raizi Abby. Mapping careers with LD and
ADD clients. New York : Columbia University Press,
c1999.
*TC HV1568.5 .J36 1999*

**VOCATIONAL GUIDANCE FOR THE
HANDICAPPED - UNITED STATES.**
Pierangelo, Roger. Complete guide to special
education transition services. West Nyack, NY :
Center for Applied Research in Education, c1997.
*TC HV1569.3.Y68 P55 1997*

**VOCATIONAL GUIDANCE - HANDBOOKS,
MANUALS, ETC.**
Encyclopedia of careers and vocational guidance. 11th
ed. Chicago : Ferguson Pub. Co., 2000.

*TC HF5381 .E52 2000*

**VOCATIONAL GUIDANCE - NEW YORK
(STATE) - NEW YORK.**
Howell, Ron. One hundred jobs :b a panorama of
work in the American city. New York : New Press :
Distributed by W.W. Norton, 1999.
*TC HF5382.5.U6 N37 1999*

**VOCATIONAL GUIDANCE - PERIODICALS.**
Journal of college placement. [Philadelphia, Pa. etc.],
The College Placement Council, inc. [etc.]

**VOCATIONAL GUIDANCE - UNITED STATES.**
Career counseling of college students. Washington,
DC : American Psychological Association, c2000.
*TC LB2343 .C3273 2000*

Carter, Carol. Majoring in the rest of your life. Upper
Saddle River, NJ : Prentice Hall, c2000.
*TC HF5382.5.U5 C373 2000*

Gray, Kenneth C. Getting real. Thousand Oaks,
Calif. : Corwin Press, c2000.
*TC HF5382.5.U5 G676 2000*

**VOCATIONAL INTERESTS.**
Janus, Raizi Abby. Mapping careers with LD and
ADD clients. New York : Columbia University Press,
c1999.
*TC HV1568.5 .J36 1999*

Janus, Raizi Abby. Mapping careers with LD and
ADD clients. New York : Columbia University Press,
c1999.
*TC HV1568.5 .J36 1999*

**VOCATIONAL INTERESTS - TESTING.**
Testing and assessment in counseling practice. 2nd ed.
Mahwah, N.J. : L. Erlbaum Associates, 2000.
*TC BF176 .T423 2000*

**VOCATIONAL NURSING.** *See* **PRACTICAL
NURSING.**

**VOCATIONAL OPPORTUNITIES.** *See*
**VOCATIONAL GUIDANCE.**

**Vocational psychology**
Testing and assessment in counseling practice. 2nd ed.
Mahwah, N.J. : L. Erlbaum Associates, 2000.
*TC BF176 .T423 2000*

**VOCATIONAL QUALIFICATIONS.**
Janus, Raizi Abby. Mapping careers with LD and
ADD clients. New York : Columbia University Press,
c1999.
*TC HV1568.5 .J36 1999*

Janus, Raizi Abby. Mapping careers with LD and
ADD clients. New York : Columbia University Press,
c1999.
*TC HV1568.5 .J36 1999*

**VOCATIONAL QUALIFICATIONS - ENGLAND.**
*See* **NATIONAL VOCATIONAL
QUALIFICATIONS (GREAT BRITAIN).**

**VOCATIONAL QUALIFICATIONS - GREAT
BRITAIN.**
Raggatt, Peter C. M. Government, markets and
vocational qualifications. London : New York :
Falmer Press, 1999.
*TC HF5381.6 .R34 1999*

**VOCATIONAL QUALIFICATIONS - WALES.** *See*
**NATIONAL VOCATIONAL
QUALIFICATIONS (GREAT BRITAIN).**

**VOCATIONAL REHABILITATION.** *See* **DEAF -
EMPLOYMENT; VOCATIONAL GUIDANCE.**

**VOCATIONAL REHABILITATION -
PITTSBURG, CALIF.**
Craddock, George W. Social disadvantagement and
dependency: Lexington, Mass., Heath Lexington
Books [1970]
*TC HD7256.U6 C438*

**VOCATIONAL REHABILITATION - UNITED
STATES - CASE STUDIES.**
Spencer, Gary. Structure and dynamics of social
intervention: Lexington, Mass., Heath Lexington
Books [1970]
*TC HV91 .S63*

**VOCATIONAL TRAINING.** *See*
**OCCUPATIONAL TRAINING;
VOCATIONAL EDUCATION.**

**Vogel, Harold L. (Harold Leslie), 1946-** Entertainment
industry economics : a guide for financial analysis /
Harold L. Vogel. 4th ed. Cambridge [England] ; New
York, NY, USA : Cambridge University Press, 1998.
xx, 490 p. : ill. ; 24 cm. Includes bibliographical references (p.
463-475) and index. ISBN 0-521-59438-3 (hardback) DDC

338.4/7791
*1. Performing arts - Finance. I. Title.*
*TC PN1590.F55 V6 1998*

**Vogele, William B.**
Protest, power, and change. New York : Garland Pub.,
1997.
*TC HM278 .P76 1997*

**Vogeli, Bruce R.** Mathematics for mastery / Bruce R.
Vogeli ... [et al.] Teacher's ed. Morristown, N. J. :
Silver Burdett, 1978. v. : col. ill. ; 24 cm. Includes index.
ISBN 0-382-01346-8 (v. 1). ISBN 0-382-01348-4 (v. 2). ISBN
0-382-01350-6 (v. 3). ISBN 0-382-01352-2 (v. 4). ISBN
0-382-01354-9 (v. 5). ISBN 0-382-01356-5 (v. 6). ISBN
0-382-01358-1 (v. 7). ISBN 0-382-01361-1 (v. 8)
*1. Mathematics. 2. Mathematics - Study and teaching
(Elementary). I. Vogeli, Bruce Ramon.*
*TC QA107 .M375 1978 Teacher's Ed.*

**Vogeli, Bruce Ramon.**
Vogeli, Bruce R. Mathematics for mastery. Teacher's
ed. Morristown, N. J. : Silver Burdett, 1978.
*TC QA107 .M375 1978 Teacher's Ed.*

**Vogelsberg, R. Timm.**
McGregor, Gail Inclusive schooling practices. [S.l.] :
Allegheny University of Health Sciences ; Balitmore :
Distributed exclusively by Paul H. Brookes
Publishing, c1998.
*TC LC4031 .M394 1998*

**Vogt, MaryEllen.**
Echevarria, Jana, 1956- Making content
comprehensible for English language learners.
Boston, MA : Allyn and Bacon, 2000.
*TC PE1128.A2 E24 2000*

**Vogtle, Laura K.**
Snell, Martha E. Social relationships and peer support.
Baltimore, Md. ; London : Paul H. Brookes Pub. Co.,
c2000.
*TC LC4069 .S54 2000*

**VOICE.** *See also* **LARYNX; PHONETICS;
SINGING; SPEECH.**
Singing development. London : Roehampton Institute,
Centre for Advanced Studies in Music Education,
Faculty of Education, [1997?]
*TC MT898 .S55 1997*

**The voice and voice therapy.**
Boone, Daniel R. 6th ed. Boston ; London : Allyn &
Bacon, c2000.
*TC RF540 .B66 2000*

**VOICE BOX.** *See* **LARYNX.**

**VOICE CULTURE.** *See* **SINGING.**

**VOICE DISORDERS.**
Boone, Daniel R. The voice and voice therapy. 6th ed.
Boston ; London : Allyn & Bacon, c2000.
*TC RF540 .B66 2000*

Stemple, Joseph C. Clinical voice pathology. 3rd ed.
San Diego : Singular Pub. Group, c2000.
*TC RF510 .S74 2000*

**VOICE DISORDERS.**
Stemple, Joseph C. Clinical voice pathology. 3rd ed.
San Diego : Singular Pub. Group, c2000.
*TC RF510 .S74 2000*

**VOICE DISORDERS.**
Voice quality measurement. San Diego : Singular Pub.
Group, c2000.
*TC RF510 .V67 2000*

**VOICE DISORDERS - DIAGNOSIS.**
Baken, R. J. (Ronald J.), 1943- Clinical measurement
of speech and voice. 2nd ed. San Diego : Singular
Thomson Learning, c2000.
*TC RC423 .B28 2000*

**VOICE DISORDERS - DIAGNOSIS.**
Boone, Daniel R. The voice and voice therapy. 6th ed.
Boston ; London : Allyn & Bacon, c2000.
*TC RF540 .B66 2000*

**VOICE DISORDERS - ETIOLOGY.**
Boone, Daniel R. The voice and voice therapy. 6th ed.
Boston ; London : Allyn & Bacon, c2000.
*TC RF540 .B66 2000*

**VOICE DISORDERS - THERAPY.**
Boone, Daniel R. The voice and voice therapy. 6th ed.
Boston ; London : Allyn & Bacon, c2000.
*TC RF540 .B66 2000*

**VOICE - MEASUREMENT.**
Baken, R. J. (Ronald J.), 1943- Clinical measurement
of speech and voice. 2nd ed. San Diego : Singular
Thomson Learning, c2000.
*TC RC423 .B28 2000*

**VOICE - PHYSIOLOGICAL ASPECTS.**
Voice quality measurement. San Diego : Singular Pub.
Group, c2000.
*TC RF510 .V67 2000*

**VOICE - PHYSIOLOGY.**
Boone, Daniel R. The voice and voice therapy. 6th ed.
Boston ; London : Allyn & Bacon, c2000.
*TC RF540 .B66 2000*

**VOICE PRODUCTION, ALARYNGEAL.**
The Artificial larynx handbook. New York : Grune &
Stratton, c1978.
*TC RF538 .A77*

**Voice quality measurement** / edited by Raymond D.
Kent, Martin J. Ball. San Diego : Singular Pub.
Group, c2000. xiii, 492 p. : ill. ; 25 cm. Includes
bibliographical references and index. ISBN 1-56593-991-3
(hbk. : alk. paper) DDC 616.85/5
*1. Voice disorders. 2. Voice - Physiological aspects. I. Kent,
Raymond D. II. Ball, Martin J. (Martin John)*
*TC RF510 .V67 2000*

**VOICE - THERAPEUTIC USE.**
Newham, Paul, 1962- Using voice and theatre in
therapy. London ; Philadelphia, Pa. : Jessica Kingsley
Publishers, 1999.
*TC RZ999 .N437 1999*

**VOICE TRAINING.**
Boone, Daniel R. The voice and voice therapy. 6th ed.
Boston ; London : Allyn & Bacon, c2000.
*TC RF540 .B66 2000*

**Voices.**
Green, Thomas F. Notre Dame, Ind. : University of
Notre Dame Press, c1999.
*TC LC268 .G667 1999*

**Voices of contemporary Australian women artists.**
Voigt, Anna. New visions, new perspectives.
Roseville East, NSW : Craftsman House, 1996.
*TC N7400.2 .V65 1996*

**Voices of the other.**
McGillis, Roderick. New York : Garland Publishing.,
Inc., c2000.
*TC PN344 .M35 2000*

**Voices unheard [videorecording].**
Juvenile sex offenders [videorecording]. Princeton,
N.J. : Films for the Humanities & Sciences, c1998.
*TC HV9067.S48 J8 1998*

**Voigt, Anna.**
Drury, Nevill, 1947- Fire and shadow. Roseville East,
NWS : Craftsman House ;Australia : United States :
G + B Arts International [distributor], c1996.
*TC N7400.2 .D78 1996*

New visions, new perspectives : voices of
contemporary Australian women artists / Anna Voigt.
Roseville East, NSW : Craftsman House, 1996. 312 p. :
col. ill. ; 30 cm. Includes bibliographical references (p. 303-
306) and index. ISBN 976-8097-92-2
*1. Art, Australian. 2. Art, Modern - 20th century - Australia. 3.
Women artists - Australia. I. Title. II. Title: Voices of
contemporary Australian women artists*
*TC N7400.2 .V65 1996*

**VOLCANISM.**
Farndon, John. Volcanoes. 1st American ed. New
York : DK Pub., 1998.
*TC QE522 .F37 1998*

**Volcanoes.**
Coleman, Satis N. (Satis Narrona), 1878-1961. New
York, The John Day Company [1946]
*TC QE522 .C56*

Farndon, John. 1st American ed. New York : DK
Pub., 1998.
*TC QE522 .F37 1998*

**VOLCANOES.**
Coleman, Satis N. (Satis Narrona), 1878-1961.
Volcanoes, New York, The John Day Company
[1946]
*TC QE522 .C56*

Farndon, John. Volcanoes. 1st American ed. New
York : DK Pub., 1998.
*TC QE522 .F37 1998*

The living machine [videorecording]. [New York,
N.Y.?] : Unapix Entertainment, Inc. [distributor],
c1996.
*TC QB631.2 .L5 1996*

**Volgy, Sandra Everett.**
Everett, Craig A. Family therapy for ADHD. New
York : Guilford Press, 1999.
*TC RJ506.H9 E94 1999*

**Volk, Mary Crawford.**
Sargent, John Singer, 1856-1925. John Singer
Sargent. Princeton : Princeton University Press, 1998.
*TC ND237.S3 A4 1998a*

**Volkwein, J. Fredericks.**
What is institutional research all about ? San
Francisco, Calif. : Jossey-Bass Publishers, c1999.
*TC LB2326.3 .W43 1999*

**VOLUNTARISM.** *See also* **ASSOCIATIONS,
INSTITUTIONS, ETC.**
Robinson, Anna Bess. Leadership development in
women's civic organizations. 1999.
*TC 06 no. 11168*

**VOLUNTARISM - NEW YORK (STATE) - NEW
YORK.**
Ostrower, Francie. Why the wealthy give. Princeton,
N.J. : Princeton University Press, c1995.
*TC HV99.N59 O85 1995*

**VOLUNTARISM - UNITED STATES.**
De Pree, Max. Leading without power. 1st ed. San
Francisco, Calif. : Jossey-Bass, c1997.
*TC HN90.V64 D4 1997*

Ladd, Everett Carll. The Ladd report. New York :
Free Press, c1999.
*TC HN90.V64 L33 1999*

**VOLUNTARY ACTION.** *See* **VOLUNTARISM.**

**VOLUNTARY ASSOCIATIONS.** *See*
**ASSOCIATIONS, INSTITUTIONS, ETC.**

**VOLUNTARY ORGANIZATIONS.** *See*
**ASSOCIATIONS, INSTITUTIONS, ETC.**

**VOLUNTARY WORKERS.**
Integrating community service into nursing education.
New York, NY : Springer Pub. Co., c1999.
*TC RT76 .I55 1999*

**VOLUNTEER WORK.** *See* **VOLUNTARISM.**

**VOLUNTEER WORKERS IN EDUCATION.**
Wachter, Joanne C. Classroom volunteers. Thousand
Oaks, Calif. : Corwin Press, c1999.
*TC LB2844.1.V6 W33 1999*

**VOLUNTEERING.** *See* **VOLUNTARISM.**

**VOLUNTEERISM.** *See* **VOLUNTARISM.**

**VOLUNTEERS.** *See* **CAREGIVERS.**

**VOMITING.** *See* **NAUSEA.**

**Von Dehsen, Christian D.**
Philosophers and religious leaders. Phoenix, Ariz. :
Oryx Press, 1999.
*TC B104 .P48 1999*

**Von Klopp, A.**
Functional categories, argument structure and
parametric variation. Edinburgh : Centre for Cognitive
Study, University of Edinburgh, c1994.
*TC P151 .F86 1994*

**Vonlanthen, A. (Andy), 1961- .
Hearing instrument technology.**
Vonlanthen, A. (Andy), 1961- Hearing instrument
technology for the hearing healthcare professional.
2nd ed. San Diego : Singular Pub. Group, c2000.
*TC RF300 .V66 2000*

Hearing instrument technology for the hearing
healthcare professional / by Andi Vonlanthen. 2nd ed.
San Diego : Singular Pub. Group, c2000. ix, 248 p. :
ill. ; 24 cm. (A Singular audiology textbook) Spine title:
Hearing instrument technology. Rev. ed. of: Hearing
instrument technology / A. Vonlanthen. [1996?] Includes
bibliographical references and index. ISBN 0-7693-0072-3
(hard cover : alk. paper) DDC 617.8/9
*1. Hearing aids. 2. Hearing disorders. 3. Audiometry. 4.
Hearing Aids. 5. Technology, Medical - instrumentation. I.
Vonlanthen, A. (Andy), 1961- . Hearing instrument technology.
II. Title. III. Title: Hearing instrument technology IV. Series:
Singular audiology text.*
*TC RF300 .V66 2000*

**Vorderman, Carol.**
Gender and the interpretation of emotion
[videorecording]. Princeton, NJ : Films for the
Humanities & Sciences, c1997.
*TC BF592.F33 G4 1997*

**Vorwerg, G. (Gisela).
Die Technik des Partnerwahiversuchs.**
Vorwerg, Manfred. Sozialpsychologische
Strukturanalysen des Kollektivs. Berlin, Deutscher
Verlag der Wissenschaften, 1966.
*TC HM291 .V6*

**Vorwerg, Manfred.** Sozialpsychologische
Strukturanalysen des Kollektivs. Mit einem Anhang
"Die Technik des Partnerwahlversuchs," von Gisela
Vorwerg. Berlin, Deutscher Verlag der
Wissenschaften, 1966. 176 p. with illus., fold. table. 22 cm.
Summaries in English, German and Russian. Bibliography: p.
165-172. DDC 301.1
*1. Social psychology. 2. Small groups. 3. Social interaction. I.
Vorwerg, G. (Gisela). Die Technik des Partnerwahiversuchs.
II. Title.*
*TC HM291 .V6*

**Vos Savant, Marilyn, 1946-** The art of spelling : the
madness and the method / by Marilyn vos Savant ;
illustrations by Joan Reilly. New York : W.W.
Norton, 2000. 204 p. : ill. ; 22 cm. Includes bibliographical
references and index. ISBN 0-393-04903-5 DDC 421/.52
*1. English language - Orthography and spelling. I. Title.*
*TC PE1143 .V67 2000*

**Vosburgh, Lynn.**
Stimolo, Bob. Introduction to school marketing.
[Haddam], Conn. : School Market Research Institute,
c1989.
*TC HF5415.122 .S75 1989*

**Vosniadou, Stella.**
Modelling changes in understanding. Amsterdam ;
New York : Pergamon, 1999.
*TC BF319 .M55 1999*

New perspectives on conceptual change. 1st ed.
Amsterdam ; New York : Oxford : Pergamon, 1999.
*TC LB1062 .N49 1999*

**VOUCHERS, EDUCATIONAL.** *See*
**EDUCATIONAL VOUCHERS.**

**VOWS.** *See* **MONASTIC AND RELIGIOUS LIFE.**

**VOYAGES AND TRAVELS.** *See* **OVERLAND
JOURNEYS TO THE PACIFIC; SEAFARING
LIFE; SHIPWRECKS.**

**VOYAGES, IMAGINARY.** *See*
**INTERPLANETARY VOYAGES.**

**VOYAGES, INTERPLANETARY.** *See*
**INTERPLANETARY VOYAGES.**

**VOYAGES TO THE MOON.** *See*
**INTERPLANETARY VOYAGES.**

**Vuchinich, Rudy E. (Rudy Eugene), 1949-.**
Reframing health behavior change with behavioral
economics. Mahwah, N.J. : London : Lawrence
Erlbaum, 2000.
*TC RA776.9 .R433 2000*

**The vulnerable observer.**
Behar, Ruth, 1956- Boston : Beacon Press, c1996.
*TC GN346.4 .B44 1996*

**Vygotskian perspectives on literacy research :**
constructing meaning through collaborative inquiry /
edited by Carol D. Lee, Peter Smagorinsky.
Cambridge, U.K. ; New York : Cambridge University
Press, 2000. xii, 280 p. : ill. ; 24 cm. (Learning in doing)
Chiefly based on papers presented at a conference entitled A
Vygotsky centennial held 1996, Chicago, Ill. Includes
bibliographical references and indexes. ISBN 0-521-63095-9
(hbk.) ISBN 0-521-63878-X (pbk.) DDC 370.15/23
*1. Vygotskiĭ, L. S. - (Lev Semenovich), - 1896-1934. 2.
Learning, Psychology of - Congresses. 3. Literacy - Social
aspects - Congresses. 4. Cognition and culture - Congresses. 5.
Sociolinguistics - Congresses. I. Lee, Carol D. II. Smagorinsky,
Peter. III. Series.*
*TC LB1060 .V95 2000*

**VYGOTSKIĬ, L. S. (LEV SEMENOVICH), 1896-
1934.**
Vygotskian perspectives on literacy research.
Cambridge, U.K. ; New York : Cambridge University
Press, 2000.
*TC LB1060 .V95 2000*

**W., BILL.**
Raphael, Matthew J. Bill W. and Mr. Wilson.
Amherst : University of Massachusetts Press, c2000.
*TC HV5032.W19 R36 2000*

**W3 (INFORMATION RETRIEVAL SYSTEM).** *See*
**WORLD WIDE WEB (INFORMATION
RETRIEVAL SYSTEM).**

**Wabi-Sabi Productions (Firm).**
Rabbit in the moon [videorecording]. San Francisco,
Calif. : Wabi-Sabi Productions, 1999.
*TC D753.8 .R3 1999*

**WACHAGA.** *See* **CHAGA (AFRICAN PEOPLE).**

**WACHAGA (AFRICAN PEOPLE).** *See* **CHAGA
(AFRICAN PEOPLE).**

**Wachowiak, Frank.** Emphasis art : a qualitative art program for elementary and middle schools / Frank Wachowiak, Robert D. Clements. 7th ed. New York ; London : Longman, c2001. xiii, 418 p. : col. ill. ; 25 x 27 cm. Includes bibliographical references (p. 402-407) and index. ISBN 0-321-02351-X DDC 372.5/2044
*1. Art - Study and teaching (Elementary) 2. Art - Study and teaching (Middle school) I. Clements, Robert D. II. Title.*
*TC N350 .W26 2001*

**Wachs, Theodore D., 1941-** Necessary but not sufficient : the respective roles of single and multiple influences on individual development / Theodore D. Wachs. 1st ed. Washington, DC : American Psychological Association, c2000. xi, 439 p. : ill. ; 27 cm. Includes bibliographical references (p. 335-405) and indexes. ISBN 1-55798-611-8 (hardcover) DDC 155.2/34
*1. Developmental psychology. I. Title.*
*TC BF713 .W33 2000*

**Wachter, Joanne C.** Classroom volunteers : uh-oh! or right on! / Joanne C. Wachter. Thousand Oaks, Calif. : Corwin Press, c1999. viii, 96 p. : ill. ; 29 cm. Includes bibliographical references. CONTENTS: Uh-oh! -- Thinking about volunteers in a new way -- Setting priorities -- Recruiting your volunteer staff -- Training volunteers -- Maintaining a smoothly running program -- Showing appreciation for volunteers -- Deciding where to go from here. ISBN 0-8039-6880-9 (perm. paper) ISBN 0-8039-6881-7 (perm. paper) DDC 371.14/124
*1. Volunteer workers in education. I. Title.*
*TC LB2844.1.V6 W33 1999*

**Wachtman, J. B. 1928-.** Ceramic innovations. Westerville, Ohio : American Ceramic Society, 1999.
*TC TP807 .C473 1999*

**Wacky wedding.** Edwards, Pamela Duncan. 1st ed. New York : Hyperion Books for Children, c1999.
*TC PZ7.E26365 Wac 1999*

**WAD (WOMEN AND DEVELOPMENT).** *See* **WOMEN IN DEVELOPMENT.**

**Waddell, Margot, 1946-** Inside lives : psychoanalysis and the development of the personality / Margot Waddell. New York : Routledge, 1998. xiii, 225 p. ; 23 cm. (Tavistock Clinic series) Includes bibliographical references (p. [219]-222) and index. ISBN 0-415-92288-7 (hardcover) ISBN 0-415-92289-5 (pbk.) DDC 155
*1. Psychoanalysis. 2. Developmental psychology. 3. Personality. I. Title. II. Series.*
*TC BF175.45 .W33 1998*

**Wade, Bonnie C.** Imaging sound : an ethnomusicological study of music, art, and culture in Mughal India / Bonnie C. Wade. Chicago : University of Chicago Press, c1998. lvi, 276 p. : ill. (some col.), maps ; 29 cm. (Chicago studies in ethnomusicology) Includes bibliographical references (p. 245-264) and indexes. ISBN 0-226-86840-0 ISBN 0-226-86841-9 (pbk.) DDC 700/.954/0903
*1. Music - India - History and criticism. 2. Music - Mogul Empire - History and criticism. 3. Music in art. I. Title. II. Series.*
*TC ML338 .W318 1998*

**Wade, Rahima Carol.** Building bridges. Washington, DC : National Council for the Social Studies, 2000.

**Wade, Suzanne E.** Inclusive education. Mahwah, N.J. : L. Erlbaum Associates, c2000.
*TC LC1201 .I527 2000*

Preparing teachers for inclusive education. Mahwah, N.J. : L. Erlbaum Associates, 2000.
*TC LC1201 .P74 2000*

**Wadelington, Charles Weldon.** Charlotte Hawkins Brown & Palmer Memorial Institute : what one young African American woman could do / Charles W. Wadelington, Richard F. Knapp. Chapel Hill ; London : University of North Carolina Press, c1999. xvi, 303 p. : ill. ; 25 cm. Includes bibliographical references (p. [227]-292) and index. ISBN 0-8078-2514-X (alk. paper) ISBN 0-8078-4794-1 (pbk. : alk. paper) DDC 371.1/0092
*1. Brown, Charlotte Hawkins, - 1883-1961. 2. Palmer Memorial Institute (Sedalia, N.C.) 3. Afro-American women teachers - North Carolina - Biography. 4. Women school administrators - North Carolina - Biography. I. Knapp, Richard F., 1945- II. Title. III. Title: Charlotte Hawkins Brown and Palmer Memorial Institute*
*TC LA2317.B598 W33 1999*

**WADSCHAGGA (AFRICAN PEOPLE).** *See* **CHAGA (AFRICAN PEOPLE).**

**The Wadsworth special educator series**
Bigge, June L. Curriculum, assessment, and instruction for students with disabilities. Belmont, CA : Wadsworth Pub., c1999.
*TC LC4031 .B46 1999*

Functional analysis of problem behavior. Belmont, CA : Wadsworth Pub. Co., c1999.
*TC RC473.B43 F85 1999*

**WAGANDA (AFRICAN PEOPLE).** *See* **GANDA (AFRICAN PEOPLE).**

**WAGER OF BATTLE.** *See* **COMBAT.**

**WAGES.** *See* **EQUAL PAY FOR EQUAL WORK.**

**The wages of seeking help.** Bohmer, Carol. Westport, Conn. ; London : Praeger, 2000.
*TC RC560.S44 B67 2000*

**Wagman, Morton.** Historical dictionary of quotations in cognitive science. Westport, Conn. : Greenwood Press, 2000.
*TC PN6084.C545 H57 2000*

The human mind according to artificial intelligence : theory, research, and implications / Morton Wagman. Westport, Conn. : Praeger, 1999. xvi, 161 p. : ill. ; 25 cm. Includes bibliographical references (p. [145]-154) and indexes. ISBN 0-275-96285-7 (alk. paper) DDC 006.3
*1. Artificial intelligence. 2. Brain. 3. Philosophy of mind. I. Title.*
*TC Q335 .W342 1999*

Scientific discovery processes in humans and computers : theory and research in psychology and artificial intelligence / Morton Wagman. Westport, CT : Praeger, 2000. xiii, 199 p. : ill. ; 25 cm. Includes bibliographical references (p. [181]-192) and indexes. ISBN 0-275-96654-2 (alk. paper) DDC 001.4/2
*1. Discoveries in science. 2. Cognitive science. 3. Artificial intelligence. I. Title.*
*TC Q180.55.D57 W34 2000*

**Wagner, Daniel A., 1946-.** The future of literacy in a changing world. Rev. ed. Cresskill, N.J. : Hampton Press, c1998.
*TC LC149 .F87 1998*

**Wagner Pacifici, Robin Erica.** Theorizing the standoff : contingency in action / Robin Wagner-Pacifici. Cambridge : Cambridge University Press, 2000. xiv, 276 p. ; 24 cm. Includes bibliographical references and index. ISBN 0-521-65244-8 ISBN 0-521-65479-3 (pbk.) DDC 303.6
*1. Social conflict. 2. Social conflict - United States - Case studies. 3. Conflict management. I. Title.*
*TC HM1121 .W34 2000*

**Wagner, Pamela Mason.** Changing lives [videorecording]. Princeton, NJ : Films for the Humanities & Sciences, c1998.
*TC RC564 .C54 1998*

**Wahl, Otto F.** Telling is risky business : mental health consumers confront stigma / Otto F. Wahl. New Brunswick, N.J. ; London : Rutgers University Press, c1999. xxi, 231 p. ; 24 cm. Includes bibliographical references (p. 207-221) and index. ISBN 0-8135-2723-6 (hbk. : alk. paper) ISBN 0-8135-2724-4 (pbk. : alk. paper) DDC 362.2
*1. Mental illness - Public opinion. 2. Psychiatry - Public opinion. 3. Stigma (Social psychology) I. Title.*
*TC RC454.4 .W327 1999*

**WAIMH handbook of infant mental health.** Handbook of infant mental health. New York : Wiley, c2000.
*TC RJ502.5 .H362 2000*

**Wainer, Howard.** Computerized adaptive testing : a primer / by Howard Wainer with Neil J. Dorans ... [et al.]. 2nd ed. Mahwah, N.J. : Lawrence Erlbaum Associates, 2000. xxiii, 335 p. : ill. ; 24 cm. Includes bibliographical references and indexes. ISBN 0-8058-3511-3 (cloth : alk. paper) DDC 371.26
*1. Computer adaptive testing. I. Dorans, Neil J. II. Title.*
*TC LB3060.32.C65 W25 2000*

**Wajcman, Judy.** The social shaping of technology. 2nd ed. Buckingham [England] ; Philadelphia : Open University Press, c1999.
*TC T14.5 .S6383 1999*

**WAKA.** Livingston, Myra Cohn. Cricket never does. New York : Margaret K. McElderry Books, c1997.
*TC PS3562.I945 C75 1997*

**WAKA, AMERICAN.** Livingston, Myra Cohn. Cricket never does. New York : Margaret K. McElderry Books, c1997.
*TC PS3562.I945 C75 1997*

**Wake Forest law review.** [Winston-Salem, N.C., Wake Forest Law Review Association, etc.] v. 25 cm. Frequency: Quarterly <, v. 21, no. 3->. Former frequency: Quarterly, 1970-77. Former frequency: Bimonthly, 1978-19. v. 7- 1970- . Indexed in its entirety by: Index to legal periodicals 0019-4077. Indexed by: Current law review. Vols. 1-10, 1965-74. 1 v.; Vols. 11-15, 1975-79 in v. 15. Continues: Intramural law review (Winston-Salem, N.C.) (OCoLC)2069753 (DLC)sf 85007001. ISSN 0043-003X DDC 340/.05
*1. Law reviews - North Carolina. I. Wake Forest University. School of Law. II. Title: Intramural law review (Winston-Salem, N.C.)*
*TC K27 .A36*

**Wake Forest University. School of Law.** Wake Forest law review. [Winston-Salem, N.C., Wake Forest Law Review Association, etc.]
*TC K27 .A36*

**Wakefield, Dan.** Selling out : a novel / by Dan Wakefield. 1st ed. Boston : Little, Brown, c1985. 300 p. ; 22 cm. ISBN 0-316-91774-5 DDC 813/.54
*I. Title.*
*TC PS3573.A413 S44 1985*

**Wakefield, Doug.** Mates, Barbara T. Adaptive technology for the Internet. Chicago, Ill. : American Library Association, 1999.
*TC Z675.B M38 1999*

**Waldfogel, Jane.** Securing the future. New York : Russell Sage Foundation, c2000.
*TC HV741 .S385 2000*

**WALDORF METHOD OF EDUCATION.** Steiner, Rudolf, 1861-1925. [Heilpädagogischer Kurs. English] Education for special needs. [New ed.]. London : Rudolf Steiner Press, 1998.
*TC LB1029.W34 S73 1998*

Steiner, Rudolf, 1861-1925. [Konferenzen mit den Lehrern der Freien Waldorfschule in Stuttgart. English] Faculty meetings with Rudolf Steiner. Hudson, NY : Anthroposophic Press, c1998.
*TC LF3195.S834 S8413 1998*

**Waldron, Karen A., 1945-.** Special education. San Francisco : EMText, c1992.
*TC LC3981 .S63 1992*

**Walk this way!.** Olien, Rebecca. Portsmouth, NH : Heinemann, c1998.
*TC LB1047 .O55 1998*

**Walker, Allan.** Quong, Terry. Values based strategic planning :. Singapore ; New York : Prentice Hall, 1998.
*TC LB2806 .Q86 1998*

**Walker Art Center.** Cole, Herbert M. The arts of Ghana. Los Angeles : Museum of Cultural History, University of California, c1977.
*TC NX589.6.G5 C64*

**Walker, Barbara J., 1946-** Diagnostic teaching of reading : techniques for instruction and assessment / Barbara J. Walker. 4th ed. Upper Saddle River, NJ : Merrill, c2000. xvi, 377 p. : ill. ; 24 cm. Includes bibliographical references (p. 361-369) and index. ISBN 0-13-083752-0 DDC 428/.4/07
*1. Reading - Remedial teaching. 2. Individualized reading instruction. 3. Reading - Ability testing. 4. Reading comprehension. I. Title.*
*TC LB1050.5 .W35 2000*

Tips for the reading team. Newark, Del. : International Reading Association, c1998.
*TC LB1573 .T57 1998*

**Walker, Bonnie L.** AGS basic English composition / by Bonnie L. Walker. Circle Pines, Minn. : American Guidance Service, c1997. v, 302 p. : ill. ; 24 cm. Includes index. ISBN 0785405380H
*1. English language - Grammar. 2. English language - Composition and exercises. I. Title. II. Title: American Guidance Service basic English composition*
*TC PE1408 .W34 1997*

AGS basic English composition / by Bonnie L. Walker. Teacher's ed. Circle Pines, Minn. : American Guidance Service, c1997. T16, vi, 321 p. : ill. ; 29 cm. Includes index. ISBN 0-7854-0540-2
*1. English language - Grammar. 2. English language - Composition and exercises. 3. English language - Study and teaching (Secondary) I. Title. II. Title: American Guidance Service basic English composition*
*TC PE1408 .W34 1997 Teacher's Ed.*

AGS basic English composition / by Bonnie L. Walker. Teacher's ed. Circle Pines, Minn. : American Guidance Service, c1997. T16, vi, 321 p. : ill. ; 29 cm.

Includes index. ISBN 0-7854-0540-2
*1. English language - Grammar. 2. English language - Composition and exercises. 3. English language - Study and teaching (Secondary) I. Title. II. Title: American Guidance Service basic English composition*
**TC PE1408 .W34 1997 Teacher's Ed.**

AGS basic English composition / by Bonnie L. Walker. Teacher's ed. Circle Pines, Minn. : American Guidance Service, c1997. T16, vi, 321 p. : ill. ; 29 cm. Includes index. ISBN 0-7854-0540-2
*1. English language - Grammar. 2. English language - Composition and exercises. 3. English language - Study and teaching (Secondary) I. Title. II. Title: American Guidance Service basic English composition*
**TC PE1408 .W34 1997 Teacher's Ed.**

AGS basic English grammar / by Bonnie L. Walker. Circle Pines, Minn. : AGS, American Guidance Service, c1997. vi, 326 p. : ill. ; 25 cm. Includes index. ISBN 0785404953H
*1. English language - Grammar. 2. English language - Composition and exercises. I. Title. II. Title: American Guidance Service basic English grammar*
**TC PE1112 .W34 1997**

AGS basic English grammar / by Bonnie L. Walker. Teacher's ed. Circle Pines, Minn. : AGS, American Guidance Service, c1997. T16, viii, 344 p. : ill. ; 25 cm. Includes index. ISBN 0-7854-0497-X
*1. English language - Grammar. 2. English language - Composition and exercises. I. Title. II. Title: American Guidance Service basic English grammar*
**TC PE1112 .W34 1997 Teacher's Ed.**

**Walker, Daniel, 1922-** Rights in conflict; convention week in Chicago, August, 25-29, 1968; a report. Special introd. by Max Frankel. New York : Dutton, c1968. xx, 362, A96 p. : ill., maps, ports. ; 22 cm. Commonly known as the Walker report. A report submitted to the National Commission on the Causes and Prevention of Violence. DDC 977.3/11/04
*1. Riots - Illinois - Chicago. 2. Police - Illinois - Chicago. 3. Democratic National Convention - (1968 : - Chicago, Ill.) I. United States. National Commission on the Causes and Prevention of Violence. II. Title. III. Title: Walker report on the violent confrontation of demonstrators and police in the parks and streets of Chicago.*
**TC F548.52 .W3 1968c**

**Walker-Hodge, Judith.** Animal hospital / written by Judith Walker-Hodge. 1st American ed. New York : DK Pub., 1999. 32 p. : col. ill. ; 24 cm. (Eyewitness readers. Level 2) SUMMARY: When two children find an injured duck and take it to a veterinarian at an animal hospital, they learn about the work of the hospital and of the doctor as she cares for the duck and other animals. ISBN 0-7894-3997-2 (hc) ISBN 0-7894-3996-4 (pbk.) DDC 636.089
*1. Veterinary hospitals - Juvenile literature. 2. Veterinary hospitals. 3. Veterinarians. 4. Animals. I. Title. II. Series.*
**TC SF604.55 .H63 1999**

**Walker, Janice R.**
Ruszkiewicz, John J., 1950- Bookmarks. New York ; Harlow, England : Longman, c2000.
**TC LB2369 .R88 2000**

**Walker, Leslie C., 1962-.**
Public and private responsibilities in long-term care. Baltimore : Johns Hopkins University Press, 1998.
**TC RA644.6 .P8 1998**

**Walker, Pam, 1953-.**
Colvin, A. Vonnie, 1951- Teaching the nuts and bolts of physical education. Champaign, IL : Human Kinetics, c2000.
**TC GV443 .C59 2000**

**Walker report on the violent confrontation of demonstrators and police in the parks and streets of Chicago.**
Walker, Daniel, 1922- Rights in conflict; convention week in Chicago, August, 25-29, 1968; New York : Dutton, c1968.
**TC F548.52 .W3 1968c**

**Walker, Rob, 1943-.**
Schratz, Michael, 1952- Research as social change. London ; New York : Routledge, 1995.
**TC H62 .S33984 1995**

**Walker, Roslyn A.**
Sieber, Roy, 1923- African art in the cycle of life. Washington, D.C. : Published for the National Museum of African Art by the Smithsonian Press, c1987.
**TC NB1091.65 .S54 1987**

**Walker's Crossing.**
Naylor, Phyllis Reynolds. New York : Atheneum Books for Young Readers, c1999.

**TC PZ7.N24 Wai 1999**

**WALL ART.** *See* **STREET ART.**

**WALL DECORATION.** *See* **MURAL PAINTING AND DECORATION.**

**WALL-PAINTING.** *See* **MURAL PAINTING AND DECORATION.**

**Wall, Vernon A.**
Toward acceptance. Lanham, Md. : University Press of America, 1999.
**TC LC192.6 .T69 1999**

**Wallace, Ian, 1950- / ill.**
Wynne-Jones, Tim. Builder of the moon. New York M.K. McElderry Books, c1988.
**TC PZ7.W993 Bu 1988**

**Wallace, Karen.** A day at Seagull beach / written by Karen Wallace. 1st American ed. New York : DK Pub., 1999. 32 p. : col. ill. ; 24 cm. (Eyewitness readers. Level 1) "Preschool-Grade 1"--Cover. SUMMARY: A seagull flies over the sea looking for something before returning to its nest. ISBN 0-7894-4003-2 (hc) ISBN 0-7894-4002-4 (pbk.) DDC [E]
*1. Gulls - Juvenile fiction. 2. Gulls - Fiction. 3. Seashore - Fiction. I. Title. II. Title: Seagull beach III. Series.*
**TC PZ10.3.W1625 Se 1999**

**Wallace, Mike.** Senior management teams in primary schools / Mike Wallace and Lynda Huckman. London : New York : Routledge, 1999. vii, 225 p. : ill. ; 24 cm. (Educational management) Includes bibliographical references (p. [215]-220) and index. ISBN 0-415-17036-2 (pbk. : alk. paper) DDC 372.12
*1. School management teams - Great Britain - Case studies. 2. Education, Elementary - Great Britain - Case studies. 3. Educational leadership - Great Britain - Case studies. I. Huckman, Lynda, 1943- II. Title. III. Series: Education management series.*
**TC LB2806.3 .W37 1999**

**Wallace, Patricia M.** The psychology of the Internet / Patricia M. Wallace. Cambridge ; New York : Cambridge University Press, 1999. xi, 264 p. ; 24 cm. Includes bibliographical references and index. ISBN 0-521-63294-3 DDC 025.04/01/9
*1. Communication - Psychological aspects. 2. Internet (Computer network) - Psychological aspects. 3. Computer networks - Psychological aspects. I. Title.*
**TC BF637.C45 W26 1999**

**Wallace, Ray.**
Reforming college composition. Westport, Conn. : Greenwood Press, 2000.
**TC PE1404 .R383 2000**

**Wallace, Susan Lewis.**
Reforming college composition. Westport, Conn. : Greenwood Press, 2000.
**TC PE1404 .R383 2000**

**Wallace, Theodore J. (Theodore Joseph), 1954-.**
Catholic school leadership. London ; New York : Falmer Press, 2000.
**TC LC501 .C3484 2000**

**Wallace, Walter L., joint author.**
Conyers, James E., 1932- Black elected officials. New York : Russell Sage Foundation, c1976.
**TC JK1924 .C65**

**Wallach, Alan.**
De Salvo, Donna M. Past imperfect. Southampton, N.Y. : Parrish Art Museum, in association with the New Press, New York, N.Y., c1993.
**TC N750 .D4**

**Wallach, Lorraine B.**
Scheinfeld, Daniel, 1933- Strengthening refugee families. Chicago, Ill. : Lyceum Books, c1997.
**TC HV640.4.U54 S34 1997**

**WALLED-IN COMMUNITIES.** *See* **GATED COMMUNITIES.**

**Wallerstein, Immanuel Maurice, 1930-** Utopistics, or, Historical choices of the twenty-first century / by Immanuel Wallerstein. New York : New Press, 1998. 93 p. ; 21 cm. "This book is a revised edition of the Sir Douglas Robb Lectures at the University of Auckland, New Zealand, given on October 16, 22, 23, 1997"--Pref. Includes bibliographical references. ISBN 1-56584-457-2 DDC 303.49/09/05
*1. World politics - 1989- - Forecasting. 2. Twenty-first century - Forecasts. I. Title. II. Title: Utopistics III. Title: Historical choices of the twenty-first century*
**TC D860 .W35 1998**

**Walling, Donovan R., 1948-.**
Hot buttons. Bloomington, Ind. : Phi Delta Kappa Educational Foundation, c1997.

**TC LA210 .H68 1997**
Rethinking how art is taught : a critical convergence / Donovan R. Walling. Thousand Oaks, Calif. : Corwin Press, c2000. xv, 109 p. ; 26 cm. ISBN 0-7619-7518-7 (cloth : acid-free paper) ISBN 0-7619-7519-5 (paper : acid-free paper) DDC 707/.1
*1. Art - Study and teaching. I. Title.*
**TC N85 .W35 2000**

**Wallis, Brian, 1953-.**
Art matters. New York : New York University Press, c1999.
**TC N72.S6 A752 1999**

**Wallner, John C., ill.**
To the zoo. 1st ed. Boston : Little, Brown, c1992.
**TC PS595.Z66 T6 1992**
Yolen, Jane. Ring of earth. 1st ed. San Diego : Harcourt Brace Jovanovich, c1986.
**TC PS3575.O43 R5 1986**

**Walls sometimes speak.**
Butler, Roger. Poster art in Australia. Canberra : National Gallery of Australia, 1993.
**TC NC1807.A78 B88 1993**

**Walmsley, Bonnie Brown.** Teaching with favorite Marc Brown books / by Bonnie Brown Walmsley and Sean A. Walmsley. New York : Scholastic Professional Books, c1998. 80 p. : ill. ; 28 cm. Includes bibliographical references (p. 78-80). SUMMARY: Engaging teaching activities and rare, inside glimpse into Marc Brown's creative process that will captivate your students almost as much as Arthur does! ISBN 0-590-31471-8
*1. Language arts (Elementary) - Activity programs - Handbooks, manuals, etc. 2. Brown, Marc Tolon - Study and teaching (Elementary) 3. Illustrators - United States - Study and teaching (Elementary) 4. Authors, American - Study and teaching (Elementary) 5. Teaching - Aids and devices. I. Walmsley, Sean A. II. Title.*
**TC LB1576 .W258 1998**

**Walmsley, Sean A.**
Walmsley, Bonnie Brown. Teaching with favorite Marc Brown books. New York : Scholastic Professional Books, c1998.
**TC LB1576 .W258 1998**

**Walsh, Anne.**
Essays on the history of Trinity College Library, Dublin. Dublin : Four Courts, c2000.
**TC Z792.5.T75 E87 2000**

**Walsh, Froma.** Strengthening family resilience / Froma Walsh. New York : Guilford Press, c1998. xiv, 338 p. ; 24 cm. (The Guilford family therapy series) Includes bibliographical references (p. 315-329) and index. ISBN 1-57230-408-1 DDC 616.89/156
*1. Family - Mental health. 2. Resilience (Personality trait) 3. Problem families. 4. Family psychotherapy. 5. Family social work. I. Title. II. Series.*
**TC RC489.F33 W34 1998**

**Walsh, Mike.** Building a successful school / Mike Walsh. London : Kogan Page, 1999. vii, 240 p. : ill. ; 24 cm. Includes index. ISBN 0-7494-3029-X
*1. School management and organization - Great Britain. 2. Educational change - Great Britain. I. Title. II. Title: Successful school*
**TC LB2900.5 .W37 1999**

**Walsh, Vivian.**
Seibold, J.otto. Going to the Getty. Los Angeles : J. Paul Getty Museum, c1997.
**TC NA6813.U6 L678 1997**

**Walsh, W. Bruce, 1936-** Tests and assessment / W. Bruce Walsh, Nancy E. Betz. 4th ed. Upper Saddle River, N.J. : Prentice Hall, c2001. ix, 481 p. : ill. ; 25 cm. Includes bibliographical references (p. 431-464) and indexes. ISBN 0-13-095947-2 DDC 150/.28/7
*1. Psychological tests. 2. Ability - Testing. 3. Psychometrics. I. Betz, Nancy E. II. Title.*
**TC BF176 .W335 2001**

**Walsh, W. Bruce, 1937-.**
Person-environment psychology. 2nd ed. Mahwah, N.J. : L. Erlbaum, 2000.
**TC BF353 .P43 2000**

**Walter, Chip.**
Fate of the earth [videorecording]. [New York, N.Y.?] : Unapix Entertainment, Inc. [distributor], c1996.
**TC QB631.2 .F3 1996**
Tales from other worlds [videorecording]. [New York, N.Y.?] : Unapix Entertainment, Inc. [distributor], c1996.

*TC QB631.2 .T3 1996*

Tales from other worlds [videorecording]. [New York, N.Y.?] : Unapix Entertainment, Inc. [distributor], c1996.
*TC QB631.2 .T3 1996*

**Walter, Chuck.**
Speiser, R. (Robert) Five women build a number system. Stamford, Conn. : Ablex Pub., c2000.
*TC QA135.5 .S5785 2000*

**Walter, John L., 1945-** Recreating brief therapy : preferences and possibilities / John L. Walter, Jane E. Peller. New York : W.W. Norton & Co., 2000. xii, 191 p. ; 25 cm. "A Norton professional book." Includes bibliographical references and index. ISBN 0-393-70325-8 DDC 616.89/14
*1. Brief therapy. 2. Psychotherapy. I. Peller, Jane E. II. Title.*
*TC RC480.5 .W276 2000*

**Walters, Glenn D.** Beyond behavior : construction of an overarching psychological theory of lifestyles / Glenn D. Walters. Westport, Conn. ; London : Praeger, 2000. xi, 229 p. : ill. ; 25 cm. Includes bibliographical references (p. [195]-224) and index. CONTENTS: I. The Precursors of Lifestyle Theory. 1. The Need for an Overarching Theory in Psychology. 2. The Conceptual Roots of Lifestyle Theory. 3. Lifestyle Theory: Three Models in One -- II. The Structural Model. 4. A Multi-Axial Classification System. 5. Anatomy of a Lifestyle. 6. Lifestyle Lineages. 7. Lifestyles in Literature: Dostoyevsky's Crime and Punishment -- III. The Functional Model: Motivation and Learning. 8. Perceiving, Processing, and Managing Threats to Survival. 9. The Lifestyle Selection Process: Incentive, Opportunity, and Choice. 10. On the Outside, Looking In. Appendix. Temperament Survey. ISBN 0-275-96992-4 (alk. paper) DDC 155.9 DDC 155.9
*1. Environmental psychology. 2. Lifestyles - Psychological aspects. I. Title.*
*TC BF353 .W356 2000*

The self-altering process : exploring the dynamic nature of lifestyle development and change / Glenn D. Walters. Westport, Conn. : Praeger, 2000. xi, 274 p. ; 25 cm. Includes bibliographical references (p. [225]-268) and index. ISBN 0-275-96993-2 (alk. paper) DDC 155.2/5
*1. Change (Psychology) 2. Lifestyles - Psychological aspects. I. Title.*
*TC BF637.C4 W35 2000*

**Walters, Ronald G.**
Primers for prudery. Updated ed. Baltimore : Johns Hopkins University Press, 2000.
*TC HQ18.U5 P75 2000*

**Walters, Thomas.** The arts : a comparative approach to the arts of painting, sculpture, architecture, music, and drama / Thomas Walters. Lanham, MD : University Press of America, 2000. 107 p. ; 22 cm. Includes bibliographical references. ISBN 0-7618-1527-9 (pbk. : alk. paper) DDC 700
*1. Arts - Comparative method. I. Title.*
*TC NX170 .W35 2000*

**Walther-Thomas, Chriss.**
Collaboration for inclusive education. Boston ; London : Allyn and Bacon, c2000.
*TC LC1201 .C63 1999*

**Walton, A. Ronald.**
Language policy and pedagogy. Philadelphia : J. Benjamins, c2000.
*TC P53 .L364 2000*

**Walton, Clarence Cyril, 1915-.**
Education, leadership, and business ethics. Boston, MA : Kluwer Academic Publishers, c1998.
*TC HF5387 .E346 1998*

**WALTON, CLARENCE CYRIL, 1915 - -CONGRESSES.**
Education, leadership, and business ethics. Boston, MA : Kluwer Academic Publishers, c1998.
*TC HF5387 .E346 1998*

**Walton, Jo Ann.**
Nursing and the experience of illness. London ; New York : Routledge, 1999.
*TC RT86 .N886 1999*

**Walton, Margaret.** Teaching reading and spelling to dyslexic children : getting to grips with words / Margaret Walton. London : D. Fulton, 1998. xi, 131 p. : ill. ; 30 cm. Includes bibliographical references and index. ISBN 1-85346-565-8
*1. Dyslexic children - Education. 2. Reading disability. 3. Spelling disability. 4. Dyslexia. I. Title.*
*TC LC4708 .W35 1998*

**Walton, Richard E.** Up and running : integrating information technology and the organization / Richard E. Walton. Boston, Mass. : Harvard Business School Press, c1989. xii, 231 p. : ill. ; 24 cm. Includes

bibliographical references (p.[219]-226) and index. ISBN 0-87584-218-6 (alk. paper) DDC 658.4038
*1. Management information systems. 2. Information technology. I. Title.*
*TC T58.6 .W345 1989*

**Walton, Sherry.**
Taylor, Kathe. Children at the center. Portsmouth, NH : Heinemann, c1998.
*TC LB3060.57 .T39 1998*

**Walz, Thomas, 1933-** The unlikely celebrity : Bill Sackter's triumph over disability / Thomas Walz ; with a foreword by Barry Morrow. Carbondale : Southern Illinois University Press, c1998. xvi, 127 p. : ill. ; 24 cm. ISBN 0-8093-2134-3 (alk. paper) ISBN 0-8093-2213-7 (pbk. : alk. paper) DDC 362.3/092
*1. Sackter, Bill. 2. Mentally handicapped - Iowa - Biography. 3. Coffee shops - Iowa - Employees - Biography. I. Title.*
*TC HV3006.S33 W35 1998*

**Wandersee, James H.**
Assessing science understanding :. San Diego, Calif. London : Academic, 2000.
*TC Q181 .A87 2000*

**Wang, Margaret C.**
Resilience across contexts. Mahwah, NJ : Lawrence Erlbaun, 2000.
*TC HQ535 .R47 2000*

**Wanting to talk** : counselling case studies in communication disorders / edited by Diana Syder. London : Whurr, c1998. xiii, 302 p. ; 24 cm. Includes bibliographical references (p. 289-296) and index. ISBN 1-86156-067-2 DDC 616.85/503
*1. Communicative disorders - Patients - Counseling of - Case studies. 2. Rehabilitative counseling - Case studies. 3. Speech disorders - Patients - Counseling of - Case studies. I. Syder, Diana.*
*TC RC423 .W26 1998*

**WAR.** *See* **MILITARISM; PEACE; SOCIOLOGY, MILITARY; WAR AND SOCIETY.**

**WAR AND EDUCATION.**
Education as a humanitarian response. London : Herndon, VA : Cassell : [s.l.] : UNESCO International Bureau of Education, 1998.
*TC LC3719 .E37 1998*

**WAR AND SOCIETY.** *See also* **SOCIOLOGY, MILITARY.**
Ethnicity and intra-state conflict. Aldershot, Hants, England : Brookfield, Vt., USA : Ashgate, c1999.
*TC GN495.6 .E83 1999*

McNeil, Elton B., ed. The nature of human conflict. Englewood Cliffs, N.J., Prentice-Hall [1965]
*TC HM36.5 .M25*

**WAR AND SOCIETY - CONGRESSES.**
Ethnicity and intra-state conflict. Aldershot, Hants, England : Brookfield, Vt., USA : Ashgate, c1999.
*TC GN495.6 .E83 1999*

**War at home [picture].**
World War II [picture]. Amawalk, NY : Jackdaw Publications, c1999.
*TC TR820.5 .W6 1999*

**The war between mentalism and behaviorism.**
Uttal, William R. Mahwah, N.J. ; London : Lawrence Erlbaum Associates, Publishers, 2000.
*TC BF199 .U77 2000*

**WAR BETWEEN THE STATES, 1861-1865.** *See* **UNITED STATES - HISTORY - CIVIL WAR, 1861-1865.**

**WAR - HISTORY - 20TH CENTURY.**
Bourke, Joanna. An intimate history of killing. [New York, NY] : Basic Books, c1999.
*TC U22.3 .B68 1999*

**WAR (INTERNATIONAL LAW).** *See* **PRISONERS OF WAR.**

**WAR MEMORIALS - AUSTRALIA.**
Hedger, Michael. Public sculpture in Australia. Roseville East, NSW : Distributed by Craftsman House : United States : G+B Arts International, c1995.
*TC NB1100 .H44 1995*

**WAR MONUMENTS.** *See* **WAR MEMORIALS.**

**WAR OF SECESSION, U.S., 1861-1865.** *See* **UNITED STATES - HISTORY - CIVIL WAR, 1861-1865.**

**WAR OF THE AMERICAN REVOLUTION.** *See* **UNITED STATES - HISTORY - REVOLUTION, 1775-1783.**

**WAR PRISONERS.** *See* **PRISONERS OF WAR.**

**WAR, PRISONERS OF.** *See* **PRISONERS OF WAR.**

**WAR - SOCIAL ASPECTS.** *See* **WAR AND SOCIETY.**

**WAR VETERANS.** *See* **VETERANS.**

**WAR VICTIMS.** *See* **PRISONERS OF WAR.**

**Ward, Alan, 1932-.**
**Experiment with series.**
Ward, Alan, 1932- Experimenting with batteries, bulbs, and wires. New York : Chelsea Juniors, c1991.
*TC QC527.2 .W37 1991*

Experimenting with batteries, bulbs, and wires / Alan Ward ; illustrated by Zena Flax. New York : Chelsea Juniors, c1991. 48 p. : ill. ; 26 cm. (Experimenting with-- series) Spine title: Batteries, bulbs, and wires. Includes index. ISBN 0-7910-1516-5 DDC 621.3/078
*1. Electricity - Experiments - Juvenile literature. 2. Electricity - Experiments. 3. Experiments. I. Flax, Zena, ill. II. Title. III. Title: Batteries, bulbs, and wires IV. Series: Ward, Alan, 1932- Experiment with-- series.*
*TC QC527.2 .W37 1991*

**Ward, Joe H., joint author.**
Bottenberg, Robert Alan. Applied multiple linear regression. Lackland Air Force Base, Texas, 6570th Personnel Research Laboratory Aerospace Medical Division, Air Force Systems Command, 1963
*TC QA276 .B67 1963*

**Ward, John (John Clarence), ill.**
Shelby, Anne. We keep a store. New York : Orchard Books, c1989.
*TC PZ7.S54125 We 1989*

Shelby, Anne. We keep a store. New York : Orchard Books, c1990.
*TC PZ7 .S54125We 1990*

**Ward, Mary Ann, 1946-** Student guidance and development / Mary Ann Ward, Dode Worsham. Larchmont, N.Y. : Eye On Education, c2000. xii, 164 p. : ill. ; 24 cm. (The school leadership library) Cover title: Student guidance & development. Includes bibliographical references (p. 163-164). ISBN 1-88300-147-1 DDC 371.4
*1. Educational counseling - United States. 2. Student assistance programs - United States. 3. Student aspirations - United States. 4. Student activities - United States. I. Worsham, Dode, 1943- II. Title. III. Title: Student guidance & development IV. Series.*
*TC LB1027.5 .W356 1998*

**Ward, Michael E., 1953-** Delegation and empowerment : leading with and through others / Michael E. Ward with Bettye MacPhail-Wilcox. Larchmont, NY : Eye on Education, c1999. xxii, 154 p. : ill. ; 24 cm. (The school leadership library) Includes bibliographical references (p. 143-154). ISBN 1-88300-176-5 DDC 371.2/012/0973
*1. School principals - United States. 2. Delegation of authority. I. MacPhail-Wilcox, Bettye. II. Title. III. Series.*
*TC LB2831.92 .W37 1999*

**Ward, Sharon M., 1938-.**
Erlandson, David A. Organizational oversight. Princeton, NJ : Eye on Education, c1996.
*TC LB2805 .E75 1996*

**Ward, Susan A.**
The physiology and pathophysiology of exercise tolerance. New York : Plenum Press, c1996.
*TC QP301 .P576 1996*

**Ward, Tony.**
Remaking relapse prevention with sex offenders. Thousand Oaks, Calif. : Sage Publications, c2000.
*TC RC560.S47 R46 2000*

**WARDS.** *See* **GUARDIAN AND WARD.**

**Ware, John.**
Teen violence [videorecording]. Princeton, NJ : Films for the Humanities & Sciences, c1998.
*TC RJ506.V56 T44 1998*

**Ware, Mark E.**
Handbook for teaching statistics and research methods. 2nd ed. Mahwah, N.J. : Lawrence Erlbaum Associates, c1999.
*TC QA276.18 .H36 1999*

Handbook of demonstrations and activities in the teaching of psychology. 2nd ed. Mahwah, N.J. : Lawrence Erlbaum Associates, c2000.
*TC BF77 .H265 2000*

**Warf, Barney, 1956-.**
Cities in the telecommunications age. New York : Routledge, 2000.

**Warhol.**
Andy Warhol [videorecording]. [Chicago, IL] : Home Vision [distributor],cc1987.
*TC N6537.W28 A45 1987*

Andy Warhol [videorecording]. [Chicago, IL] : Home Vision [distributor],cc1987.
*TC N6537.W28 A45 1987*

**Warhol, Andy, 1928-.**
Andy Warhol [videorecording]. [Chicago, IL] : Home Vision [distributor],cc1987.
*TC N6537.W28 A45 1987*

Andy Warhol [videorecording]. [Chicago, IL] : Home Vision [distributor],cc1987.
*TC N6537.W28 A45 1987*

**WARHOL, ANDY, 1928-.**
Andy Warhol [videorecording]. [Chicago, IL] : Home Vision [distributor],cc1987.
*TC N6537.W28 A45 1987*

Andy Warhol [videorecording]. [Chicago, IL] : Home Vision [distributor],cc1987.
*TC N6537.W28 A45 1987*

**WARLOCKS.** *See* **WITCHES; WIZARDS.**

**WARM-UP.** *See* **EXERCISE.**

**Warming up.** Teacher's ed. New York, N.Y. : American Book Company, c1980. xiv, 150 p. : ill. (some col.) ; 22x28 cm. (American readers ; K-1) Includes index. ISBN 0-278-46172-7
*1. Readers (Primary) 2. Reading (Primary) I. Series.*
*TC PE1119 .W37 1980 Teacher's Ed.*

**Warming up.** New York, N.Y. : American Book Company, c1980. 64 p. : col. ill. ; 22x28 cm. (American readers ; K-1) ISBN 0-278-45986-2
*1. Readers (Primary) I. Series.*
*TC PE1119 .W37 1980*

**Warming up.** Teacher's ed. Lexington, Mass. : D.C. Heath and Company, c1983. xxxii, 169 p. : ill. (some col.), music ; 22x28 cm. (American readers ; K-1) Includes index. ISBN 0-669-04914-X
*1. Readers (Primary) 2. Reading (Primary) I. Series.*
*TC PE1119 .W37 1983 Teacher's Ed.*

**Warming up.** Teacher's ed. Lexington, Mass. : D.C. Heath and Company, c1986. T30, 224 p. : ill. (some col.), music ; 22x28 cm. (Heath American readers ; K-1) Includes index. ISBN 0-669-08042-x
*1. Readers (Primary) 2. Reading (Primary) I. Series.*
*TC PE1119 .W37 1986 Teacher's Ed.*

**Warner, Carolyn.** Promoting your school : going beyond PR / Carolyn Warner. 2nd ed. Thousand Oaks, Calif. : Corwin Press, c2000. xix, 238 p. : ill. ; 30 cm. Includes bibliographical references. ISBN 0-8039-6897-3 (cloth : alk. paper) ISBN 0-8039-6898-1 (pbk. : alk. paper) DDC 659.2/9371
*1. Schools - Public relations - United States. I. Title.*
*TC LB2847 .W36 2000*

**Warner Home Video (Firm).**
Stephen Hawking's universe [videorecording]. [Alexandria, Va.] : PBS Video; Burbank, CA : Distributed by Warner Home Video, c1997.
*TC QB982 .S7 1997*

**Warner, Malcolm.**
The IEBM handbook of human resource management. 1st ed. London ; Boston : International Thomson Business Press, 1998.
*TC HF5549.17 .I33 1998*

**Warner, Mary L.**
Winning ways of coaching writing. Boston ; London : Allyn and Bacon, c2001.
*TC LB1631 .W55 2001*

**Wärneryd, Karl Erik, 1927-** The psychology of saving : a study on economic psychology / Karl-Erik Wärneryd. Northampton, Mass. : E. Elgar, c1999. ix, 389 p. : ill. ; 24 cm. Includes bibliographical references (p. 350-376) and index. ISBN 1-84064-016-2 DDC 332/.0415/019
*1. Saving and investment - Psychological aspects. 2. Economics - Psychological aspects. I. Title.*
*TC HB822 .W37 1999*

**WARPING.** *See* **WEAVING.**

**Warren, William, 1942-** Philosophical dimensions of personal construct psychology / Bill Warren. London ; New York : Routledge, 1998. viii, 200 p. ; 24 cm. Includes bibliographical references (p. [174]-191) and index. ISBN 0-415-16850-3 (hc) DDC 150.19/8
*1. Personal construct theory - Philosophy. I. Title.*
*TC BF698.9.P47 W37 1998*

**WARS.** *See* **MILITARY HISTORY; WAR.**

**Warschauer, Mark.**
Network-based language teaching. Cambridge, U.K. ; New York : Cambridge University Press, 2000.
*TC P53.285 .N48 2000*

**Washburn, Ruth Wendell, 1890-** Children have their reasons, by Ruth Wendell Washburn, with an introduction by Dorothy Canfield Fisher. New York, D. Appleton-Century, 1942. xvii, 257 p. illus., plates 20 cm. Includes index. DDC 136.7; [159.9227]
*1. Child development. I. Title.*
*TC HQ772 .W24*

**Washington and Arnold.**
The American Revolution. [videorecording]. New York, N.Y. : A&E Home Video, c1994.
*TC E208 .A447 1994*

**WASHINGTON (D.C.) - HISTORY - 20TH CENTURY - PICTORIAL WORKS.**
Visual journal. Washington, DC : Smithsonian Institution Press, c1996.
*TC TR820.5 .V57 1996*

**WASHINGTON, D.C. - HISTORY - CIVIL WAR, 1861-1865 - FICTION.**
Sappey, Maureen Stack, 1952- Letters from Vinnie. Asheville, NC : Front Street, 1999.
*TC PZ7.S2388 Le 1999*

**WASHINGTON, D.C. - HISTORY - CIVIL WAR, 1861-1865 - JUVENILE FICTION.**
Sappey, Maureen Stack, 1952- Letters from Vinnie. Asheville, NC : Front Street, 1999.
*TC PZ7.S2388 Le 1999*

**WASHINGTON (D.C.) - RACE RELATIONS.**
Moore, Jacqueline M., 1965- Leading the race. Charlottesville : University Press of Virginia, 1999.
*TC E185.93.D6 M66 1999*

**WASHINGTON (D.C.) - SOCIAL CONDITIONS - 19TH CENTURY.**
Moore, Jacqueline M., 1965- Leading the race. Charlottesville : University Press of Virginia, 1999.
*TC E185.93.D6 M66 1999*

**WASHINGTON (D.C.) - SOCIAL CONDITIONS - 20TH CENTURY.**
Moore, Jacqueline M., 1965- Leading the race. Charlottesville : University Press of Virginia, 1999.
*TC E185.93.D6 M66 1999*

**WASHINGTON, GEORGE, 1732-1799.**
Ferrie, Richard. The world turned upside down. 1st ed. New York : Holiday House, c1999.
*TC E241.Y6 F45 1999*

**WASHINGTON, GEORGE, 1732-1799 - MILITARY LEADERSHIP - JUVENILE LITERATURE.**
Ferrie, Richard. The world turned upside down. 1st ed. New York : Holiday House, c1999.
*TC E241.Y6 F45 1999*

**Washington, R. O. (Robert O.).**
Allen-Meares, Paula, 1948- Social work services in schools. 3rd ed. Boston : Allyn and Bacon, c2000.
*TC LB3013.4 .A45 2000*

**WASHINGTON (STATE) - FICTION.**
Holm, Jennifer L. Our only May Amelia. 1st ed. New York : HarperCollinsPublishers, c1999.
*TC PZ7.H732226 Ou 1999*

**Washington (State) University.**
(1) Stein, Joan W The family as a unit of study and treatment, [Seattle] Regional Rehabilitation Research Institute, University of Washington, School of Social Work [1970]
*TC RC488.5 .S88*

**Wassaja (San Francisco, Calif. : 1973).**
The Indian historian. [San Francisco, American Indian Historical Society]

**Wassaja, the Indian historian.**
The Indian historian. [San Francisco, American Indian Historical Society]

**Wasser, Henry Hirsch, 1919-** Diversification in higher education / Henry Wasser. Kassel : Wissenschaftliches Zentrum für Berufs- und Hochschulforschung der Gesamthochschule Kassel, 1999. 96 p. ; 21 cm. (Werkstattberichte ; Bd. 56) Includes bibliographical references (p. [93]-96) ISBN 3-928172-05-0
*1. Universities and colleges - Europe. 2. Universities and colleges - United States. I. Title. II. Series: Werkstattberichte (Gesamthochschule Kassel. Wissenschaftliches Zentrum für Berufs- und Hochschulforschung) ; Bd. 56.*
*TC LA622 .W37 1999*

**Wasserman, Elga R. (Elga Ruth)** The door in the dream : conversations with eminent women in science / Elga Wasserman. Washington, D.C. : Joseph Henry Press, c2000. xiv, 254 p. : ill. ; 24 cm. Includes bibliographical references and index. ISBN 0-309-06568-2 (hardcover : alk. paper) DDC 305.43/5/0973
*1. Women biologists - United States - Biography. 2. Women scientists - United States - Biography. I. Title.*
*TC QH26 .W375 2000*

**Watch IT.**
Burbules, Nicholas C. Boulder, Colo. : Westview Press, 2000.
*TC LB1028.43 .B87 2000*

**WATCHES.** *See* **CLOCKS AND WATCHES.**

**Watelet, Marilyn.**
Ecole 27 [videorecording]. Bruxelles : Paradise Films ; New York, N.Y. : [distributed by] First Run/ Icarus Films, 1997, c1996.
*TC LC746.P7 E2 1997*

**WATER.** *See also* **RIVERS.**
The nutty, nougat-filled world of human nutrition [videorecording]. [Arlington, Va.] : Cerebellum Corp., c1998.
*TC QP141 .N8 1998*

**WATER-COLOR PAINTING.** *See* **WATERCOLOR PAINTING.**

**WATER-COLOR PAINTING, AMERICAN.** *See* **WATERCOLOR PAINTING, AMERICAN.**

**WATER-COLOR PAINTING, AUSTRALIAN.** *See* **WATERCOLOR PAINTING, AUSTRALIAN.**

**WATER-COLOR PAINTINGS.** *See* **WATERCOLOR PAINTING.**

**WATER-COLORS.** *See* **WATERCOLOR PAINTING.**

**WATER-COLOUR PAINTING.** *See* **WATERCOLOR PAINTING.**

**WATER-COLOURS.** *See* **WATERCOLOR PAINTING.**

**WATER IN LANDSCAPE ARCHITECTURE.** *See* **FOUNTAINS.**

**WATER - JUVENILE LITERATURE.**
Greenfield, Eloise. Water, water. [New York?] : HarperFestival, c1999.
*TC GB662.3 .G7 1999*

**WATER - PHYSIOLOGICAL EFFECT.**
The nutty, nougat-filled world of human nutrition [videorecording]. [Arlington, Va.] : Cerebellum Corp., c1998.
*TC QP141 .N8 1998*

**Water, water.**
Greenfield, Eloise. [New York?] : HarperFestival, c1999.
*TC GB662.3 .G7 1999*

**WATERCOLOR PAINTING - 19TH CENTURY - AUSTRALIA - EXHIBITIONS.**
Kolenberg, Hendrik. Australian watercolours from the gallery's collection. Sydney, [Australia] : Art Gallery of New South Wales, 1995.
*TC ND2089 .K64 1995*

**WATERCOLOR PAINTING - 19TH CENTURY - UNITED STATES - EXHIBITIONS.**
Ferber, Linda S. Masters of color and light. Washington : Brooklyn Museum of Art in Association with Smithsonian Institution Press, c1998.
*TC ND1807 .F47 1998*

**WATERCOLOR PAINTING - 20TH CENTURY - AUSTRALIA - EXHIBITIONS.**
Kolenberg, Hendrik. Australian watercolours from the gallery's collection. Sydney, [Australia] : Art Gallery of New South Wales, 1995.
*TC ND2089 .K64 1995*

**WATERCOLOR PAINTING, AMERICAN - EXHIBITIONS.**
Ferber, Linda S. Masters of color and light. Washington : Brooklyn Museum of Art in Association with Smithsonian Institution Press, c1998.
*TC ND1807 .F47 1998*

**WATERCOLOR PAINTING, AUSTRALIAN - EXHIBITIONS.**
Kolenberg, Hendrik. Australian watercolours from the gallery's collection. Sydney, [Australia] : Art Gallery of New South Wales, 1995.
*TC ND2089 .K64 1995*

**WATERCOLOR PAINTING - NEW YORK (STATE) - NEW YORK - EXHIBITIONS.**
Ferber, Linda S. Masters of color and light.

*TC HT167 .C483 2000*

Washington : Brooklyn Museum of Art in Association with Smithsonian Institution Press, c1998.
*TC ND1807 .F47 1998*

**WATERCOLOR PAINTINGS.** *See* **WATERCOLOR PAINTING.**

**WATERCOLORS.** *See* **WATERCOLOR PAINTING.**

**The watercolors of John Singer Sargent.**
Little, Carl. Berkeley : University of California Press, c1998.
*TC ND1839.S32 L58 1998*

**WATERCOLOURS.** *See* **WATERCOLOR PAINTING.**

**Waterman, Robin.**
Purcell-Gates, Victoria. Now we read, we see, we speak. Mahwah, N.J. : L. Erlbaum Associates, Publishers, 2000.
*TC LC155.S22 P87 2000*

**Waters, Kate.** Mary Geddy's day : : a colonial girl in Williamsburg / by Kate Waters ; photographed by Russ Kendall. 1st ed. New York : Scholastic Press, 1999. 40 p. : col. ill. ; 27 cm. "In association with the Colonial Williamsburg Foundation". ISBN 0-590-92925-9
*1. Williamsburg (Va.) - History - Revolution, 1775-1783 - Juvenile fiction. 2. Williamsburg (Va.) - History - Revolution, 1775-1783 - Fiction. 3. United States - History - Revolution, 1775-1783 - Fiction. I. Kendall, Russ, ill. II. Colonial Williamsburg Foundation. III. Title.*
*TC PZ7.W26434 Mar 1999*

**Watersheds in higher education** / edited by James J. Van Patten. Lewiston, N.Y. : E. Mellen Press, c1997. 188 p. ; 24 cm. (Mellen studies in education ; v. 32) Includes bibliographical references and index. ISBN 0-7734-8605-4 DDC 378.73
*1. Education, Higher - United States - History. 2. Education, Higher - United States - Philosophy. 3. Educators - United States - Biography. I. Van Patten, James J. II. Series.*
*TC LA228 .W28 1997*

**Watkins, C. Edward.**
Testing and assessment in counseling practice. 2nd ed. Mahwah, N.J. : L. Erlbaum Associates, 2000.
*TC BF176 .T423 2000*

**Watson, David.** Mood and temperament / David Watson. New York ; London : Guilford Press, c2000. xi, 340 p. : ill. ; 24 cm. (Emotions and social behavior) Includes bibliographical references (p. 293-333) and index. ISBN 1-57230-526-6 (hardcover : alk. paper) DDC 152.4
*1. Personality and emotions. I. Title. II. Series.*
*TC BF698.9.E45 W38 2000*

**Watson, David, 1949-** Managing strategy / David Watson. Buckingham [England] ; Philadelphia : Open University Press, 2000. xix, 156 p. ; 23 cm. (Managing universities and colleges) Includes bibliographical references (p. [143]-150) and index. ISBN 0-335-20345-0 (pbk.) ISBN 0-335-20346-9 (hbk.) DDC 378.41
*1. Universities and colleges - Great Britain - Administration. 2. Strategic planning - Great Britain. 3. Education, Higher - Great Britain - Management. I. Title. II. Series.*
*TC LB2341.8.G7 W28 2000*

**Watson, Deryn.**
IFIP TC3 WG3.1/3.5 Open Conference on Communications and Networking in Education (1999 : Aulanko, Finland) Communications and networking in education. Boston : Kluwer Academic Publishers, 2000.
*TC LB1044.87 .I45 2000*

**Watson-Guptill crafts**
Taormina, Grace. The complete guide to rubber stamping. New York : Watson-Guptill Publications, c1996.
*TC TT867 .T36 1996*

**Watson-Guptill Publications.**
Jones, Mark W. (Mark Walter), 1947- Dancer's resource. New York : Watson-Guptill Publications, c1999.
*TC GV1589 .J65 1999*

**Watson, Jonathan, 1960-.**
Researching health promotion. London ; New York : Routledge, 2000.
*TC RA427.8 .R47 2000*

**Watson, Ken (Ken D.).**
Fiction, literature and media. Amsterdam : Amsterdam University Press, c1999.
*TC LB1575.8 .F53 1999*

**Watson, Linda R., 1950-** Deaf and hearing impaired pupils in mainstream schools / Linda Watson, Susan Gregory and Stephen Powers. London : David Fulton, c1999. x, 52, [2] p. ; 25 cm. Includes bibliographical

references (p. [53]) and index. ISBN 1-85346-588-7
*1. Mainstreaming in education - Great Britain. 2. Hearing impaired children - Education - Great Britain. I. Powers, Stephen, 1936- II. Gregory, Susan, 1945- III. Title.*
*TC LC1203.G7 W387 1999*

**Watson, Sam.**
Jazz dance class [videorecording]. W. Long Branch, NJ : Kultur, [1992?]
*TC GV1784 .J3 1992*

**Wattenbarger, James Lorenzo, 1922-.**
A struggle to survive. Thousand Oaks, Calif. : Corwin Press, c1996.
*TC LB2342 .S856 1996*

Where does the money go? Thousand Oaks, Calif. : Corwin Press, c1996.
*TC LB2825 .W415 1996*

**Watts, Judith.**
Luciana, James. The art of enhanced photography :. Gloucester, Mass. : Rockport Publishers, c1999.
*TC TR654 .L83 1999*

**Watts, Michael.**
Teaching economics to undergraduates. Cheltenham, UK ; Northampton, MA, USA : E. Elgar, c1998.
*TC HB74.8 .T4 1998*

**Waugh, Linda R.**
Discourse and perspective in cognitive linguistics. Amsterdam : Philadelphia : J. Benjamins, c1997.
*TC P165 .D57 1997*

**Wax, Murray Lionel, 1922-** Western rationality and the angel of dreams : self, psyche, dreaming / Murray L. Wax. Lanham, Md. ; Oxford : Rowman & Littlefield, c1999. ix, 171 p. ; 24 cm. Includes bibliographical references (p. 151-166) and index. ISBN 0-8476-9374-0 (hbk. : alk. paper) ISBN 0-8476-9375-9 (pbk. : alk. paper) DDC 154.6/
*1. Freud, Sigmund, - 1856-1939. 2. Dreams. 3. Dream interpretation. I. Title.*
*TC BF1078 .W38 1999*

**The way things are, and other poems.**
Livingston, Myra Cohn. [1st ed.]. New York, Atheneum, 1974.
*TC PZ8.3.L75 Way*

**The way we never were.**
Coontz, Stephanie. New York, NY : BasicBooks, c1992.
*TC HQ535 .C643 1992*

**Ways of knowing in science series**
Borasi, Raffaella. Reading counts. New York ; London : Teachers College Press, c2000.
*TC QA11 .B6384 2000*

Hurd, Paul DeHart, 1905- Transforming middle school science education. New York : Teachers College Press, c2000.
*TC LB1585.3 .H89 2000*

Implementing standards-based mathematics instruction. New York : Teachers College Press, c2000.
*TC QA135.5 .I525 2000*

Polman, Joseph L., 1965- Designing project-based science. New York ; London : Teachers College Press, c2000.
*TC Q181 .P4694 2000*

**We are what we eat.**
Gabaccia, Donna R., 1949- Cambridge, Mass. : Harvard University Press, 1998.
*TC GT2853.U5 G33 1998*

**We had a dream.**
Kohn, Howard. New York : Simon & Schuster, 1998.
*TC F187.P9 K64 1998*

**We keep a store.**
Shelby, Anne. New York : Orchard Books, c1989.
*TC PZ7.S54125 We 1989*

Shelby, Anne. New York : Orchard Books, c1990.
*TC PZ7 .S54125We 1990*

**We paid our dues.**
Bolles, Augusta Lynn. Washington, D.C. : Howard University Press, 1996.
*TC HD6079.2.C27 B64 1996*

**We the people simulated congressional hearing**
[videorecording] : Denver East High School State competition and Thunder Ridge Middle School non-competitive hearing 1997 / produced by the Social Science Education Consortium. [Boulder, Colo.] : Social Science Education Consortium, c1997. 1 videocassette (36 min.) : sd., col. ; 1/2 in. VHS. Catalogued from credits and cassette label. Title from cassette label. Video production by Vicki Murray-Kurzban. For educators and Social Studies teachers. SUMMARY: This video shows clips

of two simulated Congressional hearings and the students reactions to this form of pedagogy. The first takes place at Denver East High School and is part of a state competition. The second is a non-competitive hearing that takes place at Thunder Ridge Middle School. Students in both schools show an impressive grasp of the material that comprises our government and Constitution and are extremely articulate in expressing both the facts and their opinions. CONTENTS: Denver East High School Constitutional scholars simulated Congressional hearing: a performance at the Colorado "We the People" state competition, December 16, 1996 -- Unit 5: Fundamental rights -- Thunder Ridge Middle School: Lori Mable's 8th grade American studies.
*1. Legislative hearings - United States - Study and teaching - Simulation methods. 2. Constitutional law - United States - Study and teaching (Secondary) - Simulation methods - Colorado. 3. Constitutional law - United States - Study and teaching (Secondary) - Colorado - Evaluation. 4. Constitutional law - United States - Competitions - Colorado. 5. United States - Politics and government - Study and teaching (Elementary) - Simulation methods - United States. 6. United States - Politics and government - Study and teaching (Elementary) - United States - Evaluation. I. Social Science Education Consortium. II. Title: Denver East High School State competition and Thunder Ridge Middle School non-competitive hearing 1997*
*TC KF4208.5.L3 W4 1997*

**WEALTH.** *See* **POVERTY.**

**WEALTH - MORAL AND ETHICAL ASPECTS.** *See* **BUSINESS ETHICS.**

**Wealth of nations.**
Smith, Adam, 1723-1790. An inquiry into the nature and causes of the wealth of nations. Chicago : University of Chicago Press, 1976.
*TC HB161 .S65 1976*

**WEALTH - UNITED STATES - STATISTICS.**
Statistical handbook on consumption and wealth in the United States. Phoenix, Ariz. : Oryx Press, 1999.
*TC HC110.C6 S73 1999*

**WEAPONS.** *See* **FIREARMS.**

**Weapons laboratory at the end of the Cold War.**
Gusterson, Hugh. Nuclear rites. "First paperback printing 1998". Berkeley : University of California Press, 1998.
*TC U264.4.C2 G87 1998*

**WEAPONS OF MASS DESTRUCTION.** *See* **NUCLEAR WEAPONS.**

**Weare, Katherine, 1950-** Promoting mental, emotional, and social health : a whole school approach / Katherine Weare. London ; New York : Routledge, 2000. 167 p. ; 24 cm. Includes bibliographical references (p. [139]-160) and index. ISBN 0-415-16875-9 (alk. paper) ISBN 0-415-16876-7 (pbk. : alk. paper) DDC 371.7/1
*1. School children - Mental health. 2. Schools - Sociological aspects. I. Title.*
*TC LB3430 .W42 2000*

**WEARINESS.** *See* **FATIGUE.**

**WEASELS - FICTION.**
Hallensleben, Georg. Pauline. New York : Farrar, Straus & Giroux, c1999.
*TC PZ7.H15425 Pau 1999*

**WEATHER.** *See* **SNOW; WINDS.**

**WEATHER FORECASTING.**
Broad, Kenneth. Climate, culture, and values. 1999.
*TC 085 B7775*

**Weatherall, Mark.** Gentlemen, scientists, and doctors : medicine at Cambridge 1800-1940 / Mark W. Weatherall. Woodbridge, Suffolk ; Rochester, N.Y. : Boydell Press : Cambridge University Library, 2000. x, 341 p. ; 24 cm. (History of the University of Cambridge. Texts and studies, 0960-2887 ; 3) Includes bibliographical references (p. 311-332) and index. ISBN 0-85115-681-9 (hardback : acid-free paper) DDC 610/.9426/5909034
*1. Medicine - England - Cambridge - History - 19th century. 2. Medicine - England - Cambridge - History - 20th century. I. Title. II. Series.*
*TC R487 .W43 2000*

**Weatherford, Carole Boston, 1956-** The sound that jazz makes / Carole Boston Weatherford ; illustrations by Eric Velasquez. New York : Walker & Co., c2000. 1 v. (unpaged) : chiefly col. ill. ; 31 cm. SUMMARY: An illustrated history of the origins and influences of jazz, from Africa to contemporary America. ISBN 0-8027-8720-7 ISBN 0-8027-8721-5 (reinforced) DDC 781.65/09
*1. Jazz - History and criticism - Juvenile literature. 2. Jazz. I. Velasquez, Eric, ill. II. Title.*
*TC ML3506 .W42 2000*

**WEAVING.** *See also* **HAND WEAVING; TEXTILE FABRICS.**
Alexander, Marthann. Weaving on cardboard; New York, Taplinger Pub. Co. [1972]
*TC TT848 .A67*

**WEAVING - FICTION.**
Murphy, Shirley Rousseau. Wind child. New York, NY : HarperCollins, c1999.
*TC PZ8.M957 Wi 1999*

**Weaving on cardboard.**
Alexander, Marthann. New York, Taplinger Pub. Co. [1972]
*TC TT848 .A67*

**Weaving the Web.**
Berners-Lee, Tim. 1st ed. San Francisco : HarperSanFrancisco, c1999.
*TC TK5105.888 .B46 1999*

**Weaving work and motherhood.**
Garey, Anita Ilta, 1947- Philadelphia, PA : Temple University Press, 1999.
*TC HQ759.48 .G37 1999*

**Web-based learning and teaching technologies :**
opportunities and challenges / [edited by] Anil Aggarwal. Hershey, PA ; London : Idea Group Pub., c2000. vi, 372 p. : ill. ; 25 cm. Includes bibliographical references and index. ISBN 1-87828-960-8 (paper) DDC 025.06/37
*1. Education - Computer network resources. 2. Teaching - Computer network resources. 3. Internet (Computer network) in education. I. Aggarwal, Anil. 1949-*
*TC LB1044.87 .W435 2000*

**Web-based training: tactics and techniques for designing adult learning experiences.**
Driscoll, Margaret M. The application of adult education principles in the development of a manual for practitioners creating web-based training programs. 1999.
*TC 06 no. 11106*

**WEB (INFORMATION RETRIEVAL SYSTEM).** *See* **WORLD WIDE WEB (INFORMATION RETRIEVAL SYSTEM).**

**WEB PUBLISHING - SOFTWARE.**
Macromedia Dreamweaver 3 [computer file]. Version 3.0 ; Windows 95, Windows 98, Windows NT ; Education version. San Francisco, CA : Macromedia, c1999. Computer program.
*TC TK5105.8883 .M33 1999*

**Web search engines.**
Hock, Randolph, 1944- The extreme searcher's guide to Web search engines. Medford, NJ : CyberAge Books, c1999.
*TC ZA4226 .H63 1998*

Hock, Randolph, 1944- The extreme searcher's guide to Web search engines. Medford, NJ : CyberAge Books, c1999.
*TC ZA4226 .H63 1998*

**WEB SITES.** *See also* **CHILDREN'S WEB SITES.**
Alexander, Janet E. Web wisdom. Mahwah, N.J. : Lawrence Erlbaum Associates, Publishers, 1999.
*TC TK5105.888 .A376 1999*

Burwell, Helen P. Online competitive intelligence. Tempe, AZ : Facts on Demand Press, c1999.
*TC HD38.7 .B974 1999*

**WEB SITES - AUTHORING PROGRAMS.**
Macromedia Dreamweaver 3 [computer file]. Version 3.0 ; Windows 95, Windows 98, Windows NT ; Education version. San Francisco, CA : Macromedia, c1999. Computer program.
*TC TK5105.8883 .M33 1999*

**WEB SITES - DESIGN.**
Junion-Metz, Gail, 1947- Creating a power web site. New York : Neal-Schuman, c1998.
*TC Z674.75.W67 J86 1998*

The library Web. Medford, NJ : Information Today, 1997.
*TC Z674.75.W67 L53 1997*

**WEB SITES - DESIGN - SOFTWARE.**
Macromedia Dreamweaver 3 [computer file]. Version 3.0 ; Windows 95, Windows 98, Windows NT ; Education version. San Francisco, CA : Macromedia, c1999. Computer program.
*TC TK5105.8883 .M33 1999*

**WEB SITES - DIRECTORIES.**
Polly, Jean Armour. The Internet kids & family yellow pages. Millenium ed. Berkeley, Calif. : Osborne McGraw-Hill, c2000.
*TC ZA4226 .P6 2000*

The School administrator's handbook of essential Internet sites. Fourth ed. Gaithersburg, MD : Aspen Publishers.
*TC TK5105.875.I57 S3 2000*

Sharp, Richard M. The best Web sites for teachers. 3rd ed. Eugene, OR : International Society for Technology in Education, 2000.
*TC LB1044.87 .S52 2000*

**WEB SITES - UNITED STATES - DESIGN.**
Junion-Metz, Gail, 1947- Creating a power web site. New York : Neal-Schuman, c1998.
*TC Z674.75.W67 J86 1998*

The library Web. Medford, NJ : Information Today, 1997.
*TC Z674.75.W67 L53 1997*

**WEB SITES - UNITED STATES - DIRECTORIES.**
Andriot, Laurie. Internet blue pages. 1999 ed. Medford, NJ : Information Today, c1998.
*TC ZA5075 .A53 1998*

Andriot, Laurie. Uncle Sam's K-12 Web. Medford, N.J. : CyberAge Books, 1999.
*TC ZA575 .A53 1999*

**Web wisdom.**
Alexander, Janet E. Mahwah, N.J. : Lawrence Erlbaum Associates, Publishers, 1999.
*TC TK5105.888 .A376 1999*

**Webb, Eugene J., 1933-.**
Nonreactive measures in the social sciences. 2nd ed. Boston : Houghton Mifflin, c1981.
*TC H62 .N675 1981*

**Webb, Ida M.** The challenge of change in physical education : Chelsea College of Physical Education-Chelsea School, University of Brighton 1898-1998 / Ida M. Webb. London : Falmer Press, 1999. xii, 203 p. : ill., maps, ports ; 24 cm. Includes bibliographical references (p. 193-196) and index. ISBN 0-7507-0976-6
*1. Chelsea College of Physical Education. 2. University of Brighton. - Chelsea School. 3. Physical education and training - England - Brighton. 4. Physical education teachers - Training of - England - Brighton. I. Title.*
*TC GV246.E3 B79 1999*

**Webb, Lois Sinaiko.** Multicultural cookbook of life-cycle celebrations / by Lois Sinaiko Webb. Phoenix, AZ : Oryx Press, 2000. xvi, 473 p. : ill. ; 26 cm. Includes bibliographical references and index. ISBN 1-57356-290-4 DDC 641.59
*1. Cookery, International. I. Title.*
*TC TX725.A1 W43 2000*

**Webb, Norman.**
Zweizig, Douglas. Lessons from library power. Englewood, Colo. : Libraries Unlimited, 1999.
*TC Z675.S3 Z94 1999*

**WEBB, SIM - LEGENDS.**
Farmer, Nancy. Casey Jones's fireman. 1st ed. New York : Phyllis Fogelman Books, c1998.
*TC PZ8.1.F2225 Cas 1998*

Farmer, Nancy. Casey Jones's fireman. 1st ed. New York : Phyllis Fogelman Books, c1998.
*TC PZ8.1.F2225 Cas 1998*

**Webb, Virginia-Lee.**
Delivering views. Washington [D.C.] : Smithsonian Institution Press, c1998.
*TC NC1872 .D46 1998*

**Webber, Stephen L., 1967-** School, reform and society in the new Russia / Stephen L. Webber ; foreword by Anthony Jones. Houndmills [England] : Macmillan Press ; New York : St. Martin's Press in association with Centre for Russian and East European Studies, University of Birmingham, 2000. xx, 252 p. : ill. ; 23 cm. (Studies in Russian and East European history and society) Includes bibliographical references (p. 227-244) and indexes. ISBN 0-333-73396-7 (Macmillan : cloth) ISBN 0-312-22413-3 (St. Martin's : cloth) DDC 370/.947
*1. Educational change - Russia (Federation) 2. Education and state - Russia (Federation) 3. Education - Russia (Federation) I. Title. II. Series.*
*TC LA839.2 .W4 2000*

**Weber, Hartmut.** Opto-electronic storage : an alternative to filming? / by Hartmut Weber. Washington, DC : Commission on Preservation and Access, 1993. 6 p. ; 28 cm. Caption title. "Translation of a chapter from the article Verfilmen oder instandsetzen? schutz- und ersatzverfilmung im dienste der bestandserhaltung." "February 1993." "Newsletter insert." Includes bibliographical references.
*1. Documents in optical storage. 2. Documents in microform. I. Title.*
*TC Z678.93.O7 W4315 1993*

**Weber, Robert J. (Robert John), 1936-** The created self : reinventing body, persona, and spirit / Robert J. Weber. 1st ed. New York ; London : W.W. Norton, c2000. 319 p. ; 22 cm. Includes bibliographical references (p. [305]-319). ISBN 0-393-04833-0 DDC 155.2
*1. Self-presentation. 2. Change (Psychology) I. Title.*
*TC BF697.5.S44 W43 2000*

**Weber, Samuel M.**
**[Freud-Legende. English]**
The legend of Freud / Samuel Weber. Expanded ed. Stanford, Calif. : Stanford University Press, 2000. c1982. xv, 259 p. ; 22 cm. (Cultural memory in the present) Translation of: Freud-Legende. Includes bibliographical references and indexes.
*1. Psychoanalysis. 2. Freud, Sigmund. - 1856-1939. I. Title. II. Series.*
*TC BF173.F85 W2813 2000*

**Weber, Sandra.** That's funny, you don't look like a teacher! : interrogating images and identity in popular culture / Sandra Weber and Claudia Mitchell. London ; Washington, D.C. : Falmer Press, 1995. xii, 156 p. : ill. (some col.) ; 24 cm. Includes bibliographical references (p. 141-152) and index. ISBN 0-7507-0412-8 (alk. paper) ISBN 0-7507-0413-6 (pbk. : alk. paper) DDC 371.1/00941
*1. Teachers - Great Britain - Public opinion. 2. Public opinion - Great Britain. I. Mitchell, Claudia. II. Title.*
*TC LB1775.4.G7 W43 1995*

**WebSPIRS.**
[ERIC (SilverPlatter International : Online)] The ERIC database [computer file]. WebSPIRS version 3.1. [Norwood, MA] : SilverPlatter International,
*TC NETWORKED RESOURCES*

[ERIC (SilverPlatter International : Online)] The ERIC database [computer file]. WebSPIRS version 3.1. [Norwood, MA] : SilverPlatter International,
*TC NETWORKED RESOURCES*

**Webster, Douglas B., 1934-** Neuroscience of communication / Douglas B. Webster. 2nd ed. San Diego : Singular Publishing Group, c1999. xii, 379 p. : col. ill. ; 26 cm. (Singular textbook series) Includes bibliographical references and index. ISBN 1-56593-985-9 (softcover : alk. paper) DDC 612.8
*1. Neurophysiology. 2. Communicative disorders - Physiological aspects. 3. Communication. 4. Neurolinguistics. 5. Neurosciences. I. Title. II. Series.*
*TC QP355.2 .W43 1999*

**Webster, Frank.**
Robins, Kevin. Times of the technoculture. London ; New York : Routledge, 1999.
*TC T58.5 .R65 1999*

**Webster, Glenn A.**
Brencick, Janice M. Philosophy of nursing. Albany : State University of New York Press, c2000.
*TC RT84.5 .B74 2000*

**Webster, Kathy L.**
Thomas, Alice F. SLP assistant in the schools. [San Antonio, Tex.] : Communication Skill Builders, c1999.
*TC LB3454 .T46 1999*

**WEBSTER, NOAH, 1758-1843.**
**AMERICAN DICTIONARY OF THE ENGLISH LANGUAGE.**
Micklethwait, David. Noah Webster and the American dictionary. Jefferson, N.C. : McFarland, c2000.
*TC PE65.W5 M53 2000*

**WEBSTER, NOAH, 1758-1843.**
Micklethwait, David. Noah Webster and the American dictionary. Jefferson, N.C. : McFarland, c2000.
*TC PE65.W5 M53 2000*

**Webster, Wendy.** Imagining home : gender, "race," and national identity, 1945-64 / Wendy Webster. London ; Bristol, Pa. : UCL Press, 1998. xxiv, 240 p. ; 22 cm. (Women's history) Includes bibliographical references (p. 217-233) and index. ISBN 1-85728-350-3 (hb) ISBN 1-85728-351-1 (pb) DDC 305.4/0941/0904
*1. Women - Great Britain - History - 20th century. 2. Home - Great Britain - History - 20th century. I. Title. II. Series.*
*TC HQ1593 .W43 1998*

**WECHSLER ADULT INTELLIGENCE SCALE.**
Flanagan, Dawn P. The Wechsler intelligence scales and Gf-Gc theory. Boston ; London : Allyn and Bacon, c2000.
*TC BF432.5.W4 F53 2000*

**Wechsler, Henry, 1932-.**
The Horizons of health. Cambridge, Mass. : Harvard University Press, 1977.
*TC R850 .H67*

**WECHSLER INTELLIGENCE SCALE FOR CHILDREN.**
Kaufman, Alan S. Essentials of WISC-III and WPPSI-R assessment. New York ; Chichester [England] : Wiley, c2000.
*TC BF432.5.W42 K36 2000*

**The Wechsler intelligence scales and Gf-Gc theory.**
Flanagan, Dawn P. Boston ; London : Allyn and Bacon, c2000.
*TC BF432.5.W4 F53 2000*

**WECHSLER PRESCHOOL AND PRIMARY SCALE OF INTELLIGENCE.**
Kaufman, Alan S. Essentials of WISC-III and WPPSI-R assessment. New York ; Chichester [England] : Wiley, c2000.
*TC BF432.5.W42 K36 2000*

**WEDDINGS - FICTION.**
Edwards, Pamela Duncan. Wacky wedding. 1st ed. New York : Hyperion Books for Children, c1999.
*TC PZ7.E26365 Wac 1999*

Munsch, Robert N., 1945- Ribbon rescue. New York : Scholastic, 1999.
*TC PZ7.M927 Ri 1999*

**WEDDINGS - JUVENILE FICTION.**
English. Karen. Nadia's hands. 1st ed. Honesdale, PA : Boyds Mills Press, 1999.
*TC PZ7.E7232 Na 1999*

**WEDLOCK.** *See* **MARRIAGE.**

**Wedman, Judy M., 1943-.**
Issues and trends in literacy education. 2nd ed. Boston : Allyn and Bacon, c2000.
*TC LB1576 .I87 2000*

**Wee, Patricia Hachten, 1948-** Independent projects, step by step : a handbook for senior projects, graduation projects, and culminating projects / Patricia Hachten Wee. Lanham, MD : Scarecrow Press, c2000.
v, 131 p. : ill. ; 28 cm. Includes bibliographical references and index. ISBN 0-8108-3785-4 (alk. paper) DDC 373.139/43
*1. Independent study - United States - Handbooks, manuals, etc. 2. Project method in teaching - Handbooks, manuals, etc. 3. Twelfth grade (Education) - United States. I. Title.*
*TC LB1620 .W42 2000*

**Weeks, Sarah.** Little factory / written and sung by Sarah Weeks ; animated by Byron Barton. 1st ed. [New York] : Laura Geringer book, c1998. 1 v. (unpaged) : col. ill. ; 24 cm. + 1 computer optical disk (4 3/4 in.). Title from cover. "Ages 3-7"--P. [4] of cover. ISBN 0-06-027429-8 DDC [E]
*1. Factories - Fiction. 2. Air - Pollution - Fiction. 3. Solar energy - Fiction. I. Barton, Byron, ill. II. Title.*
*TC PZ7.W4125 Li 1998*

Regular Guy / Sarah Weeks. 1st ed. New York : Laura Geringer Book, c1999. 120 p. ; 22 cm. SUMMARY: Because he is so different from his eccentric parents, twelve-year-old Guy is convinced he has been switched at birth with a classmate whose parents seem more normal. ISBN 0-06-028367-X ISBN 0-06-028368-8 (lib. bdg.) DDC [Fic]
*1. Parent and child - Fiction. 2. Identity - Fiction. I. Title.*
*TC PZ7.W42215 Rg 1999*

**Weeks, Sarah T., 1926- ed.**
Hofmann, Hans, 1880-1966. Search for the real, [Rev. ed.]. Cambridge, Mass., M.I.T. Press [c1967]
*TC N7445 .H76 1967*

Hofmann, Hans, 1880-1966. Search for the real, [Rev. ed.]. Cambridge, Mass., M.I.T. Press [c1967]
*TC N7445 .H76 1967*

**Weems, Marianne.**
Art matters. New York : New York University Press, c1999.
*TC N72.S6 A752 1999*

**WEEPING.** *See* **CRYING.**

**Wehlage, Gary.**
Zweizig, Douglas. Lessons from library power. Englewood, Colo. : Libraries Unlimited, 1999.
*TC Z675.S3 Z94 1999*

**Weidenaar, Reynold, 1945-.**
Processing the signal [videorecording]. Cicero, Ill. : Roland Collection of Films on Art, c1989.
*TC N6494.V53 P7 1989*

**Weidman, John C., 1945-.**
Higher education in Korea. New York : Falmer Press, 2000.
*TC LA1333 .H54 2000*

**Weight, Bob H.**
The online teaching guide :. Boston, Mass. : Allyn and Bacon, c2000.

*TC LB1044.87 .O45 1999*

**WEIGHT CONTROL OF OBESITY.** *See* **WEIGHT LOSS.**

**WEIGHT LOSS - MANAGEMENT.**
Lean, Michael E. J. Clinical handbook of weight management. London : Martin Dunitz, Ltd. ; Malden, MA : distributed in the USA, Canada and Brazil by Blackwell Science, Ltd., c1998.
*TC RC628 .L436 1998*

**WEIGHT REDUCING.** *See* **WEIGHT LOSS.**

**WEIGHT REDUCTION.** *See* **WEIGHT LOSS.**

**Weighty issues :** fatness and thinness as social problems / Jeffery Sobal and Donna Maurer, editors. Hawthorne, N.Y. : Aldine de Gruyter, c1999. xii, 260 p. ; 24 cm. (Social problems and social issues) Includes bibliographical references and index. ISBN 0-202-30579-1 (alk. paper) ISBN 0-202-30580-5 (pbk. : alk. paper) DDC 306.4/61
*1. Obesity - Social aspects. 2. Food - Social aspects. 3. Nutrition - Social aspects. I. Sobal, Jeffery, 1950- II. Maurer, Donna, 1961- III. Series.*
*TC RA645.O23 W45 1999*

**Weikart, David P.**
Families speak. Ypsilanti, Mich. : High/Scope Press, c1994.
*TC LB1139.23 .F36 1994*

How nations serve young children. Ypsilanti, Mich. : High/Scope Press, c1989.
*TC HQ778.5 .H69 1989*

**Weil, Danny K., 1953-.**
Perspectives in critical thinking. New York : P. Lang, c2000.
*TC LB1590.3 .P476 2000*

**Weil, Ulric.** Information systems in the 80's : products, markets, and vendors / Ulric Weil. Englewood Cliffs, N.J. : Prentice-Hall, c1982. xiv, 383 p. : ill. ; 24 cm. Includes bibliographical references and index. ISBN 0-13-464560-X DDC 338.4/700164
*1. Computer industry - United States. 2. Computer industry. 3. Information storage and retrieval systems. I. Title.*
*TC HD9696.C63 U5954 1982*

**Weiler, Jeanne.** Codes and contradictions : race, gender identity, and schooling / Jeanne Drysdale Weiler. Albany : State University of New York Press, c2000. xi, 248 p. ; 24 cm. (SUNY series, power, social identity, and education) Includes bibliographical references (p. 231-245) and index. ISBN 0791445194(alk. paper) ISBN 0-7914-4520-8 (pbk. : alk. paper) DDC 373.1822/09747/1
*1. Women - Education - Social aspects - United States - Case studies. 2. Women - United States - Identity - Case studies. 3. Race awareness - United States - Case studies. 4. Feminism and education - United States. I. Title. II. Series: SUNY series, power, social identity, and education.*
*TC LC1755 .W45 2000*

**Weinberger, J.**
Democracy & the arts. Ithaca : Cornell University Press, c1999.
*TC NX180.S6 D447 1999*

**Weinberger, Jo.**
Finlay, Ann, 1944- The National Literacy Trust's international annotated bibliography of books on literacy. Stoke-on-Trent : Trentham Books, 1999.
*TC LC149 .F565 1999*

**Weiner, Annette B., 1933-.**
Cloth and human experience. Washington : Smithsonian Institution Press, c1989.
*TC GT525 .C57 1989*

**Weiner, Jonathan.** Time, love, memory : a great biologist and his quest for the origins of behavior / Jonathan Weiner. 1st ed. New York : Knopf, 1999. 300 p. : ill. ; 24 cm. "A Borzoi book." Includes bibliographical references (p. 259-283) and index. ISBN 0-679-44435-1 DDC 591.5
*1. Behavior genetics. 2. Benzer, Seymour. I. Title.*
*TC QH457 .W43 1999*

**Weiner, Jonathan. ill.**
English, Karen. Nadia's hands. Honesdale, PA : Boyds Mills Press, 1999.
*TC PZ7.E7232 Na 1999*

**Weiner, Robert, 1950-** Creativity and beyond : cultures, values, and change / Robert Paul Weiner. Albany : State University of New York Press, 2000. xii, 353 p. : ill. ; 24 cm. Includes bibliographical references and index. ISBN 0-7914-4477-5 (alk. paper) ISBN 0-7914-4478-3 (pbk. : alk. paper) DDC 153.3/5
*1. Creative thinking. 2. Creative ability. I. Title.*
*TC BF408 .W384 2000*

**Weinstein, Barbara E.** Geriatric audiology / Barbara E. Weinstein. New York : Thieme, 2000. xvi, 332 p. : ill. ; 29 cm. Includes bibliographical references and index. ISBN 0-86577-701-2 (TNY : hard cover) ISBN 3-13-108111-2 (GTV : hard cover)
*1. Hearing Disorders - Aged. 2. Aging. 3. Health Services for the Aged. 4. Hearing - physiology - Aged. I. Title.*
*TC RF291.5.A35 W44 2000*

**Weinstein, Estelle, 1937-.**
Teaching children about health. Englewood, Colo. : Morton Pub., 1999.
*TC LB1587.A3 T43 1999*

**Weinstein, Mark.**
Ballet class [videorecording]. W. Long Branch, NJ : Kultur, c1984.
*TC GV1589 .B33 1984*

**Weinstein, Miriam (Miriam H.)** Making a difference : scholarships for a better world / Miriam Weinstein. Rev. & exp. 2nd ed. Gabriola Island, BC, Can. : New Society Publishers, 2000. x, 229 p. ; 23 cm. Includes index, pp. 225-228. "An invaluable guide for students, volunteers, activists, community organizers, environmentalists...the scholarship/fellowship guide for the millions of people working to make a better world."--Cover. ISBN 0-86571-415-0 (pbk.)
*1. Scholarships - United States - Directories. 2. Social action - Scholarships, fellowships, etc. - Directories. 3. Environmentalism - Scholarships, fellowships, etc. - Directories. 4. Universities and colleges - Moral and ethical aspects - United States - Directories. I. Title. II. Title: Scholarships for a better world*
*TC LB2338 W45 2000*

**Weinstein, Sanford.** The educator's guide to substance abuse prevention / Sanford Weinstein. Mahwah, N.J. : Lawrence Erlbaum Publishers, 1999. xii, 269 ; 24 cm. Includes bibliographical references (p. 239-251) and index. ISBN 0-8058-2594-0 (cloth : alk. paper) ISBN 0-8058-2595-9 (pbk. : alk. paper) DDC 372.3/7
*1. Drug abuse - Prevention - Study and teaching (Elementary) 2. Substance abuse - Prevention - Study and teaching (Elementary) I. Title.*
*TC HV5808 .W45 1999*

**Weintraub, Robert Steven.** Informal learning in the workplace through desktop technology : a case study in a sales division of a large corporation / by Robert Steven Weintraub. 1998. ix, 214 leaves : ill. ; 29 cm. Issued also on microfilm. Thesis (Ed.D.)--Teachers College, Columbia University, 1998. Includes bibliographical references (leaves 177-188).
*1. International Business Machines Corporation - Employees - Training of. 2. Career education. 3. Educational technology. 4. Occupational training. 5. Computer-assisted instruction. 6. Adult learning. 7. Business communication - Interactive multimedia. 8. Non-formal education. 9. Adult education educators. I. International Business Machines Corporation. II. Title.*
*TC 06 no. 11003*

**Weisfeld, Glenn, 1943-** Evolutionary principles of human adolescence / Glenn E. Weisfeld. New York, NY : Basic Books, 1999. xiii, 401 p. : ill. ; 23 cm. (Lives in context) Includes bibliographical references (p. 325-377) and indexes. ISBN 0-8133-3317-2 (hardcover) ISBN 0-8133-3318-0 (pbk.) DDC 305.235
*1. Adolescent psychology. 2. Psychology, Comparative. I. Title. II. Series.*
*TC BF724 .W35 1999*

**Weiss, Carol H.** Evaluation research: methods of assessing program effectiveness [by] Carol H. Weiss. Englewood Cliffs, N.J., Prentice-Hall [1972] xii, 160 p. 23 cm. (Prentice-Hall methods of social science series) Bibliography: p. 129-154. ISBN 0-13-292193-6 DDC 001.4/33
*1. Evaluation research (Social action programs) I. Title.*
*TC H62 .W3962*

**Weiss, Gail, 1959-** Body images : embodiment as intercorporeality / Gail Weiss. New York : Routledge, 1999. x, 210 p. : ill. ; 24 cm. Includes bibliographical references (p. [195]-205) and index. ISBN 0-415-91802-2 (hardcover : alk. paper) ISBN 0-415-91803-0 (pbk. : alk. paper) DDC 128/.6
*1. Body image. 2. Body schema. I. Title.*
*TC BF697.5.B63 W45 1999*

**Weiss, Jeffrey.** Mark Rothko / Jeffrey Weiss : with contributions by John Gage ... [et al.]. Washington : National Gallery of Art ; New Haven, Conn. : Yale University Press, c1998. 376 p. : ill. (some col.) ; 32 cm. Catalogue of an exhibition held at the National Gallery of Art, Washington, D.C., 3 May-16 Aug. 1998; Whitney Museum of American Art, New York, 10 Sept.-29 Nov. 1998; Musee d'art moderne de la ville de Paris, 8 Jan.-18 April. 1999. Includes bibliographical references. ISBN 0-89468-229-6 (pbk.) ISBN 0-300-07505-7 (hardcover) DDC 760/.092
*1. Rothko, Mark, - 1903-1970 - Exhibitions. I. Gage, John. II.*

*National Gallery of Art (U.S.). III. Whitney Museum of American Art. IV. Musée d'art moderne de la ville de Paris. V. Title.*
**TC N6537.R63 A4 1998**

**Weissman, Myrna M.** Comprehensive guide to interpersonal psychotherapy / Myrna M. Weissman, John C. Markowitz, and Gerald L. Klerman. New York: Basic Books, c2000. xii, 465 p. ; 25 cm. Includes bibliographical references and index. ISBN 0-465-09566-6
*1. Psychotherapy and patient. 2. Psychotherapy. I. Markowitz, John C., 1954- II. Klerman, Gerald L., 1928- III. Title.*
**TC RC480.8 .W445 2000**

**WEIU-TV (Television Station : Charleston, Ill.).**
Grounded for life [videorecording]. Charleston, WV : Cambridge Research Group, Ltd., 1988.
**TC HQ759.4 .G7 1988**

**Wekesser, Carol, 1963-.**
Smoking. San Diego, CA : Greenhaven Press, c1997.
**TC HV5760 .S663 1997**

**Welch, Anthony R.**
Third World education. New York : Garland Pub., 2000.
**TC LC2607 .T55 2000**

**Welch, Kathleen E.** Electric rhetoric : classical rhetoric, oralism, and a new literacy / Kathleen E. Welch. Cambridge, Mass. : MIT Press, c1999. xiv, 255 p. ; 23 cm. (Digital communication) Includes bibliographical references (p. [223]-245) and index. ISBN 0-262-23202-2 (hc : alk. paper) DDC 302.2/244/01
*1. Rhetoric - Data processing. 2. Computers and literacy. 3. Rhetoric - Study and teaching - Audio-visual aids. 4. Literacy - Study and teaching - Audio-visual aids. I. Title. II. Series.*
**TC P301.5.D37 W45 1999**

**Welcome Comfort.**
Polacco, Patricia. New York : Philomel Books, 1999.
**TC PZ7.P75186 Wg 1999**

**Welfare capitalism in southeast Asia.**
Ramesh, M., 1960- New York : St. Martin's Press, c2000.
**TC HN690.8.A8 R35 2000**

**Welfare Commission for Cripples (U.S.).**
American journal of care for cripples. New York : Douglas McMurtie, 1914-1919.

**Welfare :** opposing viewpoints / Charles P. Cozic, Paul A. Winters, book editors. San Diego, CA : Greenhaven Press, c1997. 208 p. : ill. ; 23 cm. (Opposing viewpoints series) Includes bibliographical references (p. 201-202) and index. ISBN 1-56510-519-2 (pbk. : alk. paper) ISBN 1-56510-520-6 (lib. : alk. paper) DDC 362.5/8/0973
*1. Public welfare - United States - Philosophy. 2. Public welfare - Law and legislation - United States. 3. United States - Social policy. 4. United States - Economic policy. I. Cozic, Charles P., 1957- II. Winters, Paul A., 1965- III. Series: Opposing viewpoints series (Unnumbered)*
**TC HV95 .W453 1997**

**WELFARE, PUBLIC. See PUBLIC WELFARE.**

**WELFARE RECIPIENTS.**
The welfare-to-work challenge for adult literacy educators. San Francisco, CA : Jossey-Bass Publishers, 1999.
**TC LC149.7 .W43 1999**

**WELFARE REFORM. See PUBLIC WELFARE.**

**WELFARE STATE.**
Counseling and the therapeutic state. New York : Aldine de Gruyter, c1999.
**TC HV95 .C675 1999**

Crenson, Matthew A., 1943- Building the invisible orphanage. Cambridge, Mass. : Harvard University Press, 1998.
**TC HV91 .C74 1998**

**Welfare, the family, and reproductive behavior :** research perspectives / Robert A. Moffitt, editor. Washington, D.C. : National Academy Press, 1998. ix, 204 p. : ill. ; 23 cm. Includes bibliographical references. ISBN 0-309-06125-3 (pbk.) DDC 361.973
*1. Public welfare - Government policy - United states. 2. Child welfare - Government policy - United States. 3. Birth control - Government policy - United States. 4. Aid to families with dependent children programs - United States. I. Moffitt, Robert.*
**TC HV91 .W478 1998**

**The welfare-to-work challenge for adult literacy educators** / Larry G. Martin, James C. Fisher, editors. San Francisco, CA : Jossey-Bass Publishers, 1999. 104 p. ; 23 cm. (New directions for adult and continuing education ; no. 83) Includes bibliographical references and index. CONTENTS: Policy issues that drive the transformation of adult literacy / Elizabeth Hayes -- Critical issues and dilemmas for adult literacy programs under welfare reform / Barbara

Sparks -- Research on adult literacy education in the welfare-to-work transition / James C. Fisher -- Continuum of literacy program models: alternative approaches for low literate welfare recipients / Larry G. Martin -- The new world of workforce education / Eunice N. Askov, Edward E. Gordon -- The new role of community-based agencies / Daniel V. Folkman, Kalyani Rai --New skills for literacy educators / John M. Dukes -- Epilogue / Larry G. Martin, James C. Fisher.
*1. Literacy. 2. Welfare recipients. 3. Adult education - Study and teaching. I. Fisher, James C. II. Martin, Larry G. III. Series.*
**TC LC149.7 .W43 1999**

**Welfel, Elizabeth Reynolds, 1949-.**
Patterson, Lewis E. The counseling process. 5th ed. Belmont, CA : Brooks/Cole : Wadsworth, 1999.
**TC BF637.C6 P325 1999**

**WELL-KNOWN PEOPLE. See CELEBRITIES.**

**Welle, Stephen.** Human protein metabolism / Stephen Welle. New York : Springer, c1999. xi, 288 p. : ill. ; 25 cm. Includes bibliographical references (p. 228-281) and index. ISBN 0-387-98750-9 (alk. paper) DDC 612.3/98
*1. Proteins - Metabolism. I. Title.*
**TC QP551 .W43 1999**

**Weller, L. David.** Quality human resources leadership : : a principal's handbook / L. David Weller, Jr., Sylvia Weller. Lanham, Md. : Scarecrow Press, 2000. xvi, 299 p. : ill. ; 24 cm. "Technomic Books". Includes bibliographical references and index. ISBN 1-56676-850-0
*1. Educational leadership - United States. 2. School personnel management - United States. I. Weller, Sylvia. II. Title.*
**TC LB2831.92 .W45 2000**

**Weller, Sylvia.**
Weller, L. David. Quality human resources leadership :. Lanham, Md. : Scarecrow Press, 2000.
**TC LB2831.92 .W45 2000**

**Welles, Elizabeth B.**
Preparing a nation's teachers. New York : Modern Language Association of America, 1999.
**TC PE68.U5 P74 1999**

**WELLNESS. See HEALTH.**

**The wellness guide to lifelong fitness.**
White, Timothy P. New York : Rebus : Distributed by Random House, c1993.
**TC RA781 .W47 1993**

**WELLNESS PROGRAMS. See HEALTH PROMOTION.**

**Wells, Adrian.** Cognitive therapy of anxiety disorders : a practice manual and conceptual guide / Adrian Wells. Chichester ; New York : J. Wiley & Sons, c1997. xiv, 314 p. : ill. ; 25 cm. Includes bibliographical references (p. [301]-308) and index. ISBN 0-471-96474-3 (cased : acid-free paper) ISBN 0-471-96476-X (paper : acid-free paper) DDC 616.85/2230651
*1. Anxiety. 2. Cognitive therapy. I. Title.*
**TC RC531 .W43 1997**

**Wells, Jan, 1948-.**
Hart-Hewins, Linda. Better books! Better readers!. York, Me. : Stenhouse Publishers ; Markham, Ont. : Pembroke Publishers, c1999.
**TC LB1525 .H26 1999**

**Welsh, Betty L., 1925-.**
Allen-Meares, Paula, 1948- Social work services in schools. 3rd ed. Boston : Allyn and Bacon, c2000.
**TC LB3013.4 .A45 2000**

**Welsh studies**
(v. 8) Phillips, Francis R. Creating an education system for England and Wales. Lewiston, N.Y. : E. Mellen Press, 1992.
**TC LA633 .P48 1992**

**Welsh, Thomas.** Decentralization of education : Why, when, what and how / Thomas Welsh and Noel F. McGinn. Paris : International Institute for Educational Planning (IIEP) ; Paris : UNESCO, 1999. 98 p. ; 21 cm. (Fundamentals of educational planning ; 64) Includes bibliographical references. ISBN 92-803-1193-X DDC 370
*1. Educational planning. 2. School management and organization. I. McGinn, Noel F., 1934- II. Title. III. Series.*
**TC LB5 .F85 v.64**

**Wentworth, Roland A. Lubienski.** Montessori for the millennium / by Roland A. Lubienski Wentworth. Mahwah, N.J. : L. Erlbaum Associates, 1999. iii, 136 p. : ill ; 24 cm. Includes bibliographical references and index. ISBN 0-8058-3136-3 (alk. paper) DDC 371.39/2
*1. Montessori method of education. I. Title.*
**TC LB1029.M75 W46 1998**

**Wepner, Shelley B., 1951-.**
Linking literacy and technology. Newark, Del. : International Reading Association, c2000.
**TC LB1576.7 .L56 2000**

**Werkstattberichte (Gesamthochschule Kassel. Wissenschaftliches Zentrum für Berufs- und Hochschulforschung)**
(Bd. 56.) Wasser, Henry Hirsch, 1919- Diversification in higher education. Kassel : Wissenschaftliches Zentrum für Berufs- und Hochschulforschung der Gesamthochschule Kassel, 1999.
**TC LA622 .W37 1999**

**Werner, Emmy E.** Through the eyes of innocents : children witness World War II / Emmy E. Werner. Boulder, CO : Westview Press, 2000. xiv, 271 p. : ill. ; 26 cm. Includes bibliographical references and index. ISBN 0-8133-3535-3 (alk. paper)
*1. World War, 1939-1945 - Children. 2. Children - History - 20th century. I. Title.*
**TC D810.C4 W45 1999**

**Werner, Walter.** Collaborative assessment of school-based projects / Walter Werner and Roland Case. Vancouver : Pacific Educational Press, c1991. 48 p. : ill. ; 22 x 28 cm. Originally published under title: Assessing school improvement projects. ISBN 0-88865-074-4 DDC 375/.006
*1. School improvement programs - Evaluation. 2. Curriculum evaluation. 3. Enseignement - Réforme - Évaluation. 4. Programme d'études - Évaluation. I. Case, Roland, 1951- II. Title. III. Title: Assessing school improvement projects.*
**TC LB2822.8 .W47 1991**

**Werness, Hope B.** The Continuum encyclopedia of native art : worldview, symbolism, and culture in Africa, Oceania, and North America / Hope B. Werness ; line drawings by Joanne H. Benedict, Tiffany Ramsay-Lozano, and Hope B. Werness ; maps by Scott Thomas. New York : Continuum, 2000. ix, 360 p. : ill. ; 26 cm. Includes bibliographical references and index. ISBN 0-8264-1156-8 DDC 704.03
*1. Indian art - North America - Encyclopedias. 2. Art, African - Encyclopedias. 3. Art - Oceania - Encyclopedias. 4. Symbolism in art - North America - Encyclopedias. 5. Symbolism in art - Africa - Encyclopedias. 6. Symbolism in art - Oceania - Encyclopedias. 7. Indians of North America - Social life and customs - Encyclopedias. 8. Africa - Social life and customs - Encyclopedias. 9. Oceania - Social life and customs - Encyclopedias. I. Title.*
**TC E98.A7 W49 2000**

**WERNICKE-KORSAKOFF SYNDROME. See KORSAKOFF'S SYNDROME.**

**Wertheim, Margaret.** The pearly gates of cyberspace : a history of space from Dante to the Internet / Margaret Wertheim. 1st ed. New York : W.W. Norton, c1999. 336 p. ; 25 cm. Includes bibliographical references (p. 309-322) and index. ISBN 0-393-04694-X DDC 303.48/34
*1. Computers and civilization. 2. Cyberspace. 3. Internet (Computer network) I. Title.*
**TC QA76.9.C66 W48 1999**

**Wertheimer, Jack.**
Tradition renewed. 1st ed. New York, N.Y. : The Seminary, 1997.
**TC BM90.J56 T83 1997**

**Wertsch, James V.**
Communication. Stamford, Conn. : Ablex Pub. Corp., c2000.
**TC BF712 .A36 v.19**

**WEST AFRICA. See AFRICA, WEST.**

**West African Museums Programme.**
Museums & archaeology in West Africa. Washington : Smithsonian Institution Press ; Oxford : J. Currey, c1997.
**TC AM91.A358 M85 1997**

**West, Alan N.**
Spirituality, ethics, and relationship in adulthood. Madison, Conn. : Psychosocial Press, c2000.
**TC BF724.5 .S68 2000**

**WEST INDIES - RACE RELATIONS - CASE STUDIES.**
Souls looking back. New York : Routledge, 1999.
**TC E185.625 .S675 1999**

**WEST INDIES REGION. See CARIBBEAN AREA.**

**West, Jane, 1960-.**
Oldfather, Penny. Learning through children's eyes. 1st ed. Washington, DC : American Psychological Association, c1999.
**TC LB1060 .O43 1999**

**West, Lynda L.**
Kochhar, Carol. Successful inclusion. 2nd ed. Upper Saddle River, NJ : Prentice Hall, c2000.
*TC LC1201 .K63 2000*

**West, Mark I.**
Rollin, Lucy. Psychoanalytic responses to children's literature. Jefferson, N.C. : McFarland, c1999.
*TC PR990 .R65 1999*

**West, Patricia, 1958-** Domesticating history : the political origins of America's house museums / Patricia West. Washington [D.C.] : Smithsonian Institution Press, c1999. xiii, 241 p. : ill. ; 24 cm. Includes bibliographical references (p. 163-231) and index. ISBN 1-56098-811-8 (cloth : alk. paper) ISBN 1-56098-836-3 (pbk. : alk. paper) DDC 973
*1. Historical museums - United States - History. 2. Dwellings - Conservation and restoration - United States - History. 3. Mount Vernon (Va. : Estate) 4. Orchard House Museum (Concord, Mass.) 5. Monticello (Va.) 6. Booker T. Washington National Monument (Va.) I. Title.*
*TC E159 .W445 1999*

**West Publishing Company.**
West's education law digest. St. Paul : West Pub. Co., c1983-
*TC KF4110.3 .W47*

**West, Sandra S.**
Biehle, James T. NSTA guide to school science facilities. Arlington, VA : National Science Teachers Association, c1999.
*TC Q183.3.A1 B54 1999*

**WEST TURKESTAN.** *See* **ASIA, CENTRAL.**

**WEST (U. S.) - HISTORY - EXHIBITIONS.**
White, Richard, 1947- The frontier in American culture. Chicago : The Library ; Berkeley : University of California Press, c1994.
*TC F596 .W562 1994*

**WEST (U.S.) - DESCRIPTION AND TRAVEL.**
Hester, Sallie. A covered wagon girl. Mankato, Minn. : Blue Earth Books, c2000.
*TC F593 .H47 2000*

**WEST (U.S.) - DESCRIPTION AND TRAVEL - 1848-1860.** *See* **WEST (U.S.) - DESCRIPTION AND TRAVEL.**

**WEST (U.S.) - DESCRIPTION AND TRAVEL - 1860-1880.** *See* **WEST (U.S.) - DESCRIPTION AND TRAVEL.**

**WEST (U.S.) - DESCRIPTION AND TRAVEL - 1880-1950.** *See* **WEST (U.S.) - DESCRIPTION AND TRAVEL.**

**WEST (U.S.) - DESCRIPTION AND TRAVEL - 1951-1980.** *See* **WEST (U.S.) - DESCRIPTION AND TRAVEL.**

**WEST (U.S.) - DESCRIPTION AND TRAVEL - 1981-.** *See* **WEST (U.S.) - DESCRIPTION AND TRAVEL.**

**WEST (U.S.) - DESCRIPTION AND TRAVEL - JUVENILE LITERATURE.**
Hester, Sallie. A covered wagon girl. Mankato, Minn. : Blue Earth Books, c2000.
*TC F593 .H47 2000*

**WEST (U.S.) - DESCRIPTION AND TRAVEL - TO 1848.** *See* **WEST (U.S.) - DESCRIPTION AND TRAVEL.**

**WEST (U.S.) - FICTION.**
Kay, Verla. Gold fever. New York : Putnam's, c1999.
*TC PZ8.3.K225 Go 1999*

Moss, Marissa. True heart. 1st ed. San Diego : Silver Whistle, c1999.
*TC PZ7.M8535 Tr 1999*

**Westbrook, Kathleen C.**
A struggle to survive. Thousand Oaks, Calif. : Corwin Press, c1996.
*TC LB2342 .S856 1996*

**Westbury, Ian, ed.**
Research into classroom processes; New York, Teachers College Press, 1971.
*TC LB1028 .W488*

**WESTBURY PUBLIC SCHOOLS (WESTBURY, N.Y.) - STUDENTS - ATTITUDE.**
Dickerson, Pless Moore. Haitian students' perception of a school as a community of support. 1998.
*TC 06 no. 11018*

Dickerson, Pless Moore. Haitian students' perception of a school as a community of support. 1998.
*TC 06 no. 11018*

*TC 06 no. 11018*
Dickerson, Pless Moore. Haitian students' perception of a school as a community of support. 1998.
*TC 06 no. 11018*

**Westdeutscher Rundfunk.**
Monsieur René Magritte [videorecording]. [Chicago, Ill.] : Home Vision [distributor], c1978.
*TC ND673.M35 M6 1978*

**WESTERN AFRICA.** *See* **AFRICA, WEST.**

**WESTERN ART.** *See* **ART.**

**WESTERN CIVILIZATION.** *See* **CIVILIZATION, WESTERN.**

**WESTERN-EDUCATED STUDENTS.** *See* **RETURNED STUDENTS.**

**Western education and political domination in Africa.**
Bassey, Magnus O. Westport, CT : Bergin & Garvey, 1999.
*TC LC95.A2 B37 1999*

**Western, John.**
Comparative anomie research. Aldershot, Hants, England : Brookfield, Vt., USA : Ashgate, c1999.
*TC HM816 .C65 1999*

**WESTERN LITERATURE.** *See* **LITERATURE.**

**Western rationality and the angel of dreams.**
Wax, Murray Lionel, 1922- Lanham, Md. ; Oxford : Rowman & Littlefield, c1999.
*TC BF1078 .W38 1999*

**WESTERN RESERVE ACADEMY - ALUMNI AND ALUMNAE - CORRESPONDENCE.**
Remembering the boys. Kent, OH : Kent State University Press, c2000.
*TC D811.A2 R46 2000*

**WESTERN RESERVE ACADEMY - FACULTY - CORRESPONDENCE.**
Remembering the boys. Kent, OH : Kent State University Press, c2000.
*TC D811.A2 R46 2000*

**WESTERN STATES (U.S.).** *See* **WEST (U.S.).**

**Westervelt, Holly James, 1969-.**
Practitioner's guide to evaluating change with neuropsychological assessment instruments. New York : Kluwer Academic/Plenum Publishers, c2000.
*TC RC386.6.N48 P73 2000*

**Westling, David L.** Teaching students with severe disabilities / David L. Westling, Lise Fox. 2nd ed. Upper Saddle River, N.J. : Merrill, c2000. xiii, 562 p. : ill. ; 27 cm. Includes bibliographical references and indexes. ISBN 0-13-674334-X DDC 371.9/0973
*1. Handicapped children - Education - United States. 2. Handicapped youth - Education - United States. 3. Handicapped - Services for - United States. 4. Special education - Vocational guidance - United States. I. Fox, Lise. II. Title.*
*TC LC4031 .W47 2000*

**Westmoreland Museum of Art.**
Beaux, Cecilia, 1855-1942. Cecilia Beaux and the art of portraiture. Washington, DC : Published for the National Portrait Gallery by the Smithsonian Institution Press, 1995.
*TC ND1329.B39 A4 1995*

**West's education law digest.** St. Paul : West Pub. Co., c1983- v. ; 24 cm. Mar. 1983- . Education law digest. Complete index to all cases reported in: West's education law reporter, and quick access to related cases in other National Reporter System reporters. West's education law reporter. ISSN: 0744-8716. ISSN 0741-5346 DDC 344.73/07/02648 DDC 347.304702648
*1. Educational law and legislation - United States - Digests. I. West Publishing Company. II. Title: Education law digest III. Title: West's education law reporter*
*TC KF4110.3 .W47*

**West's education law reporter.**
West's education law digest. St. Paul : West Pub. Co., c1983-
*TC KF4110.3 .W47*

**Westwood, Peter S.** Spelling : : approaches to teaching and assessment / Peter Westwood. Camberwell, Vic. : ACER Press, 1999, 80 p. : ill. ; 30 cm. Includes bibliographical references (p. 73-79) and index. ISBN 0-86431-313-6
*1. English language - Orthography and spelling - Study and teaching (Elementary). I. Title.*
*TC LB1574 .W47 1999*

**Wetle, Terrie Todd, 1946-.**
Public and private responsibilities in long-term care. Baltimore : Johns Hopkins University Press, 1998.
*TC RA644.6 .P8 1998*

**Wetzel, Roberta, 1946-** Student-generated sexual harassment in secondary schools / Roberta Wetzel and Nina W. Brown ; foreword by C. Fred Bateman. Westport, Conn. : London : Bergin & Garvey, 2000. xii, 173 p. ; 22 cm. Includes bibliographical references (p. 164-170) and index. ISBN 0-89789-698-X (alk. paper) DDC 373.15/8
*1. Sexual harassment in education - United States. 2. Education, Secondary - United States. I. Brown, Nina W. II. Title.*
*TC LC212.82 .W47 2000*

**Wexberg, Erwin, 1889-** Individual psychology, by Erwin Wexberg; translated by W. Béran Wolfe. New York, Cosmopolitan Book Corporation, 1929. viii, 428 p. ; 22 cm. Includes index. Bibliography: p.417-418.
*1. Personality. 2. Personality disorders. 3. Psychology, Pathological. 4. Neuroses. I. Wolfe, Walter Béran, 1900-1935. tr. II. Title.*
*TC BF175 .W48*

**Wexler, Alice.** The art of necessity : painting and healing at the Harlem Horizon Art Studio / by Alice Wexler. 1999. vii, 327 leaves : col. ill. ; 29 cm. Issued also on microfilm. Thesis (Ed.D.)--Teachers College, Columbia University, 1999. Includes bibliographical references (leaves 285-293)
*1. Handicapped children - New York (State) - New York - Case studies. 2. Art therapy for youth. 3. Creation (Literary, artistic, etc.) - Psychological aspects. 4. Creation (Literary, artistic, etc.) - Therapeutic use. 5. Art - Psychology. 6. Harlem Horizon Art Studio. I. Harlem Horizon Art Studio. II. Title.*
*TC 06 no. 11072*

**Wexler, Kenneth.**
The development of binding. Hillsdale, N.J. : Lawrence Erlbaum , 1992.
*TC P158.2 .D5 1992*

**Wexler, Laura.**
Matthews, Sandra. Pregnant pictures. New York : Routledge, 2000.
*TC TR681.P67 M38 2000*

**WGBH Educational Foundation.**
Africans in America [videorecording]. [Boston, Mass.] : WGBH Educational Foundation ; South Burlington, VT : WGBH Boston Video [distributor], c1998.
*TC E441 .A47 1998*

Connect with English [videorecording]. S. Burlington, Vt. : The Annenberg/CPB Collection, c1997.
*TC PE1128 .C66 1997*

**WGBH (Television station : Boston, Mass.).**
Africans in America [videorecording]. [Boston, Mass.] : WGBH Educational Foundation ; South Burlington, VT : WGBH Boston Video [distributor], c1998.
*TC E441 .A47 1998*

**WGBH (Television station : Boston, Mass.). Science Unit.**
In search of human origins [videorecording]. [Boston, Mass.] : WGBH Educational Foundation, c1994.
*TC GN281 .I45 1994*

**WGBH Video (Firm).**
Africans in America [videorecording]. [Boston, Mass.] : WGBH Educational Foundation ; South Burlington, VT : WGBH Boston Video [distributor], c1998.
*TC E441 .A47 1998*

**Whaddayamean.**
Burningham, John. 1st American ed. New York : Crown Publishers, 1999.
*TC PZ7.B936 We 1999*

**WHALE FISHERIES.** *See* **WHALING.**

**Whalen, Richard E.**
Animal models of human emotion and cognition. 1st ed. Washington, DC : American Psychological Association, c1999.
*TC BF671 .A55 1999*

**WHALING.**
Jernegan, Laura, b. 1862. A whaling captain's daughter. Mankato, Minn. : Blue Earth Books, c2000.
*TC G545 .J47 2000*

**A whaling captain's daughter.**
Jernegan, Laura, b. 1862. Mankato, Minn. : Blue Earth Books, c2000.
*TC G545 .J47 2000*

**WHALING - JUVENILE LITERATURE.**
Jernegan, Laura, b. 1862. A whaling captain's daughter. Mankato, Minn. : Blue Earth Books, c2000.
***TC G545 .J47 2000***

**Whang, Gail.**
Samway, Katharine Davies. Buddy reading. Portsmouth, NH : Heinemann, c1995.
***TC LB1031.5 .S36 1995***

**What art is.**
Torres, Louis, 1938- Chicago, Ill. : Open Court, c2000.
***TC PS3535.A547 Z9 2000***

**What contributes to job satisfaction among faculty and staff** / Linda Serra Hagedorn, editor. San Francisco, Calif. : Jossey-Bass Publishers, c2000. 117 p. : ill. ; 23 cm. (New directions for institutional research, 0271-0560 ; no. 105) Spine title: Job satisfaction among faculty and staff. "Spring 2000." Includes bibliographical references and index. ISBN 0-7879-5438-1
*1. Universities and colleges - Faculty - Job satisfaction - United States. 2. College teachers - Job satisfaction - United States. 3. Universities and colleges - Employees - Job satisfaction - United States. 4. Job satisfaction - United States. I. Hagedorn, Linda Serra. II. Title: Job satisfaction among faculty and staff III. Series.*
***TC LB2331.7 .W45 2000***

**What do we know?.**
ADHD [videorecording]. New York, NY : Guilford Publications, Inc., c1992.
***TC RJ506.H9 A3 1992***

**What does a woman want?.**
André, Serge. [Que veut une femme? English] New York : Other Press, c1999.
***TC BF175 .A69613 1999***

**What every principal would like to say-- and what to say next time :** quotations for leading, learning, and living / [edited by Noah benShea]. Thousand Oaks, Calif. : Corwin Press, c2000. xi, 146 p. ; 23 cm. ISBN 0-7619-7605-1 (alk. paper) ISBN 0-7619-7606-X (pbk. : alk. paper) DDC 371.2/012/02
*1. School principals - Quotations. I. BenShea, Noah.*
***TC LB2831.9 .W53 2000***

**What has the church/synagogue to do with the academy.**
Winings, Kathy. 1996.
***TC 06 no. 10718***

**What I think.**
Stein, Herbert, 1916- Washington, D.C. : AEI Press, 1998.
***TC HC106.5 .S784 1998***

**What is a good drawing?** [videorecording] / produced, directed and edited by Anthony M. Roland ; selection and commentary by Henry M. Roland. Peasmarsh, East Sussex, Eng. : Ho-Ho-Kus, NJ : Roland Collection, [1980-1986?]. 1 videocassette (18 min.) : b&w, col. ; 1/2 in. At head of title: Anthony Roland Collection of Films on Art. VHS. Catalogued from credits, cassette label and container. Photography by Jay Singh. Addresses of the Roland Collection on cassette label: Ho-Ho-Kus, N.J. and Peasmarsh, East Sussex, Eng. Addresses on container in reverse order. For general audiences, age 12 - adult. SUMMARY: Discusses how art transcends nature, has its own rules and must have certain qualities to turn it from rote representation into a work of art.Artists' drawings from the Paleolithic period to the 20th century, from Pisanello through Holbein and Botticelli, to Barlach and Picasso, are held up as examples of how using unity of line, light, and geometric shapes, create form, volume, unity of design and expression-- the very qualities that make a drawing a work of art.
*1. Drawing. 2. Drawing - Technique. 3. Art appreciation. I. Roland, Henry Montagu. II. Roland, Anthony. III. Anthony Roland Collection of Film on Art. IV. Brighton Polytechnic. Media Services. V. Title: Anthony Roland Collection of Films on Art*
***TC NC703 .W45 1980***

**What is a woman?.**
Moi, Toril. Oxford : New York : Oxford University Press, 1999.
***TC HQ1190 .M64 1999***

**What is cognitive science?** / edited by Ernest Lepore and Zenon Pylyshyn. Malden, Mass. : Blackwell, 1999. ix, 435 p. : ill. ; 25 cm. Includes bibliographical references and index. ISBN 0-631-20493-8 (hardback : alk. paper) ISBN 0-631-20494-6 (pbk. : alk. paper) DDC 153
*1. Cognitive science. 2. Cognition. I. LePore, Ernest, 1950- II. Pylyshyn, Zenon W., 1937-*
***TC BF311 .W48 1999***

**What is indigenous knowledge? :** voices from the academy / edited by Ladislaus M. Semali, Joe L. Kincheloe. New York : Falmer Press, 1999. xvi, 381 p. ; 23 cm. (Garland reference library of social science ; v. 1191. Indigenous knowledge and schooling ; v. 2) Includes bibliographical references and index. ISBN 0-8153-3157-6 (alk. paper) ISBN 0-8153-3452-4 (pbk. : alk. paper) DDC 306.4/2
*1. Ethnoscience. I. Semali, Ladislaus, 1946- II. Kincheloe, Joe L. III. Series: Garland reference library of social science ; v. 1191. IV. Series: Garland reference library of social science. Indigenous knowledge and schooling ; v. 2.*
***TC GN476 .W47 1999***

**What is institutional research all about ? :** A critical and comprehensive assessment of the profession / J. Fredericks Volkwein, editor. San Francisco, Calif. : Jossey-Bass Publishers, c1999. 114 p. ; 23 cm. (New directions for institutional research, no. 104.) "Winter 1999." Includes bibliographical references and index. ISBN 0-7879-1406-1
*1. Education, Higher - Research - United States. 2. Research - United States. I. Volkwein, J. Fredericks. II. Series.*
***TC LB2326.3 .W43 1999***

**What is painting?.**
Bell, Julian, 1952- New York : Thames and Hudson, 1999.
***TC ND1140 .B45 1999***

**What is visual literacy?** / with Steve Moline ; produced by Straylight Media Inc. York, Maine : Stenhouse Pub., c1996. 1 videocassette (45 min.) : sd., col. ; 1/2 in. + 1 guide (12 p. : ill. ; 19 cm.). VHS. Catalogued from credits and container and accompanying material. Presenter, Steve Moline. For elementary school educators. SUMMARY: Steve Moline demonstrates some ways of teaching visual literacy in a classroom. Visual literacy is a method of teaching communication using words and pictures together. He demonstrates how the use of flow diagrams, picture glossaries, personal maps with keys, and puzzle-like webs can be used to teach reading, vocabulary, complex scientific information, as well as, drawing and writing in effective, engaging, attention-getting ways. Ms. Cecil Roy's fourth graders from Mount Pleasant Schoo, Nashua, N.H. demonstrate the principles in action. ISBN 1-57110-043-1
*1. Visual literacy. 2. Visual education. 3. Visual learning. 4. Visual communication. 5. Language arts (Elementary) 6. Vocabulary - Study and teaching (Elementary) 7. Science - Study and teaching (Elementary) I. Moline, Steve. II. Straylight Media, Inc. III. Stenhouse Publishers.*
***TC LB1068 .W45 1996***

**What kind of university? :** international perspectives on knowledge, participation and governance / edited by John Brennan ... [et al.]. 1st ed. Buckingham ; Philadelphia, PA : Society for Research into Higher Education : Open University Press, 1999. xi, 258 p. : ill. ; 24 cm. Includes bibliographical references and index. ISBN 0-335-20429-5 DDC 378
*1. Education, Higher - Aims and objectives. 2. Education, Higher - Curricula. 3. College students. 4. Universities and colleges - Administration - Case studies. I. Brennan, J. L. (John Leslie), 1947-*
***TC LB2322.2 .W43 1999***

**What our speech disrupts.**
Haake, Katharine. Urbana, Ill. : National Council of Teachers of English, c2000.
***TC PE1404 .H3 2000***

**What painting is.**
Elkins, James, 1955- New York : Routledge, 1999.
***TC ND1135 .E44 1999***

**What principals should know about-- :** a primer on school subjects / edited by Sandra Tonnsen. Springfield, Ill. : C.C. Thomas, c2000. xii, 203 p. : ill. ; 27 cm. Includes bibliographical references. ISBN 0-398-07009-1 (cloth) ISBN 0-398-07010-5 (paper) DDC 371.2/012
*1. School principals - United States. 2. Education - United States - Curricula. 3. Educational leardership - United States. I. Tonnsen, Sandra.*
***TC LB2831.92 .W52 2000***

**What reading research tells us about children with diverse learning needs :** bases and basics / edited by Deborah C. Simmons, Edward J. Kameenui. Mahwah, N.J. : Erlbaum, 1998. vi, 399 p. : ill. ; 24 cm. (The LEA series on special education and disability) Includes bibliographical references and indexes. ISBN 0-8058-2515-0 (cloth : alk. paper) ISBN 0-8058-2516-9 (pbk. : alk. paper) DDC 372.43
*1. Reading disability. 2. Reading - Research. 3. Reading - Remedial teaching. I. Simmons, Deborah C. II. Kameenui, Edward J. III. Series.*
***TC LB1050.5 .W47 1998***

**What should we expect of family literacy?.**
Paratore, Jeanne R. Newark, Del. : International Reading Association ; Chicago , Ill. : National Reading Conference, c1999.
***TC LC151 .P37 1999***

**What students say to themselves.**
Purkey, William Watson. Thousand Oaks, Calif. : Corwin Press, c2000.
***TC LB1062.6 .P87 2000***

**What teachers need to know about the "reading wars".**
In defense of good teaching. York, Me. : Stenhouse Publishers, c1998.
***TC LB1050.35 .I5 1998***

**What to look for in a classroom.**
Kohn, Alfie. 1st ed. San Francisco : Jossey-Bass, c1998.
***TC LB1775 .K643 1998***

**What works in innovation in education**
Motivating students for lifelong learning. Paris : Organisation for Economic Co-operation and Development, c2000.
***TC LB1065 .M669 2000***

**What your 5th grader needs to know.**
What your fifth grader needs to know. New York : Doubleday, c1993.
***TC LB1571 5th .W43 1993***

**What your 6th grader needs to know.**
What your sixth grader needs to know. New York : Doubleday, c1993.
***TC LB1571 6th .W43 1993***

**What your fifth grader needs to know :** fundamentals of a good fifth-grade education / edited by E.D. Hirsch, Jr. New York : Doubleday, c1993. xx, 393 p. : ill. ; 25 cm. (The Core knowledge series ; bk. 5) Cover title: What your 5th grader needs to know. Includes index. ISBN 0-385-41119-7 DDC 372.19/0973
*1. Fifth grade (Education) - United States - Curricula. 2. Curriculum planning - United States. I. Hirsch, E. D. (Eric Donald), 1928- II. Title: What your 5th grader needs to know. III. Series.*
***TC LB1571 5th .W43 1993***

**What your sixth grader needs to know :** fundamentals of a good sixth-grade education / edited by E.D. Hirsch, Jr. New York : Doubleday, c1993. xx, 392 p. : ill., maps ; 25 cm. (The Core knowledge series ; bk. 6) Cover title: What your 6th grader needs to know. Includes index. ISBN 0-385-41120-0 DDC 372.19
*1. Sixth grade (Education) - Curricula. 2. Curriculum planning - United States. I. Hirsch, E. D. (Eric Donald), 1928- II. Title: What your 6th grader needs to know III. Series: Core knowledge series ; bk. 6*
***TC LB1571 6th .W43 1993***

**Whatever happened to equal opportunities in schools? :** gender equality initiatives in education / edited by Kate Myers. Buckingham [England] ; Philadelphia : Open University Press, 2000. xiv, 241 p. ; 24 cm. Includes bibliographical references and index. ISBN 0-335-20304-3 (hbk.) ISBN 0-335-20303-5 (pbk.) DDC 379.2/6
*1. Educational equalization - Great Britain. 2. Sex discrimination in education - Great Britain. 3. Sex differences in education - Great Britain. 4. Educational change - Great Britain. I. Myers, Kate.*
***TC LC213.3.G7 W53 2000***

**What's at stake in the K-12 standards wars :** a primer for educational policy makers / edited by Sandra Stotsky. New York : P. Lang, 2000. xxiii, 369 p. : ill. ; 23 cm. Includes bibliographical references and index. ISBN 0-8204-4490-1 DDC 379.1/58/0973
*1. Education - Standards - United States. 2. Curriculum change - United States. I. Stotsky, Sandra.*
***TC LB3060.83 .W53 2000***

**What's in the picture? :** responding to illustrations in picture books / edited by Janet Evans. London : P. Chapman Pub. Ltd., c1998. xviii, 206 p. : ill. ; 24 cm. Includes bibliographical references and index. ISBN 1-85396-379-8
*1. Picture books for children - Educational aspects. I. Evans, Janet.*
***TC LB1044.9.P49 W52 1998***

**What's on my plate?.**
Gross, Ruth Belov. 1st American ed. New York : Macmillan, c1990.
***TC TX355 .G795 1990***

**What's on the menu? :** food poems / selected by Bobbye S. Goldstein ; illustrated by Chris L. Demarest. New York : Viking, 1992. 32 p. : col. ill. ; 24 cm. SUMMARY: A collection of poems about the tasty world of food, from lumpy bumpy pickles to chunky chocolate cake. ISBN 0-670-83031-3 (hard) DDC 811.008/0355
*1. Food - Juvenile poetry. 2. Children's poetry, American. 3. Food - Poetry. 4. American poetry - Collections. I. Goldstein, Bobbye S. II. Demarest, Chris L., ill.*

TC PS595.F65 W48 1992

**What's the point in discussion?.**
Bligh, Donald A. Exeter, Eng. ; Portland, OR :
Intellect, 2000.
*TC LC6519 .B555 2000*

**What's what? a guessing game/.**
Serfozo, Mary. 1st ed. New York, NY : Margaret K.
McElderry Books, c1996.
*TC PZ7.S482 Wg 1996*

**Wheale, Nigel.** Writing and society : literacy, print and
politics in Britain, 1590-1660 / Nigel Wheale.
London ; New York : Routledge, 1999. xiv, 188 p. : ill. ;
26 cm. Includes bibliographical references (p. 151-157) and
index. ISBN 0-415-08497-0 (hbk. : alk. paper) ISBN
0-415-08498-9 (pbk. : alk. paper) DDC 820.9/358
*1. English literature - Early modern, 1500-1700 - History and
criticism. 2. Politics and literature - Great Britain - History -
17th century. 3. Publishers and publishing - Great Britain -
History - 17th century. 4. Literature and society - Great
Britain - History - 17th century. 5. Written communication -
Great Britain - History - 17th century. 6. Literacy - Great
Britain - History - 17th century. 7. Printing - Great Britain -
History - 17th century. 8. Great Britain - Politics and
government - 1603-1714. I. Title.*
*TC PR438.P65 W75 1999*

**WHEAT.**
Robbins, Ken. Make me a peanut butter sandwich and
a glass of milk. New York : Scholastic, c1992.
*TC TX814.5.P38 R63 1992*

**WHEAT - JUVENILE LITERATURE.**
Robbins, Ken. Make me a peanut butter sandwich and
a glass of milk. New York : Scholastic, c1992.
*TC TX814.5.P38 R63 1992*

**WHEAT PRODUCTS.** *See* **PASTA PRODUCTS.**

**Wheatley, Margaret J.** Leadership and the new
science : discovering order in a chaotic world /
Margaret J. Wheatley. 2nd ed. San Francisco :
Berrett-Koehler Publishers, c1999. xx, 197 p. : col. ill. ;
24 cm. Includes bibliographical references (p. 178-184) and
index. ISBN 1-57675-055-8 (alk. paper) DDC 500
*1. Leadership. 2. Organization. 3. Quantum theory. 4. Self-
organizing systems. 5. Chaotic behavior in systems. I. Title.*
*TC HD57.7 .W47 1999*

**WHEATS, CULTIVATED.** *See* **WHEAT.**

**Wheelan, Susan A.** Creating effective teams : a guide
for members and leaders / Susan A. Wheelan.
Thousand Oaks, Calif. : Sage Publications, c1999. 154
p. : 24 cm. Includes bibliographical references (p. 133-147)
and index. CONTENTS: 1. Why groups? -- 2. Effective
organizational support for teams -- 3. From groups to teams :
the stages of group development -- 4. How do high
performance teams function? -- 5. Effective team members --
6. Effective team leadership -- 7. Navigating stage 1 -- 8.
Surviving stage 2 -- 9. Reorganizing at stage 3 -- 10.
Sustaining high performance. ISBN 0-7619-1816-7 (cloth : alk.
paper) ISBN 0-7619-1817-5 (pbk. : alk. paper) DDC 658.4/02
*1. Teams in the workplace. I. Title.*
*TC HD66 .W485 1999*

**Wheeler, Harvey, 1918-.**
Burdick, Eugene. Fail-safe. 1st Ecco ed. Hopewell,
N.J. : Ecco Press ; New York, NY : Distributed by
W.W. Norton, 1999.
*TC PS3552.U7116 F35 1999*

**Wheeler, James O.**
Cities in the telecommunications age. New York :
Routledge, 2000.
*TC HT167 .C483 2000*

**Wheeler, Ladd, 1937-** Interpersonal influence. Boston,
Allyn and Bacon [1970] viii, 119 p. 22 cm. (The Allyn and
Bacon series in social psychology) Bibliography: p. [115]-119.
DDC 301.1
*1. Influence (Psychology) 2. Social interaction. I. Title.*
*TC HM291 .W35*

**Wheeler, Rebecca S., 1952-.**
Language alive in the classroom. Westport, Conn. :
Praeger, 1999.
*TC P51 .L338 1999*

**Wheelis, Allen, 1915-** The listener : a psychoanalyst
examines his life / Allen Wheelis. New York : W.W.
Norton, 1999. 256 p. ; 22 cm. ISBN 0-393-04783-0 DDC
150.19/5/092
*1. Wheelis, Allen. - 1915- 2. Psychoanalysts - United States -
Biography. I. Title.*
*TC BF109.W44 A3 1999*

**WHEELIS, ALLEN, 1915-.**
Wheelis, Allen, 1915- The listener. New York : W.W.
Norton, 1999.
*TC BF109.W44 A3 1999*

**When Agnes caws.**
Fleming, Candace. 1st ed. New York : Atheneum
Books for Young Readers, 1999.
*TC PZ7.F59936 Wh 1999*

**When discourses collide.**
Lopez, Marianne Exum, 1960- New York : P. Lang,
c1999.
*TC HQ792.U5 L665 1999*

**When dreams do not work.**
Jevne, Ronna Fay. When dreams don't work.
Amityville, N.Y. : Baywood Pub., c1998.
*TC BF481 .J48 1998*

**When dreams don't work.**
Jevne, Ronna Fay. Amityville, N.Y. : Baywood Pub.,
c1998.
*TC BF481 .J48 1998*

**When father kills mother.**
Hendriks, Jean Harris. 2nd ed. London ; Philadelphia :
Routledge, 2000.
*TC RJ506.U96 .B53 2000*

**When good companies do bad things.**
Schwartz, Peter, 1946- New York : John Wiley,
c1999.
*TC HD60 .S39 1999*

**When JFK was my father.**
Gordon, Amy, 1949- Boston : Houghton Mifflin,
1999.
*TC PZ7.G65 Wh 1999*

**When juvenile crime comes to school.**
Turk, William L. Lewiston, NY : E. Mellen Press,
1999.
*TC HV6250.4.S78 T87 1999*

**When partners become parents.**
Cowan, Carolyn Pape. Mahwah, NJ : Lawrence
Erlbaum Associates, 1999.
*TC HQ755.8 .C68 1999*

**When power corrupts.**
Lewis, Lionel S. (Lionel Stanley) New Brunswick,
NJ: Transaction Publishers, c2000.
*TC LD25.8 .L49 2000*

**When schools compete.**
Fiske, Edward B. Washington, D.C. : Brookings
Institution Press, c2000.
*TC LB2822.84.N45 F58 2000*

**When self-consciousness breaks :** alien voices and
inserted thoughts / G. Lynn Stephens, George
Graham. Cambridge, Mass. : MIT Press, c2000. xii,
198 p. ; 21 cm. (Philosophical psychopathology. Disorders in
mind) "A Bradford book." Includes bibliographical references
(p. [185]-193) and index. ISBN 0-262-19437-6 (hc : alk.
paper) DDC 154.4
*1. Auditory hallucinations. 2. Thought insertion. 3. Self. 4.
Self-perception. I. Graham, George, 1945- II. Title. III. Series.*
*TC RC553.A84 S74 2000*

**When Sophie gets angry - really, really angry...**
Bang, Molly. New York : Blue Sky Press, c1999.
*TC PZ7.B2217 Wh 1999*

**When sparks fly.**
Leonard-Barton, Dorothy. Boston, Mass. : Harvard
Business School Press, 1999.
*TC HD53 .L46 1999*

**When the brain goes wrong** [videorecording] / The
Franklin Institute, Tulip Films, Inc. : a Tulip Films
Inc. Production ; [by Jonathan DAvid and Roberta
Cooks]. Short version. Boston, MA : Fanlight
Productions [dist.], c1992. 1 videocassette (ca. 45 min.) :
sd., col. : 1/2 in. + segment timing chart on inner sleeve. (Brain
series) Subtitle on container: Seven short films about brain
disorders [videorecording]. VHS. Catalogued from credits and
container. Closed-captioned. Statement of responsibility from
container. For adolescent through adult. SUMMARY: This
videorecording presents brief descriptions of seven brain
disorders: schizophrenia, manic depression, addiction,
epilepsy, stroke, head injury, and headaches. Descriptions of
each are given by physicians, clients and their families who
relate their experiences with the differenet diseases. ISBN 1-
57295-131-1
*1. Brain damage. 2. Manic-depressive illness. 3.
Schizophrenia. 4. Epilepsy. 5. Substance abuse. 6. Drug abuse.
7. Headache. 8. Cerebrovascular disease. 9. Brain - Wounds
and injuries. 10. Video recordings for the hearing impaired. I.
David, Jonathan. II. Cooks, Roberta. III. Tulip Films. IV.
Franklin Institute (Philadelphia, Pa.) V. Fanlight Productions.
VI. Title. VII. Title: Seven short films about brain disorders
[videorecording] VIII. Series.*
*TC RC386 .W54 1992*

**When the rain sings :** poems by young Native
Americans / National Museum of the American
Indian, Smithsonian Institution. New York : Simon &

Schuster Books for Young Readers, 1999. xx, 76 p. :
col. ill. ; 22 cm. Includes indexes. SUMMARY: A collection of
poems written by young Native Americans, inspired by or
matched with photographs of artifacts and people from the
National Museum of the American Indian. ISBN 0-689-
82283-9 DDC 811/.540809282/08997
*1. Indians of North America - Antiquities - Juvenile poetry. 2.
Children's poetry, American - Indian authors. 3. Children's
writings, American. 4. American poetry - 20th century. 5.
Youths' writings, American. 6. Indians of North America -
Poetry. 7. American poetry - Collections. 8. Children's
writings. I. National Museum of the American Indian (U.S.)*
*TC PS591.I55 W48 1999*

**When this world was new.**
Figueredo, D. H., 1951- 1st ed. New York : Lee &
Low Books, 1999.
*TC PZ7.F488 Wh 1999*

**When Uncle took the fiddle.**
Gray, Libba Moore. New York : Orchard Books,
1999.
*TC PZ7.G7793 Wh 1999*

**Where are the night animals?.**
Fraser, Mary Ann. 1st ed. New York : HarperCollins
Publishers, c1999.
*TC QL755.5 .F735 1999*

**Where can it be?.**
Jonas, Ann. 1st ed. New York : Greenwillow Books,
c1986.
*TC PZ7.J664 Wi 1986*

**Where does the money go? :** resource allocation in
elementary and secondary schools / editors, Lawrence
O. Picus, James L. Wattenbarger. Thousand Oaks,
Calif. : Corwin Press, c1996. xvii, 277 p. : ill. ; 23 cm.
(Annual yearbook of the American Education Finance
Association ; 16th) Includes bibliographical references and
index. ISBN 0-8039-6162-6 (alk. paper) DDC 379.1/1/0973
*1. Education - United States - Finance. 2. Resource allocation.
I. Picus, Larry, 1954- II. Wattenbarger, James Lorenzo, 1922-
III. Series.*
*TC LB2825 .W415 1996*

**Where the information is.**
Bergan, Helen, 1937- Alexandria, VA : BioGuide
Press, c1996.
*TC HD62.6 .B47 1996*

**Where the roots reach for water.**
Smith, Jeffery, 1961- New York : North Point Press,
1999.
*TC BF575.M44 S55 1999*

**Where's the bear?.**
Bruegel, Jan, 1568-1625. Los Angeles : J. Paul Getty
Museum, c1997.
*TC QL49 .B749 1997*

**Where's the fish?.**
Gomi, Tarō. [Kingyo ga nigeta. English] New York :
William Morrow, [1986], c1977.
*TC PZ7.G586 Wh 1977*

**Wherever home begins :** 100 contemporary poems /
selected by Paul B. Janeczko. New York : Orchard
Books, c1995. xiii, 114 p. ; 24 cm. "A Richard Jackson
book." Includes index. ISBN 0-531-09481-2 ISBN
0-531-08781-6 (lib. bdg.) DDC 811/.54080355
*1. Home - Juvenile poetry. 2. Children's poetry, American. 3.
Home - Poetry. 4. American poetry - Collections. I. Janeczko,
Paul B.*
*TC PS595.H645 W48 1995*

**While we run this race.**
Stroupe, Nibs. Maryknoll, N.Y. : Orbis Books, c1995.
*TC BX8949.D43 S77 1995*

**Whimbey, Arthur.** Problem solving and
comprehension / Arthur Whimbey, Jack Lochhead.
6th ed. Mahwah, N.J. : Lawrence Erlbaum Associates,
1999. ix, 387 p. : ill. ; 23 cm. Spine title: Problem solving &
comprehension. Includes bibliographical references (p. 386-
387). ISBN 0-8058-3274-2 (pbk. : alk. paper) DDC 153.4/3
*1. Problem solving - Problems, exercises, etc. 2.
Comprehension - Problems, exercises, etc. 3. Reasoning -
Problems, exercises, etc. I. Lochhead, Jack, 1944- II. Title:
Problem solving & comprehension*
*TC BF449 .W45 1999*

**Whiston, Susan C., 1953-** Principles and applications of
assessment in counseling / Susan C. Whiston.
Australia ; U.S. : Brooks/Cole, c2000. xviii, 412 p. : ill. ;
25 cm. Includes bibliographical references (p. [381]-398) and
index. ISBN 0-534-34849-1 (alk. paper) DDC 150/.28/7
*1. Counseling. 2. Psychodiagnostics. I. Title.*
*TC BF637.C6 W467 2000*

**Whitaker, Beth, 1960-.**
Whitaker, Todd, 1959- Motivating and inspiring
teachers. Larchmont, N.Y. : Eye on Education, c2000.

**TC LB2840 .W45 2000**

**Whitaker, Todd, 1959-** Motivating and inspiring teachers : the educational leader's guide for building staff morale / Todd Whitaker, Beth Whitaker, Dale Lumpa. Larchmont, N.Y. : Eye on Education, c2000. xvi, 241 p. ; 23 cm. Cover title: Motivating & inspiring teachers. Includes bibliographical references (p. 237-241). ISBN 1-88300-199-4 DDC 371.2/01
*1. Teacher morale. 2. Motivation in education. 3. School environment. 4. School management and organization. I. Whitaker, Beth, 1960- II. Lumpa, Dale, 1961- III. Title. IV. Title: Motivating & inspiring teachers*
**TC LB2840 .W45 2000**

**Whitbeck, Les B.** Nowhere to grow : homeless and runaway adolescents and their families / Les B. Whitbeck and Dan R. Hoyt. New York : Aldine de Gruyer, 1999. xi, 216 p. : ill. ; 23 cm. Includes bibliographical references and index. ISBN 0-202-30583-X (alk. paper) ISBN 0-202-30584-8 (pbk. : alk. paper) DDC 362.74
*1. Homeless youth - United States. 2. Runaway teenagers - United States. 3. Runaway teenagers - United States - Family relationships. 4. Problem families - United States. I. Hoyt, Dan R., 1949- II. Title.*
**TC HV4505 .W43 1999**

**Whitbread Education Partnership.**
Teaching and learning in cities. [S.l.] : Whitbread, 1993.
**TC LC5115 .T43 1993**

**WHITE ANTS. See TERMITES.**

**White, Betty.**
Work sight [videorecording]. Burbank, Ca. : RCA/ Columbia Pictures Home Video, c1991.
**TC HV1652 .W6 1991**

**White-collar or hoe handle.**
Sivonen, Seppo. Helsinki : Suomen Historiallinen Seura, [1995]
**TC LA1531 .S58 1995**

**WHITE COLLAR WORKERS - UNITED STATES.**
Stanback, Thomas M. Cities in transition. Totowa, N.J. : Allanheld, Osmun, 1982.
**TC HD5724 .S649 1982**

**White counsellors - Black clients.**
Banks, Nick. Aldershot, Hants, England ; Brookfield, Vt. : Ashgate, c1999.
**TC HV3177.G7 B36 1999**

**White, Edward M. (Edward Michael), 1933-.**
Assessment of writing. New York : Modern Language Association of America, 1996.
**TC PE1404 .A88 1996**

**White, Gillian, 1945-** The plague stone / Gillian White. Large print ed. Thorndike, Me., USA : G.K. Hall ; Bath, Avon, England : Chivers Press, 1996, c1990. 295 p. (large print) ; 24 cm. ISBN 0-7838-1679-0 (U.S. : softcover : alk. paper) ISBN 0-7451-4808-5 (U.K. : hardcover : alk. paper) ISBN 0-7451-4809-3 (U.K. : softcover : alk. paper) DDC 823/.914
*1. Detective and mystery stories. 2. Large type books. I. Title.*
**TC PR6073.H4925 P58 1996**

**White, Ken W.**
The online teaching guide :. Boston, Mass. : Allyn and Bacon, c2000.
**TC LB1044.87 .O45 1999**

**White knuckles and wishful thinking.**
DuWors, George Manter, 1948- 2nd rev. & expanded ed. Seattle : Hogrefe & Huber Publishers, c2000.
**TC RC565 .D79 2000**

**White, Mary Alice.** Education; a conceptual and empirical approach [by] Mary Alice White [and] Jan Duker. New York, Holt, Rinehart and Winston [1973] xi, 371 p. illus. 24 cm. Includes bibliographies and index. ISBN 0-03-080209-1 DDC 370/.8
*1. Education - Addresses, essays, lectures. I. Duker, Jan, joint author. II. Title.*
**TC LB41 .W62**

**White, Patricia, 1937-** Civic virtues and public schooling : educating citizens for a democratic society / Patricia White. New York : Teachers College Press, c1996. xii, 103 p. ; 24 cm. (Advances in contemporary educational thought series ; v. 17) Includes bibliographical references (p. 93-97) and index. ISBN 0-8077-3500-0 (hbk. : alk. paper) ISBN 0-8077-3499-3 (pbk. : alk. paper) DDC 370/.1
*1. Education, Humanistic. 2. Education - Moral and ethical aspects. 3. Social ethics - Study and teaching. I. Title. II. Series.*
**TC LC1011 .W48 1996**

**WHITE PEOPLE. See WHITES.**

**WHITE PERSONS. See WHITES.**

**WHITE POTATOES. See POTATOES.**

**White, Richard, 1947-** The frontier in American culture : an exhibition at the Newberry Library, August 26, 1994 - January 7, 1995 / essays by Richard White, Patricia Nelson Limerick ; edited by James R. Grossman. Chicago : The Library ; Berkeley : University of California Press, c1994. xiii, 116 p. : ill. (some col.) ; 26 cm. Includes bibliographical references and index. ISBN 0-520-08843-3 (alk. paper) ISBN 0-520-08844-1 (pbk. : alk. paper) DDC 978/.02/0747731
*1. Frontier and pioneer life - West (U.S.) - Exhibitions. 2. West (U.S.) - History - Exhibitions. 3. Turner, Frederick Jackson, - 1861-1932 - Exhibitions. 4. Buffalo Bill, - 1846-1917 - Exhibitions. I. Limerick, Patricia Nelson, 1951- II. Grossman, James R. III. Newberry Library. IV. Title.*
**TC F596 .W562 1994**

**WHITE SUPREMACIST MOVEMENTS. See WHITE SUPREMACY MOVEMENTS.**

**White supremacy in children's literature.**
MacCann, Donnarae. New York : Garland Pub., 1998.
**TC PS173.N4 M33 1998**

**WHITE SUPREMACY MOVEMENTS - UNITED STATES - HISTORY - 19TH CENTURY.**
MacCann, Donnarae. White supremacy in children's literature. New York : Garland Pub., 1998.
**TC PS173.N4 M33 1998**

**White teacher.**
Paley, Vivian Gussin, 1929- Cambridge, Mass. : Harvard University Press, 2000.
**TC LC2771 .P34 2000**

**White, Timothy P.** The wellness guide to lifelong fitness / by Timothy P. White and the editors of the University of California at Berkeley wellness letter. New York : Rebus : Distributed by Random House, c1993. 476 p. : col. ill. ; 27 cm. At head of title: University of California at Berkeley. Includes index. ISBN 0-929661-08-7 DDC 613.7/1
*1. Exercise. 2. Physical fitness. I. University of California, Berkeley. II. Title. III. Title: University of California, Berkeley, wellness letter.*
**TC RA781 .W47 1993**

**WHITE WORK EMBROIDERY - INDIA - LUCKNOW.**
Wilkinson-Weber, Clare M. Embroidering lives. Albany, N.Y. : State University of New York Press, c1999.
**TC HD6073.T42 I483 1999**

**Whitehead, Marian R.** Supporting language and literacy development in the early years / Marian Whitehead. Buckingham [England] ; Philadelphia : Open University Press, 1999. xi, 154 p. : ill. ; 23 cm. (Supporting early learning) Includes bibliographical references (p. [145]-150) and index. ISBN 0-335-19932-1 (hb) ISBN 0-335-19931-3 (pbk) DDC 372.6/0941
*1. Language arts (Early childhood) - Great Britain. 2. Children - Language. I. Title. II. Series.*
**TC LB1139.5.L35 W43 1999**

**Whitehouse, Peter J.**
Concepts of Alzheimer disease. Baltimore, Md. ; London : Johns Hopkins University Press, 2000.
**TC RC523 .C657 2000**

**Whitener, Cathy L.**
Whitener, Scott. A complete guide to brass. 2nd ed. New York : Schirmer Books, c1997.
**TC ML933 .W52 1997**

**Whitener, Scott.** A complete guide to brass : instruments and techniques / Scott Whitener ; illustrations by Cathy L. Whitener. 2nd ed. New York : Schirmer Books, c1997. xiii, 380 p. : ill. ; 28 cm. Includes discography (p. 344-350), bibliographical references (p. 373-377), and index. ISBN 0-02-864597-9 (alk. paper) DDC 788.9/19
*1. Brass instruments. 2. Brass instruments - Instruction and study. I. Whitener, Cathy L. II. Title.*
**TC ML933 .W52 1997**

**Whiteness :** feminist philosophical reflections / edited by Chris J. Cuomo and Kim Q. Hall. Lanham, [Md.] : Rowman & Littlefield, c1999. viii, 133 p. ; 23 cm. Includes bibliographical references (p. 119-127) and index. ISBN 0-8476-9294-9 (alk. paper) ISBN 0-8476-9295-7 (pbk. : alk. paper) DDC 305.8/00973
*1. Whites - United States - Race identity. 2. Racism - United States. 3. Feminist theory - United States. 4. United States - Race relations. I. Cuomo, Chris J. II. Hall, Kim Q., 1965-*
**TC E184.A1 W399 1999**

**WHITES - ARIZONA - CLIFTON - HISTORY - 20TH CENTURY.**
Gordon, Linda. The great Arizona orphan abduction. Cambridge, Mass. : Harvard University Press, 1999.
**TC F819.C55 G67 1999**

**WHITES IN LITERATURE.**
Mensh, Elaine, 1924- Black, white, and Huckleberry Finn. Tuscaloosa : University of Alabama Press, c2000.
**TC PS1305 .M46 2000**

**WHITES - MARYLAND - ATTITUDES - HISTORY - 19TH CENTURY.**
Fuke, Richard Paul, 1940- Imperfect equality. New York : Fordham University Press, 1999.
**TC E185.93.M2 F85 1999**

**WHITES - MICHIGAN - DETROIT - ETHNIC IDENTITY.**
Hartigan, John, 1964- Racial situations. Princeton, N.J. : Princeton University Press, c1999.
**TC F574.D49 A1 1999**

**WHITES - UNITED STATES.**
Grice, Marthe Jane. Attachment, race, and gender in late life. 1999.
**TC 085 G865**

**WHITES - UNITED STATES - RACE IDENTITY.**
Becoming and unbecoming white. Westport, Conn. : Bergin & Garvey, 1999.
**TC E184.A1 B29 1999**

Clauss, Caroline Seay. Degrees of distance. 1999.
**TC 085 C58**

Whiteness. Lanham, [Md.] : Rowman & Littlefield, c1999.
**TC E184.A1 W399 1999**

**WHITEWORK EMBROIDERY. See WHITE WORK EMBROIDERY.**

**Whitfield, Sarah, 1942-** Bonnard / essays by Sarah Whitfield and John Elderfield ; catalogue by Sarah Whitfield. New York, N.Y. : Harry N. Abrams, 1998. 269 p. : ill. (some col.) ; 31 cm. Published to accompany the exhibition ... held at the Tate Gallery, 12 February-17 May 1998 and at the Museum of Modern Art, 17 June-13 October 1998. Includes bibliographical references (p. 264-265) and index. ISBN 0-8109-4021-3 (clothbound) DDC 759.4
*1. Bonnard, Pierre, - 1867-1947 - Criticism and interpretation. I. Elderfield, John. II. Tate Gallery. III. Museum of Modern Art (New York, N.Y.) IV. Title.*
**TC ND553.B65 W45 1998**

**Whitford, Betty Lou.**
Accountability, assessment, and teacher commitment. Albany, N.Y. : State University of New York Press, 2000.
**TC LB2806.22 .A249 2000**

**Whitin, David Jackman, 1947-** It's the story that counts : more children's books for mathematical learning, K-6 / David J. Whitin, Sandra Wilde. Portsmouth, NH : Heinemann, c1995. xv, 224 p. : ill. ; 24 cm. Includes bibliographical references. ISBN 0-435-08369-4 (acid-free paper) DDC 372.7/044
*1. Mathematics - Study and teaching (Elementary) 2. Children's literature in mathematics education. I. Wilde, Sandra. II. Title. III. Title: It is the story that counts*
**TC QA135.5 .W465 1995**

Whitin, Phyllis. Math is language too. Urbana, Ill. : National Council of Teachers of English, c2000.
**TC QA8.7 .W48 2000**

**Whitin, Phyllis.** Math is language too : talking and writing in the mathematics classroom / Phyllis Whitin, David J. Whitin. Urbana, Ill. : National Council of Teachers of English, c2000. xii, 104 p. : ill. ; 26 cm. "NCTM/National Council of Teachers of Mathematics." Includes bibliographical references (p. [97]-[99]) ISBN 0-8141-2134-9 (pbk.) DDC 510/.71
*1. Mathematics - Study and teaching. I. Whitin, David Jackman, 1947- II. Title.*
**TC QA8.7 .W48 2000**

**Whitman, Mark, 1937-** The irony of desegregation law / by Mark Whitman. Princeton, NJ : M. Wiener, c1998. xi, 380 p. ; 24 cm. Includes bibliographical references (p. 371-378) and index. ISBN 1-55876-119-5 (alk. paper) ISBN 1-55876-120-9 (pbk. : alk. paper) DDC 344.73/0798
*1. Segregation in education - Law and legislation - United States - History.*
**TC KF4155 .I76 1997**

**Whitman, Nancy C.** A case study of Japanese middle schools, 1983-1998 : a reflection on practices, trends, and issues / Nancy C. Whitman. Lanham, Md. ; Oxford : University Press of America, c2000. xii, 103 p. : ill., maps ; 24 cm. Includes bibliographical references (p. [93]-99) and index. ISBN 0-7618-1760-3 (cloth : alk. paper)

ISBN 0-7618-1761-1 (paper : alk. paper) DDC 373.236/0952
*1. Middle schools - Japan - Case studies. 2. Education, Secondary - Japan - Case studies. I. Title.*
**TC LA1316 .W45 2000**

**Whitney Museum of American Art.**
Borofsky, Jonathan, 1942- Jonathan Borofsky. New York : Whitney Museum of American Art, c1984.
**TC N6537.B68 W5 1984**

Haskell, Barbara. The American century. New York : Whitney Museum of American Art in association with W.W. Norton, c1999.
**TC N6512 .H355 1999**

Livingston, Jane. The art of Richard Diebenkorn. New York : Whitney Museum of American Art ; Berkeley : University of California Press, c1997.
**TC N6537.D447 A4 1997**

Race, ethnicity and culture in the visual arts. New York : American Council for the Arts, c1993.
**TC N70 .R32 1993**

Weiss, Jeffrey. Mark Rothko. Washington : National Gallery of Art ; New Haven, Conn. : Yale University Press, c1998.
**TC N6537.R63 A4 1998**

**Whitson, Donna L.** Accessing information in a technological age / Donna L. Whitson and Donna D. Amstutz. Original ed. Malabar, Fla. : Krieger Pub. Co., 1997. ix, 180 p. : ill. ; 24 cm. (The professional practices in adult education and human resource development series) Includes bibliographical references (p. [173]-178) and index. ISBN 0-89464-934-5 (hardcover : alk. paper) DDC 025.5/24
*1. Information retrieval. 2. Research. I. Amstutz, Donna D. II. Title. III. Series.*
**TC ZA3075 .W48 1997**

**Whitt, Elizabeth J.**
Creating successful partnerships between academic and student affairs. San Francisco : Jossey-Bass Publishers, 1999.
**TC LB2342.9 .C75 1999**

**Whittier State School (Calif.). Dept. of Research.**
The Journal of delinquency. Whittier, Calif. : Whittier State School, Dept. of Research, 1916-c1928.

**Whittington-Clark, Linda E.**
Pack-Brown, Sherlon P. Images of me. Boston : Allyn and Bacon, c1998.
**TC HV1445 .P33 1998**

**WHITTLING.** *See* **WOOD-CARVING.**

**Whizbangers and wonderments.**
Abruscato, Joseph. Boston : Allyn and Bacon, c2000.
**TC Q182.3 .A27 2000**

**Who are my sisters and brothers?** : reflections on understanding and welcoming immigrants and refugees / [by the Office for the Pastoral Care of Migrants and Refugees, National Conference of Catholic Bishops and the Department of Education, United States Catholic Conference]. Washington, D.C. : The Conference, c1996. viii, 53 p. ; 28 cm. (Publication / United States Catholic Conference) ; no. 5-057) "In collaboration with National Catholic Educational Association ... [et al.]"--P. iii. Includes bibliographical references. ISBN 1-57455-057-8 (curriculum guide) DDC 261.8/32
*1. Emigration and immigration - Religious aspects - Catholic Church. 2. United States - Emigration and immigration - Religious aspects - Catholic Church. 3. Refugees - Religious life. I. Catholic Church. National Conference of Catholic Bishops. Office of Pastoral Care of Migrants and Refugees. II. United States Catholic Conference. Dept. of Education. III. National Catholic Educational Association. IV. Title. Reflections on understanding and welcoming immigrants and refugees*
**TC BX1795.E44 W46 1996**

**Who learns what from cases and how?** : the research base for teaching and learning with cases / edited by Mary A. Lundeberg, Barbara B. Levin, Helen L. Harrington. Mahwah, N.J. : L. Erlbaum Associates, 1999. xxii, 281 p. ; 24 cm. Includes bibliographical references (p. 241-257) and indexes. ISBN 0-8058-2777-3 (cloth : alk. paper) ISBN 0-8058-2778-1 (pbk. : alk. paper) DDC 370/.71/1
*1. Case method - Study and teaching - United States. 2. Teachers - Training of - United States. I. Lundeberg, Mary A. II. Levin, Barbara B. III. Harrington, Helen L.*
**TC LB1029.C37 W56 1999**

**Who plays? who pays? who cares?.**
Kenig, Sylvia. Amityville, N.Y. : Baywood Pub. Co., c1992.
**TC RA790.6 .K46 1992**

**WHOLE LANGUAGE APPROACH IN EDUCATION.** *See* **LANGUAGE EXPERIENCE APPROACH IN EDUCATION.**

**Whole music.**
Blackburn, Lois. Portsmouth, N.H. : Heinemann, c1998.
**TC MT1 .B643 1998**

**Whole to part phonics.**
Dombey, Henrietta. London : Centre for Language in Primary Education : Language Matters, c1998.
**TC LB1573.3 .D66 1998**

**WHOLESALE TRADE.** *See* **RETAIL TRADE.**

**Wholesome childhood.**
Groves, Ernest Rutherford, 1878-1946. Boston, Houghton Mifflin Company, 1924.
**TC HQ772 .G75**

**Who's sick today?.**
Cherry, Lynne. 1st ed. New York : Dutton, c1988.
**TC PZ8.3.C427 Wh 1988**

**Whose education for all?.**
Brock-Utne, Birgit, 1938- New York ; London : Falmer Press, 2000.
**TC LC67.A435 B76 2000**

**Why?.**
Camp, Lindsay. New York : Putnam, c1998.
**TC PZ7.C1475 Wf 1998**

**Why children make up stories.**
Peterson, Susan Louise, 1960- San Francisco ; London : International Scholars Publications, 1999.
**TC BF723.C57 P47 1999**

**Why do we fall ill?.**
Chiozza, Luis A. Madison, Conn. : Psychosocial Press, c1999.
**TC R726.7 .C48 1999**

**Why geese don't get obese (and we do).**
Widmaier, Eric P. New York : W. H. Freeman, c1998.
**TC QP33 .W53 1998**

**Why marriages succeed or fail.**
Gottman, John Mordechai. 1st Fireside ed. New York : Fireside, 1995.
**TC HQ536 .G68 1994**

**Why the wealthy give.**
Ostrower, Francie. Princeton, N.J. : Princeton University Press, c1995.
**TC HV99.N59 O85 1995**

**Wiberg, Hakan, 1942-.**
Ethnicity and intra-state conflict. Aldershot, Hants, England ; Brookfield, Vt., USA : Ashgate, c1999.
**TC GN495.6 .E83 1999**

**WICA.** *See* **WITCHCRAFT.**

**WICCA.** *See* **WITCHCRAFT.**

**WICCANS.** *See* **WITCHES.**

**Wick, Walter.** I spy treasure hunt : a book of picture riddles / photographs by Walter Wick ; riddles by Jean Marzollo. New York : Scholastic, c1999. 36 p. : col. ill. ; 32 cm. SUMMARY: Rhyming verses ask readers to find hidden objects in the photographs. ISBN 0-439-04244-5 DDC 793.73
*1. Picture puzzles - Juvenile literature. 2. Picture puzzles. I. Marzollo, Jean. II. Title.*
**TC GV1507.P47 W5296 1999**

**WICKET.** *See* **CRICKET.**

**WID (WOMEN IN DEVELOPMENT).** *See* **WOMEN IN DEVELOPMENT.**

**Widdowson, H. G.**
Principle & practice in applied linguistics. Oxford : Oxford University Press, 1995.
**TC P129 .P75 1995**

**WIDDOWSON, H. G.**
Principle & practice in applied linguistics. Oxford : Oxford University Press, 1995.
**TC P129 .P75 1995**

**Wide angle.**
[Wide angle (Online)] Wide angle [computer file]. Baltimore, Md. : John Hopkins University Press, c1996-
**TC EJOURNALS**

**[Wide angle (Online)]** Wide angle [computer file]. Baltimore, Md. : John Hopkins University Press, c1996- Frequency: Quarterly. 18.1 (Jan. 1996)- . Made available through: OCLC FirstSearch Electronic Collections Online. Also available in a print ed. Mode of access: World Wide Web. System requirements: World Wide Web browser software. Title from title screen. Restricted to institutions with an electronic subscription. html-encoded text and graphics (electronic journal) Digitized and made available by: Project Muse. Published in cooperation with The Ohio University College of Fine Arts and the Athens Center for Film and

Video. URL: http://muse.jhu.edu/journals/wide%5Fangle/ Available in other form: Wide angle ISSN: 0160-6840 (DLC) 78640919 (OCoLC)2757185. ISSN 1086-3354
*1. Motion pictures - Periodicals. I. Ohio University. College of Fine Arts. II. Athens Center for Film and Video. III. Project Muse. IV. Title: Wide angle*
**TC EJOURNALS**

**WIDE AREA NETWORKS (COMPUTER NETWORKS).** *See* **INTERNET (COMPUTER NETWORK).**

**Widener, Terry, ill.**
Jones, Joy. Tambourine moon. New York : Simon & Schuster, 1999.
**TC PZ7.J72025 Tam 1999**

**Widmaier, Eric P.** Why geese don't get obese (and we do) : how evolution's strategies for survival affect our everyday lives / Eric P. Widmaier. New York : W. H. Freeman, c1998. ix, 213 p. : ill. ; 25 cm. Includes index. ISBN 0-7167-3147-9 DDC 571.1
*1. Physiology, Comparative - Popular works. I. Title.*
**TC QP33 .W53 1998**

**Wiederman, Michael W.**
Keith-Spiegel, Patricia. The complete guide to graduate school admission. 2nd ed. Mahwah, N.J. ; London : L. Erlbaum Associates, 2000.
**TC BF77 .K35 2000**

**Wieler, Diana J. (Diana Jean), 1961-** Drive / Diana Wieler. Toronto : Douglas & McIntyre, 1998. A Groundwood book. ISBN 0-88899-347-1 (bound) ISBN 0-88899-348-X (pbk.) DDC jC813/.54
*I. Title.*
**TC PS8595.I53143 D74 1998**

**Wiener, Anthony J.**
Kahn, Herman, 1922- The year 2000. New York : Macmillan, c1967.
**TC CB160 .K3 1967**

**Wiener, Daniel J.**
Beyond talk therapy. 1st ed. Washington, DC : American Psychological Association, c1999.
**TC RC489.A72 B49 1999**

**Wieringen, Fons van.**
Vocational and adult education in Europe. Dordrecht ; Boston ; London : Kluwer Academic, c1999.
**TC LC1047.E8 V58 1999**

**Wiersma, William.** Research methods in education : an introduction / William Wiersma. 7th ed. Boston : Allyn and Bacon, c2000. XX, 476 p. : ill. 25 cm. + 1 computer disk. Includes bibliographical references and indexes. ISBN 0-205-28492-2 (alk. paper) DDC 370/.7/2
*1. Education - Research. I. Title.*
**TC LB1028 .W517 2000**

**Wierzbicka, Anna.** Emotions across languages and cultures : diversity and universals / Anna Wiezbicka. Cambridge : Cambridge University Press, 1999. xi, 349 p. : ill. ; 24 cm. (Studies in emotion and social interaction. Second series) Includes bibliographical references (p. 318-337). Includes index. ISBN 0-521-59042-6 ISBN 0-521-59971-7 (pbk.) DDC 152.4
*1. Emotions - Cross-cultura studies. 2. Facial expression - Cross-cultural studies. 3. Communication and culture. I. Title. II. Series.*
**TC BF531 .W54 1999**

**Wiesmüller, Dieter.**
**[Pin Kaiser und Fip Husar English]**
The adventures of Marco and Polo / Dieter Wiesmüller ; translated from the German by Beate Peter. New York : Walker & Co., 2000. 1v. (unpaged) : col. ill. ; 32 cm. SUMMARY: A penguin and a monkey become friends but realize they were not meant to live in the same climate. ISBN 0-8027-8729-0 (HC) DDC [E]
*1. Penguins - Fiction. 2. Monkeys - Fiction. I. Peter, Beate. II. Title.*
**TC PZ7.W6366 Ad 2000**

**Wiesner, David.** Sector 7 / David Wiesner. New York : Clarion Books, c1999. 1 v. (unpaged) : col. ill. ; 28 cm. SUMMARY: While on a school trip to the Empire State Building, a boy is taken by a friendly cloud to visit Sector 7, where he discovers how clouds are shaped and channeled throughout the country. ISBN 0-395-74656-6 DDC [E]
*1. Clouds - Fiction. 2. Empire State Building (New York, N.Y.) - Fiction. 3. Stories without words. I. Title. II. Title: Sector seven*
**TC PZ7.W6367 Se 1999**

**WIFE ABUSE.** *See* **ABUSED WIVES.**

**WIFE ABUSE VICTIMS.** *See* **ABUSED WIVES.**

**Wiggin, Kate Douglas Smith, 1856-1923.** Rebecca of Sunnybrook Farm / by Kate Douglas Wiggin. Boston, New York [etc.] : Houghton, Mifflin Company,

[c1903] (Cambridge, Mass. : Riverside Press) 341 p. ; 18 cm. (The Riverside literature series : [no.] 264) Cover title: Kate Douglas Wiggin's Rebecca of Sunnybrook Farm. "RLS 264"--Back cover SUMMARY: Talkative, ten-year-old Rebecca goes to live with her spinster aunts, one harsh and demanding, the other soft and sentimental, with whom she spends seven difficult but rewarding years growing up.
*1. Aunts - Fiction. 2. City and town life - New England - Fiction. 3. New England - Fiction. I. Title. II. Title: Kate Douglas Wiggin's Rebecca of Sunnybrook Farm III. Series.*
**TC PZ7.W638 Re 1903**

**Wiggins, Arthur W.**
Wynn, Charles M. The five biggest ideas in science. New York : Wiley, c1997.
**TC Q163 .W99 1997**

**Wigginton, Eliot, ed.**
Foxfire 2: ghost stories, spring wild plant foods, spinning and weaving, midwifing, burial customs, corn shuckin's, wagon making and more affairs of plain living. Garden City, N.Y., Anchor Press/ Doubleday, 1973.
**TC F291.2 .F62 1973**

Foxfire 3. 1st ed. Garden City, N.Y. : Anchor Press, 1975.
**TC F291.2 .F622 1975**

**Wijngaard, Juan, ill.**
Mark, Jan. The Midas touch. 1st U.S. ed. Cambridge, MA : Candlewick Press, 1999.
**TC BL820.M55 M33 1999**

**Wilbur, Franklin P.**
Linking America's schools and colleges. Washington, D.C. : American Association for Higher Education, 1991.
**TC LB2331.53 .L56 1991**

**Wild, Margaret, 1948-** Toby / story by Margaret Wild ; pictures by Noela Young. 1st American ed. New York : Ticknor & Fields, 1994. 1 v. (unpaged) : col. ill. ; 29 cm. SUMMARY: When Toby the dog gets old and sick and finally dies, the children who love him express their love in different ways. ISBN 0-395-67024-1 DDC [E]
*1. Death - Fiction. 2. Dogs - Fiction. I. Young, Noela, ill. II. Title.*
**TC PZ7.W64574 To 1994**

**Wild words.**
Harper, Helen J., 1957- Wild words-dangerous desires. New York : Peter Lang, c2000.
**TC LB1631 .H267 2000**

**Wild words-dangerous desires.**
Harper, Helen J., 1957- New York : Peter Lang, c2000.
**TC LB1631 .H267 2000**

**WILDCATS.** *See* **FELIDAE.**

**Wilde, Jerry, 1962-** An educators guide to difficult parents / Jerry Wilde. Huntington, N.Y. : Kroshka Books, c2000. x, 108 p. ; 23 cm. ISBN 1-56072-763-2 DDC 371.19/2
*1. Parent-teacher relationships - United States. 2. Interpersonal conflict. 3. Conflict management. I. Title.*
**TC LC225.3 .W54 2000**

**Wilde, Sandra.** Miscue analysis made easy : building on student strengths / Sandra Wilde. Portsmouth, NH : Heinemann, c2000. x, 134 p. ; 24 cm. Includes bibliographical references (p. 131-134). ISBN 0-325-00239-8 DDC 428.4
*1. Miscue analysis. 2. Reading - Language experience approach. I. Title.*
**TC LB1050.33 .W54 2000**

Whitin, David Jackman, 1947- It's the story that counts. Portsmouth, NH : Heinemann, c1995.
**TC QA135.5 .W465 1995**

**WILDLIFE.** *See* **ANIMALS; ZOOLOGY.**

**WILDLIFE UTILIZATION.** *See* **FISHERIES.**

**Wildman, Robert E. C., 1964-** Advanced human nutrition / Robert E.C. Wildman, Denis M. Medeiros. Boca Raton : CRC Press, c2000. xviii, 585 p. : ill. ; 27 cm. (CRC series in modern nutrition) Includes bibliographical references and index. CONTENTS: Foundations of the human body -- Food and the human body -- Human digestion and absorption -- Carbohydrates -- Lipids -- Protein -- Water -- Vitamins -- Major minerals -- Minor minerals -- Energy metabolism -- Body composition and obesity -- Nutrition and activity -- Nutrition supplements and nutraceuticals -- Nutrition and human reproduction -- Cardiovascular disease and nutrition -- Cancer and nutrition -- Diabetes and nutrition -- Osteoporosis and nutrition -- Nutrition research: past, present, and future -- Nutrition in the 21st century -- Appendices: Common food additives -- Growth charts -- Sweetening agents, sugar substitutes -- Normal clinical values for blood -- Some common medicinal plants. ISBN 0-8493-8566-0

*1. Nutrition. 2. Metabolism. 3. Energy metabolism. 4. Nutrition. 5. Energy Metabolism. I. Medeiros, Denis M. II. Title. III. Series: Modern nutrition (Boca Raton, Fla.)*
**TC QP141 .W512 2000**

**Wilen, William W.**
Dynamics of effective teaching. 4th ed. New York : Harlow, England : Longman, c2000.
**TC LB1737.U6 K56 2000**

**Wilens, Timothy E.** Straight talk about psychiatric medications for kids / Timothy E. Wilens. New York : Guilford Press, c1999. viii, 279 p. ; 24 cm. Includes bibliographical references and index. ISBN 1-57230-404-9 (hardcover) ISBN 1-57230-204-6 (pbk.) DDC 618.92/8918
*1. Pediatric psychopharmacology - Popular works. I. Title.*
**TC RJ504.7 .W54 1999**

**Wiles, Janet.**
Perspectives on cognitive science. Stamford, Conn. : Ablex Pub. Corp., c1999.
**TC BF311 .P373 1999**

**Wiles, Jon.** Supervision : a guide to practice / Jon Wiles, Joseph Bondi. 5th ed. Upper Saddle River, N.J. : Merrill, c2000. xviii, 395 p. ; 24 cm. Includes bibliographical references and index. ISBN 0-13-081135-1 DDC 371.2
*1. School supervision. I. Bondi, Joseph. II. Title.*
**TC LB2806.4 .W55 2000**

**Wiley encyclopedia of food science and technology.**
Encyclopedia of food science and technology. 2nd ed. / Frederick J. Francis [editor-in-chief]. New York : Wiley, c2000.
**TC TP368.2 .E62 2000**

**A Wiley publication in mathematical statistics**
Fraser, D. A. S. (Donald Alexander Stuart), 1925- Nonparametric methods in statistics. New York, Wiley [1957]
**TC QA276 .F66 1957**

**The Wiley series in clinical psychology**
Psychological problems of ageing. Chichester ; New York : Wiley, c1999.
**TC RC451.4.A5 P7774 1999**

**Wiley series in couples and family dynamics and treatment**
Goldberg, Marilee C. The art of the question. New York : Wiley, c1998.
**TC RC489.N47 G65 1998**

Handbook of family development and intervention. New York : Wiley, c2000.
**TC RC489.F33 .H36 2000**

Magnavita, Jeffrey J. Relational therapy for personality disorders. New York : Wiley, c2000.
**TC RC554 .M228 2000**

**Wiley series in culture and professional practice**
Thomas, Elwyn. Culture and schooling. Chichester, West Sussex, England ; New York : J. Wiley & Sons, c2000.
**TC LB45 .T476 2000**

**Wiley series on adulthood and aging**
Handbook of assessment in clinical gerontology. New York : Wiley, 1999.
**TC RC451.4.A5 H358 1999**

**Wilfley, Denise E., 1960-.**
Interpersonal psychotherapy for group. New York : Basic Books, 2000.
**TC RC489.I55 I584 2000**

**Wilkinson, Richard G.**
The society and population health reader. Volume I. New York, N.Y. : The New Press, c1999.
**TC RA418 .S6726 1999**

**Wilkinson-Weber, Clare M.** Embroidering lives : women's work and skill in the Lucknow embroidery industry / Clare M. Wilkinson-Weber. Albany, N.Y. : State University of New York Press, c1999. xxvi, 239 p. : ill. 3 maps ; 24 cm. (SUNY series in the anthropology of work) Portions of the text have previously been published by the journal Ethnology, Volume 36(1), Winter 1997, p. 49-65. Includes bibliographical references (p. 221-230) and index. ISBN 0-7914-4087-7 (hardcover : alk. paper) ISBN 0-7914-4088-5 (pbk. : alk. paper) DDC 331.4/874644/09542
*1. Women embroidery industry employees - India - Lucknow. 2. White work embroidery - India - Lucknow I. Title. II. Series.*
**TC HD6073.T42 1483 1999**

**WILL.** *See also* **BELIEF AND DOUBT; SELF.**
Handbook of self-regulation. San Diego : Academic, 2000.
**TC BF632 .H254 2000**

Shapiro, David, 1926- Dynamics of character. New York : Basic Books, c2000.

**TC RC455.5.T45 .S46 2000**

**Will standards save public education?** / [selected by] Deborah Meier ; foreword by Jonathan Kozol ; edited by Joshua Cohen and Joel Rogers for Boston review. Boston : Beacon Press, c2000. xvi, 90 p. ; 21 cm. (New democracy forum series) Includes bibliographical references. ISBN 0-8070-0441-3 (pbk.) DDC 371.26/2
*1. Education - Standards - United States. 2. Educational tests and measurements - United States. I. Meier, Deborah. II. Cohen, Joshua, 1951- III. Rogers, Joel, 1952- IV. Title: Boston review (Cambridge, Mass. : 1982) V. Series: New democracy forum.*
**TC LB3060.83 .W55 2000**

**Willard, Nancy.** The tale I told Sasha / Nancy Willard ; illustrated by David Christiana. 1st ed. Boston : Little, Brown, c1999. 1 v. (unpaged) : col. ill. 27 cm. SUMMARY: A yellow ball rolls out of sight, over the Bridge of Butterflies, across the Field of Lesser Beasts through painted trees to the place where all lost things are found. ISBN 0-316-94115-8 DDC [E]
*1. Lost and found possessions - Fiction. 2. Balls (Sporting goods) - Fiction. 3. Stories in rhyme. I. Christiana, David, ill. II. Title.*
**TC PZ8.3.W668 Tal 1999**

**Willats, John.** Art and representation : new principles in the analysis of pictures / John Willats. Princeton, N.J. : Princeton University Press, c1997. xiii, 394 p. : ill. (some col.) ; 25 cm. Includes bibliographical references (p. [373]-383) and index. ISBN 0-691-08737-7 (alk. paper) DDC 701/.82
*1. Visual perception. 2. Perspective. 3. Optical illusions. 4. Oblique projection. I. Title.*
**TC N7430.5 .W55 1997**

**Willert, Søren.**
Madsen, Benedicte, 1943- Survival in the organization. Aarhus [Denmark] ; Oakville, Conn. : Aarhus University Press, c1996.
**TC D805.G3 M24 1996**

**William Appleman Williams.**
Buhle, Paul, 1944- New York : Routledge, 1995.
**TC E175.5.W55 B84 1995**

**William M. Rice Institute.**
The Rice Institute pamphlet. Houston, Tex. : The Institute, 1915-1961.
**TC AS36 .W65**

**Williams, Bard.** The Internet for teachers / by Bard Williams. 3rd ed. Foster City, CA : IDG Books Worldwide, c1999. xxvi, 349 p. : ill. ; 24 cm. + 1 computer optical disc (4 3/4 in.). (--For dummies) System requirements for accompanying computer disc: 486 or faster PC with Windows 3.1 or later or Macintosh with 68020 or faster processor; System 7.5 or later; 16 MB RAM. "The A+ reference for teachers!"--Cover. Includes index. ISBN 0-7645-0623-4 (pbk. : acid-free paper) DDC 371.33/446782
*1. Teaching - Computer network resources. 2. Education - Computer network resources. 3. Internet in education. 4. Computer managed instruction. I. Title. II. Series.*
**TC LB1044.87 .W55 1999**

**Williams, C. Fred.**
Understanding the Little Rock crisis. Fayetteville, Ark : University of Arkansas Press, 1999.
**TC LC214.23.L56 U53 1999**

**Williams, Donald.** Art now : contemporary art post-1970, book two / Donald Williams, Colin Simpson. Sydney ; New York : McGraw-Hill Book Co., c1996. 208 p. : ill. (some col.) ; 28 cm. Bibliography: p. 201-202. Includes index.
*1. Art, Modern - 20th century. 2. Art, Australian. 3. Art, Modern - 20th century - Australia. 4. Art appreciation - Australia. I. Simpson, Colin, 1960- II. Title.*
**TC N6490 .W49 1996**

**Williams, Donald T.**
Duryea, E. D. (Edwin D.) The academic corporation. New York : Falmer Press, 2000.
**TC LB2341 .D79 2000**

**Williams, Donna Reilly, 1945-.**
Jevne, Ronna Fay. When dreams don't work. Amityville, N.Y. : Baywood Pub., c1998.
**TC BF481 .J48 1998**

**Williams, Drid, 1928-** Anthropology and human movement : searching for origins / Drid Williamsp.- Lanham, Md. ; London : Scarecrow Press, 2000. 305 p. : ill. ; 23 cm. (Readings in anthropology of human movement ; no. 2) Includes bibliographical references (p. [285]-305) and indexes. ISBN 0-8108-3707-2 (cloth : alk. paper) DDC 306.4/84
*1. Dance - History. 2. Sign language - History. I. Title. II. Series.*
**TC GV1595 .W53 2000**

**Williams, James D. (James Dale), 1949-** Preparing to teach writing : research, theory, and practice / James D. Williams. 2nd ed. Mahwah, N.J. : Lawrence Erlbaum Associates, 1998. xiv, 344 p. : ill. ; 23 cm. Includes bibliographical references (p. 313-330) and indexes. ISBN 0-8058-2266-6 DDC 808/.042/07
*1. English language - Rhetoric - Study and teaching - Research. 2. English language - Composition and exercises - Research. 3. Report writing - Study and teaching - Research. 4. English teachers - Training of. I. Title.*
**TC PE1404 .W54 1998**

**Williams, Joan, 1952-** Unbending gender : why family and work conflict and what to do about it / Joan Williams. Oxford ; New York : Oxford University Press, c2000. xii, 338 p. : ill. ; 24 cm. Includes bibliographical references (p. [277]-333) and index. ISBN 0-19-509464-6 (alk. paper) DDC 306.3/6
*1. Work and family - United States. 2. Sexual division of labor - United States. 3. Mothers - Employment - United States. 4. Family - Economic aspects - United States. 5. Work and family - United States - Forecasting. I. Title.*
**TC HD4904.25 .W55 2000**

**Williams, John Tyerman.**
Pooh and the ancient mysteries.
Williams, John Tyerman. Pooh and the millennium. 1st American ed. New York : Dutton Books, 1999.
**TC PR6025.I65 Z975 1999**

Pooh and the millennium : in which the bear of very little brain explores the ancient mysteries at the turn of the century / John Tyerman Williams ; with illustrations by Ernest H. Shepard. 1st American ed. New York : Dutton Books, 1999. 243 p. : ill. ; 20 cm. First published in Great Britain under title: Pooh and the ancient mysteries, 1997. ISBN 0-525-45950-2 (hc) DDC 823/.912
*1. Milne, A. A. - (Alan Alexander), - 1882-1956 - Characters - Winnie-the-Pooh. 2. Children's stories, English - History and criticism. 3. Apocalyptic literature - History and criticism. 4. Winnie-the-Pooh (Fictitious character) 5. Millennialism in literature. 6. Teddy bears in literature. 7. Occultism in literature. I. Shepard, Ernest H. (Ernest Howard), 1879-1976. II. Williams, John Tyerman. Pooh and the ancient mysteries. III. Title.*
**TC PR6025.I65 Z975 1999**

**Williams, Margot.**
Paul, Nora. Great scouts!. Medford, NJ : Information Today, c1999.
**TC ZA4201 .P38 1999**

**Williams, Mary.**
Unlocking literacy. London : David Fulton, 2000.
**TC LC149 .U485 2000**

**Williams, Michael.**
Jazz dance class [videorecording]. W. Long Branch, NJ : Kultur, [1992?]
**TC GV1784 .J3 1992**

**Williams, Steve, 1968-.**
Raggatt, Peter C. M. Government, markets and vocational qualifications. London ; New York : Falmer Press, 1999.
**TC HF5381.6 .R34 1999**

**Williams, Thomas L., 1946-** The directory of programs for students at risk / Thomas L. Williams. Larchmont, N.Y. : Eye on Education, c1999. xv, 316 p. 26 cm. Includes bibliographical references (p. 281-285) and index. ISBN 1-88300-174-9 DDC 371.826/94/0973
*1. Socially handicapped children - Education - United States. 2. Problem children - Education - United States. I. Title.*
**TC LC4091 .W55 1999**

**Williams, Wendy M. (Wendy Melissa), 1960-.**
The nature-nurture debate. Oxford ; Malden, Mass. : Blackwell, 1999.
**TC BF341 .N39 1999**

**WILLIAMS, WILLIAM APPLEMAN.**
Buhle, Paul, 1944- William Appleman Williams. New York : Routledge, 1995.
**TC E175.5.W55 B84 1995**

**WILLIAMSBURG (VA.) - HISTORY - REVOLUTION, 1775-1783 - FICTION.**
Waters, Kate. Mary Geddy's day :. 1st ed. New York : Scholastic Press, 1999.
**TC PZ7.W26434 Mar 1999**

**WILLIAMSBURG (VA.) - HISTORY - REVOLUTION, 1775-1783 - JUVENILE FICTION.**
Waters, Kate. Mary Geddy's day :. 1st ed. New York : Scholastic Press, 1999.
**TC PZ7.W26434 Mar 1999**

**Williamson, John, 1947-.**
Teacher education in the Asia-Pacific region. New York : Falmer Press, c2000.

**TC LB1727.A69 T42 2000**

**Willis, Aaron.**
Teaching government and citizenship using the Internet. Rev. ed. viii, 112 p. : ill. ; 28 cm.
**TC H61.95 .T43 2000**

**Willis, Arlette Ingram.**
Multiple and intersecting identities in qualitative research. Mahwah, N.J. ; London : L. Erlbaum Associates, 2001.
**TC LB1028.25.U6 M85 2001**

**Willis, George, 1941-.**
Marsh, Colin J. Curriculum. 2nd. ed. Upper Saddle River, N.J. : Merrill, c1999.
**TC LB1570 .M3667 1999**

**Willis-Thomas, Deborah, 1948-.**
Picturing us. New York : New Press : Distributed by W.W. Norton & Co., c1994.
**TC TR680 .P53 1994**

Visual journal. Washington, DC : Smithsonian Institution Press, c1996.
**TC TR820.5 .V57 1996**

**Wilmer, Harry A., 1917-** Quest for silence / Harry A. Wilmer. Einsiedeln, Switzerland : Daimon, c2000. 194 p. : ill. ; 22 cm. Includes bibliographical references (p. [183]-189) and index. ISBN 3-85630-593-9 (pbk.)
*1. Silence. 2. Silence - Religious aspects. I. Title.*
**TC BJ1499.S5 W556 2000**

**Wilson, Angela.** Language knowledge for primary teachers : : a guide to textual, grammatical and lexical study / Angela Wilson. London : David Fulton, 1999. ix, 166 p. : ill. ; 26 cm. Includes bibliographical references (p. [160]-163) and index. ISBN 1-85346-606-9 ISBN 1-85346-606-9
*1. English language - Study and teaching (Elementary) - Great Britain. I. Title.*
**TC LB1576 .W557 1999**

**Wilson, Catherine S.** Telling a different story : teaching and literacy in an urban preschool / Catherine Wilson ; foreword by Stacie G. Goffin. New York ; London : Teachers College Press, c2000. xiv, 105 p. : ill. ; 24 cm. (Early childhood education series) Includes bibliographical references (p. 93-100) and index. ISBN 0-8077-3899-9 (hbk. : alk. paper) ISBN 0-8077-3898-0 (pbk. : alk. paper) DDC 370/.9173/2
*1. Education, Urban - United States - Case studies. 2. Head Start programs - United States - Case studies. 3. Language arts (Preschool) - United States - Case studies. I. Title. II. Series: Early childhood education series (Teachers College Press)*
**TC LC5131 .W49 2000**

**Wilson, David E., 1955-.**
Ritchie, Joy S. Teacher narrative as critical inquiry. New York : Teachers College Press, c2000.
**TC LA2311 .R58 2000**

**Wilson, Elizabeth Laraway.** Books children love : a guide to the best children's literature / Elizabeth Laraway Wilson. Westchester, Ill. : Crossway Books, c1987. 330 p. : ill. ; 23 cm. Includes index. ISBN 0-89107-441-4 (pbk.) DDC 011/.62
*1. Best books. 2. Children's literature - Bibliography. I. Title.*
**TC Z1037 .W745 1987**

**Wilson, Frank R.**
Music and child development. St. Louis, Mo. : MMB Music, c1990.
**TC ML3820 .M87 1990**

**Wilson, Gail.** Understanding old age : : critical and global perspectives / Gail Wilson. London : Sage, 2000. 194 p. : ill. ; 24 cm. Includes bibliographical references and index. ISBN 0-7619-6011-2 ISBN 0-7619-6012-0 (pbk)
*1. Aging. I. Title.*
**TC HQ1061 .W54 2000**

**Wilson, James Q.** Moral intuitions / James Q. Wilson ; with an introduction by Emil Uddhammar. New Brunswick, N.J. : Transaction Publishers, c2000. 69 p. ; 21 cm. Based on the author's Hans L. Zetterberg lecture, delivered at the Royal Swedish Academy of the Engineering Sciences in May 1988. Includes bibliographical references (p. 68-69). ISBN 0-7658-0631-2 (paper) DDC 170
*1. Intuition - Moral and ethical aspects. I. Title.*
**TC BJ1472 .W55 2000**

**Wilson, John, 1928-** Learning to love / John Wilson. Houndmills [England] : Macmillan Press ; New York : St. Martin's Press, 2000. xiii, 301 p. ; 23 cm. Includes bibliographical references (p. 301). ISBN 0-333-77902-9 (Macmillan : hbk.) ISBN 0-333-79316-1 (Macmillan : pbk.) ISBN 0-312-22856-2 (St. Martin's : hbk.) ISBN 0-312-22857-0 (St. Martin's : pbk.) DDC 306.7
*1. Love. 2. Intimacy (Psychology) 3. Sex. I. Title.*
**TC BF575.L8 .W555 2000**

**Wilson, Keithia.** Assertion and its social context / by Keithia Wilson and Cynthia Gallois. 1st ed. Oxford ; New York : Pergamon Press, 1993. viii, 205 p. : ill. ; 23 cm. (International series in experimental social psychology) Includes bibliographical references (p. 181-193) and indexes. ISBN 0-08-041038-3 DDC 302.2
*1. Assertiveness (Psychology) 2. Interpersonal communication. I. Gallois, Cynthia. II. Title. III. Series.*
**TC BF575.A85 W55 1993**

**Wilson, Robert A. (Robert Andrew).**
Explanation and cognition. Cambridge, Mass. : MIT Press, c2000.
**TC BF311 .E886 2000**

**Wilson, Robin J.**
Oxford figures. Oxford ; New York : Oxford University Press, 2000.
**TC QA14.G73 O947 2000**

**Wilson, Rodger, 1947- ill.**
Sathre, Vivian. Three kind mice. 1st ed. San Diego : Harcourt Brace, c1997.
**TC PZ8.3.S238 Th 1997**

**Wilton, Richard.** Consciousness, free will, and the explanation of human behavior / Richard Wilton. Lewiston, N.Y. : E. Mellen Press, c2000. xii, 277 p. : ill. ; 24 cm. Includes bibliographical references (p. 269-274) and index. ISBN 0-7734-7682-2 DDC 153
*1. Mind and body. 2. Consciousness. 3. Intentionality (Philosophy) 4. Motivation (Psychology) I. Title.*
**TC BF161 .W495 2000**

**Wiltshire, Michael A.** Integrating mathematics and science for below average ninth grade students / by Michael A. Wiltshire. 1997. vii, 292 leaves : ill. ; 29 cm. Issued also on microfilm. Thesis (Ed.D.)--Teachers College, Columbia University, 1997. Includes bibliographical references (leaves 108-112).
*1. Mathematics - Study and teaching (Secondary) - Case studies. 2. Science - Study and teaching (Secondary) - Case studies. 3. Interdisciplinary approach in education. 4. Ninth grade (Education) - Curricula. 5. Slow learning children. 6. Curriculum planning. I. Title.*
**TC 06 no. 10847**

**Wimbledon School of Art.**
The dynamics of now. London : Wimbledon School of Art in association with Tate, c2000.
**TC N185 .D96 2000**

**Wimmer, Mike.**
Burleigh, Robert. Flight. New York : Philomel Books, c1991.
**TC TL540.L5 B83 1991**

**WIMMIN. See WOMEN.**

**Wimsatt, William Upski.** No more prisons : urban life, homeschooling, hip-hop leadership, the cool rich kids movement, a hitchhiker's guide to community organizing, and why philanthropy is the greatest art form of the 21st century / by William Upski Wimsatt. [New York] : Soft Skull Press, [2000?] 160 p. : ill. ; 22 cm. "A benefit for The Active Element Foundation". Includes bibliographical references. ISBN 1-88712-842-5 DDC 364.60973
*1. United States - Social conditions. 2. Youth - United States - Social conditions. 3. Alternatives to imprisonment - United States. 4. Inner cities - United States. 5. Hip-hop. 6. Home schooling - United States. 7. Community organization - United States. 8. Charity organization - United States. I. Title.*
**TC HV9276.5 .W567x 2000**

**WIND. See WINDS.**

**Wind child.**
Murphy, Shirley Rousseau. New York, NY : HarperCollins, c1999.
**TC PZ8.M957 Wi 1999**

**WIND INSTRUMENT AND PIANO MUSIC (JAZZ). See JAZZ.**

**WIND INSTRUMENTS.** See **BRASS INSTRUMENTS.**

**Windeatt, Scott.**
The Internet. Oxford ; New York : Oxford University Press, c2000.
**TC TK5105.875.I57 I57 2000**

**Windle, Michael T.** Alcohol use among adolescents / Michael Windle. Thousand Oaks : Sage Publications, c1999. x, 126 p. : ill. ; 23 cm. (Developmental clinical psychology and psychiatry ; v. 42) Includes bibliographical references (p. 103-115) and indexes. ISBN 0-7619-0919-2 (hardcover : acid-free paper) ISBN 0-7619-0920-6 (pbk. : acid-free paper) DDC 616.86/1/00835
*1. Teenagers - Alcohol use. 2. Alcoholism - Prevention. I. Title. II. Series.*
**TC RJ506.A4 W557 1999**

**WINDS - FICTION.**
Karas, G. Brian. The windy day. 1st ed. New York :
Simon & Schuster Books for Young Readers, 1998.
*TC PZ7.K1296 Wi 1998*

Murphy, Shirley Rousseau. Wind child. New York,
NY : HarperCollins, c1999.
*TC PZ8.M957 Wi 1999*

**The windy day.**
Karas, G. Brian. 1st ed. New York : Simon &
Schuster Books for Young Readers, 1998.
*TC PZ7.K1296 Wi 1998*

**Wingenbach, Kristie.**
The salsa-riffic world of Spanish [videorecording].
[Arlington, Va.] : Cerebellum Corp., c1998.
*TC PC4112.7 .S25 1998*

**Wings of an artist :** children's book illustrators talk
about their art. New York : Harry N. Abrams, 1999. 31
p. : ill. ; 32 cm. SUMMARY: More than twenty illustrators of
children's books, including James Ransome, Robert Sabuda,
Maira Kalman, and Maurice Sendak, talk about their work.
ISBN 0-8109-4552-5 DDC 741.6/42/0922
*1. Illustrators - Juvenile literature. 2. Illustrated children's
books - Juvenile literature. 3. Illustration of books - 20th
century - Juvenile literature. 4. Illustrators.*
*TC NC965 .W56 1999*

**Winings, Kathy.** What has the church/synagogue to do
with the academy : campus religious work in the
1990s / by Kathy Winings. 1996. vi, 322 leaves ; 29 cm.
Issued also on microfilm. Thesis (Ed.D.) -- Teachers College,
Columbia University, 1996. Includes bibliographical references
(leaves 309-314).
*1. College students - Religious life - History. 2. Universities
and colleges - United States - Religion - History. 3. College
chaplains. 4. Directors of religious education. 5. Jewish
college students. I. Title.*
*TC 06 no. 10718*

**Wink, Joan.** Critical pedagogy : notes from the real
world / Joan Wink. 2nd ed. New York : Longman,
c2000. xiv, 194 p. ; 24 cm. Includes bibliographical
references (p. 183-189) and index. ISBN 0-8013-3257-5 DDC
370.11/5
*1. Critical pedagogy - United States. I. Title.*
*TC LC196.5.U6 W54 2000*

**Winkler, Allan M., 1945-.**
Cayton, Andrew R. L. (Andrew Robert Lee), 1954-
America. Upper Saddle River, N.J. : Prentice Hall,
c1998.
*TC E178.1 .C364 1998*

Cayton, Andrew R. L. (Andrew Robert Lee), 1954-
America. Teacher's ed. Upper Saddle River, N.J.. :
Prentice Hall, c1998.
*TC E178.1 .C364 1998 Teacher's Ed.*

Cayton, Andrew R. L. (Andrew Robert Lee), 1954-
America. Upper Saddle River, N.J. : Prentice Hall,
c1998.
*TC E178.1 .C3643 1998*

Cayton, Andrew R. L. (Andrew Robert Lee), 1954-
America. Upper Saddle River, N.J. : Prentice Hall,
c1998.
*TC E178.1 .C3643 1998*

Cayton, Andrew R. L. (Andrew Robert Lee), 1954-
America. Teacher's ed. Upper Saddle River, N.J.. :
Prentice Hall, c1998.
*TC E178.1 .C3643 1998 Teacher's Ed.*

Cayton, Andrew R. L. (Andrew Robert Lee), 1954-
America. Upper Saddle River, N.J.. : Prentice Hall,
c1998.
*TC E178.1 .C364 1998 Teacher's Ed.*

Cayton, Andrew R. L. (Andrew Robert Lee), 1954-
America. Upper Saddle River, N.J. : Prentice Hall,
c1998.
*TC E178.1 .C364 1998*

Cayton, Andrew R. L. (Andrew Robert Lee), 1954-
America. Teacher's ed. Upper Saddle River, N.J.. :
Prentice Hall, c1998.
*TC E178.1 .C3645 1998 Teacher's Ed.*

Cayton, Andrew R. L. (Andrew Robert Lee), 1954-
America. Upper Saddle River, N.J. : Prentice Hall,
c1998.
*TC E178.1 .C3645 1998*

Cayton, Andrew R. L. (Andrew Robert Lee), 1954-
America. Upper Saddle River, N.J. : Prentice Hall,
c1998.

---

*TC E178.1 .C3645 1998*

Cayton, Andrew R. L. (Andrew Robert Lee), 1954-
America. Teacher's ed. Upper Saddle River, N.J.. :
Prentice Hall, c1998.
*TC E178.1 .C364 1998 Teacher's Ed.*

Cayton, Andrew R. L. (Andrew Robert Lee), 1954-
America. Upper Saddle River, N.J.. : Prentice Hall,
c1998.
*TC E178.1 .C364 1998*

Cayton, Andrew R. L. (Andrew Robert Lee), 1954-
America. Upper Saddle River, N.J. : Prentice Hall,
c1998.
*TC E178.1 .C364 1998*

Cayton, Andrew R. L. (Andrew Robert Lee), 1954-
America. Teacher's ed. Upper Saddle River, N.J.. :
Prentice Hall, c1998.
*TC E178.1 .C3644 1998 Teacher's Ed.*

Cayton, Andrew R. L. (Andrew Robert Lee), 1954-
America. Upper Saddle River, N.J. : Prentice Hall,
c1998.
*TC E178.1 .C364 1998*

Cayton, Andrew R. L. (Andrew Robert Lee), 1954-
America. Upper Saddle River, N.J. : Prentice Hall,
c1998.
*TC E178.1 .C3644 1998*

Cayton, Andrew R. L. (Andrew Robert Lee), 1954-
America. Upper Saddle River, N.J. : Prentice Hall,
c1998.
*TC E178.1 .C3644 1998*

Cayton, Andrew R. L. (Andrew Robert Lee), 1954-
America. Upper Saddle River, N.J. : Prentice Hall,
c1998.
*TC E178.1 .C3644 1998*

**Winkler, Barbara Scott.**
Teaching introduction to women's studies. Westport,
Conn. : Bergin & Garvey, 1999.
*TC HQ1181.U5 T43 1999*

**Winkler, Dean.**
Processing the signal [videorecording]. Cicero, Ill. :
Roland Collection of Films on Art, c1989.
*TC N6494.V53 P7 1989*

**WINNIE-THE-POOH (FICTITIOUS
CHARACTER).**
Williams, John Tyerman. Pooh and the millennium.
1st American ed. New York : Dutton Books, 1999.
*TC PR6025.I65 Z975 1999*

**WINNIE-THER-POOH (FICTITIOUS
CHARACTER).** *See* **WINNIE-THE-POOH
(FICTITIOUS CHARACTER).**

**Winning attitudes :** teacher's planning guide. New
York : Macmillan/McGraw-Hill, c1997. 1 v. (various
pagings) : col. ill. ; 31 cm. (Spotlight on literacy ; Gr.5 l.11
u.3) (The road to independent reading) Includes index. ISBN
0-02-181181-4
*1. Language arts (Elementary) 2. Reading (Elementary) I.
Series. II. Series: The road to independent reading*
*TC LB1576 .S66 1997 Gr.5 l.11 u.3*

**Winning ways of coaching writing :** a practical guide
for teaching writing, grades 6-12 / edited by Mary L.
Warner ; foreword by Leila Christenbury. Boston ;
London : Allyn and Bacon, c2001. xviii, 238 p. : ill. ; 24
cm. Includes bibliographical references and index. ISBN 0-
205-30851-1 DDC 808/.042/0712
*1. English language - Composition and exercises - Study and
teaching (Middle school) 2. English language - Composition
and exercises - Study and teaching (Secondary) I. Warner,
Mary L.*
*TC LB1631 .W55 2001*

**Winocus, Gordon.**
Cognitive neurorehabilitation. Cambridge, UK ; New
York : Cambridge University Press, c1999.
*TC RC553.C64 C654 1999*

**Winslade, John.** Narrative counseling in schools :
powerful & brief / John Winslade, Gerald Monk.
Thousand Oaks, Calif. : Corwin Press, c1999. x, 133
p. ; 23 cm. (Practical skills for counselors) Includes
bibliographical references and index. CONTENTS: What is
narrative counseling all about? We live through stories. A
narrative counseling scenario -- Doing narrative counseling : a
step-by-step guide. Starting assumptions. Attitudes to bring
into the room. Specific narrative methods -- Reworking
reputations. The discourse of schooling. School descriptions.
The power of the teacher. Deficit discourse. Resistance --
Conversations with kids who are "in trouble". Stealing trouble.
Trouble in the classroom. Combating abusive behavior.
Truancy trouble. Enrolling a new student. Counseling and
discipline -- Working in a narrative way with groups, classes,
and even communities : beyond an exclusive focus on the

---

individual. Seeking out a wider audience to the new story.
Building communities of concern. Group work programs.
Working with a whole class. Classroom lessons built on
"interviewing the problem". Starting conversations with a
school. Narrative climate in the school. ISBN 0-8039-6623-7
(cloth : acid-free paper) ISBN 0-8039-6617-2 (pbk. : acid-free
paper) DDC 371.4
*1. Educational counseling. 2. Storytelling - Therapeutic use. 3.
Interpersonal relations. I. Monk, Gerald, 1954- II. Title. III.
Series.*
*TC LB1027.5 .W535 1999*

**Winslow Homer.**
Cikovsky, Nicolai. Washington, D.C. : National
Gallery of Art, 1995.
*TC N6537.H58 A4 1995*

**Winston, Joe.** Beginning drama 4-11 / Joe Winston and
Miles Tandy. London : David Fulton Publishers,
1998. xi, 116 p. ; 25 cm. Includes bibliographical references
(p. [112]-116) ISBN 1-85346-527-5
*1. Drama - Study and teaching (Elementary) I. Tandy, Miles.
II. Title.*
*TC PN1701 .W567 1998*

Drama, literacy and moral education 5-11 / Joe
Winston. London : David Fulton, 2000. 130 p. : ill. ;
25 cm. Includes bibliographical references (p. [129]-130).
ISBN 1-85346-636-0 DDC 372.660440941
*1. Moral education (Elementary) - Great Britain. 2. Drama -
Study and teaching (Elementary) - Great Britain. 3. Literacy -
Great Britain. I. Title.*
*TC LC268 .W667 2000*

**WINSTON-SALEM (N.C.) - ANTIQUITIES.**
South, Stanley A. Historical archaeology in
Wachovia. New York : Kluwer Academic/Plenum
Publishers, c1999.
*TC F264.W8 S66 1999*

**WINSTON-SALEM (N.C.) - CHURCH HISTORY.**
South, Stanley A. Historical archaeology in
Wachovia. New York : Kluwer Academic/Plenum
Publishers, c1999.
*TC F264.W8 S66 1999*

**Winter roundtable series**
(1) Addressing cultural issues in organizations.
Thousand Oaks, Calif. : Sage Publications, 2000.
*TC E184.A1 A337 2000*

**Winter, Sarah.** Freud and the institution of
psychoanalytic knowledge / Sarah Winter. Stanford,
Calif. : Stanford University Press, 1999. xvi, 385 p. :
ill. ; 23 cm. (Cultural memory in the present) Includes
bibliographical references (p. [347]-375) and index. ISBN
0-8047-3305-8 (alk. paper) ISBN 0-8047-3306-6 (pbk. : alk.
paper) DDC 150.19/52
*1. Psychoanalysis. 2. Psychoanalysis - History. 3. Freud,
Sigmund, - 1856-1939. I. Title. II. Series.*
*TC BF173 .W5485 1999*

**Winter, Susan, ill.**
Simon, Francesca. Calling all toddlers. 1st American
ed. New York : Orchard Books, 1999.
*TC PZ8.3.S5875 Cal 1999*

**Winters, Jack M., 1957-.**
Biomechanics and neural control of posture and
movement. New York : Springer, 2000.
*TC QP303 .B5684 2000*

**Winters, Paul A., 1965-.**
Welfare. San Diego, CA : Greenhaven Press, c1997.
*TC HV95 .W453 1997*

**Wintle, Mike.** Coordinating assessment practice across
the primary school / Mike Wintle and Mike Harrison.
London ; Philadelphia, PA : Falmer Press, 1999. xi,
203 p. : ill. ; 25 cm. (Subject leader's handbooks.) Includes
bibliographical references (p. 189-196) and index. ISBN 0-
7507-0698-8
*1. Grading and marking (Students) - Great Britain. 2.
Education, Elementary - Great Britain. 3. Elementary school
administration - Great Britain. I. Harrison, Mike. (Mike A.) II.
Title. III. Series.*
*TC LB3060.37 .W56 1999*

**Winzer, M. A. (Margret A.), 1940-.**
Education in a global society. Boston : Allyn and
Bacon, c2000.
*TC LB43 .E385 2000*

**Wisconsin Symposium on Emotion (1st : 1995 :
Madison, Wis.).**
Anxiety, depression, and emotion. Oxford ; New
York : Oxford University Press, 2000.
*TC RC531 .A559 2000*

**Wisdom to action series**
Leading beyond the walls. 1st ed. San Francisco :
Jossey-Bass, c1999.

*TC HD57.7 .L4374 1999*

**The wise advisor.**
Salacuse, Jeswald W. Westport, Conn. : Praeger, 2000.
*TC BF637.C56 .S26 2000*

**Wise up.**
Claxton, Guy. 1st U.S. ed. New York, N.Y. : Bloomsbury : Distributed to the trade by St. Martin's Press, 1999.
*TC BF318 .C55 1999*

**Wise women :** reflections of teachers at midlife / editors, Phyllis R. Freeman, Jan Zlotnik Schmidt. New York ; London : Routledge, 2000. xi, 273 p. ; 24 cm. Includes bibliographical references (p. 245-261). ISBN 0-415-92302-6 (hbk.) ISBN 0-415-92303-4 (pbk.) DDC 371.1/0082 DDC 371.1/0082
*1. Women teachers - United States - Attitudes. 2. Middle age - United States. 3. Feminism and education - United States. I. Freeman, Phyllis R. II. Schmidt, Jan Zlotnik.*
*TC LB2837 .W58 2000*

**Wiseman, Dennis.**
Hunt, Gilbert. Effective teaching. 3rd ed. Springfield, Ill. : C.C. Thomas Publisher, c1999.
*TC LB1025.3 .H86 1999*

**WISHES - FICTION.**
Caines, Jeannette Franklin. I need a lunch box. New York : Macmillan/McGraw-Hill, 1988.
*TC PZ7.C12 Iaan 1988*

**Wishnietsky, Dan H.**
Wishnietsky, Dorothy Botsch. Managing chronic illness in the classroom. Bloomington, Ind. : Phi Delta Kappa Educational Foundation, c1996.
*TC LC4561 .W57 1996*

**Wishnietsky, Dorothy Botsch.** Managing chronic illness in the classroom / by Dorothy Botsch Wishnietsky and Dan H. Wishnietsky. Bloomington, Ind. : Phi Delta Kappa Educational Foundation, c1996. 102 p. ; 23 cm. ISBN 0-87367-487-1 DDC 371.91
*1. Chronically ill children - Education - United States. I. Wishnietsky, Dan H. II. Title.*
*TC LC4561 .W57 1996*

**Wisniewski, Richard.**
Reforming a college. New York : P. Lang, c2000.
*TC LD5293 .R44 2000*

**Wissenschaftsethik und Technikfolgenbeurteilung** (Bd. 4) Vision assessment. New York : Springer, 2000.
*TC T174.5 V57 2000*

**Wister, Sarah, 1761-1804.** A colonial Quaker girl : the diary of Sally Wister, 1777-1778 / edited by Megan O'Hara ; with foreword by Suzanne L. Bunkers. Mankato, Minn. : Blue Earth Books, c2000. 32 p. : ill. (some col.) ; 24 cm. (Diaries, letters, and memoirs) Includes bibliographical references (p. 31) and index. SUMMARY: Presents the diary of the sixteen-year-old daughter of a prominent Quaker family who moved with her family from British-occupied Philadelphia for the safety of the countryside during the Revolutionary War. Includes sidebars, activities, and a timeline related to this era. ISBN 0-7368-0347-5 ISBN 0-7368-0349-1 (cover) DDC 073.3/092
*1. Wister, Sarah. - 1761-1804 - Diaries - Juvenile literature. 2. Philadelphia (Pa.) - History - Revolution, 1775-1783 - Personal narratives - Juvenile literature. 3. United States - History - Revolution, 1775-1783 - Personal narratives - Juvenile literature. 4. Quakers - Pennsylvania - Philadelphia Region - Diaries - Juvenile literature. 5. Teenage girls - Pennsylvania - Philadelphia Region - Diaries - Juvenile literature. 6. Philadelphia (Pa.) - History - Revolution, 1775-1783 - Social aspects - Juvenile literature. 7. United States - History - Revolution, 1775-1783 - Social aspects - Juvenile literature. 8. Wister, Sarah. - 1761-1804. 9. Quakers. 10. United States - History - Revolution, 1775-1783 - Personal narratives. 11. United States - Social life and customs - 1775-1783. 12. Diaries. 13. Women - Biography. I. O'Hara, Megan. II. Title. III. Series.*
*TC F158.44 .W75 2000*

**WISTER, SARAH, 1761-1804.**
Wister, Sarah, 1761-1804. A colonial Quaker girl. Mankato, Minn. : Blue Earth Books, c2000.
*TC F158.44 .W75 2000*

**WISTER, SARAH, 1761-1804 - DIARIES - JUVENILE LITERATURE.**
Wister, Sarah, 1761-1804. A colonial Quaker girl. Mankato, Minn. : Blue Earth Books, c2000.
*TC F158.44 .W75 2000*

**WIT AND HUMOR.** *See* LAUGHTER; PRACTICAL JOKES.

**WIT AND HUMOR, PICTORIAL.** *See also* CARTOONING; COMIC BOOKS, STRIPS, ETC.
Comics, the 9th art [videorecording]. [S.l.] : EPISA : Cicero, Ill. : [Distributed by] The Roland Collection, 1990.
*TC PN6710 .C6 1990*

**WIT AND HUMOR, PRIMITIVE.** *See* WIT AND HUMOR.

**WIT AND HUMOR - PSYCHOLOGICAL ASPECTS.**
Humor and psyche. Hillsdale, NJ : Analytic Press, c1999.
*TC BF175 .H85 1999*

**The witch must die.**
Cashdan, Sheldon. New York : Basic Books, 1999.
*TC GR550 .C39 1999*

**WITCHCRAFT.**
Harris, Marvin, 1927- Cows, pigs, wars & witches. [1st ed.] New York : Random House, c1974.
*TC GN320 .H328 1974*

**WITCHCRAFT - MASSACHUSETTS - SALEM - HISTORY - 17TH CENTURY.**
Carlson, Laurie M., 1952- A fever in Salem. Chicago : I.R. Dee, 1999.
*TC BF1576 .C37 1999*

**Witcher, Ann E.**
Time and learning :. Bloomington, IN : Phi Delta Kappa International, c1998.
*TC LB3032 .T562 1998*

**WITCHES - FICTION.**
Rowling, J. K. Harry Potter and the sorcerer's stone. 1st American ed. New York : A.A. Levine Books, 1998.
*TC PZ7.R79835 Har 1998*

**With the phoenix rising :** lessons from ten resilient women who overcame the trauma of childhood sexual abuse / Frances K. Grossman ... [et al.]. 1st ed. San Francisco : Jossey-Bass, c1999. xi, 258 p. ; 24 cm. Includes bibliographical references (p. 243-247) and index. ISBN 0-7879-4784-9 (acid-free paper) DDC 616.85/8369
*1. Adult child sexual abuse victims - Case studies. I. Grossman, Frances Kaplan, 1939-*
*TC RC569.5.A28 W57 1999*

**Withers, Carl.** Plainville, U.S.A. / [by] James West [pseud.]. New York : Columbia University Press, [c1945] xv, 238 p. : ill. (map, plan) ; 23 cm. Includes bibiographical references.
*1. United States - Social conditions. 2. Cities and towns - United States. 3. Social surveys. I. Title.*
*TC HN57 .W58 1945*

**Without justice for all :** the new liberalism and our retreat from racial equality / edited by Adolph Reed, Jr. Boulder, Colo. : Westview Press, 1999. ix, 460 p. : ill. ; 24 cm. Includes bibliographical references (p. 353-426) and index. ISBN 0-8133-2050-X (alk. paper) DDC 305.8/00973
*1. United States - Race relations. 2. United States - Politics and government - 1993- 3. United States - Social policy - 1993- 4. Racism - Political aspects - United States - History - 20th century. 5. Afro-Americans - Civil rights - History - 20th century. 6. Liberalism - United States - History - 20th century. I. Reed, Adolph L., 1947-*
*TC E185.615 .W57 1999*

**Witt, Doris.** Black hunger : food and the politics of U.S. identity / Doris Witt. New York : Oxford University Press, 1999. xii, 292 p. : ill. ; 25 cm. (Race and American culture) Includes bibliographical references (p. 253-281) and index. ISBN 0-19-511062-5 (acid-free paper) DDC 305.8/00973
*1. Afro-American women - Race identity. 2. Afro-American women - Ethnic identity. 3. Afro-American women - Social conditions. 4. Food - Social aspects - United States - History - 20th century. 5. Racism - Social aspects - United States - History - 20th century. I. Title. II. Series.*
*TC E185.86 .W58 1999*

**Witte, John F.** The market approach to education : an analysis of America's first voucher program / John F. Witte. Princeton, N.J. : Princeton University Press, c2000. xiv, 221 p. : ill., maps ; 24 cm. Includes bibliographical references (p. [211]-218) and index. ISBN 0-691-00944-9 (cloth : alk. paper) DDC 379.1/11
*1. Educational vouchers - Wisconsin - Milwaukee - Case studies. 2. School choice - Wisconsin - Milwaukee - Case studies. 3. Education, Urban - Wisconsin - Milwaukee - Case studies. I. Title.*
*TC LB2828.85.W6 W58 2000*

**Witte, Stephen P. (Stephen Paul), 1943-.**
A Rhetoric of doing. Carbondale : Southern Illinois University Press, c1992.

*TC PE1404 .R496 1992*

**Wittenberg, Lauren G.** Peer education in eating disorder prevention : a large scale longitudinal analysis of program effectiveness / Lauren G. Wittenberg. 1999. v, 100 leaves : ill. ; 28 cm. "May, 1999." Thesis (Ph.D.)--Dartmouth College, 1999. Includes bibliographical references (leaves 60-67).
*1. Eating disorders - Prevention - Longitudinal studies. 2. Eating disorders - Treatment. 3. Peer counseling of students. I. Title.*
*TC RC552.E18 W56 1999*

**Wittgenstein.**
Peters, Michael (Michael A.), 1948- Westport, Conn. : Bergin & Garvey, 1999.
*TC B3376.W564 P388 1999*

**WITTGENSTEIN, LUDWIG, 1889-1951.**
Hagberg, Garry, 1952- Art as language. Ithaca : Cornell University Press, c1995.
*TC B3376.W564 H25 1995*

Peters, Michael (Michael A.), 1948- Wittgenstein. Westport, Conn. : Bergin & Garvey, 1999.
*TC B3376.W564 P388 1999*

**WIVES.** *See* ABUSED WIVES; HOUSEWIVES; MARRIED WOMEN.

**WIVES - EMPLOYMENT.** *See* MARRIED WOMEN - EMPLOYMENT.

**WIZARDS - FICTION.**
Rowling, J. K. Harry Potter and the Chamber of Secrets. New York : Arthur A. Levine Books, 1999.
*TC PZ7.R7968 Har 1999*

Rowling, J. K. Harry Potter and the prisoner of Azkaban. New York : Arthur A. Levine Books, 1999.
*TC PZ7.R79835 Ham 1999*

Rowling, J. K. Harry Potter and the sorcerer's stone. 1st American ed. New York : A.A. Levine Books, 1998.
*TC PZ7.R79835 Har 1998*

**WNET (Television station : New York, N.Y.).**
Changing lives [videorecording]. Princeton, NJ : Films for the Humanities & Sciences, c1998.
*TC RC564 .C54 1998*

Georgia O'Keeffe [videorecording]. [Boston?] : Home Vision c1977.
*TC ND237.O5 G4 1977*

The hijacked brain [videorecording]. Princeton, NJ : Films for the Humanities & Sciences, c1998.
*TC RC564 .H5 1998*

The Internet in action for math & science 7-12 [videorecording]. [New York] : Thirteen-WNET ; [Alexandria, Va. : distributed by] PBS Video, c1997.
*TC LB1044.87 .I453 1997*

The Internet in action for math & science K-6 [videorecording]. [New York] : Thirteen-WNET ; [Alexandria, Va. : distributed by] PBS Video, c1998.
*TC LB1044.87 .I45 1998*

Mary Cassatt [videorecording]. [Chicago, Ill.] : Home Vision, c1977.
*TC ND237.C3 M37 1977*

Nevelson in process [videorecording]. Chicago, IL : Public Media Inc., 1977.
*TC NB237.N43 N43 1977*

The next generation [videorecording]. Princeton, NJ : Films for the Humanities & Sciences, c1998.
*TC RC564 .N4 1998*

The politics of addiction [videorecording]. Princeton, NJ : Films for the Humanities & Sciences, c1998.
*TC RC564 .P59 1998*

Portrait of addiction [videorecording]. Princeton, NJ : Films for the Humanities & Sciences, c1998.
*TC HV5801 .P6 1998*

Portrait of addiction [videorecording]. Princeton, NJ : Films for the Humanities & Sciences, c1998.
*TC RC564 .P6 1998*

Stephen Hawking's universe [videorecording]. [Alexandria, Va.] : PBS Video; Burbank, CA : Distributed by Warner Home Video, c1997.
*TC QB982 .S7 1997*

**WNET (Television station : New York, N.Y.). Educational Resources Center.**
The Internet in action for math & science 7-12 [videorecording]. [New York] : Thirteen-WNET ; [Alexandria, Va. : distributed by] PBS Video, c1997.
*TC LB1044.87 .I453 1997*

The Internet in action for math & science K-6 [videorecording]. [New York] : Thirteen-WNET : [Alexandria, Va. : distributed by] PBS Video, c1998.
*TC LB1044.87 .I45 1998*

**Woburn education series**
Penn, Alan, 1926- Targeting schools. London ; Portland, OR : Woburn Press, 1999.
*TC GV443 .P388 1999*

State schools. London ; Portland, OR : Woburn Press, 1999.
*TC LC93.G7 S73 1999*

Vlaeminke, Meriel. The English higher grade schools. London ; Portland, OR : Woburn Press, 2000.
*TC LA634 .V52 2000*

**Wodin, Frederick.**
Ballet class for beginners [videorecording]. W. Long Branch, NJ : Kultur, c1981.
*TC GV1589 .B3 1981*

**Woeful afflictions.**
Klages, Mary. Philadelphia : University of Pennsylvania Press, c1999.
*TC HV1553 .K53 1999*

**Woehrle, Lynne M., 1965-.**
Social conflicts and collective identities. Lanham, Md. : Oxford : Rowman & Littlefield Publishers, c2000.
*TC HM1121 .S63 2000*

**Woellner, Elizabeth H.** Requirements for certification: teachers, counselors, librarians, administrators for elementary schools, secondary schools, junior colleges. Chicago : University of Chicago Press, 1935- v. ; 29 cm. 1st- ed.; 1935- . Title varies: Requirements for teaching certificates 1935-1938. Other slight variations in title. Vol. for 1936 (2d ed.) called revised edition. Editors: 1935-1959/60   R. C. Woellner and M. A. Wood; 1960/61-   E. H. Woellner and M. A. Wood. Editor: 1935 ed. Mary Paxton Burks. Continued by: Requirements for certification of teachers, counselors, librarians, administrators for elementary and secondary schools. ISSN 0080-1429
*1. Teachers - Certification - United States. I. Wood, Maude Aurilla, 1877- joint author. II. Woellner, Robert Carlton, 1894-1960. Requirements for teaching certificates. III. Title. IV. Title: Requirements for teaching certificates 1935-1938 V. Title: Requirements for certification of teachers, counselors, librarians, administrators for elementary and secondary schools.*
*TC LB1771 .W6*

**Woellner, Robert Carlton, 1894-1960.**
**Requirements for teaching certificates.**
Woellner, Elizabeth H. Requirements for certification: Chicago : University of Chicago Press, 1935-
*TC LB1771 .W6*

**Woff, Richard, 1953-** Bright-eyed Athena : stories from ancient Greece / Richard Woff. Los Angeles, CA : J. Paul Getty Museum, 1999. 47 p. : col. ill. ; 26 cm. SUMMARY: Retells a selection of Greek myths involving the goddess Athena including "Athena and Arachne," "Pandora's box," "Perseus and Medusa," "Demeter and Persephone," and others. ISBN 0-89236-558-7 DDC 398.2/09838/01
*1. Athena (Greek deity) - Juvenile literature. 2. Athena (Greek deity) 3. Mythology, Greek. I. Title.*
*TC BL820.M6 W64 1999*

**Wojcik-Andrews, Ian, 1952-** Children's films : history, ideology, pedagogy, theory / Ian Wojcik-Andrews. New York : Garland Pub., 2000. p. cm. (Garland reference library of the humanities ; v. 2165. Children's literature and culture ; v. 12) Filmography: p. Includes bibliographical references and index. ISBN 0-8153-3074-X (alk. paper) ISBN 0-8153-3794-9 (pbk. : alk. paper) DDC 791.43/75/083
*1. Children's films - History and criticism. I. Title. II. Series: Garland reference library of the humanities ; vol. 2165 III. Series: Garland reference library of the humanities. Children's literature and culture ; v. 12*
*TC PN1995.9.C45 W59 2000*

**Wolf and the seven little kids.**
Blades, Ann, 1947- Toronto : Douglas & McIntyre, c1999.
*TC PS8553.L33 W64 1999*

**Wolf, Dennie.**
Art works!. Portsmouth, NH : Heinemann, c1999.
*TC LB1628.5 .A78 1999*

**Wolf, Mark J. P.** Abstracting reality : art, communication, and cognition in the digital age / Mark J.P. Wolf. Lanham, Md.: University Press of America, c2000. xii, 319 p. ; 24 cm. Includes bibliographical references (p. [295]-307) and index. ISBN 0-7618-1667-4 (cloth : acid-free paper) ISBN 0-7618-1668-2 (pbk.) DDC 303.48/33

*1. Digital media - Social aspects. 2. Technology and the arts. 3. Communication and technology. 4. Technology and civilization. I. Title.*
*TC HM851 .W65 2000*

**Wolfe, David A.** Child abuse : implications for child development and psychopathology / David A. Wolfe. 2nd ed. Thousands Oaks, Calif. : Sage Publications, 1999. xii, 140 p. ; 22 cm. (Developmental clinical psychology and psychiatry ; v. 10) Includes index. Bibliography: p. 111-129. ISBN 0-8039-7227-X ISBN 0-8039-7228-8 (pbk.) DDC 362.76
*1. Child abuse. 2. Child development. 3. Parent and child. 4. Child psychopathology. I. Title. II. Series: Developmental psychology and psychiatry; v.10*
*TC HV6626.5 .W58 1999*

**Wolfe, Paula M.**
So much to say. New York : Teachers College Press, c1999.
*TC PE1128.A2 S599 1999*

**Wolfe, Walter Béran, 1900-1935, tr.**
Wexberg, Erwin, 1889- Individual psychology. New York, Cosmopolitan Book Corporation, 1929.
*TC BF175 .W48*

**Wolfendale, Sheila.**
The contribution of parents to school effectiveness. London : David Fulton Publishers, c2000.
*TC LC225.33.G7 C66 2000*

**Wolfendale, Sheila, 1939-.**
Parenting education and support. London : David Fulton, c1999.
*TC HQ755.7 .P374 1999*

**WOLFENSOHN, JAMES D.**
Our friends at the bank [videorecording]. New York, NY : First Run/Icarus Films, 1997.
*TC HG3881.5.W57 O87 1997*

**Wolfinger, Donna M.** Science in the elementary and middle school / Donna M. Wolfinger. New York : Longman, c2000. xxi, 473 p. : ill. ; 24 cm. Includes bibliographical references (p. 452-460) and index. ISBN 0-8013-2058-5 DDC 372.3/5044
*1. Science - Study and teaching (Elementary) - United States. 2. Science - Study and teaching (Middle school) - United States. I. Title.*
*TC LB1585.3 .W65 2000*

**Wolinsky, Ira.**
Energy-yielding macronutrients and energy metabolism in sports nutrition. Boca Raton, Fla. ; London : CRC Press, c2000.
*TC QP176 .E546 2000*

**Wollman-Bonilla, Julie.** Family message journals : teaching writing through family involvement / Julie E. Wollman-Bonilla. Urbana, Ill. : National Council of Teachers of English, c2000. ix, 143 p. : ill. ; 26 cm. Includes bibliographical references (p. 137-141). "NCTE stock number: 52457-3050"--T.p. verso. ISBN 0-8141-5245-7 (pbk) DDC 372.62/3044
*1. English language - Composition and exercises - Study and teaching (Elementary). 2. Education, Elementary - Parent participation. 3. Language arts (Elementary) I. Title.*
*TC LB1576 .W644 2000*

**Wollons, Roberta Lyn, 1947-.**
Kindergartens and cultures. New Haven [Conn.] ; London : Yale University Press, c2000.
*TC LB1199 .K58 2000*

**Wolves and caribou unit :** a middle-school mathematics unit / MMAP. Menlo Park, Calif. : Institute for Research on Learning, 1998, c1995. 216 p. : ill. ; 30 cm. + 1 computer disc (3 1/2 in.). Library copy is a draft copy.
*1. Mathematics - Study and teaching (Elementary) I. Middle-school Mathematics through Applications Project.*
*TC QA135.5 .W64 1995*

**WOLVES - FICTION.**
Marshall, James, 1942- Swine lake. 1st ed. [New York] : Harper Collins Publishers, 1999.
*TC PZ7.M35672 Sw 1999*

**WOMAN.** *See* WOMEN.

**WOMAN-MAN RELATIONSHIPS.** *See* MAN-WOMAN RELATIONSHIPS.

**The woman who outshone the sun.**
Cruz Martinez, Alejandro, d. 1987. [Mujer que brillaba aún más que el sol. English & Spanish] San Francisco, Calif. : Children's Book Press, c1991.
*TC F1221.Z3 C78 1991*

**WOMEN.** *See also* ABUSED WOMEN; AGED WOMEN; AUNTS; HANDICAPPED WOMEN; HOUSEWIVES; JEWISH WOMEN; LESBIANS; MARRIED WOMEN;

MENTALLY ILL WOMEN; MIDDLE CLASS WOMEN; MINORITY WOMEN; MOTHERS; MUSLIM WOMEN; OVERWEIGHT WOMEN; PREGNANT WOMEN; RURAL WOMEN; SISTERS; URBAN WOMEN; WORKING CLASS WOMEN; YOUNG WOMEN.
Mead, Margaret, 1901-1978. Male and female. London : Victor Gollancz, c1949.
*TC HQ21 .M464 1949*

Mead, Margaret, 1901-1978. Male and female. London : Victor Gollancz, c1949.
*TC HQ21 .M464 1949*

**WOMEN - ABUSE OF - UNITED STATES - PREVENTION.**
Gordon, Judith S., 1958- Helping survivors of domestic violence. New York : Garland Pub., 1998.
*TC HV6626.2 .G67 1998*

**Women afraid to eat.**
Berg, Francie M. Hettinger, ND : Healthy Weight Network, c2000.
*TC RC552.O25 B47 2000*

**WOMEN - AFRICA, SUB-SAHARAN - HISTORY - 19TH CENTURY.**
Coquery-Vidrovitch, Catherine. [Africaines. English] African women. Boulder, Colo. : WestviewPress, 1997.
*TC HQ1787 .C6613 1997*

**WOMEN - AFRICA, SUB-SAHARAN - HISTORY - 20TH CENTURY.**
Coquery-Vidrovitch, Catherine. [Africaines. English] African women. Boulder, Colo. : WestviewPress, 1997.
*TC HQ1787 .C6613 1997*

**WOMEN, AFRO-AMERICAN.** *See* AFRO-AMERICAN WOMEN.

**WOMEN AND CITY PLANNING.**
Gendering the city. Lanham [Md.] : Rowman & Littlefield, c2000.
*TC HT166 .G4614 2000*

**WOMEN AND DEVELOPMENT.** *See* WOMEN IN DEVELOPMENT.

**Women and health.**
Goldman, Marlene. San Diego, Calif. : Academic, c2000.
*TC RA564.85 .G66 2000*

**Women and human development.**
Nussbaum, Martha Craven, 1947- Cambridge, U.K. ; New York : Cambridge University Press, 2000.
*TC HQ1240 .N87 2000*

**WOMEN AND LITERATURE.**
Moi, Toril. What is a woman? Oxford ; New York : Oxford University Press, 1999.
*TC HQ1190 .M64 1999*

**WOMEN AND LITERATURE - GREAT BRITAIN - HISTORY - 18TH CENTURY.**
Pearson, Jacqueline, 1949- Women's reading in Britain, 1750-1835. Cambridge, UK ; New York : Cambridge University Press, 1999.
*TC PR756.W65 P43 1999*

**WOMEN AND LITERATURE - GREAT BRITAIN - HISTORY - 19TH CENTURY.**
Pearson, Jacqueline, 1949- Women's reading in Britain, 1750-1835. Cambridge, UK ; New York : Cambridge University Press, 1999.
*TC PR756.W65 P43 1999*

**Women and men in history**
Practical visionaries. Harlow, England ; New York : Longman, 2000.
*TC LC2042 .P72 2000*

**Women and men in organizations.**
Cleveland, Jeanette. Mahwah, N.J. ; London : Lawrence Erlbaum Associates, 2000.
*TC HD6060.65.U5 C58 2000*

**Women and minority faculty in the academic workplace.**
Aguirre, Adalberto. San Francisco, Calif. : Jossey-Bass c2000.
*TC LB2332.3 .A35 2000*

**WOMEN AND PEACE.** *See also* WOMEN PACIFISTS.
Chinn, Peggy L. Peace and power. 5th ed. Boston : Jones and Bartlett Publishers, c2001.
*TC HQ1426 .W454 2001*

**WOMEN AND PEACE - GREAT BRITAIN - HISTORY - 20TH CENTURY.**

Women in the milieu of Leonard and Virginia Woolf. New York : Pace University Press, 1998.
*TC PR6045.O72 Z925 1998*

**WOMEN AND PSYCHOANALYSIS.**
André, Serge. [Que veut une femme? English] What does a woman want? New York : Other Press, c1999.
*TC BF175 .A69613 1999*

Frosh, Stephen. The politics of psychoanalysis. 2nd ed. New York : New York University Press, 1999.
*TC BF173 .F92 1999*

Learning from our mistakes. New York : Haworth Press, c1998.
*TC RC489.F45 L43 1998*

Psychoanalysis and woman. New York : New York University Press, 2000.
*TC BF175.5.S48 P795 2000*

**Women and psychology**
Dryden, Caroline. Being married, doing gender. London ; New York : Routledge, 1999.
*TC HQ734 .D848 1999*

Stoppard, Janet M. (Janet Mary), 1945- Understanding depression. London ; New York : Routledge, 2000.
*TC RC537 .S82 2000*

**WOMEN AND RELIGION - SOUTH ASIA - HISTORY.**
Robinson, Catherine A. Tradition and liberation. New York : St. Martin's Press, 1999.
*TC HQ1735.3 .R63 1999*

**WOMEN AND RELIGION - UNITED STATES - CASE STUDIES.**
Henderson, Katharine Rhodes. The public leadership of women of faith. 2000.
*TC 06 no. 11276*

**Women and scientific employment.**
Glover, Judith, 1949- Houndmills [England] : Macmillan Press ; New York : St. Martin's Press, 2000.
*TC Q130 .G64 2000*

**Women and their vocation.**
Büchner, Louise, 1821-1877. [Frauen und ihr Beruf. English] New York : P. Lang, c1999.
*TC BJ1610 .B8313 1998*

**Women and urban change in San Juan, Puerto Rico, 1820-1868.**
Matos Rodríguez, Félix V., 1962- Gainesville, Fla. : University Press of Florida, c1999.
*TC HQ1522 .M38 1999*

**WOMEN - ANTILLES, LESSER.** *See* **BLACK CARIB WOMEN.**

**WOMEN ARCHITECTS - CANADA.**
Adams, Annmarie. Designing women. Toronto : University of Toronto Press, c2000.
*TC NA1997 A32 2000*

**WOMEN ARTISTS.** *See* **WOMEN SCULPTORS.**

**WOMEN ARTISTS - AUSTRALIA.**
Voigt, Anna. New visions, new perspectives. Roseville East, NSW : Craftsman House, 1996.
*TC N7400.2 .V65 1996*

**WOMEN ARTISTS - AUSTRALIA - BIOGRAPHY - HISTORY AND CRITICISM.**
Kirby, Sandy. Sight lines. Tortola, BVI : Craftsman House in association with Gordon and Breach ; New York : Distributed in the USA by STBS Ltd., 1992.
*TC N72.F45 K57 1992*

**WOMEN ARTISTS - PSYCHOLOGY.**
Krauss, Rosalind E. Bachelors. Cambridge, Mass. : MIT Press, c1999.
*TC NX180.F4 K73 1999*

**WOMEN AS ARCHITECTS.** *See* **WOMEN ARCHITECTS.**

**WOMEN AS ARTISTS.** *See* **WOMEN ARTISTS.**

**WOMEN AS COLLEGE TEACHERS.** *See* **WOMEN COLLEGE TEACHERS.**

**Women as learners.**
Hayes, Elisabeth. 1st ed. San Francisco : Jossey-Bass Publishers, c2000.
*TC LC5225.L42 H39 2000*

**WOMEN AS MISSIONARIES.** *See* **WOMEN MISSIONARIES.**

**WOMEN AS PHOTOGRAPHERS.** *See* **WOMEN PHOTOGRAPHERS.**

**WOMEN AS SOLDIERS.** *See* **WOMEN SOLDIERS.**

**WOMEN AS TEACHERS.** *See* **WOMEN TEACHERS.**

**Women at Michigan.**
Bordin, Ruth Birgitta Anderson, 1917- Ann Arbor : University of Michigan Press, c1999.
*TC LD3280 .B67 1999*

**WOMEN ATHLETES - LITERARY COLLECTIONS.**
Crossing boundaries. Champaign, IL : Human Kinetics, c1999.
*TC PN6071.S62 C76 1999*

**WOMEN - BIOGRAPHY.**
Berry, Carrie, b. 1854. A Confederate girl. Mankato, Minn. : Blue Earth Books, c2000.
*TC E605 .B5 2000*

Forten, Charlotte L. A free Black girl before the Civil War. Mankato, Minn. : Blue Earth Books, c2000.
*TC F74.S1 F67 2000*

Gillespie, Sarah (Sarah L.) A pioneer farm girl. Mankato, Minn. : Blue Earth Books, c2000.
*TC F629.M28 G55 2000*

Hester, Sallie. A covered wagon girl. Mankato, Minn. : Blue Earth Books, c2000.
*TC F593 .H47 2000*

Hodges, Margaret, 1911- Joan of Arc. 1st ed. New York : Holiday House, c1999.
*TC DC103.5 .H64 1999*

Jernegan, Laura, b. 1862. A whaling captain's daughter. Mankato, Minn. : Blue Earth Books, c2000.
*TC G545 .J47 2000*

Richards, Caroline Cowles, 1842-1913. A nineteenth-century schoolgirl. Mankato, Minn. : Blue Earth Books, c2000.
*TC F129.C2 R53 2000*

Wister, Sarah, 1761-1804. A colonial Quaker girl. Mankato, Minn. : Blue Earth Books, c2000.
*TC F158.44 .W75 2000*

**WOMEN BIOLOGISTS - UNITED STATES - BIOGRAPHY.**
Wasserman, Elga R. (Elga Ruth) The door in the dream. Washington, D.C. : Joseph Henry Press, c2000.
*TC QH26 .W375 2000*

**WOMEN, BLACK - BRAZIL - SOCIAL CONDITIONS.**
Race in contemporary Brazil. University Park, Pa. : Pennsylvania State University Press, 1999.
*TC F2659.N4 R245 1999*

**WOMEN, BLACK CARIB.** *See* **BLACK CARIB WOMEN.**

**WOMEN, BLACK - EDUCATION (HIGHER) - SOUTH AFRICA - CASE STUDIES.**
Makosana, I. Nokuzola Zola. Social factors in the positioning of black women in South African universities. 1997.
*TC 06 no. 10825*

**WOMEN, BLACK - EDUCATION (HIGHER) - SOUTH AFRICA - HISTORY - 20TH CENTURY.**
Makosana, I. Nokuzola Zola. Social factors in the positioning of black women in South African universities. 1997.
*TC 06 no. 10825*

**WOMEN, BLACK - GREAT BRITAIN - INTERVIEWS.**
Dove, Nah. Afrikan mothers. Albany : State University of New York Press, c1998.
*TC HQ1593 .D68 1998*

**WOMEN, BLACK - SOUTH AFRICA - BIOGRAPHY.**
McCord, Margaret (McCord Nixon) The calling of Katie Makanya. New York : J. Wiley, 1995.
*TC CT1929.M34 M38 1995*

**WOMEN, BLACK - SOUTH AFRICA - SOCIAL LIFE AND CUSTOMS.**
McCord, Margaret (McCord Nixon) The calling of Katie Makanya. New York : J. Wiley, 1995.
*TC CT1929.M34 M38 1995*

**WOMEN, BLACK - UNITED STATES - INTERVIEWS.**
Dove, Nah. Afrikan mothers. Albany : State University of New York Press, c1998.
*TC HQ1593 .D68 1998*

**WOMEN - CENTRAL AMERICA.** *See* **BLACK CARIB WOMEN.**

**WOMEN, CHINESE AMERICAN.** *See* **CHINESE AMERICAN WOMEN.**

**WOMEN CIVIC LEADERS - NEW YORK (STATE) - SUFFOLK COUNTY.**
Robinson, Anna Bess. Leadership development in women's civic organizations. 1999.
*TC 06 no. 11168*

**WOMEN CIVIC LEADERS - NEW YORK (STATE) - SUFFOLK COUNTY - TRAINING OF.**
Robinson, Anna Bess. Leadership development in women's civic organizations. 1999.
*TC 06 no. 11168*

**WOMEN - CIVIL RIGHTS.** *See* **WOMEN'S RIGHTS.**

**WOMEN - CLOTHING.** *See* **CLOTHING AND DRESS.**

**WOMEN COLLEGE PRESIDENTS - UNITED STATES.**
Tobe, Dorothy Echols. The development of cognitive leadership frames among African American female college presidents. 1999.
*TC 06 no. 11187*

**WOMEN COLLEGE STUDENTS.** *See* **LESBIAN COLLEGE STUDENTS; WOMEN SCIENCE STUDENTS.**

**WOMEN COLLEGE STUDENTS - ATTITUDES.**
Miller, Estelle L. Fears expressed by female reentry students at an urban community college : qualitative study. 1997.
*TC 06 no. 10864*

**WOMEN COLLEGE STUDENTS - DELAWARE - NEWARK - HISTORY.**
Hoffecker, Carol E. Beneath thy guiding hand. Newark, Del. : University of Delaware, c1994.
*TC LD1483 .H64 1994*

**WOMEN COLLEGE STUDENTS - NORTHEASTERN STATES - LONGITUDINAL STUDIES.**
Miller-Bernal, Leslie, 1946- Separate by degree. New York : P. Lang, c2000.
*TC LC1601 .M55 2000*

**WOMEN COLLEGE STUDENTS - SOUTHERN STATES - CONDUCT OF LIFE - HISTORY - 20TH CENTURY.**
McCandless, Amy Thompson, 1946- The past in the present. Tuscaloosa : University of Alabama Press, c1999.
*TC LC1756 .M24 1999*

**WOMEN COLLEGE TEACHERS, AFRO-AMERICAN.** *See* **AFRO-AMERICAN WOMEN COLLEGE TEACHERS.**

**WOMEN COLLEGE TEACHERS, BLACK - EMPLOYMENT - SOUTH AFRICA - CASE STUDIES.**
Makosana, I. Nokuzola Zola. Social factors in the positioning of black women in South African universities. 1997.
*TC 06 no. 10825*

**WOMEN COLLEGE TEACHERS, BLACK - SOUTH AFRICA - CASE STUDIES.**
Makosana, I. Nokuzola Zola. Social factors in the positioning of black women in South African universities. 1997.
*TC 06 no. 10825*

**WOMEN COLLEGE TEACHERS - MICHIGAN - ANN ARBOR - HISTORY.**
Bordin, Ruth Birgitta Anderson, 1917- Women at Michigan. Ann Arbor : University of Michigan Press, c1999.
*TC LD3280 .B67 1999*

**WOMEN COLLEGE TEACHERS - SELECTION AND APPOINTMENT - UNITED STATES.**
Power, race, and gender in academe. New York : Modern Language Association, 2000.
*TC LC3727 .P69 2000*

**WOMEN COLLEGE TEACHERS - UNITED STATES.** *See also* **AFRO-AMERICAN WOMEN COLLEGE TEACHERS.**
Aguirre, Adalberto. Women and minority faculty in the academic workplace. San Francisco, Calif. : Jossey-Bass c2000.
*TC LB2332.3 .A35 2000*

Power, race, and gender in academe. New York : Modern Language Association, 2000.

**TC LC3727 .P69 2000**

**WOMEN CONSUMERS.**
Nelson, Carol, 1953- Women's market handbook.
Detroit : Gale Research, c1994.
**TC HF5415 .N3495 1994**

**WOMEN - COSTUME.** *See* **COSTUME.**

**WOMEN, CROW.** *See* **CROW WOMEN.**

**WOMEN DEANS (EDUCATION) - UNITED STATES - BIOGRAPHY.**
Nidiffer, Jana, 1957- Pioneering deans of women.
New York ; London : Teachers College Press, c2000.
**TC LC1620 .N53 2000**

**WOMEN - DEVELOPING COUNTRIES.**
Nussbaum, Martha Craven, 1947- Women and human development. Cambridge, U.K. ; New York : Cambridge University Press, 2000.
**TC HQ1240 .N87 2000**

**WOMEN - DEVELOPING COUNTRIES - SOCIAL CONDITIONS - CROSS-CULTURAL STUDIES.**
Critical perspectives on schooling and fertility in the developing world. Washington, D.C. : National Academy Press, 1999.
**TC LC2572 .C75 1998**

**WOMEN, DISCRIMINATION AGAINST.** *See* **SEX DISCRIMINATION AGAINST WOMEN.**

**WOMEN - DISEASES.** *See* **DEPRESSION IN WOMEN; WOMEN - HEALTH AND HYGIENE.**

**WOMEN - DISEASES - TREATMENT.**
Healing from within. 1st ed. Washington, DC ; London : American Psychological Association, c2000.
**TC RC497 .H42 2000**

**WOMEN - DRESS.** *See* **CLOTHING AND DRESS.**

**WOMEN - EDUCATION.** *See also* **ADULT EDUCATION OF WOMEN; COEDUCATION; WOMEN COLLEGE STUDENTS; WOMEN'S COLLEGES.**
Hayes, Elisabeth. Women as learners. 1st ed. San Francisco : Jossey-Bass Publishers, c2000.
**TC LC5225.L42 H39 2000**

National Association for Women Deans, Administrators & Counselors. Journal. [Washington, D.C. : National Association for Women Deans, Administrators, & Counselors]

**WOMEN - EDUCATION - AFRICA, SUB-SAHARAN.**
Egbo, Benedicta, 1954- Gender, literacy, and life chances in Sub-Saharan Africa. Clevedon ; Buffalo : Multilingual Matters, c2000.
**TC LC2412 .E42 2000**

**WOMEN - EDUCATION - COMMONWEALTH COUNTRIES.**
Leo-Rhynie, Elsa. Gender mainstreaming in education. London : Commonwealth Secretariat, c1999.
**TC LC2572 .L46 1999**

**WOMEN - EDUCATION (CONTINUING EDUCATION) - GREAT BRITAIN - CASE STUDIES.**
Preece, Julia. Using Foucault and feminist theory to explain why some adults are excluded from British university education. Lewiston, N.Y. : E. Mellen Press, c1999.
**TC LC6256.G7 P74 1999**

**WOMEN - EDUCATION - DEVELOPING COUNTRIES.**
Gender, education, and development. London ; New York : Zed Books ; New York : Distributed in USA exclusively by St. Martin's Press, c1999.
**TC LC2607 .G46 1998**

Leo-Rhynie, Elsa. Gender mainstreaming in education. London : Commonwealth Secretariat, c1999.
**TC LC2572 .L46 1999**

**WOMEN - EDUCATION - DEVELOPING COUNTRIES - CROSS-CULTURAL STUDIES.**
Critical perspectives on schooling and fertility in the developing world. Washington, D.C. : National Academy Press, 1999.
**TC LC2572 .C75 1998**

**WOMEN - EDUCATION - GREAT BRITAIN - HISTORY - 18TH CENTURY.**
Practical visionaries. Harlow, England ; New York : Longman, 2000.
**TC LC2042 .P72 2000**

**WOMEN - EDUCATION - GREAT BRITAIN - HISTORY - 19TH CENTURY.**
Practical visionaries. Harlow, England ; New York : Longman, 2000.
**TC LC2042 .P72 2000**

**WOMEN - EDUCATION - GREAT BRITAIN - HISTORY - 20TH CENTURY.**
Practical visionaries. Harlow, England ; New York : Longman, 2000.
**TC LC2042 .P72 2000**

**WOMEN - EDUCATION (HIGHER).**
Feminist cyberscapes. Stamford, Conn. : Ablex Pub., c1999.
**TC PE1404 .F39 1999**

Haake, Katharine. What our speech disrupts. Urbana, Ill. : National Council of Teachers of English, c2000.
**TC PE1404 .H3 2000**

Morley, Louise, 1954- Organising feminisms. New York : St. Martin's Press, 1999.
**TC LC197 .M67 1999**

**WOMEN - EDUCATION (HIGHER) - GREAT BRITAIN.**
Merrill, Barbara. Gender, change and identity :. Aldershot, Hants, England ; Brookfield, Vt. : Ashgate, c1999.
**TC LC2046 .M477 1999**

**WOMEN - EDUCATION (HIGHER) - MICHIGAN - ANN ARBOR - HISTORY.**
Bordin, Ruth Birgitta Anderson, 1917- Women at Michigan. Ann Arbor : University of Michigan Press, c1999.
**TC LD3280 .B67 1999**

**WOMEN - EDUCATION (HIGHER) - SOUTHERN STATES - HISTORY - 20TH CENTURY.**
McCandless, Amy Thompson, 1946- The past in the present. Tuscaloosa : University of Alabama Press, c1999.
**TC LC1756 .M24 1999**

**WOMEN - EDUCATION (HIGHER) - UNITED STATES.**
Coming into her own. San Francisco, Calif. : Jossey-Bass, c1999.
**TC LC1503 .C65 1999**

Martin, Jane Roland, 1929- Coming of age in academe. New York ; London : Routledge, 2000.
**TC LC197 .M37 2000**

**WOMEN - EDUCATION (HIGHER) - UNITED STATES - CASE STUDIES.**
Two-year colleges for women and minorities. New York : Falmer Press, 1999.
**TC LB2328.15.U6 T96 1999**

**WOMEN - EDUCATION (HIGHER) - WISCONSIN - HISTORY.**
Transforming women's education. Madison, WI : Office of University Publications for the University of Wisconsin System, Women's Studies Consortium, 1999.
**TC HQ1181.U5 T77 1999**

**WOMEN - EDUCATION - SOCIAL ASPECTS - UNITED STATES - CASE STUDIES.**
Weiler, Jeanne. Codes and contradictions. Albany : State University of New York Press, c2000.
**TC LC1755 .W45 2000**

**WOMEN - EDUCATION - SOUTHERN STATES - CASE STUDIES.**
Key, Daphne. Literacy shutdown. Newark, Del. : International Reading Association ; Chicago, Ill. : National Reading Conference, c1998.
**TC LC1752 .K49 1998**

**WOMEN - EDUCATION - UNITED STATES.**
Coming into her own. San Francisco, Calif. : Jossey-Bass, c1999.
**TC LC1503 .C65 1999**

**WOMEN - EDUCATION - UNITED STATES - HISTORY.**
Women's philosophies of education. Upper Saddle River, N.J. : Merrill, c1999.
**TC LC1752 .T46 1999**

**WOMEN EDUCATORS.** *See* **DEANS OF WOMEN; WOMEN DEANS (EDUCATION); WOMEN TEACHERS.**

**WOMEN EDUCATORS - BIOGRAPHY.**
Practical visionaries. Harlow, England ; New York : Longman, 2000.
**TC LC2042 .P72 2000**

**WOMEN EDUCATORS - GREAT BRITAIN - BIOGRAPHY.**
Women in the milieu of Leonard and Virginia Woolf. New York : Pace University Press, 1998.
**TC PR6045.O72 Z925 1998**

**WOMEN EDUCATORS - UNITED STATES.**
Curry, Barbara K. Women in power. New York ; London : Teachers College Press, c2000.
**TC LB2831.62 .C87 2000**

**WOMEN EDUCATORS - UNITED STATES - BIOGRAPHY.**
Women's philosophies of education. Upper Saddle River, N.J. : Merrill, c1999.
**TC LC1752 .T46 1999**

**WOMEN - EGYPT - HISTORY.**
Badran, Margot. Feminists, Islam, and nation. Princeton, N.J. : Princeton University Press, c1995.
**TC HQ1793 .B33 1995**

**WOMEN - EMANCIPATION.** *See* **WOMEN'S RIGHTS.**

**WOMEN EMBROIDERY INDUSTRY EMPLOYEES - INDIA - LUCKNOW.**
Wilkinson-Weber, Clare M. Embroidering lives. Albany, N.Y. : State University of New York Press, c1999.
**TC HD6073.T42 I483 1999**

**WOMEN - EMPLOYMENT.** *See also* **EQUAL PAY FOR EQUAL WORK; SEX DISCRIMINATION IN EMPLOYMENT.**
Handbook of gender & work. Thousand Oaks, CA : Sage Publications, Inc., c1999.
**TC HQ1233 .H33 1999**

**WOMEN - EMPLOYMENT - UNITED STATES - HISTORY.**
Oldenziel, Ruth, 1958- Making technology masculine. Amsterdam : Amsterdam University Press, c1999.
**TC HD8072 .O57 1999**

**WOMEN - EMPLOYMENT - UNITED STATES - HISTORY - SOURCES.**
Women's America. 5th ed. New York : Oxford University Press, 2000.
**TC HQ1426 .W663 2000**

**WOMEN - ENCYCLOPEDIAS.**
Women's studies encyclopedia. Rev. and expanded ed. Westport, Conn. : Greenwood Press, c1999.
**TC HQ1115 .W645 1999**

**WOMEN ENTREPRENEURS.** *See* **BUSINESSWOMEN.**

**WOMEN - EVOLUTION.**
Jolly, Alison. Lucy's legacy. Cambridge, Mass. ; London : Harvard University Press, 1999.
**TC GN281 .J6 1999**

**WOMEN EXECUTIVES.**
Handbook of gender & work. Thousand Oaks, CA : Sage Publications, Inc., c1999.
**TC HQ1233 .H33 1999**

Maddock, Su. Challenging women. London ; Thousand Oaks, Calif. : Sage, 1999.
**TC HQ1236 .M342 1999**

**WOMEN - FOLKLORE.**
Mayer, Marianna. Women warriors. New York : Morrow Junior Books, 1999.
**TC PZ8.1.M46 Wo 1999**

**WOMEN, GAY.** *See* **LESBIANS.**

**WOMEN - GERMANY - CONDUCT OF LIFE.**
Büchner, Louise, 1821-1877. [Frauen und ihr Beruf. English] Women and their vocation. New York : P. Lang, c1999.
**TC BJ1610 .B8313 1998**

**WOMEN GRADUATE STUDENTS - DELAWARE - NEWARK - HISTORY.**
Hoffecker, Carol E. Beneath thy guiding hand. Newark, Del. : University of Delaware, c1994.
**TC LD1483 .H64 1994**

**WOMEN - GREAT BRITAIN - BOOKS AND READING - HISTORY - 18TH CENTURY.**
Pearson, Jacqueline, 1949- Women's reading in Britain, 1750-1835. Cambridge, UK ; New York : Cambridge University Press, 1999.
**TC PR756.W65 P43 1999**

**WOMEN - GREAT BRITAIN - BOOKS AND READING - HISTORY - 19TH CENTURY.**
Pearson, Jacqueline, 1949- Women's reading in Britain, 1750-1835. Cambridge, UK ; New York : Cambridge University Press, 1999.
**TC PR756.W65 P43 1999**

TC T61 .A56 47th 1998

**WOMEN IN THE CIVIL SERVICE.** *See also*
**WOMEN IN POLITICS; WOMEN IN PUBLIC LIFE.**
Maddock, Su. Challenging women. London ;
Thousand Oaks, Calif. : Sage, 1999.
*TC HQ1236 .M342 1999*

**WOMEN IN THE LABOR MOVEMENT.** *See*
**WOMEN LABOR LEADERS.**

**Women in the milieu of Leonard and Virginia Woolf** : peace, politics, and education / edited by
Wayne K. Chapman and Janet M. Manson. New
York : Pace University Press, 1998. 279 p. ; 24 cm.
Includes bibliographical references (p. 252-262). ISBN
0-944473-37-7 (cloth) ISBN 0-944473-38-5 (pbk.) DDC 823/
.912
*1. Woolf, Virginia, - 1882-1941 - Friends and associates. 2.
Women in education - Great Britain - History - 20th century. 3.
Women in politics - Great Britain - History - 20th century. 4.
Women and peace - Great Britain - History - 20th century. 5.
Woolf, Leonard, - 1880-1969 - Friends and associates. 6.
London (England) - Intellectual life - 20th century. 7. Women
politicians - Great Britain - Biography. 8. Women educators -
Great Britain - Biography. 9. Women pacifists - Great Britain -
Biography. 10. Bloomsbury group. I. Chapman, Wayne K. II.
Manson, Janet M.*
*TC PR6045.O72 Z925 1998*

**WOMEN IN THE MILITARY.** *See* **WOMEN SOLDIERS.**

**Women in the political economy**
Garey, Anita Ilta, 1947- Weaving work and
motherhood. Philadelphia, PA : Temple University
Press, 1999.
*TC HQ759.48 .G37 1999*

**WOMEN IN THE PROFESSIONS - UNITED STATES - CASE STUDIES.**
Henderson, Katharine Rhodes. The public leadership
of women of faith. 2000.
*TC 06 no. 11276*

**WOMEN IN THE PROFESSIONS - UNITED STATES - CONGRESSES.**
A look backward and forward at American
professional women and their families. Lanham :
University Press of America, 1999.
*TC HQ759.48 .L66 1999*

**WOMEN - JAPAN - SOCIAL CONDITIONS.**
Morley, Patricia A. The mountain is moving.
Washington Square, N.Y. : New York University
Press, 1999.
*TC HQ1762 .M64 1999*

**WOMEN, JEWISH.** *See* **JEWISH WOMEN.**

**WOMEN LABOR LEADERS - CARIBBEAN, ENGLISH-SPEAKING.**
Bolles, Augusta Lynn. We paid our dues. Washington,
D.C. : Howard University Press, 1996.
*TC HD6079.2.C27 B64 1996*

**WOMEN LABOR UNION MEMBERS - CARIBBEAN, ENGLISH-SPEAKING.**
Bolles, Augusta Lynn. We paid our dues. Washington,
D.C. : Howard University Press, 1996.
*TC HD6079.2.C27 B64 1996*

**WOMEN LABOR UNION MEMBERS - UNITED STATES.**
Deslippe, Dennis A. (Dennis Arthur), 1961- Rights,
not roses. Urbana : University of Illinois Press, c2000.
*TC HD6079.2.U5 D47 2000*

**WOMEN - LANGUAGE.**
Coates, Jennifer. Women talk. Oxford, U.K. ;
Cambridge, Mass. : Blackwell Publishers, 1996.
*TC P120.W66 C6 1996*

**WOMEN - LATIN AMERICA - SOCIAL CONDITIONS.**
Social change for women and children. Stamford,
Conn. : JAI Press, 2000.
*TC HQ1421 .S68 2000*

**WOMEN LIFE SCIENTISTS.** *See also* **WOMEN BIOLOGISTS.**
Rosser, Sue Vilhauer. Women, science, and society.
New York : Teachers College Press, c2000.
*TC QH305.5 .R67 2000*

**Women living with self-injury.**
Hyman, Jane Wegscheider. Philadelphia : Temple
University Press, 1999.
*TC RC552.S4 H95 1999*

**WOMEN-MEN RELATIONSHIPS.** *See* **MAN-WOMAN RELATIONSHIPS.**

**WOMEN - MENTAL HEALTH.** *See also*
**WOMEN - PSYCHOLOGY.**
Hyman, Jane Wegscheider. Women living with self-
injury. Philadelphia : Temple University Press, 1999.
*TC RC552.S4 H95 1999*

Woodruff, Debra, 1967- General family functioning,
parental bonding, and attachment style. 1998.
*TC 085 W858*

**WOMEN MINORITIES.** *See* **MINORITY WOMEN.**

**WOMEN MISSIONARIES - HISTORY.**
Gendered missions. Ann Arbor : University of
Michigan Press, c1999.
*TC BV2610 .G46 1999*

**WOMEN, MUSLIM.** *See* **MUSLIM WOMEN.**

**WOMEN, NEGRO.** *See* **AFRO-AMERICAN WOMEN; WOMEN, BLACK.**

**WOMEN - NEW ENGLAND - HISTORY.**
Kelly, Catherine E. In the New England fashion.
Ithaca, N.Y. : Cornell University Press, 1999.
*TC HQ1438.N35 K45 1999*

**WOMEN - OCCUPATIONS.** *See* **WOMEN - EMPLOYMENT.**

**WOMEN-OWNED BUSINESS ENTERPRISES.** *See*
**BUSINESSWOMEN.**

**WOMEN-OWNED BUSINESS ENTERPRISES - UNITED STATES - HISTORY.**
Kwolek-Folland, Angel. Incorporating women. New
York : Twayne Publishers, 1998.
*TC HD6095 .K85 1998*

**WOMEN PACIFISTS.** *See* **WOMEN AND PEACE.**

**WOMEN PACIFISTS - GREAT BRITAIN - BIOGRAPHY.**
Women in the milieu of Leonard and Virginia Woolf.
New York : Pace University Press, 1998.
*TC PR6045.O72 Z925 1998*

**WOMEN PHILANTHROPISTS - UNITED STATES.**
Shaw, Sondra C., 1936- Reinventing fundraising. 1st
ed. San Francisco : Jossey-Bass Publishers, c1995.
*TC HV41.9.U5 S53 1995*

**WOMEN PHOTOGRAPHERS - AUSTRALIA.**
Alexander, George, 1949- Julie Rrap. [Sidney] : Piper
Press, 1998.
*TC TR654 .A44 1998*

**WOMEN PHOTOGRAPHERS - UNITED STATES - BIOGRAPHY.**
Dorothea Lange--a visual life. Washington :
Smithsonian Institution Press, c1994.
*TC TR140.L3 D67 1994*

**WOMEN - PHYSIOLOGY.**
Birke, Lynda I. A. Feminism and the biological body.
New Brunswick, N.J. : Rutgers University Press,
2000.
*TC HQ1190 .B56 2000*

Brook, Barbara, 1949- Feminist perspective on the
body. New York : Longman, 1999.
*TC GT495 .B76 1999*

Vital signs. Edinburgh : Edinburgh University Press,
c1998.
*TC HQ1190 .V56 1998*

**WOMEN - POLAND - SOCIAL CONDITIONS.**
Gontarczyk, Ewa. Kobiecość i męskość jako kategorie
społeczno-kulturowe w studiach feministycznych.
Poznań : Eruditus, 1995.
*TC HQ1181.P7 G66 1995*

**WOMEN POLITICAL ACTIVISTS - UNITED STATES.**
Boehmer, Ulrike, 1959- The personal and the
political. Albany, NY : State University of New York
Press, c2000.
*TC RC280.B8 B62 2000*

**WOMEN - POLITICAL ACTIVITY.** *See* **WOMEN IN POLITICS.**

**WOMEN POLITICIANS - GREAT BRITAIN - BIOGRAPHY.**
Women in the milieu of Leonard and Virginia Woolf.
New York : Pace University Press, 1998.
*TC PR6045.O72 Z925 1998*

**Women, power, and politics**
Bush, Julia. Edwardian ladies and imperial power.
London ; New York : Leicester University Press,
2000.
*TC DA16 .B87 2000*

**WOMEN - PSYCHOLOGY.** *See also*
**LEADERSHIP IN WOMEN; SELF-ESTEEM IN WOMEN.**
André, Serge. [Que veut une femme? English] What
does a woman want? New York : Other Press, c1999.
*TC BF175 .A69613 1999*

Between the lines [videorecording]. Boston, MA :
Fanlight Productions, c1997.
*TC RC552.S4 B4 1997*

Jack, Dana Crowley. Behind the mask. Cambridge,
Mass. ; London : Harvard University Press, 1999.
*TC HQ1206 .J26 1999*

Lee, Christina. Women's health. London : Thousand
Oaks, Calif. : Sage, 1998.
*TC RA564.85 .L443 1998*

Lippert, Robin Alissa. Conflating the self with the
body. 1999.
*TC 085 L655*

Montagu, Ashley, 1905- The natural superiority of
women. 5th ed. Walnut Creek, Calif. : AltaMira Press,
c1999.
*TC HQ1206 .M65 1999*

Practicing feminist ethics in psychology. 1st ed.
Washington, DC : American Psychological
Association, c2000.
*TC BF201.4 .P73 2000*

Unger, Rhoda Kesler. Resisting gender. London ;
Thousand Oaks, Calif. : Sage Publications, 1998.
*TC BF201.4 .U544 1998*

**WOMEN PUBLIC OFFICERS.**
Maddock, Su. Challenging women. London ;
Thousand Oaks, Calif. : Sage, 1999.
*TC HQ1236 .M342 1999*

**WOMEN - PUERTO RICO - SAN JUAN - ECONOMIC CONDITIONS.**
Matos Rodríguez, Félix V., 1962- Women and urban
change in San Juan, Puerto Rico, 1820-1868.
Gainesville, Fla. : University Press of Florida, c1999.
*TC HQ1522 .M38 1999*

**WOMEN - PUERTO RICO - SAN JUAN - HISTORY.**
Matos Rodríguez, Félix V., 1962- Women and urban
change in San Juan, Puerto Rico, 1820-1868.
Gainesville, Fla. : University Press of Florida, c1999.
*TC HQ1522 .M38 1999*

**WOMEN - RELATIONS WITH MEN.** *See* **MAN-WOMAN RELATIONSHIPS.**

**WOMEN - RELIGIOUS LIFE - UNITED STATES.**
Satter, Beryl, 1959- Each mind a kingdom. Berkeley :
University of California Press, c1999.
*TC BF639 .S124 1999*

**WOMEN - RESEARCH - METHODOLOGY.**
Bloom, Leslie Rebecca. Under the sign of hope.
Albany, N.Y. : State University of New York Press,
c1998.
*TC HQ1185 .B56 1998*

**WOMEN - RESEARCH - UNITED STATES.**
Gender, culture, and ethnicity. Mountain View,
Calif. : Mayfield Pub. Co., c1999.
*TC HQ1181.U5 G45 1999*

**WOMEN - RIGHTS OF WOMEN.** *See* **WOMEN'S RIGHTS.**

**WOMEN SCHOOL ADMINISTRATORS.** *See*
**WOMEN SCHOOL PRINCIPALS.**

**WOMEN SCHOOL ADMINISTRATORS - NORTH CAROLINA - BIOGRAPHY.**
Wadelington, Charles Weldon. Charlotte Hawkins
Brown & Palmer Memorial Institute. Chapel Hill ;
London : University of North Carolina Press, c1999.
*TC LA2317.B598 W33 1999*

**WOMEN SCHOOL ADMINISTRATORS - UNITED STATES.**
Curry, Barbara K. Women in power. New York ;
London : Teachers College Press, c2000.
*TC LB2831.62 .C87 2000*

**WOMEN SCHOOL ADMINISTRATORS - UNITED STATES - INTERVIEWS.**
Gardiner, Mary E., 1953- Coloring outside the lines.
Albany : State University of New York Press, c2000.
*TC LB2831.82 .G37 2000*

**WOMEN SCHOOL PRINCIPALS - UNITED STATES.**
Villani, Susan. Are you sure you're the principal?
Thousand Oaks, Calif. : Corwin Press, c1999.
*TC LB2831.92 .V55 1999*

**WOMEN SCHOOL PRINCIPALS - UNITED STATES - CASE STUDIES.**
Smulyan, Lisa. Balancing acts. Albany : State University of New York Press, c2000.
*TC LB2831.92 .S58 2000*

**WOMEN SCHOOL SUPERINTENDENTS - TENNESSEE - BIOGRAPHY.**
McGarrh, Kellie, d. 1995. Kellie McGarrh's hangin' in tough. New York : P. Lang, c2000.
*TC LA2317.D6185 M34 2000*

**WOMEN SCHOOL SUPERINTENDENTS - UNITED STATES.**
Brunner, C. Cryss. Principles of power. Albany, NY : State University of New York Press, c2000.
*TC LB2831.72 .B78 2000*

Sacred dreams. Albany : State University of New York Press, c1999.
*TC LB2831.72 .S23 1999*

**Women, science, and society.**
Rosser, Sue Vilhauer. New York : Teachers College Press, c2000.
*TC QH305.5 .R67 2000*

**WOMEN SCIENCE STUDENTS - STUDY AND TEACHING.**
Samuels, Linda S. Girls can succeed in science!. Thousand Oaks, Calif. : Corwin Press, c1999.
*TC Q181 .S19 1999*

**WOMEN SCIENTISTS - BIOGRAPHY.**
Van der Does, Louise Q. Renaissance women in science. Lanham, Md. : University Press of America, c1999.
*TC Q141 .V25 1999*

**WOMEN SCIENTISTS - EMPLOYMENT - FRANCE.**
Glover, Judith, 1949- Women and scientific employment. Houndmills [England] : Macmillan Press ; New York : St. Martin's Press, 2000.
*TC Q130 .G64 2000*

**WOMEN SCIENTISTS - EMPLOYMENT - GREAT BRITAIN.**
Glover, Judith, 1949- Women and scientific employment. Houndmills [England] : Macmillan Press ; New York : St. Martin's Press, 2000.
*TC Q130 .G64 2000*

**WOMEN SCIENTISTS - EMPLOYMENT - UNITED STATES.**
Glover, Judith, 1949- Women and scientific employment. Houndmills [England] : Macmillan Press ; New York : St. Martin's Press, 2000.
*TC Q130 .G64 2000*

**WOMEN SCIENTISTS - UNITED STATES.**
Howes, Ruth (Ruth Hege) Their day in the sun. Philadelphia, PA : Temple University Press, 1999.
*TC QC773.3.U5 H68 1999*

**WOMEN SCIENTISTS - UNITED STATES - BIOGRAPHY.**
Wasserman, Elga R. (Elga Ruth) The door in the dream. Washington, D.C. : Joseph Henry Press, c2000.
*TC QH26 .W375 2000*

**WOMEN SCULPTORS - UNITED STATES - BIOGRAPHY.**
Nevelson in process [videorecording]. Chicago, IL : Public Media Inc., 1977.
*TC NB237.N43 N43 1977*

**WOMEN - SERVICES FOR.** *See* **SOCIAL WORK WITH WOMEN.**

**WOMEN - SEXUAL BEHAVIOR.**
Sexual behavior in the human female. Bloomington, Ind. : Indiana University Press, [1998]
*TC HQ29 .S487 1998*

**WOMEN - SEXUAL BEHAVIOR - UNITED STATES.**
Hite, Shere. The Hite report. New York : Dell, 1987.
*TC HQ29 .H57 1987*

**WOMEN SLAVES - UNITED STATES - BIOGRAPHY.**
Jacobs, Harriet A. (Harriet Ann), 1813-1897. Incidents in the life of a slave girl : written by herself. Cambridge, Mass. : Harvard University Press, 2000.
*TC E444.J17 A3 2000c*

**WOMEN - SOCIAL CONDITIONS.**
Gender and society. Oxford ; New York : Oxford University Press, 2000.
*TC HQ1075 .G4619 2000*

**WOMEN - SOCIAL CONDITIONS - STATISTICS - PERIODICALS.**
The progress of nations. New York, NY : UNICEF, 1993-
*TC RA407.A1 P76*

**WOMEN SOCIAL REFORMERS, AFRO-AMERICAN.** *See* **AFRO-AMERICAN WOMEN SOCIAL REFORMERS.**

**WOMEN SOCIAL REFORMERS - UNITED STATES.** *See* **AFRO-AMERICAN WOMEN SOCIAL REFORMERS.**

**WOMEN SOCIAL REFORMERS - UNITED STATES - CASE STUDIES.**
Henderson, Katharine Rhodes. The public leadership of women of faith. 2000.
*TC 06 no. 11276*

**WOMEN SOCIAL REFORMERS - UNITED STATES - HISTORY.**
Goodwin, Lorine Swainston, 1925- The pure food, drink, and drug crusaders, 1879-1914. Jefferson, N.C. : McFarland, 1999.
*TC HD9000.9.U5 G66 1999*

**WOMEN SOCIALISTS - FRANCE - BIOGRAPHY.**
Gordon, Felicia. Early French feminisms, 1830-1940. Cheltenham, U.K. ; Brookfield, Vt. : Edward Elgar, c1996.
*TC HQ1615.A3 G67 1996*

**WOMEN - SOCIALIZATION - UNITED STATES.**
Proweller, Amira. Constructing female identities. Albany : State University of New York Press, c1998.
*TC LC1755 .P76 1998*

**WOMEN SOLDIERS - FRANCE - BIOGRAPHY - JUVENILE LITERATURE.**
Hodges, Margaret, 1911- Joan of Arc. 1st ed. New York : Holiday House, c1999.
*TC DC103.5 .H64 1999*

**WOMEN SOLDIERS - UNITED STATES - CONGRESSES.**
A look backward and forward at American professional women and their families. Lanham : University Press of America, 1999.
*TC HQ759.48 .L66 1999*

**WOMEN - SOUTHERN STATES.**
Abbott, Shirley Womenfolks, growing up down South. Boston : Houghton Mifflin, c1998.
*TC HQ1438.S63 A33 1998*

**WOMEN - SOUTHERN STATES - HISTORY.**
Kierner, Cynthia A., 1958- Beyond the household. Ithaca, NY : Cornell University Press, 1998.
*TC HQ1391.U5 K55 1998*

**WOMEN - SOUTHERN STATES - SOCIAL CONDITIONS - CASE STUDIES.**
Key, Daphne. Literacy shutdown. Newark, Del. : International Reading Association ; Chicago, Ill. : National Reading Conference, c1998.
*TC LC1752 .K49 1998*

**WOMEN - SPORTS.** *See* **SPORTS FOR WOMEN.**

**WOMEN STUDIES.** *See* **WOMEN'S STUDIES.**

**WOMEN - STUDY AND TEACHING.** *See* **WOMEN'S STUDIES.**

**WOMEN - SUBSTANCE USE - PREVENTION.**
Cohen, Monique. Counseling addicted women. Thousand Oaks, Calif. : Sage Publications, c2000.
*TC HV4999.W65 C64 2000*

**WOMEN - SUBSTANCE USE - UNITED STATES.**
Pagliaro, Ann M. Substance use among women. Philadelphia, PA : Brunner/Mazel, c2000.
*TC RC564.5.W65 P34 2000*

**Women talk.**
Coates, Jennifer. Oxford, U.K. ; Cambridge, Mass. : Blackwell Publishers, 1996.
*TC P120.W66 C6 1996*

**WOMEN TEACHERS.** *See* **LESBIAN TEACHERS; WOMEN COLLEGE TEACHERS.**

**WOMEN TEACHERS, AFRO-AMERICAN.** *See* **AFRO-AMERICAN WOMEN TEACHERS.**

**WOMEN TEACHERS, BLACK - CANADA - SOCIAL CONDITIONS - CASE STUDIES.**
Henry, Annette, 1955- Taking back control. Albany : State University of New York Press, c1998.
*TC LB1775.4.C2 H45 1998*

**WOMEN TEACHERS - SOUTH AFRICA.**
Mahlase, Shirley Motleke. The careers of women teachers under apartheid. Harare : SAPES Books, c1997.
*TC LB2832.4.S6 M35 1997*

**Women teachers under apartheid.**
Mahlase, Shirley Motleke. The careers of women teachers under apartheid. Harare : SAPES Books, c1997.
*TC LB2832.4.S6 M35 1997*

**WOMEN TEACHERS - UNITED STATES.** *See* **AFRO-AMERICAN WOMEN TEACHERS.**

**WOMEN TEACHERS - UNITED STATES - ATTITUDES.**
Wise women. New York ; London : Routledge, 2000.
*TC LB2837 .W58 2000*

**WOMEN - UNITED STATES.** *See* **AFRO-AMERICAN WOMEN; CHINESE AMERICAN WOMEN; CROW WOMEN.**

**WOMEN - UNITED STATES - ATTITUDES - CASE STUDIES.**
Henderson, Katharine Rhodes. The public leadership of women of faith. 2000.
*TC 06 no. 11276*

**WOMEN - UNITED STATES - BIOGRAPHY.**
Kuhn, Annette. Family secrets. London ; New York : Verso, 1995.
*TC CT274 .K84 1995*

Quesnell, Quentin. The strange disappearance of Sophia Smith. Northampton [Mass.] : Smith College, c1999.
*TC LD7152.65.S45 Q84 1999*

**WOMEN - UNITED STATES - BIOGRAPHY - ENCYCLOPEDIAS.**
Her heritage [computer file]. Cambridge, MA : Pilgrim New Media, c1994. Interactive multimedia.
*TC HQ1412 .A43 1994*

**WOMEN - UNITED STATES - ENCYCLOPEDIAS.**
Women's studies encyclopedia. Rev. and expanded ed. Westport, Conn. : Greenwood Press, c1999.
*TC HQ1115 .W645 1999*

**WOMEN - UNITED STATES - HISTORIOGRAPHY.**
Quesnell, Quentin. The strange disappearance of Sophia Smith. Northampton [Mass.] : Smith College, c1999.
*TC LD7152.65.S45 Q84 1999*

**WOMEN - UNITED STATES - HISTORY - ATLASES.**
Opdycke, Sandra. The Routledge historical atlas of women in America. New York : Routledge, 2000.
*TC HQ1410 .P68 2000*

**WOMEN - UNITED STATES - HISTORY - SOURCES.**
Women's America. 5th ed. New York : Oxford University Press, 2000.
*TC HQ1426 .W663 2000*

Women's voices. Detroit : UXL, 1997.
*TC HQ1410 .W688 1997*

**WOMEN - UNITED STATES - IDENTITY - CASE STUDIES.**
Weiler, Jeanne. Codes and contradictions. Albany : State University of New York Press, c2000.
*TC LC1755 .W45 2000*

**WOMEN - UNITED STATES - PSYCHOLOGY.**
Gender, culture, and ethnicity. Mountain View, Calif. : Mayfield Pub. Co., c1999.
*TC HQ1181.U5 G45 1999*

Manton, Catherine, 1942- Fed up. Westport, Conn. : Bergin & Garvey, 1999.
*TC HQ1410 .M355 1999*

**WOMEN - UNITED STATES - SOCIAL CONDITIONS.**
Manton, Catherine, 1942- Fed up. Westport, Conn. : Bergin & Garvey, 1999.
*TC HQ1410 .M355 1999*

Social change for women and children. Stamford, Conn. : JAI Press, 2000.
*TC HQ1421 .S68 2000*

**WOMEN VOLUNTEERS IN SOCIAL SERVICES - NEW YORK (STATE) - SUFFOLK COUNTY.**
Robinson, Anna Bess. Leadership development in women's civic organizations. 1999.
*TC 06 no. 11168*

**Women warriors.**
Mayer, Marianna. New York : Morrow Junior Books, 1999.
*TC PZ8.1.M46 Wo 1999*

**Women with intellectual disabilities :** finding a place in the world / edited by Rannveig Traustadóttir and Kelley Johnson. London ; Philadelphia : Jessica Kingsley Publishers, 2000. 303 p. ; 24 cm. Includes bibliographical references (p. 284-295) and indexes. ISBN 1-85302-846-0 (pbk. : alk. paper) DDC 362.3/0082
*1. Mentally handicapped women. I. Rannveig Traustadóttir, 1950- II. Johnson, Kelley, 1947-*
*TC HV3009.5.W65 W66 2000*

**WOMEN - WOUNDS AND INJURIES.** *See* **BATTERED WOMAN SYNDROME.**

**Womenfolks, growing up down South.**
Abbott, Shirley Boston : Houghton Mifflin, c1998.
*TC HQ1438.S63 A33 1998*

**Women's America :** refocusing the past / edited by Linda K. Kerber, Jane Sherron De Hart. 5th ed. New York : Oxford University Press, 2000. xii, 660 p. : ill. ; 26cm. Includes bibliographical references and index. ISBN 0-19-512180-5 ISBN 0-19-512181-3 (pbk.) DDC 305.4/0973
*1. Women - United States - History - Sources. 2. Women - Employment - United States - History - Sources. 3. Women in politics - United States - History - Sources. 4. Women - Health and hygiene - United States - History - Sources. 5. Feminism - United States - History - Sources. I. Kerber, Linda K. II. De Hart, Jane Sherron.*
*TC HQ1426 .W663 2000*

**WOMEN'S CLOTHING.** *See* **CLOTHING AND DRESS; COSTUME.**

**WOMEN'S COLLEGES - ENGLAND - BUILDINGS.**
Vickery, Margaret Birney, 1963- Buildings for bluestockings. Newark [Del.] : University of Delaware Press ; London ; Cranbury, NJ : Associated University Presses, c1999.
*TC NA6605.G7 V53 1999*

**WOMEN'S COLLEGES - MASSACHUSETTS - NORTHAMPTON - HISTORY.**
Quesnell, Quentin. The strange disappearance of Sophia Smith. Northampton [Mass.] : Smith College, c1999.
*TC LD7152.65.S45 Q84 1999*

**WOMEN'S COLLEGES - SOCIAL ASPECTS - ENGLAND - HISTORY - 19TH CENTURY.**
Vickery, Margaret Birney, 1963- Buildings for bluestockings. Newark [Del.] : University of Delaware Press ; London ; Cranbury, NJ : Associated University Presses, c1999.
*TC NA6605.G7 V53 1999*

**WOMEN'S EDUCATION.** *See* **WOMEN - EDUCATION.**

**Women's experience series**
(10) McLeod, Ellen Mary Easton, 1945- In good hands. Montreal ; Ithaca : Published for Carleton University by McGill-Queen's University Press, c1999.
*TC NK841 .M38 1999*

**Women's health.**
Lee, Christina. London ; Thousand Oaks, Calif. : Sage, 1998.
*TC RA564.85 .L443 1998*

**WOMEN'S HEALTH.**
Goldman, Marlene. Women and health. San Diego, Calif. : Academic, c2000.
*TC RA564.85 .G66 2000*

Redman, Barbara Klug. Women's health needs in patient education. New York : Springer Pub. Co., c1999.
*TC R727.4 .R43 1999*

**Women's health needs in patient education.**
Redman, Barbara Klug. New York : Springer Pub. Co., c1999.
*TC R727.4 .R43 1999*

**Women's history**
Webster, Wendy. Imagining home. London ; Bristol, Pa. : UCL Press, 1998.
*TC HQ1593 .W43 1998*

**WOMEN'S LEADERSHIP.** *See* **LEADERSHIP IN WOMEN.**

**WOMEN'S LIB.** *See* **FEMINISM.**

**WOMEN'S LIBERATION.** *See* **WOMEN'S RIGHTS.**

**WOMEN'S LIBERATION MOVEMENT.** *See* **FEMINISM.**

**Women's market handbook.**
Nelson, Carol, 1953- Detroit : Gale Research, c1994.
*TC HF5415 .N3495 1994*

**WOMEN'S MOVEMENT.** *See* **FEMINISM.**

**Women's philosophies of education :** thinking through our mothers / edited by Connie Titone, Karen E. Maloney. Upper Saddle River, N.J. : Merrill, c1999. x, 214 p. : ill. ; 24 cm. Includes bibliographical references and index. ISBN 0-13-618042-6 DDC 371.822
*1. Women - Education - United States - History. 2. Women in education - United States - History. 3. Women educators - United States - Biography. I. Titone, Connie. II. Maloney, Karen E.*
*TC LC1752 .T46 1999*

**Women's reading in Britain, 1750-1835.**
Pearson, Jacqueline, 1949- Cambridge, UK ; New York : Cambridge University Press, 1999.
*TC PR756.W65 P43 1999*

**WOMEN'S RIGHTS.** *See* **SEX DISCRIMINATION AGAINST WOMEN.**

**WOMEN'S RIGHTS - INTERNATIONAL COOPERATION.**
Loud, proud & passionate. 1st ed. Eugene, OR : Mobility International USA, 1997.
*TC HV1569.3.W65 L68 1997*

**WOMEN'S RIGHTS - UNITED STATES - HISTORY - SOURCES.**
Women's voices. Detroit : UXL, 1997.
*TC HQ1410 .W688 1997*

**WOMEN'S STUDIES.**
Rosser, Sue Vilhauer. Women, science, and society. New York : Teachers College Press, c2000.
*TC HQ305.5 .R67 2000*

**WOMEN'S STUDIES - BIOGRAPHICAL METHODS.**
Bloom, Leslie Rebecca. Under the sign of hope. Albany, N.Y. : State University of New York Press, c1998.
*TC HQ1185 .B56 1998*

**Women's studies encyclopedia** / edited by Helen Tierney. Rev. and expanded ed. Westport, Conn. : Greenwood Press, c1999. 3 v. (xi, 1607 p.) ; 25 cm. Includes bibliographical references and index. Also available on CD-ROM. ISBN 0-313-29620-0 (set : alk. paper) ISBN 0-313-31071-8 (v. 1 : alk. paper) ISBN 0-313-31072-6 (v. 2 : alk. paper) ISBN 0-313-31073-4 (v. 3 : alk. paper) DDC 305.4/03
*1. Women - United States - Encyclopedias. 2. Women - Encyclopedias. 3. Feminism - Encyclopedias. I. Tierney, Helen.*
*TC HQ1115 .W645 1999*

**WOMEN'S STUDIES - NEW YORK (STATE).**
Mandle, Joan D. Can we wear our pearls and still be feminists? Columbia : University of Missouri Press, c2000.
*TC HQ1181.U5 M37 2000*

**WOMEN'S STUDIES - POLAND.**
Gontarczyk, Ewa. Kobiecość i męskość jako kategorie społeczno-kulturowe w studiach feministycznych. Poznań : Eruditus, 1995.
*TC HQ1181.P7 G66 1995*

**WOMEN'S STUDIES - STUDY AND TEACHING - UNITED STATES.**
Teaching introduction to women's studies. Westport, Conn. : Bergin & Garvey, 1999.
*TC HQ1181.U5 T43 1999*

**WOMEN'S STUDIES - UNITED STATES.**
Coming into her own. San Francisco, Calif. : Jossey-Bass, c1999.
*TC LC1503 .C65 1999*

Teaching introduction to women's studies. Westport, Conn. : Bergin & Garvey, 1999.
*TC HQ1181.U5 T43 1999*

**WOMEN'S STUDIES - WISCONSIN - HISTORY.**
Transforming women's education. Madison, WI : Office of University Publications for the University of Wisconsin System, Women's Studies Consortium, 1999.
*TC HQ1181.U5 T77 1999*

**Women's voices :** a documentary history of women in America / edited by Lorie Jenkins McElroy. Detroit : UXL, 1997. 2 v. (xvi, 170 p.) : ill. ; 25 cm. Includes bibliographical references and indexes. CONTENTS: v. 1. Education, abolition, suffrage -- v. 2. Property, equality, reproduction. ISBN 0-7876-0663-4 (set : acid-free paper) ISBN 0-7876-0664-2 (v. 1 : acid-free paper) ISBN 0-7876-0665-0 (v. 2 : acid-free paper) DDC 305.4/0973
*1. Women - United States - History - Sources. 2. Women's rights - United States - History - Sources. I. McElroy, Lorie Jenkins.*
*TC HQ1410 .W688 1997*

**WOMON.** *See* **WOMEN.**

**WOMYN.** *See* **WOMEN.**

**Wonders, warriors, and beasts abounding.**
Barr, Beryl. [1st ed.]. Garden City, N.Y., Doubleday [1967]
*TC N8217.G8 B33*

**The wonderworld of science.** New York : Scribner, c1952. v. : ill. (some col.) ; 21 cm. Includes index.
*1. Science - Study and teaching.*
*TC Q161.2 .W66 1952*

**Wong, Kenneth K., 1955-** Funding public schools : politics and policies / Kenneth K. Wong. Lawrence : University Press of Kansas, c1999. xi, 208 p. : ill. ; 24 cm. (Studies in government and public policy) Includes bibliographical references (p. 163-196) and index. ISBN 0-7006-0987-3 (hbk. : alk. paper) ISBN 0-7006-0988-1 (pbk. : alk. paper) DDC 379.73
*1. Education - United States - Finance. 2. Politics and education - United States. 3. Education and state - United States. I. Title. II. Series.*
*TC LB2825 .W56 1999*

**Wong, Lana.**
Shootback. London : Booth-Clibborn, 1999.
*TC HV4160.5.N34 S45 1999*

**Wong, Sau-ling Cynthia.**
New immigrants in the United States. Cambridge, U.K. ; New York : Cambridge University Press, 2000.
*TC PE1128 .N384 1999*

**Woo, Deborah Gee.**
Morrow, Lesley Mandel. Literacy instruction in half- and whole-day kindergarten. Newark, Del. : International Reading Association ; Chicago, Ill. : National Reading Conference, c1998.
*TC LB1181.2 .M67 1998*

**Woo, Kimberley Ann.** "Double happiness," double jeopardy : exploring ways in which ethnicity, gender, and high school influence the social construction of identity in Chinese American girls / by Kimberley Ann Woo. 1999. 166 leaves ; 29 cm. Typescript; issued also on microfilm. Thesis (Ed.D.)--Teachers College, Columbia University, 1999. Includes bibliographical references (leaves 148-157).
*1. Chinese American children - Education (Secondary) - New York (State) - New York - Social conditions - Case studies. 2. Girls - Ethnic identity. 3. Chinese Americans - Family relationship. 4. High school students - Social life and customs. 5. Identity (Psychology) in adolescence - Social aspects. 6. Gender identity. 7. Ethnicity. 8. Self-perception. 9. Intergenerational relations. I. Title. II. Title: Exploring ways in which ethnicity, gender, and high school influence the social construction of identity in Chinese American girls*
*TC 06 no. 11075*

**Wood, Angela.**
Richardson, Robin. Inclusive schools, inclusive society. Stoke on Trent, Staffordshire, England : Trentham Books, 1999.
*TC LC212.3.G7 R523 1999*

**WOOD-CARVING - BRITISH COLUMBIA.** *See* **KWAKIUTL WOOD-CARVING.**

**WOOD-CARVING - ENGLAND.**
Esterly, David. Grinling Gibbons and the art of carving. New York : H.N. Abrams, 1998.
*TC NK9798.G5 E88 1998*

**WOOD-CARVING, KWAKIUTL.** *See* **KWAKIUTL WOOD-CARVING.**

**WOOD-CARVING, PRIMITIVE.** *See* **WOOD-CARVING.**

**WOOD - DETERIORATION.** *See* **TERMITES.**

**WOOD-ENGRAVING, AUSTRALIAN - EXHIBITIONS.**
National Gallery of Victoria. In relief. Melbourne : National Gallery of Victoria, c1997.
*TC NE1190.25 .G72 1997*

**Wood-fired ceramics.**
Minogue, Coll. London : A & C Black ; Philadelphia : University of Pennsylvania Press, 2000.
*TC TP841 .M57 2000*

**Wood, Frank H. (Frank Henderson), 1929-.**
Punishment and aversive stimulation in special education. Reston, Va. : Council for Exceptional Children, 1982.
*TC LC4169 .P8 1982*

**WOOD FURNITURE.** *See* **FURNITURE.**

**Wood, Irene.**
CD-ROMS for kids :. [Chicago, Ill.] : American Library Association, Booklist Publications, 1997.

*TC QA76.76.C54 C47 1997*
Culturally diverse videos, audios, and CD-ROMS for children and young adults. New York : Neal-Schuman Publishers, 1999.
*TC PN1998 .M85 1999*

**Wood, Karen D.**
Promoting literacy in grades 4-9. Boston ; London : Allyn and Bacon, c2000.
*TC LB1576 .P76 2000*

**Wood, Margaret, 1957-.**
Hoy, Charles, 1939- Improving quality in education. London ; New York : Falmer Press, 2000.
*TC LB2822.84.G7 H69 1999*

**Wood, Margo, 1939-.**
O'Donnell, Michael P. Becoming a reader. 2nd ed. Boston : Allyn and Bacon, c1999.
*TC LB1050.53 .O35 1999*

**Wood, Maude Aurilla, 1877- joint author.**
Woellner, Elizabeth H. Requirements for certification: Chicago : University of Chicago Press, 1935-
*TC LB1771 .W6*

**Wood, Nigel.** Chinese glazes : their origins, chemistry, and recreation / Nigel Wood. Philadelphia, Pa. : University of Pennylvania Press, 1999. 280 p. : ill. (some col.) ; 29 cm. Includes bibliographical references and index. ISBN 0-8122-3476-6 DDC 738.1/27/0951
*1. Glazes. 2. Pottery, Oriental. I. Title.*
*TC TP812 .W65 1999*

**Wood, Robert E., 1934-** Placing aesthetics : reflections on the philosophic tradition / Robert E. Wood. Athens, OH : Ohio University Press, c1999. xvi, 413 p. : ill. ; 24 cm. (Series in Continental thought ; 26) Includes bibliographical references (p. [391]-406) and indexes. ISBN 0-8214-1280-9 (alk. paper) ISBN 0-8214-1281-7 (pbk. : alk. paper) DDC 111/.85/09
*1. Aesthetics - History. I. Title. II. Series.*
*TC BH81 .W66 1999*

**WOOD SCULPTURE, BAOULÉ.**
Ravenhill, Philip L. Dreams and reverie. Washington : Smithsonian Institution Press, c1996.
*TC NB1255.C85 R38 1996*

**WOODEN FURNITURE.** *See* **FURNITURE.**

**Woodhead, Martin.**
Making sense of social development. London ; New York : Routledge in association with the Open University, 1999.
*TC HQ783 .L57 1999*

**Woodhouse, Tom.**
Miall, Hugh. Contemporary conflict resolution. Cambridge, UK : Polity Press ; Malden, MA : Blackwell, 1999.
*TC JZ6010 .M53 1999*

**Woodring, Carl, 1919-** Literature : an embattled profession / Carl Woodring. New York : Columbia University Press, 1999. xiv, 220 p. ; 23 cm. Includes bibliographical references and index. ISBN 0-231-11522-9 (cloth) DDC 807/.1/173
*1. Literature - Study and teaching (Higher) - United States. 2. Critical theory. 3. College teachers - Tenure - United States. I. Title.*
*TC PN70 .W66 1999*

**Woodruff, Debra, 1967-** General family functioning, parental bonding, and attachment style : familial factors influencing the severity and type of symptomotology in adult women who report childhood sexual abuse and nonabused psychiatric outpatients / Debra Lynne Woodruff. 1998. vi, 93 leaves ; 29 cm. Issued also on microfilm. Thesis (Ph.D.)--Columbia University, 1998. Includes bibliographical references (leaves 87-93).
*1. Adult child sexual abuse victims - Mental health. 2. Incest victims - Mental health. 3. Women - Mental health. 4. Psychoanalysis. 5. Communication in the family. 6. Family - Psychological aspects. 7. Attachment behavior. I. Title.*
*TC 085 W858*

**Woods, David, 1942-.**
Brighouse, Tim. How to improve your school. London ; New York : Routledge, 1999.
*TC LB2822.84.G7 B75 1999*

**Woods, Peter, 1934-** Multicultural children in the early years : creative teaching, meaningful learning / Peter Woods, Mari Boyle, and Nick Hubbard. Clevedon ; Philadelphia : Multilingual Matters Ltd, c1999. x, 226 p. : ill. ; 23 cm. (Bilingual education and bilingualism ; 16) Includes bibliographical references (p. 210-219) and index. ISBN 1-85359-435-0 (alk. paper) ISBN 1-85359-434-2 (pbk. : alk. paper) DDC 370.117
*1. Children of minorities - Education (Early childhood) - Great Britain - Case studies. 2. Education, Bilingual - Great Britain -*
*Case studies. 3. Multiculturalism - Study and teaching (Early childhood) - Great Britain - Case studies. 4. Curriculum planning - Great Britain - Case studies. 5. Home and school - Great Britain - Case studies. 6. Educational change - Great Britain - Case studies. I. Boyle, Mari. II. Hubbard, Nick. III. Title. IV. Series.*
*TC LC3736.G6 W66 1999*

**Woods, Robert T.**
Psychological problems of ageing. Chichester ; New York : Wiley, c1999.
*TC RC451.4.A5 P7774 1999*

**Woodward, Diana, 1948-** Managing equal opportunities in higher education : a guide to understanding and action / Diana Woodward and Karen Ross with John Bird and Graham Upton. Buckingham [England] ; Philadelphia : Society for Research into Higher Education : Open University Press, 2000. ix, 174 p. ; 24 cm. Includes bibliographical references and index. ISBN 0-335-19561-X (hb) ISBN 0-335-19560-1 (pb) DDC 379.2/6
*1. Educational equalization - Great Britain. 2. Discrimination in higher education - Great Britain. 3. Minorities - Education (Higher) - Great Britain. I. Ross, Karen, 1957- II. Title.*
*TC LC213.3.G7 W66 2000*

**WOODWORK.** *See* **WOOD-CARVING.**

**WOODY PLANTS.** *See* **TREES.**

**WOOL.** *See* **SHEEP.**

**Woolbright, Meg, 1955-.**
Stories from the center. Urbana, Ill. National Council of Teachers of English, c2000.
*TC PE1404 .S834 2000*

**Woolf, Felicity.** Picture this century : an introduction to twentieth-century art / Felicity Woolf. New York : Doubleday Book for Young Readers, c1992. 40 p. : col. ill. ; 24 x 26 cm. Includes index. Summary: Surveys the subject matter and techniques used by various artists and movements in Europe and North America in the twentieth century, discussing such topics as cubism, abstract art, and pop art. ISBN 0-385-30852-3 DDC 709/.04
*1. Art, Modern - 20th century - Juvenile literature. 2. Art, Modern - 20th century. 3. Art appreciation. I. Title.*
*TC N6490 .W66 1992*

**WOOLF, LEONARD, 1880-1969 - FRIENDS AND ASSOCIATES.**
Women in the milieu of Leonard and Virginia Woolf. New York : Pace University Press, 1998.
*TC PR6045.O72 Z925 1998*

**WOOLF, VIRGINIA, 1882-1941 - FRIENDS AND ASSOCIATES.**
Women in the milieu of Leonard and Virginia Woolf. New York : Pace University Press, 1998.
*TC PR6045.O72 Z925 1998*

**Woolfolk, Anita.**
Readings in educational psychology. 2nd ed. Boston : Allyn and Bacon, c1998.
*TC LB1051 .R386 1998*

**Woolls, Blanche.** The school library media manager / Blanche Woolls. 2nd ed. Englewood, CO : Libraries Unlimited, 1999. xiv, 340 p. ; 26 cm. (Library and information science text series) Includes bibliographical references and index. ISBN 1-56308-772-3 (hardbound) ISBN 1-56308-702-2 (softbound) DDC 025.1/978
*1. School libraries - United States - Administration. 2. Media programs (Education) - United States - Administration. I. Title. II. Series: Library science text series.*
*TC Z675.S3 W8735 1999*

**WORD-BLINDNESS, PARTIAL.** *See* **DYSLEXIA.**

**WORD BOOKS.** *See* **VOCABULARY.**

**WORD DEAFNESS.** *See* **AUDITORY PERCEPTION.**

**Word identification strategies.**
Fox, Barbara J. 2nd ed. Upper Saddle River, N.J. : Merrill, c2000.
*TC LB1050.34 .F69 2000*

**Word matters.**
Pinnell, Gay Su. Portsmouth, NH : Heinemann, c1998.
*TC LB1573.3 .P55 1998*

**WORD PROBLEMS.**
Word problems [videorecording]. Princeton, N.J. : Video Tutor, 1988.
*TC QA139 .W6 1988*

**Word problems** [videorecording] / Video Tutor, Inc. Princeton, N.J. : Video Tutor, 1988. 1 videocassette (VHS) (ca. 63 min.) : sd., col. ; 1/2 in. + 1 student workbook & pre/post test system ([8] p. ; 19 cm.). (Video tutor instructional series) (A mathematics series) Title on container: Basic word problems [videorecording]. Title on cassette label: Video Tutor
Inc. presents basic word problems [videorecording]. VHS. Catalogued from credits, cassette label and container. John Hall, instructor. For grades 5-9 math classes.
*1. Word problems. 2. Arithmetic - Problems, exercises, etc. I. Hall, John. II. Video Tutor. III. Title: Basic word problems [videorecording] IV. Title: Video Tutor Inc. presents basic word problems [videorecording] V. Series. VI. Series: A mathematics series*
*TC QA139 .W6 1988*

**WORD PROCESSING IN EDUCATION.**
Quann, Steve. Learning computers, speaking English. Ann Arbor : University of Michigan Press, c2000.
*TC PE1128.A2 .Q83 2000*

**Word, Reagan, ill.**
Wright, Alexandra. Alice in Pastaland. Watertown, Mass. : Charlesbridge, 1997.
*TC PZ7.W9195 Al 19997*

**WORD RECOGNITION.**
Words their way. 2nd ed. Upper Saddle River, N.J. : Merrill, c2000.
*TC LB1050.44 .B43 2000*

**Word wizard.**
Falwell, Cathryn. New York : Clarion Books, c1998.
*TC PZ7.F198 Wo 1998*

**Words and pictures.**
Mikkelsen, Nina. Boston : McGraw-Hill, c2000.
*TC LB1575 .M55 2000*

**Words in the wilderness.**
Brown, Stephen Gilbert. Albany : State University of New York Press, c2000.
*TC E99.A86 B76 2000*

**Words, script, and pictures.**
Schapiro, Meyer, 1904- New York, NY : George Braziller, 1996.
*TC P93.5 .S33 1996*

**WORDS, STOCK OF.** *See* **VOCABULARY.**

**Words their way :** word study for phonics, vocabulary, and spelling instruction / Donald R. Bear ... [et al.]. 2nd ed. Upper Saddle River, N.J. : Merrill, c2000. xv, 415 p. : ill. ; 28 cm. Includes bibliographical references (p. 405-409) and index. ISBN 0-13-021339-X (pbk.) DDC 372.46/2
*1. Word recognition. 2. Reading - Phonetic method. 3. English language - Orthography and spelling. I. Bear, Donald R.*
*TC LB1050.44 .B43 2000*

**Worell, Judith, 1928-.**
Beyond appearance. 1st ed. Washington, DC : American Psychological Association, c1999.
*TC HQ798 .B43 1999*

**WORK.** *See* **LABOR; OCCUPATIONS; PERFORMANCE; QUALITY OF WORK LIFE.**

**Work and career paths of midlevel administrators.**
Understanding the work and career paths of midlevel administrators. San Francisco : Jossey-Bass, 2000.
*TC LB2341 .N5111 2000*

**WORK AND FAMILY.** *See also* **DUAL-CAREER FAMILIES.**
Organizational change & gender equity. Thousand Oaks : Sage Publications, c2000.
*TC HD58.8 .O7289 2000*

**WORK AND FAMILY - UNITED STATES.**
Williams, Joan, 1952- Unbending gender. Oxford ; New York : Oxford University Press, c2000.
*TC HD4904.25 .W55 2000*

**WORK AND FAMILY - UNITED STATES - CASE STUDIES.**
Garey, Anita Ilta, 1947- Weaving work and motherhood. Philadelphia, PA : Temple University Press, 1999.
*TC HQ759.48 .G37 1999*

**WORK AND FAMILY - UNITED STATES - CONGRESSES.**
A look backward and forward at American professional women and their families. Lanham : University Press of America, 1999.
*TC HQ759.48 .L66 1999*

**WORK AND FAMILY - UNITED STATES - FORECASTING.**
Williams, Joan, 1952- Unbending gender. Oxford ; New York : Oxford University Press, c2000.
*TC HD4904.25 .W55 2000*

**WORK AND FAMILY - UNITED STATES - PSYCHOLOGICAL ASPECTS.**
Levine, James A. Working fathers. Reading, Mass. : Addison-Wesley, c1997.

**TC HQ756 .L474 1997**

**Work and well-being :** an agenda for the 1990s / edited by Gwendolyn Puryear Keita and Steven L. Sauter. Washington, DC : American Psychological Association, c1992. viii, 228 p. : ill. ; 26 cm. Papers presented at a conference held in Washington, D.C. Nov. 15-17, 1990, sponsored by the American Psychological Association and the National Institute for Occupational Safety and Health. Includes bibliographical references and index. ISBN 1-55798-153-1 DDC 158.7
*1. Industrial psychiatry - Congresses. 2. Job stress - Congresses. I. Keita, Gwendolyn Puryear. II. Sauter, Steven L., 1946- III. American Psychological Association. IV. National Institute for Occupational Safety and Health.*
**TC RC967.5 .W67 1992**

**Work based learning.**
Raelin, Joseph A., 1948- Reading, MA : Addison-Wesley, 1999.
**TC HD30.4 .R33 1999**

**WORK ENVIRONMENT.** *See* **HOMOSEXUALITY IN THE WORKPLACE; SEX ROLE IN THE WORK ENVIRONMENT.**

**WORK ETHIC - STUDY AND TEACHING - UNITED STATES.**
Annual State of American Education Address (7th : February 22, 2000 : Durham, N.C.) The seventh annual state of American education address [videorecording. [Washington, D.C. : U.S. Dept. of Education], 2000.

**WORK EXPERIENCE.** *See* **VOCATIONAL EDUCATION.**

**WORK - FICTION.**
Hill, T. L. Morris and the kingdom of Knoll. Malibu, Calif. : J. Paul Getty Museum and Children's Library Press, c1996.
**TC PZ7.H55744 Mo 1996**

**WORK FORCE.** *See* **LABOR SUPPLY.**

**WORK GROUPS.**
Katz, Tal Y. Self-construal as a moderator of the effects of task and reward interdependence of group performance. 1999.
**TC 085 K1524**

**WORK - LAW AND LEGISLATION.** *See* **LABOR LAWS AND LEGISLATION.**

**WORK LIFE, QUALITY OF.** *See* **QUALITY OF WORK LIFE.**

**WORK, METHOD OF.** *See* **WORK.**

**The work of nature.**
Baskin, Yvonne. Washington, D.C. : Island Press, 1997.
**TC GE195 .B36 1997**

**The work of the imagination.**
Harris, Paul. L. Oxford : Blackwell Publishers, 2000.
**TC BF723.I5 H37a 2000**

**WORK - PHYSIOLOGICAL ASPECTS.** *See* **JOB STRESS.**

**WORK - PSYCHOLOGICAL ASPECTS.** *See also* **JOB STRESS.**
Grimshaw, Jennie. Employment and health. London : British Library, 1999.
**TC HF5548.85 .G75 1999**

Jevne, Ronna Fay. When dreams don't work. Amityville, N.Y. : Baywood Pub., c1998.
**TC BF481 .J48 1998**

Peterson, Nadene. The role of work in people's lives. Australia ; Belmont, Calif. : Wadsworth Pub. Co., c2000.
**TC HF5381 .P483 2000**

Rogers, Richard Randall. The impact of gay identity and perceived milieu toward gay employees on job involvement and organizational commitment of gay men. 1998.
**TC 085 R635**

**WORK SATISFACTION.** *See* **JOB SATISFACTION.**

**Work sight** [videorecording] / [Braille Institute of America]. Burbank, Ca. : RCA/Columbia Pictures Home Video, c1991. 1 videocassette (27 min.) : sd., col. ; 1/2 in. (Braille Institute insight series) VHS. Catalogued from credits and container. Photography: Brad Fowler. Introduced by Betty White. For the prospective employers of the blind and those who work with the blind. SUMMARY: This video looks at how employers and visually impaired job seekers can benefit from forming a partnership in the workplace. It also shows that being visually impaired does not have to be a barrier to finding a job. ISBN 0-8001-0872-8

*1. Blind - Employment. 2. Visually handicapped - Employment. 3. Blind - Services for. 4. Documentary television programs. I. White, Betty. II. Braille Institute of America. III. RCA/ Columbia Pictures of America. IV. Series.*
**TC HV1652 .W6 1991**

**WORK STRESS.** *See* **JOB STRESS.**

**WORK, THERAPEUTIC EFFECT OF.** *See* **OCCUPATIONAL THERAPY.**

**A Workable balance.**
Commission on Family and Medical Leave (U.S.) Washington, DC : Commission on Leave ; Women's Bureau, U.S. Dept. of Labor, [1996]
**TC HD5115.6.U5 C66 1996**

**Workbook for making choices.**
Making choices. Teacher's ed. New York, N.Y. : American Book Company, c1980.
**TC PE1121 .M34 1980 Teacher's Ed. Workbook**

**Workbook for making choices.** Teacher's ed. Lexington, Mass. : D.C. Heath Company, c1983. 142 p. : ill. (some col.) ; 28 cm. (American readers ; 6) Includes index. ISBN 0-669-05072-5
*1. Readers (Elementary) 2. Reading (Elementary) I. Series.*
**TC PE1121 .M34 1983 Teacher's Ed. Workbook**

**WORKERS.** *See* **EMPLOYEES.**

**WORKFORCE.** *See* **LABOR SUPPLY.**

**WORKFORCE DIVERSITY.** *See* **DIVERSITY IN THE WORKPLACE.**

**WORKFORCE LITERACY.** *See* **WORKPLACE LITERACY.**

**WORKING ALLIANCE (PSYCHOTHERAPY).** *See* **THERAPEUTIC ALLIANCE.**

**WORKING CLASS.** *See* **LABOR; PEASANTRY.**

**WORKING CLASS - CUBA - HISTORY - 19TH CENTURY.**
Casanovas, Joan. Bread, or bullets!. Pittsburgh : University of Pittsburgh Press, c1998.
**TC HD8206 .C33 1998**

**Working class culture, women, and Britain, 1914-1921.**
Culleton, Claire A. 1st ed. New York : St. Martin's Press, 2000.
**TC D639.W7 C79 2000**

**WORKING CLASS - EDUCATION - ENGLAND - HISTORY.**
Heathorn, Stephen J., 1965- For home, country, and race. Toronto : University of Toronto Press, 1999.
**TC LC93.E5 H42 1999**

**WORKING CLASS - EDUCATION (HIGHER) - ARKANSAS - HISTORY.**
Cobb, William H. Radical education in the rural South. Detroit : Wayne State University Press, 2000.
**TC LD1276 .C63 2000**

**WORKING CLASS - EDUCATION (SECONDARY) - NEW ZEALAND - CASE STUDIES.**
Thrupp, Martin. 1964- Schools making a difference--let's be realistic!. Buckingham [England] ; Philadelphia : Open University Press, 1999.
**TC LB2822.75 .T537 1999**

**WORKING CLASS - EMPLOYMENT.** *See* **WORKING CLASS.**

**WORKING CLASS - ENGLAND - MANCHESTER - HISTORY - 19TH CENTURY.**
Hewitt, Martin. The emergence of stability in the industrial city. Aldershot, England : Scolar Press ; Brookfield, Vt., USA : Ashgate Pub. Co., c1996.
**TC HN398.M27 H48 1996**

**WORKING CLASS - GREAT BRITAIN - LONGITUDINAL STUDIES.**
42 up. New York : The New Press : Distributed by W.W. Norton, c1998.
**TC HQ792.G7 A18 1998**

**The working class in American history**
Deslippe, Dennis A. (Dennis Arthur), 1961- Rights, not roses. Urbana : University of Illinois Press, c2000.
**TC HD6079.2.U5 D47 2000**

**WORKING CLASS IN MOTION PICTURES - GREAT BRITAIN.**
42 up. New York : The New Press : Distributed by W.W. Norton, c1998.
**TC HQ792.G7 A18 1998**

**WORKING CLASS - LEGAL STATUS, LAWS, ETC.** *See* **LABOR LAWS AND LEGISLATION.**

**WORKING CLASS - NEW YORK (STATE) - NEW YORK - PICTORIAL WORKS.**
Bernhardt, Debra E. Ordinary people, extraordinary lives. New York : New York University Press, c2000.
**TC HD8085.N53 B47 2000**

**WORKING CLASS - UNITED STATES.**
Stanback, Thomas M. Cities in transition. Totowa, N.J. : Allanheld, Osmun, 1982.
**TC HD5724 .S649 1982**

**WORKING CLASS WOMEN - GREAT BRITAIN - HISTORY - 20TH CENTURY.**
Culleton, Claire A. Working class culture, women, and Britain, 1914-1921. 1st ed. New York : St. Martin's Press, 2000.
**TC D639.W7 C79 2000**

**WORKING CLASS WOMEN - PUERTO RICO - SAN JUAN - SOCIAL CONDITIONS.**
Matos Rodríguez, Félix V., 1962- Women and urban change in San Juan, Puerto Rico, 1820-1868. Gainesville, Fla. : University Press of Florida, c1999.
**TC HQ1522 .M38 1999**

**WORKING CLASSES.** *See* **WORKING CLASS.**

**WORKING COUPLES.** *See* **DUAL-CAREER FAMILIES.**

**Working fathers.**
Levine, James A. Reading, Mass. : Addison-Wesley, c1997.
**TC HQ756 .L474 1997**

**WORKING-GIRLS.** *See* **CHILDREN - EMPLOYMENT.**

**Working it out.**
Hays, Kate F. 1st ed. Washington, DC : American Psychological Association, c1999.
**TC RC489.E9 H39 1999**

**WORKING LIFE, QUALITY OF.** *See* **QUALITY OF WORK LIFE.**

**WORKING MOTHERS.** *See also* **CHILDREN OF WORKING MOTHERS.**
Hrdy, Sarah Blaffer, 1946- Mother nature. 1st ed. New York : Pantheon Books, c1999.
**TC HQ759 .H784 1999**

**WORKING MOTHERS' CHILDREN.** *See* **CHILDREN OF WORKING MOTHERS.**

**WORKING MOTHERS - UNITED STATES.**
Hoffman, Lois Norma Wladis, 1929- Mothers at work. Cambridge ; New York : Cambridge University Press, 1999.
**TC HQ759.48 .H63 1999**

**WORKING MOTHERS - UNITED STATES - CASE STUDIES.**
Garey, Anita Ilta, 1947- Weaving work and motherhood. Philadelphia, PA : Temple University Press, 1999.
**TC HQ759.48 .G37 1999**

**WORKING MOTHERS - UNITED STATES - CONGRESSES.**
A look backward and forward at American professional women and their families. Lanham : University Press of America, 1999.
**TC HQ759.48 .L66 1999**

**Working papers in educational linguistics.**
[Philadelphia]: Language in Education Division, Graduate School of Education, University of Pennsylvania, [v.11 no.1-2; v.12 no.2] : ill. ; 28 cm. Frequency: Semiannual. Cover title: Penn working papers in educational linguistics -fall 1991. Other title: WPEL. Description based on: Vol. 6, no. 2 (fall 1990).
*1. Language and education - Periodicals. 2. Language and languages - Study and teaching - Periodicals. 3. Sociolinguistics - Periodicals. I. University of Pennsylvania. Graduate School of Education. Language in Education Division. II. Title: Penn working papers in educational linguistics -fall 1991 III. Title: WPEL*
**TC P40.8 .W675**

**Working the ruins :** feminist poststructural theory and methods in education / edited by Elizabeth A. St. Pierre and Wanda S. Pillow. New York ; London : Routledge, 2000. vi, 322 p. : ill. ; 24 cm. Includes bibliographical references and index. ISBN 0-415-92275-5 (hbk.) ISBN 0-415-92276-3 (pbk.) DDC 370.11/5
*1. Feminism and education. 2. Poststructuralism. 3. Postmodernism and education. 4. Education - Research. I. St. Pierre, Elizabeth. II. Pillow, Wanda S.*
**TC LC197 .W67 2000**

**Working together for children, young people, and their families**
Middleton, Laura. Disabled children. Malden, Mass. : Blackwell Sciences, 1999.

*TC HV888 .M53 1999*

**Working towards inclusive education.**
Mittler, Peter J. London : D. Fulton Publishers, 2000.
*TC LC1203.G7 M58 2000*

**Working with conflict** : skills and strategies for action /
Simon Fisher ... [et al.]. New York : Zed Books ;
Birmingham, UK : In association with Responding to
Conflict ; New York : Distributed in the USA
exclusively by St. Martin's Press, 2000. xvi, 185 p. :
ill. ; 29 cm. Includes bibliographical references and index.
ISBN 1-85649-836-0 (Hb) ISBN 1-85649-837-9 (Pb) DDC
303.6/9
*1. Conflict management. I. Fisher, Simon, 1948-*
*TC HM1126 .W67 2000*

**Working with groups to explore food & body
connections** : eating issues, body image, size
acceptance, self-care / Sandy Stewart Christian,
editor. Duluth, Minn. : Whole Person Associates,
c1996. xix, 188 p. : ill. ; 23 cm. Includes bibliographical
references. ISBN 1-57025-105-3 DDC 616.85/2605
*1. Eating disorders - Prevention. 2. Group counseling. 3.
Nutrition - Psychological aspects. 4. Body image. 5. Food
habits. I. Christian, Sandy Stewart. II. Title: Food & body
connections III. Title: Food and body connections*
*TC RC552.E18 W67 1996*

**Working with Latino youth.**
Koss-Chioino, Joan. 1st ed. San Francisco : Jossey-
Bass, c1999.
*TC RC451.5.H57 K67 1999*

**Working with parents of aggressive children.**
Cavell, Timothy A. 1st ed. Washington, DC :
American Psychological Association, 2000.
*TC RJ506.A35 C38 2000*

**Working with polyethylene foam and fluted plastic
sheet.**
Schlichting, Carl. Ottawa, Ontario, Canada : Canadian
Conservation Institute, Dept. of Canadian Heritage,
1994.
*TC N8554 T25 no.14*

**Working with second language learners.**
Cary, Stephen. Portsmouth, NH : Heinemann, c2000.
*TC P53 .C286 2000*

**Working with student writers** : essays on tutoring and
teaching / edited by Leonard A. Podis and JoAnne M.
Podis. New York : P. Lang, c1999. xii, 336 p. ; 23 cm.
Includes bibliographical references. ISBN 0-8204-4032-9
(pbk. : alk. paper) DDC 808/.042/07
*1. English language - Rhetoric - Study and teaching. 2. Report
writing - Study and teaching. 3. Tutors and tutoring. I. Podis,
Leonard A. II. Podis, JoAnne M.*
*TC PE1404 .W66 1999*

**WORKING WIVES.** *See* **MARRIED WOMEN -
EMPLOYMENT.**

**WORKING WOMEN IN MOTION PICTURES.**
*See* **WOMEN - EMPLOYMENT.**

**WORKOUTS (EXERCISE).** *See* **EXERCISE.**

**Workplace learning series**
Teare, Richard. The virtual university. London : New
York : Cassell, 1998.
*TC LC5215 .T42 1998*

**WORKPLACE LITERACY - UNITED STATES.**
Hollenbeck, Kevin. Classrooms in the workplace.
Kalamazoo, Mich. : W.E. Upjohn Institute for
Employment Research, 1993.
*TC HF5549.5.T7 H598 1993*

**Works on canvas.**
Rothko, Mark, 1903-1970. Mark Rothko. New
Haven : Yale University Press ; Washington, D.C. :
National Gallery of Art, c1998.
*TC ND237.R725 A4 1998*

**Workshop modules for professional development.**
Assessment in primary school science. London :
Commonwealth Secretariat, c1998.
*TC LB1585 .A87 1998*

**Workshop on Parametric Variation and Grammar
Specification (1992 : Edinburgh, Scotland).**
Functional categories, argument structure and
parametric variation. Edinburgh : Centre for Cognitive
Study, University of Edinburgh, c1994.
*TC P151 .F86 1994*

**Workshop series of the American Psychoanalytic
Association**
(monograph 9) The therapeutic alliance. Madison,
Conn. : International Universities Press, c2000.
*TC RC489.T66 T468 2000*

**WORKSHOPS.** *See* **FACTORIES.**

**WORKSHOPS (GROUP DISCUSSION).** *See*
**FORUMS (DISCUSSION AND DEBATE).**

**WORKSHOPS IN EDUCATION.** *See*
**EDUCATION - CONGRESSES.**

**World Association for Infant Mental Health.**
Handbook of infant mental health. New York : Wiley,
c2000.
*TC RJ502.5 .H362 2000*

**World at war.**
The American Revolution. [videorecording]. New
York, N.Y. : A&E Home Video, c1994.
*TC E208 .A447 1994*

**World awareness series**
Third world peoples, a Gospel perspective. Maryknoll,
NY : Maryknoll Fathers and Brothers, c1987.
*TC F1439.T54 1987*

**World Bank.** African art : the World Bank collection /
edited by Alexandre Marc. Washington, D.C. : World
Bank, c1998. xiv, 92 p. : ill. (some col.), col. map ; 30 cm.
Includes bibliographical references (p. 90-92). ISBN
0-8213-4195-2 (pbk.) DDC 709/.67/074753
*1. Art. Black - Africa. Sub-Saharan - Catalogs. 2. World Bank -
Art collections - Catalogs. 3. Art - Private collections -
Washington (D.C.) - Catalogs. I. Marc, Alexandre, 1956- II.
Title.*
*TC N7391.65 .W67 1998*

Francis, Paul A. Hard lessons. Washington, D.C. :
World Bank, c1998.
*TC LA1632 .F73 1998*

**WORLD BANK.**
Learning from experience. The Hague : Centre for the
Study of Education in Developing Countries, c1995.
*TC LC2610 .L43 1995*

Nelson, Joan M. Reforming health and education.
Washington, DC : Overseas Development Council ;
Baltimore, MD : Distributed by the Johns Hopkins
University Press, c1999.
*TC HG3881.5.W57 N447 1999*

Our friends at the bank [videorecording]. New York,
NY : First Run/Icarus Films, 1997.
*TC HG3881.5.W57 O87 1997*

A thousand flowers. Trenton, NJ : Africa World Press,
c2000, [1999].
*TC LC67.68.A35 T56 2000*

**WORLD BANK - ART COLLECTIONS -
CATALOGS.**
World Bank. African art. Washington, D.C. : World
Bank, c1998.
*TC N7391.65 .W67 1998*

**WORLD BANK - DEVELOPING COUNTRIES.**
World Bank. Human Development Network.
Education sector strategy. Washington, D.C. : World
Bank Group, c1999.
*TC LC2607 .W66 1999*

**World Bank. Europe and Central Asia Region.
Country Dept. III. Human Resources Division.**
Russia, education in the transition = [S.l.] : The World
Bank, ECA Country Development III, Human
Resources Division, 1995.
*TC LA839.2 .R87 1995*

**World Bank. Human Development Network.**
Education sector strategy / [the Human Development
Network]. Washington, D.C. : World Bank Group,
c1999. xiv, 80 p. : ill., col. maps ; 28 cm. At head of title:
Education, the World Bank. Includes bibliographical references
(p. 79-80). ISBN 0-8213-4560-5 DDC 370/.9172/4
*1. Education - Developing countries. 2. Economic
development - Effect of education on. 3. Educational
assistance - Developing countries. 4. World Bank - Developing
countries. I. Title.*
*TC LC2607 .W66 1999*

**World Bank technical paper**
(no. 420.) Francis, Paul A. Hard lessons.
Washington, D.C. : World Bank, c1998.
*TC LA1632 .F73 1998*

**World Bank technical paper. Africa region series.**
Francis, Paul A. Hard lessons. Washington, D.C. :
World Bank, c1998.
*TC LA1632 .F73 1998*

**World call.**
Worldcall. Lisse, Netherlands ; Abingdon [England] ;
Exton, PA : Swets & Zeitlinger, c1999.
*TC P53.28 .W67 1999*

**World ceramics.**
Munsterberg, Hugo, 1916- New York : Penguin
Studio Books, c1998.

*TC NK3780 .M86 1998*

**World Congress on Down Syndrome (6th : 1997 :
Madrid, Spain).**
Down syndrome. London : Whurr, 1999.
*TC RC571 .D675 1999*

**WORLD DECADE FOR CULTURAL
DEVELOPMENT, 1988-1997.** *See*
**CIVILIZATION.**

**The world food problem.**
Foster, Phillips, 1931- 2nd ed. Boulder : Lynne
Rienner Publishers, 1999.
*TC HD9018.D44 F68 1999*

**World futures general evolution studies**
(v. 13) The thirteenth labor. Amsterdam : Gordon
and Breach Publishers, c1999.
*TC Q181.3 .T45 1999*

**World geography : teacher's resource file.**
Baerwald, Thomas John. Prentice Hall world
geography. Englewood Cliffs, N.J. : Prentice Hall,
c1992.
*TC G128 .B34 1992*

**WORLD HEALTH.**
Aboud, Frances E. Health psychology in global
perspective. Thousand Oaks : Sage Publications,
c1998.
*TC R726.7 .A26 1998*

**WORLD HEALTH.**
Tulchinsky, Theodore H. The new public health. San
Diego, Calif. ; London : Academic Press, c2000.
*TC RA425 .T85 2000*

**WORLD HISTORY.** *See also* **GEOGRAPHY;
HISTORY, MODERN; MIDDLE AGES;
MIDDLE AGES - HISTORY; WORLD
POLITICS.**
Dunn, Ross E. Evanston, Ill. : McDougal, Littell &
Co. , c1988.
*TC D21 .D86 1988*

**WORLD HISTORY.**
Dunn, Ross E. World history. Evanston, Ill. :
McDougal, Littell & Co. , c1988.
*TC D21 .D86 1988*

Rogers, Lester Brown, 1875- Story of nations. New
York : H.Holt, 1965.
*TC D21 .R63 1965*

Spodek, Howard, 1941- The world's history.
Combined ed. Upper Saddle River, NJ : Prentice Hall,
1998.
*TC D20 .S77 1998*

**WORLD HISTORY - DATABASES.**
SIRS researcher [computer file] [Boca Raton, Fla.] :
SIRS Mandarin,
*TC NETWORKED RESOURCE*

**World history in documents** : a comparative reader /
edited by Peter N. Stearns. New York : New York
University Press, c1998. xi, 473 p. ; 26 cm. Includes
bibliographical references. ISBN 0-8147-8106-3 (alk. paper)
ISBN 0-8147-8107-1 (pbk. : alk. paper) DDC 909
*1. World history - Sources. I. Stearns, Peter N.*
*TC D5 .W67 1998*

**WORLD HISTORY - INDEXES.**
SIRS researcher [computer file] [Boca Raton, Fla.] :
SIRS Mandarin,
*TC NETWORKED RESOURCE*

**WORLD HISTORY, MEDIEVAL.** *See* **MIDDLE
AGES - HISTORY.**

**WORLD HISTORY, MODERN.** *See* **HISTORY,
MODERN.**

**WORLD HISTORY - SOURCES.**
World history in documents. New York : New York
University Press, c1998.
*TC D5 .W67 1998*

**WORLD HISTORY - STUDY AND TEACHING.**
*See* **HISTORY - STUDY AND TEACHING.**

**WORLD LITERATURE.** *See* **LITERATURE.**

**World literature today.**
Books abroad; Norman, Okla., The University of
Oklahoma Press.

**WORLD MAPS.** *See* **GLOBES.**

**World of art**
Allen, Christopher, 1953- Art in Australia. New York,
N.Y. : Thames and Hudson, 1997.
*TC N7400 .A45 1997*

**World of language.**
Ragno, Nancy N. [Teacher ed.]. Morristown, NJ :
Silver Burdett & Ginn, c1990.

Ragno, Nancy N. [Teacher ed.]. Morristown, NJ : Silver Burdett & Ginn, c1990.

Ragno, Nancy N. [Teacher ed.]. Morristown, NJ : Silver Burdett & Ginn, c1990.

Ragno, Nancy Nickell. Needham, Ma. : Silver Burdett Ginn, c1996.
*TC LB1576 .S4471 1996*

Ragno, Nancy Nickell. Needham, Mass. : Silver Burdett Ginn, c1996.
*TC LB1576 .S4471 1996*

**World of language** / Nancy Nickell Ragno, Marian Davies Toth, Betty G. Gray ; contributing author, Elfrieda Hiebert ... [et al.]. Needham, Mass. : Silver Burdett Ginn, c1996. 9 v. : col. ill ; 28 cm. For grades K-8. Authors' names appear in different order in some volumes. Includes indexes. For grade 7 only 1993 ed. available. ISBN 0-382-25165-2 (Gr. 1) ISBN 0-382-25166-0 (Gr. 2) ISBN 0-382-25168-7 (Gr. 3) ISBN 0-382-25101-6 (Gr. 4) ISBN 0-382-25170-9 (Gr. 5) ISBN 0-382-25171-7 (Gr. 6) ISBN 0-382-25104-0 (Gr. 7) ISBN 0-382-25173-3 (Gr. 8)
*1. Language arts (Elementary) 2. English language - Study and teaching (Elementary) 3. English language - Study and teaching (Primary) I. Ragno, Nancy Nickell. II. Toth, Marian Davies. III. Gray, Betty G. IV. Hiebert, Elfrieda. V. Silver Burdett Ginn (Firm) VI. Title.*
*TC LB1576 .S4471 1996*

**World of language** / Nancy Nickell Ragno, Marian Davies Toth, Betty G. Gray ; contributing author, Elfrieda Hiebert ... [et al.]. Teacher ed. Needham, Mass. : Silver Burdett Ginn, c1996. 9 v. : col. ill ; 28 cm. For grades K-8. Authors' names appear in different order in some volumes. Includes indexes. ISBN 0-382-25174-1 (Gr. K) ISBN 0-382-25175-x (Gr. 1) ISBN 0-382-25176-8 (Gr. 2) ISBN 0-382-25178-4 (Gr. 3) ISBN 0-382-25179-2 (Gr. 4) ISBN 0-382-25180-6 (Gr. 5) ISBN 0-382-25181-4 (Gr. 6) ISBN 0-382-25182-2 (Gr. 7) ISBN 0-382-25183-0 (Gr. 8)
*1. Language arts (Elementary) 2. English language - Study and teaching (Elementary) 3. English language - Study and teaching (Primary) I. Ragno, Nancy Nickell. II. Toth, Marian Davies. III. Gray, Betty G. IV. Hiebert, Elfrieda. V. Silver Burdett Ginn (Firm) VI. Title.*
*TC LB1576 .S4471 1996 Teacher Ed.*

**World of language** : wordless picture books. Morristown, N.J. : Silver Burdett Ginn, c1996. v. (various pagings) : col. ill ; 28 cm. 8 titles in each set. "The eight wordless books, a component of World of Language, allow children to write their own stories written directly on the pages of their books"--T.p. ISBN 0-382-10759-4 (Gr. K) ISBN 0-382-10768-3 (Gr. 1) ISBN 0-382-10836-1 (Gr. 2)
*1. Language arts (Primary) 2. English language - Study and teaching (Primary) I. Title.*
*TC LB1576 .S4471 1996 Pict. Bks.*

**The world of Washington Irving.**
Brooks, Van Wyck, 1886-1963. Philadelphia, Blakiston, 1944.
*TC PS208 .B7 1944a*

Brooks, Van Wyck, 1886-1963. [New York] E. P. Dutton & co., inc. [1944]
*TC PS208 .B7 1944*

**WORLD ORDER. See INTERNATIONAL COOPERATION; INTERNATIONAL RELATIONS.**

**WORLD POLITICS. See GEOPOLITICS; INTERNATIONAL RELATIONS.**

**WORLD POLITICS - 1945-.**
Ethnicity and intra-state conflict. Aldershot, Hants, England ; Brookfield, Vt., USA : Ashgate, c1999.
*TC GN495.6 .E83 1999*

**WORLD POLITICS - 1945- -CONGRESSES.**
Ethnicity and intra-state conflict. Aldershot, Hants, England ; Brookfield, Vt., USA : Ashgate, c1999.
*TC GN495.6 .E83 1999*

**WORLD POLITICS - 1989-.**
Tehranian, Majid. Global communication and world politics. Boulder, Colo. : Lynne Rienner Publishers, 1999.
*TC P95.8 .T44 1999*

**WORLD POLITICS - 1989- - FORECASTING.**
Wallerstein, Immanuel Maurice, 1930- Utopistics, or, Historical choices of the twenty-first century. New York : New Press, 1998.
*TC D860 .W35 1998*

**WORLD POLITICS - 20TH CENTURY - PERIODICALS.**
Foreign affairs. New York : Council on Foreign Relations, 1922-

**WORLD POLITICS - DATABASES.**
SIRS researcher [computer file] [Boca Raton, Fla.] : SIRS Mandarin,
*TC NETWORKED RESOURCE*

**WORLD POLITICS - PERIODICALS.**
Current history and Forum. New York [C-H Publishing Corporation; etc., etc., 1914-41]

[Current history (New York, N.Y. : 1916)] Current history. [New York : New York Times Co., 1916-1940]

**World population prospects as assessed in ...**
World population prospects. New York : United Nations, 1985-
*TC HA154 .W6*

**World population prospects** / Department of International Economic and Social Affairs. New York : United Nations, 1985- v. : ill., maps ; 28 cm. 1982- . (Population studies / Department of International Economic and Social Affairs) "Estimates and projections as assessed in ... " Supplemented by revisions. Has supplement: Global estimates and projections of population by sex and age,  -1988; Sex and age distributions of population, 1990- Has supplement: Global estimates and projections of population by sex and age (DLC)  90649456 (OCoLC)22136295. Has supplement: Sex and age distributions of population. Continues: World population prospects as assessed in ... (OCoLC)12389250. DDC 304.6/2/021
*1. Population - Statistics - Periodicals. 2. Population forecasting - Statistics - Periodicals. I. United Nations. Dept. of International Economic and Social Affairs. II. Title: Global estimates and projections of population by sex and age III. Title: Sex and age distributions of population IV. Title: World population prospects as assessed in ... V. Series: Population studies (New York, N.Y.)*
*TC HA154 .W6*

**World review of nutrition and dietetics**
(vol. 84) Evolutionary aspects of nutrition and health. Basel ; New York : Karger, c1999.
*TC QP141 .E95 1999*

**WORLD TRADE. See INTERNATIONAL TRADE.**

**The world turned upside down.**
Ferrie, Richard. 1st ed. New York : Holiday House, c1999.
*TC E241.Y6 F45 1999*

**WORLD WAR, 1914-1918.**
Bourke, Joanna. An intimate history of killing. [New York, NY] : Basic Books, c1999.
*TC U22.3 .B68 1999*

**WORLD WAR, 1914-1918 - PERIODICALS.**
Current history and Forum. New York [C-H Publishing Corporation; etc., etc., 1914-41]

**WORLD WAR, 1914-1918 - WOMEN - GREAT BRITAIN.**
Culleton, Claire A. Working class culture, women, and Britain, 1914-1921. 1st ed. New York : St. Martin's Press, 2000.
*TC D639.W7 C79 2000*

**WORLD WAR, 1939-1945.**
Bourke, Joanna. An intimate history of killing. [New York, NY] : Basic Books, c1999.
*TC U22.3 .B68 1999*

**WORLD WAR, 1939-1945 - AERIAL OPERATIONS, AMERICAN.**
Streb, Richard W. Life and death aboard the U.S.S. Essex. Pittsburgh, Pa. : Dorrance Pub. Co., c1999.
*TC D774.E7 S77 1999*

**WORLD WAR, 1939-1945 - ATROCITIES. See HOLOCAUST, JEWISH (1939-1945).**

**WORLD WAR, 1939-1945 - CAUSES.**
Robbins, Keith. Appeasement. Oxford, UK : New York, NY, USA : B. Blackwell, 1988.
*TC DA47.2 .R62 1988*

**WORLD WAR, 1939-1945 - CHARITIES. See WORLD WAR, 1939-1945 - WAR WORK.**

**WORLD WAR, 1939-1945 - CHILDREN.**
Werner, Emmy E. Through the eyes of innocents. Boulder, CO : Westview Press, 2000.
*TC D810.C4 W45 1999*

**WORLD WAR, 1939-1945 - CIVILIAN RELIEF. See WORLD WAR, 1939-1945 - WAR WORK.**

**WORLD WAR, 1939-1945 - DRAFT RESISTERS.**
Rabbit in the moon [videorecording]. San Francisco, Calif. : Wabi-Sabi Productions, 1999.
*TC D753.8 .R3 1999*

**WORLD WAR, 1939-1945 - ECONOMIC ASPECTS - UNITED STATES - POSTERS.**
World War II [picture]. Amawalk, NY : Jackdaw Publications, c1999.
*TC TR820.5 .W6 1999*

**WORLD WAR, 1939-1945 - EVACUATION OF CIVILIANS. See JAPANESE AMERICANS - EVACUATION AND RELOCATION, 1942-1945.**

**WORLD WAR, 1939-1945 - FINANCE. See WORLD WAR, 1939-1945 - ECONOMIC ASPECTS.**

**WORLD WAR, 1939-1945 - FRANCE - FICTION.**
Maguire, Gregory. The good liar. New York : Clarion Books, c1999.
*TC PZ7.M2762 Go 1999*

**WORLD WAR, 1939-1945 - FRANCE - JUVENILE FICTION.**
Maguire, Gregory. The good liar. New York : Clarion Books, c1999.
*TC PZ7.M2762 Go 1999*

**WORLD WAR, 1939-1945 - JAPANESE AMERICANS.**
Okihiro, Gary Y., 1945- Stories lives. Seattle : University of Washington Press, 1999.
*TC D753.8 .O38 1999*

**WORLD WAR, 1939-1945 - JAPANESE AMERICANS - PERSONAL NARRATIVES.**
Rabbit in the moon [videorecording]. San Francisco, Calif. : Wabi-Sabi Productions, 1999.
*TC D753.8 .R3 1999*

**WORLD WAR, 1939-1945 - JEWISH RESISTANCE. See HOLOCAUST, JEWISH (1939-1945).**

**WORLD WAR, 1939-1945 - JEWS. See HOLOCAUST, JEWISH (1939-1945).**

**WORLD WAR, 1939-1945 - JEWS - RESCUE - JUVENILE FICTION.**
Bat-Ami, Miriam. Two suns in the sky. 1st ed. [Chicago, IL] : Front Street/Cricket Books, 1999.
*TC PZ7.B2939 Tw 1999*

**WORLD WAR, 1939-1945 - MOTION PICTURES AND THE WAR.**
Headline stories of the century [videorecording]. Chicago, IL. : Distributed by Questar Video, Inc., c1992.
*TC D743 .H42 1992*

**WORLD WAR, 1939-1945 - NAVAL OPERATIONS, AMERICAN.**
Streb, Richard W. Life and death aboard the U.S.S. Essex. Pittsburgh, Pa. : Dorrance Pub. Co., c1999.
*TC D774.E7 S77 1999*

**WORLD WAR, 1939-1945 - PACIFIC OCEAN.**
Streb, Richard W. Life and death aboard the U.S.S. Essex. Pittsburgh, Pa. : Dorrance Pub. Co., c1999.
*TC D774.E7 S77 1999*

**WORLD WAR, 1939-1945 - PARTICIPATION, JAPANESE AMERICAN.**
Rabbit in the moon [videorecording]. San Francisco, Calif. : Wabi-Sabi Productions, 1999.
*TC D753.8 .R3 1999*

**WORLD WAR, 1939-1945 - PERSONAL NARRATIVES, AMERICAN.**
Remembering the boys. Kent, OH : Kent State University Press, c2000.
*TC D811.A2 R46 2000*

Streb, Richard W. Life and death aboard the U.S.S. Essex. Pittsburgh, Pa. : Dorrance Pub. Co., c1999.
*TC D774.E7 S77 1999*

**WORLD WAR, 1939-1945 - PRISONERS AND PRISONS, GERMAN.**
Madsen, Benedicte, 1943- Survival in the organization. Aarhus [Denmark] ; Oakville, Conn. : Aarhus University Press, c1996.
*TC D805.G3 M24 1996*

**WORLD WAR, 1939-1945 - SOCIAL ASPECTS - UNITED STATES - POSTERS.**
World War II [picture]. Amawalk, NY : Jackdaw Publications, c1999.
*TC TR820.5 .W6 1999*

**WORLD WAR, 1939-1945 - SOCIAL WORK. See WORLD WAR, 1939-1945 - WAR WORK.**

**WORLD WAR, 1939-1945 - UNITED STATES - PARTICIPATION, FEMALE - POSTERS.**
World War II [picture]. Amawalk, NY : Jackdaw Publications, c1999.
*TC TR820.5 .W6 1999*

**WORLD WAR, 1939-1945 - UNITED STATES - PARTICIPATION, JUVENILE - POSTERS.**
World War II [picture]. Amawalk, NY : Jackdaw Publications, c1999.
*TC TR820.5 .W6 1999*

**WORLD WAR, 1939-1945 - WAR WORK - UNITED STATES - POSTERS.**
World War II [picture]. Amawalk, NY : Jackdaw Publications, c1999.
*TC TR820.5 .W6 1999*

**WORLD WAR I.** *See* **WORLD WAR, 1914-1918.**

**WORLD WAR II.** *See* **WORLD WAR, 1939-1945.**

**World War II** [picture] : the war at home. Amawalk, NY : Jackdaw Publications, c1999. 12 posters : b&w ; 43 x 56 cm. + 1 leaflet ([6] p. : ill. ; 28 cm.). (Jackdaw photo collections ; PC 109) Compiled by Bill Eames; edited by Jan Morrissey. SUMMARY: 12 historical photo-posters depicting aspects of the war. CONTENTS: 1. Merchant seaman's funeral -- 2. U.S. family celebrates military service -- 3. Red Cross workers wrap bandages -- 4. School children buy defense stamps -- 5. Citizens lineup at rationing board -- 6. Gasoline rationing hits the home front -- 7. Citizens raise money for war effort -- 8. School children collect scrap metal for war -- 9. "Rosie the Riveter" -- 10. Female railroaders keep the trains running -- 11. Bomber noses fill war plant -- 12. Wall Street celebrates victory in Europe. ISBN 1-56696-170-x
*1. World War, 1939-1945 - War work - United States - Posters. 2. World War, 1939-1945 - United States - Participation, Female - Posters. 3. World War, 1939-1945 - United States - Participation, Juvenile - Posters. 4. World War, 1939-1945 - Economic aspects - United States - Posters. 5. World War, 1939-1945 - Social aspects - United States - Posters. 6. Documentary photography - United States - Posters. I. Eames, Bill. II. Morrissey, Jan. III. Jackdaw Publications. IV. Title: War at home [picture] V. Series.*
*TC TR820.5 .W6 1999*

**WORLD WIDE WEB.**
Distance learning technologies. Hershey, PA ; London : Idea Group Pub., c2000.
*TC LC5803.C65 D57 2000*

Inglis, Alistair. Delivering digitally. London : Kogan Page, c1999.
*TC LB1044.87 .I545 1999*

Instructional and cognitive impacts of Web-based education. Hershey, PA : Idea Group Pub., c2000.
*TC LB1044.87 .I545 2000*

Jody, Marilyn, 1932- Using computers to teach literature. 2nd ed. Urbana, Ill. : National Council of Teachers of English, c1998.
*TC LB1050.37 .J63 1998*

The library Web. Medford, NJ : Information Today, 1997.
*TC Z674.75.W67 L53 1997*

Owen, Bruce M. The Internet challenge to television. Cambridge, Mass. : Harvard University Press, 1999.
*TC HE8700.8 .O826 1999*

Provenzo, Eugene F. The Internet and the World Wide Web for preservice teachers. Boston : Allyn & Bacon, c1999.
*TC LB1044.87 .P763 1999*

**WORLD WIDE WEB - CONGRESSES.**
IFIP TC3 WG3.2/3.6 International Working Conference on Building University Electronic Educational Environments (1999 : Irvine, Calif.) Building university electronic educational environments. Boston : Kluwer Academic Publishers, c2000.
*TC LC5803.C65 .I352 2000*

**WORLD WIDE WEB - DIRECTORIES.**
Bigham, Vicki Smith. The Prentice Hall directory of online education resources. Paramus, N.J. : Prentice Hall, c1998.
*TC LB1044.87 .B54 1998*

**WORLD WIDE WEB - HISTORY.**
Berners-Lee, Tim. Weaving the Web. 1st ed. San Francisco : HarperSanFrancisco, c1999.
*TC TK5105.888 .B46 1999*

**WORLD WIDE WEB (INFORMATION RETRIEVAL SYSTEM).** *See also* **INTERNET (COMPUTER NETWORK).**
Alexander, Janet E. Web wisdom. Mahwah, N.J. : Lawrence Erlbaum Associates, Publishers, 1999.
*TC TK5105.888 .A376 1999*

Millhorn, Jim, 1953- Student's companion to the World Wide Web. Lanham, Md. ; London : Scarecrow Press, 1999.
*TC H61.95 .M55 1999*

Schweizer, Heidi. Designing and teaching an on-line course :. Boston : Allyn & Bacon, c1999.
*TC LB1028.3 .S377 1999*

**WORLD WIDE WEB (INFORMATION RETRIEVAL SYSTEM) - STUDY AND TEACHING.**
The Internet. Oxford ; New York : Oxford University Press, c2000.
*TC TK5105.875.I57 I57 2000*

**WORLD WIDE WEB - SOCIAL ASPECTS.**
Global literacies and the World-Wide Web. London : New York : Routledge, 2000.
*TC P94.6 .G58 2000*

**Worldcall** : global perspectives on computer-assisted language learning / edited by Robert Debski and Mike Levy. Lisse, Netherlands ; Abingdon [England] ; Exton, PA : Swets & Zeitlinger, c1999. 363 p. : ill. ; 25 cm. Cover title: World call. Includes bibliographical references and index. ISBN 90-265-1555-3 DDC 418/.00285
*1. Language and languages - Computer-assisted instruction. 2. Language and languages - Study and teaching - Technological innovations. I. Debski, Robert. II. Levy, Mike. III. Title: World call*
*TC P53.28 .W67 1999*

**Worlds apart** : acting and writing in academic and workplace contexts / Patrick Dias ... [et al.]. Mahwah, N.J. : L. Erlbaum Associates, 1999. xii, 253 p. : ill. ; 24 cm. (Rhetoric, knowledge, and society) Includes bibliographical references (p. 236-245) and indexes. ISBN 0-8058-2147-3 (cloth : alk. paper) ISBN 0-8058-2148-1 (pbk. : alk. paper) DDC 808
*1. English language - Rhetoric - Study and teaching. 2. Academic writing - Study and teaching. 3. Technical writing - Study and teaching. 4. Business writing - Study and teaching. I. Dias, Patrick. II. Series.*
*TC PE1404 .W665 1999*

**WORLD'S FAIRS.** *See* **EXHIBITIONS.**

**The world's history.**
Spodek, Howard, 1941- Combined ed. Upper Saddle River, NJ : Prentice Hall, 1998.
*TC D20 .S77 1998*

**Worlds of change** : teacher's planning guide. New York : Macmillan/McGraw-Hill, c1997. 1 v. (various pagings) : col. ill. ; 31 cm. (Spotlight on literacy ; Gr.5 l.11 u.2) (The road to independent reading) Includes index. ISBN 0-02-181180-6
*1. Language arts (Elementary) 2. Reading (Elementary) I. Series. II. Series: The road to independent reading*
*TC LB1576 .S66 1997 Gr.5 l.11 u.2*

**Worldview in painting-Art and Society.**
Schapiro, Meyer, 1904- 1st ed. New York, N.Y. : George Braziller, 1999.
*TC N72.S6 S313 1999*

**Wormser, Baron.** Teaching the art of poetry : the moves / Baron Wormser, David Cappella. Mahwah, N.J. : Lawrence Erlbaum Assoc., 2000. xviii, 373 p. ; 23 cm. Includes bibliographical references and indexes. ISBN 0-8058-3337-4 (pbk. : alk. paper) DDC 808.1/07
*1. Poetry - Study and teaching. 2. Poetry - Authorship - Study and teaching. I. Cappella, David. II. Title.*
*TC PN1101 .W67 2000*

**Worrall, Linda.**
Neurogenic communication disorders. New York : Thieme, 2000.
*TC RC423 .N48 2000*

**WORRY.** *See* **ANXIETY.**

**Worsham, Dode, 1943-.**
Ward, Mary Ann, 1946- Student guidance and development. Larchmont, N.Y. : Eye On Education, c1998.
*TC LB1027.5 .W356 1998*

**Worsham, Lynn., 1953-.**
Race, rhetoric and the postcolonial. Albany : State University of New York Press, c1999.
*TC P301.5.P67 R33 1999*

**Worsham, Murray E.**
Emmer, Edmund T. Classroom management for secondary teachers. 5th ed. Boston : Allyn and Bacon, c2000.
*TC LB3013 .C53 2000*

Evertson, Carolyn M., 1935- Classroom management for elementary teachers. 5th ed. Boston : Allyn and Bacon, c2000.
*TC LB3013 .C528 2000*

**WORSHIP.** *See* **PRAYER.**

**WORTH.** *See* **VALUES.**

**Worthman, C. M. (Carol M.), 1948-.**
Hormones, health, and behavior. Cambridge ; New York : Cambridge University Press, 1999.
*TC QP356.45 .H67 1999*

**Wosket, Val, 1954-** The therapeutic use of self : counselling practice, research, and supervision / Val Wosket. New York : Routledge, 1999. xi. 254 p. ; 22 cm. Includes bibliographical references and index. ISBN 0-415-17090-7 ISBN 0-415-17091-5 (pbk.) DDC 616.89/14
*1. Psychotherapy - Methodology. 2. Psychotherapist and patient. 3. Psychotherapists - Psychology. I. Title.*
*TC RC480.5 .W67 1999*

**Wot u lookin' at? [videorecording].**
Teen violence [videorecording]. Princeton, NJ : Films for the Humanities & Sciences, c1998.
*TC RJ506.V56 T44 1998*

**WOUNDS AND INJURIES.**
Sports injuries sourcebook ; 1st ed. Detroit, MI : Omnigraphics, c1999.
*TC RD97 .S736 1999*

**WOUNDS AND INJURIES - PSYCHOLOGY - CONGRESSES.**
Developmental perspectives on trauma. Rochester, N.Y., USA : University of Rochester Press, 1997.
*TC RJ499 .D4825 1997*

**Woven by the grandmothers** : nineteenth-century Navajo textiles from the National Museum of the American Indian = Nihimásáni deiztł'ó ... / edited by Eulalie H. Bonar ; Navajo translations by Ellavina Perkins and Esther Yazzie. Washington : Smithsonian Institution Press in association with the National Museum of the American Indian, Smithsonian Institution, c1996. xv, 214 p. : ill. (some col.) ; 26 cm. English and Navajo. Published in conjunction with an exhibition held at the National Museum of the American Indian, New York City, Oct. 1996 to Jan. 1997. Includes bibliographical references (p. 204-209) and index. ISBN 1-56098-728-6 (alk. paper) DDC 746/.089/972
*1. Navajo textile fabrics - Exhibitions. 2. Navajo Indians - Social life and customs - Exhibitions. 3. Navajo philosophy - Exhibitions. 4. National Museum of the American Indian (U.S.) - Exhibitions. I. Bonar, Eulalie H. II. National Museum of the American Indian (U.S.) III. Title: Nihimásáni deiztł'ó*
*TC E99.N3 W79 1996*

**WPEL.**
Working papers in educational linguistics. [Philadelphia]: Language in Education Division, Graduate School of Education, University of Pennsylvania,
*TC P40.8 .W675*

**WQED (Television station : Pittsburgh, Pa.).**
The blue planet [videorecording]. [New York, N.Y.?] : Unapix Entertainment, Inc. [distributor], c1996.
*TC QB631.2 .B5 1996*

The climate puzzle [videorecording]. [New York, N.Y.?] : Unapix Entertainment, Inc. [distributor], c1996.
*TC QB631.2 .C5 1996*

The living machine [videorecording]. [New York, N.Y.?] : Unapix Entertainment, Inc. [distributor], c1996.
*TC QB631.2 .L5 1996*

Fate of the earth [videorecording]. [New York, N.Y.?] : Unapix Entertainment, Inc. [distributor], c1996.
*TC QB631.2 .F3 1996*

Gifts from the earth [videorecording]. [New York, N.Y.?] : Unapix Entertainment, Inc. [distributor], c1996.
*TC QB631.2 .G5 1996*

The solar sea [videorecording]. [New York, N.Y.?] : Unapix Entertainment, Inc. [distributor], c1996.
*TC QB631.2 .S6 1996*

Tales from other worlds [videorecording]. [New York, N.Y.?] : Unapix Entertainment, Inc. [distributor], c1996.
*TC QB631.2 .T3 1996*

Tales from other worlds [videorecording]. [New York, N.Y.?] : Unapix Entertainment, Inc. [distributor], c1996.
*TC QB631.2 .T3 1996*

**Wragg, E. C. (Edward Conrad).**
Failing teachers? London ; New York : Routledge, 2000.
*TC LB1775.4.G7 F35 2000*

Improving literacy in the primary school. London : New York : Routledge, 1998.
*TC LB1573 .I56 1998*

**WRATH.** *See* **ANGER.**

**Wray, David. 1950-.**
Literacy in the secondary school. London : David Fulton, 2000.
*TC LB1632 .L587 2000*

**WRECKS.** *See* **SHIPWRECKS.**

**Wren, Carol T.** Hanging by a twig : understanding and counseling adults with learning disabilities and ADD / Carol Wren ; with psychotherapeutic commentary by Jay Einhorn. 1st ed. New York : London : Norton, c2000. xiv, 221 p. ; 25 cm. Includes bibliographical references (p. [197]-214) and index. ISBN 0-393-70315-0 DDC 616.85/889
*1. Learning disabled - Mental health. 2. Learning disabled - Counseling of. I. Einhorn, Jay. II. Title.*
*TC RC394.L37 W74 2000*

**Wren, Kevin, 1947-** Social influences / Kevin Wren. London : New York : Routledge, 1999. xi, 130 p. : ill. ; 20 cm. (Routledge modular psychology) "Social psychology"--Cover. Includes bibliographical references (p. 117-125) and index. ISBN 0-415-18658-7 (hardcover) ISBN 0-415-18659-5 (pbk). DDC 303.3/4
*1. Social influence. I. Title. II. Series: Routledge modular psychology*
*TC HM1176 .W74 1999*

**Wren, Thomas E.**
Moral sensibilities and education. Bemmel : Concorde Pub. House, 1999-
*TC BF723.M54 M684 1999*

**Wright, Alexandra.** Alice in Pastaland : a math adventure / by Alexandra Wright ; illustrated by Reagan Word. Watertown, Mass. : Charlesbridge, 1997. 32 p. : col. ill. ; 25 cm. SUMMARY: An imaginary trip through Pastaland provides Alice with opportunities to explore number concepts and basic arithmetic as she tries to help a white rabbit solve a math problem. ISBN 1-57091-151-7 (softcover) DDC [Fic]
*1. Arithmetic - Fiction. 2. Characters in literature - Fiction. 3. Pasta products - Fiction. I. Word, Reagan, ill. II. Title.*
*TC PZ7.W9195 Al 19997*

**Wright, Andrew, 1958-** Learning to teach religious education in the secondary school : a companion to school experience / Andrew Wright, Ann-Marie Brandom. London ; New York : Routledge, 2000. xviii, 314 p. : ill. ; 25 cm. (Learning to teach subjects in the secondary school) Includes bibliographical references and index. ISBN 0-415-19436-9 (pbk : alk. paper) DDC 200/.71/241
*1. Religious education - Great Britain. 2. Religion - Study and teaching (Secondary) - Great Britain. I. Brandom, Ann-Marie. II. Title. III. Series: Learning to teach subjects in the secondary school series.*
*TC LC410.G7 W75 2000*

**Wright, Cream A. H.**
Issues in education and technology :. London : Commonwealth Secretariat, c2000.
*TC LB1028.3 .I77 2000*

**Wright, David, 1947-.**
Kouki, Rafa. Telelearning via the Internet. Hershey, PA : Idea Group Pub., c1999.
*TC LC5800 .K68 1999*

**Wright, Elizur, 1804-1885.**
La Fontaine, Jean de, 1621-1695. [Fables. English. Selections] Marc Chagall. New York : New Press : Distributed by W.W. Norton, [1997]
*TC PQ1811.E3 W6 1997*

**Wright, Frank, 1948-** Two lands on one soil : Ulster politics before home rule / Frank Wright. New York : St. Martin's Press, 1996. xi, 595 p. : ill. ; maps ; 23 cm. Includes bibliographical references (p. 524-565) and index. ISBN 0-312-15924-2 DDC 941.608
*1. Ulster (Northern Ireland and Ireland) - History. 2. Social conflict - Ulster (Northern Ireland and Ireland) 3. Northern Ireland - History - 1969-1994. I. Title.*
*TC DA990.U46 W756 1996*

**Wright-Frierson, Virginia.** A North American rain forest scrapbook / Virginia Wright-Frierson. New York : Walker and Co., 1999. 1v. (unpaged) : col. ill. ; 29 cm. SUMMARY: Presented in the form of a scrapbook, describes the author's exploration of a temperate rain forest in North America, located in Washington State, and the plants and animals she found there. ISBN 0-8027-8679-0 (hardcover) ISBN 0-8027-8680-4 (reinforced) DDC 577.34/09797/94
*1. Rain forest ecology - Washington (State) - Olympic Peninsula - Juvenile literature. 2. Rain forests - Washington (State) - Olympic Peninsula - Juvenile literature. 3. Rain forest*

ecology - Washington (State) 4. Rain forests - Washington (State) 5. Ecology. 6. Scrapbooks. I. Title.
*TC QH105.W2 W75 1999*

**Wright, Ian, 1941-.**
Harrison, John, 1951- Critical challenges in social studies for upper elementary students. Vancouver : Critical Thinking Cooperative, 1999.
*TC LB1584.5.C3 H37 1999*
Trends & issues in Canadian social studies. Vancouver : Pacific Educational Press, c1997.
*TC LB1584.5.C3 T74 1997*

**Wright, Marguerite A.** I'm chocolate, you're vanilla : raising healthy Black and biracial children in a race-conscious world / Marguerite A. Wright. 1st paperback ed. San Francisco : Jossey-Bass, 2000. x, 290 p. ; 24 cm. Includes bibliographical references (p. 269-279) and index. ISBN 0-7879-5234-6
*1. Race awareness in children - United States. 2. Afro-American children - Psychology. 3. Afro-American children - Attitudes. 4. Afro-American children - Ethnic identity. 5. Racially mixed children - Psychology. 6. Racially mixed children - Attitudes. 7. Racially mixed children - Ethnic identity. I. Title. II. Title: Raising healthy Black and biracial children in a race-conscious world*
*TC BF723.R3 W75 2000*

**Wright, Nigel.**
Bottery, Mike. Teachers and the state. London ; New York : Routledge, c2000.
*TC LB1775.4.G7 B68 2000*

**Wright, Quincy, 1890-1970.**
Richardson, Lewis Fry, 1881-1953. Statistics of deadly quarrels. Pacific Grove, Ca. Boxwood Press [1960]
*TC U21.7 .R5 1960*

**Wright, Robert, 1957-** The moral animal : evolutionary psychology and everyday life / Robert Wright. 1st Vintage books ed. New York : Vintage Books, 1995, c1994. x, 466 p. : ill. ; 21 cm. Includes bibliographical references (p. 426-445) and index. ISBN 0-679-76399-6 (pbk).
*1. Sociobiology. 2. Genetic psychology. 3. Human behavior. 4. Behavior evolution. I. Title.*
*TC GN365.9 .W75 1995*

**Wright, Stanley Nathaniel.** The Beacon model : implementation of a school-based community program / by Stanley Nathaniel Wright. 1998. x, 162 leaves : ill. ; 29 cm. Includes tables. Typescript; issued also on microfilm. Thesis (Ed.D.)--Teachers College, Columbia University, 1998. Includes bibliographical references (leaves 152-155).
*1. Community and school - New York (State) - New York. 2. Interorganizational relations - New York (State) - New York. 3. School administrators - New York (State) - New York. 4. Public schools - New York (State) - New York. 5. Harlem (New York, N.Y.) - Social conditions. I. Title.*
*TC 06 no. 11007*

**A wrinkle in time by Madeleine L'Engle.**
Beech, Linda Ward. New York : Scholastic, c1997.
*TC LB1573 .B435 1997*

**The write approach.**
Stockard, Olivia. San Diego, Calif. : Academic Press, c1999.
*TC HF5718.3 .S764 1999*

**Write it!.**
Bankhead, Elizabeth. 2nd ed./MLA version. Englewood, Colo. : Libraries Unlimited, c1999.
*TC LB1047.3 .W75 1999*

**Write it.**
Bankhead, Elizabeth. Write it!. 2nd ed./MLA version. Englewood, Colo. : Libraries Unlimited, c1999.
*TC LB1047.3 .W75 1999*

**WRITERS.** *See* **AUTHORS.**

**Writers' workshop :** reflections of elementary and middle school teachers / edited by Bobbie A. Solley. Boston ; London : Allyn and Bacon, c2000. xiv, 144 p. : ill., facsims., forms ; 28 cm. Includes bibliographical references (p. 113-114) and index. ISBN 0-205-29015-9 DDC 372.62/3
*1. Creative writing (Elementary education) 2. English language - Composition and exercises - Study and teaching (Elementary) 3. Creative writing (Middle school) 4. English language - Composition and exercises - Study and teaching (Middle school) I. Solley, Bobbie A.*
*TC LB1576 .W734 2000*

**WRITING.** *See also* **ENGLISH LANGUAGE - WRITING.**
Nakanishi, Akira, 1928- [Sekai no moji. English] Writing systems of the world. 1st pbk. ed. Rutland, Vt. : C.E. Tuttle Co., 1990, c1980.

*TC Z40 .N2613 1990*
Ong, Walter J. Orality and literacy. London ; New York : Routledge, 1988.
*TC P35 .O5 1988*

**Writing across languages** / edited by Gerd Bräuer. Stamford, Conn. : Ablex Pub., c2000. xii, 191 p. ; 24 cm. (Advances in foreign and second language pedagogy ; v. 1) Includes bibliographical references and indexes. ISBN 1-56750-478-7 (cloth) ISBN 1-56750-479-5 (pbk.) DDC 418/.007
*1. Languages, Modern - Study and teaching. 2. Creative writing - Study and teaching. 3. Report writing - Study and teaching. 4. Second language acquisition. I. Bräuer, Gerd. II. Series.*
*TC PB36 .W77 2000*

**Writing and healing :** toward an informed practice / edited by Charles M. Anderson, Marian M. MacCurdy. Urbana, Ill. : National Council of Teachers of English, c2000. xvi, 476 p. ; 23 cm. (Refiguring English studies) Includes bibliographical references and index. ISBN 0-8141-5860-9 DDC 615.8/515
*1. Creative writing - Therapeutic use. 2. Psychotherapy. I. Anderson, Charles M. II. MacCurdy, Marian M. III. Series.*
*TC RC489.W75 W756 2000*

**Writing and society.**
Wheale, Nigel. London ; New York : Routledge, 1999.
*TC PR438.P65 W75 1999*

**Writing and teaching history.**
Osokoya, Israel O. (Israel Olu). Ibadan : Laurel Educational Publishers, 1996.
*TC D13 .O86 1996*

**Writing and updating technology plans.**
Cohn, John M. New York : Neal-Schuman Publishers, 2000.
*TC Z678.9.A4 U623 2000*

**WRITING (AUTHORSHIP).** *See* **AUTHORSHIP; CREATIVE WRITING.**

**WRITING CENTERS.**
Gillespie, Paula. The Allyn and Bacon guide to peer tutoring. Boston : Allyn & Bacon, c2000.
*TC LB1031.5 .G55 2000*
Stories from the center. Urbana, Ill. National Council of Teachers of English, c2000.
*TC PE1404 .S834 2000*
Taking flight with OWLs. Mahwah, N.J. : Lawrence Erlbaum Associates, Publishers, 2000.
*TC PE1404 .T24 2000*

**WRITING CENTERS - AUTOMATION.**
Coogan, David. Electronic writing centers. Stamford, Conn. : Ablex Pub. Corp., c1999.
*TC PE1404 .C6347 1999*

**WRITING (COMPOSITION).** *See* **COMPOSITION (LANGUAGE ARTS).**

**WRITING - HISTORY.**
Oauknin, Marc-Alain. [Mystères de l'alphabet. English] The mysteries of the alphabet. 1st ed. New York : Abbeville Press, c1999.
*TC P211 .O913 1999*

**WRITING LABORATORIES.** *See* **WRITING CENTERS.**

**The writing lives of children.**
Madigan, Dan. York, ME : Stenhouse Publishers, 1997.
*TC LB1042 .M24 1997*

**WRITING - MATERIALS AND INSTRUMENTS.** *See* **PAPER.**

**The writing process in action.**
Proett, Jackie, 1926- Urbana, Ill. : National Council of Teachers of English, c1986.
*TC LB1631 .P697 1986*

**Writing quality individualized education programs : what's best for students with disabilities?.**
Gibb, Gordon S. Guide to writing quality individualized education programs :. Boston : Allyn and Bacon, c2000.
*TC LC4019 .G43 2000*

**Writing rules!.**
Brusko, Mike. Portsmouth, NH : Heinemann, c1999.
*TC LB1576 .B876 1999*

**Writing science**
Naturalizing phenomenology. Stanford, Calif. : Stanford University Press, c1999.
*TC B829.5 .N38 1999*

Varela, Francisco J., 1945- [Know-how per l'etica. English] Ethical know-how. Stanford, Calif. : Stanford University Press, 1999.
*TC BJ1012 .V3813 1999*

**Writing systems of the world.**
Nakanishi, Akira, 1928- [Sekai no moji. English] 1st pbk. ed. Rutland, Vt. : C.E. Tuttle Co., 1990, c1980.
*TC Z40 .N2613 1990*

**The writing teacher's sourcebook** / edited by Edward P.J. Corbett, Nancy Myers, Gary Tate. 4th ed. New York : Oxford University Press, 2000. viii, 391 p. : ill. ; 24 cm. Includes bibliographical references. ISBN 0-19-512377-8 (alk. paper) DDC 808/.042/0711
*1. English language - Rhetoric - Study and teaching. 2. Report writing - Study and teaching. I. Corbett, Edward P. J. II. Myers, Nancy. III. Tate, Gary.*
*TC PE1404 .W74 2000*

**Writing together.**
Haines, Dawn Denham. 1st ed. New York : Berkley Pub. Group, 1997.
*TC PN145 .H28 1997*

**Writing workout.**
Huizenga, Jann. Glenview, Ill. : Scott, Foresman and Co.,,c1990.
*TC PE1128 .H84 1990*

**The writings of Clarence S. Stein.**
Stein, Clarence S. Baltimore, Md. : Johns Hopkins University Press, 1998.
*TC NA9108 .S83 1998*

**WRITINGS OF GAYS.** *See* **GAYS' WRITINGS.**

**WRITINGS OF HOMOSEXUALS.** *See* **GAYS' WRITINGS.**

**WRITTEN COMMUNICATION.** *See also* **ENGLISH LANGUAGE - WRITTEN ENGLISH.**
Jarrett, Michael, 1953- Drifting on a read. Albany, N.Y. : State University of New York Press, 1999.
*TC ML3849 .J39 1999*

A Rhetoric of doing. Carbondale : Southern Illinois University Press, c1992.
*TC PE1404 .R496 1992*

Scholes, Robert J. A linguistic approach to reading and writing. Lewiston, N.Y. : E. Mellen Press, c1999.
*TC P211 .S383 1999*

**WRITTEN COMMUNICATION - ENGLISH-SPEAKING COUNTRIES - HISTORY.**
Baron, Naomi S. Alphabet to email. London ; New York : Routledge, 2000.
*TC PE1075 .B28 2000*

**WRITTEN COMMUNICATION - GREAT BRITAIN - HISTORY - 17TH CENTURY.**
Wheale, Nigel. Writing and society. London ; New York : Routledge, 1999.
*TC PR438.P65 W75 1999*

**WRITTEN COMMUNICATION - MEDITERRANEAN REGION - HISTORY.**
Millard, A. R. (Alan Ralph) Reading and writing in the time of Jesus. New York : New York University Press, 2000.
*TC BS2555.5 .M55 2000*

**WRITTEN COMMUNICATION - SOCIAL ASPECTS.**
Global literacies and the World-Wide Web. London ; New York : Routledge, 2000.
*TC P94.6 .G58 2000*

**WRITTEN COMPOSITION.** *See* **COMPOSITION (LANGUAGE ARTS).**

**WRITTEN DISCOURSE.** *See* **WRITTEN COMMUNICATION.**

**WRITTEN ENGLISH.** *See* **ENGLISH LANGUAGE - WRITTEN ENGLISH.**

**Written expression** : the principal's survival guide / India Podsen ... [et al.]. Larchmont, NY : Eye on Education, c1997. xii, 164 p. ; 24 cm. (The school leadership library) Includes bibliographical references. ISBN 1-88300-134-X DDC 808/.042/024371
*1. Authorship - Handbooks, manuals, etc. 2. School administrators - Handbooks, manuals, etc. I. Podsen, India, 1945- II. Series.*
*TC PN145 .W78 1997*

**WRITTEN LANGUAGE.** *See* **WRITTEN COMMUNICATION.**

**Written language series**
Self-assessment and development in writing. Cresskill, N.J. : Hampton Press, c2000.

*TC PE1404 .S37 2000*

**WTM-series**
(3.) Klaassen, R. G. Effective lecturing behaviour in English-medium instruction. Delft, Netherlands : Delft University Press, 1999.
*TC LB2393 .K53 1999*

**Wu, Tzu-ming.**
International Symposium on Historical Archives of Pre-1949 Christian Higher Education in China (1993 ; Hong Kong) Chung-kuo chiao hui ta hsüeh li shih wen hsien yen t'ao hui lun wen chi. Hsiang-kang : Chung wen ta hsüeh ch'u pan she, 1995.
*TC LC432.C5 I58 1995*

**WUHANA INDIANS.** *See* **MACUNA INDIANS.**

**Wulff, Helena.** Ballet across borders : career and culture in the world of dancers / Helena Wulff. Oxford ; New York : Berg, 1998. xiii, 185 p. : ill. ; 24 cm. Includes bibliographical references (p. 169-178) and index. ISBN 1-85973-993-8 (cloth) ISBN 1-85973-998-9 (paper)
*1. Ballet. 2. Ballet dancers. 3. Ballet companies. I. Title.*
*TC GV1787 .W85 1998*

**Wurmser, Leon.**
**[Flucht vor dem Gewissen. English]**
The power of the inner judge : psychodynamic treatment of the severe neuroses / by Léon Wurmser. Northvale, N.J. : Jason Aronson Inc., c2000. xi, 356 p. ; 24 cm. Includes bibliographical references and index. ISBN 0-7657-0177-4 (alk. paper)
*1. Neuroses - Treatment. 2. Super-ego. 3. Super-ego. 4. Neurotic Disorders - therapy. 5. Defense Mechanisms. 6. Psychoanalytic Theory. 7. Psychoanalytic Therapy - methods. 8. Superego. I. Title. II. Title: Psychodynamic treatment of the severe neuroses*
*TC RC530 .W8713 2000*

**WWW (INFORMATION RETRIEVAL SYSTEM).** *See* **WORLD WIDE WEB (INFORMATION RETRIEVAL SYSTEM).**

**Wyatt, Gary, 1958-** Mythic beings : spirit art of the Northwest Coast / Gary Wyatt. Vancouver : Douglas & McIntyre ; Seattle : University of Washington Press, c1999. 144 p. : ill., maps ; 26 cm. Includes bibliographical references. ISBN 0-295-97798-1 (alk. paper) DDC 704.03/9707111
*1. Indian art - British Columbia - Pacific Coast. 2. Art, Modern - 20th century - British Columbia - Pacific Coast. 3. Indian mythology - British Columbia - Pacific Coast. 4. Legends - British Columbia - Pacific Coast. I. Title.*
*TC E78.B9 W93 1999*

**Wyatt, Robert Lee, 1940-** So you have to have a portfolio : a teacher's guide to preparation and presentation / Robert L. Wyatt III, Sandra Looper. Thousand Oaks, Calif. : Corwin Press, c1999. xiv, 110 p. ; 26 cm. Includes bibliographical references (p. 103-105) and index. ISBN 0-8039-6821-3 (cloth : acid-free paper) ISBN 0-8039-6822-1 (pbk.) DDC 370/.71/1
*1. Portfolios in education - United States. 2. Employment portfolios - United States. 3. Teachers college students - Rating of - United States. I. Looper, Sandra. II. Title.*
*TC LB1728 .W93 1999*

**Wyer, Robert S.**
Perspectives on behavioral self-regulation. Mahwah, N.J. : Lawrence Erlbaum Associates, 1999.
*TC HM291 A345 1999*

Stereotype activation and inhibition. Mahwah, N.J. : L. Erlbaum Associates, 1998.
*TC BF323.S63 S75 1998*

**Wyllie, Romy.** Caltech's architectural heritage : from Spanish tile to modern stone / Romy Wyllie. Los Angeles : Balcony Press, c2000. 287 p. : ill. (some col.) ; 29 cm. Includes bibliographical referencesand index. ISBN 1-89044-905-9
*1. California Institute of Technology - Buildings. 2. California Institute of Technology - History. 3. College buildings - California - Pasadena. 4. Pasadena (Calif.) - Buildings, structures, etc. I. Title. II. Title: California Institute of Technology's architectural heritage*
*TC NA6603 .W95 2000*

**Wyness, Michael G.** Contesting childhood / Michael G. Wyness. London ; New York : Falmer Press, 2000. 161 p. ; 23 cm. Includes bibliographical references (p. [142]-151) and index. ISBN 0-7507-0824-7 (hbk : alk. paper) ISBN 0-7507-0823-9 (pbk : alk. paper) DDC 305.23
*1. Children. 2. Child development. 3. Children - Social conditions. 4. Socialization. I. Title.*
*TC HQ767.9 .W96 2000*

**Wynn, Charles M.** The five biggest ideas in science / Charles M. Wynn and Arthur W. Wiggins ; with cartoon commentary by Sidney Harris. New York : Wiley, c1997. vii, 200 p. : ill. ; 23 cm. Includes bibliographical references (p. 185-188) and index.

SUMMARY: Presents five basic scientific hypotheses: the atomic model, the periodic law, the big bang theory, plate tectonics, and evolution. ISBN 0-471-13812-6 (pbk. : alk. paper) DDC 500
*1. Science - Miscellanea. 2. Science - Miscellanea. I. Wiggins, Arthur W. II. Harris, Sidney, ill. III. Title.*
*TC Q163 .W99 1997*

**Wynne-Jones, Tim.** Builder of the moon / by Tim Wynne-Jones ; pictures by Ian Wallace. New York M.K. McElderry Books, c1988. [32] p. : col. ill. ; 38 x 38 cm. SUMMARY: Brave block-builder David Finebloom receives a message from the moon that it is falling apart and rushes off to help. ISBN 0-02-109111-0
*1. Blocks (Toys) - Fiction. 2. Moon - Fiction. I. Wallace, Ian, 1950- / ill. II. Title.*
*TC PZ7.W993 Bu 1988*

**WYOMING - FICTION.**
Naylor, Phyllis Reynolds. Walker's Crossing. New York : Atheneum Books for Young Readers, c1999.
*TC PZ7.N24 Wai 1999*

**Wypijewski, JoAnn.**
Painting by numbers. Berkeley : University of California Press, [1999]
*TC ND1140 .P26 1999*

**Wyrwicka, Wanda.** Conditioning : situation versus intermittent stimulus / Wanda Wyrwicka. New Brunswick, N.J. : Transaction Publishers, c2000, vii, 100 p. : ill. ; 24 cm. Includes bibliographical references (p. 87-95) and indexes. ISBN 1-56000-432-0 (alk. paper) DDC 152.3/224
*1. Conditioned response. 2. Psychology, Comparative. I. Title.*
*TC BF319 .W94 2000*

**Wysong, Earl, 1944-.**
Perrucci, Robert. The new class society. Lanham, Md. : Rowman & Littlefield, 1999.
*TC HN90.S6 P47 1999*

**Wyss, Beat, 1947-**
**[Trauer der Vollendung. English]**
Hegel's art history and the critique of modernity / Beat Wyss ; translated by Caroline Dobson Saltzwedel. Cambridge, U.K. ; New York : Cambridge University Press, c1999. xv, 288 p. : ill. ; 27 cm. Includes bibliographical references (p. 265-283) and index. ISBN 0-521-59211-9 (hardback) DDC 111/.85/092
*1. Aesthetics, Modern. 2. Hegel, Georg Wilhelm Friedrich, - 1770-1831 - Aesthetics. I. Title.*
*TC BH151 .W9713 1999*

**XENOPHOBIA - UNITED STATES - HISTORY.**
Irving, Katrina. Immigrant mothers. Urbana : University of Illinois Press, c2000.
*TC HQ1419 .I75 2000*

**XINJIANG UYGUR ZIZHIQU (CHINA) - ETHNIC RELATIONS.**
Benson, Linda. China's last Nomads. Armonk, N.Y. : M.E. Sharpe, c1998.
*TC DS731.K38 B46 1998*

**XYLOPHONE AND PIANO MUSIC (JAZZ).** *See* **JAZZ.**

**YA LITERATURE.** *See* **YOUNG ADULT LITERATURE.**

**Yackel, Erna.**
Symbolizing and communicating in mathematics classrooms. Mahwah, N.J. : Lawrence Erlbaum Associates, 2000.
*TC QA11 .S873 2000*

**A Yale album.**
Benson, Richard, 1943- New Haven : Yale University in association with Yale University Press, c2000.
*TC LD6337 .B46 2000*

**Yale Center for British Art.**
Farr, Dennis, 1929- Francis Bacon. New York : Harry N. Abrams in association with the Trust for Museum Exhibitions, 1999.
*TC ND497.B16 A4 1999*

**YALE REPORT OF 1828.**
Rabil, Alison. Content, context, and continuity. 1998.
*TC 06 no. 10901*

**Yale report of 1828, its impact on antebellum higher education with implications for contemporary liberal arts programs.**
Rabil, Alison. Content, context, and continuity. 1998.
*TC 06 no. 10901*

**Yale University.**
Benson, Richard, 1943- A Yale album. New Haven : Yale University in association with Yale University Press, c2000.
*TC LD6337 .B46 2000*

**YALE UNIVERSITY - HISTORY.**
Rabil, Alison. Content, context, and continuity. 1998.
*TC 06 no. 10901*

**YALE UNIVERSITY - HISTORY - 20TH CENTURY - PICTORIAL WORKS.**
Benson, Richard, 1943- A Yale album. New Haven : Yale University in association with Yale University Press, c2000.
*TC LD6337 .B46 2000*

**Yamamoto, Hisaye.**
Rabbit in the moon [videorecording]. San Francisco, Calif. : Wabi-Sabi Productions, 1999.
*TC D753.8 .R3 1999*

**Yamusah, Salifu.** An investigation of the relative effectiveness of the composite approach and the phenomenological method for enhancing self-esteem in adults with mental retardation / Salifu Yamusah. 1998. xi, 280 leaves ; 29 cm. Typescript; issued also on microfilm. Thesis (Ph.D.)--Columbia University, 1998. Includes bibliographical references (leaves 199-218)
*1. Self-esteem. 2. Self-efficacy. 3. Mentally handicapped - Psychological testing. 4. Self psychology. 5. Adaptability (Psychology) I. Title.*
*TC 085 Y146*

**Yancey, Kathleen Blake, 1950-.**
Self-assessment and development in writing. Cresskill, N.J. : Hampton Press, c2000.
*TC PE1404 .S37 2000*

**Yang, Fang-Ying.** An analysis of 12th grade students' reasoning styles and competencies when presented with an environmental problem in a social and scientific context / by Fang-Ying Yang. 1999. xiii, 261 leaves : ill. ; 29 cm. Typescript; issued also on microfilm. Thesis (Ed.D.)--Teachers College, Columbia University, 1999. Includes bibliographical references (leaves 156-179)
*1. Reasoning - Study and teaching (Secondary) - Taiwan. 2. Reasoning - Problems, exercises, etc. 3. Science - Study and teaching (Secondary) - Taiwan - Research. 4. Social sciences - Study and teaching (Secondary) - Taiwan - Research. 5. Expertise - Social aspects. 6. Expertise - Environmental aspects. 7. Cognition and culture - Taiwan. I. Title.*
*TC 06 no. 11076*

**Yanni, Carla.** Nature's museums : Victorian science and the architecture of display / Carla Yanni. Baltimore, Md : Johns Hopkins University Press, 2000. xvi, 199 p. : ill. ; 27 cm. Includes bibliographical references (p. 187-196) and index. ISBN 0-8018-6326-0 (alk. paper)
*1. Natural history museums - History - 19th century. 2. Museum architecture - History - 19th century. 3. Architecture, Victorian. I. Title.*
*TC QH70.A1 Y25 2000*

**Yard, Sally.**
Farr, Dennis, 1929- Francis Bacon. New York : Harry N. Abrams in association with the Trust for Museum Exhibitions, 1999.
*TC ND497.B16 A4 1999*

**Yardley, Alice.** Reaching out. London : Evans Bros., 1970. 112 p. :19 cm. (Her Young children learning) Includes bibliographical references (p. 107-111) and index. DDC 372.24/1
*1. Nursery schools. I. Title.*
*TC LB1140 .Y35*

**YARIBA (AFRICAN PEOPLE).** *See* **YORUBA (AFRICAN PEOPLE).**

**Yashima, Taro, 1908-** Umbrella / by Taro Yashima. New York : Viking, 1958. 30 p. : col. ill. ; 21 x 25 cm.
*1. Umbrellas and parasols - Juvenile literature. I. Title.*
*TC PZ7.Y212 Um10*

**Yasso, Warren E.**
Brandwein, Paul F. (Paul Franz), 1912- Matter. Curie ed. New York : Harcourt Brace Jovanovich, 1980.
*TC Q161.2 .C66 1980*

**YASUTOMO, SHINICHI.**
Heart of the country [videorecording]. [New York, NY : First Run/Icarus Films, 1998].
*TC LB1565.H6 H3 1998*

**Ybarra, Silvia.**
Ardovino, Joan. Multiple measures. Thousand Oaks, Calif. : Corwin Press, c2000.
*TC LB3051 .A745 2000*

**Yeakey, Carol Camp.**
Edmund W. Gordon. Stamford, Conn. : Jai Press, c2000.
*TC HM1033 .E35 2000*

**YEAR.** *See* **MONTHS.**

**The year 2000.**
Kahn, Herman, 1922- New York : Macmillan, c1967.
*TC CB160 .K3 1967*

**YEAR-ROUND EDUCATION.** *See* **YEAR-ROUND SCHOOLS.**

**Year-round schooling.**
Shields, Carolyn M. Lanham, Md. : Scarecrow Press, 2000.
*TC LB3034 .S55 2000*

**YEAR-ROUND SCHOOLS - UNITED STATES.**
Shields, Carolyn M. Year-round schooling. Lanham, Md. : Scarecrow Press, 2000.
*TC LB3034 .S55 2000*

**Yearbook.**
Claremont Reading Conference. Claremont, Calif. : Claremont Graduate School Curriculum Laboratory, c1961-
*TC BF456.R2 A24*

**Yearbook (Council on Technology Teacher Education (U.S.))**
(47th, 1998.) Diversity in technology education. New York : Glencoe, c1998.
*TC T61 .A56 47th 1998*

(47th, 1998.) Diversity in technology education. New York : Glencoe, c1998.
*TC T61 .A56 47th 1998*

**Yearbook of the Claremont Reading Conference.**
Claremont Reading Conference. Yearbook. Claremont, Calif. : Claremont Graduate School Curriculum Laboratory, c1961-
*TC BF456.R2 A24*

**Yearbook of the College Reading Association**
(21st.) Dugan, JoAnn R. Advancing the world of literacy. Carrollton, Ga. : College Reading Association, 1999.
*TC LB2395 .C62 1999*

**Yearbook of the National Society for the Study of Education**
(99th, pt. 1.) Constructivism in education. Chicago, Ill. : NSSE : Distributed by the University of Chicago Press, 2000.
*TC LB5 .N25 99th pt. 1*

(99th, pt. 2.) American education. Chicago, Ill. : NSSE : Distributed by the University of Chicago Press, 2000.
*TC LB5 .N25 99th pt. 2*

**Yearbook of the New York Society for the Experimental Study of Education.**
Bulletin of the New York Society for the Experimental Study of Education. [New York : The Society,

**Yearbook of the Politics of Education Association**
(1998) Accuracy or advocacy. Thousand Oaks, Calif. : Corwin Press, c1999.
*TC LB1028 .A312 1999*

**Yearning.**
Hooks, Bell. Boston, MA : South End Press, c1990.
*TC E185.86 .H742 1990*

**Yellin, Jean Fagan.**
Jacobs, Harriet A. (Harriet Ann), 1813-1897. Incidents in the life of a slave girl : written by herself. Cambridge, Mass. : Harvard University Press, 2000.
*TC E444.J17 A3 2000c*

**Yenawine, Philip.**
Art matters. New York : New York University Press, c1999.
*TC N72.S6 A752 1999*

**Yeo, Frederick L.**
From nihilism to possibility. Cresskill, N.J. : Hampton Press, c1999.
*TC LC5141 .F76 1999*

**Yep, Laurence.** The case of the firecrackers / Laurence Yep. 1st ed. New York : HarperCollins, c1999. 179 p. ; 22 cm. (Chinatown mystery ; #3) SUMMARY: When a prop gun used during the making of a television show turns out to have real bullets, twelve-year-old Lily Lew and Auntie, her movie actress great-aunt, comb San Francisco's Chinatown in search of the culprit responsible for loading the gun. ISBN 0-06-024449-6 ISBN 0-06-024452-6 (lib. bdg.) DDC [Fic]
*1. Mystery and detective stories. 2. Chinese Americans - Fiction. 3. Chinatown (San Francisco, Calif.) - Fiction. I. Title. II. Series: Yep, Laurence. Chinatown ; 3.*
*TC PZ7.Y44 Cag 1999*

**Chinatown**
(3.) Yep, Laurence. The case of the firecrackers. 1st ed. New York : HarperCollins, c1999.

*TC PZ7.Y44 Cag 1999*

**Yerkes, Robert Mearns, 1876- ed.**
The Journal of animal behavior. Cambridge, Mass., H. Holt and Company; [etc., etc.], 1911-17]

**Yi, Qing.** Simulating nonmodel-fitting responses in a CAT environment / Qing Yi, Michael L. Nering. Iowa City, Iowa : ACT, 1998. ii, 26 p. : ill. ; 28 cm. (ACT research report series, 98-10). "December 1998"--Cover. Includes bibliographical references (p. 16-19).
*1. Computer adaptive testing. 2. Educational tests and measurements. 3. Examinations - Design and construction. I. Nering, Michael L. II. Title. III. Series.*
*TC LB3051 .A3 no. 98-10*

**Ying, Yu-Wen.**
Immigrant women's health. 1st ed. San Francisco : Jossey-Bass, c1999.
*TC RA448.5.I44 I44 1999*

**Yiribana.**
Art Gallery of New South Wales. 2nd ed. Sydney, Australia : The Gallery, 1998.
*TC N7401 .A765 1998*

Art Gallery of New South Wales. Yiribana. 2nd ed. Sydney, Australia : The Gallery, 1998.
*TC N7401 .A765 1998*

**Yolen, Jane.** Mouse's birthday / Jane Yolen ; illustrated by Bruce Degen. New York : Putnam's, c1993. 1 v. (unpaged) : col. ill. ; 29 cm. SUMMARY: One after another, several animals try to squeeze into Mouse's very small house to help him celebrate his birthday. ISBN 0-399-22189-1 DDC [E]
*1. Mice - Fiction. 2. Animals - Fiction. 3. Birthdays - Fiction. 4. Stories in rhyme. I. Degen, Bruce, ill. II. Title.*
*TC PZ8.3.Y76 Mo 1993*

Ring of earth : a child's book of seasons / by Jane Yolen ; illustrated by John Wallner. 1st ed. San Diego : Harcourt Brace Jovanovich, c1986. [32] p. : col. ill. ; 25 x 26 cm. SUMMARY: The four seasons are viewed in poetry from the perspectives of a weasel, spring peeper, dragonfly, and goose. ISBN 0-15-267140-4 DDC 811/.54
*1. Children's poetry, American. 2. Seasons - Juvenile poetry. 3. Animals - Juvenile poetry. 4. Seasons - Poetry. 5. Animals - Poetry. 6. American poetry. I. Wallner, John C., ill. II. Title.*
*TC PS3575.O43 R5 1986*

**YOOBA (AFRICAN PEOPLE).** *See* **YORUBA (AFRICAN PEOPLE).**

**YORKTOWN (VA.) - HISTORY - SIEGE, 1781.**
Ferrie, Richard. The world turned upside down. 1st ed. New York : Holiday House, c1999.
*TC E241.Y6 F45 1999*

**YORKTOWN (VA.) - HISTORY - SIEGE, 1781 - JUVENILE LITERATURE.**
Ferrie, Richard. The world turned upside down. 1st ed. New York : Holiday House, c1999.
*TC E241.Y6 F45 1999*

**YORUBA (AFRICAN PEOPLE) - RELIGION - INFLUENCE.**
Santería aesthetics in contemporary Latin American art. Washington : Smithsonian Institution Press, c1996.
*TC N72.R4 S26 1996*

**Yoruba, sculpture of West Africa.**
Fagg, William Buller. 1st ed. New York : Knopf : Distributed by Random House, 1982.
*TC NB1099.N5 F34*

**YORUBAS.** *See* **YORUBA (AFRICAN PEOPLE).**

**Yoshinaga-Herzig, Aiko.**
Rabbit in the moon [videorecording]. San Francisco, Calif. : Wabi-Sabi Productions, 1999.
*TC D753.8 .R3 1999*

**You eat what you are.**
Barer-Stein, Thelma. 2nd ed. Toronto : Firefly Books, 1999.
*TC GT2850 .B37 1999*

**You never asked me to read.**
Simmons, Jay, 1947- Boston : Allyn and Bacon, c2000.
*TC LB1050.46 .S535 2000*

**You sound taller on the telephone.**
Dunklee, Dennis R. Thousand Oaks, Calif. : Corwin Press, c1999.
*TC LB2831.9 .D85 1999*

**Youdell, Deborah, 1970-.**
Gillborn, David. Rationing education. Buckingham [England] ; Philadelphia : Open University Press, 2000.
*TC LC213.3.G73 L664 2000*

**You'll grow soon, Alex.**
Shavick, Andrea. New York : Walker, 2000.
*TC PZ7.S5328 Yo 2000*

**Young adolescents meet literature :** intersections for
learning / editors, Mary Clare Courtland, Trevor J.
Gambell. Vancouver : Pacific Education Press, 2000.
384 p. ; 23 cm. Includes bibliographical references and index.
ISBN 1-89576-641-9 DDC 372.64
*1. Children's literature, Canadian (English) - Study and
teaching (Elementary) 2. Young adult literature, Canadian
(English) - Study and teaching. I. Courtland, Mary Clare. II.
Gambell, Trevor J.*
*TC LB1575.5.C3 Y68 2000*

**YOUNG ADULT BOOKS.** *See* **YOUNG ADULT
LITERATURE.**

**YOUNG ADULT FICTION, AMERICAN -
HISTORY AND CRITICISM.**
Young adult science fiction. Westport, Conn. :
Greenwood Press, 1999.
*TC PS374.S35 Y63 1999*

**YOUNG ADULT FICTION - HISTORY AND
CRITICISM.**
Barnhouse, Rebecca. Recasting the past. Portsmouth,
NH : Boynton/Cook Publishers, c2000.
*TC PN3443 .B37 2000*

McCallum, Robyn. Ideologies of identity in
adolescent fiction. New York : Garland Pub., 1999.
*TC PN3443 .M38 1999*

**YOUNG ADULT FICTION - STUDY AND
TEACHING.**
Barnhouse, Rebecca. Recasting the past. Portsmouth,
NH : Boynton/Cook Publishers, c2000.
*TC PN3443 .B37 2000*

**YOUNG ADULT FILMS - CATALOGS.**
Culturally diverse videos, audios, and CD-ROMS for
children and young adults. New York : Neal-Schuman
Publishers, 1999.
*TC PN1998 .M85 1999*

**YOUNG ADULT LITERATURE.** *See* **YOUNG
ADULT FICTION.**

**YOUNG ADULT LITERATURE -
BIBLIOGRAPHY.**
Matulka, Denise I. Picture this. Westport, Conn. :
Greenwood Press, 1997.
*TC Z1033.P52 M37 1997*

**YOUNG ADULT LITERATURE - BOOK
REVIEWS.**
Gillespie, John Thomas, 1928- Characters in young
adult literature. Detroit : Gale Research, c1997.
*TC Z1037.A1 G47 1997*

**YOUNG ADULT LITERATURE, CANADIAN
(ENGLISH) - STUDY AND TEACHING.**
Young adolescents meet literature. Vancouver :
Pacific Education Press, 2000.
*TC LB1575.5.C3 Y68 2000*

**YOUNG ADULT LITERATURE, ENGLISH -
BIBLIOGRAPHY.**
Best books for young teen readers, grades 7 to 10.
New Providence, N.J. : R.R. Bowker, 2000.
*TC Z1037 .B55 2000*

**Young adult literature series (Portsmouth, N.H.).**
Barnhouse, Rebecca. Recasting the past. Portsmouth,
NH : Boynton/Cook Publishers, c2000.
*TC PN3443 .B37 2000*

**YOUNG ADULT LITERATURE, SPANISH
AMERICAN - BIBLIOGRAPHY.**
Schon, Isabel. Recommended books in Spanish for
children and young adults, 1996 through 1999.
Lanham, Md. : Scarecrow Press, 2000.
*TC Z1037.7 .S387 2000*

**YOUNG ADULT LITERATURE, SPANISH -
BIBLIOGRAPHY.**
Schon, Isabel. Recommended books in Spanish for
children and young adults, 1996 through 1999.
Lanham, Md. : Scarecrow Press, 2000.
*TC Z1037.7 .S387 2000*

**YOUNG ADULT LITERATURE - STORIES,
PLOTS, ETC.**
Gillespie, John Thomas, 1928- Characters in young
adult literature. Detroit : Gale Research, c1997.
*TC Z1037.A1 G47 1997*

**YOUNG ADULT LITERATURE - STUDY AND
TEACHING (SECONDARY).**
Rationales for teaching young adult literature.
Portland, Me. : Calendar Islands Publishers, 1999.
*TC PN59 .R33 1999*

**YOUNG ADULT LITERATURE -
TRANSLATIONS INTO SPANISH -
BIBLIOGRAPHY.**
Schon, Isabel. Recommended books in Spanish for
children and young adults, 1996 through 1999.
Lanham, Md. : Scarecrow Press, 2000.
*TC Z1037.7 .S387 2000*

**Young adult science fiction** / edited by C.W. Sullivan,
III. Westport, Conn. : Greenwood Press, 1999. xi, 247
p. : ill. ; 25 cm. (Contributions to the study of science fiction
and fantasy, 0193-6875 ; no. 79) Includes bibliographical
references (p. [181]-240) and index. ISBN 0-313-28940-9 (alk.
paper) DDC 813/.08762099283
*1. Science fiction, American - History and criticism. 2. Young
adult fiction, American - History and criticism. 3. Youth -
United States - Books and reading. I. Sullivan, Charles Wm.
(Charles William), 1944- II. Series.*
*TC PS374.S35 Y63 1999*

**YOUNG ADULTS.** *See* **YOUNG WOMEN.**

**YOUNG ADULTS - BOOKS AND READING -
UNITED STATES.**
Littlejohn, Carol. Talk that book! booktalks to
promote reading. Worthington, Ohio : Linworth
Publishing, 1999.
*TC Z1037.A2 L58 1999*

**YOUNG ADULTS - EMPLOYMENT - UNITED
STATES - CONGRESSES.**
Transitions to adulthood in a changing economy.
Westport, Conn. : Praeger, c1999.
*TC HQ799.7 .T73 1999*

**YOUNG ADULTS - MENTAL HEALTH.**
First break [videorecording]. Boston, MA : Fanlight
Productions, c1997.
*TC RC465 .F5 1997*

First break [videorecording]. Boston, MA : Fanlight
Productions, c1997.
*TC RC465 .F5 1997*

First break [videorecording]. Boston, MA : Fanlight
Productions, c1997.
*TC RC465 .F5 1997*

**YOUNG ADULTS - UNITED STATES -
ECONOMIC CONDITIONS - CONGRESSES.**
Transitions to adulthood in a changing economy.
Westport, Conn. : Praeger, c1999.
*TC HQ799.7 .T73 1999*

**YOUNG ADULTS - UNITED STATES - LIFE
SKILLS GUIDES.**
Csóti, Márianna. People skills for young adults.
London ; Philadelphia : Jessica Kingsley, 2000.
*TC HQ799.7 .C76 2000*

**YOUNG ADULTS - UNITED STATES -
PSYCHOLOGY.**
Csóti, Márianna. People skills for young adults.
London ; Philadelphia : Jessica Kingsley, 2000.
*TC HQ799.7 .C76 2000*

**YOUNG ADULTS - UNITED STATES - SOCIAL
CONDITIONS - CONGRESSES.**
Transitions to adulthood in a changing economy.
Westport, Conn. : Praeger, c1999.
*TC HQ799.7 .T73 1999*

**Young, Alma H.**
Gendering the city. Lanham [Md.] : Rowman &
Littlefield, c2000.
*TC HT166 .G4614 2000*

**Young bilingual children in nursery school.**
Thompson, Linda, 1949- Clevedon, UK ; Buffalo,
NY : Multilingual Matters, c2000.
*TC LC3723 .T47 2000*

**Young, Brian, 1940-** The making and unmaking of a
university museum : the McCord, 1921-1996 / Brian
Young. Montreal : McGill-Queen's University Press,
c2000. xvi, 224 p. : ill., geneal. tables, ports. ; 23 cm. Includes
bibliographical references and index. ISBN 0-7735-2050-3
(pbk) DDC 069/.09714/28
*1. McCord Museum of Canadian History - History. 2. Musée
McCord d'histoire canadienne - Histoire. I. Title.*
*TC FC21 .Y68 2000*

**Young children with special needs.**
Umansky, Warren. 3rd ed. Upper Saddle River, N.J. :
Merrill, c1998.
*TC LC4031 .U425 1998*

**YOUNG CONSUMERS.**
Miles, Steven. Youth lifestyles in a changing world.
Buckingham ; Philadelphia : Open University Press,
2000.
*TC HQ796 .M4783 2000*

**Young, Ila Phillip, 1947-.**
Castetter, William Benjamin, 1914- The human
resource function in educational administration. 7th
ed. Upper Saddle River, N.J. : Merrill, c2000.
*TC LB2831.58 .C37 2000*

**Young, Josephine Peyton.**
Gillet, Jean Wallace. Understanding reading
problems. 5th ed. New York : Harlow, England :
Longman, c2000.
*TC LB1050.46 .G55 2000*

**YOUNG MEN.** *See* **BOYS.**

**YOUNG MEN, AFRO-AMERICAN.** *See* **AFRO-
AMERICAN YOUNG MEN.**

**YOUNG MEN - UNITED STATES.** *See* **AFRO-
AMERICAN YOUNG MEN.**

**Young, Noela, ill.**
Wild, Margaret, 1948- Toby. 1st American ed. New
York : Ticknor & Fields, 1994.
*TC PZ7.W64574 To 1994*

**YOUNG PEOPLE.** *See* **YOUNG ADULTS;
YOUTH.**

**YOUNG PERSONS.** *See* **YOUNG ADULTS;
YOUTH.**

**Young, R. V., 1947-** At war with the word : literary
theory and liberal education / R.V. Young.
Wilmington, Del. : ISI Books, 1999. xii, 199 p. ; 24 cm.
Includes bibliographical references (p. [183]-194) and index.
ISBN 1-88292-627-7 DDC 801/.95/0904
*1. Criticism - History - 20th century. 2. Postmodernism
(Literature) 3. Deconstruction. 4. New Criticism. I. Title.*
*TC PN94 .Y68 1999*

**Young researchers.**
MALLETT, MARGARET. London ; New York :
Routledge, 1999.
*TC LB1576 .M3627 1999*

**Young, Richard E. (Richard Emerson), 1932-.**
Inventing a discipline. Urbana, Ill. : National Council
of Teachers of English, c2000.
*TC PN175 .I58 2000*

**Young, Robert L. (Robert Louis), 1949-**
Understanding misunderstandings : a practical guide
to more successful human interaction / Robert L.
Young. 1st ed. Austin : University of Texas Press,
1999. x, 172 p. ; 23 cm. Includes bibliographical references
and index. ISBN 0-292-79605-6 (alk. paper) ISBN
0-292-79606-4 (pbk. : alk. paper) DDC 153.6
*1. Miscommunication. 2. Interpersonal communication. I. Title.*
*TC BF637.C45 Y69 1999*

**Young soldiers [picture].**
Civil war [picture]. Amawalk, NY : Jackdaw
Publications, c1999.
*TC TR820.5 .C56 1999*

Civil war [picture]. Amawalk, NY : Jackdaw
Publications, c1999.
*TC TR820.5 .C56 1999*

**Young, Steven R.**
Moro, M. I. Russian grade 1 mathematics. Chicago :
University of Chicago School of Mathematics Project,
1992.
*TC QA14.R9 R8611 1992*

Moro, M. I. Russian grade 2 mathematics. Chicago :
University of Chicago School of Mathematics Project,
1992.
*TC QA14.R9 R8711 1992*

Russian grade 3 mathematics. Chicago : University of
Chicago School of Mathematics Project, 1992.
*TC QA14.R9 R8811 1992*

**Young, Sue, 1932-** The Scholastic rhyming dictionary /
Sue Young. New York : Scholastic Reference, c1994.
vii, 213 p. : ill. (some col.) ; 23 cm. "Over 15,000 words"--
Cover. Includes index. "Ages 8 and up"--Cover. ISBN 0-590-
49460-0 DDC 423/.1
*1. English language - Rhyme - Dictionaries, Juvenile. 2.
English language - Rhyme - Dictionaries. I. Scholastic Inc. II.
Title. III. Title: Rhyming dictionary*
*TC PE1519 .Y684 1994*

**YOUNG VICTIMS OF CRIME.** *See* **YOUTH -
CRIMES AGAINST.**

**YOUNG WOMEN.** *See* **GIRLS.**

**YOUNG WOMEN - BOOKS AND READING.**
O'Keefe, Deborah. Good girl messages. New York :
Continuum, 2000.
*TC PS374.G55 O44 2000*

**Youngblade, Lise M. (Lise Marie).**
Hoffman, Lois Norma Wladis, 1929- Mothers at

work. Cambridge ; New York : Cambridge University Press, 1999.
*TC HQ759.48 .H63 1999*

**Youngner, Stuart J.**
The definition of death. Baltimore : Johns Hopkins University Press, 1999.
*TC RA1063 .D44 1999*

**Youngs, Carol.**
Brownell, Gregg. A PC for the teacher. Belmont, CA : Wadsworth Pub. Co., c1999.
*TC LB1028.43 .B755 1999*

**Your anxious child.**
Dacey, John S. 1st ed. San Francisco : Jossey-Bass, c2000.
*TC BF723.A5 D33 2000*

**You're a brave man, Julius Zimmerman.**
Mills, Claudia. 1st ed. New York : Farrar Straus Giroux, c1999.
*TC PZ7.M63963 Yo 1999*

**You're only young twice.**
Morris, Timothy, 1959- Urbana : University of Illinois Press, c2000.
*TC PR990 .M67 2000*

**YOUTH.** *See also* **ARCHITECTURE AND YOUTH; ARTS AND YOUTH; DROPOUTS; HANDICAPPED YOUTH; HOMELESS YOUTH; PROBLEM YOUTH; SOCIAL WORK WITH YOUTH; TEENAGERS; URBAN YOUTH; YOUNG ADULTS.**
Adolescent behavior and society. 5th ed. Boston : McGraw-Hill, c1998.
*TC HQ796 .A3338 1998*

**YOUTH, AFRO-AMERICAN.** *See* **AFRO-AMERICAN YOUTH.**

**YOUTH AND ARCHITECTURE.** *See* **ARCHITECTURE AND YOUTH.**

**YOUTH AND PEACE - UNITED STATES.**
Peacebuilding for adolescents. New York : P. Lang, c1999.
*TC JZ5534 .P43 1999*

**YOUTH AND THE ARTS.** *See* **ARTS AND YOUTH.**

**YOUTH AND VIOLENCE - UNITED STATES.**
Garbarino, James. Lost boys. New York : Free Press, c1999.
*TC HQ799.2.V56 G37 1999*

**YOUTH AS CONSUMERS.** *See* **YOUNG CONSUMERS.**

**YOUTH - BOOKS AND READING.**
Gillespie, John Thomas, 1928- Characters in young adult literature. Detroit : Gale Research, c1997.
*TC Z1037.A1 G47 1997*

**YOUTH - CRIMES AGAINST.** *See* **SCHOOL VIOLENCE.**

**YOUTH - CRIMES AGAINST - CALIFORNIA - LOS ANGELES.**
Children of the night [videorecording]. [Charleston, W.V.] : Cambridge Educational, c1994.
*TC HV1435.C3 C45 1994*

Children of the night [videorecording]. [Charleston, W.V.] : Cambridge Educational, c1994.
*TC HV1435.C3 C45 1994*

Children of the night [videorecording]. [Charleston, W.V.] : Cambridge Educational, c1994.
*TC HV1435.C3 C45 1994*

**YOUTH - CRIMES AGAINST - NEW YORK (STATE) - NEW YORK.**
Children of the night [videorecording]. [Charleston, W.V.] : Cambridge Educational, c1994.
*TC HV1435.C3 C45 1994*

Children of the night [videorecording]. [Charleston, W.V.] : Cambridge Educational, c1994.
*TC HV1435.C3 C45 1994*

Children of the night [videorecording]. [Charleston, W.V.] : Cambridge Educational, c1994.
*TC HV1435.C3 C45 1994*

**YOUTH - DRUG USE.**
Adolescent relationships and drug use. Mahwah, N.J. ; London : Lawrence Erlbaum Associates, 2000.
*TC HV5824.Y68 A315 2000*

**YOUTH - DRUG USE - PREVENTION.**
The next generation [videorecording]. Princeton, NJ : Films for the Humanities & Sciences, c1998.
*TC RC564 .N4 1998*

**YOUTH - EDUCATION.** *See* **EDUCATION.**

**YOUTH - EMPLOYMENT - UNITED STATES.**
McCarthy, William H. Reducing urban unemployment. Washington, D.C. : National League of Cities, c1985.
*TC HD5724 .M34 1985*

**YOUTH - GOVERNMENT POLICY - UNITED STATES.**
Securing the future. New York : Russell Sage Foundation, c2000.
*TC HV741 .S385 2000*

**YOUTH, HISPANIC AMERICAN.** *See* **HISPANIC AMERICAN YOUTH.**

**YOUTH, HOMELESS.** *See* **HOMELESS YOUTH.**

**YOUTH - HOUSING.**
Homeless and working youth around the world. San Francisco : Jossey-Bass, 1999.
*TC HV4493 .H655 1999*

**YOUTH - HUNGARY - SOCIAL CONDITIONS.**
Adolescent development and rapid social change. Albany : State University of New York Press, c2000.
*TC HQ799.H8 A35 2000*

**Youth lifestyles in a changing world.**
Miles, Steven. Buckingham ; Philadelphia : Open University Press, 2000.
*TC HQ796 .M4783 2000*

**YOUTH MARKET.** *See* **YOUNG CONSUMERS.**

**YOUTH - MENTAL HEALTH.**
First break [videorecording]. Boston, MA : Fanlight Productions, c1997.
*TC RC465 .F5 1997*

First break [videorecording]. Boston, MA : Fanlight Productions, c1997.
*TC RC465 .F5 1997*

First break [videorecording]. Boston, MA : Fanlight Productions, c1997.
*TC RC465 .F5 1997*

**Youth mentoring.**
Flaxman, Erwin. New York, N.Y. : ERIC Clearinghouse on Urban Education, 1988.
*TC LC4065 .F53 1988*

**YOUTH, MEXICAN AMERICAN.** *See* **MEXICAN AMERICAN YOUTH.**

**YOUTH MOVEMENT.** *See* **STUDENT MOVEMENTS.**

**YOUTH - POLAND - SOCIAL CONDITIONS.**
Adolescent development and rapid social change. Albany : State University of New York Press, c2000.
*TC HQ799.H8 A35 2000*

**YOUTH - PSYCHOLOGICAL TESTING.**
Hoge, Robert D. Assessing adolescents in educational, counseling, and other settings. Mahwah, N.J. : Lawrence Erlbaum Associates, 1999.
*TC BF724.25 .H64 1999*

**YOUTH, PUERTO RICAN.** *See* **PUERTO RICAN YOUTH.**

**YOUTH SERVICES IN LIBRARIES.** *See* **CHILDREN'S LIBRARIES.**

**YOUTH - SOCIAL CONDITIONS.**
Miles, Steven. Youth lifestyles in a changing world. Buckingham ; Philadelphia : Open University Press, 2000.
*TC HQ796 .M4783 2000*

**YOUTH - SUBSTANCE USE - PREVENTION.**
The next generation [videorecording]. Princeton, NJ : Films for the Humanities & Sciences, c1998.
*TC RC564 .N4 1998*

**YOUTH - SUICIDAL BEHAVIOR - PREVENTION.**
Johnson, Wanda Yvonne, 1936- Youth suicide. Bloomington, Ind. : Phi Delta Kappa Educational Foundation, c1999.
*TC HV6546 .J645 1999*

**YOUTH - SUICIDAL BEHAVIOR - UNITED STATES.**
Jamison, Kay R. Night falls fast. 1st ed. New York : Knopf : Distributed by Random House, 1999.
*TC RC569 .J36 1999*

**Youth suicide.**
Johnson, Wanda Yvonne, 1936- Bloomington, Ind. : Phi Delta Kappa Educational Foundation, c1999.
*TC HV6546 .J645 1999*

**YOUTH - TOBACCO USE - PREVENTION.**
The next generation [videorecording]. Princeton, NJ : Films for the Humanities & Sciences, c1998.

*TC RC564 .N4 1998*

**YOUTH - UNITED STATES.** *See also* **AFRO-AMERICAN YOUTH; HISPANIC AMERICAN YOUTH; MEXICAN AMERICAN YOUTH; PUERTO RICAN YOUTH.**
Giroux, Henry A. Channel surfing. 1st ed. New York : St. Martin's Press, 1997.
*TC HQ799.7 .G57 1997*

**YOUTH - UNITED STATES - BOOKS AND READING.**
Young adult science fiction. Westport, Conn. : Greenwood Press, 1999.
*TC PS374.S35 Y63 1999*

**YOUTH - UNITED STATES - HISTORY.**
Childhood in America. New York : New York University Press, c2000.
*TC HQ792.U5 C4199 1999*

**YOUTH - UNITED STATES - HISTORY - SOURCES.**
Childhood in America. New York : New York University Press, c2000.
*TC HQ792.U5 C4199 1999*

**YOUTH - UNITED STATES - SEXUAL BEHAVIOR.**
Becker, Evvie. High-risk sexual behavior. New York : Plenum Press, c1998.
*TC HQ60.7.U6 B43 1998*

**YOUTH - UNITED STATES - SOCIAL CONDITIONS.**
Securing the future. New York : Russell Sage Foundation, c2000.
*TC HV741 .S385 2000*
Wimsatt, William Upski. No more prisons. [New York] : Soft Skull Press, [2000?]
*TC HV9276.5 .W567x 2000*

**YOUTHS.** *See* **YOUTH.**

**YOUTHS' WRITINGS.** *See* **COLLEGE PROSE.**

**YOUTHS' WRITINGS, AMERICAN.**
When the rain sings. New York : Simon & Schuster Books for Young Readers, 1999.
*TC PS591.I55 W48 1999*

**Yow, Deborah A.**
Humphrey, James Harry, 1911- Stress in college athletics. New York : Haworth Press, c2000.
*TC GV347 .H86 2000*

**YRE (EDUCATION).** *See* **YEAR-ROUND SCHOOLS.**

**YUCATECAN LANGUAGE.** *See* **MAYA LANGUAGE.**

**Yudonsi.**
Blake, Robert J. New York : Philomel Books, 1999.
*TC PZ7.B564 Yu 1999*

**YUGOSLAVIA - POLITICS AND GOVERNMENT - 1992-.**
[Ajmo, ajde, svi u šetnju. English.] Protest in Belgrade. Budapest, Hungary ; New York, NY, USA : Central European University Press, 1999.
*TC DR2044 .A3913 1999*

**Yukon gold.**
Jones, Charlotte Foltz. 1st ed. New York : Holiday House, c1999.
*TC F1095.K5 J66 1999*

**Zachary, Lois J.** The mentor's guide : facilitating effective learning relationships / Lois J. Zachary ; foreword by Laurent Daloz. 1st ed. San Francisco : Jossey-Bass Publishers, c2000. xxv, 195 p. : ill. ; 27 cm. (The Jossey-Bass higher and adult education series) Includes bibliographical references (p. 187-190). CONTENTS: Grounding the work : focusing on learning -- Working the ground : considering context -- To everything there is a season : predictable phases -- Tilling the soil : preparing -- Planting seeds : negotiating -- Nurturing growth : enabling -- Reaping the harvest : coming to closure -- Regenerating personal growth through mentoring. ISBN 0-7879-4742-3 (alk. paper) DDC 371.102
*1. Mentoring in education. 2. Learning, Psychology of. 3. Interpersonal relations. I. Title. II. Series.*
*TC LB1731.4 .Z23 2000*

**Zachry, Caroline Beaumont, 1894- joint author.**
Thayer, Vivian Trow, 1886- Reorganizing secondary education; New York, Appleton-Century [c1939]
*TC LB1607 .T5*

**Zahorik, John A.**
Dichanz, Horst, 1937- Changing traditions in Germany's public schools. Bloomington, Ind. : Phi Delta Kappa Educational Foundation, c1998.

**TC LA723 .D53 1998**

**Zaleski, Szymon.**
Ecole 27 [videorecording]. Bruxelles : Paradise
Films ; New York, N.Y. : [distributed by] First Run/
Icarus Films, 1997, c1996.
**TC LC746.P7 E2 1997**

**Zamorano, Ana.** Let's eat! / written by Ana Zamorano ;
illustrated by Julie Vivas. New York : Scholastic
Press, 1997. [30] p. : col. ill. ; 25 cm. SUMMARY: Each day
Antonio's Mamá tries to get everyone to sit down together to
eat, but someone is always busy elsewhere, until the family
celebrates a new arrival. ISBN 0-590-13444-2 DDC [E]
*1. Dinners and dining - Fiction. 2. Family life - Fiction. 3.
Spaniards - Fiction. I. Vivas, Julie, 1947- ill. II. Title.*
**TC PZ7.Z25455 Le 1997**

**ZAPATECO INDIANS.** *See* **ZAPOTEC INDIANS.**

**ZAPOTEC INDIANS - FOLKLORE.**
Cruz Martinez, Alejandro, d. 1987. [Mujer que
brillaba aún más que el sol. English & Spanish] The
woman who outshone the sun. San Francisco, Calif. :
Children's Book Press, c1991.
**TC F1221.Z3 C78 1991**

Cruz Martinez, Alejandro, d. 1987. [Mujer que
brillaba aún más que el sol. English & Spanish] The
woman who outshone the sun. San Francisco, Calif. :
Children's Book Press, c1991.
**TC F1221.Z3 C78 1991**

**Zarit, Steven H.**
Caregiving systems. Hillsdale, N.J. : L. Erlbaum
Associates, 1993.
**TC HV1451 .C329 1993**

**Zarrillo, James.** Teaching elementary social studies :
principles and applications / James J. Zarrillo. Upper
Saddle River, N.J. : Merrill, c2000. xviii, 398 p. : ill. ; 24
cm. Includes bibliographical references (p. 352-383) and index.
ISBN 0-02-431352-1 DDC 372.83/044/0973
*1. Social sciences - Study and teaching (Elementary) - United
States. 2. Multicultural education - United States. I. Title.*
**TC LB1584 .Z27 2000**

**Zastoupil, Lynn, 1953-.**
The Great Indian education debate. Richmond :
Curzon, 1999.
**TC LA1151 .G743 1999**

**Zavella, Patricia.**
Situated lives. New York : Routledge, 1997.
**TC GN479.65 .S57 1997**

**Zea, María Cecilia.**
Psychological interventions and research with Latino
populations. Boston : Allyn and Bacon, c1997.
**TC RC451.5.H57 P77 1997**

**Zehm, Stanley J.**
Kottler, Jeffrey A. On being a teacher. 2nd ed.
Thousand Oaks, Calif. : Corwin Press, c2000.
**TC LB1025.3 .Z44 2000**

Powell, Richard R., 1951- Classrooms under the
influence. Newbury Park, Calif. : Corwin Press,
c1995.
**TC HV5824.Y68 P69 1995**

**Zeichner, Kenneth M.**
Democratic teacher education reform in Africa.
Boulder, Colo. ; Oxford : Westview Press, 1999.
**TC LB1727.N3 D46 1999**

**Zeidner, Moshe.**
Handbook of self-regulation. San Diego : Academic,
2000.
**TC BF632 .H254 2000**

**Zeig, Jeffrey K., 1947-.**
Ericksonian approaches to hypnosis and
psychotherapy. New York : Brunner/Mazel, c1982.
**TC RC490.5.E75 E75**

**Zeitlin, Marian F.**
Strengthening the family. Tokyo ; New York : United
Nations University Press, c1995.
**TC HQ727.9 .S77 1995**

**Zeki, Semir.** Inner vision : an exploration of art and the
brain / Semir Zeki. Oxford ; New York : Oxford
University Press, c1999. x, 224 p. : ill. (some col.) ; 24 cm.
Includes bibliographical references and index. ISBN 0-19-
850519-1 DDC 612.8
*1. Art - Psychology. 2. Visual perception. 3. Art - Study and
teaching. 4. Visual cortex. 5. Brain - Physiology. I. Title.*
**TC N71 .Z45 1999**

**Zemach, Margot, ill.**
Uchida, Yoshiko. The two foolish cats. New York :
M.K. McElderry Books, c1987.
**TC PZ8.1.U35 Tw 1987**

**Zemelman, Steven.**
History comes home. York, Me. : Stenhouse
Publishers, c2000.
**TC CS49 .H57 2000**

**Zenger, John H.**
Ulrich, David, 1953- Results-based leadership.
Boston : Harvard Business School Press, 1999.
**TC HD57.7 .U45 1999**

**ZENOPHOBIA.** *See* **XENOPHOBIA.**

**ZENTENO, LUCIA (LEGENDARY
   CHARACTER) - LEGENDS.**
Cruz Martinez, Alejandro, d. 1987. [Mujer que
brillaba aún más que el sol. English & Spanish] The
woman who outshone the sun. San Francisco, Calif. :
Children's Book Press, c1991.
**TC F1221.Z3 C78 1991**

Cruz Martinez, Alejandro, d. 1987. [Mujer que
brillaba aún más que el sol. English & Spanish] The
woman who outshone the sun. San Francisco, Calif. :
Children's Book Press, c1991.
**TC F1221.Z3 C78 1991**

**Zepeda, Sally J., 1956-** Supervision and staff
development in the block : practices that empower
teachers / by Sally J. Zepeda and R. Stewart Mayers.
Larchmont, N.Y. : Eye On Education, c2000. xvii, 253
p. ; 23 cm. Includes bibliographical references and index.
ISBN 1-88300-183-8 DDC 370/.71/55
*1. Block scheduling (Education) - Planning. 2. School
supervision - Planning. 3. Teachers - In-service training. I.
Mayers, R. Stewart. 1959- II. Title.*
**TC LB3032.2 .Z46 2000**

**Zersen, David John.** Independent learning among
clergy / by David John Zersen. 1998. v, 184 leaves ; 29
cm. Typescript; issued also on microfilm. Thesis (Ed.D.)--
Teachers College, Columbia University, 1998. Includes
bibliographical references (leaves 173-178).
*1. Lutheran Church - Texas - Clergy. 2. Continuing education -
Case studies. 3. Independent study. 4. Self-evaluation. 5.
Educational evaluation. 6. Cognitive styles. 7. Adult learning -
Evaluation. I. Title.*
**TC 06 no. 11008**

**Zevin, Jack.** Social studies for the twenty-first century :
methods and materials for teaching in middle and
secondary schools / Jack Zevin. 2nd ed. Mahwah,
N.J. : L. Erlbaum Associates, c2000. xv, 439 p. : ill. ; 25
cm. Includes bibliographical references and index. ISBN
0-8058-2465-0 (p : alk. paper) DDC 300/.71/273
*1. Social sciences - Study and teaching (Secondary) - United
States. I. Title.*
**TC H62.5.U5 Z48 2000**

**Ziefert, Harriet.** Animal music / Harriet Ziefert ;
illustrated by Donald Saaf. Boston : Houghton Mifflin,
1999. 1 v. (unpaged) : col. ill. ; 30 cm. SUMMARY: An
assortment of animals playing various instruments make
different kinds of music. ISBN 0-395-95294-8 DDC [E]
*1. Bands (Music) - Fiction. 2. Animals - Fiction. 3. Stories in
rhyme. I. Saaf, Donald, ill. II. Title.*
**TC PZ8.3.Z47 An 1999**

**Zigmond, Naomi, 1941-.**
Vallecorsa, Ada, 1948- Students with mild disabilities
in general education settings. Upper Saddle River,
N.J. : Merrill, c2000.
**TC LC4705 .V35 2000**

**ZIMBABWE - CHURCH HISTORY.**
Ranger, T. O. (Terence O.) Are we not also men?
Harare : Baobab ; Portsmouth, NH : Heinemann,
1995.
**TC DT2974 .R36 1995**

**ZIMBABWE - POLITICS AND GOVERNMENT -
   1890-1965.**
Mungazi, Dickson A. The last British liberals in
Africa. Westport, Conn. : Praeger, 1999.
**TC DT2979.T63 M86 1999**

Ranger, T. O. (Terence O.) Are we not also men?
Harare : Baobab ; Portsmouth, NH : Heinemann,
1995.
**TC DT2974 .R36 1995**

**ZIMBABWE - POLITICS AND GOVERNMENT -
   1965-1979.**
Mungazi, Dickson A. The last British liberals in
Africa. Westport, Conn. : Praeger, 1999.
**TC DT2979.T63 M86 1999**

**Zimbalist, Efrem, 1923-.**
Touch 'n' go [videorecording]. Burbank, Calif. :
Columbia Tristar Home Video ; [S.l. : Distributed by]
Rank Video Services Production, c1991.
**TC HV1626 .T6 1991**

**Zimmer, Dirk, ill.**
The sky is full of song. 1st ed. New York : Harper &
Row, c1983.
**TC PS595.S42 S5 1983**

**Zimmerman, Glen.**
Management of library security. Washington, DC :
Systems and Procedures Exchange Center, Office of
Leadership and Management Services, Association of
Research Libraries, c1999.
**TC Z679.6 .M26 1999**

**Zimring, Franklin E.** American youth violence /
Franklin E. Zimring. New York : Oxford University
Press, 1998. xiii, 209 p. : ill. ; 24 cm. (Studies in crime and
public policy) Includes bibliographical references (p. 197-202)
and index. ISBN 0-19-512145-7 (alk. paper) DDC 364.36/0973
*1. Juvenile delinquency - Government policy - United States. 2.
Violent crimes - Government policy - United States. 3. Juvenile
justice. Administration of - United States. I. Title. II. Series.*
**TC HV9104 .Z57 1998**

**Zinman, M. Richard.**
Democracy & the arts. Ithaca : Cornell University
Press, c1999.
**TC NX180.S6 D447 1999**

**Zinn, Maxine Baca, 1942-** Diversity in families /
Maxine Baca Zinn, D. Stanley Eitzen. 5th ed. New
York : Longman, 1998. xvi, 543 p. : ill. ; 25 cm. Includes
bibliographical references (p. 482-519) and index. ISBN 0-
321-02279-3 DDC 306.85/0973
*1. Family - United States. 2. United States - Social conditions -
1980- I. Eitzen, D. Stanley. II. Title.*
**TC HQ536 .Z54 1998**

**ZIONISM.** *See* **JEWS - POLITICS AND
   GOVERNMENT.**

**Zola, John.**
Socratic seminar [videorecording]. [Boulder, Colo.] :
Social Science Education Consortium, c1997.
**TC LB1027.44 .S6 1997**

**Zolberg, Aristide R.**
The challenge of diversity. Aldershot, England ;
Brookfield, Vt. : Avebury, 1996.
**TC JV225 .C530 1996**

**Zolotow, Charlotte, 1915-** River winding / poems by
Charlotte Zolotow ; pictures by Kazue Mizumura. 1st
ed. New York : Crowell, [1978] [40] p. : ill. ; 23 cm.
SUMMARY: An illustrated collection of short poems about
bedtime, rivers, seasons, and other topics. ISBN 0-690-03866-
6 ISBN 0-690-03867-4 (lib. bdg.) DDC 811/.5/4
*1. American poetry. I. Mizumura, Kazue. II. Title.*
**TC PZ8.3.Z6 Ri 1978**

**ZONES OF TRANSITIONS.** *See* **INNER CITIES.**

**ZOO ANIMALS - JUVENILE POETRY.**
To the zoo. 1st ed. Boston : Little, Brown, c1992.
**TC PS595.Z66 T6 1992**

**ZOO ANIMALS - POETRY.**
To the zoo. 1st ed. Boston : Little, Brown, c1992.
**TC PS595.Z66 T6 1992**

**ZOOLOGY.** *See* **ANIMALS; NOCTURNAL
   ANIMALS; PHYSIOLOGY, COMPARATIVE;
   PSYCHOLOGY, COMPARATIVE.**

**ZOOLOGY - ICELAND.**
McMillan, Bruce. Nights of the pufflings. Boston :
Houghton Mifflin Co., 1995.
**TC QL696.C42 M39 1995**

**ZOOLOGY - NOMENCLATURE (POPULAR) -
   POLYGLOT - JUVENILE LITERATURE.**
Bruegel, Jan, 1568-1625. Where's the bear? Los
Angeles : J. Paul Getty Museum, c1997.
**TC QL49 .B749 1997**

**Zoom in** : teacher's planning guide. New York :
Macmillan/McGraw-Hill, c1997. 1 v. (various pagings) :
col. ill. ; 31 cm. (Spotlight on reading ; Gr.5 l.11 u.6) (The road
to independent reading) Includes index. ISBN 0-02-181184-9
*1. Language arts (Elementary) 2. Reading (Elementary) I.
Series. II. Series: The road to independent reading*
**TC LB1576 .S66 1997 Gr.5 l.11 u.6**

**Zoonen, Liesbet van, 1959-.**
Gender, politics and communication. Cresskill, N.J. :
Hampton Press, c2000.
**TC P94.5.W65 G46 2000**

**Zorn, Debbie.**
Caring as tenacity. Cresskill, N.J. : Hampton Press,
c2000.
**TC LC5131 .C35 2000**

**Zsidó iskolázás Magyarországon, 1780-1990.**
Felkai, László. Budapest : Országos Pedagógiai
Könyvtár és Múzeum, [1998]

*TC LC746.H8 F455 1998*

**Zuber-Skerritt, Ortrun.**
Supervising postgraduates from non-English speaking backgrounds. Buckingham ; Philadelphia : Society for Research into Higher Education : Open University Press, 1999.
*TC LB2343 .S86 1999*

**Zubizarreta-Ada, Rosalma.**
Cruz Martinez, Alejandro, d. 1987. [Mujer que brillaba aún más que el sol. English & Spanish] The woman who outshone the sun. San Francisco, Calif. : Children's Book Press, c1991.
*TC F1221.Z3 C78 1991*

**Zuelke, Dennis C.** Educational private practice : your opportunities in the changing education marketplace / Dennis C. Zuelke. Lancaster : Technomic Pub., c1996. xxiii, 223 p. ; 23 cm. Includes bibliographical references (p. 217-223). ISBN 1-56676-315-0 (pbk.)
*1. Teachers - Supplementary employment - United States - Handbooks, manuals, etc. 2. Teaching - Practice - United States - Handbooks, manuals, etc. 3. Teaching - United States - Marketing - Handbooks, manuals, etc. I. Title.*
*TC LB2844.1.S86 Z84 1996*

**ZUNI INDIANS - POTTERY.** *See* **ZUNI POTTERY.**

**ZUNI POTTERY - JUVENILE LITERATURE.**
Sullivan, Missy. The Native American look book. New York : The New Press, 1996.
*TC E98.A7 S93 1996*

**Zweites Deutsches Fernsehen.**
Ecole 27 [videorecording]. Bruxelles : Paradise Films ; New York, N.Y. : [distributed by] First Run/ Icarus Films, 1997, c1996.
*TC LC746.P7 E2 1997*

**Zweizig, Douglas.** Lessons from library power : enriching teaching and learning : final report of the evaluation of the national library power initiative : an initiative of the DeWitt Wallace-Reader's Digest Fund / Douglas L. Zweizig and Dianne McAfee Hopkins ; with Norman Lott Webb and Gary Wehlage. Englewood, Colo. : Libraries Unlimited, 1999. xiii, 281 p. ; 28 cm. Includes bibliographical references and index. ISBN 1-56308-833-9
*1. Library Power (Program) 2. School libraries - United States. 3. Libraries - United States - Gifts, legacies. 4. School libraries - United States - Finance. I. Hopkins, Dianne McAfee. II. Webb, Norman. III. Wehlage, Gary. IV. Title.*
*TC Z675.S3 Z94 1999*

**Zychowicz, James L.** Mahler's Fourth symphony / James L. Zychowicz. New York : Oxford University Press, 2000. xiii, 191 p. : ill. ; 25 cm. (Studies in musical genesis and structure) Includes bibliographical references (p.82-188) and index. DDC 784.2/184
*1. Mahler, Gustav, - 1860-1911. - Symphonies, - no. 4, - G major I. Title. II. Series: Studies in musical genesis and structure.*
*TC MT130.M25 Z93 2000*